**REFERENCE
ONLY**

PETERSON'S®
GRADUATE PROGRAMS IN THE HUMANITIES, ARTS & SOCIAL SCIENCES

2021

About Peterson's®

Peterson's® has been your trusted educational publisher for over 50 years. It's a milestone we're quite proud of, as we continue to offer the most accurate, dependable, high-quality educational content in the field, providing you with everything you need to succeed. No matter where you are on your academic or professional path, you can rely on Peterson's for its books, online information, expert test-prep tools, the most up-to-date education exploration data, and the highest quality career success resources—everything you need to achieve your education goals. For our complete line of products, visit **www.petersons.com**.

For more information about Peterson's range of educational products, contact Peterson's, 4380 S. Syracuse Street, Suite 200, Denver, CO 80237, or find us online at **www.petersons.com**.

ISSN 1093-8443
ISBN: 978-0-7689-4553-9

Printed in the United States of America

10 9 8 7 6 5 4 3 2 1   22 21 20

Fifty-fifth Edition

CONTENTS

CONTENTS

A Note from the Peterson's Editors

The six volumes of Peterson's *Graduate and Professional Programs*, the only annually updated reference work of its kind, provide wide-ranging information on the graduate and professional programs offered by accredited colleges and universities in the United States, U.S. territories, and Canada and by those institutions outside the United States that are accredited by U.S. accrediting bodies. More than 44,000 individual academic and professional programs at nearly 2,300 institutions are listed. Peterson's *Graduate and Professional Programs* have been used for more than fifty years by prospective graduate and professional students, placement counselors, faculty advisers, and all others interested in postbaccalaureate education.

Graduate & Professional Programs: An Overview contains information on institutions as a whole, while the other books in the series are devoted to specific academic and professional fields:

• *Graduate Programs in the Biological/Biomedical Sciences & Health-Related Medical Professions*

• *Graduate Programs in Business, Education, Information Studies, Law & Social Work*

• *Graduate Programs in Engineering & Applied Sciences*

• *Graduate Programs in the Humanities, Arts & Social Sciences*

• *Graduate Programs in the Physical Sciences, Mathematics, Agricultural Sciences, the Environment & Natural Resources*

The books may be used individually or as a set. For example, if you have chosen a field of study but do not know what institution you want to attend or if you have a college or university in mind but have not chosen an academic field of study, it is best to begin with the Overview guide.

Graduate & Professional Programs: An Overview presents several directories to help you identify programs of study that might interest you; you can then research those programs further in the other books in the series by using the Directory of Graduate and Professional Programs by Field, which lists 500 fields and gives the names of those institutions that offer graduate degree programs in each.

For geographical or financial reasons, you may be interested in attending a particular institution and will want to know what it has to offer. You should turn to the Directory of Institutions and Their Offerings, which lists the degree programs available at each institution. As in the Directory of Graduate and Professional Programs by Field, the level of degrees offered is also indicated.

All books in the series include advice on graduate education, including topics such as admissions tests, financial aid, and accreditation. **The Graduate Adviser** includes two essays and information about accreditation. The first essay, "The Admissions Process," discusses general admission requirements, admission tests, factors to consider when selecting a graduate school or program, when and how to apply, and how admission decisions are made. Special information for international students and tips for minority students are also included. The second essay, "Financial Support," is an overview of the broad range of support available at the graduate level. Fellowships, scholarships, and grants; assistantships and internships; federal and private loan programs, as well as Federal Work-Study; and the GI bill are detailed. This essay concludes with advice on applying for need-based financial aid. "Accreditation and Accrediting Agencies" gives information on accreditation and its purpose and lists institutional accrediting agencies first and then specialized accrediting agencies relevant to each volume's specific fields of study.

With information on more than 40,000 graduate programs in more than 500 disciplines, Peterson's *Graduate and Professional Programs* give you all the information you need about the programs that are of interest to you in three formats: **Profiles** (capsule summaries of basic information), **Displays** (information that an institution or program wants to emphasize), and **Close-Ups** (written by administrators, with more expansive information than the **Profiles**, emphasizing different aspects of the programs). By using these various formats of program information, coupled with **Appendixes** and **Indexes** covering directories and subject areas for all six books, you will find that these guides provide the most comprehensive, accurate, and up-to-date graduate study information available.

Peterson's publishes a full line of resources with information you need to guide you through the graduate admissions process. Peterson's publications can be found at college libraries and career centers and your local bookstore or library—or visit us on the Web at www.petersons.com.

Colleges and universities will be pleased to know that Peterson's helped you in your selection. Admissions staff members are more than happy to answer questions, address specific problems, and help in any way they can. The editors at Peterson's wish you great success in your graduate program search!

THE GRADUATE ADVISER

The Admissions Process

Generalizations about graduate admissions practices are not always helpful because each institution has its own set of guidelines and procedures. Nevertheless, some broad statements can be made about the admissions process that may help you plan your strategy.

Factors Involved in Selecting a Graduate School or Program

Selecting a graduate school and a specific program of study is a complex matter. Quality of the faculty; program and course offerings; the nature, size, and location of the institution; admission requirements; cost; and the availability of financial assistance are among the many factors that affect one's choice of institution. Other considerations are job placement and achievements of the program's graduates and the institution's resources, such as libraries, laboratories, and computer facilities. If you are to make the best possible choice, you need to learn as much as you can about the schools and programs you are considering before you apply.

The following steps may help you narrow your choices.

- Talk to alumni of the programs or institutions you are considering to get their impressions of how well they were prepared for work in their fields of study.
- Remember that graduate school requirements change, so be sure to get the most up-to-date information possible.
- Talk to department faculty members and the graduate adviser at your undergraduate institution. They often have information about programs of study at other institutions.
- Visit the websites of the graduate schools in which you are interested to request a graduate catalog. Contact the department chair in your chosen field of study for additional information about the department and the field.
- Visit as many campuses as possible. Call ahead for an appointment with the graduate adviser in your field of interest and be sure to check out the facilities and talk to students.

General Requirements

Graduate schools and departments have requirements that applicants for admission must meet. Typically, these requirements include undergraduate transcripts (which provide information about undergraduate grade point average and course work applied toward a major), admission test scores, and letters of recommendation. Most graduate programs also ask for an essay or personal statement that describes your personal reasons for seeking graduate study. In some fields, such as art and music, portfolios or auditions may be required in addition to other evidence of talent. Some institutions require that the applicant have an undergraduate degree in the same subject as the intended graduate major.

Most institutions evaluate each applicant on the basis of the applicant's total record, and the weight accorded any given factor varies widely from institution to institution and from program to program.

The Application Process

You should begin the application process at least one year before you expect to begin your graduate study. Find out the application deadline for each institution (many are provided in the **Profile** section of this guide). Go to the institution's website and find out if you can apply online. If not, request a paper application form. Fill out this form thoroughly and neatly. Assume that the school needs all the information it is requesting and that the admissions officer will be sensitive to the neatness and overall quality of what you submit. Do not supply more information than the school requires.

The institution may ask at least one question that will require a three- or four-paragraph answer. Compose your response on the assumption that the admissions officer is interested in both what you think and how you express yourself. Keep your statement brief and to the point, but, at the same time, include all pertinent information about your past experiences and your educational goals. Individual statements vary greatly in style and content, which helps admissions officers differentiate among applicants. Many graduate departments give considerable weight to the statement in making their admissions decisions, so be sure to take the time to prepare a thoughtful and concise statement.

If recommendations are a part of the admissions requirements, carefully choose the individuals you ask to write them. It is generally best to ask current or former professors to write the recommendations, provided they are able to attest to your intellectual ability and motivation for doing the work required of a graduate student. It is advisable to provide stamped, preaddressed envelopes to people being asked to submit recommendations on your behalf.

Completed applications, including references, transcripts, and admission test scores, should be received at the institution by the specified date.

Be advised that institutions do not usually make admissions decisions until all materials have been received. Enclose a self-addressed postcard with your application, requesting confirmation of receipt. Allow at least ten days for the return of the postcard before making further inquiries.

If you plan to apply for financial support, it is imperative that you file your application early.

ADMISSION TESTS

The major testing program used in graduate admissions is the Graduate Record Examinations (GRE®) testing program, sponsored by the GRE Board and administered by Educational Testing Service, Princeton, New Jersey.

The Graduate Record Examinations testing program consists of a General Test and six Subject Tests. The General Test measures critical thinking, verbal reasoning, quantitative reasoning, and analytical writing skills. It is offered as an Internet-based test (iBT) in the United States, Canada, and many other countries.

The GRE® revised General Test's questions were designed to reflect the kind of thinking that students need to do in graduate or business school and demonstrate that students are indeed ready for graduate-level work.

- **Verbal Reasoning**—Measures ability to analyze and evaluate written material and synthesize information obtained from it, analyze relationships among component parts of sentences, and recognize relationships among words and concepts.
- **Quantitative Reasoning**—Measures problem-solving ability, focusing on basic concepts of arithmetic, algebra, geometry, and data analysis.
- **Analytical Writing**—Measures critical thinking and analytical writing skills, specifically the ability to articulate and support complex ideas clearly and effectively.

The computer-delivered GRE® revised General Test is offered year-round at Prometric™ test centers and on specific dates at testing locations outside of the Prometric test center network. Appointments are scheduled on a first-come, first-served basis. The GRE® revised General Test is also offered as a paper-based test three times a year in areas where computer-based testing is not available.

You can take the computer-delivered GRE® revised General Test once every twenty-one days, up to five times within any continuous rolling twelve-month period (365 days)—even if you canceled your scores on a previously taken test. You may take the paper-based GRE® revised General Test as often as it is offered.

Three scores are reported on the revised General Test:

1. A **Verbal Reasoning score** is reported on a 130–170 score scale, in 1-point increments.

2. A **Quantitative Reasoning score** is reported on a 130–170 score scale, in 1-point increments.

3. An **Analytical Writing score** is reported on a 0–6 score level, in half-point increments.

The GRE® Subject Tests measure achievement and assume undergraduate majors or extensive background in the following six disciplines:

- Biology
- Chemistry
- Literature in English
- Mathematics
- Physics
- Psychology

The Subject Tests are available three times per year as paper-based administrations around the world. Testing time is approximately 2 hours and 50 minutes. You can obtain more information about the GRE® by visiting the ETS website at **www.ets.org** or consulting the *GRE® Information Bulletin*. The *Bulletin* can be obtained at many undergraduate colleges. You can also download it from the ETS website or obtain it by contacting Graduate Record Examinations, Educational Testing Service, P.O. Box 6000, Princeton, NJ 08541-6000; phone: 609-771-7670 or 866-473-4373.

If you expect to apply for admission to a program that requires any of the GRE® tests, you should select a test date well in advance of the application deadline. Scores on the computer-based General Test are reported within ten to fifteen days; scores on the paper-based Subject Tests are reported within six weeks.

Another testing program, the Miller Analogies Test® (MAT®), is administered at more than 500 Controlled Testing Centers in the United States, Canada, and other countries. The MAT® computer-based test is now available. Testing time is 60 minutes. The test consists of 120 partial analogies. You can obtain the *Candidate Information Booklet,* which contains a list of test centers and instructions for taking the test, from **www.milleranalogies.com** or by calling 800-328-5999 (toll-free).

Check the specific requirements of the programs to which you are applying.

How Admission Decisions Are Made

The program you apply to is directly involved in the admissions process. Although the final decision is usually made by the graduate dean (or an associate) or the faculty admissions committee, recommendations from faculty members in your intended field are important. At some institutions, an interview is incorporated into the decision process.

A Special Note for International Students

In addition to the steps already described, there are some special considerations for international students who intend to apply for graduate study in the United States. All graduate schools require an indication of competence in English. The purpose of the Test of English as a Foreign Language (TOEFL®) is to evaluate the English proficiency of people who are nonnative speakers of English and want to study at colleges and universities where English is the language of instruction. The TOEFL® is administered by Educational Testing Service (ETS) under the general direction of a policy board established by the College Board and the Graduate Record Examinations Board.

The TOEFL iBT® assesses four basic language skills: listening, reading, writing, and speaking. The Internet-based test is administered at secure, official test centers. The testing time is approximately 4 hours.

The TOEFL® is also offered in a paper-based format in areas of the world where internet-based testing is not available. In 2017, ETS launched a revised TOEFL® paper-based Test, that more closely aligned to the TOEFL iBT® test. This revised paper-based test consists of three sections—listening, reading, and writing. The testing time is approximately 3 hours.

You can obtain more information for both versions of the TOEFL® by visiting the ETS website at **www.ets.org/toefl**. Information can also be obtained by contacting TOEFL® Services, Educational Testing Service, P.O. Box 6151, Princeton, NJ 08541-6151. Phone: 609-771-7100 or 877-863-3546 (toll free).

International students should apply especially early because of the number of steps required to complete the admissions process. Furthermore, many United States graduate schools have a limited number of spaces for international students, and many more students apply than the schools can accommodate.

International students may find financial assistance from institutions very limited. The U.S. government requires international applicants to submit a certification of support, which is a statement attesting to the applicant's financial resources. In addition, international students *must* have health insurance coverage.

Tips for Minority Students

Indicators of a university's values in terms of diversity are found both in its recruitment programs and its resources directed to student success. Important questions: Does the institution vigorously recruit minorities for its graduate programs? Is there funding available to help with the costs associated with visiting the school? Are minorities represented in the institution's brochures or website or on their faculty rolls? What campus-based resources or services (including assistance in locating housing or career counseling and placement) are available? Is funding available to members of underrepresented groups?

At the program level, it is particularly important for minority students to investigate the "climate" of a program under consideration. How many minority students are enrolled and how many have graduated? What opportunities are there to work with diverse faculty and mentors whose research interests match yours? How are conflicts resolved or concerns addressed? How interested are faculty in building strong and supportive relations with students? "Climate" concerns should be addressed by posing questions to various individuals, including faculty members, current students, and alumni.

Information is also available through various organizations, such as the Hispanic Association of Colleges & Universities (HACU), and publications such as *Diverse Issues in Higher Education* and *Hispanic Outlook* magazine. There are also books devoted to this topic, such as *The Multicultural Student's Guide to Colleges* by Robert Mitchell.

Financial Support

The range of financial support at the graduate level is very broad. The following descriptions will give you a general idea of what you might expect and what will be expected of you as a financial support recipient.

Fellowships, Scholarships, and Grants

These are usually outright awards of a few hundred to many thousands of dollars with no service to the institution required in return. Fellowships and scholarships are usually awarded on the basis of merit and are highly competitive. Grants are made on the basis of financial need or special talent in a field of study. Many fellowships, scholarships, and grants not only cover tuition, fees, and supplies but also include stipends for living expenses with allowances for dependents. However, the terms of each should be examined because some do not permit recipients to supplement their income with outside work. Fellowships, scholarships, and grants may vary in the number of years for which they are awarded.

In addition to the availability of these funds at the university or program level, many excellent fellowship programs are available at the national level and may be applied for before and during enrollment in a graduate program. A listing of many of these programs can be found at the Council of Graduate Schools' website, **https://cgsnet.org/**. There is a wealth of information in the "Programs" and "Awards" sections.

Assistantships and Internships

Many graduate students receive financial support through assistantships, particularly involving teaching or research duties. It is important to recognize that such appointments should not be viewed simply as employment relationships but rather should constitute an integral and important part of a student's graduate education. As such, the appointments should be accompanied by strong faculty mentoring and increasingly responsible apprenticeship experiences. The specific nature of these appointments in a given program should be considered in selecting that graduate program.

TEACHING ASSISTANTSHIPS

These usually provide a salary and full or partial tuition remission and may also provide health benefits. Unlike fellowships, scholarships, and grants, which require no service to the institution, teaching assistantships require recipients to provide the institution with a specific amount of undergraduate teaching, ideally related to the student's field of study. Some teaching assistants are limited to grading papers, compiling bibliographies, taking notes, or monitoring laboratories. At some graduate schools, teaching assistants must carry lighter course loads than regular full-time students.

RESEARCH ASSISTANTSHIPS

These are very similar to teaching assistantships in the manner in which financial assistance is provided. The difference is that recipients are given basic research assignments in their disciplines rather than teaching responsibilities. The work required is normally related to the student's field of study; in most instances, the assistantship supports the student's thesis or dissertation research.

ADMINISTRATIVE INTERNSHIPS

These are similar to assistantships in application of financial assistance funds, but the student is given an assignment on a part-time basis, usually as a special assistant with one of the university's administrative offices. The assignment may not necessarily be directly related to the recipient's discipline.

RESIDENCE HALL AND COUNSELING ASSISTANTSHIPS

These assistantships are frequently assigned to graduate students in psychology, counseling, and social work, but they may be offered to students in other disciplines, especially if the student has worked in this capacity during his or her undergraduate years. Duties can vary from being available in a dean's office for a specific number of hours for consultation with undergraduates to living in campus residences and being responsible for both counseling and administrative tasks or advising student activity groups. Residence hall assistantships often include a room and board allowance and, in some cases, tuition assistance and stipends. Contact the Housing and Student Life Office for more information.

Health Insurance

The availability and affordability of health insurance is an important issue and one that should be considered in an applicant's choice of institution and program. While often included with assistantships and fellowships, this is not always the case and, even if provided, the benefits may be limited. It is important to note that the U.S. government requires international students to have health insurance.

The GI Bill

This provides financial assistance for students who are veterans of the United States armed forces. If you are a veteran, contact your local Veterans Administration office to determine your eligibility and to get full details about benefits. There are a number of programs that offer educational benefits to current military enlistees. Some states have tuition assistance programs for members of the National Guard. Contact the VA office at the college for more information.

Federal Work-Study Program (FWS)

Employment is another way some students finance their graduate studies. The federally funded Federal Work-Study Program provides eligible students with employment opportunities, usually in public and private nonprofit organizations. Federal funds pay up to 75 percent of the wages, with the remainder paid by the employing agency. FWS is available to graduate students who demonstrate financial need. Not all schools have these funds, and some only award them to undergraduates. Each school sets its application deadline and workstudy earnings limits. Wages vary and are related to the type of work done. You must file the Free Application for Federal Student Aid (FAFSA) to be eligible for this program.

Loans

Many graduate students borrow to finance their graduate programs when other sources of assistance (which do not have to be repaid) prove insufficient. You should always read and understand the terms of any loan program before submitting your application.

FEDERAL DIRECT LOANS

Federal Direct Loans. The Federal Direct Loan Program offers a variable-fixed interest rate loan to graduate students with the Department of Education acting as the lender. Students receive a new rate with each new loan, but that rate is fixed for the life of the loan. Beginning with loans made on or after July 1, 2013, the interest rate for loans made each July 1st to June 30th period are determined based on the last 10-year Treasury note auction prior to June 1st of that year, plus an added percentage. The interest rate can be no higher than 9.5%.

Beginning July 1, 2012, the Federal Direct Loan for graduate students is an unsubsidized loan. Under the *unsubsidized* program, the grad borrower pays the interest on the loan from the day proceeds are issued and is responsible for paying interest during all periods. If the borrower chooses not to pay the interest while in school, or during the grace periods, deferment, or forbearance, the interest accrues and will be capitalized.

Graduate students may borrow up to $20,500 per year through the Direct Loan Program, up to a cumulative maximum of $138,500, including undergraduate borrowing. No more than $65,500 of the $138,500 can be from subsidized loans, including loans the grad borrower may have received for periods of enrollment that began before July 1, 2012, or for prior undergraduate borrowing. You may borrow up to the cost of attendance at the school in which you are enrolled or will attend, minus estimated financial assistance from other federal, state, and private sources, up to a maximum of $20,500. Grad borrowers who reach the aggregate loan limit over the course of their education cannot receive additional loans; however, if they repay some of their loans to bring the outstanding balance below the aggregate limit, they could be eligible to borrow again, up to that limit.

Under the *subsidized* Federal Direct Loan Program, repayment begins six months after your last date of enrollment on at least a half-time basis. Under the *unsubsidized* program, repayment of interest begins within thirty days from disbursement of the loan proceeds, and repayment of the principal begins six months after your last enrollment on at least a half-time basis. Some borrowers may choose to defer interest payments while they are in school. The accrued interest is added to the loan balance when the borrower begins repayment. There are several repayment options.

Federal Perkins Loans. The Federal Perkins Loan is available to students demonstrating financial need and is administered directly by the school. Not all schools have these funds, and some may award them to undergraduates only. Eligibility is determined from the information you provide on the FAFSA. The school will notify you of your eligibility.

Eligible graduate students may borrow up to $8,000 per year, up to a maximum of $60,000, including undergraduate borrowing (even if your previous Perkins Loans have been repaid). The interest rate for Federal Perkins Loans is 5 percent, and no interest accrues while you remain in school at least half-time. Students who are attending less than half-time need to check with their school to determine the length of their grace period. There are no guarantee, loan, or disbursement fees. Repayment begins nine months after your last date of enrollment on at least a half-time basis and may extend over a maximum of ten years with no prepayment penalty.

Federal Direct Graduate PLUS Loans. Effective July 1, 2006, graduate and professional students are eligible for Graduate PLUS loans. This program allows students to borrow up to the cost of attendance, less any other aid received. These loans have a fixed interest rate (5.30% for loans first disbursed on or after July 1, 2020, and before July 1, 2021) and interest begins to accrue at the time of disbursement. Beginning with loans made on or after July 1, 2013, the interest rate for loans made each July 1st to June 30th period are determined based on the last 10-year Treasury note auction prior to June 1st of that year. The interest rate can be no higher than 10.5%. The PLUS loans do involve a credit check; a PLUS borrower may obtain a loan with a cosigner if his or her credit is not good enough. Grad PLUS loans may be deferred while a student is in school and for the six months following a drop below half-time enrollment. For more information, you should contact a representative in your college's financial aid office.

Deferring Your Federal Loan Repayments. If you borrowed under the Federal Direct Loan Program, Federal Direct PLUS Loan Program, or the Federal Perkins Loan Program for previous undergraduate or graduate study, your payments may be deferred when you return to graduate school, depending on when you borrowed and under which program.

There are other deferment options available if you are temporarily unable to repay your loan. Information about these deferments is provided at your entrance and exit interviews. If you believe you are eligible for a deferment of your loan payments, you must contact your lender or loan servicer to request a deferment. The deferment must be filed prior to the time your payment is due, and it must be re-filed when it expires if you remain eligible for deferment at that time.

SUPPLEMENTAL (PRIVATE) LOANS

Many lending institutions offer supplemental loan programs and other financing plans, such as the ones described here, to students seeking additional assistance in meeting their education expenses. Some loan programs target all types of graduate students; others are designed specifically for business, law, or medical students. In addition, you can use private loans not specifically designed for education to help finance your graduate degree.

If you are considering borrowing through a supplemental or private loan program, you should carefully consider the terms and be sure to read the fine print. Check with the program sponsor for the most current terms that will be applicable to the amounts you intend to borrow for graduate study. Most supplemental loan programs for graduate study offer unsubsidized, credit-based loans. In general, a credit-ready borrower is one who has a satisfactory credit history or no credit history at all. A creditworthy borrower generally must pass a credit test to be eligible to borrow or act as a cosigner for the loan funds.

Many supplemental loan programs have minimum and maximum annual loan limits. Some offer amounts equal to the cost of attendance minus any other aid you will receive for graduate study. If you are planning to borrow for several years of graduate study, consider whether there is a cumulative or aggregate limit on the amount you may borrow. Often this cumulative or aggregate limit will include any amounts you borrowed and have not repaid for undergraduate or previous graduate study.

The combination of the annual interest rate, loan fees, and the repayment terms you choose will determine how much you will repay over time. Compare these features in combination before you decide which loan program to use. Some loans offer interest rates that are adjusted monthly, quarterly, or annually. Some offer interest rates that are lower during the in-school, grace, and deferment periods and then increase when you begin repayment. Some programs include a loan origination fee, which is usually deducted from the principal amount you receive when the loan is disbursed and must be repaid along with the interest and other principal when you graduate, withdraw from school, or drop below half-time study. Sometimes the loan fees are reduced if you borrow with a qualified cosigner. Some programs allow you to defer interest and/or principal payments while you are enrolled in graduate school. Many programs allow you to capitalize your interest payments; the interest due on your loan is added to the outstanding balance of your loan, so you don't have to repay immediately, but this increases the amount you owe. Other programs allow you to pay the interest as you go, which reduces the amount you later have to repay. The private loan market is very competitive, and your financial aid office can help you evaluate these programs.

Applying for Need-Based Financial Aid

Schools that award federal and institutional financial assistance based on need will require you to complete the FAFSA and, in some cases, an institutional financial aid application.

If you are applying for federal student assistance, you **must** complete the FAFSA. A service of the U.S. Department of Education, the FAFSA is free to all applicants. Most applicants apply online at **www.fafsa.ed.gov**. Paper applications are available at the financial aid office of your local college.

After your FAFSA information has been processed, you will receive a Student Aid Report (SAR). If you provided an e-mail address on the FAFSA, this will be sent to you electronically; otherwise, it will be mailed to your home address.

Follow the instructions on the SAR if you need to correct information reported on your original application. If your situation changes after you file your FAFSA, contact your financial aid officer to discuss amending your information. You can also appeal your financial aid award if you have extenuating circumstances.

If you would like more information on federal student financial aid, visit the FAFSA website or download the most recent version of *Do You Need Money for College* at www.studentaid.ed.gov/sites/default/files/do-you-need-money.pdf. This guide is also available in Spanish.

The U.S. Department of Education also has a toll-free number for questions concerning federal student aid programs. The number is 1-800-4-FED AID (1-800-433-3243). If you are hearing impaired, call toll-free, 1-800-730-8913.

Summary

Remember that these are generalized statements about financial assistance at the graduate level. Because each institution allots its aid differently, you should communicate directly with the school and the specific department of interest to you. It is not unusual, for example, to find that an endowment vested within a specific department supports one or more fellowships. You may fit its requirements and specifications precisely.

Accreditation and Accrediting Agencies

Colleges and universities in the United States, and their individual academic and professional programs, are accredited by nongovernmental agencies concerned with monitoring the quality of education in this country. Agencies with both regional and national jurisdictions grant accreditation to institutions as a whole, while specialized bodies acting on a nationwide basis—often national professional associations—grant accreditation to departments and programs in specific fields.

Institutional and specialized accrediting agencies share the same basic concerns: the purpose an academic unit—whether university or program—has set for itself and how well it fulfills that purpose, the adequacy of its financial and other resources, the quality of its academic offerings, and the level of services it provides. Agencies that grant institutional accreditation take a broader view, of course, and examine university-wide or college-wide services with which a specialized agency may not concern itself.

Both types of agencies follow the same general procedures when considering an application for accreditation. The academic unit prepares a self-evaluation, focusing on the concerns mentioned above and usually including an assessment of both its strengths and weaknesses; a team of representatives of the accrediting body reviews this evaluation, visits the campus, and makes its own report; and finally, the accrediting body makes a decision on the application. Often, even when accreditation is granted, the agency makes a recommendation regarding how the institution or program can improve. All institutions and programs are also reviewed every few years to determine whether they continue to meet established standards; if they do not, they may lose their accreditation.

Accrediting agencies themselves are reviewed and evaluated periodically by the U.S. Department of Education and the Council for Higher Education Accreditation (CHEA). Recognized agencies adhere to certain standards and practices, and their authority in matters of accreditation is widely accepted in the educational community.

This does not mean, however, that accreditation is a simple matter, either for schools wishing to become accredited or for students deciding where to apply. Indeed, in certain fields the very meaning and methods of accreditation are the subject of a good deal of debate. For their part, those applying to graduate school should be aware of the safeguards provided by regional accreditation, especially in terms of degree acceptance and institutional longevity. Beyond this, applicants should understand the role that specialized accreditation plays in their field, as this varies considerably from one discipline to another. In certain professional fields, it is necessary to have graduated from a program that is accredited in order to be eligible for a license to practice, and in some fields the federal government also makes this a hiring requirement. In other disciplines, however, accreditation is not as essential, and there can be excellent programs that are not accredited. In fact, some programs choose not to seek accreditation, although most do.

Institutions and programs that present themselves for accreditation are sometimes granted the status of candidate for accreditation, or what is known as "preaccreditation." This may happen, for example, when an academic unit is too new to have met all the requirements for accreditation. Such status signifies initial recognition and indicates that the school or program in question is working to fulfill all requirements; it does not, however, guarantee that accreditation will be granted.

Institutional Accrediting Agencies—Regional

MIDDLE STATES COMMISSION ON HIGHER EDUCATION

Accredits institutions in Delaware, District of Columbia, Maryland, New Jersey, New York, Pennsylvania, Puerto Rico, and the Virgin Islands.

Dr. Elizabeth Sibolski, President
Middle States Commission on Higher Education
3624 Market Street, Second Floor West
Philadelphia, Pennsylvania 19104
Phone: 267-284-5000
Fax: 215-662-5501
E-mail: info@msche.org
Website: www.msche.org

NEW ENGLAND ASSOCIATION OF SCHOOLS AND COLLEGES

Accredits institutions in Connecticut, Maine, Massachusetts, New Hampshire, Rhode Island, and Vermont.

Dr. Barbara E. Brittingham, President/Director
Commission on Institutions of Higher Education
3 Burlington Woods Drive, Suite 100
Burlington, Massachusetts 01803-4531
Phone: 855-886-3272 or 781-425-7714
Fax: 781-425-1001
E-mail: cihe@neasc.org
Website: https://cihe.neasc.org

THE HIGHER LEARNING COMMISSION

Accredits institutions in Arizona, Arkansas, Colorado, Illinois, Indiana, Iowa, Kansas, Michigan, Minnesota, Missouri, Nebraska, New Mexico, North Dakota, Ohio, Oklahoma, South Dakota, West Virginia, Wisconsin, and Wyoming.

Dr. Barbara Gellman-Danley, President
The Higher Learning Commission
230 South LaSalle Street, Suite 7-500
Chicago, Illinois 60604-1413
Phone: 800-621-7440 or 312-263-0456
Fax: 312-263-7462
E-mail: info@hlcommission.org
Website: www.hlcommission.org

NORTHWEST COMMISSION ON COLLEGES AND UNIVERSITIES

Accredits institutions in Alaska, Idaho, Montana, Nevada, Oregon, Utah, and Washington.

Dr. Sandra E. Elman, President
8060 165th Avenue, NE, Suite 100
Redmond, Washington 98052
Phone: 425-558-4224
Fax: 425-376-0596
E-mail: selman@nwccu.org
Website: www.nwccu.org

SOUTHERN ASSOCIATION OF COLLEGES AND SCHOOLS

Accredits institutions in Alabama, Florida, Georgia, Kentucky, Louisiana, Mississippi, North Carolina, South Carolina, Tennessee, Texas, and Virginia.

Dr. Belle S. Wheelan, President
Commission on Colleges
1866 Southern Lane
Decatur, Georgia 30033-4097
Phone: 404-679-4500 Ext. 4504
Fax: 404-679-4558
E-mail: questions@sacscoc.org
Website: www.sacscoc.org

WESTERN ASSOCIATION OF SCHOOLS AND COLLEGES

Accredits institutions in California, Guam, and Hawaii.

Jamienne S. Studley, President
WASC Senior College and University Commission
985 Atlantic Avenue, Suite 100
Alameda, California 94501
Phone: 510-748-9001
Fax: 510-748-9797
E-mail: wasc@wscuc.org
Website: https://www.wscuc.org/

Institutional Accrediting Agencies—Other

ACCREDITING COUNCIL FOR INDEPENDENT COLLEGES AND SCHOOLS
Michelle Edwards, President
750 First Street NE, Suite 980
Washington, DC 20002-4223
Phone: 202-336-6780
Fax: 202-842-2593
E-mail: info@acics.org
Website: www.acics.org

DISTANCE EDUCATION ACCREDITING COMMISSION (DEAC)
Leah Matthews, Executive Director
1101 17th Street NW, Suite 808
Washington, DC 20036-4704
Phone: 202-234-5100
Fax: 202-332-1386
E-mail: info@deac.org
Website: www.deac.org

Specialized Accrediting Agencies

ACUPUNCTURE AND ORIENTAL MEDICINE
Mark S. McKenzie, LAc MsOM DiplOM, Executive Director
Accreditation Commission for Acupuncture and Oriental Medicine
8941 Aztec Drive, Suite 2
Eden Prairie, Minnesota 55347
Phone: 952-212-2434
Fax: 301-313-0912
E-mail: info@acaom.org
Website: www.acaom.org

ALLIED HEALTH
Kathleen Megivern, Executive Director
Commission on Accreditation of Allied Health Education Programs (CAAHEP)
25400 US Hwy 19 North, Suite 158
Clearwater, Florida 33763
Phone: 727-210-2350
Fax: 727-210-2354
E-mail: mail@caahep.org
Website: www.caahep.org

ART AND DESIGN
Karen P. Moynahan, Executive Director
National Association of Schools of Art and Design (NASAD)
Commission on Accreditation
11250 Roger Bacon Drive, Suite 21
Reston, Virginia 20190-5248
Phone: 703-437-0700
Fax: 703-437-6312
E-mail: info@arts-accredit.org
Website: http://nasad.arts-accredit.org

ATHLETIC TRAINING EDUCATION
Pamela Hansen, CAATE Director of Accreditation
Commission on Accreditation of Athletic Training Education (CAATE)
6850 Austin Center Blvd., Suite 100
Austin, Texas 78731-3184
Phone: 512-733-9700
E-mail: pamela@caate.net
Website: www.caate.net

AUDIOLOGY EDUCATION
Meggan Olek, Director
Accreditation Commission for Audiology Education (ACAE)
11480 Commerce Park Drive, Suite 220
Reston, Virginia 20191
Phone: 202-986-9500
Fax: 202-986-9550
E-mail: info@acaeaccred.org
Website: https://acaeaccred.org/

AVIATION
Dr. Gary J. Northam, President
Aviation Accreditation Board International (AABI)
3410 Skyway Drive
Auburn, Alabama 36830
Phone: 334-844-2431
Fax: 334-844-2432
E-mail: gary.northam@auburn.edu
Website: www.aabi.aero

BUSINESS
Stephanie Bryant, Executive Vice President and Chief Accreditation Officer
AACSB International—The Association to Advance Collegiate Schools of Business
777 South Harbour Island Boulevard, Suite 750
Tampa, Florida 33602
Phone: 813-769-6500
Fax: 813-769-6559
E-mail: stephanie.bryant@aacsb.edu
Website: www.aacsb.edu

BUSINESS EDUCATION
Dr. Phyllis Okrepkie, President
International Assembly for Collegiate Business Education (IACBE)
11374 Strang Line Road
Lenexa, Kansas 66215
Phone: 913-631-3009
Fax: 913-631-9154
E-mail: iacbe@iacbe.org
Website: www.iacbe.org

CHIROPRACTIC
Dr. Craig S. Little, President
Council on Chiropractic Education (CCE)
Commission on Accreditation
8049 North 85th Way
Scottsdale, Arizona 85258-4321
Phone: 480-443-8877 or 888-443-3506
Fax: 480-483-7333
E-mail: cce@cce-usa.org
Website: www.cce-usa.org

CLINICAL LABORATORY SCIENCES
Dianne M. Cearlock, Ph.D., Chief Executive Officer
National Accrediting Agency for Clinical Laboratory Sciences
5600 North River Road, Suite 720
Rosemont, Illinois 60018-5119
Phone: 773-714-8880 or 847-939-3597
Fax: 773-714-8886
E-mail: info@naacls.org
Website: www.naacls.org

CLINICAL PASTORAL EDUCATION
Trace Haythorn, Ph.D., Executive Director/CEO
Association for Clinical Pastoral Education, Inc.
One West Court Square, Suite 325
Decatur, Georgia 30030-2576
Phone: 678-363-6226
Fax: 404-320-0849
E-mail: acpe@acpe.edu
Website: www.acpe.edu

DANCE
Karen P. Moynahan, Executive Director
National Association of Schools of Dance (NASD)
Commission on Accreditation
11250 Roger Bacon Drive, Suite 21
Reston, Virginia 20190-5248
Phone: 703-437-0700
Fax: 703-437-6312
E-mail: info@arts-accredit.org
Website: http://nasd.arts-accredit.org

DENTISTRY
Dr. Kathleen T. O'Loughlin, Executive Director
Commission on Dental Accreditation
American Dental Association
211 East Chicago Avenue
Chicago, Illinois 60611
Phone: 312-440-2500
E-mail: accreditation@ada.org
Website: www.ada.org

DIETETICS AND NUTRITION
Mary B. Gregoire, Ph.D., Executive Director; RD, FADA, FAND
Academy of Nutrition and Dietetics
Accreditation Council for Education in Nutrition and Dietetics (ACEND)
120 South Riverside Plaza
Chicago, Illinois 60606-6995
Phone: 800-877-1600 or 312-899-0040
E-mail: acend@eatright.org
Website: www.eatright.org/cade

EDUCATION PREPARATION
Christopher Koch, President
Council for the Accreditation of Educator Preparation (CAEP)
1140 19th Street NW, Suite 400
Washington, DC 20036
Phone: 202-223-0077
Fax: 202-296-6620
E-mail: caep@caepnet.org
Website: www.caepnet.org

ENGINEERING
Michael Milligan, Ph.D., PE, Executive Director
Accreditation Board for Engineering and Technology, Inc. (ABET)
415 North Charles Street
Baltimore, Maryland 21201
Phone: 410-347-7700
E-mail: accreditation@abet.org
Website: www.abet.org

FORENSIC SCIENCES
Nancy J. Jackson, Director of Development and Accreditation
American Academy of Forensic Sciences (AAFS)
Forensic Science Education Program Accreditation Commission (FEPAC)
410 North 21st Street
Colorado Springs, Colorado 80904
Phone: 719-636-1100
Fax: 719-636-1993
E-mail: njackson@aafs.org
Website: www.fepac-edu.org

FORESTRY
Carol L. Redelsheimer
Director of Science and Education
Society of American Foresters
10100 Laureate Way
Bethesda, Maryland 20814-2198
Phone: 301-897-8720 or 866-897-8720
Fax: 301-897-3690
E-mail: membership@safnet.org
Website: www.eforester.com

HEALTHCARE MANAGEMENT
Commission on Accreditation of Healthcare Management Education (CAHME)
Anthony Stanowski, President and CEO
6110 Executive Boulevard, Suite 614
Rockville, Maryland 20852
Phone: 301-298-1820
E-mail: info@cahme.org
Website: www.cahme.org

HEALTH INFORMATICS AND HEALTH MANAGEMENT
Angela Kennedy, EdD, MBA, RHIA, Chief Executive Officer
Commission on Accreditation for Health Informatics and Information Management Education (CAHIIM)
233 North Michigan Avenue, 21st Floor
Chicago, Illinois 60601-5800
Phone: 312-233-1134
Fax: 312-233-1948
E-mail: info@cahiim.org
Website: www.cahiim.org

HUMAN SERVICE EDUCATION
Dr. Elaine Green, President
Council for Standards in Human Service Education (CSHSE)
3337 Duke Street
Alexandria, Virginia 22314
Phone: 571-257-3959
E-mail: info@cshse.org
Website: www.cshse.org

INTERIOR DESIGN
Holly Mattson, Executive Director
Council for Interior Design Accreditation
206 Grandview Avenue, Suite 350
Grand Rapids, Michigan 49503-4014
Phone: 616-458-0400
Fax: 616-458-0460
E-mail: info@accredit-id.org
Website: www.accredit-id.org

JOURNALISM AND MASS COMMUNICATIONS
Patricia Thompson, Executive Director
Accrediting Council on Education in Journalism and Mass Communications (ACEJMC)
201 Bishop Hall
P.O. Box 1848
University, MS 38677-1848
Phone: 662-915-5504
E-mail: pthomps1@olemiss.edu
Website: www.acejmc.org

LANDSCAPE ARCHITECTURE
Nancy Somerville, Executive Vice President, CEO
American Society of Landscape Architects (ASLA)
636 Eye Street, NW
Washington, DC 20001-3736
Phone: 202-898-2444
Fax: 202-898-1185
E-mail: info@asla.org
Website: www.asla.org

LAW
Barry Currier, Managing Director of Accreditation & Legal Education
American Bar Association
321 North Clark Street, 21st Floor
Chicago, Illinois 60654
Phone: 312-988-6738
Fax: 312-988-5681
E-mail: legaled@americanbar.org
Website: https://www.americanbar.org/groups/legal_education/accreditation.html

LIBRARY
Karen O'Brien, Director
Office for Accreditation
American Library Association
50 East Huron Street
Chicago, Illinois 60611-2795
Phone: 800-545-2433, ext. 2432 or 312-280-2432
Fax: 312-280-2433
E-mail: accred@ala.org
Website: http://www.ala.org/aboutala/offices/accreditation/

MARRIAGE AND FAMILY THERAPY
Tanya A. Tamarkin, Director of Educational Affairs
Commission on Accreditation for Marriage and Family Therapy
    Education (COAMFTE)
American Association for Marriage and Family Therapy
112 South Alfred Street
Alexandria, Virginia 22314-3061
Phone: 703-838-9808
Fax: 703-838-9805
E-mail: coa@aamft.org
Website: www.aamft.org

MEDICAL ILLUSTRATION
Kathleen Megivern, Executive Director
Commission on Accreditation of Allied Health Education Programs
    (CAAHEP)
25400 US Highway 19 North, Suite 158
Clearwater, Florida 33756
Phone: 727-210-2350
Fax: 727-210-2354
E-mail: mail@caahep.org
Website: www.caahep.org

MEDICINE
Liaison Committee on Medical Education (LCME)
Robert B. Hash, M.D., LCME Secretary
American Medical Association
Council on Medical Education
330 North Wabash Avenue, Suite 39300
Chicago, Illinois 60611-5885
Phone: 312-464-4933
E-mail: lcme@aamc.org
Website: www.ama-assn.org

Liaison Committee on Medical Education (LCME)
Heather Lent, M.A., Director
Accreditation Services
Association of American Medical Colleges
655 K Street, NW
Washington, DC 20001-2399
Phone: 202-828-0596
E-mail: lcme@aamc.org
Website: www.lcme.org

MUSIC
Karen P. Moynahan, Executive Director
National Association of Schools of Music (NASM)
Commission on Accreditation
11250 Roger Bacon Drive, Suite 21
Reston, Virginia 20190-5248
Phone: 703-437-0700
Fax: 703-437-6312
E-mail: info@arts-accredit.org
Website: http://nasm.arts-accredit.org/

NATUROPATHIC MEDICINE
Daniel Seitz, J.D., Ed.D., Executive Director
Council on Naturopathic Medical Education
P.O. Box 178
Great Barrington, Massachusetts 01230
Phone: 413-528-8877
E-mail: https://cnme.org/contact-us/
Website: www.cnme.org

NURSE ANESTHESIA
Francis R.Gerbasi, Ph.D., CRNA, COA Executive Director
Council on Accreditation of Nurse Anesthesia Educational Programs
    (CoA-NAEP)
American Association of Nurse Anesthetists
222 South Prospect Avenue
Park Ridge, Illinois 60068-4001
Phone: 847-655-1160
Fax: 847-692-7137
E-mail: accreditation@coa.us.com
Website: http://www.coacrna.org

NURSE EDUCATION
Jennifer L. Butlin, Executive Director
Commission on Collegiate Nursing Education (CCNE)
One Dupont Circle, NW, Suite 530
Washington, DC 20036-1120
Phone: 202-887-6791
Fax: 202-887-8476
E-mail: jbutlin@aacn.nche.edu
Website: www.aacn.nche.edu/accreditation

Marsal P. Stoll, Chief Executive Officer
Accreditation Commission for Education in Nursing (ACEN)
3343 Peachtree Road, NE, Suite 850
Atlanta, Georgia 30326
Phone: 404-975-5000
Fax: 404-975-5020
E-mail: mstoll@acenursing.org
Website: www.acenursing.org

NURSE MIDWIFERY
Heather L. Maurer, M.A., Executive Director
Accreditation Commission for Midwifery Education (ACME)
American College of Nurse-Midwives
8403 Colesville Road, Suite 1550
Silver Spring, Maryland 20910
Phone: 240-485-1800
Fax: 240-485-1818
E-mail: info@acnm.org
Website: www.midwife.org/Program-Accreditation

NURSE PRACTITIONER
Gay Johnson, CEO
National Association of Nurse Practitioners in Women's Health
Council on Accreditation
505 C Street, NE
Washington, DC 20002
Phone: 202-543-9693 Ext. 1
Fax: 202-543-9858
E-mail: info@npwh.org
Website: www.npwh.org

NURSING
Marsal P. Stoll, Chief Executive Director
Accreditation Commission for Education in Nursing (ACEN)
3343 Peachtree Road, NE, Suite 850
Atlanta, Georgia 30326
Phone: 404-975-5000
Fax: 404-975-5020
E-mail: info@acenursing.org
Website: www.acenursing.org

OCCUPATIONAL THERAPY
Heather Stagliano, DHSc, OTR/L, Executive Director
The American Occupational Therapy Association, Inc.
4720 Montgomery Lane, Suite 200
Bethesda, Maryland 20814-3449
Phone: 301-652-6611 Ext. 2682
TDD: 800-377-8555
Fax: 240-762-5150
E-mail: accred@aota.org
Website: www.aoteonline.org

OPTOMETRY
Joyce L. Urbeck, Administrative Director
Accreditation Council on Optometric Education (ACOE)
American Optometric Association
243 North Lindbergh Boulevard
St. Louis, Missouri 63141-7881
Phone: 314-991-4100, Ext. 4246
Fax: 314-991-4101
E-mail: accredit@aoa.org
Website: www.theacoe.org

OSTEOPATHIC MEDICINE
Director, Department of Accreditation
Commission on Osteopathic College Accreditation (COCA)
American Osteopathic Association
142 East Ontario Street
Chicago, Illinois 60611
Phone: 312-202-8048
Fax: 312-202-8202
E-mail: predoc@osteopathic.org
Website: www.aoacoca.org

PHARMACY
Peter H. Vlasses, PharmD, Executive Director
Accreditation Council for Pharmacy Education
135 South LaSalle Street, Suite 4100
Chicago, Illinois 60603-4810
Phone: 312-664-3575
Fax: 312-664-4652
E-mail: csinfo@acpe-accredit.org
Website: www.acpe-accredit.org

PHYSICAL THERAPY
Sandra Wise, Senior Director
Commission on Accreditation in Physical Therapy Education (CAPTE)
American Physical Therapy Association (APTA)
1111 North Fairfax Street
Alexandria, Virginia 22314-1488
Phone: 703-706-3245
Fax: 703-706-3387
E-mail: accreditation@apta.org
Website: www.capteonline.org

PHYSICIAN ASSISTANT STUDIES
Sharon L. Luke, Executive Director
Accredittion Review Commission on Education for the Physician
    Assistant, Inc. (ARC-PA)
12000 Findley Road, Suite 275
Johns Creek, Georgia 30097
Phone: 770-476-1224
Fax: 770-476-1738
E-mail: arc-pa@arc-pa.org
Website: www.arc-pa.org

PLANNING
Jesmarie Soto Johnson, Executive Director
American Institute of Certified Planners/Association of Collegiate
    Schools of Planning/American Planning Association
Planning Accreditation Board (PAB)
2334 West Lawrence Avenue, Suite 209
Chicago, Illinois 60625
Phone: 773-334-7200
E-mail: smerits@planningaccreditationboard.org
Website: www.planningaccreditationboard.org

PODIATRIC MEDICINE
Heather Stagliano, OTR/L, DHSc, Executive Director
Council on Podiatric Medical Education (CPME)
American Podiatric Medical Association (APMA)
9312 Old Georgetown Road
Bethesda, Maryland 20814-1621
Phone: 301-581-9200
Fax: 301-571-4903
Website: www.cpme.org

PSYCHOLOGY AND COUNSELING
Jacqueline Remondet, Associate Executive Director, CEO of the
Accrediting Unit,
Office of Program Consultation and Accreditation
American Psychological Association
750 First Street, NE
Washington, DC 20002-4202
Phone: 202-336-5979 or 800-374-2721
TDD/TTY: 202-336-6123
Fax: 202-336-5978
E-mail: apaaccred@apa.org
Website: www.apa.org/ed/accreditation

Kelly Coker, Executive Director
Council for Accreditation of Counseling and Related Educational
    Programs (CACREP)
1001 North Fairfax Street, Suite 510
Alexandria, Virginia 22314
Phone: 703-535-5990
Fax: 703-739-6209
E-mail: cacrep@cacrep.org
Website: www.cacrep.org

Richard M. McFall, Executive Director
Psychological Clinical Science Accreditation System (PCSAS)
1101 East Tenth Street
IU Psychology Building
Bloomington, Indiana 47405-7007
Phone: 812-856-2570
Fax: 812-322-5545
E-mail: rmmcfall@pcsas.org
Website: www.pcsas.org

PUBLIC HEALTH
Laura Rasar King, M.P.H., MCHES, Executive Director
Council on Education for Public Health
1010 Wayne Avenue, Suite 220
Silver Spring, Maryland 20910
Phone: 202-789-1050
Fax: 202-789-1895
E-mail: Lking@ceph.org
Website: www.ceph.org

PUBLIC POLICY, AFFAIRS AND ADMINISTRATION
Crystal Calarusse, Chief Accreditation Officer
Commission on Peer Review and Accreditation
Network of Schools of Public Policy, Affairs, and Administration
(NASPAA-COPRA)
1029 Vermont Avenue, NW, Suite 1100
Washington, DC 20005
Phone: 202-628-8965
Fax: 202-626-4978
E-mail: copra@naspaa.org
Website: accreditation.naspaa.org

RADIOLOGIC TECHNOLOGY
Leslie Winter, Chief Executive Officer Joint Review Committee on
Education in Radiologic Technology (JRCERT)
20 North Wacker Drive, Suite 2850
Chicago, Illinois 60606-3182
Phone: 312-704-5300
Fax: 312-704-5304
E-mail: mail@jrcert.org
Website: www.jrcert.org

REHABILITATION EDUCATION
Frank Lane, Ph.D., Executive Director
Council for Accreditation of Counseling and Related Educational
    Programs (CACREP)
1001 North Fairfax Street, Suite 510
Alexandria, Virginia 22314
Phone: 703-535-5990
Fax: 703-739-6209
E-mail: cacrep@cacrep.org
Website: www.cacrep.org

RESPIRATORY CARE
Thomas Smalling, Executive Director
Commission on Accreditation for Respiratory Care (CoARC)
1248 Harwood Road
Bedford, Texas 76021-4244
Phone: 817-283-2835
Fax: 817-354-8519
E-mail: tom@coarc.com
Website: www.coarc.com

SOCIAL WORK
Dr. Stacey Borasky, Director of Accreditation
Office of Social Work Accreditation
Council on Social Work Education
1701 Duke Street, Suite 200
Alexandria, Virginia 22314
Phone: 703-683-8080
Fax: 703-519-2078
E-mail: info@cswe.org
Website: www.cswe.org

SPEECH-LANGUAGE PATHOLOGY AND AUDIOLOGY
Kimberlee Moore, Accreditation Executive Director
American Speech-Language-Hearing Association
Council on Academic Accreditation in Audiology and Speech-Language
    Pathology
2200 Research Boulevard #310
Rockville, Maryland 20850-3289
Phone: 301-296-5700
Fax: 301-296-8750
E-mail: accreditation@asha.org
Website: http://caa.asha.org

TEACHER EDUCATION
Christopher A. Koch, President
National Council for Accreditation of Teacher Education (NCATE)
Teacher Education Accreditation Council (TEAC)
1140 19th Street, Suite 400
Washington, DC 20036
Phone: 202-223-0077
Fax: 202-296-6620
E-mail: caep@caepnet.org
Website: www.ncate.org

TECHNOLOGY
Michale S. McComis, Ed.D., Executive Director
Accrediting Commission of Career Schools and Colleges
2101 Wilson Boulevard, Suite 302
Arlington, Virginia 22201
Phone: 703-247-4212
Fax: 703-247-4533
E-mail: mccomis@accsc.org
Website: www.accsc.org

TECHNOLOGY, MANAGEMENT, AND APPLIED ENGINEERING
Kelly Schild, Director of Accreditation
The Association of Technology, Management, and Applied Engineering
(ATMAE)
275 N. York Street, Suite 401
Elmhurst, Illinois 60126
Phone: 630-433-4514
Fax: 630-563-9181
E-mail: Kelly@atmae.org
Website: www.atmae.org

THEATER
Karen P. Moynahan, Executive Director
National Association of Schools of Theatre Commission on
    Accreditation
11250 Roger Bacon Drive, Suite 21
Reston, Virginia 20190
Phone: 703-437-0700
Fax: 703-437-6312
E-mail: info@arts-accredit.org
Website: http://nast.arts-accredit.org/

THEOLOGY
Dr. Bernard Fryshman, Executive VP
Emeritus and Interim Executive Director
Association of Advanced Rabbinical and Talmudic Schools (AARTS)
Accreditation Commission
11 Broadway, Suite 405
New York, New York 10004
Phone: 212-363-1991
Fax: 212-533-5335
E-mail: k.sharfman.aarts@gmail.com

Frank Yamada, Executive Director
Association of Theological Schools in the United States and Canada
    (ATS)
Commission on Accrediting
10 Summit Park Drive
Pittsburgh, Pennsylvania 15275
Phone: 412-788-6505
Fax: 412-788-6510
E-mail: ats@ats.edu
Website: www.ats.edu

Dr. Timothy Eaton, President
Transnational Association of Christian Colleges and Schools (TRACS)
Accreditation Commission
15935 Forest Road
Forest, Virginia 24551
Phone: 434-525-9539
Fax: 434-525-9538
E-mail: info@tracs.org
Website: www.tracs.org

VETERINARY MEDICINE
Dr. Karen Brandt, Director of Education and Research
American Veterinary Medical Association (AVMA)
Council on Education
1931 North Meacham Road, Suite 100
Schaumburg, Illinois 60173-4360
Phone: 847-925-8070 Ext. 6674
Fax: 847-285-5732
E-mail: info@avma.org
Website: www.avma.org

How to Use These Guides

As you identify the particular programs and institutions that interest you, you can use both the *Graduate & Professional Programs: An Overview* volume and the specialized volumes in the series to obtain detailed information.

- *Graduate Programs in the Biological/Biomedical Sciences & Health-Related Professions*
- *Graduate Programs in Business, Education, Information Studies, Law & Social Work*
- *Graduate Programs in Engineering & Applied Sciences*
- *Graduate Programs the Humanities, Arts & Social Sciences*
- *Graduate Programs in the Physical Sciences, Mathematics, Agricultural Sciences, the Environment & Natural Resources*

Each of the specialized volumes in the series is divided into sections that contain one or more directories devoted to programs in a particular field. If you do not find a directory devoted to your field of interest in a specific volume, consult "Directories and Subject Areas" (located at the end of each volume). After you have identified the correct volume, consult the "Directories and Subject Areas in This Book" index, which shows (as does the more general directory) what directories cover subjects not specifically named in a directory or section title.

Each of the specialized volumes in the series has a number of general directories. These directories have entries for the largest unit at an institution granting graduate degrees in that field. For example, the general Engineering and Applied Sciences directory in the *Graduate Programs in Engineering & Applied Sciences* volume consists of **Profiles** for colleges, schools, and departments of engineering and applied sciences.

General directories are followed by other directories, or sections, that give more detailed information about programs in particular areas of the general field that has been covered. The general Engineering and Applied Sciences directory, in the previous example, is followed by nineteen sections with directories in specific areas of engineering, such as Chemical Engineering, Industrial/Management Engineering, and Mechanical Engineering.

Because of the broad nature of many fields, any system of organization is bound to involve a certain amount of overlap. Environmental studies, for example, is a field whose various aspects are studied in several types of departments and schools. Readers interested in such studies will find information on relevant programs in the *Graduate Programs in the Biological/Biomedical Sciences & Health-Related Professions* volume under Ecology and Environmental Biology and Environmental and Occupational Health; in the *Graduate Programs in the Physical Sciences, Mathematics, Agricultural Sciences, the Environment & Natural Resources* volume under Environmental Management and Policy and Natural Resources; and in the *Graduate Programs in Engineering & Applied Sciences* volume under Energy Management and Policy and Environmental Engineering. To help you find all of the programs of interest to you, the introduction to each section within the specialized volumes includes, if applicable, a paragraph suggesting other sections and directories with information on related areas of study.

Directory of Institutions with Programs in the Humanities, Arts & Social Sciences

This directory lists institutions in alphabetical order and includes beneath each name the academic fields in which each institution offers graduate programs. The degree level in each field is also indicated, provided that the institution has supplied that information in response to Peterson's Annual Survey of Graduate and Professional Institutions.

An M indicates that a master's degree program is offered; a D indicates that a doctoral degree program is offered; an O signifies that other advanced degrees (e.g., certificates or specialist degrees) are offered; and an * (asterisk) indicates that a **Close-Up** and/or **Display** is located in this volume. See the index, "Close-Ups and Displays," for the specific page number.

Profiles of Academic and Professional Programs in the Specialized Volumes

Each section of **Profiles** has a table of contents that lists the Program Directories, **Displays**, and **Close-Ups.** Program Directories consist of the **Profiles** of programs in the relevant fields, with **Displays** following if programs have chosen to include them. **Close-Ups,** which are more individualized statements, are also listed for those graduate schools or programs that have chosen to submit them.

The **Profiles** found in the 500 directories in the specialized volumes provide basic data about the graduate units in capsule form for quick reference. To make these directories as useful as possible, **Profiles** are generally listed for an institution's smallest academic unit within a subject area. In other words, if an institution has a College of Liberal Arts that administers many related programs, the **Profile** for the individual program (e.g., Program in History), not the entire College, appears in the directory.

Some institutions maintain a "Premium Profile" at Peterson's where prospective students can find more in-depth school program descriptions and information. You can learn more about those schools by visiting **www.petersons.com.**

There are some programs that do not fit into any current directory and are not given individual **Profiles**. The directory structure is reviewed annually in order to keep this number to a minimum and to accommodate major trends in graduate education.

The following outline describes the **Profile** information found in the guides and explains how best to use that information. Any item that does not apply to or was not provided by a graduate unit is omitted from its listing. The format of the **Profiles** is constant, making it easy to compare one institution with another and one program with another.

Identifying Information. The institution's name, in boldface type, is followed by a complete listing of the administrative structure for that field of study. (For example, University of Akron, Buchtel College of Arts and Sciences, Department of Theoretical and Applied Mathematics, Program in Mathematics.) The last unit listed is the one to which all information in the **Profile** pertains. The institution's city, state, and ZIP code follow.

Offerings. Each field of study offered by the unit is listed with all postbaccalaureate degrees awarded. Degrees that are not preceded by a specific concentration are awarded in the general field listed in the unit name. Frequently, fields of study are broken down into subspecializations, and those appear following the degrees awarded; for example, "Offerings in secondary education (M.Ed.), including English education, mathematics education, science education." Students enrolled in the M.Ed. program would be able to specialize in any of the three fields mentioned.

Professional Accreditation. Some **Profiles** indicate whether a program is professionally accredited. Because it is possible for a program to receive or lose professional accreditation at any time, students entering fields in which accreditation is important to a career should verify the status of programs by contacting either the chairperson or the appropriate accrediting association.

Jointly Offered Degrees. Explanatory statements concerning programs that are offered in cooperation with other institutions are included in the list of degrees offered. This occurs most commonly on a regional basis (for example, two state universities offering a cooperative Ph.D. in special education) or where the specialized nature of the institutions encourages joint efforts (a J.D./M.B.A. offered by a law school at an institution with no formal business programs and an institution with a business school but lacking a law school). Only programs that are truly cooperative are listed; those involving only limited course work at another institution are not. Interested students should contact the heads of such units for further information.

Program Availability. This may include the following: part-time, evening/weekend, online only, blended/hybrid learning, and/or minimal on-campus study. When information regarding the availability of part-time or evening/weekend study appears in the **Profile**, it means that students are able to earn a degree exclusively through such study. Blended/hybrid learning describes those courses in which some traditional in-class time has been replaced by online learning activities. Hybrid courses take advantage of the best features of both face-to-face and online learning.

Faculty. Figures on the number of faculty members actively involved with graduate students through teaching or research are separated into full- and part-time as well as men and women whenever the information has been supplied.

Students. Figures for the number of students enrolled in graduate and professional programs pertain to the semester of highest enrollment from the 2019-20 academic year. These figures are broken down into full-and part-time and men and women whenever the data have been supplied. Information on the number of matriculated students enrolled in the unit who are members of a minority group or are international students appears here. The average age of the matriculated students is followed by the number of applicants, the percentage accepted, and the number enrolled for fall 2019.

Degrees Awarded. The number of degrees awarded in the calendar year is listed. Many doctoral programs offer a terminal master's degree if students leave the program after completing only part of the requirements for a doctoral degree; that is indicated here. All degrees are classified into one of four types: master's, doctoral, first professional, and other advanced degrees. A unit may award one or several degrees at a given level; however, the data are only collected by type and may therefore represent several different degree programs.

Degree Requirements. The information in this section is also broken down by type of degree, and all information for a degree level pertains to all degrees of that type unless otherwise specified. Degree requirements are collected in a simplified form to provide some very basic information on the nature of the program and on foreign language, thesis or dissertation, comprehensive exam, and registration requirements. Many units also provide a short list of additional requirements, such as fieldwork or an internship. For complete information on graduation requirements, contact the graduate school or program directly.

Entrance Requirements. Entrance requirements are broken down into the four degree levels of master's, doctoral, first professional, and other advanced degrees. Within each level, information may be provided in two basic categories: entrance exams and other requirements. The entrance exams are identified by the standard acronyms used by the testing agencies, unless they are not well known. Other entrance requirements are quite varied, but they often contain an undergraduate or graduate grade point average (GPA). Unless otherwise stated, the GPA is calculated on a 4.0 scale and is listed as a minimum required for admission. Additional exam requirements/recommendations for international students may be listed here. Application deadlines for domestic and international students, the application fee, and whether electronic applications are accepted may be listed here. Note that the deadline should be used for reference only; these dates are subject to change, and students interested in applying should always contact the graduate unit directly about application procedures and deadlines.

Expenses. The typical cost of study for the 2019-20 academic year (2018-19 if 2019-20 figures were not available) is given in two basic categories: tuition and fees. Cost of study may be quite complex at a graduate institution. There are often sliding scales for part-time study, a different cost for first-year students, and other variables that make it impossible to completely cover the cost of study for each graduate program. To provide the most usable information, figures are given for full-time study for a full year where available and for part-time study in terms of a per-unit rate (per credit, per semester hour, etc.). Occasionally, variances may be noted in tuition and fees for reasons such as the type of program, whether courses are taken during the day or evening, whether courses are at the master's or doctoral level, or other institution-specific reasons. Respondents were also given the opportunity to provide more specific and detailed tuition and fees information at the unit level. When provided, this information will appear in place of any typical costs entered elsewhere on the university-level survey. Expenses are usually subject to change; for exact costs at any given time, contact your chosen schools and programs directly. Keep in mind that the tuition of Canadian institutions is usually given in Canadian dollars.

Financial Support. This section contains data on the number of awards administered by the institution and given to graduate students during the 2019-20 academic year. The first figure given represents the total number of students receiving financial support enrolled in that unit. If the unit has provided information on graduate appointments, these are broken down into three major categories: fellowships give money to graduate students to cover the cost of study and living expenses and are not based on a work obligation or research commitment, research assistantships provide stipends to graduate students for assistance in a formal research project with a faculty member, and teaching assistantships provide stipends to graduate students for teaching or for assisting faculty members in teaching undergraduate classes. Within each category, figures are given for the total number of awards, the average yearly amount per award, and whether full or partial tuition reimbursements are awarded. In addition to graduate appointments, the availability of several other financial aid sources is covered in this section. Tuition waivers are routinely part of a graduate appointment, but units sometimes waive part or all of a student's tuition even if a graduate appointment is not available. Federal Work Study is made available to students who demonstrate need and meet the federal guidelines; this form of aid normally includes 10 or more hours of work per week in an office of the institution. Institutionally sponsored loans are low-interest loans available to graduate students to cover both educational and living expenses. Career-related internships or fieldwork offer money to students who are participating in a formal off-campus research project or practicum. Grants, scholarships, traineeships, unspecified assistantships, and other awards may also be noted. The availability of financial support to part-time students is also indicated here.

Some programs list the financial aid application deadline and the forms that need to be completed for students to be eligible for financial awards. There are two forms: FAFSA, the Free Application for Federal Student Aid, which is required for federal aid, and the CSS PROFILE®.

Faculty Research. Each unit has the opportunity to list several keyword phrases describing the current research involving faculty members and graduate students. Space limitations prevent the unit from listing complete information on all research programs. The total expenditure for funded research from the previous academic year may also be included.

Unit Head and Application Contact. The head of the graduate program for each unit may be listed with academic title, phone and fax numbers, and e-mail address. In addition to the unit head's contact information, many graduate programs also list a separate contact for application and admission information, followed by the graduate school, program, or department's website. If no unit head or application contact is given, you should contact the overall institution for information on graduate admissions.

Displays and Close-Ups

Any **Displays** and **Close-Ups** are supplementary insertions submitted by deans, chairs, and other administrators who wish to offer an additional, more individualized statement to readers. A number of graduate school and program administrators have attached a **Display** ad near the **Profile** listing. Here you will find information that an institution or program wants to emphasize. The **Close-Ups** are by their very nature more expansive and flexible than the **Profiles**, and the administrators who have written them may emphasize different aspects of their programs. All of the **Close-Ups** are organized in the same way (with the exception of a few that describe research and training opportunities instead of degree programs), and in each one you will find information on the same basic topics, such as programs of study, research facilities, tuition and fees, financial aid, and application procedures. If an institution or program has submitted a **Close-Up**, a boldface cross-reference appears below its **Profile**. As with the **Displays**, all of the **Close-Ups** in the guides have been submitted by choice; the absence of a **Display** or **Close-Up** does not reflect any type of editorial judgment on the part of Peterson's, and their presence in the guides should not be taken as an indication of status, quality, or approval. Statements regarding a university's objectives and accomplishments are a reflection of its own beliefs and are not the opinions of the Peterson's editors.

Appendixes

This section contains two appendixes. The first, "Institutional Changes Since the 2020 Edition," lists institutions that have closed, merged, or changed their name or status since the last edition of the guides. The second, "Abbreviations Used in the Guides," gives abbreviations of degree names, along with what those abbreviations stand for. These appendixes are identical in all six volumes of *Peterson's Graduate and Professional Programs*.

Indexes

There are three indexes presented here, typically. When present, the first index, "Close-Ups and Displays," gives page references for all programs that have chosen to place **Close-Ups** and **Displays** in this volume. It is arranged alphabetically by institution; within institutions, the arrangement is alphabetical by subject area. It is not an index to all programs in the book's directories of **Profiles**; readers must refer to the directories themselves for **Profile** information on programs that have not submitted the additional, more individualized statements. The next index, "Directories and Subject Areas in Other Books in This Series", gives book references for the directories in the specialized volumes and also includes cross-references for subject area names not used in the directory structure, for example, "Computing Technology (see Computer Science)." The last index, "Directories and Subject Areas in This Book," gives page references for the directories in this volume and cross-references for subject area names not used in this volume's directory structure.

Data Collection Procedures

The information published in the directories and Profiles of all the books is collected through Peterson's Annual Survey of Graduate and Professional Institutions. The survey is sent each spring to nearly 2,300 institutions offering postbaccalaureate degree programs, including accredited institutions in the United States, U.S. territories, and Canada and those institutions outside the United States that are accredited by U.S. accrediting bodies. Deans and other administrators complete these surveys, providing information on programs in the 500 academic and professional fields covered in the guides as well as overall institutional information. While every effort has been made to ensure the accuracy and completeness of the data, information is sometimes unavailable or changes occur after publication deadlines. All usable information received in time for publication has been included. The omission of any particular item from a directory or Profile signifies either that the item is not applicable to the institution or program or that information was not available. Profiles of programs scheduled to begin during the 2018–19 academic year cannot, obviously, include statistics on enrollment or, in many cases, the number of faculty members. If no usable data were submitted by an institution, its name, address, and program name appear in order to indicate the availability of graduate work.

Criteria for Inclusion in This Guide

To be included in this guide, an institution must have full accreditation or be a candidate for accreditation (preaccreditation) status by an institutional or specialized accrediting body recognized by the U.S. Department of Education or the Council for Higher Education Accreditation (CHEA). Institutional accrediting bodies, which review each institution as a whole, include the six regional associations of schools and colleges (Middle States, New England, North Central, Northwest, Southern, and Western), each of which is responsible for a specified portion of the United States and its territories. Other institutional accrediting bodies are national in scope and accredit specific kinds of institutions (e.g., Bible colleges, independent colleges, and rabbinical and Talmudic schools). Program registration by the New York State Board of Regents is considered to be the equivalent of institutional accreditation, since the board requires that all programs offered by an institution meet its standards before recognition is granted. A Canadian institution must be chartered and authorized to grant degrees by the provincial government, affiliated with a chartered institution, or accredited by a recognized U.S. accrediting body. This guide also includes institutions outside the United States that are accredited by these U.S. accrediting bodies. There are recognized specialized or professional accrediting bodies in more than fifty different fields, each of which is authorized to accredit institutions or specific programs in its particular field. For specialized institutions that offer programs in one field only, we designate this to be the equivalent of institutional accreditation. A full explanation of the accrediting process and complete information on recognized institutional (regional and national) and specialized accrediting bodies can be found online at **www.chea.org** or at **www.ed.gov/admins/finaid/accred/index.html**.

DIRECTORY OF INSTITUTIONS WITH PROGRAMS IN THE HUMANITIES, ARTS & SOCIAL SCIENCES

ABILENE CHRISTIAN UNIVERSITY

Clinical Psychology	M,O
Communication—General	M
Counseling Psychology	M,O
English	M
Liberal Studies	M
Marriage and Family Therapy	M
Missions and Missiology	M,D
Pastoral Ministry and Counseling	M,D
Psychology—General	M,O
Religion	M,D
Rhetoric	M
School Psychology	M,O
Theology	M,D
Writing	M

ACADEMY FOR JEWISH RELIGION CALIFORNIA

Jewish Studies	M

ACADEMY OF ART UNIVERSITY

Applied Arts and Design—General	M
Architecture	M
Art History	M
Art/Fine Arts	M
Arts Journalism	M
Computer Art and Design	M
Film, Television, and Video Production	M
Graphic Design	M
Illustration	M
Industrial Design	M
Interior Design	M
Internet and Interactive Multimedia	M
Landscape Architecture	M
Music	M
Photography	M
Textile Design	M
Theater	M
Writing	M

ACADIA UNIVERSITY

Clinical Psychology	M
English	M
Geographic Information Systems	M
Missions and Missiology	M,D
Pastoral Ministry and Counseling	M,D
Philosophy	M
Political Science	M
Psychology—General	M
Sociology	M
Theology	M,D

ADAMS STATE UNIVERSITY

Clinical Psychology	M,D
History	M
Humanities	M
Public Administration	M
Sport Psychology	M

ADELPHI UNIVERSITY

Art/Fine Arts	M
Clinical Psychology	D
Counseling Psychology	M
Emergency Management	O
Psychology—General	M
School Psychology	M
Writing	M

ADLER UNIVERSITY

Art Therapy	M,D
Clinical Psychology	M,D
Criminal Justice and Criminology	M
Forensic Psychology	M
Health Psychology	M
Industrial and Organizational Psychology	M
Marriage and Family Therapy	M,D
Public Administration	M
Public Policy	M
Rehabilitation Counseling	M
School Psychology	M
Social Psychology	M
Sport Psychology	M

ADRIAN COLLEGE

Criminal Justice and Criminology	M

AGNES SCOTT COLLEGE

Internet and Interactive Multimedia	M
Writing	M

ALABAMA AGRICULTURAL AND MECHANICAL UNIVERSITY

Child and Family Studies	M
Clinical Psychology	M,O
Clothing and Textiles	M
Counseling Psychology	M,O
Family and Consumer Sciences-General	M
Human Development	M
Psychology—General	M,O
Rehabilitation Counseling	M,O
School Psychology	M,O
Urban and Regional Planning	M

ALABAMA STATE UNIVERSITY

Forensic Sciences	M
History	M
Rehabilitation Counseling	M

ALASKA PACIFIC UNIVERSITY

Counseling Psychology	M
Interdisciplinary Studies	M
Liberal Studies	M

ALBANY STATE UNIVERSITY

Criminal Justice and Criminology	M
Economic Development	M
Economics	M
Public Administration	M
Public Policy	M

ALBERTUS MAGNUS COLLEGE

Art Therapy	M
Criminal Justice and Criminology	M
Liberal Studies	M
Writing	M

ALBIZU UNIVERSITY - MIAMI

Clinical Psychology	M,D
Counseling Psychology	M,D
Industrial and Organizational Psychology	M,D
Marriage and Family Therapy	M,D
Psychology—General	M,D

ALBIZU UNIVERSITY - SAN JUAN

Clinical Psychology	M,D
Industrial and Organizational Psychology	M,D
Psychology—General	M,D

ALCORN STATE UNIVERSITY

Agricultural Economics and Agribusiness	M

ALFRED UNIVERSITY

Applied Arts and Design—General	M
Art/Fine Arts	M,D
Computer Art and Design	M
Counseling Psychology	M,D,O
Internet and Interactive Multimedia	M
Public Administration	M
School Psychology	M,D,O

ALLIANT INTERNATIONAL UNIVERSITY–FRESNO

Clinical Psychology	D
Forensic Psychology	D
Industrial and Organizational Psychology	M,D
Psychology—General	M,D

ALLIANT INTERNATIONAL UNIVERSITY–IRVINE

Forensic Psychology	D
Forensic Sciences	D
Marriage and Family Therapy	M,D
School Psychology	M,D,O

ALLIANT INTERNATIONAL UNIVERSITY - LOS ANGELES

Addictions/Substance Abuse Counseling	M
Clinical Psychology	D
Forensic Psychology	D
Gerontology	M
Health Psychology	D
Industrial and Organizational Psychology	M,D
Marriage and Family Therapy	M,D
Psychology—General	M,D
School Psychology	M,D,O
Social Psychology	D

ALLIANT INTERNATIONAL UNIVERSITY–SACRAMENTO

Clinical Psychology	D
Forensic Psychology	D
Marriage and Family Therapy	M,D
Psychology—General	M,D

ALLIANT INTERNATIONAL UNIVERSITY - SAN DIEGO

Clinical Psychology	M,D
Industrial and Organizational Psychology	M,D
Marriage and Family Therapy	M,D
Psychology—General	M,D
School Psychology	M,D,O

ALLIANT INTERNATIONAL UNIVERSITY–SAN FRANCISCO

Clinical Psychology	M,D,O
Criminal Justice and Criminology	M
Forensic Psychology	M,D
Industrial and Organizational Psychology	M,D
Psychology—General	M,D,O
School Psychology	M,D,O

ALVERNIA UNIVERSITY

Liberal Studies	M
Social Psychology	M

ALVERNO COLLEGE

Social Psychology	M

AMBERTON UNIVERSITY

Child and Family Studies	M
Counseling Psychology	M
Interdisciplinary Studies	M
Marriage and Family Therapy	M

AMBROSE UNIVERSITY

Pastoral Ministry and Counseling	M,O
Religion	M,O
Theology	M,O

AMERICAN BAPTIST SEMINARY OF THE WEST

Pastoral Ministry and Counseling	M
Theology	M

AMERICAN COLLEGE DUBLIN

Writing	M

AMERICAN CONSERVATORY THEATER

Theater	M,O

AMERICAN FILM INSTITUTE CONSERVATORY

Film, Television, and Video Production	M

AMERICAN GRADUATE SCHOOL IN PARIS

International Affairs	M,D

AMERICAN INTERCONTINENTAL UNIVERSITY ONLINE

Industrial and Organizational Psychology	M

AMERICAN INTERNATIONAL COLLEGE

Clinical Psychology	M,D,O
Counseling Psychology	M,D
Forensic Psychology	M,D,O
Psychology—General	M,D,O

AMERICAN JEWISH UNIVERSITY

Jewish Studies	M
Theology	M

AMERICAN MUSEUM OF NATURAL HISTORY–RICHARD GILDER GRADUATE SCHOOL

Museum Studies	D

AMERICAN PUBLIC UNIVERSITY SYSTEM

American Studies	M,D
Conflict Resolution and Mediation/Peace Studies	M,D
Criminal Justice and Criminology	M,D
History	M,D
International Affairs	M,D
Military and Defense Studies	M,D
National Security	M,D
Political Science	M,D
Public Policy	M,D

AMERICAN UNIVERSITY

American Studies	M,D,O
Anthropology	M,D,O
Applied Social Research	M,O
Art History	M
Arts Administration	M,O
Asian Studies	O
Broadcast Journalism	M
Clinical Psychology	M,D,O
Cognitive Sciences	M,D,O
Communication—General	M,D
Comparative Literature	M
Conflict Resolution and Mediation/Peace Studies	M,D,O
Corporate and Organizational Communication	M
Criminal Justice and Criminology	M,D
Cultural Studies	M,D,O
Economics	M,D,O
Ethics	M,D,O
Film, Television, and Video Production	M
French	M,O
Gender Studies	M,D,O
History	M,D
International Affairs	M,D,O
International Development	M,D,O
International Economics	M,D,O
Journalism	M
Latin American Studies	M,O
Mass Communication	M,D,O
Media Studies	M,D
Music	M,O
National Security	M,D,O
Philosophy	M
Political Science	M,D,O
Psychology—General	M,D,O
Public Administration	M,D,O
Public Policy	M,D,O
Russian	M,O
Sociology	M,O
Spanish	M,O
Sustainable Development	M,D,O
Western European Studies	M,D,O
Women's Studies	O
Writing	M

THE AMERICAN UNIVERSITY IN CAIRO

Broadcast Journalism	M,O
Communication—General	M,D,O
Comparative Literature	M,O
Economic Development	M,O
Economics	M,O
English	M,O
Gender Studies	M,O
Humanities	M,O
International Affairs	M,O
Journalism	M,O
Mass Communication	M,O
Near and Middle Eastern Languages	M,O
Near and Middle Eastern Studies	M,O
Philosophy	M,O
Psychology—General	M,O
Public Administration	M,O
Public Policy	M,O
Sustainable Development	M,D,O
Women's Studies	M,O

AMERICAN UNIVERSITY OF ARMENIA

Economics	M
International Affairs	M
Political Science	M

THE AMERICAN UNIVERSITY OF PARIS

Communication—General	M
Conflict Resolution and Mediation/Peace Studies	M
Cultural Studies	M
International Affairs	M
Near and Middle Eastern Studies	M
Public Policy	M

AMERICAN UNIVERSITY OF PUERTO RICO - BAYAMON

Criminal Justice and Criminology	M

THE AMERICAN UNIVERSITY OF ROME

Arts Administration	M
Conflict Resolution and Mediation/Peace Studies	M
Historic Preservation	M
Religion	M

AMERICAN UNIVERSITY OF SHARJAH

Translation and Interpretation	M,D
Urban and Regional Planning	M,D

AMRIDGE UNIVERSITY

Counseling Psychology	M,D
Marriage and Family Therapy	M,D
Pastoral Ministry and Counseling	M,D
Religion	M,D
Theology	M,D

ANABAPTIST MENNONITE BIBLICAL SEMINARY

Conflict Resolution and Mediation/Peace Studies	M,O
Ethics	M,O
International Affairs	M,O
Pastoral Ministry and Counseling	M,O
Public Administration	M,O
Theology	M,O

ANDERSON UNIVERSITY (IN)

Missions and Missiology	M,D
Theology	M,D

ANDERSON UNIVERSITY (SC)

Criminal Justice and Criminology	M
Pastoral Ministry and Counseling	M,D

ANDREWS UNIVERSITY

Architecture	M
Clinical Psychology	M
Communication—General	M
Counseling Psychology	M,D
Developmental Psychology	M,D
Economics	M
English	M
International Development	M
Music	M
Pastoral Ministry and Counseling	M,D,O
Psychology—General	M,D,O
School Psychology	M,O
Social Psychology	M
Theology	M,D,O
Urban and Regional Planning	M

ANGELO STATE UNIVERSITY

Communication—General	M
Criminal Justice and Criminology	M
English	M
Homeland Security	M
Industrial and Organizational Psychology	M
Media Studies	M
National Security	M
Psychology—General	M
Sociology	M

ANNA MARIA COLLEGE

Art/Fine Arts	M,O
Counseling Psychology	M
Criminal Justice and Criminology	M
Emergency Management	M,O
Industrial and Organizational Psychology	M
Public Administration	M

ANTIOCH UNIVERSITY LOS ANGELES

Clinical Psychology	M
Psychology—General	M
Sustainable Development	M

ANTIOCH UNIVERSITY NEW ENGLAND

Addictions/Substance Abuse Counseling	M,D,O
Applied Behavior Analysis	M,D,O
Applied Psychology	M,D,O
Clinical Psychology	M,D,O
Counseling Psychology	M,D,O
Interdisciplinary Studies	M,D
Marriage and Family Therapy	M,D,O
Sustainable Development	M,D
Therapies—Dance, Drama, and Music	M,D,O

ANTIOCH UNIVERSITY SANTA BARBARA

Clinical Psychology	M,D
Writing	M

ANTIOCH UNIVERSITY SEATTLE

Clinical Psychology	M,D
Marriage and Family Therapy	M,D
Therapies—Dance, Drama, and Music	M

APEX SCHOOL OF THEOLOGY

Theology	M,D

APPALACHIAN BIBLE COLLEGE

Pastoral Ministry and Counseling	M

APPALACHIAN STATE UNIVERSITY

American Studies	M
Clinical Psychology	M
Counseling Psychology	M
Cultural Studies	M
English	M
Geographic Information Systems	M
Geography	M
Health Psychology	M
History	M
Marriage and Family Therapy	M
Music	M
Political Science	M
Psychology—General	M
Public Administration	M
School Psychology	M
Therapies—Dance, Drama, and Music	M

AQUINAS INSTITUTE OF THEOLOGY

Music	M,D,O
Pastoral Ministry and Counseling	M,D,O
Theology	M,D,O

ARCADIA UNIVERSITY

Applied Behavior Analysis	M

Conflict Resolution and Mediation/Peace Studies M
Counseling Psychology M
English M
Forensic Sciences M
Marriage and Family Therapy M
Psychology—General M,D,O
Theater M,D,O
Writing M

ARGOSY UNIVERSITY, ATLANTA
Clinical Psychology M,D,O
Forensic Psychology M,D,O
Health Psychology M,D,O
Industrial and Organizational Psychology M,D,O
Marriage and Family Therapy M,D,O
Psychology—General M,D,O
Social Psychology M,D,O
Sport Psychology M,D,O

ARGOSY UNIVERSITY, CHICAGO
Clinical Psychology M,D
Counseling Psychology D
Forensic Psychology D
Health Psychology D
Human Development D
Industrial and Organizational Psychology M,D
Marriage and Family Therapy D
Psychoanalysis and Psychotherapy D
Psychology—General M,D
Public Administration M,D
Social Psychology M,D

ARGOSY UNIVERSITY, HAWAII
Addictions/Substance Abuse Counseling O
Clinical Psychology M,D,O
Counseling Psychology D
Forensic Psychology M
Marriage and Family Therapy M
Psychology—General M,D,O
School Psychology M

ARGOSY UNIVERSITY, LOS ANGELES
Clinical Psychology M,D
Counseling Psychology M,D
Forensic Psychology M,D
Marriage and Family Therapy M,D
Psychology—General M,D
Public Administration M,D

ARGOSY UNIVERSITY, NORTHERN VIRGINIA
Clinical Psychology M,D
Counseling Psychology M,D
Forensic Psychology M,D
Health Psychology M,D
Marriage and Family Therapy M,D
Psychology—General M,D
Public Administration M,D,O
Social Psychology M,D

ARGOSY UNIVERSITY, ORANGE COUNTY
Clinical Psychology M,D
Counseling Psychology M,D
Forensic Psychology M
Marriage and Family Therapy M,D
Psychology—General M,D
Public Administration M,D,O
Sport Psychology M

ARGOSY UNIVERSITY, PHOENIX
Clinical Psychology M,D
Counseling Psychology M
Forensic Psychology M
Industrial and Organizational Psychology M
Psychology—General M,D
Public Administration M,D
School Psychology M,D
Sport Psychology M,D

ARGOSY UNIVERSITY, SEATTLE
Clinical Psychology M,D,O
Counseling Psychology M,D
Psychology—General M,D,O
Public Administration M,D

ARGOSY UNIVERSITY, TAMPA
Clinical Psychology M,D
Counseling Psychology M,D
Industrial and Organizational Psychology M,D
Marriage and Family Therapy M,D
Psychology—General M,D
Public Administration M,D

ARGOSY UNIVERSITY, TWIN CITIES
Clinical Psychology M,D,O
Forensic Psychology M,D,O
Health Psychology M,D,O
Industrial and Organizational Psychology M,D,O
Marriage and Family Therapy M,D,O
Psychology—General M,D,O
Public Administration M,D

ARIZONA STATE UNIVERSITY AT TEMPE
African Studies M,D,O
Agricultural Economics and Agribusiness D
Anthropology M,D,O
Applied Arts and Design—General M,D
Applied Behavior Analysis M,D
Applied Psychology M
Archaeology M,D,O
Architectural History D
Architecture M,D
Art History M,D
Art/Fine Arts M,D
Arts Administration M,D
Building Science M,D
Child and Family Studies M,D
Chinese M,D
Clinical Psychology M,D
Cognitive Sciences M,D
Communication—General M,D
Comparative Literature M,D,O
Counseling Psychology D
Criminal Justice and Criminology M,D,O
Cultural Studies M,D
Dance M
Developmental Psychology M,D
Economics D
Emergency Management M,D
English M,D,O
Environmental Design D
Ethics M,D
Film, Television, and Video Production M
French M
Gender Studies M,D,O
Geographic Information Systems M,D,O
Geography M,D,O
German M
Gerontology M,D,O
History of Science and Technology M,D
History M,D,O
Homeland Security M,D
Human Development M,D
Interdisciplinary Studies M
Japanese M
Journalism M,D
Landscape Architecture M,D
Liberal Studies M
Linguistics M,D,O
Marriage and Family Therapy M,D
Mass Communication M,D
Media Studies M,D
Medieval and Renaissance Studies M,D,O
Museum Studies M,D,O
Music M,D
Philosophy M,D,O
Political Science M,D
Psychology—General M,D
Public Administration M,D
Public Affairs M,D
Public History M,D,O
Public Policy M,D
Publishing M,D,O
Religion M,D,O
Rhetoric M,D,O
Social Psychology M,D
Sociology M,D
Spanish M,D
Sustainable Development M,D,O
Textile Design M,D
Theater M,D
Therapies—Dance, Drama, and Music M,D
Translation and Interpretation M,D,O
Urban and Regional Planning M,D,O
Urban Design M,D
Urban Studies M,D,O
Writing M,D

ARKANSAS STATE UNIVERSITY
Addictions/Substance Abuse Counseling M,O
Clinical Psychology M,O
Communication—General M,O
Criminal Justice and Criminology M,O
Emergency Management M,O
English M,O
Gerontology M,D,O
Health Communication M,O
Historic Preservation M,D
History M,O
Journalism M
Mass Communication M
Media Studies M
Music M,O
Political Science M,O
Public Administration M,O
Rehabilitation Counseling M,O
School Psychology M,O
Sociology M,O

ARKANSAS TECH UNIVERSITY
Emergency Management M
English M
History M
Journalism M
Liberal Studies M
Psychology—General M
Sociology M

ARLINGTON BAPTIST UNIVERSITY
Theology M

ARTCENTER COLLEGE OF DESIGN
Art/Fine Arts M
Computer Art and Design M
Environmental Design M
Film, Television, and Video Production M
Graphic Design M
Industrial Design M

THE ART INSTITUTE OF DALLAS, A BRANCH OF MIAMI INTERNATIONAL UNIVERSITY OF ART & DESIGN
Applied Arts and Design—General M

ASBURY THEOLOGICAL SEMINARY
Missions and Missiology M,D,O
Pastoral Ministry and Counseling M,D,O
Theology M,D,O

ASBURY UNIVERSITY
Child and Family Studies M
Classics M
English M
French M
Spanish M
Writing M

ASHLAND THEOLOGICAL SEMINARY
Clinical Psychology M,D
Pastoral Ministry and Counseling M,D
Theology M,D

ASHLAND UNIVERSITY
Communication—General M
Corporate and Organizational Communication M
History M
Political Science M
Writing M

ASHWORTH COLLEGE
Criminal Justice and Criminology M

ASSEMBLIES OF GOD THEOLOGICAL SEMINARY
Cultural Studies M,D
Missions and Missiology M,D
Pastoral Ministry and Counseling M,D
Theology M,D

ASSUMPTION UNIVERSITY
Addictions/Substance Abuse Counseling O
Applied Behavior Analysis M,O
Child and Family Studies M,O
Counseling Psychology M,O
Economics M,O
Rehabilitation Counseling M,O
School Psychology M,O
Social Sciences O

ATHABASCA UNIVERSITY
Applied Psychology M,O
Architecture M,O
Art Therapy M,O
Counseling Psychology M,O
Cultural Studies M,O
Interdisciplinary Studies M,O
International Development M,O

THE ATHENAEUM OF OHIO
Theology M,O

ATHENS STATE UNIVERSITY
Religion M

ATLANTIC SCHOOL OF THEOLOGY
Pastoral Ministry and Counseling M,O
Theology M,O

ATLANTIC UNIVERSITY
Pastoral Ministry and Counseling O
Psychoanalysis and Psychotherapy O
Transpersonal and Humanistic Psychology M

ATLANTIC UNIVERSITY COLLEGE
Graphic Design M

A.T. STILL UNIVERSITY
Sport Psychology M,D,O

AUBURN UNIVERSITY
Agricultural Economics and Agribusiness M
Applied Economics M,D
Architecture M
Child and Family Studies M,D
Clothing and Textiles M,D
Communication—General M,O
Economics M,D
English M,D,O
Geography M
History M,D,O
Human Development M,D
Industrial Design M
Landscape Architecture M
Political Science M,D,O
Psychology—General M,D
Public Administration M,D,O
Rural Sociology M
Sociology M
Spanish M
Technical Communication M,D,O
Urban and Regional Planning M

AUBURN UNIVERSITY AT MONTGOMERY
Applied Economics M
Clinical Psychology M,O
Economics M
Geographic Information Systems M
Political Science M,D
Psychology—General M
Public Administration M,D
Public Policy M,D
School Psychology M,O
Writing M

AUGUSTANA UNIVERSITY
Genetic Counseling M

AUGUSTA UNIVERSITY
Clinical Psychology M,O
Medical Illustration M
Psychology—General M
School Psychology M,O
Social Sciences M

AURORA UNIVERSITY
Applied Behavior Analysis M,D
Homeland Security M
Public Policy M

AUSTIN PEAY STATE UNIVERSITY
Clinical Psychology M
Communication—General M
Corporate and Organizational Communication M
Counseling Psychology M
English M
Industrial and Organizational Psychology M
Media Studies M
Military and Defense Studies M
Music M
Psychology—General M

AUSTIN PRESBYTERIAN THEOLOGICAL SEMINARY
Pastoral Ministry and Counseling M,D
Theology M,D

AVE MARIA UNIVERSITY
Pastoral Ministry and Counseling M,D
Theology M,D

AVILA UNIVERSITY
Counseling Psychology M
Psychology—General M

AZUSA PACIFIC UNIVERSITY
Art/Fine Arts M
Clinical Psychology D
Developmental Psychology M
English M
Ethics M
Experimental Psychology M
Film, Television, and Video Production M
Industrial and Organizational Psychology M
Marriage and Family Therapy D
Music M
Pastoral Ministry and Counseling M
Psychology—General M
School Psychology M,D
Theology M,D
Urban Studies M

BABEL UNIVERSITY PROFESSIONAL SCHOOL OF TRANSLATION
Translation and Interpretation M

BAKER UNIVERSITY
Liberal Studies M

BAKKE GRADUATE UNIVERSITY
Pastoral Ministry and Counseling M,D
Theology M,D

BALL STATE UNIVERSITY
Anthropology M,O
Applied Behavior Analysis M
Architecture M
Art/Fine Arts M
Clinical Psychology M,D
Cognitive Sciences M
Communication—General M,O
Counseling Psychology M,D
Criminal Justice and Criminology M,O
Economic Development M,O
Emergency Management M,O
English M,D
Family and Consumer Sciences-General M
Geographic Information Systems M,O
Geography M,O
Historic Preservation M
History M
Homeland Security M,O
Human Development M,D,O
Interior Design M
Internet and Interactive Multimedia M
Journalism M
Landscape Architecture M
Linguistics M
Music M,D,O
Photography M
Political Science M
Psychology—General M
Public Administration M,O
Rehabilitation Counseling M,D
Rhetoric M,D
School Psychology M,D,O
Social Psychology M
Sociology M
Speech and Interpersonal Communication M
Sport Psychology M
Urban and Regional Planning M,O
Urban Design M
Writing M,D

BANK STREET COLLEGE OF EDUCATION
Child and Family Studies M

BAPTIST BIBLE COLLEGE
Pastoral Ministry and Counseling M
Theology M

THE BAPTIST COLLEGE OF FLORIDA
Music M
Pastoral Ministry and Counseling M
Theology M

BAPTIST MISSIONARY ASSOCIATION THEOLOGICAL SEMINARY
Theology M

BARCLAY COLLEGE
Theology M

BARD COLLEGE
Art/Fine Arts M
Economics M
English M
Film, Television, and Video Production M
History M

*M—masters degree; D—doctorate; O—other advanced degree; *—Close-Up and/or Display*

Museum Studies M
Music M,O
Photography M
Spanish M
Writing M

BARD GRADUATE CENTER
Art History M,D
Decorative Arts M,D

BARRY UNIVERSITY
Art/Fine Arts M
Clinical Psychology M,O
Liberal Studies M
Marriage and Family Therapy M,O
Pastoral Ministry and Counseling M,D
Photography M
Psychology—General M,O
Public Administration M
Rehabilitation Counseling M,O
School Psychology M,O
Sport Psychology M
Theology M,D

BARUCH COLLEGE OF THE CITY UNIVERSITY OF NEW YORK
Arts Administration M
Corporate and Organizational
  Communication M
Counseling Psychology M
Economics M
Industrial and Labor Relations M
Industrial and Organizational
  Psychology M,D
International Affairs M
International Economics M
International Trade Policy M
Public Administration M
Public Policy M
Sustainable Development M

BASTYR UNIVERSITY
Counseling Psychology M,O
Health Psychology M,O

BAYAMÓN CENTRAL UNIVERSITY
Industrial and Organizational
  Psychology M
Marriage and Family Therapy M,O
Rehabilitation Counseling M,O

BAYLOR COLLEGE OF MEDICINE
Genetic Counseling M

BAYLOR UNIVERSITY
American Studies M
Clinical Psychology D
Communication—General M
Economics M
English M,D
History M,D
Interdisciplinary Studies D
International Affairs M
Journalism M
Museum Studies M
Music M,D
Philosophy M,D
Political Science M,D
Psychology—General M,D
Religion M,D
School Psychology M,D,O
Sociology M,D
Spanish M
Theater M
Theology M,D

BAY PATH UNIVERSITY
Addictions/Substance Abuse
  Counseling M
Applied Behavior Analysis M
Clinical Psychology M
Communication—General M
Developmental Psychology M
Forensic Sciences M
Genetic Counseling M
Writing M

BECKER COLLEGE
Counseling Psychology M
Social Psychology M

BELLARMINE UNIVERSITY
Communication—General M

BELLEVUE UNIVERSITY
Corporate and Organizational
  Communication M
Criminal Justice and Criminology M
Military and Defense Studies M
National Security M
Public Administration M

BEMIDJI STATE UNIVERSITY
English M

BENEDICTINE UNIVERSITY
Clinical Psychology M
Emergency Management M

BENNINGTON COLLEGE
Dance M
Music M
Writing M

BERKLEE COLLEGE OF MUSIC
Music M,O
Theater M,O

BETHANY THEOLOGICAL SEMINARY
Conflict Resolution and
  Mediation/Peace Studies M,O
Pastoral Ministry and Counseling M,O
Religion M,O
Theology M,O

BETHEL SEMINARY
Classics M,D,O
Clinical Psychology M,D,O
Marriage and Family Therapy M,D,O
Missions and Missiology M,D,O

Near and Middle Eastern Languages M,D,O
Pastoral Ministry and Counseling M,D,O
Religion M,D,O
Theology M,D,O

BETHEL UNIVERSITY (IN)
Pastoral Ministry and Counseling M
Theology M

BETHEL UNIVERSITY (MN)
Counseling Psychology M,D,O

BETHEL UNIVERSITY (TN)
Conflict Resolution and
  Mediation/Peace Studies M

BETHESDA UNIVERSITY
Music M
Religion M
Theology M

BETH HAMEDRASH SHAAREI YOSHER INSTITUTE
Theology

BETH HATALMUD RABBINICAL COLLEGE
Theology

BETHLEHEM COLLEGE & SEMINARY
Theology M

BETH MEDRASH GOVOHA
Theology

BETHUNE-COOKMAN UNIVERSITY
Theology M

BEULAH HEIGHTS UNIVERSITY
Religion M

BEXLEY SEABURY SEMINARY
Theology M,D,O

BINGHAMTON UNIVERSITY, STATE UNIVERSITY OF NEW YORK
Anthropology M,D
Art History M,D
Asian Studies M,O
Asian-American Studies M,O
Clinical Psychology D
Cognitive Sciences D
Comparative Literature M,D
Economics M,D
English M,D
French M
Geography M
History M,D
Italian M
Liberal Studies M
Music M
Philosophy M,D
Political Science M,D
Psychology—General D
Public Administration M
Public Affairs D
Sociology M,D
Spanish M
Sustainable Development M
Theater M
Translation and Interpretation D,O
Writing M,D

BIOLA UNIVERSITY
Anthropology M,D,O
Clinical Psychology D
Cultural Studies M,D,O
Jewish Studies M,D,O
Linguistics M,D,O
Missions and Missiology M,D,O
Pastoral Ministry and Counseling M,D,O
Psychology—General D
Religion M,D,O
Theology M,D,O

BOB JONES UNIVERSITY
Art/Fine Arts M,D,O
English M,D,O
Film, Television, and Video
  Production M,D,O
Graphic Design M,D,O
History M,D,O
Illustration M,D,O
Music M,D,O
Pastoral Ministry and Counseling M,D,O
Religion M,D,O
Rhetoric M,D,O
Speech and Interpersonal
  Communication M,D,O
Theater M,D,O
Theology M,D,O

BOISE STATE UNIVERSITY
Anthropology M
Art/Fine Arts M
Communication—General M
Criminal Justice and Criminology M
Economics M
History M
Interdisciplinary Studies M
Music M
Political Science M
Public Administration M,D,O
Public Policy M,D,O
Rhetoric M
Technical Communication M

BOSTON ARCHITECTURAL COLLEGE
Architecture M
Historic Preservation M
Interior Design M
Landscape Architecture M
Sustainable Development M

BOSTON COLLEGE
Classics M
Counseling Psychology M,D
Developmental Psychology M,D
East European and Russian Studies M
Economics D

English M,D
French M
History M,D
Italian M
Linguistics M
Pastoral Ministry and Counseling M,D,O
Philosophy M,D
Political Science M,D
Psychology—General D
Russian M,D
Sociology M,D
Spanish M,D
Theology M,D,O
Western European Studies M,D

BOSTON GRADUATE SCHOOL OF PSYCHOANALYSIS
Counseling Psychology M
Developmental Psychology O
Psychoanalysis and Psychotherapy M,D,O
Psychology—General M

BOSTON UNIVERSITY
African-American Studies M
American Studies D
Anthropology M,D
Archaeology M,D
Art History M,D,O
Art/Fine Arts M
Arts Administration M,O
Classics M,D
Communication—General M
Corporate and Organizational
  Communication M
Counseling Psychology M
Criminal Justice and Criminology M
Cultural Studies M
Economic Development M
Economics M
Emergency Management M
English M,D
Film, Television, and Video
  Production M
Forensic Sciences M
Genetic Counseling M
Geographic Information Systems M,D
Health Communication M
Hispanic and Latin American
  Languages M,D
Historic Preservation M
History M,D
International Affairs M
Internet and Interactive
  Multimedia M
Journalism M
Linguistics M
Mass Communication M
Media Studies M,D,O
Museum Studies M
Music M,D,O
Philosophy M,D
Political Science D
Psychology—General M,D
Religion M,D
Romance Languages M,D
Sociology M,D
Theater M,O
Urban and Regional Planning M
Urban Studies M
Writing M

BOWIE STATE UNIVERSITY
Corporate and Organizational
  Communication M,O
Counseling Psychology M
English M
Public Administration M

BOWLING GREEN STATE UNIVERSITY
American Studies M,D
Applied Arts and Design—
  General M
Art History M
Art/Fine Arts M
Clinical Psychology M,D
Communication—General M,D
Computer Art and Design M
Criminal Justice and Criminology M
Demography and Population Studies M,D
Developmental Psychology M,D
Economics M
English M,D
Experimental Psychology M,D
Film, Television, and Video
  Production M,D
French M
German M
Graphic Design M
History M,D
Industrial and Organizational
  Psychology M,D
Interdisciplinary Studies M,D
Media Studies M,D
Music M,D
Philosophy M,D
Psychology—General M
Public Administration M
Rhetoric M,D
Social Psychology M,D
Sociology M
Spanish M
Technical Communication M
Theater M,D
Writing M,D

BRADLEY UNIVERSITY
Art/Fine Arts M
Clinical Psychology M
Counseling Psychology M
English M
Graphic Design M
Human Development M
Photography M

BRANDEIS UNIVERSITY
Anthropology M,D

Applied Economics M
Art/Fine Arts O
Child and Family Studies M,D
Chinese M
Classics M
Cognitive Sciences M,D
Conflict Resolution and
  Mediation/Peace Studies M,D
Cultural Anthropology M,D
Developmental Psychology M,D
Disability Studies D
Economics M,D
English M,D
Gender Studies M
Genetic Counseling M
History M,D
Internet and Interactive
  Multimedia M
Jewish Studies M,D
Music M,D
Near and Middle Eastern Languages M,D
Near and Middle Eastern Studies M,D
Philosophy M,D
Political Science M,D
Psychology—General M,D
Public Policy M
Social Psychology M,D
Sociology M,D
Sustainable Development M
Women's Studies M,D

BRANDMAN UNIVERSITY
Counseling Psychology M
Marriage and Family Therapy M
Psychology—General M
Public Administration M

BRANDON UNIVERSITY
Music M
Rural Planning and Studies M,O

BRENAU UNIVERSITY
Interior Design M
Psychology—General M

BRIDGEWATER STATE UNIVERSITY
Criminal Justice and Criminology M
English M
Psychology—General M
Public Administration M

BRIERCREST SEMINARY
Marriage and Family Therapy M
Missions and Missiology M
Pastoral Ministry and Counseling M
Religion M
Theology M

BRIGHAM YOUNG UNIVERSITY
Anthropology M
Art/Fine Arts M
Child and Family Studies M,D
Classics M
Clinical Psychology D
Cognitive Sciences D
Communication—General M
Comparative and Interdisciplinary
  Arts M
Comparative Literature M
Counseling Psychology M,D,O
English M
Film, Television, and Video
  Production M
Hispanic and Latin American
  Languages M
Human Development M
Humanities M
International Affairs M
Linguistics M
Marriage and Family Therapy M,D
Mass Communication M
Music M
Political Science M
Portuguese M
Psychology—General D
Public Administration M
Rhetoric M
School Psychology M,D,O
Sociology M
Spanish M
Theater M
Writing M

BRITE DIVINITY SCHOOL
Pastoral Ministry and Counseling M,D,O
Theology M,D,O

BROCK UNIVERSITY
Child and Family Studies M
Classics M
Comparative Literature M
Cultural Studies M
Disability Studies M,O
Economics M
English M
Geography M
History M
Human Development M,D
International Affairs M
Philosophy M
Political Science M
Psychology—General M,D
Public Policy M
Social Psychology M,D
Sociology M

BROOKLYN COLLEGE OF THE CITY UNIVERSITY OF NEW YORK
Art History M
Art/Fine Arts M
Arts Administration M
Counseling Psychology M,D,O
Economics M
English M
Experimental Psychology M,D
Film, Television, and Video
  Production M

Film, Television, and Video Theory and Criticism	M
French	M
History	M
Industrial and Organizational Psychology	M,D
International Affairs	M
Internet and Interactive Multimedia	M
Jewish Studies	M
Liberal Studies	M
Media Studies	M
Music	M
Photography	M
Political Science	M
Psychology—General	M,D
Public Policy	M
School Psychology	M,O
Social Psychology	M,D
Sociology	M,D
Spanish	M
Speech and Interpersonal Communication	M,D
Thanatology	M
Theater	M
Urban Studies	M
Writing	M

BROWN UNIVERSITY

American Studies	M,D
Anthropology	M,D
Archaeology	D
Art History	D
Asian Studies	D
Classics	M,D
Cognitive Sciences	M,D
Comparative Literature	D
East European and Russian Studies	M,D
Economics	D
English	M,D
French	D
German	D
Hispanic Studies	D
History of Science and Technology	D
History	M,D
Italian	D
Latin American Studies	M,D
Linguistics	M,D
Music	D
Near and Middle Eastern Studies	D
Philosophy	D
Political Science	D
Psychology—General	M,D
Public Policy	M
Publishing	M,D
Religion	D
Russian	M,D
Slavic Languages	M,D
Sociology	M,D
Theater	M,D
Western European Studies	M,D
Writing	M,D

BRYAN COLLEGE

Pastoral Ministry and Counseling	M

BRYANT UNIVERSITY

Communication—General	M,O
Corporate and Organizational Communication	M

BRYN ATHYN COLLEGE OF THE NEW CHURCH

Religion	M
Theology	M

BRYN MAWR COLLEGE

Archaeology	M,D
Art History	M,D
Classics	M,D

BUCKNELL UNIVERSITY

English	M
Psychology—General	M

BUFFALO STATE COLLEGE, STATE UNIVERSITY OF NEW YORK

Applied Economics	M
Criminal Justice and Criminology	M
Economics	M
English	M
Forensic Sciences	M
Historic Preservation	M,O
History	M
Interdisciplinary Studies	M
Museum Studies	M

BUSHNELL UNIVERSITY

Counseling Psychology	M

BUTLER UNIVERSITY

Art/Fine Arts	M
Music	M

BYZANTINE CATHOLIC SEMINARY OF SAINTS CYRIL AND METHODIUS

Theology	M

CABRINI UNIVERSITY

Communication—General	M,D
Criminal Justice and Criminology	M,D
English	M,D
History	M,D

CAIRN UNIVERSITY

Applied Behavior Analysis	M,O
Pastoral Ministry and Counseling	M
Religion	M
Theology	M

CALDWELL UNIVERSITY

Applied Behavior Analysis	M,D,O
Counseling Psychology	M,O

CALIFORNIA BAPTIST UNIVERSITY

Architecture	M
Communication—General	M
Counseling Psychology	M
English	M
Forensic Psychology	M
Music	M
Pastoral Ministry and Counseling	M
Public Administration	M
School Psychology	M

CALIFORNIA COAST UNIVERSITY

Criminal Justice and Criminology	M
Psychology—General	M

CALIFORNIA COLLEGE OF THE ARTS

Applied Arts and Design— General	M
Architecture	M
Art/Fine Arts	M
Computer Art and Design	M
Film, Television, and Video Production	M
Film, Television, and Video Theory and Criticism	M
Graphic Design	M
Illustration	M
Industrial Design	M
Museum Studies	M
Writing	M

CALIFORNIA INSTITUTE OF TECHNOLOGY

Social Sciences	M,D

CALIFORNIA INSTITUTE OF THE ARTS

Applied Arts and Design— General	M,O
Art/Fine Arts	M,O
Dance	M,O
Film, Television, and Video Production	M,O
Graphic Design	M,O
Music	M,O
Photography	M,O
Theater	M,O
Writing	M,O

CALIFORNIA LUTHERAN UNIVERSITY

Clinical Psychology	M,D
Marriage and Family Therapy	M,D
Psychology—General	M,D
Public Policy	M,O
Theology	M,D,O

CALIFORNIA POLYTECHNIC STATE UNIVERSITY, SAN LUIS OBISPO

Architecture	M
Economics	M
English	M
History	M
Political Science	M
Psychology—General	M
Urban and Regional Planning	M

CALIFORNIA STATE POLYTECHNIC UNIVERSITY, POMONA

Architecture	M
Economics	M
English	M
History	M
Interior Design	M
Landscape Architecture	M
Psychology—General	M
Public Administration	M
Urban and Regional Planning	M

CALIFORNIA STATE UNIVERSITY, CHICO

Anthropology	M
Applied Psychology	M
Art History	M
Art/Fine Arts	M
Communication—General	M
English	M
History	M
Marriage and Family Therapy	M
Museum Studies	M
Political Science	M
Psychology—General	M
Public Administration	M
School Psychology	M
Social Sciences	M

CALIFORNIA STATE UNIVERSITY, DOMINGUEZ HILLS

Applied Social Research	M
Clinical Psychology	M
Conflict Resolution and Mediation/Peace Studies	M
English	M,O
Health Psychology	M
Humanities	M
Marriage and Family Therapy	M
Psychology—General	M
Public Administration	M
Rhetoric	M,O
School Psychology	M
Sociology	M

CALIFORNIA STATE UNIVERSITY, EAST BAY

Anthropology	M
Child and Family Studies	M
Communication—General	M
Economics	M
English	M
Geography	M
History	M
Interdisciplinary Studies	M
Internet and Interactive Multimedia	M
Marriage and Family Therapy	M
Music	M

CALIFORNIA STATE UNIVERSITY, FRESNO

Applied Arts and Design— General	M
Applied Behavior Analysis	M,O
Art/Fine Arts	M
Communication—General	M
Counseling Psychology	M
Criminal Justice and Criminology	M
English	M
Experimental Psychology	M,O
History	M
Human Development	M,D
Linguistics	M
Marriage and Family Therapy	M
Music	M
Psychology—General	M,O
Public Administration	M
Rehabilitation Counseling	M
Rhetoric	M
School Psychology	M,O
Spanish	M
Sport Psychology	M
Writing	M

CALIFORNIA STATE UNIVERSITY, FULLERTON

American Studies	M
Anthropology	M
Applied Arts and Design— General	M
Art History	M
Art/Fine Arts	M
Clinical Psychology	M
Communication—General	M
Economics	M
English	M
Film, Television, and Video Production	M
Geography	M
Gerontology	M
Graphic Design	M
History	M
Illustration	M
Linguistics	M
Mass Communication	M
Museum Studies	M
Music	M
Photography	M
Political Science	M
Psychology—General	M
Public Administration	M
Social Psychology	M
Sociology	M
Spanish	M
Speech and Interpersonal Communication	M
Theater	M

CALIFORNIA STATE UNIVERSITY, LONG BEACH

African Studies	M
Anthropology	M
Art/Fine Arts	M
Asian Studies	M
Asian-American Studies	M
Communication—General	M
Criminal Justice and Criminology	M
Dance	M
Economics	M
Emergency Management	M
English	M
French	M
Geography	M
German	M
Gerontology	M
History	M
Industrial and Organizational Psychology	M
Linguistics	M,O
Marriage and Family Therapy	M,D
Music	M
Near and Middle Eastern Studies	M
Philosophy	M
Political Science	M
Psychology—General	M
Public Administration	M,O
Public Policy	M,O
Religion	M
Spanish	M
Sport Psychology	M
Theater	M
Writing	M

CALIFORNIA STATE UNIVERSITY, LOS ANGELES

Anthropology	M
Applied Arts and Design— General	M
Art History	M
Art Therapy	M
Art/Fine Arts	M
Child and Family Studies	M
Child Development	M
Communication—General	M
Criminal Justice and Criminology	M
Economics	M
English	M,O
French	M
Geography	M
Graphic Design	M
Hispanic Studies	M
History	M
Latin American Studies	M
Music	M
Philosophy	M,O
Photography	M

Public Administration	M
Public History	M
Public Policy	M
Social Psychology	M

CALIFORNIA STATE UNIVERSITY, MARITIME ACADEMY

Emergency Management	M

CALIFORNIA STATE UNIVERSITY, NORTHRIDGE

Anthropology	M
Archaeology	M
Art History	M
Art/Fine Arts	M
Clinical Psychology	M
Communication—General	M
Comparative Literature	M
English	M
Experimental Psychology	M
Family and Consumer Sciences-General	M
Film, Television, and Video Production	M
Geography	M
Hispanic Studies	M
History	M
Journalism	M
Linguistics	M
Marriage and Family Therapy	M
Mass Communication	M
Music	M
Political Science	M
Psychology—General	M
Public Administration	M,O
Rhetoric	M
School Psychology	M
Sociology	M
Spanish	M
Speech and Interpersonal Communication	M
Theater	M
Writing	M

CALIFORNIA STATE UNIVERSITY, SACRAMENTO

Anthropology	M
Applied Behavior Analysis	M
Art/Fine Arts	M
Child Development	M,D,O
Communication—General	M
Criminal Justice and Criminology	M
English	M
Industrial and Organizational Psychology	M
Music	M
Political Science	M
Psychology—General	M
Public Administration	M
Public History	M,D
Public Policy	M
School Psychology	M,D,O
Sociology	M
Writing	M

CALIFORNIA STATE UNIVERSITY, SAN BERNARDINO

Archaeology	M
Art/Fine Arts	M
Child Development	M
Clinical Psychology	M
Communication—General	M
Corporate and Organizational Communication	M
Counseling Psychology	M
Criminal Justice and Criminology	M
English	M
Industrial and Organizational Psychology	M
Interdisciplinary Studies	M
National Security	M
Psychology—General	M
Public Administration	M
Rehabilitation Counseling	M
Social Sciences	M
Spanish	M
Writing	M

CALIFORNIA STATE UNIVERSITY, SAN MARCOS

English	M
Hispanic and Latin American Languages	M
Hispanic Studies	M
History	M
Psychology—General	M
Sociology	M
Spanish	M
Writing	M

CALIFORNIA STATE UNIVERSITY, STANISLAUS

Applied Behavior Analysis	M
Counseling Psychology	M
Criminal Justice and Criminology	M
English	M,O
Genetic Counseling	M
History	M
Interdisciplinary Studies	M
Psychology—General	M
Public Administration	M
Rhetoric	M,O
Sustainable Development	M
Writing	M,O

CALIFORNIA UNIVERSITY OF MANAGEMENT AND SCIENCES

Economics	M,D

CALIFORNIA UNIVERSITY OF PENNSYLVANIA
Clinical Psychology M
Conflict Resolution and Mediation/Peace Studies M
Counseling Psychology M
Criminal Justice and Criminology M
Near and Middle Eastern Languages M
School Psychology M
Sport Psychology M

CALUMET COLLEGE OF SAINT JOSEPH
Criminal Justice and Criminology M

CALVARY UNIVERSITY
Pastoral Ministry and Counseling M
Theology M

CALVIN THEOLOGICAL SEMINARY
Missions and Missiology M,D
Pastoral Ministry and Counseling M,D
Religion M,D
Theology M,D

CAMBRIDGE COLLEGE
Addictions/Substance Abuse Counseling M,O
Conflict Resolution and Mediation/Peace Studies M
Counseling Psychology M,O
Interdisciplinary Studies M,D,O
Marriage and Family Therapy M,O
Psychology—General M,O
Rehabilitation Counseling M,O
School Psychology M,O

CAMERON UNIVERSITY
Psychology—General M

CAMPBELLSVILLE UNIVERSITY
Economics M,D
Marriage and Family Therapy M
Music M
School Psychology M
Social Sciences M
Theology M

CAMPBELL UNIVERSITY
Interdisciplinary Studies M
Pastoral Ministry and Counseling M,D
Theology M,D

CANADIAN SOUTHERN BAPTIST SEMINARY
Pastoral Ministry and Counseling M
Religion M
Theology M

CAPELLA UNIVERSITY
Addictions/Substance Abuse Counseling M,D
Applied Behavior Analysis M,D
Child and Family Studies M
Clinical Psychology M,D
Counseling Psychology M
Criminal Justice and Criminology M,D
Developmental Psychology M
Emergency Management M,D
Gerontology M
Homeland Security M
Industrial and Organizational Psychology M,D
Marriage and Family Therapy M,D
Psychology—General M,D
Public Administration M,D
School Psychology M,D
Sport Psychology M

CAPITAL UNIVERSITY
African-American Studies M
Missions and Missiology M
Music M
Pastoral Ministry and Counseling M
Theology M

CARDINAL STRITCH UNIVERSITY
Clinical Psychology M
Criminal Justice and Criminology M
Liberal Studies M
Psychology—General M

CAREY THEOLOGICAL COLLEGE
Theology M,D

CARIBBEAN UNIVERSITY
Art History M,D
Criminal Justice and Criminology M,D
Museum Studies M,D

CARLETON UNIVERSITY
Anthropology M
Architecture M
Art History M
Canadian Studies M,D
Cognitive Sciences D
Communication—General M,D
Comparative Literature D
Conflict Resolution and Mediation/Peace Studies M,O
East European and Russian Studies M,O
Economics M,D
English M,D
Film, Television, and Video Production M
French M
Geography M,D
History M,D
Industrial Design M
International Affairs M,D
Journalism M,D
Linguistics M
Music M
Philosophy M
Political Science M,D
Psychology—General M,D
Public Administration M,D
Public Policy M,D
Sociology M,D
Western European Studies M,O

CARLOW UNIVERSITY
Art/Fine Arts M
Counseling Psychology M,D,O
Forensic Sciences M
Writing M

CARNEGIE MELLON UNIVERSITY
African Studies D
African-American Studies D
Applied Arts and Design—General M,D
Architecture M,D
Art/Fine Arts M
Arts Administration M
Building Science M,D
Cognitive Sciences D
Communication—General M,D
Comparative Literature M,D
Computer Art and Design M
Corporate and Organizational Communication M
Criminal Justice and Criminology M
Cultural Studies D
Developmental Psychology D
Economics D
English M,D
Film, Television, and Video Production M
Gender Studies D
History of Science and Technology D
History D
Industrial and Labor Relations D
Linguistics M,D
Media Studies M
Music M
Philosophy M,D
Psychology—General D
Public Administration M
Public Policy M,D
Publishing M
Rhetoric M,D
Social Psychology D
Social Sciences D
Sustainable Development M,D
Technical Writing M
Theater M
Urban Design M,D
Women's Studies D
Writing M

CAROLINA CHRISTIAN COLLEGE
Pastoral Ministry and Counseling M

CARSON-NEWMAN UNIVERSITY
Theology M

CASE WESTERN RESERVE UNIVERSITY
Anthropology M,D
Art History M,D
Clinical Psychology D
Cognitive Sciences M
Comparative Literature M
Dance M
English M,D
Experimental Psychology D
French M
Genetic Counseling M,D
History M,D
Linguistics M
Museum Studies M
Music M,D
Political Science M,D
Psychology—General M,D
Sociology M,D
Theater M

CASTLETON UNIVERSITY
Forensic Psychology M
Psychology—General M

CATHOLIC DISTANCE UNIVERSITY
Theology M

CATHOLIC THEOLOGICAL UNION
Missions and Missiology M,D,O
Pastoral Ministry and Counseling M,D,O
Theology M,D,O

THE CATHOLIC UNIVERSITY OF AMERICA
American Studies M,D
Anthropology M
Applied Psychology M,D
Architecture M,O
Classics M,D,O
Clinical Psychology M,D
Criminal Justice and Criminology M
Economic Development M
English M,D,O
Experimental Psychology M,D
Hispanic Studies M,D
History M,D
International Affairs M,D
Medieval and Renaissance Studies M,D,O
Music M,D,O
Near and Middle Eastern Languages M,D
Near and Middle Eastern Studies M,D,O
Pastoral Ministry and Counseling M,D,O
Philosophy M,D,O
Political Science M,D
Psychology—General M,D
Public Policy M
Religion M,D,O
Rhetoric M,D,O
Sociology M
Spanish M,D
Sustainable Development M,O
Theater M,O
Theology M,D,O
Urban and Regional Planning M,O
Western European Studies M,D

CEDAR CREST COLLEGE
Art Therapy M
Forensic Sciences M
Writing M

CEDARVILLE UNIVERSITY
Missions and Missiology M,D
Pastoral Ministry and Counseling M,D

CENTENARY UNIVERSITY
Counseling Psychology M

CENTRAL BAPTIST THEOLOGICAL SEMINARY
Missions and Missiology M,O
Theology M,O

CENTRAL CONNECTICUT STATE UNIVERSITY
Communication—General M,O
Criminal Justice and Criminology M,O
English M,O
French M,O
Geography M
German M,O
Graphic Design M
History M,O
International Affairs M
Italian M,O
Marriage and Family Therapy M,O
Psychology—General M
Rehabilitation Counseling M,O
School Psychology M,O
Spanish M,O

CENTRAL EUROPEAN UNIVERSITY
Anthropology M,D
Cognitive Sciences D
Economics M,D
Gender Studies M,D
History M,D
International Affairs M,D
Medieval and Renaissance Studies M,D
Philosophy M,D
Political Science M,D
Public Administration M,D
Public Policy M,D
Sociology M,D

CENTRAL MICHIGAN UNIVERSITY
American Indian/Native American Studies M
American Studies M,O
Applied Psychology M,D
Child and Family Studies M,O
Clinical Psychology D
Clothing and Textiles M,O
Communication—General M
Counseling Psychology M,D,O
Cultural Studies M
Economics M
English M
Experimental Psychology M,D
Family and Consumer Sciences-General M,O
Film, Television, and Video Production M
Film, Television, and Video Theory and Criticism M
Gender Studies M
Geographic Information Systems M
Gerontology M,O
Health Psychology M,O
History M,O
Human Development M,O
Humanities M
Industrial and Organizational Psychology M,D
International Affairs M,O
Media Studies M
Music M
Philanthropic Studies M,O
Political Science M,O
Psychology—General M,D,O
Public Administration M,O
School Psychology D,O
Spanish M
Western European Studies M,O
Writing M

CENTRAL WASHINGTON UNIVERSITY
Anthropology M
Art/Fine Arts M
Child and Family Studies M
Counseling Psychology M
English M
Experimental Psychology M
Family and Consumer Sciences-General M
Geography M
Graphic Design M
History M
Interdisciplinary Studies M
Music M
Photography M
Psychology—General M,O
School Psychology O
Theater M
Writing M

CENTRAL YESHIVA TOMCHEI TMIMIM-LUBAVITCH
Jewish Studies M
Theology M

CENTRO DE ESTUDIOS AVANZADOS DE PUERTO RICO Y EL CARIBE
History M,D
Latin American Studies M,D

CHAMINADE UNIVERSITY OF HONOLULU
Child Development M
Criminal Justice and Criminology M

CHAMPLAIN COLLEGE
Conflict Resolution and Mediation/Peace Studies M
Forensic Sciences M
Internet and Interactive Multimedia M
Media Studies M

CHAPMAN UNIVERSITY
Art/Fine Arts
Communication—General M
Cultural Studies M,D,O
Disability Studies M,D,O
English M
Film, Television, and Video Production M
Holocaust and Genocide Studies M
International Affairs M
Marriage and Family Therapy M
Psychology—General M,D
School Psychology M,D,O
Writing M

CHARLESTON SOUTHERN UNIVERSITY
Criminal Justice and Criminology M

CHARLOTTE CHRISTIAN COLLEGE AND THEOLOGICAL SEMINARY
Cultural Studies M,D
Pastoral Ministry and Counseling M,D
Religion M,D
Theology M,D

CHATHAM UNIVERSITY
Communication—General M
Computer Art and Design M
Counseling Psychology M,D
Developmental Psychology M,D
Film, Television, and Video Production M
Health Communication M
Health Psychology M,D
Industrial and Organizational Psychology M,D
Interior Design M
Marriage and Family Therapy M,D
Sport Psychology M,D
Women's Studies M
Writing M

CHESTNUT HILL COLLEGE
Clinical Psychology M,D,O
Counseling Psychology M,O
Marriage and Family Therapy M,D,O
Psychology—General M,D,O

CHEYNEY UNIVERSITY OF PENNSYLVANIA
Public Administration M

THE CHICAGO SCHOOL OF PROFESSIONAL PSYCHOLOGY
Applied Behavior Analysis M,D
Clinical Psychology M,D
Forensic Psychology M,D
Industrial and Organizational Psychology M,D
Psychology—General M,D
School Psychology D,O

THE CHICAGO SCHOOL OF PROFESSIONAL PSYCHOLOGY AT DOWNTOWN LOS ANGELES
Applied Behavior Analysis M,D
Clinical Psychology M,D
Forensic Psychology D
Industrial and Organizational Psychology M
Marriage and Family Therapy M,D

THE CHICAGO SCHOOL OF PROFESSIONAL PSYCHOLOGY AT IRVINE
Clinical Psychology D
Forensic Psychology D
Marriage and Family Therapy M,D
Psychology—General D

THE CHICAGO SCHOOL OF PROFESSIONAL PSYCHOLOGY AT SAN DIEGO
Applied Behavior Analysis M,D
Applied Psychology M,D
Clinical Psychology M,D
Industrial and Organizational Psychology M,D

THE CHICAGO SCHOOL OF PROFESSIONAL PSYCHOLOGY AT WASHINGTON DC
School Psychology O

THE CHICAGO SCHOOL OF PROFESSIONAL PSYCHOLOGY AT XAVIER UNIVERSITY OF LOUISIANA
Clinical Psychology D

THE CHICAGO SCHOOL OF PROFESSIONAL PSYCHOLOGY: ONLINE
Applied Psychology M,O
Clinical Psychology M
Forensic Psychology M,O
Industrial and Organizational Psychology M,D,O
Psychology—General M,D

CHICAGO STATE UNIVERSITY
Clinical Psychology M
Criminal Justice and Criminology M
English M
Geographic Information Systems M
History M
Writing M

CHICAGO THEOLOGICAL SEMINARY
Ethics M,D
Pastoral Ministry and Counseling M,D
Religion M,D
Theology M,D

CHRISTENDOM COLLEGE
Theology M

CHRISTIAN BROTHERS UNIVERSITY
Religion M

CHRISTIAN THEOLOGICAL SEMINARY
- Marriage and Family Therapy M,D
- Pastoral Ministry and Counseling M,D
- Religion M,D
- Theology M,D

CHRISTIE'S EDUCATION
- Art History M
- Art/Fine Arts O
- Arts Administration M,O
- Museum Studies M

CHRIST THE KING SEMINARY
- Pastoral Ministry and Counseling M
- Theology M

CHURCH DIVINITY SCHOOL OF THE PACIFIC
- Theology M,D,O

CINCINNATI CHRISTIAN UNIVERSITY
- Pastoral Ministry and Counseling M
- Religion M
- Theology M

THE CITADEL, THE MILITARY COLLEGE OF SOUTH CAROLINA
- English M
- Hispanic Studies O
- History M,O
- Homeland Security M,O
- Interdisciplinary Studies M,O
- Military and Defense Studies M,O
- National Security M,O
- Political Science M
- Psychology—General M,O
- School Psychology M,O
- Social Sciences M

CITY COLLEGE OF THE CITY UNIVERSITY OF NEW YORK
- Architecture M
- Art History M
- Art/Fine Arts M
- Clinical Psychology M,D
- Computer Art and Design M
- Corporate and Organizational Communication M
- Economics M
- English M
- Graphic Design M
- History M
- International Affairs M
- Landscape Architecture M
- Media Studies M
- Museum Studies M
- Psychology—General M,D
- Public Administration M,D
- Sociology M
- Spanish M
- Sustainable Development M
- Urban Design M
- Writing M

CITY UNIVERSITY OF SEATTLE
- Counseling Psychology M

CITY VISION UNIVERSITY
- Pastoral Ministry and Counseling M

CLAREMONT GRADUATE UNIVERSITY
- African Studies M,D,O
- American Studies M,D,O
- Art/Fine Arts M
- Arts Administration M
- Cognitive Sciences M,D,O
- Comparative Literature M,D
- Computer Art and Design M
- Cultural Studies M,D,O
- Developmental Psychology M,D,O
- Economic Development M,D,O
- Economics M,D,O
- English M,D
- Ethics M,D
- Film, Television, and Video Theory and Criticism M,D
- Geographic Information Systems M,D,O
- Health Psychology M,D,O
- History M,D,O
- Human Development M,D,O
- Humanities M,D,O
- Industrial and Organizational Psychology M,D,O
- International Affairs M,D
- International Economics M,D,O
- Media Studies M,D,O
- Museum Studies M,D,O
- Music M,D
- Philosophy M,D
- Photography M
- Political Science M,D
- Psychology—General M,D,O
- Public Policy M,D,O
- Religion M,D
- Social Psychology M,D,O
- Theology M,D
- Western European Studies M,D,O
- Women's Studies M,D
- Writing M,D

CLAREMONT LINCOLN UNIVERSITY
- Ethics M
- Pastoral Ministry and Counseling M
- Religion M

CLAREMONT SCHOOL OF THEOLOGY
- Ethics M,D
- Pastoral Ministry and Counseling M,D
- Religion M,D
- Theology M,D

CLARK ATLANTA UNIVERSITY
- African-American Studies M,D
- Criminal Justice and Criminology M
- Economics M
- English M,D
- Political Science M,D
- Public Administration M
- Sociology M

CLARKSON UNIVERSITY
- Interdisciplinary Studies M,D
- Sustainable Development M,D

CLARKS SUMMIT UNIVERSITY
- Communication—General M,D
- English M
- Missions and Missiology M,D
- Pastoral Ministry and Counseling M,D
- Religion M,D
- Theology M,D

CLARK UNIVERSITY
- American Studies D
- Clinical Psychology D
- Communication—General M
- Developmental Psychology D
- Economics D
- English M
- Geographic Information Systems M
- Geography D
- History D
- Holocaust and Genocide Studies D
- International Development M
- Public Administration M,O
- Social Psychology D
- Sustainable Development M
- Urban and Regional Planning M

CLAYTON STATE UNIVERSITY
- Applied Psychology M
- Clinical Psychology M
- Criminal Justice and Criminology M
- Developmental Psychology M
- History M
- Liberal Studies M
- Psychology—General M

CLEMSON UNIVERSITY
- Anthropology M
- Applied Economics M,D
- Applied Psychology M,D
- Architecture M,D,O
- Art/Fine Arts M
- Clinical Psychology M,D,O
- Communication—General M,D
- Criminal Justice and Criminology M
- Economics M,D
- Family and Consumer Sciences-General D,O
- Historic Preservation M,O
- History M
- Industrial and Organizational Psychology M,D
- Landscape Architecture M
- Public Administration M,D,O
- Public Policy D,O
- Rhetoric M,D
- Sociology M
- Writing M,D

CLEVELAND INSTITUTE OF MUSIC
- Music M,D,O

CLEVELAND STATE UNIVERSITY
- Art History M
- Communication—General M,D,O
- Counseling Psychology M,D,O
- Economic Development M,O
- Economics M,O
- English M,O
- Geographic Information Systems M,O
- Historic Preservation M,O
- History M
- Industrial and Labor Relations M
- International Affairs M
- International Economics M
- Museum Studies M
- Music M
- Philosophy M,O
- Psychology—General M,D,O
- Public Administration M,D,O
- Public Affairs D
- Spanish M
- Sustainable Development M,O
- Urban and Regional Planning M,O
- Urban Studies M,D,O
- Writing M

COASTAL CAROLINA UNIVERSITY
- Liberal Studies M
- Writing M

COKER COLLEGE
- Criminal Justice and Criminology M

THE COLBURN SCHOOL CONSERVATORY OF MUSIC
- Music M,O

COLGATE ROCHESTER CROZER DIVINITY SCHOOL
- Conflict Resolution and Mediation/Peace Studies M,D,O
- Theology M,D,O

COLLÊGE DOMINICAIN DE PHILOSOPHIE ET DE THÊOLOGIE
- Philosophy M,D
- Theology M,D,O

COLLEGE FOR CREATIVE STUDIES
- Applied Arts and Design—General M
- Art/Fine Arts M

COLLEGE OF CHARLESTON
- Arts Administration O
- English M
- Historic Preservation M
- History M
- Public Administration M
- Urban and Regional Planning O
- Writing M

COLLEGE OF EMMANUEL AND ST. CHAD
- Theology M,D,O

THE COLLEGE OF NEW JERSEY
- Addictions/Substance Abuse Counseling M,O
- English M
- Gender Studies O
- Health Communication M
- Marriage and Family Therapy M,O

THE COLLEGE OF NEW ROCHELLE
- Art Therapy M
- Communication—General M,O
- Counseling Psychology M,O
- Marriage and Family Therapy M,O
- Public Administration M
- School Psychology M
- Thanatology M,O

COLLEGE OF SAINT ELIZABETH
- Applied Behavior Analysis M,O
- Counseling Psychology M,O
- Criminal Justice and Criminology M,O
- Holocaust and Genocide Studies M,O
- Internet and Interactive Multimedia M
- Pastoral Ministry and Counseling M,O
- Psychology—General M,D
- Public Administration M,O
- School Psychology M,D
- Theology M,O

COLLEGE OF ST. JOSEPH
- Addictions/Substance Abuse Counseling M
- Clinical Psychology M
- Counseling Psychology M
- Psychology—General M
- School Psychology M
- Social Psychology M

THE COLLEGE OF SAINT ROSE
- Counseling Psychology M,O
- School Psychology M,O

COLLEGE OF STATEN ISLAND OF THE CITY UNIVERSITY OF NEW YORK
- African Studies M
- American Studies M
- Asian Studies M
- Clinical Psychology M
- Counseling Psychology M,O
- English M
- Film, Television, and Video Theory and Criticism M
- History M
- Latin American Studies M
- Liberal Studies M
- Media Studies M
- Near and Middle Eastern Studies M
- Western European Studies M

COLORADO CHRISTIAN UNIVERSITY
- Counseling Psychology M

THE COLORADO COLLEGE
- American Studies M
- Humanities M
- Liberal Studies M

COLORADO SCHOOL OF MINES
- Humanities O
- Mineral Economics M,D
- Social Sciences O

COLORADO STATE UNIVERSITY
- Agricultural Economics and Agribusiness M,D
- Anthropology M,D
- Art History M
- Art/Fine Arts M
- Arts Administration M
- Child and Family Studies M,D
- Consumer Economics M
- Economics M,D
- English M
- Ethnic Studies M
- French M
- History M
- Human Development M,D
- Interdisciplinary Studies M,D
- Landscape Architecture M,D
- Liberal Studies M
- Marriage and Family Therapy M,D
- Media Studies M,D
- Music M
- Philosophy M
- Political Science M,D
- Psychology—General M,D
- Public History M
- Rhetoric M
- Sociology M,D
- Speech and Interpersonal Communication M,D
- Sustainable Development M,O
- Writing M

COLORADO STATE UNIVERSITY–GLOBAL CAMPUS
- Criminal Justice and Criminology M

COLORADO TECHNICAL UNIVERSITY AURORA
- Conflict Resolution and Mediation/Peace Studies M
- Criminal Justice and Criminology M

COLORADO TECHNICAL UNIVERSITY COLORADO SPRINGS
- Conflict Resolution and Mediation/Peace Studies M,D
- Criminal Justice and Criminology M

COLUMBIA COLLEGE (MO)
- Criminal Justice and Criminology M

COLUMBIA COLLEGE (SC)
- Criminal Justice and Criminology M

COLUMBIA COLLEGE CHICAGO
- Art History M
- Art/Fine Arts M
- Communication—General M
- English M
- Film, Television, and Video Production M
- Music M
- Photography M
- Writing M

COLUMBIA INTERNATIONAL UNIVERSITY
- Cultural Studies M,D,O
- Missions and Missiology M,D,O
- Pastoral Ministry and Counseling M,D,O
- Theology M,D,O

COLUMBIA SOUTHERN UNIVERSITY
- Criminal Justice and Criminology M
- Emergency Management M

COLUMBIA THEOLOGICAL SEMINARY
- Theology M,D

COLUMBIA UNIVERSITY
- African Studies M,D
- African-American Studies M,D
- American Studies M,D
- Anthropology M,D
- Archaeology M,D
- Architecture M,D
- Art History M,D
- Art/Fine Arts M,D
- Asian Studies M,D,O
- Classics M,D
- Communication—General M,D
- Comparative Literature M,D
- Conflict Resolution and Mediation/Peace Studies M
- Corporate and Organizational Communication M
- East European and Russian Studies M,D
- Economics M,D
- English M,D
- Environmental Design M,D
- Ethics M
- Film, Television, and Video Production M
- Film, Television, and Video Theory and Criticism M
- French M,D
- German M,D
- Hispanic Studies M,D
- Historic Preservation M,D,O
- History M,D
- International Affairs M,D
- Italian M,D
- Japanese M,D
- Jewish Studies M,D
- Journalism M
- Landscape Architecture M
- Latin American Studies M,D
- Media Studies M
- Medieval and Renaissance Studies M,D
- Museum Studies M,D
- Music M,D
- Near and Middle Eastern Studies M,D
- Philosophy M,D
- Political Science M,D
- Psychology—General M,D
- Public Administration M
- Public Policy M
- Religion M,D
- Romance Languages M,D
- Russian M,D
- Slavic Languages M,D
- Social Sciences M,D
- Sociology M,D
- Spanish M,D
- Sustainable Development M,D
- Theater M,D
- Translation and Interpretation M,D
- Urban and Regional Planning M,D
- Western European Studies M,D
- Writing M

COLUMBUS COLLEGE OF ART & DESIGN
- Art/Fine Arts M

COLUMBUS STATE UNIVERSITY
- Clinical Psychology M,D,O
- Criminal Justice and Criminology M
- History M,O
- Homeland Security M
- Music M,O
- Political Science M
- Public Administration M
- Theater M
- Urban Studies M

CONCORDIA LUTHERAN SEMINARY
- Theology M,O

CONCORDIA SEMINARY
- Theology M,D,O

CONCORDIA THEOLOGICAL SEMINARY
- Theology M,D

CONCORDIA UNIVERSITY (CANADA)
- Anthropology M,D

*M—masters degree; D—doctorate; O—other advanced degree; *—Close-Up and/or Display*

Applied Arts and Design—
  General — M,O
Art History — M,D
Art Therapy — M
Art/Fine Arts — M
Child and Family Studies — M
Clinical Psychology — D,O
Communication—General — M,D,O
Computer Art and Design — M,O
Cultural Anthropology — M,D
Economic Development — O
Economics — M,D,O
English — M,D
Film, Television, and Video
  Production — M,D
Film, Television, and Video
  Theory and Criticism — M,D
French — M,O
Geography — M,D,O
History — M,D
Humanities — D
Interdisciplinary Studies — M,D
Internet and Interactive
  Multimedia — M,D,O
Jewish Studies — M
Journalism — M,O
Linguistics — M,O
Media Studies — M,D,O
Music — O
Philosophy — M
Political Science — M,D
Psychology—General — M,D
Public Administration — M,D
Public Affairs — O
Public Policy — M,D
Religion — M,D
Sociology — M,D
Textile Design — M
Theology — M
Therapies—Dance, Drama, and
  Music — M,O
Translation and Interpretation — M,O
Urban and Regional Planning — O
Urban Studies — M,D,O
Writing — M

**CONCORDIA UNIVERSITY
(UNITED STATES)**
Social Psychology — M

CONCORDIA UNIVERSITY CHICAGO
Counseling Psychology — M
Gerontology — M
Music — M
Religion — M

CONCORDIA UNIVERSITY IRVINE
Applied Social Research — M
Cultural Studies — M
International Affairs — M
Religion — M
Theology — M

CONCORDIA UNIVERSITY, NEBRASKA
Pastoral Ministry and Counseling — M

**CONCORDIA UNIVERSITY
OF EDMONTON**
Religion — M
Theology — M

CONCORDIA UNIVERSITY, ST. PAUL
Child and Family Studies — M
Corporate and Organizational
  Communication — M
Criminal Justice and Criminology — M
Writing — M

CONCORDIA UNIVERSITY WISCONSIN
Child and Family Studies — M
Corporate and Organizational
  Communication — M
Music — M
Public Administration — M

**CONSERVATORIO DE MUSICA DE
PUERTO RICO**
Music — O

CONVERSE COLLEGE
English — M
History — M
Liberal Studies — M
Marriage and Family Therapy — M
Music — M
Political Science — M
Writing — M

THE CONWAY SCHOOL
Landscape Architecture — M

**COOPER UNION FOR THE
ADVANCEMENT OF SCIENCE AND ART**
Architecture — M

COPENHAGEN BUSINESS SCHOOL
Economics — M,D
Public Administration — M,D

COPPIN STATE UNIVERSITY
Addictions/Substance Abuse
  Counseling — M
Criminal Justice and Criminology — M
Rehabilitation Counseling — M

CORBAN UNIVERSITY
Pastoral Ministry and Counseling — M,D,O
Theology — M,D,O

CORNELL UNIVERSITY
African Studies — M,D
African-American Studies — M,D
Agricultural Economics and
  Agribusiness — M,D
American Studies — M,D
Anthropology — D
Applied Economics — M,D
Archaeology — M,D
Architectural History — M,D

Architecture — M
Art History — D
Art/Fine Arts — M
Asian Languages — M,D
Asian Studies — M,D
Biological Anthropology — D
Child and Family Studies — M
Classics — D
Clothing and Textiles — M
Cognitive Sciences — D
Communication—General — M,D
Comparative Literature — D
Computer Art and Design — M,D
Conflict Resolution and
  Mediation/Peace Studies — M,D
Consumer Economics — M,D
Corporate and Organizational
  Communication — M,D
Cultural Anthropology — D
Cultural Studies — M,D
Demography and Population Studies — M,D
Developmental Psychology — M,D
East European and Russian Studies — M,D
Economic Development — M,D
Economics — M,D
English — M,D
Environmental Design — M
Ethnic Studies — M,D
Experimental Psychology — D
French — D
Gender Studies — M,D
German — M,D
Health Communication — M,D
Hispanic and Latin American
  Languages — D
Historic Preservation — M,D
History of Science and Technology — M,D
History — M,D
Human Development — M,D
Industrial and Labor Relations — M,D
Interior Design — M
International Affairs — D
Italian — D
Jewish Studies — M
Landscape Architecture — M
Latin American Studies — M,D
Linguistics — M,D
Media Studies — M,D
Medieval and Renaissance Studies — M,D
Music — M,D
Near and Middle Eastern Studies — M,D
Philosophy — D
Photography — M,D
Political Science — M,D
Psychology—General — D
Public Affairs — M
Public Policy — M,D
Religion — M,D
Romance Languages — M,D
Rural Sociology — M,D
Scandinavian Languages — M,D
Slavic Languages — M,D
Social Psychology — M,D
Sociology — M,D
Spanish — D
Sustainable Development — M,D
Textile Design — M,D
Theater — D
Urban and Regional Planning — M,D
Urban Design — M,D
Western European Studies — M,D
Women's Studies — M,D
Writing — M,D

COVENANT THEOLOGICAL SEMINARY
Pastoral Ministry and Counseling — M,D,O
Theology — M,D,O

CRANBROOK ACADEMY OF ART
Architecture — M
Art/Fine Arts — M
Photography — M
Textile Design — M

CREIGHTON UNIVERSITY
Conflict Resolution and
  Mediation/Peace Studies — M,D,O
English — M
School Psychology — M
Writing — M

CRISWELL COLLEGE
Jewish Studies — M
Pastoral Ministry and Counseling — M
Theology — M

CROWN COLLEGE
Theology — M

CUMBERLAND UNIVERSITY
Public Administration — M

**CUNY CRAIG NEWMARK GRADUATE
SCHOOL OF JOURNALISM**
Journalism — M

CURRY COLLEGE
Criminal Justice and Criminology — M

CURTIS INSTITUTE OF MUSIC
Music — M

DALHOUSIE UNIVERSITY
Anthropology — M,D
Architecture — M
Classics — M,D
Clinical Psychology — M,D
Economics — M,D
English — M,D
French — M
German — M
History — M,D
Interdisciplinary Studies — D
International Development — M
Music — M
Philosophy — M
Political Science — M,D

Psychology—General — M,D
Public Administration — M,D
Rural Planning and Studies — M
Sociology — M,D
Urban and Regional Planning — M

DALLAS BAPTIST UNIVERSITY
Asian Studies — M
Communication—General — M
Conflict Resolution and
  Mediation/Peace Studies — M
Counseling Psychology — M
Criminal Justice and Criminology — M
Interdisciplinary Studies — M
International Affairs — M
Liberal Studies — M
Missions and Missiology — M
Pastoral Ministry and Counseling — M,D
Religion — M
Theology — M
Western European Studies — M

DALLAS INTERNATIONAL UNIVERSITY
Linguistics — M,O

DALLAS THEOLOGICAL SEMINARY
Child and Family Studies — M,D,O
Jewish Studies — M,D,O
Media Studies — M,D,O
Missions and Missiology — M,D,O
Pastoral Ministry and Counseling — M,D,O
Philosophy — M,D,O
Religion — M,D,O
Theology — M,D,O

**DANIEL MORGAN GRADUATE SCHOOL
OF NATIONAL SECURITY**
National Security — M

DARTMOUTH COLLEGE
Cognitive Sciences — D
Comparative Literature — M
Liberal Studies — M
Music — M
Psychology—General — D
Sustainable Development — D

DELAWARE STATE UNIVERSITY
Historic Preservation — M

DELAWARE VALLEY UNIVERSITY
Agricultural Economics and
  Agribusiness — M
Counseling Psychology — M
Criminal Justice and Criminology — M
Developmental Psychology — M
Social Psychology — M

**DELL'ARTE INTERNATIONAL SCHOOL
OF PHYSICAL THEATRE**
Theater — M

DELTA STATE UNIVERSITY
Criminal Justice and Criminology — M
Gender Studies — M
Liberal Studies — M
Philosophy — M
Religion — M
Urban and Regional Planning — M

DENVER SEMINARY
Marriage and Family Therapy — M,D,O
Pastoral Ministry and Counseling — M,D,O
Religion — M,D,O
Theology — M,D,O

DEPAUL UNIVERSITY
Applied Economics — M,D
Chinese — M
Clinical Psychology — M,D
Communication—General — M
Computer Art and Design — M,D
Corporate and Organizational
  Communication — M
Counseling Psychology — M,D
Economics — M,D
English — M
Ethnic Studies — M
Film, Television, and Video
  Production — M,D
Film, Television, and Video
  Theory and Criticism — M
French — M
Gender Studies — M
German — M
Health Communication — M
History — M
Interdisciplinary Studies — M
International Affairs — M
Internet and Interactive
  Multimedia — M,D
Italian — M
Japanese — M
Journalism — M
Liberal Studies — M
Media Studies — M
Music — M,O
Near and Middle Eastern Languages — M
Psychology—General — M,D
Public Administration — M
Public Policy — M
Publishing — M
Rhetoric — M
School Psychology — M,D
Sociology — M
Spanish — M
Sustainable Development — M
Theater — M
Urban Design — M
Women's Studies — M
Writing — M

**DEREE - THE AMERICAN
COLLEGE OF GREECE**
Applied Psychology — M
Communication—General — M

DESALES UNIVERSITY
Criminal Justice and Criminology — M,O
Forensic Sciences — M,O
Gerontology — M,D,O

DEVRY UNIVERSITY–FOLSOM CAMPUS
Public Administration — M

DIGIPEN INSTITUTE OF TECHNOLOGY
Computer Art and Design — M

DIVINE MERCY UNIVERSITY
Clinical Psychology — M,D
Psychology—General — M

DOANE UNIVERSITY
School Psychology — M,D,O

**DOMINICAN HOUSE OF STUDIES,
PONTIFICAL FACULTY OF THE
IMMACULATE CONCEPTION**
Theology — M,D

**DOMINICAN SCHOOL OF
PHILOSOPHY AND THEOLOGY**
Philosophy — M,O
Theology — M,O

**DOMINICAN UNIVERSITY OF
CALIFORNIA**
Liberal Studies — M

DRAKE UNIVERSITY
Applied Behavior Analysis — M,D,O
Communication—General — M
Public Administration — M
Public Affairs — M

DREW UNIVERSITY
American Studies — M,D,O
Art/Fine Arts — M,D,O
Conflict Resolution and
  Mediation/Peace Studies — M,D,O
Cultural Studies — M,D,O
English — M,D,O
French — M,D,O
History — M,D,O
Italian — M,D,O
Liberal Studies — M,D,O
Public History — M,D,O
Religion — M,D,O
Theology — M,D,O
Western European Studies — M,D,O
Writing — M,D,O

DREXEL UNIVERSITY
Applied Arts and Design—
  General — M,D
Applied Behavior Analysis — M,D
Art Therapy — M,O
Arts Administration — M
Clinical Psychology — D
Clothing and Textiles — M
Communication—General — M
Computer Art and Design — M,D
Corporate and Organizational
  Communication — M
Economics — M,D,O
Emergency Management — M
Film, Television, and Video
  Production — M
Forensic Psychology — D
Health Psychology — D
History of Science and Technology — M
Homeland Security — M
Interior Design — M
Marriage and Family Therapy — M,D
Mass Communication — M
Media Studies — M
Psychology—General — M
Technical Communication — M
Technical Writing — M
Textile Design — M
Therapies—Dance, Drama, and
  Music — M,O
Urban Design — M

DRURY UNIVERSITY
Communication—General — M

DUKE UNIVERSITY
Art History — M,D
Art/Fine Arts — M,D
Asian Studies — M,O
Biological Anthropology — D
Classics — D
Clinical Psychology — D
Cognitive Sciences — D
Comparative Literature — D
Cultural Anthropology — D
Developmental Psychology — D
Economics — M,D
English — D
Experimental Psychology — D
French — D
German — D
Gerontology — M,D,O
Health Psychology — D
History — M,D
Human Development — D
Humanities — M
International Development — M
Italian — D
Latin American Studies — M,D
Liberal Studies — M
Media Studies — M
Music — D
Philosophy — D
Political Science — M,D
Psychology—General — D
Public Policy — M,D
Religion — M,D
Slavic Languages — M,D
Sociology — M,D
Spanish — D
Theology — M,D

DUQUESNE UNIVERSITY
Classics — M
Clinical Psychology — M,D,O
Communication—General — M,D
Counseling Psychology — M,D,O
English — M,D
Forensic Sciences — M
History — M
Marriage and Family Therapy — M,D,O
Music — M,O
Philosophy — M,D
Psychology—General — D
Public History — M
Rhetoric — M,D
School Psychology — M,D
Theology — M,D

EARLHAM SCHOOL OF RELIGION
Pastoral Ministry and Counseling — M
Religion — M
Theology — M

EAST CAROLINA UNIVERSITY
Addictions/Substance Abuse
 Counseling — M,D,O
American Studies — M
Anthropology — M
Applied Economics — M
Art/Fine Arts — M
Child and Family Studies — M,D
Child Development — M,D
Clinical Psychology — M,D,O
Comparative Literature — M,D,O
Corporate and Organizational
 Communication — M,O
Criminal Justice and Criminology — M,O
Economic Development — M,O
English — M,D,O
Geographic Information Systems — M,O
Geography — M,O
Gerontology — M,O
Graphic Design — M
Health Communication — M
Health Psychology — M,D,O
History — M
Illustration — M
Industrial and Organizational
 Psychology — M,D,O
International Affairs — M
Linguistics — M,D,O
Marriage and Family Therapy — M,D
Military and Defense Studies — M
Music — M,O
Photography — M
Political Science — M,O
Public Administration — M,O
Public History — M
Rehabilitation Counseling — M,D,O
Rhetoric — M,D,O
Rural Planning and Studies — M,O
Social Sciences — M,D,O
Sociology — M
Technical Communication — M,D,O
Textile Design — M
Therapies—Dance, Drama, and
 Music — M,O
Urban and Regional Planning — M,O
Western European Studies — M
Writing — M,D,O

EAST CENTRAL UNIVERSITY
Clinical Psychology — M
Criminal Justice and Criminology — M
Psychology—General — M
Rehabilitation Counseling — M

EASTERN ILLINOIS UNIVERSITY
Art/Fine Arts — M
Clinical Psychology — M,O
Communication—General — M
Economics — M
English — M
Geographic Information Systems — M
Gerontology — M
History — M
Human Development — M
Music — M
Political Science — M
Psychology—General — M,O
School Psychology — M,O
Sustainable Development — M

EASTERN KENTUCKY UNIVERSITY
Clinical Psychology — M,O
Criminal Justice and Criminology — M
English — M
History — M
Industrial and Organizational
 Psychology — M
Music — M
Political Science — M
Psychology—General — M,O
Public Administration — M
School Psychology — M,O
Urban and Regional Planning — M
Writing — M

EASTERN MENNONITE UNIVERSITY
Conflict Resolution and
 Mediation/Peace Studies — M,O
Pastoral Ministry and Counseling — M,O
Religion — M,O
Theology — M,O

EASTERN MICHIGAN UNIVERSITY
African-American Studies — O
Art/Fine Arts — M
Arts Administration — M
Clinical Psychology — M,D
Clothing and Textiles — M
Communication—General — M
Corporate and Organizational
 Communication — M,O

Criminal Justice and Criminology — M
Cultural Studies — O
Dance — M
Economics — M,O
English — M,O
Gender Studies — M,O
Geographic Information Systems — M,O
Gerontology — O
Historic Preservation — M
History — M
Interior Design — M
Linguistics — M
Museum Studies — M
Music — M
Philosophy — M
Psychology—General — M,D
Public Administration — M,O
Public Policy — M,O
Social Sciences — M
Sociology — M
Sustainable Development — M,O
Technical Communication — M,O
Theater — M
Urban and Regional Planning — M,O
Women's Studies — M,O
Writing — M,O

EASTERN NAZARENE COLLEGE
Counseling Psychology — M
Marriage and Family Therapy — M

EASTERN NEW MEXICO UNIVERSITY
Anthropology — M
Communication—General — M
English — M

EASTERN UNIVERSITY
Communication—General — M,O
Music — M,O
School Psychology — M,O
Spanish — M,O
Theology — M

EASTERN VIRGINIA MEDICAL SCHOOL
Art Therapy — M
Clinical Psychology — D

EASTERN WASHINGTON UNIVERSITY
Applied Psychology — M,O
Clinical Psychology — M,O
Communication—General — M,O
Counseling Psychology — M,O
English — M
Experimental Psychology — M,O
History — M
Interdisciplinary Studies — M
Liberal Studies — M
Music — M
Psychology—General — M,O
Public Administration — M
Rhetoric — M
School Psychology — M,O
Technical Communication — M

EAST STROUDSBURG UNIVERSITY OF PENNSYLVANIA
Communication—General — M
Geography — M
History — M
Political Science — M
Public Administration — M

EAST TENNESSEE STATE UNIVERSITY
Art/Fine Arts — M
Clinical Psychology — M,D
Communication—General — M,O
Computer Art and Design — M
Criminal Justice and Criminology — M,O
Economic Development — M,O
English — M,O
Experimental Psychology — D
Geographic Information Systems — M,O
Gerontology — M,D,O
History — M,O
Liberal Studies — M,O
Marriage and Family Therapy — M
Psychology—General — D
Public Administration — M,O
School Psychology — M
Sociology — M
Translation and Interpretation — M
Urban and Regional Planning — M,O

EAST TEXAS BAPTIST UNIVERSITY
Counseling Psychology — M
Religion — M

ECCLESIA COLLEGE
Missions and Missiology — M

ECUMENICAL THEOLOGICAL SEMINARY
Pastoral Ministry and Counseling — D
Theology — M

EDEN THEOLOGICAL SEMINARY
Theology — M,D

EDINBORO UNIVERSITY OF PENNSYLVANIA
Art Therapy — M,O
Art/Fine Arts — M
Clinical Psychology — M,O
Communication—General — M
Counseling Psychology — M,O
Rehabilitation Counseling — M,O
School Psychology — M,O

ELIZABETH CITY STATE UNIVERSITY
Geographic Information Systems — M
Psychology—General — M

ELMHURST UNIVERSITY
Geographic Information Systems — M

Industrial and Organizational
 Psychology — M

ELMS COLLEGE
Applied Behavior Analysis — M,O
Religion — M
Social Sciences — M,O

ELON UNIVERSITY
Internet and Interactive
 Multimedia — M

EMBRY-RIDDLE AERONAUTICAL UNIVERSITY–PRESCOTT
Military and Defense Studies — M

EMBRY-RIDDLE AERONAUTICAL UNIVERSITY–WORLDWIDE
International Affairs — M

EMILY CARR UNIVERSITY OF ART + DESIGN
Applied Arts and Design—
 General — M
Art/Fine Arts — M
Computer Art and Design — M

EMORY & HENRY COLLEGE
American Studies — M,D
History — M,D

EMORY UNIVERSITY
Anthropology — D
Art History — D
Clinical Psychology — D
Cognitive Sciences — D
Comparative Literature — D,O
Developmental Psychology — D
Economics — D
English — D
Ethics — M,D
Film, Television, and Video
 Theory and Criticism — M,D,O
French — D
Genetic Counseling — M
History — D
Interdisciplinary Studies — D
Music — M
Pastoral Ministry and Counseling — M,D
Philosophy — D,O
Political Science — D
Portuguese — D,O
Psychology—General — D
Religion — D
Sociology — D
Spanish — D,O
Sustainable Development — M
Theology — M,D
Women's Studies — D,O

EMPORIA STATE UNIVERSITY
Art Therapy — M
Clinical Psychology — M
Counseling Psychology — M
English — M
Forensic Sciences — M,O
History — M
Industrial and Organizational
 Psychology — M
Music — M
Psychology—General — M
Rehabilitation Counseling — M
School Psychology — M,O

ENDICOTT COLLEGE
Applied Behavior Analysis — M,D,O
Emergency Management — M,O
Homeland Security — M,O
Interior Design — M

EPIC BIBLE COLLEGE
Ethics — M,D
Pastoral Ministry and Counseling — M,D

ERIKSON INSTITUTE
Child Development — M
Developmental Psychology — M,O
Human Development — M,O

ERSKINE THEOLOGICAL SEMINARY
Theology — M,D

EVANGELICAL SEMINARY
Marriage and Family Therapy — M
Missions and Missiology — M
Pastoral Ministry and Counseling — M
Theology — M

EVANGELICAL SEMINARY OF PUERTO RICO
Theology — M,D

EVANGEL UNIVERSITY
Clinical Psychology — M
Counseling Psychology — M
School Psychology — M
Social Sciences — M

THE EVERGREEN STATE COLLEGE
Public Administration — M

FAIRFIELD UNIVERSITY
Addictions/Substance Abuse
 Counseling — M,O
American Studies — M
Applied Behavior Analysis — M
Applied Psychology — M,O
Child and Family Studies — M,O
Clinical Psychology — M,O
Communication—General — M
Counseling Psychology — M,O
Internet and Interactive
 Multimedia — M,O
Marriage and Family Therapy — M,O
Pastoral Ministry and Counseling — M,O
Public Administration — M

School Psychology — M,O
Writing — M

FAIRLEIGH DICKINSON UNIVERSITY, FLORHAM CAMPUS
Clinical Psychology — M
Corporate and Organizational
 Communication — M
Counseling Psychology — M
Industrial and Organizational
 Psychology — M
Psychology—General — M,O
Public Administration — M
Writing — M

FAIRLEIGH DICKINSON UNIVERSITY, METROPOLITAN CAMPUS
Art/Fine Arts — M
Clinical Psychology — M,D
Communication—General — M
Comparative Literature — M
Criminal Justice and Criminology — M
English — M
Experimental Psychology — M,O
Forensic Psychology — M
History — M
Homeland Security — M
International Affairs — M
Media Studies — M
Political Science — M
Psychology—General — M,D,O
Public Administration — M,O
School Psychology — M,D

FAIRMONT STATE UNIVERSITY
Criminal Justice and Criminology — M

FAITH BAPTIST BIBLE COLLEGE AND THEOLOGICAL SEMINARY
Pastoral Ministry and Counseling — M
Religion — M
Theology — M

FAITH INTERNATIONAL UNIVERSITY
Theology — M,D

FAITH THEOLOGICAL SEMINARY
Theology — M,D

FASHION INSTITUTE OF TECHNOLOGY
Applied Arts and Design—
 General — M
Art History — M
Arts Administration — M
Clothing and Textiles — M
Illustration — M
Museum Studies — M

FAULKNER UNIVERSITY
Criminal Justice and Criminology — M
Humanities — M,D
Pastoral Ministry and Counseling — M,D
Theology — M,D

FAYETTEVILLE STATE UNIVERSITY
Criminal Justice and Criminology — M
Psychology—General — M
Sociology — M

FELICIAN UNIVERSITY
Counseling Psychology — M,D

FERRIS STATE UNIVERSITY
Applied Arts and Design—
 General — M
Art/Fine Arts — M
Criminal Justice and Criminology — M
Photography — M

FIELDING GRADUATE UNIVERSITY
Child Development — M,D,O
Clinical Psychology — D,O
Developmental Psychology — M,D,O
Human Development — M,D,O
Media Studies — M,D,O
Psychology—General — M,D,O

FISK UNIVERSITY
Clinical Psychology — M
Psychology—General — M

FITCHBURG STATE UNIVERSITY
Communication—General — M,O
Counseling Psychology — M
English — M,O
History — M
Interdisciplinary Studies — O
Psychology—General — O
Writing — M

FIVE TOWNS COLLEGE
Music — M,D

FLORIDA AGRICULTURAL AND MECHANICAL UNIVERSITY
Architecture — M
Criminal Justice and Criminology — M
History — M
Journalism — M
Landscape Architecture — M
Political Science — M
Psychology—General — M
Public Administration — M
Social Psychology — M
Social Sciences — M

FLORIDA ATLANTIC UNIVERSITY
Anthropology — M
Applied Arts and Design—
 General — M
Art/Fine Arts — M
Communication—General — M,O
Comparative and Interdisciplinary
 Arts — D
Comparative Literature — M
Criminal Justice and Criminology — M

M—masters degree; D—doctorate; O—other advanced degree; *—Close-Up and/or Display

Economics — M
English — M
Film, Television, and Video Production — M,O
French — M
Graphic Design — M
History — M
Linguistics — M
Media Studies — M,O
Music — M
Political Science — M
Psychology—General — M
Public Administration — M
Sociology — M
Spanish — M
Theater — M
Urban and Regional Planning — M
Women's Studies — M

FLORIDA GULF COAST UNIVERSITY
Clinical Psychology — M
Criminal Justice and Criminology — M
English — M
Forensic Sciences — M
History — M
Interdisciplinary Studies — M
Public Administration — M
School Psychology — M

FLORIDA INSTITUTE OF TECHNOLOGY
Applied Behavior Analysis — M
Clinical Psychology — D
Communication—General — M
Industrial and Organizational Psychology — M,D
Interdisciplinary Studies — M
Psychology—General — M,D
Public Administration — M

FLORIDA INTERNATIONAL UNIVERSITY
African Studies — M
Applied Behavior Analysis — M,D
Architecture — M
Art/Fine Arts — M,O
Asian Studies — M
Clinical Psychology — M,D
Cognitive Sciences — M,D
Communication—General — M
Counseling Psychology — M,D
Criminal Justice and Criminology — M,D
Developmental Psychology — M,D
Economics — M,D
Emergency Management — M
English — M
Forensic Sciences — M,D
History — M,D
Industrial and Organizational Psychology — M,D
Interior Design — M,O
International Affairs — M,D
Journalism — M
Landscape Architecture — M
Linguistics — M
Mass Communication — M
Museum Studies — M
Music — M
Political Science — M
Psychology—General — M,D
Public Administration — M
Public Affairs — M,D
Religion — M
Sociology — M,D
Spanish — M
Writing — M

FLORIDA NATIONAL UNIVERSITY
Public Administration — M

FLORIDA STATE UNIVERSITY
American Studies — M,D
Anthropology — M,D
Applied Behavior Analysis — M
Applied Economics — M,D
Applied Social Research — M,D
Archaeology — M,D
Architecture — M
Art History — M,D
Art Therapy — M,D
Art/Fine Arts — M
Arts Administration — M
Asian Studies — M
Child and Family Studies — M,D
Classics — M,D
Clinical Psychology — D
Cognitive Sciences — D
Communication—General — M,D
Corporate and Organizational Communication — M,D
Criminal Justice and Criminology — M,D
Cultural Studies — M,D
Dance — M
Demography and Population Studies — M
Developmental Psychology — D
East European and Russian Studies — M
Economics — M,D
English — M,D
Family and Consumer Sciences-General — M,D
Film, Television, and Video Production — M
French — M,D
Geographic Information Systems — M,D
Geography — M,D
German — M
History — M,D
Human Development — M,D
Interior Design — M
International Affairs — M
Italian — M
Marriage and Family Therapy — M,D
Media Studies — M,D
Museum Studies — M,D
Music — M,D
Philosophy — M,D
Political Science — M,D
Psychology—General — M,D

Public Administration — M,D
Public History — M,D
Public Policy — M,D,O
Religion — M,D
Rhetoric — M,D
Slavic Languages — M
Social Psychology — D
Sociology — M,D
Spanish — M,D
Theater — M
Therapies—Dance, Drama, and Music — M,D
Urban and Regional Planning — M,D
Writing — M,D

FONTBONNE UNIVERSITY
Art/Fine Arts — M
Family and Consumer Sciences-General — M
Health Communication — M
Theater — M

FORDHAM UNIVERSITY
Applied Psychology — M,D
Classics — M,D
Clinical Psychology — D
Communication—General — M,D
Counseling Psychology — M,D
Developmental Psychology — D
Economic Development — M,O
Economics — M,D,O
Emergency Management — M
English — M,D
Ethics — M,O
History — M,O
International Affairs — M,O
International Development — M,O
International Economics — M,D,O
Mass Communication — M
Media Studies — M,D
Medieval and Renaissance Studies — M
Pastoral Ministry and Counseling — M,D,O
Philosophy — M,D
Political Science — M
Psychology—General — M,D
Religion — M,D,O
School Psychology — M,D
Theater — M
Theology — M,D
Urban Studies — M

FORT HAYS STATE UNIVERSITY
Art/Fine Arts — M
Communication—General — M
English — M
Geography — M
History — M
Liberal Studies — M
Psychology—General — M,O
School Psychology — O

FORT VALLEY STATE UNIVERSITY
Counseling Psychology — M
Rehabilitation Counseling — M

FRAMINGHAM STATE UNIVERSITY
Counseling Psychology — M
English — M
Public Administration — M

FRANCISCAN SCHOOL OF THEOLOGY
Theology — M

FRANCISCAN UNIVERSITY OF STEUBENVILLE
Clinical Psychology — M
Counseling Psychology — M
Philosophy — M
Theology — M

FRANCIS MARION UNIVERSITY
Applied Psychology — M,O
Clinical Psychology — M,O
Counseling Psychology — M,O
Psychology—General — M,O
School Psychology — M,O

FRANKLIN UNIVERSITY
Corporate and Organizational Communication — M
Criminal Justice and Criminology — M

FREDERICK S. PARDEE RAND GRADUATE SCHOOL
Public Policy — D

FREED-HARDEMAN UNIVERSITY
Ethics — M
Pastoral Ministry and Counseling — M
Theology — M

FRESNO PACIFIC UNIVERSITY
Conflict Resolution and Mediation/Peace Studies — M,O
Interdisciplinary Studies — M
Marriage and Family Therapy — M
Missions and Missiology — M
Pastoral Ministry and Counseling — M
School Psychology — M
Theology — M
Urban Studies — M

FRIENDS UNIVERSITY
Marriage and Family Therapy — M

FROSTBURG STATE UNIVERSITY
Counseling Psychology — M
Interdisciplinary Studies — M,D
Psychology—General — M

FULLER THEOLOGICAL SEMINARY
Clinical Psychology — M,D,O
Marriage and Family Therapy — M,D,O
Missions and Missiology — M,D,O
Music — M,D,O
Pastoral Ministry and Counseling — M,D,O
Theology — M,D,O

FULL SAIL UNIVERSITY
Art/Fine Arts — M

Computer Art and Design — M
Graphic Design — M
Internet and Interactive Multimedia — M
Journalism — M
Media Studies — M
Writing — M

FUTURE GENERATIONS UNIVERSITY
Social Psychology — M
Sustainable Development — M
Urban and Regional Planning — M

GALLAUDET UNIVERSITY
Clinical Psychology — M,D,O
Counseling Psychology — M,D,O
Linguistics — M,D,O
Public Administration — M,D,O
School Psychology — M,D,O
Translation and Interpretation — M,D,O

GANNON UNIVERSITY
Clinical Psychology — M
Counseling Psychology — M
Criminal Justice and Criminology — M
English — M
Health Communication — M
Pastoral Ministry and Counseling — M,O
Public Administration — M
Theology — M,O

GARDNER-WEBB UNIVERSITY
Counseling Psychology — M
Cultural Studies — M
English — M
Missions and Missiology — M,D
Pastoral Ministry and Counseling — M,D
Psychology—General — M
School Psychology — M
Theology — M,D

GARRETT-EVANGELICAL THEOLOGICAL SEMINARY
Music — M
Pastoral Ministry and Counseling — M,D
Theology — M,D

GATEWAY SEMINARY
Pastoral Ministry and Counseling — M,D,O
Theology — M,D,O

THE GENERAL THEOLOGICAL SEMINARY
Pastoral Ministry and Counseling — M,D,O
Religion — M,D,O
Theology — M,D,O

GENEVA COLLEGE
Clinical Psychology — M
Counseling Psychology — M
Marriage and Family Therapy — M
Pastoral Ministry and Counseling — M
Psychology—General — M

GEORGE FOX UNIVERSITY
Clinical Psychology — M,D,O
Counseling Psychology — M,O
Cultural Studies — M,D,O
Marriage and Family Therapy — M,O
Pastoral Ministry and Counseling — M,D,O
School Psychology — M,O
Theology — M,D,O

GEORGE MASON UNIVERSITY
Anthropology — M,D
Art History — M
Art/Fine Arts — M
Arts Administration — M
Clinical Psychology — M,D,O
Cognitive Sciences — M,D,O
Communication—General — M,D,O
Conflict Resolution and Mediation/Peace Studies — M,D,O
Criminal Justice and Criminology — M,D
Cultural Studies — D
Developmental Psychology — M,D,O
Economics — M,D
English — M,D,O
Ethics — M
Forensic Sciences — M
French — M
Gender Studies — M
Geographic Information Systems — M
Geography — M,D,O
Graphic Design — M
History — M,D,O
Industrial and Organizational Psychology — M,D,O
Interdisciplinary Studies — M
International Affairs — M
Linguistics — M,D,O
Military and Defense Studies — M
Music — M,D
National Security — M,D,O
Near and Middle Eastern Studies — M,O
Philosophy — M
Political Science — M,D
Psychology—General — M,D,O
Public Administration — M
Public Affairs — M
Public Policy — M,D
Religion — M,D,O
Rhetoric — M,D,O
Sociology — M,D
Spanish — M
Women's Studies — M
Writing — M

GEORGETOWN UNIVERSITY
American Studies — M,D
Asian Studies — M
Communication—General — M
Comparative Literature — M,D
Conflict Resolution and Mediation/Peace Studies — M
East European and Russian Studies — M
Economic Development — D
Economics — D

Emergency Management — M,D
English — M,D
Ethics — M,D
German — M,D
History — M,D
Human Development — M,D
Humanities — M,D
Industrial and Labor Relations — D
Interdisciplinary Studies — M,D
International Affairs — M,D
International Development — M
Internet and Interactive Multimedia — M
Journalism — M,D
Latin American Studies — M,D
Liberal Studies — M,D
Linguistics — M,D
Media Studies — M,D
Medieval and Renaissance Studies — M,D
Near and Middle Eastern Languages — M,O
Near and Middle Eastern Studies — M,O
Philosophy — M,D
Political Science — M,D
Psychology—General — D
Public Policy — M,D
Religion — M,D
Spanish — M,D
Theology — D
Urban and Regional Planning — M,D
Western European Studies — M

THE GEORGE WASHINGTON UNIVERSITY
Addictions/Substance Abuse Counseling — M
American Studies — M,D
Anthropology — M,D
Applied Psychology — D
Art History — M
Art Therapy — M,O
Art/Fine Arts — M,O
Asian Studies — M
Clinical Psychology — M,D
Cognitive Sciences — D
Communication—General — M
Criminal Justice and Criminology — M,O
Dance — M,O
Decorative Arts — M
East European and Russian Studies — M
Economics — M,D
Emergency Management — M,D,O
English — M,D
Folklore — M,D
Forensic Psychology — M,D,O
Forensic Sciences — M,O
Gender Studies — O
Geography — M,O
Health Communication — M,D
Historic Preservation — M,D
History — M,D
Human Development — M
Interior Design — M
International Affairs — M,D
International Development — M,D
International Trade Policy — M
Latin American Studies — M
Mass Communication — M,O
Military and Defense Studies — M
Museum Studies — M,D,O
National Security — M,D
Near and Middle Eastern Studies — M
Philosophy — M
Photography — M,O
Political Science — M,D
Psychology—General — M,D,O
Public Administration — M,D
Public Affairs — M,O
Public Policy — M,D
Publishing — M
Rehabilitation Counseling — M
Religion — M
Social Psychology — D
Sociology — M
Theater — M,O
Western European Studies — M
Women's Studies — M,O

GEORGIA COLLEGE & STATE UNIVERSITY
Art Therapy — M
Criminal Justice and Criminology — M
English — M
Public Administration — M
Therapies—Dance, Drama, and Music — M
Writing — M

GEORGIA INSTITUTE OF TECHNOLOGY
Architecture — M,D
Building Science — M,D
Computer Art and Design — M,D
Economic Development — M,D
Economics — M,D
Geographic Information Systems — M,D
History of Science and Technology — M,D
Industrial Design — M
International Affairs — M
Internet and Interactive Multimedia — M,D
Music — M,D
Psychology—General — M,D
Public Policy — M,D
Urban and Regional Planning — M,D
Urban Design — M,D

GEORGIAN COURT UNIVERSITY
Applied Behavior Analysis — M,O
Clinical Psychology — M,O
Computer Art and Design — M,O
Counseling Psychology — M,O
Criminal Justice and Criminology — M,O
Health Psychology — M,O
Homeland Security — M,O
School Psychology — M,O
Theology — M,O

GEORGIA SOUTHERN UNIVERSITY
Applied Economics | M,O
Art/Fine Arts | M
Clinical Psychology | M,D
Corporate and Organizational Communication | M,O
Counseling Psychology | M
Criminal Justice and Criminology | M,O
English | M
Graphic Design | M
History | M,O
Music | M
Psychology—General | M,D
Public Administration | M,O
Public History | M,O
School Psychology | M,O
Sociology | M
Spanish | M,O
Writing | M,O

GEORGIA STATE UNIVERSITY
African-American Studies | M
Anthropology | M
Art History | M
Art/Fine Arts | M
Clinical Psychology | D
Clothing and Textiles | M
Cognitive Sciences | D
Communication—General | M,D
Counseling Psychology | M,O
Criminal Justice and Criminology | M,O
Cultural Studies | D
Developmental Psychology | D
Economic Development | M,D,O
Economics | M,D,O
Emergency Management | M,D,O
English | M,D
Film, Television, and Video Production | M,D
Forensic Sciences | M,O
French | M,O
Gender Studies | M,O
Geographic Information Systems | O
Geography | M,D
German | O
Gerontology | M,O
Graphic Design | M
Historic Preservation | M
History | M,D
Human Development | M,D,O
Industrial and Labor Relations | M,D
Interior Design | M
Latin American Studies | M,O
Linguistics | M,D
Mass Communication | M,D
Media Studies | M,D
Philosophy | M
Photography | M,D
Political Science | M,D
Psychology—General | D
Public Administration | M,D,O
Public History | M,D
Public Policy | M,D,O
Rehabilitation Counseling | M
Religion | M
Rhetoric | M
School Psychology | M,D,O
Social Psychology | D
Sociology | M,D
Spanish | M,O
Speech and Interpersonal Communication | M,D
Translation and Interpretation | O
Urban and Regional Planning | M,D,O
Women's Studies | M,O
Writing | M,D

GLOBAL UNIVERSITY
Missions and Missiology | M,D
Pastoral Ministry and Counseling | M,D
Theology | M,D

GODDARD COLLEGE
Art Therapy | M
Clinical Psychology | M
Comparative and Interdisciplinary Arts | M
Interdisciplinary Studies | M
Psychology—General | M
Writing | M

GOLDEN GATE UNIVERSITY
Forensic Sciences | M,O
Psychology—General | M,D,O
Public Administration | M,D,O

GONZAGA UNIVERSITY
Marriage and Family Therapy | M,D
Philosophy | M
Theology | M

GORDON-CONWELL THEOLOGICAL SEMINARY
Archaeology | M,D
Missions and Missiology | M,D
Pastoral Ministry and Counseling | M,D
Religion | M,D
Theology | M,D

GOUCHER COLLEGE
Arts Administration | M
Computer Art and Design | M
Cultural Studies | M
Historic Preservation | M
Writing | M

GOVERNORS STATE UNIVERSITY
Addictions/Substance Abuse Counseling | M
Art/Fine Arts | M
Communication—General | M
Counseling Psychology | M
Criminal Justice and Criminology | M

English | M
Film, Television, and Video Production | M
Photography | M
Political Science | M
Psychology—General | M
Public Administration | M

GRACE COLLEGE
Clinical Psychology | M

GRACE COLLEGE OF DIVINITY
Religion | M

GRACELAND UNIVERSITY (IA)
Religion | M
Theology | M

GRACE MISSION UNIVERSITY
Missions and Missiology | M,D

GRACE SCHOOL OF THEOLOGY
Theology | M

GRACE THEOLOGICAL SEMINARY
Cultural Studies | M,D,O
Missions and Missiology | M,D,O
Pastoral Ministry and Counseling | M,D,O
Theology | M,D,O
Women's Studies | M,D,O

THE GRADUATE CENTER, CITY UNIVERSITY OF NEW YORK
Anthropology | D
Archaeology | D
Architectural History | D
Art History | D
Classics | M,D
Clinical Psychology | D
Cognitive Sciences | D
Comparative Literature | M,D
Criminal Justice and Criminology | D
Cultural Anthropology | D
Developmental Psychology | D
Economics | D
English | D
Experimental Psychology | D
French | D
Geographic Information Systems | M
Hispanic and Latin American Languages | D
History | D
Humanities | M
Industrial and Organizational Psychology | D
Italian | M,D
Liberal Studies | M
Linguistics | M,D
Music | D
Philosophy | M,D
Political Science | M,D
Psychology—General | D
Publishing | M
Social Psychology | D
Social Sciences | M
Sociology | D
Theater | D

GRADUATE THEOLOGICAL UNION
Art History | M,D,O
Cultural Studies | M,D,O
Ethics | M,D,O
Jewish Studies | M,D,O
Religion | M,D,O
Social Sciences | M,D,O
Theology | M,D,O

GRAMBLING STATE UNIVERSITY
Criminal Justice and Criminology | M
English | M,D,O
Mass Communication | M
Political Science | M
Public Administration | M

GRAND CANYON UNIVERSITY
Cognitive Sciences | D
Emergency Management | M
Industrial and Organizational Psychology | D
Pastoral Ministry and Counseling | D
Psychology—General | D

GRAND RAPIDS THEOLOGICAL SEMINARY OF CORNERSTONE UNIVERSITY
Interdisciplinary Studies | M
Pastoral Ministry and Counseling | M
Religion | M
Theology | M

GRAND VALLEY STATE UNIVERSITY
Communication—General | M
Criminal Justice and Criminology | M
English | M
Linguistics | M
Public Administration | M
School Psychology | M,O

GRATZ COLLEGE
Holocaust and Genocide Studies | M,D
Jewish Studies | M,O

GREENSBORO COLLEGE
Cultural Studies | M
Ethics | M
Theology | M

GREENVILLE UNIVERSITY
Pastoral Ministry and Counseling | M

GUILFORD COLLEGE
Criminal Justice and Criminology | M

HAMLINE UNIVERSITY
Public Administration | M,D
Writing | M

HAMPTON UNIVERSITY
Liberal Studies | M,D,O
Marriage and Family Therapy | M
Pastoral Ministry and Counseling | M,D,O
Psychology—General | M

HARDING SCHOOL OF THEOLOGY
Pastoral Ministry and Counseling | M,D
Theology | M,D

HARDING UNIVERSITY
Pastoral Ministry and Counseling | M

HARDIN-SIMMONS UNIVERSITY
Counseling Psychology | M
Marriage and Family Therapy | M
Music | M
Pastoral Ministry and Counseling | M,D
Psychology—General | M
Religion | M
Theology | M

HARRISON MIDDLETON UNIVERSITY
Comparative Literature | M,D
Humanities | M,D
Interdisciplinary Studies | M,D
Philosophy | M,D
Religion | M,D
Social Sciences | M,D

HARTFORD SEMINARY
Pastoral Ministry and Counseling | M,D,O
Religion | M,D,O
Theology | M,D,O

HARVARD UNIVERSITY
African Studies | D
African-American Studies | D
American Studies | D
Anthropology | M,D
Archaeology | M,D
Architectural History | D
Architecture | M,D
Art History | D
Asian Languages | M,D
Asian Studies | M,D
Biological Anthropology | M,D
Celtic Languages | D
Chinese | D
Classics | D
Cognitive Sciences | D
Communication—General | M,D
Comparative Literature | D
Demography and Population Studies | D
Developmental Psychology | D
East European and Russian Studies | M
Economics | D
English | M,D,O
Experimental Psychology | D
French | M,D
German | D
History of Science and Technology | M,D
History | D
Human Development | M
International Affairs | D
International Development | M
Italian | M,D
Japanese | D
Jewish Studies | M,D
Journalism | M,O
Landscape Architecture | M,D
Liberal Studies | M,O
Linguistics | D
Medieval and Renaissance Studies | M
Museum Studies | M,O
Music | M,D
Near and Middle Eastern Languages | M,D
Near and Middle Eastern Studies | M,D
Philosophy | M,D
Political Science | M,D
Portuguese | M,D
Psychology—General | D
Public Administration | M
Public Policy | M,D
Religion | D
Russian | D
Scandinavian Languages | D
Slavic Languages | D
Social Psychology | D
Sociology | D
Spanish | M,D
Technical Communication | M
Theology | M
Urban and Regional Planning | M,D
Urban Design | M

HAWAII PACIFIC UNIVERSITY
Clinical Psychology | M
Communication—General | M
Liberal Studies | M
Military and Defense Studies | M
Public Administration | M
Sustainable Development | M

HAZELDEN BETTY FORD GRADUATE SCHOOL OF ADDICTION STUDIES
Addictions/Substance Abuse Counseling | M,O

HEBREW COLLEGE
Jewish Studies | M,O
Music | M,O
Theology | M

HEBREW UNION COLLEGE–JEWISH INSTITUTE OF RELIGION (NY)
Jewish Studies | M
Music | M
Near and Middle Eastern Languages | D
Theology | M,D

HEC MONTREAL
Applied Economics | M,D
Arts Administration | O

Corporate and Organizational Communication | O
Sustainable Development | O

HEIDELBERG UNIVERSITY
Counseling Psychology | M

HENDERSON STATE UNIVERSITY
Counseling Psychology | M,O
Liberal Studies | M

HENLEY-PUTNAM SCHOOL OF STRATEGIC SECURITY
Conflict Resolution and Mediation/Peace Studies | M
Homeland Security | M
Military and Defense Studies | M
National Security | D

HERITAGE CHRISTIAN UNIVERSITY
Classics | M
Pastoral Ministry and Counseling | M
Religion | M

HERITAGE COLLEGE AND SEMINARY
Theology | M,O

HERITAGE UNIVERSITY
English | M

HIGH POINT UNIVERSITY
Corporate and Organizational Communication | M,D

HILBERT COLLEGE
Criminal Justice and Criminology | M
Public Administration | M

HILLSDALE COLLEGE
Political Science | M,D

HIRAM COLLEGE
Interdisciplinary Studies | M

HODGES UNIVERSITY
Clinical Psychology | M
Counseling Psychology | M

HOFSTRA UNIVERSITY
Applied Behavior Analysis | M,D,O
Art Therapy | M,O
Clinical Psychology | M,D
Counseling Psychology | M,O
English | M
Family and Consumer Sciences-General | M,D,O
Industrial and Organizational Psychology | M,D
Journalism | M
Linguistics | M
Marriage and Family Therapy | M,O
Psychology—General | M,O
Rehabilitation Counseling | M,O
School Psychology | M,D
Social Psychology | M,D
Sustainable Development | M
Urban Design | M
Writing | M

HOLLINS UNIVERSITY
Art/Fine Arts | M
Dance | M
English | M,O
Film, Television, and Video Production | M
Film, Television, and Video Theory and Criticism | M
Humanities | M
Illustration | M,O
Interdisciplinary Studies | M
Liberal Studies | M
Music | M
Social Sciences | M
Theater | M,O
Writing | M,O

HOLMES INSTITUTE
Pastoral Ministry and Counseling | M

HOLY APOSTLES COLLEGE AND SEMINARY
Theology | M,O

HOLY CROSS GREEK ORTHODOX SCHOOL OF THEOLOGY
Theology | M

HOLY FAMILY UNIVERSITY
Counseling Psychology | M
Criminal Justice and Criminology | M

HOLY NAMES UNIVERSITY
Counseling Psychology | M
Forensic Psychology | M
Music | M,O
Pastoral Ministry and Counseling | M
Writing | M

HOOD COLLEGE
Art/Fine Arts | M,O
Clinical Psychology | M
Geographic Information Systems | M,O
Humanities | M
School Psychology | M

HOOD THEOLOGICAL SEMINARY
Theology | M,D

HOPE INTERNATIONAL UNIVERSITY
International Development | M
Marriage and Family Therapy | M
Missions and Missiology | M
Music | M
Religion | M

HOUGHTON COLLEGE
Music | M

HOUSTON BAPTIST UNIVERSITY
- Art/Fine Arts M
- English M,D
- Liberal Studies M
- Music M,D
- Near and Middle Eastern Languages M
- Philosophy M
- Spanish M
- Theology M

HOUSTON GRADUATE SCHOOL OF THEOLOGY
- Pastoral Ministry and Counseling M,D
- Theology M,D

HOWARD PAYNE UNIVERSITY
- Criminal Justice and Criminology M
- Pastoral Ministry and Counseling M
- Theology M

HOWARD UNIVERSITY
- African Studies M,D
- Applied Arts and Design—General M
- Art History M
- Art/Fine Arts M
- Clinical Psychology M,D
- Communication—General M,D
- Corporate and Organizational Communication M,D
- Counseling Psychology D
- Developmental Psychology M,D
- Economics M,D
- English M,D
- Experimental Psychology M,D
- Film, Television, and Video Production M
- French M
- History M,D
- Mass Communication M,D
- Media Studies M,D
- Music M
- Philosophy M
- Photography M
- Political Science M,D
- Psychology—General M,D
- Public Administration M
- School Psychology M,D
- Social Psychology M,D
- Sociology M,D
- Spanish M
- Theology M,D

HUMBOLDT STATE UNIVERSITY
- Anthropology M
- Counseling Psychology M
- Developmental Psychology M
- English M
- Psychology—General M
- School Psychology M
- Social Psychology M
- Social Sciences M
- Sociology M

HUNTER COLLEGE OF THE CITY UNIVERSITY OF NEW YORK
- Anthropology M
- Applied Social Research M
- Art History M
- Art/Fine Arts M
- Chinese M
- Classics M
- Comparative Literature M
- Economics M
- French M
- Geographic Information Systems M,O
- Geography M,O
- History M
- Italian M
- Media Studies M
- Music M
- Psychology—General M,O
- Rehabilitation Counseling M
- Romance Languages M
- Sociology M
- Spanish M
- Sustainable Development M,O
- Theater M
- Urban and Regional Planning M
- Urban Studies M
- Writing M

HUNTINGTON UNIVERSITY
- Pastoral Ministry and Counseling M,D

HUNTSVILLE BIBLE COLLEGE
- Pastoral Ministry and Counseling M

HUSSON UNIVERSITY
- Clinical Psychology M
- Counseling Psychology M
- Criminal Justice and Criminology M
- School Psychology M
- Social Psychology M

ICAHN SCHOOL OF MEDICINE AT MOUNT SINAI
- Genetic Counseling M,D

IDAHO STATE UNIVERSITY
- Anthropology M
- Art/Fine Arts M
- Clinical Psychology D
- Communication—General M
- Counseling Psychology M,D,O
- English M,D,O
- Experimental Psychology D
- Geographic Information Systems M,O
- History M
- Marriage and Family Therapy M,D,O
- Political Science M,D
- Psychology—General D
- Public Administration M
- School Psychology M,D,O
- Sociology M
- Theater M

IGLOBAL UNIVERSITY
- Public Administration M

ILIFF SCHOOL OF THEOLOGY
- Pastoral Ministry and Counseling M,D
- Religion M,D
- Theology M,D

ILLINOIS INSTITUTE OF TECHNOLOGY
- Applied Arts and Design—General M,D
- Architecture M,D
- Clinical Psychology M,D
- Communication—General M,D
- Corporate and Organizational Communication M
- Humanities M,D
- Industrial and Organizational Psychology M,D
- Landscape Architecture M,D
- Psychology—General M,D
- Public Administration M
- Rehabilitation Counseling M,D
- Technical Writing M,D

ILLINOIS STATE UNIVERSITY
- Agricultural Economics and Agribusiness M
- Archaeology M
- Art History M
- Art/Fine Arts M
- Clinical Psychology M,D,O
- Cognitive Sciences M,D,O
- Communication—General M
- Counseling Psychology M,D,O
- Criminal Justice and Criminology M
- Developmental Psychology M,D,O
- Economics M
- English M,D
- Family and Consumer Sciences-General M
- French M
- German M
- Graphic Design M
- History M
- Industrial and Organizational Psychology M,D,O
- Music M
- Photography M
- Political Science M
- Psychology—General M,D,O
- School Psychology M,D,O
- Sociology M
- Spanish M
- Textile Design M
- Theater M
- Writing M,D

IMMACULATA UNIVERSITY
- Clinical Psychology M,D,O
- Counseling Psychology M,D,O
- Forensic Psychology M,D,O
- Psychoanalysis and Psychotherapy M,D,O
- Psychology—General M,D,O
- School Psychology M,D,O
- Therapies—Dance, Drama, and Music M

INDIANA STATE UNIVERSITY
- Art/Fine Arts M
- Clinical Psychology M,D,O
- Communication—General M
- Criminal Justice and Criminology M
- English M
- Graphic Design M
- History M
- Linguistics M,D,O
- Media Studies M
- Music M
- Photography M
- Psychology—General M,D
- Public Administration M
- School Psychology M,D,O
- Spanish M,D,O
- Writing M

INDIANA TECH
- Psychology—General M

INDIANA UNIVERSITY BLOOMINGTON
- African Studies M
- African-American Studies M,D
- Anthropology M,D
- Applied Arts and Design—General M
- Archaeology M,D
- Architecture M,D
- Art History M,D
- Art/Fine Arts M
- Arts Administration M
- Asian Languages M,D
- Asian Studies M,D
- Chinese M,D
- Classics M,D
- Cognitive Sciences D
- Comparative Literature M,D
- Criminal Justice and Criminology M,D
- Developmental Psychology D
- East European and Russian Studies M,O
- Economic Development M,D,O
- Economics M,D
- English M,D
- Folklore M,D
- French M,D
- Gender Studies D
- Geography D
- German M,D
- Hispanic and Latin American Languages M,D
- History of Medicine M,D
- History of Science and Technology M,D
- History M,D
- International Affairs M
- International Development M,D,O
- Italian M,D
- Japanese M,D
- Jewish Studies M
- Latin American Studies M
- Linguistics M,D
- Media Studies M,D
- Medieval and Renaissance Studies M,D
- Music M,D,O
- Near and Middle Eastern Languages M,D
- Philosophy M,D
- Political Science M,D
- Portuguese M,D
- Psychology—General D
- Public Administration M,D,O
- Public Affairs M,D,O
- Public Policy M,D,O
- Religion M,D
- Rhetoric M,D
- School Psychology M,D,O
- Slavic Languages M,D
- Social Psychology D
- Social Sciences M,D,O
- Sociology M,D
- Spanish M,D
- Theater M,D
- Western European Studies M
- Writing M,D

INDIANA UNIVERSITY KOKOMO
- Public Administration M,O
- Public Policy M,O

INDIANA UNIVERSITY NORTHWEST
- Addictions/Substance Abuse Counseling M,O
- Counseling Psychology M,O
- Criminal Justice and Criminology M,O
- Gender Studies M,O
- Liberal Studies M,O
- Public Administration M,O
- Public Affairs M,O
- Urban Studies M,O

INDIANA UNIVERSITY OF PENNSYLVANIA
- Archaeology M
- Art/Fine Arts M
- Clinical Psychology M,D
- Communication—General D
- Criminal Justice and Criminology M,D
- English M,D
- Geographic Information Systems M,O
- Geography M,O
- History M
- Industrial and Labor Relations M
- Media Studies D
- Music M
- Psychology—General M,D
- Public Affairs M
- Public History M
- School Psychology D,O
- Social Psychology M
- Sociology M
- Urban and Regional Planning M

INDIANA UNIVERSITY-PURDUE UNIVERSITY INDIANAPOLIS
- American Studies M,D
- Art Therapy M
- Art/Fine Arts M
- Clinical Psychology M,D
- Communication—General M,D
- Computer Art and Design M
- Criminal Justice and Criminology M,O
- Economics M
- Emergency Management M,O
- English M,O
- Forensic Sciences M
- Geographic Information Systems M,O
- Graphic Design M
- Health Communication M,D
- History M
- Homeland Security M,O
- Industrial and Organizational Psychology M,D
- Liberal Studies M,D,O
- Museum Studies M,O
- Music M,D
- Philanthropic Studies M,D
- Philosophy M,O
- Photography M
- Political Science M
- Psychology—General M,D
- Public Administration M,O
- Public Affairs M,O
- Public History M
- Social Psychology M,D
- Social Sciences M,D,O
- Sociology M
- Technical Communication M
- Therapies—Dance, Drama, and Music M,D
- Western European Studies M
- Writing M,O

INDIANA UNIVERSITY SOUTH BEND
- Addictions/Substance Abuse Counseling M,O
- Clinical Psychology M,O
- Communication—General M,D
- Counseling Psychology M,O
- English M,O
- International Affairs M,O
- Liberal Studies M,O
- Marriage and Family Therapy M,O
- Music M,D
- Public Administration M,O
- Public Affairs M,O
- School Psychology M,O
- Writing M,O

INDIANA UNIVERSITY SOUTHEAST
- Interdisciplinary Studies M,O

INDIANA WESLEYAN UNIVERSITY
- Addictions/Substance Abuse Counseling M
- Counseling Psychology M
- Marriage and Family Therapy M
- Pastoral Ministry and Counseling M
- Social Psychology M
- Theology M

INSTITUTE FOR CHRISTIAN STUDIES
- Philosophy M,D
- Political Science M,D
- Theology M,D

INSTITUTE FOR DOCTORAL STUDIES IN THE VISUAL ARTS
- Art/Fine Arts D
- Philosophy D

INSTITUTE OF AMERICAN INDIAN ARTS
- Writing M

INSTITUTE OF PUBLIC ADMINISTRATION
- Public Administration M,O

THE INSTITUTE OF WORLD POLITICS
- Conflict Resolution and Mediation/Peace Studies M,D,O
- Homeland Security M,D,O
- International Affairs M,D,O
- International Economics M,D,O
- Military and Defense Studies M,D,O
- National Security M,D,O
- Political Science M,D,O
- Public Affairs M,D,O
- Public Policy M,D,O

INSTITUTO CENTROAMERICANO DE ADMINISTRACION DE EMPRESAS
- Agricultural Economics and Agribusiness M
- Sustainable Development M

INSTITUTO TECNOLOGICO DE SANTO DOMINGO
- Communication—General M,O
- Counseling Psychology M,O
- Economics M,O
- Gender Studies M,O
- Humanities M,O
- International Affairs M,O
- Linguistics M,O
- Marriage and Family Therapy M,O
- Sustainable Development M,O

INSTITUTO TECNOLÓGICO Y DE ESTUDIOS SUPERIORES DE MONTERREY, CAMPUS CENTRAL DE VERACRUZ
- Humanities M

INSTITUTO TECNOLÓGICO Y DE ESTUDIOS SUPERIORES DE MONTERREY, CAMPUS CIUDAD DE MÉXICO
- Economics M,D
- Humanities M,D

INSTITUTO TECNOLÓGICO Y DE ESTUDIOS SUPERIORES DE MONTERREY, CAMPUS CIUDAD JUÁREZ
- Humanities M
- Public Administration M

INSTITUTO TECNOLÓGICO Y DE ESTUDIOS SUPERIORES DE MONTERREY, CAMPUS CIUDAD OBREGÓN
- Communication—General M
- International Affairs M

INSTITUTO TECNOLÓGICO Y DE ESTUDIOS SUPERIORES DE MONTERREY, CAMPUS ESTADO DE MÉXICO
- Architecture M,D
- Humanities M,D

INSTITUTO TECNOLÓGICO Y DE ESTUDIOS SUPERIORES DE MONTERREY, CAMPUS IRAPUATO
- Architecture M,D
- Humanities M,D

INSTITUTO TECNOLÓGICO Y DE ESTUDIOS SUPERIORES DE MONTERREY, CAMPUS MONTERREY
- Communication—General M,D

INTER AMERICAN UNIVERSITY OF PUERTO RICO, AGUADILLA CAMPUS
- Counseling Psychology M
- Criminal Justice and Criminology M

INTER AMERICAN UNIVERSITY OF PUERTO RICO, BARRANQUITAS CAMPUS
- Criminal Justice and Criminology M
- History M

INTER AMERICAN UNIVERSITY OF PUERTO RICO, METROPOLITAN CAMPUS
- American Studies M,D
- Counseling Psychology M,D
- Criminal Justice and Criminology M
- English M
- History M,D
- Industrial and Labor Relations M,D
- Industrial and Organizational Psychology M,D
- Pastoral Ministry and Counseling D
- Psychology—General M,D
- School Psychology M,D
- Spanish M
- Theology D
- Women's Studies M

INTER AMERICAN UNIVERSITY OF PUERTO RICO, PONCE CAMPUS
Criminal Justice and Criminology M
Spanish M

INTER AMERICAN UNIVERSITY OF PUERTO RICO, SAN GERMÁN CAMPUS
Art/Fine Arts M
Counseling Psychology M,D
Graphic Design M
Music M
Photography M
Psychology—General M,D
School Psychology M,D

INTERDENOMINATIONAL THEOLOGICAL CENTER
Pastoral Ministry and Counseling M,D
Theology M

INTERIOR DESIGNERS INSTITUTE
Interior Design M

INTERNATIONAL BAPTIST COLLEGE AND SEMINARY
Pastoral Ministry and Counseling M,D
Theology M

INTERNATIONAL TECHNOLOGICAL UNIVERSITY
Computer Art and Design M

INTERNATIONAL UNIVERSITY IN GENEVA
Communication—General M,D
International Affairs M,D
Media Studies M,D
Public Administration M,D

IONA COLLEGE
Counseling Psychology M,O
Criminal Justice and Criminology M,O
English M
Experimental Psychology M,O
Forensic Sciences M,O
History M
Industrial and Organizational
  Psychology M,O
Marriage and Family Therapy M
Mass Communication M,O
Psychology—General M,O
School Psychology M,O
Spanish M

IOWA STATE UNIVERSITY OF SCIENCE AND TECHNOLOGY
Agricultural Economics and
  Agribusiness M,D
Anthropology M
Applied Arts and Design—
  General M,D
Architecture M
Art/Fine Arts M
Child and Family Studies M,D
Clothing and Textiles M,D
Cognitive Sciences M,D
Corporate and Organizational
  Communication M,D
Counseling Psychology M,D
Economics M,D
English M,D
Family and Consumer
  Sciences-General M
Graphic Design M
History M,D
Human Development M,D
Industrial Design M
Interdisciplinary Studies M
Interior Design M
Journalism M
Landscape Architecture M
Linguistics M,D
Mass Communication M
Political Science M
Psychology—General M,D
Public Administration M
Rhetoric M,D
Rural Planning and Studies D
Rural Sociology M,D
Social Psychology M,D
Sociology M,D
Sustainable Development M,D
Urban and Regional Planning M
Writing M,D

ITHACA COLLEGE
Art/Fine Arts M
Internet and Interactive
  Multimedia M
Music M
Photography M
Writing M

JACKSON STATE UNIVERSITY
Clinical Psychology M,D
Criminal Justice and Criminology M
English M
History M
Political Science M
Psychology—General D
Public Administration M,D
Public Affairs M,D
Public Policy M,D
School Psychology M
Sociology M
Urban and Regional Planning M

JACKSONVILLE STATE UNIVERSITY
Criminal Justice and Criminology M
Emergency Management M,D
English M
History M
Liberal Studies M
Music M

Psychology—General M
Public Administration M

JACKSONVILLE UNIVERSITY
Art/Fine Arts M
Counseling Psychology M
Dance M
Marriage and Family Therapy M
Public Policy M

JAMES MADISON UNIVERSITY
American Studies M
Applied Behavior Analysis M
Art History M
Art/Fine Arts M
Clinical Psychology D
Communication—General M
Counseling Psychology D
English M
Experimental Psychology M
Forensic Sciences M
History M
Music M,D
Photography M
Political Science M
Psychology—General M
Public Administration M
Public History M
Rhetoric M
School Psychology M,D,O
Technical Writing M
Writing M

THE JEWISH THEOLOGICAL SEMINARY
Jewish Studies M,D
Music M
Religion M,D
Theology M,D,O
Women's Studies M,D

JOHN BROWN UNIVERSITY
Clinical Psychology M,O
Counseling Psychology M,O
Ethics M,O
Marriage and Family Therapy M,O

JOHN CABOT UNIVERSITY
Art History M

JOHN CARROLL UNIVERSITY
Counseling Psychology M,O
English M
Religion M
Theology M

JOHN F. KENNEDY UNIVERSITY
Counseling Psychology M
Health Psychology M
Museum Studies O
Psychology—General M,D,O
Sport Psychology M,O
Transpersonal and Humanistic
  Psychology M

JOHN JAY COLLEGE OF CRIMINAL JUSTICE OF THE CITY UNIVERSITY OF NEW YORK
Criminal Justice and Criminology M,D
Economics M
Forensic Psychology M,D
Forensic Sciences M,D
Public Administration M
Public Policy M,D

JOHN PAUL THE GREAT CATHOLIC UNIVERSITY
Theology M

JOHNS HOPKINS UNIVERSITY
Anthropology D
Applied Economics M
Archaeology D
Art History M,D
Asian Studies M,D,O
Classics D
Clinical Psychology M,D
Cognitive Sciences M,D
Communication—General M,O
Comparative Literature M
Demography and Population Studies M,D
Economics D
English D
Film, Television, and Video
  Production M
French M,D
Genetic Counseling M,D
Geographic Information Systems M,O
German M,D
Health Communication M,D
History of Science and Technology M,D
History D
Homeland Security M,O
International Affairs M,D,O
International Development M,D,O
International Economics M,D,O
Italian M,D
Liberal Studies M,O
Media Studies M
Medical Illustration M
Museum Studies M,O
Music M,D,O
Near and Middle Eastern Languages D
Near and Middle Eastern Studies D
Philosophy M,D
Political Science M,D,O
Psychology—General D
Public Administration M,O
Public Policy M,D
Romance Languages D
Sociology D
Spanish M,D
Technical Writing M,O
Writing M,O

JOHNSON & WALES UNIVERSITY
Addictions/Substance Abuse
  Counseling M
Clinical Psychology M
Criminal Justice and Criminology M
Economic Development M
Sustainable Development M

JOHNSON UNIVERSITY
Clinical Psychology M,D,O
Cultural Studies M,D,O
Pastoral Ministry and Counseling M,D,O
Theology M,D,O

JOHNSON UNIVERSITY FLORIDA
Pastoral Ministry and Counseling M

THE JUDGE ADVOCATE GENERAL'S SCHOOL, U.S. ARMY
Military and Defense Studies M

JUDSON UNIVERSITY
Architecture M
Clinical Psychology M
Pastoral Ministry and Counseling M
Sustainable Development M
Urban Design M

THE JUILLIARD SCHOOL
Music M,D,O
Theater M,D,O

KANSAS STATE UNIVERSITY
Agricultural Economics and
  Agribusiness M,D
Architecture M
Art/Fine Arts M
Child and Family Studies M,D,O
Child Development M,D,O
Clothing and Textiles M,D
Communication—General M,D,O
Conflict Resolution and
  Mediation/Peace Studies M,D,O
Consumer Economics M,D,O
Economics M,D
English M,O
Environmental Design D
Family and Consumer
  Sciences-General M,D,O
French M
Gender Studies O
Geographic Information Systems M,D,O
Geography M,D,O
German M
Gerontology M,O
Health Communication M
History M,D
Human Development M,D,O
Interdisciplinary Studies M,O
Interior Design M
Journalism M
Landscape Architecture M
Marriage and Family Therapy M,D,O
Mass Communication M
Music M
National Security M,D
Political Science M
Psychology—General M,D
Public Administration M
Sociology M,D
Spanish M
Theater M
Urban and Regional Planning M
Women's Studies O

KEAN UNIVERSITY
Addictions/Substance Abuse
  Counseling M
Clinical Psychology M,D
Communication—General M
Counseling Psychology M
Criminal Justice and Criminology M
Forensic Psychology M
Holocaust and Genocide Studies M
Industrial and Organizational
  Psychology M
Liberal Studies M
Marriage and Family Therapy M
Psychology—General M
Public Administration M
School Psychology D,O
Writing M

KEHILATH YAKOV RABBINICAL SEMINARY
Theology M

KEISER UNIVERSITY
Criminal Justice and Criminology M
Homeland Security M
Industrial and Organizational
  Psychology M,D
Psychology—General M,D

KENNESAW STATE UNIVERSITY
American Studies M
Communication—General M
Conflict Resolution and
  Mediation/Peace Studies M,D
Criminal Justice and Criminology M
International Affairs M
Public Administration M
Writing M

KENRICK-GLENNON SEMINARY
Theology M

KENT STATE UNIVERSITY
Anthropology M
Architecture M
Art History M
Art/Fine Arts M
Biological Anthropology M,D
Broadcast Journalism M

LANCASTER BIBLE COLLEGE
Counseling Psychology M,D
Marriage and Family Therapy M,D
Pastoral Ministry and Counseling M,D,O
Theology M,D,O

Child and Family Studies M
Clinical Psychology M,D
Communication—General M
Conflict Resolution and
  Mediation/Peace Studies M,D
Counseling Psychology M
Criminal Justice and Criminology M
Economics M
English M,D
Environmental Design M
Experimental Psychology M,D
French M
Geographic Information Systems M
Geography M,D
German M,D
Gerontology M
Graphic Design M
History M,D
Human Development M,D
Illustration M
Japanese M,D
Journalism M
Landscape Architecture M
Linguistics M,D
Mass Communication M
Media Studies M
Music M,D
Near and Middle Eastern Languages M,D
Philosophy M
Photography M
Political Science M,D
Psychology—General M,D
Public Administration M
Rehabilitation Counseling M
Rhetoric M,D
Russian M
School Psychology M,D,O
Sociology M,D
Spanish M,D
Textile Design M
Theater M
Translation and Interpretation M
Urban Design M
Writing M,D

KENTUCKY CHRISTIAN UNIVERSITY
Religion M
Theology M

THE KING'S UNIVERSITY
Pastoral Ministry and Counseling M,D,O
Theology M,D,O

KINGSWOOD UNIVERSITY
Pastoral Ministry and Counseling M
Theology M

KNOX COLLEGE
Theology M,D

KNOX THEOLOGICAL SEMINARY
Classics M
Pastoral Ministry and Counseling D
Religion M
Theology M

KUTZTOWN UNIVERSITY OF PENNSYLVANIA
Arts Administration M
Counseling Psychology M
English M
Internet and Interactive
  Multimedia M
Public Administration M

LAGRANGE COLLEGE
Clinical Psychology M

LAGUNA COLLEGE OF ART & DESIGN
Art/Fine Arts M

LAKE FOREST COLLEGE
American Studies M
Art/Fine Arts M
Film, Television, and Video
  Production M
French M
History M
Liberal Studies M
Philosophy M
Spanish M
Writing M

LAKEHEAD UNIVERSITY
Clinical Psychology M,D
Economics M
English M,D
Experimental Psychology M,D
Gerontology M,D
History M
Psychology—General M,D
Sociology M
Women's Studies M,D

LAKELAND UNIVERSITY
Theology M

LAMAR UNIVERSITY
Clinical Psychology M
Counseling Psychology M
Criminal Justice and Criminology M
English M
Family and Consumer
  Sciences-General M
History M
Music M
Political Science M
Psychology—General M
Spanish M

LANCASTER THEOLOGICAL SEMINARY
Art History — M,D,O
Ethics — M,D,O
Religion — M,D,O
Theology — M,D,O

LANDER UNIVERSITY
Emergency Management — M

LANGSTON UNIVERSITY
Rehabilitation Counseling — M

LA SALLE UNIVERSITY
Clinical Psychology — M,D
Communication—General — M,O
Corporate and Organizational
  Communication — M,O
Counseling Psychology — M
Developmental Psychology — M,D
English — M,O
Forensic Sciences — M,O
Gerontology — M,D,O
Health Psychology — M,D
Hispanic Studies — M,O
Industrial and Organizational
  Psychology — M
Latin American Studies — M,O
Marriage and Family Therapy — M
Media Studies — M,O
Psychology—General — M,D
Translation and Interpretation — M,O

LASELL COLLEGE
Communication—General — M,O
Corporate and Organizational
  Communication — M,O
Criminal Justice and Criminology — M,O
Emergency Management — M,O
Health Communication — M,O
Homeland Security — M,O

LA SIERRA UNIVERSITY
Communication—General — M
English — M
Pastoral Ministry and Counseling — M
Religion — M
School Psychology — M,O
Writing — M

LAURENTIAN UNIVERSITY
Applied Psychology — M
Applied Social Research — M
Experimental Psychology — M
History — M
Human Development — M
Humanities — M
Psychology—General — M
Sociology — M
Technical Writing — O

LAWRENCE TECHNOLOGICAL UNIVERSITY
Architecture — M,O
Communication—General — M,O
Interior Design — M,O
Technical Communication — M,O
Urban Design — M,O

LEBANESE AMERICAN UNIVERSITY
International Affairs — M

LEBANON VALLEY COLLEGE
Ethics — M

LEE UNIVERSITY
Art/Fine Arts — M,O
Child Development — M
Counseling Psychology — M
Economics — M,O
English — M,O
Ethics — M
History — M,O
Music — M
Pastoral Ministry and Counseling — M
Religion — M
Spanish — M,O
Theology — M

LEHIGH UNIVERSITY
American Studies — M,D
Counseling Psychology — M,D,O
Economics — M,D
English — M,D
History — M,D
Interdisciplinary Studies — M,D
Political Science — M
Psychology—General — M,D
Public History — M,D
School Psychology — D,O
Sustainable Development — M,O

LEHMAN COLLEGE OF THE CITY UNIVERSITY OF NEW YORK
Art/Fine Arts — M
English — M
History — M
Spanish — M

LE MOYNE COLLEGE
Arts Administration — M
Urban Studies — M,O

LENOIR-RHYNE UNIVERSITY
Addictions/Substance Abuse
  Counseling — M
Clinical Psychology — M
Counseling Psychology — M
Sustainable Development — M
Theology — M
Writing — M

LESLEY UNIVERSITY
Art Therapy — M,D,O
Art/Fine Arts — M,D,O
Clinical Psychology — M,D,O
Conflict Resolution and
  Mediation/Peace Studies — M,D,O
Counseling Psychology — M,D,O
Health Psychology — M,D,O

Interdisciplinary Studies — M,D,O
International Affairs — M,D,O
Photography — M
Psychology—General — M,D,O
School Psychology — M,D,O
Social Psychology — M,D,O
Sustainable Development — M,D,O
Therapies—Dance, Drama, and
  Music — M,D,O
Urban and Regional Planning — M,D,O
Women's Studies — M,D,O
Writing — M,D,O

LETOURNEAU UNIVERSITY
Counseling Psychology — M
Marriage and Family Therapy — M
Psychology—General — M

LEWIS & CLARK COLLEGE
Addictions/Substance Abuse
  Counseling — M
Counseling Psychology — M
Marriage and Family Therapy — M
School Psychology — M

LEWIS UNIVERSITY
Clinical Psychology — M
Counseling Psychology — M
Criminal Justice and Criminology — M

LEXINGTON THEOLOGICAL SEMINARY
Theology — M,D

LIBERTY UNIVERSITY
Addictions/Substance Abuse
  Counseling — M,D,O
Applied Psychology — M,D,O
Child and Family Studies — M,D,O
Clinical Psychology — M,D,O
Communication—General — M
Counseling Psychology — M,D,O
Criminal Justice and Criminology — M,D,O
Developmental Psychology — M,D,O
Emergency Management — M,D,O
English — M
Forensic Psychology — M
History — M
Homeland Security — M
Industrial and Organizational
  Psychology — M,D,O
International Affairs — M,D
Internet and Interactive
  Multimedia — M
Marriage and Family Therapy — M,D,O
Military and Defense Studies — M,D
Missions and Missiology — M,D
Music — M,D
Pastoral Ministry and Counseling — M,D,O
Political Science — M
Psychology—General — M,D,O
Public Administration — M
Public Policy — M
Religion — M,D
School Psychology — M,D,O
Theology — M,D,O

LIM COLLEGE
Clothing and Textiles — M

LINCOLN CHRISTIAN SEMINARY
Pastoral Ministry and Counseling — M,D
Theology — M,D

LINCOLN CHRISTIAN UNIVERSITY
Cultural Studies — M
Pastoral Ministry and Counseling — M
Philosophy — M
Religion — M
Theology — M

LINCOLN UNIVERSITY (MO)
Criminal Justice and Criminology — M
History — M
Sociology — M

LINDENWOOD UNIVERSITY
Applied Behavior Analysis — M,D,O
Art History — M
Communication—General — M,O
Counseling Psychology — M,D,O
Criminal Justice and Criminology — M,O
Film, Television, and Video
  Production — M
Internet and Interactive
  Multimedia — M
Journalism — M
Mass Communication — M
Media Studies — M,O
School Psychology — M,D,O
Writing — M,O

LINDENWOOD UNIVERSITY—BELLEVILLE
Communication—General — M
Computer Art and Design — M
Criminal Justice and Criminology — M
Internet and Interactive
  Multimedia — M
Media Studies — M

LINDSEY WILSON COLLEGE
Counseling Psychology — M,D
Human Development — M,D
Internet and Interactive
  Multimedia — M

LIPSCOMB UNIVERSITY
Applied Behavior Analysis — M,D,O
Clinical Psychology — M,O
Conflict Resolution and
  Mediation/Peace Studies — M,O
Counseling Psychology — M,O
English — M,D,O
Film, Television, and Video
  Production — M
International Affairs — M,O
Marriage and Family Therapy — M,O
Pastoral Ministry and Counseling — M,D
Psychology—General — M,O

Public Administration — M
Public Policy — M
School Psychology — M,D,O
Sustainable Development — M,O
Theology — M,D
Writing — M

LOCK HAVEN UNIVERSITY OF PENNSYLVANIA
Clinical Psychology — M
Counseling Psychology — M
Sport Psychology — M

LOGOS EVANGELICAL SEMINARY
Theology — M,D,O

LOMA LINDA UNIVERSITY
Addictions/Substance Abuse
  Counseling — M,D,O
Applied Social Research — M,D
Child and Family Studies — M,D,O
Clinical Psychology — D
Criminal Justice and Criminology — M,D
Gerontology — M,D,O
Marriage and Family Therapy — M,D,O
Psychology—General — D
Religion — M

LONDON METROPOLITAN UNIVERSITY
Applied Psychology — M,D
Architecture — M,D
Arts Administration — M,D
Child and Family Studies — M,D
Clinical Psychology — M,D
Conflict Resolution and
  Mediation/Peace Studies — M,D
Counseling Psychology — M,D
Criminal Justice and Criminology — M,D
Emergency Management — M,D
Forensic Sciences — M,D
Homeland Security — M,D
Industrial and Organizational
  Psychology — M,D
International Affairs — M,D
Internet and Interactive
  Multimedia — M,D
Military and Defense Studies — M,D
Near and Middle Eastern Languages — M,D
Public Administration — M,D
Public Policy — M,D
Translation and Interpretation — M,D
Urban Design — M,D
Women's Studies — M,D
Writing — M,D

LONG ISLAND UNIVERSITY - BRENTWOOD CAMPUS
Clinical Psychology — M,O
Counseling Psychology — M,O
Criminal Justice and Criminology — M,O

LONG ISLAND UNIVERSITY - BROOKLYN
Applied Behavior Analysis — M,O
Clinical Psychology — M,D,O
Counseling Psychology — M,O
English — M,D,O
Forensic Sciences — M,D,O
Gerontology — M,O
Marriage and Family Therapy — M,O
Media Studies — M,D,O
Political Science — M,O
Psychology—General — M,D,O
Public Administration — M,O
Urban Studies — M,D,O
Writing — M,O

LONG ISLAND UNIVERSITY - HUDSON
Addictions/Substance Abuse
  Counseling — M,O
Counseling Psychology — M,O
Marriage and Family Therapy — M,O
Public Administration — M,O
School Psychology — M,O

LONG ISLAND UNIVERSITY - POST
Applied Behavior Analysis — M,O
Art Therapy — M
Art/Fine Arts — M
Clinical Psychology — M,D,O
Counseling Psychology — M,D,O
Criminal Justice and Criminology — M,O
English — M,O
Genetic Counseling — M,O
Gerontology — M,O
History — M,D,O
Interdisciplinary Studies — M,O
Internet and Interactive
  Multimedia — M
Museum Studies — M
Music — M
Political Science — M,O
Psychology—General — M,O
Public Administration — M,O
School Psychology — M,D,O
Sustainable Development — M,O
Theater — M

LONG ISLAND UNIVERSITY - RIVERHEAD
Applied Behavior Analysis — M,O
Homeland Security — M,O

LORAS COLLEGE
Applied Psychology — M
Pastoral Ministry and Counseling — M
Theology — M

LOUISIANA STATE UNIVERSITY AND AGRICULTURAL & MECHANICAL COLLEGE
Agricultural Economics and
  Agribusiness — M,D
Anthropology — M,D
Applied Arts and Design—
  General — M
Architecture — M

Art History — M
Art/Fine Arts — M
Clinical Psychology — M,D
Cognitive Sciences — M,D
Communication—General — M,D
Comparative Literature — M,D
Developmental Psychology — M,D
Economics — M,D
English — M,D
Family and Consumer
  Sciences-General — M,D
French — M,D
Geography — M,D
Graphic Design — M
Hispanic Studies — M
History — M,D
Internet and Interactive
  Multimedia — M
Landscape Architecture — M
Liberal Studies — M
Mass Communication — M,D
Media Studies — M,D
Music — M,D
Philosophy — M
Photography — M
Political Science — M,D
Psychology—General — M,D
Public Administration — M,D
School Psychology — M,D
Sociology — M,D
Theater — M,D
Writing — M,D

LOUISIANA STATE UNIVERSITY HEALTH SCIENCES CENTER
Rehabilitation Counseling — M

LOUISIANA STATE UNIVERSITY IN SHREVEPORT
Liberal Studies — M
School Psychology — O

LOUISIANA TECH UNIVERSITY
Architecture — M,D,O
Art/Fine Arts — M,D,O
Clinical Psychology — M,D,O
Counseling Psychology — M,D,O
English — M,D,O
Graphic Design — M
History — M,D,O
Industrial and Organizational
  Psychology — M,D,O
Photography — M,D,O
Technical Writing — M,D,O

LOUISVILLE PRESBYTERIAN THEOLOGICAL SEMINARY
Religion — M,D
Theology — M,D

LOURDES UNIVERSITY
Theology — M

LOYOLA MARYMOUNT UNIVERSITY
Counseling Psychology — M
English — M
Film, Television, and Video
  Production — M
Marriage and Family Therapy — M
Pastoral Ministry and Counseling — M
Philosophy — M
School Psychology — M
Theology — M
Writing — M

LOYOLA UNIVERSITY CHICAGO
Clinical Psychology — M,D,O
Communication—General — M
Corporate and Organizational
  Communication — M
Counseling Psychology — M,D,O
Criminal Justice and Criminology — M
Developmental Psychology — M
Economics — M
English — M,D
Ethics — M
Gender Studies — M
History — M,D
Humanities — M
Medieval and Renaissance Studies — M,D
Pastoral Ministry and Counseling — M,O
Philosophy — M,D
Political Science — M,D
Public History — M,D
Public Policy — M
School Psychology — D,O
Social Psychology — M,O
Sociology — M,D
Spanish — M
Theology — M,D,O
Urban Studies — M
Women's Studies — M

LOYOLA UNIVERSITY MARYLAND
Clinical Psychology — M,D,O
Counseling Psychology — M,D,O
Media Studies — M
Psychology—General — M,D,O
Theology — M

LOYOLA UNIVERSITY NEW ORLEANS
Clinical Psychology — M
Criminal Justice and Criminology — M
Marriage and Family Therapy — M
Music — M
Theology — M,O
Therapies—Dance, Drama, and
  Music — M

LUBBOCK CHRISTIAN UNIVERSITY
Theology — M

LUTHERAN SCHOOL OF THEOLOGY AT CHICAGO
Pastoral Ministry and Counseling — M,D
Theology — M,D

LUTHERAN THEOLOGICAL SEMINARY SASKATOON
Ethics — M,D
Pastoral Ministry and Counseling — M,D
Religion — M,D
Theology — M,D

LUTHER RICE COLLEGE & SEMINARY
Pastoral Ministry and Counseling — M,D
Religion — M,D
Theology — M,D

LUTHER SEMINARY
Missions and Missiology — M,D
Pastoral Ministry and Counseling — M,D
Theology — M,D

LYNN UNIVERSITY
Applied Psychology — M
Communication—General — M,O
Computer Art and Design — M,O
Counseling Psychology — M
Criminal Justice and Criminology — M
Graphic Design — M,O
Internet and Interactive Multimedia — M,O
Mass Communication — M,O
Media Studies — M,O
Music — M,O
Psychology—General — M

MACHZIKEI HADATH RABBINICAL COLLEGE
Theology — O

MADONNA UNIVERSITY
Clinical Psychology — M
Criminal Justice and Criminology — M
Liberal Studies — M
Pastoral Ministry and Counseling — M
Psychology—General — M
Theology — M

MAHARISHI INTERNATIONAL UNIVERSITY
Asian Studies — M,D
Writing — M

MAINE COLLEGE OF ART
Art/Fine Arts — M

MANHATTAN COLLEGE
Counseling Psychology — M,O
English — M,O
Marriage and Family Therapy — M

MANHATTAN SCHOOL OF MUSIC
Music — M,D,O

MANHATTANVILLE COLLEGE
Corporate and Organizational Communication — M,O
English — M,O
Spanish — M,O
Sustainable Development — M,O
Writing — M

MANSFIELD UNIVERSITY OF PENNSYLVANIA
Music — M
Psychology—General — M

MAPLE SPRINGS BAPTIST BIBLE COLLEGE AND SEMINARY
Pastoral Ministry and Counseling — M,D,O
Theology — M,D,O

MARANATHA BAPTIST UNIVERSITY
Cultural Studies — M
Pastoral Ministry and Counseling — M,D
Religion — M
Theology — M

MARIAN UNIVERSITY (IN)
Counseling Psychology — M

MARIAN UNIVERSITY (WI)
Thanatology — M

MARIETTA COLLEGE
Psychology—General — M

MARIST COLLEGE
Communication—General — M
Corporate and Organizational Communication — M
Counseling Psychology — M,O
Museum Studies — M
Psychology—General — M,O
Public Administration — M
School Psychology — M,O

MARQUETTE UNIVERSITY
Clinical Psychology — M,D
Communication—General — M,O
Counseling Psychology — M,D
Economics — M,D
English — M,D
Ethics — M,O
Health Communication — M,D
History — M,D
Interdisciplinary Studies — D
International Affairs — M,D
Journalism — M,O
Mass Communication — M,O
Philosophy — M,D
Political Science — D
Psychology—General — D
Social Psychology — M,D
Spanish — M
Speech and Interpersonal Communication — M,O
Theology — M,D

MARSHALL UNIVERSITY
Clinical Psychology — M,D,O
Communication—General — M

Criminal Justice and Criminology — M
English — M,O
Forensic Sciences — M,O
Geography — M,O
History — M,O
Humanities — M,O
Journalism — M,O
Music — M
Political Science — M
Psychology—General — M,D,O
Public Administration — M
School Psychology — O
Sociology — M

MARTIN UNIVERSITY
Pastoral Ministry and Counseling — M
Psychology—General — M
Social Psychology — M

MARY BALDWIN UNIVERSITY
Applied Behavior Analysis — M
English — M
Theater — M

MARYLAND INSTITUTE COLLEGE OF ART
Applied Arts and Design—General — M
Art/Fine Arts — M
Film, Television, and Video Production — M
Graphic Design — M
Illustration — M
Museum Studies — M
Photography — M

MARYMOUNT CALIFORNIA UNIVERSITY
International Development — M
Social Psychology — M

MARYMOUNT UNIVERSITY
Clinical Psychology — M
Counseling Psychology — M
English — M,O
Forensic Psychology — M
Interior Design — M
Pastoral Ministry and Counseling — M

MARYVILLE UNIVERSITY OF SAINT LOUIS
Addictions/Substance Abuse Counseling — M
Marriage and Family Therapy — M
Rehabilitation Counseling — M
Therapies—Dance, Drama, and Music — M

MARYWOOD UNIVERSITY
Architecture — M
Art Therapy — M,O
Art/Fine Arts — M
Clinical Psychology — M,D
Communication—General — M
Counseling Psychology — M
Criminal Justice and Criminology — M
Gerontology — M
Graphic Design — M
Human Development — D
Illustration — M
Interdisciplinary Studies — D
Interior Design — M
Photography — M
Psychology—General — M
Public Administration — M

MASSACHUSETTS COLLEGE OF ART AND DESIGN
Applied Arts and Design—General — M,O
Architecture — M
Art/Fine Arts — M,O
Film, Television, and Video Production — M,O
Interdisciplinary Studies — M,O
Media Studies — M,O
Photography — M,O
Textile Design — M,O

MASSACHUSETTS INSTITUTE OF TECHNOLOGY
Archaeology — M,D,O
Architectural History — M,D
Architecture — M,D
Art History — M,D
Cognitive Sciences — D
Economics — D
History of Science and Technology — D
Linguistics — D
Media Studies — M,D
Philosophy — D
Political Science — M,D
Social Sciences — D
Technical Writing — M
Urban and Regional Planning — M,D
Urban Studies — M,D
Writing — M

MASSACHUSETTS MARITIME ACADEMY
Emergency Management — M

THE MASTER'S UNIVERSITY
Pastoral Ministry and Counseling — M
Theology — M,D

MCCORMICK THEOLOGICAL SEMINARY
Pastoral Ministry and Counseling — M,D,O
Theology — M,D,O

MCDANIEL COLLEGE
Gerontology — M,O
Liberal Studies — M,O
Writing — M,O

MCGILL UNIVERSITY
Agricultural Economics and Agribusiness — M
Anthropology — M,D
Architecture — M,D,O
Art History — M,D
Asian Studies — M,D
Clinical Psychology — M,D
Communication—General — M,D
Counseling Psychology — M,D,O
Developmental Psychology — M,D,O
Economics — M,D
English — M,D
Experimental Psychology — M,D
Forensic Sciences — M,D
French — M,D
Genetic Counseling — M,D
Geography — M,D
German — M,D
Hispanic Studies — M,D
History of Medicine — M,D
History — M,D
International Development — M,D,O
Italian — M,D
Jewish Studies — M
Linguistics — M,D
Music — M,D
Near and Middle Eastern Studies — M,D
Philosophy — M,D
Political Science — M,D
Psychology—General — M,D
Religion — M,D
Russian — M,D
School Psychology — M,D,O
Sociology — M,D,O
Theology — M,D
Urban and Regional Planning — M,D

MCKENDREE UNIVERSITY
Clinical Psychology — M
Counseling Psychology — M

MCMASTER UNIVERSITY
Anthropology — M,D
Classics — M,D
Cultural Studies — M,D
Economics — M,D
English — M,D
French — M,D
Geography — M,D
History — M,D
Industrial and Labor Relations — M
International Affairs — M,D
Pastoral Ministry and Counseling — M,D,O
Philosophy — M,D
Political Science — M,D
Psychology—General — M,D
Public Administration — M,D
Public Affairs — M,D
Public Policy — M,D
Religion — M,D
Sociology — M,D
Theology — M,D,O

MCNEESE STATE UNIVERSITY
Applied Behavior Analysis — M,O
Counseling Psychology — M,O
Criminal Justice and Criminology — M
English — M,O
Experimental Psychology — M,O
Psychology—General — M,O
School Psychology — M,O
Writing — M

MEADVILLE LOMBARD THEOLOGICAL SCHOOL
Pastoral Ministry and Counseling — M,D
Theology — M,D

MEDAILLE COLLEGE
Clinical Psychology — M,D
Counseling Psychology — M,D
Marriage and Family Therapy — M,D
Psychology—General — M,D

MEMORIAL UNIVERSITY OF NEWFOUNDLAND
Anthropology — M,D
Archaeology — M,D
Classics — M
Clinical Psychology — M,D
Cultural Anthropology — M,D
Economics — M
English — M,D
Experimental Psychology — M,D
Folklore — M,D
French — M
Gender Studies — M,D
Geography — M,D
German — M
History — M,D
Humanities — M
Industrial and Labor Relations — M
Linguistics — M,D
Music — M,D
Philosophy — M,D
Political Science — M,D
Psychology—General — M,D
Religion — M
Sociology — M,D

MEMPHIS THEOLOGICAL SEMINARY
Theology — M,D

MERCER UNIVERSITY
Clinical Psychology — M,D
Criminal Justice and Criminology — M,D
Gerontology — M,D
Music — M,D
Pastoral Ministry and Counseling — M,D
Rehabilitation Counseling — M,D
School Psychology — M,D
Theology — M,D

MERCY COLLEGE
Counseling Psychology — M,O
English — M
Marriage and Family Therapy — M,O
Psychology—General — M
School Psychology — M

MERCYHURST UNIVERSITY
Anthropology — M
Applied Behavior Analysis — M
Archaeology — M
Biological Anthropology — M
Criminal Justice and Criminology — M,O
Forensic Sciences — M

MEREDITH COLLEGE
Industrial and Organizational Psychology — M
Psychology—General — M

MERRIMACK COLLEGE
Clinical Psychology — M,O
Public Affairs — M,O
Theology — M,O

MESIVTA OF EASTERN PARKWAY–YESHIVA ZICHRON MEILECH
Theology

MESIVTHA TIFERETH JERUSALEM OF AMERICA
Theology

MESSIAH UNIVERSITY
Clinical Psychology — M,O
Counseling Psychology — M,O
Marriage and Family Therapy — M,O
Music — M

METHODIST THEOLOGICAL SCHOOL IN OHIO
Theology — M,D

METHODIST UNIVERSITY
Criminal Justice and Criminology — M

METROPOLITAN COLLEGE OF NEW YORK
Emergency Management — M
Media Studies — M
Public Administration — M
Public Affairs — M

METROPOLITAN STATE UNIVERSITY
Addictions/Substance Abuse Counseling — M
Criminal Justice and Criminology — M
Liberal Studies — M
Public Administration — M
Public Affairs — M
Technical Writing — M

MIAMI INTERNATIONAL UNIVERSITY OF ART & DESIGN
Applied Arts and Design—General — M
Film, Television, and Video Production — M

MIAMI UNIVERSITY
Architecture — M
Art/Fine Arts — M
Child and Family Studies — M
Demography and Population Studies — M,D
Economics — M
English — M,D
French — M
Geography — M
Gerontology — M,D
History — M
Interior Design — M
Music — M
Philosophy — M
Political Science — M
Psychology—General — M,D
Spanish — M
Theater — M

MICHIGAN SCHOOL OF PSYCHOLOGY
Clinical Psychology — M,D
Psychology—General — M,D
Transpersonal and Humanistic Psychology — M,D

MICHIGAN STATE UNIVERSITY
African Studies — M,D
African-American Studies — M,D
Agricultural Economics and Agribusiness — M,D
American Studies — M,D
Anthropology — M,D
Art/Fine Arts — M
Child and Family Studies — M,D
Child Development — M,D
Communication—General — M,D
Criminal Justice and Criminology — M,D
Economics — M,D
English — M,D
Environmental Design — M,D
Forensic Sciences — M,D
French — M,D
Geography — M,D
German — M,D
Health Communication — M
Hispanic and Latin American Languages — M,D
Hispanic Studies — M,D
History — M,D
Human Development — M,D
Industrial and Labor Relations — M,D
Interior Design — M,D
Journalism — M
Latin American Studies — D
Linguistics — M,D

Media Studies	M,D
Music	M,D
Philosophy	M,D
Political Science	M,D
Psychology—General	M,D
Rehabilitation Counseling	M,D,O
Rhetoric	M,D
Romance Languages	M,D
School Psychology	M,D,O
Sociology	M,D
Spanish	M,D
Sustainable Development	M,D
Theater	M
Therapies—Dance, Drama, and Music	M,D
Urban and Regional Planning	M,D
Writing	M,D

MICHIGAN TECHNOLOGICAL UNIVERSITY

Cognitive Sciences	M,D,O
Interdisciplinary Studies	M,D,O
Mineral Economics	M

MID-AMERICA BAPTIST THEOLOGICAL SEMINARY

Missions and Missiology	M,D
Pastoral Ministry and Counseling	M,D
Theology	M,D

MID-AMERICA BAPTIST THEOLOGICAL SEMINARY NORTHEAST BRANCH

Theology	M

MID-AMERICA CHRISTIAN UNIVERSITY

Counseling Psychology	M
Marriage and Family Therapy	M
Pastoral Ministry and Counseling	M
Public Administration	M

MIDAMERICA NAZARENE UNIVERSITY

Clinical Psychology	M
Marriage and Family Therapy	M
School Psychology	M

MID-AMERICA REFORMED SEMINARY

Theology	M

MIDDLEBURY COLLEGE

Chinese	M
English	M
French	M,D
German	M,D
Italian	M,D
Near and Middle Eastern Languages	M
Russian	M,D
Spanish	M,D

MIDDLEBURY INSTITUTE OF INTERNATIONAL STUDIES AT MONTEREY

Conflict Resolution and Mediation/Peace Studies	M
International Affairs	M
International Development	M
International Trade Policy	M
Public Administration	M
Translation and Interpretation	M

MIDDLE GEORGIA STATE UNIVERSITY

Forensic Sciences	M

MIDDLE TENNESSEE STATE UNIVERSITY

Clinical Psychology	M,O
Counseling Psychology	M
Criminal Justice and Criminology	M
Economics	M,D
English	M,D
Experimental Psychology	M,O
French	M
Gender Studies	O
German	M
Gerontology	O
History	M
Industrial and Organizational Psychology	M,O
International Affairs	M
Mass Communication	M
Music	M
Political Science	M
Psychology—General	M,O
Public History	D
School Psychology	M,O
Sociology	M
Spanish	M
Women's Studies	O

MIDWESTERN BAPTIST THEOLOGICAL SEMINARY

Music	M,D,O
Pastoral Ministry and Counseling	M,D,O
Theology	M,D,O

MIDWESTERN STATE UNIVERSITY

Clinical Psychology	M
Counseling Psychology	M
Criminal Justice and Criminology	M,O
English	M,D
History	M
Philosophy	M,D
Political Science	M

MIDWESTERN UNIVERSITY, DOWNERS GROVE CAMPUS

Clinical Psychology	D

MIDWESTERN UNIVERSITY, GLENDALE CAMPUS

Clinical Psychology	D

MIDWEST UNIVERSITY

Marriage and Family Therapy	M,D
Missions and Missiology	M,D
Music	M,D
Pastoral Ministry and Counseling	M,D
Public Administration	M,D
Public Policy	M,D
Theology	M,D

MILLERSVILLE UNIVERSITY OF PENNSYLVANIA

Applied Arts and Design—General	M
Art/Fine Arts	M
Clinical Psychology	M
Emergency Management	M
English	M,O
French	M
Geographic Information Systems	M
German	M
History	M
Psychology—General	M
School Psychology	M
Spanish	M
Writing	M,O

MILLIGAN UNIVERSITY

Clinical Psychology	M,O
Missions and Missiology	M,D,O
Pastoral Ministry and Counseling	M,D,O
Religion	M,D,O
Theology	M,D,O

MILLS COLLEGE

Applied Economics	M
Art/Fine Arts	M
Dance	M
English	M,O
Illustration	M,O
Interdisciplinary Studies	M,O
Music	M
Photography	M
Public Policy	M
Translation and Interpretation	M,O
Writing	M,O

MINNEAPOLIS COLLEGE OF ART AND DESIGN

Applied Arts and Design—General	M
Art/Fine Arts	M
Film, Television, and Video Production	M
Graphic Design	M
Illustration	M
Internet and Interactive Multimedia	M
Photography	M
Sustainable Development	M

MINNESOTA STATE UNIVERSITY MANKATO

Anthropology	M
Art/Fine Arts	M
Clinical Psychology	M,D
Communication—General	M,O
Corporate and Organizational Communication	M,O
Counseling Psychology	M,D
Criminal Justice and Criminology	M
English	M,O
Ethnic Studies	M
French	M
Gender Studies	M
Geography	M
Gerontology	M
History	M
Industrial and Organizational Psychology	M,D
Interdisciplinary Studies	M
Music	M
Psychology—General	M,D
Public Administration	M
Rehabilitation Counseling	M
School Psychology	M,D
Sociology	M
Spanish	M
Technical Communication	M,O
Theater	M
Urban and Regional Planning	M,O
Urban Studies	M,O
Women's Studies	M
Writing	M,O

MINNESOTA STATE UNIVERSITY MOORHEAD

School Psychology	M,O

MINOT STATE UNIVERSITY

School Psychology	O

MIRRER YESHIVA CENTRAL INSTITUTE

Theology	

MISSIO SEMINARY

Missions and Missiology	M,D,O
Pastoral Ministry and Counseling	M,D,O
Theology	M,D,O

MISSISSIPPI COLLEGE

Art/Fine Arts	M
Communication—General	M
Corporate and Organizational Communication	M
Counseling Psychology	M,O
Criminal Justice and Criminology	M,O
English	M
History	M,O
Liberal Studies	M
Marriage and Family Therapy	M,O
Music	M
Political Science	M,O
Social Sciences	M,O

MISSISSIPPI STATE UNIVERSITY

Agricultural Economics and Agribusiness	M
Anthropology	M
Applied Psychology	M,D
Child and Family Studies	M,D
Clinical Psychology	M,D,O
Clothing and Textiles	M,D
Cognitive Sciences	M,D
Communication—General	M,D
Economics	M,D
English	M

Geography	M,D
History	M,D
Human Development	M,D
Landscape Architecture	M
Political Science	M,D
Psychology—General	M,D
Public Administration	M,D
Public Policy	M,D
Rehabilitation Counseling	M,D,O
School Psychology	M,D,O
Sociology	M,D
Sustainable Development	M,D

MISSISSIPPI VALLEY STATE UNIVERSITY

Criminal Justice and Criminology	M

MISSOURI BAPTIST UNIVERSITY

Pastoral Ministry and Counseling	M,O

MISSOURI SOUTHERN STATE UNIVERSITY

Criminal Justice and Criminology	M

MISSOURI STATE UNIVERSITY

Applied Behavior Analysis	M,O
Art/Fine Arts	M
Child and Family Studies	M
Clinical Psychology	M,O
Communication—General	M,O
Counseling Psychology	M
Criminal Justice and Criminology	M,O
English	M,O
Experimental Psychology	M,O
Film, Television, and Video Production	M,O
Geography	M,O
History	M,O
Homeland Security	M,O
Industrial and Organizational Psychology	M,O
International Affairs	M
Military and Defense Studies	M,O
Music	M
Political Science	M,O
Psychology—General	M,O
Public Administration	M,O
Religion	M,O
Urban and Regional Planning	M,O
Writing	M,O

MISSOURI UNIVERSITY OF SCIENCE AND TECHNOLOGY

Industrial and Organizational Psychology	M
Technical Communication	M

MISSOURI VALLEY COLLEGE

Social Psychology	M

MISSOURI WESTERN STATE UNIVERSITY

Forensic Sciences	M,O

MOLLOY COLLEGE

Clinical Psychology	M
Criminal Justice and Criminology	M
Therapies—Dance, Drama, and Music	M

MONMOUTH UNIVERSITY

Addictions/Substance Abuse Counseling	M,O
American Studies	M
Anthropology	M
Applied Behavior Analysis	M,D,O
Communication—General	M,O
Counseling Psychology	M,O
Criminal Justice and Criminology	M,O
English	M
History	M
Homeland Security	M,O
Media Studies	M,O
Psychology—General	M,O
Rhetoric	M
School Psychology	M,D,O
Western European Studies	M
Writing	M

MONROE COLLEGE

Criminal Justice and Criminology	M

MONTANA STATE UNIVERSITY

American Indian/Native American Studies	M
Architecture	M
Art History	M
Art/Fine Arts	M
English	M
Film, Television, and Video Production	M
History	M,D
Human Development	M
Psychology—General	M
Public Administration	M
School Psychology	M,D,O

MONTANA STATE UNIVERSITY BILLINGS

Applied Behavior Analysis	M
Communication—General	M
Counseling Psychology	M
Interdisciplinary Studies	M
Psychology—General	M
Rehabilitation Counseling	M

MONTANA TECHNOLOGICAL UNIVERSITY

Interdisciplinary Studies	M

MONTCLAIR STATE UNIVERSITY

Addictions/Substance Abuse Counseling	O
Art/Fine Arts	M
Arts Administration	M
Child and Family Studies	M,D,O
Child Development	M,O
Clinical Psychology	M

Conflict Resolution and Mediation/Peace Studies	M,O
Corporate and Organizational Communication	M
Disability Studies	M,O
English	M
Forensic Psychology	O
French	M
Geographic Information Systems	O
Industrial and Organizational Psychology	M
Internet and Interactive Multimedia	M
Linguistics	M,O
Music	M,O
Political Science	M,O
Psychology—General	M
Social Sciences	M
Spanish	M
Sustainable Development	M
Theater	M
Therapies—Dance, Drama, and Music	M,O
Translation and Interpretation	O
Writing	O

MOODY BIBLE INSTITUTE

Pastoral Ministry and Counseling	M,O
Theology	M,O
Urban Studies	M,O

MOODY THEOLOGICAL SEMINARY–MICHIGAN

Counseling Psychology	M,O
Religion	M,O
Theology	M,O

MOORE COLLEGE OF ART & DESIGN

Art/Fine Arts	M
Arts Administration	M
Communication—General	M
Interior Design	M

MORAVIAN THEOLOGICAL SEMINARY

Theology	M,O

MOREHEAD STATE UNIVERSITY

Clinical Psychology	M
Counseling Psychology	M
Criminal Justice and Criminology	M
Experimental Psychology	M
Gerontology	M
Psychology—General	M
Sociology	M

MORGAN STATE UNIVERSITY

African-American Studies	M,D
Architecture	M
Economics	M
English	M,D
Historic Preservation	M,D
History	M,D
International Affairs	M
Journalism	M
Landscape Architecture	M
Museum Studies	M,D
Music	M
Psychology—General	M,D
Sociology	M
Urban and Regional Planning	M

MOUNT ALOYSIUS COLLEGE

Social Psychology	M

MOUNT ANGEL SEMINARY

Theology	M

MOUNT MARTY UNIVERSITY

Pastoral Ministry and Counseling	M

MOUNT MARY UNIVERSITY

Art Therapy	M,D
Clinical Psychology	M,O
Counseling Psychology	M,O
English	M
Internet and Interactive Multimedia	M
Rehabilitation Counseling	M,O
Writing	M

MOUNT MERCY UNIVERSITY

Criminal Justice and Criminology	M
Marriage and Family Therapy	M

MOUNT ST. JOSEPH UNIVERSITY

Pastoral Ministry and Counseling	M,O
Religion	M,O
Theology	M,O

MOUNT SAINT MARY COLLEGE

Child Development	M,O

MOUNT SAINT MARY'S UNIVERSITY (CA)

Counseling Psychology	M,D,O
English	M,D,O
Film, Television, and Video Production	M,D,O
Humanities	M,D,O
Religion	M,D,O
Writing	M,D,O

MOUNT ST. MARY'S UNIVERSITY (MD)

Philosophy	M
Theology	M

MOUNT SAINT VINCENT UNIVERSITY

Child and Family Studies	M
Communication—General	M
Gerontology	M
School Psychology	M
Women's Studies	M

MOUNT VERNON NAZARENE UNIVERSITY

Theology	M

MULTNOMAH UNIVERSITY

Theology	M,D

MURRAY STATE UNIVERSITY
Clinical Psychology M,O
Corporate and Organizational Communication M
Economic Development M
Economics M
English M,D,O
Experimental Psychology M,O
Gender Studies M,D,O
History M
Human Development M,D,O
Interdisciplinary Studies M,O
Journalism M
Mass Communication M
Music M
Political Science M
Psychology—General M,O
School Psychology M,D,O
Sociology M
Writing M,D,O

NAROPA UNIVERSITY
Art Therapy M
Counseling Psychology M
Psychoanalysis and Psychotherapy M
Psychology—General M
Religion M
Theater M
Theology M
Therapies—Dance, Drama, and Music M
Transpersonal and Humanistic Psychology M
Writing M

NASHOTAH HOUSE THEOLOGICAL SEMINARY
Pastoral Ministry and Counseling M,D,O
Religion M,D,O
Theology M,D,O

NATIONAL AMERICAN UNIVERSITY (TX)
Criminal Justice and Criminology M,D

NATIONAL DEFENSE UNIVERSITY
Homeland Security M
Military and Defense Studies M
National Security M

NATIONAL INTELLIGENCE UNIVERSITY
Military and Defense Studies M

NATIONAL LOUIS UNIVERSITY
Human Development M,D,O
Psychology—General M,D,O
Public Policy M,D,O
School Psychology M,D,O
Writing M,D,O

NATIONAL UNIVERSITY
Applied Behavior Analysis M,O
Clinical Psychology M,O
Counseling Psychology M,O
Criminal Justice and Criminology M
Emergency Management M
English M,O
Film, Television, and Video Production M
Film, Television, and Video Theory and Criticism M,O
Forensic Sciences M,O
Homeland Security M
Internet and Interactive Multimedia M
Journalism M
Marriage and Family Therapy M,O
Public Administration M
School Psychology M,O
Writing M,O

NAVAJO TECHNICAL UNIVERSITY
American Indian/Native American Studies M

NAVAL POSTGRADUATE SCHOOL
Conflict Resolution and Mediation/Peace Studies M,D
Geographic Information Systems M,D,O
Homeland Security M,D
Military and Defense Studies M,D
National Security M,D
Pacific Area/Pacific Rim Studies M,D

NAVAL WAR COLLEGE
National Security M

NAZARENE THEOLOGICAL SEMINARY
Cultural Studies M,D,O
Theology M,D,O

NAZARETH COLLEGE OF ROCHESTER
Art Therapy M
Music M
Therapies—Dance, Drama, and Music M

NEBRASKA CHRISTIAN COLLEGE OF HOPE INTERNATIONAL UNIVERSITY
Counseling Psychology M
Missions and Missiology M
Pastoral Ministry and Counseling M
Theology M

NER ISRAEL RABBINICAL COLLEGE
Theology M,D,O

NER ISRAEL YESHIVA COLLEGE OF TORONTO
Theology

NEUMANN UNIVERSITY
Clinical Psychology M,D,O
Pastoral Ministry and Counseling M,D,O

NEW BRUNSWICK THEOLOGICAL SEMINARY
Pastoral Ministry and Counseling M,D
Theology M,D

NEW ENGLAND COLLEGE
Counseling Psychology M
International Affairs M
Public Policy M
Writing M

NEW ENGLAND COLLEGE OF BUSINESS AND FINANCE
Ethics M

NEW ENGLAND CONSERVATORY OF MUSIC
Music M,D,O

NEW HAMPSHIRE INSTITUTE OF ART
Art/Fine Arts M
Photography M
Writing M

NEW JERSEY CITY UNIVERSITY
Art/Fine Arts M
Criminal Justice and Criminology M,D,O
Music M
National Security M,D,O
Urban Studies M

NEW JERSEY INSTITUTE OF TECHNOLOGY
Architecture M,D
History M,D,O
Sustainable Development M,D,O
Technical Communication M,D,O

NEWMAN THEOLOGICAL COLLEGE
Theology M

NEWMAN UNIVERSITY
Theology M

NEW MEXICO HIGHLANDS UNIVERSITY
American Studies M
Anthropology M
Clinical Psychology M
Computer Art and Design M
Counseling Psychology M
English M
History M
Internet and Interactive Multimedia M
Media Studies M
Political Science M
Psychology—General M
Public Affairs M
Rhetoric M
Sociology M
Writing M

NEW MEXICO STATE UNIVERSITY
Agricultural Economics and Agribusiness M,D
Anthropology M,O
Art History M
Art/Fine Arts M
Clothing and Textiles M
Communication—General M
Corporate and Organizational Communication M,D
Counseling Psychology M,D,O
Criminal Justice and Criminology M
Cultural Studies M,D,O
Economic Development M,D,O
Economics M,D,O
English M,D
Family and Consumer Sciences-General M
Geography M
History M
Interdisciplinary Studies M,D
Museum Studies M,O
Music M
Political Science M
Psychology—General M,D
Public Administration M
Rhetoric M,D
School Psychology M,D,O
Sociology M
Spanish M
Writing M,D

NEW ORLEANS BAPTIST THEOLOGICAL SEMINARY
Music M,D
Pastoral Ministry and Counseling M,D
Theology M,D

NEW SAINT ANDREWS COLLEGE
Religion M,O
Theology M,O
Writing M,O

THE NEW SCHOOL
Anthropology M,D
Applied Arts and Design—General M
Applied Social Research M,D
Architecture M
Art/Fine Arts M
Clinical Psychology M,D
Clothing and Textiles M
Cognitive Sciences M,D
Computer Art and Design M
Economics M,D
History M,D
Industrial Design M
Interior Design M
International Affairs M
International Economics M,D
Internet and Interactive Multimedia M
Liberal Studies M
Lighting Design M
Media Studies M,O
Museum Studies M
Music M,O
Philosophy M,D
Photography M
Political Science M,D
Psychoanalysis and Psychotherapy M,D
Psychology—General M,D
Public Policy M,D
Social Psychology M,D
Social Sciences M,D
Sociology M,D
Textile Design M
Theater M
Urban Design M
Writing M

NEWSCHOOL OF ARCHITECTURE AND DESIGN
Architecture M

NEW YORK ACADEMY OF ART
Art/Fine Arts M

NEW YORK FILM ACADEMY
Film, Television, and Video Production M
Photography M

NEW YORK INSTITUTE OF TECHNOLOGY
Applied Arts and Design—General M
Architecture M
Art/Fine Arts M
Communication—General M
Computer Art and Design M
Graphic Design M
Industrial and Labor Relations M,O
Urban Design M

NEW YORK MEDICAL COLLEGE
Emergency Management M,D,O
Psychology—General M,D,O

NEW YORK SCHOOL OF INTERIOR DESIGN
Interior Design M
Lighting Design M
Sustainable Development M

NEW YORK STUDIO SCHOOL OF DRAWING, PAINTING AND SCULPTURE
Art/Fine Arts M,O*

NEW YORK THEOLOGICAL SEMINARY
Theology M,D

NEW YORK UNIVERSITY
African Studies M,D,O
American Studies M,D
Anthropology M,D
Applied Arts and Design—General M
Applied Economics M,D,O
Applied Psychology M,D,O
Applied Social Research M
Archaeology M,D
Architectural History M
Art History M,D
Art Therapy M
Art/Fine Arts M,D,O
Arts Administration M
Asian Studies M,D
Chinese M,D,O
Classics M,D,O
Cognitive Sciences M,D,O
Communication—General M,D
Comparative Literature M,D
Corporate and Organizational Communication M
Counseling Psychology M,D,O
Cultural Studies M,D,O
Dance M,D,O
Demography and Population Studies M,D
Developmental Psychology M,D
Economics M,D,O
English M,D
Film, Television, and Video Production M
Film, Television, and Video Theory and Criticism M,D
French M,D,O
German M,D
Historic Preservation
History M,D,O
Human Development M,D,O
Humanities M,O
Industrial and Organizational Psychology M,D,O
Interdisciplinary Studies M
International Affairs M,D
Internet and Interactive Multimedia M
Italian M,D,O
Japanese M,D,O
Jewish Studies M,D
Journalism M,D,O
Latin American Studies M
Linguistics M,D
Media Studies M,D
Museum Studies M,O
Music M,D,O
Near and Middle Eastern Studies M,D
Philosophy M,D
Political Science M,D
Portuguese M,D
Psychoanalysis and Psychotherapy M,D,O
Psychology—General M,D,O
Public Administration M,D,O
Public History M,D,O
Public Policy M
Publishing M
Religion M,O
Romance Languages M,D
Russian M
Slavic Languages M
Social Psychology M,D,O
Social Sciences M,D
Sociology M,D
Spanish M,D,O
Speech and Interpersonal Communication M,D
Sustainable Development M
Theater M,D,O
Therapies—Dance, Drama, and Music M
Translation and Interpretation M
Urban and Regional Planning M
Urban Studies M
Western European Studies M
Writing M

NIAGARA UNIVERSITY
Applied Behavior Analysis M,D,O
Counseling Psychology M,D,O
Criminal Justice and Criminology M
Forensic Sciences M
Interdisciplinary Studies M
School Psychology M

NICHOLLS STATE UNIVERSITY
Clinical Psychology M,O
School Psychology M,O

NICHOLS COLLEGE
Homeland Security M

NORFOLK STATE UNIVERSITY
Art/Fine Arts M
Clinical Psychology M
Communication—General M
Criminal Justice and Criminology M
Media Studies M
Music M
Psychology—General M,D
Social Psychology M
Urban Studies M

NORTH CAROLINA AGRICULTURAL AND TECHNICAL STATE UNIVERSITY
African-American Studies M
Agricultural Economics and Agribusiness M
Child and Family Studies M
Child Development M
Clinical Psychology M,D
English M
Environmental Design M
Family and Consumer Sciences-General M
Rehabilitation Counseling M,D

NORTH CAROLINA CENTRAL UNIVERSITY
Clinical Psychology M
Criminal Justice and Criminology M
English M
Geographic Information Systems M
History M
Music M
Psychology—General M
Public Administration M

NORTH CAROLINA STATE UNIVERSITY
Agricultural Economics and Agribusiness M,D
Anthropology M
Applied Arts and Design—General M
Applied Psychology D
Architecture M
Clothing and Textiles M,D
Cognitive Sciences D
Communication—General M
Computer Art and Design M,D
Developmental Psychology D
Economics M,D
English M
French M
Geographic Information Systems M,D
Graphic Design M
History M
Industrial and Organizational Psychology D
Industrial Design M
International Affairs M
Landscape Architecture M
Psychology—General D
Public Administration M,D
Public History M
Rhetoric M,D
School Psychology D
Social Psychology M,D
Sociology D
Spanish M
Writing M

NORTH CENTRAL COLLEGE
Cultural Studies M
Liberal Studies M

NORTHCENTRAL UNIVERSITY
Marriage and Family Therapy M,D,O
Psychology—General M,D,O

NORTH DAKOTA STATE UNIVERSITY
Agricultural Economics and Agribusiness M
Anthropology M
Architecture M
Child and Family Studies M,D,O
Child Development M
Clinical Psychology M,D
Cognitive Sciences M,D
Communication—General M,D
Consumer Economics M,O

*M—masters degree; D—doctorate; O—other advanced degree; *—Close-Up and/or Display*

Counseling Psychology M,D
Criminal Justice and Criminology M,D
Developmental Psychology D
English M,D
Family and Consumer Sciences-General M
Gerontology D,O
Health Psychology M,D
History M,D
Landscape Architecture M
Mass Communication M,D
Music M,D
Psychology—General M,D
Rhetoric M,D
School Psychology M,D
Social Psychology M,D
Sociology M
Speech and Interpersonal Communication M,D
Urban and Regional Planning M
Urban Studies M,D
Writing M,D

NORTHEASTERN ILLINOIS UNIVERSITY
Clinical Psychology M
English M
Geographic Information Systems M,O
Geography M,O
Gerontology M
History M
Latin American Studies M
Linguistics M
Marriage and Family Therapy M
Music M
Political Science M
Rehabilitation Counseling M
Speech and Interpersonal Communication M

NORTHEASTERN SEMINARY AT ROBERTS WESLEYAN COLLEGE
Theology M,D

NORTHEASTERN STATE UNIVERSITY
American Indian/Native American Studies M
Communication—General M
Criminal Justice and Criminology M
English M
Psychology—General M

NORTHEASTERN UNIVERSITY
Applied Arts and Design—General M
Applied Behavior Analysis M,D,O
Architecture M
Arts Administration M
Corporate and Organizational Communication M
Counseling Psychology M,D,O
Criminal Justice and Criminology M,D
Economic Development M
Economics M,D
English M,D
Geographic Information Systems M
History M,D
Homeland Security M,D
Interdisciplinary Studies M,D,O
International Affairs M,D
Internet and Interactive Multimedia M
Journalism M
Media Studies M
Political Science M,D
Psychology—General M,D
Public Administration M,D
Public Policy M,D,O
School Psychology M,D,O
Sociology M,D
Technical Communication M
Urban Studies M,D

NORTHEAST OHIO MEDICAL UNIVERSITY
Humanities M,D,O

NORTHERN ARIZONA UNIVERSITY
American Indian/Native American Studies O
Anthropology M
Communication—General M,O
Counseling Psychology M,D,O
Criminal Justice and Criminology M
English M,D,O
Ethnic Studies O
Gender Studies O
Geographic Information Systems M,O
Geography M,O
History M
Human Development O
Liberal Studies M
Linguistics M,D,O
Music M,O
Political Science M,D,O
Psychology—General M
Public Administration M,D,O
Rhetoric M,D,O
School Psychology M,D,O
Sociology M
Spanish M
Sustainable Development M
Urban and Regional Planning M,O
Women's Studies O
Writing M,D,O

NORTHERN ILLINOIS UNIVERSITY
Anthropology M
Art/Fine Arts M
Child and Family Studies M
Communication—General M
Dance M
Economics M,D
English M,D
French M
Geography M,D
History M,D
Music M,O
Philosophy M
Political Science M,D
Psychology—General M,D
Public Administration M
Romance Languages M
Sociology M
Spanish M
Theater M

NORTHERN KENTUCKY UNIVERSITY
Clinical Psychology M
Communication—General M,O
Counseling Psychology M
Cultural Studies M,O
English M,O
Geographic Information Systems M,O
Health Psychology M,O
Industrial and Organizational Psychology M,O
Liberal Studies M,O
Marriage and Family Therapy M,O
Media Studies M,O
Public Administration M,O
Public History M
Rhetoric M,O
Writing M,O

NORTHERN MICHIGAN UNIVERSITY
Applied Behavior Analysis M
English M,O
Psychology—General M
Theater M,O
Writing M,O

NORTHERN SEMINARY
Missions and Missiology M,D
Pastoral Ministry and Counseling M,D
Religion M,D
Theology M,D

NORTHERN STATE UNIVERSITY
Clinical Psychology M
Counseling Psychology M

NORTHERN VERMONT UNIVERSITY–JOHNSON
Addictions/Substance Abuse Counseling M
Applied Behavior Analysis M
Art/Fine Arts M
Computer Art and Design M
Photography M
School Psychology M

NORTH GREENVILLE UNIVERSITY
Pastoral Ministry and Counseling M,D

NORTH PARK THEOLOGICAL SEMINARY
Pastoral Ministry and Counseling M,O
Theology M,D

NORTH PARK UNIVERSITY
Music M

NORTHWESTERN OKLAHOMA STATE UNIVERSITY
American Studies M
Counseling Psychology M

NORTHWESTERN STATE UNIVERSITY OF LOUISIANA
Art/Fine Arts M
Clinical Psychology M
English M
Homeland Security M
Music M
Psychology—General M

NORTHWESTERN UNIVERSITY
African Studies O
African-American Studies D
American Studies M
Anthropology D
Art History D
Art/Fine Arts M
Arts Administration M
Broadcast Journalism M
Clinical Psychology D
Cognitive Sciences D
Communication—General M,D
Comparative Literature M,D
Corporate and Organizational Communication M,D
Economics D
English M,D
Ethics M
Film, Television, and Video Production M,D
French D,O
Gender Studies O
Genetic Counseling M
German D
History M,D
Human Development D
International Affairs M,D,O
Internet and Interactive Multimedia M
Italian D,O
Journalism M
Liberal Studies M
Linguistics D
Marriage and Family Therapy M
Media Studies M,D
Music M,D
Philosophy D
Political Science D
Portuguese D
Psychology—General D
Public Administration M
Public Policy M,D
Publishing M
Religion M,D
Rhetoric M,D
Slavic Languages D
Social Psychology D
Sociology D
Spanish D
Speech and Interpersonal Communication M,D
Theater M
Writing M

NORTHWEST MISSOURI STATE UNIVERSITY
Agricultural Economics and Agribusiness M
English M,O
Geographic Information Systems M,O

NORTHWEST NAZARENE UNIVERSITY
Addictions/Substance Abuse Counseling M
Clinical Psychology M
Marriage and Family Therapy M
Missions and Missiology M
Pastoral Ministry and Counseling M
Religion M
School Psychology M
Theology M

NORTHWEST UNIVERSITY
Counseling Psychology M,D
Cultural Studies M
Missions and Missiology M
Pastoral Ministry and Counseling M
Psychology—General M,D
Theology M
Urban and Regional Planning M,D

NORWICH UNIVERSITY
Conflict Resolution and Mediation/Peace Studies M
Criminal Justice and Criminology M
Emergency Management M
History M
International Affairs M
International Development M
Military and Defense Studies M
Public Administration M
Public Policy M

NOTRE DAME COLLEGE (OH)
Homeland Security M,O

NOTRE DAME DE NAMUR UNIVERSITY
Art Therapy M,D
Clinical Psychology M
Marriage and Family Therapy M
Public Administration M

NOTRE DAME OF MARYLAND UNIVERSITY
Communication—General M
Liberal Studies M

NOTRE DAME SEMINARY
Theology M

NOVA SOUTHEASTERN UNIVERSITY
Addictions/Substance Abuse Counseling M,D,O
Art/Fine Arts M,D,O
Clinical Psychology M,D,O
Conflict Resolution and Mediation/Peace Studies M,D,O
Counseling Psychology M,D,O
Criminal Justice and Criminology M,D,O
Emergency Management M,D,O
Experimental Psychology M,D,O
Forensic Psychology M,D,O
Humanities M,D,O
Interdisciplinary Studies M,D,O
Marriage and Family Therapy M,D,O
Psychology—General M,D,O
Public Administration M
School Psychology M,D,O
Social Sciences M,D,O

NSCAD UNIVERSITY
Applied Arts and Design—General M
Art/Fine Arts M

NYACK COLLEGE
Counseling Psychology M
Marriage and Family Therapy M
Missions and Missiology M,D
Pastoral Ministry and Counseling M,D
Religion M
Theology M,D

OAKLAND CITY UNIVERSITY
Pastoral Ministry and Counseling M,D
Theology M,D

OAKLAND UNIVERSITY
Applied Behavior Analysis M,O
Counseling Psychology M,D,O
Economics M,O
English M
History M
Liberal Studies M
Linguistics M,O
Music M,D
Public Administration M,O

OAKWOOD UNIVERSITY
Pastoral Ministry and Counseling M

OBERLIN COLLEGE
Music M,O

OBLATE SCHOOL OF THEOLOGY
African-American Studies M,D,O
Pastoral Ministry and Counseling M,D,O
Religion M,D,O
Theology M,D,O

OHIO CHRISTIAN UNIVERSITY
Pastoral Ministry and Counseling M
Theology M

OHIO DOMINICAN UNIVERSITY
English M
Theology M

THE OHIO STATE UNIVERSITY
African Studies M
African-American Studies M,D
Agricultural Economics and Agribusiness M,D
Anthropology M,D
Architecture M,D
Art History M,D
Art/Fine Arts M
Arts Administration M
Asian Languages M,D
Asian Studies M
Child and Family Studies M,D
Chinese M,D
Classics M,D
Clinical Psychology D
Cognitive Sciences D
Communication—General M,D
Computer Art and Design M
Dance M,D
Developmental Psychology D
East European and Russian Studies M,D
Economics M,D
English M,D
Family and Consumer Sciences-General M,D
French M,D
Gender Studies M,D
Geography M,D
German M,D
History M,D
Human Development M,D
Industrial and Labor Relations M,D
Industrial Design M
Interdisciplinary Studies M,D
Interior Design M
Internet and Interactive Multimedia M
Italian M,D
Japanese M,D
Landscape Architecture M,D
Latin American Studies M
Linguistics M,D
Music M,D
Near and Middle Eastern Languages M,D
Philosophy M,D
Political Science D
Portuguese M,D
Psychology—General D
Public Administration M,D
Public Affairs M,D
Public Policy M,D
Rural Sociology M,D
Slavic Languages M,D
Social Psychology D
Social Sciences M,D
Sociology D
Spanish M,D
Theater M,D
Urban and Regional Planning M,D
Women's Studies M,D

OHIO UNIVERSITY
African Studies M
Applied Economics M
Art History M
Art/Fine Arts M
Asian Studies M
Child and Family Studies M
Child Development M
Clinical Psychology D
Communication—General M,D
Comparative and Interdisciplinary Arts D
Consumer Economics M
Corporate and Organizational Communication M,D
Economics M
English M,D
Experimental Psychology D
Film, Television, and Video Production M
Film, Television, and Video Theory and Criticism M
French M
Geography M
Graphic Design M
Health Communication M,D
History M,D
Industrial and Organizational Psychology D
International Affairs M
International Development M
Internet and Interactive Multimedia M
Journalism M,D
Latin American Studies M
Linguistics M
Media Studies M,D
Music M,O
Philosophy M
Photography M
Political Science M
Psychology—General D
Public Administration M,O
Rehabilitation Counseling M,D
Rhetoric M,D
Social Sciences M
Sociology M
Spanish M
Speech and Interpersonal Communication M,D
Theater M
Therapies—Dance, Drama, and Music M,O

OHR HAMEIR THEOLOGICAL SEMINARY
Theology

OKLAHOMA BAPTIST UNIVERSITY
Marriage and Family Therapy M

OKLAHOMA CHRISTIAN UNIVERSITY
Theology M

OKLAHOMA CITY UNIVERSITY
Applied Behavior Analysis M
Criminal Justice and Criminology M
Music M
Photography M
Sociology M
Writing M

OKLAHOMA STATE UNIVERSITY
Agricultural Economics and Agribusiness M,D
Applied Arts and Design—General M,D
Art History M
Child and Family Studies M,D
Clinical Psychology M,D
Clothing and Textiles M,D
Consumer Economics M,D
Economics M,D
Emergency Management M,D
English M,D
Family and Consumer Sciences-General M,D
Geography M,D
Graphic Design M
History M,D
International Affairs M,D,O
Landscape Architecture M,D
Mass Communication M
Music M
Philosophy M
Political Science M,D
Psychology—General M,D
Sociology M,D
Writing M,D

OKLAHOMA STATE UNIVERSITY CENTER FOR HEALTH SCIENCES
Forensic Sciences M

OKLAHOMA WESLEYAN UNIVERSITY
Theology M

OLD DOMINION UNIVERSITY
Applied Psychology D
Clinical Psychology D
Communication—General M,O
Computer Art and Design M
Conflict Resolution and Mediation/Peace Studies M,D
Counseling Psychology M,D,O
Criminal Justice and Criminology M,D
Cultural Studies M,D,O
Economics M,D
English M,D
Gender Studies M,O
History M
Humanities M,O
Industrial and Organizational Psychology D
International Affairs M,D
International Development M,D
Linguistics M,D
Media Studies M,O
Music M
Philosophy M,O
Psychology—General M,D
Public Administration M,D
Public Policy D
Rhetoric M
School Psychology M,D,O
Sociology M
Speech and Interpersonal Communication M
Women's Studies M
Writing M

OLIVET NAZARENE UNIVERSITY
Pastoral Ministry and Counseling M
Religion M
Theology M

OMEGA GRADUATE SCHOOL
Child and Family Studies M,D
Religion M,D
Sociology M,D

OPEN UNIVERSITY
History M
Music M
Philosophy M

ORAL ROBERTS UNIVERSITY
Addictions/Substance Abuse Counseling M,D
Marriage and Family Therapy M,D
Missions and Missiology M,D
Near and Middle Eastern Languages M,D
Pastoral Ministry and Counseling M,D
Theology M,D

OREGON HEALTH & SCIENCE UNIVERSITY
Gerontology M,O

OREGON STATE UNIVERSITY
Anthropology M
Applied Economics M,D
Child and Family Studies M,D
Clinical Psychology M,D
Cognitive Sciences M,D
English M
Ethics M
Gender Studies M,D
Geographic Information Systems M
Geography M,D
Health Psychology M,D
Hispanic Studies M
History of Science and Technology M,D
Human Development M,D
Interdisciplinary Studies M
Psychology—General M,D
Public Policy M,D
Rhetoric M
School Psychology M,D
Social Sciences M,D
Women's Studies M,D
Writing M

OREGON STATE UNIVERSITY–CASCADES
School Psychology M
Social Psychology M

OTIS COLLEGE OF ART AND DESIGN
Art/Fine Arts M
Graphic Design M
Photography M
Writing M

OTTAWA UNIVERSITY
Art Therapy M
Counseling Psychology M
Marriage and Family Therapy M
Pastoral Ministry and Counseling M
School Psychology M

OUR LADY OF THE LAKE UNIVERSITY
Counseling Psychology D
English M
Marriage and Family Therapy M
Psychology—General M
School Psychology M
Sociology M
Writing M

PACE UNIVERSITY
Addictions/Substance Abuse Counseling M,D
Clinical Psychology M,D
Communication—General M
Counseling Psychology M,D
Developmental Psychology M,D
Economics O
Emergency Management M
English M,O
Forensic Sciences M
Homeland Security M
International Economics O
Internet and Interactive Multimedia M
Media Studies M
Psychology—General M
Public Administration M
Publishing M,O
School Psychology M,D
Theater M

PACIFICA GRADUATE INSTITUTE
Clinical Psychology M,D
Counseling Psychology M,D
Psychology—General M,D

PACIFIC LUTHERAN UNIVERSITY
Marriage and Family Therapy M
Writing M

PACIFIC NORTHWEST COLLEGE OF ART
Applied Arts and Design—General M
Art/Fine Arts M
Cultural Studies M

PACIFIC OAKS COLLEGE
Human Development M
Marriage and Family Therapy M

PACIFIC RIM CHRISTIAN UNIVERSITY
Pastoral Ministry and Counseling M

PACIFIC SCHOOL OF RELIGION
Religion M,D,O
Theology M,D,O

PACIFIC UNIVERSITY
Clinical Psychology M,D
Psychology—General M,D
Writing M

PALM BEACH ATLANTIC UNIVERSITY
Addictions/Substance Abuse Counseling M
Counseling Psychology M
Marriage and Family Therapy M
Theology M

PALO ALTO UNIVERSITY
Clinical Psychology M,D
Counseling Psychology M
Marriage and Family Therapy M
Psychology—General M,D

PARIS COLLEGE OF ART
Art/Fine Arts M
Interior Design M
Media Studies M
Photography M
Textile Design M

PARK UNIVERSITY
Emergency Management M,O
Music M,O
Public Administration M,O
Public Affairs M,O
Writing M,O

PAYNE THEOLOGICAL SEMINARY
Theology M

PENN STATE ERIE, THE BEHREND COLLEGE
Applied Psychology M
Clinical Psychology M

PENN STATE HARRISBURG
American Studies M,D,O
Applied Behavior Analysis M,D,O
Applied Psychology M,D,O
Clinical Psychology M,D,O
Communication—General M,D,O
Criminal Justice and Criminology M,D,O
Folklore M,D,O
Health Psychology M,D,O
Historic Preservation M,D,O
Homeland Security M,D,O
Humanities M,D,O
Museum Studies M,D,O
Psychology—General M,D,O
Public Administration M,D,O
Public Affairs M,D,O
Social Psychology M,D,O

PENN STATE UNIVERSITY PARK
Agricultural Economics and Agribusiness M,D,O
Anthropology M,D
Architecture M,D
Art History M,D
Art/Fine Arts M,D,O
Child and Family Studies M,D
Communication—General M,D
Comparative Literature M,D
Criminal Justice and Criminology M,D
Economics M,D
English M,D
Forensic Sciences M
French M,D
Geography M,D
German M,D
History M,D
Human Development M,D
Industrial and Labor Relations M
International Affairs M
Landscape Architecture M,D
Linguistics M,D
Mass Communication M,D
Media Studies M,D
Music M,D,O
Philosophy M,D
Political Science M,D
Psychology—General M,D
Rural Sociology M,D,O
Russian M,D
School Psychology M,D,O
Sociology M,D
Spanish M,D
Sustainable Development M
Theater M

PENNSYLVANIA ACADEMY OF THE FINE ARTS
Art/Fine Arts M,O

PENSACOLA CHRISTIAN COLLEGE
Art/Fine Arts M,D,O
Graphic Design M,D,O
Music M,D,O
Theater M,D,O

PENTECOSTAL THEOLOGICAL SEMINARY
Pastoral Ministry and Counseling M,D
Theology M,D

PEPPERDINE UNIVERSITY
American Studies M
Communication—General M
Economics M
Humanities M
International Affairs M
Media Studies M
Pastoral Ministry and Counseling M
Political Science M
Public Policy M
Religion M
Writing M

PERU STATE COLLEGE
Economics M

PFEIFFER UNIVERSITY
Theology M

PHILADELPHIA COLLEGE OF OSTEOPATHIC MEDICINE
Applied Behavior Analysis M,D,O
Clinical Psychology M,D,O
Counseling Psychology M,D,O
Forensic Sciences M
Industrial and Organizational Psychology M,D,O
Psychology—General M,D,O
School Psychology M,D,O

PHILLIPS GRADUATE UNIVERSITY
Art Therapy M
Marriage and Family Therapy M
Psychology—General M
School Psychology M

PHILLIPS THEOLOGICAL SEMINARY
Ethics M,D
Missions and Missiology M,D
Music M,D
Pastoral Ministry and Counseling D
Theology M,D

PHOENIX SEMINARY
Counseling Psychology M,D,O
Pastoral Ministry and Counseling M,D,O
Theology M,D,O

PIEDMONT INTERNATIONAL UNIVERSITY
Pastoral Ministry and Counseling M,D
Theology M,D

PILLAR COLLEGE
Clinical Psychology M
Marriage and Family Therapy M

PITTSBURGH THEOLOGICAL SEMINARY
Pastoral Ministry and Counseling M,D
Theology M,D

PITTSBURG STATE UNIVERSITY
Clinical Psychology M
Communication—General M
English M
Graphic Design M,O
History M
Music M
Psychology—General M
School Psychology O
Writing M

PLYMOUTH STATE UNIVERSITY
Addictions/Substance Abuse Counseling M
Clinical Psychology O
Cultural Studies M
Historic Preservation M,O
Marriage and Family Therapy M
School Psychology O

POINT LOMA NAZARENE UNIVERSITY
Clinical Psychology M
Marriage and Family Therapy M
Pastoral Ministry and Counseling M
Theology M

POINT PARK UNIVERSITY
Clinical Psychology M,D
Communication—General M
Criminal Justice and Criminology M
Journalism M
Mass Communication M
Media Studies M
Music M
Theater M

POINT UNIVERSITY
Pastoral Ministry and Counseling M

POLYTECHNIC UNIVERSITY OF PUERTO RICO
Landscape Architecture M

PONCE HEALTH SCIENCES UNIVERSITY
Clinical Psychology D

PONTIFICAL CATHOLIC UNIVERSITY OF PUERTO RICO
Art/Fine Arts M
Clinical Psychology D
Criminal Justice and Criminology M
Hispanic Studies M,O
History M
Industrial and Organizational Psychology D
Psychology—General M,D
Public Administration M
Rehabilitation Counseling M
Spanish M,O
Theology M

PONTIFICAL COLLEGE JOSEPHINUM
Theology M

PONTIFICAL JOHN PAUL II INSTITUTE FOR STUDIES ON MARRIAGE AND FAMILY
Ethics M,D,O
Marriage and Family Therapy M,D,O
Theology M,D,O

PONTIFICIA UNIVERSIDAD CATOLICA MADRE Y MAESTRA
Architecture M
Building Science M
Clinical Psychology M
Criminal Justice and Criminology M
Developmental Psychology M
Forensic Psychology M
Interior Design M
International Affairs M
Landscape Architecture M
Psychology—General M

POPE ST. JOHN XXIII NATIONAL SEMINARY
Theology M

PORTLAND STATE UNIVERSITY
American Studies M
Anthropology M,D,O
Applied Social Research M,D
Architecture M
Art/Fine Arts M
Conflict Resolution and Mediation/Peace Studies M
Criminal Justice and Criminology M
Economics M,D,O
English M
French M
Geography M,D
German M
History M
International Affairs M
Japanese M
Music M
Political Science M
Psychology—General M,D,O
Public Administration M,D,O
Public Affairs M,D,O
Public Policy M,D,O
Sociology M,D,O
Spanish M
Speech and Interpersonal Communication M,O
Theater M
Writing M

POST UNIVERSITY
Addictions/Substance Abuse Counseling M
Clinical Psychology M
Emergency Management M
Forensic Psychology M
Homeland Security M

*M—masters degree; D—doctorate; O—other advanced degree; *—Close-Up and/or Display*

Public Administration — M

PRAIRIE VIEW A&M UNIVERSITY
Architecture — M
Clinical Psychology — M,D
Forensic Psychology — M,D
Sociology — M

PRATT INSTITUTE
Applied Arts and Design—
General — M,O
Architecture — M
Art Therapy — M
Art/Fine Arts — M
Arts Administration — M
Graphic Design — M
Historic Preservation — M
Industrial Design — M
Interior Design — M
Internet and Interactive
Multimedia — M
Media Studies — M
Music — M
Sustainable Development — M
Therapies—Dance, Drama, and
Music — M
Urban and Regional Planning — M
Urban Design — M
Writing — M

PRESCOTT COLLEGE
Art Therapy — M
Art/Fine Arts — M
Counseling Psychology — M
Health Psychology — M
Humanities — M
Psychoanalysis and Psychotherapy — M

PRINCETON THEOLOGICAL SEMINARY
Religion — M,D
Theology — M,D

PRINCETON UNIVERSITY
Anthropology — D
Archaeology — D
Architecture — M,D
Asian Studies — D
Classics — D
Comparative Literature — D
Demography and Population Studies — D,O
Economics — D,O
English — D
French — D
German — D
History of Science and Technology — D
History — D
International Affairs — M,D
Music — D
Near and Middle Eastern Studies — M,D
Philosophy — D
Political Science — D
Portuguese — D
Psychology—General — D
Public Affairs — M,D,O
Public Policy — M,D
Religion — D
Russian — D
Slavic Languages — D
Sociology — D,O
Spanish — D

PROVIDENCE COLLEGE
American Studies — M
History — M
Theology — M

PROVIDENCE UNIVERSITY COLLEGE & THEOLOGICAL SEMINARY
Counseling Psychology — M,D,O
Missions and Missiology — M,D,O
Pastoral Ministry and Counseling — M,D,O
Theology — M,D,O

PURCHASE COLLEGE, STATE UNIVERSITY OF NEW YORK
Art History — M
Art/Fine Arts — M
Arts Administration — M
Computer Art and Design — M
Music — M

PURDUE UNIVERSITY
Agricultural Economics and
Agribusiness — M,D
American Studies — M,D
Anthropology — M,D
Applied Arts and Design—
General — M,D
Art/Fine Arts — M,D
Child and Family Studies — M,D
Child Development — M,D
Clinical Psychology — D
Cognitive Sciences — D
Communication—General — M,D
Comparative Literature — M,D
Computer Art and Design — M,D
Consumer Economics — M,D
Economics — D
English — M,D
French — M
German — M
History — M,D
Human Development — M,D
Industrial and Organizational
Psychology — D
Industrial Design — M,D
Interior Design — M,D
Japanese — M
Linguistics — M,D
Marriage and Family Therapy — M,D
Philosophy — M,D
Political Science — M,D
Psychology—General — D
Sociology — M,D
Spanish — M,D
Sport Psychology — D
Writing — M,D

PURDUE UNIVERSITY FORT WAYNE
Communication—General — M
English — M,O
Marriage and Family Therapy — M,O
Public Policy — M,O

PURDUE UNIVERSITY GLOBAL
Criminal Justice and Criminology — M
Political Science — M,O

PURDUE UNIVERSITY NORTHWEST
Child and Family Studies — M
Child Development — M
Communication—General — M
Counseling Psychology — M
English — M
History — M
Marriage and Family Therapy — M
School Psychology — M

QUEENS COLLEGE OF THE CITY UNIVERSITY OF NEW YORK
Applied Behavior Analysis — M
Applied Social Research — M
Art History — M
Art/Fine Arts — M
Child and Family Studies — M,O
Counseling Psychology — M,O
English — M
Family and Consumer
Sciences-General — M,O
French — M
Hispanic and Latin American
Languages — M
History — M
Italian — M
Liberal Studies — M
Linguistics — M,O
Media Studies — M
Music — M,O
Psychology—General — M
Romance Languages — M
School Psychology — M,O
Sociology — M
Spanish — M
Urban Studies — M
Writing — M

QUEEN'S UNIVERSITY AT KINGSTON
Canadian Studies — M,D
Classics — M,D
Clinical Psychology — M,D
Cognitive Sciences — M,D
Communication—General — M,D
Developmental Psychology — M,D
Economics — M,D
English — M,D
French — M,D
Gender Studies — M,D
Geography — M,D
Industrial and Labor Relations — M
International Affairs — M,D
Philosophy — M,D
Political Science — M,D
Psychology—General — M,D
Public Administration — M
Religion — M,D
Social Psychology — M,D
Sociology — M,D
Sport Psychology — M,D
Urban and Regional Planning — M
Women's Studies — M,D

QUEENS UNIVERSITY OF CHARLOTTE
Communication—General — M
Interior Design — M
Writing — M

QUINCY UNIVERSITY
Clinical Psychology — M
School Psychology — M

QUINNIPIAC UNIVERSITY
Broadcast Journalism — M
Communication—General — M
Film, Television, and Video
Production — M
Internet and Interactive
Multimedia — M
Journalism — M

RABBINICAL ACADEMY MESIVTA RABBI CHAIM BERLIN
Theology — O

RABBINICAL COLLEGE BETH SHRAGA
Theology

RABBINICAL COLLEGE BOBOVER YESHIVA B'NEI ZION
Theology — O

RABBINICAL COLLEGE OF LONG ISLAND
Theology

RABBINICAL SEMINARY OF AMERICA
Theology

RADFORD UNIVERSITY
Art/Fine Arts — M
Clinical Psychology — M
Corporate and Organizational
Communication — M
Counseling Psychology — D
Criminal Justice and Criminology — M,O
English — M
Experimental Psychology — M
Industrial and Organizational
Psychology — M
Music — M
Psychology—General — M
School Psychology — O

RANDALL UNIVERSITY
Pastoral Ministry and Counseling — M

RANDOLPH COLLEGE
Writing — M

RECONSTRUCTIONIST RABBINICAL COLLEGE
Jewish Studies — M,D,O
Theology — M,D,O
Women's Studies — M,D,O

REED COLLEGE
Liberal Studies — M

REFORMED EPISCOPAL SEMINARY
Theology

REFORMED PRESBYTERIAN THEOLOGICAL SEMINARY
Theology — M,D

REFORMED THEOLOGICAL SEMINARY–ATLANTA CAMPUS
Theology — M,D,O

REFORMED THEOLOGICAL SEMINARY–CHARLOTTE CAMPUS
Pastoral Ministry and Counseling — M,D
Religion — M,D
Theology — M,D

REFORMED THEOLOGICAL SEMINARY–DALLAS CAMPUS
Theology — M

REFORMED THEOLOGICAL SEMINARY–HOUSTON CAMPUS
Religion — M

REFORMED THEOLOGICAL SEMINARY–JACKSON CAMPUS
Marriage and Family Therapy — M,D,O
Missions and Missiology — M,D,O
Pastoral Ministry and Counseling — M,D,O
Religion — M,D,O
Theology — M,D,O

REFORMED THEOLOGICAL SEMINARY–ORLANDO CAMPUS
Pastoral Ministry and Counseling — M,D,O
Theology — M,D,O

REFORMED THEOLOGICAL SEMINARY–WASHINGTON D.C.
Religion — M
Theology — M

REFORMED UNIVERSITY
Theology — M

REGENT COLLEGE
Theology — M,O

REGENT'S UNIVERSITY LONDON
International Affairs — M

REGENT UNIVERSITY
Addictions/Substance Abuse
Counseling — M,D,O
American Studies — M
Clinical Psychology — M,D,O
Communication—General — M
Conflict Resolution and
Mediation/Peace Studies — M,D
Corporate and Organizational
Communication — M,D
Counseling Psychology — M,D,O
Criminal Justice and Criminology — M,D,O
Cultural Studies — M,D
Economics — M,D,O
Emergency Management — M
Film, Television, and Video
Production — M,D
Homeland Security — M
Interdisciplinary Studies — M,D,O
International Affairs — M,D
Journalism — M,D
Marriage and Family Therapy — M,D,O
Missions and Missiology — M,D
National Security — M,D
Pastoral Ministry and Counseling — M,D,O
Political Science — M
Public Administration — M
Public Policy — M
Religion — M,D
Theater — M,D
Theology — M,D
Writing — M,D

REGIS COLLEGE (CANADA)
Pastoral Ministry and Counseling — M,D,O
Philosophy — M,D,O
Theology — M,D,O

REGIS COLLEGE (MA)
Applied Behavior Analysis — M,D,O
Corporate and Organizational
Communication — M
Counseling Psychology — M,D,O

REGIS UNIVERSITY
Criminal Justice and Criminology — M,O
Developmental Psychology — M,D,O
Economics — M,O
Marriage and Family Therapy — M,D,O
Writing — M,O

REINHARDT UNIVERSITY
Public Administration — M
Writing — M

RENSSELAER POLYTECHNIC INSTITUTE
Architecture — M
Art/Fine Arts — D
Cognitive Sciences — M
Computer Art and Design — D
History of Science and Technology — M,D
Interdisciplinary Studies — M,D
Lighting Design — M,D
Rhetoric — M,D
Speech and Interpersonal
Communication — M,D

RHODE ISLAND COLLEGE
Art/Fine Arts — M
Arts Administration — M
Counseling Psychology — M,O
English — M,O
Health Psychology — M,O
History — M
Psychology—General — M,O
School Psychology — M,O
Writing — M,O

RHODE ISLAND SCHOOL OF DESIGN
Applied Arts and Design—
General — M
Architecture — M
Art/Fine Arts — M
Computer Art and Design — M
Graphic Design — M
Industrial Design — M
Interior Design — M
Landscape Architecture — M
Media Studies — M
Photography — M
Textile Design — M

RICE UNIVERSITY
African Studies — D
American Studies — D
Anthropology — M,D
Archaeology — M,D
Architecture — M,D
Art History — D
Cognitive Sciences — M,D
Cultural Anthropology — M,D
Economics — M,D
English — M,D
History — M,D
Industrial and Organizational
Psychology — M,D
Jewish Studies — D
Liberal Studies — M
Linguistics — M,D
Music — M,D
Near and Middle Eastern Studies — M,D
Philosophy — M,D
Political Science — D
Psychology—General — M,D
Religion — M,D
Sociology — D
Urban Design — M,D

RICHMOND, THE AMERICAN INTERNATIONAL UNIVERSITY IN LONDON
Art History — M
International Affairs — M

RICHMONT GRADUATE UNIVERSITY
Clinical Psychology — M
Marriage and Family Therapy — M
Pastoral Ministry and Counseling — M,O

RIDER UNIVERSITY
Arts Administration — M
Clinical Psychology — M,O
Corporate and Organizational
Communication — M
Health Communication — M
Homeland Security — M
Music — M
School Psychology — O

RIVIER UNIVERSITY
Clinical Psychology — M
Counseling Psychology — M,D,O
English — M
Experimental Psychology — M
Psychology—General — M
Writing — M

THE ROBERT E. WEBBER INSTITUTE FOR WORSHIP STUDIES
Religion — M,D

ROBERT MORRIS UNIVERSITY ILLINOIS
Criminal Justice and Criminology — M

ROBERTS WESLEYAN COLLEGE
Child and Family Studies — M
Clinical Psychology — M,D
Psychology—General — M,D
School Psychology — M,D

ROCHESTER INSTITUTE OF TECHNOLOGY
Architecture — M
Art/Fine Arts — M
Cognitive Sciences — O
Communication—General — M
Computer Art and Design — M
Criminal Justice and Criminology — M
Experimental Psychology — M
Film, Television, and Video
Production — M
Graphic Design — M
Industrial Design — M
Interdisciplinary Studies — M
Internet and Interactive
Multimedia — O
Media Studies — M
Medical Illustration — M
Photography — M
Psychology—General — M,O
Public Policy — M
School Psychology — M
Sustainable Development — M,D
Translation and Interpretation — M

ROCHESTER UNIVERSITY
Missions and Missiology — M

ROCKY MOUNTAIN COLLEGE OF ART + DESIGN
Arts Administration — M
Internet and Interactive
Multimedia — M

ROGER WILLIAMS UNIVERSITY
Architectural History M,O
Architecture M,O
Art History M,O
Clinical Psychology M
Criminal Justice and Criminology M
Forensic Psychology M
Historic Preservation M,O
Public Administration M
Urban and Regional Planning M,O

ROLLINS COLLEGE
Applied Behavior Analysis M
Liberal Studies M

ROOSEVELT UNIVERSITY
Arts Administration M,O
Clinical Psychology M
Communication—General M
Corporate and Organizational Communication M
Economics M
History M
Humanities M
Industrial and Organizational Psychology M,D
Music M,O
Philosophy M
Psychology—General M,D
Public Administration M
School Psychology M
Sociology M
Theater M
Writing M

ROSALIND FRANKLIN UNIVERSITY OF MEDICINE AND SCIENCE
Clinical Psychology M,D
Interdisciplinary Studies D
Psychology—General M,D

ROSEMONT COLLEGE
Counseling Psychology M
Publishing M
Writing M

ROWAN UNIVERSITY
Applied Behavior Analysis M,O
Arts Administration M
Clinical Psychology M,O
Corporate and Organizational Communication O
Criminal Justice and Criminology M
History M,O
Media Studies O
Music M
Psychology—General M,O
Publishing O
Rhetoric O
School Psychology M,O
Theater M
Writing M,O

ROYAL MILITARY COLLEGE OF CANADA
Military and Defense Studies M,D

ROYAL ROADS UNIVERSITY
Conflict Resolution and Mediation/Peace Studies M,O
Emergency Management M,O

RUTGERS UNIVERSITY - CAMDEN
Child Development M,D
Criminal Justice and Criminology M
English M
History M
International Affairs M
International Development M
Liberal Studies M
Psychology—General M
Public Administration M
Public History M
Public Policy M
Writing M

RUTGERS UNIVERSITY - NEWARK
American Studies M,D
Clothing and Textiles M
Cognitive Sciences D
Criminal Justice and Criminology M,D
Economics M,D
English M
History M
International Affairs M,D
Music M
Political Science M
Psychology—General D
Public Administration M,D
Public Policy M,D,O
Rehabilitation Counseling M,D
Social Psychology D
Urban Studies M,D
Writing M

RUTGERS UNIVERSITY - NEW BRUNSWICK
African Studies D
African-American Studies D
Agricultural Economics and Agribusiness M
Anthropology M,D
Applied Arts and Design—General M
Applied Psychology M,D
Art History M,D,O
Art/Fine Arts M
Asian Studies M,D
Classics M,D
Clinical Psychology M,D
Cognitive Sciences D
Communication—General D
Comparative Literature M,D
Counseling Psychology M
Economics M,D
Emergency Management M,D,O
English D
French M,D
Gender Studies M,D
Geography M,D
German M,D
Health Psychology D
Historic Preservation M,D,O
History of Medicine D
History of Science and Technology D
History D
Industrial and Labor Relations M,D
Interdisciplinary Studies D
International Affairs M,D
Italian M,D
Jewish Studies M,O
Landscape Architecture M
Linguistics D
Medieval and Renaissance Studies D
Music M,D,O
Philosophy D
Political Science M,D
Psychology—General D
Public Policy M,D
Religion M,O
School Psychology M,D
Social Psychology D
Sociology M,D
Spanish M,D
Theater M
Translation and Interpretation M,D
Urban and Regional Planning M,D
Women's Studies M,D
Writing M

RYERSON UNIVERSITY
Arts Administration M

SACRED HEART MAJOR SEMINARY
Pastoral Ministry and Counseling M
Theology M

SACRED HEART SEMINARY AND SCHOOL OF THEOLOGY
Theology M,O

SACRED HEART UNIVERSITY
Applied Psychology M
Communication—General M
Criminal Justice and Criminology M
Film, Television, and Video Production M
Industrial and Organizational Psychology M
Journalism M
Public Administration M
Social Psychology M

SAGE GRADUATE SCHOOL
Applied Behavior Analysis M,O
Counseling Psychology M
Forensic Psychology M,O
Gerontology M
Psychology—General M,O
Social Psychology M

SAGINAW VALLEY STATE UNIVERSITY
Chinese M
Communication—General M
Media Studies M
Public Administration M

ST. AMBROSE UNIVERSITY
Criminal Justice and Criminology M
Pastoral Ministry and Counseling M

ST. ANDREW'S COLLEGE
Theology M,D,O

ST. ANDREW'S COLLEGE IN WINNIPEG
Theology M

ST. AUGUSTINE'S SEMINARY OF TORONTO
Pastoral Ministry and Counseling M,O
Theology M,O

ST. BERNARD'S SCHOOL OF THEOLOGY AND MINISTRY
Pastoral Ministry and Counseling M,O
Theology M,O

ST. BONAVENTURE UNIVERSITY
Corporate and Organizational Communication M
Counseling Psychology M,O
Rehabilitation Counseling M,O
Social Psychology M,O

ST. CATHERINE UNIVERSITY
Pastoral Ministry and Counseling M,O
Theology M,O

SAINT CHARLES BORROMEO SEMINARY, OVERBROOK
Philosophy M
Theology M

ST. CLOUD STATE UNIVERSITY
Applied Behavior Analysis M
Applied Economics M
Archaeology M,O
Child and Family Studies M
Criminal Justice and Criminology M
Economics M
English M
Geography M,O
Gerontology M,O
Historic Preservation M,O
History M
Industrial and Organizational Psychology M
Marriage and Family Therapy M
Mass Communication M
Rhetoric M
Writing M

ST. EDWARD'S UNIVERSITY
Counseling Psychology M
Humanities M,O
Liberal Studies M,O
Sustainable Development M

ST. FRANCIS XAVIER UNIVERSITY
Cultural Studies M
Urban and Regional Planning M

ST. JOHN FISHER COLLEGE
Counseling Psychology M
French M

ST. JOHN'S COLLEGE (MD)
Liberal Studies M

ST. JOHN'S COLLEGE (NM)
Asian Languages M
Asian Studies M
Liberal Studies M

ST. JOHN'S SEMINARY (CA)
Pastoral Ministry and Counseling M
Theology M

SAINT JOHN'S SEMINARY (MA)
Religion M
Theology M

SAINT JOHN'S UNIVERSITY (MN)
Music M
Pastoral Ministry and Counseling M
Theology M

ST. JOHN'S UNIVERSITY (NY)
Asian Studies M
Clinical Psychology M,D,O
Counseling Psychology M,O
Criminal Justice and Criminology M
English M,D
History M,D
Homeland Security M
Liberal Studies M
Mass Communication M
Museum Studies M
Political Science M,O
Psychology—General M
Public Administration M,O
Public History M,D
School Psychology M,D
Sociology M
Spanish M
Theology M

ST. JOSEPH'S COLLEGE, LONG ISLAND CAMPUS
Forensic Sciences M

ST. JOSEPH'S COLLEGE, NEW YORK
Forensic Sciences M
Writing M

SAINT JOSEPH'S COLLEGE OF MAINE
Pastoral Ministry and Counseling M

ST. JOSEPH'S SEMINARY
Pastoral Ministry and Counseling M
Religion M
Theology M

SAINT JOSEPH'S UNIVERSITY
Criminal Justice and Criminology M,O
Psychology—General M,O
Writing M

SAINT LEO UNIVERSITY
Criminal Justice and Criminology M,D
Emergency Management M,D
Forensic Sciences M,D
Psychology—General M
Theology M,O
Writing M

SAINT LOUIS UNIVERSITY
American Studies M,D
Applied Behavior Analysis M,D
Clinical Psychology M,D
Communication—General M
Criminal Justice and Criminology M
Emergency Management M
English M,D
Experimental Psychology M,D
French M
History M,D
Industrial and Organizational Psychology M,D
Philosophy M,D
Political Science M
Psychology—General M,D
Spanish M
Theology M,D
Urban and Regional Planning M

SAINT LOUIS UNIVERSITY–MADRID CAMPUS
English M
Spanish M

SAINT MARTIN'S UNIVERSITY
Counseling Psychology M
Social Psychology M

SAINT MARY-OF-THE-WOODS COLLEGE
Art Therapy M,O
Therapies—Dance, Drama, and Music M

SAINT MARY'S COLLEGE OF CALIFORNIA
Conflict Resolution and Mediation/Peace Studies M
Dance M
Marriage and Family Therapy M,O
School Psychology M,O
Writing M

SAINT MARY SEMINARY AND GRADUATE SCHOOL OF THEOLOGY
Theology M,D

ST. MARY'S SEMINARY AND UNIVERSITY
Theology M,D,O

SAINT MARY'S UNIVERSITY (CANADA)
Applied Psychology M,D
Canadian Studies M,O
Criminal Justice and Criminology M
Gender Studies M
History M
Industrial and Organizational Psychology M,D
International Development M,O
Philosophy M
Psychology—General M,D
Religion M
Theology M
Women's Studies M

ST. MARY'S UNIVERSITY (UNITED STATES)
Communication—General M
Conflict Resolution and Mediation/Peace Studies M,O
Counseling Psychology M
Criminal Justice and Criminology M
English M
Homeland Security M,O
Industrial and Organizational Psychology M
International Affairs M,O
International Development M,O
Public Administration M,O
Theology M

SAINT MARY'S UNIVERSITY OF MINNESOTA
Counseling Psychology M,D,O
Geographic Information Systems M,O
Human Development M
Marriage and Family Therapy M
Philanthropic Studies M
Public Administration M

SAINT MEINRAD SCHOOL OF THEOLOGY
Theology M

SAINT MICHAEL'S COLLEGE
Clinical Psychology M

ST. NORBERT COLLEGE
Liberal Studies M
Theology M

ST. PATRICK'S SEMINARY & UNIVERSITY
Theology M,O

SAINT PAUL SCHOOL OF THEOLOGY
Theology M,D

SAINT PAUL UNIVERSITY
Conflict Resolution and Mediation/Peace Studies M
Counseling Psychology M
Marriage and Family Therapy M
Missions and Missiology M
Pastoral Ministry and Counseling M,D,O
Theology M,D,O

ST. PETER'S SEMINARY
Theology M

SAINT PETER'S UNIVERSITY
Applied Behavior Analysis M,D,O
Criminal Justice and Criminology M
Family and Consumer Sciences-General M
Public Administration M

SAINTS CYRIL AND METHODIUS SEMINARY
Pastoral Ministry and Counseling M
Theology M

ST. STEPHEN'S COLLEGE
Pastoral Ministry and Counseling M,D
Theology M,D

ST. THOMAS UNIVERSITY - FLORIDA
Arts Administration M
Communication—General M,D,O
Counseling Psychology M
Criminal Justice and Criminology M,O
Film, Television, and Video Production M
Hispanic Studies M,O
Marriage and Family Therapy M,O
Pastoral Ministry and Counseling M,D,O
Public Administration M,O
Theology M,D,O

ST. TIKHON'S ORTHODOX THEOLOGICAL SEMINARY
Theology M

ST. VINCENT DE PAUL REGIONAL SEMINARY
Theology M

SAINT VINCENT SEMINARY
Theology M

ST. VLADIMIR'S ORTHODOX THEOLOGICAL SEMINARY
Theology M,D

SAINT XAVIER UNIVERSITY
Spanish M

*M—masters degree; D—doctorate; O—other advanced degree; *—Close-Up and/or Display*

SALEM COLLEGE
Music — M

SALEM STATE UNIVERSITY
Counseling Psychology — M,O
Criminal Justice and Criminology — M
English — M
Geography — M
History — M
Psychology—General — M,O
Spanish — M

SALISBURY UNIVERSITY
American Studies — M
Conflict Resolution and
   Mediation/Peace Studies — M
English — M
Geographic Information Systems — M
History — M

SALVE REGINA UNIVERSITY
Addictions/Substance Abuse
   Counseling — M,O
Applied Behavior Analysis — M,O
Conflict Resolution and
   Mediation/Peace Studies — M,D
Counseling Psychology — M,O
Criminal Justice and Criminology — M,O
Forensic Sciences — M,O
Homeland Security — M,O
Humanities — M,D
International Affairs — M,D,O
Rehabilitation Counseling — M,O
Religion — M,D
Writing — M

SAMFORD UNIVERSITY
Music — M
Theology — M,D

SAM HOUSTON STATE UNIVERSITY
Clinical Psychology — M,D,O
Communication—General — M
Criminal Justice and Criminology — M,D
Dance — M
English — M
Family and Consumer
   Sciences-General — M
Forensic Sciences — M,D
Geographic Information Systems — M,O
History — M
Homeland Security — M
Humanities — M,D,O
Internet and Interactive
   Multimedia — M
Music — M
Political Science — M
Psychology—General — M,D,O
Public Administration — M
Publishing — M
School Psychology — M,D,O
Sociology — M
Spanish — M
Writing — M

SAN DIEGO STATE UNIVERSITY
Anthropology — M
Applied Arts and Design—
   General — M
Art/Fine Arts — M
Asian Studies — M
Child and Family Studies — M
Child Development — M
Clinical Psychology — M,D
Communication—General — M
Criminal Justice and Criminology — M
Economics — M
Emergency Management — M,D
English — M
Film, Television, and Video
   Production — M
Gender Studies — O
Geography — M,D
Gerontology — M
Graphic Design — M
Health Psychology — M,D
History — M
Industrial and Organizational
   Psychology — M,D
Interdisciplinary Studies — M
Interior Design — M
Internet and Interactive
   Multimedia — M
Latin American Studies — M
Liberal Studies — M
Linguistics — M,O
Media Studies — M
Music — M
Philosophy — M
Photography — M
Political Science — M
Psychology—General — M,D
Public Administration — M
Rehabilitation Counseling — M
Rhetoric — M
Romance Languages — M
School Psychology — M
Sociology — M
Spanish — M
Theater — M
Urban and Regional Planning — M
Western European Studies — M
Women's Studies — M
Writing — M

SAN FRANCISCO ART INSTITUTE
Art History — M
Art/Fine Arts — M,O
Museum Studies — M

SAN FRANCISCO CONSERVATORY OF MUSIC
Music — M,O

SAN FRANCISCO STATE UNIVERSITY
Anthropology — M

Applied Arts and Design—
   General — M
Archaeology — M
Art/Fine Arts — M
Asian-American Studies — M
Biological Anthropology — M
Chinese — M
Classics — M
Clinical Psychology — M,O
Comparative Literature — M
Criminal Justice and Criminology — M
Cultural Anthropology — M
Cultural Studies — M
Developmental Psychology — M,O
Economics — M
English — M,O
Ethnic Studies — M
Family and Consumer
   Sciences-General — M
Film, Television, and Video
   Production — M
Film, Television, and Video
   Theory and Criticism — M
French — M
Geographic Information Systems — M
Geography — M
German — M
Gerontology — M
History — M
Humanities — M
Industrial and Organizational
   Psychology — M,O
International Affairs — M
Italian — M
Japanese — M
Liberal Studies — M
Linguistics — M
Marriage and Family Therapy — M
Media Studies — M
Museum Studies — M
Music — M
Philosophy — M
Political Science — M
Psychology—General — M,O
Public Administration — M
Public Policy — M
School Psychology — M,O
Social Psychology — M,O
Spanish — M
Speech and Interpersonal
   Communication — M
Theater — M
Women's Studies — M
Writing — M

SAN FRANCISCO THEOLOGICAL SEMINARY
Theology — M,D

SAN JOSE STATE UNIVERSITY
Anthropology — M
Applied Economics — M
Child and Family Studies — M
Clinical Psychology — M
Communication—General — M
Criminal Justice and Criminology — M
Economics — M
Experimental Psychology — M
Film, Television, and Video
   Production — M
History — M
Industrial and Organizational
   Psychology — M
Linguistics — M,O
Mass Communication — M
Philosophy — M
Psychology—General — M
Public Administration — M
Speech and Interpersonal
   Communication — M
Theater — M

SANTA CLARA UNIVERSITY
Counseling Psychology — M,O
Ethics — M,D,O
Pastoral Ministry and Counseling — M
Religion — M,D,O
Theology — M,D,O

SARAH LAWRENCE COLLEGE
Child Development — M
Dance — M
Genetic Counseling — M
History — M
Theater — M
Women's Studies — M
Writing — M

SAVANNAH COLLEGE OF ART AND DESIGN
Applied Arts and Design—
   General — M
Architectural History — M
Architecture — M
Art History — M
Art/Fine Arts — M
Arts Administration — M
Clothing and Textiles — M
Computer Art and Design — M
Film, Television, and Video
   Production — M
Film, Television, and Video
   Theory and Criticism — M
Graphic Design — M
Historic Preservation — M
Illustration — M
Industrial Design — M
Interior Design — M
Internet and Interactive
   Multimedia — M
Media Studies — M
Music — M
Photography — M
Sustainable Development — M
Textile Design — M
Theater — M

Urban Design — M
Writing — M

SAVANNAH STATE UNIVERSITY
Public Administration — M
Urban and Regional Planning — M
Urban Studies — M

SAYBROOK UNIVERSITY
Clinical Psychology — M
Counseling Psychology — M
Health Psychology — M,D
Marriage and Family Therapy — M,D
Psychology—General — M,D
Sustainable Development — M
Transpersonal and Humanistic
   Psychology — M,D

SCHILLER INTERNATIONAL UNIVERSITY - PARIS
International Affairs — M

SCHOOL OF ADVANCED AIR AND SPACE STUDIES
Military and Defense Studies — M

SCHOOL OF ARCHITECTURE AT TALIESIN
Architecture — M

SCHOOL OF THE ART INSTITUTE OF CHICAGO
Writing — M,O

SCHOOL OF VISUAL ARTS (NY)
Applied Arts and Design—
   General — M
Art History — M
Art Therapy — M
Art/Fine Arts — M
Computer Art and Design — M
Cultural Studies — M
Film, Television, and Video
   Production — M
Graphic Design — M
Illustration — M
Internet and Interactive
   Multimedia — M
Photography — M
Writing — M

SCHREINER UNIVERSITY
Ethics — M

SEATTLE PACIFIC UNIVERSITY
Clinical Psychology — D
Industrial and Organizational
   Psychology — M,D
Marriage and Family Therapy — M,O
Religion — M,O
Theology — M,O
Writing — M

THE SEATTLE SCHOOL OF THEOLOGY AND PSYCHOLOGY
Counseling Psychology — M
Psychology—General — M
Religion — M
Theology — M

SEATTLE UNIVERSITY
Arts Administration — M
Criminal Justice and Criminology — M,O
Forensic Sciences — M,O
Marriage and Family Therapy — M
Pastoral Ministry and Counseling — M
Psychology—General — M
Public Administration — M
School Psychology — M,O
Theology — M,D,O
Transpersonal and Humanistic
   Psychology — M

SELMA UNIVERSITY
Pastoral Ministry and Counseling — M
Religion — M

SETON HALL UNIVERSITY
Asian Studies — M
Communication—General — M
Corporate and Organizational
   Communication — M
Counseling Psychology — M,D
English — M
Experimental Psychology — M
History — M
International Affairs — M,O
Jewish Studies — M,O
Museum Studies — M
Pastoral Ministry and Counseling — M,O
Psychology—General — M
Public Administration — M,O
Public Policy — M,O
Religion — M,O
School Psychology — M
Speech and Interpersonal
   Communication — M
Theology — M,O

SETON HILL UNIVERSITY
Art Therapy — M
Writing — M

SHASTA BIBLE COLLEGE
Pastoral Ministry and Counseling — M

SHAW UNIVERSITY
Theology — M

SHENANDOAH UNIVERSITY
Applied Behavior Analysis — M
Music — M,D,O
Writing — M,D,O

SHEPHERDS THEOLOGICAL SEMINARY
Pastoral Ministry and Counseling — M
Theology — M

SHILOH UNIVERSITY
Pastoral Ministry and Counseling — M,D

Theology — M,D

SHIPPENSBURG UNIVERSITY OF PENNSYLVANIA
Clinical Psychology — M,D
Communication—General — M
Criminal Justice and Criminology — M
Geography — M
History — M
Psychology—General — M
Public Administration — M
Public History — M
Sociology — M

SH'OR YOSHUV RABBINICAL COLLEGE
Theology — M

SIENA HEIGHTS UNIVERSITY
Clinical Psychology — M,O
Counseling Psychology — M,O

SILVER LAKE COLLEGE OF THE HOLY FAMILY
Music — M

SIMMONS UNIVERSITY
Applied Behavior Analysis — M,D,O
Cultural Studies — M,D,O
English — M,D,O
Gender Studies — M,D,O
History — M,D,O
Public Policy — M,D,O
Writing — M,D,O

SIMON FRASER UNIVERSITY
Anthropology — M,D
Archaeology — M,D
Communication—General — M,D
Comparative and Interdisciplinary
   Arts — M
Criminal Justice and Criminology — M,D
Cultural Studies — D
Economics — M,D
English — M,D
French — M
Gender Studies — M,D
Geography — M,D
Gerontology — M,D
History — M,D
Humanities — M
International Affairs — M
Latin American Studies — M,O
Liberal Studies — M
Linguistics — M,D
Philosophy — M,D
Political Science — M,D
Psychology—General — M,D
Public Policy — M
Publishing — M
Sociology — M,D
Urban Studies — M,O
Women's Studies — M,D

SIMPSON COLLEGE
Criminal Justice and Criminology — M

SIMPSON UNIVERSITY
Counseling Psychology — M
Missions and Missiology — M
Pastoral Ministry and Counseling — M

SIOUX FALLS SEMINARY
Marriage and Family Therapy — M
Pastoral Ministry and Counseling — M
Religion — M
Theology — M,D,O

SIT GRADUATE INSTITUTE
Conflict Resolution and
   Mediation/Peace Studies — M
International Affairs — M
Sustainable Development — M

SLIPPERY ROCK UNIVERSITY OF PENNSYLVANIA
Clinical Psychology — M
Counseling Psychology — M
Criminal Justice and Criminology — M
English — M
History — M
Therapies—Dance, Drama, and
   Music — M

SMITH COLLEGE
Dance — M
History — M
Theater — M
Women's Studies — O

SOFIA UNIVERSITY
Clinical Psychology — M,D
Counseling Psychology — M,D
Psychology—General — M,D
Transpersonal and Humanistic
   Psychology — M,D

SONOMA STATE UNIVERSITY
Anthropology — M
Clinical Psychology — M
Counseling Psychology — M
English — M
History — M
Interdisciplinary Studies — M
Political Science — M
Public Administration — M
Public History — M
School Psychology — M
Writing — M

SOTHEBY'S INSTITUTE OF ART–LONDON
Art/Fine Arts — M
Arts Administration — M
Decorative Arts — M

SOTHEBY'S INSTITUTE OF ART–NEW YORK
Art/Fine Arts — M
Arts Administration — M

Decorative Arts — M

SOUTH CAROLINA STATE UNIVERSITY
Agricultural Economics and Agribusiness — M
Child and Family Studies — M
English — M
Family and Consumer Sciences-General — M
Rehabilitation Counseling — M

SOUTH DAKOTA STATE UNIVERSITY
Communication—General — M
Consumer Economics — M
Economics — M
English — M
Family and Consumer Sciences-General — M
Geography — M
Industrial and Organizational Psychology — M
Journalism — M
Sociology — M,D

SOUTHEASTERN BAPTIST THEOLOGICAL SEMINARY
Ethics — M,D
Missions and Missiology — M,D
Music — M,D
Philosophy — M,D
Psychology—General — M,D
Theology — M,D
Women's Studies — M,D

SOUTHEASTERN LOUISIANA UNIVERSITY
Communication—General — M
English — M
Health Communication — M
History — M
Industrial and Organizational Psychology — M
Journalism — M
Music — M
Psychology—General — M
Sociology — M
Writing — M

SOUTHEASTERN OKLAHOMA STATE UNIVERSITY
Clinical Psychology — M
Counseling Psychology — M

SOUTHEASTERN UNIVERSITY (FL)
Counseling Psychology — M
Marriage and Family Therapy — M
Pastoral Ministry and Counseling — M,D
Theology — M,D
Urban and Regional Planning — M

SOUTHEAST MISSOURI STATE UNIVERSITY
Counseling Psychology — M,D,O
Criminal Justice and Criminology — M
English — M
History — M,O
Public Administration — M

SOUTHERN ADVENTIST UNIVERSITY
Counseling Psychology — M
Missions and Missiology — M
Psychology—General — M
Religion — M
Theology — M

SOUTHERN ARKANSAS UNIVERSITY–MAGNOLIA
Public Administration — M

THE SOUTHERN BAPTIST THEOLOGICAL SEMINARY
Missions and Missiology — M,D
Pastoral Ministry and Counseling — M,D
Philosophy — M,D
Religion — M,D
Theology — M,D

SOUTHERN CALIFORNIA INSTITUTE OF ARCHITECTURE
Architecture — M
Urban and Regional Planning — M
Urban Design — M

SOUTHERN CALIFORNIA SEMINARY
Counseling Psychology — M,D
Marriage and Family Therapy — M,D
Psychology—General — M,D
Religion — M,D
Theology — M,D

SOUTHERN CONNECTICUT STATE UNIVERSITY
English — M
History — M
Political Science — M
Psychology—General — M
School Psychology — M,O
Sociology — M
Women's Studies — M

SOUTHERN EVANGELICAL SEMINARY
Jewish Studies — M,D,O
Missions and Missiology — M,D,O
Near and Middle Eastern Studies — M,D,O
Pastoral Ministry and Counseling — M,D,O
Philosophy — M,D,O
Religion — M,D,O
Theology — M,D,O

SOUTHERN ILLINOIS UNIVERSITY CARBONDALE
Agricultural Economics and Agribusiness — M
Anthropology — M,D

Applied Arts and Design— General — M
Architecture — M
Art/Fine Arts — M
Clinical Psychology — M,D
Communication—General — M
Counseling Psychology — M,D
Criminal Justice and Criminology — M,D
Cultural Studies — M
Economics — M,D
English — M,D
Experimental Psychology — M,D
Geography — M,D
History — M,D
Homeland Security — M
Linguistics — M,D
Mass Communication — M,D
Media Studies — M
Music — M
Philosophy — M,D
Political Science — M,D
Psychology—General — M,D
Public Administration — M
Rhetoric — M,D
Sociology — M,D
Speech and Interpersonal Communication — M,D
Theater — M
Writing — M

SOUTHERN ILLINOIS UNIVERSITY EDWARDSVILLE
Art Therapy — M
Art/Fine Arts — M
Clinical Psychology — M
Corporate and Organizational Communication — M
Cultural Anthropology — M
Economics — M
English — M,O
Geography — M
Health Communication — M
History — M
Industrial and Organizational Psychology — M
Interdisciplinary Studies — M
Mass Communication — M
Media Studies — O
Museum Studies — M
Music — M
Psychology—General — M,O
Public Administration — M
School Psychology — O
Sociology — M
Speech and Interpersonal Communication — M
Sport Psychology — M
Sustainable Development — M
Writing — M

SOUTHERN METHODIST UNIVERSITY
Anthropology — M,D
Applied Economics — M,D
Archaeology — M,D
Art History — M,D
Art/Fine Arts — M*
Arts Administration — M
Clinical Psychology — D
Conflict Resolution and Mediation/Peace Studies — M,O
Cultural Anthropology — M,D
Economics — M,D
English — M,D
History — M,D
Liberal Studies — M,D
Medieval and Renaissance Studies — M
Music — M,D
Pastoral Ministry and Counseling — M,D
Psychology—General — D
Religion — M,D
Sustainable Development — M,D
Theater — M
Theology — M,D

SOUTHERN NAZARENE UNIVERSITY
Counseling Psychology — M
Marriage and Family Therapy — M
Psychology—General — M

SOUTHERN NEW HAMPSHIRE UNIVERSITY
Applied Economics — M,D,O
Clinical Psychology — M
Criminal Justice and Criminology — M
Economic Development — M,D,O
Economics — M,D,O
English — M
History — M
Internet and Interactive Multimedia — M,D,O
Political Science — M
Psychology—General — M
Public Administration — M,D,O
Writing — M

SOUTHERN OREGON UNIVERSITY
Counseling Psychology — M
French — M
Interdisciplinary Studies — M
Music — M
Psychology—General — M
Spanish — M
Theater — M

SOUTHERN UNIVERSITY AND AGRICULTURAL AND MECHANICAL COLLEGE
Criminal Justice and Criminology — M
History — M
Mass Communication — M
Political Science — M
Psychology—General — M

Public Administration — M
Public Policy — D
Rehabilitation Counseling — M
Social Sciences — M

SOUTHERN UNIVERSITY AT NEW ORLEANS
Criminal Justice and Criminology — M
Museum Studies — M

SOUTHERN UTAH UNIVERSITY
Arts Administration — M
Communication—General — M
Interdisciplinary Studies — M
Music — M
Public Administration — M

SOUTHERN WESLEYAN UNIVERSITY
Pastoral Ministry and Counseling — M

SOUTH FLORIDA BIBLE COLLEGE AND THEOLOGICAL SEMINARY
Theology — M

SOUTH UNIVERSITY - AUSTIN
Counseling Psychology — M

SOUTH UNIVERSITY - COLUMBIA
Counseling Psychology — M
Criminal Justice and Criminology — M

SOUTH UNIVERSITY - MONTGOMERY
Counseling Psychology — M
Criminal Justice and Criminology — M
Public Administration — M

SOUTH UNIVERSITY - RICHMOND
Counseling Psychology — M

SOUTH UNIVERSITY - SAVANNAH
Counseling Psychology — M
Criminal Justice and Criminology — M
Pastoral Ministry and Counseling — D
Public Administration — M

SOUTH UNIVERSITY - TAMPA
Criminal Justice and Criminology — M

SOUTH UNIVERSITY - VIRGINIA BEACH
Counseling Psychology — M

SOUTH UNIVERSITY - WEST PALM BEACH
Counseling Psychology — M
Criminal Justice and Criminology — M
Public Administration — M

SOUTHWESTERN ASSEMBLIES OF GOD UNIVERSITY
Counseling Psychology — M
History — M
Missions and Missiology — M
Pastoral Ministry and Counseling — M
Religion — M
Theology — M

SOUTHWESTERN BAPTIST THEOLOGICAL SEMINARY
Missions and Missiology — M,D
Music — M,D
Near and Middle Eastern Studies — M,D
Pastoral Ministry and Counseling — M,D,O
Theology — M,D

SOUTHWESTERN CHRISTIAN UNIVERSITY
Missions and Missiology — M
Pastoral Ministry and Counseling — M

SOUTHWESTERN COLLEGE (KS)
Criminal Justice and Criminology — M

SOUTHWESTERN COLLEGE (NM)
Art Therapy — M
Counseling Psychology — M,O
Health Psychology — O
Psychology—General — O
Social Psychology — O
Thanatology — O

SOUTHWESTERN OKLAHOMA STATE UNIVERSITY
Music — M
School Psychology — O
Therapies—Dance, Drama, and Music — M

SOUTHWEST UNIVERSITY
Criminal Justice and Criminology — M

SOUTHWEST UNIVERSITY OF VISUAL ARTS
Art/Fine Arts — M
Photography — M

SPALDING UNIVERSITY
Clinical Psychology — M,D
Corporate and Organizational Communication — M
Psychology—General — M,D
Writing — M

SPERTUS INSTITUTE FOR JEWISH LEARNING AND LEADERSHIP
Jewish Studies — M,D

SPRING ARBOR UNIVERSITY
Child and Family Studies — M
Communication—General — M
Counseling Psychology — M
Pastoral Ministry and Counseling — M
Theology — M

SPRINGFIELD COLLEGE
Art Therapy — M,O
Clinical Psychology — M,D,O
Counseling Psychology — M,D,O
Industrial and Organizational Psychology — M,D,O

Rehabilitation Counseling — M
Sport Psychology — M,D,O

SPRING HILL COLLEGE
Art/Fine Arts — M,O
English — M,O
Ethics — M,O
Liberal Studies — M,O
Theology — M,O

STANFORD UNIVERSITY
Anthropology — M,D
Applied Arts and Design— General — M,D,O
Archaeology — M,D
Art/Fine Arts — M,D
Asian Languages — M
Asian Studies — M
Chinese — M,D
Classics — M,D
Communication—General — M,D
Comparative Literature — D
Cultural Studies — M,D
East European and Russian Studies — M
Economics — D
English — M,D
French — M,D
German — M,D
History — M,D
Italian — M,D
Japanese — M,D
Linguistics — M,D
Music — M,D
Philosophy — M,D
Political Science — M,D
Psychology—General — D
Religion — D
Slavic Languages — D
Sociology — D
Spanish — M,D
Sustainable Development — M,D,O
Theater — D

STARR KING SCHOOL FOR THE MINISTRY
Theology — M

STATE UNIVERSITY OF NEW YORK AT FREDONIA
English — M,O
Interdisciplinary Studies — M,O
Music — M
Writing — M

STATE UNIVERSITY OF NEW YORK AT NEW PALTZ
Art/Fine Arts — M
Clinical Psychology — M,O
Counseling Psychology — M,O
English — M
French — M,O
Music — M
Psychology—General — M,O
Spanish — M,O
Therapies—Dance, Drama, and Music — M

STATE UNIVERSITY OF NEW YORK AT OSWEGO
Art/Fine Arts — M
Child and Family Studies — M
Communication—General — M
Consumer Economics — M
Corporate and Organizational Communication — M
Counseling Psychology — M
Graphic Design — M
Health Communication — M
Internet and Interactive Multimedia — M

STATE UNIVERSITY OF NEW YORK AT PLATTSBURGH
Clinical Psychology — M,O
Counseling Psychology — M,O
Psychology—General — M,O
School Psychology — M,O

STATE UNIVERSITY OF NEW YORK COLLEGE AT CORTLAND
English — M
History — M

STATE UNIVERSITY OF NEW YORK COLLEGE AT GENESEO
French — M
Spanish — M

STATE UNIVERSITY OF NEW YORK COLLEGE AT OLD WESTBURY
Counseling Psychology — M
Liberal Studies — M

STATE UNIVERSITY OF NEW YORK COLLEGE AT ONEONTA
Museum Studies — M

STATE UNIVERSITY OF NEW YORK COLLEGE AT POTSDAM
Music — M

STATE UNIVERSITY OF NEW YORK COLLEGE OF ENVIRONMENTAL SCIENCE AND FORESTRY
Economics — M,D
Geographic Information Systems — M,D
Landscape Architecture — M
Sustainable Development — M,D,O
Urban and Regional Planning — M,D
Urban Design — M

STATE UNIVERSITY OF NEW YORK EMPIRE STATE COLLEGE
Economic Development — M
Industrial and Labor Relations — M

---

*M—masters degree; D—doctorate; O—other advanced degree; *—Close-Up and/or Display*

Liberal Studies M
Public Policy M

STEPHEN F. AUSTIN STATE UNIVERSITY
Applied Arts and Design—
   General M
Art/Fine Arts M
Communication—General M
English M
Family and Consumer
   Sciences-General M
Film, Television, and Video
   Production M
Hispanic Studies M
History M
Interdisciplinary Studies M
Mass Communication M
Music M
Psychology—General M
Public Administration M
Publishing M
School Psychology M

STEPHENS COLLEGE
Addictions/Substance Abuse
   Counseling M,O
Clinical Psychology M,O
Writing M,O

STETSON UNIVERSITY
Writing M

STEVENS INSTITUTE OF TECHNOLOGY
Communication—General M,D,O
Ethics M,O
Film, Television, and Video
   Production M
Media Studies M

STEVENSON UNIVERSITY
Communication—General M
Forensic Sciences M

STOCKTON UNIVERSITY
American Studies M,O
Criminal Justice and Criminology M
Holocaust and Genocide Studies M

STONEHILL COLLEGE
Internet and Interactive
   Multimedia M

STONY BROOK UNIVERSITY, STATE UNIVERSITY OF NEW YORK
Addictions/Substance Abuse
   Counseling M,O
African Studies M,O
Anthropology M,D
Art History M,D
Art/Fine Arts M
Asian Studies M
Asian-American Studies M
Clinical Psychology D
Cognitive Sciences M
Comparative Literature M,D,O
Cultural Studies M,D,O
Economics M,D
English M,D,O
Film, Television, and Video
   Production M
French M
Gender Studies O
Geographic Information Systems O
Health Communication M,O
Health Psychology D
Hispanic and Latin American
   Languages M,D
History M,D
Italian M
Journalism M,O
Liberal Studies M,O
Linguistics M,D
Music M,D
Philosophy M,D,O
Political Science M,D
Psychology—General M,D
Public Policy M
Romance Languages D
Social Psychology D
Sociology M,D
Theater M
Women's Studies O
Writing M,O

STRATFORD UNIVERSITY (VA)
Forensic Sciences M,D

STRAYER UNIVERSITY
Public Administration M

SUFFOLK UNIVERSITY
Applied Arts and Design—
   General M
Clinical Psychology M,D,O
Corporate and Organizational
   Communication
Counseling Psychology M,D,O
Criminal Justice and Criminology M
Ethics M,O
Graphic Design M
Interior Design M
Political Science M,O
Psychology—General M,D,O
Public Administration M
Public Policy M,O

SUL ROSS STATE UNIVERSITY
Art History M
Art/Fine Arts M
Criminal Justice and Criminology M
Emergency Management M
English M
History M
Political Science M
Psychology—General M

SUM BIBLE COLLEGE & THEOLOGICAL SEMINARY
Pastoral Ministry and Counseling M
Religion M
Theology M

SUNY BROCKPORT
American Studies M
Art/Fine Arts M
Arts Administration M,O
Counseling Psychology M,O
Dance M
English M,O
Gerontology M,O
History of Medicine M,O
History M
Liberal Studies M
Psychology—General M
Public Administration M,O
Public History M
Writing M,O

SYRACUSE UNIVERSITY
Addictions/Substance Abuse
   Counseling M,O
African Studies M
African-American Studies M
Anthropology M,D
Applied Arts and Design—
   General M
Architecture M
Art History M
Art/Fine Arts M
Arts Journalism M
Broadcast Journalism M
Child and Family Studies M,D
Clinical Psychology M,D
Cognitive Sciences D
Communication—General M,D
Computer Art and Design M
Conflict Resolution and
   Mediation/Peace Studies O
Disability Studies O
Economics M,D
Emergency Management O
English M,D
Film, Television, and Video
   Production M
Forensic Sciences M,O
French M
Geography M,D
History M,D
Human Development M,D
Illustration M
International Affairs M
Journalism M
Linguistics M
Marriage and Family Therapy M,D
Mass Communication M,D
Media Studies M
Museum Studies M
Music M
Philosophy M,D
Photography M
Political Science M,D,O
Psychology—General D
Public Administration M,D
Public Affairs
Religion M,D
Rhetoric M
School Psychology M,D,O
Social Psychology D
Social Sciences M,D
Sociology M,D
Spanish M
Urban and Regional Planning O
Writing M,D

TALMUDIC UNIVERSITY
Theology M

TARLETON STATE UNIVERSITY
Applied Psychology M
Communication—General M
Counseling Psychology M
Criminal Justice and Criminology M
English M
History M
Political Science M

TAYLOR COLLEGE AND SEMINARY
Cultural Studies M,O
Missions and Missiology M,O
Theology M,O

TEACHERS COLLEGE, COLUMBIA UNIVERSITY
Anthropology M,D
Applied Behavior Analysis M,D,O
Applied Psychology M,D,O
Arts Administration M,D,O
Clinical Psychology M,D
Communication—General M,D
Counseling Psychology M,D
Developmental Psychology M,D
Economics M,D
Industrial and Organizational
   Psychology M,D
Interdisciplinary Studies M,D
International Affairs M,D,O
Linguistics M,D,O
Philosophy M,D
Political Science M,D
Psychology—General M,D
School Psychology M,D,O
Social Psychology M,D,O
Sociology M,D

TELSHE YESHIVA - CHICAGO
Jewish Studies O

TEMPLE UNIVERSITY
African-American Studies M,D
Anthropology D
Applied Behavior Analysis M,D,O
Architecture M
Art History M

Art/Fine Arts M
Arts Administration M,D
Communication—General M,D
Corporate and Organizational
   Communication M,D
Counseling Psychology M,D,O
Criminal Justice and Criminology M,D
Dance M
Economics M,D
English M,D
Film, Television, and Video
   Production M
Geographic Information Systems M,D,O
Geography M,D,O
Gerontology D
Graphic Design M
History M,D
Industrial and Labor Relations M,O
Journalism M
Media Studies M
Music M
Philosophy M,D
Photography M
Political Science M,D
Psychology—General M,D
Religion M,D
School Psychology M,D,O
Social Psychology M,D,O
Sociology M,D
Spanish M,D
Textile Design M
Theater M
Therapies—Dance, Drama, and
   Music M
Urban Studies M,D,O
Writing M

TENNESSEE STATE UNIVERSITY
Counseling Psychology M
Criminal Justice and Criminology M
Family and Consumer
   Sciences-General
Psychology—General M
Public Administration M

TENNESSEE TECHNOLOGICAL UNIVERSITY
Applied Behavior Analysis D
English M

TEXAS A&M INTERNATIONAL UNIVERSITY
Counseling Psychology M
Criminal Justice and Criminology M
English M
History M
Political Science M
Psychology—General M
Public Administration M
Social Sciences M
Sociology M
Translation and Interpretation M

TEXAS A&M UNIVERSITY
Agricultural Economics and
   Agribusiness M,D
Anthropology M,D
Architecture M,D
Art/Fine Arts M
Communication—General M,D
Counseling Psychology M,D
Cultural Studies M
Economics M,D
English M,D
Geography M,D
History M,D
International Affairs M,D
Landscape Architecture M,D
Music M
Philosophy M,D
Political Science M,D
Psychology—General M,D
Public Affairs M,O
School Psychology M,D
Sociology M,D
Spanish M
Urban and Regional Planning M,D

TEXAS A&M UNIVERSITY–CENTRAL TEXAS
Clinical Psychology M,O
Criminal Justice and Criminology M,O
Experimental Psychology M,O
History M,O
Liberal Studies M,O
Marriage and Family Therapy M,O
Political Science M,O
School Psychology M,O

TEXAS A&M UNIVERSITY–COMMERCE
Art/Fine Arts M,D,O
Criminal Justice and Criminology M,D,O
English M,D,O
Film, Television, and Video
   Theory and Criticism M,D,O
History M,D,O
Holocaust and Genocide Studies M,D,O
Homeland Security M,D,O
Linguistics M,D,O
Music M,D,O
Political Science M,D,O
Psychology—General M,D,O
Public History M,D,O
Sociology M,D,O
Spanish M,D,O
Theater M,D,O
Writing M,D,O

TEXAS A&M UNIVERSITY–CORPUS CHRISTI
Art/Fine Arts M
Clinical Psychology M
Communication—General M
English M
Geographic Information Systems M,D
History M

Human Development M,D
Psychology—General M
Public Administration M

TEXAS A&M UNIVERSITY–KINGSVILLE
Agricultural Economics and
   Agribusiness M,D
Criminal Justice and Criminology M
Cultural Studies M
English M
Family and Consumer
   Sciences-General M
Hispanic Studies D
Music M
Psychology—General M
Sociology M
Spanish M
Sustainable Development D

TEXAS A&M UNIVERSITY–SAN ANTONIO
Clinical Psychology M
English M
Marriage and Family Therapy M

TEXAS A&M UNIVERSITY–TEXARKANA
Counseling Psychology M
English M
Interdisciplinary Studies M
Psychology—General M

TEXAS CHRISTIAN UNIVERSITY
American Studies M,D
Art History M
Art/Fine Arts M
Cognitive Sciences M,D
Communication—General M
Corporate and Organizational
   Communication M
Criminal Justice and Criminology M
Developmental Psychology M,D
English M,D
Experimental Psychology M,D
Gerontology D
History M,D
Latin American Studies M,D
Liberal Studies M
Mass Communication M
Music M,D
Psychology—General M,D
Rhetoric M
Social Psychology M,D
Speech and Interpersonal
   Communication M

TEXAS SOUTHERN UNIVERSITY
Art/Fine Arts M
Communication—General M
Criminal Justice and Criminology M
English M
Family and Consumer
   Sciences-General M
History M
Music M
Psychology—General M
Public Administration M
Sociology M
Urban and Regional Planning M,D

TEXAS STATE UNIVERSITY
Anthropology M
Applied Arts and Design—
   General M
Child and Family Studies M
Clinical Psychology M
Communication—General M
Computer Art and Design M
Criminal Justice and Criminology M,D
English M
Ethics M
Family and Consumer
   Sciences-General M,D
Geographic Information Systems M,D
Geography M,D
Gerontology M
Graphic Design M
History M
Interdisciplinary Studies M
International Affairs M
Marriage and Family Therapy M
Mass Communication M
Music M
Philosophy M
Political Science M
Psychology—General M
Public Administration M
Rhetoric M
School Psychology O
Sociology M
Spanish M
Sustainable Development M
Technical Communication M
Theater M
Writing M

TEXAS TECH UNIVERSITY
Agricultural Economics and
   Agribusiness M,D
Anthropology M
Applied Economics M,D
Architecture M,D
Art History M
Art/Fine Arts M
Child and Family Studies M,D
Clinical Psychology M,D
Communication—General M
Consumer Economics M
Counseling Psychology M,D
Cultural Studies M,D
Economics M,D
English M,D
Environmental Design M,D
Experimental Psychology M,D
Geography M
Gerontology M
History M,D

Human Development	M,D
Interdisciplinary Studies	M,D
Interior Design	M,D
Landscape Architecture	M
Marriage and Family Therapy	M,D
Mass Communication	M,D
Media Studies	M,D
Museum Studies	M,D
Music	M,D
Philosophy	M
Political Science	M,D
Psychology—General	M,D
Public Administration	M,D
Rhetoric	M,D
Romance Languages	M,D
Sociology	M
Spanish	M,D
Sustainable Development	M,D
Technical Writing	M,D
Theater	M

TEXAS TECH UNIVERSITY HEALTH SCIENCES CENTER

Addictions/Substance Abuse Counseling	M
Clinical Psychology	M
Rehabilitation Counseling	M

TEXAS WOMAN'S UNIVERSITY

Art History	M
Art/Fine Arts	M
Child and Family Studies	M,D
Child Development	M,D
Counseling Psychology	M,D,O
Dance	M,D
English	M,D
Gender Studies	M,D
Graphic Design	M
History	M
Internet and Interactive Multimedia	M
Marriage and Family Therapy	M,D
Music	M
Photography	M
Political Science	M
Psychology—General	M,D,O
Rhetoric	M,D
School Psychology	M,D,O
Sociology	M,D
Theater	M
Therapies—Dance, Drama, and Music	M
Women's Studies	M,D

THEOLOGICAL UNIVERSITY OF THE CARIBBEAN

Missions and Missiology	M,D
Pastoral Ministry and Counseling	M,D

THOMAS EDISON STATE UNIVERSITY

Economic Development	M
Homeland Security	M
Industrial and Organizational Psychology	M,O
Liberal Studies	M,O
Public Administration	M
Urban and Regional Planning	M

THOMAS JEFFERSON UNIVERSITY

Applied Economics	M,D,O
Architecture	M
Art/Fine Arts	M
Clothing and Textiles	M
Emergency Management	M
Genetic Counseling	M
Geography	M
Industrial Design	M
Interior Design	M
Internet and Interactive Multimedia	M
Marriage and Family Therapy	M
Social Psychology	M
Sustainable Development	M
Textile Design	M
Urban and Regional Planning	M

THOMAS UNIVERSITY

Rehabilitation Counseling	M
Social Psychology	M

TIFFIN UNIVERSITY

Art/Fine Arts	M
Communication—General	M
Criminal Justice and Criminology	M
English	M
Film, Television, and Video Theory and Criticism	M
Forensic Psychology	M
Homeland Security	M
Humanities	M
Psychology—General	M
Writing	M

TORONTO SCHOOL OF THEOLOGY

Theology	M,D

TOURO COLLEGE

Internet and Interactive Multimedia	M

TOWSON UNIVERSITY

Art History	M
Art/Fine Arts	M
Child and Family Studies	M,O
Communication—General	M
Corporate and Organizational Communication	M
Counseling Psychology	M
Experimental Psychology	M
Forensic Sciences	M
Geography	M
Homeland Security	M,O
Humanities	M
Internet and Interactive Multimedia	M,O
Jewish Studies	M,O
Liberal Studies	M
Music	M
Psychology—General	M
School Psychology	M
Social Sciences	M
Theater	M
Women's Studies	M,O
Writing	M

TRENT UNIVERSITY

American Indian/Native American Studies	M,D
Anthropology	M
Canadian Studies	M,D
Cultural Studies	D
Geography	M,D

TREVECCA NAZARENE UNIVERSITY

Marriage and Family Therapy	M,D
Pastoral Ministry and Counseling	M
Religion	M

TRIDENT UNIVERSITY INTERNATIONAL

Conflict Resolution and Mediation/Peace Studies	M,D
Criminal Justice and Criminology	M,D
Emergency Management	M,D,O
Public Administration	M,D

TRINE UNIVERSITY

Criminal Justice and Criminology	M
Emergency Management	M

TRINITY BAPTIST COLLEGE

Religion	M

TRINITY BIBLE COLLEGE AND GRADUATE SCHOOL

Missions and Missiology	M
Pastoral Ministry and Counseling	M
Theology	M

TRINITY CHRISTIAN COLLEGE

Counseling Psychology	M

TRINITY COLLEGE (CANADA)

Music	M,D,O
Pastoral Ministry and Counseling	M,D,O
Theology	M,D,O

TRINITY COLLEGE (UNITED STATES)

American Studies	M
Cultural Studies	M
English	M
Media Studies	M
Museum Studies	M
Public Policy	M
Writing	M

TRINITY INTERNATIONAL UNIVERSITY

Archaeology	M,D,O
Counseling Psychology	M,D,O
Missions and Missiology	M,D,O
Pastoral Ministry and Counseling	M,D,O
Theology	M,D,O

TRINITY INTERNATIONAL UNIVERSITY FLORIDA

Counseling Psychology	M
Religion	M,O

TRINITY SCHOOL FOR MINISTRY

Missions and Missiology	M,D,O
Pastoral Ministry and Counseling	M,D,O
Religion	M,D,O
Theology	M,D,O

TRINITY UNIVERSITY

School Psychology	M

TRINITY WASHINGTON UNIVERSITY

Clinical Psychology	M
Communication—General	M
Counseling Psychology	M
National Security	M

TRINITY WESTERN UNIVERSITY

Counseling Psychology	M
English	M
History	M
Humanities	M
Interdisciplinary Studies	M
Linguistics	M
Pastoral Ministry and Counseling	M,D
Philosophy	M
Theology	M,D

TRI-STATE BIBLE COLLEGE

Theology	M

TROPICAL AGRICULTURE RESEARCH AND HIGHER EDUCATION CENTER

Agricultural Economics and Agribusiness	M,D

TROY UNIVERSITY

Communication—General	M
Corporate and Organizational Communication	M
Criminal Justice and Criminology	M
Economic Development	M
Economics	M
History	M
International Affairs	M
Public Administration	M
Social Sciences	M

TRUETT MCCONNELL UNIVERSITY

Counseling Psychology	M
Theology	M

TRUMAN STATE UNIVERSITY

English	M
Music	M

TUFTS UNIVERSITY

Art History	M
Art/Fine Arts	M,O
Child and Family Studies	M,D
Child Development	M,D
Classics	M
Cognitive Sciences	M,D
Economics	M,D
English	M,D
Family and Consumer Sciences-General	M,D
French	M
German	M
Health Communication	M,D,O
History	M,D
Human Development	M,D
Interdisciplinary Studies	D
International Affairs	M,D
International Development	M
Museum Studies	M,D,O
Music	M
Philosophy	M
Psychology—General	M,D
Public Administration	O
Public Policy	M,D
School Psychology	M,O
Theater	M,D
Urban and Regional Planning	M
Urban Studies	M

TULANE UNIVERSITY

Anthropology	D
Architecture	M
Art History	M
Art/Fine Arts	M
Classics	M
Dance	M
Economics	M,D
Emergency Management	M,D
English	M
French	M,D
History	M,D
Homeland Security	M
Interdisciplinary Studies	D
Latin American Studies	M,D
Liberal Studies	M
Music	M
Philosophy	M,D
Political Science	D
Portuguese	M,D
Psychology—General	M,D
Sociology	M
Spanish	M,D
Theater	M

TUSKEGEE UNIVERSITY

Agricultural Economics and Agribusiness	M

TYNDALE UNIVERSITY COLLEGE & SEMINARY

Missions and Missiology	M,O
Pastoral Ministry and Counseling	M,O
Theology	M,O

UNB FREDERICTON

Anthropology	M
Applied Economics	M
Classics	M
Economics	M
English	M,D
History	M,D
Interdisciplinary Studies	M,D
Political Science	M
Psychology—General	M,D
Public Administration	M
Sociology	M,D

UNIFICATION THEOLOGICAL SEMINARY

Theology	M,D

UNIFORMED SERVICES UNIVERSITY OF THE HEALTH SCIENCES

Clinical Psychology	D
Psychology—General	D

UNION COLLEGE (KY)

Clinical Psychology	M
Counseling Psychology	M
Psychology—General	M
School Psychology	M

UNION INSTITUTE & UNIVERSITY

Clinical Psychology	M
Cultural Studies	M,D
History	M
Humanities	D
Interdisciplinary Studies	D
Public Policy	M,D
Writing	M

UNION THEOLOGICAL SEMINARY IN THE CITY OF NEW YORK

Theology	M,D

UNION UNIVERSITY

Cultural Studies	M
Pastoral Ministry and Counseling	M,D
Religion	M,D

UNITED LUTHERAN SEMINARY

Pastoral Ministry and Counseling	M,D
Religion	M,D
Theology	M,D

UNITED LUTHERAN SEMINARY

Pastoral Ministry and Counseling	M,D,O
Religion	M,D,O
Theology	M,D,O

UNITED STATES ARMY COMMAND AND GENERAL STAFF COLLEGE

Military and Defense Studies	M

UNITED STATES INTERNATIONAL UNIVERSITY–AFRICA

Addictions/Substance Abuse Counseling	M
Conflict Resolution and Mediation/Peace Studies	M
Counseling Psychology	M
Health Psychology	M
International Affairs	M

UNITED TALMUDICAL SEMINARY

Theology	

UNITED THEOLOGICAL SEMINARY

Pastoral Ministry and Counseling	M,D
Theology	M,D

UNITED THEOLOGICAL SEMINARY OF THE TWIN CITIES

Art/Fine Arts	M,D,O
Asian Studies	M,D,O
Conflict Resolution and Mediation/Peace Studies	M,D,O
Ethnic Studies	M,D,O
Humanities	M,D,O
Pastoral Ministry and Counseling	M,D,O
Religion	M,D,O
Theology	M,D,O
Women's Studies	M,D,O

UNITY COLLEGE

Sustainable Development	M

UNIVERSIDAD AUTONOMA DE GUADALAJARA

Architecture	M,D
Computer Art and Design	M,D
Corporate and Organizational Communication	M,D
Film, Television, and Video Production	M,D
Internet and Interactive Multimedia	M,D
Philosophy	M,D
Public Policy	M,D
Spanish	M,D
Translation and Interpretation	M,D

UNIVERSIDAD CENTRAL DEL CARIBE

Addictions/Substance Abuse Counseling	M

UNIVERSIDAD DE IBEROAMERICA

Clinical Psychology	M,D
Forensic Psychology	M,D

UNIVERSIDAD DE LAS AMERICAS, A.C.

International Affairs	M
Marriage and Family Therapy	M
Psychology—General	M

UNIVERSIDAD DE LAS AMÉRICAS PUEBLA

American Studies	M
Anthropology	M
Archaeology	M
Computer Art and Design	M
Economics	M
English	M
Linguistics	M
Psychology—General	M

UNIVERSIDAD DEL ESTE

Agricultural Economics and Agribusiness	M
Criminal Justice and Criminology	M
Public Policy	M

UNIVERSIDAD DEL TURABO

Art/Fine Arts	M
Arts Administration	M
Conflict Resolution and Mediation/Peace Studies	M
Counseling Psychology	M,D,O
Criminal Justice and Criminology	M
Forensic Psychology	M,D,O
Forensic Sciences	M

UNIVERSIDAD IBEROAMERICANA

Corporate and Organizational Communication	M,D

UNIVERSIDAD METROPOLITANA

Counseling Psychology	M

UNIVERSIDAD NACIONAL PEDRO HENRIQUEZ URENA

Architecture	M
Historic Preservation	M
International Affairs	M
Political Science	M

UNIVERSITÉ DE MONCTON

Economics	M
French	M,D
History	M
Public Administration	M

UNIVERSITÉ DE MONTRÉAL

Anthropology	M,D
Art History	M,D
Classics	M
Communication—General	M,D
Comparative Literature	M,D
Criminal Justice and Criminology	M,D
Demography and Population Studies	M,D
Developmental Psychology	M,D
Economics	M,D,O
Emergency Management	O
English	M,D
Environmental Design	M,D,O
Film, Television, and Video Theory and Criticism	M,D
French	M,D
Genetic Counseling	O
Geography	M,D,O

*M—masters degree; D—doctorate; O—other advanced degree; *—Close-Up and/or Display*

German — M
Hispanic and Latin American Languages — M,D
History — M,D
Industrial and Labor Relations — M,D,O
International Affairs — M,O
Linguistics — M,D,O
Museum Studies — M
Music — M,D,O
Philosophy — M,D
Political Science — M,D
Psychology—General — M,D
Public Policy — O
Religion — M,D,O
Sociology — M
Spanish — M
Theater — M,D,O
Translation and Interpretation — M,D,O
Urban and Regional Planning — M,D,O

UNIVERSITÉ DE SAINT-BONIFACE
Canadian Studies — M

UNIVERSITÉ DE SHERBROOKE
Canadian Studies — M,D
Comparative Literature — M,D
Conflict Resolution and Mediation/Peace Studies — M,D,O
Corporate and Organizational Communication — M
Economic Development — D
Economics — M
Ethics — M,D,O
French — M,D
Geography — M
Gerontology — M
History — M
Linguistics — M,D
Philosophy — M,D,O
Psychology—General — M
Public Administration — M
Religion — M,D,O
Theater — M
Theology — M,D,O

UNIVERSITÉ DU QUÉBEC À CHICOUTIMI
Art/Fine Arts — M
Canadian Studies — M
Comparative Literature — M
Ethics — O
French — O
Linguistics — M
Theology — M,D

UNIVERSITÉ DU QUÉBEC À MONTRÉAL
Art History — M,D
Art/Fine Arts — M
Communication—General — M,D
Comparative Literature — M,D
Dance — M
Economics — M
Geographic Information Systems — O
Geography — M
History — M,D
Linguistics — M
Museum Studies — M
Philosophy — M
Political Science — M,D
Psychology—General — D
Public Administration — M
Religion — M,D
Sociology — M,D
Urban Studies — M

UNIVERSITÉ DU QUÉBEC À RIMOUSKI
Comparative Literature — M,D
Ethics — M,O
Social Psychology — M
Urban and Regional Planning — M,D,O

UNIVERSITÉ DU QUÉBEC À TROIS-RIVIÈRES
Communication—General — M,O
Comparative Literature — M
Industrial and Labor Relations — O
Philosophy — M,D
Psychology—General — D,O

UNIVERSITÉ DU QUÉBEC, ÉCOLE NATIONALE D'ADMINISTRATION PUBLIQUE
Public Administration — D,O
Urban Studies — M

UNIVERSITÉ DU QUÉBEC EN OUTAOUAIS
Industrial and Labor Relations — M,D,O
Urban and Regional Planning — M

UNIVERSITÉ DU QUÉBEC, INSTITUT NATIONAL DE LA RECHERCHE SCIENTIFIQUE
Demography and Population Studies — M,D,O
Urban Studies — M,D,O

UNIVERSITY AT ALBANY, STATE UNIVERSITY OF NEW YORK
African Studies — M
African-American Studies — M
Anthropology — M,D
Art/Fine Arts — M
Clinical Psychology — M,D
Cognitive Sciences — M,D
Communication—General — M,D
Counseling Psychology — M,D,O
Criminal Justice and Criminology — M,D
Demography and Population Studies — M,D,O
Economics — M,D,O
Emergency Management — M,D,O
English — M,D
Forensic Sciences — M
Gender Studies — M
Geographic Information Systems — M
Geography — M,O
History — M,D,O
Homeland Security — M,D,O

Industrial and Organizational Psychology — M,D
Latin American Studies — M,D,O
Philosophy — M
Political Science — M,D
Psychology—General — M
Public Administration — M,D,O
Public History — M,D
Public Policy — M,D,O
Social Psychology — M,D
Sociology — M,D,O
Spanish — M
Urban and Regional Planning — M,D
Urban Studies — M,D,O
Women's Studies — M

UNIVERSITY AT BUFFALO, THE STATE UNIVERSITY OF NEW YORK
American Studies — M,D
Anthropology — M,D
Architecture — M,D
Art History — M,D
Art/Fine Arts — M
Arts Administration — M
Canadian Studies — M,D,O
Classics — M,D,O
Communication—General — M,D
Comparative Literature — M,D
Counseling Psychology — M,D
Dance — M,D
Economic Development — M,D
Economics — M,D,O
English — M,D,O
Film, Television, and Video Theory and Criticism — M,D,O
French — M,D
Gender Studies — M,D
Geographic Information Systems — M,D
Geography — M,D
German — M,D,O
Historic Preservation — M,D,O
History — M,D
Humanities — M
Interdisciplinary Studies — M
International Trade Policy — M,D
Linguistics — M,D
Media Studies — M,D,O
Museum Studies — M,D
Music — M,D,O
Philosophy — M,D
Political Science — M,D
Psychology—General — M,D
Public History — M,D,O
Rehabilitation Counseling — M,D
Romance Languages — M,D
Social Sciences — M
Sociology — M,D
Spanish — M,D
Sustainable Development — M,D
Theater — M,D
Urban and Regional Planning — M,D,O
Urban Design — M

UNIVERSITY OF ADVANCING TECHNOLOGY
Internet and Interactive Multimedia — M

THE UNIVERSITY OF AKRON
Arts Administration — M
Child and Family Studies — M
Child Development — M
Clinical Psychology — M
Clothing and Textiles — M
Communication—General — M
Counseling Psychology — M,D
Economics — M
English — M
Gerontology — D
History — M,D
Industrial and Organizational Psychology — M,D
Marriage and Family Therapy — M
Music — M
Political Science — M
Psychology—General — M,D
Public Administration — M
Theater — M
Writing — M

THE UNIVERSITY OF ALABAMA
American Studies — M
Anthropology — M,D
Art History — M
Art/Fine Arts — M
Child and Family Studies — M
Clinical Psychology — D
Clothing and Textiles — M
Communication—General — M
Consumer Economics — M
Criminal Justice and Criminology — M
Economics — M,D
English — M,D
Experimental Psychology — D
Family and Consumer Sciences-General — M,D
French — M,D
Geographic Information Systems — M,D
Geography — M,D
German — M,D
History — M,D
Human Development — M
Journalism — M
Marriage and Family Therapy — M
Mass Communication — D
Music — M,D
Photography — M
Political Science — M,D
Psychology—General — D
Public Administration — M,D
Rhetoric — M,D
Romance Languages — M,D
Spanish — M,D
Speech and Interpersonal Communication — M

Theater — M
Women's Studies — M
Writing — M,D

THE UNIVERSITY OF ALABAMA AT BIRMINGHAM
Anthropology — M
Art History — M
Clinical Psychology — M
Communication—General — M
Criminal Justice and Criminology — M
Developmental Psychology — M,D
English — M
Forensic Sciences — M
Genetic Counseling — M
Health Psychology — M,D
History — M
Psychology—General — M,D
Public Administration — M
Rhetoric — M
Sociology — D
Sustainable Development — M
Writing — M

THE UNIVERSITY OF ALABAMA IN HUNTSVILLE
English — M,O
History — M
Industrial and Organizational Psychology — M
Psychology—General — M
Public Affairs — M
Technical Writing — M

UNIVERSITY OF ALASKA ANCHORAGE
Anthropology — M
Clinical Psychology — M,D
English — M
Psychology—General — M
Public Administration — M
Social Psychology — M,D
Writing — M

UNIVERSITY OF ALASKA FAIRBANKS
Anthropology — M
Art/Fine Arts — M
Communication—General — M
Computer Art and Design — M
Corporate and Organizational Communication — M
Criminal Justice and Criminology — M
Cultural Studies — M
Emergency Management — M
English — M
Geographic Information Systems — M
History — M
Homeland Security — M
Interdisciplinary Studies — M
Linguistics — M
Northern Studies — M
Photography — M
Rural Planning and Studies — M
Social Psychology — M,O
Sustainable Development — M,D
Writing — M

UNIVERSITY OF ALASKA SOUTHEAST
Public Administration — M

UNIVERSITY OF ALBERTA
Agricultural Economics and Agribusiness — M,D
Anthropology — M,D
Applied Arts and Design—General — M
Archaeology — M,D
Art History — M
Art/Fine Arts — M
Asian Studies — M
Chinese — M
Classics — M,D
Clothing and Textiles — M,D
Communication—General — M
Counseling Psychology — M,D
Criminal Justice and Criminology — M,D
Demography and Population Studies — M,D
East European and Russian Studies — M,D
Economics — M,D
English — M,D
Family and Consumer Sciences-General — M,D
Folklore — M,D
French — M,D
German — M,D
Hispanic Studies — M,D
History — M,D
Industrial and Labor Relations — D
Italian — M,D
Japanese — M
Linguistics — M,D
Music — M,D
Philosophy — M,D
Political Science — M,D
Psychology—General — M,D
Rural Sociology — M,D
School Psychology — M,D
Slavic Languages — M,D
Sociology — M,D
Theater — M

UNIVERSITY OF ANTELOPE VALLEY
Criminal Justice and Criminology — M

THE UNIVERSITY OF ARIZONA
African Studies — M,D,O
Agricultural Economics and Agribusiness — M
American Indian/Native American Studies — M,D
Anthropology — M,D,O
Applied Economics — M
Architecture — M
Art History — M,D
Art/Fine Arts — M
Asian Studies — M,D
Child and Family Studies — M,D,O
Classics — M

Communication—General — M,D
Counseling Psychology — M
Dance — M
Economics — M,D
English — M,D
Family and Consumer Sciences-General — D
Film, Television, and Video Theory and Criticism — M
French — M
Gender Studies — M,D,O
Geographic Information Systems — M,D,O
Geography — M,D,O
German — M,D
History — M,D,O
Human Development — M,D
Interdisciplinary Studies — M,D
Journalism — M
Landscape Architecture — M
Latin American Studies — M
Linguistics — M,D
Music — M,D
Near and Middle Eastern Studies — M,D,O
Philosophy — M,D
Political Science — M,D
Psychology—General — M,D
Public Administration — M,D,O
Public Policy — M,D,O
Rehabilitation Counseling — M,D
Rhetoric — M,D
Russian — M
School Psychology — D,O
Sociology — M,D
Spanish — M,D
Theater — M
Urban and Regional Planning — M
Women's Studies — M,D,O
Writing — M

UNIVERSITY OF ARKANSAS
Agricultural Economics and Agribusiness — M
Anthropology — M,D
Art/Fine Arts — M
Communication—General — M
Comparative Literature — M,D
Cultural Studies — M,D
Economics — M,D
English — M,D
Family and Consumer Sciences-General — M
French — M
Geography — M
German — M
History — M,D
Journalism — M
Music — M
Philosophy — M,D
Political Science — M
Psychology—General — M,D
Public Administration — M
Public Policy — D
Rehabilitation Counseling — M,D
Sociology — M
Spanish — M
Theater — M
Writing — M

UNIVERSITY OF ARKANSAS AT LITTLE ROCK
Applied Psychology — M
Art History — M
Art/Fine Arts — M
Conflict Resolution and Mediation/Peace Studies — O
Criminal Justice and Criminology — M,D
Gerontology — O
Interdisciplinary Studies — M
Mass Communication — M
Psychology—General — M
Public Administration — M
Public Affairs — M,O
Public History — M
Rehabilitation Counseling — M,O
Rhetoric — M
Speech and Interpersonal Communication — M
Technical Writing — M
Writing — M

UNIVERSITY OF ARKANSAS FOR MEDICAL SCIENCES
Genetic Counseling — M,D

UNIVERSITY OF BALTIMORE
Applied Arts and Design—General — M
Applied Psychology — M
Conflict Resolution and Mediation/Peace Studies — M
Counseling Psychology — M
Criminal Justice and Criminology — M
Graphic Design — D
Public Administration — M,D
Public Affairs — M,D
Publishing — M
Writing — M

UNIVERSITY OF BRIDGEPORT
Applied Arts and Design—General — M
Asian Studies — M
Clinical Psychology — M
Communication—General — M
Conflict Resolution and Mediation/Peace Studies — M
Counseling Psychology — M
International Affairs — M
Media Studies — M
Pacific Area/Pacific Rim Studies — M
Social Psychology — M

THE UNIVERSITY OF BRITISH COLUMBIA
Agricultural Economics and Agribusiness — M

Anthropology	M,D
Archaeology	M
Architecture	M
Art History	M,D
Art/Fine Arts	M,D
Asian Studies	M,D
Classics	M,D
Clinical Psychology	M,D
Cognitive Sciences	M,D
Counseling Psychology	M,D,O
Developmental Psychology	M,D
East European and Russian Studies	M,D
Economics	M,D
English	M,D
Ethnic Studies	M
Film, Television, and Video Production	M
Film, Television, and Video Theory and Criticism	M
French	M,D
Gender Studies	M,D
Genetic Counseling	M
Geography	M,D
German	M,D
Health Psychology	M,D
Hispanic Studies	M,D
History	M,D
Human Development	M,D,O
International Affairs	M
Internet and Interactive Multimedia	M
Journalism	M
Landscape Architecture	M
Linguistics	M,D
Museum Studies	M
Music	M,D
Pacific Area/Pacific Rim Studies	M
Philosophy	M,D
Political Science	M,D
Psychology—General	M,D
Public Policy	M
Religion	M,D
School Psychology	M,D,O
Social Psychology	M,D
Sociology	M,D
Sustainable Development	M,D
Theater	M,D
Urban and Regional Planning	M,D
Urban Design	M
Writing	M,D

UNIVERSITY OF CALGARY

Applied Psychology	M,D
Architecture	M,D
Classics	M,D
Clinical Psychology	M,D
Counseling Psychology	M,D
Environmental Design	M,D
Geography	M,D
German	M,D
History	M,D
Landscape Architecture	M,D
Linguistics	M,D
Military and Defense Studies	M,D
Music	M,D
Philosophy	M,D
Political Science	M,D
Psychology—General	M,D
Public Policy	M
Religion	M,D
School Psychology	M,D
Sociology	M,D
Sustainable Development	M,D

UNIVERSITY OF CALIFORNIA, BERKELEY

Addictions/Substance Abuse Counseling	O
African-American Studies	D
Agricultural Economics and Agribusiness	D
Anthropology	D
Applied Arts and Design—General	O
Archaeology	M,D
Architectural History	M,D
Architecture	M,D
Art History	D
Art/Fine Arts	M,O
Asian Languages	M,D
Asian Studies	M,D
Building Science	M,D
Chinese	D
Classics	M,D
Comparative Literature	D
Counseling Psychology	O
Demography and Population Studies	M,D
Economics	D
English	D
Environmental Design	M,D
Ethnic Studies	D
Film, Television, and Video Theory and Criticism	D
Folklore	M
French	D
Geography	D
German	D
Hispanic and Latin American Languages	D
History of Science and Technology	D
History	M,D
Human Development	M,D
Industrial and Labor Relations	D
Interior Design	O
International Affairs	M
Italian	D
Japanese	D
Journalism	M
Landscape Architecture	M,D,O
Linguistics	D
Music	D

Near and Middle Eastern Studies	M,D
Philosophy	D
Political Science	D
Psychology—General	D
Public Affairs	M
Public Policy	M,D
Religion	D
Rhetoric	D
Romance Languages	D
Russian	D
Scandinavian Languages	D
Slavic Languages	D
Sociology	D
Spanish	D
Sustainable Development	M,O
Theater	D
Urban and Regional Planning	M,D
Urban Design	M
Writing	O

UNIVERSITY OF CALIFORNIA, DAVIS

Agricultural Economics and Agribusiness	M,D
American Indian/Native American Studies	M,D
Anthropology	M,D
Art History	M
Art/Fine Arts	M
Child Development	M
Clothing and Textiles	M
Communication—General	M
Comparative Literature	D
Cultural Studies	M,D
Economics	M,D
English	M,D
Forensic Sciences	M
French	D
Geography	M,D
German	M,D
History	M,D
Human Development	M,D
Linguistics	M,D
Music	M,D
Philosophy	M,D
Political Science	M,D
Psychology—General	D
Sociology	M,D
Spanish	M,D
Textile Design	M
Theater	M
Urban and Regional Planning	M
Writing	M,D

UNIVERSITY OF CALIFORNIA, IRVINE

Anthropology	M,D
Art/Fine Arts	M,D
Asian Languages	M,D
Chinese	M,D
Classics	M,D
Comparative Literature	M,D
Criminal Justice and Criminology	D
Cultural Studies	D
Dance	M
Demography and Population Studies	M
Economics	M,D
English	M,D
Environmental Design	D
French	M,D
Genetic Counseling	M
German	M,D
History	M,D
Japanese	M,D
Music	M
Philosophy	M,D
Political Science	D
Psychology—General	D
Sociology	D
Spanish	M,D
Theater	M,D
Urban and Regional Planning	M,D
Urban Studies	M,D
Writing	M

UNIVERSITY OF CALIFORNIA, LOS ANGELES

African Studies	M
African-American Studies	M
American Indian/Native American Studies	M
Anthropology	M,D
Applied Arts and Design—General	M
Applied Economics	M
Archaeology	M,D
Architecture	M,D
Art History	M,D
Art/Fine Arts	M
Asian Languages	M,D
Asian Studies	M,D
Asian-American Studies	M
Classics	M,D
Comparative Literature	M,D
Dance	M,D
Economics	D
English	M,D
Film, Television, and Video Production	M,D
French	M,D
Gender Studies	M,D
Geography	M,D
German	M,D
Hispanic and Latin American Languages	D
Historic Preservation	M
History	M,D
Italian	M,D
Latin American Studies	M
Linguistics	M,D
Media Studies	M,D
Music	M,D
Near and Middle Eastern Languages	M,D
Near and Middle Eastern Studies	M,D

Philosophy	M,D
Political Science	M,D
Portuguese	M
Psychology—General	M,D
Public Affairs	M
Public Policy	M
Scandinavian Languages	M
Slavic Languages	M,D
Sociology	M,D
Spanish	M
Theater	M,D
Urban and Regional Planning	M,D
Urban Design	M,D

UNIVERSITY OF CALIFORNIA, MERCED

Cognitive Sciences	M,D
Humanities	M,D
Psychology—General	M,D
Social Sciences	M,D
Sociology	M,D

UNIVERSITY OF CALIFORNIA, RIVERSIDE

Anthropology	M,D
Applied Behavior Analysis	M,D,O
Art History	M,D
Art/Fine Arts	M
Asian Studies	M
Classics	D
Comparative Literature	M,D
Cultural Studies	D
Dance	M
Economics	M,D
English	M,D
Ethnic Studies	D
Hispanic Studies	M,D
History	M,D
Music	M,D
Philosophy	M,D
Political Science	M,D
Psychology—General	D
Public Policy	M,D
Religion	M,D
School Psychology	M,D,O
Sociology	M,D
Spanish	M,D
Writing	M

UNIVERSITY OF CALIFORNIA, SAN DIEGO

Anthropology	D
Art History	M,D
Art/Fine Arts	M,D
Clinical Psychology	D
Cognitive Sciences	D
Communication—General	D
Dance	M,D
Economics	D
English	M,D
Ethnic Studies	D
History of Science and Technology	M,D
History	M,D
International Affairs	M,D
International Development	M
International Economics	M
Jewish Studies	M,D
Latin American Studies	M
Linguistics	D
Music	M,D
Philosophy	D
Political Science	M,D
Psychology—General	D
Public Policy	M
Sociology	D
Theater	M,D
Writing	M,D

UNIVERSITY OF CALIFORNIA, SAN FRANCISCO

Anthropology	D
History of Science and Technology	M,D
Sociology	D

UNIVERSITY OF CALIFORNIA, SANTA BARBARA

African-American Studies	D
Agricultural Economics and Agribusiness	M,D
Anthropology	M,D
Art History	D
Art/Fine Arts	M
Asian Languages	M,D
Asian Studies	M,D
Classics	M,D
Clinical Psychology	M,D,O
Cognitive Sciences	D
Communication—General	D
Comparative Literature	M,D
Counseling Psychology	M,D,O
Cultural Anthropology	M,D
Cultural Studies	M,D
Economics	D
English	D
Film, Television, and Video Production	D
French	D
Geography	M,D
Hispanic and Latin American Languages	M,D
Hispanic Studies	M,D
History	D
Interdisciplinary Studies	D
International Affairs	M,D
Latin American Studies	M
Linguistics	M,D
Media Studies	M,D
Medieval and Renaissance Studies	M,D
Music	M,D
Philosophy	D
Political Science	M,D
Portuguese	M,D
Psychology—General	D

Public History	D
Religion	M,D
School Psychology	M,D,O
Social Sciences	M
Sociology	D
Spanish	M,D
Speech and Interpersonal Communication	D
Sustainable Development	M,D
Theater	M,D
Translation and Interpretation	M,D
Women's Studies	M,D
Writing	D

UNIVERSITY OF CALIFORNIA, SANTA CRUZ

Anthropology	D
Applied Economics	M
Art/Fine Arts	M,D
Communication—General	O
Comparative Literature	M
Computer Art and Design	M
Cultural Anthropology	D
Economics	D
English	M,D
Film, Television, and Video Theory and Criticism	D
History	M,D
Humanities	D
Interdisciplinary Studies	M,D
International Affairs	D
Internet and Interactive Multimedia	M,D
Linguistics	M,D
Music	M,D
Philosophy	M,D
Political Science	M,D
Psychology—General	D
Social Sciences	D
Sociology	D
Theater	O
Writing	M,D

UNIVERSITY OF CENTRAL ARKANSAS

Computer Art and Design	M
Counseling Psychology	M
Economic Development	M,O
English	M
Family and Consumer Sciences-General	M
Film, Television, and Video Production	M
Geographic Information Systems	M,O
Geography	M,O
History	M
Music	M
Psychology—General	M,D,O
School Psychology	M,D,O
Social Psychology	M
Spanish	M
Urban and Regional Planning	M,O
Writing	M

UNIVERSITY OF CENTRAL FLORIDA

Anthropology	M
Art/Fine Arts	M
Clinical Psychology	M,D
Cognitive Sciences	D
Computer Art and Design	M
Criminal Justice and Criminology	M,D,O
Economics	M,D
Emergency Management	M,O
English	M,D,O
Film, Television, and Video Production	M
History	M
Homeland Security	M,O
Industrial and Organizational Psychology	M,D
Interdisciplinary Studies	M,O
Marriage and Family Therapy	M,O
Music	M
Psychology—General	M,D
Public Administration	M,O
Public Affairs	D
School Psychology	O
Sociology	M,D
Spanish	M
Theater	M
Urban and Regional Planning	M,O

UNIVERSITY OF CENTRAL MISSOURI

Communication—General	M,D,O
Counseling Psychology	M,D,O
Criminal Justice and Criminology	M,D,O
English	M,D,O
Gerontology	M,D,O
History	M,D,O
Music	M,D,O
Psychology—General	M,D,O
Sociology	M,D,O
Theater	M,D,O

UNIVERSITY OF CENTRAL OKLAHOMA

Addictions/Substance Abuse Counseling	M
Applied Arts and Design—General	M
Child and Family Studies	M
Counseling Psychology	M
Criminal Justice and Criminology	M
English	M
Experimental Psychology	M
Family and Consumer Sciences-General	M
Forensic Psychology	M
Forensic Sciences	M
Gerontology	M
History	M
Human Development	M
Interdisciplinary Studies	M
Liberal Studies	M

*M—masters degree; D—doctorate; O—other advanced degree; *—Close-Up and/or Display*

Marriage and Family Therapy — M
Museum Studies — M
Music — M
Political Science — M
Psychology—General — M
Public Administration — M
Rhetoric — M
School Psychology — M
Sociology — M
Urban and Regional Planning — M
Writing — M

UNIVERSITY OF CHARLESTON
Forensic Sciences — M

UNIVERSITY OF CHICAGO
Anthropology — D
Archaeology — D
Art History — M,D
Art/Fine Arts — M
Asian Languages — D
Asian Studies — M,D
Classics — M,D
Comparative Literature — M,D
Economics — M,D,O
Emergency Management — M
English — M,D
Ethics — D
Film, Television, and Video Theory and Criticism — D
French — D
Gender Studies — M
German — D
History — D
Human Development — M
Humanities — M
International Affairs — M
Internet and Interactive Multimedia — M
Italian — D
Latin American Studies — M
Liberal Studies — M
Linguistics — M,D
Media Studies — M
Medieval and Renaissance Studies — D
Music — M,D
Near and Middle Eastern Languages — D
Near and Middle Eastern Studies — M,D
Pastoral Ministry and Counseling — M
Philosophy — M,D
Political Science — D
Psychology—General — D
Public Policy — M,D
Religion — M,D
Romance Languages — M,D
Slavic Languages — M
Social Sciences — M,D
Sociology — D
Spanish — D
Theater — M
Theology — D
Writing — M

UNIVERSITY OF CINCINNATI
Addictions/Substance Abuse Counseling — M,D,O
Anthropology — M
Applied Arts and Design—General — M
Applied Economics — M
Architecture — M
Art History — M
Art/Fine Arts — M
Arts Administration — M,D
Classics — M
Clinical Psychology — D
Communication—General — M
Criminal Justice and Criminology — M,D
Economics — M
English — M,D
Experimental Psychology — M,D
French — M,D
Genetic Counseling — M
Geography — M,D
German — M
Graphic Design — M
History — M,D
Industrial and Labor Relations — M
Industrial Design — M
Interdisciplinary Studies — D
Interior Design — M
Music — M,D,O
Philosophy — M,D
Political Science — M,D
Psychology—General — D
Romance Languages — M,D
School Psychology — D,O
Sociology — M,D
Spanish — M,D
Textile Design — M,D
Theater — M,D
Urban and Regional Planning — M
Women's Studies — M,O

UNIVERSITY OF COLORADO BOULDER
Anthropology — M,D
Art History — M
Art/Fine Arts — M
Asian Studies — M,D
Chinese — M,D
Classics — M,D
Communication—General — M,D
Dance — M,D
East European and Russian Studies — M,D
Economics — M,D
English — M,D
Ethnic Studies — D
Film, Television, and Video Production — M
French — M,D
Geography — M,D
German — M
Hispanic and Latin American Languages — M,D
History — M,D

Internet and Interactive Multimedia — D
Japanese — M,D
Journalism — M,D
Linguistics — M,D
Mass Communication — M,D
Media Studies — M,D
Museum Studies — M
Music — M,D
Philosophy — M,D
Photography — M
Political Science — M,D
Psychology—General — M,D
Religion — M
Sociology — D
Spanish — M,D
Theater — M,D
Writing — M,D

UNIVERSITY OF COLORADO COLORADO SPRINGS
Communication—General — M
Criminal Justice and Criminology — M
Geography — M
History — M
Interdisciplinary Studies — M
Psychology—General — M
Public Administration — M
Public Affairs — M
Sociology — M

UNIVERSITY OF COLORADO DENVER
American Studies — M
Anthropology — M
Archaeology — M
Architectural History — D
Architecture — M
Art/Fine Arts — M,O
Biological Anthropology — M
Child and Family Studies — M,D
Clinical Psychology — M
Communication—General — M
Corporate and Organizational Communication — M
Counseling Psychology — M
Criminal Justice and Criminology — M,D
Demography and Population Studies — D
Economic Development — M
Economics — M
Emergency Management — M
English — M
Ethnic Studies — M,O
Family and Consumer Sciences-General — M,D
Forensic Sciences — M
Gender Studies — M
Genetic Counseling — M
Geographic Information Systems — M,D
Health Psychology — D
Historic Preservation — M
History — M
Homeland Security — M,D
Human Development — M
Humanities — M
International Affairs — M,O
Landscape Architecture — M
Linguistics — M
Marriage and Family Therapy — M
Media Studies — M
Military and Defense Studies — M
Music — M
Political Science — M
Public Administration — M,D
Public Affairs — M
Public History — M
School Psychology — M
Sociology — M,O
Spanish — M
Sustainable Development — M,D
Urban and Regional Planning — M,D
Urban Design — M,D
Western European Studies — M
Women's Studies — M,O
Writing — M

UNIVERSITY OF CONNECTICUT
Agricultural Economics and Agribusiness — M,D
Anthropology — M,D
Applied Arts and Design—General — M
Child and Family Studies — M,D
Clinical Psychology — M,D
Cognitive Sciences — M,D
Communication—General — M,D
Counseling Psychology — M,D
Developmental Psychology — M,D
Economics — M,D
English — M,D
Experimental Psychology — M,D
Geography — M,D
History — M,D
Human Development — M,D
Industrial and Organizational Psychology — M,D
International Affairs — M,D
Jewish Studies — M,D
Landscape Architecture — M
Latin American Studies — M
Linguistics — M,D
Medieval and Renaissance Studies — M,D
Music — M,D
Philosophy — M,D
Political Science — M,D
Psychology—General — M,D
Public Administration — M
Social Psychology — M,D
Sociology — M,D
Theater — M

UNIVERSITY OF DALLAS
Pastoral Ministry and Counseling — M

UNIVERSITY OF DAYTON
Art/Fine Arts — M

Clinical Psychology — M,O
Communication—General — M
Counseling Psychology — M
Cultural Studies — M
English — M
Human Development — M,O
Interdisciplinary Studies — M
Pastoral Ministry and Counseling — M,D
Psychology—General — M
Public Administration — M
Rhetoric — M
School Psychology — M,O
Theology — M,D
Writing — M

UNIVERSITY OF DELAWARE
Agricultural Economics and Agribusiness — M
American Studies — M
Applied Arts and Design—General — M
Art History — M,D
Art/Fine Arts — M
Child and Family Studies — M,D
Chinese — M
Clinical Psychology — D
Clothing and Textiles — M
Cognitive Sciences — M,D
Communication—General — M
Criminal Justice and Criminology — M,D
Economics — M,D
Emergency Management — M
English — M,D
French — M
Geography — M,D
German — M
Historic Preservation — M
History of Science and Technology — M,D
History — M,D
Human Development — M,D
International Affairs — M,D
Liberal Studies — M
Linguistics — M,D
Music — M
Political Science — M,D
Psychology—General — D
Public Administration — M
Public Policy — M,D
School Psychology — M,D,O
Social Psychology — D
Sociology — M
Spanish — M
Theater — M
Translation and Interpretation — M
Urban Studies — M,D

UNIVERSITY OF DENVER
Anthropology — M
Archaeology — M
Art History — M
Art/Fine Arts — M
Child and Family Studies — M,D,O
Clinical Psychology — M,D,O
Communication—General — M
Computer Art and Design — M
Conflict Resolution and Mediation/Peace Studies — M,D,O
Counseling Psychology — M,D,O
Criminal Justice and Criminology — M,O
Cultural Anthropology — M
Cultural Studies — M,O
Developmental Psychology — D
Economics — M
Emergency Management — M,O
English — M,D
Forensic Psychology — M,D,O
Geographic Information Systems — M,D,O
Geography — M,D
History — M,O
Homeland Security — M
International Affairs — M,D,O
International Development — M,D
Marriage and Family Therapy — M,D,O
Mass Communication — M
Media Studies — M
Museum Studies — M
Music — M,O
Philanthropic Studies — M,O
Psychology—General — M,D,O
Public Policy — M
Religion — M,D,O
School Psychology — M,D,O
Social Psychology — D
Sport Psychology — M,D,O
Theology — D,O
Translation and Interpretation — M,O
Writing — M,D,O

UNIVERSITY OF DETROIT MERCY
Addictions/Substance Abuse Counseling — M,D,O
Clinical Psychology — M,D,O
Criminal Justice and Criminology — M,D,O
Economics — M,D,O
Ethics — M,O
Forensic Sciences — M,O
Industrial and Organizational Psychology — M,D,O
Industrial Design — M,D
Liberal Studies — M,D,O
School Psychology — M,D,O
Urban and Regional Planning — M

UNIVERSITY OF DUBUQUE
Communication—General — M
Theology — M,D

UNIVERSITY OF EVANSVILLE
Public Administration — M

THE UNIVERSITY OF FINDLAY
Linguistics — M,D
Public Administration — M
Rhetoric — M,D
Writing — M,D

UNIVERSITY OF FLORIDA
Agricultural Economics and Agribusiness — M,D
Anthropology — M,D
Architecture — M,D
Art History — M,D
Art/Fine Arts — M,D
Child Development — M
Classics — M,D
Clinical Psychology — M,D
Communication—General — M,D
Computer Art and Design — M,D
Counseling Psychology — M,D
Criminal Justice and Criminology — M,D
Economics — M,D
Emergency Management — M
English — M,D
Family and Consumer Sciences-General — M
Forensic Sciences — M,O
French — M,O
Gender Studies — M,O
Geographic Information Systems — M
Geography — M,D
German — M
Health Communication — M,D,O
Health Psychology — M,D
Historic Preservation — M,D
History — M,D
Interdisciplinary Studies — M,D
Interior Design — M,D
International Affairs — M
International Development — M,D,O
Jewish Studies — M,D
Journalism — M,D
Landscape Architecture — M,D
Latin American Studies — M,O
Linguistics — M,D,O
Marriage and Family Therapy — M,D,O
Mass Communication — M,D
Museum Studies — M,D
Music — M,D
Philosophy — M,D
Political Science — M,D,O
Psychology—General — M,D
Public Affairs — M,D,O
Religion — M,D
School Psychology — M,D
Social Sciences — M,D,O
Sociology — M,D
Spanish — M,D
Sustainable Development — M,O
Theater — M
Urban and Regional Planning — M,D
Women's Studies — M,O
Writing — M,D

UNIVERSITY OF FORT LAUDERDALE
Pastoral Ministry and Counseling — M

UNIVERSITY OF GEORGIA
Agricultural Economics and Agribusiness — M,D
Anthropology — M,D
Applied Economics — M,D
Art History — M,D
Art/Fine Arts — M,D
Child and Family Studies — M
Classics — M
Clothing and Textiles — M,D
Communication—General — M,D
Comparative Literature — M,D
Economics — M,D
English — M,D
Environmental Design — M
Family and Consumer Sciences-General — M,D
French — M,D
Geography — M,D
German — M
Gerontology — O
Historic Preservation — M
History — M,D
Interior Design — M,D
International Affairs — M,D
Italian — M,D
Journalism — M,D
Landscape Architecture — M
Linguistics — M,D
Mass Communication — M,D
Music — M,D
Philosophy — M,D
Political Science — M,D
Portuguese — D
Psychology—General — D
Public Administration — M,D
Public Policy — M,D
Religion — M
Sociology — M,D
Spanish — M,D
Sustainable Development — M,D
Theater — M,D
Women's Studies — O

UNIVERSITY OF GUAM
Art/Fine Arts — M
English — M
Graphic Design — M
Pacific Area/Pacific Rim Studies — M
Public Administration — M

UNIVERSITY OF GUELPH
Agricultural Economics and Agribusiness — M,D
Anthropology — M,D
Applied Psychology — M,D
Art/Fine Arts — M
Child and Family Studies — M,D
Clinical Psychology — M,D
Cognitive Sciences — M,D
Comparative Literature — D
Consumer Economics — M
Criminal Justice and Criminology — M,D
Demography and Population Studies — M,D
Economics — M,D

English M
French M
Geography M,D
History M,D
Human Development M,D
Industrial and Organizational Psychology M,D
International Development M,D
Landscape Architecture M
Marriage and Family Therapy M,D
Medieval and Renaissance Studies D
Philosophy M
Political Science M
Psychology—General M,D
Public Administration M
Public Policy M
Rural Planning and Studies M,D
Social Psychology M,D
Sociology M,D
Theater M
Western European Studies M

UNIVERSITY OF HARTFORD
Architecture M
Art/Fine Arts M
Clinical Psychology M,D
Communication—General M
Music M,D,O
School Psychology M

UNIVERSITY OF HAWAII AT HILO
Counseling Psychology M
Cultural Studies M

UNIVERSITY OF HAWAII AT MANOA
American Studies M,D,O
Anthropology M,D
Architecture D
Art History M
Art/Fine Arts M
Asian Languages M,D
Asian Studies O
Chinese M,D,O
Clinical Psychology M,D,O
Communication—General M,O
Conflict Resolution and Mediation/Peace Studies M,O
Cultural Studies O
Dance M,D
Demography and Population Studies O
Disability Studies O
Economics M,D
Emergency Management O
English M,D
French M
Geography M,D,O
Historic Preservation O
History M,D
International Affairs O
International Development M,D,O
Japanese M,D,O
Linguistics M,D
Museum Studies O
Music M,D
Pacific Area/Pacific Rim Studies M,O
Philosophy M,D
Political Science M,D
Psychology—General M,D,O
Public Administration M,O
Public Policy O
Religion M
Social Psychology M,D,O
Sociology M,D
Spanish M
Speech and Interpersonal Communication M
Sustainable Development M,D,O
Theater M
Urban and Regional Planning M,D,O
Women's Studies O

UNIVERSITY OF HOLY CROSS
Marriage and Family Therapy M,D
Theology M

UNIVERSITY OF HOUSTON
Anthropology M
Applied Economics M,D
Architecture M
Art History M
Art/Fine Arts M
Clinical Psychology M,D
Communication—General M
Comparative Literature M
Counseling Psychology M,D
Cultural Studies M
Developmental Psychology M,D
Economics M,D
Family and Consumer Sciences-General M
Health Communication M
Hispanic Studies M,D
History M,D
Industrial and Organizational Psychology M,D
Linguistics M,D
Mass Communication M
Music M,D
Philosophy M
Political Science M,D
Psychology—General M,D
Public Administration M,D
Public Policy M
Social Psychology M,D
Sociology M
Spanish M,D
Speech and Interpersonal Communication M
Sustainable Development M
Theater M
Urban Design M
Writing M

UNIVERSITY OF HOUSTON—CLEAR LAKE
Clinical Psychology M
Criminal Justice and Criminology M
Cultural Studies M
English M
History M
Humanities M
Marriage and Family Therapy M
Psychology—General M
School Psychology M
Sociology M

UNIVERSITY OF HOUSTON - DOWNTOWN
Criminal Justice and Criminology M
English M
Rhetoric M
Technical Communication M

UNIVERSITY OF HOUSTON—VICTORIA
Counseling Psychology M
Economic Development M
Forensic Psychology M
Forensic Sciences M
Interdisciplinary Studies M
Psychology—General M
Publishing M
School Psychology M
Writing M

UNIVERSITY OF IDAHO
Agricultural Economics and Agribusiness M
Anthropology M
Architecture M
Art/Fine Arts M
Consumer Economics M
Experimental Psychology M,D
Geography M
History M,D
Interdisciplinary Studies M
Landscape Architecture M
Music M
Philosophy M,D
Political Science M,D
Psychology—General M,D
Public Administration M,D
Rehabilitation Counseling M,O
Theater M
Urban and Regional Planning M
Writing M

UNIVERSITY OF ILLINOIS AT CHICAGO
Anthropology M,D
Applied Arts and Design—General M
Architecture M
Art History M,D
Art/Fine Arts M,D
Communication—General M,D
Criminal Justice and Criminology M,D
Developmental Psychology M,D
Disability Studies M,D
East European and Russian Studies M,D
Economics M,D
English M,D
Forensic Sciences M
French M
Geography M
German M,D
Graphic Design M
Hispanic and Latin American Languages M,D
Hispanic Studies M,D
History M,D
Human Development M,D
Interdisciplinary Studies D
Latin American Studies M
Linguistics M
Medical Illustration M
Museum Studies M,D
Philosophy M,D
Political Science M,D
Psychology—General M,D
Public Administration M,D
Slavic Languages M,D
Sociology M,D
Spanish M,D
Urban and Regional Planning M,D

UNIVERSITY OF ILLINOIS AT SPRINGFIELD
Addictions/Substance Abuse Counseling M,O
Child and Family Studies M,O
Communication—General M,O
Emergency Management M,O
English M,O
Gerontology M,O
History M
Homeland Security M,O
Human Development M
Interdisciplinary Studies M
Journalism M
Political Science M
Public Administration M,D,O
Public History M
Social Sciences M,O

UNIVERSITY OF ILLINOIS AT URBANA-CHAMPAIGN
African Studies M
Agricultural Economics and Agribusiness M,D
Anthropology M,D
Applied Arts and Design—General M
Applied Economics M,D
Architecture M,D
Art History M,D
Art/Fine Arts M

Asian Languages M,D
Asian Studies M,D
Classics M,D
Communication—General M,D
Comparative Literature M,D
Consumer Economics M,D
Corporate and Organizational Communication M
Dance M,D
East European and Russian Studies M
Economics M,D
English M,D
French M,D
Geography M,D
German M,D
Graphic Design M
History M,D
Human Development M,D
Industrial and Labor Relations M,D
Industrial Design M
Interdisciplinary Studies D
Italian M,D
Journalism M,D
Landscape Architecture M,D
Latin American Studies M,D
Linguistics M,D
Media Studies M,D
Music M,D
Near and Middle Eastern Studies M
Philosophy M,D
Photography M
Political Science M,D
Portuguese M,D
Psychology—General M,D
Religion M
Romance Languages D
Slavic Languages M,D
Sociology M,D
Spanish M,D
Theater M,D
Translation and Interpretation M
Urban and Regional Planning M,D
Western European Studies M
Writing M,D

UNIVERSITY OF INDIANAPOLIS
Addictions/Substance Abuse Counseling M
Anthropology M
Art/Fine Arts M
Clinical Psychology M,D
Counseling Psychology M,D
English M
Gerontology M,D,O
History M
International Affairs M
Psychology—General M,D
Sociology M

THE UNIVERSITY OF IOWA
American Studies M,D
Anthropology M,D
Art History M,D
Art/Fine Arts M
Asian Languages M
Asian Studies M
Chinese M
Classics M,D
Communication—General M,D
Counseling Psychology M,D,O
Dance M
Economics D
English M,D
Film, Television, and Video Production M
Film, Television, and Video Theory and Criticism M,D
French M,D
Geographic Information Systems M,D,O
Geography M,D,O
History M,D
Journalism M,D
Linguistics M,D
Marriage and Family Therapy M,D
Mass Communication M,D
Media Studies M,D
Music M,D
Philosophy D
Political Science D
Psychology—General M,D,O
Rehabilitation Counseling M,D
Religion M,D
Rhetoric M,D
School Psychology M,D,O
Sociology M,D
Spanish M,D
Speech and Interpersonal Communication M,D
Sustainable Development M
Theater M
Urban and Regional Planning M,D
Women's Studies O
Writing M,D

THE UNIVERSITY OF KANSAS
African Studies M,O
African-American Studies M,O
American Indian/Native American Studies M,O
American Studies M,D
Anthropology M,D
Applied Arts and Design—General M
Applied Behavior Analysis M,D,O
Architecture M,D,O
Art History M,D
Art/Fine Arts M,D
Asian Languages M,O
Asian Studies M,O
Classics M
Clinical Psychology M,D

Cognitive Sciences M,D
Communication—General M,D,O
Counseling Psychology M,D
Cultural Studies M,D
Developmental Psychology M,D
East European and Russian Studies M,O
Economics M,D
English M,D
Film, Television, and Video Theory and Criticism M,D
French M,D
Geographic Information Systems M,D,O
Geography M,D,O
Gerontology D
Historic Preservation M,D,O
History M,D
Interdisciplinary Studies D
International Affairs M
Journalism M,D
Latin American Studies M,O
Linguistics M,D
Media Studies M,D
Museum Studies M,O
Music M,D
Near and Middle Eastern Studies M,O
Philosophy M,D
Political Science M,D
Psychology—General M,D,O
Religion M,O
School Psychology D,O
Slavic Languages M,D
Social Psychology M,D
Sociology D
Spanish M,D
Textile Design M
Theater M,D
Therapies—Dance, Drama, and Music M,D
Urban and Regional Planning M
Urban Design M,D,O
Writing M,D

UNIVERSITY OF KENTUCKY
Agricultural Economics and Agribusiness M,D
Anthropology M,D
Applied Arts and Design—General M
Architecture M
Art History M
Art/Fine Arts M
Arts Administration M
Child and Family Studies M,D
Classics M
Counseling Psychology M,D,O
Economics M,D
English M,D
Geography M,D
German M
Gerontology D,O
Hispanic Studies M,D
Historic Preservation M
History M
Interior Design M
International Affairs M
Music M,D
Philosophy M,D
Political Science M,D
Psychology—General M,D
Public Administration M,D,O
Public Policy M,D,O
Rehabilitation Counseling M,D
School Psychology M,D,O
Sociology M,D
Therapies—Dance, Drama, and Music M,D

UNIVERSITY OF KING'S COLLEGE
Journalism M
Writing M

UNIVERSITY OF LA VERNE
Child and Family Studies M
Child Development M
Clinical Psychology D
English M,O
Gerontology M,O
Marriage and Family Therapy M,D
Psychology—General M,D
Public Administration M,D
School Psychology M,O

UNIVERSITY OF LETHBRIDGE
Addictions/Substance Abuse Counseling M,D
American Indian/Native American Studies M,D
Anthropology M,D
Archaeology M,D
Art/Fine Arts M,D
Canadian Studies M,D
Counseling Psychology M,D
Economics M,D
English M,D
French M,D
Gender Studies M,D
Geographic Information Systems M,D
Geography M,D
German M,D
Media Studies M,D
Music M,D
Philosophy M,D
Political Science M,D
Psychology—General M,D
Religion M,D
Sociology M,D
Spanish M,D
Theater M,D
Urban Studies M,D
Women's Studies M,D

M—masters degree; D—doctorate; O—other advanced degree; *—Close-Up and/or Display

UNIVERSITY OF LOUISIANA AT LAFAYETTE
American Studies M
Communication—General M
Cultural Studies M,D
English M,D
Folklore M,D
French M,D
History M,D
Latin American Studies M
Music M
Psychology—General M
Public History M
Rhetoric M,D
Sociology M,D
Western European Studies M
Writing M,D

UNIVERSITY OF LOUISIANA AT MONROE
Clinical Psychology M
Communication—General M
Counseling Psychology M
Criminal Justice and Criminology M
English M
Forensic Psychology M
Gerontology M,O
History M
Marriage and Family Therapy M,D
Psychology—General M
Public Administration M

UNIVERSITY OF LOUISVILLE
Addictions/Substance Abuse Counseling M,D,O
African Studies M
African-American Studies M
Anthropology M
Applied Arts and Design—General M,D
Applied Behavior Analysis M,D,O
Art History M,D
Art Therapy M,D
Clinical Psychology D
Cognitive Sciences D
Communication—General M
Counseling Psychology M,D
Criminal Justice and Criminology M,D
Cultural Studies M,D
Developmental Psychology D
English M,D
Experimental Psychology D
French M,O
Geography M
Gerontology M,D,O
History M,O
Humanities M,D
Interdisciplinary Studies M,D
Linguistics M,D
Marriage and Family Therapy M,D,O
Museum Studies M,D
Music M
Philosophy M,D
Political Science M
Psychology—General D
Public Administration M,D
Public Affairs M,D
Public History M,O
Public Policy M,D
Rhetoric M,D
School Psychology M,D
Sociology M,D
Spanish M,O
Theater M
Urban and Regional Planning M,D
Urban Studies M,D
Women's Studies M,O
Writing M,D

UNIVERSITY OF LYNCHBURG
Clinical Psychology M
Counseling Psychology M
Criminal Justice and Criminology M
School Psychology M

UNIVERSITY OF MAINE
Agricultural Economics and Agribusiness M
Anthropology D
Art/Fine Arts M
Communication—General M,D
Economics M
English M
French M
History M,D
Human Development M,D,O
Interdisciplinary Studies M,D
International Affairs M
Music M
Psychology—General M,D

UNIVERSITY OF MANAGEMENT AND TECHNOLOGY
Criminal Justice and Criminology M,O
Homeland Security M
Public Administration M,O

THE UNIVERSITY OF MANCHESTER
Anthropology M,D
Archaeology D
Architecture M,D
Art History D
Art/Fine Arts M,D
Arts Administration D
Asian Studies D
Chinese D
Classics D
Clinical Psychology M,D
Clothing and Textiles M,D
Conflict Resolution and Mediation/Peace Studies D
Counseling Psychology M,D
Criminal Justice and Criminology M,D
Cultural Studies M,D
Developmental Psychology M,D
East European and Russian Studies D
English D
Environmental Design M,D
French D
Geography M,D
German D
History of Medicine M,D
History of Science and Technology M,D
History D
Industrial and Labor Relations M
Industrial and Organizational Psychology M
International Affairs D
International Development M,D
Japanese D
Landscape Architecture M,D
Latin American Studies D
Linguistics D
Museum Studies D
Music D
Near and Middle Eastern Studies D
Philosophy M,D
Political Science M,D
Portuguese D
Psychology—General M,D
Religion D
Social Sciences M,D
Sociology M,D
Spanish D
Textile Design M,D
Theater D
Theology D
Translation and Interpretation D
Writing D

UNIVERSITY OF MANITOBA
Agricultural Economics and Agribusiness M,D
American Indian/Native American Studies M
Anthropology M,D
Architecture M
Canadian Studies M
Classics M
Clinical Psychology M,D
Disability Studies M
Economics M,D
English M,D
French M,D
Genetic Counseling M,D
Geography M,D
German M
History M,D
Interdisciplinary Studies M,D
Interior Design M
Landscape Architecture M
Linguistics M,D
Music M
Northern Studies M
Philosophy M
Political Science M
Psychoanalysis and Psychotherapy M
Psychology—General M,D
Public Administration M
Religion M,D
School Psychology M,D
Slavic Languages M
Sociology M,D
Urban and Regional Planning M

UNIVERSITY OF MARY HARDIN-BAYLOR
Clinical Psychology M
Counseling Psychology M
Marriage and Family Therapy M

UNIVERSITY OF MARYLAND, BALTIMORE
Ethics O
Forensic Sciences M
Genetic Counseling M
Gerontology M,D
Thanatology O

UNIVERSITY OF MARYLAND, BALTIMORE COUNTY
Applied Psychology D
Clinical Psychology M,D
Cognitive Sciences D
Communication—General M
Computer Art and Design M
Dance M
Developmental Psychology D
Economics M,D
Emergency Management M,D,O
English M
Gender Studies O
Geographic Information Systems M,O
Geography M,D
Gerontology M,D
History M
Industrial and Organizational Psychology M
Linguistics M
Music O
Psychology—General M,D
Public History M,D
Public Policy M,D,O
Social Psychology M,D
Social Sciences D
Sociology M
Theater M
Urban Studies M,D
Women's Studies O

UNIVERSITY OF MARYLAND, COLLEGE PARK
Agricultural Economics and Agribusiness M,D
American Studies M,D
Anthropology M
Architecture M
Art History M,D
Art Therapy M,D,O
Art/Fine Arts M
Broadcast Journalism M,D
Child and Family Studies M,D
Classics M
Clinical Psychology M,D
Cognitive Sciences D
Communication—General M,D
Comparative Literature M,D
Counseling Psychology M,D,O
Criminal Justice and Criminology M,D
Dance M
Developmental Psychology M,D
Economics M,D
English M,D
Experimental Psychology M,D
Family and Consumer Sciences-General M,D
French M,D
Geography M,D
German M,D
Historic Preservation M,O
History M,D
Human Development M,D
Industrial and Organizational Psychology M,D
Jewish Studies M
Journalism M,D
Landscape Architecture M
Linguistics M,D
Marriage and Family Therapy M,D
Media Studies M,D
Music M,D
Philosophy M,D
Political Science D
Portuguese M,D
Psychology—General M,D
Public Administration M
Public Policy M,D
Rehabilitation Counseling M,D,O
School Psychology M,D,O
Social Psychology M,D
Sociology M,D
Spanish M,D
Speech and Interpersonal Communication M,D
Survey Methodology M,D
Sustainable Development M
Theater M,D
Urban and Regional Planning M,D
Women's Studies M,D
Writing M,D

UNIVERSITY OF MARYLAND EASTERN SHORE
Criminal Justice and Criminology M
Rehabilitation Counseling M

UNIVERSITY OF MASSACHUSETTS AMHERST
African-American Studies M,D
Agricultural Economics and Agribusiness M,D
American Studies M,D
Anthropology M,D
Architecture M
Art History M
Art/Fine Arts M
Child and Family Studies M,D,O
Chinese M
Classics M
Clinical Psychology M,D
Cognitive Sciences M,D
Communication—General M,D
Comparative Literature M,D
Conflict Resolution and Mediation/Peace Studies M,D
Developmental Psychology M,D
Economics M,D
English M,D
French M
Geography M
German M,D
Hispanic and Latin American Languages M,D
Historic Preservation M
History M,D
Industrial and Labor Relations M
Interior Design M
Italian M
Japanese M
Landscape Architecture M
Linguistics M,D
Music M,D
Philosophy M,D
Political Science M,D
Portuguese M,D
Psychology—General M,D
Public Administration M
Public Policy M
Rhetoric M,D
Scandinavian Languages M,D
School Psychology M,D,O
Social Psychology M,D
Sociology M,D
Spanish M,D
Sustainable Development M
Theater M
Urban and Regional Planning M,D
Writing M,D

UNIVERSITY OF MASSACHUSETTS BOSTON
American Studies M
Applied Economics M
Archaeology M
Classics M
Clinical Psychology D
Cognitive Sciences M
Conflict Resolution and Mediation/Peace Studies M,O
Counseling Psychology M,D
Cultural Studies M
English M
Gerontology M,D,O
History M
International Affairs M
International Development M,D
Linguistics M,D
Marriage and Family Therapy M
Public Administration M
Public Policy M,D
Rehabilitation Counseling M
School Psychology M,D
Sociology M,D
Urban and Regional Planning M
Writing M

UNIVERSITY OF MASSACHUSETTS DARTMOUTH
Applied Behavior Analysis M,O
Art History M
Art/Fine Arts M,O
Clinical Psychology M,O
Experimental Psychology M,O
Latin American Studies M,O
Media Studies M
Portuguese M,D
Psychology—General M,O
Public Administration M,O
Public Policy M,O
Writing M,O

UNIVERSITY OF MASSACHUSETTS LOWELL
Conflict Resolution and Mediation/Peace Studies M
Criminal Justice and Criminology M
Economic Development M,O
Economics M,O
Music M
Psychology—General M
Social Psychology M
Sociology M
Urban and Regional Planning M,O

UNIVERSITY OF MASSACHUSETTS MEDICAL SCHOOL
Interdisciplinary Studies M,D

UNIVERSITY OF MEMPHIS
African-American Studies M,D,O
Anthropology M
Applied Behavior Analysis M,D,O
Archaeology M,D,O
Architecture M
Art History M,O
Art/Fine Arts M,O
Clinical Psychology M,D,O
Communication—General M,D
Comparative Literature M,D,O
Counseling Psychology M,D
Criminal Justice and Criminology M
Economics M,D
English M,D,O
Experimental Psychology M,D,O
Film, Television, and Video Production M,D
French M
Gender Studies O
Geographic Information Systems M,D,O
Geography M,D,O
Graphic Design M,O
History M,D
Interdisciplinary Studies M,D,O
Journalism M,O
Liberal Studies M,O
Linguistics M,D,O
Museum Studies M,O
Music M,D
Near and Middle Eastern Studies M,D
Philanthropic Studies M,O
Philosophy M,D
Photography M,O
Political Science M
Psychology—General M,D,O
Public Administration M,O
Public Policy M,O
Rehabilitation Counseling M,D
School Psychology M,D,O
Social Sciences M,O
Sociology M
Spanish M
Theater M
Urban and Regional Planning M,O
Writing M,D,O

UNIVERSITY OF MIAMI
Architecture M
Art History M
Art/Fine Arts M
Broadcast Journalism M,D
Clinical Psychology M,D
Communication—General M,D
Counseling Psychology D
Developmental Psychology M,D
Economics M,D
English M,D
Film, Television, and Video Production M,D
Film, Television, and Video Theory and Criticism M,D
French D
Geography M
Graphic Design M
History M,D
International Affairs M,D
Internet and Interactive Multimedia M
Journalism M,D
Latin American Studies M
Liberal Studies M
Marriage and Family Therapy M,O
Music M,D,O
Philosophy M,D
Photography M
Political Science M
Psychology—General M,D
Romance Languages D
Sociology M,D
Spanish M,D
Therapies—Dance, Drama, and Music M,D,O

Urban Design M
Writing M,D

UNIVERSITY OF MICHIGAN
African Studies M
American Studies M,D
Anthropology D
Applied Arts and Design—General M,D
Applied Economics M
Archaeology M,D
Architecture M
Art History M,D
Art/Fine Arts M
Asian Languages D
Asian Studies M,D,O
Biological Anthropology D
Classics M,D,O
Clinical Psychology D
Cognitive Sciences D
Communication—General D
Comparative Literature D
Cultural Anthropology D
Dance M
Developmental Psychology D
East European and Russian Studies M,O
Economics M,D
English M,D,O
Film, Television, and Video Theory and Criticism D,O
French D
Genetic Counseling M,D
German M,D,O
History D,O
Italian D
Jewish Studies M,D,O
Landscape Architecture M
Linguistics D
Media Studies M
Music M,D,O
Near and Middle Eastern Languages M,D
Near and Middle Eastern Studies M,D
Philosophy M,D
Political Science D
Psychology—General D,O
Public Policy M,D
Religion M,D
Slavic Languages M,D
Social Psychology D
Social Sciences D
Sociology D
Spanish D
Survey Methodology M,D,O
Sustainable Development M,D
Urban and Regional Planning M,D
Urban Design M
Women's Studies D,O
Writing M

UNIVERSITY OF MICHIGAN–DEARBORN
Applied Behavior Analysis M
Clinical Psychology M
Criminal Justice and Criminology M
Health Psychology M
Public Administration M

UNIVERSITY OF MICHIGAN–FLINT
American Studies M
Art/Fine Arts M
Arts Administration M
Criminal Justice and Criminology M
English M
Gender Studies M
Gerontology M,D,O
International Affairs M
Liberal Studies M
Museum Studies M
Music M
Political Science M
Public Administration M
Rhetoric M
Social Sciences M
Writing M

UNIVERSITY OF MINNESOTA, DULUTH
Anthropology M
Art/Fine Arts M
Criminal Justice and Criminology M
English M
Graphic Design M
Liberal Studies M
Music M
Sociology M

UNIVERSITY OF MINNESOTA, TWIN CITIES CAMPUS
American Studies D
Anthropology M,D
Applied Arts and Design—General M,D,O
Applied Economics M,D
Archaeology M,D
Architecture M
Art History M,D
Art/Fine Arts M
Asian Languages D
Asian Studies D
Child and Family Studies M,D
Child Development M,D
Classics M,D
Clinical Psychology D
Clothing and Textiles M,D,O
Cognitive Sciences D
Communication—General M,D,O
Comparative Literature D
Counseling Psychology D
Cultural Studies D
Economics M,D
English M,D
French M,D
Genetic Counseling M,D
Geographic Information Systems M,D
Geography M,D
German M,D
Hispanic and Latin American Languages M,D
History of Medicine M,D
History of Science and Technology M,D
History M,D
Industrial and Labor Relations M
Industrial and Organizational Psychology D
Interdisciplinary Studies D
Interior Design M,D,O
International Development M
Landscape Architecture M
Linguistics M,D
Marriage and Family Therapy M,D
Mass Communication M,D
Medieval and Renaissance Studies M,D
Music M,D
Philosophy M,D
Political Science D
Portuguese M,D
Psychology—General D
Public Affairs M,D
Public Policy M,D
Religion M,D
Scandinavian Languages M,D
School Psychology M,D,O
Social Psychology D
Sociology M,D
Spanish M,D
Textile Design M,D,O
Theater M,D
Urban and Regional Planning M,D
Women's Studies D

UNIVERSITY OF MISSISSIPPI
Anthropology M,D
Art/Fine Arts M,D
Criminal Justice and Criminology M,D
Economics M,D
English M,D
Experimental Psychology M,D
Film, Television, and Video Production M,D
History M,D
Journalism M
Music M,D
Philosophy M,D
Political Science M,D
Writing M,D

UNIVERSITY OF MISSOURI
Agricultural Economics and Agribusiness M,D
Anthropology M,D
Architecture M,D
Art/Fine Arts M
Child and Family Studies M,D
Classics M,D
Clothing and Textiles M,D
Communication—General M,D
Conflict Resolution and Mediation/Peace Studies M,D
Consumer Economics D
Counseling Psychology M,D,O
Economics M,D
English M,D
Family and Consumer Sciences-General M,D,O
French M,D
Geographic Information Systems M,D,O
Geography M,O
German M
Health Communication M,D
History M,D
Human Development M,D
Journalism M,D
Music M,O
Philosophy M,D
Political Science M,D,O
Psychology—General M,D,O
Public Administration M,D,O
Public Affairs M,D,O
Public Policy M,D,O
Romance Languages M,D
Rural Sociology M,D
Russian M
School Psychology M,D,O
Sociology M,D
Theater M,D

UNIVERSITY OF MISSOURI–KANSAS CITY
Art/Fine Arts M,D
Counseling Psychology M,D,O
Criminal Justice and Criminology M
Economics M,D
English M,D
French M
History M,D
Interdisciplinary Studies D
Music M,D
Political Science M
Psychology—General M,D
Public Administration M,D
Public Affairs M,D
Romance Languages M
Social Psychology M,D
Sociology M
Spanish M
Theater M
Therapies—Dance, Drama, and Music M,D

UNIVERSITY OF MISSOURI–ST. LOUIS
American Studies M,D
Clinical Psychology M,D,O
Communication—General M
Conflict Resolution and Mediation/Peace Studies M
Criminal Justice and Criminology M,D
Cultural Studies O
Economics M
English M
Gender Studies O
History M,O
Interdisciplinary Studies O
Museum Studies M,O
Philosophy M
Political Science M,D
Psychology—General M,D,O
Public Administration M,D
Public Policy M,D
School Psychology M,O
Sociology M
Writing M

UNIVERSITY OF MOBILE
Marriage and Family Therapy M
Music M,D
Theology M

UNIVERSITY OF MONTANA
Anthropology M,D
Art History M
Art/Fine Arts M
Child and Family Studies M,D,O
Clinical Psychology M,D,O
Communication—General M
Computer Art and Design M
Counseling Psychology M,D,O
Criminal Justice and Criminology M
Cultural Studies M,D,O
Developmental Psychology M,D,O
Economics M
English M
Experimental Psychology M,D,O
Film, Television, and Video Production M
French M
Geography M
German M
History M,D
Interdisciplinary Studies M,D
Internet and Interactive Multimedia M
Journalism M
Linguistics M,D
Music M
Philosophy M
Photography M
Political Science M
Psychology—General M,D,O
Public Administration M
Rural Planning and Studies M
Rural Sociology M
School Psychology M,D,O
Sociology M
Spanish M
Theater M
Writing M

UNIVERSITY OF MONTEVALLO
English M

UNIVERSITY OF NEBRASKA AT KEARNEY
Counseling Psychology M,O
English M
History M
School Psychology M,O
Writing M

UNIVERSITY OF NEBRASKA AT OMAHA
Applied Behavior Analysis M,D,O
Art/Fine Arts M
Communication—General M,O
Criminal Justice and Criminology M,D,O
Economics M
English M,O
Geographic Information Systems M,O
Geography M,O
Gerontology M,D,O
History M
Industrial and Organizational Psychology M,D,O
Music M
National Security M,O
Political Science M,O
Psychology—General M,D,O
Public Administration M,D,O
School Psychology M,D,O
Sociology M
Technical Communication M,O
Writing M,O

UNIVERSITY OF NEBRASKA–LINCOLN
Agricultural Economics and Agribusiness M,D
Anthropology M
Archaeology M,D
Architecture M,D
Art History M
Art/Fine Arts M
Child and Family Studies M,D
Child Development M,D
Classics M
Clinical Psychology M,D
Clothing and Textiles M,D
Cognitive Sciences M,D,O
Communication—General M,D
Comparative Literature M,D
Consumer Economics M,D
Corporate and Organizational Communication M,D
Counseling Psychology M,D,O
Developmental Psychology M,D,O
Economics M,D
English M,D
Family and Consumer Sciences-General M,D
French M,D
Geography M,D
German M,D
Gerontology M,D
History M,D
Human Development M,D,O
Interior Design M,D
Journalism M
Marriage and Family Therapy M,D
Mass Communication M
Music M,D
Philosophy M,D
Political Science M,D,O
Psychology—General M,D
Public Policy M,D,O
Rhetoric M,D
School Psychology M,D,O
Social Psychology M,D
Sociology M,D
Spanish M,D
Speech and Interpersonal Communication M,D
Survey Methodology M,D
Theater M
Urban and Regional Planning M,D
Writing M,D

UNIVERSITY OF NEBRASKA MEDICAL CENTER
Applied Behavior Analysis M,D
Emergency Management M

UNIVERSITY OF NEVADA, LAS VEGAS
Addictions/Substance Abuse Counseling M,D,O
Anthropology M,D
Applied Economics M,O
Architecture M,O
Art/Fine Arts M
Clinical Psychology M,D,O
Communication—General M
Counseling Psychology M,D,O
Criminal Justice and Criminology M,D
Economics M
Emergency Management M,D,O
English M,D
Film, Television, and Video Production M,O
Hispanic Studies M,O
History M,D
Journalism M
Media Studies M
Music M,D,O
Political Science M,D
Psychology—General M,D,O
Public Administration M,D,O
Public Affairs M,D,O
Public Policy M,D,O
Sociology M,D
Theater M
Translation and Interpretation M,O
Writing M,D,O

UNIVERSITY OF NEVADA, RENO
Anthropology M,D
Applied Behavior Analysis M,D
Art/Fine Arts M
Child and Family Studies M
Clinical Psychology D
Cognitive Sciences M,D
Criminal Justice and Criminology M
Economics M
English M,D
Geography M,D
History M,D
Human Development M
Journalism M
Music M
Philosophy M
Political Science M,D
Psychology—General M,D
Public Administration M
Social Psychology D
Sociology M
Spanish M
Speech and Interpersonal Communication M
Western European Studies D

UNIVERSITY OF NEW BRUNSWICK SAINT JOHN
Clinical Psychology M,D
Experimental Psychology M,D
Psychology—General M,D

UNIVERSITY OF NEW HAMPSHIRE
Addictions/Substance Abuse Counseling M,O
Child and Family Studies M,O
Economic Development M
Economics M,D
English M,D
Geographic Information Systems O
History M,D
Liberal Studies M
Linguistics M,D
Marriage and Family Therapy M,O
Museum Studies M,D
Music M
Political Science M,O
Psychology—General D
Public Administration M,O
Public Policy M
Sociology M,D
Spanish M,O
Women's Studies O
Writing M,D

UNIVERSITY OF NEW HAVEN
Conflict Resolution and Mediation/Peace Studies M,O
Criminal Justice and Criminology M,D,O
Emergency Management M,O
Forensic Psychology M,O
Forensic Sciences M,O
Geographic Information Systems M

*M—masters degree; D—doctorate; O—other advanced degree; *—Close-Up and/or Display*

Industrial and Organizational Psychology M,O
National Security M,O
Public Administration M,O
Social Psychology M,O

UNIVERSITY OF NEW MEXICO
American Indian/Native American Studies M,D
American Studies M,D
Anthropology M,D
Archaeology M,D
Architecture M,D
Art History M,D
Art/Fine Arts M
Child and Family Studies M,D
Clinical Psychology D
Cognitive Sciences D
Communication—General M,D
Comparative Literature M,D
Cultural Studies M,D
Dance M
Developmental Psychology D
Economics M,D
English M,D
Ethnic Studies M,D
French M,D
Geography M
German M,D
Health Psychology D
Historic Preservation O
History M,D
Human Development M,D
International Development M,D
International Economics M,D
Landscape Architecture M
Latin American Studies M,D
Linguistics M,D
Music M
Philosophy M,D
Photography M,D
Political Science M,D
Portuguese M,D
Psychology—General D
Public Administration M
Sociology M,D
Spanish M,D
Theater M
Urban and Regional Planning M
Writing M

UNIVERSITY OF NEW ORLEANS
Art/Fine Arts M
Arts Administration M
Economics D
English M
Film, Television, and Video Production M
History M
Music M
Political Science M,D
Psychology—General M,D
Public Administration M
Romance Languages M
Sociology M
Theater M
Urban and Regional Planning M
Urban Studies M,D
Writing M

UNIVERSITY OF NORTH ALABAMA
Child and Family Studies M
Clinical Psychology M
Criminal Justice and Criminology M
Economic Development M
English M
Geographic Information Systems M
Historic Preservation M
History M
Interdisciplinary Studies M
Political Science M
Public History M
Rhetoric M
Technical Writing M
Writing M

UNIVERSITY OF NORTH CAROLINA ASHEVILLE
Liberal Studies M,O

THE UNIVERSITY OF NORTH CAROLINA AT CHAPEL HILL
Anthropology M,D
Archaeology M,D
Art History M,D
Art/Fine Arts M
Classics M,D
Clinical Psychology D
Cognitive Sciences D
Communication—General M,D,O
Developmental Psychology D
East European and Russian Studies M
Economics M,D
English M,D
Folklore M
French M,D
Geography M,D
German D
Health Communication M,D,O
Health Psychology M,D
History M,D
International Affairs M
Italian M,D
Journalism M,D,O
Latin American Studies M,D,O
Linguistics M
Media Studies M,D,O
Music M,D
Philosophy M,D
Political Science M,D,O
Portuguese M,D
Psychology—General D
Public Administration M
Public Policy D
Religion M,D
Romance Languages M,D
School Psychology M,D
Slavic Languages D
Social Psychology D
Sociology M,D
Spanish M,D
Theater M
Urban and Regional Planning M,D

THE UNIVERSITY OF NORTH CAROLINA AT CHARLOTTE
Addictions/Substance Abuse Counseling M,D,O
African Studies O
Anthropology M
Applied Economics M,O
Architecture M
Arts Administration M,O
Child and Family Studies M,D,O
Child Development M,D,O
Cognitive Sciences M,D,O
Communication—General M
Criminal Justice and Criminology M
Cultural Studies M,O
Economics M,O
Emergency Management M,O
English M,O
Ethics M,O
Gender Studies M,D,O
Geographic Information Systems M,D
Geography M,D
Gerontology M,D,O
Health Psychology M,D,O
History M
Industrial and Organizational Psychology M,D,O
Interdisciplinary Studies M,D,O
Latin American Studies M,D,O
Liberal Studies M,D,O
Linguistics M,O
Music O
Philosophy M,O
Psychology—General M,D,O
Public Administration M,O
Public Policy M,D,O
Religion M
Sociology M
Spanish M,O
Technical Writing M,O
Theater M,D,O
Urban and Regional Planning M,O
Urban Design M
Women's Studies M,D,O
Writing M,O

THE UNIVERSITY OF NORTH CAROLINA AT GREENSBORO
Applied Economics M
Architecture M,O
Art/Fine Arts M
Child and Family Studies M,D
Classics M
Clinical Psychology M,D
Cognitive Sciences M,D
Communication—General M
Conflict Resolution and Mediation/Peace Studies M,O
Counseling Psychology M,D,O
Criminal Justice and Criminology M
Dance M
Developmental Psychology M,D
Economic Development M,D,O
Economics D
English M,D
Film, Television, and Video Production M
French M
Gender Studies M,O
Genetic Counseling M
Geographic Information Systems M,D,O
Geography M,D,O
Gerontology M,O
Hispanic and Latin American Languages M,O
Hispanic Studies M,O
Historic Preservation M,O
History M,D,O
Human Development M,D
Interior Design M,O
Liberal Studies M
Marriage and Family Therapy M,D,O
Media Studies M
Museum Studies M,D,O
Music M,D,O
Political Science M,O
Psychology—General M,D
Public Affairs M,O
Rhetoric M,D
School Psychology M,D,O
Social Psychology M,D
Sociology M
Spanish M,O
Technical Writing M,D,O
Textile Design M,D
Theater M
Women's Studies M,D,O
Writing M,D

THE UNIVERSITY OF NORTH CAROLINA AT PEMBROKE
Counseling Psychology M
Criminal Justice and Criminology M
Emergency Management M
Public Administration M

UNIVERSITY OF NORTH CAROLINA SCHOOL OF THE ARTS
Film, Television, and Video Production M
Music M,O
Theater M

THE UNIVERSITY OF NORTH CAROLINA WILMINGTON
Applied Behavior Analysis M,D
Clinical Psychology M,D
Conflict Resolution and Mediation/Peace Studies M
Criminal Justice and Criminology M
English M
Geographic Information Systems M,O
Gerontology M
Hispanic Studies M,O
History M
Liberal Studies M
Psychology—General M,D
Public Administration M
Sociology M
Spanish M,O
Writing M

UNIVERSITY OF NORTH DAKOTA
Applied Economics M
Art/Fine Arts M
Clinical Psychology M,D
Communication—General D
Counseling Psychology M,D
Criminal Justice and Criminology D
English M,D
Forensic Psychology M,D
Geographic Information Systems M
Geography M
History M,D
Linguistics M
Music M,D
Psychology—General M,D
Public Administration M
Sociology M

UNIVERSITY OF NORTHERN BRITISH COLUMBIA
Disability Studies M,D,O
Gender Studies M,D,O
History M,D,O
Interdisciplinary Studies M,D,O
International Affairs M,D,O
Political Science M,D,O
Psychology—General M,D,O

UNIVERSITY OF NORTHERN COLORADO
Art History M
Art/Fine Arts M
Clinical Psychology M
Communication—General M
Counseling Psychology D
Criminal Justice and Criminology M
English M
Gerontology M,D
History M
Music M,D
Rehabilitation Counseling M,D
School Psychology O
Sociology M
Translation and Interpretation M

UNIVERSITY OF NORTHERN IOWA
Art/Fine Arts M
Communication—General M
Counseling Psychology M
English M
Gender Studies M
Geography M
History M
Music M
Psychology—General M
Public History M
Public Policy M
School Psychology M,O
Social Sciences M
Spanish M
Women's Studies M
Writing M

UNIVERSITY OF NORTH FLORIDA
Applied Behavior Analysis M
Counseling Psychology M
Criminal Justice and Criminology M
Economics M
English M
Ethics M,O
History M
Philosophy M,O
Psychology—General M
Public Administration M,O
Translation and Interpretation M
Writing M

UNIVERSITY OF NORTH GEORGIA
Anthropology M
Counseling Psychology M
Criminal Justice and Criminology M
History M
International Affairs M
Philosophy M
Public Administration M

UNIVERSITY OF NORTH TEXAS
Anthropology M,D,O
Applied Arts and Design—General M,D,O
Applied Behavior Analysis M,D,O
Art History M,D,O
Art/Fine Arts M,D,O
Child and Family Studies M,D,O
Clinical Psychology M,D,O
Communication—General M,D,O
Counseling Psychology M,D,O
Criminal Justice and Criminology M,D,O
Economics M,D,O
Emergency Management M,D,O
English M,D,O
Film, Television, and Video Production M,D,O
French M,D,O
Geography M,D,O
Gerontology M,D,O
History M,D,O
Human Development M,D,O
Interdisciplinary Studies M,D,O
Interior Design M,D,O
International Affairs M,D,O
Internet and Interactive Multimedia M,D,O
Journalism M,D,O
Linguistics M,D,O
Music M,D,O
Philosophy M,D,O
Political Science M,D,O
Psychology—General M,D,O
Public Administration M,D,O
Rehabilitation Counseling M,D,O
Sociology M,D,O
Spanish M,D,O
Textile Design M,D,O
Writing M,D,O

UNIVERSITY OF NORTH TEXAS AT DALLAS
Clinical Psychology M
Criminal Justice and Criminology M
Public Administration M

UNIVERSITY OF NORTH TEXAS HEALTH SCIENCE CENTER AT FORT WORTH
Forensic Sciences M,D
Geographic Information Systems M,D,O

UNIVERSITY OF NORTHWESTERN–ST. PAUL
Pastoral Ministry and Counseling M
Theology M

UNIVERSITY OF NOTRE DAME
Applied Arts and Design—General M
Architecture M
Art History M
Art/Fine Arts M
Cognitive Sciences D
Comparative Literature D
Conflict Resolution and Mediation/Peace Studies M,D
Counseling Psychology D
Developmental Psychology D
Economics D
English M,D
French M
Graphic Design M
History of Science and Technology M,D
History M,D
Industrial Design M
International Affairs M
Italian M
Latin American Studies M
Medieval and Renaissance Studies M,D
Philosophy D
Photography M
Political Science D
Psychology—General D
Religion M
Romance Languages M
Sociology D
Spanish M
Sustainable Development M
Theology M,D
Writing M

UNIVERSITY OF OKLAHOMA
American Indian/Native American Studies M
Anthropology M,D
Applied Arts and Design—General M,D
Applied Behavior Analysis M,D
Applied Economics M,D
Archaeology M,D
Architecture M,D
Art History M,D
Art/Fine Arts M,D
Clinical Psychology M,O
Communication—General M,D
Corporate and Organizational Communication M,D
Criminal Justice and Criminology M,O
Cultural Studies M,D
Dance M
Economics M,D
English M,D
Film, Television, and Video Theory and Criticism M,D
French M,D
Gender Studies O
Geography M,D
German M,D
Health Communication M,D
History of Science and Technology M,D
History M,D
Interior Design M,O
International Affairs M
Landscape Architecture M
Mass Communication M,D
Museum Studies M,D
Music M,D,O
Philosophy M,D
Photography M,D
Political Science M,D
Psychology—General M,D,O
Public Administration M,D
Public Policy M,D
Rhetoric M,D
Sociology M,D
Spanish M,D
Sustainable Development M,D
Theater M
Urban and Regional Planning M,D
Women's Studies O
Writing M,D

UNIVERSITY OF OKLAHOMA HEALTH SCIENCES CENTER
Genetic Counseling M
Homeland Security M

UNIVERSITY OF OREGON
Anthropology M,D
Applied Arts and Design—General M

Architecture M
Art History M,D
Art/Fine Arts M
Asian Languages M,D
Asian Studies M
Chinese M,D
Classics M
Clinical Psychology D
Cognitive Sciences M,D
Communication—General M,D
Comparative Literature M,D
Counseling Psychology M,D
Dance M
Developmental Psychology M,D
Economics M,D
English M,D
Folklore M
French M
Geography M,D
German M,D
Historic Preservation M
History M,D
Interdisciplinary Studies M
Interior Design M
International Affairs M
Italian M
Japanese M,D
Journalism M,D
Landscape Architecture M,D
Linguistics M,D
Marriage and Family Therapy M,D
Media Studies M,D
Music M,D
Philosophy M,D
Political Science M,D
Psychology—General M,D
Public Administration M
Romance Languages M,D
Russian M
School Psychology M,D
Social Psychology M,D
Sociology M,D
Spanish M
Theater M,D
Urban and Regional Planning M
Writing M

UNIVERSITY OF OTTAWA
Anthropology M
Canadian Studies D
Classics M,D
Communication—General M
Criminal Justice and Criminology M,D
Economics M,D
English M,D
French M,D
Geography M,D
History M,D
Interdisciplinary Studies D,O
International Development M
Linguistics M,D
Music M,O
Philosophy M,D
Political Science M,D
Psychology—General D
Public Administration D,O
Religion M,D
Sociology M
Spanish M,D
Theater M
Translation and Interpretation M,D
Women's Studies M

UNIVERSITY OF PENNSYLVANIA
African Studies M,D
Anthropology M,D
Applied Economics D
Applied Psychology M
Archaeology M,D
Architecture M,D,O
Art History M,D
Art/Fine Arts M,O
Asian Studies M,D
Classics M,D
Communication—General D
Comparative Literature M,D
Computer Art and Design M,D
Counseling Psychology M,D
Criminal Justice and Criminology M,D
Demography and Population Studies M,D
Economic Development M,D
Economics M,D
English M,D
Ethics M,D
French M,D
Geographic Information Systems M,D,O
German M,D
Graphic Design M,O
Historic Preservation M,O
History of Science and Technology M,D
History M,D
Human Development M,D
International Affairs M
Internet and Interactive Multimedia M,O
Italian M,D
Landscape Architecture M,O
Liberal Studies M
Linguistics M,D
Music M,D
Near and Middle Eastern Studies M,D
Philosophy M,D
Political Science M,D,O
Psychology—General D
Public Administration M,O
Public Policy M,D
Religion D
Romance Languages M,D
Sociology M,D
Spanish M,D
Urban and Regional Planning M,D,O
Urban Design M,D,O

UNIVERSITY OF PHILOSOPHICAL RESEARCH
Psychology—General M
Theology M

UNIVERSITY OF PHOENIX - BAY AREA CAMPUS
Criminal Justice and Criminology M
Marriage and Family Therapy M
Public Administration M,D

UNIVERSITY OF PHOENIX - CENTRAL VALLEY CAMPUS
Gerontology M
Marriage and Family Therapy M
Public Administration M

UNIVERSITY OF PHOENIX - DALLAS CAMPUS
Criminal Justice and Criminology M
Public Administration M

UNIVERSITY OF PHOENIX - HAWAII CAMPUS
Gerontology M
Public Administration M

UNIVERSITY OF PHOENIX - HOUSTON CAMPUS
Public Administration M

UNIVERSITY OF PHOENIX - LAS VEGAS CAMPUS
Counseling Psychology M
Marriage and Family Therapy M
Public Administration M
School Psychology M

UNIVERSITY OF PHOENIX–ONLINE CAMPUS
Conflict Resolution and Mediation/Peace Studies M,O
Criminal Justice and Criminology M,O
Homeland Security M
Industrial and Organizational Psychology M,D,O
Psychology—General M,O
Public Administration M,O

UNIVERSITY OF PHOENIX - PHOENIX CAMPUS
Clinical Psychology M
Counseling Psychology M
Criminal Justice and Criminology M
Homeland Security M
Marriage and Family Therapy M
Psychology—General M
Public Administration M
Social Psychology M

UNIVERSITY OF PHOENIX - SACRAMENTO VALLEY CAMPUS
Public Administration M

UNIVERSITY OF PHOENIX - SAN ANTONIO CAMPUS
Criminal Justice and Criminology M
Public Administration M

UNIVERSITY OF PHOENIX - SAN DIEGO CAMPUS
Public Administration M

UNIVERSITY OF PITTSBURGH
African Studies O
Anthropology M,D
Architectural History M,D
Art History M,D
Asian Studies M,O
Chinese M,D
Clinical Psychology M,D
Communication—General M,D
Criminal Justice and Criminology M
Cultural Studies O
Developmental Psychology D
Disability Studies O
East European and Russian Studies O
Economics M,D
English M,D
Film, Television, and Video Theory and Criticism M,D,O
French M,D
Genetic Counseling M,D,O
Geographic Information Systems M,D
Health Psychology D
History of Science and Technology M,D
History M,D
Interdisciplinary Studies D
International Affairs M,D,O
International Development M,D,O
Italian M,D
Japanese M
Latin American Studies O
Linguistics M,D
Medieval and Renaissance Studies O
Military and Defense Studies M
Music M,D
Philosophy D
Political Science M,D
Psychology—General D
Public Administration M,D
Public Policy M,D
Rehabilitation Counseling M,D
Slavic Languages M,D
Social Psychology D
Sociology M,D
Spanish D
Theater M,D
Urban and Regional Planning M
Western European Studies O
Women's Studies O
Writing M,D

UNIVERSITY OF PORTLAND
Communication—General M
Corporate and Organizational Communication M

UNIVERSITY OF PRINCE EDWARD ISLAND
Geography M

UNIVERSITY OF PROVIDENCE
Counseling Psychology M
Criminal Justice and Criminology M

UNIVERSITY OF PUERTO RICO AT MAYAGÜEZ
Agricultural Economics and Agribusiness M
English M
Hispanic Studies M
Rural Sociology M

UNIVERSITY OF PUERTO RICO AT RIO PIEDRAS
Architecture M
Clinical Psychology M,D
Communication—General M
Comparative Literature M
Economic Development M
Economics M
English M,D
Family and Consumer Sciences-General M
Hispanic Studies M,D
History M,D
Industrial and Organizational Psychology M,D
Journalism M
Linguistics M,D
Mass Communication M
Philosophy M
Psychology—General M,D
Public Administration M
Public Policy M
Rehabilitation Counseling M
Social Psychology M,D
Sociology M
Translation and Interpretation M,O
Urban and Regional Planning M

UNIVERSITY OF PUERTO RICO - MEDICAL SCIENCES CAMPUS
Demography and Population Studies M
Gerontology M,O

UNIVERSITY OF PUGET SOUND
Counseling Psychology M

UNIVERSITY OF REDLANDS
Geographic Information Systems M
Music M

UNIVERSITY OF REGINA
Anthropology M
Applied Psychology M,D
Art/Fine Arts M
Clinical Psychology M,D
Criminal Justice and Criminology M
Economics M,D,O
English M,D
Experimental Psychology M,D
Film, Television, and Video Production M
French M
Geography M,D
Gerontology M
History M
Interdisciplinary Studies M
Journalism M
Music M
Philosophy M
Psychology—General M,D
Public Administration M,D,O
Public Policy M,D,O
Religion M
Social Sciences M
Sociology M
Women's Studies M
Writing M,D

UNIVERSITY OF RHODE ISLAND
Anthropology M
Archaeology M
Child and Family Studies M
Clinical Psychology M,D
Clothing and Textiles M,O
Communication—General M
Computer Art and Design M
Counseling Psychology M
Economics M,D
English M,D
Film, Television, and Video Production M,D
Forensic Sciences M,D,O
Gender Studies M,D,O
History M
Human Development M
Industrial and Labor Relations M,O
Marriage and Family Therapy M
Music M
Political Science M
Psychology—General M
Public Administration M
Public Policy M
School Psychology M,D
Spanish M
Sport Psychology M
Women's Studies O
Writing M,D

UNIVERSITY OF ROCHESTER
Art History D
Art/Fine Arts D
Clinical Psychology D
Cognitive Sciences D
Developmental Psychology D
Economics D
English M,D
History M,D
Human Development M,D
Linguistics M
Marriage and Family Therapy M
Music M,D
Philosophy D
Political Science D
Psychology—General D
Social Psychology M,D
Translation and Interpretation M,O

UNIVERSITY OF ST. FRANCIS (IL)
Forensic Sciences M,O

UNIVERSITY OF SAINT FRANCIS (IN)
Art/Fine Arts M
Clinical Psychology M,O
Counseling Psychology M,O

UNIVERSITY OF SAINT JOSEPH
Clinical Psychology M
Counseling Psychology M
Marriage and Family Therapy M

UNIVERSITY OF SAINT MARY
Counseling Psychology M
Psychology—General M

UNIVERSITY OF SAINT MARY OF THE LAKE–MUNDELEIN SEMINARY
Pastoral Ministry and Counseling M,D
Theology M,D

UNIVERSITY OF ST. MICHAEL'S COLLEGE
Jewish Studies M,D,O
Pastoral Ministry and Counseling M,D,O
Theology M,D,O

UNIVERSITY OF ST. THOMAS (MN)
Art History M,O
Counseling Psychology M,D
English M,O
Ethics M,D
Health Communication M
Human Development D
Museum Studies M,O
Music M,D
Pastoral Ministry and Counseling M
Religion M
Theology M

UNIVERSITY OF ST. THOMAS (TX)
Liberal Studies M
Music M
Pastoral Ministry and Counseling M
Philosophy M,D
Public Administration M
Public Policy M
Religion M
Theology M

UNIVERSITY OF SAN DIEGO
Conflict Resolution and Mediation/Peace Studies M
Counseling Psychology M
Criminal Justice and Criminology M
International Affairs M
Marriage and Family Therapy M
School Psychology M
Theater M

UNIVERSITY OF SAN FRANCISCO
Asian Studies M
Clinical Psychology D
Communication—General M
Counseling Psychology M
International Affairs M
International Development M
Marriage and Family Therapy M
Museum Studies M
Pacific Area/Pacific Rim Studies M
Public Administration M
Urban Studies M
Writing M

UNIVERSITY OF SASKATCHEWAN
Agricultural Economics and Agribusiness M,D,O
Anthropology M
Archaeology M
Art/Fine Arts M
Canadian Studies M,D
Counseling Psychology M,D
Cultural Studies M
Economics M,O
English M,D
French M
Geography M,D
History M,D
Linguistics M
Music M
Philosophy M
Political Science M
Psychology—General M,D
Public Policy M,D
Religion M
School Psychology M,D
Sociology M,D
Theater M

THE UNIVERSITY OF SCRANTON
Art/Fine Arts M
Clinical Psychology M
Counseling Psychology M
Rehabilitation Counseling M
Theology M

UNIVERSITY OF SOUTH AFRICA
Anthropology M,D
Archaeology M,D
Art History M,D

*M—masters degree; D—doctorate; O—other advanced degree; *—Close-Up and/or Display*

Classics M,D
Clinical Psychology M,D
Communication—General M,D
Counseling Psychology M,D
Criminal Justice and Criminology M,D
Economics M,D
English M,D
Ethics M,D
Family and Consumer
　Sciences-General M,D
French M,D
Geography M,D
German M,D
History M,D
Human Development M,D
Industrial and Organizational
　Psychology M,D
Italian M,D
Linguistics M,D
Missions and Missiology M,D
Music M,D
Near and Middle Eastern Languages M,D
Near and Middle Eastern Studies M,D
Pastoral Ministry and Counseling M,D
Philosophy M,D
Political Science M,D
Portuguese M,D
Psychology—General M,D
Public Administration M,D
Religion M,D
Romance Languages M,D
Russian M,D
Sociology M,D
Spanish M,D
Theology M,D

UNIVERSITY OF SOUTH ALABAMA
Art/Fine Arts M
Clinical Psychology M,D,O
Communication—General M
Counseling Psychology M,D,O
English M
History M
Music M
Psychology—General M
Public Administration M
Sociology M
Writing M

UNIVERSITY OF SOUTH CAROLINA
Anthropology M,D
Art History M
Art/Fine Arts M
Clinical Psychology M,D
Comparative Literature M,D
Consumer Economics M
Criminal Justice and Criminology M,D
Economics M,D
English M,D
Experimental Psychology M,D
French M
Genetic Counseling M
Geography M,D
German M,D
Gerontology O
Historic Preservation M,O
History M,D,O
International Affairs M
Journalism M
Linguistics M,D,O
Media Studies M
Museum Studies M,O
Music M,D,O
Philosophy M,D
Political Science M,D
Psychology—General M
Public Administration M
Public History M,O
Rehabilitation Counseling M
Religion M
School Psychology D
Social Psychology M,D
Sociology M,D
Spanish M,D
Speech and Interpersonal
　Communication M,D
Theater M
Women's Studies O
Writing M,D

UNIVERSITY OF SOUTH CAROLINA AIKEN
Applied Psychology M
Clinical Psychology M

UNIVERSITY OF SOUTH DAKOTA
Addictions/Substance Abuse
　Counseling M
American Indian/Native American
　Studies M,D,O
Art/Fine Arts M,D
Clinical Psychology M,D
Communication—General M
Counseling Psychology M,D,O
Criminal Justice and Criminology M,D
English M,D
Graphic Design M
History M
Human Development M,D,O
Interdisciplinary Studies M
Music M
Photography M
Psychology—General M
School Psychology M,D,O
Sustainable Development M
Theater M

UNIVERSITY OF SOUTHERN CALIFORNIA
American Studies D
Architecture M
Art History M,D,O
Art/Fine Arts M,D,O
Arts Administration M
Asian Languages M
Asian Studies M,D

Child and Family Studies M,D
Classics M,D
Clinical Psychology M,D
Cognitive Sciences M,D
Communication—General M,D
Comparative Literature D
Computer Art and Design M
Corporate and Organizational
　Communication M
Cultural Studies D
Developmental Psychology M,D
Economic Development M,D
Economics M,D
English M,D
Film, Television, and Video
　Production M
Film, Television, and Video
　Theory and Criticism M,D
Geographic Information Systems M,O
Geography M,O
Gerontology M,D,O
Health Communication M
Historic Preservation M
History D
Homeland Security M,O
International Affairs M,D
Internet and Interactive
　Multimedia M,D,O
Journalism M
Landscape Architecture M
Latin American Studies D
Linguistics M,D
Marriage and Family Therapy M
Media Studies M,D
Music M,D,O
Philosophy M
Photography M
Political Science M,D
Psychology—General M,O
Public Administration M,O
Public Policy M,D,O
Rhetoric D
Slavic Languages M,D
Social Psychology M,D
Sociology D
Spanish D
Sustainable Development M,D,O
Theater M
Urban and Regional Planning M,D,O
Writing M,D

UNIVERSITY OF SOUTHERN INDIANA
Communication—General M
Cultural Studies M
English M
Gerontology M,D,O
Liberal Studies M
Public Administration M

UNIVERSITY OF SOUTHERN MAINE
Addictions/Substance Abuse
　Counseling M,O
Applied Behavior Analysis M,O
Counseling Psychology M,O
Cultural Studies M
Music M
Public Policy M
Rehabilitation Counseling M,O
School Psychology M,O
Urban and Regional Planning M,O
Writing M

UNIVERSITY OF SOUTHERN MISSISSIPPI
Child and Family Studies M
Communication—General M
Criminal Justice and Criminology M
Economic Development M
Forensic Sciences M
Marriage and Family Therapy M
Music M,D
Psychology—General M,D

UNIVERSITY OF SOUTH FLORIDA
Addictions/Substance Abuse
　Counseling M,D
African Studies O
American Studies M
Anthropology M,D,O
Applied Behavior Analysis M,D
Archaeology M,D,O
Architecture M
Art History M
Art/Fine Arts M
Child and Family Studies M,D,O
Clinical Psychology D
Cognitive Sciences D
Communication—General M,D
Comparative Literature O
Corporate and Organizational
　Communication O
Counseling Psychology M,D,O
Criminal Justice and Criminology M,D,O
Economics M,D
Emergency Management O
English M,D,O
Film, Television, and Video
　Theory and Criticism M
Forensic Sciences M,D,O
Gender Studies M,O
Geographic Information Systems O
Geography O
Gerontology M,D,O
History M
Holocaust and Genocide Studies O
Humanities M
Industrial and Organizational
　Psychology D
Interdisciplinary Studies M,D
International Affairs O
Internet and Interactive
　Multimedia O
Journalism O
Latin American Studies O
Liberal Studies M,D

Marriage and Family Therapy M,D,O
Mass Communication M,O
Museum Studies O
Music M,D
Philosophy M,D
Political Science O
Psychology—General O
Public Administration O
Public Affairs O
Rehabilitation Counseling M,D,O
Religion M,D
Sociology M,D
Sustainable Development M
Technical Communication O
Urban and Regional Planning M
Women's Studies M
Writing M

UNIVERSITY OF SOUTH FLORIDA, ST. PETERSBURG
Computer Art and Design M
Journalism M
Liberal Studies M
Media Studies M
Psychology—General M

UNIVERSITY OF SOUTH FLORIDA SARASOTA-MANATEE
Criminal Justice and Criminology M
Liberal Studies M
Social Sciences M

THE UNIVERSITY OF TAMPA
Criminal Justice and Criminology M
Writing M

THE UNIVERSITY OF TENNESSEE
Anthropology M,D
Applied Psychology M,D
Archaeology M,D
Architecture M
Art/Fine Arts M
Biological Anthropology M,D
Child and Family Studies M,D
Clinical Psychology M,D
Clothing and Textiles M,D
Communication—General M,D
Consumer Economics M,D
Counseling Psychology M,D
Criminal Justice and Criminology M,D
Cultural Anthropology M,D
Economics M,D
English M,D
Experimental Psychology M,D
Family and Consumer
　Sciences-General D
French M,D
Geography M,D
German M,D
Gerontology M
Graphic Design M
History M,D
Industrial and Organizational
　Psychology D
Internet and Interactive
　Multimedia M,D
Italian D
Journalism M,D
Landscape Architecture M
Linguistics D
Music M
Philosophy M,D
Photography M
Political Science M,D
Portuguese D
Psychology—General M,D
Public Administration M,D
Rehabilitation Counseling M,D
Religion M,D
Russian D
School Psychology M,D,O
Sociology M,D
Spanish M,D
Theater M

THE UNIVERSITY OF TENNESSEE AT CHATTANOOGA
Criminal Justice and Criminology M
English M
Ethics M,O
Experimental Psychology M
Industrial and Organizational
　Psychology M
Psychology—General M
Public Administration M,O
Rhetoric M
School Psychology M,D,O
Social Psychology M,D,O
Writing M

THE UNIVERSITY OF TENNESSEE AT MARTIN
Addictions/Substance Abuse
　Counseling M
Agricultural Economics and
　Agribusiness M
Child and Family Studies M
Child Development M
Communication—General M
Family and Consumer
　Sciences-General M
Interdisciplinary Studies M
Social Sciences M

THE UNIVERSITY OF TEXAS AT ARLINGTON
Anthropology M
Architecture M
Art/Fine Arts M
Communication—General M
Criminal Justice and Criminology M
Economics M
English M
Experimental Psychology M,D
Film, Television, and Video
　Production M

French M
Health Psychology M,D
History M,D
Industrial and Organizational
　Psychology M,D
Landscape Architecture M
Linguistics M,D
Music M
Political Science M
Psychology—General M,D
Public Administration M
Public Policy M,D
Sociology M
Spanish M
Urban and Regional Planning D

THE UNIVERSITY OF TEXAS AT AUSTIN
African Studies M
American Studies M,D
Anthropology M,D
Applied Arts and Design—
　General M
Archaeology M,D
Architectural History M
Architecture M
Art History M,D
Art/Fine Arts M
Asian Languages M,D
Asian Studies M
Child and Family Studies M,D
Child Development M,D
Classics M,D
Clinical Psychology D
Communication—General M,D
Comparative Literature M,D
Counseling Psychology M,D
Cultural Studies M,D
Dance M,D
Developmental Psychology M,D
East European and Russian Studies M
Economics M,D
English M,D
Family and Consumer
　Sciences-General M,D
Film, Television, and Video
　Production M,D
Folklore M,D
French M,D
Geography M,D
German M,D
Hispanic and Latin American
　Languages M,D
Hispanic Studies M
Historic Preservation M
History M,D
Human Development M,D
Interior Design M
Italian M,D
Journalism M
Landscape Architecture M
Latin American Studies M
Linguistics M,D
Media Studies M,D
Mineral Economics M
Music M
Near and Middle Eastern Languages M,D
Near and Middle Eastern Studies M,D
Philosophy D
Political Science M,D
Portuguese M
Psychology—General D
Public Administration M,D
Public Affairs M,D
Public History M,D
Public Policy M,D
Rehabilitation Counseling M,D
Romance Languages M,D
School Psychology M,D
Slavic Languages M,D
Sociology M,D
Spanish M,D
Sport Psychology M,D
Sustainable Development M,D
Theater M,D
Urban and Regional Planning M,D
Urban Design M
Writing M,D

THE UNIVERSITY OF TEXAS AT DALLAS
Art History M,D
Child and Family Studies M,D
Cognitive Sciences M,D
Communication—General M,D
Comparative Literature M,D
Criminal Justice and Criminology M,D
Economics M,D
Geographic Information Systems M,D
Geography M,D
History M,D
Humanities M,D
Interdisciplinary Studies M
Internet and Interactive
　Multimedia M,D
Latin American Studies M,D
Political Science M,D
Psychology—General M,D
Public Administration M,D
Public Policy M,D

THE UNIVERSITY OF TEXAS AT EL PASO
Anthropology M,O
Applied Psychology M,O
Art/Fine Arts M
Clinical Psychology M,D
Communication—General M
Economics M
English M,D,O
Experimental Psychology M,D
History M,D
Interdisciplinary Studies M
Liberal Studies M
Linguistics M,O
Music M
Philosophy M

- Political Science M
- Psychology—General M,D
- Rehabilitation Counseling M
- Rhetoric M,D,O
- Sociology M,O
- Spanish M,O
- Writing M,D,O

THE UNIVERSITY OF TEXAS AT SAN ANTONIO
- Anthropology M,D
- Applied Behavior Analysis M,O
- Architecture M
- Art History M
- Art/Fine Arts M
- Communication—General M
- Criminal Justice and Criminology M
- Cultural Studies M,D
- Demography and Population Studies D
- Economics M
- English M,D
- History M
- Interdisciplinary Studies M,D
- Music M
- Philosophy M
- Political Science M
- Psychology—General M,D
- Public Administration M
- School Psychology M,O
- Sociology M
- Spanish M
- Urban and Regional Planning M

THE UNIVERSITY OF TEXAS AT TYLER
- Art History M
- Art/Fine Arts M
- Clinical Psychology M
- Communication—General M
- Counseling Psychology M
- Criminal Justice and Criminology M
- English M
- History M
- Interdisciplinary Studies M
- Marriage and Family Therapy M
- Psychology—General M
- Public Administration M
- School Psychology M
- Social Sciences M
- Sociology M

THE UNIVERSITY OF TEXAS HEALTH SCIENCE CENTER AT HOUSTON
- Genetic Counseling M,D

THE UNIVERSITY OF TEXAS HEALTH SCIENCE CENTER AT SAN ANTONIO
- Interdisciplinary Studies D

THE UNIVERSITY OF TEXAS MEDICAL BRANCH
- Demography and Population Studies D
- Humanities M,D

THE UNIVERSITY OF TEXAS OF THE PERMIAN BASIN
- Clinical Psychology M
- Criminal Justice and Criminology M
- English M
- Experimental Psychology M
- History M
- Political Science M
- Psychology—General M
- Spanish M

THE UNIVERSITY OF TEXAS RIO GRANDE VALLEY
- Art/Fine Arts M
- Clinical Psychology M
- Communication—General M
- Criminal Justice and Criminology M
- Emergency Management M
- English M
- Experimental Psychology M
- History M
- Interdisciplinary Studies M
- Music M
- Psychology—General M
- Public Administration M
- Public Affairs M
- Public Policy M
- Rehabilitation Counseling M,D
- School Psychology M
- Sociology M
- Spanish M
- Sustainable Development M
- Translation and Interpretation M
- Writing M

THE UNIVERSITY OF TEXAS SOUTHWESTERN MEDICAL CENTER
- Clinical Psychology D
- Rehabilitation Counseling M

THE UNIVERSITY OF THE ARTS
- Art/Fine Arts M
- Dance M
- Industrial Design M
- Museum Studies M
- Music M
- Theater M,O

UNIVERSITY OF THE CUMBERLANDS
- Clinical Psychology D
- Counseling Psychology M
- Religion M
- Theater M,D,O

UNIVERSITY OF THE DISTRICT OF COLUMBIA
- Architecture M
- Counseling Psychology M
- Homeland Security M
- Public Administration M
- Rehabilitation Counseling M

UNIVERSITY OF THE FRASER VALLEY
- Criminal Justice and Criminology M

UNIVERSITY OF THE INCARNATE WORD
- Clothing and Textiles M
- Communication—General M,D
- Industrial and Organizational Psychology M,D
- Pastoral Ministry and Counseling M

UNIVERSITY OF THE PACIFIC
- Communication—General M
- International Affairs M,D
- Music M
- Psychology—General M
- Public Policy M,D
- School Psychology M,D,O
- Therapies—Dance, Drama, and Music M

UNIVERSITY OF THE SACRED HEART
- Broadcast Journalism M,O
- Communication—General M,O
- Conflict Resolution and Mediation/Peace Studies M
- Cultural Studies M
- Film, Television, and Video Production M,O
- Internet and Interactive Multimedia M,O
- Writing M,O

UNIVERSITY OF THE SCIENCES
- Health Psychology M
- Technical Writing M,O

THE UNIVERSITY OF THE SOUTH
- English M
- Theology M,D
- Writing M

UNIVERSITY OF THE SOUTHWEST
- Counseling Psychology M

UNIVERSITY OF THE VIRGIN ISLANDS
- Liberal Studies M
- School Psychology M,D,O
- Social Sciences M

UNIVERSITY OF THE WEST
- Psychology—General M
- Religion M,D
- Theology M

THE UNIVERSITY OF TOLEDO
- Clinical Psychology M,D
- Communication—General O
- Criminal Justice and Criminology M,O
- Economics M,D,O
- Emergency Management M,O
- English M,O
- Experimental Psychology M,D
- French M
- Gender Studies O
- Geographic Information Systems M,D,O
- Geography M,D,O
- German M
- Gerontology M,O
- History M,D
- Liberal Studies M
- Music M,O
- Philosophy M
- Political Science M,O
- Psychology—General M,D
- Public Administration M,O
- School Psychology M,D,O
- Sociology M
- Spanish M
- Urban and Regional Planning M,D,O
- Women's Studies O
- Writing M,O

UNIVERSITY OF TORONTO
- Anthropology M,D
- Architecture M
- Art History M,D
- Asian Studies M,D
- Classics M,D
- Comparative Literature M,D
- Criminal Justice and Criminology M,D
- East European and Russian Studies M
- Economics M,D
- English M,D
- Film, Television, and Video Theory and Criticism M,D
- French M,D
- Gender Studies M,D
- Genetic Counseling M,D
- Geography M,D
- German M,D
- History of Science and Technology M,D
- History M,D
- Industrial and Labor Relations M,D
- International Affairs M
- Italian M,D
- Landscape Architecture M
- Linguistics M,D
- Medieval and Renaissance Studies M,D
- Museum Studies M
- Music M,D
- Near and Middle Eastern Studies M,D
- Philosophy M,D
- Political Science M,D
- Portuguese M,D
- Psychology—General M,D
- Religion M,D
- Slavic Languages M,D
- Social Sciences M,D
- Sociology M,D
- Spanish M,D
- Theater M,D
- Urban and Regional Planning M,D
- Urban Design M,D
- Women's Studies M,D
- Writing M,D

THE UNIVERSITY OF TULSA
- American Indian/Native American Studies M,D,O
- Anthropology M,D
- Clinical Psychology M,D
- English M,D
- Industrial and Organizational Psychology M,D
- Museum Studies M
- Psychology—General M,D

UNIVERSITY OF UTAH
- American Studies M,D
- Anthropology M,D
- Applied Behavior Analysis M,D
- Architecture M
- Art History M
- Art/Fine Arts M
- Asian Studies M
- Child and Family Studies M
- Clinical Psychology M,D,O
- Communication—General M,D
- Comparative Literature M,D
- Counseling Psychology M,D,O
- Cultural Studies M,D
- Dance M,O
- Developmental Psychology D
- Economics M,D
- English M,D
- Film, Television, and Video Production M
- French M,D
- Geographic Information Systems M,D
- Geography M,D
- Gerontology M,O
- Graphic Design M
- History M,D
- Human Development M
- Humanities M
- International Affairs M,D
- Internet and Interactive Multimedia M,D
- Latin American Studies M
- Linguistics M,D
- Music M,D
- Near and Middle Eastern Languages M,D
- Near and Middle Eastern Studies M,D
- Philosophy M,D
- Photography M
- Political Science M,D
- Psychology—General D
- Public Administration M,D
- Rhetoric M,D
- School Psychology M,D,O
- Social Psychology D
- Sociology M,D
- Spanish M,D
- Urban and Regional Planning M,D
- Urban Design M,D
- Writing M,D

UNIVERSITY OF VALLEY FORGE
- Music M
- Religion M
- Theology M

UNIVERSITY OF VERMONT
- Agricultural Economics and Agribusiness M
- Applied Economics M
- Classics M,O
- Clinical Psychology M,D
- Counseling Psychology M
- Developmental Psychology D
- Economics M,D,O
- English M
- Experimental Psychology D
- German M
- Historic Preservation M
- History M
- Interdisciplinary Studies M
- Psychology—General D
- Public Administration M
- School Psychology M
- Social Psychology D
- Sustainable Development M

UNIVERSITY OF VICTORIA
- Anthropology M
- Art History M,D
- Art/Fine Arts M
- Asian Studies M
- Child and Family Studies M,D
- Classics M,D
- Clinical Psychology M,D
- Computer Art and Design M
- Conflict Resolution and Mediation/Peace Studies M,D
- Counseling Psychology M,D
- Developmental Psychology M,D
- Economics M,D
- English M,D
- Experimental Psychology M,D
- Film, Television, and Video Production M
- French M
- Geography M,D
- German M
- Hispanic Studies M
- History M,D
- Human Development M,D
- Italian M
- Linguistics M,D
- Music M,D
- Pacific Area/Pacific Rim Studies M
- Philosophy M
- Photography M
- Political Science M,D
- Psychology—General M,D
- Public Administration M,D
- Social Psychology M,D
- Sociology M,D
- Theater M
- Writing M

UNIVERSITY OF VIRGINIA
- Anthropology M,D
- Architectural History M,D
- Architecture M
- Art History M,D
- Asian Studies M
- Classics M,D
- Clinical Psychology D
- Economics M,D
- English M,D
- French M,D
- German M,D
- History M,D
- Interdisciplinary Studies M,D
- International Affairs M,D
- Landscape Architecture M
- Linguistics M
- Music M,D
- Near and Middle Eastern Studies M
- Philosophy M,D
- Political Science M,D
- Psychology—General M,D
- Public Policy M
- Religion M,D
- School Psychology M,D
- Slavic Languages M,D
- Sociology M,D
- Spanish M,D
- Theater M
- Urban and Regional Planning M
- Western European Studies M
- Writing M

UNIVERSITY OF WASHINGTON
- Anthropology M,D
- Applied Arts and Design—General M
- Architecture M,D,O
- Art History M,D
- Art/Fine Arts M
- Asian Languages M,D
- Asian Studies M,D
- Chinese M,D
- Classics M,D
- Clinical Psychology M,D
- Cognitive Sciences M,D
- Communication—General M,D
- Comparative Literature M,D
- Dance M
- Developmental Psychology M,D
- East European and Russian Studies M
- Economics D
- English M,D
- French M,D
- Geography M,D
- German M,D
- Hispanic and Latin American Languages M
- Historic Preservation O
- History M,D
- Human Development M,D
- Industrial Design M
- International Affairs M,D
- Italian M,D
- Japanese M,D
- Landscape Architecture M
- Lighting Design M,D,O
- Linguistics M,D
- Museum Studies M
- Music M,D
- Near and Middle Eastern Studies M,D
- Philosophy M,D
- Photography M
- Political Science M,D
- Portuguese M
- Psychology—General M,D
- Public Administration M,D
- Public Affairs M,D
- Public Policy M,D
- Religion M,D
- Russian M,D
- Scandinavian Languages M,D
- School Psychology M,D
- Slavic Languages M,D
- Social Psychology M,D
- Social Sciences M,D
- Sociology M,D
- Spanish M
- Sustainable Development M,D
- Theater M,D
- Urban and Regional Planning M,D
- Urban Design M,D,O
- Women's Studies D
- Writing M

UNIVERSITY OF WASHINGTON, BOTHELL
- Cultural Studies M
- Public Policy M
- Writing M

UNIVERSITY OF WASHINGTON, TACOMA
- Interdisciplinary Studies M

UNIVERSITY OF WATERLOO
- Anthropology M
- Architecture M
- Art/Fine Arts M
- Economics M,D
- English M,D
- French M,D
- Geography M,D
- German M,D
- History M,D
- International Affairs M,D
- Near and Middle Eastern Studies M

*M—masters degree; D—doctorate; O—other advanced degree; *—Close-Up and/or Display*

Philosophy M,D
Political Science M,D
Psychology—General M,D
Public Affairs M
Religion D
Russian M,D
Sociology M,D
Technical Writing M,D
Urban and Regional Planning M,D

THE UNIVERSITY OF WEST ALABAMA
Child Development M,O
Clinical Psychology M
Experimental Psychology M
History M
Marriage and Family Therapy M

THE UNIVERSITY OF WESTERN ONTARIO
Anthropology M,D
Classics M
Comparative Literature M,D
Counseling Psychology M
Economics M,D
English M,D
French M,D
Geography M,D
History M,D
Interdisciplinary Studies M
Journalism M
Media Studies M,D
Music M,D
Philosophy M,D
Political Science M,D
Psychology—General M,D
Sociology M,D
Spanish M,D
Sustainable Development M,D

UNIVERSITY OF WEST FLORIDA
American Studies M
Anthropology M
Applied Behavior Analysis M
Applied Psychology M
Archaeology M
Communication—General M
Counseling Psychology M
Criminal Justice and Criminology M
English M
Experimental Psychology M
Geographic Information Systems M
History M
Industrial and Organizational Psychology M
Political Science M
Psychology—General M
Public Administration M
Public History M
Writing M

UNIVERSITY OF WINDSOR
Applied Psychology M,D
Art/Fine Arts M
Clinical Psychology M,D
Communication—General M
Criminal Justice and Criminology M,D
Economics M
English M
History M
Philosophy M
Political Science M
Psychology—General M,D
Social Psychology M,D
Sociology M,D
Writing M

THE UNIVERSITY OF WINNIPEG
History M
Marriage and Family Therapy M,O
Public Administration M
Religion M
Theology M,O

UNIVERSITY OF WISCONSIN–EAU CLAIRE
English M
History M
Psychology—General M,O
School Psychology M,O
Writing M

UNIVERSITY OF WISCONSIN–LA CROSSE
Psychology—General M,O
School Psychology M

UNIVERSITY OF WISCONSIN–MADISON
African Studies M,D
African-American Studies M
Agricultural Economics and Agribusiness M,D
American Studies M,D
Anthropology D
Applied Arts and Design—General M,D
Applied Economics M,D
Archaeology D
Art History M,D
Art/Fine Arts M
Arts Administration M
Asian Languages M,D
Asian Studies M,D
Biological Anthropology D
Child and Family Studies M,D
Chinese M,D
Classics M,D
Clinical Psychology D
Cognitive Sciences D
Communication—General M,D
Comparative Literature M,D
Consumer Economics M,D
Counseling Psychology D
Cultural Anthropology D
Demography and Population Studies M,D
Developmental Psychology D
Economics D

English M,D
Family and Consumer Sciences-General M,D
Film, Television, and Video Theory and Criticism M,D
Folklore M,D
French M,D,O
Genetic Counseling M
Geographic Information Systems M,D,O
Geography M,D,O
German M,D
History of Medicine M,D
History of Science and Technology M,D
History M,D
Human Development M,D
Italian M,D
Japanese M,D
Jewish Studies M,D
Journalism M,D
Landscape Architecture M,D
Latin American Studies M,D
Linguistics M,D
Mass Communication M,D
Media Studies M,D
Music M,D
Near and Middle Eastern Languages M,D
Near and Middle Eastern Studies M,D
Philosophy M,D
Political Science D
Portuguese M,D
Psychology—General D
Public Affairs M
Rehabilitation Counseling M,D
Rhetoric M,D
Rural Sociology M,D
Scandinavian Languages M,D
Slavic Languages M,D
Social Psychology D
Sociology M,D
Spanish M,D
Speech and Interpersonal Communication M,D
Sustainable Development M,D
Theater M,D
Urban and Regional Planning M,D
Women's Studies M,D
Writing M,D

UNIVERSITY OF WISCONSIN–MILWAUKEE
African Studies D
Anthropology M,D,O
Applied Arts and Design—General M
Architecture M,D,O
Art History M
Art/Fine Arts M,O
Classics M,O
Communication—General M,D,O
Comparative Literature M,O
Computer Art and Design M,O
Conflict Resolution and Mediation/Peace Studies M,D,O
Counseling Psychology M,D,O
Criminal Justice and Criminology M,O
Dance M,O
Developmental Psychology M,D
Economics M,D
English M,D
Film, Television, and Video Production M,D
Film, Television, and Video Theory and Criticism M,O
French M,O
Gender Studies M,O
Geographic Information Systems M,D,O
Geography M,D
German M,O
Gerontology M,D,O
History M,O
Industrial and Labor Relations M,O
Latin American Studies M,O
Liberal Studies M
Linguistics M,D,O
Media Studies M,D,O
Museum Studies M,D,O
Music M,D
Philosophy M
Political Science M,D
Portuguese M,O
Psychology—General M,D
Public Administration M
Rhetoric M,D,O
School Psychology M,D,O
Sociology M,D
Spanish M,O
Translation and Interpretation M,O
Urban and Regional Planning M
Urban Studies M,D
Women's Studies M,O
Writing M,D

UNIVERSITY OF WISCONSIN–OSHKOSH
English M
Experimental Psychology M
Industrial and Organizational Psychology M
Psychology—General M
Public Administration M

UNIVERSITY OF WISCONSIN–PARKSIDE
Clinical Psychology M

UNIVERSITY OF WISCONSIN–PLATTEVILLE
Criminal Justice and Criminology M

UNIVERSITY OF WISCONSIN–RIVER FALLS
Art/Fine Arts M
School Psychology M,O

UNIVERSITY OF WISCONSIN–STEVENS POINT
Communication—General M

Corporate and Organizational Communication M
Family and Consumer Sciences-General O
Media Studies M
Speech and Interpersonal Communication M
Sustainable Development D

UNIVERSITY OF WISCONSIN–STOUT
Applied Psychology M
Art/Fine Arts M
Clinical Psychology M
Counseling Psychology M
Marriage and Family Therapy M
Rehabilitation Counseling M
School Psychology M,O
Technical Communication M

UNIVERSITY OF WISCONSIN–SUPERIOR
Art History M
Art Therapy M
Art/Fine Arts M
Communication—General M
Mass Communication M
School Psychology M
Social Psychology M
Speech and Interpersonal Communication M
Theater M

UNIVERSITY OF WISCONSIN–WHITEWATER
Communication—General M
Corporate and Organizational Communication M
Mass Communication M
Psychology—General M,O
School Psychology M,O

UNIVERSITY OF WYOMING
Agricultural Economics and Agribusiness M
American Studies M
Anthropology M,D
Applied Economics M
Child Development M
Communication—General M
Consumer Economics M
Economics M,D
English M
French M
Geography M
German M
History M
International Affairs M
Music M
Philosophy M
Political Science M
Psychology—General M,D
Public Administration M
Rural Planning and Studies M
Sociology M
Spanish M
Writing M

UNIVERSITÉ LAVAL
Agricultural Economics and Agribusiness M,D
Anthropology M,D
Archaeology M,D
Architecture M
Art History M,D
Art/Fine Arts M
Clinical Psychology D
Comparative Literature M,D
Consumer Economics O
Economics M,D
English M,D
Ethics O
Ethnic Studies M,D
Film, Television, and Video Theory and Criticism M,D
Geographic Information Systems M,O
Geography M,D
Gerontology M
Graphic Design M
History M,D
Industrial and Labor Relations M,D
International Affairs M
Journalism O
Linguistics M,D
Mass Communication M,D
Museum Studies O
Music M,D
Philosophy M,D
Political Science M,D
Psychology—General D
Religion M,D
Rural Planning and Studies O
Social Psychology D
Sociology M,D
Spanish M,D
Theater M,D
Theology M,D
Translation and Interpretation M,O
Urban and Regional Planning M,D
Women's Studies O

UPPER IOWA UNIVERSITY
Emergency Management M
Homeland Security M
Public Administration M

URBANA UNIVERSITY–A BRANCH CAMPUS OF FRANKLIN UNIVERSITY
Criminal Justice and Criminology M

URSHAN GRADUATE SCHOOL OF THEOLOGY
Theology M

URSULINE COLLEGE
Art Therapy M
Historic Preservation M
Pastoral Ministry and Counseling M

Theology M

UTAH STATE UNIVERSITY
Agricultural Economics and Agribusiness M,D
American Studies M
Anthropology M
Applied Economics M,D
Art/Fine Arts M
Child and Family Studies M,D
Clinical Psychology M,D
Communication—General M
Consumer Economics M
Counseling Psychology M,D
Disability Studies M,D,O
Economics M
English M
Family and Consumer Sciences-General M,D
Folklore M
Geography M
History M
Human Development M
Landscape Architecture M
Marriage and Family Therapy M,D
Music M
Political Science M
Psychology—General M,D
Rehabilitation Counseling M
School Psychology M,D
Sociology M,D
Theater M
Urban and Regional Planning M,D
Writing M

UTICA COLLEGE
Criminal Justice and Criminology M

VALDOSTA STATE UNIVERSITY
English M
Industrial and Organizational Psychology M,O
Marriage and Family Therapy M,O
Psychology—General M,O
Public Administration M,D

VALPARAISO UNIVERSITY
Arts Administration M
Clinical Psychology M
Communication—General M
English M
Ethics M,O
International Economics M
International Trade Policy M
Media Studies M,O
School Psychology M,O

VANCOUVER SCHOOL OF THEOLOGY
Religion M,O
Theology M,O

VANDERBILT UNIVERSITY
Anthropology M,D
Child and Family Studies M,D
Economic Development M,D
Economics M,D
English M,D
French M,D
German M,D
History M,D
Human Development M
Latin American Studies M
Liberal Studies M
Philosophy M,D
Political Science M,D
Portuguese M,D
Psychology—General D
Public Policy D
Religion M,D
Sociology M,D
Spanish M,D
Theology M,D
Urban and Regional Planning M
Writing M

VANGUARD UNIVERSITY OF SOUTHERN CALIFORNIA
Clinical Psychology M
Industrial and Organizational Psychology M
Religion M
Theology M

VERMONT COLLEGE OF FINE ARTS
Art/Fine Arts M
Film, Television, and Video Production M
Graphic Design M
Music M
Publishing M
Translation and Interpretation M
Writing M

VICTORIA UNIVERSITY
Theology M,D,O

VILLANOVA UNIVERSITY
Classics M
Communication—General M
English M
Hispanic Studies M
History M
Liberal Studies M
Missions and Missiology M
Philosophy D
Political Science M
Psychology—General M
Public Administration M
Theater M
Theology M,D

VIRGINIA BAPTIST COLLEGE
Theology M

VIRGINIA BEACH THEOLOGICAL SEMINARY
Pastoral Ministry and Counseling M
Theology M

VIRGINIA COMMONWEALTH UNIVERSITY
Art History M,D
Art/Fine Arts M,D
Clinical Psychology D
Communication—General D
Counseling Psychology M,D
Criminal Justice and Criminology M,O
Economics M
Emergency Management M,O
English M
Film, Television, and Video Production M,D
Forensic Sciences M
Geographic Information Systems O
Gerontology M,D
Health Psychology D
History M
Homeland Security M,O
Interdisciplinary Studies M
Interior Design M,D
Journalism M
Mass Communication M
Media Studies M,D
Museum Studies M,D
Music M
Photography M,D
Political Science M,D,O
Public Administration M
Public Affairs M,D,O
Public Policy D
Rehabilitation Counseling M
Sociology M
Theater M
Urban and Regional Planning M
Writing M

VIRGINIA INTERNATIONAL UNIVERSITY
Computer Art and Design M,O
International Affairs M
Linguistics M
Public Administration M

VIRGINIA POLYTECHNIC INSTITUTE AND STATE UNIVERSITY
Agricultural Economics and Agribusiness M,D
Applied Economics M,D
Communication—General M,D,O
Economics M,D
English M,D,O
Environmental Design M,D
Geography M,D
Humanities M,D,O
Interdisciplinary Studies M,D
International Affairs M,D
Internet and Interactive Multimedia M,D
Landscape Architecture M,D
Liberal Studies M,O
National Security M,O
Political Science M,O
Psychology—General M,D
Public Administration M,D
Public Affairs M,D
Public Policy M,D
Urban and Regional Planning M,D
Urban Studies M,D
Writing M,D,O

VIRGINIA STATE UNIVERSITY
Clinical Psychology M,D
Criminal Justice and Criminology M
Economics M
Health Psychology M,D
Interdisciplinary Studies M
Media Studies M
Psychology—General M,D

VIRGINIA THEOLOGICAL SEMINARY
Theology M,D

VIRGINIA UNION UNIVERSITY
Theology M,D

VIRGINIA UNIVERSITY OF LYNCHBURG
Pastoral Ministry and Counseling M,D
Religion M,D

VITERBO UNIVERSITY
Addictions/Substance Abuse Counseling M
Counseling Psychology M
Developmental Psychology M
Ethics M,O
Health Psychology M
Pastoral Ministry and Counseling M,O

WAGNER COLLEGE
Media Studies M

WAKE FOREST UNIVERSITY
Communication—General M
English M
Liberal Studies M
Psychology—General M
Religion M
Speech and Interpersonal Communication M

WALDEN UNIVERSITY
Addictions/Substance Abuse Counseling M,D
Applied Psychology M,D,O
Child and Family Studies M,D
Clinical Psychology M,D,O
Communication—General M,D,O
Conflict Resolution and Mediation/Peace Studies M,D,O
Counseling Psychology M,D,O
Criminal Justice and Criminology M,D,O
Emergency Management M,D,O
Forensic Psychology M,D,O
Gerontology M,D
Health Psychology M,D,O
Homeland Security M,D,O
Industrial and Organizational Psychology M,D,O
Interdisciplinary Studies M,D,O
International Affairs M,D,O
International Development M,D,O
Marriage and Family Therapy M,D
Political Science M,D,O
Psychology—General M,D,O
Public Administration M,D,O
Public Policy M,D,O
Social Psychology M,D,O
Sustainable Development M,D,O

WALDORF UNIVERSITY
Criminal Justice and Criminology M
Emergency Management M
Public Administration M

WALLA WALLA UNIVERSITY
Communication—General M
Film, Television, and Video Theory and Criticism M
Internet and Interactive Multimedia M
Pastoral Ministry and Counseling M
Religion M

WALSH UNIVERSITY
Counseling Psychology M
Pastoral Ministry and Counseling M
Theology M

WARREN WILSON COLLEGE
Art/Fine Arts M
Writing M

WARTBURG THEOLOGICAL SEMINARY
Theology M

WASHBURN UNIVERSITY
Addictions/Substance Abuse Counseling M
Clinical Psychology M
Criminal Justice and Criminology M
Liberal Studies M
Psychology—General M

WASHINGTON ADVENTIST UNIVERSITY
Counseling Psychology M
Public Administration M
Religion M

WASHINGTON & JEFFERSON COLLEGE
Applied Economics M,O
Thanatology M,O
Writing M,O

WASHINGTON STATE UNIVERSITY
Agricultural Economics and Agribusiness M,D,O
American Studies M,D
Anthropology M,D
Archaeology M,D
Architecture M
Art/Fine Arts M
Clinical Psychology M,D
Clothing and Textiles M
Communication—General M,D
Corporate and Organizational Communication M,D
Counseling Psychology M,D
Criminal Justice and Criminology M,D
Cultural Anthropology M,D
Cultural Studies M,D
Economics M,D,O
English M,D
Experimental Psychology M,D
History M,D
Human Development D
Interdisciplinary Studies D
Interior Design M
Landscape Architecture M
Music M
Political Science M,D,O
Psychology—General M,D
Public Affairs M,D,O
Sociology M,D

WASHINGTON UNIVERSITY IN ST. LOUIS
Anthropology D
Archaeology M,D
Architecture M
Art History M,D
Art/Fine Arts M
Asian Languages M,D
Asian Studies M,D
Child and Family Studies M,D
Chinese M,D
Classics M,D
Comparative Literature M,D
Dance M
Developmental Psychology D
Economics D
English M,D
French D
German D
Gerontology M,D
History D
Japanese M,D
Jewish Studies M
Landscape Architecture M
Music M,D
Near and Middle Eastern Studies M
Philosophy D
Political Science D
Psychology—General D
Religion M
Romance Languages D
Spanish D
Speech and Interpersonal Communication M,D

Theater M
Urban Design M
Writing M

WATKINS COLLEGE OF ART, DESIGN, & FILM
Film, Television, and Video Production M

WAYLAND BAPTIST UNIVERSITY
Counseling Psychology M
Criminal Justice and Criminology M
History M
Homeland Security M
Humanities M
Pastoral Ministry and Counseling M
Religion M
Theology M

WAYNESBURG UNIVERSITY
Addictions/Substance Abuse Counseling M,D
Clinical Psychology M,D
Counseling Psychology M,D
Criminal Justice and Criminology M,D

WAYNE STATE COLLEGE
Communication—General M

WAYNE STATE UNIVERSITY
African-American Studies M,D,O
Anthropology M,D
Applied Behavior Analysis M,D,O
Art History M
Art/Fine Arts M
Clinical Psychology M,D
Clothing and Textiles M
Cognitive Sciences M,D
Communication—General M,D,O
Conflict Resolution and Mediation/Peace Studies M,D,O
Counseling Psychology M,D,O
Criminal Justice and Criminology M
Cultural Studies M,D
Economic Development M,D,O
Economics M,D
English M,D
Film, Television, and Video Theory and Criticism M,D
French M,D
Gender Studies M,D,O
German M,D
Gerontology M,D,O
Graphic Design M
Health Communication M,D,O
History M,D,O
Industrial and Labor Relations M,D
Industrial and Organizational Psychology M,D
Industrial Design M
Interior Design M
International Economics M,D
Italian M,D
Journalism M,D,O
Linguistics M,D
Media Studies M,D,O
Museum Studies M,D,O
Music M,O
Near and Middle Eastern Languages M,D
Near and Middle Eastern Studies M,D
Philosophy M,D
Photography M
Political Science M,D
Psychology—General M,D
Public Administration M,D
Public History M,D,O
Public Policy M,D,O
Rehabilitation Counseling M,D,O
Rhetoric M,D
Romance Languages M,D
School Psychology M,D,O
Social Psychology M,D,O
Sociology M,D
Spanish M,D
Textile Design M
Theater M
Urban and Regional Planning M,O
Urban Studies M,D,O
Women's Studies M,D,O
Writing M,D

WEBBER INTERNATIONAL UNIVERSITY
Criminal Justice and Criminology M

WEBER STATE UNIVERSITY
Communication—General M
English M

WEBSTER UNIVERSITY
Art History M
Art/Fine Arts M
Communication—General M,O
Corporate and Organizational Communication M
Counseling Psychology M
Criminal Justice and Criminology M,D,O
Forensic Sciences M
Gerontology M
International Affairs M
Internet and Interactive Multimedia M
Media Studies M
Music M
Psychology—General M
Public Administration M,D,O

WELCH COLLEGE
Pastoral Ministry and Counseling M
Theology M

WENTWORTH INSTITUTE OF TECHNOLOGY
Architecture M

WESLEYAN UNIVERSITY
Liberal Studies M,O
Music M,D
Writing M,O

WESLEY BIBLICAL SEMINARY
Linguistics M
Missions and Missiology M
Pastoral Ministry and Counseling M
Religion M
Theology M
Translation and Interpretation M

WESLEY THEOLOGICAL SEMINARY
Theology M,D

WESTERN CAROLINA UNIVERSITY
Applied Arts and Design—General M
Art/Fine Arts M
English M,O
History M
Psychology—General M
Public Affairs M
Rhetoric M,O
Technical Writing M,O
Writing M,O

WESTERN COLORADO UNIVERSITY
Film, Television, and Video Production M
Writing M

WESTERN CONNECTICUT STATE UNIVERSITY
Art/Fine Arts M
Clinical Psychology M
English M
History M
Illustration M
Writing M

WESTERN ILLINOIS UNIVERSITY
Clinical Psychology M,O
Communication—General M
Criminal Justice and Criminology M,O
Economic Development M,O
Economics M
English M,O
Experimental Psychology M,O
Geographic Information Systems M,O
Geography M,O
History M
Liberal Studies M
Museum Studies M,O
Music M
Political Science M
Psychology—General M,O
School Psychology M,O
Social Psychology M,O
Sociology M
Theater M

WESTERN KENTUCKY UNIVERSITY
Anthropology M
Applied Economics M
Clinical Psychology M,O
Communication—General M,O
Comparative Literature M
Corporate and Organizational Communication M,O
Counseling Psychology M
Criminal Justice and Criminology M
English M
Experimental Psychology M,O
French M
German M
History M
Homeland Security M
Industrial and Organizational Psychology M,O
Interdisciplinary Studies M,O
Marriage and Family Therapy M
Political Science M
Psychology—General M,O
Public Administration M
School Psychology M,O
Sociology M
Spanish M
Writing M

WESTERN MICHIGAN UNIVERSITY
Anthropology M
Applied Arts and Design—General M
Applied Economics M,D
Clinical Psychology M,D
Communication—General M
Counseling Psychology M,D
Economics M,D
English M,D
Family and Consumer Sciences-General M
Geographic Information Systems M,O
Geography M,D,O
History M,D
Industrial and Organizational Psychology M,D
International Affairs M,D
Music M,O
Philosophy M
Political Science M,D
Psychology—General M,D
Public Administration M,D,O
Public Affairs M,D,O
Religion M,O
Sociology M,D
Spanish M,D
Therapies—Dance, Drama, and Music M,O
Writing M,D

*M—masters degree; D—doctorate; O—other advanced degree; *—Close-Up and/or Display*

WESTERN MICHIGAN UNIVERSITY COOLEY LAW SCHOOL
Homeland Security — M,D
National Security — M,D

WESTERN NEW ENGLAND UNIVERSITY
Applied Behavior Analysis — M,D
Communication—General — M
Writing — M

WESTERN NEW MEXICO UNIVERSITY
Interdisciplinary Studies — M

WESTERN OREGON UNIVERSITY
Criminal Justice and Criminology — M
Music — M
Rehabilitation Counseling — M

WESTERN SEMINARY - PORTLAND
Pastoral Ministry and Counseling — M,D,O
Religion — M,O
Theology — M,O
Women's Studies — M

WESTERN SEMINARY–SACRAMENTO CAMPUS
Marriage and Family Therapy — M
Pastoral Ministry and Counseling — M
Theology — M,O
Women's Studies — O

WESTERN SEMINARY - SAN JOSE CAMPUS
Marriage and Family Therapy — M,O
Pastoral Ministry and Counseling — M,O
Theology — M,O
Women's Studies — M,O

WESTERN THEOLOGICAL SEMINARY
Pastoral Ministry and Counseling — M,D,O
Theology — M,D,O

WESTERN WASHINGTON UNIVERSITY
Anthropology — M
Counseling Psychology — M
English — M
Experimental Psychology — M
Geography — M
History — M
Music — M
Political Science — M
Psychology—General — M
Rehabilitation Counseling — M

WESTFIELD STATE UNIVERSITY
Applied Behavior Analysis — M
Counseling Psychology — M
Criminal Justice and Criminology — M
English — M
Forensic Psychology — M
Psychology—General — M
Public Administration — M

WESTMINSTER COLLEGE (UT)
Counseling Psychology — M

WESTMINSTER SEMINARY CALIFORNIA
Religion — M
Theology — M

WESTMINSTER THEOLOGICAL SEMINARY
Missions and Missiology — M,D,O
Pastoral Ministry and Counseling — M,D,O
Religion — M,D,O
Theology — M,D,O

WEST TEXAS A&M UNIVERSITY
Agricultural Economics and Agribusiness — M
Art/Fine Arts — M
Communication—General — M
Criminal Justice and Criminology — M
Economics — M
English — M
History — M
Interdisciplinary Studies — M
Music — M
Psychology—General — M

WEST VIRGINIA STATE UNIVERSITY
Criminal Justice and Criminology — M
Media Studies — M

WEST VIRGINIA UNIVERSITY
Art History — M,D
Art/Fine Arts — M,D
Clinical Psychology — M,D
Communication—General — M
Corporate and Organizational Communication — M,O
Counseling Psychology — M,D
Economics — M,D,O
English — M,D
Forensic Sciences — M,D
Geography — M,D
Graphic Design — M,D
History — M,D
Industrial and Labor Relations — M,D,O
Journalism — M,D
Landscape Architecture — M,D
Media Studies — M,O
Music — M,D
Photography — M,D
Political Science — M,D
Psychology—General — M,D
Public Administration — M,D
Rehabilitation Counseling — M,D
Sociology — M,D
Sport Psychology — M,D

Theater — M,D
Writing — M,D

WEST VIRGINIA WESLEYAN COLLEGE
Writing — M

WHEATON COLLEGE
Archaeology — M,D
Clinical Psychology — M,D
Counseling Psychology — M,D
Emergency Management — M
Marriage and Family Therapy — M
Missions and Missiology — M
Psychology—General — M,D
Theology — M,D

WHITTIER COLLEGE
Child Development — M

WHITWORTH UNIVERSITY
Missions and Missiology — M
Pastoral Ministry and Counseling — M
Theology — M

WICHITA STATE UNIVERSITY
Anthropology — M
Art/Fine Arts — M
Clinical Psychology — D
Communication—General — M
Criminal Justice and Criminology — M
Economics — M
English — M
Gerontology — M
History — M
International Economics — M
Liberal Studies — M
Music — M
Photography — M
Psychology—General — D
Public Administration — M
School Psychology — M,D,O
Social Psychology — D
Sociology — M
Spanish — M
Writing — M

WIDENER UNIVERSITY
Clinical Psychology — D
Criminal Justice and Criminology — M
Psychology—General
Public Administration — M

WILBERFORCE UNIVERSITY
Rehabilitation Counseling — M

WILFRID LAURIER UNIVERSITY
American Studies — M,D
Canadian Studies — M,D
Cognitive Sciences — M,D
Communication—General — M
Conflict Resolution and Mediation/Peace Studies — D
Criminal Justice and Criminology — M
Cultural Studies — M
Developmental Psychology — M,D
Economics — M,D
English — M,D
Film, Television, and Video Theory and Criticism — M,D
Gender Studies — M
Geography — M,D
History — M,D
International Affairs — M,D
International Economics — M
Media Studies — M
Pastoral Ministry and Counseling — M,D,O
Philosophy — M
Political Science — M,D
Psychology—General — M,D
Public Policy — M
Religion — M,D
Social Psychology — M,D
Social Sciences — M
Sociology — M
Theology — M,D,O
Therapies—Dance, Drama, and Music — M

WILLAMETTE UNIVERSITY
Conflict Resolution and Mediation/Peace Studies — M,D

WILLIAM & MARY
Marriage and Family Therapy — M,D
School Psychology — M,O

WILLIAM CAREY UNIVERSITY
Counseling Psychology — M
Psychology—General — M

WILLIAM JAMES COLLEGE
Applied Psychology — M,D,O
Clinical Psychology — M,D,O
Counseling Psychology — M,D,O
Forensic Psychology — M,D,O
Industrial and Organizational Psychology — M,D,O
Psychology—General — M,D,O
School Psychology — M,D,O

WILLIAMS COLLEGE
Art History — M
Economic Development — M

WILMINGTON UNIVERSITY
Clinical Psychology — M
Counseling Psychology — M
Criminal Justice and Criminology — M
Homeland Security — M,D
Internet and Interactive Multimedia — M

Public Administration — M,D

WILSON COLLEGE
Art/Fine Arts — M
Cultural Studies — M
Dance — M
English — M
Humanities — M
Women's Studies — M

WINEBRENNER THEOLOGICAL SEMINARY
Counseling Psychology — M,D
Theology — M,D

WINONA STATE UNIVERSITY
Addictions/Substance Abuse Counseling — M,O
Clinical Psychology — M,O
English — M

WINSTON-SALEM STATE UNIVERSITY
Rehabilitation Counseling — M

WINTHROP UNIVERSITY
Art/Fine Arts — M
Arts Administration — M
English — M
History — M
Liberal Studies — M
Music — M
Psychology—General — M,D

WISCONSIN SCHOOL OF PROFESSIONAL PSYCHOLOGY
Clinical Psychology — M,D
Psychology—General — M,D

WON INSTITUTE OF GRADUATE STUDIES
Religion — M

WOODBURY UNIVERSITY
Architecture — M

WORCESTER POLYTECHNIC INSTITUTE
Interdisciplinary Studies — M,D,O
Internet and Interactive Multimedia — M
Social Sciences — M,D,O

WORCESTER STATE UNIVERSITY
History — M
School Psychology — M,O
Spanish — M

WORLD MISSION UNIVERSITY
Music — M,D
Pastoral Ministry and Counseling — M,D
Theology — M,D

WRIGHT GRADUATE UNIVERSITY FOR THE REALIZATION OF HUMAN POTENTIAL
Human Development — M,D,O

THE WRIGHT INSTITUTE
Clinical Psychology — D
Counseling Psychology — M
Psychology—General — D

WRIGHT STATE UNIVERSITY
Applied Behavior Analysis — M
Applied Economics — M
Clinical Psychology — D
Criminal Justice and Criminology — M
Economics — M
English — M
History — M
Humanities — M
Industrial and Organizational Psychology — M,D
Psychology—General — M,D
Public Administration — M
Rehabilitation Counseling — M

WYCLIFFE COLLEGE
Religion — M,D,O
Theology — M,D,O

XAVIER UNIVERSITY
Clinical Psychology — M,D
Counseling Psychology — M
Criminal Justice and Criminology — M
English — M
Ethics — M
Industrial and Organizational Psychology — M,D
Pastoral Ministry and Counseling — M
Psychology—General — M,D
Sustainable Development — M
Theology — M

XAVIER UNIVERSITY OF LOUISIANA
Pastoral Ministry and Counseling — M
Theology — M

YALE UNIVERSITY
African Studies — M
African-American Studies — D
American Studies — M
Anthropology — M,D
Applied Arts and Design— General — M
Archaeology — M
Architecture — M,D
Art History — D
Art/Fine Arts — M
Asian Languages — D
Asian Studies — M
Classics — M,D
Clinical Psychology — D

Cognitive Sciences — D
Comparative Literature — D
Developmental Psychology — D
East European and Russian Studies — M,D
Economic Development — M
Economics — M,D
English — M,D
Environmental Design — M,D
Film, Television, and Video Theory and Criticism — D
French — M,D
German — D
Graphic Design — M
History of Medicine — M,D
History of Science and Technology — M,D
History — M,D
International Affairs — M
International Economics — M
Italian — D
Latin American Studies — D
Linguistics — D
Medieval and Renaissance Studies — M,D
Music — M,D,O
Near and Middle Eastern Languages — M,D
Near and Middle Eastern Studies — M,D
Philosophy — D
Photography — M
Political Science — D
Portuguese — D
Psychology—General — D
Religion — D
Russian — D
Slavic Languages — D
Social Psychology — D
Social Sciences — M,D
Sociology — D
Spanish — D
Theater — M,D,O
Theology — M
Writing — M,D,O

YESHIVA BETH MOSHE
Theology — O

YESHIVA DERECH CHAIM
Religion — D

YESHIVA KARLIN STOLIN
Theology — O

YESHIVA OF NITRA RABBINICAL COLLEGE
Theology — O

YESHIVA SHAAR HATORAH TALMUDIC RESEARCH INSTITUTE
Theology

YESHIVATH ZICHRON MOSHE
Theology — O

YESHIVA UNIVERSITY
Clinical Psychology — D
Conflict Resolution and Mediation/Peace Studies — M,D
Counseling Psychology — M
Economics — M
Health Psychology — D
Jewish Studies — M,D
Psychology—General — M,D
School Psychology — D

YORK UNIVERSITY
Anthropology — M,D
Applied Arts and Design— General — M
Art History — M,D
Art/Fine Arts — M,D
Communication—General — M,D
Dance — M,D
Disability Studies — M,D
Economics — M,D
Emergency Management — M
English — M,D
Film, Television, and Video Production — M,D
French — M,D
Gender Studies — M,D
Geography — M,D
History — M,D
Humanities — M,D
Interdisciplinary Studies — M
International Affairs — M
Linguistics — M,D
Music — M,D
Philosophy — M,D
Political Science — M,D
Psychology—General — M,D
Public Administration — M,D
Public Affairs — M
Public Policy — M
Sociology — M,D
Theater — M
Translation and Interpretation — M
Women's Studies — M,D

YOUNGSTOWN STATE UNIVERSITY
American Studies — M
Criminal Justice and Criminology — M
Economics — M
English — M
Gerontology — M
History — M
Music — M
School Psychology — M,D,O

ACADEMIC AND PROFESSIONAL PROGRAMS IN THE ARTS AND ARCHITECTURE

Section 1
Applied Arts and Design

This section contains a directory of institutions offering graduate work in applied arts and design, followed by in-depth entries submitted by institutions that chose to prepare detailed program descriptions. Additional information about programs listed in the directory but not augmented by an in-depth entry may be obtained by writing directly to the dean of a graduate school or chair of a department at the address given in the directory.

For programs offering related work, see also in this book *Architecture* and *Art and Art History*. In another guide in this series:

Graduate Programs in Business, Education, Information Studies, Law & Social Work

See *Advertising and Public Relations*

CONTENTS
Program Directories

Applied Arts and Design—General

Academy of Art University, Graduate Programs, School of Advertising, San Francisco, CA 94105-3410. Offers advertising (MFA); advertising and branded media technology (MA). *Program availability:* Part-time, 100% online. *Faculty:* 4 full-time (1 woman), 15 part-time/adjunct (7 women). *Students:* 51 full-time (35 women), 23 part-time (13 women); includes 16 minority (5 Black or African American, non-Hispanic/Latino; 4 Asian, non-Hispanic/Latino; 6 Hispanic/Latino; 1 Two or more races, non-Hispanic/Latino), 41 international. Average age 29. 25 applicants, 100% accepted, 18 enrolled. In 2019, 35 master's awarded. *Degree requirements:* For master's, final review. *Entrance requirements:* For master's, statement of intent; resume; portfolio/reel; official college transcripts. *Application deadline:* Applications are processed on a rolling basis. Application fee: $50. Electronic applications accepted. *Expenses: Tuition:* Full-time $1083; part-time $1083 per credit hour. *Required fees:* $860; $860 per unit. $430 per term. One-time fee: $145. Tuition and fees vary according to program. *Financial support:* Career-related internships or fieldwork, Federal Work-Study, and scholarships/grants available. Financial award application deadline: 8/10; financial award applicants required to submit FAFSA. *Application contact:* 800-544-ARTS, E-mail: info@academyart.edu.
Website: https://www.academyart.edu/academics/advertising

Alfred University, Graduate School, College of Ceramics, School of Art and Design, Alfred, NY 14802-1205. Offers ceramic art (MFA); electronic integrated arts (MFA); painting (MFA); sculpture/dimensional studies (MFA). *Accreditation:* NASAD. *Faculty:* 29 full-time (15 women), 4 part-time/adjunct (0 women). *Students:* 43 full-time (27 women); includes 4 minority (1 Asian, non-Hispanic/Latino; 2 Hispanic/Latino; 1 Two or more races, non-Hispanic/Latino), 12 international. Average age 29. 170 applicants, 24% accepted, 20 enrolled. In 2019, 18 master's awarded. *Degree requirements:* For master's, thesis or alternative, exhibit. *Entrance requirements:* For master's, portfolio. Additional exam requirements/recommendations for international students: required—TOEFL (minimum score 550 paper-based; 80 iBT), IELTS (minimum score 6). *Application deadline:* For fall admission, 1/15 for domestic and international students. Applications are processed on a rolling basis. Application fee: $60. Electronic applications accepted. Application fee is waived when completed online. *Expenses:* $23,530 per year. *Financial support:* In 2019–20, 40 students received support. Teaching assistantships with full tuition reimbursements available and tuition waivers (full) available. Financial award application deadline: 3/15; financial award applicants required to submit FAFSA. *Unit head:* Gerar Edizel, Interim Dean, 607-871-2412, E-mail: fedizel@alfred.edu. *Application contact:* Lindsey Gertin, Assistant Director of Graduate Admissions, 607-871-2017, Fax: 607-871-2198, E-mail: gradinquiry@alfred.edu.
Website: http://art.alfred.edu/graduate/

Arizona State University at Tempe, Herberger Institute for Design and the Arts, The Design School, Tempe, AZ 85287-1605. Offers architecture (M Arch); building design/built environment (MS); design (MSD), including arts, media, and engineering, healthcare and healing environments (MSD, PhD), industrial design, interaction design, interior design, new product innovation, visual communication design; design, environment and the arts (PhD), including design, digital culture, healthcare and healing environments (MSD, PhD), history, theory, and criticism; landscape architecture (MLA); urban design (MUD); MA/MBA. *Accreditation:* ASLA; NASAD. Terminal master's awarded for partial completion of doctoral program. *Degree requirements:* For master's, thesis optional, interactive Program of Study (iPOS) submitted before completing 50 percent of required credit hours; for doctorate, comprehensive exam, thesis/dissertation, interactive Program of Study (iPOS) submitted before completing 50 percent of required credit hours. *Entrance requirements:* For master's, GRE General Test, minimum GPA of 3.0 or equivalent in last 2 years of work leading to bachelor's degree, design/creative works portfolio, 3 references, statement of intent; for doctorate, GRE, master's degree in architecture, graphic design, industrial design, interior design, landscape architecture, or art history or equivalent standing; statement of purpose; 3 letters of recommendation; indication of potential faculty mentor; sample of written work. Additional exam requirements/recommendations for international students: required—TOEFL (minimum score 600 paper-based; 100 iBT). Electronic applications accepted.

The Art Institute of Dallas, a branch of Miami International University of Art & Design, Program in Design and Media Management, Dallas, TX 75231-5993. Offers MA.

Bowling Green State University, Graduate College, College of Arts and Sciences, School of Art, Bowling Green, OH 43403. Offers 2-D studio art (MA, MFA); 3-D studio art (MA, MFA); art education (MA); art history (MA); computer art (MA); design (MFA); digital arts (MFA); graphics (MFA). *Accreditation:* NASAD. *Program availability:* Part-time. *Degree requirements:* For master's, thesis or alternative, final exhibit (MFA). *Entrance requirements:* For master's, GRE General Test (for MA), slide portfolio (15-20 slides). Additional exam requirements/recommendations for international students: required—TOEFL. Electronic applications accepted.

California College of the Arts, Graduate Programs, Design Program, San Francisco, CA 94107. Offers graphic design (MFA); industrial design (MFA); interaction design (MFA). *Accreditation:* NASAD. *Degree requirements:* For master's, thesis, exhibit. *Entrance requirements:* For master's, appropriate bachelor's degree, portfolio, resume, letters of recommendation, transcripts. Additional exam requirements/recommendations for international students: required—TOEFL, IELTS, or PTE. Electronic applications accepted. *Expenses:* Contact institution.

California College of the Arts, Graduate Programs, MBA in Design Strategy Program, San Francisco, CA 94107. Offers MBA. *Accreditation:* NASAD. *Degree requirements:* For master's, thesis. *Entrance requirements:* Additional exam requirements/recommendations for international students: required—TOEFL, IELTS, or PTE. Electronic applications accepted. *Expenses:* Contact institution.

California Institute of the Arts, School of Art, Valencia, CA 91355-2340. Offers art (MFA, Adv C); graphic design (MFA, Adv C); photography (MFA, Adv C). *Accreditation:* NASAD (one or more programs are accredited). *Degree requirements:* For master's, final project. *Entrance requirements:* For master's, portfolio. Additional exam requirements/recommendations for international students: required—TOEFL. Electronic applications accepted.

California State University, Fresno, Division of Research and Graduate Studies, College of Arts and Humanities, Department of Art and Design, Fresno, CA 93740-8027. Offers art (MA). *Program availability:* Part-time, evening/weekend. *Degree requirements:* For master's, thesis or alternative. *Entrance requirements:* For master's, GRE General Test, minimum GPA of 3.0, portfolio. Additional exam requirements/recommendations for international students: required—TOEFL. Electronic applications accepted. *Expenses:* Tuition, state resident: full-time $4012; part-time $2506 per semester.

California State University, Fullerton, Graduate Studies, College of the Arts, Department of Visual Arts, Fullerton, CA 92831-3599. Offers art (MA, MFA), including art history (MA), ceramics (MFA), crafts, creative photography, exhibition design, glass, graphic design, illustration, sculpture. *Accreditation:* NASAD (one or more programs are accredited). *Program availability:* Part-time. *Entrance requirements:* For master's, minimum GPA of 2.5 in last 60 units of course work, portfolio.

California State University, Los Angeles, Graduate Studies, College of Arts and Letters, Department of Art, Los Angeles, CA 90032-8530. Offers art (MA), including art education, art history, art therapy, ceramics, metals, and textiles, design (MA, MFA), painting, sculpture, and graphic arts, photography; fine arts (MFA), including crafts, design (MA, MFA), studio arts. *Accreditation:* NASAD (one or more programs are accredited). *Program availability:* Part-time, evening/weekend. *Degree requirements:* For master's, comprehensive exam, project or thesis. *Entrance requirements:* For master's, portfolio. Additional exam requirements/recommendations for international students: required—TOEFL (minimum score 500 paper-based). Electronic applications accepted. *Expenses: Tuition, area resident:* Full-time $7176; part-time $4164 per year. Tuition, state resident: full-time $7176; part-time $4164 per year. Tuition, nonresident: full-time $14,304; part-time $8916 per year. *International tuition:* $14,304 full-time. *Required fees:* $1037.76; $1037.76 per unit. Tuition and fees vary according to degree level and program.

Carnegie Mellon University, College of Fine Arts, School of Design, Program in Design, Pittsburgh, PA 15213-3891. Offers MA, D Des, PhD. *Degree requirements:* For doctorate, one foreign language, comprehensive exam, thesis/dissertation. *Entrance requirements:* For doctorate, GRE, portfolio of relevant work. Additional exam requirements/recommendations for international students: required—TOEFL (minimum score 600 paper-based).

College for Creative Studies, Graduate Programs, Detroit, MI 48202-4034. Offers color and materials design (MFA); integrated design (MFA); interaction design (MFA); transportation design (MFA). *Accreditation:* NASAD.

Concordia University, School of Graduate Studies, Faculty of Fine Arts, Department of Design and Computation Arts, Montréal, QC H3G 1M8, Canada. Offers design (M Des); digital technologies in design art practice (Certificate).

Drexel University, Westphal College of Media Arts and Design, Philadelphia, PA 19104-2875. Offers arts administration (MS); design research (MS); digital media (MS, PhD); fashion design (MS); interior architecture and design (MS); museum leadership (MS); retail and merchandising (MS); television management (MS); urban strategy (MS); MS/MBA. *Accreditation:* NASAD. *Program availability:* Part-time, evening/weekend. *Entrance requirements:* For master's, interview. Additional exam requirements/recommendations for international students: required—TOEFL. Electronic applications accepted. *Expenses:* Contact institution.

Emily Carr University of Art + Design, Program in Applied Arts, Vancouver, BC V6H 3R9, Canada. Offers design (M Des); media arts (MAA); visual arts (MAA). *Degree requirements:* For master's, internship, thesis project. *Entrance requirements:* For master's, minimum overall GPA of 3.0, visual portfolio, 3 letters of recommendation, resume/curriculum vitae. Additional exam requirements/recommendations for international students: required—TOEFL (minimum score 570 paper-based; 84 iBT), IELTS (minimum score 6.5), Michigan English Language Assessment Battery (minimum score 81). Electronic applications accepted.

Fashion Institute of Technology, School of Graduate Studies, New York, NY 10001-5992. Offers MA, MFA, MPS. *Accreditation:* NASAD. *Program availability:* Part-time, evening/weekend. *Degree requirements:* For master's, thesis. *Entrance requirements:* For master's, portfolio, letters of recommendation, resume, interview. Additional exam requirements/recommendations for international students: required—TOEFL (minimum score 550 paper-based; 80 iBT). Electronic applications accepted.

Ferris State University, Kendall College of Art and Design, Grand Rapids, MI 49307. Offers design (MA); painting (MFA); photography (MFA); printmaking (MFA); visual and critical studies (MA). *Faculty:* 16 full-time (9 women), 6 part-time/adjunct (3 women). *Students:* 46 full-time (25 women), 18 part-time (15 women); includes 10 minority (1 Black or African American, non-Hispanic/Latino; 1 American Indian or Alaska Native, non-Hispanic/Latino; 6 Hispanic/Latino; 2 Two or more races, non-Hispanic/Latino), 8 international. Average age 33. 28 applicants, 82% accepted, 19 enrolled. In 2019, 14 master's awarded. *Degree requirements:* For master's, thesis, seminars and studio courses. *Entrance requirements:* For master's, official transcripts from all institutions of higher education attended. Letter of intent outlining proposed artistic goals. Concise artist statement that addresses the philosophical foundation of your work. CV showing successful professional experience. Portfolio of work 20 images in chosen area of emphasis. Contact information for. Additional exam requirements/recommendations for international students: required—TOEFL (minimum score 79 iBT), IELTS (minimum score 6.5). *Application deadline:* For fall admission, 2/1 priority date for domestic and international students; for spring admission, 10/15 priority date for domestic and international students. Applications are processed on a rolling basis. Application fee: $0 ($30 for international students). Electronic applications accepted. *Expenses:* $1079 per credit hour; Technology fee $175 per semester; Student Life Fee $20 per semester. *Financial support:* In 2019–20, 46 students received support, including 46 fellowships (averaging $11,736 per year); scholarships/grants and unspecified assistantships also available. Financial award application deadline: 2/1; financial award applicants required to submit FAFSA. *Unit head:* Tara McCrackin, President, 616-451-2787. *Application contact:* Thomas Post, Graduate Recruitment Specialist, 616-451-2787, Fax: 616-831-9689, E-mail: thomaspost@ferris.edu.
Website: http://www.kcad.edu/

Florida Atlantic University, Dorothy F. Schmidt College of Arts and Letters, Department of Visual Arts and Art History, Boca Raton, FL 33431-0991. Offers visual art (MFA), including ceramics, graphic design, visual art. *Faculty:* 14 full-time (10 women). *Students:* 9 full-time (7 women), 3 part-time (all women); includes 2 minority (1 Black or African American, non-Hispanic/Latino; 1 Hispanic/Latino), 1 international. Average age 41. 17 applicants, 24% accepted, 2 enrolled. In 2019, 4 master's awarded. *Degree requirements:* For master's, one foreign language, project. *Entrance requirements:* For master's, GRE General Test, minimum GPA of 3.0 during last 60 hours of course work, slide portfolio. *Application deadline:* For fall admission, 2/21 for domestic and international students; for spring admission, 10/1 for domestic and international students. Application fee: $30. Electronic applications accepted. *Expenses: Tuition:* Full-time $20,536; part-time $371.82 per credit hour. Tuition and fees vary according to program. *Financial support:* Research assistantships with full tuition reimbursements, teaching assistantships with full tuition reimbursements, career-related internships or fieldwork, Federal Work-Study, and institutionally sponsored loans available. Financial

award applicants required to submit FAFSA. *Unit head:* Dr. Eric Landes, Chair, 954-236-1106, E-mail: elandes1@fau.edu. *Application contact:* Dr. Eric Landes, Chair, 954-236-1106, E-mail: elandes1@fau.edu.
Website: http://www.fau.edu/VAAH/

Howard University, Graduate School, Division of Fine Arts, Department of Art, Program in Fine Arts, Washington, DC 20059-0002. Offers 3D reality (sculpture and ceramics) (MFA); design (MFA); electronic studio (MFA); painting (MFA); photography (MFA). *Accreditation:* NASAD. *Degree requirements:* For master's, comprehensive exam, thesis, exhibit. *Entrance requirements:* For master's, minimum GPA of 3.0, portfolio.

Illinois Institute of Technology, Graduate College, Institute of Design, Chicago, IL 60654. Offers M Des, MDM, PhD, M Des/MBA. *Program availability:* Part-time. Terminal master's awarded for partial completion of doctoral program. *Degree requirements:* For master's, comprehensive exam (for some programs), thesis (for some programs); for doctorate, one foreign language, comprehensive exam, thesis/dissertation. *Entrance requirements:* For master's, GRE (minimum score 310); GMAT (minimum score 600), bachelor's degree, minimum GPA of 3.0, official transcripts, portfolio (for applicants with design degrees), minimum of two years of professional experience; for doctorate, GRE General Test (minimum score 1000 Quantitative and Verbal, 3.5 Analytical Writing), master's degree in design from accredited institution, official transcripts, portfolio. Additional exam requirements/recommendations for international students: required—TOEFL (minimum score 100 iBT); recommended—IELTS (minimum score 7). Electronic applications accepted. *Expenses:* Contact institution.

Indiana University Bloomington, University Graduate School, College of Arts and Sciences, School of Art, Architecture and Design, Bloomington, IN 47405-7000. Offers apparel merchandising (MS); architecture (M Arch); studio art (MFA). *Accreditation:* NASAD (one or more programs are accredited). *Entrance requirements:* For master's, portfolio (MFA). Additional exam requirements/recommendations for international students: required—TOEFL. Electronic applications accepted.

Iowa State University of Science and Technology, Department of Apparel, Events, and Hospitality Management, Ames, IA 50011-1078. Offers apparel, merchandising, and design (MS, PhD); hospitality management (MS, PhD). *Program availability:* Online learning. *Degree requirements:* For doctorate, thesis/dissertation. *Entrance requirements:* For master's and doctorate, GRE General Test. Additional exam requirements/recommendations for international students: required—TOEFL (minimum score 550 paper-based; 79 iBT), IELTS (minimum score 6.5). Electronic applications accepted.

Louisiana State University and Agricultural & Mechanical College, Graduate School, College of Art and Design, Baton Rouge, LA 70803. Offers M Arch, MA, MFA, MLA. *Accreditation:* ASLA (one or more programs are accredited); NASAD (one or more programs are accredited).

Maryland Institute College of Art, Graduate Studies, Design Leadership MBA/MA Program, Baltimore, MD 21217. Offers MBA/MA. *Students:* 20 full-time (10 women); includes 7 minority (2 Black or African American, non-Hispanic/Latino; 2 Asian, non-Hispanic/Latino; 1 Hispanic/Latino; 2 Two or more races, non-Hispanic/Latino), 3 international. *Entrance requirements:* Additional exam requirements/recommendations for international students: required—TOEFL (minimum score 100 iBT) or IELTS (minimum score 7). *Application deadline:* For fall admission, 1/15 priority date for domestic and international students; for spring admission, 4/1 for domestic and international students. Applications are processed on a rolling basis. Application fee: $100. Electronic applications accepted. *Expenses:* Contact institution. *Financial support:* Scholarships/grants available. Financial award applicants required to submit FAFSA. *Unit head:* David Gracyalny, Vice Provost for Research/Dean, 410-225-5273, E-mail: dgracyalny@mica.edu. *Application contact:* Chris D. Harring, Director of Graduate Admission, 410-225-2256, Fax: 410-225-5275, E-mail: graduate@mica.edu.
Website: http://www.designleadershipmba.com/

Maryland Institute College of Art, Graduate Studies, MPS Program in Business of Art and Design, Baltimore, MD 21201. Offers MPS. *Program availability:* Part-time. *Degree requirements:* For master's, business plan presentation. *Entrance requirements:* For master's, essay, resume. Additional exam requirements/recommendations for international students: required—TOEFL (minimum score 550 paper-based; 80 iBT), IELTS (minimum score 6.5). Electronic applications accepted. *Expenses:* Contact institution.

Maryland Institute College of Art, Graduate Studies, MPS Program in Information Visualization, Baltimore, MD 21201. Offers MPS. *Program availability:* Part-time, online learning. *Entrance requirements:* For master's, curriculum vitae/resume, visualization portfolio, bachelor's degree in any field. Additional exam requirements/recommendations for international students: required—TOEFL (minimum score 550 paper-based; 80 iBT). Electronic applications accepted. *Expenses:* Contact institution.

Maryland Institute College of Art, Graduate Studies, Program in Social Design, Baltimore, MD 21201. Offers MA. *Degree requirements:* For master's, thesis, thesis project, exhibition, project presentation. *Entrance requirements:* For master's, portfolio, bachelor's degree in any field. Additional exam requirements/recommendations for international students: required—TOEFL (minimum score 550 paper-based; 80 iBT), IELTS (minimum score 6.5). Electronic applications accepted. *Expenses:* Contact institution.

Massachusetts College of Art and Design, Graduate Programs, MFA Program, Boston, MA 02115-5882. Offers 2D fine arts (MFA), including painting, printmaking; 3D fine arts (MFA), including ceramics, fibers, glass, jewelry and metalsmithing, sculpture; design (MFA, Postbaccalaureate Certificate), including dynamic media; fine arts (MFA), including interdisciplinary; media arts (MFA, Postbaccalaureate Certificate), including film/video (MFA), photography. *Accreditation:* NASAD. *Faculty:* 1 (woman) full-time, 29 part-time/adjunct (14 women). *Students:* 44 full-time (26 women), 28 part-time (17 women); includes 8 minority (5 Asian, non-Hispanic/Latino; 3 Hispanic/Latino), 18 international. 202 applicants, 44% accepted, 35 enrolled. In 2019, 30 master's, 8 other advanced degrees awarded. *Degree requirements:* For master's, thesis, thesis exhibition (for fine arts programs); thesis project and document (for design/dynamic media program). *Entrance requirements:* For master's, portfolio, college transcripts, resume, statement of purpose, letters of reference, interview, 6 credits of art history taken prior to or during MFA program; for Postbaccalaureate Certificate, portfolio, college transcripts, resume, statement of purpose, letters of reference, interview. Additional exam requirements/recommendations for international students: required—TOEFL (minimum score 550 paper-based, 85 iBT) or IELTS (6). *Application deadline:* For fall admission, 1/20 priority date for domestic and international students; for summer admission, 1/20 priority date for domestic and international students. Applications are processed on a rolling basis. Application fee: $90. Electronic applications accepted. *Expenses:* Contact institution. *Financial support:* Research assistantships, teaching assistantships, career-related internships or fieldwork, scholarships/grants, tuition waivers (partial), unspecified assistantships, and adjunct co-teaching positions available. Support available to part-time students. Financial award application deadline: 1/20; financial award applicants required to submit FAFSA. *Unit head:* Lucinda Bliss, Dean of Graduate Studies, 617-879-7157, E-mail: gradadmissions@massart.edu. *Application contact:* Stacy Petersen, Associate Director, Graduate Admissions and Operations, 617-879-7238, E-mail: gradadmissions@massart.edu.
Website: http://www.massart.edu/Admissions/Graduate_Programs.html

Massachusetts College of Art and Design, Graduate Programs, Program in Design Innovation, Boston, MA 02115-5882. Offers M Des. *Faculty:* 12 part-time/adjunct (3 women). *Students:* 18 full-time (12 women), 1 part-time (0 women); includes 3 minority (2 Asian, non-Hispanic/Latino; 1 Hispanic/Latino), 8 international. 29 applicants, 55% accepted, 4 enrolled. In 2019, 8 master's awarded. *Degree requirements:* For master's, thesis, thesis project. *Entrance requirements:* For master's, portfolio, college transcripts, resume, statement of purpose, letters of reference, interview. Additional exam requirements/recommendations for international students: required—TOEFL (minimum score 550 paper-based; 85 iBT); recommended—IELTS (minimum score 6.5). *Application deadline:* For fall admission, 1/20 priority date for domestic and international students. Application fee: $90. Electronic applications accepted. *Expenses:* Contact institution. *Financial support:* Research assistantships, teaching assistantships, career-related internships or fieldwork, scholarships/grants, and unspecified assistantships available. Support available to part-time students. Financial award application deadline: 1/20; financial award applicants required to submit FAFSA. *Unit head:* Lucinda Bliss, Dean of Graduate Studies, 617-879-7157, E-mail: lbliss@massart.edu. *Application contact:* Stacy Petersen, Associate Director of Graduate Admissions and Operations, 617-879-7238, E-mail: gradadmissions@massart.edu.
Website: http://www.massart.edu/Admissions/Graduate_Programs.html

Miami International University of Art & Design, Program in Design and Media Management, Miami, FL 33132-1418. Offers MA.

Millersville University of Pennsylvania, College of Graduate Studies and Adult Learning, College of Arts, Humanities and Social Sciences, Department of Art and Design, Millersville, PA 17551-0302. Offers art education (M Ed). *Accreditation:* NASAD; NCATE. *Program availability:* Part-time. *Faculty:* 5 full-time (4 women), 1 (woman) part-time/adjunct. *Students:* 1 (woman) full-time, 17 part-time (10 women); includes 1 minority (Hispanic/Latino). Average age 32. 6 applicants, 83% accepted, 3 enrolled. In 2019, 2 master's awarded. *Degree requirements:* For master's, comprehensive exam (for some programs), thesis (for some programs). *Entrance requirements:* For master's, teaching certificate (unless enrolled in post-bacc. Cert. concurrently), interview may be required, portfolio if not MU graduate. Additional exam requirements/recommendations for international students: required—TOEFL, IELTS (minimum score 6), PTE (minimum score 60). *Application deadline:* Applications are processed on a rolling basis. Application fee: $40. Electronic applications accepted. *Expenses: Tuition, area resident:* Part-time $516 per credit. Tuition, state resident: part-time $516 per credit. Tuition, nonresident: part-time $774 per credit. *Required fees:* $118.75 per credit. Tuition and fees vary according to course load, degree level and program. *Financial support:* In 2019–20, 1 student received support. Scholarships/grants and unspecified assistantships available. Financial award application deadline: 3/15; financial award applicants required to submit FAFSA. *Unit head:* Dr. Shauna Frischkorn, Chair, 717-871-7256, Fax: 717-871-2004, E-mail: shauna.frischkorn@millersville.edu. *Application contact:* Dr. James A. Delle, Acting Dean of College of Graduate Studies and Adult Learning/Associate Provost, Academic Administration, 717-871-7462, E-mail: James.Delle@millersville.edu.
Website: http://www.millersville.edu/art/

Minneapolis College of Art and Design, Master of Fine Arts in Visual Studies, Minneapolis, MN 55404-4347. Offers animation (MFA); comic art (MFA); drawing (MFA); filmmaking (MFA); fine arts (MFA); furniture design (MFA); graphic design (MFA); illustration (MFA); interactive media (MFA); painting (MFA); photography (MFA); printmaking (MFA); sculpture (MFA). *Accreditation:* NASAD. *Program availability:* Part-time. *Students:* 86 applicants, 44% accepted, 9 enrolled. *Degree requirements:* For master's, thesis, thesis exhibit. *Entrance requirements:* Additional exam requirements/recommendations for international students: required—TOEFL (minimum score 550 paper-based; 79 iBT), IELTS (minimum score 6.5), Duolingo English Test accepted with a minimum score of 100 *Application deadline:* For fall admission, 2/1 for domestic and international students. Application fee: $50. Electronic applications accepted. *Expenses: Tuition:* Full-time $41,344. *Required fees:* $450. One-time fee: $300 full-time. *Financial support:* In 2019–20, 15 teaching assistantships (averaging $6,000 per year) were awarded; career-related internships or fieldwork, Federal Work-Study, scholarships/grants, and unspecified assistantships also available. Support available to part-time students. Financial award application deadline: 3/15; financial award applicants required to submit FAFSA. *Unit head:* Ellen Mueller, Director, MFA Program, 612-874-3629, E-mail: emueller@mcad.edu. *Application contact:* Mary Kazura, Director of Admissions, 612-874-3668, Fax: 612-874-3701, E-mail: mkazura@mcad.edu.
Website: http://mcad.edu/mfa

The New School, Parsons Paris, Paris, NY 10011. Offers MA. *Program availability:* Part-time. *Faculty:* 5 full-time (2 women), 46 part-time/adjunct (31 women). *Students:* 41 full-time (38 women), 4 part-time (all women); includes 7 minority (4 Black or African American, non-Hispanic/Latino; 1 Asian, non-Hispanic/Latino; 2 Hispanic/Latino), 22 international. Average age 26. 36 applicants, 78% accepted, 15 enrolled. In 2019, 13 master's awarded. *Degree requirements:* For master's, one foreign language, thesis (for some programs). *Entrance requirements:* For master's, transcripts, resume, statement of purpose, recommendation letters, interviews. Additional exam requirements/recommendations for international students: required—TOEFL (minimum score 100 iBT), IELTS (minimum score 7), PTE (minimum score 68). *Application deadline:* For fall admission, 1/1 priority date for domestic and international students. Applications are processed on a rolling basis. Application fee: $50. Electronic applications accepted. *Expenses:* 1,390 per credit. *Financial support:* In 2019–20, 29 students received support. Career-related internships or fieldwork and scholarships/grants available. Financial award application deadline: 2/1; financial award applicants required to submit FAFSA. *Unit head:* Florence Leclerc-Dickler, Dean, 33-176217661, E-mail: leclercf@newschool.edu. *Application contact:* Mike Fakih, Director of Admissions, Parsons Paris, 33 176 21 76 67, E-mail: thinkparsonsparis@newschool.edu.
Website: https://www.newschool.edu/parsons-paris/

The New School, Parsons School of Design, Program in Transdisciplinary Design, New York, NY 10011. Offers MFA. *Program availability:* Part-time. *Faculty:* 12 full-time (4 women), 6 part-time/adjunct (5 women). *Students:* 43 full-time (32 women); includes 11 minority (1 Black or African American, non-Hispanic/Latino; 8 Asian, non-Hispanic/Latino; 1 Hispanic/Latino; 1 Two or more races, non-Hispanic/Latino), 20 international. Average age 27. 77 applicants, 66% accepted, 20 enrolled. In 2019, 17 master's awarded. *Degree requirements:* For master's, thesis. *Entrance requirements:* For master's, transcripts, resume, statement of purpose, recommendation letters, portfolio, interview. Additional exam requirements/recommendations for international students: required—TOEFL (minimum score 91 iBT), IELTS (minimum score 7), PTE (minimum score 63). *Application deadline:* For fall admission, 1/1 priority date for domestic and international students. Applications are processed on a rolling basis. Application fee: $50. Electronic applications accepted. *Expenses:* 1810 per credit. *Financial support:* In

2019–20, 40 students received support, including 5 fellowships (averaging $5,899 per year), 17 research assistantships (averaging $2,262 per year); career-related internships or fieldwork, scholarships/grants, and unspecified assistantships also available. Support available to part-time students. Financial award application deadline: 2/1; financial award applicants required to submit FAFSA. *Unit head:* John Bruce, Program Director, E-mail: brucej@newschool.edu. *Application contact:* Simone Varadian, Senior Director, 212-229-5150 Ext. 4117, E-mail: varadias@newschool.edu.
Website: https://www.newschool.edu/parsons/mfa-transdisciplinary-design/

New York Institute of Technology, College of Arts and Sciences, Department of Digital Art and Design, Old Westbury, NY 11568. Offers computer graphics (MFA), including animation, fine arts and technology, graphic design. *Program availability:* Part-time. *Faculty:* 10 full-time (5 women), 12 part-time/adjunct (6 women). *Students:* 31 full-time (19 women), 4 part-time (1 woman); includes 9 minority (1 Black or African American, non-Hispanic/Latino; 5 Asian, non-Hispanic/Latino; 2 Hispanic/Latino; 1 Two or more races, non-Hispanic/Latino), 19 international. Average age 27. 75 applicants, 52% accepted, 15 enrolled. In 2019, 20 master's awarded. *Degree requirements:* For master's, thesis (for some programs), thesis required for M.F.A.; senior project required for M.A. *Entrance requirements:* For master's, BFA or equivalent with minimum undergraduate GPA of 3.0; supplemental application, including digital portfolio, CV/resume (optional), personal statement (optional), and/or letters of recommendation (optional); copies of undergraduate transcripts from all schools attended and proof of degree. Additional exam requirements/recommendations for international students: required—TOEFL (minimum score 79 iBT), IELTS (minimum score 6), PTE (minimum score 53), Duolingo English Test. *Application deadline:* For fall admission, 6/1 for domestic students, 7/1 for international students; for spring admission, 12/15 for international students. Applications are processed on a rolling basis. Application fee: $50. Electronic applications accepted. *Expenses: Tuition:* Full-time $23,760; part-time $1320 per credit. *Required fees:* $260; $220 per unit. Full-time tuition and fees vary according to degree level and program. Part-time tuition and fees vary according to course load and program. *Financial support:* In 2019–20, 20 students received support. Research assistantships, teaching assistantships, Federal Work-Study, scholarships/grants, and unspecified assistantships available. Support available to part-time students. Financial award application deadline: 2/15; financial award applicants required to submit FAFSA. *Unit head:* Prof. Rosina Vavetsi, Department Chair, 516-686-7542, Fax: 212-261-1742, E-mail: rvavetsi@nyit.edu. *Application contact:* Alice Dolitsky, Director, Graduate Admissions, 800-345-6948, Fax: 516-686-1116, E-mail: admissions@nyit.edu.
Website: https://www.nyit.edu/departments/digital_art_and_design

New York University, Tisch School of the Arts, Department of Design for Stage and Film, New York, NY 10012-1019. Offers MFA. *Degree requirements:* For master's, thesis. *Entrance requirements:* For master's, interview, portfolio. Additional exam requirements/recommendations for international students: required—TOEFL (minimum score 620 paper-based; 105 iBT), IELTS. Electronic applications accepted.

North Carolina State University, Graduate School, College of Design, Department of Art and Design, Raleigh, NC 27695. Offers MAD. *Degree requirements:* For master's, thesis optional. Electronic applications accepted.

Northeastern University, College of Arts, Media and Design, Boston, MA 02115-5096. Offers architecture (M Arch); arts administration and cultural entrepreneurship (MS); experience design (MFA, MS); game science and design (MS); information design and visualization (MFA); interdisciplinary arts (MFA); journalism (MA); media advocacy (MS); music industry leadership (MS); sustainable building systems (MS); sustainable urban environments (M Des). Electronic applications accepted. *Expenses:* Contact institution.

NSCAD University, Program in Fine Arts, Halifax, NS B3J 3J6, Canada. Offers craft (MFA); design (M Des); fine and media arts (MFA). *Degree requirements:* For master's, thesis, exhibit. *Entrance requirements:* For master's, portfolio, at least 5 art history classes. Additional exam requirements/recommendations for international students: required—Michigan English Language Assessment Battery (minimum score: 80), CanTEST (minimum score: 4.5), CAEL (minimum score: 70); recommended—TOEFL (minimum score 575 paper-based; 90 iBT), IELTS (minimum score 6.5).

Oklahoma State University, College of Human Sciences, Department of Design, Housing and Merchandising, Stillwater, OK 74078. Offers MS, PhD. *Faculty:* 8 full-time (6 women). *Students:* 11 part-time (4 women); includes 2 minority (both Hispanic/Latino), 5 international. Average age 31. 9 applicants, 56% accepted, 2 enrolled. In 2019, 3 master's, 1 doctorate awarded. *Entrance requirements:* For master's and doctorate, GRE or GMAT. Additional exam requirements/recommendations for international students: required—TOEFL (minimum score 550 paper-based; 79 iBT). *Application deadline:* For fall admission, 3/1 priority date for international students; for spring admission, 8/1 priority date for international students. Applications are processed on a rolling basis. Application fee: $50 ($75 for international students). Electronic applications accepted. *Expenses: Tuition, area resident:* Full-time $4148.10; part-time $2765.40 per credit hour. Tuition, state resident: full-time $4148.10; part-time $2765.40 per credit hour. Tuition, nonresident: full-time $15,775; part-time $10,516.80 per credit hour. *International tuition:* $15,775.20 full-time. *Required fees:* $2196.90; $122.05 per credit hour. Tuition and fees vary according to course load, campus/location and program. *Financial support:* In 2019–20, 2 research assistantships (averaging $1,660 per year), 4 teaching assistantships (averaging $1,788 per year) were awarded; career-related internships or fieldwork, Federal Work-Study, scholarships/grants, health care benefits, tuition waivers (partial), and unspecified assistantships also available. Support available to part-time students. Financial award application deadline: 3/1; financial award applicants required to submit FAFSA. *Unit head:* Dr. Lynn Boorady, Department Head, 405-744-5035, Fax: 405-744-6910, E-mail: lynn.m.boorady@okstate.edu. *Application contact:* Dr. Sheryl Tucker, Vice Prov/Dean/Prof, 405-744-6368, E-mail: gradi@okstate.edu.
Website: https://education.okstate.edu/

Pacific Northwest College of Art, Program in Applied Craft and Design, Portland, OR 97209. Offers MFA. *Accreditation:* NASAD. *Entrance requirements:* For master's, resume, 2 letters of recommendation, portfolio.

Pacific Northwest College of Art, Program in Collaborative Design, Portland, OR 97209. Offers MFA.

Pratt Institute, School of Art, Brooklyn, NY 11205-3899. Offers MA, MFA, MPS, MS, Adv C, MS/MFA. *Accreditation:* NASAD (one or more programs are accredited). *Program availability:* Part-time. *Faculty:* 27 full-time (15 women), 11 part-time/adjunct (5 women). *Students:* 284 full-time (229 women), 88 part-time (75 women); includes 93 minority (24 Black or African American, non-Hispanic/Latino; 18 Asian, non-Hispanic/Latino; 39 Hispanic/Latino; 12 Two or more races, non-Hispanic/Latino), 163 international. Average age 27. 1,001 applicants, 52% accepted, 169 enrolled. In 2019, 150 master's, 2 other advanced degrees awarded. *Degree requirements:* For master's, thesis. *Entrance requirements:* For master's, portfolio. Additional exam requirements/recommendations for international students: required—TOEFL (minimum score 550 paper-based; 79 iBT). *Application deadline:* For fall admission, 1/5 for domestic and international students; for spring admission, 10/1 for domestic and international students. Application fee: $50 ($90 for international students). Electronic applications accepted. *Expenses: Tuition:* Full-time $33,246; part-time $1847 per credit. *Required fees:* $1980. *Financial support:* Career-related internships or fieldwork, Federal Work-Study, institutionally sponsored loans, scholarships/grants, health care benefits, and unspecified assistantships available. Support available to part-time students. Financial award application deadline: 2/1; financial award applicants required to submit FAFSA. *Unit head:* Jorge Oliver, Acting Dean, 718-636-3619, E-mail: joliver6@pratt.edu. *Application contact:* Natalie Capannelli, Director of Graduate Admissions, 718-636-3551, Fax: 718-399-4242, E-mail: ncapanne@pratt.edu.
Website: https://www.pratt.edu/academics/school-of-art/graduate-school-of-art/

Pratt Institute, School of Design, Brooklyn, NY 11205-3899. Offers MFA, MID, MS. *Program availability:* Part-time. *Faculty:* 17 full-time (8 women), 248 part-time/adjunct (111 women). *Students:* 405 full-time (310 women), 12 part-time (7 women); includes 42 minority (5 Black or African American, non-Hispanic/Latino; 18 Asian, non-Hispanic/Latino; 12 Hispanic/Latino; 1 Native Hawaiian or other Pacific Islander, non-Hispanic/Latino; 6 Two or more races, non-Hispanic/Latino), 321 international. Average age 24. 987 applicants, 52% accepted, 194 enrolled. In 2019, 151 master's awarded. *Degree requirements:* For master's, thesis. *Entrance requirements:* For master's, letters of recommendation, portfolio. Additional exam requirements/recommendations for international students: required—TOEFL (minimum score 575 paper-based; 90 iBT). *Application deadline:* For fall admission, 1/5 for domestic and international students; for spring admission, 10/1 for domestic and international students. Application fee: $50 ($90 for international students). Electronic applications accepted. *Expenses: Tuition:* Full-time $33,246; part-time $1847 per credit. *Required fees:* $1980. *Financial support:* Career-related internships or fieldwork, Federal Work-Study, institutionally sponsored loans, scholarships/grants, health care benefits, and unspecified assistantships available. Support available to part-time students. Financial award application deadline: 2/1; financial award applicants required to submit FAFSA. *Unit head:* Anita Cooney, Dean, School of Design, 718-687-5744, Fax: 718-636-3410, E-mail: acooney@pratt.edu. *Application contact:* Natalie Capannelli, Director of Graduate Admissions, 718-636-3551, Fax: 718-636-3670, E-mail: ncapanne@pratt.edu.
Website: https://www.pratt.edu/academics/school-of-design/graduate-school-of-design/

Purdue University, Graduate School, College of Liberal Arts, Department of Art and Design, West Lafayette, IN 47907. Offers art education (MA, PhD); industrial design (MFA); interior design (MFA); visual communications design (MFA). *Accreditation:* NASAD; NAST. *Program availability:* Part-time. *Faculty:* 4 full-time (1 woman). *Students:* 37 full-time (21 women), 3 part-time (2 women); includes 9 minority (1 Black or African American, non-Hispanic/Latino; 3 Asian, non-Hispanic/Latino; 4 Hispanic/Latino; 1 Two or more races, non-Hispanic/Latino), 14 international. Average age 28. 144 applicants, 23% accepted, 14 enrolled. In 2019, 24 master's awarded. *Degree requirements:* For master's, terminal exhibit, project, or thesis. *Entrance requirements:* For master's, GRE General Test (for art education), minimum undergraduate GPA of 3.0 or equivalent; 9 undergraduate hours in an art or design history; BA in art (for MA in art education); for doctorate, GRE General Test (minimum scores 600 in verbal and 1000 total), master's degree in art education or art with teaching certification; 3 years of teaching experience at the K-12 level. Additional exam requirements/recommendations for international students: required—TOEFL (minimum score 550 paper-based; 77 iBT). *Application deadline:* For fall admission, 2/1 for domestic students, 2/1 priority date for international students. Applications are processed on a rolling basis. Application fee: $60 ($75 for international students). Electronic applications accepted. *Financial support:* Teaching assistantships with tuition reimbursements and career-related internships or fieldwork available. Support available to part-time students. Financial award applicants required to submit FAFSA. *Unit head:* Arne R. Flaten, Head of the Graduate Program, 765-494-3056, E-mail: aflaten@purdue.edu. *Application contact:* Kathryn Evans, Graduate Contact, 765-494-7666, E-mail: kathy@purdue.edu.
Website: https://www.cla.purdue.edu/vpa/ad/

Rhode Island School of Design, Department of Furniture Design, Providence, RI 02903-2784. Offers MFA. *Students:* 18 full-time (10 women); includes 2 minority (1 Hispanic/Latino; 1 Two or more races, non-Hispanic/Latino), 11 international. Average age 28. 36 applicants, 50% accepted, 9 enrolled. In 2019, 11 master's awarded. *Degree requirements:* For master's, thesis, exhibition. *Entrance requirements:* For master's, portfolio, statement of purpose, 3 letters of recommendation. Additional exam requirements/recommendations for international students: required—TOEFL (minimum score 580 paper-based; 93 iBT), IELTS (minimum score 6.5), Duolingo. *Application deadline:* For fall admission, 1/10 for domestic and international students. Application fee: $60. Electronic applications accepted. *Expenses: Tuition:* Full-time $51,800. *Required fees:* $1060. *Financial support:* Fellowships, research assistantships, teaching assistantships, Federal Work-Study, scholarships/grants, and unspecified assistantships available. Financial award application deadline: 2/1; financial award applicants required to submit FAFSA. *Unit head:* Chris Specce, Department Head, 401-454-6102, E-mail: furniture@risd.edu. *Application contact:* Molly Pettengill, Associate Director for Graduate Recruitment, 401-454-6312, Fax: 401-454-6309, E-mail: mpetteng@risd.edu.
Website: http://www.risd.edu/academics/furniture-design/

Rutgers University - New Brunswick, Mason Gross School of the Arts, Theater Department, New Brunswick, NJ 08901. Offers acting (MFA); design (MFA); playwriting (MFA); stage management (MFA); technical direction (MFA). *Degree requirements:* For master's, thesis (for some programs), performance project. *Entrance requirements:* For master's, audition, interview, portfolio. Additional exam requirements/recommendations for international students: required—TOEFL (minimum score 550 paper-based), IELTS (minimum score 7). Electronic applications accepted.

San Diego State University, Graduate and Research Affairs, College of Professional Studies and Fine Arts, School of Art and Design, San Diego, CA 92182. Offers studio arts (MA, MFA), including applied design, graphic design, interior architecture, multimedia and photography, painting and printmaking, sculpture. *Accreditation:* NASAD (one or more programs are accredited). *Degree requirements:* For master's, variable foreign language requirement, thesis. *Entrance requirements:* For master's, GRE General Test, bachelor's degree in related field, slide portfolio, typed slide information sheet, 2 letters of recommendation. Additional exam requirements/recommendations for international students: required—TOEFL. Electronic applications accepted.

San Francisco State University, Division of Graduate Studies, College of Liberal and Creative Arts, School of Design, San Francisco, CA 94132-1722. Offers industrial arts (MA). *Expenses: Tuition, area resident:* Full-time $7176; part-time $4164 per year. Tuition, state resident: full-time $7176; part-time $4164 per year. Tuition, nonresident: full-time $16,680; part-time $396 per unit. *International tuition:* $16,680 full-time. *Required fees:* $1524; $1524 per unit. $762 per semester. Tuition and fees vary according to degree level and program. *Unit head:* Prof. Mari Hulick, Director, 415-338-2211, Fax: 415-338-6159, E-mail: design@sfsu.edu. *Application contact:* Prof. Hsiao-Yun Chu, Graduate Coordinator, 415-338-2430, Fax: 415-338-6159, E-mail: hychu@sfsu.edu.
Website: http://design.sfsu.edu/

Savannah College of Art and Design, Program in Service Design, Savannah, GA 31402-3146. Offers MFA. *Program availability:* Part-time. *Degree requirements:* For master's, thesis. *Entrance requirements:* For master's, GRE (recommended), portfolio (submitted in digital format), audition or writing submission, resume, statement of purpose, two letters of recommendation. Additional exam requirements/ recommendations for international students: recommended—TOEFL (minimum score 550 paper-based; 85 iBT), IELTS (minimum score 6.5). Electronic applications accepted.

School of Visual Arts, Graduate Programs, Design Department, New York, NY 10010-3994. Offers MFA. *Accreditation:* NASAD. *Degree requirements:* For master's, thesis, 60 credits; minimum cumulative GPA of 3.0; residency of two academic years. *Entrance requirements:* For master's, portfolio that reflects wide range of design work and fluency in type and typography. Additional exam requirements/recommendations for international students: required—TOEFL (minimum score 550 paper-based; 79 iBT). *Expenses:* Contact institution.

School of Visual Arts, Graduate Programs, Design for Social Innovation Department, New York, NY 10010-3994. Offers MFA. *Degree requirements:* For master's, thesis, 60 credits with minimum cumulative GPA of 3.0; residency of two academic years. *Entrance requirements:* For master's, resume/curriculum vitae; statement of purpose; portfolio; personal interview. Additional exam requirements/ recommendations for international students: required—TOEFL (minimum score 550 paper-based; 79 iBT). Electronic applications accepted. *Expenses:* Contact institution.

School of Visual Arts, Graduate Programs, Products of Design Department, New York, NY 10010-3994. Offers MFA. *Degree requirements:* For master's, thesis, 60 credits; minimum cumulative GPA of 3.0; residency of two academic years. *Entrance requirements:* For master's, portfolio. Additional exam requirements/recommendations for international students: required—TOEFL (minimum score 550 paper-based; 79 iBT). Electronic applications accepted.

School of Visual Arts, Graduate Programs, Program in Branding, New York, NY 10010-3994. Offers MPS. *Degree requirements:* For master's, thesis, 36 credits; minimum cumulative GPA of 3.0; residency of one academic year. *Entrance requirements:* For master's, writing sample, statement of purpose. Additional exam requirements/recommendations for international students: required—TOEFL (minimum score 550 paper-based; 79 iBT). *Expenses:* Contact institution.

School of Visual Arts, Graduate Programs, Program in Design Research, Writing and Criticism, New York, NY 10010-3994. Offers MA. *Degree requirements:* For master's, thesis, 64 credits with minimum cumulative GPA of 3.0; residency of two academic years. *Entrance requirements:* For master's, short essay critiquing design object, event or concept; writing sample of published or unpublished writing between 1,000 and 2,000 words; personal interview. Additional exam requirements/ recommendations for international students: required—TOEFL (minimum score 550 paper-based; 79 iBT). Electronic applications accepted.

Southern Illinois University Carbondale, Graduate School, College of Liberal Arts, School of Art and Design, Carbondale, IL 62901-4701. Offers drawing (MFA); fiber/ weaving (MFA); glass (MFA); metalsmithing/blacksmithing (MFA); painting (MFA). *Accreditation:* NASAD. *Degree requirements:* For master's, thesis or alternative. *Entrance requirements:* For master's, minimum GPA of 2.7, portfolio, slides. Additional exam requirements/recommendations for international students: required—TOEFL.

Stanford University, School of Engineering, Department of Civil and Environmental Engineering, Stanford, CA 94305-2004. Offers atmosphere and energy (MS, PhD); construction (MS), including construction engineering and management, design-construction integration, sustainable design and construction; environmental engineering and science (MS, PhD); environmental fluid mechanics and hydrology (PhD); structural engineering (MS). *Expenses: Tuition:* Full-time $52,479; part-time $34,110 per unit. *Required fees:* $672; $224 per quarter. Tuition and fees vary according to program and student level.
Website: http://www-ce.stanford.edu/

Stephen F. Austin State University, Graduate School, College of Fine Arts, School of Art, Nacogdoches, TX 75962. Offers art (MA); art education (MAAE); design (MFA); drawing (MFA); filmmaking (MFA); painting (MFA); sculpture (MFA). *Accreditation:* NASAD. *Program availability:* Part-time. *Degree requirements:* For master's, comprehensive exam, thesis, exhibit. *Entrance requirements:* For master's, GRE General Test, portfolio. Additional exam requirements/recommendations for international students: required—TOEFL.

Suffolk University, New England School of Art and Design, Boston, MA 02108-2770. Offers graphic design (MA); interior architecture (MA). *Accreditation:* CIDA. *Program availability:* Part-time, evening/weekend. *Faculty:* 2 full-time (1 woman), 2 part-time/adjunct (1 woman). *Students:* 36 full-time (31 women), 6 part-time (all women); includes 7 minority (2 Black or African American, non-Hispanic/Latino; 2 Asian, non-Hispanic/Latino; 3 Hispanic/Latino), 14 international. Average age 26. 81 applicants, 79% accepted, 25 enrolled. In 2019, 20 master's awarded. *Entrance requirements:* For master's, GRE (for MFA), art portfolio, interview, 2 letters of recommendation, resume; letter of intent (for MFA). Additional exam requirements/recommendations for international students: required—TOEFL (minimum score 550 paper-based; 80 iBT). *Application deadline:* For fall admission, 3/15 priority date for domestic and international students; for spring admission, 10/15 priority date for domestic and international students. Applications are processed on a rolling basis. Application fee: $50. Electronic applications accepted. *Expenses:* Contact institution. *Financial support:* In 2019–20, 36 students received support, including 7 fellowships (averaging $2,829 per year); career-related internships or fieldwork, Federal Work-Study, institutionally sponsored loans, scholarships/grants, and unspecified assistantships also available. Financial award application deadline: 4/1; financial award applicants required to submit FAFSA. *Unit head:* Audrey Goldstein, Department Chair, 617-997-4290, E-mail: agoldstein@suffolk.edu. *Application contact:* Mara Marzocchi, Associate Director of Graduate Admissions, 617-573-8302, Fax: 617-305-1733, E-mail: grad.admission@suffolk.edu.
Website: http://www.suffolk.edu/nesad/

Syracuse University, College of Visual and Performing Arts, MFA Program in Art Video, Syracuse, NY 13244. Offers MFA. *Accreditation:* NASAD. *Program availability:* Part-time, online learning. *Entrance requirements:* For master's, portfolio, artist statement, three letters of recommendation, transcripts, personal statement/essay, resume. Additional exam requirements/recommendations for international students: required—TOEFL (minimum score 100 iBT), IELTS. Electronic applications accepted.

Texas State University, The Graduate College, College of Fine Arts and Communication, Program in Theatre Arts, San Marcos, TX 78666. Offers design (MFA); directing (MFA); dramatic writing (MFA); theatre history, dramatic criticism and dramaturgy (MA). *Program availability:* Part-time, evening/weekend. *Degree requirements:* For master's, comprehensive exam, thesis (for some programs). *Entrance requirements:* For master's, official GRE (general test only) required with competitive scores in the verbal reasoning and quantitative reasoning sections, baccalaureate degree from regionally-accredited institution with minimum GPA of 2.75 in last 60 hours of undergraduate course work, 2 letters of recommendation, statement of purpose, curriculum vitae/resume; writing sample (for playwriting applicants only); interview (for directing applicants only). Additional exam requirements/recommendations for international students: required—TOEFL (minimum score 550 paper-based; 78 iBT), IELTS (minimum score 6). Electronic applications accepted.

University of Alberta, Faculty of Graduate Studies and Research, Department of Art and Design, Edmonton, AB T6G 2E1, Canada. Offers drawing (MFA); history of art, design, and visual culture (MA); industrial design (M Des); painting (MFA); printmaking (MFA); sculpture (MFA); visual communication design (M Des). *Degree requirements:* For master's, thesis. *Entrance requirements:* For master's, portfolio (MFA and MDES). Additional exam requirements/recommendations for international students: required—TOEFL (minimum score 550 paper-based).

University of Baltimore, Graduate School, Yale Gordon College of Arts and Sciences, Program in Integrated Design, Baltimore, MD 21201-5779. Offers MA, MFA. *Program availability:* Part-time, evening/weekend. *Entrance requirements:* Additional exam requirements/recommendations for international students: required—TOEFL (minimum score 550 paper-based). Electronic applications accepted. *Expenses:* Contact institution.

University of Bridgeport, Shintaro Akatsu School of Design, Bridgeport, CT 06604. Offers design management (MPS). *Program availability:* Part-time, evening/ weekend. *Entrance requirements:* Additional exam requirements/recommendations for international students: recommended—TOEFL (minimum score 550 paper-based; 80 iBT), IELTS (minimum score 6.5). Electronic applications accepted.

University of California, Berkeley, UC Berkeley Extension, Certificate Programs in Art and Design, Berkeley, CA 94720. Offers interior design and interior architecture (Certificate); landscape architecture (Certificate); visual arts (Postbaccalaureate Certificate).

University of California, Los Angeles, Graduate Division, School of the Arts and Architecture, Department of Design Media Arts, Los Angeles, CA 90095. Offers MFA. *Degree requirements:* For master's, comprehensive exam. *Entrance requirements:* For master's, bachelor's degree; minimum undergraduate GPA of 3.0 (or its equivalent if letter grade system not used); portfolio. Additional exam requirements/ recommendations for international students: required—TOEFL. Electronic applications accepted. *Expenses:* Contact institution.

University of Central Oklahoma, The Jackson College of Graduate Studies, College of Fine Arts and Design, Department of Design, Edmond, OK 73034-5209. Offers design (MFA). *Accreditation:* NASAD. *Program availability:* Part-time. *Degree requirements:* For master's, thesis. *Entrance requirements:* For master's, essay, portfolio. Additional exam requirements/recommendations for international students: required—TOEFL (minimum score 550 paper-based; 79 iBT), IELTS (minimum score 6.5). Electronic applications accepted.

University of Cincinnati, Graduate School, College of Design, Architecture, Art, and Planning, School of Design, Cincinnati, OH 45221. Offers fashion design (M Des); graphic design (M Des); industrial design (M Des); interaction design (M Des); product development (M Des). *Accreditation:* NASAD. *Degree requirements:* For master's, thesis. *Entrance requirements:* For master's, undergraduate degree in design or related field, 2 years of work experience in design or related field. Additional exam requirements/recommendations for international students: required—TOEFL. Electronic applications accepted.

University of Connecticut, Graduate School, School of Fine Arts, Department of Dramatic Arts, Storrs, CT 06269. Offers acting (MA, MFA); design (MA, MFA); puppetry (MA, MFA); technical direction (MA, MFA). *Degree requirements:* For master's, comprehensive exam. *Entrance requirements:* Additional exam requirements/ recommendations for international students: required—TOEFL (minimum score 550 paper-based). Electronic applications accepted.

University of Delaware, College of Arts and Sciences, Department of Art, Newark, DE 19716. Offers MA, MFA. *Degree requirements:* For master's, exposition paper final exhibition. *Entrance requirements:* For master's, portfolio of creative work. Electronic applications accepted.

University of Illinois at Chicago, College of Architecture, Design and the Arts, School of Design, Chicago, IL 60607-7128. Offers graphic design (M Des); industrial design (M Des). *Degree requirements:* For master's, thesis, exhibit. *Entrance requirements:* For master's, MAT, portfolio. Additional exam requirements/ recommendations for international students: required—TOEFL. Electronic applications accepted. *Expenses:* Contact institution.

University of Illinois at Urbana-Champaign, Graduate College, College of Fine and Applied Arts, School of Art and Design, Champaign, IL 61820. Offers Ed M, MA, MFA, PhD. *Accreditation:* NASAD. *Entrance requirements:* For master's, minimum GPA of 3.0.

The University of Kansas, Graduate Studies, School of Architecture and Design, Department of Design, Lawrence, KS 66045. Offers design management (MA); interaction design (MA). *Accreditation:* NASAD. *Program availability:* Part-time. *Students:* 4 full-time (3 women), 11 part-time (5 women); includes 1 minority (Asian, non-Hispanic/Latino), 3 international. Average age 35. 10 applicants, 70% accepted, 3 enrolled. In 2019, 5 master's awarded. *Entrance requirements:* For master's, GRE (preferred), curriculum vitae or resume; statement of design philosophy and approach; official transcripts; three recommendations; portfolio of design work or, if previous degree was not in design-related discipline, samples of written work or other creative artifacts produced. Additional exam requirements/recommendations for international students: required—TOEFL, IELTS. *Application deadline:* For fall admission, 4/15 priority date for domestic and international students; for spring admission, 11/15 priority date for domestic and international students. Application fee: $65 ($85 for international students). Electronic applications accepted. *Expenses:* Tuition, state resident: full-time $9989. Tuition, nonresident: full-time $23,950. *International tuition:* $23,950 full-time. *Required fees:* $984; $81.99 per credit hour. Tuition and fees vary according to course load, campus/location and program. *Financial support:* Fellowships, teaching assistantships, Federal Work-Study, scholarships/grants, and unspecified assistantships available. Financial award application deadline: 2/1; financial award applicants required to submit FAFSA. *Unit head:* Frank Zilm, Dean, 816-561-7186, E-mail: frankzilm@ku.edu. *Application contact:* Joan Weaver, Graduate Admissions Contact, 785-864-3709, E-mail: jweaver@ku.edu.
Website: http://design.ku.edu/

University of Kentucky, Graduate School, College of Design, Lexington, KY 40506-0032. Offers M Arch, MAIDM, MHP, MSIDM. *Accreditation:* NASAD. *Entrance requirements:* For master's, GRE, minimum GPA of 2.75. Additional exam requirements/ recommendations for international students: required—TOEFL (minimum score 550 paper-based). Electronic applications accepted.

University of Louisville, Graduate School, College of Arts and Sciences, Department of Fine Arts, Louisville, KY 40292. Offers art history (MA, PhD); curatorial studies (MA); studio art (MFA), including design. *Program availability:* Part-time. *Faculty:*

20 full-time (9 women), 21 part-time/adjunct (14 women). *Students:* 19 full-time (16 women), 1 (woman) part-time; includes 5 minority (1 Black or African American, non-Hispanic/Latino; 2 Asian, non-Hispanic/Latino; 1 Hispanic/Latino; 1 Two or more races, non-Hispanic/Latino), 3 international. Average age 34. 21 applicants, 62% accepted, 10 enrolled. In 2019, 11 master's, 2 doctorates awarded. *Degree requirements:* For master's, one foreign language, thesis. *Entrance requirements:* For master's, Two letters of reference, official transcripts. Additional exam requirements/recommendations for international students: required—TOEFL (minimum score 550 paper-based; 79 iBT), IELTS can be taken in place of the TOEFL; recommended—IELTS (minimum score 6.5). *Application deadline:* For fall admission, 3/1 priority date for domestic students, 3/1 for international students. Applications are processed on a rolling basis. Application fee: $65. Electronic applications accepted. *Expenses: Tuition, area resident:* Full-time $13,000; part-time $723 per credit hour. Tuition, state resident: full-time $13,000; part-time $723 per credit hour. Tuition, nonresident: full-time $27,114; part-time $1507 per credit hour. *International tuition:* $27,114 full-time. *Required fees:* $196. Tuition and fees vary according to program and reciprocity agreements. *Financial support:* In 2019–20, 13 students received support, including 9 teaching assistantships with full tuition reimbursements available (averaging $14,000 per year); fellowships, research assistantships, scholarships/grants, health care benefits, and unspecified assistantships also available. Financial award application deadline: 3/1. *Unit head:* Dr. Scott L. Massey, Associate Professor and Chair, 502-852-6794, Fax: 502-852-6791, E-mail: s.massey@louisville.edu. *Application contact:* Theresa Berbet, Academic Coordinator, Senior, 502-852-6147, Fax: 502-852-6791, E-mail: theresa.berbet@louisville.edu.
Website: http://art.louisville.edu

University of Louisville, Graduate School, College of Arts and Sciences, Department of Theatre Arts, Louisville, KY 40292-0001. Offers design (MFA); performance (MFA). *Accreditation:* NAST. *Program availability:* Part-time. *Faculty:* 12 full-time (4 women), 7 part-time/adjunct (4 women). *Students:* 12 full-time (6 women); includes 9 minority (all Black or African American, non-Hispanic/Latino), 1 international. Average age 27. 10 applicants, 40% accepted, 4 enrolled. In 2019, 3 master's awarded. *Degree requirements:* For master's, performance project and monograph. *Entrance requirements:* For master's, audition or portfolio, 2 letters of reference, official transcripts. Additional exam requirements/recommendations for international students: required—TOEFL (minimum score 550 paper-based; 79 iBT), IELTS can be used in place of the TOEFL; recommended—IELTS (minimum score 6.5). *Application deadline:* For fall admission, 4/15 for domestic and international students. Applications are processed on a rolling basis. Application fee: $65. Electronic applications accepted. *Expenses: Tuition, area resident:* Full-time $13,000; part-time $723 per credit hour. Tuition, state resident: full-time $13,000; part-time $723 per credit hour. Tuition, nonresident: full-time $27,114; part-time $1507 per credit hour. *International tuition:* $27,114 full-time. *Required fees:* $196. Tuition and fees vary according to program and reciprocity agreements. *Financial support:* In 2019–20, 10 students received support, including 10 teaching assistantships with full tuition reimbursements available (averaging $14,000 per year); fellowships, research assistantships, health care benefits, and unspecified assistantships also available. *Unit head:* Dr. Nefertiti Burton, Professor and Chair, 502-852-7682, E-mail: nefertiti.burton@louisville.edu. *Application contact:* Dr. Nefertiti Burton, Professor and Chair, 502-852-7682, E-mail: nefertiti.burton@louisville.edu.
Website: http://louisville.edu/theatrearts/

University of Michigan, College of Engineering, Department of Integrative Systems and Design, Ann Arbor, MI 48109. Offers automotive engineering (M Eng); design science (MS, PhD); energy systems engineering (M Eng, MS); global automotive and manufacturing engineering (M Eng); manufacturing engineering (M Eng, D Eng); pharmaceutical engineering (M Eng); robotics and autonomous vehicles (M Eng); systems engineering and design (M Eng); MBA/M Eng; MSE/MS. *Program availability:* Part-time, online learning. Terminal master's awarded for partial completion of doctoral program. *Degree requirements:* For master's, capstone project; for doctorate, thesis/dissertation. *Entrance requirements:* For master's and doctorate, GRE. Additional exam requirements/recommendations for international students: required—TOEFL. Electronic applications accepted.

University of Michigan, Rackham Graduate School, Penny W. Stamps School of Art and Design, Ann Arbor, MI 48109. Offers art and design (MFA); integrative design (M Des). *Accreditation:* NASAD. *Degree requirements:* For master's, thesis, exhibit (MFA), slide lecture. *Entrance requirements:* For master's, portfolio. Additional exam requirements/recommendations for international students: required—TOEFL (minimum score 560 paper-based; 84 iBT), IELTS (minimum score 6.5). Electronic applications accepted.

University of Minnesota, Twin Cities Campus, Graduate School, College of Design, Department of Design, Housing, and Apparel, Minneapolis, MN 55455-0213. Offers apparel (MA, MS, PhD); design communication (MA, MS, PhD); housing studies (MA, MS, PhD, Postbaccalaureate Certificate); interactive design (MFA); interior design (MA, MS, PhD). *Program availability:* Part-time. *Degree requirements:* For master's and Postbaccalaureate Certificate, comprehensive exam, thesis (for some programs); for doctorate, comprehensive exam, thesis/dissertation. *Entrance requirements:* For master's, GRE General Test, minimum GPA of 3.0 (preferred), portfolio, 3 letters of recommendation; for doctorate, GRE General Test, minimum GPA of 3.0 (preferred), portfolio, 3 letters of recommendation, writing sample; for Postbaccalaureate Certificate, GRE General Test, minimum GPA of 3.0 (preferred). Additional exam requirements/recommendations for international students: required—TOEFL (minimum score 550 paper-based; 79 iBT). Electronic applications accepted.

University of North Texas, Toulouse Graduate School, Denton, TX 76203-5459. Offers accounting (MS); applied anthropology (MA, MS); applied behavior analysis (Certificate); applied geography (MA); applied technology and performance improvement (M Ed, MS); art education (MA); art history (MA); arts leadership (Certificate); audiology (Au D); behavior analysis (MS); behavioral science (PhD); biochemistry and molecular biology (MS); biology (MA, MS); biomedical engineering (MS); business analysis (MS); chemistry (MS); clinical health psychology (PhD); communication studies (MA, MS); computer engineering (MS); computer science (MS); counseling (M Ed, MS), including clinical mental health counseling (MS), college and university counseling, elementary school counseling, secondary school counseling; creative writing (MA); criminal justice (MS); curriculum and instruction (M Ed); decision sciences (MBA); design (MA, MFA), including fashion design (MFA), innovation studies, interior design (MFA); early childhood studies (MS); economics (MS); educational leadership (M Ed, Ed D); educational psychology (MS, PhD), including family studies (MS), gifted and talented (MS), human development (MS), learning and cognition (MS), research, measurement and evaluation (MS); electrical engineering (MS); emergency management (MPA); engineering technology (MS); English (MA); English as a second language (MA); environmental science (MS); finance (MBA, MS); financial management (MPA); French (MA); health services management (MBA); higher education (M Ed, Ed D); history (MA, MS); hospitality management (MS); human resources management (MPA); information science (MS); information systems (PhD); information technologies (MBA); interdisciplinary studies (MA, MS); international studies (MA); international sustainable tourism (MS); jazz studies (MM); journalism (MA, MJ, Graduate Certificate), including interactive and virtual digital communication (Graduate Certificate), narrative journalism (Graduate Certificate), public relations (Graduate Certificate); kinesiology (MS); linguistics (MA); local government management (MPA); logistics (PhD); logistics and supply chain management (MBA); long-term care, senior housing, and aging services (MA); management (PhD); marketing (MBA); mathematics (MA, MS); mechanical and energy engineering (MS, PhD); music (MA), including ethnomusicology, music theory, musicology, performance; music composition (PhD); music education (MM Ed, PhD); nonprofit management (MPA); operations and supply chain management (MBA); performance (MM, DMA); philosophy (MA); political science (MA); professional and technical communication (MA); radio, television and film (MA, MFA); rehabilitation counseling (Certificate); sociology (MA); Spanish (MA); special education (M Ed); speech-language pathology (MA); strategic management (MBA); studio art (MFA); teaching (M Ed); MBA/MS. *Program availability:* Part-time, evening/weekend, online learning. Terminal master's awarded for partial completion of doctoral program. *Degree requirements:* For master's, variable foreign language requirement, comprehensive exam (for some programs), thesis (for some programs); for doctorate, variable foreign language requirement, comprehensive exam (for some programs), thesis/dissertation; for other advanced degree, variable foreign language requirement, comprehensive exam (for some programs). *Entrance requirements:* For master's and doctorate, GRE, GMAT. Additional exam requirements/recommendations for international students: required—TOEFL (minimum score 550 paper-based; 79 iBT). Electronic applications accepted.

University of Notre Dame, The Graduate School, College of Arts and Letters, Department of Art, Art History, and Design, Notre Dame, IN 46556. Offers art history (MA); design (MFA), including graphic design, industrial design; studio art (MFA), including ceramics, painting, photography, printmaking, sculpture. *Accreditation:* NASAD. *Degree requirements:* For master's, comprehensive exam (for some programs), thesis. *Entrance requirements:* For master's, GRE General Test, minimum GPA of 3.0. Additional exam requirements/recommendations for international students: required—TOEFL (minimum score 600 paper-based; 80 iBT). Electronic applications accepted.

University of Oklahoma, Weitzenhoffer Family College of Fine Arts, School of Visual Arts, Norman, OK 73019. Offers art (MFA), including art and technology, ceramics, film, painting, photography, printmaking, sculpture, video, visual communication; art history (MA, PhD), including art history (MA), art of the American West (PhD), Native American art (PhD); design (MFA). *Degree requirements:* For master's, 2 foreign languages, comprehensive exam (for some programs), thesis (for some programs); for doctorate, 2 foreign languages, comprehensive exam, thesis/dissertation. *Entrance requirements:* For master's and doctorate, GRE. Additional exam requirements/recommendations for international students: required—TOEFL (minimum score 79 iBT) or IELTS (minimum score 6.5). Electronic applications accepted. *Expenses:* Tuition, state resident: full-time $6583.20; part-time $274.30 per credit hour. Tuition, nonresident: full-time $21,242; part-time $885.10 per credit hour. *International tuition:* $21,242.40 full-time. *Required fees:* $1994.20; $72.55 per credit hour. $126.50 per semester. Tuition and fees vary according to course load and degree level.

University of Oregon, Graduate School, College of Design, Department of Product Design, Eugene, OR 97403. Offers sports product design (MS).

The University of Texas at Austin, Graduate School, College of Fine Arts, Department of Art and Art History, Program in Design, Austin, TX 78712-1111. Offers MFA. *Accreditation:* NASAD. *Degree requirements:* For master's, thesis, oral exam, exhibition. *Entrance requirements:* For master's, minimum GPA of 3.0, portfolio. Electronic applications accepted.

University of Washington, Graduate School, College of Arts and Sciences, School of Art, Division of Design, Seattle, WA 98195. Offers industrial design (MFA); visual communication design (MFA).

University of Wisconsin–Madison, Graduate School, School of Human Ecology, Program in Design Studies, Madison, WI 53706. Offers MFA, MS, PhD. *Degree requirements:* For master's, thesis (for some programs); for doctorate, comprehensive exam, thesis/dissertation. *Entrance requirements:* For master's, portfolio, scholarly paper, 3 letters of recommendation from faculty; for doctorate, letters of recommendation, scholarly paper. Additional exam requirements/recommendations for international students: required—TOEFL (minimum score 580 paper-based; 92 iBT).

University of Wisconsin–Milwaukee, Graduate School, College of Health Sciences, Department of Occupational Science and Technology, Milwaukee, WI 53201-0413. Offers assistive technology and design (MS); disability and occupation (MS); ergonomics (MS); therapeutic recreation (MS). *Accreditation:* AOTA. *Entrance requirements:* Additional exam requirements/recommendations for international students: required—TOEFL (minimum score 550 paper-based; 79 iBT), IELTS (minimum score 6.5).

Western Carolina University, Graduate School, College of Fine and Performing Arts, School of Art and Design, Cullowhee, NC 28723. Offers MFA. *Accreditation:* NASAD. *Program availability:* Part-time. *Degree requirements:* For master's, thesis. *Entrance requirements:* For master's, GRE, appropriate undergraduate degree, portfolio, letters of recommendation. Additional exam requirements/recommendations for international students: required—TOEFL (minimum score 550 paper-based; 79 iBT). *Expenses: Tuition, area resident:* Full-time $2217.50; part-time $1664 per semester. Tuition, state resident: full-time $2217.50; part-time $1664 per semester. Tuition, nonresident: full-time $7421; part-time $5566 per semester. *International tuition:* $7421 full-time. *Required fees:* $5598; $1954 per semester. Tuition and fees vary according to course load, campus/location and program.

Western Michigan University, Graduate College, College of Fine Arts, Gwen Frostic School of Art, Kalamazoo, MI 49008. Offers art education (MA). *Accreditation:* NASAD. *Degree requirements:* For master's, thesis or alternative.

Yale University, School of Art, New Haven, CT 06520-8339. Offers graphic design (MFA); painting/printmaking (MFA); photography (MFA); sculpture (MFA). *Degree requirements:* For master's, thesis (for some programs). *Entrance requirements:* Additional exam requirements/recommendations for international students: required—TOEFL (minimum score 550 paper-based; 100 iBT). Electronic applications accepted. *Expenses:* Contact institution.

York University, Faculty of Graduate Studies, Faculty of Fine Arts, Program in Design, Toronto, ON M3J 1P3, Canada. Offers M Des. Electronic applications accepted.

Computer Art and Design

Academy of Art University, Graduate Programs, School of Graphic Design, San Francisco, CA 94105-3410. Offers graphic design (MFA); graphic design and digital media (MA). *Accreditation:* NASAD. *Program availability:* Part-time, 100% online. *Faculty:* 5 full-time (1 woman), 19 part-time/adjunct (9 women). *Students:* 142 full-time (99 women), 119 part-time (82 women); includes 31 minority (9 Black or African American, non-Hispanic/Latino; 6 Asian, non-Hispanic/Latino; 13 Hispanic/Latino; 1 Native Hawaiian or other Pacific Islander, non-Hispanic/Latino; 2 Two or more races, non-Hispanic/Latino), 166 international. Average age 28. 125 applicants, 100% accepted, 80 enrolled. In 2019, 105 master's awarded. *Degree requirements:* For master's, final review. *Entrance requirements:* For master's, statement of intent; resume; portfolio/reel; official college transcripts. *Application deadline:* Applications are processed on a rolling basis. Application fee: $50. Electronic applications accepted. *Expenses: Tuition:* Full-time $1083; part-time $1083 per credit hour. *Required fees:* $860; $860 per unit. $430 per term. One-time fee: $145. Tuition and fees vary according to program. *Financial support:* Career-related internships or fieldwork, Federal Work-Study, and scholarships/grants available. Financial award application deadline: 8/10; financial award applicants required to submit FAFSA.
Website: https://www.academyart.edu/academics/graphic-design

Academy of Art University, Graduate Programs, School of Visual Development, San Francisco, CA 94105-3410. Offers MA, MFA. *Program availability:* Part-time, 100% online. *Faculty:* 4 full-time (0 women), 8 part-time/adjunct (1 woman). *Students:* 66 full-time (48 women), 41 part-time (30 women); includes 16 minority (4 Black or African American, non-Hispanic/Latino; 1 American Indian or Alaska Native, non-Hispanic/Latino; 4 Asian, non-Hispanic/Latino; 6 Hispanic/Latino; 1 Two or more races, non-Hispanic/Latino), 47 international. Average age 28. 34 applicants, 100% accepted, 33 enrolled. In 2019, 53 master's awarded. *Degree requirements:* For master's, final review. *Entrance requirements:* For master's, statement of intent; resume; portfolio/reel; official college transcripts. *Application deadline:* Applications are processed on a rolling basis. Application fee: $50. Electronic applications accepted. *Expenses: Tuition:* Full-time $1083; part-time $1083 per credit hour. *Required fees:* $860; $860 per unit. $430 per term. One-time fee: $145. Tuition and fees vary according to program. *Financial support:* Career-related internships or fieldwork, Federal Work-Study, and scholarships/grants available. Financial award application deadline: 8/10; financial award applicants required to submit FAFSA.
Website: https://www.academyart.edu/academics/visual-development

Academy of Art University, Graduate Programs, School of Web Design and New Media, San Francisco, CA 94105-3410. Offers MA, MFA. *Program availability:* Part-time, 100% online. *Faculty:* 6 full-time (2 women), 23 part-time/adjunct (5 women). *Students:* 203 full-time (158 women), 113 part-time (82 women); includes 38 minority (4 Black or African American, non-Hispanic/Latino; 24 Asian, non-Hispanic/Latino; 5 Hispanic/Latino; 1 Native Hawaiian or other Pacific Islander, non-Hispanic/Latino; 4 Two or more races, non-Hispanic/Latino), 228 international. Average age 29. 87 applicants, 100% accepted, 71 enrolled. In 2019, 163 master's awarded. *Degree requirements:* For master's, final review. *Entrance requirements:* For master's, statement of intent; resume; portfolio/reel; official college transcripts. *Application deadline:* Applications are processed on a rolling basis. Application fee: $50. Electronic applications accepted. *Expenses: Tuition:* Full-time $1083; part-time $1083 per credit hour. *Required fees:* $860; $860 per unit. $430 per term. One-time fee: $145. Tuition and fees vary according to program. *Financial support:* Career-related internships or fieldwork, Federal Work-Study, and scholarships/grants available. Financial award application deadline: 8/10; financial award applicants required to submit FAFSA. *Application contact:* 800-544-ARTS, E-mail: info@academyart.edu.
Website: http://www.academyart.edu/computer-arts-school/index.html

Alfred University, Graduate School, College of Ceramics, School of Art and Design, Alfred, NY 14802-1205. Offers ceramic art (MFA); electronic integrated arts (MFA); painting (MFA); sculpture/dimensional studies (MFA). *Accreditation:* NASAD. *Faculty:* 29 full-time (15 women), 4 part-time/adjunct (0 women). *Students:* 43 full-time (27 women); includes 4 minority (1 Asian, non-Hispanic/Latino; 2 Hispanic/Latino; 1 Two or more races, non-Hispanic/Latino), 12 international. Average age 29. 170 applicants, 24% accepted, 20 enrolled. In 2019, 18 master's awarded. *Degree requirements:* For master's, thesis or alternative, exhibit. *Entrance requirements:* For master's, portfolio. Additional exam requirements/recommendations for international students: required—TOEFL (minimum score 550 paper-based; 80 iBT), IELTS (minimum score 6). *Application deadline:* For fall admission, 1/15 for domestic and international students. Applications are processed on a rolling basis. Application fee: $60. Electronic applications accepted. Application fee is waived when completed online. *Expenses:* $23,530 per year. *Financial support:* In 2019–20, 40 students received support. Teaching assistantships with full tuition reimbursements available and tuition waivers (full) available. Financial award application deadline: 3/15; financial award applicants required to submit FAFSA. *Unit head:* Gerar Edizel, Interim Dean, 607-871-2412, E-mail: fedizel@alfred.edu. *Application contact:* Lindsey Gertin, Assistant Director of Graduate Admissions, 607-871-2017, Fax: 607-871-2198, E-mail: gradinquiry@alfred.edu.
Website: http://art.alfred.edu/graduate/

ArtCenter College of Design, Graduate Media Design Practices Program, Pasadena, CA 91103. Offers MFA. *Accreditation:* NASAD.

Bowling Green State University, Graduate College, College of Arts and Sciences, School of Art, Bowling Green, OH 43403. Offers 2-D studio art (MA, MFA); 3-D studio art (MA, MFA); art education (MA); art history (MA); computer art (MA); design (MFA); digital arts (MFA); graphics (MFA). *Accreditation:* NASAD. *Program availability:* Part-time. *Degree requirements:* For master's, thesis or alternative, final exhibit (MFA). *Entrance requirements:* For master's, GRE General Test (for MA), slide portfolio (15-20 slides). Additional exam requirements/recommendations for international students: required—TOEFL. Electronic applications accepted.

California College of the Arts, Graduate Programs, Design Program, San Francisco, CA 94107. Offers graphic design (MFA); industrial design (MFA); interaction design (MFA). *Accreditation:* NASAD. *Degree requirements:* For master's, thesis, exhibit. *Entrance requirements:* For master's, appropriate bachelor's degree, portfolio, resume, letters of recommendation, transcripts. Additional exam requirements/recommendations for international students: required—TOEFL, IELTS, or PTE. Electronic applications accepted. *Expenses:* Contact institution.

Carnegie Mellon University, College of Fine Arts, School of Design, Program in Design for Interactions, Pittsburgh, PA 15213-3891. Offers M Des. *Program availability:* Part-time. *Degree requirements:* For master's, thesis. *Entrance requirements:* For master's, GRE, portfolio of relevant work. Additional exam requirements/

recommendations for international students: required—TOEFL (minimum score 600 paper-based).

Chatham University, Program in Film and Digital Technology, Pittsburgh, PA 15232-2826. Offers MFA. *Program availability:* Part-time, evening/weekend. *Degree requirements:* For master's, thesis, capstone project. *Entrance requirements:* Additional exam requirements/recommendations for international students: required—TOEFL (minimum score 600 paper-based; 100 iBT), IELTS (minimum score 7), TWE. Electronic applications accepted. Application fee is waived when completed online. *Expenses: Tuition:* Part-time $1017 per credit. *Required fees:* $30 per credit. Tuition and fees vary according to program.

City College of the City University of New York, Graduate School, Division of Humanities and the Arts, Department of Art, Program in Fine Arts, New York, NY 10031-9198. Offers advertising design (MFA); ceramic design (MFA); digital and interdisciplinary art practice (MFA); painting (MFA); printmaking (MFA); sculpture (MFA); wood and metal design (MFA). *Degree requirements:* For master's, thesis exhibit. *Entrance requirements:* For master's, 20-slide portfolio. Additional exam requirements/recommendations for international students: required—TOEFL (minimum score 577 paper-based; 90 iBT). Electronic applications accepted.

Claremont Graduate University, Graduate Programs, School of Arts and Humanities, Department of Art, Claremont, CA 91711. Offers digital media (MFA); drawing (MFA); installation (MFA); painting (MFA); performance (MFA); photography (MFA); sculpture (MFA); studio (MFA). *Program availability:* Part-time. *Degree requirements:* For master's, final project show. *Entrance requirements:* For master's, BA in art or BFA, slide review. Additional exam requirements/recommendations for international students: required—TOEFL (minimum score 75 iBT). Electronic applications accepted. *Expenses:* Contact institution.

Concordia University, School of Graduate Studies, Faculty of Fine Arts, Department of Design and Computation Arts, Montréal, QC H3G 1M8, Canada. Offers design (M Des); digital technologies in design art practice (Certificate).

Cornell University, Graduate School, Graduate Fields of Architecture, Art and Planning, Field of Architecture, Ithaca, NY 14853. Offers architectural design (M Arch); architectural science (MS); computer graphics (MS); history of architecture (MA, PhD); history of urban development (MA, PhD); theory and criticism of architecture (M Arch); urban design (M Arch). *Degree requirements:* For master's, one foreign language, thesis (MA, MS); for doctorate, 2 foreign languages, comprehensive exam, thesis/dissertation. *Entrance requirements:* For master's, GRE General Test, 5-year bachelor's degree in architecture, portfolio (M Arch), 3 letters of recommendation; for doctorate, GRE General Test, 3 letters of recommendation. Additional exam requirements/recommendations for international students: required—TOEFL (minimum score 600 paper-based; 77 iBT). Electronic applications accepted.

DePaul University, College of Computing and Digital Media, Chicago, IL 60604. Offers animation (MA, MFA); applied technology (MS); business information technology (MS); computational finance (MS); computer and information sciences (PhD); computer science (MS); creative producing (MFA); cybersecurity (MS); data science (MS); digital communication and media arts (MA); documentary (MFA); e-commerce technology (MS); experience design (MA); film and television (MS); film and television directing (MFA); game design (MFA); game programming (MS); health informatics (MS); human centered design (PhD); human-computer interaction (MS); information systems (MS); network engineering and security (MS); product innovation and computing (MS); screenwriting (MFA); software engineering (MS); JD/MS. *Program availability:* Part-time, evening/weekend, online learning. *Degree requirements:* For master's, thesis (for some programs); for doctorate, comprehensive exam, thesis/dissertation. *Entrance requirements:* For master's, GRE or GMAT (for MS in computational finance only), bachelor's degree, resume (MS in predictive analytics only), IT experience (MS in information technology project management only), portfolio review (all MFA programs and MA in animation); for doctorate, GRE, master's degree in computer science. Additional exam requirements/recommendations for international students: required—TOEFL (minimum score 590 paper-based; 80 iBT), IELTS (minimum score 6.5), PTE (minimum score 53). Electronic applications accepted. *Expenses:* Contact institution.

DigiPen Institute of Technology, Graduate Programs, Redmond, WA 98052. Offers computer science (MS); digital art and animation (MFA). *Program availability:* Part-time. *Degree requirements:* For master's, comprehensive exam (for some programs), thesis (for some programs). *Entrance requirements:* For master's, GRE General Test (for MSCS), art portfolio (for MFA); official transcripts from all post-secondary education including final transcript indicating degree earned, statement of purpose, and 2 letters of recommendation. Additional exam requirements/recommendations for international students: required—TOEFL (minimum score 550 paper-based; 80 iBT). Electronic applications accepted. *Expenses:* Contact institution.

Drexel University, Westphal College of Media Arts and Design, Program in Digital Media, Philadelphia, PA 19104-2875. Offers MS, PhD. *Degree requirements:* For master's, thesis (including oral presentation, written statement, and copy of completed media work). *Entrance requirements:* For master's, interview. Additional exam requirements/recommendations for international students: required—TOEFL. Electronic applications accepted.

East Tennessee State University, College of Graduate and Continuing Studies, College of Business and Technology, Department of Engineering, Engineering Technology, and Surveying, Johnson City, TN 37614. Offers technology (MS). *Program availability:* Part-time. *Degree requirements:* For master's, comprehensive exam, thesis optional, capstone. *Entrance requirements:* For master's, bachelor's degree in technical or related area, minimum GPA of 3.0, undergraduate course in probability and statistics. Additional exam requirements/recommendations for international students: required—TOEFL (minimum score 550 paper-based; 79 iBT). Electronic applications accepted.

Emily Carr University of Art + Design, Program in Digital Media, Vancouver, BC V5T 0C6, Canada. Offers MDM. *Degree requirements:* For master's, internship. *Entrance requirements:* For master's, portfolio, minimum undergraduate B+ average, 3 reference letters. Additional exam requirements/recommendations for international students: required—TOEFL (minimum score 93 iBT), IELTS (minimum score 6.5), PTE (minimum score 62). Electronic applications accepted.

Full Sail University, Game Design Master of Science Program - Campus, Winter Park, FL 32792-7437. Offers MS.

Georgia Institute of Technology, Graduate Studies, Ivan Allen College of Liberal Arts, School of Literature, Media, and Communication, Atlanta, GA 30332. Offers digital media (MS, PhD). *Program availability:* Part-time. *Faculty:* 16 full-time (7 women). *Students:* 67 full-time (43 women), 4 part-time (2 women); includes 19 minority (9 Black

or African American, non-Hispanic/Latino; 8 Asian, non-Hispanic/Latino; 2 Two or more races, non-Hispanic/Latino), 29 international. Average age 28. 129 applicants, 43% accepted, 32 enrolled. In 2019, 16 master's, 3 doctorates awarded. Terminal master's awarded for partial completion of doctoral program. *Degree requirements:* For master's, thesis optional, project studio, paid internship, responsible conduct of research training; for doctorate, comprehensive exam, thesis/dissertation, portfolio review, responsible conduct of research training. *Entrance requirements:* For master's and doctorate, GRE, three letters of recommendation, transcripts from each college/university attended, design portfolio, statement of purpose. Additional exam requirements/recommendations for international students: required—TOEFL (minimum score 650 paper-based; 114 iBT), IELTS, TOEFL is the preferred method with the requirements shown on the programs. *Application deadline:* For fall admission, 1/8 priority date for domestic and international students. Applications are processed on a rolling basis. Application fee: $75 ($85 for international students). Electronic applications accepted. *Expenses: Tuition, area resident:* Full-time $14,064; part-time $586 per credit hour. Tuition, state resident: full-time $14,064; part-time $586 per credit hour. Tuition, nonresident: full-time $29,140; part-time $1215 per credit hour. *International tuition:* $29,140 full-time. *Required fees:* $2024; $840 per semester. $2096. Tuition and fees vary according to course load. *Financial support:* In 2019–20, 6 research assistantships, 2 teaching assistantships were awarded; fellowships, career-related internships or fieldwork, Federal Work-Study, institutionally sponsored loans, tuition waivers (full and partial), and unspecified assistantships also available. Support available to part-time students. Financial award application deadline: 7/1; financial award applicants required to submit FAFSA. *Unit head:* Richard Utz, School Chair, 404-894-2730, Fax: 404-894-1287, E-mail: richard.utz@lmc.gatech.edu. *Application contact:* Marla Bruner, Director of Graduate Studies, 404-894-1610, Fax: 404-894-1609, E-mail: gradinfo@mail.gatech.edu.
Website: http://lmc.gatech.edu

Georgian Court University, School of Business and Digital Media, Lakewood, NJ 08701. Offers business (MBA); business essentials (Certificate); nonprofit management (Certificate). *Program availability:* Part-time, evening/weekend. *Faculty:* 7 full-time (3 women), 5 part-time/adjunct (2 women). *Students:* 22 full-time (9 women), 21 part-time (14 women); includes 13 minority (5 Black or African American, non-Hispanic/Latino; 1 Asian, non-Hispanic/Latino; 6 Hispanic/Latino; 1 Native Hawaiian or other Pacific Islander, non-Hispanic/Latino), 1 international. Average age 28. 37 applicants, 57% accepted, 15 enrolled. In 2019, 23 master's, 3 other advanced degrees awarded. *Degree requirements:* For master's, comprehensive exam (for some programs), thesis (for some programs); for Certificate, comprehensive exam (for some programs). *Entrance requirements:* For master's, GMAT or CPA exam, 3 letters of recommendation. Additional exam requirements/recommendations for international students: required—TOEFL (minimum score 550 paper-based; 79 iBT). *Application deadline:* For fall admission, 8/15 for domestic students, 5/1 for international students; for spring admission, 1/15 for domestic students, 10/1 for international students. Applications are processed on a rolling basis. Application fee: $40. Electronic applications accepted. *Financial support:* Scholarships/grants, health care benefits, and unspecified assistantships available. Financial award application deadline: 4/15; financial award applicants required to submit FAFSA. *Unit head:* Dr. Jennifer Edmonds, Dean School of Business and Digital Media, 732-987-2662, Fax: 732-987-2024, E-mail: jedmonds@georgian.edu. *Application contact:* Dr. Jennifer Edmonds, Dean School of Business and Digital Media, 732-987-2662, Fax: 732-987-2024, E-mail: jedmonds@georgian.edu.
Website: https://georgian.edu/academics/school-of-business-digital-media/

Goucher College, MA and MFA Programs, Baltimore, MD 21204-2794. Offers art and technology (MFA); arts administration (MA); cultural sustainability (MA); digital arts (MA); historic preservation (MA); nonfiction (MFA). *Program availability:* Part-time, evening/weekend, blended/hybrid learning. *Degree requirements:* For master's, thesis, e-portfolio. *Entrance requirements:* For master's, digital portfolio (for MA, MFA in digital arts); writing sample (for MFA in creative nonfiction). Additional exam requirements/recommendations for international students: required—TOEFL (minimum score 550 paper-based; 80 iBT). Electronic applications accepted. *Expenses:* Contact institution.

Indiana University-Purdue University Indianapolis, Herron School of Art and Design, Indianapolis, IN 46202. Offers art therapy (MA); visual art (MFA), including ceramics, furniture design, painting and drawing, photography and intermedia, printmaking, sculpture; visual communication design (MFA). *Degree requirements:* For master's, thesis. *Entrance requirements:* For master's, personal statement, resume, recommendations, portfolio, transcripts (18 credit hours of studio art and 12 credit hours of psychology, including 3 credit hours of developmental psychology and 3 credit hours of abnormal psychology for MA). Additional exam requirements/recommendations for international students: recommended—TOEFL (minimum score 550 paper-based; 79 iBT), IELTS (minimum score 6.5). Electronic applications accepted. *Expenses:* Contact institution.

International Technological University, Program in Digital Arts, San Jose, CA 95134. Offers MA. *Program availability:* Part-time. *Degree requirements:* For master's, capstone project. *Entrance requirements:* Additional exam requirements/recommendations for international students: required—TOEFL, IELTS. Electronic applications accepted.

Lindenwood University–Belleville, Graduate Programs, Belleville, IL 62226. Offers business administration (MBA); communications (MA), including digital and multimedia, media management, promotions, training and development; counseling (MA); criminal justice administration (MS); education (MA); healthcare administration (MS); human resource management (MS); school administration (MA); teaching (MAT).

Lynn University, Eugene M. and Christine E. Lynn College of Communication and Design, Boca Raton, FL 33431-5598. Offers communication and media (MS); digital media (Certificate); digital media and design (MS); graphic and Web design (MFA); visual effects animation (MFA). *Program availability:* Part-time, evening/weekend. *Faculty:* 17 full-time (6 women), 3 part-time/adjunct (2 women). *Students:* 28 full-time (15 women), 32 part-time (16 women); includes 15 minority (8 Black or African American, non-Hispanic/Latino; 6 Hispanic/Latino; 1 Two or more races, non-Hispanic/Latino), 19 international. Average age 28. 36 applicants, 92% accepted, 20 enrolled. In 2019, 30 master's awarded. *Degree requirements:* For master's, thesis (for some programs), completion of degree in four calendar years; minimum cumulative GPA of 3.0 and C grade or higher in each course; orientation seminar (one credit); 36 credits of foundation and specialization or a thesis. *Entrance requirements:* For master's, Bachelor's degree from accredited institution, minimum undergraduate GPA of 3.0, official undergraduate transcripts, letter of recommendation from academic or professional source, writing sample demonstrating capacity to perform at graduate level. Additional exam requirements/recommendations for international students: required—TOEFL (minimum score 550 paper-based; 80 iBT), IELTS (minimum score 6.5). *Application deadline:* For fall admission, 8/10 for domestic students, 7/31 for international students; for spring admission, 12/18 for domestic students, 12/2 for international students; for summer admission, 4/12 for domestic students, 4/2 for international students. Applications are processed on a rolling basis. Application fee: $45. Electronic applications accepted. *Expenses:* $740.00 per hour. *Financial support:* In 2019–20, 15 students received support. Career-related internships or fieldwork, Federal Work-Study, scholarships/grants, tuition waivers (full and partial), and unspecified assistantships available. Support available to part-time students. Financial award application deadline: 3/1; financial award applicants required to submit FAFSA. *Unit head:* Dr. David L. Jaffe, Dean, 561-237-7099, Fax: 561-237-7097, E-mail: djaffe@lynn.edu. *Application contact:* Steven Pruitt, Director of Graduate Admission, 561-237-7834, Fax: 561-237-7100, E-mail: admission@lynn.edu.
Website: https://www.lynn.edu/academics/colleges-schools/communication-and-design

New Mexico Highlands University, Graduate Studies, School of Business, Media and Technology, Department of Media Arts and Technology, Las Vegas, NM 87701. Offers media arts and computer science (MA), including media arts.

The New School, Parsons School of Design, Program in Design and Technology, New York, NY 10011. Offers MFA. *Program availability:* Part-time. *Faculty:* 16 full-time, 112 part-time/adjunct. *Students:* 179 full-time (132 women), 4 part-time (1 woman); includes 22 minority (5 Black or African American, non-Hispanic/Latino; 8 Asian, non-Hispanic/Latino; 6 Hispanic/Latino; 3 Two or more races, non-Hispanic/Latino), 137 international. Average age 25. 453 applicants, 45% accepted, 80 enrolled. In 2019, 91 master's awarded. *Degree requirements:* For master's, thesis or alternative. *Entrance requirements:* For master's, transcripts, resume, statement of purpose, recommendation letters, portfolio, interview. Additional exam requirements/recommendations for international students: required—TOEFL (minimum score 92 iBT), IELTS (minimum score 7), PTE (minimum score 63). *Application deadline:* For fall admission, 1/1 for domestic students, 1/1 priority date for international students; for summer admission, 1/1 priority date for domestic and international students. Applications are processed on a rolling basis. Application fee: $50. Electronic applications accepted. *Expenses:* 1810 per credit. *Financial support:* In 2019–20, 163 students received support, including 1 fellowship (averaging $2,081 per year), 35 research assistantships (averaging $2,326 per year), 8 teaching assistantships (averaging $5,442 per year); career-related internships or fieldwork, Federal Work-Study, scholarships/grants, and travel funding; tuition waivers for students who are also New School employees also available. Support available to part-time students. Financial award application deadline: 2/1; financial award applicants required to submit FAFSA. *Unit head:* John Sharp, Program Director, E-mail: sharp@newschool.edu. *Application contact:* Simone Varadian, Senior Director, 212-229-5150 Ext. 4117, E-mail: varadias@newschool.edu.
Website: https://www.newschool.edu/parsons/mfa-design-technology/

New York Institute of Technology, College of Arts and Sciences, Department of Digital Art and Design, Old Westbury, NY 11568. Offers computer graphics (MFA), including animation, fine arts and technology, graphic design. *Program availability:* Part-time. *Faculty:* 10 full-time (5 women), 12 part-time/adjunct (6 women). *Students:* 31 full-time (19 women), 4 part-time (1 woman); includes 9 minority (1 Black or African American, non-Hispanic/Latino; 5 Asian, non-Hispanic/Latino; 2 Hispanic/Latino; 1 Two or more races, non-Hispanic/Latino), 19 international. Average age 27. 75 applicants, 52% accepted, 15 enrolled. In 2019, 20 master's awarded. *Degree requirements:* For master's, thesis (for some programs), thesis required for M.F.A; senior project required for M.A. *Entrance requirements:* For master's, BFA or equivalent with minimum undergraduate GPA of 3.0; supplemental application, including digital portfolio, CV/resume (optional), personal statement (optional), and/or letters of recommendation (optional); copies of undergraduate transcripts from all schools attended and proof of degree. Additional exam requirements/recommendations for international students: required—TOEFL (minimum score 79 iBT), IELTS (minimum score 6), PTE (minimum score 53), Duolingo English Test. *Application deadline:* For fall admission, 6/1 for domestic students, 7/1 for international students; for spring admission, 12/15 for international students. Applications are processed on a rolling basis. Application fee: $50. Electronic applications accepted. *Expenses: Tuition:* Full-time $23,760; part-time $1320 per credit. *Required fees:* $260; $220 per unit. Full-time tuition and fees vary according to degree level and program. Part-time tuition and fees vary according to course load and program. *Financial support:* In 2019–20, 20 students received support. Research assistantships, teaching assistantships, Federal Work-Study, scholarships/grants, and unspecified assistantships available. Support available to part-time students. Financial award application deadline: 2/15; financial award applicants required to submit FAFSA. *Unit head:* Prof. Rosina Vavetsi, Department Chair, 516-686-7542, Fax: 212-261-1742, E-mail: rvavetsi@nyit.edu. *Application contact:* Alice Dolitsky, Director, Graduate Admissions, 800-345-6948, Fax: 516-686-1116, E-mail: admissions@nyit.edu.
Website: https://www.nyit.edu/departments/digital_art_and_design

North Carolina State University, Graduate School, College of Humanities and Social Sciences, Program in Communication, Rhetoric, and Digital Media, Raleigh, NC 27695. Offers MS, PhD.

Northern Vermont University–Johnson, Program in Studio Arts, Johnson, VT 05656. Offers ceramics (MFA); digital media (MFA); drawing (MFA); painting (MFA); photography (MFA); printmaking (MFA); sculpture (MFA). *Program availability:* Part-time, online learning. *Degree requirements:* For master's, thesis. *Entrance requirements:* For master's, portfolio. Additional exam requirements/recommendations for international students: required—TOEFL. Electronic applications accepted. *Expenses:* Contact institution.

The Ohio State University, Graduate School, College of Arts and Sciences, Division of Arts and Humanities, Department of Design, Columbus, OH 43210. Offers design (MA); design research and development (MFA); digital animation and interactive media (MFA). *Accreditation:* NASAD. *Program availability:* Part-time. *Entrance requirements:* For master's, GRE General Test (for all applicants with cumulative GPA below 3.0), portfolio. Additional exam requirements/recommendations for international students: recommended—TOEFL (minimum score 550 paper-based; 79 iBT). Electronic applications accepted.

Old Dominion University, College of Arts and Letters, Program in Lifespan and Digital Communication, Norfolk, VA 23529. Offers MA. *Accreditation:* NASAD. *Program availability:* Part-time, evening/weekend. *Degree requirements:* For master's, thesis or capstone project. *Entrance requirements:* For master's, GRE. Additional exam requirements/recommendations for international students: required—TOEFL (minimum score 550 paper-based; 79 iBT). Electronic applications accepted. *Expenses:* Contact institution.

Purchase College, State University of New York, School of Art and Design, Purchase, NY 10577-1400. Offers art history/visual arts (MA); visual arts (MFA). *Accreditation:* NASAD. *Students:* 17 full-time (12 women); includes 3 minority (2 Asian, non-Hispanic/Latino; 1 Hispanic/Latino), 4 international. Average age 31. 46 applicants, 41% accepted, 8 enrolled. *Degree requirements:* For master's, thesis, exhibit. *Entrance requirements:* For master's, portfolio. Additional exam requirements/recommendations for international students: required—TOEFL (minimum score 550 paper-based; 80 iBT), IELTS (minimum score 6.5). *Application deadline:* For fall admission, 2/15 for domestic students. Applications are processed on a rolling basis. Application fee: $85. Electronic applications accepted. *Expenses: Tuition, area resident:* Full-time $11,310. Tuition, state resident: full-time $11,310. Tuition, nonresident: full-time $23,100. *Required fees:* $1883. *Financial support:* Fellowships, teaching assistantships, Federal Work-Study,

scholarships/grants, and tuition waivers (partial) available. Support available to part-time students. Financial award application deadline: 3/15; financial award applicants required to submit FAFSA. *Unit head:* Christopher Robbins, Director, 914-251-6750, Fax: 914-251-6793, E-mail: christopher.robbins@purchase.edu. *Application contact:* Beatriz Martin-Ruiz, Assistant Director of Admissions, 914-251-6304, Fax: 914-251-6314, E-mail: admissn@purchase.edu.
Website: https://www.purchase.edu/academics/art-and-design/

Purdue University, Graduate School, Purdue Polytechnic Institute, Department of Computer Graphics Technology, West Lafayette, IN 47907. Offers MS, PhD. *Faculty:* 23 full-time (5 women), 2 part-time/adjunct (0 women). *Students:* 49 full-time (17 women), 19 part-time (8 women); includes 7 minority (5 Asian, non-Hispanic/Latino; 1 Hispanic/Latino; 1 Two or more races, non-Hispanic/Latino), 41 international. Average age 24. 103 applicants, 60% accepted, 19 enrolled. In 2019, 21 master's awarded. *Degree requirements:* For master's, thesis; for doctorate, thesis/dissertation. *Entrance requirements:* For master's, GRE (minimum scores: 50th percentile, 150 on verbal, 150 on quantitative, 4.0 analytical). Additional exam requirements/recommendations for international students: required—TOEFL (minimum score 550 paper-based; 77 iBT); recommended—TWE. *Application deadline:* For fall admission, 4/1 for domestic and international students; for spring admission, 10/1 for domestic students, 9/1 for international students; for summer admission, 4/1 for domestic students, 2/15 for international students. Applications are processed on a rolling basis. Application fee: $60 ($75 for international students). Electronic applications accepted. *Financial support:* Research assistantships and teaching assistantships available. *Unit head:* Nathan W. Hartman, Interim Head of the Graduate Program, 765-496-6104, E-mail: nhartman@purdue.edu. *Application contact:* Chasity Kuxhausen, Graduate Contact, 765-496-6368, E-mail: ckuxhaus@purdue.edu.
Website: http://www.tech.purdue.edu/cgt/

Rensselaer Polytechnic Institute, Graduate School, School of Humanities, Arts, and Social Sciences, Program in Electronic Arts, Troy, NY 12180-3590. Offers PhD. *Faculty:* 25 full-time (10 women), 9 part-time/adjunct (5 women). *Students:* 20 full-time (10 women), 1 part-time (0 women); includes 2 minority (1 Asian, non-Hispanic/Latino; 1 Hispanic/Latino), 7 international. Average age 34. 23 applicants, 26% accepted, 4 enrolled. In 2019, 1 doctorate awarded. *Degree requirements:* For doctorate, comprehensive exam. *Entrance requirements:* For doctorate, portfolio, research proposal, writing sample. Additional exam requirements/recommendations for international students: required—TOEFL (minimum score 570 paper-based; 88 iBT), IELTS (minimum score 6.5), PTE (minimum score 60). *Application deadline:* For fall admission, 1/1 priority date for domestic and international students. Applications are processed on a rolling basis. Application fee: $75. Electronic applications accepted. *Financial support:* In 2019–20, research assistantships (averaging $23,000 per year), teaching assistantships with full tuition reimbursements (averaging $23,000 per year) were awarded; scholarships/grants also available. Financial award application deadline: 1/1. *Unit head:* Dr. Tomie Hahn, Graduate Program Director, 518-276-2379, E-mail: hahnt@rpi.edu. *Application contact:* Jarron Decker, Director of Graduate Admissions, 518-276-6216, Fax: 518-276-4072, E-mail: gradadmissions@rpi.edu.
Website: http://www.arts.rpi.edu/pl/graduate-programs

Rhode Island School of Design, Department of Digital and Media, Providence, RI 02903-2784. Offers MFA. *Students:* 19 full-time (14 women); includes 2 minority (both Hispanic/Latino), 11 international. Average age 27. 161 applicants, 17% accepted, 11 enrolled. In 2019, 11 master's awarded. *Degree requirements:* For master's, thesis, exhibition. *Entrance requirements:* For master's, portfolio, statement of purpose, 3 letters of recommendation. Additional exam requirements/recommendations for international students: required—TOEFL (minimum score 580 paper-based; 93 iBT), IELTS (minimum score 6.5), Duolingo. *Application deadline:* For fall admission, 1/10 for domestic and international students. Application fee: $60. Electronic applications accepted. *Expenses: Tuition:* Full-time $51,800. *Required fees:* $1060. *Financial support:* Fellowships, research assistantships, teaching assistantships, Federal Work-Study, scholarships/grants, and unspecified assistantships available. Financial award application deadline: 2/1; financial award applicants required to submit FAFSA. *Unit head:* Shawn Greenlee, Department Head and Graduate Program Director, 401-454-6139, Fax: 401-277-4966, E-mail: digital@risd.edu. *Application contact:* Molly Pettengill, Associate Director for Graduate Recruitment, 401-454-6312, Fax: 401-454-6309, E-mail: mpetteng@risd.edu.
Website: http://www.risd.edu/academics/digital-media/

Rochester Institute of Technology, Graduate Enrollment Services, College of Imaging Arts and Sciences, School of Design, MFA Program in Visual Communication Design, Rochester, NY 14623-5603. Offers MFA. *Accreditation:* NASAD. *Program availability:* Part-time. *Degree requirements:* For master's, thesis, thesis exhibition. *Entrance requirements:* For master's, portfolio, personal statement, three letters of recommendation. Additional exam requirements/recommendations for international students: required—TOEFL (minimum score 550 paper-based; 90 iBT), IELTS (minimum score 7), PTE (minimum score 58). Electronic applications accepted.

Rochester Institute of Technology, Graduate Enrollment Services, College of Imaging Arts and Sciences, School of Film and Animation, MFA Program in Film and Animation, Rochester, NY 14623-5603. Offers MFA. *Program availability:* Part-time. *Degree requirements:* For master's, thesis. *Entrance requirements:* For master's, portfolio, two-to-three minute online self-portrait video, personal statement, two letters of recommendation. Additional exam requirements/recommendations for international students: required—TOEFL (minimum score 550 paper-based; 88 iBT), IELTS (minimum score 6.5), PTE (minimum score 58). Electronic applications accepted.

Savannah College of Art and Design, Program in Animation, Savannah, GA 31402-3146. Offers MA, MFA. *Program availability:* Part-time, 100% online. *Degree requirements:* For master's, final project (for MA); thesis (for MFA). *Entrance requirements:* For master's, GRE (recommended), portfolio (submitted in digital format), audition or writing submission, resume, statement of purpose, two letters of recommendation. Additional exam requirements/recommendations for international students: recommended—TOEFL (minimum score 550 paper-based; 85 iBT), IELTS (minimum score 6.5). Electronic applications accepted.

Savannah College of Art and Design, Program in Interactive Design and Game Development, Savannah, GA 31402-3146. Offers MA, MFA. *Program availability:* Part-time, 100% online. *Degree requirements:* For master's, final project (for MA); thesis (for MFA). *Entrance requirements:* For master's, GRE (recommended), portfolio (submitted in digital format), audition or writing submission, resume, statement of purpose, two letters of recommendation. Additional exam requirements/recommendations for international students: recommended—TOEFL (minimum score 550 paper-based; 85 iBT), IELTS (minimum score 6.5). Electronic applications accepted.

Savannah College of Art and Design, Program in Motion Media Design, Savannah, GA 31402-3146. Offers MA, MFA. *Program availability:* Part-time, 100% online. *Degree requirements:* For master's, final project (for MA); thesis (for MFA). *Entrance requirements:* For master's, GRE (recommended), portfolio (submitted in digital format), audition or writing submission, resume, statement of purpose, two letters of recommendation. Additional exam requirements/recommendations for international students: recommended—TOEFL (minimum score 550 paper-based; 85 iBT), IELTS (minimum score 6.5). Electronic applications accepted.

School of Visual Arts, Graduate Programs, Computer Art Department, New York, NY 10010-3994. Offers MFA. *Accreditation:* NASAD. *Degree requirements:* For master's, thesis, 60 credits; minimum GPA of 3.0; matriculation of two academic years. *Entrance requirements:* For master's, portfolio; 3-5 minute sample reel showing best work; statement of purpose; official transcript; 3 letters of recommendation; resume/curriculum vitae. Additional exam requirements/recommendations for international students: required—TOEFL (minimum score 550 paper-based; 79 iBT). Electronic applications accepted. *Expenses:* Contact institution.

Syracuse University, College of Visual and Performing Arts, MFA Program in Computer Art, Syracuse, NY 13244. Offers MFA. *Entrance requirements:* For master's, portfolio, artist statement, three letters of recommendation, transcripts, personal statement/essay, resume. Additional exam requirements/recommendations for international students: required—TOEFL (minimum score 100 iBT), IELTS. Electronic applications accepted.

Texas State University, The Graduate College, College of Fine Arts and Communication, Program in Communication Design, San Marcos, TX 78666. Offers MFA. *Program availability:* Part-time. *Degree requirements:* For master's, comprehensive exam, thesis. *Entrance requirements:* For master's, related baccalaureate degree from regionally-accredited institution with minimum GPA of 2.75 in last 60 hours of undergraduate course work, 3 letters of recommendation, academic and professional statement of purpose, online portfolio showcasing at least 20 works in communication design. Additional exam requirements/recommendations for international students: required—TOEFL (minimum score 550 paper-based; 78 iBT), IELTS (minimum score 6), TOEFL (minimum iBT scores: 19 listening, 19 reading, 19 speaking, 18 writing). Electronic applications accepted.

Universidad Autonoma de Guadalajara, Graduate Programs, Guadalajara, Mexico. Offers administrative law and justice (LL M); advertising and corporate communications (MA); architecture (M Arch); business (MBA); computational science (MCC); education (Ed M, Ed D); English-Spanish translation (MA); entrepreneurship and management (MBA); integrated management of digital animation (MA); international business (MIB); international corporate law (LL M); Internet technologies (MS); manufacturing systems (MMS); occupational health (MS); philosophy (MA, PhD); power electronics (MS); quality systems (MQS); renewable energy (MS); social evaluation of projects (MBA); strategic market research (MBA); tax law (MA); teaching mathematics (MA).

Universidad de las Américas Puebla, Division of Graduate Studies, School of Humanities, Program in Information Design, Puebla, Mexico. Offers MA. *Program availability:* Part-time, evening/weekend. *Degree requirements:* For master's, one foreign language, thesis. *Entrance requirements:* Additional exam requirements/recommendations for international students: required—TOEFL.

University of Alaska Fairbanks, College of Liberal Arts, Department of Art, Fairbanks, AK 99775-5640. Offers art (MFA); ceramics (MFA); computer art (MFA); drawing (MFA); painting (MFA); photography (MFA); printmaking (MFA); sculpture (MFA). *Program availability:* Part-time. *Degree requirements:* For master's, comprehensive exam, oral defense of project or thesis. *Entrance requirements:* For master's, portfolio of work including about 20 slides or appropriate equivalent depending on field of study. Additional exam requirements/recommendations for international students: required—TOEFL (minimum score 550 paper-based; 79 iBT), IELTS (minimum score 6.5). Electronic applications accepted.

University of California, Santa Cruz, Division of Graduate Studies, Division of the Arts, Department of Film and Digital Media, Santa Cruz, CA 95064. Offers PhD. *Degree requirements:* For doctorate, one foreign language, thesis/dissertation, qualifying exams. *Entrance requirements:* For doctorate, GRE. Additional exam requirements/recommendations for international students: required—TOEFL (minimum score 550 paper-based; 83 iBT); recommended—IELTS (minimum score 8). Electronic applications accepted.

University of California, Santa Cruz, Division of Graduate Studies, Division of the Arts, Program in Digital Arts and New Media, Santa Cruz, CA 95064. Offers MFA. *Degree requirements:* For master's, thesis, written paper. *Entrance requirements:* Additional exam requirements/recommendations for international students: required—TOEFL (minimum score 550 paper-based; 83 iBT); recommended—IELTS (minimum score 8). Electronic applications accepted.

University of Central Arkansas, Graduate School, College of Fine Arts and Communication, Program in Digital Filmmaking, Conway, AR 72035-0001. Offers MFA. *Accreditation:* NASAD. *Degree requirements:* For master's, thesis. *Entrance requirements:* For master's, GRE General Test, minimum GPA of 2.7. Additional exam requirements/recommendations for international students: required—TOEFL (minimum score 550 paper-based). Electronic applications accepted.

University of Central Florida, College of Arts and Humanities, School of Visual Arts and Design, Orlando, FL 32816. Offers digital media (MA); emerging media (MFA), including animation and visual effects, digital media, entrepreneurial digital cinema, studio art and the computer. *Program availability:* Part-time. *Students:* 41 full-time (17 women), 5 part-time (2 women); includes 23 minority (6 Black or African American, non-Hispanic/Latino; 1 Asian, non-Hispanic/Latino; 15 Hispanic/Latino; 1 Two or more races, non-Hispanic/Latino), 2 international. Average age 30. 41 applicants, 56% accepted, 18 enrolled. In 2019, 5 master's awarded. *Degree requirements:* For master's, comprehensive exam, thesis or alternative. *Entrance requirements:* For master's, GRE, letter of recommendation. Additional exam requirements/recommendations for international students: required—TOEFL. *Application deadline:* For fall admission, 7/1 for domestic students. Application fee: $30. Electronic applications accepted. *Financial support:* In 2019–20, 22 students received support, including 10 fellowships with partial tuition reimbursements available (averaging $7,400 per year), 15 teaching assistantships with partial tuition reimbursements available (averaging $5,226 per year); scholarships/grants, health care benefits, and unspecified assistantships also available. Financial award application deadline: 3/1; financial award applicants required to submit FAFSA. *Unit head:* Dr. Rudy McDaniel, Director, 407-823-3145, E-mail: rudy@ucf.edu. *Application contact:* Associate Director, Graduate Admissions, 407-823-2766, Fax: 407-823-6442, E-mail: gradadmissions@ucf.edu.
Website: http://svad.cah.ucf.edu/

University of Denver, Division of Arts, Humanities and Social Sciences, Program in Emergent Digital Practices, Denver, CO 80208. Offers MA, MFA. *Program availability:* Part-time. *Faculty:* 1 (woman) full-time, 2 part-time/adjunct (1 woman). *Students:* 8 full-time (5 women), 333 part-time (193 women); includes 80 minority (18 Black or African American, non-Hispanic/Latino; 6 American Indian or Alaska Native, non-Hispanic/Latino; 3 Asian, non-Hispanic/Latino; 38 Hispanic/Latino; 2 Native Hawaiian or other Pacific Islander, non-Hispanic/Latino; 13 Two or more races, non-Hispanic/Latino), 4 international. Average age 30. 233 applicants, 89% accepted, 123 enrolled. In 2019, 105 master's awarded. *Degree requirements:* For master's, thesis (for some programs), project, thesis, or exhibition. *Entrance requirements:* For master's, GRE General Test,

bachelor's degree (BFA for MFA recommended), transcripts, personal statement, resume or curriculum vitae, three letters of recommendation, portfolio for MFA. Additional exam requirements/recommendations for international students: required—TOEFL (minimum score 550 paper-based; 80 iBT). *Application deadline:* For fall admission, 1/21 priority date for domestic and international students. Applications are processed on a rolling basis. Application fee: $65. Electronic applications accepted. *Expenses:* Contact institution. *Financial support:* In 2019–20, 15 students received support, including 8 teaching assistantships with tuition reimbursements available (averaging $6,433 per year); Federal Work-Study, scholarships/grants, and unspecified assistantships also available. Financial award application deadline: 2/15; financial award applicants required to submit FAFSA. *Unit head:* Dr. Bill Depper, Teaching Professor/Program Director, 303-871-4661, E-mail: wdepper@du.edu. *Application contact:* Dr. Christopher Coleman, Professor/Graduate Director, 303-871-7423, E-mail: christopher.coleman@du.edu.
Website: http://www.du.edu/ahss/edp

University of Florida, Graduate School, College of The Arts, School of Art and Art History, Gainesville, FL 32611. Offers art (MA), including digital arts and sciences; art education (MA); art history (MA, PhD); museology (MA), including historic preservation. *Accreditation:* NASAD. *Program availability:* Online learning. *Degree requirements:* For master's, project or thesis (MFA); 1 foreign language (MA in art history); for doctorate, 2 foreign languages, comprehensive exam, thesis/dissertation. *Entrance requirements:* For master's, GRE General Test, portfolio (MFA), writing sample (MA), minimum GPA 3.0; for doctorate, GRE General Test, minimum GPA of 3.0. Additional exam requirements/recommendations for international students: required—TOEFL (minimum score 550 paper-based; 80 iBT), IELTS (minimum score 6). Electronic applications accepted.

University of Florida, Graduate School, Herbert Wertheim College of Engineering, Department of Computer and Information Science and Engineering, Gainesville, FL 32611. Offers computer engineering (ME, MS, PhD); computer science (MS); digital arts and sciences (MS). *Program availability:* Part-time, online learning. Terminal master's awarded for partial completion of doctoral program. *Degree requirements:* For master's, comprehensive exam, thesis optional; for doctorate, comprehensive exam, thesis/dissertation. *Entrance requirements:* For master's and doctorate, minimum GPA of 3.0. Additional exam requirements/recommendations for international students: required—TOEFL (minimum score 550 paper-based; 80 iBT), IELTS (minimum score 6). Electronic applications accepted.

University of Maryland, Baltimore County, The Graduate School, College of Arts, Humanities and Social Sciences, Department of Visual Arts, MFA in Intermedia and Digital Arts Program, Baltimore, MD 21250. Offers MFA. *Faculty:* 24 full-time (13 women), 15 part-time/adjunct (7 women). *Students:* 15 full-time (9 women), 1 (woman) part-time; includes 6 minority (1 Black or African American, non-Hispanic/Latino; 3 Hispanic/Latino; 2 Two or more races, non-Hispanic/Latino), 2 international. Average age 33. 15 applicants, 40% accepted, 5 enrolled. In 2019, 5 master's awarded. *Degree requirements:* For master's, oral defense, exhibition, written thesis. *Entrance requirements:* For master's, minimum GPA of 3.0, portfolio. Additional exam requirements/recommendations for international students: required—TOEFL. *Application deadline:* For fall admission, 2/1 for domestic and international students. Applications are processed on a rolling basis. Application fee: $50. Electronic applications accepted. *Expenses:* $14,382 per year. *Financial support:* In 2019–20, 14 students received support, including 14 research assistantships with partial tuition reimbursements available (averaging $22,325 per year); institutionally sponsored loans, scholarships/grants, health care benefits, and unspecified assistantships also available. Financial award application deadline: 2/1. *Unit head:* Prof. Lisa Moren, Graduate Program Director, 410-455-2490, Fax: 410-455-1053, E-mail: lmoren@umbc.edu. *Application contact:* Prof. Lisa Moren, Graduate Program Director, 410-455-2490, Fax: 410-455-1053, E-mail: lmoren@umbc.edu.
Website: http://imda.umbc.edu

University of Montana, Graduate School, College of Visual and Performing Arts, School of Media Arts, Missoula, MT 59812. Offers digital filmmaking (MFA); integrated digital media (MFA).

University of Pennsylvania, School of Engineering and Applied Science, Department of Computer and Information Science, Philadelphia, PA 19104. Offers computer and information science (MSE, PhD); computer and information technology (MCIT); computer graphics and game technology (MSE). *Program availability:* Part-time. *Faculty:* 61 full-time (9 women), 9 part-time/adjunct (0 women). *Students:* 250 full-time (63 women), 23 part-time (2 women); includes 36 minority (6 Black or African American, non-Hispanic/Latino; 27 Asian, non-Hispanic/Latino; 2 Hispanic/Latino; 1 Two or more races, non-Hispanic/Latino), 173 international. Average age 26. 2,124 applicants, 12% accepted, 103 enrolled. In 2019, 87 master's, 18 doctorates awarded. Terminal master's awarded for partial completion of doctoral program. *Degree requirements:* For master's, comprehensive exam, thesis optional; for doctorate, comprehensive exam, thesis/dissertation. *Entrance requirements:* For master's and doctorate, GRE, bachelor's degree, letters of recommendation, resume, personal statement. Additional exam requirements/recommendations for international students: required—TOEFL (minimum score 100 iBT), IELTS (minimum score 7). *Application deadline:* For fall admission, 12/15 priority date for domestic and international students. Application fee: $80. Electronic

applications accepted. *Expenses:* Contact institution. *Application contact:* Associate Director of Graduate Admissions, 215-898-4542, Fax: 215-573-5577, E-mail: admissions2@upenn.edu.
Website: http://www.cis.upenn.edu/prospective-students/graduate/

University of Rhode Island, Graduate School, College of Arts and Sciences, Graduate School of Library and Information Studies, Kingston, RI 02881. Offers libraries, leadership and transforming communities (MLIS); organization of digital media (MLIS); school library media (MLIS); MLIS/MA; MLIS/MPA. *Accreditation:* ALA (one or more programs are accredited). *Program availability:* Part-time. *Faculty:* 4 full-time (all women). *Students:* 15 full-time (7 women), 89 part-time (78 women); includes 8 minority (4 Asian, non-Hispanic/Latino; 2 Hispanic/Latino; 2 Two or more races, non-Hispanic/Latino). 54 applicants, 80% accepted, 20 enrolled. In 2019, 37 master's awarded. *Entrance requirements:* For master's, GRE or MAT if undergraduate GPA below 3.3, 2 letters of recommendation. Additional exam requirements/recommendations for international students: required—TOEFL. *Application deadline:* For fall admission, 6/15 for domestic students, 2/1 for international students; for spring admission, 10/15 for domestic students, 7/15 for international students; for summer admission, 3/15 for domestic students. Application fee: $65. Electronic applications accepted. *Expenses:* Tuition, area resident: Full-time $13,734; part-time $763 per credit. Tuition, state resident: full-time $13,734; part-time $763 per credit. Tuition, nonresident: full-time $26,512; part-time $1473 per credit. International tuition: $26,512 full-time. *Required fees:* $1780; $52 per credit. $35 per term. One-time fee: $165. *Financial support:* Application deadline: 1/15; applicants required to submit FAFSA. *Unit head:* Dr. Valerie Karno, Chair, 401-874-4682, Fax: 401-874-4127, E-mail: karno@uri.edu. *Application contact:* Dr. Valerie Karno, Chair, 401-874-4682, Fax: 401-874-4127, E-mail: karno@uri.edu.
Website: http://www.uri.edu/artsci/lsc/

University of Southern California, Graduate School, School of Cinematic Arts, John C. Hench Division of Animation and Digital Arts, Los Angeles, CA 90089. Offers MFA. *Degree requirements:* For master's, thesis, digital media and research documentation. *Entrance requirements:* Additional exam requirements/recommendations for international students: recommended—TOEFL. Electronic applications accepted. *Expenses:* Contact institution.

University of South Florida, St. Petersburg, College of Arts and Sciences, St. Petersburg, FL 33701. Offers digital journalism and design (MA); environmental science and policy (MA, MS); Florida studies (MLA); journalism and media studies (MA); liberal studies (MLA); psychology (MA). *Program availability:* Part-time, online learning. *Degree requirements:* For master's, comprehensive exam, thesis or project. *Entrance requirements:* For master's, GRE, LSAT, MCAT (varies by program), letter of intent, 3 letters of recommendation, writing samples, bachelor's degree from regionally-accredited institution with minimum GPA of 3.0 overall or in upper two years. Additional exam requirements/recommendations for international students: required—TOEFL (minimum score 550 paper-based; 79 iBT); recommended—IELTS. Electronic applications accepted.

University of Victoria, Faculty of Graduate Studies, Faculty of Fine Arts, Department of Visual Arts, Victoria, BC V8W 2Y2, Canada. Offers digital multimedia (MFA); drawing (MFA); painting (MFA); photography (MFA); sculpture (MFA); video (MFA). *Degree requirements:* For master's, exhibit, oral exam. *Entrance requirements:* For master's, portfolio, BFA. Additional exam requirements/recommendations for international students: required—TOEFL (minimum score 575 paper-based), IELTS (minimum score 7). Electronic applications accepted.

University of Wisconsin–Milwaukee, Graduate School, Peck School of the Arts, Milwaukee, WI 53201-0413. Offers art education (MS); chamber music (CAS); conducting (MM); dance (MFA); design entrepreneurship and innovation (MA); film, video, animation, and new genres (MFA); music education (MM); music history and literature (MM); performance (MM); string pedagogy (MM); studio art (MA, MFA); theory and composition (MM). *Program availability:* Part-time. *Degree requirements:* For master's, comprehensive exam, thesis or alternative. *Entrance requirements:* For master's, portfolio. Additional exam requirements/recommendations for international students: required—TOEFL (minimum score 550 paper-based; 79 iBT), IELTS (minimum score 6.5). Electronic applications accepted.

Virginia International University, School of Computer Information Systems, Fairfax, VA 22030. Offers business intelligence (Graduate Certificate); business intelligence and data analytics (MIS); computer science (MS), including computer animation and gaming, cybersecurity, data management networking, intelligent systems, software applications development, software engineering; cybersecurity (MIS); data management (MIS); enterprise project management (MIS); health informatics (MIS); information assurance (MIS); information systems (Graduate Certificate); information systems management (MS, Graduate Certificate); information technology (MS); information technology audit and compliance (Graduate Certificate); knowledge management (MIS); software engineering (MS). *Program availability:* Part-time, online learning. *Entrance requirements:* For master's, bachelor's degree. Additional exam requirements/recommendations for international students: required—TOEFL (minimum score 550 paper-based; 80 iBT), IELTS. Electronic applications accepted.

Graphic Design

Academy of Art University, Graduate Programs, School of Graphic Design, San Francisco, CA 94105-3410. Offers graphic design (MFA); graphic design and digital media (MA). *Accreditation:* NASAD. *Program availability:* Part-time, 100% online. *Faculty:* 5 full-time (1 woman), 19 part-time/adjunct (9 women). *Students:* 142 full-time (99 women), 119 part-time (82 women); includes 31 minority (9 Black or African American, non-Hispanic/Latino; 6 Asian, non-Hispanic/Latino; 13 Hispanic/Latino; 1 Native Hawaiian or other Pacific Islander, non-Hispanic/Latino; 2 Two or more races, non-Hispanic/Latino), 166 international. Average age 28. 125 applicants, 100% accepted, 80 enrolled. In 2019, 105 master's awarded. *Degree requirements:* For master's, final review. *Entrance requirements:* For master's, statement of intent; resume; portfolio/reel; official college transcripts. *Application deadline:* Applications are processed on a rolling basis. Application fee: $50. Electronic applications accepted. *Expenses: Tuition:* Full-time $1083; part-time $1083 per credit hour. *Required fees:* $860; $860 per unit. $430 per term. One-time fee: $145. Tuition and fees vary according to program. *Financial support:* Career-related internships or fieldwork, Federal Work-Study, and scholarships/grants available. Financial award application deadline: 8/10;

financial award applicants required to submit FAFSA.
Website: https://www.academyart.edu/academics/graphic-design

ArtCenter College of Design, Graduate Graphic Design Program, Pasadena, CA 91103. Offers MFA.

Atlantic University College, Program in Graphic Arts, Guaynabo, PR 00970. Offers digital graphic design (MGD). *Program availability:* Part-time. *Degree requirements:* For master's, thesis. *Entrance requirements:* For master's, minimum GPA of 3.0, 2 letters of recommendation, portfolio, interview.

Bob Jones University, Graduate Programs, Greenville, SC 29614. Offers accountancy (MS); Bible (MA); Bible translation (MA); Biblical studies (Certificate); business administration (MBA); church history (MA, PhD); church ministries (MA); church music (MM); cinema and video production (MA); counseling (MS); curriculum and instruction (Ed D); divinity (M Div); dramatic production (MA); educational leadership (MS, Ed D, Ed S); elementary education (M Ed, MAT); English (M Ed, MA, MAT); fine arts (MA); graphic design (MA); history (M Ed, MA); illustration (MA); interpretative speech (MA); mathematics (M Ed, MAT); medical missions (Certificate);

ministry (MM, D Min); multi-categorical special education (M Ed, MAT); music (M Ed); New Testament interpretation (PhD); Old Testament interpretation (PhD); orchestral instrument performance (MM); organ performance (MM); pastoral studies (MA); personnel services (MS, Ed S); piano pedagogy (MM); piano performance (MM); platform arts (MA); rhetoric and public address (MA); secondary education (M Ed); studio art (MA); teaching Bible (MA); theology (MA, PhD); voice performance (MM); youth ministries (MA); M Div/MM.

Bowling Green State University, Graduate College, College of Arts and Sciences, School of Art, Bowling Green, OH 43403. Offers 2-D studio art (MA, MFA); 3-D studio art (MA, MFA); art education (MA); art history (MA); computer art (MA); design (MFA); digital arts (MFA); graphics (MFA). *Accreditation:* NASAD. *Program availability:* Part-time. *Degree requirements:* For master's, thesis or alternative, final exhibit (MFA). *Entrance requirements:* For master's, GRE General Test (for MA), slide portfolio (15-20 slides). Additional exam requirements/recommendations for international students: required—TOEFL. Electronic applications accepted.

Bradley University, The Graduate School, Slane College of Communications and Fine Arts, Department of Art, Peoria, IL 61625-0002. Offers ceramics (MA, MFA); drawing (MA, MFA); graphic design (MA, MFA); painting (MA, MFA); photography (MA, MFA); printmaking (MA, MFA); sculpture (MA, MFA). *Accreditation:* NASAD. *Program availability:* Part-time. *Faculty:* 10 full-time (4 women). *Students:* 4 full-time (2 women), 2 part-time (both women); includes 1 minority (American Indian or Alaska Native, non-Hispanic/Latino). Average age 42. 3 applicants, 33% accepted. In 2019, 6 master's awarded. *Degree requirements:* For master's, comprehensive exam, thesis, final exhibit. *Entrance requirements:* For master's, portfolio, 2 letters of recommendation. Additional exam requirements/recommendations for international students: required—TOEFL (minimum score 550 paper-based; 79 iBT), PTE (minimum score 58). *Application deadline:* For fall admission, 4/1 priority date for domestic and international students; for spring admission, 11/1 priority date for domestic and international students. Applications are processed on a rolling basis. Application fee: $40 ($50 for international students). Electronic applications accepted. *Expenses: Tuition:* Part-time $930 per credit hour. *Financial support:* In 2019–20, 2 students received support. Teaching assistantships, scholarships/grants, tuition waivers (partial), and unspecified assistantships available. Support available to part-time students. Financial award application deadline: 4/1. *Unit head:* Gary Will, Chairperson, 309-677-2967, E-mail: gwill@bradley.edu. *Application contact:* Rachel Webb, Director of On-Campus Graduate Admissions and International Student and Scholar Services, 309-677-2375, E-mail: rkwebb@bradley.edu.
Website: http://www.bradley.edu/academic/departments/art/

California College of the Arts, Graduate Programs, Design Program, San Francisco, CA 94107. Offers graphic design (MFA); industrial design (MFA); interaction design (MFA). *Accreditation:* NASAD. *Degree requirements:* For master's, thesis, exhibit. *Entrance requirements:* For master's, appropriate bachelor's degree, portfolio, resume, letters of recommendation, transcripts. Additional exam requirements/recommendations for international students: required—TOEFL, IELTS, or PTE. Electronic applications accepted. *Expenses:* Contact institution.

California Institute of the Arts, School of Art, Valencia, CA 91355-2340. Offers art (MFA, Adv C); graphic design (MFA, Adv C); photography (MFA, Adv C). *Accreditation:* NASAD (one or more programs are accredited). *Degree requirements:* For master's, final project. *Entrance requirements:* For master's, portfolio. Additional exam requirements/recommendations for international students: required—TOEFL. Electronic applications accepted.

California State University, Fullerton, Graduate Studies, College of the Arts, Department of Visual Arts, Fullerton, CA 92831-3599. Offers art (MA, MFA), including art history (MA), ceramics (MFA), crafts, creative photography, exhibition design, glass, graphic design, illustration, sculpture. *Accreditation:* NASAD (one or more programs are accredited). *Program availability:* Part-time. *Entrance requirements:* For master's, minimum GPA of 2.5 in last 60 units of course work, portfolio.

California State University, Los Angeles, Graduate Studies, College of Arts and Letters, Department of Art, Los Angeles, CA 90032-8530. Offers art (MA), including art education, art history, art therapy, ceramics, metals, and textiles, design (MA, MFA), painting, sculpture, and graphic arts, photography; fine arts (MFA), including crafts, design (MA, MFA), studio arts. *Accreditation:* NASAD (one or more programs are accredited). *Program availability:* Part-time, evening/weekend. *Degree requirements:* For master's, comprehensive exam, project or thesis. *Entrance requirements:* For master's, portfolio. Additional exam requirements/recommendations for international students: required—TOEFL (minimum score 500 paper-based). Electronic applications accepted. *Expenses: Tuition, area resident:* Full-time $7176; part-time $4164 per year. Tuition, state resident: full-time $7176; part-time $4164 per year. Tuition, nonresident: full-time $14,304; part-time $8916 per year. *International tuition:* $14,304 full-time. *Required fees:* $1037.76; $1037.76 per unit. Tuition and fees vary according to degree level and program.

Central Connecticut State University, School of Graduate Studies, College of Liberal Arts and Social Sciences, Department of Design, New Britain, CT 06050-4010. Offers information design (MA). *Program availability:* Part-time, evening/weekend. *Degree requirements:* For master's, thesis or alternative, research project. *Entrance requirements:* For master's, portfolio, minimum undergraduate GPA of 3.0, essay. Additional exam requirements/recommendations for international students: required—TOEFL (minimum score 550 paper-based; 79 iBT); recommended—IELTS (minimum score 6.5). Electronic applications accepted.

Central Washington University, School of Graduate Studies and Research, College of Arts and Humanities, Department of Art and Design, Ellensburg, WA 98926. Offers ceramics (MFA); computer arts (MFA); jewelry and metalsmithing (MFA); painting and drawing (MFA); photography (MFA); sculpture (MFA). *Entrance requirements:* For master's, minimum GPA of 3.0, portfolio. Additional exam requirements/recommendations for international students: required—TOEFL (minimum score 550 paper-based; 79 iBT) or IELTS (minimum score 6.5). Electronic applications accepted.

City College of the City University of New York, Graduate School, Division of Humanities and the Arts, Department of Art, Program in Fine Arts, New York, NY 10031-9198. Offers advertising design (MFA); ceramic design (MFA); digital and interdisciplinary art practice (MFA); painting (MFA); printmaking (MFA); sculpture (MFA); wood and metal design (MFA). *Degree requirements:* For master's, thesis exhibit. *Entrance requirements:* For master's, 20-slide portfolio. Additional exam requirements/recommendations for international students: required—TOEFL (minimum score 577 paper-based; 90 iBT). Electronic applications accepted.

East Carolina University, Graduate School, College of Fine Arts and Communication, School of Art and Design, Greenville, NC 27858-4353. Offers art education (MA Ed); ceramics (MFA); graphic design (MFA); illustration (MFA); metal design (MFA); painting and drawing (MFA); photography (MFA); printmaking (MFA); sculpture (MFA); textile design (MFA); wood design (MFA). *Accreditation:* NASAD (one or more programs are accredited). *Program availability:* Part-time, evening/weekend. *Application deadline:* For fall admission, 2/1 for domestic students; for spring admission, 10/1 for domestic students. *Expenses: Tuition, area resident:* Full-time $4749; part-time $185 per credit hour. Tuition, state resident: full-time $4749; part-time $185 per credit hour. Tuition, nonresident: full-time $17,898; part-time $864 per credit hour. *International tuition:* $17,898 full-time. *Required fees:* $2787. *Financial support:* Application deadline: 6/1. *Unit head:* Dr. Kate Bukowski, Director, 252-328-6665, E-mail: bukowskik16@ecu.edu. *Application contact:* Graduate School Admissions, 252-328-6012, E-mail: gradschool@ecu.edu.
Website: https://art.ecu.edu/

Florida Atlantic University, Dorothy F. Schmidt College of Arts and Letters, Department of Visual Arts and Art History, Boca Raton, FL 33431-0991. Offers visual art (MFA), including ceramics, graphic design, visual art. *Faculty:* 14 full-time (10 women). *Students:* 9 full-time (7 women), 3 part-time (all women); includes 2 minority (1 Black or African American, non-Hispanic/Latino; 1 Hispanic/Latino), 1 international. Average age 41. 17 applicants, 24% accepted, 2 enrolled. In 2019, 4 master's awarded. *Degree requirements:* For master's, one foreign language, project. *Entrance requirements:* For master's, GRE General Test, minimum GPA of 3.0 during last 60 hours of course work, slide portfolio. *Application deadline:* For fall admission, 2/21 for domestic and international students; for spring admission, 10/1 for domestic and international students. Application fee: $30. Electronic applications accepted. *Expenses: Tuition:* Full-time $20,536; part-time $371.82 per credit hour. Tuition and fees vary according to program. *Financial support:* Research assistantships with full tuition reimbursements, teaching assistantships with full tuition reimbursements, career-related internships or fieldwork, Federal Work-Study, and institutionally sponsored loans available. Financial award applicants required to submit FAFSA. *Unit head:* Dr. Eric Landes, Chair, 954-236-1106, E-mail: elandes1@fau.edu. *Application contact:* Dr. Eric Landes, Chair, 954-236-1106, E-mail: elandes1@fau.edu.
Website: http://www.fau.edu/VAAH/

Full Sail University, Game Design Master of Science Program - Campus, Winter Park, FL 32792-7437. Offers MS.

George Mason University, College of Visual and Performing Arts, Program in Graphic Design, Fairfax, VA 22030. Offers MA. *Degree requirements:* For master's, thesis, exhibition, publication, or portfolio. *Entrance requirements:* For master's, portfolio presentation; artist statement; recommendations; transcript. Additional exam requirements/recommendations for international students: required—TOEFL (minimum score 575 paper-based; 88 iBT), IELTS (minimum score 6.5), PTE (minimum score 59). Electronic applications accepted.

George Mason University, College of Visual and Performing Arts, Program in Visual and Performing Arts, Fairfax, VA 22030. Offers MFA. *Accreditation:* NASAD. *Entrance requirements:* For master's, official transcripts; 3 letters of recommendation; letter of intent; resume; professional goals statement. Additional exam requirements/recommendations for international students: required—TOEFL (minimum score 575 paper-based; 88 iBT), IELTS (minimum score 6.5), PTE (minimum score 59). Electronic applications accepted.

Georgia Southern University, Jack N. Averitt College of Graduate Studies, College of Arts and Humanities, Program in Art, Statesboro, GA 30460. Offers fine arts (MFA), including 2D graphic design, 2D studio art, 3D studio art. *Accreditation:* NASAD. *Program availability:* Part-time. *Faculty:* 27 full-time (12 women). *Students:* 16 full-time (12 women), 3 part-time (2 women); includes 2 minority (1 Black or African American, non-Hispanic/Latino; 1 Hispanic/Latino), 5 international. Average age 29. 7 applicants, 86% accepted, 6 enrolled. In 2019, 2 master's awarded. *Degree requirements:* For master's, thesis, exhibition. *Entrance requirements:* For master's, minimum GPA of 3.0; 18 semester hours of course work in studio art, 9 in art history; portfolio; letters of reference. Additional exam requirements/recommendations for international students: required—TOEFL (minimum score 550 paper-based; 80 iBT), IELTS (minimum score 6). *Application deadline:* For fall admission, 3/1 priority date for domestic and international students; for spring admission, 10/1 priority date for domestic students, 10/1 for international students. Applications are processed on a rolling basis. Application fee: $50. Electronic applications accepted. *Expenses: Tuition, area resident:* Full-time $4986; part-time $277 per credit hour. Tuition, nonresident: full-time $19,890; part-time $1105 per credit hour. *International tuition:* $19,890 full-time. *Required fees:* $2114; $1057 per semester. $1057 per semester. Tuition and fees vary according to course load, campus/location and program. *Financial support:* In 2019–20, 10 students received support, including 4 fellowships with full tuition reimbursements available (averaging $7,750 per year); career-related internships or fieldwork, Federal Work-Study, scholarships/grants, tuition waivers (full), and unspecified assistantships also available. Support available to part-time students. Financial award application deadline: 4/15; financial award applicants required to submit FAFSA. *Unit head:* Dr. Robert Farber, Department Chair, 912-478-5358, Fax: 912-478-5104, E-mail: rfarber@georgiasouthern.edu.
Website: http://class.georgiasouthern.edu/art

Georgia State University, College of Arts, Ernest G. Welch School of Art and Design, Program in Studio Art, Atlanta, GA 30302-3083. Offers ceramics (MFA); drawing and painting (MFA); graphic design (MFA); interior design (MFA); photography (MFA); printmaking (MFA); sculpture (MFA); textiles (MFA). *Accreditation:* NASAD. Application fee: $50. Electronic applications accepted. *Expenses: Tuition, area resident:* Full-time $7164; part-time $398 per credit hour. Tuition, state resident: full-time $7164; part-time $398 per credit hour. Tuition, nonresident: full-time $22,662; part-time $1259 per credit hour. *International tuition:* $22,662 full-time. *Required fees:* $2128; $312 per credit hour. Tuition and fees vary according to course load and program. *Financial support:* Fellowships, research assistantships, teaching assistantships, scholarships/grants, and unspecified assistantships available. Financial award application deadline: 4/15; financial award applicants required to submit FAFSA. *Unit head:* Joseph Peragine, Director, Welch School of Art and Design, 404-413-5229, E-mail: jperagine@gsu.edu. *Application contact:* Joseph Peragine, Director, Welch School of Art and Design, 404-413-5229, E-mail: jperagine@gsu.edu.
Website: http://artdesign.gsu.edu/graduate/admissions/masters-of-fine-arts-in-studio/

Illinois State University, Graduate School, Wonsook Kim College of Fine Arts, School of Art, Normal, IL 61790. Offers art history (MA, MS); ceramics (MFA, MS); drawing (MFA, MS); fibers (MFA, MS); glass (MFA, MS); graphic design (MFA, MS); metals (MFA, MS); painting (MFA, MS); photography (MFA, MS); printmaking (MFA, MS); sculpture (MFA, MS). *Accreditation:* NASAD (one or more programs are accredited). *Faculty:* 34 full-time (18 women), 15 part-time/adjunct (11 women). *Students:* 25 full-time (16 women), 5 part-time (4 women). Average age 31. 32 applicants, 66% accepted, 12 enrolled. In 2019, 11 master's awarded. *Degree requirements:* For master's, thesis or alternative, internship. *Entrance requirements:* For master's, portfolio, sample of scholarly writing. *Application deadline:* Applications are processed on a rolling basis. Application fee: $50. *Expenses: Tuition, area resident:* Full-time $7956; part-time $9767 per year. Tuition, nonresident: full-time $9233; part-time $17,592 per year. *Required fees:* $1797. *Financial support:* In 2019–20, 20 teaching assistantships were awarded; career-related internships or fieldwork, Federal Work-Study, tuition waivers (full and partial), and unspecified assistantships also available. Support available to part-time students. Financial award application deadline: 4/1. *Unit head:* Mike Wille, Director of Art School, 309-438-5610, E-mail: mjwill4@ilstu.edu. *Application contact:* Tyler Lotz, Graduate Coordinator, 309-438-8301, E-mail:

tlotz@ilstu.edu.
Website: http://www.arts.ilstu.edu/art/

Indiana State University, College of Graduate and Professional Studies, College of Arts and Sciences, Department of Art and Design, Terre Haute, IN 47809. Offers ceramics (MA, MFA); drawing (MA, MFA); graphic design (MA, MFA); painting (MA, MFA); photography (MA, MFA); printmaking (MA, MFA); sculpture (MA, MFA). *Accreditation:* NASAD (one or more programs are accredited). *Program availability:* Part-time. *Degree requirements:* For master's, thesis or alternative, departmental qualifying exam. *Entrance requirements:* For master's, portfolio. Additional exam requirements/recommendations for international students: required—TOEFL (minimum score 550 paper-based).

Indiana University-Purdue University Indianapolis, Herron School of Art and Design, Indianapolis, IN 46202. Offers art therapy (MA); visual art (MFA), including ceramics, furniture design, painting and drawing, photography and intermedia, printmaking, sculpture; visual communication design (MFA). *Degree requirements:* For master's, thesis. *Entrance requirements:* For master's, personal statement, resume, recommendations, portfolio, transcripts (18 credit hours of studio art and 12 credit hours of psychology, including 3 credit hours of developmental psychology and 3 credit hours of abnormal psychology for MA). Additional exam requirements/recommendations for international students: recommended—TOEFL (minimum score 550 paper-based; 79 iBT), IELTS (minimum score 6.5). Electronic applications accepted. *Expenses:* Contact institution.

Inter American University of Puerto Rico, San Germán Campus, Graduate Studies Center, Program in Fine Arts, San Germán, PR 00683-5008. Offers drawing (MFA); graphic design (MFA); painting (MFA); photography (MFA); printmaking (MFA); sculpture (MFA). *Program availability:* Part-time, evening/weekend. *Degree requirements:* For master's, comprehensive exam, thesis. *Entrance requirements:* For master's, GRE General Test or EXADEP, minimum GPA of 3.0.

Iowa State University of Science and Technology, Program in Graphic Design, Ames, IA 50011. Offers MA, MFA. *Accreditation:* NASAD. *Entrance requirements:* Additional exam requirements/recommendations for international students: required—TOEFL (minimum score 550 paper-based; 79 iBT), IELTS (minimum score 6). Electronic applications accepted.

Kent State University, College of Communication and Information, School of Visual Communication Design, Kent, OH 44242-0001. Offers MA, MFA. *Accreditation:* NASAD. *Program availability:* Part-time. *Faculty:* 9 full-time (4 women), 5 part-time/adjunct (1 woman). *Students:* 20 full-time (10 women), 11 part-time (6 women); includes 6 minority (3 Black or African American, non-Hispanic/Latino; 2 Asian, non-Hispanic/Latino; 1 Two or more races, non-Hispanic/Latino), 5 international. Average age 31. 29 applicants, 66% accepted, 9 enrolled. In 2019, 4 master's awarded. *Degree requirements:* For master's, thesis, project (MA); thesis (MFA). *Entrance requirements:* For master's, undergraduate degree in design or closely-related program, minimum major GPA of 3.0, goal statement, autobiographical statement, 2 letters of recommendation (3 for MFA), resume, transcripts, link to personal online portfolio (for MFA). Additional exam requirements/recommendations for international students: required—TOEFL (minimum score 94 iBT), IELTS (minimum score 7), PTE (minimum score 65), Michigan English Language Assessment Battery (minimum score 82). *Application deadline:* For fall admission, 3/1 for domestic and international students; for spring admission, 10/1 for domestic and international students. Applications are processed on a rolling basis. Application fee: $45 ($70 for international students). Electronic applications accepted. *Financial support:* Scholarships/grants and unspecified assistantships available. Financial award application deadline: 3/5; financial award applicants required to submit FAFSA. *Unit head:* Dr. Daniel Alenquer, Director, 330-672-7856, E-mail: dalenque@kent.edu. *Application contact:* Ken Visocky O'Grady, Graduate Coordinator and Professor, 330-672-1353, E-mail: kogrady@kent.edu.
Website: http://www.kent.edu/vcd/

Louisiana State University and Agricultural & Mechanical College, Graduate School, College of Art and Design, School of Art, Program in Studio Art, Baton Rouge, LA 70803. Offers ceramics (MFA); graphic design (MFA); painting and drawing (MFA); photography (MFA); printmaking (MFA); sculpture (MFA). *Accreditation:* NASAD.

Louisiana Tech University, Graduate School, College of Liberal Arts, Ruston, LA 71272. Offers architecture (M Arch); art (MFA), including graphic design, photography, studio; audiology (Au D); communication (MA), including speech communication, theatre; English (MA), including literature, technical writing; history (MA); speech pathology (MA); technical writing and communication (Graduate Certificate). *Accreditation:* ASHA. *Program availability:* Part-time. *Degree requirements:* For master's, thesis (for some programs); for doctorate, thesis/dissertation. *Entrance requirements:* For master's, GRE General Test; for doctorate, GRE General Test, bachelor's degree, minimum GPA of 3.0 or 3.2 on last 60 hours attempted. Additional exam requirements/recommendations for international students: required—TOEFL (minimum score 550 paper-based; 80 iBT), IELTS (minimum score 6.5). Electronic applications accepted. *Expenses: Tuition, area resident:* Full-time $6592; part-time $400 per credit. Tuition, state resident: full-time $6592; part-time $400 per credit. Tuition, nonresident: full-time $13,333; part-time $681 per credit. *International tuition:* $13,333 full-time. *Required fees:* $3011; $3011 per unit.

Lynn University, Eugene M. and Christine E. Lynn College of Communication and Design, Boca Raton, FL 33431-5598. Offers communication and media (MS); digital media (Certificate); digital media and design (MS); graphic and Web design (MFA); visual effects animation (MFA). *Program availability:* Part-time, evening/weekend. *Faculty:* 17 full-time (6 women), 3 part-time/adjunct (2 women). *Students:* 28 full-time (15 women), 32 part-time (16 women); includes 15 minority (8 Black or African American, non-Hispanic/Latino; 6 Hispanic/Latino; 1 Two or more races, non-Hispanic/Latino), 19 international. Average age 28. 36 applicants, 92% accepted, 20 enrolled. In 2019, 30 master's awarded. *Degree requirements:* For master's, thesis (for some programs), completion of degree in four calendar years; minimum cumulative GPA of 3.0 and C grade or higher in each course; orientation seminar (one credit); 36 credits of foundation and specialization or a thesis. *Entrance requirements:* For master's, Bachelor's degree from accredited institution, minimum undergraduate GPA of 3.0, official undergraduate transcripts, letter of recommendation from academic or professional source, writing sample demonstrating capacity to perform at graduate level. Additional exam requirements/recommendations for international students: required—TOEFL (minimum score 550 paper-based; 80 iBT), IELTS (minimum score 6.5). *Application deadline:* For fall admission, 8/10 for domestic students, 7/31 for international students; for spring admission, 12/18 for domestic students, 12/2 for international students; for summer admission, 4/12 for domestic students, 4/2 for international students. Applications are processed on a rolling basis. Application fee: $45. Electronic applications accepted. *Expenses:* $740.00 per hour. *Financial support:* In 2019–20, 15 students received support. Career-related internships or fieldwork, Federal Work-Study, scholarships/grants, tuition waivers (full and partial), and unspecified assistantships available. Support available to part-time students. Financial award application deadline: 3/1; financial award applicants required to submit FAFSA. *Unit head:* Dr. David L. Jaffe, Dean, 561-237-7099, Fax: 561-237-7097, E-mail: djaffe@lynn.edu. *Application contact:* Steven Pruitt, Director of Graduate Admission, 561-237-7834, Fax: 561-237-7100, E-mail: admission@lynn.edu.
Website: https://www.lynn.edu/academics/colleges-schools/communication-and-design

Maryland Institute College of Art, Graduate Studies, MA Program in Graphic Design, Baltimore, MD 21201. Offers MA. *Entrance requirements:* Additional exam requirements/recommendations for international students: required—TOEFL (minimum score 550 paper-based; 80 iBT), IELTS (minimum score 6.5). Electronic applications accepted. *Expenses: Tuition:* Full-time $50,160. One-time fee: $150 full-time. Full-time tuition and fees vary according to degree level.

Maryland Institute College of Art, Graduate Studies, MFA Program in Graphic Design, Baltimore, MD 21201. Offers MFA. *Degree requirements:* For master's, thesis, exhibit and thesis documentation. *Entrance requirements:* For master's, portfolio, bachelor's degree in any field. Additional exam requirements/recommendations for international students: required—TOEFL (minimum score 550 paper-based; 80 iBT), IELTS (minimum score 6.5). Electronic applications accepted. *Expenses:* Contact institution.

Marywood University, Academic Affairs, Insalaco College of Creative and Performing Arts, Art Department, Program in Visual Arts, Scranton, PA 18509-1598. Offers clay (MFA); graphic design (MFA); illustration (MFA); painting (MFA); photography (MFA); printmaking (MFA); sculpture (MFA). *Accreditation:* NASAD. *Program availability:* Part-time. Electronic applications accepted. *Expenses:* Contact institution.

Minneapolis College of Art and Design, Master of Arts in Graphic and Web Design, Minneapolis, MN 55404-4347. Offers MA. *Program availability:* Part-time, evening/weekend. *Students:* 22 applicants, 82% accepted, 14 enrolled. *Entrance requirements:* For master's, No exams are required for the MA in Graphic and Web Design, MA students must hold an undergraduate degree before enrolling. Other admissions requirements can be found online here: https://mcad.edu/admissions-and-aid/master-of-arts/application-checklist. Additional exam requirements/recommendations for international students: required—TOEFL (minimum score 550 paper-based; 79 iBT), IELTS (minimum score 6.5), MCAD also accepts the Duolingo Exam for English Language requirement. A score of 100 or higher is required. *Application deadline:* For fall admission, 4/1 priority date for domestic and international students; for spring admission, 11/1 priority date for domestic and international students. Applications are processed on a rolling basis. Application fee: $50. Electronic applications accepted. *Expenses: Tuition:* Full-time $41,344. *Required fees:* $450. One-time fee: $300 full-time. *Financial support:* Career-related internships or fieldwork available. Support available to part-time students. Financial award application deadline: 3/15; financial award applicants required to submit FAFSA. *Unit head:* Lafe Smith, Director, Master of Arts in Graphic and Web Design, E-mail: lsmith257@mcad.edu. *Application contact:* Mary Kazura, Director of Admissions, 612-874-3668, E-mail: mkazura@mcad.edu.
Website: https://mcad.edu/academic-programs/graphic-and-web-design

Minneapolis College of Art and Design, Master of Fine Arts in Visual Studies, Minneapolis, MN 55404-4347. Offers animation (MFA); comic art (MFA); drawing (MFA); filmmaking (MFA); fine arts (MFA); furniture design (MFA); graphic design (MFA); illustration (MFA); interactive media (MFA); painting (MFA); photography (MFA); printmaking (MFA); sculpture (MFA). *Accreditation:* NASAD. *Program availability:* Part-time. *Students:* 86 applicants, 44% accepted, 9 enrolled. *Degree requirements:* For master's, thesis, thesis exhibit. *Entrance requirements:* Additional exam requirements/recommendations for international students: required—TOEFL (minimum score 550 paper-based; 79 iBT), IELTS (minimum score 6.5), Duolingo English Test accepted with a minimum score of 100 *Application deadline:* For fall admission, 2/1 for domestic and international students. Application fee: $50. Electronic applications accepted. *Expenses: Tuition:* Full-time $41,344. *Required fees:* $450. One-time fee: $300 full-time. *Financial support:* In 2019–20, 15 teaching assistantships (averaging $6,000 per year) were awarded; career-related internships or fieldwork, Federal Work-Study, scholarships/grants, and unspecified assistantships also available. Support available to part-time students. Financial award application deadline: 3/15; financial award applicants required to submit FAFSA. *Unit head:* Ellen Mueller, Director, MFA Program, 612-874-3629, E-mail: emueller@mcad.edu. *Application contact:* Mary Kazura, Director of Admissions, 612-874-3668, Fax: 612-874-3701, E-mail: mkazura@mcad.edu.
Website: http://mcad.edu/mfa

New York Institute of Technology, College of Arts and Sciences, Department of Digital Art and Design, Old Westbury, NY 11568. Offers computer graphics (MFA), including animation, fine arts and technology, graphic design. *Program availability:* Part-time. *Faculty:* 10 full-time (5 women), 12 part-time/adjunct (6 women). *Students:* 31 full-time (19 women), 4 part-time (1 woman); includes 9 minority (1 Black or African American, non-Hispanic/Latino; 5 Asian, non-Hispanic/Latino; 2 Hispanic/Latino; 1 Two or more races, non-Hispanic/Latino), 19 international. Average age 27. 75 applicants, 52% accepted, 15 enrolled. In 2019, 20 master's awarded. *Degree requirements:* For master's, thesis (for some programs), thesis required for M.F.A.; senior project required for M.A. *Entrance requirements:* For master's, BFA or equivalent with minimum undergraduate GPA of 3.0; supplemental application, including digital portfolio, CV/resume (optional), personal statement (optional), and/or letters of recommendation (optional); copies of undergraduate transcripts from all schools attended and proof of degree. Additional exam requirements/recommendations for international students: required—TOEFL (minimum score 79 iBT), IELTS (minimum score 6), PTE (minimum score 53), Duolingo English Test. *Application deadline:* For fall admission, 6/1 for domestic students, 7/1 for international students; for spring admission, 12/15 for international students. Applications are processed on a rolling basis. Application fee: $50. Electronic applications accepted. *Expenses: Tuition:* Full-time $23,760; part-time $1320 per credit. *Required fees:* $260; $220 per unit. Full-time tuition and fees vary according to degree level and program. Part-time tuition and fees vary according to course load and program. *Financial support:* In 2019–20, 20 students received support. Research assistantships, teaching assistantships, Federal Work-Study, scholarships/grants, and unspecified assistantships available. Support available to part-time students. Financial award application deadline: 2/15; financial award applicants required to submit FAFSA. *Unit head:* Prof. Rosina Vavetsi, Department Chair, 516-686-7542, Fax: 212-261-1742, E-mail: rvavetsi@nyit.edu. *Application contact:* Alice Dolitsky, Director, Graduate Admissions, 800-345-6948, Fax: 516-686-1116, E-mail: admissions@nyit.edu.
Website: https://www.nyit.edu/departments/digital_art_and_design

North Carolina State University, Graduate School, College of Design, Department of Graphic Design, Raleigh, NC 27695. Offers MGD. *Accreditation:* NASAD. *Degree requirements:* For master's, thesis optional, oral exam. *Entrance requirements:* For master's, GRE General Test, portfolio. Electronic applications accepted.

Ohio University, Graduate College, College of Fine Arts, School of Art, Athens, OH 45701-2979. Offers art history (MA); ceramics (MFA); graphic design (MFA); painting (MFA); photography (MFA); printmaking (MFA); sculpture (MFA). *Program availability:* Part-time. *Degree requirements:* For master's, thesis. *Entrance requirements:* For master's, portfolio. Additional exam requirements/recommendations for international students: required—TOEFL (minimum score 550 paper-based; 80 iBT) or IELTS (minimum score 6.5). Electronic applications accepted.

Oklahoma State University, College of Arts and Sciences, Department of Art, Graphic Design and Art History, Stillwater, OK 74078. Offers art history (MA); graphic design (MA). *Faculty:* 15 full-time (8 women), 1 (woman) part-time/adjunct. *Students:* 5 full-time (all women), 3 part-time (2 women); includes 3 minority (1 Asian, non-Hispanic/Latino; 2 Hispanic/Latino), 3 international. Average age 30. 9 applicants, 33% accepted, 2 enrolled. In 2019, 4 master's awarded. *Entrance requirements:* For master's, GRE or GMAT. Additional exam requirements/recommendations for international students: required—TOEFL (minimum score 550 paper-based; 79 iBT). *Application deadline:* For fall admission, 3/1 for domestic students; for spring admission, 8/1 for domestic students. Application fee: $50 ($75 for international students). Electronic applications accepted. *Expenses:* Tuition, area resident: Full-time $4148.10; part-time $2765.40 per credit hour. Tuition, state resident: full-time $4148.10; part-time $2765.40 per credit hour. Tuition, nonresident: full-time $15,775; part-time $10,516.80 per credit hour. International tuition: $15,775.20 full-time. *Required fees:* $2196.90; $122.05 per credit hour. Tuition and fees vary according to course load, campus/location and program. *Financial support:* In 2019–20, 8 teaching assistantships (averaging $1,330 per year) were awarded; research assistantships, career-related internships or fieldwork, Federal Work-Study, scholarships/grants, health care benefits, tuition waivers, and unspecified assistantships also available. Support available to part-time students. Financial award application deadline: 3/1; financial award applicants required to submit FAFSA. *Unit head:* Liz Roth, Interim Head, 405-744-6016, E-mail: liz.roth@okstate.edu. *Application contact:* Dr. Sheryl Tucker, Dean, 405-744-6368, Fax: 405-744-0355, E-mail: gradi@okstate.edu.
Website: http://art.okstate.edu/

Otis College of Art and Design, Program in Graphic Design, Los Angeles, CA 90045-9785. Offers MFA. *Entrance requirements:* Additional exam requirements/recommendations for international students: required—TOEFL (minimum score 600 paper-based). Electronic applications accepted.

Pensacola Christian College, Graduate Studies, Pensacola, FL 32503-2267. Offers business administration (MBA); curriculum and instruction (MS, Ed D, Ed S); dramatics (MFA); educational leadership (MS, Ed D, Ed S); graphic design (MA, MFA); music (MA); nursing (MSN); performance studies (MA); studio art (MA, MFA).

Pittsburg State University, Graduate School, College of Technology, Department of Technology and Workforce Learning, Pittsburg, KS 66762. Offers career and technical education (MS); human resource development (MS); technology (MS), including automotive technology, construction management, graphic design, graphics management, information technology, innovation in technology, personnel development, technology management, workforce learning; workforce development and education (Ed S). *Program availability:* Part-time, evening/weekend, 100% online, blended/hybrid learning. *Degree requirements:* For master's, thesis or alternative; for Ed S, thesis optional. *Entrance requirements:* Additional exam requirements/recommendations for international students: required—TOEFL (minimum score 520 paper-based; 68 iBT), IELTS (minimum score 6), PTE (minimum score 47). Electronic applications accepted. *Expenses:* Contact institution.

Pratt Institute, School of Art, Program in Digital Arts, Brooklyn, NY 11205-3899. Offers MFA, MS/MFA. *Accreditation:* NASAD. *Students:* 53 full-time (41 women), 10 part-time (5 women); includes 6 minority (3 Asian, non-Hispanic/Latino; 3 Hispanic/Latino), 51 international. Average age 24. 259 applicants, 36% accepted, 25 enrolled. In 2019, 14 master's awarded. *Degree requirements:* For master's, thesis, exhibit. *Entrance requirements:* For master's, portfolio or video, letters of recommendation. Additional exam requirements/recommendations for international students: required—TOEFL (minimum score 550 paper-based; 79 iBT). *Application deadline:* For fall admission, 1/5 for domestic and international students; for spring admission, 10/1 for domestic and international students. Application fee: $50 ($90 for international students). Electronic applications accepted. *Expenses:* Tuition: Full-time $33,246; part-time $1847 per credit. *Required fees:* $1980. *Financial support:* Career-related internships or fieldwork, Federal Work-Study, institutionally sponsored loans, scholarships/grants, health care benefits, and unspecified assistantships available. Support available to part-time students. Financial award application deadline: 2/1; financial award applicants required to submit FAFSA. *Unit head:* Peter Patchen, Chair, 718-636-3693, Fax: 718-399-4494, E-mail: ppatchen@pratt.edu. *Application contact:* Natalie Capannelli, Director of Graduate Admissions, 718-636-3551, Fax: 718-399-4242, E-mail: ncapanne@pratt.edu.
Website: https://www.pratt.edu/academics/school-of-art/graduate-school-of-art/digital-arts-grad/

Pratt Institute, School of Design, Program in Communications Design, Brooklyn, NY 10011. Offers MFA. *Accreditation:* NASAD. *Program availability:* Part-time. *Students:* 150 full-time (122 women); includes 12 minority (3 Black or African American, non-Hispanic/Latino; 4 Asian, non-Hispanic/Latino; 3 Hispanic/Latino; 1 Native Hawaiian or other Pacific Islander, non-Hispanic/Latino; 1 Two or more races, non-Hispanic/Latino), 125 international. Average age 24. 386 applicants, 59% accepted, 80 enrolled. In 2019, 68 master's awarded. *Degree requirements:* For master's, thesis. *Entrance requirements:* For master's, portfolio, letters of recommendation. Additional exam requirements/recommendations for international students: required—TOEFL (minimum score 575 paper-based; 90 iBT). *Application deadline:* For fall admission, 1/5 for domestic and international students; for spring admission, 10/1 for domestic and international students. Application fee: $50 ($90 for international students). Electronic applications accepted. *Expenses:* Tuition: Full-time $33,246; part-time $1847 per credit. *Required fees:* $1980. *Financial support:* Career-related internships or fieldwork, Federal Work-Study, institutionally sponsored loans, scholarships/grants, health care benefits, and unspecified assistantships available. Support available to part-time students. Financial award application deadline: 2/1; financial award applicants required to submit FAFSA. *Unit head:* Santiago Piedrafita Iglesias, Chairperson, 212-687-5313, Fax: 718-399-4495, E-mail: spiedraf@pratt.edu. *Application contact:* Natalie Capannelli, Director of Graduate Admissions, 718-636-3551, Fax: 718-399-4242, E-mail: ncapanne@pratt.edu.
Website: https://www.pratt.edu/academics/school-of-design/graduate-school-of-design/grad-communications-design/

Rhode Island School of Design, Department of Graphic Design, Providence, RI 02903-2784. Offers MFA. *Accreditation:* NASAD. *Students:* 37 full-time (19 women); includes 7 minority (5 Asian, non-Hispanic/Latino; 1 Hispanic/Latino; 1 Two or more races, non-Hispanic/Latino), 13 international. Average age 28. 315 applicants, 9% accepted, 16 enrolled. In 2019, 16 master's awarded. *Degree requirements:* For master's, thesis, exhibition. *Entrance requirements:* For master's, portfolio, statement of purpose, 3 letters of recommendation. Additional exam requirements/recommendations for international students: required—TOEFL (minimum score 580 paper-based; 93 iBT), IELTS (minimum score 6.5), Duolingo. *Application deadline:* For fall admission, 1/10 for domestic and international students. Application fee: $60. Electronic applications accepted. *Expenses:* Tuition: Full-time $51,800. *Required fees:* $1060. *Financial support:* Fellowships, research assistantships, teaching assistantships, Federal Work-Study, scholarships/grants, and unspecified assistantships available. Financial award

application deadline: 2/1; financial award applicants required to submit FAFSA. *Unit head:* Lucy Hitchcock, Department Head, 401-454-6171, Fax: 401-454-6117, E-mail: gd@risd.edu. *Application contact:* Molly Pettengill, Associate Director for Graduate Recruitment, 401-454-6312, Fax: 401-454-6309, E-mail: mpetteng@risd.edu.
Website: http://www.risd.edu/academics/graphic-design/

Rochester Institute of Technology, Graduate Enrollment Services, College of Imaging Arts and Sciences, School of Design, MFA Program in Visual Communication Design, Rochester, NY 14623-5603. Offers MFA. *Accreditation:* NASAD. *Program availability:* Part-time. *Degree requirements:* For master's, thesis, thesis exhibition. *Entrance requirements:* For master's, portfolio, personal statement, three letters of recommendation. Additional exam requirements/recommendations for international students: required—TOEFL (minimum score 550 paper-based; 90 iBT), IELTS (minimum score 7), PTE (minimum score 58). Electronic applications accepted.

Rochester Institute of Technology, Graduate Enrollment Services, College of Imaging Arts and Sciences, School of Media Sciences, MS Program in Print Media, Rochester, NY 14623-5603. Offers MS. *Program availability:* Part-time. *Degree requirements:* For master's, thesis. *Entrance requirements:* For master's, GRE, minimum GPA of 3.0 (recommended), personal statement, resume, two letters of recommendation. Additional exam requirements/recommendations for international students: required—TOEFL (minimum score 550 paper-based; 79 iBT), IELTS (minimum score 6.5), PTE (minimum score 58). Electronic applications accepted.

San Diego State University, Graduate and Research Affairs, College of Professional Studies and Fine Arts, School of Art and Design, San Diego, CA 92182. Offers studio arts (MA, MFA), including applied design, graphic design, interior architecture, multimedia and photography, painting and printmaking, sculpture. *Accreditation:* NASAD (one or more programs are accredited). *Degree requirements:* For master's, variable foreign language requirement, thesis. *Entrance requirements:* For master's, GRE General Test, bachelor's degree in related field, slide portfolio, typed slide information sheet, 2 letters of recommendation. Additional exam requirements/recommendations for international students: required—TOEFL. Electronic applications accepted.

Savannah College of Art and Design, Program in Advertising, Savannah, GA 31402-3146. Offers MA, MFA. *Program availability:* Part-time. *Degree requirements:* For master's, final project (for MA); thesis (for MFA). *Entrance requirements:* For master's, GRE (recommended), portfolio (submitted in digital format), audition or writing submission, resume, statement of purpose, two letters of recommendation. Additional exam requirements/recommendations for international students: recommended—TOEFL (minimum score 550 paper-based; 85 iBT), IELTS (minimum score 6.5). Electronic applications accepted.

Savannah College of Art and Design, Program in Graphic Design and Visual Experience, Savannah, GA 31402-3146. Offers MA, MFA. *Program availability:* Part-time, 100% online. *Degree requirements:* For master's, capstone course (for MA); thesis (for MFA). *Entrance requirements:* For master's, GRE (recommended), portfolio (submitted in digital format), audition or writing submission, resume, statement of purpose, two letters of recommendation. Additional exam requirements/recommendations for international students: recommended—TOEFL (minimum score 550 paper-based; 85 iBT), IELTS (minimum score 6.5). Electronic applications accepted.

School of Visual Arts, Graduate Programs, Program in Visual Narrative, New York, NY 10010-3994. Offers MFA. *Degree requirements:* For master's, thesis, 60 credits. *Entrance requirements:* For master's, portfolio; statement of purpose; unique and complete short story/visual narrative (minimum 2-5 pages/images, or 2-5 minutes for video or animation submissions). Additional exam requirements/recommendations for international students: required—TOEFL (minimum score 550 paper-based; 79 iBT). Electronic applications accepted.

State University of New York at Oswego, Graduate Studies, Department of Art, Oswego, NY 13126. Offers art (MA); graphic design and digital media (MA). *Accreditation:* NASAD. *Program availability:* Part-time. *Students:* 4. In 2019, 4 master's awarded. *Degree requirements:* For master's, exhibit, final presentation. *Entrance requirements:* For master's, slides of previous work. Additional exam requirements/recommendations for international students: required—TOEFL (minimum score 560 paper-based). *Application deadline:* For fall admission, 4/1 for domestic students; for spring admission, 10/1 for domestic students. Applications are processed on a rolling basis. Application fee: $65. Electronic applications accepted. *Financial support:* Teaching assistantships with full and partial tuition reimbursements, career-related internships or fieldwork, Federal Work-Study, institutionally sponsored loans, scholarships/grants, health care benefits, tuition waivers (partial), and unspecified assistantships available. Support available to part-time students. Financial award application deadline: 4/1; financial award applicants required to submit FAFSA. *Unit head:* Kelly Roe, Chair, 315-312-2850, E-mail: kelly.roe@oswego.edu. *Application contact:* Juan Perdiguero, Program Coordinator, 315-312-3240, E-mail: juan.perdiguero@oswego.edu.
Website: http://www.oswego.edu/academics/colleges_and_departments/departments/art.html

Suffolk University, New England School of Art and Design, Boston, MA 02108-2770. Offers graphic design (MA); interior architecture (MA). *Accreditation:* CIDA. *Program availability:* Part-time, evening/weekend. *Faculty:* 2 full-time (1 woman), 2 part-time/adjunct (1 woman). *Students:* 36 full-time (31 women), 6 part-time (all women); includes 7 minority (2 Black or African American, non-Hispanic/Latino; 2 Asian, non-Hispanic/Latino; 3 Hispanic/Latino), 14 international. Average age 26. 81 applicants, 79% accepted, 25 enrolled. In 2019, 20 master's awarded. *Entrance requirements:* For master's, GRE (for MFA), art portfolio, interview, 2 letters of recommendation, resume; letter of intent (for MFA). Additional exam requirements/recommendations for international students: required—TOEFL (minimum score 550 paper-based; 80 iBT). *Application deadline:* For fall admission, 3/15 priority date for domestic and international students; for spring admission, 10/15 priority date for domestic and international students. Applications are processed on a rolling basis. Application fee: $50. Electronic applications accepted. *Expenses:* Contact institution. *Financial support:* In 2019–20, 36 students received support, including 7 fellowships (averaging $2,829 per year); career-related internships or fieldwork, Federal Work-Study, institutionally sponsored loans, scholarships/grants, and unspecified assistantships also available. Financial award application deadline: 4/1; financial award applicants required to submit FAFSA. *Unit head:* Audrey Goldstein, Department Chair, 617-997-4290, E-mail: agoldstein@suffolk.edu. *Application contact:* Mara Marzocchi, Associate Director of Graduate Admissions, 617-573-8302, Fax: 617-305-1733, E-mail: grad.admission@suffolk.edu.
Website: http://www.suffolk.edu/nesad/

Temple University, Tyler School of Art and Architecture, Department of Graphic Arts and Design, Philadelphia, PA 19122-6096. Offers graphic and interactive design (MFA); photography (MFA); printmaking (MFA). *Students:* 123 applicants, 15% accepted, 12 enrolled. In 2019, 8 master's awarded. *Degree requirements:* For master's, thesis, written statement, slide portfolio. *Entrance requirements:* For master's, 3 letters of

recommendation, portfolio, 40 credits in studio art, 12 credits in art history, resume, statement of goals. Additional exam requirements/recommendations for international students: required—TOEFL (minimum score 79 iBT), IELTS (minimum score 6.5), PTE (minimum score 53), one of three is required. *Application deadline:* For fall admission, 1/15 for domestic students, 12/15 for international students. Application fee: $60. Electronic applications accepted. *Expenses:* Contact institution. *Financial support:* Fellowships, teaching assistantships, Federal Work-Study, and health care benefits available. Financial award applicants required to submit FAFSA. *Unit head:* Dermot Mac Cormack, Associate Professor and Department Chair of Graphic and Interactive Design, 610-653-8227, E-mail: dermot@temple.edu. *Application contact:* Tamryn McDermott, Director of Admissions, 215-777-9159, E-mail: tyleradmissions@temple.edu.
Website: https://tyler.temple.edu/programs/graphic-interactive-design

Texas State University, The Graduate College, College of Fine Arts and Communication, Program in Communication Design, San Marcos, TX 78666. Offers MFA. *Program availability:* Part-time. *Degree requirements:* For master's, comprehensive exam, thesis. *Entrance requirements:* For master's, related baccalaureate degree from regionally-accredited institution with minimum GPA of 2.75 in last 60 hours of undergraduate course work, 3 letters of recommendation, academic and professional statement of purpose, online portfolio showcasing at least 20 works in communication design. Additional exam requirements/recommendations for international students: required—TOEFL (minimum score 550 paper-based; 78 iBT), IELTS (minimum score 6), TOEFL (minimum iBT scores: 19 listening, 19 reading, 19 speaking, 18 writing). Electronic applications accepted.

Texas Woman's University, Graduate School, College of Arts and Sciences, School of the Arts, Department of Visual Arts, Denton, TX 76204. Offers art (MA, MAT, MFA), including art education (MA, MAT), art history (MA), ceramics (MFA), graphic design (MA), intermedia (MFA), painting (MFA), photography (MFA), sculpture (MFA). *Faculty:* 6 full-time (5 women). *Students:* 13 full-time (9 women), 8 part-time (5 women); includes 5 minority (1 Asian, non-Hispanic/Latino; 3 Hispanic/Latino; 1 Two or more races, non-Hispanic/Latino), 1 international. Average age 36. 15 applicants, 80% accepted, 9 enrolled. In 2019, 8 master's awarded. *Degree requirements:* For master's, comprehensive exam, thesis (for some programs), exhibit (MFA), oral exam, thesis or professional paper (MA). *Entrance requirements:* For master's, portfolio, interview, current curriculum vitae, letter of intent, 3 letters of recommendation, artist statement, separate application. Additional exam requirements/recommendations for international students: required—TOEFL (minimum score 79 iBT); recommended—IELTS (minimum score 6.5), TSE (minimum score 53). *Application deadline:* For fall admission, 2/15 for domestic and international students; for spring admission, 11/15 for domestic and international students. Application fee: $50 ($75 for international students). Electronic applications accepted. *Expenses: Tuition, area resident:* Full-time $4973.40; part-time $276.30 per semester hour. Tuition, state resident: full-time $4973.40; part-time $276.30 per semester hour. Tuition, nonresident: full-time $12,569; part-time $698.30 per semester hour. *International tuition:* $12,569.40 full-time. *Required fees:* $2524.30. Tuition and fees vary according to course level, course load, degree level and program. *Financial support:* In 2019–20, 15 students received support, including 12 teaching assistantships (averaging $4,968 per year); career-related internships or fieldwork, scholarships/grants, health care benefits, and unspecified assistantships also available. Support available to part-time students. Financial award application deadline: 3/1; financial award applicants required to submit FAFSA. *Unit head:* Dr. Vagner Whitehead, Chair, 940-898-2530, Fax: 940-898-2496, E-mail: visualarts@twu.edu. *Application contact:* Korie Hawkins, Associate Director of Admissions, Graduate Recruitment, 940-898-3188, Fax: 940-898-3081, E-mail: admissions@twu.edu.
Website: http://www.twu.edu/visual-arts/

University of Baltimore, Graduate School, Yale Gordon College of Arts and Sciences, Doctoral Program in Information and Interaction Design, Baltimore, MD 21201-5779. Offers DS. *Program availability:* Part-time, evening/weekend. *Entrance requirements:* For doctorate, minimum GPA of 3.2, previous graduate study in related discipline, portfolio, resume. Electronic applications accepted.

University of Cincinnati, Graduate School, College of Design, Architecture, Art, and Planning, School of Design, Cincinnati, OH 45221. Offers fashion design (M Des); graphic design (M Des); industrial design (M Des); interaction design (M Des); product development (M Des). *Accreditation:* NASAD. *Degree requirements:* For master's, thesis. *Entrance requirements:* For master's, undergraduate degree in design or related field, 2 years of work experience in design or related field. Additional exam requirements/recommendations for international students: required—TOEFL. Electronic applications accepted.

University of Guam, Office of Graduate Studies, College of Liberal Arts and Social Sciences, Division of Fine Arts, Mangilao, GU 96923. Offers ceramics (MA); graphics (MA); painting (MA). *Degree requirements:* For master's, thesis or alternative, exhibit, final oral exam. *Entrance requirements:* For master's, GRE General Test, portfolio. Additional exam requirements/recommendations for international students: required—TOEFL.

University of Illinois at Chicago, College of Architecture, Design and the Arts, School of Design, Chicago, IL 60607-7128. Offers graphic design (M Des); industrial design (M Des). *Degree requirements:* For master's, thesis, exhibit. *Entrance requirements:* For master's, MAT, portfolio. Additional exam requirements/recommendations for international students: required—TOEFL. Electronic applications accepted. *Expenses:* Contact institution.

University of Illinois at Urbana-Champaign, Graduate College, College of Fine and Applied Arts, School of Art and Design, Program in Design and Media, Champaign, IL 61820. Offers art and design (MFA), including new media; graphic design (MFA); industrial design (MFA). *Accreditation:* NASAD.

University of Memphis, Graduate School, College of Communication and Fine Arts, Department of Art, Memphis, TN 38152. Offers art history (MA), including Egyptian art and archaeology, general art history; ceramics (MFA); graphic design (MFA); museum studies (Graduate Certificate); painting (MFA); printmaking/photography (MFA); sculpture (MFA). *Accreditation:* NASAD (one or more programs are accredited). *Program availability:* Part-time. *Students:* 28 full-time (21 women), 5 part-time (4 women); includes 9 minority (3 Black or African American, non-Hispanic/Latino; 1 Asian, non-Hispanic/Latino; 3 Hispanic/Latino; 2 Two or more races, non-Hispanic/Latino), 2 international. Average age 30. 36 applicants, 69% accepted, 13 enrolled. In 2019, 11 master's, 4 other advanced degrees awarded. *Degree requirements:* For master's, variable foreign language requirement, comprehensive exam, thesis, image identification exam, qualifying exam; for Graduate Certificate, internship. *Entrance requirements:* For master's, GRE General Test or MAT, portfolio (MFA), letter of intent, sample of undergraduate writing, two letters of recommendation; for Graduate Certificate, three letters of recommendation, letter of intent. *Application deadline:* For fall admission, 2/15 for domestic students; for spring admission, 11/1 for domestic students. Applications are processed on a rolling basis. Application fee: $35 ($60 for international students). *Expenses: Tuition, area resident:* Full-time $9216; part-time $512 per credit hour. Tuition, state resident: full-time $9216; part-time $512 per credit hour. Tuition, nonresident: full-time $12,672; part-time $704 per credit hour. *International tuition:* $16,128 full-time. *Required fees:* $1530; $85 per credit hour. Tuition and fees vary according to program. *Financial support:* Research assistantships with full tuition reimbursements, teaching assistantships with full tuition reimbursements, Federal Work-Study, scholarships/grants, and unspecified assistantships available. Financial award application deadline: 2/1; financial award applicants required to submit FAFSA. *Unit head:* Richard Lou, Chair, 901-678-2217, Fax: 901-678-2735, E-mail: ralou@memphis.edu. *Application contact:* Richard Lou, Chair, 901-678-2217, Fax: 901-678-2735, E-mail: ralou@memphis.edu.
Website: http://memphis.edu/art/

University of Miami, Graduate School, College of Arts and Sciences, Department of Art and Art History, Coral Gables, FL 33124. Offers art history (MA); ceramics/glass (MFA); graphic design/multimedia (MFA); painting (MFA); photography/digital imaging (MFA); printmaking (MFA); sculpture (MFA). *Program availability:* Part-time. *Degree requirements:* For master's, variable foreign language requirement, thesis, exhibit (MFA), comprehensive exam (MA). *Entrance requirements:* For master's, GRE General Test (MA), research paper (MA), slide portfolio (MFA). Additional exam requirements/recommendations for international students: required—TOEFL. Electronic applications accepted.

University of Minnesota, Duluth, Graduate School, School of Fine Arts, Department of Art and Design, Duluth, MN 55812-2496. Offers graphic design (MFA). *Accreditation:* NASAD. *Program availability:* Part-time. *Degree requirements:* For master's, final exhibit, project, supporting paper. *Entrance requirements:* For master's, minimum GPA of 3.0, writing sample, slide portfolio. Additional exam requirements/recommendations for international students: required—TOEFL (minimum score 550 paper-based).

University of Notre Dame, The Graduate School, College of Arts and Letters, Department of Art, Art History, and Design, Notre Dame, IN 46556. Offers art history (MA); design (MFA), including graphic design, industrial design; studio art (MFA), including ceramics, painting, photography, printmaking, sculpture. *Accreditation:* NASAD. *Degree requirements:* For master's, comprehensive exam (for some programs), thesis. *Entrance requirements:* For master's, GRE General Test, minimum GPA of 3.0. Additional exam requirements/recommendations for international students: required—TOEFL (minimum score 600 paper-based; 80 iBT). Electronic applications accepted.

University of Pennsylvania, Stuart Weitzman School of Design, Department of Fine Arts, Philadelphia, PA 19104. Offers emerging design and research (Certificate); fine arts (MFA); time-based and interactive media (Certificate). *Faculty:* 7 full-time (3 women), 1 part-time/adjunct (0 women). *Students:* 34 full-time (19 women), 1 (woman) part-time; includes 11 minority (3 Black or African American, non-Hispanic/Latino; 2 Asian, non-Hispanic/Latino; 4 Hispanic/Latino; 2 Two or more races, non-Hispanic/Latino), 10 international. Average age 27. 88 applicants, 48% accepted, 17 enrolled. In 2019, 11 master's, 3 other advanced degrees awarded. *Application deadline:* Applications are processed on a rolling basis. Application fee: $80. Electronic applications accepted. *Financial support:* In 2019–20, 30 students received support, including teaching assistantships (averaging $6,000 per year); fellowships with full tuition reimbursements available, research assistantships, Federal Work-Study, scholarships/grants, health care benefits, and unspecified assistantships also available. Financial award applicants required to submit FAFSA. *Application contact:* Joan Weston, Director of Admissions & Financial Aid, 215-898-6520, E-mail: weston@design.upenn.edu.
Website: http://www.design.upenn.edu/mfa

University of South Dakota, Graduate School, College of Fine Arts, Department of Art, Vermillion, SD 57069. Offers art education (MFA); ceramics (MFA); graphic design (MFA); painting (MFA); photography (MFA); printmaking (MFA); sculpture (MFA). *Accreditation:* NASAD. *Degree requirements:* For master's, thesis or alternative. *Entrance requirements:* For master's, portfolio, minimum GPA of 2.7. Additional exam requirements/recommendations for international students: required—TOEFL (minimum score 550 paper-based; 79 iBT). Electronic applications accepted.

The University of Tennessee, Graduate School, College of Arts and Sciences, School of Art, Knoxville, TN 37996. Offers ceramics (MFA); drawing (MFA); graphic design (MFA); inter-area studies (MFA); media arts (MFA); painting (MFA); printmaking (MFA); sculpture (MFA); watercolor (MFA). *Accreditation:* NASAD. *Degree requirements:* For master's, thesis or alternative, exhibit. *Entrance requirements:* For master's, portfolio, minimum GPA of 2.7. Additional exam requirements/recommendations for international students: required—TOEFL. Electronic applications accepted.

University of Utah, Graduate School, College of Fine Arts, Department of Art and Art History, Salt Lake City, UT 84112-0380. Offers art history (MA); ceramics (MFA); community-based art education (MFA); drawing (MFA); graphic design (MFA); painting (MFA); photography/digital imaging (MFA); printmaking (MFA); sculpture/intermedia (MFA). *Degree requirements:* For master's, variable foreign language requirement, comprehensive exam (for some programs), thesis or alternative, exhibit and final project paper (for MFA). *Entrance requirements:* For master's, CD portfolio (MFA), writing sample (MA), curriculum vitae, letters of recommendation, letter of intent. Additional exam requirements/recommendations for international students: required—TOEFL (minimum score 575 paper-based; 75 iBT). Electronic applications accepted. *Expenses:* Contact institution.

Université Laval, Faculty of Architecture, Planning and Visual Arts, School of Visual Arts, Programs in Visual Arts, Québec, QC G1K 7P4, Canada. Offers graphic design and multimedia (MA); visual arts (MA). *Degree requirements:* For master's, thesis (for some programs). *Entrance requirements:* For master's, technical exam, interview, mastery of pertinent software, knowledge of French. Electronic applications accepted.

Vermont College of Fine Arts, MFA in Graphic Design Program, Montpelier, VT 05602. Offers MFA. *Accreditation:* NASAD. Electronic applications accepted. *Expenses:* Contact institution.

Wayne State University, College of Fine, Performing and Communication Arts, James Pearson Duffy Department of Art and Art History, Detroit, MI 48202. Offers art (MA, MFA), including ceramics, drawing, fashion design and merchandising (MA), fibers, graphic design, industrial design (MA), interior design (MA), metalsmithing, painting, photography, printmaking, sculpture; art history (MA). *Degree requirements:* For master's, thesis (for some programs), essay or thesis. *Entrance requirements:* For master's, BFA or another degree and equivalent course work, portfolio, personal interview, reference letters, statement of intent (except for art history program). Additional exam requirements/recommendations for international students: required—TOEFL (minimum score 550 paper-based; 79 iBT), TWE (minimum score 5.5), Michigan English Language Assessment Battery (minimum score 85); recommended—IELTS (minimum score 6.5). Electronic applications accepted. *Expenses:* Contact institution.

West Virginia University, College of Creative Arts, Morgantown, WV 26506. Offers acting (MFA); art education (MA); art history (MA); ceramics (MFA); collaborative piano (MM, DMA); composition (MM, DMA); conducting (MM, DMA); costume design and technology (MFA); graphic design (MFA); intermedia and photography (MFA); jazz pedagogy (MM); lighting design and technology (MFA); music (PhD); music education (MM, PhD); music industry (MA); music theory (MM); musicology (MA); painting and printmaking (MFA); performance (MM, DMA); piano pedagogy (MM); scenic design and technology (MFA); sculpture (MFA); studio art (MA); technical direction (MFA); vocal pedagogy and performance (DMA). *Program availability:* Part-time. *Degree requirements:* For master's, thesis, recitals; for doctorate, comprehensive exam, thesis/dissertation, recitals (DMA). *Entrance requirements:* For doctorate, minimum GPA of 3.0, audition. Additional exam requirements/recommendations for international students: required—TOEFL. Electronic applications accepted.

Yale University, School of Art, New Haven, CT 06520-8339. Offers graphic design (MFA); painting/printmaking (MFA); photography (MFA); sculpture (MFA). *Degree requirements:* For master's, thesis (for some programs). *Entrance requirements:* Additional exam requirements/recommendations for international students: required—TOEFL (minimum score 550 paper-based; 100 iBT). Electronic applications accepted. *Expenses:* Contact institution.

Illustration

Academy of Art University, Graduate Programs, School of Illustration, San Francisco, CA 94105-3410. Offers MA, MFA. *Accreditation:* NASAD. *Program availability:* Part-time, 100% online. *Faculty:* 10 full-time (2 women), 27 part-time/adjunct (12 women). *Students:* 79 full-time (59 women), 83 part-time (66 women); includes 30 minority (11 Black or African American, non-Hispanic/Latino; 2 American Indian or Alaska Native, non-Hispanic/Latino; 8 Asian, non-Hispanic/Latino; 9 Hispanic/Latino), 67 international. Average age 32. 62 applicants, 100% accepted, 27 enrolled. In 2019, 68 master's awarded. *Degree requirements:* For master's, final review. *Entrance requirements:* For master's, statement of intent; resume; portfolio/reel; official college transcripts. *Application deadline:* Applications are processed on a rolling basis. Application fee: $50. Electronic applications accepted. *Expenses: Tuition:* Full-time $1083; part-time $1083 per credit hour. *Required fees:* $860; $860 per unit. $430 per term. One-time fee: $145. Tuition and fees vary according to program. *Financial support:* Career-related internships or fieldwork, Federal Work-Study, and scholarships/grants available. Financial award application deadline: 8/10; financial award applicants required to submit FAFSA.
Website: http://www.academyart.edu/illustration-school/index.html

Bob Jones University, Graduate Programs, Greenville, SC 29614. Offers accountancy (MS); Bible (MA); Bible translation (MA); Biblical studies (Certificate); business administration (MBA); church history (MA, PhD); church ministries (MA); church music (MM); cinema and video production (MA); counseling (MS); curriculum and instruction (Ed D); divinity (M Div); dramatic production (MA); educational leadership (MS, Ed D, Ed S); elementary education (M Ed, MAT); English (M Ed, MA, MAT); fine arts (MA); graphic design (MA); history (M Ed, MA); illustration (MA); interpretative speech (MA); mathematics (M Ed, MAT); medical missions (Certificate); ministry (MM, D Min); multi-categorical special education (M Ed, MAT); music (M Ed); New Testament interpretation (PhD); Old Testament interpretation (PhD); orchestral instrument performance (MM); organ performance (MM); pastoral studies (MA); personnel services (MS, Ed S); piano pedagogy (MM); piano performance (MM); platform arts (MA); rhetoric and public address (MA); secondary education (M Ed); studio art (MA); teaching Bible (MA); theology (MA, PhD); voice performance (MM); youth ministries (MA); M Div/MM.

California College of the Arts, Graduate Programs, MFA in Comics Program, San Francisco, CA 94107. Offers MFA. *Program availability:* Part-time-only. *Degree requirements:* For master's, thesis. *Entrance requirements:* For master's, portfolio, personal essay, resume, two letters of recommendation, college transcripts, interview. Additional exam requirements/recommendations for international students: required—TOEFL, IELTS, or PTE. Electronic applications accepted. *Expenses:* Contact institution.

California State University, Fullerton, Graduate Studies, College of the Arts, Department of Visual Arts, Fullerton, CA 92831-3599. Offers art (MA, MFA), including art history (MA), ceramics (MFA), crafts, creative photography, exhibition design, glass, graphic design, illustration, sculpture. *Accreditation:* NASAD (one or more programs are accredited). *Program availability:* Part-time. *Entrance requirements:* For master's, minimum GPA of 2.5 in last 60 units of course work, portfolio.

East Carolina University, Graduate School, College of Fine Arts and Communication, School of Art and Design, Greenville, NC 27858-4353. Offers art education (MA Ed); ceramics (MFA); graphic design (MFA); illustration (MFA); metal design (MFA); painting and drawing (MFA); photography (MFA); printmaking (MFA); sculpture (MFA); textile design (MFA); wood design (MFA). *Accreditation:* NASAD (one or more programs are accredited). *Program availability:* Part-time, evening/weekend. *Application deadline:* For fall admission, 2/1 for domestic students; for spring admission, 10/1 for domestic students. *Expenses: Tuition, area resident:* Full-time $4749; part-time $185 per credit hour. Tuition, state resident: full-time $4749; part-time $185 per credit hour. Tuition, nonresident: full-time $17,898; part-time $864 per credit hour. *International tuition:* $17,898 full-time. *Required fees:* $2787. *Financial support:* Application deadline: 6/1. *Unit head:* Dr. Kate Bukowski, Director, 252-328-6665, E-mail: bukowskik16@ecu.edu. *Application contact:* Graduate School Admissions, 252-328-6012, E-mail: gradschool@ecu.edu.
Website: https://art.ecu.edu/

Fashion Institute of Technology, School of Graduate Studies, Program in Illustration, New York, NY 10001-5992. Offers MFA. *Degree requirements:* For master's, thesis. *Entrance requirements:* Additional exam requirements/recommendations for international students: required—TOEFL (minimum score 550 paper-based). Electronic applications accepted.

Hollins University, Graduate Programs, Graduate Programs in Children's Literature, Roanoke, VA 24020. Offers children's book illustration (Certificate); children's book writing and illustrating (MFA); children's literature (MA, MFA). *Program availability:* Part-time. *Degree requirements:* For master's, one foreign language, thesis. *Entrance requirements:* For master's, transcripts, letters of recommendation, portfolio, personal statement of educational objectives. Additional exam requirements/recommendations for international students: required—TOEFL (minimum score 550 paper-based; 79 iBT), IELTS (minimum score 6.5). Electronic applications accepted. *Expenses:* Contact institution.

Kent State University, College of Communication and Information, School of Visual Communication Design, Kent, OH 44242-0001. Offers MA, MFA. *Accreditation:* NASAD. *Program availability:* Part-time. *Faculty:* 9 full-time (4 women), 5 part-time/adjunct (1 woman). *Students:* 20 full-time (10 women), 11 part-time (6 women); includes 6 minority (3 Black or African American, non-Hispanic/Latino; 2 Asian, non-Hispanic/Latino; 1 Two or more races, non-Hispanic/Latino), 5 international. Average age 31. 29 applicants, 66% accepted, 9 enrolled. In 2019, 4 master's awarded. *Degree requirements:* For master's, thesis, project (MA); thesis (MFA). *Entrance requirements:* For master's, undergraduate degree in design or closely-related program, minimum major GPA of 3.0, goal statement, autobiographical statement, 2 letters of recommendation (3 for MFA), resume, transcripts, link to personal online portfolio (for MFA). Additional exam

requirements/recommendations for international students: required—TOEFL (minimum score 94 iBT), IELTS (minimum score 7), PTE (minimum score 65), Michigan English Language Assessment Battery (minimum score 82). *Application deadline:* For fall admission, 3/1 for domestic and international students; for spring admission, 10/1 for domestic and international students. Applications are processed on a rolling basis. Application fee: $45 ($70 for international students). Electronic applications accepted. *Financial support:* Scholarships/grants and unspecified assistantships available. Financial award application deadline: 3/5; financial award applicants required to submit FAFSA. *Unit head:* Dr. Daniel Alenquer, Director, 330-672-7856, E-mail: dalenque@kent.edu. *Application contact:* Ken Visocky O'Grady, Graduate Coordinator and Professor, 330-672-1353, E-mail: kogrady@kent.edu.
Website: http://www.kent.edu/vcd/

Maryland Institute College of Art, Graduate Studies, Program in Illustration Practice, Baltimore, MD 21201. Offers MFA. *Degree requirements:* For master's, thesis, exhibition. *Entrance requirements:* For master's, portfolio, writing sample, bachelor's degree in any field. Additional exam requirements/recommendations for international students: required—TOEFL (minimum score 550 paper-based; 80 iBT), IELTS (minimum score 6.5). Electronic applications accepted. *Expenses:* Contact institution.

Marywood University, Academic Affairs, Insalaco College of Creative and Performing Arts, Art Department, Program in Visual Arts, Scranton, PA 18509-1598. Offers clay (MFA); graphic design (MFA); illustration (MFA); painting (MFA); photography (MFA); printmaking (MFA); sculpture (MFA). *Accreditation:* NASAD. *Program availability:* Part-time. Electronic applications accepted. *Expenses:* Contact institution.

Mills College, Graduate Studies, Department of English, Oakland, CA 94613-1000. Offers book art and creative writing (MFA); literature (MA); poetry (MFA); prose (MFA); Spanish creative writing (Certificate); translation (MFA). *Program availability:* Part-time. *Degree requirements:* For master's, comprehensive exam, thesis. *Entrance requirements:* For master's, 15-20 page writing sample. Additional exam requirements/recommendations for international students: required—TOEFL (minimum score 600 paper-based; 100 iBT), IELTS (minimum score 7). Electronic applications accepted. *Expenses:* Contact institution.

Mills College, Graduate Studies, Program in Book Art and Creative Writing, Oakland, CA 94613-1000. Offers MFA. *Program availability:* Part-time. *Degree requirements:* For master's, thesis project. *Entrance requirements:* For master's, visual portfolio of 15-25 images, written portfolio sample (for creative writing program). Additional exam requirements/recommendations for international students: required—TOEFL (minimum score 600 paper-based; 100 iBT), IELTS (minimum score 7). Electronic applications accepted.

Minneapolis College of Art and Design, Master of Fine Arts in Visual Studies, Minneapolis, MN 55404-4347. Offers animation (MFA); comic art (MFA); drawing (MFA); filmmaking (MFA); fine arts (MFA); furniture design (MFA); graphic design (MFA); illustration (MFA); interactive media (MFA); painting (MFA); photography (MFA); printmaking (MFA); sculpture (MFA). *Accreditation:* NASAD. *Program availability:* Part-time. *Students:* 86 applicants, 44% accepted, 9 enrolled. *Degree requirements:* For master's, thesis, thesis exhibit. *Entrance requirements:* Additional exam requirements/recommendations for international students: required—TOEFL (minimum score 550 paper-based; 79 iBT), IELTS (minimum score 6.5), Duolingo English Test accepted with a minimum score of 100 *Application deadline:* For fall admission, 2/1 for domestic and international students. Application fee: $50. Electronic applications accepted. *Expenses: Tuition:* Full-time $41,344. *Required fees:* $450. One-time fee: $300 full-time. *Financial support:* In 2019–20, 15 teaching assistantships (averaging $6,000 per year) were awarded; career-related internships or fieldwork, Federal Work-Study, scholarships/grants, and unspecified assistantships also available. Support available to part-time students. Financial award application deadline: 3/15; financial award applicants required to submit FAFSA. *Unit head:* Ellen Mueller, Director, MFA Program, 612-874-3629, E-mail: emueller@mcad.edu. *Application contact:* Mary Kazura, Director of Admissions, 612-874-3668, Fax: 612-874-3701, E-mail: mkazura@mcad.edu.
Website: http://mcad.edu/mfa

Savannah College of Art and Design, Program in Illustration, Savannah, GA 31402-3146. Offers MA, MFA. *Program availability:* Part-time, 100% online. *Degree requirements:* For master's, final project (for MA); thesis (for MFA). *Entrance requirements:* For master's, GRE (recommended), portfolio (submitted in digital format), audition or writing submission, resume, statement of purpose, two letters of recommendation. Additional exam requirements/recommendations for international students: recommended—TOEFL (minimum score 550 paper-based; 85 iBT), IELTS (minimum score 6.5). Electronic applications accepted.

Savannah College of Art and Design, Program in Sequential Art, Savannah, GA 31402-3146. Offers MA, MFA. *Program availability:* Part-time. *Degree requirements:* For master's, final project (for MA); thesis (for MFA). *Entrance requirements:* For master's, GRE (recommended), portfolio (submitted in digital format), audition or writing submission, resume, statement of purpose, two letters of recommendation. Additional exam requirements/recommendations for international students: recommended—TOEFL (minimum score 550 paper-based; 85 iBT), IELTS (minimum score 6.5). Electronic applications accepted.

School of Visual Arts, Graduate Programs, Illustration as Visual Essay Department, New York, NY 10010-3994. Offers MFA. *Accreditation:* NASAD. *Degree requirements:* For master's, thesis, 60 credits; residency of two academic years. *Entrance requirements:* For master's, portfolio of work (still images) submitted through SlideRoom. Additional exam requirements/recommendations for international students: required—TOEFL (minimum score 100 iBT). Electronic applications accepted.

Syracuse University, College of Visual and Performing Arts, MFA Program in Illustration, Syracuse, NY 13244. Offers MFA. *Entrance requirements:* For master's, portfolio, artist statement, three letters of recommendation, academic transcripts, personal statement/essay, resume. Additional exam requirements/recommendations for international students: required—TOEFL (minimum score 100 iBT), IELTS. Electronic applications accepted.

Western Connecticut State University, Division of Graduate Studies, School of Visual and Performing Arts, Department of Art, Danbury, CT 06810-6885. Offers illustration (MFA); painting (MFA). *Program availability:* Part-time. *Entrance requirements:* For master's, portfolio review, minimum GPA of 2.5. Additional exam requirements/recommendations for international students: recommended—TOEFL (minimum score 550 paper-based; 79 iBT), IELTS (minimum score 6). *Expenses:* Contact institution.

Industrial Design

Academy of Art University, Graduate Programs, School of Industrial Design, San Francisco, CA 94105-3410. Offers MA, MFA. *Program availability:* Part-time, 100% online. *Faculty:* 4 full-time (0 women), 25 part-time/adjunct (3 women). *Students:* 41 full-time (16 women), 48 part-time (19 women); includes 9 minority (2 Black or African American, non-Hispanic/Latino; 2 Asian, non-Hispanic/Latino; 3 Hispanic/Latino; 2 Two or more races, non-Hispanic/Latino), 63 international. Average age 28. 52 applicants, 100% accepted, 27 enrolled. In 2019, 37 master's awarded. *Degree requirements:* For master's, final review. *Entrance requirements:* For master's, statement of intent; resume; portfolio/reel; official college transcripts. *Application deadline:* Applications are processed on a rolling basis. Application fee: $50. Electronic applications accepted. *Expenses: Tuition:* Full-time $1083; part-time $1083 per credit hour. *Required fees:* $860; $860 per unit. $430 per term. One-time fee: $145. Tuition and fees vary according to program. *Financial support:* Career-related internships or fieldwork, Federal Work-Study, and scholarships/grants available. Financial award application deadline: 8/10; financial award applicants required to submit FAFSA. *Application contact:* 800-544-ARTS, E-mail: info@academyart.edu.
Website: http://www.academyart.edu/industrial-design-school/index.html

ArtCenter College of Design, Graduate Industrial Design Program, Pasadena, CA 91103. Offers MS. *Accreditation:* NASAD.

Auburn University, Graduate School, College of Architecture, Design, and Construction, School of Industrial and Graphic Design, Auburn, AL 36849. Offers MID. *Accreditation:* NASAD. *Program availability:* Part-time. *Faculty:* 20 full-time (5 women), 4 part-time/adjunct (1 woman). *Students:* 34 full-time (17 women), 2 part-time (1 woman); includes 2 minority (1 Asian, non-Hispanic/Latino; 1 Hispanic/Latino), 27 international. Average age 25. 39 applicants, 44% accepted, 12 enrolled. In 2019, 13 master's awarded. *Degree requirements:* For master's, thesis (for some programs). *Entrance requirements:* For master's, GRE General Test. Additional exam requirements/recommendations for international students: required—TOEFL (minimum score 550 paper-based; 79 iBT), iTEP; recommended—IELTS (minimum score 6.5). *Application deadline:* Applications are processed on a rolling basis. Application fee: $60 ($70 for international students). Electronic applications accepted. *Expenses:* $546 per credit hour state resident tuition, $1638 per credit hour nonresident tuition, $680 student services fee for GRA/GTA, $2160 per semester. *Financial support:* In 2019–20, 5 teaching assistantships with partial tuition reimbursements (averaging $7,344 per year) were awarded; Federal Work-Study also available. Support available to part-time students. Financial award application deadline: 3/15; financial award applicants required to submit FAFSA. *Unit head:* Clark E. Lundell, Head, 334-844-2369, E-mail: lundece@auburn.edu. *Application contact:* Dr. George Flowers, Dean of the Graduate School, 334-844-2125.
Website: http://www.auburn.edu/academic/architecture/ind/menu.html

California College of the Arts, Graduate Programs, Design Program, San Francisco, CA 94107. Offers graphic design (MFA); industrial design (MFA); interaction design (MFA). *Accreditation:* NASAD. *Degree requirements:* For master's, thesis, exhibit. *Entrance requirements:* For master's, appropriate bachelor's degree, portfolio, resume, letters of recommendation, transcripts. Additional exam requirements/recommendations for international students: required—TOEFL, IELTS, or PTE. Electronic applications accepted. *Expenses:* Contact institution.

Carleton University, Faculty of Graduate Studies, Faculty of Engineering and Design, School of Industrial Design, Ottawa, ON K1S 5B6, Canada. Offers M Des. *Degree requirements:* For master's, thesis optional. *Entrance requirements:* For master's, honors degree. Additional exam requirements/recommendations for international students: required—TOEFL.

Georgia Institute of Technology, Graduate Studies, College of Design, School of Industrial Design, Atlanta, GA 30332-0001. Offers MID. *Accreditation:* NASAD. *Degree requirements:* For master's, thesis optional. *Expenses: Tuition, area resident:* Full-time $14,064; part-time $586 per credit hour. *Tuition, state resident:* full-time $14,064; part-time $586 per credit hour. *Tuition, nonresident:* full-time $29,140; part-time $1215 per credit hour. *International tuition:* $29,140 full-time. *Required fees:* $2024; $840 per semester. $2096. Tuition and fees vary according to course load.

Iowa State University of Science and Technology, Program in Industrial Design, Ames, IA 50011. Offers MID. *Accreditation:* NASAD. *Entrance requirements:* For master's, GRE, curriculum vitae, portfolio, letters of recommendation, interview. Additional exam requirements/recommendations for international students: required—TOEFL (minimum score 587 paper-based; 95 iBT), IELTS (minimum score 7). Electronic applications accepted.

The New School, Parsons School of Design, Program in Industrial Design, New York, NY 10011. Offers MFA. *Program availability:* Part-time. *Faculty:* 6 full-time (0 women), 57 part-time/adjunct. *Students:* 50 full-time (29 women); includes 8 minority (5 Asian, non-Hispanic/Latino; 3 Hispanic/Latino), 29 international. Average age 27. 170 applicants, 34% accepted, 25 enrolled. In 2019, 23 master's awarded. *Degree requirements:* For master's, thesis. *Entrance requirements:* For master's, transcripts, resume, statement of purpose, recommendation letters, portfolio, interview. Additional exam requirements/recommendations for international students: required—TOEFL (minimum score 92 iBT), IELTS (minimum score 7), PTE (minimum score 63). *Application deadline:* For fall admission, 1/1 priority date for domestic and international students; for summer admission, 1/1 priority date for domestic and international students. Applications are processed on a rolling basis. Application fee: $50. Electronic applications accepted. *Expenses:* 1810 per credit. *Financial support:* In 2019–20, 36 students received support, including 7 research assistantships (averaging $1,736 per year), 6 teaching assistantships (averaging $3,589 per year); career-related internships or fieldwork, scholarships/grants, unspecified assistantships, and travel funding; tuition waivers for students who are also New School employees also available. Support available to part-time students. Financial award application deadline: 2/1; financial award applicants required to submit FAFSA. *Unit head:* Yvette Chaparro, E-mail: chaparry@newschool.edu. *Application contact:* Simone Varadian, Senior Director, 212-229-5150 Ext. 4117, E-mail: varadias@newschool.edu.
Website: https://www.newschool.edu/parsons/mfa-industrial-design/

North Carolina State University, Graduate School, College of Design, Department of Industrial Design, Raleigh, NC 27695. Offers MID. *Accreditation:* NASAD. *Program availability:* Part-time. *Degree requirements:* For master's, thesis optional, oral exam, project. *Entrance requirements:* For master's, GRE General Test (recommended), portfolio. Electronic applications accepted.

The Ohio State University, Graduate School, College of Arts and Sciences, Division of Arts and Humanities, Department of Design, Columbus, OH 43210. Offers design (MA); design research and development (MFA); digital animation and interactive media (MFA). *Accreditation:* NASAD. *Program availability:* Part-time. *Entrance requirements:* For master's, GRE General Test (for all applicants with cumulative GPA below 3.0), portfolio. Additional exam requirements/recommendations for international students: recommended—TOEFL (minimum score 550 paper-based; 79 iBT). Electronic applications accepted.

Pratt Institute, School of Design, Program in Industrial Design, Brooklyn, NY 11205-3899. Offers MID. *Accreditation:* NASAD. *Program availability:* Part-time. *Students:* 69 full-time (36 women), 4 part-time (2 women); includes 9 minority (5 Asian, non-Hispanic/Latino; 4 Hispanic/Latino), 48 international. Average age 25. 279 applicants, 35% accepted, 33 enrolled. In 2019, 21 master's awarded. *Degree requirements:* For master's, thesis. *Entrance requirements:* For master's, portfolio, letters of recommendation. Additional exam requirements/recommendations for international students: required—TOEFL (minimum score 565 paper-based; 85 iBT). *Application deadline:* For fall admission, 1/5 for domestic and international students; for spring admission, 10/1 for domestic and international students. Application fee: $50 ($90 for international students). Electronic applications accepted. *Expenses: Tuition:* Full-time $33,246; part-time $1847 per credit. *Required fees:* $1980. *Financial support:* Career-related internships or fieldwork, Federal Work-Study, institutionally sponsored loans, scholarships/grants, health care benefits, and unspecified assistantships available. Support available to part-time students. Financial award application deadline: 2/1; financial award applicants required to submit FAFSA. *Unit head:* Constantin Boym, Chairperson, 718-636-3520, Fax: 718-636-3553, E-mail: cboym@pratt.edu. *Application contact:* Natalie Capannelli, Director of Graduate Admissions, 718-636-3551, Fax: 718-399-4242, E-mail: ncapanne@pratt.edu.
Website: https://www.pratt.edu/academics/school-of-design/graduate-school-of-design/industrial-design-grad/

Pratt Institute, School of Design, Program in Package Design, Brooklyn, NY 10011. Offers MS. *Accreditation:* NASAD. *Program availability:* Part-time. *Students:* 49 full-time (41 women), 3 part-time (2 women); includes 5 minority (1 Black or African American, non-Hispanic/Latino; 2 Asian, non-Hispanic/Latino; 1 Hispanic/Latino; 1 Two or more races, non-Hispanic/Latino), 40 international. Average age 25. 53 applicants, 91% accepted, 28 enrolled. In 2019, 14 master's awarded. *Degree requirements:* For master's, thesis. *Entrance requirements:* For master's, portfolio, letters of recommendation. Additional exam requirements/recommendations for international students: required—TOEFL (minimum score 575 paper-based; 90 iBT). *Application deadline:* For fall admission, 1/5 for domestic and international students; for spring admission, 10/1 for domestic and international students. Application fee: $50 ($90 for international students). Electronic applications accepted. *Expenses: Tuition:* Full-time $33,246; part-time $1847 per credit. *Required fees:* $1980. *Financial support:* Career-related internships or fieldwork, Federal Work-Study, institutionally sponsored loans, scholarships/grants, health care benefits, and unspecified assistantships available. Support available to part-time students. Financial award application deadline: 2/1; financial award applicants required to submit FAFSA. *Unit head:* Santiago Piedrafita Iglesias, Chairperson, 718-648-5313, Fax: 718-399-4495, E-mail: spiedraf@pratt.edu. *Application contact:* Natalie Capannelli, Director of Graduate Admissions, 718-636-3551, Fax: 718-399-4242, E-mail: ncapanne@pratt.edu.
Website: https://www.pratt.edu/academics/school-of-design/graduate-school-of-design/grad-communications-design/package-design-ms/

Purdue University, Graduate School, College of Liberal Arts, Department of Art and Design, West Lafayette, IN 47907. Offers art education (MA, PhD); industrial design (MFA); interior design (MFA); visual communications design (MFA). *Accreditation:* NASAD; NAST. *Program availability:* Part-time. *Faculty:* 4 full-time (1 woman). *Students:* 37 full-time (21 women), 3 part-time (2 women); includes 9 minority (1 Black or African American, non-Hispanic/Latino; 3 Asian, non-Hispanic/Latino; 4 Hispanic/Latino; 1 Two or more races, non-Hispanic/Latino), 14 international. Average age 28. 144 applicants, 23% accepted, 14 enrolled. In 2019, 24 master's awarded. *Degree requirements:* For master's, terminal exhibit, project, or thesis. *Entrance requirements:* For master's, GRE General Test (for art education), minimum undergraduate GPA of 3.0 or equivalent; 9 undergraduate hours in an art or design history; BA in art (for MA in art education); for doctorate, GRE General Test (minimum scores 600 in verbal and 1000 total), master's degree in art education or art with teaching certification; 3 years of teaching experience at the K-12 level. Additional exam requirements/recommendations for international students: required—TOEFL (minimum score 550 paper-based; 77 iBT). *Application deadline:* For fall admission, 2/1 for domestic students, 2/1 priority date for international students. Applications are processed on a rolling basis. Application fee: $60 ($75 for international students). Electronic applications accepted. *Financial support:* Teaching assistantships with tuition reimbursements and career-related internships or fieldwork available. Support available to part-time students. Financial award applicants required to submit FAFSA. *Unit head:* Arne R. Flaten, Head of the Graduate Program, 765-494-3056, E-mail: aflaten@purdue.edu. *Application contact:* Kathryn Evans, Graduate Contact, 765-494-7666, E-mail: kathy@purdue.edu.
Website: https://www.cla.purdue.edu/vpa/ad/

Rhode Island School of Design, Department of Industrial Design, Providence, RI 02903-2784. Offers MID. *Accreditation:* NASAD. *Students:* 50 full-time (24 women); includes 6 minority (4 Asian, non-Hispanic/Latino; 2 Hispanic/Latino), 31 international. Average age 26. 255 applicants, 17% accepted, 9 enrolled. In 2019, 14 master's

awarded. *Degree requirements:* For master's, thesis, exhibition. *Entrance requirements:* For master's, portfolio, statement of purpose, 3 letters of recommendation. Additional exam requirements/recommendations for international students: required—TOEFL (minimum score 580 paper-based; 93 iBT), IELTS (minimum score 6.5), Duolingo. *Application deadline:* For fall admission, 1/10 for domestic and international students. Application fee: $60. Electronic applications accepted. *Expenses: Tuition:* Full-time $51,800. *Required fees:* $1060. *Financial support:* Fellowships, research assistantships, teaching assistantships, Federal Work-Study, scholarships/grants, and unspecified assistantships available. Financial award application deadline: 2/1; financial award applicants required to submit FAFSA. *Unit head:* Khipra Nichols, Department Head, 401-454-6160, Fax: 401-454-6157, E-mail: idgradprogram@risd.edu. *Application contact:* Molly Pettengill, Associate Director for Graduate Recruitment, 401-454-6312, Fax: 401-454-6309, E-mail: mpetteng@risd.edu.
Website: http://www.risd.edu/academics/industrial-design/

Rochester Institute of Technology, Graduate Enrollment Services, College of Imaging Arts and Sciences, School of Design, MFA Program in Industrial Design, Rochester, NY 14623-5603. Offers MFA. *Accreditation:* NASAD. *Program availability:* Part-time. *Degree requirements:* For master's, thesis, thesis exhibition. *Entrance requirements:* For master's, portfolio and artist's statement, resume, three letters of recommendation. Additional exam requirements/recommendations for international students: required—TOEFL (minimum score 550 paper-based; 88 iBT), IELTS (minimum score 6.5), PTE (minimum score 58). Electronic applications accepted.

Savannah College of Art and Design, Program in Industrial Design, Savannah, GA 31402-3146. Offers MA, MFA. *Program availability:* Part-time. *Degree requirements:* For master's, final project (for MA); thesis (for MFA). *Entrance requirements:* For master's, GRE (recommended), portfolio (submitted in digital format), audition or writing submission, resume, statement of purpose, two letters of recommendation. Additional exam requirements/recommendations for international students: recommended—TOEFL (minimum score 550 paper-based; 85 iBT), IELTS (minimum score 6.5). Electronic applications accepted.

Thomas Jefferson University, Kanbar College of Design, Engineering and Commerce, Program in Industrial Design, Philadelphia, PA 19107. Offers MS. *Accreditation:* NASAD. *Program availability:* Part-time, evening/weekend. *Degree requirements:* For master's, project. *Entrance requirements:* For master's, essay; portfolio (recommended). Additional exam requirements/recommendations for international students: required—TOEFL (minimum score 79 iBT), IELTS (minimum score 6.5).

University of Cincinnati, Graduate School, College of Design, Architecture, Art, and Planning, School of Design, Cincinnati, OH 45221. Offers fashion design (M Des); graphic design (M Des); industrial design (M Des); interaction design (M Des); product development (M Des). *Accreditation:* NASAD. *Degree requirements:* For master's, thesis. *Entrance requirements:* For master's, undergraduate degree in design or related field, 2 years of work experience in design or related field. Additional exam requirements/recommendations for international students: required—TOEFL. Electronic applications accepted.

University of Detroit Mercy, College of Engineering and Science, Detroit, MI 48221. Offers chemistry (MS); civil and environmental engineering (DE); electrical and computer engineering (ME); electrical engineering (DE); engineering management (M Eng Mgt); environmental engineering (MEE); mechanical engineering (MME, DE); product development (MS); software engineering (MSSE); teaching of mathematics (MATM). *Program availability:* Part-time, evening/weekend. *Degree requirements:* For doctorate, thesis/dissertation. Electronic applications accepted. Application fee is waived when completed online. *Expenses:* Contact institution.

University of Illinois at Urbana-Champaign, Graduate College, College of Fine and Applied Arts, School of Art and Design, Program in Design and Media, Champaign, IL 61820. Offers art and design (MFA), including new media; graphic design (MFA); industrial design (MFA). *Accreditation:* NASAD.

University of Notre Dame, The Graduate School, College of Arts and Letters, Department of Art, Art History, and Design, Notre Dame, IN 46556. Offers art history (MA); design (MFA), including graphic design, industrial design; studio art (MFA), including ceramics, painting, photography, printmaking, sculpture. *Accreditation:* NASAD. *Degree requirements:* For master's, comprehensive exam (for some programs), thesis. *Entrance requirements:* For master's, GRE General Test, minimum GPA of 3.0. Additional exam requirements/recommendations for international students: required—TOEFL (minimum score 600 paper-based; 80 iBT). Electronic applications accepted.

The University of the Arts, College of Art, Media and Design, Department of Product Design, Philadelphia, PA 19102-4944. Offers M Des. *Accreditation:* NASAD. *Degree requirements:* For master's, thesis. *Entrance requirements:* For master's, portfolio of 20 pieces that showcases self-generated projects, professional assignments or projects developed in a previous program; official transcripts; three letters of recommendation; one- to two-page statement of professional plans and goals; personal interview; resume or curriculum vitae; statement of intent. Additional exam requirements/recommendations for international students: required—TOEFL (minimum score 580 paper-based, 92 iBT) or IELTS (minimum score 6.5).

University of Washington, Graduate School, College of Arts and Sciences, School of Art, Division of Design, Seattle, WA 98195. Offers industrial design (MFA); visual communication design (MFA).

Wayne State University, College of Fine, Performing and Communication Arts, James Pearson Duffy Department of Art and Art History, Detroit, MI 48202. Offers art (MA, MFA), including ceramics, drawing, fashion design and merchandising (MA), fibers, graphic design, industrial design (MA), interior design (MA), metalsmithing, painting, photography, printmaking, sculpture; art history (MA). *Degree requirements:* For master's, thesis (for some programs), essay or thesis. *Entrance requirements:* For master's, BFA or another degree and equivalent course work, portfolio, personal interview, reference letters, statement of intent (except for art history program). Additional exam requirements/recommendations for international students: required—TOEFL (minimum score 550 paper-based; 79 iBT), TWE (minimum score 5.5), Michigan English Language Assessment Battery (minimum score 85); recommended—IELTS (minimum score 6.5). Electronic applications accepted. *Expenses:* Contact institution.

Interior Design

Academy of Art University, Graduate Programs, School of Interior Architecture and Design, San Francisco, CA 94105-3410. Offers MA, MFA. *Accreditation:* CIDA. *Program availability:* Part-time, 100% online. *Faculty:* 4 full-time (3 women), 28 part-time/adjunct (14 women). *Students:* 107 full-time (95 women), 157 part-time (143 women); includes 44 minority (11 Black or African American, non-Hispanic/Latino; 1 American Indian or Alaska Native, non-Hispanic/Latino; 10 Asian, non-Hispanic/Latino; 20 Hispanic/Latino; 2 Two or more races, non-Hispanic/Latino), 79 international. Average age 33. 110 applicants, 100% accepted, 82 enrolled. In 2019, 98 master's awarded. *Degree requirements:* For master's, final review. *Entrance requirements:* For master's, statement of intent; resume; portfolio/reel; official college transcripts. *Application deadline:* Applications are processed on a rolling basis. Application fee: $50. Electronic applications accepted. *Expenses: Tuition:* Full-time $1083; part-time $1083 per credit hour. *Required fees:* $860; $860 per unit. $430 per term. One-time fee: $145. Tuition and fees vary according to program. *Financial support:* Career-related internships or fieldwork, Federal Work-Study, and scholarships/grants available. Financial award application deadline: 8/10; financial award applicants required to submit FAFSA. *Application contact:* 800-544-ARTS, E-mail: info@academyart.edu.
Website: http://www.academyart.edu/interior-design-school/index.html

Ball State University, Graduate School, Teachers College, Department of Family, Consumer, and Technology Education, Muncie, IN 47306. Offers family and consumer science (MS), including apparel design (MA, MS), fashion merchandising (MA, MS), interior design (MA, MS), residential property management (MA, MS); family and consumer sciences (MA), including apparel design (MA, MS), fashion merchandising (MA, MS), interior design (MA, MS), residential property management (MA, MS); nutrition and dietetics (MA, MS). *Program availability:* Part-time, evening/weekend, 100% online. *Entrance requirements:* For master's, letter of intent, resume, two letters of recommendation, portfolio (for interior design option). Additional exam requirements/recommendations for international students: required—TOEFL (minimum score 550 paper-based; 79 iBT), IELTS (minimum score 6.5). Electronic applications accepted. *Expenses: Tuition, area resident:* Full-time $7506; part-time $417 per credit hour. Tuition, nonresident: full-time $20,610; part-time $1145 per credit hour. *Required fees:* $2126. Tuition and fees vary according to course load, campus/location and program.

Boston Architectural College, Graduate Programs, Boston, MA 02115-2795. Offers architecture (M Arch); historic preservation (MDS); interior design (MID); landscape architecture (MLA); sustainable design (MDS). *Accreditation:* CIDA. *Degree requirements:* For master's, thesis. *Entrance requirements:* For master's, portfolio (recommended). Electronic applications accepted.

Brenau University, Sydney O. Smith Graduate School, College of Fine Arts and Humanities, Gainesville, GA 30501. Offers interior design (MID). *Accreditation:* CIDA. *Program availability:* Part-time, evening/weekend. *Faculty:* 3 full-time (2 women). *Students:* 1 (woman) full-time, 6 part-time (all women); includes 3 minority (1 Black or African American, non-Hispanic/Latino; 2 Hispanic/Latino). Average age 37. 8 applicants, 50% accepted, 1 enrolled. In 2019, 10 master's awarded. *Degree requirements:* For master's, internship for MID which is in teachout; Thesis for MFA. *Entrance requirements:* For master's, GMAT, GRE, or MAT, portfolio review, minimum GPA of 3.0, resume. Additional exam requirements/recommendations for international students: required—TOEFL (minimum score 497 paper-based; 71 iBT); recommended—IELTS (minimum score 5.5). *Application deadline:* Applications are processed on a rolling basis. Application fee: $35. Electronic applications accepted. *Expenses: Tuition:* Full-time $7339.65; part-time $3685.36 per year. *Required fees:* $740 per semester. Tuition and fees vary according to course load, degree level and program. *Financial support:* Applicants required to submit FAFSA. *Unit head:* Dr. Andrea Birch, Dean, College of Fine Arts & Humanities, 770-718-5325, E-mail: abirch@brenau.edu. *Application contact:* Nathan Goss, Assistant Vice President for Recruitment, 770-534-6162, Fax: 770-718-5338.
Website: http://www.brenau.edu/fineartshumanities/

California State Polytechnic University, Pomona, Program in Interior Architecture, Pomona, CA 91768-2557. Offers interior architecture (MIA). *Accreditation:* CIDA. *Program availability:* Part-time, evening/weekend. *Entrance requirements:* Additional exam requirements/recommendations for international students: required—TOEFL (minimum score 550 paper-based). Electronic applications accepted. *Expenses:* Contact institution.

Chatham University, Program in Interior Architecture, Pittsburgh, PA 15232-2826. Offers MIA. *Accreditation:* CIDA. *Program availability:* Part-time, evening/weekend, online learning. *Entrance requirements:* Additional exam requirements/recommendations for international students: required—TOEFL (minimum score 600 paper-based; 100 iBT), IELTS (minimum score 7), TWE. Electronic applications accepted. Application fee is waived when completed online. *Expenses: Tuition:* Part-time $1017 per credit. *Required fees:* $30 per credit. Tuition and fees vary according to program.

Cornell University, Graduate School, Graduate Fields of Human Ecology, Field of Design and Environmental Analysis, Ithaca, NY 14853. Offers applied research in human-environment relations (MS); facilities planning and management (MS); housing and design (MS); human factors and ergonomics (MS); human-environment relations (MS); interior design (MA, MPS). *Degree requirements:* For master's, thesis. *Entrance requirements:* For master's, GRE General Test, portfolio or slides of recent work; bachelor's degree in interior design, architecture or related design discipline; 2 letters of recommendation. Additional exam requirements/recommendations for international students: required—TOEFL (minimum score 600 paper-based; 105 iBT). Electronic applications accepted.

Drexel University, Westphal College of Media Arts and Design, Program in Interior Architecture and Design, Philadelphia, PA 19104-2875. Offers MS. *Accreditation:* CIDA; NASAD. *Degree requirements:* For master's, comprehensive exam, thesis. *Entrance requirements:* For master's, interview. Additional exam requirements/recommendations for international students: required—TOEFL. Electronic applications accepted.

Eastern Michigan University, Graduate School, College of Engineering and Technology, School of Visual and Built Environments, Program in Interior Design, Ypsilanti, MI 48197. Offers MS. *Program availability:* Part-time, evening/weekend, online learning. *Students:* 6 full-time (all women), 4 part-time (3 women); includes 1 minority (Black or African American, non-Hispanic/Latino), 4 international. Average age 27. 16 applicants, 56% accepted, 4 enrolled. In 2019, 5 master's awarded. *Entrance requirements:* Additional exam requirements/recommendations for international students: required—TOEFL. *Application deadline:* Applications are processed on a rolling basis. Application fee: $45. *Financial support:* Fellowships, research assistantships with full tuition reimbursements, teaching assistantships with full tuition reimbursements, career-related internships or fieldwork, Federal Work-Study, institutionally sponsored loans, scholarships/grants, tuition waivers (partial), and unspecified assistantships available. Support available to part-time students. Financial award applicants required to submit FAFSA. *Application contact:* Dr. Deb de Laski-Smith, Graduate Program Coordinator, 734-487-8254, Fax: 734-487-8755, E-mail: ddelaski@emich.edu.

Endicott College, School of Performing and Visual Arts, Program in Interior Architecture, Beverly, MA 01915. Offers MA, MFA. *Accreditation:* NASAD. *Program availability:* Part-time, evening/weekend. *Faculty:* 1 (woman) full-time, 12 part-time/adjunct (8 women). *Students:* 14 full-time (12 women), 2 part-time (1 woman); includes 3 minority (all Asian, non-Hispanic/Latino). Average age 32. 9 applicants, 33% accepted, 2 enrolled. In 2019, 7 master's awarded. *Degree requirements:* For master's, thesis. *Entrance requirements:* For master's, official transcript of all post-secondary academic work; 250-500 word essay on specified topic; 2 letters of recommendation; design portfolio required with a minimum of 15 pieces of design work (only for some programs). Additional exam requirements/recommendations for international students: required—TOEFL (minimum score 550 paper-based; 79 iBT). *Application deadline:* Applications are processed on a rolling basis. Application fee: $50. Electronic applications accepted. *Expenses:* Tuition varies by program. *Financial support:* Applicants required to submit FAFSA. *Unit head:* Myoung Joo Chun, Director of Graduate Interior Design Programs, 978-232-2545, Fax: 978-232-3000, E-mail: mchun@endicott.edu. *Application contact:* Ian Menchini, Director, Graduate Enrollment and Advising, 978-232-5292, Fax: 978-232-3000, E-mail: imenchin@endicott.edu.
Website: https://www.endicott.edu/academics/schools/visual-performing-arts/graduate-programs

Florida International University, College of Communication, Architecture and The Arts, Department of Interior Architecture, Miami, FL 33199. Offers MA, MIA, Certificate. *Accreditation:* CIDA. *Faculty:* 4 full-time (3 women), 8 part-time/adjunct (all women). *Students:* 48 full-time (40 women), 5 part-time (4 women); includes 43 minority (1 Black or African American, non-Hispanic/Latino; 40 Hispanic/Latino; 2 Two or more races, non-Hispanic/Latino), 6 international. Average age 27. 19 applicants, 42% accepted, 5 enrolled. In 2019, 30 master's awarded. *Entrance requirements:* For master's, GRE or minimum GPA of 3.0 in upper-level undergraduate work, portfolio. Additional exam requirements/recommendations for international students: required—TOEFL (minimum score 550 paper-based; 80 iBT). *Application deadline:* For fall admission, 2/1 for domestic and international students. Application fee: $30. Electronic applications accepted. *Expenses: Tuition, area resident:* Full-time $8912; part-time $446 per credit hour. Tuition, state resident: full-time $8912; part-time $446 per credit hour. Tuition, nonresident: full-time $21,393; part-time $992 per credit hour. *Required fees:* $2194. *Financial support:* Institutionally sponsored loans and scholarships/grants available. Financial award application deadline: 3/1; financial award applicants required to submit FAFSA. *Unit head:* Newton Dsouza Prabhu, Chair, 305-348-1875, E-mail: newton.dsouza@fiu.edu. *Application contact:* Nanett Rojas, Manager, Admissions Operations, 305-348-7464, Fax: 305-348-7441, E-mail: gradadm@fiu.edu.

Florida State University, The Graduate School, College of Fine Arts, Department of Interior Architecture and Design, Tallahassee, FL 32306. Offers MFA, MS. *Accreditation:* NASAD (one or more programs are accredited). *Program availability:* Part-time. *Students:* Average age 25. 37 applicants, 54% accepted, 9 enrolled. In 2019, 25 master's awarded. *Entrance requirements:* For master's, GRE General Test, minimum GPA of 3.0 during previous 2 years. Additional exam requirements/recommendations for international students: required—TOEFL (minimum score 550 paper-based; 80 iBT). *Application deadline:* For fall admission, 7/1 for domestic students, 5/1 for international students; for summer admission, 3/1 for domestic and international students. Applications are processed on a rolling basis. Application fee: $30. Electronic applications accepted. *Financial support:* In 2019–20, 13 teaching assistantships with tuition reimbursements (averaging $5,000 per year) were awarded; career-related internships or fieldwork and unspecified assistantships also available. Financial award applicants required to submit FAFSA. *Unit head:* Dr. Jill Pable, Chair, 850-644-8326, Fax: 850-644-3112, E-mail: jpable@fsu.edu. *Application contact:* Dr. Steven Webber, Director of Graduate Studies, E-mail: swebber@fsu.edu.
Website: http://interiordesign.fsu.edu/

The George Washington University, Columbian College of Arts and Sciences, Corcoran School of the Arts and Design, Washington, DC 20007. Offers art and the book (MA); art education (MA, MAT); decorative arts and design history (MA); exhibition design (MA); interior design (MA); new media photojournalism (MA). *Accreditation:* NASAD. *Program availability:* Part-time. *Entrance requirements:* Additional exam requirements/recommendations for international students: required—TOEFL (minimum score 95 iBT).

The George Washington University, Columbian College of Arts and Sciences, Department of Fine Arts and Art History, Program in Interior Design, Washington, DC 20052. Offers MA, MFA. *Accreditation:* CIDA. *Entrance requirements:* Additional exam requirements/recommendations for international students: required—TOEFL (minimum score 550 paper-based; 80 iBT).

Georgia State University, College of Arts, Ernest G. Welch School of Art and Design, Program in Studio Art, Atlanta, GA 30302-3083. Offers ceramics (MFA); drawing and painting (MFA); graphic design (MFA); interior design (MFA); photography (MFA); printmaking (MFA); sculpture (MFA); textiles (MFA). *Accreditation:* NASAD. Application fee: $50. Electronic applications accepted. *Expenses: Tuition, area resident:* Full-time $7164; part-time $398 per credit hour. Tuition, state resident: full-time $7164; part-time $398 per credit hour. Tuition, nonresident: full-time $22,662; part-time $1259 per credit hour. *International tuition:* $22,662 full-time. *Required fees:* $2128; $312 per credit hour. Tuition and fees vary according to course load and program. *Financial support:* Fellowships, research assistantships, teaching assistantships, scholarships/grants, and unspecified assistantships available. Financial award application deadline: 4/15; financial award applicants required to submit FAFSA. *Unit head:* Joseph Peragine, Director, Welch School of Art and Design, 404-413-5229, E-mail: jperagine@gsu.edu. *Application contact:* Joseph Peragine, Director, Welch School of Art and Design, 404-413-5229, E-mail: jperagine@gsu.edu.
Website: http://artdesign.gsu.edu/graduate/admissions/masters-of-fine-arts-in-studio/

Interior Designers Institute, Graduate Program, Newport Beach, CA 92660. Offers MA.

Iowa State University of Science and Technology, Program in Interior Design, Ames, IA 50011. Offers MA, MFA. *Accreditation:* NASAD. *Entrance requirements:* For master's, GRE. Additional exam requirements/recommendations for international students: required—TOEFL (minimum score 550 paper-based; 79 iBT), IELTS (minimum score 6.5). Electronic applications accepted.

Kansas State University, Graduate School, College of Architecture, Planning and Design, Department of Interior Architecture and Product Design, Manhattan, KS 66506. Offers MIAPD. *Accreditation:* CIDA. *Degree requirements:* For master's, thesis, oral exam, culminating project. *Entrance requirements:* For master's, minimum GPA of 3.0, portfolio. Additional exam requirements/recommendations for international students: required—TOEFL (minimum score 600 paper-based; 95 iBT) or IELTS (minimum score 7). Electronic applications accepted.

Lawrence Technological University, College of Architecture and Design, Southfield, MI 48075-1058. Offers architecture (M Arch, MA), including interior architecture (M Arch); build information modeling (Graduate Certificate); interior design (MID); public interest design (Graduate Certificate); social practice (MFA); urban design (MUD). *Accreditation:* NASAD. *Program availability:* Part-time, evening/weekend. *Faculty:* 10 full-time (1 woman), 7 part-time/adjunct (4 women). *Students:* 6 full-time (3 women), 149 part-time (70 women); includes 18 minority (7 Black or African American, non-Hispanic/Latino; 3 Asian, non-Hispanic/Latino; 6 Hispanic/Latino; 2 Two or more races, non-Hispanic/Latino), 21 international. Average age 30. 214 applicants, 84% accepted, 94 enrolled. In 2019, 54 master's awarded. *Degree requirements:* For master's, thesis optional. *Entrance requirements:* Additional exam requirements/recommendations for international students: required—TOEFL (minimum score 550 paper-based; 79 iBT). *Application deadline:* For fall admission, 5/24 for international students; for spring admission, 10/13 for international students; for summer admission, 2/18 for international students. Applications are processed on a rolling basis. Application fee: $50. Electronic applications accepted. *Expenses: Tuition:* Full-time $16,618; part-time $8309 per year. *Required fees:* $600; $600. *Financial support:* In 2019–20, 39 students received support, including 8 research assistantships with partial tuition reimbursements available (averaging $6,000 per year); career-related internships or fieldwork, scholarships/grants, and unspecified assistantships also available. Financial award application deadline: 4/1; financial award applicants required to submit FAFSA. *Unit head:* Prof. Karl Daubmann, Dean/Professor, 248-204-2805, E-mail: archdean@ltu.edu. *Application contact:* Jane Rohrback, Director of Admissions, 248-204-3160, Fax: 248-204-2228, E-mail: admissions@ltu.edu.
Website: http://www.ltu.edu/architecture_and_design/index.asp

Marymount University, School of Design, Arts, and Humanities, Program in Interior Design, Arlington, VA 22207-4299. Offers interior design (MA). *Accreditation:* CIDA. *Program availability:* Part-time, evening/weekend. *Faculty:* 6 full-time (4 women), 6 part-time/adjunct (5 women). *Students:* 43 full-time (41 women), 28 part-time (27 women); includes 22 minority (13 Black or African American, non-Hispanic/Latino; 5 Asian, non-Hispanic/Latino; 3 Hispanic/Latino; 1 Two or more races, non-Hispanic/Latino), 15 international. Average age 36. 29 applicants, 86% accepted, 14 enrolled. In 2019, 23 master's awarded. *Degree requirements:* For master's, thesis, 3-6 semesters of applied design studio work. *Entrance requirements:* For master's, First-Professional Track: 2 letters of recommendation, resume, personal statement, transcripts with minimum of 30 credits in liberal arts and sciences coursework (or credits will be made up during the program). Post-Professional Track: 2 letters of recommendation, resume, bachelor's in Interior Design or Architecture, personal statement, portfolio. Additional exam requirements/recommendations for international students: required—TOEFL (minimum score 600 paper-based; 96 iBT), IELTS (minimum score 6.5), PTE (minimum score 58). *Application deadline:* For fall admission, 7/16 priority date for domestic and international students; for spring admission, 11/16 priority date for domestic and international students; for summer admission, 4/16 priority date for domestic and international students. Applications are processed on a rolling basis. Application fee: $40. Electronic applications accepted. *Expenses: Tuition:* Part-time $1050 per credit. *Required fees:* $22 per credit. One-time fee: $270 part-time. Tuition and fees vary according to program. *Financial support:* In 2019–20, 7 students received support. Research assistantships, teaching assistantships, career-related internships or fieldwork, scholarships/grants, and unspecified assistantships available. Support available to part-time students. Financial award application deadline: 3/1; financial award applicants required to submit FAFSA. *Unit head:* Douglas Seidler, Chair, Interior Design, 703-284-6515, E-mail: douglas.seidler@marymount.edu. *Application contact:* Fiona McDonnell, Administrative Assistant, 703-284-5901, E-mail: gadmissi@marymount.edu.
Website: https://www.marymount.edu/Academics/School-of-Design-Arts-and-Humanities/Graduate-Programs/Interior-Design-MA

Marywood University, Academic Affairs, School of Architecture, Program in Interior Architecture/Design, Scranton, PA 18509-1598. Offers MA. *Degree requirements:* For master's, thesis. *Entrance requirements:* For master's, resume, personal essay, portfolio.

Miami University, College of Creative Arts, Department of Architecture and Interior Design, Oxford, OH 45056. Offers M Arch. *Accreditation:* NASAD.

Michigan State University, The Graduate School, College of Agriculture and Natural Resources and College of Social Science, School of Planning, Design and Construction, East Lansing, MI 48824. Offers construction management (MS, PhD); environmental design (MA); interior design and facilities management (MA); international planning studies (MIPS); urban and regional planning (MURP). *Degree requirements:* For master's, thesis or alternative. *Entrance requirements:* Additional exam requirements/recommendations for international students: required—TOEFL. Electronic applications accepted.

Moore College of Art & Design, Program in Interior Design, Philadelphia, PA 19103. Offers MFA. *Accreditation:* NASAD. *Program availability:* Evening/weekend. *Degree requirements:* For master's, thesis, internship, thesis exhibition. *Entrance requirements:* For master's, minimum GPA of 3.0, on-site interview, portfolio, 3 letters of recommendation, resume.

The New School, Parsons School of Design, Program in Interior Design, New York, NY 10011. Offers MFA. *Program availability:* Part-time. *Faculty:* 24 full-time, 36 part-time/adjunct. *Students:* 39 full-time (36 women), 1 (woman) part-time; includes 4 minority (1 Black or African American, non-Hispanic/Latino; 1 Asian, non-Hispanic/Latino; 2 Hispanic/Latino), 22 international. Average age 26. 183 applicants, 32% accepted, 20 enrolled. In 2019, 17 master's awarded. *Degree requirements:* For master's, thesis. *Entrance requirements:* For master's, transcripts, resume, statement of purpose, recommendation letters, portfolio, interviews. Additional exam requirements/recommendations for international students: required—TOEFL (minimum score 92 iBT), IELTS (minimum score 7), PTE (minimum score 63). *Application deadline:* For fall admission, 1/1 priority date for domestic and international students; for summer admission, 1/1 for domestic students, 1/1 priority date for international students. Applications are processed on a rolling basis. Application fee: $50. Electronic applications accepted. *Expenses:* 1810 per credit. *Financial support:* In 2019–20, 33 students received support, including 3 teaching assistantships (averaging $3,745 per year); career-related internships or fieldwork, scholarships/grants, and unspecified assistantships also available. Support available to part-time students. Financial award application deadline: 2/1; financial award applicants required to submit FAFSA. *Unit head:* Rosie Scott, PhD, E-mail: scottr@newschool.edu. *Application contact:* Simone Varadian, Senior Director, 212-229-5150 Ext. 4117, E-mail: varadias@newschool.edu.
Website: https://www.newschool.edu/parsons/mfa-interior-design/

New York School of Interior Design, Program in Healthcare Interior Design, New York, NY 10021-5110. Offers MPS. *Entrance requirements:* For master's, portfolio, resume, undergraduate degree in interior design or closely-related field. Additional exam requirements/recommendations for international students: required—TOEFL (minimum score 550 paper-based; 79 iBT). Electronic applications accepted.

New York School of Interior Design, Program in Interior Design (Post-Professional Level), New York, NY 10021-5110. Offers MFA. *Degree requirements:* For master's, thesis. *Entrance requirements:* For master's, portfolio, resume, undergraduate degree in interior design or closely-related field. Additional exam requirements/recommendations for international students: required—TOEFL (minimum score 550 paper-based; 79 iBT). Electronic applications accepted.

New York School of Interior Design, Program in Interior Design (Professional-Level), New York, NY 10021-5110. Offers MFA. *Accreditation:* CIDA; NASAD. *Degree requirements:* For master's, thesis. *Entrance requirements:* For master's, portfolio, resume, undergraduate degree in interior design or closely-related field. Additional exam requirements/recommendations for international students: required—TOEFL (minimum score 550 paper-based; 79 iBT). Electronic applications accepted.

The Ohio State University, Graduate School, College of Arts and Sciences, Division of Arts and Humanities, Department of Design, Columbus, OH 43210. Offers design (MA); design research and development (MFA); digital animation and interactive media (MFA). *Accreditation:* NASAD. *Program availability:* Part-time. *Entrance requirements:* For master's, GRE General Test (for all applicants with cumulative GPA below 3.0), portfolio. Additional exam requirements/recommendations for international students: recommended—TOEFL (minimum score 550 paper-based; 79 iBT). Electronic applications accepted.

Paris College of Art, Graduate Programs, Paris, France. Offers accessories design (MA); fashion design: new materials and technologies (MA); fashion film and photography (MA); interior design (MA); transdisciplinary new media (MA, MFA). *Entrance requirements:* Additional exam requirements/recommendations for international students: required—TOEFL or IELTS.

Pontificia Universidad Catolica Madre y Maestra, Graduate School, Faculty of Sciences and Humanities, Santiago, Dominican Republic. Offers architecture (M Arch), including architecture of interiors, architecture of tourist lodgings, landscaping; early childhood education (M Ed).

Pratt Institute, School of Design, Program in Interior Design, Brooklyn, NY 11205-3899. Offers MFA. *Accreditation:* NASAD. *Program availability:* Part-time. *Students:* 137 full-time (111 women), 5 part-time (3 women); includes 16 minority (1 Black or African American, non-Hispanic/Latino; 7 Asian, non-Hispanic/Latino; 4 Hispanic/Latino; 4 Two or more races, non-Hispanic/Latino), 108 international. Average age 25. 269 applicants, 52% accepted, 53 enrolled. In 2019, 48 master's awarded. *Degree requirements:* For master's, thesis. *Entrance requirements:* For master's, portfolio, letters of recommendation. Additional exam requirements/recommendations for international students: required—TOEFL (minimum score 575 paper-based; 90 iBT). *Application deadline:* For fall admission, 1/5 for domestic and international students; for spring admission, 10/1 for domestic and international students. Application fee: $50 ($90 for international students). Electronic applications accepted. *Expenses: Tuition:* Full-time $33,246; part-time $1847 per credit. *Required fees:* $1980. *Financial support:* Career-related internships or fieldwork, Federal Work-Study, institutionally sponsored loans, scholarships/grants, health care benefits, and unspecified assistantships available. Support available to part-time students. Financial award application deadline: 2/1; financial award applicants required to submit FAFSA. *Unit head:* David Foley, Acting Chair, 718-636-3630, Fax: 718-636-3410, E-mail: dfoley@pratt.edu. *Application contact:* Natalie Capannelli, Director of Graduate Admissions, 718-636-3551, Fax: 718-636-3670, E-mail: ncapanne@pratt.edu.
Website: https://www.pratt.edu/academics/school-of-design/graduate-school-of-design/interior-design-grad/

Purdue University, Graduate School, College of Liberal Arts, Department of Art and Design, West Lafayette, IN 47907. Offers art education (MA, PhD); industrial design (MFA); interior design (MFA); visual communications design (MFA). *Accreditation:* NASAD; NAST. *Program availability:* Part-time. *Faculty:* 4 full-time (1 woman). *Students:* 37 full-time (21 women), 3 part-time (2 women); includes 9 minority (1 Black or African American, non-Hispanic/Latino; 3 Asian, non-Hispanic/Latino; 4 Hispanic/Latino; 1 Two or more races, non-Hispanic/Latino), 14 international. Average age 28. 144 applicants, 23% accepted, 14 enrolled. In 2019, 24 master's awarded. *Degree requirements:* For master's, terminal exhibit, project, or thesis. *Entrance requirements:* For master's, GRE General Test (for art education), minimum undergraduate GPA of 3.0 or equivalent; 9 undergraduate hours in an art or design history; BA in art (for MA in art education); for doctorate, GRE General Test (minimum scores 600 in verbal and 1000 total), master's degree in art education or art with teaching certification; 3 years of teaching experience at the K-12 level. Additional exam requirements/recommendations for international students: required—TOEFL (minimum score 550 paper-based; 77 iBT). *Application deadline:* For fall admission, 2/1 for domestic students, 2/1 priority date for international students. Applications are processed on a rolling basis. Application fee: $60 ($75 for international students). Electronic applications accepted. *Financial support:* Teaching assistantships with tuition reimbursements and career-related internships or fieldwork available. Support available to part-time students. Financial award applicants required to submit FAFSA. *Unit head:* Arne R. Flaten, Head of the Graduate Program, 765-494-3056, E-mail: aflaten@purdue.edu. *Application contact:* Kathryn Evans, Graduate Contact, 765-494-7666, E-mail: kathy@purdue.edu.
Website: https://www.cla.purdue.edu/vpa/ad/

Queens University of Charlotte, College of Arts and Sciences, Charlotte, NC 28274-0002. Offers creative writing (MFA); interior design (MA). *Program availability:* Part-time, online learning. Electronic applications accepted.

Rhode Island School of Design, Department of Interior Architecture, Providence, RI 02903-2784. Offers exhibition and narrative environments (M Des); interior studies/adaptive reuse (M Des, MA). *Students:* 69 full-time (58 women); includes 3 minority (all Asian, non-Hispanic/Latino), 59 international. Average age 25. 200 applicants, 46% accepted, 37 enrolled. In 2019, 44 master's awarded. *Degree requirements:* For master's, thesis, exhibition. *Entrance requirements:* For master's, portfolio, statement of purpose, 3 letters of recommendation. Additional exam requirements/recommendations for international students: required—TOEFL (minimum score 580 paper-based; 93 iBT), IELTS (minimum score 6.5), Duolingo. *Application deadline:* For fall admission, 1/10 for domestic and international students. Application fee: $60. Electronic applications accepted. *Expenses: Tuition:* Full-time $51,800. *Required fees:* $1060. *Financial support:* Fellowships, research assistantships, teaching assistantships, Federal Work-Study, scholarships/grants, and unspecified assistantships available. Financial award application deadline: 2/1; financial award applicants required to submit FAFSA. *Unit head:* Liliane Wong, Department Head, 401-454-6272, Fax: 401-277-4962, E-mail: lwong@risd.edu. *Application contact:* Molly Pettengill, Associate Director for Graduate Recruitment, 401-454-6312, Fax: 401-454-6309, E-mail: mpetteng@risd.edu.
Website: http://www.risd.edu/academics/interior-architecture/

San Diego State University, Graduate and Research Affairs, College of Professional Studies and Fine Arts, School of Art and Design, San Diego, CA 92182. Offers studio arts (MA, MFA), including applied design, graphic design, interior architecture, multimedia and photography, painting and printmaking, sculpture. *Accreditation:* NASAD (one or more programs are accredited). *Degree requirements:* For master's, variable foreign language requirement, thesis. *Entrance requirements:* For master's, GRE General Test, bachelor's degree in related field, slide portfolio, typed slide information sheet, 2 letters of recommendation. Additional exam requirements/recommendations for international students: required—TOEFL. Electronic applications accepted.

Savannah College of Art and Design, Program in Interior Design, Savannah, GA 31402-3146. Offers MA, MFA. *Program availability:* Part-time, 100% online. *Degree requirements:* For master's, final project (for MA); thesis (for MFA). *Entrance requirements:* For master's, GRE (recommended), portfolio (submitted in digital format), audition or writing submission, resume, statement of purpose, two letters of recommendation. Additional exam requirements/recommendations for international students: recommended—TOEFL (minimum score 550 paper-based; 85 iBT), IELTS (minimum score 6.5). Electronic applications accepted.

Suffolk University, New England School of Art and Design, Boston, MA 02108-2770. Offers graphic design (MA); interior architecture (MA). *Accreditation:* CIDA. *Program availability:* Part-time, evening/weekend. *Faculty:* 2 full-time (1 woman), 2 part-time/adjunct (1 woman). *Students:* 36 full-time (31 women), 6 part-time (all women); includes 7 minority (2 Black or African American, non-Hispanic/Latino; 2 Asian, non-Hispanic/Latino; 3 Hispanic/Latino), 14 international. Average age 26. 81 applicants, 79% accepted, 25 enrolled. In 2019, 20 master's awarded. *Entrance requirements:* For master's, GRE (for MFA), art portfolio, interview, 2 letters of recommendation, resume; letter of intent (for MFA). Additional exam requirements/recommendations for international students: required—TOEFL (minimum score 550 paper-based; 80 iBT). *Application deadline:* For fall admission, 3/15 priority date for domestic and international students; for spring admission, 10/15 priority date for domestic and international students. Applications are processed on a rolling basis. Application fee: $50. Electronic applications accepted. *Expenses:* Contact institution. *Financial support:* In 2019–20, 36 students received support, including 7 fellowships (averaging $2,829 per year); career-related internships or fieldwork, Federal Work-Study, institutionally sponsored loans, scholarships/grants, and unspecified assistantships also available. Financial award application deadline: 4/1; financial award applicants required to submit FAFSA. *Unit head:* Audrey Goldstein, Department Chair, 617-997-4290, E-mail: agoldstein@suffolk.edu. *Application contact:* Mara Marzocchi, Associate Director of Graduate Admissions, 617-573-8302, Fax: 617-305-1733, E-mail: grad.admission@suffolk.edu.
Website: http://www.suffolk.edu/nesad/

Texas Tech University, Graduate School, College of Human Sciences, Department of Design, Lubbock, TX 79409-1220. Offers environmental design (MS); interior and environmental design (PhD). *Program availability:* Part-time. *Faculty:* 12 full-time (10 women). *Students:* 19 full-time (13 women), 8 part-time (5 women); includes 4 minority (3 Hispanic/Latino; 1 Two or more races, non-Hispanic/Latino), 16 international. Average age 35. 8 applicants, 38% accepted, 1 enrolled. In 2019, 7 master's, 2 doctorates awarded. *Degree requirements:* For master's, comprehensive exam, thesis or alternative; for doctorate, comprehensive exam, thesis/dissertation. *Entrance requirements:* For master's, 3 recommendation letters, design portfolio, 500-word written statement (reason for pursuing degree), resume; for doctorate, 3 recommendation letters, 500-word written statement (reason for pursuing degree), resume. Design portfolio required for those wishing to apply for teaching assistantships. Additional exam requirements/recommendations for international students: required—TOEFL (minimum score 550 paper-based; 79 iBT), Required to take either IELTS or TOEFL. Minimum for IELTS is 6.5. *Application deadline:* For fall admission, 6/1 priority date for domestic students, 1/15 priority date for international students; for spring admission, 9/1 priority date for domestic students, 6/15 priority date for international students. Applications are processed on a rolling basis. Application fee: $65. Electronic applications accepted. *Expenses:* Contact institution. *Financial support:* In 2019–20, 13 students received support, including 11 fellowships (averaging $9,664 per year), 6 research assistantships (averaging $7,638 per year); teaching assistantships, scholarships/grants, and unspecified assistantships also available. Financial award application deadline: 4/15; financial award applicants required to submit FAFSA. *Unit head:* Dr. Sharran F. Parkinson, Professor, Graduate Program Director, Department Chairperson, 806-742-3031, Fax: 806-742-1639, E-mail: sharran.parkinson@ttu.edu. *Application contact:* Erin Rebecca Sopronyi, Senior Office Manager, 806-742-3050, Fax: 806-742-1639, E-mail: erin.r.sopronyi@ttu.edu.
Website: www.dod.ttu.edu

Thomas Jefferson University, College of Architecture and the Built Environment, Program in Interior Architecture, Philadelphia, PA 19107. Offers MS.

University of California, Berkeley, UC Berkeley Extension, Certificate Programs in Art and Design, Berkeley, CA 94720. Offers interior design and interior architecture (Certificate); landscape architecture (Certificate); visual arts (Postbaccalaureate Certificate).

University of Cincinnati, Graduate School, College of Design, Architecture, Art, and Planning, School of Architecture and Interior Design, Cincinnati, OH 45221. Offers architecture (M Arch). *Accreditation:* NASAD. *Degree requirements:* For master's, one foreign language, thesis. *Entrance requirements:* Additional exam requirements/recommendations for international students: required—TOEFL.

University of Cincinnati, Graduate School, College of Design, Architecture, Art, and Planning, School of Architecture and Interior Design, Program in Interior Design, Cincinnati, OH 45221. Offers M Des. *Degree requirements:* For master's, one foreign language, thesis. *Entrance requirements:* For master's, undergraduate degree in design or related field, 2 years of work experience in design or related field.

University of Florida, Graduate School, College of Design, Construction and Planning, Department of Interior Design, Gainesville, FL 32611. Offers historic preservation (MID); interior design (MID); sustainable design (MID). *Degree requirements:* For master's, thesis. *Entrance requirements:* For master's, GRE General Test, minimum GPA of 3.0. Additional exam requirements/recommendations for international students: required—TOEFL (minimum score 550 paper-based; 80 iBT), IELTS (minimum score 6).

University of Florida, Graduate School, College of Design, Construction and Planning, Doctoral Program in Design, Construction and Planning, Gainesville, FL 32611. Offers construction management (PhD); design, construction and planning (PhD); geographic information systems (PhD); historic preservation (PhD); interior design (PhD); landscape architecture (PhD); urban and regional planning (PhD). *Degree requirements:* For doctorate, thesis/dissertation. *Entrance requirements:* For doctorate, GRE General Test, minimum GPA of 3.0. Additional exam requirements/recommendations for international students: required—TOEFL (minimum score 550 paper-based; 80 iBT), IELTS (minimum score 6). Electronic applications accepted.

University of Georgia, College of Family and Consumer Sciences, Department of Textiles, Merchandising, and Interiors, Athens, GA 30602. Offers historical and cultural aspects of dress and textiles (MS); interior environments (MS); international merchandising (PhD); merchandising and international trade (MS); polymer, fiber and textile science (MS); polymer, fiber, and textile sciences (PhD). *Accreditation:* NASAD.

Interior Design

Degree requirements: For master's, thesis; for doctorate, thesis/dissertation. *Entrance requirements:* For master's and doctorate, GRE General Test. Electronic applications accepted.

University of Kentucky, Graduate School, College of Design, Program in Interior Design, Merchandising, and Textiles, Lexington, KY 40506-0032. Offers interior design (MA). *Degree requirements:* For master's, comprehensive exam, thesis optional. *Entrance requirements:* For master's, GRE General Test, minimum undergraduate GPA of 2.75. Additional exam requirements/recommendations for international students: required—TOEFL (minimum score 550 paper-based). Electronic applications accepted.

University of Manitoba, Faculty of Graduate Studies, Faculty of Architecture, Department of Interior Design, Winnipeg, MB R3T 2N2, Canada. Offers MID. *Accreditation:* CIDA.

University of Massachusetts Amherst, Graduate School, College of Humanities and Fine Arts, Department of Architecture, Amherst, MA 01003. Offers architecture (M Arch); design (MS); design in historic preservation (MS). *Program availability:* Part-time. *Degree requirements:* For master's, thesis or alternative, project. *Entrance requirements:* For master's, GRE General Test (for M Arch only), 3 letters of recommendation (M Arch only); portfolio. Additional exam requirements/recommendations for international students: required—TOEFL (minimum score 550 paper-based; 80 iBT), IELTS (minimum score 6.5). Electronic applications accepted.

University of Minnesota, Twin Cities Campus, Graduate School, College of Design, Department of Design, Housing, and Apparel, Minneapolis, MN 55455-0213. Offers apparel (MA, MS, PhD); design communication (MA, MS, PhD); housing studies (MA, MS, PhD, Postbaccalaureate Certificate); interactive design (MFA); interior design (MA, MS, PhD). *Program availability:* Part-time. *Degree requirements:* For master's and Postbaccalaureate Certificate, comprehensive exam, thesis (for some programs); for doctorate, comprehensive exam, thesis/dissertation. *Entrance requirements:* For master's, GRE General Test, minimum GPA of 3.0 (preferred), portfolio, 3 letters of recommendation; for doctorate, GRE General Test, minimum GPA of 3.0 (preferred), portfolio, 3 letters of recommendation, writing sample; for Postbaccalaureate Certificate, GRE General Test, minimum GPA of 3.0 (preferred). Additional exam requirements/recommendations for international students: required—TOEFL (minimum score 550 paper-based; 79 iBT). Electronic applications accepted.

University of Nebraska–Lincoln, Graduate College, College of Architecture, Department of Architecture, Lincoln, NE 68588. Offers architecture (M Arch, MS, PhD); interior design (MS); M Arch/MBA; M Arch/MCRP. *Entrance requirements:* Additional exam requirements/recommendations for international students: required—TOEFL. Electronic applications accepted.

The University of North Carolina at Greensboro, Graduate School, College of Arts and Sciences, Department of Interior Architecture, Greensboro, NC 27412-5001. Offers historic preservation (Certificate); interior architecture (MS); museum studies (Certificate). *Degree requirements:* For master's, thesis. *Entrance requirements:* For master's, GRE General Test or MAT, bachelor's degree in interior design, interview, portfolio. Additional exam requirements/recommendations for international students: required—TOEFL. Electronic applications accepted.

University of North Texas, Toulouse Graduate School, Denton, TX 76203-5459. Offers accounting (MS); applied anthropology (MA, MS); applied behavior analysis (Certificate); applied geography (MA); applied technology and performance improvement (M Ed, MS); art education (MA); art history (MA); arts leadership (Certificate); audiology (Au D); behavior analysis (MS); behavioral science (PhD); biochemistry and molecular biology (MS); biology (MA, MS); biomedical engineering (MS); business analysis (MS); chemistry (MS); clinical health psychology (PhD); communication studies (MA, MS); computer engineering (MS); computer science (MS); counseling (M Ed, MS), including clinical mental health counseling (MS), college and university counseling, elementary school counseling, secondary school counseling; creative writing (MA); criminal justice (MS); curriculum and instruction (M Ed); decision sciences (MBA); design (MA, MFA), including fashion design (MFA), innovation studies, interior design (MFA); early childhood studies (MS); economics (MS); educational leadership (M Ed, Ed D); educational psychology (MS, PhD), including family studies (MS), gifted and talented (MS), human development (MS), learning and cognition (MS), research, measurement and evaluation (MS); electrical engineering (MS); emergency management (MPA); engineering technology (MS); English (MA); English as a second language (MA); environmental science (MS); finance (MBA, MS); financial management (MPA); French (MA); health services management (MBA); higher education (M Ed, Ed D); history (MA, MS); hospitality management (MS); human resources management (MPA); information science (MS); information systems (PhD); information technologies (MBA); interdisciplinary studies (MA, MS); international studies (MA); international sustainable tourism (MS); jazz studies (MM); journalism (MA, MJ, Graduate Certificate), including interactive and virtual digital communication (Graduate Certificate), narrative journalism (Graduate Certificate), public relations (Graduate Certificate); kinesiology (MS); linguistics (MA); local government management (MPA); logistics (PhD); logistics and supply chain management (MBA); long-term care, senior housing, and aging services (MA); management (PhD); marketing (MBA); mathematics (MA, MS); mechanical and energy engineering (MS, PhD); music (MA), including ethnomusicology, music theory, musicology, performance; music composition (PhD); music education (MM Ed, PhD); nonprofit management (MPA); operations and supply chain management (MBA); performance (MM, DMA); philosophy (MA); political science (MA); professional and technical communication (MA); radio, television and film (MA, MFA); rehabilitation counseling (Certificate); sociology (MA); Spanish (MA); special education (M Ed); speech-language pathology (MA); strategic management (MBA); studio art (MFA); teaching (M Ed); MBA/MS. *Program availability:* Part-time, evening/weekend, online learning. Terminal master's awarded for partial completion of doctoral program. *Degree requirements:* For master's, variable foreign language requirement, comprehensive exam (for some programs), thesis (for some programs); for doctorate, variable foreign language requirement, comprehensive exam (for some programs), thesis/dissertation; for other advanced degree, variable foreign language requirement, comprehensive exam (for some programs). *Entrance requirements:* For master's and doctorate, GRE, GMAT. Additional exam requirements/recommendations for international students: required—TOEFL (minimum score 550 paper-based; 79 iBT). Electronic applications accepted.

University of Oklahoma, Christopher C. Gibbs College of Architecture, Division of Interior Design, Norman, OK 73019-0390. Offers interior design (MS); professional applications of interior design (Graduate Certificate). *Program availability:* Part-time. *Degree requirements:* For master's, comprehensive exam, project or thesis. *Entrance requirements:* For master's, graduate degree in interior design or related field, portfolio of design work, letter of intent limited to 500 words, three letters of recommendation; for Graduate Certificate, undergraduate degree in interior design or related field, portfolio of design work, letter of intent limited to 500 words, three letters of recommendation. Additional exam requirements/recommendations for international students: required—TOEFL (minimum score 79 iBT) or IELTS (minimum score 6.5). Electronic applications accepted. *Expenses:* Tuition, state resident: full-time $6583.20; part-time $274.30 per credit hour. Tuition, nonresident: full-time $21,242; part-time $885.10 per credit hour. *International tuition:* $21,242.40 full-time. *Required fees:* $1994.20; $72.55 per credit hour. $126.50 per semester. Tuition and fees vary according to course load and degree level.

University of Oregon, Graduate School, College of Design, Department of Architecture, Eugene, OR 97403. Offers architecture (M Arch); interior architecture (MI Arch). *Accreditation:* CIDA. *Degree requirements:* For master's, thesis (for some programs). *Entrance requirements:* For master's, GRE General Test. Additional exam requirements/recommendations for international students: required—TOEFL.

University of Oregon, Graduate School, College of Design, Department of Interior Architecture, Eugene, OR 97403. Offers MI Arch, MS.

The University of Texas at Austin, Graduate School, School of Architecture, Program in Interior Design, Austin, TX 78712-1111. Offers MID.

Virginia Commonwealth University, Graduate School, School of the Arts, Richmond, VA 23284-9005. Offers art education (MAE, PhD); art history (MA, PhD), including curatorial (PhD), historical studies, museum studies (MA); ceramics (MFA); design (MFA), including interior environments, visual communications; fibers (MFA); furniture design (MFA); glassworking (MFA); jewelry/metalworking (MFA); kinetic imaging (MFA); music (MM), including music education; painting (MFA); photography and film (MFA); printmaking (MFA); sculpture (MFA); theatre (MFA), including costume design, pedagogy/literature, pedagogy/performance, scene design/technical theatre. *Accreditation:* CIDA. *Program availability:* Part-time. *Entrance requirements:* For doctorate, GRE General Test, writing sample. Additional exam requirements/recommendations for international students: required—TOEFL (minimum score 600 paper-based; 100 iBT). Electronic applications accepted.

Washington State University, College of Agricultural, Human, and Natural Resource Sciences, Program in Interior Design and Landscape Architecture, Pullman, WA 99164-2220. Offers MA, MS. *Program availability:* Part-time. *Degree requirements:* For master's, comprehensive exam, thesis (for some programs), oral exam. *Entrance requirements:* For master's, portfolio. Additional exam requirements/recommendations for international students: required—TOEFL or IELTS. Electronic applications accepted.

Wayne State University, College of Fine, Performing and Communication Arts, James Pearson Duffy Department of Art and Art History, Detroit, MI 48202. Offers art (MA, MFA), including ceramics, drawing, fashion design and merchandising (MA), fibers, graphic design, industrial design (MA), interior design (MA), metalsmithing, painting, photography, printmaking, sculpture; art history (MA). *Degree requirements:* For master's, thesis (for some programs), essay or thesis. *Entrance requirements:* For master's, BFA or another degree and equivalent course work, portfolio, personal interview, reference letters, statement of intent (except for art history program). Additional exam requirements/recommendations for international students: required—TOEFL (minimum score 550 paper-based; 79 iBT), TWE (minimum score 5.5), Michigan English Language Assessment Battery (minimum score 85); recommended—IELTS (minimum score 6.5). Electronic applications accepted. *Expenses:* Contact institution.

Medical Illustration

Augusta University, College of Allied Health Sciences, Program in Medical Illustration, Augusta, GA 30912. Offers MS. *Accreditation:* ARCMI. *Degree requirements:* For master's, thesis or alternative, project. *Entrance requirements:* For master's, GRE General Test, portfolio. Additional exam requirements/recommendations for international students: required—TOEFL (minimum score 550 paper-based; 79 iBT). Electronic applications accepted.

Johns Hopkins University, School of Medicine, Graduate Programs in Medicine, Department of Art as Applied to Medicine, Baltimore, MD 21205. Offers medical and biological illustration (MA). *Accreditation:* ARCMI. *Degree requirements:* For master's, thesis. *Entrance requirements:* For master's, GRE General Test (encouraged). Additional exam requirements/recommendations for international students: recommended—TOEFL, IELTS. Electronic applications accepted.

Rochester Institute of Technology, Graduate Enrollment Services, College of Health Sciences and Technology, Health Sciences Department, MFA Program in Medical Illustration, Rochester, NY 14623-5603. Offers MFA. *Program availability:* Part-time. *Degree requirements:* For master's, thesis. *Entrance requirements:* For master's, portfolio, minimum GPA of 3.0 (recommended). Additional exam requirements/recommendations for international students: required—TOEFL (minimum score 550 paper-based; 79 iBT), IELTS (minimum score 6.5), PTE (minimum score 58). Electronic applications accepted.

University of Illinois at Chicago, College of Applied Health Sciences, Program in Biomedical Visualization, Chicago, IL 60607-7128. Offers MS. *Accreditation:* ARCMI. *Degree requirements:* For master's, thesis. *Entrance requirements:* For master's, GRE General Test, minimum GPA of 2.75. Additional exam requirements/recommendations for international students: required—TOEFL. Electronic applications accepted. *Expenses:* Contact institution.

Photography

Academy of Art University, Graduate Programs, School of Photography, San Francisco, CA 94105-3410. Offers MA, MFA. *Accreditation:* NASAD. *Program availability:* Part-time, 100% online. *Faculty:* 6 full-time (3 women), 26 part-time/adjunct (9 women). *Students:* 100 full-time (50 women), 93 part-time (57 women); includes 40 minority (14 Black or African American, non-Hispanic/Latino; 2 American Indian or Alaska Native, non-Hispanic/Latino; 5 Asian, non-Hispanic/Latino; 12 Hispanic/Latino; 1 Native Hawaiian or other Pacific Islander, non-Hispanic/Latino; 6 Two or more races, non-Hispanic/Latino), 56 international. Average age 38. 50 applicants, 100% accepted, 43 enrolled. In 2019, 69 master's awarded. *Degree requirements:* For master's, final review. *Entrance requirements:* For master's, statement of intent; resume; portfolio/reel; official college transcripts. *Application deadline:* Applications are processed on a rolling basis. *Application fee:* $50. Electronic applications accepted. *Expenses: Tuition:* Full-time $1083; part-time $1083 per credit hour. *Required fees:* $860; $860 per unit. $430 per term. One-time fee: $145. Tuition and fees vary according to program. *Financial support:* Career-related internships or fieldwork, Federal Work-Study, and scholarships/grants available. Financial award application deadline: 8/10; financial award applicants required to submit FAFSA. *Application contact:* 800-544-ARTS, E-mail: info@academyart.edu.
Website: http://www.academyart.edu/photography-school/index.html

Ball State University, Graduate School, College of Fine Arts, School of Art, Muncie, IN 47306. Offers fine arts (MFA), including animation, glass; visual arts studio (MA), including ceramics, drawing, metals, painting, photography and intermedia arts, printmaking, sculpture. *Accreditation:* NASAD. *Program availability:* Part-time. *Entrance requirements:* For master's, minimum baccalaureate GPA of 2.75 or 3.0 in latter half of baccalaureate, goals statement, digital portfolio of artwork, resume, transcripts of all college-level course work, three letters of recommendation. Additional exam requirements/recommendations for international students: required—TOEFL (minimum score 550 paper-based; 79 iBT), IELTS (minimum score 6.5). Electronic applications accepted. *Expenses: Tuition, area resident:* Full-time $7506; part-time $417 per credit hour. Tuition, nonresident: full-time $20,610; part-time $1145 per credit hour. *Required fees:* $2126. Tuition and fees vary according to course load, campus/location and program.

Bard College, International Center of Photography, Annandale-on-Hudson, NY 12504. Offers advanced photographic studies (MFA).

Bard College, Milton Avery Graduate School of the Arts, Annandale-on-Hudson, NY 12504. Offers film/video (MFA); music/sound (MFA); painting (MFA); photography (MFA); sculpture (MFA); writing (MFA). *Degree requirements:* For master's, thesis, project, 8-week summer residency, independent study. *Entrance requirements:* For master's, interview, portfolio, 2 letters of recommendation, history of work in the arts. Additional exam requirements/recommendations for international students: required—TOEFL (minimum score 550 paper-based). Electronic applications accepted. *Expenses:* Contact institution.

Barry University, College of Arts and Sciences, Department of Fine Arts, Miami Shores, FL 33161-6695. Offers photography (MA, MFA). *Degree requirements:* For master's, thesis (for some programs). *Entrance requirements:* For master's, GRE General Test, minimum GPA of 3.0. Electronic applications accepted.

Bradley University, The Graduate School, Slane College of Communications and Fine Arts, Department of Art, Peoria, IL 61625-0002. Offers ceramics (MA, MFA); drawing (MA, MFA); graphic design (MA, MFA); painting (MA, MFA); photography (MA, MFA); printmaking (MA, MFA); sculpture (MA, MFA). *Accreditation:* NASAD. *Program availability:* Part-time. *Faculty:* 10 full-time (4 women). *Students:* 4 full-time (2 women), 2 part-time (both women); includes 1 minority (American Indian or Alaska Native, non-Hispanic/Latino). Average age 42. 3 applicants, 33% accepted. In 2019, 6 master's awarded. *Degree requirements:* For master's, comprehensive exam, thesis, final exhibit. *Entrance requirements:* For master's, portfolio, 2 letters of recommendation. Additional exam requirements/recommendations for international students: required—TOEFL (minimum score 550 paper-based; 79 iBT), PTE (minimum score 58). *Application deadline:* For fall admission, 4/1 priority date for domestic and international students; for spring admission, 11/1 priority date for domestic and international students. Applications are processed on a rolling basis. Application fee: $40 ($50 for international students). Electronic applications accepted. *Expenses: Tuition:* Part-time $930 per credit hour. *Financial support:* In 2019–20, 2 students received support. Teaching assistantships, scholarships/grants, tuition waivers (partial), and unspecified assistantships available. Support available to part-time students. Financial award application deadline: 4/1. *Unit head:* Gary Will, Chairperson, 309-677-2967, E-mail: gwill@bradley.edu. *Application contact:* Rachel Webb, Director of On-Campus Graduate Admissions and International Student and Scholar Services, 309-677-2375, E-mail: rkwebb@bradley.edu.
Website: http://www.bradley.edu/academic/departments/art/

Brooklyn College of the City University of New York, School of Visual, Media and Performing Arts, Department of Art, Brooklyn, NY 11210-2889. Offers art history (MA); digital art (MFA); drawing and painting (MFA); photography (MFA); printmaking (MFA); sculpture (MFA). *Program availability:* Part-time. *Degree requirements:* For master's, thesis. *Entrance requirements:* For master's, bachelor's degree in art, portfolio, 2 letters of recommendation. Additional exam requirements/recommendations for international students: required—TOEFL (minimum score 500 paper-based; 61 iBT). Electronic applications accepted.

California Institute of the Arts, School of Art, Valencia, CA 91355-2340. Offers art (MFA, Adv C); graphic design (MFA, Adv C); photography (MFA, Adv C). *Accreditation:* NASAD (one or more programs are accredited). *Degree requirements:* For master's, final project. *Entrance requirements:* For master's, portfolio. Additional exam requirements/recommendations for international students: required—TOEFL. Electronic applications accepted.

California State University, Fullerton, Graduate Studies, College of the Arts, Department of Visual Arts, Fullerton, CA 92831-3599. Offers art (MA, MFA), including art history (MA), ceramics (MFA), crafts, creative photography, exhibition design, glass, graphic design, illustration, sculpture. *Accreditation:* NASAD (one or more programs are accredited). *Program availability:* Part-time. *Entrance requirements:* For master's, minimum GPA of 2.5 in last 60 units of course work, portfolio.

California State University, Los Angeles, Graduate Studies, College of Arts and Letters, Department of Art, Los Angeles, CA 90032-8530. Offers art (MA), including art education, art history, art therapy, ceramics, metals, and textiles, design (MA, MFA), painting, sculpture, and graphic arts, photography; fine arts (MFA), including crafts, design (MA, MFA), studio arts. *Accreditation:* NASAD (one or more programs are accredited). *Program availability:* Part-time, evening/weekend. *Degree requirements:* For master's, comprehensive exam, project or thesis. *Entrance requirements:* For master's, portfolio. Additional exam requirements/recommendations for international students: required—TOEFL (minimum score 500 paper-based). Electronic applications accepted. *Expenses: Tuition, area resident:* Full-time $7176; part-time $4164 per year. Tuition, state resident: full-time $7176; part-time $4164 per year. Tuition, nonresident: full-time $14,304; part-time $8916 per year. *International tuition:* $14,304 full-time. *Required fees:* $1037.76; $1037.76 per unit. Tuition and fees vary according to degree level and program.

Central Washington University, School of Graduate Studies and Research, College of Arts and Humanities, Department of Art and Design, Ellensburg, WA 98926. Offers ceramics (MFA); computer arts (MFA); jewelry and metalsmithing (MFA); painting and drawing (MFA); photography (MFA); sculpture (MFA). *Entrance requirements:* For master's, minimum GPA of 3.0, portfolio. Additional exam requirements/recommendations for international students: required—TOEFL (minimum score 550 paper-based; 79 iBT) or IELTS (minimum score 6.5). Electronic applications accepted.

Claremont Graduate University, Graduate Programs, School of Arts and Humanities, Department of Art, Claremont, CA 91711. Offers digital media (MFA); drawing (MFA); installation (MFA); painting (MFA); performance (MFA); photography (MFA); sculpture (MFA); studio (MFA). *Program availability:* Part-time. *Degree requirements:* For master's, final project show. *Entrance requirements:* For master's, BA in art or BFA, slide review. Additional exam requirements/recommendations for international students: required—TOEFL (minimum score 75 iBT). Electronic applications accepted. *Expenses:* Contact institution.

Columbia College Chicago, School of Graduate Studies, Photography Department, Chicago, IL 60605-1996. Offers MFA. *Program availability:* Part-time. *Degree requirements:* For master's, thesis. *Entrance requirements:* For master's, self-assessment essay, portfolio, resume, letters of recommendation, transcripts. Additional exam requirements/recommendations for international students: required—TOEFL, IELTS. Electronic applications accepted. *Expenses:* Contact institution.

Cornell University, Graduate School, Graduate Fields of Architecture, Art and Planning, Field of Art, Ithaca, NY 14853. Offers creative visual arts (MFA), including painting, photography, printmaking, sculpture. *Degree requirements:* For master's, thesis, exhibit. *Entrance requirements:* For master's, slide portfolio of 10-20 slides, 3 letters of recommendation, resume. Additional exam requirements/recommendations for international students: required—TOEFL (minimum score 550 paper-based; 77 iBT). Electronic applications accepted.

Cornell University, Graduate School, Graduate Fields of Arts and Sciences, Field of History of Art, Archaeology and Visual Studies, Ithaca, NY 14853. Offers 19th century art (PhD); African, African American and African diaspora (PhD); American art (PhD); ancient art and archaeology (PhD); Asian American art (PhD); Baroque art (PhD); Comparative Modernities (PhD); digital art (PhD); East Asian art (PhD); history of photography (PhD); Islamic art (PhD); Latin American art (PhD); medieval art (PhD); modern art (PhD); Renaissance art (PhD); Southeast Asian art (PhD); theory and criticism (PhD); visual studies (PhD). *Degree requirements:* For doctorate, one foreign language, comprehensive exam, thesis/dissertation, general exams in 3 areas. *Entrance requirements:* For doctorate, GRE General Test, sample of written work, 3 letters of recommendation. Additional exam requirements/recommendations for international students: required—TOEFL (minimum score 550 paper-based; 77 iBT). Electronic applications accepted.

Cranbrook Academy of Art, Program in Fine Arts, Bloomfield Hills, MI 48303-0801. Offers 2d design (MFA); 3d design (MFA); ceramics (MFA); fiber (MFA); metalsmithing (MFA); painting (MFA); photography (MFA); print media (MFA); sculpture (MFA). *Accreditation:* NASAD. *Degree requirements:* For master's, thesis, exhibit. *Entrance requirements:* Additional exam requirements/recommendations for international students: required—TOEFL (minimum score 85 iBT). Electronic applications accepted.

East Carolina University, Graduate School, College of Fine Arts and Communication, School of Art and Design, Greenville, NC 27858-4353. Offers art education (MA Ed); ceramics (MFA); graphic design (MFA); illustration (MFA); metal design (MFA); painting and drawing (MFA); photography (MFA); printmaking (MFA); sculpture (MFA); textile design (MFA); wood design (MFA). *Accreditation:* NASAD (one or more programs are accredited). *Program availability:* Part-time, evening/weekend. *Application deadline:* For fall admission, 2/1 for domestic students; for spring admission, 10/1 for domestic students. *Expenses: Tuition, area resident:* Full-time $4749; part-time $185 per credit hour. Tuition, state resident: full-time $4749; part-time $185 per credit hour. Tuition, nonresident: full-time $17,898; part-time $864 per credit hour. *International tuition:* $17,898 full-time. *Required fees:* $2787. *Financial support:* Application deadline: 6/1. *Unit head:* Dr. Kate Bukowski, Director, 252-328-6665, E-mail: bukowskik16@ecu.edu. *Application contact:* Graduate School Admissions, 252-328-6012, E-mail: gradschool@ecu.edu.
Website: https://art.ecu.edu/

Ferris State University, Kendall College of Art and Design, Grand Rapids, MI 49307. Offers design (MA); painting (MFA); photography (MFA); printmaking (MFA); visual and critical studies (MA). *Faculty:* 16 full-time (9 women), 6 part-time/adjunct (3 women). *Students:* 46 full-time (25 women), 18 part-time (15 women); includes 10 minority (1 Black or African American, non-Hispanic/Latino; 1 American Indian or Alaska Native, non-Hispanic/Latino; 6 Hispanic/Latino; 2 Two or more races, non-Hispanic/Latino), 8 international. Average age 33. 28 applicants, 82% accepted, 19 enrolled. In 2019, 14 master's awarded. *Degree requirements:* For master's, thesis, seminars and studio courses. *Entrance requirements:* For master's, official transcripts from all institutions of higher education attended. Letter of intent outlining proposed artistic goals. Concise artist statement that addresses the philosophical foundation of your work. CV showing successful professional experience. Portfolio of work 20 images in chosen area of emphasis. Contact information for. Additional exam requirements/recommendations for international students: required—TOEFL (minimum score 79 iBT), IELTS (minimum score 6.5). *Application deadline:* For fall admission, 2/1 priority date for domestic and international students; for spring admission, 10/15 priority date for domestic and international students. Applications are processed on a rolling basis. Application fee: $0 ($30 for international students). Electronic applications accepted. *Expenses:* $1079 per credit hour; Technology fee $175 per semester; Student Life Fee $20 per semester. *Financial support:* In 2019–20, 46 students received support, including 46 fellowships (averaging $11,736 per year); scholarships/grants and unspecified assistantships also available. Financial award application deadline: 2/1; financial award applicants required to submit FAFSA. *Unit head:* Tara McCrackin, President, 616-451-2787. *Application contact:* Thomas Post, Graduate Recruitment Specialist, 616-451-2787, Fax: 616-831-9689, E-mail: thomaspost@ferris.edu.
Website: http://www.kcad.edu/

Photography

The George Washington University, Columbian College of Arts and Sciences, Corcoran School of the Arts and Design, Washington, DC 20007. Offers art and the book (MA); art education (MA, MAT); decorative arts and design history (MA); exhibition design (MA); interior design (MA); new media photojournalism (MA). *Accreditation:* NASAD. *Program availability:* Part-time. *Entrance requirements:* Additional exam requirements/recommendations for international students: required—TOEFL (minimum score 95 iBT).

The George Washington University, Columbian College of Arts and Sciences, Department of Fine Arts and Art History, Washington, DC 20052. Offers art history (MA), including art history, museum training; ceramics (MFA); drawing/painting (MFA); interior design (MFA), including interior architecture and design; new media (MFA); photography (MFA); sculpture (MFA). *Accreditation:* CIDA. *Program availability:* Part-time, evening/weekend. *Entrance requirements:* For master's, GRE General Test, bachelor's degree in field, minimum GPA of 3.0. Additional exam requirements/recommendations for international students: required—TOEFL (minimum score 550 paper-based; 80 iBT). Electronic applications accepted.

Georgia State University, College of Arts and Sciences, Department of Communication, Atlanta, GA 30302-3083. Offers film, video, and digital imaging (MA), including critical studies, production, screenwriting; human communication and social influence (MA); mass communication (MA); media and society (PhD); moving image studies (PhD); public communication (PhD); rhetoric and politics (PhD). *Program availability:* Part-time. *Faculty:* 22 full-time (16 women), 1 part-time/adjunct (0 women). *Students:* 67 full-time (46 women), 26 part-time (17 women); includes 44 minority (40 Black or African American, non-Hispanic/Latino; 1 Asian, non-Hispanic/Latino; 1 Hispanic/Latino; 1 Native Hawaiian or other Pacific Islander, non-Hispanic/Latino; 1 Two or more races, non-Hispanic/Latino), 12 international. Average age 36. 82 applicants, 49% accepted, 22 enrolled. In 2019, 9 master's, 5 doctorates awarded. *Degree requirements:* For master's, variable foreign language requirement, thesis (for some programs); for doctorate, comprehensive exam, thesis/dissertation. *Entrance requirements:* For master's and doctorate, GRE. Additional exam requirements/recommendations for international students: required—TOEFL (minimum score 550 paper-based; 80 iBT), IELTS (minimum score 6.5). *Application deadline:* For fall admission, 2/10 for domestic and international students; for spring admission, 10/15 for domestic and international students. Application fee: $50. Electronic applications accepted. *Expenses: Tuition, area resident:* Full-time $7164; part-time $398 per credit hour. Tuition, state resident: full-time $7164; part-time $398 per credit hour. Tuition, nonresident: full-time $22,662; part-time $1259 per credit hour. *International tuition:* $22,662 full-time. *Required fees:* $2128; $312 per credit hour. Tuition and fees vary according to course load and program. *Financial support:* In 2019–20, fellowships with tuition reimbursements (averaging $15,000 per year), teaching assistantships with tuition reimbursements (averaging $15,000 per year) were awarded; career-related internships or fieldwork and unspecified assistantships also available. Financial award applicants required to submit FAFSA. *Unit head:* Dr. Greg Lisby, Chair, 404-413-5639, Fax: 404-413-5634, E-mail: glisby@gsu.edu. *Application contact:* Dr. Greg Lisby, Chair, 404-413-5639, Fax: 404-413-5634, E-mail: glisby@gsu.edu.
Website: http://communication.gsu.edu

Georgia State University, College of Arts, Ernest G. Welch School of Art and Design, Program in Studio Art, Atlanta, GA 30302-3083. Offers ceramics (MFA); drawing and painting (MFA); graphic design (MFA); interior design (MFA); photography (MFA); printmaking (MFA); sculpture (MFA); textiles (MFA). *Accreditation:* NASAD. Application fee: $50. Electronic applications accepted. *Expenses: Tuition, area resident:* Full-time $7164; part-time $398 per credit hour. Tuition, state resident: full-time $7164; part-time $398 per credit hour. Tuition, nonresident: full-time $22,662; part-time $1259 per credit hour. *International tuition:* $22,662 full-time. *Required fees:* $2128; $312 per credit hour. Tuition and fees vary according to course load and program. *Financial support:* Fellowships, research assistantships, teaching assistantships, scholarships/grants, and unspecified assistantships available. Financial award application deadline: 4/15; financial award applicants required to submit FAFSA. *Unit head:* Joseph Peragine, Director, Welch School of Art and Design, 404-413-5229, E-mail: jperagine@gsu.edu. *Application contact:* Joseph Peragine, Director, Welch School of Art and Design, 404-413-5229, E-mail: jperagine@gsu.edu.
Website: http://artdesign.gsu.edu/graduate/admissions/masters-of-fine-arts-in-studio/

Governors State University, College of Arts and Sciences, Program in Independent Film and Digital Imaging, University Park, IL 60484. Offers MFA. *Program availability:* Part-time. *Faculty:* 57 full-time (33 women), 72 part-time/adjunct (40 women). *Students:* 8 full-time (5 women), 8 part-time (3 women); includes 10 minority (9 Black or African American, non-Hispanic/Latino; 1 Two or more races, non-Hispanic/Latino). Average age 41. 2 applicants, 50% accepted, 1 enrolled. In 2019, 6 master's awarded. *Application deadline:* For fall admission, 4/1 for domestic students. Applications are processed on a rolling basis. Application fee: $50. Electronic applications accepted. *Expenses: Tuition, area resident:* Full-time $8472; part-time $353 per credit hour. Tuition, state resident: full-time $8472; part-time $353 per credit hour. Tuition, nonresident: full-time $16,944; part-time $706 per credit hour. *International tuition:* $16,944 full-time. *Required fees:* $2520; $105 per credit hour. $38 per term. Tuition and fees vary according to course load, degree level and program. *Financial support:* Application deadline: 5/1; applicants required to submit FAFSA. *Unit head:* Jason Zingsheim, Chair, Division of Arts and Letters, 708-534-5000 Ext. 7493, E-mail: jzingsheim@govst.edu. *Application contact:* Jason Zingsheim, Chair, Division of Arts and Letters, 708-534-5000 Ext. 7493, E-mail: jzingsheim@govst.edu.

Howard University, Graduate School, Division of Fine Arts, Department of Art, Program in Fine Arts, Washington, DC 20059-0002. Offers 3D reality (sculpture and ceramics) (MFA); design (MFA); electronic studio (MFA); painting (MFA); photography (MFA). *Accreditation:* NASAD. *Degree requirements:* For master's, comprehensive exam, thesis, exhibit. *Entrance requirements:* For master's, minimum GPA of 3.0, portfolio.

Illinois State University, Graduate School, Wonsook Kim College of Fine Arts, School of Art, Normal, IL 61790. Offers art history (MA, MS); ceramics (MFA, MS); drawing (MFA, MS); fibers (MFA, MS); glass (MFA, MS); graphic design (MFA, MS); metals (MFA, MS); painting (MFA, MS); photography (MFA, MS); printmaking (MFA, MS); sculpture (MFA, MS). *Accreditation:* NASAD (one or more programs are accredited). *Faculty:* 34 full-time (18 women), 15 part-time/adjunct (11 women). *Students:* 25 full-time (16 women), 5 part-time (4 women). Average age 31. 32 applicants, 66% accepted, 12 enrolled. In 2019, 11 master's awarded. *Degree requirements:* For master's, thesis or alternative, internship. *Entrance requirements:* For master's, portfolio, sample of scholarly writing. *Application deadline:* Applications are processed on a rolling basis. Application fee: $50. *Expenses: Tuition, area resident:* Full-time $7956; part-time $9767 per year. Tuition, nonresident: full-time $9233; part-time $17,592 per year. *Required fees:* $1797. *Financial support:* In 2019–20, 20 teaching assistantships were awarded; career-related internships or fieldwork, Federal Work-Study, tuition waivers (full and partial), and unspecified assistantships also available. Support available to part-time students. Financial award application deadline: 4/1. *Unit head:* Mike Wille, Director of Art School, 309-438-5610, E-mail: mjwill4@ilstu.edu. *Application contact:* Tyler Lotz, Graduate Coordinator, 309-438-8301, E-mail: tlotz@ilstu.edu.
Website: http://www.arts.ilstu.edu/art/

Indiana State University, College of Graduate and Professional Studies, College of Arts and Sciences, Department of Art and Design, Terre Haute, IN 47809. Offers ceramics (MA, MFA); drawing (MA, MFA); graphic design (MA, MFA); painting (MA, MFA); photography (MA, MFA); printmaking (MA, MFA); sculpture (MA, MFA). *Accreditation:* NASAD (one or more programs are accredited). *Program availability:* Part-time. *Degree requirements:* For master's, thesis or alternative, departmental qualifying exam. *Entrance requirements:* For master's, portfolio. Additional exam requirements/recommendations for international students: required—TOEFL (minimum score 550 paper-based).

Indiana University-Purdue University Indianapolis, Herron School of Art and Design, Indianapolis, IN 46202. Offers art therapy (MA); visual art (MFA), including ceramics, furniture design, painting and drawing, photography and intermedia, printmaking, sculpture; visual communication design (MFA). *Degree requirements:* For master's, thesis. *Entrance requirements:* For master's, personal statement, resume, recommendations, portfolio, transcripts (18 credit hours of studio art and 12 credit hours of psychology, including 3 credit hours of developmental psychology and 3 credit hours of abnormal psychology for MA). Additional exam requirements/recommendations for international students: recommended—TOEFL (minimum score 550 paper-based; 79 iBT), IELTS (minimum score 6.5). Electronic applications accepted. *Expenses:* Contact institution.

Inter American University of Puerto Rico, San Germán Campus, Graduate Studies Center, Program in Fine Arts, San Germán, PR 00683-5008. Offers drawing (MFA); graphic design (MFA); painting (MFA); photography (MFA); printmaking (MFA); sculpture (MFA). *Program availability:* Part-time, evening/weekend. *Degree requirements:* For master's, comprehensive exam, thesis. *Entrance requirements:* For master's, GRE General Test or EXADEP, minimum GPA of 3.0.

Ithaca College, Roy H. Park School of Communications, Program in Image Text, Ithaca, NY 14850. Offers MFA. *Program availability:* Part-time-only. *Faculty:* 12 full-time (3 women). *Students:* 7 part-time (4 women); includes 2 minority (1 Black or African American, non-Hispanic/Latino; 1 Two or more races, non-Hispanic/Latino), 1 international. Average age 37. 22 applicants, 91% accepted, 5 enrolled. In 2019, 8 master's awarded. *Entrance requirements:* Additional exam requirements/recommendations for international students: required—TOEFL (minimum score 550 paper-based; 80 iBT). *Application deadline:* For fall admission, 2/1 for domestic and international students. Applications are processed on a rolling basis. Application fee: $40. Electronic applications accepted. *Expenses:* Contact institution. *Financial support:* In 2019–20, 7 students received support, including 7 fellowships (averaging $6,490 per year); Federal Work-Study and scholarships/grants also available. Support available to part-time students. Financial award application deadline: 3/1; financial award applicants required to submit FAFSA. *Unit head:* Nicholas Muellner, Co-Director, Image Text Program, 607-274-1984, E-mail: nmuellner@ithaca.edu. *Application contact:* Nicole Eversley Bradwell, Director, Office of Admission, 800-429-4274, Fax: 607-274-1263, E-mail: admission@ithaca.edu.
Website: https://www.ithaca.edu/admission/graduate-admission/graduate-study-image-text

James Madison University, The Graduate School, College of Visual and Performing Arts, School of Art, Design and Art History, Harrisonburg, VA 22807. Offers art education (MA); studio art (MA, MFA), including ceramics (MFA), drawing/painting (MFA), intermedia (MFA), metal/jewelry (MFA), photography (MFA), sculpture (MFA). *Accreditation:* NASAD. *Program availability:* Part-time. *Students:* 7 full-time (6 women), 1 (woman) part-time. Average age 30. In 2019, 3 master's awarded. Application fee: $60. Electronic applications accepted. *Financial support:* In 2019–20, 7 students received support, including 2 teaching assistantships with full tuition reimbursements available (averaging $9,284 per year); Federal Work-Study and assistantships (averaging $7911) also available. Financial award application deadline: 3/1; financial award applicants required to submit FAFSA. *Unit head:* Dr. Kathy A. Schwartz, Director of School of Art, Design and Art History, 540-568-6216, E-mail: schwarka@jmu.edu. *Application contact:* Lynette D. Michael, Director of Graduate Student Admissions, 540-568-6131 Ext. 6395, Fax: 540-568-7860, E-mail: michaeld@jmu.edu.
Website: http://www.jmu.edu/artandarthistory/

Kent State University, College of the Arts, School of Art, Kent, OH 44242-0001. Offers art education (MA); art history (MA); crafts (MA), including glass (MA, MFA); fine arts (MA), including fashion; studio art (MFA), including ceramics, drawing, glass (MA, MFA), jewelry, metals and enameling, painting, print media and photography, sculpture, textiles. *Accreditation:* NASAD (one or more programs are accredited). *Program availability:* Part-time, 100% online, blended/hybrid learning. *Faculty:* 22 full-time (13 women), 5 part-time/adjunct (4 women). *Students:* 36 full-time (27 women), 24 part-time (22 women); includes 4 minority (3 Black or African American, non-Hispanic/Latino; 1 Hispanic/Latino), 2 international. Average age 30. 52 applicants, 67% accepted, 20 enrolled. In 2019, 15 master's awarded. *Degree requirements:* For master's, comprehensive exam, thesis (for some programs), 1 foreign language (for art history); final project (for crafts and fine arts). *Entrance requirements:* For master's, bachelors's degree min 3.0 GPA on 4.0 scale, transcripts, goal statement, 3 letters of recommendation, curriculum vitae, for MA and MFA in Studio Art: portfolio, artist statement;l MA Art Education: goal statement that focuses on philosophy of art education. Additional exam requirements/recommendations for international students: required—TOEFL (minimum score 79 iBT), IELTS (minimum score 6.5), PTE (minimum score 58), Michigan English Language Assessment Battery (minimum score 77). *Application deadline:* For fall admission, 2/2 priority date for domestic students, 2/2 for international students; for spring admission, 10/15 for domestic and international students. Applications are processed on a rolling basis. Application fee: $45 ($70 for international students). Electronic applications accepted. *Financial support:* Career-related internships or fieldwork, scholarships/grants, and unspecified assistantships available. Financial award application deadline: 3/1. *Unit head:* Marie Bukowski, Director, 330-672-2192, E-mail: mbukows1@kent.edu. *Application contact:* Peter Christian Johnson, Graduate Coordinator and Associate Professor Ceramics, 330-672-3360, E-mail: pjohns35@kent.edu.
Website: http://www.kent.edu/art

Lesley University, College of Art and Design, Cambridge, MA 02138-2790. Offers photography (MFA); visual arts (MFA). *Program availability:* Part-time. *Degree requirements:* For master's, thesis, final exhibition of thesis work. *Entrance requirements:* For master's, portfolio, resume, personal statement. Additional exam requirements/recommendations for international students: required—TOEFL (minimum score 550 paper-based; 80 iBT). Electronic applications accepted.

Louisiana State University and Agricultural & Mechanical College, Graduate School, College of Art and Design, School of Art, Program in Studio Art, Baton Rouge, LA 70803. Offers ceramics (MFA); graphic design (MFA); painting and drawing (MFA); photography (MFA); printmaking (MFA); sculpture (MFA). *Accreditation:* NASAD.

Louisiana Tech University, Graduate School, College of Liberal Arts, Ruston, LA 71272. Offers architecture (M Arch); art (MFA), including graphic design, photography, studio; audiology (Au D); communication (MA), including speech communication, theatre; English (MA), including literature, technical writing; history (MA); speech pathology (MA); technical writing and communication (Graduate Certificate). *Accreditation:* ASHA. *Program availability:* Part-time. *Degree requirements:* For master's, thesis (for some programs); for doctorate, thesis/dissertation. *Entrance requirements:* For master's, GRE General Test; for doctorate, GRE General Test, bachelor's degree, minimum GPA of 3.0 or 3.2 on last 60 hours attempted. Additional exam requirements/recommendations for international students: required—TOEFL (minimum score 550 paper-based; 80 iBT), IELTS (minimum score 6.5). Electronic applications accepted. *Expenses:* Tuition, area resident: Full-time $6592; part-time $400 per credit. Tuition, state resident: full-time $6592; part-time $400 per credit. Tuition, nonresident: full-time $13,333; part-time $681 per credit. *International tuition:* $13,333 full-time. *Required fees:* $3011; $3011 per unit.

Maryland Institute College of Art, Graduate Studies, MFA Program in Photographic and Electronic Media, Baltimore, MD 21201. Offers MFA. *Accreditation:* NASAD. *Degree requirements:* For master's, thesis, exhibit and thesis documentation. *Entrance requirements:* For master's, portfolio, bachelor's degree in any field. Additional exam requirements/recommendations for international students: required—TOEFL (minimum score 550 paper-based; 80 iBT), IELTS (minimum score 6.5). Electronic applications accepted. *Expenses:* Contact institution.

Marywood University, Academic Affairs, Insalaco College of Creative and Performing Arts, Art Department, Program in Studio Art, Scranton, PA 18509-1598. Offers clay (MA); painting (MA); photography (MA); printmaking (MA); sculpture (MA). *Accreditation:* NASAD. Electronic applications accepted.

Marywood University, Academic Affairs, Insalaco College of Creative and Performing Arts, Art Department, Program in Visual Arts, Scranton, PA 18509-1598. Offers clay (MFA); graphic design (MFA); illustration (MFA); painting (MFA); photography (MFA); printmaking (MFA); sculpture (MFA). *Accreditation:* NASAD. *Program availability:* Part-time. Electronic applications accepted. *Expenses:* Contact institution.

Massachusetts College of Art and Design, Graduate Programs, MFA Program, Boston, MA 02115-5882. Offers 2D fine arts (MFA), including painting, printmaking; 3D fine arts (MFA), including ceramics, fibers, glass, jewelry and metalsmithing, sculpture; design (MFA, Postbaccalaureate Certificate), including dynamic media; fine arts (MFA), including interdisciplinary; media arts (MFA, Postbaccalaureate Certificate), including film/video (MFA), photography. *Accreditation:* NASAD. *Faculty:* 1 (woman) full-time, 29 part-time/adjunct (14 women). *Students:* 44 full-time (26 women), 28 part-time (17 women); includes 8 minority (5 Asian, non-Hispanic/Latino; 3 Hispanic/Latino), 18 international. 202 applicants, 44% accepted, 35 enrolled. In 2019, 30 master's, 8 other advanced degrees awarded. *Degree requirements:* For master's, thesis, thesis exhibition (for fine arts programs); thesis project and document (for design/dynamic media program). *Entrance requirements:* For master's, portfolio, college transcripts, resume, statement of purpose, letters of reference, interview, 6 credits of art history taken prior to or during MFA program; for Postbaccalaureate Certificate, portfolio, college transcripts, resume, statement of purpose, letters of reference, interview. Additional exam requirements/recommendations for international students: required—TOEFL (minimum score 550 paper-based, 85 iBT) or IELTS (6). *Application deadline:* For fall admission, 1/20 priority date for domestic and international students; for summer admission, 1/20 priority date for domestic and international students. Applications are processed on a rolling basis. Application fee: $90. Electronic applications accepted. *Expenses:* Contact institution. *Financial support:* Research assistantships, teaching assistantships, career-related internships or fieldwork, scholarships/grants, tuition waivers (partial), unspecified assistantships, and adjunct co-teaching positions available. Support available to part-time students. Financial award application deadline: 1/20; financial award applicants required to submit FAFSA. *Unit head:* Lucinda Bliss, Dean of Graduate Studies, 617-879-7157, E-mail: gradadmissions@massart.edu. *Application contact:* Stacy Petersen, Associate Director, Graduate Admissions and Operations, 617-879-7238, E-mail: gradadmissions@massart.edu.
Website: http://www.massart.edu/Admissions/Graduate_Programs.html

Mills College, Graduate Studies, Department of Art, Oakland, CA 94613-1000. Offers art (MFA); ceramics (MFA); intermedia (MFA); painting (MFA); photography (MFA); sculpture (MFA). *Degree requirements:* For master's, thesis or alternative, exhibit. *Entrance requirements:* For master's, portfolio, artist statement. Additional exam requirements/recommendations for international students: required—TOEFL (minimum score 550 paper-based; 80 iBT) or IELTS (minimum score 6). Electronic applications accepted. *Expenses:* Contact institution.

Minneapolis College of Art and Design, Master of Fine Arts in Visual Studies, Minneapolis, MN 55404-4347. Offers animation (MFA); comic art (MFA); drawing (MFA); filmmaking (MFA); fine arts (MFA); furniture design (MFA); graphic design (MFA); illustration (MFA); interactive media (MFA); painting (MFA); photography (MFA); printmaking (MFA); sculpture (MFA). *Accreditation:* NASAD. *Program availability:* Part-time. *Students:* 86 applicants, 44% accepted, 9 enrolled. *Degree requirements:* For master's, thesis, thesis exhibit. *Entrance requirements:* Additional exam requirements/recommendations for international students: required—TOEFL (minimum score 550 paper-based; 79 iBT), IELTS (minimum score 6.5), Duolingo English Test accepted with a minimum score of 100 *Application deadline:* For fall admission, 2/1 for domestic and international students. Application fee: $50. Electronic applications accepted. *Expenses:* Tuition: Full-time $41,344. *Required fees:* $450. One-time fee: $300 full-time. *Financial support:* In 2019–20, 15 teaching assistantships (averaging $6,000 per year) were awarded; career-related internships or fieldwork, Federal Work-Study, scholarships/grants, and unspecified assistantships also available. Support available to part-time students. Financial award application deadline: 3/15; financial award applicants required to submit FAFSA. *Unit head:* Ellen Mueller, Director, MFA Program, 612-874-3629, E-mail: emueller@mcad.edu. *Application contact:* Mary Kazura, Director of Admissions, 612-874-3668, Fax: 612-874-3701, E-mail: mkazura@mcad.edu.
Website: http://mcad.edu/mfa

New Hampshire Institute of Art, Graduate Studies, Manchester, NH 03104. Offers art education (MA); creative writing (MFA); photography (MFA); teaching visual arts (MAT); visual arts (MFA). *Accreditation:* NASAD. *Degree requirements:* For master's, thesis, corresponding exhibition and artist talk. *Entrance requirements:* For master's, writing sample or visual art portfolio; curriculum vitae; transcripts; letters of recommendation. Additional exam requirements/recommendations for international students: required—TOEFL (minimum score 550 paper-based; 80 iBT), IELTS (minimum score 6.5). Electronic applications accepted. *Expenses:* Contact institution.

The New School, Parsons School of Design, Program in Photography, New York, NY 10011. Offers MFA. *Program availability:* Part-time. *Faculty:* 4 full-time (1 woman), 181 part-time/adjunct. *Students:* 21 full-time (11 women), 7 part-time (4 women); includes 8 minority (4 Black or African American, non-Hispanic/Latino; 1 Asian, non-Hispanic/Latino; 3 Hispanic/Latino), 14 international. Average age 27. 108 applicants, 31% accepted, 15 enrolled. In 2019, 18 master's awarded. *Degree requirements:* For master's, thesis. *Entrance requirements:* For master's, transcripts, resume, statement of

purpose, recommendation letters, portfolio, interview. Additional exam requirements/recommendations for international students: required—TOEFL (minimum score 92 iBT), IELTS (minimum score 7), PTE (minimum score 63). *Application deadline:* For fall admission, 1/1 priority date for domestic and international students; for summer admission, 1/1 priority date for domestic and international students. Applications are processed on a rolling basis. Application fee: $50. Electronic applications accepted. *Expenses:* 1625 per credit. *Financial support:* In 2019–20, 21 students received support, including 8 research assistantships (averaging $2,029 per year), 9 teaching assistantships (averaging $6,866 per year); career-related internships or fieldwork, scholarships/grants, unspecified assistantships, and travel funding; tuition waivers for students who are also New School employees also available. Support available to part-time students. Financial award application deadline: 2/1; financial award applicants required to submit FAFSA. *Unit head:* James Ramer, Program Director, 212-229-8923 Ext. 4243, E-mail: ramerj@newschool.edu. *Application contact:* Simone Varadian, Senior Director, 212-229-5150 Ext. 4117, E-mail: varadias@newschool.edu. Website: https://www.newschool.edu/parsons/mfa-photography/

New York Film Academy, Program in Filmmaking–Los Angeles, Burbank, CA 91505. Offers acting for film (MFA); cinematography (MFA); documentary film (MFA); film and media production (MA); filmmaking (MFA); game design (MFA); photography (MFA); producing (MA, MFA); screenwriting (MA, MFA). *Accreditation:* NASAD.

New York Film Academy, Program in Filmmaking–South Beach, Florida, Miami Beach, FL 33139. Offers acting for film (MFA); cinematography (MFA); documentary film (MFA); film and media production (MA); filmmaking (MFA); game design (MFA); photography (MFA); producing (MA, MFA); screenwriting (MA, MFA).

Northern Vermont University–Johnson, Program in Studio Arts, Johnson, VT 05656. Offers ceramics (MFA); digital media (MFA); drawing (MFA); painting (MFA); photography (MFA); printmaking (MFA); sculpture (MFA). *Program availability:* Part-time, online learning. *Degree requirements:* For master's, thesis. *Entrance requirements:* For master's, portfolio. Additional exam requirements/recommendations for international students: required—TOEFL. Electronic applications accepted. *Expenses:* Contact institution.

Ohio University, Graduate College, College of Fine Arts, School of Art, Athens, OH 45701-2979. Offers art history (MA); ceramics (MFA); graphic design (MFA); painting (MFA); photography (MFA); printmaking (MFA); sculpture (MFA). *Program availability:* Part-time. *Degree requirements:* For master's, thesis. *Entrance requirements:* For master's, portfolio. Additional exam requirements/recommendations for international students: required—TOEFL (minimum score 550 paper-based; 80 iBT) or IELTS (minimum score 6.5). Electronic applications accepted.

Ohio University, Graduate College, Scripps College of Communication, School of Visual Communication, Athens, OH 45701-2979. Offers MA. *Entrance requirements:* For master's, minimum GPA of 2.5, portfolio. Additional exam requirements/recommendations for international students: required—TOEFL (minimum score 600 paper-based; 100 iBT) or IELTS (minimum score 7). Electronic applications accepted.

Oklahoma City University, Petree College of Arts and Sciences, Oklahoma City, OK 73106-1402. Offers applied behavioral studies (M Ed); applied sociology: nonprofit leadership (MA); creative writing (MFA); criminology (MS); early childhood education (M Ed); elementary education (M Ed); general studies (MLA); leadership/management (MLA); moving image arts (MFA); professional counseling (M Ed); teaching (MA); teaching English to speakers of other languages (MA). *Program availability:* Part-time, evening/weekend. *Degree requirements:* For master's, capstone/practicum. *Entrance requirements:* For master's, bachelor's degree from accredited institution with minimum GPA of 3.0, essay, recommendation letters. Additional exam requirements/recommendations for international students: required—TOEFL (minimum score 550 paper-based; 80 iBT). Electronic applications accepted. *Expenses:* Contact institution.

Otis College of Art and Design, Program in Fine Arts, Los Angeles, CA 90045-9785. Offers new genres (MFA); painting (MFA); photography (MFA); sculpture (MFA). *Accreditation:* NASAD. *Degree requirements:* For master's, thesis. *Entrance requirements:* For master's, portfolio. Additional exam requirements/recommendations for international students: required—TOEFL (minimum score 600 paper-based). Electronic applications accepted.

Paris College of Art, Graduate Programs, Paris, France. Offers accessories design (MA); fashion design: new materials and technologies (MA); fashion film and photography (MA); interior design (MA); transdisciplinary new media (MA, MFA). *Entrance requirements:* Additional exam requirements/recommendations for international students: required—TOEFL or IELTS.

Rhode Island School of Design, Department of Photography, Providence, RI 02903-2784. Offers MFA. *Accreditation:* NASAD. *Students:* 14 full-time (10 women); includes 2 minority (both Hispanic/Latino), 4 international. Average age 27. 123 applicants, 17% accepted, 8 enrolled. In 2019, 9 master's awarded. *Degree requirements:* For master's, thesis, exhibition. *Entrance requirements:* For master's, portfolio, statement of purpose, 3 letters of recommendation. Additional exam requirements/recommendations for international students: required—TOEFL (minimum score 580 paper-based; 93 iBT), IELTS (minimum score 6.5), Duolingo. *Application deadline:* For fall admission, 1/10 for domestic and international students. Application fee: $60. Electronic applications accepted. *Expenses:* Tuition: Full-time $51,800. *Required fees:* $1060. *Financial support:* Fellowships, research assistantships, teaching assistantships, Federal Work-Study, scholarships/grants, and unspecified assistantships available. Financial award application deadline: 2/1; financial award applicants required to submit FAFSA. *Unit head:* Steven Smith, Department Head, 401-454-6122, Fax: 401-454-6385, E-mail: photo@risd.edu. *Application contact:* Molly Pettengill, Associate Director for Graduate Recruitment, 401-454-6312, Fax: 401-454-6309, E-mail: mpetteng@risd.edu.
Website: http://www.risd.edu/academics/photography/

Rochester Institute of Technology, Graduate Enrollment Services, College of Imaging Arts and Sciences, School of Photographic Arts and Sciences, MFA Program in Photography and Related Media, Rochester, NY 14623-5603. Offers MFA. *Accreditation:* NASAD. *Program availability:* Part-time. *Degree requirements:* For master's, thesis, exhibit. *Entrance requirements:* For master's, portfolio and artist's statement, personal statement, resume, three letters of recommendation. Additional exam requirements/recommendations for international students: required—TOEFL (minimum score 550 paper-based; 88 iBT), IELTS (minimum score 6.5), PTE (minimum score 58). Electronic applications accepted.

San Diego State University, Graduate and Research Affairs, College of Professional Studies and Fine Arts, School of Art and Design, San Diego, CA 92182. Offers studio arts (MA, MFA), including applied design, graphic design, interior architecture, multimedia and photography, painting and printmaking, sculpture. *Accreditation:* NASAD (one or more programs are accredited). *Degree requirements:* For master's, variable foreign language requirement, thesis. *Entrance requirements:* For master's, GRE General Test, bachelor's degree in related field, slide portfolio, typed slide information sheet, 2 letters of recommendation. Additional exam requirements/

recommendations for international students: required—TOEFL. Electronic applications accepted.

Savannah College of Art and Design, Program in Photography, Savannah, GA 31402-3146. Offers MA, MFA. *Program availability:* Part-time, 100% online. *Degree requirements:* For master's, final portfolio (for MA); thesis (for MFA). *Entrance requirements:* For master's, GRE (recommended), portfolio (submitted in digital format), audition or writing submission, resume, statement of purpose, two letters of recommendation. Additional exam requirements/recommendations for international students: recommended—TOEFL (minimum score 550 paper-based; 85 iBT), IELTS (minimum score 6.5). Electronic applications accepted.

School of Visual Arts, Graduate Programs, Digital Photography Department, New York, NY 10010-3994. Offers MPS. *Program availability:* Part-time, online learning. *Degree requirements:* For master's, thesis, 33 credits; minimum GPA of 3.0; thesis project culminating in online project, printed book and exhibition. *Entrance requirements:* For master's, image portfolio which represents 1-3 photographically cohesive bodies of work based on style, concept and execution. Additional exam requirements/ recommendations for international students: required—TOEFL (minimum score 550 paper-based; 79 iBT). Electronic applications accepted.

School of Visual Arts, Graduate Programs, Fashion Photography Department, New York, NY 10010-3994. Offers MPS. *Degree requirements:* For master's, 30 credits; minimum cumulative GPA of 3.0; original, challenging and provocative portfolio of images. *Entrance requirements:* For master's, portfolio, writing sample. Additional exam requirements/recommendations for international students: required—TOEFL (minimum score 550 paper-based; 79 iBT). Electronic applications accepted. *Expenses:* Contact institution.

School of Visual Arts, Graduate Programs, Program in Photography, Video and Related Media, New York, NY 10010-3994. Offers MFA. *Accreditation:* NASAD. *Degree requirements:* For master's, thesis, 60 credits; minimum GPA of 3.3; thesis project. *Entrance requirements:* For master's, portfolio (still images and/or videos) submitted through SlideRoom. Additional exam requirements/recommendations for international students: required—TOEFL (minimum score 550 paper-based; 79 iBT). Electronic applications accepted.

Southwest University of Visual Arts, MFA Programs, Tucson, AZ 85716-2505. Offers motion arts (MFA); painting and drawing (MFA); photography (MFA).

Syracuse University, College of Visual and Performing Arts, MFA Program in Art Photography, Syracuse, NY 13244. Offers MFA. *Accreditation:* NASAD. *Entrance requirements:* For master's, personal statement, portfolio, three letters of recommendation, transcripts. Additional exam requirements/recommendations for international students: required—TOEFL (minimum score 100 iBT). Electronic applications accepted.

Syracuse University, S. I. Newhouse School of Public Communications, MS in Photography Program, Syracuse, NY 13244. Offers MS. *Degree requirements:* For master's, thesis optional, special project. *Entrance requirements:* For master's, portfolio, resume, official transcripts, personal statement, three letters of recommendation. Additional exam requirements/recommendations for international students: required—TOEFL (minimum score 600 paper-based; 100 iBT). Electronic applications accepted.

Temple University, Tyler School of Art and Architecture, Department of Graphic Arts and Design, Philadelphia, PA 19122-6096. Offers graphic and interactive design (MFA); photography (MFA); printmaking (MFA). *Students:* 123 applicants, 15% accepted, 12 enrolled. In 2019, 8 master's awarded. *Degree requirements:* For master's, thesis, written statement, slide portfolio. *Entrance requirements:* For master's, 3 letters of recommendation, portfolio, 40 credits in studio art, 12 credits in art history, resume, statement of goals. Additional exam requirements/recommendations for international students: required—TOEFL (minimum score 79 iBT), IELTS (minimum score 6.5), PTE (minimum score 53), one of three is required. *Application deadline:* For fall admission, 1/15 for domestic students, 12/15 for international students. Application fee: $60. Electronic applications accepted. *Expenses:* Contact institution. *Financial support:* Fellowships, teaching assistantships, Federal Work-Study, and health care benefits available. Financial award applicants required to submit FAFSA. *Unit head:* Dermot Mac Cormack, Associate Professor and Department Chair of Graphic and Interactive Design, 610-653-8227, E-mail: dermot@temple.edu. *Application contact:* Tamryn McDermott, Director of Admissions, 215-777-9159, E-mail: tyleradmissions@temple.edu.
Website: https://tyler.temple.edu/programs/graphic-interactive-design

Texas Woman's University, Graduate School, College of Arts and Sciences, School of the Arts, Department of Visual Arts, Denton, TX 76204. Offers art (MA, MAT, MFA), including art education (MA, MAT), art history (MA), ceramics (MFA), graphic design (MA), intermedia (MFA), painting (MFA), photography (MFA), sculpture (MFA). *Faculty:* 6 full-time (5 women). *Students:* 13 full-time (9 women), 8 part-time (5 women); includes 5 minority (1 Asian, non-Hispanic/Latino; 3 Hispanic/Latino; 1 Two or more races, non-Hispanic/Latino), 1 international. Average age 36. 15 applicants, 80% accepted, 9 enrolled. In 2019, 8 master's awarded. *Degree requirements:* For master's, comprehensive exam, thesis (for some programs), exhibit (MFA), oral exam, thesis or professional paper (MA). *Entrance requirements:* For master's, portfolio, interview, current curriculum vitae, letter of intent, 3 letters of recommendation, artist statement, separate application. Additional exam requirements/recommendations for international students: required—TOEFL (minimum score 79 iBT); recommended—IELTS (minimum score 6.5), TSE (minimum score 53). *Application deadline:* For fall admission, 2/15 for domestic and international students; for spring admission, 11/15 for domestic and international students. Application fee: $50 ($75 for international students). Electronic applications accepted. *Expenses: Tuition, area resident:* Full-time $4973.40; part-time $276.30 per semester hour. Tuition, state resident: full-time $4973.40; part-time $276.30 per semester hour. Tuition, nonresident: full-time $12,569; part-time $698.30 per semester hour. *International tuition:* $12,569.40 full-time. *Required fees:* $2524.30. Tuition and fees vary according to course level, course load, degree level and program. *Financial support:* In 2019–20, 15 students received support, including 12 teaching assistantships (averaging $4,968 per year); career-related internships or fieldwork, scholarships/grants, health care benefits, and unspecified assistantships also available. Support available to part-time students. Financial award application deadline: 3/1; financial award applicants required to submit FAFSA. *Unit head:* Dr. Vagner Whitehead, Chair, 940-898-2530, Fax: 940-898-2496, E-mail: visualarts@twu.edu. *Application contact:* Korie Hawkins, Associate Director of Admissions, Graduate Recruitment, 940-898-3188, Fax: 940-898-3081, E-mail: admissions@twu.edu.
Website: http://www.twu.edu/visual-arts/

The University of Alabama, Graduate School, College of Arts and Sciences, Department of Art and Art History, Tuscaloosa, AL 35487. Offers art history (MA); studio art (MA, MFA), including ceramics, painting, photography, printmaking, sculpture. *Accreditation:* NASAD. *Program availability:* Part-time. *Faculty:* 9 full-time (3 women). *Students:* 20 full-time (16 women), 3 part-time (1 woman); includes 3 minority (1 Black or African American, non-Hispanic/Latino; 2 Hispanic/Latino), 4 international. Average age 29. 22 applicants, 59% accepted, 8 enrolled. In 2019, 6 master's awarded. *Degree requirements:* For master's, one foreign language, comprehensive exam (for some programs), oral exam, thesis statement, exhibit (studio art), thesis (art history). *Entrance requirements:* For master's, GRE General Test or MAT (art history), minimum GPA of 3.0, BFA or equivalent (studio art). Additional exam requirements/recommendations for international students: required—TOEFL (minimum score 550 paper-based). *Application deadline:* For fall admission, 3/15 for domestic and international students; for spring admission, 10/15 for domestic and international students. Applications are processed on a rolling basis. Application fee: $50 ($60 for international students). Electronic applications accepted. *Expenses: Tuition, area resident:* Full-time $10,780; part-time $440 per credit hour. Tuition, nonresident: full-time $30,250; part-time $1550 per credit hour. *Financial support:* In 2019–20, 8 students received support, including 2 fellowships with full tuition reimbursements available, 14 teaching assistantships with tuition reimbursements available (averaging $15,427 per year); career-related internships or fieldwork, institutionally sponsored loans, scholarships/grants, and unspecified assistantships also available. Financial award application deadline: 7/1. *Unit head:* Jason Guynes, Chair, 205-348-9944, Fax: 205-348-0287, E-mail: jguynes@ua.edu. *Application contact:* Allison Grant, Studio Art Graduate Program Director, 205-348-5968, Fax: 205-348-5967, E-mail: agrant4@ua.edu.
Website: http://www.art.ua.edu/

University of Alaska Fairbanks, College of Liberal Arts, Department of Art, Fairbanks, AK 99775-5640. Offers art (MFA); ceramics (MFA); computer art (MFA); drawing (MFA); painting (MFA); photography (MFA); printmaking (MFA); sculpture (MFA). *Program availability:* Part-time. *Degree requirements:* For master's, comprehensive exam, oral defense of project or thesis. *Entrance requirements:* For master's, portfolio of work including about 20 slides or appropriate equivalent depending on field of study. Additional exam requirements/recommendations for international students: required—TOEFL (minimum score 550 paper-based; 79 iBT), IELTS (minimum score 6.5). Electronic applications accepted.

University of Colorado Boulder, Graduate School, College of Arts and Sciences, Department of Art and Art History, Boulder, CO 80309. Offers art history (MA), including contemporary art criticism, early twentieth-century art, nineteenth-century art, Russian and Soviet art; ceramics (MFA); photography and media arts (MFA); printmaking (MFA); sculpture (MFA). Terminal master's awarded for partial completion of doctoral program. *Degree requirements:* For master's, variable foreign language requirement, comprehensive exam, thesis (for some programs). *Entrance requirements:* For master's, GRE General Test, minimum undergraduate GPA of 3.0, portfolio. Electronic applications accepted. Application fee is waived when completed online.

University of Illinois at Urbana-Champaign, Graduate College, College of Fine and Applied Arts, School of Art and Design, Program in Studio Arts, Champaign, IL 61820. Offers art and design (MFA); crafts (MFA); metals (MFA); painting (MFA); photography (MFA); sculpture (MFA). *Accreditation:* NASAD. *Entrance requirements:* For master's, minimum GPA of 3.0.

University of Memphis, Graduate School, College of Communication and Fine Arts, Department of Art, Memphis, TN 38152. Offers art history (MA), including Egyptian art and archaeology, general art history; ceramics (MFA); graphic design (MFA); museum studies (Graduate Certificate); painting (MFA); printmaking/photography (MFA); sculpture (MFA). *Accreditation:* NASAD (one or more programs are accredited). *Program availability:* Part-time. *Students:* 28 full-time (21 women), 5 part-time (4 women); includes 9 minority (3 Black or African American, non-Hispanic/Latino; 1 Asian, non-Hispanic/Latino; 3 Hispanic/Latino; 2 Two or more races, non-Hispanic/Latino), 2 international. Average age 30. 36 applicants, 69% accepted, 13 enrolled. In 2019, 11 master's, 4 other advanced degrees awarded. *Degree requirements:* For master's, variable foreign language requirement, comprehensive exam, thesis, image identification exam, qualifying exam; for Graduate Certificate, internship. *Entrance requirements:* For master's, GRE General Test or MAT, portfolio (MFA), letter of intent, sample of undergraduate writing, two letters of recommendation; for Graduate Certificate, three letters of recommendation, letter of intent. *Application deadline:* For fall admission, 2/15 for domestic students; for spring admission, 11/1 for domestic students. Applications are processed on a rolling basis. Application fee: $35 ($60 for international students). *Expenses: Tuition, area resident:* Full-time $9216; part-time $512 per credit hour. Tuition, state resident: full-time $9216; part-time $512 per credit hour. Tuition, nonresident: full-time $12,672; part-time $704 per credit hour. *International tuition:* $16,128 full-time. *Required fees:* $1530; $85 per credit hour. Tuition and fees vary according to program. *Financial support:* Research assistantships with full tuition reimbursements, teaching assistantships with full tuition reimbursements, Federal Work-Study, scholarships/grants, and unspecified assistantships available. Financial award application deadline: 2/1; financial award applicants required to submit FAFSA. *Unit head:* Richard Lou, Chair, 901-678-2217, Fax: 901-678-2735, E-mail: ralou@memphis.edu. *Application contact:* Richard Lou, Chair, 901-678-2217, Fax: 901-678-2735, E-mail: ralou@memphis.edu.
Website: http://memphis.edu/art/

University of Miami, Graduate School, College of Arts and Sciences, Department of Art and Art History, Coral Gables, FL 33124. Offers art history (MA); ceramics/glass (MFA); graphic design/multimedia (MFA); painting (MFA); photography/digital imaging (MFA); printmaking (MFA); sculpture (MFA). *Program availability:* Part-time. *Degree requirements:* For master's, variable foreign language requirement, thesis, exhibit (MFA), comprehensive exam (MA). *Entrance requirements:* For master's, GRE General Test (MA), research paper (MA), slide portfolio (MFA). Additional exam requirements/ recommendations for international students: required—TOEFL. Electronic applications accepted.

University of Montana, Graduate School, College of Visual and Performing Arts, School of Art, Missoula, MT 59812. Offers fine arts (MA), including art, art history; photography (MFA). *Accreditation:* NASAD (one or more programs are accredited). *Degree requirements:* For master's, thesis exhibit. *Entrance requirements:* For master's, GRE General Test, portfolio.

University of New Mexico, Graduate Studies, College of Fine Arts, Program in Art History, Albuquerque, NM 87131-2039. Offers art history (MA); art of the Americas (MA); history of architecture (PhD); history of graphic arts (PhD); history of photography (PhD); modern Latin American art (PhD); Native American art (PhD); Pre-Columbian art and architecture (PhD); Spanish colonial art (PhD). *Program availability:* Part-time. *Degree requirements:* For master's, one foreign language, comprehensive exam (for some programs), thesis, symposium; for doctorate, 2 foreign languages, comprehensive exam, thesis/dissertation, symposium. *Entrance requirements:* Additional exam requirements/recommendations for international students: required—TOEFL (minimum score 550 paper-based), IELTS (minimum score 6). Electronic applications accepted. *Expenses:* Tuition, state resident: full-time $7633; part-time $972 per year. Tuition, nonresident: full-time $22,586; part-time $3840 per year. *International tuition:* $23,292 full-time. *Required fees:* $8608. Tuition and fees vary according to course level, course load, degree level, program and student level.

University of Notre Dame, The Graduate School, College of Arts and Letters, Department of Art, Art History, and Design, Notre Dame, IN 46556. Offers art history (MA); design (MFA), including graphic design, industrial design; studio art (MFA), including ceramics, painting, photography, printmaking, sculpture. *Accreditation:* NASAD. *Degree requirements:* For master's, comprehensive exam (for some programs), thesis. *Entrance requirements:* For master's, GRE General Test, minimum GPA of 3.0. Additional exam requirements/recommendations for international students: required—TOEFL (minimum score 600 paper-based; 80 iBT). Electronic applications accepted.

University of Oklahoma, Weitzenhoffer Family College of Fine Arts, School of Visual Arts, Norman, OK 73019. Offers art (MFA), including art and technology, ceramics, film, painting, photography, printmaking, sculpture, video, visual communication; art history (MA, PhD), including art history (MA), art of the American West (PhD), Native American art (PhD); design (MFA). *Degree requirements:* For master's, 2 foreign languages, comprehensive exam (for some programs), thesis (for some programs); for doctorate, 2 foreign languages, comprehensive exam, thesis/dissertation. *Entrance requirements:* For master's and doctorate, GRE. Additional exam requirements/recommendations for international students: required—TOEFL (minimum score 79 iBT) or IELTS (minimum score 6.5). Electronic applications accepted. *Expenses:* Tuition, state resident: full-time $6583.20; part-time $274.30 per credit hour. Tuition, nonresident: full-time $21,242; part-time $885.10 per credit hour. *International tuition:* $21,242.40 full-time. *Required fees:* $1994.20; $72.55 per credit hour. $126.50 per semester. Tuition and fees vary according to course load and degree level.

University of South Dakota, Graduate School, College of Fine Arts, Department of Art, Vermillion, SD 57069. Offers art education (MFA); ceramics (MFA); graphic design (MFA); painting (MFA); photography (MFA); printmaking (MFA); sculpture (MFA). *Accreditation:* NASAD. *Degree requirements:* For master's, thesis or alternative. *Entrance requirements:* For master's, portfolio, minimum GPA of 2.7. Additional exam requirements/recommendations for international students: required—TOEFL (minimum score 550 paper-based; 79 iBT). Electronic applications accepted.

University of Southern California, Graduate School, Roski School of Art and Design, Graduate Programs in Fine Arts, Los Angeles, CA 90089. Offers new genres (MFA); painting/drawing (MFA); photography (MFA); sculpture (MFA). *Degree requirements:* For master's, thesis. *Entrance requirements:* For master's, portfolio, artist statement, 3 letters of recommendation. Additional exam requirements/recommendations for international students: required—TOEFL (minimum score 600 paper-based; 100 iBT). Electronic applications accepted.

The University of Tennessee, Graduate School, College of Arts and Sciences, School of Art, Knoxville, TN 37996. Offers ceramics (MFA); drawing (MFA); graphic design (MFA); inter-area studies (MFA); media arts (MFA); painting (MFA); printmaking (MFA); sculpture (MFA); watercolor (MFA). *Accreditation:* NASAD. *Degree requirements:* For master's, thesis or alternative, exhibit. *Entrance requirements:* For master's, portfolio, minimum GPA of 2.7. Additional exam requirements/recommendations for international students: required—TOEFL. Electronic applications accepted.

University of Utah, Graduate School, College of Fine Arts, Department of Art and Art History, Salt Lake City, UT 84112-0380. Offers art history (MA); ceramics (MFA); community-based art education (MFA); drawing (MFA); graphic design (MFA); painting (MFA); photography/digital imaging (MFA); printmaking (MFA); sculpture/intermedia (MFA). *Degree requirements:* For master's, variable foreign language requirement, comprehensive exam (for some programs), thesis or alternative, exhibit and final project paper (for MFA). *Entrance requirements:* For master's, CD portfolio (MFA), writing sample (MA), curriculum vitae, letters of recommendation, letter of intent. Additional exam requirements/recommendations for international students: required—TOEFL (minimum score 575 paper-based; 75 iBT). Electronic applications accepted. *Expenses:* Contact institution.

University of Victoria, Faculty of Graduate Studies, Faculty of Fine Arts, Department of Visual Arts, Victoria, BC V8W 2Y2, Canada. Offers digital multimedia (MFA); drawing (MFA); painting (MFA); photography (MFA); sculpture (MFA); video (MFA). *Degree requirements:* For master's, exhibit, oral exam. *Entrance requirements:* For master's, portfolio, BFA. Additional exam requirements/recommendations for international students: required—TOEFL (minimum score 575 paper-based), IELTS (minimum score 7). Electronic applications accepted.

University of Washington, Graduate School, College of Arts and Sciences, School of Art, Division of Art, Seattle, WA 98195. Offers painting and drawing (MFA); photography (MFA). *Degree requirements:* For master's, thesis, exhibit. *Entrance requirements:* For master's, BFA or equivalent academic work in art, 20 slide portfolio. Additional exam requirements/recommendations for international students: required—TOEFL. Electronic applications accepted.

Virginia Commonwealth University, Graduate School, School of the Arts, Richmond, VA 23284-9005. Offers art education (MAE, PhD); art history (MA, PhD), including curatorial (PhD), historical studies, museum studies (MA); ceramics (MFA); design (MFA), including interior environments, visual communications; fibers (MFA); furniture design (MFA); glassworking (MFA); jewelry/metalworking (MFA); kinetic imaging (MFA); music (MM), including music education; painting (MFA); photography and film (MFA); printmaking (MFA); sculpture (MFA); theatre (MFA), including costume design, pedagogy/literature, pedagogy/performance, scene design/technical theatre. *Accreditation:* CIDA. *Program availability:* Part-time. *Entrance requirements:* For doctorate, GRE General Test, writing sample. Additional exam requirements/recommendations for international students: required—TOEFL (minimum score 600 paper-based; 100 iBT). Electronic applications accepted.

Wayne State University, College of Fine, Performing and Communication Arts, James Pearson Duffy Department of Art and Art History, Detroit, MI 48202. Offers art (MA, MFA), including ceramics, drawing, fashion design and merchandising (MA), fibers, graphic design, industrial design (MA), interior design (MA), metalsmithing, painting, photography, printmaking, sculpture; art history (MA). *Degree requirements:* For master's, thesis (for some programs), essay or thesis. *Entrance requirements:* For master's, BFA or another degree and equivalent course work, portfolio, personal interview, reference letters, statement of intent (except for art history program). Additional exam requirements/recommendations for international students: required—TOEFL (minimum score 550 paper-based; 79 iBT), TWE (minimum score 5.5), Michigan English Language Assessment Battery (minimum score 85); recommended—IELTS (minimum score 6.5). Electronic applications accepted. *Expenses:* Contact institution.

West Virginia University, College of Creative Arts, Morgantown, WV 26506. Offers acting (MFA); art education (MA); art history (MA); ceramics (MFA); collaborative piano (MM, DMA); composition (MM, DMA); conducting (MM, DMA); costume design and technology (MFA); graphic design (MFA); intermedia and photography (MFA); jazz pedagogy (MM); lighting design and technology (MFA); music (PhD); music education (MM, PhD); music industry (MA); music theory (MM); musicology (MA); painting and printmaking (MFA); performance (MM, DMA); piano pedagogy (MM); scenic design and technology (MFA); sculpture (MFA); studio art (MA); technical direction (MFA); vocal pedagogy and performance (DMA). *Program availability:* Part-time. *Degree requirements:* For master's, thesis, recitals; for doctorate, comprehensive exam, thesis/dissertation, recitals (DMA). *Entrance requirements:* For doctorate, minimum GPA of 3.0, audition. Additional exam requirements/recommendations for international students: required—TOEFL. Electronic applications accepted.

Wichita State University, Graduate School, College of Fine Arts, School of Art, Design and Creative Industries, Wichita, KS 67260. Offers studio arts (MFA), including ceramics, painting, photo media, printmaking, sculpture. *Accreditation:* NASAD.

Yale University, School of Art, New Haven, CT 06520-8339. Offers graphic design (MFA); painting/printmaking (MFA); photography (MFA); sculpture (MFA). *Degree requirements:* For master's, thesis (for some programs). *Entrance requirements:* Additional exam requirements/recommendations for international students: required—TOEFL (minimum score 550 paper-based; 100 iBT). Electronic applications accepted. *Expenses:* Contact institution.

Textile Design

Academy of Art University, Graduate Programs, Program in Costume Design, San Francisco, CA 94105-3410. Offers MA, MFA. *Program availability:* Part-time, evening/weekend, 100% online. *Faculty:* 22 full-time (16 women), 54 part-time/adjunct (40 women). *Students:* 12 full-time (all women), 14 part-time (13 women); includes 7 minority (3 Black or African American, non-Hispanic/Latino; 2 Asian, non-Hispanic/Latino; 1 Hispanic/Latino; 1 Two or more races, non-Hispanic/Latino), 7 international. Average age 36. 4 applicants, 100% accepted, 2 enrolled. In 2019, 7 master's awarded. *Degree requirements:* For master's, final review. *Entrance requirements:* For master's, statement of intent; resume; portfolio/reel; official college transcripts. *Application deadline:* Applications are processed on a rolling basis. Application fee: $50. Electronic applications accepted. *Expenses: Tuition:* Full-time $1083; part-time $1083 per credit hour. *Required fees:* $860; $860 per unit. $430 per term. One-time fee: $145. Tuition and fees vary according to program. *Financial support:* Career-related internships or fieldwork, Federal Work-Study, and scholarships/grants available. Financial award application deadline: 8/10; financial award applicants required to submit FAFSA.
Website: http://www.academyart.edu/academics/fashion/graduate-degrees

Academy of Art University, Graduate Programs, School of Fashion, San Francisco, CA 94105-3410. Offers fashion (MA, MFA); fashion merchandising (MA); fashion merchandising and management (MFA); fashion product development (MFA); knitwear design (MFA); textile design (MFA). *Program availability:* Part-time, 100% online. *Faculty:* 22 full-time (16 women), 54 part-time/adjunct (40 women). *Students:* 199 full-time (173 women), 136 part-time (126 women); includes 66 minority (30 Black or African American, non-Hispanic/Latino; 1 American Indian or Alaska Native, non-Hispanic/Latino; 17 Asian, non-Hispanic/Latino; 12 Hispanic/Latino; 6 Two or more races, non-Hispanic/Latino), 185 international. Average age 30. 154 applicants, 100% accepted, 89 enrolled. In 2019, 181 master's awarded. *Degree requirements:* For master's, final review. *Entrance requirements:* For master's, statement of intent; resume; portfolio/reel; official college transcripts. *Application deadline:* Applications are processed on a rolling basis. Application fee: $50. Electronic applications accepted. *Expenses: Tuition:* Full-time $1083; part-time $1083 per credit hour. *Required fees:* $860; $860 per unit. $430 per term. One-time fee: $145. Tuition and fees vary according to program. *Financial support:* Career-related internships or fieldwork, Federal Work-Study, and scholarships/grants available. Financial award application deadline: 8/10; financial award applicants required to submit FAFSA.
Website: http://www.academyart.edu/fashion-school/index.html

Arizona State University at Tempe, Herberger Institute for Design and the Arts, School of Art, Tempe, AZ 85287-1505. Offers art education (MA); art history (MA); ceramics (MFA); design, environment and the arts (PhD), including history, theory and criticism; drawing (MFA); fibers (MFA); intermedia (MFA); metals (MFA); museum studies (MFA); painting (MFA); printmaking (MFA); sculpture (MFA); wood (MFA); MFA/MA. Terminal master's awarded for partial completion of doctoral program. *Degree requirements:* For master's, thesis/exhibition (MFA, MA in art education); interactive Program of Study (iPOS) submitted before completing 50 percent of required credit hours; for doctorate, comprehensive exam, thesis/dissertation, interactive Program of Study (iPOS) submitted before completing 50 percent of required credit hours. *Entrance requirements:* For master's, GRE or MAT, minimum GPA of 3.0 or equivalent in last 2 years of work leading to bachelor's degree; for doctorate, GRE, master's degree in architecture, graphic design, industrial design, interior design, landscape architecture, or art history or equivalent standing; statement of purpose; 3 letters of recommendation; indication of potential faculty mentor; sample of written work. Additional exam requirements/recommendations for international students: required—TOEFL, IELTS, or PTE. Electronic applications accepted.

California State University, Los Angeles, Graduate Studies, College of Arts and Letters, Department of Art, Los Angeles, CA 90032-8530. Offers art (MA), including art education, art history, art therapy, ceramics, metals, and textiles, design (MA, MFA), painting, sculpture, and graphic arts, photography; fine arts (MFA), including crafts, design (MA, MFA), studio arts. *Accreditation:* NASAD (one or more programs are accredited). *Program availability:* Part-time, evening/weekend. *Degree requirements:* For master's, comprehensive exam, project or thesis. *Entrance requirements:* For master's, portfolio. Additional exam requirements/recommendations for international students: required—TOEFL (minimum score 500 paper-based). Electronic applications accepted. *Expenses: Tuition, area resident:* Full-time $7176; part-time $4164 per year. Tuition, state resident: full-time $7176; part-time $4164 per year. Tuition, nonresident: full-time $14,304; part-time $8916 per year. *International tuition:* $14,304 full-time. *Required fees:* $1037.76; $1037.76 per unit. Tuition and fees vary according to degree level and program.

Concordia University, School of Graduate Studies, Faculty of Fine Arts, Department of Studio Arts, Montréal, QC H3G 1M8, Canada. Offers studio arts (MFA), including fibers and material practices, film production, intermedia, painting and drawing, photography, print media, sculpture. *Degree requirements:* For master's, thesis or alternative. *Entrance requirements:* For master's, portfolio.

Cornell University, Graduate School, Graduate Fields of Human Ecology, Field of Fiber Science and Apparel Design, Ithaca, NY 14853. Offers apparel design (MA, MPS); fiber science (MS, PhD); polymer science (MS, PhD); textile science (MS, PhD). *Degree* *requirements:* For master's, thesis (MA, MS), project paper (MPS); for doctorate, comprehensive exam, thesis/dissertation. *Entrance requirements:* For master's, GRE General Test, 2 letters of recommendation, portfolio (for functional apparel design); for doctorate, GRE General Test, 2 letters of recommendation. Additional exam requirements/recommendations for international students: required—TOEFL (minimum score 600 paper-based; 77 iBT). Electronic applications accepted.

Cranbrook Academy of Art, Program in Fine Arts, Bloomfield Hills, MI 48303-0801. Offers 2d design (MFA); 3d design (MFA); ceramics (MFA); fiber (MFA); metalsmithing (MFA); painting (MFA); photography (MFA); print media (MFA); sculpture (MFA). *Accreditation:* NASAD. *Degree requirements:* For master's, thesis, exhibit. *Entrance requirements:* Additional exam requirements/recommendations for international students: required—TOEFL (minimum score 85 iBT). Electronic applications accepted.

Drexel University, Westphal College of Media Arts and Design, Program in Fashion Design, Philadelphia, PA 19104-2875. Offers MS. *Accreditation:* NASAD. *Degree requirements:* For master's, thesis, portfolio review. *Entrance requirements:* For master's, interview. Additional exam requirements/recommendations for international students: required—TOEFL. Electronic applications accepted.

East Carolina University, Graduate School, College of Fine Arts and Communication, School of Art and Design, Greenville, NC 27858-4353. Offers art education (MA Ed); ceramics (MFA); graphic design (MFA); illustration (MFA); metal design (MFA); painting and drawing (MFA); photography (MFA); printmaking (MFA); sculpture (MFA); textile design (MFA); wood design (MFA). *Accreditation:* NASAD (one or more programs are accredited). *Program availability:* Part-time, evening/weekend. *Application deadline:* For fall admission, 2/1 for domestic students; for spring admission, 10/1 for domestic students. *Expenses: Tuition, area resident:* Full-time $4749; part-time $185 per credit hour. Tuition, state resident: full-time $4749; part-time $185 per credit hour. Tuition, nonresident: full-time $17,898; part-time $864 per credit hour. *International tuition:* $17,898 full-time. *Required fees:* $2787. *Financial support:* Application deadline: 6/1. *Unit head:* Dr. Kate Bukowski, Director, 252-328-6665, E-mail: bukowskik16@ecu.edu. *Application contact:* Graduate School Admissions, 252-328-6012, E-mail: gradschool@ecu.edu.
Website: https://art.ecu.edu/

Illinois State University, Graduate School, Wonsook Kim College of Fine Arts, School of Art, Normal, IL 61790. Offers art history (MA, MS); ceramics (MFA, MS); drawing (MFA, MS); fibers (MFA, MS); glass (MFA, MS); graphic design (MFA, MS); metals (MFA, MS); painting (MFA, MS); photography (MFA, MS); printmaking (MFA, MS); sculpture (MFA, MS). *Accreditation:* NASAD (one or more programs are accredited). *Faculty:* 34 full-time (18 women), 15 part-time/adjunct (11 women). *Students:* 25 full-time (16 women), 5 part-time (4 women). Average age 31. 32 applicants, 66% accepted, 12 enrolled. In 2019, 11 master's awarded. *Degree requirements:* For master's, thesis or alternative, internship. *Entrance requirements:* For master's, portfolio, sample of scholarly writing. *Application deadline:* Applications are processed on a rolling basis. Application fee: $50. *Expenses: Tuition, area resident:* Full-time $7956; part-time $9767 per year. Tuition, nonresident: full-time $9233; part-time $17,592 per year. *Required fees:* $1797. *Financial support:* In 2019–20, 20 teaching assistantships were awarded; career-related internships or fieldwork, Federal Work-Study, tuition waivers (full and partial), and unspecified assistantships also available. Support available to part-time students. Financial award application deadline: 4/1. *Unit head:* Mike Wille, Director of Art School, 309-438-5610, E-mail: mjwill4@ilstu.edu. *Application contact:* Tyler Lotz, Graduate Coordinator, 309-438-8301, E-mail: tlotz@ilstu.edu.
Website: http://www.arts.ilstu.edu/art/

Kent State University, College of the Arts, School of Art, Kent, OH 44242-0001. Offers art education (MA); art history (MA); crafts (MA), including glass (MA, MFA); fine arts (MA), including fashion; studio art (MFA), including ceramics, drawing, glass (MA, MFA), jewelry, metals and enameling, painting, print media and photography, sculpture, textiles. *Accreditation:* NASAD (one or more programs are accredited). *Program availability:* Part-time, 100% online, blended/hybrid learning. *Faculty:* 22 full-time (13 women), 5 part-time/adjunct (4 women). *Students:* 36 full-time (27 women), 24 part-time (22 women); includes 4 minority (3 Black or African American, non-Hispanic/Latino; 1 Hispanic/Latino), 2 international. Average age 30. 52 applicants, 67% accepted, 20 enrolled. In 2019, 15 master's awarded. *Degree requirements:* For master's, comprehensive exam, thesis (for some programs), 1 foreign language (for art history); final project (for crafts and fine arts). *Entrance requirements:* For master's, bachelors's degree min 3.0 GPA on 4.0 scale, transcripts, goal statement, 3 letters of recommendation, curriculum vitae, for MA and MFA in Studio Art: portfolio, artist statement;l MA Art Education: goal statement that focuses on philosophy of art education. Additional exam requirements/recommendations for international students: required—TOEFL (minimum score 79 iBT), IELTS (minimum score 6.5), PTE (minimum score 58), Michigan English Language Assessment Battery (minimum score 77). *Application deadline:* For fall admission, 2/2 priority date for domestic students, 2/2 for international students; for spring admission, 10/15 for domestic and international students. Applications are processed on a rolling basis. Application fee: $45 ($70 for international students). Electronic applications accepted. *Financial support:* Career-related internships or fieldwork, scholarships/grants, and unspecified assistantships available. Financial award application deadline: 3/1. *Unit head:* Marie Bukowski, Director, 330-672-2192, E-mail: mbukows1@kent.edu. *Application contact:* Peter Christian Johnson, Graduate Coordinator and Associate Professor Ceramics, 330-672-3360, E-mail: pjohns35@kent.edu.
Website: http://www.kent.edu/art

Massachusetts College of Art and Design, Graduate Programs, MFA Program, Boston, MA 02115-5882. Offers 2D fine arts (MFA), including painting, printmaking; 3D fine arts (MFA), including ceramics, fibers, glass, jewelry and metalsmithing, sculpture; design (MFA, Postbaccalaureate Certificate), including dynamic media; fine arts (MFA), including interdisciplinary; media arts (MFA, Postbaccalaureate Certificate), including film/video (MFA), photography. *Accreditation:* NASAD. *Faculty:* 1 (woman) full-time, 29 part-time/adjunct (14 women). *Students:* 44 full-time (26 women), 28 part-time (17 women); includes 8 minority (5 Asian, non-Hispanic/Latino; 3 Hispanic/Latino), 18 international. 202 applicants, 44% accepted, 35 enrolled. In 2019, 30 master's, 8 other advanced degrees awarded. *Degree requirements:* For master's, thesis, thesis exhibition (for fine arts programs); thesis project and document (for design/dynamic media program). *Entrance requirements:* For master's, portfolio, college transcripts, resume, statement of purpose, letters of reference, interview, 6 credits of art history taken prior to or during MFA program; for Postbaccalaureate Certificate, portfolio, college transcripts, resume, statement of purpose, letters of reference, interview. Additional exam requirements/recommendations for international students: required—TOEFL (minimum score 550 paper-based, 85 iBT) or IELTS (6). *Application deadline:* For fall admission, 1/20 priority date for domestic and international students; for summer admission, 1/20 priority date for domestic and international students. Applications are processed on a rolling basis. Application fee: $90. Electronic applications accepted. *Expenses:* Contact institution. *Financial support:* Research assistantships, teaching assistantships, career-related internships or fieldwork, scholarships/grants, tuition waivers (partial), unspecified assistantships, and adjunct co-teaching positions available. Support available to part-time students. Financial award application deadline: 1/20; financial award applicants required to submit FAFSA. *Unit head:* Lucinda Bliss, Dean of Graduate Studies, 617-879-7157, E-mail: gradadmissions@massart.edu. *Application contact:* Stacy Petersen, Associate Director, Graduate Admissions and Operations, 617-879-7238, E-mail: gradadmissions@massart.edu.
Website: http://www.massart.edu/Admissions/Graduate_Programs.html

The New School, Parsons School of Design, Program in Fashion Design and Society, New York, NY 10011. Offers MFA. *Program availability:* Part-time. *Faculty:* 3 full-time (1 woman), 5 part-time/adjunct (3 women). *Students:* 36 full-time (26 women), 1 (woman) part-time; includes 1 minority (Asian, non-Hispanic/Latino), 33 international. Average age 25. 244 applicants, 10% accepted, 16 enrolled. In 2019, 14 master's awarded. *Degree requirements:* For master's, thesis. *Entrance requirements:* For master's, transcripts, resume, statement of purpose, recommendation letters, portfolio. Additional exam requirements/recommendations for international students: required—TOEFL (minimum score 92 iBT), IELTS (minimum score 7), PTE (minimum score 63). *Application deadline:* For fall admission, 1/1 priority date for domestic and international students; for summer admission, 1/1 for domestic students, 1/1 priority date for international students. Applications are processed on a rolling basis. Application fee: $50. Electronic applications accepted. *Expenses:* 1810. *Financial support:* In 2019–20, 31 students received support. Career-related internships or fieldwork, scholarships/grants, and unspecified assistantships available. Support available to part-time students. Financial award application deadline: 2/1; financial award applicants required to submit FAFSA. *Unit head:* Shelley Fox, Program Director, 212-229-8966 Ext. 2746, E-mail: foxs@newschool.edu. *Application contact:* Simone Varadine, Senior Director, 212-229-5150 Ext. 4117, E-mail: varadias@newschool.edu.
Website: https://www.newschool.edu/parsons/mfa-fashion-design-society/

The New School, Parsons School of Design, Program in Fashion Studies, New York, NY 10011. Offers MA. *Program availability:* Part-time. *Faculty:* 16 full-time, 16 part-time/adjunct. *Students:* 41 full-time (37 women), 2 part-time (both women); includes 15 minority (4 Black or African American, non-Hispanic/Latino; 2 Asian, non-Hispanic/Latino; 8 Hispanic/Latino; 1 Two or more races, non-Hispanic/Latino), 17 international. Average age 25. 93 applicants, 53% accepted, 19 enrolled. In 2019, 34 master's awarded. *Degree requirements:* For master's, thesis. *Entrance requirements:* For master's, transcripts, resume, statement of purpose, recommendation letters, interview. Additional exam requirements/recommendations for international students: required—TOEFL (minimum score 92 iBT), IELTS (minimum score 7), PTE (minimum score 63). *Application deadline:* For fall admission, 1/1 priority date for domestic and international students; for summer admission, 1/1 priority date for domestic and international students. Applications are processed on a rolling basis. Application fee: $50. Electronic applications accepted. *Expenses:* 1810 per credit. *Financial support:* In 2019–20, 32 students received support, including 10 research assistantships (averaging $2,714 per year), 6 teaching assistantships (averaging $9,597 per year); career-related internships or fieldwork, scholarships/grants, unspecified assistantships, and travel funding; tuition waivers for students who are also New School employees also available. Support available to part-time students. Financial award application deadline: 2/1; financial award applicants required to submit FAFSA. *Unit head:* Heike Jenss, Program Director, 212-229-8990 Ext. 4190, E-mail: jenssh@newschool.edu. *Application contact:* Simone Varadian, Senior Director, 212-229-5150 Ext. 4117, E-mail: varadias@newschool.edu.
Website: https://www.newschool.edu/parsons/ma-fashion-studies/

Paris College of Art, Graduate Programs, Paris, France. Offers accessories design (MA); fashion design: new materials and technologies (MA); fashion film and photography (MA); interior design (MA); transdisciplinary new media (MA, MFA). *Entrance requirements:* Additional exam requirements/recommendations for international students: required—TOEFL or IELTS.

Rhode Island School of Design, Department of Textiles, Providence, RI 02903-2784. Offers MFA. *Accreditation:* NASAD. *Students:* 10 full-time (8 women), 8 international. Average age 27. 46 applicants, 22% accepted, 4 enrolled. In 2019, 5 master's awarded. *Degree requirements:* For master's, thesis, exhibition. *Entrance requirements:* For master's, portfolio, statement of purpose, 3 letters of recommendation. Additional exam requirements/recommendations for international students: required—TOEFL (minimum score 580 paper-based; 93 iBT), IELTS (minimum score 6.5), Duolingo. *Application deadline:* For fall admission, 1/10 for domestic and international students. Application fee: $60. Electronic applications accepted. *Expenses:* Tuition: Full-time $51,800. *Required fees:* $1060. *Financial support:* Fellowships, research assistantships, teaching assistantships, Federal Work-Study, scholarships/grants, and unspecified assistantships available. Financial award application deadline: 2/1; financial award applicants required to submit FAFSA. *Unit head:* Mary Anne Friel, Department Head, 401-427-6967, Fax: 401-277-4883, E-mail: textiles@risd.edu. *Application contact:* Molly Pettengill, Associate Director for Graduate Recruitment, 401-454-6312, Fax: 401-454-6309, E-mail: mpetteng@risd.edu.
Website: http://www.risd.edu/academics/textiles/

Savannah College of Art and Design, Program in Fashion, Savannah, GA 31402-3146. Offers MA, MFA. *Program availability:* Part-time, 100% online. *Degree requirements:* For master's, final project (for MA); thesis (for MFA). *Entrance requirements:* For master's, GRE (recommended), portfolio (submitted in digital format), audition or writing submission, resume, statement of purpose, two letters of recommendation. Additional exam requirements/recommendations for international students: recommended—TOEFL (minimum score 550 paper-based; 85 iBT), IELTS (minimum score 6.5). Electronic applications accepted.

Savannah College of Art and Design, Program in Fibers, Savannah, GA 31402-3146. Offers MA, MFA. *Program availability:* Part-time. *Degree requirements:* For master's, final project (for MA); thesis (for MFA). *Entrance requirements:* For master's, GRE (recommended), portfolio (submitted in digital format), audition or writing submission, resume, statement of purpose, two letters of recommendation. Additional exam requirements/recommendations for international students: recommended—TOEFL (minimum score 550 paper-based; 85 iBT), IELTS (minimum score 6.5). Electronic applications accepted.

Savannah College of Art and Design, Program in Luxury and Fashion Management, Savannah, GA 31402-3146. Offers MA, MFA. *Program availability:* Part-time, 100% online. *Degree requirements:* For master's, final project (for MA); thesis (for MFA). *Entrance requirements:* For master's, GRE (recommended), portfolio (submitted in digital format), audition or writing submission, resume, statement of purpose, two letters of recommendation. Additional exam requirements/recommendations for international students: recommended—TOEFL (minimum score 550 paper-based; 85 iBT), IELTS (minimum score 6.5). Electronic applications accepted.

Temple University, Tyler School of Art and Architecture, Department of Art, Philadelphia, PA 19122-6096. Offers ceramics/glass (MFA); fibers and material studies (MFA); glass (MFA); metals/jewelry/CAD-CAM (MFA). *Faculty:* 27 full-time (14 women), 41 part-time/adjunct (22 women). *Students:* 47 full-time (33 women); includes 10 minority (3 Black or African American, non-Hispanic/Latino; 2 Asian, non-Hispanic/

Latino; 4 Hispanic/Latino; 1 Two or more races, non-Hispanic/Latino), 8 international. 165 applicants, 26% accepted, 23 enrolled. In 2019, 13 master's awarded. *Entrance requirements:* Additional exam requirements/recommendations for international students: required—TOEFL (minimum score 79 iBT), IELTS (minimum score 6.5), PTE (minimum score 53), one of three is required. *Application deadline:* For fall admission, 1/6 for domestic students. Application fee: $60. Electronic applications accepted. *Expenses:* Contact institution. *Financial support:* Fellowships, teaching assistantships, Federal Work-Study, and health care benefits available. Financial award applicants required to submit FAFSA. *Unit head:* Susan E Cahan, Dean, 215-777-9000, E-mail: tyler@temple.edu. *Application contact:* Lauren O'Neill, Director of Admissions, 215-777-9159, E-mail: tyleradmissions@temple.edu.
Website: https://tyler.temple.edu/academic-programs

Thomas Jefferson University, Kanbar College of Design, Engineering and Commerce, Program in Textile Design, Philadelphia, PA 19107. Offers MS. *Program availability:* Part-time. *Entrance requirements:* For master's, GRE or MAT, minimum GPA of 2.8. Additional exam requirements/recommendations for international students: required—TOEFL (minimum score 550 paper-based; 79 iBT). Electronic applications accepted.

University of California, Davis, Graduate Studies, Program in Textile Arts and Costume Design, Davis, CA 95616. Offers MFA. *Degree requirements:* For master's, presentation of an individual project/body of work. *Entrance requirements:* For master's, minimum GPA of 3.0, portfolio. Additional exam requirements/recommendations for international students: required—TOEFL (minimum score 550 paper-based). Electronic applications accepted.

University of Cincinnati, Graduate School, College of Design, Architecture, Art, and Planning, School of Design, Cincinnati, OH 45221. Offers fashion design (M Des); graphic design (M Des); industrial design (M Des); interaction design (M Des); product development (M Des). *Accreditation:* NASAD. *Degree requirements:* For master's, thesis. *Entrance requirements:* For master's, undergraduate degree in design or related field, 2 years of work experience in design or related field. Additional exam requirements/recommendations for international students: required—TOEFL. Electronic applications accepted.

The University of Kansas, Graduate Studies, College of Liberal Arts and Sciences, Department of Visual Art, Lawrence, KS 66045. Offers ceramics (MFA); drawing and painting (MFA); expanded media (MFA); metalsmithing/jewelry (MFA); sculpture (MFA); textiles/fibers (MFA); visual art education (MA). *Accreditation:* NASAD. *Program availability:* Part-time. *Students:* 20 full-time (10 women), 1 (woman) part-time; includes 8 minority (1 Black or African American, non-Hispanic/Latino; 4 Hispanic/Latino; 3 Two or more races, non-Hispanic/Latino). Average age 30. 36 applicants, 39% accepted, 11 enrolled. In 2019, 9 master's awarded. *Entrance requirements:* For master's, portfolio, official transcript, minimum GPA of 3.0, 3 letters of recommendation. Additional exam requirements/recommendations for international students: required—TOEFL, IELTS. *Application deadline:* For fall admission, 2/1 for domestic and international students. Application fee: $65 ($85 for international students). Electronic applications accepted. *Expenses:* Tuition, state resident: full-time $9989. Tuition, nonresident: full-time $23,950. *International tuition:* $23,950 full-time. *Required fees:* $984; $81.99 per credit hour. Tuition and fees vary according to course load, campus/location and program. *Financial support:* Fellowships, teaching assistantships, Federal Work-Study, scholarships/grants, and unspecified assistantships available. Financial award application deadline: 2/1; financial award applicants required to submit FAFSA. *Unit head:* Marshall Maude, Associate Chair, E-mail: maude@ku.edu. *Application contact:* Julia Reilly, Graduate Admissions Contact, 785-864-9488, E-mail: juliareilly@ku.edu.
Website: http://art.ku.edu/

The University of Manchester, School of Materials, Manchester, United Kingdom. Offers advanced aerospace materials engineering (M Sc); advanced metallic systems (PhD); biomedical materials (M Phil, M Sc, PhD); ceramics and glass (M Phil, M Sc, PhD); composite materials (M Sc, PhD); corrosion and protection (M Phil, M Sc, PhD); materials (M Phil, PhD); metallic materials (M Phil, M Sc, PhD); nanostructural materials (M Phil, M Sc, PhD); paper science (M Phil, M Sc, PhD); polymer science and engineering (M Phil, M Sc, PhD); technical textiles (M Sc); textile design, fashion and management (M Phil, M Sc, PhD); textile science and technology (M Phil, M Sc, PhD); textiles (M Phil, PhD); textiles and fashion (M Ent).

University of Minnesota, Twin Cities Campus, Graduate School, College of Design, Department of Design, Housing, and Apparel, Minneapolis, MN 55455-0213. Offers apparel (MA, MS, PhD); design communication (MA, MS, PhD); housing studies (MA, MS, PhD, Postbaccalaureate Certificate); interactive design (MFA); interior design (MA, MS, PhD). *Program availability:* Part-time. *Degree requirements:* For master's and Postbaccalaureate Certificate, comprehensive exam, thesis (for some programs); for doctorate, comprehensive exam, thesis/dissertation. *Entrance requirements:* For master's, GRE General Test, minimum GPA of 3.0 (preferred), portfolio, 3 letters of recommendation; for doctorate, GRE General Test, minimum GPA of 3.0 (preferred), portfolio, 3 letters of recommendation, writing sample; for Postbaccalaureate Certificate, GRE General Test, minimum GPA of 3.0 (preferred). Additional exam requirements/recommendations for international students: required—TOEFL (minimum score 550 paper-based; 79 iBT). Electronic applications accepted.

The University of North Carolina at Greensboro, Graduate School, Bryan School of Business and Economics, Department of Consumer, Apparel, and Retail Studies, Greensboro, NC 27412-5001. Offers MS, PhD. *Degree requirements:* For master's, one foreign language; for doctorate, one foreign language, thesis/dissertation. *Entrance requirements:* For master's and doctorate, GRE General Test. Additional exam requirements/recommendations for international students: required—TOEFL. Electronic applications accepted.

University of North Texas, Toulouse Graduate School, Denton, TX 76203-5459. Offers accounting (MS); applied anthropology (MA, MS); applied behavior analysis (Certificate); applied geography (MA); applied technology and performance improvement (M Ed, MS); art education (MA); art history (MA); arts leadership (Certificate); audiology (Au D); behavior analysis (MS); behavioral science (PhD); biochemistry and molecular biology (MS); biology (MA, MS); biomedical engineering (MS); business analysis (MS); chemistry (MS); clinical health psychology (PhD); communication studies (MA, MS); computer engineering (MS); computer science (MS); counseling (M Ed, MS), including clinical mental health counseling (MS), college and university counseling, elementary school counseling, secondary school counseling; creative writing (MA); criminal justice (MS); curriculum and instruction (M Ed); decision sciences (MBA); design (MA, MFA), including fashion design (MFA), innovation studies, interior design (MFA); early childhood studies (MS); economics (MS); educational leadership (M Ed, Ed D); educational psychology (MS, PhD), including family studies (MS), gifted and talented (MS), human development (MS), learning and cognition (MS), research, measurement and evaluation (MS); electrical engineering (MS); emergency management (MPA); engineering technology (MS); English (MA); English as a second language (MA); environmental science (MS); finance (MBA, MS); financial management (MPA); French (MA); health services management (MBA); higher education (M Ed, Ed D); history (MA, MS); hospitality management (MS); human resources management (MPA); information science (MS); information systems (PhD); information technologies (MBA); interdisciplinary studies (MA, MS); international studies (MA); international sustainable tourism (MS); jazz studies (MM); journalism (MA, MJ, Graduate Certificate), including interactive and virtual digital communication (Graduate Certificate), narrative journalism (Graduate Certificate), public relations (Graduate Certificate); kinesiology (MS); linguistics (MA); local government management (MPA); logistics (PhD); logistics and supply chain management (MBA); long-term care, senior housing, and aging services (MA); management (PhD); marketing (MBA); mathematics (MA, MS); mechanical and energy engineering (MS, PhD); music (MA), including ethnomusicology, music theory, musicology, performance; music composition (PhD); music education (MM Ed, PhD); nonprofit management (MPA); operations and supply chain management (MBA); performance (MM, DMA); philosophy (MA); political science (MA); professional and technical communication (MA); radio, television and film (MA, MFA); rehabilitation counseling (Certificate); sociology (MA); Spanish (MA); special education (M Ed); speech-language pathology (MA); strategic management (MBA); studio art (MFA); teaching (M Ed); MBA/MS. *Program availability:* Part-time, evening/weekend, online learning. Terminal master's awarded for partial completion of doctoral program. *Degree requirements:* For master's, variable foreign language requirement, comprehensive exam (for some programs), thesis (for some programs); for doctorate, variable foreign language requirement, comprehensive exam (for some programs), thesis/dissertation; for other advanced degree, variable foreign language requirement, comprehensive exam (for some programs). *Entrance requirements:* For master's and doctorate, GRE, GMAT. Additional exam requirements/recommendations for international students: required—TOEFL (minimum score 550 paper-based; 79 iBT). Electronic applications accepted.

Wayne State University, College of Fine, Performing and Communication Arts, James Pearson Duffy Department of Art and Art History, Detroit, MI 48202. Offers art (MA, MFA), including ceramics, drawing, fashion design and merchandising (MA), fibers, graphic design, industrial design (MA), interior design (MA), metalsmithing, painting, photography, printmaking, sculpture; art history (MA). *Degree requirements:* For master's, thesis (for some programs), essay or thesis. *Entrance requirements:* For master's, BFA or another degree and equivalent course work, portfolio, personal interview, reference letters, statement of intent (except for art history program). Additional exam requirements/recommendations for international students: required—TOEFL (minimum score 550 paper-based; 79 iBT), TWE (minimum score 5.5), Michigan English Language Assessment Battery (minimum score 85); recommended—IELTS (minimum score 6.5). Electronic applications accepted. *Expenses:* Contact institution.

Section 2
Architecture

This section contains a directory of institutions offering graduate work in architecture, followed by in-depth entries submitted by institutions that chose to prepare detailed program descriptions. Additional information about programs listed in the directory but not augmented by an in-depth entry may be obtained by writing directly to the dean of a graduate school or chair of a department at the address given in the directory.

For programs offering related work, see also in this book *Applied Arts and Design, Art and Art History,* and *Public, Regional, and Industrial Affairs.* In another guide in this series:

Graduate Programs in Engineering & Applied Sciences
See *Civil and Environmental Engineering*

CONTENTS

Program Directories

Architectural History

Arizona State University at Tempe, Herberger Institute for Design and the Arts, The Design School, PhD Program in Design, Environment and the Arts, Tempe, AZ 85287-2105. Offers design (PhD); digital culture (PhD); healthcare and healing environments (PhD); history, theory, and criticism (PhD). *Degree requirements:* For doctorate, comprehensive exam, thesis/dissertation, interactive Program of Study (iPOS) submitted before completing 50 percent of required credit hours. *Entrance requirements:* For doctorate, GRE, master's degree in architecture, graphic design, industrial design, interior design, landscape architecture, or art history or equivalent standing; statement of purpose; 3 letters of recommendation; indication of potential faculty mentor; sample of written work. Additional exam requirements/recommendations for international students: required—TOEFL, IELTS, or PTE. Electronic applications accepted. *Expenses:* Contact institution.

Cornell University, Graduate School, Graduate Fields of Architecture, Art and Planning, Field of Architecture, Ithaca, NY 14853. Offers architectural design (M Arch); architectural science (MS); computer graphics (MS); history of architecture (MA, PhD); history of urban development (MA, PhD); theory and criticism of architecture (M Arch); urban design (M Arch). *Degree requirements:* For master's, one foreign language, thesis (MA, MS); for doctorate, 2 foreign languages, comprehensive exam, thesis/dissertation. *Entrance requirements:* For master's, GRE General Test, 5-year bachelor's degree in architecture, portfolio (M Arch), 3 letters of recommendation; for doctorate, GRE General Test, 3 letters of recommendation. Additional exam requirements/recommendations for international students: required—TOEFL (minimum score 600 paper-based; 77 iBT). Electronic applications accepted.

The Graduate Center, City University of New York, Graduate Studies, Program in Art History, New York, NY 10016-4039. Offers architecture (PhD); graphic arts (PhD); painting (PhD); photography (PhD); sculpture (PhD). *Degree requirements:* For doctorate, 2 foreign languages, thesis/dissertation. *Entrance requirements:* For doctorate, GRE General Test. Additional exam requirements/recommendations for international students: required—TOEFL. Electronic applications accepted.

Harvard University, Graduate School of Arts and Sciences, Department of History of Art and Architecture, Cambridge, MA 02138. Offers ancient art (PhD); ancient Near Eastern art (PhD); Baroque art (PhD); Byzantine art (PhD); classical art (PhD); Indian art (PhD); Islamic art (PhD); Japanese and Chinese art (PhD); medieval art (PhD); modern art (PhD); Renaissance and modern architecture (PhD); Renaissance art (PhD). *Degree requirements:* For doctorate, variable foreign language requirement, thesis/dissertation, general exams; reading exams in French, German, and Italian. *Entrance requirements:* For doctorate, GRE General Test. Additional exam requirements/recommendations for international students: required—TOEFL.

Massachusetts Institute of Technology, School of Architecture and Planning, Department of Architecture, Cambridge, MA 02139. Offers architecture (M Arch, PhD), including building technology (PhD), design and computation (PhD), history and theory of architecture (PhD), history and theory of art (PhD); architecture studies (SM Arch S); art, culture and technology (SMACT); building technology (SMBT). *Degree requirements:* For master's, thesis; for doctorate, comprehensive exam, thesis/dissertation. *Entrance requirements:* For master's and doctorate, GRE General Test. Additional exam requirements/recommendations for international students: required—TOEFL, IELTS. Electronic applications accepted.

New York University, Graduate School of Arts and Science, Program in Historical and Sustainable Architecture, New York, NY 10012-1019. Offers MA. *Entrance requirements:* For master's, GRE, writing sample. Additional exam requirements/recommendations for international students: required—TOEFL, IELTS.

Roger Williams University, School of Architecture, Art and Historic Preservation, Bristol, RI 02809. Offers architecture (M Arch); art and architectural history (MA); historical preservation (MS, Certificate); urban and regional planning (Certificate). *Program availability:* Part-time. *Faculty:* 8 full-time (4 women), 6 part-time/adjunct (1 woman). *Students:* 97 full-time (46 women), 10 part-time (0 women); includes 15 minority (1 Black or African American, non-Hispanic/Latino; 1 American Indian or Alaska Native, non-Hispanic/Latino; 1 Asian, non-Hispanic/Latino; 8 Hispanic/Latino; 4 Two or more races, non-Hispanic/Latino), 5 international. Average age 23. 97 applicants, 92% accepted, 54 enrolled. In 2019, 48 master's awarded. *Degree requirements:* For master's, thesis. *Entrance requirements:* For master's, letter of intent, transcripts, 2 letters of recommendation, portfolio (Architecture only), writing sample (Preservation only); for Certificate, transcripts. Additional exam requirements/recommendations for international students: required—TOEFL (minimum score 85 paper-based), IELTS (minimum score 6.5). *Application deadline:* For fall admission, 1/15 for domestic students, 5/1 for international students. Application fee: $50. Electronic applications accepted. *Expenses:* Tuition per credit hour: Architecture: $1579, Preservation: $951. *Financial support:* In 2019–20, 103 students received support. Scholarships/grants and unspecified assistantships available. Financial award application deadline: 3/15;

financial award applicants required to submit FAFSA. *Unit head:* Stephen White, Dean, 401-254-3607, E-mail: swhite@rwu.edu. *Application contact:* Gregory Laramie, Associate Dean, 401-254-3743, E-mail: glaramie@rwu.edu.
Website: https://www.rwu.edu/academics/schools-and-colleges/saahp

Savannah College of Art and Design, Program in Architectural History, Savannah, GA 31402-3146. Offers MFA. *Program availability:* Part-time. *Degree requirements:* For master's, thesis. *Entrance requirements:* For master's, GRE (recommended), portfolio (submitted in digital format), audition or writing submission, resume, statement of purpose, two letters of recommendation. Additional exam requirements/recommendations for international students: recommended—TOEFL (minimum score 550 paper-based; 85 iBT), IELTS (minimum score 6.5). Electronic applications accepted.

University of California, Berkeley, Graduate Division, College of Environmental Design, Department of Architecture, Berkeley, CA 94720. Offers architecture (M Arch); building science (MS, PhD); building structures, construction and materials (MS, PhD); design theories, methods, and practices (MS, PhD); environmental design in developing countries (MS, PhD); history of architecture and urbanism (MS, PhD); social and cultural processes in architecture and urbanism (MS, PhD); M Arch/MCP; M Arch/MS; MLA/M Arch. *Degree requirements:* For master's, thesis; for doctorate, thesis/dissertation, qualifying exam. *Entrance requirements:* For master's and doctorate, GRE General Test, minimum GPA of 3.0, 3 letters of recommendation. Additional exam requirements/recommendations for international students: required—TOEFL (minimum score 570 paper-based; 90 iBT). Electronic applications accepted. Application fee is waived when completed online.

University of Colorado Denver, College of Architecture and Planning, Program in Design and Planning, Denver, CO 80217. Offers history of architecture, landscape and urbanism (PhD); sustainable and healthy environments (PhD). *Program availability:* Part-time. *Degree requirements:* For doctorate, comprehensive exam, thesis/dissertation. *Entrance requirements:* For doctorate, GRE (minimum score of 158 for both verbal and quantitative; writing 4.0), minimum undergraduate GPA of 3.0, graduate 3.5; writing sample; three letters of recommendation; statement of personal and professional goals. Additional exam requirements/recommendations for international students: required—TOEFL (minimum score 80 iBT); recommended—IELTS (minimum score 6.8). Electronic applications accepted. *Expenses:* Contact institution.

University of Pittsburgh, Kenneth P. Dietrich School of Arts and Sciences, Department of History of Art and Architecture, Pittsburgh, PA 15260. Offers MA, PhD. *Faculty:* 17 full-time (9 women). *Students:* 38 full-time (31 women); includes 15 minority (4 Asian, non-Hispanic/Latino; 7 Hispanic/Latino; 1 Native Hawaiian or other Pacific Islander, non-Hispanic/Latino; 3 Two or more races, non-Hispanic/Latino). Average age 33. 42 applicants, 17% accepted, 5 enrolled. In 2019, 2 doctorates awarded. *Degree requirements:* For master's, one foreign language, thesis or alternative, MA paper; for doctorate, 2 foreign languages, comprehensive exam, thesis/dissertation, teaching portfolio. *Entrance requirements:* For master's and doctorate, Personal statement, Writing sample, Electronic transcripts of all college-level work to date, 3 letters of recommendation, Foreign language questionnaire. Additional exam requirements/recommendations for international students: required—TOEFL (minimum score 550 paper-based; 90 iBT). *Application deadline:* For fall admission, 12/15 for domestic and international students. Application fee: $50. Electronic applications accepted. *Financial support:* In 2019–20, 32 students received support, including 9 fellowships with full tuition reimbursements available (averaging $23,688 per year), 5 research assistantships with full tuition reimbursements available (averaging $20,250 per year), 6 teaching assistantships with full tuition reimbursements available (averaging $20,250 per year); scholarships/grants, health care benefits, tuition waivers (partial), and unspecified assistantships also available. Financial award application deadline: 12/15. *Unit head:* Dr. Jennifer Josten, Interim Department Chair and Associate Professor, 412-648-2417, Fax: 412-648-2792, E-mail: jej40@pitt.edu. *Application contact:* Karoline Swinotek, Academic and Fiscal Manager, 412-648-2400, Fax: 412-648-2792, E-mail: karoline@pitt.edu.
Website: http://www.haa.pitt.edu

The University of Texas at Austin, Graduate School, School of Architecture, Program in Architectural History, Austin, TX 78712-1111. Offers MA, PhD. *Degree requirements:* For doctorate, thesis/dissertation.

University of Virginia, School of Architecture, Department of Architectural History, Charlottesville, VA 22903. Offers M Arch H, PhD. *Degree requirements:* For master's, one foreign language, thesis. *Entrance requirements:* For master's, GRE General Test, 3 letters of recommendation. Additional exam requirements/recommendations for international students: required—TOEFL (minimum score 600 paper-based; 90 iBT). Electronic applications accepted.

Architecture

Academy of Art University, Graduate Programs, School of Architecture, San Francisco, CA 94105-3410. Offers advanced architectural design (MA); architecture (M Arch). *Program availability:* Part-time, 100% online. *Faculty:* 9 full-time (4 women), 29 part-time/adjunct (8 women). *Students:* 88 full-time (46 women), 78 part-time (36 women); includes 35 minority (9 Black or African American, non-Hispanic/Latino; 7 Asian, non-Hispanic/Latino; 19 Hispanic/Latino), 43 international. Average age 35. 68 applicants, 100% accepted, 37 enrolled. In 2019, 25 master's awarded. *Degree requirements:* For master's, final review. *Entrance requirements:* For master's, statement of intent; resume; portfolio/reel; official college transcripts. *Application deadline:* Applications are processed on a rolling basis. Application fee: $50. Electronic applications accepted. *Expenses: Tuition:* Full-time $1083; part-time $1083 per credit hour. *Required fees:* $860; $860 per unit $430 per term. One-time fee: $145. Tuition and fees vary according to program. *Financial support:* Career-related internships or fieldwork, Federal Work-Study, and scholarships/grants available. Financial award application deadline: 8/10; financial award applicants required to submit FAFSA. Website: http://www.academyart.edu/architecture-school/index.html

Andrews University, College of Health and Human Services, School of Architecture and Interior Design, Berrien Springs, MI 49104. Offers M Arch. *Faculty:* 9 full-time (3 women), 1 (woman) part-time/adjunct. *Students:* 13 full-time (9 women), 1 (woman) part-time; includes 8 minority (4 Black or African American, non-Hispanic/Latino; 1 Asian, non-Hispanic/Latino; 3 Hispanic/Latino), 4 international. Average age 24. In 2019, 14 master's awarded. *Entrance requirements:* For master's, GRE. Additional exam requirements/recommendations for international students: required—TOEFL (minimum score 550 paper-based). *Application deadline:* Applications are processed on a rolling basis. Application fee: $60. Electronic applications accepted. *Financial support:* Research assistantships, Federal Work-Study, institutionally sponsored loans, scholarships/grants, and health care benefits available. *Unit head:* Ariel Solis, Dean, 269-471-6003. *Application contact:* Jillian Panigot, Supervisor of Graduate Admission, 800-253-2874, Fax: 269-471-6321, E-mail: graduate@andrews.edu.

Arizona State University at Tempe, Herberger Institute for Design and the Arts, The Design School, Tempe, AZ 85287-1605. Offers architecture (M Arch); building design/built environment (MS); design (MSD), including arts, media, and engineering, healthcare and healing environments (MSD, PhD), industrial design, interaction design, interior design, new product innovation, visual communication design; design, environment and the arts (PhD), including design, digital culture, healthcare and healing environments (MSD, PhD), history, theory, and criticism; landscape architecture (MLA); urban design (MUD); MA/MBA. *Accreditation:* ASLA; NASAD. Terminal master's awarded for partial completion of doctoral program. *Degree requirements:* For master's, thesis optional, interactive Program of Study (iPOS) submitted before completing 50 percent of required credit hours; for doctorate, comprehensive exam, thesis/dissertation, interactive Program of Study (iPOS) submitted before completing 50 percent of required credit hours. *Entrance requirements:* For master's, GRE General Test, minimum GPA of 3.0 or equivalent in last 2 years of work leading to bachelor's degree, design/creative works portfolio, 3 references, statement of intent; for doctorate, GRE, master's degree in architecture, graphic design, industrial design, interior design, landscape architecture, or art history or equivalent standing; statement of purpose; 3 letters of recommendation; indication of potential faculty mentor; sample of written work. Additional exam requirements/recommendations for international students: required—TOEFL (minimum score 600 paper-based; 100 iBT). Electronic applications accepted.

Athabasca University, Faculty of Science and Technology, Athabasca, AB T9S 3A3, Canada. Offers architecture (Postgraduate Diploma); information systems (M Sc). *Program availability:* Part-time, online learning. *Degree requirements:* For master's, thesis optional. *Entrance requirements:* For master's, B Sc in computing or other bachelor's degree and IT experience. Electronic applications accepted. *Expenses:* Contact institution.

Auburn University, Graduate School, College of Architecture, Design, and Construction, Auburn, AL 36849. Offers MBC, MCP, MID, ML Arch, MPA/MCP. *Program availability:* Part-time. *Faculty:* 71 full-time (20 women), 15 part-time/adjunct (4 women). *Students:* 73 full-time (35 women), 106 part-time (21 women); includes 35 minority (18 Black or African American, non-Hispanic/Latino; 1 American Indian or Alaska Native, non-Hispanic/Latino; 5 Asian, non-Hispanic/Latino; 10 Hispanic/Latino; 1 Native Hawaiian or other Pacific Islander, non-Hispanic/Latino), 42 international. Average age 34. 170 applicants, 81% accepted, 87 enrolled. In 2019, 68 master's awarded. *Degree requirements:* For master's, thesis (for some programs). *Entrance requirements:* For master's, GRE General Test. Additional exam requirements/recommendations for international students: required—TOEFL (minimum score 550 paper-based; 79 iBT), iTEP; recommended—IELTS (minimum score 6.5). *Application deadline:* Applications are processed on a rolling basis. Application fee: $60 ($70 for international students). Electronic applications accepted. *Expenses:* $546 per credit hour state resident tuition, $1638 per credit hour nonresident tuition, $680 student services fee for GRA/GTA, $2160 per semester. *Financial support:* In 2019–20, 11 fellowships with full tuition reimbursements (averaging $3,845 per year) were awarded; Federal Work-Study, scholarships/grants, and unspecified assistantships also available. Support available to part-time students. Financial award application deadline: 3/15; financial award applicants required to submit FAFSA. *Unit head:* Dr. Vini Nathan, Dean/Chair, 334-844-4529, E-mail: vzn0007@auburn.edu. *Application contact:* Dr. George Flowers, Dean of the Graduate School, 334-844-2125.
Website: http://www.cadc.auburn.edu/

Ball State University, Graduate School, College of Architecture and Planning, Department of Architecture, Program in Architecture, Muncie, IN 47306. Offers architecture (M Arch, M Arch II). *Program availability:* Part-time. *Degree requirements:* For master's, thesis. *Entrance requirements:* For master's, GRE (if cumulative baccalaureate GPA is below 3.0), minimum baccalaureate GPA of 2.75 or 3.0 in latter half of baccalaureate, resume, statement of purpose, portfolio, three letters of reference. Additional exam requirements/recommendations for international students: required—TOEFL (minimum score 550 paper-based; 79 iBT), IELTS (minimum score 6.5). Electronic applications accepted. *Expenses:* Contact institution.

Boston Architectural College, Graduate Programs, Boston, MA 02115-2795. Offers architecture (M Arch); historic preservation (MDS); interior design (MID); landscape architecture (MLA); sustainable design (MDS). *Accreditation:* CIDA. *Degree requirements:* For master's, thesis. *Entrance requirements:* For master's, portfolio (recommended). Electronic applications accepted.

California Baptist University, Program in Architecture, Riverside, CA 92504-3206. Offers M Arch. *Degree requirements:* For master's, thesis, internship, professional practice, minimum cumulative GPA of 2.75 by the end of the first semester of the third year, progress review after the fifth full-time semester in the program. *Entrance requirements:* Additional exam requirements/recommendations for international students: required—TOEFL (minimum score 80 iBT). Electronic applications accepted. *Expenses:* Contact institution.

California College of the Arts, Graduate Programs, Architecture Programs, San Francisco, CA 94107. Offers advanced architecture design (MAAD); architecture (M Arch). *Degree requirements:* For master's, thesis. *Entrance requirements:* For master's, appropriate bachelor's degree, portfolio, resume, minimum 2 letters of recommendation, essay, transcripts. Additional exam requirements/recommendations for international students: required—TOEFL, IELTS, or PTE. Electronic applications accepted. *Expenses:* Contact institution.

California Polytechnic State University, San Luis Obispo, College of Architecture and Environmental Design, Department of Architecture, San Luis Obispo, CA 93407. Offers MS. *Program availability:* Part-time. *Faculty:* 3 full-time (2 women). *Students:* 3 full-time (2 women), 1 international. Average age 24. 16 applicants, 38% accepted, 1 enrolled. In 2019, 1 master's awarded. *Degree requirements:* For master's, comprehensive exam (for some programs), thesis. *Entrance requirements:* For master's, GRE. Additional exam requirements/recommendations for international students: required—TOEFL (minimum score 80 iBT). *Application deadline:* For fall admission, 4/1 for domestic and international students. Applications are processed on a rolling basis. Application fee: $55. Electronic applications accepted. *Expenses:* Tuition, state resident: full-time $7176; part-time $4164 per year. Tuition, nonresident: full-time $18,690; part-time $8916 per year. *Required fees:* $4206; $3185 per unit. $1061 per term. *Financial support:* Fellowships, research assistantships, teaching assistantships, and institutionally sponsored loans available. Financial award application deadline: 3/2; financial award applicants required to submit FAFSA. *Unit head:* Thomas Fowler, Graduate Coordinator, 805-756-2981, E-mail: tfowler@calpoly.edu. *Application contact:* Thomas Fowler, Graduate Coordinator, 805-756-2981, E-mail: tfowler@calpoly.edu.
Website: http://www.architecture.calpoly.edu/

California State Polytechnic University, Pomona, Program in Architecture, Pomona, CA 91768-2557. Offers architecture (M Arch). *Program availability:* Part-time, evening/weekend. *Entrance requirements:* Additional exam requirements/recommendations for international students: required—TOEFL (minimum score 550 paper-based). Electronic applications accepted. *Expenses:* Contact institution.

Carleton University, Faculty of Graduate Studies, Faculty of Engineering and Design, School of Architecture, Ottawa, ON K1S 5B6, Canada. Offers design studies (M Arch). *Degree requirements:* For master's, thesis. *Entrance requirements:* For master's, honors degree. Additional exam requirements/recommendations for international students: required—TOEFL.

Carnegie Mellon University, College of Fine Arts, School of Architecture, Pittsburgh, PA 15213-3891. Offers architecture (MSA); architecture, engineering, and construction management (PhD); building performance and diagnostics (MS, PhD); computational design (MS, PhD); engineering construction management (MSA); tangible interaction design (MTID); urban design (MUD). Terminal master's awarded for partial completion of doctoral program. *Degree requirements:* For doctorate, thesis/dissertation. *Entrance requirements:* For master's and doctorate, GRE General Test. Additional exam requirements/recommendations for international students: required—TOEFL.

The Catholic University of America, School of Architecture and Planning, Washington, DC 20064. Offers architecture and planning (M Arch, MS Arch St); city and regional planning (M Arch); facilities management (MS Arch); regional development (Certificate); sustainable design (M Arch, Certificate). *Program availability:* Part-time. *Degree requirements:* For master's, thesis. *Entrance requirements:* For master's, GRE (minimum score: 1000), minimum GPA of 2.8, portfolio, statement of purpose, official copies of academic transcripts, three letters of recommendation. Additional exam requirements/recommendations for international students: required—TOEFL (minimum score 550 paper-based; 80 iBT). Electronic applications accepted. *Expenses:* Contact institution.

City College of the City University of New York, Graduate School, The Bernard and Anne Spitzer School of Architecture, Program in Architecture, New York, NY 10031-9198. Offers M Arch. *Entrance requirements:* For master's, GRE. Additional exam requirements/recommendations for international students: required—TOEFL (minimum score 550 paper-based).

Clemson University, Graduate School, College of Architecture, Arts, and Humanities, School of Architecture, Clemson, SC 29634. Offers architecture (M Arch, MS, Certificate), including community build (Certificate); architecture and health (M Arch); digital ecologies (Certificate); historic preservation (MS, Certificate); integrated project delivery (Certificate); planning, design and the built environment (PhD); resilient urban design (MRUD). *Accreditation:* ASLA. *Students:* Average age 26. 275 applicants, 77% accepted, 75 enrolled. In 2019, 59 master's, 4 doctorates, 9 other advanced degrees awarded. *Degree requirements:* For master's, thesis (for some programs); for doctorate, comprehensive exam, thesis/dissertation. *Entrance requirements:* For master's, GRE General Test, design portfolio, unofficial transcripts, letters of recommendation, personal statement. Additional exam requirements/recommendations for international students: required—TOEFL (minimum score 80 paper-based; 80 iBT); recommended—IELTS (minimum score 6.5), TSE (minimum score 54). *Application deadline:* For fall admission, 4/15 for international students; for spring admission, 10/15 for international students. Applications are processed on a rolling basis. Application fee: $80 ($90 for international students). Electronic applications accepted. *Expenses:* Contact institution. *Financial support:* In 2019–20, 120 students received support, including 42 fellowships with full and partial tuition reimbursements available (averaging $2,307 per year), 20 research assistantships with full and partial tuition reimbursements available (averaging $4,248 per year), 19 teaching assistantships with full and partial tuition reimbursements available (averaging $18,468 per year); career-related internships or fieldwork and unspecified assistantships also available. *Unit head:* Kate Schwennsen, School Director, 864-656-3895, E-mail: kschwen@clemson.edu. *Application contact:* Dr. Dan Harding, Graduate Director, 864-606-6645, E-mail: hardin4@clemson.edu.
Website: https://www.clemson.edu/caah/departments/architecture/index.html

Columbia University, Graduate School of Architecture, Planning, and Preservation, Program in Advanced Architectural Design, New York, NY 10027. Offers MS. *Entrance requirements:* For master's, GRE General Test. *Expenses: Tuition:* Full-time $47,600; part-time $1880 per credit. One-time fee: $105.

Columbia University, Graduate School of Architecture, Planning, and Preservation, Program in Architecture, New York, NY 10027. Offers M Arch, PhD, M Arch/MS. *Degree requirements:* For master's, thesis optional. *Entrance requirements:* For master's, GRE General Test. *Expenses: Tuition:* Full-time $47,600; part-time $1880 per credit. One-time fee: $105.

Cooper Union for the Advancement of Science and Art, Irwin S. Chanin School of Architecture, New York, NY 10003. Offers M Arch II. *Degree requirements:* For master's, thesis. *Entrance requirements:* For master's, GRE, official transcripts from all colleges and universities from which applicant received credit; three recommendation letters; resume/curriculum vitae; written essay, portfolio, examples of written work. Additional exam requirements/recommendations for international students: required—TOEFL (minimum score 600 paper-based; 100 iBT). Electronic applications accepted. *Expenses:* Contact institution.

Cornell University, Graduate School, Graduate Fields of Architecture, Art and Planning, Field of Architecture, Ithaca, NY 14853. Offers architectural design (M Arch); architectural science (MS); computer graphics (MS); history of architecture (MA, PhD); history of urban development (MA, PhD); theory and criticism of architecture (M Arch); urban design (M Arch). *Degree requirements:* For master's, one foreign language, thesis (MA, MS); for doctorate, 2 foreign languages, comprehensive exam, thesis/dissertation. *Entrance requirements:* For master's, GRE General Test, 5-year bachelor's degree in architecture, portfolio (M Arch), 3 letters of recommendation; for doctorate, GRE General Test, 3 letters of recommendation. Additional exam requirements/recommendations for international students: required—TOEFL (minimum score 600 paper-based; 77 iBT). Electronic applications accepted.

Cranbrook Academy of Art, Program in Architecture, Bloomfield Hills, MI 48303-0801. Offers M Arch. *Degree requirements:* For master's, thesis, exhibit. *Entrance requirements:* Additional exam requirements/recommendations for international students: required—TOEFL (minimum score 85 iBT). Electronic applications accepted.

Dalhousie University, Faculty of Architecture and Planning, Halifax, NS B3J 2X4, Canada. Offers M Arch, M Eng, M Plan, MEDS, MPS. *Degree requirements:* For master's, thesis. *Entrance requirements:* Additional exam requirements/recommendations for international students: required—1 of 5 approved tests: TOEFL, IELTS, CANTEST, CAEL, Michigan English Language Assessment Battery. Electronic applications accepted.

Florida Agricultural and Mechanical University, Division of Graduate Studies, Research, and Continuing Education, School of Architecture, Tallahassee, FL 32307-3200. Offers architectural studies (MS Arch); architecture (professional) (M Arch); landscape architecture (MLA). *Program availability:* Part-time. *Degree requirements:* For master's, thesis. *Entrance requirements:* For master's, GRE General Test, minimum GPA of 3.0, portfolio. Additional exam requirements/recommendations for international students: required—TOEFL (minimum score 550 paper-based).

Florida International University, College of Communication, Architecture and The Arts, Department of Architecture, Miami, FL 33199. Offers M Arch, MA. *Program availability:* Part-time, evening/weekend. *Faculty:* 14 full-time (2 women), 22 part-time/adjunct (14 women). *Students:* 193 full-time (114 women), 17 part-time (6 women); includes 154 minority (13 Black or African American, non-Hispanic/Latino; 5 Asian, non-Hispanic/Latino; 135 Hispanic/Latino; 1 Two or more races, non-Hispanic/Latino), 32 international. Average age 26. 95 applicants, 46% accepted, 21 enrolled. In 2019, 91 master's awarded. *Entrance requirements:* For master's, GRE or minimum GPA of 3.0 in upper-level undergraduate work, portfolio. Additional exam requirements/recommendations for international students: required—TOEFL (minimum score 550 paper-based; 80 iBT). *Application deadline:* For fall admission, 2/1 for domestic and international students. Application fee: $30. Electronic applications accepted. *Expenses: Tuition, area resident:* Full-time $8912; part-time $446 per credit hour. Tuition, state resident: full-time $8912; part-time $446 per credit hour. Tuition, nonresident: full-time $21,393; part-time $992 per credit hour. *Required fees:* $2194. *Financial support:* Institutionally sponsored loans and scholarships/grants available. Financial award application deadline: 3/1; financial award applicants required to submit FAFSA. *Unit head:* Jason Chandler, Chair, 305-348-6913, E-mail: jason.chandler@fiu.edu. *Application contact:* Nanett Rojas, Manager, Admissions Operations, 305-348-7464, Fax: 305-348-7441, E-mail: gradadm@fiu.edu.

Florida State University, The Graduate School, College of Fine Arts, Department of Interior Architecture and Design, Tallahassee, FL 32306. Offers MFA, MS. *Accreditation:* NASAD (one or more programs are accredited). *Program availability:* Part-time. *Students:* Average age 25. 37 applicants, 54% accepted, 9 enrolled. In 2019, 25 master's awarded. *Entrance requirements:* For master's, GRE General Test, minimum GPA of 3.0 during previous 2 years. Additional exam requirements/recommendations for international students: required—TOEFL (minimum score 550 paper-based; 80 iBT). *Application deadline:* For fall admission, 7/1 for domestic students, 5/1 for international students; for summer admission, 3/1 for domestic and international students. Applications are processed on a rolling basis. Application fee: $30. Electronic applications accepted. *Financial support:* In 2019–20, 13 teaching assistantships with tuition reimbursements (averaging $5,000 per year) were awarded; career-related internships or fieldwork and unspecified assistantships also available. Financial award applicants required to submit FAFSA. *Unit head:* Dr. Jill Pable, Chair, 850-644-8326, Fax: 850-644-3112, E-mail: jpable@fsu.edu. *Application contact:* Dr. Steven Webber, Director of Graduate Studies, E-mail: swebber@fsu.edu.
Website: http://interiordesign.fsu.edu/

Georgia Institute of Technology, Graduate Studies, College of Design, Doctoral Program in Architecture, Atlanta, GA 30332-0001. Offers PhD. *Program availability:* Part-time, online learning. *Degree requirements:* For doctorate, comprehensive exam, thesis/dissertation. *Entrance requirements:* For doctorate, GRE General Test. Additional exam requirements/recommendations for international students: required—TOEFL (minimum score 600 paper-based). Electronic applications accepted. *Expenses: Tuition, area resident:* Full-time $14,064; part-time $586 per credit hour. Tuition, state resident: full-time $14,064; part-time $586 per credit hour. Tuition, nonresident: full-time $29,140; part-time $1215 per credit hour. *International tuition:* $29,140 full-time. *Required fees:* $2024; $840 per semester. $2096. Tuition and fees vary according to course load.

Georgia Institute of Technology, Graduate Studies, College of Design, Master's Program in Architecture, Atlanta, GA 30332-0001. Offers M Arch, MS, M Arch/MCRP. *Program availability:* Part-time. *Degree requirements:* For master's, thesis or alternative. *Entrance requirements:* For master's, GRE General Test. Additional exam requirements/recommendations for international students: required—TOEFL (minimum score 600 paper-based). Electronic applications accepted. *Expenses: Tuition, area resident:* Full-time $14,064; part-time $586 per credit hour. Tuition, state resident: full-time $14,064; part-time $586 per credit hour. Tuition, nonresident: full-time $29,140; part-time $1215 per credit hour. *International tuition:* $29,140 full-time. *Required fees:* $2024; $840 per semester. $2096. Tuition and fees vary according to course load.

Georgia Institute of Technology, Graduate Studies, College of Design, School of City and Regional Planning, Atlanta, GA 30332-0001. Offers city and regional planning (PhD); economic development (MCRP); environmental planning and management (MCRP); geographic information systems (MCRP); land and community development (MCRP); land use planning (MCRP); transportation (MCRP); urban design (MCRP); MCP/MSCE. *Accreditation:* ACSP. *Degree requirements:* For master's, thesis, internship. *Entrance requirements:* For master's, GRE General Test, minimum GPA of 2.7. Additional exam requirements/recommendations for international students: required—TOEFL. Electronic applications accepted. *Expenses: Tuition, area resident:* Full-time $14,064; part-time $586 per credit hour. Tuition, state resident: full-time $14,064; part-time $586 per credit hour. Tuition, nonresident: full-time $29,140; part-time $1215 per credit hour. *International tuition:* $29,140 full-time. *Required fees:* $2024; $840 per semester. $2096. Tuition and fees vary according to course load.

Harvard University, Graduate School of Arts and Sciences, Committee on Architecture, Landscape Architecture, and Urban Planning, Cambridge, MA 02138. Offers architecture (PhD); landscape architecture (PhD); urban planning (PhD). *Accreditation:* ACSP. *Degree requirements:* For doctorate, one foreign language, thesis/dissertation, oral exam. *Entrance requirements:* For doctorate, GRE General Test. Additional exam requirements/recommendations for international students: required—TOEFL.

Harvard University, Graduate School of Design, Department of Architecture, Cambridge, MA 02138. Offers M Arch. *Degree requirements:* For master's, thesis (for some programs). *Entrance requirements:* For master's, GRE General Test. Additional exam requirements/recommendations for international students: required—TOEFL (minimum score 600 paper-based; 104 iBT). Electronic applications accepted.

Harvard University, Graduate School of Design, Program in Design, Cambridge, MA 02138. Offers Dr DES. *Entrance requirements:* For doctorate, GRE General Test. Additional exam requirements/recommendations for international students: required—TOEFL (minimum score 600 paper-based; 104 iBT). Electronic applications accepted.

Harvard University, Graduate School of Design, Program in Design Studies, Cambridge, MA 02138. Offers M Des S. *Entrance requirements:* For master's, GRE General Test. Additional exam requirements/recommendations for international students: required—TOEFL (minimum score 600 paper-based; 104 iBT). Electronic applications accepted.

Illinois Institute of Technology, Graduate College, College of Architecture, Chicago, IL 60616. Offers M Arch, MLA, MS Arch, PhD, MLA/M Arch. *Accreditation:* ASLA. *Program availability:* Part-time. Terminal master's awarded for partial completion of doctoral program. *Degree requirements:* For master's, comprehensive exam (for some programs), thesis (for some programs); for doctorate, comprehensive exam, thesis/dissertation. *Entrance requirements:* For master's, GRE General Test (minimum score 292 Quantitative and Verbal, 2.5 Analytical Writing), minimum college GPA of 3.0, official transcripts, portfolio, 3 letters of recommendation, professional statement; for doctorate, GRE General Test (minimum score 900 Quantitative and Verbal, 2.5 Analytical Writing), minimum GPA of 3.5, official transcripts, portfolio, 3 letters of recommendation, professional statement. Additional exam requirements/recommendations for international students: required—TOEFL (minimum score 550 paper-based; 80 iBT). Electronic applications accepted.

Indiana University Bloomington, University Graduate School, College of Arts and Sciences, School of Art, Architecture and Design, Bloomington, IN 47405-7000. Offers apparel merchandising (MS); architecture (M Arch); studio art (MFA). *Accreditation:* NASAD (one or more programs are accredited). *Entrance requirements:* For master's, portfolio (MFA). Additional exam requirements/recommendations for international students: required—TOEFL. Electronic applications accepted.

Instituto Tecnológico y de Estudios Superiores de Monterrey, Campus Estado de México, Professional and Graduate Division, Estado de Mexico, Mexico. Offers administration of information technologies (MITA); architecture (M Arch); business administration (GMBA, MBA); computer sciences (MCS, PhD); education (M Ed); educational institution administration (MAD); educational technology and innovation (PhD); electronic commerce (MEC); environmental systems (MS); finance (MAF); humanistic studies (MHS); information sciences and knowledge management (MISKM); information systems (MS); manufacturing systems (MS); marketing (MEM); quality systems and productivity (MS); science and materials engineering (PhD); telecommunications management (MTM). *Program availability:* Part-time, online learning. *Degree requirements:* For master's, one foreign language, thesis (for some programs); for doctorate, one foreign language, thesis/dissertation. *Entrance requirements:* For master's, E-PAEP 500, interview; for doctorate, E-PAEP 500, research proposal. Additional exam requirements/recommendations for international students: required—TOEFL (minimum score 550 paper-based).

Instituto Tecnológico y de Estudios Superiores de Monterrey, Campus Irapuato, Graduate Programs, Irapuato, Mexico. Offers administration (MBA); administration of information technology (MAIT); administration of telecommunications (MAT); architecture (M Arch); computer science (MCS); education (M Ed); educational administration (MEA); educational innovation and technology (DEIT); educational technology (MET); electronic commerce (MBA); environmental administration and planning (MEAP); environmental systems (MES); finances (MBA); humanistic studies (MHS); international management for Latin American executives (MIMLAE); library and information science (MLIS); manufacturing quality management (MMQM); marketing research (MBA).

Iowa State University of Science and Technology, Department of Architecture, Ames, IA 50011. Offers architectural studies (MSAS); architecture (M Arch, MS); M Arch/MBA; M Arch/MCRP; M Arch/MS. *Degree requirements:* For master's, thesis (for some programs). *Entrance requirements:* For master's, GRE General Test, portfolio, letters of reference. Additional exam requirements/recommendations for international students: required—TOEFL (minimum score 600 paper-based; 79 iBT), IELTS (minimum score 7). Electronic applications accepted.

Judson University, Master of Architecture Program, Elgin, IL 60123. Offers architecture (M Arch); sustainable design (M Arch); traditional architecture and urbanism (M Arch). *Program availability:* Part-time. *Faculty:* 4 full-time (0 women), 2 part-time/adjunct (0 women). *Students:* 11 full-time (4 women), 1 part-time (0 women); includes 10 minority (all Hispanic/Latino). Average age 24. 12 applicants, 100% accepted, 12 enrolled. In 2019, 18 master's awarded. *Degree requirements:* For master's, thesis optional, 1600-hour practicum/preceptorship completed prior to enrollment. *Entrance requirements:* For master's, GRE, BA in Architecture or equivalent; transcripts, 1600 hours under a licensed architect, portfolio, minimum cumulative undergraduate GPA of 2.75, 3.0 in architecture; 3 letters of recommendation, letter of intent. Additional exam requirements/recommendations for international students: required—TOEFL (minimum score 550 paper-based), IELTS (minimum score 6.5). *Application deadline:* For fall admission, 2/15 priority date for domestic and international students; for winter admission, 11/15 for domestic students; for spring admission, 11/15 for domestic and international students. Applications are processed on a rolling basis. Application fee: $100. Electronic applications accepted. *Expenses:* Contact institution. *Financial support:* In 2019–20, 9 students received support. Fellowships, research assistantships, teaching assistantships, scholarships/grants, and 8 assistantships available. Financial award application deadline: 5/1; financial award applicants required to submit FAFSA. *Unit head:* Dr. Curtis Sartor, Interim Chair, 847-628-1017, E-mail: csartor@judsonu.edu. *Application contact:* Annelise Pollard, Admissions Representative, 847-628-2519, E-mail: annelise.pollard@judsonu.edu.
Website: http://www.judsonu.edu/ArchMaster/

Kansas State University, Graduate School, College of Architecture, Planning and Design, Department of Architecture, Manhattan, KS 66506. Offers M Arch, MS Arch. *Program availability:* Part-time. *Degree requirements:* For master's, thesis optional, residency. *Entrance requirements:* For master's, portfolio, minimum GPA of 3.0. Additional exam requirements/recommendations for international students: required—TOEFL (minimum score 95 iBT), IELTS (minimum score 7). Electronic applications accepted.

Kent State University, College of Architecture and Environmental Design, Kent, OH 44242-0001. Offers architecture (M Arch); architecture and environmental design (MS); health care design (MHCD); landscape architecture (MLA); urban design (MUD); M Arch/MBA; M Arch/MUD. *Accreditation:* ASLA. *Program availability:* Part-time. *Faculty:* 19 full-time (5 women), 9 part-time/adjunct (3 women). *Students:* 62 full-time (29 women), 12 part-time (9 women); includes 8 minority (3 Black or African American, non-Hispanic/Latino; 1 Asian, non-Hispanic/Latino; 2 Hispanic/Latino; 2 Two or more races, non-Hispanic/Latino), 11 international. Average age 26. 149 applicants, 87% accepted, 69 enrolled. In 2019, 66 master's awarded. *Degree requirements:* For master's, thesis (for some programs), capstone project (for some programs). *Entrance requirements:* For master's, GRE with minimum scores 151 (460) verbal reasoning, 150 (620) quantitative reasoning, and 4.25 analytical writing (except for MHCD), letters of recommendation, portfolio. Additional exam requirements/recommendations for international students: required—TOEFL (minimum score 80 iBT), IELTS (minimum score 6.5), PTE (minimum score 54), Michigan English Language Assessment Battery (minimum score 77). *Application deadline:* For fall admission, 1/15 for domestic students; for spring admission, 6/1 for domestic students. Applications are processed on a rolling basis. Application fee: $45 ($70 for international students). Electronic applications accepted. *Financial support:* Research assistantships with full tuition reimbursements, teaching assistantships with full tuition reimbursements, Federal Work-Study, scholarships/grants, and unspecified assistantships available. Financial award application deadline: 2/1; financial award applicants required to submit FAFSA. *Unit head:* Mark Mistur, Dean, 330-672-2917, E-mail: mmistur1@kent.edu. *Application contact:* Bill Willoughby, Associate Dean, 330-672-2917, E-mail: wwilloug@kenk.edu.
Website: http://www.kent.edu/caed

Lawrence Technological University, College of Architecture and Design, Southfield, MI 48075-1058. Offers architecture (M Arch, MA), including interior architecture (M Arch); build information modeling (Graduate Certificate); interior design (MID); public interest design (Graduate Certificate); social practice (MFA); urban design (MUD). *Accreditation:* NASAD. *Program availability:* Part-time, evening/weekend. *Faculty:* 10 full-time (1 woman), 7 part-time/adjunct (4 women). *Students:* 6 full-time (3 women), 149 part-time (70 women); includes 18 minority (7 Black or African American, non-Hispanic/Latino; 3 Asian, non-Hispanic/Latino; 6 Hispanic/Latino; 2 Two or more races, non-Hispanic/Latino), 21 international. Average age 30. 214 applicants, 84% accepted, 94 enrolled. In 2019, 54 master's awarded. *Degree requirements:* For master's, thesis optional. *Entrance requirements:* Additional exam requirements/recommendations for international students: required—TOEFL (minimum score 550 paper-based; 79 iBT). *Application deadline:* For fall admission, 5/24 for international students; for spring admission, 10/13 for international students; for summer admission,

2/18 for international students. Applications are processed on a rolling basis. Application fee: $50. Electronic applications accepted. *Expenses: Tuition:* Full-time $16,618; part-time $8309 per year. *Required fees:* $600; $600. *Financial support:* In 2019–20, 39 students received support, including 8 research assistantships with partial tuition reimbursements available (averaging $6,000 per year); career-related internships or fieldwork, scholarships/grants, and unspecified assistantships also available. Financial award application deadline: 4/1; financial award applicants required to submit FAFSA. *Unit head:* Prof. Karl Daubmann, Dean/Professor, 248-204-2805, E-mail: archdean@ltu.edu. *Application contact:* Jane Rohrback, Director of Admissions, 248-204-3160, Fax: 248-204-2228, E-mail: admissions@ltu.edu.
Website: http://www.ltu.edu/architecture_and_design/index.asp

London Metropolitan University, Graduate Programs, London, United Kingdom. Offers applied psychology (M Sc); architecture (MA); biomedical science (M Sc); blood science (M Sc); cancer pharmacology (M Sc); computer networking and cyber security (M Sc); computing and information systems (M Sc); conference interpreting (MA); counter-terrorism studies (M Sc); creative, digital and professional writing (MA); crime, violence and prevention (M Sc); criminology (M Sc); curating contemporary art (MA); data analytics (M Sc); digital media (MA); early childhood studies (MA); education (MA, Ed D); financial services law, regulation and compliance (LL M); food science (M Sc); forensic psychology (M Sc); health and social care management and policy (M Sc); human nutrition (M Sc); human resource management (MA); human rights and international conflict (MA); information technology (M Sc); intelligence and security studies (M Sc); international oil, gas and energy law (LL M); international relations (MA); interpreting (MA); learning and teaching in higher education (MA); legal practice (LL M); media and entertainment law (LL M); organizational and consumer psychology (M Sc); psychological therapy (M Sc); psychology of mental health (M Sc); public health (M Sc); public policy and management (MPA); security studies (M Sc); social work (M Sc); spatial planning and urban design (MA); sports therapy (M Sc); supporting older children and young people with dyslexia (MA); teaching languages (MA), including Arabic, English; translation (MA); woman and child abuse (MA).

Louisiana State University and Agricultural & Mechanical College, Graduate School, College of Art and Design, School of Architecture, Baton Rouge, LA 70803. Offers M Arch.

Louisiana Tech University, Graduate School, College of Liberal Arts, Ruston, LA 71272. Offers architecture (M Arch); art (MFA), including graphic design, photography, studio; audiology (Au D); communication (MA), including speech communication, theatre; English (MA), including literature, technical writing; history (MA); speech pathology (MA); technical writing and communication (Graduate Certificate). *Accreditation:* ASHA. *Program availability:* Part-time. *Degree requirements:* For master's, thesis (for some programs); for doctorate, thesis/dissertation. *Entrance requirements:* For master's, GRE General Test; for doctorate, GRE General Test, bachelor's degree, minimum GPA of 3.0 or 3.2 on last 60 hours attempted. Additional exam requirements/recommendations for international students: required—TOEFL (minimum score 550 paper-based; 80 iBT), IELTS (minimum score 6.5). Electronic applications accepted. *Expenses: Tuition, area resident:* Full-time $6592; part-time $400 per credit. Tuition, state resident: full-time $6592; part-time $400 per credit. Tuition, nonresident: full-time $13,333; part-time $681 per credit. *International tuition:* $13,333 full-time. *Required fees:* $3011; $3011 per unit.

Marywood University, Academic Affairs, School of Architecture, Program in Architecture, Scranton, PA 18509-1598. Offers M Arch. *Program availability:* Part-time. *Degree requirements:* For master's, thesis project.

Massachusetts College of Art and Design, Graduate Programs, Program in Architecture, Boston, MA 02115-5882. Offers M Arch. *Faculty:* 1 (woman) full-time, 11 part-time/adjunct (3 women). *Students:* 18 full-time (8 women), 2 part-time (1 woman); includes 8 minority (3 Black or African American, non-Hispanic/Latino; 2 Asian, non-Hispanic/Latino; 3 Hispanic/Latino), 6 international. 30 applicants, 87% accepted, 10 enrolled. In 2019, 9 master's awarded. *Entrance requirements:* For master's, portfolio, college transcripts, resume, statement of purpose, letters of reference, interview. Additional exam requirements/recommendations for international students: required—TOEFL (minimum score 550 paper-based; 85 iBT); recommended—IELTS (minimum score 6). *Application deadline:* For summer admission, 1/20 priority date for domestic and international students. Application fee: $90. Electronic applications accepted. *Expenses:* Contact institution. *Financial support:* Research assistantships, teaching assistantships, career-related internships or fieldwork, scholarships/grants, tuition waivers (partial), and unspecified assistantships available. Support available to part-time students. Financial award application deadline: 1/20; financial award applicants required to submit FAFSA. *Unit head:* Lucinda Bliss, Dean of Graduate Studies, 617-879-7157, E-mail: lbliss@massart.edu. *Application contact:* Stacy Petersen, Associate Director of Graduate Admissions and Operations, 617-879-7238, E-mail: gradadmissions@massart.edu.
Website: http://www.massart.edu/Admissions/Graduate_Programs.html

Massachusetts Institute of Technology, School of Architecture and Planning, Department of Architecture, Cambridge, MA 02139. Offers architecture (M Arch, PhD), including building technology (PhD), design and computation (PhD), history and theory of architecture (PhD), history and theory of art (PhD); architecture studies (SM Arch S); art, culture and technology (SMACT); building technology (SMBT). *Degree requirements:* For master's, thesis; for doctorate, comprehensive exam, thesis/dissertation. *Entrance requirements:* For master's and doctorate, GRE General Test. Additional exam requirements/recommendations for international students: required—TOEFL, IELTS. Electronic applications accepted.

McGill University, Faculty of Graduate and Postdoctoral Studies, Faculty of Engineering, School of Architecture, Montréal, QC H3A 2T5, Canada. Offers affordable homes (M Arch II, Diploma); architectural history and theory (M Arch II); architecture (PhD); domestic environment (M Arch II); domestic environments (Diploma); minimum cost housing in developing countries (M Arch II, Diploma); professional architecture (M Arch I).

Miami University, College of Creative Arts, Department of Architecture and Interior Design, Oxford, OH 45056. Offers M Arch. *Accreditation:* NASAD.

Montana State University, The Graduate School, College of Arts and Architecture, School of Architecture, Bozeman, MT 59717. Offers M Arch. *Program availability:* Part-time. *Degree requirements:* For master's, comprehensive exam. *Entrance requirements:* For master's, GRE General Test, minimum cumulative GPA of 3.0, portfolio, 3 letters of recommendation. Additional exam requirements/recommendations for international students: required—TOEFL (minimum score 550 paper-based). Electronic applications accepted.

Morgan State University, School of Graduate Studies, School of Architecture and Planning, Program in Architecture, Baltimore, MD 21251. Offers M Arch. *Program availability:* Part-time, evening/weekend. *Faculty:* 6 full-time (1 woman), 3 part-time/adjunct (all women). *Students:* 27 full-time (7 women), 6 part-time (3 women); includes 18 minority (10 Black or African American, non-Hispanic/Latino; 3 Asian, non-Hispanic/Latino; 5 Hispanic/Latino), 2 international. Average age 32. 6 applicants, 100% accepted, 3 enrolled. In 2019, 16 master's awarded. *Degree requirements:* For master's, thesis or alternative. *Entrance requirements:* For master's, GRE, Minimum GPA=3.0. Additional exam requirements/recommendations for international students: required—TOEFL (minimum score 550 paper-based; 70 iBT), IELTS (minimum score 6). *Application deadline:* For fall admission, 5/1 for domestic students. Applications are processed on a rolling basis. Application fee: $50 ($70 for international students). Electronic applications accepted. *Expenses:* Tuition, state resident: full-time $455; part-time $455 per credit hour. Tuition, nonresident: full-time $894; part-time $894 per credit hour. *Required fees:* $82; $82 per credit hour. *Financial support:* In 2019–20, 5 students received support. Fellowships with full tuition reimbursements available, research assistantships with full tuition reimbursements available, teaching assistantships with full tuition reimbursements available, career-related internships or fieldwork, Federal Work-Study, institutionally sponsored loans, scholarships/grants, and tuition waivers (full and partial) available. Support available to part-time students. Financial award application deadline: 2/1. *Unit head:* Dr. Mohammad Gharipour, Graduate Program Director, 443-885-3910, E-mail: mohammad.gharipour@morgan.edu. *Application contact:* Dr. Jahmaine Smith, Director of Admissions, 443-885-3185, Fax: 443-885-8226, E-mail: gradapply@morgan.edu.
Website: https://morgan.edu/sap/arch

New Jersey Institute of Technology, J. Robert and Barbara A. Hillier College of Architecture and Design, Newark, NJ 07102. Offers architecture (M Arch); infrastructure planning (MIP); urban systems (PhD). *Program availability:* Part-time, evening/weekend. *Faculty:* 24 full-time (9 women), 35 part-time/adjunct (16 women). *Students:* 51 full-time (33 women), 2 part-time (1 woman); includes 13 minority (1 Black or African American, non-Hispanic/Latino; 1 Asian, non-Hispanic/Latino; 8 Hispanic/Latino; 3 Two or more races, non-Hispanic/Latino), 19 international. Average age 29. 71 applicants, 63% accepted, 20 enrolled. In 2019, 27 master's awarded. Terminal master's awarded for partial completion of doctoral program. *Degree requirements:* For master's, thesis (for some programs); for doctorate, thesis/dissertation. *Entrance requirements:* For master's, GRE General Test, Minimum GPA of 3.0, personal statement, 3 letters of recommendation, design portfolio and transcripts; for doctorate, GRE General Test, Personal statement, 3 letters of recommendation, design portfolio and transcripts. Additional exam requirements/recommendations for international students: required—TOEFL (minimum score 550 paper-based; 79 iBT), IELTS (minimum score 6.5). *Application deadline:* For fall admission, 6/1 priority date for domestic students, 5/1 priority date for international students; for spring admission, 11/15 priority date for domestic and international students. Applications are processed on a rolling basis. Application fee: $75. Electronic applications accepted. *Expenses:* $23,828 per year (in-state), $33,744 per year (out-of-state). *Financial support:* In 2019–20, 36 students received support, including fellowships with full tuition reimbursements available (averaging $24,000 per year), 1 research assistantship with full tuition reimbursement available (averaging $24,000 per year), 7 teaching assistantships with full tuition reimbursements available (averaging $24,000 per year); career-related internships or fieldwork, Federal Work-Study, scholarships/grants, traineeships, unspecified assistantships, and studio assistantships (1 averaging $10,000) also available. Financial award application deadline: 1/15. *Unit head:* Dr. Branko Kolarevic, Dean, 973-596-3080, E-mail: branko.r.kolarevic@njit.edu. *Application contact:* Stephen Eck, Executive Director of University Admissions, 973-596-3300, Fax: 973-596-3461, E-mail: admissions@njit.edu.
Website: http://architecture.njit.edu/

The New School, Parsons School of Design, Program in Architecture, New York, NY 10011. Offers M Arch, M Arch/MFA. *Faculty:* 11 full-time, 50 part-time/adjunct. *Students:* 58 full-time (38 women); includes 19 minority (7 Black or African American, non-Hispanic/Latino; 5 Asian, non-Hispanic/Latino; 5 Hispanic/Latino; 2 Two or more races, non-Hispanic/Latino), 20 international. Average age 26. 153 applicants, 73% accepted, 20 enrolled. In 2019, 19 master's awarded. *Degree requirements:* For master's, thesis. *Entrance requirements:* For master's, GRE, transcripts, resume, statement of purpose, recommendation letters, portfolio, interview. Additional exam requirements/recommendations for international students: required—TOEFL (minimum score 92 iBT), IELTS (minimum score 7), PTE (minimum score 63). *Application deadline:* For fall admission, 1/1 for domestic and international students. Applications are processed on a rolling basis. Application fee: $50. Electronic applications accepted. *Expenses:* 1810 per credit. *Financial support:* In 2019–20, 50 students received support, including 8 research assistantships (averaging $3,605 per year), 5 teaching assistantships (averaging $1,873 per year); career-related internships or fieldwork, Federal Work-Study, scholarships/grants, unspecified assistantships, and travel funding; tuition waivers for students who are also New School employees also available. Support available to part-time students. Financial award application deadline: 2/1; financial award applicants required to submit FAFSA. *Unit head:* Mark Gardner, Program Head, 212-229-890 Ext. 4859, E-mail: gardnerm@newschool.edu. *Application contact:* Simone Varadian, Senior Director I, 212-229-5150 Ext. 4117, E-mail: thinkparsonsgrad@newschool.edu.
Website: https://www.newschool.edu/parsons/masters-architecture/

NewSchool of Architecture and Design, Program in Architecture, San Diego, CA 92101-6634. Offers M Arch, MS. *Program availability:* Part-time, online learning. *Degree requirements:* For master's, thesis. *Entrance requirements:* For master's, portfolio, interview. Additional exam requirements/recommendations for international students: required—TOEFL, IELTS.

New York Institute of Technology, School of Architecture and Design, Old Westbury, NY 11568-8000. Offers architecture (M Arch); architecture, urban and regional design (MS). *Program availability:* Part-time. *Entrance requirements:* For master's, For M.Arch: Varies depending on track; see website for details. For M.S. Architecture, Urban & Regional Design: professional architecture or landscape architecture degree from accredited college or university approved by NAAB; minimum undergraduate GPA 3.0; digital portfolio; C.V. Additional exam requirements/recommendations for international students: required—TOEFL (minimum score 79 iBT), IELTS (minimum score 6), PTE (minimum score 53). Electronic applications accepted. *Expenses: Tuition:* Full-time $23,760; part-time $1320 per credit. *Required fees:* $260; $220 per unit. Full-time tuition and fees vary according to degree level and program. Part-time tuition and fees vary according to course load and program.

North Carolina State University, Graduate School, College of Design, School of Architecture, Raleigh, NC 27695. Offers M Arch. *Degree requirements:* For master's, thesis optional, oral exam, project. *Entrance requirements:* For master's, GRE General Test, portfolio. Electronic applications accepted.

North Dakota State University, College of Graduate and Interdisciplinary Studies, College of Arts, Humanities and Social Sciences, Department of Architecture and Landscape Architecture, Fargo, ND 58102. Offers architecture (M Arch); landscape architecture (MLA). Electronic applications accepted. Tuition and fees vary according to program and reciprocity agreements.

Northeastern University, College of Arts, Media and Design, Boston, MA 02115-5096. Offers architecture (M Arch); arts administration and cultural entrepreneurship (MS); experience design (MFA, MS); game science and design (MS); information design and visualization (MFA); interdisciplinary arts (MFA); journalism (MA); media advocacy (MS); music industry leadership (MS); sustainable building systems (MS); sustainable urban environments (M Des). Electronic applications accepted. *Expenses:* Contact institution.

The Ohio State University, Graduate School, College of Engineering, Austin E. Knowlton School of Architecture, Columbus, OH 43210. Offers architecture (M Arch); city and regional planning (MCRP, PhD); landscape architecture (M Land Arch). *Accreditation:* ACSP; ASLA. *Entrance requirements:* For master's, GRE or GMAT (city and regional planning), portfolio (for architecture and landscape architecture); for doctorate, GRE or GMAT (city and regional planning), example of research or written work. Additional exam requirements/recommendations for international students: required—TOEFL (minimum score 600 paper-based; 100 iBT), Michigan English Language Assessment Battery (minimum score 86); recommended—IELTS (minimum score 8). Electronic applications accepted.

Penn State University Park, Graduate School, College of Arts and Architecture, Stuckeman School of Architecture and Landscape Architecture, University Park, PA 16802. Offers architecture (M Arch, MS, PhD); landscape architecture (MLA, MS). *Accreditation:* ASLA.

Pontificia Universidad Catolica Madre y Maestra, Graduate School, Faculty of Sciences and Humanities, Santiago, Dominican Republic. Offers architecture (M Arch), including architecture of interiors, architecture of tourist lodgings, landscaping; early childhood education (M Ed).

Portland State University, Graduate Studies, College of the Arts, School of Architecture, Portland, OR 97207-0751. Offers M Arch. *Faculty:* 13 full-time (5 women), 15 part-time/adjunct (6 women). *Students:* 44 full-time (24 women), 4 part-time (all women); includes 12 minority (3 Asian, non-Hispanic/Latino; 4 Hispanic/Latino; 5 Two or more races, non-Hispanic/Latino), 6 international. Average age 30. 45 applicants, 82% accepted, 6 enrolled. In 2019, 14 master's awarded. *Degree requirements:* For master's, thesis optional. *Entrance requirements:* For master's, GRE General Test, statement of intent, resume, 3 letters of recommendation, writing sample, portfolio. Additional exam requirements/recommendations for international students: required—TOEFL (minimum score 550 paper-based; 80 iBT), IELTS (minimum score 6.5). *Application deadline:* For fall admission, 6/22 for domestic students; for summer admission, 5/23 for domestic students. Applications are processed on a rolling basis. Application fee: $65. Electronic applications accepted. *Expenses:* Contact institution. *Financial support:* In 2019–20, 22 students received support, including 1 research assistantship with tuition reimbursement available (averaging $7,209 per year), 5 teaching assistantships with tuition reimbursements available (averaging $7,204 per year); Federal Work-Study, institutionally sponsored loans, scholarships/grants, and unspecified assistantships also available. Support available to part-time students. *Unit head:* Prof. Clive Knights, Director, 503-725-3349, E-mail: knightsc@pdx.edu. *Application contact:* Prof. Clive Knights, Director, 503-725-3349, E-mail: knightsc@pdx.edu.
Website: https://www.pdx.edu/architecture/

Prairie View A&M University, School of Architecture, Prairie View, TX 77446. Offers M Arch, MCD. *Program availability:* Part-time, evening/weekend. *Faculty:* 6 full-time (1 woman), 1 (woman) part-time/adjunct. *Students:* 30 full-time (15 women), 17 part-time (8 women); includes 39 minority (31 Black or African American, non-Hispanic/Latino; 1 Asian, non-Hispanic/Latino; 7 Hispanic/Latino), 4 international. Average age 31. 21 applicants, 95% accepted, 15 enrolled. In 2019, 29 master's awarded. *Degree requirements:* For master's, comprehensive exam, thesis. *Entrance requirements:* For master's, GRE General Test, portfolio (M Arch), minimum GPA of 2.75. Additional exam requirements/recommendations for international students: required—TOEFL (minimum score 550 paper-based; 79 iBT). *Application deadline:* For fall admission, 5/1 priority date for domestic and international students; for spring admission, 10/1 priority date for domestic students, 9/1 priority date for international students; for summer admission, 3/1 priority date for domestic students, 2/1 priority date for international students. Applications are processed on a rolling basis. Application fee: $50. Electronic applications accepted. *Expenses: Tuition, area resident:* Full-time $5479.68. Tuition, state resident: full-time $5479.68. Tuition, nonresident: full-time $15,439. *International tuition:* $15,439 full-time. *Required fees:* $2149.32. *Financial support:* In 2019–20, 10 students received support, including 5 research assistantships (averaging $14,400 per year); career-related internships or fieldwork, institutionally sponsored loans, scholarships/grants, unspecified assistantships, and out of state waiver- $1000 each also available. Support available to part-time students. Financial award application deadline: 4/1; financial award applicants required to submit FAFSA. *Unit head:* Dr. Ikhlas Sabouni, Dean, 936-261-9800, Fax: 936-261-2350, E-mail: isabouni@pvamu.edu. *Application contact:* Pauline Walker, Administrative Assistant II, Research and Graduate Studies, 936-261-3521, Fax: 936-261-3529, E-mail: pmwalker@pvamu.edu.

Pratt Institute, School of Architecture, Program in Architecture, Brooklyn, NY 11205-3899. Offers architecture (first-professional) (M Arch); architecture (post-professional) (MS Arch). *Students:* 192 full-time (102 women); includes 36 minority (1 Black or African American, non-Hispanic/Latino; 15 Asian, non-Hispanic/Latino; 18 Hispanic/Latino; 2 Two or more races, non-Hispanic/Latino), 104 international. Average age 25. 531 applicants, 89% accepted, 76 enrolled. In 2019, 38 master's awarded. *Degree requirements:* For master's, thesis. *Entrance requirements:* For master's, GRE (for M Arch only), B Arch (for MS Arch only), portfolio, letters of recommendation. Additional exam requirements/recommendations for international students: required—TOEFL (minimum score 550 paper-based; 79 iBT). *Application deadline:* For fall admission, 1/5 for domestic and international students; for spring admission, 10/1 for domestic and international students. Application fee: $50 ($90 for international students). Electronic applications accepted. *Expenses: Tuition:* Full-time $33,246; part-time $1847 per credit. *Required fees:* $1980. *Financial support:* Career-related internships or fieldwork, Federal Work-Study, institutionally sponsored loans, scholarships/grants, health care benefits, and unspecified assistantships available. Support available to part-time students. Financial award application deadline: 2/1; financial award applicants required to submit FAFSA. *Unit head:* David Erdman, Chairperson, 718-399-4327, E-mail: derdman@pratt.edu. *Application contact:* Natalie Capannelli, Director of Graduate Admissions, 718-636-3551, Fax: 718-399-4242, E-mail: ncapanne@pratt.edu.
Website: https://www.pratt.edu/academics/architecture/grad-arch-urban-design/grad-dept-architecture/

Princeton University, Graduate School, School of Architecture, Princeton, NJ 08544-1019. Offers M Arch, PhD. Terminal master's awarded for partial completion of doctoral program. *Degree requirements:* For master's, thesis; for doctorate, 2 foreign languages, comprehensive exam, thesis/dissertation. *Entrance requirements:* For master's, GRE General Test, design portfolio, math, 2 semesters of physics, and art/architecture survey; for doctorate, GRE General Test, samples of written work. Additional exam requirements/recommendations for international students: required—TOEFL (minimum score 600 paper-based). Electronic applications accepted.

Rensselaer Polytechnic Institute, Graduate School, School of Architecture, Program in Architecture, Troy, NY 12180-3590. Offers M Arch. *Faculty:* 33 full-time (8 women), 13 part-time/adjunct (1 woman). *Students:* 16 full-time (6 women); includes 3 minority (1 Black or African American, non-Hispanic/Latino; 1 Hispanic/Latino; 1 Two or more races, non-Hispanic/Latino), 4 international. Average age 27. 69 applicants, 86% accepted, 6 enrolled. In 2019, 13 master's awarded. *Degree requirements:* For master's, thesis. *Entrance requirements:* For master's, GRE, portfolio. Additional exam requirements/recommendations for international students: required—TOEFL (minimum score 570 paper-based; 88 iBT), IELTS (minimum score 6.5), PTE (minimum score 60). *Application deadline:* For fall admission, 1/1 priority date for domestic and international students; for summer admission, 1/1 priority date for domestic and international students. Applications are processed on a rolling basis. Application fee: $75. Electronic applications accepted. *Financial support:* Scholarships/grants available. Financial award application deadline: 1/1. *Unit head:* Lonn Combs, Graduate Program Director, 518-276-8718, E-mail: combsl@rpi.edu. *Application contact:* Jarron Decker, Director of Graduate Admissions, 518-276-6216, Fax: 518-276-4072, E-mail: gradadmissions@rpi.edu.
Website: http://march1.arch.rpi.edu/

Rensselaer Polytechnic Institute, Graduate School, School of Architecture, Program in Lighting, Troy, NY 12180-3590. Offers MS. *Faculty:* 33 full-time (8 women), 13 part-time/adjunct (1 woman). *Students:* 7 full-time (3 women), 5 international. Average age 28. 6 applicants, 83% accepted, 4 enrolled. In 2019, 4 master's awarded. *Degree requirements:* For master's, comprehensive exam, thesis. *Entrance requirements:* For master's, GRE. Additional exam requirements/recommendations for international students: required—TOEFL (minimum score 570 paper-based; 88 iBT), IELTS (minimum score 6.5), PTE (minimum score 60). *Application deadline:* For fall admission, 1/1 priority date for domestic and international students. Applications are processed on a rolling basis. Application fee: $75. Electronic applications accepted. *Financial support:* Scholarships/grants available. Financial award application deadline: 1/1. *Unit head:* Nadarajah Narendran, Graduate Program Director, 518-687-7100, E-mail: narenn2@rpi.edu. *Application contact:* Jarron Decker, Director of Graduate Admissions, 518-276-6216, Fax: 518-276-4072, E-mail: gradadmissions@rpi.edu.
Website: http://www.arch.rpi.edu/academic/graduate/lighting/

Rhode Island School of Design, Department of Architecture, Providence, RI 02903-2784. Offers M Arch. *Students:* 98 full-time (52 women); includes 19 minority (5 Black or African American, non-Hispanic/Latino; 4 Asian, non-Hispanic/Latino; 7 Hispanic/Latino; 3 Two or more races, non-Hispanic/Latino), 42 international. Average age 25. 313 applicants, 68% accepted, 41 enrolled. In 2019, 28 master's awarded. *Degree requirements:* For master's, thesis, exhibition. *Entrance requirements:* For master's, portfolio, statement of purpose, 3 letters of recommendation. Additional exam requirements/recommendations for international students: required—TOEFL (minimum score 580 paper-based; 93 iBT), IELTS (minimum score 6.5). *Application deadline:* For fall admission, 1/10 for domestic and international students. Application fee: $60. Electronic applications accepted. *Expenses: Tuition:* Full-time $51,800. *Required fees:* $1060. *Financial support:* Fellowships, research assistantships, teaching assistantships, Federal Work-Study, and unspecified assistantships available. Financial award application deadline: 2/1; financial award applicants required to submit FAFSA. *Unit head:* Amy Kulper, Department Head, 401-454-6281, Fax: 401-454-6299, E-mail: archgrad@risd.edu. *Application contact:* Molly Pettengill, Assistant Director for Graduate Recruitment, 401-454-6312, Fax: 401-454-6309, E-mail: mpetteng@risd.edu.
Website: http://www.risd.edu/academics/architecture/

Rice University, Graduate Programs, School of Architecture, Houston, TX 77251-1892. Offers architecture (M Arch, D Arch); urban design (M Arch). *Degree requirements:* For master's, thesis optional; for doctorate, thesis/dissertation. *Entrance requirements:* For master's and doctorate, GRE. Additional exam requirements/recommendations for international students: required—TOEFL (minimum score 600 paper-based; 100 iBT). Electronic applications accepted.

Rochester Institute of Technology, Graduate Enrollment Services, Golisano Institute for Sustainability, Architecture and Sustainability Department, M Arch Program in Architecture, Rochester, NY 14623-5603. Offers M Arch. *Degree requirements:* For master's, thesis. *Entrance requirements:* For master's, GRE, minimum GPA of 3.0 (recommended), portfolio, personal statement, complete at least 1 semester each of college-level math and science, 2 letters of recommendation. Additional exam requirements/recommendations for international students: required—TOEFL (minimum score 550 paper-based; 79 iBT), IELTS (minimum score 6.5), PTE (minimum score 58). Electronic applications accepted.

Roger Williams University, School of Architecture, Art and Historic Preservation, Bristol, RI 02809. Offers architecture (M Arch); art and architectural history (MA); historical preservation (MS, Certificate); urban and regional planning (Certificate). *Program availability:* Part-time. *Faculty:* 8 full-time (4 women), 6 part-time/adjunct (1 woman). *Students:* 97 full-time (46 women), 10 part-time (0 women); includes 15 minority (1 Black or African American, non-Hispanic/Latino; 1 American Indian or Alaska Native, non-Hispanic/Latino; 1 Asian, non-Hispanic/Latino; 8 Hispanic/Latino; 4 Two or more races, non-Hispanic/Latino), 5 international. Average age 23. 97 applicants, 92% accepted, 54 enrolled. In 2019, 48 master's awarded. *Degree requirements:* For master's, thesis. *Entrance requirements:* For master's, letter of intent, transcripts, 2 letters of recommendation, portfolio (Architecture only), writing sample (Preservation only); for Certificate, transcripts. Additional exam requirements/recommendations for international students: required—TOEFL (minimum score 85 paper-based), IELTS (minimum score 6.5). *Application deadline:* For fall admission, 1/15 for domestic students, 5/1 for international students. Application fee: $50. Electronic applications accepted. *Expenses:* Tuition per credit hour: Architecture: $1579, Preservation: $951. *Financial support:* In 2019–20, 103 students received support. Scholarships/grants and unspecified assistantships available. Financial award application deadline: 3/15; financial award applicants required to submit FAFSA. *Unit head:* Stephen White, Dean, 401-254-3607, E-mail: swhite@rwu.edu. *Application contact:* Gregory Laramie, Associate Dean, 401-254-3743, E-mail: glaramie@rwu.edu.
Website: https://www.rwu.edu/academics/schools-and-colleges/saahp

Savannah College of Art and Design, Program in Architecture, Savannah, GA 31402-3146. Offers M Arch. *Program availability:* Part-time. *Degree requirements:* For master's, thesis. *Entrance requirements:* For master's, GRE (recommended), portfolio (submitted in digital format), audition or writing submission, resume, statement of purpose, two letters of recommendation. Additional exam requirements/recommendations for international students: recommended—TOEFL (minimum score 550 paper-based; 85 iBT), IELTS (minimum score 6.5). Electronic applications accepted.

School of Architecture at Taliesin, Graduate Program, Scottsdale, AZ 85259. Offers M Arch. *Degree requirements:* For master's, thesis or alternative. *Entrance requirements:* For master's, interviews, portfolio, statement of purpose, resume, 3 letters of recommendation, transcripts. Additional exam requirements/recommendations for international students: required—TOEFL, IELTS. Electronic applications accepted. Application fee is waived when completed online. *Expenses:* Contact institution.

Southern California Institute of Architecture, Center for Advanced Studies, Los Angeles, CA 90013. Offers architectural technologies (MS); design of cities (MS); design theory and pedagogy (MS); fiction and entertainment (MS).

Southern California Institute of Architecture, Graduate Program in Architecture, Los Angeles, CA 90013. Offers M Arch. *Degree requirements:* For master's, thesis, final thesis project. *Entrance requirements:* For master's, GRE General Test, portfolio, 3 letters of recommendation, transcripts, statement of purpose, resume.

Additional exam requirements/recommendations for international students: required—TOEFL (minimum score 583 paper-based, 90 iBT) or IELTS (minimum score 6.5). Electronic applications accepted.

Southern Illinois University Carbondale, Graduate School, College of Applied Science, School of Architecture, Carbondale, IL 62901-4701. Offers M Arch. *Entrance requirements:* Additional exam requirements/recommendations for international students: required—TOEFL (minimum score 550 paper-based; 80 iBT). Electronic applications accepted.

Syracuse University, School of Architecture, Master of Architecture Program, Syracuse, NY 13210. Offers M Arch. *Faculty:* 41 full-time (15 women), 10 part-time/adjunct (2 women). *Students:* 73 full-time (38 women), 50 international. In 2019, 39 master's awarded. *Degree requirements:* For master's, thesis. *Entrance requirements:* For master's, GRE, online portfolio of creative and/or professional work in architecture, the visual arts, design, and/or affiliated fields; personal statement; official transcripts; three letters of recommendation. Optional video response. Additional exam requirements/recommendations for international students: required—TOEFL, IELTS, PTE. *Application deadline:* For fall admission, 1/3 priority date for domestic and international students. Applications are processed on a rolling basis. Application fee: $75. Electronic applications accepted. *Financial support:* Fellowships, research assistantships, teaching assistantships, scholarships/grants, and health care benefits available. Financial award application deadline: 4/15. *Unit head:* Brian Lonsway, Chair, 315-443-2316, E-mail: blonsway@syr.edu. *Application contact:* Lauren Mintier, Graduate Program Manager, 315-443-1041, E-mail: lmintier@syr.edu. Website: http://soa.syr.edu/programs/march/

Syracuse University, School of Architecture, MS in Architecture Program, Syracuse, NY 13210. Offers MS. *Faculty:* 41 full-time (15 women), 10 part-time/adjunct (2 women). *Students:* 17 full-time (11 women), all international. In 2019, 5 master's awarded. *Degree requirements:* For master's, thesis. *Entrance requirements:* For master's, GRE (recommended), online portfolio of creative and/or professional work in architecture, the visual arts, design, and/or affiliated fields; essay; writing sample; official transcripts; three letters of recommendation. Additional exam requirements/recommendations for international students: required—TOEFL, IELTS. *Application deadline:* For fall admission, 1/3 priority date for domestic and international students. Applications are processed on a rolling basis. Application fee: $75. Electronic applications accepted. *Financial support:* Fellowships, research assistantships, teaching assistantships, scholarships/grants, and health care benefits available. Financial award application deadline: 4/15. *Unit head:* Brian Lonsway, Associate Professor/Graduate Chair, 315-443-2316, E-mail: blonsway@syr.edu. *Application contact:* Vittoria Buccina, Asst. Dean, Enrollment Management, 315-443-5074, E-mail: vabuccin@syr.edu. Website: http://soa.syr.edu/programs/post-professional-ms/

Temple University, Tyler School of Art and Architecture, Department of Architecture and Environmental Design, Philadelphia, PA 19122-6096. Offers M Arch. *Program availability:* Part-time. *Faculty:* 21 full-time (7 women), 45 part-time/adjunct (19 women). *Students:* 76 full-time (48 women), 12 part-time (4 women); includes 12 minority (5 Black or African American, non-Hispanic/Latino; 3 Asian, non-Hispanic/Latino; 2 Hispanic/Latino; 2 Two or more races, non-Hispanic/Latino), 13 international. 73 applicants, 89% accepted, 27 enrolled. In 2019, 24 master's awarded. *Degree requirements:* For master's, thesis optional, design studio project, capstone course. *Entrance requirements:* For master's, GRE, statement of goals, 3 letters of recommendation, portfolio, resume. Additional exam requirements/recommendations for international students: required—TOEFL (minimum score 79 iBT), IELTS (minimum score 6.5), PTE (minimum score 53), one of three is required. *Application deadline:* For fall admission, 1/6 for domestic students; for spring admission, 11/1 for domestic students. Applications are processed on a rolling basis. Application fee: $60. Electronic applications accepted. *Expenses:* Contact institution. *Financial support:* Federal Work-Study and scholarships/grants available. Financial award applicants required to submit FAFSA. *Unit head:* Rashida Ng, Associate Professor and Chair of Architecture, 215-204-8813, Fax: 215-204-5481, E-mail: architecture@temple.edu. *Application contact:* Lauren O'Neill, Director of Admissions, 215-777-9159, E-mail: tyleradmissions@temple.edu. Website: https://tyler.temple.edu/programs/architecture

Texas A&M University, College of Architecture, Department of Architecture, College Station, TX 77843. Offers architecture (M Arch, MS). *Faculty:* 44. *Students:* 155 full-time (79 women), 7 part-time (5 women); includes 35 minority (5 Black or African American, non-Hispanic/Latino; 6 Asian, non-Hispanic/Latino; 24 Hispanic/Latino), 85 international. Average age 30. 144 applicants, 69% accepted, 40 enrolled. In 2019, 42 master's, 6 doctorates awarded. *Degree requirements:* For master's, comprehensive exam, thesis (for some programs); for doctorate, comprehensive exam, thesis/dissertation. *Entrance requirements:* For master's, GRE General Test, portfolio, letters of recommendation; for doctorate, GRE General Test. Additional exam requirements/recommendations for international students: required—TOEFL (minimum score 550 paper-based; 80 iBT), IELTS (minimum score 6), PTE (minimum score 53). *Application deadline:* For fall admission, 12/15 priority date for domestic and international students. Applications are processed on a rolling basis. Application fee: $65 ($90 for international students). Electronic applications accepted. *Expenses:* Contact institution. *Financial support:* In 2019–20, 134 students received support, including 5 fellowships with tuition reimbursements available (averaging $8,860 per year), 47 research assistantships with tuition reimbursements available (averaging $9,914 per year), 64 teaching assistantships with tuition reimbursements available (averaging $9,136 per year); career-related internships or fieldwork, institutionally sponsored loans, scholarships/grants, traineeships, health care benefits, tuition waivers (full and partial), and unspecified assistantships also available. Support available to part-time students. Financial award application deadline: 3/15; financial award applicants required to submit FAFSA. *Unit head:* Dr. Robert Warden, Interim Department Head, E-mail: r-warden@tamu.edu. *Application contact:* Graduate Admissions, 979-845-1060, E-mail: graduate-admissions@tamu.edu. Website: http://dept.arch.tamu.edu/

Texas Tech University, Graduate School, College of Architecture, Lubbock, TX 79409-2091. Offers architecture (M Arch, MS); land-use planning, management, and design (PhD); MBA/M Arch. *Program availability:* Part-time. *Faculty:* 35 full-time (13 women), 14 part-time/adjunct (4 women). *Students:* 67 full-time (30 women), 6 part-time (0 women); includes 38 minority (1 Black or African American, non-Hispanic/Latino; 36 Hispanic/Latino; 1 Two or more races, non-Hispanic/Latino), 6 international. Average age 25. 50 applicants, 72% accepted, 24 enrolled. In 2019, 41 master's awarded. *Degree requirements:* For master's, comprehensive exam (for some programs), thesis (for some programs); for doctorate, comprehensive exam, thesis/dissertation. *Entrance requirements:* For master's, GRE General Test, portfolio; for doctorate, GRE General Test. Additional exam requirements/recommendations for international students: required—TOEFL (minimum score 550 paper-based; 79 iBT). *Application deadline:* For fall admission, 6/1 priority date for domestic students, 1/15 priority date for international students; for spring admission, 9/1 priority date for domestic students, 6/15 priority date for international students. Applications are processed on a rolling basis. Application fee: $65. Electronic applications accepted. *Expenses:* Contact institution. *Financial support:* In 2019–20, 73 students received support, including 56 fellowships (averaging $3,795

per year), 11 teaching assistantships (averaging $9,155 per year); research assistantships, career-related internships or fieldwork, Federal Work-Study, institutionally sponsored loans, scholarships/grants, traineeships, health care benefits, and unspecified assistantships also available. Support available to part-time students. Financial award application deadline: 2/1; financial award applicants required to submit FAFSA. *Unit head:* Prof. James P. Williamson, Dean, 806-742-3136, Fax: 806-742-1400, E-mail: james.p.williamson@ttu.edu. *Application contact:* Sarah Hatley, Unit Manager, College Advising, 806-834-5704, Fax: 806-742-1400, E-mail: sarah.hatley@ttu.edu. Website: arch.ttu.edu/

Thomas Jefferson University, College of Architecture and the Built Environment, Program in Architecture, Philadelphia, PA 19107. Offers M Arch, MS. *Entrance requirements:* For master's, bachelor's degree, official undergraduate transcripts, current resume, two letters of recommendation, portfolio of relevant work, personal essay describing intended research.

Tulane University, School of Architecture, New Orleans, LA 70118-5669. Offers M Arch, M Arch II, MPS, MSRED. *Program availability:* Part-time. *Degree requirements:* For master's, thesis. *Entrance requirements:* For master's, GRE, portfolio. Additional exam requirements/recommendations for international students: required—TOEFL. *Expenses:* Contact institution.

Universidad Autonoma de Guadalajara, Graduate Programs, Guadalajara, Mexico. Offers administrative law and justice (LL M); advertising and corporate communications (MA); architecture (M Arch); business (MBA); computational science (MCC); education (Ed M, Ed D); English-Spanish translation (MA); entrepreneurship and management (MBA); integrated management of digital animation (MA); international business (MIB); international corporate law (LL M); Internet technologies (MS); manufacturing systems (MMS); occupational health (MS); philosophy (MA, PhD); power electronics (MS); quality systems (MQS); renewable energy (MS); social evaluation of projects (MBA); strategic market research (MBA); tax law (MA); teaching mathematics (MA).

Universidad Nacional Pedro Henriquez Urena, Graduate School, Santo Domingo, Dominican Republic. Offers agricultural diversity (MS), including horticultural/fruit production, tropical animal production; conservation of monuments and cultural assets (M Arch); ecology and environment (MS); environmental engineering (MEE); international relations (MA); natural resource management (MS); political science (MA); project feasibility (MPM); project management (MPM); project optimization (MPM); sanitation engineering (ME); science for teachers (MS); tropical Caribbean architecture (M Arch).

University at Buffalo, the State University of New York, Graduate School, School of Architecture and Planning, Department of Architecture, Buffalo, NY 14260. Offers architecture (M Arch); ecological practices, inclusive design, situated technologies, historic preservation (MS Arch); M Arch/MBA; M Arch/MFA; M Arch/MUP. *Program availability:* Part-time. *Faculty:* 30 full-time (10 women), 7 part-time/adjunct (4 women). *Students:* 122 full-time (55 women), 9 part-time (6 women); includes 25 minority (6 Black or African American, non-Hispanic/Latino; 11 Asian, non-Hispanic/Latino; 7 Hispanic/Latino; 1 Two or more races, non-Hispanic/Latino), 32 international. Average age 25. 170 applicants, 43% accepted, 57 enrolled. In 2019, 45 master's awarded. *Degree requirements:* For master's, thesis or alternative, project, portfolio. *Entrance requirements:* For master's, portfolio, two letters of recommendation, transcripts, personal statement. Additional exam requirements/recommendations for international students: required—TOEFL (minimum score 79 iBT), IELTS (minimum score 6.5). *Application deadline:* For fall admission, 1/1 priority date for domestic and international students. Application fee: $75. Electronic applications accepted. *Expenses:* Contact institution. *Financial support:* In 2019–20, 86 students received support, including 4 fellowships with full tuition reimbursements available (averaging $15,600 per year), 2 research assistantships with partial tuition reimbursements available (averaging $15,814 per year), 40 teaching assistantships with partial tuition reimbursements available (averaging $5,756 per year); career-related internships or fieldwork, Federal Work-Study, scholarships/grants, health care benefits, tuition waivers (full and partial), and unspecified assistantships also available. Financial award application deadline: 3/1; financial award applicants required to submit FAFSA. *Unit head:* Dr. Korydon Smith, Professor and Chair, 716-829-5908, Fax: 716-829-3256, E-mail: khsmith@buffalo.edu. *Application contact:* Stacey Komendat, Graduate Programs Coordinator, 716-829-3671, Fax: 716-829-3256, E-mail: staceyga@buffalo.edu. Website: http://www.ap.buffalo.edu/architecture/

The University of Arizona, College of Architecture, Planning, and Landscape Architecture, School of Architecture, Tucson, AZ 85721. Offers M Arch, MS. *Entrance requirements:* For master's, GRE, 3 letters of recommendation, statement of purpose, portfolio, resume. Additional exam requirements/recommendations for international students: required—TOEFL (minimum score 550 paper-based; 79 iBT). Electronic applications accepted.

The University of British Columbia, Faculty of Applied Science, School of Architecture and Landscape Architecture, Vancouver, BC V6T 1Z2, Canada. Offers architecture (M Arch, MASA); landscape architecture (MASLA, MLA, MUD), including advanced studies in landscape architecture (MASLA), landscape architecture (MLA), urban design (MUD); M Arch/MLA. *Degree requirements:* For master's, thesis. *Entrance requirements:* For master's, portfolio, resume, statement of interest, 3 reference letters. Additional exam requirements/recommendations for international students: required—TOEFL, IELTS. Electronic applications accepted. *Expenses:* Contact institution.

University of Calgary, School of Architecture, Planning and Landscaping, Program in Environmental Design, Calgary, AB T2N 1N4, Canada. Offers architecture (M Arch); environmental design (M Env Des, PhD); landscape architecture (MLA); planning (M Plan). *Degree requirements:* For master's, thesis; for doctorate, thesis/dissertation. *Entrance requirements:* For master's, minimum GPA of 3.0; for doctorate, minimum GPA of 3.5. Additional exam requirements/recommendations for international students: required—TOEFL (minimum score 550 paper-based).

University of California, Berkeley, Graduate Division, College of Environmental Design, Department of Architecture, Berkeley, CA 94720. Offers architecture (M Arch); building science (MS, PhD); building structures, construction and materials (MS, PhD); design theories, methods, and practices (MS, PhD); environmental design in developing countries (MS, PhD); history of architecture and urbanism (MS, PhD); social and cultural processes in architecture and urbanism (MS, PhD); M Arch/MCP; M Arch/MS; MLA/M Arch. *Degree requirements:* For master's, thesis; for doctorate, thesis/dissertation, qualifying exam. *Entrance requirements:* For master's and doctorate, GRE General Test, minimum GPA of 3.0, 3 letters of recommendation. Additional exam requirements/recommendations for international students: required—TOEFL (minimum score 570 paper-based; 90 iBT). Electronic applications accepted. Application fee is waived when completed online.

University of California, Los Angeles, Graduate Division, School of the Arts and Architecture, Department of Architecture and Urban Design, Los Angeles, CA 90095. Offers M Arch, MA, PhD. *Degree requirements:* For master's, comprehensive exam (M Arch I, II); thesis (MA); for doctorate, 2 foreign languages, thesis/dissertation, oral and written qualifying exams. *Entrance requirements:* For master's, GRE General Test, bachelor's degree; minimum undergraduate GPA of 3.0 (or its equivalent if letter grade system not used); writing sample (MA only); portfolio (M Arch only); for doctorate, GRE General Test, bachelor's degree; minimum undergraduate GPA of 3.5 (or its equivalent if letter grade system not used); writing sample. Additional exam requirements/recommendations for international students: required—TOEFL. Electronic applications accepted. *Expenses:* Contact institution.

University of Cincinnati, Graduate School, College of Design, Architecture, Art, and Planning, School of Architecture and Interior Design, Cincinnati, OH 45221. Offers architecture (M Arch). *Accreditation:* NASAD. *Degree requirements:* For master's, one foreign language, thesis. *Entrance requirements:* Additional exam requirements/recommendations for international students: required—TOEFL.

University of Cincinnati, Graduate School, College of Design, Architecture, Art, and Planning, School of Architecture and Interior Design, PhD Program in Architecture, Cincinnati, OH 45221. Offers MS Arch. *Degree requirements:* For master's, one foreign language, thesis.

University of Colorado Denver, College of Architecture and Planning, Program in Architecture, Denver, CO 80217. Offers M Arch. *Program availability:* Part-time. *Degree requirements:* For master's, thesis optional. *Entrance requirements:* For master's, GRE, portfolio; sample of writing or work project; three letters of recommendation; statement of purpose. Additional exam requirements/recommendations for international students: required—TOEFL (minimum score 75 iBT). Electronic applications accepted. *Expenses:* Contact institution.

University of Florida, Graduate School, College of Design, Construction and Planning, Doctoral Program in Design, Construction and Planning, Gainesville, FL 32611. Offers construction management (PhD); design, construction and planning (PhD); geographic information systems (PhD); historic preservation (PhD); interior design (PhD); landscape architecture (PhD); urban and regional planning (PhD). *Degree requirements:* For doctorate, thesis/dissertation. *Entrance requirements:* For doctorate, GRE General Test, minimum GPA of 3.0. Additional exam requirements/recommendations for international students: required—TOEFL (minimum score 550 paper-based; 80 iBT), IELTS (minimum score 6). Electronic applications accepted.

University of Florida, Graduate School, College of Design, Construction and Planning, School of Architecture, Gainesville, FL 32611. Offers architecture (M Arch, MSAS); historic preservation (M Arch, MSAS); sustainable architecture (M Arch, MSAS); sustainable design (M Arch, MSAS). *Program availability:* Online learning. *Entrance requirements:* For master's, GRE General Test, minimum GPA of 3.0. Additional exam requirements/recommendations for international students: required—TOEFL (minimum score 550 paper-based; 80 iBT), IELTS (minimum score 6).

University of Hartford, College of Engineering, Technology and Architecture, Program in Architecture, West Hartford, CT 06117-1599. Offers M Arch. *Faculty:* 2 full-time (0 women), 4 part-time/adjunct (1 woman). *Students:* 13 full-time (8 women), 6 part-time (0 women); includes 5 minority (2 Black or African American, non-Hispanic/Latino; 3 Hispanic/Latino), 6 international. Average age 26. 12 applicants, 58% accepted, 2 enrolled. In 2019, 13 master's awarded. *Entrance requirements:* For master's, 3 letters of recommendation, portfolio. Additional exam requirements/recommendations for international students: required—TOEFL (minimum score 550 paper-based). *Application deadline:* For fall admission, 2/15 priority date for domestic students. Application fee: $45. *Expenses: Tuition:* Full-time $23,700; part-time $645 per credit. *Required fees:* $510; $510 per unit. Tuition and fees vary according to course load, degree level and program. *Financial support:* In 2019–20, 1 teaching assistantship (averaging $8,000 per year) was awarded. *Unit head:* Michael J. Crosbiu, Chair, 860-768-5136. *Application contact:* Renee Murphy, Assistant Director of Graduate Admissions, 860-768-4371, Fax: 860-768-5160, E-mail: gettoknow@hartford.edu.
Website: http://admission.hartford.edu/graduate/

University of Hawaii at Manoa, School of Architecture, Honolulu, HI 96822. Offers D Arch. *Program availability:* Part-time. *Entrance requirements:* Additional exam requirements/recommendations for international students: required—TOEFL, IELTS.

University of Houston, Gerald D. Hines College of Architecture and Design, Houston, TX 77204. Offers architectural studies (MA); architecture (M Arch, MS), including media and fabrication (MS), sustainable design (MS), sustainable urban systems (MS), urban design (MS); industrial design (MS). *Faculty:* 15 full-time (4 women), 13 part-time/adjunct (3 women). *Students:* 92 full-time (40 women), 6 part-time (2 women); includes 23 minority (1 Black or African American, non-Hispanic/Latino; 1 American Indian or Alaska Native, non-Hispanic/Latino; 9 Asian, non-Hispanic/Latino; 9 Hispanic/Latino; 3 Two or more races, non-Hispanic/Latino), 20 international. Average age 28. 192 applicants, 45% accepted, 47 enrolled. In 2019, 21 master's awarded. *Degree requirements:* For master's, thesis (for some programs). *Entrance requirements:* For master's, GRE General Test, digital portfolio. Additional exam requirements/recommendations for international students: required—TOEFL (minimum score 550 paper-based; 79 iBT), IELTS (minimum score 6.5). *Application deadline:* For fall admission, 2/1 priority date for domestic students, 2/1 for international students. Applications are processed on a rolling basis. Application fee: $50. Electronic applications accepted. *Expenses:* M.Arch + 3 is $50,825.70; M.Arch + 2 is $33,883.80. *Financial support:* In 2019–20, 8 students received support, including 8 research assistantships with tuition reimbursements available (averaging $1,358 per year), 5 teaching assistantships (averaging $3,487 per year); career-related internships or fieldwork, institutionally sponsored loans, scholarships/grants, and unspecified assistantships also available. Financial award application deadline: 1/1; financial award applicants required to submit FAFSA. *Unit head:* Patricia Belton Oliver, Dean, 713-743-2400, Fax: 713-743-2358, E-mail: poliver@central.uh.edu. *Application contact:* Trang Phan, Assistant Dean, 713-743-2400, Fax: 713-743-2358, E-mail: tphan@uh.edu. Website: http://www.uh.edu/architecture/

University of Idaho, College of Graduate Studies, College of Art and Architecture, Moscow, ID 83844-2282. Offers architecture (M Arch); art and design (MFA); bioregional planning and community design (MS); integrated architecture and design (MS); landscape architecture (MLA). *Accreditation:* NASAD. *Students:* 73 full-time, 10 part-time. Average age 28. 105 applicants, 76% accepted, 38 enrolled. In 2019, 32 master's awarded. *Entrance requirements:* For master's, minimum GPA of 3.0. Additional exam requirements/recommendations for international students: required—TOEFL (minimum score 79 iBT). *Application deadline:* For fall admission, 7/30 for domestic students; for spring admission, 12/1 for domestic students. Applications are processed on a rolling basis. Application fee: $60. Electronic applications accepted. *Expenses:* Tuition, state resident: full-time $7753.80; part-time $502 per credit hour. Tuition, nonresident: full-time $26,990; part-time $1571 per credit hour. *Required fees:* $2122.20; $47 per credit hour. *Financial support:* Applicants required to submit FAFSA. *Unit head:* Dr. Shauna Corry, Dean, 208-885-4409, E-mail: caa@uidaho.edu. *Application contact:* Dr. Shauna Corry, Dean, 208-885-4409, E-mail: caa@uidaho.edu. Website: http://www.uidaho.edu/caa

University of Illinois at Chicago, College of Architecture, Design and the Arts, School of Architecture, Chicago, IL 60607-7128. Offers M Arch, MA, MS, MS Arch. *Entrance requirements:* For master's, GRE General Test, portfolio, minimum GPA of 3.0

in the last 60 hours of coursework, 3 letters of recommendation, statement of intent. Additional exam requirements/recommendations for international students: required—TOEFL or IELTS. Electronic applications accepted. *Expenses:* Contact institution.

University of Illinois at Urbana-Champaign, Graduate College, College of Fine and Applied Arts, School of Architecture, Champaign, IL 61820. Offers architectural studies (MS); architecture (M Arch, PhD); M Arch/MBA; M Arch/MS; M Arch/MUP; MCS/M Arch.

The University of Kansas, Graduate Studies, School of Architecture and Design, Department of Architecture, Lawrence, KS 66045. Offers architectural acoustics (Certificate); architecture (M Arch, PhD); health and wellness (Certificate); historic preservation (Certificate); urban design (Certificate). *Students:* 93 full-time (45 women), 23 part-time (13 women); includes 20 minority (4 Black or African American, non-Hispanic/Latino; 5 Asian, non-Hispanic/Latino; 4 Hispanic/Latino; 7 Two or more races, non-Hispanic/Latino), 23 international. Average age 25. 91 applicants, 59% accepted, 30 enrolled. In 2019, 70 master's, 2 doctorates, 8 other advanced degrees awarded. Terminal master's awarded for partial completion of doctoral program. *Entrance requirements:* For master's, GRE, transcript; resume; minimum GPA of 3.0; statement of purpose; letters of recommendation; portfolio of design work, or samples of written work or other creative artifacts produced if previous degree was not in a design-related discipline; for doctorate, GRE, transcript, resume, minimum GPA of 3.0, statement of purpose, letters of recommendation, research-informed writing sample, exhibit of work illustrating applicant's interests and abilities in areas related to the design disciplines. Additional exam requirements/recommendations for international students: required—TOEFL, IELTS. *Application deadline:* For fall admission, 1/15 priority date for domestic and international students; for summer admission, 1/15 priority date for domestic and international students. Application fee: $65 ($85 for international students). Electronic applications accepted. *Expenses:* Tuition, state resident: full-time $9989. Tuition, nonresident: full-time $23,950. *International tuition:* $23,950 full-time. *Required fees:* $984; $81.99 per credit hour. Tuition and fees vary according to course load, campus/location and program. *Financial support:* Fellowships, research assistantships, teaching assistantships, scholarships/grants, health care benefits, and unspecified assistantships available. Financial award application deadline: 1/15; financial award applicants required to submit FAFSA. *Unit head:* Frank Zilm, Dean, 816-561-7186, E-mail: frankzilm@ku.edu. *Application contact:* Joan Weaver, Graduate Admissions Contact, 785-864-3709, Fax: 785-864-5185, E-mail: jweaver@ku.edu. Website: http://architecture.ku.edu/

University of Kentucky, Graduate School, College of Design, School of Architecture, Lexington, KY 40506-0032. Offers M Arch. *Degree requirements:* For master's, comprehensive exam. *Entrance requirements:* For master's, GRE General Test, minimum undergraduate GPA of 2.75. Additional exam requirements/recommendations for international students: required—TOEFL (minimum score 550 paper-based). Electronic applications accepted.

The University of Manchester, School of Environment, Education and Development, Manchester, United Kingdom. Offers architecture (M Phil, PhD); development policy and management (M Phil, PhD); human geography (M Phil, PhD); physical geography (M Phil, PhD); planning and landscape (M Phil, PhD).

University of Manitoba, Faculty of Graduate Studies, Faculty of Architecture, Department of Architecture, Winnipeg, MB R3T 2N2, Canada. Offers M Arch. *Degree requirements:* For master's, thesis or alternative.

University of Maryland, College Park, Academic Affairs, School of Architecture, Planning and Preservation, Program in Architecture, College Park, MD 20742. Offers M Arch, M Arch/MCP. *Program availability:* Part-time, evening/weekend. *Entrance requirements:* For master's, GRE General Test, portfolio, minimum GPA of 3.0, letters of recommendation. Additional exam requirements/recommendations for international students: required—TOEFL. Electronic applications accepted.

University of Massachusetts Amherst, Graduate School, College of Humanities and Fine Arts, Department of Architecture, Amherst, MA 01003. Offers architecture (M Arch); design (MS); design in historic preservation (MS). *Program availability:* Part-time. *Degree requirements:* For master's, thesis or alternative, project. *Entrance requirements:* For master's, GRE General Test (for M Arch only), 3 letters of recommendation (M Arch only); portfolio. Additional exam requirements/recommendations for international students: required—TOEFL (minimum score 550 paper-based; 80 iBT), IELTS (minimum score 6.5). Electronic applications accepted.

University of Memphis, Graduate School, College of Communication and Fine Arts, Department of Architecture, Memphis, TN 38152. Offers M Arch. *Program availability:* Part-time. *Students:* 10 full-time (3 women), 2 part-time (0 women); includes 2 minority (1 Black or African American, non-Hispanic/Latino; 1 Hispanic/Latino), 3 international. Average age 29. 7 applicants, 100% accepted, 2 enrolled. In 2019, 5 master's awarded. *Degree requirements:* For master's, thesis or alternative. *Entrance requirements:* For master's, portfolio; letters of recommendation; statement of intent; pre-professional undergraduate degree in architecture, environmental design, or equivalent. Additional exam requirements/recommendations for international students: required—TOEFL (minimum score 550 paper-based; 79 iBT). *Application deadline:* For fall admission, 3/15 for domestic students. Application fee: $35 ($60 for international students). Electronic applications accepted. *Expenses: Tuition, area resident:* Full-time $9216; part-time $512 per credit hour. Tuition, state resident: full-time $9216; part-time $512 per credit hour. Tuition, nonresident: full-time $12,672; part-time $704 per credit hour. *International tuition:* $16,128 full-time. *Required fees:* $1530; $85 per credit hour. Tuition and fees vary according to program. *Financial support:* Research assistantships with full tuition reimbursements, teaching assistantships with full tuition reimbursements, Federal Work-Study, scholarships/grants, and unspecified assistantships available. Financial award application deadline: 2/1; financial award applicants required to submit FAFSA. *Unit head:* Michael D. Hagge, Chair, 901-678-2677, Fax: 901-678-1755, E-mail: mdhagge@memphis.edu. *Application contact:* Jennifer Barker, Director of Graduate Studies, 901-678-3097, Fax: 901-678-1755, E-mail: jlbrker1@memphis.edu. Website: https://www.memphis.edu/architecture/

University of Miami, Graduate School, School of Architecture, Professional Program in Architecture, Coral Gables, FL 33124. Offers M Arch. *Entrance requirements:* For master's, GRE General Test, minimum GPA of 3.0, portfolio. Additional exam requirements/recommendations for international students: required—TOEFL. Electronic applications accepted.

University of Michigan, Taubman College of Architecture and Urban Planning, Master of Architecture Program, Ann Arbor, MI 48109-2069. Offers M Arch, M Arch/M Eng, M Arch/MSE, M Arch/MUD, MBA/M Arch. *Degree requirements:* For master's, thesis or alternative, thesis studio. *Entrance requirements:* Additional exam requirements/recommendations for international students: required—TOEFL (minimum score 100 iBT), GRE. Electronic applications accepted. *Expenses:* Contact institution.

University of Michigan, Taubman College of Architecture and Urban Planning, Master of Science in Architecture Design and Research Program, Ann Arbor, MI 48109. Offers design and health (MS); digital materials technologies (MS); material systems (MS). *Degree requirements:* For master's, thesis or alternative, capstone studio.

Entrance requirements: Additional exam requirements/recommendations for international students: required—TOEFL (minimum score 100 iBT), GRE. Electronic applications accepted. *Expenses:* Contact institution.

University of Minnesota, Twin Cities Campus, Graduate School, College of Design, School of Architecture, Minneapolis, MN 55455-0213. Offers architecture (M Arch); sustainable design (MS). *Degree requirements:* For master's, thesis (for some programs). *Entrance requirements:* For master's, GRE General Test, suggested GPA of 3.0, portfolio. Additional exam requirements/recommendations for international students: required—TOEFL (minimum score 550 paper-based; 79 iBT). *Expenses:* Contact institution.

University of Missouri, Office of Research and Graduate Studies, College of Human Environmental Sciences, Department of Architectural Studies, Columbia, MO 65211. Offers MS, PhD. *Entrance requirements:* For master's, GRE General Test, minimum GPA of 3.0. Additional exam requirements/recommendations for international students: required—TOEFL (minimum score 500 paper-based; 61 iBT). Electronic applications accepted.

University of Nebraska–Lincoln, Graduate College, College of Architecture, Department of Architecture, Graduate Program in Architecture, Lincoln, NE 68588. Offers MS, PhD. *Degree requirements:* For master's, comprehensive exam, thesis. *Entrance requirements:* For master's, GRE General Test. Additional exam requirements/recommendations for international students: required—TOEFL (minimum score 550 paper-based). Electronic applications accepted.

University of Nebraska–Lincoln, Graduate College, College of Architecture, Department of Architecture, Professional Program in Architecture, Lincoln, NE 68588. Offers M Arch, M Arch/MBA, M Arch/MCRP. *Entrance requirements:* For master's, GRE General Test. Additional exam requirements/recommendations for international students: required—TOEFL.

University of Nevada, Las Vegas, Graduate College, College of Fine Arts, School of Architecture, Las Vegas, NV 89154. Offers architecture (M Arch); healthcare interior design (MHID); hospitality design (Certificate). *Program availability:* Part-time. *Faculty:* 9 full-time (2 women), 2 part-time/adjunct (0 women). *Students:* 39 full-time (15 women), 4 part-time (3 women); includes 24 minority (1 Black or African American, non-Hispanic/Latino; 8 Asian, non-Hispanic/Latino; 14 Hispanic/Latino; 1 Two or more races, non-Hispanic/Latino), 4 international. Average age 28. 36 applicants, 92% accepted, 25 enrolled. In 2019, 19 master's awarded. *Degree requirements:* For master's, thesis (for some programs), professional project; for Certificate, defense of design/research presentation. *Entrance requirements:* For master's, GRE General Test, design portfolio; writing sample; bachelor's degree with minimum GPA of 3.0; for Certificate, portfolio of original work. Additional exam requirements/recommendations for international students: required—TOEFL (minimum score 550 paper-based; 80 iBT), IELTS (minimum score 7). *Application deadline:* For fall admission, 1/15 for domestic and international students. Application fee: $60 ($95 for international students). Electronic applications accepted. *Expenses:* Contact institution. *Financial support:* In 2019–20, 14 students received support, including 5 research assistantships with full tuition reimbursements available (averaging $15,000 per year), 12 teaching assistantships with full tuition reimbursements available (averaging $14,875 per year); institutionally sponsored loans, scholarships/grants, health care benefits, and unspecified assistantships also available. Financial award application deadline: 3/15; financial award applicants required to submit FAFSA. *Unit head:* Dr. Daniel Ortega, Chair, 702-895-1908, Fax: 702-895-1119, E-mail: architecture.chair@unlv.edu. *Application contact:* Dr. Joshua Vermillion, Graduate Coordinator, 702-895-1905, Fax: 702-895-1119, E-mail: architecture.gradcoord@unlv.edu.
Website: http://architecture.unlv.edu/

University of New Mexico, Graduate Studies, College of Fine Arts, Program in Art History, Albuquerque, NM 87131-2039. Offers art history (MA); art of the Americas (MA); history of architecture (PhD); history of graphic arts (PhD); history of photography (PhD); modern Latin American art (PhD); Native American art (PhD); Pre-Columbian art and architecture (PhD); Spanish colonial art (PhD). *Program availability:* Part-time. *Degree requirements:* For master's, one foreign language, comprehensive exam (for some programs), thesis, symposium; for doctorate, 2 foreign languages, comprehensive exam, thesis/dissertation, symposium. *Entrance requirements:* Additional exam requirements/recommendations for international students: required—TOEFL (minimum score 550 paper-based), IELTS (minimum score 6). Electronic applications accepted. *Expenses:* Tuition, state resident: full-time $7633; part-time $972 per year. Tuition, nonresident: full-time $22,586; part-time $3840 per year. *International tuition:* $23,292 full-time. *Required fees:* $8608. Tuition and fees vary according to course level, course load, degree level, program and student level.

University of New Mexico, Graduate Studies, School of Architecture and Planning, Program in Architecture, Albuquerque, NM 87131-2039. Offers M Arch. *Entrance requirements:* For master's, experience in field. Additional exam requirements/recommendations for international students: required—TOEFL (minimum score 550 paper-based; 79 iBT). Electronic applications accepted. *Expenses:* Tuition, state resident: full-time $7633; part-time $972 per year. Tuition, nonresident: full-time $22,586; part-time $3840 per year. *International tuition:* $23,292 full-time. *Required fees:* $8608. Tuition and fees vary according to course level, course load, degree level, program and student level.

The University of North Carolina at Charlotte, College of Arts and Architecture, School of Architecture, Charlotte, NC 28223-0001. Offers architecture (M Arch I, M Arch II, MS); urban design (MUD). *Faculty:* 25 full-time (11 women), 4 part-time/adjunct (0 women). *Students:* 79 full-time (35 women), 7 part-time (2 women); includes 25 minority (11 Black or African American, non-Hispanic/Latino; 3 Asian, non-Hispanic/Latino; 8 Hispanic/Latino; 3 Two or more races, non-Hispanic/Latino), 13 international. Average age 26. 119 applicants, 87% accepted, 36 enrolled. In 2019, 62 master's awarded. *Entrance requirements:* For master's, Official GRE Test scores (TOEFL scores where applicable), official transcripts from all previous college-level institution(s); statement of purpose explaining reasons for wanting to study in the School of Architecture; three recommendations from persons familiar with the applicant's personal and professional qualifications; resume or curriculum vitae; portfolio. Additional exam requirements/recommendations for international students: required—TOEFL (minimum score 557 paper-based; 83 iBT), IELTS (minimum score 6.5), TOEFL (minimum score 557 paper-based, 83 iBT) or IELTS (6.5). *Application deadline:* For fall admission, 1/15 priority date for domestic students. Applications are processed on a rolling basis. Application fee: $75. Electronic applications accepted. *Expenses:* Contact institution. *Financial support:* In 2019–20, 20 students received support, including 12 research assistantships (averaging $6,113 per year), 8 teaching assistantships (averaging $3,170 per year); institutionally sponsored loans, scholarships/grants, unspecified assistantships, and administrative assistantship also available. Financial award application deadline: 3/1; financial award applicants required to submit FAFSA. *Unit head:* Peter Wong, Director, Graduate School Programs, 704-687-0134, E-mail: plwong@uncc.edu. *Application contact:* Kathy B. Giddings, Director of Graduate Admissions, 704-687-5503, Fax: 704-687-1668, E-mail: gradadm@uncc.edu.
Website: http://coaa.uncc.edu/academics/school-of-architecture

The University of North Carolina at Greensboro, Graduate School, College of Arts and Sciences, Department of Interior Architecture, Greensboro, NC 27412-5001. Offers historic preservation (Certificate); interior architecture (MS); museum studies (Certificate). *Degree requirements:* For master's, thesis. *Entrance requirements:* For master's, GRE General Test or MAT, bachelor's degree in interior design, interview, portfolio. Additional exam requirements/recommendations for international students: required—TOEFL. Electronic applications accepted.

University of Notre Dame, The Graduate School, School of Architecture, Notre Dame, IN 46556. Offers architectural design and urbanism (M ADU); architecture (M Arch). *Degree requirements:* For master's, thesis or alternative. *Entrance requirements:* For master's, GRE General Test, portfolio. Additional exam requirements/recommendations for international students: required—TOEFL (minimum score 600 paper-based; 80 iBT). Electronic applications accepted.

University of Oklahoma, Christopher C. Gibbs College of Architecture, Division of Architecture, Norman, OK 73019-0390. Offers architecture (MS); data and digital representation (M Arch); design entrepreneurship and real estate (M Arch); planning, design and construction (PhD); resilient planning, design, and construction (M Arch). *Program availability:* Part-time. Terminal master's awarded for partial completion of doctoral program. *Degree requirements:* For master's, variable foreign language requirement; for doctorate, variable foreign language requirement, comprehensive exam, thesis/dissertation. *Entrance requirements:* Additional exam requirements/recommendations for international students: required—TOEFL (minimum score 79 iBT) or IELTS (minimum score 6.5). Electronic applications accepted. *Expenses:* Tuition, state resident: full-time $6583.20; part-time $274.30 per credit hour. Tuition, nonresident: full-time $21,242; part-time $885.10 per credit hour. *International tuition:* $21,242.40 full-time. *Required fees:* $1994.20; $72.55 per credit hour. $126.50 per semester. Tuition and fees vary according to course load and degree level.

University of Oregon, Graduate School, College of Design, Department of Architecture, Eugene, OR 97403. Offers architecture (M Arch); interior architecture (MI Arch). *Accreditation:* CIDA. *Degree requirements:* For master's, thesis (for some programs). *Entrance requirements:* For master's, GRE General Test. Additional exam requirements/recommendations for international students: required—TOEFL.

University of Pennsylvania, Stuart Weitzman School of Design, Department of Architecture, Philadelphia, PA 19104. Offers architecture (M Arch, PhD); ecological architecture (Certificate); environmental building design (MEBD). *Program availability:* Part-time. *Faculty:* 14 full-time (5 women), 12 part-time/adjunct (3 women). *Students:* 380 full-time (208 women), 1 (woman) part-time; includes 44 minority (2 Black or African American, non-Hispanic/Latino; 17 Asian, non-Hispanic/Latino; 22 Hispanic/Latino; 3 Two or more races, non-Hispanic/Latino), 263 international. Average age 26. 893 applicants, 43% accepted, 136 enrolled. In 2019, 134 master's, 2 doctorates, 33 other advanced degrees awarded. Application fee: $80. *Application contact:* Lauren Hoover, Admission & Recruitment Coordinator, 215-898-6520, E-mail: lhoover@design.upenn.edu.

University of Puerto Rico at Rio Piedras, School of Architecture, San Juan, PR 00931-3300. Offers M Arch. *Program availability:* Part-time. *Degree requirements:* For master's, comprehensive exam, thesis, design project. *Entrance requirements:* For master's, PAEG or GRE, bachelor's degree in architecture, interview, minimum GPA of 3.0, portfolio, 2 letters of recommendation.

University of Southern California, Graduate School, School of Architecture, Los Angeles, CA 90089. Offers architecture (M Arch); building science (MBS); heritage conservation (MHP); landscape architecture and urbanism (MLA); M Arch/M Pl; MLA/M Pl. Terminal master's awarded for partial completion of doctoral program. *Degree requirements:* For master's, thesis (for some programs). *Entrance requirements:* For master's, GRE. Additional exam requirements/recommendations for international students: required—TOEFL (minimum score 100 iBT). Electronic applications accepted.

University of South Florida, College of The Arts, School of Architecture and Community Design, Tampa, FL 33620-9951. Offers architecture (M Arch). *Faculty:* 8 full-time (0 women). *Students:* 74 full-time (40 women), 19 part-time (8 women); includes 33 minority (7 Black or African American, non-Hispanic/Latino; 9 Asian, non-Hispanic/Latino; 14 Hispanic/Latino; 3 Two or more races, non-Hispanic/Latino), 19 international. Average age 26. 59 applicants, 39% accepted, 17 enrolled. In 2019, 42 master's awarded. *Degree requirements:* For master's, comprehensive exam, thesis. *Entrance requirements:* For master's, GRE General Test, three letters of recommendation; portfolio or creative work; written statement of intent; prerequisite courses in physics, calculus, and AutoCAD. Additional exam requirements/recommendations for international students: required—TOEFL, TOEFL (minimum score 550 paper-based; 79 iBT) or IELTS (minimum score 6.5). *Application deadline:* For fall admission, 2/1 priority date for domestic students, 2/1 for international students. Applications are processed on a rolling basis. Application fee: $30. Electronic applications accepted. *Financial support:* In 2019–20, 43 students received support, including 3 teaching assistantships with tuition reimbursements available (averaging $9,360 per year); Federal Work-Study, scholarships/grants, and unspecified assistantships also available. *Unit head:* Dr. Robert MacLeod, Director and Professor, School of Architecture and Community Design, 813-974-6015, Fax: 813-974-2557, E-mail: rmacleod@arch.usf.edu. *Application contact:* Mildred Abreu, Academic Advisor, 813-974-1216, Fax: 813-974-2557, E-mail: abreu@arch.usf.edu.
Website: http://www.arch.usf.edu/

The University of Tennessee, Graduate School, College of Architecture and Design, Program in Architecture, Knoxville, TN 37996. Offers architecture (professional) (M Arch); architecture (research) (M Arch). *Degree requirements:* For master's, thesis. *Entrance requirements:* For master's, GRE General Test, minimum GPA of 3.0, 3 letters of recommendation, samples of portfolio work (highly recommended for professional track). Additional exam requirements/recommendations for international students: required—TOEFL (minimum score 550 paper-based).

The University of Texas at Arlington, Graduate School, College of Architecture, Planning and Public Affairs, Program in Architecture, Arlington, TX 76019. Offers M Arch. *Degree requirements:* For master's, thesis. *Entrance requirements:* For master's, GRE General Test, minimum GPA of 3.0, portfolio (for those with previous design degrees). Additional exam requirements/recommendations for international students: required—TOEFL (minimum score 575 paper-based; 91 iBT).

The University of Texas at Austin, Graduate School, School of Architecture, Program in Architecture, Austin, TX 78712-1111. Offers M Arch, MSAS. *Entrance requirements:* For master's, GRE, transcripts, portfolio, statement of interest, references.

The University of Texas at San Antonio, College of Architecture, Construction and Planning, Department of Architecture, San Antonio, TX 78249-0617. Offers M Arch, MS Arch. *Program availability:* Part-time. *Degree requirements:* For master's, comprehensive exam (for some programs), thesis optional. *Entrance requirements:* For master's, GRE General Test, bachelor's degree with 18 credit hours in field of study or in another appropriate field of study, 2 letters of recommendation, statement of purpose. Additional exam requirements/recommendations for international students: required—

TOEFL (minimum score 550 paper-based; 79 iBT), IELTS (minimum score 6.5). Electronic applications accepted.

University of the District of Columbia, College of Agriculture, Urban Sustainability and Environmental Sciences, Program in Architecture, Washington, DC 20008-1175. Offers M Arch, M Arch II.

University of Toronto, School of Graduate Studies, John H. Daniels Faculty of Architecture, Landscape, and Design, Toronto, ON M5S 1A1, Canada. Offers M Arch, MLA, MUD, MVS. *Entrance requirements:* For master's, minimum B average; 3 letters of reference; resume; 3 writing samples; 5 samples of design work, drawing, or work in a related field, statement of interest. Additional exam requirements/recommendations for international students: required—TOEFL (minimum score 580 paper-based; 93 iBT), IELTS (minimum score 7), TWE (minimum score 5), Michigan English Language Assessment Battery (minimum score 85), COPE (minimum score 76). Electronic applications accepted. *Expenses:* Contact institution.

University of Utah, Graduate School, College of Architecture and Planning, Department of Architecture, Salt Lake City, UT 84112. Offers architectural studies (MS); architecture (M Arch). *Faculty:* 10 full-time (4 women), 3 part-time/adjunct (0 women). *Students:* 70 full-time (28 women); includes 23 minority (3 Asian, non-Hispanic/Latino; 16 Hispanic/Latino; 4 Two or more races, non-Hispanic/Latino), 3 international. Average age 27. 76 applicants, 82% accepted, 42 enrolled. In 2019, 28 master's awarded. *Degree requirements:* For master's, final project. *Entrance requirements:* For master's, GRE, minimum undergraduate GPA of 3.0; portfolio; statement of purpose; letters of recommendation; resume. Additional exam requirements/recommendations for international students: required—TOEFL (minimum score 80 paper-based). *Application deadline:* For fall admission, 1/10 priority date for domestic and international students. Applications are processed on a rolling basis. Application fee: $55 ($65 for international students). Electronic applications accepted. Application fee is waived when completed online. *Expenses:* Approximately $8000 per semester for residents; approximately $18,000 per semester for non-residents. *Financial support:* In 2019–20, 47 students received support, including 17 fellowships (averaging $9,412 per year), 33 teaching assistantships with partial tuition reimbursements available (averaging $4,818 per year); unspecified assistantships also available. Financial award application deadline: 4/15. *Unit head:* Lisa Henry, Interim Chair, 801-581-8353, E-mail: henry@arch.utah.edu. *Application contact:* Linda Bastyr, Administrative Officer/Advisor, 801-585-5354, E-mail: bastyr@arch.utah.edu.
Website: http://www.arch.utah.edu/?school_of_architecture

University of Virginia, School of Architecture, Department of Architecture, Charlottesville, VA 22903. Offers M Arch. *Entrance requirements:* For master's, GRE General Test, 3 letters of recommendation; portfolio. Additional exam requirements/recommendations for international students: required—TOEFL (minimum score 600 paper-based; 90 iBT). Electronic applications accepted.

University of Washington, Graduate School, College of Built Environments, Department of Architecture, Seattle, WA 98195. Offers architecture (M Arch, MS); built environment (PhD); design computing (Certificate); design firm leadership and management (Certificate); historic preservation (Certificate); lighting (Certificate); urban design (Certificate). *Degree requirements:* For master's, thesis. *Entrance requirements:* For master's, GRE General Test, minimum GPA of 3.0, portfolio, 3 letters of recommendation. Additional exam requirements/recommendations for international students: required—TOEFL.

University of Waterloo, Graduate Studies and Postdoctoral Affairs, Faculty of Engineering, School of Architecture, Waterloo, ON N2L 3G1, Canada. Offers M Arch. *Program availability:* Part-time. *Degree requirements:* For master's, thesis. *Entrance requirements:* For master's, bachelor's degree in pre-professional architecture. Additional exam requirements/recommendations for international students: required—TOEFL, IELTS, PTE. Electronic applications accepted.

University of Wisconsin–Milwaukee, Graduate School, School of Architecture and Urban Planning, Department of Architecture, Milwaukee, WI 53201-0413. Offers architecture (M Arch, MS Arch, PhD); geographic information systems (Graduate Certificate). *Degree requirements:* For master's, comprehensive exam, thesis; for doctorate, comprehensive exam, thesis/dissertation. *Entrance requirements:* For master's, GRE General Test, portfolio. Additional exam requirements/recommendations for international students: required—TOEFL (minimum score 600 paper-based; 100 iBT), IELTS (minimum score 7). Electronic applications accepted.

Université Laval, Faculty of Architecture, Planning and Visual Arts, School of Architecture, Program in Architecture, Québec, QC G1K 7P4, Canada. Offers M Arch, M Sc. *Program availability:* Part-time. *Degree requirements:* For master's, thesis (for some programs). *Entrance requirements:* For master's, mastery of software (CAO), knowledge of French and English. Electronic applications accepted.

Washington State University, Voiland College of Engineering and Architecture, Program in Architecture, Pullman, WA 99164-2220. Offers architecture (M Arch). *Degree requirements:* For master's, comprehensive exam, thesis, oral exam. *Entrance requirements:* For master's, minimum GPA of 3.0, 3 letters of recommendation, personal statement, portfolio. Additional exam requirements/recommendations for international students: required—TOEFL (minimum score 80 iBT), IELTS.

Washington University in St. Louis, Sam Fox School of Design and Visual Arts, Program in Architecture, St. Louis, MO 63130-4899. Offers M Arch, MLA, M Arch/MBA, M Arch/MCM, M Arch/MSW, M Arch/MUD, MLA/M Arch. *Degree requirements:* For master's, final project. *Entrance requirements:* For master's, GRE General Test, portfolio. Additional exam requirements/recommendations for international students: required—TOEFL (minimum score 550 paper-based; 80 iBT), TWE. Electronic applications accepted.

Wentworth Institute of Technology, Department of Architecture, Boston, MA 02115-5998. Offers M Arch. *Degree requirements:* For master's, thesis project. *Entrance requirements:* For master's, GRE, statement of objectives, resume or curriculum vitae, recommendation letters, official transcripts, portfolio. Additional exam requirements/recommendations for international students: required—TOEFL (minimum score 525 paper-based). Electronic applications accepted. *Expenses:* Contact institution.

Woodbury University, School of Architecture, Burbank, CA 91504-1052. Offers M Arch, MIA, MS Arch. *Degree requirements:* For master's, thesis. *Entrance requirements:* For master's, GRE (if undergraduate GPA is below 3.0), 3 letters of recommendation, portfolio, essay, interview, resume, academic transcripts. Additional exam requirements/recommendations for international students: required—TOEFL (minimum score 550 paper-based; 83 iBT), IELTS (minimum score 6.5). *Expenses:* Contact institution.

Yale University, School of Architecture, New Haven, CT 06520. Offers M Arch, M Env Des, MEM, PhD, M Arch/M Env Des, M Arch/MBA. *Entrance requirements:* For master's, GRE General Test, design portfolio. Additional exam requirements/recommendations for international students: required—TOEFL. Electronic applications accepted. *Expenses:* Contact institution.

Building Science

Arizona State University at Tempe, Herberger Institute for Design and the Arts, The Design School, Tempe, AZ 85287-1605. Offers architecture (M Arch); building design/built environment (MS); design (MSD), including arts, media, and engineering, healthcare and healing environments (MSD, PhD), industrial design, interaction design, interior design, new product innovation, visual communication design; design, environment and the arts (PhD), including design, digital culture, healthcare and healing environments (MSD, PhD), history, theory, and criticism; landscape architecture (MLA); urban design (MUD); MA/MBA. *Accreditation:* ASLA; NASAD. Terminal master's awarded for partial completion of doctoral program. *Degree requirements:* For master's, thesis optional, interactive Program of Study (iPOS) submitted before completing 50 percent of required credit hours; for doctorate, comprehensive exam, thesis/dissertation, interactive Program of Study (iPOS) submitted before completing 50 percent of required credit hours. *Entrance requirements:* For master's, GRE General Test, minimum GPA of 3.0 or equivalent in last 2 years of work leading to bachelor's degree, design/creative works portfolio, 3 references, statement of intent; for doctorate, GRE, master's degree in architecture, graphic design, industrial design, interior design, landscape architecture, or art history or equivalent standing; statement of purpose; 3 letters of recommendation; indication of potential faculty mentor; sample of written work. Additional exam requirements/recommendations for international students: required—TOEFL (minimum score 600 paper-based; 100 iBT). Electronic applications accepted.

Carnegie Mellon University, College of Fine Arts, School of Architecture, Pittsburgh, PA 15213-3891. Offers architecture (MSA); architecture, engineering, and construction management (PhD); building performance and diagnostics (MS, PhD); computational design (MS, PhD); engineering construction management (MSA); tangible interaction design (MTID); urban design (MUD). Terminal master's awarded for partial completion of doctoral program. *Degree requirements:* For doctorate, thesis/dissertation. *Entrance requirements:* For master's and doctorate, GRE General Test. Additional exam requirements/recommendations for international students: required—TOEFL.

Georgia Institute of Technology, Graduate Studies, College of Design, School of Building Construction, Atlanta, GA 30332-0001. Offers building construction (PhD); integrated facility and property management (MS); integrated project delivery systems (MS); program management (MS); residential construction development (MS). *Program availability:* Part-time, evening/weekend. *Entrance requirements:* For master's and doctorate, GRE or GMAT. Additional exam requirements/recommendations for international students: required—TOEFL (minimum score 550 paper-based). Electronic applications accepted. *Expenses: Tuition, area resident:* Full-time $14,064; part-time $586 per credit hour. Tuition, state resident: full-time $14,064; part-time $586 per credit hour. Tuition, nonresident: full-time $29,140; part-time $1215 per credit hour. *International tuition:* $29,140 full-time. *Required fees:* $2024; $840 per semester. $2096. Tuition and fees vary according to course load.

Pontificia Universidad Catolica Madre y Maestra, Graduate School, Faculty of Engineering Sciences, Santiago, Dominican Republic. Offers earthquake engineering (ME); logistics management (ME).

University of California, Berkeley, Graduate Division, College of Environmental Design, Department of Architecture, Berkeley, CA 94720. Offers architecture (M Arch); building science (MS, PhD); building structures, construction and materials (MS, PhD); design theories, methods, and practices (MS, PhD); environmental design in developing countries (MS, PhD); history of architecture and urbanism (MS, PhD); social and cultural processes in architecture and urbanism (MS, PhD); M Arch/MCP; M Arch/MS; MLA/M Arch. *Degree requirements:* For master's, thesis; for doctorate, thesis/dissertation, qualifying exam. *Entrance requirements:* For master's and doctorate, GRE General Test, minimum GPA of 3.0, 3 letters of recommendation. Additional exam requirements/recommendations for international students: required—TOEFL (minimum score 570 paper-based; 90 iBT). Electronic applications accepted. Application fee is waived when completed online.

Environmental Design

Arizona State University at Tempe, Herberger Institute for Design and the Arts, The Design School, PhD Program in Design, Environment and the Arts, Tempe, AZ 85287-2105. Offers design (PhD); digital culture (PhD); healthcare and healing environments (PhD); history, theory, and criticism (PhD). *Degree requirements:* For doctorate, comprehensive exam, thesis/dissertation, interactive Program of Study (iPOS) submitted before completing 50 percent of required credit hours. *Entrance requirements:* For doctorate, GRE, master's degree in architecture, graphic design, industrial design, interior design, landscape architecture, or art history or equivalent standing; statement of purpose; 3 letters of recommendation; indication of potential faculty mentor; sample of written work. Additional exam requirements/recommendations for international students: required—TOEFL, IELTS, or PTE. Electronic applications accepted. *Expenses:* Contact institution.

ArtCenter College of Design, Graduate Environmental Design Program, Pasadena, CA 91103. Offers furniture and fixtures (MS); spatial experience (MS).

Columbia University, School of Professional Studies, Program in Landscape Design, New York, NY 10027. Offers MS. *Program availability:* Part-time. *Entrance requirements:* For master's, minimum undergraduate GPA of 3.0. Additional exam requirements/recommendations for international students: required—American Language Program placement test. *Expenses: Tuition:* Full-time $47,600; part-time $1880 per credit. One-time fee: $105.

Cornell University, Graduate School, Graduate Fields of Human Ecology, Field of Design and Environmental Analysis, Ithaca, NY 14853. Offers applied research in human-environment relations (MS); facilities planning and management (MS); housing and design (MS); human factors and ergonomics (MS); human-environment relations (MS); interior design (MA, MPS). *Degree requirements:* For master's, thesis. *Entrance requirements:* For master's, GRE General Test, portfolio or slides of recent work; bachelor's degree in interior design, architecture or related design discipline; 2 letters of recommendation. Additional exam requirements/recommendations for international students: required—TOEFL (minimum score 600 paper-based; 105 iBT). Electronic applications accepted.

Kansas State University, Graduate School, College of Architecture, Planning and Design, Interdisciplinary Doctoral Program in Environmental Design and Planning, Manhattan, KS 66506. Offers PhD. *Degree requirements:* For doctorate, comprehensive exam, thesis/dissertation, preliminary exam, oral exam. *Entrance requirements:* For doctorate, GRE, transcript(s), statement of intent, three letters of recommendation, portfolio. Additional exam requirements/recommendations for international students: required—TOEFL (minimum score 600 paper-based; 100 iBT), IELTS (minimum score 7), PTE (minimum score 70). Electronic applications accepted.

Kent State University, College of Architecture and Environmental Design, Kent, OH 44242-0001. Offers architecture (M Arch); architecture and environmental design (MS); health care design (MHCD); landscape architecture (MLA); urban design (MUD); M Arch/MBA; M Arch/MUD. *Accreditation:* ASLA. *Program availability:* Part-time. *Faculty:* 19 full-time (5 women), 9 part-time/adjunct (3 women). *Students:* 62 full-time (29 women), 12 part-time (9 women); includes 8 minority (3 Black or African American, non-Hispanic/Latino; 1 Asian, non-Hispanic/Latino; 2 Hispanic/Latino; 2 Two or more races, non-Hispanic/Latino), 11 international. Average age 26. 149 applicants, 87% accepted, 69 enrolled. In 2019, 66 master's awarded. *Degree requirements:* For master's, thesis (for some programs), capstone project (for some programs). *Entrance requirements:* For master's, GRE with minimum scores 151 (460) verbal reasoning, 150 (620) quantitative reasoning, and 4.25 analytical writing (except for MHCD), letters of recommendation, portfolio. Additional exam requirements/recommendations for international students: required—TOEFL (minimum score 80 iBT), IELTS (minimum score 6.5), PTE (minimum score 54), Michigan English Language Assessment Battery (minimum score 77). *Application deadline:* For fall admission, 1/15 for domestic students; for spring admission, 6/1 for domestic students. Applications are processed on a rolling basis. Application fee: $45 ($70 for international students). Electronic applications accepted. *Financial support:* Research assistantships with full tuition reimbursements, teaching assistantships with full tuition reimbursements, Federal Work-Study, scholarships/grants, and unspecified assistantships available. Financial award application deadline: 2/1; financial award applicants required to submit FAFSA. *Unit head:* Mark Mistur, Dean, 330-672-2917, E-mail: mmistur1@kent.edu. *Application contact:* Bill Willoughby, Associate Dean, 330-672-2917, E-mail: wwilloug@kenk.edu. Website: http://www.kent.edu/caed

Michigan State University, The Graduate School, College of Agriculture and Natural Resources and College of Social Science, School of Planning, Design and Construction, East Lansing, MI 48824. Offers construction management (MS, PhD); environmental design (MA); interior design and facilities management (MA); international planning studies (MIPS); urban and regional planning (MURP). *Degree requirements:* For master's, thesis or alternative. *Entrance requirements:* Additional exam requirements/recommendations for international students: required—TOEFL. Electronic applications accepted.

North Carolina Agricultural and Technical State University, The Graduate College, College of Agriculture and Environmental Sciences, Department of Natural Resources and Environmental Design, Greensboro, NC 27411. Offers plant, soil and environmental science (MS). *Program availability:* Part-time, evening/weekend. *Degree requirements:* For master's, comprehensive exam, thesis optional, qualifying exam. *Entrance requirements:* For master's, GRE General Test, minimum GPA of 3.0.

Texas Tech University, Graduate School, College of Human Sciences, Department of Design, Lubbock, TX 79409-1220. Offers environmental design (MS); interior and environmental design (PhD). *Program availability:* Part-time. *Faculty:* 12 full-time (10 women). *Students:* 19 full-time (13 women), 8 part-time (5 women); includes 4 minority (3 Hispanic/Latino; 1 Two or more races, non-Hispanic/Latino), 16 international. Average age 35. 8 applicants, 38% accepted, 1 enrolled. In 2019, 7 master's, 2 doctorates awarded. *Degree requirements:* For master's, comprehensive exam, thesis or alternative; for doctorate, comprehensive exam, thesis/dissertation. *Entrance requirements:* For master's, 3 recommendation letters, design portfolio, 500-word written statement (reason for pursuing degree); resume; for doctorate, 3 recommendation letters, 500-word written statement (reason for pursuing degree), resume. Design portfolio required for those wishing to apply for teaching assistantships. Additional exam requirements/recommendations for international students: required—TOEFL (minimum score 550 paper-based; 79 iBT), Required to take either IELTS or TOEFL. Minimum for IELTS is 6.5. *Application deadline:* For fall admission, 6/1 priority date for domestic students, 1/15 priority date for international students; for spring admission, 9/1 priority date for domestic students, 6/15 priority date for international students. Applications are processed on a rolling basis. Application fee: $65. Electronic applications accepted. *Expenses:* Contact institution. *Financial support:* In 2019–20, 13 students received

support, including 11 fellowships (averaging $9,664 per year), 6 research assistantships (averaging $7,638 per year); teaching assistantships, scholarships/grants, and unspecified assistantships also available. Financial award application deadline: 4/15; financial award applicants required to submit FAFSA. *Unit head:* Dr. Sharran F. Parkinson, Professor, Graduate Program Director, Department Chairperson, 806-742-3031, Fax: 806-742-1639, E-mail: sharran.parkinson@ttu.edu. *Application contact:* Erin Rebecca Sopronyi, Senior Office Manager, 806-742-3050, Fax: 806-742-1639, E-mail: erin.r.sopronyi@ttu.edu. Website: www.dod.ttu.edu

Université de Montréal, Faculty of Environmental Design and Planning, Montréal, QC H3C 3J7, Canada. Offers environmental design and planning (M Sc A, PhD); environmental planning and design projects (DESS); game design (DESS); urban management for developing countries (DESS); urban planning (M Urb). *Accreditation:* ACSP. *Degree requirements:* For doctorate, thesis/dissertation, general exam. Electronic applications accepted. *Expenses:* Contact institution.

University of Calgary, School of Architecture, Planning and Landscaping, Program in Environmental Design, Calgary, AB T2N 1N4, Canada. Offers architecture (M Arch); environmental design (M Env Des, PhD); landscape architecture (MLA); planning (M Plan). *Degree requirements:* For master's, thesis; for doctorate, thesis/dissertation. *Entrance requirements:* For master's, minimum GPA of 3.0; for doctorate, minimum GPA of 3.5. Additional exam requirements/recommendations for international students: required—TOEFL (minimum score 550 paper-based).

University of California, Berkeley, Graduate Division, College of Environmental Design, Department of Landscape Architecture and Environmental Planning, Berkeley, CA 94720. Offers landscape architecture (MLA), including environmental planning, landscape design and site planning, urban and community design; landscape architecture and environmental planning (PhD); MLA/M Arch; MLA/MCP. *Accreditation:* ASLA (one or more programs are accredited). *Degree requirements:* For master's, comprehensive exam (for some programs), thesis (for some programs), professional project or thesis; for doctorate, one foreign language, thesis/dissertation, qualifying exam. *Entrance requirements:* For master's, GRE General Test, minimum GPA of 3.0, portfolio; for doctorate, GRE General Test, master's degree (strongly recommended), minimum GPA of 3.0, sample of written work, 3 letters of recommendation. Additional exam requirements/recommendations for international students: required—TOEFL (minimum score 570 paper-based; 90 iBT). Electronic applications accepted.

University of California, Irvine, School of Social Ecology, Programs in Social Ecology, Irvine, CA 92697. Offers environmental analysis and design (PhD); epidemiology and public health (PhD); social ecology (PhD). *Students:* 19 full-time (15 women); includes 7 minority (3 Black or African American, non-Hispanic/Latino; 1 Asian, non-Hispanic/Latino; 2 Hispanic/Latino; 1 Two or more races, non-Hispanic/Latino), 2 international. Average age 29. 36 applicants, 28% accepted, 6 enrolled. In 2019, 1 doctorate awarded. Application fee: $120 ($140 for international students). *Unit head:* Tim-Allen Bruckner, Professor, 949-824-5797, Fax: 949-824-1845, E-mail: tim.bruckner@uci.edu. *Application contact:* Jennifer Craig, Director of Graduate Student Services, 949-824-5918, Fax: 949-824-1845, E-mail: craigj@uci.edu. Website: http://socialecology.uci.edu/core/graduate-se-core-programs

University of Georgia, College of Environment and Design, Athens, GA 30602. Offers environmental planning and design (MEPD); historic preservation (MHP); landscape architecture (MLA). *Accreditation:* ACSP; ASLA.

The University of Manchester, School of Environment, Education and Development, Manchester, United Kingdom. Offers architecture (M Phil, PhD); development policy and management (M Phil, PhD); human geography (M Phil, PhD); physical geography (M Phil, PhD); planning and landscape (M Phil, PhD).

Virginia Polytechnic Institute and State University, Graduate School, College of Architecture and Urban Studies, Blacksburg, VA 24061. Offers architecture (M Arch, MS); architecture and design research (PhD); building construction science management (MS); creative technologies (MFA); environmental design and planning (PhD); government and international affairs (MPIA); landscape architecture (MLA, PhD); planning, governance, and globalization (PhD); public administration and public affairs (MPA, PhD); urban and regional planning (MURPL). *Accreditation:* ASLA (one or more programs are accredited). *Faculty:* 145 full-time (58 women), 2 part-time/adjunct (1 woman). *Students:* 304 full-time (156 women), 180 part-time (77 women); includes 90 minority (40 Black or African American, non-Hispanic/Latino; 19 Asian, non-Hispanic/Latino; 24 Hispanic/Latino; 7 Two or more races, non-Hispanic/Latino), 130 international. Average age 33. 475 applicants, 72% accepted, 126 enrolled. In 2019, 130 master's, 23 doctorates awarded. *Degree requirements:* For master's, comprehensive exam (for some programs), thesis (for some programs); for doctorate, comprehensive exam (for some programs), thesis/dissertation (for some programs). *Entrance requirements:* For master's and doctorate, GRE/GMAT. Additional exam requirements/recommendations for international students: required—TOEFL (minimum score 90 iBT). *Application deadline:* For fall admission, 8/1 for domestic students, 4/1 for international students; for spring admission, 1/1 for domestic students, 9/1 for international students. Applications are processed on a rolling basis. Application fee: $75. Electronic applications accepted. *Expenses: Tuition,* state resident: full-time $13,700; part-time $761.25 per credit hour. *Tuition,* nonresident: full-time $27,614; part-time $1534 per credit hour. *Required fees:* $886.50 per term. Tuition and fees vary according to campus/location and program. *Financial support:* In 2019–20, 2 fellowships with full tuition reimbursements (averaging $24,875 per year), 35 research assistantships with full tuition reimbursements (averaging $16,344 per year), 126 teaching assistantships with full tuition reimbursements (averaging $11,525 per year) were awarded; scholarships/grants and unspecified assistantships also available. Financial award application deadline: 3/1; financial award applicants required to submit FAFSA. *Unit head:* Dr. Richard Blythe, Dean, 540-231-6416, Fax: 540-231-6332, E-mail: richbl1@vt.edu. *Application contact:* Christine Mattsson-Coon, Executive Assistant, 540-231-6416, Fax: 540-231-6332, E-mail: cmattsso@vt.edu. Website: http://www.caus.vt.edu/

Yale University, School of Architecture, New Haven, CT 06520. Offers M Arch, M Env Des, MEM, PhD, M Arch/M Env Des, M Arch/MBA. *Entrance requirements:* For master's, GRE General Test, design portfolio. Additional exam requirements/recommendations for international students: required—TOEFL. Electronic applications accepted. *Expenses:* Contact institution.

Historic Preservation

The American University of Rome, Graduate School, Rome, Italy. Offers arts management (MA); food studies (MA); peace studies (MA); sustainable cultural heritage (MA). *Degree requirements:* For master's, thesis, internship. *Entrance requirements:* For master's, bachelor's degree in the liberal arts, humanities or social sciences; minimum GPA of 2.75. Additional exam requirements/recommendations for international students: required—TOEFL (minimum score 550 paper-based; 80 iBT), IELTS (minimum score 6.5). Electronic applications accepted.

Arkansas State University, Graduate School, College of Humanities and Social Sciences, Heritage Studies Program, State University, AR 72467. Offers heritage studies (MA, PhD). *Program availability:* Part-time. *Degree requirements:* For master's, comprehensive exam, thesis or alternative, portfolio; for doctorate, comprehensive exam, thesis/dissertation, portfolio. *Entrance requirements:* For master's, GRE, MAT or GMAT, appropriate bachelor's degree, letters of reference, official transcript, interview, letter of interest, writing sample, immunization records; for doctorate, GRE, MAT, or GMAT, appropriate bachelor's or master's degree, interview, letters of reference, official transcript, letter of interest, writing sample, immunization records. Additional exam requirements/recommendations for international students: required—TOEFL (minimum score 550 paper-based; 79 iBT), IELTS (minimum score 6), PTE (minimum score 56). Electronic applications accepted.

Ball State University, Graduate School, College of Architecture and Planning, Department of Architecture, Program in Historic Preservation, Muncie, IN 47306. Offers MS. *Program availability:* Part-time. *Entrance requirements:* For master's, minimum baccalaureate GPA of 2.75 or 3.0 in latter half of baccalaureate, resume, statement of purpose, academic writing sample, three letters of recommendation. Additional exam requirements/recommendations for international students: required—TOEFL (minimum score 550 paper-based; 79 iBT), IELTS (minimum score 6.5). Electronic applications accepted. *Expenses:* Contact institution.

Boston Architectural College, Graduate Programs, Boston, MA 02115-2795. Offers architecture (M Arch); historic preservation (MDS); interior design (MID); landscape architecture (MLA); sustainable design (MDS). *Accreditation:* CIDA. *Degree requirements:* For master's, thesis. *Entrance requirements:* For master's, portfolio (recommended). Electronic applications accepted.

Boston University, Graduate School of Arts and Sciences, Program in Preservation Studies, Boston, MA 02215. Offers MA, JD/MA. *Students:* 8 full-time (4 women), 2 international. Average age 26. 16 applicants, 94% accepted, 6 enrolled. *Degree requirements:* For master's, thesis or alternative, internship, major project. *Entrance requirements:* For master's, GRE General Test, scholarly writing sample, 3 letters of recommendation, transcripts, curriculum vitae, personal statement. Additional exam requirements/recommendations for international students: required—TOEFL (minimum score 550 paper-based; 84 iBT). *Application deadline:* For fall admission, 1/15 for domestic and international students; for spring admission, 4/15 for domestic and international students. Application fee: $95. Electronic applications accepted. *Financial support:* In 2019–20, 9 students received support. Career-related internships or fieldwork, Federal Work-Study, scholarships/grants, and unspecified assistantships available. Support available to part-time students. Financial award application deadline: 1/15. *Unit head:* Daniel Bluestone, Director, 617-358-7332, Fax: 617-353-2556, E-mail: dblues@bu.edu. *Application contact:* Julia Kline, Senior Program Coordinator, 617-353-2948, Fax: 617-353-2556, E-mail: jgawle@bu.edu.
Website: http://www.bu.edu/amnesp/academics/graduate/preservation-studies-ma/

Buffalo State College, State University of New York, The Graduate School, School of Arts and Humanities, Patricia H. and Richard E. Garman Department of Art Conservation, Buffalo, NY 14222-1095. Offers art conservation (CAS); conservation of historic works and art works (MA). *Degree requirements:* For master's, final oral exam; for CAS, internship. *Entrance requirements:* For master's, GRE General Test, minimum GPA of 2.8. Additional exam requirements/recommendations for international students: required—TOEFL (minimum score 550 paper-based).

Clemson University, Graduate School, College of Architecture, Arts, and Humanities, School of Architecture, Master of Science Program in Historic Preservation, Charleston, SC 29634. Offers MS, Certificate. *Faculty:* 6 full-time (3 women), 6 part-time/adjunct (3 women). *Students:* 8 full-time (5 women), 1 part-time (0 women); all minorities (8 Black or African American, non-Hispanic/Latino; 1 Hispanic/Latino). Average age 27. 30 applicants, 97% accepted, 10 enrolled. In 2019, 10 master's awarded. *Expenses:* Full-Time Student per Semester: Tuition: $15750, Fees: $286; Part-Time Student Per Credit Hour: $724 (in-state), $1050, Fees: $46. *Financial support:* In 2019–20, 7 students received support, including 7 fellowships with full and partial tuition reimbursements available (averaging $5,857 per year); career-related internships or fieldwork also available. *Unit head:* Dr. Jon Marcoux, Director of Graduate Programs, 864-937-9567, E-mail: jbmarco@clemson.edu. *Application contact:* Amanda Tucker, Program Coordinator, 843-937-9596.
Website: http://www.clemson.edu/caah/departments/historic-preservation/

Cleveland State University, College of Graduate Studies, Maxine Goodman Levin College of Urban Affairs, Program in Urban Planning and Development, Cleveland, OH 44115. Offers economic development (MUPD); environmental sustainability (MUPD); historic preservation (MUPD); housing and neighborhood development (MUPD); real estate development and finance (MUPD); urban economic development (Certificate); urban geographic information systems (MUPD); JD/MUPDD. *Accreditation:* ACSP. *Program availability:* Part-time, evening/weekend. *Degree requirements:* For master's, thesis or alternative, exit project. *Entrance requirements:* For master's, GRE General Test (minimum score: 50th percentile combined verbal and quantitative, 4.0 analytical writing), minimum GPA of 3.0. Additional exam requirements/recommendations for international students: required—TOEFL (minimum score 550 paper-based; 78 iBT), IELTS (6.0), or International Test of English Proficiency (iTEP). Electronic applications accepted. *Expenses:* Contact institution.

College of Charleston, Graduate School, School of the Arts, Program in Historic Preservation, Charleston, SC 29424-0001. Offers MS. *Degree requirements:* For master's, thesis optional. *Entrance requirements:* For master's, GRE. Additional exam requirements/recommendations for international students: required—TOEFL (minimum score 81 iBT). Electronic applications accepted.

Columbia University, Graduate School of Architecture, Planning, and Preservation, Program in Historic Preservation, New York, NY 10027. Offers MS, PhD, Certificate, M Arch/MS, MS/MS. *Degree requirements:* For master's, thesis. *Entrance requirements:* For master's, GRE General Test. *Expenses: Tuition:* Full-time $47,600; part-time $1880 per credit. One-time fee: $105.

Cornell University, Graduate School, Graduate Fields of Architecture, Art and Planning, Field of City and Regional Planning, Ithaca, NY 14853. Offers city and regional planning (MRP, PhD); environmental planning and design (MRP, PhD); historic preservation planning (MA); international development planning (MRP, PhD); planning theory and systems analysis (MRP, PhD); regional economics and development planning (MRP, PhD); regional science (MRP, PhD); social and health systems planning (MRP, PhD); urban and regional theory (MRP, PhD); urban planning history (MRP, PhD). *Accreditation:* ACSP (one or more programs are accredited). *Degree requirements:* For master's, thesis (MA); for doctorate, comprehensive exam, thesis/dissertation. *Entrance requirements:* For master's and doctorate, GRE General Test, 2 letters of recommendation. Additional exam requirements/recommendations for international students: required—TOEFL (minimum score 600 paper-based; 77 iBT). Electronic applications accepted.

Delaware State University, Graduate Programs, Department of History, Philosophy and Political Sciences, Dover, DE 19901-2277. Offers historic preservation (MA). *Entrance requirements:* Additional exam requirements/recommendations for international students: required—TOEFL (minimum score 550 paper-based). Electronic applications accepted.

Eastern Michigan University, Graduate School, College of Arts and Sciences, Department of Geography and Geology, Programs in Historic Preservation, Ypsilanti, MI 48197. Offers heritage interpretation and museum practice (MS); historic preservation (Graduate Certificate); preservation planning and administration (MS); recording, documentation and digital cultural heritage (MS). *Program availability:* Part-time, evening/weekend, online learning. *Students:* 7 full-time (5 women), 22 part-time (15 women); includes 2 minority (both Hispanic/Latino). Average age 36. 13 applicants, 100% accepted, 8 enrolled. In 2019, 16 master's, 1 other advanced degree awarded. *Entrance requirements:* Additional exam requirements/recommendations for international students: required—TOEFL. *Application deadline:* Applications are processed on a rolling basis. Application fee: $45. *Financial support:* Fellowships, research assistantships with full tuition reimbursements, teaching assistantships with full tuition reimbursements, career-related internships or fieldwork, Federal Work-Study, institutionally sponsored loans, scholarships/grants, tuition waivers (partial), and unspecified assistantships available. Support available to part-time students. Financial award applicants required to submit FAFSA. *Application contact:* Dr. Ted Ligibel, Program Director, 734-487-0232, Fax: 734-487-6979, E-mail: tligibel@emich.edu.

The George Washington University, Columbian College of Arts and Sciences, Department of American Studies, Washington, DC 20052. Offers American studies (PhD); folk life (MA); historic preservation (MA); material culture (MA). *Program availability:* Part-time, evening/weekend. Terminal master's awarded for partial completion of doctoral program. *Degree requirements:* For master's, comprehensive exam; for doctorate, one foreign language, thesis/dissertation, general exam. *Entrance requirements:* For master's and doctorate, GRE General Test, minimum GPA of 3.0. Additional exam requirements/recommendations for international students: required—TOEFL (minimum score 550 paper-based; 80 iBT).

Georgia State University, College of Arts and Sciences, Department of History, Program in Heritage Preservation, Atlanta, GA 30302-3083. Offers MHP. *Program availability:* Part-time. *Entrance requirements:* For master's, GRE General Test, statement of purpose, three letters of recommendation, official transcripts. Additional exam requirements/recommendations for international students: required—TOEFL (minimum score 550 paper-based; 80 iBT). *Application deadline:* Applications are processed on a rolling basis. Application fee: $50. Electronic applications accepted. *Expenses: Tuition, area resident:* Full-time $7164; part-time $398 per credit hour. Tuition, state resident: full-time $7164; part-time $398 per credit hour. Tuition, nonresident: full-time $22,662; part-time $1259 per credit hour. *International tuition:* $22,662 full-time. *Required fees:* $2128; $312 per credit hour. Tuition and fees vary according to course load and program. *Financial support:* Fellowships, research assistantships, career-related internships or fieldwork, Federal Work-Study, scholarships/grants, and unspecified assistantships available. Support available to part-time students. Financial award application deadline: 7/15. *Unit head:* Dr. Michelle Brattain, Chair, 404-413-6352, E-mail: mbrattain@gsu.edu. *Application contact:* Richard Laub, Director of Heritage Preservation Program, 404-413-6365, E-mail: rlaub@gsu.edu.
Website: https://history.gsu.edu/

Goucher College, MA and MFA Programs, Baltimore, MD 21204-2794. Offers art and technology (MFA); arts administration (MA); cultural sustainability (MA); digital arts (MA); historic preservation (MA); nonfiction (MFA). *Program availability:* Part-time, evening/weekend, blended/hybrid learning. *Degree requirements:* For master's, thesis, e-portfolio. *Entrance requirements:* For master's, digital portfolio (for MA, MFA in digital arts); writing sample (for MFA in creative nonfiction). Additional exam requirements/recommendations for international students: required—TOEFL (minimum score 550 paper-based; 80 iBT). Electronic applications accepted. *Expenses:* Contact institution.

Morgan State University, School of Graduate Studies, James H. Gilliam Jr College of Liberal Arts, Department of History and Geography, Baltimore, MD 21251. Offers African-American studies (MA); history (MA, PhD); museum studies and historic preservation (MA). *Program availability:* Part-time, evening/weekend. *Faculty:* 20 full-time (5 women), 1 part-time/adjunct (0 women). *Students:* 37 full-time (24 women), 8 part-time (6 women); includes 41 minority (36 Black or African American, non-Hispanic/Latino; 5 Hispanic/Latino), 3 international. Average age 37. 13 applicants, 92% accepted, 4 enrolled. In 2019, 4 master's, 4 doctorates awarded. *Degree requirements:* For master's, comprehensive exam, thesis; for doctorate, comprehensive exam, thesis/dissertation. *Entrance requirements:* For master's, GRE, minimum GPA of 2.5; for doctorate, GRE or MAT, minimum GPA of 3.0. Additional exam requirements/recommendations for international students: required—TOEFL (minimum score 550 paper-based). *Application deadline:* For fall admission, 2/1 priority date for domestic students, 4/1 for international students; for spring admission, 11/15 for domestic students, 10/1 for international students. Applications are processed on a rolling basis. Application fee: $50 ($70 for international students). Electronic applications accepted. *Expenses:* Tuition, state resident: full-time $455; part-time $455 per credit hour. Tuition, nonresident: full-time $894; part-time $894 per credit hour. *Required fees:* $82; $82 per credit hour. *Financial support:* In 2019–20, 5 students received support. Fellowships with full and partial tuition reimbursements available, research assistantships with full and partial tuition reimbursements available, teaching assistantships with full and partial tuition reimbursements available, career-related internships or fieldwork, Federal Work-Study, scholarships/grants, tuition waivers (full and partial), and unspecified assistantships available. Support available to part-time students. Financial award application deadline: 2/1. *Unit head:* Dr. Jeremiah I. Dibua, Interim Chair of Department, 443-885-3190, Fax: 443-885-8227, E-mail: jeremiah.dibua@morgan.edu. *Application contact:* Dr. Jahmaine Smith, Director of Admissions, 443-885-3185, Fax: 443-885-

8226, E-mail: gradapply@morgan.edu.
Website: https://morgan.edu/college_of_liberal_arts/departments/history_geography_and_museum_studies/graduate_program_handbook.html

New York University, Graduate School of Arts and Science, Institute of Fine Arts, Program in Conservation Training, New York, NY 10012-1019. Offers MA/Diploma. *Entrance requirements:* Additional exam requirements/recommendations for international students: required—TOEFL, IELTS.

Penn State Harrisburg, Graduate School, School of Humanities, Middletown, PA 17057. Offers American studies (MA, PhD); communications (MA); folklore and ethnography (Certificate); heritage and museum practice (Certificate); humanities (MA). *Program availability:* Evening/weekend.

Plymouth State University, Program in Historic Preservation, Plymouth, NH 03264-1595. Offers MA, Graduate Certificate.

Pratt Institute, School of Architecture, Program in Historic Preservation, New York, NY 10011. Offers MS. *Program availability:* Part-time. *Students:* 12 full-time (8 women), 2 part-time (1 woman); includes 1 minority (Hispanic/Latino), 5 international. Average age 28. 24 applicants, 96% accepted, 6 enrolled. In 2019, 13 master's awarded. *Degree requirements:* For master's, thesis. *Entrance requirements:* For master's, writing sample, bachelor's degree, transcripts, letters of recommendation, portfolio. Additional exam requirements/recommendations for international students: required—TOEFL (minimum score 575 paper-based; 90 iBT). *Application deadline:* For fall admission, 1/5 for domestic and international students; for spring admission, 10/1 for domestic and international students. Application fee: $50 ($90 for international students). Electronic applications accepted. *Expenses:* Tuition: Full-time $33,246; part-time $1847 per credit. *Required fees:* $1980. *Financial support:* Career-related internships or fieldwork, Federal Work-Study, institutionally sponsored loans, scholarships/grants, health care benefits, and unspecified assistantships available. Support available to part-time students. Financial award application deadline: 2/1; financial award applicants required to submit FAFSA. *Unit head:* Vicki Weiner, Director, 718-637-8645, E-mail: vweiner@pratt.edu. *Application contact:* Natalie Capannelli, Director of Graduate Admissions, 718-636-3551, Fax: 718-399-4242, E-mail: ncapanne@pratt.edu. Website: https://www.pratt.edu/academics/architecture/historic-preservation/

Roger Williams University, School of Architecture, Art and Historic Preservation, Bristol, RI 02809. Offers architecture (M Arch); art and architectural history (MA); historical preservation (MS, Certificate); urban and regional planning (Certificate). *Program availability:* Part-time. *Faculty:* 8 full-time (4 women), 6 part-time/adjunct (1 woman). *Students:* 97 full-time (46 women), 10 part-time (0 women); includes 15 minority (1 Black or African American, non-Hispanic/Latino; 1 American Indian or Alaska Native, non-Hispanic/Latino; 1 Asian, non-Hispanic/Latino; 8 Hispanic/Latino; 4 Two or more races, non-Hispanic/Latino), 5 international. Average age 23. 97 applicants, 92% accepted, 54 enrolled. In 2019, 48 master's awarded. *Degree requirements:* For master's, thesis. *Entrance requirements:* For master's, letter of intent, transcripts, 2 letters of recommendation, portfolio (Architecture only), writing sample (Preservation only); for Certificate, transcripts. Additional exam requirements/recommendations for international students: required—TOEFL (minimum score 85 paper-based), IELTS (minimum score 6.5). *Application deadline:* For fall admission, 1/15 for domestic students, 5/1 for international students. Application fee: $50. Electronic applications accepted. *Expenses:* Tuition per credit hour: Architecture: $1579, Preservation: $951. *Financial support:* In 2019–20, 103 students received support. Scholarships/grants and unspecified assistantships available. Financial award application deadline: 3/15; financial award applicants required to submit FAFSA. *Unit head:* Stephen White, Dean, 401-254-3607, E-mail: swhite@rwu.edu. *Application contact:* Gregory Laramie, Associate Dean, 401-254-3743, E-mail: glaramie@rwu.edu. Website: https://www.rwu.edu/academics/schools-and-colleges/saahp

Rutgers University - New Brunswick, Graduate School-New Brunswick, Program in Art History, Piscataway, NJ 08854-8097. Offers art history (MA, PhD); curatorial studies (Certificate); historic preservation (Certificate). *Program availability:* Part-time. Terminal master's awarded for partial completion of doctoral program. *Degree requirements:* For master's, one foreign language, comprehensive exam; for doctorate, 2 foreign languages, comprehensive exam, thesis/dissertation. *Entrance requirements:* For master's and doctorate, GRE General Test, writing sample. Additional exam requirements/recommendations for international students: required—TOEFL (minimum score 550 paper-based). Electronic applications accepted.

Rutgers University - New Brunswick, Graduate School-New Brunswick, Program in Cultural Heritage and Preservation Studies, Piscataway, NJ 08854-8097. Offers cultural heritage and preservation studies (MA); historic preservation (Certificate).

St. Cloud State University, School of Graduate Studies, College of Social Sciences, Program in Cultural Resource Management Archeology, St. Cloud, MN 56301-4498. Offers MS, Graduate Certificate. *Entrance requirements:* For master's, GRE General Test, minimum GPA of 2.75. Additional exam requirements/recommendations for international students: required—Michigan English Language Assessment Battery; recommended—TOEFL (minimum score 550 paper-based).

Savannah College of Art and Design, Program in Preservation Design, Savannah, GA 31402-3146. Offers MA, MFA. *Program availability:* Part-time, 100% online. *Degree requirements:* For master's, thesis (for some programs), preservation practicum (for MA); thesis (for MFA). *Entrance requirements:* For master's, GRE (recommended), portfolio (submitted in digital format), audition or writing submission, resume, statement of purpose, two letters of recommendation. Additional exam requirements/recommendations for international students: recommended—TOEFL (minimum score 550 paper-based; 85 iBT), IELTS (minimum score 6.5). Electronic applications accepted.

Universidad Nacional Pedro Henriquez Urena, Graduate School, Santo Domingo, Dominican Republic. Offers agricultural diversity (MS), including horticultural/fruit production, tropical animal production; conservation of monuments and cultural assets (M Arch); ecology and environment (MS); environmental engineering (MEE); international relations (MA); natural resource management (MS); political science (MA); project feasibility (MPM); project management (MPM); project optimization (MPM); sanitation engineering (ME); science for teachers (MS); tropical Caribbean architecture (M Arch).

University at Buffalo, the State University of New York, Graduate School, School of Architecture and Planning, Department of Urban and Regional Planning, Buffalo, NY 14214. Offers economic development (MUP); environment/land use (MUP); health and food systems (MUP); historic preservation (MUP, Certificate); neighborhood/community development (MUP); real estate development (MSRED); urban and regional planning (PhD); urban design (MUP); JD/MUP; M Arch/MUP. *Accreditation:* ACSP. *Program availability:* Part-time. *Faculty:* 11 full-time (4 women), 15 part-time/adjunct (6 women). *Students:* 88 full-time (40 women), 25 part-time (10 women); includes 32 minority (16 Black or African American, non-Hispanic/Latino; 2 Asian, non-Hispanic/Latino; 7 Hispanic/Latino; 7 Two or more races, non-Hispanic/Latino), 13 international. Average age 26. 146 applicants, 40% accepted, 40 enrolled. In 2019, 31 master's, 1 doctorate, 4 other advanced degrees awarded. *Degree requirements:* For master's,

thesis or alternative, project; for doctorate, comprehensive exam, thesis/dissertation, dissertation. *Entrance requirements:* For master's, resume, two letters of recommendation, personal statement, transcripts; for doctorate, GRE, transcripts, three letters of recommendation, resume, research statement, writing sample. Additional exam requirements/recommendations for international students: required—TOEFL (minimum score 79 iBT), IELTS (minimum score 6.5). *Application deadline:* For fall admission, 3/1 priority date for domestic and international students; for spring admission, 10/31 priority date for domestic students, 10/1 priority date for international students. Applications are processed on a rolling basis. Application fee: $75. Electronic applications accepted. *Expenses:* Tuition, area resident: Full-time $11,310; part-time $471 per credit hour. Tuition, state resident: full-time $11,310; part-time $471 per credit hour. Tuition, nonresident: full-time $23,100; part-time $963 per credit hour. *International tuition:* $23,100 full-time. *Required fees:* $2820. *Financial support:* In 2019–20, 54 students received support, including 5 fellowships with full tuition reimbursements available (averaging $22,560 per year), 1 research assistantship with partial tuition reimbursement available (averaging $16,027 per year), 20 teaching assistantships with partial tuition reimbursements available (averaging $6,912 per year); career-related internships or fieldwork, Federal Work-Study, institutionally sponsored loans, scholarships/grants, health care benefits, tuition waivers (full and partial), and unspecified assistantships also available. Financial award application deadline: 3/1; financial award applicants required to submit FAFSA. *Unit head:* Dr. Daniel B. Hess, Professor and Chair, 716-829-5326, Fax: 716-829-3256, E-mail: dbhess@buffalo.edu. *Application contact:* Norma Everett, Graduate Programs Coordinator, 716-829-3283, Fax: 716-829-3256, E-mail: norma.everett@buffalo.edu. Website: http://www.ap.buffalo.edu/planning/

University of California, Los Angeles, Graduate Division, College of Letters and Science, Interdepartmental Program in Conservation of Archaeological and Ethnographic Materials, Los Angeles, CA 90095. Offers MA. *Degree requirements:* For master's, one foreign language, thesis, eleven-month internship. *Entrance requirements:* For master's, GRE General Test, bachelor's degree; minimum undergraduate GPA of 3.0 (or its equivalent if letter grade system not used); proficiency in one foreign language; portfolio; writing sample; documented practical experience; interview. Additional exam requirements/recommendations for international students: required—TOEFL.

University of Colorado Denver, College of Architecture and Planning, Program in Historic Preservation, Denver, CO 80217. Offers MS. *Degree requirements:* For master's, thesis, 45 credit hours. *Entrance requirements:* For master's, GRE (recommended, especially for students with an undergraduate GPA of less than 3.0), portfolio of creative work; sample of writing or work project. Additional exam requirements/recommendations for international students: required—TOEFL (minimum score 75 iBT). Electronic applications accepted. *Expenses:* Contact institution.

University of Delaware, College of Arts and Sciences, Department of Art Conservation, Newark, DE 19716. Offers art conservation (MS); preservation studies (PhD). *Degree requirements:* For master's, internship, portfolio, oral exam, oral presentation. *Entrance requirements:* For master's, GRE General Test, course work in chemistry, art history/anthropology and studio art; minimum of 400 hours of conservation experience. Additional exam requirements/recommendations for international students: recommended—TOEFL. Electronic applications accepted.

University of Delaware, College of Arts and Sciences, School of Public Policy and Administration, Program in Urban Affairs and Public Policy, Newark, DE 19716. Offers governance planning and management (PhD); historic preservation (MA); social and urban policy (PhD); technology, environment and society (PhD); urban affairs and public policy (MA). *Program availability:* Part-time. Terminal master's awarded for partial completion of doctoral program. *Degree requirements:* For master's, analytical paper or thesis; for doctorate, thesis/dissertation. *Entrance requirements:* For master's, GRE General Test, minimum GPA of 3.0; for doctorate, GRE General Test, minimum GPA of 3.5. Additional exam requirements/recommendations for international students: required—TOEFL. Electronic applications accepted.

University of Florida, Graduate School, College of Liberal Arts and Sciences, Department of History, Gainesville, FL 32611. Offers historic preservation (MA, PhD); history (MA, PhD); Jewish studies (MA); women's and gender studies (PhD); JD/MA; JD/PhD. *Program availability:* Part-time. Terminal master's awarded for partial completion of doctoral program. *Degree requirements:* For master's, variable foreign language requirement, thesis optional, 30 credit hours; for doctorate, variable foreign language requirement, comprehensive exam, thesis/dissertation, 90 credit hours. *Entrance requirements:* For master's and doctorate, GRE General Test, minimum GPA of 3.0. Additional exam requirements/recommendations for international students: required—TOEFL (minimum score 550 paper-based; 80 iBT), IELTS (minimum score 6). Electronic applications accepted.

University of Georgia, College of Environment and Design, Athens, GA 30602. Offers environmental planning and design (MEPD); historic preservation (MHP); landscape architecture (MLA). *Accreditation:* ACSP; ASLA.

University of Hawaii at Manoa, Office of Graduate Education, College of Arts and Humanities, Department of American Studies, Program in Historic Preservation, Honolulu, HI 96822. Offers Graduate Certificate. *Program availability:* Part-time. *Entrance requirements:* Additional exam requirements/recommendations for international students: required—TOEFL (minimum score 600 paper-based; 100 iBT), IELTS (minimum score 7).

The University of Kansas, Graduate Studies, School of Architecture and Design, Department of Architecture, Lawrence, KS 66045. Offers architectural acoustics (Certificate); architecture (M Arch, PhD); health and wellness (Certificate); historic preservation (Certificate); urban design (Certificate). *Students:* 93 full-time (45 women), 23 part-time (13 women); includes 20 minority (4 Black or African American, non-Hispanic/Latino; 5 Asian, non-Hispanic/Latino; 4 Hispanic/Latino; 7 Two or more races, non-Hispanic/Latino), 23 international. Average age 25. 91 applicants, 59% accepted, 30 enrolled. In 2019, 70 master's, 2 doctorates, 8 other advanced degrees awarded. Terminal master's awarded for partial completion of doctoral program. *Entrance requirements:* For master's, GRE, transcript; resume; minimum GPA of 3.0; statement of purpose; letters of recommendation; portfolio of design work, or samples of written work or other creative artifacts produced if previous degree was not in a design-related discipline; for doctorate, GRE, transcript, resume, minimum GPA of 3.0, statement of purpose, letters of recommendation, research-informed writing sample, exhibit of work illustrating applicant's interests and abilities in areas related to the design disciplines. Additional exam requirements/recommendations for international students: required—TOEFL, IELTS. *Application deadline:* For fall admission, 1/15 priority date for domestic and international students; for summer admission, 1/15 priority date for domestic and international students. Application fee: $65 ($85 for international students). Electronic applications accepted. *Expenses:* Tuition, state resident: full-time $9989. Tuition, nonresident: full-time $23,950. *International tuition:* $23,950 full-time. *Required fees:* $984; $81.99 per credit hour. Tuition and fees vary according to course load, campus/location and program. *Financial support:* Fellowships, research assistantships, teaching assistantships, scholarships/grants, health care benefits, and unspecified assistantships

available. Financial award application deadline: 1/15; financial award applicants required to submit FAFSA. *Unit head:* Frank Zilm, Dean, 816-561-7186, E-mail: frankzilm@ku.edu. *Application contact:* Joan Weaver, Graduate Admissions Contact, 785-864-3709, Fax: 785-864-5185, E-mail: jweaver@ku.edu.
Website: http://architecture.ku.edu/

University of Kentucky, Graduate School, College of Design, Department of Historic Preservation, Lexington, KY 40506-0032. Offers MHP. *Degree requirements:* For master's, comprehensive exam. *Entrance requirements:* For master's, GRE General Test, minimum undergraduate GPA of 2.75. Additional exam requirements/recommendations for international students: required—TOEFL (minimum score 550 paper-based). Electronic applications accepted.

University of Maryland, College Park, Academic Affairs, School of Architecture, Planning and Preservation, Program in Historic Preservation, College Park, MD 20742. Offers MHP, Certificate. *Degree requirements:* For Certificate, thesis. *Entrance requirements:* For master's, GRE, minimum GPA of 3.0, 3 letters of recommendation, writing sample. Additional exam requirements/recommendations for international students: required—TOEFL. Electronic applications accepted.

University of Massachusetts Amherst, Graduate School, College of Humanities and Fine Arts, Department of Architecture, Amherst, MA 01003. Offers architecture (M Arch); design (MS); design in historic preservation (MS). *Program availability:* Part-time. *Degree requirements:* For master's, thesis or alternative, project. *Entrance requirements:* For master's, GRE General Test (for M Arch only), 3 letters of recommendation (M Arch only); portfolio. Additional exam requirements/recommendations for international students: required—TOEFL (minimum score 550 paper-based; 80 iBT), IELTS (minimum score 6.5). Electronic applications accepted.

University of New Mexico, Graduate Studies, School of Architecture and Planning, Program in Historic Preservation and Regionalism, Albuquerque, NM 87131-2039. Offers Graduate Certificate. *Program availability:* Part-time, evening/weekend. Electronic applications accepted. *Expenses:* Tuition, state resident: full-time $7633; part-time $972 per year. Tuition, nonresident: full-time $22,586; part-time $3840 per year. *International tuition:* $23,292 full-time. *Required fees:* $8608. Tuition and fees vary according to course level, course load, degree level, program and student level.

University of North Alabama, College of Arts and Sciences, Department of History, Program in Public History, Florence, AL 35632-0001. Offers historic preservation (MA); historical administration (MA). *Program availability:* Part-time. *Degree requirements:* For master's, comprehensive exam (for some programs), thesis optional. *Entrance requirements:* For master's, GRE, three letters of recommendation; essay; writing sample. Additional exam requirements/recommendations for international students: required—TOEFL (minimum score 79 iBT), IELTS (minimum score 6), TWE, PTE (minimum score 54). Electronic applications accepted.

The University of North Carolina at Greensboro, Graduate School, College of Arts and Sciences, Department of Interior Architecture, Greensboro, NC 27412-5001. Offers historic preservation (Certificate); interior architecture (MS); museum studies (Certificate). *Degree requirements:* For master's, thesis. *Entrance requirements:* For master's, GRE General Test or MAT, bachelor's degree in interior design, interview, portfolio. Additional exam requirements/recommendations for international students: required—TOEFL. Electronic applications accepted.

University of Oregon, Graduate School, College of Design, Program in Historic Preservation, Eugene, OR 97403. Offers MS. *Degree requirements:* For master's, thesis, internship. *Entrance requirements:* For master's, participation in Pacific Northwest Field School. Additional exam requirements/recommendations for international students: required—TOEFL.

University of Pennsylvania, Stuart Weitzman School of Design, Program in Historic Preservation, Philadelphia, PA 19104. Offers MS, Certificate. *Faculty:* 3 full-time (0 women), 3 part-time/adjunct (1 woman). *Students:* 41 full-time (30 women); includes 7 minority (1 Black or African American, non-Hispanic/Latino; 2 Asian, non-Hispanic/Latino; 3 Hispanic/Latino; 1 Two or more races, non-Hispanic/Latino), 13 international. Average age 27. 46 applicants, 96% accepted, 20 enrolled. In 2019, 26 master's awarded. *Entrance requirements:* For master's, GRE, official academic transcripts, 3 letters of recommendation, course in computer-aided drafting (preferably AutoCad). Additional exam requirements/recommendations for international students: required—TOEFL (minimum score 600 paper-based; 100 iBT). *Application deadline:* For fall admission, 1/12 for domestic students. Application fee: $80. *Financial support:* Research assistantships, teaching assistantships, career-related internships or fieldwork, Federal Work-Study, institutionally sponsored loans, scholarships/grants, and unspecified assistantships available. Financial award application deadline: 4/15; financial award applicants required to submit FAFSA. *Application contact:* Joan Weston, Director of Admissions & Financial Aid, 215-898-6520, E-mail: weston@design.upenn.edu.
Website: http://www.design.upenn.edu/historic-preservation

University of South Carolina, The Graduate School, College of Arts and Sciences, Department of History, Program in Public History, Columbia, SC 29208. Offers archive management (MA); historic preservation (MA); museum administration (MA); museum management (Certificate); MLIS/MA. *Degree requirements:* For master's, one foreign language, thesis, internship. *Entrance requirements:* For master's, GRE General Test, writing sample. Additional exam requirements/recommendations for international students: required—TOEFL. Electronic applications accepted.

University of Southern California, Graduate School, School of Architecture, Los Angeles, CA 90089. Offers architecture (M Arch); building science (MBS); heritage conservation (MHP); landscape architecture and urbanism (MLA); M Arch/M Pl; MLA/M Pl. Terminal master's awarded for partial completion of doctoral program. *Degree requirements:* For master's, thesis (for some programs). *Entrance requirements:* For master's, GRE. Additional exam requirements/recommendations for international students: required—TOEFL (minimum score 100 iBT). Electronic applications accepted.

The University of Texas at Austin, Graduate School, School of Architecture, Program in Historic Preservation, Austin, TX 78712-1111. Offers M Arch, MS, MSCRP.

University of Vermont, Graduate College, College of Arts and Sciences, Program in Historic Preservation, Burlington, VT 05405. Offers MS. *Entrance requirements:* For master's, GRE General Test, writing sample or sample project. Additional exam requirements/recommendations for international students: required—TOEFL (minimum score 550 paper-based, 90 iBT) or IELTS (6.5). Electronic applications accepted. *Expenses:* Contact institution.

University of Washington, Graduate School, College of Built Environments, Interdisciplinary Program in Historic Preservation, Seattle, WA 98195. Offers Certificate. *Program availability:* Part-time. Electronic applications accepted.

Ursuline College, School of Graduate and Professional Studies, Program in Historic Preservation, Pepper Pike, OH 44124-4398. Offers MA. *Program availability:* Part-time. *Faculty:* 1 (woman) full-time. *Students:* 3 full-time (all women), 2 part-time (1 woman); includes 1 minority (American Indian or Alaska Native, non-Hispanic/Latino). Average age 39. 1 applicant, 100% accepted. In 2019, 1 master's awarded. *Degree requirements:* For master's, thesis. *Entrance requirements:* For master's, minimum undergraduate GPA of 3.0. Additional exam requirements/recommendations for international students: required—TOEFL (minimum score 500 paper-based; 80 iBT), or GRE. *Application deadline:* For fall admission, 8/1 priority date for domestic students. Applications are processed on a rolling basis. Application fee: $25. Electronic applications accepted. *Expenses:* 42 credit hours at $1,174. *Financial support:* In 2019–20, 1 student received support. Scholarships/grants available. Financial award application deadline: 3/1; financial award applicants required to submit FAFSA. *Unit head:* Dr. Bari Stith, Director, 440-646-8135, Fax: 440-684-6088, E-mail: bstith@ursuline.edu. *Application contact:* Melanie Steele, Director, Graduate Admission, 440-646-8146, Fax: 440-684-6138, E-mail: graduateadmissions@ursuline.edu.

Landscape Architecture

Academy of Art University, Graduate Programs, School of Landscape Architecture, San Francisco, CA 94105-3410. Offers MA, MFA. *Program availability:* Part-time, 100% online. *Faculty:* 2 full-time (1 woman), 10 part-time/adjunct (3 women). *Students:* 12 full-time (7 women), 11 part-time (6 women); includes 2 minority (both Hispanic/Latino), 15 international. Average age 35. 20 applicants, 100% accepted, 9 enrolled. In 2019, 9 master's awarded. *Degree requirements:* For master's, final review. *Entrance requirements:* For master's, statement of intent; resume; portfolio/reel; official college transcripts. *Application deadline:* Applications are processed on a rolling basis. Application fee: $50. Electronic applications accepted. *Expenses: Tuition:* Full-time $1083; part-time $1083 per credit hour. *Required fees:* $860; $860 per unit. $430 per term. One-time fee: $145. Tuition and fees vary according to program. *Financial support:* Career-related internships or fieldwork, Federal Work-Study, and scholarships/grants available. Financial award application deadline: 8/10; financial award applicants required to submit FAFSA.
Website: http://www.academyart.edu/landscape-architecture-school/index.html

Arizona State University at Tempe, Herberger Institute for Design and the Arts, The Design School, Tempe, AZ 85287-1605. Offers architecture (M Arch); building design/built environment (MS); design (MSD), including arts, media, and engineering, healthcare and healing environments (MSD, PhD), industrial design, interaction design, interior design, new product innovation, visual communication design; design, environment and the arts (PhD), including design, digital culture, healthcare and healing environments (MSD, PhD), history, theory, and criticism; landscape architecture (MLA); urban design (MUD); MA/MBA. *Accreditation:* ASLA; NASAD. Terminal master's awarded for partial completion of doctoral program. *Degree requirements:* For master's, thesis optional, interactive Program of Study (iPOS) submitted before completing 50 percent of required credit hours; for doctorate, comprehensive exam, thesis/dissertation, interactive Program of Study (iPOS) submitted before completing 50 percent of required credit hours. *Entrance requirements:* For master's, GRE General Test, minimum GPA of 3.0 or equivalent in last 2 years of work leading to bachelor's degree, design/creative works portfolio, 3 references, statement of intent; for doctorate, GRE, master's degree in architecture, graphic design, industrial design, interior design, landscape architecture, or art history or equivalent standing; statement of purpose; 3 letters of recommendation; indication of potential faculty mentor; sample of written work. Additional exam requirements/recommendations for international students: required—TOEFL (minimum score 600 paper-based; 100 iBT). Electronic applications accepted.

Auburn University, Graduate School, College of Architecture, Design, and Construction, Program in Landscape Architecture, Auburn, AL 36849. Offers ML Arch. *Accreditation:* ASLA. *Faculty:* 23 full-time (8 women), 8 part-time/adjunct (0 women). *Students:* 25 full-time (14 women), 1 part-time (0 women); includes 2 minority (both Black or African American, non-Hispanic/Latino), 9 international. Average age 27. 29 applicants, 83% accepted, 17 enrolled. In 2019, 8 master's awarded. *Entrance requirements:* For master's, 3 letters of recommendation. Additional exam requirements/recommendations for international students: required—TOEFL (minimum score 550 paper-based; 79 iBT), iTEP; recommended—IELTS (minimum score 6.5). *Application deadline:* Applications are processed on a rolling basis. Application fee: $60 ($70 for international students). Electronic applications accepted. *Expenses:* $546 per credit hour state resident tuition, $1638 per credit hour nonresident tuition, $680 student services fee for GRA/GTA, $2160 per semester. *Financial support:* In 2019–20, 18 research assistantships with partial tuition reimbursements (averaging $9,059 per year) were awarded. Financial award application deadline: 3/15; financial award applicants required to submit FAFSA. *Unit head:* Dr. David Hill, Chair, 334-844-5434, E-mail: hill@auburn.edu. *Application contact:* Dr. George Flowers, Dean of the Graduate School, 334-844-2125.
Website: https://cadc.auburn.edu/architecture/architecture-degrees-programs/program-of-landscape-architecture/

Ball State University, Graduate School, College of Architecture and Planning, Department of Landscape Architecture, Muncie, IN 47306. Offers MLA. *Accreditation:* ASLA. *Program availability:* Part-time. *Entrance requirements:* For master's, minimum baccalaureate GPA of 2.75 or 3.0 in latter half of baccalaureate, resume, three letters of reference, copies of all transcripts, portfolio, writing sample. Additional exam requirements/recommendations for international students: required—TOEFL (minimum score 550 paper-based; 79 iBT), IELTS (minimum score 6.5). Electronic applications accepted. *Expenses:* Contact institution.

Boston Architectural College, Graduate Programs, Boston, MA 02115-2795. Offers architecture (M Arch); historic preservation (MDS); interior design (MID); landscape architecture (MLA); sustainable design (MDS). *Accreditation:* CIDA. *Degree requirements:* For master's, thesis. *Entrance requirements:* For master's, portfolio (recommended). Electronic applications accepted.

California State Polytechnic University, Pomona, Program in Landscape Architecture, Pomona, CA 91768-2557. Offers landscape architecture (M Land Arch).

Accreditation: ASLA. *Program availability:* Part-time, evening/weekend. *Entrance requirements:* Additional exam requirements/recommendations for international students: required—TOEFL (minimum score 550 paper-based). Electronic applications accepted. *Expenses:* Contact institution.

City College of the City University of New York, Graduate School, The Bernard and Anne Spitzer School of Architecture, Program in Landscape Architecture, New York, NY 10031-9198. Offers MLA. *Accreditation:* ASLA.

Clemson University, Graduate School, College of Architecture, Arts, and Humanities, Department of Landscape Architecture, Clemson, SC 29634. Offers MLA. *Accreditation:* ASLA. *Degree requirements:* For master's, thesis or alternative. *Entrance requirements:* For master's, GRE General Test, unofficial transcripts, letters of recommendation, portfolio of creative and design work. Additional exam requirements/recommendations for international students: required—TOEFL (minimum score 80 iBT), IELTS (minimum score 6.5). Electronic applications accepted. *Expenses:* Contact institution.

Colorado State University, College of Agricultural Sciences, Department of Horticulture and Landscape Architecture, Fort Collins, CO 80523-1173. Offers MLA, MS, PhD. *Students:* Average age 34. 50 applicants, 52% accepted, 4 enrolled. In 2019, 11 master's awarded. Terminal master's awarded for partial completion of doctoral program. *Degree requirements:* For master's, thesis (for some programs), research paper; for doctorate, thesis/dissertation. *Entrance requirements:* For master's, GRE General Test (minimum score of 300 combined Verbal and Quantitative sections), minimum GPA of 3.0, letters of reference, transcripts, resume/curriculum vitae, statement of purpose; for doctorate, GRE General Test (minimum score of 300 combined Verbal and Quantitative sections), minimum GPA of 3.0, letters of reference, statement of purpose, resume/curriculum vitae, transcripts. Additional exam requirements/recommendations for international students: required—TOEFL (minimum score 550 paper-based), IELTS. *Application deadline:* For fall admission, 4/1 for domestic and international students; for spring admission, 9/1 for domestic and international students; for summer admission, 1/1 for domestic and international students. Application fee: $60 ($70 for international students). Electronic applications accepted. *Expenses:* Tuition, state resident: full-time $10,520; part-time $5844 per credit hour. Tuition, nonresident: full-time $25,791; part-time $14,328 per credit hour. *International tuition:* $25,791 full-time. *Required fees:* $2512.80. Part-time tuition and fees vary according to course level, course load, degree level, program and student level. *Financial support:* In 2019–20, 9 research assistantships with partial tuition reimbursements (averaging $19,924 per year), 6 teaching assistantships with partial tuition reimbursements (averaging $13,068 per year) were awarded; scholarships/grants and unspecified assistantships also available. Financial award application deadline: 2/15. *Unit head:* Dr. Jessica G. Davis, Department Head/Professor, 970-491-7018, Fax: 970-491-7745, E-mail: jessica.davis@colostate.edu. *Application contact:* Kathi Nietfeld, Graduate Coordinator, 970-491-7018, Fax: 970-491-7745, E-mail: kathi.nietfeld@colostate.edu.
Website: http://hortla.agsci.colostate.edu

Columbia University, School of Professional Studies, Program in Landscape Design, New York, NY 10027. Offers MS. *Program availability:* Part-time. *Entrance requirements:* For master's, minimum undergraduate GPA of 3.0. Additional exam requirements/recommendations for international students: required—American Language Program placement test. *Expenses: Tuition:* Full-time $47,600; part-time $1880 per credit. One-time fee: $105.

The Conway School, Program in Ecological Design, Conway, MA 01341-0179. Offers MS. *Degree requirements:* For master's, projects. *Expenses:* Contact institution.

Cornell University, Graduate School, Graduate Fields of Agriculture and Life Sciences and Graduate Fields of Architecture, Art and Planning, Field of Landscape Architecture, Ithaca, NY 14853. Offers MLA, MPS. *Accreditation:* ASLA. *Degree requirements:* For master's, project or thesis. *Entrance requirements:* For master's, GRE General Test (recommended), portfolio, 2 letters of recommendation. Additional exam requirements/recommendations for international students: required—TOEFL (minimum score 550 paper-based; 77 iBT). Electronic applications accepted.

Florida Agricultural and Mechanical University, Division of Graduate Studies, Research, and Continuing Education, School of Architecture, Tallahassee, FL 32307-3200. Offers architectural studies (MS Arch); architecture (professional) (M Arch); landscape architecture (MLA). *Program availability:* Part-time. *Degree requirements:* For master's, thesis. *Entrance requirements:* For master's, GRE General Test, minimum GPA of 3.0, portfolio. Additional exam requirements/recommendations for international students: required—TOEFL (minimum score 550 paper-based).

Florida International University, College of Communication, Architecture and The Arts, Department of Landscape Architecture, Miami, FL 33199. Offers MLA. *Accreditation:* ASLA. *Program availability:* Part-time. *Faculty:* 4 full-time (1 woman), 5 part-time/adjunct (3 women). *Students:* 29 full-time (13 women), 3 part-time (2 women); includes 29 minority (1 Black or African American, non-Hispanic/Latino; 27 Hispanic/Latino; 1 Two or more races, non-Hispanic/Latino), 5 international. Average age 28. 19 applicants, 37% accepted, 3 enrolled. In 2019, 18 master's awarded. *Entrance requirements:* For master's, GRE or minimum GPA of 3.0 in upper-level undergraduate work, portfolio. Additional exam requirements/recommendations for international students: required—TOEFL (minimum score 550 paper-based; 80 iBT). *Application deadline:* For fall admission, 2/1 for domestic and international students. Application fee: $30. Electronic applications accepted. *Expenses: Tuition, area resident:* Full-time $8912; part-time $446 per credit hour. Tuition, state resident: full-time $8912; part-time $446 per credit hour. Tuition, nonresident: full-time $21,393; part-time $992 per credit hour. *Required fees:* $2194. *Financial support:* Institutionally sponsored loans and scholarships/grants available. Financial award application deadline: 3/1; financial award applicants required to submit FAFSA. *Unit head:* David Rifkind, Chair, 305-348-1867, E-mail: David.Rifkind@fiu.edu. *Application contact:* Nanett Rojas, Manager, Admissions Operations, 305-348-7464, Fax: 305-348-7441, E-mail: gradadm@fiu.edu.
Website: http://carta.fiu.edu/landscape/

Harvard University, Graduate School of Arts and Sciences, Committee on Architecture, Landscape Architecture, and Urban Planning, Cambridge, MA 02138. Offers architecture (PhD); landscape architecture (PhD); urban planning (PhD). *Accreditation:* ACSP. *Degree requirements:* For doctorate, one foreign language, thesis/dissertation, oral exam. *Entrance requirements:* For doctorate, GRE General Test. Additional exam requirements/recommendations for international students: required—TOEFL.

Harvard University, Graduate School of Design, Department of Landscape Architecture, Cambridge, MA 02138. Offers MLA. *Accreditation:* ASLA. *Entrance requirements:* For master's, GRE General Test. Additional exam requirements/recommendations for international students: required—TOEFL (minimum score 600 paper-based; 104 iBT). Electronic applications accepted.

Illinois Institute of Technology, Graduate College, College of Architecture, Chicago, IL 60616. Offers M Arch, MLA, MS Arch, PhD, MLA/M Arch. *Accreditation:* ASLA. *Program availability:* Part-time. Terminal master's awarded for partial completion of doctoral program. *Degree requirements:* For master's, comprehensive exam (for some programs), thesis (for some programs); for doctorate, comprehensive exam, thesis/dissertation. *Entrance requirements:* For master's, GRE General Test (minimum score 292 Quantitative and Verbal, 2.5 Analytical Writing), minimum college GPA of 3.0, official transcripts, portfolio, 3 letters of recommendation, professional statement; for doctorate, GRE General Test (minimum score 900 Quantitative and Verbal, 2.5 Analytical Writing), minimum GPA of 3.5, official transcripts, portfolio, 3 letters of recommendation, professional statement. Additional exam requirements/recommendations for international students: required—TOEFL (minimum score 550 paper-based; 80 iBT). Electronic applications accepted.

Iowa State University of Science and Technology, Department of Landscape Architecture, Ames, IA 50011. Offers MLA, MS, MCRP/MLA. *Accreditation:* ASLA. *Program availability:* Part-time. *Degree requirements:* For master's, thesis. *Entrance requirements:* For master's, GRE (highly recommended), portfolio. Additional exam requirements/recommendations for international students: required—TOEFL (minimum score 600 paper-based; 79 iBT), IELTS (minimum score 7). Electronic applications accepted.

Kansas State University, Graduate School, College of Architecture, Planning and Design, Department of Landscape Architecture and Regional and Community Planning, Manhattan, KS 66506. Offers community development (MS); landscape architecture (MLA); regional and community planning (MRCP). *Accreditation:* ACSP; ASLA. *Program availability:* Part-time, 100% online. Terminal master's awarded for partial completion of doctoral program. *Degree requirements:* For master's, thesis, oral exam. *Entrance requirements:* Additional exam requirements/recommendations for international students: required—TOEFL (minimum score 600 paper-based), IELTS (minimum score 6.5). Electronic applications accepted.

Kent State University, College of Architecture and Environmental Design, Kent, OH 44242-0001. Offers architecture (M Arch); architecture and environmental design (MS); health care design (MHCD); landscape architecture (MLA); urban design (MUD); M Arch/MBA; M Arch/MUD. *Accreditation:* ASLA. *Program availability:* Part-time. *Faculty:* 19 full-time (5 women), 9 part-time/adjunct (3 women). *Students:* 62 full-time (29 women), 12 part-time (9 women); includes 8 minority (3 Black or African American, non-Hispanic/Latino; 1 Asian, non-Hispanic/Latino; 2 Hispanic/Latino; 2 Two or more races, non-Hispanic/Latino), 11 international. Average age 26. 149 applicants, 87% accepted, 69 enrolled. In 2019, 66 master's awarded. *Degree requirements:* For master's, thesis (for some programs), capstone project (for some programs). *Entrance requirements:* For master's, GRE with minimum scores 151 (460) verbal reasoning, 150 (620) quantitative reasoning, and 4.25 analytical writing (except for MHCD), letters of recommendation, portfolio. Additional exam requirements/recommendations for international students: required—TOEFL (minimum score 80 iBT), IELTS (minimum score 6.5), PTE (minimum score 54), Michigan English Language Assessment Battery (minimum score 77). *Application deadline:* For fall admission, 1/15 for domestic students; for spring admission, 6/1 for domestic students. Applications are processed on a rolling basis. Application fee: $45 ($70 for international students). Electronic applications accepted. *Financial support:* Research assistantships with full tuition reimbursements, teaching assistantships with full tuition reimbursements, Federal Work-Study, scholarships/grants, and unspecified assistantships available. Financial award application deadline: 2/1; financial award applicants required to submit FAFSA. *Unit head:* Mark Mistur, Dean, 330-672-2917, E-mail: mmistur1@kent.edu. *Application contact:* Bill Willoughby, Associate Dean, 330-672-2917, E-mail: wwilloug@kenk.edu.
Website: http://www.kent.edu/caed

Louisiana State University and Agricultural & Mechanical College, Graduate School, College of Art and Design, Robert Reich School of Landscape Architecture, Baton Rouge, LA 70803. Offers MLA. *Accreditation:* ASLA.

Mississippi State University, College of Agriculture and Life Sciences, Department of Landscape Architecture, Mississippi State, MS 39762. Offers MLA. *Accreditation:* ASLA. *Program availability:* Part-time. *Faculty:* 9 full-time (1 woman). *Students:* 8 full-time (1 woman), 2 part-time (1 woman); includes 2 minority (both Hispanic/Latino), 2 international. Average age 31. 7 applicants, 100% accepted, 2 enrolled. *Degree requirements:* For master's, thesis. *Entrance requirements:* For master's, GRE or minimum GPA of 3.0 in upper-division major emphasis courses from accredited university, minimum GPA of 2.8 on bachelor's degree. Additional exam requirements/recommendations for international students: required—TOEFL (minimum score 600 paper-based; 100 iBT); recommended—IELTS (minimum score 7.5). *Application deadline:* For fall admission, 7/1 for domestic students, 5/1 for international students; for spring admission, 10/1 for domestic students, 9/1 for international students. Applications are processed on a rolling basis. Application fee: $60 ($80 for international students). Electronic applications accepted. *Expenses: Tuition, area resident:* Full-time $8880; part-time $456 per credit hour. Tuition, state resident: full-time $8880. Tuition, nonresident: full-time $23,840; part-time $1236 per credit hour. *Required fees:* $110; $11.12 per credit hour. Tuition and fees vary according to course load. *Financial support:* In 2019–20, 3 research assistantships with full tuition reimbursements (averaging $11,513 per year), 4 teaching assistantships with partial tuition reimbursements (averaging $7,120 per year) were awarded; Federal Work-Study, institutionally sponsored loans, tuition waivers (partial), and unspecified assistantships also available. Financial award application deadline: 4/1; financial award applicants required to submit FAFSA. *Unit head:* Dr. Sadik C. Artunc, Professor and Department Head, 662-325-3012, Fax: 662-325-7893, E-mail: sa305@msstate.edu. *Application contact:* Ryan King, Admissions and Enrollment Assistant, 662-325-8951, Fax: 662-325-7893, E-mail: rjk@grad.msstate.edu.
Website: http://www.lalc.msstate.edu

Morgan State University, School of Graduate Studies, School of Architecture and Planning, Program in Landscape Architecture, Baltimore, MD 21251. Offers MLA. *Accreditation:* ASLA. *Program availability:* Part-time, evening/weekend, online learning. *Faculty:* 4 full-time (3 women). *Students:* 9 full-time (6 women), 3 part-time (2 women); includes 4 minority (2 Black or African American, non-Hispanic/Latino; 1 Asian, non-Hispanic/Latino; 1 Two or more races, non-Hispanic/Latino). Average age 32. 6 applicants, 100% accepted, 6 enrolled. In 2019, 5 master's awarded. *Entrance requirements:* For master's, GPA 3.0. Additional exam requirements/recommendations for international students: required—TOEFL (minimum score 550 paper-based; 70 iBT), IELTS (minimum score 6). *Application deadline:* For fall admission, 7/1 for domestic students; for spring admission, 10/1 priority date for domestic students. Application fee: $50 ($70 for international students). Electronic applications accepted. *Expenses:* Tuition, state resident: full-time $455; part-time $455 per credit hour. Tuition, nonresident: full-time $894; part-time $894 per credit hour. *Required fees:* $82; $82 per credit hour. *Financial support:* In 2019–20, 2 students received support. Fellowships with full and partial tuition reimbursements available, research assistantships with full and partial tuition reimbursements available, teaching assistantships with full and partial tuition reimbursements available, scholarships/grants, health care benefits, tuition waivers (full and partial), and unspecified assistantships available. Support available to part-time students. Financial award application deadline: 2/1; financial award applicants required to submit FAFSA. *Unit head:* Laurel Mcsherry, Program Director, 443-885-1861. *Application contact:* Dr. Jahmaine Smith, Director of Admissions, 443-885-3185,

Fax: 443-885-8226.
Website: https://morgan.edu/sap/laar

North Carolina State University, Graduate School, College of Design, Department of Landscape Architecture, Raleigh, NC 27695. Offers MLA. *Accreditation:* ASLA. *Degree requirements:* For master's, thesis optional, oral exam, project. *Entrance requirements:* For master's, GRE General Test (recommended), portfolio. Electronic applications accepted.

North Dakota State University, College of Graduate and Interdisciplinary Studies, College of Arts, Humanities and Social Sciences, Department of Architecture and Landscape Architecture, Fargo, ND 58102. Offers architecture (M Arch); landscape architecture (MLA). Electronic applications accepted. Tuition and fees vary according to program and reciprocity agreements.

The Ohio State University, Graduate School, College of Engineering, Austin E. Knowlton School of Architecture, Columbus, OH 43210. Offers architecture (M Arch); city and regional planning (MCRP, PhD); landscape architecture (M Land Arch). *Accreditation:* ACSP; ASLA. *Entrance requirements:* For master's, GRE or GMAT (city and regional planning), portfolio (for architecture and landscape architecture); for doctorate, GRE or GMAT (city and regional planning), example of research or written work. Additional exam requirements/recommendations for international students: required—TOEFL (minimum score 600 paper-based; 100 iBT), Michigan English Language Assessment Battery (minimum score 86); recommended—IELTS (minimum score 8). Electronic applications accepted.

Oklahoma State University, College of Agricultural Science and Natural Resources, Department of Horticulture and Landscape Architecture, Stillwater, OK 74078. Offers crop science (PhD); horticulture (M Ag, MS). *Faculty:* 11 full-time (1 woman), 1 (woman) part-time/adjunct. *Students:* 6 full-time (3 women), 18 part-time (11 women); includes 6 minority (2 Black or African American, non-Hispanic/Latino; 2 American Indian or Alaska Native, non-Hispanic/Latino; 2 Hispanic/Latino), 10 international. Average age 26. 8 applicants, 75% accepted, 6 enrolled. In 2019, 4 master's awarded. *Entrance requirements:* For master's and doctorate, GRE or GMAT. Additional exam requirements/recommendations for international students: required—TOEFL (minimum score 550 paper-based; 79 iBT). *Application deadline:* For fall admission, 3/1 priority date for international students; for spring admission, 8/1 priority date for international students. Applications are processed on a rolling basis. Application fee: $50 ($75 for international students). Electronic applications accepted. *Expenses: Tuition, area resident:* Full-time $4148.10; part-time $2765.40 per credit hour. Tuition, state resident: full-time $4148.10; part-time $2765.40 per credit hour. Tuition, nonresident: full-time $15,775; part-time $10,516.80 per credit hour. *International tuition:* $15,775.20 full-time. *Required fees:* $2196.90; $122.05 per credit hour. Tuition and fees vary according to course load, campus/location and program. *Financial support:* In 2019–20, 8 research assistantships (averaging $1,333 per year), 2 teaching assistantships (averaging $1,220 per year) were awarded; career-related internships or fieldwork, Federal Work-Study, scholarships/grants, health care benefits, tuition waivers (partial), and unspecified assistantships also available. Support available to part-time students. Financial award application deadline: 3/1; financial award applicants required to submit FAFSA. *Unit head:* Dr. Justin Moss, Department Head, 405-744-5729, E-mail: mossjq@okstate.edu. *Application contact:* Dr. Sheryl Tucker, Dean, 405-744-7099, Fax: 405-744-0355, E-mail: gradi@okstate.edu.
Website: http://www.hortla.okstate.edu/academics/academics/graduate-program

Penn State University Park, Graduate School, College of Arts and Architecture, Stuckeman School of Architecture and Landscape Architecture, University Park, PA 16802. Offers architecture (M Arch, MS, PhD); landscape architecture (MLA, MS). *Accreditation:* ASLA.

Polytechnic University of Puerto Rico, Graduate School, Hato Rey, PR 00918. Offers business administration (MBA), including computer information systems, general management, management of information systems, management of international enterprises; civil engineering (ME, MS); computer engineering (ME, MS); computer science (MCS, MS); electrical engineering (ME, MS); engineering management (MEM); environmental management (MEM); landscape architecture (M Land Arch); manufacturing competitiveness (MMC, MS); manufacturing engineering (ME, MS); mechanical engineering (M Mech E). *Accreditation:* ASLA. *Program availability:* Part-time, evening/weekend. *Entrance requirements:* For master's, 3 letters of recommendation.

Pontificia Universidad Catolica Madre y Maestra, Graduate School, Faculty of Sciences and Humanities, Santiago, Dominican Republic. Offers architecture (M Arch), including architecture of interiors, architecture of tourist lodgings, landscaping; early childhood education (M Ed).

Rhode Island School of Design, Department of Landscape Architecture, Providence, RI 02903-2784. Offers MLA. *Accreditation:* ASLA. *Students:* 77 full-time (55 women); includes 1 minority (Asian, non-Hispanic/Latino), 66 international. Average age 24. 144 applicants, 63% accepted, 29 enrolled. In 2019, 26 master's awarded. *Degree requirements:* For master's, thesis, exhibition. *Entrance requirements:* For master's, portfolio, statement of purpose, 3 letters of recommendation. Additional exam requirements/recommendations for international students: required—TOEFL (minimum score 580 paper-based; 93 iBT), IELTS (minimum score 6.5), Duolingo. *Application deadline:* For fall admission, 1/10 for domestic and international students. Application fee: $60. Electronic applications accepted. *Expenses: Tuition:* Full-time $51,800. *Required fees:* $1060. *Financial support:* Fellowships, research assistantships, teaching assistantships, Federal Work-Study, scholarships/grants, and unspecified assistantships available. Financial award application deadline: 2/1; financial award applicants required to submit FAFSA. *Unit head:* Johanna Barthmeier-Payne, Department Head, 401-454-6282, Fax: 401-454-6299, E-mail: ldardept@risd.edu. *Application contact:* Molly Pettengill, Associate Director for Graduate Recruitment, 401-454-6312, Fax: 401-454-6309, E-mail: mpetteng@risd.edu.
Website: http://www.risd.edu/academics/landscape-architecture/

Rutgers University - New Brunswick, Graduate School-New Brunswick, Department of Landscape Architecture, Piscataway, NJ 08854-8097. Offers MLA.

State University of New York College of Environmental Science and Forestry, Department of Landscape Architecture, Syracuse, NY 13210-2779. Offers community design and planning (MLA, MS); cultural landscape studies and conservation (MLA, MS); landscape and urban ecology (MLA, MS). *Accreditation:* ASLA (one or more programs are accredited). *Program availability:* Part-time. *Faculty:* 10 full-time (4 women), 7 part-time/adjunct (5 women). *Students:* 19 full-time (13 women), 5 international. Average age 27. 21 applicants, 95% accepted, 7 enrolled. In 2019, 9 master's awarded. *Degree requirements:* For master's, comprehensive exam (for some programs), thesis (for some programs). *Entrance requirements:* For master's, GRE General Test, minimum GPA of 3.0. Additional exam requirements/recommendations for international students: required—TOEFL (minimum score 550 paper-based; 80 iBT), IELTS (minimum score 6), or STEP Eiken (grade 1). *Application deadline:* For fall admission, 2/1 priority date for domestic and international students; for spring admission, 11/1 priority date for domestic and international students. Applications are processed on a rolling basis. Application fee: $60. Electronic applications accepted. *Expenses:* Tuition, state resident: full-time $11,310; part-time $472 per credit hour. Tuition, nonresident: full-time $23,100; part-time $963 per credit hour. *Required fees:* $1890; $95.21 per credit hour. *Financial support:* In 2019–20, 10 students received support. Unspecified assistantships available. Financial award application deadline: 6/30; financial award applicants required to submit FAFSA. *Unit head:* Dr. Douglas Johnston, Chair, 315-470-6544, Fax: 315-470-6540, E-mail: dmjohnst@esf.edu. *Application contact:* Scott Shannon, Associate Provost for Instruction/Dean of the Graduate School, 315-470-6599, Fax: 315-470-6978, E-mail: esfgrad@esf.edu.
Website: http://www.esf.edu/la/

Texas A&M University, College of Architecture, Department of Landscape Architecture and Urban Planning, College Station, TX 77843. Offers land and property development (MLPD); landscape architecture (MLA); urban and regional planning (MUP); urban and regional science (PhD). *Accreditation:* ACSP (one or more programs are accredited); ASLA (one or more programs are accredited). *Faculty:* 33. *Students:* 151 full-time (75 women), 14 part-time (6 women); includes 33 minority (6 Black or African American, non-Hispanic/Latino; 1 American Indian or Alaska Native, non-Hispanic/Latino; 8 Asian, non-Hispanic/Latino; 18 Hispanic/Latino), 70 international. Average age 28. 179 applicants, 64% accepted, 49 enrolled. In 2019, 68 master's, 5 doctorates awarded. Terminal master's awarded for partial completion of doctoral program. *Degree requirements:* For master's, comprehensive exam (for some programs), thesis (for some programs), professional internship; for doctorate, comprehensive exam, thesis/dissertation, seminar. *Entrance requirements:* For master's, GRE General Test, portfolio (MLA), letters of recommendation; for doctorate, GRE General Test, writing sample (URSC), letters of recommendation. Additional exam requirements/recommendations for international students: required—TOEFL (minimum score 550 paper-based; 80 iBT), IELTS (minimum score 6), PTE (minimum score 53). *Application deadline:* For fall admission, 12/1 priority date for domestic and international students. Applications are processed on a rolling basis. Application fee: $65 ($90 for international students). Electronic applications accepted. *Expenses:* Contact institution. *Financial support:* In 2019–20, 125 students received support, including 3 fellowships with tuition reimbursements available (averaging $21,706 per year), 38 research assistantships with tuition reimbursements available (averaging $10,851 per year), 14 teaching assistantships with tuition reimbursements available (averaging $12,905 per year); career-related internships or fieldwork, institutionally sponsored loans, scholarships/grants, traineeships, health care benefits, tuition waivers (full and partial), and unspecified assistantships also available. Support available to part-time students. Financial award application deadline: 12/1; financial award applicants required to submit FAFSA. *Unit head:* Dr. Shannon Van Zandt, Head, 979-458-1223, E-mail: svanzandt@tamu.edu. *Application contact:* Brandi Blankenship, Administrative Coordinator & Graduate Advisor, E-mail: bblankenship@arch.tamu.edu.
Website: http://laup.arch.tamu.edu/

Texas Tech University, Graduate School, College of Agricultural Sciences and Natural Resources, Department of Landscape Architecture, Lubbock, TX 79409-2121. Offers MLA. *Accreditation:* ASLA. *Program availability:* Part-time. *Faculty:* 5 full-time (1 woman), 3 part-time/adjunct (0 women). *Students:* 2 full-time (0 women), 2 part-time (1 woman); includes 1 minority (Hispanic/Latino), 1 international. Average age 29. 5 applicants, 40% accepted, 1 enrolled. In 2019, 1 master's awarded. Terminal master's awarded for partial completion of doctoral program. *Degree requirements:* For master's, thesis or alternative. *Entrance requirements:* For master's, formal approval from departmental committee. Additional exam requirements/recommendations for international students: required—TOEFL (minimum score 550 paper-based; 79 iBT). *Application deadline:* For fall admission, 6/1 priority date for domestic students, 1/15 priority date for international students; for spring admission, 9/1 priority date for domestic students, 6/15 priority date for international students. Applications are processed on a rolling basis. Application fee: $65. Electronic applications accepted. *Expenses:* Contact institution. *Financial support:* In 2019–20, 5 students received support. Fellowships, research assistantships, teaching assistantships, career-related internships or fieldwork, scholarships/grants, and unspecified assistantships available. Financial award application deadline: 4/15; financial award applicants required to submit FAFSA. *Unit head:* Prof. Eric A. Bernard, Professor and Chairperson, 806-834-3482, Fax: 806-742-0770, E-mail: eric.bernard@ttu.edu. *Application contact:* Prof. Eric A. Bernard, Professor and Chairperson, 806-834-3482, Fax: 806-742-0770, E-mail: eric.bernard@ttu.edu.
Website: www.larc.ttu.edu/

The University of Arizona, College of Architecture, Planning, and Landscape Architecture, Landscape Architecture Program, Tucson, AZ 85721. Offers ML Arch. *Accreditation:* ASLA. *Degree requirements:* For master's, thesis. *Entrance requirements:* For master's, minimum GPA of 3.2, 3 letters of reference, statement of intent, portfolio, transcripts. Additional exam requirements/recommendations for international students: required—TOEFL (minimum score 600 paper-based). Electronic applications accepted.

The University of British Columbia, Faculty of Applied Science, School of Architecture and Landscape Architecture, Program in Landscape Architecture, Vancouver, BC V6T 1Z2, Canada. Offers advanced studies in landscape architecture (MASLA); landscape architecture (MLA); urban design (MUD); M Arch/MLA. *Accreditation:* ASLA. *Degree requirements:* For master's, comprehensive exam or thesis. *Entrance requirements:* For master's, portfolio. Additional exam requirements/recommendations for international students: required—TOEFL. Electronic applications accepted. *Expenses:* Contact institution.

University of Calgary, School of Architecture, Planning and Landscaping, Program in Environmental Design, Calgary, AB T2N 1N4, Canada. Offers architecture (M Arch); environmental design (M Env Des, PhD); landscape architecture (MLA); planning (M Plan). *Degree requirements:* For master's, thesis; for doctorate, thesis/dissertation. *Entrance requirements:* For master's, minimum GPA of 3.0; for doctorate, minimum GPA of 3.5. Additional exam requirements/recommendations for international students: required—TOEFL (minimum score 550 paper-based).

University of California, Berkeley, Graduate Division, College of Environmental Design, Department of Landscape Architecture and Environmental Planning, Berkeley, CA 94720. Offers landscape architecture (MLA), including environmental planning, landscape design and site planning, urban and community design; landscape architecture and environmental planning (PhD); MLA/M Arch; MLA/MCP. *Accreditation:* ASLA (one or more programs are accredited). *Degree requirements:* For master's, comprehensive exam (for some programs), thesis (for some programs), professional project or thesis; for doctorate, one foreign language, thesis/dissertation, qualifying exam. *Entrance requirements:* For master's, GRE General Test, minimum GPA of 3.0, portfolio; for doctorate, GRE General Test, master's degree (strongly recommended), minimum GPA of 3.0, sample of written work, 3 letters of recommendation. Additional exam requirements/recommendations for international students: required—TOEFL (minimum score 570 paper-based; 90 iBT). Electronic applications accepted.

University of California, Berkeley, UC Berkeley Extension, Certificate Programs in Art and Design, Berkeley, CA 94720. Offers interior design and interior architecture (Certificate); landscape architecture (Certificate); visual arts (Postbaccalaureate Certificate).

University of Colorado Denver, College of Architecture and Planning, Program in Landscape Architecture, Denver, CO 80217. Offers MLA. *Accreditation:* ASLA. *Program availability:* Part-time. *Degree requirements:* For master's, thesis optional, six-semester sequence of course work totaling 90 semester hours. *Entrance requirements:* For master's, GRE (recommended for students with an undergraduate GPA of 3.0 or lower), portfolio of creative work; statement of purpose; three letters of recommendation. Additional exam requirements/recommendations for international students: required—TOEFL (minimum score 75 iBT). Electronic applications accepted. *Expenses:* Contact institution.

University of Connecticut, Graduate School, College of Agriculture, Health and Natural Resources, Department of Plant Science and Landscape Architecture, Storrs, CT 06269. Offers MS, PhD. Terminal master's awarded for partial completion of doctoral program. *Degree requirements:* For master's, comprehensive exam; for doctorate, thesis/dissertation. *Entrance requirements:* For master's and doctorate, GRE General Test, GRE Subject Test. Additional exam requirements/recommendations for international students: required—TOEFL (minimum score 550 paper-based). Electronic applications accepted.

University of Florida, Graduate School, College of Design, Construction and Planning, Department of Landscape Architecture, Gainesville, FL 32611. Offers geographic information systems (MLA); historic preservation (MLA); landscape architecture (MLA); sustainable design (MLA); wetland sciences (MLA). *Accreditation:* ASLA. *Program availability:* Part-time. *Degree requirements:* For master's, thesis, internship. *Entrance requirements:* For master's, GRE General Test, minimum GPA of 3.0. Additional exam requirements/recommendations for international students: required—TOEFL (minimum score 550 paper-based; 80 iBT), IELTS (minimum score 6). Electronic applications accepted.

University of Florida, Graduate School, College of Design, Construction and Planning, Doctoral Program in Design, Construction and Planning, Gainesville, FL 32611. Offers construction management (PhD); design, construction and planning (PhD); geographic information systems (PhD); historic preservation (PhD); interior design (PhD); landscape architecture (PhD); urban and regional planning (PhD). *Degree requirements:* For doctorate, thesis/dissertation. *Entrance requirements:* For doctorate, GRE General Test, minimum GPA of 3.0. Additional exam requirements/recommendations for international students: required—TOEFL (minimum score 550 paper-based; 80 iBT), IELTS (minimum score 6). Electronic applications accepted.

University of Georgia, College of Environment and Design, Athens, GA 30602. Offers environmental planning and design (MEPD); historic preservation (MHP); landscape architecture (MLA). *Accreditation:* ACSP; ASLA.

University of Guelph, Office of Graduate and Postdoctoral Studies, Ontario Agricultural College, School of Environmental Design and Rural Development, Landscape Architecture Program, Guelph, ON N1G 2W1, Canada. Offers MLA. *Degree requirements:* For master's, thesis. *Entrance requirements:* For master's, minimum B-average during previous 2 years of honors degree, portfolio and questionnaire. Additional exam requirements/recommendations for international students: required—TOEFL (minimum score 600 paper-based; 89 iBT), IELTS (minimum score 7), Canadian Academic Language Assessment, Michigan English Language Assessment Battery. Electronic applications accepted.

University of Idaho, College of Graduate Studies, College of Art and Architecture, Moscow, ID 83844-2282. Offers architecture (M Arch); art and design (MFA); bioregional planning and community design (MS); integrated architecture and design (MS); landscape architecture (MLA). *Accreditation:* NASAD. *Students:* 73 full-time, 10 part-time. Average age 28. 105 applicants, 76% accepted, 38 enrolled. In 2019, 32 master's awarded. *Entrance requirements:* For master's, minimum GPA of 3.0. Additional exam requirements/recommendations for international students: required—TOEFL (minimum score 79 iBT). *Application deadline:* For fall admission, 7/30 for domestic students; for spring admission, 12/1 for domestic students. Applications are processed on a rolling basis. Application fee: $60. Electronic applications accepted. *Expenses:* Tuition, state resident: full-time $7753.80; part-time $502 per credit hour. Tuition, nonresident: full-time $26,990; part-time $1571 per credit hour. *Required fees:* $2122.20; $47 per credit hour. *Financial support:* Applicants required to submit FAFSA. *Unit head:* Dr. Shauna Corry, Dean, 208-885-4409, E-mail: caa@uidaho.edu. *Application contact:* Dr. Shauna Corry, Dean, 208-885-4409, E-mail: caa@uidaho.edu. Website: http://www.uidaho.edu/caa

University of Illinois at Urbana-Champaign, Graduate College, College of Fine and Applied Arts, Department of Landscape Architecture, Champaign, IL 61820. Offers MLA, PhD, MLA/MUP. *Accreditation:* ASLA.

The University of Manchester, School of Environment, Education and Development, Manchester, United Kingdom. Offers architecture (M Phil, PhD); development policy and management (M Phil, PhD); human geography (M Phil, PhD); physical geography (M Phil, PhD); planning and landscape (M Phil, PhD).

University of Manitoba, Faculty of Graduate Studies, Faculty of Architecture, Department of Landscape Architecture, Winnipeg, MB R3T 2N2, Canada. Offers M Land Arch. *Accreditation:* ASLA. *Degree requirements:* For master's, thesis or alternative.

University of Maryland, College Park, Academic Affairs, College of Agriculture and Natural Resources, Department of Plant Science and Landscape Architecture, Landscape Architecture Program, College Park, MD 20742. Offers MLA. *Accreditation:* ASLA. *Entrance requirements:* Additional exam requirements/recommendations for international students: required—TOEFL. Electronic applications accepted.

University of Massachusetts Amherst, Graduate School, College of Social and Behavioral Sciences, Department of Landscape Architecture and Regional Planning, Dual Degree Program in Landscape Architecture and Regional Planning, Amherst, MA 01003. Offers MLA/MRP. *Accreditation:* ACSP; ASLA. *Program availability:* Part-time. *Entrance requirements:* Additional exam requirements/recommendations for international students: required—TOEFL (minimum score 550 paper-based; 80 iBT), IELTS (minimum score 6.5). Electronic applications accepted.

University of Massachusetts Amherst, Graduate School, College of Social and Behavioral Sciences, Department of Landscape Architecture and Regional Planning, Program in Landscape Architecture, Amherst, MA 01003. Offers MLA, MLA/M Arch. *Accreditation:* ASLA. *Program availability:* Part-time. *Degree requirements:* For master's, thesis or alternative. *Entrance requirements:* For master's, GRE General Test, portfolio. Additional exam requirements/recommendations for international students: required—TOEFL (minimum score 550 paper-based; 80 iBT), IELTS (minimum score 6.5). Electronic applications accepted.

University of Michigan, School for Environment and Sustainability, Program in Landscape Architecture, Ann Arbor, MI 48109. Offers MLA, MLA/M Arch, MLA/MBA, MURP/MLA. *Accreditation:* ASLA (one or more programs are accredited). *Degree requirements:* For master's, thesis, practicum, or group project. *Entrance requirements:* For master's, GRE General Test (must be taken within 5 years of application submission). Additional exam requirements/recommendations for international students:

required—TOEFL (minimum score 560 paper-based; 84 iBT). Electronic applications accepted.

University of Minnesota, Twin Cities Campus, Graduate School, College of Design, Department of Landscape Architecture, Minneapolis, MN 55455-0213. Offers MLA, MS. *Accreditation:* ASLA (one or more programs are accredited). *Degree requirements:* For master's, thesis (MS). *Entrance requirements:* For master's, GRE General Test (MS), suggested GPA of 3.0. Additional exam requirements/recommendations for international students: required—TOEFL (minimum score 550 paper-based; 79 iBT). Electronic applications accepted. *Expenses:* Contact institution.

University of New Mexico, Graduate Studies, School of Architecture and Planning, Department of Landscape Architecture, Albuquerque, NM 87131-2039. Offers MLA. *Accreditation:* ASLA. *Program availability:* Part-time. *Degree requirements:* For master's, comprehensive exam, thesis optional, portfolio review, thesis studio. *Entrance requirements:* For master's, minimum GPA of 3.0. Additional exam requirements/recommendations for international students: required—TOEFL. Electronic applications accepted. *Expenses:* Contact institution.

University of Oklahoma, Christopher C. Gibbs College of Architecture, Division of Landscape Architecture, Norman, OK 73019-0390. Offers landscape architectural studies (MLA); landscape architecture (MLA); MRCP/MLA. *Accreditation:* ASLA. Terminal master's awarded for partial completion of doctoral program. *Entrance requirements:* Additional exam requirements/recommendations for international students: required—TOEFL (minimum score 79 iBT) or IELTS (minimum score 6.5). Electronic applications accepted. *Expenses:* Tuition, state resident: full-time $6583.20; part-time $274.30 per credit hour. Tuition, nonresident: full-time $21,242; part-time $885.10 per credit hour. *International tuition:* $21,242.40 full-time. *Required fees:* $1994.20; $72.55 per credit hour. $126.50 per semester. Tuition and fees vary according to course load and degree level.

University of Oregon, Graduate School, College of Design, Department of Landscape Architecture, Eugene, OR 97403. Offers MLA, PhD. *Accreditation:* ASLA. *Degree requirements:* For master's, thesis or alternative, project. *Entrance requirements:* For master's, portfolio. Additional exam requirements/recommendations for international students: required—TOEFL.

University of Pennsylvania, Stuart Weitzman School of Design, Department of Landscape Architecture, Philadelphia, PA 19104. Offers landscape architecture (MLA); landscape studies (Certificate). *Accreditation:* ASLA (one or more programs are accredited). *Program availability:* Part-time. *Faculty:* 6 full-time (2 women), 5 part-time/ adjunct (2 women). *Students:* 131 full-time (93 women), 2 part-time (both women); includes 11 minority (1 Black or African American, non-Hispanic/Latino; 6 Asian, non-Hispanic/Latino; 4 Hispanic/Latino), 92 international. Average age 26. 337 applicants, 37% accepted, 60 enrolled. In 2019, 48 master's, 10 Certificates awarded. Application fee: $80. *Financial support:* Teaching assistantships available. Financial award application deadline: 2/1. *Application contact:* Joan Weston, Director of Admissions & Financial Aid, 215-898-6520, E-mail: weston@design.upenn.edu.

University of Southern California, Graduate School, School of Architecture, Los Angeles, CA 90089. Offers architecture (M Arch); building science (MBS); heritage conservation (MHP); landscape architecture and urbanism (MLA); M Arch/M Pl; MLA/M Pl. Terminal master's awarded for partial completion of doctoral program. *Degree requirements:* For master's, thesis (for some programs). *Entrance requirements:* For master's, GRE. Additional exam requirements/recommendations for international students: required—TOEFL (minimum score 100 iBT). Electronic applications accepted.

The University of Tennessee, Graduate School, College of Architecture and Design, Program in Landscape Architecture, Knoxville, TN 37996. Offers landscape architecture (MLA); landscape architecture (research) (MA, MS). *Accreditation:* ASLA. *Degree requirements:* For master's, oral exam, project and thesis optional (MLA), oral exam and thesis (MA, MS). *Entrance requirements:* For master's, GRE General Test, minimum GPA of 3.0, 3 letters of recommendation, samples of portfolio work. Additional exam requirements/recommendations for international students: required—TOEFL (minimum score 550 paper-based).

The University of Texas at Arlington, Graduate School, College of Architecture, Planning and Public Affairs, Program in Landscape Architecture, Arlington, TX 76019. Offers MLA. *Accreditation:* ASLA. *Program availability:* Part-time, evening/weekend. *Degree requirements:* For master's, thesis. *Entrance requirements:* For master's, GRE General Test, minimum GPA of 3.0, portfolio. Additional exam requirements/recommendations for international students: required—TOEFL (minimum score 575 paper-based; 80 iBT).

The University of Texas at Austin, Graduate School, School of Architecture, Program in Landscape Architecture, Austin, TX 78712-1111. Offers MLA. *Accreditation:* ASLA.

University of Toronto, School of Graduate Studies, John H. Daniels Faculty of Architecture, Landscape, and Design, Toronto, ON M5S 1A1, Canada. Offers M Arch, MLA, MUD, MVS. *Entrance requirements:* For master's, minimum B average; 3 letters of reference; resume; 3 writing samples; 5 samples of design work, drawing, or work in a related field, statement of interest. Additional exam requirements/recommendations for international students: required—TOEFL (minimum score 580 paper-based; 93 iBT), IELTS (minimum score 7), TWE (minimum score 5), Michigan English Language Assessment Battery (minimum score 85), COPE (minimum score 76). Electronic applications accepted. *Expenses:* Contact institution.

University of Virginia, School of Architecture, Department of Landscape Architecture, Charlottesville, VA 22903. Offers M Land Arch. *Accreditation:* ASLA. *Entrance requirements:* For master's, GRE General Test, 3 letters of recommendation; portfolio. Additional exam requirements/recommendations for international students: required—TOEFL (minimum score 600 paper-based; 90 iBT). Electronic applications accepted.

University of Washington, Graduate School, College of Built Environments, Department of Landscape Architecture, Seattle, WA 98195. Offers MLA. *Accreditation:* ASLA. *Degree requirements:* For master's, thesis. *Entrance requirements:* For master's, GRE, minimum GPA of 3.0. Additional exam requirements/recommendations for international students: required—TOEFL.

University of Wisconsin–Madison, Graduate School, College of Letters and Science, Department of Planning and Landscape Architecture, Madison, WI 53706-1380. Offers landscape architecture (MS); urban and regional planning (MS, PhD). *Accreditation:* ACSP (one or more programs are accredited). *Program availability:* Part-time. *Degree requirements:* For master's, thesis optional, internship; for doctorate, thesis/dissertation, 3 preliminary exams. *Entrance requirements:* For master's, GRE, minimum GPA of 3.0, previous course work in statistics; for doctorate, 1 year of experience, master's degree in related field. Electronic applications accepted.

Utah State University, School of Graduate Studies, College of Agriculture and Applied Sciences, Department of Landscape Architecture and Environmental Planning, Logan, UT 84322. Offers bioregional planning (MS); landscape architecture (MLA). *Accreditation:* ASLA (one or more programs are accredited). *Degree requirements:* For master's, thesis. *Entrance requirements:* For master's, GRE General Test, minimum GPA of 3.0. Additional exam requirements/recommendations for international students: required—TOEFL.

Virginia Polytechnic Institute and State University, Graduate School, College of Architecture and Urban Studies, Blacksburg, VA 24061. Offers architecture (M Arch, MS); architecture and design research (PhD); building construction science management (MS); creative technologies (MFA); environmental design and planning (PhD); government and international affairs (MPIA); landscape architecture (MLA, PhD); planning, governance, and globalization (PhD); public administration and public affairs (MPA, PhD); urban and regional planning (MURPL). *Accreditation:* ASLA (one or more programs are accredited). *Faculty:* 145 full-time (58 women), 2 part-time/adjunct (1 woman). *Students:* 304 full-time (156 women), 180 part-time (77 women); includes 90 minority (40 Black or African American, non-Hispanic/Latino; 19 Asian, non-Hispanic/Latino; 24 Hispanic/Latino; 7 Two or more races, non-Hispanic/Latino), 130 international. Average age 33. 475 applicants, 72% accepted, 126 enrolled. In 2019, 130 master's, 23 doctorates awarded. *Degree requirements:* For master's, comprehensive exam (for some programs), thesis (for some programs); for doctorate, comprehensive exam (for some programs), thesis/dissertation (for some programs). *Entrance requirements:* For master's and doctorate, GRE/GMAT. Additional exam requirements/recommendations for international students: required—TOEFL (minimum score 90 iBT). *Application deadline:* For fall admission, 8/1 for domestic students, 4/1 for international students; for spring admission, 1/1 for domestic students, 9/1 for international students. Applications are processed on a rolling basis. Application fee: $75. Electronic applications accepted. *Expenses:* Tuition, state resident: full-time $13,700; part-time $761.25 per credit hour. Tuition, nonresident: full-time $27,614; part-time $1534 per credit hour. *Required fees:* $886.50 per term. Tuition and fees vary according to campus/location and program. *Financial support:* In 2019–20, 2 fellowships with full tuition reimbursements (averaging $24,875 per year), 35 research assistantships with full tuition reimbursements (averaging $16,344 per year), 126 teaching assistantships with full tuition reimbursements (averaging $11,525 per year) were awarded; scholarships/grants and unspecified assistantships also available. Financial award application deadline: 3/1; financial award applicants required to submit FAFSA. *Unit head:* Dr. Richard Blythe, Dean, 540-231-6416, Fax: 540-231-6332, E-mail: richbl1@vt.edu. *Application contact:* Christine Mattsson-Coon, Executive Assistant, 540-231-6416, Fax: 540-231-6332, E-mail: cmattsso@vt.edu.
Website: http://www.caus.vt.edu/

Washington State University, College of Agricultural, Human, and Natural Resource Sciences, Program in Interior Design and Landscape Architecture, Pullman, WA 99164-2220. Offers MA, MS. *Program availability:* Part-time. *Degree requirements:* For master's, comprehensive exam, thesis (for some programs), oral exam. *Entrance requirements:* For master's, portfolio. Additional exam requirements/recommendations for international students: required—TOEFL or IELTS. Electronic applications accepted.

Washington University in St. Louis, Sam Fox School of Design and Visual Arts, Program in Landscape Architecture, St. Louis, MO 63130-4899. Offers MLA.

West Virginia University, Davis College of Agriculture, Forestry and Consumer Sciences, Morgantown, WV 26506. Offers agricultural and extension education (MS, PhD); agriculture and resource management (MS); agriculture, natural resources and design (M Agr); agronomy (MS); animal and food science (PhD); animal physiology (MS); applied and environmental microbiology (MS); design and merchandising (MS); entomology (MS); forest resource science (PhD); forestry (MSF); genetics and developmental biology (MS, PhD); horticulture (MS); human and community development (PhD); landscape architecture (MLA); natural resource economics (PhD); nutritional and food science (MS); plant and soil science (PhD); plant pathology (MS); recreation, parks and tourism resources (MS); reproductive physiology (MS, PhD); wildlife and fisheries resources (PhD). *Accreditation:* ASLA. *Program availability:* Part-time. *Degree requirements:* For master's, thesis; for doctorate, thesis/dissertation. *Entrance requirements:* Additional exam requirements/recommendations for international students: required—TOEFL (minimum score 550 paper-based). Electronic applications accepted.

Lighting Design

The New School, Parsons School of Design, Program in Lighting Design, New York, NY 10011. Offers MFA, M Arch/MFA. *Faculty:* 6 full-time (1 woman), 62 part-time/adjunct. *Students:* 28 full-time (24 women), 2 part-time (both women); includes 4 minority (1 Asian, non-Hispanic/Latino; 2 Hispanic/Latino; 1 Two or more races, non-Hispanic/Latino), 22 international. Average age 27. 37 applicants, 81% accepted, 12 enrolled. In 2019, 7 master's awarded. *Degree requirements:* For master's, thesis. *Entrance requirements:* For master's, transcripts, resume, statement of purpose, recommendation letters, portfolio, interviews. Additional exam requirements/recommendations for international students: required—TOEFL (minimum score 92 iBT), IELTS (minimum score 7), PTE (minimum score 63). *Application deadline:* For fall admission, 1/1 priority date for domestic and international students; for summer admission, 1/1 priority date for domestic and international students. Applications are processed on a rolling basis. Application fee: $50. Electronic applications accepted. *Expenses:* 1810 per credit. *Financial support:* In 2019–20, 20 students received support, including 2 research assistantships (averaging $5,302 per year), 1 teaching assistantship (averaging $1,404 per year); career-related internships or fieldwork, scholarships/grants, and unspecified assistantships also available. Support available to part-time students. Financial award application deadline: 2/1; financial award applicants required to submit FAFSA. *Unit head:* Craig Bernecker, 212-229-8900 Ext. 4866, E-mail: berneckc@newschool.edu. *Application contact:* Simone Varadian, Senior Director, 212-229-5150 Ext. 4117, E-mail: varadias@newschool.edu.
Website: https://www.newschool.edu/parsons/lighting-design/

New York School of Interior Design, Program in Interior Lighting Design, New York, NY 10021-5110. Offers MPS. *Entrance requirements:* For master's, portfolio, resume, undergraduate degree in interior design or closely-related field. Additional exam requirements/recommendations for international students: required—TOEFL (minimum score 79 iBT). Electronic applications accepted.

Rensselaer Polytechnic Institute, Graduate School, School of Architecture, Program in Architectural Sciences, Troy, NY 12180-3590. Offers architectural acoustics (PhD); built ecologies (PhD); lighting (PhD). *Faculty:* 33 full-time (8 women), 13 part-time/adjunct (1 woman). *Students:* 21 full-time (5 women), 2 part-time (both women); includes 4 minority (1 Black or African American, non-Hispanic/Latino; 1 Asian, non-Hispanic/Latino; 2 Two or more races, non-Hispanic/Latino), 7 international. Average age 28. 28 applicants, 57% accepted, 5 enrolled. In 2019, 4 doctorates awarded. *Degree requirements:* For doctorate, comprehensive exam (for some programs), thesis/dissertation. *Entrance requirements:* For doctorate, GRE, portfolio/personal statement. Additional exam requirements/recommendations for international students: required—TOEFL (minimum score 570 paper-based; 88 iBT), IELTS (minimum score 6.5), PTE (minimum score 60). *Application deadline:* For fall admission, 1/1 priority date for domestic and international students. Applications are processed on a rolling basis. Application fee: $75. Electronic applications accepted. *Financial support:* In 2019–20, research assistantships (averaging $23,000 per year), teaching assistantships with full tuition reimbursements (averaging $23,000 per year) were awarded; fellowships also available. Financial award application deadline: 1/1. *Unit head:* Evan Douglis, Dean, School of Architecture, 518-276-3034, E-mail: douglis@rpi.edu. *Application contact:* Jarron Decker, Director of Graduate Admissions, 518-276-6216, Fax: 518-276-4072, E-mail: gradadmissions@rpi.edu.
Website: http://www.arch.rpi.edu/academic/graduate/phd-program/

Rensselaer Polytechnic Institute, Graduate School, School of Architecture, Program in Lighting, Troy, NY 12180-3590. Offers MS. *Faculty:* 33 full-time (8 women), 13 part-time/adjunct (1 woman). *Students:* 7 full-time (3 women), 5 international. Average age 28. 6 applicants, 83% accepted, 4 enrolled. In 2019, 4 master's awarded. *Degree requirements:* For master's, comprehensive exam, thesis. *Entrance requirements:* For master's, GRE. Additional exam requirements/recommendations for international students: required—TOEFL (minimum score 570 paper-based; 88 iBT), IELTS (minimum score 6.5), PTE (minimum score 60). *Application deadline:* For fall admission, 1/1 priority date for domestic and international students. Applications are processed on a rolling basis. Application fee: $75. Electronic applications accepted. *Financial support:* Scholarships/grants available. Financial award application deadline: 1/1. *Unit head:* Nadarajah Narendran, Graduate Program Director, 518-687-7100, E-mail: narenn2@rpi.edu. *Application contact:* Jarron Decker, Director of Graduate Admissions, 518-276-6216, Fax: 518-276-4072, E-mail: gradadmissions@rpi.edu.
Website: http://www.arch.rpi.edu/academic/graduate/lighting/

University of Washington, Graduate School, College of Built Environments, Department of Architecture, Seattle, WA 98195. Offers architecture (M Arch, MS); built environment (PhD); design computing (Certificate); design firm leadership and management (Certificate); historic preservation (Certificate); lighting (Certificate); urban design (Certificate). *Degree requirements:* For master's, thesis. *Entrance requirements:* For master's, GRE General Test, minimum GPA of 3.0, portfolio, 3 letters of recommendation. Additional exam requirements/recommendations for international students: required—TOEFL.

Urban Design

Arizona State University at Tempe, Herberger Institute for Design and the Arts, The Design School, Tempe, AZ 85287-1605. Offers architecture (M Arch); building design/built environment (MS); design (MSD), including arts, media, and engineering, healthcare and healing environments (MSD, PhD), industrial design, interaction design, interior design, new product innovation, visual communication design; design, environment and the arts (PhD), including design, digital culture, healthcare and healing environments (MSD, PhD), history, theory, and criticism; landscape architecture (MLA); urban design (MUD); MA/MBA. *Accreditation:* ASLA; NASAD. Terminal master's awarded for partial completion of doctoral program. *Degree requirements:* For master's, thesis optional, interactive Program of Study (iPOS) submitted before completing 50 percent of required credit hours; for doctorate, comprehensive exam, thesis/dissertation, interactive Program of Study (iPOS) submitted before completing 50 percent of required credit hours. *Entrance requirements:* For master's, GRE General Test, minimum GPA of 3.0 or equivalent in last 2 years of work leading to bachelor's degree, design/creative works portfolio, 3 references, statement of intent; for doctorate, GRE, master's degree in architecture, graphic design, industrial design, interior design, landscape architecture, or art history or equivalent standing; statement of purpose; 3 letters of recommendation; indication of potential faculty mentor; sample of written work. Additional exam requirements/recommendations for international students: required—TOEFL (minimum score 600 paper-based; 100 iBT). Electronic applications accepted.

Ball State University, Graduate School, College of Architecture and Planning, Interdepartmental Program in Urban Design, Muncie, IN 47306. Offers MUD. *Entrance requirements:* For master's, minimum cumulative baccalaureate GPA of 2.75 or 3.0 for latter half of baccalaureate, curriculum vitae or resume, statement of professional intent, portfolio of professional/academic work, writing sample. Additional exam requirements/recommendations for international students: required—TOEFL (minimum score 550 paper-based; 79 iBT), IELTS (minimum score 6.5). Electronic applications accepted. *Expenses:* Contact institution.

Carnegie Mellon University, College of Fine Arts, School of Architecture, Pittsburgh, PA 15213-3891. Offers architecture (MSA); architecture, engineering, and construction management (PhD); building performance and diagnostics (MS, PhD); computational design (MS, PhD); engineering construction management (MSA); tangible interaction design (MTID); urban design (MUD). Terminal master's awarded for partial completion of doctoral program. *Degree requirements:* For doctorate, thesis/

dissertation. *Entrance requirements:* For master's and doctorate, GRE General Test. Additional exam requirements/recommendations for international students: required—TOEFL.

City College of the City University of New York, Graduate School, The Bernard and Anne Spitzer School of Architecture, Program in Urban Design, New York, NY 10031-9198. Offers MUP. *Program availability:* Part-time. *Degree requirements:* For master's, thesis. *Entrance requirements:* For master's, portfolio, professional degree in architecture or equivalent. Additional exam requirements/recommendations for international students: required—TOEFL (minimum score 550 paper-based).

Cornell University, Graduate School, Graduate Fields of Architecture, Art and Planning, Field of Architecture, Ithaca, NY 14853. Offers architectural design (M Arch); architectural science (MS); computer graphics (MS); history of architecture (MA, PhD); history of urban development (MA, PhD); theory and criticism of architecture (M Arch); urban design (M Arch). *Degree requirements:* For master's, one foreign language, thesis (MA, MS); for doctorate, 2 foreign languages, comprehensive exam, thesis/dissertation. *Entrance requirements:* For master's, GRE General Test, 5-year bachelor's degree in architecture, portfolio (M Arch), 3 letters of recommendation; for doctorate, GRE General Test, 3 letters of recommendation. Additional exam requirements/recommendations for international students: required—TOEFL (minimum score 600 paper-based; 77 iBT). Electronic applications accepted.

DePaul University, College of Liberal Arts and Social Sciences, Chicago, IL 60614. Offers Arabic (MA); Chinese (MA); critical ethnic studies (MA); English (MA); French (MA); German (MA); history (MA); interdisciplinary studies (MA, MS); international public service (MS); international studies (MA); Italian (MA); Japanese (MA); liberal studies (MA); nonprofit management (MNM); public administration (MPA); public health (MPH); public policy (MPP); public service management (MS); refugee and forced migration studies (MS); social work (MSW); sociology (MA); Spanish (MA); sustainable urban development (MA); women's and gender studies (MA); writing and publishing (MA); writing, rhetoric and discourse (MA); MA/PhD. *Accreditation:* CEPH. *Program availability:* Part-time, evening/weekend, online learning. Terminal master's awarded for partial completion of doctoral program. *Degree requirements:* For master's, variable foreign language requirement, comprehensive exam (for some programs), thesis (for some programs). Electronic applications accepted.

Drexel University, Westphal College of Media Arts and Design, Program in Urban Strategy, Philadelphia, PA 19104-2875. Offers MS.

Georgia Institute of Technology, Graduate Studies, College of Design, School of City and Regional Planning, Atlanta, GA 30332-0001. Offers city and regional planning (PhD); economic development (MCRP); environmental planning and management (MCRP); geographic information systems (MCRP); land and community development (MCRP); land use planning (MCRP); transportation (MCRP); urban design (MCRP); MCP/MSCE. *Accreditation:* ACSP. *Degree requirements:* For master's, thesis, internship. *Entrance requirements:* For master's, GRE General Test, minimum GPA of 2.7. Additional exam requirements/recommendations for international students: required—TOEFL. Electronic applications accepted. *Expenses: Tuition, area resident:* Full-time $14,064; part-time $586 per credit hour. Tuition, state resident: full-time $14,064; part-time $586 per credit hour. Tuition, nonresident: full-time $29,140; part-time $1215 per credit hour. *International tuition:* $29,140 full-time. *Required fees:* $2024; $840 per semester. $2096. Tuition and fees vary according to course load.

Harvard University, Graduate School of Design, Department of Urban Planning and Design, Cambridge, MA 02138. Offers urban planning (MUP); urban planning and design (MAUD, MLAUD). *Accreditation:* ACSP (one or more programs are accredited). *Entrance requirements:* For master's, GRE General Test. Additional exam requirements/recommendations for international students: required—TOEFL (minimum score 600 paper-based; 104 iBT). Electronic applications accepted.

Hofstra University, College of Liberal Arts and Sciences, Programs in Biology, Hempstead, NY 11549. Offers biology (MA, MS); urban ecology (MA, MS). *Program availability:* Part-time, evening/weekend. *Students:* 5 full-time (3 women), 4 part-time (all women); includes 4 minority (1 Asian, non-Hispanic/Latino; 2 Hispanic/Latino; 1 Two or more races, non-Hispanic/Latino). Average age 25. 21 applicants, 71% accepted, 5 enrolled. In 2019, 9 master's awarded. *Degree requirements:* For master's, thesis, minimum GPA of 3.0. *Entrance requirements:* For master's, GRE, bachelor's degree in biology or equivalent, 2 letters of recommendation, essay. Additional exam requirements/recommendations for international students: required—TOEFL (minimum score 550 paper-based; 80 iBT); recommended—IELTS (minimum score 6.5). *Application deadline:* Applications are processed on a rolling basis. Application fee: $75. Electronic applications accepted. *Expenses: Tuition:* Full-time $25,164; part-time $1398 per credit. *Required fees:* $580; $165 per semester. Tuition and fees vary according to course load, degree level and program. *Financial support:* In 2019–20, 11 students received support, including 8 fellowships with full and partial tuition reimbursements available (averaging $7,443 per year); research assistantships with full and partial tuition reimbursements available, career-related internships or fieldwork, Federal Work-Study, institutionally sponsored loans, scholarships/grants, tuition waivers (full and partial), unspecified assistantships, and scholarships and endowed scholarships also available. Support available to part-time students. Financial award applicants required to submit FAFSA. *Unit head:* Dr. Peter Daniel, Chairperson, 516-463-6718, Fax: 516-463-5112, E-mail: peter.c.daniel@hofstra.edu. *Application contact:* Sunil Samuel, Assistant Vice President of Admissions, 516-463-4723, Fax: 516-463-4664, E-mail: graduateadmission@hofstra.edu.
Website: http://www.hofstra.edu/hclas

Judson University, Master of Architecture Program, Elgin, IL 60123. Offers architecture (M Arch); sustainable design (M Arch); traditional architecture and urbanism (M Arch). *Program availability:* Part-time. *Faculty:* 4 full-time (0 women), 2 part-time/adjunct (0 women). *Students:* 11 full-time (4 women), 1 part-time (0 women); includes 10 minority (all Hispanic/Latino). Average age 24. 12 applicants, 100% accepted, 12 enrolled. In 2019, 18 master's awarded. *Degree requirements:* For master's, thesis optional, 1600-hour practicum/preceptorship completed prior to enrollment. *Entrance requirements:* For master's, GRE, BA in Architecture or equivalent; transcripts, 1600 hours under a licensed architect, portfolio, minimum cumulative undergraduate GPA of 2.75, 3.0 in architecture; 3 letters of recommendation, letter of intent. Additional exam requirements/recommendations for international students: required—TOEFL (minimum score 550 paper-based), IELTS (minimum score 6.5). *Application deadline:* For fall admission, 2/15 priority date for domestic and international students; for winter admission, 11/15 for domestic students; for spring admission, 11/15 for domestic and international students. Applications are processed on a rolling basis. Application fee: $100. Electronic applications accepted. *Expenses:* Contact institution. *Financial support:* In 2019–20, 9 students received support. Fellowships, research assistantships, teaching assistantships, scholarships/grants, and 8 assistantships available. Financial award application deadline: 5/1; financial award applicants required to submit FAFSA. *Unit head:* Dr. Curtis Sartor, Interim Chair, 847-628-1017, E-mail: csartor@judsonu.edu. *Application contact:* Annelise Pollard, Admissions Representative, 847-628-2519, E-mail: annelise.pollard@judsonu.edu.
Website: http://www.judsonu.edu/ArchMaster/

Kent State University, College of Architecture and Environmental Design, Kent, OH 44242-0001. Offers architecture (M Arch); architecture and environmental design (MS); health care design (MHCD); landscape architecture (MLA); urban design (MUD); M Arch/MBA; M Arch/MUD. *Accreditation:* ASLA. *Program availability:* Part-time. *Faculty:* 19 full-time (5 women), 9 part-time/adjunct (3 women). *Students:* 62 full-time (29 women), 12 part-time (9 women); includes 8 minority (3 Black or African American, non-Hispanic/Latino; 1 Asian, non-Hispanic/Latino; 2 Hispanic/Latino; 2 Two or more races, non-Hispanic/Latino), 11 international. Average age 26. 149 applicants, 87% accepted, 69 enrolled. In 2019, 66 master's awarded. *Degree requirements:* For master's, thesis (for some programs), capstone project (for some programs). *Entrance requirements:* For master's, GRE with minimum scores 151 (460) verbal reasoning, 150 (620) quantitative reasoning, and 4.25 analytical writing (except for MHCD), letters of recommendation, portfolio. Additional exam requirements/recommendations for international students: required—TOEFL (minimum score 80 iBT), IELTS (minimum score 6.5), PTE (minimum score 54), Michigan English Language Assessment Battery (minimum score 77). *Application deadline:* For fall admission, 1/15 for domestic students; for spring admission, 6/1 for domestic students. Applications are processed on a rolling basis. Application fee: $45 ($70 for international students). Electronic applications accepted. *Financial support:* Research assistantships with full tuition reimbursements, teaching assistantships with full tuition reimbursements, Federal Work-Study, scholarships/grants, and unspecified assistantships available. Financial award application deadline: 2/1; financial award applicants required to submit FAFSA. *Unit head:* Mark Mistur, Dean, 330-672-2917, E-mail: mmistur1@kent.edu. *Application contact:* Bill Willoughby, Associate Dean, 330-672-2917, E-mail: wwilloug@kenk.edu.
Website: http://www.kent.edu/caed

Lawrence Technological University, College of Architecture and Design, Southfield, MI 48075-1058. Offers architecture (M Arch, MA), including interior architecture (M Arch); build information modeling (Graduate Certificate); interior design (MID); public interest design (Graduate Certificate); social practice (MFA); urban design (MUD). *Accreditation:* NASAD. *Program availability:* Part-time, evening/weekend. *Faculty:* 10 full-time (1 woman), 7 part-time/adjunct (4 women). *Students:* 6 full-time (3 women), 149 part-time (70 women); includes 18 minority (7 Black or African American, non-Hispanic/Latino; 3 Asian, non-Hispanic/Latino; 6 Hispanic/Latino; 2 Two or more races, non-Hispanic/Latino), 21 international. Average age 30. 214 applicants, 84% accepted, 94 enrolled. In 2019, 54 master's awarded. *Degree requirements:* For master's, thesis optional. *Entrance requirements:* Additional exam requirements/recommendations for international students: required—TOEFL (minimum score 550 paper-based; 79 iBT). *Application deadline:* For fall admission, 5/24 for international students; for spring admission, 10/13 for international students; for summer admission, 2/18 for international students. Applications are processed on a rolling basis. Application fee: $50. Electronic applications accepted. *Expenses: Tuition:* Full-time $16,618; part-time $8309 per year. *Required fees:* $600; $600. *Financial support:* In 2019–20, 39 students received support, including 8 research assistantships with partial tuition reimbursements available (averaging $6,000 per year); career-related internships or fieldwork, scholarships/grants, and unspecified assistantships also available. Financial award application deadline: 4/1; financial award applicants required to submit FAFSA. *Unit head:* Prof. Karl Daubmann, Dean/Professor, 248-204-2805, E-mail: archdean@ltu.edu. *Application contact:* Jane Rohrback, Director of Admissions, 248-204-3160, Fax: 248-204-2228, E-mail: admissions@ltu.edu.
Website: http://www.ltu.edu/architecture_and_design/index.asp

London Metropolitan University, Graduate Programs, London, United Kingdom. Offers applied psychology (M Sc); architecture (MA); biomedical science (M Sc); blood science (M Sc); cancer pharmacology (M Sc); computer networking and cyber security (M Sc); computing and information systems (M Sc); conference interpreting (MA); counter-terrorism studies (M Sc); creative, digital and professional writing (MA); crime, violence and prevention (M Sc); criminology (M Sc); curating contemporary art (MA); data analytics (M Sc); digital media (MA); early childhood studies (MA); education (MA, Ed D); financial services law, regulation and compliance (LL M); food science (M Sc); forensic psychology (M Sc); health and social care management and policy (M Sc); human nutrition (M Sc); human resource management (MA); human rights and international conflict (MA); information technology (M Sc); intelligence and security studies (M Sc); international oil, gas and energy law (LL M); international relations (MA); interpreting (MA); learning and teaching in higher education (MA); legal practice (LL M); media and entertainment law (LL M); organizational and consumer psychology (M Sc); psychological therapy (M Sc); psychology of mental health (M Sc); public health (M Sc); public policy and management (MPA); security studies (M Sc); social work (M Sc); spatial planning and urban design (MA); sports therapy (M Sc); supporting older children and young people with dyslexia (MA); teaching languages (MA), including Arabic, English; translation (MA); woman and child abuse (MA).

The New School, Parsons School of Design, Program in Design and Urban Ecologies, New York, NY 10011. Offers MS. *Program availability:* Part-time. *Faculty:* 8 full-time (4 women), 4 part-time/adjunct. *Students:* 21 full-time (16 women), 1 (woman) part-time; includes 7 minority (2 Black or African American, non-Hispanic/Latino; 3 Hispanic/Latino; 1 Native Hawaiian or other Pacific Islander, non-Hispanic/Latino; 1 Two or more races, non-Hispanic/Latino), 8 international. Average age 28. 39 applicants, 92% accepted, 7 enrolled. In 2019, 16 master's awarded. *Degree requirements:* For master's, thesis. *Entrance requirements:* For master's, transcripts, resume, statement of purpose, recommendation letters, portfolio, interview. Additional exam requirements/recommendations for international students: required—TOEFL (minimum score 92 iBT), IELTS (minimum score 7), PTE (minimum score 63). *Application deadline:* For fall admission, 1/1 priority date for domestic and international students; for summer admission, 1/1 priority date for domestic and international students. Applications are processed on a rolling basis. Application fee: $50. Electronic applications accepted. *Expenses:* 1810 per credit. *Financial support:* In 2019–20, 29 students received support, including 9 research assistantships (averaging $6,005 per year), 2 teaching assistantships (averaging $4,682 per year); career-related internships or fieldwork, Federal Work-Study, scholarships/grants, unspecified assistantships, and travel funding; tuition waivers for students who are also New School employees also available. Support available to part-time students. Financial award application deadline: 2/1; financial award applicants required to submit FAFSA. *Unit head:* Miodrag Mitrasinovic, Chair, Urban Council, E-mail: mitrasim@newschool.edu. *Application contact:* Simone Varadian, Senior Director, 212-229-5150 Ext. 4117, E-mail: thinkparsonsgrad@newschool.edu.
Website: https://www.newschool.edu/parsons/ms-design-urban-ecology/

The New School, Parsons School of Design, Program in Theories of Urban Practice, New York, NY 10011. Offers MA. *Program availability:* Part-time. *Faculty:* 8 full-time (4 women), 4 part-time/adjunct. *Students:* 8 full-time (3 women), 2 part-time (both women); includes 3 minority (2 Black or African American, non-Hispanic/Latino; 1 Hispanic/Latino), 4 international. Average age 27. 12 applicants, 92% accepted, 5 enrolled. In 2019, 8 master's awarded. *Degree requirements:* For master's, thesis. *Entrance requirements:* For master's, transcripts, resume, statement of purpose, recommendation letters, portfolio or writing sample, interview. Additional exam requirements/recommendations for international students: required—TOEFL (minimum score 92 iBT), IELTS (minimum score 7), PTE (minimum score 63). *Application deadline:* For fall

admission, 1/1 priority date for domestic and international students. Applications are processed on a rolling basis. Application fee: $50. Electronic applications accepted. *Expenses:* 1810 per credit. *Financial support:* In 2019–20, 8 students received support, including 1 research assistantship (averaging $1,977 per year); career-related internships or fieldwork, scholarships/grants, and unspecified assistantships also available. Support available to part-time students. Financial award application deadline: 2/1; financial award applicants required to submit FAFSA. *Unit head:* Miodrag Mitrasinovic, Co-Chair, Urban Council, 212-229-8970 Ext. 4722, E-mail: mitrasim@newschool.edu. *Application contact:* Simone Varadian, Senior Director, 212-229-5150 Ext. 4011, E-mail: varadias@newschool.edu.
Website: https://www.newschool.edu/parsons/ma-theories-urban-research/

New York Institute of Technology, School of Architecture and Design, Old Westbury, NY 11568-8000. Offers architecture (M Arch); architecture, urban and regional design (MS). *Program availability:* Part-time. *Entrance requirements:* For master's, For M.Arch: Varies depending on track; see website for details. For M.S. Architecture, Urban & Regional Design: professional architecture or landscape architecture degree from accredited college or university approved by NAAB; minimum undergraduate GPA 3.0; digital portfolio; C.V. Additional exam requirements/recommendations for international students: required—TOEFL (minimum score 79 iBT), IELTS (minimum score 6), PTE (minimum score 53). Electronic applications accepted. *Expenses: Tuition:* Full-time $23,760; part-time $1320 per credit. *Required fees:* $260; $220 per unit. Full-time tuition and fees vary according to degree level and program. Part-time tuition and fees vary according to course load and program.

Pratt Institute, School of Architecture, Program in Architecture and Urban Design, Brooklyn, NY 11205-3899. Offers MS. *Students:* 10 full-time (5 women); includes 2 minority (1 Black or African American, non-Hispanic/Latino; 1 Hispanic/Latino), 8 international. Average age 25. 69 applicants, 74% accepted, 10 enrolled. In 2019, 6 master's awarded. *Degree requirements:* For master's, thesis. *Entrance requirements:* For master's, portfolio, letters of recommendation. Additional exam requirements/recommendations for international students: required—TOEFL (minimum score 550 paper-based; 79 iBT). *Application deadline:* For fall admission, 1/5 for domestic and international students; for spring admission, 10/1 for domestic and international students. Application fee: $50 ($90 for international students). Electronic applications accepted. *Expenses: Tuition:* Full-time $33,246; part-time $1847 per credit. *Required fees:* $1980. *Financial support:* Career-related internships or fieldwork, Federal Work-Study, institutionally sponsored loans, scholarships/grants, health care benefits, and unspecified assistantships available. Support available to part-time students. Financial award application deadline: 2/1; financial award applicants required to submit FAFSA. *Unit head:* David Erdman, Chairperson, 718-399-4327, E-mail: derdman@pratt.edu. *Application contact:* Natalie Capannelli, Director of Graduate Admissions, 718-636-3551, Fax: 718-399-4242, E-mail: ncapanne@pratt.edu.
Website: https://www.pratt.edu/academics/architecture/grad-arch-urban-design/

Rice University, Graduate Programs, School of Architecture, Houston, TX 77251-1892. Offers architecture (M Arch, D Arch); urban design (M Arch). *Degree requirements:* For master's, thesis optional; for doctorate, thesis/dissertation. *Entrance requirements:* For master's and doctorate, GRE. Additional exam requirements/recommendations for international students: required—TOEFL (minimum score 600 paper-based; 100 iBT). Electronic applications accepted.

Savannah College of Art and Design, Program in Urban Design, Savannah, GA 31402-3146. Offers MUD. *Program availability:* Part-time. *Degree requirements:* For master's, thesis. *Entrance requirements:* For master's, GRE (recommended), portfolio (submitted in digital format), audition or writing submission, resume, statement of purpose, two letters of recommendation. Additional exam requirements/recommendations for international students: recommended—TOEFL (minimum score 550 paper-based; 85 iBT), IELTS (minimum score 6.5). Electronic applications accepted.

Southern California Institute of Architecture, Center for Advanced Studies, Los Angeles, CA 90013. Offers architectural technologies (MS); design of cities (MS); design theory and pedagogy (MS); fiction and entertainment (MS).

State University of New York College of Environmental Science and Forestry, Department of Landscape Architecture, Syracuse, NY 13210-2779. Offers community design and planning (MLA, MS); cultural landscape studies and conservation (MLA, MS); landscape and urban ecology (MLA, MS). *Accreditation:* ASLA (one or more programs are accredited). *Program availability:* Part-time. *Faculty:* 10 full-time (4 women), 7 part-time/adjunct (5 women). *Students:* 19 full-time (13 women), 5 international. Average age 27. 21 applicants, 95% accepted, 7 enrolled. In 2019, 9 master's awarded. *Degree requirements:* For master's, comprehensive exam (for some programs), thesis (for some programs). *Entrance requirements:* For master's, GRE General Test, minimum GPA of 3.0. Additional exam requirements/recommendations for international students: required—TOEFL (minimum score 550 paper-based; 80 iBT), IELTS (minimum score 6), or STEP Eiken (grade 1). *Application deadline:* For fall admission, 2/1 priority date for domestic and international students; for spring admission, 11/1 priority date for domestic and international students. Applications are processed on a rolling basis. Application fee: $60. Electronic applications accepted. *Expenses:* Tuition, state resident: full-time $11,310; part-time $472 per credit hour. Tuition, nonresident: full-time $23,100; part-time $963 per credit hour. *Required fees:* $1890; $95.21 per credit hour. *Financial support:* In 2019–20, 10 students received support. Unspecified assistantships available. Financial award application deadline: 6/30; financial award applicants required to submit FAFSA. *Unit head:* Dr. Douglas Johnston, Chair, 315-470-6544, Fax: 315-470-6540, E-mail: dmjohnst@esf.edu. *Application contact:* Scott Shannon, Associate Provost for Instruction/Dean of the Graduate School, 315-470-6599, Fax: 315-470-6978, E-mail: esfgrad@esf.edu.
Website: http://www.esf.edu/la/

University at Buffalo, the State University of New York, Graduate School, School of Architecture and Planning, Department of Urban and Regional Planning, Buffalo, NY 14214. Offers economic development (MUP); environment/land use (MUP); health and food systems (MUP); historic preservation (MUP, Certificate); neighborhood/community development (MUP); real estate development (MSRED); urban and regional planning (PhD); urban design (MUP); JD/MUP; M Arch/MUP. *Accreditation:* ACSP. *Program availability:* Part-time. *Faculty:* 11 full-time (4 women), 15 part-time/adjunct (6 women). *Students:* 88 full-time (40 women), 25 part-time (10 women); includes 32 minority (16 Black or African American, non-Hispanic/Latino; 2 Asian, non-Hispanic/Latino; 7 Hispanic/Latino; 7 Two or more races, non-Hispanic/Latino), 13 international. Average age 26. 146 applicants, 40% accepted, 40 enrolled. In 2019, 31 master's, 1 doctorate, 4 other advanced degrees awarded. *Degree requirements:* For master's, thesis or alternative, project; for doctorate, comprehensive exam, thesis/dissertation, dissertation. *Entrance requirements:* For master's, resume, two letters of recommendation, personal statement, transcripts; for doctorate, GRE, transcripts, three letters of recommendation, resume, research statement, writing sample. Additional exam requirements/recommendations for international students: required—TOEFL (minimum score 79 iBT), IELTS (minimum score 6.5). *Application deadline:* For fall admission, 3/1 priority date for domestic and international students; for spring admission, 10/31 priority date for domestic students, 10/1 priority date for international students. Applications are processed on a rolling basis. Application fee: $75. Electronic applications accepted. *Expenses: Tuition, area resident:* Full-time $11,310; part-time $471 per credit hour. Tuition, state resident: full-time $11,310; part-time $471 per credit hour. Tuition, nonresident: full-time $23,100; part-time $963 per credit hour. *International tuition:* $23,100 full-time. *Required fees:* $2820. *Financial support:* In 2019–20, 54 students received support, including 5 fellowships with full tuition reimbursements available (averaging $22,560 per year), 1 research assistantship with partial tuition reimbursement available (averaging $16,027 per year), 20 teaching assistantships with partial tuition reimbursements available (averaging $6,912 per year); career-related internships or fieldwork, Federal Work-Study, institutionally sponsored loans, scholarships/grants, health care benefits, tuition waivers (full and partial), and unspecified assistantships also available. Financial award application deadline: 3/1; financial award applicants required to submit FAFSA. *Unit head:* Dr. Daniel B. Hess, Professor and Chair, 716-829-5326, Fax: 716-829-3256, E-mail: dbhess@buffalo.edu. *Application contact:* Norma Everett, Graduate Programs Coordinator, 716-829-3283, Fax: 716-829-3256, E-mail: norma.everett@buffalo.edu.
Website: http://www.ap.buffalo.edu/planning/

The University of British Columbia, Faculty of Applied Science, School of Architecture and Landscape Architecture, Program in Landscape Architecture, Vancouver, BC V6T 1Z2, Canada. Offers advanced studies in landscape architecture (MASLA); landscape architecture (MLA); urban design (MUD); M Arch/MLA. *Accreditation:* ASLA. *Degree requirements:* For master's, comprehensive exam or thesis. *Entrance requirements:* For master's, portfolio. Additional exam requirements/recommendations for international students: required—TOEFL. Electronic applications accepted. *Expenses:* Contact institution.

University of California, Berkeley, Graduate Division, College of Environmental Design, Department of Architecture, Berkeley, CA 94720. Offers architecture (M Arch); building science (MS, PhD); building structures, construction and materials (MS, PhD); design theories, methods, and practices (MS, PhD); environmental design in developing countries (MS, PhD); history of architecture and urbanism (MS, PhD); social and cultural processes in architecture and urbanism (MS, PhD); M Arch/MCP; M Arch/MS; MLA/M Arch. *Degree requirements:* For master's, thesis; for doctorate, thesis/dissertation, qualifying exam. *Entrance requirements:* For master's and doctorate, GRE General Test, minimum GPA of 3.0, 3 letters of recommendation. Additional exam requirements/recommendations for international students: required—TOEFL (minimum score 570 paper-based; 90 iBT). Electronic applications accepted. Application fee is waived when completed online.

University of California, Berkeley, Graduate Division, College of Environmental Design, Department of Landscape Architecture and Environmental Planning, Berkeley, CA 94720. Offers landscape architecture (MLA), including environmental planning, landscape design and site planning, urban and community design; landscape architecture and environmental planning (PhD); MLA/M Arch; MLA/MCP. *Accreditation:* ASLA (one or more programs are accredited). *Degree requirements:* For master's, comprehensive exam (for some programs), thesis (for some programs), professional project or thesis; for doctorate, one foreign language, thesis/dissertation, qualifying exam. *Entrance requirements:* For master's, GRE General Test, minimum GPA of 3.0, portfolio; for doctorate, GRE General Test, master's degree (strongly recommended), minimum GPA of 3.0, sample of written work, 3 letters of recommendation. Additional exam requirements/recommendations for international students: required—TOEFL (minimum score 570 paper-based; 90 iBT). Electronic applications accepted.

University of California, Berkeley, Graduate Division, College of Environmental Design, Group in Urban Design, Berkeley, CA 94720. Offers MUD. *Degree requirements:* For master's, thesis (for some programs), professional project or thesis. *Entrance requirements:* For master's, GRE General Test, minimum GPA of 3.0, portfolio, 3 letters of recommendation. Additional exam requirements/recommendations for international students: required—TOEFL (minimum score 570 paper-based; 90 iBT). Electronic applications accepted.

University of California, Los Angeles, Graduate Division, School of the Arts and Architecture, Department of Architecture and Urban Design, Los Angeles, CA 90095. Offers M Arch, MA, PhD. *Degree requirements:* For master's, comprehensive exam (M Arch I, II); thesis (MA); for doctorate, 2 foreign languages, thesis/dissertation, oral and written qualifying exams. *Entrance requirements:* For master's, GRE General Test, bachelor's degree; minimum undergraduate GPA of 3.0 (or its equivalent if letter grade system not used); writing sample (MA only); portfolio (M Arch only); for doctorate, GRE General Test, bachelor's degree; minimum undergraduate GPA of 3.5 (or its equivalent if letter grade system not used); writing sample. Additional exam requirements/recommendations for international students: required—TOEFL. Electronic applications accepted. *Expenses:* Contact institution.

University of Colorado Denver, College of Architecture and Planning, Program in Design and Planning, Denver, CO 80217. Offers history of architecture, landscape and urbanism (PhD); sustainable and healthy environments (PhD). *Program availability:* Part-time. *Degree requirements:* For doctorate, comprehensive exam, thesis/dissertation. *Entrance requirements:* For doctorate, GRE (minimum score of 158 for both verbal and quantitative; writing 4.0), minimum undergraduate GPA of 3.0, graduate 3.5; writing sample; three letters of recommendation; statement of personal and professional goals. Additional exam requirements/recommendations for international students: required—TOEFL (minimum score 80 iBT); recommended—IELTS (minimum score 6.8). Electronic applications accepted. *Expenses:* Contact institution.

University of Colorado Denver, College of Architecture and Planning, Program in Urban Design, Denver, CO 80217. Offers MUD. *Program availability:* Part-time. *Entrance requirements:* For master's, GRE (for students with an undergraduate GPA below 3.0), BA in related field; prior professional degree; portfolio of creative work; statement of purpose; resume. *Expenses:* Contact institution.

University of Colorado Denver, School of Education and Human Development, Program in Educational Leadership and Innovation, Denver, CO 80217. Offers educational studies and research (PhD), including administrative leadership and policy, early childhood special education, math education, research, assessment and evaluation, science education, urban ecologies. *Program availability:* Part-time, evening/weekend. *Degree requirements:* For doctorate, comprehensive exam, thesis/dissertation, 75 credit hours (for PhD). *Entrance requirements:* For doctorate, GRE or equivalent, resume or curriculum vitae, letters of recommendation, master's degree or equivalent, completion of basic or advanced statistics course with minimum B grade. Additional exam requirements/recommendations for international students: required—TOEFL (minimum score 537 paper-based; 75 iBT); recommended—IELTS (minimum score 6.5). Electronic applications accepted. Tuition and fees vary according to course load, program and reciprocity agreements.

University of Houston, Gerald D. Hines College of Architecture and Design, Houston, TX 77204. Offers architectural studies (MA); architecture (M Arch, MS), including media and fabrication (MS), sustainable design (MS), sustainable urban systems (MS), urban design (MS); industrial design (MS). *Faculty:* 15 full-time (4 women), 13 part-time/adjunct (3 women). *Students:* 92 full-time (40 women), 6 part-time (2 women); includes 23 minority (1 Black or African American, non-Hispanic/Latino; 1

American Indian or Alaska Native, non-Hispanic/Latino; 9 Asian, non-Hispanic/Latino; 9 Hispanic/Latino; 3 Two or more races, non-Hispanic/Latino), 20 international. Average age 28. 192 applicants, 45% accepted, 47 enrolled. In 2019, 21 master's awarded. *Degree requirements:* For master's, thesis (for some programs). *Entrance requirements:* For master's, GRE General Test, digital portfolio. Additional exam requirements/recommendations for international students: required—TOEFL (minimum score 550 paper-based; 79 iBT), IELTS (minimum score 6.5). *Application deadline:* For fall admission, 2/1 priority date for domestic students, 2/1 for international students. Applications are processed on a rolling basis. Application fee: $50. Electronic applications accepted. *Expenses:* M.Arch + 3 is $50,825.70; M.Arch + 2 is $33,883.80. *Financial support:* In 2019–20, 8 students received support, including 8 research assistantships with tuition reimbursements available (averaging $1,358 per year), 5 teaching assistantships (averaging $3,487 per year); career-related internships or fieldwork, institutionally sponsored loans, scholarships/grants, and unspecified assistantships also available. Financial award application deadline: 1/1; financial award applicants required to submit FAFSA. *Unit head:* Patricia Belton Oliver, Dean, 713-743-2400, Fax: 713-743-2358, E-mail: poliver@central.uh.edu. *Application contact:* Trang Phan, Assistant Dean, 713-743-2400, Fax: 713-743-2358, E-mail: tphan@uh.edu.
Website: http://www.uh.edu/architecture/

The University of Kansas, Graduate Studies, School of Architecture and Design, Department of Architecture, Lawrence, KS 66045. Offers architectural acoustics (Certificate); architecture (M Arch, PhD); health and wellness (Certificate); historic preservation (Certificate); urban design (Certificate). *Students:* 93 full-time (45 women), 23 part-time (13 women); includes 20 minority (4 Black or African American, non-Hispanic/Latino; 5 Asian, non-Hispanic/Latino; 4 Hispanic/Latino; 7 Two or more races, non-Hispanic/Latino), 23 international. Average age 25. 91 applicants, 59% accepted, 30 enrolled. In 2019, 70 master's, 2 doctorates, 8 other advanced degrees awarded. Terminal master's awarded for partial completion of doctoral program. *Entrance requirements:* For master's, GRE, transcript; resume; minimum GPA of 3.0; statement of purpose; letters of recommendation; portfolio of design work, or samples of written work or other creative artifacts produced if previous degree was not in a design-related discipline; for doctorate, GRE, transcript, resume, minimum GPA of 3.0, statement of purpose, letters of recommendation, research-informed writing sample, exhibit of work illustrating applicant's interests and abilities in areas related to the design disciplines. Additional exam requirements/recommendations for international students: required—TOEFL, IELTS. *Application deadline:* For fall admission, 1/15 priority date for domestic and international students; for summer admission, 1/15 priority date for domestic and international students. Application fee: $65 ($85 for international students). Electronic applications accepted. *Expenses:* Tuition, state resident: full-time $9989. Tuition, nonresident: full-time $23,950. *International tuition:* $23,950 full-time. *Required fees:* $984; $81.99 per credit hour. Tuition and fees vary according to course load, campus/location and program. *Financial support:* Fellowships, research assistantships, teaching assistantships, scholarships/grants, health care benefits, and unspecified assistantships available. Financial award application deadline: 1/15; financial award applicants required to submit FAFSA. *Unit head:* Frank Zilm, Dean, 816-561-7186, E-mail: frankzilm@ku.edu. *Application contact:* Joan Weaver, Graduate Admissions Contact, 785-864-3709, Fax: 785-864-5185, E-mail: jweaver@ku.edu.
Website: http://architecture.ku.edu/

University of Miami, Graduate School, School of Architecture, Program in Suburb and Town Design, Coral Gables, FL 33124. Offers M Arch. *Entrance requirements:* For master's, GRE General Test, minimum GPA of 3.0, portfolio. Additional exam requirements/recommendations for international students: required—TOEFL. Electronic applications accepted.

University of Michigan, Taubman College of Architecture and Urban Planning, Master of Urban Design Program, Ann Arbor, MI 48109-2069. Offers architecture (MUD/M Arch); MUD/M Arch. *Degree requirements:* For master's, thesis or alternative. *Entrance requirements:* Additional exam requirements/recommendations for international students: required—TOEFL (minimum score 100 iBT), GRE. Electronic applications accepted. *Expenses:* Contact institution.

The University of North Carolina at Charlotte, College of Arts and Architecture, School of Architecture, Charlotte, NC 28223-0001. Offers architecture (M Arch I, M Arch II, MS); urban design (MUD). *Faculty:* 25 full-time (11 women), 4 part-time/adjunct (0 women). *Students:* 79 full-time (35 women), 7 part-time (2 women); includes 25 minority (11 Black or African American, non-Hispanic/Latino; 3 Asian, non-Hispanic/Latino; 8 Hispanic/Latino; 3 Two or more races, non-Hispanic/Latino), 13 international. Average age 26. 119 applicants, 87% accepted, 36 enrolled. In 2019, 62 master's awarded. *Entrance requirements:* For master's, Official GRE Test scores (TOEFL scores where applicable), official transcripts from all previous college-level institution(s); statement of purpose explaining reasons for wanting to study in the School of Architecture; three recommendations from persons familiar with the applicant's personal and professional qualifications; resume or curriculum vitae; portfolio. Additional exam requirements/recommendations for international students: required—TOEFL (minimum score 557 paper-based; 83 iBT), IELTS (minimum score 6.5), TOEFL (minimum score 557 paper-based, 83 iBT) or IELTS (6.5). *Application deadline:* For fall admission, 1/15 priority date for domestic students. Applications are processed on a rolling basis. Application fee: $75. Electronic applications accepted. *Expenses:* Contact institution. *Financial support:* In 2019–20, 20 students received support, including 12 research assistantships (averaging $6,113 per year), 8 teaching assistantships (averaging $3,170 per year); institutionally sponsored loans, scholarships/grants, unspecified assistantships, and administrative assistantship also available. Financial award application deadline: 3/1; financial award applicants required to submit FAFSA. *Unit head:* Peter Wong, Director, Graduate School Programs, 704-687-0134, E-mail: plwong@uncc.edu. *Application contact:* Kathy B. Giddings, Director of Graduate Admissions, 704-687-5503, Fax: 704-687-1668, E-mail: gradadm@uncc.edu.
Website: http://coaa.uncc.edu/academics/school-of-architecture

University of Pennsylvania, Stuart Weitzman School of Design, Department of City and Regional Planning, Philadelphia, PA 19104. Offers city and regional planning (PhD); city planning (MCP); GIS and spatial analysis (Certificate); land preservation (Certificate); urban design (Certificate); urban redevelopment (Certificate); urban spatial analytics (MUSA). *Accreditation:* ACSP (one or more programs are accredited). *Program availability:* Part-time. *Faculty:* 24 full-time (10 women), 4 part-time/adjunct (0 women). *Students:* 191 full-time (120 women), 6 part-time (3 women); includes 40 minority (14 Black or African American, non-Hispanic/Latino; 13 Asian, non-Hispanic/Latino; 8 Hispanic/Latino; 5 Two or more races, non-Hispanic/Latino), 94 international. Average age 26. 433 applicants, 59% accepted, 119 enrolled. In 2019, 92 master's, 1 doctorate, 7 other advanced degrees awarded. *Entrance requirements:* Additional exam requirements/recommendations for international students: required—TOEFL (minimum score 100 iBT); recommended—IELTS (minimum score 7), TSE (minimum score 68). *Application deadline:* For spring admission, 1/12 for domestic students. Application fee: $80. Electronic applications accepted. *Financial support:* In 2019–20, 39 teaching assistantships (averaging $2,000 per year) were awarded; fellowships, research assistantships, and Federal Work-Study also available. Financial award application deadline: 2/15; financial award applicants required to submit FAFSA. *Application contact:* Lauren Hoover, Admissions & Recruitment Coordinator, 215-898-6520, E-mail: lhoover@design.upenn.edu.
Website: https://www.design.upenn.edu/city-regional-planning

The University of Texas at Austin, Graduate School, School of Architecture, Program in Urban Design, Austin, TX 78712-1111. Offers M Arch, MSUD.

University of Toronto, School of Graduate Studies, Faculty of Arts and Science, Department of Geography, Program in Planning, Toronto, ON M5S 1A1, Canada. Offers M Sc Pl, MUDS, PhD. *Program availability:* Part-time. *Degree requirements:* For master's, summer internship. *Entrance requirements:* For master's, bachelor's degree in planning, geography, social science or a closely related professional field, minimum B+ average in final year, 3 letters of reference; for doctorate, minimum A- or equivalent standing in previous master's program. Additional exam requirements/recommendations for international students: required—TOEFL (minimum score 580 paper-based; 93 iBT), TWE (minimum score 5). Electronic applications accepted. *Expenses:* Contact institution.

University of Toronto, School of Graduate Studies, John H. Daniels Faculty of Architecture, Landscape, and Design, Toronto, ON M5S 1A1, Canada. Offers M Arch, MLA, MUD, MVS. *Entrance requirements:* For master's, minimum B average; 3 letters of reference; resume; 3 writing samples; 5 samples of design work, drawing, or work in a related field, statement of interest. Additional exam requirements/recommendations for international students: required—TOEFL (minimum score 580 paper-based; 93 iBT), IELTS (minimum score 7), TWE (minimum score 5), Michigan English Language Assessment Battery (minimum score 85), COPE (minimum score 76). Electronic applications accepted. *Expenses:* Contact institution.

University of Utah, Graduate School, College of Architecture and Planning, Department of City and Metropolitan Planning, Salt Lake City, UT 84112. Offers city and metropolitan planning (MCMP), including ecological planning, small town and resort planning, smart growth and transportation, urban design; metropolitan planning, policy and design (PhD). *Accreditation:* ACSP. *Program availability:* Part-time. *Faculty:* 7 full-time (5 women), 6 part-time/adjunct (1 woman). *Students:* 40 full-time (23 women), 10 part-time (5 women); includes 8 minority (2 Asian, non-Hispanic/Latino; 4 Hispanic/Latino; 2 Two or more races, non-Hispanic/Latino), 16 international. Average age 31. In 2019, 21 master's awarded. *Degree requirements:* For master's, thesis or alternative, comprehensive project; for doctorate, thesis/dissertation. *Entrance requirements:* For master's, GRE, minimum undergraduate GPA of 3.0; for doctorate, GRE, minimum GPA of 3.5. Additional exam requirements/recommendations for international students: required—TOEFL (minimum score 500 paper-based; 61 iBT); recommended—IELTS (minimum score 6). *Application deadline:* For fall admission, 1/15 priority date for domestic and international students; for spring admission, 11/1 for domestic and international students. Applications are processed on a rolling basis. Electronic applications accepted. *Expenses:* Contact institution. *Financial support:* In 2019–20, 25 students received support, including 11 fellowships (averaging $14,273 per year), 6 research assistantships (averaging $19,500 per year), 17 teaching assistantships (averaging $17,765 per year); career-related internships or fieldwork, Federal Work-Study, scholarships/grants, health care benefits, and unspecified assistantships also available. Financial award application deadline: 1/15; financial award applicants required to submit FAFSA. *Unit head:* Reid Ewing, Chair, 801-585-3745, Fax: 801-581-8217, E-mail: ewing@arch.utah.edu. *Application contact:* Saolo Utu, Recruitment and Admissions Advisor, 801-581-2361, Fax: 801-581-8217, E-mail: recruitment@arch.utah.edu.
Website: http://www.plan.utah.edu/

University of Washington, Graduate School, College of Built Environments, Department of Urban Design and Planning, Seattle, WA 98195. Offers urban design and planning (PhD); urban planning (MUP). *Accreditation:* ACSP (one or more programs are accredited). *Degree requirements:* For master's, thesis or alternative; for doctorate, thesis/dissertation. *Entrance requirements:* For master's and doctorate, GRE General Test, minimum GPA of 3.0. Additional exam requirements/recommendations for international students: required—TOEFL.

University of Washington, Graduate School, College of Built Environments, Interdisciplinary Program in Urban Design, Seattle, WA 98195. Offers Certificate. Electronic applications accepted.

Washington University in St. Louis, Sam Fox School of Design and Visual Arts, Program in Urban Design, St. Louis, MO 63130-4899. Offers MUD, M Arch/MUD, MUD/MSW. *Entrance requirements:* For master's, GRE General Test, portfolio. Additional exam requirements/recommendations for international students: required—TOEFL (minimum score 600 paper-based; 100 iBT), TWE.

Section 3
Art and Art History

This section contains a directory of institutions offering graduate work in art and art history, followed by in-depth entries submitted by institutions that chose to prepare detailed program descriptions. Additional information about programs listed in the directory but not augmented by an in-depth entry may be obtained by writing directly to the dean of a graduate school or chair of a department at the address given in the directory.

For programs offering related work, see also in this book *Applied Arts and Design; Architecture; Area and Cultural Studies; Film, Television, and Video; Performing Arts;* and *Sociology, Anthropology, and Archaeology.* In another guide in this series:

Graduate Programs in Business, Education, Information Studies, Law & Social Work

See *Subject Areas (Art Education)*

CONTENTS

Art/Fine Arts

Academy of Art University, Graduate Programs, School of Fine Art, San Francisco, CA 94105-3410. Offers figurative painting (MFA). *Accreditation:* NASAD. *Program availability:* Part-time, 100% online. *Faculty:* 12 full-time (6 women), 24 part-time/adjunct (13 women). *Students:* 63 full-time (41 women), 104 part-time (79 women); includes 28 minority (3 Black or African American, non-Hispanic/Latino; 2 American Indian or Alaska Native, non-Hispanic/Latino; 9 Asian, non-Hispanic/Latino; 7 Hispanic/Latino; 3 Native Hawaiian or other Pacific Islander, non-Hispanic/Latino; 4 Two or more races, non-Hispanic/Latino), 45 international. Average age 42. 44 applicants, 100% accepted, 29 enrolled. In 2019, 71 master's awarded. *Degree requirements:* For master's, final review. *Entrance requirements:* For master's, statement of intent; resume; portfolio/reel; official college transcripts. *Application deadline:* Applications are processed on a rolling basis. Application fee: $50. Electronic applications accepted. *Expenses: Tuition:* Full-time $1083; part-time $1083 per credit hour. *Required fees:* $860; $860 per unit. $430 per term. One-time fee: $145. Tuition and fees vary according to program. *Financial support:* Career-related internships or fieldwork, Federal Work-Study, and scholarships/grants available. Financial award application deadline: 8/10; financial award applicants required to submit FAFSA. Website: http://www.academyart.edu/fine-art-school/index.html

Academy of Art University, Graduate Programs, School of Jewelry and Metal Arts, San Francisco, CA 94105-3410. Offers MA, MFA. *Program availability:* Part-time, 100% online. *Faculty:* 2 full-time (both women), 8 part-time/adjunct (6 women). *Students:* 16 full-time (14 women), 13 part-time (10 women); includes 2 minority (1 Asian, non-Hispanic/Latino; 1 Hispanic/Latino), 16 international. Average age 35. 14 applicants, 100% accepted, 10 enrolled. In 2019, 11 master's awarded. *Degree requirements:* For master's, final review. *Entrance requirements:* For master's, statement of intent; resume; portfolio/reel; official college transcripts. *Application deadline:* Applications are processed on a rolling basis. Application fee: $50. Electronic applications accepted. *Expenses: Tuition:* Full-time $1083; part-time $1083 per credit hour. *Required fees:* $860; $860 per unit. $430 per term. One-time fee: $145. Tuition and fees vary according to program. *Financial support:* Career-related internships or fieldwork, Federal Work-Study, and scholarships/grants available. Financial award application deadline: 8/10; financial award applicants required to submit FAFSA. Website: http://www.academyart.edu/jewelry-and-metal-arts-school/

Adelphi University, College of Arts and Sciences, Department of Art and Art History, Garden City, NY 11530-0701. Offers studio art (MA). *Program availability:* Part-time. *Entrance requirements:* For master's, essay, portfolio, 2 letters of recommendation. Additional exam requirements/recommendations for international students: required—TOEFL (minimum score 550 paper-based; 80 iBT), IELTS (minimum score 6.5). Electronic applications accepted. *Expenses:* Contact institution.

Alfred University, Graduate School, College of Ceramics, Inamori School of Engineering, Alfred, NY 14802-1205. Offers biomaterials engineering (MS); ceramic engineering (MS, PhD); electrical engineering (MS); glass science (MS, PhD); materials science and engineering (MS, PhD); mechanical engineering (MS). *Program availability:* Part-time. *Faculty:* 27 full-time (4 women), 2 part-time/adjunct (both women). *Students:* 30 full-time (11 women), 15 part-time (5 women); includes 2 minority (both Asian, non-Hispanic/Latino), 12 international. Average age 28. 24 applicants, 83% accepted, 18 enrolled. In 2019, 8 master's, 5 doctorates awarded. *Degree requirements:* For master's, comprehensive exam, thesis; for doctorate, comprehensive exam, thesis/dissertation. *Entrance requirements:* Additional exam requirements/recommendations for international students: required—TOEFL (minimum score 590 paper-based; 90 iBT), IELTS (minimum score 6.5). *Application deadline:* For fall admission, 3/1 priority date for domestic students, 3/15 for international students; for spring admission, 10/1 priority date for domestic students, 10/1 for international students. Applications are processed on a rolling basis. Application fee: $60. Electronic applications accepted. Application fee is waived when completed online. *Expenses:* $23,530 per year. *Financial support:* In 2019–20, 31 students received support. Fellowships with full tuition reimbursements available, research assistantships with full tuition reimbursements available, teaching assistantships with full tuition reimbursements available, tuition waivers (full and partial), and unspecified assistantships available. Financial award application deadline: 3/15; financial award applicants required to submit FAFSA. *Unit head:* Dr. Gabrielle Gaustad, Dean, 607-871-2953, E-mail: gaustad@alfred.edu. *Application contact:* Lindsey Gertin, Assistant Director of Graduate Admissions, 607-871-2017, Fax: 607-871-2198, E-mail: gradinquiry@alfred.edu.
Website: http://engineering.alfred.edu/grad/

Alfred University, Graduate School, College of Ceramics, School of Art and Design, Alfred, NY 14802-1205. Offers ceramic art (MFA); electronic integrated arts (MFA); painting (MFA); sculpture/dimensional studies (MFA). *Accreditation:* NASAD. *Faculty:* 29 full-time (15 women), 4 part-time/adjunct (0 women). *Students:* 43 full-time (27 women); includes 4 minority (1 Asian, non-Hispanic/Latino; 2 Hispanic/Latino; 1 Two or more races, non-Hispanic/Latino), 12 international. Average age 29. 170 applicants, 24% accepted, 20 enrolled. In 2019, 18 master's awarded. *Degree requirements:* For master's, thesis or alternative, exhibit. *Entrance requirements:* For master's, portfolio. Additional exam requirements/recommendations for international students: required—TOEFL (minimum score 550 paper-based; 80 iBT), IELTS (minimum score 6). *Application deadline:* For fall admission, 1/15 for domestic and international students. Applications are processed on a rolling basis. Application fee: $60. Electronic applications accepted. Application fee is waived when completed online. *Expenses:* $23,530 per year. *Financial support:* In 2019–20, 40 students received support. Teaching assistantships with full tuition reimbursements available and tuition waivers (full) available. Financial award application deadline: 3/15; financial award applicants required to submit FAFSA. *Unit head:* Gerar Edizel, Interim Dean, 607-871-2412, E-mail: fedizel@alfred.edu. *Application contact:* Lindsey Gertin, Assistant Director of Graduate Admissions, 607-871-2017, Fax: 607-871-2198, E-mail: gradinquiry@alfred.edu.
Website: http://art.alfred.edu/graduate/

Anna Maria College, Graduate Division, Program in Education, Paxton, MA 01612. Offers early childhood education (M Ed); education (CAGS); elementary education (M Ed); English language arts (M Ed); visual arts (M Ed). *Program availability:* Part-time, evening/weekend. *Entrance requirements:* For master's, bachelor's degree in liberal arts or sciences, minimum GPA of 3.0. Additional exam requirements/recommendations for international students: required—TOEFL (minimum score 500 paper-based). Electronic applications accepted.

Arizona State University at Tempe, Herberger Institute for Design and the Arts, School of Art, Tempe, AZ 85287-1505. Offers art education (MA); art history (MA); ceramics (MFA); design, environment and the arts (PhD), including history, theory and criticism; drawing (MFA); fibers (MFA); intermedia (MFA); metals (MFA); museum studies (MFA); painting (MFA); printmaking (MFA); sculpture (MFA); wood (MFA); MFA/MA. Terminal master's awarded for partial completion of doctoral program. *Degree requirements:* For master's, thesis/exhibition (MFA, MA in art education); interactive Program of Study (iPOS) submitted before completing 50 percent of required credit hours; for doctorate, comprehensive exam, thesis/dissertation, interactive Program of Study (iPOS) submitted before completing 50 percent of required credit hours. *Entrance requirements:* For master's, GRE or MAT, minimum GPA of 3.0 or equivalent in last 2 years of work leading to bachelor's degree; for doctorate, GRE, master's degree in architecture, graphic design, industrial design, interior design, landscape architecture, or art history or equivalent standing; statement of purpose; 3 letters of recommendation; indication of potential faculty mentor; sample of written work. Additional exam requirements/recommendations for international students: required—TOEFL, IELTS, or PTE. Electronic applications accepted.

ArtCenter College of Design, Graduate Art Program, Pasadena, CA 91103. Offers MFA. *Accreditation:* NASAD.

Azusa Pacific University, College of Music and the Arts, Azusa, CA 91702-7000. Offers composition (M Mus); conducting (M Mus); education (M Mus); modern art history, theory, and criticism (MA); music entrepreneurial studies (MA); performance (M Mus); screenwriting (MA); visual art (MFA). *Accreditation:* NASAD; NASM. *Program availability:* Part-time, evening/weekend. *Degree requirements:* For master's, recital. *Entrance requirements:* For master's, interview, audition. Additional exam requirements/recommendations for international students: required—TOEFL (minimum score 550 paper-based).

Ball State University, Graduate School, College of Fine Arts, School of Art, Muncie, IN 47306. Offers fine arts (MFA), including animation, glass; visual arts studio (MA), including ceramics, drawing, metals, painting, photography and intermedia arts, printmaking, sculpture. *Accreditation:* NASAD. *Program availability:* Part-time. *Entrance requirements:* For master's, minimum baccalaureate GPA of 2.75 or 3.0 in latter half of baccalaureate, goals statement, digital portfolio of artwork, resume, transcripts of all college-level course work, three letters of recommendation. Additional exam requirements/recommendations for international students: required—TOEFL (minimum score 550 paper-based; 79 iBT), IELTS (minimum score 6.5). Electronic applications accepted. *Expenses: Tuition, area resident:* Full-time $7506; part-time $417 per credit hour. Tuition, nonresident: full-time $20,610; part-time $1145 per credit hour. *Required fees:* $2126. Tuition and fees vary according to course load, campus/location and program.

Bard College, Milton Avery Graduate School of the Arts, Annandale-on-Hudson, NY 12504. Offers film/video (MFA); music/sound (MFA); painting (MFA); photography (MFA); sculpture (MFA); writing (MFA). *Degree requirements:* For master's, thesis, project, 8-week summer residency, independent study. *Entrance requirements:* For master's, interview, portfolio, 2 letters of recommendation, history of work in the arts. Additional exam requirements/recommendations for international students: required—TOEFL (minimum score 550 paper-based). Electronic applications accepted. *Expenses:* Contact institution.

Barry University, College of Arts and Sciences, Department of Fine Arts, Miami Shores, FL 33161-6695. Offers photography (MA, MFA). *Degree requirements:* For master's, thesis (for some programs). *Entrance requirements:* For master's, GRE General Test, minimum GPA of 3.0. Electronic applications accepted.

Bob Jones University, Graduate Programs, Greenville, SC 29614. Offers accountancy (MS); Bible (MA); Bible translation (MA); Biblical studies (Certificate); business administration (MBA); church history (MA, PhD); church ministries (MA); church music (MM); cinema and video production (MA); counseling (MS); curriculum and instruction (Ed D); divinity (M Div); dramatic production (MA); educational leadership (MS, Ed D, Ed S); elementary education (M Ed, MAT); English (M Ed, MA, MAT); fine arts (MA); graphic design (MA); history (M Ed, MA); illustration (MA); interpretative speech (MA); mathematics (M Ed, MAT); medical missions (Certificate); ministry (MM, D Min); multi-categorical special education (M Ed, MAT); music (M Ed); New Testament interpretation (PhD); Old Testament interpretation (PhD); orchestral instrument performance (MM); organ performance (MM); pastoral studies (MA); personnel services (MS, Ed S); piano pedagogy (MM); piano performance (MM); platform arts (MA); rhetoric and public address (MA); secondary education (M Ed); studio art (MA); teaching Bible (MA); theology (MA, PhD); voice performance (MM); youth ministries (MA); M Div/MM.

Boise State University, College of Arts and Sciences, Art, Design, and Visual Studies, Boise, ID 83725-0399. Offers visual arts (MFA). *Program availability:* Part-time. *Students:* 8 full-time (5 women), 2 part-time (both women); includes 1 minority (Two or more races, non-Hispanic/Latino), 2 international. *Degree requirements:* For master's, thesis optional. *Entrance requirements:* For master's, minimum GPA of 3.0, portfolio. Additional exam requirements/recommendations for international students: required—TOEFL, IELTS. Electronic applications accepted. *Expenses: Tuition, area resident:* Full-time $7110; part-time $470 per credit hour. Tuition, state resident: full-time $7110; part-time $470 per credit hour. Tuition, nonresident: full-time $24,030; part-time $827 per credit hour. *International tuition:* $24,030 full-time. *Required fees:* $2536. Tuition and fees vary according to course load and program. *Financial support:* Teaching assistantships, scholarships/grants, and unspecified assistantships available. Financial award applicants required to submit FAFSA. *Unit head:* Dr. Dan Scott, Department Chair, 208-426-4070, E-mail: dannyscott@boisestate.edu. *Application contact:* Chad Erpelding, Graduate Program Coordinator, 208-426-4081, E-mail: chaderpelding@boisestate.edu.
Website: https://www.boisestate.edu/art/

Boston University, College of Fine Arts, School of Visual Arts, Boston, MA 02215. Offers sculpture (MFA); studio teaching (MA). *Faculty:* 17 full-time, 4 part-time/adjunct. *Students:* 145 full-time (121 women); includes 23 minority (4 Black or African American, non-Hispanic/Latino; 1 American Indian or Alaska Native, non-Hispanic/Latino; 7 Asian, non-Hispanic/Latino; 10 Hispanic/Latino; 1 Two or more races, non-Hispanic/Latino), 37 international. Average age 30. 270 applicants, 56% accepted, 49 enrolled. In 2019, 13 master's awarded. *Entrance requirements:* For master's, portfolio. Additional exam requirements/recommendations for international students: required—TOEFL (minimum score 90 iBT), IELTS (minimum score 7), DuoLingo. *Application deadline:* For fall admission, 2/1 for domestic and international students. Applications are processed on a rolling basis. Application fee: $95. *Expenses:* Contact institution. *Financial support:* In 2019–20, 36 students received support. Fellowships, teaching assistantships, scholarships/grants, and unspecified assistantships available. Financial award application deadline: 2/1. *Unit head:* Dana Clancy, Director, 617-353-3371. *Application contact:* Jessica Caccamo, Assistant Director of Admissions, 617-353-3371, E-mail: visuarts@bu.edu.

Bowling Green State University, Graduate College, College of Arts and Sciences, School of Art, Bowling Green, OH 43403. Offers 2-D studio art (MA, MFA); 3-D studio art (MA, MFA); art education (MA); art history (MA); computer art (MA); design (MFA); digital arts (MFA); graphics (MFA). *Accreditation:* NASAD. *Program availability:* Part-time. *Degree requirements:* For master's, thesis or alternative, final exhibit (MFA). *Entrance requirements:* For master's, GRE General Test (for MA), slide portfolio (15-20 slides). Additional exam requirements/recommendations for international students: required—TOEFL. Electronic applications accepted.

Bradley University, The Graduate School, Slane College of Communications and Fine Arts, Department of Art, Peoria, IL 61625-0002. Offers ceramics (MA, MFA); drawing (MA, MFA); graphic design (MA, MFA); painting (MA, MFA); photography (MA, MFA); printmaking (MA, MFA); sculpture (MA, MFA). *Accreditation:* NASAD. *Program availability:* Part-time. *Faculty:* 10 full-time (4 women). *Students:* 4 full-time (2 women), 2 part-time (both women); includes 1 minority (American Indian or Alaska Native, non-Hispanic/Latino). Average age 42. 3 applicants, 33% accepted. In 2019, 6 master's awarded. *Degree requirements:* For master's, comprehensive exam, thesis, final exhibit. *Entrance requirements:* For master's, portfolio, 2 letters of recommendation. Additional exam requirements/recommendations for international students: required—TOEFL (minimum score 550 paper-based; 79 iBT), PTE (minimum score 58). *Application deadline:* For fall admission, 4/1 priority date for domestic and international students; for spring admission, 11/1 priority date for domestic and international students. Applications are processed on a rolling basis. Application fee: $40 ($50 for international students). Electronic applications accepted. *Expenses: Tuition:* Part-time $930 per credit hour. *Financial support:* In 2019–20, 2 students received support. Teaching assistantships, scholarships/grants, tuition waivers (partial), and unspecified assistantships available. Support available to part-time students. Financial award application deadline: 4/1. *Unit head:* Gary Will, Chairperson, 309-677-2967, E-mail: gwill@bradley.edu. *Application contact:* Rachel Webb, Director of On-Campus Graduate Admissions and International Student and Scholar Services, 309-677-2375, E-mail: rkwebb@bradley.edu.
Website: http://www.bradley.edu/academic/departments/art/

Brandeis University, Graduate School of Arts and Sciences, Department of Fine Arts, Waltham, MA 02454-9110. Offers studio art (Postbaccalaureate Certificate). *Program availability:* Part-time. *Faculty:* 14 full-time (9 women), 3 part-time/adjunct (1 woman). *Students:* 7 full-time (5 women), 3 international. Average age 24. 6 applicants, 100% accepted, 4 enrolled. In 2019, 4 Postbaccalaureate Certificates awarded. *Degree requirements:* For Postbaccalaureate Certificate, exhibit of work. *Entrance requirements:* For degree, transcripts, letters of recommendation, resume, 12 images of recent works. and statement of purpose. Additional exam requirements/recommendations for international students: required—TOEFL, IELTS, PTE. *Application deadline:* For fall admission, 6/15 for domestic and international students; for spring admission, 12/15 for domestic and international students. Applications are processed on a rolling basis. Application fee: $75. Electronic applications accepted. *Financial support:* Scholarships/grants and unspecified assistantships available. *Unit head:* Ariel Freiberg, Director of Graduate Studies, 781-736-2660, E-mail: afreiberg@brandeis.edu. *Application contact:* Christine Kahn, Administrator, 781-736-2655, E-mail: cdunant@brandeis.edu.
Website: http://www.brandeis.edu/gsas/programs/studio_art.html

Brigham Young University, Graduate Studies, College of Fine Arts and Communications, Department of Art, Provo, UT 84602-6414. Offers art education (MA); studio arts (MFA). *Accreditation:* NASAD. *Faculty:* 13 full-time (2 women). *Students:* 22 full-time (19 women); includes 4 minority (2 Asian, non-Hispanic/Latino; 1 Hispanic/Latino; 1 Two or more races, non-Hispanic/Latino). Average age 36. 25 applicants, 40% accepted, 10 enrolled. In 2019, 9 master's awarded. *Degree requirements:* For master's, comprehensive exam, thesis, selected project (for MFA); curriculum project (for art education). *Entrance requirements:* For master's, TOEFL or IELTS required for International (non-native english speaking) students. MFA-Art applications require a portfolio of 15-20 examples of artwork, cover letter, CV, and artist statement. MA-Art Education applications require a portfolio of 20 pieces, 1-2 written papers, certification to teach in public schools, and a resume. Additional exam requirements/recommendations for international students: required—TOEFL (minimum score 580 paper-based; 80 iBT), TOEFL (minimum score 580 paper-based, 85 iBT) or IELTS (7); recommended—IELTS (minimum score 7). *Application deadline:* For fall admission, 2/1 for domestic and international students. Application fee: $50. Electronic applications accepted. *Financial support:* In 2019–20, 15 students received support. Teaching assistantships with partial tuition reimbursements available and scholarships/grants available. Financial award application deadline: 2/1. *Unit head:* Prof. Joseph Ostraff, Chair, 801-422-4468, Fax: 801-422-0695, E-mail: joseph_ostraff@byu.edu. *Application contact:* Maddison Colvin, Secretary, 801-422-4429, Fax: 801-422-0695, E-mail: maddison_colvin@byu.edu.
Website: http://art.byu.edu

Brooklyn College of the City University of New York, School of Visual, Media and Performing Arts, Department of Art, Brooklyn, NY 11210-2889. Offers art history (MA); digital art (MFA); drawing and painting (MFA); photography (MFA); printmaking (MFA); sculpture (MFA). *Program availability:* Part-time. *Degree requirements:* For master's, thesis. *Entrance requirements:* For master's, bachelor's degree in art, portfolio, 2 letters of recommendation. Additional exam requirements/recommendations for international students: required—TOEFL (minimum score 500 paper-based; 61 iBT). Electronic applications accepted.

Butler University, Jordan College of the Arts, Indianapolis, IN 46208-3485. Offers composition (MM); conducting (MM), including choral, instrumental; music education (MM); musicology (MA); performance (MM); piano pedagogy (MM). *Accreditation:* NASM. *Program availability:* Part-time, evening/weekend, blended/hybrid learning. *Faculty:* 18 full-time (4 women), 12 part-time/adjunct (7 women). *Students:* 20 full-time (9 women), 26 part-time (13 women); includes 6 minority (2 Black or African American, non-Hispanic/Latino; 1 Asian, non-Hispanic/Latino; 2 Hispanic/Latino; 1 Two or more races, non-Hispanic/Latino), 1 international. Average age 27. 43 applicants, 63% accepted, 19 enrolled. In 2019, 13 master's awarded. *Degree requirements:* For master's, variable foreign language requirement, comprehensive exam, thesis (for some programs). *Entrance requirements:* For master's, Music Theory diagnostic exam, Music History diagnostic exam, audition, interview. Additional exam requirements/recommendations for international students: required—TOEFL (minimum score 550 paper-based; 79 iBT), IELTS. *Application deadline:* For fall admission, 2/1 for domestic and international students; for spring admission, 12/15 for domestic and international students; for summer admission, 4/15 for domestic and international students. Applications are processed on a rolling basis. Application fee: $0. Electronic applications accepted. Application fee is waived when completed online. *Expenses:* $595 per credit hour. *Financial support:* In 2019–20, 21 students received support. Scholarships/grants, tuition waivers (full and partial), and unspecified assistantships available. Financial award applicants required to submit FAFSA. *Unit head:* David Patrick Murray, Director - School of Music, 317-940-9988, Fax: 317-9409658, E-mail: dmurray@butler.edu. *Application contact:* Dr. Nicholas Dean Johnson, Director of Graduate Studies, 317-9409064, E-mail: ndjohns1@butler.edu.
Website: http://www.butler.edu/jca/

California College of the Arts, Graduate Programs, Fine Arts Programs, San Francisco, CA 94107. Offers film (MFA); fine arts (MFA). *Accreditation:* NASAD. *Degree requirements:* For master's, thesis, exhibit. *Entrance requirements:* For master's, appropriate bachelor's degree, portfolio, resume, 2 letters of recommendation, transcript. Additional exam requirements/recommendations for international students: required—TOEFL, IELTS, or PTE. Electronic applications accepted. *Expenses:* Contact institution.

California College of the Arts, Graduate Programs, Visual and Critical Studies Program, San Francisco, CA 94107. Offers visual and critical studies (MA), including curatorial practice, fine arts, writing. *Degree requirements:* For master's, thesis. *Entrance requirements:* For master's, portfolio, resume, 2 letters of recommendation, transcripts, essay, interview. Additional exam requirements/recommendations for international students: required—TOEFL, IELTS, or PTE. Electronic applications accepted. *Expenses:* Contact institution.

California Institute of the Arts, School of Art, Valencia, CA 91355-2340. Offers art (MFA, Adv C); graphic design (MFA, Adv C); photography (MFA, Adv C). *Accreditation:* NASAD (one or more programs are accredited). *Degree requirements:* For master's, final project. *Entrance requirements:* For master's, portfolio. Additional exam requirements/recommendations for international students: required—TOEFL. Electronic applications accepted.

California State University, Chico, Office of Graduate Studies, College of Humanities and Fine Arts, Department of Art and Art History, Program in Fine Arts, Chico, CA 95929-0722. Offers art studio (MFA). *Accreditation:* NASAD. *Degree requirements:* For master's, thesis or alternative, exhibition with written evaluation of work. *Entrance requirements:* For master's, MFA application due by March 1st. 3 letters of recommendation, resume, statement of purpose and media portfolio. Additional exam requirements/recommendations for international students: required—TOEFL (minimum score 550 paper-based; 80 iBT), IELTS (minimum score 6.5), PTE (minimum score 59). Electronic applications accepted.

California State University, Fresno, Division of Research and Graduate Studies, College of Arts and Humanities, Department of Art and Design, Fresno, CA 93740-8027. Offers art (MA). *Program availability:* Part-time, evening/weekend. *Degree requirements:* For master's, thesis or alternative. *Entrance requirements:* For master's, GRE General Test, minimum GPA of 3.0, portfolio. Additional exam requirements/recommendations for international students: required—TOEFL. Electronic applications accepted. *Expenses:* Tuition, state resident: full-time $4012; part-time $2506 per semester.

California State University, Fullerton, Graduate Studies, College of the Arts, Department of Visual Arts, Fullerton, CA 92831-3599. Offers art (MA, MFA), including art history (MA), ceramics (MFA), crafts, creative photography, exhibition design, glass, graphic design, illustration, sculpture. *Accreditation:* NASAD (one or more programs are accredited). *Program availability:* Part-time. *Entrance requirements:* For master's, minimum GPA of 2.5 in last 60 units of course work, portfolio.

California State University, Long Beach, Graduate Studies, College of the Arts, Department of Art, Long Beach, CA 90840. Offers art education (MA); studio art (MFA). *Accreditation:* NASAD. *Program availability:* Part-time. *Degree requirements:* For master's, thesis (for some programs). *Entrance requirements:* For master's, minimum GPA of 3.0 in last 60 hours. Electronic applications accepted.

California State University, Los Angeles, Graduate Studies, College of Arts and Letters, Department of Art, Los Angeles, CA 90032-8530. Offers art (MA), including art education, art history, art therapy, ceramics, metals, and textiles, design (MA, MFA), painting, sculpture, and graphic arts, photography; fine arts (MFA), including crafts, design (MA, MFA), studio arts. *Accreditation:* NASAD (one or more programs are accredited). *Program availability:* Part-time, evening/weekend. *Degree requirements:* For master's, comprehensive exam, project or thesis. *Entrance requirements:* For master's, portfolio. Additional exam requirements/recommendations for international students: required—TOEFL (minimum score 500 paper-based). Electronic applications accepted. *Expenses: Tuition, area resident:* Full-time $7176; part-time $4164 per year. Tuition, state resident: full-time $7176; part-time $4164 per year. Tuition, nonresident: full-time $14,304; part-time $8916 per year. *International tuition:* $14,304 full-time. *Required fees:* $1037.76; $1037.76 per unit. Tuition and fees vary according to degree level and program.

California State University, Northridge, Graduate Studies, Mike Curb College of Arts, Media, and Communication, Department of Art, Northridge, CA 91330. Offers art education (MA); art history (MA); studio art (MA, MFA); visual communications (MA, MFA). *Accreditation:* NASAD.

California State University, Sacramento, College of Arts and Letters, Department of Art, Sacramento, CA 95819. Offers studio art (MA). *Accreditation:* NASAD. *Program availability:* Part-time. *Students:* Average age 31. 16 applicants, 38% accepted, 2 enrolled. In 2019, 2 master's awarded. *Degree requirements:* For master's, comprehensive exam, thesis, culminating exhibition of student's work; passage of writing proficiency examination or approved waiver. *Entrance requirements:* For master's, BA in art or its equivalent, including 12 units in art history; minimum GPA of 2.5 in last 60 units attempted; approval by studio faculty review of other submitted materials. Additional exam requirements/recommendations for international students: required—TOEFL (minimum score 550 paper-based; 80 iBT); recommended—IELTS (minimum score 7). *Application deadline:* For fall admission, 2/15 for domestic students, 1/15 for international students; for spring admission, 9/15 for domestic students, 8/15 for international students. Applications are processed on a rolling basis. Application fee: $70. Electronic applications accepted. *Expenses:* Contact institution. *Financial support:* Career-related internships or fieldwork and Federal Work-Study available. Support available to part-time students. Financial award application deadline: 3/1; financial award applicants required to submit FAFSA. *Unit head:* Carolyn Gibbs, Chair, 916-278-7515, Fax: 916-278-7287, E-mail: carolyng@csus.edu. *Application contact:* Jose Martinez, Graduate Admissions Supervisor, 916-278-7871, E-mail: martinj@skymail.csus.edu.
Website: http://www.al.csus.edu/art

California State University, San Bernardino, Graduate Studies, College of Arts and Letters, Program in Studio Art, San Bernardino, CA 92407. Offers MA. *Accreditation:* NASAD; NCATE. *Faculty:* 3 full-time (2 women). *Students:* 11 full-time (0 women), 1 (woman) part-time; includes 8 minority (1 Black or African American, non-Hispanic/Latino; 1 Asian, non-Hispanic/Latino; 5 Hispanic/Latino; 1 Two or more races, non-Hispanic/Latino). Average age 32. 11 applicants, 45% accepted, 4 enrolled. In 2019, 4 master's awarded. *Entrance requirements:* Additional exam requirements/recommendations for international students: required—TOEFL. Application fee: $55. *Unit head:* Dr. Matthew Poole, Chair, 909-537-5808, E-mail: matthew.poole@csusb.edu. *Application contact:* Dr. Dorota Huizinga, Dean of Graduate Studies, 909-537-5058, E-mail: dodrota.huizinga@csusb.edu.

Carlow University, College of Learning and Innovation, Program in Art, Pittsburgh, PA 15213-3165. Offers MA. *Program availability:* Part-time, evening/weekend. *Students:* 2 full-time (both women), 1 (woman) part-time; includes 1 minority (Two or more races, non-Hispanic/Latino). Average age 41. 1 applicant, 100% accepted, 1 enrolled. In 2019, 1 master's awarded. *Entrance requirements:* For master's, personal essay; resume or curriculum vitae; 2 recommendations; official transcripts; interview; minimum undergraduate GPA of 3.0. Additional exam requirements/recommendations for international students: required—TOEFL (minimum score 550 paper-based). *Application deadline:* Applications are processed on a rolling basis. Electronic applications accepted. *Expenses: Tuition:* Full-time $13,666; part-time $902 per credit hour. *Required fees:* $15; $15 per credit. Tuition and fees vary according to degree level and program. *Financial support:* Application deadline: 4/1; applicants required to submit FAFSA. *Unit head:* Dale Huffman, Chair, 412-578-6033, E-mail: dhuffman@carlow.edu. *Application contact:* Dale Huffman, Chair, 412-578-6033, E-mail: dhuffman@carlow.edu. Website: http://www.carlow.edu/MA_art.aspx

Carnegie Mellon University, College of Fine Arts, School of Art, Pittsburgh, PA 15213-3891. Offers MFA. *Degree requirements:* For master's, thesis, exhibit. *Entrance requirements:* For master's, portfolio. Additional exam requirements/recommendations for international students: required—TOEFL.

Central Washington University, School of Graduate Studies and Research, College of Arts and Humanities, Department of Art and Design, Ellensburg, WA 98926. Offers ceramics (MFA); computer arts (MFA); jewelry and metalsmithing (MFA); painting and drawing (MFA); photography (MFA); sculpture (MFA). *Entrance requirements:* For master's, minimum GPA of 3.0, portfolio. Additional exam requirements/recommendations for international students: required—TOEFL (minimum score 550 paper-based; 79 iBT) or IELTS (minimum score 6.5). Electronic applications accepted.

Chapman University, The College of Performing Arts, Orange, CA 92866. Offers MBA/MM. *Program availability:* Part-time. *Students:* 1 part-time. Average age 23. 1 applicant, 100% accepted, 1 enrolled. *Entrance requirements:* Additional exam requirements/recommendations for international students: required—TOEFL, IELTS, PTE. *Application deadline:* Applications are processed on a rolling basis. Application fee: $60. Electronic applications accepted. *Expenses:* Contact institution. *Application contact:* Melissa Liberman, Admission Counselor, 714-628-2847, Fax: 714-997-6713, E-mail: liberman@chapman.edu.

Christie's Education, Certificate Program in Modern and Contemporary Art in New York, New York, NY 10020. Offers Certificate. *Program availability:* Part-time. *Expenses:* Contact institution.

City College of the City University of New York, Graduate School, Division of Humanities and the Arts, Department of Art, Program in Fine Arts, New York, NY 10031-9198. Offers advertising design (MFA); ceramic design (MFA); digital and interdisciplinary art practice (MFA); painting (MFA); printmaking (MFA); sculpture (MFA); wood and metal design (MFA). *Degree requirements:* For master's, thesis exhibit. *Entrance requirements:* For master's, 20-slide portfolio. Additional exam requirements/recommendations for international students: required—TOEFL (minimum score 577 paper-based; 90 iBT). Electronic applications accepted.

Claremont Graduate University, Graduate Programs, School of Arts and Humanities, Department of Art, Claremont, CA 91711. Offers digital media (MFA); drawing (MFA); installation (MFA); painting (MFA); performance (MFA); photography (MFA); sculpture (MFA); studio (MFA). *Program availability:* Part-time. *Degree requirements:* For master's, final project show. *Entrance requirements:* For master's, BA in art or BFA, slide review. Additional exam requirements/recommendations for international students: required—TOEFL (minimum score 75 iBT). Electronic applications accepted. *Expenses:* Contact institution.

Clemson University, Graduate School, College of Architecture, Arts, and Humanities, Department of Art, Clemson, SC 29634. Offers visual arts (MFA). *Accreditation:* NASAD. *Faculty:* 13 full-time (6 women), 5 part-time/adjunct (2 women). *Students:* 16 full-time (14 women). Average age 29. 26 applicants, 23% accepted, 6 enrolled. In 2019, 8 master's awarded. *Expenses: Tuition, area resident:* Full-time $10,600; part-time $8688 per semester. Tuition, state resident: full-time $10,600; part-time $8688 per semester. Tuition, nonresident: full-time $22,050; part-time $17,412 per semester. *International tuition:* $22,050 full-time. *Required fees:* $1196; $617 per semester. $617 per semester. Tuition and fees vary according to course load, degree level, campus/location and program. *Financial support:* In 2019–20, 20 students received support, including 4 fellowships with full and partial tuition reimbursements available (averaging $2,500 per year), 7 teaching assistantships with full and partial tuition reimbursements available (averaging $3,485 per year); career-related internships or fieldwork and unspecified assistantships also available. *Unit head:* Valarie Zimany, Department Chair, 864-656-3880, E-mail: vzimany@clemson.edu. *Application contact:* David Detrich, Graduate Program Coordinator, 864-656-3890, E-mail: ddavid@clemson.edu.
Website: http://www.clemson.edu/caah/departments/art/index.html

College for Creative Studies, Graduate Programs, Detroit, MI 48202-4034. Offers color and materials design (MFA); integrated design (MFA); interaction design (MFA); transportation design (MFA). *Accreditation:* NASAD.

Colorado State University, College of Liberal Arts, Department of Art and Art History, Fort Collins, CO 80523-1779. Offers studio art (MFA). *Program availability:* Part-time. *Faculty:* 16 full-time (8 women), 2 part-time/adjunct (both women). *Students:* 15 full-time (5 women), 3 part-time (all women); includes 8 minority (1 Black or African American, non-Hispanic/Latino; 5 Hispanic/Latino; 2 Two or more races, non-Hispanic/Latino). Average age 31. 39 applicants, 23% accepted, 5 enrolled. In 2019, 3 master's awarded. *Degree requirements:* For master's, comprehensive exam (for some programs), thesis, exhibition. *Entrance requirements:* For master's, portfolio, three letters of recommendation, transcripts, statement of purpose, resume, artist statement; 20 images of work (including video, if applicable). Additional exam requirements/recommendations for international students: required—TOEFL (minimum score 550 paper-based; 80 iBT). *Application deadline:* For fall admission, 2/1 priority date for domestic and international students. Applications are processed on a rolling basis. Application fee: $60 ($70 for international students). Electronic applications accepted. *Expenses:* Tuition, state resident: full-time $10,520; part-time $5844 per credit hour. Tuition, nonresident: full-time $25,791; part-time $14,328 per credit hour. *International tuition:* $25,791 full-time. *Required fees:* $2512.80. Part-time tuition and fees vary according to course level, course load, degree level, program and student level. *Financial support:* In 2019–20, 2 students received support, including 10 teaching assistantships with full tuition reimbursements available (averaging $12,397 per year); fellowships with partial tuition reimbursements available, scholarships/grants, and unspecified assistantships also available. Financial award applicants required to submit FAFSA. *Unit head:* Dr. Eleanor Moseman, Department Chair/Associate Professor, 970-491-5451, Fax: 970-491-0505, E-mail: EleanorMoseman@colostate.edu. *Application contact:* Haley Bates, Graduate Contact, 970-491-6775, E-mail: haley.bates@colostate.edu.
Website: http://art.colostate.edu/

Columbia College Chicago, School of Graduate Studies, Art and Art History Department, Chicago, IL 60605-1996. Offers fine arts (MFA). *Program availability:* Part-time, evening/weekend. *Degree requirements:* For master's, thesis. *Entrance requirements:* For master's, self-assessment essay, work sample, interview, letters of recommendation, transcripts. Additional exam requirements/recommendations for international students: required—TOEFL, IELTS. Electronic applications accepted.

Columbia University, Graduate School of Arts and Sciences, New York, NY 10027. Offers African-American studies (MA); American studies (MA); anthropology (MA, PhD); art history and archaeology (MA, PhD); astronomy (PhD); biological sciences (PhD); biotechnology (MA); chemical physics (PhD); chemistry (PhD); classical studies (MA, PhD); classics (MA, PhD); climate and society (MA); conservation biology (MA); earth and environmental sciences (PhD); East Asia: regional studies (MA); East Asian languages and cultures (MA, PhD); ecology, evolution and environmental biology (MA), including conservation biology; ecology, evolution, and environmental biology (PhD), including ecology and evolutionary biology, evolutionary primatology; economics (MA, PhD); English and comparative literature (MA, PhD); French and Romance philology (MA, PhD); Germanic languages (MA, PhD); global French studies (MA); global thought (MA); Hispanic cultural studies (MA); history (PhD); history and literature (MA); human rights studies (MA); Islamic studies (MA); Italian (MA, PhD); Japanese pedagogy (MA); Jewish studies (MA); Latin America and the Caribbean: regional studies (MA); Latin American and Iberian cultures (PhD); mathematics (MA, PhD), including finance (MA); medieval and Renaissance studies (MA); Middle Eastern, South Asian, and African studies (MA, PhD); modern art: critical and curatorial studies (MA); modern European studies (MA); museum anthropology (MA); music (DMA, PhD); oral history (MA); philosophical foundations of physics (MA); philosophy (MA, PhD); physics (PhD); political science (MA, PhD); psychology (PhD); quantitative methods in the social sciences (MA); religion (MA, PhD); Russia, Eurasia and East Europe: regional studies (MA); Russian translation (MA); Slavic cultures (MA); Slavic languages (MA, PhD); sociology (MA, PhD); South Asian studies (MA); statistics (MA, PhD); theatre (PhD). *Program availability:* Part-time. *Students:* 3,506 full-time (1,844 women), 208 part-time (121 women); includes 864 minority (110 Black or African American, non-Hispanic/Latino; 5 American Indian or Alaska Native, non-Hispanic/Latino; 416 Asian, non-Hispanic/Latino; 147 Hispanic/Latino; 6 Native Hawaiian or other Pacific Islander, non-Hispanic/Latino; 180 Two or more races, non-Hispanic/Latino), 2,065 international. 14,545 applicants, 25% accepted, 1,429 enrolled. In 2019, 1,262 master's, 363 doctorates awarded. Terminal master's awarded for partial completion of doctoral program. *Degree requirements:* For master's, variable foreign language requirement, comprehensive exam (for some programs), thesis (for some programs); for doctorate, variable foreign language requirement, comprehensive exam (for some programs), thesis/dissertation. *Entrance requirements:* For master's and doctorate, GRE General Test, GRE Subject Test (for some programs). Additional exam requirements/recommendations for international students: required—TOEFL (minimum score 600 paper-based; 100 iBT), IELTS (minimum score 7.5). Application fee: $115. Electronic applications accepted. *Expenses: Tuition:* Full-time $47,600; part-time $1880 per credit. One-time fee: $105. *Financial support:* Fellowships, research assistantships, teaching assistantships, career-related internships or fieldwork, Federal Work-Study, institutionally sponsored loans, scholarships/grants, traineeships, health care benefits, tuition waivers, and unspecified assistantships available. Support available to part-time students. Financial award application deadline: 12/15. *Unit head:* Dr. Carlos J. Alonso, Dean of the Graduate School of Arts and Sciences and Vice President for Graduate Education, 212-854-2861, E-mail: gsas-dean@columbia.edu. *Application contact:* GSAS Office of Admissions, 212-854-6729, E-mail: gsas-admissions@columbia.edu.
Website: http://gsas.columbia.edu/

Columbia University, School of the Arts, Sound Art Program, New York, NY 10027. Offers MFA. *Degree requirements:* For master's, thesis. *Entrance requirements:* For master's, Undergraduate transcript, 3 letters of recommendation, statement of intent, work sample. Additional exam requirements/recommendations for international students: required—Either the TOEFL or the IELTS is required. Electronic applications accepted. *Expenses: Tuition:* Full-time $47,600; part-time $1880 per credit. One-time fee: $105.

Columbia University, School of the Arts, Visual Arts Program, New York, NY 10027. Offers new genres (MFA). *Degree requirements:* For master's, thesis. *Entrance requirements:* For master's, Undergraduate transcript, 3 letters of recommendation, statement of intent, portfolio, resume. Additional exam requirements/recommendations for international students: required—Either the TOEFL or the IELTS is required. Electronic applications accepted. *Expenses: Tuition:* Full-time $47,600; part-time $1880 per credit. One-time fee: $105.

Columbus College of Art & Design, Graduate Programs, Columbus, OH 43215-1758. Offers integrative design (M Des); visual arts (MFA). *Accreditation:* NASAD. *Program availability:* Part-time. *Degree requirements:* For master's, thesis, thesis exhibition. *Entrance requirements:* For master's, portfolio, resume/curriculum vitae, three letters of recommendation, minimum GPA of 3.0. Additional exam requirements/recommendations for international students: required—TOEFL (minimum score 80 iBT), IELTS (minimum score 6.5). Electronic applications accepted.

Concordia University, School of Graduate Studies, Faculty of Fine Arts, Department of Studio Arts, Montréal, QC H3G 1M8, Canada. Offers studio arts (MFA), including fibers and material practices, film production, intermedia, painting and drawing, photography, print media, sculpture. *Degree requirements:* For master's, thesis or alternative. *Entrance requirements:* For master's, portfolio.

Cornell University, Graduate School, Graduate Fields of Architecture, Art and Planning, Field of Art, Ithaca, NY 14853. Offers creative visual arts (MFA), including painting, photography, printmaking, sculpture. *Degree requirements:* For master's, thesis, exhibit. *Entrance requirements:* For master's, slide portfolio of 10-20 slides, 3 letters of recommendation, resume. Additional exam requirements/recommendations for international students: required—TOEFL (minimum score 550 paper-based; 77 iBT). Electronic applications accepted.

Cranbrook Academy of Art, Program in Fine Arts, Bloomfield Hills, MI 48303-0801. Offers 2d design (MFA); 3d design (MFA); ceramics (MFA); fiber (MFA); metalsmithing (MFA); painting (MFA); photography (MFA); print media (MFA); sculpture (MFA). *Accreditation:* NASAD. *Degree requirements:* For master's, thesis, exhibit. *Entrance requirements:* Additional exam requirements/recommendations for international students: required—TOEFL (minimum score 85 iBT). Electronic applications accepted.

Drew University, Caspersen School of Graduate Studies, Madison, NJ 07940-1493. Offers conflict resolution and leadership (Certificate), including community leadership, moderation, peace building; education (M Ed); finance (MA); history and culture (MA, PhD), including American history, book history, British history, European history, intellectual history, Irish history, print culture, public history; K-12 education (MAT), including art, biology, chemistry, elementary education, English, French, Italian, math, secondary education, special education, teacher of students with disabilities; liberal studies (M Litt, D Litt), including history, Irish/Irish-American studies, literature (M Litt, MMH, D Litt, DMH, CMH), religion, spirituality, teaching in the two-year college, writing; medical humanities (MMH, DMH, CMH), including arts, health, healthcare, literature (M Litt, MMH, D Litt, DMH, CMH), scientific research; poetry (MFA). *Program availability:* Part-time, evening/weekend. Terminal master's awarded for partial completion of doctoral program. *Degree requirements:* For master's and other advanced degree, thesis (for some programs); for doctorate, one foreign language, comprehensive exam (for some programs), thesis/dissertation. *Entrance requirements:* For master's, PRAXIS Core and Subject Area tests (for MAT), GRE/GMAT (for MFin MS in Data Analytics), resume, transcripts, writing sample, personal statement, letters of recommendation; for doctorate, GRE (PhD in history and culture), resume, transcripts, writing sample, personal statement, letters of recommendation; for other advanced degree, resume, transcripts, personal statement. Additional exam requirements/recommendations for international students: required—TOEFL (minimum score 587 paper-based; 80 iBT), IELTS (minimum score 6), TWE (minimum score 4). Electronic applications accepted.

Duke University, Graduate School, Department of Art, Art History and Visual Studies, Durham, NC 27708-0764. Offers historical and cultural visualization (MA); history of art (PhD). *Degree requirements:* For doctorate, thesis/dissertation. *Entrance requirements:* For doctorate, GRE General Test. Additional exam requirements/recommendations for international students: required—TOEFL (minimum score 577 paper-based; 90 iBT) or IELTS (minimum score 7). Electronic applications accepted.

East Carolina University, Graduate School, College of Fine Arts and Communication, School of Art and Design, Greenville, NC 27858-4353. Offers art education (MA Ed); ceramics (MFA); graphic design (MFA); illustration (MFA); metal design (MFA); painting and drawing (MFA); photography (MFA); printmaking (MFA); sculpture (MFA); textile design (MFA); wood design (MFA). *Accreditation:* NASAD (one or more programs are accredited). *Program availability:* Part-time, evening/weekend. *Application deadline:* For fall admission, 2/1 for domestic students; for spring admission, 10/1 for domestic students. *Expenses: Tuition,* area resident: Full-time $4749; part-time $185 per credit hour. Tuition, state resident: full-time $4749; part-time $185 per credit hour. Tuition, nonresident: full-time $17,898; part-time $864 per credit hour. *International tuition:* $17,898 full-time. *Required fees:* $2787. *Financial support:* Application deadline: 6/1. *Unit head:* Dr. Kate Bukowski, Director, 252-328-6665, E-mail: bukowskik16@ecu.edu. *Application contact:* Graduate School Admissions, 252-328-6012, E-mail: gradschool@ecu.edu.
Website: https://art.ecu.edu/

Eastern Illinois University, Graduate School, College of Liberal Arts and Sciences, Department of Art, Charleston, IL 61920. Offers art (MA); art education (MA); community arts (MA). *Accreditation:* NASAD. *Program availability:* Part-time, evening/weekend, online learning. *Degree requirements:* For master's, comprehensive exam (for some programs), thesis (for some programs). *Entrance requirements:* For master's, GMAT or GRE. Additional exam requirements/recommendations for international students: required—TOEFL (minimum score 500 paper-based; 61 iBT), IELTS (minimum score 6). Electronic applications accepted.

Eastern Michigan University, Graduate School, College of Arts and Sciences, School of Art and Design, Program in Studio Art, Ypsilanti, MI 48197. Offers MA, MFA. *Accreditation:* NASAD. *Program availability:* Part-time, evening/weekend, online learning. *Students:* 10 full-time (6 women), 8 part-time (7 women); includes 3 minority (all Two or more races, non-Hispanic/Latino), 1 international. Average age 40. 15 applicants, 53% accepted, 5 enrolled. In 2019, 1 master's awarded. *Application deadline:* Applications are processed on a rolling basis. Application fee: $45. *Financial support:* Fellowships, research assistantships with full tuition reimbursements, teaching assistantships with full tuition reimbursements, career-related internships or fieldwork, Federal Work-Study, institutionally sponsored loans, scholarships/grants, and unspecified assistantships available. Support available to part-time students. *Application contact:* Michael Reedy, Graduate Coordinator, 734-487-1268, Fax: 734-487-2324, E-mail: mreedy@emich.edu.

East Tennessee State University, College of Graduate and Continuing Studies, College of Arts and Sciences, Department of Art and Design, Johnson City, TN 37614. Offers studio art (MFA). *Accreditation:* NASAD. *Degree requirements:* For master's, thesis, exhibit, oral exam. *Entrance requirements:* For master's, GRE General Test, portfolio, bachelor's degree in art, minimum GPA of 3.0, three letters of recommendation. Additional exam requirements/recommendations for international students: required—TOEFL (minimum score 550 paper-based; 79 iBT). Electronic applications accepted.

Edinboro University of Pennsylvania, Department of Art, Edinboro, PA 16444. Offers art education (MA); fine arts (MFA), including ceramics (MA, MFA), metals/jewelry, painting (MA, MFA), printmaking (MA, MFA), sculpture (MA, MFA); studio art (MA), including ceramics (MA, MFA), jewelry/metals, painting (MA, MFA), printmaking (MA, MFA), sculpture (MA, MFA). *Accreditation:* NASAD. *Program availability:* Evening/weekend. *Faculty:* 11 full-time (5 women), 1 part-time/adjunct. *Students:* 21 full-time (15 women), 29 part-time (26 women); includes 4 minority (2 Asian, non-Hispanic/Latino; 2 Hispanic/Latino). Average age 31. 39 applicants, 44% accepted, 16 enrolled. In 2019, 13 master's awarded. *Degree requirements:* For master's, comprehensive exam, thesis or alternative, competency exam, exhibit, portfolio. *Entrance requirements:* For master's, GRE or MAT, interview, minimum QPA of 2.5, portfolio. Additional exam requirements/recommendations for international students: required—TOEFL (minimum score 550 paper-based; 79 iBT), IELTS (minimum score 6.5). *Application deadline:* Applications are processed on a rolling basis. Application fee: $30. Electronic applications accepted. *Expenses: Tuition,* area resident: Full-time $11,261; part-time $625.60 per credit. Tuition, state resident: full-time $11,261; part-time $625.60 per credit. Tuition, nonresident: full-time $16,850; part-time $936.10 per credit. *International tuition:* $16,850 full-time. *Required fees:* $57.75 per credit. *Financial support:* In 2019–20, 19 students received support. Research assistantships with tuition reimbursements available, Federal Work-Study, scholarships/grants, and unspecified assistantships available. Financial award application deadline: 2/15; financial award applicants required to submit FAFSA. *Unit head:* Suzanne Proulx, Chairperson, 814-732-1184, E-mail: sproulx@edinboro.edu. *Application contact:* Suzanne Proulx, Chairperson, 814-732-1184, E-mail: sproulx@edinboro.edu.
Website: http://art.edinboro.edu/

Emily Carr University of Art + Design, Program in Applied Arts, Vancouver, BC V6H 3R9, Canada. Offers design (M Des); media arts (MAA); visual arts (MAA). *Degree requirements:* For master's, internship, thesis project. *Entrance requirements:* For master's, minimum overall GPA of 3.0, visual portfolio, 3 letters of recommendation, resume/curriculum vitae. Additional exam requirements/recommendations for international students: required—TOEFL (minimum score 570 paper-based; 84 iBT), IELTS (minimum score 6.5), Michigan English Language Assessment Battery (minimum score 81). Electronic applications accepted.

Fairleigh Dickinson University, Metropolitan Campus, University College: Arts, Sciences, and Professional Studies, School of Art and Media Studies, Teaneck, NJ 07666-1914. Offers MA.

Ferris State University, Kendall College of Art and Design, Grand Rapids, MI 49307. Offers design (MA); painting (MFA); photography (MFA); printmaking (MFA); visual and critical studies (MA). *Faculty:* 16 full-time (9 women), 6 part-time/adjunct (3 women). *Students:* 46 full-time (25 women), 18 part-time (15 women); includes 10 minority (1 Black or African American, non-Hispanic/Latino; 1 American Indian or Alaska Native, non-Hispanic/Latino; 6 Hispanic/Latino; 2 Two or more races, non-Hispanic/Latino), 8 international. Average age 33. 28 applicants, 82% accepted, 19 enrolled. In 2019, 14 master's awarded. *Degree requirements:* For master's, thesis, seminars and studio courses. *Entrance requirements:* For master's, official transcripts from all institutions of higher education attended. Letter of intent outlining proposed artistic goals. Concise artist statement that addresses the philosophical foundation of your work. CV showing successful professional experience. Portfolio of work 20 images in chosen area of emphasis. Contact information for. Additional exam requirements/recommendations for international students: required—TOEFL (minimum score 79 iBT), IELTS (minimum score 6.5). *Application deadline:* For fall admission, 2/1 priority date for domestic and international students; for spring admission, 10/15 priority date for domestic and international students. Applications are processed on a rolling basis. Application fee: $0 ($30 for international students). Electronic applications accepted. *Expenses:* $1079 per credit hour; Technology fee $175 per semester; Student Life Fee $20 per semester. *Financial support:* In 2019–20, 46 students received support, including 46 fellowships (averaging $11,736 per year); scholarships/grants and unspecified assistantships also available. Financial award application deadline: 2/1; financial award applicants required to submit FAFSA. *Unit head:* Tara McCrackin, President, 616-451-2787. *Application contact:* Thomas Post, Graduate Recruitment Specialist, 616-451-2787, Fax: 616-831-9689, E-mail: thomaspost@ferris.edu. Website: http://www.kcad.edu/

Florida Atlantic University, Dorothy F. Schmidt College of Arts and Letters, Department of Visual Arts and Art History, Boca Raton, FL 33431-0991. Offers visual art (MFA), including ceramics, graphic design, visual art. *Faculty:* 14 full-time (10 women). *Students:* 9 full-time (7 women), 3 part-time (all women); includes 2 minority (1 Black or African American, non-Hispanic/Latino; 1 Hispanic/Latino), 1 international. Average age 41. 17 applicants, 24% accepted, 2 enrolled. In 2019, 4 master's awarded. *Degree requirements:* For master's, one foreign language, project. *Entrance requirements:* For master's, GRE General Test, minimum GPA of 3.0 during last 60 hours of course work, slide portfolio. *Application deadline:* For fall admission, 2/21 for domestic and international students; for spring admission, 10/1 for domestic and international students. Application fee: $30. Electronic applications accepted. *Expenses: Tuition:* Full-time $20,536; part-time $371.82 per credit hour. Tuition and fees vary according to program. *Financial support:* Research assistantships with full tuition reimbursements, teaching assistantships with full tuition reimbursements, career-related internships or fieldwork, Federal Work-Study, and institutionally sponsored loans available. Financial award applicants required to submit FAFSA. *Unit head:* Dr. Eric Landes, Chair, 954-236-1106, E-mail: elandes1@fau.edu. *Application contact:* Dr. Eric Landes, Chair, 954-236-1106, E-mail: elandes1@fau.edu.
Website: http://www.fau.edu/VAAH/

Florida International University, College of Communication, Architecture and The Arts, Department of Art and Art History, Miami, FL 33199. Offers museum studies (Graduate Certificate); studio art (MFA). *Accreditation:* NASAD. *Program availability:* Part-time, evening/weekend. *Faculty:* 15 full-time (7 women), 23 part-time/adjunct (11 women). *Students:* 20 full-time (17 women), 9 part-time (all women); includes 21 minority (3 Black or African American, non-Hispanic/Latino; 18 Hispanic/Latino), 3 international. Average age 32. 20 applicants, 70% accepted, 7 enrolled. In 2019, 8 master's awarded. *Entrance requirements:* For master's, minimum GPA of 3.0 in upper-level coursework, 3 letters of recommendation, 20 slides of creative work. Additional exam requirements/recommendations for international students: required—TOEFL (minimum score 550 paper-based; 80 iBT). *Application deadline:* For fall admission, 2/1 for domestic and international students. Application fee: $30. Electronic applications accepted. *Expenses: Tuition,* area resident: Full-time $8912; part-time $446 per credit hour. Tuition, state resident: full-time $8912; part-time $446 per credit hour. Tuition, nonresident: full-time $21,393; part-time $992 per credit hour. *Required fees:* $2194. *Financial support:* Institutionally sponsored loans and scholarships/grants available. Financial award application deadline: 3/1; financial award applicants required to submit FAFSA. *Unit head:* Dr. David Chang, Chair, 305-348-2897, Fax: 305-348-0513, E-mail: David.Chang@fiu.edu. *Application contact:* Nanett Rojas, Manager, Admissions Operations, 305-348-7464, Fax: 305-348-7441, E-mail: gradadm@fiu.edu.
Website: http://carta.fiu.edu/arts/

Florida State University, The Graduate School, College of Fine Arts, Department of Art, Tallahassee, FL 32301. Offers MFA. *Accreditation:* NASAD. *Faculty:* 20 full-time (12 women), 33 part-time/adjunct (22 women). *Students:* 25 full-time (17 women); includes 6 minority (1 Black or African American, non-Hispanic/Latino; 5 Hispanic/Latino), 1 international. Average age 26. 63 applicants, 32% accepted, 12 enrolled. In 2019, 11 master's awarded. *Degree requirements:* For master's, thesis, creative thesis project, short thesis paper. *Entrance requirements:* Additional exam requirements/recommendations for international students: required—TOEFL (minimum score 550 paper-based). *Application deadline:* For fall admission, 2/1 priority date for domestic and international students. Application fee: $30. Electronic applications accepted. *Financial support:* In 2019–20, 30 students received support, including 30 teaching assistantships (averaging $5,900 per year); fellowships, Federal Work-Study, scholarships/grants, tuition waivers (full), and unspecified assistantships also available. *Unit head:* Stephanie James, Department Chair, 850-644-2932, E-mail: sljames@fsu.edu. *Application contact:* Tenee' Hart, Graduate Advisor & Coordinator, 540-220-5629, E-mail: tahart@fsu.edu.
Website: http://art.fsu.edu/

Fontbonne University, Graduate Programs, St. Louis, MO 63105-3098. Offers accounting (MBA, MS); art (MA); art (K-12) (MAT); business (MBA); computer science (MS); deaf education (MA); early intervention in deaf education (MA); education (MA), including autism spectrum disorders, curriculum and instruction, diverse learners, early childhood education, reading, special education; elementary education (MAT); family and consumer sciences (MA), including multidisciplinary health communication studies; fine arts (MFA); instructional design and technology (MS); management and leadership (MM); middle school education (MAT); secondary education (MAT); special education (MAT); speech-language pathology (MS); supply chain management (MS); theatre (MA). *Accreditation:* ASHA. *Program availability:* Part-time, evening/weekend, online learning. *Degree requirements:* For master's, comprehensive exam (for some programs), thesis (for some programs). *Entrance requirements:* Additional exam requirements/recommendations for international students: required—TOEFL (minimum score 500 paper-based; 65 iBT). Electronic applications accepted. *Expenses: Tuition:* Full-time $6975; part-time $775 per credit hour. *Required fees:* $225; $25 per credit hour. Tuition and fees vary according to degree level and program.

Fort Hays State University, Graduate School, College of Arts, Humanities, and Social Sciences, Department of Art and Design, Hays, KS 67601-4099. Offers studio art (MFA). *Program availability:* Part-time. *Degree requirements:* For master's, comprehensive exam, thesis. *Entrance requirements:* For master's, slides. Additional exam requirements/recommendations for international students: required—TOEFL (minimum score 550 paper-based; 79 iBT). Electronic applications accepted.

Full Sail University, Education Media Design and Technology Master of Science Program - Online, Winter Park, FL 32792-7437. Offers MS. *Program availability:* Online learning. *Entrance requirements:* Additional exam requirements/recommendations for international students: required—TOEFL (minimum score 550 paper-based; 79 iBT).

Art/Fine Arts

Full Sail University, Media Design Master of Fine Arts Program - Online, Winter Park, FL 32792-7437. Offers MFA. *Program availability:* Online learning.

George Mason University, College of Visual and Performing Arts, Program in Visual and Performing Arts, Fairfax, VA 22030. Offers MFA. *Accreditation:* NASAD. *Entrance requirements:* For master's, official transcripts; 3 letters of recommendation; letter of intent; resume; professional goals statement. Additional exam requirements/recommendations for international students: required—TOEFL (minimum score 575 paper-based; 88 iBT), IELTS (minimum score 6.5), PTE (minimum score 59). Electronic applications accepted.

The George Washington University, Columbian College of Arts and Sciences, Department of Fine Arts and Art History, Washington, DC 20052. Offers art history (MA), including art history, museum training; ceramics (MFA); drawing/painting (MFA); interior design (MFA), including interior architecture and design; new media (MFA); photography (MFA); sculpture (MFA). *Accreditation:* CIDA. *Program availability:* Part-time, evening/weekend. *Entrance requirements:* For master's, GRE General Test, bachelor's degree in field, minimum GPA of 3.0. Additional exam requirements/recommendations for international students: required—TOEFL (minimum score 550 paper-based; 80 iBT). Electronic applications accepted.

Georgia Southern University, Jack N. Averitt College of Graduate Studies, College of Arts and Humanities, Program in Art, Statesboro, GA 30460. Offers fine arts (MFA), including 2D graphic design, 2D studio art, 3D studio art. *Accreditation:* NASAD. *Program availability:* Part-time. *Faculty:* 27 full-time (12 women). *Students:* 16 full-time (12 women), 3 part-time (2 women); includes 2 minority (1 Black or African American, non-Hispanic/Latino; 1 Hispanic/Latino), 5 international. Average age 29. 7 applicants, 86% accepted, 6 enrolled. In 2019, 2 master's awarded. *Degree requirements:* For master's, thesis, exhibition. *Entrance requirements:* For master's, minimum GPA of 3.0; 18 semester hours of course work in studio art, 9 in art history; portfolio; letters of reference. Additional exam requirements/recommendations for international students: required—TOEFL (minimum score 550 paper-based; 80 iBT), IELTS (minimum score 6). *Application deadline:* For fall admission, 3/1 priority date for domestic and international students; for spring admission, 10/1 priority date for domestic students, 10/1 for international students. Applications are processed on a rolling basis. Application fee: $50. Electronic applications accepted. *Expenses: Tuition, area resident:* Full-time $4986; part-time $277 per credit hour. Tuition, nonresident: full-time $19,890; part-time $1105 per credit hour. *International tuition:* $19,890 full-time. *Required fees:* $2114; $1057 per semester. $1057 per semester. Tuition and fees vary according to course load, campus/location and program. *Financial support:* In 2019–20, 10 students received support, including 4 fellowships with full tuition reimbursements available (averaging $7,750 per year); career-related internships or fieldwork, Federal Work-Study, scholarships/grants, tuition waivers (full), and unspecified assistantships also available. Support available to part-time students. Financial award application deadline: 4/15; financial award applicants required to submit FAFSA. *Unit head:* Dr. Robert Farber, Department Chair, 912-478-5358, Fax: 912-478-5104, E-mail: rfarber@georgiasouthern.edu.
Website: http://class.georgiasouthern.edu/art

Georgia State University, College of Arts, Ernest G. Welch School of Art and Design, Program in Studio Art, Atlanta, GA 30302-3083. Offers ceramics (MFA); drawing and painting (MFA); graphic design (MFA); interior design (MFA); photography (MFA); printmaking (MFA); sculpture (MFA); textiles (MFA). *Accreditation:* NASAD. Application fee: $50. Electronic applications accepted. *Expenses: Tuition, area resident:* Full-time $7164; part-time $398 per credit hour. Tuition, state resident: full-time $7164; part-time $398 per credit hour. Tuition, nonresident: full-time $22,662; part-time $1259 per credit hour. *International tuition:* $22,662 full-time. *Required fees:* $2128; $312 per credit hour. Tuition and fees vary according to course load and program. *Financial support:* Fellowships, research assistantships, teaching assistantships, scholarships/grants, and unspecified assistantships available. Financial award application deadline: 4/15; financial award applicants required to submit FAFSA. *Unit head:* Joseph Peragine, Director, Welch School of Art and Design, 404-413-5229, E-mail: jperagine@gsu.edu. *Application contact:* Joseph Peragine, Director, Welch School of Art and Design, 404-413-5229, E-mail: jperagine@gsu.edu.
Website: http://artdesign.gsu.edu/graduate/admissions/masters-of-fine-arts-in-studio/

Governors State University, College of Arts and Sciences, Program in Art, University Park, IL 60484. Offers MA. *Program availability:* Part-time. *Faculty:* 57 full-time (33 women), 72 part-time/adjunct (40 women). *Students:* 2 full-time (both women), 1 (woman) part-time. Average age 52. 5 applicants, 40% accepted, 2 enrolled. *Application deadline:* For fall admission, 4/1 for domestic students. Applications are processed on a rolling basis. Application fee: $50. Electronic applications accepted. *Expenses: Tuition, area resident:* Full-time $8472; part-time $353 per credit hour. Tuition, state resident: full-time $8472; part-time $353 per credit hour. Tuition, nonresident: full-time $16,944; part-time $706 per credit hour. *International tuition:* $16,944 full-time. *Required fees:* $2520; $105 per credit hour. $38 per term. Tuition and fees vary according to course load, degree level and program. *Financial support:* Application deadline: 5/1; applicants required to submit FAFSA. *Unit head:* Jason Zingsheim, Chair, Division of Arts and Letters, 708-534-5000 Ext. 7493, E-mail: jzingsheim@govst.edu. *Application contact:* Jason Zingsheim, Chair, Division of Arts and Letters, 708-534-5000 Ext. 7493, E-mail: jzingsheim@govst.edu.

Hollins University, Graduate Programs, Program in Liberal Studies, Roanoke, VA 24020. Offers humanities (MALS); interdisciplinary studies (MALS); leadership (MALS); social sciences (MALS); visual and performing arts (MALS). *Program availability:* Part-time, evening/weekend, 100% online, blended/hybrid learning. *Degree requirements:* For master's, thesis. *Entrance requirements:* For master's, three letters of recommendation, interview, bachelor's degree, undergraduate transcripts, statement of educational objectives. Additional exam requirements/recommendations for international students: required—TOEFL (minimum score 550 paper-based; 80 iBT), IELTS (minimum score 6.5). Electronic applications accepted. *Expenses:* Contact institution.

Hood College, Graduate School, Program in Ceramic Arts, Frederick, MD 21701-8575. Offers ceramic arts (Certificate); ceramics (MA, MFA). *Program availability:* Part-time, evening/weekend. *Degree requirements:* For master's, thesis (for some programs), capstone project. *Entrance requirements:* For master's, minimum GPA of 2.75, official transcripts, artist statement, resume, 2 letters of recommendation, portfolio of 20 images; for Certificate, official transcripts, artist statement, portfolio of 12 images. Additional exam requirements/recommendations for international students: required—TOEFL (minimum score 575 paper-based; 89 iBT), IELTS (minimum score 6.5). Electronic applications accepted.

Houston Baptist University, School of Fine Arts, Houston, TX 77074-3298. Offers studio art (MFA). *Program availability:* Part-time, evening/weekend. *Degree requirements:* For master's, comprehensive exam. *Entrance requirements:* For master's, minimum GPA of 2.5, essay/personal statement, resume, bachelor's degree transcript, digital portfolio. Additional exam requirements/recommendations for international students: required—TOEFL (minimum score 80 iBT), IELTS (minimum score 6.5). Electronic applications accepted. Application fee is waived when completed online. *Expenses:* Contact institution.

Howard University, Graduate School, Division of Fine Arts, Department of Art, Program in Fine Arts, Washington, DC 20059-0002. Offers 3D reality (sculpture and ceramics) (MFA); design (MFA); electronic studio (MFA); painting (MFA); photography (MFA). *Accreditation:* NASAD. *Degree requirements:* For master's, comprehensive exam, thesis, exhibit. *Entrance requirements:* For master's, minimum GPA of 3.0, portfolio.

Hunter College of the City University of New York, Graduate School, School of Arts and Sciences, Department of Art and Art History, Program in Studio Art, New York, NY 10013. Offers MFA. *Program availability:* Part-time, evening/weekend. *Degree requirements:* For master's, exhibit, project. *Entrance requirements:* For master's, minimum of 24 credits of course work in studio art, 9 in art history; portfolio; minimum GPA of 3.0 overall and in art courses; statement of purpose; two letters of recommendation. Additional exam requirements/recommendations for international students: required—TOEFL (minimum score 550 paper-based; 60 iBT).

Idaho State University, Graduate School, College of Arts and Letters, Department of Art, Pocatello, ID 83209-8004. Offers MFA. *Program availability:* Part-time. *Degree requirements:* For master's, comprehensive exam, thesis, exhibit, 2 year minimum participation in program, oral exam. *Entrance requirements:* For master's, GRE General Test, GMAT or MAT, minimum GPA of 3.0 in all upper-division classes, portfolio of work, 3 letters of recommendation. Additional exam requirements/recommendations for international students: required—TOEFL (minimum score 550 paper-based; 80 iBT). Electronic applications accepted.

Illinois State University, Graduate School, Wonsook Kim College of Fine Arts, Creative Technologies, Normal, IL 61790. Offers MS. *Accreditation:* NASAD. *Faculty:* 113 full-time (55 women), 37 part-time/adjunct (20 women). *Students:* 14 full-time (7 women), 4 part-time (2 women). Average age 31. 8 applicants, 100% accepted, 7 enrolled. In 2019, 7 master's awarded. *Degree requirements:* For master's, thesis or alternative. Application fee: $50. *Expenses: Tuition, area resident:* Full-time $7956; part-time $9767 per year. Tuition, nonresident: full-time $9233; part-time $17,592 per year. *Required fees:* $1797. *Financial support:* In 2019–20, 5 teaching assistantships were awarded. Financial award application deadline: 4/1. *Unit head:* Dr. Aaron Paolucci, Director of Arts Technology, 309-438-2875, E-mail: ampaolu@ilstu.edu. *Application contact:* Jody DeCremer, Assistant Director, 309-438-3921, E-mail: decremer@ilstu.edu.
Website: http://www.arts.ilstu.edu/artstech/

Illinois State University, Graduate School, Wonsook Kim College of Fine Arts, School of Art, Normal, IL 61790. Offers art history (MA, MS); ceramics (MFA, MS); drawing (MFA, MS); fibers (MFA, MS); glass (MFA, MS); graphic design (MFA, MS); metals (MFA, MS); painting (MFA, MS); photography (MFA, MS); printmaking (MFA, MS); sculpture (MFA, MS). *Accreditation:* NASAD (one or more programs are accredited). *Faculty:* 34 full-time (18 women), 15 part-time/adjunct (11 women). *Students:* 25 full-time (16 women), 5 part-time (4 women). Average age 31. 32 applicants, 66% accepted, 12 enrolled. In 2019, 11 master's awarded. *Degree requirements:* For master's, thesis or alternative, internship. *Entrance requirements:* For master's, portfolio, sample of scholarly writing. *Application deadline:* Applications are processed on a rolling basis. Application fee: $50. *Expenses: Tuition, area resident:* Full-time $7956; part-time $9767 per year. Tuition, nonresident: full-time $9233; part-time $17,592 per year. *Required fees:* $1797. *Financial support:* In 2019–20, 20 teaching assistantships were awarded; career-related internships or fieldwork, Federal Work-Study, tuition waivers (full and partial), and unspecified assistantships also available. Support available to part-time students. Financial award application deadline: 4/1. *Unit head:* Mike Wille, Director of Art School, 309-438-5610, E-mail: mjwill4@ilstu.edu. *Application contact:* Tyler Lotz, Graduate Coordinator, 309-438-8301, E-mail: tlotz@ilstu.edu.
Website: http://www.arts.ilstu.edu/art/

Indiana State University, College of Graduate and Professional Studies, College of Arts and Sciences, Department of Art and Design, Terre Haute, IN 47809. Offers ceramics (MA, MFA); drawing (MA, MFA); graphic design (MA, MFA); painting (MA, MFA); photography (MA, MFA); printmaking (MA, MFA); sculpture (MA, MFA). *Accreditation:* NASAD (one or more programs are accredited). *Program availability:* Part-time. *Degree requirements:* For master's, thesis or alternative, departmental qualifying exam. *Entrance requirements:* For master's, portfolio. Additional exam requirements/recommendations for international students: required—TOEFL (minimum score 550 paper-based).

Indiana University Bloomington, University Graduate School, College of Arts and Sciences, School of Art, Architecture and Design, Bloomington, IN 47405-7000. Offers apparel merchandising (MS); architecture (M Arch); studio art (MFA). *Accreditation:* NASAD (one or more programs are accredited). *Entrance requirements:* For master's, portfolio (MFA). Additional exam requirements/recommendations for international students: required—TOEFL. Electronic applications accepted.

Indiana University of Pennsylvania, School of Graduate Studies and Research, College of Fine Arts, Department of Art, MA Program in Art, Indiana, PA 15705. Offers MA. *Accreditation:* NASAD. *Program availability:* Part-time. *Faculty:* 7 full-time (3 women), 7 part-time/adjunct (3 women). *Students:* 3 part-time (all women). Average age 27. 3 applicants, 100% accepted, 2 enrolled. In 2019, 3 master's awarded. *Degree requirements:* For master's, thesis optional. *Entrance requirements:* For master's, 3 letters of recommendation, portfolio, official transcripts, goal statement. Additional exam requirements/recommendations for international students: required—TOEFL (minimum score 540 paper-based; 76 iBT); recommended—IELTS (minimum score 6). *Application deadline:* For fall admission, 4/15 priority date for domestic students. Applications are processed on a rolling basis. Application fee: $50. Electronic applications accepted. *Expenses: Tuition, area resident:* Full-time $9288; part-time $516 per credit. Tuition, nonresident: full-time $13,932; part-time $774 per credit. *Required fees:* $4454. One-time fee: $115 full-time. Tuition and fees vary according to course load and program. *Financial support:* In 2019–20, 1 fellowship (averaging $300 per year), 1 research assistantship with tuition reimbursement (averaging $6,000 per year) were awarded; career-related internships or fieldwork, Federal Work-Study, scholarships/grants, and unspecified assistantships also available. Support available to part-time students. Financial award application deadline: 4/15; financial award applicants required to submit FAFSA. *Unit head:* Dr. Susan Palmisano, Graduate Coordinator, 724-357-2536, E-mail: Susan.Palmisano@iup.edu. *Application contact:* Dr. Susan Palmisano, Graduate Coordinator, 724-357-2536, E-mail: Susan.Palmisano@iup.edu.
Website: http://www.iup.edu/art/grad/default.aspx

Indiana University of Pennsylvania, School of Graduate Studies and Research, College of Fine Arts, Department of Art, Master of Fine Arts Program, Indiana, PA 15705. Offers MFA. *Program availability:* Part-time. *Faculty:* 7 full-time (3 women), 7 part-time/adjunct (3 women). *Students:* 7 full-time (4 women), 2 part-time (0 women); includes 1 minority (Hispanic/Latino), 2 international. Average age 30. 9 applicants, 89% accepted, 4 enrolled. In 2019, 6 master's awarded. *Degree requirements:* For master's, thesis/exhibition. *Entrance requirements:* For master's, 2 letters of recommendation, art

slides, official transcripts, goal statement. Additional exam requirements/recommendations for international students: required—TOEFL (minimum score 540 paper-based; 76 iBT); recommended—IELTS (minimum score 6). *Application deadline:* For fall admission, 2/15 priority date for domestic students. Applications are processed on a rolling basis. Application fee: $50. Electronic applications accepted. *Expenses: Tuition, area resident:* Full-time $9288; part-time $516 per credit. Tuition, nonresident: full-time $13,932; part-time $774 per credit. *Required fees:* $4454. One-time fee: $115 full-time. Tuition and fees vary according to course load and program. *Financial support:* In 2019–20, 8 research assistantships with tuition reimbursements (averaging $5,500 per year) were awarded; fellowships with full tuition reimbursements, career-related internships or fieldwork, Federal Work-Study, scholarships/grants, and unspecified assistantships also available. Support available to part-time students. Financial award application deadline: 4/15; financial award applicants required to submit FAFSA. *Unit head:* Dr. Susan Palmisano, Graduate Coordinator, 724-357-2536, E-mail: Susan.Palmisano@iup.edu. *Application contact:* Dr. Susan Palmisano, Graduate Coordinator, 724-357-2536, E-mail: Susan.Palmisano@iup.edu.
Website: http://www.iup.edu/art/grad/default.aspx

Indiana University-Purdue University Indianapolis, Herron School of Art and Design, Indianapolis, IN 46202. Offers art therapy (MA); visual art (MFA), including ceramics, furniture design, painting and drawing, photography and intermedia, printmaking, sculpture; visual communication design (MFA). *Degree requirements:* For master's, thesis. *Entrance requirements:* For master's, personal statement, resume, recommendations, portfolio, transcripts (18 credit hours of studio art and 12 credit hours of psychology, including 3 credit hours of developmental psychology and 3 credit hours of abnormal psychology for MA). Additional exam requirements/recommendations for international students: recommended—TOEFL (minimum score 550 paper-based; 79 iBT), IELTS (minimum score 6.5). Electronic applications accepted. *Expenses:* Contact institution.

Institute for Doctoral Studies in the Visual Arts, PhD Program in Visual Art: Philosophy, Aesthetics, and Art Theory, Portland, ME 04102. Offers art theory (PhD); art theory, philosophy and aesthetics (PhD); philosophy (PhD). *Program availability:* Blended/hybrid learning. *Degree requirements:* For doctorate, comprehensive exam, thesis/dissertation, dissertation defense. *Entrance requirements:* For doctorate, curriculum vitae, writing sample, portfolio, interview. Electronic applications accepted. Application fee is waived when completed online. *Expenses: Tuition:* Full-time $42,600.

Inter American University of Puerto Rico, San Germán Campus, Graduate Studies Center, Program in Fine Arts, San Germán, PR 00683-5008. Offers drawing (MFA); graphic design (MFA); painting (MFA); photography (MFA); printmaking (MFA); sculpture (MFA). *Program availability:* Part-time, evening/weekend. *Degree requirements:* For master's, comprehensive exam, thesis. *Entrance requirements:* For master's, GRE General Test or EXADEP, minimum GPA of 3.0.

Iowa State University of Science and Technology, Program in Integrated Visual Arts, Ames, IA 50011. Offers MFA. *Accreditation:* NASAD. *Entrance requirements:* Additional exam requirements/recommendations for international students: required—TOEFL (minimum score 550 paper-based; 79 iBT), IELTS (minimum score 6.5).

Ithaca College, Roy H. Park School of Communications, Program in Image Text, Ithaca, NY 14850. Offers MFA. *Program availability:* Part-time-only. *Faculty:* 12 full-time (3 women). *Students:* 7 part-time (4 women); includes 2 minority (1 Black or African American, non-Hispanic/Latino; 1 Two or more races, non-Hispanic/Latino), 1 international. Average age 37. 22 applicants, 91% accepted, 5 enrolled. In 2019, 8 master's awarded. *Entrance requirements:* Additional exam requirements/recommendations for international students: required—TOEFL (minimum score 550 paper-based; 80 iBT). *Application deadline:* For fall admission, 2/1 for domestic and international students. Applications are processed on a rolling basis. Application fee: $40. Electronic applications accepted. *Expenses:* Contact institution. *Financial support:* In 2019–20, 7 students received support, including 7 fellowships (averaging $6,490 per year); Federal Work-Study and scholarships/grants also available. Support available to part-time students. Financial award application deadline: 3/1; financial award applicants required to submit FAFSA. *Unit head:* Nicholas Muellner, Co-Director, Image Text Program, 607-274-1984, E-mail: nmuellner@ithaca.edu. *Application contact:* Nicole Eversley Bradwell, Director, Office of Admission, 800-429-4274, Fax: 607-274-1263, E-mail: admission@ithaca.edu.
Website: https://www.ithaca.edu/admission/graduate-admission/graduate-study-image-text

Jacksonville University, College of Fine Arts, MFA in Visual Arts Program, Jacksonville, FL 32211. Offers MFA. *Accreditation:* NASAD. *Program availability:* Blended/hybrid learning. *Students:* 5 full-time (2 women), 7 part-time (6 women); includes 3 minority (2 Black or African American, non-Hispanic/Latino; 1 American Indian or Alaska Native, non-Hispanic/Latino). Average age 37. 18 applicants, 61% accepted, 7 enrolled. In 2019, 4 master's awarded. *Degree requirements:* For master's, thesis, portfolio. *Entrance requirements:* For master's, portfolio, artist statement of intent, undergraduate degree, three current references, official transcripts of academic work, sample of selected works (12 minutes maximum). Additional exam requirements/recommendations for international students: recommended—TOEFL (minimum score 540 paper-based; 76 iBT). *Application deadline:* Applications are processed on a rolling basis. Application fee: $50. Electronic applications accepted. *Expenses:* Contact institution. *Financial support:* In 2019–20, 1 fellowship (averaging $35,700 per year) was awarded; institutionally sponsored loans, scholarships/grants, and health care benefits also available. Support available to part-time students. Financial award application deadline: 3/1; financial award applicants required to submit FAFSA. *Unit head:* Cari Coble, Professor of Dance and MFA Coordinator, 904-256-7398, E-mail: ccoble@ju.edu. *Application contact:* Kyrstin Creswell, Assistant Director of Graduate Admissions, 904-256-7002, E-mail: kcreswe@ju.edu.
Website: https://www.ju.edu/cfa/mfavisualarts/index.php

James Madison University, The Graduate School, College of Visual and Performing Arts, School of Art, Design and Art History, Harrisonburg, VA 22807. Offers art education (MA); studio art (MA, MFA), including ceramics (MFA), drawing/painting (MFA), intermedia (MFA), metal/jewelry (MFA), photography (MFA), sculpture (MFA). *Accreditation:* NASAD. *Program availability:* Part-time. *Students:* 7 full-time (6 women), 1 (woman) part-time. Average age 30. In 2019, 3 master's awarded. Application fee: $60. Electronic applications accepted. *Financial support:* In 2019–20, 7 students received support, including 2 teaching assistantships with full tuition reimbursements available (averaging $9,284 per year); Federal Work-Study and assistantships (averaging $7911) also available. Financial award application deadline: 3/1; financial award applicants required to submit FAFSA. *Unit head:* Dr. Kathy A. Schwartz, Director of School of Art, Design and Art History, 540-568-6216, E-mail: schwarka@jmu.edu. *Application contact:* Lynette D. Michael, Director of Graduate Student Admissions, 540-568-6131 Ext. 6395, Fax: 540-568-7860, E-mail: michaeld@jmu.edu.
Website: http://www.jmu.edu/artandarthistory/

Kansas State University, Graduate School, College of Arts and Sciences, Department of Art, Manhattan, KS 66506. Offers MFA. *Accreditation:* NASAD. *Degree requirements:* For master's, thesis, gallery exhibit. *Entrance requirements:* For master's, slides of artistic work, portfolio, official transcripts, recommendation form/letters, statement of purpose. Additional exam requirements/recommendations for international students: required—TOEFL (minimum score 550 paper-based; 79 iBT). Electronic applications accepted.

Kent State University, College of the Arts, School of Art, Kent, OH 44242-0001. Offers art education (MA); art history (MA); crafts (MA), including glass (MA, MFA); fine arts (MA), including fashion; studio art (MFA), including ceramics, drawing, glass (MA, MFA), jewelry, metals and enameling, painting, print media and photography, sculpture, textiles. *Accreditation:* NASAD (one or more programs are accredited). *Program availability:* Part-time, 100% online, blended/hybrid learning. *Faculty:* 22 full-time (13 women), 5 part-time/adjunct (4 women). *Students:* 36 full-time (27 women), 24 part-time (22 women); includes 4 minority (3 Black or African American, non-Hispanic/Latino; 1 Hispanic/Latino), 2 international. Average age 30. 52 applicants, 67% accepted, 20 enrolled. In 2019, 15 master's awarded. *Degree requirements:* For master's, comprehensive exam, thesis (for some programs), 1 foreign language (for art history); final project (for crafts and fine arts). *Entrance requirements:* For master's, bachelors's degree min 3.0 GPA on 4.0 scale, transcripts, goal statement, 3 letters of recommendation, curriculum vitae, for MA and MFA in Studio Art: portfolio, artist statement;l MA Art Education: goal statement that focuses on philosophy of art education. Additional exam requirements/recommendations for international students: required—TOEFL (minimum score 79 iBT), IELTS (minimum score 6.5), PTE (minimum score 58), Michigan English Language Assessment Battery (minimum score 77). *Application deadline:* For fall admission, 2/2 priority date for domestic students, 2/2 for international students; for spring admission, 10/15 for domestic and international students. Applications are processed on a rolling basis. Application fee: $45 ($70 for international students). Electronic applications accepted. *Financial support:* Career-related internships or fieldwork, scholarships/grants, and unspecified assistantships available. Financial award application deadline: 3/1. *Unit head:* Marie Bukowski, Director, 330-672-2192, E-mail: mbukows1@kent.edu. *Application contact:* Peter Christian Johnson, Graduate Coordinator and Associate Professor Ceramics, 330-672-3360, E-mail: pjohns35@kent.edu.
Website: http://www.kent.edu/art

Laguna College of Art & Design, Graduate Program, Laguna Beach, CA 92651-1136. Offers painting (MFA). *Accreditation:* NASAD. *Entrance requirements:* For master's, BA with a studio concentration or BFA, minimum GPA of 3.0 in studio subjects, portfolio, resume. Additional exam requirements/recommendations for international students: required—TOEFL (minimum score 550 paper-based). Electronic applications accepted.

Lake Forest College, Graduate Program in Liberal Studies, Lake Forest, IL 60045. Offers American studies (MLS); cinema in East Asia (MLS); environmental studies (MLS); history (MLS); Medieval and Renaissance art (MLS); philosophy (MLS); Spanish (MLS); writing (MLS). *Program availability:* Part-time, evening/weekend. *Faculty:* 10 full-time (4 women). *Students:* 24 part-time (14 women). Average age 45. 10 applicants, 80% accepted, 3 enrolled. In 2019, 5 master's awarded. *Degree requirements:* For master's, thesis optional, 8 courses, including at least 3 interdisciplinary seminars. *Entrance requirements:* For master's, transcript, essay, interview. Additional exam requirements/recommendations for international students: required—TOEFL (minimum score 550 paper-based; 83 iBT); recommended—IELTS (minimum score 6.5). *Application deadline:* For fall admission, 8/15 priority date for domestic students, 7/15 priority date for international students; for spring admission, 12/15 priority date for domestic students, 11/15 priority date for international students. Applications are processed on a rolling basis. Application fee: $30. Electronic applications accepted. Application fee is waived when completed online. *Expenses:* Application fee = $30 — no other fees; tuition = $2,700/course. *Financial support:* In 2019–20, 2 students received support. Partial tuition grants (for full-time teachers) available. *Unit head:* Prof. D. L. LeMahieu, Director, 847-735-5133, Fax: 847-735-6291, E-mail: lemahieu@lakeforest.edu. *Application contact:* Prof. Carol Gayle, Associate Director, 847-735-5083, Fax: 847-735-6291, E-mail: gayle@lakeforest.edu.
Website: http://www.lakeforest.edu/academics/programs/mls/

Lake Forest College, Master of Arts in Teaching Program, Lake Forest, IL 60045. Offers elementary education (MAT); K-12 French (MAT); K-12 music (MAT); K-12 Spanish (MAT); K-12 visual art (MAT); secondary biology (MAT); secondary chemistry (MAT); secondary English (MAT); secondary history (MAT); secondary mathematics (MAT). *Degree requirements:* For master's, comprehensive exam, portfolio. *Entrance requirements:* For master's, GRE. *Expenses: Tuition:* Full-time $29,600; part-time $3200 per course.

Lee University, Program in Education, Cleveland, TN 37320-3450. Offers art (MAT); curriculum and instruction (M Ed, Ed S); early childhood (MAT); educational leadership (M Ed, Ed S); elementary education (MAT); English and math (MAT); English and science (MAT); English and social studies (MAT); higher education administration (MS); history (MAT); history and economics (MAT); math and science (MAT); math and social studies (MAT); middle grades (MAT); science and social studies (MASW); secondary education (MAT); Spanish (MAT); special education (M Ed, MAT); TESOL (MAT). *Accreditation:* NCATE. *Program availability:* Part-time. *Faculty:* 13 full-time (5 women), 9 part-time/adjunct (6 women). *Students:* 24 full-time (15 women), 72 part-time (46 women); includes 14 minority (8 Black or African American, non-Hispanic/Latino; 1 Hispanic/Latino; 5 Two or more races, non-Hispanic/Latino), 1 international. Average age 29. 44 applicants, 86% accepted, 33 enrolled. In 2019, 60 master's, 3 other advanced degrees awarded. *Degree requirements:* For master's, variable foreign language requirement, thesis optional, internship. *Entrance requirements:* For master's, MAT or GRE General Test, minimum undergraduate GPA of 2.75, 3 letters of recommendation, interview, writing sample, official transcripts, background check; for Ed S, minimum undergraduate and master's GPA of 2.75, official transcripts for undergraduate and master's degrees. Additional exam requirements/recommendations for international students: required—TOEFL (minimum score 61 iBT). *Application deadline:* For fall admission, 6/1 priority date for domestic and international students; for spring admission, 11/1 priority date for domestic and international students; for summer admission, 4/1 priority date for domestic and international students. Applications are processed on a rolling basis. Application fee: $25. Electronic applications accepted. *Expenses: Tuition:* Full-time $13,590; part-time $755 per credit hour. *Required fees:* $25. Tuition and fees vary according to program. *Financial support:* In 2019–20, 40 students received support. Career-related internships or fieldwork, Federal Work-Study, institutionally sponsored loans, scholarships/grants, and unspecified assistantships available. Financial award application deadline: 3/1; financial award applicants required to submit FAFSA. *Unit head:* Dr. William Kamm, Director, 423-614-8544, E-mail: wkamm@leeuniversity.edu. *Application contact:* Jeffery McGirt, Director of Graduate Enrollment, 423-614-8691, Fax: 423-614-8317, E-mail: jmcgirt@leeuniversity.edu.
Website: http://www.leeuniversity.edu/academics/graduate/education

Lehman College of the City University of New York, School of Arts and Humanities, Department of Art, Bronx, NY 10468-1589. Offers art education (MA); art studio (MA, MFA). *Program availability:* Part-time, evening/weekend. *Entrance requirements:* For master's, 33 undergraduate credits in art, interview, portfolio.

Expenses: Tuition, area resident: Full-time $5545; part-time $470 per credit. Tuition, nonresident: part-time $855 per credit. *Required fees:* $240.

Lesley University, College of Art and Design, Cambridge, MA 02138-2790. Offers photography (MFA); visual arts (MFA). *Program availability:* Part-time. *Degree requirements:* For master's, thesis, final exhibition of thesis work. *Entrance requirements:* For master's, portfolio, resume, personal statement. Additional exam requirements/recommendations for international students: required—TOEFL (minimum score 550 paper-based; 80 iBT). Electronic applications accepted.

Lesley University, Graduate School of Education, Cambridge, MA 02138-2790. Offers arts, community, and education (M Ed); autism studies (Certificate); curriculum and instruction (M Ed, CAGS); early childhood education (M Ed); ecological teaching and learning (MS); educational studies (PhD), including adult learning, educational leadership, individually designed; elementary education (M Ed); emergent technologies for educators (Certificate); ESLArts: language learning through the arts (M Ed); high school education (M Ed); individually designed (M Ed); integrated teaching through the arts (M Ed); literacy for K-8 classroom teachers (M Ed); mathematics education (M Ed); middle school education (M Ed); moderate disabilities (M Ed); online learning (Certificate); reading (CAGS); science in education (M Ed); severe disabilities (M Ed); special needs (CAGS); specialist teacher of reading (M Ed); teacher of visual art (M Ed); technology in education (M Ed, CAGS). *Accreditation:* TEAC. *Program availability:* Part-time, evening/weekend, online learning. *Degree requirements:* For master's, practicum; for doctorate, thesis/dissertation. *Entrance requirements:* For master's, Massachusetts Tests for Educator Licensure (MTEL), transcripts, statement of purpose, recommendations; interview (for special education); for doctorate, GRE General Test, transcripts, statement of purpose, recommendations, interview, master's degree, resume; for other advanced degree, interview, master's degree. Additional exam requirements/recommendations for international students: required—TOEFL (minimum score 550 paper-based; 80 iBT). Electronic applications accepted.

Long Island University - Post, College of Arts, Communications and Design, Brookville, NY 11548-1300. Offers art (MA); clinical art therapy (MA); clinical art therapy and counseling (MA); digital game design and development (MA); fine arts and design (MFA); interactive multimedia arts (MA); museum studies (MA); music (MA); theatre (MFA). *Degree requirements:* For master's, variable foreign language requirement, comprehensive exam (for some programs), thesis. *Entrance requirements:* For master's, performance audition or portfolio. Additional exam requirements/recommendations for international students: required—TOEFL (minimum score 550 paper-based; 79 iBT). Electronic applications accepted.

Louisiana State University and Agricultural & Mechanical College, Graduate School, College of Art and Design, School of Art, Program in Studio Art, Baton Rouge, LA 70803. Offers ceramics (MFA); graphic design (MFA); painting and drawing (MFA); photography (MFA); printmaking (MFA); sculpture (MFA). *Accreditation:* NASAD.

Louisiana Tech University, Graduate School, College of Liberal Arts, Ruston, LA 71272. Offers architecture (M Arch); art (MFA), including graphic design, photography, studio; audiology (Au D); communication (MA), including speech communication, theatre; English (MA), including literature, technical writing; history (MA); speech pathology (MA); technical writing and communication (Graduate Certificate). *Accreditation:* ASHA. *Program availability:* Part-time. *Degree requirements:* For master's, thesis (for some programs); for doctorate, thesis/dissertation. *Entrance requirements:* For master's, GRE General Test; for doctorate, GRE General Test, bachelor's degree, minimum GPA of 3.0 or 3.2 on last 60 hours attempted. Additional exam requirements/recommendations for international students: required—TOEFL (minimum score 550 paper-based; 80 iBT), IELTS (minimum score 6.5). Electronic applications accepted. *Expenses: Tuition, area resident:* Full-time $6592; part-time $400 per credit. Tuition, state resident: full-time $6592; part-time $400 per credit. Tuition, nonresident: full-time $13,333; part-time $681 per credit. *International tuition:* $13,333 full-time. *Required fees:* $3011; $3011 per unit.

Maine College of Art, Program in Studio Art, Portland, ME 04101. Offers MA, MFA. *Accreditation:* NASAD. *Faculty:* 8 full-time (5 women), 7 part-time/adjunct (5 women). *Students:* 38 full-time (24 women). 105 applicants, 67% accepted, 23 enrolled. In 2019, 20 master's awarded. *Degree requirements:* For master's, thesis, studio thesis exhibition. *Entrance requirements:* Additional exam requirements/recommendations for international students: required—TOEFL (minimum score 550 paper-based). *Application deadline:* For fall admission, 2/22 for domestic students; for summer admission, 2/22 priority date for domestic students, 2/22 for international students. Applications are processed on a rolling basis. Application fee: $50 ($70 for international students). Electronic applications accepted. *Expenses: Tuition:* Full-time $36,850. *Required fees:* $1280. One-time fee: $50 full-time. *Financial support:* In 2019–20, 13 teaching assistantships with partial tuition reimbursements (averaging $3,000 per year) were awarded; Federal Work-Study, scholarships/grants, and resident advisor positions also available. Financial award application deadline: 3/1; financial award applicants required to submit FAFSA. *Unit head:* Rachel Katz, Administrative Director, Graduate Programs, 207-699-5030, Fax: 207-775-5069, E-mail: rkatz@meca.edu. *Application contact:* Joel Tsui, Graduate Admissions Counselor, 207-699-5021, Fax: 207-775-5069, E-mail: joel.tsui-staff@meca.edu.
Website: http://www.meca.edu/mfa/

Maryland Institute College of Art, Graduate Studies, LeRoy E. Hoffberger School of Painting, Baltimore, MD 21217. Offers MFA. *Accreditation:* NASAD. *Faculty:* 1 (woman) full-time, 2 part-time/adjunct (0 women). *Students:* 20 full-time (12 women); includes 4 minority (1 Black or African American, non-Hispanic/Latino; 1 Asian, non-Hispanic/Latino; 1 Hispanic/Latino; 1 Two or more races, non-Hispanic/Latino), 4 international. Average age 27. 200 applicants, 10% accepted, 10 enrolled. In 2019, 10 master's awarded. *Degree requirements:* For master's, thesis, exhibit and thesis documentation. *Entrance requirements:* For master's, portfolio, bachelor's degree in any field. Additional exam requirements/recommendations for international students: required—TOEFL (minimum score 550 paper-based; 80 iBT), IELTS (minimum score 6.5). *Application deadline:* For fall admission, 1/15 for domestic and international students. Application fee: $75. Electronic applications accepted. *Expenses:* Contact institution. *Financial support:* In 2019–20, 20 students received support, including 20 fellowships (averaging $13,000 per year), 20 teaching assistantships (averaging $3,200 per year); career-related internships or fieldwork and scholarships/grants also available. Financial award application deadline: 1/15; financial award applicants required to submit FAFSA. *Unit head:* Joan Waltemath, Director, 410-225-5274, Fax: 410-225-5275, E-mail: graduate@mica.edu. *Application contact:* Chris D. Harring, Director of Graduate Admission, 410-225-2256, Fax: 410-225-5275, E-mail: graduate@mica.edu.
Website: http://www.mica.edu/Programs_of_Study/Graduate_Programs/Hoffberger_School_of_Painting.html

Maryland Institute College of Art, Graduate Studies, Mount Royal School of Art, Baltimore, MD 21217. Offers painting (MFA). *Degree requirements:* For master's, thesis, exhibit and thesis documentation. *Entrance requirements:* For master's, 40 credits in studio art, bachelor's degree in any field. Additional exam requirements/recommendations for international students: required—TOEFL (minimum score 550 paper-based; 80 iBT), IELTS (minimum score 6.5). Electronic applications accepted. *Expenses:* Contact institution.

Maryland Institute College of Art, Graduate Studies, MPS Program in Business of Art and Design, Baltimore, MD 21201. Offers MPS. *Program availability:* Part-time. *Degree requirements:* For master's, business plan presentation. *Entrance requirements:* For master's, essay, resume. Additional exam requirements/recommendations for international students: required—TOEFL (minimum score 550 paper-based; 80 iBT), IELTS (minimum score 6.5). Electronic applications accepted. *Expenses:* Contact institution.

Maryland Institute College of Art, Graduate Studies, Program in Community Arts, Baltimore, MD 21201. Offers MFA. *Program availability:* Part-time. *Degree requirements:* For master's, thesis, exhibition and thesis documentation. *Entrance requirements:* For master's, portfolio, bachelor's degree in any field. Additional exam requirements/recommendations for international students: required—TOEFL (minimum score 550 paper-based; 80 iBT), IELTS (minimum score 6.5). Electronic applications accepted. *Expenses:* Contact institution.

Maryland Institute College of Art, Graduate Studies, Program in Studio Art, Baltimore, MD 21201. Offers MFA. *Degree requirements:* For master's, thesis, exhibition, final paper. *Entrance requirements:* For master's, portfolio, 40 studio credits, 6 credits in art history, bachelor's degree in any field. Additional exam requirements/recommendations for international students: required—TOEFL (minimum score 550 paper-based; 80 iBT), IELTS (minimum score 6.5). Electronic applications accepted. *Expenses:* Contact institution.

Maryland Institute College of Art, Graduate Studies, Rinehart School of Sculpture, Baltimore, MD 21201. Offers MFA. *Accreditation:* NASAD. *Degree requirements:* For master's, thesis, exhibition. *Entrance requirements:* For master's, portfolio, bachelor's degree in any field. Additional exam requirements/recommendations for international students: required—TOEFL (minimum score 550 paper-based; 80 iBT), IELTS (minimum score 6.5). Electronic applications accepted. *Expenses:* Contact institution.

Marywood University, Academic Affairs, Insalaco College of Creative and Performing Arts, Art Department, Program in Studio Art, Scranton, PA 18509-1598. Offers clay (MA); painting (MA); photography (MA); printmaking (MA); sculpture (MA). *Accreditation:* NASAD. Electronic applications accepted.

Marywood University, Academic Affairs, Insalaco College of Creative and Performing Arts, Art Department, Program in Visual Arts, Scranton, PA 18509-1598. Offers clay (MFA); graphic design (MFA); illustration (MFA); painting (MFA); photography (MFA); printmaking (MFA); sculpture (MFA). *Accreditation:* NASAD. *Program availability:* Part-time. Electronic applications accepted. *Expenses:* Contact institution.

Massachusetts College of Art and Design, Graduate Programs, MFA Program, Boston, MA 02115-5882. Offers 2D fine arts (MFA), including painting, printmaking; 3D fine arts (MFA), including ceramics, fibers, glass, jewelry and metalsmithing, sculpture; design (MFA, Postbaccalaureate Certificate), including dynamic media; fine arts (MFA), including interdisciplinary; media arts (MFA, Postbaccalaureate Certificate), including film/video (MFA), photography. *Accreditation:* NASAD. *Faculty:* 1 (woman) full-time, 29 part-time/adjunct (14 women). *Students:* 44 full-time (26 women), 28 part-time (17 women); includes 8 minority (5 Asian, non-Hispanic/Latino; 3 Hispanic/Latino), 18 international. 202 applicants, 44% accepted, 35 enrolled. In 2019, 30 master's, 8 other advanced degrees awarded. *Degree requirements:* For master's, thesis, thesis exhibition (for fine arts programs); thesis project and document (for design/dynamic media program). *Entrance requirements:* For master's, portfolio, college transcripts, resume, statement of purpose, letters of reference, interview, 6 credits of art history taken prior to or during MFA program; for Postbaccalaureate Certificate, portfolio, college transcripts, resume, statement of purpose, letters of reference, interview. Additional exam requirements/recommendations for international students: required—TOEFL (minimum score 550 paper-based, 85 iBT) or IELTS (6). *Application deadline:* For fall admission, 1/20 priority date for domestic and international students; for summer admission, 1/20 priority date for domestic and international students. Applications are processed on a rolling basis. Application fee: $90. Electronic applications accepted. *Expenses:* Contact institution. *Financial support:* Research assistantships, teaching assistantships, career-related internships or fieldwork, scholarships/grants, tuition waivers (partial), unspecified assistantships, and adjunct co-teaching positions available. Support available to part-time students. Financial award application deadline: 1/20; financial award applicants required to submit FAFSA. *Unit head:* Lucinda Bliss, Dean of Graduate Studies, 617-879-7157, E-mail: gradadmissions@massart.edu. *Application contact:* Stacy Petersen, Associate Director, Graduate Admissions and Operations, 617-879-7238, E-mail: gradadmissions@massart.edu.
Website: http://www.massart.edu/Admissions/Graduate_Programs.html

Miami University, College of Creative Arts, Department of Art, Oxford, OH 45056. Offers art education (MA); studio art (MFA). *Accreditation:* NASAD (one or more programs are accredited).

Michigan State University, The Graduate School, College of Arts and Letters, Department of Art, Art History and Design, East Lansing, MI 48824. Offers studio art (MFA). *Entrance requirements:* For master's, minimum GPA of 3.0, portfolio, resume. Additional exam requirements/recommendations for international students: required—TOEFL, Michigan State University ELT (minimum score 85), Michigan English Language Assessment Battery (minimum score 83). Electronic applications accepted.

Millersville University of Pennsylvania, College of Graduate Studies and Adult Learning, College of Arts, Humanities and Social Sciences, Department of Art and Design, Millersville, PA 17551-0302. Offers art education (M Ed). *Accreditation:* NASAD; NCATE. *Program availability:* Part-time. *Faculty:* 5 full-time (4 women), 1 (woman) part-time/adjunct. *Students:* 1 (woman) full-time, 17 part-time (10 women); includes 1 minority (Hispanic/Latino). Average age 32. 6 applicants, 83% accepted, 3 enrolled. In 2019, 2 master's awarded. *Degree requirements:* For master's, comprehensive exam (for some programs), thesis (for some programs). *Entrance requirements:* For master's, teaching certificate (unless enrolled in post-bacc. Cert. concurrently), interview may be required, portfolio if not MU graduate. Additional exam requirements/recommendations for international students: required—TOEFL, IELTS (minimum score 6), PTE (minimum score 60). *Application deadline:* Applications are processed on a rolling basis. Application fee: $40. Electronic applications accepted. *Expenses: Tuition, area resident:* Part-time $516 per credit. Tuition, state resident: part-time $516 per credit. Tuition, nonresident: part-time $774 per credit. *Required fees:* $118.75 per credit. Tuition and fees vary according to course load, degree level and program. *Financial support:* In 2019–20, 1 student received support. Scholarships/grants and unspecified assistantships available. Financial award application deadline: 3/15; financial award applicants required to submit FAFSA. *Unit head:* Dr. Shauna Frischkorn, Chair, 717-871-7256, Fax: 717-871-2004, E-mail: shauna.frischkorn@millersville.edu. *Application contact:* Dr. James A. Delle, Acting Dean of College of Graduate Studies and Adult Learning/Associate Provost, Academic Administration, 717-871-7462, E-mail:

James.Delle@millersville.edu.
Website: http://www.millersville.edu/art/

Mills College, Graduate Studies, Department of Art, Oakland, CA 94613-1000. Offers art (MFA); ceramics (MFA); intermedia (MFA); painting (MFA); photography (MFA); sculpture (MFA). *Degree requirements:* For master's, thesis or alternative, exhibit. *Entrance requirements:* For master's, portfolio, artist statement. Additional exam requirements/recommendations for international students: required—TOEFL (minimum score 550 paper-based; 80 iBT) or IELTS (minimum score 6). Electronic applications accepted. *Expenses:* Contact institution.

Minneapolis College of Art and Design, Master of Fine Arts in Visual Studies, Minneapolis, MN 55404-4347. Offers animation (MFA); comic art (MFA); drawing (MFA); filmmaking (MFA); fine arts (MFA); furniture design (MFA); graphic design (MFA); illustration (MFA); interactive media (MFA); painting (MFA); photography (MFA); printmaking (MFA); sculpture (MFA). *Accreditation:* NASAD. *Program availability:* Part-time. *Students:* 86 applicants, 44% accepted, 9 enrolled. *Degree requirements:* For master's, thesis, thesis exhibit. *Entrance requirements:* Additional exam requirements/recommendations for international students: required—TOEFL (minimum score 550 paper-based; 79 iBT), IELTS (minimum score 6.5), Duolingo English Test accepted with a minimum score of 100 *Application deadline:* For fall admission, 2/1 for domestic and international students. Application fee: $50. Electronic applications accepted. *Expenses: Tuition:* Full-time $41,344. *Required fees:* $450. One-time fee: $300 full-time. *Financial support:* In 2019–20, 15 teaching assistantships (averaging $6,000 per year) were awarded; career-related internships or fieldwork, Federal Work-Study, scholarships/grants, and unspecified assistantships also available. Support available to part-time students. Financial award application deadline: 3/15; financial award applicants required to submit FAFSA. *Unit head:* Ellen Mueller, Director, MFA Program, 612-874-3629, E-mail: emueller@mcad.edu. *Application contact:* Mary Kazura, Director of Admissions, 612-874-3668, Fax: 612-874-3701, E-mail: mkazura@mcad.edu.
Website: http://mcad.edu/mfa

Minnesota State University Mankato, College of Graduate Studies and Research, College of Arts and Humanities, Department of Art, Mankato, MN 56001. Offers art (MA); art education (MAT). *Accreditation:* NASAD (one or more programs are accredited). *Program availability:* Part-time. *Degree requirements:* For master's, one foreign language, comprehensive exam, thesis or alternative. *Entrance requirements:* For master's, portfolio, three letters of reference. Additional exam requirements/recommendations for international students: required—TOEFL. Electronic applications accepted.

Mississippi College, Graduate School, College of Arts and Sciences, School of Christian Studies and the Arts, Department of Art, Clinton, MS 39058. Offers M Ed, MA, MFA. *Program availability:* Part-time, evening/weekend. *Degree requirements:* For master's, one foreign language, comprehensive exam, thesis (for some programs). *Entrance requirements:* For master's, GRE or NTE, minimum GPA of 2.5. Additional exam requirements/recommendations for international students: recommended—TOEFL, IELTS. Electronic applications accepted.

Missouri State University, Graduate College, College of Arts and Letters, Department of Art and Design, Springfield, MO 65897. Offers visual studies (MFA). *Program availability:* Part-time. *Degree requirements:* For master's, comprehensive exam, thesis, exhibition. *Entrance requirements:* For master's, digital portfolio; 300- to 800-word statement describing reasons and goals behind applicant's interest in graduate study and direction of intended research; at least three letters of recommendation from individuals able to speak of applicant's academic achievements and potential. Additional exam requirements/recommendations for international students: required—TOEFL (minimum score 550 paper-based; 79 iBT), IELTS (minimum score 6). Electronic applications accepted. *Expenses: Tuition,* area resident: Full-time $2600; part-time $1735 per credit hour. Tuition, nonresident: full-time $5240; part-time $3495 per credit hour. *International tuition:* $5240 full-time. *Required fees:* $530; $438 per credit hour. Tuition and fees vary according to class time, course level, course load, degree level, campus/location and program.

Montana State University, The Graduate School, College of Arts and Architecture, School of Art, Bozeman, MT 59717. Offers art (MFA); art history (MA). *Accreditation:* NASAD (one or more programs are accredited). *Program availability:* Part-time. *Degree requirements:* For master's, comprehensive exam, thesis. *Entrance requirements:* For master's, GRE General Test, undergraduate degree in art. Additional exam requirements/recommendations for international students: required—TOEFL (minimum score 550 paper-based). Electronic applications accepted.

Montclair State University, The Graduate School, College of the Arts, Program in Fine Art, Montclair, NJ 07043-1624. Offers museum management (MA); studio (MA). *Accreditation:* NASAD. *Program availability:* Part-time, evening/weekend. *Degree requirements:* For master's, project. *Entrance requirements:* For master's, GRE or MAT, 2 letters of recommendation, essay. Electronic applications accepted.

Montclair State University, The Graduate School, College of the Arts, Program in Studio Art, Montclair, NJ 07043-1624. Offers MFA. *Accreditation:* NASAD. *Program availability:* Part-time, evening/weekend. *Degree requirements:* For master's, project. *Entrance requirements:* For master's, 2 letters of recommendation, essay. Additional exam requirements/recommendations for international students: required—TOEFL (minimum score 83 iBT), IELTS (minimum score 6.5). Electronic applications accepted.

Moore College of Art & Design, Program in Studio Art, Philadelphia, PA 19103. Offers MFA. *Accreditation:* NASAD. *Degree requirements:* For master's, thesis. *Entrance requirements:* For master's, bachelor's degree in visual arts or another field with completion of 15 art history credits; minimum GPA of 3.0; on-site interview; portfolio; 3 letters of recommendation; resume.

New Hampshire Institute of Art, Graduate Studies, Manchester, NH 03104. Offers art education (MA); creative writing (MFA); photography (MFA); teaching visual arts (MAT); visual arts (MFA). *Accreditation:* NASAD. *Degree requirements:* For master's, thesis, corresponding exhibition and artist talk. *Entrance requirements:* For master's, writing sample or visual art portfolio; curriculum vitae; transcripts; letters of recommendation. Additional exam requirements/recommendations for international students: required—TOEFL (minimum score 550 paper-based; 80 iBT), IELTS (minimum score 6.5). Electronic applications accepted. *Expenses:* Contact institution.

New Jersey City University, William J. Maxwell College of Arts and Sciences, Department of Art, Jersey City, NJ 07305-1597. Offers art (MFA); art education (MA); studio art (MFA). *Accreditation:* NASAD. *Program availability:* Part-time, evening/weekend. *Degree requirements:* For master's, thesis or alternative, exhibit. *Entrance requirements:* For master's, portfolio. Additional exam requirements/recommendations for international students: required—TOEFL (minimum score 79 iBT).

New Mexico State University, College of Arts and Sciences, Department of Art, Las Cruces, NM 88003-8001. Offers art history (MA); studio art (MFA). *Program availability:* Part-time. *Faculty:* 8 full-time (6 women), 1 (woman) part-time/adjunct. *Students:* 13 full-time (9 women), 2 part-time (both women); includes 8 minority (7 Hispanic/Latino; 1 Two or more races, non-Hispanic/Latino), 1 international. Average age 30. 8 applicants, 75% accepted, 5 enrolled. In 2019, 4 master's awarded. *Degree requirements:* For master's, one foreign language, comprehensive exam (for some programs), thesis, thesis exhibit. *Entrance requirements:* For master's, portfolio (for MFA); 10-20 page paper (for MA). Additional exam requirements/recommendations for international students: required—TOEFL (minimum score 550 paper-based; 79 iBT), IELTS (minimum score 6.5). *Application deadline:* For fall admission, 1/20 for domestic students; for spring admission, 11/15 for domestic students. Application fee: $40 ($50 for international students). Electronic applications accepted. *Financial support:* In 2019–20, 12 students received support, including 1 fellowship (averaging $4,844 per year), 11 teaching assistantships (averaging $17,508 per year); career-related internships or fieldwork, Federal Work-Study, scholarships/grants, traineeships, health care benefits, and unspecified assistantships also available. Support available to part-time students. Financial award application deadline: 3/1. *Unit head:* Dr. Julia Barello, Department Head, 575-646-2728, Fax: 575-646-8036, E-mail: jbarello@nmsu.edu. *Application contact:* Dr. Julia Barello, Department Head, 575-646-2728, Fax: 575-646-8036, E-mail: jbarello@nmsu.edu.
Website: http://artdepartment.nmsu.edu/

The New School, Parsons School of Design, Program in Fine Arts, New York, NY 10011. Offers MFA. *Program availability:* Part-time. *Faculty:* 7 full-time (4 women), 214 part-time/adjunct. *Students:* 45 full-time (36 women); includes 10 minority (5 Black or African American, non-Hispanic/Latino; 2 Asian, non-Hispanic/Latino; 2 Hispanic/Latino; 1 Two or more races, non-Hispanic/Latino), 28 international. Average age 26. 131 applicants, 45% accepted, 25 enrolled. In 2019, 18 master's awarded. *Degree requirements:* For master's, thesis. *Entrance requirements:* For master's, transcripts, resume, statement of purpose, recommendation letters, portfolio, interview. Additional exam requirements/recommendations for international students: required—TOEFL (minimum score 92 iBT), IELTS (minimum score 7), PTE (minimum score 63). *Application deadline:* For fall admission, 1/1 priority date for domestic and international students; for summer admission, 1/1 priority date for domestic and international students. Applications are processed on a rolling basis. Application fee: $50. Electronic applications accepted. *Expenses:* 1810 per credit. *Financial support:* In 2019–20, 34 students received support, including 13 research assistantships (averaging $2,017 per year), 12 teaching assistantships (averaging $4,174 per year); career-related internships or fieldwork, scholarships/grants, and unspecified assistantships also available. Support available to part-time students. Financial award application deadline: 2/1; financial award applicants required to submit FAFSA. *Unit head:* Anthony Aziz, 212-229-8942 Ext. 2949, E-mail: aziza@newschool.edu. *Application contact:* Simone Varadian, Senior Director 1, 212-229-5150 Ext. 4117, E-mail: varadias@newschool.edu.
Website: https://www.newschool.edu/parsons/mfa-fine-arts/

New York Academy of Art, Master of Fine Arts Program, New York, NY 10013-2911. Offers anatomy (MFA); drawing (MFA); fine arts (MFA), including anatomy; painting (MFA); printmaking (MFA); sculpture (MFA). *Accreditation:* NASAD. *Degree requirements:* For master's, thesis. *Entrance requirements:* For master's, portfolio, essay, two letters of recommendation, curriculum vitae or resume, official undergraduate transcripts. Additional exam requirements/recommendations for international students: required—TOEFL (minimum score 550 paper-based; 80 iBT), IELTS (minimum score 6.5). Electronic applications accepted. Application fee is waived when completed online. *Expenses:* Contact institution.

New York Institute of Technology, College of Arts and Sciences, Department of Digital Art and Design, Old Westbury, NY 11568. Offers computer graphics (MFA), including animation, fine arts and technology, graphic design. *Program availability:* Part-time. *Faculty:* 10 full-time (5 women), 12 part-time/adjunct (6 women). *Students:* 31 full-time (19 women), 4 part-time (1 woman); includes 9 minority (1 Black or African American, non-Hispanic/Latino; 5 Asian, non-Hispanic/Latino; 2 Hispanic/Latino; 1 Two or more races, non-Hispanic/Latino), 19 international. Average age 27. 75 applicants, 52% accepted, 15 enrolled. In 2019, 20 master's awarded. *Degree requirements:* For master's, thesis (for some programs), thesis required for M.F.A.; senior project required for M.A. *Entrance requirements:* For master's, BFA or equivalent with minimum undergraduate GPA of 3.0; supplemental application, including digital portfolio, CV/resume (optional), personal statement (optional), and/or letters of recommendation (optional); copies of undergraduate transcripts from all schools attended and proof of degree. Additional exam requirements/recommendations for international students: required—TOEFL (minimum score 79 iBT), IELTS (minimum score 6), PTE (minimum score 53), Duolingo English Test. *Application deadline:* For fall admission, 6/1 for domestic students, 7/1 for international students; for spring admission, 12/15 for international students. Applications are processed on a rolling basis. Application fee: $50. Electronic applications accepted. *Expenses: Tuition:* Full-time $23,760; part-time $1320 per credit. *Required fees:* $260; $220 per unit. Full-time tuition and fees vary according to degree level and program. Part-time tuition and fees vary according to course load and program. *Financial support:* In 2019–20, 20 students received support. Research assistantships, teaching assistantships, Federal Work-Study, scholarships/grants, and unspecified assistantships available. Support available to part-time students. Financial award application deadline: 2/15; financial award applicants required to submit FAFSA. *Unit head:* Prof. Rosina Vavetsi, Department Chair, 516-686-7542, Fax: 212-261-1742, E-mail: rvavetsi@nyit.edu. *Application contact:* Alice Dolitsky, Director, Graduate Admissions, 800-345-6948, Fax: 516-686-1116, E-mail: admissions@nyit.edu.
Website: https://www.nyit.edu/departments/digital_art_and_design

New York Studio School of Drawing, Painting and Sculpture, Certificate Program, New York, NY 10011. Offers studio art (Certificate). *Expenses: Tuition:* Full-time $25,375.

New York Studio School of Drawing, Painting and Sculpture, MFA Program, New York, NY 10011. Offers painting (MFA); sculpture (MFA). *Expenses: Tuition:* Full-time $25,375.

See Display on page 118 and Close-Up on page 153.

New York University, Graduate School of Arts and Science, Institute of Fine Arts, New York, NY 10012-1019. Offers art history and archaeology (MA, PhD), including architectural studies (PhD), art history and archaeology, classical art and archaeology (PhD), curatorial studies (PhD), East and South Asian art (PhD), Near Eastern art and archaeology (PhD); MA/Diploma; PhD/Certificate. *Program availability:* Part-time. Terminal master's awarded for partial completion of doctoral program. *Degree requirements:* For master's, 2 foreign languages, thesis or alternative, 2 qualifying papers; for doctorate, 2 foreign languages, thesis/dissertation. *Entrance requirements:* For master's, GRE General Test; for doctorate, GRE General Test, MA. Additional exam requirements/recommendations for international students: required—TOEFL, IELTS.

New York University, Steinhardt School of Culture, Education, and Human Development, Department of Art and Art Professions, Program in Studio Art, New York, NY 10003. Offers MA, MFA, Advanced Certificate. *Program availability:* Part-time. *Entrance requirements:* For master's, portfolio, interview, presentation. Additional exam requirements/recommendations for international students: required—TOEFL (minimum score 100 iBT). Electronic applications accepted.

New York University, Steinhardt School of Culture, Education, and Human Development, Department of Art and Art Professions, Program in Visual Culture, New

Art/Fine Arts

York, NY 10012. Offers costume studies (MA); MA/MS. *Program availability:* Part-time. *Entrance requirements:* Additional exam requirements/recommendations for international students: required—TOEFL (minimum score 100 iBT). Electronic applications accepted.

New York University, Tisch School of the Arts, Masters in Arts Politics, New York, NY 10012. Offers MA. *Entrance requirements:* For master's, professional resume, writing sample, statement of purpose. Additional exam requirements/recommendations for international students: required—TOEFL. Electronic applications accepted.

Norfolk State University, School of Graduate Studies, School of Liberal Arts, Department of Fine Arts, Norfolk, VA 23504. Offers visual studies (MA, MFA). *Program availability:* Part-time. *Degree requirements:* For master's, thesis or alternative. *Entrance requirements:* For master's, portfolio, interview, letters of recommendation. Additional exam requirements/recommendations for international students: required—TOEFL (minimum score 500 paper-based).

Northern Illinois University, Graduate School, College of Visual and Performing Arts, School of Art, De Kalb, IL 60115-2854. Offers MA, MFA, MS. *Accreditation:* NASAD (one or more programs are accredited). *Program availability:* Part-time, evening/weekend. *Faculty:* 36 full-time (15 women), 1 (woman) part-time/adjunct. *Students:* 29 full-time (18 women), 27 part-time (18 women); includes 10 minority (2 Black or African American, non-Hispanic/Latino; 2 Asian, non-Hispanic/Latino; 4 Hispanic/Latino; 2 Two or more races, non-Hispanic/Latino), 4 international. Average age 33. 40 applicants, 68% accepted, 13 enrolled. In 2019, 20 master's awarded. *Degree requirements:* For master's, variable foreign language requirement, comprehensive exam, thesis (for some programs), show or project. *Entrance requirements:* For master's, GRE General Test, minimum GPA of 2.75, portfolio. Additional exam requirements/recommendations for international students: required—TOEFL (minimum score 550 paper-based). *Application deadline:* For fall and spring admission, 3/1 for domestic and international students. Applications are processed on a rolling basis. Application fee: $40. Electronic applications accepted. *Financial support:* In 2019–20, 25 research assistantships with full tuition reimbursements, 15 teaching assistantships with full tuition reimbursements were awarded; fellowships with full tuition reimbursements, career-related internships or fieldwork, Federal Work-Study, scholarships/grants, tuition waivers (full), and staff assistantships also available. Support available to part-time students. Financial award applicants required to submit FAFSA. *Unit head:* Douglas Boughton, Acting Director, 815-753-7850, Fax: 815-753-7701. *Application contact:* Kurt Schultz, Graduate Coordinator, 815-753-1473, E-mail: artgradcoordinator@niu.edu. Website: http://www.niu.edu/art/

Northern Vermont University–Johnson, Program in Studio Arts, Johnson, VT 05656. Offers ceramics (MFA); digital media (MFA); drawing (MFA); painting (MFA); photography (MFA); printmaking (MFA); sculpture (MFA). *Program availability:* Part-time, online learning. *Degree requirements:* For master's, thesis. *Entrance requirements:* For master's, portfolio. Additional exam requirements/recommendations for international students: required—TOEFL. Electronic applications accepted. *Expenses:* Contact institution.

Northwestern State University of Louisiana, Graduate Studies and Research, School of Creative and Performing Arts, Program in Art, Natchitoches, LA 71497. Offers fine and graphic arts (MA). *Accreditation:* NASAD. *Degree requirements:* For master's, comprehensive exam, thesis or alternative. *Entrance requirements:* For master's, GRE General Test, minimum undergraduate GPA of 2.5. Additional exam requirements/recommendations for international students: required—TOEFL. Electronic applications accepted.

Northwestern University, The Graduate School, Judd A. and Marjorie Weinberg College of Arts and Sciences, Department of Art Theory and Practice, Evanston, IL 60208. Offers visual arts (MFA). *Degree requirements:* For master's, essay, exhibit. *Entrance requirements:* For master's, 20 slides of recent work. Additional exam requirements/recommendations for international students: required—TOEFL. Electronic applications accepted.

Nova Southeastern University, College of Arts, Humanities, and Social Sciences, Fort Lauderdale, FL 33314-7796. Offers advanced conflict resolution practice (Graduate Certificate); child protection (MHS); college student affairs (MS); conflict analysis and resolution (MS, PhD); criminal justice (MS, PhD); cross-disciplinary studies (MA); developmental disabilities (MS); family studies (Graduate Certificate); family systems health care (Graduate Certificate); family therapy (MS, PhD); marriage and family therapy (DMFT); peace studies (Graduate Certificate); qualitative research (Graduate Certificate); solution focused coaching (Graduate Certificate). *Accreditation:* AAMFT/COAMFTE (one or more programs are accredited). *Program availability:* Part-time, evening/weekend, 100% online, blended/hybrid learning. *Faculty:* 60 full-time (37 women), 88 part-time/adjunct (65 women). *Students:* 201 full-time (157 women), 418 part-time (297 women); includes 365 minority (180 Black or African American, non-Hispanic/Latino; 4 American Indian or Alaska Native, non-Hispanic/Latino; 15 Asian, non-Hispanic/Latino; 141 Hispanic/Latino; 25 Two or more races, non-Hispanic/Latino), 49 international. Average age 37. 303 applicants, 84% accepted, 197 enrolled. In 2019, 125 master's, 63 doctorates, 24 other advanced degrees awarded. *Degree requirements:* For master's, comprehensive exam (for some programs), thesis optional, comprehensive exams, portfolios (for some programs), table-top exams (for some programs); for doctorate, comprehensive exam, thesis/dissertation, qualifying exams, portfolios (for some programs). *Entrance requirements:* For master's, interview, minimum GPA of 3.0, writing sample; for doctorate, interview, minimum GPA of 3.5, master's degree in related field, writing sample; for Graduate Certificate, minimum GPA of 3.0. Additional exam requirements/recommendations for international students: required—TOEFL (minimum score 79 paper-based). *Application deadline:* Applications are processed on a rolling basis. Application fee: $50. Electronic applications accepted. *Expenses:* Contact institution. *Financial support:* In 2019–20, 170 students received support. Career-related internships or fieldwork, Federal Work-Study, scholarships/grants, and unspecified assistantships available. Financial award application deadline: 4/1; financial award applicants required to submit FAFSA. *Unit head:* Dr. Honggang Yang, Dean, 954-262-3016, Fax: 954-262-3968, E-mail: yangh@nova.edu. *Application contact:* Marcia Arango, Student Recruitment Coordinator, 954-262-3006, Fax: 954-262-3968, E-mail: marango@nsu.nova.edu. Website: http://cahss.nova.edu/

NSCAD University, Program in Fine Arts, Halifax, NS B3J 3J6, Canada. Offers craft (MFA); design (M Des); fine and media arts (MFA). *Degree requirements:* For master's, thesis, exhibit. *Entrance requirements:* For master's, portfolio, at least 5 art history classes. Additional exam requirements/recommendations for international students: required—Michigan English Language Assessment Battery (minimum score: 80), CanTEST (minimum score: 4.5), CAEL (minimum score: 70); recommended—TOEFL (minimum score 575 paper-based; 90 iBT), IELTS (minimum score 6.5).

The Ohio State University, Graduate School, College of Arts and Sciences, Division of Arts and Humanities, Department of Art, Columbus, OH 43210. Offers MFA. *Accreditation:* NASAD. *Degree requirements:* For master's, thesis, exhibit, oral exams. *Entrance requirements:* For master's, GRE General Test (if GPA cumulative average is less than 3.0), electronic portfolio. Additional exam requirements/recommendations for international students: required—Michigan English Language Assessment Battery (minimum score 82); recommended—TOEFL (minimum score 550 paper-based; 79 iBT), IELTS (minimum score 7). Electronic applications accepted.

Ohio University, Graduate College, College of Fine Arts, School of Art, Athens, OH 45701-2979. Offers art history (MA); ceramics (MFA); graphic design (MFA); painting (MFA); photography (MFA); printmaking (MFA); sculpture (MFA). *Program availability:* Part-time. *Degree requirements:* For master's, thesis. *Entrance requirements:* For master's, portfolio. Additional exam requirements/recommendations for international students: required—TOEFL (minimum score 550 paper-based; 80 iBT) or IELTS (minimum score 6.5). Electronic applications accepted.

Otis College of Art and Design, Program in Fine Arts, Los Angeles, CA 90045-9785. Offers new genres (MFA); painting (MFA); photography (MFA); sculpture (MFA). *Accreditation:* NASAD. *Degree requirements:* For master's, thesis. *Entrance requirements:* For master's, portfolio. Additional exam requirements/recommendations for international students: required—TOEFL (minimum score 600 paper-based). Electronic applications accepted.

Otis College of Art and Design, Program in Public Practice, Los Angeles, CA 90045-9785. Offers MFA. *Entrance requirements:* Additional exam requirements/recommendations for international students: required—TOEFL (minimum score 600 paper-based). Electronic applications accepted.

Pacific Northwest College of Art, Program in Print Media, Portland, OR 97209. Offers MFA.

Pacific Northwest College of Art, Program in Visual Studies, Portland, OR 97209. Offers MFA. *Accreditation:* NASAD.

Paris College of Art, Graduate Programs, Paris, France. Offers accessories design (MA); fashion design: new materials and technologies (MA); fashion film and photography (MA); interior design (MA); transdisciplinary new media (MA, MFA). *Entrance requirements:* Additional exam requirements/recommendations for international students: required—TOEFL or IELTS.

Penn State University Park, Graduate School, College of Arts and Architecture, School of Visual Arts, University Park, PA 16802. Offers art (MFA); art education (MS, PhD, Certificate).

Pennsylvania Academy of the Fine Arts, Division of Graduate Studies, Philadelphia, PA 19102. Offers painting (MFA, Postbaccalaureate Certificate); printmaking (MFA, Postbaccalaureate Certificate); sculpture (MFA, Postbaccalaureate Certificate); studio art (MFA, Postbaccalaureate Certificate). *Accreditation:* NASAD (one or more programs are accredited). *Degree requirements:* For master's, thesis, thesis exhibit. *Entrance requirements:* For master's and Postbaccalaureate Certificate, Portfolio of 20 images submitted on SlideRoom, 2 letters of recommendation, official transcripts showing bachelor's degree (or degree in-progress), statement of purpose. Additional exam requirements/recommendations for international students: required—TOEFL (minimum score 600 paper-based; 80 iBT), IELTS (minimum score 6.5). Electronic applications accepted.

Pensacola Christian College, Graduate Studies, Pensacola, FL 32503-2267. Offers business administration (MBA); curriculum and instruction (MS, Ed D, Ed S); dramatics (MFA); educational leadership (MS, Ed D, Ed S); graphic design (MA, MFA); music (MA); nursing (MSN); performance studies (MA); studio art (MA, MFA).

Pontifical Catholic University of Puerto Rico, College of Arts and Humanities, Department of Fine Arts, Ponce, PR 00717-0777. Offers painting and drawing (MA).

Portland State University, Graduate Studies, College of the Arts, School of Art and Design, Portland, OR 97207-0751. Offers contemporary art practice: art and social practice (MFA); contemporary art practice: studio practice (MFA). *Faculty:* 22 full-time (14 women), 52 part-time/adjunct (37 women). *Students:* 24 full-time (13 women), 1 (woman) part-time; includes 6 minority (1 Black or African American, non-Hispanic/Latino; 1 Asian, non-Hispanic/Latino; 2 Hispanic/Latino; 2 Two or more races, non-Hispanic/Latino), 1 international. Average age 33. 45 applicants, 56% accepted, 11 enrolled. In 2019, 3 master's awarded. *Degree requirements:* For master's, variable foreign language requirement, thesis, exhibition project. *Entrance requirements:* For master's, minimum GPA of 3.0 in upper-division course work or 2.75 overall, digital portfolio, 3 letters of recommendation, statement of intent. Additional exam requirements/recommendations for international students: required—TOEFL (minimum score 550 paper-based; 80 iBT), IELTS (minimum score 6.5). *Application deadline:* For fall admission, 3/1 for domestic and international students. Application fee: $65. *Expenses:* Contact institution. *Financial support:* In 2019–20, 16 students received support, including 6 teaching assistantships with full and partial tuition reimbursements available (averaging $7,206 per year); research assistantships with full and partial tuition reimbursements available, Federal Work-Study, scholarships/grants, and unspecified assistantships also available. Support available to part-time students. Financial award application deadline: 3/1; financial award applicants required to submit FAFSA. *Unit head:* Patricia Boas, Director, 503-725-8980, Fax: 503-725-4541, E-mail: boasp@pdx.edu. *Application contact:* Ellen Wack, Program Coordinator, 503-725-8450, E-mail: wacke@pdx.edu.
Website: https://www.pdx.edu/art-design/

Pratt Institute, School of Art, Program in Fine Arts, Brooklyn, NY 11205-3899. Offers MFA. *Accreditation:* NASAD. *Program availability:* Part-time. *Students:* 75 full-time (51 women), 3 part-time (2 women); includes 17 minority (3 Black or African American, non-Hispanic/Latino; 3 Asian, non-Hispanic/Latino; 7 Hispanic/Latino; 4 Two or more races, non-Hispanic/Latino), 31 international. Average age 27. 277 applicants, 44% accepted, 40 enrolled. In 2019, 33 master's awarded. *Degree requirements:* For master's, thesis, exhibit. *Entrance requirements:* For master's, portfolio, letters of recommendation. Additional exam requirements/recommendations for international students: required—TOEFL (minimum score 550 paper-based; 79 iBT). *Application deadline:* For fall admission, 1/5 for domestic and international students; for spring admission, 10/1 for domestic and international students. Application fee: $50 ($90 for international students). Electronic applications accepted. *Expenses:* Tuition: Full-time $33,246; part-time $1847 per credit. *Required fees:* $1980. *Financial support:* Career-related internships or fieldwork, Federal Work-Study, institutionally sponsored loans, scholarships/grants, health care benefits, and unspecified assistantships available. Support available to part-time students. Financial award application deadline: 2/1; financial award applicants required to submit FAFSA. *Unit head:* Jane South, Chairperson, 718-636-3634, E-mail: jsouth@pratt.edu. *Application contact:* Natalie Capannelli, Director of Graduate Admissions, 718-636-3551, Fax: 718-399-4242, E-mail: ncapanne@pratt.edu.
Website: https://www.pratt.edu/academics/school-of-art/graduate-school-of-art/graduate-fine-arts/

Prescott College, Graduate Programs, Program in Arts and Humanities, Prescott, AZ 86301. Offers humanities (MA); social justice and human rights (MA); student-directed independent study (MA). *Program availability:* Part-time, online learning. *Degree requirements:* For master's, thesis, fieldwork or internship, practicum. *Entrance requirements:* For master's, 2 letters of recommendation, resume, essay. Additional exam requirements/recommendations for international students: required—TOEFL (minimum score 500 paper-based). Electronic applications accepted.

Purchase College, State University of New York, School of Art and Design, Purchase, NY 10577-1400. Offers art history/visual arts (MA); visual arts (MFA).

Accreditation: NASAD. *Students:* 17 full-time (12 women); includes 3 minority (2 Asian, non-Hispanic/Latino; 1 Hispanic/Latino), 4 international. Average age 31. 46 applicants, 41% accepted, 8 enrolled. *Degree requirements:* For master's, thesis, exhibit. *Entrance requirements:* For master's, portfolio. Additional exam requirements/recommendations for international students: required—TOEFL (minimum score 550 paper-based; 80 iBT), IELTS (minimum score 6.5). *Application deadline:* For fall admission, 2/15 for domestic students. Applications are processed on a rolling basis. Application fee: $85. Electronic applications accepted. *Expenses: Tuition, area resident:* Full-time $11,310. Tuition, state resident: full-time $11,310. Tuition, nonresident: full-time $23,100. *Required fees:* $1883. *Financial support:* Fellowships, teaching assistantships, Federal Work-Study, scholarships/grants, and tuition waivers (partial) available. Support available to part-time students. Financial award application deadline: 3/15; financial award applicants required to submit FAFSA. *Unit head:* Christopher Robbins, Director, 914-251-6750, Fax: 914-251-6793, E-mail: christopher.robbins@purchase.edu. *Application contact:* Beatriz Martin-Ruiz, Assistant Director of Admissions, 914-251-6304, Fax: 914-251-6314, E-mail: admissn@purchase.edu.
Website: https://www.purchase.edu/academics/art-and-design/

Purdue University, Graduate School, College of Liberal Arts, Department of Art and Design, West Lafayette, IN 47907. Offers art education (MA, PhD); industrial design (MFA); interior design (MFA); visual communications design (MFA). *Accreditation:* NASAD; NAST. *Program availability:* Part-time. *Faculty:* 4 full-time (1 woman). *Students:* 37 full-time (21 women), 3 part-time (2 women); includes 9 minority (1 Black or African American, non-Hispanic/Latino; 3 Asian, non-Hispanic/Latino; 4 Hispanic/Latino; 1 Two or more races, non-Hispanic/Latino), 14 international. Average age 28. 144 applicants, 23% accepted, 14 enrolled. In 2019, 24 master's awarded. *Degree requirements:* For master's, terminal exhibit, project, or thesis. *Entrance requirements:* For master's, GRE General Test (for art education), minimum undergraduate GPA of 3.0 or equivalent; 9 undergraduate hours in an art or design history; BA in art (for MA in art education); for doctorate, GRE General Test (minimum scores 600 in verbal and 1000 total), master's degree in art education or art with teaching certification; 3 years of teaching experience at the K-12 level. Additional exam requirements/recommendations for international students: required—TOEFL (minimum score 550 paper-based; 77 iBT). *Application deadline:* For fall admission, 2/1 for domestic students, 2/1 priority date for international students. Applications are processed on a rolling basis. Application fee: $60 ($75 for international students). Electronic applications accepted. *Financial support:* Teaching assistantships with tuition reimbursements and career-related internships or fieldwork available. Support available to part-time students. Financial award applicants required to submit FAFSA. *Unit head:* Arne R. Flaten, Head of the Graduate Program, 765-494-3056, E-mail: aflaten@purdue.edu. *Application contact:* Kathryn Evans, Graduate Contact, 765-494-7666, E-mail: kathy@purdue.edu.
Website: https://www.cla.purdue.edu/vpa/ad/

Queens College of the City University of New York, Arts and Humanities Division, Department of Art, Flushing, NY 11367. Offers art history (MA); studio art (MFA). *Program availability:* Part-time. *Faculty:* 18 full-time (5 women), 57 part-time/adjunct (31 women). *Students:* 1 (woman) full-time. Average age 36. 3 applicants. In 2019, 2 master's awarded. *Degree requirements:* For master's, 2 foreign languages, comprehensive exam, thesis optional, comprehensive exam (for art history program). *Entrance requirements:* For master's, Qualifying Exam, minimum GPA of 3.0. Additional exam requirements/recommendations for international students: required—TOEFL (minimum score 600 paper-based), IELTS. *Application deadline:* For fall admission, 4/1 for domestic students; for spring admission, 11/1 for domestic students. Applications are processed on a rolling basis. Application fee: $125. Electronic applications accepted. *Financial support:* Fellowships and career-related internships or fieldwork available. Financial award application deadline: 4/1; financial award applicants required to submit FAFSA. *Unit head:* Michael Nelson, Chair, 718-997-4800, E-mail: michael.nelson@qc.cuny.edu. *Application contact:* Elizabeth D'Amico-Ramirez, Assistant Director of Graduate Admissions, 718-997-5203, E-mail: elizabeth.damicoramirez@qc.cuny.edu.
Website: http://art.qc.cuny.edu/

Radford University, College of Graduate Studies and Research, Art, MFA, Radford, VA 24142. Offers MFA. *Accreditation:* NASAD. *Program availability:* Part-time. *Degree requirements:* For master's, comprehensive exam. *Entrance requirements:* For master's, statement of philosophy; minimum GPA of 2.75, 2 letters of reference, BFA or commensurate collegiate course work, 20 slides or CD of recent work, resume, and official transcripts (for studio art); minimum GPA of 3.0 (preferred) and three letters of reference (for design thinking). Additional exam requirements/recommendations for international students: required—TOEFL (minimum score 550 paper-based; 79 iBT), IELTS (minimum score 6.5). Electronic applications accepted. *Expenses:* Contact institution.

Rensselaer Polytechnic Institute, Graduate School, School of Humanities, Arts, and Social Sciences, Program in Electronic Arts, Troy, NY 12180-3590. Offers PhD. *Faculty:* 25 full-time (10 women), 9 part-time/adjunct (5 women). *Students:* 20 full-time (10 women), 1 part-time (0 women); includes 2 minority (1 Asian, non-Hispanic/Latino; 1 Hispanic/Latino), 7 international. Average age 34. 23 applicants, 26% accepted, 4 enrolled. In 2019, 1 doctorate awarded. *Degree requirements:* For doctorate, comprehensive exam. *Entrance requirements:* For doctorate, portfolio, research proposal, writing sample. Additional exam requirements/recommendations for international students: required—TOEFL (minimum score 570 paper-based; 88 iBT), IELTS (minimum score 6.5), PTE (minimum score 60). *Application deadline:* For fall admission, 1/1 priority date for domestic and international students. Applications are processed on a rolling basis. Application fee: $75. Electronic applications accepted. *Financial support:* In 2019–20, research assistantships (averaging $23,000 per year), teaching assistantships with full tuition reimbursements (averaging $23,000 per year) were awarded; scholarships/grants also available. Financial award application deadline: 1/1. *Unit head:* Dr. Tomie Hahn, Graduate Program Director, 518-276-2379, E-mail: hahnt@rpi.edu. *Application contact:* Jarron Decker, Director of Graduate Admissions, 518-276-6216, Fax: 518-276-4072, E-mail: gradadmissions@rpi.edu.
Website: http://www.arts.rpi.edu/pl/graduate-programs

Rhode Island College, School of Graduate Studies, Faculty of Arts and Sciences, Department of Art, Providence, RI 02908-1991. Offers art education (MA, MAT); media studies (MA). *Accreditation:* NASAD (one or more programs are accredited). *Program availability:* Part-time, evening/weekend. *Faculty:* 4 full-time (3 women), 1 (woman) part-time/adjunct. *Students:* 4 part-time (all women). Average age 35. In 2019, 1 master's awarded. *Degree requirements:* For master's, thesis. *Entrance requirements:* For master's, GRE General Test, portfolio (MA), 3 letters of recommendation, interview. Additional exam requirements/recommendations for international students: required—TOEFL (minimum score 550 paper-based; 80 iBT). *Application deadline:* For fall admission, 3/1 for domestic students. Applications are processed on a rolling basis. Application fee: $50. Electronic applications accepted. *Expenses: Tuition, area resident:* Part-time $462 per credit hour. Tuition, state resident: part-time $462 per credit hour. *Required fees:* $720. One-time fee: $140. *Financial support:* Teaching assistantships, career-related internships or fieldwork, Federal Work-Study, scholarships/grants, health care benefits, and unspecified assistantships available. Support available to part-time

students. Financial award application deadline: 5/15; financial award applicants required to submit FAFSA. *Unit head:* Prof. Douglas Bosch, Chair, 401-456-8054. *Application contact:* Prof. Douglas Bosch, Chair, 401-456-8054.
Website: http://www.ric.edu/art/Pages/M.A.T.-in-Art-Education.aspx

Rhode Island School of Design, Department of Ceramics, Providence, RI 02903-2784. Offers MFA. *Accreditation:* NASAD. *Students:* 9 full-time (5 women); includes 3 minority (1 Black or African American, non-Hispanic/Latino; 2 Asian, non-Hispanic/Latino), 2 international. Average age 27. 24 applicants, 54% accepted, 5 enrolled. In 2019, 6 master's awarded. *Degree requirements:* For master's, thesis, exhibition. *Entrance requirements:* For master's, portfolio, statement of purpose, 3 letters of recommendation. Additional exam requirements/recommendations for international students: required—TOEFL (minimum score 580 paper-based; 93 iBT), IELTS (minimum score 6.5), Duolingo. *Application deadline:* For fall admission, 1/10 for domestic and international students. Application fee: $60. Electronic applications accepted. *Expenses: Tuition:* Full-time $51,800. *Required fees:* $1060. *Financial support:* Fellowships, research assistantships, teaching assistantships, Federal Work-Study, scholarships/grants, and unspecified assistantships available. Financial award application deadline: 2/1; financial award applicants required to submit FAFSA. *Unit head:* Lesley Baker, Department Head and Graduate Coordinator, 401-454-6190, Fax: 401-454-6191, E-mail: ceramics@risd.edu. *Application contact:* Molly Pettengill, Associate Director for Graduate Recruitment, 401-454-6312, Fax: 401-454-6309, E-mail: ceramics@risd.edu.
Website: http://www.risd.edu/academics/ceramics/

Rhode Island School of Design, Department of Glass, Providence, RI 02903-2784. Offers MFA. *Accreditation:* NASAD. *Students:* 6 full-time (5 women); includes 2 minority (1 Asian, non-Hispanic/Latino; 1 Two or more races, non-Hispanic/Latino), 3 international. Average age 28. 5 applicants, 60% accepted, 3 enrolled. In 2019, 5 master's awarded. *Degree requirements:* For master's, thesis, exhibition. *Entrance requirements:* For master's, portfolio, statement of purpose, 3 letters of recommendation. Additional exam requirements/recommendations for international students: required—TOEFL (minimum score 580 paper-based; 93 iBT), IELTS (minimum score 6.5), Duolingo. *Application deadline:* For fall admission, 1/10 for domestic and international students. Application fee: $60. Electronic applications accepted. *Expenses: Tuition:* Full-time $51,800. *Required fees:* $1060. *Financial support:* Fellowships, research assistantships, teaching assistantships, Federal Work-Study, scholarships/grants, and unspecified assistantships available. Financial award application deadline: 2/1; financial award applicants required to submit FAFSA. *Unit head:* Jocelyne Prince, Department Head and Graduate Program Director, 401-454-6190, Fax: 401-454-6680, E-mail: jprince@risd.edu. *Application contact:* Molly Pettengill, Associate Director for Graduate Recruitment, 401-454-6312, Fax: 401-454-6309, E-mail: mpetteng@risd.edu.
Website: http://www.risd.edu/academics/glass/

Rhode Island School of Design, Department of Jewelry and Metalsmithing, Providence, RI 02903-2784. Offers MFA. *Accreditation:* NASAD. *Students:* 10 full-time (8 women); includes 1 minority (Asian, non-Hispanic/Latino), 6 international. Average age 25. 41 applicants, 24% accepted, 6 enrolled. In 2019, 4 master's awarded. *Degree requirements:* For master's, thesis, exhibition. *Entrance requirements:* For master's, portfolio, statement of purpose, 3 letters of recommendation. Additional exam requirements/recommendations for international students: required—TOEFL (minimum score 580 paper-based; 93 iBT), IELTS (minimum score 6.5), Duolingo. *Application deadline:* For fall admission, 1/10 for domestic and international students. Application fee: $60. Electronic applications accepted. *Expenses: Tuition:* Full-time $51,800. *Required fees:* $1060. *Financial support:* Fellowships, research assistantships, teaching assistantships, Federal Work-Study, scholarships/grants, and unspecified assistantships available. Financial award application deadline: 2/1; financial award applicants required to submit FAFSA. *Unit head:* Tracy Steepy, Department Head, 401-454-6190, Fax: 401-454-6191, E-mail: jewelry@risd.edu. *Application contact:* Molly Pettengill, Associate Director for Graduate Recruitment, 401-454-6312, Fax: 401-454-6309, E-mail: mpetteng@risd.edu.
Website: http://www.risd.edu/academics/jewelry-metalsmithing/

Rhode Island School of Design, Department of Painting, Providence, RI 02903-2784. Offers MFA. *Accreditation:* NASAD. *Students:* 19 full-time (10 women); includes 2 minority (1 Black or African American, non-Hispanic/Latino; 1 Asian, non-Hispanic/Latino), 1 international. Average age 27. 216 applicants, 11% accepted, 9 enrolled. In 2019, 9 master's awarded. *Degree requirements:* For master's, thesis, exhibition. *Entrance requirements:* For master's, portfolio, statement of purpose, 3 letters of recommendation. Additional exam requirements/recommendations for international students: required—TOEFL (minimum score 580 paper-based; 93 iBT), IELTS (minimum score 6.5), Duolingo. *Application deadline:* For fall admission, 1/10 for domestic and international students. Application fee: $60. Electronic applications accepted. *Expenses: Tuition:* Full-time $51,800. *Required fees:* $1060. *Financial support:* Fellowships, research assistantships, teaching assistantships, Federal Work-Study, scholarships/grants, and unspecified assistantships available. Financial award application deadline: 2/1; financial award applicants required to submit FAFSA. *Unit head:* Kevin Zucker, Department Head, 401-454-6158, Fax: 401-454-6681, E-mail: painting@risd.edu. *Application contact:* Molly Pettengill, Associate Director for Graduate Recruitment, 401-454-6312, Fax: 401-454-6309, E-mail: mpetteng@risd.edu.
Website: http://www.risd.edu/academics/painting/

Rhode Island School of Design, Department of Printmaking, Providence, RI 02903-2784. Offers MFA. *Students:* 14 full-time (11 women); includes 3 minority (1 Hispanic/Latino; 2 Two or more races, non-Hispanic/Latino), 3 international. Average age 26. 40 applicants, 25% accepted, 6 enrolled. In 2019, 5 master's awarded. *Degree requirements:* For master's, thesis, exhibition. *Entrance requirements:* For master's, portfolio, statement of purpose, 3 letters of recommendation. Additional exam requirements/recommendations for international students: required—TOEFL (minimum score 580 paper-based; 93 iBT), IELTS (minimum score 6.5), Duolingo. *Application deadline:* For fall admission, 1/10 for domestic and international students. Application fee: $60. Electronic applications accepted. *Expenses: Tuition:* Full-time $51,800. *Required fees:* $1060. *Financial support:* Fellowships, research assistantships, teaching assistantships, Federal Work-Study, scholarships/grants, and unspecified assistantships available. Financial award application deadline: 2/1; financial award applicants required to submit FAFSA. *Unit head:* Cornelia McSheehy, Department Head, 401-454-6224, Fax: 401-454-6707, E-mail: printmaking@risd.edu. *Application contact:* Molly Pettengill, Associate Director for Graduate Recruitment, 401-454-6312, Fax: 401-454-6309, E-mail: mpetteng@risd.edu.
Website: http://www.risd.edu/academics/printmaking/

Rhode Island School of Design, Department of Sculpture, Providence, RI 02903-2784. Offers MFA. *Accreditation:* NASAD. *Students:* 10 full-time (8 women); includes 2 minority (1 Hispanic/Latino; 1 Two or more races, non-Hispanic/Latino), 7 international. Average age 27. 68 applicants, 26% accepted, 5 enrolled. In 2019, 9 master's awarded. *Degree requirements:* For master's, thesis, exhibition. *Entrance requirements:* For master's, portfolio, statement of purpose, 3 letters of recommendation. Additional exam requirements/recommendations for international students: required—TOEFL (minimum score 580 paper-based; 93 iBT), IELTS (minimum score 6.5), Duolingo. *Application deadline:* For fall admission, 1/10 for domestic and international students. Application fee: $60. Electronic applications accepted. *Expenses: Tuition:* Full-time $51,800. *Required fees:* $1060. *Financial support:* Fellowships, research assistantships, teaching assistantships, Federal Work-Study, scholarships/grants, and unspecified assistantships available. Financial award application deadline: 2/1; financial award applicants required to submit FAFSA. *Unit head:* Lisi Raskin, Department Head, 401-454-6425, Fax: 401-454-6191, E-mail: sculpture@risd.edu. *Application contact:* Molly Pettengill, Associate Director for Graduate Recruitment, 401-454-6312, Fax: 401-454-6309, E-mail: mpetteng@risd.edu.
Website: http://www.risd.edu/academics/sculpture/

Rochester Institute of Technology, Graduate Enrollment Services, College of Imaging Arts and Sciences, School for American Crafts, MFA Program in Ceramics, Rochester, NY 14623. Offers MFA. *Accreditation:* NASAD. *Program availability:* Part-time. *Degree requirements:* For master's, thesis. *Entrance requirements:* For master's, portfolio, Undergraduate degree should include 50 semester hours in studio courses. Additional exam requirements/recommendations for international students: required—TOEFL (minimum score 550 paper-based; 80 iBT), IELTS (minimum score 6.5), PTE (minimum score 58). Electronic applications accepted.

Rochester Institute of Technology, Graduate Enrollment Services, College of Imaging Arts and Sciences, School for American Crafts, MFA Program in Furniture Design, Rochester, NY 14623-5603. Offers MFA. *Program availability:* Part-time. *Degree requirements:* For master's, thesis, thesis project/exhibition. *Entrance requirements:* For master's, portfolio, undergraduate degree should include 50 semester hours in studio courses. Additional exam requirements/recommendations for international students: required—TOEFL (minimum score 570 paper-based; 80 iBT), IELTS (minimum score 6.5), PTE (minimum score 58). Electronic applications accepted.

Rochester Institute of Technology, Graduate Enrollment Services, College of Imaging Arts and Sciences, School for American Crafts, MFA Program in Glass, Rochester, NY 14623-5603. Offers MFA. *Accreditation:* NASAD. *Program availability:* Part-time. *Degree requirements:* For master's, thesis. *Entrance requirements:* For master's, portfolio, undergraduate degree should include 50 semester hours of studio courses. Additional exam requirements/recommendations for international students: required—TOEFL (minimum score 540 paper-based; 80 iBT), IELTS (minimum score 6.5), PTE (minimum score 58). Electronic applications accepted.

Rochester Institute of Technology, Graduate Enrollment Services, College of Imaging Arts and Sciences, School for American Crafts, MFA Program in Metals and Jewelry Design, Rochester, NY 14623-5603. Offers MFA. *Accreditation:* NASAD. *Program availability:* Part-time. *Degree requirements:* For master's, thesis. *Entrance requirements:* For master's, portfolio, undergraduate degree should include 50 semester hours of studio courses. Additional exam requirements/recommendations for international students: required—TOEFL (minimum score 550 paper-based; 79 iBT), IELTS (minimum score 6.5), PTE (minimum score 58). Electronic applications accepted.

Rochester Institute of Technology, Graduate Enrollment Services, College of Imaging Arts and Sciences, School of Art, MFA Program in Fine Arts Studio, Rochester, NY 14623. Offers fine arts studio (MFA). *Accreditation:* NASAD. *Program availability:* Part-time. *Entrance requirements:* For master's, portfolio. Additional exam requirements/recommendations for international students: required—TOEFL (minimum score 550 paper-based; 80 iBT), IELTS (minimum score 6.5), PTE (minimum score 58). Electronic applications accepted. *Expenses:* Contact institution.

Rutgers University - New Brunswick, Mason Gross School of the Arts, Visual Arts Department, New Brunswick, NJ 08901. Offers drawing (MFA); painting (MFA); sculpture (MFA); visual arts (MFA). *Accreditation:* NASAD. *Degree requirements:* For master's, thesis, exhibit. *Entrance requirements:* For master's, portfolio. Additional exam requirements/recommendations for international students: required—TOEFL (minimum score 550 paper-based), IELTS (minimum score 7). Electronic applications accepted.

San Diego State University, Graduate and Research Affairs, College of Professional Studies and Fine Arts, School of Art and Design, San Diego, CA 92182. Offers studio arts (MA, MFA), including applied design, graphic design, interior architecture, multimedia and photography, painting and printmaking, sculpture. *Accreditation:* NASAD (one or more programs are accredited). *Degree requirements:* For master's, variable foreign language requirement, thesis. *Entrance requirements:* For master's, GRE General Test, bachelor's degree in related field, slide portfolio, typed slide information sheet, 2 letters of recommendation. Additional exam requirements/recommendations for international students: required—TOEFL. Electronic applications accepted.

San Francisco Art Institute, Master of Fine Arts Programs, San Francisco, CA 94133. Offers studio art (MFA, Certificate), including art and technology (MFA), film (MFA), new genres (MFA), painting (MFA), photography (MFA), printmaking (MFA), sculpture (MFA); MFA/MA. *Accreditation:* NASAD. *Degree requirements:* For master's, thesis. *Entrance requirements:* For master's and Certificate, portfolio. Additional exam requirements/recommendations for international students: required—TOEFL (minimum score 580 paper-based; 92 iBT), IELTS (minimum score 7). Electronic applications accepted.

San Francisco State University, Division of Graduate Studies, College of Liberal and Creative Arts, School of Art, San Francisco, CA 94132-1722. Offers art (MFA); museum studies (MA). *Accreditation:* NASAD (one or more programs are accredited). *Expenses: Tuition, area resident:* Full-time $7176; part-time $4164 per year. Tuition, state resident: full-time $7176; part-time $4164 per year. Tuition, nonresident: full-time $16,680; part-time $396 per unit. *International tuition:* $16,680 full-time. *Required fees:* $1524; $1524 per unit. $762 per semester. Tuition and fees vary according to degree level and program. *Unit head:* Prof. Gwen Allen, Director, 415-338-2176, Fax: 415-338-6537, E-mail: gwen@sfsu.edu. *Application contact:* Prof. Chris Finley, Graduate Coordinator, 415-338-6318, Fax: 415-338-6537, E-mail: cfinley@sfsu.edu.
Website: http://www.art.sfsu.edu

Savannah College of Art and Design, Program in Accessory Design, Savannah, GA 31402-3146. Offers MA, MFA. *Program availability:* Part-time. *Degree requirements:* For master's, final project (for MA); thesis (for MFA). *Entrance requirements:* For master's, GRE (recommended), portfolio (submitted in digital format), audition or writing submission, resume, statement of purpose, two letters of recommendation. Additional exam requirements/recommendations for international students: recommended—TOEFL (minimum score 550 paper-based; 85 iBT), IELTS (minimum score 6.5). Electronic applications accepted.

Savannah College of Art and Design, Program in Furniture Design, Savannah, GA 31402-3146. Offers MA, MFA. *Program availability:* Part-time. *Degree requirements:* For master's, final project (for MA); thesis (for MFA). *Entrance requirements:* For master's, GRE (recommended), portfolio (submitted in digital format), audition or writing submission, resume, statement of purpose, two letters of recommendation. Additional exam requirements/recommendations for international students: recommended—TOEFL (minimum score 550 paper-based; 85 iBT), IELTS (minimum score 6.5). Electronic applications accepted.

Savannah College of Art and Design, Program in Jewelry, Savannah, GA 31402-3146. Offers MA, MFA. *Program availability:* Part-time. *Degree requirements:* For master's, final project (for MA); thesis (for MFA). *Entrance requirements:* For master's, GRE (recommended), portfolio (submitted in digital format), audition or writing submission, resume, statement of purpose, two letters of recommendation. Additional exam requirements/recommendations for international students: recommended—TOEFL (minimum score 550 paper-based; 85 iBT), IELTS (minimum score 6.5). Electronic applications accepted.

Savannah College of Art and Design, Program in Painting, Savannah, GA 31402-3146. Offers MA, MFA. *Program availability:* Part-time, 100% online. *Degree requirements:* For master's, final project (for MA); thesis (for MFA). *Entrance requirements:* For master's, GRE (recommended), portfolio (submitted in digital format), audition or writing submission, resume, statement of purpose, two letters of recommendation. Additional exam requirements/recommendations for international students: recommended—TOEFL (minimum score 550 paper-based; 85 iBT), IELTS (minimum score 6.5). Electronic applications accepted.

Savannah College of Art and Design, Program in Sculpture, Savannah, GA 31402-3146. Offers MA, MFA. *Program availability:* Part-time. *Degree requirements:* For master's, final project (for MA); thesis (for MFA). *Entrance requirements:* For master's, GRE (recommended), portfolio (submitted in digital format), audition or writing submission, resume, statement of purpose, two letters of recommendation. Additional exam requirements/recommendations for international students: recommended—TOEFL (minimum score 550 paper-based; 85 iBT), IELTS (minimum score 6.5). Electronic applications accepted.

Savannah College of Art and Design, Program in Visual Effects, Savannah, GA 31402-3146. Offers MA, MFA. *Program availability:* Part-time. *Degree requirements:* For master's, final project (for MA); thesis (for MFA). *Entrance requirements:* For master's, GRE (recommended), portfolio (submitted in digital format), audition or writing submission, resume, statement of purpose, two letters of recommendation. Additional exam requirements/recommendations for international students: recommended—TOEFL (minimum score 550 paper-based; 85 iBT), IELTS (minimum score 6.5). Electronic applications accepted.

School of Visual Arts, Graduate Programs, Art Practice Department, New York, NY 10010-3994. Offers MFA. *Degree requirements:* For master's, thesis. *Entrance requirements:* For master's, portfolio submitted through SlideRoom; 500- to 750-word writing sample. Additional exam requirements/recommendations for international students: required—TOEFL (minimum score 550 paper-based; 100 iBT), IELTS (minimum score 8). Electronic applications accepted.

School of Visual Arts, Graduate Programs, Design Department, New York, NY 10010-3994. Offers MFA. *Accreditation:* NASAD. *Degree requirements:* For master's, thesis, 60 credits; minimum cumulative GPA of 3.0; residency of two academic years. *Entrance requirements:* For master's, portfolio that reflects wide range of design work and fluency in type and typography. Additional exam requirements/recommendations for international students: required—TOEFL (minimum score 550 paper-based; 79 iBT). *Expenses:* Contact institution.

School of Visual Arts, Graduate Programs, Illustration as Visual Essay Department, New York, NY 10010-3994. Offers MFA. *Accreditation:* NASAD. *Degree requirements:* For master's, thesis, 60 credits; residency of two academic years. *Entrance requirements:* For master's, portfolio of work (still images) submitted through SlideRoom. Additional exam requirements/recommendations for international students: required—TOEFL (minimum score 100 iBT). Electronic applications accepted.

School of Visual Arts, Graduate Programs, Program in Fine Arts, New York, NY 10010-3994. Offers MFA. *Accreditation:* NASAD. *Degree requirements:* For master's, thesis, 60 credits; residency of two academic years. *Entrance requirements:* For master's, CD portfolio of work with exactly 12 images. Additional exam requirements/recommendations for international students: required—TOEFL (minimum score 550 paper-based; 79 iBT). Electronic applications accepted.

Sotheby's Institute of Art–London, Graduate Programs, London, United Kingdom. Offers art business (MA); contemporary art (MA); fine and decorative art and design (MA); modern and contemporary Asian art (MA). *Degree requirements:* For master's, thesis. *Entrance requirements:* Additional exam requirements/recommendations for international students: required—IELTS (minimum score 7). Electronic applications accepted.

Sotheby's Institute of Art–New York, Graduate Programs, New York, NY 10021. Offers art business (MA); contemporary art (MA); fine and decorative art and design (MA). *Accreditation:* NASAD. *Entrance requirements:* For master's, academic transcripts, two letters of academic reference, personal statement, writing sample, curriculum vitae/resume, interview. Additional exam requirements/recommendations for international students: required—TOEFL (minimum score 100 iBT), IELTS (minimum score 7). Electronic applications accepted.

Southern Illinois University Carbondale, Graduate School, College of Liberal Arts, School of Art and Design, Carbondale, IL 62901-4701. Offers drawing (MFA); fiber/weaving (MFA); glass (MFA); metalsmithing/blacksmithing (MFA); painting (MFA). *Accreditation:* NASAD. *Degree requirements:* For master's, thesis or alternative. *Entrance requirements:* For master's, minimum GPA of 2.7, portfolio, slides. Additional exam requirements/recommendations for international students: required—TOEFL.

Southern Illinois University Edwardsville, Graduate School, College of Arts and Sciences, Department of Art and Design, Program in Art Studio, Edwardsville, IL 62026. Offers MFA. *Accreditation:* NASAD. *Program availability:* Part-time. *Degree requirements:* For master's, thesis, exhibition. *Entrance requirements:* For master's, portfolio. Additional exam requirements/recommendations for international students: required—TOEFL (minimum score 550 paper-based; 79 iBT), IELTS (minimum score 6.5). Electronic applications accepted.

Southern Methodist University, Meadows School of the Arts, Division of Art, Dallas, TX 75275. Offers studio art (MFA), including ceramics. *Accreditation:* NASAD. *Degree requirements:* For master's, thesis or alternative, exhibit. *Entrance requirements:* For master's, BFA or equivalent, letters of recommendation, portfolio. Additional exam requirements/recommendations for international students: required—TOEFL (minimum score 550 paper-based; 80 iBT).

Southwest University of Visual Arts, MFA Programs, Tucson, AZ 85716-2505. Offers motion arts (MFA); painting and drawing (MFA); photography (MFA).

Spring Hill College, Graduate Programs, Program in Liberal Arts, Mobile, AL 36608-1791. Offers fine arts (MLA); leadership and ethics (MLA, Postbaccalaureate Certificate); literature (MLA). *Program availability:* Part-time, evening/weekend. *Faculty:* 3 full-time (0 women), 2 part-time/adjunct (both women). *Students:* 3 full-time (2 women), 12 part-time (5 women); includes 1 minority (Hispanic/Latino), 4 international. Average age 35. In 2019, 9 master's awarded. *Degree requirements:* For master's, capstone course, completion of program within 6 years of initial admittance. *Entrance requirements:* For master's, bachelor's degree with minimum undergraduate GPA of 3.0 or graduate/professional degree. Additional exam requirements/recommendations for international students: required—TOEFL (minimum score 550 paper-based; 80 iBT), IELTS (minimum score 6.5), CPE or CAE (minimum score C), Michigan English Language Assessment Battery (minimum score 90). *Application deadline:* For fall admission, 8/1 priority date for domestic and international students; for spring admission, 12/1 priority date for domestic and international students. Applications are processed on a rolling basis. Application fee: $25 ($35 for international students). Electronic applications accepted. *Expenses:* Contact institution. *Financial support:* Fellowships, research assistantships, teaching assistantships, and tuition waivers available. Financial award applicants required to submit FAFSA. *Unit head:* Dr. Thomas J. Hoffman, Director, 251-380-4184, Fax: 251-460-2115, E-mail: thoffman@shc.edu. *Application contact:* Gary Bracken, Vice President of Enrollment Management, 251-380-3038, Fax: 251-460-2186, E-mail: gbracken@shc.edu.
Website: http://ug.shc.edu/graduate-degrees/master-liberal-arts/

Stanford University, School of Humanities and Sciences, Department of Art and Art History, Stanford, CA 94305-2004. Offers MFA, PhD, MS/MFA. *Expenses: Tuition:* Full-time $52,479; part-time $34,110 per unit. *Required fees:* $672; $224 per quarter. Tuition and fees vary according to program and student level.
Website: http://www.stanford.edu/dept/art/

State University of New York at New Paltz, Graduate and Extended Learning School, School of Fine and Performing Arts, Department of Fine Arts, New Paltz, NY 12561. Offers ceramics (MFA); metal (MFA); painting-drawing (MFA); printmaking (MFA); sculpture (MFA). *Accreditation:* NASAD. *Program availability:* Part-time, evening/weekend. *Faculty:* 19 full-time (12 women), 2 part-time/adjunct (1 woman). *Students:* 40 full-time (29 women), 1 (woman) part-time; includes 10 minority (1 Black or African American, non-Hispanic/Latino; 3 Asian, non-Hispanic/Latino; 4 Hispanic/Latino; 2 Two or more races, non-Hispanic/Latino), 7 international. 99 applicants, 41% accepted, 23 enrolled. In 2019, 18 master's awarded. *Degree requirements:* For master's, thesis, portfolio, exhibit (MFA). *Entrance requirements:* For master's, minimum GPA of 3.0, portfolio. Additional exam requirements/recommendations for international students: required—TOEFL (minimum score 550 paper-based; 80 iBT), IELTS (minimum score 6.5). *Application deadline:* For fall admission, 2/15 priority date for domestic and international students. Applications are processed on a rolling basis. Application fee: $50. Electronic applications accepted. *Expenses: Tuition, area resident:* Full-time $11,310; part-time $471 per credit. Tuition, state resident: full-time $11,310; part-time $471 per credit. Tuition, nonresident: full-time $23,100; part-time $963 per credit. *International tuition:* $23,100 full-time. *Required fees:* $1432; $41.83 per credit. *Financial support:* In 2019–20, 8 research assistantships with partial tuition reimbursements (averaging $5,000 per year), 7 teaching assistantships with partial tuition reimbursements (averaging $5,000 per year) were awarded. Financial award application deadline: 8/1. *Unit head:* Prof. Anne Galperin, Chair, 845-257-3833, E-mail: galperia@newpaltz.edu. *Application contact:* Prof. Matthew Friday, Graduate Coordinator, 845-257-2609, E-mail: fridaym@newpaltz.edu.
Website: http://www.newpaltz.edu/art/

State University of New York at Oswego, Graduate Studies, Department of Art, Oswego, NY 13126. Offers art (MA); graphic design and digital media (MA). *Accreditation:* NASAD. *Program availability:* Part-time. *Students:* 4. In 2019, 4 master's awarded. *Degree requirements:* For master's, exhibit, final presentation. *Entrance requirements:* For master's, slides of previous work. Additional exam requirements/recommendations for international students: required—TOEFL (minimum score 560 paper-based). *Application deadline:* For fall admission, 4/1 for domestic students; for spring admission, 10/1 for domestic students. Applications are processed on a rolling basis. Application fee: $65. Electronic applications accepted. *Financial support:* Teaching assistantships with full and partial tuition reimbursements, career-related internships or fieldwork, Federal Work-Study, institutionally sponsored loans, scholarships/grants, health care benefits, tuition waivers (partial), and unspecified assistantships available. Support available to part-time students. Financial award application deadline: 4/1; financial award applicants required to submit FAFSA. *Unit head:* Kelly Roe, Chair, 315-312-2850, E-mail: kelly.roe@oswego.edu. *Application contact:* Juan Perdiguero, Program Coordinator, 315-312-3240, E-mail: juan.perdiguero@oswego.edu.
Website: http://www.oswego.edu/academics/colleges_and_departments/departments/art.html

Stephen F. Austin State University, Graduate School, College of Fine Arts, School of Art, Nacogdoches, TX 75962. Offers art (MA); art education (MAAE); design (MFA); drawing (MFA); filmmaking (MFA); painting (MFA); sculpture (MFA). *Accreditation:* NASAD. *Program availability:* Part-time. *Degree requirements:* For master's, comprehensive exam, thesis, exhibit. *Entrance requirements:* For master's, GRE General Test, portfolio. Additional exam requirements/recommendations for international students: required—TOEFL.

Stony Brook University, State University of New York, Graduate School, College of Arts and Sciences, Department of Art, Program in Studio Art, Stony Brook, NY 11794. Offers MFA. *Students:* 11 full-time (7 women); includes 1 minority (Hispanic/Latino), 2 international. Average age 32. 9 applicants, 78% accepted, 5 enrolled. In 2019, 2 master's awarded. *Degree requirements:* For master's, comprehensive exam, thesis, reading knowledge of German, French, or Italian; exhibition. *Entrance requirements:* For master's, GRE General Test, minimum undergraduate GPA of 3.0. Additional exam requirements/recommendations for international students: required—TOEFL (minimum score 550 paper-based; 90 iBT), IELTS (minimum score 6.5). *Application deadline:* For fall admission, 1/15 priority date for domestic students; for spring admission, 10/1 for domestic students. Application fee: $100. *Expenses:* Contact institution. *Financial support:* In 2019–20, 5 teaching assistantships were awarded. *Unit head:* Prof. Isak Berbic, Director, 631-632-7250, E-mail: Isak.Berbic@stonybrook.edu. *Application contact:* Lisa Perez, Coordinator, 631-632-7270, Fax: 631-632-7261, E-mail: lisa.perez@stonybrook.edu.
Website: http://art.stonybrook.edu/graduate/g-ars/

Sul Ross State University, College of Arts and Sciences, Department of Fine Arts and Communication, Alpine, TX 79832. Offers art history (MA); studio art (MA), including art education. *Program availability:* Part-time. *Degree requirements:* For master's, oral or written exam. *Entrance requirements:* For master's, GRE General Test, minimum GPA of 2.5 in last 60 hours of undergraduate work.

SUNY Brockport, School of Arts and Sciences, Visual Studies Workshop, Brockport, NY 14420-2997. Offers MFA. *Faculty:* 2 full-time (1 woman). *Students:* 6 full-time (3 women), 10 part-time (6 women); includes 2 minority (both Black or African American, non-Hispanic/Latino). 6 applicants, 50% accepted, 3 enrolled. In 2019, 2 master's awarded. *Degree requirements:* For master's, thesis or alternative, internship, final project. *Entrance requirements:* For master's, slides, portfolio, video or CD/DVD, including work description; letters of recommendation; minimum GPA of 3.0; statement of objectives. Additional exam requirements/recommendations for international students: required—TOEFL (minimum score 550 paper-based; 79 iBT), IELTS (minimum score 6.5). *Application deadline:* For fall admission, 2/15 priority date for domestic and international students. Application fee: $50. Electronic applications accepted. *Expenses: Tuition, area resident:* Part-time $471 per credit hour. Tuition, nonresident: part-time $963 per credit hour. *Financial support:* Federal Work-Study and

scholarships/grants available. Support available to part-time students. Financial award application deadline: 3/15; financial award applicants required to submit FAFSA. *Unit head:* Tate Shaw, Graduate Director, 585-442-8676, Fax: 585-442-1992, E-mail: tshaw@brockport.edu. *Application contact:* Danielle A. Welch, Graduate Admissions Counselor, 585-395-5465, Fax: 585-395-2515.
Website: https://www.brockport.edu/academics/visual/graduate/masters.html

Syracuse University, College of Visual and Performing Arts, MFA Program in Studio Arts, Syracuse, NY 13244. Offers MFA. *Accreditation:* NASAD. *Program availability:* Part-time. *Entrance requirements:* For master's, portfolio, three letters of recommendation, resume, personal statement. Additional exam requirements/recommendations for international students: required—TOEFL (minimum score 100 iBT). Electronic applications accepted.

Temple University, Tyler School of Art and Architecture, Department of Art, Philadelphia, PA 19122-6096. Offers ceramics/glass (MFA); fibers and material studies (MFA); glass (MFA); metals/jewelry/CAD-CAM (MFA). *Faculty:* 27 full-time (14 women), 41 part-time/adjunct (22 women). *Students:* 47 full-time (33 women); includes 10 minority (3 Black or African American, non-Hispanic/Latino; 2 Asian, non-Hispanic/Latino; 4 Hispanic/Latino; 1 Two or more races, non-Hispanic/Latino), 8 international. 165 applicants, 26% accepted, 23 enrolled. In 2019, 13 master's awarded. *Entrance requirements:* Additional exam requirements/recommendations for international students: required—TOEFL (minimum score 79 iBT), IELTS (minimum score 6.5), PTE (minimum score 53), one of three is required. *Application deadline:* For fall admission, 1/6 for domestic students. Application fee: $60. Electronic applications accepted. *Expenses:* Contact institution. *Financial support:* Fellowships, teaching assistantships, Federal Work-Study, and health care benefits available. Financial award applicants required to submit FAFSA. *Unit head:* Susan E Cahan, Dean, 215-777-9000, E-mail: tyler@temple.edu. *Application contact:* Lauren O'Neill, Director of Admissions, 215-777-9159, E-mail: tyleradmissions@temple.edu.
Website: https://tyler.temple.edu/academic-programs

Temple University, Tyler School of Art and Architecture, Department of Graphic Arts and Design, Philadelphia, PA 19122-6096. Offers graphic and interactive design (MFA); photography (MFA); printmaking (MFA). *Students:* 123 applicants, 15% accepted, 12 enrolled. In 2019, 8 master's awarded. *Degree requirements:* For master's, thesis, written statement, slide portfolio. *Entrance requirements:* For master's, 3 letters of recommendation, portfolio, 40 credits in studio art, 12 credits in art history, resume, statement of goals. Additional exam requirements/recommendations for international students: required—TOEFL (minimum score 79 iBT), IELTS (minimum score 6.5), PTE (minimum score 53), one of three is required. *Application deadline:* For fall admission, 1/15 for domestic students, 12/15 for international students. Application fee: $60. Electronic applications accepted. *Expenses:* Contact institution. *Financial support:* Fellowships, teaching assistantships, Federal Work-Study, and health care benefits available. Financial award applicants required to submit FAFSA. *Unit head:* Dermot Mac Cormack, Associate Professor and Department Chair of Graphic and Interactive Design, 610-653-8227, E-mail: dermot@temple.edu. *Application contact:* Tamryn McDermott, Director of Admissions, 215-777-9159, E-mail: tyleradmissions@temple.edu.
Website: https://tyler.temple.edu/programs/graphic-interactive-design

Texas A&M University, College of Architecture, Department of Visualization, College Station, TX 77843. Offers visualization (MS). *Faculty:* 16. *Students:* 37 full-time (24 women), 24 part-time (13 women); includes 15 minority (2 Black or African American, non-Hispanic/Latino; 6 Asian, non-Hispanic/Latino; 7 Hispanic/Latino), 19 international. Average age 27. 28 applicants, 82% accepted, 19 enrolled. In 2019, 21 master's awarded. *Degree requirements:* For master's, thesis (for some programs). *Entrance requirements:* For master's, portfolio. Additional exam requirements/recommendations for international students: required—TOEFL (minimum score 550 paper-based; 80 iBT), TWE, PTE (minimum score 53). *Application deadline:* For fall admission, 12/15 priority date for domestic students. Application fee: $65 ($90 for international students). *Expenses:* Contact institution. *Financial support:* In 2019–20, 53 students received support, including 1 fellowship with tuition reimbursement available (averaging $13,000 per year), 12 research assistantships with tuition reimbursements available (averaging $6,247 per year), 38 teaching assistantships with tuition reimbursements available (averaging $6,713 per year); career-related internships or fieldwork, institutionally sponsored loans, scholarships/grants, traineeships, health care benefits, tuition waivers (full and partial), and unspecified assistantships also available. Support available to part-time students. Financial award application deadline: 12/15; financial award applicants required to submit FAFSA. *Unit head:* Dr. Tim McLaughlin, Department Head, 979-845-3465, E-mail: timm@viz.tamu.edu. *Application contact:* Dr. Tim McLaughlin, Department Head, 979-845-3465, E-mail: timm@viz.tamu.edu.
Website: http://viz.arch.tamu.edu/

Texas A&M University–Commerce, College of Humanities, Social Sciences and Arts, Commerce, TX 75429. Offers applied criminology (MS); applied linguistics (MA, MS); art (MA, MFA); christianity in history (Graduate Certificate); computational linguistics (Graduate Certificate); creative writing (Graduate Certificate); criminal justice management (Graduate Certificate); criminal justice studies (Graduate Certificate); English (MA, MS, PhD); film studies (Graduate Certificate); history (MA, MS); Holocaust studies (Graduate Certificate); homeland security (Graduate Certificate); music (MM); music performance (MM); political science (MA, MS); public history (Graduate Certificate); sociology (MS); Spanish (MA); studies in children's and adolescent literature and culture (Graduate Certificate); teaching English to speakers of other languages (Graduate Certificate); theater (MA, MS); world history (Graduate Certificate). *Program availability:* Part-time. *Faculty:* 49 full-time (28 women), 8 part-time/adjunct (2 women). *Students:* 34 full-time (21 women), 427 part-time (302 women); includes 175 minority (66 Black or African American, non-Hispanic/Latino; 1 American Indian or Alaska Native, non-Hispanic/Latino; 13 Asian, non-Hispanic/Latino; 79 Hispanic/Latino; 16 Two or more races, non-Hispanic/Latino), 15 international. Average age 38. 193 applicants, 49% accepted, 78 enrolled. In 2019, 122 master's, 6 doctorates awarded. *Degree requirements:* For master's, one foreign language, comprehensive exam, thesis (for some programs); for doctorate, one foreign language, comprehensive exam, thesis/dissertation, departmental qualifying exam. *Entrance requirements:* For master's, GRE General Test, official transcripts, letters of recommendation, resume, statement of goals; for doctorate, GRE General Test, official transcripts, letters of recommendation, statement of goals, writing samples, writing sessions, resumes. Additional exam requirements/recommendations for international students: required—TOEFL (minimum score 550 paper-based; 79 iBT), IELTS (minimum score 6), PTE (minimum score 53). *Application deadline:* For fall admission, 6/1 priority date for international students; for spring admission, 10/15 priority date for international students; for summer admission, 3/15 priority date for international students. Applications are processed on a rolling basis. Application fee: $50 ($75 for international students). Electronic applications accepted. *Expenses: Tuition, area resident:* Full-time $3630; part-time $202 per credit hour. Tuition, state resident: full-time $3630; part-time $202 per credit hour. Tuition, nonresident: full-time $11,232; part-time $624 per credit hour. *International tuition:* $11,232 full-time. *Required fees:* $2948. *Financial support:* In 2019–20, 30 students received support, including 18 research assistantships with partial tuition reimbursements available (averaging $3,231 per year), 136 teaching assistantships with partial tuition reimbursements available (averaging $4,053 per year); Federal Work-Study, institutionally sponsored loans, scholarships/grants, health care benefits, and unspecified assistantships also available. Financial award application deadline: 5/1; financial award applicants required to submit FAFSA. *Unit head:* Dr. William F. Kuracina, Interim Dean, 903-886-5166, Fax: 903-886-5774, E-mail: william.kuracina@tamuc.edu. *Application contact:* Rebecca Stevens, Graduate Student Services Coordinator, 903-468-6049, E-mail: rebecca.stevens@tamuc.edu.
Website: http://www.tamuc.edu/academics/colleges/humanitiesSocialSciencesArts/

Texas A&M University–Corpus Christi, College of Graduate Studies, College of Liberal Arts, Program in Studio Art, Corpus Christi, TX 78412. Offers MFA. *Program availability:* Part-time, evening/weekend. *Degree requirements:* For master's, comprehensive exam, thesis. *Entrance requirements:* For master's, essay (300-500 words); 3 letters of recommendation; portfolio of applicant's works (up to 20 .jpg image files of at least 150 dpi). Additional exam requirements/recommendations for international students: required—TOEFL (minimum score 550 paper-based; 79 iBT), IELTS (minimum score 6.5). Electronic applications accepted.

Texas Christian University, College of Fine Arts, School of Art, Fort Worth, TX 76129. Offers art history (MA); studio art (MFA), including painting. *Accreditation:* NASAD. *Faculty:* 12 full-time (6 women), 2 part-time/adjunct (1 woman). *Students:* 21 full-time (13 women); includes 6 minority (2 Asian, non-Hispanic/Latino; 4 Hispanic/Latino), 2 international. Average age 27. 36 applicants, 31% accepted, 9 enrolled. In 2019, 9 master's awarded. *Degree requirements:* For master's, variable foreign language requirement, comprehensive exam, thesis. *Entrance requirements:* For master's, GRE General Test (for MA). Additional exam requirements/recommendations for international students: required—TOEFL (minimum score 550 paper-based; 80 iBT). *Application deadline:* For fall admission, 2/1 for domestic and international students. Application fee: $60. Electronic applications accepted. *Expenses:* Contact institution. *Financial support:* In 2019–20, 21 students received support, including 21 teaching assistantships (averaging $10,000 per year); institutionally sponsored loans, scholarships/grants, health care benefits, tuition waivers (full and partial), and unspecified assistantships also available. Financial award application deadline: 2/1. *Unit head:* Richard Lane, Director, 817-257-7643, E-mail: r.lane@tcu.edu. *Application contact:* Donna Smolik, TCU College of Fine Arts Graduate Office, 817-257-7603, Fax: 817-257-5672, E-mail: cfagradinfo@tcu.edu.
Website: http://www.art.tcu.edu/

Texas Southern University, College of Liberal Arts and Behavioral Sciences, Department of Fine Arts, Houston, TX 77004-4584. Offers fine arts (MA); music (MA). *Program availability:* Part-time. *Degree requirements:* For master's, one foreign language, comprehensive exam, recital. *Entrance requirements:* For master's, GRE General Test, minimum GPA of 2.5. Additional exam requirements/recommendations for international students: required—TOEFL. Electronic applications accepted.

Texas Tech University, Graduate School, J.T. and Margaret Talkington College of Visual and Performing Arts, Fine Arts Doctoral Program, Lubbock, TX 79409-5060. Offers PhD. *Accreditation:* NAST. *Students:* 42 full-time (23 women), 34 part-time (22 women); includes 11 minority (2 Black or African American, non-Hispanic/Latino; 1 Asian, non-Hispanic/Latino; 5 Hispanic/Latino; 3 Two or more races, non-Hispanic/Latino), 14 international. Average age 38. 23 applicants, 48% accepted, 7 enrolled. In 2019, 8 doctorates awarded. *Degree requirements:* For doctorate, variable foreign language requirement, comprehensive exam, thesis/dissertation. *Entrance requirements:* For doctorate, GRE General Test (for some tracks). Additional exam requirements/recommendations for international students: required—TOEFL (minimum score 550 paper-based; 79 iBT). *Application deadline:* For fall admission, 6/1 priority date for domestic students, 1/15 priority date for international students; for spring admission, 9/1 priority date for domestic students, 6/15 priority date for international students. Applications are processed on a rolling basis. Application fee: $65. Electronic applications accepted. *Expenses:* Contact institution. *Financial support:* In 2019–20, 51 students received support, including 51 fellowships (averaging $3,886 per year), 41 teaching assistantships (averaging $11,819 per year); research assistantships, Federal Work-Study, institutionally sponsored loans, scholarships/grants, health care benefits, tuition waivers (partial), unspecified assistantships, and competitive grants to support graduate research also available. Financial award application deadline: 2/1; financial award applicants required to submit FAFSA. *Unit head:* Dr. Brian D. Steele, Director/Associate Dean, Talkington College of Visual and Performing Arts, 806-742-0700, Fax: 806-742-0695, E-mail: brian.steele@ttu.edu. *Application contact:* Dr. Brian D. Steele, Director/Associate Dean, Talkington College of Visual and Performing Arts, 806-742-0700, Fax: 806-742-0695, E-mail: brian.steele@ttu.edu.
Website: www.fadp.vpa.ttu.edu

Texas Tech University, Graduate School, J.T. and Margaret Talkington College of Visual and Performing Arts, School of Art, Lubbock, TX 79409-2081. Offers art (MFA); art education (MAE); art history (MA). *Accreditation:* NASAD (one or more programs are accredited). *Program availability:* Part-time, blended/hybrid learning. *Faculty:* 31 full-time (16 women), 6 part-time/adjunct (5 women). *Students:* 28 full-time (20 women), 14 part-time (all women); includes 11 minority (1 Black or African American, non-Hispanic/Latino; 1 Asian, non-Hispanic/Latino; 8 Hispanic/Latino; 1 Two or more races, non-Hispanic/Latino), 2 international. Average age 35. 30 applicants, 67% accepted, 17 enrolled. In 2019, 15 master's awarded. *Degree requirements:* For master's, variable foreign language requirement, comprehensive exam, thesis (for some programs). *Entrance requirements:* For master's, GRE (for MA). Additional exam requirements/recommendations for international students: required—TOEFL (minimum score 550 paper-based; 79 iBT), IELTS (minimum score 6.5). *Application deadline:* For fall admission, 6/1 priority date for domestic students, 1/15 priority date for international students; for spring admission, 9/1 priority date for domestic students, 6/15 priority date for international students. Applications are processed on a rolling basis. Application fee: $65. Electronic applications accepted. *Expenses:* Contact institution. *Financial support:* In 2019–20, 35 students received support, including 35 fellowships (averaging $4,789 per year), 24 teaching assistantships (averaging $10,257 per year); research assistantships, Federal Work-Study, institutionally sponsored loans, scholarships/grants, health care benefits, tuition waivers (partial), and unspecified assistantships also available. Financial award application deadline: 1/15; financial award applicants required to submit FAFSA. *Unit head:* Prof. Robin D. Germany, Interim Director, 806-834-6440, E-mail: robin.d.germany@ttu.edu. *Application contact:* Linda Rumbelow, Academic Advisor, 806-742-3825 Ext. 222, E-mail: linda.rumbelow@ttu.edu.
Website: www.art.ttu.edu

Texas Woman's University, Graduate School, College of Arts and Sciences, School of the Arts, Department of Visual Arts, Denton, TX 76204. Offers art (MA, MAT, MFA), including art education (MA, MAT), art history (MA), ceramics (MFA), graphic design (MA), intermedia (MFA), painting (MFA), photography (MFA), sculpture (MFA). *Faculty:* 6 full-time (5 women). *Students:* 13 full-time (9 women), 8 part-time (5 women); includes 5 minority (1 Asian, non-Hispanic/Latino; 3 Hispanic/Latino; 1 Two or more races, non-Hispanic/Latino), 1 international. Average age 36. 15 applicants, 80% accepted, 9 enrolled. In 2019, 8 master's awarded. *Degree requirements:* For master's, comprehensive exam, thesis (for some programs), exhibit (MFA), oral exam, thesis or professional paper (MA). *Entrance requirements:* For master's, portfolio, interview,

current curriculum vitae, letter of intent, 3 letters of recommendation, artist statement, separate application. Additional exam requirements/recommendations for international students: required—TOEFL (minimum score 79 iBT); recommended—IELTS (minimum score 6.5), TSE (minimum score 53). *Application deadline:* For fall admission, 2/15 for domestic and international students; for spring admission, 11/15 for domestic and international students. Application fee: $50 ($75 for international students). Electronic applications accepted. *Expenses: Tuition, area resident:* Full-time $4973.40; part-time $276.30 per semester hour. Tuition, state resident: full-time $4973.40; part-time $276.30 per semester hour. Tuition, nonresident: full-time $12,569; part-time $698.30 per semester hour. *International tuition:* $12,569.40 full-time. *Required fees:* $2524.30. Tuition and fees vary according to course level, course load, degree level and program. *Financial support:* In 2019–20, 15 students received support, including 12 teaching assistantships (averaging $4,968 per year); career-related internships or fieldwork, scholarships/grants, health care benefits, and unspecified assistantships also available. Support available to part-time students. Financial award application deadline: 3/1; financial award applicants required to submit FAFSA. *Unit head:* Dr. Vagner Whitehead, Chair, 940-898-2530, Fax: 940-898-2496, E-mail: visualarts@twu.edu. *Application contact:* Korie Hawkins, Associate Director of Admissions, Graduate Recruitment, 940-898-3188, Fax: 940-898-3081, E-mail: admissions@twu.edu.
Website: http://www.twu.edu/visual-arts/

Thomas Jefferson University, Kanbar College of Design, Engineering and Commerce, Program in Surface Imaging, Philadelphia, PA 19107. Offers MS.

Tiffin University, Program in Humanities, Tiffin, OH 44883-2161. Offers art and visual media (MH); communication (MH); creative writing (MH); English (MH); film studies (MH); humanities (MH); individualized studies (MH). *Program availability:* Part-time, evening/weekend, online only, 100% online, blended/hybrid learning. *Entrance requirements:* For master's, work experience. Additional exam requirements/recommendations for international students: required—TOEFL (minimum score 550 paper-based; 79 iBT). Electronic applications accepted. Application fee is waived when completed online. *Expenses:* Contact institution.

Towson University, College of Fine Arts and Communication, Program in Studio Art, Towson, MD 21252-0001. Offers MFA. *Students:* 18 full-time (11 women), 6 part-time (4 women); includes 6 minority (3 Black or African American, non-Hispanic/Latino; 1 Hispanic/Latino; 2 Two or more races, non-Hispanic/Latino), 2 international. *Entrance requirements:* For master's, bachelor's degree, preferably in art; portfolio; minimum GPA of 3.0; letter of intent; current resume; 2 letters of recommendation. *Application deadline:* For fall admission, 1/17 for domestic students, 5/15 for international students; for spring admission, 10/15 for domestic students, 12/1 for international students. Applications are processed on a rolling basis. Application fee: $45. Electronic applications accepted. *Expenses: Tuition, area resident:* Full-time $7920; part-time $439 per credit. Tuition, nonresident: full-time $16,344; part-time $908 per credit. *International tuition:* $16,344 full-time. *Required fees:* $2628; $146 per credit. $876 per term. *Financial support:* Application deadline: 4/1. *Unit head:* Prof. Tonia Matthews, Graduate Program Director, 410-704-2803, E-mail: tmatthews@towson.edu. *Application contact:* Coverley Beidleman, Assistant Director of Graduate Admissions, 410-704-5630, Fax: 410-704-3030, E-mail: grads@towson.edu.
Website: https://www.towson.edu/cofac/departments/art/grad/studio/

Tufts University, School of the Museum of Fine Arts at Tufts University, Boston, MA 02155. Offers art education (MAT); studio art (MFA, Postbaccalaureate Certificate), including museum studies (MFA). *Faculty:* 31 full-time (19 women), 23 part-time/adjunct (16 women). *Students:* 55 full-time. Average age 25. In 2019, 44 master's, 15 other advanced degrees awarded. Terminal master's awarded for partial completion of doctoral program. *Degree requirements:* For master's, thesis, thesis exhibition. *Entrance requirements:* For master's, BFA (preferred) or bachelor's degree or equivalent in related area; portfolio; for Postbaccalaureate Certificate, portfolio, BFA or equivalent. Additional exam requirements/recommendations for international students: required—TOEFL (minimum score 85 iBT), IELTS (minimum score 6.5). *Application deadline:* For fall admission, 1/15 priority date for domestic and international students. Applications are processed on a rolling basis. Application fee: $85. Electronic applications accepted. *Expenses:* Contact institution. *Financial support:* Fellowships, teaching assistantships, Federal Work-Study, and scholarships/grants available. Financial award application deadline: 1/15. *Unit head:* Lisa Bynoe, Associate Director of Graduate Programs, 617-627-0031, E-mail: lisa.bynoe@tufts.edu. *Application contact:* Office of Graduate Admissions, 617-627-3395, E-mail: gradadmissions@tufts.edu.
Website: https://smfa.tufts.edu/

Tulane University, School of Liberal Arts, Department of Art, New Orleans, LA 70118-5669. Offers history of art (MA); studio art (MFA). *Degree requirements:* For master's, one foreign language, thesis. *Entrance requirements:* For master's, GRE General Test, minimum B average in undergraduate course work. Additional exam requirements/recommendations for international students: required—TOEFL. Electronic applications accepted. *Expenses: Tuition:* Full-time $57,004; part-time $3167 per credit hour. *Required fees:* $2086; $44.50 per credit hour. $80 per term. Tuition and fees vary according to course load, degree level and program.

United Theological Seminary of the Twin Cities, Graduate Programs, New Brighton, MN 55112-2598. Offers advanced theological studies (Diploma); justice and peace studies (M Div, MA); leadership toward racial justice (M Div, MA, Certificate); Methodist studies (M Div, MA, Certificate); ministry (D Min); ministry renewal and professional development (Certificate); pastoral care and counseling (M Div, MA, MARL); religion and theology (MA); theological and religious studies (Certificate); theology and the arts (M Div, MA); urban ministry (M Div, MA, MARL); women's studies: religion, theology and ministry (M Div, MA). *Accreditation:* ACIPE; ATS. *Program availability:* Part-time, evening/weekend. *Degree requirements:* For master's, thesis; for doctorate, comprehensive exam, thesis/dissertation. *Entrance requirements:* For master's, minimum GPA of 2.75; strong analytical, reflective thinking and writing skills; vocational and academic goals compatible with those of Seminary; for doctorate, M Div or equivalent, minimum GPA of 3.0, 3 years experience in professional ministry; for other advanced degree, BA or equivalent life experience; strong analytical, reflective thinking and writing skills (Certificate); proficiency in English language, previous study of theology at a theological school, recommendation of student's denomination (Diploma). Additional exam requirements/recommendations for international students: required—TOEFL (minimum score 550 paper-based).

Universidad del Turabo, Graduate Programs, Programs in Education, Program in Teaching of Fine Arts, Gurabo, PR 00778-3030. Offers M Ed. *Entrance requirements:* For master's, GRE, EXADEP, GMAT, interview, official transcript, essay, recommendation letters. Electronic applications accepted.

Université du Québec à Chicoutimi, Graduate Programs, Program in Fine Arts, Chicoutimi, QC G7H 2B1, Canada. Offers MA. *Program availability:* Part-time. *Degree requirements:* For master's, thesis optional. *Entrance requirements:* For master's, appropriate bachelor's degree, proficiency in French.

Université du Québec à Montréal, Graduate Programs, Program in Fine Arts, Montréal, QC H3C 3P8, Canada. Offers MA. *Program availability:* Part-time. *Degree requirements:* For master's, thesis optional. *Entrance requirements:* For master's, appropriate bachelor's degree or equivalent, proficiency in French.

University at Albany, State University of New York, College of Arts and Sciences, Department of Art and Art History, Albany, NY 12222-0001. Offers art (MA, MFA). *Program availability:* Part-time. *Faculty:* 13 full-time (9 women), 18 part-time/adjunct (10 women). *Students:* 10 full-time (0 women), 17 part-time (0 women); includes 7 minority (1 Black or African American, non-Hispanic/Latino; 2 Asian, non-Hispanic/Latino; 1 Native Hawaiian or other Pacific Islander, non-Hispanic/Latino; 3 Two or more races, non-Hispanic/Latino), 2 international. Average age 26. 33 applicants, 73% accepted, 19 enrolled. In 2019, 17 master's awarded. *Degree requirements:* For master's, exhibit. *Entrance requirements:* For master's, portfolio, transcripts of all schools attended, statement of background and goals, resume, names and contact information for 3 recommenders. Additional exam requirements/recommendations for international students: required—TOEFL (minimum score 550 paper-based). *Application deadline:* For fall admission, 1/15 for domestic students, 4/15 for international students; for spring admission, 11/15 for domestic and international students. Application fee: $75. *Expenses: Tuition, area resident:* Full-time $11,530; part-time $480 per credit hour. Tuition, nonresident: full-time $23,530; part-time $980 per credit hour. *International tuition:* $23,530 full-time. *Required fees:* $2185; $96 per credit hour. Part-time tuition and fees vary according to course load and program. *Financial support:* Federal Work-Study available. Financial award application deadline: 4/1. *Unit head:* Sarah Cohen, Chair, 518-442-4020, Fax: 518-442-4807. *Application contact:* Michael DeRensis, Director, Graduate Admissions, 518-442-3980, Fax: 518-442-3922, E-mail: graduate@albany.edu.
Website: http://www.albany.edu/finearts/

University at Buffalo, the State University of New York, Graduate School, College of Arts and Sciences, Department of Art, Program in Studio Art, Buffalo, NY 14260. Offers MFA. *Degree requirements:* For master's, thesis, thesis exhibition or equivalent public defense. *Entrance requirements:* For master's, portfolio of 20 slides or CD, 3 letters of reference, curriculum vitae. Additional exam requirements/recommendations for international students: required—TOEFL (minimum score 550 paper-based; 79 iBT). Electronic applications accepted. *Expenses:* Contact institution.

The University of Alabama, Graduate School, College of Arts and Sciences, Department of Art and Art History, Tuscaloosa, AL 35487. Offers art history (MA); studio art (MA, MFA), including ceramics, painting, photography, printmaking, sculpture. *Accreditation:* NASAD. *Program availability:* Part-time. *Faculty:* 9 full-time (3 women). *Students:* 20 full-time (16 women), 3 part-time (1 woman); includes 3 minority (1 Black or African American, non-Hispanic/Latino; 2 Hispanic/Latino), 4 international. Average age 29. 22 applicants, 59% accepted, 8 enrolled. In 2019, 6 master's awarded. *Degree requirements:* For master's, one foreign language, comprehensive exam (for some programs), oral exam, thesis statement, exhibit (studio art), thesis (art history). *Entrance requirements:* For master's, GRE General Test or MAT (art history), minimum GPA of 3.0, BFA or equivalent (studio art). Additional exam requirements/recommendations for international students: required—TOEFL (minimum score 550 paper-based). *Application deadline:* For fall admission, 3/15 for domestic and international students; for spring admission, 10/15 for domestic and international students. Applications are processed on a rolling basis. Application fee: $50 ($60 for international students). Electronic applications accepted. *Expenses: Tuition, area resident:* Full-time $10,780; part-time $440 per credit hour. Tuition, nonresident: full-time $30,250; part-time $1550 per credit hour. *Financial support:* In 2019–20, 8 students received support, including 2 fellowships with full tuition reimbursements available, 14 teaching assistantships with tuition reimbursements available (averaging $15,427 per year); career-related internships or fieldwork, institutionally sponsored loans, scholarships/grants, and unspecified assistantships also available. Financial award application deadline: 7/1. *Unit head:* Jason Guynes, Chair, 205-348-9944, Fax: 205-348-0287, E-mail: jguynes@ua.edu. *Application contact:* Allison Grant, Studio Art Graduate Program Director, 205-348-5968, Fax: 205-348-5967, E-mail: agrant4@ua.edu.
Website: http://www.art.ua.edu/

University of Alaska Fairbanks, College of Liberal Arts, Department of Art, Fairbanks, AK 99775-5640. Offers art (MFA); ceramics (MFA); computer art (MFA); drawing (MFA); painting (MFA); photography (MFA); printmaking (MFA); sculpture (MFA). *Program availability:* Part-time. *Degree requirements:* For master's, comprehensive exam, oral defense of project or thesis. *Entrance requirements:* For master's, portfolio of work including about 20 slides or appropriate equivalent depending on field of study. Additional exam requirements/recommendations for international students: required—TOEFL (minimum score 550 paper-based; 79 iBT), IELTS (minimum score 6.5). Electronic applications accepted.

University of Alberta, Faculty of Graduate Studies and Research, Department of Art and Design, Edmonton, AB T6G 2E1, Canada. Offers drawing (MFA); history of art, design, and visual culture (MA); industrial design (M Des); painting (MFA); printmaking (MFA); sculpture (MFA); visual communication design (M Des). *Degree requirements:* For master's, thesis. *Entrance requirements:* For master's, portfolio (MFA and MDES). Additional exam requirements/recommendations for international students: required—TOEFL (minimum score 550 paper-based).

The University of Arizona, College of Fine Arts, School of Art, Program in Art, Tucson, AZ 85721. Offers MFA. *Entrance requirements:* Additional exam requirements/recommendations for international students: required—TOEFL (minimum score 550 paper-based; 79 iBT). Electronic applications accepted.

University of Arkansas, Graduate School, J. William Fulbright College of Arts and Sciences, School of Art, Fayetteville, AR 72701. Offers MFA. *Accreditation:* NASAD. *Students:* 33 full-time (17 women), 1 part-time (0 women); includes 8 minority (3 Black or African American, non-Hispanic/Latino; 1 American Indian or Alaska Native, non-Hispanic/Latino; 2 Hispanic/Latino; 2 Two or more races, non-Hispanic/Latino), 6 international. 116 applicants, 16% accepted. In 2019, 6 master's awarded. *Application deadline:* For fall admission, 8/1 for domestic students, 4/1 for international students; for spring admission, 12/1 for domestic students, 10/1 for international students; for summer admission, 4/15 for domestic students, 3/1 for international students. Applications are processed on a rolling basis. Application fee: $60. Electronic applications accepted. *Financial support:* In 2019–20, 11 research assistantships were awarded; fellowships, teaching assistantships, career-related internships or fieldwork, and Federal Work-Study also available. Support available to part-time students. Financial award application deadline: 4/1; financial award applicants required to submit FAFSA. *Unit head:* Gerry Snyder, Executive Director, 479-575-5202, E-mail: gwsnyder@uark.edu. *Application contact:* Donna Jones, Director of Outreach and Recruitment, 479-575-5202, E-mail: donnas@uark.edu.
Website: https://fulbright.uark.edu/departments/art/

University of Arkansas at Little Rock, Graduate School, College of Arts, Letters, and Sciences, Department of Art, Little Rock, AR 72204-1099. Offers art education (MA); art history (MA); studio art (MA). *Accreditation:* NASAD. *Program availability:* Part-time. *Degree requirements:* For master's, 4 foreign languages, oral exam, oral defense of thesis or exhibit. *Entrance requirements:* For master's, portfolio review or term paper evaluation, minimum GPA of 2.7.

Art/Fine Arts

The University of British Columbia, Faculty of Arts, Department of Art History, Visual Art, and Theory, Vancouver, BC V6T 1Z2, Canada. Offers art history (MA, PhD); critical and curatorial studies (MA); visual art (MFA). *Degree requirements:* For master's, one foreign language, thesis, final exhibition (MFA, MA in critical and curatorial studies); for doctorate, 2 foreign languages, comprehensive exam, thesis/dissertation. *Entrance requirements:* For master's, bachelor's degree with minimum B+ average (MFA, MA in critical and curatorial studies), A- (MA in art history); for doctorate, master's degree with minimum A- average. Additional exam requirements/recommendations for international students: required—TOEFL. Electronic applications accepted. *Expenses:* Contact institution.

University of California, Berkeley, Graduate Division, College of Letters and Science, Department of Art Practice, Berkeley, CA 94720. Offers MFA. *Entrance requirements:* For master's, GRE General Test, minimum GPA of 3.0, sample of work, 3 letters of recommendation. Additional exam requirements/recommendations for international students: required—TOEFL (minimum score 570 paper-based; 90 iBT). Electronic applications accepted.

University of California, Berkeley, UC Berkeley Extension, Certificate Programs in Art and Design, Berkeley, CA 94720. Offers interior design and interior architecture (Certificate); landscape architecture (Certificate); visual arts (Postbaccalaureate Certificate).

University of California, Davis, Graduate Studies, Program in Art, Davis, CA 95616. Offers MFA. *Degree requirements:* For master's, final exhibit. *Entrance requirements:* For master's, minimum GPA of 3.0, portfolio. Additional exam requirements/recommendations for international students: required—TOEFL (minimum score 550 paper-based). Electronic applications accepted.

University of California, Irvine, Claire Trevor School of the Arts, Department of Art, Irvine, CA 92697. Offers MFA. *Students:* 28 full-time (12 women), 1 part-time (0 women); includes 13 minority (1 Black or African American, non-Hispanic/Latino; 5 Asian, non-Hispanic/Latino; 3 Hispanic/Latino; 4 Two or more races, non-Hispanic/Latino), 2 international. Average age 33. 178 applicants, 7% accepted, 9 enrolled. In 2019, 12 master's awarded. *Entrance requirements:* For master's, minimum GPA of 3.0. *Application deadline:* For fall admission, 1/15 for domestic and international students. Applications are processed on a rolling basis. Application fee: $120 ($140 for international students). Electronic applications accepted. *Financial support:* Fellowships with tuition reimbursements, research assistantships with tuition reimbursements, teaching assistantships with tuition reimbursements, institutionally sponsored loans, traineeships, health care benefits, and unspecified assistantships available. Financial award application deadline: 3/1; financial award applicants required to submit FAFSA. *Unit head:* Kevin Appel, Chair, Fax: 949-824-5297, E-mail: kappel@uci.edu. *Application contact:* John Medina, Department Manager, 949-824-4917, Fax: 949-824-5297, E-mail: jcmedina@uci.edu.
Website: http://www.arts.uci.edu/ctsa-academic-departments-art-department

University of California, Irvine, School of Humanities, Department of Art History, Irvine, CA 92697. Offers visual studies (MA, PhD). *Students:* 28 full-time (18 women), 1 (woman) part-time; includes 15 minority (4 Black or African American, non-Hispanic/Latino; 4 Asian, non-Hispanic/Latino; 5 Hispanic/Latino; 2 Two or more races, non-Hispanic/Latino), 3 international. Average age 32. 81 applicants, 15% accepted, 8 enrolled. In 2019, 5 master's, 5 doctorates awarded. *Entrance requirements:* For master's, GRE, minimum GPA of 3.0; for doctorate, GRE General Test, writing sample. Additional exam requirements/recommendations for international students: required—TOEFL (minimum score 550 paper-based). *Application deadline:* For fall admission, 12/15 for domestic and international students. Application fee: $120 ($140 for international students). Electronic applications accepted. *Financial support:* Fellowships, teaching assistantships, institutionally sponsored loans, traineeships, health care benefits, and unspecified assistantships available. Financial award application deadline: 3/1; financial award applicants required to submit FAFSA. *Unit head:* Prof. Cecile Whiting, Chair, 949-824-2464, E-mail: cwhiting@uci.edu. *Application contact:* Lucas Hilderbrand, Director of Graduate Studies for Visual Studies, 949-824-1124, Fax: 949-824-2865, E-mail: lucas.h@uci.edu.
Website: http://www.hnet.uci.edu/arthistory/

University of California, Los Angeles, Graduate Division, School of the Arts and Architecture, Department of Art, Los Angeles, CA 90095. Offers MFA. *Degree requirements:* For master's, comprehensive exam. *Entrance requirements:* For master's, bachelor's degree; minimum undergraduate GPA of 3.0 (or its equivalent if letter grade system not used); portfolio. Additional exam requirements/recommendations for international students: required—TOEFL. Electronic applications accepted. *Expenses:* Contact institution.

University of California, Riverside, Graduate Division, Program in Visual Arts, Riverside, CA 92521-0102. Offers MFA. *Degree requirements:* For master's, thesis. *Entrance requirements:* For master's, portfolio, minimum GPA of 3.2. Additional exam requirements/recommendations for international students: required—TOEFL (minimum score 550 paper-based; 80 iBT). Electronic applications accepted.

University of California, San Diego, Graduate Division, Department of Visual Arts, La Jolla, CA 92093. Offers art history, theory, and criticism (PhD); visual arts (MFA). *Students:* 69 full-time (47 women), 1 (woman) part-time. 116 applicants, 25% accepted, 17 enrolled. In 2019, 16 master's, 5 doctorates awarded. *Degree requirements:* For master's, comprehensive exam, thesis; for doctorate, 2 foreign languages, comprehensive exam, thesis/dissertation, reading knowledge of at least two of the foreign languages commonly used by scholars engaged in the advanced study in art history, theory, and criticism. *Entrance requirements:* For master's, electronic portfolio; for doctorate, GRE General Test, electronic portfolio. Additional exam requirements/recommendations for international students: required—TOEFL (minimum score 550 paper-based; 80 iBT), IELTS (minimum score 7). *Application deadline:* For fall admission, 1/3 for domestic students. Application fee: $105 ($125 for international students). Electronic applications accepted. *Financial support:* Fellowships, research assistantships, teaching assistantships, career-related internships or fieldwork, scholarships/grants, and readerships available. Financial award applicants required to submit FAFSA. *Unit head:* Amy Adler, Chair, 858-534-0418, E-mail: aadler@ucsd.edu. *Application contact:* Katherine Edwards, Graduate Program Coordinator, 858-822-3882, E-mail: vis-grad@ucsd.edu.
Website: http://visarts.ucsd.edu/

University of California, Santa Barbara, Graduate Division, College of Letters and Sciences, Division of Humanities and Fine Arts, Department of Art, Santa Barbara, CA 93106-7120. Offers MFA. *Degree requirements:* For master's, thesis, exhibition. *Entrance requirements:* Additional exam requirements/recommendations for international students: required—TOEFL (minimum score 550 paper-based; 80 iBT), IELTS (minimum score 7). Electronic applications accepted.

University of California, Santa Cruz, Division of Graduate Studies, Division of the Arts, Program in Digital Arts and New Media, Santa Cruz, CA 95064. Offers MFA. *Degree requirements:* For master's, thesis, written paper. *Entrance requirements:* Additional exam requirements/recommendations for international students: required—

TOEFL (minimum score 550 paper-based; 83 iBT); recommended—IELTS (minimum score 8). Electronic applications accepted.

University of California, Santa Cruz, Division of Graduate Studies, Division of the Arts, Program in Visual Studies, Santa Cruz, CA 95064. Offers PhD. *Degree requirements:* For doctorate, one foreign language, thesis/dissertation, qualifying exams. *Entrance requirements:* For doctorate, GRE, writing sample under 20 pages, 3 letters of recommendation. Additional exam requirements/recommendations for international students: required—TOEFL (minimum score 550 paper-based; 83 iBT); recommended—IELTS (minimum score 8). Electronic applications accepted.

University of Central Florida, College of Arts and Humanities, School of Visual Arts and Design, Orlando, FL 32816. Offers digital media (MA); emerging media (MFA), including animation and visual effects, digital media, entrepreneurial digital cinema, studio art and the computer. *Program availability:* Part-time. *Students:* 41 full-time (17 women), 5 part-time (2 women); includes 23 minority (6 Black or African American, non-Hispanic/Latino; 1 Asian, non-Hispanic/Latino; 15 Hispanic/Latino; 1 Two or more races, non-Hispanic/Latino), 2 international. Average age 30. 41 applicants, 56% accepted, 18 enrolled. In 2019, 5 master's awarded. *Degree requirements:* For master's, comprehensive exam, thesis or alternative. *Entrance requirements:* For master's, GRE, letter of recommendation. Additional exam requirements/recommendations for international students: required—TOEFL. *Application deadline:* For fall admission, 7/1 for domestic students. Application fee: $30. Electronic applications accepted. *Financial support:* In 2019–20, 22 students received support, including 10 fellowships with partial tuition reimbursements available (averaging $7,400 per year), 15 teaching assistantships with partial tuition reimbursements available (averaging $5,226 per year); scholarships/grants, health care benefits, and unspecified assistantships also available. Financial award application deadline: 3/1; financial award applicants required to submit FAFSA. *Unit head:* Dr. Rudy McDaniel, Director, 407-823-3145, E-mail: rudy@ucf.edu. *Application contact:* Associate Director, Graduate Admissions, 407-823-2766, Fax: 407-823-6442, E-mail: gradadmissions@ucf.edu.
Website: http://svad.cah.ucf.edu/

University of Chicago, Division of the Humanities, Department of Visual Arts, Chicago, IL 60637. Offers MFA. *Degree requirements:* For master's, thesis presentation and exhibition. *Entrance requirements:* For master's, portfolio, artist's statement, 3 letters of recommendation, transcripts for all previous degrees and institutions attended. Additional exam requirements/recommendations for international students: required—TOEFL (minimum score 104 iBT), IELTS (minimum score 7). Electronic applications accepted.

University of Cincinnati, Graduate School, College of Design, Architecture, Art, and Planning, School of Art, Program in Fine Arts, Cincinnati, OH 45221. Offers MFA. *Accreditation:* NASAD. *Program availability:* Part-time. *Degree requirements:* For master's, thesis, oral exam. *Entrance requirements:* Additional exam requirements/recommendations for international students: required—TOEFL. Electronic applications accepted.

University of Colorado Boulder, Graduate School, College of Arts and Sciences, Department of Art and Art History, Boulder, CO 80309. Offers art history (MA), including contemporary art criticism, early twentieth-century art, nineteenth-century art, Russian and Soviet art; ceramics (MFA); photography and media arts (MFA); printmaking (MFA); sculpture (MFA). Terminal master's awarded for partial completion of doctoral program. *Degree requirements:* For master's, variable foreign language requirement, comprehensive exam, thesis (for some programs). *Entrance requirements:* For master's, GRE General Test, minimum undergraduate GPA of 3.0, portfolio. Electronic applications accepted. Application fee is waived when completed online.

University of Colorado Denver, College of Liberal Arts and Sciences, Program in Humanities, Denver, CO 80217. Offers community health (MSS); ethnic studies (MH, MSS); humanities (MH, Graduate Certificate); international studies (MSS); philosophy and theory (MH); social justice (MH, MSS); society and the environment (MSS); visual studies (MH); women's and gender studies (MH, MSS). *Program availability:* Part-time, evening/weekend. *Degree requirements:* For master's, 36 credit hours, project or thesis. *Entrance requirements:* For master's, writing sample, statement of purpose/letter of intent, three letters of recommendation. Additional exam requirements/recommendations for international students: required—TOEFL (minimum score 537 paper-based; 75 iBT); recommended—IELTS (minimum score 6.5). Electronic applications accepted. Tuition and fees vary according to course load, program and reciprocity agreements.

University of Dayton, Department of Teacher Education, Dayton, OH 45469. Offers adolescence to young adult education (MS Ed); early childhood leadership and advocacy (MS Ed); interdisciplinary education (MS Ed), including visual arts; interdisciplinary education studies (MS Ed); leadership in educational systems (MS Ed); literacy (MS Ed); mathematics education (MS Ed); middle childhood education (MS Ed); multi-age education (MS Ed), including world languages; music education (MS Ed); teacher as leader (MS Ed); teacher education (MS Ed); technology-enhanced learning (MS Ed); trans-disciplinary early childhood education (MS Ed). *Program availability:* Part-time, 100% online. *Degree requirements:* For master's, variable foreign language requirement, thesis or alternative, internship (for teaching licensure or endorsement). *Entrance requirements:* For master's, GRE (minimum score of 149 verbal, 4 on writing) or MAT (minimum score of 396) if undergraduate GPA was under 2.75, minimum GPA of 2.75, 3 letters of recommendation, personal statement or resume, official transcripts. Additional exam requirements/recommendations for international students: required—TOEFL (minimum score 550 paper-based; 80 iBT); recommended—IELTS (minimum score 6.5). Electronic applications accepted. *Expenses:* Contact institution.

University of Delaware, College of Arts and Sciences, Department of Art, Newark, DE 19716. Offers MA, MFA. *Degree requirements:* For master's, exposition paper final exhibition. *Entrance requirements:* For master's, portfolio of creative work. Electronic applications accepted.

University of Denver, Division of Arts, Humanities and Social Sciences, School of Art and Art History, Denver, CO 80208. Offers art history (MA); museum studies (MA). *Accreditation:* NASAD. *Program availability:* Part-time. *Faculty:* 16 full-time (11 women), 6 part-time/adjunct (5 women). *Students:* 11 full-time (all women), 10 part-time (7 women); includes 6 minority (1 Black or African American, non-Hispanic/Latino; 1 Asian, non-Hispanic/Latino; 4 Hispanic/Latino). Average age 27. 21 applicants, 86% accepted, 12 enrolled. In 2019, 13 master's awarded. *Degree requirements:* For master's, one foreign language, comprehensive exam, research paper. *Entrance requirements:* For master's, GRE General Test, transcripts, personal statement, writing sample, three letters of recommendation. Additional exam requirements/recommendations for international students: required—TOEFL (minimum score 550 paper-based; 80 iBT). *Application deadline:* For fall admission, 1/31 priority date for domestic and international students. Applications are processed on a rolling basis. Application fee: $65. Electronic applications accepted. *Expenses:* Contact institution. *Financial support:* In 2019–20, 20 students received support, including 8 teaching assistantships with tuition reimbursements available (averaging $8,177 per year); research assistantships with tuition reimbursements available, career-related internships or fieldwork, Federal Work-Study, institutionally sponsored loans, scholarships/grants, and unspecified

assistantships also available. Support available to part-time students. Financial award application deadline: 2/15; financial award applicants required to submit FAFSA. *Unit head:* Annabeth Headrick, Associate Professor and Director, 303-871-3574, E-mail: annabeth.headrick@du.edu. *Application contact:* Jason Kellermeyer, Coordinator of Academic Programs, 303-871-2846, E-mail: jason.kellermeyer@du.edu.
Website: http://www.du.edu/ahss/art/index.html

University of Florida, Graduate School, College of The Arts, School of Art and Art History, Gainesville, FL 32611. Offers art (MA), including digital arts and sciences; art education (MA); art history (MA, PhD); museology (MA), including historic preservation. *Accreditation:* NASAD. *Program availability:* Online learning. *Degree requirements:* For master's, project or thesis (MFA); 1 foreign language (MA in art history); for doctorate, 2 foreign languages, comprehensive exam, thesis/dissertation. *Entrance requirements:* For master's, GRE General Test, portfolio (MFA), writing sample (MA), minimum GPA 3.0; for doctorate, GRE General Test, minimum GPA of 3.0. Additional exam requirements/recommendations for international students: required—TOEFL (minimum score 550 paper-based; 80 iBT), IELTS (minimum score 6). Electronic applications accepted.

University of Georgia, Franklin College of Arts and Sciences, Lamar Dodd School of Art, Athens, GA 30602. Offers art (MFA, PhD); art history (MA). *Accreditation:* NASAD (one or more programs are accredited). *Degree requirements:* For doctorate, one foreign language, thesis/dissertation. *Entrance requirements:* For master's and doctorate, GRE General Test. Electronic applications accepted.

University of Guam, Office of Graduate Studies, College of Liberal Arts and Social Sciences, Division of Fine Arts, Mangilao, GU 96923. Offers ceramics (MA); graphics (MA); painting (MA). *Degree requirements:* For master's, thesis or alternative, exhibit, final oral exam. *Entrance requirements:* For master's, GRE General Test, portfolio. Additional exam requirements/recommendations for international students: required—TOEFL.

University of Guelph, Office of Graduate and Postdoctoral Studies, College of Arts, School of Fine Art and Music, Guelph, ON N1G 2W1, Canada. Offers studio art (MFA). *Degree requirements:* For master's, exhibition, support paper, oral defense. *Entrance requirements:* For master's, minimum B- average during previous 2 years of course work. Additional exam requirements/recommendations for international students: required—TOEFL. Electronic applications accepted.

University of Hartford, Hartford Art School, West Hartford, CT 06117-1599. Offers MFA. *Program availability:* Part-time. *Faculty:* 3 full-time (1 woman), 2 part-time/adjunct (0 women). *Students:* 41 full-time (21 women); includes 13 minority (2 Black or African American, non-Hispanic/Latino; 3 Asian, non-Hispanic/Latino; 6 Hispanic/Latino; 2 Two or more races, non-Hispanic/Latino), 1 international. Average age 37. 22 applicants, 18% accepted, 2 enrolled. In 2019, 21 master's awarded. *Degree requirements:* For master's, thesis. *Entrance requirements:* For master's, portfolio, 3 letters of recommendation. Additional exam requirements/recommendations for international students: required—TOEFL (minimum score 550 paper-based). *Application deadline:* For fall admission, 3/1 priority date for domestic students. Applications are processed on a rolling basis. Application fee: $45. Electronic applications accepted. *Expenses:* Contact institution. *Financial support:* In 2019–20, 10 fellowships with partial tuition reimbursements (averaging $6,000 per year) were awarded; teaching assistantships and Federal Work-Study also available. Support available to part-time students. Financial award application deadline: 6/1; financial award applicants required to submit FAFSA. *Unit head:* Power Boothe, Dean, 860-768-4391. *Application contact:* Ellen Carey, Director, 860-768-4616, Fax: 860-768-5160, E-mail: ecarey@mail.hartford.edu.
Website: http://www.hartfordartschool.org/

University of Hawaii at Manoa, Office of Graduate Education, College of Arts and Humanities, Department of Art and Art History, Honolulu, HI 96822. Offers art history (MA); visual arts (MFA). *Program availability:* Part-time. *Degree requirements:* For master's, thesis optional. *Entrance requirements:* For master's, GRE General Test, BFA, 18 hours of course work in art history. Additional exam requirements/recommendations for international students: required—TOEFL (minimum score 550 paper-based; 79 iBT), IELTS (minimum score 7).

University of Houston, Kathrine G. McGovern College of the Arts, School of Art, Houston, TX 77204. Offers art history (MA); interdisciplinary practice and emerging forms (MFA); painting (MFA); studio art (MFA). *Entrance requirements:* For master's, baccalaureate degree, portfolio. Electronic applications accepted.

University of Idaho, College of Graduate Studies, College of Art and Architecture, Moscow, ID 83844-2282. Offers architecture (M Arch); art and design (MFA); bioregional planning and community design (MS); integrated architecture and design (MS); landscape architecture (MLA). *Accreditation:* NASAD. *Students:* 73 full-time, 10 part-time. Average age 28. 105 applicants, 76% accepted, 38 enrolled. In 2019, 32 master's awarded. *Entrance requirements:* For master's, minimum GPA of 3.0. Additional exam requirements/recommendations for international students: required—TOEFL (minimum score 79 iBT). *Application deadline:* For fall admission, 7/30 for domestic students; for spring admission, 12/1 for domestic students. Applications are processed on a rolling basis. Application fee: $60. Electronic applications accepted. *Expenses:* Tuition, state resident: full-time $7753.80; part-time $502 per credit hour. Tuition, nonresident: full-time $26,990; part-time $1571 per credit hour. *Required fees:* $2122.20; $47 per credit hour. *Financial support:* Applicants required to submit FAFSA. *Unit head:* Dr. Shauna Corry, Dean, 208-885-4409, E-mail: caa@uidaho.edu. *Application contact:* Dr. Shauna Corry, Dean, 208-885-4409, E-mail: caa@uidaho.edu.
Website: http://www.uidaho.edu/caa

University of Illinois at Chicago, College of Architecture, Design and the Arts, School of Art and Art History, Chicago, IL 60607-7128. Offers art history (MA); electronic visualization (MFA); museum and exhibition studies (MA); new media arts (MFA). *Program availability:* Part-time, evening/weekend. Terminal master's awarded for partial completion of doctoral program. *Degree requirements:* For master's, one foreign language, thesis or alternative; for doctorate, thesis/dissertation. *Entrance requirements:* For master's, GRE General Test, minimum GPA of 2.75, 3 letters of recommendation; for doctorate, GRE General Test, MA in art history or equivalent, minimum GPA of 3.0. Additional exam requirements/recommendations for international students: required—TOEFL. Electronic applications accepted. *Expenses:* Contact institution.

University of Illinois at Urbana-Champaign, Graduate College, College of Fine and Applied Arts, School of Art and Design, Program in Design and Media, Champaign, IL 61820. Offers art and design (MFA), including new media; graphic design (MFA); industrial design (MFA). *Accreditation:* NASAD.

University of Illinois at Urbana-Champaign, Graduate College, College of Fine and Applied Arts, School of Art and Design, Program in Studio Arts, Champaign, IL 61820. Offers art and design (MFA); crafts (MFA); metals (MFA); painting (MFA); photography (MFA); sculpture (MFA). *Accreditation:* NASAD. *Entrance requirements:* For master's, minimum GPA of 3.0.

University of Indianapolis, Graduate Programs, Shaheen College of Arts and Sciences, Department of Art, Indianapolis, IN 46227-3697. Offers MA. *Accreditation:* NASAD. *Program availability:* Part-time, evening/weekend. *Entrance requirements:* For master's, GRE Subject Test, 3 letters of recommendation, portfolio. Additional exam requirements/recommendations for international students: required—TOEFL.

The University of Iowa, Graduate College, College of Liberal Arts and Sciences, School of Art and Art History, Program in Art, Iowa City, IA 52242-1316. Offers MA, MFA. *Faculty:* 18 full-time (8 women), 17 part-time/adjunct (10 women). *Students:* 54 full-time (29 women), 5 part-time (3 women); includes 12 minority (5 Black or African American, non-Hispanic/Latino; 3 Asian, non-Hispanic/Latino; 1 Hispanic/Latino; 3 Two or more races, non-Hispanic/Latino), 8 international. Average age 31. 137 applicants, 33% accepted, 39 enrolled. In 2019, 42 master's awarded. *Degree requirements:* For master's, thesis (for some programs), final exam and thesis. *Entrance requirements:* For master's, portfolio. Additional exam requirements/recommendations for international students: required—TOEFL (minimum score 550 paper-based; 81 iBT). *Application deadline:* For fall admission, 2/1 for domestic and international students. Application fee: $60 ($100 for international students). Electronic applications accepted. *Financial support:* In 2019–20, 59 students received support, including 4 fellowships with full and partial tuition reimbursements available (averaging $18,500 per year), 2 research assistantships with full and partial tuition reimbursements available (averaging $9,618 per year), 53 teaching assistantships with full and partial tuition reimbursements available (averaging $9,618 per year); career-related internships or fieldwork, Federal Work-Study, institutionally sponsored loans, scholarships/grants, health care benefits, and unspecified assistantships also available. Support available to part-time students. Financial award application deadline: 2/1. *Unit head:* Prof. Isabel Barbuzza, Director of Graduate Studies, 319-335-1789, E-mail: art@uiowa.edu. *Application contact:* Laura Jorgensen, Graduate Program Coordinator, 319-335-1758, E-mail: art@uiowa.edu.
Website: https://art.uiowa.edu/

The University of Kansas, Graduate Studies, College of Liberal Arts and Sciences, Department of English, Lawrence, KS 66045. Offers creative writing (MFA), including fine arts/creative writing; English (MA, PhD). *Program availability:* Part-time. *Students:* 80 full-time (54 women), 2 part-time (1 woman); includes 21 minority (7 Black or African American, non-Hispanic/Latino; 4 Asian, non-Hispanic/Latino; 6 Hispanic/Latino; 4 Two or more races, non-Hispanic/Latino), 9 international. Average age 31. 186 applicants, 10% accepted, 12 enrolled. In 2019, 13 master's, 12 doctorates awarded. *Entrance requirements:* For master's and doctorate, GRE General Test, two examples of academic writing; resume; statement of approximately 500 words describing interests, training, experience (including teaching experience), academic ability, and goals; three letters of recommendation; official transcripts. Additional exam requirements/recommendations for international students: required—TOEFL, IELTS, TOEFL or IELTS. *Application deadline:* For fall admission, 12/31 for domestic and international students. Application fee: $65 ($85 for international students). Electronic applications accepted. *Expenses:* Tuition, state resident: full-time $9989. Tuition, nonresident: full-time $23,950. *International tuition:* $23,950 full-time. *Required fees:* $984; $81.99 per credit hour. Tuition and fees vary according to course load, campus/location and program. *Financial support:* Fellowships, research assistantships, teaching assistantships, and unspecified assistantships available. *Unit head:* Kathryn Conrad, Chair, 785-864-2572, E-mail: kconrad@ku.edu. *Application contact:* Mary Strickell, Graduate Admissions Contact, 785-864-9438, E-mail: maryj@ku.edu.
Website: http://www.english.ku.edu

The University of Kansas, Graduate Studies, College of Liberal Arts and Sciences, Department of Visual Art, Program in Visual Art Education, Lawrence, KS 66045. Offers MA. *Program availability:* Part-time. *Students:* 3 full-time (2 women), 4 part-time (3 women). Average age 33. 4 applicants, 75% accepted, 1 enrolled. In 2019, 2 master's awarded. *Entrance requirements:* For master's, portfolio, 3 letters of recommendation, minimum GPA of 3.0. Additional exam requirements/recommendations for international students: required—TOEFL, IELTS, TOEFL (minimum score 570 paper-based) or IELTS (minimum score 6.5). *Application deadline:* For fall admission, 5/1 for domestic and international students; for spring admission, 12/1 for domestic and international students. Application fee: $65 ($85 for international students). Electronic applications accepted. *Expenses:* Tuition, state resident: full-time $9989. Tuition, nonresident: full-time $23,950. *International tuition:* $23,950 full-time. *Required fees:* $984; $81.99 per credit hour. Tuition and fees vary according to course load, campus/location and program. *Financial support:* Teaching assistantships, Federal Work-Study, scholarships/grants, and unspecified assistantships available. *Unit head:* Marshall Maude, Associate Chair, E-mail: maude@ku.edu. *Application contact:* Julia Reilly, Graduate Admissions Contact, 785-864-9488, E-mail: juliareilly@ku.edu.
Website: http://art.ku.edu/programs/visual_art_education/

University of Kentucky, Graduate School, College of Fine Arts, Program in Art Studio, Lexington, KY 40506-0032. Offers MFA. *Accreditation:* NASAD. *Degree requirements:* For master's, comprehensive exam. *Entrance requirements:* For master's, GRE General Test, minimum undergraduate GPA of 2.75. Additional exam requirements/recommendations for international students: required—TOEFL (minimum score 550 paper-based). Electronic applications accepted.

University of Lethbridge, School of Graduate Studies, Lethbridge, AB T1K 3M4, Canada. Offers addictions counseling (M Sc); agricultural biotechnology (M Sc); agricultural studies (M Sc, MA); anthropology (MA); archaeology (M Sc, MA); art (MA, MFA); biochemistry (M Sc); biological sciences (M Sc); biomolecular science (PhD); biosystems and biodiversity (PhD); Canadian studies (MA); chemistry (M Sc); computer science (M Sc); computer science and geographical information science (M Sc); counseling (MC); counseling psychology (M Ed); dramatic arts (MA); earth, space, and physical science (PhD); economics (MA); education (MA, PhD); educational leadership (M Ed); English (MA); environmental science (M Sc); evolution and behavior (PhD); exercise science (M Sc); French (MA); French/German (MA); French/Spanish (MA); general education (M Ed); geography (M Sc, MA); German (MA); health sciences (M Sc); individualized multidisciplinary (M Sc, MA); kinesiology (M Sc, MA); management (M Sc), including accounting, finance, human resource management and labor relations, information systems, international management, marketing, policy and strategy; mathematics (M Sc); music (M Mus, MA); Native American studies (MA); neuroscience (M Sc, PhD); new media (MA, MFA); nursing (M Sc, MN); philosophy (MA); physics (M Sc); political science (MA); psychology (M Sc, MA); religious studies (MA); sociology (MA); theatre and dramatic arts (MFA); theoretical and computational science (PhD); urban and regional studies (MA); women and gender studies (MA). *Program availability:* Part-time, evening/weekend. *Degree requirements:* For master's, thesis (for some programs); for doctorate, comprehensive exam, thesis/dissertation. *Entrance requirements:* For master's, GMAT (for M Sc in management), bachelor's degree in related field, minimum GPA of 3.0 during previous 20 graded semester courses, 2 years' teaching or related experience (M Ed); for doctorate, master's degree, minimum graduate GPA of 3.5. Additional exam requirements/recommendations for international students: required—TOEFL (minimum score 580 paper-based; 93 iBT). Electronic applications accepted.

University of Maine, Graduate School, Intermedia Program, Orono, ME 04469. Offers MFA. *Accreditation:* NASAD. *Faculty:* 9 full-time (4 women), 4 part-time/adjunct (3 women). *Students:* 23 full-time (12 women), 3 part-time (all women); includes 3 minority (1 American Indian or Alaska Native, non-Hispanic/Latino; 1 Hispanic/Latino; 1 Two or more races, non-Hispanic/Latino), 3 international. Average age 39. 14 applicants, 100%

accepted, 11 enrolled. In 2019, 4 master's awarded. Terminal master's awarded for partial completion of doctoral program. *Degree requirements:* For master's, comprehensive exam, thesis. *Entrance requirements:* For master's, portfolio. Additional exam requirements/recommendations for international students: required—TOEFL. Application fee: $65. *Expenses: Tuition, area resident:* Full-time $8100; part-time $450 per credit hour. Tuition, state resident: full-time $8100; part-time $450 per credit hour. Tuition, nonresident: full-time $26,388; part-time $1466 per credit hour. *International tuition:* $26,388 full-time. *Required fees:* $1257; $278 per semester. Tuition and fees vary according to course load. *Financial support:* In 2019–20, 23 students received support, including 1 research assistantship with full tuition reimbursement available (averaging $8,000 per year), 6 teaching assistantships with full tuition reimbursements available (averaging $15,825 per year); Federal Work-Study, scholarships/grants, health care benefits, and unspecified assistantships also available. Financial award application deadline: 3/1; financial award applicants required to submit FAFSA. *Unit head:* Dr. Owen Smith, Director, 207-581-4389, E-mail: owen.smith@umit.maine.edu. *Application contact:* Scott G. Delcourt, Assistant Vice President for Graduate Studies and Senior Associate Dean, 207-581-3291, Fax: 207-581-3232, E-mail: graduate@maine.edu.
Website: http://intermediamfa.org

The University of Manchester, School of Arts, Languages and Cultures, Manchester, United Kingdom. Offers anthropology, media and performance (PhD); applied theatre (PhD); Arab world studies (PhD); archaeology (PhD); art history and visual studies (PhD); arts and cultural management (PhD); arts management and cultural policy (PhD); Chinese studies (PhD); classics and ancient history (PhD); composition (PhD); creative writing (PhD); drama (PhD); East Asian studies (PhD); electroacoustic composition (PhD); English and American studies (PhD); English language (PhD); French studies (PhD); German studies (PhD); history (PhD); humanitarianism and conflict response (PhD); interpreting studies (PhD); Japanese studies (PhD); Latin American cultural studies (PhD); linguistics (PhD); Middle Eastern studies (PhD); museology (PhD); museum practice (PhD); music (PhD); musicology (PhD); Polish studies (PhD); Portuguese studies (PhD); religions and theology (PhD); Russian studies (PhD); Spanish studies (PhD); translation and intercultural studies (PhD).

The University of Manchester, School of Materials, Manchester, United Kingdom. Offers advanced aerospace materials engineering (M Sc); advanced metallic systems (PhD); biomedical materials (M Phil, M Sc, PhD); ceramics and glass (M Phil, M Sc, PhD); composite materials (M Sc, PhD); corrosion and protection (M Phil, M Sc, PhD); materials (M Phil, PhD); metallic materials (M Phil, M Sc, PhD); nanostructural materials (M Phil, M Sc, PhD); paper science (M Phil, M Sc, PhD); polymer science and engineering (M Phil, M Sc, PhD); technical textiles (M Sc); textile design, fashion and management (M Phil, M Sc, PhD); textile science and technology (M Phil, M Sc, PhD); textiles (M Phil, PhD); textiles and fashion (M Ent).

University of Maryland, College Park, Academic Affairs, College of Arts and Humanities, Department of Art, College Park, MD 20742. Offers MFA. *Degree requirements:* For master's, thesis, oral defense. *Entrance requirements:* For master's, minimum GPA of 3.0, portfolio, 20 digital images, 3 letters of recommendation. Electronic applications accepted.

University of Massachusetts Amherst, Graduate School, College of Humanities and Fine Arts, Department of Art, Amherst, MA 01003. Offers art (MA, MFA), including art education (MA), studio art (MFA). *Program availability:* Part-time. *Degree requirements:* For master's, comprehensive exam (for some programs), thesis (for some programs). *Entrance requirements:* For master's, portfolio. Additional exam requirements/recommendations for international students: required—TOEFL (minimum score 550 paper-based; 80 iBT), IELTS (minimum score 6.5). Electronic applications accepted.

University of Massachusetts Dartmouth, Graduate School, College of Visual and Performing Arts, Department of Art and Design, North Dartmouth, MA 02747-2300. Offers artisanry (MFA, Postbaccalaureate Certificate); fine arts (MFA, Postbaccalaureate Certificate); visual design (MFA). *Accreditation:* NASAD. *Program availability:* Part-time. *Faculty:* 33 full-time (16 women), 12 part-time/adjunct (8 women). *Students:* 25 full-time (20 women), 8 part-time (5 women); includes 5 minority (1 Asian, non-Hispanic/Latino; 3 Hispanic/Latino; 1 Two or more races, non-Hispanic/Latino), 6 international. Average age 33. 82 applicants, 51% accepted, 12 enrolled. In 2019, 10 master's awarded. *Degree requirements:* For master's, thesis, visual and written thesis. *Entrance requirements:* For master's, statement of purpose (minimum of 300 words), resume, 2 letters of recommendation, official transcripts, portfolio (20 images) representing applicant's art work, process of thinking, implementation of concepts and studio production; for Postbaccalaureate Certificate, statement of purpose (minimum of 300 words), resume, 3 letters of recommendation, official transcripts, portfolio (10 images representing applicant's art work, process of thinking, implementation of concepts and studio production). Additional exam requirements/recommendations for international students: required—TOEFL (minimum score 533 paper-based; 72 iBT). *Application deadline:* For fall admission, 8/15 for domestic students, 7/15 for international students; for spring admission, 10/15 for domestic students, 9/15 for international students. Application fee: $60. Electronic applications accepted. *Expenses: Tuition, area resident:* Full-time $16,390; part-time $682.92 per credit. Tuition, state resident: full-time $16,390; part-time $682.92 per credit. Tuition, nonresident: full-time $29,578; part-time $1232.42 per credit. *Required fees:* $575. *Financial support:* Application deadline: 3/1; applicants required to submit FAFSA. *Unit head:* Thomas Stubblefield, Interim Associate Dean of College and Visual and Performing Arts, 508-999-8565, E-mail: tstubblefield@umassd.edu. *Application contact:* Scott Webster, Director of Graduate Studies and Admissions, 508-999-8604, Fax: 508-999-8183, E-mail: graduate@umassd.edu.
Website: http://www.umassd.edu/cvpa/programs

University of Memphis, Graduate School, College of Communication and Fine Arts, Department of Art, Memphis, TN 38152. Offers art history (MA), including Egyptian art and archaeology, general art history; ceramics (MFA); graphic design (MFA); museum studies (Graduate Certificate); painting (MFA); printmaking/photography (MFA); sculpture (MFA). *Accreditation:* NASAD (one or more programs are accredited). *Program availability:* Part-time. *Students:* 28 full-time (21 women), 5 part-time (4 women); includes 9 minority (3 Black or African American, non-Hispanic/Latino; 1 Asian, non-Hispanic/Latino; 3 Hispanic/Latino; 2 Two or more races, non-Hispanic/Latino), 2 international. Average age 30. 36 applicants, 69% accepted, 13 enrolled. In 2019, 11 master's, 4 other advanced degrees awarded. *Degree requirements:* For master's, variable foreign language requirement, comprehensive exam, thesis, image identification exam, qualifying exam; for Graduate Certificate, internship. *Entrance requirements:* For master's, GRE General Test or MAT, portfolio (MFA), letter of intent, sample of undergraduate writing, two letters of recommendation; for Graduate Certificate, three letters of recommendation, letter of intent. *Application deadline:* For fall admission, 2/15 for domestic students; for spring admission, 11/1 for domestic students. Applications are processed on a rolling basis. Application fee: $35 ($60 for international students). *Expenses: Tuition, area resident:* Full-time $9216; part-time $512 per credit hour. Tuition, state resident: full-time $9216; part-time $512 per credit hour. Tuition, nonresident: full-time $12,672; part-time $704 per credit hour. *International tuition:* $16,128 full-time. *Required fees:* $1530; $85 per credit hour. Tuition and fees vary according to program. *Financial support:* Research assistantships with full tuition reimbursements, teaching assistantships with full tuition reimbursements, Federal Work-Study, scholarships/grants, and unspecified assistantships available. Financial award application deadline: 2/1; financial award applicants required to submit FAFSA. *Unit head:* Richard Lou, Chair, 901-678-2217, Fax: 901-678-2735, E-mail: ralou@memphis.edu. *Application contact:* Richard Lou, Chair, 901-678-2217, Fax: 901-678-2735, E-mail: ralou@memphis.edu.
Website: http://memphis.edu/art/

University of Miami, Graduate School, College of Arts and Sciences, Department of Art and Art History, Coral Gables, FL 33124. Offers art history (MA); ceramics/glass (MFA); graphic design/multimedia (MFA); painting (MFA); photography/digital imaging (MFA); printmaking (MFA); sculpture (MFA). *Program availability:* Part-time. *Degree requirements:* For master's, variable foreign language requirement, thesis, exhibit (MFA), comprehensive exam (MA). *Entrance requirements:* For master's, GRE General Test (MA), research paper (MA), slide portfolio (MFA). Additional exam requirements/recommendations for international students: required—TOEFL. Electronic applications accepted.

University of Michigan, Rackham Graduate School, Penny W. Stamps School of Art and Design, Ann Arbor, MI 48109. Offers art and design (MFA); integrative design (M Des). *Accreditation:* NASAD. *Degree requirements:* For master's, thesis, exhibit (MFA), slide lecture. *Entrance requirements:* For master's, portfolio. Additional exam requirements/recommendations for international students: required—TOEFL (minimum score 560 paper-based; 84 iBT), IELTS (minimum score 6.5). Electronic applications accepted.

University of Michigan–Flint, Graduate Programs, Program in Arts Administration, Flint, MI 48502-1950. Offers performance (MA), including museum and visual arts, performance. *Program availability:* Part-time. *Faculty:* 7 full-time (3 women), 11 part-time/adjunct (7 women). *Students:* 11 part-time (7 women); includes 5 minority (4 Black or African American, non-Hispanic/Latino; 1 Asian, non-Hispanic/Latino). Average age 40. 11 applicants, 82% accepted, 2 enrolled. In 2019, 2 master's awarded. *Degree requirements:* For master's, thesis. *Entrance requirements:* For master's, bachelor degree in the arts (visual art, theatre, dance, music, etc.) from regionally-accredited institution; minimum cumulative undergraduate GPA of 3.0 on 4.0 scale. Additional exam requirements/recommendations for international students: required—TOEFL (minimum score 84 iBT), IELTS (minimum score 6.5). *Application deadline:* For fall admission, 8/1 for domestic students, 5/1 for international students; for winter admission, 11/15 for domestic students, 10/1 for international students. Applications are processed on a rolling basis. Application fee: $55. Electronic applications accepted. *Expenses:* Contact institution. *Financial support:* Federal Work-Study, institutionally sponsored loans, scholarships/grants, and unspecified assistantships available. Support available to part-time students. Financial award application deadline: 3/1; financial award applicants required to submit FAFSA. *Unit head:* Nicole Broughton, Director, 810-237-6522, E-mail: broughn@umflint.edu. *Application contact:* Matt Bohlen, Associate Director of Graduate Admissions, 810-762-3171, Fax: 810-766-6789, E-mail: mbohlen@umflint.edu.
Website: http://www.umflint.edu/graduateprograms/arts-administration-ma

University of Minnesota, Duluth, Graduate School, School of Fine Arts, Department of Art and Design, Duluth, MN 55812-2496. Offers graphic design (MFA). *Accreditation:* NASAD. *Program availability:* Part-time. *Degree requirements:* For master's, final exhibit, project, supporting paper. *Entrance requirements:* For master's, minimum GPA of 3.0, writing sample, slide portfolio. Additional exam requirements/recommendations for international students: required—TOEFL (minimum score 550 paper-based).

University of Minnesota, Twin Cities Campus, Graduate School, College of Liberal Arts, Department of Art, Minneapolis, MN 55455. Offers MFA. *Degree requirements:* For master's, oral exam, supporting paper, thesis exhibit. *Entrance requirements:* For master's, portfolio, letters of recommendation, minimum GPA of 3.0. Additional exam requirements/recommendations for international students: required—TOEFL (minimum score 550 paper-based; 79 iBT); recommended—IELTS (minimum score 6.5). Electronic applications accepted.

University of Mississippi, Graduate School, College of Liberal Arts, University, MS 38677. Offers anthropology (MA); biology (MS, PhD); chemistry (MS, DA, PhD); creative writing (MFA); documentary expression (MFA); economics (MA, PhD); English (MA, PhD); experimental psychology (PhD); history (MA, PhD); mathematics (MS, PhD); modern languages (MA); music (MM); philosophy (MA); physics (MA, MS, PhD); political science (MA, PhD); Southern studies (MA); studio art (MFA). *Program availability:* Part-time. *Faculty:* 481 full-time (215 women), 71 part-time/adjunct (40 women). *Students:* 509 full-time (258 women), 55 part-time (21 women); includes 89 minority (40 Black or African American, non-Hispanic/Latino; 13 Asian, non-Hispanic/Latino; 25 Hispanic/Latino; 11 Two or more races, non-Hispanic/Latino), 157 international. Average age 29. In 2019, 119 master's, 51 doctorates awarded. *Degree requirements:* For doctorate, thesis/dissertation. *Entrance requirements:* For master's, GRE General Test, minimum GPA of 3.0; for doctorate, GRE General Test. Additional exam requirements/recommendations for international students: required—TOEFL. *Application deadline:* Applications are processed on a rolling basis. Application fee: $50. Electronic applications accepted. *Expenses:* Tuition, state resident: full-time $8718; part-time $484.25 per credit hour. Tuition, nonresident: full-time $24,990; part-time $1388.25 per credit hour. *Required fees:* $100; $4.16 per credit hour. *Financial support:* Fellowships, research assistantships, teaching assistantships, career-related internships or fieldwork, Federal Work-Study, institutionally sponsored loans, scholarships/grants, and unspecified assistantships available. Financial award application deadline: 3/1; financial award applicants required to submit FAFSA. *Unit head:* Dr. Lee Michael Cohen, Dean, 662-915-7177, Fax: 662-915-5792, E-mail: libarts@olemiss.edu. *Application contact:* Tameka Smith, Graduate Activities Specialist for Admissions, 662-915-7474, Fax: 662-915-7577, E-mail: gschool@olemiss.edu.
Website: ventress@olemiss.edu

University of Missouri, Office of Research and Graduate Studies, College of Arts and Science, Department of Art, Columbia, MO 65211. Offers MFA. *Entrance requirements:* For master's, GRE General Test, minimum GPA of 3.0.

University of Missouri–Kansas City, College of Arts and Sciences, Department of Art and Art History, Kansas City, MO 64110-2499. Offers MA, PhD. *Program availability:* Part-time. Terminal master's awarded for partial completion of doctoral program. *Degree requirements:* For master's, thesis, qualifying exam; for doctorate, thesis/dissertation, exams. *Entrance requirements:* For master's, good general education in the humanities. Additional exam requirements/recommendations for international students: required—TOEFL (minimum score 550 paper-based; 80 iBT). Electronic applications accepted.

University of Montana, Graduate School, College of Visual and Performing Arts, School of Art, Missoula, MT 59812. Offers fine arts (MA), including art, art history; photography (MFA). *Accreditation:* NASAD (one or more programs are accredited).

Degree requirements: For master's, thesis exhibit. *Entrance requirements:* For master's, GRE General Test, portfolio.

University of Nebraska at Omaha, Graduate Studies, College of Communication, Fine Arts and Media, School of the Arts, Omaha, NE 68182. Offers MA. *Accreditation:* NASAD. *Program availability:* Part-time. *Degree requirements:* For master's, comprehensive exam, thesis (for some programs). *Entrance requirements:* For master's, minimum GPA of 3.0, statement of purpose, writing sample, 2 letters of recommendation, transcripts. Additional exam requirements/recommendations for international students: required—TOEFL, IELTS, PTE. Electronic applications accepted.

University of Nebraska–Lincoln, Graduate College, College of Fine and Performing Arts, Department of Art and Art History, Lincoln, NE 68588. Offers art history (MA); studio art (MFA). *Accreditation:* NASAD. *Degree requirements:* For master's, thesis. *Entrance requirements:* For master's, slide portfolio. Additional exam requirements/recommendations for international students: required—TOEFL (minimum score 550 paper-based). Electronic applications accepted.

University of Nevada, Las Vegas, Graduate College, College of Fine Arts, Department of Art, Las Vegas, NV 89154-5013. Offers MFA. *Accreditation:* NASAD. *Program availability:* Part-time. *Faculty:* 7 full-time (1 woman), 4 part-time/adjunct (3 women). *Students:* 12 full-time (7 women); includes 5 minority (2 American Indian or Alaska Native, non-Hispanic/Latino; 3 Hispanic/Latino), 1 international. Average age 38. 28 applicants, 29% accepted, 7 enrolled. In 2019, 6 master's awarded. *Degree requirements:* For master's, thesis. *Entrance requirements:* For master's, bachelor's degree, 20 slides of work. Additional exam requirements/recommendations for international students: required—TOEFL (minimum score 550 paper-based; 80 iBT), IELTS (minimum score 7). *Application deadline:* For fall admission, 2/1 for domestic and international students. Application fee: $60 ($95 for international students). Electronic applications accepted. *Expenses:* Contact institution. *Financial support:* In 2019–20, 9 students received support, including 9 research assistantships with full tuition reimbursements available (averaging $15,000 per year), 3 teaching assistantships with full tuition reimbursements available (averaging $15,000 per year); institutionally sponsored loans, scholarships/grants, health care benefits, and unspecified assistantships also available. Financial award application deadline: 3/15; financial award applicants required to submit FAFSA. *Unit head:* Dr. Marcus Civin, Chair/Professor, 702-895-3237, Fax: 702-895-4346, E-mail: art.chair@unlv.edu. *Application contact:* Wendy Kveck, Graduate Coordinator, 702-895-4346, E-mail: art.gradcoord@unlv.edu. Website: http://art.unlv.edu/

University of Nevada, Reno, Graduate School, College of Liberal Arts, Program in Fine Arts, Reno, NV 89557. Offers MFA. *Degree requirements:* For master's, thesis optional. *Entrance requirements:* For master's, minimum GPA of 2.75. Additional exam requirements/recommendations for international students: required—TOEFL (minimum score 500 paper-based; 61 iBT), IELTS (minimum score 6). Electronic applications accepted.

University of New Mexico, Graduate Studies, College of Fine Arts, Program in Studio Art, Albuquerque, NM 87131-2039. Offers MFA. *Degree requirements:* For master's, comprehensive exam, thesis or alternative, studio reviews, qualifying exams. *Entrance requirements:* Additional exam requirements/recommendations for international students: required—TOEFL (minimum score 550 paper-based), IELTS (minimum score 6). Electronic applications accepted. *Expenses:* Tuition, state resident: full-time $7633; part-time $972 per year. Tuition, nonresident: full-time $22,586; part-time $3840 per year. *International tuition:* $23,292 full-time. *Required fees:* $8608. Tuition and fees vary according to course level, course load, degree level, program and student level.

University of New Orleans, Graduate School, College of Liberal Arts, Education and Human Development, Department of Fine Arts, New Orleans, LA 70148. Offers MFA. *Accreditation:* NASAD. *Degree requirements:* For master's, thesis. *Entrance requirements:* For master's, GRE General Test, slide review. Additional exam requirements/recommendations for international students: required—TOEFL (minimum score 550 paper-based; 79 iBT), IELTS (minimum score 6.5). Electronic applications accepted.

The University of North Carolina at Chapel Hill, Graduate School, College of Arts and Sciences, Department of Art, Studio Art Program, Chapel Hill, NC 27599. Offers MFA. *Degree requirements:* For master's, variable foreign language requirement. *Entrance requirements:* For master's, minimum GPA of 3.0, portfolio. Electronic applications accepted.

The University of North Carolina at Greensboro, Graduate School, College of Arts and Sciences, Department of Art, Greensboro, NC 27412-5001. Offers studio arts (MFA). *Degree requirements:* For master's, thesis (for some programs). *Entrance requirements:* For master's, GRE General Test, 39 hours of course work in studio art, 15 hours of course work in art history, portfolio. Additional exam requirements/recommendations for international students: required—TOEFL. Electronic applications accepted.

University of North Dakota, Graduate School, College of Arts and Sciences, Department of Visual Arts, Grand Forks, ND 58202. Offers MFA. *Accreditation:* NASAD. *Degree requirements:* For master's, thesis or alternative, comprehensive evaluation, professional exhibition. *Entrance requirements:* For master's, minimum GPA of 3.0. Additional exam requirements/recommendations for international students: required—TOEFL (minimum score 550 paper-based; 79 iBT), IELTS (minimum score 6.5). Electronic applications accepted.

University of Northern Colorado, Graduate School, College of Performing and Visual Arts, School of Art and Design, Greeley, CO 80639. Offers art education (MA); art history (MA); studio art (MA). *Accreditation:* NASAD. *Program availability:* Part-time. *Degree requirements:* For master's, comprehensive exam, thesis. *Entrance requirements:* For master's, GRE General Test, portfolio, 3 letters of recommendation, minimum undergraduate GPA of 3.0. Electronic applications accepted.

University of Northern Iowa, Graduate College, College of Humanities, Arts and Sciences, Department of Art, Cedar Falls, IA 50614. Offers art education (MA). *Program availability:* Part-time, evening/weekend. *Degree requirements:* For master's, comprehensive exam (for some programs), thesis or alternative. *Entrance requirements:* For master's, minimum GPA of 3.0, portfolio. Additional exam requirements/recommendations for international students: required—TOEFL (minimum score 500 paper-based; 61 iBT). Electronic applications accepted.

University of North Texas, Toulouse Graduate School, Denton, TX 76203-5459. Offers accounting (MS); applied anthropology (MA, MS); applied behavior analysis (Certificate); applied geography (MA); applied technology and performance improvement (M Ed, MS); art education (MA); art history (MA); arts leadership (Certificate); audiology (Au D); behavior analysis (MS); behavioral science (PhD); biochemistry and molecular biology (MS); biology (MA, MS); biomedical engineering (MS); business analysis (MS); chemistry (MS); clinical health psychology (PhD); communication studies (MA, MS); computer engineering (MS); computer science (MS); counseling (M Ed, MS), including clinical mental health counseling (MS), college and university counseling, elementary school counseling, secondary school counseling;

creative writing (MA); criminal justice (MS); curriculum and instruction (M Ed); decision sciences (MBA); design (MA, MFA), including fashion design (MFA), innovation studies, interior design (MFA); early childhood studies (MS); economics (MS); educational leadership (M Ed, Ed D); educational psychology (MS, PhD), including family studies (MS), gifted and talented (MS), human development (MS), learning and cognition (MS), research, measurement and evaluation (MS); electrical engineering (MS); emergency management (MPA); engineering technology (MS); English (MA); English as a second language (MA); environmental science (MS); finance (MBA, MS); financial management (MPA); French (MA); health services management (MBA); higher education (M Ed, Ed D); history (MA, MS); hospitality management (MS); human resources management (MPA); information science (MS); information systems (PhD); information technologies (MBA); interdisciplinary studies (MA, MS); international studies (MA); international sustainable tourism (MS); jazz studies (MM); journalism (MA, MJ, Graduate Certificate), including interactive and virtual digital communication (Graduate Certificate), narrative journalism (Graduate Certificate), public relations (Graduate Certificate); kinesiology (MS); linguistics (MA); local government management (MPA); logistics (PhD); logistics and supply chain management (MBA); long-term care, senior housing, and aging services (MA); management (PhD); marketing (MBA); mathematics (MA, MS); mechanical and energy engineering (MS, PhD); music (MA), including ethnomusicology, music theory, musicology, performance; music composition (PhD); music education (MM Ed, PhD); nonprofit management (MPA); operations and supply chain management (MBA); performance (MM, DMA); philosophy (MA); political science (MA); professional and technical communication (MA); radio, television and film (MA, MFA); rehabilitation counseling (Certificate); sociology (MA); Spanish (MA); special education (M Ed); speech-language pathology (MA); strategic management (MBA); studio art (MFA); teaching (M Ed); MBA/MS. *Program availability:* Part-time, evening/weekend, online learning. Terminal master's awarded for partial completion of doctoral program. *Degree requirements:* For master's, variable foreign language requirement, comprehensive exam (for some programs), thesis (for some programs); for doctorate, variable foreign language requirement, comprehensive exam (for some programs), thesis/dissertation; for other advanced degree, variable foreign language requirement, comprehensive exam (for some programs). *Entrance requirements:* For master's and doctorate, GRE, GMAT. Additional exam requirements/recommendations for international students: required—TOEFL (minimum score 550 paper-based; 79 iBT). Electronic applications accepted.

University of Notre Dame, The Graduate School, College of Arts and Letters, Department of Art, Art History, and Design, Notre Dame, IN 46556. Offers art history (MA); design (MFA), including graphic design, industrial design; studio art (MFA), including ceramics, painting, photography, printmaking, sculpture. *Accreditation:* NASAD. *Degree requirements:* For master's, comprehensive exam (for some programs), thesis. *Entrance requirements:* For master's, GRE General Test, minimum GPA of 3.0. Additional exam requirements/recommendations for international students: required—TOEFL (minimum score 600 paper-based; 80 iBT). Electronic applications accepted.

University of Oklahoma, Weitzenhoffer Family College of Fine Arts, School of Visual Arts, Norman, OK 73019. Offers art (MFA), including art and technology, ceramics, film, painting, photography, printmaking, sculpture, video, visual communication; art history (MA, PhD), including art history (MA), art of the American West (PhD), Native American art (PhD); design (MFA). *Degree requirements:* For master's, 2 foreign languages, comprehensive exam (for some programs), thesis (for some programs); for doctorate, 2 foreign languages, comprehensive exam, thesis/dissertation. *Entrance requirements:* For master's and doctorate, GRE. Additional exam requirements/recommendations for international students: required—TOEFL (minimum score 79 iBT) or IELTS (minimum score 6.5). Electronic applications accepted. *Expenses:* Tuition, state resident: full-time $6583.20; part-time $274.30 per credit hour. Tuition, nonresident: full-time $21,242; part-time $885.10 per credit hour. *International tuition:* $21,242.40 full-time. *Required fees:* $1994.20; $72.55 per credit hour. $126.50 per semester. Tuition and fees vary according to course load and degree level.

University of Oregon, Graduate School, College of Design, Department of Art, Eugene, OR 97403. Offers MFA. *Accreditation:* NASAD. *Degree requirements:* For master's, thesis or alternative. *Entrance requirements:* For master's, BFA or equivalent. Additional exam requirements/recommendations for international students: required—TOEFL.

University of Pennsylvania, Stuart Weitzman School of Design, Department of Fine Arts, Philadelphia, PA 19104. Offers emerging design and research (Certificate); fine arts (MFA); time-based and interactive media (Certificate). *Faculty:* 7 full-time (3 women), 1 part-time/adjunct (0 women). *Students:* 34 full-time (19 women), 1 (woman) part-time; includes 11 minority (3 Black or African American, non-Hispanic/Latino; 2 Asian, non-Hispanic/Latino; 4 Hispanic/Latino; 2 Two or more races, non-Hispanic/Latino), 10 international. Average age 27. 88 applicants, 48% accepted, 17 enrolled. In 2019, 11 master's, 3 other advanced degrees awarded. *Application deadline:* Applications are processed on a rolling basis. Application fee: $80. Electronic applications accepted. *Financial support:* In 2019–20, 30 students received support, including teaching assistantships (averaging $6,000 per year); fellowships with full tuition reimbursements available, research assistantships, Federal Work-Study, scholarships/grants, health care benefits, and unspecified assistantships also available. Financial award applicants required to submit FAFSA. *Application contact:* Joan Weston, Director of Admissions & Financial Aid, 215-898-6520, E-mail: weston@design.upenn.edu. Website: http://www.design.upenn.edu/mfa

University of Regina, Faculty of Graduate Studies and Research, Faculty of Media, Art, and Performance, Department of Visual Arts, Regina, SK S4S 0A2, Canada. Offers ceramics (MFA); drawing (MFA); interdisciplinary studies (MA, MFA); intermedia (MFA); painting (MFA); sculpture (MFA). *Program availability:* Part-time. *Faculty:* 11 full-time (6 women), 3 part-time/adjunct (1 woman). *Students:* 6 full-time (3 women), 3 part-time (2 women). Average age 30. 19 applicants, 11% accepted. In 2019, 2 master's awarded. *Degree requirements:* For master's, exhibition, support paper, oral defense. *Entrance requirements:* For master's, submit documentation (CD, DVD or URL's.) of recent work (20 images or equivalent) accompanied by a corresponding sheet indicating: (a) title of each work; (b) media; (c) date; (d) dimensions (if applicable). Other relevant documentation may be included. Additional exam requirements/recommendations for international students: required—TOEFL (minimum score 600 paper-based; 92 iBT), IELTS (minimum score 6.5), PTE (minimum score 65), other options are CAEL, MELAB, Cantest and U of R ESL. *Application deadline:* For fall admission, 1/15 for domestic and international students. Application fee: $100. Electronic applications accepted. *Expenses:* Tuition: Full-time $6684 Canadian dollars. *Required fees:* $100 Canadian dollars; $3351.45 Canadian dollars per trimester. $1117.15 Canadian dollars per semester. Tuition and fees vary according to course level, course load, degree level and program. *Financial support:* Fellowships, research assistantships, teaching assistantships, career-related internships or fieldwork, Federal Work-Study, scholarships/grants, unspecified assistantships, and travel award and Graduate Scholarship Base Funds available. Support available to part-time students. Financial award application deadline: 9/30. *Unit head:* Dr. Risa Horowitz, Department Head, 306-

585-5641, Fax: 306-585-5526, E-mail: risa.horowitz@uregina.ca. *Application contact:* Dr. Ruth Chambers, Graduate Coordinator, Visual Arts, 306-585-5575, Fax: 306-585-5526, E-mail: ruth.chambers@uregina.ca.

University of Rochester, School of Arts and Sciences, Department of Art and Art History, Rochester, NY 14627. Offers visual and cultural studies (PhD). *Faculty:* 11 full-time (6 women). *Students:* 29 full-time (18 women); includes 8 minority (2 Black or African American, non-Hispanic/Latino; 1 Asian, non-Hispanic/Latino; 4 Hispanic/Latino; 1 Two or more races, non-Hispanic/Latino), 11 international. Average age 31. 47 applicants, 19% accepted, 5 enrolled. In 2019, 1 doctorate awarded. Terminal master's awarded for partial completion of doctoral program. *Degree requirements:* For doctorate, thesis/dissertation, qualifying exam. *Entrance requirements:* For doctorate, GRE General Test, personal statement, three letters of recommendation, official undergraduate and graduate transcripts, writing sample. Additional exam requirements/recommendations for international students: required—TOEFL. *Application deadline:* For fall admission, 1/15 for domestic and international students. Application fee: $60. Electronic applications accepted. *Financial support:* Research assistantships, teaching assistantships with full tuition reimbursements, and tuition waivers (full) available. *Unit head:* Rachel Haidu, Associate Professor and Chair, 585-275-4112, E-mail: rachel.haidu@rochester.edu. *Application contact:* Martin Collier, Administrator, 585-275-7451, E-mail: marty.collier@rochester.edu.
Website: http://www.sas.rochester.edu/aah/graduate/index.html

University of Saint Francis, Graduate School, Division of Creative Arts, Fort Wayne, IN 46808-3994. Offers studio art (MA, MFA). *Accreditation:* NASAD. *Program availability:* Part-time, evening/weekend, blended/hybrid learning. *Faculty:* 1 (woman) full-time, 1 (woman) part-time/adjunct. *Students:* 3 full-time (1 woman). Average age 57. 6 applicants, 100% accepted. In 2019, 1 master's awarded. *Entrance requirements:* Additional exam requirements/recommendations for international students: required—TOEFL (minimum score 550 paper-based), IELTS (minimum score 6.5). *Application deadline:* Applications are processed on a rolling basis. Application fee: $0. Electronic applications accepted. *Expenses:* $650 per semester hour. *Financial support:* Applicants required to submit FAFSA. *Unit head:* Colleen Huddleson, Creative Arts Division Executive Director, 260-399-7700 Ext. 8004, E-mail: chuddleson@sf.edu. *Application contact:* Kyle Richardson, Associate Director of Enrollment Management, 260-399-7700 Ext. 6310, Fax: 260-399-8152, E-mail: krichardson@sf.edu.
Website: https://www.sf.edu/academics/school-of-creative-arts/

University of Saskatchewan, College of Graduate and Postdoctoral Studies, College of Arts and Science, Department of Art and Art History, Saskatoon, SK S7N 5A2, Canada. Offers studio (MFA). *Program availability:* Part-time. *Degree requirements:* For master's, thesis. *Entrance requirements:* Additional exam requirements/recommendations for international students: required—TOEFL (minimum score 80 iBT); recommended—IELTS (minimum score 6.5).

The University of Scranton, College of Arts and Sciences, Scranton, PA 18510. Offers MA, MS. *Program availability:* Part-time, evening/weekend, 100% online. *Degree requirements:* For master's, comprehensive exam (for some programs), thesis (for some programs), capstone experience. *Entrance requirements:* For master's, GMAT (for MBA), minimum GPA of 3.0, three letters of reference. Additional exam requirements/recommendations for international students: required—TOEFL (minimum score 500 paper-based; 80 iBT), IELTS (minimum score 6.5). Electronic applications accepted.

University of South Alabama, College of Arts and Sciences, Department of Visual Arts, Mobile, AL 36688-0002. Offers creative technologies and practice (MFA). *Faculty:* 8 full-time (4 women), 2 part-time/adjunct (both women). *Students:* 12 full-time (8 women); includes 1 minority (Black or African American, non-Hispanic/Latino). Average age 36. 5 applicants, 100% accepted, 4 enrolled. In 2019, 3 master's awarded. *Degree requirements:* For master's, thesis. *Entrance requirements:* Additional exam requirements/recommendations for international students: required—TOEFL (minimum score 525 paper-based; 71 iBT), IELTS (minimum score 6). *Application deadline:* For fall admission, 7/15 priority date for domestic students, 6/15 for international students. Applications are processed on a rolling basis. Application fee: $35. Electronic applications accepted. *Expenses: Tuition, area resident:* Part-time $442 per credit hour. Tuition, state resident: full-time $10,608; part-time $442 per credit hour. Tuition, nonresident: full-time $21,216; part-time $884 per credit hour. *Financial support:* In 2019–20, teaching assistantships with tuition reimbursements (averaging $8,000 per year) were awarded; fellowships, career-related internships or fieldwork, and unspecified assistantships also available. Financial award application deadline: 3/31; financial award applicants required to submit FAFSA. *Unit head:* Dr. Susan Fitzsimmons, Chairperson, 251-461-1438, E-mail: sgfitzsimmons@southalabama.edu. *Application contact:* Diane Gibbs, Graduate Coordinator, 251-461-1696, Fax: 251-461-1744, E-mail: dgibbs@southalabama.edu.
Website: http://www.southalabama.edu/colleges/artsandsci/art/

University of South Carolina, The Graduate School, College of Arts and Sciences, Department of Art, Columbia, SC 29208. Offers art education (IMA, MA, MAT); art history (MA); art studio (MA); media arts (MMA); studio art (MFA). *Accreditation:* NASAD. *Degree requirements:* For master's, comprehensive exam (for some programs), thesis (for some programs). *Entrance requirements:* For master's, GRE General Test or MAT, portfolio. Additional exam requirements/recommendations for international students: required—TOEFL. Electronic applications accepted.

University of South Dakota, Graduate School, College of Fine Arts, Department of Art, Vermillion, SD 57069. Offers art education (MFA); ceramics (MFA); graphic design (MFA); painting (MFA); photography (MFA); printmaking (MFA); sculpture (MFA). *Accreditation:* NASAD. *Degree requirements:* For master's, thesis or alternative. *Entrance requirements:* For master's, portfolio, minimum GPA of 2.7. Additional exam requirements/recommendations for international students: required—TOEFL (minimum score 550 paper-based; 79 iBT). Electronic applications accepted.

University of Southern California, Graduate School, Dana and David Dornsife College of Letters, Arts and Sciences, Department of Art History, Los Angeles, CA 90089. Offers art history (MA, PhD); visual studies (Graduate Certificate). *Degree requirements:* For doctorate, 2 foreign languages, comprehensive exam, thesis/dissertation, 60 units. *Entrance requirements:* For doctorate, GRE. Additional exam requirements/recommendations for international students: required—TOEFL.

University of Southern California, Graduate School, Roski School of Art and Design, Graduate Programs in Fine Arts, Los Angeles, CA 90089. Offers new genres (MFA); painting/drawing (MFA); photography (MFA); sculpture (MFA). *Degree requirements:* For master's, thesis. *Entrance requirements:* For master's, portfolio, artist statement, 3 letters of recommendation. Additional exam requirements/recommendations for international students: required—TOEFL (minimum score 600 paper-based; 100 iBT). Electronic applications accepted.

University of South Florida, College of The Arts, School of Art and Art History, Tampa, FL 33620-9951. Offers MA, MFA. *Accreditation:* NASAD. *Program availability:* Part-time. *Faculty:* 17 full-time (8 women). *Students:* 45 full-time (25 women), 1 (woman) part-time; includes 11 minority (1 Black or African American, non-Hispanic/Latino; 8 Hispanic/Latino; 2 Two or more races, non-Hispanic/Latino), 4 international. Average age 30. 69 applicants, 32% accepted, 20 enrolled. In 2019, 13 master's awarded. *Degree requirements:* For master's, comprehensive exam, thesis, exhibition (for MFA). *Entrance requirements:* For master's, GRE General Test, bachelor's degree from regionally-accredited institution with minimum GPA of 3.0; portfolio; goals statement (for MA in art history). Additional exam requirements/recommendations for international students: required—TOEFL, TOEFL (minimum score 550 paper-based; 79 iBT) or IELTS (minimum score 6.5). *Application deadline:* For fall admission, 1/15 priority date for domestic students, 2/1 for international students. Application fee: $30. Electronic applications accepted. *Financial support:* In 2019–20, 42 students received support, including 37 teaching assistantships with partial tuition reimbursements available (averaging $9,440 per year); scholarships/grants, health care benefits, and unspecified assistantships also available. Support available to part-time students. Financial award application deadline: 2/15; financial award applicants required to submit FAFSA. *Unit head:* Prof. Wallace Wilson, Director, 813-974-2360, Fax: 813-974-9226, E-mail: wwilson2@usf.edu. *Application contact:* Prof. Neil Bender, Associate Professor and Graduate Program Director, 813-974-2360, Fax: 813-974-9226, E-mail: nb2@usf.edu.
Website: http://www.art.usf.edu

The University of Tennessee, Graduate School, College of Arts and Sciences, School of Art, Knoxville, TN 37996. Offers ceramics (MFA); drawing (MFA); graphic design (MFA); inter-area studies (MFA); media arts (MFA); painting (MFA); printmaking (MFA); sculpture (MFA); watercolor (MFA). *Accreditation:* NASAD. *Degree requirements:* For master's, thesis or alternative, exhibit. *Entrance requirements:* For master's, portfolio, minimum GPA of 2.7. Additional exam requirements/recommendations for international students: required—TOEFL. Electronic applications accepted.

The University of Texas at Arlington, Graduate School, College of Liberal Arts, Department of Art and Art History, Arlington, TX 76019. Offers film and video (MFA); glass (MFA); intermedia (MFA); visual communication (MFA). *Accreditation:* NASAD. *Degree requirements:* For master's, thesis or alternative, mid- and final program reviews; exhibition. *Entrance requirements:* For master's, GRE, minimum GPA of 3.0, 3 letters of recommendation, portfolio, resume. Additional exam requirements/recommendations for international students: required—TOEFL (minimum score 550 paper-based). Electronic applications accepted.

The University of Texas at Austin, Graduate School, College of Fine Arts, Department of Art and Art History, Program in Studio Art, Austin, TX 78712-1111. Offers MFA. *Accreditation:* NASAD. *Degree requirements:* For master's, thesis, oral exam. *Entrance requirements:* For master's, minimum GPA of 3.0, portfolio of 15 slides. Electronic applications accepted.

The University of Texas at El Paso, Graduate School, College of Liberal Arts, Department of Art, El Paso, TX 79968-0001. Offers art education (MA); studio art (MA). *Program availability:* Part-time, evening/weekend. *Degree requirements:* For master's, thesis optional. *Entrance requirements:* For master's, minimum GPA of 3.0, digital portfolio, letters of recommendation. Additional exam requirements/recommendations for international students: required—TOEFL; recommended—IELTS. Electronic applications accepted.

The University of Texas at San Antonio, College of Liberal and Fine Arts, Department of Art and Art History, San Antonio, TX 78249-0617. Offers art (MFA); art history (MA). *Accreditation:* NASAD (one or more programs are accredited). *Entrance requirements:* For master's, GRE General Test, portfolio, minimum GPA of 3.0 in last 60 hours, 3 letters of recommendation, statement of purpose. Additional exam requirements/recommendations for international students: required—TOEFL (minimum score 550 paper-based; 79 iBT), IELTS (minimum score 6.5). Electronic applications accepted.

The University of Texas at Tyler, College of Arts and Sciences, Department of Art and Art History, Tyler, TX 75799-0001. Offers art history (MA); interdisciplinary (MAIS); studio art (MFA). *Faculty:* 5 full-time (4 women), 5 part-time/adjunct (4 women). *Students:* 12 full-time (9 women), 3 part-time (1 woman); includes 2 minority (1 Hispanic/Latino; 1 Two or more races, non-Hispanic/Latino). Average age 38. 3 applicants, 100% accepted, 2 enrolled. In 2019, 5 master's awarded. *Degree requirements:* For master's, thesis, graduate committee review. *Entrance requirements:* For master's, minimum GPA of 3.0. Additional exam requirements/recommendations for international students: required—TOEFL. *Application deadline:* For fall admission, 8/17 priority date for domestic students, 7/1 priority date for international students; for spring admission, 12/21 priority date for domestic students, 11/1 priority date for international students. Applications are processed on a rolling basis. Application fee: $25 ($50 for international students). *Financial support:* Application deadline: 7/1; applicants required to submit FAFSA. *Unit head:* Dr. Merrie Wright, Chair, 903-566-7423, Fax: 903-566-7062, E-mail: mewright@uttyler.edu. *Application contact:* Dr. Merrie Wright, Chair, 903-566-7423, Fax: 903-566-7062, E-mail: mewright@uttyler.edu.
Website: https://www.uttyler.edu/art/

The University of Texas Rio Grande Valley, College of Fine Arts, School of Art, Edinburg, TX 78539. Offers MFA. *Faculty:* 4 full-time (0 women). *Students:* 5 full-time (4 women), 16 part-time (13 women); includes 19 minority (1 Asian, non-Hispanic/Latino; 18 Hispanic/Latino). Average age 33. 3 applicants, 67% accepted, 1 enrolled. In 2019, 9 master's awarded. *Expenses: Tuition, area resident:* Full-time $5959; part-time $440 per credit hour. Tuition, state resident: full-time $5959. Tuition, nonresident: full-time $5959. *International tuition:* $13,321 full-time. *Required fees:* $1169; $185 per credit hour.

The University of the Arts, College of Art, Media and Design, Department of Art and Education, Philadelphia, PA 19102-4944. Offers visual arts (MAT), including art education. *Accreditation:* NASAD. *Program availability:* Part-time. *Degree requirements:* For master's, student teaching (MAT); thesis (MA). *Entrance requirements:* For master's, portfolio, official transcripts from each undergraduate or graduate school attended, three letters of recommendation, one- to two-page statement of professional plans and goals, personal interview, writing sample. Additional exam requirements/recommendations for international students: required—TOEFL (minimum score 580 paper-based, 92 iBT) or IELTS (minimum score 6.5).

The University of the Arts, College of Art, Media and Design, Program in Book Arts and Printmaking, Philadelphia, PA 19102-4944. Offers MFA. *Accreditation:* NASAD. *Degree requirements:* For master's, thesis. *Entrance requirements:* For master's, portfolio of 20-30 digital images showing work that represents applicant's full range of studio experience, preferably including printmaking and book arts; official transcripts from each undergraduate or graduate school attended; three letters of recommendation; one- to two-page statement of professional plans and goals; personal interview. Additional exam requirements/recommendations for international students: required—TOEFL (minimum score 580 paper-based, 92 iBT) or IELTS (minimum score 6.5).

The University of the Arts, College of Art, Media and Design, Program in Studio Art, Philadelphia, PA 19102-4944. Offers MFA. *Degree requirements:* For master's, thesis, summer residency. *Entrance requirements:* For master's, official transcripts from each undergraduate or graduate school attended, three letters of recommendation, one- to two-page statement of professional plans and goals, personal interview, portfolio. Additional exam requirements/recommendations for international students: required—TOEFL (minimum score 580 paper-based, 92 iBT) or IELTS (minimum score 6.5).

University of Utah, Graduate School, College of Fine Arts, Department of Art and Art History, Salt Lake City, UT 84112-0380. Offers art history (MA); ceramics (MFA); community-based art education (MFA); drawing (MFA); graphic design (MFA); painting (MFA); photography/digital imaging (MFA); printmaking (MFA); sculpture/intermedia (MFA). *Degree requirements:* For master's, variable foreign language requirement, comprehensive exam (for some programs), thesis or alternative, exhibit and final project paper (for MFA). *Entrance requirements:* For master's, CD portfolio (MFA), writing sample (MA), curriculum vitae, letters of recommendation, letter of intent. Additional exam requirements/recommendations for international students: required—TOEFL (minimum score 575 paper-based; 75 iBT). Electronic applications accepted. *Expenses:* Contact institution.

University of Victoria, Faculty of Graduate Studies, Faculty of Fine Arts, Department of Visual Arts, Victoria, BC V8W 2Y2, Canada. Offers digital multimedia (MFA); drawing (MFA); painting (MFA); photography (MFA); sculpture (MFA); video (MFA). *Degree requirements:* For master's, exhibit, oral exam. *Entrance requirements:* For master's, portfolio, BFA. Additional exam requirements/recommendations for international students: required—TOEFL (minimum score 575 paper-based), IELTS (minimum score 7). Electronic applications accepted.

University of Washington, Graduate School, College of Arts and Sciences, School of Art, Division of Art, Seattle, WA 98195. Offers painting and drawing (MFA); photography (MFA). *Degree requirements:* For master's, thesis, exhibit. *Entrance requirements:* For master's, BFA or equivalent academic work in art, 20 slide portfolio. Additional exam requirements/recommendations for international students: required—TOEFL. Electronic applications accepted.

University of Waterloo, Graduate Studies and Postdoctoral Affairs, Faculty of Arts, Department of Fine Arts, Waterloo, ON N2L 3G1, Canada. Offers studio art (MFA). *Degree requirements:* For master's, thesis exhibit. *Entrance requirements:* For master's, honors degree, minimum A- average, sample of work. Additional exam requirements/recommendations for international students: required—TOEFL, IELTS, PTE. Electronic applications accepted.

University of Windsor, Faculty of Graduate Studies, Faculty of Arts and Social Sciences, School of Visual Arts, Windsor, ON N9B 3P4, Canada. Offers MFA. *Degree requirements:* For master's, thesis. *Entrance requirements:* For master's, minimum B average, portfolio. Additional exam requirements/recommendations for international students: required—TOEFL (minimum score 560 paper-based). Electronic applications accepted.

University of Wisconsin–Madison, Graduate School, School of Education, Department of Art, Madison, WI 53706-1380. Offers MFA. *Accreditation:* NASAD. Electronic applications accepted.

University of Wisconsin–Milwaukee, Graduate School, Peck School of the Arts, Milwaukee, WI 53201-0413. Offers art education (MS); chamber music (CAS); conducting (MM); dance (MFA); design entrepreneurship and innovation (MA); film, video, animation, and new genres (MFA); music education (MM); music history and literature (MM); performance (MM); string pedagogy (MM); studio art (MA, MFA); theory and composition (MM). *Program availability:* Part-time. *Degree requirements:* For master's, comprehensive exam, thesis or alternative. *Entrance requirements:* For master's, portfolio. Additional exam requirements/recommendations for international students: required—TOEFL (minimum score 550 paper-based; 79 iBT), IELTS (minimum score 6.5). Electronic applications accepted.

University of Wisconsin–River Falls, Outreach and Graduate Studies, College of Arts and Science, Program in Fine Arts, River Falls, WI 54022. Offers MSE.

University of Wisconsin–Stout, Graduate School, College of Arts, Humanities and Social Sciences, Menomonie, WI 54751. Offers design (MFA); technical and professional communication (MS). *Accreditation:* NASAD.

University of Wisconsin–Superior, Graduate Division, Department of Visual Arts, Superior, WI 54880-4500. Offers art education (MA); art history (MA); art therapy (MA); studio arts (MA). *Program availability:* Part-time. *Degree requirements:* For master's, comprehensive exam, exhibit. *Entrance requirements:* For master's, minimum GPA of 2.75, portfolio. Electronic applications accepted.

Université Laval, Faculty of Architecture, Planning and Visual Arts, School of Visual Arts, Programs in Visual Arts, Québec, QC G1K 7P4, Canada. Offers graphic design and multimedia (MA); visual arts (MA). *Degree requirements:* For master's, thesis (for some programs). *Entrance requirements:* For master's, technical exam, interview, mastery of pertinent software, knowledge of French. Electronic applications accepted.

Utah State University, School of Graduate Studies, Caine College of the Arts, Department of Art and Design, Logan, UT 84322. Offers MFA. *Accreditation:* NASAD. *Degree requirements:* For master's, thesis, exhibit. *Entrance requirements:* For master's, GRE General Test or MAT, minimum GPA of 3.0, slide portfolio of art. Additional exam requirements/recommendations for international students: required—TOEFL.

Vermont College of Fine Arts, MFA in Visual Art Program, Montpelier, VT 05602. Offers MFA. *Accreditation:* NASAD. *Entrance requirements:* For master's, BFA, BA, or BS from accredited college or university, or Diploma from recognized professional art school; substantial experience in making art; thirty semester hours in undergraduate study (preferred). Electronic applications accepted. *Expenses:* Contact institution.

Virginia Commonwealth University, Graduate School, College of Humanities and Sciences, Richard T. Robertson School of Media and Culture, Program in Media, Art, and Text, Richmond, VA 23284-9005. Offers PhD. *Entrance requirements:* For doctorate, GRE. Additional exam requirements/recommendations for international students: required—TOEFL (minimum score 600 paper-based; 100 iBT); recommended—IELTS (minimum score 6.5). Electronic applications accepted.

Virginia Commonwealth University, Graduate School, School of the Arts, Richmond, VA 23284-9005. Offers art education (MAE, PhD); art history (MA, PhD), including curatorial (PhD), historical studies, museum studies (MA); ceramics (MFA); design (MFA), including interior environments, visual communications; fibers (MFA); furniture design (MFA); glassworking (MFA); jewelry/metalworking (MFA); kinetic imaging (MFA); music (MM), including music education; painting (MFA); photography and film (MFA); printmaking (MFA); sculpture (MFA); theatre (MFA), including costume design, pedagogy/literature, pedagogy/performance, scene design/technical theatre. *Accreditation:* CIDA. *Program availability:* Part-time. *Entrance requirements:* For doctorate, GRE General Test, writing sample. Additional exam requirements/recommendations for international students: required—TOEFL (minimum score 600 paper-based; 100 iBT). Electronic applications accepted.

Warren Wilson College, Master of Arts Program in Critical and Historical Craft Studies, Asheville, NC 28815-9000. Offers MA. *Entrance requirements:* For master's, written response to a craft piece, personal essay, letters of reference, official transcripts for previous undergraduate/graduate degrees. Electronic applications accepted. *Expenses: Tuition:* Full-time $18,800.

Washington State University, College of Arts and Sciences, Department of Fine Arts, Pullman, WA 99164. Offers MFA. *Degree requirements:* For master's, comprehensive exam (for some programs), thesis, exhibit, oral exam. *Entrance requirements:* For master's, statement of intent, portfolio of no more than 15 images on CD/DVD. Additional exam requirements/recommendations for international students: required—TOEFL (minimum score 550 paper-based), IELTS. Electronic applications accepted.

Washington University in St. Louis, Sam Fox School of Design and Visual Arts, Graduate School of Art, St. Louis, MO 63130-4899. Offers visual art (MFA). *Accreditation:* NASAD. *Degree requirements:* For master's, thesis, exhibition. *Entrance requirements:* For master's, portfolio, resume, transcripts, 3 letters of recommendation. Additional exam requirements/recommendations for international students: required—TOEFL (minimum score 577 paper-based; 90 iBT), IELTS (minimum score 7.5). Electronic applications accepted. *Expenses:* Contact institution.

Wayne State University, College of Fine, Performing and Communication Arts, James Pearson Duffy Department of Art and Art History, Detroit, MI 48202. Offers art (MA, MFA), including ceramics, drawing, fashion design and merchandising (MA), fibers, graphic design, industrial design (MA), interior design (MA), metalsmithing, painting, photography, printmaking, sculpture; art history (MA). *Degree requirements:* For master's, thesis (for some programs), essay or thesis. *Entrance requirements:* For master's, BFA or another degree and equivalent course work, portfolio, personal interview, reference letters, statement of intent (except for art history program). Additional exam requirements/recommendations for international students: required—TOEFL (minimum score 550 paper-based; 79 iBT), TWE (minimum score 5.5), Michigan English Language Assessment Battery (minimum score 85); recommended—IELTS (minimum score 6.5). Electronic applications accepted. *Expenses:* Contact institution.

Webster University, Leigh Gerdine College of Fine Arts, Department of Art, Design, and Art History, St. Louis, MO 63119-3194. Offers art history and criticism (MA). *Program availability:* Part-time. *Degree requirements:* For master's, thesis. *Entrance requirements:* For master's, BA or BFA in related field, interview, portfolio. Additional exam requirements/recommendations for international students: required—TOEFL.

Western Carolina University, Graduate School, College of Fine and Performing Arts, Cullowhee, NC 28723. Offers MFA. *Accreditation:* NASAD. *Program availability:* Part-time. *Degree requirements:* For master's, comprehensive exam, thesis optional. *Entrance requirements:* For master's, GRE, appropriate undergraduate degree, portfolio, letters of recommendation, letter of intent, live audition and/or interview. Additional exam requirements/recommendations for international students: required—TOEFL (minimum score 550 paper-based; 79 iBT). *Expenses: Tuition, area resident:* Full-time $2217.50; part-time $1664 per semester. Tuition, state resident: full-time $2217.50; part-time $1664 per semester. Tuition, nonresident: full-time $7421; part-time $5566 per semester. *International tuition:* $7421 full-time. *Required fees:* $5598; $1954 per semester. Tuition and fees vary according to course load, campus/location and program.

Western Connecticut State University, Division of Graduate Studies, School of Visual and Performing Arts, Department of Art, Danbury, CT 06810-6885. Offers illustration (MFA); painting (MFA). *Program availability:* Part-time. *Entrance requirements:* For master's, portfolio review, minimum GPA of 2.5. Additional exam requirements/recommendations for international students: recommended—TOEFL (minimum score 550 paper-based; 79 iBT), IELTS (minimum score 6). *Expenses:* Contact institution.

West Texas A&M University, College of Fine Arts and Humanities, Department of Art, Theatre and Dance, Canyon, TX 79015. Offers studio art (MFA). *Program availability:* Part-time. *Degree requirements:* For master's, comprehensive exam, thesis optional. *Entrance requirements:* For master's, GRE General Test. Additional exam requirements/recommendations for international students: required—TOEFL (minimum score 550 paper-based). Electronic applications accepted.

West Virginia University, College of Creative Arts, Morgantown, WV 26506. Offers acting (MFA); art education (MA); art history (MA); ceramics (MFA); collaborative piano (MM, DMA); composition (MM, DMA); conducting (MM, DMA); costume design and technology (MFA); graphic design (MFA); intermedia and photography (MFA); jazz pedagogy (MM); lighting design and technology (MFA); music (PhD); music education (MM, PhD); music industry (MA); music theory (MM); musicology (MA); painting and printmaking (MFA); performance (MM, DMA); piano pedagogy (MM); scenic design and technology (MFA); sculpture (MFA); studio art (MA); technical direction (MFA); vocal pedagogy and performance (DMA). *Program availability:* Part-time. *Degree requirements:* For master's, thesis, recitals; for doctorate, comprehensive exam, thesis/dissertation, recitals (DMA). *Entrance requirements:* For doctorate, minimum GPA of 3.0, audition. Additional exam requirements/recommendations for international students: required—TOEFL. Electronic applications accepted.

Wichita State University, Graduate School, College of Fine Arts, School of Art, Design and Creative Industries, Wichita, KS 67260. Offers studio arts (MFA), including ceramics, painting, photo media, printmaking, sculpture. *Accreditation:* NASAD.

Wilson College, Graduate Programs, Chambersburg, PA 17201-1285. Offers accounting (M Acc); choreography and visual art (MFA); education (M Ed); educational technology (MET); healthcare administration (MHA); humanities (MA), including art and culture, critical/cultural theory, English language and literature, women's studies; management (MSM); nursing (MSN), including nursing education, nursing leadership and management; special education (MSE). *Program availability:* Evening/weekend. *Degree requirements:* For master's, project. *Entrance requirements:* For master's, PRAXIS, minimum undergraduate cumulative GPA of 3.0, 2 letters of recommendation, current certification for eligibility to teach in grades K-12, resume, personal interview. Electronic applications accepted.

Winthrop University, College of Visual and Performing Arts, Department of Art, Rock Hill, SC 29733. Offers art (MFA); art administration (MA); art education (MA). *Accreditation:* NASAD. *Program availability:* Part-time. *Degree requirements:* For master's, comprehensive exam (for some programs), thesis (for some programs), documented exhibit, oral exam. *Entrance requirements:* For master's, GRE General Test or MAT, PRAXIS (for MA), minimum GPA of 3.0, resume, slide portfolio, teaching certificate (MA). Additional exam requirements/recommendations for international students: required—TOEFL (minimum score 550 paper-based; 79 iBT), IELTS (minimum score 6). Electronic applications accepted. *Expenses: Tuition, area resident:* Full-time $7659; part-time $641 per credit hour. Tuition, state resident: full-time $7659; part-time $641 per credit hour. Tuition, nonresident: full-time $14,753; part-time $1234 per credit hour.

Yale University, School of Art, New Haven, CT 06520-8339. Offers graphic design (MFA); painting/printmaking (MFA); photography (MFA); sculpture (MFA). *Degree requirements:* For master's, thesis (for some programs). *Entrance requirements:* Additional exam requirements/recommendations for international students: required—TOEFL (minimum score 550 paper-based; 100 iBT). Electronic applications accepted. *Expenses:* Contact institution.

York University, Faculty of Graduate Studies, Faculty of Fine Arts, Program in Visual Arts, Toronto, ON M3J 1P3, Canada. Offers MFA, PhD. *Degree requirements:* For master's, thesis. *Entrance requirements:* For master's, portfolio. Electronic applications accepted.

Art History

Academy of Art University, Graduate Programs, School of Art History, San Francisco, CA 94105-3410. Offers MA. *Program availability:* Part-time, 100% online. *Faculty:* 1 (woman) full-time, 3 part-time/adjunct (2 women). *Students:* 2 full-time (both women), 27 part-time (24 women); includes 4 minority (1 Black or African American, non-Hispanic/Latino; 2 Hispanic/Latino; 1 Two or more races, non-Hispanic/Latino), 2 international. Average age 38. 9 applicants, 100% accepted, 5 enrolled. In 2019, 12 master's awarded. *Degree requirements:* For master's, final review. *Entrance requirements:* For master's, statement of intent; resume; portfolio/reel; official college transcripts. *Application deadline:* Applications are processed on a rolling basis. Application fee: $50. Electronic applications accepted. *Expenses: Tuition:* Full-time $1083; part-time $1083 per credit hour. *Required fees:* $860; $860 per unit. $430 per term. One-time fee: $145. Tuition and fees vary according to program. *Financial support:* Career-related internships or fieldwork, Federal Work-Study, and scholarships/grants available. Financial award application deadline: 8/10; financial award applicants required to submit FAFSA.
Website: http://www.academyart.edu/art-history/

American University, College of Arts and Sciences, Department of Art, Washington, DC 20016-8004. Offers art history (MA); studio art (MFA). *Program availability:* Part-time. *Degree requirements:* For master's, comprehensive exam. *Entrance requirements:* For master's, GRE, Please visit website: https://www.american.edu/cas/art/, portfolio or writing sample, statement of purpose, transcripts, 2 letters of recommendation. Additional exam requirements/recommendations for international students: required—TOEFL. *Expenses:* Contact institution.

Arizona State University at Tempe, Herberger Institute for Design and the Arts, School of Art, Tempe, AZ 85287-1505. Offers art education (MA); art history (MA); ceramics (MFA); design, environment and the arts (PhD), including history, theory and criticism; drawing (MFA); fibers (MFA); intermedia (MFA); metals (MFA); museum studies (MFA); painting (MFA); printmaking (MFA); sculpture (MFA); wood (MFA); MFA/MA. Terminal master's awarded for partial completion of doctoral program. *Degree requirements:* For master's, thesis/exhibition (MFA, MA in art education); interactive Program of Study (iPOS) submitted before completing 50 percent of required credit hours; for doctorate, comprehensive exam, thesis/dissertation, interactive Program of Study (iPOS) submitted before completing 50 percent of required credit hours. *Entrance requirements:* For master's, GRE or MAT, minimum GPA of 3.0 or equivalent in last 2 years of work leading to bachelor's degree; for doctorate, GRE, master's degree in architecture, graphic design, industrial design, interior design, landscape architecture, or art history or equivalent standing; statement of purpose; 3 letters of recommendation; indication of potential faculty mentor; sample of written work. Additional exam requirements/recommendations for international students: required—TOEFL, IELTS, or PTE. Electronic applications accepted.

Bard Graduate Center, Graduate Studies, New York, NY 10024-3602. Offers MA, PhD. *Program availability:* Part-time. *Degree requirements:* For master's, one foreign language, thesis, internship; for doctorate, 2 foreign languages, thesis/dissertation, 3 field exams. *Entrance requirements:* For master's, GRE General Test, writing sample, 3 letters of recommendation; for doctorate, GRE General Test, MA, master's thesis or equivalent, 3 letters of recommendation. Additional exam requirements/recommendations for international students: required—TOEFL.

Binghamton University, State University of New York, Graduate School, Harpur College of Arts and Sciences, Department of Art History, Binghamton, NY 13902-6000. Offers MA, PhD. *Program availability:* Part-time. Terminal master's awarded for partial completion of doctoral program. *Degree requirements:* For master's, one foreign language, comprehensive exam, thesis; for doctorate, 2 foreign languages, comprehensive exam, thesis/dissertation. *Entrance requirements:* For master's and doctorate, GRE General Test, writing sample. Additional exam requirements/recommendations for international students: required—TOEFL (minimum score 80 iBT). Electronic applications accepted.

Boston University, Graduate School of Arts and Sciences, Department of History of Art and Architecture, Boston, MA 02215. Offers history of art and architecture (MA, PhD); museum studies (Certificate). *Accreditation:* NASAD. *Students:* 48 full-time (40 women), 5 part-time (4 women); includes 5 minority (2 Asian, non-Hispanic/Latino; 3 Hispanic/Latino), 10 international. Average age 28. 132 applicants, 41% accepted, 10 enrolled. In 2019, 5 master's, 5 doctorates awarded. Terminal master's awarded for partial completion of doctoral program. *Degree requirements:* For master's, one foreign language, comprehensive exam, thesis or alternative, scholarly paper; for doctorate, 2 foreign languages, comprehensive exam, thesis/dissertation. *Entrance requirements:* For master's and doctorate, GRE General Test, 3 letters of recommendation, transcripts, personal statement, curriculum vitae, writing sample, foreign language proficiency. Additional exam requirements/recommendations for international students: required—TOEFL (minimum score 550 paper-based; 84 iBT). *Application deadline:* For fall admission, 1/5 for domestic and international students; for spring admission, 10/15 for domestic and international students. Application fee: $95. Electronic applications accepted. *Financial support:* In 2019–20, 50 students received support, including 19 fellowships with full tuition reimbursements available (averaging $23,340 per year), 14 teaching assistantships with full tuition reimbursements available (averaging $23,340 per year); career-related internships or fieldwork, Federal Work-Study, scholarships/grants, health care benefits, and unspecified assistantships also available. Financial award application deadline: 1/5. *Unit head:* Alice Tseng, Chair, 617-353-1458, Fax: 617-353-3243, E-mail: aytseng@bu.edu. *Application contact:* Cheryl Crombie, Administrative Assistant, 617-353-2522, Fax: 617-353-3243, E-mail: ccrombie@bu.edu.
Website: http://www.bu.edu/AH/

Bowling Green State University, Graduate College, College of Arts and Sciences, School of Art, Bowling Green, OH 43403. Offers 2-D studio art (MA, MFA); 3-D studio art (MA, MFA); art education (MA); art history (MA); computer art (MA); design (MFA); digital arts (MFA); graphics (MFA). *Accreditation:* NASAD. *Program availability:* Part-time. *Degree requirements:* For master's, thesis or alternative, final exhibit (MFA). *Entrance requirements:* For master's, GRE General Test (for MA), slide portfolio (15-20 slides). Additional exam requirements/recommendations for international students: required—TOEFL. Electronic applications accepted.

Brooklyn College of the City University of New York, School of Visual, Media and Performing Arts, Department of Art, Brooklyn, NY 11210-2889. Offers art history (MA); digital art (MFA); drawing and painting (MFA); photography (MFA); printmaking (MFA); sculpture (MFA). *Program availability:* Part-time. *Degree requirements:* For master's, thesis. *Entrance requirements:* For master's, bachelor's degree in art, portfolio, 2 letters of recommendation. Additional exam requirements/recommendations for international students: required—TOEFL (minimum score 500 paper-based; 61 iBT). Electronic applications accepted.

Brown University, Graduate School, Department of History of Art and Architecture, Providence, RI 02912. Offers PhD. *Degree requirements:* For doctorate, 2 foreign languages, thesis/dissertation, oral exam. *Entrance requirements:* For doctorate, GRE General Test, MA with distinction.

Brown University, Graduate School, Joukowsky Institute for Archaeology and the Ancient World, Providence, RI 02912. Offers PhD. *Degree requirements:* For doctorate, thesis/dissertation.

Bryn Mawr College, Graduate School of Arts and Sciences, Department of History of Art, Bryn Mawr, PA 19010-2899. Offers MA, PhD. *Program availability:* Part-time. Terminal master's awarded for partial completion of doctoral program. *Degree requirements:* For master's, 2 foreign languages, thesis; for doctorate, 2 foreign languages, comprehensive exam, thesis/dissertation. *Entrance requirements:* For master's and doctorate, GRE General Test, transcripts, three letters of recommendation, statement of interest, resume or curriculum vitae. Additional exam requirements/recommendations for international students: required—TOEFL (minimum score 600 paper-based; 100 iBT), IELTS (minimum score 7). Electronic applications accepted.

California State University, Chico, Office of Graduate Studies, College of Humanities and Fine Arts, Department of Art and Art History, Program in Art History, Chico, CA 95929-0722. Offers MA. *Accreditation:* NASAD. *Degree requirements:* For master's, thesis, thesis. *Entrance requirements:* For master's, MA Art Two letters of recommendation, statement of purpose, writing samples, and two upper division art history papers. Additional exam requirements/recommendations for international students: required—TOEFL (minimum score 550 paper-based; 80 iBT), IELTS (minimum score 6.5), PTE (minimum score 59). Electronic applications accepted.

California State University, Fullerton, Graduate Studies, College of the Arts, Department of Visual Arts, Fullerton, CA 92831-3599. Offers art (MA, MFA), including art history (MA), ceramics (MFA), crafts, creative photography, exhibition design, glass, graphic design, illustration, sculpture. *Accreditation:* NASAD (one or more programs are accredited). *Program availability:* Part-time. *Entrance requirements:* For master's, minimum GPA of 2.5 in last 60 units of course work, portfolio.

California State University, Los Angeles, Graduate Studies, College of Arts and Letters, Department of Art, Los Angeles, CA 90032-8530. Offers art (MA), including art education, art history, art therapy, ceramics, metals, and textiles, design (MA, MFA), painting, sculpture, and graphic arts, photography; fine arts (MFA), including crafts, design (MA, MFA), studio arts. *Accreditation:* NASAD (one or more programs are accredited). *Program availability:* Part-time, evening/weekend. *Degree requirements:* For master's, comprehensive exam, project or thesis. *Entrance requirements:* For master's, portfolio. Additional exam requirements/recommendations for international students: required—TOEFL (minimum score 500 paper-based). Electronic applications accepted. *Expenses: Tuition, area resident:* Full-time $7176; part-time $4164 per year. Tuition, state resident: full-time $7176; part-time $4164 per year. Tuition, nonresident: full-time $14,304; part-time $8916 per year. *International tuition:* $14,304 full-time. *Required fees:* $1037.76; $1037.76 per unit. Tuition and fees vary according to degree level and program.

California State University, Northridge, Graduate Studies, Mike Curb College of Arts, Media, and Communication, Department of Art, Northridge, CA 91330. Offers art education (MA); art history (MA); studio art (MA, MFA); visual communications (MA, MFA). *Accreditation:* NASAD.

Caribbean University, Graduate School, Bayamón, PR 00960-0493. Offers administration and supervision (MA Ed); criminal justice (MA); curriculum and instruction (MA Ed, PhD), including elementary education (MA Ed), English education (MA Ed), history education (MA Ed), mathematics education (MA Ed), primary education (MA Ed), science education (MA Ed), Spanish education (MA Ed); educational technology in instructional systems (MA Ed); gerontology (MSN); human resources (MBA); museology, archiving and art history (MA Ed); neonatal pediatrics (MSN); physical education (MA Ed); special education (MA Ed). *Entrance requirements:* For master's, interview, minimum GPA of 2.5.

Carleton University, Faculty of Graduate Studies, Faculty of Arts and Social Sciences, School for Studies in Art and Culture, Program in Art History: Art and its Institutions, Ottawa, ON K1S 5B6, Canada. Offers MA. *Degree requirements:* For master's, thesis. *Entrance requirements:* For master's, honors degree.

Case Western Reserve University, School of Graduate Studies, Department of Art History and Art, Program in Art History, Cleveland, OH 44106. Offers MA, PhD. *Program availability:* Part-time. *Faculty:* 8 full-time (7 women), 5 part-time/adjunct (3 women). *Students:* 21 full-time (18 women), 1 (woman) part-time; includes 3 minority (1 Hispanic/Latino; 2 Two or more races, non-Hispanic/Latino), 3 international. Average age 29. 34 applicants, 79% accepted, 7 enrolled. In 2019, 8 master's, 1 doctorate awarded. *Degree requirements:* For master's, one foreign language, comprehensive exam; for doctorate, 2 foreign languages, comprehensive exam, thesis/dissertation. *Entrance requirements:* For master's, GRE General Test, 2 samples of written work; 3 letters of recommendation; for doctorate, GRE General Test, 2 samples of written work, MA thesis. Additional exam requirements/recommendations for international students: required—TOEFL (minimum score 600 paper-based; 100 iBT). *Application deadline:* For fall admission, 1/1 priority date for domestic students. Applications are processed on a rolling basis. Application fee: $50. Electronic applications accepted. *Financial support:* Fellowships, research assistantships, teaching assistantships, career-related internships or fieldwork, health care benefits, and tuition waivers available. Financial award application deadline: 1/1; financial award applicants required to submit FAFSA. *Unit head:* Elizabeth Bolman, Professor of Art History and Chair, 216-368-4039, Fax: 216-368-4681, E-mail: elizabeth.bolman@case.edu. *Application contact:* Deborah Tenenbaum, Department Assistant, 216-368-4118, Fax: 216-368-4681, E-mail:

deborah.tenenbaum@case.edu.
Website: http://arthistory.case.edu/graduate/art-history/

Christie's Education, MA Program in Modern and Contemporary Art and the Market, New York, NY 10020. Offers MA. *Program availability:* Part-time. *Degree requirements:* For master's, one foreign language, thesis, internship. *Entrance requirements:* For master's, writing sample, 3 letters of recommendation. Additional exam requirements/recommendations for international students: required—TOEFL. *Expenses:* Contact institution.

City College of the City University of New York, Graduate School, Division of Humanities and the Arts, Department of Art, Programs in Art History and Museum Studies, New York, NY 10031-9198. Offers art history (MA); art museum education (MA); museum studies (MA). *Program availability:* Part-time. *Degree requirements:* For master's, one foreign language, thesis. *Entrance requirements:* For master's, minimum GPA of 3.0, portfolio, art history paper. Additional exam requirements/recommendations for international students: required—TOEFL (minimum score 577 paper-based; 90 iBT). Electronic applications accepted.

Cleveland State University, College of Graduate Studies, College of Liberal Arts and Social Sciences, Department of History, Cleveland, OH 44115. Offers art history (MA); museum studies (MA). *Program availability:* Part-time, evening/weekend. *Students:* Average age 32. 21 applicants, 90% accepted, 6 enrolled. In 2019, 9 master's awarded. *Entrance requirements:* For master's, minimum GPA of 3.0, bachelor's degree in history (or related field for art history). Additional exam requirements/recommendations for international students: required—TOEFL (minimum score 550 paper-based; 78 iBT). *Application deadline:* Applications are processed on a rolling basis. Application fee: $40. Electronic applications accepted. *Expenses:* Tuition, state resident: full-time $10,215; part-time $6810 per credit hour. Tuition, nonresident: full-time $17,496; part-time $11,664 per credit hour. *International tuition:* $19,316 full-time. Tuition and fees vary according to degree level and program. *Financial support:* In 2019–20, 7 students received support. Research assistantships, career-related internships or fieldwork, tuition waivers (full and partial), and unspecified assistantships available. Financial award application deadline: 4/15. *Unit head:* Dr. Elizabeth A. Lehfeldt, Chairperson, 216-687-3920, Fax: 216-687-5592, E-mail: e.lehfeldt@csuohio.edu. *Application contact:* Dr. Karen Sotiropoulos, Graduate Director, 216-687-3940, E-mail: r.s.shelton@csuohio.edu.
Website: http://www.csuohio.edu/history/

Colorado State University, College of Liberal Arts, Department of Art and Art History, Fort Collins, CO 80523-1779. Offers studio art (MFA). *Program availability:* Part-time. *Faculty:* 16 full-time (8 women), 2 part-time/adjunct (both women). *Students:* 15 full-time (5 women), 3 part-time (all women); includes 8 minority (1 Black or African American, non-Hispanic/Latino; 5 Hispanic/Latino; 2 Two or more races, non-Hispanic/Latino). Average age 31. 39 applicants, 23% accepted, 5 enrolled. In 2019, 3 master's awarded. *Degree requirements:* For master's, comprehensive exam (for some programs), thesis, exhibition. *Entrance requirements:* For master's, portfolio, three letters of recommendation, transcripts, statement of purpose, resume, artist statement; 20 images of work (including video, if applicable). Additional exam requirements/recommendations for international students: required—TOEFL (minimum score 550 paper-based; 80 iBT). *Application deadline:* For fall admission, 2/1 priority date for domestic and international students. Applications are processed on a rolling basis. Application fee: $60 ($70 for international students). Electronic applications accepted. *Expenses:* Tuition, state resident: full-time $10,520; part-time $5844 per credit hour. Tuition, nonresident: full-time $25,791; part-time $14,328 per credit hour. *International tuition:* $25,791 full-time. *Required fees:* $2512.80. Part-time tuition and fees vary according to course level, course load, degree level, program and student level. *Financial support:* In 2019–20, 2 students received support, including 10 teaching assistantships with full tuition reimbursements available (averaging $12,397 per year); fellowships with partial tuition reimbursements available, scholarships/grants, and unspecified assistantships also available. Financial award applicants required to submit FAFSA. *Unit head:* Dr. Eleanor Moseman, Department Chair/Associate Professor, 970-491-5451, Fax: 970-491-0505, E-mail: EleanorMoseman@colostate.edu. *Application contact:* Haley Bates, Graduate Contact, 970-491-6775, E-mail: haley.bates@colostate.edu.
Website: http://art.colostate.edu/

Columbia College Chicago, School of Graduate Studies, Art and Art History Department, Chicago, IL 60605-1996. Offers fine arts (MFA). *Program availability:* Part-time, evening/weekend. *Degree requirements:* For master's, thesis. *Entrance requirements:* For master's, self-assessment essay, work sample, interview, letters of recommendation, transcripts. Additional exam requirements/recommendations for international students: required—TOEFL, IELTS. Electronic applications accepted.

Columbia University, Graduate School of Arts and Sciences, New York, NY 10027. Offers African-American studies (MA); American studies (MA); anthropology (MA, PhD); art history and archaeology (MA, PhD); astronomy (PhD); biological sciences (PhD); biotechnology (MA); chemical physics (PhD); chemistry (PhD); classical studies (MA, PhD); classics (MA, PhD); climate and society (MA); conservation biology (MA); earth and environmental sciences (PhD); East Asia: regional studies (MA); East Asian languages and cultures (MA, PhD); ecology, evolution and environmental biology (MA), including conservation biology; ecology, evolution, and environmental biology (PhD), including ecology and evolutionary biology, evolutionary primatology; economics (MA, PhD); English and comparative literature (MA, PhD); French and Romance philology (MA, PhD); Germanic languages (MA, PhD); global French studies (MA); global thought (MA); Hispanic cultural studies (MA); history (PhD); history and literature (MA); human rights studies (MA); Islamic studies (MA); Italian (MA, PhD); Japanese pedagogy (MA); Jewish studies (MA); Latin America and the Caribbean: regional studies (MA); Latin American and Iberian cultures (PhD); mathematics (MA, PhD), including finance (MA); medieval and Renaissance studies (MA); Middle Eastern, South Asian, and African studies (MA, PhD); modern art: critical and curatorial studies (MA); modern European studies (MA); museum anthropology (MA); music (DMA, PhD); oral history (MA); philosophical foundations of physics (MA); philosophy (MA, PhD); physics (PhD); political science (MA, PhD); psychology (PhD); quantitative methods in the social sciences (MA); religion (MA, PhD); Russia, Eurasia and East Europe: regional studies (MA); Russian translation (MA); Slavic cultures (MA); Slavic languages (MA, PhD); sociology (MA, PhD); South Asian studies (MA); statistics (MA, PhD); theatre (PhD). *Program availability:* Part-time. *Students:* 3,506 full-time (1,844 women), 208 part-time (121 women); includes 864 minority (110 Black or African American, non-Hispanic/Latino; 5 American Indian or Alaska Native, non-Hispanic/Latino; 416 Asian, non-Hispanic/Latino; 147 Hispanic/Latino; 6 Native Hawaiian or other Pacific Islander, non-Hispanic/Latino; 180 Two or more races, non-Hispanic/Latino), 2,065 international. 14,545 applicants, 25% accepted, 1,429 enrolled. In 2019, 1,262 master's, 363 doctorates awarded. Terminal master's awarded for partial completion of doctoral program. *Degree requirements:* For master's, variable foreign language requirement, comprehensive exam (for some programs), thesis (for some programs); for doctorate, variable foreign language requirement, comprehensive exam (for some programs), thesis/dissertation. *Entrance requirements:* For master's and doctorate, GRE General Test, GRE Subject Test (for some programs). Additional exam requirements/recommendations for international students: required—TOEFL (minimum score 600 paper-based; 100 iBT), IELTS (minimum score 7.5). Application fee: $115. Electronic applications accepted. *Expenses: Tuition:* Full-time $47,600; part-time $1880 per credit. One-time fee: $105. *Financial support:* Fellowships, research assistantships, teaching assistantships, career-related internships or fieldwork, Federal Work-Study, institutionally sponsored loans, scholarships/grants, traineeships, health care benefits, tuition waivers, and unspecified assistantships available. Support available to part-time students. Financial award application deadline: 12/15. *Unit head:* Dr. Carlos J. Alonso, Dean of the Graduate School of Arts and Sciences and Vice President for Graduate Education, 212-854-2861, E-mail: gsas-dean@columbia.edu. *Application contact:* GSAS Office of Admissions, 212-854-6729, E-mail: gsas-admissions@columbia.edu.
Website: http://gsas.columbia.edu/

Concordia University, School of Graduate Studies, Faculty of Fine Arts, Department of Art History, Montréal, QC H3G 1M8, Canada. Offers MA, PhD. *Degree requirements:* For master's, one foreign language, thesis. *Entrance requirements:* For master's, BFA or equivalent, minimum B average in major.

Cornell University, Graduate School, Graduate Fields of Arts and Sciences, Field of History of Art, Archaeology and Visual Studies, Ithaca, NY 14853. Offers 19th century art (PhD); African, African American and African diaspora (PhD); American art (PhD); ancient art and archaeology (PhD); Asian American art (PhD); Baroque art (PhD); Comparative Modernities (PhD); digital art (PhD); East Asian art (PhD); history of photography (PhD); Islamic art (PhD); Latin American art (PhD); medieval art (PhD); modern art (PhD); Renaissance art (PhD); Southeast Asian art (PhD); theory and criticism (PhD); visual studies (PhD). *Degree requirements:* For doctorate, one foreign language, comprehensive exam, thesis/dissertation, general exams in 3 areas. *Entrance requirements:* For doctorate, GRE General Test, sample of written work, 3 letters of recommendation. Additional exam requirements/recommendations for international students: required—TOEFL (minimum score 550 paper-based; 77 iBT). Electronic applications accepted.

Duke University, Graduate School, Department of Art, Art History and Visual Studies, Durham, NC 27708-0764. Offers historical and cultural visualization (MA); history of art (PhD). *Degree requirements:* For doctorate, thesis/dissertation. *Entrance requirements:* For doctorate, GRE General Test. Additional exam requirements/recommendations for international students: required—TOEFL (minimum score 577 paper-based; 90 iBT) or IELTS (minimum score 7). Electronic applications accepted.

Emory University, Laney Graduate School, Department of Art History, Atlanta, GA 30322-1100. Offers PhD. *Degree requirements:* For doctorate, 2 foreign languages, comprehensive exam, thesis/dissertation, oral exam. *Entrance requirements:* For doctorate, GRE General Test. Additional exam requirements/recommendations for international students: required—TOEFL. Electronic applications accepted.

Fashion Institute of Technology, School of Graduate Studies, Program in Art Market Studies, New York, NY 10001-5992. Offers MA. *Accreditation:* NASAD. *Degree requirements:* For master's, thesis or alternative, internship. *Entrance requirements:* For master's, GRE General Test, previous course work in art history, 4 semesters of a foreign language. Additional exam requirements/recommendations for international students: required—TOEFL (minimum score 550 paper-based). Electronic applications accepted.

Florida State University, The Graduate School, College of Fine Arts, Department of Art History, Tallahassee, FL 32306. Offers history and criticism of art (MA, PhD). *Accreditation:* NASAD. *Program availability:* Part-time. *Faculty:* 13 full-time (6 women), 10 part-time/adjunct (6 women). *Students:* 39 full-time (38 women), 7 part-time (all women); includes 7 minority (2 Black or African American, non-Hispanic/Latino; 1 Asian, non-Hispanic/Latino; 3 Hispanic/Latino; 1 Two or more races, non-Hispanic/Latino). Average age 29. 43 applicants, 81% accepted, 15 enrolled. In 2019, 13 master's awarded. Terminal master's awarded for partial completion of doctoral program. *Degree requirements:* For master's, one foreign language, thesis (for some programs), capstone project (for some programs); for doctorate, 2 foreign languages, comprehensive exam, thesis/dissertation. *Entrance requirements:* For master's, GRE General Test, minimum GPA of 3.0; for doctorate, GRE General Test, minimum GPA of 3.5. Additional exam requirements/recommendations for international students: required—TOEFL (minimum score 550 paper-based; 80 iBT), IELTS (minimum score 6.5). *Application deadline:* For fall admission, 7/1 for domestic and international students. Applications are processed on a rolling basis. Application fee: $35. Electronic applications accepted. *Expenses:* Contact institution. *Financial support:* In 2019–20, 37 students received support, including 16 fellowships with full tuition reimbursements available (averaging $6,200 per year), 14 research assistantships with full tuition reimbursements available (averaging $5,100 per year), 9 teaching assistantships with full tuition reimbursements available (averaging $7,140 per year); career-related internships or fieldwork, Federal Work-Study, institutionally sponsored loans, scholarships/grants, tuition waivers (full), and unspecified assistantships also available. Financial award application deadline: 1/1; financial award applicants required to submit FAFSA. *Unit head:* Dr. Adam Jolles, Associate Professor of Art History/Department Chair, 850-644-7066, E-mail: ajolles@fsu.edu. *Application contact:* Juan Barcelo-Gonzalez, Academic Program Specialist/Graduate Student Advisor, 850-644-8207, Fax: 850-644-7065, E-mail: juan.barcelo@fsu.edu.
Website: http://arthistory.fsu.edu/

George Mason University, College of Humanities and Social Sciences, Department of History and Art History, Program in Art History, Fairfax, VA 22030. Offers MA. *Accreditation:* NASAD. *Degree requirements:* For master's, variable foreign language requirement, comprehensive exam, thesis optional. *Entrance requirements:* For master's, GRE (waived for those who hold another graduate degree or received their undergraduate degree 10 or more years ago), expanded goals statement; 2 letters of recommendation; resume; official transcript. Additional exam requirements/recommendations for international students: required—TOEFL (minimum score 575 paper-based; 88 iBT), IELTS (minimum score 6.5), PTE (minimum score 59). Electronic applications accepted.

The George Washington University, Columbian College of Arts and Sciences, Department of Fine Arts and Art History, Program in Art History, Washington, DC 20052. Offers art history (MA); museum training (MA). *Program availability:* Part-time, evening/weekend. *Degree requirements:* For master's, one foreign language, comprehensive exam, thesis or alternative. *Entrance requirements:* For master's, GRE General Test, bachelor's degree in field, minimum GPA of 3.0. Additional exam requirements/recommendations for international students: required—TOEFL (minimum score 550 paper-based; 80 iBT). Electronic applications accepted.

Georgia State University, College of Arts, Ernest G. Welch School of Art and Design, Program in Art History, Atlanta, GA 30302-3083. Offers MA. *Accreditation:* NASAD. Application fee: $50. Electronic applications accepted. *Expenses: Tuition, area resident:* Full-time $7164; part-time $398 per credit hour. Tuition, state resident: full-time $7164; part-time $398 per credit hour. Tuition, nonresident: full-time $22,662; part-time $1259 per credit hour. *International tuition:* $22,662 full-time. *Required fees:* $2128; $312 per credit hour. Tuition and fees vary according to course load and program. *Financial support:* Fellowships, research assistantships, scholarships/grants, and

unspecified assistantships available. Financial award application deadline: 4/15; financial award applicants required to submit FAFSA. *Unit head:* Joseph Peragine, Director, Welch School of Art and Design, 404-413-5229, E-mail: jperagine@gsu.edu. *Application contact:* Joseph Peragine, Director, Welch School of Art and Design, 404-413-5229, E-mail: jperagine@gsu.edu.
Website: http://artdesign.gsu.edu/graduate/admissions/master-of-arts-in-art-history/

The Graduate Center, City University of New York, Graduate Studies, Program in Art History, New York, NY 10016-4039. Offers architecture (PhD); graphic arts (PhD); painting (PhD); photography (PhD); sculpture (PhD). *Degree requirements:* For doctorate, 2 foreign languages, thesis/dissertation. *Entrance requirements:* For doctorate, GRE General Test. Additional exam requirements/recommendations for international students: required—TOEFL. Electronic applications accepted.

Graduate Theological Union, Graduate Programs, Berkeley, CA 94709-1212. Offers art and religion (MA, PhD, Th D); biblical languages (MA); Biblical studies (PhD, Th D); biblical studies (MA); Buddhist studies (MA); Christian spirituality (MA, PhD, Th D); cultural and historical studies of religions (MA, PhD, Th D); ethics and social theory (PhD, Th D); history (MA, PhD, Th D); homiletics (MA, PhD, Th D); interdisciplinary studies (PhD, Th D); Jewish studies (MA, PhD, Th D, Certificate); liturgical studies (MA, PhD, Th D); Near Eastern religions (PhD, Th D); Orthodox Christian studies (MA); religion and psychology (MA, PhD, Th D); religion and society/ethics and social theory (MA); systematic and philosophical theology (MA, PhD, Th D). *Accreditation:* ATS. Terminal master's awarded for partial completion of doctoral program. *Degree requirements:* For master's, one foreign language, thesis; for doctorate, one foreign language, comprehensive exam, thesis/dissertation. *Entrance requirements:* For master's, GRE General Test; for doctorate, GRE General Test, MA or M Div. Additional exam requirements/recommendations for international students: required—TOEFL. Electronic applications accepted.

Harvard University, Graduate School of Arts and Sciences, Department of History of Art and Architecture, Cambridge, MA 02138. Offers ancient art (PhD); ancient Near Eastern art (PhD); Baroque art (PhD); Byzantine art (PhD); classical art (PhD); Indian art (PhD); Islamic art (PhD); Japanese and Chinese art (PhD); medieval art (PhD); modern art (PhD); Renaissance and modern architecture (PhD); Renaissance art (PhD). *Degree requirements:* For doctorate, variable foreign language requirement, thesis/dissertation, general exams; reading exams in French, German, and Italian. *Entrance requirements:* For doctorate, GRE General Test. Additional exam requirements/recommendations for international students: required—TOEFL.

Howard University, Graduate School, Division of Fine Arts, Department of Art, Program in Art History, Washington, DC 20059-0002. Offers art history (MA); history of art and visual culture (MA). *Accreditation:* NASAD. *Program availability:* Part-time. *Degree requirements:* For master's, comprehensive exam, thesis. *Entrance requirements:* For master's, GRE General Test, minimum GPA of 3.0, BA in art history or related field, portfolio.

Hunter College of the City University of New York, Graduate School, School of Arts and Sciences, Department of Art and Art History, Program in Art History, New York, NY 10065-5085. Offers MA. *Program availability:* Part-time, evening/weekend. *Degree requirements:* For master's, one foreign language, comprehensive exam, thesis. *Entrance requirements:* For master's, GRE General Test, minimum 12 credits of course work in art history, reading knowledge of a foreign language (Italian, French, German, or Spanish), 2 letters of recommendation, statement of purpose, writing sample. Additional exam requirements/recommendations for international students: required—TOEFL (minimum score 550 paper-based; 60 iBT).

Illinois State University, Graduate School, Wonsook Kim College of Fine Arts, School of Art, Normal, IL 61790. Offers art history (MA, MS); ceramics (MFA, MS); drawing (MFA, MS); fibers (MFA, MS); glass (MFA, MS); graphic design (MFA, MS); metals (MFA, MS); painting (MFA, MS); photography (MFA, MS); printmaking (MFA, MS); sculpture (MFA, MS). *Accreditation:* NASAD (one or more programs are accredited). *Faculty:* 34 full-time (18 women), 15 part-time/adjunct (11 women). *Students:* 25 full-time (16 women), 5 part-time (4 women). Average age 31. 32 applicants, 66% accepted, 12 enrolled. In 2019, 11 master's awarded. *Degree requirements:* For master's, thesis or alternative, internship. *Entrance requirements:* For master's, portfolio, sample of scholarly writing. *Application deadline:* Applications are processed on a rolling basis. Application fee: $50. *Expenses: Tuition, area resident:* Full-time $7956; part-time $9767 per year. Tuition, nonresident: full-time $9233; part-time $17,592 per year. *Required fees:* $1797. *Financial support:* In 2019–20, 20 teaching assistantships were awarded; career-related internships or fieldwork, Federal Work-Study, tuition waivers (full and partial), and unspecified assistantships also available. Support available to part-time students. Financial award application deadline: 4/1. *Unit head:* Mike Wille, Director of Art School, 309-438-5610, E-mail: mjwill4@ilstu.edu. *Application contact:* Tyler Lotz, Graduate Coordinator, 309-438-8301, E-mail: tlotz@ilstu.edu.
Website: http://www.arts.ilstu.edu/art/

Indiana University Bloomington, University Graduate School, College of Arts and Sciences, Department of Art History, Bloomington, IN 47405-7000. Offers MA, PhD, MA/MLS. *Accreditation:* NASAD. *Degree requirements:* For master's, one foreign language, thesis; for doctorate, 2 foreign languages, comprehensive exam, thesis/dissertation. *Entrance requirements:* For master's, GRE, writing sample, 3 letters of recommendation, transcript; for doctorate, GRE, transcript, writing samples, 3 letters of recommendation. Additional exam requirements/recommendations for international students: required—TOEFL (minimum score 550 paper-based).

James Madison University, The Graduate School, College of Visual and Performing Arts, School of Art, Design and Art History, Harrisonburg, VA 22807. Offers art education (MA); studio art (MA, MFA), including ceramics (MFA), drawing/painting (MFA), intermedia (MFA), metal/jewelry (MFA), photography (MFA), sculpture (MFA). *Accreditation:* NASAD. *Program availability:* Part-time. *Students:* 7 full-time (6 women), 1 (woman) part-time. Average age 30. In 2019, 3 master's awarded. Application fee: $60. Electronic applications accepted. *Financial support:* In 2019–20, 7 students received support, including 2 teaching assistantships with full tuition reimbursements available (averaging $9,284 per year); Federal Work-Study and assistantships (averaging $7911) also available. Financial award application deadline: 3/1; financial award applicants required to submit FAFSA. *Unit head:* Dr. Kathy A. Schwartz, Director of School of Art, Design and Art History, 540-568-6216, E-mail: schwarka@jmu.edu. *Application contact:* Lynette D. Michael, Director of Graduate Student Admissions, 540-568-6131 Ext. 6395, Fax: 540-568-7860, E-mail: michaeld@jmu.edu.
Website: http://www.jmu.edu/artandarthistory/

John Cabot University, John Cabot University - Graduate School, Rome, Italy. Offers art history (MA). *Degree requirements:* For master's, one foreign language, comprehensive exam, thesis. *Entrance requirements:* Additional exam requirements/recommendations for international students: required—IELTS (minimum score 7), PTE (minimum score 70), CAE Cambridge (optional), CPE Cambridge (optional), GRE Scores (recommended). Electronic applications accepted. Application fee is waived when completed online.

Johns Hopkins University, Zanvyl Krieger School of Arts and Sciences, Department of History of Art, Baltimore, MD 21218. Offers MA, PhD. Terminal master's awarded for partial completion of doctoral program. *Degree requirements:* For master's, 2 foreign languages; for doctorate, 2 foreign languages, comprehensive exam, thesis/dissertation. *Entrance requirements:* For doctorate, GRE General Test. Additional exam requirements/recommendations for international students: required—TOEFL (minimum score 600 paper-based; 100 iBT), IELTS. Electronic applications accepted. *Expenses:* Contact institution.

Kent State University, College of the Arts, School of Art, Kent, OH 44242-0001. Offers art education (MA); art history (MA); crafts (MA), including glass (MA, MFA); fine arts (MA), including fashion; studio art (MFA), including ceramics, drawing, glass (MA, MFA), jewelry, metals and enameling, painting, print media and photography, sculpture, textiles. *Accreditation:* NASAD (one or more programs are accredited). *Program availability:* Part-time, 100% online, blended/hybrid learning. *Faculty:* 22 full-time (13 women), 5 part-time/adjunct (4 women). *Students:* 36 full-time (27 women), 24 part-time (22 women); includes 4 minority (3 Black or African American, non-Hispanic/Latino; 1 Hispanic/Latino), 2 international. Average age 30. 52 applicants, 67% accepted, 20 enrolled. In 2019, 15 master's awarded. *Degree requirements:* For master's, comprehensive exam, thesis (for some programs), 1 foreign language (for art history); final project (for crafts and fine arts). *Entrance requirements:* For master's, bachelors's degree min 3.0 GPA on 4.0 scale, transcripts, goal statement, 3 letters of recommendation, curriculum vitae, for MA and MFA in Studio Art: portfolio, artist statement;l MA Art Education: goal statement that focuses on philosophy of art education. Additional exam requirements/recommendations for international students: required—TOEFL (minimum score 79 iBT), IELTS (minimum score 6.5), PTE (minimum score 58), Michigan English Language Assessment Battery (minimum score 77). *Application deadline:* For fall admission, 2/2 priority date for domestic students, 2/2 for international students; for spring admission, 10/15 for domestic and international students. Applications are processed on a rolling basis. Application fee: $45 ($70 for international students). Electronic applications accepted. *Financial support:* Career-related internships or fieldwork, scholarships/grants, and unspecified assistantships available. Financial award application deadline: 3/1. *Unit head:* Marie Bukowski, Director, 330-672-2192, E-mail: mbukows1@kent.edu. *Application contact:* Peter Christian Johnson, Graduate Coordinator and Associate Professor Ceramics, 330-672-3360, E-mail: pjohns35@kent.edu.
Website: http://www.kent.edu/art

Lancaster Theological Seminary, Graduate and Professional Programs, Lancaster, PA 17603-2812. Offers biblical studies (MAR); Christian education (MAR); Christianity and the arts (MAR); church history (MAR); congregational life (MAR); lay leadership (Certificate); theological studies (M Div); theology (D Min); theology and ethics (MAR). *Accreditation:* ACIPE; ATS. *Degree requirements:* For doctorate, thesis/dissertation.

Lindenwood University, Graduate Programs, School of Arts, Media, and Communications, St. Charles, MO 63301-1695. Offers advertising (MA); art history (MA); cinema and media arts (MFA); communications (MA); digital and Web design (MA); fashion and business design (MS); journalism (MA); mass communications (MA); social media and digital content (MS). *Program availability:* Part-time, 100% online. *Faculty:* 20 full-time (5 women), 15 part-time/adjunct (6 women). *Students:* 64 full-time (42 women), 76 part-time (57 women); includes 43 minority (20 Black or African American, non-Hispanic/Latino; 13 Hispanic/Latino; 10 Two or more races, non-Hispanic/Latino), 8 international. Average age 33. 145 applicants, 46% accepted, 56 enrolled. In 2019, 11 master's awarded. *Degree requirements:* For master's, thesis (for some programs), minimum cumulative GPA of 3.0. *Entrance requirements:* For master's, audition or interview, minimum GPA of 3.0, portfolio, letter of recommendation. Additional exam requirements/recommendations for international students: required—TOEFL (minimum score 553 paper-based; 81 iBT); recommended—IELTS (minimum score 6.5). *Application deadline:* For fall admission, 8/9 priority date for domestic students, 6/1 priority date for international students; for spring admission, 12/20 for domestic students, 11/1 priority date for international students; for summer admission, 5/15 priority date for domestic students, 3/27 priority date for international students. Applications are processed on a rolling basis. Application fee: $0 ($100 for international students). Electronic applications accepted. *Expenses: Tuition:* Full-time $8910; part-time $495 per credit. Tuition and fees vary according to course load, degree level and program. *Financial support:* In 2019–20, 23 students received support. Career-related internships or fieldwork, institutionally sponsored loans, scholarships/grants, tuition waivers (partial), and unspecified assistantships available. Financial award application deadline: 6/30; financial award applicants required to submit FAFSA. *Unit head:* Dr. Jason Lively, Dean, School of Arts, Media, and Communications, 636-949-4164, Fax: 636-949-4910, E-mail: JLively@lindenwood.edu. *Application contact:* Kara Schilli, Assistant Vice President, University Admissions, 636-949-4349, Fax: 636-949-4109, E-mail: adultadmissions@lindenwood.edu.
Website: https://www.lindenwood.edu/academics/academic-schools/school-of-arts-media-and-communications/

Louisiana State University and Agricultural & Mechanical College, Graduate School, College of Art and Design, School of Art, Program in Art History, Baton Rouge, LA 70803. Offers MA. *Accreditation:* NASAD.

Massachusetts Institute of Technology, School of Architecture and Planning, Department of Architecture, Cambridge, MA 02139. Offers architecture (M Arch, PhD), including building technology (PhD), design and computation (PhD), history and theory of architecture (PhD), history and theory of art (PhD); architecture studies (SM Arch S); art, culture and technology (SMACT); building technology (SMBT). *Degree requirements:* For master's, thesis; for doctorate, comprehensive exam, thesis/dissertation. *Entrance requirements:* For master's and doctorate, GRE General Test. Additional exam requirements/recommendations for international students: required—TOEFL, IELTS. Electronic applications accepted.

McGill University, Faculty of Graduate and Postdoctoral Studies, Faculty of Arts, Department of Art History and Communication Studies, Montréal, QC H3A 2T5, Canada. Offers MA, PhD.

Montana State University, The Graduate School, College of Arts and Architecture, School of Art, Bozeman, MT 59717. Offers art (MFA); art history (MA). *Accreditation:* NASAD (one or more programs are accredited). *Program availability:* Part-time. *Degree requirements:* For master's, comprehensive exam, thesis. *Entrance requirements:* For master's, GRE General Test, undergraduate degree in art. Additional exam requirements/recommendations for international students: required—TOEFL (minimum score 550 paper-based). Electronic applications accepted.

New Mexico State University, College of Arts and Sciences, Department of Art, Las Cruces, NM 88003-8001. Offers art history (MA); studio art (MFA). *Program availability:* Part-time. *Faculty:* 8 full-time (6 women), 1 (woman) part-time/adjunct. *Students:* 13 full-time (9 women), 2 part-time (both women); includes 8 minority (7 Hispanic/Latino; 1 Two or more races, non-Hispanic/Latino), 1 international. Average age 30. 8 applicants, 75% accepted, 5 enrolled. In 2019, 4 master's awarded. *Degree requirements:* For master's, one foreign language, comprehensive exam (for some

programs), thesis, thesis exhibit. *Entrance requirements:* For master's, portfolio (for MFA); 10-20 page paper (for MA). Additional exam requirements/recommendations for international students: required—TOEFL (minimum score 550 paper-based; 79 iBT), IELTS (minimum score 6.5). *Application deadline:* For fall admission, 1/20 for domestic students; for spring admission, 11/15 for domestic students. Application fee: $40 ($50 for international students). Electronic applications accepted. *Financial support:* In 2019-20, 12 students received support, including 1 fellowship (averaging $4,844 per year), 11 teaching assistantships (averaging $17,508 per year); career-related internships or fieldwork, Federal Work-Study, scholarships/grants, traineeships, health care benefits, and unspecified assistantships also available. Support available to part-time students. Financial award application deadline: 3/1. *Unit head:* Dr. Julia Barello, Department Head, 575-646-2728, Fax: 575-646-8036, E-mail: jbarello@nmsu.edu. *Application contact:* Dr. Julia Barello, Department Head, 575-646-2728, Fax: 575-646-8036, E-mail: jbarello@nmsu.edu.
Website: http://artdepartment.nmsu.edu/

New York University, Graduate School of Arts and Science, Institute of Fine Arts, Program in Art History and Archaeology, New York, NY 10012-1019. Offers architectural studies (PhD); art history and archaeology (MA, PhD); classical art and archaeology (PhD); curatorial studies (PhD); East and South Asian art (PhD); Near Eastern art and archaeology (PhD); MA/Diploma; PhD/Certificate. *Program availability:* Part-time. Terminal master's awarded for partial completion of doctoral program. *Degree requirements:* For master's, 2 foreign languages, thesis or alternative, 2 qualifying papers; for doctorate, 2 foreign languages, thesis/dissertation. *Entrance requirements:* For master's, GRE General Test; for doctorate, GRE General Test, MA. Additional exam requirements/recommendations for international students: required—TOEFL, IELTS.

Northwestern University, The Graduate School, Judd A. and Marjorie Weinberg College of Arts and Sciences, Department of Art History, Evanston, IL 60208. Offers PhD. *Degree requirements:* For doctorate, 2 foreign languages, comprehensive exam, thesis/dissertation, major and minor field exercises. *Entrance requirements:* For doctorate, GRE General Test. Additional exam requirements/recommendations for international students: required—TOEFL. Electronic applications accepted.

The Ohio State University, Graduate School, College of Arts and Sciences, Division of Arts and Humanities, Department of History of Art, Columbus, OH 43210. Offers MA, PhD. *Accreditation:* NASAD. Terminal master's awarded for partial completion of doctoral program. *Degree requirements:* For master's, one foreign language, thesis optional; for doctorate, 2 foreign languages, thesis/dissertation. *Entrance requirements:* For master's and doctorate, GRE General Test. Additional exam requirements/recommendations for international students: required—TOEFL (minimum score 550 paper-based; 79 iBT), Michigan English Language Assessment Battery (minimum score 82); recommended—IELTS (minimum score 7). Electronic applications accepted.

Ohio University, Graduate College, College of Fine Arts, School of Art, Athens, OH 45701-2979. Offers art history (MA); ceramics (MFA); graphic design (MFA); painting (MFA); photography (MFA); printmaking (MFA); sculpture (MFA). *Program availability:* Part-time. *Degree requirements:* For master's, thesis. *Entrance requirements:* For master's, portfolio. Additional exam requirements/recommendations for international students: required—TOEFL (minimum score 550 paper-based; 80 iBT) or IELTS (minimum score 6.5). Electronic applications accepted.

Oklahoma State University, College of Arts and Sciences, Department of Art, Graphic Design and Art History, Stillwater, OK 74078. Offers art history (MA); graphic design (MA). *Faculty:* 15 full-time (8 women), 1 (woman) part-time/adjunct. *Students:* 5 full-time (all women), 3 part-time (2 women); includes 3 minority (1 Asian, non-Hispanic/Latino; 2 Hispanic/Latino), 3 international. Average age 30. 9 applicants, 33% accepted, 2 enrolled. In 2019, 4 master's awarded. *Entrance requirements:* For master's, GRE or GMAT. Additional exam requirements/recommendations for international students: required—TOEFL (minimum score 550 paper-based; 79 iBT). *Application deadline:* For fall admission, 3/1 for domestic students; for spring admission, 8/1 for domestic students. Application fee: $50 ($75 for international students). Electronic applications accepted. *Expenses: Tuition, area resident:* Full-time $4148.10; part-time $2765.40 per credit hour. Tuition, state resident: full-time $4148.10; part-time $2765.40 per credit hour. Tuition, nonresident: full-time $15,775; part-time $10,516.80 per credit hour. *International tuition:* $15,775.20 full-time. *Required fees:* $2196.90; $122.05 per credit hour. Tuition and fees vary according to course load, campus/location and program. *Financial support:* In 2019-20, 8 teaching assistantships (averaging $1,330 per year) were awarded; research assistantships, career-related internships or fieldwork, Federal Work-Study, scholarships/grants, health care benefits, tuition waivers, and unspecified assistantships also available. Support available to part-time students. Financial award application deadline: 3/1; financial award applicants required to submit FAFSA. *Unit head:* Liz Roth, Interim Head, 405-744-6016, E-mail: liz.roth@okstate.edu. *Application contact:* Dr. Sheryl Tucker, Dean, 405-744-6368, Fax: 405-744-0355, E-mail: gradi@okstate.edu.
Website: http://art.okstate.edu/

Penn State University Park, Graduate School, College of Arts and Architecture, Department of Art History, University Park, PA 16802. Offers MA, PhD.

Purchase College, State University of New York, School of Humanities, Purchase, NY 10577-1400. Offers art history (MA). *Accreditation:* NASAD. *Students:* 7 full-time (6 women), 4 part-time (2 women); includes 5 minority (1 Black or African American, non-Hispanic/Latino; 3 Hispanic/Latino; 1 Two or more races, non-Hispanic/Latino). Average age 36. 16 applicants, 88% accepted, 5 enrolled. *Degree requirements:* For master's, one foreign language, thesis. *Entrance requirements:* For master's, BA or BFA, previous course work in art history, three letters of recommendation, personal statement, 1-2 writing samples, official transcripts. Additional exam requirements/recommendations for international students: required—TOEFL (minimum score 550 paper-based; 80 iBT), IELTS (minimum score 6.5). *Application deadline:* For fall admission, 3/1 for domestic students. Application fee: $85. Electronic applications accepted. *Expenses: Tuition, area resident:* Full-time $11,310. Tuition, state resident: full-time $11,310. Tuition, nonresident: full-time $23,100. *Required fees:* $1883. *Financial support:* Fellowships, Federal Work-Study, scholarships/grants, and tuition waivers (partial) available. Support available to part-time students. Financial award application deadline: 3/15; financial award applicants required to submit FAFSA. *Unit head:* Ross Daly, Chair, 914-251-6550. *Application contact:* Beatriz Martin-Ruiz, Assistant Director of Admissions, 914-251-6304, Fax: 914-251-6314, E-mail: admissn@purchase.edu.
Website: https://www.purchase.edu/academics/school-of-humanities/

Queens College of the City University of New York, Arts and Humanities Division, Department of Art, Flushing, NY 11367. Offers art history (MA); studio art (MFA). *Program availability:* Part-time. *Faculty:* 18 full-time (5 women), 57 part-time/adjunct (31 women). *Students:* 1 (woman) full-time. Average age 36. 3 applicants. In 2019, 2 master's awarded. *Degree requirements:* For master's, 2 foreign languages, comprehensive exam, thesis optional, comprehensive exam (for art history program). *Entrance requirements:* For master's, Qualifying Exam, minimum GPA of 3.0. Additional exam requirements/recommendations for international students: required—TOEFL (minimum score 600 paper-based), IELTS. *Application deadline:* For fall admission, 4/1 for domestic students; for spring admission, 11/1 for domestic students. Applications are processed on a rolling basis. Application fee: $125. Electronic applications accepted. *Financial support:* Fellowships and career-related internships or fieldwork available. Financial award application deadline: 4/1; financial award applicants required to submit FAFSA. *Unit head:* Michael Nelson, Chair, 718-997-4800, E-mail: michael.nelson@qc.cuny.edu. *Application contact:* Elizabeth D'Amico-Ramirez, Assistant Director of Graduate Admissions, 718-997-5203, E-mail: elizabeth.damicoramirez@qc.cuny.edu.
Website: http://art.qc.cuny.edu/

Rice University, Graduate Programs, School of Humanities, Department of Art History, Houston, TX 77251-1892. Offers PhD.

Richmond, The American International University in London, MA in Art History Program, Richmond, United Kingdom. Offers MA. *Program availability:* Part-time. *Degree requirements:* For master's, thesis. *Entrance requirements:* For master's, minimum GPA of 3.0. Additional exam requirements/recommendations for international students: required—TOEFL, IELTS. Electronic applications accepted. *Expenses:* Contact institution.

Roger Williams University, School of Architecture, Art and Historic Preservation, Bristol, RI 02809. Offers architecture (M Arch); art and architectural history (MA); historical preservation (MS, Certificate); urban and regional planning (Certificate). *Program availability:* Part-time. *Faculty:* 8 full-time (4 women), 6 part-time/adjunct (1 woman). *Students:* 97 full-time (46 women), 10 part-time (0 women); includes 15 minority (1 Black or African American, non-Hispanic/Latino; 1 American Indian or Alaska Native, non-Hispanic/Latino; 1 Asian, non-Hispanic/Latino; 8 Hispanic/Latino; 4 Two or more races, non-Hispanic/Latino), 5 international. Average age 23. 97 applicants, 92% accepted, 54 enrolled. In 2019, 48 master's awarded. *Degree requirements:* For master's, thesis. *Entrance requirements:* For master's, letter of intent, transcripts, 2 letters of recommendation, portfolio (Architecture only), writing sample (Preservation only); for Certificate, transcripts. Additional exam requirements/recommendations for international students: required—TOEFL (minimum score 85 paper-based), IELTS (minimum score 6.5). *Application deadline:* For fall admission, 1/15 for domestic students, 5/1 for international students. Application fee: $50. Electronic applications accepted. *Expenses:* Tuition per credit hour: Architecture $1579, Preservation: $951. *Financial support:* In 2019-20, 103 students received support. Scholarships/grants and unspecified assistantships available. Financial award application deadline: 3/15; financial award applicants required to submit FAFSA. *Unit head:* Stephen White, Dean, 401-254-3607, E-mail: swhite@rwu.edu. *Application contact:* Gregory Laramie, Associate Dean, 401-254-3743, E-mail: glaramie@rwu.edu.
Website: https://www.rwu.edu/academics/schools-and-colleges/saahp

Rutgers University - New Brunswick, Graduate School-New Brunswick, Program in Art History, Piscataway, NJ 08854-8097. Offers art history (MA, PhD); curatorial studies (Certificate); historic preservation (Certificate). *Program availability:* Part-time. Terminal master's awarded for partial completion of doctoral program. *Degree requirements:* For master's, one foreign language, comprehensive exam; for doctorate, 2 foreign languages, comprehensive exam, thesis/dissertation. *Entrance requirements:* For master's and doctorate, GRE General Test, writing sample. Additional exam requirements/recommendations for international students: required—TOEFL (minimum score 550 paper-based). Electronic applications accepted.

San Francisco Art Institute, Master of Arts Programs, San Francisco, CA 94133. Offers exhibition and museum studies (MA); history and theory of contemporary art (MA). *Degree requirements:* For master's, thesis. *Entrance requirements:* For master's, statement of purpose, writing samples. Additional exam requirements/recommendations for international students: required—TOEFL (minimum score 600 paper-based; 100 iBT), IELTS (minimum score 7.5). Electronic applications accepted.

Savannah College of Art and Design, Program in Art History, Savannah, GA 31402-3146. Offers MA. *Program availability:* Part-time. *Degree requirements:* For master's, one foreign language, comprehensive exam, thesis. *Entrance requirements:* For master's, GRE (recommended), portfolio (submitted in digital format), audition or writing submission, resume, statement of purpose, two letters of recommendation. Additional exam requirements/recommendations for international students: recommended—TOEFL (minimum score 550 paper-based; 85 iBT), IELTS (minimum score 6.5). Electronic applications accepted.

School of Visual Arts, Graduate Programs, Program in Art Writing, New York, NY 10010-3994. Offers MFA. *Degree requirements:* For master's, thesis, 60 credits; residency of two academic years. *Entrance requirements:* For master's, typed writing sample between 2,500 and 3,000 words in length; personal interviews. Additional exam requirements/recommendations for international students: required—TOEFL (minimum score 550 paper-based; 79 iBT). Electronic applications accepted.

School of Visual Arts, Graduate Programs, Program in Curatorial Practice, New York, NY 10010-3994. Offers MA.

Southern Methodist University, Meadows School of the Arts, Division of Art History, Dallas, TX 75275. Offers art history (MA); rhetorics of art, space and culture (PhD). *Program availability:* Part-time, evening/weekend. *Degree requirements:* For master's, one foreign language, thesis, translation exam. *Entrance requirements:* For master's, GRE, 12 upper-level hours in art history, sample research paper. Additional exam requirements/recommendations for international students: required—TOEFL (minimum score 550 paper-based; 80 iBT).

Stony Brook University, State University of New York, Graduate School, College of Arts and Sciences, Department of Art, Program in Art History and Criticism, Stony Brook, NY 11794. Offers MA, PhD. *Program availability:* Part-time. *Students:* 30 full-time (24 women), 2 part-time (0 women); includes 7 minority (3 Asian, non-Hispanic/Latino; 3 Hispanic/Latino; 1 Two or more races, non-Hispanic/Latino), 2 international. Average age 32. 41 applicants, 80% accepted, 7 enrolled. In 2019, 11 master's, 4 doctorates awarded. *Degree requirements:* For master's, comprehensive exam, thesis, reading knowledge of German or French; for doctorate, comprehensive exam, thesis/dissertation, qualifying paper, reading knowledge of German and French, qualifying examination. *Entrance requirements:* For master's, GRE General Test, minimum undergraduate GPA of 3.0; for doctorate, GRE General Test, minimum graduate GPA of 3.0. Additional exam requirements/recommendations for international students: required—TOEFL (minimum score 550 paper-based), IELTS (minimum score 6.5). *Application deadline:* For fall admission, 1/15 for domestic students; for spring admission, 10/1 for domestic students. Application fee: $100. *Expenses:* Contact institution. *Financial support:* In 2019-20, 16 teaching assistantships were awarded; fellowships and research assistantships also available. Financial award applicants required to submit FAFSA. *Unit head:* Dr. Shoki Goodarzi, Director of Graduate Studies, 631-632-7250, E-mail: Shoki.Goodarzi@stonybrook.edu. *Application contact:* Lisa Perez, Coordinator, 631-632-7270, E-mail: lisa.a.perez@stonybrook.edu.
Website: http://art.stonybrook.edu/graduate/g-arhc/

Sul Ross State University, College of Arts and Sciences, Department of Fine Arts and Communication, Alpine, TX 79832. Offers art history (MA); studio art (MA), including art education. *Program availability:* Part-time. *Degree requirements:* For master's, oral or written exam. *Entrance requirements:* For master's, GRE General Test, minimum GPA of 2.5 in last 60 hours of undergraduate work.

Syracuse University, College of Arts and Sciences, MA Program in Art History, Syracuse, NY 13244. Offers MA. *Degree requirements:* For master's, one foreign language, symposium presentation. *Entrance requirements:* For master's, GRE, competency exam in the history of art, bachelor's degree, normally as art history major, at accredited institution; academic transcripts of all undergraduate studies. Additional exam requirements/recommendations for international students: required—TOEFL (minimum score 100 iBT). Electronic applications accepted.

Temple University, Tyler School of Art and Architecture, Department of Art History, Philadelphia, PA 19122-6096. Offers MA, PhD. *Program availability:* Part-time. *Faculty:* 11 full-time (8 women), 8 part-time/adjunct (5 women). *Students:* 48 full-time (37 women), 3 part-time (all women); includes 11 minority (1 Black or African American, non-Hispanic/Latino; 2 Asian, non-Hispanic/Latino; 5 Hispanic/Latino; 3 Two or more races, non-Hispanic/Latino), 5 international. 31 applicants, 68% accepted, 7 enrolled. In 2019, 9 master's, 3 doctorates awarded. *Degree requirements:* For master's, one foreign language, thesis (for some programs), internship (fine arts administration track); for doctorate, 2 foreign languages, thesis/dissertation. *Entrance requirements:* For master's, GRE, 3 letters of recommendation, 5 courses in art history, statement of goals, resume/curriculum vitae, writing sample; for doctorate, GRE, 3 letters of recommendation, statement of goals, resume/curriculum vitae, writing sample. Additional exam requirements/recommendations for international students: required—TOEFL (minimum score 79 iBT), IELTS (minimum score 6.5), PTE (minimum score 53), one of three is required. *Application deadline:* For fall admission, 12/15 for domestic students; for spring admission, 11/1 for domestic students. Application fee: $60. Electronic applications accepted. *Financial support:* Fellowships, research assistantships, teaching assistantships, career-related internships or fieldwork, Federal Work-Study, and health care benefits available. Financial award application deadline: 12/15; financial award applicants required to submit FAFSA. *Unit head:* Dr. Jane DeRose Evans, Chair, 215-777-9165, Fax: 215-204-6951, E-mail: jevans@temple.edu. *Application contact:* Lauren O'Neill, Director of Admissions, 215-777-9159, E-mail: tyleradmissions@temple.edu.
Website: https://tyler.temple.edu/programs/art-history

Texas Christian University, College of Fine Arts, School of Art, Fort Worth, TX 76129. Offers art history (MA); studio art (MFA), including painting. *Accreditation:* NASAD. *Faculty:* 12 full-time (6 women), 2 part-time/adjunct (1 woman). *Students:* 21 full-time (13 women); includes 6 minority (2 Asian, non-Hispanic/Latino; 4 Hispanic/Latino), 2 international. Average age 27. 36 applicants, 31% accepted, 9 enrolled. In 2019, 9 master's awarded. *Degree requirements:* For master's, variable foreign language requirement, comprehensive exam, thesis. *Entrance requirements:* For master's, GRE General Test (for MA). Additional exam requirements/recommendations for international students: required—TOEFL (minimum score 550 paper-based; 80 iBT). *Application deadline:* For fall admission, 2/1 for domestic and international students. Application fee: $60. Electronic applications accepted. *Expenses:* Contact institution. *Financial support:* In 2019–20, 21 students received support, including 21 teaching assistantships (averaging $10,000 per year); institutionally sponsored loans, scholarships/grants, health care benefits, tuition waivers (full and partial), and unspecified assistantships also available. Financial award application deadline: 2/1. *Unit head:* Richard Lane, Director, 817-257-7643, E-mail: r.lane@tcu.edu. *Application contact:* Donna Smolik, TCU College of Fine Arts Graduate Office, 817-257-7603, Fax: 817-257-5672, E-mail: cfagradinfo@tcu.edu.
Website: http://www.art.tcu.edu/

Texas Tech University, Graduate School, J.T. and Margaret Talkington College of Visual and Performing Arts, School of Art, Lubbock, TX 79409-2081. Offers art (MFA); art education (MAE); art history (MA). *Accreditation:* NASAD (one or more programs are accredited). *Program availability:* Part-time, blended/hybrid learning. *Faculty:* 31 full-time (16 women), 6 part-time/adjunct (5 women). *Students:* 28 full-time (20 women), 14 part-time (all women); includes 11 minority (1 Black or African American, non-Hispanic/Latino; 1 Asian, non-Hispanic/Latino; 8 Hispanic/Latino; 1 Two or more races, non-Hispanic/Latino), 2 international. Average age 35. 30 applicants, 67% accepted, 17 enrolled. In 2019, 15 master's awarded. *Degree requirements:* For master's, variable foreign language requirement, comprehensive exam, thesis (for some programs). *Entrance requirements:* For master's, GRE (for MA). Additional exam requirements/recommendations for international students: required—TOEFL (minimum score 550 paper-based; 79 iBT), IELTS (minimum score 6.5). *Application deadline:* For fall admission, 6/1 priority date for domestic students, 1/15 priority date for international students; for spring admission, 9/1 priority date for domestic students, 6/15 priority date for international students. Applications are processed on a rolling basis. Application fee: $65. Electronic applications accepted. *Expenses:* Contact institution. *Financial support:* In 2019–20, 35 students received support, including 35 fellowships (averaging $4,789 per year), 24 teaching assistantships (averaging $10,257 per year); research assistantships, Federal Work-Study, institutionally sponsored loans, scholarships/grants, health care benefits, tuition waivers (partial), and unspecified assistantships also available. Financial award application deadline: 1/15; financial award applicants required to submit FAFSA. *Unit head:* Prof. Robin D. Germany, Interim Director, 806-834-6440, E-mail: robin.d.germany@ttu.edu. *Application contact:* Linda Rumbelow, Academic Advisor, 806-742-3825 Ext. 222, E-mail: linda.rumbelow@ttu.edu.
Website: www.art.ttu.edu

Texas Woman's University, Graduate School, College of Arts and Sciences, School of the Arts, Department of Visual Arts, Denton, TX 76204. Offers art (MA, MAT, MFA), including art education (MA, MAT), art history (MA), ceramics (MFA), graphic design (MA), intermedia (MFA), painting (MFA), photography (MFA), sculpture (MFA). *Faculty:* 6 full-time (5 women). *Students:* 13 full-time (9 women), 8 part-time (5 women); includes 5 minority (1 Asian, non-Hispanic/Latino; 3 Hispanic/Latino; 1 Two or more races, non-Hispanic/Latino), 1 international. Average age 36. 15 applicants, 80% accepted, 9 enrolled. In 2019, 8 master's awarded. *Degree requirements:* For master's, comprehensive exam, thesis (for some programs), exhibit (MFA), oral exam, thesis or professional paper (MA). *Entrance requirements:* For master's, portfolio, interview, current curriculum vitae, letter of intent, 3 letters of recommendation, artist statement, separate application. Additional exam requirements/recommendations for international students: required—TOEFL (minimum score 79 iBT); recommended—IELTS (minimum score 6.5), TSE (minimum score 53). *Application deadline:* For fall admission, 2/15 for domestic and international students; for spring admission, 11/15 for domestic and international students. Application fee: $50 ($75 for international students). Electronic applications accepted. *Expenses: Tuition, area resident:* Full-time $4973.40; part-time $276.30 per semester hour. Tuition, state resident: full-time $4973.40; part-time $276.30 per semester hour. Tuition, nonresident: full-time $12,569; part-time $698.30 per semester hour. *International tuition:* $12,569.40 full-time. *Required fees:* $2524.30. Tuition and fees vary according to course level, course load, degree level and program. *Financial support:* In 2019–20, 15 students received support, including 12 teaching assistantships (averaging $4,968 per year); career-related internships or fieldwork, scholarships/grants, health care benefits, and unspecified assistantships also available. Support available to part-time students. Financial award application deadline: 3/1; financial award applicants required to submit FAFSA. *Unit head:* Dr. Vagner Whitehead, Chair, 940-898-2530, Fax: 940-898-2496, E-mail: visualarts@twu.edu. *Application contact:* Korie Hawkins, Associate Director of Admissions, Graduate Recruitment, 940-898-3188, Fax: 940-898-3081, E-mail: admissions@twu.edu.
Website: http://www.twu.edu/visual-arts/

Towson University, College of Liberal Arts, Program in Professional Studies, Towson, MD 21252-0001. Offers art history (MA); individualized plan of study (MA). *Program availability:* Part-time, evening/weekend. *Students:* 10 full-time (8 women), 13 part-time (7 women); includes 10 minority (8 Black or African American, non-Hispanic/Latino; 1 Hispanic/Latino; 1 Two or more races, non-Hispanic/Latino), 1 international. *Entrance requirements:* For master's, minimum GPA of 3.0, essay. *Application deadline:* For fall admission, 1/17 for domestic students, 5/15 for international students; for spring admission, 10/15 for domestic students, 12/1 for international students. Applications are processed on a rolling basis. Application fee: $45. Electronic applications accepted. *Expenses: Tuition, area resident:* Full-time $7920; part-time $439 per credit. Tuition, nonresident: full-time $16,344; part-time $908 per credit. *International tuition:* $16,344 full-time. *Required fees:* $2628; $146 per credit. $876 per term. *Financial support:* Application deadline: 4/1. *Unit head:* Dr. Karen Eskow, Program Director, 410-704-2128, E-mail: keskow@towson.edu. *Application contact:* Coverley Beidleman, Assistant Director of Graduate Admissions, 410-704-5630, Fax: 410-704-3030, E-mail: grads@towson.edu.
Website: https://www.towson.edu/cla/departments/interdisciplinary/grad/professional/

Tufts University, Graduate School of Arts and Sciences, Department of Art and Art History, Medford, MA 02155. Offers art history (MA); art history and museum studies (MA). *Degree requirements:* For master's, one foreign language, thesis (for some programs). *Entrance requirements:* For master's, GRE General Test. Additional exam requirements/recommendations for international students: required—TOEFL (minimum score 550 paper-based; 80 iBT), IELTS (minimum score 6.5). Electronic applications accepted. *Expenses:* Contact institution.

Tulane University, School of Liberal Arts, Department of Art, New Orleans, LA 70118-5669. Offers history of art (MA); studio art (MFA). *Degree requirements:* For master's, one foreign language, thesis. *Entrance requirements:* For master's, GRE General Test, minimum B average in undergraduate course work. Additional exam requirements/recommendations for international students: required—TOEFL. Electronic applications accepted. *Expenses: Tuition:* Full-time $57,004; part-time $3167 per credit hour. *Required fees:* $2086; $44.50 per credit hour. $80 per term. Tuition and fees vary according to course load, degree level and program.

Université de Montréal, Faculty of Arts and Sciences, Department of Art History and Film Studies, Montréal, QC H3C 3J7, Canada. Offers art history (MA, PhD); film studies (MA, PhD). *Degree requirements:* For master's, thesis. Electronic applications accepted.

Université du Québec à Montréal, Graduate Programs, Program in Art Studies, Montréal, QC H3C 3P8, Canada. Offers art history (PhD); art studies (MA); study and practices of the arts (PhD). *Program availability:* Part-time. *Degree requirements:* For master's, thesis; for doctorate, thesis/dissertation. *Entrance requirements:* For master's, appropriate bachelor's degree or equivalent, proficiency in French; for doctorate, appropriate master's degree or equivalent, proficiency in French.

University at Buffalo, the State University of New York, Graduate School, College of Arts and Sciences, Department of Art, Program in Visual Studies, Buffalo, NY 14260. Offers critical museum studies (MA); visual studies (MA, PhD). *Program availability:* Part-time. *Degree requirements:* For master's, thesis, field exam; for doctorate, one foreign language, thesis/dissertation. *Entrance requirements:* Additional exam requirements/recommendations for international students: required—TOEFL (minimum score 79 iBT). Electronic applications accepted. *Expenses: Tuition, area resident:* Full-time $11,310; part-time $471 per credit hour. Tuition, state resident: full-time $11,310; part-time $471 per credit hour. Tuition, nonresident: full-time $23,100; part-time $963 per credit hour. *International tuition:* $23,100 full-time. *Required fees:* $2820.

The University of Alabama, Graduate School, College of Arts and Sciences, Department of Art and Art History, Tuscaloosa, AL 35487. Offers art history (MA); studio art (MA, MFA), including ceramics, painting, photography, printmaking, sculpture. *Accreditation:* NASAD. *Program availability:* Part-time. *Faculty:* 9 full-time (3 women). *Students:* 20 full-time (16 women), 3 part-time (1 woman); includes 3 minority (1 Black or African American, non-Hispanic/Latino; 2 Hispanic/Latino), 4 international. Average age 29. 22 applicants, 59% accepted, 8 enrolled. In 2019, 6 master's awarded. *Degree requirements:* For master's, one foreign language, comprehensive exam (for some programs), oral exam, thesis statement, exhibit (studio art), thesis (art history). *Entrance requirements:* For master's, GRE General Test or MAT (art history), minimum GPA of 3.0, BFA or equivalent (studio art). Additional exam requirements/recommendations for international students: required—TOEFL (minimum score 550 paper-based). *Application deadline:* For fall admission, 3/15 for domestic and international students; for spring admission, 10/15 for domestic and international students. Applications are processed on a rolling basis. Application fee: $50 ($60 for international students). Electronic applications accepted. *Expenses: Tuition, area resident:* Full-time $10,780; part-time $440 per credit hour. Tuition, nonresident: full-time $30,250; part-time $1550 per credit hour. *Financial support:* In 2019–20, 8 students received support, including 2 fellowships with full tuition reimbursements available, 14 teaching assistantships with tuition reimbursements available (averaging $15,427 per year); career-related internships or fieldwork, institutionally sponsored loans, scholarships/grants, and unspecified assistantships also available. Financial award application deadline: 7/1. *Unit head:* Jason Guynes, Chair, 205-348-9944, Fax: 205-348-0287, E-mail: jguynes@ua.edu. *Application contact:* Allison Grant, Studio Art Graduate Program Director, 205-348-5968, Fax: 205-348-5967, E-mail: agrant4@ua.edu.
Website: http://www.art.ua.edu/

The University of Alabama at Birmingham, College of Arts and Sciences, Program in Art History, Birmingham, AL 35294. Offers MA. *Accreditation:* NASAD. *Program availability:* Part-time, evening/weekend. *Faculty:* 4 full-time (all women). *Students:* 3 full-time (all women), 3 part-time (2 women); includes 1 minority (Hispanic/Latino), 2 international. Average age 36. 3 applicants, 67% accepted. In 2019, 4 master's awarded. Terminal master's awarded for partial completion of doctoral program. *Degree requirements:* For master's, one foreign language, comprehensive exam, thesis. *Entrance requirements:* For master's, GRE General Test, minimum GPA of 3.0. Additional exam requirements/recommendations for international students: required—TOEFL. *Application deadline:* For fall admission, 4/1 for domestic students; for spring admission, 10/1 for domestic students. Applications are processed on a rolling basis. Electronic applications accepted. *Financial support:* In 2019–20, 3 students received support, including 1 fellowship with partial tuition reimbursement available, 2 research assistantships with partial tuition reimbursements available; Federal Work-Study and tuition waivers (partial) also available. Financial award application deadline: 5/1; financial award applicants required to submit FAFSA. *Unit head:* Dr. Cathleen Cummings, Graduate Advisor, 205-934-4941, E-mail: cathleen@uab.edu. *Application*

contact: Susan Noblitt Banks, Director of Graduate School Operations, 205-934-8227, Fax: 205-934-8413, E-mail: gradschool@uab.edu.
Website: http://www.uab.edu/cas/art/areas-of-study/ma-art-history

University of Alberta, Faculty of Graduate Studies and Research, Department of Art and Design, Edmonton, AB T6G 2E1, Canada. Offers drawing (MFA); history of art, design, and visual culture (MA); industrial design (M Des); painting (MFA); printmaking (MFA); sculpture (MFA); visual communication design (M Des). *Degree requirements:* For master's, thesis. *Entrance requirements:* For master's, portfolio (MFA and MDES). Additional exam requirements/recommendations for international students: required—TOEFL (minimum score 550 paper-based).

The University of Arizona, College of Fine Arts, School of Art, Program in Art History, Tucson, AZ 85721. Offers MA. *Accreditation:* NASAD. *Program availability:* Part-time. Terminal master's awarded for partial completion of doctoral program. *Degree requirements:* For master's, one foreign language, thesis. *Entrance requirements:* For master's, GRE, 3 letters of recommendation, resume or curriculum vitae, writing sample. Additional exam requirements/recommendations for international students: required—TOEFL (minimum score 550 paper-based; 79 iBT). Electronic applications accepted.

The University of Arizona, College of Fine Arts, School of Art, Program in Art History and Education, Tucson, AZ 85721. Offers PhD. *Degree requirements:* For doctorate, thesis/dissertation. *Entrance requirements:* Additional exam requirements/recommendations for international students: required—TOEFL (minimum score 550 paper-based; 79 iBT). Electronic applications accepted.

The University of Arizona, College of Fine Arts, School of Art, Program in History and Theory of Art, Tucson, AZ 85721. Offers PhD. *Entrance requirements:* Additional exam requirements/recommendations for international students: required—TOEFL (minimum score 550 paper-based; 79 iBT).

University of Arkansas at Little Rock, Graduate School, College of Arts, Letters, and Sciences, Department of Art, Little Rock, AR 72204-1099. Offers art education (MA); art history (MA); studio art (MA). *Accreditation:* NASAD. *Program availability:* Part-time. *Degree requirements:* For master's, 4 foreign languages, oral exam, oral defense of thesis or exhibit. *Entrance requirements:* For master's, portfolio review or term paper evaluation, minimum GPA of 2.7.

The University of British Columbia, Faculty of Arts, Department of Art History, Visual Art, and Theory, Vancouver, BC V6T 1Z2, Canada. Offers art history (MA, PhD); critical and curatorial studies (MA); visual art (MFA). *Degree requirements:* For master's, one foreign language, thesis, final exhibition (MFA, MA in critical and curatorial studies); for doctorate, 2 foreign languages, comprehensive exam, thesis/dissertation. *Entrance requirements:* For master's, bachelor's degree with minimum B+ average (MFA, MA in critical and curatorial studies), A- (MA in art history); for doctorate, master's degree with minimum A- average. Additional exam requirements/recommendations for international students: required—TOEFL. Electronic applications accepted. *Expenses:* Contact institution.

University of California, Berkeley, Graduate Division, College of Letters and Science, Department of History of Art, Berkeley, CA 94720. Offers PhD. *Degree requirements:* For doctorate, 2 foreign languages, thesis/dissertation, qualifying exam. *Entrance requirements:* For doctorate, GRE General Test, minimum GPA of 3.0, 3 letters of recommendation. Additional exam requirements/recommendations for international students: required—TOEFL (minimum score 570 paper-based; 90 iBT). Electronic applications accepted.

University of California, Davis, Graduate Studies, Program in Art History, Davis, CA 95616. Offers MA. *Degree requirements:* For master's, thesis. *Entrance requirements:* For master's, GRE, minimum GPA of 3.0, writing sample. Additional exam requirements/recommendations for international students: required—TOEFL (minimum score 550 paper-based). Electronic applications accepted.

University of California, Los Angeles, Graduate Division, College of Letters and Science, Department of Art History, Los Angeles, CA 90095. Offers MA, PhD. Terminal master's awarded for partial completion of doctoral program. *Degree requirements:* For master's, one foreign language, thesis; for doctorate, one foreign language, thesis/dissertation, oral and written qualifying exams. *Entrance requirements:* For doctorate, GRE General Test, master's degree; minimum undergraduate GPA of 3.0 (or its equivalent if letter grade system not used); thesis or research paper, language survey. Additional exam requirements/recommendations for international students: required—TOEFL. Electronic applications accepted.

University of California, Riverside, Graduate Division, Department of Art History, Riverside, CA 92521-0102. Offers MA, PhD. *Program availability:* Part-time. *Degree requirements:* For master's, one foreign language, thesis. *Entrance requirements:* For master's, GRE General Test, sample of written work, minimum GPA of 3.2. Additional exam requirements/recommendations for international students: required—TOEFL (minimum score 550 paper-based; 80 iBT). Electronic applications accepted.

University of California, San Diego, Graduate Division, Department of Visual Arts, La Jolla, CA 92093. Offers art history, theory, and criticism (PhD); visual arts (MFA). *Students:* 69 full-time (47 women), 1 (woman) part-time. 116 applicants, 25% accepted, 17 enrolled. In 2019, 16 master's, 5 doctorates awarded. *Degree requirements:* For master's, comprehensive exam, thesis; for doctorate, 2 foreign languages, comprehensive exam, thesis/dissertation, reading knowledge of at least two of the foreign languages commonly used by scholars engaged in the advanced study in art history, theory, and criticism. *Entrance requirements:* For master's, electronic portfolio; for doctorate, GRE General Test, electronic portfolio. Additional exam requirements/recommendations for international students: required—TOEFL (minimum score 550 paper-based; 80 iBT), IELTS (minimum score 7). *Application deadline:* For fall admission, 1/3 for domestic students. Application fee: $105 ($125 for international students). Electronic applications accepted. *Financial support:* Fellowships, research assistantships, teaching assistantships, career-related internships or fieldwork, scholarships/grants, and readerships available. Financial award applicants required to submit FAFSA. *Unit head:* Amy Adler, Chair, 858-534-0418, E-mail: aadler@ucsd.edu. *Application contact:* Katherine Edwards, Graduate Program Coordinator, 858-822-3882, E-mail: vis-grad@ucsd.edu.
Website: http://visarts.ucsd.edu/

University of California, Santa Barbara, Graduate Division, College of Letters and Sciences, Division of Humanities and Fine Arts, Department of History of Art and Architecture, Santa Barbara, CA 93106-2014. Offers art history (PhD), including art history, European medieval studies, feminist studies; MA/PhD. Terminal master's awarded for partial completion of doctoral program. *Degree requirements:* For doctorate, 2 foreign languages, comprehensive exam, thesis/dissertation. *Entrance requirements:* For doctorate, GRE. Additional exam requirements/recommendations for international students: required—TOEFL (minimum score 550 paper-based; 80 iBT), IELTS (minimum score 7). Electronic applications accepted.

University of Chicago, Division of the Humanities, Department of Art History, Chicago, IL 60637. Offers PhD. Terminal master's awarded for partial completion of doctoral program. *Degree requirements:* For doctorate, variable foreign language requirement, comprehensive exam, thesis/dissertation. *Entrance requirements:* For doctorate, GRE General Test, 15-20 page writing sample, statement of purpose, 3 letters of recommendation, transcripts for all previous degrees and institutions attended. Additional exam requirements/recommendations for international students: required—TOEFL (minimum score 104 iBT), IELTS (minimum score 7). Electronic applications accepted.

University of Chicago, Division of the Humanities, Master of Arts Program in the Humanities, Chicago, IL 60637. Offers art history (MA); cinema and media studies (MA); classic languages (MA); comparative literature (MA); creative writing (MA); cultural policy studies (MA); digital humanities (MA); East Asian languages and civilizations (MA); English language and literature (MA); gender and sexuality studies (MA); Germanic studies (MA); linguistics (MA); music (MA); near Eastern languages and civilizations (MA); philosophy (MA); poetics (MA); race, politics and culture (MA); Romance languages and literatures (MA); Slavic languages and literatures (MA); South Asian languages and civilizations (MA); theater and performance studies (MA). *Degree requirements:* For master's, thesis. *Entrance requirements:* For master's, GRE General Test, 10-15 page writing sample, statement of purpose, 3 letters of recommendation, transcripts for all previous degrees and institutions attended. Additional exam requirements/recommendations for international students: required—TOEFL (minimum score 104 iBT), IELTS (minimum score 7). Electronic applications accepted. *Expenses:* Contact institution.

University of Cincinnati, Graduate School, College of Design, Architecture, Art, and Planning, School of Art, Cincinnati, OH 45221. Offers art history (MA); fine arts (MFA); visual arts education (MA). *Accreditation:* NASAD (one or more programs are accredited). *Program availability:* Part-time. Electronic applications accepted.

University of Colorado Boulder, Graduate School, College of Arts and Sciences, Department of Art and Art History, Boulder, CO 80309. Offers art history (MA), including contemporary art criticism, early twentieth-century art, nineteenth-century art, Russian and Soviet art; ceramics (MFA); photography and media arts (MFA); printmaking (MFA); sculpture (MFA). Terminal master's awarded for partial completion of doctoral program. *Degree requirements:* For master's, variable foreign language requirement, comprehensive exam, thesis (for some programs). *Entrance requirements:* For master's, GRE General Test, minimum undergraduate GPA of 3.0, portfolio. Electronic applications accepted. Application fee is waived when completed online.

University of Delaware, College of Arts and Sciences, Department of Art History, Newark, DE 19716. Offers MA, PhD. *Program availability:* Part-time. *Degree requirements:* For master's, one foreign language, thesis; for doctorate, 2 foreign languages, comprehensive exam, thesis/dissertation. *Entrance requirements:* For master's and doctorate, GRE General Test, writing sample. Additional exam requirements/recommendations for international students: required—TOEFL. Electronic applications accepted.

University of Denver, Division of Arts, Humanities and Social Sciences, School of Art and Art History, Denver, CO 80208. Offers art history (MA); museum studies (MA). *Accreditation:* NASAD. *Program availability:* Part-time. *Faculty:* 16 full-time (11 women), 6 part-time/adjunct (5 women). *Students:* 11 full-time (all women), 10 part-time (7 women); includes 6 minority (1 Black or African American, non-Hispanic/Latino; 1 Asian, non-Hispanic/Latino; 4 Hispanic/Latino). Average age 27. 21 applicants, 86% accepted, 12 enrolled. In 2019, 13 master's awarded. *Degree requirements:* For master's, one foreign language, comprehensive exam, research paper. *Entrance requirements:* For master's, GRE General Test, transcripts, personal statement, writing sample, three letters of recommendation. Additional exam requirements/recommendations for international students: required—TOEFL (minimum score 550 paper-based; 80 iBT). *Application deadline:* For fall admission, 1/31 priority date for domestic and international students. Applications are processed on a rolling basis. Application fee: $65. Electronic applications accepted. *Expenses:* Contact institution. *Financial support:* In 2019–20, 20 students received support, including 8 teaching assistantships with tuition reimbursements available (averaging $8,177 per year); research assistantships with tuition reimbursements available, career-related internships or fieldwork, Federal Work-Study, institutionally sponsored loans, scholarships/grants, and unspecified assistantships also available. Support available to part-time students. Financial award application deadline: 2/15; financial award applicants required to submit FAFSA. *Unit head:* Annabeth Headrick, Associate Professor and Director, 303-871-3574, E-mail: annabeth.headrick@du.edu. *Application contact:* Jason Kellermeyer, Coordinator of Academic Programs, 303-871-2846, E-mail: jason.kellermeyer@du.edu.
Website: http://www.du.edu/ahss/art/index.html

University of Florida, Graduate School, College of The Arts, School of Art and Art History, Gainesville, FL 32611. Offers art (MA), including digital arts and sciences; art education (MA); art history (MA, PhD); museology (MA), including historic preservation. *Accreditation:* NASAD. *Program availability:* Online learning. *Degree requirements:* For master's, project or thesis (MFA); 1 foreign language (MA in art history); for doctorate, 2 foreign languages, comprehensive exam, thesis/dissertation. *Entrance requirements:* For master's, GRE General Test, portfolio (MFA), writing sample (MA), minimum GPA 3.0; for doctorate, GRE General Test, minimum GPA of 3.0. Additional exam requirements/recommendations for international students: required—TOEFL (minimum score 550 paper-based; 80 iBT), IELTS (minimum score 6). Electronic applications accepted.

University of Georgia, Franklin College of Arts and Sciences, Lamar Dodd School of Art, Athens, GA 30602. Offers art (MFA, PhD); art history (MA). *Accreditation:* NASAD (one or more programs are accredited). *Degree requirements:* For doctorate, one foreign language, thesis/dissertation. *Entrance requirements:* For master's and doctorate, GRE General Test. Electronic applications accepted.

University of Hawaii at Manoa, Office of Graduate Education, College of Arts and Humanities, Department of Art and Art History, Program in Art History, Honolulu, HI 96822. Offers MA. *Program availability:* Part-time. *Entrance requirements:* Additional exam requirements/recommendations for international students: required—TOEFL (minimum score 600 paper-based; 100 iBT); recommended—IELTS.

University of Houston, Kathrine G. McGovern College of the Arts, School of Art, Houston, TX 77204. Offers art history (MA); interdisciplinary practice and emerging forms (MFA); painting (MFA); studio art (MFA). *Entrance requirements:* For master's, baccalaureate degree, portfolio. Electronic applications accepted.

University of Illinois at Chicago, College of Architecture, Design and the Arts, School of Art and Art History, Chicago, IL 60607-7128. Offers art history (MA); electronic visualization (MFA); museum and exhibition studies (MA); new media arts (MFA). *Program availability:* Part-time, evening/weekend. Terminal master's awarded for partial completion of doctoral program. *Degree requirements:* For master's, one foreign language, thesis or alternative; for doctorate, thesis/dissertation. *Entrance requirements:* For master's, GRE General Test, minimum GPA of 2.75, 3 letters of recommendation; for doctorate, GRE General Test, MA in art history or equivalent, minimum GPA of 3.0. Additional exam requirements/recommendations for international students: required—TOEFL. Electronic applications accepted. *Expenses:* Contact institution.

Art History

University of Illinois at Urbana-Champaign, Graduate College, College of Fine and Applied Arts, School of Art and Design, Program in Art History, Champaign, IL 61820. Offers MA, PhD. *Accreditation:* NASAD.

The University of Iowa, Graduate College, College of Liberal Arts and Sciences, School of Art and Art History, Program in Art History, Iowa City, IA 52242. Offers MA, PhD. *Faculty:* 9 full-time (5 women), 1 part-time/adjunct (0 women). *Students:* 16 full-time (12 women), 2 part-time (both women); includes 1 minority (Hispanic/Latino), 2 international. Average age 34. 20 applicants, 45% accepted, 8 enrolled. In 2019, 4 master's, 2 doctorates awarded. *Degree requirements:* For master's, one foreign language, thesis or alternative, substantial paper and exam; for doctorate, 2 foreign languages, comprehensive exam, thesis/dissertation, final exams and dissertation. *Entrance requirements:* For master's, GRE General Test; for doctorate, GRE General Test, MA in art history. Additional exam requirements/recommendations for international students: required—TOEFL (minimum score 550 paper-based; 81 iBT). *Application deadline:* For fall admission, 12/15 for domestic and international students. Application fee: $60 ($100 for international students). Electronic applications accepted. *Financial support:* In 2019–20, 16 students received support, including 1 fellowship (averaging $10,000 per year), 15 teaching assistantships with full and partial tuition reimbursements available (averaging $19,236 per year); research assistantships, career-related internships or fieldwork, Federal Work-Study, institutionally sponsored loans, scholarships/grants, health care benefits, and unspecified assistantships also available. Support available to part-time students. Financial award application deadline: 12/15. *Unit head:* Brenda Longfellow, Area Head for Art History, 319-335-3795, E-mail: brenda-longfellow@uiowa.edu. *Application contact:* Laura Jorgensen, Graduate Program Coordinator, 319-335-1758, E-mail: art@uiowa.edu.
Website: https://art.uiowa.edu/

The University of Kansas, Graduate Studies, College of Liberal Arts and Sciences, The Kress Foundation Department of Art History, Lawrence, KS 66045. Offers MA, PhD, PhD/MA. *Program availability:* Part-time. *Students:* 41 full-time (35 women), 2 part-time (both women); includes 1 minority (Asian, non-Hispanic/Latino), 15 international. Average age 29. 33 applicants, 70% accepted, 10 enrolled. In 2019, 11 master's, 5 doctorates awarded. Terminal master's awarded for partial completion of doctoral program. *Entrance requirements:* For master's and doctorate, GRE, resume or curriculum vitae, one-page statement of educational and career objectives, writing sample (preferably an art history paper), copy or scan of official transcripts. Additional exam requirements/recommendations for international students: required—TOEFL, IELTS. *Application deadline:* For fall admission, 1/1 for domestic and international students. Application fee: $65 ($85 for international students). Electronic applications accepted. *Expenses:* Tuition, state resident: full-time $9989. Tuition, nonresident: full-time $23,950. *International tuition:* $23,950 full-time. *Required fees:* $984; $81.99 per credit hour. Tuition and fees vary according to course load, campus/location and program. *Financial support:* Fellowships, research assistantships, teaching assistantships, career-related internships or fieldwork, scholarships/grants, health care benefits, and unspecified assistantships available. Financial award application deadline: 1/1. *Unit head:* David Cateforis, Chair, 785-864-1491, E-mail: dcat@ku.edu. *Application contact:* Bethany Harris, Graduate Admissions Contact, 785-864-0778, E-mail: bethanyharris@ku.edu.
Website: http://arthistory.ku.edu/

University of Kentucky, Graduate School, College of Fine Arts, Program in Art History, Lexington, KY 40506-0032. Offers MA. *Accreditation:* NASAD. *Degree requirements:* For master's, 2 foreign languages, comprehensive exam, thesis. *Entrance requirements:* For master's, GRE General Test, minimum undergraduate GPA of 2.75. Additional exam requirements/recommendations for international students: required—TOEFL (minimum score 550 paper-based). Electronic applications accepted.

University of Louisville, Graduate School, College of Arts and Sciences, Department of Fine Arts, Louisville, KY 40292. Offers art history (MA, PhD); curatorial studies (MA); studio art (MFA), including design. *Program availability:* Part-time. *Faculty:* 20 full-time (9 women), 21 part-time/adjunct (14 women). *Students:* 19 full-time (16 women), 1 (woman) part-time; includes 5 minority (1 Black or African American, non-Hispanic/Latino; 2 Asian, non-Hispanic/Latino; 1 Hispanic/Latino; 1 Two or more races, non-Hispanic/Latino), 3 international. Average age 34. 21 applicants, 62% accepted, 10 enrolled. In 2019, 11 master's, 2 doctorates awarded. *Degree requirements:* For master's, one foreign language, thesis. *Entrance requirements:* For master's, Two letters of reference, official transcripts. Additional exam requirements/recommendations for international students: required—TOEFL (minimum score 550 paper-based; 79 iBT), IELTS can be taken in place of the TOEFL; recommended—IELTS (minimum score 6.5). *Application deadline:* For fall admission, 3/1 priority date for domestic students, 3/1 for international students. Applications are processed on a rolling basis. Application fee: $65. Electronic applications accepted. *Expenses: Tuition, area resident:* Full-time $13,000; part-time $723 per credit hour. Tuition, state resident: full-time $13,000; part-time $723 per credit hour. Tuition, nonresident: full-time $27,114; part-time $1507 per credit hour. *International tuition:* $27,114 full-time. *Required fees:* $196. Tuition and fees vary according to program and reciprocity agreements. *Financial support:* In 2019–20, 13 students received support, including 9 teaching assistantships with full tuition reimbursements available (averaging $14,000 per year); fellowships, research assistantships, scholarships/grants, health care benefits, and unspecified assistantships also available. Financial award application deadline: 3/1. *Unit head:* Dr. Scott L. Massey, Associate Professor and Chair, 502-852-6794, Fax: 502-852-6791, E-mail: s.massey@louisville.edu. *Application contact:* Theresa Berbet, Academic Coordinator, Senior, 502-852-6147, Fax: 502-852-6791, E-mail: theresa.berbet@louisville.edu.
Website: http://art.louisville.edu

The University of Manchester, School of Arts, Languages and Cultures, Manchester, United Kingdom. Offers anthropology, media and performance (PhD); applied theatre (PhD); Arab world studies (PhD); archaeology (PhD); art history and visual studies (PhD); arts and cultural management (PhD); arts management and cultural policy (PhD); Chinese studies (PhD); classics and ancient history (PhD); composition (PhD); creative writing (PhD); drama (PhD); East Asian studies (PhD); electroacoustic composition (PhD); English and American studies (PhD); English language (PhD); French studies (PhD); German studies (PhD); history (PhD); humanitarianism and conflict response (PhD); interpreting studies (PhD); Japanese studies (PhD); Latin American cultural studies (PhD); linguistics (PhD); Middle Eastern studies (PhD); museology (PhD); museum practice (PhD); music (PhD); musicology (PhD); Polish studies (PhD); Portuguese studies (PhD); religions and theology (PhD); Russian studies (PhD); Spanish studies (PhD); translation and intercultural studies (PhD).

University of Maryland, College Park, Academic Affairs, College of Arts and Humanities, Department of Art History and Archaeology, College Park, MD 20742. Offers art history (MA, PhD). *Degree requirements:* For master's, one foreign language, thesis, oral exam; for doctorate, 2 foreign languages, thesis/dissertation, oral exam. *Entrance requirements:* For master's, GRE General Test, minimum GPA of 3.0, writing sample, 3 letters of recommendation. Additional exam requirements/recommendations for international students: required—TOEFL. Electronic applications accepted.

University of Massachusetts Amherst, Graduate School, College of Humanities and Fine Arts, Department of the History of Art and Architecture, Amherst, MA 01003. Offers MA. *Accreditation:* NASAD. *Program availability:* Part-time. *Degree requirements:* For master's, comprehensive exam, journal-level knowledge of French, German, or Italian. *Entrance requirements:* For master's, GRE General Test, 7-20 page writing sample. Additional exam requirements/recommendations for international students: required—TOEFL (minimum score 550 paper-based; 80 iBT), IELTS (minimum score 6.5). Electronic applications accepted.

University of Massachusetts Dartmouth, Graduate School, College of Visual and Performing Arts, Department of Art Education, Art History and Media Studies, North Dartmouth, MA 02747-2300. Offers MAE. *Accreditation:* NASAD. *Program availability:* Part-time. *Faculty:* 5 full-time (all women), 3 part-time/adjunct (all women). *Students:* 2 full-time (both women), 14 part-time (10 women); includes 1 minority (Hispanic/Latino). Average age 32. 3 applicants, 100% accepted, 1 enrolled. In 2019, 6 master's awarded. *Degree requirements:* For master's, thesis. *Entrance requirements:* For master's, MTEL (per program description), statement of professional goals and program intent, resume, 2 letters of recommendation, official transcripts, portfolio demonstrating capability for advanced work within a chosen discipline. Additional exam requirements/recommendations for international students: required—TOEFL (minimum score 550 paper-based; 79 iBT). *Application deadline:* For fall admission, 8/15 for domestic students, 7/15 for international students; for spring admission, 10/15 for domestic students, 9/15 for international students. Application fee: $60. Electronic applications accepted. *Expenses: Tuition, area resident:* Full-time $16,390; part-time $682.92 per credit. Tuition, state resident: full-time $16,390; part-time $682.92 per credit. Tuition, nonresident: full-time $29,578; part-time $1232.42 per credit. *Required fees:* $575. *Financial support:* In 2019–20, 1 teaching assistantship (averaging $2,040 per year) was awarded. Financial award application deadline: 3/1; financial award applicants required to submit FAFSA. *Unit head:* Cathy Smilan, Graduate Program Director, Art Education, 508-910-6594, Fax: 508-999-8901, E-mail: csmilan@umassd.edu. *Application contact:* Scott Webster, Director of Graduate Studies and Admissions, 508-999-8604, Fax: 508-999-8183, E-mail: graduate@umassd.edu.
Website: http://www.umassd.edu/cvpa/programs

University of Memphis, Graduate School, College of Communication and Fine Arts, Department of Art, Memphis, TN 38152. Offers art history (MA), including Egyptian art and archaeology, general art history; ceramics (MFA); graphic design (MFA); museum studies (Graduate Certificate); painting (MFA); printmaking/photography (MFA); sculpture (MFA). *Accreditation:* NASAD (one or more programs are accredited). *Program availability:* Part-time. *Students:* 28 full-time (21 women), 5 part-time (4 women); includes 9 minority (3 Black or African American, non-Hispanic/Latino; 1 Asian, non-Hispanic/Latino; 3 Hispanic/Latino; 2 Two or more races, non-Hispanic/Latino), 2 international. Average age 30. 36 applicants, 69% accepted, 13 enrolled. In 2019, 11 master's, 4 other advanced degrees awarded. *Degree requirements:* For master's, variable foreign language requirement, comprehensive exam, thesis, image identification exam, qualifying exam; for Graduate Certificate, internship. *Entrance requirements:* For master's, GRE General Test or MAT, portfolio (MFA), letter of intent, sample of undergraduate writing, two letters of recommendation; for Graduate Certificate, three letters of recommendation, letter of intent. *Application deadline:* For fall admission, 2/15 for domestic students; for spring admission, 11/1 for domestic students. Applications are processed on a rolling basis. Application fee: $35 ($60 for international students). *Expenses: Tuition, area resident:* Full-time $9216; part-time $512 per credit hour. Tuition, state resident: full-time $9216; part-time $512 per credit hour. Tuition, nonresident: full-time $12,672; part-time $704 per credit hour. *International tuition:* $16,128 full-time. *Required fees:* $1530; $85 per credit hour. Tuition and fees vary according to program. *Financial support:* Research assistantships with full tuition reimbursements, teaching assistantships with full tuition reimbursements, Federal Work-Study, scholarships/grants, and unspecified assistantships available. Financial award application deadline: 2/1; financial award applicants required to submit FAFSA. *Unit head:* Richard Lou, Chair, 901-678-2217, Fax: 901-678-2735, E-mail: ralou@memphis.edu. *Application contact:* Richard Lou, Chair, 901-678-2217, Fax: 901-678-2735, E-mail: ralou@memphis.edu.
Website: http://memphis.edu/art/

University of Miami, Graduate School, College of Arts and Sciences, Department of Art and Art History, Coral Gables, FL 33124. Offers art history (MA); ceramics/glass (MFA); graphic design/multimedia (MFA); painting (MFA); photography/digital imaging (MFA); printmaking (MFA); sculpture (MFA). *Program availability:* Part-time. *Degree requirements:* For master's, variable foreign language requirement, thesis, exhibit (MFA), comprehensive exam (MA). *Entrance requirements:* For master's, GRE General Test (MA), research paper (MA), slide portfolio (MFA). Additional exam requirements/recommendations for international students: required—TOEFL. Electronic applications accepted.

University of Michigan, Rackham Graduate School, College of Literature, Science, and the Arts, Department of History of Art, Ann Arbor, MI 48109-1357. Offers PhD. *Degree requirements:* For doctorate, 2 foreign languages, thesis/dissertation, preliminary examinations, oral defense of written dissertation. *Entrance requirements:* For doctorate, GRE General Test. Additional exam requirements/recommendations for international students: recommended—TOEFL. Electronic applications accepted. *Expenses:* Contact institution.

University of Michigan, Rackham Graduate School, College of Literature, Science, and the Arts, Interdepartmental Program in Classical Art and Archaeology, Ann Arbor, MI 48109-1390. Offers MA, PhD. *Degree requirements:* For doctorate, 4 foreign languages, comprehensive exam, thesis/dissertation, ancient history exam, qualifying exam, preliminary exam. *Entrance requirements:* For doctorate, GRE General Test. Additional exam requirements/recommendations for international students: required—TOEFL (minimum score 560 paper-based; 84 iBT). Electronic applications accepted.

University of Minnesota, Twin Cities Campus, Graduate School, College of Liberal Arts, Department of Art History, Minneapolis, MN 55455. Offers MA, PhD. Terminal master's awarded for partial completion of doctoral program. *Degree requirements:* For master's, one foreign language, comprehensive exam, thesis or alternative; for doctorate, 2 foreign languages, comprehensive exam, thesis/dissertation. *Entrance requirements:* For master's, GRE, 3 letters of recommendation, writing sample, statement of purpose; for doctorate, transcripts, 3 letters of recommendation, writing sample. Additional exam requirements/recommendations for international students: required—TOEFL (minimum score 79 iBT). Electronic applications accepted.

University of Minnesota, Twin Cities Campus, Graduate School, College of Liberal Arts, Department of Classical and Near Eastern Studies, Minneapolis, MN 55455-0213. Offers ancient and medieval art and archaeology (MA, PhD); classics (MA, PhD); Greek (MA, PhD); Latin (MA, PhD); religions in antiquity (MA). *Program availability:* Part-time. Terminal master's awarded for partial completion of doctoral program. *Degree requirements:* For master's, 2 foreign languages, comprehensive exam, thesis or alternative; for doctorate, variable foreign language requirement, comprehensive exam, thesis/dissertation. *Entrance requirements:* For master's and doctorate, GRE, 3 letters of recommendation, writing sample, copies of transcripts, personal statement. Additional exam requirements/recommendations for international students: required—TOEFL. Electronic applications accepted.

University of Montana, Graduate School, College of Visual and Performing Arts, School of Art, Missoula, MT 59812. Offers fine arts (MA), including art, art history; photography (MFA). *Accreditation:* NASAD (one or more programs are accredited). *Degree requirements:* For master's, thesis exhibit. *Entrance requirements:* For master's, GRE General Test, portfolio.

University of Nebraska–Lincoln, Graduate College, College of Fine and Performing Arts, Department of Art and Art History, Lincoln, NE 68588. Offers art history (MA); studio art (MFA). *Accreditation:* NASAD. *Degree requirements:* For master's, thesis. *Entrance requirements:* For master's, slide portfolio. Additional exam requirements/recommendations for international students: required—TOEFL (minimum score 550 paper-based). Electronic applications accepted.

University of New Mexico, Graduate Studies, College of Fine Arts, Program in Art History, Albuquerque, NM 87131-2039. Offers art history (MA); art of the Americas (MA); history of architecture (PhD); history of graphic arts (PhD); history of photography (PhD); modern Latin American art (PhD); Native American art (PhD); Pre-Columbian art and architecture (PhD); Spanish colonial art (PhD). *Program availability:* Part-time. *Degree requirements:* For master's, one foreign language, comprehensive exam (for some programs), thesis, symposium; for doctorate, 2 foreign languages, comprehensive exam, thesis/dissertation, symposium. *Entrance requirements:* Additional exam requirements/recommendations for international students: required—TOEFL (minimum score 550 paper-based), IELTS (minimum score 6). Electronic applications accepted. *Expenses:* Tuition, state resident: full-time $7633; part-time $972 per year. Tuition, nonresident: full-time $22,586; part-time $3840 per year. *International tuition:* $23,292 full-time. *Required fees:* $8608. Tuition and fees vary according to course level, course load, degree level, program and student level.

The University of North Carolina at Chapel Hill, Graduate School, College of Arts and Sciences, Department of Art, Program in Art History, Chapel Hill, NC 27599. Offers MA, PhD. *Degree requirements:* For master's, one foreign language, comprehensive exam, thesis; for doctorate, one foreign language, comprehensive exam, thesis/dissertation. *Entrance requirements:* For master's and doctorate, GRE General Test, minimum GPA of 3.0.

University of Northern Colorado, Graduate School, College of Performing and Visual Arts, School of Art and Design, Greeley, CO 80639. Offers art education (MA); art history (MA); studio art (MA). *Accreditation:* NASAD. *Program availability:* Part-time. *Degree requirements:* For master's, comprehensive exam, thesis. *Entrance requirements:* For master's, GRE General Test, portfolio, 3 letters of recommendation, minimum undergraduate GPA of 3.0. Electronic applications accepted.

University of North Texas, Toulouse Graduate School, Denton, TX 76203-5459. Offers accounting (MS); applied anthropology (MA, MS); applied behavior analysis (Certificate); applied geography (MA); applied technology and performance improvement (M Ed, MS); art education (MA); art history (MA); arts leadership (Certificate); audiology (Au D); behavior analysis (MS); behavioral science (PhD); biochemistry and molecular biology (MS); biology (MA, MS); biomedical engineering (MS); business analysis (MS); chemistry (MS); clinical health psychology (PhD); communication studies (MA, MS); computer engineering (MS); computer science (MS); counseling (M Ed, MS), including clinical mental health counseling (MS), college and university counseling, elementary school counseling, secondary school counseling; creative writing (MA); criminal justice (MS); curriculum and instruction (M Ed); decision sciences (MBA); design (MA, MFA), including fashion design (MFA), innovation studies, interior design (MFA); early childhood studies (MS); economics (MS); educational leadership (M Ed, Ed D); educational psychology (MS, PhD), including family studies (MS), gifted and talented (MS), human development (MS), learning and cognition (MS), research, measurement and evaluation (MS); electrical engineering (MS); emergency management (MPA); engineering technology (MS); English (MA); English as a second language (MA); environmental science (MS); finance (MBA, MS); financial management (MPA); French (MA); health services management (MBA); higher education (M Ed, Ed D); history (MA, MS); hospitality management (MS); human resources management (MPA); information science (MS); information systems (PhD); information technologies (MBA); interdisciplinary studies (MA, MS); international studies (MA); international sustainable tourism (MS); jazz studies (MM); journalism (MA, MJ, Graduate Certificate), including interactive and virtual digital communication (Graduate Certificate), narrative journalism (Graduate Certificate), public relations (Graduate Certificate); kinesiology (MS); linguistics (MA); local government management (MPA); logistics (PhD); logistics and supply chain management (MBA); long-term care, senior housing, and aging services (MA); management (PhD); marketing (MBA); mathematics (MA, MS); mechanical and energy engineering (MS, PhD); music (MA), including ethnomusicology, music theory, musicology, performance; music composition (PhD); music education (MM Ed, PhD); nonprofit management (MPA); operations and supply chain management (MBA); performance (MM, DMA); philosophy (MA); political science (MA); professional and technical communication (MA); radio, television and film (MA, MFA); rehabilitation counseling (Certificate); sociology (MA); Spanish (MA); special education (M Ed); speech-language pathology (MA); strategic management (MBA); studio art (MFA); teaching (M Ed); MBA/MS. *Program availability:* Part-time, evening/weekend, online learning. Terminal master's awarded for partial completion of doctoral program. *Degree requirements:* For master's, variable foreign language requirement, comprehensive exam (for some programs), thesis (for some programs); for doctorate, variable foreign language requirement, comprehensive exam (for some programs), thesis/dissertation; for other advanced degree, variable foreign language requirement, comprehensive exam (for some programs). *Entrance requirements:* For master's and doctorate, GRE, GMAT. Additional exam requirements/recommendations for international students: required—TOEFL (minimum score 550 paper-based; 79 iBT). Electronic applications accepted.

University of Notre Dame, The Graduate School, College of Arts and Letters, Department of Art, Art History, and Design, Notre Dame, IN 46556. Offers art history (MA); design (MFA), including graphic design, industrial design; studio art (MFA), including ceramics, painting, photography, printmaking, sculpture. *Accreditation:* NASAD. *Degree requirements:* For master's, comprehensive exam (for some programs), thesis. *Entrance requirements:* For master's, GRE General Test, minimum GPA of 3.0. Additional exam requirements/recommendations for international students: required—TOEFL (minimum score 600 paper-based; 80 iBT). Electronic applications accepted.

University of Oklahoma, Weitzenhoffer Family College of Fine Arts, School of Visual Arts, Norman, OK 73019. Offers art (MFA), including art and technology, ceramics, film, painting, photography, printmaking, sculpture, video, visual communication; art history (MA, PhD), including art history (MA), art of the American West (PhD), Native American art (PhD); design (MFA). *Degree requirements:* For master's, 2 foreign languages, comprehensive exam (for some programs), thesis (for some programs); for doctorate, 2 foreign languages, comprehensive exam, thesis/dissertation. *Entrance requirements:* For master's and doctorate, GRE. Additional exam requirements/recommendations for international students: required—TOEFL (minimum score 79 iBT) or IELTS (minimum score 6.5). Electronic applications accepted. *Expenses:* Tuition, state resident: full-time $6583.20; part-time $274.30 per credit hour. Tuition, nonresident: full-time $21,242; part-time $885.10 per credit hour. *International tuition:* $21,242.40 full-time. *Required fees:* $1994.20; $72.55 per credit hour. $126.50 per semester. Tuition and fees vary according to course load and degree level.

University of Oregon, Graduate School, College of Design, Department of the History of Art and Architecture, Eugene, OR 97403. Offers art history (MA, PhD). *Degree requirements:* For master's, one foreign language, thesis or alternative; for doctorate, 2 foreign languages, thesis/dissertation. *Entrance requirements:* For master's, GRE General Test, minimum GPA of 3.0; for doctorate, minimum GPA of 3.0. Additional exam requirements/recommendations for international students: required—TOEFL.

University of Pennsylvania, School of Arts and Sciences, Graduate Group in the History of Art, Philadelphia, PA 19104. Offers AM, PhD. *Faculty:* 27 full-time (15 women), 15 part-time/adjunct (7 women). *Students:* 40 full-time (27 women); includes 10 minority (4 Black or African American, non-Hispanic/Latino; 1 Asian, non-Hispanic/Latino; 2 Hispanic/Latino; 3 Two or more races, non-Hispanic/Latino), 7 international. Average age 30. 168 applicants, 5% accepted, 5 enrolled. In 2019, 4 master's, 10 doctorates awarded. Terminal master's awarded for partial completion of doctoral program. Application fee: $90.
Website: http://www.sas.upenn.edu/arthistory/graduate/about-the-program

University of Pittsburgh, Kenneth P. Dietrich School of Arts and Sciences, Department of History of Art and Architecture, Pittsburgh, PA 15260. Offers MA, PhD. *Faculty:* 17 full-time (9 women). *Students:* 38 full-time (31 women); includes 15 minority (4 Asian, non-Hispanic/Latino; 7 Hispanic/Latino; 1 Native Hawaiian or other Pacific Islander, non-Hispanic/Latino; 3 Two or more races, non-Hispanic/Latino). Average age 33. 42 applicants, 17% accepted, 5 enrolled. In 2019, 2 doctorates awarded. *Degree requirements:* For master's, one foreign language, thesis or alternative, MA paper; for doctorate, 2 foreign languages, comprehensive exam, thesis/dissertation, teaching portfolio. *Entrance requirements:* For master's and doctorate, Personal statement, Writing sample, Electronic transcripts of all college-level work to date, 3 letters of recommendation, Foreign language questionnaire. Additional exam requirements/recommendations for international students: required—TOEFL (minimum score 550 paper-based; 90 iBT). *Application deadline:* For fall admission, 12/15 for domestic and international students. Application fee: $50. Electronic applications accepted. *Financial support:* In 2019–20, 32 students received support, including 9 fellowships with full tuition reimbursements available (averaging $23,688 per year), 5 research assistantships with full tuition reimbursements available (averaging $20,250 per year), 6 teaching assistantships with full tuition reimbursements available (averaging $20,250 per year); scholarships/grants, health care benefits, tuition waivers (partial), and unspecified assistantships also available. Financial award application deadline: 12/15. *Unit head:* Dr. Jennifer Josten, Interim Department Chair and Associate Professor, 412-648-2417, Fax: 412-648-2792, E-mail: jej40@pitt.edu. *Application contact:* Karoline Swinotek, Academic and Fiscal Manager, 412-648-2400, Fax: 412-648-2792, E-mail: karoline@pitt.edu.
Website: http://www.haa.pitt.edu

University of Rochester, School of Arts and Sciences, Department of Art and Art History, Rochester, NY 14627. Offers visual and cultural studies (PhD). *Faculty:* 11 full-time (6 women). *Students:* 29 full-time (18 women); includes 8 minority (2 Black or African American, non-Hispanic/Latino; 1 Asian, non-Hispanic/Latino; 4 Hispanic/Latino; 1 Two or more races, non-Hispanic/Latino), 11 international. Average age 31. 47 applicants, 19% accepted, 5 enrolled. In 2019, 1 doctorate awarded. Terminal master's awarded for partial completion of doctoral program. *Degree requirements:* For doctorate, thesis/dissertation, qualifying exam. *Entrance requirements:* For doctorate, GRE General Test, personal statement, three letters of recommendation, official undergraduate and graduate transcripts, writing sample. Additional exam requirements/recommendations for international students: required—TOEFL. *Application deadline:* For fall admission, 1/15 for domestic and international students. Application fee: $60. Electronic applications accepted. *Financial support:* Research assistantships, teaching assistantships with full tuition reimbursements, and tuition waivers (full) available. *Unit head:* Rachel Haidu, Associate Professor and Chair, 585-275-4112, E-mail: rachel.haidu@rochester.edu. *Application contact:* Martin Collier, Administrator, 585-275-7451, E-mail: marty.collier@rochester.edu.
Website: http://www.sas.rochester.edu/aah/graduate/index.html

University of St. Thomas, College of Arts and Sciences, Department of Art History, St. Paul, MN 55105-1096. Offers art history (MA); museum studies (Graduate Certificate). *Program availability:* Part-time, evening/weekend. *Degree requirements:* For master's, one foreign language, thesis, oral exam, reading proficiency in 1 foreign language. *Entrance requirements:* For master's, Bachelor's degree in art history or related field; 3 letters of recommendation; writing sample; personal statement; transcript; for Graduate Certificate, Bachelor's degree; 1 letter of recommendation; personal statement; transcript. Additional exam requirements/recommendations for international students: required—TOEFL (minimum score 80 iBT). Electronic applications accepted. *Expenses:* Contact institution.

University of South Africa, College of Human Sciences, Pretoria, South Africa. Offers adult education (M Ed); African languages (MA, PhD); African politics (MA, PhD); Afrikaans (MA, PhD); ancient history (MA, PhD); ancient Near Eastern studies (MA, PhD); anthropology (MA, PhD); applied linguistics (MA); Arabic (MA, PhD); archaeology (MA); art history (MA); Biblical archaeology (MA); Biblical studies (M Th, D Th, PhD); Christian spirituality (M Th, D Th); church history (M Th, D Th); classical studies (MA, PhD); clinical psychology (MA); communication (MA, PhD); comparative education (M Ed, Ed D); consulting psychology (D Admin, D Com, PhD); curriculum studies (M Ed, Ed D); development studies (M Admin, MA, D Admin, PhD); didactics (M Ed, Ed D); education (M Tech); education management (M Ed, Ed D); educational psychology (M Ed); English (MA); environmental education (M Ed); French (MA, PhD); German (MA, PhD); Greek (MA); guidance and counseling (M Ed); health studies (MA, PhD), including health sciences education (MA), health services management (MA), medical and surgical nursing science (critical care general) (MA), midwifery and neonatal nursing science (MA), trauma and emergency care (MA); history (MA, PhD); history of education (Ed D); inclusive education (M Ed, Ed D); information and communications technology policy and regulation (MA); information science (MA, MIS, PhD); international politics (MA, PhD); Islamic studies (MA, PhD); Italian (MA, PhD); Judaica (MA, PhD); linguistics (MA, PhD); mathematical education (M Ed); mathematics education (MA); missiology (M Th, D Th); modern Hebrew (MA, PhD); musicology (MA, MMus, D Mus, PhD); natural science education (M Ed); New Testament (M Th, D Th); Old Testament (D Th); pastoral therapy (M Th, D Th); philosophy (MA); philosophy of education (M Ed, Ed D); politics (MA, PhD); Portuguese (MA, PhD); practical theology (M Th, D Th); psychology (MA, MS, PhD); psychology of education (M Ed, Ed D); public health (MA); religious studies (MA, D Th, PhD); Romance languages (MA); Russian (MA, PhD); Semitic languages (MA, PhD); social behavior studies in HIV/AIDS (MA); social science (mental health) (MA); social science in development studies (MA); social science in psychology (MA); social science in social work (MA); social science in sociology (MA); social work (MSW, DSW, PhD); socio-education (M Ed, Ed D); sociolinguistics (MA); sociology (MA, PhD); Spanish (MA, PhD); systematic theology (M Th, D Th); TESOL (teaching English to speakers of other languages) (MA); theological ethics (M Th, D Th); theory of literature (MA, PhD); urban ministries (D Th); urban ministry (M Th).

University of South Carolina, The Graduate School, College of Arts and Sciences, Department of Art, Program in Art History, Columbia, SC 29208. Offers MA. *Accreditation:* NASAD. *Program availability:* Part-time. *Degree requirements:* For master's, one foreign language, comprehensive exam, thesis. *Entrance requirements:* For master's, GRE General Test or MAT, writing sample. Additional exam requirements/recommendations for international students: required—TOEFL. Electronic applications accepted.

University of Southern California, Graduate School, Dana and David Dornsife College of Letters, Arts and Sciences, Department of Art History, Los Angeles, CA 90089. Offers art history (MA, PhD); visual studies (Graduate Certificate). *Degree requirements:* For doctorate, 2 foreign languages, comprehensive exam, thesis/dissertation, 60 units. *Entrance requirements:* For doctorate, GRE. Additional exam requirements/recommendations for international students: required—TOEFL.

University of South Florida, College of The Arts, School of Art and Art History, Tampa, FL 33620-9951. Offers MA, MFA. *Accreditation:* NASAD. *Program availability:* Part-time. *Faculty:* 17 full-time (8 women). *Students:* 45 full-time (25 women), 1 (woman) part-time; includes 11 minority (1 Black or African American, non-Hispanic/Latino; 8 Hispanic/Latino; 2 Two or more races, non-Hispanic/Latino), 4 international. Average age 30. 69 applicants, 32% accepted, 20 enrolled. In 2019, 13 master's awarded. *Degree requirements:* For master's, comprehensive exam, thesis, exhibition (for MFA). *Entrance requirements:* For master's, GRE General Test, bachelor's degree from regionally-accredited institution with minimum GPA of 3.0; portfolio; goals statement (for MA in art history). Additional exam requirements/recommendations for international students: required—TOEFL, TOEFL (minimum score 550 paper-based; 79 iBT) or IELTS (minimum score 6.5). *Application deadline:* For fall admission, 1/15 priority date for domestic students, 2/1 for international students. Application fee: $30. Electronic applications accepted. *Financial support:* In 2019–20, 42 students received support, including 37 teaching assistantships with partial tuition reimbursements available (averaging $9,440 per year); scholarships/grants, health care benefits, and unspecified assistantships also available. Support available to part-time students. Financial award application deadline: 2/15; financial award applicants required to submit FAFSA. *Unit head:* Prof. Wallace Wilson, Director, 813-974-2360, Fax: 813-974-9226, E-mail: wwilson2@usf.edu. *Application contact:* Prof. Neil Bender, Associate Professor and Graduate Program Director, 813-974-2360, Fax: 813-974-9226, E-mail: nb2@usf.edu. Website: http://www.art.usf.edu

The University of Texas at Austin, Graduate School, College of Fine Arts, Department of Art and Art History, Program in Art History, Austin, TX 78712-1111. Offers MA, PhD. *Accreditation:* NASAD. *Program availability:* Part-time. *Degree requirements:* For master's, one foreign language, thesis; for doctorate, 2 foreign languages, thesis/dissertation, oral and written qualifying exam. *Entrance requirements:* For master's, GRE General Test, 2 samples of written work; for doctorate, GRE General Test, minimum GPA of 3.0, 2 samples of written work. Electronic applications accepted.

The University of Texas at Dallas, School of Arts and Humanities, Richardson, TX 75080. Offers art history (MA); history (MA); humanities (MA, PhD), including aesthetic studies, history of ideas, studies in literature; Latin American studies (MA). *Program availability:* Part-time, evening/weekend. *Faculty:* 48 full-time (19 women), 11 part-time/adjunct (6 women). *Students:* 123 full-time (76 women), 116 part-time (71 women); includes 62 minority (14 Black or African American, non-Hispanic/Latino; 3 American Indian or Alaska Native, non-Hispanic/Latino; 9 Asian, non-Hispanic/Latino; 25 Hispanic/Latino; 11 Two or more races, non-Hispanic/Latino), 27 international. Average age 40. 130 applicants, 60% accepted, 59 enrolled. In 2019, 30 master's, 16 doctorates awarded. *Degree requirements:* For master's, one foreign language, portfolio; for doctorate, one foreign language, thesis/dissertation. *Entrance requirements:* For master's and doctorate, minimum GPA of 3.0 in undergraduate course work in field. Additional exam requirements/recommendations for international students: required—TOEFL (minimum score 550 paper-based). *Application deadline:* For fall admission, 7/15 for domestic students, 5/1 priority date for international students; for spring admission, 11/15 for domestic students, 9/1 priority date for international students. Applications are processed on a rolling basis. Application fee: $50 ($100 for international students). Electronic applications accepted. *Expenses: Tuition, area resident:* Full-time $16,504. Tuition, state resident: full-time $16,504. Tuition, nonresident: full-time $34,266. Tuition and fees vary according to course load. *Financial support:* In 2019–20, 87 students received support, including 9 fellowships (averaging $5,074 per year), 14 research assistantships with partial tuition reimbursements available (averaging $26,575 per year), 69 teaching assistantships with partial tuition reimbursements available (averaging $14,961 per year); Federal Work-Study, institutionally sponsored loans, scholarships/grants, and unspecified assistantships also available. Support available to part-time students. Financial award application deadline: 4/30; financial award applicants required to submit FAFSA. *Unit head:* Dr. Nils Roemer, Interim Dean, 972-883-2984, Fax: 972-883-2989, E-mail: nroemer@utdallas.edu. *Application contact:* Dr. John Gooch, Associate Dean of Graduate Studies, 972-883-2756, Fax: 972-883-2989, E-mail: john.gooch@utdallas.edu. Website: http://www.utdallas.edu/ah/

The University of Texas at San Antonio, College of Liberal and Fine Arts, Department of Art and Art History, San Antonio, TX 78249-0617. Offers art (MFA); art history (MA). *Accreditation:* NASAD (one or more programs are accredited). *Entrance requirements:* For master's, GRE General Test, portfolio, minimum GPA of 3.0 in last 60 hours, 3 letters of recommendation, statement of purpose. Additional exam requirements/recommendations for international students: required—TOEFL (minimum score 550 paper-based; 79 iBT), IELTS (minimum score 6.5). Electronic applications accepted.

The University of Texas at Tyler, College of Arts and Sciences, Department of Art and Art History, Tyler, TX 75799-0001. Offers art history (MA); interdisciplinary (MAIS); studio art (MFA). *Faculty:* 5 full-time (4 women), 5 part-time/adjunct (4 women). *Students:* 12 full-time (9 women), 3 part-time (1 woman); includes 2 minority (1 Hispanic/Latino; 1 Two or more races, non-Hispanic/Latino). Average age 38. 3 applicants, 100% accepted, 2 enrolled. In 2019, 5 master's awarded. *Degree requirements:* For master's, thesis, graduate committee review. *Entrance requirements:* For master's, minimum GPA of 3.0. Additional exam requirements/recommendations for international students: required—TOEFL. *Application deadline:* For fall admission, 8/17 priority date for domestic students, 7/1 priority date for international students; for spring admission, 12/21 priority date for domestic students, 11/1 priority date for international students. Applications are processed on a rolling basis. Application fee: $25 ($50 for international students). *Financial support:* Application deadline: 7/1; applicants required to submit FAFSA. *Unit head:* Dr. Merrie Wright, Chair, 903-566-7423, Fax: 903-566-7062, E-mail: mewright@uttyler.edu. *Application contact:* Dr. Merrie Wright, Chair, 903-566-7423, Fax: 903-566-7062, E-mail: mewright@uttyler.edu. Website: https://www.uttyler.edu/art/

University of Toronto, School of Graduate Studies, Faculty of Arts and Science, Department of Art, Toronto, ON M5S 1A1, Canada. Offers art history (MA, PhD). *Program availability:* Part-time. *Degree requirements:* For master's, 2 foreign languages, language proficiency exams; for doctorate, 2 foreign languages, comprehensive exam, thesis/dissertation. *Entrance requirements:* For master's, coursework in a foreign language, 3 letters of reference, sample research paper, minimum B+ average in senior art history and/or humanities courses; for doctorate, minimum A- average in senior art history and/or humanities courses, 2 letters of reference, sample research paper. Electronic applications accepted.

University of Utah, Graduate School, College of Fine Arts, Department of Art and Art History, Program in Art History, Salt Lake City, UT 84112-0380. Offers MA. Terminal master's awarded for partial completion of doctoral program. *Degree requirements:* For master's, one foreign language, comprehensive exam, qualifying paper, thesis or project defense. *Entrance requirements:* For master's, curriculum vitae, academic writing sample, letters of recommendation. Additional exam requirements/recommendations for international students: required—TOEFL (minimum score 80 iBT). Electronic applications accepted. *Expenses:* Tuition, state resident: full-time $7085; part-time $272.51 per credit hour. Tuition, nonresident: full-time $24,937; part-time $959.12 per credit hour. *Required fees:* $880.52; $880.52 per semester. Tuition and fees vary according to degree level, program and student level.

University of Victoria, Faculty of Graduate Studies, Faculty of Fine Arts, Department of History in Art, Victoria, BC V8W 2Y2, Canada. Offers MA, PhD. *Degree requirements:* For master's, one foreign language, thesis (for some programs), oral defense; for doctorate, 2 foreign languages, comprehensive exam, thesis/dissertation, oral defense. *Entrance requirements:* For master's, minimum B+ average in undergraduate course work; for doctorate, minimum B+ average in graduate course work. Additional exam requirements/recommendations for international students: required—TOEFL (minimum score 575 paper-based), IELTS (minimum score 7). Electronic applications accepted.

University of Virginia, College and Graduate School of Arts and Sciences, Program in Art and Architectural History, Charlottesville, VA 22903. Offers MA, PhD. *Degree requirements:* For master's, one foreign language, comprehensive exam, thesis; for doctorate, 2 foreign languages, thesis/dissertation, oral exam. *Entrance requirements:* For master's and doctorate, GRE, 2 letters of recommendation. Electronic applications accepted.

University of Washington, Graduate School, College of Arts and Sciences, School of Art, Division of Art History, Seattle, WA 98195. Offers MA, PhD. Terminal master's awarded for partial completion of doctoral program. *Degree requirements:* For master's, 2 foreign languages, practicum or thesis; for doctorate, 2 foreign languages, thesis/dissertation. *Entrance requirements:* For master's, GRE General Test, minimum undergraduate GPA of 3.0, undergraduate major in art history or equivalent; for doctorate, GRE General Test, MA in art history, minimum graduate GPA of 3.0. Additional exam requirements/recommendations for international students: required—TOEFL (minimum score 580 paper-based). Electronic applications accepted.

University of Wisconsin–Madison, Graduate School, College of Letters and Science, Department of Art History, Madison, WI 53706-1380. Offers MA, PhD. *Program availability:* Part-time. Terminal master's awarded for partial completion of doctoral program. *Degree requirements:* For master's, one foreign language; for doctorate, 2 foreign languages, thesis/dissertation. *Entrance requirements:* For master's and doctorate, GRE. Additional exam requirements/recommendations for international students: required—TOEFL. Electronic applications accepted.

University of Wisconsin–Milwaukee, Graduate School, College of Letters and Science, Department of Art History, Milwaukee, WI 53201-0413. Offers art history (MA); art history and criticism (MA); art museum studies (MA). *Program availability:* Part-time. *Degree requirements:* For master's, one foreign language, comprehensive exam, thesis or alternative. *Entrance requirements:* For master's, GRE. Additional exam requirements/recommendations for international students: required—TOEFL (minimum score 550 paper-based; 79 iBT), IELTS (minimum score 6.5). Electronic applications accepted.

University of Wisconsin–Superior, Graduate Division, Department of Visual Arts, Superior, WI 54880-4500. Offers art education (MA); art history (MA); art therapy (MA); studio arts (MA). *Program availability:* Part-time. *Degree requirements:* For master's, comprehensive exam, exhibit. *Entrance requirements:* For master's, minimum GPA of 2.75, portfolio. Electronic applications accepted.

Université Laval, Faculty of Letters, Department of History, Programs in Art History, Québec, QC G1K 7P4, Canada. Offers MA, PhD. Terminal master's awarded for partial completion of doctoral program. *Degree requirements:* For master's, thesis; for doctorate, comprehensive exam, thesis/dissertation. *Entrance requirements:* For master's, English test (comprehension of written English), knowledge of French; for doctorate, English test (comprehension of written English), knowledge of French and English, knowledge of a third language. Electronic applications accepted.

Virginia Commonwealth University, Graduate School, School of the Arts, Department of Art History, Richmond, VA 23284-9005. Offers curatorial (PhD); historical studies (MA, PhD); museum studies (MA). *Accreditation:* NASAD. *Degree requirements:* For master's, thesis; for doctorate, comprehensive exam, thesis/dissertation. *Entrance requirements:* For master's and doctorate, GRE General Test. Electronic applications accepted.

Washington University in St. Louis, The Graduate School, Department of Art History and Archaeology, St. Louis, MO 63130-4899. Offers AM, PhD. *Degree requirements:* For doctorate, 2 foreign languages, comprehensive exam, thesis/dissertation. *Entrance requirements:* For master's and doctorate, GRE General Test, sample of written work. Electronic applications accepted.

Wayne State University, College of Fine, Performing and Communication Arts, James Pearson Duffy Department of Art and Art History, Detroit, MI 48202. Offers art (MA, MFA), including ceramics, drawing, fashion design and merchandising (MA), fibers, graphic design, industrial design (MA), interior design (MA), metalsmithing, painting, photography, printmaking, sculpture; art history (MA). *Degree requirements:* For master's, thesis (for some programs), essay or thesis. *Entrance requirements:* For master's, BFA or another degree and equivalent course work, portfolio, personal interview, reference letters, statement of intent (except for art history program). Additional exam requirements/recommendations for international students: required—TOEFL (minimum score 550 paper-based; 79 iBT), TWE (minimum score 5.5), Michigan English Language Assessment Battery (minimum score 85); recommended—IELTS (minimum score 6.5). Electronic applications accepted. *Expenses:* Contact institution.

Webster University, Leigh Gerdine College of Fine Arts, Department of Art, Design, and Art History, St. Louis, MO 63119-3194. Offers art history and criticism (MA). *Program availability:* Part-time. *Degree requirements:* For master's, thesis. *Entrance requirements:* For master's, BA or BFA in related field, interview, portfolio. Additional exam requirements/recommendations for international students: required—TOEFL.

West Virginia University, College of Creative Arts, Morgantown, WV 26506. Offers acting (MFA); art education (MA); art history (MA); ceramics (MFA); collaborative piano (MM, DMA); composition (MM, DMA); conducting (MM, DMA); costume design and technology (MFA); graphic design (MFA); intermedia and photography (MFA); jazz pedagogy (MM); lighting design and technology (MFA); music (PhD); music education (MM, PhD); music industry (MA); music theory (MM); musicology (MA); painting and printmaking (MFA); performance (MM, DMA); piano pedagogy (MM); scenic design and technology (MFA); sculpture (MFA); studio art (MA); technical direction (MFA); vocal pedagogy and performance (DMA). *Program availability:* Part-time. *Degree requirements:* For master's, thesis, recitals; for doctorate, comprehensive exam, thesis/ dissertation, recitals (DMA). *Entrance requirements:* For doctorate, minimum GPA of 3.0, audition. Additional exam requirements/recommendations for international students: required—TOEFL. Electronic applications accepted.

Williams College, Graduate Program in the History of Art, Williamstown, MA 01267. Offers development economics (MA); history of art (MA). *Degree requirements:* For master's, 2 foreign languages, symposium paper and lecture. *Entrance requirements:*

For master's, GRE General Test. Additional exam requirements/recommendations for international students: required—TOEFL. Electronic applications accepted. *Expenses:* Tuition: Full-time $55,140.

Yale University, Graduate School of Arts and Sciences, Department of History of Art, New Haven, CT 06520. Offers PhD. *Degree requirements:* For doctorate, 2 foreign languages, thesis/dissertation. *Entrance requirements:* For doctorate, GRE General Test.

York University, Faculty of Graduate Studies, Faculty of Fine Arts, Program in Art History, Toronto, ON M3J 1P3, Canada. Offers MA, PhD. *Program availability:* Part-time. *Degree requirements:* For master's, one foreign language, thesis or alternative. Electronic applications accepted.

Arts Administration

American University, College of Arts and Sciences, Department of Performing Arts, Washington, DC 20016-8053. Offers art management (MA); audio production (Certificate); audio technology (MA); international arts management (Certificate); technology in arts management (Certificate). *Program availability:* Part-time, evening/ weekend. *Degree requirements:* For master's, comprehensive exam, thesis or alternative. *Entrance requirements:* For master's, GRE; Please visits website: https:// www.american.edu/cas/performing-arts/index.cfm, minimum GPA of 3.0, statement of purpose, transcripts, 2 letters of recommendation, resume, art portfolio; for Certificate, bachelor's degree, statement of purpose, transcripts, resume, art portfolio. Additional exam requirements/recommendations for international students: required—TOEFL. *Expenses:* Contact institution.

The American University of Rome, Graduate School, Rome, Italy. Offers arts management (MA); food studies (MA); peace studies (MA); sustainable cultural heritage (MA). *Degree requirements:* For master's, thesis, internship. *Entrance requirements:* For master's, bachelor's degree in the liberal arts, humanities or social sciences; minimum GPA of 2.75. Additional exam requirements/recommendations for international students: required—TOEFL (minimum score 550 paper-based; 80 iBT), IELTS (minimum score 6.5). Electronic applications accepted.

Arizona State University at Tempe, Herberger Institute for Design and the Arts, School of Film, Dance and Theatre, Tempe, AZ 85287-2002. Offers dance (MFA), including dance, interdisciplinary digital media and performance; theatre (MA, MFA, PhD), including arts entrepreneurship and management (MFA), directing (MFA), dramatic writing (MFA), interdisciplinary digital media and performance (MFA), performance (MFA), performance design (MFA), theatre (MFA), theatre and performance of the Americas (PhD), theatre for youth (MFA, PhD). Terminal master's awarded for partial completion of doctoral program. *Degree requirements:* For master's, comprehensive exam (for some programs), thesis (for some programs), applied project (for some programs); interactive Program of Study (iPOS) submitted before completing 50 percent of required credit hours; for doctorate, comprehensive exam, thesis/ dissertation, interactive Program of Study (iPOS) submitted before completing 50 percent of required credit hours. *Entrance requirements:* For master's, GRE or MAT, minimum GPA of 3.0 in last 2 years of work leading to bachelor's degree (depending on program); for doctorate, GRE, minimum GPA of 3.0 or equivalent in last 2 years of work leading to bachelor's degree, 3 letters of recommendation, resume, scholarly writing sample, statement of purpose. Additional exam requirements/recommendations for international students: required—TOEFL, IELTS, or PTE. Electronic applications accepted.

Baruch College of the City University of New York, Weissman School of Arts and Sciences, Program in Arts Administration, New York, NY 10010-5585. Offers MA. *Program availability:* Part-time, evening/weekend. *Degree requirements:* For master's, thesis or alternative, arts consultancy project. *Entrance requirements:* For master's, GRE/GMAT. Additional exam requirements/recommendations for international students: required—TOEFL or IELTS. Electronic applications accepted.

Boston University, Metropolitan College, Program in Arts Administration, Boston, MA 02215. Offers arts administration (MS, Graduate Certificate); fundraising management (Graduate Certificate). *Program availability:* Part-time, evening/weekend. *Faculty:* 1 full-time (0 women), 15 part-time/adjunct (8 women). *Students:* 19 full-time (17 women), 49 part-time (38 women); includes 5 minority (1 Black or African American, non-Hispanic/Latino; 2 Asian, non-Hispanic/Latino; 1 Hispanic/Latino; 1 Two or more races, non-Hispanic/Latino), 29 international. Average age 27. 119 applicants, 66% accepted, 27 enrolled. In 2019, 42 master's awarded. *Entrance requirements:* Additional exam requirements/recommendations for international students: required—TOEFL (minimum score 95 iBT). *Application deadline:* For fall admission, 4/1 priority date for domestic students, 2/1 priority date for international students; for spring admission, 11/ 15 priority date for domestic and international students. Applications are processed on a rolling basis. Application fee: $85. Electronic applications accepted. *Expenses:* Contact institution. *Financial support:* In 2019–20, 3 research assistantships (averaging $8,400 per year) were awarded; career-related internships or fieldwork, unspecified assistantships, and 6 office assistantships (averaging $4200) also available. Support available to part-time students. Financial award applicants required to submit FAFSA. *Unit head:* Dr. Douglas DeNatale, Associate Professor of the Practice and Director, 617-353-4064, E-mail: artsad@bu.edu. *Application contact:* Sameera Palkar, Program Manager, 617-353-4064, E-mail: artsad@bu.edu. Website: http://www.bu.edu/artsadmin/programs/

Brooklyn College of the City University of New York, School of Visual, Media and Performing Arts, Department of Theater, Brooklyn, NY 11210-2889. Offers acting (MFA); design and technical theater (MFA); directing (MFA); performing arts management (MFA); theater history and criticism (MA). *Program availability:* Part-time. *Degree requirements:* For master's, thesis, professional residency. *Entrance requirements:* For master's, audition or interview, 18 credits in theater, 2 letters of recommendation, essay. Additional exam requirements/recommendations for international students: required—TOEFL. Electronic applications accepted.

Carnegie Mellon University, Heinz College, School of Public Policy and Management, Master of Arts Management Program, Pittsburgh, PA 15213-3891. Offers MAM. *Degree requirements:* For master's, internship. *Entrance requirements:* For master's, GRE or GMAT, college-level course in advanced algebra/pre-calculus; college-level courses in economics and statistics (recommended). Additional exam requirements/recommendations for international students: required—TOEFL or IELTS. Electronic applications accepted.

Christie's Education, Certificate Program in Art Business, New York, NY 10020. Offers Certificate. Electronic applications accepted. *Expenses:* Contact institution.

Christie's Education, MA Program in Art, Law and Business, New York, NY 10020. Offers MA. *Degree requirements:* For master's, capstone project, internship. *Entrance requirements:* For master's, bachelor's degree or equivalent international degree, official transcripts from all post-secondary institutions attended. Additional exam requirements/ recommendations for international students: required—TOEFL.

Claremont Graduate University, Graduate Programs, Peter F. Drucker and Masatoshi Ito Graduate School of Management, Program in Art Business, Claremont, CA 91711-6160. Offers MA. *Degree requirements:* For master's, project seminar. *Entrance requirements:* Additional exam requirements/recommendations for international students: required—TOEFL (minimum score 75 iBT). Electronic applications accepted.

Claremont Graduate University, Graduate Programs, Program in Arts Management, Claremont, CA 91711. Offers MA. *Entrance requirements:* For master's, GRE General Test. Additional exam requirements/recommendations for international students: required—TOEFL (minimum score 75 iBT). Electronic applications accepted.

College of Charleston, Graduate School, School of the Arts, Program in Arts Management, Charleston, SC 29424-0001. Offers Certificate. *Program availability:* Part-time, evening/weekend. *Entrance requirements:* For degree, minimum GPA of 3.0, writing sample. Additional exam requirements/recommendations for international students: required—TOEFL (minimum score 81 iBT).

Colorado State University, College of Liberal Arts, LEAP Institute for the Arts, Fort Collins, CO 80523-1778. Offers arts leadership and cultural management (MALCM). *Program availability:* Part-time, evening/weekend, 100% online. *Degree requirements:* For master's, comprehensive exam, internship. *Entrance requirements:* For master's, official transcripts, 3 letters of recommendation, personal statement, resume. Additional exam requirements/recommendations for international students: required—TOEFL (minimum score 550 paper-based; 80 iBT). Electronic applications accepted. *Expenses:* Contact institution.

Drexel University, Westphal College of Media Arts and Design, Program in Arts Administration, Philadelphia, PA 19104-2875. Offers MS. *Accreditation:* NASAD. *Program availability:* Part-time, evening/weekend. *Degree requirements:* For master's, thesis, internship. *Entrance requirements:* For master's, GRE, interview, minimum GPA of 3.0, previous course work in arts and business. Additional exam requirements/ recommendations for international students: required—TOEFL. Electronic applications accepted.

Eastern Michigan University, Graduate School, College of Arts and Sciences, School of Communication, Media and Theatre Arts, Program in Arts Administration, Ypsilanti, MI 48197. Offers MA. *Program availability:* Part-time, evening/weekend, online learning. *Students:* 2 full-time (both women), 8 part-time (6 women); includes 3 minority (2 Hispanic/Latino; 1 Two or more races, non-Hispanic/Latino), 1 international. Average age 30. 7 applicants, 86% accepted, 2 enrolled. In 2019, 2 master's awarded. *Entrance requirements:* Additional exam requirements/recommendations for international students: required—TOEFL. *Application deadline:* Applications are processed on a rolling basis. Application fee: $45. *Financial support:* Fellowships, research assistantships with full tuition reimbursements, teaching assistantships with full tuition reimbursements, career-related internships or fieldwork, Federal Work-Study, institutionally sponsored loans, scholarships/grants, tuition waivers (partial), and unspecified assistantships available. Support available to part-time students. Financial award applicants required to submit FAFSA. *Unit head:* Dr. Susan Booth, Coordinator, 734-487-1220, Fax: 734-487-3443, E-mail: sbooth1@emich.edu. *Application contact:* Dr. Susan Booth, Coordinator, 734-487-1220, Fax: 734-487-3443, E-mail: sbooth1@emich.edu.

Fashion Institute of Technology, School of Graduate Studies, Program in Art Market Studies, New York, NY 10001-5992. Offers MA. *Accreditation:* NASAD. *Degree requirements:* For master's, thesis or alternative, internship. *Entrance requirements:* For master's, GRE General Test, previous course work in art history, 4 semesters of a foreign language. Additional exam requirements/recommendations for international students: required—TOEFL (minimum score 550 paper-based). Electronic applications accepted.

Florida State University, The Graduate School, College of Fine Arts, Department of Art Education, Tallahassee, FL 32306. Offers art education (MA, MS, Ed D, PhD); art therapy (PhD); arts administration (PhD). *Accreditation:* NASAD (one or more programs are accredited). *Program availability:* Part-time, evening/weekend, 100% online. *Faculty:* 11 full-time (8 women), 11 part-time/adjunct (9 women). *Students:* 58 full-time (53 women), 33 part-time (28 women); includes 32 minority (6 Black or African American, non-Hispanic/Latino; 1 American Indian or Alaska Native, non-Hispanic/Latino; 10 Asian, non-Hispanic/Latino; 12 Hispanic/Latino; 3 Two or more races, non-Hispanic/ Latino), 10 international. Average age 31. 116 applicants, 51% accepted, 33 enrolled. In 2019, 38 master's, 8 doctorates awarded. *Degree requirements:* For master's, comprehensive exam, thesis (for some programs); for doctorate, thesis/dissertation. *Entrance requirements:* For master's, GRE (can apply for waiver with GPA greater than 3.0, there is no GRE waiver available for the Art Therapy Program); minimum GPA of 3.0 in last 2 years; for doctorate, GRE. Additional exam requirements/recommendations for international students: required—TOEFL (minimum score 550 paper-based; 80 iBT), Students can take the TOEFL or IELTS; recommended—IELTS (minimum score 6.5), TSE (minimum score 55). *Application deadline:* For fall admission, 2/1 priority date for domestic and international students; for spring admission, 10/1 priority date for domestic

and international students. Applications are processed on a rolling basis. Application fee: $30. Electronic applications accepted. *Financial support:* In 2019–20, 20 students received support, including 16 research assistantships with full tuition reimbursements available (averaging $6,345 per year), 4 teaching assistantships with full tuition reimbursements available (averaging $8,742 per year); fellowships, career-related internships or fieldwork, Federal Work-Study, scholarships/grants, health care benefits, tuition waivers (full), and unspecified assistantships also available. Financial award application deadline: 2/1; financial award applicants required to submit FAFSA. *Unit head:* Victoria Cole, Program Associate, 850-644-2147, E-mail: vcole@fsu.edu. *Application contact:* Vicki Barr, Academic Support Assistant, 850-644-5473, Fax: 850-644-6067, E-mail: vbarr@fsu.edu.
Website: http://arted.fsu.edu/

Florida State University, The Graduate School, College of Music, Tallahassee, FL 32306. Offers accompanying (MM); arts administration (MA); choral conducting (MM); composition (MM, DM); ethnomusicology (MM); general music (MA); historical musicology (PhD); instrumental accompanying (MM); instrumental conducting (MM); jazz studies (MM); music theory (MM, PhD); music therapy (MM); musicology (MM); opera (MM); performance (MM, DM); piano pedagogy (MM); piano technology (MA); vocal accompanying (MM). *Accreditation:* NASM. *Program availability:* Part-time. *Faculty:* 77 full-time (28 women). *Students:* 355 full-time (169 women); includes 94 minority (30 Black or African American, non-Hispanic/Latino; 1 American Indian or Alaska Native, non-Hispanic/Latino; 29 Asian, non-Hispanic/Latino; 33 Hispanic/Latino; 1 Native Hawaiian or other Pacific Islander, non-Hispanic/Latino). Average age 26. 789 applicants, 44% accepted, 153 enrolled. In 2019, 98 master's, 36 doctorates awarded. *Degree requirements:* For master's, variable foreign language requirement, comprehensive exam (for some programs), thesis (for some programs), comprehensive exam; for doctorate, variable foreign language requirement, comprehensive exam (for some programs), thesis/dissertation, preliminary exam, treatise/dissertation defense. *Entrance requirements:* For master's, GRE General Test (for some programs), audition, minimum GPA of 3.0; for doctorate, GRE General Test (for some programs), audition, master's degree, minimum GPA of 3.0. Additional exam requirements/recommendations for international students: required—TOEFL (minimum score 590 paper-based; 97 iBT), IELTS (minimum score 7.5). *Application deadline:* For fall admission, 7/1 for domestic and international students; for spring admission, 11/1 for domestic and international students; for summer admission, 3/1 for domestic students. Applications are processed on a rolling basis. Application fee: $30. Electronic applications accepted. *Financial support:* In 2019–20, 235 students received support, including 2 fellowships with full tuition reimbursements available (averaging $15,000 per year), 14 research assistantships with full and partial tuition reimbursements available (averaging $7,400 per year), 201 teaching assistantships with full and partial tuition reimbursements available (averaging $7,400 per year); career-related internships or fieldwork, scholarships/grants, tuition waivers (full and partial), and unspecified assistantships also available. Support available to part-time students. Financial award application deadline: 2/28; financial award applicants required to submit FAFSA. *Unit head:* Dr. Patricia Flowers, Dean, 850-644-4361, Fax: 850-644-2033, E-mail: pjflowers@fsu.edu. *Application contact:* Kristopher Watson, Director of Admissions, 850-645-2126, Fax: 850-644-2033, E-mail: krwatson@fsu.edu.
Website: http://www.music.fsu.edu/

George Mason University, College of Visual and Performing Arts, Program in Arts Management, Fairfax, VA 22030. Offers MA. *Accreditation:* NASAD. *Entrance requirements:* For master's, GRE (recommended), undergraduate degree with minimum GPA of 3.0, official transcripts, 2 letters of recommendation, statement of purpose, resume. Additional exam requirements/recommendations for international students: required—TOEFL (minimum score 575 paper-based; 88 iBT), IELTS (minimum score 6.5), PTE (minimum score 59). Electronic applications accepted.

Goucher College, MA and MFA Programs, Baltimore, MD 21204-2794. Offers art and technology (MFA); arts administration (MA); cultural sustainability (MA); digital arts (MA); historic preservation (MA); nonfiction (MFA). *Program availability:* Part-time, evening/weekend, blended/hybrid learning. *Degree requirements:* For master's, thesis, e-portfolio. *Entrance requirements:* For master's, digital portfolio (for MA, MFA in digital arts); writing sample (for MFA in creative nonfiction). Additional exam requirements/recommendations for international students: required—TOEFL (minimum score 550 paper-based; 80 iBT). Electronic applications accepted. *Expenses:* Contact institution.

HEC Montreal, School of Business Administration, Graduate Diploma Programs in Administration, Program in Management of Cultural Organizations, Montréal, QC H3T 2A7, Canada. Offers Graduate Diploma. *Entrance requirements:* For degree, bachelor's degree (not in administration, preferably cultural field), one year of work experience. Electronic applications accepted.

Indiana University Bloomington, School of Public and Environmental Affairs, Program in Arts Administration, Bloomington, IN 47405-7000. Offers MAAA. *Program availability:* Part-time. *Degree requirements:* For master's, final internship. *Entrance requirements:* For master's, GRE or GMAT. Additional exam requirements/recommendations for international students: required—TOEFL or IELTS. Electronic applications accepted.

Kutztown University of Pennsylvania, College of Visual and Performing Arts, Program in Arts Administration, Kutztown, PA 19530-0730. Offers MA. *Program availability:* Evening/weekend, 100% online, blended/hybrid learning. *Faculty:* 1 full-time (0 women). *Students:* 1 (woman) full-time, 19 part-time (17 women); includes 1 minority (Two or more races, non-Hispanic/Latino). Average age 28. 14 applicants, 86% accepted, 9 enrolled. In 2019, 4 master's awarded. *Entrance requirements:* For master's, official transcripts; professional resume; related work/volunteer experience in arts administration or two reference letters. Additional exam requirements/recommendations for international students: required—TOEFL (minimum score 550 paper-based, 79 iBT), IELTS (minimum score 6.5), or PTE (minimum score 53). *Application deadline:* For fall admission, 8/1 for domestic and international students; for spring admission, 12/1 for domestic and international students. Application fee: $35. Electronic applications accepted. *Expenses: Tuition, area resident:* Full-time $9288; part-time $515 per credit. Tuition, state resident: full-time $9288. Tuition, nonresident: full-time $13,932; part-time $774 per credit. *Required fees:* $1688; $94 per credit. *Financial support:* Career-related internships or fieldwork, Federal Work-Study, and unspecified assistantships available. Financial award application deadline: 3/1; financial award applicants required to submit FAFSA. *Unit head:* Dr. Julia L. Hovanec, Dept. Chair, 610-683-4815, E-mail: hovanec@kutztown.edu. *Application contact:* Dr. Julia L. Hovanec, Dept. Chair, 610-683-4815, E-mail: hovanec@kutztown.edu.
Website: https://www.kutztown.edu/academics/graduate-programs/arts-administration.htm

Le Moyne College, Program in Arts Administration, Syracuse, NY 13214. Offers arts administration (MS). *Program availability:* Part-time, evening/weekend. *Faculty:* 1 full-time (0 women), 2 part-time/adjunct (both women). *Students:* 8 full-time (6 women), 6 part-time (4 women); includes 4 minority (2 Black or African American, non-Hispanic/Latino; 1 Hispanic/Latino; 1 Two or more races, non-Hispanic/Latino). Average age 26. 16 applicants, 88% accepted, 13 enrolled. In 2019, 7 master's awarded. *Degree requirements:* For master's, capstone consulting practicum. *Entrance requirements:* For master's, official transcript, bachelor's degree with minimum GPA of 2.8, two letters of recommendation, personal statement, resume or CV, interview. Additional exam requirements/recommendations for international students: required—TOEFL (minimum score 79 iBT); recommended—IELTS (minimum score 6.5). *Application deadline:* For fall admission, 3/1 priority date for domestic and international students; for spring admission, 11/1 priority date for domestic and international students; for summer admission, 4/1 priority date for domestic and international students. Applications are processed on a rolling basis. Electronic applications accepted. *Expenses:* $746 per credit hour, $75 fee per semester. *Financial support:* In 2019–20, 8 students received support. Career-related internships or fieldwork, Federal Work-Study, scholarships/grants, and health care benefits available. Support available to part-time students. Financial award applicants required to submit FAFSA. *Unit head:* Travis Newton, Associate Professor and Director of Arts Administration, 315-445-4201, E-mail: newtontm@lemoyne.edu. *Application contact:* Travis Newton, Director of Graduate Admission, 315-445-4201, E-mail: artsadmin@lemoyne.edu.
Website: http://www.lemoyne.edu/Learn/Colleges-Schools-Centers/College-of-Arts-Sciences/Majors-Minors/Arts-Administration

London Metropolitan University, Graduate Programs, London, United Kingdom. Offers applied psychology (M Sc); architecture (MA); biomedical science (M Sc); blood science (M Sc); cancer pharmacology (M Sc); computer networking and cyber security (M Sc); computing and information systems (M Sc); conference interpreting (MA); counter-terrorism studies (M Sc); creative, digital and professional writing (MA); crime, violence and prevention (M Sc); criminology (M Sc); curating contemporary art (MA); data analytics (M Sc); digital media (MA); early childhood studies (MA); education (MA, Ed D); financial services law, regulation and compliance (LL M); food science (M Sc); forensic psychology (M Sc); health and social care management and policy (M Sc); human nutrition (M Sc); human resource management (MA); human rights and international conflict (MA); information technology (M Sc); intelligence and security studies (M Sc); international oil, gas and energy law (LL M); international relations (MA); interpreting (MA); learning and teaching in higher education (MA); legal practice (LL M); media and entertainment law (LL M); organizational and consumer psychology (M Sc); psychological therapy (M Sc); psychology of mental health (M Sc); public health (M Sc); public policy and management (MPA); security studies (M Sc); social work (M Sc); spatial planning and urban design (MA); sports therapy (M Sc); supporting older children and young people with dyslexia (MA); teaching languages (MA), including Arabic, English; translation (MA); woman and child abuse (MA).

Montclair State University, The Graduate School, College of the Arts, MA Program in Theatre, Montclair, NJ 07043-1624. Offers arts management (MA); production/stage management (MA); theatre studies (MA). *Accreditation:* NAST. *Program availability:* Part-time, evening/weekend. *Degree requirements:* For master's, comprehensive exam, thesis or alternative. *Entrance requirements:* For master's, GRE General Test, 2 letters of recommendation. Additional exam requirements/recommendations for international students: required—TOEFL (minimum score 83 iBT) or IELTS (minimum score 6.5). Electronic applications accepted.

Moore College of Art & Design, Program in Community Practice, Philadelphia, PA 19103. Offers MFA. *Degree requirements:* For master's, thesis.

New York University, Steinhardt School of Culture, Education, and Human Development, Department of Art and Art Professions, Program in Visual Arts Administration, New York, NY 10003. Offers MA. *Program availability:* Part-time. *Entrance requirements:* For master's, interview. Additional exam requirements/recommendations for international students: required—TOEFL (minimum score 100 iBT). Electronic applications accepted.

New York University, Steinhardt School of Culture, Education, and Human Development, Department of Music and Performing Arts Professions, Program in Performing Arts Administration, New York, NY 10012. Offers MA. *Program availability:* Part-time. *Entrance requirements:* For master's, interview. Additional exam requirements/recommendations for international students: required—TOEFL (minimum score 100 iBT). Electronic applications accepted.

New York University, Tisch School of the Arts, Masters in Arts Politics, New York, NY 10012. Offers MA. *Entrance requirements:* For master's, professional resume, writing sample, statement of purpose. Additional exam requirements/recommendations for international students: required—TOEFL. Electronic applications accepted.

Northeastern University, College of Arts, Media and Design, Boston, MA 02115-5096. Offers architecture (M Arch); arts administration and cultural entrepreneurship (MS); experience design (MFA, MS); game science and design (MS); information design and visualization (MFA); interdisciplinary arts (MFA); journalism (MA); media advocacy (MS); music industry leadership (MS); sustainable building systems (MS); sustainable urban environments (M Des). Electronic applications accepted. *Expenses:* Contact institution.

Northwestern University, The Graduate School, School of Communication, Program in Leadership for Creative Enterprises, Evanston, IL 60208. Offers MS.

The Ohio State University, Graduate School, College of Arts and Sciences, Division of Arts and Humanities, Department of Arts Administration, Education and Policy, Program in Arts Policy and Administration, Columbus, OH 43210. Offers MA. *Degree requirements:* For master's, thesis. *Entrance requirements:* For master's, GRE General Test. Additional exam requirements/recommendations for international students: required—TOEFL (minimum score 600 paper-based; 100 iBT); recommended—IELTS (minimum score 8). Electronic applications accepted.

Pratt Institute, School of Art, Program in Arts and Cultural Management, New York, NY 10011. Offers MPS. *Program availability:* Part-time, evening/weekend. *Students:* 29 full-time (24 women), 13 part-time (11 women); includes 8 minority (4 Black or African American, non-Hispanic/Latino; 2 Hispanic/Latino; 2 Two or more races, non-Hispanic/Latino), 33 international. Average age 25. 121 applicants, 75% accepted, 26 enrolled. In 2019, 16 master's awarded. *Degree requirements:* For master's, thesis. *Entrance requirements:* For master's, statement of purpose. Additional exam requirements/recommendations for international students: required—TOEFL (minimum iBT score of 82) or IELTS (6.5). *Application deadline:* For fall admission, 1/5 for domestic and international students; for spring admission, 10/1 for domestic and international students. Application fee: $50 ($90 for international students). Electronic applications accepted. *Expenses: Tuition:* Full-time $33,246; part-time $1847 per credit. *Required fees:* $1980. *Financial support:* Career-related internships or fieldwork, Federal Work-Study, institutionally sponsored loans, scholarships/grants, health care benefits, and unspecified assistantships available. Support available to part-time students. Financial award application deadline: 2/1; financial award applicants required to submit FAFSA. *Unit head:* Dr. Mary McBride, Director, 212-647-7538, Fax: 212-367-2480, E-mail: mmcb1033@pratt.edu. *Application contact:* Natalie Capannelli, Director of Graduate Admissions, 718-636-3551, Fax: 718-399-4242, E-mail: ncapanne@pratt.edu.
Website: https://www.pratt.edu/academics/school-of-art/graduate-school-of-art/arts-cultural-management/

Pratt Institute, School of Art, Program in Design Management, New York, NY 10011. Offers MPS. *Program availability:* Part-time. *Students:* 31 full-time (25 women), 15 part-

time (11 women); includes 11 minority (3 Black or African American, non-Hispanic/Latino; 4 Asian, non-Hispanic/Latino; 2 Hispanic/Latino; 2 Two or more races, non-Hispanic/Latino), 31 international. Average age 26. 114 applicants, 76% accepted, 29 enrolled. In 2019, 21 master's awarded. *Degree requirements:* For master's, thesis. *Entrance requirements:* For master's, statement of purpose; undergraduate degree in one of the design disciplines, or another discipline with an interest in working in creative enterprise; resume. Additional exam requirements/recommendations for international students: required—TOEFL (minimum iBT score of 82) or IELTS (6.5). *Application deadline:* For fall admission, 1/5 for domestic and international students; for spring admission, 10/1 for domestic and international students. Application fee: $50 ($90 for international students). Electronic applications accepted. *Expenses: Tuition:* Full-time $33,246; part-time $1847 per credit. *Required fees:* $1980. *Financial support:* Career-related internships or fieldwork, Federal Work-Study, institutionally sponsored loans, scholarships/grants, health care benefits, and unspecified assistantships available. Support available to part-time students. Financial award application deadline: 2/1; financial award applicants required to submit FAFSA. *Unit head:* Dr. Mary McBride, Chairperson, 212-647-7538, Fax: 212-367-2480, E-mail: mmcb1033@pratt.edu. *Application contact:* Natalie Capannelli, Director of Graduate Admissions, 718-636-3551, Fax: 718-399-4242, E-mail: ncapanne@pratt.edu.
Website: https://www.pratt.edu/academics/school-of-art/graduate-school-of-art/design-management/

Purchase College, State University of New York, School of the Arts, Purchase, NY 10577-1400. Offers entrepreneurship in the arts (MA). *Program availability:* Part-time. *Students:* 13 full-time (10 women), 3 part-time; includes 3 minority (1 Black or African American, non-Hispanic/Latino; 2 Hispanic/Latino), 3 international. Average age 29. 18 applicants, 94% accepted, 11 enrolled. *Degree requirements:* For master's, thesis. *Entrance requirements:* Additional exam requirements/recommendations for international students: required—TOEFL (minimum score 550 paper-based; 80 iBT), IELTS (minimum score 6.5). *Application deadline:* For fall admission, 3/1 for domestic students. Applications are processed on a rolling basis. Application fee: $85. Electronic applications accepted. Application fee is waived when completed online. *Expenses: Tuition, area resident:* Full-time $11,310. Tuition, state resident: full-time $11,310. Tuition, nonresident: full-time $23,100. *Required fees:* $1883. *Application contact:* Beatriz Martin-Ruiz, 914-251-6304, Fax: 914-251-6314, E-mail: admissn@purchase.edu.
Website: https://www.purchase.edu/academics/arts/

Rhode Island College, School of Graduate Studies, Faculty of Arts and Sciences, Department of Art, Providence, RI 02908-1991. Offers art education (MA, MAT); media studies (MA). *Accreditation:* NASAD (one or more programs are accredited). *Program availability:* Part-time, evening/weekend. *Faculty:* 4 full-time (3 women), 1 (woman) part-time/adjunct. *Students:* 4 part-time (all women). Average age 35. In 2019, 1 master's awarded. *Degree requirements:* For master's, thesis. *Entrance requirements:* For master's, GRE General Test, portfolio (MA), 3 letters of recommendation, interview. Additional exam requirements/recommendations for international students: required—TOEFL (minimum score 550 paper-based; 80 iBT). *Application deadline:* For fall admission, 3/1 for domestic students. Applications are processed on a rolling basis. Application fee: $50. Electronic applications accepted. *Expenses: Tuition, area resident:* Part-time $462 per credit hour. Tuition, state resident: part-time $462 per credit hour. *Required fees:* $720. One-time fee: $140. *Financial support:* Teaching assistantships, career-related internships or fieldwork, Federal Work-Study, scholarships/grants, health care benefits, and unspecified assistantships available. Support available to part-time students. Financial award application deadline: 5/15; financial award applicants required to submit FAFSA. *Unit head:* Prof. Douglas Bosch, Chair, 401-456-8054. *Application contact:* Prof. Douglas Bosch, Chair, 401-456-8054.
Website: http://www.ric.edu/art/Pages/M.A.T.-in-Art-Education.aspx

Rider University, School of Fine and Performing Arts, Lawrenceville, NJ 08648-3001. Offers arts management and executive leadership (MA).

Rocky Mountain College of Art + Design, Program in Education, Leadership + Emerging Technologies, Lakewood, CO 80214. Offers MA. *Accreditation:* NASAD. *Program availability:* Online learning.

Roosevelt University, Graduate Division, Chicago College of Performing Arts, Music Conservatory, Chicago, IL 60605. Offers brass (Diploma); brass performance (MM); classical guitar (MM, Diploma); music (MM); music composition (MM); opera (Diploma); orchestral studies (MM, Diploma); percussion (MM, Diploma); performing arts administration (MA); piano (Diploma); piano performance (MM); strings (MM, Diploma); voice (MM); woodwinds (MM, Diploma). Electronic applications accepted. *Expenses:* Contact institution.

Rowan University, Graduate School, College of Performing Arts, Department of Theatre and Dance, Glassboro, NJ 08028-1701. Offers theatre arts administration (MA). *Accreditation:* NASAD. Electronic applications accepted. *Expenses: Tuition, area resident:* Part-time $715.50 per semester hour. Tuition, state resident: part-time $715.50 per semester hour. Tuition, nonresident: part-time $715.50 per semester hour. *Required fees:* $161.55 per semester hour.

Ryerson University, School of Graduate Studies, Program in Photographic Preservation and Collections Management, Toronto, ON M5B 2K3, Canada. Offers MA.

St. Thomas University - Florida, School of Leadership Studies, Program in Art Management, Miami Gardens, FL 33054-6459. Offers MA.

Savannah College of Art and Design, Creative Business Leadership, Savannah, GA 31402-3146. Offers MA. *Program availability:* Part-time, 100% online. *Degree requirements:* For master's, final project. *Entrance requirements:* For master's, GRE (recommended), portfolio (submitted in digital format), audition or writing submission, resume, statement of purpose, two letters of recommendation. Additional exam requirements/recommendations for international students: recommended—TOEFL (minimum score 550 paper-based; 85 iBT), IELTS (minimum score 6.5). Electronic applications accepted.

Savannah College of Art and Design, Program in Design Management, Savannah, GA 31402-3146. Offers MA, MFA. *Program availability:* Part-time, 100% online. *Degree requirements:* For master's, final project (for MA); thesis (for MFA). *Entrance requirements:* For master's, GRE (recommended), portfolio (submitted in digital format), audition or writing submission, resume, statement of purpose, two letters of recommendation. Additional exam requirements/recommendations for international students: recommended—TOEFL (minimum score 550 paper-based; 85 iBT), IELTS (minimum score 6.5). Electronic applications accepted.

Seattle University, College of Arts and Sciences, Program in Arts Leadership, Seattle, WA 98122-1090. Offers MFA. *Program availability:* Part-time, evening/weekend. *Faculty:* 10 full-time (4 women), 7 part-time/adjunct (6 women). *Students:* 1 (woman) full-time, 25 part-time (22 women); includes 5 minority (2 Black or African American, non-Hispanic/Latino; 2 Asian, non-Hispanic/Latino; 1 Two or more races, non-Hispanic/Latino), 2 international. Average age 30. 47 applicants, 72% accepted, 15 enrolled. In 2019, 30 master's awarded. *Entrance requirements:* For master's, minimum GPA of 3.0; 2 years of management in nonprofit, comparable work, or volunteer experience. Additional exam requirements/recommendations for international students: required—TOEFL, IELTS. *Application deadline:* For fall admission, 3/15 for domestic students, 4/1 for international students. Applications are processed on a rolling basis. Application fee: $55. Electronic applications accepted. *Financial support:* In 2019–20, 24 students received support. Application deadline: 3/15; applicants required to submit FAFSA. *Unit head:* Kevin Maifeld, Director, 206-296-5370, E-mail: maifeldk@seattleu.edu. *Application contact:* Janet Shandley, Associate Dean of Graduate Admissions, 206-296-5900, Fax: 206-298-5656, E-mail: grad_admissions@seattleu.edu.
Website: https://www.seattleu.edu/artsci/mfa/

Sotheby's Institute of Art–London, Graduate Programs, London, United Kingdom. Offers art business (MA); contemporary art (MA); fine and decorative art and design (MA); modern and contemporary Asian art (MA). *Degree requirements:* For master's, thesis. *Entrance requirements:* Additional exam requirements/recommendations for international students: required—IELTS (minimum score 7). Electronic applications accepted.

Sotheby's Institute of Art–New York, Graduate Programs, New York, NY 10021. Offers art business (MA); contemporary art (MA); fine and decorative art and design (MA). *Accreditation:* NASAD. *Entrance requirements:* For master's, academic transcripts, two letters of academic reference, personal statement, writing sample, curriculum vitae/resume, interview. Additional exam requirements/recommendations for international students: required—TOEFL (minimum score 100 iBT), IELTS (minimum score 7). Electronic applications accepted.

Southern Methodist University, Meadows School of the Arts, Division of Arts Management and Arts Entrepreneurship, Dallas, TX 75275. Offers international arts management (MM); MA/MBA. *Entrance requirements:* For master's, GMAT. Additional exam requirements/recommendations for international students: required—TOEFL (minimum score 600 paper-based; 100 iBT). Electronic applications accepted.

Southern Utah University, Program in Arts Administration, Cedar City, UT 84720-2498. Offers MA, MFA. *Program availability:* Part-time, 100% online. *Entrance requirements:* For master's, bachelor's degree, interview, 3 letters of recommendation, resume, minimum undergraduate GPA of 3.0, written statement of purpose, transcripts. Additional exam requirements/recommendations for international students: required—TOEFL (minimum score 550 paper-based; 79 iBT), TOEFL (minimum score 550 paper-based, 79 iBT) or IELTS (minimum score 6); recommended—IELTS (minimum score 6). Electronic applications accepted. *Expenses:* Contact institution.

SUNY Brockport, School of Business and Management, Department of Public Administration, Brockport, NY 14420-2997. Offers arts administration (AGC); nonprofit management (AGC); public administration (MPA), including health care management, nonprofit management, poverty studies, public management, public safety. *Accreditation:* NASPAA. *Program availability:* Part-time, evening/weekend. *Faculty:* 5 full-time (3 women), 7 part-time/adjunct (0 women). *Students:* 35 full-time (23 women), 92 part-time (56 women); includes 15 minority (10 Black or African American, non-Hispanic/Latino; 1 Asian, non-Hispanic/Latino; 3 Hispanic/Latino; 1 Native Hawaiian or other Pacific Islander, non-Hispanic/Latino). 41 applicants, 78% accepted, 23 enrolled. In 2019, 104 master's, 6 other advanced degrees awarded. *Degree requirements:* For master's, thesis or alternative. *Entrance requirements:* For master's, GRE or minimum GPA of 3.0, letters of recommendation, statement of objectives, current resume. Additional exam requirements/recommendations for international students: required—TOEFL (minimum score 550 paper-based; 79 iBT), IELTS (minimum score 6.5). *Application deadline:* For fall admission, 8/15 priority date for domestic and international students; for spring admission, 1/15 priority date for domestic and international students; for summer admission, 4/15 priority date for domestic and international students. Application fee: $50. Electronic applications accepted. *Expenses: Tuition, area resident:* Part-time $471 per credit hour. Tuition, nonresident: part-time $963 per credit hour. *Financial support:* In 2019–20, 1 fellowship with full tuition reimbursement (averaging $7,500 per year), 1 teaching assistantship with full tuition reimbursement (averaging $6,000 per year) were awarded; Federal Work-Study, scholarships/grants, and unspecified assistantships also available. Support available to part-time students. Financial award application deadline: 3/15; financial award applicants required to submit FAFSA. *Unit head:* Dr. Wendy Wright, Graduate Director, 585-395-5570, Fax: 585-395-2172, E-mail: wwright@brockport.edu. *Application contact:* Danielle A. Welch, Graduate Admissions Counselor, 585-395-2525, Fax: 585-395-2515.
Website: https://www.brockport.edu/academics/public_administration/graduate/masters.html

Teachers College, Columbia University, Department of Arts and Humanities, New York, NY 10027. Offers applied linguistics (MA, Ed D); art and art education (Ed M, MA, Ed D, Ed DCT); arts administration (MA); bilingual and bicultural education (MA); global competence (Certificate); history and education (Ed D, PhD); music and music education (Ed DCT); philosophy and education (MA, Ed D, PhD); social studies education (Ed M, PhD); teaching English to speakers of other languages (Ed M); teaching of English and English education (Ed M, MA, Ed D, PhD), including English education (Ed M, Ed D, PhD), teaching of English (MA); teaching of social studies (MA); TESOL (MA, Ed D). *Faculty:* 26 full-time (17 women). *Students:* 426 full-time (358 women), 390 part-time (259 women); includes 222 minority (44 Black or African American, non-Hispanic/Latino; 2 American Indian or Alaska Native, non-Hispanic/Latino; 94 Asian, non-Hispanic/Latino; 65 Hispanic/Latino; 17 Two or more races, non-Hispanic/Latino), 252 international. 957 applicants, 66% accepted, 375 enrolled. *Unit head:* Dr. ZhaoHong Han, Department Chair, E-mail: zhh2@tc.columbia.edu. *Application contact:* Kelly Sutton-Skinner, Director of Admissions and New Student Enrollment, 212-678-3710, E-mail: kms2237@tc.columbia.edu.

Temple University, Tyler School of Art and Architecture, Department of Art History, Philadelphia, PA 19122-6096. Offers MA, PhD. *Program availability:* Part-time. *Faculty:* 11 full-time (8 women), 8 part-time/adjunct (5 women). *Students:* 48 full-time (37 women), 3 part-time (all women); includes 11 minority (1 Black or African American, non-Hispanic/Latino; 2 Asian, non-Hispanic/Latino; 5 Hispanic/Latino; 3 Two or more races, non-Hispanic/Latino), 5 international. 31 applicants, 68% accepted, 7 enrolled. In 2019, 9 master's, 3 doctorates awarded. *Degree requirements:* For master's, one foreign language, thesis (for some programs), internship (fine arts administration track); for doctorate, 2 foreign languages, thesis/dissertation. *Entrance requirements:* For master's, GRE, 3 letters of recommendation, 5 courses in art history, statement of goals, resume/curriculum vitae, writing sample; for doctorate, GRE, 3 letters of recommendation, statement of goals, resume/curriculum vitae, writing sample. Additional exam requirements/recommendations for international students: required—TOEFL (minimum score 79 iBT), IELTS (minimum score 6.5), PTE (minimum score 53), one of three is required. *Application deadline:* For fall admission, 12/15 for domestic students; for spring admission, 11/1 for domestic students. Application fee: $60. Electronic applications accepted. *Financial support:* Fellowships, research assistantships, teaching assistantships, career-related internships or fieldwork, Federal Work-Study, and health care benefits available. Financial award application deadline: 12/15; financial award applicants required to submit FAFSA. *Unit head:* Dr. Jane DeRose Evans, Chair, 215-777-9165, Fax: 215-204-6951, E-mail: jevans@temple.edu. *Application contact:* Lauren O'Neill, Director of Admissions, 215-777-9159, E-mail:

tyleradmissions@temple.edu.
Website: https://tyler.temple.edu/programs/art-history

Universidad del Turabo, Graduate Programs, School of Social Sciences and Humanities, Programs in Public Affairs, Program in Arts Administration, Gurabo, PR 00778-3030. Offers MPA. *Entrance requirements:* For master's, GRE, EXADEP or GMAT, interview, essay, official transcript, recommendation letters. Electronic applications accepted.

University at Buffalo, the State University of New York, Graduate School, College of Arts and Sciences, Arts Management Program, Buffalo, NY 14260. Offers MA. *Program availability:* Part-time. *Faculty:* 2 full-time (both women), 6 part-time/adjunct (2 women). *Students:* 11 full-time (8 women), 1 (woman) part-time; includes 1 minority (Black or African American, non-Hispanic/Latino), 8 international. Average age 24. 36 applicants, 44% accepted, 8 enrolled. In 2019, 1 master's awarded. *Degree requirements:* For master's, thesis. *Entrance requirements:* For master's, curriculum vitae, academic essay, personal statement, 2 letters of recommendation, official transcripts; bank statements, supporting documentation, and passport (for international students). Additional exam requirements/recommendations for international students: required—TOEFL (minimum score 550 paper-based; 79 iBT), TOEFL or IELTS. *Application deadline:* For fall admission, 1/31 priority date for domestic and international students. Applications are processed on a rolling basis. Application fee: $75. Electronic applications accepted. *Expenses:* Overall dollar amount includes standard tuition and fee rates for an in state, graduate student at the University at Buffalo plus the Arts Management Program fee ($500). This additional fee covers a portion of travel costs associated with site visits students make during their time in the Program. Standard out of state tuition and fees for a graduate student, plus the Arts Management Program fee, is $42,689. *Financial support:* Application deadline: 8/15; applicants required to submit FAFSA. *Unit head:* Dr. Cristanne Miller, Director, 716-645-2437, E-mail: artsmgmt@buffalo.edu. *Application contact:* Kevin Leary, Assistant Director, 716-645-0766, E-mail: artsmgmt@buffalo.edu.
Website: http://www.buffalo.edu/cas/arts_management.html

The University of Akron, Graduate School, Buchtel College of Arts and Sciences, School of Dance, Theatre, and Arts Administration, Program in Arts Administration, Akron, OH 44325. Offers MA. *Accreditation:* NASAD. *Degree requirements:* For master's, thesis. *Entrance requirements:* For master's, minimum GPA of 2.75, 300-word statement of intent summarizing student background and outlining career goals. Additional exam requirements/recommendations for international students: required—TOEFL (minimum score 79 iBT), IELTS (minimum score 6.5). Electronic applications accepted.

University of Cincinnati, Graduate School, College-Conservatory of Music, Division of Theatre Arts, Production and Arts Administration, Cincinnati, OH 45221. Offers arts administration (MA); directing (MFA); theater design and production (MFA); voice and opera (MM, DMA); MBA/MA. *Accreditation:* NAST (one or more programs are accredited). *Degree requirements:* For master's, final project. *Entrance requirements:* For master's, GMAT (MA), audition/interview. Additional exam requirements/recommendations for international students: required—TOEFL (minimum score 520 paper-based). Electronic applications accepted.

University of Kentucky, Graduate School, College of Fine Arts, Program in Arts Administration, Lexington, KY 40506-0032. Offers MA.

The University of Manchester, School of Arts, Languages and Cultures, Manchester, United Kingdom. Offers anthropology, media and performance (PhD); applied theatre (PhD); Arab world studies (PhD); archaeology (PhD); art history and visual studies (PhD); arts and cultural management (PhD); arts management and cultural policy (PhD); Chinese studies (PhD); classics and ancient history (PhD); composition (PhD); creative writing (PhD); drama (PhD); East Asian studies (PhD); electroacoustic composition (PhD); English and American studies (PhD); English language (PhD); French studies (PhD); German studies (PhD); history (PhD); humanitarianism and conflict response (PhD); interpreting studies (PhD); Japanese studies (PhD); Latin American cultural studies (PhD); linguistics (PhD); Middle Eastern studies (PhD); museology (PhD); museum practice (PhD); music (PhD); musicology (PhD); Polish studies (PhD); Portuguese studies (PhD); religions and theology (PhD); Russian studies (PhD); Spanish studies (PhD); translation and intercultural studies (PhD).

University of Michigan–Flint, Graduate Programs, Program in Arts Administration, Flint, MI 48502-1950. Offers performance (MA), including museum and visual arts, performance. *Program availability:* Part-time. *Faculty:* 7 full-time (3 women), 11 part-time/adjunct (7 women). *Students:* 11 part-time (7 women); includes 5 minority (4 Black or African American, non-Hispanic/Latino; 1 Asian, non-Hispanic/Latino). Average age 40. 11 applicants, 82% accepted, 2 enrolled. In 2019, 2 master's awarded. *Degree requirements:* For master's, thesis. *Entrance requirements:* For master's, bachelor degree in the arts (visual art, theatre, dance, music, etc.) from regionally-accredited institution; minimum cumulative undergraduate GPA of 3.0 on 4.0 scale. Additional exam requirements/recommendations for international students: required—TOEFL (minimum score 84 iBT), IELTS (minimum score 6.5). *Application deadline:* For fall admission, 8/1 for domestic students, 5/1 for international students; for winter admission, 11/15 for domestic students, 10/1 for international students. Applications are processed on a rolling basis. Application fee: $55. Electronic applications accepted. *Expenses:* Contact institution. *Financial support:* Federal Work-Study, institutionally sponsored loans, scholarships/grants, and unspecified assistantships available. Support available to part-time students. Financial award application deadline: 3/1; financial award applicants required to submit FAFSA. *Unit head:* Nicole Broughton, Director, 810-237-6522, E-mail: broughn@umflint.edu. *Application contact:* Matt Bohlen, Associate Director of Graduate Admissions, 810-762-3171, Fax: 810-766-6789, E-mail: mbohlen@umflint.edu.
Website: http://www.umflint.edu/graduateprograms/arts-administration-ma

University of New Orleans, Graduate School, College of Liberal Arts, Education and Human Development, Program in Arts Administration, New Orleans, LA 70148. Offers MA. *Program availability:* Part-time. *Degree requirements:* For master's, internship. *Entrance requirements:* For master's, GRE General Test. Additional exam requirements/recommendations for international students: required—TOEFL (minimum score 550 paper-based; 79 iBT), IELTS (minimum score 6.5). Electronic applications accepted.

The University of North Carolina at Charlotte, College of Liberal Arts and Sciences, Department of Political Science and Public Administration, Charlotte, NC 28223-0001. Offers emergency management (Graduate Certificate); non-profit management (Graduate Certificate); public administration (MPA), including arts administration, emergency management, non-profit management, public budgeting and finance, urban management and policy; public budgeting and finance (Graduate Certificate); urban management and policy (Graduate Certificate). *Accreditation:* NASPAA. *Program availability:* Part-time, evening/weekend. *Faculty:* 20 full-time (10 women), 5 part-time/adjunct (1 woman). *Students:* 30 full-time (21 women), 45 part-time (29 women); includes 23 minority (15 Black or African American, non-Hispanic/Latino; 1 American Indian or Alaska Native, non-Hispanic/Latino; 5 Hispanic/Latino; 2 Two or more races, non-Hispanic/Latino), 2 international. Average age 30. 38 applicants, 68% accepted, 21 enrolled. In 2019, 18 master's, 13 other advanced degrees awarded. *Degree requirements:* For master's, thesis or alternative. *Entrance requirements:* For master's, GRE General Test, bachelor's degree, or its equivalent, from accredited college or university; minimum undergraduate GPA of 3.0; 3 letters of recommendation; statement of purpose; for Graduate Certificate, one official transcript from each post-secondary institution; three letters of recommendation from academic or professional sources; overall undergraduate GPA of 3.0 on a 4.0 scale; statement of purpose (1-2 pages in length) in which the applicant explains his/her career goals, how the Certificate fits into achieving those goals, and any relevant w. Additional exam requirements/recommendations for international students: required—TOEFL (minimum score 557 paper-based; 83 iBT), IELTS (minimum score 6.5), TOEFL (minimum score 557paper-based, 83 iBT) or IELTS (6.5). *Application deadline:* For fall admission, 8/15 for domestic students; for spring admission, 12/1 for domestic students; for summer admission, 5/11 for domestic students. Applications are processed on a rolling basis. Application fee: $75. Electronic applications accepted. *Expenses:* Tuition, state resident: full-time $4337. Tuition, nonresident: full-time $17,771. *Required fees:* $3093. Tuition and fees vary according to course load, degree level and program. *Financial support:* In 2019–20, 16 students received support, including 1 fellowship (averaging $55,000 per year), 15 research assistantships (averaging $8,583 per year); teaching assistantships, career-related internships or fieldwork, institutionally sponsored loans, scholarships/grants, and unspecified assistantships also available. Support available to part-time students. Financial award applicants required to submit FAFSA. *Unit head:* Dr. Cheryl L. Brown, Interim Chair, Undergraduate Coordinator, & Associate Professor, 704-687-7574, E-mail: cbrown@uncc.edu. *Application contact:* Kathy B. Giddings, Director of Graduate Admissions, 704-687-5503, Fax: 704-687-1668, E-mail: gradadm@uncc.edu.
Website: http://politicalscience.uncc.edu/

University of Southern California, Graduate School, Roski School of Art and Design, Art and Curatorial Practices in the Public Sphere Program, Los Angeles, CA 90089. Offers MA. *Degree requirements:* For master's, thesis, practicum exhibition. *Entrance requirements:* For master's, GRE, personal statement, writing sample, three letters of recommendation. Additional exam requirements/recommendations for international students: required—TOEFL (minimum score 600 paper-based; 100 iBT). Electronic applications accepted.

University of Wisconsin–Madison, Graduate School, Wisconsin School of Business, Wisconsin Full-Time MBA Program, Madison, WI 53706-1380. Offers applied security analysis (MBA); arts administration (MBA); brand and product management (MBA); corporate finance and investment banking (MBA); marketing research (MBA); operations and technology management (MBA); real estate (MBA); risk management and insurance (MBA); strategic human resource management (MBA); supply chain management (MBA). *Faculty:* 131 full-time (35 women), 33 part-time/adjunct (11 women). *Students:* 146 full-time (51 women); includes 21 minority (2 Black or African American, non-Hispanic/Latino; 1 American Indian or Alaska Native, non-Hispanic/Latino; 6 Asian, non-Hispanic/Latino; 8 Hispanic/Latino; 4 Two or more races, non-Hispanic/Latino), 41 international. Average age 28. 314 applicants, 44% accepted, 67 enrolled. In 2019, 104 master's awarded. *Entrance requirements:* For master's, GMAT or GRE, U.S. active military, U.S. veterans, candidates with terminal degrees (JD, PhD) or those with 5 years of work experience can apply for a GMAT or GRE waiver, bachelor's degree, standardized test scores (GMAT or GRE), English proficiency test (TOEFL, IELTS, or PTE for applicants whose native language is not English or whose undergraduate instruction was not in English), 2 years of work experience preferred, 1 completed recommendation, resume, essays (one required, one recommended, one optional). Additional exam requirements/recommendations for international students: required—TOEFL (minimum score 100 iBT), IELTS (minimum score 7.5), TOEFL is not required for international students whose undergraduate training was in English. *Application deadline:* For fall admission, 11/1 for domestic and international students; for winter admission, 1/10 for domestic and international students; for spring admission, 3/1 for domestic and international students; for summer admission, 4/27 for domestic students, 4/27 priority date for international students. Applications are processed on a rolling basis. Application fee: $75 ($81 for international students). Electronic applications accepted. *Expenses:* $43,061 in-state tuition and fees for 2-year program; $82,214 out-of-state tuition and fees for the 2-year program. *Financial support:* Fellowships, research assistantships, teaching assistantships, scholarships/grants, health care benefits, tuition waivers (full and partial), and unspecified assistantships available. Financial award application deadline: 1/10. *Unit head:* Dr. Enno Siemsen, Associate Dean of the MBA and Masters Programs, 608-890-3130, E-mail: esiemsen@wisc.edu. *Application contact:* Betsy Kacizak, Director of Admissions and Recruitment, Full-Time MBA and Masters Programs, 608-262-8948, E-mail: betsy.kacizak@wisc.edu.
Website: https://wsb.wisc.edu/

Valparaiso University, Graduate School and Continuing Education, Program in Arts and Entertainment Administration, Valparaiso, IN 46383. Offers MA. *Program availability:* Part-time, evening/weekend. *Degree requirements:* For master's, internship or research project. *Entrance requirements:* Additional exam requirements/recommendations for international students: required—TOEFL (minimum score 550 paper-based; 80 iBT), IELTS (minimum score 6). Electronic applications accepted.

Winthrop University, College of Visual and Performing Arts, Department of Art, Rock Hill, SC 29733. Offers art (MFA); art administration (MA); art education (MA). *Accreditation:* NASAD. *Program availability:* Part-time. *Degree requirements:* For master's, comprehensive exam (for some programs), thesis (for some programs), documented exhibit, oral exam. *Entrance requirements:* For master's, GRE General Test or MAT, PRAXIS (for MA), minimum GPA of 3.0, resume, slide portfolio, teaching certificate (MA). Additional exam requirements/recommendations for international students: required—TOEFL (minimum score 550 paper-based; 79 iBT), IELTS (minimum score 6). Electronic applications accepted. *Expenses: Tuition, area resident:* Full-time $7659; part-time $641 per credit hour. Tuition, state resident: full-time $7659; part-time $641 per credit hour. Tuition, nonresident: full-time $14,753; part-time $1234 per credit hour.

Art Therapy

Adler University, Master of Arts (M.A.) in Counseling: Art Therapy/Ph.D. in Art Therapy, Chicago, IL 60602. Offers PhD. *Program availability:* Part-time. In 2019, 1 doctorate awarded. *Degree requirements:* For doctorate, comprehensive exam, Dissertation Required, Practicum; Internship. *Unit head:* Phyllis Horton, Director of Admissions, 312-662-4100, E-mail: admissions@adler.edu. *Application contact:* Phyllis Horton, Director of Admissions, 312-662-4100, E-mail: admissions@adler.edu.

Adler University, Master of Counselling Psychology: Art Therapy, Vancouver, BC V6B 3J5, Canada. Offers MCP. In 2019, 1 master's awarded. *Degree requirements:* For master's, Social Justice Practicum. *Unit head:* Michelle Brice, Associate Vice President of Admissions, 236-521-2409, E-mail: vanadmissions@adler.edu. *Application contact:* Michelle Brice, Associate Vice President of Admissions, 236-521-2409, E-mail: vanadmissions@adler.edu.

Albertus Magnus College, Master of Arts in Art Therapy and Counseling Program, New Haven, CT 06511-1189. Offers MA. *Students:* 10 full-time (9 women), 20 part-time (all women); includes 7 minority (2 Asian, non-Hispanic/Latino; 5 Hispanic/Latino). Average age 29. *Unit head:* Dr. Stephen Joy, Director of M.A.A.T.C Program, 203-773-8555, E-mail: sjoy@albertus.edu. *Application contact:* Annette Bosley-Boyce, Dean of the Division of Professional and Graduate Studies, 203-672-6685, E-mail: abosleyboyce@albertus.edu.
Website: https://www.albertus.edu/art-therapy/ms/

Athabasca University, Program in Counseling, Athabasca, AB T9S 3A3, Canada. Offers applied psychology (Post Master's Certificate); art therapy (MC); career counseling (MC); counseling (Advanced Certificate); counseling psychology (MC); school counseling (MC).

California State University, Los Angeles, Graduate Studies, College of Arts and Letters, Department of Art, Los Angeles, CA 90032-8530. Offers art (MA), including art education, art history, art therapy, ceramics, metals, and textiles, design (MA, MFA), painting, sculpture, and graphic arts, photography; fine arts (MFA), including crafts, design (MA, MFA), studio arts. *Accreditation:* NASAD (one or more programs are accredited). *Program availability:* Part-time, evening/weekend. *Degree requirements:* For master's, comprehensive exam, project or thesis. *Entrance requirements:* For master's, portfolio. Additional exam requirements/recommendations for international students: required—TOEFL (minimum score 500 paper-based). Electronic applications accepted. *Expenses: Tuition, area resident:* Full-time $7176; part-time $4164 per year. Tuition, state resident: full-time $7176; part-time $4164 per year. Tuition, nonresident: full-time $14,304; part-time $8916 per year. *International tuition:* $14,304 full-time. *Required fees:* $1037.76; $1037.76 per unit. Tuition and fees vary according to degree level and program.

Cedar Crest College, Program in Art Therapy, Allentown, PA 18104-6196. Offers MA. *Program availability:* Part-time, evening/weekend, blended/hybrid learning. Electronic applications accepted. *Expenses:* Contact institution.

The College of New Rochelle, Graduate School, Division of Art and Communication Studies, Program in Art Therapy, New Rochelle, NY 10805-2308. Offers art therapy (MS); art therapy/counseling (MS). *Program availability:* Part-time, evening/weekend. *Degree requirements:* For master's, thesis, practicum, fieldwork, internship. *Entrance requirements:* For master's, 12 credits in psychology, portfolio.

Concordia University, School of Graduate Studies, Faculty of Fine Arts, Department of Creative Arts Therapies, Montréal, QC H3G 1M8, Canada. Offers art therapy (MA); drama therapy (MA); music therapy (MA).

Drexel University, College of Nursing and Health Professions, Department of Creative Arts Therapies, Specialization in Art Therapy, Philadelphia, PA 19104-2875. Offers MA, PMC. *Accreditation:* NASAD. *Degree requirements:* For master's, comprehensive exam, thesis. *Entrance requirements:* For master's, GRE General Test or MAT, interview, minimum GPA of 2.75, portfolio. Electronic applications accepted.

Eastern Virginia Medical School, Graduate Art Therapy and Counseling Program, Norfolk, VA 23501-1980. Offers MS. *Degree requirements:* For master's, thesis, internship. *Entrance requirements:* For master's, 12 credit hours in psychology, including abnormal and developmental; 18 credit hours in studio art; face-to-face interview; portfolio (diverse media preferred). Electronic applications accepted. *Expenses:* Contact institution.

Edinboro University of Pennsylvania, Department of Counseling, School Psychology and Special Education, Edinboro, PA 16444. Offers counseling (MA), including art therapy, clinical mental health counseling, college counseling, rehabilitation counseling, school counseling; educational psychology (M Ed); school psychology (Ed S); special education (M Ed), including autism, behavior management. *Accreditation:* ACA. *Program availability:* Part-time, evening/weekend. *Faculty:* 19 full-time (13 women), 2 part-time/adjunct (1 woman). *Students:* 180 full-time (146 women), 215 part-time (186 women); includes 42 minority (18 Black or African American, non-Hispanic/Latino; 2 American Indian or Alaska Native, non-Hispanic/Latino; 4 Asian, non-Hispanic/Latino; 12 Hispanic/Latino; 1 Native Hawaiian or other Pacific Islander, non-Hispanic/Latino; 5 Two or more races, non-Hispanic/Latino), 3 international. Average age 31. 197 applicants, 63% accepted, 71 enrolled. In 2019, 87 master's, 8 other advanced degrees awarded. *Degree requirements:* For master's, thesis or alternative, competency exam; for Ed S, thesis or alternative. *Entrance requirements:* For master's and Ed S, GRE or MAT, minimum QPA of 2.5. Additional exam requirements/recommendations for international students: required—TOEFL (minimum score 550 paper-based; 213 iBT), IELTS (minimum score 6.5). *Application deadline:* Applications are processed on a rolling basis. Application fee: $30. Electronic applications accepted. *Expenses: Tuition, area resident:* Full-time $11,261; part-time $625.60 per credit. Tuition, state resident: full-time $11,261; part-time $625.60 per credit. Tuition, nonresident: full-time $16,850; part-time $936.10 per credit. *International tuition:* $16,850 full-time. *Required fees:* $57.75 per credit. *Financial support:* In 2019–20, 35 students received support. Research assistantships with tuition reimbursements available, career-related internships or fieldwork, Federal Work-Study, scholarships/grants, and unspecified assistantships available. Support available to part-time students. Financial award application deadline: 2/15; financial award applicants required to submit FAFSA. *Unit head:* Dr. Penelope Orr, Chairperson, 814-732-1684, E-mail: porr@edinboro.edu. *Application contact:* Dr. Penelope Orr, Chairperson, 814-732-1684, E-mail: porr@edinboro.edu.
Website: https://www.edinboro.edu/academics/schools-and-departments/soe/departments/cspe/

Emporia State University, Program in Art Therapy, Emporia, KS 66801-5415. Offers MS. *Accreditation:* NASAD. *Program availability:* Part-time. *Degree requirements:* For master's, comprehensive exam or thesis, internship. *Entrance requirements:* For master's, GRE General Test or MAT, essay exam, appropriate bachelor's degree. Additional exam requirements/recommendations for international students: required—TOEFL (minimum score 520 paper-based; 68 iBT). Electronic applications accepted. *Expenses: Tuition, area resident:* Full-time $6394; part-time $266.41 per credit hour. Tuition, state resident: full-time $6394; part-time $266.41 per credit hour. Tuition, nonresident: full-time $20,128; part-time $828.66 per credit hour. *International tuition:* $20,128 full-time. *Required fees:* $2183; $90.95 per credit hour. Tuition and fees vary according to campus/location and program.

Florida State University, The Graduate School, College of Fine Arts, Department of Art Education, Tallahassee, FL 32306. Offers art education (MA, MS, Ed D, PhD); art therapy (PhD); arts administration (PhD). *Accreditation:* NASAD (one or more programs are accredited). *Program availability:* Part-time, evening/weekend, 100% online. *Faculty:* 11 full-time (8 women), 11 part-time/adjunct (9 women). *Students:* 58 full-time (53 women), 33 part-time (28 women); includes 32 minority (6 Black or African American, non-Hispanic/Latino; 1 American Indian or Alaska Native, non-Hispanic/Latino; 10 Asian, non-Hispanic/Latino; 12 Hispanic/Latino; 3 Two or more races, non-Hispanic/Latino), 10 international. Average age 31. 116 applicants, 51% accepted, 33 enrolled. In 2019, 38 master's, 8 doctorates awarded. *Degree requirements:* For master's, comprehensive exam, thesis (for some programs); for doctorate, thesis/dissertation. *Entrance requirements:* For master's, GRE (can apply for waiver with GPA greater than 3.0, there is no GRE waiver available for the Art Therapy Program); minimum GPA of 3.0 in last 2 years; for doctorate, GRE. Additional exam requirements/recommendations for international students: required—TOEFL (minimum score 550 paper-based; 80 iBT), Students can take the TOEFL or IELTS; recommended—IELTS (minimum score 6.5), TSE (minimum score 55). *Application deadline:* For fall admission, 2/1 priority date for domestic and international students; for spring admission, 10/1 priority date for domestic and international students. Applications are processed on a rolling basis. Application fee: $30. Electronic applications accepted. *Financial support:* In 2019–20, 20 students received support, including 16 research assistantships with full tuition reimbursements available (averaging $6,345 per year), 4 teaching assistantships with full tuition reimbursements available (averaging $8,742 per year); fellowships, career-related internships or fieldwork, Federal Work-Study, scholarships/grants, health care benefits, tuition waivers (full), and unspecified assistantships also available. Financial award application deadline: 2/1; financial award applicants required to submit FAFSA. *Unit head:* Victoria Cole, Program Associate, 850-644-2147, E-mail: vcole@fsu.edu. *Application contact:* Vicki Barr, Academic Support Assistant, 850-644-5473, Fax: 850-644-6067, E-mail: vbarr@fsu.edu.
Website: http://arted.fsu.edu/

The George Washington University, Columbian College of Arts and Sciences, Program in Art Therapy, Washington, DC 20052. Offers MA, Graduate Certificate. *Entrance requirements:* For master's, GRE General Test, interview, minimum GPA of 3.0; for Graduate Certificate, interview, minimum GPA of 3.0. Additional exam requirements/recommendations for international students: required—TOEFL (minimum score 550 paper-based; 80 iBT).

Georgia College & State University, The Graduate School, College of Health Sciences, Program in Art Therapy, Milledgeville, GA 31061. Offers MA. *Students:* 6 full-time (all women). Average age 23. 8 applicants, 75% accepted, 6 enrolled. In 2019, 2 master's awarded. *Degree requirements:* For master's, comprehensive exam, thesis or alternative, Each student admitted to the degree program must successfully complete the program requirements within 12 months of admission. *Entrance requirements:* For master's, 3 letters of recommendation; minimum undergraduate GPA of 2.75; official transcript; 12 credit hours in psychology, 18 in studio art; 12 pieces of recent artwork; essay; interview. Application fee: $40. *Expenses:* $2646 per semester full-time in-state tuition, $1011 per semester full-time in-state fees, $9423 per semester full-time out-of-state tuition, $1011 per semester full-time out-of-state fees. *Financial support:* Application deadline: 3/1; applicants required to submit FAFSA. *Unit head:* Carrie Elder, Program Coordinator, Art Therapy, 478-445-2645, Fax: 478-445-4532, E-mail: carrie.elder@gcsu.edu. *Application contact:* Kate Marshall, Graduate Admissions Coordinator, 478-445-1184, Fax: 478-445-1336, E-mail: grad-admit@gcsu.edu.

Goddard College, Graduate Division, Master of Arts in Psychology Program, Plainfield, VT 05667-9432. Offers expressive arts therapy (MA); psychology (MA); sexual orientation (MA). *Program availability:* Part-time, online learning. *Degree requirements:* For master's, thesis or alternative, clinical internship. *Entrance requirements:* For master's, eight specific undergraduate prerequisite courses taken within previous five years (or preparatory semester at Goddard), statement of purpose, 3 letters of recommendation, interview. Electronic applications accepted.

Hofstra University, School of Health Professions and Human Services, Programs in Counseling, Hempstead, NY 11549. Offers counseling (MS Ed, PD); creative arts therapy (MA); interdisciplinary transition specialist (Advanced Certificate); marriage and family therapy (MA); mental health counseling (MA, Advanced Certificate); rehabilitation administration (PD); rehabilitation counseling (MS Ed, Advanced Certificate); rehabilitation counseling in mental health (MS Ed, Advanced Certificate). *Accreditation:* ACA. *Program availability:* Part-time, evening/weekend. *Students:* 124 full-time (105 women), 69 part-time (64 women); includes 68 minority (23 Black or African American, non-Hispanic/Latino; 10 Asian, non-Hispanic/Latino; 32 Hispanic/Latino; 3 Native Hawaiian or other Pacific Islander, non-Hispanic/Latino), 4 international. Average age 28. 188 applicants, 77% accepted, 75 enrolled. In 2019, 58 master's, 3 other advanced degrees awarded. *Degree requirements:* For master's, comprehensive exam (for some programs), thesis (for some programs), internship, practicum, student teaching, seminars, minimum GPA of 3.0. *Entrance requirements:* For master's, GRE, interview, letters of recommendation, portfolio, essay, professional experience, certification; for other advanced degree, GRE, interview, letters of recommendation, essay, professional experience, resume, master's degree. Additional exam requirements/recommendations for international students: required—TOEFL (minimum score 550 paper-based; 80 iBT); recommended—IELTS (minimum score 6.5). *Application deadline:* Applications are processed on a rolling basis. Application fee: $75. Electronic applications accepted. *Expenses: Tuition:* Full-time $25,164; part-time $1398 per credit. *Required fees:* $580; $165 per semester. Tuition and fees vary according to course load, degree level and program. *Financial support:* In 2019–20, 77 students received support, including 44 fellowships with full and partial tuition reimbursements available (averaging $3,811 per year), 9 research assistantships with full and partial tuition reimbursements available (averaging $6,586 per year); career-related internships or fieldwork, Federal Work-Study, institutionally sponsored loans, scholarships/grants, traineeships, tuition waivers (full and partial), unspecified assistantships, and scholarships and endowed scholarships also available. Support available to part-time students. Financial award applicants required to submit FAFSA. *Unit head:* Dr. Jamie Mitus, Chairperson, 516-463-5759, E-mail: jamie.s.mitus@hofstra.edu. *Application contact:* Sunil Samuel, Assistant Vice President of Admissions, 516-463-4723, Fax: 516-463-4664, E-mail:

graduateadmission@hofstra.edu.
Website: http://www.hofstra.edu/academics/colleges/healthscienceshumanservices/

Indiana University-Purdue University Indianapolis, Herron School of Art and Design, Indianapolis, IN 46202. Offers art therapy (MA); visual art (MFA), including ceramics, furniture design, painting and drawing, photography and intermedia, printmaking, sculpture; visual communication design (MFA). *Degree requirements:* For master's, thesis. *Entrance requirements:* For master's, personal statement, resume, recommendations, portfolio, transcripts (18 credit hours of studio art and 12 credit hours of psychology, including 3 credit hours of developmental psychology and 3 credit hours of abnormal psychology for MA). Additional exam requirements/recommendations for international students: recommended—TOEFL (minimum score 550 paper-based; 79 iBT), IELTS (minimum score 6.5). Electronic applications accepted. *Expenses:* Contact institution.

Lesley University, Graduate School of Arts and Social Sciences, Cambridge, MA 02138-2790. Offers clinical mental health counseling (MA), including holistic counseling, school and community counseling, trauma studies; counseling psychology (MA, CAGS), including professional counseling (MA), school counseling (MA); creative writing (MFA); expressive therapies (MA, PhD, CAGS), including art (MA), clinical mental health counseling (MA), dance (MA), expressive therapies (MA), music (MA); independent studies (CAGS); independent study (MA); intercultural relations (MA, CAGS); interdisciplinary studies (MA), including individualized studies, integrative holistic health, mindfulness studies, peace and conflict transformation, trauma sensitive assessment, intervention, and consultation, women's studies; urban environmental leadership (MA). *Program availability:* Part-time, online learning. *Degree requirements:* For master's, internship, practicum, thesis (for expressive therapies); for doctorate, thesis/dissertation, arts apprenticeship, field placement; for CAGS, thesis, internship (for counseling psychology, expressive therapies). *Entrance requirements:* For master's, MAT (counseling psychology), interview, writing samples, art portfolio; for doctorate, GRE or MAT, interview, master's degree; for CAGS, interview, master's degree. Additional exam requirements/recommendations for international students: required—TOEFL (minimum score 550 paper-based; 80 iBT). Electronic applications accepted.

Long Island University - Post, College of Arts, Communications and Design, Brookville, NY 11548-1300. Offers art (MA); clinical art therapy (MA); clinical art therapy and counseling (MA); digital game design and development (MA); fine arts and design (MFA); interactive multimedia arts (MA); museum studies (MA); music (MA); theatre (MFA). *Degree requirements:* For master's, variable foreign language requirement, comprehensive exam (for some programs), thesis. *Entrance requirements:* For master's, performance audition or portfolio. Additional exam requirements/recommendations for international students: required—TOEFL (minimum score 550 paper-based; 79 iBT). Electronic applications accepted.

Marywood University, Academic Affairs, Insalaco College of Creative and Performing Arts, Art Department, Program in Art Therapy, Scranton, PA 18509-1598. Offers MA, Graduate Certificate. *Accreditation:* NASAD. *Program availability:* Part-time. Electronic applications accepted.

Mount Mary University, Graduate Programs, Program in Art Therapy, Milwaukee, WI 53222-4597. Offers MS, DAT. *Program availability:* Part-time, evening/weekend. *Degree requirements:* For master's, thesis or alternative, internship; for doctorate, culminating project and pre-graduation defense. *Entrance requirements:* For master's, minimum GPA of 3.0; for doctorate, minimum GPA of 3.5. Additional exam requirements/recommendations for international students: required—TOEFL (minimum score 550 paper-based; 80 iBT); recommended—IELTS (minimum score 6.5). Electronic applications accepted. *Expenses:* Contact institution.

Naropa University, Graduate Programs, Program in Clinical Mental Health Counseling, Concentration in Transpersonal Art Therapy, Boulder, CO 80302-6697. Offers MA. *Degree requirements:* For master's, internship, 190 direct art contact hours of studio-based work, counseling practicum. *Entrance requirements:* For master's, interview, visual art portfolio, statement of interest, 2 letters of recommendation, transcripts. Additional exam requirements/recommendations for international students: required—TOEFL (minimum score 550 paper-based; 80 iBT). Electronic applications accepted. *Expenses:* Contact institution.

Nazareth College of Rochester, Graduate Studies, Department of Creative Arts Therapy, Rochester, NY 14618. Offers art therapy (MS); music therapy (MS). *Program availability:* Part-time. *Entrance requirements:* For master's, minimum GPA of 3.0; portfolio review (art therapy); audition (music therapy). Additional exam requirements/recommendations for international students: required—TOEFL (minimum score 550 paper-based, 79 iBT) or IELTS (6.5). Electronic applications accepted.

New York University, Steinhardt School of Culture, Education, and Human Development, Department of Art and Art Professions, Program in Art Therapy, New York, NY 10003. Offers MA. *Program availability:* Part-time. *Entrance requirements:* For master's, interview, portfolio. Additional exam requirements/recommendations for international students: required—TOEFL (minimum score 100 iBT). Electronic applications accepted.

Notre Dame de Namur University, Division of Academic Affairs, School of Education and Psychology, Program in Art Therapy, Belmont, CA 94002-1908. Offers art therapy (MA); art therapy psychology (PhD). *Program availability:* Part-time, evening/weekend. Terminal master's awarded for partial completion of doctoral program. *Degree requirements:* For master's, thesis, oral presentation, portfolio; for doctorate, thesis/dissertation. *Entrance requirements:* For master's, interview, minimum GPA of 2.5; for doctorate, master's degree from accredited university in art therapy or in a related field; minimum of two years of clinical work in the field; portfolio; three professional recommendations; one published article or scholarly academic writing on an art therapy subject in publication-acceptable form; interview. Additional exam requirements/recommendations for international students: required—TOEFL (minimum score 550 paper-based; 79 iBT). Electronic applications accepted.

Ottawa University, Graduate Studies-Arizona, Program in Professional Counseling, Ottawa, KS 66067-3399. Offers Christian counseling (MA); expressive arts therapy (MA); marriage and family therapy (MA); treatment of trauma, abuse and deprivation (MA). *Program availability:* Part-time, evening/weekend, online learning. *Degree requirements:* For master's, comprehensive exam, thesis or alternative, field experience, practicum. *Entrance requirements:* For master's, minimum undergraduate GPA of 3.0; course work in theories of personality, abnormal psychology, and human growth and development. Additional exam requirements/recommendations for international students: required—TOEFL (minimum score 550 paper-based).

Phillips Graduate University, Master's Program in Psychology, Chatsworth, CA 91311. Offers art therapy (MA); marriage and family therapy (MA); school counseling (MA); school psychology (MA). *Program availability:* Evening/weekend. *Degree requirements:* For master's, comprehensive exam, thesis. *Entrance requirements:* For master's, minimum GPA of 2.5. Electronic applications accepted.

Pratt Institute, School of Art, Programs in Creative Arts Therapy, Brooklyn, NY 11205-3899. Offers art therapy and creativity development (MPS); dance/movement therapy (MS). *Accreditation:* NASAD (one or more programs are accredited). *Program* availability: Part-time. *Students:* 67 full-time (63 women), 41 part-time (all women); includes 41 minority (11 Black or African American, non-Hispanic/Latino; 7 Asian, non-Hispanic/Latino; 19 Hispanic/Latino; 4 Two or more races, non-Hispanic/Latino), 7 international. Average age 30. 112 applicants, 69% accepted, 31 enrolled. In 2019, 43 master's awarded. *Degree requirements:* For master's, thesis. *Entrance requirements:* For master's, letters of recommendation, portfolio. Additional exam requirements/recommendations for international students: required—TOEFL (minimum score 600 paper-based; 100 iBT). *Application deadline:* For fall admission, 1/5 for domestic and international students; for spring admission, 10/1 for domestic and international students. Applications are processed on a rolling basis. Application fee: $50 ($90 for international students). Electronic applications accepted. *Expenses: Tuition:* Full-time $33,246; part-time $1847 per credit. *Required fees:* $1980. *Financial support:* Career-related internships or fieldwork, Federal Work-Study, institutionally sponsored loans, scholarships/grants, health care benefits, and unspecified assistantships available. Support available to part-time students. Financial award application deadline: 2/1; financial award applicants required to submit FAFSA. *Unit head:* Julie Miller, Chairperson, 718-399-4532, Fax: 718-636-3597, E-mail: jmiller2@pratt.edu. *Application contact:* Natalie Capannelli, Director of Graduate Admissions, 718-636-3551, Fax: 718-399-4242, E-mail: ncapanne@pratt.edu.
Website: https://www.pratt.edu/academics/school-of-art/graduate-school-of-art/creative-arts-therapy/

Prescott College, Graduate Programs, Program in Counseling and Psychology, Prescott, AZ 86301. Offers adventure-based psychotherapy (MA); counseling psychology (MA); ecopsychology (MA); ecotherapy (MA); equine-assisted mental health (MA); expressive arts therapy (MA); somatic psychology (MA); student-directed independent study (MA). *Program availability:* Part-time, online learning. Terminal master's awarded for partial completion of doctoral program. *Degree requirements:* For master's, thesis, fieldwork or internship, practicum. *Entrance requirements:* For master's, 2 letters of recommendation, resume. Additional exam requirements/recommendations for international students: required—TOEFL (minimum score 500 paper-based). Electronic applications accepted.

Saint Mary-of-the-Woods College, Master of Arts in Art Therapy Program, Saint Mary of the Woods, IN 47876. Offers MA, Post-Master's Certificate. *Program availability:* Part-time. *Faculty:* 5 full-time (all women). *Students:* 123 full-time (118 women), 19 part-time (all women); includes 32 minority (7 Black or African American, non-Hispanic/Latino; 1 American Indian or Alaska Native, non-Hispanic/Latino; 2 Asian, non-Hispanic/Latino; 3 Hispanic/Latino; 19 Two or more races, non-Hispanic/Latino), 1 international. Average age 34. 68 applicants, 62% accepted, 32 enrolled. In 2019, 27 master's awarded. *Degree requirements:* For master's, thesis, three supervised clinical experiences. *Entrance requirements:* For degree, 12 credit hours each in general psychology, abnormal psychology, theories of personality, and developmental psychology; 18 credit hours in studio art skills. *Application deadline:* For fall admission, 4/30 priority date for domestic and international students; for winter admission, 10/31 priority date for domestic and international students. Applications are processed on a rolling basis. Application fee: $0. Electronic applications accepted. *Expenses:* $750 per credit hour. *Financial support:* In 2019–20, 38 students received support. Scholarships/grants available. Financial award applicants required to submit FAFSA. *Unit head:* Dr. Tracy Richardson, Dean of Graduate Therapy and Counseling Programs, 812-535-5154, E-mail: trichardson@smwc.edu. *Application contact:* Crystal Cox, Associate Director of Admissions, 812-535-5263, E-mail: graduate@smwc.edu.
Website: http://www.smwc.edu/graduate/maat/

School of Visual Arts, Graduate Programs, Art Therapy Department, New York, NY 10010-3994. Offers MPS. *Degree requirements:* For master's, thesis, 60 credits; minimum cumulative GPA of 3.0; residency of two academic years; internship. *Entrance requirements:* For master's, interview; 18 credits (or equivalent) in studio art and 12 credits in psychology (developmental and abnormal required; courses in introduction to psychology and theories of personality recommended); 15 to 20 digital images on CD. Additional exam requirements/recommendations for international students: required—TOEFL (minimum score 550 paper-based; 79 iBT). Electronic applications accepted.

Seton Hill University, MA Program in Art Therapy, Greensburg, PA 15601. Offers MA. *Program availability:* Part-time. *Students:* 49. Average age 35. 35 applicants, 57% accepted, 18 enrolled. *Entrance requirements:* For master's, portfolio; 3 letters of recommendation; letter of intent; transcripts; writing sample (APA style); resume. Additional exam requirements/recommendations for international students: required—TOEFL (minimum score 650 paper-based; 114 iBT), IELTS (minimum score 7). *Application deadline:* For fall admission, 7/1 for domestic and international students; for spring admission, 11/30 for domestic and international students. Applications are processed on a rolling basis. Application fee: $0. Electronic applications accepted. Application fee is waived when completed online. *Expenses: Tuition:* Full-time $29,196; part-time $811 per credit. *Required fees:* $550; $100 per unit. $25 per semester. Tuition and fees vary according to class time, course level, course load, degree level, campus/location, program, reciprocity agreements, student level and student's religious affiliation. *Financial support:* Federal Work-Study, scholarships/grants, and tuition discounts available. Financial award application deadline: 8/15; financial award applicants required to submit FAFSA. *Unit head:* Dr. Julie Barris, Director, Graduate & Adult Studies, E-mail: jbarris@setonhill.edu. *Application contact:* Dr. Julie Barris, Director, Graduate & Adult Studies, E-mail: jbarris@setonhill.edu.
Website: http://www.setonhill.edu/academics/graduate_programs/art_therapy

Southern Illinois University Edwardsville, Graduate School, College of Arts and Sciences, Department of Art and Design, Program in Art Therapy Counseling, Edwardsville, IL 62026. Offers MA. *Program availability:* Part-time. *Degree requirements:* For master's, thesis or alternative, project. *Entrance requirements:* For master's, MAT, portfolio. Additional exam requirements/recommendations for international students: required—TOEFL (minimum score 550 paper-based; 79 iBT), IELTS (minimum score 6.5). Electronic applications accepted.

Southwestern College, Program in Art Therapy/Counseling, Santa Fe, NM 87502-4788. Offers MA. *Program availability:* Part-time, evening/weekend. *Degree requirements:* For master's, internship. *Entrance requirements:* For master's, resume, slide portfolio, interview, 3 letters of reference. Additional exam requirements/recommendations for international students: required—TOEFL.

Springfield College, Graduate Programs, Program in Art Therapy, Springfield, MA 01109-3797. Offers M Ed, MS, CAGS. *Program availability:* Part-time. *Degree requirements:* For master's, thesis or alternative, research project, final art exhibition. *Entrance requirements:* For master's, portfolio. Additional exam requirements/recommendations for international students: required—TOEFL (minimum score 90 iBT); recommended—IELTS (minimum score 7). Electronic applications accepted.

University of Louisville, Graduate School, College of Education and Human Development, Department of Counseling and Human Development, Louisville, KY 40292-0001. Offers counseling and personnel services (M Ed, PhD), including art therapy (M Ed), college student personnel, counseling psychology, counselor education and supervision (PhD), educational psychology, measurement, and evaluation (PhD), mental health counseling (M Ed), school counseling (M Ed). *Accreditation:* APA;

NCATE. *Program availability:* Part-time. *Faculty:* 11 full-time (7 women), 10 part-time/adjunct (6 women). *Students:* 118 full-time (95 women), 60 part-time (45 women); includes 54 minority (32 Black or African American, non-Hispanic/Latino; 1 American Indian or Alaska Native, non-Hispanic/Latino; 2 Asian, non-Hispanic/Latino; 12 Hispanic/Latino; 1 Native Hawaiian or other Pacific Islander, non-Hispanic/Latino; 6 Two or more races, non-Hispanic/Latino), 3 international. Average age 29. 118 applicants, 52% accepted, 43 enrolled. In 2019, 61 master's, 11 doctorates awarded. Terminal master's awarded for partial completion of doctoral program. *Degree requirements:* For master's, thesis optional; for doctorate, comprehensive exam, thesis/dissertation. *Entrance requirements:* For master's, professional statement, recommendation letters, resume, transcripts; for doctorate, GRE, professional statement, recommendation letters, resume, transcripts. Additional exam requirements/recommendations for international students: required—TOEFL (minimum score 550 paper-based; 79 iBT); recommended—IELTS (minimum score 6.5). *Application deadline:* For fall admission, 3/1 priority date for domestic and international students; for spring admission, 10/1 priority date for domestic and international students; for summer admission, 3/1 priority date for domestic and international students. Application fee: $65. Electronic applications accepted. *Expenses: Tuition, area resident:* Full-time $13,000; part-time $723 per credit hour. Tuition, state resident: full-time $13,000; part-time $723 per credit hour. Tuition, nonresident: full-time $27,114; part-time $1507 per credit hour. *International tuition:* $27,114 full-time. *Required fees:* $196. Tuition and fees vary according to program and reciprocity agreements. *Financial support:* In 2019–20, 73 students received support, including 3 fellowships with full tuition reimbursements available (averaging $21,024 per year), 5 research assistantships with full tuition reimbursements available (averaging $21,024 per year), 3 teaching assistantships with full tuition reimbursements available (averaging $21,024 per year); scholarships/grants, health care benefits, and unspecified assistantships also available. Financial award application deadline: 3/1; financial award applicants required to submit FAFSA. *Unit head:* Dr. Mark M. Leach, Department Chair, 502-852-0588, Fax: 502-852-0629, E-mail: m.leach@louisville.edu. *Application contact:* Dr. Margaret Pentecost, Assistant Dean for Graduate Student Success, 502-852-2628, Fax: 502-852-1417, E-mail: gedadm@louisville.edu.
Website: http://www.louisville.edu/education/departments/ecpy

University of Maryland, College Park, Academic Affairs, College of Education, Department of Counseling, Higher Education and Special Education, College Park, MD 20742. Offers college student personnel (M Ed, MA); college student personnel administration (PhD); community counseling (CAGS); community/career counseling (M Ed, MA); counseling and personnel services (M Ed, MA, PhD), including art therapy (M Ed), college student personnel (M Ed), counseling and personnel services (PhD); counseling psychology (M Ed), mental health counseling (M Ed), school counseling (M Ed); counseling psychology (PhD); counselor education (PhD); rehabilitation counseling (M Ed, MA, AGSC); school counseling (M Ed, MA); school psychology (M Ed, MA, PhD). *Accreditation:* APA (one or more programs are accredited); NCATE. *Program availability:* Part-time, evening/weekend, online learning. *Degree requirements:* For master's, thesis (for some programs); for doctorate, thesis/dissertation. *Entrance requirements:* For master's, GRE General Test or MAT, minimum GPA of 3.0, 3 letters of recommendation; for doctorate, GRE General Test or MAT, minimum GPA of 3.5, 3 letters of recommendation. Additional exam requirements/recommendations for international students: required—TOEFL. Electronic applications accepted.

University of Wisconsin–Superior, Graduate Division, Department of Visual Arts, Superior, WI 54880-4500. Offers art education (MA); art history (MA); art therapy (MA); studio arts (MA). *Program availability:* Part-time. *Degree requirements:* For master's, comprehensive exam, exhibit. *Entrance requirements:* For master's, minimum GPA of 2.75, portfolio. Electronic applications accepted.

Ursuline College, School of Graduate and Professional Studies, Program in Counseling and Art Therapy, Pepper Pike, OH 44124-4398. Offers MA. *Program availability:* Part-time. *Faculty:* 6 full-time (5 women), 6 part-time/adjunct (5 women). *Students:* 70 full-time (62 women), 19 part-time (17 women); includes 17 minority (12 Black or African American, non-Hispanic/Latino; 2 Asian, non-Hispanic/Latino; 2 Hispanic/Latino; 1 Two or more races, non-Hispanic/Latino). Average age 29. 132 applicants, 99% accepted, 20 enrolled. In 2019, 19 master's awarded. *Degree requirements:* For master's, thesis, 700-hour internship. *Entrance requirements:* For master's, BA in psychology, social sciences, or related field; minimum undergraduate GPA of 3.0; portfolio; work experience with human service agency. Additional exam requirements/recommendations for international students: required—TOEFL (minimum score 500 paper-based; 80 iBT). *Application deadline:* For fall admission, 8/1 priority date for domestic students. Applications are processed on a rolling basis. Application fee: $25. Electronic applications accepted. *Expenses:* 65 Credit hours at $1,174 per. *Financial support:* In 2019–20, 18 students received support. Federal Work-Study, scholarships/grants, and Housing discount available. Financial award application deadline: 3/1; financial award applicants required to submit FAFSA. *Unit head:* Gail Rule-Hoffman, Director, 440-646-8138, Fax: 440-684-6135. *Application contact:* Melanie Steele, Director, Graduate Admission, 440-646-8119, Fax: 440-684-6138, E-mail: graduateadmissions@ursuline.edu.

Decorative Arts

Bard Graduate Center, Graduate Studies, New York, NY 10024-3602. Offers MA, PhD. *Program availability:* Part-time. *Degree requirements:* For master's, one foreign language, thesis, internship; for doctorate, 2 foreign languages, thesis/dissertation, 3 field exams. *Entrance requirements:* For master's, GRE General Test, writing sample, 3 letters of recommendation; for doctorate, GRE General Test, MA, master's thesis or equivalent, 3 letters of recommendation. Additional exam requirements/recommendations for international students: required—TOEFL.

The George Washington University, Columbian College of Arts and Sciences, Corcoran School of the Arts and Design, Washington, DC 20007. Offers art and the book (MA); art education (MA, MAT); decorative arts and design history (MA); exhibition design (MA); interior design (MA); new media photojournalism (MA). *Accreditation:* NASAD. *Program availability:* Part-time. *Entrance requirements:* Additional exam requirements/recommendations for international students: required—TOEFL (minimum score 95 iBT).

Sotheby's Institute of Art–London, Graduate Programs, London, United Kingdom. Offers art business (MA); contemporary art (MA); fine and decorative art and design (MA); modern and contemporary Asian art (MA). *Degree requirements:* For master's, thesis. *Entrance requirements:* Additional exam requirements/recommendations for international students: required—IELTS (minimum score 7). Electronic applications accepted.

Sotheby's Institute of Art–New York, Graduate Programs, New York, NY 10021. Offers art business (MA); contemporary art (MA); fine and decorative art and design (MA). *Accreditation:* NASAD. *Entrance requirements:* For master's, academic transcripts, two letters of academic reference, personal statement, writing sample, curriculum vitae/resume, interview. Additional exam requirements/recommendations for international students: required—TOEFL (minimum score 100 iBT), IELTS (minimum score 7). Electronic applications accepted.

Museum Studies

American Museum of Natural History–Richard Gilder Graduate School, Program in Comparative Biology, New York, NY 10024. Offers PhD. *Degree requirements:* For doctorate, thesis/dissertation, qualifying examination. *Entrance requirements:* For doctorate, GRE General Test (taken within the past five years); GRE Subject Test (recommended), BA, BS, or equivalent degree from accredited institution; official transcripts; essay. Additional exam requirements/recommendations for international students: required—TOEFL (minimum score 600 paper-based; 100 iBT), IELTS (minimum score 7).

Arizona State University at Tempe, College of Liberal Arts and Sciences, School of Human Evolution and Social Change, Tempe, AZ 85287-2402. Offers anthropology (MA, PhD), including anthropology (PhD), archaeology (PhD), bioarchaeology (PhD), evolutionary (PhD), museum studies (MA), sociocultural (PhD); applied mathematics for the life and social sciences (PhD); environmental social science (PhD), including environmental social science, urbanism; global health (MA, PhD), including complex adaptive systems science (PhD), evolutionary global health sciences (PhD), health and culture (PhD), urbanism (PhD); immigration studies (Graduate Certificate). Terminal master's awarded for partial completion of doctoral program. *Degree requirements:* For master's, thesis or alternative, interactive Program of Study (iPOS) submitted before completing 50 percent of required credit hours; for doctorate, comprehensive exam, thesis/dissertation, interactive Program of Study (iPOS) submitted before completing 50 percent of required credit hours. *Entrance requirements:* For master's and doctorate, GRE, minimum GPA of 3.0 or equivalent in last 2 years of work leading to bachelor's degree. Additional exam requirements/recommendations for international students: required—TOEFL, IELTS, or PTE. Electronic applications accepted.

Arizona State University at Tempe, Herberger Institute for Design and the Arts, School of Art, Tempe, AZ 85287-1505. Offers art education (MA); art history (MA); ceramics (MFA); design, environment and the arts (PhD), including history, theory and criticism; drawing (MFA); fibers (MFA); intermedia (MFA); metals (MFA); museum studies (MFA); painting (MFA); printmaking (MFA); sculpture (MFA); wood (MFA); MFA/MA. Terminal master's awarded for partial completion of doctoral program. *Degree requirements:* For master's, thesis/exhibition (MFA, MA in art education); interactive Program of Study (iPOS) submitted before completing 50 percent of required credit hours; for doctorate, comprehensive exam, thesis/dissertation, interactive Program of Study (iPOS) submitted before completing 50 percent of required credit hours. *Entrance requirements:* For master's, GRE or MAT, minimum GPA of 3.0 or equivalent in last 2 years of work leading to bachelor's degree; for doctorate, GRE, master's degree in architecture, graphic design, industrial design, interior design, landscape architecture, or art history or equivalent standing; statement of purpose; 3 letters of recommendation; indication of potential faculty mentor; sample of written work. Additional exam requirements/recommendations for international students: required—TOEFL, IELTS, or PTE. Electronic applications accepted.

Bard College, Center for Curatorial Studies, Annandale-on-Hudson, NY 12504. Offers MA. *Degree requirements:* For master's, thesis, exhibition. *Entrance requirements:* For master's, exhibition review, 3 letters of recommendation. Additional exam requirements/recommendations for international students: required—TOEFL (minimum score 550 paper-based). Electronic applications accepted. *Expenses:* Contact institution.

Baylor University, Graduate School, College of Arts and Sciences, Department of Museum Studies, Waco, TX 76798. Offers MA. *Program availability:* Part-time. *Degree requirements:* For master's, comprehensive exam, thesis or alternative. *Entrance requirements:* For master's, GRE General Test. Additional exam requirements/recommendations for international students: required—TOEFL (minimum score 550 paper-based; 80 iBT). Electronic applications accepted.

Boston University, Graduate School of Arts and Sciences, Department of History of Art and Architecture, Boston, MA 02215. Offers history of art and architecture (MA, PhD); museum studies (Certificate). *Accreditation:* NASAD. *Students:* 48 full-time (40 women), 5 part-time (4 women); includes 5 minority (2 Asian, non-Hispanic/Latino; 3 Hispanic/Latino), 10 international. Average age 28. 132 applicants, 41% accepted, 10 enrolled. In 2019, 5 master's, 5 doctorates awarded. Terminal master's awarded for partial completion of doctoral program. *Degree requirements:* For master's, one foreign language, comprehensive exam, thesis or alternative, scholarly paper; for doctorate, 2 foreign languages, comprehensive exam, thesis/dissertation. *Entrance requirements:* For master's and doctorate, GRE General Test, 3 letters of recommendation, transcripts, personal statement, curriculum vitae, writing sample, foreign language proficiency.

Additional exam requirements/recommendations for international students: required—TOEFL (minimum score 550 paper-based; 84 iBT). *Application deadline:* For fall admission, 1/5 for domestic and international students; for spring admission, 10/15 for domestic and international students. Application fee: $95. Electronic applications accepted. *Financial support:* In 2019–20, 50 students received support, including 19 fellowships with full tuition reimbursements available (averaging $23,340 per year), 14 teaching assistantships with full tuition reimbursements available (averaging $23,340 per year); career-related internships or fieldwork, Federal Work-Study, scholarships/grants, health care benefits, and unspecified assistantships also available. Financial award application deadline: 1/5. *Unit head:* Alice Tseng, Chair, 617-353-1458, Fax: 617-353-3243, E-mail: aytseng@bu.edu. *Application contact:* Cheryl Crombie, Administrative Assistant, 617-353-2522, Fax: 617-353-3243, E-mail: ccrombie@bu.edu.
Website: http://www.bu.edu/AH/

Buffalo State College, State University of New York, The Graduate School, School of Natural and Social Sciences, Department of History and Social Studies Education, Buffalo, NY 14222-1095. Offers history (MA); museum studies (MA); secondary education (MS Ed), including social studies. *Program availability:* Part-time, evening/weekend. *Degree requirements:* For master's, one foreign language, thesis (for some programs), project (MS Ed). *Entrance requirements:* For master's, minimum GPA of 2.75, 30 hours in history (MA), 36 hours in history or social sciences (MS Ed). Additional exam requirements/recommendations for international students: required—TOEFL (minimum score 550 paper-based).

California College of the Arts, Graduate Programs, Curatorial Practice Program, San Francisco, CA 94107. Offers curatorial practice (MA), including visual and critical studies. *Degree requirements:* For master's, thesis, exhibit. *Entrance requirements:* For master's, appropriate bachelor's degree, portfolio, resume, letters of recommendation, transcript. Additional exam requirements/recommendations for international students: required—TOEFL, IELTS, or PTE. Electronic applications accepted. *Expenses:* Contact institution.

California State University, Chico, Office of Graduate Studies, College of Behavioral and Social Sciences, Department of Anthropology, Chico, CA 95929-0722. Offers anthropology (MA); museum studies (MA). *Degree requirements:* For master's, comprehensive exam, thesis, Thesis, project or oral examination. *Entrance requirements:* For master's, GRE General Test, Deadline for January 10th. Fall admission only. Two letters of recommendation, statement of purpose, curriculum vitae, writing sample, and department letter of recommendation to access waiver form. Additional exam requirements/recommendations for international students: required—TOEFL (minimum score 550 paper-based; 80 iBT), IELTS (minimum score 6.5), PTE (minimum score 59). Electronic applications accepted.

California State University, Fullerton, Graduate Studies, College of the Arts, Department of Visual Arts, Fullerton, CA 92831-3599. Offers art (MA, MFA), including art history (MA), ceramics (MFA), crafts, creative photography, exhibition design, glass, graphic design, illustration, sculpture. *Accreditation:* NASAD (one or more programs are accredited). *Program availability:* Part-time. *Entrance requirements:* For master's, minimum GPA of 2.5 in last 60 units of course work, portfolio.

Caribbean University, Graduate School, Bayamón, PR 00960-0493. Offers administration and supervision (MA Ed); criminal justice (MA); curriculum and instruction (MA Ed, PhD), including elementary education (MA Ed), English education (MA Ed), history education (MA Ed), mathematics education (MA Ed), primary education (MA Ed), science education (MA Ed), Spanish education (MA Ed); educational technology in instructional systems (MA Ed); gerontology (MSN); human resources (MBA); museology, archiving and art history (MA Ed); neonatal pediatrics (MSN); physical education (MA Ed); special education (MA Ed). *Entrance requirements:* For master's, interview, minimum GPA of 2.5.

Case Western Reserve University, School of Graduate Studies, Department of Art History and Art, Program in Art History and Museum Studies, Cleveland, OH 44106. Offers MA. *Program availability:* Part-time. *Degree requirements:* For master's, one foreign language, comprehensive exam. *Entrance requirements:* For master's, GRE General Test, 2 samples of written work; 3 letters of recommendation. Additional exam requirements/recommendations for international students: required—TOEFL (minimum score 600 paper-based; 100 iBT). Electronic applications accepted.

Christie's Education, MA Program in Modern and Contemporary Art and the Market, New York, NY 10020. Offers MA. *Program availability:* Part-time. *Degree requirements:* For master's, one foreign language, thesis, internship. *Entrance requirements:* For master's, writing sample, 3 letters of recommendation. Additional exam requirements/recommendations for international students: required—TOEFL. *Expenses:* Contact institution.

City College of the City University of New York, Graduate School, Division of Humanities and the Arts, Department of Art, Programs in Art History and Museum Studies, New York, NY 10031-9198. Offers art history (MA); art museum education (MA); museum studies (MA). *Program availability:* Part-time. *Degree requirements:* For master's, one foreign language, thesis. *Entrance requirements:* For master's, minimum GPA of 3.0, portfolio, art history paper. Additional exam requirements/recommendations for international students: required—TOEFL (minimum score 577 paper-based; 90 iBT). Electronic applications accepted.

Claremont Graduate University, Graduate Programs, School of Arts and Humanities, Department of Cultural Studies, Claremont, CA 91711-6160. Offers Africana studies (Certificate); cultural studies (MA, PhD); media studies (MA, PhD); museum studies (MA). *Program availability:* Part-time. *Entrance requirements:* For master's and doctorate, GRE General Test. Additional exam requirements/recommendations for international students: required—TOEFL (minimum score 75 iBT). Electronic applications accepted.

Cleveland State University, College of Graduate Studies, College of Liberal Arts and Social Sciences, Department of History, Cleveland, OH 44115. Offers art history (MA); museum studies (MA). *Program availability:* Part-time, evening/weekend. *Students:* Average age 32. 21 applicants, 90% accepted, 6 enrolled. In 2019, 9 master's awarded. *Entrance requirements:* For master's, minimum GPA of 3.0, bachelor's degree in history (or related field for art history). Additional exam requirements/recommendations for international students: required—TOEFL (minimum score 550 paper-based; 78 iBT). *Application deadline:* Applications are processed on a rolling basis. Application fee: $40. Electronic applications accepted. *Expenses:* Tuition, state resident: full-time $10,215; part-time $6810 per credit hour. Tuition, nonresident: full-time $17,496; part-time $11,664 per credit hour. *International tuition:* $19,316 full-time. Tuition and fees vary according to degree level and program. *Financial support:* In 2019–20, 7 students received support. Research assistantships, career-related internships or fieldwork, tuition waivers (full and partial), and unspecified assistantships available. Financial award application deadline: 4/15. *Unit head:* Dr. Elizabeth A. Lehfeldt, Chairperson, 216-687-3920, Fax: 216-687-5592, E-mail: e.lehfeldt@csuohio.edu. *Application contact:* Dr. Karen Sotiropoulos, Graduate Director, 216-687-3940, E-mail: r.s.shelton@csuohio.edu.
Website: http://www.csuohio.edu/history/

Columbia University, Graduate School of Arts and Sciences, New York, NY 10027. Offers African-American studies (MA); American studies (MA); anthropology (MA, PhD); art history and archaeology (MA, PhD); astronomy (PhD); biological sciences (PhD); biotechnology (MA); chemical physics (PhD); chemistry (PhD); classical studies (MA, PhD); classics (MA, PhD); climate and society (MA); conservation biology (MA); earth and environmental sciences (PhD); East Asia: regional studies (MA); East Asian languages and cultures (MA, PhD); ecology, evolution and environmental biology (MA), including conservation biology; ecology, evolution, and environmental biology (PhD), including ecology and evolutionary biology, evolutionary primatology; economics (MA, PhD); English and comparative literature (MA, PhD); French and Romance philology (MA, PhD); Germanic languages (MA, PhD); global French studies (MA); global thought (MA); Hispanic cultural studies (MA); history (PhD); history and literature (MA); human rights studies (MA); Islamic studies (MA); Italian (MA, PhD); Japanese pedagogy (MA); Jewish studies (MA); Latin America and the Caribbean: regional studies (MA); Latin American and Iberian cultures (PhD); mathematics (MA, PhD), including finance (MA); medieval and Renaissance studies (MA); Middle Eastern, South Asian, and African studies (MA, PhD); modern art: critical and curatorial studies (MA); modern European studies (MA); museum anthropology (MA); music (DMA, PhD); oral history (MA); philosophical foundations of physics (MA); philosophy (MA, PhD); physics (PhD); political science (MA, PhD); psychology (PhD); quantitative methods in the social sciences (MA); religion (MA, PhD); Russia, Eurasia and East Europe: regional studies (MA); Russian translation (MA); Slavic cultures (MA); Slavic languages (MA, PhD); sociology (MA, PhD); South Asian studies (MA); statistics (MA, PhD); theatre (PhD). *Program availability:* Part-time. *Students:* 3,506 full-time (1,844 women), 208 part-time (121 women); includes 864 minority (110 Black or African American, non-Hispanic/Latino; 5 American Indian or Alaska Native, non-Hispanic/Latino; 416 Asian, non-Hispanic/Latino; 147 Hispanic/Latino; 6 Native Hawaiian or other Pacific Islander, non-Hispanic/Latino; 180 Two or more races, non-Hispanic/Latino), 2,065 international. 14,545 applicants, 25% accepted, 1,429 enrolled. In 2019, 1,262 master's, 363 doctorates awarded. Terminal master's awarded for partial completion of doctoral program. *Degree requirements:* For master's, variable foreign language requirement, comprehensive exam (for some programs), thesis (for some programs); for doctorate, variable foreign language requirement, comprehensive exam (for some programs), thesis/dissertation. *Entrance requirements:* For master's and doctorate, GRE General Test, GRE Subject Test (for some programs). Additional exam requirements/recommendations for international students: required—TOEFL (minimum score 600 paper-based; 100 iBT), IELTS (minimum score 7.5). Application fee: $115. Electronic applications accepted. *Expenses: Tuition:* Full-time $47,600; part-time $1880 per credit. One-time fee: $105. *Financial support:* Fellowships, research assistantships, teaching assistantships, career-related internships or fieldwork, Federal Work-Study, institutionally sponsored loans, scholarships/grants, traineeships, health care benefits, tuition waivers, and unspecified assistantships available. Support available to part-time students. Financial award application deadline: 12/15. *Unit head:* Dr. Carlos J. Alonso, Dean of the Graduate School of Arts and Sciences and Vice President for Graduate Education, 212-854-2861, E-mail: gsas-dean@columbia.edu. *Application contact:* GSAS Office of Admissions, 212-854-6729, E-mail: gsas-admissions@columbia.edu.
Website: http://gsas.columbia.edu/

Eastern Michigan University, Graduate School, College of Arts and Sciences, Department of Geography and Geology, Programs in Historic Preservation, Ypsilanti, MI 48197. Offers heritage interpretation and museum practice (MS); historic preservation (Graduate Certificate); preservation planning and administration (MS); recording, documentation and digital cultural heritage (MS). *Program availability:* Part-time, evening/weekend, online learning. *Students:* 7 full-time (5 women), 22 part-time (15 women); includes 2 minority (both Hispanic/Latino). Average age 36. 13 applicants, 100% accepted, 8 enrolled. In 2019, 16 master's, 1 other advanced degree awarded. *Entrance requirements:* Additional exam requirements/recommendations for international students: required—TOEFL. *Application deadline:* Applications are processed on a rolling basis. Application fee: $45. *Financial support:* Fellowships, research assistantships with full tuition reimbursements, teaching assistantships with full tuition reimbursements, career-related internships or fieldwork, Federal Work-Study, institutionally sponsored loans, scholarships/grants, tuition waivers (partial), and unspecified assistantships available. Support available to part-time students. Financial award applicants required to submit FAFSA. *Application contact:* Dr. Ted Ligibel, Program Director, 734-487-0232, Fax: 734-487-6979, E-mail: tligibel@emich.edu.

Fashion Institute of Technology, School of Graduate Studies, Exhibition and Experience Design Program, New York, NY 10001-5992. Offers MA. *Degree requirements:* For master's, qualifying project. *Entrance requirements:* Additional exam requirements/recommendations for international students: required—TOEFL (minimum score 550 paper-based). Electronic applications accepted.

Fashion Institute of Technology, School of Graduate Studies, Program in Fashion and Textile Studies: History, Theory, Museum Practice, New York, NY 10001-5992. Offers MA. *Accreditation:* NASAD. *Degree requirements:* For master's, one foreign language, thesis, internship. *Entrance requirements:* For master's, GRE General Test or GRE Subject Test, previous course work in art history and chemistry, 4 semesters of a foreign language. Additional exam requirements/recommendations for international students: required—TOEFL (minimum score 550 paper-based). Electronic applications accepted.

Florida International University, College of Communication, Architecture and The Arts, Department of Art and Art History, Miami, FL 33199. Offers museum studies (Graduate Certificate); studio art (MFA). *Accreditation:* NASAD. *Program availability:* Part-time, evening/weekend. *Faculty:* 15 full-time (7 women), 23 part-time/adjunct (11 women). *Students:* 20 full-time (17 women), 9 part-time (all women); includes 21 minority (3 Black or African American, non-Hispanic/Latino; 18 Hispanic/Latino), 3 international. Average age 32. 20 applicants, 70% accepted, 7 enrolled. In 2019, 8 master's awarded. *Entrance requirements:* For master's, minimum GPA of 3.0 in upper-level coursework, 3 letters of recommendation, 20 slides of creative work. Additional exam requirements/recommendations for international students: required—TOEFL (minimum score 550 paper-based; 80 iBT). *Application deadline:* For fall admission, 2/1 for domestic and international students. Application fee: $30. Electronic applications accepted. *Expenses: Tuition, area resident:* Full-time $8912; part-time $446 per credit hour. Tuition, state resident: full-time $8912; part-time $446 per credit hour. Tuition, nonresident: full-time $21,393; part-time $992 per credit hour. *Required fees:* $2194. *Financial support:* Institutionally sponsored loans and scholarships/grants available. Financial award application deadline: 3/1; financial award applicants required to submit FAFSA. *Unit head:* Dr. David Chang, Chair, 305-348-2897, Fax: 305-348-0513, E-mail: David.Chang@fiu.edu. *Application contact:* Nanett Rojas, Manager, Admissions Operations, 305-348-7464, Fax: 305-348-7441, E-mail: gradadm@fiu.edu.
Website: http://carta.fiu.edu/arts/

Florida State University, The Graduate School, College of Fine Arts, Department of Art History, Tallahassee, FL 32306. Offers history and criticism of art (MA, PhD). *Accreditation:* NASAD. *Program availability:* Part-time. *Faculty:* 13 full-time (6 women), 10 part-time/adjunct (6 women). *Students:* 39 full-time (38 women), 7 part-time (all women); includes 7 minority (2 Black or African American, non-Hispanic/Latino; 1 Asian,

non-Hispanic/Latino; 3 Hispanic/Latino; 1 Two or more races, non-Hispanic/Latino). Average age 29. 43 applicants, 81% accepted, 15 enrolled. In 2019, 13 master's awarded. Terminal master's awarded for partial completion of doctoral program. *Degree requirements:* For master's, one foreign language, thesis (for some programs), capstone project (for some programs); for doctorate, 2 foreign languages, comprehensive exam, thesis/dissertation. *Entrance requirements:* For master's, GRE General Test, minimum GPA of 3.0; for doctorate, GRE General Test, minimum GPA of 3.5. Additional exam requirements/recommendations for international students: required—TOEFL (minimum score 550 paper-based; 80 iBT), IELTS (minimum score 6.5). *Application deadline:* For fall admission, 7/1 for domestic and international students. Applications are processed on a rolling basis. Application fee: $35. Electronic applications accepted. *Expenses:* Contact institution. *Financial support:* In 2019–20, 37 students received support, including 16 fellowships with full tuition reimbursements available (averaging $6,200 per year), 14 research assistantships with full tuition reimbursements available (averaging $5,100 per year), 9 teaching assistantships with full tuition reimbursements available (averaging $7,140 per year); career-related internships or fieldwork, Federal Work-Study, institutionally sponsored loans, scholarships/grants, tuition waivers (full), and unspecified assistantships also available. Financial award application deadline: 1/1; financial award applicants required to submit FAFSA. *Unit head:* Dr. Adam Jolles, Associate Professor of Art History/Department Chair, 850-644-7066, E-mail: ajolles@fsu.edu. *Application contact:* Juan Barcelo-Gonzalez, Academic Program Specialist/Graduate Student Advisor, 850-644-8207, Fax: 850-644-7065, E-mail: juan.barcelo@fsu.edu.
Website: http://arthistory.fsu.edu/

The George Washington University, Columbian College of Arts and Sciences, Department of Anthropology, Washington, DC 20052. Offers anthropology (MA, PhD); international development (MA); medical anthropology (MA); museum training (MA). *Program availability:* Part-time, evening/weekend. *Degree requirements:* For master's, one foreign language, comprehensive exam, thesis or alternative. *Entrance requirements:* For master's, GRE General Test, minimum GPA of 3.0. Additional exam requirements/recommendations for international students: required—TOEFL (minimum score 550 paper-based; 80 iBT). Electronic applications accepted.

The George Washington University, Columbian College of Arts and Sciences, Department of Fine Arts and Art History, Program in Art History, Washington, DC 20052. Offers art history (MA); museum training (MA). *Program availability:* Part-time, evening/weekend. *Degree requirements:* For master's, one foreign language, comprehensive exam, thesis or alternative. *Entrance requirements:* For master's, GRE General Test, bachelor's degree in field, minimum GPA of 3.0. Additional exam requirements/recommendations for international students: required—TOEFL (minimum score 550 paper-based; 80 iBT). Electronic applications accepted.

The George Washington University, Columbian College of Arts and Sciences, Program in Museum Studies, Washington, DC 20052. Offers museum collections management and care (Graduate Certificate); museum studies (MA). *Program availability:* Part-time, evening/weekend. *Degree requirements:* For master's, comprehensive exam, internship. *Entrance requirements:* For master's, GRE General Test, minimum GPA of 3.0. Additional exam requirements/recommendations for international students: required—TOEFL (minimum score 550 paper-based; 80 iBT). Electronic applications accepted.

Harvard University, Extension School, Cambridge, MA 02138-3722. Offers applied sciences (CAS); biotechnology (ALM); educational technologies (ALM); educational technology (CET); English for graduate and professional studies (DGP); environmental management (ALM, CEM); information technology (ALM); journalism (ALM); liberal arts (ALM); management (ALM, CM); mathematics for teaching (ALM); museum studies (ALM); premedical studies (Diploma); publication and communication (CPC). *Program availability:* Part-time, evening/weekend. *Degree requirements:* For master's, thesis. *Entrance requirements:* For master's, 3 completed graduate courses with grade of B or higher. Additional exam requirements/recommendations for international students: required—TOEFL (minimum score 600 paper-based), TWE (minimum score 5). *Expenses:* Contact institution.

Indiana University-Purdue University Indianapolis, School of Liberal Arts, Museum Studies Program, Indianapolis, IN 46202. Offers MA, Certificate. *Entrance requirements:* For master's, GRE.

John F. Kennedy University, College of Business and Professional Studies, Program in Museum Studies, Pleasant Hill, CA 94523-4817. Offers museum studies (Certificate), including collections management, education and interpretation. *Program availability:* Part-time, online only, 100% online. *Entrance requirements:* Additional exam requirements/recommendations for international students: required—TOEFL, TWE.

Johns Hopkins University, Advanced Academic Programs, Program in Museum Studies, Washington, DC 21218. Offers digital curation (Certificate); museum studies (MA). *Program availability:* Part-time, evening/weekend, online learning. *Entrance requirements:* For master's, minimum GPA of 3.0. Additional exam requirements/recommendations for international students: required—TOEFL (minimum score 100 iBT). Electronic applications accepted.

Long Island University - Post, College of Arts, Communications and Design, Brookville, NY 11548-1300. Offers art (MA); clinical art therapy (MA); clinical art therapy and counseling (MA); digital game design and development (MA); fine arts and design (MFA); interactive multimedia arts (MA); museum studies (MA); music (MA); theatre (MFA). *Degree requirements:* For master's, variable foreign language requirement, comprehensive exam (for some programs), thesis. *Entrance requirements:* For master's, performance audition or portfolio. Additional exam requirements/recommendations for international students: required—TOEFL (minimum score 550 paper-based; 79 iBT). Electronic applications accepted.

Marist College, Graduate Programs, School of Communication and the Arts, Poughkeepsie, NY 12601-1387. Offers communication (MA); integrated marketing communication (MA); museum studies (MA). *Program availability:* Part-time, online learning. *Degree requirements:* For master's, thesis or comprehensive exam. *Entrance requirements:* For master's, GRE, minimum undergraduate GPA of 3.0, resume, 3 letters of recommendation. Additional exam requirements/recommendations for international students: required—TOEFL (minimum score 550 paper-based; 80 iBT), recommended—IELTS (minimum score 6.5). Electronic applications accepted.

Maryland Institute College of Art, Graduate Studies, MFA Program in Curatorial Practice, Baltimore, MD 21201. Offers MFA. *Degree requirements:* For master's, thesis, exhibit and thesis documentation. *Entrance requirements:* For master's, portfolio, bachelor's degree in any field. Additional exam requirements/recommendations for international students: required—TOEFL (minimum score 550 paper-based; 80 iBT), IELTS (minimum score 6.5). Electronic applications accepted. *Expenses:* Contact institution.

Morgan State University, School of Graduate Studies, James H. Gilliam Jr College of Liberal Arts, Department of History and Geography, Baltimore, MD 21251. Offers African-American studies (MA); history (MA, PhD); museum studies and historic preservation (MA). *Program availability:* Part-time, evening/weekend. *Faculty:* 20 full-

time (5 women), 1 part-time/adjunct (0 women). *Students:* 37 full-time (24 women), 8 part-time (6 women); includes 41 minority (36 Black or African American, non-Hispanic/Latino; 5 Hispanic/Latino), 3 international. Average age 37. 13 applicants, 92% accepted, 4 enrolled. In 2019, 4 master's, 4 doctorates awarded. *Degree requirements:* For master's, comprehensive exam, thesis; for doctorate, comprehensive exam, thesis/dissertation. *Entrance requirements:* For master's, GRE, minimum GPA of 2.5; for doctorate, GRE or MAT, minimum GPA of 3.0. Additional exam requirements/recommendations for international students: required—TOEFL (minimum score 550 paper-based). *Application deadline:* For fall admission, 2/1 priority date for domestic students, 4/1 for international students; for spring admission, 11/15 for domestic students, 10/1 for international students. Applications are processed on a rolling basis. Application fee: $50 ($70 for international students). Electronic applications accepted. *Expenses:* Tuition, state resident: full-time $455; part-time $455 per credit hour. Tuition, nonresident: full-time $894; part-time $894 per credit hour. *Required fees:* $82; $82 per credit hour. *Financial support:* In 2019–20, 5 students received support. Fellowships with full and partial tuition reimbursements available, research assistantships with full and partial tuition reimbursements available, teaching assistantships with full and partial tuition reimbursements available, career-related internships or fieldwork, Federal Work-Study, scholarships/grants, tuition waivers (full and partial), and unspecified assistantships available. Support available to part-time students. Financial award application deadline: 2/1. *Unit head:* Dr. Jeremiah I. Dibua, Interim Chair of Department, 443-885-3190, Fax: 443-885-8227, E-mail: jeremiah.dibua@morgan.edu. *Application contact:* Dr. Jahmaine Smith, Director of Admissions, 443-885-3185, Fax: 443-885-8226, E-mail: gradapply@morgan.edu.
Website: https://morgan.edu/college_of_liberal_arts/departments/history_geography_and_museum_studies/graduate_program_handbook.html

New Mexico State University, College of Arts and Sciences, Department of Anthropology, Las Cruces, NM 88003-8001. Offers anthropology (MA); cultural resource management (Graduate Certificate); museum studies (Graduate Certificate). *Program availability:* Part-time. *Faculty:* 9 full-time (6 women), 1 part-time/adjunct (0 women). *Students:* 24 full-time (15 women), 21 part-time (15 women); includes 20 minority (1 Black or African American, non-Hispanic/Latino; 2 American Indian or Alaska Native, non-Hispanic/Latino; 1 Asian, non-Hispanic/Latino; 13 Hispanic/Latino; 3 Two or more races, non-Hispanic/Latino), 2 international. Average age 32. 19 applicants, 79% accepted, 12 enrolled. In 2019, 15 master's, 21 other advanced degrees awarded. *Degree requirements:* For master's, thesis optional, non-theses option will complete an internship or special research project; for Graduate Certificate, graduate certificate in cultural resource management; graduate certificate in museum studies-available via secondary application. *Entrance requirements:* For master's and Graduate Certificate, minimum undergraduate GPA of 3.0. Additional exam requirements/recommendations for international students: required—TOEFL (minimum score 550 paper-based; 79 iBT), IELTS (minimum score 6.5). *Application deadline:* For fall admission, 2/1 priority date for domestic and international students; for spring admission, 10/1 priority date for domestic and international students. Applications are processed on a rolling basis. Application fee: $40 ($50 for international students). Electronic applications accepted. *Financial support:* In 2019–20, 24 students received support, including 2 research assistantships (averaging $9,081 per year), 10 teaching assistantships (averaging $11,274 per year); career-related internships or fieldwork, Federal Work-Study, scholarships/grants, traineeships, health care benefits, and unspecified assistantships also available. Support available to part-time students. Financial award application deadline: 3/1. *Unit head:* Dr. Rani Alexander, Department Head, 575-646-5809, E-mail: raalexan@nmsu.edu. *Application contact:* Dr. Lois Stanford, Graduate Advisor, 575-646-6092, E-mail: lstanfor@nmsu.edu.
Website: http://anthropology.nmsu.edu

The New School, Parsons School of Design, Program in the History of Design and Curatorial Studies, New York, NY 10011. Offers MA. *Program availability:* Part-time. *Faculty:* 16 full-time, 13 part-time/adjunct. *Students:* 25 full-time (22 women), 20 part-time (19 women); includes 14 minority (2 Black or African American, non-Hispanic/Latino; 2 Asian, non-Hispanic/Latino; 8 Hispanic/Latino; 2 Two or more races, non-Hispanic/Latino), 7 international. Average age 32. 51 applicants, 78% accepted, 14 enrolled. In 2019, 16 master's awarded. *Degree requirements:* For master's, thesis. *Entrance requirements:* For master's, transcripts, resume, statement of purpose, recommendation letters. Additional exam requirements/recommendations for international students: required—TOEFL (minimum score 92 iBT), IELTS (minimum score 7), PTE (minimum score 63). *Application deadline:* For fall admission, 1/1 priority date for domestic and international students; for summer admission, 1/1 priority date for domestic and international students. Applications are processed on a rolling basis. Application fee: $50. Electronic applications accepted. *Expenses:* 1810 per credit. *Financial support:* In 2019–20, 24 students received support, including 4 research assistantships (averaging $2,716 per year), 10 teaching assistantships (averaging $8,895 per year); career-related internships or fieldwork, scholarships/grants, and unspecified assistantships also available. Support available to part-time students. Financial award application deadline: 2/1; financial award applicants required to submit FAFSA. *Unit head:* Sarah Lichtman, Program Director, E-mail: lichtmas@newschool.edu. *Application contact:* Simone Varadian, Senior Director, 212-229-5150 Ext. 4117, E-mail: varadias@newschool.edu.
Website: https://www.newschool.edu/parsons/ma-history-design-curatorial-studies/

New York University, Graduate School of Arts and Science, Program in Museum Studies, New York, NY 10012-1019. Offers museum studies (Advanced Certificate). *Program availability:* Part-time, evening/weekend. *Entrance requirements:* For master's, GRE General Test; for Advanced Certificate, master's degree or PhD. Additional exam requirements/recommendations for international students: required—TOEFL, IELTS.

Penn State Harrisburg, Graduate School, School of Humanities, Middletown, PA 17057. Offers American studies (MA, PhD); communications (MA); folklore and ethnography (Certificate); heritage and museum practice (Certificate); humanities (MA). *Program availability:* Evening/weekend.

St. John's University, St. John's College of Liberal Arts and Sciences, Department of Art and Design, Queens, NY 11439. Offers museum administration (MA). *Program availability:* Part-time, evening/weekend, 100% online, blended/hybrid learning. *Degree requirements:* For master's, curated exhibition; one-semester internship; 21 credits of required courses and 15 credits of electives. *Entrance requirements:* For master's, GRE General Test, letters of recommendation, transcripts, resume, personal statement. Additional exam requirements/recommendations for international students: required—TOEFL (minimum score 80 iBT), IELTS (minimum score 6.5). Electronic applications accepted.

San Francisco Art Institute, Master of Arts Programs, San Francisco, CA 94133. Offers exhibition and museum studies (MA); history and theory of contemporary art (MA). *Degree requirements:* For master's, thesis. *Entrance requirements:* For master's, statement of purpose, writing samples. Additional exam requirements/recommendations for international students: required—TOEFL (minimum score 600 paper-based; 100 iBT), IELTS (minimum score 7.5). Electronic applications accepted.

San Francisco State University, Division of Graduate Studies, College of Liberal and Creative Arts, School of Art, Museum Studies Program, San Francisco, CA 94132-

1722. Offers MA. *Program availability:* Part-time. *Expenses: Tuition, area resident:* Full-time $7176; part-time $4164 per year. Tuition, state resident: full-time $7176; part-time $4164 per year. Tuition, nonresident: full-time $16,680; part-time $396 per unit. *International tuition:* $16,680 full-time. *Required fees:* $1524; $1524 per unit. $762 per semester. Tuition and fees vary according to degree level and program. *Financial support:* Career-related internships or fieldwork and Federal Work-Study available. *Unit head:* Dr. Edward Luby, Program Director, 415-338-3163, Fax: 415-338-6159, E-mail: emluby@sfsu.edu. *Application contact:* Dr. Edward Luby, Program Director, 415-338-3163, Fax: 415-338-6159, E-mail: emluby@sfsu.edu.
Website: http://museum.sfsu.edu/

Seton Hall University, College of Communication and the Arts, Program in Museum Professions, South Orange, NJ 07079-2697. Offers exhibition development (MA); museum management (MA); museum registration (MA). *Program availability:* Part-time, evening/weekend, online learning. *Degree requirements:* For master's, thesis (for some programs). *Entrance requirements:* For master's, GRE or MAT, official transcripts, resume, personal statement, 3 letters of recommendation. Additional exam requirements/recommendations for international students: required—TOEFL (minimum iBT score 80) or IELTS (6.5). Electronic applications accepted.

Southern Illinois University Edwardsville, Graduate School, College of Arts and Sciences, Department of Historical Studies, Program in Museum Studies, Edwardsville, IL 62026. Offers Postbaccalaureate Certificate. *Program availability:* Part-time, evening/weekend. *Entrance requirements:* Additional exam requirements/recommendations for international students: required—TOEFL (minimum score 550 paper-based; 79 iBT), IELTS (minimum score 6.5). Electronic applications accepted.

Southern University at New Orleans, School of Graduate Studies, New Orleans, LA 70126-1009. Offers criminal justice (MA); management information systems (MS); museum studies (MA); social work (MSW). *Accreditation:* CSWE. *Program availability:* Part-time, evening/weekend. *Degree requirements:* For master's, thesis. *Entrance requirements:* For master's, GRE/GMAT. Additional exam requirements/recommendations for international students: required—TOEFL.

State University of New York College at Oneonta, Graduate Programs, Cooperstown Graduate Program in Museum Studies, Cooperstown, NY 13326. Offers history museum studies (MA); science museum studies (MA). *Degree requirements:* For master's, research paper or thesis. *Entrance requirements:* For master's, GRE General Test. *Expenses:* Contact institution.

Syracuse University, College of Visual and Performing Arts, MA Program in Museum Studies, Syracuse, NY 13244. Offers MA. *Accreditation:* NASAD. *Entrance requirements:* For master's, three letters of recommendation, academic transcripts, personal statement/essay, academic writing sample, resume. Additional exam requirements/recommendations for international students: required—TOEFL (minimum score 100 iBT), IELTS. Electronic applications accepted.

Texas Tech University, Graduate School, Interdisciplinary Programs, Lubbock, TX 79409-1030. Offers arid land studies (MS); biotechnology (MS); heritage and museum sciences (MA); interdisciplinary studies (MA, MS); wind science and engineering (PhD); JD/MS. *Program availability:* Part-time, 100% online, blended/hybrid learning. *Faculty:* 5 full-time (3 women). *Students:* 114 full-time (46 women), 94 part-time (59 women); includes 72 minority (30 Black or African American, non-Hispanic/Latino; 3 Asian, non-Hispanic/Latino; 31 Hispanic/Latino; 8 Two or more races, non-Hispanic/Latino), 34 international. Average age 31. 118 applicants, 85% accepted, 66 enrolled. In 2019, 57 master's, 4 doctorates awarded. Terminal master's awarded for partial completion of doctoral program. *Degree requirements:* For master's, comprehensive exam (for some programs), thesis (for some programs); for doctorate, comprehensive exam, thesis/dissertation (for some programs). *Entrance requirements:* Additional exam requirements/recommendations for international students: required—TOEFL (minimum score 550 paper-based; 79 iBT), IELTS (minimum score 6.5), PTE (minimum score 60), Cambridge Advanced (B), Cambridge Proficiency (C), ELS English for Academic Purposes (Level 112), Duolingo English Test (100). *Application deadline:* For fall admission, 6/1 priority date for domestic students, 1/15 priority date for international students; for spring admission, 9/1 priority date for domestic students, 6/15 priority date for international students. Applications are processed on a rolling basis. Application fee: $65. Electronic applications accepted. *Expenses:* Tuition, state resident: full-time $7944; part-time $331 per credit hour. Tuition, nonresident: full-time $17,904; part-time $746 per credit hour. *Required fees:* $2556; $55.50 per credit hour. $612 per semester. Tuition and fees vary according to program. *Financial support:* In 2019–20, 150 students received support, including 138 fellowships (averaging $5,639 per year), 26 research assistantships (averaging $18,634 per year), 16 teaching assistantships (averaging $13,404 per year); scholarships/grants and unspecified assistantships also available. Financial award application deadline: 4/15; financial award applicants required to submit FAFSA. *Unit head:* Dr. Mark A. Sheridan, Vice Provost for Graduate and Postdoctoral Affairs/Dean of the Graduate School, 806-834-5537, Fax: 806-742-1746, E-mail: mark.sheridan@ttu.edu. *Application contact:* Dr. David Doerfert, Associate Dean, 806-834-4477, Fax: 806-742-4038, E-mail: david.doerfert@ttu.edu.
Website: www.gradschool.ttu.edu

Trinity College, Graduate Programs, Program in American Studies, Hartford, CT 06106-3100. Offers American culture studies (MA); museums and communities (MA). *Program availability:* Part-time, evening/weekend. *Degree requirements:* For master's, thesis or alternative. *Entrance requirements:* For master's, minimum GPA of 3.0.

Tufts University, Graduate School of Arts and Sciences, Department of Art and Art History, Medford, MA 02155. Offers art history (MA); art history and museum studies (MA). *Degree requirements:* For master's, one foreign language, thesis (for some programs). *Entrance requirements:* For master's, GRE General Test. Additional exam requirements/recommendations for international students: required—TOEFL (minimum score 550 paper-based; 80 iBT), IELTS (minimum score 6.5). Electronic applications accepted. *Expenses:* Contact institution.

Tufts University, Graduate School of Arts and Sciences, Department of History, Medford, MA 02155. Offers history (MA, PhD), including global history (PhD); history and museum studies (MA). Terminal master's awarded for partial completion of doctoral program. *Degree requirements:* For master's, one foreign language, thesis optional; for doctorate, 2 foreign languages, comprehensive exam, thesis/dissertation. *Entrance requirements:* For master's and doctorate, GRE General Test, writing sample. Additional exam requirements/recommendations for international students: required—TOEFL (minimum score 550 paper-based; 80 iBT), IELTS (minimum score 6.5). Electronic applications accepted. *Expenses:* Contact institution.

Tufts University, Graduate School of Arts and Sciences, Graduate Certificate Programs, Museum Studies Program, Medford, MA 02155. Offers Certificate. *Program availability:* Part-time, evening/weekend. *Expenses:* Contact institution.

Tufts University, School of the Museum of Fine Arts at Tufts University, Boston, MA 02155. Offers art education (MAT); studio art (MFA, Postbaccalaureate Certificate), including museum studies (MFA). *Faculty:* 31 full-time (19 women), 23 part-time/adjunct (16 women). *Students:* 55 full-time. Average age 25. In 2019, 44 master's, 15 other advanced degrees awarded. Terminal master's awarded for partial completion of doctoral program. *Degree requirements:* For master's, thesis, thesis exhibition. *Entrance requirements:* For master's, BFA (preferred) or bachelor's degree or equivalent in related area; portfolio; for Postbaccalaureate Certificate, portfolio, BFA or equivalent. Additional exam requirements/recommendations for international students: required—TOEFL (minimum score 85 iBT), IELTS (minimum score 6.5). *Application deadline:* For fall admission, 1/15 priority date for domestic and international students. Applications are processed on a rolling basis. Application fee: $85. Electronic applications accepted. *Expenses:* Contact institution. *Financial support:* Fellowships, teaching assistantships, Federal Work-Study, and scholarships/grants available. Financial award application deadline: 1/15. *Unit head:* Lisa Bynoe, Associate Director of Graduate Programs, 617-627-0031, E-mail: lisa.bynoe@tufts.edu. *Application contact:* Office of Graduate Admissions, 617-627-3395, E-mail: gradadmissions@tufts.edu.
Website: https://smfa.tufts.edu/

Université de Montréal, Faculty of Arts and Sciences, Program in Museology, Montréal, QC H3C 3J7, Canada. Offers MA. Electronic applications accepted.

Université du Québec à Montréal, Graduate Programs, Program in Museology, Montréal, QC H3C 3P8, Canada. Offers MA. *Program availability:* Part-time. *Entrance requirements:* For master's, appropriate bachelor's degree or equivalent and proficiency in French.

University at Buffalo, the State University of New York, Graduate School, College of Arts and Sciences, Department of Art, Program in Visual Studies, Buffalo, NY 14260. Offers critical museum studies (MA); visual studies (MA, PhD). *Program availability:* Part-time. *Degree requirements:* For master's, thesis, field exam; for doctorate, one foreign language, thesis/dissertation. *Entrance requirements:* Additional exam requirements/recommendations for international students: required—TOEFL (minimum score 79 iBT). Electronic applications accepted. *Expenses: Tuition, area resident:* Full-time $11,310; part-time $471 per credit hour. Tuition, state resident: full-time $11,310; part-time $471 per credit hour. Tuition, nonresident: full-time $23,100; part-time $963 per credit hour. *International tuition:* $23,100 full-time. *Required fees:* $2820.

The University of British Columbia, Faculty of Arts, Department of Art History, Visual Art, and Theory, Vancouver, BC V6T 1Z2, Canada. Offers art history (MA, PhD); critical and curatorial studies (MA); visual art (MFA). *Degree requirements:* For master's, one foreign language, thesis, final exhibition (MFA, MA in critical and curatorial studies); for doctorate, 2 foreign languages, comprehensive exam, thesis/dissertation. *Entrance requirements:* For master's, bachelor's degree with minimum B+ average (MFA, MA in critical and curatorial studies), A- (MA in art history); for doctorate, master's degree with minimum A- average. Additional exam requirements/recommendations for international students: required—TOEFL. Electronic applications accepted. *Expenses:* Contact institution.

University of Central Oklahoma, The Jackson College of Graduate Studies, College of Liberal Arts, Department of History, Edmond, OK 73034-5209. Offers museum studies (MA). *Program availability:* Part-time. *Degree requirements:* For master's, one foreign language, comprehensive exam (for some programs), thesis (for some programs). *Entrance requirements:* For master's, writing sample, essay. Additional exam requirements/recommendations for international students: required—TOEFL (minimum score 550 paper-based; 79 iBT), IELTS (minimum score 6.5). Electronic applications accepted.

University of Colorado Boulder, Graduate School, Museum and Field Studies Program, Boulder, CO 80309. Offers MS. Terminal master's awarded for partial completion of doctoral program. *Degree requirements:* For master's, comprehensive exam, thesis or alternative. *Entrance requirements:* For master's, GRE General Test, GRE Subject Test, minimum undergraduate GPA of 3.0. Electronic applications accepted. Application fee is waived when completed online.

University of Denver, Division of Arts, Humanities and Social Sciences, Department of Anthropology, Denver, CO 80208. Offers archaeology (MA); cultural anthropology (MA); museum and heritage studies (MA). *Program availability:* Part-time. *Faculty:* 8 full-time (4 women), 1 part-time/adjunct (0 women). *Students:* 2 full-time (both women), 21 part-time (16 women); includes 7 minority (2 Black or African American, non-Hispanic/Latino; 1 Asian, non-Hispanic/Latino; 3 Hispanic/Latino; 1 Two or more races, non-Hispanic/Latino). Average age 27. 35 applicants, 57% accepted, 11 enrolled. In 2019, 12 master's awarded. *Degree requirements:* For master's, comprehensive exam, thesis (for some programs). *Entrance requirements:* For master's, GRE General Test, bachelor's degree, transcripts, personal statement, two letters of recommendation. Additional exam requirements/recommendations for international students: required—TOEFL (minimum score 550 paper-based; 80 iBT). *Application deadline:* For fall admission, 2/28 for domestic and international students. Applications are processed on a rolling basis. Application fee: $65. Electronic applications accepted. *Expenses:* Contact institution. *Financial support:* In 2019–20, 22 students received support, including 12 teaching assistantships with tuition reimbursements available (averaging $5,233 per year); career-related internships or fieldwork, Federal Work-Study, institutionally sponsored loans, scholarships/grants, and unspecified assistantships also available. Support available to part-time students. Financial award application deadline: 2/15; financial award applicants required to submit FAFSA. *Unit head:* Dr. Larry Conyers, Professor, Director of Graduate Program, 303-871-2684, E-mail: lconyers@du.edu. *Application contact:* Dr. Larry Conyers, Professor, Director of Graduate Program, 303-871-2684, E-mail: lconyers@du.edu.
Website: http://www.du.edu/ahss/anthropology

University of Denver, Division of Arts, Humanities and Social Sciences, School of Art and Art History, Denver, CO 80208. Offers art history (MA); museum studies (MA). *Accreditation:* NASAD. *Program availability:* Part-time. *Faculty:* 16 full-time (11 women), 6 part-time/adjunct (5 women). *Students:* 11 full-time (all women), 10 part-time (7 women); includes 6 minority (1 Black or African American, non-Hispanic/Latino; 1 Asian, non-Hispanic/Latino; 4 Hispanic/Latino). Average age 27. 21 applicants, 86% accepted, 12 enrolled. In 2019, 13 master's awarded. *Degree requirements:* For master's, one foreign language, comprehensive exam, research paper. *Entrance requirements:* For master's, GRE General Test, transcripts, personal statement, writing sample, three letters of recommendation. Additional exam requirements/recommendations for international students: required—TOEFL (minimum score 550 paper-based; 80 iBT). *Application deadline:* For fall admission, 1/31 priority date for domestic and international students. Applications are processed on a rolling basis. Application fee: $65. Electronic applications accepted. *Expenses:* Contact institution. *Financial support:* In 2019–20, 20 students received support, including 8 teaching assistantships with tuition reimbursements available (averaging $8,177 per year); research assistantships with tuition reimbursements available, career-related internships or fieldwork, Federal Work-Study, institutionally sponsored loans, scholarships/grants, and unspecified assistantships also available. Support available to part-time students. Financial award application deadline: 2/15; financial award applicants required to submit FAFSA. *Unit head:* Annabeth Headrick, Associate Professor and Director, 303-871-3574, E-mail: annabeth.headrick@du.edu. *Application contact:* Jason Kellermeyer, Coordinator of Academic Programs, 303-871-2846, E-mail: jason.kellermeyer@du.edu.
Website: http://www.du.edu/ahss/art/index.html

University of Florida, Graduate School, College of The Arts, School of Art and Art History, Gainesville, FL 32611. Offers art (MA), including digital arts and sciences; art education (MA); art history (MA, PhD); museology (MA), including historic preservation. *Accreditation:* NASAD. *Program availability:* Online learning. *Degree requirements:* For master's, project or thesis (MFA); 1 foreign language (MA in art history); for doctorate, 2 foreign languages, comprehensive exam, thesis/dissertation. *Entrance requirements:* For master's, GRE General Test, portfolio (MFA), writing sample (MA), minimum GPA 3.0; for doctorate, GRE General Test, minimum GPA of 3.0. Additional exam requirements/recommendations for international students: required—TOEFL (minimum score 550 paper-based; 80 iBT), IELTS (minimum score 6). Electronic applications accepted.

University of Hawaii at Manoa, Office of Graduate Education, College of Arts and Humanities, Department of American Studies, Program in Museum Studies, Honolulu, HI 96822. Offers Graduate Certificate. *Program availability:* Part-time. *Entrance requirements:* Additional exam requirements/recommendations for international students: required—TOEFL (minimum score 600 paper-based; 100 iBT), IELTS (minimum score 7).

University of Illinois at Chicago, College of Architecture, Design and the Arts, School of Art and Art History, Chicago, IL 60607-7128. Offers art history (MA); electronic visualization (MFA); museum and exhibition studies (MA); new media arts (MFA). *Program availability:* Part-time, evening/weekend. Terminal master's awarded for partial completion of doctoral program. *Degree requirements:* For master's, one foreign language, thesis or alternative; for doctorate, thesis/dissertation. *Entrance requirements:* For master's, GRE General Test, minimum GPA of 2.75, 3 letters of recommendation; for doctorate, GRE General Test, MA in art history or equivalent, minimum GPA of 3.0. Additional exam requirements/recommendations for international students: required—TOEFL. Electronic applications accepted. *Expenses:* Contact institution.

The University of Kansas, Graduate Studies, College of Liberal Arts and Sciences, Museum Studies Program, Lawrence, KS 66045-7545. Offers MA, Graduate Certificate. *Program availability:* Part-time. *Students:* 28 full-time (22 women), 3 part-time (1 woman); includes 5 minority (3 Black or African American, non-Hispanic/Latino; 2 Two or more races, non-Hispanic/Latino). Average age 27. 29 applicants, 69% accepted, 14 enrolled. In 2019, 8 master's, 3 other advanced degrees awarded. *Entrance requirements:* For master's, GRE, 3 letters of recommendation, resume, writing sample, statement of purpose, official transcripts. Additional exam requirements/recommendations for international students: required—TOEFL, IELTS. *Application deadline:* For fall admission, 1/15 priority date for domestic and international students. Application fee: $65 ($85 for international students). Electronic applications accepted. *Expenses:* Tuition, state resident: full-time $9989. Tuition, nonresident: full-time $23,950. *International tuition:* $23,950 full-time. *Required fees:* $984; $81.99 per credit hour. Tuition and fees vary according to course load, campus/location and program. *Financial support:* Research assistantships, career-related internships or fieldwork, and unspecified assistantships available. Financial award application deadline: 1/15. *Unit head:* Mary Madden, Director, 785-864-5702, E-mail: mmadden@kshs.org. *Application contact:* Bethany Harris, Graduate Admissions Contact, 785-864-0778, E-mail: bethanyharris@ku.edu.
Website: http://museumstudies.ku.edu/

University of Louisville, Graduate School, College of Arts and Sciences, Department of Fine Arts, Louisville, KY 40292. Offers art history (MA, PhD); curatorial studies (MA); studio art (MFA), including design. *Program availability:* Part-time. *Faculty:* 20 full-time (9 women), 21 part-time/adjunct (14 women). *Students:* 19 full-time (16 women), 1 (woman) part-time; includes 5 minority (1 Black or African American, non-Hispanic/Latino; 2 Asian, non-Hispanic/Latino; 1 Hispanic/Latino; 1 Two or more races, non-Hispanic/Latino), 3 international. Average age 34. 21 applicants, 62% accepted, 10 enrolled. In 2019, 11 master's, 2 doctorates awarded. *Degree requirements:* For master's, one foreign language, thesis. *Entrance requirements:* For master's, Two letters of reference, official transcripts. Additional exam requirements/recommendations for international students: required—TOEFL (minimum score 550 paper-based; 79 iBT), IELTS can be taken in place of the TOEFL; recommended—IELTS (minimum score 6.5). *Application deadline:* For fall admission, 3/1 priority date for domestic students, 3/1 for international students. Applications are processed on a rolling basis. Application fee: $65. Electronic applications accepted. *Expenses: Tuition, area resident:* Full-time $13,000; part-time $723 per credit hour. Tuition, state resident: full-time $13,000; part-time $723 per credit hour. Tuition, nonresident: full-time $27,114; part-time $1507 per credit hour. *International tuition:* $27,114 full-time. *Required fees:* $196. Tuition and fees vary according to program and reciprocity agreements. *Financial support:* In 2019–20, 13 students received support, including 9 teaching assistantships with full tuition reimbursements available (averaging $14,000 per year); fellowships, research assistantships, scholarships/grants, health care benefits, and unspecified assistantships also available. Financial award application deadline: 3/1. *Unit head:* Dr. Scott L. Massey, Associate Professor and Chair, 502-852-6794, Fax: 502-852-6791, E-mail: s.massey@louisville.edu. *Application contact:* Theresa Berbet, Academic Coordinator, Senior, 502-852-6147, Fax: 502-852-6791, E-mail: theresa.berbet@louisville.edu.
Website: http://art.louisville.edu

The University of Manchester, School of Arts, Languages and Cultures, Manchester, United Kingdom. Offers anthropology, media and performance (PhD); applied theatre (PhD); Arab world studies (PhD); archaeology (PhD); art history and visual studies (PhD); arts and cultural management (PhD); arts management and cultural policy (PhD); Chinese studies (PhD); classics and ancient history (PhD); composition (PhD); creative writing (PhD); drama (PhD); East Asian studies (PhD); electroacoustic composition (PhD); English and American studies (PhD); English language (PhD); French studies (PhD); German studies (PhD); history (PhD); humanitarianism and conflict response (PhD); interpreting studies (PhD); Japanese studies (PhD); Latin American cultural studies (PhD); linguistics (PhD); Middle Eastern studies (PhD); museology (PhD); museum practice (PhD); music (PhD); musicology (PhD); Polish studies (PhD); Portuguese studies (PhD); religions and theology (PhD); Russian studies (PhD); Spanish studies (PhD); translation and intercultural studies (PhD).

University of Memphis, Graduate School, College of Arts and Sciences, Program in Interdisciplinary Studies, Memphis, TN 38152. Offers museum studies (Graduate Certificate); women's and gender studies (Graduate Certificate). *Students:* 10 full-time (7 women), 5 part-time (1 woman); includes 6 minority (2 Black or African American, non-Hispanic/Latino; 3 Asian, non-Hispanic/Latino; 1 Two or more races, non-Hispanic/Latino), 3 international. Average age 31. 4 applicants, 100% accepted, 1 enrolled. In 2019, 2 Graduate Certificates awarded. *Degree requirements:* For Graduate Certificate, minimum GPA of 3.0. *Entrance requirements:* For degree, GRE, letter of interest, undergraduate transcript. Additional exam requirements/recommendations for international students: required—TOEFL (minimum score 550 paper-based). *Application deadline:* For fall admission, 4/3 for domestic students. Application fee: $35 ($60 for international students). *Expenses: Tuition, area resident:* Full-time $9216; part-time $512 per credit hour. Tuition, state resident: full-time $9216; part-time $512 per credit hour. Tuition, nonresident: full-time $12,672; part-time $704 per credit hour. *International tuition:* $16,128 full-time. *Required fees:* $1530; $85 per credit hour. Tuition and fees vary according to program. *Financial support:* Research assistantships with full tuition reimbursements, teaching assistantships with full tuition reimbursements, Federal Work-Study, scholarships/grants, and unspecified assistantships available. Financial award application deadline: 2/1; financial award applicants required to submit FAFSA. *Unit head:* Dr. Robert Marczynski, Director, 901-678-3516, E-mail: marczyns@memphis.edu. *Application contact:* Dr. Robert Marczynski, Director, 901-678-3516, E-mail: marczyns@memphis.edu.
Website: http://www.memphis.edu/isc/

University of Memphis, Graduate School, College of Communication and Fine Arts, Department of Art, Memphis, TN 38152. Offers art history (MA), including Egyptian art and archaeology, general art history; ceramics (MFA); graphic design (MFA); museum studies (Graduate Certificate); painting (MFA); printmaking/photography (MFA); sculpture (MFA). *Accreditation:* NASAD (one or more programs are accredited). *Program availability:* Part-time. *Students:* 28 full-time (21 women), 5 part-time (4 women); includes 9 minority (3 Black or African American, non-Hispanic/Latino; 1 Asian, non-Hispanic/Latino; 3 Hispanic/Latino; 2 Two or more races, non-Hispanic/Latino), 2 international. Average age 30. 36 applicants, 69% accepted, 13 enrolled. In 2019, 11 master's, 4 other advanced degrees awarded. *Degree requirements:* For master's, variable foreign language requirement, comprehensive exam, thesis, image identification exam, qualifying exam; for Graduate Certificate, internship. *Entrance requirements:* For master's, GRE General Test or MAT, portfolio (MFA), letter of intent, sample of undergraduate writing, two letters of recommendation; for Graduate Certificate, three letters of recommendation, letter of intent. *Application deadline:* For fall admission, 2/15 for domestic students; for spring admission, 11/1 for domestic students. Applications are processed on a rolling basis. Application fee: $35 ($60 for international students). *Expenses: Tuition, area resident:* Full-time $9216; part-time $512 per credit hour. Tuition, state resident: full-time $9216; part-time $512 per credit hour. Tuition, nonresident: full-time $12,672; part-time $704 per credit hour. *International tuition:* $16,128 full-time. *Required fees:* $1530; $85 per credit hour. Tuition and fees vary according to program. *Financial support:* Research assistantships with full tuition reimbursements, teaching assistantships with full tuition reimbursements, Federal Work-Study, scholarships/grants, and unspecified assistantships available. Financial award application deadline: 2/1; financial award applicants required to submit FAFSA. *Unit head:* Richard Lou, Chair, 901-678-2217, Fax: 901-678-2735, E-mail: ralou@memphis.edu. *Application contact:* Richard Lou, Chair, 901-678-2217, Fax: 901-678-2735, E-mail: ralou@memphis.edu.
Website: http://memphis.edu/art/

University of Michigan–Flint, Graduate Programs, Program in Arts Administration, Flint, MI 48502-1950. Offers performance (MA), including museum and visual arts, performance. *Program availability:* Part-time. *Faculty:* 7 full-time (3 women), 11 part-time/adjunct (7 women). *Students:* 11 part-time (7 women); includes 5 minority (4 Black or African American, non-Hispanic/Latino; 1 Asian, non-Hispanic/Latino). Average age 40. 11 applicants, 82% accepted, 2 enrolled. In 2019, 2 master's awarded. *Degree requirements:* For master's, thesis. *Entrance requirements:* For master's, bachelor degree in the arts (visual art, theatre, dance, music, etc.) from regionally-accredited institution; minimum cumulative undergraduate GPA of 3.0 on 4.0 scale. Additional exam requirements/recommendations for international students: required—TOEFL (minimum score 84 iBT), IELTS (minimum score 6.5). *Application deadline:* For fall admission, 8/1 for domestic students, 5/1 for international students; for winter admission, 11/15 for domestic students, 10/1 for international students. Applications are processed on a rolling basis. Application fee: $55. Electronic applications accepted. *Expenses:* Contact institution. *Financial support:* Federal Work-Study, institutionally sponsored loans, scholarships/grants, and unspecified assistantships available. Support available to part-time students. Financial award application deadline: 3/1; financial award applicants required to submit FAFSA. *Unit head:* Nicole Broughton, Director, 810-237-6522, E-mail: broughn@umflint.edu. *Application contact:* Matt Bohlen, Associate Director of Graduate Admissions, 810-762-3171, Fax: 810-766-6789, E-mail: mbohlen@umflint.edu.
Website: http://www.umflint.edu/graduateprograms/arts-administration-ma

University of Missouri–St. Louis, College of Arts and Sciences, Department of History, St. Louis, MO 63121. Offers history (MA); history education (Certificate); museum studies (MA, Certificate). *Program availability:* Part-time, evening/weekend. *Degree requirements:* For master's, thesis (for some programs). *Entrance requirements:* For master's, writing sample; minimum GPA of 2.75 (for history), 3.2 (for museum studies). Additional exam requirements/recommendations for international students: required—TOEFL (minimum score 550 paper-based; 79 iBT), IELTS (minimum score 6.5). Electronic applications accepted. *Expenses: Tuition, area resident:* Full-time $9005.40; part-time $6003.60 per credit hour. Tuition, state resident: full-time $9005.40; part-time $6003.60 per credit hour. Tuition, nonresident: full-time $22,108; part-time $14,738.40 per credit hour. *International tuition:* $22,108 full-time. Tuition and fees vary according to course load.

University of New Hampshire, Graduate School, College of Liberal Arts, Department of History, Durham, NH 03824. Offers history (MA, PhD); history: museum studies (MA). *Program availability:* Part-time. *Students:* 28 full-time (12 women), 10 part-time (6 women); includes 1 minority (Two or more races, non-Hispanic/Latino), 1 international. Average age 31. 30 applicants, 63% accepted, 10 enrolled. In 2019, 10 master's, 2 doctorates awarded. *Entrance requirements:* For master's and doctorate, GRE General Test, writing sample. Additional exam requirements/recommendations for international students: required—TOEFL (minimum score 550 paper-based; 80 iBT), IELTS, PTE. *Application deadline:* For fall admission, 2/1 for domestic students. Application fee: $65. Electronic applications accepted. *Financial support:* In 2019–20, 21 students received support, including 1 fellowship, 13 teaching assistantships; research assistantships, career-related internships or fieldwork, Federal Work-Study, scholarships/grants, and tuition waivers (full and partial) also available. Support available to part-time students. Financial award application deadline: 2/15. *Unit head:* Kurk Dorsey, Chair, 603-862-3022. *Application contact:* Lara Demarest, Administrative Assistant, 603-862-1765, E-mail: history.grad@unh.edu.
Website: http://cola.unh.edu/history

The University of North Carolina at Greensboro, Graduate School, College of Arts and Sciences, Department of History, Greensboro, NC 27412-5001. Offers historic preservation (Certificate); history (MA); museum studies (Certificate); U.S. history (PhD). *Program availability:* Part-time. *Entrance requirements:* For master's, GRE General Test. Additional exam requirements/recommendations for international students: required—TOEFL. Electronic applications accepted.

The University of North Carolina at Greensboro, Graduate School, College of Arts and Sciences, Department of Interior Architecture, Greensboro, NC 27412-5001. Offers historic preservation (Certificate); interior architecture (MS); museum studies (Certificate). *Degree requirements:* For master's, thesis. *Entrance requirements:* For master's, GRE General Test or MAT, bachelor's degree in interior design, interview, portfolio. Additional exam requirements/recommendations for international students: required—TOEFL. Electronic applications accepted.

University of Oklahoma, College of Professional and Continuing Studies, Norman, OK 73019. Offers administrative leadership (MA, Graduate Certificate), including government and military leadership (MA), organizational leadership (MA), volunteer and non-profit leadership (MA); corrections management (Graduate Certificate); criminal justice (MS); integrated studies (MA), including human and health services administration, integrated studies; museum studies (MA); prevention science (MPS); restorative justice administration (Graduate Certificate). *Program availability:* Part-time, 100% online, blended/hybrid learning. *Degree requirements:* For master's, comprehensive exam, thesis optional, 33 credit hours; project/internship (for museum studies program only); for Graduate Certificate, 12 graduate credit hours (for Graduate Certificate). *Entrance requirements:* For master's and Graduate Certificate, minimum GPA of 3.0 in last 60 undergraduate hours; statement of goals; resume. Additional exam requirements/recommendations for international students: required—TOEFL (minimum score 79 iBT) or IELTS (minimum score 6.5). Electronic applications accepted. *Expenses:* Tuition, state resident: full-time $6583.20; part-time $274.30 per credit hour. Tuition, nonresident: full-time $21,242; part-time $885.10 per credit hour. *International tuition:* $21,242.40 full-time. *Required fees:* $1994.20; $72.55 per credit hour. $126.50 per semester. Tuition and fees vary according to course load and degree level.

University of St. Thomas, College of Arts and Sciences, Department of Art History, St. Paul, MN 55105-1096. Offers art history (MA); museum studies (Graduate Certificate). *Program availability:* Part-time, evening/weekend. *Degree requirements:* For master's, one foreign language, thesis, oral exam, reading proficiency in 1 foreign language. *Entrance requirements:* For master's, Bachelor's degree in art history or related field; 3 letters of recommendation; writing sample; personal statement; transcript; for Graduate Certificate, Bachelor's degree; 1 letter of recommendation; personal statement; transcript. Additional exam requirements/recommendations for international students: required—TOEFL (minimum score 80 iBT). Electronic applications accepted. *Expenses:* Contact institution.

University of San Francisco, College of Arts and Sciences, Museum Studies Program, San Francisco, CA 94117. Offers MA. *Program availability:* Part-time, evening/weekend. *Faculty:* 3 full-time (all women), 2 part-time/adjunct (both women). *Students:* 29 full-time (26 women), 15 part-time (14 women); includes 10 minority (1 Black or African American, non-Hispanic/Latino; 1 American Indian or Alaska Native, non-Hispanic/Latino; 6 Hispanic/Latino; 2 Two or more races, non-Hispanic/Latino), 13 international. Average age 28. 81 applicants, 72% accepted, 21 enrolled. In 2019, 22 master's awarded. *Entrance requirements:* Additional exam requirements/recommendations for international students: required—TOEFL (minimum score 90 iBT), IELTS (minimum score 6.5), PTE (minimum score 61). *Application deadline:* For fall admission, 2/1 for domestic and international students. Applications are processed on a rolling basis. Application fee: $55. Electronic applications accepted. Application fee is waived when completed online. *Financial support:* Teaching assistantships with partial tuition reimbursements, career-related internships or fieldwork, and scholarships/grants available. Financial award applicants required to submit FAFSA. *Unit head:* Dr. Marjorie Schwarzer, Graduate Director, 415-422-5685, E-mail: muse@usfca.edu. *Application contact:* Information Contact, 415-422-5101, E-mail: asgraduate@usfca.edu.
Website: https://www.usfca.edu/arts-sciences/graduate-programs/museum-studies

University of South Carolina, The Graduate School, College of Arts and Sciences, Department of History, Program in Public History, Columbia, SC 29208. Offers archive management (MA); historic preservation (MA); museum administration (MA); museum management (Certificate); MLIS/MA. *Degree requirements:* For master's, one foreign language, thesis, internship. *Entrance requirements:* For master's, GRE General Test, writing sample. Additional exam requirements/recommendations for international students: required—TOEFL. Electronic applications accepted.

University of South Florida, Innovative Education, Tampa, FL 33620-9951. Offers adult, career and higher education (Graduate Certificate), including college teaching, leadership in developing human resources, leadership in higher education; Africana studies (Graduate Certificate), including diasporas and health disparities, genocide and human rights; aging studies (Graduate Certificate), including gerontology; art research (Graduate Certificate), including museum studies; business foundations (Graduate Certificate); chemical and biomedical engineering (Graduate Certificate), including materials science and engineering, water, health and sustainability; child and family studies (Graduate Certificate), including positive behavior support; civil and industrial engineering (Graduate Certificate), including transportation systems analysis; community and family health (Graduate Certificate), including maternal and child health, social marketing and public health, violence and injury: prevention and intervention, women's health; criminology (Graduate Certificate), including criminal justice administration; data science for public administration (Graduate Certificate); digital humanities (Graduate Certificate); educational measurement and research (Graduate Certificate), including evaluation; English (Graduate Certificate), including comparative literary studies, creative writing, professional and technical communication; entrepreneurship (Graduate Certificate); environmental health (Graduate Certificate), including safety management; epidemiology and biostatistics (Graduate Certificate), including applied biostatistics, biostatistics, concepts and tools of epidemiology, epidemiology, epidemiology of infectious diseases; geography, environment and planning (Graduate Certificate), including community development, environmental policy and management, geographical information systems; geology (Graduate Certificate), including hydrogeology; global health (Graduate Certificate), including disaster management, global health and Latin American and Caribbean studies, global health practice, humanitarian assistance, infection control; government and international affairs (Graduate Certificate), including Cuban studies, globalization studies; health policy and management (Graduate Certificate), including health management and leadership, public health policy and programs; hearing specialist: early intervention (Graduate Certificate); industrial and management systems engineering (Graduate Certificate), including systems engineering, technology management; information studies (Graduate Certificate), including school library media specialist; information systems/decision sciences (Graduate Certificate), including analytics and business intelligence; instructional technology (Graduate Certificate), including distance education, Florida digital/virtual educator, instructional design, multimedia design, Web design; internal medicine, bioethics and medical humanities (Graduate Certificate), including biomedical ethics; Latin American and Caribbean studies (Graduate Certificate); leadership for coastal resiliency planning (Graduate Certificate); mass communications (Graduate Certificate), including multimedia journalism; mathematics and statistics (Graduate Certificate), including mathematics; medicine (Graduate Certificate), including aging and neuroscience, bioinformatics, biotechnology, brain fitness and memory management, clinical investigation, hand and upper limb rehabilitation, health informatics, health sciences, integrative weight management, intellectual property, medicine and gender, metabolic and nutritional medicine, metabolic cardiology, pharmacy sciences; national and competitive intelligence (Graduate Certificate); nursing (Graduate Certificate), including simulation based academic fellowship in advanced pain management; psychological and social foundations (Graduate Certificate), including career counseling, college teaching, diversity in education, mental health counseling, school counseling; public affairs (Graduate Certificate), including nonprofit management, public management, research administration; public health (Graduate Certificate), including assessing chemical toxicity and public health risks, health equity, pharmacoepidemiology, public health generalist, toxicology, translational research in adolescent behavioral health; public health practices (Graduate Certificate), including planning for healthy communities; rehabilitation and mental health counseling (Graduate Certificate), including integrative mental health care, marriage and family therapy, rehabilitation technology; secondary education (Graduate Certificate), including ESOL, foreign language education: culture and content, foreign language education: professional; social work (Graduate Certificate), including geriatric social work/clinical gerontology; special education (Graduate Certificate), including autism spectrum disorder, disabilities education: severe/profound; world languages (Graduate Certificate), including teaching English as a second language (TESL) or foreign language. *Unit head:* Dr. Cynthia DeLuca, Associate Vice President and Assistant Vice Provost, 813-974-3077, Fax: 813-974-7061, E-mail: deluca@usf.edu. *Application contact:* Owen Hooper, Director, Summer and Alternative Calendar Programs, 813-974-6917, E-mail: hooper@usf.edu.
Website: http://www.usf.edu/innovative-education/

The University of the Arts, College of Art, Media and Design, Department of Museum Studies, Philadelphia, PA 19102-4944. Offers museum education (MA); museum exhibition planning and design (MFA); museum studies (MA). *Accreditation:* NASAD. *Degree requirements:* For master's, thesis, internship. *Entrance requirements:* For master's, official transcripts, three letters of recommendation, personal interview; academic writing sample and examples of work (for museum communication); two examples of academic and professional writing (for museum education); portfolio and/or writing samples (for museum exhibition planning and design). Additional exam requirements/recommendations for international students: required—TOEFL (minimum score 580 paper-based, 92 iBT) or IELTS (minimum score 6.5).

University of Toronto, School of Graduate Studies, Faculty of Information, Program in Museum Studies, Toronto, ON M5S 1A1, Canada. Offers MM St. *Entrance requirements:* Additional exam requirements/recommendations for international students: required—TOEFL (minimum score 580 paper-based; 93 iBT), TWE (minimum score 5). Electronic applications accepted. *Expenses:* Contact institution.

The University of Tulsa, Graduate School, Program in Museum Science and Management, Tulsa, OK 74104-3189. Offers MA. *Program availability:* Part-time. *Degree requirements:* For master's, final semester internship or independent research project. *Entrance requirements:* For master's, GRE General Test. Additional exam requirements/recommendations for international students: required—TOEFL (minimum score 575 paper-based; 91 iBT), IELTS (minimum score 6.5). Electronic applications accepted. *Expenses: Tuition:* Full-time $22,896; part-time $1272 per credit hour. *Required fees:* $6 per credit hour. Tuition and fees vary according to course load and program.

University of Washington, Graduate School, Museology Graduate Program, Seattle, WA 98195. Offers museum evaluation (MA). *Faculty:* 4 full-time (3 women), 8 part-time/adjunct (5 women). *Students:* 69 full-time (59 women); includes 21 minority (1 American Indian or Alaska Native, non-Hispanic/Latino; 6 Asian, non-Hispanic/Latino; 7 Hispanic/Latino; 1 Native Hawaiian or other Pacific Islander, non-Hispanic/Latino; 6 Two or more races, non-Hispanic/Latino), 2 international. Average age 28. 138 applicants, 48% accepted, 34 enrolled. In 2019, 32 master's awarded. *Degree requirements:* For master's, thesis. *Entrance requirements:* For master's, baccalaureate degree; minimum GPA of 3.0 during last 2 years (60 semester credits and 90 quarter credits) of courses. Additional exam requirements/recommendations for international students: required—TOEFL (minimum score 580 paper-based; 92 iBT). *Application deadline:* For fall admission, 1/15 for domestic and international students. Application fee: $85. Electronic applications accepted. *Expenses:* $6,496 per quarter tuition, $55 per quarter registration fee, $243 per quarter student fees, $38 per quarter technology fees. *Financial support:* In 2019–20, 2 students received support. Career-related internships or fieldwork, Federal Work-Study, scholarships/grants, and Conference and research travel scholarships available. Financial award application deadline: 1/15; financial award applicants required to submit FAFSA. *Unit head:* Dr. Jessica Luke, Director, 206-685-3496, E-mail: uwmuse@uw.edu. *Application contact:* Dylan High, Graduate Advisor, 206-221-0713, E-mail: uwmuse@uw.edu.
Website: http://www.washington.edu/museology/

University of Wisconsin–Milwaukee, Graduate School, College of Letters and Science, Department of Anthropology, Milwaukee, WI 53201-0413. Offers anthropology (MS, PhD); museum studies (Graduate Certificate). *Degree requirements:* For master's, thesis or alternative; for doctorate, one foreign language, thesis/dissertation, departmental qualifying exam. *Entrance requirements:* For master's, GRE; for doctorate, GRE, minimum GPA of 3.0, master's degree. Additional exam requirements/recommendations for international students: required—TOEFL (minimum score 550 paper-based; 79 iBT), IELTS (minimum score 6.5). Electronic applications accepted.

Université Laval, Faculty of Letters, Department of History, Program in Museology, Québec, QC G1K 7P4, Canada. Offers Diploma. *Program availability:* Part-time. *Entrance requirements:* For degree, English exam (comprehension of English), knowledge of French. Electronic applications accepted.

Virginia Commonwealth University, Graduate School, School of the Arts, Department of Art History, Richmond, VA 23284-9005. Offers curatorial (PhD); historical studies (MA, PhD); museum studies (MA). *Accreditation:* NASAD. *Degree requirements:* For master's, thesis; for doctorate, comprehensive exam, thesis/dissertation. *Entrance requirements:* For master's and doctorate, GRE General Test. Electronic applications accepted.

Wayne State University, College of Liberal Arts and Sciences, Tracy Neumann, Detroit, MI 48202. Offers history (MA, PhD); public history (MA), including African American history and culture, cultural resource management, gender, sexuality, and women's studies, labor and urban history, museum studies, public policy; world history (Graduate Certificate); JD/MA; M Ed/MA; MLIS/MA. *Program availability:* Evening/weekend. *Faculty:* 23 full-time (11 women). *Students:* 18 full-time (7 women), 16 part-time (7 women); includes 4 minority (2 Black or African American, non-Hispanic/Latino; 2 Two or more races, non-Hispanic/Latino). Average age 37. 38 applicants, 34% accepted, 13 enrolled. In 2019, 7 master's, 3 doctorates awarded. *Degree requirements:* For master's, thesis (for some programs), final oral exam on thesis or essay and seminar; internship and project (for public history); for doctorate, variable foreign language requirement, comprehensive exam, thesis/dissertation, qualifying exam in 4 fields of history. *Entrance requirements:* For master's, GRE General Test, minimum undergraduate GPA of 3.25 in history, 3.0 overall; at least 18 credits in history and related subjects at the advanced undergraduate level; foreign language; letter of intent; research paper; at least two letters of recommendation from former instructors; for doctorate, GRE General Test, minimum GPA of 3.0, 3.25 in minimum of 18 semester credits in history and related subjects; letter of intent; research paper; at least three letters of recommendation from former professors; for Graduate Certificate, baccalaureate degree from accredited college or university; minimum GPA of 3.0, 3.25 in a minimum of eighteen semester credits in history and related subjects at the advanced undergraduate level. Additional exam requirements/recommendations for international students: required—TOEFL (minimum score 550 paper-based; 79 iBT), TWE (minimum score 5.5), Michigan English Language Assessment Battery (minimum score 85); recommended—IELTS (minimum score 6.5). *Application deadline:* For fall admission, 1/15 priority date for domestic and international students; for winter admission, 4/15 for domestic students, 4/15 priority date for international students; for spring admission, 10/15 for domestic students, 10/15 priority date for international students. Application fee: $50. Electronic applications accepted. *Expenses: Tuition:* Full-time $34,567. *Financial support:* In 2019–20, 18 students received support, including 2 fellowships with tuition reimbursements available (averaging $20,797 per year), 2 research assistantships with tuition reimbursements available (averaging $23,960 per year), 7 teaching assistantships with tuition reimbursements available (averaging $19,967 per year); scholarships/grants, health care benefits, and unspecified assistantships also available. Financial award applicants required to submit FAFSA. *Unit head:* Dr. Elizabeth V. Faue, Professor/Chair, 313-577-2525, E-mail: evfaue@wayne.edu. *Application contact:* Dr. Tracy Neumann, Associate Professor and Director of Graduate Studies, 313-577-2525, E-mail: tracyneumann@wayne.edu. Website: http://clas.wayne.edu/history/

Western Illinois University, School of Graduate Studies, College of Fine Arts and Communication, Program in Museum Studies, Macomb, IL 61455-1390. Offers MA, Certificate. *Accreditation:* NASAD. *Program availability:* Part-time. *Entrance requirements:* For master's, minimum GPA of 3.0. Additional exam requirements/recommendations for international students: required—TOEFL (minimum score 600 paper-based; 100 iBT). Electronic applications accepted.

NEW YORK STUDIO SCHOOL OF DRAWING, PAINTING & SCULPTURE

Master of Fine Arts Program

Programs of Study

The New York Studio School is committed to providing aspiring artists with a significant education that will last a lifetime. Students are encouraged to question rigorously and to think deeply about the practice of drawing, painting, and sculpture. Master of Fine Arts (MFA) students graduate from the program with an ambitious studio practice, a developed understanding of the language of art, and an enlarged imagination stirred by an established work ethic.

During the first year of study, students choose a core faculty member with whom they work alongside within an Atelier model. Faculty members are present in the classrooms two days each week, and students are expected to work on the objectives set by the instructors throughout the week. As students develop independence in their second year, MFA candidates work in private and semi-private studios toward the completion of their individual thesis projects.

The MFA programs are offered with concentrations in painting or in sculpture and are based on maintaining a full-time, rigorous studio practice. Students typically work a minimum of 40 hours per week for the duration of their two years at the School. Studio practice is balanced with Critical Studies courses and instructed critiques. Lectures and seminars are held throughout the semester, as well as small group discussion with current and visiting faculty. Students must complete 60 credits to successfully achieve the Master of Fine Arts degree and credits must include all required courses. A residency of at least two academic years is necessary to complete the degree. Students have access to their studios on a full-time basis. New York City's museums, arts organizations, and culture serve as a profound additional resource to all students.

The School's internationally recognized Marathon Programs were developed in 1988 by Dean Graham Nickson as a way of generating momentum, subject matter, and drawing strategies for the semester to follow. The program has since expanded to become a core component of the School's curriculum. The interest in the Marathon Programs has led to a wider audience of participants outside the full-time student body. Renowned artists, art historians, dealers, collectors, art educators, writers, journalists, and students of all levels and affiliations have since experienced the intensity of the program. The Marathons are offered throughout the year, both in-person and virtually.

Research Facilities

The John McEnroe Library's mission is to support the New York Studio School's programs and courses by providing materials and information for students, faculty, staff, and visiting lecturers. Holdings include monographs on artists, art historical texts, art periodicals, and exhibition catalogs, as well as an extensive lecture archive, comprising audio and video recordings of lectures from the past thirty years, featuring artists, historians, critics, and philosophers.

The library provides an online catalog to check the holdings of the collection, as well as access to research databases and indexes that aid in scholarly research.

Financial Aid

The financial aid programs are part of the School's desire to attract qualified students from diverse backgrounds. Any student who would like to be considered for financial assistance from the School must complete a financial aid application and submit it to Student Services by the deadline date each year. Financial aid scholarships are contingent on the continuation of satisfactory progress in all enrolled courses and are available to all full-time enrolled students. Scholarships are available for part-time students during the summer session.

Cost of Study

For the 2019–20 academic year, the cost for the MFA program was $12,687.50 per semester. The cost for the Certificate program was $8,675 per semester. For additional, up-to-date cost information, prospective students should visit www.nyss.org/admissions-services/tuition-fees/.

Living and Housing Costs

The School does not have housing facilities. Upon acceptance, students receive information on housing opportunities in New York, including listings of temporary accommodations and help on searching for suitable living situations. The School is easily accessible by public transport from the outer boroughs and New Jersey. Rents in the outer boroughs tend to be lower than in Manhattan. Less expensive situations can be found through sublets or by living with roommates. Students should plan to find proper accommodations prior to enrolling.

Student Group

The Studio School welcomes a diverse demographic of students of varying ages and geographical origins; one third of the full-time student body is composed of international students. All students are encouraged to develop work and cultivate studio skills which will support them and allow them to continue an independent studio practice long after they have graduated from the School. At the School, the pursuit of authenticity tends to subdue the distractions of style or the rush for novelty. Response to the contemporary does not lessen the excitement of discovery within the art of the past. No dichotomy between realism and abstraction is assumed at the School. On the contrary, perceptual experience is encouraged to lead the student to the discovery of abstract equivalents, to a deepening grasp of the plastic means.

Location

The School is located on West 8th Street, between Sixth Avenue/Avenue of the Americas and Fifth Avenue. It is accessible by subway or the PATH train. The School occupies eight historic buildings with an extraordinary cultural and artistic history. Occupied by various artists, and the original site of the Whitney Museum of American Art from 1931 to 1954, the School's physical home has been a place where art has been created, discussed, and displayed for over a century. In the fifty plus years that the School has been on West 8th Street, artists and students alike have found both inspiration and comfort in continuing the tradition of drawing, painting, and sculpting in the historic spaces that have played such an important role in the history of art in America.

New York Studio School of Drawing, Painting & Sculpture

Applying

The application deadline for MFA applicants is January 15. Late applications are reviewed on a case-by-case basis; however late applicants may not be eligible for financial aid. MFA candidates are accepted exclusively for enrollment in the fall semester. Applicants must have a bachelor's degree or equivalent to be considered for admission. Forms must be completed online at https://nyss.slideroom.com/#/Login.

Completed applications include the application form, two required essays, a $70 nonrefundable application fee, two letters of recommendation, 20 jpeg images of student work with an image list accompanying the images, and official transcripts from all previous institutions that resulted in the applicant's undergraduate degree. Detailed instructions are available as part of the application form. Partial applications will not be considered. Prospective candidates will be invited for an interview with the Admissions Committee.

For additional information, prospective students should visit http://www.nyss.org/academics/mfa-program/.

Correspondence and Information

New York Studio School
8 West 8th Street
New York, New York 10011
United States
Phone: 212-673-6466
Fax: 212-777-0996
E-mail: info@nyss.org
Website: http://www.nyss.org

candidates begin in the fall and spring semesters with either a Drawing or Sculpture Marathon.

THE FACULTY

Lourdes Bernard, painter, educated at Syracuse University and the New York Studio School.

David Cohen, art critic; publisher of artcritical.com.

Bruce Gagnier, sculptor; M.F.A., Columbia. National Academician represented by Lori Bookstein Fine Art.

Bill Jensen, painter; B.F.A. and M.F.A., University of Minnesota. Represented by Cheim & Read Gallery, New York.

Elisa Jensen, painter; M.A., Smith College and the New York Studio School.

Jilaine Jones, sculptor, College of Ceramics, Alfred University; M.A. School of the Museum of Fina Arts.

John Lees, painter; B.F.A. and M.F.A., Otis Art Institute. Represented by Betty Cuningham Gallery.

Leonid Lerman, sculptor: Odessa School of Art; M.F.A. Mukhina College of Art and Design.

Margrit Lewczuk, painter; studied at Queens College and the Brooklyn Museum Art School.

John Newman, sculptor; B.A., Oberlin College; M.F.A., Yale School of Art.

Graham Nickson, painting and drawing; B.A., Camberwell School of Arts & Crafts; M.A., Royal College of Art (London).

Jennifer Samet, art historian and curator: B.A., Bard College and Ph.D. at the Graduate Center, CUNY, director at Eric Firestone Gallery.

Kyle Staver, painter; B.A., Minneapolis College of Art and Design; M.F.A., Yale School of Art.

Clintel Steed, painting and drawing; B.F.A., Art Institute of Chicago; M.F.A., Indiana University.

Lee Tribe, sculptor; educated at Saint Martin's School of Art and Birmingham School of Art (England) and the New York Studio School.

Karen Wilkin, art historian and critic; educated at Barnard College and Columbia University. Fulbright and Woodrow Wilson Fellow.

Second-year MFA candidates are provided with semi-private to private studios, allowing for growth and development of their creative practice.

The School's internationally recognized Marathon programs were developed by Dean Graham Nickson, initially as a measure for the rest of the semester at the start of the program year. All MFA and Certificate

Section 4
Comparative and Interdisciplinary Arts

This section contains a directory of institutions offering graduate work in comparative and interdisciplinary arts. Additional information about programs listed in the directory may be obtained by writing directly to the dean of a graduate school or chair of a department at the address given in the directory.

For programs offering related work, see also in this book *Applied Arts and Design, Architecture, Art and Art History,* and *Performing Arts.* In another guide in this series:

Graduate Programs in Business, Education, Information Studies, Law & Social Work
See *Subject Areas (Art Education)*

CONTENTS

Program Directory

Comparative and Interdisciplinary Arts

Brigham Young University, Graduate Studies, College of Humanities, Department of Comparative Arts and Letters, Provo, UT 84602-1001. Offers comparative studies (MA). *Program availability:* Part-time. *Faculty:* 29 full-time (7 women), 4 part-time/adjunct (2 women). *Students:* 15 full-time (10 women), 1 (woman) part-time; includes 1 minority (Asian, non-Hispanic/Latino). Average age 29. 15 applicants, 60% accepted, 8 enrolled. In 2019, 8 master's awarded. *Degree requirements:* For master's, 2 foreign languages, comprehensive exam, thesis, Coursework à?33 credit hours in seminars at graduate level and other courses by approval. *Entrance requirements:* For master's, GRE, minimum GPA of 3.0 in last 60 hours, writing sample, foreign language experience, undergraduate degree or experience in a humanities discipline, proficiency in a language of scholarship or other spoken language. Additional exam requirements/recommendations for international students: required—TOEFL (minimum score 580 paper-based; 85 iBT), E3PT (to obtain the required minimum English language proficieny scores for the E3PT, IELTS, or TOEFL tests; or to obtain waiver "í".) *Application deadline:* For fall admission, 3/1 for domestic and international students. Application fee: $50. Electronic applications accepted. *Financial support:* In 2019–20, 15 students received support, including 1 research assistantship, 15 teaching assistantships (averaging $5,000 per year); scholarships/grants, tuition waivers (partial), unspecified assistantships, and student instructorships also available. Support available to part-time students. Financial award application deadline: 9/1. *Unit head:* Dr. Julie Allen, Graduate Coordinator/Professor of Classical Studies, 801-422-7891, Fax: 801-422-0305, E-mail: julie_allen@byu.edu. *Application contact:* Andrea Kristensen, Graduate Program Manager, 801-422-2996, Fax: 801-422-0305, E-mail: andrea_kristensen@byu.edu.
Website: http://cal.byu.edu/

Florida Atlantic University, Dorothy F. Schmidt College of Arts and Letters, Program in Comparative Studies, Boca Raton, FL 33431-0991. Offers PhD. *Program availability:* Part-time. *Students:* 24 full-time (14 women), 27 part-time (19 women); includes 20 minority (5 Black or African American, non-Hispanic/Latino; 14 Hispanic/Latino; 1 Two or more races, non-Hispanic/Latino), 5 international. Average age 41. 24 applicants, 88% accepted, 15 enrolled. In 2019, 9 doctorates awarded. *Degree requirements:* For doctorate, one foreign language, comprehensive exam, thesis/dissertation. *Entrance requirements:* For doctorate, GRE, minimum GPA of 3.5, 3 references. Additional exam requirements/recommendations for international students: required—TOEFL (minimum score 500 paper-based; 61 iBT), IELTS (minimum score 6). *Application deadline:* For fall admission, 2/1 priority date for domestic and international students. Applications are processed on a rolling basis. Application fee: $30. *Expenses: Tuition:* Full-time $20,536; part-time $371.82 per credit hour. Tuition and fees vary according to program. *Financial support:* Teaching assistantships available. *Unit head:* Dr. Eric Berlatsky, Associate Dean, 561-297-3831, E-mail: eberlats@fau.edu. *Application contact:* Dr. Eric Berlatsky, Associate Dean, 561-297-3831, E-mail: eberlats@fau.edu.
Website: http://www.fau.edu/comparativestudies/

Goddard College, Graduate Division, Master of Fine Arts in Interdisciplinary Arts Program, Plainfield, VT 05667-9432. Offers MFA. *Program availability:* Online learning. *Degree requirements:* For master's, thesis. *Entrance requirements:* For master's, relevant undergraduate degree, 3 letters of recommendation, interview, portfolio, artistic resume. Electronic applications accepted.

Ohio University, Graduate College, College of Fine Arts, School of Interdisciplinary Arts, Athens, OH 45701-2979. Offers PhD. *Degree requirements:* For doctorate, 2 foreign languages, comprehensive exam, thesis/dissertation. *Entrance requirements:* For doctorate, GRE and MAT, master's degree. Additional exam requirements/recommendations for international students: required—TOEFL (minimum score 575 paper-based; 91 iBT) or IELTS (minimum score 7). Electronic applications accepted.

Simon Fraser University, Office of Graduate Studies and Postdoctoral Fellows, Faculty of Communication, Art and Technology, School for the Contemporary Arts, Vancouver, BC V6B 5K3, Canada. Offers MA, MFA. *Degree requirements:* For master's, thesis or alternative. *Entrance requirements:* For master's, portfolio; minimum GPA of 3.0 (on scale of 4.33) or 3.33 based on last 60 credits of undergraduate courses. Additional exam requirements/recommendations for international students: recommended—TOEFL (minimum score 580 paper-based; 93 iBT), IELTS (minimum score 7), TWE (minimum score 5). Electronic applications accepted.

Section 5
Film, Television, and Video

This section contains a directory of institutions offering graduate work in film, television, and video. Additional information about programs listed in the directory but not augmented by an in-depth entry may be obtained by writing directly to the dean of a graduate school or chair of a department at the address given in the directory.

For programs offering related work, see also in this book *Art and Art History* and *Communication and Media.* In the other guides in this series:

Graduate Programs in Engineering & Applied Sciences
See *Telecommunications*

Graduate Programs in Business, Education, Information Studies, Law & Social Work
See *Advertising and Public Relations*

CONTENTS

Program Directories

Film, Television, and Video Production

Academy of Art University, Graduate Programs, School of Animation and Visual Effects, San Francisco, CA 94105-3410. Offers 3D animation (MFA). *Program availability:* Part-time, 100% online. *Faculty:* 16 full-time (3 women), 51 part-time/adjunct (12 women). *Students:* 215 full-time (113 women), 122 part-time (59 women); includes 59 minority (18 Black or African American, non-Hispanic/Latino; 12 Asian, non-Hispanic/Latino; 23 Hispanic/Latino; 1 Native Hawaiian or other Pacific Islander, non-Hispanic/Latino; 5 Two or more races, non-Hispanic/Latino), 193 international. Average age 29. 112 applicants, 100% accepted, 84 enrolled. In 2019, 135 master's awarded. *Degree requirements:* For master's, final review. *Entrance requirements:* For master's, statement of intent; resume; portfolio/reel; official college transcripts. *Application deadline:* Applications are processed on a rolling basis. Application fee: $50. Electronic applications accepted. *Expenses: Tuition:* Full-time $1083; part-time $1083 per credit hour. *Required fees:* $860; $860 per unit. $430 per term. One-time fee: $145. Tuition and fees vary according to program. *Financial support:* Career-related internships or fieldwork, Federal Work-Study, and scholarships/grants available. Financial award application deadline: 8/10; financial award applicants required to submit FAFSA. Website: http://www.academyart.edu/animation-school/index.html

Academy of Art University, Graduate Programs, School of Motion Pictures and Television, San Francisco, CA 94105-3410. Offers motion pictures and television (MFA); writing and directing for film (MA). *Program availability:* Part-time, 100% online. *Faculty:* 8 full-time (3 women), 37 part-time/adjunct (13 women). *Students:* 88 full-time (40 women), 38 part-time (15 women); includes 22 minority (9 Black or African American, non-Hispanic/Latino; 1 American Indian or Alaska Native, non-Hispanic/Latino; 3 Asian, non-Hispanic/Latino; 8 Hispanic/Latino; 1 Two or more races, non-Hispanic/Latino), 71 international. Average age 32. 55 applicants, 100% accepted, 23 enrolled. In 2019, 73 master's awarded. *Degree requirements:* For master's, final review. *Entrance requirements:* For master's, statement of intent; resume; portfolio/reel; official college transcripts. *Application deadline:* Applications are processed on a rolling basis. Application fee: $50. Electronic applications accepted. *Expenses: Tuition:* Full-time $1083; part-time $1083 per credit hour. *Required fees:* $860; $860 per unit. $430 per term. One-time fee: $145. Tuition and fees vary according to program. *Financial support:* Career-related internships or fieldwork, Federal Work-Study, and scholarships/grants available. Financial award application deadline: 8/10; financial award applicants required to submit FAFSA. *Application contact:* 800-544-ARTS, E-mail: info@academyart.edu. Website: http://www.academyart.edu/film-school/index.html

Academy of Art University, Graduate Programs, School of Music Production and Sound Design for Visual Media, San Francisco, CA 94105-3410. Offers music scoring and composition (MA, MFA); sound design (MA, MFA). *Program availability:* Part-time, 100% online. *Faculty:* 1 full-time (0 women), 26 part-time/adjunct (4 women). *Students:* 73 full-time (33 women), 23 part-time (7 women); includes 16 minority (7 Black or African American, non-Hispanic/Latino; 1 Asian, non-Hispanic/Latino; 4 Hispanic/Latino; 4 Two or more races, non-Hispanic/Latino), 54 international. Average age 30. 44 applicants, 100% accepted, 31 enrolled. In 2019, 34 master's awarded. *Degree requirements:* For master's, final review. *Entrance requirements:* For master's, statement of intent; resume; portfolio/reel; official college transcripts. *Application deadline:* Applications are processed on a rolling basis. Application fee: $50. Electronic applications accepted. *Expenses: Tuition:* Full-time $1083; part-time $1083 per credit hour. *Required fees:* $860; $860 per unit. $430 per term. One-time fee: $145. Tuition and fees vary according to program. *Financial support:* Career-related internships or fieldwork, Federal Work-Study, and scholarships/grants available. Financial award application deadline: 8/10; financial award applicants required to submit FAFSA. Website: http://www.academyart.edu/music-for-visual-media/index.html

Academy of Art University, Graduate Programs, School of Writing for Film, Television and Digital Media, San Francisco, CA 94105-3410. Offers MFA. *Program availability:* Part-time, 100% online. *Faculty:* 8 full-time (3 women), 37 part-time/adjunct (13 women). *Students:* 21 full-time (15 women), 27 part-time (18 women); includes 15 minority (10 Black or African American, non-Hispanic/Latino; 3 Hispanic/Latino; 2 Two or more races, non-Hispanic/Latino), 6 international. Average age 36. 13 applicants, 100% accepted, 12 enrolled. In 2019, 3 master's awarded. *Degree requirements:* For master's, final review. *Entrance requirements:* For master's, statement of intent; resume; portfolio/reel; official college transcripts. *Application deadline:* Applications are processed on a rolling basis. Application fee: $50. Electronic applications accepted. *Expenses: Tuition:* Full-time $1083; part-time $1083 per credit hour. *Required fees:* $860; $860 per unit. $430 per term. One-time fee: $145. Tuition and fees vary according to program. *Financial support:* Career-related internships or fieldwork, Federal Work-Study, and scholarships/grants available. Financial award application deadline: 8/10; financial award applicants required to submit FAFSA. Website: http://www.academyart.edu/academics/writing-film-television-digital-media

American Film Institute Conservatory, Graduate Program, Los Angeles, CA 90027-1657. Offers cinematography (MFA); directing (MFA); editing (MFA); producing (MFA); production design (MFA); screenwriting (MFA). *Degree requirements:* For master's, thesis. *Entrance requirements:* For master's, resume, two letters of recommendation, official transcripts. Additional exam requirements/recommendations for international students: required—TOEFL (minimum score 600 paper-based; 100 iBT), IELTS (minimum score 7). Electronic applications accepted.

American University, School of Communication, Film and Media Arts Division, Washington, DC 20016-8001. Offers art in entertainment (MFA); environmental and wildlife filmmaking (MFA); film and media arts (MFA); game design (MA); games and interactive media (MFA); games and interactivity (MFA); political, cultural, and social impact (MFA); producing film, television and video (MA). *Program availability:* Part-time, evening/weekend. *Degree requirements:* For master's, comprehensive exam, thesis or alternative. *Entrance requirements:* Additional exam requirements/recommendations for international students: required—TOEFL (minimum score 600 paper-based; 100 iBT), IELTS (minimum score 7). Electronic applications accepted.

Arizona State University at Tempe, College of Liberal Arts and Sciences, Department of English, Program in Film and Media Studies, Tempe, AZ 85287-0402. Offers American media and popular culture (MAS). *Program availability:* Part-time, evening/weekend, online learning. *Degree requirements:* For master's, integrated project. *Entrance requirements:* For master's, minimum GPA of 3.0 or equivalent in last 2 years of work leading to bachelor's degree. Additional exam requirements/recommendations for international students: required—TOEFL, IELTS, or PTE. Electronic applications accepted. *Expenses:* Contact institution.

ArtCenter College of Design, Graduate Film Program, Pasadena, CA 91103. Offers MFA. *Accreditation:* NASAD.

Azusa Pacific University, College of Music and the Arts, Azusa, CA 91702-7000. Offers composition (M Mus); conducting (M Mus); education (M Mus); modern art

history, theory, and criticism (MA); music entrepreneurial studies (MA); performance (M Mus); screenwriting (MA); visual art (MFA). *Accreditation:* NASAD; NASM. *Program availability:* Part-time, evening/weekend. *Degree requirements:* For master's, recital. *Entrance requirements:* For master's, interview, audition. Additional exam requirements/recommendations for international students: required—TOEFL (minimum score 550 paper-based).

Bard College, Milton Avery Graduate School of the Arts, Annandale-on-Hudson, NY 12504. Offers film/video (MFA); music/sound (MFA); painting (MFA); photography (MFA); sculpture (MFA); writing (MFA). *Degree requirements:* For master's, thesis, project, 8-week summer residency, independent study. *Entrance requirements:* For master's, interview, portfolio, 2 letters of recommendation, history of work in the arts. Additional exam requirements/recommendations for international students: required—TOEFL (minimum score 550 paper-based). Electronic applications accepted. *Expenses:* Contact institution.

Bob Jones University, Graduate Programs, Greenville, SC 29614. Offers accountancy (MS); Bible (MA); Bible translation (MA); Biblical studies (Certificate); business administration (MBA); church history (MA, PhD); church ministries (MA); church music (MM); cinema and video production (MA); counseling (MS); curriculum and instruction (Ed D); divinity (M Div); dramatic production (MA); educational leadership (MS, Ed D, Ed S); elementary education (M Ed, MAT); English (M Ed, MA, MAT); fine arts (MA); graphic design (MA); history (M Ed, MA); illustration (MA); interpretative speech (MA); mathematics (M Ed, MAT); medical missions (Certificate); ministry (MM, D Min); multi-categorical special education (M Ed, MAT); music (M Ed); New Testament interpretation (PhD); Old Testament interpretation (PhD); orchestral instrument performance (MM); organ performance (MM); pastoral studies (MA); personnel services (MS, Ed S); piano pedagogy (MM); piano performance (MM); platform arts (MA); rhetoric and public address (MA); secondary education (M Ed); studio art (MA); teaching Bible (MA); theology (MA, PhD); voice performance (MM); youth ministries (MA); M Div/MM.

Boston University, College of Communication, Department of Film and Television, Boston, MA 02215. Offers MFA, MS. *Program availability:* Part-time. *Faculty:* 17 full-time, 25 part-time/adjunct. *Students:* 79 full-time (54 women), 5 part-time (2 women); includes 14 minority (5 Black or African American, non-Hispanic/Latino; 3 Asian, non-Hispanic/Latino; 5 Hispanic/Latino; 1 Two or more races, non-Hispanic/Latino), 21 international. Average age 25. 275 applicants, 46% accepted, 55 enrolled. In 2019, 61 master's awarded. *Degree requirements:* For master's, thesis (for some programs). *Entrance requirements:* For master's, transcript(s), resume/CV, writing and creative samples, letters of recommendation. Additional exam requirements/recommendations for international students: required—TOEFL (minimum score 600 paper-based; 100 iBT), either TOEFL or IELTS; recommended—IELTS (minimum score 7). *Application deadline:* For fall admission, 5/1 for domestic and international students. Applications are processed on a rolling basis. Application fee: $95. Electronic applications accepted. *Financial support:* Research assistantships, teaching assistantships with partial tuition reimbursements, career-related internships or fieldwork, Federal Work-Study, scholarships/grants, and unspecified assistantships available. Support available to part-time students. Financial award application deadline: 5/1; financial award applicants required to submit FAFSA. *Unit head:* Paul Schneider, Chairman, 617-353-3483, Fax: 617-353-1084, E-mail: ftvchair@bu.edu. *Application contact:* Jackie Cummings, Admission and Financial Aid Counselor, 617-353-3481, E-mail: comgrad@bu.edu. Website: http://www.bu.edu/com/academics/film-tv/

Bowling Green State University, Graduate College, College of Arts and Sciences, Department of Theatre and Film, Bowling Green, OH 43403. Offers MA, PhD. *Accreditation:* NAST. *Program availability:* Part-time. Terminal master's awarded for partial completion of doctoral program. *Degree requirements:* For master's, thesis or alternative; for doctorate, comprehensive exam, thesis/dissertation, 9-hour research tool. *Entrance requirements:* For master's and doctorate, GRE General Test. Additional exam requirements/recommendations for international students: required—TOEFL. Electronic applications accepted.

Brigham Young University, Graduate Studies, College of Fine Arts and Communications, Department of Theatre and Media Arts, Provo, UT 84602-6404. Offers media and performance studies (MA). *Accreditation:* NAST. *Faculty:* 7 full-time (3 women). *Students:* 9 full-time (6 women); includes 2 minority (1 Asian, non-Hispanic/Latino; 1 Hispanic/Latino). Average age 28. 9 applicants, 44% accepted, 2 enrolled. *Degree requirements:* For master's, comprehensive exam, thesis, 32 hours, oral defense. *Entrance requirements:* For master's, two samples of scholarly writing, letter of intent, three letters of recommendation. Additional exam requirements/recommendations for international students: required—TOEFL (minimum score 580 paper-based; 85 iBT). *Application deadline:* For fall admission, 2/15 priority date for domestic and international students. Application fee: $50. Electronic applications accepted. *Financial support:* In 2019–20, 9 students received support, including 3 research assistantships with partial tuition reimbursements available (averaging $1,000 per year), 8 teaching assistantships with partial tuition reimbursements available (averaging $2,000 per year); scholarships/grants, health care benefits, tuition waivers (partial), and unspecified assistantships also available. Financial award application deadline: 2/15. *Unit head:* Dr. Kimball Jensen, Graduate Coordinator, 801-422-6648, E-mail: kimball_jensen@byu.edu. *Application contact:* Katie Tolman, Graduate Secretary, 801-422-3750. Website: http://cfac.byu.edu/departments/tma

Brooklyn College of the City University of New York, School of Visual, Media and Performing Arts, Department of Television and Radio, Brooklyn, NY 11210-2889. Offers media studies (MS); television production (MFA). *Program availability:* Part-time, evening/weekend. *Degree requirements:* For master's, comprehensive exam. *Entrance requirements:* For master's, GRE General Test or MAT, 12 credits in television/radio with a minimum B average, 2 letters of recommendation. Additional exam requirements/recommendations for international students: required—TOEFL (minimum score 580 paper-based; 92 iBT). Electronic applications accepted.

Brooklyn College of the City University of New York, School of Visual, Media and Performing Arts, Feirstein Graduate School of Cinema, Brooklyn, NY 11210-2889. Offers cinema arts (MFA); cinema studies (MA).

California College of the Arts, Graduate Programs, Fine Arts Programs, San Francisco, CA 94107. Offers film (MFA); fine arts (MFA). *Accreditation:* NASAD. *Degree requirements:* For master's, thesis, exhibit. *Entrance requirements:* For master's, appropriate bachelor's degree, portfolio, resume, 2 letters of recommendation, transcript. Additional exam requirements/recommendations for international students: required—TOEFL, IELTS, or PTE. Electronic applications accepted. *Expenses:* Contact institution.

California Institute of the Arts, School of Film/Video, Valencia, CA 91355-2340. Offers experimental animation (MFA); film directing (MFA, Adv C); film/video (Adv C). *Entrance requirements:* For master's, portfolio. Additional exam requirements/recommendations for international students: required—TOEFL. Electronic applications accepted.

California State University, Fullerton, Graduate Studies, College of Communications, Department of Cinema and Television Arts, Fullerton, CA 92831-3599. Offers screenwriting (MFA). *Entrance requirements:* For master's, bachelor's degree from accredited university; samples of competent and creative writing, such as original screenplays, teleplays, theatrical plays, or other narrative work; essay; three letters of recommendation. Electronic applications accepted.

California State University, Northridge, Graduate Studies, Mike Curb College of Arts, Media, and Communication, Department of Cinema and Television Arts, Northridge, CA 91330. Offers screenwriting (MA). *Entrance requirements:* For master's, GRE (if cumulative undergraduate GPA less than 3.0).

Carleton University, Faculty of Graduate Studies, Faculty of Arts and Social Sciences, School for Studies in Art and Culture, Program in Film Studies, Ottawa, ON K1S 5B6, Canada. Offers MA. *Degree requirements:* For master's, thesis. *Entrance requirements:* For master's, honors degree. Additional exam requirements/recommendations for international students: required—TOEFL.

Carnegie Mellon University, College of Fine Arts, School of Drama, Pittsburgh, PA 15213-3891. Offers design (MFA); directing (MFA); dramatic writing (MFA); production technology and management (MFA); video and media design (MFA). *Degree requirements:* For master's, thesis (for some programs). *Entrance requirements:* For master's, audition, portfolio review, interview. Additional exam requirements/recommendations for international students: required—TOEFL.

Carnegie Mellon University, School of Computer Science and College of Fine Arts, Program in Entertainment Technology, Pittsburgh, PA 15213-3891. Offers MET.

Central Michigan University, College of Graduate Studies, College of the Arts and Media, School of Broadcast and Cinematic Arts, Mount Pleasant, MI 48859. Offers electronic media management (MA); electronic media production (MA); electronic media studies (MA); film theory and criticism (MA). *Program availability:* Part-time. *Degree requirements:* For master's, thesis or alternative. *Entrance requirements:* For master's, undergraduate degree in broadcasting, film studies, or an associated discipline with minimum GPA of 2.7. Electronic applications accepted. *Expenses: Tuition, area resident:* Full-time $12,267; part-time $8178 per year. Tuition, state resident: full-time $12,267; part-time $8178 per year. Tuition, nonresident: full-time $12,267; part-time $8178 per year. *International tuition:* $16,110 full-time. *Required fees:* $225 per semester. Tuition and fees vary according to degree level and program.

Chapman University, Dodge College of Film and Media Arts, Orange, CA 92866. Offers documentary filmmaking (MFA); film and television producing (MFA); film production (MFA); film studies (MA); production design (MFA); screenwriting (MFA); television writing and producing (MFA); JD/MFA; MBA/MFA. *Faculty:* 53 full-time (16 women), 110 part-time/adjunct (36 women). *Students:* 290 full-time (137 women), 5 part-time (3 women); includes 81 minority (14 Black or African American, non-Hispanic/Latino; 21 Asian, non-Hispanic/Latino; 24 Hispanic/Latino; 1 Native Hawaiian or other Pacific Islander, non-Hispanic/Latino; 21 Two or more races, non-Hispanic/Latino), 132 international. Average age 26. 669 applicants, 44% accepted, 117 enrolled. In 2019, 100 master's awarded. *Degree requirements:* For master's, thesis. *Entrance requirements:* For master's, creative portfolio. Additional exam requirements/recommendations for international students: required—TOEFL (minimum score 80 iBT), IELTS (minimum score 6.5), PTE (minimum score 53). *Application deadline:* For fall admission, 12/1 for domestic students. Application fee: $60. Electronic applications accepted. *Expenses:* Contact institution. *Financial support:* Fellowships, Federal Work-Study, and scholarships/grants available. Financial award applicants required to submit FAFSA. *Unit head:* Stephen Galloway, Dean, 714-997-6715, E-mail: sgalloway@chapman.edu. *Application contact:* Priscilla Campos, Associate Director of Admissions, 714-997-6996, E-mail: pcampos@chapman.edu.
Website: https://www.chapman.edu/dodge/index.aspx

Chatham University, Program in Film and Digital Technology, Pittsburgh, PA 15232-2826. Offers MFA. *Program availability:* Part-time, evening/weekend. *Degree requirements:* For master's, thesis, capstone project. *Entrance requirements:* Additional exam requirements/recommendations for international students: required—TOEFL (minimum score 600 paper-based; 100 iBT), IELTS (minimum score 7), TWE. Electronic applications accepted. Application fee is waived when completed online. *Expenses: Tuition:* Part-time $1017 per credit. *Required fees:* $30 per credit. Tuition and fees vary according to program.

Columbia College Chicago, School of Graduate Studies, Cinema and Television Arts Department, Chicago, IL 60605-1996. Offers cinema directing (MFA); creative producing (MFA). *Degree requirements:* For master's, thesis. *Entrance requirements:* For master's, self-assessment essay, work samples, interview, case study, letters of recommendation, transcripts, resume. Additional exam requirements/recommendations for international students: required—TOEFL, IELTS. Electronic applications accepted.

Columbia University, School of the Arts, Film Program, New York, NY 10027. Offers film (MFA), including creative producing, screenwriting/directing. *Degree requirements:* For master's, thesis. *Entrance requirements:* For master's, Undergraduate transcript, 3 letters of recommendation, dramatic writing sample, completion of a scene from a prompt, autobiographical essay, feature film treatment, current resume (for Producing students), optional visual submission. Additional exam requirements/recommendations for international students: required—Either the TOEFL or the IELTS is required. Electronic applications accepted. *Expenses:* Contact institution.

Concordia University, School of Graduate Studies, Faculty of Fine Arts, Department of Studio Arts, Montréal, QC H3G 1M8, Canada. Offers studio arts (MFA), including fibers and material practices, film production, intermedia, painting and drawing, photography, print media, sculpture. *Degree requirements:* For master's, thesis or alternative. *Entrance requirements:* For master's, portfolio.

Concordia University, School of Graduate Studies, Faculty of Fine Arts, Mel Hoppenheim School of Cinema, Montréal, QC H3G 1M8, Canada. Offers film and moving image studies (PhD); film production (MFA); film studies (MA).

DePaul University, College of Computing and Digital Media, Chicago, IL 60604. Offers animation (MA, MFA); applied technology (MS); business information technology (MS); computational finance (MS); computer and information sciences (PhD); computer science (MS); creative producing (MFA); cybersecurity (MS); data science (MS); digital communication and media arts (MA); documentary (MFA); e-commerce technology (MS); experience design (MA); film and television (MS); film and television directing (MFA); game design (MFA); game programming (MS); health informatics (MS); human centered design (PhD); human-computer interaction (MS); information systems (MS); network engineering and security (MS); product innovation and computing (MS); screenwriting (MFA); software engineering (MS); JD/MS. *Program availability:* Part-time, evening/weekend, online learning. *Degree requirements:* For master's, thesis (for some programs); for doctorate, comprehensive exam, thesis/dissertation. *Entrance requirements:* For master's, GRE or GMAT (for MS in computational finance only), bachelor's degree, resume (MS in predictive analytics only), IT experience (MS in information technology project management only), portfolio review (all MFA programs and MA in animation); for doctorate, GRE, master's degree in computer science. Additional exam requirements/recommendations for international students: required—TOEFL (minimum score 590 paper-based; 80 iBT), IELTS (minimum score 6.5), PTE (minimum score 53). Electronic applications accepted. *Expenses:* Contact institution.

Drexel University, Westphal College of Media Arts and Design, Program in Television Management, Philadelphia, PA 19104-2875. Offers MS, MS/MBA.

Florida Atlantic University, Dorothy F. Schmidt College of Arts and Letters, School of Communication and Multimedia Studies, Boca Raton, FL 33431-0991. Offers communication studies (MA); film and video (Certificate); media, technology and entertainment (MFA). *Program availability:* Part-time. *Faculty:* 23 full-time (9 women). *Students:* 30 full-time (19 women), 13 part-time (5 women); includes 22 minority (9 Black or African American, non-Hispanic/Latino; 1 Asian, non-Hispanic/Latino; 6 Hispanic/Latino; 6 Two or more races, non-Hispanic/Latino), 7 international. Average age 30. 32 applicants, 66% accepted, 19 enrolled. In 2019, 8 master's awarded. *Degree requirements:* For master's, one foreign language, comprehensive exam (for some programs), thesis (for some programs). *Entrance requirements:* For master's, GRE General Test, minimum GPA of 3.0, essay, letters of recommendation. *Application deadline:* For fall admission, 7/1 priority date for domestic students, 4/1 for international students; for spring admission, 11/1 for domestic students, 10/1 for international students. Applications are processed on a rolling basis. Application fee: $30. Electronic applications accepted. *Expenses: Tuition:* Full-time $20,536; part-time $371.82 per credit hour. Tuition and fees vary according to program. *Financial support:* Teaching assistantships with partial tuition reimbursements, Federal Work-Study, institutionally sponsored loans, scholarships/grants, and unspecified assistantships available. Support available to part-time students. Financial award application deadline: 3/1; financial award applicants required to submit FAFSA. *Unit head:* Dr. Carol Bishop Mills, Director, 561-297-0042, Fax: 561-297-2615, E-mail: millsc@fau.edu. *Application contact:* Dr. Stephen Charbonneau, Graduate Director, 561-297-3856, Fax: 561-297-2615, E-mail: scharbo1@fau.edu.
Website: http://www.fau.edu/scms/

Florida State University, The Graduate School, College of Motion Picture Arts, Tallahassee, FL 32306-2350. Offers film production (MFA); screenwriting (MFA). *Faculty:* 28 full-time (8 women), 3 part-time/adjunct (1 woman). *Students:* 64 full-time (33 women); includes 20 minority (10 Black or African American, non-Hispanic/Latino; 1 American Indian or Alaska Native, non-Hispanic/Latino; 4 Asian, non-Hispanic/Latino; 3 Hispanic/Latino; 2 Two or more races, non-Hispanic/Latino), 14 international. Average age 25. 217 applicants, 15% accepted, 32 enrolled. In 2019, 30 master's awarded. *Degree requirements:* For master's, thesis, Thesis film project. *Entrance requirements:* For master's, minimum GPA of 3.0, resume, statement of purpose, writing sample, 3 letters of recommendation, creative portfolio, video pitch. Additional exam requirements/recommendations for international students: required—TOEFL (minimum score 550 paper-based; 80 iBT). *Application deadline:* For fall admission, 12/1 for domestic and international students. Application fee: $30. Electronic applications accepted. *Expenses:* Contact institution. *Financial support:* In 2019–20, 20 students received support, including 20 teaching assistantships with partial tuition reimbursements available (averaging $5,500 per year); institutionally sponsored loans, tuition waivers, and unspecified assistantships also available. Financial award application deadline: 7/1; financial award applicants required to submit FAFSA. *Unit head:* Reb Braddock, Dean, 850-644-8712, Fax: 850-644-2626. *Application contact:* Paige Roberts, Head of Admissions, 850-644-8524, Fax: 850-644-2626, E-mail: proberts@fsu.edu.
Website: http://film.fsu.edu/

Georgia State University, College of Arts and Sciences, Department of Communication, Atlanta, GA 30302-3083. Offers film, video, and digital imaging (MA), including critical studies, production, screenwriting; human communication and social influence (MA); mass communication (MA); media and society (PhD); moving image studies (PhD); public communication (PhD); rhetoric and politics (PhD). *Program availability:* Part-time. *Faculty:* 22 full-time (16 women), 1 part-time/adjunct (0 women). *Students:* 67 full-time (46 women), 26 part-time (17 women); includes 44 minority (40 Black or African American, non-Hispanic/Latino; 1 Asian, non-Hispanic/Latino; 1 Hispanic/Latino; 1 Native Hawaiian or other Pacific Islander, non-Hispanic/Latino; 1 Two or more races, non-Hispanic/Latino), 12 international. Average age 36. 82 applicants, 49% accepted, 22 enrolled. In 2019, 9 master's, 5 doctorates awarded. *Degree requirements:* For master's, variable foreign language requirement, thesis (for some programs); for doctorate, comprehensive exam, thesis/dissertation. *Entrance requirements:* For master's and doctorate, GRE. Additional exam requirements/recommendations for international students: required—TOEFL (minimum score 550 paper-based; 80 iBT), IELTS (minimum score 6.5). *Application deadline:* For fall admission, 2/10 for domestic and international students; for spring admission, 10/15 for domestic and international students. Application fee: $50. Electronic applications accepted. *Expenses: Tuition, area resident:* Full-time $7164; part-time $398 per credit hour. Tuition, state resident: full-time $7164; part-time $398 per credit hour. Tuition, nonresident: full-time $22,662; part-time $1259 per credit hour. *International tuition:* $22,662 full-time. *Required fees:* $2128; $312 per credit hour. Tuition and fees vary according to course load and program. *Financial support:* In 2019–20, fellowships with tuition reimbursements (averaging $15,000 per year), teaching assistantships with tuition reimbursements (averaging $15,000 per year) were awarded; career-related internships or fieldwork and unspecified assistantships also available. Financial award applicants required to submit FAFSA. *Unit head:* Dr. Greg Lisby, Chair, 404-413-5639, Fax: 404-413-5634, E-mail: glisby@gsu.edu. *Application contact:* Dr. Greg Lisby, Chair, 404-413-5639, Fax: 404-413-5634, E-mail: glisby@gsu.edu.
Website: http://communication.gsu.edu

Governors State University, College of Arts and Sciences, Program in Independent Film and Digital Imaging, University Park, IL 60484. Offers MFA. *Program availability:* Part-time. *Faculty:* 57 full-time (33 women), 72 part-time/adjunct (40 women). *Students:* 8 full-time (5 women), 8 part-time (3 women); includes 10 minority (9 Black or African American, non-Hispanic/Latino; 1 Two or more races, non-Hispanic/Latino). Average age 41. 2 applicants, 50% accepted, 1 enrolled. In 2019, 6 master's awarded. *Application deadline:* For fall admission, 4/1 for domestic students. Applications are processed on a rolling basis. Application fee: $50. Electronic applications accepted. *Expenses: Tuition, area resident:* Full-time $8472; part-time $353 per credit hour. Tuition, state resident: full-time $8472; part-time $353 per credit hour. Tuition, nonresident: full-time $16,944; part-time $706 per credit hour. *International tuition:* $16,944 full-time. *Required fees:* $2520; $105 per credit hour. $38 per term. Tuition and fees vary according to course load, degree level and program. *Financial support:* Application deadline: 5/1; applicants required to submit FAFSA. *Unit head:* Jason Zingsheim, Chair, Division of Arts and Letters, 708-534-5000 Ext. 7493, E-mail: jzingsheim@govst.edu. *Application contact:* Jason Zingsheim, Chair, Division of Arts and Letters, 708-534-5000 Ext. 7493, E-mail: jzingsheim@govst.edu.

Hollins University, Graduate Programs, Program in Screenwriting and Film Studies, Roanoke, VA 24020. Offers screenwriting (MFA); screenwriting and film studies (MA). *Program availability:* Part-time. *Degree requirements:* For master's, one foreign language, comprehensive exam, thesis. *Entrance requirements:* For master's, letters of recommendation, manuscript, transcript review, personal statement. Additional exam requirements/recommendations for international students: required—TOEFL (minimum score 550 paper-based; 80 iBT), IELTS (minimum score 6.5). Electronic applications accepted. *Expenses:* Contact institution.

Howard University, Cathy Hughes School of Communications, Department of Media, Journalism and Film, Washington, DC 20059-0002. Offers film (MFA). *Program availability:* Part-time. *Degree requirements:* For master's, thesis optional. *Entrance requirements:* For master's, GRE General Test, minimum GPA of 3.0.

Johns Hopkins University, Advanced Academic Programs, Program in Film and Media, Baltimore, MD 21218. Offers MA. *Program availability:* Part-time.

Lake Forest College, Graduate Program in Liberal Studies, Lake Forest, IL 60045. Offers American studies (MLS); cinema in East Asia (MLS); environmental studies (MLS); history (MLS); Medieval and Renaissance art (MLS); philosophy (MLS); Spanish (MLS); writing (MLS). *Program availability:* Part-time, evening/weekend. *Faculty:* 10 full-time (4 women). *Students:* 24 part-time (14 women). Average age 45. 10 applicants, 80% accepted, 3 enrolled. In 2019, 5 master's awarded. *Degree requirements:* For master's, thesis optional, 8 courses, including at least 3 interdisciplinary seminars. *Entrance requirements:* For master's, transcript, essay, interview. Additional exam requirements/recommendations for international students: required—TOEFL (minimum score 550 paper-based; 83 iBT); recommended—IELTS (minimum score 6.5). *Application deadline:* For fall admission, 8/15 priority date for domestic students, 7/15 priority date for international students; for spring admission, 12/15 priority date for domestic students, 11/15 priority date for international students. Applications are processed on a rolling basis. Application fee: $30. Electronic applications accepted. Application fee is waived when completed online. *Expenses:* Application fee = $30 — no other fees; tuition = $2,700/course. *Financial support:* In 2019–20, 2 students received support. Partial tuition grants (for full-time teachers) available. *Unit head:* Prof. D. L. LeMahieu, Director, 847-735-5133, Fax: 847-735-6291, E-mail: lemahieu@lakeforest.edu. *Application contact:* Prof. Carol Gayle, Associate Director, 847-735-5083, Fax: 847-735-6291, E-mail: gayle@lakeforest.edu.
Website: http://www.lakeforest.edu/academics/programs/mls/

Lindenwood University, Graduate Programs, School of Arts, Media, and Communications, St. Charles, MO 63301-1695. Offers advertising (MA); art history (MA); cinema and media arts (MFA); communications (MA); digital and Web design (MA); fashion and business design (MS); journalism (MA); mass communications (MA); social media and digital content (MS). *Program availability:* Part-time, 100% online. *Faculty:* 20 full-time (5 women), 15 part-time/adjunct (6 women). *Students:* 64 full-time (42 women), 76 part-time (57 women); includes 43 minority (20 Black or African American, non-Hispanic/Latino; 13 Hispanic/Latino; 10 Two or more races, non-Hispanic/Latino), 8 international. Average age 33. 145 applicants, 46% accepted, 56 enrolled. In 2019, 11 master's awarded. *Degree requirements:* For master's, thesis (for some programs), minimum cumulative GPA of 3.0. *Entrance requirements:* For master's, audition or interview, minimum GPA of 3.0, portfolio, letter of recommendation. Additional exam requirements/recommendations for international students: required—TOEFL (minimum score 553 paper-based; 81 iBT); recommended—IELTS (minimum score 6.5). *Application deadline:* For fall admission, 8/9 priority date for domestic students, 6/1 priority date for international students; for spring admission, 12/20 for domestic students, 11/1 priority date for international students; for summer admission, 5/15 priority date for domestic students, 3/27 priority date for international students. Applications are processed on a rolling basis. Application fee: $0 ($100 for international students). Electronic applications accepted. *Expenses: Tuition:* Full-time $8910; part-time $495 per credit. Tuition and fees vary according to course load, degree level and program. *Financial support:* In 2019–20, 23 students received support. Career-related internships or fieldwork, institutionally sponsored loans, scholarships/grants, tuition waivers (partial), and unspecified assistantships available. Financial award application deadline: 6/30; financial award applicants required to submit FAFSA. *Unit head:* Dr. Jason Lively, Dean, School of Arts, Media, and Communications, 636-949-4164, Fax: 636-949-4910, E-mail: JLively@lindenwood.edu. *Application contact:* Kara Schilli, Assistant Vice President, University Admissions, 636-949-4349, Fax: 636-949-4109, E-mail: adultadmissions@lindenwood.edu.
Website: https://www.lindenwood.edu/academics/academic-schools/school-of-arts-media-and-communications/

Lipscomb University, Program in Film and Creative Media, Nashville, TN 37204-3951. Offers writer/director (MFA); MFA/MBA. *Program availability:* Part-time, evening/weekend. *Degree requirements:* For master's, professional practicum, portfolio. *Entrance requirements:* For master's, GRE or MAT, 2 references, resume, video portfolio. Additional exam requirements/recommendations for international students: required—TOEFL (minimum score 570 paper-based; 80 iBT). Electronic applications accepted. *Expenses:* Contact institution.

Loyola Marymount University, School of Film and Television, Program in Film and Television Production, Los Angeles, CA 90094. Offers MFA. *Students:* 115 full-time (54 women); includes 46 minority (16 Black or African American, non-Hispanic/Latino; 8 Asian, non-Hispanic/Latino; 17 Hispanic/Latino; 5 Two or more races, non-Hispanic/Latino), 46 international. Average age 26. 361 applicants, 30% accepted. In 2019, 22 master's awarded. *Entrance requirements:* For master's, GRE Score (waived with GPA 3.0+), graduate application, personal statement, 2 letters of recommendation (one from current employer), official transcripts, visual samples, creative samples, video recording, portfolio list, 1-page resume, $500 deposit. Additional exam requirements/recommendations for international students: required—TOEFL, IELTS. *Application deadline:* For fall admission, 12/4 for domestic students. Application fee: $50. Electronic applications accepted. *Financial support:* Career-related internships or fieldwork, Federal Work-Study, scholarships/grants, and unspecified assistantships available. Financial award applicants required to submit FAFSA. *Unit head:* Dr. Eugene Brancolini, Director, Film and Television Production, 310-258-8891, E-mail: ebrancol@lmu.edu. *Application contact:* Ammar Dalal, Assistant Vice Provost for Graduate Enrollment, 310-338-2721, Fax: 310-338-6086, E-mail: graduateadmission@lmu.edu.
Website: http://sftv.lmu.edu/academics/graduateprograms/filmandtvproduction

Loyola Marymount University, School of Film and Television, Program in Writing and Producing for Television, Los Angeles, CA 90094. Offers MFA. *Students:* 50 full-time (38 women); includes 18 minority (10 Black or African American, non-Hispanic/Latino; 3 Hispanic/Latino; 5 Two or more races, non-Hispanic/Latino), 1 international. Average age 25. 83 applicants, 37% accepted. In 2019, 12 master's awarded. *Entrance requirements:* For master's, GRE Score (waived with GPA 3.0+), graduate application, personal statement, 2 letters of recommendation (one from current employer), official transcripts, visual samples, creative samples, video recording, portfolio list, 1-page resume, $500 deposit. Additional exam requirements/recommendations for international students: required—TOEFL, IELTS. *Application deadline:* For fall admission, 12/4 for domestic students. Application fee: $50. Electronic applications accepted. *Financial support:* Career-related internships or fieldwork, Federal Work-Study, scholarships/grants, and unspecified assistantships available. Financial award applicants required to submit FAFSA. *Unit head:* Patricia Meyer, Director, Writing and Producing for Television, E-mail: Patricia.Meyer@lmu.edu. *Application contact:* Ammar Dalal, Assistant Vice Provost for Graduate Enrollment, 310-338-2721, Fax: 310-338-6086, E-mail: graduateadmission@lmu.edu.
Website: http://sftv.lmu.edu/academics/graduateprograms/writingandproducingfortv

Maryland Institute College of Art, Graduate Studies, Program in Filmmaking, Baltimore, MD 21201. Offers MFA. *Degree requirements:* For master's, thesis film and screening, written thesis. *Entrance requirements:* For master's, portfolio, writing samples, bachelor's degree in any field. Additional exam requirements/recommendations for international students: required—TOEFL (minimum score 550 paper-based; 80 iBT), IELTS (minimum score 6.5). Electronic applications accepted. *Expenses:* Contact institution.

Massachusetts College of Art and Design, Graduate Programs, MFA Program, Boston, MA 02115-5882. Offers 2D fine arts (MFA), including painting, printmaking; 3D fine arts (MFA), including ceramics, fibers, glass, jewelry and metalsmithing, sculpture; design (MFA, Postbaccalaureate Certificate), including dynamic media; fine arts (MFA), including interdisciplinary; media arts (MFA, Postbaccalaureate Certificate), including film/video (MFA), photography. *Accreditation:* NASAD. *Faculty:* 1 (woman) full-time, 29 part-time/adjunct (14 women). *Students:* 44 full-time (26 women), 28 part-time (17 women); includes 8 minority (5 Asian, non-Hispanic/Latino; 3 Hispanic/Latino), 18 international. 202 applicants, 44% accepted, 35 enrolled. In 2019, 30 master's, 8 other advanced degrees awarded. *Degree requirements:* For master's, thesis, thesis exhibition (for fine arts programs); thesis project and document (for design/dynamic media program). *Entrance requirements:* For master's, portfolio, college transcripts, resume, statement of purpose, letters of reference, interview, 6 credits of art history taken prior to or during MFA program; for Postbaccalaureate Certificate, portfolio, college transcripts, resume, statement of purpose, letters of reference, interview. Additional exam requirements/recommendations for international students: required—TOEFL (minimum score 550 paper-based, 85 iBT) or IELTS (6). *Application deadline:* For fall admission, 1/20 priority date for domestic and international students; for summer admission, 1/20 priority date for domestic and international students. Applications are processed on a rolling basis. Application fee: $90. Electronic applications accepted. *Expenses:* Contact institution. *Financial support:* Research assistantships, teaching assistantships, career-related internships or fieldwork, scholarships/grants, tuition waivers (partial), unspecified assistantships, and adjunct co-teaching positions available. Support available to part-time students. Financial award application deadline: 1/20; financial award applicants required to submit FAFSA. *Unit head:* Lucinda Bliss, Dean of Graduate Studies, 617-879-7157, E-mail: gradadmissions@massart.edu. *Application contact:* Stacy Petersen, Associate Director, Graduate Admissions and Operations, 617-879-7238, E-mail: gradadmissions@massart.edu.
Website: http://www.massart.edu/Admissions/Graduate_Programs.html

Miami International University of Art & Design, Program in Film, Miami, FL 33132-1418. Offers MFA. *Program availability:* Online learning.

Minneapolis College of Art and Design, Master of Fine Arts in Visual Studies, Minneapolis, MN 55404-4347. Offers animation (MFA); comic art (MFA); drawing (MFA); filmmaking (MFA); fine arts (MFA); furniture design (MFA); graphic design (MFA); illustration (MFA); interactive media (MFA); painting (MFA); photography (MFA); printmaking (MFA); sculpture (MFA). *Accreditation:* NASAD. *Program availability:* Part-time. *Students:* 86 applicants, 44% accepted, 9 enrolled. *Degree requirements:* For master's, thesis, thesis exhibit. *Entrance requirements:* Additional exam requirements/recommendations for international students: required—TOEFL (minimum score 550 paper-based; 79 iBT), IELTS (minimum score 6.5), Duolingo English Test accepted with a minimum score of 100 *Application deadline:* For fall admission, 2/1 for domestic and international students. Application fee: $50. Electronic applications accepted. *Expenses: Tuition:* Full-time $41,344. *Required fees:* $450. One-time fee: $300 full-time. *Financial support:* In 2019–20, 15 teaching assistantships (averaging $6,000 per year) were awarded; career-related internships or fieldwork, Federal Work-Study, scholarships/grants, and unspecified assistantships also available. Support available to part-time students. Financial award application deadline: 3/15; financial award applicants required to submit FAFSA. *Unit head:* Ellen Mueller, Director, MFA Program, 612-874-3629, E-mail: emueller@mcad.edu. *Application contact:* Mary Kazura, Director of Admissions, 612-874-3668, Fax: 612-874-3701, E-mail: mkazura@mcad.edu.
Website: http://mcad.edu/mfa

Missouri State University, Graduate College, Interdisciplinary Program in Professional Studies, Springfield, MO 65897. Offers administrative studies (Certificate); applied communication (MS); criminal justice (MS); environmental management (MS); homeland security (MS); individualized (MS); professional studies (MS); screenwriting and producing (MS); sports management (MS). *Program availability:* Part-time, evening/weekend, 100% online, blended/hybrid learning. *Degree requirements:* For master's, comprehensive exam, thesis or alternative. *Entrance requirements:* For master's, GRE, GMAT (if GPA less than 3.0). Additional exam requirements/recommendations for international students: required—TOEFL (minimum score 550 paper-based; 79 iBT), IELTS (minimum score 6). Electronic applications accepted. *Expenses: Tuition, area resident:* Full-time $2600; part-time $1735 per credit hour. Tuition, nonresident: full-time $5240; part-time $3495 per credit hour. *International tuition:* $5240 full-time. *Required fees:* $530; $438 per credit hour. Tuition and fees vary according to class time, course level, course load, degree level, campus/location and program.

Montana State University, The Graduate School, College of Arts and Architecture, School of Film and Photography, Bozeman, MT 59717. Offers science and natural history filmmaking (MFA). *Program availability:* Part-time. *Degree requirements:* For master's, comprehensive exam. *Entrance requirements:* For master's, GRE General Test, minimum GPA of 3.0, resume, 3 letters of recommendation. Additional exam requirements/recommendations for international students: required—TOEFL (minimum score 550 paper-based). Electronic applications accepted.

Mount Saint Mary's University, Graduate Division, Los Angeles, CA 90049. Offers business administration (MBA); counseling psychology (MS); creative writing (MFA); education (MS, Certificate); film and television (MFA); health policy and management (MS); humanities (MA); nursing (MSN, Certificate); physical therapy (DPT); religious studies (MA). *Program availability:* Part-time, evening/weekend. *Entrance requirements:* Additional exam requirements/recommendations for international students: required—TOEFL. Electronic applications accepted. *Expenses: Tuition:* Full-time $18,648; part-time $9324 per year. *Required fees:* $540; $540 per unit.

National University, School of Professional Studies, La Jolla, CA 92037-1011. Offers criminal justice (MCJ); digital cinema production (MFA); digital journalism (MA); homeland security and emergency management (MS); juvenile justice (MS); professional screenwriting (MFA); public administration (MPA), including human resource management, organizational leadership. *Program availability:* Part-time, evening/weekend, 100% online, blended/hybrid learning. *Degree requirements:* For master's, thesis (for some programs). *Entrance requirements:* For master's, interview, minimum GPA of 2.5. Additional exam requirements/recommendations for international students: required—TOEFL (minimum score 550 paper-based; 79 iBT), IELTS (minimum score 6). Electronic applications accepted. *Expenses: Tuition:* Full-time $442; part-time $442 per unit.

New York Film Academy, Program in Filmmaking–Los Angeles, Burbank, CA 91505. Offers acting for film (MFA); cinematography (MFA); documentary film (MFA); film and media production (MA); filmmaking (MFA); game design (MFA); photography (MFA); producing (MA, MFA); screenwriting (MA, MFA). *Accreditation:* NASAD.

New York Film Academy, Program in Filmmaking–South Beach, Florida, Miami Beach, FL 33139. Offers acting for film (MFA); cinematography (MFA); documentary film (MFA); film and media production (MA); filmmaking (MFA); game design (MFA); photography (MFA); producing (MA, MFA); screenwriting (MA, MFA).

New York University, Tisch School of the Arts, Kanbar Institute of Film and Television, New York, NY 10012-1019. Offers MFA. *Degree requirements:* For master's, 4 films. *Entrance requirements:* For master's, artistic portfolio, personal essay, bachelor's degree. Additional exam requirements/recommendations for international students: required—TOEFL, IELTS (minimum score 7). Electronic applications accepted.

New York University, Tisch School of the Arts, Program in Moving Image Archiving and Preservation, New York, NY 10012. Offers MA. *Degree requirements:* For master's, thesis. *Entrance requirements:* Additional exam requirements/recommendations for international students: required—TOEFL. Electronic applications accepted. *Expenses:* Contact institution.

Northwestern University, The Graduate School, School of Communication, Department of Radio, Television and Film, Evanston, IL 60208. Offers documentary media (MFA); screen cultures (MA, PhD); writing for the screen and stage (MFA). *Program availability:* Part-time. Terminal master's awarded for partial completion of doctoral program. *Degree requirements:* For master's, comprehensive exam or thesis; for doctorate, thesis/dissertation, qualifying exam. *Entrance requirements:* For master's and doctorate, GRE General Test. Additional exam requirements/recommendations for international students: required—TOEFL. Electronic applications accepted.

Ohio University, Graduate College, College of Fine Arts, School of Film, Athens, OH 45701-2979. Offers film (MFA); film studies (MA). *Degree requirements:* For master's, one foreign language, thesis. *Entrance requirements:* Additional exam requirements/recommendations for international students: required—TOEFL (minimum score 550 paper-based; 80 iBT) or IELTS (minimum score 6.5). Electronic applications accepted.

Quinnipiac University, School of Communications, Program in Interactive Media and Communications, Hamden, CT 06518-1940. Offers interactive media (MS); media design (MS); social media (MS); UX design (MS). *Program availability:* Part-time, evening/weekend, online only, 100% online. *Entrance requirements:* For master's, minimum GPA of 3.0, portfolio or writing sample. Additional exam requirements/recommendations for international students: required—TOEFL (minimum score 575 paper-based; 90 iBT), IELTS (minimum score 6.5). Electronic applications accepted. *Expenses:* Contact institution.

Regent University, Graduate School, School of Communication and the Arts, Virginia Beach, VA 23464-9800. Offers acting (MFA); communication (MA, PhD), including media and arts management and promotion (MA), political communication (MA), strategic communication (MA), technical communication (MA); film and TV (MA), including producing (MA, MFA), production, script writing; film-television (MFA), including directing, producing (MA, MFA), script and screenwriting; journalism (MA); theatre (MA). *Program availability:* Part-time, evening/weekend, 100% online, blended/hybrid learning. *Degree requirements:* For master's, thesis or alternative; for doctorate, thesis/dissertation. *Entrance requirements:* For master's, transcripts, writing sample, resume, audition (for MFA programs); for doctorate, GRE General Test, resume, writing sample, recommendations, interview, transcripts, personal goals statement. Additional exam requirements/recommendations for international students: required—TOEFL (minimum score 577 paper-based). Electronic applications accepted. *Expenses:* Contact institution.

Rochester Institute of Technology, Graduate Enrollment Services, College of Imaging Arts and Sciences, School of Film and Animation, MFA Program in Film and Animation, Rochester, NY 14623-5603. Offers MFA. *Program availability:* Part-time. *Degree requirements:* For master's, thesis. *Entrance requirements:* For master's, portfolio, two-to-three minute online self-portrait video, personal statement, two letters of recommendation. Additional exam requirements/recommendations for international students: required—TOEFL (minimum score 550 paper-based; 88 iBT), IELTS (minimum score 6.5), PTE (minimum score 58). Electronic applications accepted.

Rochester Institute of Technology, Graduate Enrollment Services, College of Imaging Arts and Sciences, School of Photographic Arts and Sciences, MFA Program in Photography and Related Media, Rochester, NY 14623-5603. Offers MFA. *Accreditation:* NASAD. *Program availability:* Part-time. *Degree requirements:* For master's, thesis, exhibit. *Entrance requirements:* For master's, portfolio and artist's statement, personal statement, resume, three letters of recommendation. Additional exam requirements/recommendations for international students: required—TOEFL (minimum score 550 paper-based; 88 iBT), IELTS (minimum score 6.5), PTE (minimum score 58). Electronic applications accepted.

Sacred Heart University, Graduate Programs, College of Arts and Sciences, Department of Communication, Fairfield, CT 06825. Offers corporate communications and public relations (MA Comm); digital multimedia journalism (MA Comm); digital multimedia production (MA Comm); film and television production (MA); media literacy and digital culture (MA), including children, health and media, media and social justice, political action and media production; sports communication and media (MA), including athletic communications and promotions, sports broadcasting. *Program availability:* Part-time, evening/weekend. *Degree requirements:* For master's, thesis or alternative. *Entrance requirements:* For master's, bachelor's degree. Additional exam requirements/recommendations for international students: required—TOEFL (minimum score 570 paper-based, 80 iBT), TWE, or IELTS (6.5). Electronic applications accepted. *Expenses:* Contact institution.

St. Thomas University - Florida, School of Leadership Studies, Program in Electronic Media, Miami Gardens, FL 33054-6459. Offers MA.

San Diego State University, Graduate and Research Affairs, College of Professional Studies and Fine Arts, School of Theater, Television and Film, Program in Film and Television Production, San Diego, CA 92182. Offers MFA. *Entrance requirements:* For master's, GRE General Test, 3 letters of recommendation, resume, sample reel, influential book list, influential films list, hobby list. Additional exam requirements/recommendations for international students: required—TOEFL. Electronic applications accepted.

San Francisco State University, Division of Graduate Studies, College of Liberal and Creative Arts, School of Cinema, San Francisco, CA 94132-1722. Offers MA, MFA. *Expenses: Tuition, area resident:* Full-time $7176; part-time $4164 per year. Tuition, state resident: full-time $7176; part-time $4164 per year. Tuition, nonresident: full-time $16,680; part-time $396 per unit. *International tuition:* $16,680 full-time. *Required fees:* $1524; $1524 per unit. $762 per semester. Tuition and fees vary according to degree level and program. *Unit head:* Dr. Celine Shimizu, Director, 415-338-1629, Fax: 415-338-6159, E-mail: shimizu@sfsu.edu. *Application contact:* Prof. Steve Choe, MA Coordinator, 415-338-1072, Fax: 415-338-6159, E-mail: stevec3@sfsu.edu.
Website: http://www.cinema.sfsu.edu/

San Jose State University, Program in Film and Theatre, San Jose, CA 95192-0001. Offers theatre arts (MA). *Accreditation:* NAST. *Degree requirements:* For master's, written exam. *Entrance requirements:* Additional exam requirements/recommendations for international students: required—TOEFL (minimum score 570 paper-based). Electronic applications accepted. *Expenses: Tuition, area resident:* Full-time $7176; part-time $4164 per credit hour. Tuition, state resident: full-time $7176; part-time $4164 per credit hour. Tuition, nonresident: full-time $7176; part-time $4165 per credit hour. *International tuition:* $7176 full-time. *Required fees:* $2110; $2110.

Savannah College of Art and Design, Program in Animation, Savannah, GA 31402-3146. Offers MA, MFA. *Program availability:* Part-time, 100% online. *Degree requirements:* For master's, final project (for MA); thesis (for MFA). *Entrance requirements:* For master's, GRE (recommended), portfolio (submitted in digital format), audition or writing submission, resume, statement of purpose, two letters of recommendation. Additional exam requirements/recommendations for international students: recommended—TOEFL (minimum score 550 paper-based; 85 iBT), IELTS (minimum score 6.5). Electronic applications accepted.

Savannah College of Art and Design, Program in Film and Television, Savannah, GA 31402-3146. Offers MA, MFA. *Program availability:* Part-time. *Degree requirements:* For master's, final project (for MA); thesis (for MFA). *Entrance requirements:* For master's, GRE (recommended), portfolio (submitted in digital format), audition or writing submission, resume, statement of purpose, two letters of recommendation. Additional exam requirements/recommendations for international students: recommended—TOEFL (minimum score 550 paper-based; 85 iBT), IELTS (minimum score 6.5). Electronic applications accepted.

Savannah College of Art and Design, Program in Sound Design, Savannah, GA 31402-3146. Offers MA, MFA. *Program availability:* Part-time. *Degree requirements:* For master's, final project (for MA); thesis (for MFA). *Entrance requirements:* For master's, GRE (recommended), portfolio (submitted in digital format), audition or writing submission, resume, statement of purpose, two letters of recommendation. Additional exam requirements/recommendations for international students: recommended—TOEFL (minimum score 550 paper-based; 85 iBT), IELTS (minimum score 6.5). Electronic applications accepted.

School of Visual Arts, Graduate Programs, Directing Department, New York, NY 10010-3994. Offers MPS. *Degree requirements:* For master's, thesis, 36 credits; minimum GPA of 3.0; completion and marketing of own thesis film. *Entrance requirements:* For master's, portfolio. Additional exam requirements/recommendations for international students: required—TOEFL (minimum score 550 paper-based; 79 iBT).

School of Visual Arts, Graduate Programs, Program in Photography, Video and Related Media, New York, NY 10010-3994. Offers MFA. *Accreditation:* NASAD. *Degree requirements:* For master's, thesis, 60 credits; minimum GPA of 3.3; thesis project. *Entrance requirements:* For master's, portfolio (still images and/or videos) submitted through SlideRoom. Additional exam requirements/recommendations for international students: required—TOEFL (minimum score 550 paper-based; 79 iBT). Electronic applications accepted.

School of Visual Arts, Graduate Programs, Social Documentary Film Department, New York, NY 10010-3994. Offers MFA. *Degree requirements:* For master's, thesis, 60 credits; minimum cumulative GPA of 3.0; residency of two academic years. *Entrance requirements:* For master's, concise treatment for documentary film production; video work or still imagery; visual documentation of a subject (for applicants without prior filmmaking experience). Additional exam requirements/recommendations for international students: required—TOEFL (minimum score 550 paper-based; 79 iBT). Electronic applications accepted. *Expenses:* Contact institution.

Stephen F. Austin State University, Graduate School, College of Fine Arts, School of Art, Nacogdoches, TX 75962. Offers art (MA); art education (MAAE); design (MFA); drawing (MFA); filmmaking (MFA); painting (MFA); sculpture (MFA). *Accreditation:* NASAD. *Program availability:* Part-time. *Degree requirements:* For master's, comprehensive exam, thesis, exhibit. *Entrance requirements:* For master's, GRE General Test, portfolio. Additional exam requirements/recommendations for international students: required—TOEFL.

Stevens Institute of Technology, Graduate School, Charles V. Schaefer Jr. School of Engineering and Science, Interdisciplinary Program, Hoboken, NJ 07030. Offers MS. *Program availability:* Part-time, evening/weekend. *Faculty:* 276 full-time (74 women), 168 part-time/adjunct (33 women). *Students:* 4 full-time (3 women), 2 part-time (0 women), 3 international. Average age 29. In 2019, 1 master's awarded. *Degree requirements:* For master's, thesis optional, minimum B average in major field and overall. *Entrance requirements:* For master's, International applicants must submit TOEFL/IELTS scores and fulfill the English Language Proficiency Requirement. Applicants to full-time programs who do not qualify for a score waiver are required to submit GRE/GMAT scores. Additional exam requirements/recommendations for international students: required—TOEFL (minimum score 74 iBT), IELTS (minimum score 6). *Application deadline:* For fall admission, 4/15 for domestic and international students; for spring admission, 11/1 for domestic and international students; for summer admission, 5/1 for domestic students. Applications are processed on a rolling basis. Electronic applications accepted. *Expenses: Tuition:* Full-time $52,134. *Required fees:* $1880. Tuition and fees vary according to course load. *Financial support:* Fellowships, research assistantships, teaching assistantships, career-related internships or fieldwork, Federal Work-Study, scholarships/grants, and unspecified assistantships available. Financial award application deadline: 2/15; financial award applicants required to submit FAFSA. *Unit head:* Dr. Jean Zu, Dean of SES, 201-216.8233, Fax: 201-216.8372, E-mail: Jean.Zu@stevens.edu. *Application contact:* Graduate Admissions, 888-783-8367, Fax: 888-555-1306, E-mail: graduate@stevens.edu.

Stony Brook University, State University of New York, Stony Brook Southampton, Program in Film, Stony Brook, NY 11794. Offers MFA. *Faculty:* 7 full-time (4 women), 10 part-time/adjunct (3 women). *Students:* 35 full-time (16 women), 24 part-time (15 women); includes 11 minority (3 Black or African American, non-Hispanic/Latino; 6 Asian, non-Hispanic/Latino; 1 Hispanic/Latino; 1 Two or more races, non-Hispanic/Latino), 5 international. 45 applicants, 67% accepted, 18 enrolled. In 2019, 7 master's awarded. *Entrance requirements:* Additional exam requirements/recommendations for international students: required—TOEFL (minimum score 85 iBT), IELTS (minimum score 6.5). *Application deadline:* For fall admission, 1/15 for domestic students; for spring admission, 10/1 for domestic students. Application fee: $100. *Expenses:* Contact institution. *Financial support:* Research assistantships and teaching assistantships available. *Unit head:* Magdalene Brandeis, Director, 631-632-5030, Fax: 631-982-7318, E-mail: magdalene.brandeis@stonybrook.edu. *Application contact:* Margaret S. Grigonis, Administrative Coordinator, 631-632-5028, Fax: 631-982-7318, E-mail: margaret.grigonis@stonybrook.edu.
Website: http://www.stonybrook.edu/southampton/mfa/film/index.html

Film, Television, and Video Production

Syracuse University, College of Visual and Performing Arts, MFA Program in Film, Syracuse, NY 13244. Offers MFA. *Entrance requirements:* For master's, portfolio, artist statement, three letters of recommendation, academic transcripts, personal statement/essay, resume. Additional exam requirements/recommendations for international students: required—TOEFL (minimum score 100 iBT). Electronic applications accepted.

Temple University, Center for the Performing and Cinematic Arts, School of Theater, Film and Media Arts, Department of Film and Media Arts, Philadelphia, PA 19122-6096. Offers MA, MFA. *Program availability:* Part-time. *Faculty:* 20 full-time (10 women), 23 part-time/adjunct (5 women). *Students:* 37 full-time (18 women), 4 part-time (2 women); includes 12 minority (5 Black or African American, non-Hispanic/Latino; 1 Asian, non-Hispanic/Latino; 2 Hispanic/Latino; 4 Two or more races, non-Hispanic/Latino), 14 international. 66 applicants, 47% accepted, 17 enrolled. In 2019, 10 master's awarded. *Degree requirements:* For master's, comprehensive exam (for some programs). *Entrance requirements:* For master's, standardized test scores (optional), statement of goals, portfolio. Additional exam requirements/recommendations for international students: required—TOEFL (minimum score 600 paper-based; 100 iBT), IELTS, PTE, one of three is required. *Application deadline:* For fall admission, 1/11 for domestic students, 12/1 for international students. Application fee: $60. Electronic applications accepted. *Expenses:* Contact institution. *Financial support:* Fellowships, teaching assistantships, Federal Work-Study, and unspecified assistantships available. Financial award application deadline: 3/1; financial award applicants required to submit FAFSA. *Unit head:* Paul Swann, Chair, Department of Film and Media Arts; Professor, 215-204-1735, E-mail: paul.swann@temple.edu. *Application contact:* Paury Flowers, Recruitment Coordinator, CPCA: Admin. Office, 215-777-9135, E-mail: pflowers@temple.edu.
Website: https://tfma.temple.edu/fma

Universidad Autonoma de Guadalajara, Graduate Programs, Guadalajara, Mexico. Offers administrative law and justice (LL M); advertising and corporate communications (MA); architecture (M Arch); business (MBA); computational science (MCC); education (Ed M, Ed D); English-Spanish translation (MA); entrepreneurship and management (MBA); integrated management of digital animation (MA); international business (MIB); international corporate law (LL M); Internet technologies (MS); manufacturing systems (MMS); occupational health (MS); philosophy (MA, PhD); power electronics (MS); quality systems (MQS); renewable energy (MS); social evaluation of projects (MBA); strategic market research (MBA); tax law (MA); teaching mathematics (MA).

The University of British Columbia, Faculty of Arts, Creative Writing Program, Vancouver, BC V6T 1Z1, Canada. Offers creative writing (MFA); creative writing and theatre (MFA); film production and creative writing (MFA). *Program availability:* Part-time, online learning. *Degree requirements:* For master's, thesis. *Entrance requirements:* For master's, sample of written work. Additional exam requirements/recommendations for international students: required—TOEFL. Electronic applications accepted. *Expenses:* Contact institution.

The University of British Columbia, Faculty of Arts, Department of Theatre and Film, Film Program, Vancouver, BC V6T 1Z2, Canada. Offers film production (MFA); film studies (MA). *Degree requirements:* For master's, variable foreign language requirement, comprehensive exam, thesis (MA); thesis or project (MFA). *Entrance requirements:* For master's, portfolio (MFA). Additional exam requirements/recommendations for international students: required—TOEFL. *Expenses:* Contact institution.

University of California, Los Angeles, Graduate Division, School of Theater, Film and Television, Department of Film, Television, and Digital Media, Los Angeles, CA 90034. Offers animation (MFA); cinema and media studies (MA, PhD); cinematography (MFA); production (MFA); screenwriting (MFA). *Degree requirements:* For master's, comprehensive exam; for doctorate, one foreign language, thesis/dissertation, oral and written qualifying exams. *Entrance requirements:* For master's, GRE General Test (for MA applicants), bachelor's degree; minimum undergraduate GPA of 3.0 (or its equivalent if letter grade system not used); writing sample (for MA); for doctorate, GRE General Test, master's degree; minimum undergraduate GPA of 3.0 (or its equivalent if letter grade system not used); writing sample. Additional exam requirements/recommendations for international students: required—TOEFL. Electronic applications accepted. *Expenses:* Contact institution.

University of California, Los Angeles, Graduate Division, School of Theater, Film and Television, Interdepartmental Program in Moving Image Archive Studies, Los Angeles, CA 90095. Offers MA. *Degree requirements:* For master's, comprehensive exam, thesis. *Entrance requirements:* For master's, bachelor's degree; minimum undergraduate GPA of 3.0 (or its equivalent if letter grade system not used); writing sample. Additional exam requirements/recommendations for international students: required—TOEFL. Electronic applications accepted.

University of California, Santa Barbara, Graduate Division, College of Letters and Sciences, Division of Humanities and Fine Arts, Department of Film and Media Studies, Santa Barbara, CA 93106-4010. Offers PhD, MA/PhD. Terminal master's awarded for partial completion of doctoral program. *Degree requirements:* For doctorate, one foreign language, comprehensive exam, thesis/dissertation. *Entrance requirements:* For doctorate, GRE, MA in film/media studies or equivalent. Additional exam requirements/recommendations for international students: required—TOEFL (minimum score 600 paper-based; 100 iBT), IELTS (minimum score 7). Electronic applications accepted.

University of Central Arkansas, Graduate School, College of Fine Arts and Communication, Program in Digital Filmmaking, Conway, AR 72035-0001. Offers MFA. *Accreditation:* NASAD. *Degree requirements:* For master's, thesis. *Entrance requirements:* For master's, GRE General Test, minimum GPA of 2.7. Additional exam requirements/recommendations for international students: required—TOEFL (minimum score 550 paper-based). Electronic applications accepted.

University of Central Florida, College of Arts and Humanities, School of Visual Arts and Design, Orlando, FL 32816. Offers digital media (MA); emerging media (MFA), including animation and visual effects, digital media, entrepreneurial digital cinema, studio art and the computer. *Program availability:* Part-time. *Students:* 41 full-time (17 women), 5 part-time (2 women); includes 23 minority (6 Black or African American, non-Hispanic/Latino; 1 Asian, non-Hispanic/Latino; 15 Hispanic/Latino; 1 Two or more races, non-Hispanic/Latino), 2 international. Average age 30. 41 applicants, 56% accepted, 18 enrolled. In 2019, 5 master's awarded. *Degree requirements:* For master's, comprehensive exam, thesis or alternative. *Entrance requirements:* For master's, GRE, letter of recommendation. Additional exam requirements/recommendations for international students: required—TOEFL. *Application deadline:* For fall admission, 7/1 for domestic students. Application fee: $30. Electronic applications accepted. *Financial support:* In 2019–20, 22 students received support, including 10 fellowships with partial tuition reimbursements available (averaging $7,400 per year), 15 teaching assistantships with partial tuition reimbursements available (averaging $5,226 per year); scholarships/grants, health care benefits, and unspecified assistantships also available. Financial award application deadline: 3/1; financial award applicants required to submit FAFSA. *Unit head:* Dr. Rudy McDaniel, Director, 407-823-3145, E-mail: rudy@ucf.edu. *Application contact:* Associate Director, Graduate Admissions, 407-823-2766, Fax: 407-823-6442, E-mail: gradadmissions@ucf.edu.
Website: http://svad.cah.ucf.edu/

University of Colorado Boulder, Graduate School, College of Media, Communication and Information, Program in Critical Media Practices, Boulder, CO 80309. Offers interdisciplinary documentary media practices (MFA). Electronic applications accepted. Application fee is waived when completed online.

The University of Iowa, Graduate College, College of Liberal Arts and Sciences, Department of Cinema and Comparative Literature, Program in Film and Video Production, Iowa City, IA 52242-1316. Offers MFA. *Degree requirements:* For master's, thesis (for some programs), exam. *Entrance requirements:* For master's, GRE General Test, minimum GPA of 3.0. Additional exam requirements/recommendations for international students: required—TOEFL (minimum score 550 paper-based; 81 iBT). Electronic applications accepted.

University of Memphis, Graduate School, College of Communication and Fine Arts, Department of Communication and Film, Memphis, TN 38152. Offers communication (MA); communication arts (PhD); film and video production (MA). *Program availability:* Part-time. *Students:* 13 full-time (10 women), 31 part-time (18 women); includes 16 minority (13 Black or African American, non-Hispanic/Latino; 1 Asian, non-Hispanic/Latino; 1 Hispanic/Latino; 1 Two or more races, non-Hispanic/Latino), 2 international. Average age 36. 20 applicants, 100% accepted, 11 enrolled. In 2019, 9 master's, 3 doctorates awarded. *Degree requirements:* For master's, comprehensive exam, thesis or alternative, culminating project; for doctorate, comprehensive exam, thesis/dissertation. *Entrance requirements:* For master's and doctorate, GRE General Test, personal goal statement, letters of recommendation, writing sample. Additional exam requirements/recommendations for international students: required—TOEFL (minimum score 600 paper-based). *Application deadline:* For fall admission, 1/13 priority date for domestic students. Applications are processed on a rolling basis. Application fee: $35 ($60 for international students). *Expenses: Tuition, area resident:* Full-time $9216; part-time $512 per credit hour. Tuition, state resident: full-time $9216; part-time $512 per credit hour. Tuition, nonresident: full-time $12,672; part-time $704 per credit hour. *International tuition:* $16,128 full-time. *Required fees:* $1530; $85 per credit hour. Tuition and fees vary according to program. *Financial support:* Research assistantships with full tuition reimbursements, teaching assistantships with full tuition reimbursements, Federal Work-Study, scholarships/grants, and unspecified assistantships available. Financial award application deadline: 2/1; financial award applicants required to submit FAFSA. *Unit head:* Dr. Wendy Atkins-Sayre, Department Chair, 901-678-3012, E-mail: wltknssy@memphis.edu. *Application contact:* Dr. Marina Levina, Director of Graduate Studies, 901-678-3185, Fax: 901-678-4331, E-mail: mlevina@memphis.edu.
Website: https://www.memphis.edu/communication/

University of Miami, Graduate School, School of Communication, Coral Gables, FL 33124. Offers communication (PhD); communication studies (MA); film studies (MA, PhD); motion pictures (MFA), including production, producing, and screenwriting; print journalism (MA); public relations (MA); Spanish language journalism (MA); television broadcast journalism (MA). *Program availability:* Part-time. *Degree requirements:* For master's, comprehensive exam (for some programs), thesis (for some programs); for doctorate, comprehensive exam, thesis/dissertation. *Entrance requirements:* For master's, GRE General Test; for doctorate, GRE General Test, master's thesis or scholarly research. Additional exam requirements/recommendations for international students: required—TOEFL (minimum score 600 paper-based; 100 iBT). Electronic applications accepted.

University of Mississippi, Graduate School, College of Liberal Arts, University, MS 38677. Offers anthropology (MA); biology (MS, PhD); chemistry (MS, DA, PhD); creative writing (MFA); documentary expression (MFA); economics (MA, PhD); English (MA, PhD); experimental psychology (PhD); history (MA, PhD); mathematics (MS, PhD); modern languages (MA); music (MM); philosophy (MA); physics (MA, MS, PhD); political science (MA, PhD); Southern studies (MA); studio art (MFA). *Program availability:* Part-time. *Faculty:* 481 full-time (215 women), 71 part-time/adjunct (40 women). *Students:* 509 full-time (258 women), 55 part-time (21 women); includes 89 minority (40 Black or African American, non-Hispanic/Latino; 13 Asian, non-Hispanic/Latino; 25 Hispanic/Latino; 11 Two or more races, non-Hispanic/Latino), 157 international. Average age 29. In 2019, 119 master's, 51 doctorates awarded. *Degree requirements:* For doctorate, thesis/dissertation. *Entrance requirements:* For master's, GRE General Test, minimum GPA of 3.0; for doctorate, GRE General Test. Additional exam requirements/recommendations for international students: required—TOEFL. *Application deadline:* Applications are processed on a rolling basis. Application fee: $50. Electronic applications accepted. *Expenses:* Tuition, state resident: full-time $8718; part-time $484.25 per credit hour. Tuition, nonresident: full-time $24,990; part-time $1388.25 per credit hour. *Required fees:* $100; $4.16 per credit hour. *Financial support:* Fellowships, research assistantships, teaching assistantships, career-related internships or fieldwork, Federal Work-Study, institutionally sponsored loans, scholarships/grants, and unspecified assistantships available. Financial award application deadline: 3/1; financial award applicants required to submit FAFSA. *Unit head:* Dr. Lee Michael Cohen, Dean, 662-915-7177, Fax: 662-915-5792, E-mail: libarts@olemiss.edu. *Application contact:* Tameka Smith, Graduate Activities Specialist for Admissions, 662-915-7474, Fax: 662-915-7577, E-mail: gschool@olemiss.edu.
Website: ventress@olemiss.edu

University of Montana, Graduate School, College of Visual and Performing Arts, School of Media Arts, Missoula, MT 59812. Offers digital filmmaking (MFA); integrated digital media (MFA).

University of Nevada, Las Vegas, Graduate College, College of Fine Arts, Department of Film, Las Vegas, NV 89154-5015. Offers film/writing for dramatic media (MFA); writing for dramatic media (Certificate). *Program availability:* Part-time. *Faculty:* 3 full-time (0 women). *Students:* 7 full-time (4 women); includes 1 minority (Two or more races, non-Hispanic/Latino), 1 international. Average age 34. 13 applicants, 15% accepted, 2 enrolled. In 2019, 2 master's awarded. *Degree requirements:* For master's, thesis, creative project and defense; for Certificate, creative project and defense. *Entrance requirements:* For master's, writing sample. Additional exam requirements/recommendations for international students: required—TOEFL (minimum score 550 paper-based; 80 iBT), IELTS (minimum score 7). *Application deadline:* For fall admission, 1/15 for domestic and international students. Application fee: $60 ($95 for international students). Electronic applications accepted. *Expenses:* Contact institution. *Financial support:* In 2019–20, 8 students received support, including 8 teaching assistantships with full tuition reimbursements available (averaging $15,250 per year); institutionally sponsored loans, scholarships/grants, health care benefits, and unspecified assistantships also available. Financial award application deadline: 3/15; financial award applicants required to submit FAFSA. *Unit head:* Dr. Heather Addison, Chair/Professor, 702-895-3547, Fax: 702-895-4395, E-mail: film.chair@unlv.edu. *Application contact:* Sean Clark, Graduate Coordinator, 702-895-4210, Fax: 702-895-4194, E-mail: film.gradcoord@unlv.edu.
Website: http://film.unlv.edu/

University of New Orleans, Graduate School, College of Liberal Arts, Education and Human Development, Department of Film and Theatre, New Orleans, LA 70148. Offers design (MFA); film production (MFA); theatre performance (MFA), including acting, directing. *Accreditation:* NAST. *Degree requirements:* For master's, comprehensive exam, thesis. *Entrance requirements:* Additional exam requirements/recommendations for international students: required—TOEFL (minimum score 550 paper-based; 79 iBT), IELTS (minimum score 6.5). Electronic applications accepted.

The University of North Carolina at Greensboro, Graduate School, College of Arts and Sciences, Department of Media Studies, Greensboro, NC 27412-5001. Offers film and video production (MFA).

University of North Carolina School of the Arts, School of Filmmaking, Winston-Salem, NC 27127-2738. Offers creative producing (MFA); film music composition (MFA); screenwriting (MFA). *Entrance requirements:* For master's, audition, performance, portfolio, interview. Additional exam requirements/recommendations for international students: required—TOEFL. Electronic applications accepted.

University of North Texas, Toulouse Graduate School, Denton, TX 76203-5459. Offers accounting (MS); applied anthropology (MA, MS); applied behavior analysis (Certificate); applied geography (MA); applied technology and performance improvement (M Ed, MS); art education (MA); art history (MA); arts leadership (Certificate); audiology (Au D); behavior analysis (MS); behavioral science (PhD); biochemistry and molecular biology (MS); biology (MA, MS); biomedical engineering (MS); business analysis (MS); chemistry (MS); clinical health psychology (PhD); communication studies (MA, MS); computer engineering (MS); computer science (MS); counseling (M Ed, MS), including clinical mental health counseling (MS), college and university counseling, elementary school counseling, secondary school counseling; creative writing (MA); criminal justice (MS); curriculum and instruction (M Ed); decision sciences (MBA); design (MA, MFA), including fashion design (MFA), innovation studies, interior design (MFA); early childhood studies (MS); economics (MS); educational leadership (M Ed, Ed D); educational psychology (MS, PhD), including family studies (MS), gifted and talented (MS), human development (MS), learning and cognition (MS), research, measurement and evaluation (MS); electrical engineering (MS); emergency management (MPA); engineering technology (MS); English (MA); English as a second language (MA); environmental science (MS); finance (MBA, MS); financial management (MPA); French (MA); health services management (MBA); higher education (M Ed, Ed D); history (MA, MS); hospitality management (MS); human resources management (MPA); information science (MS); information systems (PhD); information technologies (MBA); interdisciplinary studies (MA, MS); international studies (MA); international sustainable tourism (MS); jazz studies (MM); journalism (MA, MJ, Graduate Certificate), including interactive and virtual digital communication (Graduate Certificate), narrative journalism (Graduate Certificate), public relations (Graduate Certificate); kinesiology (MS); linguistics (MA); local government management (MPA); logistics (PhD); logistics and supply chain management (MBA); long-term care, senior housing, and aging services (MA); management (PhD); marketing (MBA); mathematics (MA, MS); mechanical and energy engineering (MS, PhD); music (MA), including ethnomusicology, music theory, musicology, performance; music composition (PhD); music education (MM Ed, PhD); nonprofit management (MPA); operations and supply chain management (MBA); performance (MM, DMA); philosophy (MA); political science (MA); professional and technical communication (MA); radio, television and film (MA, MFA); rehabilitation counseling (Certificate); sociology (MA); Spanish (MA); special education (M Ed); speech-language pathology (MA); strategic management (MBA); studio art (MFA); teaching (M Ed); MBA/MS. *Program availability:* Part-time, evening/weekend, online learning. Terminal master's awarded for partial completion of doctoral program. *Degree requirements:* For master's, variable foreign language requirement, comprehensive exam (for some programs), thesis (for some programs); for doctorate, variable foreign language requirement, comprehensive exam (for some programs), thesis/dissertation; for other advanced degree, variable foreign language requirement, comprehensive exam (for some programs). *Entrance requirements:* For master's and doctorate, GRE, GMAT. Additional exam requirements/recommendations for international students: required—TOEFL (minimum score 550 paper-based; 79 iBT). Electronic applications accepted.

University of Regina, Faculty of Graduate Studies and Research, Faculty of Media, Art, and Performance, Department of Film, Regina, SK S4S 0A2, Canada. Offers media production (MFA); media studies (MA). *Program availability:* Part-time. *Faculty:* 17 full-time (8 women). *Students:* 21 full-time (15 women), 7 part-time (5 women). Average age 30. 23 applicants, 30% accepted. In 2019, 3 master's awarded. *Degree requirements:* For master's, thesis (for some programs), project. *Entrance requirements:* For master's, two writing samples (for MA); media-based support material (for MFA). Additional exam requirements/recommendations for international students: required—TOEFL (minimum score 600 paper-based; 93 iBT), IELTS (minimum score 7), PTE (minimum score 65), other options are CAEL, MELAB, Cantest and U of R ESL. *Application deadline:* For fall admission, 1/15 for domestic and international students. Application fee: $100 Canadian dollars. Electronic applications accepted. *Expenses: Tuition:* Full-time $6684 Canadian dollars. *Required fees:* $100 Canadian dollars; $3351.45 Canadian dollars per trimester. $1117.15 Canadian dollars per semester. Tuition and fees vary according to course level, course load, degree level and program. *Financial support:* Fellowships, research assistantships, teaching assistantships, career-related internships or fieldwork, Federal Work-Study, scholarships/grants, unspecified assistantships, and travel award and Graduate Scholarship Base funds available. Support available to part-time students. Financial award application deadline: 9/30. *Unit head:* Dr. Mark Wihak, Department Head, 306-337-2233, E-mail: mark.wihak@uregina.ca. *Application contact:* Dr. Christina Stojanova, Graduate Coordinator, 306-585-5690, E-mail: christina.stojanova@uregina.ca.

University of Rhode Island, Graduate School, College of Arts and Sciences, Department of English, Kingston, RI 02881. Offers American literature and culture (PhD); British literature and culture (PhD); creative writing (PhD); critical theories (PhD); English (MA); film (PhD); gender studies (PhD); MLIS/MA. *Program availability:* Part-time. *Faculty:* 18 full-time (10 women). *Students:* 29 full-time (19 women), 11 part-time (7 women); includes 2 minority (both Black or African American, non-Hispanic/Latino), 8 international. 15 applicants, 40% accepted, 6 enrolled. In 2019, 2 master's, 9 doctorates awarded. *Entrance requirements:* Additional exam requirements/recommendations for international students: required—TOEFL (minimum score 91 iBT). *Application deadline:* For fall admission, 1/15 for domestic and international students. Application fee: $65. Electronic applications accepted. *Expenses: Tuition, area resident:* Full-time $13,734; part-time $763 per credit. Tuition, state resident: full-time $13,734; part-time $763 per credit. Tuition, nonresident: full-time $26,512; part-time $1473 per credit. *International tuition:* $26,512 full-time. *Required fees:* $1780; $52 per credit. $35 per term. One-time fee: $165. *Financial support:* In 2019–20, 24 teaching assistantships with tuition reimbursements (averaging $19,520 per year) were awarded. Financial award application deadline: 1/15; financial award applicants required to submit FAFSA. *Unit head:* Dr. Travis Williams, Chair, 401-874-9501, E-mail: tdwilliams@uri.edu. *Application contact:* Dr. David Faflik, Director of Graduate Studies, 401-874-4670, E-mail: faflik@uri.edu.
Website: http://www.uri.edu/artsci/eng/

University of Southern California, Graduate School, School of Cinematic Arts, Division of Film and Television Production, Los Angeles, CA 90089. Offers MFA. Terminal master's awarded for partial completion of doctoral program. *Degree requirements:* For master's, advanced project. *Entrance requirements:* Additional exam requirements/recommendations for international students: required—TOEFL (minimum score 600 paper-based). Electronic applications accepted.

University of Southern California, Graduate School, School of Cinematic Arts, John C. Hench Division of Animation and Digital Arts, Los Angeles, CA 90089. Offers MFA. *Degree requirements:* For master's, thesis, digital media and research documentation. *Entrance requirements:* Additional exam requirements/recommendations for international students: recommended—TOEFL. Electronic applications accepted. *Expenses:* Contact institution.

University of Southern California, Graduate School, School of Cinematic Arts, John Wells Division of Writing for Screen and Television, Los Angeles, CA 90089. Offers MFA. *Degree requirements:* For master's, thesis or alternative. *Entrance requirements:* For master's, GRE. Additional exam requirements/recommendations for international students: required—TOEFL. Electronic applications accepted.

University of Southern California, Graduate School, School of Cinematic Arts, The Peter Stark Producing Program, Los Angeles, CA 90089. Offers motion picture producing (MFA). *Degree requirements:* For master's, thesis, set curriculum, oral examination. *Entrance requirements:* For master's, GRE. Additional exam requirements/recommendations for international students: required—TOEFL (minimum score 600 paper-based; 100 iBT), IELTS (minimum score 7). Electronic applications accepted.

The University of Texas at Arlington, Graduate School, College of Liberal Arts, Department of Art and Art History, Arlington, TX 76019. Offers film and video (MFA); glass (MFA); intermedia (MFA); visual communication (MFA). *Accreditation:* NASAD. *Degree requirements:* For master's, thesis or alternative, mid- and final program reviews; exhibition. *Entrance requirements:* For master's, GRE, minimum GPA of 3.0, 3 letters of recommendation, portfolio, resume. Additional exam requirements/recommendations for international students: required—TOEFL (minimum score 550 paper-based). Electronic applications accepted.

The University of Texas at Austin, Graduate School, College of Communication, Department of Radio-Television-Film, Austin, TX 78712-1111. Offers film and media production (MFA); media studies (MA, PhD); screenwriting (MFA). *Degree requirements:* For master's, thesis (for some programs); for doctorate, thesis/dissertation. *Entrance requirements:* For master's and doctorate, GRE General Test. Electronic applications accepted.

The University of Texas at Austin, Graduate School, Michener Center for Writers, Austin, TX 78712-1111. Offers fiction (MFA); playwriting (MFA); poetry (MFA); screenwriting (MFA). Electronic applications accepted.

University of the Sacred Heart, Graduate Programs, Department of Communication, San Juan, PR 00914-0383. Offers contemporary culture and media (MA); digital journalism (MA, Certificate); editing for media (MA, Certificate); public relations (MA, Certificate); publicity (MA, Certificate); scriptwriting (MA, Certificate). *Program availability:* Part-time, evening/weekend. *Degree requirements:* For master's, thesis.

University of Utah, Graduate School, College of Fine Arts, Film and Media Arts Department, Salt Lake City, UT 84112-0380. Offers MFA. *Faculty:* 15 full-time (7 women), 1 part-time/adjunct (0 women). *Students:* 15 full-time (5 women); includes 2 minority (1 American Indian or Alaska Native, non-Hispanic/Latino; 1 Asian, non-Hispanic/Latino), 2 international. Average age 29. 12 applicants, 25% accepted, 2 enrolled. In 2019, 6 master's awarded. *Degree requirements:* For master's, Creative Project. *Entrance requirements:* For master's, creative reel and critical writing sample. Additional exam requirements/recommendations for international students: required—TOEFL (minimum score 80 paper-based), IELTS (minimum score 6.5). *Application deadline:* For fall admission, 12/31 for domestic and international students. Application fee: $55 ($65 for international students). *Expenses:* Tuition, state resident: full-time $7085; part-time $272.51 per credit hour. Tuition, nonresident: full-time $24,937; part-time $959.12 per credit hour. *Required fees:* $880.52; $880.52 per semester. Tuition and fees vary according to degree level, program and student level. *Financial support:* In 2019–20, 11 students received support, including 1 fellowship (averaging $15,000 per year), 17 teaching assistantships (averaging $15,000 per year). *Unit head:* Dr. Andrew Patrick Nelson, PhD, Chair, 801-585-1601, Fax: 801-585-3192, E-mail: ap.nelson@utah.edu. *Application contact:* Paula Joy Lee, Program Manger, 801-581-5127, E-mail: paula.lee@utah.edu.
Website: http://www.film.utah.edu

University of Victoria, Faculty of Graduate Studies, Faculty of Fine Arts, Department of Visual Arts, Victoria, BC V8W 2Y2, Canada. Offers digital multimedia (MFA); drawing (MFA); painting (MFA); photography (MFA); sculpture (MFA); video (MFA). *Degree requirements:* For master's, exhibit, oral exam. *Entrance requirements:* For master's, portfolio, BFA. Additional exam requirements/recommendations for international students: required—TOEFL (minimum score 575 paper-based), IELTS (minimum score 7). Electronic applications accepted.

University of Wisconsin–Milwaukee, Graduate School, Peck School of the Arts, Milwaukee, WI 53201-0413. Offers art education (MS); chamber music (CAS); conducting (MM); dance (MFA); design entrepreneurship and innovation (MA); film, video, animation, and new genres (MFA); music education (MM); music history and literature (MM); performance (MM); string pedagogy (MM); studio art (MA, MFA); theory and composition (MM). *Program availability:* Part-time. *Degree requirements:* For master's, comprehensive exam, thesis or alternative. *Entrance requirements:* For master's, portfolio. Additional exam requirements/recommendations for international students: required—TOEFL (minimum score 550 paper-based; 79 iBT), IELTS (minimum score 6.5). Electronic applications accepted.

Vermont College of Fine Arts, MFA in Film Program, Montpelier, VT 05602. Offers MFA. *Degree requirements:* For master's, thesis. *Entrance requirements:* For master's, bachelor's degree. Electronic applications accepted. *Expenses:* Contact institution.

Virginia Commonwealth University, Graduate School, School of the Arts, Richmond, VA 23284-9005. Offers art education (MAE, PhD); art history (MA, PhD), including curatorial (PhD), historical studies, museum studies (MA); ceramics (MFA); design (MFA), including interior environments, visual communications; fibers (MFA); furniture design (MFA); glassworking (MFA); jewelry/metalworking (MFA); kinetic imaging (MFA); music (MM), including music education; painting (MFA); photography and film (MFA); printmaking (MFA); sculpture (MFA); theatre (MFA), including costume design, pedagogy/literature, pedagogy/performance, scene design/technical theatre. *Accreditation:* CIDA. *Program availability:* Part-time. *Entrance requirements:* For doctorate, GRE General Test, writing sample. Additional exam requirements/recommendations for international students: required—TOEFL (minimum score 600 paper-based; 100 iBT). Electronic applications accepted.

Film, Television, and Video Production

Watkins College of Art, Design, & Film, Program in Film, Nashville, TN 37228. Offers MFA. *Program availability:* Evening/weekend. *Degree requirements:* For master's, thesis.

Western Colorado University, Program in Creative Writing, Gunnison, CO 81231. Offers mainstream genre fiction (MFA); poetry (MFA); screenwriting (MFA). *Program availability:* Online learning. *Degree requirements:* For master's, thesis.

York University, Faculty of Graduate Studies, Faculty of Fine Arts, Program in Film, Toronto, ON M3J 1P3, Canada. Offers MA, MFA, PhD. *Degree requirements:* For master's, thesis. *Entrance requirements:* For master's, portfolio. Electronic applications accepted.

Film, Television, and Video Theory and Criticism

Brooklyn College of the City University of New York, School of Visual, Media and Performing Arts, Feirstein Graduate School of Cinema, Brooklyn, NY 11210-2889. Offers cinema arts (MFA); cinema studies (MA).

California College of the Arts, Graduate Programs, Visual and Critical Studies Program, San Francisco, CA 94107. Offers visual and critical studies (MA), including curatorial practice, fine arts, writing. *Degree requirements:* For master's, thesis. *Entrance requirements:* For master's, portfolio, resume, 2 letters of recommendation, transcripts, essay, interview. Additional exam requirements/recommendations for international students: required—TOEFL, IELTS, or PTE. Electronic applications accepted. *Expenses:* Contact institution.

Central Michigan University, College of Graduate Studies, College of the Arts and Media, School of Broadcast and Cinematic Arts, Mount Pleasant, MI 48859. Offers electronic media management (MA); electronic media production (MA); electronic media studies (MA); film theory and criticism (MA). *Program availability:* Part-time. *Degree requirements:* For master's, thesis or alternative. *Entrance requirements:* For master's, undergraduate degree in broadcasting, film studies, or an associated discipline with minimum GPA of 2.7. Electronic applications accepted. *Expenses: Tuition, area resident:* Full-time $12,267; part-time $8178 per year. Tuition, state resident: full-time $12,267; part-time $8178 per year. Tuition, nonresident: full-time $12,267; part-time $8178 per year. *International tuition:* $16,110 full-time. *Required fees:* $225 per semester. Tuition and fees vary according to degree level and program.

Claremont Graduate University, Graduate Programs, School of Arts and Humanities, Department of English, Claremont, CA 91711-6160. Offers American studies (MA, PhD); critical theory (MA, PhD); early modern studies (MA, PhD); English (M Phil, MA, PhD); literary theory (PhD); literature (MA, PhD); literature and creative writing (MA); literature and film (MA); MBA/MA; MBA/PhD. *Program availability:* Part-time. *Entrance requirements:* For master's and doctorate, GRE General Test. Additional exam requirements/recommendations for international students: required—TOEFL (minimum score 75 iBT). Electronic applications accepted.

College of Staten Island of the City University of New York, Graduate Programs, Division of Humanities and Social Sciences, Program in Cinema and Media Studies, Staten Island, NY 10314-6600. Offers MA. *Program availability:* Part-time, evening/weekend. *Faculty:* 1. *Students:* 5. 12 applicants. In 2019, 5 master's awarded. *Degree requirements:* For master's, comprehensive exam (for some programs), thesis optional, 36 credits in graduate cinema and media studies courses, remaining credits are to be fulfilled, following advisement, through electives offered in the graduate program in Cinema and Media Studies. A written thesis, or a production thesis, or an examination is to be completed. *Entrance requirements:* For master's, bachelor's degree with minimum B average in undergraduate cinema studies or communications courses; 10-12 page writing sample; three letters of recommendation; 1-2 page statement of intent detailing interest in the field, background in film and media studies, and/or research interests; three letters of recommendation. Additional exam requirements/recommendations for international students: required—TOEFL (minimum score 550 paper-based; 79 iBT), IELTS (minimum score 6.5). *Application deadline:* For fall admission, 6/15 priority date for domestic students, 6/15 for international students; for spring admission, 11/25 priority date for domestic students, 11/25 for international students. Applications are processed on a rolling basis. Application fee: $75. Electronic applications accepted. *Expenses: Tuition, area resident:* Full-time $11,090; part-time $470 per credit. Tuition, state resident: full-time $11,090; part-time $470 per credit. Tuition, nonresident: full-time $20,520; part-time $855 per credit. *International tuition:* $20,520 full-time. *Required fees:* $559; $181 per semester. Tuition and fees vary according to program. *Unit head:* Bilge Yesil, Graduate Program Coordinator, 718-982-2549, E-mail: cinemamasters@csi.cuny.edu. *Application contact:* Sasha Spence, Associate Director for Graduate Admissions, 718-982-2019, Fax: 718-982-2500, E-mail: sasha.spence@csi.cuny.edu.
Website: https://www.csi.cuny.edu/academics-and-research/departments-programs/media-culture

Columbia University, School of the Arts, Film and Media Studies Program, New York, NY 10027. Offers MA. *Program availability:* Part-time. Terminal master's awarded for partial completion of doctoral program. *Degree requirements:* For master's, thesis. *Entrance requirements:* For master's, undergraduate transcript, 3 letters of recommendation, autobiographical essay, 2 samples of scholarly writing, graduate transcript (if applicable). Additional exam requirements/recommendations for international students: required—Either the TOEFL or the IELTS is required. Electronic applications accepted. *Expenses:* Contact institution.

Concordia University, School of Graduate Studies, Faculty of Fine Arts, Mel Hoppenheim School of Cinema, Montréal, QC H3G 1M8, Canada. Offers film and moving image studies (PhD); film production (MFA); film studies (MA).

DePaul University, College of Communication, Chicago, IL 60604. Offers digital communication and media arts (MA); health communication (MA); journalism (MA); media and cinema studies (MA); multicultural communication (MA); organizational communication (MA); public relations and advertising (MA); relational communication (MA). *Program availability:* Part-time, evening/weekend. *Entrance requirements:* Additional exam requirements/recommendations for international students: required—TOEFL (minimum score 590 paper-based; 96 iBT), IELTS (minimum score 7.5) or PTE. Electronic applications accepted.

Emory University, Laney Graduate School, Department of Film Studies, Atlanta, GA 30322-1100. Offers MA, PhD/Certificate. *Degree requirements:* For master's, comprehensive exam, thesis or alternative. *Entrance requirements:* For master's, GRE General Test, 3 letters of reference, 2 writing samples. Additional exam requirements/recommendations for international students: required—TOEFL. Electronic applications accepted.

Emory University, Laney Graduate School, Department of Spanish and Portuguese, Atlanta, GA 30322-1100. Offers comparative literature (Certificate); film studies (Certificate); Spanish (PhD); women's studies (Certificate). *Degree requirements:* For

doctorate, 2 foreign languages, comprehensive exam, thesis/dissertation. *Entrance requirements:* For doctorate, GRE General Test. Additional exam requirements/recommendations for international students: required—TOEFL. Electronic applications accepted.

Hollins University, Graduate Programs, Program in Screenwriting and Film Studies, Roanoke, VA 24020. Offers screenwriting (MFA); screenwriting and film studies (MA). *Program availability:* Part-time. *Degree requirements:* For master's, one foreign language, comprehensive exam, thesis. *Entrance requirements:* For master's, letters of recommendation, manuscript, transcript review, personal statement. Additional exam requirements/recommendations for international students: required—TOEFL (minimum score 550 paper-based; 80 iBT), IELTS (minimum score 6.5). Electronic applications accepted. *Expenses:* Contact institution.

National University, College of Letters and Sciences, La Jolla, CA 92037-1011. Offers biology (MS); counseling psychology (MA), including licensed professional clinical counseling, marriage and family therapy; creative writing (MFA); English (MA); film studies (MA); forensic and crime scene investigations (Certificate); forensic sciences (MFS); human behavior (MA); mathematics for educators (MS); performance psychology (MA); strategic communications (MA). *Program availability:* Part-time, evening/weekend, 100% online, blended/hybrid learning. *Degree requirements:* For master's, thesis (for some programs). *Entrance requirements:* For master's, interview, minimum GPA of 2.5. Additional exam requirements/recommendations for international students: required—TOEFL (minimum score 550 paper-based; 79 iBT), IELTS (minimum score 6). Electronic applications accepted. *Expenses: Tuition:* Full-time $442; part-time $442 per unit.

New York University, Tisch School of the Arts and Graduate School of Arts and Science, Department of Cinema Studies, New York, NY 10002. Offers cinema studies (MA, PhD); moving image archiving and preservation (MA). *Degree requirements:* For master's, comprehensive exam; for doctorate, one foreign language, thesis/dissertation, 3 comprehensive exams. *Entrance requirements:* For master's, sample of written work; for doctorate, master's degree, writing sample. Additional exam requirements/recommendations for international students: required—TOEFL, IELTS, TOEFL or IELTS. Electronic applications accepted. *Expenses:* Contact institution.

Ohio University, Graduate College, College of Fine Arts, School of Film, Athens, OH 45701-2979. Offers film (MFA); film studies (MA). *Degree requirements:* For master's, one foreign language, thesis. *Entrance requirements:* Additional exam requirements/recommendations for international students: required—TOEFL (minimum score 550 paper-based; 80 iBT) or IELTS (minimum score 6.5). Electronic applications accepted.

San Francisco State University, Division of Graduate Studies, College of Liberal and Creative Arts, School of Cinema, San Francisco, CA 94132-1722. Offers MA, MFA. *Expenses: Tuition, area resident:* Full-time $7176; part-time $4164 per year. Tuition, state resident: full-time $7176; part-time $4164 per year. Tuition, nonresident: full-time $16,680; part-time $396 per unit. *International tuition:* $16,680 full-time. *Required fees:* $1524; $1524 per unit. $762 per semester. Tuition and fees vary according to degree level and program. *Unit head:* Dr. Celine Shimizu, Director, 415-338-1629, Fax: 415-338-6159, E-mail: shimizu@sfsu.edu. *Application contact:* Prof. Steve Choe, MA Coordinator, 415-338-1072, Fax: 415-338-6159, E-mail: stevec3@sfsu.edu. Website: http://www.cinema.sfsu.edu/

Savannah College of Art and Design, Program in Cinema Studies, Savannah, GA 31402-3146. Offers MA. *Program availability:* Part-time. *Degree requirements:* For master's, thesis. *Entrance requirements:* For master's, GRE (recommended), portfolio (submitted in digital format), audition or writing submission, resume, statement of purpose, two letters of recommendation. Additional exam requirements/recommendations for international students: recommended—TOEFL (minimum score 550 paper-based; 85 iBT), IELTS (minimum score 6.5). Electronic applications accepted.

Texas A&M University–Commerce, College of Humanities, Social Sciences and Arts, Commerce, TX 75429. Offers applied criminology (MS); applied linguistics (MA, MS); art (MA, MFA); christianity in history (Graduate Certificate); computational linguistics (Graduate Certificate); creative writing (Graduate Certificate); criminal justice management (Graduate Certificate); criminal justice studies (Graduate Certificate); English (MA, MS, PhD); film studies (Graduate Certificate); history (MA, MS); Holocaust studies (Graduate Certificate); homeland security (Graduate Certificate); music (MM); music performance (MM); political science (MA, MS); public history (Graduate Certificate); sociology (MS); Spanish (MA); studies in children's and adolescent literature and culture (Graduate Certificate); teaching English to speakers of other languages (Graduate Certificate); theater (MA, MS); world history (Graduate Certificate). *Program availability:* Part-time. *Faculty:* 49 full-time (28 women), 8 part-time/adjunct (2 women). *Students:* 34 full-time (21 women), 427 part-time (302 women); includes 175 minority (66 Black or African American, non-Hispanic/Latino; 1 American Indian or Alaska Native, non-Hispanic/Latino; 13 Asian, non-Hispanic/Latino; 79 Hispanic/Latino; 16 Two or more races, non-Hispanic/Latino), 15 international. Average age 38. 193 applicants, 49% accepted, 78 enrolled. In 2019, 122 master's, 6 doctorates awarded. *Degree requirements:* For master's, one foreign language, comprehensive exam, thesis (for some programs); for doctorate, one foreign language, comprehensive exam, thesis/dissertation, departmental qualifying exam. *Entrance requirements:* For master's, GRE General Test, official transcripts, letters of recommendation, resume, statement of goals; for doctorate, GRE General Test, official transcripts, letters of recommendation, statement of goals, writing samples, writing sessions, resumes. Additional exam requirements/recommendations for international students: required—TOEFL (minimum score 550 paper-based; 79 iBT), IELTS (minimum score 6), PTE (minimum score 53). *Application deadline:* For fall admission, 6/1 priority date for international students; for spring admission, 10/15 priority date for international students; for summer admission, 3/15 priority date for international students. Applications are processed on a rolling basis. Application fee: $50 ($75 for international students). Electronic applications accepted. *Expenses: Tuition, area resident:* Full-time $3630; part-time $202 per credit hour. Tuition, state resident: full-time $3630; part-time $202 per credit hour. Tuition,

nonresident: full-time $11,232; part-time $624 per credit hour. *International tuition:* $11,232 full-time. *Required fees:* $2948. *Financial support:* In 2019–20, 30 students received support, including 18 research assistantships with partial tuition reimbursements available (averaging $3,231 per year), 136 teaching assistantships with partial tuition reimbursements available (averaging $4,053 per year); Federal Work-Study, institutionally sponsored loans, scholarships/grants, health care benefits, and unspecified assistantships also available. Financial award application deadline: 5/1; financial award applicants required to submit FAFSA. *Unit head:* Dr. William F. Kuracina, Interim Dean, 903-886-5166, Fax: 903-886-5774, E-mail: william.kuracina@tamuc.edu. *Application contact:* Rebecca Stevens, Graduate Student Services Coordinator, 903-468-6049, E-mail: rebecca.stevens@tamuc.edu.
Website: http://www.tamuc.edu/academics/colleges/humanitiesSocialSciencesArts/

Tiffin University, Program in Humanities, Tiffin, OH 44883-2161. Offers art and visual media (MH); communication (MH); creative writing (MH); English (MH); film studies (MH); humanities (MH); individualized studies (MH). *Program availability:* Part-time, evening/weekend, online only, 100% online, blended/hybrid learning. *Entrance requirements:* For master's, work experience. Additional exam requirements/recommendations for international students: required—TOEFL (minimum score 550 paper-based; 79 iBT). Electronic applications accepted. Application fee is waived when completed online. *Expenses:* Contact institution.

Université de Montréal, Faculty of Arts and Sciences, Department of Art History and Film Studies, Montréal, QC H3C 3J7, Canada. Offers art history (MA, PhD); film studies (MA, PhD). *Degree requirements:* For master's, thesis. Electronic applications accepted.

University at Buffalo, the State University of New York, Graduate School, College of Arts and Sciences, Department of Media Study, Buffalo, NY 14260. Offers architecture and media (M Arch/MFA); film and media study (MAH); media arts production (MFA); media study (PhD); new media design (Certificate); social media (MAH); M Arch/MFA. *Faculty:* 13 full-time (7 women). *Students:* 36 full-time (18 women); includes 19 minority (1 Black or African American, non-Hispanic/Latino; 14 Asian, non-Hispanic/Latino; 4 Hispanic/Latino). Average age 31. 80 applicants, 30% accepted, 8 enrolled. In 2019, 5 master's, 1 doctorate awarded. Terminal master's awarded for partial completion of doctoral program. *Degree requirements:* For master's, thesis, media project; for doctorate, comprehensive exam, thesis/dissertation, qualifying exam, media project. *Entrance requirements:* For master's, portfolio; for doctorate, GRE, portfolio. Additional exam requirements/recommendations for international students: required—TOEFL (minimum score 550 paper-based; 79 iBT). *Application deadline:* For fall admission, 1/5 priority date for domestic and international students. Applications are processed on a rolling basis. Application fee: $75. Electronic applications accepted. *Expenses:* Approximately $15,000 per year in state tuition + fees, same as normal for institution, with some courses having small (about $100) additional equipment fees; many students are on TAship and pay no tuition, about $1500 per semester in fees; generally 2 years for MAH, 3 for MFA, and 5 for PhD, though not all of PhD years require full courseload. *Financial support:* In 2019–20, 14 students received support, including 10 teaching assistantships with full tuition reimbursements available (averaging $16,000 per year); fellowships, career-related internships or fieldwork, Federal Work-Study, scholarships/grants, and unspecified assistantships also available. Support available to part-time students. Financial award application deadline: 1/5; financial award applicants required to submit FAFSA. *Unit head:* Prof. Tom Feeley, Chair, 716-645-1160, Fax: 716-645-6979, E-mail: thfeeley@buffalo.edu. *Application contact:* Bradley Hendricks, Assistant to the Chair for Student Programs, 716-645-0945, Fax: 716-645-6979, E-mail: bhendric@buffalo.edu.
Website: http://mediastudy.buffalo.edu/

The University of Arizona, College of Fine Arts, School of Theatre, Film and Television, Tucson, AZ 85721. Offers MFA. *Accreditation:* NAST. *Degree requirements:* For master's, comprehensive exam (for some programs), thesis (for some programs), production monograph. *Entrance requirements:* For master's, 3 letters of recommendation, portfolio. Additional exam requirements/recommendations for international students: required—TOEFL (minimum score 550 paper-based; 79 iBT). Electronic applications accepted.

The University of British Columbia, Faculty of Arts, Department of Theatre and Film, Film Program, Vancouver, BC V6T 1Z2, Canada. Offers film production (MFA); film studies (MA). *Degree requirements:* For master's, variable foreign language requirement, comprehensive exam, thesis (MA); thesis or project (MFA). *Entrance requirements:* For master's, portfolio (MFA). Additional exam requirements/recommendations for international students: required—TOEFL. *Expenses:* Contact institution.

University of California, Berkeley, Graduate Division, College of Letters and Science, Department of Film and Media, Berkeley, CA 94720-2670. Offers PhD. *Degree requirements:* For doctorate, thesis/dissertation, qualifying exam. *Entrance requirements:* Additional exam requirements/recommendations for international students: required—TOEFL (minimum score 570 paper-based; 90 iBT). Electronic applications accepted.

University of California, Santa Cruz, Division of Graduate Studies, Division of the Arts, Department of Film and Digital Media, Santa Cruz, CA 95064. Offers PhD. *Degree requirements:* For doctorate, one foreign language, thesis/dissertation, qualifying exams. *Entrance requirements:* For doctorate, GRE. Additional exam requirements/recommendations for international students: required—TOEFL (minimum score 550 paper-based; 83 iBT); recommended—IELTS (minimum score 8). Electronic applications accepted.

University of Chicago, Division of the Humanities, Department of Cinema and Media Studies, Chicago, IL 60637. Offers PhD. *Degree requirements:* For doctorate, 2 foreign languages, comprehensive exam, thesis/dissertation. *Entrance requirements:* For doctorate, GRE General Test, 15-20 page writing sample, statement of purpose, 3 letters of recommendation, transcripts for all previous degrees and institutions attended. Additional exam requirements/recommendations for international students: required—TOEFL (minimum score 104 iBT), IELTS (minimum score 7). Electronic applications accepted.

The University of Iowa, Graduate College, College of Liberal Arts and Sciences, Department of Cinema and Comparative Literature, Program in Film Studies, Iowa City, IA 52242-1316. Offers MA, PhD. *Degree requirements:* For master's, thesis optional, exam; for doctorate, comprehensive exam, thesis/dissertation. *Entrance requirements:* For master's and doctorate, GRE General Test, minimum GPA of 3.0. Additional exam requirements/recommendations for international students: required—TOEFL (minimum score 550 paper-based; 81 iBT). Electronic applications accepted.

The University of Kansas, Graduate Studies, College of Liberal Arts and Sciences, Department of Film and Media Studies, Lawrence, KS 66045. Offers MA, PhD. *Students:* 12 full-time (8 women); includes 5 minority (1 Black or African American, non-Hispanic/Latino; 2 American Indian or Alaska Native, non-Hispanic/Latino; 1 Asian, non-Hispanic/Latino; 1 Two or more races, non-Hispanic/Latino), 1 international. Average age 32. 13 applicants, 31% accepted, 2 enrolled. In 2019, 1 master's, 3 doctorates awarded. *Entrance requirements:* For master's, GRE General Test, three recent letters of recommendation, current resume, statement of personal goals, writing sample; for doctorate, GRE General Test, MA in film or related field; three recent letters of recommendation; current resume; statement of personal goals; writing sample; minimum GPA of 3.2 undergraduate, 3.5 graduate. Additional exam requirements/recommendations for international students: required—TOEFL, IELTS, TOEFL or IELTS. *Application deadline:* For fall admission, 1/1 priority date for domestic and international students. Application fee: $65 ($85 for international students). Electronic applications accepted. *Expenses:* Tuition, state resident: full-time $9989. Tuition, nonresident: full-time $23,950. *International tuition:* $23,950 full-time. *Required fees:* $984; $81.99 per credit hour. Tuition and fees vary according to course load, campus/location and program. *Financial support:* Fellowships, research assistantships, teaching assistantships, scholarships/grants, and unspecified assistantships available. Financial award application deadline: 1/1; financial award applicants required to submit FAFSA. *Unit head:* Dr. Michael Baskett, Chair, 785-864-1384, E-mail: eiga@ku.edu. *Application contact:* Julia Reilly, Graduate Admissions Contact, 785-864-9488, E-mail: juliareilly@ku.edu.
Website: http://film.ku.edu/

University of Miami, Graduate School, School of Communication, Coral Gables, FL 33124. Offers communication (PhD); communication studies (MA); film studies (MA, PhD); motion pictures (MFA), including production, producing, and screenwriting; print journalism (MA); public relations (MA); Spanish language journalism (MA); television broadcast journalism (MA). *Program availability:* Part-time. *Degree requirements:* For master's, comprehensive exam (for some programs), thesis (for some programs); for doctorate, comprehensive exam, thesis/dissertation. *Entrance requirements:* For master's, GRE General Test; for doctorate, GRE General Test, master's thesis or scholarly research. Additional exam requirements/recommendations for international students: required—TOEFL (minimum score 600 paper-based; 100 iBT). Electronic applications accepted.

University of Michigan, Rackham Graduate School, College of Literature, Science, and the Arts, Department of Film, Television, and Media, Ann Arbor, MI 48109. Offers PhD, Certificate. *Degree requirements:* For doctorate, one foreign language, comprehensive exam, thesis/dissertation; for Certificate, 15 credit hours. *Entrance requirements:* For doctorate, GRE. Additional exam requirements/recommendations for international students: required—TOEFL. Electronic applications accepted.

University of Oklahoma, Weitzenhoffer Family College of Fine Arts, School of Visual Arts, Norman, OK 73019. Offers art (MFA), including art and technology, ceramics, film, painting, photography, printmaking, sculpture, video, visual communication; art history (MA, PhD), including art history (MA), art of the American West (PhD), Native American art (PhD); design (MFA). *Degree requirements:* For master's, 2 foreign languages, comprehensive exam (for some programs), thesis (for some programs); for doctorate, 2 foreign languages, comprehensive exam, thesis/dissertation. *Entrance requirements:* For master's and doctorate, GRE. Additional exam requirements/recommendations for international students: required—TOEFL (minimum score 79 iBT) or IELTS (minimum score 6.5). Electronic applications accepted. *Expenses:* Tuition, state resident: full-time $6583.20; part-time $274.30 per credit hour. Tuition, nonresident: full-time $21,242; part-time $885.10 per credit hour. *International tuition:* $21,242.40 full-time. *Required fees:* $1994.20; $72.55 per credit hour. $126.50 per semester. Tuition and fees vary according to course load and degree level.

University of Pittsburgh, Kenneth P. Dietrich School of Arts and Sciences, Department of French and Italian Languages and Literatures, Pittsburgh, PA 15260. Offers French (MA, PhD), including film studies (PhD), French (MA), Romance languages and literatures (PhD); Italian (MA). *Program availability:* Part-time. *Faculty:* 8 full-time (3 women). *Students:* 16 full-time (6 women); includes 3 minority (2 Black or African American, non-Hispanic/Latino; 1 Asian, non-Hispanic/Latino). Average age 29. 18 applicants, 22% accepted, 3 enrolled. In 2019, 2 master's, 1 doctorate awarded. Terminal master's awarded for partial completion of doctoral program. *Degree requirements:* For master's, one foreign language, comprehensive exam; for doctorate, one foreign language, comprehensive exam, thesis/dissertation. *Entrance requirements:* For doctorate, application must be completed through Apply Yourself; 3 letters of recommendation; unofficial transcripts of all post-secondary academic work, and official translations if these are not in English; personal statement (1-3 pages single-spaced) written in English outlining goals and reasons for pursuing graduate education in French. Additional exam requirements/recommendations for international students: required—TOEFL (minimum score 90 iBT) or IELTS (minimum score 7). *Application deadline:* For fall admission, 1/10 priority date for domestic and international students. Application fee: $50. Electronic applications accepted. *Financial support:* In 2019–20, 88 students received support, including 2 fellowships with full tuition reimbursements available (averaging $23,690 per year), 8 teaching assistantships with full tuition reimbursements available (averaging $20,250 per year); scholarships/grants, health care benefits, tuition waivers (full), and unspecified assistantships also available. Financial award application deadline: 1/10. *Unit head:* Dr. Todd Reeser, Department Chair, 412-624-6258, E-mail: reeser@pitt.edu. *Application contact:* Keanna Cash, Graduate Administrator, 412-624-5227, Fax: 412-624-6263, E-mail: kec176@pitt.edu.
Website: http://frenchanditalian.pitt.edu

University of Pittsburgh, Kenneth P. Dietrich School of Arts and Sciences, Department of Slavic Languages and Literatures, Pittsburgh, PA 15260. Offers film studies (PhD), including Russian literature and culture; Russian literature and culture (MA, PhD). *Faculty:* 5 full-time (2 women), 6 part-time/adjunct (5 women). *Students:* 11 full-time (8 women); includes 1 minority (Asian, non-Hispanic/Latino). Average age 30. 13 applicants, 23% accepted, 2 enrolled. In 2019, 1 master's, 2 doctorates awarded. Terminal master's awarded for partial completion of doctoral program. *Degree requirements:* For master's, 2 foreign languages, comprehensive exam; for doctorate, 3 foreign languages, comprehensive exam, thesis/dissertation. *Entrance requirements:* For doctorate, personal statement, transcript copies, 3 letters of recommendation (online submissions), writing sample (in English); a Russian sample can also be submitted (optional). Additional exam requirements/recommendations for international students: required—either the IELTS or TOEFL are required; recommended—TOEFL (minimum score 90 iBT), IELTS (minimum score 7). *Application deadline:* For fall admission, 1/15 priority date for domestic and international students. Application fee: $50. Electronic applications accepted. *Expenses:* $24,480 in-state, $40,848 out-of-state. *Financial support:* In 2019–20, 100 students received support, including 5 fellowships with full tuition reimbursements available (averaging $22,170 per year), 6 teaching assistantships with full tuition reimbursements available (averaging $20,250 per year); career-related internships or fieldwork, scholarships/grants, health care benefits, tuition waivers (full), and unspecified assistantships also available. Financial award application deadline: 1/15. *Unit head:* Dr. Bella Grigoryan, Department Chair, 412-624-9958, Fax: 412-624-9714, E-mail: grigoryan@pitt.edu. *Application contact:* Keanna Cash, Graduate Administrator, 412-624-5227, E-mail: kec176@pitt.edu.
Website: http://www.slavic.pitt.edu

University of Pittsburgh, Kenneth P. Dietrich School of Arts and Sciences, Film and Media Studies Program, Pittsburgh, PA 15260-0001. Offers PhD, Certificate. *Faculty:* 21 full-time (6 women). *Students:* 22 full-time (11 women); includes 8 minority (5 Asian, non-Hispanic/Latino; 3 Hispanic/Latino). Average age 31. 84 applicants, 8%

accepted, 5 enrolled. In 2019, 4 doctorates awarded. Terminal master's awarded for partial completion of doctoral program. *Degree requirements:* For doctorate, one foreign language, comprehensive exam, thesis/dissertation; for Certificate, Certificate paper. *Entrance requirements:* Additional exam requirements/recommendations for international students: required—TOEFL (minimum score 80 paper-based). *Application deadline:* For fall admission, 12/10 for domestic students, 12/6 for international students. Application fee: $50. Electronic applications accepted. *Financial support:* In 2019–20, 22 students received support, including 22 fellowships with full tuition reimbursements available (averaging $23,000 per year); teaching assistantships, scholarships/grants, and health care benefits also available. *Unit head:* Dr. Randall Halle, Klaus W. Jonas Professor of German Film and Cultural Studies, Program, 412-648-2614, Fax: 412-624-6318, E-mail: rhalle@pitt.edu. *Application contact:* Dr. Mark Lynn Anderson, Associate Professor of English, Director of Graduate Studies for Film and Media Studies Program, 412-624-6514, Fax: 412-624-6639, E-mail: andersml@pitt.edu.
Website: http://www.filmstudies.pitt.edu/

University of Southern California, Graduate School, School of Cinematic Arts, Division of Cinema and Media Studies, Los Angeles, CA 90089. Offers MA, PhD. *Degree requirements:* For master's, comprehensive exam; for doctorate, comprehensive exam, thesis/dissertation. *Entrance requirements:* For master's and doctorate, GRE. Additional exam requirements/recommendations for international students: required—TOEFL (minimum score 100 iBT). Electronic applications accepted.

University of South Florida, College of Arts and Sciences, Department of Humanities and Cultural Studies, Tampa, FL 33620-9951. Offers liberal arts (MA), including American studies, film studies, humanities. *Program availability:* Part-time, evening/weekend. *Faculty:* 8 full-time (3 women). *Students:* 19 full-time (7 women), 6 part-time (4 women); includes 7 minority (2 Black or African American, non-Hispanic/Latino; 2 Asian, non-Hispanic/Latino; 3 Hispanic/Latino), 1 international. Average age 29. 21 applicants, 71% accepted, 15 enrolled. In 2019, 8 master's awarded. *Degree requirements:* For master's, comprehensive exam, thesis, language (for humanities subconcentration). *Entrance requirements:* For master's, GRE Recommended. Contact department for advising, minimum GPA of 3.0, writing sample. Personal statement, letters of recommendation are recommended. Students must select a concentration at the time of application. Additional exam requirements/recommendations for international students: required—TOEFL, TOEFL (minimum score 550 paper-based) or IELTS (minimum score 6.5). *Application deadline:* For fall admission, 2/15 priority date for domestic students, 2/15 for international students; for spring admission, 10/15 priority date for domestic students, 9/15 for international students; for summer admission, 2/15 for domestic students, 1/15 for international students. Application fee: $30. Electronic applications accepted. *Financial support:* In 2019–20, 5 students received support, including 15 teaching assistantships with tuition reimbursements available (averaging $12,437 per year); scholarships/grants also available. Financial award application deadline: 4/1. *Unit head:* Dr. Andrew Berish, Associate Professor and Chair, 813-974-9380, E-mail: aberish@usf.edu. *Application contact:* Dr. Maria Cizmic, Associate Professor and Graduate Program Director, 813-974-9380, E-mail: mcizmic@usf.edu. Website: http://humanities.usf.edu/

University of Toronto, School of Graduate Studies, Faculty of Arts and Science, Cinema Studies Institute, Toronto, ON M5S 1A1, Canada. Offers MA, PhD. *Entrance requirements:* For master's, minimum B+ in final year or over a year's worth of senior courses, successful completion of minimum of six full-course equivalents in cinema studies or comparable program preparation. Additional exam requirements/recommendations for international students: required—TOEFL (minimum score 580 paper-based; 93 iBT), TWE (minimum score 5). Electronic applications accepted.

University of Wisconsin–Madison, Graduate School, College of Letters and Science, Department of Communication Arts, Madison, WI 53706-1380. Offers communication science (MA, PhD); film (MA, PhD); media and cultural studies (MA, PhD); rhetoric (MA, PhD). Terminal master's awarded for partial completion of doctoral program. *Degree requirements:* For master's, one foreign language, thesis (for some programs); for doctorate, one foreign language, thesis/dissertation. *Entrance requirements:* For master's and doctorate, GRE General Test, minimum GPA of 3.5. Electronic applications accepted.

University of Wisconsin–Milwaukee, Graduate School, College of Letters and Science, Department of English, Milwaukee, WI 53201-0413. Offers English (MA, PhD), including creative writing, English language and linguistics, English secondary education, literary and critical studies, literature and cultural theory (PhD), literature and language studies, literature, culture, and media, media, cinema and digital studies, professional and technical communication (MA), professional and technical writing, professional writing (PhD), rhetoric and composition (PhD), rhetoric and writing. *Degree*

requirements: For master's, thesis or alternative; for doctorate, one foreign language, thesis/dissertation. *Entrance requirements:* For master's, GRE General Test, GRE Subject Test; for doctorate, GRE. Additional exam requirements/recommendations for international students: required—TOEFL (minimum score 550 paper-based; 79 iBT), IELTS (minimum score 6.5). Electronic applications accepted.

Université Laval, Faculty of Letters, Department of Literature, Programs in Literature and Arts of the Screen and Stage, Québec, QC G1K 7P4, Canada. Offers MA, PhD. *Program availability:* Part-time. Terminal master's awarded for partial completion of doctoral program. *Degree requirements:* For master's, thesis; for doctorate, comprehensive exam, thesis/dissertation. *Entrance requirements:* For master's and doctorate, linguistics exams, knowledge of French, knowledge of a second language. Electronic applications accepted.

Walla Walla University, Graduate Studies, Center for Cinema, Religion, and Worldview, College Place, WA 99324. Offers Web and interactive media (MA). *Entrance requirements:* For master's, three professional references, transcripts, personal statement.

Wayne State University, College of Liberal Arts and Sciences, Department of English, Detroit, MI 48202. Offers English (MA); film and media studies (PhD); literary and cultural studies (PhD); rhetoric and composition studies (PhD). *Faculty:* 27. *Students:* 59 full-time (36 women), 31 part-time (24 women); includes 17 minority (4 Black or African American, non-Hispanic/Latino; 4 Asian, non-Hispanic/Latino; 3 Hispanic/Latino; 6 Two or more races, non-Hispanic/Latino), 4 international. Average age 33. 87 applicants, 44% accepted, 17 enrolled. In 2019, 12 master's, 9 doctorates awarded. Terminal master's awarded for partial completion of doctoral program. *Degree requirements:* For master's, variable foreign language requirement, essay, thesis, or portfolio of work approved by Director of Graduate Studies; for doctorate, one foreign language, comprehensive exam, thesis/dissertation. *Entrance requirements:* For master's, statement of purpose; two academic letters of reference; sample essay from previous English course; for doctorate, statement of purpose; two academic letters of reference; sample of scholarly or critical writing. Additional exam requirements/recommendations for international students: required—TOEFL (minimum score 550 paper-based; 79 iBT), TWE (minimum score 5.5), Michigan English Language Assessment Battery (minimum score 85); recommended—IELTS (minimum score 6.5). *Application deadline:* For fall admission, 1/15 for domestic students. Applications are processed on a rolling basis. Application fee: $50. Electronic applications accepted. *Expenses:* Tuition: Full-time $34,567. *Financial support:* In 2019–20, 54 students received support, including 5 fellowships with tuition reimbursements available (averaging $21,500 per year), 1 research assistantship with tuition reimbursement available (averaging $19,967 per year), 28 teaching assistantships with tuition reimbursements available (averaging $19,967 per year); scholarships/grants, health care benefits, and unspecified assistantships also available. Financial award applicants required to submit FAFSA. *Unit head:* Dr. Caroline Maun, Chair and Associate Professor, 313-577-7692, E-mail: av4495@wayne.edu. *Application contact:* Dr. Richard Marback, Director of Graduate Studies, 313-577-7694, E-mail: aa4749@wayne.edu. Website: http://clas.wayne.edu/english/

Wilfrid Laurier University, Faculty of Graduate and Postdoctoral Studies, Faculty of Arts, Department of English and Film Studies, Waterloo, ON N2L 3C5, Canada. Offers English (MA); English and film (PhD). *Degree requirements:* For master's, thesis optional; for doctorate, thesis/dissertation. *Entrance requirements:* For master's, honours BA or the equivalent in English, minimum B+ in English courses above first year level; for doctorate, MA in English, minimum A- average in graduate work. Additional exam requirements/recommendations for international students: recommended—TOEFL (minimum score 89 iBT). Electronic applications accepted.

Yale University, Graduate School of Arts and Sciences, Department of East Asian Languages and Literatures, New Haven, CT 06520. Offers East Asian languages and literatures (PhD); East Asian languages and literatures and film studies (PhD). *Degree requirements:* For doctorate, 2 foreign languages, thesis/dissertation. *Entrance requirements:* For doctorate, GRE General Test.

Yale University, Graduate School of Arts and Sciences, Department of Slavic Languages and Literatures, New Haven, CT 06520. Offers medieval Slavic literature and philology (PhD); Polish literature (PhD); Russian literature (PhD); Slavic languages and literatures and film studies (PhD). *Degree requirements:* For doctorate, 3 foreign languages, thesis/dissertation. *Entrance requirements:* For doctorate, GRE General Test.

Yale University, Graduate School of Arts and Sciences, Interdisciplinary Program in Film Studies, New Haven, CT 06520. Offers PhD.

Section 6
Performing Arts

This section contains a directory of institutions offering graduate work in performing arts, followed by an in-depth entry submitted by an institution that chose to prepare a detailed program description. Additional information about programs listed in the directory but not augmented by an in-depth entry may be obtained by writing directly to the dean of a graduate school or chair of a department at the address given in the directory.

For programs offering related work, see also in this book *Area and Cultural Studies, Art and Art History, Communication and Media,* and *Film, Television, and Video.* In another guide in this series:

Graduate Programs in Business, Education, Information Studies, Law & Social Work

See *Leisure Studies and Recreation, Subject Areas (Music Education),* and *Physical Education and Kinesiology*

CONTENTS

Program Directories

Dance

Arizona State University at Tempe, Herberger Institute for Design and the Arts, School of Film, Dance and Theatre, Department of Dance, Tempe, AZ 85287-0304. Offers dance (MFA); interdisciplinary digital media and performance (MFA). *Degree requirements:* For master's, thesis optional, project, written document and oral defense, interactive Program of Study (iPOS) submitted before completing 50 percent of required credit hours. *Entrance requirements:* For master's, personal statement relating to school's core values, resume, 3 letters of recommendation from professionals in the dance field. Electronic applications accepted.

Bennington College, Graduate Programs, MFA in Dance Program, Bennington, VT 05201. Offers MFA. *Program availability:* Part-time. *Degree requirements:* For master's, performances. *Entrance requirements:* Additional exam requirements/recommendations for international students: recommended—TOEFL. Electronic applications accepted. *Expenses:* Contact institution.

California Institute of the Arts, The Sharon Disney Lund School of Dance, Valencia, CA 91355-2340. Offers MFA, Adv C. *Accreditation:* NASD. *Degree requirements:* For master's, thesis presentation. *Entrance requirements:* For master's, audition, video of choreography. Additional exam requirements/recommendations for international students: required—TOEFL.

California State University, Long Beach, Graduate Studies, College of the Arts, Department of Dance, Long Beach, CA 90840. Offers MA, MFA. *Accreditation:* NASD. *Program availability:* Part-time. *Degree requirements:* For master's, thesis. Electronic applications accepted.

Case Western Reserve University, School of Graduate Studies, Department of Dance, Cleveland, OH 44106. Offers MA, MFA. *Degree requirements:* For master's, thesis, performance thesis. *Entrance requirements:* For master's, professional video, statement of goals and objectives, audition, interview. Additional exam requirements/recommendations for international students: required—TOEFL (minimum score 577 paper-based; 90 iBT); recommended—IELTS (minimum score 7). Electronic applications accepted.

Eastern Michigan University, Graduate School, College of Arts and Sciences, School of Music and Dance, Ypsilanti, MI 48197. Offers MM. *Accreditation:* NASM. *Program availability:* Part-time, evening/weekend, online learning. *Faculty:* 26 full-time (12 women). *Students:* 4 full-time (3 women), 11 part-time (6 women); includes 2 minority (1 Black or African American, non-Hispanic/Latino; 1 Asian, non-Hispanic/Latino), 3 international. Average age 31. 30 applicants, 43% accepted, 6 enrolled. In 2019, 1 master's awarded. *Entrance requirements:* Additional exam requirements/recommendations for international students: required—TOEFL. *Application deadline:* Applications are processed on a rolling basis. Application fee: $45. *Financial support:* Fellowships, research assistantships with full tuition reimbursements, teaching assistantships with full tuition reimbursements, career-related internships or fieldwork, Federal Work-Study, institutionally sponsored loans, scholarships/grants, tuition waivers (partial), and unspecified assistantships available. Support available to part-time students. Financial award applicants required to submit FAFSA. *Unit head:* Dr. Christopher Barrick, Director, 734-487-0244, Fax: 734-487-6939, E-mail: cbarrick@emich.edu. *Application contact:* Dr. David Pierce, Coordinator of Music Advising, 734-487-4114, Fax: 734-487-6939, E-mail: david.pierce@emich.edu. Website: http://www.emich.edu/musicdance

Florida State University, The Graduate School, College of Fine Arts, School of Dance, Tallahassee, FL 32306-2120. Offers dance (MA, MFA). *Accreditation:* NASD. *Faculty:* 19 full-time (13 women), 3 part-time/adjunct (all women). *Students:* 26 full-time (15 women); includes 12 minority (8 Black or African American, non-Hispanic/Latino; 1 Asian, non-Hispanic/Latino; 2 Hispanic/Latino; 1 Two or more races, non-Hispanic/Latino). Average age 28. 45 applicants, 33% accepted, 12 enrolled. In 2019, 12 master's awarded. *Degree requirements:* For master's, comprehensive exam (for some programs), thesis (for some programs), 1 foreign language (for MA in American dance studies). *Entrance requirements:* For master's, letters of recommendation, statement of purpose, transcripts, writing sample, CV/resume, (an audition is also required for MFA and MA in studio and related studies applicants). Additional exam requirements/recommendations for international students: required—TOEFL (minimum score 550 paper-based, 80 iBT), IELTS (minimum score 6.5) or Michigan English Language Assessment Battery (minimum score 77). *Application deadline:* For fall admission, 1/1 priority date for domestic and international students. Applications are processed on a rolling basis. Application fee: $30. Electronic applications accepted. *Financial support:* In 2019–20, 21 students received support, including 2 fellowships with full tuition reimbursements available (averaging $10,000 per year), 9 research assistantships with full tuition reimbursements available (averaging $6,098 per year), 12 teaching assistantships with full tuition reimbursements available (averaging $6,098 per year); scholarships/grants, health care benefits, tuition waivers (full), and unspecified assistantships also available. Financial award application deadline: 1/1; financial award applicants required to submit FAFSA. *Unit head:* Prof. Anjali Austin, Professor and Chair, 850-644-1024, Fax: 850-644-1277, E-mail: aaustin@fsu.edu. *Application contact:* Dr. Jeff Bray, Academic Program Manager, 850-644-1023, Fax: 850-644-1277, E-mail: jbray@fsu.edu. Website: http://dance.fsu.edu/

The George Washington University, Columbian College of Arts and Sciences, Department of Theatre and Dance, Washington, DC 20052. Offers classical acting (MFA); dance (MFA); exhibit design (Graduate Certificate); production design (MFA). *Program availability:* Part-time, evening/weekend. *Entrance requirements:* For master's, minimum GPA of 3.0, portfolio. Additional exam requirements/recommendations for international students: required—TOEFL (minimum score 550 paper-based; 80 iBT). Electronic applications accepted.

Hollins University, Graduate Programs, Program in Dance, Roanoke, VA 24020. Offers dance (MFA). *Degree requirements:* For master's, thesis. *Entrance requirements:* For master's, DVD of selected works, 3 letters of recommendation, undergraduate transcript(s), personal statement of educational objectives. Additional exam requirements/recommendations for international students: required—TOEFL (minimum score 550 paper-based; 80 iBT), IELTS (minimum score 6.5). Electronic applications accepted. *Expenses:* Contact institution.

Jacksonville University, College of Fine Arts, MFA in Choreography Program, Jacksonville, FL 32211. Offers MFA. *Accreditation:* NASD. *Program availability:* Blended/hybrid learning. *Students:* 7 full-time (all women), 14 part-time (11 women); includes 4 minority (1 Black or African American, non-Hispanic/Latino; 3 Hispanic/Latino). Average age 37. 12 applicants, 83% accepted, 7 enrolled. In 2019, 17 master's awarded. *Degree requirements:* For master's, thesis. *Entrance requirements:* For master's, portfolio, artist statement of intent, undergraduate degree, three current

references, official transcripts of academic work, sample of selected works (12 minutes maximum). Additional exam requirements/recommendations for international students: recommended—TOEFL (minimum score 540 paper-based; 76 iBT). *Application deadline:* Applications are processed on a rolling basis. Application fee: $50. Electronic applications accepted. *Expenses:* Contact institution. *Financial support:* Fellowships, institutionally sponsored loans, scholarships/grants, and health care benefits available. Support available to part-time students. Financial award application deadline: 3/1; financial award applicants required to submit FAFSA. *Unit head:* Cari Coble, Professor of Dance and MFA Coordinator, 904-256-7398, E-mail: ccoble@ju.edu. *Application contact:* Kyrstin Creswell, Assistant Director of Graduate Admissions, 904-256-7002, E-mail: kcreswe@ju.edu. Website: https://www.ju.edu/cfa/mfadance/index.php

Mills College, Graduate Studies, Department of Dance, Oakland, CA 94613-1000. Offers MA, MFA. *Program availability:* Part-time. *Degree requirements:* For master's, comprehensive exam, thesis, performance. *Entrance requirements:* For master's, audition, DVD recording of original choreography of up to two choreographic works (for MFA); writing sample with topic related to field of dance studies (for MA). Additional exam requirements/recommendations for international students: required—TOEFL (minimum score 550 paper-based; 80 iBT) or IELTS (minimum score 6). Electronic applications accepted.

New York University, Steinhardt School of Culture, Education, and Human Development, Department of Music and Performing Arts Professions, Program in Dance Education, New York, NY 10012. Offers teaching dance in the professions (MA), including American Ballet Theatre ballet pedagogy, teaching dance in the professions; teaching dance, all grades (MA, Advanced Certificate); MA/MA. *Program availability:* Part-time. *Entrance requirements:* For master's, audition, interview. Additional exam requirements/recommendations for international students: required—TOEFL (minimum score 100 iBT). Electronic applications accepted.

New York University, Tisch School of the Arts, Department of Dance, New York, NY 10012-1019. Offers MFA. *Entrance requirements:* For master's, audition. Electronic applications accepted.

New York University, Tisch School of the Arts and Graduate School of Arts and Science, Department of Performance Studies, New York, NY 10003. Offers MA, PhD. *Degree requirements:* For doctorate, one foreign language, comprehensive exam, thesis/dissertation, dissertation defense, qualifying exam. *Entrance requirements:* For master's, sample of written work; for doctorate, master's degree, writing sample. Additional exam requirements/recommendations for international students: required—TOEFL (minimum score 105 paper-based). Electronic applications accepted. *Expenses:* Contact institution.

Northern Illinois University, Graduate School, College of Visual and Performing Arts, School of Theatre and Dance, De Kalb, IL 60115-2854. Offers MFA. *Program availability:* Part-time. *Faculty:* 16 full-time (9 women). *Students:* 25 full-time (12 women), 1 part-time (0 women); includes 6 minority (2 Black or African American, non-Hispanic/Latino; 1 Asian, non-Hispanic/Latino; 2 Hispanic/Latino; 1 Two or more races, non-Hispanic/Latino). Average age 26. 52 applicants, 48% accepted, 3 enrolled. In 2019, 17 master's awarded. *Degree requirements:* For master's, comprehensive exam, final project and defense. *Entrance requirements:* For master's, minimum GPA of 2.75, audition or portfolio. Additional exam requirements/recommendations for international students: required—TOEFL (minimum score 550 paper-based). *Application deadline:* For fall admission, 4/1 priority date for domestic students, 5/1 for international students; for spring admission, 10/15 priority date for domestic students, 10/1 for international students. Applications are processed on a rolling basis. Application fee: $40. Electronic applications accepted. *Financial support:* In 2019–20, 28 teaching assistantships with full tuition reimbursements were awarded; fellowships with full tuition reimbursements, research assistantships with full tuition reimbursements, career-related internships or fieldwork, Federal Work-Study, scholarships/grants, tuition waivers (full), and staff assistantships also available. Support available to part-time students. Financial award applicants required to submit FAFSA. *Unit head:* Alexander Gelman, Director, 815-753-8253, Fax: 815-753-8415, E-mail: agelman@niu.edu. *Application contact:* Graduate School Office, 815-753-0395, E-mail: gradsch@niu.edu. Website: http://www.niu.edu/theatre/

The Ohio State University, Graduate School, College of Arts and Sciences, Division of Arts and Humanities, Department of Dance, Columbus, OH 43210. Offers choreography (MFA); dance (MFA, PhD); dance and technology (MFA); dance studies (PhD); history, theory and literature (MFA); lighting and production (MFA); movement analysis, Laban studies, notation and dance documentation (MFA); performance (MFA). *Accreditation:* NASD. *Degree requirements:* For master's, thesis optional. *Entrance requirements:* For master's, GRE General Test (for all applicants with cumulative GPA below 3.0), audition; for doctorate, GRE General Test, invitation-only interview. Additional exam requirements/recommendations for international students: required—Michigan English Language Assessment Battery (minimum score 82); recommended—TOEFL (minimum score 550 paper-based; 79 iBT), IELTS (minimum score 7). Electronic applications accepted.

Saint Mary's College of California, School of Liberal Arts, MFA Program in Dance, Moraga, CA 94575. Offers dance: creative practice (MFA); dance: design and production (MFA).

Sam Houston State University, College of Fine Arts and Mass Communication, Department of Dance, Huntsville, TX 77341. Offers MFA. *Program availability:* Part-time. *Degree requirements:* For master's, comprehensive exam, thesis, project. *Entrance requirements:* For master's, GRE General Test, writing sample, interview, audition, resume, video portfolio, letters of recommendation. Additional exam requirements/recommendations for international students: required—TOEFL (minimum score 550 paper-based; 79 iBT), IELTS (minimum score 6.5). Electronic applications accepted.

Sarah Lawrence College, Graduate Studies, Program in Dance, Bronxville, NY 10708-5999. Offers MFA. *Degree requirements:* For master's, performance. *Entrance requirements:* For master's, audition, minimum B average in undergraduate course work. Additional exam requirements/recommendations for international students: required—TOEFL. Electronic applications accepted.

Sarah Lawrence College, Graduate Studies, Program in Dance/Movement Therapy, Bronxville, NY 10708-5999. Offers MS. *Degree requirements:* For master's, thesis, practicum.

Smith College, Graduate and Special Programs, Department of Dance, Northampton, MA 01063. Offers MFA. *Students:* 7 full-time (5 women); includes 1 minority (Hispanic/Latino), 1 international. Average age 31. 16 applicants, 31%

accepted, 4 enrolled. In 2019, 4 master's awarded. *Degree requirements:* For master's, thesis performance. *Entrance requirements:* For master's, audition. Additional exam requirements/recommendations for international students: required—TOEFL (minimum score 595 paper-based; 97 iBT), IELTS (minimum score 7.5). *Application deadline:* For fall admission, 1/15 for domestic and international students. Application fee: $60. *Expenses: Tuition:* Full-time $36,940; part-time $1690 per credit. *Required fees:* $90. Full-time tuition and fees vary according to course load, degree level and program. *Financial support:* In 2019–20, 7 students received support, including 7 teaching assistantships with full tuition reimbursements available (averaging $13,850 per year). Financial award application deadline: 1/15; financial award applicants required to submit CSS PROFILE or FAFSA. *Unit head:* Chris Aiken, Graduate Adviser, 413-585-3241, E-mail: caiken@smith.edu. *Application contact:* Ruth Morgan, Program Coordinator, 413-585-3050, E-mail: rmorgan@smith.edu.
Website: http://www.smith.edu/dance/

SUNY Brockport, School of Arts and Sciences, Department of Dance, Brockport, NY 14420-2997. Offers dance (MA, MFA), including choreography/performance, dance studies (MA). *Program availability:* Part-time. *Faculty:* 7 full-time (6 women), 5 part-time/adjunct (3 women). *Students:* 8 full-time (all women), 4 part-time (all women); includes 2 minority (both Black or African American, non-Hispanic/Latino). 20 applicants, 30% accepted, 3 enrolled. In 2019, 7 master's awarded. *Entrance requirements:* For master's, audition/interview, minimum GPA of 3.0, letters of recommendation, local writing assessment. Additional exam requirements/recommendations for international students: required—TOEFL (minimum score 550 paper-based; 79 iBT), IELTS (minimum score 6.5). *Application deadline:* For fall admission, 4/15 priority date for domestic and international students. Application fee: $50. Electronic applications accepted. *Expenses: Tuition, area resident:* Part-time $471 per credit hour. Tuition, nonresident: part-time $963 per credit hour. *Financial support:* In 2019–20, 1 fellowship with full tuition reimbursement (averaging $7,500 per year), 4 teaching assistantships with full tuition reimbursements (averaging $6,000 per year) were awarded; Federal Work-Study, scholarships/grants, and unspecified assistantships also available. Support available to part-time students. Financial award application deadline: 3/15; financial award applicants required to submit FAFSA. *Unit head:* Mariah Maloney, Graduate Director, 585-395-2493, Fax: 585-395-5134, E-mail: mmaloney@brockport.edu. *Application contact:* Danielle A. Welch, Graduate Counselor, 585-395-5430, Fax: 585-395-2115, E-mail: dwelch@brockport.edu.
Website: https://www.brockport.edu/academics/dance/

Temple University, Center for the Performing and Cinematic Arts, Boyer College of Music and Dance, Department of Dance, Philadelphia, PA 19122-6096. Offers MA, MFA, PhD. *Accreditation:* NASD. *Program availability:* Part-time. *Faculty:* 8 full-time (5 women), 13 part-time/adjunct (8 women). *Students:* 36 full-time (31 women); includes 11 minority (9 Black or African American, non-Hispanic/Latino; 2 Hispanic/Latino), 10 international. 33 applicants, 70% accepted, 8 enrolled. In 2019, 11 master's, 6 doctorates awarded. *Degree requirements:* For master's, comprehensive exam (for some programs), thesis (for some programs); for doctorate, thesis/dissertation. *Entrance requirements:* For master's and doctorate, audition/interview, academic writing sample, dance questionnaire. Additional exam requirements/recommendations for international students: required—TOEFL, IELTS, PTE, one of three is required. *Application deadline:* For fall admission, 1/2 for domestic students, 1/1 for international students. Application fee: $60. Electronic applications accepted. *Expenses:* Contact institution. *Financial support:* Fellowships with tuition reimbursements, research assistantships with tuition reimbursements, teaching assistantships with tuition reimbursements, career-related internships or fieldwork, Federal Work-Study, scholarships/grants, tuition waivers, and unspecified assistantships available. Financial award application deadline: 3/1; financial award applicants required to submit FAFSA. *Unit head:* Karen Bond, Chair, Assoc. Professor, Interim Coordinator of Graduate Studies, 215-204-6280, E-mail: karen.bond@temple.edu. *Application contact:* Norma Porter, Dance Admissions and Recruitment, 215-204-0533, Fax: 215-204-0533, E-mail: norma.porter@temple.edu.
Website: http://www.temple.edu/boyer/academicprograms/dance/

Texas Woman's University, Graduate School, College of Arts and Sciences, School of the Arts, Department of Dance, Denton, TX 76204. Offers MA, MFA, PhD. *Accreditation:* NASD. *Faculty:* 6 full-time (4 women), 1 (woman) part-time/adjunct. *Students:* 22 full-time (19 women), 23 part-time (22 women); includes 21 minority (12 Black or African American, non-Hispanic/Latino; 2 Asian, non-Hispanic/Latino; 3 Hispanic/Latino; 4 Two or more races, non-Hispanic/Latino), 1 international. Average age 34. 14 applicants, 79% accepted, 8 enrolled. In 2019, 7 master's, 2 doctorates awarded. *Degree requirements:* For master's, comprehensive exam, thesis or alternative, choreography portfolio, professional paper/thesis; for doctorate, comprehensive exam, thesis/dissertation, dissertation, written and oral exam. *Entrance requirements:* For master's, audition, 3 letters of recommendation, interview, writing sample, resume, personal essay, separate Dept of Dance Graduate Application Form, video portfolio; for doctorate, interview, 3 letters of recommendation, curriculum vitae, statement of purpose, separate PhD in Dance Application, writing sample. Additional exam requirements/recommendations for international students: required—TOEFL (minimum score 550 paper-based; 79 iBT), recommended—IELTS (minimum score 6.5), TSE (minimum score 53). *Application deadline:* For fall admission, 12/15 for domestic students, 6/15 priority date for international students. Application fee: $50 ($75 for international students). Electronic applications accepted. *Expenses: Tuition, area resident:* Full-time $4973.40; part-time $276.30 per semester hour. Tuition, state resident: Full-time $4973.40; part-time $276.30 per semester hour. Tuition, nonresident: full-time $12,569; part-time $698.30 per semester hour. *International tuition:* $12,569.40 full-time. *Required fees:* $2524.30. Tuition and fees vary according to course level, course load, degree level and program. *Financial support:* In 2019–20, 26 students received support, including 9 teaching assistantships (averaging $11,311 per year); career-related internships or fieldwork, scholarships/grants, health care benefits, and unspecified assistantships also available. Support available to part-time students. Financial award application deadline: 3/1; financial award applicants required to submit FAFSA. *Unit head:* Mary Williford-Shade, Chair, 940-898-2086, Fax: 940-898-2098, E-mail: dance@twu.edu. *Application contact:* Korie Hawkins, Associate Director of Admissions, Graduate Recruitment, 940-898-3188, Fax: 940-898-3081, E-mail: admissions@twu.edu.
Website: http://www.twu.edu/dance/

Tulane University, School of Liberal Arts, Department of Theatre and Dance, New Orleans, LA 70118-5669. Offers design and technical production (MFA). *Entrance requirements:* For master's, GRE General Test, minimum B average in undergraduate course work. Additional exam requirements/recommendations for international students: required—TOEFL. Electronic applications accepted. *Expenses: Tuition:* Full-time $57,004; part-time $3167 per credit hour. *Required fees:* $2086; $44.50 per credit hour. $80 per term. Tuition and fees vary according to course load, degree level and program.

Université du Québec à Montréal, Graduate Programs, Program in Dance, Montréal, QC H3C 3P8, Canada. Offers MA. *Program availability:* Part-time. *Degree requirements:* For master's, thesis optional. *Entrance requirements:* For master's, appropriate bachelor's degree or equivalent and proficiency in French.

University at Buffalo, the State University of New York, Graduate School, College of Arts and Sciences, Department of Theatre and Dance, Buffalo, NY 14260. Offers dance (MFA); theatre and performance (MA, PhD). *Program availability:* Part-time. *Faculty:* 10 full-time (7 women). *Students:* 14 full-time (11 women), 5 part-time (3 women). Average age 36. 34 applicants, 44% accepted, 9 enrolled. In 2019, 4 master's, 1 doctorate awarded. *Degree requirements:* For master's, comprehensive exam (for some programs), thesis project or written thesis; for doctorate, one foreign language, comprehensive exam, thesis/dissertation. *Entrance requirements:* For master's, statement of purpose; academic writing sample (e.g., scholarly essay, performance or book review); 3 letters of recommendation (sent electronically); portfolio of creative work; resume; BA, BFA, or BS; audition and sample of choreographic work (for MFA); for doctorate, GRE, statement of purpose; academic writing sample (e.g., scholarly essay, performance or book review); 3 letters of recommendation (sent electronically); portfolio of creative work; resume; master's degree. Additional exam requirements/recommendations for international students: required—TOEFL (minimum score 550 paper-based), IELTS. *Application deadline:* For fall admission, 1/15 priority date for domestic and international students. Applications are processed on a rolling basis. Application fee: $75. Electronic applications accepted. *Expenses: Tuition, area resident:* Full-time $11,310; part-time $471 per credit hour. Tuition, state resident: full-time $11,310; part-time $471 per credit hour. Tuition, nonresident: full-time $23,100; part-time $963 per credit hour. *International tuition:* $23,100 full-time. *Required fees:* $2820. *Financial support:* In 2019–20, 2 fellowships (averaging $4,000 per year), 7 teaching assistantships with full tuition reimbursements (averaging $13,400 per year) were awarded; scholarships/grants also available. Financial award application deadline: 1/2. *Unit head:* Prof. Anne H. Burnidge, Chair, 716-645-6897, E-mail: burnidge@buffalo.edu. *Application contact:* Rachel Olszewski, Graduate Studies Staff Assistant, 716-645-6076, E-mail: rachelol@buffalo.edu.
Website: http://www.theatredance.buffalo.edu/

The University of Arizona, College of Fine Arts, School of Dance, Tucson, AZ 85721. Offers MFA. *Accreditation:* NASD. *Entrance requirements:* Additional exam requirements/recommendations for international students: required—TOEFL (minimum score 550 paper-based; 79 iBT). Electronic applications accepted.

University of California, Irvine, Claire Trevor School of the Arts, Department of Dance, Irvine, CA 92697. Offers MFA. *Students:* 15 full-time (8 women); includes 8 minority (2 Black or African American, non-Hispanic/Latino; 4 Asian, non-Hispanic/Latino; 1 Hispanic/Latino; 1 Two or more races, non-Hispanic/Latino), 2 international. Average age 31. 42 applicants, 19% accepted, 7 enrolled. In 2019, 10 master's awarded. *Entrance requirements:* For master's, minimum GPA of 3.0. *Application deadline:* For fall admission, 1/15 priority date for domestic students, 1/15 for international students. Applications are processed on a rolling basis. Application fee: $120 ($140 for international students). Electronic applications accepted. *Financial support:* Fellowships, teaching assistantships, institutionally sponsored loans, traineeships, health care benefits, and unspecified assistantships available. Financial award application deadline: 3/1; financial award applicants required to submit FAFSA. *Unit head:* Molly Lynch, Chair, 949-824-7226, Fax: 949-824-4563, E-mail: mlynch@uci.edu. *Application contact:* Robert Warner, Department Manager, 949-824-2692, Fax: 949-824-4563, E-mail: r.warner@uci.edu.
Website: http://dance.arts.uci.edu/

University of California, Los Angeles, Graduate Division, School of the Arts and Architecture, Department of World Arts and Cultures, Los Angeles, CA 90095. Offers culture and performance (MA, PhD); dance (MFA). *Degree requirements:* For master's, 1 foreign language, and comprehensive exam or thesis (MA); comprehensive exam (MFA); for doctorate, one foreign language, thesis/dissertation, oral and written qualifying exams. *Entrance requirements:* For master's, bachelor's degree; minimum undergraduate GPA of 3.0 (or its equivalent if letter grade system not used); audition and interview (MFA); writing sample (MA); for doctorate, master's degree; minimum undergraduate GPA of 3.0 (or its equivalent if letter grade system not used); writing sample. Additional exam requirements/recommendations for international students: required—TOEFL. Electronic applications accepted.

University of California, Riverside, Graduate Division, Department of Dance, Riverside, CA 92521. Offers experimental choreography (MFA). *Entrance requirements:* For master's, stable electronic link (such as Vimeo/YouTube) of a choreographed piece (for MFA program only). Additional exam requirements/recommendations for international students: required—TOEFL (minimum score 550 paper-based; 80 iBT). Electronic applications accepted.

University of California, San Diego, Graduate Division, Department of Theatre and Dance, La Jolla, CA 92093. Offers acting (MFA); dance theatre (MFA); design (MFA); directing (MFA); drama and theatre (PhD); playwriting (MFA); stage management (MFA). *Students:* 73 full-time (42 women). 523 applicants, 6% accepted, 19 enrolled. In 2019, 20 master's, 4 doctorates awarded. *Degree requirements:* For master's, thesis; for doctorate, comprehensive exam, thesis/dissertation, 4 quarters of teaching. *Entrance requirements:* For master's, GRE General Test (for playwriting only), minimum GPA of 3.5; audition or interview; for doctorate, GRE General Test, minimum GPA of 3.5, audition and/or interview, two samples of critical writing. Additional exam requirements/recommendations for international students: required—TOEFL (minimum score 550 paper-based; 80 iBT), IELTS (minimum score 7). *Application deadline:* For fall admission, 1/10 for domestic students. Application fee: $105 ($125 for international students). Electronic applications accepted. *Financial support:* Fellowships, teaching assistantships, and scholarships/grants available. Financial award applicants required to submit FAFSA. *Unit head:* Allan Havis, Chair, 858-534-8208, E-mail: ahavis@ucsd.edu. *Application contact:* Marybeth Ward, Graduate Coordinator, 858-534-1046, E-mail: meward@ucsd.edu.
Website: http://theatre.ucsd.edu/

University of Colorado Boulder, Graduate School, College of Arts and Sciences, Department of Theatre and Dance, Boulder, CO 80309. Offers dance (MFA); theatre (MA, PhD). Terminal master's awarded for partial completion of doctoral program. *Degree requirements:* For master's, comprehensive exam, thesis; for doctorate, one foreign language, thesis/dissertation. *Entrance requirements:* For master's, GRE General Test (MA), audition (MFA), minimum undergraduate GPA of 2.75. Electronic applications accepted. Application fee is waived when completed online.

University of Hawaii at Manoa, Office of Graduate Education, College of Arts and Humanities, Department of Theatre and Dance, Honolulu, HI 96822. Offers dance (MA, MFA); theatre (MA, MFA, PhD). *Program availability:* Part-time. *Degree requirements:* For master's, one foreign language, thesis optional; for doctorate, one foreign language, comprehensive exam, thesis/dissertation. *Entrance requirements:* For master's and doctorate, GRE General Test. Additional exam requirements/recommendations for international students: required—TOEFL (minimum score 600 paper-based; 100 iBT), IELTS (minimum score 7).

University of Illinois at Urbana-Champaign, Graduate College, College of Fine and Applied Arts, Department of Dance, Champaign, IL 61820. Offers MFA. *Accreditation:* NASD.

Dance

The University of Iowa, Graduate College, College of Liberal Arts and Sciences, Department of Dance, Iowa City, IA 52242-1316. Offers MFA. *Accreditation:* NASD. *Degree requirements:* For master's, thesis, exam. *Entrance requirements:* For master's, minimum GPA of 3.0. Additional exam requirements/recommendations for international students: required—TOEFL (minimum score 550 paper-based; 81 iBT). Electronic applications accepted.

University of Maryland, Baltimore County, The Graduate School, College of Arts, Humanities and Social Sciences, Department of Education, Program in Teaching, Baltimore, MD 21250. Offers early childhood education (MAT); elementary education (MAT); teaching (MAT), including art, biology, chemistry, choral music, classical foreign language, dance, earth/space science, English, instrumental music, mathematics, modern foreign language, physical science, physics, social studies, theatre. *Program availability:* Part-time, evening/weekend. *Faculty:* 24 full-time (18 women), 25 part-time/adjunct (19 women). *Students:* 25 full-time (19 women), 15 part-time (8 women); includes 14 minority (5 Black or African American, non-Hispanic/Latino; 1 American Indian or Alaska Native, non-Hispanic/Latino; 5 Asian, non-Hispanic/Latino; 1 Hispanic/Latino; 2 Two or more races, non-Hispanic/Latino). Average age 32. 34 applicants, 79% accepted, 18 enrolled. In 2019, 23 master's awarded. *Degree requirements:* For master's, comprehensive exam (for some programs), thesis (for some programs). *Entrance requirements:* For master's, PRAXIS Core Examination or GRE (minimum score of 1000), minimum GPA of 3.0. Additional exam requirements/recommendations for international students: required—TOEFL. *Application deadline:* For fall admission, 6/1 for domestic and international students; for spring admission, 11/1 for domestic and international students. Applications are processed on a rolling basis. Application fee: $50. Electronic applications accepted. *Expenses: Tuition, area resident:* Full-time $659. Tuition, state resident: full-time $659. Tuition, nonresident: full-time $1132. *International tuition:* $1132 full-time. *Required fees:* $140; $140 per credit hour. *Financial support:* In 2019–20, 6 students received support, including 1 research assistantship with tuition reimbursement available (averaging $12,000 per year), 5 teaching assistantships with tuition reimbursements available (averaging $12,000 per year); career-related internships or fieldwork, Federal Work-Study, scholarships/grants, tuition waivers, and unspecified assistantships also available. Financial award application deadline: 3/15. *Unit head:* Dr. Susan M. Blunck, Graduate Program Director, 410-455-2869, Fax: 410-455-3986, E-mail: blunck@umbc.edu. *Application contact:* Cheryl Johnson, MAT Program Specialist, 410-455-3388, E-mail: blackwel@umbc.edu.
Website: http://www.umbc.edu/education/

University of Maryland, College Park, Academic Affairs, College of Arts and Humanities, School of Theatre, Dance and Performance Studies, Program in Dance, College Park, MD 20742. Offers MFA. *Accreditation:* NASD. *Degree requirements:* For master's, final project. *Entrance requirements:* For master's, audition/interview, video tapes/writing sample, 3 letters of recommendation. Additional exam requirements/recommendations for international students: required—TOEFL. Electronic applications accepted.

University of Michigan, Rackham Graduate School, School of Music, Theatre, and Dance, Department of Dance, Ann Arbor, MI 48109-2217. Offers modern dance performance and choreography (MFA). *Accreditation:* NASD. *Entrance requirements:* For master's, audition. Additional exam requirements/recommendations for international students: required—TOEFL. Electronic applications accepted.

University of New Mexico, Graduate Studies, College of Fine Arts, Department of Theatre and Dance, Albuquerque, NM 87131-2039. Offers dance (MFA); dance history (MA); dramatic writing (MFA); theatre education and outreach (MA). *Accreditation:* NASD; NAST. *Degree requirements:* For master's, comprehensive exam (for some programs), thesis (for some programs). *Entrance requirements:* For master's, minimum GPA of 3.0; undergraduate major in theatre, dance or closely-related field; 3 letters of recommendation; letter of intent; BA, BFA, BS, or MA in dance movement science or related field, or equivalent experience (for MFA in dance). Electronic applications accepted. *Expenses:* Tuition, state resident: full-time $7633; part-time $972 per year. Tuition, nonresident: full-time $22,586; part-time $3840 per year. *International tuition:* $23,292 full-time. *Required fees:* $8608. Tuition and fees vary according to course level, course load, degree level, program and student level.

The University of North Carolina at Greensboro, Graduate School, School of Music, Theatre and Dance, Department of Dance, Greensboro, NC 27412-5001. Offers MA, MFA. *Accreditation:* NASD. *Degree requirements:* For master's, thesis. *Entrance requirements:* For master's, GRE General Test or MAT, audition or video (MFA). Additional exam requirements/recommendations for international students: required—TOEFL. Electronic applications accepted.

University of Oklahoma, Weitzenhoffer Family College of Fine Arts, School of Dance, Norman, OK 73019. Offers dance (MFA); modern dance (MFA). *Entrance requirements:* For master's, BFA in dance, audition, interview, writing sample, letters of recommendation. Additional exam requirements/recommendations for international students: required—TOEFL (minimum score 79 iBT) or IELTS (minimum score 6.5). Electronic applications accepted. *Expenses:* Tuition, state resident: full-time $6583.20; part-time $274.30 per credit hour. Tuition, nonresident: full-time $21,242; part-time $885.10 per credit hour. *International tuition:* $21,242.40 full-time. *Required fees:* $1994.20; $72.55 per credit hour. $126.50 per semester. Tuition and fees vary according to course load and degree level.

University of Oregon, Graduate School, School of Music, Department of Dance, Eugene, OR 97403. Offers MA, MS. *Degree requirements:* For master's, thesis or alternative. *Entrance requirements:* For master's, minimum GPA of 3.0. Additional exam requirements/recommendations for international students: required—TOEFL.

The University of Texas at Austin, Graduate School, College of Fine Arts, Department of Theatre and Dance, Austin, TX 78712-1111. Offers acting (MFA); dance (MFA); directing (MFA); drama and theatre for youth (MFA); performance as public practice (MA, MFA, PhD); playwriting (MFA); theatre technology (MFA); theatrical design (MFA). *Degree requirements:* For master's, thesis; for doctorate, variable foreign language requirement, thesis/dissertation. *Entrance requirements:* For master's and doctorate, GRE General Test.

The University of the Arts, College of Performing Arts, School of Dance, Philadelphia, PA 19102-4944. Offers MFA.

University of Utah, Graduate School, College of Fine Arts, School of Dance, Salt Lake City, UT 84112-0280. Offers MFA, Certificate. *Accreditation:* NASD. *Program availability:* Blended/hybrid learning. *Faculty:* 10 full-time (7 women). *Students:* 12 full-time (10 women), 1 (woman) part-time; includes 2 minority (1 Black or African American, non-Hispanic/Latino; 1 Hispanic/Latino). Average age 30. 15 applicants, 20% accepted, 3 enrolled. In 2019, 7 master's awarded. *Degree requirements:* For master's, thesis, Candidates must maintain at least a 3.0 grade point average with no required classes graded below B-. *Entrance requirements:* For master's, Ballet: applicants must submit a video of themselves teaching a ballet class, a curriculum vitae, and 1000-2000 word essay/statement of purpose in addition to University application requirements. Modern Dance: an in-person audition is required and offered twice a year in January and February; video auditions are accepted, but only students audition; for Certificate, Screendance: applicants will need to fill out and submit the Screendance Certificate Application found on the School of Dance website, a curriculum vitae, a DVD or online link to work samples and 2 letters of recommendation to the program director electronically or through the mail. Additional exam requirements/recommendations for international students: required—TOEFL (minimum score 80 paper-based; 80 iBT), IELTS (minimum score 6.5). *Application deadline:* For fall admission, 1/25 priority date for domestic and international students. Application fee: $105 ($115 for international students). Electronic applications accepted. *Expenses:* Contact institution. *Financial support:* In 2019–20, 12 students received support, including 12 teaching assistantships (averaging $164,032 per year). Financial award application deadline: 1/25; financial award applicants required to submit FAFSA. *Unit head:* Luc Vanier, Director, School of Dance, 801-581-7327, Fax: 801-581-5442, E-mail: luc.vanier@utah.edu. *Application contact:* Eric Handman, Director of Graduate Studies, 801-587-9813, Fax: 801-581-5442, E-mail: eric.handman@utah.edu.
Website: http://www.dance.utah.edu

University of Washington, Graduate School, College of Arts and Sciences, Program in Dance, Seattle, WA 98195-1150. Offers MFA. *Degree requirements:* For master's, performance, project, course development. *Entrance requirements:* For master's, 8 years of professional dance experience, resume, performance DVD or VHS tape, 3 letters of reference. Additional exam requirements/recommendations for international students: required—TOEFL. Electronic applications accepted.

University of Wisconsin–Milwaukee, Graduate School, Peck School of the Arts, Milwaukee, WI 53201-0413. Offers art education (MS); chamber music (CAS); conducting (MM); dance (MFA); design entrepreneurship and innovation (MA); film, video, animation, and new genres (MFA); music education (MM); music history and literature (MM); performance (MM); string pedagogy (MM); studio art (MA, MFA); theory and composition (MM). *Program availability:* Part-time. *Degree requirements:* For master's, comprehensive exam, thesis or alternative. *Entrance requirements:* For master's, portfolio. Additional exam requirements/recommendations for international students: required—TOEFL (minimum score 550 paper-based; 79 iBT), IELTS (minimum score 6.5). Electronic applications accepted.

Washington University in St. Louis, The Graduate School, Department of Performing Arts, St. Louis, MO 63130-4899. Offers dance (MFA); theater and performance studies (MA). *Degree requirements:* For master's, thesis optional. *Entrance requirements:* For master's, GRE General Test, sample of written work. Additional exam requirements/recommendations for international students: required—TOEFL. Electronic applications accepted.

Wilson College, Graduate Programs, Chambersburg, PA 17201-1285. Offers accounting (M Acc); choreography and visual art (MFA); education (M Ed); educational technology (MET); healthcare administration (MHA); humanities (MA), including art and culture, critical/cultural theory, English language and literature, women's studies; management (MSM); nursing (MSN), including nursing education, nursing leadership and management; special education (MSE). *Program availability:* Evening/weekend. *Degree requirements:* For master's, project. *Entrance requirements:* For master's, PRAXIS, minimum undergraduate cumulative GPA of 3.0, 2 letters of recommendation, current certification for eligibility to teach in grades K-12, resume, personal interview. Electronic applications accepted.

York University, Faculty of Graduate Studies, Faculty of Fine Arts, Program in Dance, Toronto, ON M3J 1P3, Canada. Offers MA, MFA, PhD. *Degree requirements:* For master's, thesis or alternative. Electronic applications accepted.

Music

Academy of Art University, Graduate Programs, School of Music Production and Sound Design for Visual Media, San Francisco, CA 94105-3410. Offers music scoring and composition (MA, MFA); sound design (MA, MFA). *Program availability:* Part-time, 100% online. *Faculty:* 1 full-time (0 women), 26 part-time/adjunct (4 women). *Students:* 73 full-time (33 women), 23 part-time (7 women); includes 16 minority (7 Black or African American, non-Hispanic/Latino; 1 Asian, non-Hispanic/Latino; 4 Hispanic/Latino; 4 Two or more races, non-Hispanic/Latino), 54 international. Average age 30. 44 applicants, 100% accepted, 31 enrolled. In 2019, 34 master's awarded. *Degree requirements:* For master's, final review. *Entrance requirements:* For master's, statement of intent; resume; portfolio/reel; official college transcripts. *Application deadline:* Applications are processed on a rolling basis. Application fee: $50. Electronic applications accepted. *Expenses:* Tuition: Full-time $1083; part-time $1083 per credit hour. *Required fees:* $860; $860 per unit. $430 per term. One-time fee: $145. Tuition and fees vary according to program. *Financial support:* Career-related internships or fieldwork, Federal Work-Study, and scholarships/grants available. Financial award application deadline: 8/10; financial award applicants required to submit FAFSA.
Website: http://www.academyart.edu/music-for-visual-media/index.html

American University, College of Arts and Sciences, Department of Performing Arts, Washington, DC 20016-8053. Offers art management (MA); audio production (Certificate); audio technology (MA); international arts management (Certificate); technology in arts management (Certificate). *Program availability:* Part-time, evening/weekend. *Degree requirements:* For master's, comprehensive exam, thesis or alternative. *Entrance requirements:* For master's, GRE; Please visits website: https://www.american.edu/cas/performing-arts/index.cfm, minimum GPA of 3.0, statement of purpose, transcripts, 2 letters of recommendation, resume, art portfolio; for Certificate, bachelor's degree, statement of purpose, transcripts, resume, art portfolio. Additional exam requirements/recommendations for international students: required—TOEFL. *Expenses:* Contact institution.

Andrews University, School of Graduate Studies, College of Arts and Sciences, Department of Music, Berrien Springs, MI 49104. Offers M Mus, MA. *Accreditation:* NASM. *Faculty:* 10 full-time (4 women). *Students:* 4 full-time (2 women), 10 part-time (5 women); includes 2 minority (1 Black or African American, non-Hispanic/Latino; 1 Hispanic/Latino), 9 international. Average age 29. In 2019, 4 master's awarded. *Degree* *requirements:* For master's, variable foreign language requirement. *Entrance requirements:* For master's, GRE Subject Test, minimum undergraduate GPA of 2.6. Additional exam requirements/recommendations for international students: required—TOEFL (minimum score 550 paper-based). *Application deadline:* Applications are processed on a rolling basis. Application fee: $60. Electronic applications accepted. *Financial support:* Research assistantships, teaching assistantships, Federal Work-Study, institutionally sponsored loans, and scholarships/grants available. *Unit head:* Dr. Adriana Perera, Chairman, 269-471-3555. *Application contact:* Jillian Panigot, Director, University Admissions, 800-253-2874, Fax: 269-471-6321, E-mail: graduate@andrews.edu.

Appalachian State University, Cratis D. Williams School of Graduate Studies, School of Music, Boone, NC 28608. Offers music performance (MM); music therapy (MMT). *Accreditation:* NASM. *Program availability:* Part-time. *Degree requirements:* For master's, comprehensive exam, thesis or alternative. *Entrance requirements:* For master's, GRE General Test, 3 letters of reference, audition. Additional exam requirements/recommendations for international students: required—TOEFL (minimum score 550 paper-based; 79 iBT), IELTS (minimum score 6.5). Electronic applications accepted.

Aquinas Institute of Theology, Graduate and Professional Programs, St. Louis, MO 63108. Offers biblical studies (Certificate); church music (MM); health care mission (MAHCM); ministry (M Div); pastoral care (Certificate); pastoral ministry (MAPM); pastoral studies (MAPS); preaching (D Min); spiritual direction (Certificate); theology (M Div, MA); Thomistic studies (Certificate); M Div/MA; MA/PhD; MAPS/MSW. *Accreditation:* ATS (one or more programs are accredited). *Program availability:* Part-time, evening/weekend, online learning. *Degree requirements:* For master's, variable foreign language requirement, comprehensive exam (for some programs), thesis (for some programs); for doctorate, thesis/dissertation. *Entrance requirements:* For master's and Certificate, MAT; for doctorate, 3 years of ministerial experience, 6 hours of graduate course work in homiletics, M Div or the equivalent, minimum GPA of 3.0. Additional exam requirements/recommendations for international students: required—TOEFL. *Expenses:* Contact institution.

Arizona State University at Tempe, Herberger Institute for Design and the Arts, School of Film, Dance and Theatre, Tempe, AZ 85287-2002. Offers dance (MFA), including dance, interdisciplinary digital media and performance; theatre (MA, MFA, PhD), including arts entrepreneurship and management (MFA), directing (MFA), dramatic writing (MFA), interdisciplinary digital media and performance (MFA), performance (MFA), performance design (MFA), theatre (MFA), theatre and performance of the Americas (PhD), theatre for youth (MFA, PhD). Terminal master's awarded for partial completion of doctoral program. *Degree requirements:* For master's, comprehensive exam (for some programs), thesis (for some programs), applied project (for some programs); interactive Program of Study (iPOS) submitted before completing 50 percent of required credit hours; for doctorate, comprehensive exam, thesis/dissertation, interactive Program of Study (iPOS) submitted before completing 50 percent of required credit hours. *Entrance requirements:* For master's, GRE or MAT, minimum GPA of 3.0 in last 2 years of work leading to bachelor's degree (depending on program); for doctorate, GRE, minimum GPA of 3.0 or equivalent in last 2 years of work leading to bachelor's degree, 3 letters of recommendation, resume, scholarly writing sample, statement of purpose. Additional exam requirements/recommendations for international students: required—TOEFL, IELTS, or PTE. Electronic applications accepted.

Arizona State University at Tempe, Herberger Institute for Design and the Arts, School of Music, Tempe, AZ 85287-0405. Offers composition (MM, DMA); conducting (DMA); ethnomusicology (MA); interdisciplinary digital media/performance (DMA); music education (MM, PhD); music history and literature (MA); music therapy (MM); performance (MM, DMA). *Accreditation:* NASM. Terminal master's awarded for partial completion of doctoral program. *Degree requirements:* For master's, thesis (for some programs), interactive Program of Study (iPOS) submitted before completing 50 percent of required credit hours; for doctorate, comprehensive exam, thesis/dissertation, interactive Program of Study (iPOS) submitted before completing 50 percent of required credit hours. *Entrance requirements:* For master's, minimum GPA of 3.0 or equivalent in last 2 years of work leading to bachelor's degree, 3 letters of recommendation, resume; for doctorate, GRE or MAT, minimum GPA of 3.0 or equivalent in last 2 years of work leading to bachelor's degree, 3 letters of recommendation, curriculum vitae, statement of intent. Additional exam requirements/recommendations for international students: required—TOEFL, IELTS, or PTE. Electronic applications accepted.

Arkansas State University, Graduate School, College of Fine Arts, Department of Music, State University, AR 72467. Offers music education (MME, SCCT); music performance (MM). *Accreditation:* NASM (one or more programs are accredited). *Program availability:* Part-time. *Degree requirements:* For master's, 2 foreign languages, comprehensive exam, thesis or alternative; for SCCT, comprehensive exam. *Entrance requirements:* For master's, GRE General Test or MAT, university entrance exam, appropriate bachelor's degree, audition, letters of recommendation, teaching experience, official transcripts, immunization records, valid teaching certificate; for SCCT, GRE General Test or MAT, interview, master's degree, official transcript, immunization records, letters of recommendation. Additional exam requirements/recommendations for international students: required—TOEFL (minimum score 550 paper-based; 79 iBT), IELTS (minimum score 6), PTE (minimum score 56). Electronic applications accepted.

Austin Peay State University, College of Graduate Studies, College of Arts and Letters, Department of Music, Clarksville, TN 37044. Offers music education (M Mu); music performance (M Mu). *Accreditation:* NASM. *Program availability:* Part-time. *Faculty:* 17 full-time (8 women), 4 part-time/adjunct (2 women). *Students:* 21 full-time (7 women), 9 part-time (7 women); includes 7 minority (4 Black or African American, non-Hispanic/Latino; 1 Asian, non-Hispanic/Latino; 2 Hispanic/Latino), 1 international. Average age 26. 17 applicants, 100% accepted, 12 enrolled. In 2019, 14 master's awarded. *Degree requirements:* For master's, comprehensive exam, thesis optional. *Entrance requirements:* For master's, GRE General Test, diagnostic exams, audition, interview, bachelor's degree, 3 letters of recommendation. Additional exam requirements/recommendations for international students: required—TOEFL (minimum score 500 paper-based). *Application deadline:* For fall admission, 8/5 priority date for domestic students. Applications are processed on a rolling basis. Application fee: $45 ($55 for international students). Electronic applications accepted. *Financial support:* Research assistantships with full tuition reimbursements, career-related internships or fieldwork, Federal Work-Study, institutionally sponsored loans, scholarships/grants, and unspecified assistantships available. Support available to part-time students. Financial award application deadline: 7/1; financial award applicants required to submit FAFSA. *Unit head:* Dr. Eric Branscome, Chair, 931-221-7811, Fax: 931-221-7529, E-mail: branscomee@apsu.edu. *Application contact:* Megan Mitchell, Coordinator of Graduate Admissions, 931-221-6189, Fax: 931-221-7641, E-mail: mitchellm@apsu.edu. Website: http://www.apsu.edu/music/

Azusa Pacific University, College of Music and the Arts, Azusa, CA 91702-7000. Offers composition (M Mus); conducting (M Mus); education (M Mus); modern art history, theory, and criticism (MA); music entrepreneurial studies (MA); performance

(M Mus); screenwriting (MA); visual art (MFA). *Accreditation:* NASAD; NASM. *Program availability:* Part-time, evening/weekend. *Degree requirements:* For master's, recital. *Entrance requirements:* For master's, interview, audition. Additional exam requirements/recommendations for international students: required—TOEFL (minimum score 550 paper-based).

Ball State University, Graduate School, College of Fine Arts, School of Music, Muncie, IN 47306. Offers music (MA, MM, DA, Artist Diploma), including conducting (MM, DA), music education (MA, MM, DA), music history and musicology (MA, MM, DA), music performance (MA, MM, DA), music theory (MA), music theory and composition (DA), piano chamber music/accompanying (MM, DA), piano performance and pedagogy (MM), woodwinds (MM). *Accreditation:* NASM; NCATE (one or more programs are accredited). *Degree requirements:* For doctorate, thesis/dissertation. *Entrance requirements:* For master's, placement tests in history and theory, minimum baccalaureate GPA of 2.75 or 3.0 in latter half of baccalaureate, resume, audition; for doctorate, GRE General Test, minimum graduate GPA of 3.2, interview, audition, resume, three professional letters of reference. Additional exam requirements/recommendations for international students: required—TOEFL (minimum score 550 paper-based; 79 iBT), IELTS (minimum score 6.5). Electronic applications accepted. *Expenses:* Contact institution.

The Baptist College of Florida, Graduate Programs, Graceville, FL 32440. Offers Christian studies (MA); music and worship leadership (MA). *Program availability:* Part-time, 100% online, blended/hybrid learning. *Faculty:* 13 full-time (2 women). *Students:* 33 full-time (6 women); includes 2 minority (1 Black or African American, non-Hispanic/Latino; 1 Hispanic/Latino). Average age 28. 10 applicants, 100% accepted, 10 enrolled. In 2019, 3 master's awarded. *Degree requirements:* For master's, variable foreign language requirement, comprehensive exam (for some programs), thesis (for some programs). *Entrance requirements:* For master's, regionally-accredited undergraduate degree, undergraduate courses in field, minimum GPA of 2.5. Additional exam requirements/recommendations for international students: required—TOEFL. *Application deadline:* For fall admission, 8/10 for domestic and international students; for spring admission, 1/20 for domestic and international students. Applications are processed on a rolling basis. Application fee: $25. Electronic applications accepted. *Expenses:* Tuition: Full-time $4320; part-time $360 per credit hour. *Financial support:* In 2019–20, 2 students received support. Applicants required to submit FAFSA. *Unit head:* Dr. Robin Jumper, Academic Dean, 850-263-3261 Ext. 425, Fax: 850-263-2141, E-mail: grjumper@baptistcollege.edu. *Application contact:* Sandra Richards, Director of Student Life and Marketing, 850-263-3261 Ext. 415, Fax: 850-263-9026, E-mail: skrichards@baptistcollege.edu.
Website: http://www.baptistcollege.edu

Bard College, Conservatory of Music, The Conductors Institute, Annandale-on-Hudson, NY 12504. Offers choral conducting (MM); orchestral conducting (MM). *Entrance requirements:* For master's, resume, 3 letters of recommendation.

Bard College, Conservatory of Music, Graduate Program in Vocal Arts, Annandale-on-Hudson, NY 12504. Offers MM. *Entrance requirements:* For master's, portfolio, 2 letters of recommendation, headshot, repertoire list. *Expenses:* Contact institution.

Bard College, Longy School of Music of Bard College, Cambridge, MA 02138. Offers chamber music (Artist Diploma); collaborative piano (MM, Artist Diploma, GPD); composition (MM); opera (MM, GPD); organ (MM, Artist Diploma, GPD); piano (MM, Artist Diploma, GPD); voice (MM, Artist Diploma, GPD). *Program availability:* Part-time. *Degree requirements:* For master's, thesis (for some programs), recital; for other advanced degree, recital. *Entrance requirements:* For master's and other advanced degree, audition. Additional exam requirements/recommendations for international students: required—TOEFL (minimum score 550 paper-based; 79 iBT). Electronic applications accepted.

Baylor University, Graduate School, School of Music, Waco, TX 76798. Offers church music (MM, DMA); conducting (MM); musicology (MM); M Div/MM. *Accreditation:* NASM. *Faculty:* 57 full-time (23 women), 6 part-time/adjunct (4 women). *Students:* 27 full-time (9 women), 44 part-time (21 women); includes 13 minority (2 Black or African American, non-Hispanic/Latino; 9 Hispanic/Latino; 2 Two or more races, non-Hispanic/Latino), 13 international. Average age 26. 88 applicants, 67% accepted, 33 enrolled. In 2019, 23 master's, 2 doctorates awarded. *Degree requirements:* For master's, variable foreign language requirement, comprehensive exam, thesis (for some programs); for doctorate, one foreign language, comprehensive exam, thesis/dissertation (for some programs). *Entrance requirements:* For master's, GRE for Music Theory, Musicology, purpose statement; transcripts; resume; 3 letters of recommendation; audition for performance degrees; teaching video for Piano Pedagogy; 2 conducting videos (Rehearsal & Performance) for Conducting and Church Music with Conducting Emphasis; writing sample of 10 pages for Musicology, Music Theory, and Church Music; portfolio for Composition; for doctorate, GRE, purpose statement; 25 page writing sample; audition for DMA; resume; transcripts; 3 letters of recommendation; 2 conducting videos (Rehearsal & Performance) for DMA with Conducting Emphasis. Additional exam requirements/recommendations for international students: required—TOEFL (minimum score 550 paper-based; 80 iBT), IELTS (minimum score 6.5), Either TOEFL or IELTS is required. *Application deadline:* For fall admission, 2/15 for domestic and international students; for spring admission, 10/15 for domestic and international students. Application fee: $80. Electronic applications accepted. *Financial support:* In 2019–20, 66 students received support, including 16 teaching assistantships with full tuition reimbursements available (averaging $7,546 per year); Federal Work-Study, scholarships/grants, and unspecified assistantships also available. Financial award application deadline: 2/15. *Unit head:* Dr. Timothy McKinney, Associate Dean for Graduate Studies, 254-710-6498, Fax: 254-710-1191, E-mail: Timothy_McKinney@baylor.edu. *Application contact:* Melinda G. Coats, Administrative Associate for Graduate and Academic Studies, 254-710-2360, Fax: 254-710-1491, E-mail: melinda_coats@baylor.edu.
Website: http://www.baylor.edu/music/

Bennington College, Graduate Programs, MFA in Music Program, Bennington, VT 05201. Offers MFA. *Program availability:* Part-time. *Degree requirements:* For master's, thesis, concert performances. *Entrance requirements:* Additional exam requirements/recommendations for international students: recommended—TOEFL. Electronic applications accepted. *Expenses:* Contact institution.

Berklee College of Music, Berklee Graduate Programs, Boston, MA 46013, Spain. Offers contemporary performance (MM), including global jazz, production; global entertainment and music business (MA); music production, technology, and innovation (MM); scoring for film, television, and video games (MM). *Program availability:* Part-time. *Faculty:* 18 full-time (6 women), 46 part-time/adjunct (11 women). *Students:* 212 full-time (94 women), 1 part-time (0 women); includes 40 minority (11 Black or African American, non-Hispanic/Latino; 7 Asian, non-Hispanic/Latino; 17 Hispanic/Latino; 5 Two or more races, non-Hispanic/Latino), 123 international. Average age 27. 683 applicants, 39% accepted, 167 enrolled. In 2019, 141 master's awarded. *Degree requirements:* For master's, thesis, culminating experience project. *Entrance requirements:* Additional exam requirements/recommendations for international students: required—TOEFL (minimum score 600 paper-based; 100 iBT), IELTS (minimum score 7.5), PTE

(minimum score 73), Business English Certificate, Certificate in Advanced English, Duolingo. *Application deadline:* For fall admission, 1/15 for domestic and international students. Application fee: 150 euros for international students. Electronic applications accepted. *Expenses:* Contact institution. *Financial support:* Fellowships with full and partial tuition reimbursements, research assistantships, career-related internships or fieldwork, scholarships/grants, and tuition waivers (full and partial) available. Support available to part-time students. Financial award application deadline: 1/15; financial award applicants required to submit CSS PROFILE or FAFSA. *Unit head:* Rob Lagueux, PhD, Associate Vice President for Academic Affairs, 617-747-6908, E-mail: rlagueux@berklee.edu. *Application contact:* Office of Admissions, 617-747-2221, E-mail: admissions@berklee.edu.
Website: https://www.berklee.edu/graduate

Berklee College of Music, The Boston Conservatory at Berklee, Boston, MA 02215-3693. Offers bassoon performance (MM); cello performance (MM); choral conducting (MM); clarinet performance (MM); collaborative piano (MM); composition (MM); contemporary music performance (MM); double bass performance (MM); flute performance (MM); harp performance (MM); horn performance (MM); marimba performance (MM); music and autism (Certificate); music education (MM); music education and autism (MM); music performance (ADP); musical theater (MFA); oboe performance (MM); opera performance (MM); orchestral conducting (MM); percussion performance (MM); piano performance (MM); saxophone performance (MM); trombone performance (MM); trumpet performance (MM). *Program availability:* Part-time. *Faculty:* 20 full-time (11 women), 26 part-time/adjunct (15 women). *Students:* 232 full-time (134 women), 2 part-time (1 woman); includes 45 minority (10 Black or African American, non-Hispanic/Latino; 2 American Indian or Alaska Native, non-Hispanic/Latino; 8 Asian, non-Hispanic/Latino; 10 Hispanic/Latino; 15 Two or more races, non-Hispanic/Latino), 92 international. Average age 26. 769 applicants, 38% accepted, 110 enrolled. In 2019, 117 master's, 14 other advanced degrees awarded. *Degree requirements:* For master's, recital or performance; for other advanced degree, recital. *Entrance requirements:* For master's and other advanced degree, audition. Additional exam requirements/recommendations for international students: required—TOEFL (minimum score 550 paper-based; 79 iBT), IELTS (minimum score 6.5), Duolingo. *Application deadline:* For fall admission, 12/1 for domestic and international students. Application fee: $150. Electronic applications accepted. *Expenses:* MM & MFA: $45,280/year tuition, $1040 fee. *Financial support:* Research assistantships, teaching assistantships, and scholarships/grants available. Financial award application deadline: 12/1; financial award applicants required to submit FAFSA. *Unit head:* Robert Lagueux, PhD, Associate Vice President, Academic Affairs, 617-747-6908, E-mail: rlagueux@berklee.edu. *Application contact:* Director of Admissions, 617-912-9153, Fax: 617-912-9217, E-mail: admissions@bostonconservatory.edu.
Website: http://www.bostonconservatory.edu/

Bethesda University, Graduate and Professional Programs, Anaheim, CA 92801. Offers biblical studies (MA); music (MA); theology (M Div). *Entrance requirements:* For master's, interview. Additional exam requirements/recommendations for international students: recommended—TOEFL.

Binghamton University, State University of New York, Graduate School, Harpur College of Arts and Sciences, Department of Music, Binghamton, NY 13902-6000. Offers MM. *Accreditation:* NASM. *Program availability:* Part-time. *Degree requirements:* For master's, variable foreign language requirement, comprehensive exam, thesis (for some programs). *Entrance requirements:* For master's, GRE (for music history and literature applicants), portfolio, writing sample. Additional exam requirements/recommendations for international students: required—TOEFL (minimum score 550 paper-based; 80 iBT). Electronic applications accepted.

Bob Jones University, Graduate Programs, Greenville, SC 29614. Offers accountancy (MS); Bible (MA); Bible translation (MA); Biblical studies (Certificate); business administration (MBA); church history (MA, PhD); church ministries (MA); church music (MM); cinema and video production (MA); counseling (MS); curriculum and instruction (Ed D); divinity (M Div); dramatic production (MA); educational leadership (MS, Ed D, Ed S); elementary education (M Ed, MAT); English (M Ed, MA, MAT); fine arts (MA); graphic design (MA); history (M Ed, MA); illustration (MA); interpretative speech (MA); mathematics (M Ed, MAT); medical missions (Certificate); ministry (MM, D Min); multi-categorical special education (M Ed, MAT); music (M Ed); New Testament interpretation (PhD); Old Testament interpretation (PhD); orchestral instrument performance (MM); organ performance (MM); pastoral studies (MA); personnel services (MS, Ed S); piano pedagogy (MM); piano performance (MM); platform arts (MA); rhetoric and public address (MA); secondary education (M Ed); studio art (MA); teaching Bible (MA); theology (MA, PhD); voice performance (MM); youth ministries (MA); M Div/MM.

Boise State University, College of Arts and Sciences, Department of Music, Boise, ID 83725-0399. Offers music education (MM); music performance (MM). *Accreditation:* NASM. *Program availability:* Part-time. *Students:* 16 full-time (9 women), 5 part-time (3 women); includes 4 minority (1 Black or African American, non-Hispanic/Latino; 2 Hispanic/Latino; 1 Two or more races, non-Hispanic/Latino), 2 international. 9 applicants. *Degree requirements:* For master's, thesis optional. *Entrance requirements:* For master's, minimum GPA of 3.0, performance demonstration. Additional exam requirements/recommendations for international students: required—TOEFL, IELTS. Electronic applications accepted. *Expenses: Tuition, area resident:* Full-time $7110; part-time $470 per credit hour. Tuition, state resident: full-time $7110; part-time $470 per credit hour. Tuition, nonresident: full-time $24,030; part-time $827 per credit hour. *International tuition:* $24,030 full-time. *Required fees:* $2536. Tuition and fees vary according to course load and program. *Financial support:* Teaching assistantships, scholarships/grants, and unspecified assistantships available. Financial award applicants required to submit FAFSA. *Unit head:* Dr. Linda Kline, Chair, 208-426-3665, E-mail: lkline@boisestate.edu. *Application contact:* Dr. Jeanne Belfy, Graduate Program Coordinator, 208-426-1216, E-mail: jbelfy@boisestate.edu.
Website: https://www.boisestate.edu/music/graduate/

Boston University, College of Fine Arts, Department of Musicology and Ethnomusicology, Boston, MA 02215. Offers ethnomusicology (PhD); historical musicology (PhD); musicology (MA). *Accreditation:* NASM. *Students:* 16 full-time (8 women), 1 (woman) part-time; includes 3 minority (1 Black or African American, non-Hispanic/Latino; 1 Asian, non-Hispanic/Latino; 1 Two or more races, non-Hispanic/Latino), 2 international. Average age 30. 29 applicants, 21% accepted, 3 enrolled. In 2019, 1 doctorate awarded. Terminal master's awarded for partial completion of doctoral program. *Degree requirements:* For master's, 2 foreign languages, comprehensive exam, thesis; for doctorate, 2 foreign languages, comprehensive exam, thesis/dissertation. *Entrance requirements:* For master's, GRE General Test, musical composition or research paper, 3 letters of recommendation, transcripts, personal statement, curriculum vitae. Additional exam requirements/recommendations for international students: required—TOEFL (minimum score 550 paper-based; 90 iBT), IELTS. *Application deadline:* For fall admission, 1/15 for domestic and international students. Application fee: $95. Electronic applications accepted. *Financial support:* In 2019–20, 13 students received support. Research assistantships, teaching assistantships, Federal Work-Study, scholarships/grants, health care benefits, and unspecified assistantships available. Financial award application deadline: 12/1. *Unit head:* Victor Coelho, Director, 617-358-0628, Fax: 617-353-7455, E-mail: blues@bu.edu. *Application contact:* Victor Coelho, Director, 617-358-0628, Fax: 617-353-7455, E-mail: blues@bu.edu.
Website: http://www.bu.edu/musicology/

Boston University, College of Fine Arts, School of Music, Boston, MA 02215. Offers choral conducting (MM); composition and theory (DMA); conducting (Performance Diploma); music education (MM, DMA, CAS); musicology (MA, PhD). *Accreditation:* NASM. *Program availability:* Part-time, 100% online. *Faculty:* 36 full-time, 21 part-time/adjunct. *Students:* 248 full-time (129 women), 7 part-time (3 women); includes 30 minority (4 Black or African American, non-Hispanic/Latino; 2 American Indian or Alaska Native, non-Hispanic/Latino; 9 Asian, non-Hispanic/Latino; 8 Hispanic/Latino; 7 Two or more races, non-Hispanic/Latino), 108 international. Average age 26. 830 applicants, 38% accepted, 100 enrolled. In 2019, 53 master's, 26 doctorates awarded. *Degree requirements:* For master's, thesis; for doctorate, 2 foreign languages, thesis/dissertation. *Entrance requirements:* Additional exam requirements/recommendations for international students: required—TOEFL (minimum score 90 iBT), IELTS (minimum score 7), DuoLingo. *Application deadline:* For fall admission, 12/1 priority date for domestic and international students. Application fee: $95. Electronic applications accepted. *Expenses:* 27,400. *Financial support:* In 2019–20, 175 teaching assistantships (averaging $3,500 per year) were awarded; fellowships, scholarships/grants, and unspecified assistantships also available. Financial award application deadline: 12/1. *Unit head:* Gregory Melchor-Barz, Director, 617-353-3341, Fax: 617-353-7455, E-mail: cfamusic@bu.edu. *Application contact:* Laura Conyers, Director of Admissions, 617-353-3341, E-mail: arts@bu.edu.

Bowling Green State University, Graduate College, College of Musical Arts, Bowling Green, OH 43403. Offers composition (MM); contemporary music (DMA), including composition, performance; ethnomusicology (MM); music education (MM), including choral music education, comprehensive music education, instrumental music education; music history (MM); music theory (MM); performance (MM). *Accreditation:* NASM. *Program availability:* Part-time. *Degree requirements:* For master's, thesis or alternative, recitals; for doctorate, comprehensive exam, thesis/dissertation. *Entrance requirements:* For master's, GRE General Test, diagnostic placement exams in music history and theory, audition, interview. Additional exam requirements/recommendations for international students: required—TOEFL. Electronic applications accepted.

Brandeis University, Graduate School of Arts and Sciences, Department of Music, Waltham, MA 02454-9110. Offers composition and theory (MA, MFA, PhD); musicology (MA, MFA, PhD). *Program availability:* Part-time. *Faculty:* 7 full-time (4 women), 13 part-time/adjunct (3 women). *Students:* 28 full-time (5 women), 2 part-time (1 woman); includes 5 minority (3 Asian, non-Hispanic/Latino; 1 Hispanic/Latino; 1 Two or more races, non-Hispanic/Latino), 5 international. Average age 30. 78 applicants, 22% accepted, 6 enrolled. In 2019, 4 master's, 4 doctorates awarded. Terminal master's awarded for partial completion of doctoral program. *Degree requirements:* For master's, variable foreign language requirement, comprehensive exam (for some programs), thesis or alternative, project, thesis; for doctorate, one foreign language, comprehensive exam, thesis/dissertation. *Entrance requirements:* For master's and doctorate, General GRE is recommended, transcripts, letters of recommendation, resume, portfolio, music composition exam, and statement of purpose. Additional exam requirements/recommendations for international students: required—TOEFL, IELTS, PTE. *Application deadline:* For fall admission, 1/15 priority date for domestic and international students. Applications are processed on a rolling basis. Application fee: $75. Electronic applications accepted. *Financial support:* In 2019–20, 20 fellowships with full tuition reimbursements (averaging $25,000 per year), 19 teaching assistantships (averaging $3,550 per year) were awarded; scholarships/grants, health care benefits, and tuition waivers also available. *Unit head:* Dr. Karen Desmond, Director of Graduate Study, 781-736-3329, E-mail: kdesmond@brandeis.edu. *Application contact:* Mark Kagan, Administrator, 781-736-3311, E-mail: kagan@brandeis.edu.
Website: http://www.brandeis.edu/gsas/programs/music.html

Brandon University, School of Music, Brandon, MB R7A 6A9, Canada. Offers composition (M Mus); music education (M Mus); performance and literature (M Mus), including clarinet, conducting, jazz, low brass, piano, strings, trumpet. *Program availability:* Part-time. *Degree requirements:* For master's, comprehensive exam (for some programs), thesis (for some programs), 2 recitals. *Entrance requirements:* For master's, B Mus. Additional exam requirements/recommendations for international students: required—TOEFL (minimum score 580 paper-based), IELTS (minimum score 7). Electronic applications accepted. *Expenses:* Contact institution.

Brigham Young University, Graduate Studies, College of Fine Arts and Communications, School of Music, Provo, UT 84602-1001. Offers composition (MM); conducting, choral (MM); music education (MA, MM); performance (MM). *Accreditation:* NASM. *Faculty:* 44 full-time (7 women). *Students:* 21 full-time (13 women), 25 part-time (16 women); includes 5 minority (1 American Indian or Alaska Native, non-Hispanic/Latino; 2 Asian, non-Hispanic/Latino; 2 Hispanic/Latino). Average age 28. 42 applicants, 62% accepted, 21 enrolled. In 2019, 13 master's awarded. *Degree requirements:* For master's, comprehensive exam (for some programs), thesis (for some programs), composition, project, recital, or thesis (for some programs). *Entrance requirements:* For master's, School of Music Entrance Exam, minimum GPA of 3.0, undergraduate degree in music, supplemental material and/or audition. Additional exam requirements/recommendations for international students: required—TOEFL (minimum score 580 paper-based; 85 iBT), IELTS (minimum score 7), E3PT, TOEFL, or IELTS are accepted; only one is required to show English proficiency for non-native English speakers. *Application deadline:* For fall admission, 12/15 priority date for domestic and international students. Application fee: $50. Electronic applications accepted. *Expenses:* Contact institution. *Financial support:* In 2019–20, 41 students received support. Institutionally sponsored loans, scholarships/grants, and unspecified assistantships available. Financial award application deadline: 12/15; financial award applicants required to submit FAFSA. *Unit head:* Dr. Kirt R. Saville, Director, 801-422-6304, Fax: 801-422-0533, E-mail: kirt_saville@byu.edu. *Application contact:* Dr. A. Claudine Bigelow, Associate Director, Graduate Studies, 801-422-1315, E-mail: claudine_bigelow@byu.edu.
Website: https://music.byu.edu

Brooklyn College of the City University of New York, School of Visual, Media and Performing Arts, Conservatory of Music, Brooklyn, NY 11210-2889. Offers composition (MM); music teacher (MA); musicology (MA); performance (MM). *Program availability:* Part-time. *Degree requirements:* For master's, one foreign language, comprehensive exam, thesis. *Entrance requirements:* For master's, placement exam, 36 credits in music, audition, completed composition, writing sample. Additional exam requirements/recommendations for international students: required—TOEFL (minimum score 550 paper-based; 79 iBT). Electronic applications accepted.

Brooklyn College of the City University of New York, School of Visual, Media and Performing Arts, Program in Performance and Interactive Media Arts, Brooklyn, NY 11210-2889. Offers MFA. *Entrance requirements:* For master's, 2 letters of recommendation, resume, portfolio, interview. Additional exam requirements/

recommendations for international students: required—TOEFL (minimum score 550 paper-based; 61 iBT). Electronic applications accepted.

Brown University, Graduate School, Department of Music, Providence, RI 02912. Offers computer music and multimedia (PhD); ethnomusicology (PhD). *Degree requirements:* For doctorate, 2 foreign languages, comprehensive exam, thesis/ dissertation, departmental qualifying exam. *Entrance requirements:* For doctorate, GRE General Test.

Butler University, Jordan College of the Arts, Indianapolis, IN 46208-3485. Offers composition (MM); conducting (MM), including choral, instrumental; music education (MM); musicology (MA); performance (MM); piano pedagogy (MM). *Accreditation:* NASM. *Program availability:* Part-time, evening/weekend, blended/hybrid learning. *Faculty:* 18 full-time (4 women), 12 part-time/adjunct (7 women). *Students:* 20 full-time (9 women), 26 part-time (13 women); includes 6 minority (2 Black or African American, non-Hispanic/Latino; 1 Asian, non-Hispanic/Latino; 2 Hispanic/Latino; 1 Two or more races, non-Hispanic/Latino), 1 international. Average age 27. 43 applicants, 63% accepted, 19 enrolled. In 2019, 13 master's awarded. *Degree requirements:* For master's, variable foreign language requirement, comprehensive exam, thesis (for some programs). *Entrance requirements:* For master's, Music Theory diagnostic exam, Music History diagnostic exam, audition, interview. Additional exam requirements/ recommendations for international students: required—TOEFL (minimum score 550 paper-based; 79 iBT), IELTS. *Application deadline:* For fall admission, 2/1 for domestic and international students; for spring admission, 12/15 for domestic and international students; for summer admission, 4/15 for domestic and international students. Applications are processed on a rolling basis. Application fee: $0. Electronic applications accepted. Application fee is waived when completed online. *Expenses:* $595 per credit hour. *Financial support:* In 2019–20, 21 students received support. Scholarships/grants, tuition waivers (full and partial), and unspecified assistantships available. Financial award applicants required to submit FAFSA. *Unit head:* David Patrick Murray, Director - School of Music, 317-940-9988, Fax: 317-9409658, E-mail: dmurray@butler.edu. *Application contact:* Dr. Nicholas Dean Johnson, Director of Graduate Studies, 317-9409064, E-mail: ndjohns1@butler.edu.
Website: http://www.butler.edu/jca/

California Baptist University, Program in Music, Riverside, CA 92504-3206. Offers conducting (MM); music education (MM); performance (MM). *Accreditation:* NASM. *Program availability:* Part-time. *Degree requirements:* For master's, comprehensive exam or thesis. *Entrance requirements:* For master's, minimum undergraduate GPA of 2.75; bachelor's degree in music; three recommendations; comprehensive essay; interview/audition. Additional exam requirements/ recommendations for international students: required—TOEFL (minimum score 80 iBT). Electronic applications accepted. *Expenses:* Contact institution.

California Institute of the Arts, The Herb Alpert School of Music, Valencia, CA 91355-2340. Offers African music (MFA, Adv C); composition (MFA, Adv C); composition/new media (MFA, Adv C); Indonesian music (MFA, Adv C); jazz (MFA, Adv C); North Indian music (MFA, Adv C); performance (MFA, Adv C); performer/ composer (MFA, Adv C); voice (MFA, Adv C); world music performance (MFA). *Program availability:* Part-time. *Degree requirements:* For master's, composition or recital. *Entrance requirements:* For master's, audition or portfolio. Additional exam requirements/recommendations for international students: required—TOEFL. Electronic applications accepted.

California State University, East Bay, Office of Graduate Studies, College of Letters, Arts, and Social Sciences, Department of Music, Hayward, CA 94542-3000. Offers MA. *Accreditation:* NASM. *Program availability:* Part-time. *Degree requirements:* For master's, variable foreign language requirement, comprehensive exam, project, recital, or thesis. *Entrance requirements:* For master's, minimum GPA of 3.0 in field; audition or work sample; 2 letters of recommendation. Additional exam requirements/ recommendations for international students: required—TOEFL (minimum score 550 paper-based). Electronic applications accepted.

California State University, Fresno, Division of Research and Graduate Studies, College of Arts and Humanities, Department of Music, Fresno, CA 93740-8027. Offers music (MA); music education (MA); performance (MA). *Accreditation:* NASM. *Program availability:* Part-time. *Degree requirements:* For master's, thesis or alternative. *Entrance requirements:* For master's, GRE General Test, BA in music, minimum GPA of 3.0. Additional exam requirements/recommendations for international students: required—TOEFL. Electronic applications accepted. *Expenses:* Tuition, state resident: full-time $4012; part-time $2506 per semester.

California State University, Fullerton, Graduate Studies, College of the Arts, Department of Music, Fullerton, CA 92831-3599. Offers music education (MA); performance (MM). *Accreditation:* NASM. *Program availability:* Part-time. *Degree requirements:* For master's, comprehensive exam, project or thesis. *Entrance requirements:* For master's, audition, major in music or related field, minimum GPA of 2.5 in last 60 units of course work.

California State University, Long Beach, Graduate Studies, College of the Arts, Department of Music, Long Beach, CA 90840. Offers composition (MM); music (MA). *Accreditation:* NASM. *Program availability:* Part-time. *Degree requirements:* For master's, thesis or alternative, departmental qualifying exam. Electronic applications accepted.

California State University, Los Angeles, Graduate Studies, College of Arts and Letters, Department of Music, Los Angeles, CA 90032-8530. Offers music composition (MM); music education (MA); musicology (MA); performance (MM). *Accreditation:* NASM. *Program availability:* Part-time, evening/weekend. *Degree requirements:* For master's, comprehensive exam, project or thesis. *Entrance requirements:* For master's, audition. Additional exam requirements/recommendations for international students: required—TOEFL (minimum score 500 paper-based). Electronic applications accepted. *Expenses: Tuition, area resident:* Full-time $7176; part-time $4164 per year. Tuition, state resident: full-time $7176; part-time $4164 per year. Tuition, nonresident: full-time $14,304; part-time $8916 per year. *International tuition:* $14,304 full-time. *Required fees:* $1037.76; $1037.76 per unit. Tuition and fees vary according to degree level and program.

California State University, Northridge, Graduate Studies, Mike Curb College of Arts, Media, and Communication, Department of Music, Northridge, CA 91330. Offers composition (MM); conducting (MM); music education (MA); performance (MM). *Accreditation:* NASM. *Degree requirements:* For master's, thesis. *Entrance requirements:* For master's, audition, GRE General Test or minimum GPA of 3.0. Additional exam requirements/recommendations for international students: required—TOEFL.

California State University, Sacramento, College of Arts and Letters, Department of Music, Sacramento, CA 95819. Offers composition (MM); conducting (MM); performance (MM). *Accreditation:* NASM. *Program availability:* Part-time. *Students:* 16 full-time (8 women), 5 part-time (0 women); includes 4 minority (1 American Indian or Alaska Native, non-Hispanic/Latino; 3 Hispanic/Latino). Average age 32. 23 applicants, 48% accepted, 9 enrolled. In 2019, 6 master's awarded. *Degree requirements:* For master's, comprehensive exam, thesis optional, thesis or project, writing proficiency exam. *Entrance requirements:* For master's, GRE, music exam, BA in music or equivalent, minimum GPA of 3.0 during previous 2 years of course work. Additional exam requirements/recommendations for international students: required—TOEFL (minimum score 550 paper-based; 80 iBT); recommended—IELTS. *Application deadline:* For fall admission, 3/1 for domestic students, 2/1 for international students; for spring admission, 9/15 for domestic students, 8/15 for international students. Applications are processed on a rolling basis. Application fee: $70. Electronic applications accepted. *Expenses:* Contact institution. *Financial support:* Teaching assistantships, career-related internships or fieldwork, Federal Work-Study, and scholarships/grants available. Support available to part-time students. Financial award application deadline: 3/1; financial award applicants required to submit FAFSA. *Unit head:* Dr. Ernie Hills, Chair, 916-278-5191, E-mail: hills@csus.edu. *Application contact:* Jose Martinez, Graduate Admissions Supervisor, 916-278-7871, E-mail: martinj@skymail.csus.edu.
Website: http://www.csus.edu/music

Campbellsville University, School of Music, Campbellsville, KY 42718-2799. Offers music (MA); music education (MM), including conducting, instrumental performance, vocal performance and pedagogy; musicology (MA); worship (MA). *Accreditation:* NASM. *Program availability:* Part-time, 100% online, blended/hybrid learning. *Degree requirements:* For master's, comprehensive exam, thesis (for some programs), paper or recital. *Entrance requirements:* For master's, GRE General Test or PRAXIS, minimum GPA of 2.75, college transcripts. Additional exam requirements/ recommendations for international students: required—TOEFL (minimum score 550 paper-based; 79 iBT); recommended—IELTS (minimum score 6). Electronic applications accepted. Application fee is waived when completed online. *Expenses:* Contact institution.

Capital University, Conservatory of Music, Columbus, OH 43209-2394. Offers music education (MM), including instrumental emphasis, Kodály emphasis. *Accreditation:* NASM. *Program availability:* Part-time. *Degree requirements:* For master's, comprehensive exam, thesis or alternative, chamber performance exam. *Entrance requirements:* For master's, music theory exam, minimum undergraduate GPA of 3.0. Additional exam requirements/recommendations for international students: required—TOEFL (minimum score 550 paper-based; 80 iBT). Electronic applications accepted. *Expenses:* Contact institution.

Capital University, Trinity Lutheran Seminary, Columbus, OH 43209-2394. Offers African American studies (MTS); Biblical studies (MTS, STM); Christian education (MA); Christian spirituality (STM); church in the world (MTS); church music (MA); divinity (M Div); general theological studies (MTS); mission and evangelism (STM); pastoral leadership and practice (STM); youth and family ministry (MA); MSN/MTS; MTS/JD. *Accreditation:* ACIPE; ATS. *Program availability:* Part-time. *Degree requirements:* For master's, variable foreign language requirement, comprehensive exam (for some programs), thesis (for some programs), field experience (for some programs). *Entrance requirements:* For master's, BA or equivalent (for MA, M Div, MTS); M Div, MTS, or equivalent (for STM); audition (for MACM). Additional exam requirements/ recommendations for international students: required—TOEFL. Electronic applications accepted. *Expenses:* Contact institution.

Carleton University, Faculty of Graduate Studies, Faculty of Arts and Social Sciences, School for Studies in Art and Culture, Program in Music and Culture, Ottawa, ON K1S 5B6, Canada. Offers MA.

Carnegie Mellon University, College of Fine Arts, School of Music, Pittsburgh, PA 15213-3891. Offers collaborative piano (MM); composition (MM); instrumental performance (MM); music and technology (MS); music education (MM); vocal performance (MM). *Accreditation:* NASM. *Program availability:* Part-time. *Degree requirements:* For master's, comprehensive exam, recital. *Entrance requirements:* For master's, audition.

Case Western Reserve University, School of Graduate Studies, Department of Music, Program in Historical Musicology, Cleveland, OH 44106. Offers historical musicology (PhD); music history (MA). *Degree requirements:* For master's, thesis. *Entrance requirements:* Additional exam requirements/recommendations for international students: required—TOEFL (minimum score 577 paper-based; 90 iBT); recommended—IELTS (minimum score 7).

Case Western Reserve University, School of Graduate Studies, Department of Music, Program in Historical Performance Practice, Cleveland, OH 44106. Offers MA, DMA, PhD. Terminal master's awarded for partial completion of doctoral program. *Degree requirements:* For master's, one foreign language, comprehensive exam (for some programs), ensemble participation; juried lecture-recital; for doctorate, 2 foreign languages, comprehensive exam (for some programs), thesis/dissertation, ensemble participation; juried lecture-recital. *Entrance requirements:* For master's, GRE, statement of purpose; audio/video recording of a performance; two writing samples; three letters of recommendation; live audition; for doctorate, GRE, statement of purpose; two writing samples; curriculum vitae; three letters of recommendation. Additional exam requirements/recommendations for international students: required—TOEFL (minimum score 577 paper-based; 90 iBT); recommended—IELTS (minimum score 7). Electronic applications accepted.

The Catholic University of America, Benjamin T. Rome School of Music, Washington, DC 20064. Offers cello (Artist Diploma); chamber music (piano) (MM, DMA); composition (MM, DMA), including concert music (MM), stage music (MM); music (MAT); musicology (MA, PhD); orchestral conducting (MM, DMA, Artist Diploma); orchestral instruments/guitar (MM, DMA); piano (Artist Diploma); piano pedagogy (MM, DMA); piano performance (MM, DMA); sacred music (MMSM, DMA); violin (Artist Diploma); vocal accompanying (MM, DMA); vocal pedagogy (MM, DMA); vocal performance (MM, DMA); voice (Artist Diploma); MA/MSLIS. *Accreditation:* NASM. *Program availability:* Part-time. *Faculty:* 31 full-time (9 women), 67 part-time/adjunct (48 women). *Students:* 41 full-time (31 women), 85 part-time (55 women); includes 39 minority (10 Black or African American, non-Hispanic/Latino; 12 Asian, non-Hispanic/ Latino; 10 Hispanic/Latino; 7 Two or more races, non-Hispanic/Latino), 27 international. Average age 32. 105 applicants, 64% accepted, 26 enrolled. In 2019, 16 master's, 11 doctorates awarded. *Degree requirements:* For master's, variable foreign language requirement, comprehensive exam (for some programs), thesis (for some programs), final recital (for some programs); for doctorate, variable foreign language requirement, comprehensive exam (for some programs), thesis/dissertation (for some programs), final recital (for some programs); for Artist Diploma, variable foreign language requirement, final recital (for some programs). *Entrance requirements:* For master's, music theory and music history placement examinations, statement of purpose, 2 letters of recommendation, minimum undergraduate B average, audition (for all performance degrees), official copy of academic transcript showing completed and conferred BM; for doctorate, music theory and music history placement examinations, 2 letters of recommendation, minimum B average in all previous course work and degrees, official copies of academic transcripts showing completion and conferral of all previous degrees, audition (for all performance degrees); for Artist Diploma, music theory and music history placement examinations, statement of purpose, 2 letters of

recommendation, minimum B average in all previous course work and degrees, BM, audition, official copies of academic transcripts showing completion and conferral of all previous degrees. Additional exam requirements/recommendations for international students: required—TOEFL (minimum score 550 paper-based; 80 iBT). *Application deadline:* For fall admission, 7/15 priority date for domestic students, 7/1 for international students; for spring admission, 11/15 priority date for domestic students, 11/1 for international students. Applications are processed on a rolling basis. Application fee: $55. Electronic applications accepted. *Expenses:* Contact institution. *Financial support:* Fellowships, research assistantships, teaching assistantships, Federal Work-Study, scholarships/grants, tuition waivers (full and partial), and unspecified assistantships available. Financial award application deadline: 2/1; financial award applicants required to submit FAFSA. *Unit head:* Jacqueline Leary-Warsaw, Dean, 202-319-5417, Fax: 202-319-6280, E-mail: cua-music@cua.edu. *Application contact:* Dr. Steven Brown, Director of Graduate Admissions, 202-319-5247, Fax: 202-319-6174, E-mail: cua-graduatestudies@cua.edu.
Website: https://music.catholic.edu/

Central Michigan University, College of Graduate Studies, College of the Arts and Media, School of Music, Mount Pleasant, MI 48859. Offers composition (MM); conducting (MM); music education (MM); performance (MM). *Accreditation:* NASM. *Program availability:* Part-time. *Degree requirements:* For master's, thesis or alternative. Electronic applications accepted. *Expenses: Tuition, area resident:* Full-time $12,267; part-time $8178 per year. Tuition, state resident: full-time $12,267; part-time $8178 per year. Tuition, nonresident: full-time $12,267; part-time $8178 per year. *International tuition:* $16,110 full-time. *Required fees:* $225 per semester. Tuition and fees vary according to degree level and program.

Central Washington University, School of Graduate Studies and Research, College of Arts and Humanities, Department of Music, Ellensburg, WA 98926. Offers composition (MM); conducting (MM); music education (MM); pedagogy (MM); performance (MM). *Accreditation:* NASM. *Entrance requirements:* For master's, minimum GPA of 3.0. Additional exam requirements/recommendations for international students: required—TOEFL (minimum score 550 paper-based; 79 iBT) or IELTS (minimum score 6.5). Electronic applications accepted.

Claremont Graduate University, Graduate Programs, School of Arts and Humanities, Department of Music, Claremont, CA 91711-6160. Offers church music (MA, DCM); composition (MA, DMA); historical performance practices (MA, DMA); musicology (MA, PhD); performance (MA, DMA); MBA/PhD. *Program availability:* Part-time. Terminal master's awarded for partial completion of doctoral program. *Degree requirements:* For master's, one foreign language, comprehensive exam, thesis (for some programs), oral and written qualifying exams, recitals; for doctorate, 2 foreign languages, comprehensive exam, thesis/dissertation (for some programs), oral and written qualifying exams, oral defense of dissertation, recitals. *Entrance requirements:* For master's and doctorate, GRE General Test, auditions, compositions, or papers. Additional exam requirements/recommendations for international students: required—TOEFL (minimum score 75 iBT). Electronic applications accepted.

Cleveland Institute of Music, Graduate Programs, Cleveland, OH 44106-1776. Offers MM, DMA, AD, CPS. *Accreditation:* NASM (one or more programs are accredited). *Faculty:* 29 full-time (12 women), 75 part-time/adjunct (22 women). *Students:* 151 full-time (88 women), 7 part-time (4 women); includes 26 minority (4 Black or African American, non-Hispanic/Latino; 14 Asian, non-Hispanic/Latino; 8 Hispanic/Latino), 39 international. Average age 24. 1,041 applicants, 32% accepted, 115 enrolled. In 2019, 53 master's, 5 doctorates, 14 ADs awarded. *Degree requirements:* For master's, comprehensive exam, recital; for doctorate, comprehensive exam, thesis/dissertation (for some programs), final projects; for other advanced degree, recital. *Entrance requirements:* For master's, theory placement tests, audition; for doctorate, diagnostic exams, theory placement test, audition; for other advanced degree, audition. Additional exam requirements/recommendations for international students: required—TOEFL (minimum score 550 paper-based; 79 iBT), IELTS (minimum score 6.5), PTE (minimum score 60). *Application deadline:* For fall admission, 12/1 for domestic and international students. Application fee: $110. Electronic applications accepted. *Expenses: Tuition:* Full-time $40,000; part-time $1967 per credit hour. *Required fees:* $4336; $4336 per unit. One-time fee: $250 full-time. *Financial support:* In 2019–20, 142 students received support. Federal Work-Study, scholarships/grants, and unspecified assistantships available. Financial award application deadline: 2/1; financial award applicants required to submit CSS PROFILE or FAFSA. *Unit head:* David Cerone, President, 216-791-5000. *Application contact:* E. William Fay, Director of Admissions, 216-795-3107, E-mail: cimadmission@po.cwru.edu.

Cleveland State University, College of Graduate Studies, College of Liberal Arts and Social Sciences, Department of Music, Cleveland, OH 44115. Offers composition (MM); music education (MM). *Accreditation:* NASM. *Program availability:* Part-time, evening/weekend. *Faculty:* 9 full-time (2 women), 19 part-time/adjunct (6 women). *Students:* 3 full-time (1 woman), 17 part-time (4 women); includes 4 minority (1 Black or African American, non-Hispanic/Latino; 2 Hispanic/Latino; 1 Two or more races, non-Hispanic/Latino), 4 international. Average age 26. 34 applicants, 91% accepted, 19 enrolled. In 2019, 11 master's awarded. *Entrance requirements:* For master's, departmental assessment in music history, minimum undergraduate GPA of 2.75, audition on primary instrument, or submission of composition portfolio or written samples (for music education). Additional exam requirements/recommendations for international students: required—TOEFL (minimum score 550 paper-based; 78 iBT). *Application deadline:* For fall admission, 7/1 priority date for domestic students, 5/15 for international students; for spring admission, 11/15 for domestic students, 11/1 for international students; for summer admission, 4/1 for domestic students, 3/15 for international students. Applications are processed on a rolling basis. Application fee: $40. Electronic applications accepted. *Expenses:* Tuition, state resident: full-time $10,215; part-time $6810 per credit hour. Tuition, nonresident: full-time $17,496; part-time $11,664 per credit hour. *International tuition:* $19,316 full-time. Tuition and fees vary according to degree level and program. *Financial support:* In 2019–20, 14 students received support. Scholarships/grants, tuition waivers (partial), and unspecified assistantships available. Financial award application deadline: 3/15; financial award applicants required to submit FAFSA. *Unit head:* Dr. John Perrine, Chairperson/Associate Professor, 216-687-3959, Fax: 216-687-9279, E-mail: j.m.perrine@csuohio.edu. *Application contact:* Kate Bill, Music Admission Specialist, 216-687-5039, Fax: 216-687-9279, E-mail: m.c.bill@csuohio.edu.
Website: http://www.csuohio.edu/music/

The Colburn School Conservatory of Music, Graduate Programs, Los Angeles, CA 90012. Offers music (AD); performance (MM). *Accreditation:* NASM. *Expenses: Required fees:* $5905.

Colorado State University, College of Liberal Arts, School of Music, Theatre and Dance, Fort Collins, CO 80523-1779. Offers collaborative piano (MM). *Accreditation:* NASM. *Program availability:* Part-time. *Degree requirements:* For master's, recital. *Entrance requirements:* For master's, diagnostic exams in music theory and music history, minimum GPA of 3.0; audition. Additional exam requirements/recommendations for international students: recommended—TOEFL (minimum score 550 paper-based; 80 iBT), IELTS (minimum score 6.5). Electronic applications accepted. *Expenses:* Tuition, state resident: full-time $10,520; part-time $5844 per credit hour. Tuition, nonresident: full-time $25,791; part-time $14,328 per credit hour. *International tuition:* $25,791 full-time. *Required fees:* $2512.80. Part-time tuition and fees vary according to course level, course load, degree level, program and student level.

Columbia College Chicago, School of Graduate Studies, Music Department, Chicago, IL 60605-1996. Offers MFA. *Entrance requirements:* For master's, self-assessment essay, work samples, resume, letters of recommendation, transcripts. Additional exam requirements/recommendations for international students: required—TOEFL, IELTS. Electronic applications accepted. *Expenses:* Contact institution.

Columbia University, Graduate School of Arts and Sciences, New York, NY 10027. Offers African-American studies (MA); American studies (MA); anthropology (MA, PhD); art history and archaeology (MA, PhD); astronomy (PhD); biological sciences (PhD); biotechnology (MA); chemical physics (PhD); chemistry (PhD); classical studies (MA, PhD); classics (MA, PhD); climate and society (MA); conservation biology (MA); earth and environmental sciences (PhD); East Asia: regional studies (MA); East Asian languages and cultures (MA, PhD); ecology, evolution and environmental biology (MA), including conservation biology; ecology, evolution, and environmental biology (PhD), including ecology and evolutionary biology, evolutionary primatology; economics (MA, PhD); English and comparative literature (MA, PhD); French and Romance philology (MA, PhD); Germanic languages (MA, PhD); global French studies (MA); global thought (MA); Hispanic cultural studies (MA); history (PhD); history and literature (MA); human rights studies (MA); Islamic studies (MA); Italian (MA, PhD); Japanese pedagogy (MA); Jewish studies (MA); Latin America and the Caribbean: regional studies (MA); Latin American and Iberian cultures (PhD); mathematics (MA, PhD), including finance (MA); medieval and Renaissance studies (MA); Middle Eastern, South Asian, and African studies (MA, PhD); modern art: critical and curatorial studies (MA); modern European studies (MA); museum anthropology (MA); music (DMA, PhD); oral history (MA); philosophical foundations of physics (MA); philosophy (MA, PhD); physics (PhD); political science (MA, PhD); psychology (PhD); quantitative methods in the social sciences (MA); religion (MA, PhD); Russia, Eurasia and East Europe: regional studies (MA); Russian translation (MA); Slavic cultures (MA); Slavic languages (MA, PhD); sociology (MA, PhD); South Asian studies (MA); statistics (MA, PhD); theatre (PhD). *Program availability:* Part-time. *Students:* 3,506 full-time (1,844 women), 208 part-time (121 women); includes 864 minority (110 Black or African American, non-Hispanic/Latino; 5 American Indian or Alaska Native, non-Hispanic/Latino; 416 Asian, non-Hispanic/Latino; 147 Hispanic/Latino; 6 Native Hawaiian or other Pacific Islander, non-Hispanic/Latino; 180 Two or more races, non-Hispanic/Latino), 2,065 international. 14,545 applicants, 25% accepted, 1,429 enrolled. In 2019, 1,262 master's, 363 doctorates awarded. Terminal master's awarded for partial completion of doctoral program. *Degree requirements:* For master's, variable foreign language requirement, comprehensive exam (for some programs), thesis (for some programs); for doctorate, variable foreign language requirement, comprehensive exam (for some programs), thesis/dissertation. *Entrance requirements:* For master's and doctorate, GRE General Test, GRE Subject Test (for some programs). Additional exam requirements/recommendations for international students: required—TOEFL (minimum score 600 paper-based; 100 iBT), IELTS (minimum score 7.5). Application fee: $115. Electronic applications accepted. *Expenses: Tuition:* Full-time $47,600; part-time $1880 per credit. One-time fee: $105. *Financial support:* Fellowships, research assistantships, teaching assistantships, career-related internships or fieldwork, Federal Work-Study, institutionally sponsored loans, scholarships/grants, traineeships, health care benefits, tuition waivers, and unspecified assistantships available. Support available to part-time students. Financial award application deadline: 12/15. *Unit head:* Dr. Carlos J. Alonso, Dean of the Graduate School of Arts and Sciences and Vice President for Graduate Education, 212-854-2861, E-mail: gsas-dean@columbia.edu. *Application contact:* GSAS Office of Admissions, 212-854-6729, E-mail: gsas-admissions@columbia.edu.
Website: http://gsas.columbia.edu/

Columbia University, School of the Arts, Sound Art Program, New York, NY 10027. Offers MFA. *Degree requirements:* For master's, thesis. *Entrance requirements:* For master's, Undergraduate transcript, 3 letters of recommendation, statement of intent, work sample. Additional exam requirements/recommendations for international students: required—Either the TOEFL or the IELTS is required. Electronic applications accepted. *Expenses: Tuition:* Full-time $47,600; part-time $1880 per credit. One-time fee: $105.

Columbus State University, Graduate Studies, College of the Arts, Schwob School of Music, Columbus, GA 31907-5645. Offers music (Artist Diploma); music education (MM); music performance (MM). *Accreditation:* NASM; NCATE (one or more programs are accredited). *Program availability:* Part-time. *Degree requirements:* For master's, exit exam. *Entrance requirements:* For master's, audition, letters of recommendation, undergraduate degree in music with minimum GPA of 2.5. Additional exam requirements/recommendations for international students: required—TOEFL (minimum score 550 paper-based; 79 iBT). Electronic applications accepted. *Expenses: Tuition, area resident:* Full-time $210; part-time $210 per credit hour. Tuition, state resident: full-time $210; part-time $210 per credit hour. Tuition, nonresident: full-time $817; part-time $817 per credit hour. *International tuition:* $817 full-time. *Required fees:* $802.50. Tuition and fees vary according to course load, degree level and program.

Concordia University, School of Graduate Studies, Faculty of Fine Arts, Department of Music, Montréal, QC H3G 1M8, Canada. Offers advanced music performance studies (Diploma). *Degree requirements:* For Diploma, performance, 2 recitals.

Concordia University Chicago, College of Graduate Studies, Program in Church Music, River Forest, IL 60305-1499. Offers MCM. *Accreditation:* NASM. *Program availability:* Part-time. *Degree requirements:* For master's, composition, recital, or thesis. *Entrance requirements:* For master's, minimum GPA of 2.9, audition. Additional exam requirements/recommendations for international students: required—TOEFL (minimum score 550 paper-based). Electronic applications accepted.

Concordia University Chicago, College of Graduate Studies, Program in Music, River Forest, IL 60305-1499. Offers MA. *Program availability:* Part-time. *Degree requirements:* For master's, composition, recital, or thesis. *Entrance requirements:* For master's, minimum GPA of 2.9, audition. Additional exam requirements/recommendations for international students: required—TOEFL (minimum score 550 paper-based). Electronic applications accepted.

Concordia University Wisconsin, Graduate Programs, School of Arts and Sciences, Program in Church Music, Mequon, WI 53097-2402. Offers MCM. *Degree requirements:* For master's, comprehensive exam, thesis or alternative. *Entrance requirements:* For master's, minimum GPA of 3.0. Additional exam requirements/recommendations for international students: required—TOEFL.

Conservatorio de Musica de Puerto Rico, Program in Musical Performance, San Juan, PR 00907. Offers guitar (Diploma); orchestral instruments (Diploma); piano (Diploma); vocal performance (Diploma). *Entrance requirements:* For degree, 3 letters of recommendation, audition, degree in music, minimum GPA of 2.5.

Converse College, Petrie School of Music, Spartanburg, SC 29302. Offers music education (M Mus); performance (M Mus). *Accreditation:* NASM. *Program availability:*

Part-time, evening/weekend. *Degree requirements:* For master's, variable foreign language requirement, comprehensive exam, thesis (for some programs), recitals. *Entrance requirements:* For master's, NTE (music education), audition, 3 letters of recommendation. Additional exam requirements/recommendations for international students: required—TOEFL. Electronic applications accepted.

Cornell University, Graduate School, Graduate Fields of Arts and Sciences, Field of Music, Ithaca, NY 14853. Offers composition (DMA); musicology (PhD); performance practice (DMA); theory of music (MA). *Degree requirements:* For doctorate, comprehensive exam, thesis/dissertation, 1 foreign language (DMA), 2 foreign languages (PhD). *Entrance requirements:* For doctorate, GRE General Test, 2 music papers (PhD); 2 recent scores with recording and 1 music paper (DMA in composition); 1 music paper, recording and audition (DMA in performance practice). Additional exam requirements/recommendations for international students: required—TOEFL (minimum score 600 paper-based; 77 iBT). Electronic applications accepted.

Curtis Institute of Music, Graduate Studies, Philadelphia, PA 19103-6107. Offers opera (MM). *Accreditation:* NASM. *Entrance requirements:* For master's, audition or performance in 2 or more principal roles or 6 major scenes.

Dalhousie University, Faculty of Arts and Social Sciences, Fountain School of Performing Arts, Halifax, NS B3H 4R2, Canada. Offers musicology (MA). *Entrance requirements:* Additional exam requirements/recommendations for international students: required—TOEFL, IELTS, CANTEST, CAEL, or Michigan English Language Assessment Battery. Electronic applications accepted.

Dartmouth College, Guarini School of Graduate and Advanced Studies, Department of Music, Hanover, NH 03755. Offers MA. *Entrance requirements:* Additional exam requirements/recommendations for international students: required—TOEFL. Electronic applications accepted.

DePaul University, School of Music, Chicago, IL 60614. Offers composition (MM); jazz studies (MM); music education (MM); music performance (MM); performance (Certificate). *Accreditation:* NASM (one or more programs are accredited). *Program availability:* Part-time, evening/weekend. *Degree requirements:* For master's, comprehensive exam. *Entrance requirements:* For master's, bachelor's degree in music or related field, minimum GPA of 3.0, auditions (performance), scores (composition); for Certificate, master's degree in performance or related field, auditions (for performance majors). Additional exam requirements/recommendations for international students: required—TOEFL (minimum score 550 paper-based; 80 iBT). Electronic applications accepted. *Expenses:* Contact institution.

Duke University, Graduate School, Department of Music, Durham, NC 27708. Offers music composition (PhD); musicology (PhD); performance practice (PhD). *Program availability:* Part-time. Terminal master's awarded for partial completion of doctoral program. *Degree requirements:* For doctorate, 3 foreign languages, thesis/dissertation. *Entrance requirements:* For doctorate, GRE General Test, paper on musical topic (for musicology); samples of compositions (for music composition). Additional exam requirements/recommendations for international students: required—TOEFL (minimum score 577 paper-based; 90 iBT) or IELTS (minimum score 7). Electronic applications accepted.

Duquesne University, Mary Pappert School of Music, Pittsburgh, PA 15282-0001. Offers music education (MM). *Accreditation:* NASM. *Program availability:* Part-time. *Degree requirements:* For master's, comprehensive exam, thesis (for some programs), recital (music performance); for AD, recital. *Entrance requirements:* For master's, audition, minimum undergraduate QPA of 3.0 in music, portfolio of original compositions, or music education experience; for AD, audition. Additional exam requirements/recommendations for international students: required—TOEFL (minimum score 550 paper-based; 79 iBT), IELTS (minimum score 6.5). Electronic applications accepted. Application fee is waived when completed online. *Expenses:* Contact institution.

East Carolina University, Graduate School, College of Fine Arts and Communication, School of Music, Greenville, NC 27858-4353. Offers advanced performance studies (Certificate); composition (MM); music education (MM), including choral conducting, instrumental conducting, music theory/composition, music therapy, performance, Suzuki pedagogy; music therapy (MM); Suzuki pedagogy (Certificate); theory (MM); woodwind specialist (MM), including accompanying, choral conducting, instrumental, instrumental conducting, jazz studies, keyboard, organ, piano pedagogy, Suzuki string pedagogy, vocal pedagogy, voice, woodwind specialist. *Accreditation:* NASM. *Program availability:* Part-time. *Application deadline:* For fall admission, 6/1 priority date for domestic students. *Expenses: Tuition, area resident:* Full-time $4749; part-time $185 per credit hour. Tuition, state resident: full-time $4749; part-time $185 per credit hour. Tuition, nonresident: full-time $17,898; part-time $864 per credit hour. *International tuition:* $17,898 full-time. *Required fees:* $2787. *Financial support:* Application deadline: 6/1. *Unit head:* Christopher Ulffers, Director, 252-328-4270, E-mail: ulffersj@ecu.edu. *Application contact:* Graduate School Admissions, 252-328-6012, Fax: 252-328-6071, E-mail: gradschool@ecu.edu.
Website: https://music.ecu.edu/

Eastern Illinois University, Graduate School, College of Liberal Arts and Sciences, Department of Music, Charleston, IL 61920. Offers composition (MA); conducting (MA); music education (MA); performance (MA). *Accreditation:* NASM. *Program availability:* Part-time, evening/weekend, online learning. *Degree requirements:* For master's, comprehensive exam (for some programs), thesis (for some programs). *Entrance requirements:* For master's, personal statement, resume, three letters of recommendation. Additional exam requirements/recommendations for international students: required—TOEFL (minimum score 500 paper-based; 61 iBT), IELTS (minimum score 6). Electronic applications accepted.

Eastern Kentucky University, The Graduate School, College of Arts and Sciences, Department of Music, Richmond, KY 40475-3102. Offers choral conducting (MM); performance (MM); theory/composition (MM). *Accreditation:* NASM. *Program availability:* Part-time. *Degree requirements:* For master's, thesis optional. *Entrance requirements:* For master's, GRE General Test, minimum GPA of 2.5.

Eastern Michigan University, Graduate School, College of Arts and Sciences, School of Music and Dance, Ypsilanti, MI 48197. Offers MM. *Accreditation:* NASM. *Program availability:* Part-time, evening/weekend, online learning. *Faculty:* 26 full-time (12 women). *Students:* 4 full-time (3 women), 11 part-time (6 women); includes 2 minority (1 Black or African American, non-Hispanic/Latino; 1 Asian, non-Hispanic/Latino), 3 international. Average age 31. 30 applicants, 43% accepted, 6 enrolled. In 2019, 1 master's awarded. *Entrance requirements:* Additional exam requirements/recommendations for international students: required—TOEFL. *Application deadline:* Applications are processed on a rolling basis. Application fee: $45. *Financial support:* Fellowships, research assistantships with full tuition reimbursements, teaching assistantships with full tuition reimbursements, career-related internships or fieldwork, Federal Work-Study, institutionally sponsored loans, scholarships/grants, tuition waivers (partial), and unspecified assistantships available. Support available to part-time students. Financial award applicants required to submit FAFSA. *Unit head:* Dr. Christopher Barrick, Director, 734-487-0244, Fax: 734-487-6939, E-mail: cbarrick@emich.edu. *Application contact:* Dr. David Pierce, Coordinator of Music Advising, 734-487-4114, Fax: 734-487-6939, E-mail: david.pierce@emich.edu.
Website: http://www.emich.edu/musicdance

Eastern University, Graduate Education Programs, St. Davids, PA 19087-3696. Offers ESL program specialist (K-12) (Certificate); general supervisor (PreK-12) (Certificate); health and physical education (K-12) (Certificate); middle level (4-8) (Certificate); multicultural education (M Ed); music (K-12) (Certificate); Pre K-4 (Certificate); Pre K-4 with special education (Certificate); reading (M Ed); reading specialist (K-12) (Certificate); reading supervisor (K-12) (Certificate); school counseling (MA, CAGS); school principalship (preK-12) (Certificate); school psychology (MS, CAGS); secondary biology education (7-12) (Certificate); secondary chemistry education (7-12) (Certificate); secondary communication education (7-12) (Certificate); secondary English education (7-12) (Certificate); secondary math education (7-12) (Certificate); secondary social studies education (7-12) (Certificate); special education (M Ed); special education (7-12) (Certificate); special education (Pre K-8) (Certificate); special education supervisor (K-12) (Certificate); TESOL (M Ed); world language (Certificate), including Spanish. *Program availability:* Part-time, evening/weekend, online learning. *Students:* 54 full-time (45 women), 149 part-time (134 women); includes 75 minority (54 Black or African American, non-Hispanic/Latino; 3 Asian, non-Hispanic/Latino; 15 Hispanic/Latino; 3 Two or more races, non-Hispanic/Latino). Average age 33. In 2019, 89 master's, 10 other advanced degrees awarded. *Entrance requirements:* Additional exam requirements/recommendations for international students: required—TOEFL. *Application deadline:* Applications are processed on a rolling basis. Application fee: $35. Electronic applications accepted. Application fee is waived when completed online. *Expenses:* Contact institution. *Unit head:* Michael Dziedziak, Executive Director of Enrollment, 800-452-0996, E-mail: gpsadmissions@eastern.edu. *Application contact:* Michael Dziedziak, Executive Director of Enrollment, 800-452-0996, E-mail: gpsadmissions@eastern.edu.
Website: https://www.eastern.edu/academics/programs/education-department-graduate-programs/graduate-programs

Eastern Washington University, Graduate Studies, College of Arts, Letters and Education, Department of Music, Cheney, WA 99004-2431. Offers composition (MA); instrumental/vocal performance (MA); jazz pedagogy (MA); liberal arts (MA); music education (MA). *Accreditation:* NASM. *Program availability:* Part-time. *Faculty:* 16 full-time (10 women). *Students:* 8 full-time (4 women), 4 part-time (1 woman); includes 1 minority (Hispanic/Latino), 1 international. Average age 29. 9 applicants, 89% accepted, 4 enrolled. In 2019, 5 master's awarded. *Degree requirements:* For master's, comprehensive exam, thesis or alternative. *Entrance requirements:* For master's, GRE General Test, minimum GPA of 3.0. Additional exam requirements/recommendations for international students: required—TOEFL (minimum score 580 paper-based; 92 iBT), IELTS (minimum score 7), TWE, PTE (minimum score 63). *Application deadline:* For fall admission, 4/1 priority date for domestic students; for spring admission, 1/15 for domestic students. Applications are processed on a rolling basis. Application fee: $75. Electronic applications accepted. *Financial support:* In 2019–20, 8 students received support, including teaching assistantships with partial tuition reimbursements available (averaging $10,000 per year); career-related internships or fieldwork, Federal Work-Study, institutionally sponsored loans, scholarships/grants, health care benefits, tuition waivers (partial), and unspecified assistantships also available. Support available to part-time students. Financial award application deadline: 2/1; financial award applicants required to submit FAFSA. *Unit head:* Dr. Jody Graves, Director of Keyboard Studies, 509-359-6119, E-mail: jgraves@ewu.edu. *Application contact:* Dr. Jody Graves, Director of Keyboard Studies, 509-359-6119, E-mail: jgraves@ewu.edu.
Website: http://www.ewu.edu/cale/programs/music.xml

Emory University, Laney Graduate School, Department of Music, Atlanta, GA 30322-1100. Offers choral conducting (MM, MSM); organ performance (MM, MSM). Terminal master's awarded for partial completion of doctoral program. *Degree requirements:* For master's, comprehensive exam, recital or worship service. *Entrance requirements:* For master's, GRE General Test, audition, interview. Additional exam requirements/recommendations for international students: required—TOEFL. Electronic applications accepted.

Emporia State University, Department of Music, Emporia, KS 66801-5415. Offers MM. *Accreditation:* NASM. *Program availability:* Part-time. *Degree requirements:* For master's, comprehensive exam or thesis. *Entrance requirements:* For master's, music qualifying exam, appropriate undergraduate degree. Additional exam requirements/recommendations for international students: required—TOEFL (minimum score 520 paper-based; 68 iBT). Electronic applications accepted. *Expenses: Tuition, area resident:* Full-time $6394; part-time $266.41 per credit hour. Tuition, state resident: full-time $6394; part-time $266.41 per credit hour. Tuition, nonresident: full-time $20,128; part-time $828.66 per credit hour. *International tuition:* $20,128 full-time. *Required fees:* $2183; $90.95 per credit hour. Tuition and fees vary according to campus/location and program.

Five Towns College, Graduate Programs, Dix Hills, NY 11746-6055. Offers childhood education (MS Ed); composition and arranging (DMA); jazz/commercial music (MM); music education (MM, DMA); music history and literature (DMA); music performance (DMA). *Program availability:* Part-time. *Degree requirements:* For master's, thesis, exams, major composition or capstone project, recital; for doctorate, comprehensive exam, thesis/dissertation, final oral exam. *Entrance requirements:* For master's, audition (for MM); New York state teaching certification (for MS Ed); personal statement, two letters of recommendation; for doctorate, 3 letters of recommendation, audition, essay. Additional exam requirements/recommendations for international students: required—TOEFL (minimum score 520 paper-based; 85 iBT); recommended—IELTS (minimum score 7). Electronic applications accepted.

Florida Atlantic University, Dorothy F. Schmidt College of Arts and Letters, Department of Music, Boca Raton, FL 33431-0991. Offers MM. *Accreditation:* NASM. *Program availability:* Part-time. *Faculty:* 15 full-time (6 women), 8 part-time/adjunct (5 women). *Students:* 11 full-time (4 women), 2 part-time (0 women); includes 8 minority (1 Black or African American, non-Hispanic/Latino; 6 Hispanic/Latino; 1 Two or more races, non-Hispanic/Latino), 5 international. Average age 36. 16 applicants, 75% accepted, 8 enrolled. In 2019, 6 master's awarded. *Degree requirements:* For master's, one foreign language, comprehensive exam, thesis (for some programs), lecture/recital or thesis. *Entrance requirements:* For master's, placement evaluations in music history and theory, audition, minimum GPA of 3.0 in last 60 hours of course work. Additional exam requirements/recommendations for international students: required—TOEFL (minimum score 500 paper-based; 61 iBT), IELTS (minimum score 6). *Application deadline:* For fall admission, 7/1 priority date for domestic students, 2/15 for international students; for spring admission, 11/1 for domestic students, 7/15 for international students. Applications are processed on a rolling basis. Application fee: $30. *Expenses: Tuition:* Full-time $20,536; part-time $371.82 per credit hour. Tuition and fees vary according to program. *Financial support:* Fellowships with partial tuition reimbursements, teaching assistantships with partial tuition reimbursements, career-related internships or fieldwork, Federal Work-Study, and scholarships/grants available. Financial award application deadline: 5/1. *Unit head:* Dr. Kevin Wilt, Chair, 561-297-3337, E-mail: wiltk@fau.edu. *Application contact:* Dr. Kevin Wilt, Chair, 561-297-3337, E-mail:

wiltk@fau.edu.
Website: http://www.fau.edu/music/

Florida International University, College of Communication, Architecture and The Arts, School of Music, Miami, FL 33199. Offers music (MM); music education (MS). *Accreditation:* NASM. *Program availability:* Part-time, evening/weekend. *Faculty:* 25 full-time (5 women), 36 part-time/adjunct (14 women). *Students:* 28 full-time (12 women), 17 part-time (5 women); includes 33 minority (4 Black or African American, non-Hispanic/Latino; 28 Hispanic/Latino; 1 Two or more races, non-Hispanic/Latino), 6 international. Average age 33. 33 applicants, 67% accepted, 15 enrolled. In 2019, 12 master's awarded. *Entrance requirements:* For master's, GRE (depending on program), statement of intent; 2 letters of recommendation; audition, interview and/or writing sample (depending on the area). Additional exam requirements/recommendations for international students: required—TOEFL (minimum score 550 paper-based; 80 iBT). *Application deadline:* For fall admission, 6/1 for domestic students, 4/1 for international students; for spring admission, 10/1 for domestic students, 9/1 for international students. Applications are processed on a rolling basis. Application fee: $30. Electronic applications accepted. *Expenses: Tuition, area resident:* Full-time $8912; part-time $446 per credit hour. Tuition, state resident: full-time $8912; part-time $446 per credit hour. Tuition, nonresident: full-time $21,393; part-time $992 per credit hour. *Required fees:* $2194. *Financial support:* Institutionally sponsored loans and scholarships/grants available. Financial award application deadline: 3/1; financial award applicants required to submit FAFSA. *Unit head:* Joel Galand, Program Director, 305-348-7078, E-mail: Joel.Galand@fiu.edu. *Application contact:* Nanett Rojas, Manager, Admissions Operations, 305-348-7464, Fax: 305-348-7441, E-mail: gradadm@fiu.edu.
Website: http://carta.fiu.edu/music/

Florida State University, The Graduate School, College of Music, Tallahassee, FL 32306. Offers accompanying (MM); arts administration (MA); choral conducting (MM); composition (MM, DM); ethnomusicology (MM); general music (MA); historical musicology (PhD); instrumental accompanying (MM); instrumental conducting (MM); jazz studies (MM); music theory (MM, PhD); music therapy (MM); musicology (MM); opera (MM); performance (MM, DM); piano pedagogy (MM); piano technology (MA); vocal accompanying (MM). *Accreditation:* NASM. *Program availability:* Part-time. *Faculty:* 77 full-time (28 women). *Students:* 355 full-time (169 women); includes 94 minority (30 Black or African American, non-Hispanic/Latino; 1 American Indian or Alaska Native, non-Hispanic/Latino; 29 Asian, non-Hispanic/Latino; 33 Hispanic/Latino; 1 Native Hawaiian or other Pacific Islander, non-Hispanic/Latino). Average age 26. 789 applicants, 44% accepted, 153 enrolled. In 2019, 98 master's, 36 doctorates awarded. *Degree requirements:* For master's, variable foreign language requirement, comprehensive exam (for some programs), thesis (for some programs), comprehensive exam; for doctorate, variable foreign language requirement, comprehensive exam (for some programs), thesis/dissertation, preliminary exam, treatise/dissertation defense. *Entrance requirements:* For master's, GRE General Test (for some programs), audition, minimum GPA of 3.0; for doctorate, GRE General Test (for some programs), audition, master's degree, minimum GPA of 3.0. Additional exam requirements/recommendations for international students: required—TOEFL (minimum score 590 paper-based; 97 iBT), IELTS (minimum score 7.5). *Application deadline:* For fall admission, 7/1 for domestic and international students; for spring admission, 11/1 for domestic and international students; for summer admission, 3/1 for domestic students. Applications are processed on a rolling basis. Application fee: $30. Electronic applications accepted. *Financial support:* In 2019–20, 235 students received support, including 2 fellowships with full tuition reimbursements available (averaging $15,000 per year), 14 research assistantships with full and partial tuition reimbursements available (averaging $7,400 per year), 201 teaching assistantships with full and partial tuition reimbursements available (averaging $7,400 per year); career-related internships or fieldwork, scholarships/grants, tuition waivers (full and partial), and unspecified assistantships also available. Support available to part-time students. Financial award application deadline: 2/28; financial award applicants required to submit FAFSA. *Unit head:* Dr. Patricia Flowers, Dean, 850-644-4361, Fax: 850-644-2033, E-mail: pjflowers@fsu.edu. *Application contact:* Kristopher Watson, Director of Admissions, 850-645-2126, Fax: 850-644-2033, E-mail: krwatson@fsu.edu.
Website: http://www.music.fsu.edu/

Fuller Theological Seminary, Graduate Programs, Pasadena, CA 91182. Offers Christian leadership (MACL); clinical psychology (PhD, Psy D); family studies (MA); global leadership (MA); global ministries (D Min); global ministries (Korean language) (D Min); intercultural studies (MA, Th M, PhD); intercultural studies (Korean language) (MA); marital and family therapy (MS); marriage and family enrichment (Certificate); ministry (M Div, D Min); missiology (D Miss); missiology (Korean language) (Th M); theology (MA, Th M, PhD), including evangelism (MA), family life education (MA), pastoral ministry (MA), recovery ministry (MA), worship music ministry (MA), worship, theology, and the arts (MA), youth, family, and culture (MA); theology and ministry (MA).

Garrett-Evangelical Theological Seminary, Graduate and Professional Programs, Evanston, IL 60201-3298. Offers Bible and culture (PhD); Christian education (MA); Christian education and congregational studies (PhD); contemporary theology and culture (PhD); divinity (M Div); ethics, church, and society (MA); liturgical studies (PhD); ministry (D Min); music ministry (MA); pastoral care and counseling (MA); pastoral theology, personality, and culture (PhD); spiritual formation and evangelism (MA); theological studies (MTS); M Div/MSW. *Accreditation:* ACIPE; ATS (one or more programs are accredited). *Program availability:* Part-time. *Degree requirements:* For master's, thesis (for some programs); for doctorate, thesis/dissertation. *Entrance requirements:* For doctorate, GRE (PhD). Additional exam requirements/recommendations for international students: required—TOEFL (minimum score 560 paper-based). Electronic applications accepted.

George Mason University, College of Visual and Performing Arts, School of Music, Program in Music, Fairfax, VA 22030. Offers composition (MM); conducting (MM); jazz studies (MM); music education (MM); pedagogy (MM); performance (MM). *Accreditation:* NASM. *Entrance requirements:* For master's, expanded goals statement; 2 letters of recommendation; official transcript. Additional exam requirements/recommendations for international students: required—TOEFL (minimum score 575 paper-based; 88 iBT), IELTS (minimum score 6.5), PTE (minimum score 59). Electronic applications accepted.

George Mason University, College of Visual and Performing Arts, School of Music, Program in Musical Arts, Fairfax, VA 22030. Offers composition (DMA); conducting (DMA); performance (DMA). *Degree requirements:* For doctorate, one foreign language, comprehensive exam, thesis/dissertation. *Entrance requirements:* For doctorate, GRE, master's degree in music; minimum GPA of 3.0 in master's coursework, 3.25 in courses related to field of study; 3 letters of recommendation; writing sample; audition or portfolio (depending on area of study). Additional exam requirements/recommendations for international students: required—TOEFL (minimum score 575 paper-based; 88 iBT), IELTS (minimum score 6.5), PTE (minimum score 59). Electronic applications accepted.

Georgia Institute of Technology, Graduate Studies, College of Design, School of Music, Atlanta, GA 30332-0001. Offers music technology (MS, PhD). *Expenses: Tuition, area resident:* Full-time $14,064; part-time $586 per credit hour. Tuition, state resident: full-time $14,064; part-time $586 per credit hour. Tuition, nonresident: full-time $29,140; part-time $1215 per credit hour. *International tuition:* $29,140 full-time. *Required fees:* $2024; $840 per semester. $2096. Tuition and fees vary according to course load.

Georgia Southern University, Jack N. Averitt College of Graduate Studies, College of Arts and Humanities, Program in Music, Statesboro, GA 30460. Offers composition (MM); conducting (MM); music education (MM); music technology (MM); performance (MM). *Accreditation:* NASM. *Program availability:* Part-time, evening/weekend. *Faculty:* 30 full-time (11 women), 4 part-time/adjunct (0 women). *Students:* 12 full-time (6 women), 12 part-time (4 women); includes 6 minority (5 Black or African American, non-Hispanic/Latino; 1 Two or more races, non-Hispanic/Latino), 4 international. Average age 26. 17 applicants, 100% accepted, 9 enrolled. In 2019, 5 master's awarded. *Degree requirements:* For master's, comprehensive exam, recital or final project. *Entrance requirements:* For master's, minimum GPA of 2.5, audition, letters of recommendation. Additional exam requirements/recommendations for international students: required—TOEFL (minimum score 550 paper-based; 80 iBT), IELTS (minimum score 6). *Application deadline:* For fall admission, 3/1 priority date for domestic and international students; for spring admission, 10/1 priority date for domestic students, 10/1 for international students. Applications are processed on a rolling basis. Application fee: $50. Electronic applications accepted. *Expenses: Tuition, area resident:* Full-time $4986; part-time $277 per credit hour. Tuition, nonresident: full-time $19,890; part-time $1105 per credit hour. *International tuition:* $19,890 full-time. *Required fees:* $2114; $1057 per semester. $1057 per semester. Tuition and fees vary according to course load, campus/location and program. *Financial support:* In 2019–20, 15 students received support, including 10 fellowships with full tuition reimbursements available (averaging $7,750 per year), 3 teaching assistantships with full tuition reimbursements available (averaging $7,750 per year); Federal Work-Study, scholarships/grants, tuition waivers (full), and unspecified assistantships also available. Support available to part-time students. Financial award application deadline: 4/15; financial award applicants required to submit FAFSA. *Unit head:* Dr. Greg Harwood, Graduate Director, 912-478-5813, Fax: 912-478-1295, E-mail: gharwood@georgiasouthern.edu.
Website: http://class.georgiasouthern.edu/music/

The Graduate Center, City University of New York, Graduate Studies, Program in Music, New York, NY 10016-4039. Offers DMA, PhD. *Degree requirements:* For doctorate, 2 foreign languages, thesis/dissertation. *Entrance requirements:* For doctorate, GRE General Test. Additional exam requirements/recommendations for international students: required—TOEFL. Electronic applications accepted.

Hardin-Simmons University, Graduate School, College of Fine Arts, Abilene, TX 79698-0001. Offers church music (MM); music education (MM); music performance (MM); theory and composition (MM). *Accreditation:* NASM. *Program availability:* Part-time. *Degree requirements:* For master's, comprehensive exam, thesis (for some programs). *Entrance requirements:* For master's, minimum undergraduate GPA of 3.0 in major, 2.7 overall; writing sample; demonstrated knowledge in chosen area. Additional exam requirements/recommendations for international students: required—TOEFL (minimum score 550 paper-based; 79 iBT). Electronic applications accepted.

Harvard University, Graduate School of Arts and Sciences, Department of Music, Cambridge, MA 02138. Offers composition (AM, PhD); musicology (AM); musicology and ethnomusicology (PhD); theory (AM, PhD). *Degree requirements:* For doctorate, 3 foreign languages, thesis/dissertation, composition, analytical paper. *Entrance requirements:* For master's and doctorate, GRE General Test. Additional exam requirements/recommendations for international students: required—TOEFL.

Hebrew College, Program in Jewish Studies, Newton Centre, MA 02459. Offers Jewish liturgical music (Certificate); Jewish music education (Certificate); Jewish studies (MA). *Program availability:* Part-time, evening/weekend, online learning. *Degree requirements:* For master's, one foreign language. *Entrance requirements:* For master's, GRE, interview. Additional exam requirements/recommendations for international students: required—TOEFL.

Hebrew Union College–Jewish Institute of Religion, School of Sacred Music, New York, NY 10012-1186. Offers MSM. *Degree requirements:* For master's, one foreign language, thesis, recital. *Entrance requirements:* For master's, GRE, minimum 2 years of college-level Hebrew, bachelor's degree in music or related area, trained singing voice. Additional exam requirements/recommendations for international students: required—TOEFL. *Expenses:* Contact institution.

Hollins University, Graduate Programs, Program in Liberal Studies, Roanoke, VA 24020. Offers humanities (MALS); interdisciplinary studies (MALS); leadership (MALS); social sciences (MALS); visual and performing arts (MALS). *Program availability:* Part-time, evening/weekend, 100% online, blended/hybrid learning. *Degree requirements:* For master's, thesis. *Entrance requirements:* For master's, three letters of recommendation, interview, bachelor's degree, undergraduate transcripts, statement of educational objectives. Additional exam requirements/recommendations for international students: required—TOEFL (minimum score 550 paper-based; 80 iBT), IELTS (minimum score 6.5). Electronic applications accepted. *Expenses:* Contact institution.

Holy Names University, Graduate Division, Department of Music, Oakland, CA 94619-1699. Offers Kodaly (Certificate); music education with Kodaly emphasis (MM); piano pedagogy (MM); vocal pedagogy (MM). *Degree requirements:* For master's, comprehensive exam, recital. *Entrance requirements:* For master's, audition; minimum undergraduate GPA of 2.6 overall, 3.0 in major. Additional exam requirements/recommendations for international students: required—TOEFL (minimum score 550 paper-based; 79 iBT). Electronic applications accepted.

Hope International University, School of Graduate and Professional Studies, Programs in Ministry, Fullerton, CA 92831-3138. Offers Christian leadership (MCM); church music (MA); church music (Korean track) (MCM); church planting (MCM); intercultural studies (MCM); worship (MCM). *Program availability:* Part-time, evening/weekend, online learning. *Degree requirements:* For master's, thesis (for some programs), project. *Entrance requirements:* For master's, minimum GPA of 3.0, MCM program requires an undergraduate degree in music, 2 references. Additional exam requirements/recommendations for international students: required—TOEFL (minimum score 550 paper-based; 86 iBT); recommended—IELTS (minimum score 6.5). Electronic applications accepted. *Expenses:* Contact institution.

Houghton College, Greatbatch School of Music, Houghton, NY 14744. Offers collaborative performance (MMus); composition (MMus); conducting (MMus); music (MA); performance (MMus); world music with theology and intercultural studies (MA). *Accreditation:* NASM. *Degree requirements:* For master's, comprehensive exam (for some programs), thesis (for some programs), recitals (for some programs). *Entrance requirements:* For master's, B Mus or equivalent. Additional exam requirements/recommendations for international students: required—TOEFL (minimum score 600 paper-based). Electronic applications accepted.

Houston Baptist University, College of Education and Behavioral Sciences, Programs in Education, Houston, TX 77074-3298. Offers bilingual education (M Ed); counselor education (M Ed); curriculum and instruction (M Ed); curriculum and instruction (EC-6 bilingual) (M Ed); curriculum and instruction in all-level art, Spanish, music, or physical education (M Ed); curriculum and instruction in EC-6 and special education (EC-12) (M Ed); curriculum and instruction in instructional technology (M Ed); curriculum and instruction in mathematics, science, or social studies (4-8) (M Ed); curriculum and instruction with EC-6 generalist (M Ed); curriculum and instruction with English language arts and reading (4-8) (M Ed); educational administration (M Ed); educational diagnostician (M Ed); executive educational leadership (Ed D); higher education in business management (M Ed); higher education in Christian studies (M Ed); higher education in counseling (M Ed); higher education in educational technology (M Ed); reading (M Ed); special educational leadership (Ed D). *Program availability:* Part-time, evening/weekend, 100% online, blended/hybrid learning. *Degree requirements:* For master's, comprehensive exam; for doctorate, thesis/dissertation. *Entrance requirements:* For master's, minimum GPA of 2.75, two recommendations, resume, bachelor's degree conferred transcript; interview (for non-certified teachers); for doctorate, GRE, 5 letters of recommendation. Additional exam requirements/recommendations for international students: required—TOEFL (minimum score 80 iBT), IELTS (minimum score 6.5). Electronic applications accepted. Application fee is waived when completed online. *Expenses:* Contact institution.

Howard University, Graduate School, Division of Fine Arts, Department of Music, Washington, DC 20059-0002. Offers applied music (MM); instrument (MM Ed); jazz studies (MM); organ (MM Ed); piano (MM Ed); voice (MM Ed). *Accreditation:* NASM. *Program availability:* Part-time. *Degree requirements:* For master's, comprehensive exam, thesis or alternative, departmental qualifying exam, recital. *Entrance requirements:* For master's, minimum GPA of 3.0, bachelor's degree in music or music education. Additional exam requirements/recommendations for international students: required—TOEFL.

Hunter College of the City University of New York, Graduate School, School of Arts and Sciences, Department of Music, New York, NY 10065-5085. Offers composition (MA); ethnomusicology (MA); music history (MA); music theory (MA); performance (MA). *Program availability:* Part-time, evening/weekend. *Degree requirements:* For master's, one foreign language, thesis, composition, essay, or recital; proficiency exam. *Entrance requirements:* For master's, undergraduate major in music (minimum 24 credits) or equivalent, sample of work, research paper. Additional exam requirements/recommendations for international students: required—TOEFL.

Illinois State University, Graduate School, Wonsook Kim College of Fine Arts, School of Music, Normal, IL 61790. Offers MM, MM Ed. *Accreditation:* NASM. *Faculty:* 52 full-time (24 women), 18 part-time/adjunct (6 women). *Students:* 55 full-time (29 women), 18 part-time (10 women). Average age 27. 71 applicants, 68% accepted, 30 enrolled. In 2019, 35 master's awarded. *Degree requirements:* For master's, thesis or alternative, performance. *Entrance requirements:* For master's, minimum GPA of 3.00 in music, 2.8 overall; auditions. *Application deadline:* Applications are processed on a rolling basis. Application fee: $50. *Expenses: Tuition, area resident:* Full-time $7956; part-time $9767 per year. Tuition, nonresident: full-time $9233; part-time $17,592 per year. *Required fees:* $1797. *Financial support:* In 2019–20, 32 teaching assistantships were awarded; tuition waivers (full) and unspecified assistantships also available. Financial award application deadline: 4/1. *Unit head:* Dr. Stephen Parsons, Director of Music, 309-438-8959, E-mail: sbpars@ilstu.edu. *Application contact:* Angelo Favis, 309-438-8960, E-mail: musgrad@ilstu.edu.
Website: http://www.arts.ilstu.edu/music/

Indiana State University, College of Graduate and Professional Studies, College of Arts and Sciences, School of Music, Terre Haute, IN 47809. Offers conducting (MM); music education (MM); music performance (MM). *Accreditation:* NASM. *Degree requirements:* For master's, comprehensive exam, thesis, qualifying exam. Electronic applications accepted.

Indiana University Bloomington, Jacobs School of Music, Bloomington, IN 47405-7000. Offers MA, MM, MME, MS, DM, DME, PhD, Artist Diploma, Performance Diploma, Spec, MA/MLS, MM/MLS. *Degree requirements:* For master's, comprehensive exam (for some programs); for doctorate, comprehensive exam, thesis/dissertation. *Entrance requirements:* For master's and doctorate, GRE, audition, 3 letters of recommendation. Additional exam requirements/recommendations for international students: required—TOEFL; recommended—IELTS. Electronic applications accepted. *Expenses:* Contact institution.

Indiana University Bloomington, University Graduate School, College of Arts and Sciences, Department of Folklore and Ethnomusicology, Bloomington, IN 47405. Offers ethnomusicology (MA, PhD), including folklore. Terminal master's awarded for partial completion of doctoral program. *Degree requirements:* For master's, one foreign language, comprehensive exam, project, thesis, or exam; for doctorate, 2 foreign languages, comprehensive exam, thesis/dissertation. *Entrance requirements:* For master's, GRE General Test (minimum scores: 151 for Verbal, 150 for Quantitative, 4.5 for Analytical), minimum GPA of 3.0, writing sample, curriculum vitae, 3 letters of recommendation, personal statement; for doctorate, GRE General Test (minimum scores: 151 for Verbal, 150 for Quantitative, 4.5 for Analytical), minimum GPA of 3.0, writing sample, curriculum vitae, 3 letters of recommendation, personal statement, MA. Additional exam requirements/recommendations for international students: required—TOEFL (minimum score 550 paper-based; 79 iBT). Electronic applications accepted. *Expenses:* Contact institution.

Indiana University of Pennsylvania, School of Graduate Studies and Research, College of Fine Arts, Department of Music, Program in Music Performance, Indiana, PA 15705. Offers MA. *Accreditation:* NASM. *Program availability:* Part-time. *Faculty:* 13 full-time (3 women), 1 (woman) part-time/adjunct. *Students:* 10 full-time (4 women), 7 part-time (2 women); includes 3 minority (all Hispanic/Latino), 1 international. Average age 29. 18 applicants, 100% accepted, 9 enrolled. In 2019, 4 master's awarded. *Degree requirements:* For master's, thesis optional. *Entrance requirements:* For master's, 2 letters of recommendation, audition, official transcripts, goal statement. Additional exam requirements/recommendations for international students: required—TOEFL (minimum score 550 paper-based; 80 iBT); recommended—IELTS (minimum score 6.5). *Application deadline:* Applications are processed on a rolling basis. Application fee: $50. Electronic applications accepted. *Expenses: Tuition, area resident:* Full-time $9288; part-time $516 per credit. Tuition, nonresident: full-time $13,932; part-time $774 per credit. *Required fees:* $4454. One-time fee: $115 full-time. Tuition and fees vary according to course load and program. *Financial support:* In 2019–20, 1 fellowship with tuition reimbursement (averaging $700 per year), 10 research assistantships with tuition reimbursements (averaging $3,994 per year) were awarded; career-related internships or fieldwork, Federal Work-Study, scholarships/grants, and unspecified assistantships also available. Support available to part-time students. Financial award application deadline: 4/15; financial award applicants required to submit FAFSA. *Unit head:* Dr. Matthew Baumer, Graduate Coordinator, 724-357-5646, E-mail: mbaumer@iup.edu. *Application contact:* Dr. Matthew Baumer, Graduate Coordinator, 724-357-5646, E-mail: mbaumer@iup.edu.
Website: http://www.iup.edu/music/grad/default.aspx

Indiana University-Purdue University Indianapolis, School of Engineering and Technology, Department of Music and Arts Technology, Indianapolis, IN 46202. Offers music technology (MS, PhD); music therapy (MS). *Accreditation:* NASM. *Program availability:* Part-time, evening/weekend, online learning. *Degree requirements:* For master's, thesis optional, internship or final project; for doctorate, thesis/dissertation. *Entrance requirements:* For master's, GRE, interview, audition, minimum GPA of 3.0; for doctorate, GRE, three letters of recommendation; research adviser letter; statement of purpose; writing samples; transcripts; portfolio. Additional exam requirements/recommendations for international students: required—TOEFL (minimum score 550 paper-based; 79 iBT); recommended—IELTS (minimum score 6.5). Electronic applications accepted. *Expenses:* Contact institution.

Indiana University South Bend, Ernestine M. Raclin School of the Arts, South Bend, IN 46615. Offers communication studies (MA); music (MM), including composition, performance; music performance (AD). *Accreditation:* NASM. *Program availability:* Part-time. *Entrance requirements:* For master's, performance audition. Additional exam requirements/recommendations for international students: required—TOEFL (minimum score 600 paper-based; 90 iBT). Electronic applications accepted. *Expenses:* Contact institution.

Inter American University of Puerto Rico, San Germán Campus, Graduate Studies Center, Program in Music Education, San Germán, PR 00683-5008. Offers music (MA); music teacher education (MA). *Accreditation:* TEAC. *Program availability:* Part-time, evening/weekend.

Ithaca College, School of Music, Programs in Music and Music Education, Ithaca, NY 14850. Offers composition (MM); music education (MS); performance (MM). *Accreditation:* NASM. *Program availability:* Part-time. *Faculty:* 69 full-time (25 women), 3 part-time/adjunct (all women). *Students:* 9 full-time (6 women), 29 part-time (14 women); includes 8 minority (1 Black or African American, non-Hispanic/Latino; 4 Asian, non-Hispanic/Latino; 3 Hispanic/Latino), 9 international. Average age 24. 114 applicants, 46% accepted, 16 enrolled. In 2019, 23 master's awarded. *Entrance requirements:* For master's, GRE for Music Education applicants. Additional exam requirements/recommendations for international students: required—TOEFL (minimum score 550 paper-based; 80 iBT). *Application deadline:* For fall admission, 12/1 for domestic and international students. Applications are processed on a rolling basis. Application fee: $40. Electronic applications accepted. *Expenses:* Contact institution. *Financial support:* In 2019–20, 37 students received support, including 37 teaching assistantships (averaging $10,451 per year); Federal Work-Study and scholarships/grants also available. Support available to part-time students. Financial award application deadline: 3/1; financial award applicants required to submit FAFSA. *Unit head:* Dr. Les Black, Chair, Graduate Studies in Music, 607-274-7997, E-mail: lblack@ithaca.edu. *Application contact:* Nicole Eversley Bradwell, Director, Office of Admission, 800-429-4247, Fax: 607-274-1263, E-mail: admission@ithaca.edu.
Website: https://www.ithaca.edu/academics/school-music/graduate-study

Jacksonville State University, Graduate Studies, School of Arts and Humanities, Department of Music, Jacksonville, AL 36265-1602. Offers MA. *Accreditation:* NASM. *Program availability:* Part-time, evening/weekend. *Degree requirements:* For master's, comprehensive exam, thesis (for some programs). *Entrance requirements:* For master's, GRE General Test or MAT. Additional exam requirements/recommendations for international students: required—TOEFL (minimum score 500 paper-based; 61 iBT). Electronic applications accepted.

James Madison University, The Graduate School, College of Visual and Performing Arts, Doctor of Musical Arts Program, Harrisonburg, VA 22807. Offers conducting (DMA); performance (DMA). *Program availability:* Part-time. *Students:* 28 full-time (18 women), 13 part-time (5 women); includes 3 minority (1 Asian, non-Hispanic/Latino; 2 Hispanic/Latino), 17 international. Average age 30. In 2019, 6 doctorates awarded. Application fee: $60. Electronic applications accepted. *Financial support:* In 2019–20, 24 students received support. Fellowships, Federal Work-Study, unspecified assistantships, and doctoral assistantships (averaging $12,935) available. Financial award application deadline: 3/1; financial award applicants required to submit FAFSA. *Unit head:* Dr. Jeffrey Bush, Director of the School of Music, 540-568-3614, E-mail: bushje@jmu.edu. *Application contact:* Lynette D. Michael, Director of Graduate Admissions, 540-568-6131 Ext. 6395, Fax: 540-568-7860, E-mail: michaeld@jmu.edu.
Website: http://www.jmu.edu/music/degree-programs/dma.shtml

James Madison University, The Graduate School, College of Visual and Performing Arts, Master of Music Program, Harrisonburg, VA 22807. Offers composition (MM); conducting (MM); music education (MM); performance (MM). *Accreditation:* NASM. *Program availability:* Part-time. *Students:* 20 full-time (9 women), 8 part-time (4 women); includes 5 minority (3 Black or African American, non-Hispanic/Latino; 1 Asian, non-Hispanic/Latino; 1 Two or more races, non-Hispanic/Latino), 2 international. Average age 30. In 2019, 8 master's awarded. Application fee: $60. Electronic applications accepted. *Financial support:* In 2019–20, 13 students received support, including teaching assistantships with full tuition reimbursements available (averaging $8,837 per year); fellowships, Federal Work-Study, and assistantships (averaging $7911) also available. Financial award application deadline: 3/1; financial award applicants required to submit FAFSA. *Unit head:* Dr. Jeffrey Bush, Director of the School of Music, 540-568-3614, E-mail: bushje@jmu.edu. *Application contact:* Lynette D. Michael, Director of Graduate Admissions, 540-568-6131 Ext. 6395, Fax: 540-568-7860, E-mail: michaeld@jmu.edu.
Website: http://www.jmu.edu/music/

The Jewish Theological Seminary, H. L. Miller Cantorial School and College of Jewish Music, New York, NY 10027-4649. Offers MSM. *Degree requirements:* For master's, one foreign language, comprehensive exam, departmental qualifying exam, recitals. *Entrance requirements:* For master's, music aptitude test, audition, interview, 3 letters of recommendation. Additional exam requirements/recommendations for international students: required—TOEFL. *Expenses:* Contact institution.

Johns Hopkins University, Peabody Conservatory, Baltimore, MD 21218. Offers MA, MM, DMA, AD, GPD. *Degree requirements:* For master's, thesis (for some programs), departmental qualifying exam, recital; for doctorate, one foreign language, comprehensive exam, thesis/dissertation (for some programs), departmental qualifying exam, recitals; for other advanced degree, recitals. *Entrance requirements:* For master's and other advanced degree, audition; for doctorate, audition, interview. Additional exam requirements/recommendations for international students: required—TOEFL (minimum score 550 paper-based; 79 iBT), IELTS (minimum score 6.5). Electronic applications accepted. *Expenses:* Contact institution.

The Juilliard School, Graduate Programs, New York, NY 10023-6588. Offers acting (MFA); jazz studies (Artist Diploma); music (MM, DMA, Diploma); music performance (Artist Diploma); opera studies (Artist Diploma); string quartet (Artist Diploma). *Degree requirements:* For master's and other advanced degree, performance jury, recital; for doctorate, one foreign language, thesis/dissertation, performance jury, 3 recitals. *Entrance requirements:* For master's and other advanced degree, audition; for doctorate, audition, interview. Additional exam requirements/recommendations for international students: required—TOEFL (minimum score 570 paper-based; 89 iBT). Electronic applications accepted.

Kansas State University, Graduate School, College of Arts and Sciences, School of Music, Theatre and Dance, Manhattan, KS 66506. Offers MA, MM. *Accreditation:* NASM; NAST. *Program availability:* Part-time, online learning. *Degree requirements:* For master's, thesis optional. *Entrance requirements:* For master's, GRE, audition (in person or recording), interview (for music education). Additional exam requirements/recommendations for international students: required—TOEFL (minimum score 600 paper-based). Electronic applications accepted.

Kent State University, College of the Arts, Hugh A. Glauser School of Music, Kent, OH 44242-0001. Offers conducting (MM), including choral conducting; ethnomusicology (MA); music composition (MA); music education (MM, PhD); music theory (MA); music theory-composition (PhD); performance (MM), including chamber music. *Accreditation:* NASM. *Program availability:* Part-time, 100% online. *Faculty:* 36 full-time (12 women), 23 part-time/adjunct (15 women). *Students:* 57 full-time (28 women), 186 part-time (118 women); includes 21 minority (12 Black or African American, non-Hispanic/Latino; 1 Asian, non-Hispanic/Latino; 4 Hispanic/Latino; 1 Native Hawaiian or other Pacific Islander, non-Hispanic/Latino; 3 Two or more races, non-Hispanic/Latino), 30 international. Average age 31. 106 applicants, 90% accepted, 68 enrolled. In 2019, 94 master's, 4 doctorates awarded. *Degree requirements:* For master's, comprehensive exam (for some programs), thesis (for some programs), capstone project or thesis (for MM in music education); for doctorate, comprehensive exam, thesis/dissertation. *Entrance requirements:* For master's, transcripts; minimum GPA of 3.0; 3 letters of recommendation; goal statement; resume; writing sample (for MA in ethnomusicology); portfolio of original composition (for MA in composition); audition (for MM in conducting, performance); prior degree, teaching certificate, and 1 year of teaching experience (for MM in music education); for doctorate, master's degree, 3 letters of recommendation, resume or curriculum vitae, transcripts, minimum GPA of 3.0; See Music Theory Ph.D. for further requirements and Music Education Ph.D. for further requirements. Additional exam requirements/recommendations for international students: required—TOEFL (minimum score 71 iBT), IELTS (minimum score 6), PTE (minimum score 50), Michigan English Language Assessment Battery (minimum score 74). *Application deadline:* Applications are processed on a rolling basis. Application fee: $45 ($70 for international students). Electronic applications accepted. *Financial support:* Teaching assistantships with full and partial tuition reimbursements, scholarships/grants, and unspecified assistantships available. Financial award application deadline: 3/1. *Unit head:* Kent McWilliams, Director, Hugh A. Glausser School of Music, 330-672-2172, E-mail: kmcwill2@kent.edu. *Application contact:* Michael Chunn, Graduate Coordinator/Trumpet Professor, 330-672-9234, Fax: 330-672-7837, E-mail: mchunn@kent.edu.
Website: http://www.kent.edu/music/

Lamar University, College of Graduate Studies, College of Fine Arts and Communication, Mary Morgan Moore Department of Music, Beaumont, TX 77710. Offers MM. *Accreditation:* NASM. *Faculty:* 22 full-time (5 women), 6 part-time/adjunct (2 women). *Students:* 7 part-time (2 women); includes 4 minority (2 Black or African American, non-Hispanic/Latino; 1 Hispanic/Latino; 1 Two or more races, non-Hispanic/Latino), 1 international. Average age 28. 3 applicants, 67% accepted, 2 enrolled. In 2019, 4 master's awarded. *Degree requirements:* For master's, comprehensive exam, thesis optional. *Entrance requirements:* For master's, GRE General Test, theory placement exams, audition. Additional exam requirements/recommendations for international students: required—TOEFL (minimum score 550 paper-based; 79 iBT), IELTS (minimum score 6.5). *Application deadline:* Applications are processed on a rolling basis. Application fee: $25 ($50 for international students). Electronic applications accepted. *Expenses: Tuition, area resident:* Full-time $6324; part-time $351 per credit. Tuition, state resident: full-time $6324; part-time $351 per credit. Tuition, nonresident: full-time $13,920; part-time $773 per credit. *International tuition:* $13,920 full-time. *Required fees:* $2462; $327 per credit. Tuition and fees vary according to course load, campus/location and reciprocity agreements. *Financial support:* In 2019–20, 3 students received support. Fellowships with tuition reimbursements available, teaching assistantships, institutionally sponsored loans, and tuition waivers (partial) available. Support available to part-time students. Financial award applicants required to submit FAFSA. *Unit head:* Dr. Brian Shook, Interim Chair, 409-880-8144, Fax: 409-880-8143. *Application contact:* Celeste Contreas, Director, Admissions and Academic Services, 409-880-8888, Fax: 409-880-7419, E-mail: gradmissions@lamar.edu.
Website: http://fineartscomm.lamar.edu/music

Lee University, Program in Music, Cleveland, TN 37320-3450. Offers music education (MM); music performance (MM); religious studies (MCM). *Accreditation:* NASM. *Program availability:* Part-time, online only, 100% online. *Faculty:* 20 full-time (5 women), 9 part-time/adjunct (4 women). *Students:* 16 full-time (7 women), 8 part-time (3 women); includes 2 minority (1 Black or African American, non-Hispanic/Latino; 1 Asian, non-Hispanic/Latino), 6 international. Average age 28. 20 applicants, 100% accepted, 13 enrolled. In 2019, 12 master's awarded. *Degree requirements:* For master's, variable foreign language requirement, comprehensive exam, thesis, internship. *Entrance requirements:* For master's, placement exercises in music theory, music history, diction, and piano proficiency, audition, resume, interview, minimum GPA of 2.75, official transcripts, essay, 3 recommendations, immunization forms. Additional exam requirements/recommendations for international students: required—TOEFL (minimum score 61 iBT). *Application deadline:* For fall admission, 4/1 priority date for domestic and international students; for spring admission, 10/1 priority date for domestic and international students. Applications are processed on a rolling basis. Application fee: $25. Electronic applications accepted. *Expenses: Tuition:* Full-time $13,590; part-time $755 per credit hour. *Required fees:* $25. Tuition and fees vary according to program. *Financial support:* In 2019–20, 32 students received support. Career-related internships or fieldwork, Federal Work-Study, institutionally sponsored loans, scholarships/grants, and unspecified assistantships available. Financial award application deadline: 3/1; financial award applicants required to submit FAFSA. *Unit head:* Dr. Ron Brendle, Director, 423-614-8240, Fax: 423-614-8245, E-mail: gradmusic@leeuniversity.edu. *Application contact:* Jeffery McGirt, Director of Graduate Enrollment, 423-614-8691, Fax: 423-614-8317, E-mail: jmcgirt@leeuniversity.edu.
Website: http://www.leeuniversity.edu/academics/graduate/music

Liberty University, School of Music, Lynchburg, VA 24515. Offers ethnomusicology (MA); music and worship (MA); music education (MA); worship studies (MA, DWS), including ethnomusicology (MA), leadership (MA), pastoral counseling (MA), worship techniques (MA). *Accreditation:* NASM. *Program availability:* Part-time, online learning. *Students:* 147 full-time (72 women), 220 part-time (103 women); includes 104 minority (61 Black or African American, non-Hispanic/Latino; 1 American Indian or Alaska Native, non-Hispanic/Latino; 15 Asian, non-Hispanic/Latino; 21 Hispanic/Latino; 6 Two or more races, non-Hispanic/Latino), 17 international. Average age 37. 537 applicants, 30% accepted, 89 enrolled. In 2019, 44 master's, 11 doctorates awarded. *Entrance requirements:* For master's, minimum GPA of 3.0; interview; letter of recommendation; statement of purpose; bachelor's/master's degree in music, worship, or related field, or 5 years of experience. Additional exam requirements/recommendations for international students: required—TOEFL (minimum score 600 paper-based; 100 iBT). *Application deadline:* Applications are processed on a rolling basis. Application fee: $50. Electronic applications accepted. *Expenses: Tuition:* Full-time $545; part-time $410 per credit hour. One-time fee: $50. *Financial support:* In 2019–20, 619 students received support. Federal Work-Study available. Financial award applicants required to submit FAFSA. *Unit head:* Dr. Stephen W. Müller,, Dean, 434-5823459, E-mail: swmuller@liberty.edu. *Application contact:* Jay Bridge, Director of Admissions, 800-424-9595, Fax: 800-628-7977, E-mail: gradadmissions@liberty.edu.
Website: https://www.liberty.edu/music/

Long Island University - Post, College of Arts, Communications and Design, Brookville, NY 11548-1300. Offers art (MA); clinical art therapy (MA); clinical art therapy and counseling (MA); digital game design and development (MA); fine arts and design (MFA); interactive multimedia arts (MA); museum studies (MA); music (MA); theatre (MFA). *Degree requirements:* For master's, variable foreign language requirement, comprehensive exam (for some programs), thesis. *Entrance requirements:* For master's, performance audition or portfolio. Additional exam requirements/recommendations for international students: required—TOEFL (minimum score 550 paper-based; 79 iBT). Electronic applications accepted.

Louisiana State University and Agricultural & Mechanical College, Graduate School, College of Music and Dramatic Arts, School of Music, Baton Rouge, LA 70803. Offers music (MM, DMA, PhD); music education (PhD). *Accreditation:* NASM.

Loyola University New Orleans, College of Music and Media, New Orleans, LA 70118. Offers music therapy (MMT); performance (MM). *Accreditation:* NASM. *Program availability:* Part-time. *Faculty:* 13 full-time (6 women), 17 part-time/adjunct (7 women). *Students:* 15 full-time (6 women), 31 part-time (24 women); includes 16 minority (7 Black or African American, non-Hispanic/Latino; 6 Hispanic/Latino; 3 Two or more races, non-Hispanic/Latino). Average age 28. 43 applicants, 93% accepted, 26 enrolled. In 2019, 14 master's awarded. *Entrance requirements:* For master's, performance audition, appropriate bachelor's degree, transcripts, minimum GPA of 3.0, 2 letters of recommendation, resume. Additional exam requirements/recommendations for international students: required—TOEFL (minimum score 550 paper-based; 79 iBT). *Application deadline:* For fall admission, 8/15 priority date for domestic and international students; for spring admission, 1/1 priority date for domestic and international students. Applications are processed on a rolling basis. Application fee: $20. Electronic applications accepted. *Expenses:* Contact institution. *Financial support:* In 2019–20, 43 students received support. Career-related internships or fieldwork, Federal Work-Study, institutionally sponsored loans, scholarships/grants, unspecified assistantships, and talent-based music scholarships available. Support available to part-time students. Financial award application deadline: 5/1; financial award applicants required to submit FAFSA. *Unit head:* Dr. Kern Maass, Dean, 504-865-3039, Fax: 504-865-2852, E-mail: kdmaass@loyno.edu. *Application contact:* Dr. Kern Maass, Dean, 504-865-3039, Fax: 504-865-2852, E-mail: kdmaass@loyno.edu.
Website: https://www.loyno.edu/academics/colleges/college-music-media

Lynn University, Conservatory of Music, Boca Raton, FL 33431-5598. Offers composition (MM); instrumental collaborative piano (MM); performance (MM); professional performance (Certificate). *Accreditation:* NASM. *Program availability:* Part-time, evening/weekend. *Faculty:* 6 full-time (2 women), 1 part-time/adjunct (0 women). *Students:* 24 full-time (13 women), 25 part-time (8 women); includes 11 minority (3 Asian, non-Hispanic/Latino; 8 Hispanic/Latino), 23 international. Average age 26. 59 applicants, 44% accepted, 26 enrolled. In 2019, 17 master's, 13 Certificates awarded. *Degree requirements:* For master's, comprehensive exam, completion of program in 4 calendar years, minimum GPA of 3.0, performance forum. *Entrance requirements:* For master's, Bachelor's degree from accredited institution, official undergraduate transcripts, two conservatory recommendation forms, audition (for performance and instrumental collaborative piano majors), portfolio of three original compositions and, if available, recordings (for composition majors). Additional exam requirements/recommendations for international students: required—TOEFL (minimum score 550 paper-based; 80 iBT), IELTS (minimum score 6.5). *Application deadline:* For fall admission, 8/10 for domestic students, 7/31 for international students; for spring admission, 12/18 for domestic students, 12/2 for international students; for summer admission, 4/12 for domestic students, 4/2 for international students. Applications are processed on a rolling basis. Application fee: $50. Electronic applications accepted. *Expenses:* $740.00 per credit hour. *Financial support:* In 2019–20, 49 students received support. Career-related internships or fieldwork, Federal Work-Study, scholarships/grants, tuition waivers (full and partial), and unspecified assistantships available. Support available to part-time students. Financial award application deadline: 3/1; financial award applicants required to submit FAFSA. *Unit head:* Dr. Jon Robertson, Dean, 561-237-7702, Fax: 561-237-9002, E-mail: jrobertson@lynn.edu. *Application contact:* Steven Pruitt, Director of Graduate Admissions, 561-237-7834, Fax: 561-237-7100, E-mail: admission@lynn.edu.
Website: http://www.lynn.edu/academics/colleges/conservatory

Manhattan School of Music, Graduate Programs, New York, NY 10027-4698. Offers composition (MM, DMA); jazz (MM, DMA); music performance (MM, DMA); orchestral performance (MM). *Degree requirements:* For master's, recital; for doctorate, variable foreign language requirement, thesis/dissertation, departmental qualifying exam, recitals. *Entrance requirements:* For master's, audition, pre-screen CD, bachelor's degree; for doctorate, departmental exam, audition, interview, pre-screen CD, master's degree. Additional exam requirements/recommendations for international students: required—TOEFL (minimum score 550 paper-based; 79 iBT). Electronic applications accepted.

Manhattan School of Music, Professional Studies Certificate Program, New York, NY 10027-4698. Offers instrumental music (CPS), including accompanying, brass, composition, guitar, orchestral performance, organ, piano, strings, voice, woodwinds; vocal music (CPS), including accompanying, brass, composition, guitar, orchestral performance, organ, piano, strings, voice, woodwinds. *Degree requirements:* For CPS, recital. *Entrance requirements:* For degree, audition, pre-screen CD. Additional exam requirements/recommendations for international students: required—TOEFL (minimum score 550 paper-based). Electronic applications accepted.

Mansfield University of Pennsylvania, Graduate Studies, Department of Music, Mansfield, PA 16933. Offers band conducting (MA); choral conducting (MA); performance (MA). *Accreditation:* NASM. *Program availability:* Part-time, evening/weekend. *Degree requirements:* For master's, comprehensive exam, thesis optional. *Entrance requirements:* For master's, minimum GPA of 3.0, audition. Additional exam requirements/recommendations for international students: required—TOEFL (minimum score 550 paper-based). Electronic applications accepted.

Marshall University, Academic Affairs Division, College of Arts and Media, Program in Music, Huntington, WV 25755. Offers music (MA), including music composition. *Accreditation:* NASM. *Program availability:* Evening/weekend. *Degree requirements:* For master's, thesis optional.

McGill University, Faculty of Graduate and Postdoctoral Studies, Schulich School of Music, Montréal, QC H3A 2T5, Canada. Offers composition (M Mus, D Mus, PhD); music education (MA, PhD); music technology (MA, PhD); musicology (MA, PhD); performance (M Mus); performance studies (D Mus); sound recording (M Mus, PhD); theory (MA, PhD).

Memorial University of Newfoundland, School of Graduate Studies, Interdisciplinary Program in Ethnomusicology, St. John's, NL A1C 5S7, Canada. Offers MA, PhD. *Program availability:* Part-time. *Degree requirements:* For master's, research paper or thesis; for doctorate, one foreign language, comprehensive exam, thesis/dissertation, oral defense of thesis. *Entrance requirements:* For master's, minimum B+ average with B Mus or humanities/social sciences degree; for doctorate, MA in ethnomusicology or a related field. Electronic applications accepted.

Memorial University of Newfoundland, School of Graduate Studies, School of Music, St. John's, NL A1C 5S7, Canada. Offers conducting (MMus); performance pedagogy (MMus); performing (MMus). *Entrance requirements:* For master's, diagnostic exams measuring skills and knowledge in musical literacy, B Mus with first-class standing, audition. Electronic applications accepted.

Mercer University, Graduate Studies, Macon Campus, Townsend School of Music, Macon, GA 31207. Offers choral conducting (MM); church music (MM); collaborative piano (MM), including instrumental, vocal; instrumental conducting (MM); performance (MM). *Faculty:* 12 full-time (4 women), 2 part-time/adjunct (1 woman). *Students:* 10 full-time (4 women), 1 (woman) part-time; includes 1 minority (Hispanic/Latino), 1 international. Average age 25. 25 applicants, 48% accepted, 9 enrolled. In 2019, 2 master's awarded. *Degree requirements:* For master's, comprehensive exam, recitals. *Entrance requirements:* For master's, Please see https://music.mercer.edu/admissions/, audition. Additional exam requirements/recommendations for international students: required—TOEFL (minimum score 550 paper-based; 80 iBT). *Application deadline:* For fall admission, 6/1 for domestic students, 5/1 for international students. Applications are processed on a rolling basis. Application fee: $100. *Expenses:* Contact institution. *Financial support:* In 2019–20, 14 students received support. Tuition waivers (full) and unspecified assistantships available. Financial award application deadline: 6/1; financial award applicants required to submit FAFSA. *Unit head:* Dr. Richard G. Kosowski, Director of Graduate Studies, 478-301-4167, Fax: 478-301-5633, E-mail: kosowski_rg@mercer.edu. *Application contact:* Dr. Richard G. Kosowski, Director of Graduate Studies, 478-301-4167, E-mail: kosowski_rg@mercer.edu. Website: http://music.mercer.edu

Messiah University, Program in Conducting, Mechanicsburg, PA 17055. Offers choral conducting (MM); orchestral conducting (MM); wind conducting (MM). *Accreditation:* NASM. *Program availability:* Part-time, online learning. *Degree requirements:* For master's, advanced conducting project. Electronic applications accepted.

Miami University, College of Creative Arts, Department of Music, Oxford, OH 45056. Offers music education (MM); music performance (MM). *Accreditation:* NASM.

Michigan State University, The Graduate School, College of Music, East Lansing, MI 48824. Offers collaborative piano (M Mus); jazz studies (M Mus); music (PhD); music composition (M Mus, DMA); music conducting (M Mus, DMA); music education (M Mus); music performance (M Mus, DMA); music theory (M Mus); music therapy (M Mus); musicology (MA); piano pedagogy (M Mus). *Accreditation:* NASM. *Entrance requirements:* Additional exam requirements/recommendations for international students: required—TOEFL. Electronic applications accepted.

Middle Tennessee State University, College of Graduate Studies, College of Liberal Arts, School of Music, Murfreesboro, TN 37132. Offers MA. *Accreditation:* NASM. *Program availability:* Part-time, evening/weekend, online learning. *Degree requirements:* For master's, one foreign language, comprehensive exam, thesis optional. *Entrance requirements:* For master's, GRE or MAT. Additional exam requirements/recommendations for international students: required—TOEFL (minimum score 525 paper-based; 71 iBT) or IELTS (minimum score 6). Electronic applications accepted.

Middle Tennessee State University, College of Graduate Studies, College of Mass Communication, Department of Recording Industry, Murfreesboro, TN 37132. Offers recording arts and technologies (MFA). *Program availability:* Part-time, evening/weekend, online learning. *Degree requirements:* For master's, comprehensive exam, thesis or alternative. *Entrance requirements:* For master's, GRE. Additional exam requirements/recommendations for international students: required—TOEFL (minimum score 525 paper-based; 71 iBT) or IELTS (minimum score 6).

Midwestern Baptist Theological Seminary, Graduate and Professional Programs, Kansas City, MO 64118-4697. Offers Christian education (MACE); Christian foundations (Graduate Certificate); church music (MCM); counseling (MA); ministry (D Ed Min, D Min); Old or New Testament studies (PhD); theology (M Div). *Accreditation:* ATS. *Program availability:* Part-time, online learning. *Degree requirements:* For doctorate, thesis/dissertation. *Entrance requirements:* For doctorate, MAT. Electronic applications accepted.

Midwest University, Graduate Programs, Wentzville, MO 63385. Offers asset management/investment/real estate (MBA); Christian counseling (D Min); Christian education (D Min); counseling (MA), including marriage and family counseling, school counseling; divinity (M Div); education (MA), including brain and gifted education, Christian education; global business management (MBA); global leadership (MBA); leadership (PhD), including brain and gifted educational leadership, entrepreneurial leadership, international aviation leadership, organizational leadership, political leadership; mission studies (D Min); music (MM, DMA); pastoral theology (D Min); public policy/administration (MBA); teaching English to speakers of other languages (MA). *Program availability:* Part-time, online learning. *Degree requirements:* For master's, thesis (for some programs); for doctorate, thesis/dissertation. *Entrance requirements:* Additional exam requirements/recommendations for international students: recommended—TOEFL (minimum score 550 paper-based).

Mills College, Graduate Studies, Department of Music, Oakland, CA 94613-1000. Offers composition (MA); electronic music and recording media (MFA); music performance and literature (MFA). *Program availability:* Part-time. *Degree requirements:* For master's, variable foreign language requirement, thesis, performance or recital. *Entrance requirements:* For master's, portfolio or audition. Additional exam requirements/recommendations for international students: required—TOEFL (minimum score 550 paper-based; 80 iBT) or IELTS (minimum score 6). Electronic applications accepted.

Minnesota State University Mankato, College of Graduate Studies and Research, College of Arts and Humanities, Department of Music, Mankato, MN 56001. Offers choral conducting (MM); music education (MAT); piano performance (MM); wind band conducting (MM). *Accreditation:* NASM. *Degree requirements:* For master's, comprehensive exam, thesis or alternative. *Entrance requirements:* For master's, minimum GPA of 3.0 during previous 2 years, audition or test. Additional exam requirements/recommendations for international students: required—TOEFL. Electronic applications accepted.

Mississippi College, Graduate School, College of Arts and Sciences, School of Christian Studies and the Arts, Department of Music, Clinton, MS 39058. Offers applied music performance (MM); conducting (MM); music education (MM); music performance: organ (MM); vocal pedagogy (MM). *Accreditation:* NASM. *Program availability:* Part-time, evening/weekend. *Degree requirements:* For master's, comprehensive exam, recital. *Entrance requirements:* For master's, GRE, minimum GPA of 2.5. Additional exam requirements/recommendations for international students: recommended—TOEFL, IELTS. Electronic applications accepted.

Missouri State University, Graduate College, College of Arts and Letters, Department of Music, Springfield, MO 65897. Offers MM, MS Ed. *Accreditation:* NASM. *Program availability:* Part-time. *Degree requirements:* For master's, comprehensive exam, thesis or alternative. *Entrance requirements:* For master's, GRE, interview/

audition (MM), 9-12 teaching certification (MS Ed). Additional exam requirements/recommendations for international students: required—TOEFL (minimum score 550 paper-based; 79 iBT), IELTS (minimum score 6). Electronic applications accepted. *Expenses: Tuition, area resident:* Full-time $2600; part-time $1735 per credit hour. Tuition, nonresident: full-time $5240; part-time $3495 per credit hour. *International tuition:* $5240 full-time. *Required fees:* $530; $438 per credit hour. Tuition and fees vary according to class time, course level, course load, degree level, campus/location and program.

Montclair State University, The Graduate School, College of the Arts, John J. Cali School of Music, Artist's Diploma Program, Montclair, NJ 07043-1624. Offers AD. *Accreditation:* NASM. *Program availability:* Part-time, evening/weekend. *Entrance requirements:* For degree, essay. Additional exam requirements/recommendations for international students: required—TOEFL (minimum score 83 iBT), IELTS (minimum score 6.5). Electronic applications accepted.

Montclair State University, The Graduate School, College of the Arts, John J. Cali School of Music, Performer's Certificate Program, Montclair, NJ 07043-1624. Offers Performer's Certificate.

Montclair State University, The Graduate School, College of the Arts, John J. Cali School of Music, Program in Music, Montclair, NJ 07043-1624. Offers music education (MA); music therapy (MA); performance (MA); theory/composition (MA). *Program availability:* Part-time, evening/weekend. *Degree requirements:* For master's, thesis. *Entrance requirements:* For master's, GRE General Test, 2 letters of recommendation, essay. Additional exam requirements/recommendations for international students: required—TOEFL (minimum score 83 iBT), IELTS (minimum score 6.5). Electronic applications accepted.

Morgan State University, School of Graduate Studies, James H. Gilliam Jr College of Liberal Arts, Department of Fine and Performing Arts, Baltimore, MD 21251. Offers music (MA), including choral, conducting, instrumental, piano, sacred music, vocal. *Accreditation:* NASM. *Program availability:* Part-time, evening/weekend. *Faculty:* 21 full-time (10 women), 13 part-time/adjunct (3 women). *Students:* 3 full-time (2 women), 5 part-time (4 women); all minorities (7 Black or African American, non-Hispanic/Latino; 1 Two or more races, non-Hispanic/Latino). Average age 28. 8 applicants, 88% accepted, 5 enrolled. In 2019, 6 master's awarded. *Degree requirements:* For master's, comprehensive exam, thesis. *Entrance requirements:* For master's, Minimum GPA 3.0, GRE. Additional exam requirements/recommendations for international students: required—TOEFL (minimum score 550 paper-based), IELTS (minimum score 6). *Application deadline:* For fall admission, 2/1 priority date for domestic students, 4/1 for international students; for spring admission, 11/15 for domestic students, 10/1 for international students. Applications are processed on a rolling basis. Application fee: $50 ($70 for international students). Electronic applications accepted. *Expenses:* Tuition, state resident: full-time $455; part-time $455 per credit hour. Tuition, nonresident: full-time $894; part-time $894 per credit hour. *Required fees:* $82; $82 per credit hour. *Financial support:* In 2019–20, 1 student received support. Fellowships with full and partial tuition reimbursements available, research assistantships with full and partial tuition reimbursements available, teaching assistantships with full and partial tuition reimbursements available, career-related internships or fieldwork, Federal Work-Study, scholarships/grants, tuition waivers (full and partial), and unspecified assistantships available. Support available to part-time students. Financial award application deadline: 2/1. *Unit head:* Dr. Eric Conway, Chairperson, 443-885-3598, E-mail: eric.conway@morgan.edu. *Application contact:* Dr. Jahmaine Smith, Director of Admissions, 443-885-3185, Fax: 443-885-8226, E-mail: gradapply@morgan.edu. Website: https://morgan.edu/college_of_liberal_arts/departments/fine_and_performing_arts/music/graduate_degree_program.html

Murray State University, College of Humanities and Fine Arts, Department of Music, Murray, KY 42071. Offers music education (MME). *Accreditation:* NASM. *Program availability:* Part-time. *Entrance requirements:* For master's, GRE or GMAT, minimum university GPA of 2.75. Additional exam requirements/recommendations for international students: required—TOEFL (minimum score 527 paper-based; 71 iBT). Electronic applications accepted.

Nazareth College of Rochester, Graduate Studies, Department of Music, Rochester, NY 14618. Offers music education (MS Ed); music performance and pedagogy (MM). *Program availability:* Part-time, evening/weekend. *Entrance requirements:* For master's, GRE or MAT (for music education program), audition, minimum GPA of 3.0. Additional exam requirements/recommendations for international students: required—TOEFL (minimum score 550 paper-based, 79 iBT) or IELTS (6.5). Electronic applications accepted.

New England Conservatory of Music, Graduate Program in Music, Boston, MA 02115. Offers MM, DMA, Diploma. *Faculty:* 92 full-time (31 women), 106 part-time/adjunct (37 women). *Students:* 323 full-time (157 women), 23 part-time (10 women); includes 58 minority (8 Black or African American, non-Hispanic/Latino; 27 Asian, non-Hispanic/Latino; 9 Hispanic/Latino; 14 Two or more races, non-Hispanic/Latino), 152 international. Average age 23. 1,301 applicants, 33% accepted, 168 enrolled. In 2019, 147 master's, 10 doctorates awarded. *Degree requirements:* For master's, variable foreign language requirement, comprehensive exam, thesis (for some programs), recital; for doctorate, one foreign language, comprehensive exam, thesis/dissertation, qualifying exams, recital. *Entrance requirements:* For master's and Diploma, audition; for doctorate, music theory and musicology exam, audition. Additional exam requirements/recommendations for international students: required—TOEFL (minimum score 550 paper-based; 79 iBT). *Application deadline:* For fall admission, 12/1 priority date for domestic and international students; for spring admission, 10/15 for domestic and international students. Applications are processed on a rolling basis. Application fee: $115. Electronic applications accepted. *Expenses: Tuition:* Full-time $49,580; part-time $3180 per credit. *Required fees:* $880. *Financial support:* Fellowships with partial tuition reimbursements, teaching assistantships, Federal Work-Study, scholarships/grants, and tuition waivers (partial) available. Support available to part-time students. Financial award application deadline: 12/1; financial award applicants required to submit FAFSA. *Unit head:* Novak, Vice President and Provost, 617-585-1308, Fax: 617-585-1303, E-mail: tom.novak@necmusic.edu. *Application contact:* Alex Powell, Dean of Admissions and Financial Aid, 617-585-1101, Fax: 617-585-1115, E-mail: alex.powell@newenglandconservatory.edu. Website: www.necmusic.edu

New Jersey City University, William J. Maxwell College of Arts and Sciences, Department of Music, Dance and Theatre, Jersey City, NJ 07305-1597. Offers music education (MA); performance (MM). *Accreditation:* NASM. *Program availability:* Part-time, evening/weekend. *Degree requirements:* For master's, thesis optional, recital. *Entrance requirements:* Additional exam requirements/recommendations for international students: required—TOEFL (minimum score 79 iBT).

New Mexico State University, College of Arts and Sciences, Department of Music, Las Cruces, NM 88003-8001. Offers conducting (MM); music education (MM); performance (MM). *Accreditation:* NASM. *Program availability:* Part-time-only, online learning. *Faculty:* 17 full-time (7 women), 1 part-time/adjunct (0 women). *Students:* 11 full-time (7 women), 8 part-time (4 women); includes 7 minority (all Hispanic/Latino), 5

international. Average age 33. 17 applicants, 82% accepted, 6 enrolled. In 2019, 10 master's awarded. *Degree requirements:* For master's, comprehensive exam, thesis (for some programs), recital. *Entrance requirements:* For master's, 2 initial review courses, audition, bachelor's degree or equivalent from an accredited institution. Additional exam requirements/recommendations for international students: required—TOEFL (minimum score 550 paper-based; 79 iBT), IELTS (minimum score 6.5). *Application deadline:* For fall admission, 7/1 priority date for domestic students; for spring admission, 11/1 for domestic students; for summer admission, 3/1 for domestic students. Applications are processed on a rolling basis. Application fee: $40 ($50 for international students). Electronic applications accepted. *Financial support:* In 2019–20, 12 students received support, including 2 fellowships (averaging $2,824 per year), 8 teaching assistantships (averaging $15,893 per year); career-related internships or fieldwork, Federal Work-Study, scholarships/grants, traineeships, health care benefits, and unspecified assistantships also available. Support available to part-time students. Financial award application deadline: 3/1. *Unit head:* Dr. Lon W. Chaffin, Department Head, 575-646-2421, Fax: 575-646-8199, E-mail: lchaffin@nmsu.edu. *Application contact:* Dr. James Shearer, Coordinator of Graduate Studies, 575-646-2601, Fax: 575-646-8199, E-mail: jshearer@nmsu.edu.
Website: http://music.nmsu.edu

New Orleans Baptist Theological Seminary, Graduate and Professional Programs, Division of Church Music Ministries, New Orleans, LA 70126-4858. Offers M Div, MMCM, DMA. *Accreditation:* NASM. *Program availability:* Online learning. *Degree requirements:* For doctorate, one foreign language, thesis/dissertation. *Entrance requirements:* For doctorate, GRE General Test. Additional exam requirements/recommendations for international students: required—TOEFL.

The New School, College of Performing Arts, Mannes School of Music, New York, NY 10011. Offers composition (MM, Advanced Diploma); guitar (MM, Advanced Diploma); harpsichord (MM, Advanced Diploma); music theory (MM); orchestral conducting (MM, Advanced Diploma); orchestral instruments (MM, Advanced Diploma); piano (MM, Advanced Diploma); piano and collaborative piano (MM, Advanced Diploma); theory (Advanced Diploma); voice (MM, Advanced Diploma). *Program availability:* Part-time. *Faculty:* 9 full-time (4 women), 128 part-time/adjunct (53 women). *Students:* 315 full-time (200 women), 3 part-time (0 women); includes 35 minority (4 Black or African American, non-Hispanic/Latino; 17 Asian, non-Hispanic/Latino; 10 Hispanic/Latino; 4 Two or more races, non-Hispanic/Latino), 192 international. Average age 25. 894 applicants, 44% accepted, 318 enrolled. In 2019, 103 master's, 27 Advanced Diplomas awarded. *Degree requirements:* For master's, performance examination. *Entrance requirements:* For master's, transcripts, recommendation letter, essay, live audition. Additional exam requirements/recommendations for international students: required—TOEFL (minimum score 79 iBT), IELTS (minimum score 6.5), PTE (minimum score 53). *Application deadline:* For fall admission, 12/1 priority date for domestic and international students; for spring admission, 10/15 priority date for domestic and international students. Applications are processed on a rolling basis. Application fee: $50. Electronic applications accepted. *Expenses:* 1680 per credit. *Financial support:* In 2019–20, 303 students received support, including 4 fellowships (averaging $4,994 per year), 4 research assistantships (averaging $2,887 per year), 4 teaching assistantships (averaging $7,022 per year); career-related internships or fieldwork, Federal Work-Study, scholarships/grants, and unspecified assistantships also available. Support available to part-time students. Financial award application deadline: 2/1; financial award applicants required to submit FAFSA. *Unit head:* Richard Kessler, Executive Dean, College of Performing Arts, 212-580-0210 Ext. 4848, E-mail: richardkessler@newschool.edu. *Application contact:* Amanda Hosking, Director of Admission, College of Performing Arts, 212-229-5150 Ext. 4805, E-mail: performingarts@newschool.edu.
Website: http://www.newschool.edu/mannes/

New York University, Graduate School of Arts and Science, Department of Music, New York, NY 10012-1019. Offers composition and theory (MA, PhD); early music performance (Advanced Certificate); ethnomusicology (MA, PhD). Terminal master's awarded for partial completion of doctoral program. *Degree requirements:* For master's, one foreign language, thesis (for some programs), general exam; for doctorate, 2 foreign languages, thesis/dissertation, general and special exams. *Entrance requirements:* For master's, GRE General Test, bachelor's degree in liberal arts or music; for doctorate, GRE General Test, master's degree in music. Additional exam requirements/recommendations for international students: required—TOEFL, IELTS.

New York University, Steinhardt School of Culture, Education, and Human Development, Department of Music and Performing Arts Professions, Program in Music Business, New York, NY 10012. Offers music business (MA); music technology (MA). *Program availability:* Part-time. *Entrance requirements:* For master's, interview. Additional exam requirements/recommendations for international students: required—TOEFL (minimum score 100 iBT). Electronic applications accepted.

New York University, Steinhardt School of Culture, Education, and Human Development, Department of Music and Performing Arts Professions, Program in Music Performance and Composition, New York, NY 10012. Offers instrumental performance (MM), including instrumental performance, jazz instrumental performance; music performance and composition (PhD), including music performance and composition; music theory and composition (MM), including composition for film and multimedia, composition for music theater, computer music composition, music theory and composition, songwriting; piano performance (MM), including collaborative piano, solo piano; vocal pedagogy (Advanced Certificate); vocal performance (MM), including classical voice, musical theatre performance. *Program availability:* Part-time. *Entrance requirements:* For master's, audition; for doctorate, GRE General Test, audition, interview. Additional exam requirements/recommendations for international students: required—TOEFL (minimum score 100 iBT). Electronic applications accepted.

New York University, Steinhardt School of Culture, Education, and Human Development, Department of Music and Performing Arts Professions, Program in Music Technology, New York, NY 10012. Offers MM, PhD. *Program availability:* Part-time. *Entrance requirements:* For master's, portfolio; for doctorate, essay, 3 letters of recommendation, master's degree. Additional exam requirements/recommendations for international students: required—TOEFL (minimum score 100 iBT). Electronic applications accepted.

New York University, Tisch School of the Arts, Graduate Musical Theatre Writing Program, New York, NY 10003. Offers MFA. *Degree requirements:* For master's, full-length musical theatre work. *Entrance requirements:* For master's, interview, portfolio. Additional exam requirements/recommendations for international students: recommended—TOEFL, IELTS. Electronic applications accepted. *Expenses:* Contact institution.

Norfolk State University, School of Graduate Studies, School of Liberal Arts, Department of Music, Norfolk, VA 23504. Offers music (MM); music education (MM); performance (MM); theory and composition (MM). *Accreditation:* NASM. *Program availability:* Part-time. *Degree requirements:* For master's, thesis or alternative. *Entrance requirements:* For master's, minimum GPA of 2.7, letters of recommendation. Additional exam requirements/recommendations for international students: required—TOEFL.

North Carolina Central University, College of Arts and Sciences, Department of Music, Durham, NC 27707-3129. Offers jazz studies (MM).

North Dakota State University, College of Graduate and Interdisciplinary Studies, College of Arts, Humanities and Social Sciences, Challey School of Music, Fargo, ND 58102. Offers conducting (MM, DMA); music education (MM); performance (MM, DMA). *Accreditation:* NASM. *Degree requirements:* For master's, 2 foreign languages, comprehensive exam, thesis or alternative, recitals; for doctorate, 2 foreign languages, comprehensive exam, thesis/dissertation or alternative, recitals. *Entrance requirements:* For master's and doctorate, music history, music theory, performance audition. Additional exam requirements/recommendations for international students: required—TOEFL (minimum score 525 paper-based; 71 iBT). Electronic applications accepted. Tuition and fees vary according to program and reciprocity agreements.

Northeastern Illinois University, College of Graduate Studies and Research, College of Arts and Sciences, Program in Music, Chicago, IL 60625. Offers music (MA), including applied music pedagogy. *Accreditation:* NASM. *Program availability:* Part-time, evening/weekend. *Degree requirements:* For master's, comprehensive exam, thesis optional. *Entrance requirements:* For master's, departmental exam, audition, minimum GPA of 2.75. Additional exam requirements/recommendations for international students: required—TOEFL (minimum score 550 paper-based; 79 iBT). Electronic applications accepted.

Northern Arizona University, College of Arts and Letters, School of Music, Flagstaff, AZ 86011. Offers music (MM); music performance (Graduate Certificate). *Accreditation:* NASM. *Program availability:* Part-time. *Degree requirements:* For master's, variable foreign language requirement, comprehensive exam (for some programs), thesis (for some programs). *Entrance requirements:* For master's, bachelor's degree in music, minimum cumulative GPA of 3.0, audition, major professor and/or area approval for the candidate's sub-plan. Additional exam requirements/recommendations for international students: required—TOEFL (minimum score 80 iBT), IELTS (minimum score 6.5). Electronic applications accepted.

Northern Illinois University, Graduate School, College of Visual and Performing Arts, School of Music, De Kalb, IL 60115-2854. Offers MM, Performer's Certificate. *Accreditation:* NASM. *Program availability:* Part-time. *Faculty:* 33 full-time (3 women), 14 part-time/adjunct (3 women). *Students:* 39 full-time (16 women), 35 part-time (16 women); includes 14 minority (2 Black or African American, non-Hispanic/Latino; 3 Asian, non-Hispanic/Latino; 7 Hispanic/Latino; 2 Two or more races, non-Hispanic/Latino), 34 international. Average age 28. 67 applicants, 64% accepted, 25 enrolled. In 2019, 28 master's, 8 other advanced degrees awarded. *Degree requirements:* For master's, comprehensive exam, thesis optional, recital or project; for Performer's Certificate, recitals. *Entrance requirements:* For master's, minimum GPA of 2.75, appropriate bachelor's degree, audition, interview; for Performer's Certificate, minimum GPA of 2.75 (undergraduate), 3.2 (graduate); audition. Additional exam requirements/recommendations for international students: required—TOEFL (minimum score 550 paper-based). *Application deadline:* For fall admission, 4/1 for domestic students, 5/1 for international students; for spring admission, 11/1 for domestic students, 10/1 for international students. Applications are processed on a rolling basis. Application fee: $40. Electronic applications accepted. *Financial support:* In 2019–20, 4 research assistantships with full tuition reimbursements, 30 teaching assistantships with full tuition reimbursements were awarded; fellowships with full tuition reimbursements, Federal Work-Study, scholarships/grants, tuition waivers (full), and staff assistantships also available. Support available to part-time students. Financial award applicants required to submit FAFSA. *Unit head:* Dr. Andrew Glendening, Director, 815-753-7954, Fax: 815-753-1759. *Application contact:* Lynn Slater, Coordinator of Admissions and Public Relations, 815-753-1546, E-mail: lslater@niu.edu.
Website: http://www.niu.edu/music/

North Park University, School of Music, Chicago, IL 60625-4895. Offers vocal performance (MM). *Accreditation:* NASM.

Northwestern State University of Louisiana, Graduate Studies and Research, School of Creative and Performing Arts, Program in Music, Natchitoches, LA 71497. Offers MM. *Accreditation:* NASM. *Degree requirements:* For master's, comprehensive exam, thesis or alternative. *Entrance requirements:* For master's, GRE General Test, minimum undergraduate GPA of 2.5. Additional exam requirements/recommendations for international students: required—TOEFL. Electronic applications accepted.

Northwestern University, The Graduate School, School of Communication, Department of Performance Studies, Evanston, IL 60208. Offers MA, PhD. *Program availability:* Part-time. Terminal master's awarded for partial completion of doctoral program. *Degree requirements:* For master's, recital; for doctorate, one foreign language, thesis/dissertation, recital. *Entrance requirements:* For master's and doctorate, GRE General Test. Additional exam requirements/recommendations for international students: required—TOEFL.

Northwestern University, Henry and Leigh Bienen School of Music, Department of Music Performance, Evanston, IL 60208. Offers brass performance (MM, DMA); conducting (MM, DMA); jazz studies (MM); percussion performance (MM, DMA); performance (MM); piano pedagogy (MME); piano performance (MM, DMA); piano performance and collaborative arts (MM, DMA); piano performance and pedagogy (MM, DMA); string performance (MM, DMA); voice and opera performance (MM, DMA); woodwind performance (MM, DMA). *Accreditation:* NASM. *Degree requirements:* For master's, recital; for doctorate, comprehensive exam, thesis/dissertation, 3 recitals. *Entrance requirements:* For master's, audition, prescreening auditions where required; for doctorate, audition, preliminary tapes. Additional exam requirements/recommendations for international students: required—TOEFL (minimum score 80 iBT).

Northwestern University, Henry and Leigh Bienen School of Music, Department of Music Studies, Evanston, IL 60208. Offers composition (DMA); music education (MME, PhD); music theory and cognition (PhD); musicology (MM, PhD); theory (MM). *Accreditation:* NASM. *Degree requirements:* For doctorate, comprehensive exam, thesis/dissertation. *Entrance requirements:* For master's, portfolio or research papers; for doctorate, GRE General Test (for PhD), portfolio, research papers. Additional exam requirements/recommendations for international students: required—TOEFL (minimum score 600 paper-based; 80 iBT).

Oakland University, School of Music, Theatre and Dance, Rochester, MI 48309-4401. Offers music (MM); music education (PhD). *Accreditation:* NASM. *Entrance requirements:* Additional exam requirements/recommendations for international students: required—TOEFL (minimum score 550 paper-based; 79 iBT), IELTS (minimum score 6.5). Electronic applications accepted. *Expenses:* Contact institution.

Oberlin College, Conservatory of Music, Oberlin, OH 44074-1588. Offers conducting (MM); contemporary chamber music (MM); historical performance (MM); performance (AD); piano technology (AD). *Degree requirements:* For master's, 2 recitals. *Entrance requirements:* For master's and AD, audition. Additional exam requirements/recommendations for international students: recommended—TOEFL, IELTS. Electronic applications accepted.

The Ohio State University, Graduate School, College of Arts and Sciences, Division of Arts and Humanities, School of Music, Columbus, OH 43210. Offers MA,

MM, DMA, PhD. *Accreditation:* NASM. *Program availability:* Part-time. *Degree requirements:* For master's, thesis optional; for doctorate, 2 foreign languages, thesis/dissertation. *Entrance requirements:* For master's, GRE General Test (for all MA applicants and for MM applicants if GPA is below 3.0), pre-screen video audition (for piano and voice); for doctorate, GRE General Test (for all PhD applicants and for DMA applicants if GPA is below 3.0), pre-screen video audition (for piano and voice). Additional exam requirements/recommendations for international students: required—TOEFL (minimum score 550 paper-based; 79 iBT), Michigan English Language Assessment Battery (minimum score 82); recommended—IELTS (minimum score 7). Electronic applications accepted.

Ohio University, Graduate College, College of Fine Arts, School of Music, Athens, OH 45701-2979. Offers accompanying (MM); composition (MM); conducting (MM); history/literature (MM); music education (MM); music therapy (MM); performance (MM, Certificate); performance/pedagogy (MM); theory (MM). *Accreditation:* NASM. *Program availability:* Part-time, evening/weekend, online learning. *Degree requirements:* For master's, comprehensive exam, thesis (for some programs), oral exam. *Entrance requirements:* For master's, audition, interview, portfolio, recordings (varies by program). Additional exam requirements/recommendations for international students: required—TOEFL (minimum score 550 paper-based; 80 iBT) or IELTS (minimum score 6.5). Electronic applications accepted.

Oklahoma City University, Wanda L. Bass School of Music, Oklahoma City, OK 73106-1402. Offers composition (MM); conducting (MM); musical theatre (MM); opera performance (MM); performance (MM); vocal coaching (MM). *Accreditation:* NASM. *Program availability:* Part-time. *Degree requirements:* For master's, thesis, departmental qualifying exam, recital. *Entrance requirements:* For master's, audition, bachelor's degree in music from NASM-accredited institution, minimum GPA of 3.0. Additional exam requirements/recommendations for international students: required—TOEFL (minimum score 550 paper-based; 80 iBT). Electronic applications accepted. *Expenses:* Contact institution.

Oklahoma State University, College of Arts and Sciences, Michael and Anne Greenwood School of Music, Stillwater, OK 74078. Offers pedagogy and performance (MM). *Accreditation:* NASM. *Faculty:* 28 full-time (9 women), 7 part-time/adjunct (2 women). *Students:* 14 full-time (7 women), 9 part-time (4 women); includes 2 minority (both Hispanic/Latino), 3 international. Average age 25. 47 applicants, 55% accepted, 9 enrolled. In 2019, 12 master's awarded. *Entrance requirements:* For master's, GRE, audition. Additional exam requirements/recommendations for international students: required—TOEFL (minimum score 550 paper-based; 79 iBT). *Application deadline:* For fall admission, 3/1 priority date for international students; for spring admission, 8/1 priority date for international students. Applications are processed on a rolling basis. Application fee: $50 ($75 for international students). Electronic applications accepted. *Expenses:* Tuition, area resident: Full-time $4148.10; part-time $2765.40 per credit hour. Tuition, state resident: full-time $4148.10; part-time $2765.40 per credit hour. Tuition, nonresident: full-time $15,775; part-time $10,516.80 per credit hour. *International tuition:* $15,775.20 full-time. *Required fees:* $2196.90; $122.05 per credit hour. Tuition and fees vary according to course load, campus/location and program. *Financial support:* In 2019–20, 22 teaching assistantships (averaging $1,302 per year) were awarded; research assistantships, career-related internships or fieldwork, Federal Work-Study, scholarships/grants, health care benefits, tuition waivers (partial), and unspecified assistantships also available. Support available to part-time students. Financial award application deadline: 3/1; financial award applicants required to submit FAFSA. *Unit head:* Dr. Jeff Loeffert, Director, 405-744-8997, Fax: 405-744-9324, E-mail: osumusic@okstate.edu. *Application contact:* Dr. Sheryl Tucker, Dean, 405-744-6368, Fax: 405-744-0355, E-mail: gradi@okstate.edu. Website: http://music.okstate.edu/

Old Dominion University, College of Arts and Letters, Master of Music Education Program, Norfolk, VA 23529. Offers applied studies or conducting (MME); pedagogy (MME); research (MME). *Accreditation:* NASM. *Program availability:* Part-time, evening/weekend. *Degree requirements:* For master's, comprehensive exam, thesis (for some programs), performance recital (for applied studies or conducting), ePortfolio (for pedagogy). *Entrance requirements:* For master's, music theory exam, diagnostic examination, GRE or MAT, baccalaureate degree in music education, music theory, music history, or applied music; audition (for applied music areas). Additional exam requirements/recommendations for international students: required—TOEFL. Electronic applications accepted. *Expenses:* Contact institution.

Open University, Graduate Programs, Milton Keynes, United Kingdom. Offers business (MBA); education (M Ed); engineering (M Eng); history (MA); music (MA); philosophy (MA).

Park University, School of Graduate and Professional Studies, Kansas City, MO 54105. Offers adult education (M Ed); business and government leadership (Graduate Certificate); business, government, and global society (MPA); communication and leadership (MA); creative and life writing (Graduate Certificate); disaster and emergency management (MPA, Graduate Certificate); educational leadership (M Ed); finance (MBA, Graduate Certificate); general business (MBA); global business (Graduate Certificate); healthcare administration (MHA); healthcare services management and leadership (Graduate Certificate); international business (MBA); language and literacy (M Ed), including English for speakers of other languages, special reading teacher/literacy coach; leadership of international healthcare organizations (Graduate Certificate); management information systems (MBA, Graduate Certificate); music performance (ADP, Graduate Certificate), including cello (MM, ADP), piano (MM, ADP), viola (MM, ADP), violin (MM, ADP); nonprofit and community services management (MPA); nonprofit leadership (Graduate Certificate); performance (MM), including cello (MM, ADP), piano (MM, ADP), viola (MM, ADP), violin (MM, ADP); public management (MPA); social work (MSW); teacher leadership (M Ed), including curriculum and assessment, instructional leader. *Program availability:* Part-time, evening/weekend, online learning. *Degree requirements:* For master's, comprehensive exam (for some programs), thesis (for some programs), internship (for some programs); exam (for some programs). *Entrance requirements:* For master's, GRE or GMAT (for some programs), teacher certification (for some M Ed programs), letters of recommendation, essay, resume (for some programs). Additional exam requirements/recommendations for international students: required—TOEFL (minimum score 550 paper-based; 79 iBT), IELTS (minimum score 6). Electronic applications accepted.

Penn State University Park, Graduate School, College of Arts and Architecture, School of Music, University Park, PA 16802. Offers composition-theory (M Mus); conducting (M Mus); music (MA); music education (MME, PhD, Certificate); pedagogy and performance (M Mus); performance (M Mus); piano performance (DMA). *Accreditation:* NASM.

Pensacola Christian College, Graduate Studies, Pensacola, FL 32503-2267. Offers business administration (MBA); curriculum and instruction (MS, Ed D, Ed S); dramatics (MFA); educational leadership (MS, Ed D, Ed S); graphic design (MA, MFA); music (MA); nursing (MSN); performance studies (MA); studio art (MA, MFA).

Phillips Theological Seminary, Programs in Theology, Tulsa, OK 74116. Offers administration of church agencies (M Div); campus ministry (M Div); church-related

social work (M Div); college and seminary teaching (M Div); global mission work (M Div); institutional chaplaincy (M Div); ministerial vocations in Christian education (M Div); ministry (D Min), including parish ministry, pastoral counseling, practices of ministry; ministry and culture (MAMC), including Christian education, congregational leadership, history and practice of Christian spirituality, theology, ethics, and culture; ministry of music (M Div); pastoral care and counseling (M Div); pastoral ministry (M Div); theological studies (MTS). *Accreditation:* ATS. *Program availability:* Part-time, online learning. *Degree requirements:* For master's, thesis (for some programs); for doctorate, thesis/dissertation. *Entrance requirements:* For master's, minimum GPA of 2.5; for doctorate, M Div, minimum GPA of 3.0.

Pittsburg State University, Graduate School, College of Arts and Sciences, Department of Music, Pittsburg, KS 66762. Offers conducting (MM), including choral, instrumental - orchestral, instrumental - wind, organ, piano, voice; education (MM), including instrumental, vocal; performance (MM), including harpsichord, percussion, strings, winds. *Accreditation:* NASM. *Degree requirements:* For master's, thesis or alternative. *Entrance requirements:* Additional exam requirements/recommendations for international students: required—TOEFL (minimum score 520 paper-based; 68 iBT), IELTS (minimum score 6), PTE (minimum score 47). Electronic applications accepted. *Expenses:* Contact institution.

Point Park University, Conservatory of Performing Arts, Pittsburgh, PA 15222-1984. Offers screenwriting and playwriting (MFA). *Program availability:* Blended/hybrid learning. *Degree requirements:* For master's, comprehensive exam (for some programs), thesis or alternative. *Entrance requirements:* For master's, interview, undergraduate degree in related field, theatre experience. Additional exam requirements/recommendations for international students: required—TOEFL (minimum score 550 paper-based; 79 iBT). Electronic applications accepted.

Portland State University, Graduate Studies, College of the Arts, School of Music and Theater, Portland, OR 97207-0751. Offers conducting (Mus M); jazz studies (Mus M); music (Mus M); performance (Mus M). *Accreditation:* NASM. *Program availability:* Part-time. *Faculty:* 30 full-time (14 women), 60 part-time/adjunct (25 women). *Students:* 25 full-time (12 women), 6 part-time (1 woman); includes 6 minority (1 Asian, non-Hispanic/Latino; 3 Hispanic/Latino; 2 Two or more races, non-Hispanic/Latino), 4 international. Average age 30. 43 applicants, 72% accepted, 15 enrolled. In 2019, 9 master's awarded. *Degree requirements:* For master's, variable foreign language requirement, exit exam. *Entrance requirements:* For master's, GRE General Test, music diagnostic entrance examination, minimum GPA of 3.0 in graduate coursework or 2.75 overall undergraduate, audition. Additional exam requirements/recommendations for international students: required—TOEFL (minimum score 550 paper-based). *Application deadline:* For fall admission, 4/15 priority date for domestic students, 4/15 for international students; for winter admission, 10/1 for domestic and international students; for spring admission, 12/1 for domestic and international students; for summer admission, 1/15 for domestic and international students. Application fee: $65. *Expenses:* Contact institution. *Financial support:* In 2019–20, 24 students received support, including 10 teaching assistantships with full and partial tuition reimbursements available (averaging $7,203 per year); Federal Work-Study, scholarships/grants, and unspecified assistantships also available. Support available to part-time students. Financial award application deadline: 3/1; financial award applicants required to submit FAFSA. *Unit head:* Bonnie Miksch, Director, 503-725-3063, Fax: 503-725-8215, E-mail: bonnie@pdx.edu. *Application contact:* Bonnie Miksch, Director, 503-725-3063, Fax: 503-725-8215, E-mail: bonnie@pdx.edu. Website: https://www.pdx.edu/music/

Pratt Institute, School of Liberal Arts and Sciences, Program in Performance and Performance Studies, Brooklyn, NY 11205-3899. Offers MFA. *Students:* 7 full-time (6 women), 1 part-time (0 women); includes 3 minority (1 Black or African American, non-Hispanic/Latino; 1 Hispanic/Latino; 1 Two or more races, non-Hispanic/Latino). Average age 31. 23 applicants, 96% accepted, 1 enrolled. In 2019, 13 master's awarded. *Degree requirements:* For master's, thesis. *Entrance requirements:* Additional exam requirements/recommendations for international students: required—TOEFL. *Application deadline:* For fall admission, 1/5 for domestic and international students; for spring admission, 10/1 for domestic and international students. Application fee: $50 ($90 for international students). Electronic applications accepted. *Expenses: Tuition:* Full-time $33,246; part-time $1847 per credit. *Required fees:* $1980. *Financial support:* Career-related internships or fieldwork, Federal Work-Study, institutionally sponsored loans, scholarships/grants, health care benefits, and unspecified assistantships available. Support available to part-time students. Financial award application deadline: 2/1; financial award applicants required to submit FAFSA. *Unit head:* Jennifer Miller, Coordinator, 718-636-3421, E-mail: jmille11@pratt.edu. *Application contact:* Natalie Capannelli, Director of Graduate Admissions, 718-636-3551, Fax: 718-399-4242, E-mail: ncapanne@pratt.edu. Website: https://www.pratt.edu/academics/liberal-arts-and-sciences/performance-and-performance-studies/

Princeton University, Graduate School, Department of Music, Princeton, NJ 08544-1019. Offers composition (PhD); musicology (PhD). *Degree requirements:* For doctorate, variable foreign language requirement, thesis/dissertation. *Entrance requirements:* For doctorate, GRE General Test, sample of written work. Additional exam requirements/recommendations for international students: required—TOEFL (minimum score 600 paper-based). Electronic applications accepted.

Purchase College, State University of New York, Conservatory of Music, Purchase, NY 10577-1400. Offers classical composition (MM); instrumental performance (MM); jazz studies (MM); studio composition (MM); voice and opera studies (MM). *Students:* 53 full-time (22 women), 2 part-time (1 woman); includes 13 minority (2 Black or African American, non-Hispanic/Latino; 5 Asian, non-Hispanic/Latino; 5 Hispanic/Latino; 1 Two or more races, non-Hispanic/Latino), 19 international. Average age 28. 120 applicants, 57% accepted, 21 enrolled. *Degree requirements:* For master's, thesis or alternative, composition, performance. *Entrance requirements:* For master's, audition. Additional exam requirements/recommendations for international students: required—TOEFL (minimum score 550 paper-based; 80 iBT), IELTS (minimum score 6.5). *Application deadline:* For fall admission, 1/15 for domestic students; for spring admission, 10/15 for domestic students. Applications are processed on a rolling basis. Application fee: $142. Electronic applications accepted. *Expenses: Tuition,* area resident: Full-time $11,310. Tuition, state resident: full-time $11,310. Tuition, nonresident: full-time $23,100. *Required fees:* $1883. *Financial support:* Fellowships, teaching assistantships, career-related internships or fieldwork, Federal Work-Study, scholarships/grants, and tuition waivers (partial) available. Support available to part-time students. Financial award application deadline: 3/15; financial award applicants required to submit FAFSA. *Unit head:* Jennifer Undercofler, Director, 914-251-6700, Fax: 914-251-6739, E-mail: jennifer.undercofler@purchase.edu. *Application contact:* Beatriz Martin-Ruiz, Assistant Director of Admissions, 914-251-6304, Fax: 914-251-6316, E-mail: admissn@purchase.edu. Website: https://www.purchase.edu/academics/music/

Queens College of the City University of New York, Arts and Humanities Division, Aaron Copland School of Music, Queens, NY 11367-1597. Offers classical performance (MM, Advanced Diploma); jazz studies (MM); music (MA); music education

(MS Ed, Advanced Certificate). *Program availability:* Part-time. *Faculty:* 25 full-time (7 women), 74 part-time/adjunct (28 women). *Students:* 21 full-time (6 women), 153 part-time (75 women); includes 60 minority (8 Black or African American, non-Hispanic/Latino; 1 American Indian or Alaska Native, non-Hispanic/Latino; 22 Asian, non-Hispanic/Latino; 22 Hispanic/Latino; 7 Two or more races, non-Hispanic/Latino), 33 international. Average age 30. 72 applicants, 63% accepted, 19 enrolled. In 2019, 50 master's, 5 other advanced degrees awarded. *Degree requirements:* For master's, comprehensive exam (for some programs), thesis (for some programs), Graduation Recital for MM Performance Classical Programs. *Entrance requirements:* For master's, for Master of Music (Classical), all applicants must pass the Theory Quiz, audition, bachelor's degree in music, minimum GPA of 3.0; for other advanced degree, for all classical music performance certificates, all applicants are required to audition. Additional exam requirements/recommendations for international students: required—TOEFL (minimum score 550 paper-based; 79 iBT), IELTS (minimum score 6). *Application deadline:* For fall admission, 4/1 for domestic students; for spring admission, 11/1 for domestic students. Applications are processed on a rolling basis. Application fee: $125. Electronic applications accepted. *Financial support:* In 2019–20, 20 students received support. Career-related internships or fieldwork, Federal Work-Study, institutionally sponsored loans, and scholarships/grants available. Financial award application deadline: 4/1; financial award applicants required to submit FAFSA. *Unit head:* Michael Lipsey, Chair, 718-997-3800, E-mail: Michael.Lipsey@qc.cuny.edu. *Application contact:* Elizabeth D'Amico-Ramirez, Assistant Director of Graduate Admissions, 718-997-5203, E-mail: elizabeth.damicoramirez@qc.cuny.edu.
Website: http://qcpages.qc.cuny.edu/music/

Radford University, College of Graduate Studies and Research, Music, MA/MS, Radford, VA 24142. Offers MA, MS. *Accreditation:* NASM. *Program availability:* Part-time. *Degree requirements:* For master's, comprehensive exam, thesis or alternative. *Entrance requirements:* For master's, GRE or PRAXIS II (music content knowledge); written diagnostic exams in music, minimum GPA of 2.75, 2 letters of reference, resume, official transcripts. Additional exam requirements/recommendations for international students: required—TOEFL (minimum score 550 paper-based; 79 iBT), IELTS (minimum score 6.5). Electronic applications accepted.

Rice University, Graduate Programs, Shepherd School of Music, Houston, TX 77251-1892. Offers composition (MM, DMA); conducting (MM); musicology (MM); performance (MM, DMA); theory (MM). *Degree requirements:* For master's, thesis (for some programs), 2 recitals; for doctorate, one foreign language, comprehensive exam, thesis/dissertation, 4 recitals. *Entrance requirements:* For master's, GRE General Test (musicology); for doctorate, GRE General Test. Additional exam requirements/recommendations for international students: required—TOEFL (minimum score 600 paper-based; 100 iBT), IELTS (minimum score 7).

Rider University, Westminster Choir College, Programs in Music, Lawrenceville, NJ 08648-3001. Offers American and public musicology (MM); choral conducting (MM); composition (MM); organ performance (MM); piano accompanying and coaching (MM); piano pedagogy and performance (MM); piano performance (MM); sacred music (MM); voice pedagogy and performance (MM, MVP). *Program availability:* Part-time. *Degree requirements:* For master's, variable foreign language requirement, departmental qualifying exam. *Entrance requirements:* For master's, audition, interview, repertoire list, 2 letters of reference, resume, Applications must be received at least three weeks in advance of the requested audition date, official transcripts, personal statement. Additional exam requirements/recommendations for international students: required—TOEFL (minimum score 540 paper-based; 79 iBT). Electronic applications accepted.

Roosevelt University, Graduate Division, Chicago College of Performing Arts, Music Conservatory, Chicago, IL 60605. Offers brass (Diploma); brass performance (MM); classical guitar (MM, Diploma); music (MM); music composition (MM); opera (Diploma); orchestral studies (MM, Diploma); percussion (MM, Diploma); performing arts administration (MA); piano (Diploma); piano performance (MM); strings (MM, Diploma); voice (MM); woodwinds (MM, Diploma). Electronic applications accepted. *Expenses:* Contact institution.

Rowan University, Graduate School, College of Performing Arts, Program in Performance, Glassboro, NJ 08028-1701. Offers MM. *Accreditation:* NASM. *Program availability:* Part-time, evening/weekend. *Degree requirements:* For master's, thesis (for some programs). *Entrance requirements:* For master's, GRE General Test. Additional exam requirements/recommendations for international students: required—TOEFL. Electronic applications accepted. *Expenses: Tuition, area resident:* Part-time $715.50 per semester hour. Tuition, state resident: part-time $715.50 per semester hour. Tuition, nonresident: part-time $715.50 per semester hour. *Required fees:* $161.55 per semester hour.

Rutgers University - Newark, Graduate School, Program in Jazz History and Research, Newark, NJ 07102. Offers MA. *Entrance requirements:* For master's, GRE, minimum B average. Electronic applications accepted.

Rutgers University - New Brunswick, Mason Gross School of the Arts, Music Department, New Brunswick, NJ 08901. Offers collaborative piano (MM, DMA); conducting: choral (MM, DMA); conducting: instrumental (MM, DMA); conducting: orchestral (MM, DMA); jazz studies (MM); music (DMA, AD); music education (MM, DMA); music performance (MM). *Accreditation:* NASM. *Degree requirements:* For doctorate, one foreign language. *Entrance requirements:* For master's and doctorate, audition. Additional exam requirements/recommendations for international students: required—TOEFL (minimum score 550 paper-based), IELTS (minimum score 7). Electronic applications accepted.

Saint John's University, Saint John's School of Theology and Seminary, Collegeville, MN 56321. Offers divinity (M Div); liturgical music (MA); liturgical studies (MA); pastoral ministry (MA); theology (MA), including church history, liturgy, monastic studies, scripture, spirituality, systematics; M Div/MA. *Program availability:* Part-time, online learning. *Degree requirements:* For master's, one foreign language, comprehensive exam (for some programs), thesis (for some programs). *Entrance requirements:* For master's, GRE General Test or MAT. Electronic applications accepted.

Salem College, Graduate Studies, Winston-Salem, NC 27101. Offers art education (MAT); elementary education (M Ed, MAT); language and literacy (M Ed); middle school education (MAT); organ (MM); piano (MM); school counseling (M Ed); second language studies (MAT); secondary education (MAT); special education (M Ed, MAT). *Accreditation:* NCATE. *Program availability:* Part-time, evening/weekend, online learning. *Degree requirements:* For master's, practicum (MAT), action research project (M Ed). *Entrance requirements:* For master's, minimum GPA of 3.0, two academic/professional recommendations, acceptable criminal background check. Additional exam requirements/recommendations for international students: recommended—TOEFL. Electronic applications accepted. *Expenses: Tuition:* Full-time $2700; part-time $450 per semester hour. *Required fees:* $300.

Samford University, School of the Arts, Birmingham, AL 35229. Offers church music (MM), including conducting, performance, thesis; instrumental performance (MM); piano performance and pedagogy (MM); vocal performance (MM); vocal/choral (MME). *Accreditation:* NASM. *Program availability:* Part-time. *Faculty:* 9 full-time (3 women), 6 part-time/adjunct (4 women). *Students:* 11 full-time (6 women), 1 (woman) part-time; includes 1 minority (Black or African American, non-Hispanic/Latino), 2 international. Average age 26. 17 applicants, 82% accepted, 3 enrolled. In 2019, 6 master's awarded. *Degree requirements:* For master's, comprehensive exam, thesis/dissertation varies; recital. *Entrance requirements:* For master's, placement examinations, 3 letters of recommendation, audition/interview. Additional exam requirements/recommendations for international students: required—TOEFL (minimum score 550 paper-based; 79 iBT). *Application deadline:* For fall admission, 1/17 for domestic and international students; for spring admission, 10/18 for domestic and international students. Applications are processed on a rolling basis. Application fee: $35. Electronic applications accepted. *Expenses: Tuition:* Full-time $17,754; part-time $862 per credit hour. *Required fees:* $550; $550 per unit. Full-time tuition and fees vary according to course load, program and student level. *Financial support:* In 2019–20, 11 students received support. Scholarships/grants available. Financial award application deadline: 1/17; financial award applicants required to submit FAFSA. *Unit head:* Dr. Mark Lackey, Associate Professor, 205-726-4623, E-mail: mlackey@samford.edu. *Application contact:* Dr. Mark Lackey, Associate Professor, 205-726-4623, E-mail: mlackey@samford.edu.
Website: http://www.samford.edu/arts/

Sam Houston State University, College of Fine Arts and Mass Communication, School of Music, Huntsville, TX 77341. Offers MM. *Accreditation:* NASM. *Program availability:* Part-time. *Degree requirements:* For master's, comprehensive exam, thesis, departmental qualifying exam. *Entrance requirements:* For master's, GRE General Test, letters of recommendation, audition/interview. Additional exam requirements/recommendations for international students: required—TOEFL (minimum score 550 paper-based; 79 iBT), IELTS (minimum score 6.5). Electronic applications accepted.

San Diego State University, Graduate and Research Affairs, College of Professional Studies and Fine Arts, School of Music and Dance, San Diego, CA 92182. Offers composition (acoustic and electronic) (MM); conducting (MM); ethnomusicology (MA); jazz studies (MM); musicology (MA); performance (MM); piano pedagogy (MA); theory (MA). *Degree requirements:* For master's, comprehensive exam (for some programs), thesis (for some programs). *Entrance requirements:* For master's, GRE General Test, bachelor's degree in related field, 2 letters of reference. Additional exam requirements/recommendations for international students: required—TOEFL. Electronic applications accepted.

San Francisco Conservatory of Music, Graduate Division, San Francisco, CA 94102. Offers brass (MM), including bass trombone, horn, tenor trombone, trumpet, tuba; chamber music (MM, Artist Certificate), including cello (MM, Artist Certificate, Artist Diploma), piano (MM, Artist Certificate, Artist Diploma), preformed string quartet, viola (MM, Artist Certificate, Artist Diploma), violin (MM, Artist Certificate, Artist Diploma); composition (MM); conducting (MM); guitar (MM); harp (MM); historical performance (MM), including harpsichord (MM, MM); percussion (MM), including percussion; piano (MM, MM, Artist Diploma), including collaborative piano (MM), harpsichord (MM, MM), organ (MM), piano (MM, Artist Certificate, Artist Diploma); strings (MM, Artist Diploma), including cello (MM, Artist Certificate, Artist Diploma), double bass (MM), viola (MM, Artist Certificate, Artist Diploma), violin (MM, Artist Certificate, Artist Diploma); voice (MM, Postgraduate Diploma); woodwinds (MM), including bassoon, clarinet, flute, oboe. *Degree requirements:* For master's and other advanced degree, variable foreign language requirement, 1-2 recitals, 1-3 juried performances. *Entrance requirements:* For master's and other advanced degree, recommendations, transcripts, audition. Additional exam requirements/recommendations for international students: required—TOEFL (minimum score 500 paper-based; 80 iBT). Electronic applications accepted. *Expenses:* Contact institution.

San Francisco State University, Division of Graduate Studies, College of Liberal and Creative Arts, School of Music, San Francisco, CA 94132-1722. Offers chamber music (MM); classical performance (MM); composition (MA); conducting (MM); music education (MA); music history (MA). *Accreditation:* NASM. *Expenses: Tuition, area resident:* Full-time $7176; part-time $4164 per year. Tuition, state resident: full-time $7176; part-time $4164 per year. Tuition, nonresident: full-time $16,680; part-time $396 per unit. *International tuition:* $16,680 full-time. *Required fees:* $1524; $1524 per unit. $762 per semester. Tuition and fees vary according to degree level and program. *Unit head:* Dr. Cyrus Ginwala, Director, 415-338-7613, Fax: 415-338-6159, E-mail: cginwala@sfsu.edu. *Application contact:* Dr. Benjamin Sabey, Graduate Coordinator, 415-338-7613, Fax: 415-338-6159, E-mail: sabey@sfsu.edu.
Website: http://music.sfsu.edu/

Savannah College of Art and Design, Program in Performing Arts, Savannah, GA 31402-3146. Offers MFA. *Program availability:* Part-time. *Degree requirements:* For master's, thesis. *Entrance requirements:* For master's, GRE (recommended), portfolio (submitted in digital format), audition or writing submission, resume, statement of purpose, two letters of recommendation. Additional exam requirements/recommendations for international students: recommended—TOEFL (minimum score 550 paper-based; 85 iBT), IELTS (minimum score 6.5). Electronic applications accepted.

Shenandoah University, Shenandoah Conservatory, Winchester, VA 22601. Offers music (Artist Diploma). *Accreditation:* NASM. *Program availability:* Part-time, 100% online. *Faculty:* 40 full-time (14 women), 15 part-time/adjunct (7 women). *Students:* 73 full-time (51 women), 66 part-time (41 women); includes 24 minority (11 Black or African American, non-Hispanic/Latino; 10 Hispanic/Latino; 3 Two or more races, non-Hispanic/Latino), 18 international. Average age 30. 127 applicants, 84% accepted, 52 enrolled. In 2019, 39 master's, 4 doctorates, 8 other advanced degrees awarded. *Degree requirements:* For master's, comprehensive exam (for some programs), thesis or alternative; for doctorate, comprehensive exam, thesis/dissertation. *Entrance requirements:* For master's, successful audition or interview; Master of Music Therapy; baccalaureate degree in music therapy with a minimum GPA of 3.0; Master of Science in Performing Arts Leadership Management: baccalaureate degree in the arts (or equivalent) with a minimum GPA of 2.5; all other master degrees: baccalaureate degree in music with a minimum GPA of 2.5; for doctorate, successful audition/interview, baccalaureate degree in music, master degree in music with a minimum GPA of 3.25; for other advanced degree, successful interview. Professional Studies Program for Music Therapy Certificate Eligibility baccalaureate degree in music or related field with a minimum GPA of 3.0. Additional exam requirements/recommendations for international students: required—Duolingo (min. 55 on 100-pt. scale; min. 105 on 160-pt. scale); recommended—TOEFL (minimum score 21 paper-based; 79 iBT), IELTS (minimum score 6.5), TSE (minimum score 53). *Application deadline:* For fall admission, 1/15 for domestic and international students; for spring admission, 12/1 for domestic and international students; for summer admission, 4/15 for domestic and international students. Applications are processed on a rolling basis. Application fee: $30. Electronic applications accepted. *Expenses:* All fees $2480 a year. *Financial support:* In 2019–20, 43 students received support, including 12 teaching assistantships with full tuition reimbursements available (averaging $9,000 per year); tuition waivers (partial) and unspecified assistantships also available. Financial award application deadline: 8/1; financial award applicants required to submit FAFSA. *Unit head:* Dr. Michael J. Stepniak, Dean, 540-542-6201, Fax: 540-665-5402, E-mail: mstepnia@su.edu. *Application contact:* Andrew Woodall, Executive Director of Recruitment and

Advancement, 540-665-4581, Fax: 540-665-4627, E-mail: admit@su.edu.
Website: http://www.su.edu/conservatory/

Silver Lake College of the Holy Family, Graduate School, Graduate Music Program, Manitowoc, WI 54220-9319. Offers music education-Kodaly emphasis (MM). *Accreditation:* NASM. *Program availability:* Part-time, online learning. *Degree requirements:* For master's, comprehensive exam, thesis, capstone culminating project, comprehensive portfolio, public presentation of skills, or thesis research. *Entrance requirements:* For master's, ACT (preferred) or SAT, minimum undergraduate GPA of 3.0. Additional exam requirements/recommendations for international students: required—TOEFL (minimum score 550 paper-based; 89 iBT). Electronic applications accepted. *Expenses:* Contact institution.

Southeastern Baptist Theological Seminary, Graduate and Professional Programs, Wake Forest, NC 27587. Offers advanced biblical studies (M Div); Christian education (M Div, MACE); Christian ethics (PhD); Christian ministry (M Div); Christian planting (M Div); church music (MACM); counseling (MACO); evangelism (PhD); language (M Div); ministry (D Min); New Testament (PhD); Old Testament (PhD); philosophy (PhD); theology (Th M, PhD); women's studies (M Div). *Accreditation:* ACIPE; ATS (one or more programs are accredited). *Degree requirements:* For master's, thesis (for some programs), oral exam; for doctorate, thesis/dissertation, fieldwork. *Entrance requirements:* For master's, Cooperative English Test, minimum GPA of 2.0, M Div or equivalent (Th M); for doctorate, GRE General Test or MAT, Cooperative English Test, M Div or equivalent, 3 years of professional experience.

Southeastern Louisiana University, College of Arts, Humanities and Social Sciences, Department of Music and Performing Arts, Hammond, LA 70402. Offers choral conducting (M Mus); instrumental conducting (M Mus); music performance (M Mus); music theory (M Mus). *Accreditation:* NASM. *Program availability:* Part-time. *Faculty:* 7 full-time (1 woman). *Students:* 15 full-time (5 women); includes 5 minority (3 Hispanic/Latino; 2 Two or more races, non-Hispanic/Latino), 4 international. Average age 25. 12 applicants, 100% accepted, 9 enrolled. In 2019, 5 master's awarded. *Degree requirements:* For master's, comprehensive exam, thesis (for some programs), recital required for most programs. *Entrance requirements:* For master's, auditions and/or interviews; Bachelor of Music, Bachelor of Music Education, Bachelor of Arts in Music, or a Bachelor of Science in Music degree. Additional exam requirements/recommendations for international students: required—TOEFL (minimum score 500 paper-based; 61 iBT). *Application deadline:* For fall admission, 2/1 priority date for domestic and international students; for spring admission, 12/1 priority date for domestic students, 10/1 priority date for international students. Applications are processed on a rolling basis. Application fee: $20 ($30 for international students). Electronic applications accepted. *Expenses: Tuition, area resident:* Full-time $6684; part-time $489 per credit hour. Tuition, state resident: full-time $6684; part-time $489 per credit hour. Tuition, nonresident: full-time $19,162; part-time $1183 per credit hour. *International tuition:* $19,162 full-time. *Required fees:* $2124. *Financial support:* In 2019–20, 16 students received support, including 11 teaching assistantships with tuition reimbursements available (averaging $10,127 per year); institutionally sponsored loans, traineeships, and unspecified assistantships also available. Financial award application deadline: 5/1; financial award applicants required to submit FAFSA. *Unit head:* Dr. Jeffrey Wright, Department Head, 985-549-2184, Fax: 985-549-2892, E-mail: jeffrey.wright-3@southeastern.edu. *Application contact:* Office of Admissions, 985-549-5637, Fax: 985-549-5632, E-mail: admissions@southeastern.edu.
Website: https://www.southeastern.edu/acad_research/depts/mus/index.html

Southern Illinois University Carbondale, Graduate School, College of Liberal Arts, School of Music, Carbondale, IL 62901-4701. Offers MM. *Accreditation:* NASM. *Program availability:* Part-time. *Degree requirements:* For master's, one foreign language, thesis or alternative. *Entrance requirements:* For master's, audition, minimum GPA of 2.7. Additional exam requirements/recommendations for international students: required—TOEFL.

Southern Illinois University Edwardsville, Graduate School, College of Arts and Sciences, Department of Music, Program in Music, Edwardsville, IL 62026. Offers music education (MM); music performance (MM). *Accreditation:* NASM. *Program availability:* Part-time. *Degree requirements:* For master's, one foreign language, thesis (for some programs), recital. *Entrance requirements:* Additional exam requirements/recommendations for international students: required—TOEFL (minimum score 550 paper-based; 79 iBT), IELTS (minimum score 6.5). Electronic applications accepted.

Southern Methodist University, Meadows School of the Arts, Division of Music, Dallas, TX 75275. Offers composition (MM); conducting (MM), including choral, instrumental; music education (MM); musicology (MM); performance (MM), including organ, piano, piano performance and pedagogy, voice; theory pedagogy (MM). *Accreditation:* NASM. *Program availability:* Part-time. *Degree requirements:* For master's, variable foreign language requirement, comprehensive exam, project, recital, or thesis. *Entrance requirements:* For master's, placement exams in music history and theory, audition; bachelor's degree in music or equivalent; minimum GPA of 3.0; research paper in history/theory/education. Additional exam requirements/recommendations for international students: required—TOEFL (minimum score 550 paper-based; 80 iBT). Electronic applications accepted.

Southern Methodist University, Perkins School of Theology, Dallas, TX 75275. Offers ministry (M Div, D Min); sacred music (MSM); theological studies (MTS). *Accreditation:* ACIPE. *Program availability:* Part-time. *Degree requirements:* For master's, thesis (for some programs), internship; for doctorate, internship, oral exam, professional project. *Entrance requirements:* For master's, minimum GPA of 2.75; for doctorate, minimum graduate GPA of 3.0, M Div or equivalent, 3 years of ministry experience. Additional exam requirements/recommendations for international students: required—TOEFL (minimum score 600 paper-based; 100 iBT), TWE. *Expenses:* Contact institution.

Southern Oregon University, Graduate Studies, Department of Music, Ashland, OR 97520. Offers performance (MM). *Accreditation:* NASM. *Program availability:* Part-time. *Entrance requirements:* For master's, undergraduate degree with music major, audition, three letters of recommendation.

Southern Utah University, Program in Music, Cedar City, UT 84720-2498. Offers performance technology (MMus). *Accreditation:* NASM. *Program availability:* Part-time, 100% online. *Entrance requirements:* Additional exam requirements/recommendations for international students: required—TOEFL (minimum score 550 paper-based; 79 iBT), IELTS (minimum score 6). *Expenses:* Contact institution.

Southwestern Baptist Theological Seminary, School of Church Music, Fort Worth, TX 76122-0000. Offers MACM, MAWSHP, MM, DMA, PhD. *Accreditation:* NASM. *Program availability:* Part-time. Terminal master's awarded for partial completion of doctoral program. *Degree requirements:* For master's, comprehensive exam, thesis; for doctorate, comprehensive exam, thesis/dissertation. *Entrance requirements:* For master's, audition; for doctorate, MM or equivalent. Additional exam requirements/recommendations for international students: required—TOEFL. Electronic applications accepted.

Southwestern Oklahoma State University, College of Arts and Sciences, Department of Music, Weatherford, OK 73096-3098. Offers music education (MM); music performance (MM); music therapy (MM). *Accreditation:* NASM. *Program availability:* Part-time. *Degree requirements:* For master's, comprehensive exam, recital (music performance). *Entrance requirements:* For master's, minimum GPA of 2.5. Additional exam requirements/recommendations for international students: required—TOEFL (minimum score 550 paper-based), IELTS (minimum score 6.5).

Stanford University, School of Humanities and Sciences, Department of Music, Stanford, CA 94305-2004. Offers composition (DMA); musicology (PhD). *Expenses: Tuition:* Full-time $52,479; part-time $34,110 per unit. *Required fees:* $672; $224 per quarter. Tuition and fees vary according to program and student level.
Website: http://music.stanford.edu/

State University of New York at Fredonia, School of Music, Fredonia, NY 14063-1136. Offers music education (MM); music performance (MM); music theory/composition (MM); music therapy (MM). *Accreditation:* NASM. *Program availability:* Part-time. *Degree requirements:* For master's, comprehensive exam (for some programs), thesis or final project/recital. *Entrance requirements:* For master's, audition. Additional exam requirements/recommendations for international students: required—TOEFL (minimum score 79 iBT), IELTS (minimum score 6.5). Electronic applications accepted.

State University of New York at New Paltz, Graduate and Extended Learning School, School of Fine and Performing Arts, Department of Music, New Paltz, NY 12561. Offers music therapy (MS). *Accreditation:* NASM. *Program availability:* Part-time. *Faculty:* 4 full-time (3 women), 5 part-time/adjunct (1 woman). *Students:* 22 full-time (16 women), 20 part-time (16 women); includes 5 minority (1 Black or African American, non-Hispanic/Latino; 1 Asian, non-Hispanic/Latino; 3 Hispanic/Latino), 4 international. 31 applicants, 65% accepted, 14 enrolled. In 2019, 21 master's awarded. *Degree requirements:* For master's, thesis. *Entrance requirements:* For master's, audition, minimum GPA of 3.0. Additional exam requirements/recommendations for international students: required—TOEFL (minimum score 550 paper-based; 80 iBT), IELTS (minimum score 6.5). *Application deadline:* For fall admission, 5/15 for domestic and international students; for spring admission, 11/15 for domestic and international students. Applications are processed on a rolling basis. Application fee: $50. Electronic applications accepted. *Expenses: Tuition, area resident:* Full-time $11,310; part-time $471 per credit. Tuition, state resident: full-time $11,310; part-time $471 per credit. Tuition, nonresident: full-time $23,100; part-time $963 per credit. *International tuition:* $23,100 full-time. *Required fees:* $1432; $41.83 per credit. *Financial support:* In 2019–20, 4 teaching assistantships with partial tuition reimbursements (averaging $5,000 per year) were awarded. Financial award application deadline: 8/1. *Unit head:* Kathleen Murphy, Program Director, 845-257-2708, E-mail: murphyk@newpaltz.edu. *Application contact:* Vika Shock, Director of Graduate Admissions, 845-257-3286, Fax: 845-257-3284, E-mail: gradstudies@newpaltz.edu.
Website: http://www.newpaltz.edu/music/

State University of New York College at Potsdam, Crane School of Music, Potsdam, NY 13676. Offers music education (MM); music performance (MM). *Program availability:* Part-time. *Degree requirements:* For master's, variable foreign language requirement, thesis (for some programs). *Entrance requirements:* For master's, audition, minimum GPA of 3.0. Additional exam requirements/recommendations for international students: required—TOEFL (minimum score 550 paper-based; 80 iBT), IELTS (minimum score 6). Electronic applications accepted.

Stephen F. Austin State University, Graduate School, College of Fine Arts, School of Music, Nacogdoches, TX 75962. Offers MA, MM. *Accreditation:* NASM (one or more programs are accredited). *Program availability:* Part-time. *Degree requirements:* For master's, comprehensive exam, thesis optional. *Entrance requirements:* For master's, GRE General Test, audition. Additional exam requirements/recommendations for international students: required—TOEFL.

Stony Brook University, State University of New York, Graduate School, College of Arts and Sciences, Department of Music, Program in Music History/Theory, Stony Brook, NY 11794. Offers MA, PhD. *Students:* 30 full-time (8 women), 7 part-time (2 women); includes 4 minority (1 Black or African American, non-Hispanic/Latino; 1 Asian, non-Hispanic/Latino; 2 Two or more races, non-Hispanic/Latino), 5 international. Average age 30. 43 applicants, 37% accepted, 8 enrolled. In 2019, 2 master's, 3 doctorates awarded. *Entrance requirements:* For master's and doctorate, GRE General Test. Additional exam requirements/recommendations for international students: required—TOEFL (minimum score 90 iBT). *Application deadline:* For fall admission, 1/15 for domestic students; for spring admission, 10/1 for domestic students. Application fee: $100. Electronic applications accepted. *Expenses:* Contact institution. *Financial support:* In 2019–20, 23 teaching assistantships were awarded. *Unit head:* Dr. Perry Goldstein, Chair, 631-632-7340, E-mail: perry.goldstein@stonybrook.edu. *Application contact:* Monica Gentile, Coordinator, 631-632-7340, Fax: 631-632-7404, E-mail: monica.gentile@stonybrook.edu.

Stony Brook University, State University of New York, Graduate School, College of Arts and Sciences, Department of Music, Program in Music Performance, Stony Brook, NY 11794. Offers MM, DMA. *Students:* 152 full-time (82 women), 7 part-time (4 women); includes 27 minority (1 Black or African American, non-Hispanic/Latino; 15 Asian, non-Hispanic/Latino; 6 Hispanic/Latino; 5 Two or more races, non-Hispanic/Latino), 55 international. 257 applicants, 38% accepted, 37 enrolled. In 2019, 15 master's, 51 doctorates awarded. *Entrance requirements:* For master's and doctorate, GRE General Test. Additional exam requirements/recommendations for international students: required—TOEFL (minimum score 90 iBT). *Application deadline:* For fall admission, 1/15 for domestic students; for spring admission, 10/1 for domestic students. Application fee: $100. Electronic applications accepted. *Expenses:* Contact institution. *Financial support:* In 2019–20, 1 research assistantship, 53 teaching assistantships were awarded. *Unit head:* Dr. Perry Goldstein, Chair, 631-632-7340, E-mail: perry.goldstein@stonybrook.edu. *Application contact:* Monica Gentile, Coordinator, 631-632-7330, Fax: 631-632-7404, E-mail: monica.gentile@stonybrook.edu.
Website: http://www.stonybrook.edu/commcms/music/degree_programs/graduate/performance.html

Syracuse University, College of Visual and Performing Arts, MM in Music and Performance Program, Syracuse, NY 13244. Offers music and performance (MM), including organ, percussion, piano, strings, voice, wind instruments. *Entrance requirements:* For master's, audition, three letters of recommendation, academic transcript, personal statement/essay, resume. Additional exam requirements/recommendations for international students: required—TOEFL (minimum score 100 iBT). Electronic applications accepted.

Syracuse University, College of Visual and Performing Arts, MM Program in Composition, Syracuse, NY 13244. Offers MM. *Entrance requirements:* For master's, audition, three letters of recommendation, academic transcript, personal statement/essay, resume. Additional exam requirements/recommendations for international students: required—TOEFL (minimum score 100 iBT). Electronic applications accepted.

Syracuse University, College of Visual and Performing Arts, MM Program in Conducting, Syracuse, NY 13244. Offers MM. *Accreditation:* NASM. *Entrance* *requirements:* For master's, audition, interview, three letters of recommendation, transcripts, personal statement, resume. Additional exam requirements/recommendations for international students: required—TOEFL (minimum score 100 iBT). Electronic applications accepted.

Temple University, Center for the Performing and Cinematic Arts, Boyer College of Music and Dance, Department of Instrumental Studies, Philadelphia, PA 19122-6079. Offers MM, DMA. *Program availability:* Part-time. *Faculty:* 1 (woman) full-time. *Students:* 95 full-time (53 women), 6 part-time (5 women); includes 10 minority (2 Black or African American, non-Hispanic/Latino; 3 Asian, non-Hispanic/Latino; 2 Hispanic/Latino; 3 Two or more races, non-Hispanic/Latino), 48 international. 235 applicants, 42% accepted, 45 enrolled. In 2019, 36 master's, 6 doctorates awarded. *Degree requirements:* For master's, Professional Development such as touring. *Entrance requirements:* For master's, written analysis, Diagnostic Examinations, professional resume. Instrumental teaching experience at the secondary level, community ensemble level, collegiate level, semi-professional level, or professionally is highly encouraged and is favorably viewed in the decision process. Additional exam requirements/recommendations for international students: required—TOEFL (minimum score 79 iBT), IELTS (minimum score 6.5), PTE (minimum score 53), one of the three. *Application deadline:* For fall admission, 12/15 for international students; for spring admission, 8/1 for international students. Applications are processed on a rolling basis. Application fee: $50. Electronic applications accepted. *Financial support:* Fellowships, scholarships/grants, and unspecified assistantships available. Financial award application deadline: 2/1; financial award applicants required to submit FAFSA. *Unit head:* Prof. Terell Stafford, Chair, 215-204-5527, E-mail: jsolow@temple.edu. *Application contact:* James Short, Director of Undergraduate and Graduate Admissions, 215-204-8598, Fax: 215-204-4957, E-mail: james.short@temple.edu.
Website: https://www.temple.edu/academics/degree-programs/instrumental-conducting-wind-band-mm-bc-icwb-mmus

Temple University, Center for the Performing and Cinematic Arts, Boyer College of Music and Dance, Department of Music, Philadelphia, PA 19122-6096. Offers choral conducting (MM); collaborative piano/chamber music (MM); collaborative piano/opera coaching (MM); composition (MM, PhD); instrumental conducting (MM); music education (MM, PhD); music history (MM); music performance (MM, DMA), including instrumental studies (MM), keyboard (DMA), keyboard studies (MM), voice (DMA), voice and opera (MM); music studies (PhD); music theory (MM, PhD); music therapy (MMT, PhD); musicology (MM, PhD); opera (MM); piano pedagogy (MM); string pedagogy (MM). *Accreditation:* NASM. *Program availability:* Part-time, evening/weekend, online learning. Terminal master's awarded for partial completion of doctoral program. *Degree requirements:* For doctorate, thesis/dissertation (for some programs). *Entrance requirements:* Additional exam requirements/recommendations for international students: required—TOEFL, IELTS, PTE, one of three is required. Electronic applications accepted. *Expenses:* Contact institution.

Temple University, Center for the Performing and Cinematic Arts, Boyer College of Music and Dance, Department of Music Studies, Philadelphia, PA 19122-6079. Offers composition (MM, DMA); music history (MM); music theory (MM). *Accreditation:* NASM. *Program availability:* Part-time. *Faculty:* 18 full-time (5 women), 23 part-time/adjunct (2 women). *Students:* 46 full-time (20 women), 2 part-time (1 woman); includes 10 minority (4 Black or African American, non-Hispanic/Latino; 2 Hispanic/Latino; 4 Two or more races, non-Hispanic/Latino), 12 international. 114 applicants, 52% accepted, 24 enrolled. In 2019, 12 master's, 3 doctorates awarded. *Degree requirements:* For master's, Culminating Event; for doctorate, 2 foreign languages, thesis/dissertation. *Entrance requirements:* For master's, audition, resume; for doctorate, GRE/MAT, auditions, resume, statement of goals. Additional exam requirements/recommendations for international students: required—TOEFL, IELTS, PTE, one of three. Application fee: $60. *Financial support:* Fellowships, scholarships/grants, and unspecified assistantships available. Financial award application deadline: 2/1; financial award applicants required to submit FAFSA. *Unit head:* Dr. Cynthia Folio, Chairperson, 215-204-8316, E-mail: cynthia.folio@temple.edu. *Application contact:* James Short, Director of Undergraduate and Graduate Admissions, 215-204-8598, Fax: 215-204-4957, E-mail: jshort@temple.edu.

Texas A&M University, College of Liberal Arts, Department of Performance Studies, College Station, TX 77843. Offers performance studies (MA). *Faculty:* 12. *Students:* 8 full-time (5 women); includes 2 minority (1 Black or African American, non-Hispanic/Latino; 1 Asian, non-Hispanic/Latino), 4 international. Average age 29. 4 applicants, 100% accepted, 3 enrolled. In 2019, 6 master's awarded. *Degree requirements:* For master's, comprehensive exam (for some programs), thesis optional. *Entrance requirements:* For master's, GRE General Test, letters of recommendation, curriculum vitae. Additional exam requirements/recommendations for international students: required—TOEFL (minimum score 550 paper-based; 80 iBT), IELTS (minimum score 6), PTE (minimum score 53). Application fee: $65 ($90 for international students). Electronic applications accepted. *Expenses:* Contact institution. *Financial support:* In 2019–20, 44 students received support, including 2 fellowships (averaging $18,627 per year), 17 teaching assistantships (averaging $19,558 per year); unspecified assistantships also available. Financial award application deadline: 3/15; financial award applicants required to submit FAFSA. *Unit head:* Dr. Steven Oberhelman, Interim Department Head, 979-847-5816, E-mail: s-oberhelman@tamu.edu. *Application contact:* Dr. Leonardo Cardoso, Director of Graduate Studies, E-mail: cardoso@tamu.edu.
Website: https://liberalarts.tamu.edu/performancestudies/

Texas A&M University–Commerce, College of Humanities, Social Sciences and Arts, Commerce, TX 75429. Offers applied criminology (MS); applied linguistics (MA, MS); art (MA, MFA); christianity in history (Graduate Certificate); computational linguistics (Graduate Certificate); creative writing (Graduate Certificate); criminal justice management (Graduate Certificate); criminal justice studies (Graduate Certificate); English (MA, MS, PhD); film studies (Graduate Certificate); history (MA, MS); Holocaust studies (Graduate Certificate); homeland security (Graduate Certificate); music (MM); music performance (MM); political science (MA, MS); public history (Graduate Certificate); sociology (MS); Spanish (MA); studies in children's and adolescent literature and culture (Graduate Certificate); teaching English to speakers of other languages (Graduate Certificate); theater (MA, MS); world history (Graduate Certificate). *Program availability:* Part-time. *Faculty:* 49 full-time (28 women), 8 part-time/adjunct (2 women). *Students:* 34 full-time (21 women), 427 part-time (302 women); includes 175 minority (66 Black or African American, non-Hispanic/Latino; 1 American Indian or Alaska Native, non-Hispanic/Latino; 13 Asian, non-Hispanic/Latino; 79 Hispanic/Latino; 16 Two or more races, non-Hispanic/Latino), 15 international. Average age 38. 193 applicants, 49% accepted, 78 enrolled. In 2019, 122 master's, 6 doctorates awarded. *Degree requirements:* For master's, one foreign language, comprehensive exam, thesis (for some programs); for doctorate, one foreign language, comprehensive exam, thesis/dissertation, departmental qualifying exam. *Entrance requirements:* For master's, GRE General Test, official transcripts, letters of recommendation, resume, statement of goals; for doctorate, GRE General Test, official transcripts, letters of recommendation, statement of goals, writing samples, writing sessions, resumes. Additional exam requirements/recommendations for international students: required—TOEFL (minimum

score 550 paper-based; 79 iBT), IELTS (minimum score 6), PTE (minimum score 53). *Application deadline:* For fall admission, 6/1 priority date for international students; for spring admission, 10/15 priority date for international students; for summer admission, 3/15 priority date for international students. Applications are processed on a rolling basis. Application fee: $50 ($75 for international students). Electronic applications accepted. *Expenses: Tuition, area resident:* Full-time $3630; part-time $202 per credit hour. *Tuition, state resident:* full-time $3630; part-time $202 per credit hour. *Tuition, nonresident:* full-time $11,232; part-time $624 per credit hour. *International tuition:* $11,232 full-time. *Required fees:* $2948. *Financial support:* In 2019–20, 30 students received support, including 18 research assistantships with partial tuition reimbursements available (averaging $3,231 per year), 136 teaching assistantships with partial tuition reimbursements available (averaging $4,053 per year); Federal Work-Study, institutionally sponsored loans, scholarships/grants, health care benefits, and unspecified assistantships also available. Financial award application deadline: 5/1; financial award applicants required to submit FAFSA. *Unit head:* Dr. William F. Kuracina, Interim Dean, 903-886-5166, Fax: 903-886-5774, E-mail: william.kuracina@tamuc.edu. *Application contact:* Rebecca Stevens, Graduate Student Services Coordinator, 903-468-6049, E-mail: rebecca.stevens@tamuc.edu.
Website: http://www.tamuc.edu/academics/colleges/humanitiesSocialSciencesArts/

Texas A&M University–Kingsville, College of Graduate Studies, College of Arts and Sciences, Department of Music, Program in Music, Kingsville, TX 78363. Offers instrumental performance (MM); vocal performance (MM).

Texas Christian University, College of Fine Arts, School of Music, Doctoral Programs in Music, Fort Worth, TX 76129. Offers composition (DMA), including music history; conducting (DMA), including music history, music theory; performance (DMA), including music history, music theory, piano pedagogy; piano pedagogy (DMA). *Accreditation:* NASM. *Faculty:* 43 full-time (10 women), 15 part-time/adjunct (7 women). *Students:* 9 full-time (3 women), 6 part-time (1 woman); includes 1 minority (Two or more races, non-Hispanic/Latino), 5 international. Average age 33. 44 applicants, 25% accepted, 2 enrolled. In 2019, 3 doctorates awarded. *Degree requirements:* For doctorate, comprehensive exam, thesis/dissertation. *Entrance requirements:* For doctorate, GRE General Test, Music Theory and Music History Diagnostic Exams; audition; interview. Additional exam requirements/recommendations for international students: required—TOEFL (minimum score 100 iBT). *Application deadline:* For spring admission, 12/1 for domestic and international students. Application fee: $80. Electronic applications accepted. Full-time tuition and fees vary according to program. *Financial support:* In 2019–20, 10 students received support, including 10 research assistantships with full tuition reimbursements available (averaging $10,000 per year); career-related internships or fieldwork, institutionally sponsored loans, scholarships/grants, tuition waivers (full and partial), and unspecified assistantships also available. Financial award application deadline: 12/1; financial award applicants required to submit CSS PROFILE or FAFSA. *Unit head:* Dr. Kristen A. Queen, Interim Director, 817-257-6606, Fax: 817-257-5818, E-mail: k.queen@tcu.edu. *Application contact:* Donna Smolik, TCU College of Fine Arts Graduate Office, 817-257-7603, Fax: 817-257-5672, E-mail: cfagradinfo@tcu.edu.
Website: http://www.music.tcu.edu

Texas Christian University, College of Fine Arts, School of Music, Master's Programs in Music, Fort Worth, TX 76129-0002. Offers conducting (M Mus); music education (MM Ed). *Faculty:* 44 full-time (10 women), 14 part-time/adjunct (6 women). *Students:* 45 full-time (20 women), 1 (woman) part-time; includes 6 minority (1 Black or African American, non-Hispanic/Latino; 4 Hispanic/Latino; 1 Two or more races, non-Hispanic/Latino), 18 international. Average age 25. 96 applicants, 35% accepted, 22 enrolled. In 2019, 21 master's awarded. *Degree requirements:* For master's, comprehensive exam. *Entrance requirements:* For master's, GRE General Test for some programs, Music Theory Diagnostic Exam. Additional exam requirements/recommendations for international students: required—TOEFL (minimum score 80 iBT). *Application deadline:* For fall admission, 2/15 for domestic and international students. Application fee: $80. Electronic applications accepted. Full-time tuition and fees vary according to program. *Financial support:* In 2019–20, 60 students received support, including 60 research assistantships with full tuition reimbursements available (averaging $6,000 per year); career-related internships or fieldwork, institutionally sponsored loans, scholarships/grants, tuition waivers (full and partial), and unspecified assistantships also available. Financial award application deadline: 2/15; financial award applicants required to submit CSS PROFILE or FAFSA. *Unit head:* Dr. Kristen A. Queen, Interim Director, 817-257-6606, Fax: 817-257-5818, E-mail: music@tcu.edu. *Application contact:* Donna Smolik, TCU College of Fine Arts Graduate Office, 817-257-7603, Fax: 817-257-5672, E-mail: cfagradinfo@tcu.edu.
Website: http://www.music.tcu.edu

Texas Southern University, College of Liberal Arts and Behavioral Sciences, Department of Fine Arts, Houston, TX 77004-4584. Offers fine arts (MA); music (MA). *Program availability:* Part-time. *Degree requirements:* For master's, one foreign language, comprehensive exam, recital. *Entrance requirements:* For master's, GRE General Test, minimum GPA of 2.5. Additional exam requirements/recommendations for international students: required—TOEFL. Electronic applications accepted.

Texas State University, The Graduate College, College of Fine Arts and Communication, Program in Music, San Marcos, TX 78666. Offers MM. *Accreditation:* NASM. *Program availability:* Part-time. *Degree requirements:* For master's, comprehensive exam, thesis (for some programs). *Entrance requirements:* For master's, baccalaureate degree in music from regionally-accredited institution with minimum GPA of 2.75 in last 60 hours of undergraduate course work, resume, 3 letters of recommendation; music portfolio (for composition, theory and history concentrations). Additional exam requirements/recommendations for international students: required—TOEFL (minimum score 550 paper-based; 78 iBT), IELTS (minimum score 6). Electronic applications accepted.

Texas Tech University, Graduate School, J.T. and Margaret Talkington College of Visual and Performing Arts, School of Music, Lubbock, TX 79409-2033. Offers music (MM, DMA); music education (MM Ed). *Accreditation:* NASM. *Program availability:* Part-time. *Faculty:* 56 full-time (25 women), 10 part-time/adjunct (4 women). *Students:* 125 full-time (54 women), 28 part-time (9 women); includes 31 minority (3 Black or African American, non-Hispanic/Latino; 3 Asian, non-Hispanic/Latino; 19 Hispanic/Latino; 6 Two or more races, non-Hispanic/Latino), 53 international. Average age 29. 160 applicants, 62% accepted, 60 enrolled. In 2019, 31 master's, 20 doctorates awarded. *Degree requirements:* For master's, one foreign language, thesis or alternative; for doctorate, 2 foreign languages, comprehensive exam (for some programs), thesis/dissertation. *Entrance requirements:* For master's, BM or BME or BA, performance audition or portfolio presentation; for doctorate, BM, MM or comparable experience and accomplishment. Additional exam requirements/recommendations for international students: required—TOEFL (minimum score 550 paper-based; 79 iBT). *Application deadline:* For fall admission, 6/1 priority date for domestic students, 1/15 priority date for international students; for spring admission, 9/1 priority date for domestic students, 6/15 priority date for international students. Applications are processed on a rolling basis. Application fee: $65. Electronic applications accepted. *Expenses:* Contact institution. *Financial support:* In 2019–20, 171 students received support, including 152 fellowships

(averaging $3,062 per year), 110 teaching assistantships (averaging $10,933 per year); research assistantships, career-related internships or fieldwork, Federal Work-Study, institutionally sponsored loans, scholarships/grants, health care benefits, tuition waivers (partial), and unspecified assistantships also available. Financial award application deadline: 4/15; financial award applicants required to submit FAFSA. *Unit head:* Prof. Kim Walker, Director, 806-834-7420, E-mail: kim.walker@ttu.edu. *Application contact:* Kimberly Calvert-Gibson, Graduate and International Student Academic Coordinator, 806-834-0616, Fax: 806-742-2294, E-mail: Kimberly.Calvert@ttu.edu.
Website: www.music.ttu.edu

Texas Woman's University, Graduate School, College of Arts and Sciences, School of the Arts, Department of Music and Theatre, Denton, TX 76204. Offers drama (MA); music (MA), including music education, music therapy, pedagogy, performance. *Accreditation:* NASM. *Program availability:* Part-time. *Faculty:* 18 full-time (9 women), 9 part-time/adjunct (5 women). *Students:* 63 full-time (52 women), 31 part-time (24 women); includes 35 minority (7 Black or African American, non-Hispanic/Latino; 3 Asian, non-Hispanic/Latino; 23 Hispanic/Latino; 2 Two or more races, non-Hispanic/Latino), 11 international. Average age 29. 38 applicants, 92% accepted, 24 enrolled. In 2019, 21 master's awarded. *Degree requirements:* For master's, comprehensive exam, thesis (for some programs), project, recital, professional paper, professional paper or thesis (for music education). *Entrance requirements:* For master's, music history/theory placement exam (for music only), audition and/or design portfolio, interview, resume, writing sample (for drama only), letter of intent, minimum undergraduate GPA of 3.0. Additional exam requirements/recommendations for international students: required—TOEFL (minimum score 550 paper-based; 79 iBT); recommended—IELTS (minimum score 6.5), TSE (minimum score 53). *Application deadline:* For fall admission, 3/1 priority date for domestic and international students; for spring admission, 11/1 priority date for domestic students, 7/1 for international students; for summer admission, 4/30 for domestic students, 2/1 priority date for international students. Application fee: $50 ($75 for international students). Electronic applications accepted. *Expenses:* All are estimates. Tuition for 10 hours = $2,763; Fees for 10 hours = $1,342. Music courses require additional $35/SCH. *Financial support:* In 2019–20, 50 students received support, including 1 research assistantship, 6 teaching assistantships; career-related internships or fieldwork, scholarships/grants, health care benefits, and unspecified assistantships also available. Support available to part-time students. Financial award application deadline: 3/1; financial award applicants required to submit FAFSA. *Unit head:* Dr. Pamela Youngblood, Chair of Music and Theatre, 940-898-2500, Fax: 940-898-2494, E-mail: music@twu.edu. *Application contact:* Korie Hawkins, Associate Director of Admissions, Graduate Recruitment, 940-898-3188, Fax: 940-898-3081, E-mail: admissions@twu.edu.

Towson University, College of Fine Arts and Communication, Program in Music Performance and Composition, Towson, MD 21252-0001. Offers MM. *Accreditation:* NASM. *Program availability:* Part-time, evening/weekend. *Students:* 6 full-time (0 women), 5 part-time (1 woman); includes 3 minority (all Hispanic/Latino), 1 international. *Entrance requirements:* For master's, audition, bachelor's degree in music, minimum GPA of 3.0. Additional exam requirements/recommendations for international students: required—TOEFL (minimum score 550 paper-based). *Application deadline:* For fall admission, 1/17 for domestic students, 5/15 for international students; for spring admission, 10/15 for domestic students, 12/1 for international students. Applications are processed on a rolling basis. Application fee: $45. Electronic applications accepted. *Expenses: Tuition, area resident:* Full-time $7920; part-time $439 per credit. Tuition, nonresident: full-time $16,344; part-time $908 per credit. *International tuition:* $16,344 full-time. *Required fees:* $2628; $146 per credit. $876 per term. *Financial support:* Application deadline: 4/1. *Unit head:* Dr. Terry Ewell, Program Coordinator, 410-704-2824, E-mail: tewell@towson.edu. *Application contact:* Coverley Beidleman, Assistant Director of Graduate Admissions, 410-704-5630, Fax: 410-704-3030, E-mail: grads@towson.edu.
Website: https://www.towson.edu/cofac/departments/music/programs/

Trinity College, Faculty of Divinity, Toronto, ON M5S 1H8, Canada. Offers ministry (Diploma); ministry for church musicians (Diploma); theology (M Div, MA, MTS, Th M, D Min, PhD, Th D, Diploma, L Th); M Div/MA. *Accreditation:* ATS. *Program availability:* Part-time. *Degree requirements:* For master's, 2 foreign languages, thesis (for some programs); for doctorate, 3 foreign languages, comprehensive exam, thesis/dissertation; for other advanced degree, thesis (for some programs). *Entrance requirements:* For master's, 1 language (modern or ancient), interview; for doctorate, 2 languages (modern and ancient). Additional exam requirements/recommendations for international students: required—TOEFL, TWE.

Truman State University, Office of Graduate Studies, School of Arts and Letters, Program in Music, Kirksville, MO 63501-4221. Offers MA. *Accreditation:* NASM. *Degree requirements:* For master's, comprehensive exam, thesis or alternative. *Entrance requirements:* For master's, GRE General Test, minimum GPA of 3.0. Additional exam requirements/recommendations for international students: required—TOEFL (minimum score 550 paper-based). Electronic applications accepted. Application fee is waived when completed online. *Expenses:* Tuition, state resident: full-time $4630; part-time $385.50 per credit hour. Tuition, nonresident: full-time $8018; part-time $668 per credit hour. *International tuition:* $8018 full-time. *Required fees:* $324. Full-time tuition and fees vary according to course level, course load, program and reciprocity agreements.

Tufts University, Graduate School of Arts and Sciences, Department of Music, Medford, MA 02155. Offers composition (MA); ethnomusicology (MA); music theory (MA). *Program availability:* Part-time. *Degree requirements:* For master's, one foreign language, thesis. *Entrance requirements:* For master's, GRE General Test, writing sample or musical score. Additional exam requirements/recommendations for international students: required—TOEFL (minimum score 550 paper-based; 80 iBT), IELTS (minimum score 6.5). Electronic applications accepted. *Expenses:* Contact institution.

Tulane University, School of Liberal Arts, Department of Music, New Orleans, LA 70118-5669. Offers MA, MFA. *Degree requirements:* For master's, one foreign language, thesis (for some programs), recital or composition (MA). *Entrance requirements:* For master's, GRE General Test, minimum B average in undergraduate course work. Additional exam requirements/recommendations for international students: required—TOEFL. Electronic applications accepted. *Expenses: Tuition:* Full-time $57,004; part-time $3167 per credit hour. *Required fees:* $2086; $44.50 per credit hour. $80 per term. Tuition and fees vary according to course load, degree level and program.

Université de Montréal, Faculty of Music, Montréal, QC H3C 3J7, Canada. Offers composition (M Mus, D Mus); interpretation (M Mus, D Mus, DESS); music (MA, PhD); orchestral repertoire (DESS). *Degree requirements:* For doctorate, thesis/dissertation, general exam. Electronic applications accepted.

University at Buffalo, the State University of New York, Graduate School, College of Arts and Sciences, Department of Music, Buffalo, NY 14260. Offers contemporary performance (Advanced Certificate); historical musicology and music theory (PhD); music composition (MA, PhD); music history (MA); music performance (MM); music theory (MA). Terminal master's awarded for partial completion of doctoral program. *Degree requirements:* For master's, variable foreign language requirement, comprehensive exam (for some programs), thesis (for some programs), recitals (for MM); projects and/or thesis (for MA); for doctorate, variable foreign language requirement, comprehensive exam, thesis/dissertation; for Advanced Certificate, recitals. *Entrance requirements:* For master's, audition (for MM), compositions, writing sample(s), essay, letters of recommendation; for doctorate, GRE General Test, compositions, writing sample(s), essay, letters of recommendation; for Advanced Certificate, audition. Additional exam requirements/recommendations for international students: required—TOEFL (minimum score 550 paper-based; 79 iBT), IELTS. Electronic applications accepted. *Expenses: Tuition, area resident:* Full-time $11,310; part-time $471 per credit hour. Tuition, state resident: full-time $11,310; part-time $471 per credit hour. Tuition, nonresident: full-time $23,100; part-time $963 per credit hour. *International tuition:* $23,100 full-time. *Required fees:* $2820.

The University of Akron, Graduate School, Buchtel College of Arts and Sciences, School of Music, Program in Accompanying, Akron, OH 44325. Offers MM. *Entrance requirements:* For master's, minimum GPA of 2.75, three letters of recommendation, audition. Additional exam requirements/recommendations for international students: required—TOEFL (minimum score 79 iBT), IELTS (minimum score 6.5).

The University of Akron, Graduate School, Buchtel College of Arts and Sciences, School of Music, Program in Composition, Akron, OH 44325. Offers MM. *Degree requirements:* For master's, comprehensive exam, thesis optional. *Entrance requirements:* For master's, theory diagnostic exam, minimum GPA of 2.75, three letters of recommendation, sample of scholarly writing, composition portfolio, interview. Additional exam requirements/recommendations for international students: required—TOEFL (minimum score 79 iBT), IELTS (minimum score 6.5). Electronic applications accepted.

The University of Akron, Graduate School, Buchtel College of Arts and Sciences, School of Music, Program in Music Technology, Akron, OH 44325. Offers MM. *Degree requirements:* For master's, comprehensive exam, thesis optional. *Entrance requirements:* For master's, minimum GPA of 2.75, three letters of recommendation, interview. Additional exam requirements/recommendations for international students: required—TOEFL (minimum score 79 iBT), IELTS (minimum score 6.5). Electronic applications accepted.

The University of Akron, Graduate School, Buchtel College of Arts and Sciences, School of Music, Program in Performance, Akron, OH 44325. Offers MM. *Degree requirements:* For master's, comprehensive exam. *Entrance requirements:* For master's, minimum GPA of 2.75, three letters of recommendation, audition. Additional exam requirements/recommendations for international students: required—TOEFL (minimum score 79 iBT), IELTS (minimum score 6.5). Electronic applications accepted.

The University of Akron, Graduate School, Buchtel College of Arts and Sciences, School of Music, Program in Theory, Akron, OH 44325. Offers MM. *Degree requirements:* For master's, comprehensive exam, thesis optional. *Entrance requirements:* For master's, minimum GPA of 2.75, interview, three letters of recommendation. Additional exam requirements/recommendations for international students: required—TOEFL (minimum score 79 iBT), IELTS (minimum score 6.5). Electronic applications accepted.

The University of Alabama, Graduate School, College of Arts and Sciences, Department of Music, Tuscaloosa, AL 35487. Offers arranging (MM); choral conducting (MM, DMA); church music (MM); composition (MM, DMA); music education (MA, PhD); musicology (MM); performance (MM, DMA); theory (MM); wind conducting (MM, DMA). *Accreditation:* NASM. *Faculty:* 37 full-time (9 women). *Students:* 52 full-time (18 women), 11 part-time (2 women); includes 11 minority (5 Black or African American, non-Hispanic/Latino; 1 American Indian or Alaska Native, non-Hispanic/Latino; 2 Asian, non-Hispanic/Latino; 3 Hispanic/Latino), 8 international. Average age 29. 77 applicants, 73% accepted, 22 enrolled. In 2019, 18 master's, 18 doctorates awarded. *Degree requirements:* For master's, variable foreign language requirement, comprehensive exam (for some programs), thesis (for some programs), recital; for doctorate, variable foreign language requirement, comprehensive exam, thesis/dissertation, oral exam; recital (for some majors). *Entrance requirements:* For master's and doctorate, audition exam, audition in the major instrument or area. Additional exam requirements/recommendations for international students: required—PTE (minimum score 59), TOEFL (minimum score 550 paper-based, 79 iBT) or IELTS (minimum score 6.5). *Application deadline:* For fall admission, 3/15 priority date for domestic and international students; for winter admission, 9/1 priority date for domestic and international students; for spring admission, 9/1 priority date for domestic and international students. Applications are processed on a rolling basis. Application fee: $50 ($60 for international students). Electronic applications accepted. *Expenses: Tuition, area resident:* Full-time $10,780; part-time $440 per credit hour. Tuition, nonresident: full-time $30,250; part-time $1550 per credit hour. *Financial support:* Fellowships with full tuition reimbursements, teaching assistantships with tuition reimbursements, institutionally sponsored loans, scholarships/grants, health care benefits, and unspecified assistantships available. Financial award application deadline: 3/15. *Unit head:* Charles G. Snead, Director, 205-348-7110, Fax: 205-348-1473, E-mail: ssnead@music.ua.edu. *Application contact:* Dr. Jon Noffsinger, Director of Graduate Studies, 205-348-1475, Fax: 205-348-1473, E-mail: jnoffsin@ua.edu.
Website: http://music.ua.edu/

University of Alberta, Faculty of Graduate Studies and Research, Department of Music, Edmonton, AB T6G 2E1, Canada. Offers applied music (M Mus); choral conducting (M Mus); composition (M Mus); music (PhD); organ and choral conductors (D Mus); piano (D Mus). *Degree requirements:* For master's, one foreign language, thesis; for doctorate, one foreign language, thesis/dissertation. *Entrance requirements:* Additional exam requirements/recommendations for international students: required—TOEFL (minimum score 550 paper-based). Electronic applications accepted.

The University of Arizona, College of Fine Arts, School of Music, Program in Music, Tucson, AZ 85721. Offers composition (MM); ethnomusicology (MM); music education (MM, PhD); music theory (MM, PhD); musicology (MM); performance (MM), including conducting - choral, conducting - instrumental, instrumental, keyboard, piano accompanying, piano and dance accompanying, vocal. *Entrance requirements:* Additional exam requirements/recommendations for international students: required—TOEFL (minimum score 550 paper-based; 79 iBT). Electronic applications accepted.

The University of Arizona, College of Fine Arts, School of Music, Program in Musical Arts, Tucson, AZ 85721. Offers composition (DMA); conducting (DMA); performance (DMA), including instrumental, keyboard, vocal. *Entrance requirements:* Additional exam requirements/recommendations for international students: required—TOEFL (minimum score 550 paper-based; 79 iBT). Electronic applications accepted.

University of Arkansas, Graduate School, J. William Fulbright College of Arts and Sciences, Department of Music, Fayetteville, AR 72701. Offers MM. *Accreditation:* NASM. *Students:* 32 full-time (12 women), 7 part-time (4 women); includes 11 minority (6 Black or African American, non-Hispanic/Latino; 3 Asian, non-Hispanic/Latino; 2 Hispanic/Latino), 4 international. 41 applicants, 93% accepted. In 2019, 14 master's awarded. *Entrance requirements:* For master's, GRE General Test. *Application deadline:* For fall admission, 8/1 for domestic students, 4/1 for international students; for spring admission, 12/1 for domestic students, 10/1 for international students; for summer

admission, 4/15 for domestic students, 3/1 for international students. Applications are processed on a rolling basis. Application fee: $60. Electronic applications accepted. *Financial support:* In 2019–20, 2 research assistantships, 24 teaching assistantships were awarded; fellowships, career-related internships or fieldwork, and Federal Work-Study also available. Support available to part-time students. Financial award application deadline: 4/1; financial award applicants required to submit FAFSA. *Unit head:* Dr. Ronda M. Mains, Department Chair, 479-575-4701, Fax: 479-575-5409, E-mail: rmains@uark.edu. *Application contact:* Er-Gene Kahng, Associate Professor, Violin, 479-575-6270, Fax: 479-575-5409, E-mail: ekahng@uark.edu.
Website: https://fulbright.uark.edu/departments/music/

The University of British Columbia, Faculty of Arts, School of Music, Vancouver, BC V6T 1Z2, Canada. Offers M Mus, MA, DMA, PhD. *Program availability:* Part-time. *Degree requirements:* For master's, recital (M Mus), thesis (MA); for doctorate, one foreign language, comprehensive exam, public performance or composition (DMA), dissertation (PhD). *Entrance requirements:* For master's, audition/performance (M Mus); for doctorate, audition/performance (DMA). Additional exam requirements/recommendations for international students: required—TOEFL. Electronic applications accepted. *Expenses:* Contact institution.

University of Calgary, Faculty of Graduate Studies, Faculty of Arts, Program in Music, Calgary, AB T2N 1N4, Canada. Offers M Mus, MA, PhD. *Degree requirements:* For master's, one foreign language, thesis; for doctorate, 2 foreign languages, thesis/dissertation. *Entrance requirements:* For master's, audition (performance), 3 compositions. Additional exam requirements/recommendations for international students: required—TOEFL. Electronic applications accepted.

University of California, Berkeley, Graduate Division, College of Letters and Science, Department of Music, Berkeley, CA 94720. Offers composition (PhD); ethnomusicology (PhD); musicology (PhD). *Degree requirements:* For doctorate, 2 foreign languages, thesis/dissertation, qualifying exam. *Entrance requirements:* For doctorate, GRE General Test, minimum GPA of 3.0, examples of work, 3 letters of recommendation. Additional exam requirements/recommendations for international students: required—TOEFL (minimum score 570 paper-based; 90 iBT). Electronic applications accepted.

University of California, Davis, Graduate Studies, Program in Music, Davis, CA 95616. Offers composition (MA, PhD); conducting (MA, PhD); musicology (MA, PhD). Terminal master's awarded for partial completion of doctoral program. *Degree requirements:* For master's, one foreign language, thesis; for doctorate, 2 foreign languages, thesis/dissertation. *Entrance requirements:* For master's, minimum GPA of 3.0; for doctorate, GRE, minimum GPA of 3.0. Additional exam requirements/recommendations for international students: required—TOEFL (minimum score 550 paper-based). Electronic applications accepted.

University of California, Davis, Graduate Studies, Program in Performance Studies, Davis, CA 95616. Offers dramatic art (PhD). *Degree requirements:* For doctorate, 2 foreign languages, thesis/dissertation. *Entrance requirements:* For doctorate, GRE, minimum GPA of 3.25. Additional exam requirements/recommendations for international students: required—TOEFL (minimum score 550 paper-based). Electronic applications accepted.

University of California, Irvine, Claire Trevor School of the Arts, Department of Music, Irvine, CA 92697. Offers accompanying (MFA); choral conducting (MFA); composition and technology (MFA); guitar/lute performance (MFA); instrumental performance (MFA); piano performance (MFA); vocal performance (MFA). *Students:* 30 full-time (8 women), 2 part-time (1 woman); includes 9 minority (2 Black or African American, non-Hispanic/Latino; 1 Asian, non-Hispanic/Latino; 1 Hispanic/Latino; 5 Two or more races, non-Hispanic/Latino), 7 international. Average age 31. 41 applicants, 27% accepted, 8 enrolled. In 2019, 9 master's awarded. *Degree requirements:* For master's, one foreign language, thesis. *Entrance requirements:* For master's, minimum GPA of 3.0. *Application deadline:* For fall admission, 1/15 priority date for domestic students, 1/15 for international students. Applications are processed on a rolling basis. Application fee: $120 ($140 for international students). Electronic applications accepted. *Financial support:* Fellowships, teaching assistantships, institutionally sponsored loans, traineeships, health care benefits, and unspecified assistantships available. Financial award application deadline: 3/1; financial award applicants required to submit FAFSA. *Unit head:* Michael Dessen, Chair of Music, Fax: 949-824-4914, E-mail: mdessen@uci.edu. *Application contact:* Peter Chang, Department Manager, 949-824-4281, Fax: 949-824-4914, E-mail: pechang@uci.edu.
Website: http://www.arts.uci.edu/ctsa-academic-departments-music

University of California, Los Angeles, Graduate Division, College of Letters and Science, Department of Musicology, Los Angeles, CA 90095. Offers MA, PhD. Terminal master's awarded for partial completion of doctoral program. *Degree requirements:* For master's, one foreign language, comprehensive exam, thesis; for doctorate, one foreign language, thesis/dissertation, oral and written qualifying exams. *Entrance requirements:* For master's and doctorate, GRE General Test (recommended), bachelor's degree; minimum undergraduate GPA of 3.0 (or its equivalent if letter grade system not used); writing sample. Additional exam requirements/recommendations for international students: required—TOEFL. Electronic applications accepted.

University of California, Los Angeles, Graduate Division, School of the Arts and Architecture, Department of Ethnomusicology, Los Angeles, CA 90095. Offers MA, PhD. *Degree requirements:* For master's, one foreign language, comprehensive exam; for doctorate, 2 foreign languages, thesis/dissertation, oral and written qualifying exams. *Entrance requirements:* For master's, bachelor's degree; minimum undergraduate GPA of 3.0 (or its equivalent if letter grade system not used); writing sample; for doctorate, master's degree; minimum undergraduate GPA of 3.0 (or its equivalent if letter grade system not used); writing sample. Additional exam requirements/recommendations for international students: required—TOEFL. Electronic applications accepted.

University of California, Los Angeles, Graduate Division, School of the Arts and Architecture, Department of Music, Los Angeles, CA 90095. Offers composition (MA, PhD); performance (MM, DMA). *Degree requirements:* For master's, one foreign language, thesis, final recital (for MM); for doctorate, one foreign language, thesis/dissertation, oral and written qualifying exams; recital (DMA). *Entrance requirements:* For master's, departmental assessment exams, bachelor's degree; minimum undergraduate GPA of 3.0 (or its equivalent if letter grade system not used); portfolio; interview; audition; for doctorate, departmental assessment exams, master's degree; minimum undergraduate GPA of 3.0 (or its equivalent if letter grade system not used); portfolio; interview. Additional exam requirements/recommendations for international students: required—TOEFL. Electronic applications accepted.

University of California, Riverside, Graduate Division, Department of Music, Riverside, CA 92521-0102. Offers composition (PhD); ethnomusicology (MA). Terminal master's awarded for partial completion of doctoral program. *Degree requirements:* For master's, one foreign language, comprehensive exam, thesis (for some programs), oral exams; for doctorate, 2 foreign languages, comprehensive exam, thesis/dissertation, written and oral qualifying examination. *Entrance requirements:* For master's and doctorate, GRE General Test, minimum GPA of 3.0. Additional exam requirements/recommendations for international students: required—TOEFL (minimum score 550 paper-based; 80 iBT). Electronic applications accepted.

University of California, San Diego, Graduate Division, Department of Music, La Jolla, CA 92093. Offers contemporary music performance (DMA); music (MA, PhD). *Students:* 77 full-time (31 women), 1 part-time (0 women). 134 applicants, 22% accepted, 15 enrolled. In 2019, 6 master's, 15 doctorates awarded. *Degree requirements:* For master's, thesis; for doctorate, comprehensive exam (for some programs), thesis/dissertation (for some programs), 6 credit units of apprentice teaching; major composition (for some programs); major recital (for some programs). *Entrance requirements:* For master's, GRE General Test, musical portfolio; for doctorate, GRE General Test, master's degree; supporting musical portfolio. Additional exam requirements/recommendations for international students: required—TOEFL (minimum score 550 paper-based; 80 iBT), IELTS (minimum score 7). *Application deadline:* For fall admission, 12/10 for domestic students. Application fee: $105 ($125 for international students). Electronic applications accepted. *Financial support:* Fellowships, research assistantships, teaching assistantships, scholarships/grants, unspecified assistantships, and readerships available. Financial award applicants required to submit FAFSA. *Unit head:* David Borgo, Chair, 858-822-4957, E-mail: dborgo@ucsd.edu. *Application contact:* Dimple Bhatt, Graduate Coordinator, 858-534-3279, E-mail: mus-grad@ucsd.edu.
Website: http://musicweb.ucsd.edu/

University of California, Santa Barbara, Graduate Division, College of Letters and Sciences, Division of Humanities and Fine Arts, Department of Music, Santa Barbara, CA 93106-2014. Offers brass (MM); composition (MA, PhD); conducting (MM, DMA); ethnomusicology (MA, PhD); keyboard (MM, DMA); musicology (MA, PhD); piano accompanying (MM); strings (MM, DMA); theory (MA, PhD); voice (MM, DMA); woodwinds (MM); MA/PhD; MM/DMA. *Degree requirements:* For master's, variable foreign language requirement, comprehensive exam (for some programs), thesis (for some programs); for doctorate, variable foreign language requirement, comprehensive exam, thesis/dissertation. *Entrance requirements:* For master's and doctorate, GRE. Additional exam requirements/recommendations for international students: required—TOEFL (minimum score 550 paper-based; 80 iBT), IELTS (minimum score 7). Electronic applications accepted.

University of California, Santa Cruz, Division of Graduate Studies, Division of the Arts, Department of Music, Santa Cruz, CA 95064. Offers ethnomusicology (MA); music (PhD), including cross-cultural and interdisciplinary studies; music composition (MA, DMA), including world music composition (DMA); music composition (DMA), including computer-assisted (algorithmic) composition; performance practice (MA). *Degree requirements:* For master's, one foreign language, thesis, recital; for doctorate, one foreign language, thesis/dissertation, qualifying and final examinations. *Entrance requirements:* For master's, GRE General Test, 3 letters of recommendation, writing or composition sample, 10-20 minute unedited recording; for doctorate, GRE General Test, 3 letters of recommendation, writing sample. Additional exam requirements/recommendations for international students: required—TOEFL (minimum score 550 paper-based; 83 iBT); recommended—IELTS (minimum score 8). Electronic applications accepted.

University of Central Arkansas, Graduate School, College of Fine Arts and Communication, Department of Music, Conway, AR 72035-0001. Offers choral conducting (MM); instrumental conducting (MM); music (PC); music education (MM); music theory (MM); performance (MM). *Accreditation:* NASM. *Program availability:* Part-time. *Degree requirements:* For master's, comprehensive exam, thesis optional. *Entrance requirements:* For master's, GRE General Test, minimum GPA of 2.7. Additional exam requirements/recommendations for international students: required—TOEFL (minimum score 550 paper-based). Electronic applications accepted.

University of Central Florida, College of Arts and Humanities, School of Performing Arts, Orlando, FL 32816. Offers music (MA); theatre (MA, MFA), including acting (MFA), theatre for young audiences (MFA). *Accreditation:* NASM; NCATE. *Program availability:* Part-time. *Students:* 65 full-time (32 women), 20 part-time (5 women); includes 22 minority (6 Black or African American, non-Hispanic/Latino; 1 Asian, non-Hispanic/Latino; 12 Hispanic/Latino; 3 Two or more races, non-Hispanic/Latino), 1 international. Average age 31. 76 applicants, 64% accepted, 37 enrolled. In 2019, 17 master's awarded. *Degree requirements:* For master's, comprehensive exam, thesis or alternative. *Entrance requirements:* For master's, GRE General Test, letters of recommendation, writing sample. Additional exam requirements/recommendations for international students: required—TOEFL. *Application deadline:* For fall admission, 7/15 for domestic students; for spring admission, 12/1 for domestic students. Application fee: $30. Electronic applications accepted. *Financial support:* In 2019–20, 35 students received support, including 6 fellowships with partial tuition reimbursements available (averaging $8,333 per year), 8 research assistantships with partial tuition reimbursements available (averaging $2,808 per year), 30 teaching assistantships with partial tuition reimbursements available (averaging $4,695 per year); career-related internships or fieldwork, Federal Work-Study, institutionally sponsored loans, health care benefits, tuition waivers (partial), and unspecified assistantships also available. Financial award application deadline: 3/1; financial award applicants required to submit FAFSA. *Unit head:* Dr. Michael Wainstein, Director, 407-823-2519, Fax: 407-823-3378, E-mail: michael.wainstein@ucf.edu. *Application contact:* Associate Director, Graduate Admissions, 407-823-2766, Fax: 407-823-6442, E-mail: gradadmissions@ucf.edu.
Website: http://performingarts.cah.ucf.edu/

University of Central Missouri, The Graduate School, Warrensburg, MO 64093. Offers accountancy (MA); accounting (MBA); applied mathematics (MS); aviation safety (MA); biology (MS); business administration (MBA); career and technology education (MS); college student personnel administration (MS); communication (MA); computer information systems and information technology (MS); computer science (MS); counseling (MS); criminal justice and criminology (MS); educational leadership (Ed S); educational leadership and policy analysis (Ed D); educational technology (MS, Ed S); elementary and early childhood education (MSE); English (MA); english language learners - teaching english as a second language (MA); environmental studies (MA); finance (MBA); history (MA); industrial hygiene (MS); industrial management (MS); information systems (MBA); kinesiology (MS); library science and information services (MS); literacy education (MSE); marketing (MBA); mathematics (MS); music (MA); occupational safety management (MS); professional leadership - adult, career, and technical education (Ed S); professional leadership - counseling (Ed S); psychology (MS); rural family nursing (MS); school administration (MSE); social gerontology (MS); sociology (MA); special education (MSE); speech language pathology (MS); teaching (MAT); technology (MS); technology management (PhD); theatre (MA). *Accreditation:* ASHA. *Program availability:* Part-time, 100% online, blended/hybrid learning. *Faculty:* 236 full-time (113 women), 97 part-time/adjunct (61 women). *Students:* 787 full-time (448 women), 1,459 part-time (997 women); includes 213 minority (72 Black or African American, non-Hispanic/Latino; 5 American Indian or Alaska Native, non-Hispanic/Latino; 27 Asian, non-Hispanic/Latino; 59 Hispanic/Latino; 50 Two or more races, non-Hispanic/Latino), 574 international. Average age 30. 1,477 applicants, 68% accepted, 664 enrolled. In 2019, 831 master's, 93 other advanced degrees awarded. *Degree requirements:* For master's and Ed S, comprehensive exam (for some programs), thesis

(for some programs). *Entrance requirements:* For master's, A GRE or GMAT test score may be required by some of the programs, A minimum GPA, letters of recommendation, a statement of purpose may be required by some of the programs; for Ed S, A master's degree is required for the application of an Education Specialist's degree program. Additional exam requirements/recommendations for international students: required—TOEFL (minimum score 550 paper-based; 79 iBT). *Application deadline:* For fall admission, 6/1 priority date for domestic and international students; for spring admission, 10/15 priority date for domestic and international students; for summer admission, 4/1 priority date for domestic and international students. Applications are processed on a rolling basis. Application fee: $30 ($75 for international students). Electronic applications accepted. *Expenses: Tuition, area resident:* Full-time $7524; part-time $313.50 per credit hour. Tuition, state resident: full-time $7524; part-time $313.50 per credit hour. Tuition, nonresident: full-time $15,048; part-time $627 per credit hour. *International tuition:* $15,048 full-time. *Required fees:* $915; $30.50 per credit hour. *Financial support:* In 2019–20, 89 students received support. Research assistantships, teaching assistantships, career-related internships or fieldwork, Federal Work-Study, scholarships/grants, unspecified assistantships, and administrative and laboratory assistantships available. Support available to part-time students. Financial award application deadline: 4/1; financial award applicants required to submit FAFSA. *Unit head:* Shellie Hewitt, Director of Graduate and International Student Services, 660-543-4621, Fax: 660-543-4778, E-mail: hewitt@ucmo.edu. *Application contact:* Shellie Hewitt, Director of Graduate and International Student Services, 660-543-4621, Fax: 660-543-4778, E-mail: hewitt@ucmo.edu.
Website: http://www.ucmo.edu/graduate/

University of Central Oklahoma, The Jackson College of Graduate Studies, College of Fine Arts and Design, Department of Music, Edmond, OK 73034-5209. Offers jazz studies (MM), including music production, performance; music (MM), including collaborative piano, composition, conducting, instrumental performance, music education, musical theatre, piano pedagogy, piano performance, vocal pedagogy, vocal performance. *Accreditation:* NASM. *Program availability:* Part-time. *Degree requirements:* For master's, comprehensive exam, recital or project. *Entrance requirements:* For master's, interview, audition. Additional exam requirements/ recommendations for international students: required—TOEFL (minimum score 550 paper-based; 79 iBT), IELTS (minimum score 6.5). Electronic applications accepted.

University of Chicago, Division of the Humanities, Department of Music, Chicago, IL 60637. Offers composition (PhD); ethnomusicology (PhD); music history and theory (PhD). Terminal master's awarded for partial completion of doctoral program. *Degree requirements:* For doctorate, 3 foreign languages, comprehensive exam, thesis/ dissertation. *Entrance requirements:* For doctorate, GRE General Test, 15-20 page writing sample, statement of purpose, 3 letters of recommendation, transcripts for all previous degrees and institutions attended. Additional exam requirements/ recommendations for international students: required—TOEFL (minimum score 104 iBT), IELTS (minimum score 7). Electronic applications accepted.

University of Chicago, Division of the Humanities, Master of Arts Program in the Humanities, Chicago, IL 60637. Offers art history (MA); cinema and media studies (MA); classic languages (MA); comparative literature (MA); creative writing (MA); cultural policy studies (MA); digital humanities (MA); East Asian languages and civilizations (MA); English language and literature (MA); gender and sexuality studies (MA); Germanic studies (MA); linguistics (MA); music (MA); near Eastern languages and civilizations (MA); philosophy (MA); poetics (MA); race, politics and culture (MA); Romance languages and literatures (MA); Slavic languages and literatures (MA); South Asian languages and civilizations (MA); theater and performance studies (MA). *Degree requirements:* For master's, thesis. *Entrance requirements:* For master's, GRE General Test, 10-15 page writing sample, statement of purpose, 3 letters of recommendation, transcripts for all previous degrees and institutions attended. Additional exam requirements/recommendations for international students: required—TOEFL (minimum score 104 iBT), IELTS (minimum score 7). Electronic applications accepted. *Expenses:* Contact institution.

University of Cincinnati, Graduate School, College-Conservatory of Music, Division of Composition, Musicology and Theory, Cincinnati, OH 45221. Offers composition (MM, DMA); music history (MM); music theory (MM, PhD); musicology (PhD). *Accreditation:* NASM. *Degree requirements:* For master's, variable foreign language requirement, comprehensive exam, thesis; for doctorate, variable foreign language requirement, comprehensive exam, thesis/dissertation. *Entrance requirements:* For master's and doctorate, GRE General Test, interview. Additional exam requirements/recommendations for international students: required—TOEFL (minimum score 520 paper-based). Electronic applications accepted.

University of Cincinnati, Graduate School, College-Conservatory of Music, Division of Ensembles and Conducting, Cincinnati, OH 45221. Offers choral conducting (MM, DMA); orchestral conducting (MM, DMA); wind conducting (MM, DMA). *Accreditation:* NASM. *Degree requirements:* For master's, comprehensive exam, conducting performances; for doctorate, one foreign language, comprehensive exam, thesis/dissertation, conducting performances, lecture recital. *Entrance requirements:* For master's and doctorate, GRE General Test, audition, interview. Additional exam requirements/recommendations for international students: required—TOEFL (minimum score 520 paper-based). Electronic applications accepted.

University of Cincinnati, Graduate School, College-Conservatory of Music, Division of Keyboard Studies, Cincinnati, OH 45221-0003. Offers MM, DMA, AD. *Degree requirements:* For master's, comprehensive exam, Two recitals; for doctorate, one foreign language, comprehensive exam, thesis/dissertation, Lecture recital. Either a project or a document. *Entrance requirements:* For master's, GRE General Test, audition; for doctorate, GRE General Test, audition, entrance test; for AD, audition. Additional exam requirements/recommendations for international students: required—TOEFL (minimum score 520 paper-based). Electronic applications accepted.

University of Cincinnati, Graduate School, College-Conservatory of Music, Division of Performance Studies, Cincinnati, OH 45221. Offers performance (MM, DMA, AD). *Accreditation:* NASM. *Degree requirements:* For master's, comprehensive exam, recitals; for doctorate, one foreign language, comprehensive exam, thesis/dissertation, recitals; for AD, recitals. *Entrance requirements:* For master's and doctorate, GRE General Test, audition. Additional exam requirements/recommendations for international students: required—TOEFL (minimum score 520 paper-based). Electronic applications accepted.

University of Cincinnati, Graduate School, College-Conservatory of Music, Division of Theatre Arts, Production and Arts Administration, Cincinnati, OH 45221. Offers arts administration (MA); directing (MFA); theater design and production (MFA); voice and opera (MM, DMA); MBA/MA. *Accreditation:* NAST (one or more programs are accredited). *Degree requirements:* For master's, final project. *Entrance requirements:* For master's, GMAT (MA), audition/interview. Additional exam requirements/ recommendations for international students: required—TOEFL (minimum score 520 paper-based). Electronic applications accepted.

University of Colorado Boulder, Graduate School, College of Music, Boulder, CO 80309. Offers composition (M Mus, D Mus A); conducting (M Mus); instrumental conducting and literature (D Mus A); literature and performance of choral music (D Mus A); music education (M Mus Ed, PhD), including choral or wind instrument conducting (M Mus Ed), general (M Mus Ed), Kodaly concepts (M Mus Ed), piano pedagogy (M Mus Ed), primary instruments (M Mus Ed), secondary instruments (M Mus Ed), voice pedagogy (M Mus Ed); music theory (M Mus); performance (M Mus, D Mus A); performance and pedagogy (M Mus, D Mus A). *Accreditation:* NASM. Terminal master's awarded for partial completion of doctoral program. *Degree requirements:* For master's, variable foreign language requirement, comprehensive exam, thesis or alternative, recital; for doctorate, variable foreign language requirement, thesis/dissertation. *Entrance requirements:* For master's, GRE General Test, GRE Subject Test (music literature), minimum undergraduate GPA of 2.75; for doctorate, GRE General Test, GRE Subject Test, audition, sample of research. Electronic applications accepted. Application fee is waived when completed online.

University of Colorado Denver, College of Arts and Media, Denver, CO 80217-3364. Offers recording arts (MS), including media forensics, recording arts. *Accreditation:* NASM. *Program availability:* Part-time, evening/weekend. *Degree requirements:* For master's, 34 credits, thesis/portfolio. *Entrance requirements:* For master's, GRE General Test (minimum scores higher than 50th percentile for all sections), minimum undergraduate GPA of 3.0, portfolio, resume, interview, 3 letters of recommendation. Additional exam requirements/recommendations for international students: required—TOEFL (minimum score 70 iBT). Electronic applications accepted. Tuition and fees vary according to course load, program and reciprocity agreements.

University of Connecticut, Graduate School, School of Fine Arts, Department of Music, Storrs, CT 06269. Offers conducting (M Mus, DMA); historical musicology (MA); music theory (MA); music theory and history (PhD); performance (M Mus, DMA). *Accreditation:* NASM. Terminal master's awarded for partial completion of doctoral program. *Degree requirements:* For master's, comprehensive exam; for doctorate, thesis/dissertation. *Entrance requirements:* For master's, GRE General Test, GRE Subject Test, audition; for doctorate, GRE Subject Test, MAT, audition. Additional exam requirements/recommendations for international students: required—TOEFL (minimum score 550 paper-based).

University of Delaware, College of Arts and Sciences, Department of Music, Newark, DE 19716. Offers composition (MM); music education (MM); performance (MM). *Accreditation:* NASM. *Program availability:* Part-time. *Entrance requirements:* For master's, audition. Additional exam requirements/recommendations for international students: required—TOEFL. Electronic applications accepted.

University of Denver, Division of Arts, Humanities and Social Sciences, Lamont School of Music, Denver, CO 80208. Offers composition (MM); composition - jazz emphasis (MM); conducting (MM, Certificate); jazz studies (Certificate); music theory (MA); musicology (MA); orchestral studies (Certificate); pedagogy (MM); performance (MM, Certificate); performance - jazz emphasis (MM); Suzuki teaching (Certificate). *Accreditation:* NASM. *Program availability:* Part-time. *Faculty:* 30 full-time (10 women), 30 part-time/adjunct (14 women). *Students:* 25 full-time (12 women), 78 part-time (38 women); includes 20 minority (3 Black or African American, non-Hispanic/Latino; 1 American Indian or Alaska Native, non-Hispanic/Latino; 3 Asian, non-Hispanic/Latino; 9 Hispanic/Latino; 4 Two or more races, non-Hispanic/Latino), 16 international. Average age 28. 186 applicants, 83% accepted, 58 enrolled. In 2019, 33 master's, 7 other advanced degrees awarded. *Degree requirements:* For master's, one foreign language, comprehensive exam, recital or project (for performance), thesis (for musicology, music theory, piano pedagogy). *Entrance requirements:* For master's, GRE General Test (for MA only), bachelor's degree, transcripts, personal statement, resume, three letters of recommendation, pre-screen audition (for performance), portfolio (for composition), essay or research paper (for MA only); for Certificate, bachelor's degree, transcripts, personal statement, resume, letters of recommendation, pre-screen video recording or music audition. Additional exam requirements/recommendations for international students: required—TOEFL (minimum score 550 paper-based; 80 iBT). *Application deadline:* For fall admission, 1/15 priority date for domestic and international students. Applications are processed on a rolling basis. Application fee: $65. Electronic applications accepted. *Expenses:* Contact institution. *Financial support:* In 2019–20, 80 students received support, including 39 teaching assistantships with tuition reimbursements available (averaging $6,709 per year); career-related internships or fieldwork, Federal Work-Study, institutionally sponsored loans, scholarships/grants, tuition waivers, and unspecified assistantships also available. Support available to part-time students. Financial award application deadline: 2/15; financial award applicants required to submit FAFSA. *Unit head:* Dr. Keith Ward, Professor and Director, 303-871-6986, E-mail: Keith.Ward@du.edu. *Application contact:* Stephen Campbell, Director of Admission, 303-871-6973, E-mail: stephen.l.campbell@du.edu.
Website: http://www.du.edu/ahss/lamont/index.html

University of Florida, Graduate School, College of The Arts, School of Music, Gainesville, FL 32611. Offers choral conducting (MM); composition (MM, PhD); electronic music (MM); ethnomusicology (MM); instrumental conducting (MM); music (MM, PhD); music education (MM, PhD), including choral conducting (MM), composition (MM), electronic music (MM), ethnomusicology (MM), instrumental conducting (MM), music education (MM), music history and literature (MM), music theory (MM), performance (MM), piano pedagogy (MM); music history and literature (MM, PhD); music theory (MM); performance (MM); sacred music (MM). *Accreditation:* NASM. *Degree requirements:* For master's, variable foreign language requirement, comprehensive exam, thesis, recital; for doctorate, thesis/dissertation. *Entrance requirements:* For master's and doctorate, GRE General Test, audition, minimum GPA of 3.0. Additional exam requirements/recommendations for international students: required—TOEFL (minimum score 550 paper-based; 80 iBT), IELTS (minimum score 6). Electronic applications accepted.

University of Georgia, Franklin College of Arts and Sciences, Hugh Hodgson School of Music, Athens, GA 30602. Offers composition (MM, DMA); conducting (MM, DMA); music (PhD); music education (MM Ed, Ed D); musicology (MA); performance (MM, DMA). *Accreditation:* NASM. *Degree requirements:* For master's, variable foreign language requirement, thesis (MA); for doctorate, variable foreign language requirement, thesis/dissertation. *Entrance requirements:* For master's and doctorate, GRE General Test. Electronic applications accepted.

University of Hartford, The Hartt School, West Hartford, CT 06117-1599. Offers choral conducting (MM Ed); composition (MM, DMA, Artist Diploma, Diploma); conducting (MM, DMA, Artist Diploma, Diploma), including choral (MM, Diploma), instrumental (MM, Diploma); early childhood education (MM Ed); instrumental conducting (MM Ed); Kodály (MM Ed); music (CAGS); music education (DMA, PhD); music history (MM); music theory (MM); pedagogy (MM Ed); performance (MM, MM Ed, DMA, Artist Diploma, Diploma); research (MM Ed); technology (MM Ed). *Program availability:* Part-time. *Faculty:* 36 full-time (5 women), 31 part-time/adjunct (13 women). *Students:* 155 full-time (85 women), 31 part-time (13 women); includes 22 minority (3 Black or African American, non-Hispanic/Latino; 7 Asian, non-Hispanic/Latino; 5 Hispanic/Latino; 7 Two or more races, non-Hispanic/Latino), 86 international. Average age 27. 186 applicants, 58% accepted, 49 enrolled. In 2019, 46 master's, 7 doctorates, 10 other advanced degrees awarded. *Degree requirements:* For master's, variable foreign language requirement, thesis (for some programs), recital; for doctorate, variable

foreign language requirement, thesis/dissertation (for some programs), recital; for other advanced degree, recital. *Entrance requirements:* For master's, audition, letters of recommendation; for doctorate, proficiency exam, audition, interview, research paper; for other advanced degree, audition. Additional exam requirements/recommendations for international students: required—TOEFL. *Application deadline:* For fall admission, 4/1 priority date for domestic students. Applications are processed on a rolling basis. Application fee: $45. Electronic applications accepted. *Expenses:* Contact institution. *Financial support:* Fellowships, teaching assistantships, and Federal Work-Study available. Support available to part-time students. Financial award application deadline: 6/1; financial award applicants required to submit FAFSA. *Unit head:* Dr. Malcolm Morrison, Dean, 860-768-4468, E-mail: morrison@mail.hartford.edu. *Application contact:* Lynne Johnson, Director of Admissions, 860-768-4115, Fax: 860-768-4441, E-mail: johnson@hartford.edu.
Website: http://www.hartford.edu/hartt/

University of Hawaii at Manoa, Office of Graduate Education, College of Arts and Humanities, Department of Music, Honolulu, HI 96822. Offers M Mus, MA, PhD. *Accreditation:* NASM. *Program availability:* Part-time. *Degree requirements:* For master's, variable foreign language requirement, thesis optional; for doctorate, variable foreign language requirement, comprehensive exam, thesis/dissertation. *Entrance requirements:* For master's, GRE General Test, diagnostic exams in acoustics theory; for doctorate, diagnostic exams in music history and theory, GRE General Test. Additional exam requirements/recommendations for international students: required—TOEFL (minimum score 540 paper-based; 76 iBT), IELTS (minimum score 5).

University of Houston, Kathrine G. McGovern College of the Arts, Moores School of Music, Houston, TX 77204. Offers accompanying and chamber music (MM); applied music (MM); composition (MM); music education (DMA); music theory (MM); performance (DMA). *Accreditation:* NASM. *Program availability:* Part-time. *Degree requirements:* For master's, one foreign language, comprehensive exam, recital; for doctorate, one foreign language, comprehensive exam, thesis/dissertation. *Entrance requirements:* For master's, audition, resume, 3 letters of recommendation; for doctorate, writing sample, audition, statement of purpose, resume. Additional exam requirements/recommendations for international students: required—TOEFL (minimum score 550 paper-based; 79 iBT), IELTS (minimum score 6.5). Electronic applications accepted.

University of Idaho, College of Graduate Studies, College of Letters, Arts and Social Sciences, Lionel Hampton School of Music, Moscow, ID 83844-2282. Offers M Mus, MA. *Accreditation:* NASM. *Faculty:* 20. *Students:* 16. Average age 27. In 2019, 7 master's awarded. *Entrance requirements:* For master's, minimum GPA of 3.0. Additional exam requirements/recommendations for international students: required—TOEFL (minimum score 88 iBT). *Application deadline:* For fall admission, 5/1 for domestic students. Applications are processed on a rolling basis. Application fee: $60. Electronic applications accepted. *Expenses:* Tuition, state resident: full-time $7753.80; part-time $502 per credit hour. Tuition, nonresident: full-time $26,990; part-time $1571 per credit hour. *Required fees:* $2122.20; $47 per credit hour. *Financial support:* Research assistantships and teaching assistantships available. Financial award applicants required to submit FAFSA. *Unit head:* Dr. Vanessa Sielert, Director, 208-885-6231, E-mail: music@uidaho.edu. *Application contact:* Dr. Vanessa Sielert, Director, 208-885-6231, E-mail: music@uidaho.edu.
Website: https://www.uidaho.edu/class/music

University of Illinois at Urbana-Champaign, Graduate College, College of Fine and Applied Arts, School of Music, Champaign, IL 61820. Offers music (M Mus, AD, DMA); music education (MME, PhD); musicology (PhD). *Accreditation:* NASM.

The University of Iowa, Graduate College, College of Liberal Arts and Sciences, School of Music, Iowa City, IA 52242-1316. Offers MA, MFA, DMA, PhD. *Accreditation:* NASM. *Degree requirements:* For master's, thesis (for some programs), exam; for doctorate, comprehensive exam, thesis/dissertation. *Entrance requirements:* For master's and doctorate, minimum GPA of 3.0. Additional exam requirements/recommendations for international students: required—TOEFL (minimum score 550 paper-based; 81 iBT). Electronic applications accepted.

The University of Kansas, Graduate Studies, School of Music, Program in Music, Lawrence, KS 66045. Offers MM, DMA, PhD. *Program availability:* Part-time. *Students:* 124 full-time (55 women), 11 part-time (7 women); includes 9 minority (1 Black or African American, non-Hispanic/Latino; 3 Asian, non-Hispanic/Latino; 4 Hispanic/Latino; 1 Two or more races, non-Hispanic/Latino), 53 international. Average age 30. 236 applicants, 55% accepted, 54 enrolled. In 2019, 29 master's, 28 doctorates awarded. *Entrance requirements:* For master's, KU Musicology and Music Theory diagnostic exam, minimum GPA of 3.0, resume/curriculum vitae, 3 letters of reference, official transcripts, statement of purpose; for doctorate, GRE (for PhD); KU Musicology and Music Theory diagnostic exam, minimum GPA of 3.0, audition (for DMA), resume/curriculum vitae, 3 letters of reference, official transcripts, statement of purpose. Additional exam requirements/recommendations for international students: required—TOEFL, IELTS. *Application deadline:* For fall admission, 12/1 priority date for domestic and international students; for summer admission, 4/15 for domestic students, 2/15 for international students. Application fee: $65 ($85 for international students). Electronic applications accepted. *Expenses:* Tuition, state resident: full-time $9989. Tuition, nonresident: full-time $23,950. *International tuition:* $23,950 full-time. *Required fees:* $984; $81.99 per credit hour. Tuition and fees vary according to course load, campus/location and program. *Financial support:* Fellowships, teaching assistantships, institutionally sponsored loans, scholarships/grants, and unspecified assistantships available. Financial award application deadline: 12/1; financial award applicants required to submit FAFSA. *Unit head:* Dr. Martin Bergee, Associate Dean for Academic Affairs, 785-864-3421, Fax: 785-864-5866, E-mail: music@ku.edu. *Application contact:* Amara Simons, Graduate Admissions Contact, 785-864-4466, E-mail: aksimons@ku.edu.
Website: http://www.music.ku.edu

University of Kentucky, Graduate School, College of Fine Arts, Program in Music, Lexington, KY 40506-0032. Offers composition (MM, DMA); conducting (MM, DMA); music education (MM, PhD); music theory (MA, PhD); music therapy (MM); musicology (MA, PhD); performance (MM, DMA); sacred music (MM). *Accreditation:* NASM. *Program availability:* Part-time, evening/weekend. *Degree requirements:* For master's, variable foreign language requirement, comprehensive exam, thesis (for some programs); for doctorate, variable foreign language requirement, comprehensive exam, thesis/dissertation. *Entrance requirements:* For master's, GRE General Test, minimum undergraduate GPA of 2.75; for doctorate, GRE General Test, minimum undergraduate GPA of 2.75, graduate 3.0. Additional exam requirements/recommendations for international students: required—TOEFL (minimum score 550 paper-based). Electronic applications accepted.

University of Lethbridge, School of Graduate Studies, Lethbridge, AB T1K 3M4, Canada. Offers addictions counseling (M Sc); agricultural biotechnology (M Sc); agricultural studies (M Sc, MA); anthropology (MA); archaeology (M Sc, MA); art (MA, MFA); biochemistry (M Sc); biological sciences (M Sc); biomolecular science (PhD); biosystems and biodiversity (PhD); Canadian studies (MA); chemistry (M Sc); computer science (M Sc); computer science and geographical information science (M Sc); counseling (MC); counseling psychology (M Ed); dramatic arts (MA); earth, space, and physical science (PhD); economics (MA); education (MA, PhD); educational leadership (M Ed); English (MA); environmental science (M Sc); evolution and behavior (PhD); exercise science (M Sc); French (MA); French/German (MA); French/Spanish (MA); general education (M Ed); geography (M Sc, MA); German (MA); health sciences (M Sc); individualized multidisciplinary (M Sc, MA); kinesiology (M Sc, MA); management (M Sc), including accounting, finance, human resource management and labor relations, information systems, international management, marketing, policy and strategy; mathematics (M Sc); music (M Mus, MA); Native American studies (MA); neuroscience (M Sc, PhD); new media (MA, MFA); nursing (M Sc, MN); philosophy (MA); physics (M Sc); political science (MA); psychology (M Sc, MA); religious studies (MA); sociology (MA); theatre and dramatic arts (MFA); theoretical and computational science (PhD); urban and regional studies (MA); women and gender studies (MA). *Program availability:* Part-time, evening/weekend. *Degree requirements:* For master's, thesis (for some programs); for doctorate, comprehensive exam, thesis/dissertation. *Entrance requirements:* For master's, GMAT (for M Sc in management), bachelor's degree in related field, minimum GPA of 3.0 during previous 20 graded semester courses, 2 years' teaching or related experience (M Ed); for doctorate, master's degree, minimum graduate GPA of 3.5. Additional exam requirements/recommendations for international students: required—TOEFL (minimum score 580 paper-based; 93 iBT). Electronic applications accepted.

University of Louisiana at Lafayette, College of the Arts, School of Music, Lafayette, LA 70504. Offers conducting (MM); music education (MM); performance (MM); performance pedagogy (MM); theory/composition (MM). *Accreditation:* NASM. *Entrance requirements:* For master's, GRE General Test, minimum GPA of 2.75. Additional exam requirements/recommendations for international students: required—TOEFL (minimum score 550 paper-based). Electronic applications accepted. *Expenses: Tuition, area resident:* Full-time $5511; part-time $1630 per credit hour. Tuition, state resident: full-time $5511; part-time $1630 per credit hour. Tuition, nonresident: full-time $19,239; part-time $2409 per credit hour. *Required fees:* $46,637.

University of Louisville, Graduate School, School of Music, Louisville, KY 40292-0001. Offers composition (MM); electronic composition (MM); music education (MME); music history and literature (MM); music performance (MM), including choral conducting, instrumental, jazz composition, jazz performance, orchestral conducting, organ performance, piano pedagogy, piano performance, string pedagogy, vocal performance, wind band performance, wind conducting; music theory (MM). *Accreditation:* NASM. *Program availability:* Part-time. *Faculty:* 41 full-time (13 women), 33 part-time/adjunct (16 women). *Students:* 56 full-time (19 women), 3 part-time (1 woman); includes 10 minority (2 Black or African American, non-Hispanic/Latino; 1 American Indian or Alaska Native, non-Hispanic/Latino; 4 Asian, non-Hispanic/Latino; 2 Hispanic/Latino; 1 Two or more races, non-Hispanic/Latino), 8 international. Average age 27. 75 applicants, 76% accepted, 31 enrolled. In 2019, 23 master's awarded. *Degree requirements:* For master's, variable foreign language requirement, comprehensive exam, thesis (for some programs). *Entrance requirements:* For master's, Music History Entrance Exam, Music Theory Entrance Exam, Jazz History, Theory and Piano Proficiency Entrance Exam. Additional exam requirements/recommendations for international students: required—TOEFL (minimum score 79 iBT). Application fee: $65. Electronic applications accepted. *Expenses: Tuition, area resident:* Full-time $13,000; part-time $723 per credit hour. Tuition, state resident: full-time $13,000; part-time $723 per credit hour. Tuition, nonresident: full-time $27,114; part-time $1507 per credit hour. *International tuition:* $27,114 full-time. *Required fees:* $196. Tuition and fees vary according to program and reciprocity agreements. *Financial support:* In 2019–20, 40 students received support, including 2 fellowships with full tuition reimbursements available (averaging $12,000 per year), 12 teaching assistantships with full tuition reimbursements available (averaging $12,000 per year); Federal Work-Study, scholarships/grants, health care benefits, tuition waivers (full), and unspecified assistantships also available. Financial award application deadline: 3/1. *Unit head:* Dr. Teresa L. Reed, Dean, School of Music, 502-852-6907, Fax: 502-852-0520, E-mail: teresa.reed@louisville.edu. *Application contact:* Laura Angermeier, Admissions Counselor/Senior Advising Counselor, 502-852-1623, Fax: 502-852-0520, E-mail: leange01@louisville.edu.
Website: http://www.louisville.edu/music/

University of Maine, Graduate School, College of Liberal Arts and Sciences, School of Performing Arts, Orono, ME 04469. Offers MM. *Accreditation:* NASM. *Program availability:* Part-time. *Faculty:* 10 full-time (3 women), 5 part-time/adjunct (2 women). *Students:* 4 full-time (2 women), 3 part-time (1 woman); includes 1 minority (Hispanic/Latino). Average age 32. 5 applicants, 80% accepted, 3 enrolled. In 2019, 3 master's awarded. *Entrance requirements:* For master's, audition. Additional exam requirements/recommendations for international students: required—TOEFL. *Application deadline:* For fall admission, 2/1 priority date for domestic students. Applications are processed on a rolling basis. Application fee: $65. Electronic applications accepted. *Expenses: Tuition, area resident:* Full-time $8100; part-time $450 per credit hour. Tuition, state resident: full-time $8100; part-time $450 per credit hour. Tuition, nonresident: full-time $26,388; part-time $1466 per credit hour. *International tuition:* $26,388 full-time. *Required fees:* $1257; $278 per semester. Tuition and fees vary according to course load. *Financial support:* In 2019–20, 3 students received support, including 3 teaching assistantships with full tuition reimbursements available (averaging $10,550 per year); career-related internships or fieldwork, Federal Work-Study, institutionally sponsored loans, scholarships/grants, and tuition waivers (full and partial) also available. Support available to part-time students. Financial award application deadline: 3/1; financial award applicants required to submit FAFSA. *Unit head:* Dr. Beth Wiemann, Chair, 207-581-1244, Fax: 207-581-4701. *Application contact:* Scott G. Delcourt, Assistant Vice President for Graduate Studies and Senior Associate Dean, 207-581-3291, Fax: 207-581-3232, E-mail: graduate@maine.edu.
Website: http://umaine.edu/spa/

The University of Manchester, School of Arts, Languages and Cultures, Manchester, United Kingdom. Offers anthropology, media and performance (PhD); applied theatre (PhD); Arab world studies (PhD); archaeology (PhD); art history and visual studies (PhD); arts and cultural management (PhD); arts management and cultural policy (PhD); Chinese studies (PhD); classics and ancient history (PhD); composition (PhD); creative writing (PhD); drama (PhD); East Asian studies (PhD); electroacoustic composition (PhD); English and American studies (PhD); English language (PhD); French studies (PhD); German studies (PhD); history (PhD); humanitarianism and conflict response (PhD); interpreting studies (PhD); Japanese studies (PhD); Latin American cultural studies (PhD); linguistics (PhD); Middle Eastern studies (PhD); museology (PhD); museum practice (PhD); music (PhD); musicology (PhD); Polish studies (PhD); Portuguese studies (PhD); religions and theology (PhD); Russian studies (PhD); Spanish studies (PhD); translation and intercultural studies (PhD).

University of Manitoba, Faculty of Graduate Studies, Desautels Faculty of Music, Winnipeg, MB R3T 2N2, Canada. Offers M Mus.

University of Maryland, Baltimore County, The Graduate School, College of Arts, Humanities and Social Sciences, Department of Music, Baltimore, MD 21250.

Offers American contemporary music (Postbaccalaureate Certificate). *Accreditation:* NASM. *Program availability:* Part-time. *Faculty:* 3 full-time (2 women). *Students:* 2 full-time (1 woman), 1 (woman) part-time; includes 1 minority (Asian, non-Hispanic/Latino). Average age 22. 3 applicants, 67% accepted, 2 enrolled. In 2019, 1 Postbaccalaureate Certificate awarded. *Degree requirements:* For Postbaccalaureate Certificate, solo recital. *Entrance requirements:* For degree, minimum GPA of 3.0, resume, reference letters, DVD of performance, BM. Additional exam requirements/recommendations for international students: recommended—TOEFL. *Application deadline:* For fall admission, 12/1 for domestic and international students; for winter admission, 1/30 for domestic and international students; for spring admission, 5/15 priority date for domestic students, 4/15 for international students. Applications are processed on a rolling basis. Application fee: $50. Electronic applications accepted. *Expenses:* $14,382 per year. *Financial support:* Scholarships/grants available. Financial award applicants required to submit FAFSA. *Application contact:* Dr. Lisa Cella, Director, Certificate Program in American Contemporary Music, 410-455-1405, Fax: 410-455-1181, E-mail: cella@umbc.edu. Website: http://music.umbc.edu/degrees-certificates/american-contemporary-music/

University of Maryland, College Park, Academic Affairs, College of Arts and Humanities, School of Music, Program in Ethnomusicology, College Park, MD 20742. Offers MA. *Degree requirements:* For master's, comprehensive exam, thesis optional, oral defense. *Entrance requirements:* Additional exam requirements/recommendations for international students: required—TOEFL.

University of Maryland, College Park, Academic Affairs, College of Arts and Humanities, School of Music, Program in Music, College Park, MD 20742. Offers M Ed, MA, MM, DMA, Ed D, PhD. *Accreditation:* NASM. *Entrance requirements:* For master's, GRE General Test (for ethnomusicology, historical musicology and music theory), 3 letters of recommendation, audition/interview. Additional exam requirements/recommendations for international students: required—TOEFL.

University of Massachusetts Amherst, Graduate School, College of Humanities and Fine Arts, Department of Music and Dance, Amherst, MA 01003. Offers collaborative piano (MM); composition (MM); conducting (MM); jazz composition/arranging (MM); music education (MM, PhD); music history (MM); music theory (PhD); performance (MM). *Accreditation:* NASM. *Program availability:* Part-time. Terminal master's awarded for partial completion of doctoral program. *Degree requirements:* For master's, thesis or alternative; for doctorate, comprehensive exam, thesis/dissertation. *Entrance requirements:* For master's and doctorate, placement tests, original scores, research, audition or tape. Additional exam requirements/recommendations for international students: required—TOEFL (minimum score 550 paper-based; 80 iBT), IELTS (minimum score 6.5). Electronic applications accepted.

University of Massachusetts Lowell, College of Fine Arts, Humanities and Social Sciences, Department of Music, Lowell, MA 01854. Offers music education (MM). *Accreditation:* NASM. *Program availability:* Part-time. *Degree requirements:* For master's, one foreign language, thesis. *Entrance requirements:* For master's, MAT, audition. Electronic applications accepted.

University of Memphis, Graduate School, College of Communication and Fine Arts, Rudi E. Scheidt School of Music, Memphis, TN 38152. Offers composition (M Mu, DMA); conducting (M Mu, DMA); jazz and studio music (M Mu); music education (M Mu, PhD); music theory (DCC); musicology (PhD); Orff-Schulwerk (M Mu); pedagogy (M Mu); performance (M Mu, DMA). *Accreditation:* NASM. *Program availability:* Part-time. *Students:* 68 full-time (25 women), 54 part-time (29 women); includes 29 minority (11 Black or African American, non-Hispanic/Latino; 4 Asian, non-Hispanic/Latino; 12 Hispanic/Latino; 2 Two or more races, non-Hispanic/Latino), 12 international. Average age 31. 125 applicants, 74% accepted, 42 enrolled. In 2019, 20 master's, 7 doctorates awarded. Terminal master's awarded for partial completion of doctoral program. *Degree requirements:* For master's, variable foreign language requirement, comprehensive exam, thesis or alternative; for doctorate, one foreign language, comprehensive exam, thesis/dissertation, qualifying exam. *Entrance requirements:* For master's, audition; for doctorate, GRE General Test or MAT, proficiency exam, audition, work sample, master's degree. Additional exam requirements/recommendations for international students: required—TOEFL (minimum score 550 paper-based; 79 iBT). *Application deadline:* For fall admission, 8/1 for domestic students; for spring admission, 12/1 for domestic students. Applications are processed on a rolling basis. Application fee: $35 ($60 for international students). Electronic applications accepted. *Expenses: Tuition, area resident:* Full-time $9216; part-time $512 per credit hour. *Tuition, state resident:* full-time $9216; part-time $512 per credit hour. *Tuition, nonresident:* full-time $12,672; part-time $704 per credit hour. *International tuition:* $16,128 full-time. *Required fees:* $1530; $85 per credit hour. Tuition and fees vary according to program. *Financial support:* Research assistantships with tuition reimbursements, teaching assistantships with tuition reimbursements, Federal Work-Study, scholarships/grants, and unspecified assistantships available. Financial award application deadline: 2/1; financial award applicants required to submit FAFSA. *Unit head:* Dr. Kevin Sanders, Director, 901-678-3625, Fax: 901-678-3096, E-mail: kevin.sanders@memphis.edu. *Application contact:* Dr. Kevin Sanders, Director, 901-678-3625, Fax: 901-678-3096, E-mail: kevin.sanders@memphis.edu. Website: http://www.memphis.edu/music/

University of Miami, Graduate School, Frost School of Music, Department of Instrumental Performance, Coral Gables, FL 33124. Offers instrumental conducting (MM, DMA); instrumental performance (MM, DMA, AD); multiple woodwinds (MM, DMA). *Accreditation:* NASM. *Degree requirements:* For master's, thesis, recital paper, recital; for doctorate, thesis/dissertation, essay, 2 research tools, 3 recitals. *Entrance requirements:* For master's and doctorate, GRE General Test, audition. Additional exam requirements/recommendations for international students: required—TOEFL (minimum score 550 paper-based; 59 iBT). Electronic applications accepted.

University of Miami, Graduate School, Frost School of Music, Department of Keyboard Performance, Coral Gables, FL 33124. Offers accompanying and chamber music (MM, DMA); keyboard performance and pedagogy (MM, DMA); piano performance (MM, DMA, AD). *Accreditation:* NASM. *Degree requirements:* For master's, thesis, recital paper, recital; for doctorate, thesis/dissertation, essay, 2 research tools, 3 recitals. *Entrance requirements:* For master's and doctorate, GRE General Test, audition. Additional exam requirements/recommendations for international students: required—TOEFL (minimum score 555 paper-based; 59 iBT). Electronic applications accepted.

University of Miami, Graduate School, Frost School of Music, Department of Music Media and Industry, Coral Gables, FL 33124. Offers music business and entertainment industries (MM); music engineering (MS). *Accreditation:* NASM. *Degree requirements:* For master's, thesis, internship (MM); research project (MS). *Entrance requirements:* For master's, GRE General Test. Additional exam requirements/recommendations for international students: required—TOEFL (minimum score 550 paper-based; 59 iBT). Electronic applications accepted.

University of Miami, Graduate School, Frost School of Music, Department of Musicology, Coral Gables, FL 33124. Offers MM. *Accreditation:* NASM. *Degree requirements:* For master's, thesis. *Entrance requirements:* For master's, GRE General Test. Additional exam requirements/recommendations for international students: required—TOEFL (minimum score 550 paper-based; 59 iBT). Electronic applications accepted.

University of Miami, Graduate School, Frost School of Music, Department of Music Theory and Composition, Coral Gables, FL 33124. Offers composition (MM, DMA); electronic music (MM); media writing and production (MM); music theory (MM). *Accreditation:* NASM. *Degree requirements:* For master's, thesis; for doctorate, thesis/dissertation, essay. *Entrance requirements:* For master's and doctorate, GRE General Test, portfolio. Additional exam requirements/recommendations for international students: required—TOEFL (minimum score 550 paper-based; 59 iBT). Electronic applications accepted.

University of Miami, Graduate School, Frost School of Music, Department of Studio Music and Jazz, Coral Gables, FL 33124. Offers jazz composition (DMA); jazz pedagogy (MM); jazz performance (MM, DMA); studio jazz writing (MM). *Accreditation:* NASM. *Degree requirements:* For master's, thesis. *Entrance requirements:* For master's and doctorate, GRE General Test, portfolio. Additional exam requirements/recommendations for international students: required—TOEFL (minimum score 550 paper-based; 59 iBT). Electronic applications accepted.

University of Miami, Graduate School, Frost School of Music, Department of Vocal Performance, Coral Gables, FL 33124. Offers choral conducting (MM, DMA); vocal pedagogy (DMA); vocal performance (MM, DMA, AD). *Accreditation:* NASM. *Degree requirements:* For master's, 2 foreign languages, thesis, recital paper; for doctorate, thesis/dissertation, essay. *Entrance requirements:* For master's and doctorate, GRE General Test, audition. Additional exam requirements/recommendations for international students: required—TOEFL (minimum score 550 paper-based; 59 iBT). Electronic applications accepted.

University of Michigan, Rackham Graduate School, School of Music, Theatre, and Dance, Program in Composition, Ann Arbor, MI 48109-2217. Offers MA, MM, A Mus D. *Degree requirements:* For doctorate, one foreign language, thesis/dissertation, oral exam, composition. *Entrance requirements:* For master's and doctorate, portfolio. Additional exam requirements/recommendations for international students: required—TOEFL.

University of Michigan, Rackham Graduate School, School of Music, Theatre, and Dance, Program in Composition and Theory, Ann Arbor, MI 48109-2085. Offers PhD. *Degree requirements:* For doctorate, one foreign language, thesis/dissertation, oral exam, composition. *Entrance requirements:* For doctorate, GRE, portfolio. Additional exam requirements/recommendations for international students: required—TOEFL. Electronic applications accepted.

University of Michigan, Rackham Graduate School, School of Music, Theatre, and Dance, Program in Conducting, Ann Arbor, MI 48109-2085. Offers MM, A Mus D. *Degree requirements:* For doctorate, one foreign language, thesis/dissertation, 3 concerts, oral exam. *Entrance requirements:* For doctorate, audition, portfolio. Additional exam requirements/recommendations for international students: required—TOEFL. Electronic applications accepted.

University of Michigan, Rackham Graduate School, School of Music, Theatre, and Dance, Program in Musicology, Ann Arbor, MI 48109-2085. Offers MA, PhD. *Degree requirements:* For doctorate, 2 foreign languages, thesis/dissertation, oral exam. *Entrance requirements:* For master's and doctorate, GRE General Test, writing sample. Additional exam requirements/recommendations for international students: required—TOEFL. Electronic applications accepted.

University of Michigan, Rackham Graduate School, School of Music, Theatre, and Dance, Program in Music Theory, Ann Arbor, MI 48109-2085. Offers PhD. *Degree requirements:* For doctorate, one foreign language, thesis/dissertation, oral exam. *Entrance requirements:* For doctorate, GRE, writing sample. Additional exam requirements/recommendations for international students: required—TOEFL. Electronic applications accepted.

University of Michigan, Rackham Graduate School, School of Music, Theatre, and Dance, Program in Performance, Ann Arbor, MI 48109-2085. Offers MM, A Mus D, Spec M. *Degree requirements:* For doctorate, one foreign language, thesis/dissertation, 3 concerts, oral exam. *Entrance requirements:* For doctorate, audition. Additional exam requirements/recommendations for international students: required—TOEFL. Electronic applications accepted.

University of Michigan–Flint, Graduate Programs, Program in Arts Administration, Flint, MI 48502-1950. Offers performance (MA), including museum and visual arts, performance. *Program availability:* Part-time. *Faculty:* 7 full-time (3 women), 11 part-time/adjunct (7 women). *Students:* 11 part-time (7 women); includes 5 minority (4 Black or African American, non-Hispanic/Latino; 1 Asian, non-Hispanic/Latino). Average age 40. 11 applicants, 82% accepted, 2 enrolled. In 2019, 2 master's awarded. *Degree requirements:* For master's, thesis. *Entrance requirements:* For master's, bachelor degree in the arts (visual art, theatre, dance, music, etc.) from regionally-accredited institution; minimum cumulative undergraduate GPA of 3.0 on 4.0 scale. Additional exam requirements/recommendations for international students: required—TOEFL (minimum score 84 iBT), IELTS (minimum score 6.5). *Application deadline:* For fall admission, 8/1 for domestic students, 5/1 for international students; for winter admission, 11/15 for domestic students, 10/1 for international students. Applications are processed on a rolling basis. Application fee: $55. Electronic applications accepted. *Expenses:* Contact institution. *Financial support:* Federal Work-Study, institutionally sponsored loans, scholarships/grants, and unspecified assistantships available. Support available to part-time students. Financial award application deadline: 3/1; financial award applicants required to submit FAFSA. *Unit head:* Nicole Broughton, Director, 810-237-6522, E-mail: broughn@umflint.edu. *Application contact:* Matt Bohlen, Associate Director of Graduate Admissions, 810-762-3171, Fax: 810-766-6789, E-mail: mbohlen@umflint.edu. Website: http://www.umflint.edu/graduateprograms/arts-administration-ma

University of Minnesota, Duluth, Graduate School, School of Fine Arts, Department of Music, Duluth, MN 55812-2496. Offers music education (MM); performance (MM). *Accreditation:* NASM. *Program availability:* Part-time. *Degree requirements:* For master's, comprehensive exam, thesis (for some programs), recital (MM in performance). *Entrance requirements:* For master's, audition, minimum GPA of 3.0, sample of written work, interview, bachelor's degree in music, video of teaching. Additional exam requirements/recommendations for international students: required—TOEFL (minimum score 550 paper-based).

University of Minnesota, Twin Cities Campus, Graduate School, College of Liberal Arts, School of Music, Minneapolis, MN 55455-0213. Offers MA, MM, DMA, PhD. *Accreditation:* NASM. *Degree requirements:* For master's, comprehensive exam, thesis (for some programs), foreign language (MA), recital (MM); for doctorate, comprehensive exam, 5 recitals (DMA); 2 foreign languages or computer languages, dissertation (PhD). *Entrance requirements:* For master's, GRE (MA); for doctorate, GRE (PhD). Additional exam requirements/recommendations for international students: required—TOEFL (minimum score 550 paper-based; 79 iBT: 21 writing, 19 reading), IELTS (minimum score 6.5). Electronic applications accepted.

Music

University of Mississippi, Graduate School, College of Liberal Arts, University, MS 38677. Offers anthropology (MA); biology (MS, PhD); chemistry (MS, DA, PhD); creative writing (MFA); documentary expression (MFA); economics (MA, PhD); English (MA, PhD); experimental psychology (PhD); history (MA, PhD); mathematics (MS, PhD); modern languages (MA); music (MM); philosophy (MA); physics (MA, MS, PhD); political science (MA, PhD); Southern studies (MA); studio art (MFA). *Program availability:* Part-time. *Faculty:* 481 full-time (215 women), 71 part-time/adjunct (40 women). *Students:* 509 full-time (258 women), 55 part-time (21 women); includes 89 minority (40 Black or African American, non-Hispanic/Latino; 13 Asian, non-Hispanic/Latino; 25 Hispanic/Latino; 11 Two or more races, non-Hispanic/Latino), 157 international. Average age 29. In 2019, 119 master's, 51 doctorates awarded. *Degree requirements:* For doctorate, thesis/dissertation. *Entrance requirements:* For master's, GRE General Test, minimum GPA of 3.0; for doctorate, GRE General Test. Additional exam requirements/recommendations for international students: required—TOEFL. *Application deadline:* Applications are processed on a rolling basis. Application fee: $50. Electronic applications accepted. *Expenses:* Tuition, state resident: full-time $8718; part-time $484.25 per credit hour. Tuition, nonresident: full-time $24,990; part-time $1388.25 per credit hour. *Required fees:* $100; $4.16 per credit hour. *Financial support:* Fellowships, research assistantships, teaching assistantships, career-related internships or fieldwork, Federal Work-Study, institutionally sponsored loans, scholarships/grants, and unspecified assistantships available. Financial award application deadline: 3/1; financial award applicants required to submit FAFSA. *Unit head:* Dr. Lee Michael Cohen, Dean, 662-915-7177, Fax: 662-915-5792, E-mail: libarts@olemiss.edu. *Application contact:* Tameka Smith, Graduate Activities Specialist for Admissions, 662-915-7474, Fax: 662-915-7577, E-mail: gschool@olemiss.edu.
Website: ventress@olemiss.edu

University of Missouri, Office of Research and Graduate Studies, College of Arts and Science, School of Music, Columbia, MO 65211. Offers MA, Certificate. *Accreditation:* NASM. *Entrance requirements:* For master's, minimum GPA of 3.0. Additional exam requirements/recommendations for international students: required—TOEFL.

University of Missouri–Kansas City, Conservatory of Music and Dance, Kansas City, MO 64110-2499. Offers composition (MM, DMA); conducting (MM, DMA); music (MA); music education (MME, PhD); music history and literature (MM); music theory (MM); music therapy (MA); performance (MM, DMA). *Accreditation:* NASM. *Program availability:* Part-time. *Degree requirements:* For master's, variable foreign language requirement, comprehensive exam, thesis (for some programs); for doctorate, variable foreign language requirement, comprehensive exam, thesis/dissertation or alternative. *Entrance requirements:* For master's, minimum GPA of 3.0 in major, auditions (for MM in performance); for doctorate, minimum graduate GPA of 3.5, auditions (for DMA in performance), portfolio of compositions. Additional exam requirements/recommendations for international students: required—TOEFL (minimum score 550 paper-based; 80 iBT).

University of Mobile, Graduate Studies, Programs in Piano and Vocal Performance, Mobile, AL 36613. Offers piano performance (MM); vocal performance (MM, DMA). *Program availability:* Part-time. *Degree requirements:* For master's, comprehensive exam, thesis; for doctorate, comprehensive exam, thesis/dissertation. Electronic applications accepted.

University of Montana, Graduate School, College of Visual and Performing Arts, School of Music, Missoula, MT 59812. Offers performance (MM). *Accreditation:* NASM. *Entrance requirements:* For master's, GRE General Test, GRE Subject Test, portfolio.

University of Nebraska at Omaha, Graduate Studies, College of Communication, Fine Arts and Media, School of Music, Omaha, NE 68182. Offers MM. *Accreditation:* NASM. *Program availability:* Part-time, evening/weekend. *Degree requirements:* For master's, comprehensive exam (for some programs), thesis (for some programs). *Entrance requirements:* For master's, departmental diagnostic exam, minimum GPA of 3.0, resume, transcripts. Additional exam requirements/recommendations for international students: required—TOEFL, IELTS, PTE. Electronic applications accepted.

University of Nebraska–Lincoln, Graduate College, College of Fine and Performing Arts, School of Music, Lincoln, NE 68588. Offers composition (MM, DMA); conducting (MM, DMA); music education (MM, PhD); music history (MM); music theory (MM); performance (MM, DMA); piano pedagogy (MM); woodwind specialties (MM). *Accreditation:* NASM. *Degree requirements:* For master's, thesis optional; for doctorate, comprehensive exam, thesis/dissertation. *Entrance requirements:* For master's and doctorate, audition. Additional exam requirements/recommendations for international students: required—TOEFL. Electronic applications accepted.

University of Nevada, Las Vegas, Graduate College, College of Fine Arts, School of Music, Las Vegas, NV 89154-5025. Offers K-12 music (Certificate); music (MM); musical arts (DMA). *Accreditation:* NASM. *Program availability:* Part-time. *Faculty:* 27 full-time (8 women), 13 part-time/adjunct (5 women). *Students:* 61 full-time (30 women), 30 part-time (19 women); includes 22 minority (8 Black or African American, non-Hispanic/Latino; 5 Asian, non-Hispanic/Latino; 5 Hispanic/Latino; 4 Two or more races, non-Hispanic/Latino), 18 international. Average age 33. 59 applicants, 81% accepted, 27 enrolled. In 2019, 16 master's, 6 doctorates awarded. *Degree requirements:* For master's, oral and/or written comprehensive exam; for doctorate, one foreign language, comprehensive exam, thesis/dissertation, lecture-recital and document. *Entrance requirements:* For master's, placement examinations, bachelor's degree with minimum GPA 3.0; statement of purpose; 2 letters of recommendation; portfolio of compositions; for doctorate, music history placement exam, music theory and aural skills/sight-singing placement examination, master's degree in music; for Certificate, PRAXIS I Pre-Professional Skills Test, bachelor's degree. Additional exam requirements/recommendations for international students: required—TOEFL (minimum score 550 paper-based; 80 iBT), IELTS (minimum score 7). *Application deadline:* For fall admission, 5/1 for domestic and international students; for spring admission, 11/15 for domestic students, 10/1 for international students; for summer admission, 5/15 for domestic students, 3/1 for international students. Application fee: $60 ($95 for international students). Electronic applications accepted. *Expenses:* Contact institution. *Financial support:* In 2019–20, 40 students received support, including 3 research assistantships with full tuition reimbursements available (averaging $15,000 per year), 37 teaching assistantships with full tuition reimbursements available (averaging $13,885 per year); institutionally sponsored loans, scholarships/grants, health care benefits, and unspecified assistantships also available. Financial award application deadline: 3/15; financial award applicants required to submit FAFSA. *Unit head:* Dr. Susan Mueller, Chair/Professor, 702-895-5776, Fax: 702-895-4239, E-mail: music.chair@unlv.edu. *Application contact:* Dr. Richard Miller, Graduate Coordinator, 702-895-3332, E-mail: music.gradcoord@unlv.edu.
Website: http://music.unlv.edu/

University of Nevada, Reno, Graduate School, College of Liberal Arts, Department of Music, Reno, NV 89557. Offers MA, MM. *Accreditation:* NASM. *Degree requirements:* For master's, thesis optional. *Entrance requirements:* For master's, minimum GPA of 2.75. Additional exam requirements/recommendations for international students: required—TOEFL (minimum score 500 paper-based; 61 iBT), IELTS (minimum score 6). Electronic applications accepted.

University of New Hampshire, Graduate School, College of Liberal Arts, Department of Music, Durham, NH 03824. Offers music composition (MA); music conducting (MA); musicology (MA). *Accreditation:* NASM. *Students:* 6 full-time (3 women), 1 part-time (0 women); includes 1 minority (Asian, non-Hispanic/Latino), 1 international. Average age 30. 7 applicants, 71% accepted, 4 enrolled. In 2019, 4 master's awarded. *Entrance requirements:* For master's, entrance exam, writing sample, portfolio, audition. Additional exam requirements/recommendations for international students: required—TOEFL (minimum score 550 paper-based; 80 iBT), IELTS, PTE. *Application deadline:* For fall admission, 7/1 for domestic students, 4/1 for international students; for spring admission, 12/1 for domestic students. Application fee: $65. Electronic applications accepted. *Financial support:* In 2019–20, 6 students received support, including 4 teaching assistantships; fellowships, research assistantships, career-related internships or fieldwork, Federal Work-Study, scholarships/grants, and tuition waivers (full and partial) also available. Support available to part-time students. Financial award application deadline: 2/15. *Unit head:* Robert Haskins, Chair, 603-862-3987. *Application contact:* Alexis Zaricki, Administrative Assistant, 603-862-2418, E-mail: grad.music@unh.edu.
Website: http://cola.unh.edu/music

University of New Mexico, Graduate Studies, College of Fine Arts, Program in Music, Albuquerque, NM 87131-0001. Offers collaborative piano (M Mu); conducting (M Mu); music education (M Mu); music history and literature (M Mu); performance (M Mu); theory and composition (M Mu). *Accreditation:* NASM. *Program availability:* Part-time. *Degree requirements:* For master's, variable foreign language requirement, comprehensive exam, thesis (for some programs), recital (for some programs). *Entrance requirements:* For master's, placement exams in music history and theory. Additional exam requirements/recommendations for international students: required—TOEFL (minimum score 550 paper-based). Electronic applications accepted. *Expenses:* Tuition, state resident: full-time $7633; part-time $972 per year. Tuition, nonresident: full-time $22,586; part-time $3840 per year. *International tuition:* $23,292 full-time. *Required fees:* $8608. Tuition and fees vary according to course level, course load, degree level, program and student level.

University of New Orleans, Graduate School, College of Liberal Arts, Education and Human Development, Department of Music, New Orleans, LA 70148. Offers MM. *Accreditation:* NASM. *Program availability:* Evening/weekend. *Degree requirements:* For master's, recital. *Entrance requirements:* For master's, GRE General Test, audition. Additional exam requirements/recommendations for international students: required—TOEFL (minimum score 550 paper-based; 79 iBT), IELTS (minimum score 6.5). Electronic applications accepted.

The University of North Carolina at Chapel Hill, Graduate School, College of Arts and Sciences, Department of Music, Chapel Hill, NC 27599. Offers MA, PhD. Terminal master's awarded for partial completion of doctoral program. *Degree requirements:* For master's, one foreign language, thesis, theory and keyboard exams; for doctorate, 2 foreign languages, comprehensive exam, thesis/dissertation, theory and keyboard exams. *Entrance requirements:* For master's and doctorate, GRE General Test, department diagnostic exam, minimum GPA of 3.0. Additional exam requirements/recommendations for international students: required—TOEFL. Electronic applications accepted. *Expenses:* Contact institution.

The University of North Carolina at Charlotte, College of Arts and Architecture, Department of Music, Charlotte, NC 28223-0001. Offers vocal pedagogy (Graduate Certificate). *Accreditation:* NASM. *Program availability:* Part-time. *Faculty:* 2 full-time (1 woman). *Entrance requirements:* For degree, placement tests in music theory, ear training, and piano; diagnostic vocal pedagogy exam, bachelor's degree in music from accredited university or conservatory; official transcripts; formal audition. Additional exam requirements/recommendations for international students: required—TOEFL (minimum score 557 paper-based; 83 iBT), IELTS (minimum score 6.5), TOEFL (minimum score 557 paper-based, 83 iBT) or IELTS (6.5). *Application deadline:* Applications are processed on a rolling basis. Application fee: $75. Electronic applications accepted. *Expenses:* Tuition, state resident: full-time $4337. Tuition, nonresident: full-time $17,771. *Required fees:* $3093. Tuition and fees vary according to course load, degree level and program. *Financial support:* Career-related internships or fieldwork and unspecified assistantships available. Financial award application deadline: 3/1; financial award applicants required to submit FAFSA. *Unit head:* Dr. Fred P. Spano, Interim Chair, 704-687-0263, E-mail: jagrymes@uncc.edu. *Application contact:* Kathy B. Giddings, Director of Graduate Admissions, 704-687-5503, Fax: 704-687-1668, E-mail: gradadm@uncc.edu.
Website: http://coaa.uncc.edu/academics/department-of-music

The University of North Carolina at Greensboro, Graduate School, School of Music, Theatre and Dance, Greensboro, NC 27412-5001. Offers composition (MM); dance (MA, MFA); education (MM); music education (PhD); performance (MM, DMA); theatre (M Ed, MFA), including acting (MFA), design (MFA), directing (MFA), theatre education (M Ed), theatre for youth (MFA); theory (MM). *Accreditation:* NASM. *Degree requirements:* For master's, variable foreign language requirement, thesis (for some programs), recital; for doctorate, comprehensive exam, thesis/dissertation, diagnostic exam, recital. *Entrance requirements:* For master's, GRE General Test, NTE, audition; for doctorate, GRE General Test, GRE Subject Test (music), audition. Additional exam requirements/recommendations for international students: required—TOEFL. Electronic applications accepted.

University of North Carolina School of the Arts, School of Filmmaking, Winston-Salem, NC 27127-2738. Offers creative producing (MFA); film music composition (MFA); screenwriting (MFA). *Entrance requirements:* For master's, audition, performance, portfolio, interview. Additional exam requirements/recommendations for international students: required—TOEFL. Electronic applications accepted.

University of North Carolina School of the Arts, School of Music, Winston-Salem, NC 27127-2738. Offers music (Artist Certificate); music performance (MM), including chamber music performance; vocal performance (MM). *Entrance requirements:* For master's, audition (music performance), interview, original score. Additional exam requirements/recommendations for international students: required—TOEFL. Electronic applications accepted.

University of North Dakota, Graduate School, College of Arts and Sciences, Department of Music, Grand Forks, ND 58202. Offers music (MM); music education (PhD). *Accreditation:* NASM. *Program availability:* Part-time. *Degree requirements:* For master's, comprehensive exam, thesis or alternative. *Entrance requirements:* For master's, minimum GPA of 3.0. Additional exam requirements/recommendations for international students: required—TOEFL (minimum score 550 paper-based; 79 iBT), IELTS (minimum score 6.5). Electronic applications accepted.

University of Northern Colorado, Graduate School, College of Performing and Visual Arts, School of Music, Greeley, CO 80639. Offers collaborative piano (MM, DA); composition (DA); conducting (MM, DA); instrumental performance (MM); jazz studies (MM, DA); music education (MM, DA); music history and literature (MM, DA); music theory and composition (MM); performance (DA); vocal performance (MM).

Accreditation: NASM; NCATE (one or more programs are accredited). *Program availability:* Part-time. *Degree requirements:* For master's, comprehensive exam, thesis or alternative; for doctorate, comprehensive exam, thesis/dissertation. *Entrance requirements:* For master's, audition; for doctorate, GRE General Test, audition, 3 letters of recommendation. Electronic applications accepted.

University of Northern Iowa, Graduate College, College of Humanities, Arts and Sciences, School of Music, MA Program in Music, Cedar Falls, IA 50614. Offers MA. *Accreditation:* NASM. *Degree requirements:* For master's, comprehensive exam, thesis or alternative. *Entrance requirements:* For master's, written diagnostic exam in theory, music history, expository writing skills, and in the area of claimed competency, portfolio, tape recordings of compositions, in-person auditions, minimum GPA of 3.0. Additional exam requirements/recommendations for international students: required—TOEFL (minimum score 500 paper-based; 61 iBT). Electronic applications accepted.

University of Northern Iowa, Graduate College, College of Humanities, Arts and Sciences, School of Music, MM Program in Composition, Cedar Falls, IA 50614. Offers MM. *Degree requirements:* For master's, comprehensive exam. *Entrance requirements:* For master's, portfolio, recordings of compositions.

University of Northern Iowa, Graduate College, College of Humanities, Arts and Sciences, School of Music, MM Program in Conducting, Cedar Falls, IA 50614. Offers MM. *Degree requirements:* For master's, comprehensive exam. *Entrance requirements:* For master's, audition, interview.

University of Northern Iowa, Graduate College, College of Humanities, Arts and Sciences, School of Music, MM Program in Music History, Cedar Falls, IA 50614. Offers MM. *Entrance requirements:* For master's, scholarly paper.

University of Northern Iowa, Graduate College, College of Humanities, Arts and Sciences, School of Music, MM Program in Performance, Cedar Falls, IA 50614. Offers percussion (MM); piano/organ (MM); strings (MM); voice (MM); woodwind (MM). *Degree requirements:* For master's, comprehensive exam. *Entrance requirements:* For master's, audition.

University of Northern Iowa, Graduate College, College of Humanities, Arts and Sciences, School of Music, MM Program in Piano Performance and Pedagogy, Cedar Falls, IA 50614. Offers MM.

University of North Texas, Toulouse Graduate School, Denton, TX 76203-5459. Offers accounting (MS); applied anthropology (MA, MS); applied behavior analysis (Certificate); applied geography (MA); applied technology and performance improvement (M Ed, MS); art education (MA); art history (MA); arts leadership (Certificate); audiology (Au D); behavior analysis (MS); behavioral science (PhD); biochemistry and molecular biology (MS); biology (MA, MS); biomedical engineering (MS); business analysis (MS); chemistry (MS); clinical health psychology (PhD); communication studies (MA, MS); computer engineering (MS); computer science (MS); counseling (M Ed, MS), including clinical mental health counseling (MS), college and university counseling, elementary school counseling, secondary school counseling; creative writing (MA); criminal justice (MS); curriculum and instruction (M Ed); decision sciences (MBA); design (MA, MFA), including fashion design (MFA), innovation studies, interior design (MFA); early childhood studies (MS); economics (MS); educational leadership (M Ed, Ed D); educational psychology (MS, PhD), including family studies (MS), gifted and talented (MS), human development (MS), learning and cognition (MS), research, measurement and evaluation (MS); electrical engineering (MS); emergency management (MPA); engineering technology (MS); English (MA); English as a second language (MA); environmental science (MS); finance (MBA, MS); financial management (MPA); French (MA); health services management (MBA); higher education (M Ed, Ed D); history (MA, MS); hospitality management (MS); human resources management (MPA); information science (MS); information systems (PhD); information technologies (MBA); interdisciplinary studies (MA, MS); international studies (MA); international sustainable tourism (MS); jazz studies (MM); journalism (MA, MJ, Graduate Certificate), including interactive and virtual digital communication (Graduate Certificate), narrative journalism (Graduate Certificate), public relations (Graduate Certificate); kinesiology (MS); linguistics (MA); local government management (MPA); logistics (PhD); logistics and supply chain management (MBA); long-term care, senior housing, and aging services (MA); management (PhD); marketing (MBA); mathematics (MA, MS); mechanical and energy engineering (MS, PhD); music (MA), including ethnomusicology, music theory, musicology, performance; music composition (PhD); music education (MM Ed, PhD); nonprofit management (MPA); operations and supply chain management (MBA); performance (MM, DMA); philosophy (MA); political science (MA); professional and technical communication (MA); radio, television and film (MA, MFA); rehabilitation counseling (Certificate); sociology (MA); Spanish (MA); special education (M Ed); speech-language pathology (MA); strategic management (MBA); studio art (MFA); teaching (M Ed); MBA/MS. *Program availability:* Part-time, evening/weekend, online learning. Terminal master's awarded for partial completion of doctoral program. *Degree requirements:* For master's, variable foreign language requirement, comprehensive exam (for some programs), thesis (for some programs); for doctorate, variable foreign language requirement, comprehensive exam (for some programs), thesis/dissertation; for other advanced degree, variable foreign language requirement, comprehensive exam (for some programs). *Entrance requirements:* For master's and doctorate, GRE, GMAT. Additional exam requirements/recommendations for international students: required—TOEFL (minimum score 550 paper-based; 79 iBT). Electronic applications accepted.

University of Oklahoma, Weitzenhoffer Family College of Fine Arts, School of Music, Norman, OK 73019. Offers choral conducting (M Mus), including church music (M Mus, DMA), standard; composition (M Mus); conducting (M Mus Ed, DMA), including choral (M Mus Ed), choral conducting (DMA), church music (M Mus, DMA), instrumental (M Mus Ed), orchestral conducting (DMA), wind conducting (DMA); general (M Mus Ed), including Kodaly concepts (M Mus Ed, PhD), vocal/general; instrumental (M Mus Ed), including primary instrument, secondary instrument; instrumental conducting (M Mus); music composition (DMA); music education (PhD), including choral or wind instrument conducting, general, Kodaly concepts (M Mus Ed, PhD), piano pedagogy; music performance (Graduate Certificate); music theory (M Mus); musicology (M Mus); organ (M Mus, DMA), including church music, organ - standard (DMA), organ technology (M Mus), standard (M Mus); piano (M Mus, DMA), including performance, performance and pedagogy; piano pedagogy (M Mus Ed); voice (M Mus, DMA), including opera (M Mus), performance; wind/percussion/string (M Mus); wind/percussion/string instruments (DMA), including performance (M Mus, DMA). *Accreditation:* NASM. *Degree requirements:* For master's, variable foreign language requirement, comprehensive exam (for some programs), thesis (for some programs), final recital (for M Mus performance, conducting, and composition degrees); for doctorate, variable foreign language requirement, comprehensive exam, thesis/dissertation, three recitals and/or workshops (two recitals for DMA in composition); for Graduate Certificate, variable foreign language requirement, two recitals. *Entrance requirements:* For master's, bachelor's degree in music, music education, or the equivalent; transcripts; resume; personal statement; 3 letters of recommendation; audition and/or other practical application materials as appropriate to intended degree; sample of scholarly writing (for M Mus in musicology and in music theory); for doctorate, master's degree in music, music education, or the equivalent; transcripts; resume; personal statement; 3 letters of recommendation; sample of scholarly writing; audition and/or other practical application materials as appropriate to intended degree; for Graduate Certificate, bachelor's degree in music, music education, or the equivalent; transcripts; resume; personal statement; 3 letters of recommendation; audition. Additional exam requirements/recommendations for international students: required—TOEFL (minimum score 79 iBT) or IELTS (minimum score 6.5). Electronic applications accepted. *Expenses:* Tuition, state resident: full-time $6583.20; part-time $274.30 per credit hour. Tuition, nonresident: full-time $21,242; part-time $885.10 per credit hour. *International tuition:* $21,242.40 full-time. *Required fees:* $1994.20; $72.55 per credit hour. $126.50 per semester. Tuition and fees vary according to course load and degree level.

University of Oregon, Graduate School, School of Music, Program in Music, Eugene, OR 97403. Offers composition (M Mus, DMA, PhD); conducting (M Mus); jazz studies (M Mus); music (MA), including music history, music theory; music history (PhD); music theory (PhD); performance (M Mus, DMA); piano pedagogy (M Mus). *Entrance requirements:* For master's, minimum GPA of 3.0, audition (performance applicants), videotape or interview (conducting applicants); for doctorate, GRE General Test, minimum GPA of 3.0, audition (performance applicants), videotape or interview (conducting applicants). Additional exam requirements/recommendations for international students: required—TOEFL.

University of Ottawa, Faculty of Graduate and Postdoctoral Studies, Faculty of Arts, Department of Music, Ottawa, ON K1N 6N5, Canada. Offers music (M Mus, MA); orchestral studies (Certificate); piano pedagogy research (Certificate). *Degree requirements:* For master's, thesis optional. *Entrance requirements:* For master's, honors degree or equivalent, minimum B+ average. Electronic applications accepted.

University of Pennsylvania, School of Arts and Sciences, Graduate Group in Music, Philadelphia, PA 19104. Offers AM, PhD. *Faculty:* 13 full-time (5 women), 2 part-time/adjunct (0 women). *Students:* 31 full-time (16 women); includes 2 minority (1 Black or African American, non-Hispanic/Latino; 1 Asian, non-Hispanic/Latino), 10 international. Average age 30. 80 applicants, 6% accepted, 2 enrolled. In 2019, 2 master's, 6 doctorates awarded. Terminal master's awarded for partial completion of doctoral program. Application fee: $80.
Website: http://www.sas.upenn.edu/graduate-division

University of Pittsburgh, Kenneth P. Dietrich School of Arts and Sciences, Department of Music, Pittsburgh, PA 15260. Offers composition and theory (PhD); ethnomusicology (PhD); historical musicology (PhD); jazz studies (PhD); music (MA). *Faculty:* 16 full-time (7 women), 3 part-time/adjunct (1 woman). *Students:* 40 full-time (15 women); includes 7 minority (3 Black or African American, non-Hispanic/Latino; 4 Two or more races, non-Hispanic/Latino), 11 international. Average age 33. 63 applicants, 10% accepted, 5 enrolled. In 2019, 2 master's, 5 doctorates awarded. Terminal master's awarded for partial completion of doctoral program. *Degree requirements:* For master's, variable foreign language requirement, comprehensive exam, thesis; for doctorate, variable foreign language requirement, comprehensive exam, thesis/dissertation. *Entrance requirements:* Additional exam requirements/recommendations for international students: required—TOEFL (minimum score 90 iBT), IELTS (minimum score 7). *Application deadline:* For fall admission, 1/5 for domestic and international students. Application fee: $50. Electronic applications accepted. *Financial support:* In 2019–20, 30 students received support, including 23 fellowships with full tuition reimbursements available (averaging $20,709 per year), 1 teaching assistantship with full tuition reimbursement available (averaging $18,910 per year); health care benefits and unspecified assistantships also available. Financial award application deadline: 1/5. *Unit head:* Dr. Mathew Rosenblum, Professor and Chair, 412-624-4199, Fax: 412-624-4186, E-mail: rosenblu@pitt.edu. *Application contact:* Dr. Amy Williams, Associate Professor, 412-624-4120, Fax: 412-624-4186, E-mail: amywill@pitt.edu.
Website: http://www.music.pitt.edu/

University of Redlands, College of Arts and Sciences, School of Music, Redlands, CA 92373-0999. Offers MM. *Accreditation:* NASM. *Program availability:* Part-time. *Degree requirements:* For master's, comprehensive exam, thesis, 3 recitals, major conducted ensemble. *Entrance requirements:* For master's, GRE, bachelor's degree in music, minimum GPA of 2.75, audition, original scores. Additional exam requirements/recommendations for international students: required—TOEFL (minimum score 550 paper-based). *Expenses:* Contact institution.

University of Regina, Faculty of Graduate Studies and Research, Faculty of Media, Art, and Performance, Department of Music, Regina, SK S4S 0A2, Canada. Offers composition (MMus); conducting (MMus); music theory (MA); musicology (MA); performance (MMus), including piano, organ, voice, and orchestral instruments. *Program availability:* Part-time. *Faculty:* 8 full-time (4 women). *Students:* 3 full-time (all women), 1 (woman) part-time. Average age 30. 5 applicants. In 2019, 2 master's awarded. *Degree requirements:* For master's, thesis (for some programs), recital, oral exam, jury examinations. *Entrance requirements:* For master's, B Mus or equivalent; recent compositions (composers only); audition; singing ability in French, Italian, German (vocalists only); DVDs; scores. Additional exam requirements/recommendations for international students: required—TOEFL (minimum score 600 paper-based; 92 iBT), IELTS (minimum score 6.5), PTE (minimum score 65), other options are CAEL, MELAB, Cantest and U of R ESL. *Application deadline:* For fall admission, 1/15 for domestic and international students. Application fee: $100 Canadian dollars. Electronic applications accepted. *Expenses: Tuition:* Full-time $6684 Canadian dollars. *Required fees:* $100 Canadian dollars; $3351.45 Canadian dollars per trimester. $1117.15 Canadian dollars per semester. Tuition and fees vary according to course level, course load, degree level and program. *Financial support:* Fellowships, research assistantships, teaching assistantships, career-related internships or fieldwork, Federal Work-Study, scholarships/grants, unspecified assistantships, and travel award and Graduate Scholarship Base Funds available. Support available to part-time students. Financial award application deadline: 9/30. *Unit head:* Brent Ghiglione, Department Head, 306-585-5542, Fax: 306-585-5549, E-mail: brent.ghiglione@uregina.ca. *Application contact:* Dr. Helen Pridmore, Graduate Coordinator in Music, 306-585-5540, Fax: 306-585-5544, E-mail: helen.pridmore@uregina.ca.

University of Rhode Island, Graduate School, College of Arts and Sciences, Department of Music, Kingston, RI 02881. Offers music education (MM), including composition, conducting, performance, thesis; music performance (MM), including composition, conducting, voice or instrument. *Accreditation:* NASM. *Program availability:* Part-time. *Faculty:* 14 full-time (6 women). *Students:* 8 full-time (0 women), 2 part-time (both women); includes 1 minority (Black or African American, non-Hispanic/Latino). 8 applicants, 88% accepted, 5 enrolled. In 2019, 4 master's awarded. *Entrance requirements:* For master's, 2 letters of recommendation, audition. Additional exam requirements/recommendations for international students: required—TOEFL. *Application deadline:* For fall admission, 7/15 for domestic students, 2/1 for international students; for spring admission, 11/15 for domestic students, 7/15 for international students. Application fee: $65. Electronic applications accepted. *Expenses: Tuition, area resident:* Full-time $13,734; part-time $763 per credit. Tuition, state resident: full-time $13,734; part-time $763 per credit. Tuition, nonresident: full-time $26,512; part-time $1473 per credit. *International tuition:* $26,512 full-time. *Required fees:* $1780; $52 per credit. $35 per term. One-time fee: $165. *Financial support:* In 2019–20, 3 teaching assistantships with tuition reimbursements (averaging $18,986 per year) were awarded. Financial award application deadline: 2/1; financial award applicants required to submit FAFSA. *Unit head:* Dr. Mark Conley, Chair, 401-874-2431, E-mail: mconley@uri.edu. *Application contact:* Dr. Mark Conley, Department Chair, E-mail: mconley@uri.edu. Website: https://web.uri.edu/music/

University of Rochester, Eastman School of Music, Program in Ethnomusicology, Rochester, NY 14627. Offers MA.

University of Rochester, Eastman School of Music, Program in Music Theory Pedagogy, Rochester, NY 14627. Offers MA.

University of Rochester, Eastman School of Music, Programs in Music Composition, Rochester, NY 14627. Offers MA, MM, DMA, PhD.

University of Rochester, Eastman School of Music, Programs in Musicology, Rochester, NY 14627. Offers PhD.

University of Rochester, Eastman School of Music, Programs in Music Theory, Rochester, NY 14627. Offers PhD.

University of St. Thomas, College of Arts and Sciences, Graduate Programs in Music Education, St. Paul, MN 55105-1096. Offers choral (MA); instrumental (MA); Kodaly (MA); leadership in music education (Ed D); Orff Schulwerk (MA); piano pedagogy (MA). *Accreditation:* NASM; NCATE. *Program availability:* Part-time. *Degree requirements:* For master's, comprehensive exam, thesis, music history theory and diagnostic exam, piano recital (for piano pedagogy students), oral exam. *Entrance requirements:* For master's, performance assessment hearing, interview. Additional exam requirements/recommendations for international students: required—TOEFL (minimum score 550 paper-based; 80 iBT). Electronic applications accepted. *Expenses:* Contact institution.

University of St. Thomas, School of Arts and Sciences, Houston, TX 77006-4696. Offers public policy administration (MPPA); sacred music (MSM). *Program availability:* Part-time-only, evening/weekend. *Faculty:* 44 full-time (14 women), 49 part-time/adjunct (15 women). *Students:* 8 full-time (4 women), 94 part-time (67 women); includes 87 minority (1 Black or African American, non-Hispanic/Latino; 2 Asian, non-Hispanic/Latino; 84 Hispanic/Latino), 9 international. Average age 44. 164 applicants, 70% accepted, 58 enrolled. In 2019, 35 master's awarded. *Degree requirements:* For master's, Number of Foreign Languages-S, Comprehensive Exam -S, Thesis/Dissertation -A. *Entrance requirements:* For master's, Letters of recommendation required, undergraduate GPA of 3.0, essay requirement, transcripts from all undergraduate and graduate institutions, GRE/GMAT recommended but not required for most programs. Additional exam requirements/recommendations for international students: recommended—TOEFL, IELTS. *Application deadline:* For fall admission, 7/15 priority date for domestic and international students; for spring admission, 12/15 priority date for domestic and international students; for summer admission, 4/15 priority date for domestic and international students. Applications are processed on a rolling basis. Application fee: $35. Electronic applications accepted. Application fee is waived when completed online. *Expenses: Tuition:* Full-time $30,800; part-time $1163 per credit hour. *Required fees:* $250; $210 per semester. One-time fee: $660. Tuition and fees vary according to degree level and program. *Financial support:* Fellowships, research assistantships, teaching assistantships, career-related internships or fieldwork, Federal Work-Study, institutionally sponsored loans, scholarships/grants, tuition waivers, and unspecified assistantships available. Support available to part-time students. Financial award application deadline: 7/15; financial award applicants required to submit FAFSA. *Unit head:* George A. Harne, PhD, Executive Dean of the School of Arts and Sciences, 713-942-3419, E-mail: harneg@stthom.edu. *Application contact:* Christopher S Cheek, Graduate Admissions Manager, 713-525-3817, E-mail: cheekc@stthom.edu. Website: http://www.stthom.edu/Academics/School_of_Arts_and_Sciences/Index.aqf

University of Saskatchewan, College of Graduate and Postdoctoral Studies, College of Arts and Science, Department of Music, Saskatoon, SK S7N 5A2, Canada. Offers M Mus, MA. *Degree requirements:* For master's, thesis. *Entrance requirements:* Additional exam requirements/recommendations for international students: required—TOEFL (minimum score 80 iBT); recommended—IELTS (minimum score 6.5). Electronic applications accepted.

University of South Africa, College of Human Sciences, Pretoria, South Africa. Offers adult education (M Ed); African languages (MA, PhD); African politics (MA, PhD); Afrikaans (MA, PhD); ancient history (MA, PhD); ancient Near Eastern studies (MA, PhD); anthropology (MA, PhD); applied linguistics (MA); Arabic (MA, PhD); archaeology (MA); art history (MA); Biblical archaeology (MA); Biblical studies (M Th, D Th, PhD); Christian spirituality (M Th, D Th); church history (M Th, D Th); classical studies (MA, PhD); clinical psychology (MA); communication (MA, PhD); comparative education (M Ed, Ed D); consulting psychology (D Admin, D Com, PhD); curriculum studies (M Ed, Ed D); development studies (M Admin, MA, D Admin, PhD); didactics (M Ed, Ed D); education (M Tech); education management (M Ed, Ed D); educational psychology (M Ed); English (MA); environmental education (M Ed); French (MA, PhD); German (MA, PhD); Greek (MA); guidance and counseling (M Ed); health studies (MA, PhD), including health sciences education (MA), health services management (MA), medical and surgical nursing science (critical care general) (MA), midwifery and neonatal nursing science (MA), trauma and emergency care (MA); history (MA, PhD); history of education (Ed D); inclusive education (M Ed, Ed D); information and communications technology policy and regulation (MA); information science (MA, MIS, PhD); international politics (MA, PhD); Islamic studies (MA, PhD); Italian (MA, PhD); Judaica (MA, PhD); linguistics (MA, PhD); mathematical education (M Ed); mathematics education (MA); missiology (M Th, D Th); modern Hebrew (MA, PhD); musicology (MA, MMus, D Mus, PhD); natural science education (M Ed); New Testament (M Th, D Th); Old Testament (D Th); pastoral therapy (M Th, D Th); philosophy (MA); philosophy of education (M Ed, Ed D); politics (MA, PhD); Portuguese (MA, PhD); practical theology (M Th, D Th); psychology (MA, MS, PhD); psychology of education (M Ed, Ed D); public health (MA); religious studies (MA, D Th, PhD); Romance languages (MA); Russian (MA, PhD); Semitic languages (MA, PhD); social behavior studies in HIV/AIDS (MA); social science (mental health) (MA); social science in development studies (MA); social science in psychology (MA); social science in social work (MA); social science in sociology (MA); social work (MSW, DSW, PhD); socio-education (M Ed, Ed D); sociolinguistics (MA); sociology (MA, PhD); Spanish (MA, PhD); systematic theology (M Th, D Th); TESOL (teaching English to speakers of other languages) (MA); theological ethics (M Th, D Th); theory of literature (MA, PhD); urban ministries (D Th); urban ministry (M Th).

University of South Alabama, College of Arts and Sciences, Department of Music, Mobile, AL 36688-0002. Offers collaborative keyboard (MM); music education (MM); performance (MM). *Faculty:* 7 full-time (3 women), 1 part-time/adjunct (0 women). *Students:* 8 full-time (5 women), 1 part-time (0 women); includes 1 minority (Black or African American, non-Hispanic/Latino), 1 international. Average age 24. 5 applicants, 100% accepted, 4 enrolled. In 2019, 4 master's awarded. *Degree requirements:* For master's, comprehensive exam. *Entrance requirements:* For master's, GRE/GMAT. Additional exam requirements/recommendations for international students: required—TOEFL (minimum score 525 paper-based; 71 iBT). *Application deadline:* For fall admission, 7/1 priority date for domestic students, 6/1 priority date for international students; for spring admission, 12/1 priority date for domestic students, 11/1 priority date for international students; for summer admission, 5/1 priority date for domestic students, 4/1 priority date for international students. Applications are processed on a rolling basis. Application fee: $35. Electronic applications accepted. *Expenses: Tuition, area resident:* Part-time $442 per credit hour. Tuition, state resident: full-time $10,608; part-time $442 per credit hour. Tuition, nonresident: full-time $21,216; part-time $884 per credit hour. *Financial support:* Fellowships, research assistantships, teaching assistantships, career-related internships or fieldwork, Federal Work-Study, institutionally sponsored loans, scholarships/grants, and unspecified assistantships available. Support available to part-time students. Financial award application deadline: 3/31; financial award applicants required to submit FAFSA. *Unit head:* Dr. Laura Moore, Interim Chair, Music, 251-460-6136, E-mail: lauramoore@southalabama.edu. *Application contact:* Dr. Thomas Rowell, Graduate Coordinator, Music, 251-460-6136, E-mail: trowell@southalabama.edu. Website: http://www.southalabama.edu/colleges/music/

University of South Carolina, The Graduate School, School of Music, Columbia, SC 29208. Offers composition (MM, DMA); conducting (MM, DMA); jazz studies (MM); music education (MM Ed, PhD); music history (MM); music performance (Certificate); music theory (MM); opera theater (MM); performance (MM, DMA); piano pedagogy (MM, DMA). *Accreditation:* NASM. *Program availability:* Part-time. *Degree requirements:* For master's, 5 foreign languages, comprehensive exam, thesis (for some programs); for doctorate, one foreign language, comprehensive exam, thesis/dissertation; for Certificate, recitals. *Entrance requirements:* For master's and doctorate, GRE General Test or MAT, music diagnostic exam. Additional exam requirements/recommendations for international students: required—TOEFL (minimum score 570 paper-based). Electronic applications accepted. *Expenses:* Contact institution.

University of South Dakota, Graduate School, College of Fine Arts, Department of Music, Vermillion, SD 57069. Offers collaborative piano (MM); conducting (MM); history of musical instruments (MM); music education (MM); music history (MM); music performance (MM). *Accreditation:* NASM. *Degree requirements:* For master's, thesis or alternative. *Entrance requirements:* For master's, minimum GPA of 2.7, audition or performance tape. Additional exam requirements/recommendations for international students: required—TOEFL (minimum score 550 paper-based; 79 iBT). Electronic applications accepted.

University of Southern California, Graduate School, Thornton School of Music, Los Angeles, CA 90089. Offers brass performance (MM, DMA, Graduate Certificate); choral and sacred music (MM, DMA); classical guitar (MM, DMA, Graduate Certificate); composition (MM, DMA); early music (MA, DMA); harp performance (MM, DMA, Graduate Certificate); historical musicology (PhD); jazz studies (MM, DMA, Graduate Certificate); keyboard collaborative arts (MM, DMA, Graduate Certificate); music education (MM, DMA); organ performance (MM, DMA, Graduate Certificate); percussion performance (MM, DMA, Graduate Certificate); piano performance (MM, DMA, Graduate Certificate); scoring for motion pictures and television (Graduate Certificate); strings performance (MM, DMA, Graduate Certificate); studio jazz guitar (MM, DMA, Graduate Certificate); teaching music (MA); vocal arts (classical voice/opera) (MM, DMA, Graduate Certificate); woodwind performance (MM, DMA, Graduate Certificate). *Program availability:* Part-time, evening/weekend. Terminal master's awarded for partial completion of doctoral program. *Degree requirements:* For master's, variable foreign language requirement, comprehensive exam (for some programs), thesis (for some programs); for doctorate, variable foreign language requirement, comprehensive exam, thesis/dissertation (for some programs). *Entrance requirements:* For master's, GRE (for MA in early music and MM in music education); for doctorate, GRE (for DMA). Additional exam requirements/recommendations for international students: required—TOEFL (minimum score 560 paper-based; 83 iBT). Electronic applications accepted. *Expenses:* Contact institution.

University of Southern Maine, College of Arts, Humanities, and Social Sciences, School of Music, Portland, ME 04103. Offers composition (MM); conducting (MM); jazz studies (MM); music education (MM); performance (MM). *Accreditation:* NASM. *Expenses: Tuition, area resident:* Full-time $864; part-time $432 per credit hour. Tuition, state resident: full-time $864; part-time $432 per credit hour. Tuition, nonresident: full-time $2372; part-time $1186 per credit hour. *Required fees:* $141; $108 per credit hour. Tuition and fees vary according to course load.

University of Southern Mississippi, College of Arts and Sciences, School of Music, Hattiesburg, MS 39406-0001. Offers conducting (DMA); music education (MME); performance and pedagogy (DMA); piano accompanying (MM); theory (MM); woodwind performance and pedagogy (MM). *Accreditation:* NASM. *Program availability:* Blended/hybrid learning. *Students:* 83 full-time (43 women), 57 part-time (13 women); includes 20 minority (12 Black or African American, non-Hispanic/Latino; 1 American Indian or Alaska Native, non-Hispanic/Latino; 4 Hispanic/Latino; 3 Two or more races, non-Hispanic/Latino), 37 international. 103 applicants, 53% accepted, 24 enrolled. In 2019, 20 master's, 9 doctorates awarded. Terminal master's awarded for partial completion of doctoral program. *Degree requirements:* For master's, comprehensive exam, thesis (for some programs); for doctorate, comprehensive exam, thesis/dissertation. *Entrance requirements:* For master's, GRE General Test, minimum GPA of 2.75 in last 60 hours; for doctorate, GRE General Test, minimum GPA of 3.5. Additional exam requirements/recommendations for international students: required—TOEFL, IELTS. *Application deadline:* For fall admission, 6/1 for domestic students; for spring admission, 11/1 for domestic students; for summer admission, 3/1 for domestic students. Applications are processed on a rolling basis. Application fee: $60. *Expenses: Tuition, area resident:* Full-time $4393; part-time $488 per credit hour. Tuition, nonresident: full-time $5393; part-time $600 per credit hour. *Required fees:* $6 per semester. *Financial support:* Fellowships with full tuition reimbursements, research assistantships, teaching assistantships with full tuition reimbursements, Federal Work-Study, institutionally sponsored loans, scholarships/grants, health care benefits, tuition waivers (partial), and unspecified assistantships available. Financial award application deadline: 2/1; financial award applicants required to submit FAFSA. *Unit head:* Dr. Jay Dean, Director, 601-266-4001, E-mail: Jay.Dean@usm.edu. *Application contact:* Dr. Jay Dean, Director, 601-266-4001, E-mail: Jay.Dean@usm.edu. Website: https://www.usm.edu/music

University of South Florida, College of The Arts, School of Music, Tampa, FL 33620-9951. Offers MA, MM, PhD. *Accreditation:* NASM. *Program availability:* Part-time, evening/weekend. *Faculty:* 23 full-time (7 women), 1 part-time/adjunct (0 women). *Students:* 58 full-time (27 women), 18 part-time (9 women); includes 11 minority (3 Black or African American, non-Hispanic/Latino; 3 Hispanic/Latino; 5 Two or more races, non-Hispanic/Latino), 29 international. Average age 28. 76 applicants, 55% accepted, 28 enrolled. In 2019, 34 master's, 2 doctorates awarded. *Degree requirements:* For master's, comprehensive exam, thesis optional; for doctorate, comprehensive exam, thesis/dissertation. *Entrance requirements:* For master's, minimum GPA of 3.0 in upper-division courses and music courses for bachelor's degree; resume; three letters of recommendation; at least 2 years of K-12 music teaching experience (for MA in music education); audition or interview (for MM); for doctorate, GRE General Test, master's degree from accredited institution with minimum GPA of 3.5, 3.0 in upper-division undergraduate courses; at least 2 years of K-12 music teaching experience; interview with faculty; 3 letters of recommendation; academic writing sample; curriculum vitae; personal goals statement; 15-20 minute video of applicant teaching music. Additional

exam requirements/recommendations for international students: required—TOEFL, TOEFL (minimum score 550 paper-based; 79 iBT) or IELTS (minimum score 6.5). *Application deadline:* For fall admission, 2/15 priority date for domestic students, 2/1 for international students; for spring admission, 10/15 for domestic students, 9/15 for international students; for summer admission, 2/15 for domestic students, 1/15 for international students. Application fee: $30. Electronic applications accepted. *Financial support:* In 2019–20, 40 students received support, including 1 research assistantship with tuition reimbursement available (averaging $15,724 per year), 46 teaching assistantships with tuition reimbursements available (averaging $10,099 per year); unspecified assistantships also available. Financial award application deadline: 2/15. *Unit head:* Dr. Karen Bryan, Director, 813-974-2311, Fax: 813-974-8721, E-mail: kmbryan@usf.edu. *Application contact:* Dr. David Williams, Associate Director/ Associate Professor of Music Education, 813-974-9166, Fax: 813-974-8721, E-mail: davidw@usf.edu.
Website: http://music.arts.usf.edu/

The University of Tennessee, Graduate School, College of Arts and Sciences, School of Music, Knoxville, TN 37996. Offers accompanying (MM); choral conducting (MM); composition (MM); instrumental conducting (MM); jazz (MM); music education (MM); music theory (MM); musicology (MM); performance (MM); piano pedagogy and literature (MM). *Accreditation:* NASM. *Program availability:* Part-time. *Degree requirements:* For master's, thesis (for some programs). *Entrance requirements:* For master's, audition, minimum GPA of 2.7. Additional exam requirements/ recommendations for international students: required—TOEFL. Electronic applications accepted.

The University of Texas at Arlington, Graduate School, College of Liberal Arts, Department of Music, Arlington, TX 76019. Offers education (MM); performance (MM). *Accreditation:* NASM. *Program availability:* Part-time, evening/weekend. *Degree requirements:* For master's, comprehensive exam, thesis optional. *Entrance requirements:* For master's, GRE, 3 letters of recommendation, minimum GPA of 3.0 in last 60 hours of course work. Additional exam requirements/recommendations for international students: required—TOEFL (minimum score 550 paper-based). Electronic applications accepted.

The University of Texas at Austin, Graduate School, College of Fine Arts, Sarah and Ernest Butler School of Music, Austin, TX 78712-1111. Offers band and wind conducting (M Music, DMA); brass/woodwind/percussion (MM, DMA); chamber music (MM); choral conducting (MM, DMA); collaborative piano (MM, DMA); composition (MM, DMA), including composition, jazz, jazz (DMA); ethnomusicology (MM, PhD); literature and pedagogy (MM); music and human learning (MM, PhD); music and human learning (DMA), including jazz (MM, DMA), piano pedagogy; musicology (MM, PhD); opera performance (MM, DMA); orchestral conducting (MM, DMA); organ (MM), including sacred music; organ performance (MM, DMA); performance (MM), including jazz (MM, DMA); performance (DMA), including jazz (MM, DMA); piano (DMA), including jazz (MM, DMA); piano literature and pedagogy (MM); piano performance (MM, DMA); string performance (MM, DMA); theory (MM, PhD); vocal performance (MM, DMA); voice (DMA), including opera; voice performance pedagogy (DMA); woodwind, brass, percussion performance (MM). *Accreditation:* NASM. *Program availability:* Part-time. *Degree requirements:* For master's, one foreign language, comprehensive exam, thesis (for some programs), recital (performance or composition majors); for doctorate, one foreign language, comprehensive exam, thesis/dissertation (for some programs), recital (for performance or composition majors). *Entrance requirements:* For master's and doctorate, GRE General Test (except for performance or composition majors), audition (performance majors). Electronic applications accepted.

The University of Texas at El Paso, Graduate School, College of Liberal Arts, Department of Music, El Paso, TX 79968-0001. Offers music education (MM); music performance (MM). *Accreditation:* NASM. *Program availability:* Part-time, evening/ weekend. *Degree requirements:* For master's, thesis optional. *Entrance requirements:* For master's, audition, interview, letters of recommendation. Additional exam requirements/recommendations for international students: required—TOEFL; recommended—IELTS. Electronic applications accepted.

The University of Texas at San Antonio, College of Liberal and Fine Arts, Department of Music, San Antonio, TX 78249-0617. Offers MM. *Accreditation:* NASM. *Program availability:* Part-time. *Degree requirements:* For master's, comprehensive exam, thesis (for some programs). *Entrance requirements:* For master's, GRE, audition, 3 letters of recommendation. Additional exam requirements/recommendations for international students: required—TOEFL (minimum score 550 paper-based; 79 iBT), IELTS (minimum score 6.5). Electronic applications accepted.

The University of Texas Rio Grande Valley, College of Fine Arts, School of Music, Edinburg, TX 78539. Offers MM. *Accreditation:* NASM. *Faculty:* 20 full-time (6 women), 2 part-time/adjunct (0 women). *Students:* 13 full-time (4 women), 4 part-time (1 woman); includes 11 minority (all Hispanic/Latino), 4 international. Average age 30. 11 applicants, 64% accepted, 5 enrolled. In 2019, 5 master's awarded. *Entrance requirements:* Additional exam requirements/recommendations for international students: required—TOEFL or IELTS. *Expenses: Tuition, area resident:* Full-time $5959; part-time $440 per credit hour. Tuition, state resident: full-time $5959. Tuition, nonresident: full-time $5959. *International tuition:* $13,321 full-time. *Required fees:* $1169; $185 per credit hour.

The University of the Arts, College of Performing Arts, School of Music, Program in Jazz Studies, Philadelphia, PA 19102-4944. Offers MM. *Degree requirements:* For master's, recital, thesis/project. *Entrance requirements:* For master's, audition consisting of a performance, interview and written examination to measure aural, theoretical, arranging and historical skills and knowledge; official transcripts from each undergraduate or graduate school attended; three letters of recommendation; one- to two-page statement of professional plans and goals. Additional exam requirements/ recommendations for international students: required—TOEFL (minimum score 580 paper-based, 92 iBT) or IELTS (minimum score 6.5).

University of the Pacific, Conservatory of Music, Stockton, CA 95211-0197. Offers music education (MM); music therapy (MA). *Entrance requirements:* For master's, GRE General Test. Additional exam requirements/recommendations for international students: required—TOEFL.

The University of Toledo, College of Graduate Studies, College of Communication and the Arts, Department of Music, Toledo, OH 43606-3390. Offers music (Certificate); music performance (MMP). *Accreditation:* NASM. *Degree requirements:* For master's, comprehensive exam, diagnostic theory exam. *Entrance requirements:* For master's, GRE if GPA less than 2.7, minimum cumulative point-hour ratio of 2.7 for all previous academic work, audition. Additional exam requirements/recommendations for international students: required—TOEFL (minimum score 550 paper-based; 80 iBT). Electronic applications accepted.

University of Toronto, School of Graduate Studies, Faculty of Music, Toronto, ON M5S 1A1, Canada. Offers composition (M Mus, DMA); ethnomusicology (MA, PhD); jazz (M Mus); music education (MA, PhD); musicology/theory (MA, PhD); opera (M Mus); performance (M Mus, DMA). *Program availability:* Part-time. *Degree requirements:* For master's, comprehensive exam (for some programs), oral examination (M Mus in composition), 1 foreign language (MA); for doctorate, recital of original works (DMA), thesis (PhD). *Entrance requirements:* For master's, BM in area of specialization with minimum B average in final 2 years, original compositions (M Mus in composition); for doctorate, master's degree in area of specialization, minimum B+ average, at least 2 extended compositions (DMA). Additional exam requirements/ recommendations for international students: required—TOEFL (minimum score 580 paper-based; 93 iBT), TWE (minimum score 5). Electronic applications accepted.

University of Utah, Graduate School, College of Fine Arts, School of Music, Salt Lake City, UT 84112. Offers choral conducting (M Mus, DMA); collaborative piano (M Mus); composition (M Mus, PhD); instrumental conducting (M Mus, DMA); instrumental performance (M Mus, DMA); jazz studies (M Mus); music education (M Mus, PhD); music history and literature (M Mus); musicology (MA); organ performance (M Mus); piano performance (M Mus, DMA); piano performance and pedagogy (M Mus); string performance and pedagogy (M Mus); theory (M Mus); vocal performance (DMA). *Accreditation:* NASM. *Faculty:* 36 full-time (13 women), 17 part-time/adjunct (5 women). *Students:* 75 full-time (39 women), 21 part-time (14 women); includes 14 minority (5 Asian, non-Hispanic/Latino; 6 Hispanic/Latino; 3 Two or more races, non-Hispanic/Latino), 20 international. Average age 32. 121 applicants, 55% accepted, 31 enrolled. In 2019, 15 master's, 12 doctorates awarded. *Degree requirements:* For master's, thesis or alternative; for doctorate, comprehensive exam (for some programs), thesis/dissertation (for some programs). *Entrance requirements:* For master's, placement exams, minimum GPA of 3.0, audition, bachelor's degree in music; for doctorate, placement exams, minimum GPA of 3.0, audition, master's degree in music. Additional exam requirements/recommendations for international students: required—TOEFL (minimum score 85 iBT), IELTS (minimum score 6.5), We require either a TOEFL score of 85 or above OR an IELTS score of 6.5 or above. *Application deadline:* For fall admission, 2/15 for domestic students, 1/15 for international students; for spring admission, 10/1 for domestic students, 9/1 for international students; for summer admission, 3/15 for domestic students, 2/15 for international students. Applications are processed on a rolling basis. Application fee: $55 ($65 for international students). Electronic applications accepted. *Expenses:* Contact institution. *Financial support:* In 2019–20, 62 students received support, including 55 teaching assistantships (averaging $17,273 per year). Financial award application deadline: 2/15. *Unit head:* Miguel Chuaqui, Director, 801-585-3720, E-mail: m.chauqui@utah.edu. *Application contact:* Cassie Wagstaff, Academic Coordinator, 801-585-6972, Fax: 801-581-5683, E-mail: cassandra.wagstaff@utah.edu.
Website: http://www.music.utah.edu/

University of Valley Forge, Program in Music Technology, Phoenixville, PA 19460. Offers MM. *Program availability:* Online learning.

University of Victoria, Faculty of Graduate Studies, Faculty of Fine Arts, School of Music, Victoria, BC V8W 2Y2, Canada. Offers composition (M Mus); musicology (MA, PhD); musicology with performance (MA); performance (M Mus). *Degree requirements:* For master's, 2 foreign languages, thesis; for doctorate, 2 foreign languages, thesis/ dissertation, candidacy exam. *Entrance requirements:* For master's, theory placement test, audition or sample papers and compositions; for doctorate, audition or sample papers and compositions. Additional exam requirements/recommendations for international students: required—TOEFL (minimum score 575 paper-based), IELTS (minimum score 7). Electronic applications accepted.

University of Virginia, College and Graduate School of Arts and Sciences, Department of Music, Charlottesville, VA 22903. Offers MA, PhD. *Degree requirements:* For master's, one foreign language, article-length paper; for doctorate, one foreign language, comprehensive exam, thesis/dissertation. *Entrance requirements:* For master's and doctorate, GRE General Test, 2 writing samples or portfolio. Additional exam requirements/recommendations for international students: required—TOEFL (minimum score 600 paper-based; 90 iBT), IELTS (minimum score 7). Electronic applications accepted.

University of Washington, Graduate School, College of Arts and Sciences, School of Music, Concentration in Choral Conducting, Seattle, WA 98195. Offers MM, DMA.

University of Washington, Graduate School, College of Arts and Sciences, School of Music, Concentration in Ethnomusicology, Seattle, WA 98195. Offers MA.

University of Washington, Graduate School, College of Arts and Sciences, School of Music, Concentration in Music History, Seattle, WA 98195. Offers MA, PhD.

University of Washington, Graduate School, College of Arts and Sciences, School of Music, Department of Choral Music, Seattle, WA 98195. Offers choral conducting (MM, DMA).

The University of Western Ontario, School of Graduate and Postdoctoral Studies, Don Wright Faculty of Music, London, ON N6A 3K7, Canada. Offers music (M Mus, PhD); popular music and culture (MA). *Program availability:* Part-time. Terminal master's awarded for partial completion of doctoral program. *Degree requirements:* For master's, 2 foreign languages, thesis (for some programs), recital; for doctorate, 2 foreign languages, thesis/dissertation. *Entrance requirements:* For master's, honors degree in music; minimum A average in proposed area of concentration, B average overall; for doctorate, MA or equivalent.

University of Wisconsin–Madison, Graduate School, College of Letters and Science, School of Music, Program in Composition, Madison, WI 53706-1380. Offers MM, DMA. *Accreditation:* NASM. *Degree requirements:* For doctorate, thesis/ dissertation.

University of Wisconsin–Madison, Graduate School, College of Letters and Science, School of Music, Program in Conducting, Madison, WI 53706-1380. Offers choral (MM, DMA); instrumental (MM, DMA); orchestral (MM, DMA). *Accreditation:* NASM. *Degree requirements:* For doctorate, thesis/dissertation.

University of Wisconsin–Madison, Graduate School, College of Letters and Science, School of Music, Program in Musicology and Ethnomusicology, Madison, WI 53706-1380. Offers ethnomusicology (MA, PhD); historical musicology (PhD); music history (MA). *Accreditation:* NASM. *Degree requirements:* For doctorate, 2 foreign languages, thesis/dissertation. *Entrance requirements:* For doctorate, GRE General Test.

University of Wisconsin–Madison, Graduate School, College of Letters and Science, School of Music, Program in Music Performance, Madison, WI 53706-1380. Offers MM, DMA. *Accreditation:* NASM. *Degree requirements:* For doctorate, one foreign language, thesis/dissertation.

University of Wisconsin–Madison, Graduate School, College of Letters and Science, School of Music, Program in Music Theory, Madison, WI 53706-1380. Offers MA, PhD. *Accreditation:* NASM. *Degree requirements:* For master's, thesis, 1 foreign language (MA); for doctorate, 2 foreign languages, thesis/dissertation. *Entrance requirements:* For master's, GRE General Test (MA); for doctorate, GRE General Test.

University of Wisconsin–Milwaukee, Graduate School, Peck School of the Arts, Milwaukee, WI 53201-0413. Offers art education (MS); chamber music (CAS); conducting (MM); dance (MFA); design entrepreneurship and innovation (MA); film, video, animation, and new genres (MFA); music education (MM); music history and literature (MM); performance (MM); string pedagogy (MM); studio art (MA, MFA); theory and composition (MM). *Program availability:* Part-time. *Degree requirements:* For master's, comprehensive exam, thesis or alternative. *Entrance requirements:* For master's, portfolio. Additional exam requirements/recommendations for international students: required—TOEFL (minimum score 550 paper-based; 79 iBT), IELTS (minimum score 6.5). Electronic applications accepted.

University of Wyoming, College of Arts and Sciences, Department of Music, Laramie, WY 82071. Offers music education (MME); performance (MM). *Accreditation:* NASM. *Degree requirements:* For master's, comprehensive exam, thesis or alternative. *Entrance requirements:* For master's, minimum GPA of 3.0. Additional exam requirements/recommendations for international students: required—TOEFL (minimum score 540 paper-based). Electronic applications accepted.

Université Laval, Faculty of Music, Programs in Music, Québec, QC G1K 7P4, Canada. Offers composition (M Mus); instrumental didactics (M Mus); interpretation (M Mus); music education (M Mus, PhD); musicology (M Mus, PhD). Terminal master's awarded for partial completion of doctoral program. *Degree requirements:* For master's, thesis (for some programs); for doctorate, comprehensive exam, thesis/dissertation. *Entrance requirements:* For master's, English exam, audition, knowledge of French; for doctorate, English exam, knowledge of French, third language. Electronic applications accepted.

Utah State University, School of Graduate Studies, Caine College of the Arts, Department of Music, Logan, UT 84322. Offers guitar performance (MM); piano performance and pedagogy (MM).

Vermont College of Fine Arts, MFA in Music Composition Program, Montpelier, VT 05602. Offers MFA. *Entrance requirements:* For master's, resume of education and relevant professional experience, three samples of original compositions, official transcripts of all previous undergraduate and graduate coursework, two letters of recommendation, statement of purpose. *Expenses:* Contact institution.

Virginia Commonwealth University, Graduate School, School of the Arts, Department of Music, Richmond, VA 23284-9005. Offers music education (MM). *Accreditation:* NASM. *Degree requirements:* For master's, departmental qualifying exam, recital. *Entrance requirements:* For master's, department examination, audition or tapes, portfolio. Additional exam requirements/recommendations for international students: required—TOEFL (minimum score 600 paper-based; 100 iBT). Electronic applications accepted.

Washington State University, College of Arts and Sciences, School of Music, Pullman, WA 99164-5300. Offers MA. *Accreditation:* NASM. *Program availability:* Part-time. *Degree requirements:* For master's, one foreign language, comprehensive exam, thesis (for some programs), oral exam. *Entrance requirements:* For master's, audition, minimum GPA of 3.0, 3 letters of recommendation, composition portfolio and recording (for composition); writing sample and written philosophy (for music education); writing sample (for music history); in-depth audition (for performance). Additional exam requirements/recommendations for international students: required—TOEFL, IELTS. Electronic applications accepted.

Washington University in St. Louis, The Graduate School, Department of Music, St. Louis, MO 63130-4899. Offers MA, PhD. Terminal master's awarded for partial completion of doctoral program. *Degree requirements:* For master's, thesis or alternative; for doctorate, thesis/dissertation. *Entrance requirements:* For master's, GRE General Test, departmental exam; for doctorate, departmental exam, GRE General Test. Additional exam requirements/recommendations for international students: required—TOEFL. Electronic applications accepted.

Wayne State University, College of Fine, Performing and Communication Arts, Department of Music, Detroit, MI 48202. Offers composition/theory (MA, MM); conducting (MA, MM); jazz performance (MA, MM); music education (MA, MM); orchestral studies (Certificate); performance (MA, MM). *Accreditation:* NASM. *Degree requirements:* For master's, thesis (for some programs), oral examination (for some programs), recital with program notes (for some programs). *Entrance requirements:* For master's, diagnostic exam in theory and history, undergraduate degree in same field as desired field of graduate study or equivalent in course work, private study, or experience; audition/interview; for Certificate, undergraduate degree in same field as desired field of graduate study or equivalent in course work, private study, or experience; audition/interview. Additional exam requirements/recommendations for international students: required—TOEFL (minimum score 550 paper-based; 79 iBT), Michigan English Language Assessment Battery (minimum score 85); recommended—IELTS (minimum score 6.5), TWE (minimum score 5.5). Electronic applications accepted. *Expenses:* Contact institution.

Webster University, Leigh Gerdine College of Fine Arts, Department of Music, St. Louis, MO 63119-3194. Offers church music (MM); composition (MM); jazz studies (MM); music (MA); music education (MM); organ (MM); performance (MM); piano (MM); voice (MM). *Accreditation:* NASM. *Entrance requirements:* Additional exam requirements/recommendations for international students: required—TOEFL.

Wesleyan University, Graduate Studies, Department of Music, Middletown, CT 06459. Offers composition (MA); ethnomusicology (MA, PhD). *Degree requirements:* For master's, one foreign language, thesis; for doctorate, 2 foreign languages, comprehensive exam, thesis/dissertation. *Entrance requirements:* For master's, undergraduate music major or its equivalent; for doctorate, MA. Additional exam requirements/recommendations for international students: required—TOEFL. Electronic applications accepted.

Western Illinois University, School of Graduate Studies, College of Fine Arts and Communication, School of Music, Macomb, IL 61455-1390. Offers MM. *Accreditation:* NASM. *Program availability:* Part-time. *Degree requirements:* For master's, comprehensive exam, thesis or alternative. *Entrance requirements:* For master's, audition. Additional exam requirements/recommendations for international students: required—TOEFL (minimum score 550 paper-based; 80 iBT). Electronic applications accepted.

Western Michigan University, Graduate College, College of Fine Arts, School of Music, Kalamazoo, MI 49008. Offers music (MA); music composition (MM); music conducting (MM); music education (MM); music performance (MM); music therapy (MM). *Accreditation:* NASM.

Western Oregon University, Graduate Programs, College of Liberal Arts and Sciences, Division of Creative Arts, Monmouth, OR 97361. Offers contemporary music (MM). *Accreditation:* NASM. *Entrance requirements:* Additional exam requirements/recommendations for international students: required—TOEFL (minimum score 550 paper-based; 79 iBT), IELTS (minimum score 6.5).

Western Washington University, Graduate School, College of Fine and Performing Arts, Department of Music, Bellingham, WA 98225-5996. Offers M Mus. *Accreditation:* NASM. *Program availability:* Part-time. *Degree requirements:* For master's, thesis. *Entrance requirements:* For master's, GRE General Test, department placement exams, audition, portfolio, minimum GPA of 3.0 in last 60 semester hours or last 90 quarter hours of course work. Additional exam requirements/recommendations for international students: required—TOEFL (minimum score 567 paper-based). Electronic applications accepted.

West Texas A&M University, College of Fine Arts and Humanities, School of Music, Program in Music, Canyon, TX 79015. Offers MA. *Accreditation:* NASM. *Program availability:* Part-time. *Degree requirements:* For master's, comprehensive exam, thesis optional. *Entrance requirements:* For master's, GRE General Test. Additional exam requirements/recommendations for international students: required—TOEFL (minimum score 550 paper-based). Electronic applications accepted.

West Texas A&M University, College of Fine Arts and Humanities, School of Music, Program in Performance, Canyon, TX 79015. Offers MM. *Accreditation:* NASM. *Program availability:* Part-time. *Degree requirements:* For master's, comprehensive exam, thesis optional. *Entrance requirements:* For master's, GRE General Test. Additional exam requirements/recommendations for international students: required—TOEFL (minimum score 550 paper-based). Electronic applications accepted.

West Virginia University, College of Creative Arts, Morgantown, WV 26506. Offers acting (MFA); art education (MA); art history (MA); ceramics (MFA); collaborative piano (MM, DMA); composition (MM, DMA); conducting (MM, DMA); costume design and technology (MFA); graphic design (MFA); intermedia and photography (MFA); jazz pedagogy (MM); lighting design and technology (MFA); music (PhD); music education (MM, PhD); music industry (MA); music theory (MM); musicology (MA); painting and printmaking (MFA); performance (MM, DMA); piano pedagogy (MM); scenic design and technology (MFA); sculpture (MFA); studio art (MA); technical direction (MFA); vocal pedagogy and performance (DMA). *Program availability:* Part-time. *Degree requirements:* For master's, thesis, recitals; for doctorate, comprehensive exam, thesis/dissertation, recitals (DMA). *Entrance requirements:* For doctorate, minimum GPA of 3.0, audition. Additional exam requirements/recommendations for international students: required—TOEFL. Electronic applications accepted.

Wichita State University, Graduate School, College of Fine Arts, School of Music, Wichita, KS 67260. Offers music (MM); music education (MME). *Accreditation:* NASM. *Program availability:* Part-time.

Winthrop University, College of Visual and Performing Arts, Department of Music, Rock Hill, SC 29733. Offers conducting (MM); music education (MME); performance (MM). *Accreditation:* NASM. *Program availability:* Part-time. *Degree requirements:* For master's, comprehensive exam (for some programs), oral and written exams, recital (MM). *Entrance requirements:* For master's, GRE General Test, audition, minimum GPA of 3.0, 2 recitals. Additional exam requirements/recommendations for international students: required—TOEFL (minimum score 550 paper-based; 79 iBT), IELTS (minimum score 6). Electronic applications accepted. *Expenses: Tuition, area resident:* Full-time $7659; part-time $641 per credit hour. Tuition, state resident: full-time $7659; part-time $641 per credit hour. Tuition, nonresident: full-time $14,753; part-time $1234 per credit hour.

World Mission University, Graduate Programs, Los Angeles, CA 90020. Offers biblical preaching (M Div); Christian counseling (M Div, MACC); church ministry (M Div); church music (M Div, DCM); ministry (D Min); music (MA); theology (MAT). *Program availability:* Online learning.

Yale University, Graduate School of Arts and Sciences, Department of Music, New Haven, CT 06520. Offers music history (MA); music theory (MA). Terminal master's awarded for partial completion of doctoral program. *Degree requirements:* For master's, one foreign language; for doctorate, 3 foreign languages, thesis/dissertation. *Entrance requirements:* For doctorate, GRE General Test, GRE Subject Test.

Yale University, School of Music, New Haven, CT 06520-8246. Offers MM, MMA, DMA, AD, Certificate. *Faculty:* 29 full-time (9 women), 31 part-time/adjunct (7 women). *Students:* 232 full-time (105 women); includes 47 minority (3 Black or African American, non-Hispanic/Latino; 22 Asian, non-Hispanic/Latino; 15 Hispanic/Latino; 7 Two or more races, non-Hispanic/Latino). Average age 25. 1,481 applicants, 12% accepted, 116 enrolled. In 2019, 73 master's, 6 doctorates, 30 ADs awarded. *Degree requirements:* For master's and other advanced degree, recitals; for doctorate, comprehensive exam, thesis/dissertation, oral and written exam, recitals. *Entrance requirements:* For master's and other advanced degree, departmental exams, audition; for doctorate, entrance exam in music history, analysis, and musicianship, audition. Additional exam requirements/recommendations for international students: required—TOEFL (minimum score 567 paper-based; 86 iBT). *Application deadline:* For fall admission, 12/1 for domestic and international students. Application fee: $150. Electronic applications accepted. *Expenses:* Contact institution. *Financial support:* In 2019–20, 211 students received support, including 211 fellowships (averaging $38,000 per year); Federal Work-Study, scholarships/grants, and unspecified assistantships also available. Financial award application deadline: 5/30; financial award applicants required to submit FAFSA. *Unit head:* Robert Blocker, Dean, 203-432-4160, Fax: 203-432-7542. *Application contact:* Suzanne M. Stringer, Director of Student Services, 203-432-1962, Fax: 203-432-7448, E-mail: suzanne.stringer@yale.edu.
Website: http://music.yale.edu/

York University, Faculty of Graduate Studies, Faculty of Fine Arts, Program in Music, Toronto, ON M3J 1P3, Canada. Offers composition (MA); music (PhD); musicology and ethnomusicology (MA). *Program availability:* Part-time. *Degree requirements:* For master's, one foreign language, thesis optional; for doctorate, 2 foreign languages, comprehensive exam, thesis/dissertation. *Entrance requirements:* For master's, portfolio. Electronic applications accepted.

Youngstown State University, College of Graduate Studies, Cliffe College of Creative Arts and Communication, Dana School of Music, Youngstown, OH 44555-0001. Offers jazz studies (MM); music education (MM); music history and literature (MM); music theory and composition (MM); performance (MM). *Accreditation:* NASM. *Program availability:* Part-time, evening/weekend. *Degree requirements:* For master's, one foreign language, thesis optional, final qualifying exam. *Entrance requirements:* For master's, audition; GRE General Test or minimum GPA of 2.7. Additional exam requirements/recommendations for international students: required—TOEFL.

Theater

Academy of Art University, Graduate Programs, School of Acting, San Francisco, CA 94105-3410. Offers MA, MFA. *Program availability:* Part-time. *Faculty:* 1 (woman) full-time, 8 part-time/adjunct (3 women). *Students:* 25 full-time (13 women), 4 part-time (2 women); includes 8 minority (6 Black or African American, non-Hispanic/Latino; 2 Hispanic/Latino), 9 international. Average age 28. 36 applicants, 100% accepted, 6 enrolled. In 2019, 9 master's awarded. *Degree requirements:* For master's, final review. *Entrance requirements:* For master's, statement of intent; resume; portfolio/reel; official college transcripts. *Application deadline:* Applications are processed on a rolling basis. Application fee: $50. Electronic applications accepted. *Expenses: Tuition:* Full-time $1083; part-time $1083 per credit hour. *Required fees:* $860; $860 per unit. $430 per term. One-time fee: $145. Tuition and fees vary according to program. *Financial support:* Career-related internships or fieldwork, Federal Work-Study, and scholarships/grants available. Financial award application deadline: 8/10; financial award applicants required to submit FAFSA.
Website: http://www.academyart.edu/acting-school/index.html

American Conservatory Theater, Program in Acting, San Francisco, CA 94108-5800. Offers MFA, Certificate. *Degree requirements:* For master's, thesis (for some programs), stage performance. *Entrance requirements:* For master's, audition, interview, bachelor's degree from an accredited institution, 2 confidential letters of recommendation.

Arcadia University, School of Education, Glenside, PA 19038-3295. Offers art education (M Ed); computer education (CAS); curriculum (CAS); curriculum studies (M Ed); early childhood education (M Ed), including individualized, master teacher, research in child development; educational leadership (M Ed, Ed D, CAS); elementary education (M Ed); English education (MA Ed); environmental education (MA Ed); instructional technology (M Ed); language arts (M Ed); library science (M Ed); mathematics education (M Ed, MA Ed); music education (MA Ed); psychology (MA Ed); reading (M Ed, CAS); science education (M Ed, CAS); secondary education (M Ed, CAS); special education (M Ed, Ed D, CAS); theater arts (MA Ed); written communication (MA Ed). *Accreditation:* NASAD. *Program availability:* Part-time, evening/weekend, online learning. *Faculty:* 13 full-time (9 women). *Students:* 32 full-time (28 women), 260 part-time (202 women); includes 66 minority (45 Black or African American, non-Hispanic/Latino; 11 Asian, non-Hispanic/Latino; 5 Hispanic/Latino; 5 Two or more races, non-Hispanic/Latino), 2 international. In 2019, 148 master's, 8 doctorates, 163 CASs awarded. *Entrance requirements:* Additional exam requirements/recommendations for international students: required—Official results from the TOEFL or IELTS are required. *Application deadline:* Applications are processed on a rolling basis. Application fee: $25. Electronic applications accepted. *Expenses:* Contact institution. *Financial support:* Career-related internships or fieldwork, tuition waivers (partial), and unspecified assistantships available. *Unit head:* Kimberly Dean, Chair, 215-572-8629. *Application contact:* 215-572-2925, Fax: 215-572-2126, E-mail: grad@arcadia.edu.

Arizona State University at Tempe, Herberger Institute for Design and the Arts, School of Film, Dance and Theatre, Tempe, AZ 85287-2002. Offers dance (MFA), including dance, interdisciplinary digital media and performance; theatre (MA, MFA, PhD), including arts entrepreneurship and management (MFA), directing (MFA), dramatic writing (MFA), interdisciplinary digital media and performance (MFA), performance (MFA), performance design (MFA), theatre (MFA), theatre and performance of the Americas (PhD), theatre for youth (MFA, PhD). Terminal master's awarded for partial completion of doctoral program. *Degree requirements:* For master's, comprehensive exam (for some programs), thesis (for some programs), applied project (for some programs); interactive Program of Study (iPOS) submitted before completing 50 percent of required credit hours; for doctorate, comprehensive exam, thesis/dissertation, interactive Program of Study (iPOS) submitted before completing 50 percent of required credit hours. *Entrance requirements:* For master's, GRE or MAT, minimum GPA of 3.0 in last 2 years of work leading to bachelor's degree (depending on program); for doctorate, GRE, minimum GPA of 3.0 or equivalent in last 2 years of work leading to bachelor's degree, 3 letters of recommendation, resume, scholarly writing sample, statement of purpose. Additional exam requirements/recommendations for international students: required—TOEFL, IELTS, or PTE. Electronic applications accepted.

Baylor University, Graduate School, College of Arts and Sciences, Department of Theatre Arts, Waco, TX 76798. Offers MA, MFA. *Accreditation:* NAST. *Faculty:* 6 full-time (2 women). *Students:* 9 full-time (6 women); includes 2 minority (both Hispanic/Latino). 188 applicants, 2% accepted, 3 enrolled. In 2019, 2 master's awarded. *Entrance requirements:* For master's, MA needs the GRE, MFA applicants need a play anlysis, statement of purpose, and directing portolio. *Financial support:* In 2019–20, 6 teaching assistantships with full tuition reimbursements (averaging $15,000 per year) were awarded; health care benefits and tuition waivers (full) also available. *Unit head:* Dr. David Jortner, Graduate Program Director, 254-710-6452, E-mail: David_Jortner@Baylor.edu. *Application contact:* Renee Cluke, Administrative Assistant, 254-710-1861, Fax: 254-710-1765, E-mail: renee_cluke@baylor.edu.
Website: http://www.baylor.edu/Theatre_Arts/

Berklee College of Music, The Boston Conservatory at Berklee, Boston, MA 02215-3693. Offers bassoon performance (MM); cello performance (MM); choral conducting (MM); clarinet performance (MM); collaborative piano (MM); composition (MM); contemporary music performance (MM); double bass performance (MM); flute performance (MM); harp performance (MM); horn performance (MM); marimba performance (MM); music and autism (Certificate); music education (MM); music education and autism (MM); music performance (ADP); musical theater (MFA); oboe performance (MM); opera performance (MM); orchestral conducting (MM); percussion performance (MM); piano performance (MM); saxophone performance (MM); trombone performance (MM); trumpet performance (MM). *Program availability:* Part-time. *Faculty:* 20 full-time (11 women), 26 part-time/adjunct (15 women). *Students:* 232 full-time (134 women), 2 part-time (1 woman); includes 45 minority (10 Black or African American, non-Hispanic/Latino; 2 American Indian or Alaska Native, non-Hispanic/Latino; 8 Asian, non-Hispanic/Latino; 10 Hispanic/Latino; 15 Two or more races, non-Hispanic/Latino), 92 international. Average age 26. 769 applicants, 38% accepted, 110 enrolled. In 2019, 117 master's, 14 other advanced degrees awarded. *Degree requirements:* For master's, recital or performance; for other advanced degree, recital. *Entrance requirements:* For master's and other advanced degree, audition. Additional exam requirements/recommendations for international students: required—TOEFL (minimum score 550 paper-based; 79 iBT), IELTS (minimum score 6.5), Duolingo. *Application deadline:* For fall admission, 12/1 for domestic and international students. Application fee: $150. Electronic applications accepted. *Expenses:* MM & MFA: $45,280/year tuition, $1040 fee. *Financial support:* Research assistantships, teaching assistantships, and scholarships/grants available. Financial award application deadline: 12/1; financial award applicants required to submit FAFSA. *Unit head:* Robert Lagueux, PhD, Associate Vice President, Academic Affairs, 617-747-6908, E-mail: rlagueux@berklee.edu. *Application contact:* Director of Admissions, 617-912-9153, Fax: 617-912-9217, E-mail: admissions@bostonconservatory.edu.
Website: http://www.bostonconservatory.edu/

Binghamton University, State University of New York, Graduate School, Harpur College of Arts and Sciences, Department of Theatre, Binghamton, NY 13902-6000. Offers MA. *Program availability:* Part-time. *Degree requirements:* For master's, thesis. *Entrance requirements:* For master's, GRE General Test, writing sample, portfolio. Additional exam requirements/recommendations for international students: required—TOEFL (minimum score 550 paper-based; 80 iBT). Electronic applications accepted.

Bob Jones University, Graduate Programs, Greenville, SC 29614. Offers accountancy (MS); Bible (MA); Bible translation (MA); Biblical studies (Certificate); business administration (MBA); church history (MA, PhD); church ministries (MA); church music (MM); cinema and video production (MA); counseling (MS); curriculum and instruction (Ed D); divinity (M Div); dramatic production (MA); educational leadership (MS, Ed D, Ed S); elementary education (M Ed, MAT); English (M Ed, MA, MAT); fine arts (MA); graphic design (MA); history (M Ed, MA); illustration (MA); interpretative speech (MA); mathematics (M Ed, MAT); medical missions (Certificate); ministry (MM, D Min); multi-categorical special education (M Ed, MAT); music (M Ed); New Testament interpretation (PhD); Old Testament interpretation (PhD); orchestral instrument performance (MM); organ performance (MM); pastoral studies (MA); personnel services (MS, Ed S); piano pedagogy (MM); piano performance (MM); platform arts (MA); rhetoric and public address (MA); secondary education (M Ed); studio art (MA); teaching Bible (MA); theology (MA, PhD); voice performance (MM); youth ministries (MA); M Div/MM.

Boston University, College of Fine Arts, School of Theatre, Boston, MA 02215. Offers design (MFA); lighting crafts (Certificate); management (MFA); production (MFA); scenic painting (Certificate). *Program availability:* Part-time. *Faculty:* 16 full-time, 9 part-time/adjunct. *Students:* 52 full-time (34 women), 2 part-time (0 women); includes 5 minority (1 Black or African American, non-Hispanic/Latino; 2 Asian, non-Hispanic/Latino; 2 Two or more races, non-Hispanic/Latino), 4 international. Average age 28. 139 applicants, 20% accepted, 19 enrolled. In 2019, 13 master's awarded. *Entrance requirements:* For master's, application, two recommendations, transcripts from all colleges attended. Personal statement. Additional writing required for MFA-Directing and MFA-Theatre Education candidates, interview, portfolio. Additional exam requirements/recommendations for international students: required—TOEFL (minimum score 90 iBT), IELTS (minimum score 7), DuoLingo. *Application deadline:* For fall admission, 2/1 priority date for domestic and international students. Application fee: $95. Electronic applications accepted. *Expenses:* Contact institution. *Financial support:* In 2019–20, 16 students received support, including 16 teaching assistantships (averaging $3,000 per year); scholarships/grants, unspecified assistantships, and stipends also available. Financial award application deadline: 2/1. *Unit head:* Susan Mickey, Director, 617-353-3390. *Application contact:* McCaela Donovan, Assistant Director, School of Theatre, 617-353-3390, E-mail: mccaela@bu.edu.

Bowling Green State University, Graduate College, College of Arts and Sciences, Department of Theatre and Film, Bowling Green, OH 43403. Offers MA, PhD. *Accreditation:* NAST. *Program availability:* Part-time. Terminal master's awarded for partial completion of doctoral program. *Degree requirements:* For master's, thesis or alternative; for doctorate, comprehensive exam, thesis/dissertation, 9-hour research tool. *Entrance requirements:* For master's and doctorate, GRE General Test. Additional exam requirements/recommendations for international students: required—TOEFL. Electronic applications accepted.

Brigham Young University, Graduate Studies, College of Fine Arts and Communications, Department of Theatre and Media Arts, Provo, UT 84602-6404. Offers media and performance studies (MA). *Accreditation:* NAST. *Faculty:* 7 full-time (3 women). *Students:* 9 full-time (6 women); includes 2 minority (1 Asian, non-Hispanic/Latino; 1 Hispanic/Latino). Average age 28. 9 applicants, 44% accepted, 2 enrolled. *Degree requirements:* For master's, comprehensive exam, thesis, 32 hours, oral defense. *Entrance requirements:* For master's, two samples of scholarly writing, letter of intent, three letters of recommendation. Additional exam requirements/recommendations for international students: required—TOEFL (minimum score 580 paper-based; 85 iBT). *Application deadline:* For fall admission, 2/15 priority date for domestic and international students. Application fee: $50. Electronic applications accepted. *Financial support:* In 2019–20, 9 students received support, including 3 research assistantships with partial tuition reimbursements available (averaging $1,000 per year), 8 teaching assistantships with partial tuition reimbursements available (averaging $2,000 per year); scholarships/grants, health care benefits, tuition waivers (partial), and unspecified assistantships also available. Financial award application deadline: 2/15. *Unit head:* Dr. Kimball Jensen, Graduate Coordinator, 801-422-6648, E-mail: kimball_jensen@byu.edu. *Application contact:* Katie Tolman, Graduate Secretary, 801-422-3750.
Website: http://cfac.byu.edu/departments/tma

Brooklyn College of the City University of New York, School of Visual, Media and Performing Arts, Department of Theater, Brooklyn, NY 11210-2889. Offers acting (MFA); design and technical theater (MFA); directing (MFA); performing arts management (MFA); theater history and criticism (MA). *Program availability:* Part-time. *Degree requirements:* For master's, thesis, professional residency. *Entrance requirements:* For master's, audition or interview, 18 credits in theater, 2 letters of recommendation, essay. Additional exam requirements/recommendations for international students: required—TOEFL. Electronic applications accepted.

Brown University, Graduate School, Department of Theatre Arts and Performance Studies, Providence, RI 02912. Offers acting and directing (MFA); playwriting (MFA); theatre and performance studies (PhD). *Degree requirements:* For master's, thesis or alternative. *Entrance requirements:* For master's, GRE General Test.

California Institute of the Arts, School of Theater, Valencia, CA 91355-2340. Offers acting (MFA, Adv C); creative producing and management (MFA); design and production (MFA); design and technology (Adv C); directing (MFA); theater management (Adv C). *Degree requirements:* For master's, thesis (for some programs), faculty review, performance or portfolio. *Entrance requirements:* For master's, audition or portfolio, interview. Additional exam requirements/recommendations for international students: required—TOEFL. Electronic applications accepted.

California State University, Fullerton, Graduate Studies, College of the Arts, Department of Theatre and Dance, Fullerton, CA 92831-3599. Offers theatre arts (MFA), including acting. *Accreditation:* NAST. *Program availability:* Part-time. *Entrance requirements:* For master's, major in theatre or related field, audition or interview, minimum GPA of 2.5 in last 60 units of course work.

California State University, Long Beach, Graduate Studies, College of the Arts, Department of Theatre Arts, Long Beach, CA 90840. Offers acting (MFA); MBA/MFA. *Accreditation:* NAST. *Program availability:* Part-time. *Degree requirements:* For master's, thesis or alternative. Electronic applications accepted.

California State University, Los Angeles, Graduate Studies, College of Arts and Letters, Department of Theatre Arts and Dance, Los Angeles, CA 90032-8530. Offers theater arts (MA). *Program availability:* Part-time, evening/weekend. *Degree requirements:* For master's, comprehensive exam, project or thesis. *Entrance requirements:* For master's, minimum GPA of 2.5, 30 units of course work in theater. Additional exam requirements/recommendations for international students: required—TOEFL (minimum score 500 paper-based). Electronic applications accepted. *Expenses: Tuition, area resident:* Full-time $7176; part-time $4164 per year. Tuition, state resident: full-time $7176; part-time $4164 per year. Tuition, nonresident: full-time $14,304; part-time $8916 per year. *International tuition:* $14,304 full-time. *Required fees:* $1037.76; $1037.76 per unit. Tuition and fees vary according to degree level and program.

California State University, Northridge, Graduate Studies, Mike Curb College of Arts, Media, and Communication, Department of Theatre, Northridge, CA 91330. Offers MA. *Accreditation:* NAST. *Degree requirements:* For master's, thesis. *Entrance requirements:* For master's, GRE General Test or minimum GPA of 3.0. Additional exam requirements/recommendations for international students: required—TOEFL.

Carnegie Mellon University, College of Fine Arts, School of Drama, Pittsburgh, PA 15213-3891. Offers design (MFA); directing (MFA); dramatic writing (MFA); production technology and management (MFA); video and media design (MFA). *Degree requirements:* For master's, thesis (for some programs). *Entrance requirements:* For master's, audition, portfolio review, interview. Additional exam requirements/recommendations for international students: required—TOEFL.

Case Western Reserve University, School of Graduate Studies, Department of Theater, Cleveland, OH 44106. Offers acting (MFA); theater (MA). *Faculty:* 6 full-time (3 women), 3 part-time/adjunct (2 women). *Students:* 18 full-time (9 women), 1 part-time (0 women); includes 7 minority (4 Black or African American, non-Hispanic/Latino; 1 Asian, non-Hispanic/Latino; 2 Hispanic/Latino). Average age 25. 13 applicants, 69% accepted, 8 enrolled. In 2019, 2 master's awarded. *Degree requirements:* For master's, comprehensive exam, thesis, oral presentation and defense, portfolio, thesis concert production and presentation (for MFA). *Entrance requirements:* For master's, audition, interview, letter of intent, three recommendations, headshots, resume. Additional exam requirements/recommendations for international students: required—TOEFL (minimum score 577 paper-based; 90 iBT); recommended—IELTS (minimum score 7). *Application deadline:* Applications are processed on a rolling basis. Application fee: $50. Electronic applications accepted. *Financial support:* Fellowships, scholarships/grants, health care benefits, tuition waivers (full and partial), and stipends available. Financial award application deadline: 3/1; financial award applicants required to submit FAFSA. *Unit head:* Jerrold Scott, Professor/Chair/Artistic Director, 216-368-6140, Fax: 216-368-5184, E-mail: jerrold.scott@case.edu. *Application contact:* DeBorah Hamilton, Department Assistant, 216-368-4868, Fax: 216-368-5184, E-mail: deborah.hamilton@case.edu.
Website: http://theater.case.edu

The Catholic University of America, School of Arts and Sciences, Department of Drama, Washington, DC 20064. Offers acting (MFA); creative teaching through drama (Certificate); directing (MFA); playwriting (MFA); theatre education (MA); theatre history and criticism (MA). *Program availability:* Part-time. *Faculty:* 8 full-time (4 women), 8 part-time/adjunct (4 women). *Students:* 8 full-time (7 women), 19 part-time (17 women); includes 9 minority (5 Black or African American, non-Hispanic/Latino; 2 Hispanic/Latino; 2 Two or more races, non-Hispanic/Latino). Average age 31. 14 applicants, 64% accepted, 5 enrolled. In 2019, 5 master's awarded. *Degree requirements:* For master's, variable foreign language requirement, comprehensive exam, thesis or alternative. *Entrance requirements:* For master's, GRE General Test, statement of purpose, official copies of academic transcripts, three letters of recommendation. Additional exam requirements/recommendations for international students: required—TOEFL (minimum score 550 paper-based; 80 iBT). *Application deadline:* For fall admission, 7/15 priority date for domestic students, 7/1 for international students; for spring admission, 11/15 priority date for domestic students, 11/1 for international students. Applications are processed on a rolling basis. Application fee: $55. Electronic applications accepted. *Expenses:* Contact institution. *Financial support:* Fellowships, research assistantships, teaching assistantships, Federal Work-Study, scholarships/grants, tuition waivers (full and partial), and unspecified assistantships available. Financial award application deadline: 2/1; financial award applicants required to submit FAFSA. *Unit head:* Dr. Eleanor Holdridge, Chair, 202-319-5358, Fax: 202-319-5359, E-mail: holdridge@cua.edu. *Application contact:* Dr. Steven Brown, Director of Graduate Admissions, 202-319-5057, Fax: 202-319-6533, E-mail: cua-admissions@cua.edu.
Website: http://drama.cua.edu/

Central Washington University, School of Graduate Studies and Research, College of Arts and Humanities, Department of Theatre Arts, Ellensburg, WA 98926. Offers theatre production (MA); theatre studies (MA). *Program availability:* Part-time. *Entrance requirements:* For master's, minimum GPA of 3.0. Additional exam requirements/recommendations for international students: required—TOEFL (minimum score 550 paper-based; 79 iBT). Electronic applications accepted.

Columbia University, Graduate School of Arts and Sciences, New York, NY 10027. Offers African-American studies (MA); American studies (MA); anthropology (MA, PhD); art history and archaeology (MA, PhD); astronomy (PhD); biological sciences (PhD); biotechnology (MA); chemical physics (PhD); chemistry (PhD); classical studies (MA, PhD); classics (MA, PhD); climate and society (MA); conservation biology (MA); earth and environmental sciences (PhD); East Asia: regional studies (MA); East Asian languages and cultures (MA, PhD); ecology, evolution and environmental biology (MA), including conservation biology; ecology, evolution, and environmental biology (PhD), including ecology and evolutionary biology, evolutionary primatology; economics (MA, PhD); English and comparative literature (MA, PhD); French and Romance philology (MA, PhD); Germanic languages (MA, PhD); global French studies (MA); global thought (MA); Hispanic cultural studies (MA); history (PhD); history and literature (MA); human rights studies (MA); Islamic studies (MA); Italian (MA, PhD); Japanese pedagogy (MA); Jewish studies (MA); Latin America and the Caribbean: regional studies (MA); Latin American and Iberian cultures (PhD); mathematics (MA, PhD), including finance (MA); medieval and Renaissance studies (MA); Middle Eastern, South Asian, and African studies (MA, PhD); modern art: critical and curatorial studies (MA); modern European studies (MA); museum anthropology (MA); music (DMA, PhD); oral history (MA); philosophical foundations of physics (MA); philosophy (MA, PhD); physics (PhD); political science (MA, PhD); psychology (PhD); quantitative methods in the social sciences (MA); religion (MA, PhD); Russia, Eurasia and East Europe: regional studies (MA); Russian translation (MA); Slavic cultures (MA); Slavic languages (MA, PhD); sociology (MA, PhD); South Asian studies (MA); statistics (MA, PhD); theatre (PhD). *Program availability:* Part-time. *Students:* 3,506 full-time (1,844 women), 208 part-time (121 women); includes 864 minority (110 Black or African American, non-Hispanic/Latino; 5 American Indian or Alaska Native, non-Hispanic/Latino; 416 Asian, non-Hispanic/Latino; 147 Hispanic/Latino; 6 Native Hawaiian or other Pacific Islander, non-Hispanic/Latino; 180 Two or more races, non-Hispanic/Latino), 2,065 international. 14,545 applicants, 25% accepted, 1,429 enrolled. In 2019, 1,262 master's, 363 doctorates awarded. Terminal master's awarded for partial completion of doctoral program. *Degree requirements:* For master's, variable foreign language requirement, comprehensive exam (for some programs), thesis (for some programs); for doctorate, variable foreign language requirement, comprehensive exam (for some programs), thesis/dissertation. *Entrance requirements:* For master's and doctorate, GRE General Test, GRE Subject Test (for some programs). Additional exam requirements/recommendations for international students: required—TOEFL (minimum score 600 paper-based; 100 iBT), IELTS (minimum score 7.5). Application fee: $115. Electronic applications accepted. *Expenses: Tuition:* Full-time $47,600; part-time $1880 per credit. One-time fee: $105. *Financial support:* Fellowships, research assistantships, teaching assistantships, career-related internships or fieldwork, Federal Work-Study, institutionally sponsored loans, scholarships/grants, traineeships, health care benefits, tuition waivers, and unspecified assistantships available. Support available to part-time students. Financial award application deadline: 12/15. *Unit head:* Dr. Carlos J. Alonso, Dean of the Graduate School of Arts and Sciences and Vice President for Graduate Education, 212-854-2861, E-mail: gsas-dean@columbia.edu. *Application contact:* GSAS Office of Admissions, 212-854-6729, E-mail: gsas-admissions@columbia.edu.
Website: http://gsas.columbia.edu/

Columbia University, School of the Arts, Theatre Program, New York, NY 10027. Offers theatre (MFA), including acting, directing, dramaturgy, playwriting, stage management, theatre management and producing; JD/MFA. *Degree requirements:* For master's, thesis, 2 internships (3 for theatre management and producing; none required for acting). *Entrance requirements:* For master's, undergraduate transcript, 3 letters of recommendation, theatrical resume, brief autobiography, statement of theatrical and personal objectives, creative materials appropriate to intended concentration (see web for details). Additional exam requirements/recommendations for international students: required—Either the TOEFL or the IELTS is required. Electronic applications accepted. *Expenses: Tuition:* Full-time $47,600; part-time $1880 per credit. One-time fee: $105.

Columbus State University, Graduate Studies, College of the Arts, Department of Theatre, Columbus, GA 31907-5645. Offers theatre education (M Ed, MAT). *Accreditation:* NAST. *Entrance requirements:* For master's, audition, letters of recommendation, minimum GPA of 2.75. Additional exam requirements/recommendations for international students: required—TOEFL (minimum score 550 paper-based; 79 iBT). Electronic applications accepted. *Expenses: Tuition, area resident:* Full-time $210; part-time $210 per credit hour. Tuition, state resident: full-time $210; part-time $210 per credit hour. Tuition, nonresident: full-time $817; part-time $817 per credit hour. *International tuition:* $817 full-time. *Required fees:* $802.50. Tuition and fees vary according to course load, degree level and program.

Cornell University, Graduate School, Graduate Fields of Arts and Sciences, Field of Theatre Arts, Ithaca, NY 14853. Offers drama and the theatre (PhD); theatre history (PhD); theatre theory and aesthetics (PhD). *Degree requirements:* For doctorate, 2 foreign languages, comprehensive exam, thesis/dissertation. *Entrance requirements:* For doctorate, GRE General Test, sample of written work, 3 letters of recommendation. Additional exam requirements/recommendations for international students: required—TOEFL (minimum score 600 paper-based; 77 iBT). Electronic applications accepted.

Dell'Arte International School of Physical Theatre, MFA Program, Blue Lake, CA 95525. Offers ensemble based physical theatre (MFA). *Accreditation:* NAST. *Degree requirements:* For master's, thesis. *Entrance requirements:* For master's, undergraduate degree, audition. Electronic applications accepted.

DePaul University, The Theatre School, Chicago, IL 60614. Offers acting (MFA); arts leadership (MFA); directing (MFA). *Degree requirements:* For master's, comprehensive exam, thesis. *Entrance requirements:* For master's, audition or interview, official transcripts, three letters of recommendation, resume, written statements (for directing program). Additional exam requirements/recommendations for international students: required—TOEFL (minimum score 550 paper-based; 80 iBT), IELTS (minimum score 6.5). Electronic applications accepted. *Expenses:* Contact institution.

Eastern Michigan University, Graduate School, College of Arts and Sciences, School of Communication, Media and Theatre Arts, Programs in Applied Drama/Theatre for the Young, Ypsilanti, MI 48197. Offers MA, MFA. *Program availability:* Part-time, online learning. *Students:* 3 full-time (all women), 3 part-time (2 women); includes 1 minority (Black or African American, non-Hispanic/Latino). Average age 29. 10 applicants, 50% accepted, 2 enrolled. In 2019, 3 master's awarded. *Entrance requirements:* Additional exam requirements/recommendations for international students: required—TOEFL. *Application deadline:* Applications are processed on a rolling basis. Application fee: $45. *Financial support:* Fellowships, research assistantships with full tuition reimbursements, teaching assistantships with full tuition reimbursements, career-related internships or fieldwork, Federal Work-Study, institutionally sponsored loans, scholarships/grants, tuition waivers (partial), and unspecified assistantships available. Support available to part-time students. Financial award applicants required to submit FAFSA. *Application contact:* Dr. Christine Tanner, Coordinator, 734-487-0332, Fax: 734-487-3443, E-mail: christine.tanner@emich.edu.

Eastern Michigan University, Graduate School, College of Arts and Sciences, School of Communication, Media and Theatre Arts, Programs in Theatre Arts, Ypsilanti, MI 48197. Offers interpretation/performance studies (MA); theatre arts (MA), including drama/theatre for the young, general. *Program availability:* Part-time, evening/weekend, online learning. *Students:* 4 full-time (1 woman), 4 part-time (2 women); includes 1 minority (Black or African American, non-Hispanic/Latino), 1 international. Average age 27. 7 applicants, 86% accepted, 3 enrolled. In 2019, 1 master's awarded. *Entrance requirements:* Additional exam requirements/recommendations for international students: required—TOEFL. *Application deadline:* Applications are processed on a rolling basis. Application fee: $45. *Financial support:* Fellowships, research assistantships with full tuition reimbursements, teaching assistantships with full tuition reimbursements, career-related internships or fieldwork, Federal Work-Study, institutionally sponsored loans, scholarships/grants, and unspecified assistantships available. Support available to part-time students. Financial award applicants required to submit FAFSA. *Application contact:* Dr. Lee Stille, Coordinator, 734-487-6846, Fax: 734-487-3443, E-mail: lstille@emich.edu.

Florida Atlantic University, Dorothy F. Schmidt College of Arts and Letters, Department of Theatre and Dance, Boca Raton, FL 33431-0991. Offers acting (MFA); design and technology (MFA). *Faculty:* 7 full-time (2 women). *Students:* 12 full-time (7 women), 2 part-time (0 women); includes 4 minority (3 Black or African American, non-Hispanic/Latino; 1 Hispanic/Latino). Average age 30. 5 applicants, 60% accepted, 2 enrolled. In 2019, 3 master's awarded. *Degree requirements:* For master's, thesis, production. *Entrance requirements:* For master's, GRE General Test, minimum GPA of 3.0 during last 60 hours of undergraduate course work. *Application deadline:* For fall admission, 8/15 priority date for domestic students, 8/15 for international students. Applications are processed on a rolling basis. Application fee: $30. *Expenses: Tuition:* Full-time $20,536; part-time $371.82 per credit hour. Tuition and fees vary according to program. *Financial support:* Fellowships, teaching assistantships with full tuition reimbursements, career-related internships or fieldwork, Federal Work-Study, and institutionally sponsored loans available. Support available to part-time students. Financial award application deadline: 3/31. *Unit head:* Dr. Thomas Shorrock, Chair, 561-297-3886, Fax: 561-297-2180, E-mail: shorrock@fau.edu. *Application contact:* Dr. Thomas Shorrock, Chair, 561-297-3886, Fax: 561-297-2180, E-mail: shorrock@fau.edu. Website: http://www.fau.edu/theatre/

Florida State University, The Graduate School, College of Fine Arts, School of Theatre, Tallahassee, FL 32306. Offers acting (MFA); costume design (MFA); directing (MFA); technical production (MFA); theatre (MA, PhD); theatre management (MFA). *Accreditation:* NAST. *Faculty:* 12 full-time (5 women). *Students:* 84 full-time (41 women); includes 14 minority (8 Black or African American, non-Hispanic/Latino; 6 Hispanic/Latino), 1 international. Average age 28. 125 applicants, 24% accepted, 24 enrolled. In 2019, 19 master's, 3 doctorates awarded. *Degree requirements:* For master's, one foreign language, comprehensive exam (for some programs), thesis (for some programs); for doctorate, one foreign language, comprehensive exam, thesis/dissertation. *Entrance requirements:* For master's, GRE General Test, writing sample (MA); interview and portfolio (MFA); minimum undergraduate GPA of 3.0; audition (MFA in acting). Additional exam requirements/recommendations for international students: required—TOEFL. *Application deadline:* For fall admission, 2/15 priority date for domestic and international students. Applications are processed on a rolling basis. Application fee: $30. Electronic applications accepted. *Financial support:* In 2019–20, 83 students received support, including 1 fellowship with full tuition reimbursement available (averaging $18,000 per year), 32 research assistantships with full tuition reimbursements available (averaging $18,000 per year), 24 teaching assistantships with full tuition reimbursements available (averaging $18,000 per year); career-related internships or fieldwork, institutionally sponsored loans, scholarships/grants, health care benefits, and unspecified assistantships also available. Financial award application deadline: 1/1; financial award applicants required to submit FAFSA. *Unit head:* Bradley Brock, Director, 850-644-7257, Fax: 850-644-7408, E-mail: bbrock@admin.fsu.edu. *Application contact:* Barbara Thomas, Program Assistant, 850-644-7234, Fax: 850-644-7246, E-mail: bgthomas@admin.fsu.edu. Website: http://theatre.fsu.edu/

Fontbonne University, Graduate Programs, St. Louis, MO 63105-3098. Offers accounting (MBA, MS); art (MA); art (K-12) (MAT); business (MBA); computer science (MS); deaf education (MA); early intervention in deaf education (MA); education (MA), including autism spectrum disorders, curriculum and instruction, diverse learners, early childhood education, reading, special education; elementary education (MAT); family and consumer sciences (MA), including multidisciplinary health communication studies; fine arts (MFA); instructional design and technology (MS); management and leadership (MM); middle school education (MAT); secondary education (MAT); special education (MAT); speech-language pathology (MS); supply chain management (MS); theatre (MA). *Accreditation:* ASHA. *Program availability:* Part-time, evening/weekend, online learning. *Degree requirements:* For master's, comprehensive exam (for some programs), thesis (for some programs). *Entrance requirements:* Additional exam requirements/recommendations for international students: required—TOEFL (minimum score 500 paper-based; 65 iBT). Electronic applications accepted. *Expenses: Tuition:* Full-time $6975; part-time $775 per credit hour. *Required fees:* $225; $25 per credit hour. Tuition and fees vary according to degree level and program.

Fordham University, Graduate School of Arts and Sciences, Program in Playwriting, New York, NY 10458. Offers MFA. *Students:* 19 applicants, 11% accepted, 2 enrolled. In 2019, 2 master's awarded. *Entrance requirements:* For master's, 3 letters of recommendation, resume/curriculum vitae, statement of intent, official transcripts, playwriting portfolio, bachelor's degree. Additional exam requirements/recommendations for international students: required—TOEFL. *Application deadline:* Applications are processed on a rolling basis. Application fee: $70. Electronic applications accepted. *Unit head:* Matthew Maguire, Director, 212-636-6306, E-mail: mmaguire@fordham.edu. *Application contact:* Garrett Marino, Director of Graduate Admissions, 718-817-4419, Fax: 718-817-3566, E-mail: gmarino10@fordham.edu. Website: http://www.fordham.edu/info/21309/playwriting_mfa/2561/playwriting_mfa_application_information

The George Washington University, Columbian College of Arts and Sciences, Department of Theatre and Dance, Washington, DC 20052. Offers classical acting (MFA); dance (MFA); exhibit design (Graduate Certificate); production design (MFA). *Program availability:* Part-time, evening/weekend. *Entrance requirements:* For master's, minimum GPA of 3.0, portfolio. Additional exam requirements/recommendations for international students: required—TOEFL (minimum score 550 paper-based; 80 iBT). Electronic applications accepted.

The Graduate Center, City University of New York, Graduate Studies, Program in Theatre, New York, NY 10016-4039. Offers PhD. *Degree requirements:* For doctorate, 2 foreign languages, thesis/dissertation. *Entrance requirements:* For doctorate, GRE General Test, writing sample. Additional exam requirements/recommendations for international students: required—TOEFL. Electronic applications accepted.

Hollins University, Graduate Programs, Program in Playwriting, Roanoke, VA 24020. Offers new play directing (Certificate); new play performance (Certificate); playwriting (MFA). *Program availability:* Part-time. *Degree requirements:* For master's, comprehensive exam, thesis. *Entrance requirements:* For master's, letters of recommendation, bachelor's degree, undergraduate transcripts, manuscript. Additional exam requirements/recommendations for international students: required—TOEFL (minimum score 550 paper-based; 80 iBT), IELTS (minimum score 6.5). Electronic applications accepted. *Expenses:* Contact institution.

Hunter College of the City University of New York, Graduate School, School of Arts and Sciences, Department of Theatre, Program in Theatre, New York, NY 10065-5085. Offers MA.

Idaho State University, Graduate School, College of Arts and Letters, Program in Theatre, Pocatello, ID 83209-8006. Offers MA. *Accreditation:* NAST. *Program availability:* Part-time. *Degree requirements:* For master's, comprehensive exam, thesis optional, oral and written exam. *Entrance requirements:* For master's, GRE General Test (35th percentile or above on one of the 3 sections). Additional exam requirements/recommendations for international students: required—TOEFL (minimum score 550 paper-based; 80 iBT). Electronic applications accepted.

Illinois State University, Graduate School, Wonsook Kim College of Fine Arts, School of Theatre, Normal, IL 61790. Offers MA, MFA, MS. *Accreditation:* NAST. *Program availability:* Part-time. *Faculty:* 27 full-time (13 women), 4 part-time/adjunct (3 women). *Students:* 20 full-time (13 women), 6 part-time (4 women). Average age 28. 39 applicants, 51% accepted, 10 enrolled. In 2019, 9 master's awarded. *Degree requirements:* For master's, variable foreign language requirement, thesis or alternative. *Entrance requirements:* For master's, GRE, sample of written work, minimum GPA of

3.0 in last 60 hours of course work. *Application deadline:* Applications are processed on a rolling basis. Application fee: $50. *Expenses: Tuition, area resident:* Full-time $7956; part-time $9767 per year. Tuition, nonresident: full-time $9233; part-time $17,592 per year. *Required fees:* $1797. *Financial support:* In 2019–20, 21 teaching assistantships were awarded; career-related internships or fieldwork, Federal Work-Study, institutionally sponsored loans, tuition waivers (full and partial), and unspecified assistantships also available. Financial award application deadline: 4/1. *Unit head:* Dr. Ann Haugo, Interim Director of Theatre. *Application contact:* Ann Haugo, 309-438-3955, E-mail: ahaugo@ilstu.edu. Website: http://www.arts.ilstu.edu/theatre/theatre.html/

Indiana University Bloomington, University Graduate School, College of Arts and Sciences, Department of Theatre, Drama, and Contemporary Dance, Bloomington, IN 47405. Offers acting (MFA); design and technology (MFA); directing (MFA); playwriting (MFA); theatre history, theory, and literature (MA, PhD). *Accreditation:* NAST. Terminal master's awarded for partial completion of doctoral program. *Degree requirements:* For master's, one foreign language, comprehensive exam, thesis, 30 credit hours; for doctorate, 2 foreign languages, comprehensive exam, thesis/dissertation, 90 credit hours. *Entrance requirements:* For master's, audition, interview, portfolio or script analysis; for doctorate, GRE General Test. Additional exam requirements/recommendations for international students: required—TOEFL (minimum score 550 paper-based, 80 iBT) or IELTS. Electronic applications accepted. *Expenses:* Contact institution.

The Juilliard School, Graduate Programs, New York, NY 10023-6588. Offers acting (MFA); jazz studies (Artist Diploma); music (MM, DMA, Diploma); music performance (Artist Diploma); opera studies (Artist Diploma); string quartet (Artist Diploma). *Degree requirements:* For master's and other advanced degree, performance jury, recital; for doctorate, one foreign language, thesis/dissertation, performance jury, 3 recitals. *Entrance requirements:* For master's and other advanced degree, audition; for doctorate, audition, interview. Additional exam requirements/recommendations for international students: required—TOEFL (minimum score 570 paper-based; 89 iBT). Electronic applications accepted.

Kansas State University, Graduate School, College of Arts and Sciences, School of Music, Theatre and Dance, Manhattan, KS 66506. Offers MA, MM. *Accreditation:* NASM; NAST. *Program availability:* Part-time, online learning. *Degree requirements:* For master's, thesis optional. *Entrance requirements:* For master's, GRE, audition (in person or recording), interview (for music education). Additional exam requirements/recommendations for international students: required—TOEFL (minimum score 600 paper-based). Electronic applications accepted.

Kent State University, College of the Arts, School of Theatre and Dance, Kent, OH 44242-0001. Offers theatre studies (MFA), including acting, design/technology. *Accreditation:* NAST. *Program availability:* Part-time. *Faculty:* 12 full-time (8 women), 2 part-time/adjunct (0 women). *Students:* 17 full-time (6 women), 1 part-time (0 women); includes 2 minority (1 Black or African American, non-Hispanic/Latino; 1 Two or more races, non-Hispanic/Latino), 2 international. Average age 36. 10 applicants, 80% accepted, 7 enrolled. In 2019, 6 master's awarded. *Degree requirements:* For master's, thesis, comprehensive project. *Entrance requirements:* For master's, GRE if grade point below 3.0, Bachelor's degree, transcripts, 3 letters of recommendation, goal statement, resume; audition (for acting); portfolio (for design/technology), minimum GPA 3.0 on 4.0 scale, interview, evidence of professional experience (for acting). Additional exam requirements/recommendations for international students: required—TOEFL (minimum score 71 iBT), IELTS (minimum score 6), PTE (minimum score 50), Michigan English Language Assessment Battery (minimum score 74). *Application deadline:* Applications are processed on a rolling basis. Application fee: $45 ($70 for international students). Electronic applications accepted. *Financial support:* Teaching assistantships with full tuition reimbursements, career-related internships or fieldwork, Federal Work-Study, scholarships/grants, and unspecified assistantships available. Financial award application deadline: 5/1. *Unit head:* Eric van Baars, Director and Associate Professor, 330-672-0102, E-mail: fvanbaar@kent.edu. *Application contact:* Yuko Kurahashi, Graduate Coordinator and Associate Professor of Theatre, 330-672-9483, E-mail: ykurahas@kent.edu. Website: http://www.kent.edu/theatredance

Long Island University - Post, College of Arts, Communications and Design, Brookville, NY 11548-1300. Offers art (MA); clinical art therapy (MA); clinical art therapy and counseling (MA); digital game design and development (MA); fine arts and design (MFA); interactive multimedia arts (MA); museum studies (MA); music (MA); theatre (MFA). *Degree requirements:* For master's, variable foreign language requirement, comprehensive exam (for some programs), thesis. *Entrance requirements:* For master's, performance audition or portfolio. Additional exam requirements/recommendations for international students: required—TOEFL (minimum score 550 paper-based; 79 iBT). Electronic applications accepted.

Louisiana State University and Agricultural & Mechanical College, Graduate School, College of Music and Dramatic Arts, Department of Theatre, Baton Rouge, LA 70803. Offers acting (MFA); directing (MFA); theatre (PhD); theatre design/technology (MFA). *Accreditation:* NAST.

Mary Baldwin University, Graduate Studies, Program in Shakespeare and Performance, Staunton, VA 24401-3610. Offers acting (M Litt); directing (M Litt); dramaturgy (M Litt); Shakespeare and performance (MFA); teaching (M Litt). *Entrance requirements:* For master's, GRE (M Litt).

Miami University, College of Creative Arts, Department of Theatre, Oxford, OH 45056. Offers MA. *Accreditation:* NAST.

Michigan State University, The Graduate School, College of Arts and Letters, Department of Theatre, East Lansing, MI 48824. Offers MA, MFA. *Entrance requirements:* Additional exam requirements/recommendations for international students: required—TOEFL. Electronic applications accepted.

Minnesota State University Mankato, College of Graduate Studies and Research, College of Arts and Humanities, Department of Theatre and Dance, Mankato, MN 56001. Offers theatre arts (MA, MFA). *Degree requirements:* For master's, one foreign language, comprehensive exam, thesis. *Entrance requirements:* For master's, minimum GPA of 3.0 during previous 2 years, 3 letters of recommendation, resume of theatre work, audition. Additional exam requirements/recommendations for international students: required—TOEFL. Electronic applications accepted.

Montclair State University, The Graduate School, College of the Arts, MA Program in Theatre, Montclair, NJ 07043-1624. Offers arts management (MA); production/stage management (MA); theatre studies (MA). *Accreditation:* NAST. *Program availability:* Part-time, evening/weekend. *Degree requirements:* For master's, comprehensive exam, thesis or alternative. *Entrance requirements:* For master's, GRE General Test, 2 letters of recommendation. Additional exam requirements/recommendations for international students: required—TOEFL (minimum score 83 iBT) or IELTS (minimum score 6.5). Electronic applications accepted.

Naropa University, Graduate Programs, Program in Theater: Contemporary Performance, Boulder, CO 80302-6697. Offers MFA. *Degree requirements:* For master's, thesis, culminating projects and performances. *Entrance requirements:* For master's, interview/audition; headshot; resume/curriculum vitae with pertinent academic, employment and volunteer activities; transcripts; 2 letters of recommendation; letter of interest. Additional exam requirements/recommendations for international students: required—TOEFL (minimum score 550 paper-based; 80 iBT). Electronic applications accepted. *Expenses:* Contact institution.

The New School, College of Performing Arts, School of Drama, New York, NY 10014. Offers acting (MFA); directing (MFA); playwriting (MFA). *Program availability:* Part-time. *Faculty:* 6 full-time (0 women), 141 part-time/adjunct. *Students:* 63 full-time (37 women); includes 30 minority (17 Black or African American, non-Hispanic/Latino; 12 Hispanic/Latino; 1 Two or more races, non-Hispanic/Latino), 8 international. Average age 28. 131 applicants, 24% accepted, 25 enrolled. In 2019, 18 master's awarded. *Degree requirements:* For master's, thesis, involvement in theatrical production and presentation. *Entrance requirements:* For master's, official transcripts, recommendation letters, statement of purpose; artistic resume and photograph (for directing and acting); writing sample (for directing); auditions (for acting). Additional exam requirements/recommendations for international students: required—TOEFL (minimum score 100 iBT), IELTS (minimum score 7), PTE (minimum score 68). *Application deadline:* For fall admission, 12/1 priority date for domestic and international students; for spring admission, 1/15 for domestic students, 1/15 priority date for international students. Applications are processed on a rolling basis. Application fee: $50. Electronic applications accepted. *Expenses:* 2195 per credit. *Financial support:* In 2019–20, 60 students received support, including 1 fellowship (averaging $6,243 per year), 1 teaching assistantship (averaging $4,682 per year); career-related internships or fieldwork, Federal Work-Study, scholarships/grants, and unspecified assistantships also available. Support available to part-time students. Financial award application deadline: 2/1; financial award applicants required to submit FAFSA. *Unit head:* Pippin Parker, Dean, School of Drama, 212-229-5859 Ext. 2636, E-mail: parkerp@newschool.edu. *Application contact:* Marlon Meikle, Assistant Director of Admissions, College of Performing Arts, 212-229-5859 Ext. 4828, E-mail: performingarts@newschool.edu.
Website: https://www.newschool.edu/drama

New York University, Steinhardt School of Culture, Education, and Human Development, Department of Music and Performing Arts Professions, Program in Educational Theatre, New York, NY 10012. Offers educational theatre and English 7-12 (MA); educational theatre and social studies 7-12 (MA); educational theatre in colleges and communities (MA, Ed D, PhD); educational theatre, all grades (MA). *Program availability:* Part-time. *Entrance requirements:* For master's, audition; for doctorate, GRE General Test, interview. Additional exam requirements/recommendations for international students: required—TOEFL (minimum score 100 iBT). Electronic applications accepted.

New York University, Steinhardt School of Culture, Education, and Human Development, Department of Music and Performing Arts Professions, Program in Music Performance and Composition, New York, NY 10012. Offers instrumental performance (MM), including instrumental performance, jazz instrumental performance; music performance and composition (PhD), including music performance and composition; music theory and composition (MM), including composition for film and multimedia, composition for music theater, computer music composition, music theory and composition, songwriting; piano performance (MM), including collaborative piano, solo piano; vocal pedagogy (Advanced Certificate); vocal performance (MM), including classical voice, musical theatre performance. *Program availability:* Part-time. *Entrance requirements:* For master's, audition; for doctorate, GRE General Test, audition, interview. Additional exam requirements/recommendations for international students: required—TOEFL (minimum score 100 iBT). Electronic applications accepted.

New York University, Tisch School of the Arts and Graduate School of Arts and Science, Department of Performance Studies, New York, NY 10003. Offers MA, PhD. *Degree requirements:* For doctorate, one foreign language, comprehensive exam, thesis/dissertation, dissertation defense, qualifying exam. *Entrance requirements:* For master's, sample of written work; for doctorate, master's degree, writing sample. Additional exam requirements/recommendations for international students: required—TOEFL (minimum score 105 paper-based). Electronic applications accepted. *Expenses:* Contact institution.

New York University, Tisch School of the Arts, Graduate Acting Program, New York, NY 10012-1019. Offers MFA. *Entrance requirements:* For master's, bachelor's degree, audition. Electronic applications accepted.

Northern Illinois University, Graduate School, College of Visual and Performing Arts, School of Theatre and Dance, De Kalb, IL 60115-2854. Offers MFA. *Program availability:* Part-time. *Faculty:* 16 full-time (9 women). *Students:* 25 full-time (12 women), 1 part-time (0 women); includes 6 minority (2 Black or African American, non-Hispanic/Latino; 1 Asian, non-Hispanic/Latino; 2 Hispanic/Latino; 1 Two or more races, non-Hispanic/Latino). Average age 26. 52 applicants, 48% accepted, 3 enrolled. In 2019, 17 master's awarded. *Degree requirements:* For master's, comprehensive exam, final project and defense. *Entrance requirements:* For master's, minimum GPA of 2.75, audition or portfolio. Additional exam requirements/recommendations for international students: required—TOEFL (minimum score 550 paper-based). *Application deadline:* For fall admission, 4/1 priority date for domestic students, 5/1 for international students; for spring admission, 10/15 priority date for domestic students, 10/1 for international students. Applications are processed on a rolling basis. Application fee: $40. Electronic applications accepted. *Financial support:* In 2019–20, 28 teaching assistantships with full tuition reimbursements were awarded; fellowships with full tuition reimbursements, research assistantships with full tuition reimbursements, career-related internships or fieldwork, Federal Work-Study, scholarships/grants, tuition waivers (full), and staff assistantships also available. Support available to part-time students. Financial award applicants required to submit FAFSA. *Unit head:* Alexander Gelman, Director, 815-753-8253, Fax: 815-753-8415, E-mail: agelman@niu.edu. *Application contact:* Graduate School Office, 815-753-0395, E-mail: gradsch@niu.edu.
Website: http://www.niu.edu/theatre/

Northern Michigan University, Office of Graduate Education and Research, College of Arts and Sciences, Department of English, Marquette, MI 49855-5301. Offers creative writing (MFA); literature (MA); pedagogy (MA); teaching English to speakers of other languages (Graduate Certificate); theater (MA); writing (MA). *Program availability:* Part-time. *Degree requirements:* For master's, thesis (for some programs), capstone project: thesis, practicum or portfolio (for MA); thesis (for MFA). *Entrance requirements:* For master's, minimum GPA of 3.0; bachelor's degree in English or minimum of 30 credit hours in undergraduate English; statement of purpose; resume; critical essay; creative writing sample (for MFA); 3 letters of recommendation; for Graduate Certificate, bachelor's degree. Additional exam requirements/recommendations for international students: required—TOEFL (minimum score 500 paper-based; 61 iBT), IELTS (minimum score 6). *Application deadline:* For fall admission, 2/1 for domestic students; for winter admission, 2/1 for domestic students; for summer admission, 3/17 for domestic students. Applications are processed on a rolling basis. Application fee: $50. Electronic applications accepted. *Financial support:* Teaching assistantships, career-related internships or fieldwork, scholarships/grants, and unspecified assistantships available. Financial award application deadline: 3/1; financial award applicants required to submit FAFSA. *Unit head:* Dr. Lynn Domina, Department Head and Professor, 906-227-1759, E-mail: ldomina@nmu.edu. *Application contact:* Dr. Lesley Larkin, Director of MA Program and Professor, 906-227-1794, E-mail: llarkin@nmu.edu.
Website: http://www.nmu.edu/english/

Northwestern University, The Graduate School, School of Communication, Department of Theatre, Evanston, IL 60208. Offers directing (MFA); stage design (MFA); theatre and drama (PhD). *Degree requirements:* For master's, thesis (MFA). *Entrance requirements:* For master's, GRE General Test. Additional exam requirements/recommendations for international students: required—TOEFL.

Northwestern University, The Graduate School, School of Communication, Interdisciplinary PhD Program in Theatre and Drama, Evanston, IL 60208. Offers PhD. *Degree requirements:* For doctorate, thesis/dissertation, qualifying and final oral exams. *Entrance requirements:* For doctorate, GRE General Test, sample of written work. Additional exam requirements/recommendations for international students: required—TOEFL. Electronic applications accepted.

The Ohio State University, Graduate School, College of Arts and Sciences, Division of Arts and Humanities, Department of Theatre, Columbus, OH 43210. Offers acting (MFA); design (MFA); theatre (PhD); theatre studies (MA). *Accreditation:* NAST. Terminal master's awarded for partial completion of doctoral program. *Degree requirements:* For master's, thesis (for some programs); for doctorate, one foreign language, thesis/dissertation. *Entrance requirements:* For master's, GRE General Test (for all MA applicants and MFA applicants with GPA below 3.0), audition (for MFA in acting); electronic design portfolio (for MFA in design); sample of published or unpublished research work (for MA); for doctorate, GRE General Test. Additional exam requirements/recommendations for international students: required—Michigan English Language Assessment Battery (minimum score 82); recommended—TOEFL (minimum score 550 paper-based; 79 iBT), IELTS (minimum score 7). Electronic applications accepted.

Ohio University, Graduate College, College of Fine Arts, School of Theater, Athens, OH 45701-2979. Offers MA, MFA. *Accreditation:* NAST. *Degree requirements:* For master's, thesis or alternative. *Entrance requirements:* For master's, minimum GPA of 3.0. Additional exam requirements/recommendations for international students: required—TOEFL (minimum score 550 paper-based; 80 iBT) or IELTS (minimum score 6.5). Electronic applications accepted.

Pace University, Dyson College of Arts and Sciences, The Actors Studio MFA Program, New York, NY 10038. Offers acting (MFA); directing (MFA); playwriting (MFA). *Degree requirements:* For master's, thesis. *Entrance requirements:* For master's, artistic resume, 2 letters of recommendation (theater, academic and/or professional), official transcripts; audition (for actors); interview and portfolio (for directors and playwrights). Additional exam requirements/recommendations for international students: required—TOEFL (minimum score 88 iBT), IELTS (minimum score 7) or PTE (minimum score 60).

Penn State University Park, Graduate School, College of Arts and Architecture, School of Theatre, University Park, PA 16802. Offers MFA. *Accreditation:* NAST.

Pensacola Christian College, Graduate Studies, Pensacola, FL 32503-2267. Offers business administration (MBA); curriculum and instruction (MS, Ed D, Ed S); dramatics (MFA); educational leadership (MS, Ed D, Ed S); graphic design (MA, MFA); music (MA); nursing (MSN); performance studies (MA); studio art (MA, MFA).

Point Park University, Conservatory of Performing Arts, Pittsburgh, PA 15222-1984. Offers screenwriting and playwriting (MFA). *Program availability:* Blended/hybrid learning. *Degree requirements:* For master's, comprehensive exam (for some programs), thesis or alternative. *Entrance requirements:* For master's, interview, undergraduate degree in related field, theatre experience. Additional exam requirements/recommendations for international students: required—TOEFL (minimum score 550 paper-based; 79 iBT). Electronic applications accepted.

Portland State University, Graduate Studies, College of the Arts, School of Music and Theater, Portland, OR 97207-0751. Offers conducting (Mus M); jazz studies (Mus M); music (Mus M); performance (Mus M). *Accreditation:* NASM. *Program availability:* Part-time. *Faculty:* 30 full-time (14 women), 60 part-time/adjunct (25 women). *Students:* 25 full-time (12 women), 6 part-time (1 woman); includes 6 minority (1 Asian, non-Hispanic/Latino; 3 Hispanic/Latino; 2 Two or more races, non-Hispanic/Latino), 4 international. Average age 30. 43 applicants, 72% accepted, 15 enrolled. In 2019, 9 master's awarded. *Degree requirements:* For master's, variable foreign language requirement, exit exam. *Entrance requirements:* For master's, GRE General Test, music diagnostic entrance examination, minimum GPA of 3.0 in graduate coursework or 2.75 overall undergraduate, audition. Additional exam requirements/recommendations for international students: required—TOEFL (minimum score 550 paper-based). *Application deadline:* For fall admission, 4/15 priority date for domestic students, 4/15 for international students; for winter admission, 10/1 for domestic and international students; for spring admission, 12/1 for domestic and international students; for summer admission, 1/15 for domestic and international students. Application fee: $65. *Expenses:* Contact institution. *Financial support:* In 2019–20, 24 students received support, including 10 teaching assistantships with full and partial tuition reimbursements available (averaging $7,203 per year); Federal Work-Study, scholarships/grants, and unspecified assistantships also available. Support available to part-time students. Financial award application deadline: 3/1; financial award applicants required to submit FAFSA. *Unit head:* Bonnie Miksch, Director, 503-725-3063, Fax: 503-725-8215, E-mail: bonnie@pdx.edu. *Application contact:* Bonnie Miksch, Director, 503-725-3063, Fax: 503-725-8215, E-mail: bonnie@pdx.edu.
Website: https://www.pdx.edu/music/

Regent University, Graduate School, School of Communication and the Arts, Virginia Beach, VA 23464-9800. Offers acting (MFA); communication (MA, PhD), including media and arts management and promotion (MA), political communication (MA), strategic communication (MA), technical communication (MA); film and TV (MA), including producing (MA, MFA), production, script writing; film-television (MFA), including directing, producing (MA, MFA), script and screenwriting; journalism (MA); theatre (MA). *Program availability:* Part-time, evening/weekend, 100% online, blended/hybrid learning. *Degree requirements:* For master's, thesis or alternative; for doctorate, thesis/dissertation. *Entrance requirements:* For master's, transcripts, writing sample, resume, audition (for MFA programs); for doctorate, GRE General Test, resume, writing sample, recommendations, interview, transcripts, personal goals statement. Additional exam requirements/recommendations for international students: required—TOEFL (minimum score 577 paper-based). Electronic applications accepted. *Expenses:* Contact institution.

Roosevelt University, Graduate Division, Chicago College of Performing Arts, Theatre Conservatory, Chicago, IL 60605. Offers theatre directing (MA). Electronic applications accepted. *Expenses:* Contact institution.

Rowan University, Graduate School, College of Education, Department of Language, Literacy, and Sociocultural Education, Program in Theatre Education, Glassboro, NJ 08028-1701. Offers MST. *Accreditation:* NAST. Electronic applications accepted. *Expenses: Tuition, area resident:* Part-time $715.50 per semester hour.

Tuition, state resident: part-time $715.50 per semester hour. Tuition, nonresident: part-time $715.50 per semester hour. *Required fees:* $161.55 per semester hour.

Rowan University, Graduate School, College of Performing Arts, Department of Theatre and Dance, Glassboro, NJ 08028-1701. Offers theatre arts administration (MA). *Accreditation:* NASAD. Electronic applications accepted. *Expenses: Tuition, area resident:* Part-time $715.50 per semester hour. Tuition, state resident: part-time $715.50 per semester hour. Tuition, nonresident: part-time $715.50 per semester hour. *Required fees:* $161.55 per semester hour.

Rutgers University - New Brunswick, Mason Gross School of the Arts, Theater Department, New Brunswick, NJ 08901. Offers acting (MFA); design (MFA); playwriting (MFA); stage management (MFA); technical direction (MFA). *Degree requirements:* For master's, thesis (for some programs), performance project. *Entrance requirements:* For master's, audition, interview, portfolio. Additional exam requirements/recommendations for international students: required—TOEFL (minimum score 550 paper-based), IELTS (minimum score 7). Electronic applications accepted.

San Diego State University, Graduate and Research Affairs, College of Professional Studies and Fine Arts, School of Theater, Television and Film, San Diego, CA 92182. Offers design and technology (MFA); film and television production (MFA); musical theatre (MFA); theatre arts (MA). *Accreditation:* NAST. *Program availability:* Part-time. *Degree requirements:* For master's, thesis. *Entrance requirements:* For master's, GRE General Test, 3 letters of recommendation, interview. Additional exam requirements/recommendations for international students: required—TOEFL. Electronic applications accepted.

San Francisco State University, Division of Graduate Studies, College of Liberal and Creative Arts, School of Theatre and Dance, San Francisco, CA 94132-1722. Offers theatre arts (MA, MFA). *Accreditation:* NAST. *Expenses: Tuition, area resident:* Full-time $7176; part-time $4164 per year. Tuition, state resident: full-time $7176; part-time $4164 per year. Tuition, nonresident: full-time $16,680; part-time $396 per unit. *International tuition:* $16,680 full-time. *Required fees:* $1524; $1524 per unit. $762 per semester. Tuition and fees vary according to degree level and program. *Unit head:* Prof. Kim Schwartz, Director, 415-338-1341, Fax: 415-338-6159, E-mail: ks@sfsu.edu. *Application contact:* Dr. Bruce Avery, Graduate Coordinator, 415- 338-3100, Fax: 415-338-6159, E-mail: bravery@sfsu.edu.
Website: http://www.theatre.sfsu.edu

San Jose State University, Program in Film and Theatre, San Jose, CA 95192-0001. Offers theatre arts (MA). *Accreditation:* NAST. *Degree requirements:* For master's, written exam. *Entrance requirements:* Additional exam requirements/recommendations for international students: required—TOEFL (minimum score 570 paper-based). Electronic applications accepted. *Expenses: Tuition, area resident:* Full-time $7176; part-time $4164 per credit hour. Tuition, state resident: full-time $7176; part-time $4164 per credit hour. Tuition, nonresident: full-time $7176; part-time $4165 per credit hour. *International tuition:* $7176 full-time. *Required fees:* $2110; $2110.

Sarah Lawrence College, Graduate Studies, Program in Theater, Bronxville, NY 10708-5999. Offers MFA. *Degree requirements:* For master's, portfolio. *Entrance requirements:* For master's, interview, minimum B average in undergraduate course work. Additional exam requirements/recommendations for international students: required—TOEFL (minimum score 600 paper-based). Electronic applications accepted.

Savannah College of Art and Design, Program in Dramatic Writing, Savannah, GA 31402-3146. Offers MFA. *Program availability:* Part-time. *Degree requirements:* For master's, thesis. *Entrance requirements:* For master's, GRE (recommended), portfolio (submitted in digital format), audition or writing submission, resume, statement of purpose, two letters of recommendation. Additional exam requirements/recommendations for international students: recommended—TOEFL (minimum score 550 paper-based; 85 iBT), IELTS (minimum score 6.5). Electronic applications accepted.

Savannah College of Art and Design, Program in Production Design, Savannah, GA 31402-3146. Offers MA, MFA. *Program availability:* Part-time. *Degree requirements:* For master's, final project (for MA); thesis (for MFA). *Entrance requirements:* For master's, GRE (recommended), portfolio (submitted in digital format), audition or writing submission, resume, statement of purpose, two letters of recommendation. Additional exam requirements/recommendations for international students: recommended—TOEFL (minimum score 550 paper-based; 85 iBT), IELTS (minimum score 6.5). Electronic applications accepted.

Smith College, Graduate and Special Programs, Department of Theatre, Northampton, MA 01063. Offers theatre (MFA), including playwriting. *Program availability:* Part-time. *Students:* 2 full-time (both women). Average age 57. 3 applicants, 67% accepted, 1 enrolled. *Degree requirements:* For master's, thesis. *Entrance requirements:* For master's, full-length play. Additional exam requirements/recommendations for international students: required—TOEFL (minimum score 595 paper-based; 97 iBT), IELTS (minimum score 7.5). *Application deadline:* For fall admission, 4/1 for domestic students, 1/15 for international students; for spring admission, 12/1 for domestic students. Application fee: $60. *Expenses: Tuition:* Full-time $36,940; part-time $1690 per credit. *Required fees:* $90. Full-time tuition and fees vary according to course load, degree level and program. *Financial support:* In 2019–20, 2 students received support. Scholarships/grants and human resources employee benefit available. Financial award application deadline: 1/15; financial award applicants required to submit CSS PROFILE or FAFSA. *Unit head:* Leonard Berkman, Graduate Student Adviser, 413-585-3206, E-mail: lberkman@smith.edu. *Application contact:* Ruth Morgan, Program Coordinator, 413-585-3050, Fax: 413-585-3054, E-mail: rmorgan@smith.edu.
Website: http://www.smith.edu/theatre/

Southern Illinois University Carbondale, Graduate School, College of Liberal Arts, Theater Department, Carbondale, IL 62901-4701. Offers speech/theater (PhD); theater (MFA). *Accreditation:* NAST (one or more programs are accredited). *Program availability:* Part-time. *Degree requirements:* For master's, thesis; for doctorate, thesis/dissertation. *Entrance requirements:* For master's, minimum GPA of 2.7; for doctorate, minimum GPA of 3.25. Additional exam requirements/recommendations for international students: required—TOEFL.

Southern Methodist University, Meadows School of the Arts, Division of Theatre, Dallas, TX 75275. Offers acting (MFA); design (MFA). *Accreditation:* NAST. *Entrance requirements:* For master's, audition or interview. Additional exam requirements/recommendations for international students: required—TOEFL (minimum score 550 paper-based; 80 iBT). Electronic applications accepted.

Southern Oregon University, Graduate Studies, Ashland Center for Theatre Studies, Ashland, OR 97520. Offers MTS. *Program availability:* Part-time. *Degree requirements:* For master's, thesis (for some programs). *Entrance requirements:* For master's, GRE General Test, minimum cumulative GPA of 3.0 in the last 90 quarter credits (60 semester credits) of undergraduate coursework. Additional exam requirements/recommendations for international students: required—TOEFL (minimum score 540 paper-based; 76 iBT), IELTS (minimum score 6), ELPT (minimum score 964) or ELS (minimum score 112). Electronic applications accepted.

Stanford University, School of Humanities and Sciences, Department of Theater and Performance Studies, Stanford, CA 94305-2004. Offers PhD. *Expenses: Tuition:* Full-time $52,479; part-time $34,110 per unit. *Required fees:* $672; $224 per quarter. Tuition and fees vary according to program and student level.
Website: http://taps.stanford.edu/

Stony Brook University, State University of New York, Graduate School, College of Arts and Sciences, Department of Theatre Arts, Program in Dramaturgy, Stony Brook, NY 11794. Offers MFA. *Degree requirements:* For master's, one foreign language, thesis. *Entrance requirements:* For master's, GRE General Test. Additional exam requirements/recommendations for international students: required—TOEFL. *Application deadline:* For fall admission, 1/15 for domestic students; for spring admission, 10/1 for domestic students. Application fee: $100. *Expenses:* Contact institution. *Unit head:* Prof. Nick Mangano, Chair, 631-632-7245, E-mail: Nick.Mangano@stonybrook.edu. *Application contact:* Lisa Perez, Coordinator, 631-632-7270, Fax: 631-632-7261, E-mail: lisa.perez@stonybrook.edu.

Stony Brook University, State University of New York, Graduate School, College of Arts and Sciences, Department of Theatre Arts, Program in Theatre Arts, Stony Brook, NY 11794. Offers MA. *Program availability:* Evening/weekend. *Students:* Average age 35. In 2019, 1 master's awarded. *Degree requirements:* For master's, one foreign language, thesis. *Entrance requirements:* For master's, GRE General Test. Additional exam requirements/recommendations for international students: required—TOEFL. *Application deadline:* For fall admission, 1/15 for domestic students; for spring admission, 10/1 for domestic students. Application fee: $100. *Expenses:* Contact institution. *Unit head:* Prof. Nick Mangano, Chair, 631-632-7245, E-mail: Nick.Mangano@stonybrook.edu. *Application contact:* Lisa Perez, Coordinator, 631-632-7270, Fax: 631-632-7258, E-mail: lisa.perez@stonybrook.edu.
Website: https://www.stonybrook.edu/commcms/theatre-arts/

Temple University, Center for the Performing and Cinematic Arts, School of Theater, Film and Media Arts, Department of Theater, Philadelphia, PA 19122-6096. Offers acting (MFA); design (MFA); directing (MFA); musical theater collaboration (MFA); musical theater studies (MA); playwriting (MFA). *Accreditation:* NAST. *Program availability:* Part-time. *Faculty:* 14 full-time (5 women), 26 part-time/adjunct (14 women). *Students:* 25 full-time (13 women); includes 6 minority (2 Black or African American, non-Hispanic/Latino; 1 American Indian or Alaska Native, non-Hispanic/Latino; 3 Hispanic/Latino), 3 international. 21 applicants, 71% accepted, 9 enrolled. In 2019, 6 master's awarded. *Entrance requirements:* For master's, audition/interview, portfolio, or samples of written work. Additional exam requirements/recommendations for international students: required—TOEFL, IELTS, PTE, one of three is required. Application fee: $60. Electronic applications accepted. *Expenses:* Contact institution. *Financial support:* Fellowships, teaching assistantships with full tuition reimbursements, Federal Work-Study, scholarships/grants, health care benefits, and unspecified assistantships available. Financial award application deadline: 3/1; financial award applicants required to submit FAFSA. *Unit head:* Fred M. Duer, Chair, Department of Theater; Head of Design and Professor (Scenic Design), 215-204-2804, E-mail: fred.duer@temple.edu. *Application contact:* Paury Flowers, Recruitment Coordinator, CPCA: Admin. Office, 215-777-9135, E-mail: pflowers@temple.edu.
Website: https://tfma.temple.edu/theater

Texas A&M University–Commerce, College of Humanities, Social Sciences and Arts, Commerce, TX 75429. Offers applied criminology (MS); applied linguistics (MA, MS); art (MA, MFA); christianity in history (Graduate Certificate); computational linguistics (Graduate Certificate); creative writing (Graduate Certificate); criminal justice management (Graduate Certificate); criminal justice studies (Graduate Certificate); English (MA, MS, PhD); film studies (Graduate Certificate); history (MA, MS); Holocaust studies (Graduate Certificate); homeland security (Graduate Certificate); music (MM); music performance (MM); political science (MA, MS); public history (Graduate Certificate); sociology (MS); Spanish (MA); studies in children's and adolescent literature and culture (Graduate Certificate); teaching English to speakers of other languages (Graduate Certificate); theater (MA, MS); world history (Graduate Certificate). *Program availability:* Part-time. *Faculty:* 49 full-time (28 women), 8 part-time/adjunct (2 women). *Students:* 34 full-time (21 women), 427 part-time (302 women); includes 175 minority (66 Black or African American, non-Hispanic/Latino; 1 American Indian or Alaska Native, non-Hispanic/Latino; 13 Asian, non-Hispanic/Latino; 79 Hispanic/Latino; 16 Two or more races, non-Hispanic/Latino), 15 international. Average age 38. 193 applicants, 49% accepted, 78 enrolled. In 2019, 122 master's, 6 doctorates awarded. *Degree requirements:* For master's, one foreign language, comprehensive exam, thesis (for some programs); for doctorate, one foreign language, comprehensive exam, thesis/dissertation, departmental qualifying exam. *Entrance requirements:* For master's, GRE General Test, official transcripts, letters of recommendation, resume, statement of goals; for doctorate, GRE General Test, official transcripts, letters of recommendation, statement of goals, writing samples, writing sessions, resumes. Additional exam requirements/recommendations for international students: required—TOEFL (minimum score 550 paper-based; 79 iBT), IELTS (minimum score 6), PTE (minimum score 53). *Application deadline:* For fall admission, 6/1 priority date for international students; for spring admission, 10/15 priority date for international students; for summer admission, 3/15 priority date for international students. Applications are processed on a rolling basis. Application fee: $50 ($75 for international students). Electronic applications accepted. *Expenses: Tuition, area resident:* Full-time $3630; part-time $202 per credit hour. Tuition, state resident: full-time $3630; part-time $202 per credit hour. Tuition, nonresident: full-time $11,232; part-time $624 per credit hour. *International tuition:* $11,232 full-time. *Required fees:* $2948. *Financial support:* In 2019–20, 30 students received support, including 18 research assistantships with partial tuition reimbursements available (averaging $3,231 per year), 136 teaching assistantships with partial tuition reimbursements available (averaging $4,053 per year); Federal Work-Study, institutionally sponsored loans, scholarships/grants, health care benefits, and unspecified assistantships also available. Financial award application deadline: 5/1; financial award applicants required to submit FAFSA. *Unit head:* Dr. William F. Kuracina, Interim Dean, 903-886-5166, Fax: 903-886-5774, E-mail: william.kuracina@tamuc.edu. *Application contact:* Rebecca Stevens, Graduate Student Services Coordinator, 903-468-6049, E-mail: rebecca.stevens@tamuc.edu.
Website: http://www.tamuc.edu/academics/colleges/humanitiesSocialSciencesArts/

Texas State University, The Graduate College, College of Fine Arts and Communication, Program in Theatre Arts, San Marcos, TX 78666. Offers design (MFA); directing (MFA); dramatic writing (MFA); theatre history, dramatic criticism and dramaturgy (MA). *Program availability:* Part-time, evening/weekend. *Degree requirements:* For master's, comprehensive exam, thesis (for some programs). *Entrance requirements:* For master's, official GRE (general test only) required with competitive scores in the verbal reasoning and quantitative reasoning sections, baccalaureate degree from regionally-accredited institution with minimum GPA of 2.75 in last 60 hours of undergraduate course work, 2 letters of recommendation, statement of purpose, curriculum vitae/resume; writing sample (for playwriting applicants only); interview (for directing applicants only). Additional exam requirements/recommendations for international students: required—TOEFL (minimum score 550 paper-based; 78 iBT), IELTS (minimum score 6). Electronic applications accepted.

Theater

Texas Tech University, Graduate School, J.T. and Margaret Talkington College of Visual and Performing Arts, School of Theatre and Dance, Lubbock, TX 79409-2061. Offers dance studies (MA); theatre arts (MA, MFA). *Accreditation:* NAST. *Program availability:* Part-time. *Faculty:* 24 full-time (13 women). *Students:* 40 full-time (18 women), 3 part-time (2 women); includes 8 minority (2 Black or African American, non-Hispanic/Latino; 2 Hispanic/Latino; 4 Two or more races, non-Hispanic/Latino), 1 international. Average age 29. 30 applicants, 50% accepted, 14 enrolled. In 2019, 13 master's awarded. *Degree requirements:* For master's, variable foreign language requirement, comprehensive exam (for some programs), thesis (for some programs), direct a production (for some programs). *Entrance requirements:* For master's, GRE, samples of artistic work in area of interest and/or interview/audition with faculty (for MFA). Additional exam requirements/recommendations for international students: required—TOEFL (minimum score 550 paper-based; 79 iBT), IELTS (minimum score 6.5), PTE (minimum score 60). *Application deadline:* For fall admission, 6/1 priority date for domestic students, 1/15 priority date for international students; for spring admission, 9/1 priority date for domestic students, 6/15 priority date for international students. Applications are processed on a rolling basis. Application fee: $65. Electronic applications accepted. *Expenses:* Contact institution. *Financial support:* In 2019–20, 40 students received support, including 34 fellowships (averaging $4,405 per year), 39 teaching assistantships (averaging $9,893 per year); research assistantships, Federal Work-Study, scholarships/grants, tuition waivers (partial), and unspecified assistantships also available. Financial award application deadline: 4/15; financial award applicants required to submit FAFSA. *Unit head:* Dr. Mark Charney, Director of Theatre and Dance, 806-742-3601, Fax: 806-742-1338, E-mail: mark.charney@ttu.edu. *Application contact:* Sarah Midgley, Graduate Admissions and Recruitment Coordinator, 806-834-5405, Fax: 806-742-1338, E-mail: sarah.midgley@ttu.edu.
Website: www.depts.ttu.edu/theatreanddance/

Texas Woman's University, Graduate School, College of Arts and Sciences, School of the Arts, Department of Music and Theatre, Denton, TX 76204. Offers drama (MA); music (MA), including music education, music therapy, pedagogy, performance. *Accreditation:* NASM. *Program availability:* Part-time. *Faculty:* 18 full-time (9 women), 9 part-time/adjunct (5 women). *Students:* 63 full-time (52 women), 31 part-time (24 women); includes 35 minority (7 Black or African American, non-Hispanic/Latino; 3 Asian, non-Hispanic/Latino; 23 Hispanic/Latino; 2 Two or more races, non-Hispanic/Latino), 11 international. Average age 29. 38 applicants, 92% accepted, 24 enrolled. In 2019, 21 master's awarded. *Degree requirements:* For master's, comprehensive exam, thesis (for some programs), project, recital, professional paper, professional paper or thesis (for music education). *Entrance requirements:* For master's, music history/theory placement exam (for music only), audition and/or design portfolio, interview, resume, writing sample (for drama only), letter of intent, minimum undergraduate GPA of 3.0. Additional exam requirements/recommendations for international students: required—TOEFL (minimum score 550 paper-based; 79 iBT); recommended—IELTS (minimum score 6.5), TSE (minimum score 53). *Application deadline:* For fall admission, 3/1 priority date for domestic and international students; for spring admission, 11/1 priority date for domestic students, 7/1 for international students; for summer admission, 4/30 for domestic students, 2/1 priority date for international students. Application fee: $50 ($75 for international students). Electronic applications accepted. *Expenses:* All are estimates. Tuition for 10 hours = $2,763; Fees for 10 hours = $1,342. Music courses require additional $35/SCH. *Financial support:* In 2019–20, 50 students received support, including 1 research assistantship, 6 teaching assistantships; career-related internships or fieldwork, scholarships/grants, health care benefits, and unspecified assistantships also available. Support available to part-time students. Financial award application deadline: 3/1; financial award applicants required to submit FAFSA. *Unit head:* Dr. Pamela Youngblood, Chair of Music and Theatre, 940-898-2500, Fax: 940-898-2494, E-mail: music@twu.edu. *Application contact:* Korie Hawkins, Associate Director of Admissions, Graduate Recruitment, 940-898-3188, Fax: 940-898-3081, E-mail: admissions@twu.edu.

Towson University, College of Fine Arts and Communication, Program in Theatre, Towson, MD 21252-0001. Offers MFA. *Accreditation:* NAST. *Students:* 7 full-time (4 women); includes 1 minority (Two or more races, non-Hispanic/Latino), 1 international. *Entrance requirements:* For master's, minimum GPA of 3.0, bachelor's degree, 3 letters of recommendation, artistic statement, current professional resume, 3 references, portfolio, interview. *Application deadline:* For fall admission, 1/17 for domestic students, 5/15 for international students; for spring admission, 10/15 for domestic students, 12/1 for international students. Applications are processed on a rolling basis. Application fee: $45. Electronic applications accepted. *Expenses: Tuition, area resident:* Full-time $7920; part-time $439 per credit. Tuition, nonresident: full-time $16,344; part-time $908 per credit. *International tuition:* $16,344 full-time. *Required fees:* $2628; $146 per credit. $876 per term. *Financial support:* Application deadline: 4/1. *Unit head:* Dr. Robyn Quick, Department Chair, 410-704-4519, E-mail: theatremfainfo@towson.edu. *Application contact:* Coverley Beidleman, Assistant Director of Graduate Admissions, 410-704-5630, Fax: 410-704-3030, E-mail: grads@towson.edu.
Website: https://www.towson.edu/cofac/departments/theatre/gradtheatre/

Tufts University, Graduate School of Arts and Sciences, Department of Drama and Dance, Medford, MA 02155. Offers theatre and performance studies (MA, PhD). Terminal master's awarded for partial completion of doctoral program. *Degree requirements:* For master's, one foreign language, thesis; for doctorate, one foreign language, thesis/dissertation, oral exam, written general exam. *Entrance requirements:* For master's and doctorate, GRE General Test, writing sample. Additional exam requirements/recommendations for international students: required—TOEFL (minimum score 600 paper-based; 80 iBT), IELTS (minimum score 6.5). Electronic applications accepted. *Expenses:* Contact institution.

Tulane University, School of Liberal Arts, Department of Theatre and Dance, New Orleans, LA 70118-5669. Offers design and technical production (MFA). *Entrance requirements:* For master's, GRE General Test, minimum B average in undergraduate course work. Additional exam requirements/recommendations for international students: required—TOEFL. Electronic applications accepted. *Expenses: Tuition:* Full-time $57,004; part-time $3167 per credit hour. *Required fees:* $2086; $44.50 per credit hour. $80 per term. Tuition and fees vary according to course load, degree level and program.

Université de Sherbrooke, Faculty of Letters and Human Sciences, Department of Letters and Communications, Sherbrooke, QC J1K 2R1, Canada. Offers comparative Canadian literature (MA, PhD); French literature (MA, PhD); linguistics (MA); theatre (MA). *Degree requirements:* For master's, thesis or alternative; for doctorate, thesis/dissertation. *Entrance requirements:* For master's, minimum GPA of 2.8; for doctorate, minimum GPA of 3.0.

University at Buffalo, the State University of New York, Graduate School, College of Arts and Sciences, Department of Theatre and Dance, Buffalo, NY 14260. Offers dance (MFA); theatre and performance (MA, PhD). *Program availability:* Part-time. *Faculty:* 10 full-time (7 women). *Students:* 14 full-time (11 women), 5 part-time (3 women). Average age 36. 34 applicants, 44% accepted, 9 enrolled. In 2019, 4 master's, 1 doctorate awarded. *Degree requirements:* For master's, comprehensive exam (for some programs), thesis project or written thesis; for doctorate, one foreign language, comprehensive exam, thesis/dissertation. *Entrance requirements:* For master's, statement of purpose; academic writing sample (e.g., scholarly essay, performance or book review); 3 letters of recommendation (sent electronically); portfolio of creative work; resume; BA, BFA, or BS; audition and sample of choreographic work (for MFA); for doctorate, GRE, statement of purpose; academic writing sample (e.g., scholarly essay, performance or book review); 3 letters of recommendation (sent electronically); portfolio of creative work; resume; master's degree. Additional exam requirements/recommendations for international students: required—TOEFL (minimum score 550 paper-based), IELTS. *Application deadline:* For fall admission, 1/15 priority date for domestic and international students. Applications are processed on a rolling basis. Application fee: $75. Electronic applications accepted. *Expenses: Tuition, area resident:* Full-time $11,310; part-time $471 per credit hour. Tuition, state resident: full-time $11,310; part-time $471 per credit hour. Tuition, nonresident: full-time $23,100; part-time $963 per credit hour. *International tuition:* $23,100 full-time. *Required fees:* $2820. *Financial support:* In 2019–20, 2 fellowships (averaging $4,000 per year), 7 teaching assistantships with full tuition reimbursements (averaging $13,400 per year) were awarded; scholarships/grants also available. Financial award application deadline: 1/2. *Unit head:* Prof. Anne H. Burnidge, Chair, 716-645-6897, E-mail: burnidge@buffalo.edu. *Application contact:* Rachel Olszewski, Graduate Studies Staff Assistant, 716-645-6076, E-mail: rachelol@buffalo.edu.
Website: http://www.theatredance.buffalo.edu/

The University of Akron, Graduate School, Buchtel College of Arts and Sciences, School of Dance, Theatre, and Arts Administration, Akron, OH 44325. Offers arts administration (MA); theatre arts (MA). *Program availability:* Part-time, evening/weekend. *Degree requirements:* For master's, thesis. *Entrance requirements:* For master's, minimum GPA of 2.75, 300-word statement of intent summarizing student background and outlining career goals. Additional exam requirements/recommendations for international students: required—TOEFL (minimum score 79 iBT), IELTS (minimum score 6.5). Electronic applications accepted.

The University of Alabama, Graduate School, College of Arts and Sciences, Department of Theatre and Dance, Tuscaloosa, AL 35487. Offers acting (MFA); costume design (MFA); directing (MFA); scene design/technical production (MFA); stage management (MFA); theatre (MFA); theatre management/administration (MFA). *Accreditation:* NAST. *Faculty:* 11 full-time (4 women). *Students:* 33 full-time (19 women), 1 part-time (0 women); includes 4 minority (2 Black or African American, non-Hispanic/Latino; 1 Hispanic/Latino; 1 Two or more races, non-Hispanic/Latino), 1 international. Average age 28. 34 applicants, 50% accepted, 12 enrolled. In 2019, 8 master's awarded. *Degree requirements:* For master's, thesis project. *Entrance requirements:* For master's, audition and/or portfolio review. *Application deadline:* For fall admission, 4/1 priority date for domestic students, 3/1 priority date for international students. Applications are processed on a rolling basis. Application fee: $50 ($60 for international students). Electronic applications accepted. *Expenses: Tuition, area resident:* Full-time $10,780; part-time $440 per credit hour. Tuition, nonresident: full-time $30,250; part-time $1550 per credit hour. *Financial support:* In 2019–20, 38 students received support, including research assistantships with full tuition reimbursements available (averaging $18,300 per year), teaching assistantships with full tuition reimbursements available (averaging $18,300 per year); career-related internships or fieldwork, health care benefits, and unspecified assistantships also available. Financial award application deadline: 4/15. *Unit head:* Prof. Sarah Barry, Chair and Professor, 205-348-8699, Fax: 205-348-9048, E-mail: smbarry@ua.edu. *Application contact:* Nancy Calvert, Recruiting Contact, 205-348-5283, Fax: 205-348-9048, E-mail: ncalvert@ua.edu.
Website: http://www.as.ua.edu/theatre/

University of Alberta, Faculty of Graduate Studies and Research, Department of Drama, Edmonton, AB T6G 2E1, Canada. Offers design (MFA); directing (MFA); drama (MA). *Degree requirements:* For master's, one foreign language, production thesis.

The University of Arizona, College of Fine Arts, School of Theatre, Film and Television, Tucson, AZ 85721. Offers MFA. *Accreditation:* NAST. *Degree requirements:* For master's, comprehensive exam (for some programs), thesis (for some programs), production monograph. *Entrance requirements:* For master's, 3 letters of recommendation, portfolio. Additional exam requirements/recommendations for international students: required—TOEFL (minimum score 550 paper-based; 79 iBT). Electronic applications accepted.

University of Arkansas, Graduate School, J. William Fulbright College of Arts and Sciences, Department of Theatre, Fayetteville, AR 72701. Offers MA, MFA. *Students:* 16 full-time (8 women); includes 6 minority (2 Black or African American, non-Hispanic/Latino; 1 American Indian or Alaska Native, non-Hispanic/Latino; 3 Hispanic/Latino), 1 international. 18 applicants, 67% accepted. In 2019, 15 master's awarded. *Application deadline:* For fall admission, 8/1 for domestic students, 4/1 for international students; for spring admission, 12/1 for domestic students, 10/1 for international students; for summer admission, 4/15 for domestic students, 3/1 for international students. Applications are processed on a rolling basis. Application fee: $60. Electronic applications accepted. *Financial support:* In 2019–20, 9 research assistantships, 11 teaching assistantships were awarded; fellowships with tuition reimbursements, career-related internships or fieldwork, and Federal Work-Study also available. Support available to part-time students. Financial award application deadline: 4/1; financial award applicants required to submit FAFSA. *Unit head:* Michael Riha, Department Chair, 479-575-3612, Fax: 479-575-7602, E-mail: mriha@uark.edu. *Application contact:* Weston Wilkerson, 479-575-3645, Fax: 479-575-7602, E-mail: wrwilker@uark.edu.
Website: https://fulbright.uark.edu/departments/theatre/

The University of British Columbia, Faculty of Arts, Creative Writing Program, Vancouver, BC V6T 1Z1, Canada. Offers creative writing (MFA); creative writing and theatre (MFA); film production and creative writing (MFA). *Program availability:* Part-time, online learning. *Degree requirements:* For master's, thesis. *Entrance requirements:* For master's, sample of written work. Additional exam requirements/recommendations for international students: required—TOEFL. Electronic applications accepted. *Expenses:* Contact institution.

The University of British Columbia, Faculty of Arts, Department of Theatre and Film, Theatre Program, Vancouver, BC V6T 1Z2, Canada. Offers theatre (MA, PhD); theatre design (MFA); theatre directing (MFA). Terminal master's awarded for partial completion of doctoral program. *Degree requirements:* For master's, variable foreign language requirement, comprehensive exam, thesis; for doctorate, one foreign language, comprehensive exam, thesis/dissertation. *Entrance requirements:* For master's, portfolio (MFA); for doctorate, MA or equivalent. Additional exam requirements/recommendations for international students: required—TOEFL (minimum score 550 paper-based for MFA; 600 for MA and PhD). *Expenses:* Contact institution.

University of California, Berkeley, Graduate Division, College of Letters and Science, Group in Performance Studies, Berkeley, CA 94720. Offers PhD. *Degree requirements:* For doctorate, one foreign language, thesis/dissertation, qualifying exam. *Entrance requirements:* For doctorate, GRE General Test, sample of critical writing, 3 letters of recommendation. Additional exam requirements/recommendations for international students: required—TOEFL. Electronic applications accepted.

University of California, Davis, Graduate Studies, Program in Dramatic Art, Davis, CA 95616. Offers acting (MFA); dramatic art (PhD). *Entrance requirements:* For master's, minimum GPA of 3.0, portfolio. Additional exam requirements/recommendations for international students: required—TOEFL (minimum score 550 paper-based). Electronic applications accepted.

University of California, Davis, Graduate Studies, Program in Performance Studies, Davis, CA 95616. Offers dramatic art (PhD). *Degree requirements:* For doctorate, 2 foreign languages, thesis/dissertation. *Entrance requirements:* For doctorate, GRE, minimum GPA of 3.25. Additional exam requirements/recommendations for international students: required—TOEFL (minimum score 550 paper-based). Electronic applications accepted.

University of California, Irvine, Claire Trevor School of the Arts, Department of Drama, Irvine, CA 92697. Offers acting (MFA); design and stage management (MFA); directing (MFA); drama (MFA); drama and theatre (PhD). *Students:* 70 full-time (38 women), 1 (woman) part-time; includes 27 minority (11 Black or African American, non-Hispanic/Latino; 4 Asian, non-Hispanic/Latino; 6 Hispanic/Latino; 6 Two or more races, non-Hispanic/Latino), 5 international. Average age 28. 170 applicants, 15% accepted, 23 enrolled. In 2019, 21 master's, 5 doctorates awarded. *Degree requirements:* For master's, comprehensive exam, thesis; for doctorate, one foreign language, thesis/dissertation. *Entrance requirements:* For master's, audition, interview, or portfolio; minimum GPA of 3.0; for doctorate, GRE, minimum GPA of 3.5, critical writing samples. *Application deadline:* For fall admission, 1/15 priority date for domestic students, 1/15 for international students. Applications are processed on a rolling basis. Application fee: $120 ($140 for international students). Electronic applications accepted. *Financial support:* Fellowships, teaching assistantships, institutionally sponsored loans, traineeships, health care benefits, and unspecified assistantships available. Financial award application deadline: 3/1; financial award applicants required to submit FAFSA. *Unit head:* Don Hill, Acting Chair of Drama, 949-824-3882, Fax: 949-824-3475, E-mail: donhill@uci.edu. *Application contact:* Marcus Beeman, Department Manager, 949-824-6332, E-mail: mbeeman@uci.edu.
Website: http://www.arts.uci.edu/ctsa-academic-departments-drama

University of California, Los Angeles, Graduate Division, School of Theater, Film and Television, Department of Theater, Los Angeles, CA 90095. Offers theater (MA, MFA); theater and performance studies (PhD). *Accreditation:* NAST. *Degree requirements:* For master's, comprehensive exam or thesis; for doctorate, one foreign language, thesis/dissertation, oral and written qualifying exams. *Entrance requirements:* For master's, bachelor's degree; minimum undergraduate GPA of 3.0 (or its equivalent if letter grade system not used); portfolio (MFA); writing sample (MA); for doctorate, GRE General Test, bachelor's degree; minimum undergraduate GPA of 3.0 (or its equivalent if letter grade system not used); writing sample. Additional exam requirements/recommendations for international students: required—TOEFL. Electronic applications accepted. *Expenses:* Contact institution.

University of California, San Diego, Graduate Division, Department of Theatre and Dance, La Jolla, CA 92093. Offers acting (MFA); dance theatre (MFA); design (MFA); directing (MFA); drama and theatre (PhD); playwriting (MFA); stage management (MFA). *Students:* 73 full-time (42 women). 523 applicants, 6% accepted, 19 enrolled. In 2019, 20 master's, 4 doctorates awarded. *Degree requirements:* For master's, thesis; for doctorate, comprehensive exam, thesis/dissertation, 4 quarters of teaching. *Entrance requirements:* For master's, GRE General Test (for playwriting only), minimum GPA of 3.5; audition or interview; for doctorate, GRE General Test, minimum GPA of 3.5, audition and/or interview, two samples of critical writing. Additional exam requirements/recommendations for international students: required—TOEFL (minimum score 550 paper-based; 80 iBT), IELTS (minimum score 7). *Application deadline:* For fall admission, 1/10 for domestic students. Application fee: $105 ($125 for international students). Electronic applications accepted. *Financial support:* Fellowships, teaching assistantships, and scholarships/grants available. Financial award applicants required to submit FAFSA. *Unit head:* Allan Havis, Chair, 858-534-8208, E-mail: ahavis@ucsd.edu. *Application contact:* Marybeth Ward, Graduate Coordinator, 858-534-1046, E-mail: meward@ucsd.edu.
Website: http://theatre.ucsd.edu/

University of California, Santa Barbara, Graduate Division, College of Letters and Sciences, Division of Humanities and Fine Arts, Department of Theater and Dance, Santa Barbara, CA 93106-7060. Offers theater studies (MA, PhD), including European medieval studies (PhD), feminist studies (PhD), theatre studies (PhD); MA/PhD. Terminal master's awarded for partial completion of doctoral program. *Degree requirements:* For master's, comprehensive exam, thesis; for doctorate, one foreign language, comprehensive exam, thesis/dissertation. *Entrance requirements:* For master's and doctorate, GRE. Additional exam requirements/recommendations for international students: required—TOEFL (minimum score 550 paper-based; 80 iBT), IELTS (minimum score 7). Electronic applications accepted.

University of California, Santa Cruz, Division of Graduate Studies, Division of the Arts, Department of Theater Arts, Santa Cruz, CA 95064. Offers Certificate. *Entrance requirements:* Additional exam requirements/recommendations for international students: required—TOEFL (minimum score 550 paper-based; 83 iBT); recommended—IELTS (minimum score 8). Electronic applications accepted.

University of Central Florida, College of Arts and Humanities, School of Performing Arts, Orlando, FL 32816. Offers music (MA); theatre (MA, MFA), including acting (MFA), theatre for young audiences (MFA). *Accreditation:* NASM; NCATE. *Program availability:* Part-time. *Students:* 65 full-time (32 women), 20 part-time (5 women); includes 22 minority (6 Black or African American, non-Hispanic/Latino; 1 Asian, non-Hispanic/Latino; 12 Hispanic/Latino; 3 Two or more races, non-Hispanic/Latino), 1 international. Average age 31. 76 applicants, 64% accepted, 37 enrolled. In 2019, 17 master's awarded. *Degree requirements:* For master's, comprehensive exam, thesis or alternative. *Entrance requirements:* For master's, GRE General Test, letters of recommendation, writing sample. Additional exam requirements/recommendations for international students: required—TOEFL. *Application deadline:* For fall admission, 7/15 for domestic students; for spring admission, 12/1 for domestic students. Application fee: $30. Electronic applications accepted. *Financial support:* In 2019–20, 35 students received support, including 6 fellowships with partial tuition reimbursements available (averaging $8,333 per year), 8 research assistantships with partial tuition reimbursements available (averaging $2,808 per year), 30 teaching assistantships with partial tuition reimbursements available (averaging $4,695 per year); career-related internships or fieldwork, Federal Work-Study, institutionally sponsored loans, health care benefits, tuition waivers (partial), and unspecified assistantships also available. Financial award application deadline: 3/1; financial award applicants required to submit FAFSA. *Unit head:* Dr. Michael Wainstein, Director, 407-823-2519, Fax: 407-823-3378, E-mail: michael.wainstein@ucf.edu. *Application contact:* Associate Director, Graduate Admissions, 407-823-2766, Fax: 407-823-6442, E-mail: gradadmissions@ucf.edu.
Website: http://performingarts.cah.ucf.edu/

University of Central Missouri, The Graduate School, Warrensburg, MO 64093. Offers accountancy (MA); accounting (MBA); applied mathematics (MS); aviation safety (MA); biology (MS); business administration (MBA); career and technology education (MS); college student personnel administration (MS); communication (MA); computer information systems and information technology (MS); computer science (MS); counseling (MS); criminal justice and criminology (MS); educational leadership (Ed S); educational leadership and policy analysis (Ed D); educational technology (MS, Ed S); elementary and early childhood education (MSE); English (MA); english language learners - teaching english as a second language (MA); environmental studies (MA); finance (MBA); history (MA); industrial hygiene (MS); industrial management (MS); information systems (MBA); kinesiology (MS); library science and information services (MS); literacy education (MSE); marketing (MBA); mathematics (MS); music (MA); occupational safety management (MS); professional leadership - adult, career, and technical education (Ed S); professional leadership - counseling (Ed S); psychology (MS); rural family nursing (MS); school administration (MSE); social gerontology (MS); sociology (MA); special education (MSE); speech language pathology (MS); teaching (MAT); technology (MS); technology management (PhD); theatre (MA). *Accreditation:* ASHA. *Program availability:* Part-time, 100% online, blended/hybrid learning. *Faculty:* 236 full-time (113 women), 97 part-time/adjunct (61 women). *Students:* 787 full-time (448 women), 1,459 part-time (997 women); includes 213 minority (72 Black or African American, non-Hispanic/Latino; 5 American Indian or Alaska Native, non-Hispanic/Latino; 27 Asian, non-Hispanic/Latino; 59 Hispanic/Latino; 50 Two or more races, non-Hispanic/Latino), 574 international. Average age 30. 1,477 applicants, 68% accepted, 664 enrolled. In 2019, 831 master's, 93 other advanced degrees awarded. *Degree requirements:* For master's and Ed S, comprehensive exam (for some programs), thesis (for some programs). *Entrance requirements:* For master's, A GRE or GMAT test score may be required by some of the programs, A minimum GPA, letters of recommendation, a statement of purpose may be required by some of the programs; for Ed S, A master's degree is required for the application of an Education Specialist's degree program. Additional exam requirements/recommendations for international students: required—TOEFL (minimum score 550 paper-based; 79 iBT). *Application deadline:* For fall admission, 6/1 priority date for domestic and international students; for spring admission, 10/15 priority date for domestic and international students; for summer admission, 4/1 priority date for domestic and international students. Applications are processed on a rolling basis. Application fee: $30 ($75 for international students). Electronic applications accepted. *Expenses: Tuition, area resident:* Full-time $7524; part-time $313.50 per credit hour. Tuition, state resident: full-time $7524; part-time $313.50 per credit hour. Tuition, nonresident: full-time $15,048; part-time $627 per credit hour. *International tuition:* $15,048 full-time. *Required fees:* $915; $30.50 per credit hour. *Financial support:* In 2019–20, 89 students received support. Research assistantships, teaching assistantships, career-related internships or fieldwork, Federal Work-Study, scholarships/grants, unspecified assistantships, and administrative and laboratory assistantships available. Support available to part-time students. Financial award application deadline: 4/1; financial award applicants required to submit FAFSA. *Unit head:* Shellie Hewitt, Director of Graduate and International Student Services, 660-543-4621, Fax: 660-543-4778, E-mail: hewitt@ucmo.edu. *Application contact:* Shellie Hewitt, Director of Graduate and International Student Services, 660-543-4621, Fax: 660-543-4778, E-mail: hewitt@ucmo.edu.
Website: http://www.ucmo.edu/graduate/

University of Chicago, Division of the Humanities, Master of Arts Program in the Humanities, Chicago, IL 60637. Offers art history (MA); cinema and media studies (MA); classic languages (MA); comparative literature (MA); creative writing (MA); cultural policy studies (MA); digital humanities (MA); East Asian languages and civilizations (MA); English language and literature (MA); gender and sexuality studies (MA); Germanic studies (MA); linguistics (MA); music (MA); near Eastern languages and civilizations (MA); philosophy (MA); poetics (MA); race, politics and culture (MA); Romance languages and literatures (MA); Slavic languages and literatures (MA); South Asian languages and civilizations (MA); theater and performance studies (MA). *Degree requirements:* For master's, thesis. *Entrance requirements:* For master's, GRE General Test, 10-15 page writing sample, statement of purpose, 3 letters of recommendation, transcripts for all previous degrees and institutions attended. Additional exam requirements/recommendations for international students: required—TOEFL (minimum score 104 iBT), IELTS (minimum score 7). Electronic applications accepted. *Expenses:* Contact institution.

University of Cincinnati, Graduate School, College-Conservatory of Music, Division of Theatre Arts, Production and Arts Administration, Cincinnati, OH 45221. Offers arts administration (MA); directing (MFA); theater design and production (MFA); voice and opera (MM, DMA); MBA/MA. *Accreditation:* NAST (one or more programs are accredited). *Degree requirements:* For master's, final project. *Entrance requirements:* For master's, GMAT (MA), audition/interview. Additional exam requirements/recommendations for international students: required—TOEFL (minimum score 520 paper-based). Electronic applications accepted.

University of Colorado Boulder, Graduate School, College of Arts and Sciences, Department of Theatre and Dance, Boulder, CO 80309. Offers dance (MFA); theatre (MA, PhD). Terminal master's awarded for partial completion of doctoral program. *Degree requirements:* For master's, comprehensive exam, thesis; for doctorate, one foreign language, thesis/dissertation. *Entrance requirements:* For master's, GRE General Test (MA), audition (MFA), minimum undergraduate GPA of 2.75. Electronic applications accepted. Application fee is waived when completed online.

University of Connecticut, Graduate School, School of Fine Arts, Department of Dramatic Arts, Storrs, CT 06269. Offers acting (MA, MFA); design (MA, MFA); puppetry (MA, MFA); technical direction (MA, MFA). *Degree requirements:* For master's, comprehensive exam. *Entrance requirements:* Additional exam requirements/recommendations for international students: required—TOEFL (minimum score 550 paper-based). Electronic applications accepted.

University of Delaware, College of Arts and Sciences, Professional Theatre Training Program, Newark, DE 19716. Offers acting (MFA); stage management (MFA); technical production (MFA). *Entrance requirements:* For master's, audition, interview. Electronic applications accepted.

University of Florida, Graduate School, College of The Arts, School of Theatre and Dance, Gainesville, FL 32611. Offers theatre (MFA), including acting, costume design, lighting design, scene design. *Accreditation:* NAST. *Program availability:* Online learning. *Degree requirements:* For master's, thesis, creative project. *Entrance requirements:* For master's, GRE General Test, audition/portfolio, bachelor's degree in theatre, interview, minimum GPA 3.0. Additional exam requirements/recommendations for international students: required—TOEFL (minimum score 550 paper-based; 80 iBT), IELTS (minimum score 6). Electronic applications accepted.

University of Georgia, Franklin College of Arts and Sciences, Department of Theatre and Film Studies, Athens, GA 30602. Offers theatre (MFA, PhD). *Accreditation:* NAST. *Degree requirements:* For master's, comprehensive exam; for doctorate, one foreign language, comprehensive exam, thesis/dissertation. *Entrance requirements:* For master's and doctorate, GRE General Test. Additional exam requirements/recommendations for international students: required—TOEFL (minimum score 550 paper-based). Electronic applications accepted.

University of Guelph, Office of Graduate and Postdoctoral Studies, College of Arts, School of English and Theatre Studies, Program in Drama, Guelph, ON N1G 2W1, Canada. Offers MA. *Program availability:* Part-time. *Degree requirements:* For master's, thesis (for some programs). *Entrance requirements:* For master's, 2 letters of reference, 4 year honours undergraduate degree in English or drama. Additional exam requirements/recommendations for international students: required—TOEFL. Electronic applications accepted.

University of Hawaii at Manoa, Office of Graduate Education, College of Arts and Humanities, Department of Theatre and Dance, Honolulu, HI 96822. Offers dance (MA, MFA); theatre (MA, MFA, PhD). *Program availability:* Part-time. *Degree requirements:* For master's, one foreign language, thesis optional; for doctorate, one foreign language, comprehensive exam, thesis/dissertation. *Entrance requirements:* For master's and doctorate, GRE General Test. Additional exam requirements/recommendations for international students: required—TOEFL (minimum score 600 paper-based; 100 iBT), IELTS (minimum score 7).

University of Houston, Kathrine G. McGovern College of the Arts, School of Theatre and Dance, Houston, TX 77204. Offers theatre (MA, MFA). *Program availability:* Part-time. *Degree requirements:* For master's, thesis optional. *Entrance requirements:* For master's, GRE General Test, audition/interview (for MFA). Electronic applications accepted.

University of Idaho, College of Graduate Studies, College of Letters, Arts and Social Sciences, Department of Theatre Arts, Moscow, ID 83844-2282. Offers MFA. *Faculty:* 9 full-time. *Students:* 35. Average age 38. In 2019, 18 master's awarded. *Entrance requirements:* For master's, minimum GPA of 3.0. Additional exam requirements/recommendations for international students: required—TOEFL (minimum score 79 iBT). *Application deadline:* For fall admission, 7/30 for domestic students; for spring admission, 12/1 for domestic students. Applications are processed on a rolling basis. Application fee: $60. Electronic applications accepted. *Expenses:* Tuition, state resident: full-time $7753.80; part-time $502 per credit hour. Tuition, nonresident: full-time $26,990; part-time $1571 per credit hour. *Required fees:* $2122.20; $47 per credit hour. *Financial support:* Research assistantships and teaching assistantships available. Financial award applicants required to submit FAFSA. *Unit head:* Robert Caisley, Chair, 208-885-6465, E-mail: theatre@uidaho.edu. *Application contact:* Robert Caisley, Chair, 208-885-6465, E-mail: theatre@uidaho.edu.
Website: https://www.uidaho.edu/class/theatre

University of Illinois at Urbana-Champaign, Graduate College, College of Fine and Applied Arts, Department of Theatre, Champaign, IL 61820. Offers MA, MFA, PhD.

The University of Iowa, Graduate College, College of Liberal Arts and Sciences, Department of Theatre Arts, Iowa City, IA 52242-1316. Offers MFA. *Accreditation:* NAST. *Degree requirements:* For master's, thesis, exam. *Entrance requirements:* For master's, minimum GPA of 3.0. Additional exam requirements/recommendations for international students: required—TOEFL (minimum score 550 paper-based; 81 iBT). Electronic applications accepted.

The University of Kansas, Graduate Studies, College of Liberal Arts and Sciences, Department of Theatre and Dance, Lawrence, KS 66045. Offers scenography (MFA), including scenography; theatre studies (MA, PhD). *Program availability:* Part-time. *Students:* 14 full-time (9 women), 1 (woman) part-time; includes 5 minority (1 Black or African American, non-Hispanic/Latino; 1 American Indian or Alaska Native, non-Hispanic/Latino; 1 Hispanic/Latino; 2 Two or more races, non-Hispanic/Latino). Average age 31. 7 applicants, 57% accepted, 1 enrolled. In 2019, 2 master's, 1 doctorate awarded. *Entrance requirements:* For master's and doctorate, GRE General Test, official transcript, three recent letters of recommendation, current resume, statement of personal goals, writing sample. Additional exam requirements/recommendations for international students: required—TOEFL, IELTS. *Application deadline:* For fall admission, 2/15 for domestic and international students. Application fee: $65 ($85 for international students). Electronic applications accepted. *Expenses:* Tuition, state resident: full-time $9989. Tuition, nonresident: full-time $23,950. *International tuition:* $23,950 full-time. *Required fees:* $984; $81.99 per credit hour. Tuition and fees vary according to course load, campus/location and program. *Financial support:* Fellowships, research assistantships, teaching assistantships, Federal Work-Study, scholarships/grants, and unspecified assistantships available. Financial award application deadline: 1/1. *Unit head:* Henry Bial, Chair, 785-864-4225, E-mail: hbial@ku.edu. *Application contact:* Julia Reilly, Graduate Admissions Contact, 785-864-9488, E-mail: juliareilly@ku.edu.
Website: https://theatredance.ku.edu/

University of Lethbridge, School of Graduate Studies, Lethbridge, AB T1K 3M4, Canada. Offers addictions counseling (M Sc); agricultural biotechnology (M Sc); agricultural studies (M Sc, MA); anthropology (MA); archaeology (M Sc, MA); art (MA, MFA); biochemistry (M Sc); biological sciences (M Sc); biomolecular science (PhD); biosystems and biodiversity (PhD); Canadian studies (MA); chemistry (M Sc); computer science (M Sc); computer science and geographical information science (M Sc); counseling (MC); counseling psychology (M Ed); dramatic arts (MA); earth, space, and physical science (PhD); economics (MA); education (MA, PhD); educational leadership (M Ed); English (MA); environmental science (M Sc); evolution and behavior (PhD); exercise science (M Sc); French (MA); French/German (MA); French/Spanish (MA); general education (M Ed); geography (M Sc, MA); German (MA); health sciences (M Sc); individualized multidisciplinary (M Sc, MA); kinesiology (M Sc, MA); management (M Sc), including accounting, finance, human resource management and labor relations, information systems, international management, marketing, policy and strategy; mathematics (M Sc); music (M Mus, MA); Native American studies (MA); neuroscience (M Sc, PhD); new media (MA, MFA); nursing (M Sc, MN); philosophy (MA); physics (M Sc); political science (MA); psychology (M Sc, MA); religious studies (MA); sociology (MA); theatre and dramatic arts (MFA); theoretical and computational science (PhD); urban and regional studies (MA); women and gender studies (MA). *Program availability:* Part-time, evening/weekend. *Degree requirements:* For master's, thesis (for some programs); for doctorate, comprehensive exam, thesis/dissertation. *Entrance requirements:* For master's, GMAT (for M Sc in management), bachelor's degree in related field, minimum GPA of 3.0 during previous 20 graded semester courses, 2 years' teaching or related experience (M Ed); for doctorate, master's degree, minimum graduate GPA of 3.5. Additional exam requirements/recommendations for international students: required—TOEFL (minimum score 580 paper-based; 93 iBT). Electronic applications accepted.

University of Louisville, Graduate School, College of Arts and Sciences, Department of Theatre Arts, Louisville, KY 40292-0001. Offers design (MFA); performance (MFA). *Accreditation:* NAST. *Program availability:* Part-time. *Faculty:* 12 full-time (4 women), 7 part-time/adjunct (4 women). *Students:* 12 full-time (6 women); includes 9 minority (all Black or African American, non-Hispanic/Latino), 1 international. Average age 27. 10 applicants, 40% accepted, 4 enrolled. In 2019, 3 master's awarded. *Degree requirements:* For master's, performance project and monograph. *Entrance requirements:* For master's, audition or portfolio, 2 letters of reference, official transcripts. Additional exam requirements/recommendations for international students: required—TOEFL (minimum score 550 paper-based; 79 iBT), IELTS can be used in place of the TOEFL; recommended—IELTS (minimum score 6.5). *Application deadline:* For fall admission, 4/15 for domestic and international students. Applications are processed on a rolling basis. Application fee: $65. Electronic applications accepted. *Expenses: Tuition, area resident:* Full-time $13,000; part-time $723 per credit hour. Tuition, state resident: full-time $13,000; part-time $723 per credit hour. Tuition, nonresident: full-time $27,114; part-time $1507 per credit hour. *International tuition:* $27,114 full-time. *Required fees:* $196. Tuition and fees vary according to program and reciprocity agreements. *Financial support:* In 2019–20, 10 students received support, including 10 teaching assistantships with full tuition reimbursements available (averaging $14,000 per year); fellowships, research assistantships, health care benefits, and unspecified assistantships also available. *Unit head:* Dr. Nefertiti Burton, Professor and Chair, 502-852-7682, E-mail: nefertiti.burton@louisville.edu. *Application contact:* Dr. Nefertiti Burton, Professor and Chair, 502-852-7682, E-mail: nefertiti.burton@louisville.edu.
Website: http://louisville.edu/theatrearts/

The University of Manchester, School of Arts, Languages and Cultures, Manchester, United Kingdom. Offers anthropology, media and performance (PhD); applied theatre (PhD); Arab world studies (PhD); archaeology (PhD); art history and visual studies (PhD); arts and cultural management (PhD); arts management and cultural policy (PhD); Chinese studies (PhD); classics and ancient history (PhD); composition (PhD); creative writing (PhD); drama (PhD); East Asian studies (PhD); electroacoustic composition (PhD); English and American studies (PhD); English language (PhD); French studies (PhD); German studies (PhD); history (PhD); humanitarianism and conflict response (PhD); interpreting studies (PhD); Japanese studies (PhD); Latin American cultural studies (PhD); linguistics (PhD); Middle Eastern studies (PhD); museology (PhD); museum practice (PhD); music (PhD); musicology (PhD); Polish studies (PhD); Portuguese studies (PhD); religions and theology (PhD); Russian studies (PhD); Spanish studies (PhD); translation and intercultural studies (PhD).

University of Maryland, Baltimore County, The Graduate School, College of Arts, Humanities and Social Sciences, Department of Education, Program in Teaching, Baltimore, MD 21250. Offers early childhood education (MAT); elementary education (MAT); teaching (MAT), including art, biology, chemistry, choral music, classical foreign language, dance, earth/space science, English, instrumental music, mathematics, modern foreign language, physical science, physics, social studies, theatre. *Program availability:* Part-time, evening/weekend. *Faculty:* 24 full-time (18 women), 25 part-time/adjunct (19 women). *Students:* 25 full-time (19 women), 15 part-time (8 women); includes 14 minority (5 Black or African American, non-Hispanic/Latino; 1 American Indian or Alaska Native, non-Hispanic/Latino; 5 Asian, non-Hispanic/Latino; 1 Hispanic/Latino; 2 Two or more races, non-Hispanic/Latino). Average age 32. 34 applicants, 79% accepted, 18 enrolled. In 2019, 23 master's awarded. *Degree requirements:* For master's, comprehensive exam (for some programs), thesis (for some programs). *Entrance requirements:* For master's, PRAXIS Core Examination or GRE (minimum score of 1000), minimum GPA of 3.0. Additional exam requirements/recommendations for international students: required—TOEFL. *Application deadline:* For fall admission, 6/1 for domestic and international students; for spring admission, 11/1 for domestic and international students. Applications are processed on a rolling basis. Application fee: $50. Electronic applications accepted. *Expenses: Tuition, area resident:* Full-time $659. Tuition, state resident: full-time $659. Tuition, nonresident: full-time $1132. *International tuition:* $1132 full-time. *Required fees:* $140; $140 per credit hour. *Financial support:* In 2019–20, 6 students received support, including 1 research assistantship with tuition reimbursement available (averaging $12,000 per year), 5 teaching assistantships with tuition reimbursements available (averaging $12,000 per year); career-related internships or fieldwork, Federal Work-Study, scholarships/grants, tuition waivers, and unspecified assistantships also available. Financial award application deadline: 3/15. *Unit head:* Dr. Susan M. Blunck, Graduate Program Director, 410-455-2869, Fax: 410-455-3986, E-mail: blunck@umbc.edu. *Application contact:* Cheryl Johnson, MAT Program Specialist, 410-455-3388, E-mail: blackwel@umbc.edu.
Website: http://www.umbc.edu/education/

University of Maryland, College Park, Academic Affairs, College of Arts and Humanities, School of Theatre, Dance and Performance Studies, Theatre Program, College Park, MD 20742. Offers performance (MFA); theatre and performance studies (MA, PhD); theatre design (MFA). *Degree requirements:* For master's, comprehensive exam, thesis optional. *Entrance requirements:* For master's, GRE General Test, portfolio, writing sample, 3 letters of recommendation. Additional exam requirements/recommendations for international students: required—TOEFL. Electronic applications accepted.

University of Massachusetts Amherst, Graduate School, College of Humanities and Fine Arts, Department of Theater, Amherst, MA 01003. Offers costume design (MFA); directing (MFA); dramaturgy (MFA); lighting design (MFA); scenic design (MFA). *Program availability:* Part-time. *Degree requirements:* For master's, thesis. *Entrance requirements:* For master's, GRE (for dramaturgy and costume design only), two critical essays or design portfolios, resume of production experience. Additional exam requirements/recommendations for international students: required—TOEFL (minimum score 550 paper-based; 80 iBT), IELTS (minimum score 6.5). Electronic applications accepted.

University of Memphis, Graduate School, College of Communication and Fine Arts, Department of Theatre and Dance, Memphis, TN 38152. Offers theatre (MFA). *Accreditation:* NAST. *Students:* 15 full-time (7 women), 4 part-time (2 women); includes 3 minority (1 Asian, non-Hispanic/Latino; 1 Hispanic/Latino; 1 Two or more races, non-Hispanic/Latino), 1 international. Average age 37. 30 applicants, 27% accepted, 8 enrolled. In 2019, 6 master's awarded. *Degree requirements:* For master's, comprehensive exam, practicum, internship. *Entrance requirements:* For master's, minimum GPA of 3.0 in major, 2.5 overall, interview/audition. *Application deadline:* For fall admission, 8/1 priority date for domestic students; for spring admission, 12/1 priority date for domestic students. Applications are processed on a rolling basis. Application fee: $35 ($60 for international students). Electronic applications accepted. *Expenses: Tuition, area resident:* Full-time $9216; part-time $512 per credit hour. Tuition, state resident: full-time $9216; part-time $512 per credit hour. Tuition, nonresident: full-time $12,672; part-time $704 per credit hour. *International tuition:* $16,128 full-time. *Required fees:* $1530; $85 per credit hour. Tuition and fees vary according to program. *Financial support:* Research assistantships with full tuition reimbursements, teaching assistantships with full tuition reimbursements, career-related internships or fieldwork, Federal Work-Study, institutionally sponsored loans, scholarships/grants, and unspecified assistantships available. Financial award application deadline: 2/1; financial award applicants required to submit FAFSA. *Unit head:* Holly Lau, Chair, 901-678-2523, Fax: 901-678-1350, E-mail: hclau@memphis.edu. *Application contact:* Sarah Brown, Coordinator of Graduate Studies, 901-678-3137, Fax: 901-678-1350, E-mail: sbrown8@memphis.edu.
Website: http://www.memphis.edu/theatre/

University of Minnesota, Twin Cities Campus, Graduate School, College of Liberal Arts, Department of Theatre Arts and Dance, Minneapolis, MN 55455. Offers design technology (MFA); theatre arts (MA, PhD). Terminal master's awarded for partial completion of doctoral program. *Degree requirements:* For master's, thesis (for some programs), final creative project (MFA), foreign language (MA); for doctorate, one foreign language, thesis/dissertation, oral defense, written exams. *Entrance* *requirements:* For master's, GRE General Test (for MA), minimum GPA of 3.0 or portfolio; for doctorate, GRE General Test, minimum GPA of 3.0, writing sample, 1 foreign language. Additional exam requirements/recommendations for international students: required—TOEFL (minimum score 550 paper-based; 79 iBT). Electronic applications accepted.

University of Missouri, Office of Research and Graduate Studies, College of Arts and Science, Department of Theatre, Columbia, MO 65211. Offers MA, PhD. *Program availability:* Part-time. *Entrance requirements:* For master's, GRE General Test, minimum GPA of 3.0 overall and in last 60 hours; for doctorate, GRE General Test, minimum GPA of 3.0 overall and in last 60 hours, 3.5 in master's program.

University of Missouri–Kansas City, College of Arts and Sciences, Theatre Department, Kansas City, MO 64110-2499. Offers MA, MFA. *Accreditation:* NAST. *Degree requirements:* For master's, thesis. *Entrance requirements:* For master's, audition or portfolio, interview. Additional exam requirements/recommendations for international students: required—TOEFL (minimum score 550 paper-based; 80 iBT). Electronic applications accepted.

University of Montana, Graduate School, College of Visual and Performing Arts, School of Theatre and Dance, Missoula, MT 59812. Offers design/technology (MFA); theatre (MA). *Accreditation:* NAST (one or more programs are accredited). *Degree requirements:* For master's, thesis or alternative. *Entrance requirements:* For master's, GRE General Test, audition, portfolio, production notebook.

University of Nebraska–Lincoln, Graduate College, College of Fine and Performing Arts, Johnny Carson School of Theatre and Film, Lincoln, NE 68588. Offers acting (MFA); costume (MFA); directing (MFA); stage design (MFA). *Accreditation:* NAST. *Degree requirements:* For master's, thesis. *Entrance requirements:* For master's, audition, portfolio. Additional exam requirements/recommendations for international students: required—TOEFL (minimum score 500 paper-based). Electronic applications accepted.

University of Nevada, Las Vegas, Graduate College, College of Fine Arts, Department of Theatre, Las Vegas, NV 89154-5036. Offers MA, MFA. *Program availability:* Part-time. *Faculty:* 6 full-time (4 women), 5 part-time/adjunct (2 women). *Students:* 19 full-time (10 women), 1 (woman) part-time; includes 3 minority (1 Hispanic/Latino; 2 Two or more races, non-Hispanic/Latino). Average age 30. 21 applicants, 43% accepted, 8 enrolled. In 2019, 15 master's awarded. *Degree requirements:* For master's, comprehensive exam (for some programs), thesis (for some programs), creative project, oral exam. *Entrance requirements:* For master's, sample research paper or research statement; statement of purpose; 2 letters of recommendation. Additional exam requirements/recommendations for international students: required—TOEFL (minimum score 550 paper-based; 80 iBT), IELTS (minimum score 7). *Application deadline:* For fall admission, 8/1 for domestic students, 5/1 for international students. Application fee: $60 ($95 for international students). Electronic applications accepted. *Expenses:* Contact institution. *Financial support:* In 2019–20, 27 students received support, including 18 research assistantships with full tuition reimbursements available (averaging $15,000 per year), 1 teaching assistantship with full tuition reimbursement available (averaging $15,000 per year); institutionally sponsored loans, scholarships/grants, health care benefits, and unspecified assistantships also available. Financial award application deadline: 3/15; financial award applicants required to submit FAFSA. *Unit head:* Norma Saldivar, Chair/Professor, 702-895-3666, E-mail: theatre.chair@unlv.edu. *Application contact:* Norma Saldivar, Chair/Professor, 702-895-3666, E-mail: theatre.chair@unlv.edu.
Website: http://theatre.unlv.edu/

University of New Mexico, Graduate Studies, College of Fine Arts, Department of Theatre and Dance, Albuquerque, NM 87131-2039. Offers dance (MFA); dance history (MA); dramatic writing (MFA); theatre education and outreach (MA). *Accreditation:* NASD; NAST. *Degree requirements:* For master's, comprehensive exam (for some programs), thesis (for some programs). *Entrance requirements:* For master's, minimum GPA of 3.0; undergraduate major in theatre, dance or closely-related field; 3 letters of recommendation; letter of intent; BA, BFA, BS, or MA in dance movement science or related field, or equivalent experience (for MFA in dance). Electronic applications accepted. *Expenses:* Tuition, state resident: full-time $7633; part-time $972 per year. Tuition, nonresident: full-time $22,586; part-time $3840 per year. *International tuition:* $23,292 full-time. *Required fees:* $8608. Tuition and fees vary according to course level, course load, degree level, program and student level.

University of New Orleans, Graduate School, College of Liberal Arts, Education and Human Development, Department of Film and Theatre, New Orleans, LA 70148. Offers design (MFA); film production (MFA); theatre performance (MFA), including acting, directing. *Accreditation:* NAST. *Degree requirements:* For master's, comprehensive exam, thesis. *Entrance requirements:* Additional exam requirements/recommendations for international students: required—TOEFL (minimum score 550 paper-based; 79 iBT), IELTS (minimum score 6.5). Electronic applications accepted.

The University of North Carolina at Chapel Hill, Graduate School, College of Arts and Sciences, Department of Dramatic Art, Chapel Hill, NC 27599. Offers acting (MFA); costume production (MFA); technical production (MFA). *Entrance requirements:* For master's, audition or portfolio.

The University of North Carolina at Charlotte, Cato College of Education, Interdisciplinary Education Programs, Charlotte, NC 28223-0001. Offers art education (Graduate Certificate); child and family development: early childhood development (MAT); curriculum and instruction (PhD); elementary education (MAT); foreign language education (MAT); middle grades education (MAT); secondary education (MAT); special education (MAT); teachin (Graduate Certificate); teaching English as a second language (MAT); theatre education (Graduate Certificate). *Program availability:* Part-time, 100% online, blended/hybrid learning. *Students:* 52 full-time (42 women), 647 part-time (526 women); includes 266 minority (172 Black or African American, non-Hispanic/Latino; 2 American Indian or Alaska Native, non-Hispanic/Latino; 11 Asian, non-Hispanic/Latino; 56 Hispanic/Latino; 25 Two or more races, non-Hispanic/Latino), 8 international. Average age 34. 590 applicants, 84% accepted, 382 enrolled. In 2019, 84 master's, 15 doctorates, 156 other advanced degrees awarded. *Degree requirements:* For master's, capstone/portfolio. *Entrance requirements:* For master's, GRE or MAT, bachelor's degree, or its U.S. equivalent, from regionally-accredited college or university; minimum overall GPA of 3.0 on all previous work beyond high school; statement of purpose (essay); at least three recommendation forms; for doctorate, GRE or MAT, bachelor's degree or its U.S. equivalent from regionally-accredited college or university; minimum overall GPA of 3.5 in master's degree program; for Graduate Certificate, bachelor's degree from regionally-accredited university; minimum GPA of 2.75 on all post-secondary work attempted; transcripts; personal statement outlining why the applicant seeks admission to the program. Additional exam requirements/recommendations for international students: required—TOEFL (minimum score 557 paper-based; 83 iBT), IELTS (minimum score 6.5), TOEFL (minimum score 557 paper-based, 83 iBT) or IELTS (6.5). *Application deadline:* Applications are processed on a rolling basis. Application fee: $75. Electronic applications accepted. *Expenses:* Tuition, state resident: full-time $4337. Tuition, nonresident: full-time $17,771. *Required fees:* $3093. Tuition and fees vary according to course load, degree level and program. *Financial*

support: Career-related internships or fieldwork, institutionally sponsored loans, scholarships/grants, and unspecified assistantships available. Support available to part-time students. Financial award application deadline: 3/1; financial award applicants required to submit FAFSA. *Unit head:* Dr. Ellen McIntyre, Dean, 704-687-8722, E-mail: ellen.mcintyre@uncc.edu. *Application contact:* Kathy B. Giddings, Director of Graduate Admissions, 704-687-5503, Fax: 704-687-1668, E-mail: gradadm@uncc.edu.
Website: http://education.uncc.edu/academic-programs

The University of North Carolina at Greensboro, Graduate School, School of Music, Theatre and Dance, Department of Theatre, Greensboro, NC 27412-5001. Offers acting (MFA); design (MFA); directing (MFA); theater education (M Ed); theater for youth (MFA). *Accreditation:* NAST. *Entrance requirements:* For master's, portfolio, interviews. Electronic applications accepted.

University of North Carolina School of the Arts, School of Design and Production, Winston-Salem, NC 27127-2738. Offers costume design (MFA); costume technology (MFA); scene design (MFA); scenic art (MFA); sound design (MFA); stage automation (MFA); stage properties (MFA); technical direction (MFA); wig and makeup design (MFA). *Degree requirements:* For master's, thesis (for some programs), project. *Entrance requirements:* For master's, interview, portfolio. Additional exam requirements/recommendations for international students: required—TOEFL. Electronic applications accepted.

University of Oklahoma, Weitzenhoffer Family College of Fine Arts, Helmerich School of Drama, Norman, OK 73019. Offers MA. *Degree requirements:* For master's, thesis. *Entrance requirements:* For master's, BFA in drama. Additional exam requirements/recommendations for international students: required—TOEFL (minimum score 79 iBT) or IELTS (minimum score 6.5). Electronic applications accepted. *Expenses:* Tuition, state resident: full-time $6583.20; part-time $274.30 per credit hour. Tuition, nonresident: full-time $21,242; part-time $885.10 per credit hour. *International tuition:* $21,242.40 full-time. *Required fees:* $1994.20; $72.55 per credit hour. $126.50 per semester. Tuition and fees vary according to course load and degree level.

University of Oregon, Graduate School, College of Arts and Sciences, Department of Theater Arts, Eugene, OR 97403. Offers MA, MFA, MS, PhD. *Degree requirements:* For master's, variable foreign language requirement, thesis or alternative; for doctorate, variable foreign language requirement, thesis/dissertation. *Entrance requirements:* For master's and doctorate, minimum GPA of 3.0. Additional exam requirements/recommendations for international students: required—TOEFL.

University of Ottawa, Faculty of Graduate and Postdoctoral Studies, Faculty of Arts, Department of Theatre, Ottawa, ON K1N 6N5, Canada. Offers directing for theatre (MA). Electronic applications accepted.

University of Pittsburgh, Kenneth P. Dietrich School of Arts and Sciences, Department of Theatre Arts, Pittsburgh, PA 15260. Offers MA, MFA, PhD. *Accreditation:* NAST. *Faculty:* 10 full-time (7 women). *Students:* 16 full-time (12 women); includes 2 minority (1 Black or African American, non-Hispanic/Latino; 1 Asian, non-Hispanic/Latino). Average age 27. 33 applicants, 9% accepted, 2 enrolled. In 2019, 1 doctorate awarded. Terminal master's awarded for partial completion of doctoral program. *Degree requirements:* For master's, comprehensive exam, thesis; for doctorate, one foreign language, comprehensive exam, thesis/dissertation. *Entrance requirements:* For master's, personal statement, transcripts, CV, 3 letters of recommendation, 1 writing sample, head shot, resume; audition or interview in second stage of application process; for doctorate, personal statement, transcripts, 3 letters of recommendation, 2 writing samples. Additional exam requirements/recommendations for international students: required—TOEFL (minimum score 100 paper-based), IELTS (minimum score 7). *Application deadline:* For fall admission, 1/15 for domestic and international students. Application fee: $75. Electronic applications accepted. *Financial support:* In 2019–20, 12 students received support, including 1 fellowship (averaging $23,628 per year), 11 teaching assistantships (averaging $19,480 per year); Federal Work-Study, scholarships/grants, and health care benefits also available. Financial award application deadline: 1/15; financial award applicants required to submit FAFSA. *Unit head:* Annmarie Duggan, Department Chair, 412-624-7284, Fax: 412-624-6338, E-mail: duggan@pitt.edu. *Application contact:* Joshua Oliver, Graduate Student Administrator, 412-624-6568, Fax: 412-624-6338, E-mail: jjo48@pitt.edu.
Website: http://www.play.pitt.edu/

University of San Diego, College of Arts and Sciences, The Old Globe and University of San Diego Shiley Graduate Theatre Program, San Diego, CA 92110-2492. Offers MFA. *Faculty:* 5 full-time (1 woman), 1 (woman) part-time/adjunct. *Students:* 14 full-time (7 women); includes 8 minority (3 Black or African American, non-Hispanic/Latino; 5 Hispanic/Latino). Average age 29. 319 applicants, 3% accepted, 7 enrolled. In 2019, 7 master's awarded. *Entrance requirements:* For master's, audition. Additional exam requirements/recommendations for international students: required—TOEFL (minimum score 580 paper-based; 83 iBT), TWE. *Application deadline:* For fall admission, 1/5 for domestic and international students. Application fee: $55. *Financial support:* In 2019–20, 14 students received support, including 14 fellowships with full tuition reimbursements available; career-related internships or fieldwork, Federal Work-Study, and institutionally sponsored loans also available. Financial award applicants required to submit FAFSA. *Unit head:* Jesse Perez, Graduate Program Director, 619-260-7934, Fax: 619-260-8810, E-mail: theatrearts@sandiego.edu. *Application contact:* Erika Garwood, Associate Director of Graduate Admissions, 619-260-4524, Fax: 619-260-4158, E-mail: grads@sandiego.edu.
Website: http://www.graduateacting.com/

University of Saskatchewan, College of Graduate and Postdoctoral Studies, College of Arts and Science, Department of Drama, Saskatoon, SK S7N 5A2, Canada. Offers MA. *Degree requirements:* For master's, thesis. *Entrance requirements:* Additional exam requirements/recommendations for international students: required—TOEFL (minimum score 80 iBT); recommended—IELTS (minimum score 6.5). Electronic applications accepted.

University of South Carolina, The Graduate School, College of Arts and Sciences, Department of Theatre and Dance, Columbia, SC 29208. Offers theatre (MA, MAT, MFA). *Accreditation:* NAST (one or more programs are accredited). *Degree requirements:* For master's, comprehensive exam, thesis. *Entrance requirements:* For master's, GRE General Test, GRE or MAT (MAT), audition, interview (for MFA). Additional exam requirements/recommendations for international students: required—TOEFL. Electronic applications accepted.

University of South Carolina, The Graduate School, College of Education, Department of Instruction and Teacher Education, Program in Secondary Education, Columbia, SC 29208. Offers art education (IMA, MAT); business education (IMA, MAT); English (MAT); foreign language (MAT); health education (MAT); mathematics (MAT); science (IMA, MAT); secondary (Ed D); secondary education (MT, PhD); social studies (MAT); theatre and speech (MAT). *Accreditation:* NCATE. *Degree requirements:* For master's, comprehensive exam, thesis (for some programs), foreign language (MA); for doctorate, one foreign language, comprehensive exam, thesis/dissertation. *Entrance requirements:* For master's, GRE General Test or MAT, teaching certificate (IMA, M Ed), interview; for doctorate, GRE General Test or MAT, interview.

University of South Dakota, Graduate School, College of Fine Arts, Department of Theatre, Vermillion, SD 57069. Offers design/technology (MFA); directing (MFA); theatre (MA). *Accreditation:* NAST. *Degree requirements:* For master's, thesis or alternative. *Entrance requirements:* For master's, GRE (for MA), minimum GPA of 2.7, portfolio. Additional exam requirements/recommendations for international students: required—TOEFL (minimum score 550 paper-based; 79 iBT). Electronic applications accepted.

University of Southern California, Graduate School, School of Dramatic Arts, Los Angeles, CA 90089. Offers acting (MFA); dramatic writing (MFA). *Degree requirements:* For master's, comprehensive exam. *Entrance requirements:* For master's, GRE. Additional exam requirements/recommendations for international students: required—TOEFL. Electronic applications accepted.

The University of Tennessee, Graduate School, College of Arts and Sciences, Department of Theatre, Knoxville, TN 37996. Offers acting (MFA); costume design (MFA); lighting design (MFA); scene design (MFA). *Accreditation:* NAST. *Degree requirements:* For master's, thesis or alternative. *Entrance requirements:* For master's, audition, minimum GPA of 2.7. Additional exam requirements/recommendations for international students: required—TOEFL. Electronic applications accepted.

The University of Texas at Austin, Graduate School, College of Fine Arts, Department of Theatre and Dance, Austin, TX 78712-1111. Offers acting (MFA); dance (MFA); directing (MFA); drama and theatre for youth (MFA); performance as public practice (MA, MFA, PhD); playwriting (MFA); theatre technology (MFA); theatrical design (MFA). *Degree requirements:* For master's, thesis; for doctorate, variable foreign language requirement, thesis/dissertation. *Entrance requirements:* For master's and doctorate, GRE General Test.

The University of Texas at Austin, Graduate School, Michener Center for Writers, Austin, TX 78712-1111. Offers fiction (MFA); playwriting (MFA); poetry (MFA); screenwriting (MFA). Electronic applications accepted.

The University of the Arts, College of Performing Arts, Program in Devised Performance, Philadelphia, PA 19102-4944. Offers MFA, Certificate.

University of the Cumberlands, Graduate Programs in Education, Williamsburg, KY 40769-1372. Offers all grades (P-12) (M Ed); business and marketing (MA Ed, MAT); counselor education and supervision (Ed D); director of pupil personnel (Certificate); director of special education (Certificate); educational administration and supervision (Ed S); educational leadership (Ed D); elementary education (MA Ed, MAT); instructional leadership - principalship (MA Ed); instructional leadership - school principal (Certificate); middle school education (MA Ed, MAT); reading and writing (MA Ed); school counseling (MA Ed); school superintendent (Certificate); secondary education (MA Ed, MAT); special education (MAT); supervisor of instruction (Certificate); teacher leader (MA Ed). *Program availability:* Part-time, evening/weekend, online learning. *Degree requirements:* For master's, comprehensive exam. Electronic applications accepted.

University of Toronto, School of Graduate Studies, Faculty of Arts and Science, Centre for Drama, Theatre and Performance Studies, Toronto, ON M5S 1A1, Canada. Offers MA, PhD. *Program availability:* Part-time. *Entrance requirements:* For master's, minimum B+ average, significant coursework in drama and related disciplines, resume, 2 letters of recommendation. Additional exam requirements/recommendations for international students: required—TOEFL (minimum score 580 paper-based; 93 iBT), TWE (minimum score 5). Electronic applications accepted.

University of Victoria, Faculty of Graduate Studies, Faculty of Fine Arts, Department of Theatre, Victoria, BC V8W 2Y2, Canada. Offers design (MFA); directing (MFA); theatre history (MA). *Degree requirements:* For master's, thesis. *Entrance requirements:* Additional exam requirements/recommendations for international students: required—TOEFL (minimum score 575 paper-based), IELTS (minimum score 7). Electronic applications accepted.

University of Virginia, College and Graduate School of Arts and Sciences, Department of Drama, Charlottesville, VA 22903. Offers MFA. *Degree requirements:* For master's, thesis project. *Entrance requirements:* For master's, GRE General Test, resume; 3 letters of recommendation. Additional exam requirements/recommendations for international students: required—TOEFL (minimum score 600 paper-based; 90 iBT), IELTS (minimum score 7). Electronic applications accepted.

University of Washington, Graduate School, College of Arts and Sciences, School of Drama, Seattle, WA 98195. Offers acting (MFA); costume design (MFA); directing (MFA); dramatic theory (PhD); lighting design (MFA); scenic design (MFA); theatre and performance history (PhD). *Degree requirements:* For master's, thesis; for doctorate, one foreign language, comprehensive exam, thesis/dissertation. *Entrance requirements:* For master's, interview, minimum GPA of 3.0, portfolio; for doctorate, GRE General Test, minimum GPA of 3.0, writing sample. Additional exam requirements/recommendations for international students: required—TOEFL.

University of Wisconsin–Madison, Graduate School, College of Letters and Science, Department of Theatre and Drama, Madison, WI 53706-1380. Offers MA, MFA, PhD. *Accreditation:* NAST. *Program availability:* Part-time. *Degree requirements:* For master's, thesis; for doctorate, thesis/dissertation. *Entrance requirements:* For master's and doctorate, GRE. Electronic applications accepted.

University of Wisconsin–Superior, Graduate Division, Department of Communicating Arts, Superior, WI 54880-4500. Offers mass communication (MA); speech communication (MA); theater (MA). *Program availability:* Part-time. *Degree requirements:* For master's, comprehensive exam, thesis or alternative, position paper or project. *Entrance requirements:* For master's, minimum GPA of 2.75. Electronic applications accepted.

Université Laval, Faculty of Letters, Department of Literature, Programs in Literature and Arts of the Screen and Stage, Québec, QC G1K 7P4, Canada. Offers MA, PhD. *Program availability:* Part-time. Terminal master's awarded for partial completion of doctoral program. *Degree requirements:* For master's, thesis; for doctorate, comprehensive exam, thesis/dissertation. *Entrance requirements:* For master's and doctorate, linguistics exams, knowledge of French, knowledge of a second language. Electronic applications accepted.

Utah State University, School of Graduate Studies, Caine College of the Arts, Department of Theatre Arts, Logan, UT 84322. Offers design (MFA). *Degree requirements:* For master's, variable foreign language requirement, thesis (for some programs), summer internship. *Entrance requirements:* For master's, GRE General Test or MAT, portfolio, minimum GPA of 3.0, interview, BS or 20 semester credits. Additional exam requirements/recommendations for international students: required—TOEFL.

Villanova University, Graduate School of Liberal Arts and Sciences, Department of Theatre, Villanova, PA 19085-1699. Offers MA. *Program availability:* Part-time, evening/weekend. *Degree requirements:* For master's, comprehensive exam. *Entrance requirements:* For master's, GRE, minimum GPA of 3.0, resume, statement of goals, headshot. Additional exam requirements/recommendations for international students: required—TOEFL. Electronic applications accepted.

Virginia Commonwealth University, Graduate School, School of the Arts, Department of Theatre, Richmond, VA 23284-9005. Offers costume design (MFA); pedagogy/literature (MFA); pedagogy/performance (MFA); scene design/technical theatre (MFA). *Accreditation:* NAST. *Degree requirements:* For master's, thesis (for some programs). *Entrance requirements:* For master's, audition, portfolio. Additional exam requirements/recommendations for international students: required—TOEFL (minimum score 600 paper-based; 100 iBT). Electronic applications accepted.

Washington University in St. Louis, The Graduate School, Department of Performing Arts, St. Louis, MO 63130-4899. Offers dance (MFA); theater and performance studies (MA). *Degree requirements:* For master's, thesis optional. *Entrance requirements:* For master's, GRE General Test, sample of written work. Additional exam requirements/recommendations for international students: required—TOEFL. Electronic applications accepted.

Wayne State University, College of Fine, Performing and Communication Arts, Maggie Allesee Department of Theatre and Dance, Detroit, MI 48202. Offers theatre (MFA), including acting, stage costume design, stage lighting design, stage management, theatre management, theatre stage design; theatre and dance (MA). *Accreditation:* NAST. *Program availability:* 100% online, blended/hybrid learning. *Degree requirements:* For master's, comprehensive exam, thesis (for some programs), final project (for MFA). *Entrance requirements:* For master's, minimum GPA of 3.0; auditions and head shots (for MFA in acting only); interviews, resume, letters of recommendation, samples of work (except for MFA in acting and MA). Additional exam requirements/recommendations for international students: required—TOEFL (minimum score 550 paper-based; 79 iBT), TWE (minimum score 5.5), Michigan English Language Assessment Battery (minimum score 85); recommended—IELTS (minimum score 6.5). Electronic applications accepted. *Expenses:* Contact institution.

Western Illinois University, School of Graduate Studies, College of Fine Arts and Communication, Department of Theatre and Dance, Macomb, IL 61455-1390. Offers theatre (MFA), including acting, design, directing. *Accreditation:* NAST. *Program availability:* Part-time. *Degree requirements:* For master's, comprehensive exam, thesis or alternative, creative project, written exam. *Entrance requirements:* For master's, audition or interview. Additional exam requirements/recommendations for international students: required—TOEFL (minimum score 550 paper-based; 80 iBT). Electronic applications accepted.

West Virginia University, College of Creative Arts, Morgantown, WV 26506. Offers acting (MFA); art education (MA); art history (MA); ceramics (MFA); collaborative piano (MM, DMA); composition (MM, DMA); conducting (MM, DMA); costume design and technology (MFA); graphic design (MFA); intermedia and photography (MFA); jazz pedagogy (MM); lighting design and technology (MFA); music (PhD); music education (MM, PhD); music industry (MA); music theory (MM); musicology (MA); painting and printmaking (MFA); performance (MM, DMA); piano pedagogy (MM); scenic design and technology (MFA); sculpture (MFA); studio art (MA); technical direction (MFA); vocal pedagogy and performance (DMA). *Program availability:* Part-time. *Degree requirements:* For master's, thesis, recitals; for doctorate, comprehensive exam, thesis/dissertation, recitals (DMA). *Entrance requirements:* For doctorate, minimum GPA of 3.0, audition. Additional exam requirements/recommendations for international students: required—TOEFL. Electronic applications accepted.

Yale University, School of Drama, New Haven, CT 06520. Offers acting (MFA, Certificate); design (MFA, Certificate), including costume design, lighting design, projection design, set design; directing (MFA, Certificate); dramaturgy and dramatic criticism (MFA, DFA); playwriting (MFA, Certificate); sound design (MFA, Certificate); stage management (MFA, Certificate); technical design and production (MFA, Certificate); theater management (MFA); MFA/MBA. *Degree requirements:* For master's, comprehensive exam (for some programs), thesis (for some programs); for doctorate, thesis/dissertation, oral and written comprehensive exams. *Entrance requirements:* For master's, GRE (verbal, quantitative, and analytical), in-person audition (for acting); portfolio review (for design). Additional exam requirements/recommendations for international students: required—TOEFL. Electronic applications accepted.

York University, Faculty of Graduate Studies, Faculty of Fine Arts, Program in Theatre, Toronto, ON M3J 1P3, Canada. Offers MFA. *Degree requirements:* For master's, thesis. Electronic applications accepted.

York University, Faculty of Graduate Studies, Faculty of Fine Arts, Program in Theatre and Performance Studies, Toronto, ON M3J 1P3, Canada. Offers MA, PhD.

Therapies—Dance, Drama, and Music

Antioch University New England, Graduate School, Department of Applied Psychology, Keene, NH 03431-3552. Offers autism spectrum disorders (Certificate), including applied behavioral analysis internship, autism spectrum disorders; clinical mental health counseling (MA), including clinical mental health counseling, substance abuse counseling; dance/movement therapy and counseling (M Ed, MA, PMC); marriage and family therapy (MA, PhD, Certificate). *Faculty:* 15 full-time (12 women), 30 part-time/adjunct (25 women). *Students:* 264 full-time (217 women), 79 part-time (64 women); includes 67 minority (25 Black or African American, non-Hispanic/Latino; 2 American Indian or Alaska Native, non-Hispanic/Latino; 8 Asian, non-Hispanic/Latino; 27 Hispanic/Latino; 5 Two or more races, non-Hispanic/Latino), 5 international. Average age 35. 149 applicants, 52% accepted, 77 enrolled. In 2019, 49 master's awarded. *Degree requirements:* For master's, internship, practicum. *Entrance requirements:* For master's, previous course work and work experience in psychology. Additional exam requirements/recommendations for international students: required—TOEFL (minimum score 550 paper-based). *Application deadline:* For fall admission, 7/15 for domestic and international students; for spring admission, 12/1 for domestic and international

students. Applications are processed on a rolling basis. Application fee: $50. Electronic applications accepted. *Expenses:* Contact institution. *Financial support:* In 2019–20, 56 students received support. Fellowships, research assistantships, career-related internships or fieldwork, Federal Work-Study, and scholarships/grants available. Financial award application deadline: 6/1; financial award applicants required to submit FAFSA. *Unit head:* Dr. Kevin Lyness, Department Chair, 603-283-2149, E-mail: klyness@antioch.edu. *Application contact:* Admissions, 800-552-8380, Fax: 603-357-0718, E-mail: admissions.ane@antioch.edu.
Website: https://www.antioch.edu/new-england/degrees-programs/counseling-wellness/

Antioch University Seattle, Program in Education, Seattle, WA 98121. Offers adult education (MA); drama therapy (MA); individualized studies (MA); leadership in edible education (MA); teaching (MAT); urban environmental education (MA). *Program availability:* Part-time, evening/weekend. *Faculty:* 9 full-time (all women), 6 part-time/adjunct (all women). *Students:* 60 full-time (46 women), 24 part-time (21 women); includes 20 minority (8 Black or African American, non-Hispanic/Latino; 1 American Indian or Alaska Native, non-Hispanic/Latino; 2 Asian, non-Hispanic/Latino; 4 Hispanic/Latino; 5 Two or more races, non-Hispanic/Latino), 2 international. Average age 36. 15 applicants, 100% accepted, 13 enrolled. *Degree requirements:* For master's, comprehensive exam (for some programs), thesis. *Entrance requirements:* For master's, WEST-B, WEST-E, current resume, transcripts of undergraduate degree and coursework (or for highest degree completed), two letters of recommendation, proof of fingerprinting and background check, moral character with fitness statement of understanding, documentation of 40 hours' experience in school classroom(s). *Application deadline:* Applications are processed on a rolling basis. Application fee: $50. *Expenses:* Contact institution. *Financial support:* Research assistantships, Federal Work-Study, scholarships/grants, and unspecified assistantships available. Financial award application deadline: 6/15. *Unit head:* Sue Byers, Director, E-mail: sbyers@antioch.edu. *Application contact:* Sue Byers, Director, E-mail: sbyers@antioch.edu.
Website: https://www.antioch.edu/seattle/degrees-programs/education-degrees/

Appalachian State University, Cratis D. Williams School of Graduate Studies, School of Music, Boone, NC 28608. Offers music performance (MM); music therapy (MMT). *Accreditation:* NASM. *Program availability:* Part-time. *Degree requirements:* For master's, comprehensive exam, thesis or alternative. *Entrance requirements:* For master's, GRE General Test, 3 letters of reference, audition. Additional exam requirements/recommendations for international students: required—TOEFL (minimum score 550 paper-based; 79 iBT), IELTS (minimum score 6.5). Electronic applications accepted.

Arizona State University at Tempe, Herberger Institute for Design and the Arts, School of Music, Tempe, AZ 85287-0405. Offers composition (MM, DMA); conducting (DMA); ethnomusicology (MA); interdisciplinary digital media/performance (DMA); music education (MM, PhD); music history and literature (MA); music therapy (MM); performance (MM, DMA). *Accreditation:* NASM. Terminal master's awarded for partial completion of doctoral program. *Degree requirements:* For master's, thesis (for some programs), interactive Program of Study (iPOS) submitted before completing 50 percent of required credit hours; for doctorate, comprehensive exam, thesis/dissertation, interactive Program of Study (iPOS) submitted before completing 50 percent of required credit hours. *Entrance requirements:* For master's, minimum GPA of 3.0 or equivalent in last 2 years of work leading to bachelor's degree, 3 letters of recommendation, resume; for doctorate, GRE or MAT, minimum GPA of 3.0 or equivalent in last 2 years of work leading to bachelor's degree, 3 letters of recommendation, curriculum vitae, statement of intent. Additional exam requirements/recommendations for international students: required—TOEFL, IELTS, or PTE. Electronic applications accepted.

Concordia University, School of Graduate Studies, Faculty of Fine Arts, Department of Creative Arts Therapies, Montréal, QC H3G 1M8, Canada. Offers art therapy (MA); drama therapy (MA); music therapy (MA).

Drexel University, College of Nursing and Health Professions, Department of Creative Arts Therapies, Specialization in Dance/Movement Therapy, Philadelphia, PA 19104-2875. Offers MA, PMC. *Program availability:* Part-time. *Degree requirements:* For master's, comprehensive exam, thesis. *Entrance requirements:* For master's, GRE General Test or MAT, audition, interview, minimum GPA of 2.75. Electronic applications accepted.

Drexel University, College of Nursing and Health Professions, Department of Creative Arts Therapies, Specialization in Music Therapy, Philadelphia, PA 19104-2875. Offers MA, PMC. *Program availability:* Part-time. *Degree requirements:* For master's, comprehensive exam, thesis. *Entrance requirements:* For master's, GRE General Test or MAT, audition, interview, minimum GPA of 2.75. Electronic applications accepted.

East Carolina University, Graduate School, College of Fine Arts and Communication, School of Music, Greenville, NC 27858-4353. Offers advanced performance studies (Certificate); composition (MM); music education (MM), including choral conducting, instrumental conducting, music theory/composition, music therapy, performance, Suzuki pedagogy; music therapy (MM); Suzuki pedagogy (Certificate); theory (MM); woodwind specialist (MM), including accompanying, choral conducting, instrumental, instrumental conducting, jazz studies, keyboard, organ, piano pedagogy, Suzuki string pedagogy, vocal pedagogy, voice, woodwind specialist. *Accreditation:* NASM. *Program availability:* Part-time. *Application deadline:* For fall admission, 6/1 priority date for domestic students. *Expenses: Tuition, area resident:* Full-time $4749; part-time $185 per credit hour. Tuition, state resident: full-time $4749; part-time $185 per credit hour. Tuition, nonresident: full-time $17,898; part-time $864 per credit hour. *International tuition:* $17,898 full-time. *Required fees:* $2787. *Financial support:* Application deadline: 6/1. *Unit head:* Christopher Ulffers, Director, 252-328-4270, E-mail: ulffersj@ecu.edu. *Application contact:* Graduate School Admissions, 252-328-6012, Fax: 252-328-6071, E-mail: gradschool@ecu.edu.
Website: https://music.ecu.edu/

Florida State University, The Graduate School, College of Music, Tallahassee, FL 32306. Offers accompanying (MM); arts administration (MA); choral conducting (MM); composition (MM, DM); ethnomusicology (MM); general music (MA); historical musicology (PhD); instrumental accompanying (MM); instrumental conducting (MM); jazz studies (MM); music theory (MM, PhD); music therapy (MM); musicology (MM); opera (MM); performance (MM, DM); piano pedagogy (MM); piano technology (MA); vocal accompanying (MM). *Accreditation:* NASM. *Program availability:* Part-time. *Faculty:* 77 full-time (28 women). *Students:* 355 full-time (169 women); includes 94 minority (30 Black or African American, non-Hispanic/Latino; 1 American Indian or Alaska Native, non-Hispanic/Latino; 29 Asian, non-Hispanic/Latino; 33 Hispanic/Latino; 1 Native Hawaiian or other Pacific Islander, non-Hispanic/Latino). Average age 26. 789 applicants, 44% accepted, 153 enrolled. In 2019, 98 master's, 36 doctorates awarded. *Degree requirements:* For master's, variable foreign language requirement, comprehensive exam (for some programs), thesis (for some programs), comprehensive exam; for doctorate, variable foreign language requirement, comprehensive exam (for some programs), thesis/dissertation, preliminary exam, treatise/dissertation defense. *Entrance requirements:* For master's, GRE General Test (for some programs), audition, minimum GPA of 3.0; for doctorate, GRE General Test (for some programs), audition, master's degree, minimum GPA of 3.0. Additional exam requirements/recommendations for international students: required—TOEFL (minimum score 590 paper-based; 97 iBT), IELTS (minimum score 7.5). *Application deadline:* For fall admission, 7/1 for domestic and international students; for spring admission, 11/1 for domestic and international students; for summer admission, 3/1 for domestic students. Applications are processed on a rolling basis. Application fee: $30. Electronic applications accepted. *Financial support:* In 2019–20, 235 students received support, including 2 fellowships with full tuition reimbursements available (averaging $15,000 per year), 14 research assistantships with full and partial tuition reimbursements available (averaging $7,400 per year), 201 teaching assistantships with full and partial tuition reimbursements available (averaging $7,400 per year); career-related internships or fieldwork, scholarships/grants, tuition waivers (full and partial), and unspecified assistantships also available. Support available to part-time students. Financial award application deadline: 2/28; financial award applicants required to submit FAFSA. *Unit head:* Dr. Patricia Flowers, Dean, 850-644-4361, Fax: 850-644-2033, E-mail: pjflowers@fsu.edu. *Application contact:* Kristopher Watson, Director of Admissions, 850-645-2126, Fax: 850-644-2033, E-mail: krwatson@fsu.edu.
Website: http://www.music.fsu.edu/

Georgia College & State University, The Graduate School, College of Health Sciences, Program in Music Therapy, Milledgeville, GA 31061. Offers MMT. *Program availability:* Part-time, evening/weekend, online only, 100% online. *Students:* 9 full-time (7 women), 6 part-time (4 women); includes 7 minority (5 Black or African American, non-Hispanic/Latino; 1 Asian, non-Hispanic/Latino; 1 Hispanic/Latino). Average age 31. 6 applicants, 100% accepted, 5 enrolled. In 2019, 2 master's awarded. *Degree requirements:* For master's, comprehensive exam, thesis or alternative, minimum GPA of 3.0, complete program within 6 years from starting. *Entrance requirements:* For master's, bachelor's degree in music therapy or equivalent, minimum undergraduate GPA of 2.75, 3 references, essay, interview, audition, resume. Additional exam requirements/recommendations for international students: required—English proficiency demonstrated by one of the following: minimum TOEFL score of 79 on internet test or 550 paper test OR IELTS score of 6.5. *Application deadline:* For fall admission, 7/1 priority date for domestic students; for spring admission, 11/1 priority date for domestic students; for summer admission, 4/1 priority date for domestic students. Applications are processed on a rolling basis. Application fee: $40. Electronic applications accepted. *Expenses:* Full time enrollment, per semester: $3042 tuition and $343 fees. *Financial support:* Application deadline: 3/1; applicants required to submit FAFSA. *Unit head:* Dr. Don Parker, Chair, Depart of Music, 478-445-8289, Fax: 478-445-1633, E-mail: don.parker@gcsu.edu. *Application contact:* Kate Marshall, Graduate Admissions Coordinator, 478-445-1184, Fax: 478-445-1336, E-mail: grad-admit@gcsu.edu.
Website: http://gcsu.edu/health/therapy/music-therapy-mmt

Immaculata University, College of Graduate Studies, Program in Music Therapy, Immaculata, PA 19345. Offers MA. *Accreditation:* NASM. *Program availability:* Part-time, evening/weekend. *Degree requirements:* For master's, comprehensive exam, thesis optional. *Entrance requirements:* For master's, GRE General Test or MAT, minimum GPA of 3.0. Additional exam requirements/recommendations for international students: required—TOEFL. Electronic applications accepted.

Indiana University-Purdue University Indianapolis, School of Engineering and Technology, Department of Music and Arts Technology, Indianapolis, IN 46202. Offers music technology (MS, PhD); music therapy (MS). *Accreditation:* NASM. *Program availability:* Part-time, evening/weekend, online learning. *Degree requirements:* For master's, thesis optional, internship or final project; for doctorate, thesis/dissertation. *Entrance requirements:* For master's, GRE, interview, audition, minimum GPA of 3.0; for doctorate, GRE, three letters of recommendation; research adviser letter; statement of purpose; writing samples; transcripts; portfolio. Additional exam requirements/recommendations for international students: required—TOEFL (minimum score 550 paper-based; 79 iBT); recommended—IELTS (minimum score 6.5). Electronic applications accepted. *Expenses:* Contact institution.

Lesley University, Graduate School of Arts and Social Sciences, Cambridge, MA 02138-2790. Offers clinical mental health counseling (MA), including holistic counseling, school and community counseling, trauma studies; counseling psychology (MA, CAGS), including professional counseling (MA), school counseling (MA); creative writing (MFA); expressive therapies (MA, PhD, CAGS), including art (MA), clinical mental health counseling (MA), dance (MA), expressive therapies (MA), music (MA); independent studies (CAGS); independent study (MA); intercultural relations (MA, CAGS); interdisciplinary studies (MA), including individualized studies, integrative holistic health, mindfulness studies, peace and conflict transformation, trauma sensitive assessment, intervention, and consultation, women's studies; urban environmental leadership (MA). *Program availability:* Part-time, online learning. *Degree requirements:* For master's, internship, practicum, thesis (for expressive therapies); for doctorate, thesis/dissertation, arts apprenticeship, field placement; for CAGS, thesis, internship (for counseling psychology, expressive therapies). *Entrance requirements:* For master's, MAT (counseling psychology), interview, writing samples, art portfolio; for doctorate, GRE or MAT, interview, master's degree; for CAGS, interview, master's degree. Additional exam requirements/recommendations for international students: required—TOEFL (minimum score 550 paper-based; 80 iBT). Electronic applications accepted.

Loyola University New Orleans, College of Music and Media, New Orleans, LA 70118. Offers music therapy (MMT); performance (MM). *Accreditation:* NASM. *Program availability:* Part-time. *Faculty:* 13 full-time (6 women), 17 part-time/adjunct (7 women). *Students:* 15 full-time (6 women), 31 part-time (24 women); includes 16 minority (7 Black or African American, non-Hispanic/Latino; 6 Hispanic/Latino; 3 Two or more races, non-Hispanic/Latino). Average age 28. 43 applicants, 93% accepted, 26 enrolled. In 2019, 14 master's awarded. *Entrance requirements:* For master's, performance audition, appropriate bachelor's degree, transcripts, minimum GPA of 3.0, 2 letters of recommendation, resume. Additional exam requirements/recommendations for international students: required—TOEFL (minimum score 550 paper-based; 79 iBT). *Application deadline:* For fall admission, 8/15 priority date for domestic and international students; for spring admission, 1/1 priority date for domestic and international students. Applications are processed on a rolling basis. Application fee: $20. Electronic applications accepted. *Expenses:* Contact institution. *Financial support:* In 2019–20, 43 students received support. Career-related internships or fieldwork, Federal Work-Study, institutionally sponsored loans, scholarships/grants, unspecified assistantships, and talent-based music scholarships available. Support available to part-time students. Financial award application deadline: 5/1; financial award applicants required to submit FAFSA. *Unit head:* Dr. Kern Maass, Dean, 504-865-3039, Fax: 504-865-2852, E-mail: kdmaass@loyno.edu. *Application contact:* Dr. Kern Maass, Dean, 504-865-3039, Fax: 504-865-2852, E-mail: kdmaass@loyno.edu.
Website: https://www.loyno.edu/academics/colleges/college-music-media

Maryville University of Saint Louis, Myrtle E. and Earl E. Walker College of Health Professions, Music Therapy, St. Louis, MO 63141-7299. Offers MMT. *Accreditation:* NASM. *Program availability:* Part-time. *Faculty:* 2 full-time (both women). *Students:* 4 full-time (all women), 7 part-time (6 women); includes 1 minority (Two or more races, non-Hispanic/Latino). Average age 28. In 2019, 2 master's awarded. *Entrance requirements:* For master's, application for admission, official transcripts,

career goal statement, music audition, interview, minimum undergraduate GPA of 3.0, 3 letters of recommendation. Additional exam requirements/recommendations for international students: required—TOEFL (minimum score 92 iBT). *Application deadline:* Applications are processed on a rolling basis. Electronic applications accepted. *Expenses:* Contact institution. *Financial support:* Application deadline: 4/1; applicants required to submit FAFSA. *Unit head:* Laura Beer, Director Music Therapy, 314-529-9441, Fax: 314-529-9495, E-mail: lbeer@maryville.edu. *Application contact:* Jeannie DeLuca, Director, Admissions and Advising, 314-529-9355, Fax: 314-529-9927, E-mail: jdeluca@maryville.edu.
Website: http://www.maryville.edu/hp/music-therapy/

Michigan State University, The Graduate School, College of Music, East Lansing, MI 48824. Offers collaborative piano (M Mus); jazz studies (M Mus); music (PhD); music composition (M Mus, DMA); music conducting (M Mus, DMA); music education (M Mus); music performance (M Mus, DMA); music theory (M Mus); music therapy (M Mus); musicology (MA); piano pedagogy (M Mus). *Accreditation:* NASM. *Entrance requirements:* Additional exam requirements/recommendations for international students: required—TOEFL. Electronic applications accepted.

Molloy College, Graduate Music Therapy Program, Rockville Centre, NY 11571. Offers music therapy (MS). *Program availability:* Part-time, evening/weekend. *Faculty:* 5 full-time (4 women), 5 part-time/adjunct (3 women). *Students:* 20 full-time (17 women), 10 part-time (7 women); includes 11 minority (1 Black or African American, non-Hispanic/Latino; 2 Asian, non-Hispanic/Latino; 7 Hispanic/Latino; 1 Two or more races, non-Hispanic/Latino), 8 international. Average age 29. 12 applicants, 50% accepted, 2 enrolled. In 2019, 12 master's awarded. *Entrance requirements:* For master's, Minimum 3.0 undergraduate GPA, students with a GPA between 2.8 and 3.0 may be accepted on a probationary status; Three letters of recommendation; Official transcripts from undergraduate institution; Music department audition; Personal interview and written essay. Additional exam requirements/recommendations for international students: required—TOEFL (minimum score 500 paper-based; 61 iBT). *Application deadline:* Applications are processed on a rolling basis. Application fee: $60. Electronic applications accepted. *Expenses: Tuition:* Full-time $21,510; part-time $1195 per credit hour. *Required fees:* $1100. Tuition and fees vary according to course load, degree level and program. *Financial support:* Application deadline: 3/1; applicants required to submit FAFSA. *Unit head:* Suzanne Sorel, Associate Dean, Director of Graduate Music Therapy, 516-323-3322, E-mail: ssorel@molloy.edu. *Application contact:* Faye Hood, Assistant Director for Admissions, 516-323-4009, E-mail: fhood@molloy.edu.
Website: https://www.molloy.edu/academics/graduate-programs/graduate-music-therapy

Montclair State University, The Graduate School, College of the Arts, John J. Cali School of Music, Post Baccalaureate Certificate Program in Music Therapy, Montclair, NJ 07043-1624. Offers Postbaccalaureate Certificate. *Program availability:* Part-time, evening/weekend. *Entrance requirements:* For degree, 2 letters of recommendation, essay. Additional exam requirements/recommendations for international students: required—TOEFL (minimum score 83 iBT), IELTS (minimum score 6.5). Electronic applications accepted.

Montclair State University, The Graduate School, College of the Arts, John J. Cali School of Music, Program in Music, Montclair, NJ 07043-1624. Offers music education (MA); music therapy (MA); performance (MA); theory/composition (MA). *Program availability:* Part-time, evening/weekend. *Degree requirements:* For master's, thesis. *Entrance requirements:* For master's, GRE General Test, 2 letters of recommendation, essay. Additional exam requirements/recommendations for international students: required—TOEFL (minimum score 83 iBT), IELTS (minimum score 6.5). Electronic applications accepted.

Naropa University, Graduate Programs, Program in Clinical Mental Health Counseling, Concentration in Somatic Counseling: Dance/Movement Therapy, Boulder, CO 80302-6697. Offers MA. *Degree requirements:* For master's, internship, clinical practicum. *Entrance requirements:* For master's, BA (preferably in field related to the helping professions); minimum of 100 hours of paid or volunteer experience in mental health field or community facility/service organization; interview; state of interest essay; supplemental essays; 2 letters of recommendation; transcripts. Additional exam requirements/recommendations for international students: required—TOEFL (minimum score 550 paper-based; 80 iBT). Electronic applications accepted. *Expenses:* Contact institution.

Nazareth College of Rochester, Graduate Studies, Department of Creative Arts Therapy, Rochester, NY 14618. Offers art therapy (MS); music therapy (MS). *Program availability:* Part-time. *Entrance requirements:* For master's, minimum GPA of 3.0; portfolio review (art therapy); audition (music therapy). Additional exam requirements/recommendations for international students: required—TOEFL (minimum score 550 paper-based, 79 iBT) or IELTS (6.5). Electronic applications accepted.

New York University, Steinhardt School of Culture, Education, and Human Development, Department of Music and Performing Arts Professions, Program in Drama Therapy, New York, NY 10012. Offers MA. *Program availability:* Part-time. *Entrance requirements:* For master's, audition, interview. Additional exam requirements/recommendations for international students: required—TOEFL (minimum score 100 iBT). Electronic applications accepted.

New York University, Steinhardt School of Culture, Education, and Human Development, Department of Music and Performing Arts Professions, Program in Music Therapy, New York, NY 10012. Offers MA. *Program availability:* Part-time. *Entrance requirements:* For master's, audition, interview. Additional exam requirements/recommendations for international students: required—TOEFL (minimum score 100 iBT). Electronic applications accepted.

Ohio University, Graduate College, College of Fine Arts, School of Music, Athens, OH 45701-2979. Offers accompanying (MM); composition (MM); conducting (MM); history/literature (MM); music education (MM); music therapy (MM); performance (MM, Certificate); performance/pedagogy (MM); theory (MM). *Accreditation:* NASM. *Program availability:* Part-time, evening/weekend, online learning. *Degree requirements:* For master's, comprehensive exam, thesis (for some programs), oral exam. *Entrance requirements:* For master's, audition, interview, portfolio, recordings (varies by program). Additional exam requirements/recommendations for international students: required—TOEFL (minimum score 550 paper-based; 80 iBT) or IELTS (minimum score 6.5). Electronic applications accepted.

Pratt Institute, School of Art, Programs in Creative Arts Therapy, Brooklyn, NY 11205-3899. Offers art therapy and creativity development (MPS); dance/movement therapy (MS). *Accreditation:* NASAD (one or more programs are accredited). *Program availability:* Part-time. *Students:* 67 full-time (63 women), 41 part-time (all women); includes 41 minority (11 Black or African American, non-Hispanic/Latino; 7 Asian, non-Hispanic/Latino; 19 Hispanic/Latino; 4 Two or more races, non-Hispanic/Latino), 7 international. Average age 30. 112 applicants, 69% accepted, 31 enrolled. In 2019, 43 master's awarded. *Degree requirements:* For master's, thesis. *Entrance requirements:* For master's, letters of recommendation, portfolio. Additional exam requirements/recommendations for international students: required—TOEFL (minimum score 600 paper-based; 100 iBT). *Application deadline:* For fall admission, 1/5 for domestic and international students; for spring admission, 10/1 for domestic and international students. Applications are processed on a rolling basis. Application fee: $50 ($90 for international students). Electronic applications accepted. *Expenses: Tuition:* Full-time $33,246; part-time $1847 per credit. *Required fees:* $1980. *Financial support:* Career-related internships or fieldwork, Federal Work-Study, institutionally sponsored loans, scholarships/grants, health care benefits, and unspecified assistantships available. Support available to part-time students. Financial award application deadline: 2/1; financial award applicants required to submit FAFSA. *Unit head:* Julie Miller, Chairperson, 718-399-4532, Fax: 718-636-3597, E-mail: jmiller2@pratt.edu. *Application contact:* Natalie Capannelli, Director of Graduate Admissions, 718-636-3551, Fax: 718-399-4242, E-mail: ncapanne@pratt.edu.
Website: https://www.pratt.edu/academics/school-of-art/graduate-school-of-art/creative-arts-therapy/

Saint Mary-of-the-Woods College, Master of Arts in Music Therapy Program, Saint Mary of the Woods, IN 47876. Offers MA. *Accreditation:* NASM. *Program availability:* Part-time, blended/hybrid learning. *Faculty:* 2 full-time (both women), 7 part-time/adjunct (6 women). *Students:* 26 full-time (24 women); includes 7 minority (1 Black or African American, non-Hispanic/Latino; 1 Asian, non-Hispanic/Latino; 5 Two or more races, non-Hispanic/Latino). Average age 32. 17 applicants, 47% accepted, 7 enrolled. In 2019, 7 master's awarded. *Degree requirements:* For master's, thesis, qualifying exam, portfolio. *Entrance requirements:* For master's, diagnostic music exam, audition. *Application deadline:* For fall admission, 4/30 priority date for domestic and international students; for winter admission, 10/31 priority date for domestic students, 10/30 priority date for international students. Applications are processed on a rolling basis. Application fee: $0. Electronic applications accepted. *Expenses:* $750 per credit hour. *Financial support:* In 2019–20, 21 students received support. Career-related internships or fieldwork, scholarships/grants, and unspecified assistantships available. Financial award applicants required to submit FAFSA. *Unit head:* Dr. Tracy Richardson, Dean of Graduate Therapy and Counseling Programs, 812-535-5154, E-mail: trichardson@smwc.edu. *Application contact:* Crystal Cox, Associate Director of Admissions, 812-535-5263, E-mail: graduate@smwc.edu.
Website: http://www.smwc.edu

Slippery Rock University of Pennsylvania, Graduate Studies (Recruitment), College of Liberal Arts, Department of Music, Slippery Rock, PA 16057-1383. Offers music therapy (MMT). *Program availability:* Part-time, blended/hybrid learning, interactive online classes and face-to-face intensives. *Faculty:* 2 full-time (1 woman). *Students:* 18 full-time (17 women), 13 part-time (6 women); includes 7 minority (4 Black or African American, non-Hispanic/Latino; 2 Hispanic/Latino; 1 Two or more races, non-Hispanic/Latino). Average age 28. 19 applicants, 68% accepted, 13 enrolled. In 2019, 6 master's awarded. *Degree requirements:* For master's, thesis or alternative. *Entrance requirements:* For master's, bachelor's degree in music therapy with minimum GPA of 3.0, resume, statement of professional goals, video-recording of three songs accompanied on piano and three songs accompanied on guitar, video interview, official transcripts. Additional exam requirements/recommendations for international students: required—TOEFL (minimum score 550 paper-based; 80 iBT). *Application deadline:* For fall admission, 5/1 priority date for domestic students, 3/1 priority date for international students; for spring admission, 10/1 priority date for domestic students, 9/1 priority date for international students. Applications are processed on a rolling basis. Application fee: $25 ($30 for international students). Electronic applications accepted. *Expenses:* $516 per credit in-state tuition, $173.61 per credit in-state fees; $774 per credit out-of-state tuition, $224.31 per credit out-of-state fees; $516 per credit in-state tuition, $105.40 per credit in-state fees (for distance education); $526 per credit out-of-state tuition, $118.90 per credit out-of-state fees (for distance education). *Financial support:* In 2019–20, 1 student received support. Career-related internships or fieldwork, Federal Work-Study, institutionally sponsored loans, scholarships/grants, tuition waivers (partial), and unspecified assistantships available. Support available to part-time students. Financial award application deadline: 5/1; financial award applicants required to submit FAFSA. *Unit head:* Dr. Susan Hadley, Program Director, 724-738-2063, Fax: 724-738-2263, E-mail: susan.hadley@sru.edu. *Application contact:* Brandi Weber-Mortimer, Director of Graduate Admissions, 724-738-4340, E-mail: graduate.admissions@sru.edu.
Website: http://www.sru.edu/academics/colleges-and-departments/cla/departments/music

Southwestern Oklahoma State University, College of Arts and Sciences, Department of Music, Weatherford, OK 73096-3098. Offers music education (MM); music performance (MM); music therapy (MM). *Accreditation:* NASM. *Program availability:* Part-time. *Degree requirements:* For master's, comprehensive exam, recital (music performance). *Entrance requirements:* For master's, minimum GPA of 2.5. Additional exam requirements/recommendations for international students: required—TOEFL (minimum score 550 paper-based), IELTS (minimum score 6.5).

State University of New York at New Paltz, Graduate and Extended Learning School, School of Fine and Performing Arts, Department of Music, New Paltz, NY 12561. Offers music therapy (MS). *Accreditation:* NASM. *Program availability:* Part-time. *Faculty:* 4 full-time (3 women), 5 part-time/adjunct (1 woman). *Students:* 22 full-time (16 women), 20 part-time (16 women); includes 5 minority (1 Black or African American, non-Hispanic/Latino; 1 Asian, non-Hispanic/Latino; 3 Hispanic/Latino), 4 international. 31 applicants, 65% accepted, 14 enrolled. In 2019, 21 master's awarded. *Degree requirements:* For master's, thesis. *Entrance requirements:* For master's, audition, minimum GPA of 3.0. Additional exam requirements/recommendations for international students: required—TOEFL (minimum score 550 paper-based; 80 iBT), IELTS (minimum score 6.5). *Application deadline:* For fall admission, 5/15 for domestic and international students; for spring admission, 11/15 for domestic and international students. Applications are processed on a rolling basis. Application fee: $50. Electronic applications accepted. *Expenses: Tuition, area resident:* Full-time $11,310; part-time $471 per credit. Tuition, state resident: full-time $11,310; part-time $471 per credit. Tuition, nonresident: full-time $23,100; part-time $963 per credit. *International tuition:* $23,100 full-time. *Required fees:* $1432; $41.83 per credit. *Financial support:* In 2019–20, 4 teaching assistantships with partial tuition reimbursements (averaging $5,000 per year) were awarded. Financial award application deadline: 8/1. *Unit head:* Kathleen Murphy, Program Director, 845-257-2708, E-mail: murphyk@newpaltz.edu. *Application contact:* Vika Shock, Director of Graduate Admissions, 845-257-3286, Fax: 845-257-3284, E-mail: gradstudies@newpaltz.edu.
Website: http://www.newpaltz.edu/music/

Temple University, Center for the Performing and Cinematic Arts, Boyer College of Music and Dance, Department of Music, Philadelphia, PA 19122-6096. Offers choral conducting (MM); collaborative piano/chamber music (MM); collaborative piano/opera coaching (MM); composition (MM, PhD); instrumental conducting (MM); music education (MM, PhD); music history (MM); music performance (MM, DMA), including instrumental studies (MM), keyboard (DMA), keyboard studies (MM), voice (DMA), voice and opera (MM); music studies (PhD); music theory (MM, PhD); music therapy (MMT, PhD); musicology (MM, PhD); opera (MM); piano pedagogy (MM); string pedagogy (MM). *Accreditation:* NASM. *Program availability:* Part-time, evening/weekend, online learning. Terminal master's awarded for partial completion of doctoral program. *Degree requirements:* For doctorate, thesis/dissertation (for some programs). *Entrance* *requirements:* Additional exam requirements/recommendations for international students: required—TOEFL, IELTS, PTE, one of three is required. Electronic applications accepted. *Expenses:* Contact institution.

Texas Woman's University, Graduate School, College of Arts and Sciences, School of the Arts, Department of Music and Theatre, Denton, TX 76204. Offers drama (MA); music (MA), including music education, music therapy, pedagogy, performance. *Accreditation:* NASM. *Program availability:* Part-time. *Faculty:* 18 full-time (9 women), 9 part-time/adjunct (5 women). *Students:* 63 full-time (52 women), 31 part-time (24 women); includes 35 minority (7 Black or African American, non-Hispanic/Latino; 3 Asian, non-Hispanic/Latino; 23 Hispanic/Latino; 2 Two or more races, non-Hispanic/Latino; 11 international. Average age 29. 38 applicants, 92% accepted, 24 enrolled. In 2019, 21 master's awarded. *Degree requirements:* For master's, comprehensive exam, thesis (for some programs), project, recital, professional paper, professional paper or thesis (for music education). *Entrance requirements:* For master's, music history/theory placement exam (for music only), audition and/or design portfolio, interview, resume, writing sample (for drama only), letter of intent, minimum undergraduate GPA of 3.0. Additional exam requirements/recommendations for international students: required—TOEFL (minimum score 550 paper-based; 79 iBT); recommended—IELTS (minimum score 6.5), TSE (minimum score 53). *Application deadline:* For fall admission, 3/1 priority date for domestic and international students; for spring admission, 11/1 priority date for domestic students, 7/1 for international students; for summer admission, 4/30 for domestic students, 2/1 priority date for international students. Application fee: $50 ($75 for international students). Electronic applications accepted. *Expenses:* All are estimates. Tuition for 10 hours = $2,763; Fees for 10 hours = $1,342. Music courses require additional $35/SCH. *Financial support:* In 2019–20, 50 students received support, including 1 research assistantship, 6 teaching assistantships; career-related internships or fieldwork, scholarships/grants, health care benefits, and unspecified assistantships also available. Support available to part-time students. Financial award application deadline: 3/1; financial award applicants required to submit FAFSA. *Unit head:* Dr. Pamela Youngblood, Chair of Music and Theatre, 940-898-2500, Fax: 940-898-2494, E-mail: music@twu.edu. *Application contact:* Korie Hawkins, Associate Director of Admissions, Graduate Recruitment, 940-898-3188, Fax: 940-898-3081, E-mail: admissions@twu.edu.

The University of Kansas, Graduate Studies, School of Music, Program in Music Therapy, Lawrence, KS 66045. Offers MME, PhD. *Program availability:* Part-time. *Students:* 11 full-time (all women), 8 part-time (all women); includes 2 minority (1 Asian, non-Hispanic/Latino; 1 Two or more races, non-Hispanic/Latino), 2 international. Average age 28. 7 applicants, 100% accepted, 5 enrolled. In 2019, 8 master's awarded. *Entrance requirements:* For master's, GRE General Test, minimum undergraduate GPA of 3.0, video, reference letters, transcripts; for doctorate, GRE General Test, MEMT Diagnostic Exam, minimum graduate GPA of 3.5, video, reference letters, transcripts, writing sample, proof of professional experience. Additional exam requirements/recommendations for international students: required—TOEFL, IELTS. *Application deadline:* For fall admission, 12/1 priority date for domestic and international students. Application fee: $65 ($85 for international students). Electronic applications accepted. *Expenses:* Tuition, state resident: full-time $9989. Tuition, nonresident: full-time $23,950. *International tuition:* $23,950 full-time. *Required fees:* $984; $81.99 per credit hour. Tuition and fees vary according to course load, campus/location and program. *Financial support:* Fellowships, research assistantships, teaching assistantships, institutionally sponsored loans, scholarships/grants, and unspecified assistantships available. Financial award application deadline: 12/1; financial award applicants required to submit FAFSA. *Unit head:* Dr. Robert Walzel, Dean, 785-864-3421, E-mail: Robert.Walzel@ku.edu. *Application contact:* Lois Elmer, Administrative Professional for

Music, 785-864-2862, Fax: 785-864-9640, E-mail: elmer@ku.edu. Website: http://www.memt.ku.edu

University of Kentucky, Graduate School, College of Fine Arts, Program in Music, Lexington, KY 40506-0032. Offers composition (MM, DMA); conducting (MM, DMA); music education (MM, PhD); music theory (MA, PhD); music therapy (MM); musicology (MA, PhD); performance (MM, DMA); sacred music (MM). *Accreditation:* NASM. *Program availability:* Part-time, evening/weekend. *Degree requirements:* For master's, variable foreign language requirement, comprehensive exam, thesis (for some programs); for doctorate, variable foreign language requirement, comprehensive exam, thesis/dissertation. *Entrance requirements:* For master's, GRE General Test, minimum undergraduate GPA of 2.75; for doctorate, GRE General Test, minimum undergraduate GPA of 2.75, graduate 3.0. Additional exam requirements/recommendations for international students: required—TOEFL (minimum score 550 paper-based). Electronic applications accepted.

University of Miami, Graduate School, Frost School of Music, Department of Music Education and Music Therapy, Coral Gables, FL 33124. Offers music education (MM, PhD, Spec M); music therapy (MM). *Accreditation:* NASM. *Degree requirements:* For master's, thesis; for doctorate, thesis/dissertation, 2 research tools; for Spec M, thesis, research project. *Entrance requirements:* For master's and doctorate, GRE General Test. Additional exam requirements/recommendations for international students: required—TOEFL (minimum score 550 paper-based; 59 iBT). Electronic applications accepted.

University of Missouri–Kansas City, Conservatory of Music and Dance, Kansas City, MO 64110-2499. Offers composition (MM, DMA); conducting (MM, DMA); music (MA); music education (MME, PhD); music history and literature (MM); music theory (MM); music therapy (MA); performance (MM, DMA). *Accreditation:* NASM. *Program availability:* Part-time. *Degree requirements:* For master's, variable foreign language requirement, comprehensive exam, thesis (for some programs); for doctorate, variable foreign language requirement, comprehensive exam, thesis/dissertation or alternative. *Entrance requirements:* For master's, minimum GPA of 3.0 in major, auditions (for MM in performance); for doctorate, minimum graduate GPA of 3.5, auditions (for DMA in performance), portfolio of compositions. Additional exam requirements/recommendations for international students: required—TOEFL (minimum score 550 paper-based; 80 iBT).

University of the Pacific, Conservatory of Music, Stockton, CA 95211-0197. Offers music education (MM); music therapy (MA). *Entrance requirements:* For master's, GRE General Test. Additional exam requirements/recommendations for international students: required—TOEFL.

Western Michigan University, Graduate College, College of Fine Arts, School of Music, Kalamazoo, MI 49008. Offers music (MA); music composition (MM); music conducting (MM); music education (MM); music performance (MM); music therapy (MM). *Accreditation:* NASM.

Wilfrid Laurier University, Faculty of Graduate and Postdoctoral Studies, Faculty of Music, Waterloo, ON N2L 3C5, Canada. Offers MMT. *Entrance requirements:* For master's, 4-year honours BA in music therapy with minimum B average in final year, grade 6 RCM and grade 10 performance ability (for 1-year program); 4-year honours BA in allied area (music or psychology) with minimum B average in final year, grade 6 RCM, grade 10 performance ability (for 2-year program). Additional exam requirements/recommendations for international students: required—TOEFL (minimum score 89 iBT). Electronic applications accepted.

ACADEMIC AND PROFESSIONAL PROGRAMS IN THE HUMANITIES

Section 7
History

This section contains a directory of institutions offering graduate work in history. Additional information about programs listed in the directory may be obtained by writing directly to the dean of a graduate school or chair of a department at the address given in the directory.

For programs offering related work, see also in this book *Area and Cultural Studies, Architecture, Humanities, Political Science and International Affairs,* and *Sociology, Anthropology, and Archaeology.*

CONTENTS

Program Directories

History

Adams State University, Office of Graduate Studies, Department of History, Government and Philosophy, Alamosa, CO 81101. Offers humanities (MA), including cultural resource management, public administration, U.S. history. *Degree requirements:* For master's, thesis. Application fee: $30. *Unit head:* Chair, 719-587-7771, Fax: 719-587-7176. *Application contact:* Chair, 719-587-7771, Fax: 719-587-7176.
Website: https://www.adams.edu/academics/graduate/humanities/

Alabama State University, College of Liberal Arts and Social Sciences, Department of History and Political Science, Montgomery, AL 36101-0271. Offers history (MA). *Program availability:* Part-time. *Faculty:* 2 full-time (1 woman), 1 part-time/adjunct (0 women). *Students:* 3 applicants. *Degree requirements:* For master's, one foreign language, comprehensive exam, thesis. *Entrance requirements:* For master's, GRE General Test, writing competency test or MAT. Additional exam requirements/recommendations for international students: recommended—TOEFL (minimum score 500 paper-based). *Application deadline:* For fall admission, 7/15 for domestic students; for spring admission, 12/15 for domestic students. Applications are processed on a rolling basis. Application fee: $25. Electronic applications accepted. *Financial support:* Fellowships, research assistantships, teaching assistantships, Federal Work-Study, scholarships/grants, tuition waivers (partial), and unspecified assistantships available. Financial award application deadline: 6/30. *Unit head:* Dr. Derryn Moten, Acting Chair, 334-229-4433, E-mail: dmoten@alasu.edu. *Application contact:* Dr. Derryn Moten, Acting Chair, 334-229-4433, E-mail: dmoten@alasu.edu.

American Public University System, AMU/APU Graduate Programs, Charles Town, WV 25414. Offers accounting (MS); applied business analytics (MS); business administration (MBA); criminal justice (MA); cybersecurity studies (MS); educational leadership (M Ed); environmental policy and management (MS); global security (DGS); health information management (MS); history (MA), including American military history, American Revolution, civil war, war since 1945, World War II; information technology (MS); international relations and conflict resolution (MA), including American politics and government, comparative government and development, general, international relations, public policy; national security studies (MA); nursing (MSN); political science (MA); public policy (MPP); reverse logistics management (MA), including comparative and security issues, conflict resolution, international and transnational security issues, peacekeeping; space studies (MS); sports management (MS); strategic intelligence (DSI); teaching (M Ed), including secondary social studies; transportation and logistics management (MA). *Program availability:* Part-time, evening/weekend, online only, 100% online. *Students:* 461 full-time (193 women), 7,322 part-time (3,127 women); includes 3,089 minority (1,404 Black or African American, non-Hispanic/Latino; 30 American Indian or Alaska Native, non-Hispanic/Latino; 210 Asian, non-Hispanic/Latino; 753 Hispanic/Latino; 445 Native Hawaiian or other Pacific Islander, non-Hispanic/Latino; 247 Two or more races, non-Hispanic/Latino), 117 international. Average age 37. In 2019, 2,681 master's awarded. *Degree requirements:* For master's, comprehensive exam or practicum; for doctorate, practicum. *Entrance requirements:* For master's, official transcript showing earned bachelor's degree from institution accredited by recognized accrediting body. Additional exam requirements/recommendations for international students: required—TOEFL (minimum score 550 paper-based), IELTS (minimum score 6.5). *Application deadline:* Applications are processed on a rolling basis. Application fee: $0. Electronic applications accepted. *Financial support:* Scholarships/grants available. Financial award applicants required to submit FAFSA. *Unit head:* Dr. Wallace Boston, President, 877-468-6268, Fax: 304-728-2348, E-mail: president@apus.edu. *Application contact:* Yoci Deal, Associate Vice President, Graduate and International Admissions, 877-468-6268, Fax: 304-724-3764, E-mail: info@apus.edu.
Website: http://www.apus.edu

American University, College of Arts and Sciences, Department of History, Washington, DC 20016-8038. Offers MA, PhD. *Program availability:* Part-time, evening/weekend. *Degree requirements:* For master's, comprehensive exam, thesis or alternative; for doctorate, thesis/dissertation. *Entrance requirements:* For master's, GRE; Visit website: https://www.american.edu/cas/history/, personal statement, transcripts, 2 letters of recommendation, resume, writing sample; for doctorate, GRE, sample of written work, personal statement, transcripts, 3 letters of recommendation, resume. Additional exam requirements/recommendations for international students: required—TOEFL. Electronic applications accepted. *Expenses:* Contact institution.

Appalachian State University, Cratis D. Williams School of Graduate Studies, Department of History, Boone, NC 28608. Offers general history (MA). *Program availability:* Part-time, online learning. *Degree requirements:* For master's, one foreign language, comprehensive exam, thesis (for some programs). *Entrance requirements:* For master's, GRE General Test, 3 letters of recommendation. Additional exam requirements/recommendations for international students: required—TOEFL (minimum score 570 paper-based; 79 iBT), IELTS (minimum score 6.5). Electronic applications accepted.

Arizona State University at Tempe, College of Liberal Arts and Sciences, School of Historical, Philosophical and Religious Studies, Tempe, AZ 85287-4301. Offers European history (MA, PhD); medieval studies (Graduate Certificate); North American history (MA, PhD); philosophy (MA, PhD); public history (MA); religious studies (MA, PhD); Renaissance studies (Graduate Certificate); scholarly publishing (Graduate Certificate). *Program availability:* Part-time. Terminal master's awarded for partial completion of doctoral program. *Degree requirements:* For master's, thesis or alternative, interactive Program of Study (iPOS) submitted before completing 50 percent of required credit hours; for doctorate, variable foreign language requirement, comprehensive exam, thesis/dissertation, interactive Program of Study (iPOS) submitted before completing 50 percent of required credit hours. *Entrance requirements:* For master's and doctorate, GRE, minimum GPA of 3.0 or equivalent in last 2 years of work leading to bachelor's degree. Additional exam requirements/recommendations for international students: required—TOEFL, IELTS, or PTE. Electronic applications accepted.

Arkansas State University, Graduate School, College of Humanities and Social Sciences, Department of History, State University, AR 72467. Offers history (MA); history education (SCCT); social science education (MSE). *Program availability:* Part-time. *Degree requirements:* For master's, comprehensive exam, thesis or alternative; for SCCT, comprehensive exam. *Entrance requirements:* For master's, GRE General Test or MAT, GMAT, appropriate bachelor's degree, letters of reference, official transcript, valid teaching certificate (for MSE), immunization records; for SCCT, GRE General Test or MAT, interview, master's degree, letters of reference, official transcript, immunization records. Additional exam requirements/recommendations for international students: required—TOEFL (minimum score 550 paper-based; 79 iBT), IELTS (minimum score 6), PTE (minimum score 56). Electronic applications accepted.

Arkansas Tech University, College of Arts and Humanities, Russellville, AR 72801. Offers applied sociology (MS); English (M Ed, MA); history (MA); liberal arts (MLA); multi-media journalism (MA); psychology (MS); teaching English as a second language (MA). *Program availability:* Part-time, 100% online, blended/hybrid learning. *Students:* 32 full-time (19 women), 102 part-time (70 women); includes 22 minority (5 Black or African American, non-Hispanic/Latino; 1 American Indian or Alaska Native, non-Hispanic/Latino; 1 Asian, non-Hispanic/Latino; 12 Hispanic/Latino; 3 Two or more races, non-Hispanic/Latino), 9 international. Average age 32. In 2019, 89 master's awarded. *Degree requirements:* For master's, comprehensive exam (for some programs), thesis (for some programs), project. *Entrance requirements:* Additional exam requirements/recommendations for international students: required—TOEFL (minimum score 550 paper-based; 79 iBT), IELTS (minimum score 6.5), PTE (minimum score 58). *Application deadline:* For fall admission, 3/1 priority date for domestic students, 5/1 priority date for international students; for spring admission, 10/1 priority date for domestic and international students. Applications are processed on a rolling basis. Application fee: $40 ($90 for international students). Electronic applications accepted. *Expenses: Tuition, area resident:* Full-time $7008; part-time $292 per credit hour. Tuition, state resident: full-time $7008; part-time $292 per credit hour. Tuition, nonresident: full-time $14,016; part-time $584 per credit hour. *International tuition:* $14,016 full-time. *Required fees:* $343 per term. *Financial support:* In 2019–20, research assistantships with full and partial tuition reimbursements (averaging $4,800 per year), teaching assistantships with full and partial tuition reimbursements (averaging $4,800 per year) were awarded; career-related internships or fieldwork, Federal Work-Study, scholarships/grants, health care benefits, and unspecified assistantships also available. Support available to part-time students. Financial award application deadline: 4/15; financial award applicants required to submit FAFSA. *Unit head:* Dr. Jeffrey Cass, Dean of College of Arts and Humanities, 479-968-0274, Fax: 479-964-0812, E-mail: jcass@atu.edu. *Application contact:* Dr. Richard Schoephoerster, Dean of Graduate College and Research, 479-968-0398, Fax: 479-964-0542, E-mail: gradcollege@atu.edu.
Website: http://www.atu.edu/humanities/

Ashland University, College of Arts and Sciences, Program in American History and Government, Ashland, OH 44805-3702. Offers American history and government (MAHG). *Program availability:* Part-time, evening/weekend, 100% online, blended/hybrid learning. *Degree requirements:* For master's, capstone project, thesis, or comprehensive exam. *Entrance requirements:* For master's, minimum undergraduate GPA of 2.75, 3.0 graduate. Electronic applications accepted. *Expenses:* Contact institution.

Auburn University, Graduate School, College of Liberal Arts, Department of History, Auburn, AL 36849. Offers MA, PhD, Graduate Certificate. *Program availability:* Part-time. *Faculty:* 33 full-time (12 women), 7 part-time/adjunct (1 woman). *Students:* 20 full-time (7 women), 23 part-time (9 women); includes 6 minority (4 Black or African American, non-Hispanic/Latino; 1 Hispanic/Latino; 1 Two or more races, non-Hispanic/Latino). Average age 36. 40 applicants, 53% accepted, 9 enrolled. In 2019, 3 master's, 7 doctorates awarded. *Degree requirements:* For master's, thesis, oral exam; for doctorate, 2 foreign languages, thesis/dissertation. *Entrance requirements:* For master's, GRE General Test; for doctorate, GRE General Test, master's degree with thesis. Additional exam requirements/recommendations for international students: required—iTEP; recommended—TOEFL (minimum score 550 paper-based; 79 iBT), IELTS (minimum score 6.5). *Application deadline:* Applications are processed on a rolling basis. Application fee: $60 ($70 for international students). Electronic applications accepted. *Expenses: Tuition, area resident:* Full-time $9828; part-time $546 per credit hour. Tuition, state resident: full-time $9828; part-time $546 per credit hour. Tuition, nonresident: full-time $29,484; part-time $1638 per credit hour. *International tuition:* $29,744 full-time. Tuition and fees vary according to course load, program and reciprocity agreements. *Financial support:* In 2019–20, 55 fellowships with tuition reimbursements, 29 teaching assistantships with tuition reimbursements (averaging $20,828 per year) were awarded; Federal Work-Study also available. Support available to part-time students. Financial award application deadline: 3/15; financial award applicants required to submit FAFSA. *Unit head:* David Lucsko, Chair, 334-844-4328, E-mail: dnl0006@auburn.edu. *Application contact:* Dr. George Flowers, Dean of the Graduate School, 334-844-2125.

Ball State University, Graduate School, College of Sciences and Humanities, Department of History, Muncie, IN 47306. Offers MA. *Program availability:* Part-time. *Entrance requirements:* For master's, minimum baccalaureate GPA of 2.75 or 3.0 in latter half of baccalaureate, resume or curriculum vitae, two letters of recommendation, undergraduate transcripts, writing sample, goal statement. Additional exam requirements/recommendations for international students: required—TOEFL (minimum score 550 paper-based; 79 iBT), IELTS (minimum score 6.5). Electronic applications accepted. *Expenses: Tuition, area resident:* Full-time $7506; part-time $417 per credit hour. Tuition, nonresident: full-time $20,610; part-time $1145 per credit hour. *Required fees:* $2126. Tuition and fees vary according to course load, campus/location and program.

Bard College, Master of Arts in Teaching Program, Annandale-on-Hudson, NY 12504. Offers secondary education (MAT), including biology, history, literature, mathematics, Spanish; MS/MAT. *Program availability:* Part-time. *Degree requirements:* For master's, year-long teaching residencies in area middle and high schools. *Entrance requirements:* For master's, GRE General Test, resume, 3 letters of recommendation, personal statement, official transcripts. Additional exam requirements/recommendations for international students: required—TOEFL. Electronic applications accepted. Application fee is waived when completed online.

Baylor University, Graduate School, College of Arts and Sciences, Department of History, Waco, TX 76798. Offers MA, PhD. Terminal master's awarded for partial completion of doctoral program. *Entrance requirements:* For master's and doctorate, GRE General Test, 18 semester hours in history. Additional exam requirements/recommendations for international students: required—TOEFL. Electronic applications accepted.

Binghamton University, State University of New York, Graduate School, Harpur College of Arts and Sciences, Department of History, Binghamton, NY 13902-6000. Offers MA, PhD. *Program availability:* Part-time. Terminal master's awarded for partial completion of doctoral program. *Degree requirements:* For master's, variable foreign language requirement, comprehensive exam, thesis; for doctorate, variable foreign language requirement, comprehensive exam, thesis/dissertation. *Entrance requirements:* For master's and doctorate, GRE General Test, writing sample. Additional exam requirements/recommendations for international students: required—TOEFL (minimum score 550 paper-based; 80 iBT). Electronic applications accepted.

Bob Jones University, Graduate Programs, Greenville, SC 29614. Offers accountancy (MS); Bible (MA); Bible translation (MA); Biblical studies (Certificate); business administration (MBA); church history (MA, PhD); church ministries (MA); church music (MM); cinema and video production (MA); counseling (MS); curriculum and instruction (Ed D); divinity (M Div); dramatic production (MA); educational leadership (MS, Ed D, Ed S); elementary education (M Ed, MAT); English (M Ed, MA, MAT); fine arts (MA); graphic design (MA); history (M Ed, MA); illustration (MA); interpretative speech (MA); mathematics (M Ed, MAT); medical missions (Certificate); ministry (MM, D Min); multi-categorical special education (M Ed, MAT); music (M Ed); New Testament interpretation (PhD); Old Testament interpretation (PhD); orchestral instrument performance (MM); organ performance (MM); pastoral studies (MA); personnel services (MS, Ed S); piano pedagogy (MM); piano performance (MM); platform arts (MA); rhetoric and public address (MA); secondary education (M Ed); studio art (MA); teaching Bible (MA); theology (MA, PhD); voice performance (MM); youth ministries (MA); M Div/MM.

Boise State University, College of Arts and Sciences, Department of History, Boise, ID 83725-0399. Offers applied historical research (MAHR); history (MA). *Program availability:* Part-time. *Students:* 10 full-time (4 women), 15 part-time (5 women); includes 1 minority (Hispanic/Latino), 1 international. *Degree requirements:* For master's, thesis (for MA); applied research project (for MAHR). *Entrance requirements:* For master's, GRE General Test, minimum GPA of 3.0. Additional exam requirements/recommendations for international students: required—TOEFL, IELTS. Electronic applications accepted. *Expenses: Tuition, area resident:* Full-time $7110; part-time $470 per credit hour. Tuition, state resident: full-time $7110; part-time $470 per credit hour. Tuition, nonresident: full-time $24,030; part-time $827 per credit hour. *International tuition:* $24,030 full-time. *Required fees:* $2536. Tuition and fees vary according to course load and program. *Financial support:* Research assistantships, teaching assistantships, scholarships/grants, and unspecified assistantships available. Financial award applicants required to submit FAFSA. *Unit head:* Dr. Nick Miller, Department Chair, 208-426-3902, E-mail: nmiller@boisestate.edu. *Application contact:* Dr. Lisa McClain, Graduate Coordinator, 208-426-1985, E-mail: lisamcclain@boisestate.edu. Website: https://www.boisestate.edu/history/graduate/

Boston College, Morrissey Graduate School of Arts and Sciences, Department of History, Chestnut Hill, MA 02467-3800. Offers European national studies (MA); history (MA, PhD); medieval studies (MA). Terminal master's awarded for partial completion of doctoral program. *Degree requirements:* For master's, one foreign language, comprehensive exam, thesis optional; for doctorate, 2 foreign languages, comprehensive exam, thesis/dissertation. *Entrance requirements:* For master's and doctorate, GRE General Test, writing sample. Additional exam requirements/recommendations for international students: required—TOEFL (minimum score 600 paper-based; 100 iBT), IELTS (minimum score 8). Electronic applications accepted.

Boston University, Graduate School of Arts and Sciences, Department of History, Boston, MA 02215. Offers MA, PhD, JD/MA. *Students:* 36 full-time (14 women), 3 part-time (all women); includes 2 minority (1 Hispanic/Latino; 1 Two or more races, non-Hispanic/Latino), 1 international. Average age 39. 103 applicants, 23% accepted, 11 enrolled. In 2019, 4 master's, 2 doctorates awarded. Terminal master's awarded for partial completion of doctoral program. *Degree requirements:* For master's, one foreign language, thesis or alternative, major research paper; for doctorate, 2 foreign languages, comprehensive exam, thesis/dissertation. *Entrance requirements:* For master's and doctorate, 3 letters of recommendation, writing sample, transcripts, personal statement, curriculum vitae, foreign language proficiency. Additional exam requirements/recommendations for international students: required—TOEFL (minimum score 550 paper-based; 84 iBT). *Application deadline:* For fall admission, 12/20 for domestic and international students. Application fee: $95. Electronic applications accepted. *Financial support:* In 2019–20, 38 students received support, including 19 fellowships with full tuition reimbursements available (averaging $23,340 per year), 1 research assistantship with full tuition reimbursement available (averaging $23,340 per year), 9 teaching assistantships with full tuition reimbursements available (averaging $23,340 per year); Federal Work-Study, scholarships/grants, health care benefits, and unspecified assistantships also available. Financial award application deadline: 12/20. *Unit head:* Nina Silber, Chair, Fax: 617-353-2556, E-mail: nsilber@bu.edu. *Application contact:* Cady Steinberg, Department Administrator, 617-353-2555, Fax: 617-353-2556, E-mail: cady8590@bu.edu. Website: http://www.bu.edu/history/

Bowling Green State University, Graduate College, College of Arts and Sciences, Department of History, Bowling Green, OH 43403. Offers history (MA, MAT, PhD); public history (MA); MA/MA. *Program availability:* Part-time. *Degree requirements:* For master's, thesis or alternative; for doctorate, one foreign language, comprehensive exam, thesis/dissertation. *Entrance requirements:* For master's and doctorate, GRE General Test. Additional exam requirements/recommendations for international students: required—TOEFL. Electronic applications accepted.

Brandeis University, Graduate School of Arts and Sciences, Department of History, Waltham, MA 02454-9110. Offers MA, PhD. *Program availability:* Part-time. *Faculty:* 16 full-time (6 women), 3 part-time/adjunct (0 women). *Students:* 31 full-time (18 women), 2 part-time (both women); includes 5 minority (3 Black or African American, non-Hispanic/Latino; 1 Asian, non-Hispanic/Latino; 1 Two or more races, non-Hispanic/Latino), 2 international. Average age 31. 93 applicants, 17% accepted, 8 enrolled. In 2019, 4 master's, 2 doctorates awarded. Terminal master's awarded for partial completion of doctoral program. *Degree requirements:* For master's, thesis or alternative, thesis, capstone, or paper; for doctorate, one foreign language, comprehensive exam, thesis/dissertation. *Entrance requirements:* For master's and doctorate, GRE General, transcripts, letters of recommendation, resume, statement of purpose, and writing sample. Additional exam requirements/recommendations for international students: required—TOEFL, IELTS, PTE. *Application deadline:* For fall admission, 1/15 priority date for domestic students, 1/15 for international students. Applications are processed on a rolling basis. Application fee: $75. Electronic applications accepted. *Financial support:* In 2019–20, 21 fellowships with full tuition reimbursements (averaging $30,170 per year), 21 teaching assistantships (averaging $3,550 per year) were awarded; scholarships/grants, health care benefits, and tuition waivers also available. *Unit head:* Dr. Paul Jankowski, Director of Graduate Studies, 781-736-2274, E-mail: jankowski@brandeis.edu. *Application contact:* Dona DeLorenzo, Administrator, 781-736-2270, E-mail: delorenz@brandeis.edu. Website: http://www.brandeis.edu/gsas/programs/history.html

Brock University, Faculty of Graduate Studies, Faculty of Humanities, Program in History, St. Catharines, ON L2S 3A1, Canada. Offers MA. *Program availability:* Part-time. *Degree requirements:* For master's, thesis optional. *Entrance requirements:* For master's, honors degree in history. Additional exam requirements/recommendations for international students: required—TOEFL (minimum score 550 paper-based; 80 iBT), IELTS (minimum score 6.5), TWE (minimum score 4). Electronic applications accepted.

Brooklyn College of the City University of New York, School of Humanities and Social Sciences, Department of History, Brooklyn, NY 11210-2889. Offers MA. *Program availability:* Part-time, evening/weekend. *Degree requirements:* For master's, 30 credits. *Entrance requirements:* For master's, 12 credits in history, minimum GPA of 3.0 in major, 2 letters of recommendation. Additional exam requirements/recommendations for international students: required—TOEFL (minimum score 650 paper-based; 114 iBT). Electronic applications accepted.

Brown University, Graduate School, Department of History, Providence, RI 02912. Offers MA, PhD. *Degree requirements:* For master's, thesis or alternative; for doctorate, variable foreign language requirement, thesis/dissertation, preliminary exam.

Buffalo State College, State University of New York, The Graduate School, School of Natural and Social Sciences, Department of History and Social Studies Education, Buffalo, NY 14222-1095. Offers history (MA); museum studies (MA); secondary education (MS Ed), including social studies. *Program availability:* Part-time, evening/weekend. *Degree requirements:* For master's, one foreign language, thesis (for some programs), project (MS Ed). *Entrance requirements:* For master's, minimum GPA of 2.75, 30 hours in history (MA), 36 hours in history or social sciences (MS Ed). Additional exam requirements/recommendations for international students: required—TOEFL (minimum score 550 paper-based).

Cabrini University, Academic Affairs, Radnor, PA 19087. Offers accounting (M Acc); autism spectrum disorder (M Ed); biological sciences (MS), including civic leadership; criminology and criminal justice (MA); curriculum, instruction, and assessment (M Ed); educational leadership (M Ed, Ed D), including curriculum and instructional leadership (Ed D), preK-12 leadership (Ed D); English as a second language (M Ed); organizational leadership (DBA, PhD); preK to 4 (M Ed); reading specialist (M Ed); secondary education (M Ed), including biology, chemistry, English, English/communication, mathematics, social studies; special education grades 7-12 (M Ed); special education preK-8 (M Ed); teaching and learning (M Ed). *Program availability:* Part-time, evening/weekend. *Degree requirements:* For master's, comprehensive exam (for some programs), thesis (for some programs); for doctorate, comprehensive exam (for some programs), thesis/dissertation. *Entrance requirements:* For master's, professional resume, personal statement, two recommendations, official transcripts; for doctorate, official transcripts, minimum master's GPA of 3.0, two recommendations, interview with admissions committee. Additional exam requirements/recommendations for international students: required—TOEFL (minimum score 80 iBT). Electronic applications accepted. Application fee is waived when completed online. *Expenses:* Contact institution.

California Polytechnic State University, San Luis Obispo, College of Liberal Arts, Department of History, San Luis Obispo, CA 93407. Offers MA. *Program availability:* Part-time. *Faculty:* 5 full-time (2 women). *Students:* 2 full-time (both women), 9 part-time (6 women); includes 3 minority (2 Hispanic/Latino; 1 Two or more races, non-Hispanic/Latino). Average age 29. 14 applicants, 93% accepted, 4 enrolled. In 2019, 7 master's awarded. *Entrance requirements:* Additional exam requirements/recommendations for international students: required—TOEFL (minimum score 80 iBT). *Application deadline:* For fall admission, 4/1 for domestic and international students. Applications are processed on a rolling basis. Application fee: $55. Electronic applications accepted. *Expenses:* Tuition, state resident: full-time $7176; part-time $4164 per year. Tuition, nonresident: full-time $18,690; part-time $8916 per year. *Required fees:* $4206; $3185 per unit. $1061 per term. *Financial support:* Research assistantships, Federal Work-Study, scholarships/grants, and unspecified assistantships available. Support available to part-time students. Financial award application deadline: 3/2; financial award applicants required to submit FAFSA. *Unit head:* Dr. Andrew Morris, Graduate Coordinator, 805-756-2761, E-mail: admorris@calpoly.edu. *Application contact:* Dr. Andrew Morris, Graduate Coordinator, 805-756-2761, E-mail: admorris@calpoly.edu. Website: http://cla.calpoly.edu/hist.html

California State Polytechnic University, Pomona, Program in History, Pomona, CA 91768-2557. Offers history (MA). *Program availability:* Part-time, evening/weekend. *Entrance requirements:* Additional exam requirements/recommendations for international students: required—TOEFL (minimum score 550 paper-based). Electronic applications accepted. *Expenses:* Contact institution.

California State University, Chico, Office of Graduate Studies, College of Humanities and Fine Arts, Department of History, Chico, CA 95929-0722. Offers MA. *Program availability:* Part-time. *Degree requirements:* For master's, thesis, Thesis or oral exam. *Entrance requirements:* For master's, GRE General Test, 2 letters of recommendation, statement of purpose, writing sample, department letter of recommendation access waiver form. Additional exam requirements/recommendations for international students: required—TOEFL (minimum score 550 paper-based; 80 iBT), IELTS (minimum score 6.5), PTE (minimum score 59). Electronic applications accepted.

California State University, East Bay, Office of Graduate Studies, College of Letters, Arts, and Social Sciences, Department of History, Hayward, CA 94542-3000. Offers history (MA); public history (MA); teaching (MA). *Program availability:* Part-time, evening/weekend. *Degree requirements:* For master's, one foreign language, comprehensive exam, project, thesis, or exam. *Entrance requirements:* For master's, GRE (strongly recommended), minimum GPA of 3.0 in field, 3.3 in history; 2 letters of recommendation; writing sample. Additional exam requirements/recommendations for international students: required—TOEFL (minimum score 550 paper-based). Electronic applications accepted.

California State University, Fresno, Division of Research and Graduate Studies, College of Social Sciences, Department of History, Fresno, CA 93740-8027. Offers history (MA); history teaching (MA). *Program availability:* Part-time, evening/weekend. *Degree requirements:* For master's, project; thesis or comprehensive examination. *Entrance requirements:* For master's, GRE General Test, minimum GPA of 3.0. Additional exam requirements/recommendations for international students: required—TOEFL. Electronic applications accepted. *Expenses:* Tuition, state resident: full-time $4012; part-time $2506 per semester.

California State University, Fullerton, Graduate Studies, College of Humanities and Social Sciences, Department of History, Fullerton, CA 92831-3599. Offers MA. *Program availability:* Part-time. *Degree requirements:* For master's, comprehensive exam, project or thesis. *Entrance requirements:* For master's, undergraduate major in history or related field, minimum GPA of 3.0.

California State University, Long Beach, Graduate Studies, College of Liberal Arts, Department of History, Long Beach, CA 90840. Offers Africa and the Middle East (MA). *Program availability:* Part-time, evening/weekend. *Degree requirements:* For master's, one foreign language, comprehensive exam or thesis. Electronic applications accepted.

California State University, Los Angeles, Graduate Studies, College of Natural and Social Sciences, Department of History, Los Angeles, CA 90032-8530. Offers MA. *Program availability:* Part-time, evening/weekend. *Degree requirements:* For master's, one foreign language, comprehensive exam or thesis. *Entrance requirements:* For master's, minimum GPA of 3.0, undergraduate major in history. Additional exam requirements/recommendations for international students: required—TOEFL (minimum score 500 paper-based). Electronic applications accepted. *Expenses: Tuition, area resident:* Full-time $7176; part-time $4164 per year. Tuition, state resident: full-time $7176; part-time $4164 per year. Tuition, nonresident: full-time $14,304; part-time $8916 per year. *International tuition:* $14,304 full-time. *Required fees:* $1037.76; $1037.76 per unit. Tuition and fees vary according to degree level and program.

History

California State University, Northridge, Graduate Studies, College of Social and Behavioral Sciences, Department of History, Northridge, CA 91330. Offers MA. *Degree requirements:* For master's, one foreign language. *Entrance requirements:* For master's, GRE General Test or minimum GPA of 3.0, 2 letters of recommendation. Additional exam requirements/recommendations for international students: required—TOEFL.

California State University, San Marcos, College of Humanities, Arts, Behavioral and Social Sciences, Program in History, San Marcos, CA 92096-0001. Offers MA. *Entrance requirements:* For master's, GRE General Test, three letters of recommendation, minimum GPA of 3.0 overall and in major, academic writing sample. Additional exam requirements/recommendations for international students: required—TOEFL (minimum score 500 paper-based). *Expenses:* Tuition, area resident: Full-time $7176. Tuition, state resident: full-time $7176. Tuition, nonresident: full-time $18,640. *International tuition:* $18,640 full-time. *Required fees:* $1960.

California State University, Stanislaus, College of the Arts, Humanities and Social Sciences, Master of Arts in History Program, Turlock, CA 95382. Offers MA. *Program availability:* Part-time. *Degree requirements:* For master's, comprehensive exam, thesis or alternative. *Entrance requirements:* For master's, GRE, minimum GPA of 3.0, personal statement. Additional exam requirements/recommendations for international students: required—TOEFL (minimum score 575 paper-based). Electronic applications accepted.

Carleton University, Faculty of Graduate Studies, Faculty of Arts and Social Sciences, Department of History, Ottawa, ON K1S 5B6, Canada. Offers MA, PhD. *Degree requirements:* For master's, one foreign language, thesis; for doctorate, one foreign language, thesis/dissertation. *Entrance requirements:* For master's, honors degree; for doctorate, master's degree. Additional exam requirements/recommendations for international students: required—TOEFL.

Carnegie Mellon University, Dietrich College of Humanities and Social Sciences, Department of History, Pittsburgh, PA 15213-3891. Offers African and African-American diaspora (PhD); culture and power (PhD); labor, politics and social movements (PhD); technology, environment, science and health (PhD); women, gender and the family (PhD). *Program availability:* Part-time. *Degree requirements:* For doctorate, oral and written comprehensive exams, dissertation defense. *Entrance requirements:* For doctorate, GRE General Test. Additional exam requirements/recommendations for international students: required—TOEFL. Electronic applications accepted.

Case Western Reserve University, School of Graduate Studies, Department of History, Cleveland, OH 44106. Offers MA, PhD. *Program availability:* Part-time. *Faculty:* 15 full-time (5 women), 2 part-time/adjunct (1 woman). *Students:* 18 full-time (12 women); includes 1 minority (Asian, non-Hispanic/Latino), 3 international. Average age 35. 11 applicants, 18% accepted, 2 enrolled. In 2019, 1 doctorate awarded. Terminal master's awarded for partial completion of doctoral program. *Degree requirements:* For master's, thesis; for doctorate, thesis/dissertation. *Entrance requirements:* For master's and doctorate, GRE General Test, statement of objectives; three letters of recommendation; curriculum vitae; writing sample; short essay. Additional exam requirements/recommendations for international students: required—TOEFL (minimum score 577 paper-based; 90 iBT); recommended—IELTS (minimum score 7). *Application deadline:* For fall admission, 1/31 priority date for domestic students. Application fee: $50. Electronic applications accepted. *Financial support:* Fellowships, research assistantships, teaching assistantships, career-related internships or fieldwork, health care benefits, tuition waivers (full and partial), and unspecified assistantships available. Financial award application deadline: 1/31; financial award applicants required to submit FAFSA. *Unit head:* Kenneth Ledford, Associate Professor and Chair, 216-368-4144, Fax: 216-368-4681, E-mail: kenneth.ledford@case.edu. *Application contact:* Daniel Cohen, Associate Professor, 216-368-4165, Fax: 216-368-4681, E-mail: daniel.a.cohen@case.edu.
Website: http://history.case.edu/

The Catholic University of America, School of Arts and Sciences, Department of History, Washington, DC 20064. Offers history (MA, PhD), including early modern European history, medieval history, modern European history, U.S. history; religion and society in the late medieval and early modern world (MA); MA/JD; MSLS/MA. *Program availability:* Part-time. *Faculty:* 14 full-time (6 women). *Students:* 5 full-time (4 women), 17 part-time (6 women); includes 3 minority (all Two or more races, non-Hispanic/Latino), 2 international. Average age 30. 14 applicants, 57% accepted, 3 enrolled. In 2019, 3 master's, 1 doctorate awarded. Terminal master's awarded for partial completion of doctoral program. *Degree requirements:* For master's, one foreign language, comprehensive exam, thesis optional, 2 languages (for medievalists), one of which must be Latin; for doctorate, 2 foreign languages, comprehensive exam, thesis/dissertation, 3 languages (for medievalists), one of which must be Latin. *Entrance requirements:* For master's and doctorate, GRE General Test, statement of purpose, official copies of academic transcripts, three letters of recommendation, writing sample. Additional exam requirements/recommendations for international students: required—TOEFL (minimum score 550 paper-based; 80 iBT). *Application deadline:* For fall admission, 7/15 priority date for domestic students, 7/1 for international students; for spring admission, 11/15 priority date for domestic students, 11/1 for international students. Applications are processed on a rolling basis. Application fee: $55. Electronic applications accepted. *Expenses:* Contact institution. *Financial support:* Fellowships, research assistantships, teaching assistantships, Federal Work-Study, scholarships/grants, tuition waivers (full and partial), and unspecified assistantships available. Financial award application deadline: 2/1; financial award applicants required to submit FAFSA. *Unit head:* Dr. Michael Kimmage, Chair, 202-319-5484, Fax: 202-319-5569, E-mail: kimmage@cua.edu. *Application contact:* Dr. Steven Brown, Director of Graduate Admissions, 202-319-5057, Fax: 202-319-6533, E-mail: cua-admissions@cua.edu.
Website: http://history.cua.edu/

Central Connecticut State University, School of Graduate Studies, College of Liberal Arts and Social Sciences, Department of History, New Britain, CT 06050-4010. Offers MA, Certificate. *Program availability:* Part-time, evening/weekend. *Degree requirements:* For master's, comprehensive exam, thesis or alternative; for Certificate, qualifying exam. *Entrance requirements:* For master's, minimum undergraduate GPA of 3.0, essays, letters of recommendation. Additional exam requirements/recommendations for international students: required—TOEFL (minimum score 550 paper-based; 79 iBT); recommended—IELTS (minimum score 6.5). Electronic applications accepted.

Central European University, Department of History, Budapest, Hungary. Offers MA, PhD. Terminal master's awarded for partial completion of doctoral program. *Degree requirements:* For master's, one foreign language, thesis; for doctorate, one foreign language, comprehensive exam, thesis/dissertation. *Entrance requirements:* For master's and doctorate, essay, statement of purpose, interview. Additional exam requirements/recommendations for international students: required—TOEFL (minimum score 570 paper-based); recommended—IELTS (minimum score 6.5). Electronic applications accepted.

Central Michigan University, College of Graduate Studies, College of Liberal Arts and Social Sciences, Department of History, Mount Pleasant, MI 48859. Offers European history (Graduate Certificate); history (MA); modern history (Graduate Certificate); United States history (Graduate Certificate); MA/PhD. *Program availability:* Part-time.

Degree requirements: For master's, thesis or alternative. Electronic applications accepted. *Expenses:* Tuition, area resident: Full-time $12,267; part-time $8178 per year. Tuition, state resident: full-time $12,267; part-time $8178 per year. Tuition, nonresident: full-time $12,267; part-time $8178 per year. *International tuition:* $16,110 full-time. *Required fees:* $225 per semester. Tuition and fees vary according to degree level and program.

Central Washington University, School of Graduate Studies and Research, College of Arts and Humanities, Department of History, Ellensburg, WA 98926. Offers MA. *Entrance requirements:* For master's, GRE General Test, minimum GPA of 3.0, writing sample. Additional exam requirements/recommendations for international students: required—TOEFL (minimum score 550 paper-based; 79 iBT). Electronic applications accepted.

Centro de Estudios Avanzados de Puerto Rico y el Caribe, Graduate Program in Puerto Rican and Caribbean Studies, Old San Juan, PR 00902-3970. Offers Puerto Rican and Caribbean history (MA, PhD); Puerto Rican and Caribbean literature (MA, PhD); Puerto Rican studies (MA). *Program availability:* Part-time, evening/weekend. *Degree requirements:* For master's, comprehensive exam, thesis; for doctorate, 2 foreign languages, comprehensive exam, thesis/dissertation. *Entrance requirements:* For master's and doctorate, interview.

Chicago State University, School of Graduate and Professional Studies, College of Arts and Sciences, Department of Geography, Sociology, History, African-American Studies and Anthropology, Chicago, IL 60628. Offers geographic information systems (MA); history (MA). *Entrance requirements:* For master's, minimum GPA of 3.0.

The Citadel, The Military College of South Carolina, Citadel Graduate College, School of Humanities and Social Sciences, Department of History, Charleston, SC 29409. Offers history (MA); history and teaching content (Graduate Certificate). *Program availability:* Part-time, evening/weekend, 100% online, blended/hybrid learning. *Faculty:* 14 full-time (6 women), 6 part-time/adjunct (1 woman). *Students:* 13 part-time (3 women); includes 1 minority (Hispanic/Latino). In 2019, 2 master's awarded. *Degree requirements:* For master's, thesis optional. *Entrance requirements:* For master's, MA History: GRE. MA Military History: GRE or MAT, MA History: submission of an official transcript reflecting the highest degree earned from a regionally accredited college or university, UG cumulative GPA of 2.5 and major GPA of 3.0, 3 letters of recommendation, and a writing sample. MA Military History: submission of official transcripts from all degrees earned from previous colleges or univers; for Graduate Certificate, Certificate in History and Teaching Content: Submission of an official transcript reflecting the highest degree earned from a regionally accredited college or university, letter of intent, 3 references, and either a Baccalaureate degree in Elementary Education, Social Studies, Education or History or a Baccalaureate degree in a related Social Studi. Additional exam requirements/recommendations for international students: required—TOEFL (minimum score 550 paper-based; 79 iBT). Application fee: $40. Electronic applications accepted. *Expenses:* MA Military History: $695 per credit hour. $165 per semester in fees ($75 Technology Fee + $75 Infrastructure Fee + $15 Registration Fee). *Financial support:* Federal Work-Study, scholarships/grants, tuition waivers (partial), and Athletics available. Financial award applicants required to submit FAFSA. *Unit head:* Joelle Neulander, Department Head of History, 843-953-5073, Fax: 843-953-1663, E-mail: neulanderj1@citadel.edu. *Application contact:* Caroline Schlatt, Assistant Director of Enrollment Management, 843-953-5073, Fax: 843-953-7630, E-mail: cschlatt@citadel.edu.
Website: http://www.citadel.edu/root/history-masters-program

City College of the City University of New York, Graduate School, Division of Humanities and the Arts, Department of History, New York, NY 10031-9198. Offers MA. *Program availability:* Part-time. *Degree requirements:* For master's, one foreign language, comprehensive exam, thesis. *Entrance requirements:* Additional exam requirements/recommendations for international students: required—TOEFL (minimum score 600 paper-based; 100 iBT). Electronic applications accepted.

Claremont Graduate University, Graduate Programs, School of Arts and Humanities, Department of History, Claremont, CA 91711-6160. Offers Africana history (Certificate); American studies and U.S. history (MA, PhD); archival studies (MA); early modern studies (MA, PhD); European studies (MA, PhD); oral history (MA, PhD); MBA/MA; MBA/PhD. Terminal master's awarded for partial completion of doctoral program. *Entrance requirements:* For master's and doctorate, GRE General Test. Additional exam requirements/recommendations for international students: required—TOEFL (minimum score 75 iBT). Electronic applications accepted.

Clark University, Graduate School, Department of History, Program in United States and Atlantic History, Worcester, MA 01610-1477. Offers history of the Atlantic world (PhD); history of the United States (PhD). *Expenses:* Tuition: Full-time $47,650; part-time $4765 per course. *Required fees:* $1850.

Clayton State University, School of Graduate Studies, College of Arts and Sciences, Program in Education, Morrow, GA 30260-0285. Offers biology (MAT); English (MAT); history (MAT); mathematics (MAT). *Accreditation:* NCATE. *Entrance requirements:* For master's, GRE, GACE, 2 official copies of transcripts, 3 recommendation letters, statement of purpose. Additional exam requirements/recommendations for international students: required—TOEFL (minimum score 550 paper-based). Electronic applications accepted.

Clemson University, Graduate School, College of Architecture, Arts, and Humanities, Department of History, Clemson, SC 29634. Offers MA. *Faculty:* 24 full-time (9 women), 1 (woman) part-time/adjunct. *Students:* 17 full-time (9 women), 5 part-time (1 woman); includes 3 minority (2 Black or African American, non-Hispanic/Latino; 1 Hispanic/Latino). Average age 34. 18 applicants, 61% accepted, 8 enrolled. In 2019, 3 master's awarded. *Expenses:* Tuition, area resident: Full-time $10,600; part-time $8688 per semester. Tuition, state resident: full-time $10,600; part-time $8688 per semester. Tuition, nonresident: full-time $22,050; part-time $17,412 per semester. *International tuition:* $22,050 full-time. *Required fees:* $1196; $617 per semester. $617 per semester. Tuition and fees vary according to course load, degree level, campus/location and program. *Financial support:* In 2019–20, 16 students received support, including 15 teaching assistantships with full and partial tuition reimbursements available (averaging $10,087 per year); unspecified assistantships also available. *Unit head:* Dr. Amit Bein, Interim Department Chair, 864-656-3153, E-mail: abein@clemson.edu. *Application contact:* Dr. Michael Meng, Graduate Studies Director, 864-656-3153, E-mail: mmeng@clemson.edu.
Website: https://www.clemson.edu/caah/departments/history/

Cleveland State University, College of Graduate Studies, College of Liberal Arts and Social Sciences, Department of History, Cleveland, OH 44115. Offers art history (MA); museum studies (MA). *Program availability:* Part-time, evening/weekend. *Students:* Average age 32. 21 applicants, 90% accepted, 6 enrolled. In 2019, 9 master's awarded. *Entrance requirements:* For master's, minimum GPA of 3.0, bachelor's degree in history (or related field for art history). Additional exam requirements/recommendations for international students: required—TOEFL (minimum score 550 paper-based; 78 iBT). *Application deadline:* Applications are processed on a rolling basis. Application fee: $40. Electronic applications accepted. *Expenses:* Tuition, state resident: full-time $10,215; part-time $6810 per credit hour. Tuition, nonresident: full-time $17,496; part-time

$11,664 per credit hour. *International tuition:* $19,316 full-time. Tuition and fees vary according to degree level and program. *Financial support:* In 2019–20, 7 students received support. Research assistantships, career-related internships or fieldwork, tuition waivers (full and partial), and unspecified assistantships available. Financial award application deadline: 4/15. *Unit head:* Dr. Elizabeth A. Lehfeldt, Chairperson, 216-687-3920, Fax: 216-687-5592, E-mail: e.lehfeldt@csuohio.edu. *Application contact:* Dr. Karen Sotiropoulos, Graduate Director, 216-687-3940, E-mail: r.s.shelton@csuohio.edu.
Website: http://www.csuohio.edu/history/

College of Charleston, Graduate School, School of Humanities and Social Sciences, Program in History, Charleston, SC 29424-0001. Offers MA. *Program availability:* Part-time, evening/weekend. *Degree requirements:* For master's, comprehensive exam, thesis optional. *Entrance requirements:* For master's, GRE General Test or MAT, writing sample. Additional exam requirements/recommendations for international students: required—TOEFL (minimum score 81 iBT). Electronic applications accepted.

College of Staten Island of the City University of New York, Graduate Programs, Division of Humanities and Social Sciences, Program in History, Staten Island, NY 10314-6600. Offers history (MA), including Africa and the Middle East, Asia, Europe, Latin America and the Caribbean, United States. *Program availability:* Part-time, evening/weekend. *Faculty:* 5. *Students:* 17. 12 applicants, 67% accepted, 8 enrolled. In 2019, 1 master's awarded. *Degree requirements:* For master's, comprehensive exam (for some programs), thesis or alternative, the MA in History requires 32 graduate credits at the 700-level, with all graduate courses designated at four credits, for a total of eight courses. Students must take at least one course in each of four of the program's five areas of concentration, rigorous thesis option or portfolio option. *Entrance requirements:* For master's, bachelor's degree with minimum GPA of 3.0 overall and in undergraduate history courses, two letters of recommendation, letter of interest, research-based writing sample. Additional exam requirements/recommendations for international students: required—TOEFL (minimum score 550 paper-based; 79 iBT), IELTS (minimum score 6.5). *Application deadline:* For fall admission, 5/10 priority date for domestic students, 4/25 for international students; for spring admission, 12/2 priority date for domestic students, 11/23 for international students. Applications are processed on a rolling basis. Application fee: $75. Electronic applications accepted. *Expenses: Tuition, area resident:* Full-time $11,090; part-time $470 per credit. Tuition, state resident: full-time $11,090; part-time $470 per credit. Tuition, nonresident: full-time $20,520; part-time $855 per credit. *International tuition:* $20,520 full-time. *Required fees:* $559; $181 per semester. Tuition and fees vary according to program. *Unit head:* Susan Smith-Peter, Graduate Program Coordinator, 718-982-3290, E-mail: susan.smithpeter@csi.cuny.edu. *Application contact:* Sasha Spence, Associate Director for Graduate Admissions, 718-982-2019, Fax: 718-982-2500, E-mail: sasha.spence@csi.cuny.edu.
Website: https://www.csi.cuny.edu/academics-and-research/departments-programs/history/master-arts-history

College of Staten Island of the City University of New York, Graduate Programs, School of Education, Program in Adolescence Education, Staten Island, NY 10314-6600. Offers adolescence education (MS Ed), including biology, English, mathematics, social studies. *Program availability:* Part-time, evening/weekend. *Faculty:* 24. *Students:* 82. 36 applicants, 83% accepted, 25 enrolled. In 2019, 30 master's awarded. *Degree requirements:* For master's, thesis, educational research project supervised by faculty; Sequence 1 consists of a minimum of 33-38 graduate credits among 11 courses. Sequence 2 consists of a minimum of 46-53 graduate credits. *Entrance requirements:* For master's, The candidate must also take the General Test of the Graduate Record Examination (GRE) or an approved equivalent examination and request the submission of official scores to the College. The CSI Code is 2778. Applicants should apply directly to the Educational Testing Service (ETS) to take the examination, Sequence 1: NYS initial teaching; Sequence 2: 32 approved academic credits in appropriate subject area. Relevant bachelors degree, overall GPA at or above 3.0, two letters of recommendation, one-or-two-page personal statement. Additional exam requirements/recommendations for international students: required—TOEFL (minimum score 550 paper-based; 79 iBT), IELTS (minimum score 6.5). *Application deadline:* For fall admission, 4/25 for domestic and international students; for spring admission, 11/25 for domestic and international students. Applications are processed on a rolling basis. Application fee: $75. Electronic applications accepted. *Expenses: Tuition, area resident:* Full-time $11,090; part-time $470 per credit. Tuition, state resident: full-time $11,090; part-time $470 per credit. Tuition, nonresident: full-time $20,520; part-time $855 per credit. *International tuition:* $20,520 full-time. *Required fees:* $559; $181 per semester. Tuition and fees vary according to program. *Unit head:* Diane Brescia, 718-982-3877, E-mail: diane.brescia@csi.cuny.edu. *Application contact:* Sasha Spence, Associate Director for Graduate Admissions, 718-982-2019, Fax: 718-982-2500, E-mail: sasha.spence@csi.cuny.edu.
Website: http://csicuny.smartcatalogiq.com/en/current/Graduate-Catalog/Graduate-Programs-Disciplines-and-Offerings-in-Selected-Disciplines/Adolescence-Educatio

Colorado State University, College of Liberal Arts, Department of History, Fort Collins, CO 80523-1776. Offers liberal arts (MA); public history (MA). *Program availability:* Part-time. *Faculty:* 6 full-time (3 women), 1 (woman) part-time/adjunct. *Students:* 22 full-time (13 women), 1 part-time (0 women); includes 2 minority (1 Hispanic/Latino; 1 Two or more races, non-Hispanic/Latino). Average age 26. 28 applicants, 57% accepted, 12 enrolled. In 2019, 15 master's awarded. *Degree requirements:* For master's, variable foreign language requirement, comprehensive exam, thesis (for some programs). *Entrance requirements:* For master's, GRE, 21 undergraduate credits in history; minimum undergraduate GPA of 3.0; personal statement; 3 letters of reference. Additional exam requirements/recommendations for international students: required—TOEFL, IELTS. *Application deadline:* For winter admission, 2/1 for domestic and international students. Application fee: $60 ($70 for international students). Electronic applications accepted. *Expenses:* Tuition, state resident: full-time $10,520; part-time $5844 per credit hour. Tuition, nonresident: full-time $25,791; part-time $14,328 per credit hour. *International tuition:* $25,791 full-time. *Required fees:* $2512.80. Part-time tuition and fees vary according to course level, course load, degree level, program and student level. *Financial support:* In 2019–20, 22 students received support, including 22 teaching assistantships (averaging $15,210 per year); health care benefits also available. Financial award application deadline: 2/1; financial award applicants required to submit FAFSA. *Unit head:* Dr. Robert Gudmestad, Department Chair, 970-491-6050, Fax: 970-491-2941, E-mail: doug.yarrington@colostate.edu. *Application contact:* Nancy Rehe, Administrative Assistant, 970-491-6334, E-mail: nancy.rehe@colostate.edu.
Website: http://history.colostate.edu/

Columbia University, Graduate School of Arts and Sciences, New York, NY 10027. Offers African-American studies (MA); American studies (MA); anthropology (MA, PhD); art history and archaeology (MA, PhD); astronomy (PhD); biological sciences (PhD); biotechnology (MA); chemical physics (PhD); chemistry (PhD); classical studies (MA, PhD); classics (MA, PhD); climate and society (MA); conservation biology (MA); earth and environmental sciences (PhD); East Asia: regional studies (MA); East Asian languages and cultures (MA, PhD); ecology, evolution and environmental biology (MA), including conservation biology; ecology, evolution, and environmental biology (PhD), including ecology and evolutionary biology, evolutionary primatology; economics (MA, PhD); English and comparative literature (MA, PhD); French and Romance philology (MA, PhD); Germanic languages (MA, PhD); global French studies (MA); global thought (MA); Hispanic cultural studies (MA); history (PhD); history and literature (MA); human rights studies (MA); Islamic studies (MA); Italian (MA, PhD); Japanese pedagogy (MA); Jewish studies (MA); Latin America and the Caribbean: regional studies (MA); Latin American and Iberian cultures (PhD); mathematics (MA, PhD), including finance (MA); medieval and Renaissance studies (MA); Middle Eastern, South Asian, and African studies (MA, PhD); modern art: critical and curatorial studies (MA); modern European studies (MA); museum anthropology (MA); music (DMA, PhD); oral history (MA); philosophical foundations of physics (MA); philosophy (MA, PhD); physics (PhD); political science (MA, PhD); psychology (PhD); quantitative methods in the social sciences (MA); religion (MA, PhD); Russia, Eurasia and East Europe: regional studies (MA); Russian translation (MA); Slavic cultures (MA); Slavic languages (MA, PhD); sociology (MA, PhD); South Asian studies (MA); statistics (MA, PhD); theatre (PhD). *Program availability:* Part-time. *Students:* 3,506 full-time (1,844 women), 208 part-time (121 women); includes 864 minority (110 Black or African American, non-Hispanic/Latino; 5 American Indian or Alaska Native, non-Hispanic/Latino; 416 Asian, non-Hispanic/Latino; 147 Hispanic/Latino; 6 Native Hawaiian or other Pacific Islander, non-Hispanic/Latino; 180 Two or more races, non-Hispanic/Latino), 2,065 international. 14,545 applicants, 25% accepted, 1,429 enrolled. In 2019, 1,262 master's, 363 doctorates awarded. Terminal master's awarded for partial completion of doctoral program. *Degree requirements:* For master's, variable foreign language requirement, comprehensive exam (for some programs), thesis (for some programs); for doctorate, variable foreign language requirement, comprehensive exam (for some programs), thesis/dissertation. *Entrance requirements:* For master's and doctorate, GRE General Test, GRE Subject Test (for some programs). Additional exam requirements/recommendations for international students: required—TOEFL (minimum score 600 paper-based; 100 iBT), IELTS (minimum score 7.5). Application fee: $115. Electronic applications accepted. *Expenses: Tuition:* Full-time $47,600; part-time $1880 per credit. One-time fee: $105. *Financial support:* Fellowships, research assistantships, teaching assistantships, career-related internships or fieldwork, Federal Work-Study, institutionally sponsored loans, scholarships/grants, traineeships, health care benefits, tuition waivers, and unspecified assistantships available. Support available to part-time students. Financial award application deadline: 12/15. *Unit head:* Dr. Carlos J. Alonso, Dean of the Graduate School of Arts and Sciences and Vice President for Graduate Education, 212-854-2861, E-mail: gsas-dean@columbia.edu. *Application contact:* GSAS Office of Admissions, 212-854-6729, E-mail: gsas-admissions@columbia.edu.
Website: http://gsas.columbia.edu/

Columbus State University, Graduate Studies, College of Education and Health Professions, Department of Teacher Education, Columbus, GA 31907-5645. Offers curriculum and instruction in accomplished teaching (M Ed); early childhood education (M Ed, MAT, Ed S); middle grades education (M Ed, MAT, Ed S); secondary education (M Ed, MAT, Ed S), including biology (MAT), chemistry (MAT), earth and space science (MAT), English/language arts, general science (M Ed), history (MAT), mathematics, science (Ed S), social science (M Ed, Ed S); special education (M Ed, MAT, Ed S), including general curriculum (M Ed, MAT); teacher leadership (M Ed). *Accreditation:* NCATE. *Program availability:* Part-time, evening/weekend, 100% online, blended/hybrid learning. *Degree requirements:* For Ed S, thesis or alternative. *Entrance requirements:* For master's, GRE General Test, minimum undergraduate GPA of 2.75; for Ed S, GRE General Test, minimum undergraduate GPA of 2.75, graduate 3.0. Additional exam requirements/recommendations for international students: required—TOEFL (minimum score 550 paper-based; 79 iBT). Electronic applications accepted. *Expenses: Tuition, area resident:* Full-time $210; part-time $210 per credit hour. Tuition, state resident: full-time $210; part-time $210 per credit hour. Tuition, nonresident: full-time $817; part-time $817 per credit hour. *International tuition:* $817 full-time. *Required fees:* $802.50. Tuition and fees vary according to course load, degree level and program.

Columbus State University, Graduate Studies, College of Letters and Sciences, Department of History and Geography, Columbus, GA 31907-5645. Offers history (MA), including race, ethnicity and society. *Program availability:* Evening/weekend. *Degree requirements:* For master's, thesis. *Entrance requirements:* For master's, GRE, minimum GPA of 3.0, writing sample, statement of purpose, two letters of recommendation. Additional exam requirements/recommendations for international students: required—TOEFL (minimum score 550 paper-based; 79 iBT). Electronic applications accepted. *Expenses: Tuition, area resident:* Full-time $210; part-time $210 per credit hour. Tuition, state resident: full-time $210; part-time $210 per credit hour. Tuition, nonresident: full-time $817; part-time $817 per credit hour. *International tuition:* $817 full-time. *Required fees:* $802.50. Tuition and fees vary according to course load, degree level and program.

Concordia University, School of Graduate Studies, Faculty of Arts and Science, Department of History, Montréal, QC H3G 1M8, Canada. Offers MA, PhD. *Degree requirements:* For master's, one foreign language, thesis optional; for doctorate, one foreign language, comprehensive exam, thesis/dissertation. *Entrance requirements:* For master's, honors degree in history or equivalent.

Converse College, Program in Liberal Arts, Spartanburg, SC 29302. Offers English (MLA); history (MLA); political science (MLA). *Degree requirements:* For master's, capstone paper. *Entrance requirements:* For master's, minimum GPA of 3.0, 2 recommendations.

Cornell University, Graduate School, Graduate Fields of Arts and Sciences, Field of History, Ithaca, NY 14853. Offers African history (MA, PhD); American history (MA, PhD); ancient Greek history (PhD); ancient history (MA, PhD); ancient Roman history (PhD); early modern European history (MA, PhD); English history (MA, PhD); French history (MA, PhD); German history (MA, PhD); history of science (MA, PhD); Korean history (PhD); Latin American history (MA, PhD); medieval Chinese history (MA, PhD); medieval history (MA, PhD); modern Chinese history (MA, PhD); modern European history (MA, PhD); modern Japanese history (MA, PhD); modern Middle Eastern history (PhD); premodern Islamic history (MA, PhD); premodern Japanese history (MA, PhD); Renaissance history (MA, PhD); Russian history (MA, PhD); South Asian history (PhD); Southeast Asian history (MA, PhD). Terminal master's awarded for partial completion of doctoral program. *Degree requirements:* For master's, thesis; for doctorate, 2 foreign languages, comprehensive exam, thesis/dissertation, 1 year of teaching experience. *Entrance requirements:* For master's and doctorate, GRE General Test, writing sample, 3 letters of recommendation. Additional exam requirements/recommendations for international students: required—TOEFL (minimum score 550 paper-based; 77 iBT). Electronic applications accepted.

Dalhousie University, Faculty of Arts and Social Sciences, Department of History, Halifax, NS B3H 4R2, Canada. Offers MA, PhD. *Entrance requirements:* Additional exam requirements/recommendations for international students: required—TOEFL, IELTS, CANTEST, CAEL, or Michigan English Language Assessment Battery. Electronic applications accepted.

DePaul University, College of Liberal Arts and Social Sciences, Chicago, IL 60614. Offers Arabic (MA); Chinese (MA); critical ethnic studies (MA); English (MA); French (MA); German (MA); history (MA); interdisciplinary studies (MA, MS); international public service (MS); international studies (MA); Italian (MA); Japanese (MA); liberal studies

(MA); nonprofit management (MNM); public administration (MPA); public health (MPH); public policy (MPP); public service management (MS); refugee and forced migration studies (MS); social work (MSW); sociology (MA); Spanish (MA); sustainable urban development (MA); women's and gender studies (MA); writing and publishing (MA); writing, rhetoric and discourse (MA); MA/PhD. *Accreditation:* CEPH. *Program availability:* Part-time, evening/weekend, online learning. Terminal master's awarded for partial completion of doctoral program. *Degree requirements:* For master's, variable foreign language requirement, comprehensive exam (for some programs), thesis (for some programs). Electronic applications accepted.

Drew University, Caspersen School of Graduate Studies, Madison, NJ 07940-1493. Offers conflict resolution and leadership (Certificate), including community leadership, moderation, peace building; education (M Ed); finance (MA); history and culture (MA, PhD), including American history, book history, British history, European history, intellectual history, Irish history, print culture, public history; K-12 education (MAT), including art, biology, chemistry, elementary education, English, French, Italian, math, secondary education, special education, teacher of students with disabilities; liberal studies (M Litt, D Litt), including history, Irish/Irish-American studies, literature (M Litt, MMH, D Litt, DMH, CMH), religion, spirituality, teaching in the two-year college, writing; medical humanities (MMH, DMH, CMH), including arts, health, healthcare, literature (M Litt, MMH, D Litt, DMH, CMH), scientific research; poetry (MFA). *Program availability:* Part-time, evening/weekend. Terminal master's awarded for partial completion of doctoral program. *Degree requirements:* For master's and other advanced degree, thesis (for some programs); for doctorate, one foreign language, comprehensive exam (for some programs), thesis/dissertation. *Entrance requirements:* For master's, PRAXIS Core and Subject Area tests (for MAT), GRE/GMAT (for MFin MS in Data Analytics), resume, transcripts, writing sample, personal statement, letters of recommendation; for doctorate, GRE (PhD in history and culture), resume, transcripts, writing sample, personal statement, letters of recommendation; for other advanced degree, resume, transcripts, personal statement. Additional exam requirements/recommendations for international students: required—TOEFL (minimum score 587 paper-based; 80 iBT), IELTS (minimum score 6), TWE (minimum score 4). Electronic applications accepted.

Duke University, Graduate School, Department of History, Durham, NC 27708. Offers history (AM, PhD); Latin American studies (PhD); JD/AM. *Degree requirements:* For doctorate, 2 foreign languages, thesis/dissertation. *Entrance requirements:* For doctorate, GRE General Test. Additional exam requirements/recommendations for international students: required—TOEFL (minimum score 577 paper-based; 90 iBT) or IELTS (minimum score 7). Electronic applications accepted.

Duquesne University, Graduate School of Liberal Arts, Department of History, Pittsburgh, PA 15282-0001. Offers historical studies (MA); public history (MA). *Program availability:* Part-time, evening/weekend. *Degree requirements:* For master's, comprehensive exam (for some programs), thesis optional. *Entrance requirements:* For master's, GRE General Test, writing sample. Additional exam requirements/recommendations for international students: required—TOEFL. Electronic applications accepted.

East Carolina University, Graduate School, Thomas Harriot College of Arts and Sciences, Department of History, Greenville, NC 27858-4353. Offers American history (MA); Atlantic world (MA); European history (MA); maritime studies (MA); military history (MA); public history (MA). *Program availability:* Part-time. *Application deadline:* For fall admission, 4/1 priority date for domestic and international students; for spring admission, 10/15 priority date for domestic and international students. *Expenses: Tuition, area resident:* Full-time $4749; part-time $185 per credit hour. Tuition, state resident: full-time $4749; part-time $185 per credit hour. Tuition, nonresident: full-time $17,898; part-time $864 per credit hour. *International tuition:* $17,898 full-time. *Required fees:* $2787. *Financial support:* Application deadline: 1/15. *Unit head:* Dr. Christopher Oakley, Chair, 252-328-1025, E-mail: oakleyc@ecu.edu. *Application contact:* Graduate School Admissions, 252-328-6012, E-mail: gradschool@ecu.edu.
Website: https://history.ecu.edu/

Eastern Illinois University, Graduate School, College of Liberal Arts and Sciences, Department of History, Charleston, IL 61920. Offers history (MA). *Program availability:* Part-time, evening/weekend. *Degree requirements:* For master's, comprehensive exam (for some programs), thesis (for some programs). *Entrance requirements:* For master's, GMAT or GRE. Additional exam requirements/recommendations for international students: required—TOEFL (minimum score 500 paper-based; 61 iBT), IELTS (minimum score 6). Electronic applications accepted.

Eastern Kentucky University, The Graduate School, College of Arts and Sciences, Department of History, Richmond, KY 40475-3102. Offers MA. *Program availability:* Part-time. *Degree requirements:* For master's, comprehensive exam, thesis optional. *Entrance requirements:* For master's, GRE General Test, GRE Subject Test, minimum GPA of 2.5.

Eastern Michigan University, Graduate School, College of Arts and Sciences, Department of History and Philosophy, Program in History, Ypsilanti, MI 48197. Offers MA. *Program availability:* Part-time, evening/weekend, online learning. *Students:* 4 full-time (all women), 27 part-time (12 women); includes 6 minority (2 Black or African American, non-Hispanic/Latino; 4 Hispanic/Latino). Average age 33. 19 applicants, 84% accepted, 6 enrolled. In 2019, 13 master's awarded. *Entrance requirements:* Additional exam requirements/recommendations for international students: required—TOEFL. *Application deadline:* Applications are processed on a rolling basis. Application fee: $45. *Financial support:* Fellowships, research assistantships with full tuition reimbursements, teaching assistantships with full tuition reimbursements, career-related internships or fieldwork, Federal Work-Study, institutionally sponsored loans, scholarships/grants, tuition waivers (partial), and unspecified assistantships available. Support available to part-time students. Financial award applicants required to submit FAFSA. *Application contact:* Dr. John McCurdy, Graduate Coordinator, 734-487-1018, Fax: 734-487-6835, E-mail: jmccurdy@emich.edu.

Eastern Washington University, Graduate Studies, College of Social Sciences, Department of History, Cheney, WA 99004-2431. Offers MA. *Faculty:* 4 full-time (0 women). *Students:* 9 full-time (2 women), 7 part-time (4 women); includes 5 minority (1 Black or African American, non-Hispanic/Latino; 3 American Indian or Alaska Native, non-Hispanic/Latino; 1 Asian, non-Hispanic/Latino). Average age 36. 9 applicants, 67% accepted, 5 enrolled. In 2019, 6 master's awarded. *Degree requirements:* For master's, comprehensive exam, thesis optional. *Entrance requirements:* For master's, minimum GPA of 3.0. Additional exam requirements/recommendations for international students: required—TOEFL (minimum score 580 paper-based; 92 iBT), IELTS (minimum score 7), TWE, PTE (minimum score 63). *Application deadline:* For fall admission, 4/1 priority date for domestic students; for spring admission, 1/15 for domestic students. Applications are processed on a rolling basis. Application fee: $75. *Financial support:* In 2019–20, 6 students received support. Teaching assistantships with partial tuition reimbursements available, career-related internships or fieldwork, Federal Work-Study, institutionally sponsored loans, scholarships/grants, health care benefits, tuition waivers (partial), and unspecified assistantships available. Support available to part-time students. Financial award application deadline: 2/1; financial award applicants required to submit FAFSA. *Unit head:* Dr. Liping Zhu, Chair, 509-359-6086, E-mail: lzhu@ewu.edu. *Application contact:* Dr. Michael Conlin, Director of Graduate Programs, 509-359-7851.

East Stroudsburg University of Pennsylvania, Graduate and Extended Studies, College of Arts and Sciences, Department of History and Geography, East Stroudsburg, PA 18301-2999. Offers M Ed, MA. *Program availability:* Part-time, evening/weekend. *Degree requirements:* For master's, comprehensive exam, thesis, thesis defense. *Entrance requirements:* For master's, Bachelor's degree in History is preferable. Additional exam requirements/recommendations for international students: recommended—TOEFL (minimum score 560 paper-based; 83 iBT), IELTS. Electronic applications accepted.

East Tennessee State University, College of Graduate and Continuing Studies, College of Arts and Sciences, Department of Appalachian Studies, Johnson City, TN 37614. Offers Appalachian communities (MA); Appalachian heritage and culture (MA); Appalachian studies (Postbaccalaureate Certificate). *Program availability:* Part-time. *Degree requirements:* For master's, thesis optional. *Entrance requirements:* For master's, GRE General Test, minimum undergraduate GPA of 3.0, writing sample, 3 letters of recommendation; for Postbaccalaureate Certificate, minimum undergraduate GPA of 3.0, writing sample. Additional exam requirements/recommendations for international students: required—TOEFL (minimum score 550 paper-based; 79 iBT). Electronic applications accepted.

East Tennessee State University, College of Graduate and Continuing Studies, College of Arts and Sciences, Department of History, Johnson City, TN 37614. Offers MA. *Program availability:* Part-time, evening/weekend. *Degree requirements:* For master's, comprehensive exam, thesis optional. *Entrance requirements:* For master's, bachelor's degree in history, minimum GPA of 3.0, three letters of recommendation, minimum of 27 credit hours of study in history. Additional exam requirements/recommendations for international students: required—TOEFL (minimum score 550 paper-based; 79 iBT). Electronic applications accepted.

Emory & Henry College, Graduate Programs, Emory, VA 24327. Offers American history (MA Ed); education professional studies (M Ed); occupational therapy (MOT); organizational leadership (MCOL); physical therapy (DPT); physician assistant studies (MPAS); reading specialist (MA Ed). *Program availability:* Part-time. *Degree requirements:* For master's, thesis optional; for doctorate, thesis/dissertation optional. *Entrance requirements:* For master's, GRE or PRAXIS I, official transcripts from all colleges previously attended, three professional recommendations, essay. Additional exam requirements/recommendations for international students: recommended—TOEFL, IELTS (minimum score 6). Electronic applications accepted. *Expenses:* Contact institution.

Emory University, Laney Graduate School, Department of History, Atlanta, GA 30322-1100. Offers PhD. *Degree requirements:* For doctorate, 2 foreign languages, comprehensive exam, thesis/dissertation. *Entrance requirements:* For doctorate, GRE General Test, minimum GPA of 3.0. Additional exam requirements/recommendations for international students: recommended—TOEFL. Electronic applications accepted.

Emporia State University, Program in History, Emporia, KS 66801-5415. Offers American history (MA); world history (MA). *Program availability:* Part-time. *Degree requirements:* For master's, comprehensive exam or thesis. *Entrance requirements:* For master's, 12 credit hours in history, minimum undergraduate GPA of 2.5, writing sample. Additional exam requirements/recommendations for international students: required—TOEFL (minimum score 520 paper-based; 68 iBT). Electronic applications accepted. *Expenses: Tuition, area resident:* Full-time $6394; part-time $266.41 per credit hour. Tuition, state resident: full-time $6394; part-time $266.41 per credit hour. Tuition, nonresident: full-time $20,128; part-time $828.66 per credit hour. *International tuition:* $20,128 full-time. *Required fees:* $2183; $90.95 per credit hour. Tuition and fees vary according to campus/location and program.

Fairleigh Dickinson University, Metropolitan Campus, University College: Arts, Sciences, and Professional Studies, School of History, Political and International Studies, Program in History, Teaneck, NJ 07666-1914. Offers MA.

Fitchburg State University, Division of Graduate and Continuing Education, Program in Middle School Education, Fitchburg, MA 01420-2697. Offers English (M Ed); general science (M Ed); history (M Ed); math (M Ed). *Accreditation:* NCATE. *Program availability:* Part-time, evening/weekend. *Entrance requirements:* Additional exam requirements/recommendations for international students: required—TOEFL (minimum score 550 paper-based; 79 iBT). Electronic applications accepted. *Expenses:* Contact institution.

Fitchburg State University, Division of Graduate and Continuing Education, Programs in History and Teaching History (Secondary Level), Fitchburg, MA 01420-2697. Offers MA. *Accreditation:* NCATE. *Program availability:* Part-time, evening/weekend. *Entrance requirements:* Additional exam requirements/recommendations for international students: required—TOEFL (minimum score 550 paper-based; 79 iBT). Electronic applications accepted. *Expenses:* Contact institution.

Florida Agricultural and Mechanical University, Division of Graduate Studies, Research, and Continuing Education, College of Social Sciences, Arts and Humanities, Department of History and Political Science, Program in Applied Social Science, Tallahassee, FL 32307-3200. Offers criminal justice (MASS); history (MASS); political science (MASS); public administration (MASS). *Program availability:* Part-time. *Degree requirements:* For master's, thesis optional. *Entrance requirements:* For master's, GRE General Test, minimum GPA of 3.0.

Florida Atlantic University, Dorothy F. Schmidt College of Arts and Letters, Department of History, Boca Raton, FL 33431-0991. Offers MA. *Program availability:* Part-time. *Faculty:* 19 full-time (7 women). *Students:* 8 full-time (3 women), 12 part-time (5 women); includes 7 minority (2 Black or African American, non-Hispanic/Latino; 2 Asian, non-Hispanic/Latino; 3 Hispanic/Latino). Average age 37. 10 applicants, 80% accepted, 7 enrolled. In 2019, 12 master's awarded. *Degree requirements:* For master's, one foreign language, thesis optional. *Entrance requirements:* For master's, GRE General Test, minimum GPA of 3.0. Additional exam requirements/recommendations for international students: required—TOEFL (minimum score 500 paper-based; 61 iBT), IELTS (minimum score 6). *Application deadline:* For fall admission, 6/1 priority date for domestic students, 2/15 for international students; for spring admission, 10/15 for domestic students, 8/15 for international students. Applications are processed on a rolling basis. Application fee: $30. Electronic applications accepted. *Expenses: Tuition:* Full-time $20,536; part-time $371.82 per credit hour. Tuition and fees vary according to program. *Financial support:* Fellowships, research assistantships, teaching assistantships, career-related internships or fieldwork, Federal Work-Study, and tuition waivers (partial) available. Support available to part-time students. Financial award application deadline: 3/1. *Unit head:* Dr. Douglas Kanter, Director, Graduate Studies Program, 561-297-3840, E-mail: dkanter1@fau.edu. *Application contact:* Dr. Douglas Kanter, Director, Graduate Studies Program, 561-297-3840, E-mail: dkanter1@fau.edu.
Website: http://www.fau.edu/history/

Florida Gulf Coast University, College of Arts and Sciences, Program in History, Fort Myers, FL 33965-6565. Offers MA. *Program availability:* Part-time, evening/weekend. *Entrance requirements:* Additional exam requirements/recommendations for international students: required—TOEFL (minimum score 550 paper-based). Electronic applications accepted. *Expenses: Tuition, area resident:* Full-time $6974; part-time $4350 per credit hour. Tuition, state resident: full-time $6974; part-time $4350 per credit hour. Tuition, nonresident: full-time $28,169; part-time $17,595 per credit hour. *International tuition:* $28,169 full-time. *Required fees:* $2027; $1267 per credit hour. $507 per semester. Tuition and fees vary according to course load.

Florida International University, Steven J. Green School of International and Public Affairs, Department of History, Miami, FL 33199. Offers Atlantic history (PhD); history (MA). *Program availability:* Part-time, evening/weekend. *Faculty:* 25 full-time (15 women), 15 part-time/adjunct (9 women). *Students:* 35 full-time (17 women), 20 part-time (7 women); includes 33 minority (7 Black or African American, non-Hispanic/Latino; 26 Hispanic/Latino), 7 international. Average age 38. 30 applicants, 60% accepted, 11 enrolled. In 2019, 5 master's, 4 doctorates awarded. *Degree requirements:* For master's, one foreign language, thesis optional; for doctorate, 2 foreign languages, comprehensive exam, thesis/dissertation. *Entrance requirements:* For master's, 12 credits of history courses (non-history majors), 2 letters of recommendation, writing sample, minimum GPA of 3.25; for doctorate, GRE General Test (minimum score of 1120), two letters of recommendation, statement of purpose, curriculum vitae, writing sample, minimum GPA of 3.25. Additional exam requirements/recommendations for international students: required—TOEFL (minimum score 575 paper-based; 90 iBT). *Application deadline:* For fall admission, 1/15 priority date for domestic students, 1/15 for international students. Application fee: $30. Electronic applications accepted. *Expenses: Tuition, area resident:* Full-time $8912; part-time $446 per credit hour. Tuition, state resident: full-time $8912; part-time $446 per credit hour. Tuition, nonresident: full-time $21,393; part-time $992 per credit hour. *Required fees:* $2194. *Financial support:* Institutionally sponsored loans, scholarships/grants, and unspecified assistantships available. Financial award application deadline: 3/1; financial award applicants required to submit FAFSA. *Unit head:* Dr. Victor Uribe, Chair, 305-348-2961, Fax: 305-348-3561, E-mail: victor.uribe@fiu.edu. *Application contact:* Nanett Rojas, Manager, Admissions Operations, 305-348-7464, Fax: 305-348-7441, E-mail: gradadm@fiu.edu. Website: http://history.fiu.edu/

Florida State University, The Graduate School, Department of Anthropology, Department of Classics, Tallahassee, FL 32306-1510. Offers ancient history (MA); classical archaeology (MA); classical civilization (MA); classics (PhD), including classical archaeology, classics; Greek (MA); Greek and Latin (MA); Latin (MA). *Faculty:* 18 full-time (8 women), 1 (woman) part-time/adjunct. *Students:* 31 full-time (22 women); includes 4 minority (1 Asian, non-Hispanic/Latino; 3 Two or more races, non-Hispanic/Latino). Average age 27. 41 applicants, 32% accepted, 13 enrolled. In 2019, 16 master's, 4 doctorates awarded. Terminal master's awarded for partial completion of doctoral program. *Degree requirements:* For master's, 2 foreign languages, comprehensive exam, thesis or alternative; for doctorate, 4 foreign languages, comprehensive exam, thesis/dissertation. *Entrance requirements:* For master's and doctorate, GRE General Test, minimum GPA of 3.0, official transcripts, resume/CV, statement of purpose, writing sample. Additional exam requirements/recommendations for international students: required—TOEFL (minimum score 550 paper-based; 80 iBT). *Application deadline:* For fall admission, 12/15 priority date for domestic students, 12/15 for international students. Applications are processed on a rolling basis. Application fee: $30. Electronic applications accepted. *Financial support:* In 2019–20, 39 students received support, including 1 fellowship with full tuition reimbursement available (averaging $18,000 per year), 2 research assistantships with full tuition reimbursements available (averaging $12,000 per year), 24 teaching assistantships with full tuition reimbursements available (averaging $12,400 per year); Federal Work-Study, scholarships/grants, tuition waivers (full), and unspecified assistantships also available. Financial award application deadline: 1/15; financial award applicants required to submit FAFSA. *Unit head:* Dr. John Marincola, Chair, 850-644-0304, Fax: 850-644-4073, E-mail: jmarinco@fsu.edu. *Application contact:* Dr. Jessica Clark, Admissions Director, 850-644-4259, Fax: 850-644-4073, E-mail: jhclark@fsu.edu. Website: http://classics.fsu.edu/

Florida State University, The Graduate School, Department of Anthropology, Department of History, Tallahassee, FL 32306. Offers history (MA, MS, PhD); public history (MA). *Program availability:* Part-time. *Faculty:* 27 full-time (10 women), 3 part-time/adjunct (2 women). *Students:* 43 full-time (16 women), 28 part-time (9 women); includes 12 minority (2 Black or African American, non-Hispanic/Latino; 2 Asian, non-Hispanic/Latino; 8 Two or more races, non-Hispanic/Latino). Average age 30. 39 applicants, 87% accepted, 22 enrolled. In 2019, 23 master's, 15 doctorates awarded. *Degree requirements:* For master's, one foreign language, comprehensive exam (for some programs), thesis (for some programs), internships; for doctorate, one foreign language, comprehensive exam, thesis/dissertation. *Entrance requirements:* For master's, GRE General Test, minimum GPA of 3.3, minimum 18 hours of course work in history; for doctorate, GRE General Test, master's degree, minimum graduate GPA of 3.65. Additional exam requirements/recommendations for international students: required—TOEFL (minimum score 550 paper-based; 80 iBT). *Application deadline:* For fall admission, 12/1 for domestic and international students. Applications are processed on a rolling basis. Application fee: $30. Electronic applications accepted. *Financial support:* In 2019–20, 49 students received support, including 7 fellowships with full tuition reimbursements available (averaging $19,000 per year), 5 research assistantships with full tuition reimbursements available (averaging $15,500 per year), 5 teaching assistantships with full tuition reimbursements available (averaging $18,000 per year); Federal Work-Study, institutionally sponsored loans, scholarships/grants, tuition waivers (full and partial), and unspecified assistantships also available. Financial award application deadline: 12/1; financial award applicants required to submit FAFSA. *Unit head:* Dr. Edward Gray, Chair, 850-644-5888, Fax: 850-644-6402, E-mail: egray@fsu.edu. *Application contact:* Anne Kozar, Academic Program Specialist, 850-644-4494, E-mail: mkozar@fsu.edu. Website: http://history.fsu.edu/

Fordham University, Graduate School of Arts and Sciences, Department of History, New York, NY 10458. Offers MA, PhD. *Program availability:* Part-time, evening/weekend. *Students:* Average age 33. 37 applicants, 54% accepted, 7 enrolled. In 2019, 4 master's, 4 doctorates awarded. Terminal master's awarded for partial completion of doctoral program. *Degree requirements:* For master's, one foreign language, thesis optional; for doctorate, 2 foreign languages, comprehensive exam, thesis/dissertation. *Entrance requirements:* For master's and doctorate, GRE General Test. Additional exam requirements/recommendations for international students: required—TOEFL (minimum score 650 paper-based). *Application deadline:* For fall admission, 1/4 priority date for domestic students; for spring admission, 11/1 for domestic students. Application fee: $70. Electronic applications accepted. *Financial support:* In 2019–20, 23 students received support, including 3 fellowships with tuition reimbursements available (averaging $27,622 per year), 16 teaching assistantships with tuition reimbursements available (averaging $16,806 per year); research assistantships, institutionally sponsored loans, tuition waivers (full and partial), and unspecified assistantships also available. Financial award application deadline: 1/4; financial award applicants required to submit FAFSA. *Unit head:* Dr. Grace Shen, Director of Graduate Studies, 718-817-3925, Fax: 718-817-4680, E-mail: gshen1@fordham.edu. *Application contact:* Garrett

Marino, Director of Graduate Admissions, 718-817-4419, Fax: 718-817-3566, E-mail: gmarino10@fordham.edu.

Fort Hays State University, Graduate School, College of Arts, Humanities, and Social Sciences, Department of History, Hays, KS 67601-4099. Offers MA. *Degree requirements:* For master's, comprehensive exam, thesis or alternative. *Entrance requirements:* For master's, minimum undergraduate GPA of 3.0. Additional exam requirements/recommendations for international students: required—TOEFL (minimum score 550 paper-based). Electronic applications accepted.

George Mason University, College of Humanities and Social Sciences, Department of History and Art History, Program in History, Fairfax, VA 22030. Offers digital public humanities (Certificate); history (MA, PhD). *Degree requirements:* For master's, comprehensive exam, thesis or alternative, translation language exam; for doctorate, comprehensive exam, thesis/dissertation; for Certificate, comprehensive exam, thesis or alternative, internship in applied history. *Entrance requirements:* For master's, goals statement, writing sample, letters of recommendation; for doctorate, GRE, goals statement, writing sample, letters of recommendation. Additional exam requirements/recommendations for international students: required—TOEFL (minimum score 575 paper-based; 88 iBT), IELTS (minimum score 6.5), PTE (minimum score 59). Electronic applications accepted.

Georgetown University, Graduate School of Arts and Sciences, Department of History, Washington, DC 20057-1305. Offers global history (MA); global, international and comparative history (MA); history (MA, PhD); MA/PhD; MS/MA. *Degree requirements:* For master's, thesis (for some programs); for doctorate, 2 foreign languages, comprehensive exam, thesis/dissertation. *Entrance requirements:* For master's and doctorate, GRE General Test. Additional exam requirements/recommendations for international students: required—TOEFL.

Georgetown University, Graduate School of Arts and Sciences, School of Continuing Studies, Washington, DC 20057. Offers American studies (MALS); applied intelligence (MPS); Catholic studies (MALS); classical civilizations (MALS); emergency and disaster management (MPS); ethics and the professions (MALS); global strategic communications (MPS); hospitality management (MPS); human resources management (MPS); humanities (MALS); individualized study (MALS); integrated marketing communications (MPS); international affairs (MALS); Islam and Muslim-Christian relations (MALS); journalism (MPS); liberal studies (DLS); literature and society (MALS); medieval and early modern European studies (MALS); public relations and corporate communications (MPS); real estate (MPS); religious studies (MALS); social and public policy (MALS); sports industry management (MPS); systems engineering management (MPS); technology management (MPS); the theory and practice of American democracy (MALS); urban and regional planning (MPS); visual culture (MALS). *Entrance requirements:* Additional exam requirements/recommendations for international students: required—TOEFL.

The George Washington University, Columbian College of Arts and Sciences, Department of History, Washington, DC 20052. Offers MA, PhD. *Program availability:* Part-time, evening/weekend. Terminal master's awarded for partial completion of doctoral program. *Degree requirements:* For master's, one foreign language, comprehensive exam, thesis or alternative; for doctorate, 2 foreign languages, thesis/dissertation, general exam. *Entrance requirements:* For master's and doctorate, GRE General Test, minimum GPA of 3.0. Additional exam requirements/recommendations for international students: required—TOEFL (minimum score 550 paper-based; 80 iBT). Electronic applications accepted.

Georgia Southern University, Jack N. Averitt College of Graduate Studies, College of Arts and Humanities, Program in History, Statesboro, GA 30460. Offers history (MA); public history (Graduate Certificate). *Program availability:* Part-time. *Faculty:* 36 full-time (11 women), 5 part-time/adjunct (0 women). *Students:* 21 full-time (14 women), 5 part-time (1 woman); includes 3 minority (1 Black or African American, non-Hispanic/Latino; 1 Hispanic/Latino; 1 Two or more races, non-Hispanic/Latino). Average age 34. 20 applicants, 85% accepted, 8 enrolled. In 2019, 12 master's awarded. *Degree requirements:* For master's, one foreign language, thesis optional, terminal exams. *Entrance requirements:* For master's, GRE General Test, minimum GPA of 3.0, undergraduate major in history or equivalent, letters of reference. Additional exam requirements/recommendations for international students: required—TOEFL (minimum score 550 paper-based; 80 iBT), IELTS (minimum score 6). *Application deadline:* For fall admission, 3/1 priority date for domestic and international students; for spring admission, 10/1 priority date for domestic students, 10/1 for international students. Applications are processed on a rolling basis. Application fee: $50. Electronic applications accepted. *Expenses: Tuition, area resident:* Full-time $4986; part-time $277 per credit hour. Tuition, nonresident: full-time $19,890; part-time $1105 per credit hour. *International tuition:* $19,890 full-time. *Required fees:* $2114; $1057 per semester. $1057 per semester. Tuition and fees vary according to course load, campus/location and program. *Financial support:* In 2019–20, 21 students received support, including 14 fellowships with full tuition reimbursements available (averaging $7,750 per year), 1 teaching assistantship with full tuition reimbursement available (averaging $7,750 per year); career-related internships or fieldwork, Federal Work-Study, scholarships/grants, tuition waivers (full), and unspecified assistantships also available. Support available to part-time students. Financial award application deadline: 4/15; financial award applicants required to submit FAFSA. *Unit head:* Dr. Timothy Teeter, Graduate Program Director, 912-478-0239, Fax: 912-478-0377, E-mail: tmteeter@georgiasouthern.edu. Website: http://class.georgiasouthern.edu/history/

Georgia State University, College of Arts and Sciences, Department of History, Atlanta, GA 30302-3083. Offers heritage preservation (MHP); history (MA, PhD), including historic preservation (MA), history (PhD), public history (MA), world history (MA). *Program availability:* Part-time, evening/weekend. *Faculty:* 13 full-time (3 women), 5 part-time/adjunct (2 women). *Students:* 65 full-time (37 women), 61 part-time (35 women); includes 32 minority (15 Black or African American, non-Hispanic/Latino; 4 Asian, non-Hispanic/Latino; 9 Hispanic/Latino; 4 Two or more races, non-Hispanic/Latino), 4 international. Average age 41. 55 applicants, 82% accepted, 25 enrolled. In 2019, 14 master's, 6 doctorates awarded. Terminal master's awarded for partial completion of doctoral program. *Entrance requirements:* For master's, GRE, BA in history; statement of purpose; writing sample; three letters of recommendation; official transcripts; for doctorate, GRE, MA in history; master's thesis; statement of purpose; writing sample; three letters of recommendation; official transcripts; appropriate language skills. Additional exam requirements/recommendations for international students: required—TOEFL (minimum score 550 paper-based; 80 iBT). *Application deadline:* For fall admission, 3/15 for domestic and international students; for spring admission, 10/15 for domestic and international students. Applications are processed on a rolling basis. Application fee: $50. Electronic applications accepted. *Expenses: Tuition, area resident:* Full-time $7164; part-time $398 per credit hour. Tuition, state resident: full-time $7164; part-time $398 per credit hour. Tuition, nonresident: full-time $22,662; part-time $1259 per credit hour. *International tuition:* $22,662 full-time. *Required fees:* $2128; $312 per credit hour. Tuition and fees vary according to course load and program. *Financial support:* In 2019–20, research assistantships with tuition reimbursements (averaging $6,240 per year), teaching assistantships with tuition reimbursements (averaging $14,700 per year) were awarded; scholarships/grants also

available. Financial award application deadline: 2/15. *Unit head:* Dr. Michelle Brattain, Chair, 404-413-6374, Fax: 404-413-6384, E-mail: mbrattain@gsu.edu. *Application contact:* Dr. Joe Perry, Director of Graduate Studies, 404-413-6374, Fax: 404-413-6384, E-mail: jbperry@gsu.edu.
Website: https://history.gsu.edu/

Georgia State University, College of Education and Human Development, Department of Middle and Secondary Education, Atlanta, GA 30302-3083. Offers curriculum and instruction (Ed D); English education (MAT); mathematics education (M Ed, MAT); middle level education (MAT); reading, language and literacy education (M Ed, MAT), including reading instruction (M Ed); science education (M Ed, MAT), including biology (MAT), broad field science (MAT), chemistry (MAT), earth science (MAT), physics (MAT); social studies education (M Ed, MAT), including economics (MAT), geography (MAT), history (MAT), political science (MAT); teaching and learning (PhD), including language and literacy, mathematics education, music education, science education, social studies education, teaching and teacher education. *Accreditation:* NCATE. *Program availability:* Part-time, evening/weekend, online learning. *Faculty:* 20 full-time (16 women), 8 part-time/adjunct (all women). *Students:* 184 full-time (117 women), 195 part-time (144 women); includes 218 minority (157 Black or African American, non-Hispanic/Latino; 22 Asian, non-Hispanic/Latino; 27 Hispanic/Latino; 12 Two or more races, non-Hispanic/Latino), 3 international. Average age 34. 123 applicants, 61% accepted, 46 enrolled. In 2019, 122 master's, 18 doctorates awarded. *Entrance requirements:* For master's, GRE; GACE I (for initial teacher preparation programs), baccalaureate degree or equivalent, resume, goals statement, two letters of recommendation, minimum undergraduate GPA of 2.5; proof of initial teacher certification in the content area (for M Ed); for doctorate, GRE, resume, goals statement, writing sample, two letters of recommendation, minimum graduate GPA of 3.3, interview. *Application deadline:* For fall admission, 1/15 priority date for domestic and international students; for spring admission, 10/1 for domestic and international students. Application fee: $50. Electronic applications accepted. *Expenses: Tuition, area resident:* Full-time $7164; part-time $398 per credit hour. Tuition, state resident: full-time $7164; part-time $398 per credit hour. Tuition, nonresident: full-time $22,662; part-time $1259 per credit hour. *International tuition:* $22,662 full-time. *Required fees:* $2128; $312 per credit hour. Tuition and fees vary according to course load and program. *Financial support:* In 2019–20, fellowships with full tuition reimbursements (averaging $19,667 per year), research assistantships with full tuition reimbursements (averaging $5,436 per year), teaching assistantships with full tuition reimbursements (averaging $2,779 per year) were awarded; career-related internships or fieldwork, Federal Work-Study, scholarships/grants, health care benefits, tuition waivers (full and partial), and unspecified assistantships also available. Financial award application deadline: 3/15. *Unit head:* Dr. Gertrude Marilyn Tinker Sachs, Chair, 404-413-8384, Fax: 404-413-8063, E-mail: gtinkersachs@gsu.edu. *Application contact:* Shaleen Tibbs, Administrative Specialist, 404-413-8385, Fax: 404-413-8063, E-mail: stibbs@gsu.edu.
Website: http://mse.education.gsu.edu/

The Graduate Center, City University of New York, Graduate Studies, Program in History, New York, NY 10016-4039. Offers PhD. *Degree requirements:* For doctorate, one foreign language, thesis/dissertation. *Entrance requirements:* For doctorate, GRE General Test, writing sample (15 pages). Additional exam requirements/recommendations for international students: required—TOEFL. Electronic applications accepted.

Harvard University, Graduate School of Arts and Sciences, Department of History, Cambridge, MA 02138. Offers African history (PhD); American history (PhD); ancient, medieval, early modern, and modern Europe (PhD), including Central Europe, Russia, Southeastern Europe, Western Europe; diplomatic history (PhD); East Asian history (PhD); economic and social history (PhD); intellectual history (PhD); Latin American history (PhD); Near Eastern history (PhD); oceanic history (PhD). *Degree requirements:* For doctorate, variable foreign language requirement, thesis/dissertation, oral general exam. *Entrance requirements:* For doctorate, GRE General Test, proficiency in 2 languages. Additional exam requirements/recommendations for international students: required—TOEFL.

Howard University, Graduate School, Department of History, Washington, DC 20059-0002. Offers African diaspora (MA, PhD); African history (MA, PhD); Latin America and the Caribbean (MA, PhD); public history (MA); United States history (MA, PhD). *Program availability:* Part-time. Terminal master's awarded for partial completion of doctoral program. *Degree requirements:* For master's, one foreign language, thesis optional; for doctorate, 2 foreign languages, comprehensive exam, thesis/dissertation. *Entrance requirements:* For master's, GRE General Test, minimum GPA of 3.0, 3 letters of recommendation; for doctorate, GRE General Test, minimum GPA of 3.5, 3 letters of recommendation. Additional exam requirements/recommendations for international students: required—TOEFL. Electronic applications accepted.

Hunter College of the City University of New York, Graduate School, School of Arts and Sciences, Department of History, New York, NY 10065-5085. Offers MA. *Degree requirements:* For master's, one foreign language, comprehensive exam, thesis, essay, language exam. *Entrance requirements:* For master's, GRE General Test, minimum of 18 credits in undergraduate history or related field. Additional exam requirements/recommendations for international students: required—TOEFL.

Idaho State University, Graduate School, College of Arts and Letters, Department of History, Pocatello, ID 83209-8079. Offers historical resources management (MA). *Program availability:* Part-time. *Degree requirements:* For master's, comprehensive exam, thesis optional, internship. *Entrance requirements:* For master's, GRE, 3 letters of recommendation, minimum of 18 upper division history credits. Additional exam requirements/recommendations for international students: required—TOEFL (minimum score 550 paper-based; 80 iBT). Electronic applications accepted.

Illinois State University, Graduate School, College of Arts and Sciences, Department of History, Normal, IL 61790. Offers MA, MS. *Faculty:* 27 full-time (13 women), 14 part-time/adjunct (6 women). *Students:* 14 full-time (8 women), 22 part-time (6 women). Average age 32. 20 applicants, 85% accepted, 11 enrolled. In 2019, 8 master's awarded. *Degree requirements:* For master's, thesis or alternative. *Entrance requirements:* For master's, GRE General Test, minimum GPA of 2.6 in last 60 hours of course work. *Application deadline:* Applications are processed on a rolling basis. Application fee: $50. *Expenses: Tuition, area resident:* Full-time $7956; part-time $9767 per year. Tuition, nonresident: full-time $9233; part-time $17,592 per year. *Required fees:* $1797. *Financial support:* In 2019–20, 15 teaching assistantships were awarded; tuition waivers (full) also available. Financial award application deadline: 4/1. *Unit head:* Dr. Ross Kennedy, Department Chair, 309-438-5015, E-mail: rkenned@IllinoisState.edu. *Application contact:* Faith Ten Haken, Graduate Secretary, 309-438-5685, E-mail: fatenha@IllinoisState.edu.
Website: http://www.history.ilstu.edu/

Indiana State University, College of Graduate and Professional Studies, College of Arts and Sciences, Department of History, Terre Haute, IN 47809. Offers MA, MS. *Program availability:* Part-time, evening/weekend. *Degree requirements:* For master's, comprehensive exam (for some programs), thesis or alternative. *Entrance requirements:* For master's, GRE, equivalent of minor in geography or geology. Additional exam requirements/recommendations for international students: required—TOEFL (minimum score 550 paper-based).

Indiana University Bloomington, University Graduate School, College of Arts and Sciences, Department of History, Bloomington, IN 47405. Offers MA, MAT, PhD, MA/MLS. Terminal master's awarded for partial completion of doctoral program. *Degree requirements:* For master's, one foreign language, thesis optional; for doctorate, variable foreign language requirement, comprehensive exam, thesis/dissertation. *Entrance requirements:* For master's and doctorate, GRE General Test. Additional exam requirements/recommendations for international students: required—TOEFL. Electronic applications accepted.

Indiana University of Pennsylvania, School of Graduate Studies and Research, College of Humanities and Social Sciences, Department of History, Program in History, Indiana, PA 15705. Offers MA. *Program availability:* Part-time. In 2019, 2 master's awarded. *Degree requirements:* For master's, thesis optional. *Entrance requirements:* For master's, GRE, 2 letters of recommendation. Additional exam requirements/recommendations for international students: required—TOEFL (minimum score 540 paper-based). *Application deadline:* Applications are processed on a rolling basis. Application fee: $50. Electronic applications accepted. *Expenses: Tuition, area resident:* Full-time $9288; part-time $516 per credit. Tuition, nonresident: full-time $13,932; part-time $774 per credit. *Required fees:* $4454. One-time fee: $115 full-time. Tuition and fees vary according to course load and program. *Financial support:* Fellowships, research assistantships with tuition reimbursements, career-related internships or fieldwork, Federal Work-Study, scholarships/grants, and unspecified assistantships available. Support available to part-time students. Financial award application deadline: 4/15; financial award applicants required to submit FAFSA. *Unit head:* Dr. Jeanine Mazak-Kahne, Graduate Coordinator, 724-357-2436, E-mail: jmkahne@iup.edu. *Application contact:* Dr. Jeanine Mazak-Kahne, Graduate Coordinator, 724-357-2436, E-mail: jmkahne@iup.edu.
Website: http://www.iup.edu/grad/history/default.aspx

Indiana University-Purdue University Indianapolis, School of Liberal Arts, Department of History, Indianapolis, IN 46202. Offers European history (MA); public history (MA); United States history (MA); MA/MA; MA/MLS. *Program availability:* Part-time, evening/weekend. *Degree requirements:* For master's, one foreign language, thesis. *Entrance requirements:* For master's, GRE General Test, minimum GPA of 3.0. Electronic applications accepted.

Inter American University of Puerto Rico, Barranquitas Campus, Program in Education, Barranquitas, PR 00794. Offers curriculum and teaching (M Ed), including biology, English as a second language, history, Spanish; educational leadership and management (MA); elementary education (M Ed); information and library service technology (M Ed); special education (MA). *Accreditation:* TEAC. *Program availability:* Part-time, evening/weekend. *Degree requirements:* For master's, 2 foreign languages, comprehensive exam, thesis (for some programs). *Entrance requirements:* For master's, GRE or EXADEP, bachelor's degree or its equivalent from accredited institution, official academic transcript from institution that conferred bachelor's degree, minimum GPA of 2.5, two recommendation letters, interview (for some programs), essay (for some programs). Electronic applications accepted. *Expenses:* Contact institution.

Inter American University of Puerto Rico, Metropolitan Campus, Graduate Programs, Program in History, San Juan, PR 00919-1293. Offers American history (PhD); history (MA, PhD).

Inter American University of Puerto Rico, Metropolitan Campus, Graduate Programs, Program in History Education, San Juan, PR 00919-1293. Offers MA.

Iona College, School of Arts and Science, Department of History, New Rochelle, NY 10801-1890. Offers MA. *Program availability:* Part-time, evening/weekend. *Faculty:* 2 full-time (0 women). *Students:* 1. 14 applicants, 100% accepted, 7 enrolled. In 2019, 4 master's awarded. *Degree requirements:* For master's, one foreign language, comprehensive exam, 27 credits of coursework and culminating project or 24 credits of coursework and thesis. *Entrance requirements:* For master's, undergraduate major in history or related field, minimum GPA of 3.0. Additional exam requirements/recommendations for international students: required—TOEFL (minimum score 550 paper-based; 80 iBT), IELTS (minimum score 6.5). *Application deadline:* For fall admission, 8/1 priority date for domestic students, 5/1 priority date for international students; for spring admission, 1/1 priority date for domestic students, 8/1 priority date for international students. Applications are processed on a rolling basis. Electronic applications accepted. *Financial support:* Scholarships/grants and unspecified assistantships available. Financial award application deadline: 4/15; financial award applicants required to submit FAFSA. *Unit head:* Michael Hughes, PhD, Chairman, 914-633-2586, E-mail: mjhughes@iona.edu. *Application contact:* RoseDeline Martinez, Director of Graduate Admissions, School of Arts and Science, 914-633-2427, Fax: 914-633-2277, E-mail: rmartinez@iona.edu.
Website: http://www.iona.edu/Academics/School-of-Arts-Science/Departments/History/Graduate-Programs.aspx

Iowa State University of Science and Technology, Department of History, Ames, IA 50011. Offers history (MA); rural, agricultural, technological, and environmental history (PhD). *Degree requirements:* For master's, thesis or alternative; for doctorate, thesis/dissertation. *Entrance requirements:* For master's and doctorate, GRE General Test. Additional exam requirements/recommendations for international students: required—TOEFL (minimum score 600 paper-based; 79 iBT), IELTS (minimum score 7). Electronic applications accepted.

Jackson State University, Graduate School, College of Liberal Arts, Department of History and Philosophy, Jackson, MS 39217. Offers history (MA). *Program availability:* Part-time, evening/weekend, 100% online, blended/hybrid learning. *Degree requirements:* For master's, comprehensive exam, thesis or alternative. *Entrance requirements:* For master's, GRE General Test. Additional exam requirements/recommendations for international students: required—TOEFL (minimum score 520 paper-based; 67 iBT). Electronic applications accepted. *Expenses:* Contact institution.

Jacksonville State University, Graduate Studies, School of Arts and Humanities, Department of History, Jacksonville, AL 36265-1602. Offers MA. *Program availability:* Part-time, evening/weekend. *Degree requirements:* For master's, comprehensive exam, thesis (for some programs). *Entrance requirements:* For master's, GRE General Test or MAT. Additional exam requirements/recommendations for international students: required—TOEFL (minimum score 500 paper-based; 61 iBT). Electronic applications accepted.

James Madison University, The Graduate School, College of Arts and Letters, Program in History, Harrisonburg, VA 22807. Offers public history (MA); U.S. history (MA); world history (MA). *Program availability:* Part-time. *Students:* 20 full-time (11 women), 6 part-time (3 women); includes 2 minority (1 Asian, non-Hispanic/Latino; 1 Two or more races, non-Hispanic/Latino). Average age 30. In 2019, 6 master's awarded. *Degree requirements:* For master's, one foreign language, comprehensive exam, thesis. Application fee: $60. Electronic applications accepted. *Financial support:* In 2019–20, 10 students received support, including 3 teaching assistantships with full tuition reimbursements available (averaging $9,284 per year); fellowships, Federal Work-

Study, and assistantships (averaging $7911) also available. Financial award application deadline: 3/1; financial award applicants required to submit FAFSA. *Unit head:* Dr. Gabrielle Lanier, Department Head, 540-568-6132, E-mail: laniergm@jmu.edu. *Application contact:* Lynette D. Michael, Director of Graduate Admissions, 540-568-6131 Ext. 6395, Fax: 540-568-7860, E-mail: michaeld@jmu.edu.
Website: http://www.jmu.edu/history

Johns Hopkins University, Zanvyl Krieger School of Arts and Sciences, Department of History, Baltimore, MD 21218. Offers PhD. *Degree requirements:* For doctorate, variable foreign language requirement, comprehensive exam, thesis/dissertation. *Entrance requirements:* For doctorate, GRE General Test. Additional exam requirements/recommendations for international students: required—TOEFL (minimum score 600 paper-based; 100 iBT), IELTS. Electronic applications accepted.

Kansas State University, Graduate School, College of Arts and Sciences, Department of History, Manhattan, KS 66506. Offers MA, PhD. *Program availability:* Part-time. *Degree requirements:* For master's, thesis (for some programs); for doctorate, one foreign language, thesis/dissertation, qualifying exam. *Entrance requirements:* For master's, GRE General Test, minimum undergraduate GPA of 3.0; for doctorate, GRE General Test. Additional exam requirements/recommendations for international students: required—TOEFL (minimum score 600 paper-based). Electronic applications accepted.

Kent State University, College of Arts and Sciences, Department of History, Kent, OH 44242-0001. Offers history (MA, PhD), including history (MA), history for teachers (MA). *Program availability:* Part-time. *Faculty:* 9 full-time (4 women). *Students:* 20 full-time (5 women), 4 part-time (1 woman); includes 2 minority (1 Hispanic/Latino; 1 Two or more races, non-Hispanic/Latino), 3 international. Average age 35. 20 applicants, 30% accepted, 4 enrolled. In 2019, 6 master's, 5 doctorates awarded. *Degree requirements:* For master's, one foreign language, thesis (for some programs), must be able to demonstrate reading knowledge of a foreign language; Thesis or Capstone; for doctorate, one foreign language, comprehensive exam, thesis/dissertation, must be able to demonstrate reading knowledge of a foreign language; must successfully complete written and oral examinations in the three elected fields of history. *Entrance requirements:* For master's, GRE, Bachelor's degree in History, minimum 3.0 GPA on 4.0 scale, official transcript(s), statement of purpose describing professional objectives and proposed field of study, significant piece of written work that integrates primary and secondary sources, three letters of recommendation (preferably academic); for doctorate, GRE, official transcript(s), master's degree in history or related discipline, minimum 3.0 GPA on a 4.0 scale, statement of purpose describing professional objectives and proposed field of study, significant piece of written work, three letters of recommendation (preferably academic). Additional exam requirements/recommendations for international students: required—TOEFL (minimum score 79 iBT), IELTS (minimum score 6.5), PTE (minimum score 58), Michigan English Language Assessment Battery (minimum score 77). *Application deadline:* For fall admission, 2/1 for domestic and international students. Applications are processed on a rolling basis. Application fee: $45 ($70 for international students). Electronic applications accepted. *Financial support:* Teaching assistantships with full tuition reimbursements and unspecified assistantships available. Financial award application deadline: 2/1. *Unit head:* Dr. Kevin Adams, Associate Professor and Chair, 330-672-8902, E-mail: kadams9@kent.edu. *Application contact:* Dr. Mary Ann Heiss, Associate Professor and Graduate Coordinator, 330-672-8905, E-mail: mheiss@kent.edu.
Website: https://www.kent.edu/history/

Lake Forest College, Graduate Program in Liberal Studies, Lake Forest, IL 60045. Offers American studies (MLS); cinema in East Asia (MLS); environmental studies (MLS); history (MLS); Medieval and Renaissance art (MLS); philosophy (MLS); Spanish (MLS); writing (MLS). *Program availability:* Part-time, evening/weekend. *Faculty:* 10 full-time (4 women). *Students:* 24 part-time (14 women). Average age 45. 10 applicants, 80% accepted, 3 enrolled. In 2019, 5 master's awarded. *Degree requirements:* For master's, thesis optional, 8 courses, including at least 3 interdisciplinary seminars. *Entrance requirements:* For master's, transcript, essay, interview. Additional exam requirements/recommendations for international students: required—TOEFL (minimum score 550 paper-based; 83 iBT); recommended—IELTS (minimum score 6.5). *Application deadline:* For fall admission, 8/15 priority date for domestic students, 7/15 priority date for international students; for spring admission, 12/15 priority date for domestic students, 11/15 priority date for international students. Applications are processed on a rolling basis. Application fee: $30. Electronic applications accepted. Application fee is waived when completed online. *Expenses:* Application fee = $30 — no other fees; tuition = $2,700/course. *Financial support:* In 2019–20, 2 students received support. Partial tuition grants (for full-time teachers) available. *Unit head:* Prof. D. L. LeMahieu, Director, 847-735-5133, Fax: 847-735-6291, E-mail: lemahieu@lakeforest.edu. *Application contact:* Prof. Carol Gayle, Associate Director, 847-735-5083, Fax: 847-735-6291, E-mail: gayle@lakeforest.edu.
Website: http://www.lakeforest.edu/academics/programs/mls/

Lakehead University, Graduate Studies, Faculty of Social Sciences and Humanities, Department of History, Thunder Bay, ON P7B 5E1, Canada. Offers gerontology (MA); history (MA); women's studies (MA). *Program availability:* Part-time. *Degree requirements:* For master's, one foreign language, thesis. *Entrance requirements:* For master's, minimum B average. Additional exam requirements/recommendations for international students: required—TOEFL.

Lamar University, College of Graduate Studies, College of Arts and Sciences, Department of History, Beaumont, TX 77710. Offers MA. *Program availability:* Part-time. *Faculty:* 13 full-time (5 women), 2 part-time/adjunct (1 woman). *Students:* 1 full-time (0 women). Average age 25. 4 applicants. In 2019, 4 master's awarded. *Degree requirements:* For master's, comprehensive exam (for some programs), thesis (for some programs). *Entrance requirements:* For master's, GRE General Test, minimum GPA of 2.5 in last 60 hours of undergraduate course work. Additional exam requirements/recommendations for international students: required—TOEFL (minimum score 550 paper-based; 79 iBT), IELTS (minimum score 6.5). *Application deadline:* Applications are processed on a rolling basis. Application fee: $25 ($50 for international students). Electronic applications accepted. *Expenses: Tuition, area resident:* Full-time $6324; part-time $351 per credit. Tuition, state resident: full-time $6324; part-time $351 per credit. Tuition, nonresident: full-time $13,920; part-time $773 per credit. *International tuition:* $13,920 full-time. *Required fees:* $2462; $327 per credit. Tuition and fees vary according to course load, campus/location and reciprocity agreements. *Financial support:* In 2019–20, 1 student received support, including teaching assistantships (averaging $2,000 per year); fellowships also available. *Unit head:* Dr. Rebecca Boone, Department Chair, 409-880-8511, Fax: 409-880-8710. *Application contact:* Celeste Contreas, Director, Admissions and Academic Services, 409-880-8888, Fax: 409-880-7419, E-mail: gradmissions@lamar.edu.
Website: http://artssciences.lamar.edu/history/

Laurentian University, School of Graduate Studies and Research, Programme in History, Sudbury, ON P3E 2C6, Canada. Offers European history (MA); history of Northern Ontario (MA); North American history (MA). *Program availability:* Part-time. *Degree requirements:* For master's, thesis or alternative. *Entrance requirements:* For master's, honors degree with minimum second class.

Lee University, Program in Education, Cleveland, TN 37320-3450. Offers art (MAT); curriculum and instruction (M Ed, Ed S); early childhood (MAT); educational leadership (M Ed, Ed S); elementary education (MAT); English and math (MAT); English and science (MAT); English and social studies (MAT); higher education administration (MS); history (MAT); history and economics (MAT); math and science (MAT); math and social studies (MAT); middle grades (MAT); science and social studies (MASW); secondary education (MAT); Spanish (MAT); special education (M Ed, MAT); TESOL (MAT). *Accreditation:* NCATE. *Program availability:* Part-time. *Faculty:* 13 full-time (5 women), 9 part-time/adjunct (6 women). *Students:* 24 full-time (15 women), 72 part-time (46 women); includes 14 minority (8 Black or African American, non-Hispanic/Latino; 1 Hispanic/Latino; 5 Two or more races, non-Hispanic/Latino), 1 international. Average age 29. 44 applicants, 86% accepted, 33 enrolled. In 2019, 60 master's, 3 other advanced degrees awarded. *Degree requirements:* For master's, variable foreign language requirement, thesis optional, internship. *Entrance requirements:* For master's, MAT or GRE General Test, minimum undergraduate GPA of 2.75, 3 letters of recommendation, interview, writing sample, official transcripts, background check; for Ed S, minimum undergraduate and master's GPA of 2.75, official transcripts for undergraduate and master's degrees. Additional exam requirements/recommendations for international students: required—TOEFL (minimum score 61 iBT). *Application deadline:* For fall admission, 6/1 priority date for domestic and international students; for spring admission, 11/1 priority date for domestic and international students; for summer admission, 4/1 priority date for domestic and international students. Applications are processed on a rolling basis. Application fee: $25. Electronic applications accepted. *Expenses: Tuition:* Full-time $13,590; part-time $755 per credit hour. *Required fees:* $25. Tuition and fees vary according to program. *Financial support:* In 2019–20, 40 students received support. Career-related internships or fieldwork, Federal Work-Study, institutionally sponsored loans, scholarships/grants, and unspecified assistantships available. Financial award application deadline: 3/1; financial award applicants required to submit FAFSA. *Unit head:* Dr. William Kamm, Director, 423-614-8544, E-mail: wkamm@leeuniversity.edu. *Application contact:* Jeffery McGirt, Director of Graduate Enrollment, 423-614-8691, Fax: 423-614-8317, E-mail: jmcgirt@leeuniversity.edu.
Website: http://www.leeuniversity.edu/academics/graduate/education

Lehigh University, College of Arts and Sciences, Department of History, Bethlehem, PA 18015. Offers Atlantic world (PhD); British history (PhD); history (MA); industrial and modern America (PhD); public history (MA). *Program availability:* Part-time. *Faculty:* 11 full-time (5 women), 1 (woman) part-time/adjunct. *Students:* 15 full-time (6 women), 16 part-time (4 women); includes 2 minority (1 Black or African American, non-Hispanic/Latino; 1 Two or more races, non-Hispanic/Latino), 2 international. Average age 35. 11 applicants, 45% accepted, 3 enrolled. In 2019, 1 master's, 1 doctorate awarded. Terminal master's awarded for partial completion of doctoral program. *Degree requirements:* For master's, comprehensive exam (for some programs), thesis (for some programs), comprehensive exam or thesis; for doctorate, comprehensive exam, thesis/dissertation. *Entrance requirements:* For master's, GRE General Test, recommendations, writing sample; for doctorate, GRE General Test, recommendations, writing samples. Additional exam requirements/recommendations for international students: required—TOEFL. *Application deadline:* For fall admission, 2/15 for domestic and international students. Applications are processed on a rolling basis. Application fee: $75. *Financial support:* In 2019–20, 1 fellowship with full tuition reimbursement (averaging $22,500 per year) was awarded; research assistantships, teaching assistantships with full tuition reimbursements, scholarships/grants, health care benefits, tuition waivers (full and partial), and unspecified assistantships also available. Financial award application deadline: 1/15. *Unit head:* Prof. Rick Matthews, Chairman, 610-758-3360, Fax: 610-758-6554, E-mail: rm02@lehigh.edu. *Application contact:* Ellen Zimmer Lewis, Graduate Coordinator, 610-758-3360, Fax: 610-758-3360, E-mail: ell414@lehigh.edu.
Website: http://history.cas2.lehigh.edu/

Lehman College of the City University of New York, School of Arts and Humanities, Department of History, Bronx, NY 10468-1589. Offers MA. *Program availability:* Part-time, evening/weekend. *Degree requirements:* For master's, comprehensive exam, thesis. *Entrance requirements:* For master's, 18 undergraduate credits in history, minimum GPA of 2.7. *Expenses: Tuition, area resident:* Full-time $5545; part-time $470 per credit. Tuition, nonresident: part-time $855 per credit. *Required fees:* $240.

Liberty University, College of Arts and Sciences, Lynchburg, VA 24515. Offers English (MA); history (MA); professional writing (MA). *Accreditation:* AACN. *Program availability:* Part-time, online learning. *Students:* 382 full-time (203 women), 499 part-time (272 women); includes 161 minority (82 Black or African American, non-Hispanic/Latino; 4 American Indian or Alaska Native, non-Hispanic/Latino; 4 Asian, non-Hispanic/Latino; 43 Hispanic/Latino; 1 Native Hawaiian or other Pacific Islander, non-Hispanic/Latino; 27 Two or more races, non-Hispanic/Latino), 9 international. Average age 38. 1,716 applicants, 32% accepted, 320 enrolled. In 2019, 253 master's awarded. *Degree requirements:* For master's, comprehensive exam (for some programs), thesis (for some programs). *Entrance requirements:* For master's, GRE, minimum undergraduate GPA of 3.0, letters of recommendation, statement of purpose. Additional exam requirements/recommendations for international students: required—TOEFL (minimum score 600 paper-based; 100 iBT). *Application deadline:* For fall admission, 6/1 for domestic students; for spring admission, 11/1 for domestic students. Applications are processed on a rolling basis. Application fee: $50. Electronic applications accepted. *Expenses: Tuition:* Full-time $545; part-time $410 per credit hour. One-time fee: $50. *Financial support:* In 2019–20, 659 students received support. Teaching assistantships with tuition reimbursements available and Federal Work-Study available. *Unit head:* Dr. Roger Schultz, Dean, 434-592-4031, Fax: 434-522-0430, E-mail: rschultz@liberty.edu. *Application contact:* Chris Jones, Director of Admissions, 434-592-3966, Fax: 434-522-0430, E-mail: gradadmissions@liberty.edu.
Website: https://www.liberty.edu/arts-sciences/

Lincoln University, Graduate Studies, Jefferson City, MO 65101. Offers accounting (MBA); counseling (M Ed), including addictions counseling; environmental science (MS); higher education (MA), including hbcu; history (MA); natural sciences (MS); school teaching middle school with certification (M Ed); school teaching-elementary (M Ed); school teaching-secondary (M Ed); sociology (MA); sociology/criminal justice (MA); sustainable agriculture (MS). *Program availability:* Part-time, evening/weekend, 100% online, blended/hybrid learning. *Students:* 47 full-time (33 women), 62 part-time (35 women); includes 42 minority (39 Black or African American, non-Hispanic/Latino; 1 American Indian or Alaska Native, non-Hispanic/Latino; 1 Asian, non-Hispanic/Latino; 1 Native Hawaiian or other Pacific Islander, non-Hispanic/Latino), 13 international. Average age 33. In 2019, 32 master's awarded. *Degree requirements:* For master's, comprehensive exam, thesis optional. *Entrance requirements:* For master's, GRE, MAT, or GMAT, minimum GPA of 2.75 overall, 3.0 in courses related to specialization; 3 letters of recommendation; minimum C average in English composition; personal statement of purpose. Additional exam requirements/recommendations for international students: required—TOEFL (minimum score 500 paper-based; 61 iBT), IELTS (minimum score 5.5), Michigan English Language Assessment Battery (minimum score 80). *Application deadline:* For fall admission, 7/1 priority date for domestic students, 5/1 priority date for international students; for spring admission, 11/1 priority date for domestic students, 10/1 priority date for international students; for summer admission, 6/

1 priority date for domestic students. Applications are processed on a rolling basis. Application fee: $30. Electronic applications accepted. *Expenses: Tuition, area resident:* Full-time $511; part-time $511 per credit hour. Tuition, state resident: full-time $511; part-time $511 per credit hour. Tuition, nonresident: full-time $886; part-time $886 per credit hour. *International tuition:* $886 full-time. *Required fees:* $20; $20 per credit hour. $381.10 per semester. *Financial support:* In 2019–20, 8 fellowships (averaging $4,017 per year), 6 research assistantships (averaging $18,500 per year) were awarded; Federal Work-Study, scholarships/grants, and unspecified assistantships also available. Support available to part-time students. Financial award application deadline: 3/1; financial award applicants required to submit FAFSA. *Unit head:* Dr. Benjamin Arnold, Assistant Vice President of Academic Affairs, 573-681-5247, Fax: 573-681-5106, E-mail: gradschool@lincolnu.edu. *Application contact:* James Kendall, Graduate Admission Coordinator/Recruiter, 573-681-5150, Fax: 573-681-5106, E-mail: gradschool@lincolnu.edu.
Website: http://www.lincolnu.edu/web/graduate-studies/graduate-studies

Long Island University - Post, College of Liberal Arts and Sciences, Brookville, NY 11548-1300. Offers applied mathematics (MS); behavior analysis (MA); biology (MS); criminal justice (MS); earth science (MS); English (MA); environmental sustainability (MS); genetic counseling (MS); history (MA); interdisciplinary studies (MA, MS); political science (MA); psychology (MA). *Program availability:* Part-time, evening/weekend, blended/hybrid learning. Terminal master's awarded for partial completion of doctoral program. *Degree requirements:* For master's, comprehensive exam (for some programs), thesis (for some programs). *Entrance requirements:* Additional exam requirements/recommendations for international students: required—TOEFL, IELTS, or PTE. Electronic applications accepted.

Louisiana State University and Agricultural & Mechanical College, Graduate School, College of Humanities and Social Sciences, Department of History, Baton Rouge, LA 70803. Offers MA, PhD.

Louisiana Tech University, Graduate School, College of Liberal Arts, Ruston, LA 71272. Offers architecture (M Arch); art (MFA), including graphic design, photography, studio; audiology (Au D); communication (MA), including speech communication, theatre; English (MA), including literature, technical writing; history (MA); speech pathology (MA); technical writing and communication (Graduate Certificate). *Accreditation:* ASHA. *Program availability:* Part-time. *Degree requirements:* For master's, thesis (for some programs); for doctorate, thesis/dissertation. *Entrance requirements:* For master's, GRE General Test; for doctorate, GRE General Test, bachelor's degree, minimum GPA of 3.0 or 3.2 on last 60 hours attempted. Additional exam requirements/recommendations for international students: required—TOEFL (minimum score 550 paper-based; 80 iBT), IELTS (minimum score 6.5). Electronic applications accepted. *Expenses: Tuition, area resident:* Full-time $6592; part-time $400 per credit. Tuition, state resident: full-time $6592; part-time $400 per credit. Tuition, nonresident: full-time $13,333; part-time $681 per credit. *International tuition:* $13,333 full-time. *Required fees:* $3011; $3011 per unit.

Loyola University Chicago, Graduate School, Department of History, Chicago, IL 60660. Offers history (MA, PhD); public history (MA). *Program availability:* Part-time. *Faculty:* 38 full-time (21 women), 9 part-time/adjunct (6 women). *Students:* 42 full-time (25 women), 10 part-time (6 women); includes 4 minority (1 Black or African American, non-Hispanic/Latino; 3 Hispanic/Latino), 1 international. Average age 30. 67 applicants, 63% accepted, 16 enrolled. In 2019, 12 master's, 6 doctorates awarded. Terminal master's awarded for partial completion of doctoral program. *Degree requirements:* For master's, one foreign language, comprehensive exam, thesis optional, portfolio (for public history program); for doctorate, 2 foreign languages, comprehensive exam, thesis/dissertation. *Entrance requirements:* For master's, research paper/writing sample; for doctorate, seminar paper or master's thesis. Additional exam requirements/recommendations for international students: required—TOEFL (minimum score 550 paper-based), IELTS. *Application deadline:* For fall admission, 5/1 for domestic students; for spring admission, 10/1 for domestic students. Applications are processed on a rolling basis. Electronic applications accepted. Application fee is waived when completed online. *Expenses:* 1033 per credit hour, student development 85-125, technology 30-125, dissertation supervision 1935. *Financial support:* In 2019–20, 20 students received support, including 1 fellowship with full tuition reimbursement available (averaging $20,000 per year), 3 research assistantships with full tuition reimbursements available (averaging $18,000 per year), 14 teaching assistantships with full tuition reimbursements available (averaging $18,000 per year); Federal Work-Study, scholarships/grants, health care benefits, and unspecified assistantships also available. Financial award application deadline: 1/1; financial award applicants required to submit FAFSA. *Unit head:* Dr. Paticia Mooney-Melvin, Director, Graduate Programs, 773-508-2228, Fax: 773-508-3693, E-mail: pmooney@luc.edu. *Application contact:* Dr. Patricia Mooney-Melvin, Director, Graduate Programs, 773-508-2228, Fax: 773-508-3693, E-mail: pmooney@luc.edu.
Website: http://www.luc.edu/history/

Marquette University, Graduate School, College of Arts and Sciences, Department of History, Milwaukee, WI 53201-1881. Offers European history (MA, PhD); global studies (MA); United States history (MA, PhD). *Program availability:* Part-time. *Degree requirements:* For master's, comprehensive exam, essay, 2 classes of research seminars (6 hours); for doctorate, one foreign language, comprehensive exam, thesis/dissertation, 2 research seminars, dissertation seminar. *Entrance requirements:* For master's, GRE General Test, official transcripts from all current and previous colleges/universities except Marquette, one-page statement of purpose, three letters of recommendation from former teachers; for doctorate, GRE General Test, official transcripts from all current and previous colleges/universities except Marquette, one-page statement of purpose, three letters of recommendation from former teachers, writing sample. Additional exam requirements/recommendations for international students: required—TOEFL. Electronic applications accepted.

Marshall University, Academic Affairs Division, College of Liberal Arts, Department of History, Huntington, WV 25755. Offers MA, Certificate. *Entrance requirements:* For master's, GRE.

McGill University, Faculty of Graduate and Postdoctoral Studies, Faculty of Arts, Department of History and Classical Studies, Montréal, QC H3A 2T5, Canada. Offers history (MA, PhD); history of medicine (MA).

McMaster University, School of Graduate Studies, Faculty of Humanities, Department of History, Hamilton, ON L8S 4M2, Canada. Offers MA, PhD. *Program availability:* Part-time. *Degree requirements:* For master's, one foreign language, thesis or alternative; for doctorate, one foreign language, comprehensive exam, thesis/dissertation. *Entrance requirements:* For master's, honors BA in history, minimum B+ average. Additional exam requirements/recommendations for international students: required—TOEFL (minimum score 580 paper-based).

Memorial University of Newfoundland, School of Graduate Studies, Department of History, St. John's, NL A1C 5S7, Canada. Offers MA, PhD. *Program availability:* Part-time. *Degree requirements:* For master's, thesis or comprehensive exam; for doctorate, one foreign language, comprehensive exam, thesis/dissertation, oral defense of thesis. *Entrance requirements:* For master's, honors degree or equivalent; for doctorate, master's degree. Electronic applications accepted.

Miami University, College of Arts and Science, Department of History, Oxford, OH 45056. Offers MA.

Michigan State University, The Graduate School, College of Social Science, Department of History, East Lansing, MI 48824. Offers history (MA, PhD); history-secondary school teaching (MA). *Entrance requirements:* Additional exam requirements/recommendations for international students: required—TOEFL. Electronic applications accepted.

Middle Tennessee State University, College of Graduate Studies, College of Liberal Arts, Department of History, Program in History, Murfreesboro, TN 37132. Offers MA. *Program availability:* Part-time, evening/weekend, online learning. *Degree requirements:* For master's, one foreign language, comprehensive exam, thesis optional. *Entrance requirements:* For master's, GRE. Additional exam requirements/recommendations for international students: required—TOEFL (minimum score 525 paper-based; 71 iBT) or IELTS (minimum score 6).

Midwestern State University, Billie Doris McAda Graduate School, Prothro-Yeager College of Humanities and Social Sciences, Department of History, Wichita Falls, TX 76308. Offers MA. *Program availability:* Part-time. *Degree requirements:* For master's, one foreign language, thesis. *Entrance requirements:* For master's, GRE General Test. Additional exam requirements/recommendations for international students: required—TOEFL (minimum score 550 paper-based). Electronic applications accepted.

Millersville University of Pennsylvania, College of Graduate Studies and Adult Learning, College of Arts, Humanities and Social Sciences, Department of History, Millersville, PA 17551-0302. Offers history (MA). *Program availability:* Part-time, evening/weekend. *Faculty:* 3 full-time (2 women). *Students:* 5 part-time (2 women); includes 1 minority (Hispanic/Latino). Average age 34. 5 applicants, 100% accepted, 3 enrolled. In 2019, 3 master's awarded. *Degree requirements:* For master's, comprehensive exam, thesis optional. *Entrance requirements:* For master's, GRE, required only if cumulative GPA is lower than 2.85, 8-12 page academic writing sample. Additional exam requirements/recommendations for international students: required—TOEFL, IELTS (minimum score 6), PTE (minimum score 60). *Application deadline:* Applications are processed on a rolling basis. Application fee: $40. Electronic applications accepted. *Expenses: Tuition, area resident:* Part-time $516 per credit. Tuition, state resident: part-time $516 per credit. Tuition, nonresident: part-time $774 per credit. *Required fees:* $118.75 per credit. Tuition and fees vary according to course load, degree level and program. *Financial support:* In 2019–20, 2 students received support. Scholarships/grants and unspecified assistantships available. Financial award application deadline: 3/15; financial award applicants required to submit FAFSA. *Unit head:* Dr. John M. MacLarnon, III, Department Chair, 717-871-7193, Fax: 717-871-7939, E-mail: john.mclarnon@millersville.edu. *Application contact:* Dr. James A. Delle, Acting Dean of College of Graduate Studies and Adult Learning/Associate Provost, Academic Administration, 717-871-7462, E-mail: James.Delle@millersville.edu.
Website: http://www.millersville.edu/history/graduate-program.php

Minnesota State University Mankato, College of Graduate Studies and Research, College of Social and Behavioral Sciences, Department of History, Mankato, MN 56001. Offers history (MA, MS); social studies (MAT). *Degree requirements:* For master's, one foreign language, comprehensive exam, thesis or alternative. *Entrance requirements:* For master's, minimum GPA of 3.0, statement of purpose. Additional exam requirements/recommendations for international students: required—TOEFL (minimum score 600 paper-based). Electronic applications accepted.

Mississippi College, Graduate School, College of Arts and Sciences, School of Humanities and Social Sciences, Department of History and Political Science, Clinton, MS 39058. Offers administration of justice (MSS); history (M Ed, MA, MSS); paralegal studies (Certificate); political science (MSS); social sciences (M Ed, MSS). *Program availability:* Part-time. *Degree requirements:* For master's, one foreign language, comprehensive exam, thesis (for some programs). *Entrance requirements:* For master's, GRE or NTE, minimum GPA of 2.5. Additional exam requirements/recommendations for international students: recommended—TOEFL, IELTS. Electronic applications accepted.

Mississippi State University, College of Arts and Sciences, Department of History, Mississippi State, MS 39762. Offers Africa (MA, PhD); Asia (MA, PhD); Europe (MA, PhD); Latin America (MA, PhD); United States (MA, PhD); world history (MA, PhD). *Program availability:* Part-time. *Faculty:* 22 full-time (9 women). *Students:* 37 full-time (10 women), 11 part-time (2 women); includes 8 minority (3 Black or African American, non-Hispanic/Latino; 2 Hispanic/Latino; 3 Two or more races, non-Hispanic/Latino), 1 international. Average age 30. 26 applicants, 73% accepted, 11 enrolled. In 2019, 10 master's, 3 doctorates awarded. *Degree requirements:* For master's, one foreign language, comprehensive exam, thesis optional; for doctorate, 2 foreign languages, thesis/dissertation, comprehensive oral and written exam. *Entrance requirements:* For master's, minimum GPA of 3.0 on last two years of undergraduate courses; for doctorate, GRE, writing sample, minimum graduate GPA of 3.0. Additional exam requirements/recommendations for international students: required—TOEFL (minimum score 550 paper-based). *Application deadline:* For fall admission, 4/1 for domestic students, 5/1 for international students; for spring admission, 11/1 for domestic students, 9/1 for international students. Applications are processed on a rolling basis. Application fee: $60 ($80 for international students). Electronic applications accepted. *Expenses: Tuition, area resident:* Full-time $8880; part-time $456 per credit hour. Tuition, state resident: full-time $8880. Tuition, nonresident: full-time $23,840; part-time $1236 per credit hour. *Required fees:* $110; $11.12 per credit hour. Tuition and fees vary according to course load. *Financial support:* In 2019–20, 34 teaching assistantships with full tuition reimbursements (averaging $14,498 per year) were awarded; Federal Work-Study, institutionally sponsored loans, scholarships/grants, and unspecified assistantships also available. Financial award application deadline: 4/1; financial award applicants required to submit FAFSA. *Unit head:* Dr. Alan I. Marcus, Professor and Head, 662-325-7075, Fax: 662-325-1139, E-mail: aim10@msstate.edu. *Application contact:* Ryan King, Admissions and Enrollment Assistant, 662-325-8951, E-mail: rjk101@msstate.edu.
Website: http://www.history.msstate.edu

Missouri State University, Graduate College, College of Humanities and Public Affairs, Department of History, Springfield, MO 65897. Offers history (MA); history education (MS Ed); history for teachers (Certificate). *Program availability:* Part-time, 100% online, blended/hybrid learning. *Degree requirements:* For master's, comprehensive exam, thesis or alternative. *Entrance requirements:* For master's, minimum GPA of 2.75, 24 hours of undergraduate course work in history (MA), 9-12 teaching certification (MS Ed). Additional exam requirements/recommendations for international students: required—TOEFL (minimum score 550 paper-based; 79 iBT), IELTS (minimum score 6). Electronic applications accepted. *Expenses: Tuition, area resident:* Full-time $2600; part-time $1735 per credit hour. Tuition, nonresident: full-time $5240; part-time $3495 per credit hour. *International tuition:* $5240 full-time. *Required fees:* $530; $438 per credit hour. Tuition and fees vary according to class time, course level, course load, degree level, campus/location and program.

Monmouth University, Graduate Studies, Program in History, West Long Branch, NJ 07764-1898. Offers European history (MA); United States history (MA). *Program availability:* Part-time, evening/weekend. *Faculty:* 9 full-time (2 women). *Students:* 2 full-time (1 woman), 24 part-time (9 women); includes 2 minority (1 Black or African American, non-Hispanic/Latino; 1 Hispanic/Latino). Average age 33. In 2019, 10 master's awarded. *Degree requirements:* For master's, comprehensive exam (for some programs), thesis (for some programs). *Entrance requirements:* For master's, minimum GPA of 3.0 in major, 2.5 overall; two letters of recommendation; statement describing historical areas of interest and how graduate study will contribute to professional and academic goals. Additional exam requirements/recommendations for international students: required—TOEFL (minimum score 550 paper-based; 79 iBT), IELTS (minimum score 6) or Michigan English Language Assessment Battery (minimum score 77). *Application deadline:* For fall admission, 7/15 priority date for domestic students, 6/1 for international students; for spring admission, 12/15 priority date for domestic students, 11/1 for international students. Applications are processed on a rolling basis. Application fee: $50. Electronic applications accepted. *Expenses: Tuition:* Full-time $22,194; part-time $14,796 per credit. *Required fees:* $712; $178 per semester. $178 per semester. Tuition and fees vary according to course load. *Financial support:* In 2019–20, 22 students received support. Research assistantships, teaching assistantships, scholarships/grants, and unspecified assistantships available. Support available to part-time students. Financial award applicants required to submit FAFSA. *Unit head:* Dr. Maryann Rhett, Program Director, 732-263-5768, Fax: 732-263-5112, E-mail: mrhett@monmouth.edu. *Application contact:* Kevin New, Graduate Admission Counselor, 732-571-3452, Fax: 732-263-5123, E-mail: gradadm@monmouth.edu.
Website: https://www.monmouth.edu/graduate/ma-history/

Montana State University, The Graduate School, College of Letters and Science, Department of History, Bozeman, MT 59717. Offers MA, PhD. *Program availability:* Part-time. *Degree requirements:* For master's, comprehensive exam; for doctorate, comprehensive exam, thesis/dissertation. *Entrance requirements:* For master's, GRE General Test, transcripts, 3 letters of recommendation, writing sample, statement of interest; for doctorate, GRE General Test, MA, transcripts, 3 letters of recommendation, writing sample, statement of interest. Additional exam requirements/recommendations for international students: required—TOEFL (minimum score 550 paper-based). Electronic applications accepted.

Morgan State University, School of Graduate Studies, James H. Gilliam Jr College of Liberal Arts, Department of History and Geography, Baltimore, MD 21251. Offers African-American studies (MA); history (MA, PhD); museum studies and historic preservation (MA). *Program availability:* Part-time, evening/weekend. *Faculty:* 20 full-time (5 women), 1 part-time/adjunct (0 women). *Students:* 37 full-time (24 women), 8 part-time (6 women); includes 41 minority (36 Black or African American, non-Hispanic/Latino; 5 Hispanic/Latino), 3 international. Average age 37. 13 applicants, 92% accepted, 4 enrolled. In 2019, 4 master's, 4 doctorates awarded. *Degree requirements:* For master's, comprehensive exam, thesis; for doctorate, comprehensive exam, thesis/dissertation. *Entrance requirements:* For master's, GRE, minimum GPA of 2.5; for doctorate, GRE or MAT, minimum GPA of 3.0. Additional exam requirements/recommendations for international students: required—TOEFL (minimum score 550 paper-based). *Application deadline:* For fall admission, 2/1 priority date for domestic students, 4/1 for international students; for spring admission, 11/15 for domestic students, 10/1 for international students. Applications are processed on a rolling basis. Application fee: $50 ($70 for international students). Electronic applications accepted. *Expenses:* Tuition, state resident: full-time $455; part-time $455 per credit hour. Tuition, nonresident: full-time $894; part-time $894 per credit hour. *Required fees:* $82; $82 per credit hour. *Financial support:* In 2019–20, 5 students received support. Fellowships with full and partial tuition reimbursements available, research assistantships with full and partial tuition reimbursements available, teaching assistantships with full and partial tuition reimbursements available, career-related internships or fieldwork, Federal Work-Study, scholarships/grants, tuition waivers (full and partial), and unspecified assistantships available. Support available to part-time students. Financial award application deadline: 2/1. *Unit head:* Dr. Jeremiah I. Dibua, Interim Chair of Department, 443-885-3190, Fax: 443-885-8227, E-mail: jeremiah.dibua@morgan.edu. *Application contact:* Dr. Jahmaine Smith, Director of Admissions, 443-885-3185, Fax: 443-885-8226, E-mail: gradapply@morgan.edu.
Website: https://morgan.edu/college_of_liberal_arts/departments/history_geography_and_museum_studies/graduate_program_handbook.html

Murray State University, College of Humanities and Fine Arts, Department of History, Murray, KY 42071. Offers MA. *Program availability:* Part-time. *Entrance requirements:* For master's, GRE or GMAT, minimum university GPA of 2.75. Additional exam requirements/recommendations for international students: required—TOEFL (minimum score 527 paper-based; 71 iBT). Electronic applications accepted.

New Jersey Institute of Technology, College of Science and Liberal Arts, Newark, NJ 07102. Offers applied mathematics (MS); applied physics (MS, PhD); applied statistics (MS, Certificate); biology (MS, PhD); biostatistics (MS); chemistry (MS, PhD); environmental and sustainability policy (MS); environmental science (MS, PhD); history (MA, MAT); materials science and engineering (MS, PhD); mathematical and computational finance (MS); mathematical sciences (PhD); pharmaceutical chemistry (MS); professional and technical communications (MS); technical communication essentials (Certificate). *Program availability:* Part-time, evening/weekend. *Faculty:* 159 full-time (42 women), 156 part-time/adjunct (61 women). *Students:* 197 full-time (80 women), 58 part-time (14 women); includes 58 minority (18 Black or African American, non-Hispanic/Latino; 22 Asian, non-Hispanic/Latino; 16 Hispanic/Latino; 2 Two or more races, non-Hispanic/Latino), 130 international. Average age 29. 401 applicants, 63% accepted, 73 enrolled. In 2019, 54 master's, 10 doctorates, 1 other advanced degree awarded. Terminal master's awarded for partial completion of doctoral program. *Degree requirements:* For master's, thesis (for some programs); for doctorate, thesis/dissertation. *Entrance requirements:* For master's and doctorate, GRE General Test, Minimum GPA of 3.0, personal statement, 3 letters of recommendation, and transcripts. Additional exam requirements/recommendations for international students: required—TOEFL (minimum score 550 paper-based; 79 iBT), IELTS (minimum score 6.5). *Application deadline:* For fall admission, 6/1 priority date for domestic students, 5/1 priority date for international students; for spring admission, 11/15 priority date for domestic and international students. Applications are processed on a rolling basis. Application fee: $75. Electronic applications accepted. *Expenses:* $23,828 per year (in-state), $33,744 per year (out-of-state). *Financial support:* In 2019–20, 147 students received support, including 13 fellowships with full tuition reimbursements available (averaging $24,000 per year), 41 research assistantships with full tuition reimbursements available (averaging $24,000 per year), 87 teaching assistantships with full tuition reimbursements available (averaging $24,000 per year); scholarships/grants, traineeships, health care benefits, and unspecified assistantships also available. Financial award application deadline: 1/15. *Unit head:* Dr. Kevin Belfield, Dean, 973-596-3676, Fax: 973-565-0586, E-mail: kevin.d.belfield@njit.edu. *Application contact:* Stephen Eck, Director of Admissions, 973-596-3300, Fax: 973-596-3461, E-mail: admissions@njit.edu.
Website: http://csla.njit.edu/

New Mexico Highlands University, Graduate Studies, College of Arts and Sciences, Department of History, Political Science, and Languages and Culture, Las Vegas, NM 87701. Offers public affairs (MA), including historical and cross-cultural perspectives, history/political science, political and governmental processes. *Degree requirements:* For master's, comprehensive exam, thesis or alternative. *Entrance requirements:* Additional exam requirements/recommendations for international students: required—TOEFL (minimum score 540 paper-based).

New Mexico State University, College of Arts and Sciences, Department of History, Las Cruces, NM 88003-8001. Offers history (MA); public history (MA). *Program availability:* Part-time. *Faculty:* 9 full-time (5 women). *Students:* 8 full-time (3 women), 11 part-time (2 women); includes 8 minority (all Hispanic/Latino). Average age 36. 9 applicants, 67% accepted, 3 enrolled. In 2019, 5 master's awarded. *Degree requirements:* For master's, comprehensive exam, thesis (for some programs). *Entrance requirements:* For master's, minimum of 12 upper-division history credits, writing sample, minimum GPA of 3.0. Additional exam requirements/recommendations for international students: required—TOEFL (minimum score 550 paper-based; 79 iBT), IELTS (minimum score 6.5). *Application deadline:* For fall admission, 7/1 priority date for domestic students; for spring admission, 11/1 for domestic students. Applications are processed on a rolling basis. Application fee: $40 ($50 for international students). Electronic applications accepted. *Financial support:* In 2019–20, 10 students received support, including 6 teaching assistantships (averaging $18,162 per year); career-related internships or fieldwork, Federal Work-Study, scholarships/grants, traineeships, health care benefits, and unspecified assistantships also available. Support available to part-time students. Financial award application deadline: 3/1. *Unit head:* Dr. Mark Cioc-Ortega, Department Head, 575-646-4601, Fax: 575-646-6096, E-mail: mcioc@nmsu.edu. *Application contact:* Dr. Margaret Malamud, Director of Graduate Studies, 575-646-4310, Fax: 575-646-6096, E-mail: mmalamud@nmsu.edu.
Website: http://history.nmsu.edu

The New School, The New School for Social Research, Department of Historical Studies, New York, NY 10003. Offers historical studies (MA); politics (PhD), including historical studies; sociology (PhD), including historical studies. *Program availability:* Part-time, evening/weekend. *Faculty:* 1 (woman) full-time, 2 part-time/adjunct (both women). *Students:* 10 full-time (3 women), 4 part-time (2 women); includes 1 minority (Asian, non-Hispanic/Latino), 4 international. Average age 28. 8 applicants, 100% accepted, 6 enrolled. In 2019, 7 master's awarded. *Degree requirements:* For master's, thesis. *Entrance requirements:* For master's, GRE, two letters of recommendation, writing sample, essays, transcripts. Additional exam requirements/recommendations for international students: required—TOEFL (minimum score 100 iBT), IELTS (minimum score 7), PTE (minimum score 68). *Application deadline:* For fall admission, 1/15 priority date for domestic and international students; for spring admission, 10/15 priority date for domestic and international students. Applications are processed on a rolling basis. Application fee: $50. Electronic applications accepted. *Expenses:* 2260 per credit. *Financial support:* In 2019–20, 11 students received support, including 6 research assistantships (averaging $5,723 per year), 4 teaching assistantships (averaging $7,022 per year); Federal Work-Study, scholarships/grants, traineeships, health care benefits, and tuition waivers (full and partial) also available. Support available to part-time students. Financial award application deadline: 2/1; financial award applicants required to submit FAFSA. *Unit head:* Dr. Oz Frankel, Department Chair, 212-229-5376 Ext. 4924, E-mail: frankelo@newschool.edu. *Application contact:* Merida Gasbarro, Director of Graduate Admission, 212-229-5600 Ext. 1108, E-mail: escandom@newschool.edu.
Website: http://www.newschool.edu/nssr/historical-studies/

The New School, The New School for Social Research, Department of Sociology, New York, NY 10003. Offers historical studies (PhD); sociology (M Phil, MA). *Program availability:* Part-time. *Faculty:* 11 full-time (5 women), 1 (woman) part-time/adjunct. *Students:* 76 full-time (43 women), 7 part-time (4 women); includes 13 minority (4 Black or African American, non-Hispanic/Latino; 2 Asian, non-Hispanic/Latino; 6 Hispanic/Latino; 1 Two or more races, non-Hispanic/Latino), 45 international. Average age 34. 68 applicants, 65% accepted, 21 enrolled. In 2019, 25 master's, 10 doctorates awarded. Terminal master's awarded for partial completion of doctoral program. *Degree requirements:* For master's, comprehensive exam; for doctorate, one foreign language, thesis/dissertation. *Entrance requirements:* For master's and doctorate, GRE, letters of recommendation, writing sample, essays, transcripts. Additional exam requirements/recommendations for international students: required—TOEFL (minimum score 92 iBT), IELTS (minimum score 7), PTE (minimum score 68). *Application deadline:* For fall admission, 5/5 priority date for domestic students, 6/15 priority date for international students; for spring admission, 10/15 priority date for domestic and international students. Applications are processed on a rolling basis. Application fee: $50. Electronic applications accepted. *Expenses:* 2260. *Financial support:* In 2019–20, 62 students received support, including 8 fellowships (averaging $7,023 per year), 24 research assistantships (averaging $4,958 per year), 16 teaching assistantships (averaging $10,026 per year); Federal Work-Study, scholarships/grants, and tuition waivers (full and partial) also available. Support available to part-time students. Financial award application deadline: 2/1; financial award applicants required to submit FAFSA. *Unit head:* Dr. Benoit Challand, 212-229-5747 Ext. 3034, E-mail: challanb@newschool.edu. *Application contact:* Merida Gasbarro, Director of Graduate Admission, 212-229-5600 Ext. 1108, E-mail: escandom@newschool.edu.
Website: https://www.newschool.edu/nssr/sociology/

New York University, Graduate School of Arts and Science, Department of History, New York, NY 10012-1019. Offers African diaspora (PhD); African history (PhD); archival management (Advanced Certificate); Atlantic history (PhD); French studies/history (PhD); Hebrew and Judaic studies/history (PhD); history (MA, PhD), including Europe (PhD), Latin America and the Caribbean (PhD), United States (PhD), women's history (MA); Middle Eastern history (MA); Middle Eastern studies/history (PhD); public history (Advanced Certificate); world history (MA); JD/MA; MA/Advanced Certificate. *Program availability:* Part-time. Terminal master's awarded for partial completion of doctoral program. *Degree requirements:* For master's, seminar paper; for doctorate, one foreign language, thesis/dissertation, oral and written exams; for Advanced Certificate, internship. *Entrance requirements:* For master's, GRE General Test, minimum GPA of 3.0, writing sample; for doctorate, GRE. Additional exam requirements/recommendations for international students: required—TOEFL.

New York University, Graduate School of Arts and Science, Institute for the Study of the Ancient World, New York, NY 10012-1019. Offers PhD. *Degree requirements:* For doctorate, 4 foreign languages, comprehensive exam, thesis/dissertation, fieldwork, teaching experience. *Entrance requirements:* For doctorate, GRE General Test. Additional exam requirements/recommendations for international students: required—TOEFL, IELTS. Electronic applications accepted.

North Carolina Central University, College of Arts and Sciences, Department of History, Durham, NC 27707-3129. Offers MA. *Program availability:* Part-time, evening/weekend. *Degree requirements:* For master's, one foreign language, comprehensive exam, thesis. *Entrance requirements:* For master's, GRE, minimum GPA of 3.0 in major, 2.5 overall. Additional exam requirements/recommendations for international students: required—TOEFL.

History

North Carolina State University, Graduate School, College of Humanities and Social Sciences, Department of History, Raleigh, NC 27695. Offers history (MA); public history (MA). *Program availability:* Part-time, evening/weekend. *Degree requirements:* For master's, thesis. *Entrance requirements:* For master's, GRE General Test. Electronic applications accepted.

North Dakota State University, College of Graduate and Interdisciplinary Studies, College of Arts, Humanities and Social Sciences, Department of History, Philosophy, and Religious Studies, Fargo, ND 58102. Offers history (MA, MS, PhD). *Program availability:* Part-time, evening/weekend. *Degree requirements:* For master's, one foreign language, comprehensive exam, thesis optional; for doctorate, 2 foreign languages, comprehensive exam, thesis/dissertation. *Entrance requirements:* For master's and doctorate, GRE General Test. Additional exam requirements/recommendations for international students: required—TOEFL (minimum score 600 paper-based; 100 iBT). Electronic applications accepted. Tuition and fees vary according to program and reciprocity agreements.

Northeastern Illinois University, College of Graduate Studies and Research, College of Arts and Sciences, Program in History, Chicago, IL 60625. Offers MA. *Program availability:* Part-time, evening/weekend. *Degree requirements:* For master's, comprehensive exam, thesis optional. *Entrance requirements:* For master's, 24 undergraduate hours in history, minimum GPA of 2.75. Additional exam requirements/recommendations for international students: required—TOEFL (minimum score 550 paper-based; 79 iBT). Electronic applications accepted.

Northeastern University, College of Social Sciences and Humanities, Boston, MA 02115. Offers criminology and criminal justice (MSCJ); criminology and justice policy (PhD); economics (MA, PhD); English (MA, PhD); international affairs (MA); law and public policy (PhD); political science (MA, PhD); public administration (MPA); public policy (MPP); security and resilience studies (MS); sociology (MA, PhD); urban and regional policy (MS); urban informatics (MS); world history (MA, PhD). *Program availability:* Online learning. *Degree requirements:* For doctorate, variable foreign language requirement, comprehensive exam, thesis/dissertation. *Entrance requirements:* For master's and doctorate, GRE. Additional exam requirements/recommendations for international students: required—TOEFL, IELTS. Electronic applications accepted. *Expenses:* Contact institution.

Northern Arizona University, College of Arts and Letters, Department of History, Flagstaff, AZ 86011. Offers MA. *Program availability:* Part-time. *Degree requirements:* For master's, variable foreign language requirement, comprehensive exam (for some programs), thesis (for some programs). *Entrance requirements:* For master's, GRE General Test. Additional exam requirements/recommendations for international students: required—TOEFL (minimum score 80 iBT), IELTS (minimum score 6.5). Electronic applications accepted.

Northern Illinois University, Graduate School, College of Liberal Arts and Sciences, Department of History, De Kalb, IL 60115-2854. Offers MA, PhD. *Program availability:* Part-time. *Faculty:* 18 full-time (8 women), 2 part-time/adjunct (0 women). *Students:* 22 full-time (9 women), 19 part-time (9 women); includes 5 minority (2 Black or African American, non-Hispanic/Latino; 1 Asian, non-Hispanic/Latino; 1 Hispanic/Latino; 1 Two or more races, non-Hispanic/Latino), 2 international. Average age 34. 33 applicants, 76% accepted, 9 enrolled. In 2019, 5 master's, 2 doctorates awarded. Terminal master's awarded for partial completion of doctoral program. *Degree requirements:* For master's, variable foreign language requirement, comprehensive exam, thesis optional, research seminars; for doctorate, variable foreign language requirement, thesis/dissertation, candidacy exam, dissertation defense, research seminars. *Entrance requirements:* For master's, GRE General Test, minimum GPA of 2.75; for doctorate, GRE General Test, minimum undergraduate GPA of 2.75, graduate 3.2. Additional exam requirements/recommendations for international students: required—TOEFL (minimum score 550 paper-based). *Application deadline:* For fall admission, 6/1 for domestic students, 5/1 for international students; for spring admission, 11/1 for domestic students, 10/1 for international students. Applications are processed on a rolling basis. Application fee: $40. Electronic applications accepted. *Financial support:* In 2019–20, 2 research assistantships with full tuition reimbursements, 16 teaching assistantships with full tuition reimbursements were awarded; fellowships with full tuition reimbursements, career-related internships or fieldwork, Federal Work-Study, scholarships/grants, tuition waivers (full), and unspecified assistantships also available. Support available to part-time students. Financial award applicants required to submit FAFSA. *Unit head:* Dr. Valerie Garver, Chair, 815-753-0131, Fax: 815-753-6302, E-mail: vgarver@niu.edu. *Application contact:* Dr. Andy Bruno, Director of Graduate Studies, 815-753-0131, E-mail: history@niu.edu.
Website: http://www.niu.edu/history/

Northwestern University, The Graduate School, Judd A. and Marjorie Weinberg College of Arts and Sciences, Department of History, Evanston, IL 60208. Offers PhD, JD/PhD. *Degree requirements:* For doctorate, variable foreign language requirement, thesis/dissertation, major and minor field exams. *Entrance requirements:* For doctorate, sample of written work. Additional exam requirements/recommendations for international students: required—TOEFL. Electronic applications accepted.

Northwestern University, School of Professional Studies, Program in Liberal Studies, Evanston, IL 60208. Offers American studies (MA); history (MA); religious and ethical studies (MA). *Program availability:* Part-time, evening/weekend.

Norwich University, College of Graduate and Continuing Studies, Master of Arts in History Program, Northfield, VT 05663. Offers history (MA), including American history, world history. *Program availability:* Evening/weekend, online only, mostly all online with a week-long residency requirement. *Degree requirements:* For master's, thesis optional, capstone. *Entrance requirements:* For master's, minimum undergraduate GPA of 2.75. Additional exam requirements/recommendations for international students: required—TOEFL (minimum score 550 paper-based; 80 iBT), IELTS (minimum score 6.5). Electronic applications accepted. *Expenses:* Contact institution.

Oakland University, Graduate Study and Lifelong Learning, College of Arts and Sciences, Department of History, Rochester, MI 48309-4401. Offers MA. *Program availability:* Part-time, evening/weekend. *Degree requirements:* For master's, comprehensive exam (for some programs), thesis (for some programs). *Entrance requirements:* For master's, Applicants should have a minimum GPA of 3.5 (on a 4.0 scale) in undergraduate history courses with a cumulative GPA of 3.2, Detailed statement of purpose or justification for entering the graduate program, Academic writing sample. Additional exam requirements/recommendations for international students: required—TOEFL (minimum score 550 paper-based; 79 iBT), IELTS (minimum score 6.5). Electronic applications accepted. *Expenses: Tuition, area resident:* Full-time $12,328; part-time $770.50 per credit hour. Tuition, state resident: full-time $12,328; part-time $770.50 per credit hour. Tuition, nonresident: full-time $16,432; part-time $1027 per credit hour. *International tuition:* $16,432 full-time. Tuition and fees vary according to degree level and program.

The Ohio State University, Graduate School, College of Arts and Sciences, Division of Arts and Humanities, Department of History, Columbus, OH 43210. Offers MA, PhD. Terminal master's awarded for partial completion of doctoral program. *Degree requirements:* For master's, thesis optional; for doctorate, variable foreign language

requirement, thesis/dissertation. *Entrance requirements:* For master's and doctorate, GRE General Test. Additional exam requirements/recommendations for international students: required—TOEFL (minimum score 550 paper-based; 79 iBT), GRE General Test (strongly recommended). Electronic applications accepted.

Ohio University, Graduate College, College of Arts and Sciences, Department of History, Athens, OH 45701-2979. Offers MA, PhD. *Degree requirements:* For master's, one foreign language, thesis optional; for doctorate, 2 foreign languages, comprehensive exam, thesis/dissertation. *Entrance requirements:* For master's, GRE, minimum GPA of 3.0; for doctorate, GRE, minimum GPA of 3.0, MA. Additional exam requirements/recommendations for international students: required—TOEFL (minimum score 550 paper-based; 80 iBT) or IELTS (minimum score 6.5). Electronic applications accepted.

Oklahoma State University, College of Arts and Sciences, Department of History, Stillwater, OK 74078. Offers MA, PhD. *Faculty:* 19 full-time (10 women), 1 part-time/adjunct (0 women). *Students:* 11 full-time (7 women), 17 part-time (6 women); includes 8 minority (1 Black or African American, non-Hispanic/Latino; 1 American Indian or Alaska Native, non-Hispanic/Latino; 1 Hispanic/Latino; 5 Two or more races, non-Hispanic/Latino). Average age 33. 19 applicants, 53% accepted, 7 enrolled. In 2019, 2 master's, 3 doctorates awarded. *Entrance requirements:* For master's and doctorate, GRE. Additional exam requirements/recommendations for international students: required—TOEFL (minimum score 550 paper-based; 79 iBT). *Application deadline:* For fall admission, 3/1 priority date for international students; for spring admission, 8/1 priority date for international students. Applications are processed on a rolling basis. Application fee: $50 ($75 for international students). Electronic applications accepted. *Expenses: Tuition, area resident:* Full-time $4148.10; part-time $2765.40 per credit hour. Tuition, state resident: full-time $4148.10; part-time $2765.40 per credit hour. Tuition, nonresident: full-time $15,775; part-time $10,516.80 per credit hour. *International tuition:* $15,775.20 full-time. Required fees: $2196.90; $122.05 per credit hour. Tuition and fees vary according to course load, campus/location and program. *Financial support:* In 2019–20, 17 teaching assistantships (averaging $1,848 per year) were awarded; career-related internships or fieldwork, Federal Work-Study, scholarships/grants, health care benefits, tuition waivers (partial), and unspecified assistantships also available. Support available to part-time students. Financial award application deadline: 3/1; financial award applicants required to submit FAFSA. *Unit head:* Dr. Brian Hosmer, Department Head, 405-744-8188, Fax: 405-744-5400, E-mail: brian.hosmer@okstate.edu. *Application contact:* Dr. Sheryl Tucker, Dean, 405-744-6368, Fax: 405-744-0355, E-mail: gradi@okstate.edu.
Website: http://history.okstate.edu/

Old Dominion University, College of Arts and Letters, Program in History, Norfolk, VA 23529. Offers MA. *Program availability:* Part-time, evening/weekend. *Degree requirements:* For master's, comprehensive exam, thesis optional. *Entrance requirements:* For master's, GRE General Test, 24 credits in history with minimum GPA of 3.0. Additional exam requirements/recommendations for international students: recommended—TOEFL. Electronic applications accepted.

Open University, Graduate Programs, Milton Keynes, United Kingdom. Offers business (MBA); education (M Ed); engineering (M Eng); history (MA); music (MA); philosophy (MA).

Penn State University Park, Graduate School, College of the Liberal Arts, Department of History, University Park, PA 16802. Offers MA, PhD.

Pittsburg State University, Graduate School, College of Arts and Sciences, Department of History, Pittsburg, KS 66762. Offers MA. *Program availability:* Part-time, 100% online, blended/hybrid learning. *Degree requirements:* For master's, thesis or alternative. *Entrance requirements:* Additional exam requirements/recommendations for international students: required—TOEFL (minimum score 520 paper-based; 68 iBT), IELTS (minimum score 6), PTE (minimum score 47). Electronic applications accepted. *Expenses:* Contact institution.

Pontifical Catholic University of Puerto Rico, College of Arts and Humanities, Department of History, Ponce, PR 00717-0777. Offers MA. *Entrance requirements:* For master's, GRE General Test, minimum GPA of 2.75, 2 letters of recommendation.

Portland State University, Graduate Studies, College of Liberal Arts and Sciences, Department of History, Portland, OR 97207-0751. Offers MA. *Program availability:* Part-time. *Faculty:* 21 full-time (6 women), 2 part-time/adjunct (1 woman). *Students:* 17 full-time (7 women), 18 part-time (10 women); includes 5 minority (2 American Indian or Alaska Native, non-Hispanic/Latino; 2 Hispanic/Latino; 1 Two or more races, non-Hispanic/Latino). Average age 36. 19 applicants, 68% accepted, 8 enrolled. In 2019, 7 master's awarded. *Degree requirements:* For master's, one foreign language, comprehensive exam, thesis, oral and written exams. *Entrance requirements:* For master's, GRE General Test, minimum GPA of 3.5 in upper-division history courses, overall 3.25; 2 letters of recommendation; BA/BS in history; statement of intent; writing samples. Additional exam requirements/recommendations for international students: required—TOEFL (minimum score 550 paper-based; 80 iBT). *Application deadline:* For fall admission, 2/15 for domestic and international students; for winter admission, 9/1 for domestic students, 6/1 for international students; for spring admission, 11/1 for domestic and international students; for summer admission, 2/1 for domestic and international students. Application fee: $65. Electronic applications accepted. *Expenses:* $429 per credit resident, $645 per credit non-resident. *Financial support:* In 2019–20, 1 teaching assistantship was awarded; research assistantships, career-related internships or fieldwork, Federal Work-Study, scholarships/grants, and unspecified assistantships also available. Support available to part-time students. Financial award application deadline: 3/1; financial award applicants required to submit FAFSA. *Unit head:* Dr. John Ott, Chair, 503-725-3917, E-mail: ott@pdx.edu. *Application contact:* Dr. Richard Beyler, Graduate Coordinator, 503-725-3996, Fax: 503-725-3953, E-mail: r.beyler@pdx.edu.
Website: https://www.pdx.edu/history/

Princeton University, Graduate School, Department of Classics, Princeton, NJ 08544-1019. Offers classical and Hellenic studies (PhD); classical philosophy (PhD); history (the ancient world) (PhD); literature and philology (PhD). *Degree requirements:* For doctorate, thesis/dissertation. *Entrance requirements:* For doctorate, GRE General Test, sample of written work. Additional exam requirements/recommendations for international students: required—TOEFL (minimum score 600 paper-based). Electronic applications accepted.

Princeton University, Graduate School, Department of History, Princeton, NJ 08544-1019. Offers history (PhD); history of science (PhD). *Degree requirements:* For doctorate, variable foreign language requirement, comprehensive exam, thesis/dissertation. *Entrance requirements:* For doctorate, GRE General Test, sample of written work. Additional exam requirements/recommendations for international students: required—TOEFL (minimum score 600 paper-based). Electronic applications accepted.

Providence College, Department of History, Providence, RI 02918. Offers American history (MA); modern European history (MA). *Program availability:* Part-time, evening/weekend. *Degree requirements:* For master's, comprehensive exam, thesis optional. *Entrance requirements:* Additional exam requirements/recommendations for international students: required—TOEFL (minimum score 577 paper-based; 90 iBT). *Expenses:* Contact institution.

Purdue University, Graduate School, College of Liberal Arts, Department of History, West Lafayette, IN 47907. Offers MA, PhD. *Program availability:* Part-time. *Faculty:* 29 full-time (12 women), 1 part-time/adjunct (0 women). *Students:* 29 full-time (15 women), 10 part-time (4 women); includes 2 minority (1 Black or African American, non-Hispanic/Latino; 1 Two or more races, non-Hispanic/Latino), 5 international. Average age 31. 55 applicants, 44% accepted, 9 enrolled. In 2019, 1 master's, 4 doctorates awarded. *Degree requirements:* For master's, thesis optional; for doctorate, one foreign language, thesis/dissertation. *Entrance requirements:* For master's, GRE General Test, minimum undergraduate GPA of 3.0 or equivalent; for doctorate, GRE General Test, minimum undergraduate GPA of 3.0 or equivalent; master's degree with minimum GPA of 3.0 or equivalent. Additional exam requirements/recommendations for international students: required—TOEFL (minimum score 550 paper-based; 77 iBT), TWE. *Application deadline:* For fall admission, 1/1 priority date for domestic and international students; for spring admission, 9/1 for domestic and international students. Applications are processed on a rolling basis. Application fee: $60 ($75 for international students). Electronic applications accepted. *Financial support:* In 2019–20, 37 students received support. Fellowships with full tuition reimbursements available and teaching assistantships with full tuition reimbursements available available. Support available to part-time students. Financial award application deadline: 1/15; financial award applicants required to submit FAFSA. *Unit head:* Dr. Federick R. Davis, Head, 765-494-4132, E-mail: doughurt@purdue.edu. *Application contact:* Fay M. Chan, Graduate Contact, 765-494-4126, E-mail: chanf@purdue.edu.
Website: http://www.cla.purdue.edu/history/

Purdue University Northwest, Graduate Studies Office, School of Liberal Arts and Social Sciences, Department of History and Political Science, Hammond, IN 46323-2094. Offers history (MA). *Program availability:* Part-time, evening/weekend. *Entrance requirements:* Additional exam requirements/recommendations for international students: required—TOEFL.

Queens College of the City University of New York, School of Social Sciences, Department of History, Queens, NY 11367-1597. Offers MA. *Program availability:* Part-time, evening/weekend. *Degree requirements:* For master's, comprehensive exam, thesis optional. *Entrance requirements:* For master's, minimum GPA of 3.0. Additional exam requirements/recommendations for international students: required—TOEFL (minimum score 90 iBT), IELTS (minimum score 6.5). Electronic applications accepted.

Rhode Island College, School of Graduate Studies, Faculty of Arts and Sciences, Department of History, Providence, RI 02908-1991. Offers MA. *Program availability:* Part-time, evening/weekend. *Faculty:* 3 full-time (0 women). *Students:* 1 full-time (0 women), 2 part-time (1 woman). Average age 28. In 2019, 1 master's awarded. *Degree requirements:* For master's, oral exam or thesis. *Entrance requirements:* For master's, GRE General and Subject Tests, 3 letters of recommendation, interview. Additional exam requirements/recommendations for international students: required—TOEFL (minimum score 550 paper-based; 80 iBT). *Application deadline:* For fall admission, 3/1 for domestic students; for spring admission, 11/1 for domestic students. Applications are processed on a rolling basis. Application fee: $50. Electronic applications accepted. *Expenses: Tuition, area resident:* Part-time $462 per credit hour. Tuition, state resident: part-time $462 per credit hour. *Required fees:* $720. One-time fee: $140. *Financial support:* Teaching assistantships, Federal Work-Study, scholarships/grants, health care benefits, and unspecified assistantships available. Support available to part-time students. Financial award application deadline: 5/15; financial award applicants required to submit FAFSA. *Unit head:* Dr. Karl Benziger, Chair, 401-456-8039. *Application contact:* Dr. Karl Benziger, Chair, 401-456-8039.
Website: http://www.ric.edu/history/Pages/graduate-programs.aspx

Rice University, Graduate Programs, School of Humanities, Department of History, Houston, TX 77251-1892. Offers MA, PhD. Terminal master's awarded for partial completion of doctoral program. *Degree requirements:* For doctorate, variable foreign language requirement, comprehensive exam, thesis/dissertation, 4 semesters of coursework. *Entrance requirements:* For doctorate, GRE, writing samples, letters of recommendation, personal statement, transcripts. Additional exam requirements/recommendations for international students: required—TOEFL (minimum score 600 paper-based; 90 iBT) or IELTS (minimum score 7). Electronic applications accepted.

Roosevelt University, Graduate Division, College of Arts and Sciences, Department of History and Philosophy, Chicago, IL 60605. Offers history (MA). *Program availability:* Part-time, evening/weekend. Electronic applications accepted.

Rowan University, Graduate School, College of Humanities and Social Sciences, Department of History, Glassboro, NJ 08028-1701. Offers history (MA, CGS). *Expenses: Tuition, area resident:* Part-time $715.50 per semester hour. Tuition, state resident: part-time $715.50 per semester hour. Tuition, nonresident: part-time $715.50 per semester hour. *Required fees:* $161.55 per semester hour.

Rowan University, Graduate School, College of Humanities and Social Sciences, Program in History, Glassboro, NJ 08028-1701. Offers MA, CGS. *Degree requirements:* For master's, thesis optional. *Entrance requirements:* For master's, GRE, statement of objectives; current resume; official transcript demonstrating that applicant has earned undergraduate degree from accredited institution with minimum GPA of 3.0; two letters of recommendation from undergraduate professors or other qualified professionals; writing sample. Additional exam requirements/recommendations for international students: required—TOEFL (minimum score 90 iBT). Electronic applications accepted. *Expenses: Tuition, area resident:* Part-time $715.50 per semester hour. Tuition, state resident: part-time $715.50 per semester hour. Tuition, nonresident: part-time $715.50 per semester hour. *Required fees:* $161.55 per semester hour.

Rutgers University - Camden, Graduate School of Arts and Sciences, Program in American and Public History, Camden, NJ 08102. Offers MA. *Program availability:* Part-time, evening/weekend. *Degree requirements:* For master's, comprehensive exam, thesis optional, 30 credits. *Entrance requirements:* For master's, GRE General Test (for full-time applicants), 3 letters of recommendation; history or related undergraduate degree (preferred). Additional exam requirements/recommendations for international students: required—TOEFL, IELTS. Electronic applications accepted.

Rutgers University - Newark, Graduate School, Program in History, Newark, NJ 07102. Offers MA, MAT. *Program availability:* Part-time, evening/weekend. *Degree requirements:* For master's, one foreign language, comprehensive exam, thesis optional. *Entrance requirements:* For master's, GRE, minimum undergraduate B average.

Rutgers University - New Brunswick, Graduate School-New Brunswick, Program in History, Piscataway, NJ 08854-8097. Offers African-American history (PhD); early American history (PhD); early modern European history (PhD); east Asian history (PhD); global and comparative history (PhD); history (PhD); history of diplomacy and foreign relations (PhD); history of technology, environment and health (PhD); history of the Atlantic cultures and African diaspora (PhD); Latin American history (PhD); medieval history (PhD); modern European history (PhD); nineteenth and twentieth century American history (PhD); women's and gender history (PhD). *Degree requirements:* For doctorate, thesis/dissertation. *Entrance requirements:* For doctorate, GRE General Test, sample of written work. Electronic applications accepted.

St. Cloud State University, School of Graduate Studies, College of Liberal Arts, Department of History, St. Cloud, MN 56301-4498. Offers MA, MS. *Program availability:* Part-time. *Degree requirements:* For master's, thesis or alternative. *Entrance requirements:* For master's, GRE General Test, GRE Subject Test, minimum GPA of 2.75. Additional exam requirements/recommendations for international students: required—Michigan English Language Assessment Battery; recommended—TOEFL (minimum score 550 paper-based), IELTS (minimum score 6.5).

St. John's University, St. John's College of Liberal Arts and Sciences, Department of History, Queens, NY 11439. Offers history (MA, PhD); public history (MA). *Program availability:* Part-time, evening/weekend. Terminal master's awarded for partial completion of doctoral program. *Degree requirements:* For master's, variable foreign language requirement, comprehensive exam, thesis optional; for doctorate, variable foreign language requirement, thesis/dissertation, annual portfolio, internships. *Entrance requirements:* For master's, letters of recommendation, transcripts, resume, personal statement; for doctorate, GRE General Test, letters of recommendation, transcripts, resume, personal statement. Additional exam requirements/recommendations for international students: required—TOEFL (minimum score 80 iBT), IELTS (minimum score 6.5). Electronic applications accepted.

Saint Louis University, Graduate Programs, College of Arts and Sciences, Department of History, St. Louis, MO 63103. Offers MA, MA-R, PhD. *Program availability:* Part-time. *Degree requirements:* For master's, one foreign language, comprehensive exam, thesis optional, comprehensive oral exam; for doctorate, 2 foreign languages, comprehensive exam, thesis/dissertation, preliminary oral and written exams. *Entrance requirements:* For master's, GRE General Test, letters of recommendation, resume, writing sample; for doctorate, GRE General Test, letters of recommendation, resumé, writing sample, goal statement, transcripts. Additional exam requirements/recommendations for international students: required—TOEFL (minimum score 525 paper-based). Electronic applications accepted.

Saint Mary's University, Faculty of Arts, Department of History, Halifax, NS B3H 3C3, Canada. Offers MA. *Program availability:* Part-time. *Degree requirements:* For master's, one foreign language, comprehensive exam, thesis. *Entrance requirements:* For master's, honors degree. *Expenses:* Contact institution.

Salem State University, School of Graduate Studies, Program in History, Salem, MA 01970-5353. Offers MA, MAT. *Program availability:* Part-time, evening/weekend. *Entrance requirements:* For master's, GRE or MAT. Additional exam requirements/recommendations for international students: required—TOEFL (minimum score 550 paper-based; 80 iBT) or IELTS (minimum score 5.5).

Salisbury University, Department of History, Salisbury, MD 21801-6837. Offers history (MA), including Colonial and Revolutionary American history, history of the Chesapeake Bay region, United States history in the 19th and 20th centuries, world history. *Program availability:* Part-time, evening/weekend. *Faculty:* 5 full-time (1 woman). *Students:* 6 full-time (3 women), 5 part-time (2 women); includes 2 minority (both Two or more races, non-Hispanic/Latino). Average age 33. 9 applicants, 89% accepted, 8 enrolled. In 2019, 5 master's awarded. *Degree requirements:* For master's, comprehensive exam, must take history methods and theory course. *Entrance requirements:* For master's, transcripts; resume or CV; personal statement; writing sample if undergraduate degree is from a different institution; minimum GPA of 3.0; three letters of recommendation; if student does not have a history BA, it is requested they take a history methods course upon admission. Additional exam requirements/recommendations for international students: recommended—TOEFL (minimum score 550 paper-based; 79 iBT). *Application deadline:* For fall admission, 4/15 priority date for domestic and international students; for spring admission, 11/15 priority date for domestic and international students. Applications are processed on a rolling basis. Application fee: $65. Electronic applications accepted. *Expenses:* Contact institution. *Financial support:* In 2019–20, 3 students received support, including 4 research assistantships with full tuition reimbursements available (averaging $8,000 per year); career-related internships or fieldwork and scholarships/grants also available. Support available to part-time students. Financial award application deadline: 3/1; financial award applicants required to submit FAFSA. *Unit head:* Dr. Celine Carayon, Graduate Program Director, 410-677-4601, E-mail: cxcarayon@salisbury.edu. *Application contact:* Dr. Celine Carayon, Graduate Program Director, 410-677-4601, E-mail: cxcarayon@salisbury.edu.
Website: https://www.salisbury.edu/explore-academics/programs/graduate-degree-programs/history-masters/

Sam Houston State University, College of Humanities and Social Sciences, Department of History, Huntsville, TX 77341. Offers MA. *Program availability:* Part-time, evening/weekend. *Degree requirements:* For master's, comprehensive exam, thesis optional. *Entrance requirements:* For master's, GRE General Test. Additional exam requirements/recommendations for international students: required—TOEFL (minimum score 550 paper-based; 79 iBT), IELTS (minimum score 6.5). Electronic applications accepted.

San Diego State University, Graduate and Research Affairs, College of Arts and Letters, Department of History, San Diego, CA 92182. Offers MA. *Degree requirements:* For master's, one foreign language. *Entrance requirements:* For master's, GRE General Test, bachelor's degree in related field. Additional exam requirements/recommendations for international students: required—TOEFL. Electronic applications accepted.

San Francisco State University, Division of Graduate Studies, College of Liberal and Creative Arts, Department of History, San Francisco, CA 94132-1722. Offers MA. *Expenses: Tuition, area resident:* Full-time $7176; part-time $4164 per year. Tuition, state resident: full-time $7176; part-time $4164 per year. Tuition, nonresident: full-time $16,680; part-time $396 per unit. *International tuition:* $16,680 full-time. *Required fees:* $1524; $1524 per unit. $762 per semester. Tuition and fees vary according to degree level and program. *Unit head:* Dr. Laura Lisy-Wagner, Chair, 415-338-1604, Fax: 415-338-6159, E-mail: lalisy@sfsu.edu. *Application contact:* Dr. Sarah Curtis, Graduate Coordinator, 415-338-2250, Fax: 415-338-6159, E-mail: scurtis@sfsu.edu.
Website: http://history.sfsu.edu/

San Jose State University, Program in History, San Jose, CA 95192-0117. Offers history (MA); history education (MA). *Program availability:* Part-time, evening/weekend. *Faculty:* 8 full-time (6 women), 2 part-time/adjunct (both women). *Students:* 7 full-time (2 women), 32 part-time (12 women); includes 17 minority (6 Asian, non-Hispanic/Latino; 11 Hispanic/Latino). Average age 36. 15 applicants, 87% accepted, 9 enrolled. In 2019, 12 master's awarded. *Degree requirements:* For master's, variable foreign language requirement, comprehensive exam, thesis optional. *Entrance requirements:* For master's, undergraduate degree and transcripts, statement of purpose, writing sample, 2 letters of recommendation. Additional exam requirements/recommendations for international students: recommended—TOEFL. *Application deadline:* For fall admission, 4/1 for domestic and international students; for spring admission, 11/1 for domestic and international students. Applications are processed on a rolling basis. Application fee: $70. Electronic applications accepted. *Expenses: Tuition, area resident:* Full-time $7176; part-time $4164 per credit hour. Tuition, state resident: full-time $7176; part-time $4164 per credit hour. Tuition, nonresident: full-time $7176; part-time $4165 per credit

hour. *International tuition:* $7176 full-time. *Required fees:* $2110; $2110. *Financial support:* In 2019–20, 9 students received support. Scholarships/grants and Instructional Student Assistants available. Financial award application deadline: 5/1; financial award applicants required to submit FAFSA. *Unit head:* Glen Gendzel, Department Chair, 408-924-5514, Fax: 408-924-5531, E-mail: glen.gendzel@sjsu.edu. *Application contact:* Libra Hilde, Graduate Advisor, 408-924-5512, Fax: 408-9244-5531, E-mail: libra.hilde@sjsu.edu.
Website: http://www.sjsu.edu/depts/history/

Sarah Lawrence College, Graduate Studies, Program in Women's History, Bronxville, NY 10708-5999. Offers MA. *Program availability:* Part-time. *Degree requirements:* For master's, thesis. *Entrance requirements:* For master's, previous course work in history, minimum B average in undergraduate course work. Additional exam requirements/recommendations for international students: required—TOEFL (minimum score 600 paper-based). Electronic applications accepted.

Seton Hall University, College of Arts and Sciences, Department of History, South Orange, NJ 07079-2697. Offers history (MA), including Catholic history, European history, global history, United States history. *Program availability:* Part-time. *Degree requirements:* For master's, thesis or comprehensive exam. *Entrance requirements:* For master's, GRE. Additional exam requirements/recommendations for international students: required—TOEFL. Electronic applications accepted.

Shippensburg University of Pennsylvania, School of Graduate Studies, College of Arts and Sciences, Department of History and Philosophy, Shippensburg, PA 17257-2299. Offers applied history (MA). *Program availability:* Part-time, evening/weekend. *Faculty:* 5 full-time (1 woman). *Students:* 10 full-time (7 women), 6 part-time (4 women); includes 2 minority (1 Black or African American, non-Hispanic/Latino; 1 Two or more races, non-Hispanic/Latino). Average age 33. 23 applicants, 78% accepted, 9 enrolled. In 2019, 12 master's awarded. *Degree requirements:* For master's, thesis, thesis, internship, or student teaching and professional practicum. *Entrance requirements:* For master's, 500-word statement of purpose; interview or minimum GPA of 2.75. Additional exam requirements/recommendations for international students: required—TOEFL (minimum score 550 paper-based; 68 iBT), IELTS (minimum score 6), TOEFL (minimum score 550 paper-based, 68 iBT) or IELTS (minimum score 6). *Application deadline:* For fall admission, 2/15 for domestic and international students; for spring admission, 9/15 for domestic and international students; for summer admission, 2/15 for domestic and international students. Applications are processed on a rolling basis. Application fee: $45. Electronic applications accepted. *Expenses:* Tuition, state resident: part-time $516 per credit. Tuition, nonresident: part-time $774 per credit. *Required fees:* $149 per credit. *Financial support:* In 2019–20, 11 students received support. Career-related internships or fieldwork, scholarships/grants, unspecified assistantships, and resident hall director and student payroll positions available. Support available to part-time students. Financial award application deadline: 3/1; financial award applicants required to submit FAFSA. *Unit head:* Dr. John D. Bloom, Professor and Program Coordinator, 717-477-1621, Fax: 717-477-4062, E-mail: jdbloo@ship.edu. *Application contact:* Maya T. Mapp, Director of Admissions, 717-477-1231, Fax: 717-477-4016, E-mail: mtmapp@ship.edu.
Website: http://www.ship.edu/history/

Shippensburg University of Pennsylvania, School of Graduate Studies, College of Education and Human Services, Department of Teacher Education, Shippensburg, PA 17257-2299. Offers curriculum and instruction (M Ed), including biology, early childhood education, elementary education, geography/earth science, global languages, history, mathematics, middle school education; literacy, technology & reading (M Ed), including reading specialist. *Accreditation:* NCATE. *Program availability:* Part-time, evening/weekend, 100% online, blended/hybrid learning. *Faculty:* 12 full-time (9 women), 3 part-time/adjunct (all women). *Students:* 14 full-time (11 women), 54 part-time (51 women); includes 4 minority (all Hispanic/Latino). Average age 31. 50 applicants, 74% accepted, 23 enrolled. In 2019, 29 master's awarded. *Degree requirements:* For master's, comprehensive exam (for some programs), thesis optional, practicum or internship; capstone seminar (for some programs). *Entrance requirements:* For master's, MAT or GRE (if GPA less than 2.75), interview, 3 letters of reference, questionnaire of teaching background and future goals, resume. Additional exam requirements/recommendations for international students: required—TOEFL (minimum score 550 paper-based; 68 iBT), IELTS (minimum score 6), TOEFL (minimum score 550 paper-based, 68 iBT) or IELTS (minimum score 6). *Application deadline:* For fall admission, 4/1 priority date for domestic students, 4/30 for international students; for spring admission, 9/1 priority date for domestic students, 9/30 for international students; for summer admission, 2/1 priority date for domestic students. Applications are processed on a rolling basis. Application fee: $45. Electronic applications accepted. *Expenses:* Tuition, state resident: part-time $516 per credit. Tuition, nonresident: part-time $774 per credit. *Required fees:* $149 per credit. *Financial support:* In 2019–20, 6 students received support. Career-related internships or fieldwork, scholarships/grants, unspecified assistantships, and resident hall director and student payroll positions available. Support available to part-time students. Financial award application deadline: 3/1; financial award applicants required to submit FAFSA. *Unit head:* Dr. Janet M. Bufalino, Department Chairperson, 717-477-1688, Fax: 717-477-4046, E-mail: jmbufa@ship.edu. *Application contact:* Maya T. Mapp, Director of Admissions, 717-477-1231, Fax: 717-477-4016, E-mail: mtmapp@ship.edu.
Website: http://www.ship.edu/teacher/

Simmons University, Gwen Ifill College of Media, Arts, and Humanities, Boston, MA 02115. Offers behavior analysis (MS, PhD, Ed S); children's literature (MA); dietetics (Certificate); elementary education (MAT); English (MA); gender/cultural studies (MA); history (MA); nutrition and health promotion (MS); physical therapy (DPT); public health (MPH); public policy (MPP); special education: moderate and severe disabilities (MS Ed); sports nutrition (Certificate); writing for children (MFA). *Program availability:* Part-time. *Faculty:* 10 full-time (9 women), 7 part-time/adjunct (6 women). *Students:* 2 full-time (both women), 67 part-time (57 women); includes 13 minority (3 Black or African American, non-Hispanic/Latino; 4 Asian, non-Hispanic/Latino; 3 Hispanic/Latino; 3 Two or more races, non-Hispanic/Latino), 1 international. Average age 31. 42 applicants, 62% accepted, 23 enrolled. In 2019, 24 master's awarded. *Degree requirements:* For master's, thesis optional. *Entrance requirements:* For master's, GRE, bachelor's degree from accredited college or university; minimum B average (preferred). Additional exam requirements/recommendations for international students: required—TOEFL (minimum score 600 paper-based; 100 iBT). *Application deadline:* For fall admission, 8/1 for domestic and international students; for spring admission, 12/15 for domestic and international students; for summer admission, 5/1 for domestic and international students. Applications are processed on a rolling basis. Application fee: $35. Electronic applications accepted. *Expenses:* Contact institution. *Financial support:* In 2019–20, 14 students received support, including 1 fellowship (averaging $15,360 per year), 13 teaching assistantships (averaging $2,000 per year); scholarships/grants also available. Financial award applicants required to submit FAFSA. *Unit head:* Dr. Brian Norman, Dean, 617-521-2472, E-mail: brian.norman@simmons.edu. *Application contact:* Patricia Flaherty, Director, Graduate Studies Admission, 617-521-3902, Fax: 617-521-3058, E-mail: gsa@simmons.edu.
Website: https://www.simmons.edu/academics/colleges-schools-departments/ifill

Simon Fraser University, Office of Graduate Studies and Postdoctoral Fellows, Faculty of Arts and Social Sciences, Department of History, Burnaby, BC V5A 1S6, Canada. Offers MA, PhD. *Degree requirements:* For master's, one foreign language, thesis, language exam; for doctorate, one foreign language, comprehensive exam, thesis/dissertation, language exam. *Entrance requirements:* For master's, minimum GPA of 3.0 (on scale of 4.33) or 3.33 based on last 60 credits of undergraduate courses; for doctorate, minimum GPA of 3.5 (on scale of 4.33). Additional exam requirements/recommendations for international students: recommended—TOEFL (minimum score 580 paper-based; 93 iBT), IELTS (minimum score 7), TWE (minimum score 5). Electronic applications accepted.

Slippery Rock University of Pennsylvania, Graduate Studies (Recruitment), College of Liberal Arts, Department of History, Slippery Rock, PA 16057-1383. Offers MA. *Program availability:* Part-time, evening/weekend, online only, 100% online. *Faculty:* 6 full-time (3 women). *Students:* 44 part-time (20 women); includes 5 minority (2 Black or African American, non-Hispanic/Latino; 1 American Indian or Alaska Native, non-Hispanic/Latino; 1 Asian, non-Hispanic/Latino; 1 Hispanic/Latino). Average age 34. 60 applicants, 42% accepted, 13 enrolled. In 2019, 7 master's awarded. *Degree requirements:* For master's, comprehensive exam, thesis (for some programs). *Entrance requirements:* For master's, transcripts (undergraduate/graduate), minimum GPA of 3.0, personal statement. Additional exam requirements/recommendations for international students: required—TOEFL (minimum score 550 paper-based; 80 iBT). *Application deadline:* For fall admission, 3/1 priority date for domestic students, 5/1 priority date for international students; for spring admission, 11/1 priority date for domestic students, 9/1 priority date for international students. Applications are processed on a rolling basis. Application fee: $25 ($30 for international students). Electronic applications accepted. *Expenses:* $516 per credit in-state tuition, $173.61 per credit in-state fees; $774 per credit out-of-state tuition, $224.31 per credit out-of-state fees; $516 per credit in-state tuition, $105.40 per credit in-state fees (for distance education); $526 per credit out-of-state tuition, $118.90 per credit out-of-state fees (for distance education). *Financial support:* In 2019–20, 1 student received support. Career-related internships or fieldwork, Federal Work-Study, institutionally sponsored loans, scholarships/grants, tuition waivers (partial), and unspecified assistantships available. Support available to part-time students. Financial award application deadline: 5/1; financial award applicants required to submit FAFSA. *Unit head:* Dr. Paula Rieder, Graduate Coordinator, 724-738-4923, Fax: 724-738-4762, E-mail: paula.rieder@sru.edu. *Application contact:* Brandi Weber-Mortimer, Director of Graduate Admissions, 724-738-2051, Fax: 724-738-2146, E-mail: graduate.admissions@sru.edu.
Website: http://www.sru.edu/academics/graduate-programs/history-master-of-arts

Smith College, Graduate and Special Programs, Department of History, Northampton, MA 01063. Offers secondary education (MAT), including history education. *Program availability:* Part-time. *Students:* 1 full-time (0 women), 1 part-time (0 women). Average age 28. 2 applicants, 100% accepted, 1 enrolled. In 2019, 2 master's awarded. *Entrance requirements:* Additional exam requirements/recommendations for international students: required—TOEFL (minimum score 595 paper-based; 97 iBT), IELTS (minimum score 7.5). *Application deadline:* For fall admission, 4/15 for domestic students, 1/15 for international students; for spring admission, 12/1 for domestic students. Applications are processed on a rolling basis. Application fee: $60. *Expenses:* The total tuition cost to each M.A.T. student is $18,500. This is the full 'program fee' after awarding of the automatic scholarship. *Financial support:* In 2019–20, 2 students received support, including 1 fellowship with full tuition reimbursement available; scholarships/grants also available. Support available to part-time students. Financial award application deadline: 4/15; financial award applicants required to submit CSS PROFILE or FAFSA. *Unit head:* Elizabeth Pryor, Graduate Student Adviser, 413-585-3701, E-mail: epryor@smith.edu. *Application contact:* Ruth Morgan, Program Coordinator, 413-585-3050, Fax: 413-585-3054, E-mail: gradstdy@smith.edu.
Website: http://www.smith.edu/history/

Sonoma State University, School of Social Sciences, Department of History, Rohnert Park, CA 94928-3609. Offers MA. *Program availability:* Part-time. *Entrance requirements:* For master's, GRE General Test or GRE Subject Test, minimum GPA of 3.0. Additional exam requirements/recommendations for international students: required—TOEFL (minimum score 500 paper-based).

Southeastern Louisiana University, College of Arts, Humanities and Social Sciences, Department of History and Political Science, Hammond, LA 70402. Offers history (MA). *Program availability:* Part-time. *Faculty:* 10 full-time (4 women), 1 part-time/adjunct (0 women). *Students:* 3 full-time (2 women), 29 part-time (7 women); includes 3 minority (2 Hispanic/Latino; 1 Two or more races, non-Hispanic/Latino). Average age 26. 10 applicants, 100% accepted, 9 enrolled. In 2019, 10 master's awarded. *Degree requirements:* For master's, comprehensive exam, thesis optional. *Entrance requirements:* For master's, GRE General Test (minimum score of 290 combined verbal and quantitative), at least 30 undergraduate hours of history, minimum undergraduate GPA 2.5 or 2.75 gpa on upper division undergraduate coursework. Additional exam requirements/recommendations for international students: required—TOEFL (minimum score 500 paper-based; 61 iBT). *Application deadline:* For fall admission, 4/1 priority date for domestic and international students; for spring admission, 12/1 priority date for domestic students, 10/1 priority date for international students. Applications are processed on a rolling basis. Application fee: $20 ($30 for international students). Electronic applications accepted. *Expenses: Tuition, area resident:* Full-time $6684; part-time $489 per credit hour. Tuition, state resident: full-time $6684; part-time $489 per credit hour. Tuition, nonresident: full-time $19,162; part-time $1183 per credit hour. *International tuition:* $19,162 full-time. *Required fees:* $2124. *Financial support:* In 2019–20, 20 students received support, including 3 research assistantships with tuition reimbursements available (averaging $9,367 per year), 8 teaching assistantships with tuition reimbursements available (averaging $9,275 per year); career-related internships or fieldwork, institutionally sponsored loans, and unspecified assistantships also available. Financial award application deadline: 5/1; financial award applicants required to submit FAFSA. *Unit head:* Dr. William Robison, Department Head, 985-549-2109, Fax: 985-549-2012, E-mail: hips@southeastern.edu. *Application contact:* Office of Admissions, 985-549-5637, Fax: 985-549-5632, E-mail: admissions@southeastern.edu.
Website: http://www.southeastern.edu/acad_research/depts/hist_ps/index.html

Southeast Missouri State University, School of Graduate Studies, Department of History and Anthropology, Cape Girardeau, MO 63701. Offers MA, Certificate. *Program availability:* Part-time, evening/weekend. *Faculty:* 12 full-time (5 women). *Students:* 8 full-time (4 women), 4 part-time (2 women). Average age 31. 10 applicants, 90% accepted, 6 enrolled. In 2019, 8 master's awarded. *Degree requirements:* For master's, comprehensive exam (for some programs), thesis or comprehensive exams plus a capstone project/paper (for history); thesis or internship plus advanced project in applied history and comprehensive exams (for public history). *Entrance requirements:* Additional exam requirements/recommendations for international students: required—TOEFL (minimum score 550 paper-based; 79 iBT), IELTS (minimum score 6), PTE (minimum score 53). *Application deadline:* For fall admission, 8/1 for domestic students, 7/1 priority date for international students; for spring admission, 11/21 for domestic students, 11/1 priority date for international students; for summer admission, 5/15 for domestic students. Applications are processed on a rolling basis. Application fee: $30 ($40 for

international students). Electronic applications accepted. *Expenses:* Tuition, state resident: full-time $6989; part-time $291.20 per credit hour. Tuition, nonresident: full-time $13,061; part-time $544.20 per credit hour. *International tuition:* $13,061 full-time. *Required fees:* $955; $39.80 per credit hour. Tuition and fees vary according to degree level. *Financial support:* In 2019–20, 5 students received support, including 2 teaching assistantships with full tuition reimbursements available; career-related internships or fieldwork, Federal Work-Study, scholarships/grants, traineeships, tuition waivers (full), and unspecified assistantships also available. Financial award application deadline: 2/1; financial award applicants required to submit FAFSA. *Unit head:* Dr. Toni Alexander, Chairperson/Professor of History, 573-651-2146, Fax: 573-651-5114, E-mail: talexander@semo.edu. *Application contact:* Dr. Vicky McAlister, Graduate Coordinator/Assistant Professor of History, 573-651-2763, Fax: 573-651-5114, E-mail: vmcalister@semo.edu.
Website: https://semo.edu/history-anthropology/index.html

Southern Connecticut State University, School of Graduate Studies, School of Arts and Sciences, Department of History, New Haven, CT 06515-1355. Offers MA, MS. *Program availability:* Part-time, evening/weekend. *Degree requirements:* For master's, one foreign language, thesis. *Entrance requirements:* For master's, interview, undergraduate major or minor in history. Electronic applications accepted.

Southern Illinois University Carbondale, Graduate School, College of Liberal Arts, Department of History, Carbondale, IL 62901-4701. Offers MA, PhD. *Program availability:* Part-time. *Degree requirements:* For master's, one foreign language, research papers or thesis, written exams; for doctorate, 2 foreign languages, thesis/dissertation. *Entrance requirements:* For master's, GRE General Test, minimum GPA of 3.0; for doctorate, GRE General Test, minimum GPA of 3.25. Additional exam requirements/recommendations for international students: required—TOEFL.

Southern Illinois University Edwardsville, Graduate School, College of Arts and Sciences, Department of Historical Studies, Program in History, Edwardsville, IL 62026. Offers MA. *Program availability:* Part-time, evening/weekend. *Degree requirements:* For master's, one foreign language, thesis (for some programs), final exam. *Entrance requirements:* For master's, GRE. Additional exam requirements/recommendations for international students: required—TOEFL (minimum score 550 paper-based; 79 iBT), IELTS (minimum score 6.5). Electronic applications accepted.

Southern Methodist University, Dedman College of Humanities and Sciences, William P. Clements Department of History, Dallas, TX 75275. Offers American history (MA, PhD); global history (MA). *Program availability:* Part-time. Terminal master's awarded for partial completion of doctoral program. *Degree requirements:* For master's, one foreign language, thesis, oral exam, thesis defense; for doctorate, one foreign language, thesis/dissertation, oral exam, dissertation defense. *Entrance requirements:* For master's and doctorate, GRE General Test, minimum GPA of 3.0, 12 undergraduate hours in advanced level history, writing sample. Additional exam requirements/recommendations for international students: required—TOEFL. Electronic applications accepted.

Southern New Hampshire University, School of Arts and Sciences, Manchester, NH 03106-1045. Offers clinical mental health counseling (MS); creative writing (MA); criminal justice (MS); cyber security (MS); English (MA); fiction and nonfiction (MFA); history (MA); political science (MS); psychology (MS). *Program availability:* Part-time, evening/weekend. *Degree requirements:* For master's, one foreign language, thesis. *Entrance requirements:* For master's, minimum GPA of 3.0 (for MFA). Additional exam requirements/recommendations for international students: required—TOEFL (minimum score 550 paper-based; 79 iBT), IELTS (minimum score 6.5), TWE (minimum score 5). Electronic applications accepted. *Expenses:* Contact institution.

Southern University and Agricultural and Mechanical College, Graduate School, Nelson Mandela College of Government and Social Sciences, Department of History, Baton Rouge, LA 70813. Offers social sciences (MA). *Program availability:* Part-time. *Degree requirements:* For master's, thesis. *Entrance requirements:* For master's, GRE General Test. Additional exam requirements/recommendations for international students: required—TOEFL (minimum score 525 paper-based).

Southwestern Assemblies of God University, Thomas F. Harrison School of Graduate Studies, Program in History, Waxahachie, TX 75165-5735. Offers MA.

Stanford University, School of Humanities and Sciences, Department of History, Stanford, CA 94305-2004. Offers MA, PhD. *Expenses:* Tuition: Full-time $52,479; part-time $34,110 per unit. *Required fees:* $672; $224 per quarter. Tuition and fees vary according to program and student level.
Website: http://www.stanford.edu/dept/history/

State University of New York College at Cortland, Graduate Studies, School of Arts and Sciences, Department of History, Cortland, NY 13045. Offers MA. *Program availability:* Part-time, evening/weekend. *Degree requirements:* For master's, one foreign language, comprehensive exam, thesis optional. *Entrance requirements:* Additional exam requirements/recommendations for international students: required—TOEFL.

Stephen F. Austin State University, Graduate School, College of Liberal and Applied Arts, Department of History, Nacogdoches, TX 75962. Offers MA. *Program availability:* Part-time, evening/weekend. *Degree requirements:* For master's, comprehensive exam. *Entrance requirements:* For master's, GRE General Test. Additional exam requirements/recommendations for international students: required—TOEFL.

Stony Brook University, State University of New York, Graduate School, College of Arts and Sciences, Department of History, Stony Brook, NY 11794. Offers MA, PhD. *Program availability:* Evening/weekend. *Faculty:* 27 full-time (13 women), 2 part-time/adjunct (both women). *Students:* 48 full-time (22 women), 8 part-time (3 women); includes 8 minority (2 Black or African American, non-Hispanic/Latino; 1 Asian, non-Hispanic/Latino; 4 Hispanic/Latino; 1 Two or more races, non-Hispanic/Latino), 11 international. Average age 32. 31 applicants, 52% accepted, 7 enrolled. In 2019, 5 master's, 4 doctorates awarded. *Entrance requirements:* For master's and doctorate, GRE General Test. Additional exam requirements/recommendations for international students: required—TOEFL. *Application deadline:* For fall admission, 1/15 for domestic students; for spring admission, 10/1 for domestic students. Application fee: $100. Electronic applications accepted. *Expenses:* Contact institution. *Financial support:* In 2019–20, 4 fellowships, 27 teaching assistantships were awarded; research assistantships also available. *Unit head:* Dr. Sara Lipton, Interim Chair, 631-632-7500, Fax: 631-632-7367, E-mail: sara.lipton@stonybrook.edu. *Application contact:* Roxanne Fernandez, Coordinator, 631-632-7490, Fax: 631-632-7367, E-mail: roxanne.fernandez@stonybrook.edu.
Website: http://www.sunysb.edu/history/

Sul Ross State University, College of Arts and Sciences, Department of Behavioral and Social Sciences, Program in History, Alpine, TX 79832. Offers MA. *Program availability:* Part-time, evening/weekend. *Degree requirements:* For master's, thesis optional. *Entrance requirements:* For master's, GRE General Test, minimum GPA of 2.5 in last 60 hours of undergraduate work.

SUNY Brockport, School of Arts and Sciences, Department of History, Brockport, NY 14420-2997. Offers history (MA), including American and world history, American

history, American public history, world history. *Program availability:* Part-time, evening/weekend. *Faculty:* 9 full-time (4 women), 1 part-time/adjunct (0 women). *Students:* 6 full-time (2 women), 33 part-time (17 women); includes 2 minority (both Black or African American, non-Hispanic/Latino). 11 applicants, 91% accepted, 5 enrolled. In 2019, 17 master's awarded. *Entrance requirements:* For master's, minimum GPA of 3.0, writing sample, letters of recommendation, statement of objectives. Additional exam requirements/recommendations for international students: required—TOEFL (minimum score 550 paper-based; 79 iBT), IELTS (minimum score 6.5). *Application deadline:* For fall admission, 7/1 priority date for domestic and international students; for spring admission, 11/15 priority date for domestic and international students; for summer admission, 4/15 for domestic and international students. Application fee: $50. Electronic applications accepted. *Expenses: Tuition, area resident:* Part-time $471 per credit hour. Tuition, nonresident: part-time $963 per credit hour. *Financial support:* In 2019–20, 1 fellowship with tuition reimbursement (averaging $3,750 per year), 2 teaching assistantships with full tuition reimbursements (averaging $6,000 per year) were awarded; Federal Work-Study, scholarships/grants, and unspecified assistantships also available. Support available to part-time students. Financial award application deadline: 3/15; financial award applicants required to submit FAFSA. *Unit head:* Dr. Jose Torre, Chairperson, 585-395-5698, Fax: 585-395-2620, E-mail: jrtorre@brockport.edu. *Application contact:* Dr. Carl Davila, Graduate Director, 585-395-5699, Fax: 585-395-2620, E-mail: cdavila@brockport.edu.
Website: https://www.brockport.edu/academics/history/graduate/masters.html

Syracuse University, Maxwell School of Citizenship and Public Affairs, Programs in History, Syracuse, NY 13244. Offers MA, PhD. *Program availability:* Part-time. Terminal master's awarded for partial completion of doctoral program. *Degree requirements:* For master's, comprehensive exam, thesis or alternative; for doctorate, 2 foreign languages, comprehensive exam, thesis/dissertation. *Entrance requirements:* For master's and doctorate, GRE General Test, sample of written work, resume, personal statement, three letters of recommendation. Additional exam requirements/recommendations for international students: required—TOEFL (minimum score 100 iBT). Electronic applications accepted.

Tarleton State University, College of Graduate Studies, College of Liberal and Fine Arts, History, Sociology and Geography, Stephenville, TX 76402. Offers history (MA). *Program availability:* Part-time. *Faculty:* 20 full-time (8 women), 2 part-time/adjunct (0 women). *Students:* 2 full-time (0 women), 11 part-time (6 women); includes 4 minority (1 Asian, non-Hispanic/Latino; 3 Hispanic/Latino). Average age 29. 60 applicants, 77% accepted, 33 enrolled. *Degree requirements:* For master's, comprehensive exam, thesis optional. *Entrance requirements:* For master's, GRE General Test, minimum GPA of 2.5. Additional exam requirements/recommendations for international students: required—TOEFL (minimum score 520 paper-based; 69 iBT); recommended—IELTS (minimum score 6), TSE (minimum score 50). *Application deadline:* For fall admission, 8/15 priority date for domestic students; for spring admission, 1/7 for domestic students. Applications are processed on a rolling basis. Application fee: $50 ($130 for international students). Electronic applications accepted. *Expenses:* Tuition, state resident: part-time $221.73 per credit hour. Tuition, nonresident: part-time $636.73 per credit hour. *Required fees:* $198 per credit hour. $100 per semester. Tuition and fees vary according to degree level. *Financial support:* Research assistantships, teaching assistantships, career-related internships or fieldwork, and Federal Work-Study available. Support available to part-time students. Financial award application deadline: 5/1; financial award applicants required to submit FAFSA. *Unit head:* Dr. Opeyemi Zubair, Department Head, 254-968-9029, E-mail: zubair@tarleton.edu. *Application contact:* Wendy Weiss, Graduate Admissions Coordinator, 254-968-9104, Fax: 254-968-9670, E-mail: weiss@tarleton.edu.
Website: https://www.tarleton.edu/hsgg/index.html

Temple University, College of Liberal Arts, Department of History, Philadelphia, PA 19122-6096. Offers MA, PhD. *Program availability:* Part-time. *Faculty:* 21 full-time (8 women), 4 part-time/adjunct (0 women). *Students:* 51 full-time (17 women), 6 part-time (4 women); includes 7 minority (1 Black or African American, non-Hispanic/Latino; 1 American Indian or Alaska Native, non-Hispanic/Latino; 1 Asian, non-Hispanic/Latino; 3 Hispanic/Latino; 1 Two or more races, non-Hispanic/Latino), 4 international. 75 applicants, 55% accepted, 14 enrolled. In 2019, 8 master's, 11 doctorates awarded. *Degree requirements:* For master's, thesis optional; for doctorate, one foreign language, thesis/dissertation, general exam. *Entrance requirements:* For master's and doctorate, GRE, 3 letters of recommendation, statement of goals, writing sample. Additional exam requirements/recommendations for international students: required—TOEFL (minimum score 79 iBT), IELTS, PTE, one of three is required. Application fee: $60. Electronic applications accepted. *Financial support:* Fellowships, teaching assistantships, Federal Work-Study, and health care benefits available. Financial award applicants required to submit FAFSA. *Unit head:* Jay Lockenour, Chairperson, 215-204-7437, E-mail: jay.lockenour@temple.edu. *Application contact:* Djuna Witherspoon, Coordinator, 215-204-7839, E-mail: djuna@temple.edu.
Website: http://www.cla.temple.edu/history/

Texas A&M International University, Office of Graduate Studies and Research, College of Arts and Sciences, Department of Humanities, Laredo, TX 78041. Offers English (MA); history and political thought (MA); language, literature and translation (MA). *Degree requirements:* For master's, comprehensive exam (for some programs), thesis (for some programs). *Entrance requirements:* For master's, GRE General Test. Additional exam requirements/recommendations for international students: required—TOEFL (minimum score 550 paper-based; 79 iBT).

Texas A&M International University, Office of Graduate Studies and Research, College of Arts and Sciences, Department of Social Sciences, Laredo, TX 78041. Offers criminal justice (MS); history and political thought (MA); public administration (MPA); sociology (MA). *Degree requirements:* For master's, comprehensive exam (for some programs), thesis (for some programs). *Entrance requirements:* For master's, GRE General Test. Additional exam requirements/recommendations for international students: required—TOEFL (minimum score 550 paper-based; 79 iBT).

Texas A&M University, College of Liberal Arts, Department of History, College Station, TX 77843. Offers history (PhD). *Faculty:* 32. *Students:* 31 full-time (10 women), 19 part-time (6 women); includes 9 minority (all Hispanic/Latino), 1 international. Average age 35. 45 applicants, 40% accepted, 8 enrolled. In 2019, 1 master's, 6 doctorates awarded. Terminal master's awarded for partial completion of doctoral program. *Degree requirements:* For master's, one foreign language, comprehensive exam, thesis optional; for doctorate, one foreign language, comprehensive exam, thesis/dissertation. *Entrance requirements:* For master's and doctorate, GRE General Test, letters of recommendation, curriculum vitae, writing sample. Additional exam requirements/recommendations for international students: required—TOEFL (minimum score 550 paper-based; 80 iBT), IELTS (minimum score 6), PTE (minimum score 53). *Application deadline:* For fall admission, 12/15 for domestic students. Application fee: $65 ($90 for international students). Electronic applications accepted. *Expenses:* Contact institution. *Financial support:* In 2019–20, 37 students received support, including 4 fellowships with tuition reimbursements available (averaging $11,200 per year), 2 research assistantships with tuition reimbursements available (averaging $24,030 per year), 29 teaching assistantships with tuition reimbursements available (averaging $16,452 per

year); career-related internships or fieldwork, institutionally sponsored loans, scholarships/grants, traineeships, health care benefits, tuition waivers (full and partial), and unspecified assistantships also available. Support available to part-time students. Financial award application deadline: 3/15; financial award applicants required to submit FAFSA. *Unit head:* Dr. Carlos Blanton, Department Head, E-mail: ckblanton@tamu.edu. *Application contact:* Dr. Walter Kamphoefner, Director of Graduate Studies, 979-862-1314, E-mail: waltkamp@tamu.edu.
Website: https://liberalarts.tamu.edu/history/

Texas A&M University–Central Texas, Graduate Studies and Research, Killeen, TX 76549. Offers accounting (MS); business administration (MBA); clinical mental health counseling (MS); criminal justice (MCJ); curriculum and instruction (M Ed); educational administration (M Ed); educational psychology - experimental psychology (MS); history (MA); human resource management (MS); information systems (MS); liberal studies (MS); management and leadership (MS); marriage and family therapy (MS); mathematics (MS); political science (MA); school counseling (M Ed); school psychology (Ed S).

Texas A&M University–Commerce, College of Humanities, Social Sciences and Arts, Commerce, TX 75429. Offers applied criminology (MS); applied linguistics (MA, MS); art (MA, MFA); christianity in history (Graduate Certificate); computational linguistics (Graduate Certificate); creative writing (Graduate Certificate); criminal justice management (Graduate Certificate); criminal justice studies (Graduate Certificate); English (MA, MS, PhD); film studies (Graduate Certificate); history (MA, MS); Holocaust studies (Graduate Certificate); homeland security (Graduate Certificate); music (MM); music performance (MM); political science (MA, MS); public history (Graduate Certificate); sociology (MS); Spanish (MA); studies in children's and adolescent literature and culture (Graduate Certificate); teaching English to speakers of other languages (Graduate Certificate); theater (MA, MS); world history (Graduate Certificate). *Program availability:* Part-time. *Faculty:* 49 full-time (28 women), 8 part-time/adjunct (2 women). *Students:* 34 full-time (21 women), 427 part-time (302 women); includes 175 minority (66 Black or African American, non-Hispanic/Latino; 1 American Indian or Alaska Native, non-Hispanic/Latino; 13 Asian, non-Hispanic/Latino; 79 Hispanic/Latino; 16 Two or more races, non-Hispanic/Latino), 15 international. Average age 38. 193 applicants, 49% accepted, 78 enrolled. In 2019, 122 master's, 6 doctorates awarded. *Degree requirements:* For master's, one foreign language, comprehensive exam, thesis (for some programs); for doctorate, one foreign language, comprehensive exam, thesis/dissertation, departmental qualifying exam. *Entrance requirements:* For master's, GRE General Test, official transcripts, letters of recommendation, resume, statement of goals; for doctorate, GRE General Test, official transcripts, letters of recommendation, statement of goals, writing samples, writing sessions, resumes. Additional exam requirements/recommendations for international students: required—TOEFL (minimum score 550 paper-based; 79 iBT), IELTS (minimum score 6), PTE (minimum score 53). *Application deadline:* For fall admission, 6/1 priority date for international students; for spring admission, 10/15 priority date for international students; for summer admission, 3/15 priority date for international students. Applications are processed on a rolling basis. Application fee: $50 ($75 for international students). Electronic applications accepted. *Expenses: Tuition, area resident:* Full-time $3630; part-time $202 per credit hour. Tuition, state resident: full-time $3630; part-time $202 per credit hour. Tuition, nonresident: full-time $11,232; part-time $624 per credit hour. *International tuition:* $11,232 full-time. *Required fees:* $2948. *Financial support:* In 2019–20, 30 students received support, including 18 research assistantships with partial tuition reimbursements available (averaging $3,231 per year), 136 teaching assistantships with partial tuition reimbursements available (averaging $4,053 per year); Federal Work-Study, institutionally sponsored loans, scholarships/grants, health care benefits, and unspecified assistantships also available. Financial award application deadline: 5/1; financial award applicants required to submit FAFSA. *Unit head:* Dr. William F. Kuracina, Interim Dean, 903-886-5166, Fax: 903-886-5774, E-mail: william.kuracina@tamuc.edu. *Application contact:* Rebecca Stevens, Graduate Student Services Coordinator, 903-468-6049, E-mail: rebecca.stevens@tamuc.edu.
Website: http://www.tamuc.edu/academics/colleges/humanitiesSocialSciencesArts/

Texas A&M University–Corpus Christi, College of Graduate Studies, College of Liberal Arts, Corpus Christi, TX 78412. Offers communication (MA); English (MA); history (MA); psychology (MA), including clinical psychology, general psychology; public administration (MPA); studio art (MFA). *Program availability:* Part-time, evening/weekend. *Degree requirements:* For master's, comprehensive exam (for some programs). *Entrance requirements:* For master's, portfolio. Additional exam requirements/recommendations for international students: required—TOEFL (minimum score 550 paper-based; 79 iBT), IELTS (minimum score 6.5). Electronic applications accepted.

Texas Christian University, AddRan College of Liberal Arts, Department of History, Fort Worth, TX 76129-0002. Offers Latin America (MA, PhD); United States (MA, PhD). *Faculty:* 16 full-time (6 women). *Students:* 47 full-time (20 women); includes 8 minority (1 Black or African American, non-Hispanic/Latino; 6 Hispanic/Latino; 1 Two or more races, non-Hispanic/Latino), 2 international. Average age 35. 25 applicants, 48% accepted, 8 enrolled. In 2019, 2 master's, 3 doctorates awarded. Terminal master's awarded for partial completion of doctoral program. *Degree requirements:* For master's, comprehensive exam, thesis or alternative; for doctorate, one foreign language, comprehensive exam, thesis/dissertation. *Entrance requirements:* For master's and doctorate, GRE General Test. Additional exam requirements/recommendations for international students: recommended—TOEFL. *Application deadline:* 2/1 for domestic and international students; for summer admission, 2/1 for domestic and international students. Application fee: $60. Electronic applications accepted. Full-time tuition and fees vary according to program. *Financial support:* In 2019–20, 50 students received support, including 3 fellowships with full tuition reimbursements available (averaging $25,000 per year), 15 research assistantships with full tuition reimbursements available (averaging $20,000 per year), 5 teaching assistantships with full tuition reimbursements available (averaging $20,000 per year); tuition waivers (full) also available. Financial award application deadline: 2/1. *Unit head:* Dr. William Meier, Associate Professor, 817-257-5882, Fax: 817-257-5650, E-mail: w.meier@tcu.edu. *Application contact:* Heather Confessore, Administrative Assistant, 817-257-7288, Fax: 817-257-5650, E-mail: h.confessore@tcu.edu.
Website: https://addran.tcu.edu/history/academics/areas-of-study/graduate-programs/

Texas Southern University, College of Liberal Arts and Behavioral Sciences, Department of History and Geography, Houston, TX 77004-4584. Offers history (MA). *Program availability:* Part-time, evening/weekend. *Degree requirements:* For master's, comprehensive exam, thesis optional. *Entrance requirements:* For master's, GRE General Test, minimum GPA of 2.5. Additional exam requirements/recommendations for international students: required—TOEFL. Electronic applications accepted.

Texas State University, The Graduate College, College of Liberal Arts, Program in History, San Marcos, TX 78666. Offers M Ed, MA. *Program availability:* Part-time. *Degree requirements:* For master's, comprehensive exam, thesis optional. *Entrance requirements:* For master's, official GRE (general test only) required with competitive scores in the verbal reasoning section, baccalaureate degree from regionally-accredited university with minimum GPA of 2.75 on last 60 undergraduate semester hours, 3.25 on 24 hours of undergraduate history course work; description of foreign language competencies; resume; statement of purpose describing interest in history and work experience; 2 letters of recommendation. Additional exam requirements/recommendations for international students: required—TOEFL (minimum score 550 paper-based; 78 iBT), IELTS (minimum score 6.5). Electronic applications accepted.

Texas Tech University, Graduate School, College of Arts and Sciences, Department of History, Lubbock, TX 79409-1013. Offers MA, PhD. *Program availability:* Part-time, evening/weekend. *Faculty:* 31 full-time (11 women), 2 part-time/adjunct (0 women). *Students:* 60 full-time (29 women), 21 part-time (4 women); includes 20 minority (3 Black or African American, non-Hispanic/Latino; 1 American Indian or Alaska Native, non-Hispanic/Latino; 1 Asian, non-Hispanic/Latino; 10 Hispanic/Latino; 1 Native Hawaiian or other Pacific Islander, non-Hispanic/Latino; 4 Two or more races, non-Hispanic/Latino), 8 international. Average age 33. 26 applicants, 73% accepted, 13 enrolled. In 2019, 10 master's, 1 doctorate awarded. *Degree requirements:* For master's, one foreign language, comprehensive exam (for some programs), thesis optional; for doctorate, one foreign language, comprehensive exam, thesis/dissertation. *Entrance requirements:* For master's and doctorate, GRE, statement of purpose, 3 letters of reference, writing sample. Additional exam requirements/recommendations for international students: required—TOEFL (minimum score 550 paper-based; 79 iBT). *Application deadline:* For fall admission, 6/1 priority date for domestic students, 1/15 priority date for international students; for spring admission, 9/1 priority date for domestic students, 6/15 priority date for international students. Applications are processed on a rolling basis. Application fee: $65. Electronic applications accepted. *Expenses:* Contact institution. *Financial support:* In 2019–20, 65 students received support, including 63 fellowships (averaging $2,781 per year), 58 teaching assistantships (averaging $15,898 per year); research assistantships, scholarships/grants, health care benefits, and unspecified assistantships also available. Financial award application deadline: 3/15; financial award applicants required to submit FAFSA. *Unit head:* Dr. Sean P. Cunningham, Associate Professor and Chair, 806-742-3744, Fax: 806-742-1060, E-mail: sean.cunningham@ttu.edu. *Application contact:* Dr. Richard Verrone, Graduate Program Coordinator, 806-742-3744, Fax: 806-742-1060, E-mail: richard.verrone@ttu.edu.
Website: www.history.ttu.edu

Texas Woman's University, Graduate School, College of Arts and Sciences, Department of History and Political Science, Denton, TX 76204. Offers government (MA); history (MA). *Program availability:* Part-time, evening/weekend. *Faculty:* 8 full-time (3 women), 1 part-time/adjunct (0 women). *Students:* 8 full-time (5 women), 19 part-time (13 women); includes 11 minority (4 Black or African American, non-Hispanic/Latino; 1 American Indian or Alaska Native, non-Hispanic/Latino; 3 Asian, non-Hispanic/Latino; 2 Hispanic/Latino; 1 Two or more races, non-Hispanic/Latino). Average age 31. 11 applicants, 91% accepted, 8 enrolled. In 2019, 5 master's awarded. *Degree requirements:* For master's, comprehensive exam, thesis or alternative, professional paper or thesis; exam is a defense of the thesis or professional paper. *Entrance requirements:* For master's, minimum GPA of 3.25 on last 60 undergraduate hours, writing sample, curriculum vitae, 3 references. Additional exam requirements/recommendations for international students: required—TOEFL (minimum score 79 iBT); recommended—IELTS (minimum score 6.5), TSE (minimum score 53). *Application deadline:* For fall admission, 3/1 priority date for domestic and international students; for spring admission, 11/1 priority date for domestic students, 7/1 priority date for international students; for summer admission, 5/1 priority date for domestic students, 2/1 priority date for international students. Applications are processed on a rolling basis. Application fee: $50 ($75 for international students). Electronic applications accepted. *Expenses: Tuition, area resident:* Full-time $4973.40; part-time $276.30 per semester hour. Tuition, state resident: full-time $4973.40; part-time $276.30 per semester hour. Tuition, nonresident: full-time $12,569; part-time $698.30 per semester hour. *International tuition:* $12,569.40 full-time. *Required fees:* $2524.30. Tuition and fees vary according to course level, course load, degree level and program. *Financial support:* In 2019–20, 14 students received support, including 12 teaching assistantships (averaging $10,385 per year); career-related internships or fieldwork, scholarships/grants, health care benefits, and unspecified assistantships also available. Support available to part-time students. Financial award application deadline: 3/1; financial award applicants required to submit FAFSA. *Unit head:* Dr. Jonathan Olsen, Chair, 940-898-2133, Fax: 940-898-2130, E-mail: historygov@twu.edu. *Application contact:* Korie Hawkins, Associate Director of Admissions, Graduate Recruitment, 940-898-3188, Fax: 940-898-3081, E-mail: admissions@twu.edu.
Website: http://www.twu.edu/history-government/

Trinity Western University, School of Graduate Studies, Master of Arts in Interdisciplinary Humanities, Langley, BC V2Y 1Y1, Canada. Offers general humanities (MAIH); specialized (MAIH), including English, history, philosophy. *Program availability:* Part-time. *Degree requirements:* For master's, thesis or alternative, 30 semester hours. *Entrance requirements:* For master's, Strong undergraduate degree in humanities or English, history or philosophy. Additional exam requirements/recommendations for international students: required—TOEFL (minimum score 105 iBT), IELTS (minimum score 7.5), DuoLingo. *Application deadline:* Applications are processed on a rolling basis. Electronic applications accepted. *Expenses:* Contact institution. *Financial support:* Fellowships, research assistantships, teaching assistantships, career-related internships or fieldwork, scholarships/grants, and unspecified assistantships available. Support available to part-time students. Financial award application deadline: 4/1. *Unit head:* Dr. Bruce Shelvey, Director, E-mail: bruce.shelvey@twu.ca. *Application contact:* Phil Kay, Director, Graduate Admissions, 604-513-2121 Ext. 3444, E-mail: phil.kay@twu.ca.
Website: http://www.twu.ca/academics/

Troy University, Graduate School, College of Arts and Sciences, Program in History, Troy, AL 36082. Offers American history (MA); European history (MA). *Program availability:* Part-time, evening/weekend. *Faculty:* 1 full-time (0 women), 1 part-time/adjunct (0 women). *Students:* 4 part-time (0 women); includes 1 minority (Two or more races, non-Hispanic/Latino). Average age 34. 1 applicant, 100% accepted. *Degree requirements:* For master's, variable foreign language requirement, comprehensive exam, thesis optional. *Entrance requirements:* For master's, GRE 290 (recommended:150 verbal, 140 quantitative) and GRE writing score. If student has taken the MCAT (recommended: 487), DAT (recommended: 16) or equivalent professional exam, then this may be substituted for the GRE, bachelor's degree, minimum undergraduate GPA of 2.5 or 3.0 on last 30 semester hours, letter of recommendation. Additional exam requirements/recommendations for international students: required—TOEFL (minimum score 523 paper-based; 70 iBT), IELTS (minimum score 6); recommended—TWE. *Application deadline:* For fall admission, 6/1 for international students; for spring admission, 10/15 for international students. Applications are processed on a rolling basis. Application fee: $50. Electronic applications accepted. *Expenses: Tuition, area resident:* Full-time $7650; part-time $2550 per semester hour. Tuition, state resident: full-time $7650; part-time $2550 per semester hour. Tuition, nonresident: full-time $15,300; part-time $5100 per semester hour. *International tuition:* $15,300 full-time. *Required fees:* $856; $352 per semester hour. $176 per semester. *Financial support:* Fellowships, research assistantships, teaching assistantships, career-related internships or fieldwork, Federal Work-Study, scholarships/grants, traineeships, tuition waivers, and unspecified assistantships available. Support available to part-time students. Financial award application deadline: 3/1; financial award applicants required to submit FAFSA. *Unit head:* Dr. Allen E. Jones, Jr., Chairman, 334-670-3512, E-mail: ajones@troy.edu. *Application contact:* Haley McKinnon, Director of Graduate Admissions, 334-670-3178, Fax: 334-670-3733, E-mail: hmckinnon@troy.edu. Website: https://www.troy.edu/academics/academic-programs/college-arts-sciences-programs.php

Tufts University, Graduate School of Arts and Sciences, Department of History, Medford, MA 02155. Offers history (MA, PhD), including global history (PhD); history and museum studies (MA). Terminal master's awarded for partial completion of doctoral program. *Degree requirements:* For master's, one foreign language, thesis optional; for doctorate, 2 foreign languages, comprehensive exam, thesis/dissertation. *Entrance requirements:* For master's and doctorate, GRE General Test, writing sample. Additional exam requirements/recommendations for international students: required—TOEFL (minimum score 550 paper-based; 80 iBT), IELTS (minimum score 6.5). Electronic applications accepted. *Expenses:* Contact institution.

Tulane University, School of Liberal Arts, Department of History, New Orleans, LA 70118-5669. Offers MA, PhD. *Degree requirements:* For master's, one foreign language, thesis; for doctorate, variable foreign language requirement, thesis/dissertation. *Entrance requirements:* For master's, GRE General Test, minimum B average in undergraduate course work; for doctorate, GRE General Test. Additional exam requirements/recommendations for international students: required—TOEFL. Electronic applications accepted. *Expenses:* Tuition: Full-time $57,004; part-time $3167 per credit hour. *Required fees:* $2086; $44.50 per credit hour. $80 per term. Tuition and fees vary according to course load, degree level and program.

UNB Fredericton, School of Graduate Studies, Faculty of Arts - Saint John, Department of History, Fredericton, NB E3B 5A3, Canada. Offers MA, PhD. *Program availability:* Part-time. *Faculty:* 13 full-time (8 women), 3 part-time/adjunct (2 women). *Students:* 27 full-time (14 women), 15 part-time (2 women), 4 international. Average age 39. In 2019, 5 master's awarded. *Degree requirements:* For master's, one foreign language, thesis, language depends on subject nationality, canadian history subject specialist require english and french; for doctorate, one foreign language, thesis/dissertation, language depends on subject nationality, canadian history subject specialist require english and french. *Entrance requirements:* For master's, minimum GPA of 3.0, resume, writing sample, statement of research interests, honors degree in history or equivalent; for doctorate, minimum GPA of 3.0, statement of research interests, writing sample, master's degree in history. Additional exam requirements/recommendations for international students: required—TWE (minimum score 5.5), TOEFL (minimum paper-based score 600) or IELTS (minimum score 7). *Application deadline:* For fall admission, 3/1 for domestic students; for winter admission, 1/15 priority date for domestic and international students. Applications are processed on a rolling basis. Application fee: $50 Canadian dollars. Electronic applications accepted. *Expenses:* Tuition, area resident: Full-time $6975 Canadian dollars; part-time $3423 Canadian dollars per year. Tuition, state resident: full-time $6975 Canadian dollars; part-time $3423 Canadian dollars per year. Tuition, Canadian resident: full-time $6975 Canadian dollars; part-time $3423 Canadian dollars per year. *International tuition:* $12,435 Canadian dollars full-time. *Required fees:* $92.25 Canadian dollars per term. Full-time tuition and fees vary according to degree level, campus/location, program, reciprocity agreements and student level. *Financial support:* Fellowships, research assistantships, teaching assistantships, and scholarships/grants available. Financial award application deadline: 1/31. *Unit head:* Dr. Lisa Todd, Director of Graduate Studies, 506-458 7421, Fax: 506-453-5068, E-mail: ltodd@unb.ca. *Application contact:* Elizabeth Arnold, Graduate Secretary, 506-458-7471, Fax: 506-453-5068, E-mail: eliz@unb.ca. Website: http://go.unb.ca/gradprograms

Union Institute & University, Master of Arts Program, Cincinnati, OH 45206-1925. Offers creativity studies (MA); health and wellness (MA); history and culture (MA); leadership, public policy, and social issues (MA); literature and writing (MA). *Program availability:* Part-time, online only, 100% online. *Degree requirements:* For master's, thesis. *Entrance requirements:* For master's, transcript, essay, 3 letters of recommendation, resume. Additional exam requirements/recommendations for international students: recommended—TOEFL. Electronic applications accepted. *Expenses:* Contact institution.

Université de Moncton, Faculty of Arts and Social Sciences, Department of History and Geography, Moncton, NB E1A 3E9, Canada. Offers history (MA). *Degree requirements:* For master's, thesis, proficiency in English and French. *Entrance requirements:* For master's, honors degree in history, minimum GPA of 2.7. Electronic applications accepted.

Université de Montréal, Faculty of Arts and Sciences, Department of History, Montréal, QC H3C 3J7, Canada. Offers MA, PhD. *Degree requirements:* For master's, thesis; for doctorate, thesis/dissertation, general exam. *Entrance requirements:* For doctorate, master's degree in related field. Electronic applications accepted.

Université de Sherbrooke, Faculty of Letters and Human Sciences, Department of Human Sciences, Sherbrooke, QC J1K 2R1, Canada. Offers history (MA); philosophy (MA). *Degree requirements:* For master's, thesis. *Entrance requirements:* For master's, minimum GPA of 2.75.

Université du Québec à Montréal, Graduate Programs, Program in History, Montréal, QC H3C 3P8, Canada. Offers MA, PhD. *Program availability:* Part-time. *Degree requirements:* For master's, thesis; for doctorate, thesis/dissertation. *Entrance requirements:* For master's, appropriate bachelor's degree or equivalent, proficiency in French; for doctorate, appropriate master's degree or equivalent, proficiency in French.

University at Albany, State University of New York, College of Arts and Sciences, Department of History, Albany, NY 12222-0001. Offers history (MA, PhD); public history (Certificate). *Program availability:* Part-time, blended/hybrid learning. *Faculty:* 21 full-time (7 women), 14 part-time/adjunct (11 women). *Students:* 24 full-time (11 women), 50 part-time (19 women); includes 7 minority (2 Black or African American, non-Hispanic/Latino; 1 Asian, non-Hispanic/Latino; 2 Hispanic/Latino; 2 Two or more races, non-Hispanic/Latino), 3 international. 30 applicants, 70% accepted, 15 enrolled. In 2019, 7 master's, 4 doctorates awarded. *Degree requirements:* For master's, variable foreign language requirement, exam, research paper or thesis; for doctorate, thesis/dissertation. *Entrance requirements:* For master's, minimum GPA of 3.0, transcripts of all schools attended, statement of background and goals, departmental questionnaire, resume, names and contact information for 3 recommenders; for doctorate, GRE General Test, minimum GPA of 3.0, transcripts of all schools attended, statement of background and goals, departmental questionnaire, resume, names and contact information for 3 recommenders. Additional exam requirements/recommendations for international students: required—TOEFL (minimum score 550 paper-based). *Application deadline:* For fall admission, 7/15 for domestic students, 5/1 for international students; for spring admission, 11/15 for domestic students, 11/1 for international students. Applications are processed on a rolling basis. Application fee: $75. Electronic applications accepted. *Expenses:* Tuition, area resident: Full-time $11,530; part-time $480 per credit hour. Tuition, nonresident: full-time $23,530; part-time $980 per credit hour. *International tuition:* $23,530 full-time. *Required fees:* $2185; $96 per credit hour. Part-time tuition

and fees vary according to course load and program. *Financial support:* Teaching assistantships and career-related internships or fieldwork available. Financial award application deadline: 3/1. *Unit head:* Patrick Nold, Chair, 518-442-5300, Fax: 518-442-5301, E-mail: rhamm@albany.edu. *Application contact:* Michael DeRensis, Director, Graduate Admissions, 518-442-3980, Fax: 518-442-3922, E-mail: graduate@albany.edu. Website: https://www.albany.edu/history/

University at Buffalo, the State University of New York, Graduate School, College of Arts and Sciences, Department of History, Buffalo, NY 14260. Offers history (MA, PhD, Advanced Certificate); public history (MA). *Program availability:* Part-time. Terminal master's awarded for partial completion of doctoral program. *Degree requirements:* For master's, project; for doctorate, one foreign language, comprehensive exam, thesis/dissertation. *Entrance requirements:* For doctorate, GRE General Test. Additional exam requirements/recommendations for international students: required—TOEFL (minimum score 550 paper-based; 79 iBT). Electronic applications accepted. *Expenses:* Contact institution.

The University of Akron, Graduate School, Buchtel College of Arts and Sciences, Department of History, Akron, OH 44325. Offers MA, PhD. *Program availability:* Part-time. *Entrance requirements:* For master's, GRE General Test, minimum GPA of 3.0, writing sample, three letters of recommendation, letter of intent; for doctorate, GRE General Test, minimum GPA of 3.5, three letters of recommendation, personal statement, writing sample, evidence of reading knowledge in one foreign language. Additional exam requirements/recommendations for international students: required—TOEFL (minimum score 92 iBT). Electronic applications accepted.

The University of Alabama, Graduate School, College of Arts and Sciences, Department of History, Tuscaloosa, AL 35487. Offers MA, PhD. *Faculty:* 17 full-time (8 women). *Students:* 48 full-time (23 women), 2 part-time (0 women); includes 4 minority (2 Black or African American, non-Hispanic/Latino; 1 Hispanic/Latino; 1 Two or more races, non-Hispanic/Latino), 2 international. Average age 30. 39 applicants, 62% accepted, 12 enrolled. In 2019, 14 master's, 2 doctorates awarded. Terminal master's awarded for partial completion of doctoral program. *Degree requirements:* For master's, one foreign language, thesis optional, oral exam; for doctorate, 2 foreign languages, comprehensive exam, thesis/dissertation, oral exams, written exam. *Entrance requirements:* For master's and doctorate, GRE General Test. Additional exam requirements/recommendations for international students: required—TOEFL (minimum score 79 paper-based), IELTS (minimum score 6.5), PTE (minimum score 59), Duolingo during Covid-19 crisis. *Application deadline:* For fall admission, 12/15 for domestic and international students. Applications are processed on a rolling basis. Application fee: $50 ($60 for international students). *Expenses: Tuition, area resident:* Full-time $10,780; part-time $440 per credit hour. Tuition, nonresident: full-time $30,250; part-time $1550 per credit hour. *Financial support:* In 2019–20, 37 students received support, including fellowships with full tuition reimbursements available (averaging $10,000 per year), research assistantships (averaging $10,000 per year), teaching assistantships with full tuition reimbursements available (averaging $10,200 per year); institutionally sponsored loans and unspecified assistantships also available. Financial award application deadline: 12/15; financial award applicants required to submit FAFSA. *Unit head:* Dr. Andrew Huebner, Interim Chair and Professor, 205-348-1864, E-mail: ahuebner@ua.edu. *Application contact:* Dr. Daniel Riches, Director of Graduate Studies, 205-348-1825, E-mail: dlriches@ua.edu.

The University of Alabama at Birmingham, College of Arts and Sciences, Program in History, Birmingham, AL 35294. Offers MA. *Program availability:* Part-time. *Faculty:* 15 full-time (5 women). *Students:* 8 full-time (5 women), 5 part-time (1 woman). Average age 37. 5 applicants, 100% accepted, 4 enrolled. In 2019, 9 master's awarded. *Degree requirements:* For master's, variable foreign language requirement, thesis or alternative. *Entrance requirements:* For master's, GRE General Test. Additional exam requirements/recommendations for international students: required—TOEFL, TWE. *Application deadline:* For fall admission, 7/1 for domestic students; for spring admission, 11/1 for domestic students. Applications are processed on a rolling basis. Application fee: $45 ($60 for international students). Electronic applications accepted. *Financial support:* Research assistantships, teaching assistantships, and institutionally sponsored loans available. *Unit head:* Dr. John Van Sant, Program Director, 205-975-6520, E-mail: jvansant@uab.edu. *Application contact:* Susan Noblitt Banks, Director of Graduate School Operations, 205-934-8227, Fax: 205-934-8413, E-mail: gradschool@uab.edu. Website: http://www.uab.edu/cas/history/graduate-program

The University of Alabama in Huntsville, School of Graduate Studies, College of Arts, Humanities, and Social Sciences, Department of History, Huntsville, AL 35899. Offers MA. *Program availability:* Part-time. *Degree requirements:* For master's, one foreign language, comprehensive exam, thesis or alternative, oral and written exams. *Entrance requirements:* For master's, GRE General Test, minimum GPA of 3.0, bachelor's degree in history or related area. Additional exam requirements/recommendations for international students: required—TOEFL (minimum score 500 paper-based; 80 iBT), IELTS (minimum score 6.5). Electronic applications accepted.

University of Alaska Fairbanks, College of Liberal Arts, Department of Arctic and Northern Studies, Fairbanks, AK 99775-6460. Offers Arctic policy (MA); environmental politics and policy (MA); Northern history (MA). *Program availability:* Part-time, blended/hybrid learning. *Degree requirements:* For master's, comprehensive exam, oral defense of project or thesis. *Entrance requirements:* For master's, bachelor's degree from accredited institution, preference given to applicants with 3.0 GPA or higher. Additional exam requirements/recommendations for international students: required—TOEFL (minimum score 550 paper-based; 79 iBT), IELTS (minimum score 6.5). Electronic applications accepted.

University of Alberta, Faculty of Graduate Studies and Research, Department of History and Classics, Edmonton, AB T6G 2E1, Canada. Offers ancient history (PhD); classical archaeology (MA, PhD); classical literature (PhD); classics (MA); history (MA, PhD). *Program availability:* Part-time, evening/weekend. *Degree requirements:* For master's, one foreign language, thesis (for some programs); for doctorate, one foreign language, thesis/dissertation. *Entrance requirements:* For master's, minimum B+ average; for doctorate, minimum A- average. Additional exam requirements/recommendations for international students: required—TOEFL (minimum score 580 paper-based). Electronic applications accepted.

The University of Arizona, College of Social and Behavioral Sciences, Department of History, Tucson, AZ 85721. Offers MA, PhD, Graduate Certificate. *Program availability:* Part-time. Terminal master's awarded for partial completion of doctoral program. *Degree requirements:* For master's, one foreign language, comprehensive exam, thesis optional; for doctorate, 2 foreign languages, comprehensive exam, thesis/dissertation. *Entrance requirements:* For master's, GRE General Test, 3 letters of recommendation, writing sample; for doctorate, GRE General Test, 3 letters of recommendation, statement of purpose, 2 writing samples. Additional exam requirements/recommendations for international students: required—TOEFL (minimum score 550 paper-based; 79 iBT). Electronic applications accepted.

University of Arkansas, Graduate School, J. William Fulbright College of Arts and Sciences, Department of History, Fayetteville, AR 72701. Offers MA, PhD. *Program*

availability: Part-time. *Students:* 27 full-time (12 women), 14 part-time (6 women); includes 4 minority (1 Black or African American, non-Hispanic/Latino; 1 Asian, non-Hispanic/Latino; 2 Two or more races, non-Hispanic/Latino), 4 international. 17 applicants, 71% accepted. In 2019, 2 master's, 7 doctorates awarded. *Degree requirements:* For master's, thesis optional; for doctorate, 2 foreign languages, thesis/dissertation. *Entrance requirements:* For master's, GRE General Test; for doctorate, GRE General Test, GRE Subject Test. *Application deadline:* For fall admission, 8/1 for domestic students, 4/1 for international students; for spring admission, 12/1 for domestic students, 10/1 for international students; for summer admission, 4/15 for domestic students, 3/1 for international students. Applications are processed on a rolling basis. Application fee: $60. Electronic applications accepted. *Financial support:* In 2019–20, 9 research assistantships, 9 teaching assistantships were awarded; fellowships with tuition reimbursements, career-related internships or fieldwork, and Federal Work-Study also available. Support available to part-time students. Financial award application deadline: 4/1; financial award applicants required to submit FAFSA. *Unit head:* Dr. Jim Gigantino, II, Department Chair, 479-575-7332, E-mail: jgiganti@uark.edu. *Application contact:* Dr. Todd Cleveland, Associate Chair and Dir. of Graduate Studies, 479-575-7596, E-mail: tcclevel@uark.edu.
Website: https://fulbright.uark.edu/departments/history/

The University of British Columbia, Faculty of Arts, Department of History, Vancouver, BC V6T 1Z1, Canada. Offers history (MA, PhD). *Faculty:* 33 full-time (11 women). *Students:* 51 full-time (21 women). 105 applicants, 22% accepted, 14 enrolled. In 2019, 11 master's, 1 doctorate awarded. *Degree requirements:* For master's, one foreign language, thesis, six 3-credit courses; for doctorate, one foreign language, comprehensive exam, thesis/dissertation, five 3-credit courses. *Entrance requirements:* For master's, four-year bachelor's degree; for doctorate, master's degree (or equivalent) in history, first-class (A) standing in graduate courses, language relevant to dissertation research. Additional exam requirements/recommendations for international students: required—TOEFL (minimum score 90 iBT). *Application deadline:* For fall admission, 12/15 for domestic and international students. Application fee: $104 Canadian dollars ($168 Canadian dollars for international students). Electronic applications accepted. *Financial support:* In 2019–20, 36 students received support, including 15 fellowships with partial tuition reimbursements available (averaging $18,000 per year), 3 research assistantships (averaging $3,000 per year), 30 teaching assistantships (averaging $12,000 per year); scholarships/grants, tuition waivers (partial), and unspecified assistantships also available. *Unit head:* Dr. John Roosa, Department Head, 604-822-5175, Fax: 604-822-6658, E-mail: jroosa@mail.ubc.ca. *Application contact:* Jason Wu, Graduate Student Support, 604-822-6070, Fax: 604-822-6658, E-mail: hist.grad@ubc.ca.
Website: https://www.history.ubc.ca/

University of Calgary, Faculty of Graduate Studies, Faculty of Arts, Program in History, Calgary, AB T2N 1N4, Canada. Offers MA, PhD. *Program availability:* Part-time. *Degree requirements:* For master's, one foreign language, thesis; for doctorate, one foreign language, thesis/dissertation, 3 written comprehensive exams, oral candidacy exam. *Entrance requirements:* For master's, minimum GPA of 3.4, writing sample; for doctorate, sample of written work, master's degree in history. Additional exam requirements/recommendations for international students: recommended—TOEFL. Electronic applications accepted.

University of California, Berkeley, Graduate Division, College of Letters and Science, Department of History, Berkeley, CA 94720-2550. Offers PhD. *Degree requirements:* For doctorate, variable foreign language requirement, comprehensive exam, thesis/dissertation. *Entrance requirements:* For doctorate, GRE General Test, minimum GPA of 3.0, 3 letters of recommendation, writing sample (not to exceed 10 pages), academic transcripts, 2 essays (statement of purpose, personal statement). Additional exam requirements/recommendations for international students: required—TOEFL (minimum score 570 paper-based; 68 iBT). Electronic applications accepted.

University of California, Berkeley, Graduate Division, College of Letters and Science, Group in Ancient History and Mediterranean Archaeology, Berkeley, CA 94720. Offers MA, PhD. Terminal master's awarded for partial completion of doctoral program. *Degree requirements:* For master's, one foreign language, exam or thesis; for doctorate, 2 foreign languages, thesis/dissertation, qualifying exam. *Entrance requirements:* For master's and doctorate, GRE General Test, minimum GPA of 3.0, 3 letters of recommendation. Additional exam requirements/recommendations for international students: required—TOEFL (minimum score 570 paper-based; 90 iBT), TWE. Electronic applications accepted.

University of California, Davis, Graduate Studies, Program in History, Davis, CA 95616. Offers MA, PhD. Terminal master's awarded for partial completion of doctoral program. *Degree requirements:* For master's, one foreign language, comprehensive exam (for some programs), thesis (for some programs); for doctorate, 2 foreign languages, thesis/dissertation. *Entrance requirements:* For master's, GRE General Test, minimum GPA of 3.0, writing sample; for doctorate, GRE General Test, master's degree, writing sample. Additional exam requirements/recommendations for international students: required—TOEFL (minimum score 550 paper-based). Electronic applications accepted.

University of California, Irvine, School of Humanities, Department of History, Irvine, CA 92697. Offers MA, PhD. *Students:* 41 full-time (20 women); includes 15 minority (2 Black or African American, non-Hispanic/Latino; 4 Asian, non-Hispanic/Latino; 6 Hispanic/Latino; 3 Two or more races, non-Hispanic/Latino), 12 international. Average age 31. 80 applicants, 26% accepted, 10 enrolled. In 2019, 2 master's, 8 doctorates awarded. *Entrance requirements:* For master's and doctorate, GRE General Test, minimum GPA of 3.0. Additional exam requirements/recommendations for international students: required—TOEFL (minimum score 550 paper-based). *Application deadline:* For fall admission, 1/2 priority date for domestic students, 1/2 for international students. Application fee: $120 ($140 for international students). Electronic applications accepted. *Financial support:* Fellowships, research assistantships with full tuition reimbursements, teaching assistantships, institutionally sponsored loans, traineeships, health care benefits, and unspecified assistantships available. Financial award application deadline: 3/1; financial award applicants required to submit FAFSA. *Unit head:* Prof. David Igler, Chair, 949-824-9313, E-mail: digler@uci.edu. *Application contact:* Yuting Wu, Graduate Coordinator, 949-824-5891, E-mail: yutingw6@uci.edu.
Website: http://www.hnet.uci.edu/history/

University of California, Los Angeles, Graduate Division, College of Letters and Science, Department of History, Los Angeles, CA 90095. Offers MA, PhD, MLIS/MA. Terminal master's awarded for partial completion of doctoral program. *Degree requirements:* For master's, one foreign language, comprehensive exam; for doctorate, variable foreign language requirement, thesis/dissertation, oral and written qualifying exams. *Entrance requirements:* For doctorate, GRE General Test, bachelor's degree; minimum undergraduate GPA of 3.0, 3.5 graduate (or its equivalent if letter grade system not used). Additional exam requirements/recommendations for international students: required—TOEFL. Electronic applications accepted.

University of California, Riverside, Graduate Division, Department of History, Riverside, CA 92521-0102. Offers archival management (MA); history (PhD). *Program availability:* Part-time. Terminal master's awarded for partial completion of doctoral program. *Degree requirements:* For master's, one foreign language, comprehensive exam, internship report and oral exams, or thesis; for doctorate, 2 foreign languages, thesis/dissertation, qualifying exams. *Entrance requirements:* For master's and doctorate, GRE General Test, minimum GPA of 3.2. Additional exam requirements/recommendations for international students: required—TOEFL (minimum score 550 paper-based; 80 iBT). Electronic applications accepted.

University of California, San Diego, Graduate Division, Department of History, La Jolla, CA 92093. Offers history (MA, PhD); Judaic studies (MA). *Students:* 74 full-time (32 women), 1 (woman) part-time. 121 applicants, 21% accepted, 7 enrolled. In 2019, 7 master's, 12 doctorates awarded. *Degree requirements:* For master's, one foreign language, comprehensive exam; for doctorate, one foreign language, comprehensive exam, thesis/dissertation. *Entrance requirements:* For master's, GRE General Test, minimum GPA of 3.0; for doctorate, GRE General Test, writing sample (7-15 pages long), preferably in a history course. Additional exam requirements/recommendations for international students: required—TOEFL (minimum score 550 paper-based; 80 iBT), IELTS (minimum score 7). *Application deadline:* For fall admission, 1/4 for domestic students. Application fee: $105 ($125 for international students). Electronic applications accepted. *Financial support:* Fellowships, research assistantships, teaching assistantships, career-related internships or fieldwork, scholarships/grants, and readerships available. Financial award applicants required to submit FAFSA. *Unit head:* Edward Watts, Chair, 858-534-2733, E-mail: ewatts@ucsd.edu. *Application contact:* Sally Hargate, Graduate Coordinator, 858-822-0664, E-mail: shargate@ucsd.edu.
Website: http://history.ucsd.edu

University of California, Santa Barbara, Graduate Division, College of Letters and Sciences, Division of Humanities and Fine Arts, Department of History, Santa Barbara, CA 93106-9410. Offers European medieval studies (PhD); global studies (PhD); public historical studies (PhD); technology and society (PhD); women's studies (PhD); MA/PhD. *Degree requirements:* For doctorate, variable foreign language requirement, comprehensive exam, thesis/dissertation. *Entrance requirements:* For doctorate, GRE. Additional exam requirements/recommendations for international students: required—TOEFL (minimum score 550 paper-based; 80 iBT), IELTS (minimum score 7). Electronic applications accepted.

University of California, Santa Cruz, Division of Graduate Studies, Division of Humanities, Department of History, Santa Cruz, CA 95064. Offers MA, PhD. *Degree requirements:* For doctorate, variable foreign language requirement, comprehensive exam, thesis/dissertation, qualifying exam. *Entrance requirements:* For master's and doctorate, GRE, writing sample of up to 30 pages. Additional exam requirements/recommendations for international students: required—TOEFL (minimum score 550 paper-based; 83 iBT); recommended—IELTS (minimum score 8). Electronic applications accepted.

University of Central Arkansas, Graduate School, College of Liberal Arts, Department of History, Conway, AR 72035-0001. Offers MA. *Program availability:* Part-time. *Degree requirements:* For master's, one foreign language, comprehensive exam, thesis optional. *Entrance requirements:* For master's, GRE General Test, minimum GPA of 2.7. Additional exam requirements/recommendations for international students: required—TOEFL (minimum score 550 paper-based). Electronic applications accepted.

University of Central Florida, College of Arts and Humanities, Department of History, Orlando, FL 32816. Offers MA. *Program availability:* Part-time, evening/weekend. *Students:* 26 full-time (11 women), 25 part-time (7 women); includes 10 minority (2 Black or African American, non-Hispanic/Latino; 1 American Indian or Alaska Native, non-Hispanic/Latino; 6 Hispanic/Latino; 1 Two or more races, non-Hispanic/Latino), 1 international. Average age 30. 24 applicants, 92% accepted, 12 enrolled. In 2019, 11 master's awarded. *Degree requirements:* For master's, thesis, written exam. *Entrance requirements:* For master's, GRE General Test, minimum GPA of 3.0 in last 60 hours. Additional exam requirements/recommendations for international students: required—TOEFL. *Application deadline:* For fall admission, 6/1 for domestic students; for spring admission, 12/1 for domestic students; for summer admission, 4/15 for domestic students. Application fee: $30. Electronic applications accepted. *Financial support:* In 2019–20, 11 students received support, including 2 fellowships with partial tuition reimbursements available (averaging $5,000 per year), 6 research assistantships with partial tuition reimbursements available (averaging $2,863 per year), 10 teaching assistantships with partial tuition reimbursements available (averaging $4,439 per year); career-related internships or fieldwork, Federal Work-Study, institutionally sponsored loans, health care benefits, tuition waivers (partial), and unspecified assistantships also available. Financial award application deadline: 3/1; financial award applicants required to submit FAFSA. *Unit head:* Dr. Peter Larson, Chair, 407-823-6466, E-mail: peter.larson@ucf.edu. *Application contact:* Associate Director, Graduate Admissions, 407-823-2766, Fax: 407-823-6442, E-mail: gradadmissions@ucf.edu.
Website: http://history.cah.ucf.edu/

University of Central Missouri, The Graduate School, Warrensburg, MO 64093. Offers accountancy (MA); accounting (MBA); applied mathematics (MS); aviation safety (MA); biology (MS); business administration (MBA); career and technology education (MS); college student personnel administration (MS); communication (MA); computer information systems and information technology (MS); computer science (MS); counseling (MS); criminal justice and criminology (MS); educational leadership (Ed S); educational leadership and policy analysis (Ed D); educational technology (MS, Ed S); elementary and early childhood education (MSE); English (MA); english language learners - teaching english as a second language (MA); environmental studies (MA); finance (MBA); history (MA); industrial hygiene (MS); industrial management (MS); information systems (MBA); kinesiology (MS); library science and information services (MS); literacy education (MSE); marketing (MBA); mathematics (MS); music (MA); occupational safety management (MS); professional leadership - adult, career, and technical education (Ed S); professional leadership - counseling (Ed S); psychology (MS); rural family nursing (MS); school administration (MSE); social gerontology (MS); sociology (MA); special education (MSE); speech language pathology (MS); teaching (MAT); technology (MS); technology management (PhD); theatre (MA). *Accreditation:* ASHA. *Program availability:* Part-time, 100% online, blended/hybrid learning. *Faculty:* 236 full-time (113 women), 97 part-time/adjunct (61 women). *Students:* 787 full-time (448 women), 1,459 part-time (997 women); includes 213 minority (72 Black or African American, non-Hispanic/Latino; 5 American Indian or Alaska Native, non-Hispanic/Latino; 27 Asian, non-Hispanic/Latino; 59 Hispanic/Latino; 50 Two or more races, non-Hispanic/Latino), 574 international. Average age 30. 1,477 applicants, 68% accepted, 664 enrolled. In 2019, 831 master's, 93 other advanced degrees awarded. *Degree requirements:* For master's and Ed S, comprehensive exam (for some programs), thesis (for some programs). *Entrance requirements:* For master's, A GRE or GMAT test score may be required by some of the programs, A minimum GPA, letters of recommendation, a statement of purpose may be required by some of the programs; for Ed S, A master's degree is required for the application of an Education Specialist's degree program. Additional exam requirements/recommendations for international students: required—TOEFL (minimum score 550 paper-based; 79 iBT). *Application deadline:* For fall admission, 6/1 priority date for domestic and international students; for spring admission, 10/15 priority date for domestic and international students; for summer

admission, 4/1 priority date for domestic and international students. Applications are processed on a rolling basis. Application fee: $30 ($75 for international students). Electronic applications accepted. *Expenses: Tuition, area resident:* Full-time $7524; part-time $313.50 per credit hour. Tuition, state resident: full-time $7524; part-time $313.50 per credit hour. Tuition, nonresident: full-time $15,048; part-time $627 per credit hour. *International tuition:* $15,048 full-time. *Required fees:* $915; $30.50 per credit hour. *Financial support:* In 2019–20, 89 students received support. Research assistantships, teaching assistantships, career-related internships or fieldwork, Federal Work-Study, scholarships/grants, unspecified assistantships, and administrative and laboratory assistantships available. Support available to part-time students. Financial award application deadline: 4/1; financial award applicants required to submit FAFSA. *Unit head:* Shellie Hewitt, Director of Graduate and International Student Services, 660-543-4621, Fax: 660-543-4778, E-mail: hewitt@ucmo.edu. *Application contact:* Shellie Hewitt, Director of Graduate and International Student Services, 660-543-4621, Fax: 660-543-4778, E-mail: hewitt@ucmo.edu.
Website: http://www.ucmo.edu/graduate/

University of Central Oklahoma, The Jackson College of Graduate Studies, College of Liberal Arts, Department of History, Edmond, OK 73034-5209. Offers museum studies (MA). *Program availability:* Part-time. *Degree requirements:* For master's, one foreign language, comprehensive exam (for some programs), thesis (for some programs). *Entrance requirements:* For master's, writing sample, essay. Additional exam requirements/recommendations for international students: required—TOEFL (minimum score 550 paper-based; 79 iBT), IELTS (minimum score 6.5). Electronic applications accepted.

University of Chicago, Division of the Social Sciences, Department of History, Chicago, IL 60637. Offers PhD. *Degree requirements:* For doctorate, variable foreign language requirement, thesis/dissertation, oral exams in 3 fields. *Entrance requirements:* For doctorate, GRE General Test, 3 letters of recommendation, statement of purpose, transcripts, resume or curriculum vitae, writing sample (dependent on department). Additional exam requirements/recommendations for international students: required—TOEFL (minimum score 104 iBT), IELTS (minimum score 7). Electronic applications accepted.

University of Cincinnati, Graduate School, McMicken College of Arts and Sciences, Department of History, Cincinnati, OH 45221. Offers MA, PhD. Terminal master's awarded for partial completion of doctoral program. *Degree requirements:* For master's, comprehensive exam, thesis optional; for doctorate, comprehensive exam, thesis/dissertation. *Entrance requirements:* For master's, GRE General Test, BA in history; for doctorate, GRE General Test, MA in history. Additional exam requirements/recommendations for international students: required—TOEFL (minimum score 600 paper-based). Electronic applications accepted.

University of Colorado Boulder, Graduate School, College of Arts and Sciences, Department of History, Boulder, CO 80309. Offers MA, PhD. Terminal master's awarded for partial completion of doctoral program. *Degree requirements:* For master's, comprehensive exam, thesis optional; for doctorate, one foreign language, thesis/dissertation. *Entrance requirements:* For master's, GRE General Test, minimum undergraduate GPA of 2.75; for doctorate, GRE General Test. Electronic applications accepted. Application fee is waived when completed online.

University of Colorado Colorado Springs, College of Letters, Arts and Sciences, Department of History, Colorado Springs, CO 80918. Offers history (MA). *Program availability:* Part-time, evening/weekend. *Faculty:* 10 full-time (5 women), 8 part-time/adjunct (5 women). *Students:* 7 full-time (3 women), 40 part-time (14 women); includes 11 minority (1 Black or African American, non-Hispanic/Latino; 1 American Indian or Alaska Native, non-Hispanic/Latino; 5 Hispanic/Latino; 4 Two or more races, non-Hispanic/Latino). Average age 35. 20 applicants, 85% accepted, 17 enrolled. In 2019, 8 master's awarded. *Degree requirements:* For master's, portfolio of 3-4 research projects, oral exam. *Entrance requirements:* For master's, minimum GPA of 3.0, writing sample. Additional exam requirements/recommendations for international students: recommended—TOEFL (minimum score 80 iBT), IELTS (minimum score 6.5). *Application deadline:* Applications are processed on a rolling basis. Application fee: $60 ($100 for international students). Electronic applications accepted. *Expenses:* Contact institution. *Financial support:* In 2019–20, 15 students received support, including 2 research assistantships (averaging $1,500 per year), 4 teaching assistantships (averaging $2,125 per year); Federal Work-Study, scholarships/grants, and unspecified assistantships also available. Support available to part-time students. Financial award application deadline: 3/1; financial award applicants required to submit FAFSA. *Unit head:* Dr. Roger Martinez-Davila, Director of Graduate Studies, 719-255-4070, Fax: 719-255-4068, E-mail: rmartin8@uccs.edu. *Application contact:* Ian Smith, Administrative Assistant, 719-255-4069, Fax: 719-255-4068, E-mail: ismith2@uccs.edu.
Website: https://www.uccs.edu/history/graduate

University of Colorado Denver, College of Liberal Arts and Sciences, Department of History, Denver, CO 80217. Offers European history (MA); global history (MA); public history (MA); U.S. history (MA). *Program availability:* Part-time, evening/weekend. *Degree requirements:* For master's, comprehensive exam, thesis optional, 36 semester hours (12 courses). *Entrance requirements:* For master's, GRE General Test, writing sample, minimum undergraduate GPA of 3.25, three letters of recommendation, statement of purpose addressing any weaknesses in academic record. Additional exam requirements/recommendations for international students: required—TOEFL (minimum score 537 paper-based; 75 iBT); recommended—IELTS (minimum score 6.5). Electronic applications accepted. Tuition and fees vary according to course load, program and reciprocity agreements.

University of Connecticut, Graduate School, College of Liberal Arts and Sciences, Department of History, Storrs, CT 06269. Offers MA, PhD. Terminal master's awarded for partial completion of doctoral program. *Degree requirements:* For master's, comprehensive exam; for doctorate, thesis/dissertation. *Entrance requirements:* For master's and doctorate, GRE General Test, GRE Subject Test. Additional exam requirements/recommendations for international students: required—TOEFL (minimum score 550 paper-based). Electronic applications accepted.

University of Delaware, College of Arts and Sciences, Department of History, Hagley Program in the History of Technology and Industrialization, Newark, DE 19716. Offers MA, PhD. *Degree requirements:* For master's, thesis optional; for doctorate, comprehensive exam, thesis/dissertation. *Entrance requirements:* For master's and doctorate, interview. Electronic applications accepted.

University of Denver, University College, Denver, CO 80208. Offers arts and culture (MA, Certificate); communication management (MS, Certificate), including translation studies (Certificate), world history and culture (Certificate); environmental policy and management (MS); geographic information systems (MS); global affairs (MA, Certificate), including human capital in organizations (Certificate), philanthropic leadership (Certificate), project management (Certificate), strategic innovation and change (Certificate); healthcare leadership (MS); information communications and technology (MS); leadership and organizations (MS); professional creative writing (MA, Certificate), including emergency planning and response (Certificate), organizational security (Certificate); security management (MS, Certificate); strategic human resources

(Certificate). *Program availability:* Part-time, evening/weekend, 100% online, blended/hybrid learning. *Faculty:* 104 part-time/adjunct (52 women). *Students:* 59 full-time (33 women), 1,893 part-time (1,210 women); includes 545 minority (133 Black or African American, non-Hispanic/Latino; 16 American Indian or Alaska Native, non-Hispanic/Latino; 64 Asian, non-Hispanic/Latino; 252 Hispanic/Latino; 4 Native Hawaiian or other Pacific Islander, non-Hispanic/Latino; 76 Two or more races, non-Hispanic/Latino), 78 international. Average age 32. 1,290 applicants, 91% accepted, 752 enrolled. In 2019, 457 master's, 181 other advanced degrees awarded. *Degree requirements:* For master's, capstone project. *Entrance requirements:* For master's, baccalaureate degree, transcripts, two letters of recommendation, personal statement, resume, writing sample (Master of Arts in Professional Creative Writing). Additional exam requirements/recommendations for international students: required—TOEFL (minimum score 550 paper-based; 80 iBT). *Application deadline:* For fall admission, 6/19 priority date for domestic students, 6/14 priority date for international students; for winter admission, 10/25 priority date for domestic students, 9/27 priority date for international students; for spring admission, 2/7 priority date for domestic students, 1/10 priority date for international students; for summer admission, 4/24 priority date for domestic students, 3/27 priority date for international students. Applications are processed on a rolling basis. Application fee: $75. Electronic applications accepted. *Expenses:* Contact institution. *Financial support:* In 2019–20, 56 students received support. Teaching assistantships available. Financial award applicants required to submit FAFSA. *Unit head:* Dr. Michael McGuire, Dean, 303-871-3518, E-mail: michael.mcguire@du.edu. *Application contact:* Admission Team, 303-871-2291, E-mail: ucoladm@du.edu.
Website: http://universitycollege.du.edu/

University of Florida, Graduate School, College of Liberal Arts and Sciences, Department of History, Gainesville, FL 32611. Offers historic preservation (MA, PhD); history (MA, PhD); Jewish studies (MA); women's and gender studies (PhD); JD/MA; JD/PhD. *Program availability:* Part-time. Terminal master's awarded for partial completion of doctoral program. *Degree requirements:* For master's, variable foreign language requirement, thesis optional, 30 credit hours; for doctorate, variable foreign language requirement, comprehensive exam, thesis/dissertation, 90 credit hours. *Entrance requirements:* For master's and doctorate, GRE General Test, minimum GPA of 3.0. Additional exam requirements/recommendations for international students: required—TOEFL (minimum score 550 paper-based; 80 iBT), IELTS (minimum score 6). Electronic applications accepted.

University of Georgia, Franklin College of Arts and Sciences, Department of History, Athens, GA 30602. Offers MA, PhD. *Degree requirements:* For master's, one foreign language, thesis; for doctorate, one foreign language, thesis/dissertation. *Entrance requirements:* For master's and doctorate, GRE General Test. Electronic applications accepted.

University of Guelph, Office of Graduate and Postdoctoral Studies, College of Arts, Department of History, Guelph, ON N1G 2W1, Canada. Offers MA, PhD. *Program availability:* Part-time. *Degree requirements:* For master's, one foreign language, thesis (for some programs); for doctorate, one foreign language, thesis/dissertation, 3 qualifying fields. *Entrance requirements:* For master's, minimum B+ average during previous 2 years of course work; for doctorate, minimum A- average in MA. Additional exam requirements/recommendations for international students: required—TOEFL (minimum score 550 paper-based). Electronic applications accepted.

University of Hawaii at Manoa, Office of Graduate Education, College of Arts and Humanities, Department of History, Honolulu, HI 96822. Offers MA, PhD. *Program availability:* Part-time. *Degree requirements:* For master's, 2 foreign languages, thesis optional; for doctorate, 2 foreign languages, comprehensive exam, thesis/dissertation. *Entrance requirements:* For master's, GRE, minimum GPA of 3.0, writing sample; for doctorate, GRE, MA, sample of written work. Additional exam requirements/recommendations for international students: required—TOEFL (minimum score 580 paper-based; 92 iBT), IELTS (minimum score 5).

University of Houston, College of Liberal Arts and Social Sciences, Department of History, Houston, TX 77204. Offers MA, PhD. *Program availability:* Part-time. Terminal master's awarded for partial completion of doctoral program. *Degree requirements:* For master's, one foreign language, thesis (for some programs); for doctorate, one foreign language, comprehensive exam, thesis/dissertation. *Entrance requirements:* For master's, GRE General Test, minimum GPA of 3.3; for doctorate, GRE General Test, minimum GPA of 3.67. Additional exam requirements/recommendations for international students: required—TOEFL. Electronic applications accepted.

University of Houston–Clear Lake, School of Human Sciences and Humanities, Programs in Humanities and Fine Arts, Houston, TX 77058-1002. Offers history (MA); humanities (MA); literature (MA). *Program availability:* Part-time, evening/weekend, online learning. *Degree requirements:* For master's, thesis or alternative. *Entrance requirements:* For master's, GRE General Test. Additional exam requirements/recommendations for international students: required—TOEFL (minimum score 550 paper-based).

University of Idaho, College of Graduate Studies, College of Letters, Arts and Social Sciences, Department of History, Moscow, ID 83844-2282. Offers MA, PhD. *Students:* 11 full-time, 10 part-time. Average age 35. In 2019, 1 master's, 1 doctorate awarded. *Degree requirements:* For doctorate, thesis/dissertation. *Entrance requirements:* For master's and doctorate, minimum GPA of 3.0. Additional exam requirements/recommendations for international students: required—TOEFL (minimum score 88 iBT). *Application deadline:* For fall admission, 7/30 for domestic students; for spring admission, 12/1 for domestic students. Applications are processed on a rolling basis. Application fee: $60. Electronic applications accepted. *Expenses:* Tuition, state resident: full-time $7753.80; part-time $502 per credit hour. Tuition, nonresident: full-time $26,990; part-time $1571 per credit hour. *Required fees:* $2122.20; $47 per credit hour. *Financial support:* Research assistantships and teaching assistantships available. Financial award applicants required to submit FAFSA. *Unit head:* Dr. Ellen Kittell, Interim Chair, 208-885-6253, E-mail: history@uidaho.edu. *Application contact:* Dr. Ellen Kittell, Interim Chair, 208-885-6253, E-mail: history@uidaho.edu.
Website: https://www.uidaho.edu/class/history

University of Illinois at Chicago, College of Liberal Arts and Sciences, Department of History, Chicago, IL 60607-7128. Offers MA, MAT, PhD. *Program availability:* Part-time, evening/weekend. *Degree requirements:* For master's, one foreign language, comprehensive exam; for doctorate, 2 foreign languages, comprehensive exam, thesis/dissertation. *Entrance requirements:* For master's and doctorate, GRE General Test, previous course work in a foreign language, minimum GPA of 3.0. Additional exam requirements/recommendations for international students: required—TOEFL. Electronic applications accepted.

University of Illinois at Springfield, Graduate Programs, College of Liberal Arts and Sciences, Program in History, Springfield, IL 62703-5407. Offers MA. *Program availability:* Part-time. *Faculty:* 9 full-time (4 women). *Students:* 6 full-time (4 women), 14 part-time (9 women); includes 1 minority (Black or African American, non-Hispanic/Latino), 1 international. Average age 31. 14 applicants, 71% accepted, 5 enrolled. In 2019, 10 master's awarded. *Degree requirements:* For master's, internship; closure exercise; position paper and historiography; thesis or project. *Entrance requirements:*

History

For master's, BA in history or related field, minimum undergraduate cumulative GPA of 2.50 from an accredited college or university, writing sample, statement of purpose. Additional exam requirements/recommendations for international students: required—TOEFL (minimum score 500 paper-based; 61 iBT). *Application deadline:* Applications are processed on a rolling basis. Application fee: $60 ($75 for international students). Electronic applications accepted. *Expenses: Tuition, area resident:* Full-time $7896; part-time $329 per credit hour. Tuition, nonresident: full-time $16,200; part-time $675 per credit hour. *Required fees:* $2735.60; $130.65 per credit hour. *Financial support:* In 2019–20, research assistantships with full tuition reimbursements (averaging $10,562 per year), teaching assistantships with full tuition reimbursements (averaging $10,652 per year) were awarded; fellowships, career-related internships or fieldwork, Federal Work-Study, scholarships/grants, health care benefits, and unspecified assistantships also available. Support available to part-time students. Financial award application deadline: 11/15; financial award applicants required to submit FAFSA. *Unit head:* Dr. John Barker, Program Administrator, 217-206-6512, Fax: 217-206-6217, E-mail: jbark3@uis.edu. *Application contact:* Dr. John Barker, Program Administrator, 217-206-6512, Fax: 217-206-6217, E-mail: jbark3@uis.edu.
Website: his@uis.edu

University of Illinois at Urbana-Champaign, Graduate College, College of Liberal Arts and Sciences, Department of History, Champaign, IL 61820. Offers MA, PhD.

University of Indianapolis, Graduate Programs, Shaheen College of Arts and Sciences, Department of History and Political Science, Indianapolis, IN 46227-3697. Offers history (MA); international relations (MA). *Program availability:* Part-time, evening/weekend. *Degree requirements:* For master's, thesis optional. *Entrance requirements:* For master's, GRE Subject Test, minimum GPA of 3.0, 3 letters of recommendation. Additional exam requirements/recommendations for international students: required—TOEFL (minimum score 550 paper-based). Electronic applications accepted.

The University of Iowa, Graduate College, College of Liberal Arts and Sciences, Department of History, Iowa City, IA 52242-1316. Offers MA, PhD. *Degree requirements:* For master's, thesis optional, exam; for doctorate, comprehensive exam, thesis/dissertation. *Entrance requirements:* For master's and doctorate, GRE General Test, minimum GPA of 3.0. Additional exam requirements/recommendations for international students: required—TOEFL (minimum score 550 paper-based; 81 iBT). Electronic applications accepted.

The University of Kansas, Graduate Studies, College of Liberal Arts and Sciences, Department of History, Lawrence, KS 66045. Offers MA, PhD. *Program availability:* Part-time. *Students:* 37 full-time (11 women), 3 part-time (1 woman); includes 7 minority (1 Black or African American, non-Hispanic/Latino; 3 Hispanic/Latino; 3 Two or more races, non-Hispanic/Latino), 5 international. Average age 34. 34 applicants, 38% accepted, 4 enrolled. In 2019, 6 master's, 6 doctorates awarded. *Entrance requirements:* For master's and doctorate, GRE General Test, two-page statement of objectives, writing sample (20-25 pages maximum), three letters of reference, transcripts, curriculum vitae. Additional exam requirements/recommendations for international students: required—TOEFL, IELTS, TOEFL or IELTS. *Application deadline:* For fall admission, 1/1 for domestic and international students. Application fee: $65 ($85 for international students). Electronic applications accepted. *Expenses:* Tuition, state resident: full-time $9989. Tuition, nonresident: full-time $23,950. *International tuition:* $23,950 full-time. *Required fees:* $984; $81.99 per credit hour. Tuition and fees vary according to course load, campus/location and program. *Financial support:* Fellowships, research assistantships, teaching assistantships, and unspecified assistantships available. Financial award application deadline: 1/1. *Unit head:* Eve Levin, Chair, 785-864-9463, E-mail: evelevin@ku.edu. *Application contact:* Mary Strickell, Graduate Admissions Contact, 785-864-9438, E-mail: maryj@ku.edu.
Website: http://www.history.ku.edu/

University of Kentucky, Graduate School, College of Arts and Sciences, Program in History, Lexington, KY 40506-0032. Offers MA, PhD. *Program availability:* Part-time. *Degree requirements:* For master's, one foreign language, comprehensive exam, thesis optional; for doctorate, variable foreign language requirement, comprehensive exam, thesis/dissertation. *Entrance requirements:* For master's, GRE General Test, minimum undergraduate GPA of 2.75; for doctorate, GRE General Test, minimum graduate GPA of 3.0. Additional exam requirements/recommendations for international students: required—TOEFL (minimum score 550 paper-based). Electronic applications accepted.

University of Louisiana at Lafayette, College of Liberal Arts, Department of English, Lafayette, LA 70504. Offers American culture (MA, PhD), including history, sociology; American literature and language (PhD); creative writing (MA, PhD), including creative writing (MA), folklore (MA), rhetoric (MA); folklore (MA, PhD); linguistic studies (MA, PhD); professional writing (PhD); rhetoric (MA, PhD); TESOL studies (MA, PhD). *Program availability:* Part-time. Terminal master's awarded for partial completion of doctoral program. *Degree requirements:* For master's, one foreign language, thesis or alternative; for doctorate, 2 foreign languages, comprehensive exam, thesis/dissertation. *Entrance requirements:* For master's, GRE General Test, minimum GPA of 2.75; for doctorate, GRE General Test, minimum GPA of 3.0. Additional exam requirements/recommendations for international students: required—TOEFL (minimum score 550 paper-based). Electronic applications accepted. *Expenses: Tuition, area resident:* Full-time $5511; part-time $1630 per credit hour. Tuition, state resident: full-time $5511; part-time $1630 per credit hour. Tuition, nonresident: full-time $19,239; part-time $2409 per credit hour. *Required fees:* $46,637.

University of Louisiana at Lafayette, College of Liberal Arts, Department of History, Geography and Philosophy, Lafayette, LA 70504. Offers history (MA), including American history, European history, Latin American history, public history. *Program availability:* Part-time. *Degree requirements:* For master's, one foreign language, thesis or alternative. *Entrance requirements:* For master's, GRE General Test, minimum GPA of 2.75. Additional exam requirements/recommendations for international students: required—TOEFL (minimum score 550 paper-based). Electronic applications accepted. *Expenses: Tuition, area resident:* Full-time $5511; part-time $1630 per credit hour. Tuition, state resident: full-time $5511; part-time $1630 per credit hour. Tuition, nonresident: full-time $19,239; part-time $2409 per credit hour. *Required fees:* $46,637.

University of Louisiana at Monroe, Graduate School, College of Arts, Education, and Sciences, Department of History, Monroe, LA 71209-0001. Offers MA. *Program availability:* Part-time, evening/weekend, online learning. *Faculty:* 3 full-time (0 women). *Students:* 7 full-time (6 women), 19 part-time (10 women); includes 3 minority (1 Black or African American, non-Hispanic/Latino; 2 Hispanic/Latino), 1 international. Average age 34. 30 applicants, 70% accepted, 14 enrolled. In 2019, 3 master's awarded. *Degree requirements:* For master's, thesis optional. *Entrance requirements:* For master's, GRE General Test (minimum score of verbal and quantitative of 283), minimum undergraduate GPA of 2.5. Additional exam requirements/recommendations for international students: required—TOEFL (minimum score 500 paper-based; 61 iBT); recommended—IELTS (minimum score 5.5). *Application deadline:* For fall admission, 8/1 for domestic students, 6/1 for international students; for spring admission, 1/1 for domestic students, 11/1 for international students; for summer admission, 6/1 for domestic students, 3/1 for international students. Applications are processed on a rolling basis. Application fee: $40. Electronic applications accepted. *Expenses: Tuition, area resident:* Full-time $6489. Tuition, state resident: full-time $6489. Tuition, nonresident: full-time $18,989. *Required fees:* $2748. Tuition and fees vary according to course load and program. *Financial support:* In 2019–20, 13 students received support. Research assistantships with full tuition reimbursements available, teaching assistantships with full tuition reimbursements available, career-related internships or fieldwork, Federal Work-Study, scholarships/grants, and unspecified assistantships available. Financial award application deadline: 2/15; financial award applicants required to submit FAFSA. *Unit head:* Dr. Jeffrey Anderson, Program & Graduate Coordinator, 318-342-1370, E-mail: jeanderson@ulm.edu. *Application contact:* Dr. Jeffrey Anderson, Program & Graduate Coordinator, 318-342-1370, E-mail: jeanderson@ulm.edu.
Website: http://www.ulm.edu/history/

University of Louisville, Graduate School, College of Arts and Sciences, Department of History, Louisville, KY 40292-0001. Offers history (MA); public history (Certificate). *Program availability:* Part-time. *Faculty:* 17 full-time (8 women), 4 part-time/adjunct (2 women). *Students:* 11 full-time (5 women), 10 part-time (3 women); includes 4 minority (3 Black or African American, non-Hispanic/Latino; 1 Two or more races, non-Hispanic/Latino). Average age 32. 9 applicants, 100% accepted, 7 enrolled. In 2019, 6 master's, 2 other advanced degrees awarded. *Degree requirements:* For master's, comprehensive exam (for some programs), thesis. *Entrance requirements:* For master's, GRE General Test, 2 letters of reference, official transcripts, statement of purpose, not to exceed 500 words, which describes in reasonably specific terms, academic and career objectives and how they can be advanced through work in program. Additional exam requirements/recommendations for international students: required—TOEFL (minimum score 550 paper-based; 79 iBT), IELTS can be used in place of the TOEFL; recommended—IELTS (minimum score 6.5). *Application deadline:* For fall admission, 2/15 for domestic and international students; for spring admission, 12/1 for domestic and international students. Applications are processed on a rolling basis. Application fee: $65. Electronic applications accepted. *Expenses: Tuition, area resident:* Full-time $13,000; part-time $723 per credit hour. Tuition, state resident: full-time $13,000; part-time $723 per credit hour. Tuition, nonresident: full-time $27,114; part-time $1507 per credit hour. *International tuition:* $27,114 full-time. *Required fees:* $196. Tuition and fees vary according to program and reciprocity agreements. *Financial support:* In 2019–20, 6 students received support. Fellowships, research assistantships, teaching assistantships, health care benefits, and unspecified assistantships available. Financial award application deadline: 2/15. *Unit head:* Dr. Blake Beattie, Chairperson/Associate Professor, 502-852-6818, Fax: 502-852-0770, E-mail: history@louisville.edu. *Application contact:* Dr. Jennifer T. Westerfeld, Director of Graduate Studies/Assoc. Prof, 502-852-3756, E-mail: histgrad@louisville.edu.
Website: http://louisville.edu/history/

University of Maine, Graduate School, College of Liberal Arts and Sciences, Department of History, Orono, ME 04469. Offers MA, PhD. *Faculty:* 14 full-time (3 women), 9 part-time/adjunct (2 women). *Students:* 27 full-time (15 women), 6 part-time (0 women); includes 2 minority (1 Hispanic/Latino; 1 Two or more races, non-Hispanic/Latino), 2 international. Average age 39. 16 applicants, 88% accepted, 8 enrolled. In 2019, 5 master's, 2 doctorates awarded. *Degree requirements:* For master's, variable foreign language requirement, thesis optional; for doctorate, one foreign language, comprehensive exam, thesis/dissertation. *Entrance requirements:* For master's and doctorate, GRE General Test. Additional exam requirements/recommendations for international students: required—TOEFL (minimum score 79 iBT). *Application deadline:* For fall admission, 1/15 priority date for domestic and international students; for spring admission, 10/15 for domestic students, 10/15 priority date for international students. Applications are processed on a rolling basis. Application fee: $65. Electronic applications accepted. *Expenses: Tuition, area resident:* Full-time $8100; part-time $450 per credit hour. Tuition, state resident: full-time $8100; part-time $450 per credit hour. Tuition, nonresident: full-time $26,388; part-time $1466 per credit hour. *International tuition:* $26,388 full-time. *Required fees:* $1257; $278 per semester. Tuition and fees vary according to course load. *Financial support:* In 2019–20, 20 students received support, including 1 fellowship with full tuition reimbursement available (averaging $16,700 per year), 17 teaching assistantships with full tuition reimbursements available (averaging $15,825 per year); career-related internships or fieldwork, Federal Work-Study, scholarships/grants, tuition waivers (full and partial), and unspecified assistantships also available. Support available to part-time students. Financial award application deadline: 3/1; financial award applicants required to submit FAFSA. *Unit head:* Dr. Stephen Miller, Chair, 207-581-1905, Fax: 207-581-1817, E-mail: stephen.miller@maine.edu. *Application contact:* Scott G. Delcourt, Assistant Vice President for Graduate Studies and Senior Associate Dean, 207-581-3291, Fax: 207-581-3232, E-mail: graduate@maine.edu.
Website: http://www.umaine.edu/history/

The University of Manchester, School of Arts, Languages and Cultures, Manchester, United Kingdom. Offers anthropology, media and performance (PhD); applied theatre (PhD); Arab world studies (PhD); archaeology (PhD); art history and visual studies (PhD); arts and cultural management (PhD); arts management and cultural policy (PhD); Chinese studies (PhD); classics and ancient history (PhD); composition (PhD); creative writing (PhD); drama (PhD); East Asian studies (PhD); electroacoustic composition (PhD); English and American studies (PhD); English language (PhD); French studies (PhD); German studies (PhD); history (PhD); humanitarianism and conflict response (PhD); interpreting studies (PhD); Japanese studies (PhD); Latin American cultural studies (PhD); linguistics (PhD); Middle Eastern studies (PhD); museology (PhD); museum practice (PhD); music (PhD); musicology (PhD); Polish studies (PhD); Portuguese studies (PhD); religions and theology (PhD); Russian studies (PhD); Spanish studies (PhD); translation and intercultural studies (PhD).

University of Manitoba, Faculty of Graduate Studies, Faculty of Arts, Department of History, Winnipeg, MB R3T 2N2, Canada. Offers archival studies (MA); history (MA, PhD). *Degree requirements:* For master's, thesis; for doctorate, one foreign language, thesis/dissertation.

University of Maryland, Baltimore County, The Graduate School, College of Arts, Humanities and Social Sciences, Department of History, Program in Historical Studies, Baltimore, MD 21250. Offers MA. *Program availability:* Part-time, evening/weekend. *Faculty:* 16 full-time (10 women), 8 part-time/adjunct (5 women). *Students:* 17 full-time (5 women), 10 part-time (5 women); includes 4 minority (1 Black or African American, non-Hispanic/Latino; 1 Hispanic/Latino; 2 Two or more races, non-Hispanic/Latino), 2 international. Average age 29. 33 applicants, 70% accepted, 13 enrolled. In 2019, 10 master's awarded. *Degree requirements:* For master's, thesis. *Entrance requirements:* For master's, GRE General Test, minimum GPA of 3.0. Additional exam requirements/recommendations for international students: required—TOEFL. *Application deadline:* For fall admission, 2/15 priority date for domestic students, 1/1 for international students. Application fee: $50. Electronic applications accepted. *Expenses:* $14,382 per year. *Financial support:* In 2019–20, 11 students received support, including 3 research assistantships with full tuition reimbursements available (averaging $12,874 per year), 8 teaching assistantships with tuition reimbursements available (averaging $12,874 per year); career-related internships or fieldwork, health care benefits, tuition waivers (partial), and unspecified assistantships also available. Financial award application

deadline: 2/15; financial award applicants required to submit FAFSA. *Unit head:* Dr. Daniel Ritschel, Graduate Program Director, 410-455-2034, Fax: 410-455-1045, E-mail: ritschel@umbc.edu. *Application contact:* Carla S. Ison, Graduate Program Coordinator, 410-455-4178, Fax: 410-455-1045, E-mail: ison@umbc.edu.
Website: http://www.umbc.edu/history

University of Maryland, College Park, Academic Affairs, College of Arts and Humanities, Department of History, College Park, MD 20742. Offers MA, PhD. *Degree requirements:* For master's, comprehensive exam, thesis optional; for doctorate, one foreign language, thesis/dissertation, oral and written exams. *Entrance requirements:* For master's, GRE General Test, minimum GPA of 3.25, writing sample, 3 letters of recommendation, statements of goals and research interests and experiences; for doctorate, GRE General Test, minimum GPA of 3.5. Additional exam requirements/recommendations for international students: required—TOEFL. Electronic applications accepted.

University of Maryland, College Park, Academic Affairs, Program in History, Library, and Information Services, College Park, MD 20742. Offers MA/MLS. *Entrance requirements:* Additional exam requirements/recommendations for international students: required—TOEFL. Electronic applications accepted.

University of Massachusetts Amherst, Graduate School, College of Humanities and Fine Arts, Department of History, Amherst, MA 01003. Offers MA, PhD. *Program availability:* Part-time. Terminal master's awarded for partial completion of doctoral program. *Degree requirements:* For master's, one foreign language, thesis or alternative; for doctorate, one foreign language, comprehensive exam, thesis/dissertation. *Entrance requirements:* For master's and doctorate, GRE General Test, writing sample. Additional exam requirements/recommendations for international students: required—TOEFL (minimum score 550 paper-based; 80 iBT), IELTS (minimum score 6.5). Electronic applications accepted.

University of Massachusetts Boston, College of Liberal Arts, Program in History, Boston, MA 02125-3393. Offers archival methods (MA). *Program availability:* Part-time, evening/weekend. *Entrance requirements:* For master's, minimum GPA of 2.75. Electronic applications accepted.

University of Memphis, Graduate School, College of Arts and Sciences, Department of History, Memphis, TN 38152. Offers ancient Egyptian history (MA, PhD). *Program availability:* 100% online. *Students:* 21 full-time (13 women), 41 part-time (29 women); includes 15 minority (12 Black or African American, non-Hispanic/Latino; 1 Asian, non-Hispanic/Latino; 2 Hispanic/Latino), 1 international. Average age 35. 27 applicants, 81% accepted, 9 enrolled. In 2019, 9 master's, 7 doctorates awarded. *Degree requirements:* For master's, comprehensive exam, thesis optional; for doctorate, one foreign language, comprehensive exam, thesis/dissertation, 60 credits plus 12 dissertation credits, 2 research seminars. *Entrance requirements:* For master's, GRE General Test or MAT, 18 undergraduate hours of course work in history with minimum GPA of 3.0, 2 letters of recommendation, writing sample, statement of research interest; for doctorate, GRE General Test, GRE Subject Test, MA in history or related field, three letters of recommendation, writing sample, statement of purpose. Additional exam requirements/recommendations for international students: required—TOEFL (minimum score 550 paper-based; 79 iBT). *Application deadline:* For fall admission, 1/15 for domestic students; for spring admission, 9/15 for domestic students. Applications are processed on a rolling basis. Application fee: $35 ($60 for international students). Electronic applications accepted. *Expenses: Tuition, area resident:* Full-time $9216; part-time $512 per credit hour. Tuition, state resident: full-time $9216; part-time $512 per credit hour. Tuition, nonresident: full-time $12,672; part-time $704 per credit hour. *International tuition:* $16,128 full-time. *Required fees:* $1530; $85 per credit hour. Tuition and fees vary according to program. *Financial support:* Research assistantships with full tuition reimbursements, teaching assistantships with full tuition reimbursements, career-related internships or fieldwork, Federal Work-Study, scholarships/grants, and unspecified assistantships available. Financial award application deadline: 2/1; financial award applicants required to submit FAFSA. *Unit head:* Dr. Daniel Unowsky, Chair, 901-678-3385, Fax: 901-678-2720, E-mail: dunowsky@memphis.edu. *Application contact:* Dr. Andrew Daily, Graduate Coordinator, 901-678-2868, Fax: 901-678-2720, E-mail: amdaily@memphis.edu.
Website: https://www.memphis.edu/history

University of Miami, Graduate School, College of Arts and Sciences, Department of History, Coral Gables, FL 33124. Offers MA, PhD. *Program availability:* Part-time. Terminal master's awarded for partial completion of doctoral program. *Degree requirements:* For master's, one foreign language, comprehensive exam, thesis optional; for doctorate, one foreign language, comprehensive exam, thesis/dissertation. *Entrance requirements:* For master's and doctorate, GRE General Test, GRE Subject Test. Additional exam requirements/recommendations for international students: required—TOEFL (minimum score 550 paper-based; 59 iBT). Electronic applications accepted.

University of Michigan, Rackham Graduate School, College of Literature, Science, and the Arts, Department of History, Ann Arbor, MI 48109. Offers PhD. *Degree requirements:* For doctorate, 2 foreign languages, thesis/dissertation, oral defense of dissertation, preliminary exam. *Entrance requirements:* For doctorate, GRE General Test, writing sample. Additional exam requirements/recommendations for international students: required—TOEFL. Electronic applications accepted.

University of Michigan, Rackham Graduate School, College of Literature, Science, and the Arts, Department of Women's Studies, Ann Arbor, MI 48109. Offers English and women's studies (PhD); history and women's studies (PhD); LGBTQ studies (Certificate); psychology and women's studies (PhD); women's studies (Certificate). *Degree requirements:* For doctorate, variable foreign language requirement, comprehensive exam (for some programs), thesis/dissertation. *Entrance requirements:* For doctorate, previous undergraduate coursework in women's studies. Electronic applications accepted.

University of Michigan, Rackham Graduate School, College of Literature, Science, and the Arts, Doctoral Program in Anthropology and History, Ann Arbor, MI 48109. Offers PhD. *Degree requirements:* For doctorate, 2 foreign languages, thesis/dissertation, oral defense of dissertation, preliminary exam. *Entrance requirements:* For doctorate, GRE General Test, writing sample. Additional exam requirements/recommendations for international students: required—TOEFL. Electronic applications accepted.

University of Michigan, Rackham Graduate School, College of Literature, Science, and the Arts, Interdepartmental Program in Greek and Roman History, Ann Arbor, MI 48109. Offers PhD, Certificate. *Degree requirements:* For doctorate, 4 foreign languages, comprehensive exam, thesis/dissertation, oral defense of dissertation, dissertation prospectus, preliminary exams, qualifying exams. *Entrance requirements:* For doctorate, GRE, strict minimum of 2 years each of classical Greek and Latin. Additional exam requirements/recommendations for international students: required—TOEFL (minimum score 560 paper-based). Electronic applications accepted.

University of Minnesota, Twin Cities Campus, Graduate School, College of Liberal Arts, Department of Classical and Near Eastern Studies, Minneapolis, MN 55455-0213. Offers ancient and medieval art and archaeology (MA, PhD); classics (MA, PhD); Greek (MA, PhD); Latin (MA, PhD); religions in antiquity (MA). *Program availability:* Part-time. Terminal master's awarded for partial completion of doctoral program. *Degree requirements:* For master's, 2 foreign languages, comprehensive exam, thesis or alternative; for doctorate, variable foreign language requirement, comprehensive exam, thesis/dissertation. *Entrance requirements:* For master's and doctorate, GRE, 3 letters of recommendation, writing sample, copies of transcripts, personal statement. Additional exam requirements/recommendations for international students: required—TOEFL. Electronic applications accepted.

University of Minnesota, Twin Cities Campus, Graduate School, College of Liberal Arts, Department of History, Minneapolis, MN 55455-0213. Offers MA, PhD. *Degree requirements:* For master's, one foreign language, comprehensive exam, thesis or alternative; for doctorate, 2 foreign languages, comprehensive exam, thesis/dissertation. *Entrance requirements:* For doctorate, GRE General Test, writing sample, letters of recommendation. Additional exam requirements/recommendations for international students: required—TOEFL (minimum score 550 paper-based). Electronic applications accepted.

University of Mississippi, Graduate School, College of Liberal Arts, University, MS 38677. Offers anthropology (MA); biology (MS, PhD); chemistry (MS, DA, PhD); creative writing (MFA); documentary expression (MFA); economics (MA, PhD); English (MA, PhD); experimental psychology (PhD); history (MA, PhD); mathematics (MS, PhD); modern languages (MA); music (MM); philosophy (MA); physics (MA, MS, PhD); political science (MA, PhD); Southern studies (MA); studio art (MFA). *Program availability:* Part-time. *Faculty:* 481 full-time (215 women), 71 part-time/adjunct (40 women). *Students:* 509 full-time (258 women), 55 part-time (21 women); includes 89 minority (40 Black or African American, non-Hispanic/Latino; 13 Asian, non-Hispanic/Latino; 25 Hispanic/Latino; 11 Two or more races, non-Hispanic/Latino), 157 international. Average age 29. In 2019, 119 master's, 51 doctorates awarded. *Degree requirements:* For doctorate, thesis/dissertation. *Entrance requirements:* For master's, GRE General Test, minimum GPA of 3.0; for doctorate, GRE General Test. Additional exam requirements/recommendations for international students: required—TOEFL. *Application deadline:* Applications are processed on a rolling basis. Application fee: $50. Electronic applications accepted. *Expenses:* Tuition, state resident: full-time $8718; part-time $484.25 per credit hour. Tuition, nonresident: full-time $24,990; part-time $1388.25 per credit hour. *Required fees:* $100; $4.16 per credit hour. *Financial support:* Fellowships, research assistantships, teaching assistantships, career-related internships or fieldwork, Federal Work-Study, institutionally sponsored loans, scholarships/grants, and unspecified assistantships available. Financial award application deadline: 3/1; financial award applicants required to submit FAFSA. *Unit head:* Dr. Lee Michael Cohen, Dean, 662-915-7177, Fax: 662-915-5792, E-mail: libarts@olemiss.edu. *Application contact:* Tameka Smith, Graduate Activities Specialist for Admissions, 662-915-7474, Fax: 662-915-7577, E-mail: gschool@olemiss.edu.
Website: ventress@olemiss.edu

University of Missouri, Office of Research and Graduate Studies, College of Arts and Science, Department of History, Columbia, MO 65211. Offers MA, PhD. *Entrance requirements:* For master's, GRE General Test, minimum GPA of 3.0 in last 60 hours, 3.3 in undergraduate history courses; at least 18 hours in history; BA or BS; for doctorate, GRE General Test, minimum GPA of 3.0; MA in history (strongly preferred); master's thesis or research seminar paper.

University of Missouri–Kansas City, College of Arts and Sciences, Department of History, Kansas City, MO 64110-2499. Offers MA, PhD. *Program availability:* Part-time. *Degree requirements:* For master's, thesis optional; for doctorate, one foreign language, thesis/dissertation. *Entrance requirements:* For master's, GRE General Test, minimum GPA of 3.0, 2 writing samples, 3 letters of recommendation; for doctorate, GRE General Test. Additional exam requirements/recommendations for international students: required—TOEFL (minimum score 550 paper-based; 80 iBT). Electronic applications accepted.

University of Missouri–St. Louis, College of Arts and Sciences, Department of History, St. Louis, MO 63121. Offers history (MA); history education (Certificate); museum studies (MA, Certificate). *Program availability:* Part-time, evening/weekend. *Degree requirements:* For master's, thesis (for some programs). *Entrance requirements:* For master's, writing sample; minimum GPA of 2.75 (for history), 3.2 (for museum studies). Additional exam requirements/recommendations for international students: required—TOEFL (minimum score 550 paper-based; 79 iBT), IELTS (minimum score 6.5). Electronic applications accepted. *Expenses: Tuition, area resident:* Full-time $9005.40; part-time $6003.60 per credit hour. Tuition, state resident: full-time $9005.40; part-time $6003.60 per credit hour. Tuition, nonresident: full-time $22,108; part-time $14,738.40 per credit hour. *International tuition:* $22,108 full-time. Tuition and fees vary according to course load.

University of Montana, Graduate School, College of Humanities and Sciences, Department of History, Missoula, MT 59812. Offers MA, PhD. *Degree requirements:* For master's, thesis or additional course work/professional paper. *Entrance requirements:* For master's, GRE General Test. Additional exam requirements/recommendations for international students: required—TOEFL.

University of Nebraska at Kearney, College of Natural and Social Sciences, College of Arts & Sciences, Kearney, NE 68849. Offers MA. *Program availability:* Part-time, evening/weekend, 100% online, blended/hybrid learning. *Faculty:* 12 full-time (3 women). *Students:* 8 full-time (3 women), 116 part-time (46 women); includes 8 minority (5 Hispanic/Latino; 3 Two or more races, non-Hispanic/Latino). Average age 36. 48 applicants, 100% accepted, 31 enrolled. In 2019, 43 master's awarded. *Degree requirements:* For master's, comprehensive exam, thesis optional. *Entrance requirements:* For master's, letters of recommendation, writing sample, letter of interest. Additional exam requirements/recommendations for international students: required—TOEFL (minimum score 550 paper-based; 79 iBT), IELTS (minimum score 6.5). *Application deadline:* For fall admission, 7/10 for domestic students, 5/10 for international students; for spring admission, 11/10 for domestic students, 9/10 for international students; for summer admission, 4/10 for domestic students, 1/10 for international students. Applications are processed on a rolling basis. Application fee: $45. Electronic applications accepted. *Expenses: Tuition, area resident:* Full-time $4662; part-time $259 per credit hour. Tuition, nonresident: full-time $10,242; part-time $569 per credit hour. *International tuition:* $10,242 full-time. *Required fees:* $1222; $381.50 per term. Full-time tuition and fees vary according to course load, campus/location and program. *Financial support:* In 2019–20, 6 students received support, including 6 teaching assistantships with full tuition reimbursements available (averaging $10,980 per year); career-related internships or fieldwork, scholarships/grants, health care benefits, and unspecified assistantships also available. Support available to part-time students. Financial award application deadline: 2/28; financial award applicants required to submit FAFSA. *Unit head:* Dr. Doug Biggs, Graduate Program Director, 308-865-8509, E-mail: biggsdl@unk.edu. *Application contact:* Amber Alexander, Advisor, Graduate History Program, 308-865-8766, E-mail: alexanderaj@unk.edu.
Website: https://www.unk.edu/academics/history/index.php

History

University of Nebraska at Omaha, Graduate Studies, College of Arts and Sciences, Department of History, Omaha, NE 68182. Offers MA. *Program availability:* Part-time, evening/weekend. *Degree requirements:* For master's, comprehensive exam, thesis (for some programs). *Entrance requirements:* For master's, minimum GPA of 3.0, 21 hours of course work in history, 2 letters of recommendation, resume, statement of purpose, writing sample, official transcripts. Additional exam requirements/recommendations for international students: required—TOEFL, IELTS, PTE. Electronic applications accepted.

University of Nebraska–Lincoln, Graduate College, College of Arts and Sciences, Department of History, Lincoln, NE 68588. Offers MA, PhD. *Degree requirements:* For master's, thesis optional; for doctorate, one foreign language, comprehensive exam, thesis/dissertation. *Entrance requirements:* For master's and doctorate, GRE General Test, GRE Subject Test, writing sample. Additional exam requirements/recommendations for international students: required—TOEFL (minimum score 575 paper-based). Electronic applications accepted.

University of Nevada, Las Vegas, Graduate College, College of Liberal Arts, Department of History, Las Vegas, NV 89154-5020. Offers MA, PhD. *Program availability:* Part-time. *Faculty:* 12 full-time (3 women). *Students:* 20 full-time (15 women), 14 part-time (6 women); includes 9 minority (1 American Indian or Alaska Native, non-Hispanic/Latino; 1 Asian, non-Hispanic/Latino; 4 Hispanic/Latino; 3 Two or more races, non-Hispanic/Latino), 1 international. Average age 40. 22 applicants, 45% accepted, 9 enrolled. In 2019, 6 master's, 1 doctorate awarded. *Degree requirements:* For master's, one foreign language, comprehensive exam (for some programs), thesis (for some programs); for doctorate, 2 foreign languages, comprehensive exam, thesis/dissertation, written and oral examinations. *Entrance requirements:* For master's, minimum overall GPA of 3.0, 3.3 in history courses; 2 recommendations; statement of purpose; writing sample; for doctorate, GRE General Test, completion of significant course work at upper-division or graduate level in history; 3 recommendations; minimum overall GPA of 3.75 undergraduate, 3.5 graduate; statement of purpose; writing sample. Additional exam requirements/recommendations for international students: required—TOEFL (minimum score 550 paper-based; 80 iBT), IELTS (minimum score 7). *Application deadline:* For fall admission, 4/15 for domestic and international students; for spring admission, 11/1 for domestic students, 10/1 for international students. Application fee: $60 ($95 for international students). Electronic applications accepted. *Expenses:* Contact institution. *Financial support:* In 2019–20, 22 students received support, including 1 research assistantship with full tuition reimbursement available (averaging $15,000 per year), 21 teaching assistantships with full tuition reimbursements available (averaging $14,272 per year); institutionally sponsored loans, scholarships/grants, health care benefits, and unspecified assistantships also available. Financial award application deadline: 3/15; financial award applicants required to submit FAFSA. *Unit head:* Dr. Andrew Kirk, Chair/Professor, 702-895-3349, Fax: 702-895-1782, E-mail: history.chair@unlv.edu. *Application contact:* Dr. William Bauer, Graduate Coordinator, 702-895-0918, Fax: 702-895-1782, E-mail: history.gradcoord@unlv.edu.
Website: http://history.unlv.edu/graduate.html

University of Nevada, Reno, Graduate School, College of Liberal Arts, Department of History, Reno, NV 89557. Offers MA, PhD. Terminal master's awarded for partial completion of doctoral program. *Degree requirements:* For master's, thesis optional; for doctorate, one foreign language, thesis/dissertation. *Entrance requirements:* For master's, GRE General Test, minimum GPA of 2.75; for doctorate, GRE General Test, minimum GPA of 3.0. Additional exam requirements/recommendations for international students: required—TOEFL (minimum score 500 paper-based; 61 iBT), IELTS (minimum score 6). Electronic applications accepted.

University of New Hampshire, Graduate School, College of Liberal Arts, Department of History, Durham, NH 03824. Offers history (MA, PhD); history: museum studies (MA). *Program availability:* Part-time. *Students:* 28 full-time (12 women), 10 part-time (6 women); includes 1 minority (Two or more races, non-Hispanic/Latino), 1 international. Average age 31. 30 applicants, 63% accepted, 10 enrolled. In 2019, 10 master's, 2 doctorates awarded. *Entrance requirements:* For master's and doctorate, GRE General Test, writing sample. Additional exam requirements/recommendations for international students: required—TOEFL (minimum score 550 paper-based; 80 iBT), IELTS, PTE. *Application deadline:* For fall admission, 2/1 for domestic students. Application fee: $65. Electronic applications accepted. *Financial support:* In 2019–20, 21 students received support, including 1 fellowship, 13 teaching assistantships; research assistantships, career-related internships or fieldwork, Federal Work-Study, scholarships/grants, and tuition waivers (full and partial) also available. Support available to part-time students. Financial award application deadline: 2/15. *Unit head:* Kurk Dorsey, Chair, 603-862-3022. *Application contact:* Lara Demarest, Administrative Assistant, 603-862-1765, E-mail: history.grad@unh.edu.
Website: http://cola.unh.edu/history

University of New Mexico, Graduate Studies, College of Arts and Sciences, Program in History, Albuquerque, NM 87131-2039. Offers MA, PhD. *Program availability:* Part-time. Terminal master's awarded for partial completion of doctoral program. *Degree requirements:* For master's, one foreign language, comprehensive exam, thesis optional; for doctorate, 2 foreign languages, comprehensive exam, thesis/dissertation. *Entrance requirements:* For master's, GRE, BA in history or equivalent; for doctorate, GRE, MA in history or equivalent. Additional exam requirements/recommendations for international students: required—TOEFL. Electronic applications accepted. *Expenses:* Tuition, state resident: full-time $7633; part-time $972 per year. Tuition, nonresident: full-time $22,586; part-time $3840 per year. *International tuition:* $23,292 full-time. *Required fees:* $8608. Tuition and fees vary according to course level, course load, degree level, program and student level.

University of New Orleans, Graduate School, College of Liberal Arts, Education and Human Development, Department of History, New Orleans, LA 70148. Offers MA. *Entrance requirements:* For master's, GRE General Test. Additional exam requirements/recommendations for international students: required—TOEFL (minimum score 550 paper-based; 79 iBT), IELTS (minimum score 6.5). Electronic applications accepted.

University of North Alabama, College of Arts and Sciences, Department of History, Program in History, Florence, AL 35632-0001. Offers MA. *Program availability:* Part-time, 100% online. *Degree requirements:* For master's, comprehensive exam (for some programs), thesis optional. *Entrance requirements:* For master's, GRE, three letters of recommendation; essay; writing sample. Additional exam requirements/recommendations for international students: required—TOEFL (minimum score 79 iBT), IELTS (minimum score 6), PTE (minimum score 54). Electronic applications accepted.

The University of North Carolina at Chapel Hill, Graduate School, College of Arts and Sciences, Department of History, Chapel Hill, NC 27599. Offers MA, PhD. Terminal master's awarded for partial completion of doctoral program. *Degree requirements:* For master's, one foreign language, thesis, oral thesis defense; for doctorate, 2 foreign languages, comprehensive exam, thesis/dissertation, oral dissertation defense. *Entrance requirements:* For master's and doctorate, GRE General Test, minimum GPA of 3.0. Electronic applications accepted.

The University of North Carolina at Charlotte, College of Liberal Arts and Sciences, Department of History, Charlotte, NC 28223-0001. Offers history (MA), including public history. *Program availability:* Part-time, evening/weekend. *Faculty:* 29 full-time (14 women), 2 part-time/adjunct (0 women). *Students:* 15 full-time (9 women), 29 part-time (13 women); includes 5 minority (3 Black or African American, non-Hispanic/Latino; 2 Two or more races, non-Hispanic/Latino), 1 international. Average age 31. 23 applicants, 78% accepted, 9 enrolled. In 2019, 17 master's awarded. *Degree requirements:* For master's, thesis optional. *Entrance requirements:* For master's, GRE General Test, minimum undergraduate GPA of 3.0 in history or related discipline; personal statement (1-2 pages) detailing experiences, interests, and goals in history; three letters of recommendation, at least two of which should be from professors in history or related field; writing sample; curriculum vitae/resume. Additional exam requirements/recommendations for international students: required—TOEFL (minimum score 557 paper-based; 83 iBT), IELTS (minimum score 6.5), TOEFL (minimum score 557 paper-based, 83 iBT) or IELTS (6.5). *Application deadline:* For fall admission, 2/1 priority date for domestic students; for spring admission, 11/1 priority date for domestic students; for summer admission, 4/1 priority date for domestic students. Applications are processed on a rolling basis. Application fee: $75. Electronic applications accepted. *Expenses:* Tuition, state resident: full-time $4337. Tuition, nonresident: full-time $17,771. *Required fees:* $3093. Tuition and fees vary according to course load, degree level and program. *Financial support:* In 2019–20, 11 students received support, including 4 research assistantships (averaging $9,000 per year), 7 teaching assistantships (averaging $10,571 per year); career-related internships or fieldwork, Federal Work-Study, institutionally sponsored loans, scholarships/grants, and unspecified assistantships also available. Support available to part-time students. Financial award application deadline: 2/1; financial award applicants required to submit FAFSA. *Unit head:* Dr. Jurgen Buchenau, Professor and Chair, 704-687-5136, E-mail: jbuchenau@uncc.edu. *Application contact:* Kathy B. Giddings, Director of Graduate Admissions, 704-687-5530, Fax: 704-687-1668, E-mail: gradadm@uncc.edu.
Website: http://history.uncc.edu/

The University of North Carolina at Greensboro, Graduate School, College of Arts and Sciences, Department of History, Greensboro, NC 27412-5001. Offers historic preservation (Certificate); history (MA); museum studies (Certificate); U.S. history (PhD). *Program availability:* Part-time. *Entrance requirements:* For master's, GRE General Test. Additional exam requirements/recommendations for international students: required—TOEFL. Electronic applications accepted.

The University of North Carolina Wilmington, College of Arts and Sciences, Department of History, Wilmington, NC 28403-3297. Offers MA. *Program availability:* Part-time, 100% online. *Faculty:* 26 full-time (8 women). *Students:* 11 full-time (5 women), 46 part-time (27 women); includes 6 minority (3 Black or African American, non-Hispanic/Latino; 1 American Indian or Alaska Native, non-Hispanic/Latino; 2 Hispanic/Latino). Average age 33. 43 applicants, 86% accepted, 30 enrolled. In 2019, 19 master's awarded. *Degree requirements:* For master's, comprehensive exam, thesis or alternative. *Entrance requirements:* For master's, GRE General Test, 3 recommendations, essay, writing sample (research paper preferred). Additional exam requirements/recommendations for international students: required—TOEFL (minimum score 79 iBT), IELTS (minimum score 6.5). *Application deadline:* For fall admission, 7/1 for domestic students. Applications are processed on a rolling basis. Application fee: $75. Electronic applications accepted. *Expenses: Tuition, area resident:* Full-time $4719; part-time $326 per credit hour. Tuition, state resident: full-time $4719; part-time $326 per credit hour. Tuition, nonresident: full-time $18,548; part-time $1099 per credit hour. *Required fees:* $2738. Tuition and fees vary according to program. *Financial support:* Teaching assistantships, scholarships/grants, and out-of-state tuition remission available. Financial award application deadline: 1/1; financial award applicants required to submit FAFSA. *Unit head:* Dr. Lynn Mollenauer, Chair, 910-962-3308, Fax: 910-962-7011, E-mail: mollenauerl@uncw.edu. *Application contact:* Dr. W. Taylor Fain, Graduate Director, 910-962-3305, Fax: 910-962-7011, E-mail: fainwt@uncw.edu.
Website: http://www.uncw.edu/hst/graduate/index.html

University of North Dakota, Graduate School, College of Arts and Sciences, Department of History, Grand Forks, ND 58202. Offers M Ed, MA, DA, PhD. *Program availability:* Part-time. *Degree requirements:* For master's, comprehensive exam (for some programs), thesis (for some programs), final exam; for doctorate, comprehensive exam, thesis/dissertation, final exam. *Entrance requirements:* For master's, minimum GPA of 3.0; for doctorate, minimum GPA of 3.5. Additional exam requirements/recommendations for international students: required—TOEFL (minimum score 550 paper-based; 79 iBT), IELTS (minimum score 6.5). Electronic applications accepted.

University of Northern British Columbia, Office of Graduate Studies, Prince George, BC V2N 4Z9, Canada. Offers business administration (Diploma); community health science (M Sc); disability management (MA); education (M Ed); first nations studies (MA); gender studies (MA); history (MA); interdisciplinary studies (MA); international studies (MA); mathematical, computer and physical sciences (M Sc); natural resources and environmental studies (M Sc, MA, MNRES, PhD); political science (MA); psychology (M Sc, PhD); social work (MSW). *Program availability:* Part-time, evening/weekend, online learning. *Degree requirements:* For master's, thesis; for doctorate, thesis/dissertation. *Entrance requirements:* For master's, GRE, minimum B average in undergraduate course work; for doctorate, candidacy exam, minimum A average in graduate course work.

University of Northern Colorado, Graduate School, College of Humanities and Social Sciences, Department of History, Greeley, CO 80639. Offers MA. *Program availability:* Part-time. *Degree requirements:* For master's, comprehensive exam, thesis or alternative. *Entrance requirements:* For master's, GRE, 3 letters of recommendation. Electronic applications accepted.

University of Northern Iowa, Graduate College, College of Social and Behavioral Sciences, Department of History, Cedar Falls, IA 50614. Offers history (MA); public history (MA). *Program availability:* Part-time. *Degree requirements:* For master's, comprehensive exam (for some programs), thesis or alternative. *Entrance requirements:* For master's, minimum GPA of 3.2. Additional exam requirements/recommendations for international students: required—TOEFL (minimum score 500 paper-based; 61 iBT). Electronic applications accepted.

University of North Florida, College of Arts and Sciences, Department of History, Jacksonville, FL 32224. Offers European history (MA); U.S. history (MA). *Program availability:* Part-time. *Degree requirements:* For master's, comprehensive exam (for some programs), thesis optional. *Entrance requirements:* For master's, GRE General Test, 3 letters of recommendation, minimum GPA of 3.0 in last 60 hours of course work. Additional exam requirements/recommendations for international students: required—TOEFL (minimum score 500 paper-based; 61 iBT). Electronic applications accepted.

University of North Georgia, Department of History, Anthropology and Philosophy, Dahlonega, GA 30597. Offers history (MA), including American history, military history, world history. *Unit head:* Dr. Jeff Pardue, Department Head, 678-717-3867. *Application contact:* Cory Thornton, Director of Graduate Admissions, 706-867-2077, E-mail: cory.thornton@ung.edu.
Website: http://ung.edu/history-anthropology-philosophy/

University of North Texas, Toulouse Graduate School, Denton, TX 76203-5459. Offers accounting (MS); applied anthropology (MA, MS); applied behavior analysis (Certificate); applied geography (MA); applied technology and performance improvement (M Ed, MS); art education (MA); art history (MA); arts leadership (Certificate); audiology (Au D); behavior analysis (MS); behavioral science (PhD); biochemistry and molecular biology (MS); biology (MA, MS); biomedical engineering (MS); business analysis (MS); chemistry (MS); clinical health psychology (PhD); communication studies (MA, MS); computer engineering (MS); computer science (MS); counseling (M Ed, MS), including clinical mental health counseling (MS), college and university counseling, elementary school counseling, secondary school counseling; creative writing (MA); criminal justice (MS); curriculum and instruction (M Ed); decision sciences (MBA); design (MA, MFA), including fashion design (MFA), innovation studies, interior design (MFA); early childhood studies (MS); economics (MS); educational leadership (M Ed, Ed D); educational psychology (MS, PhD), including family studies (MS), gifted and talented (MS), human development (MS), learning and cognition (MS), research, measurement and evaluation (MS); electrical engineering (MS); emergency management (MPA); engineering technology (MS); English (MA); English as a second language (MA); environmental science (MS); finance (MBA, MS); financial management (MPA); French (MA); health services management (MBA); higher education (M Ed, Ed D); history (MA, MS); hospitality management (MS); human resources management (MPA); information science (MS); information systems (PhD); information technologies (MBA); interdisciplinary studies (MA, MS); international studies (MA); international sustainable tourism (MS); jazz studies (MM); journalism (MA, MJ, Graduate Certificate), including interactive and virtual digital communication (Graduate Certificate), narrative journalism (Graduate Certificate), public relations (Graduate Certificate); kinesiology (MS); linguistics (MA); local government management (MPA); logistics (PhD); logistics and supply chain management (MBA); long-term care, senior housing, and aging services (MA); management (PhD); marketing (MBA); mathematics (MA, MS); mechanical and energy engineering (MS, PhD); music (MA), including ethnomusicology, music theory, musicology, performance; music composition (PhD); music education (MM Ed, PhD); nonprofit management (MPA); operations and supply chain management (MBA); performance (MM, DMA); philosophy (MA); political science (MA); professional and technical communication (MA); radio, television and film (MA, MFA); rehabilitation counseling (Certificate); sociology (MA); Spanish (MA); special education (M Ed); speech-language pathology (MA); strategic management (MBA); studio art (MFA); teaching (M Ed); MBA/MS. *Program availability:* Part-time, evening/weekend, online learning. Terminal master's awarded for partial completion of doctoral program. *Degree requirements:* For master's, variable foreign language requirement, comprehensive exam (for some programs), thesis (for some programs); for doctorate, variable foreign language requirement, comprehensive exam (for some programs), thesis/dissertation; for other advanced degree, variable foreign language requirement, comprehensive exam (for some programs). *Entrance requirements:* For master's and doctorate, GRE, GMAT. Additional exam requirements/recommendations for international students: required—TOEFL (minimum score 550 paper-based; 79 iBT). Electronic applications accepted.

University of Notre Dame, The Graduate School, College of Arts and Letters, Division of Humanities, Department of History, Notre Dame, IN 46556. Offers MA, PhD. *Degree requirements:* For doctorate, one foreign language, thesis/dissertation, candidacy exam. *Entrance requirements:* For doctorate, GRE General Test. Additional exam requirements/recommendations for international students: required—TOEFL (minimum score 600 paper-based; 80 iBT). Electronic applications accepted.

University of Oklahoma, College of Arts and Sciences, Department of History, Norman, OK 73019. Offers MA, PhD. *Degree requirements:* For master's, comprehensive exam (for some programs), thesis (for some programs), 30 hours for thesis option; 34 hours for non-thesis option plus a 4-hour written exam; for doctorate, one foreign language, comprehensive exam, thesis/dissertation. *Entrance requirements:* For master's, GRE, 3 letters of reference, preferably from applicant's professors; statement of purpose; writing sample; minimum GPA of 3.5; for doctorate, GRE, 3 letters of reference, preferably from applicant's history professors; statement of purpose; writing sample; minimum GPA of 3.5. Additional exam requirements/recommendations for international students: required—TOEFL (minimum score 79 iBT) or IELTS (minimum score 6.5). Electronic applications accepted. *Expenses:* Tuition, state resident: full-time $6583.20; part-time $274.30 per credit hour. Tuition, nonresident: full-time $21,242; part-time $885.10 per credit hour. *International tuition:* $21,242.40 full-time. *Required fees:* $1994.20; $72.55 per credit hour. $126.50 per semester. Tuition and fees vary according to course load and degree level.

University of Oregon, Graduate School, College of Arts and Sciences, Department of History, Eugene, OR 97403. Offers MA, PhD. *Degree requirements:* For master's, one foreign language, thesis or alternative, written exam; for doctorate, 2 foreign languages, thesis/dissertation, oral and written exams. *Entrance requirements:* For master's and doctorate, GRE General Test, minimum GPA of 3.0. Additional exam requirements/recommendations for international students: required—TOEFL.

University of Ottawa, Faculty of Graduate and Postdoctoral Studies, Faculty of Arts, Department of History, Ottawa, ON K1N 6N5, Canada. Offers MA, PhD. *Degree requirements:* For master's, 2 foreign languages, thesis or alternative; for doctorate, 2 foreign languages, thesis/dissertation, oral exam. *Entrance requirements:* For master's, honors degree or equivalent, minimum B average; for doctorate, master's degree, minimum B+ average. Electronic applications accepted.

University of Pennsylvania, School of Arts and Sciences, Graduate Group in Ancient History, Philadelphia, PA 19104. Offers AM, PhD. *Faculty:* 19 full-time (6 women), 2 part-time/adjunct (0 women). *Students:* 12 full-time (2 women); includes 1 minority (Hispanic/Latino), 2 international. Average age 28. 24 applicants, 17% accepted. In 2019, 1 doctorate awarded. Application fee: $90.
Website: http://www.sas.upenn.edu/graduate-division

University of Pennsylvania, School of Arts and Sciences, Graduate Group in History, Philadelphia, PA 19104. Offers AM, PhD. *Faculty:* 69 full-time (32 women), 9 part-time/adjunct (3 women). *Students:* 72 full-time (34 women), 2 part-time (1 woman); includes 12 minority (3 Black or African American, non-Hispanic/Latino; 2 Asian, non-Hispanic/Latino; 4 Hispanic/Latino; 3 Two or more races, non-Hispanic/Latino), 22 international. Average age 30. 254 applicants, 11% accepted, 11 enrolled. In 2019, 8 master's, 10 doctorates awarded. Terminal master's awarded for partial completion of doctoral program. Application fee: $90.
Website: http://www.sas.upenn.edu/graduate-division

University of Pittsburgh, Kenneth P. Dietrich School of Arts and Sciences, Department of History, Pittsburgh, PA 15260. Offers MA, PhD. *Faculty:* 33 full-time (15 women). *Students:* 23 full-time (9 women), 1 part-time (0 women); includes 4 minority (2 Black or African American, non-Hispanic/Latino; 2 Hispanic/Latino), 6 international. Average age 25. 54 applicants, 20% accepted, 3 enrolled. In 2019, 3 master's, 6 doctorates awarded. Terminal master's awarded for partial completion of doctoral program. *Degree requirements:* For master's, one foreign language, comprehensive exam, thesis; for doctorate, one foreign language, comprehensive exam, thesis/dissertation. *Entrance requirements:* For master's and doctorate, writing sample. Additional exam requirements/recommendations for international students: required—TOEFL (minimum score 550 paper-based; 90 iBT), IELTS (minimum score 7). *Application deadline:* For fall admission, 1/15 for domestic and international students. Application fee: $75. Electronic applications accepted. *Financial support:* In 2019–20, 18 students received support, including 10 fellowships with full tuition reimbursements available (averaging $23,000 per year), 11 teaching assistantships with full tuition reimbursements available (averaging $19,000 per year); scholarships/grants, health care benefits, tuition waivers (full and partial), and unspecified assistantships also available. Financial award application deadline: 1/15. *Unit head:* Dr. Diego Holstein, Professor & Chair, 412-648-7452, Fax: 412-648-9074, E-mail: holstein@pitt.edu. *Application contact:* Patty Landon, Academic Administrator, 412-687-7450, Fax: 412-648-9074, E-mail: pal14@pitt.edu.
Website: http://www.history.pitt.edu

University of Puerto Rico at Río Piedras, College of Humanities, Department of History, San Juan, PR 00931-3300. Offers Caribbean history (PhD); history (MA); Puerto Rican history (PhD). *Program availability:* Part-time. *Degree requirements:* For master's, one foreign language, comprehensive exam, thesis; for doctorate, one foreign language, comprehensive exam, thesis/dissertation. *Entrance requirements:* For master's, PAEG or GRE, interview, minimum GPA of 3.0, 2 letters of recommendation; for doctorate, PAEG or GRE, interview, master's degree, minimum GPA of 3.0, 2 letters of recommendation.

University of Regina, Faculty of Graduate Studies and Research, Faculty of Arts, Department of History, Regina, SK S4S 0A2, Canada. Offers MA. *Program availability:* Part-time. *Faculty:* 12 full-time (5 women), 2 part-time/adjunct (0 women). *Students:* 8 full-time (3 women), 1 part-time (0 women). Average age 30. 16 applicants, 38% accepted. In 2019, 2 master's awarded. *Degree requirements:* For master's, thesis. *Entrance requirements:* For master's, transcript, degree certificate and 2 letters of recommendation. Additional exam requirements/recommendations for international students: required—TOEFL (minimum score 580 paper-based; 80 iBT), IELTS (minimum score 6.5), PTE (minimum score 59), other options are CANTEST, MELAB, CAEL and U of R ESL; GRE is required for Psychology. *Application deadline:* For fall admission, 3/31 for domestic and international students. Application fee: $100. Electronic applications accepted. *Expenses: Tuition:* Full-time $6684 Canadian dollars. *Required fees:* $100 Canadian dollars; $3351.45 Canadian dollars per trimester. $1117.15 Canadian dollars per semester. Tuition and fees vary according to course level, course load, degree level and program. *Financial support:* Fellowships, research assistantships, teaching assistantships, career-related internships or fieldwork, scholarships/grants, unspecified assistantships, and travel award and Graduate Scholarship Base funds available. Support available to part-time students. Financial award application deadline: 9/30. *Unit head:* Dr. Raymond Blake, Department Head, 306-585-5431, Fax: 306-585-4827, E-mail: raymond.blake@uregina.ca. *Application contact:* Dr. Philip Charrier, Graduate Program Coordinator, 306-585-4215, Fax: 306-585-4827, E-mail: philip.charrier@uregina.ca.
Website: http://www.uregina.ca/arts/history

University of Rhode Island, Graduate School, College of Arts and Sciences, Department of History, Kingston, RI 02881. Offers archaeology and anthropology (MA); European history (MA), including European history, United States history; MLIS/MA. *Program availability:* Part-time. *Faculty:* 16 full-time (7 women). *Students:* 7 full-time (2 women), 10 part-time (5 women). 11 applicants, 91% accepted, 4 enrolled. In 2019, 5 master's awarded. *Entrance requirements:* Additional exam requirements/recommendations for international students: required—TOEFL. *Application deadline:* For fall admission, 7/15 for domestic students; for spring admission, 11/15 for domestic students. Application fee: $65. Electronic applications accepted. *Expenses: Tuition, area resident:* Full-time $13,734; part-time $763 per credit. Tuition, state resident: full-time $13,734; part-time $763 per credit. Tuition, nonresident: full-time $26,512; part-time $1473 per credit. *International tuition:* $26,512 full-time. *Required fees:* $1780; $52 per credit. $35 per term. One-time fee: $165. *Financial support:* In 2019–20, 4 teaching assistantships with tuition reimbursements (averaging $18,986 per year) were awarded. Financial award application deadline: 2/1; financial award applicants required to submit FAFSA. *Unit head:* Dr. Rod Mather, Chair, 401-874-4093, E-mail: rodmather@uri.edu. *Application contact:* Dr. Evelyn Sterne, Director of Graduate Studies, 401-874-4074, E-mail: sterne@uri.edu.
Website: http://www.uri.edu/artsci/his/

University of Rochester, School of Arts and Sciences, Department of History, Rochester, NY 14627. Offers MA, PhD. *Faculty:* 19 full-time (5 women). *Students:* 33 full-time (20 women); includes 4 minority (1 Asian, non-Hispanic/Latino; 2 Hispanic/Latino; 1 Two or more races, non-Hispanic/Latino), 4 international. Average age 33. 21 applicants, 33% accepted, 3 enrolled. In 2019, 5 master's, 1 doctorate awarded. Terminal master's awarded for partial completion of doctoral program. *Degree requirements:* For master's, thesis optional, essay; for doctorate, 2 foreign languages, comprehensive exam, thesis/dissertation, first- and second-year essays, teaching assistant for two semesters. *Entrance requirements:* For master's and doctorate, GRE General Test, statement of purpose, transcripts, three letters of recommendation, writing sample. Additional exam requirements/recommendations for international students: required—TOEFL (minimum score 100 iBT), IELTS (minimum score 8). *Application deadline:* For fall admission, 1/15 for domestic and international students. Application fee: $60. Electronic applications accepted. *Financial support:* In 2019–20, 9 students received support, including 3 fellowships (averaging $19,400 per year), 6 teaching assistantships (averaging $20,000 per year); scholarships/grants, tuition waivers (full and partial), and unspecified assistantships also available. Financial award application deadline: 3/15. *Unit head:* Laura Smoller, Professor and Chair, 585-275-7721, E-mail: laura.smoller@rochester.edu. *Application contact:* Chelsea Kuhn, Graduate Coordinator, 585-275-2053, E-mail: chelsea.kuhn@rochester.edu.
Website: https://www.sas.rochester.edu/his/graduate/index.html

University of Saskatchewan, College of Graduate and Postdoctoral Studies, College of Arts and Science, Department of History, Saskatoon, SK S7N 5A2, Canada. Offers MA, PhD. *Program availability:* Part-time. *Degree requirements:* For master's, thesis; for doctorate, comprehensive exam (for some programs), thesis/dissertation. *Entrance requirements:* Additional exam requirements/recommendations for international students: required—TOEFL (minimum score 80 iBT); recommended—IELTS (minimum score 6.5). Electronic applications accepted.

University of South Africa, College of Human Sciences, Pretoria, South Africa. Offers adult education (M Ed); African languages (MA, PhD); African politics (MA, PhD); Afrikaans (MA, PhD); ancient history (MA, PhD); ancient Near Eastern studies (MA, PhD); anthropology (MA, PhD); applied linguistics (MA); Arabic (MA, PhD); archaeology (MA); art history (MA); Biblical archaeology (MA); Biblical studies (M Th, D Th, PhD); Christian spirituality (M Th, D Th); church history (M Th, D Th); classical studies (MA, PhD); clinical psychology (MA); communication (MA, PhD); comparative education (M Ed, Ed D); consulting psychology (D Admin, D Com, PhD); curriculum studies (M Ed, Ed D); development studies (M Admin, MA, D Admin, PhD); didactics (M Ed, Ed D); education (M Tech); education management (M Ed, Ed D); educational psychology (M Ed); English (MA); environmental education (M Ed); French (MA, PhD); German (MA, PhD); Greek (MA); guidance and counseling (M Ed); health studies (MA, PhD), including health sciences education (MA), health services management (MA), medical and surgical nursing science (critical care general) (MA), midwifery and neonatal nursing science (MA), trauma and emergency care (MA); history (MA, PhD); history of education (Ed D); inclusive education (M Ed, Ed D); information and communications technology policy and regulation (MA); information science (MA, MIS, PhD); international politics

(MA, PhD); Islamic studies (MA, PhD); Italian (MA, PhD); Judaica (MA, PhD); linguistics (MA, PhD); mathematical education (M Ed); mathematics education (MA); missiology (M Th, D Th); modern Hebrew (MA, PhD); musicology (MA, MMus, D Mus, PhD); natural science education (M Ed); New Testament (M Th, D Th); Old Testament (D Th); pastoral therapy (M Th, D Th); philosophy (MA); philosophy of education (M Ed, Ed D); politics (MA, PhD); Portuguese (MA, PhD); practical theology (M Th, D Th); psychology (MA, MS, PhD); psychology of education (M Ed, Ed D); public health (MA); religious studies (MA, D Th, PhD); Romance languages (MA); Russian (MA, PhD); Semitic languages (MA, PhD); social behavior studies in HIV/AIDS (MA); social science (mental health) (MA); social science in development studies (MA); social science in psychology (MA); social science in social work (MA); social science in sociology (MA); social work (MSW, DSW, PhD); socio-education (M Ed, Ed D); sociolinguistics (MA); sociology (MA, PhD); Spanish (MA, PhD); systematic theology (M Th, D Th); TESOL (teaching English to speakers of other languages) (MA); theological ethics (M Th, D Th); theory of literature (MA, PhD); urban ministries (D Th); urban ministry (M Th).

University of South Alabama, College of Arts and Sciences, Department of History, Mobile, AL 36688. Offers MA. *Program availability:* Part-time, evening/weekend. *Faculty:* 7 full-time (4 women). *Students:* 3 full-time (all women), 7 part-time (4 women). Average age 34. 2 applicants, 100% accepted, 1 enrolled. In 2019, 3 master's awarded. *Degree requirements:* For master's, comprehensive exam, thesis optional. *Entrance requirements:* For master's, GRE. Additional exam requirements/recommendations for international students: required—TOEFL (minimum score 525 paper-based; 71 iBT). *Application deadline:* For fall admission, 7/10 priority date for domestic students, 6/15 priority date for international students; for spring admission, 11/20 priority date for domestic students, 11/1 priority date for international students; for summer admission, 4/20 for domestic students, 3/20 for international students. Applications are processed on a rolling basis. Application fee: $35. Electronic applications accepted. *Expenses: Tuition, area resident:* Part-time $442 per credit hour. Tuition, state resident: full-time $10,608; part-time $442 per credit hour. Tuition, nonresident: full-time $21,216; part-time $884 per credit hour. *Financial support:* Fellowships, research assistantships, teaching assistantships, career-related internships or fieldwork, Federal Work-Study, institutionally sponsored loans, scholarships/grants, and unspecified assistantships available. Support available to part-time students. Financial award application deadline: 3/31; financial award applicants required to submit FAFSA. *Unit head:* Dr. David Messenger, Chair, History, 251-460-6210, E-mail: davidamessenger@southalabama.edu. *Application contact:* Dr. Marsha Hamilton, Director of Graduate Studies, History, 251-460-7611, E-mail: mhamilton@southalabama.edu.
Website: http://www.southalabama.edu/colleges/artsandsci/history/gradprogram.html

University of South Carolina, The Graduate School, College of Arts and Sciences, Department of History, Columbia, SC 29208. Offers history (MA, PhD); public history (MA, Certificate), including archive management (MA), historic preservation (MA), museum administration (MA), museum management (Certificate); MLIS/MA. *Program availability:* Part-time. Terminal master's awarded for partial completion of doctoral program. *Degree requirements:* For master's, one foreign language, thesis; for doctorate, one foreign language, thesis/dissertation. *Entrance requirements:* For master's and doctorate, GRE General Test. Additional exam requirements/recommendations for international students: required—TOEFL. Electronic applications accepted.

University of South Dakota, Graduate School, College of Arts and Sciences, Department of History, Vermillion, SD 57069. Offers MA, JD/MA. *Program availability:* Part-time. *Degree requirements:* For master's, thesis (for some programs). *Entrance requirements:* For master's, GRE General Test, minimum GPA of 2.7. Additional exam requirements/recommendations for international students: required—TOEFL (minimum score 550 paper-based; 79 iBT). Electronic applications accepted.

University of Southern California, Graduate School, Dana and David Dornsife College of Letters, Arts and Sciences, Department of History, Los Angeles, CA 90089. Offers PhD. *Degree requirements:* For doctorate, 2 foreign languages, comprehensive exam, thesis/dissertation, 60 semester units of acceptable coursework. *Entrance requirements:* For doctorate, GRE General Test. Additional exam requirements/recommendations for international students: recommended—TOEFL. Electronic applications accepted.

University of South Florida, College of Arts and Sciences, Department of History, Tampa, FL 33620-9951. Offers MA, PhD. *Program availability:* Part-time, evening/weekend. *Faculty:* 17 full-time (8 women). *Students:* 36 full-time (11 women), 20 part-time (11 women); includes 4 minority (1 American Indian or Alaska Native, non-Hispanic/Latino; 2 Hispanic/Latino; 1 Two or more races, non-Hispanic/Latino), 1 international. Average age 33. 35 applicants, 60% accepted, 13 enrolled. In 2019, 13 master's, 5 doctorates awarded. *Degree requirements:* For master's, one foreign language, comprehensive exam, thesis optional; for doctorate, one foreign language, comprehensive exam, thesis/dissertation. *Entrance requirements:* For master's, minimum GPA of 3.0, two letters of recommendation, 2-page statement of purpose, writing sample; for doctorate, three letters of recommendation, statement of purpose, writing sample, foreign language proficiency in the field of study. Additional exam requirements/recommendations for international students: required—TOEFL, TOEFL (minimum score 550 paper-based; 79 iBT) or IELTS (minimum score 6.5). *Application deadline:* For fall admission, 12/1 priority date for domestic students, 12/1 for international students. Applications are processed on a rolling basis. Application fee: $30. Electronic applications accepted. *Financial support:* In 2019–20, 17 students received support, including 17 teaching assistantships with tuition reimbursements available (averaging $12,750 per year); unspecified assistantships also available. Financial award application deadline: 1/15. *Unit head:* Dr. Fraser Ottanelli, Professor and Chair, 813-974-6209, Fax: 813-974-6228, E-mail: ottanelli@usf.edu. *Application contact:* Dr. Kees Boterbloem, Professor and Graduate Program Director, 813-974-2807, E-mail: cboterbl@usf.edu.
Website: http://history.usf.edu

The University of Tennessee, Graduate School, College of Arts and Sciences, Department of History, Knoxville, TN 37996. Offers American history (PhD); European history (PhD); history (MA). *Program availability:* Part-time. *Degree requirements:* For master's, thesis or alternative; for doctorate, one foreign language, thesis/dissertation. *Entrance requirements:* For master's and doctorate, GRE General Test, minimum GPA of 2.7. Additional exam requirements/recommendations for international students: required—TOEFL. Electronic applications accepted.

The University of Texas at Arlington, Graduate School, College of Liberal Arts, Department of History, Arlington, TX 76019. Offers history (MA); transatlantic history (PhD). *Program availability:* Part-time, evening/weekend. *Degree requirements:* For master's, one foreign language, comprehensive exam (for some programs), thesis (for some programs); for doctorate, one foreign language, comprehensive exam, thesis/dissertation. *Entrance requirements:* For master's, GRE General Test, minimum GPA of 3.0 in last 60 hours, 3 letters of recommendation; for doctorate, GRE General Test, minimum graduate GPA of 3.5, 3 letters of recommendation, academic writing sample. Additional exam requirements/recommendations for international students: required—TOEFL (minimum score 550 paper-based). Electronic applications accepted.

The University of Texas at Austin, Graduate School, College of Liberal Arts, Department of History, Austin, TX 78712-1111. Offers MA, PhD. *Degree requirements:* For doctorate, thesis/dissertation. *Entrance requirements:* For master's and doctorate, GRE General Test. Electronic applications accepted.

The University of Texas at Dallas, School of Arts and Humanities, Richardson, TX 75080. Offers art history (MA); history (MA); humanities (MA, PhD), including aesthetic studies, history of ideas, studies in literature; Latin American studies (MA). *Program availability:* Part-time, evening/weekend. *Faculty:* 48 full-time (19 women), 11 part-time/adjunct (6 women). *Students:* 123 full-time (76 women), 116 part-time (71 women); includes 62 minority (14 Black or African American, non-Hispanic/Latino; 3 American Indian or Alaska Native, non-Hispanic/Latino; 9 Asian, non-Hispanic/Latino; 25 Hispanic/Latino; 11 Two or more races, non-Hispanic/Latino), 27 international. Average age 40. 130 applicants, 60% accepted, 59 enrolled. In 2019, 30 master's, 16 doctorates awarded. *Degree requirements:* For master's, one foreign language, portfolio; for doctorate, one foreign language, thesis/dissertation. *Entrance requirements:* For master's and doctorate, minimum GPA of 3.0 in undergraduate course work in field. Additional exam requirements/recommendations for international students: required—TOEFL (minimum score 550 paper-based). *Application deadline:* For fall admission, 7/15 for domestic students, 5/1 priority date for international students; for spring admission, 11/15 for domestic students, 9/1 priority date for international students. Applications are processed on a rolling basis. Application fee: $50 ($100 for international students). Electronic applications accepted. *Expenses: Tuition, area resident:* Full-time $16,504. Tuition, state resident: full-time $16,504. Tuition, nonresident: full-time $34,266. Tuition and fees vary according to course load. *Financial support:* In 2019–20, 87 students received support, including 9 fellowships (averaging $5,074 per year), 14 research assistantships with partial tuition reimbursements available (averaging $26,575 per year), 69 teaching assistantships with partial tuition reimbursements available (averaging $14,961 per year); Federal Work-Study, institutionally sponsored loans, scholarships/grants, and unspecified assistantships also available. Support available to part-time students. Financial award application deadline: 4/30; financial award applicants required to submit FAFSA. *Unit head:* Dr. Nils Roemer, Interim Dean, 972-883-2984, Fax: 972-883-2989, E-mail: nroemer@utdallas.edu. *Application contact:* Dr. John Gooch, Associate Dean of Graduate Studies, 972-883-2756, Fax: 972-883-2989, E-mail: john.gooch@utdallas.edu.
Website: http://www.utdallas.edu/ah/

The University of Texas at El Paso, Graduate School, College of Liberal Arts, Department of History, El Paso, TX 79968-0001. Offers borderlands history (MA, PhD); history (MA). *Program availability:* Part-time. *Degree requirements:* For master's, thesis optional; for doctorate, 2 foreign languages, thesis/dissertation. *Entrance requirements:* For master's, GRE, minimum GPA of 3.0, writing sample, letters of recommendation, transcripts; for doctorate, GRE, statement of purpose, writing sample, letters of recommendation, transcripts. Additional exam requirements/recommendations for international students: required—TOEFL; recommended—IELTS.

The University of Texas at San Antonio, College of Liberal and Fine Arts, Department of History, San Antonio, TX 78249-0617. Offers MA. *Program availability:* Part-time. *Degree requirements:* For master's, comprehensive exam, thesis optional, minimum of 30 credit hours. *Entrance requirements:* For master's, GRE, bachelor's degree with 18 credit hours in field of study or in another appropriate field of study (12 of these hours must be at the upper-division level with minimum GPA of 3.0 in last 60 hours), statement of purpose. Additional exam requirements/recommendations for international students: required—TOEFL (minimum score 550 paper-based; 79 iBT), IELTS (minimum score 6.5). Electronic applications accepted. *Expenses:* Contact institution.

The University of Texas at Tyler, College of Arts and Sciences, Department of History and Political Science, Tyler, TX 75799-0001. Offers MA. *Program availability:* Part-time, evening/weekend. *Faculty:* 8 full-time (2 women), 8 part-time/adjunct (2 women). *Students:* 9 full-time (8 women), 19 part-time (10 women); includes 9 minority (5 Black or African American, non-Hispanic/Latino; 1 Asian, non-Hispanic/Latino; 1 Hispanic/Latino; 2 Two or more races, non-Hispanic/Latino), 1 international. Average age 32. 21 applicants, 100% accepted, 11 enrolled. In 2019, 9 master's awarded. *Degree requirements:* For master's, one foreign language, comprehensive exam, thesis optional. *Entrance requirements:* For master's, GRE General Test, minimum GPA of 3.0. Additional exam requirements/recommendations for international students: required—TOEFL. *Application deadline:* For fall admission, 8/17 priority date for domestic students, 7/1 priority date for international students; for spring admission, 12/21 priority date for domestic students, 11/1 priority date for international students. Applications are processed on a rolling basis. Application fee: $25 ($50 for international students). Electronic applications accepted. *Financial support:* Federal Work-Study and unspecified assistantships available. Support available to part-time students. Financial award application deadline: 7/1; financial award applicants required to submit FAFSA. *Unit head:* Dr. Marcus Stadelmann, Chair, 903-566-7412, E-mail: mstadelmann@uttyler.edu. *Application contact:* Dr. Marcus Stadelmann, Chair, 903-566-7412, E-mail: mstadelmann@uttyler.edu.
Website: https://www.uttyler.edu/cas/advising/graduate/masters-degrees.php

The University of Texas of the Permian Basin, Office of Graduate Studies, College of Arts and Sciences, Department of History, Odessa, TX 79762-0001. Offers MA. *Program availability:* Part-time, evening/weekend. *Degree requirements:* For master's, comprehensive exam (for some programs), thesis (for some programs). *Entrance requirements:* For master's, GRE General Test. Additional exam requirements/recommendations for international students: required—TOEFL (minimum score 550 paper-based).

The University of Texas Rio Grande Valley, College of Liberal Arts, Department of History, Edinburg, TX 78539. Offers MA, MAIS. *Faculty:* 14 full-time (6 women). *Students:* 6 full-time (1 woman), 28 part-time (12 women); includes 28 minority (all Hispanic/Latino). Average age 32. 3 applicants, 100% accepted, 3 enrolled. In 2019, 6 master's awarded. *Expenses: Tuition, area resident:* Full-time $5959; part-time $440 per credit hour. Tuition, state resident: full-time $5959. Tuition, nonresident: full-time $5959. *International tuition:* $13,321 full-time. *Required fees:* $1169; $185 per credit hour.
Website: utrgv.edu/history/index.htm

The University of Toledo, College of Graduate Studies, College of Languages, Literature and Social Sciences, Department of History, Toledo, OH 43606-3390. Offers MA, PhD. *Program availability:* Part-time. *Degree requirements:* For master's, comprehensive exam (for some programs), thesis or comprehensive exam; for doctorate, thesis/dissertation, oral and written exams. *Entrance requirements:* For master's and doctorate, GRE General Test, minimum cumulative point-hour ratio of 2.7 for all previous academic work, three letters of recommendation. Additional exam requirements/recommendations for international students: required—TOEFL (minimum score 550 paper-based; 80 iBT). Electronic applications accepted.

University of Toronto, School of Graduate Studies, Faculty of Arts and Science, Department of History, Toronto, ON M5S 1A1, Canada. Offers MA, PhD. *Program availability:* Part-time. *Degree requirements:* For master's, one foreign language, thesis or research essay, French language exam; for doctorate, comprehensive exam, thesis/

dissertation, oral examination/thesis defense. *Entrance requirements:* For master's, minimum B+ average or GPA of 3.3, 6 full academic year history courses; for doctorate, MA in history, minimum A- average or GPA of 3.7. Additional exam requirements/recommendations for international students: required—TOEFL (minimum score 580 paper-based; 93 iBT), TWE (minimum score 5). Electronic applications accepted.

University of Utah, Graduate School, College of Humanities, Department of History, Salt Lake City, UT 84112. Offers MA, MS, PhD. *Program availability:* Part-time. *Faculty:* 15 full-time (6 women). *Students:* 21 full-time (14 women), 18 part-time (7 women); includes 7 minority (2 American Indian or Alaska Native, non-Hispanic/Latino; 3 Hispanic/Latino; 2 Two or more races, non-Hispanic/Latino). Average age 36. 30 applicants, 50% accepted, 12 enrolled. In 2019, 6 master's awarded. *Degree requirements:* For master's, one foreign language, thesis (for some programs); for doctorate, one foreign language, comprehensive exam, thesis/dissertation. *Entrance requirements:* Additional exam requirements/recommendations for international students: required—TOEFL (minimum score 80 paper-based; 80 iBT). *Application deadline:* For fall admission, 12/1 for domestic and international students. Application fee: $55 ($65 for international students). Electronic applications accepted. *Expenses:* Tuition, state resident: full-time $7085; part-time $272.51 per credit hour. Tuition, nonresident: full-time $24,937; part-time $959.12 per credit hour. *Required fees:* $880.52; $880.52 per semester. Tuition and fees vary according to degree level, program and student level. *Financial support:* In 2019–20, 19 students received support, including 2 fellowships (averaging $6,500 per year), 16 teaching assistantships with full tuition reimbursements available (averaging $12,000 per year). Financial award application deadline: 11/1. *Unit head:* Benjamin Cohen, Department Chair, 801-581-6121, Fax: 801-585-0580, E-mail: isabel.moreira@utah.edu. *Application contact:* Amarilys Scott, Academic Advisor, 801-581-6121, Fax: 801-585-0580, E-mail: amarilys.scott@utah.edu.
Website: http://history.utah.edu

University of Utah, Graduate School, College of Humanities, Program in Middle East Studies, Salt Lake City, UT 84112. Offers Arabic (MA, PhD); Hebrew (MA); history (MA, PhD); Persian (MA, PhD); political science (MA, PhD). In 2019, 2 doctorates awarded. *Entrance requirements:* For master's, GRE General Test, minimum GPA of 3.2; for doctorate, GRE General Test, MA in Middle East studies or equivalent, minimum GPA of 3.2. Additional exam requirements/recommendations for international students: required—TOEFL (minimum score 580 paper-based; 92 iBT); recommended—IELTS (minimum score 7). Application fee: $55 ($65 for international students). *Expenses:* Tuition, state resident: full-time $7085; part-time $272.51 per credit hour. Tuition, nonresident: full-time $24,937; part-time $959.12 per credit hour. *Required fees:* $880.52; $880.52 per semester. Tuition and fees vary according to degree level, program and student level. *Unit head:* Johanna Watzinger-Tharp, Director, 801-581-7148, Fax: 801-581-6105, E-mail: j.tharp@utah.edu. *Application contact:* Kellie Hubbard, Academic Advisor, 801-581-5362, Fax: 801-581-6105, E-mail: kellie.hubbard@utah.edu.
Website: http://www.mec.utah.edu

University of Vermont, Graduate College, College of Arts and Sciences, Program in History, Burlington, VT 05405. Offers MA. *Degree requirements:* For master's, thesis. *Entrance requirements:* For master's, GRE General Test, writing sample (10 pages using primary sources). Additional exam requirements/recommendations for international students: required—TOEFL (minimum score 550 paper-based, 90 iBT) or IELTS (6.5). Electronic applications accepted. *Expenses:* Contact institution.

University of Victoria, Faculty of Graduate Studies, Faculty of Humanities, Department of History, Victoria, BC V8W 2Y2, Canada. Offers MA, PhD. *Program availability:* Part-time. *Degree requirements:* For master's, one foreign language, thesis; for doctorate, one foreign language, comprehensive exam, thesis/dissertation. *Entrance requirements:* Additional exam requirements/recommendations for international students: required—TOEFL (minimum score 600 paper-based), TWE. Electronic applications accepted.

University of Virginia, College and Graduate School of Arts and Sciences, Corcoran Department of History, Charlottesville, VA 22903. Offers MA, PhD, JD/MA. *Degree requirements:* For master's, one foreign language, essay; for doctorate, variable foreign language requirement, comprehensive exam, thesis/dissertation. *Entrance requirements:* For master's and doctorate, GRE General Test, 2 or more letters of recommendation. Additional exam requirements/recommendations for international students: required—TOEFL (minimum score 600 paper-based; 90 iBT), IELTS (minimum score 7). Electronic applications accepted.

University of Washington, Graduate School, College of Arts and Sciences, Department of History, Seattle, WA 98195. Offers MA, PhD. *Program availability:* Part-time. *Degree requirements:* For master's, one foreign language, comprehensive exam, thesis optional; for doctorate, one foreign language, comprehensive exam, thesis/dissertation. *Entrance requirements:* For master's and doctorate, GRE, minimum GPA of 3.0. Additional exam requirements/recommendations for international students: required—TOEFL. Electronic applications accepted.

University of Waterloo, Graduate Studies and Postdoctoral Affairs, Faculty of Arts, Department of Classical Studies, Waterloo, ON N2L 3G1, Canada. Offers ancient Mediterranean cultures (MA). *Degree requirements:* For master's, one foreign language.

University of Waterloo, Graduate Studies and Postdoctoral Affairs, Faculty of Arts, Department of History, Waterloo, ON N2L 3G1, Canada. Offers MA, PhD. *Program availability:* Part-time, evening/weekend. *Degree requirements:* For master's, one foreign language, thesis optional; for doctorate, one foreign language, thesis/dissertation. *Entrance requirements:* For master's, honors degree, minimum B+ average, resume; for doctorate, master's degree, minimum A average, resume, writing sample. Additional exam requirements/recommendations for international students: required—TOEFL, IELTS, PTE. Electronic applications accepted.

The University of West Alabama, School of Graduate Studies, College of Education, Program in Secondary Education, Livingston, AL 35470. Offers biology (MAT); English language arts (MAT); high school 6-12 (M Ed); history (MAT); mathematics (MAT); science (MAT); social science (MAT). *Program availability:* Part-time, evening/weekend, 100% online. *Faculty:* 15 full-time (5 women), 8 part-time/adjunct (2 women). *Students:* 237 full-time (161 women), 19 part-time (14 women); includes 47 minority (33 Black or African American, non-Hispanic/Latino; 3 American Indian or Alaska Native, non-Hispanic/Latino; 3 Hispanic/Latino; 8 Two or more races, non-Hispanic/Latino), 3 international. Average age 31. 71 applicants, 85% accepted, 52 enrolled. In 2019, 114 master's awarded. *Degree requirements:* For master's, comprehensive exam, thesis optional. *Entrance requirements:* For master's, GRE, minimum GPA of 2.75, verification of background clearance/fingerprints, valid bachelor's-level Professional Educator Certificate in same teaching field. Additional exam requirements/recommendations for international students: required—TOEFL (minimum score 500 paper-based; 61 iBT). *Application deadline:* Applications are processed on a rolling basis. Application fee: $40. Electronic applications accepted. *Expenses: Required fees:* $380; $130. *Financial support:* Teaching assistantships, Federal Work-Study, scholarships/grants, and unspecified assistantships available. Support available to part-time students. Financial award application deadline: 3/1; financial award applicants required to submit FAFSA. *Unit head:* Dr. Jodie Winship, Chair of College of Education, 205-652-5415, Fax: 205-652-3706, E-mail: jwinship@uwa.edu. *Application contact:* Dr. Jodie Winship, Chair of College of Education, 205-652-5415, Fax: 205-652-3706, E-mail: jwinship@uwa.edu.

The University of Western Ontario, School of Graduate and Postdoctoral Studies, Faculty of Social Science, Department of History, London, ON N6A 3K7, Canada. Offers MA, PhD. *Program availability:* Part-time. *Degree requirements:* For master's, one foreign language, thesis (for some programs); for doctorate, one foreign language, thesis/dissertation. *Entrance requirements:* For master's, minimum B+ average on last 10 senior courses; for doctorate, minimum A- average on MA or last year honors degree. Additional exam requirements/recommendations for international students: required—TOEFL.

University of West Florida, College of Arts, Social Sciences, and Humanities, Department of History, Pensacola, FL 32514-5750. Offers early American studies (MA); public history (MA); traditional history (MA). *Program availability:* Part-time, evening/weekend. *Degree requirements:* For master's, thesis or alternative. *Entrance requirements:* For master's, GRE (minimum score: verbal 500, writing 3.5) or MAT (minimum score 415), minimum GPA of 3.0; minimum 15 hours of upper-level history courses; official transcripts; letter of intent; writing sample (undergraduate research paper preferred). Additional exam requirements/recommendations for international students: required—TOEFL (minimum score 550 paper-based).

University of Windsor, Faculty of Graduate Studies, Faculty of Arts and Social Sciences, Department of History, Windsor, ON N9B 3P4, Canada. Offers MA. *Program availability:* Part-time. *Degree requirements:* For master's, thesis (for some programs). *Entrance requirements:* For master's, minimum B average. Additional exam requirements/recommendations for international students: required—TOEFL (minimum score 600 paper-based). Electronic applications accepted.

The University of Winnipeg, Faculty of Graduate Studies, Department of History, Winnipeg, MB R3B 2E9, Canada. Offers MA. *Program availability:* Part-time, evening/weekend. *Degree requirements:* For master's, one foreign language, comprehensive exam or thesis.

University of Wisconsin–Eau Claire, College of Arts and Sciences, Department of History, Eau Claire, WI 54702-4004. Offers public history (MA). *Program availability:* Part-time. *Degree requirements:* For master's, comprehensive exam, thesis optional, oral and written exams. *Entrance requirements:* For master's, minimum GPA of 3.15 during last 2 years, 3.3 in history, or 3.0 overall; research paper; bachelor's degree with minimum of 24 credits in history. Additional exam requirements/recommendations for international students: required—TOEFL (minimum score 79 iBT).

University of Wisconsin–Madison, Graduate School, College of Letters and Science, Department of History, Madison, WI 53706-1380. Offers African history (MA, PhD); Central Asian history (MA, PhD); comparative world history (MA, PhD); East Asian history (MA, PhD); European history (MA, PhD); gender and women's history (MA, PhD); Latin American and Caribbean history (MA, PhD); Middle Eastern history (MA, PhD); South Asian history (MA, PhD); Southeast Asian history (MA, PhD); United States history (MA, PhD). Terminal master's awarded for partial completion of doctoral program. *Degree requirements:* For master's, thesis (for some programs); for doctorate, variable foreign language requirement, thesis/dissertation. *Entrance requirements:* For master's and doctorate, GRE General Test. Additional exam requirements/recommendations for international students: required—Michigan English Language Assessment Battery or TOEFL. Electronic applications accepted.

University of Wisconsin–Milwaukee, Graduate School, College of Letters and Science, Department of History, Milwaukee, WI 53201-0413. Offers MA, PhD. *Program availability:* Part-time. *Degree requirements:* For master's, comprehensive exam, thesis or alternative; for doctorate, thesis/dissertation. *Entrance requirements:* For master's and doctorate, GRE General Test. Additional exam requirements/recommendations for international students: required—TOEFL (minimum score 550 paper-based; 79 iBT), IELTS (minimum score 6.5). Electronic applications accepted.

University of Wyoming, College of Arts and Sciences, Department of History, Laramie, WY 82071. Offers MA, MAT. *Program availability:* Part-time. *Degree requirements:* For master's, one foreign language, thesis (for some programs). *Entrance requirements:* For master's, GRE General Test, minimum GPA of 3.0, 12 semester hours of undergraduate course work in history. Additional exam requirements/recommendations for international students: required—TOEFL. Electronic applications accepted.

Université Laval, Faculty of Letters, Department of History, Programs in History, Québec, QC G1K 7P4, Canada. Offers MA, PhD. Terminal master's awarded for partial completion of doctoral program. *Degree requirements:* For master's, thesis (for some programs); for doctorate, comprehensive exam, thesis/dissertation. *Entrance requirements:* For master's and doctorate, English exam (comprehension of written English), knowledge of French. Electronic applications accepted.

Université Laval, Faculty of Letters, Department of Literature, Programs in Ancient Civilization, Québec, QC G1K 7P4, Canada. Offers MA, PhD. *Program availability:* Part-time. Terminal master's awarded for partial completion of doctoral program. *Degree requirements:* For master's, thesis; for doctorate, comprehensive exam, thesis/dissertation. *Entrance requirements:* For master's and doctorate, English test (comprehension of written English), knowledge of French, knowledge of an ancient language. Electronic applications accepted.

Utah State University, School of Graduate Studies, College of Humanities and Social Sciences, Department of History, Logan, UT 84322. Offers MA, MS. *Program availability:* Part-time, evening/weekend. *Degree requirements:* For master's, one foreign language, thesis. *Entrance requirements:* For master's, GRE General Test, minimum GPA of 3.0. Additional exam requirements/recommendations for international students: required—TOEFL. Electronic applications accepted.

Vanderbilt University, Department of History, Nashville, TN 37240-1001. Offers MA, MAT, PhD. *Faculty:* 36 full-time (12 women). *Students:* 48 full-time (23 women), 1 part-time (0 women); includes 8 minority (1 Black or African American, non-Hispanic/Latino; 1 American Indian or Alaska Native, non-Hispanic/Latino; 4 Hispanic/Latino; 2 Two or more races, non-Hispanic/Latino), 12 international. Average age 29. 124 applicants, 17% accepted, 8 enrolled. In 2019, 2 master's, 11 doctorates awarded. Terminal master's awarded for partial completion of doctoral program. *Degree requirements:* For doctorate, one foreign language, comprehensive exam, thesis/dissertation, final and qualifying exams. *Entrance requirements:* For doctorate, GRE General Test, sample of written work (recommended). Additional exam requirements/recommendations for international students: required—TOEFL (minimum score 570 paper-based; 88 iBT). *Application deadline:* For fall admission, 1/15 for domestic and international students. Application fee: $0. Electronic applications accepted. *Expenses: Tuition:* Full-time $51,018; part-time $2087 per hour. *Required fees:* $542. Tuition and fees vary according to program. *Financial support:* Fellowships with full tuition reimbursements, teaching assistantships with full tuition reimbursements, Federal Work-Study, institutionally sponsored loans, scholarships/grants, and health care benefits available. Financial award application deadline: 1/15; financial award applicants required to submit CSS PROFILE or FAFSA. *Unit head:* Dr. Joel Harrington, Chair, 615-322-2575, Fax: 615-343-6002, E-mail: joel.harrington@vanderbilt.edu. *Application contact:* Samira Sheikh, Director of Graduate Studies, 615-322-4740, Fax: 615-343-6002, E-mail:

samira.sheikh@vanderbilt.edu.
Website: http://www.vanderbilt.edu/historydept/graduate.html

Villanova University, Graduate School of Liberal Arts and Sciences, Department of History, Villanova, PA 19085-1699. Offers MA. *Program availability:* Part-time, evening/weekend. *Degree requirements:* For master's, comprehensive exam, thesis optional. *Entrance requirements:* For master's, GRE General Test, minimum GPA of 3.0, 3 letters of recommendation, personal statement. Additional exam requirements/recommendations for international students: required—TOEFL. Electronic applications accepted.

Virginia Commonwealth University, Graduate School, College of Humanities and Sciences, Department of History, Richmond, VA 23284-9005. Offers MA. *Program availability:* Part-time. *Degree requirements:* For master's, thesis optional. *Entrance requirements:* For master's, GRE General Test, 30 undergraduate credits in history. Additional exam requirements/recommendations for international students: required—TOEFL (minimum score 600 paper-based; 100 iBT); recommended—IELTS (minimum score 6.5). Electronic applications accepted.

Washington State University, College of Arts and Sciences, Department of History, Pullman, WA 99164. Offers MA, PhD. *Program availability:* Part-time. *Degree requirements:* For master's, comprehensive exam, thesis optional, oral exam; for doctorate, one foreign language, comprehensive exam, thesis/dissertation, oral and written exam. *Entrance requirements:* For master's and doctorate, GRE General Test, official transcripts from all universities attended; three letters of recommendation; statement of purpose; writing sample; Preferred Fields of Study form; Language Background form. Additional exam requirements/recommendations for international students: required—TOEFL (minimum score 550 paper-based), IELTS. Electronic applications accepted.

Washington University in St. Louis, The Graduate School, Department of History, St. Louis, MO 63130-4899. Offers PhD. *Degree requirements:* For doctorate, 2 foreign languages, thesis/dissertation. *Entrance requirements:* For doctorate, GRE General Test. Additional exam requirements/recommendations for international students: required—TOEFL. Electronic applications accepted.

Wayland Baptist University, Graduate Programs, Programs in Behavioral and Social Sciences, Plainview, TX 79072-6998. Offers counseling (MA); criminal justice (MACJ); government administration (MPA); history (MA); homeland security (MPA); humanities (MAH); justice administration (MPA). *Program availability:* Part-time, evening/weekend, 100% online, blended/hybrid learning. *Degree requirements:* For master's, comprehensive exam. *Entrance requirements:* For master's, GRE, MAT. Additional exam requirements/recommendations for international students: required—TOEFL (minimum score 500 paper-based; 61 iBT). Electronic applications accepted. *Expenses: Tuition:* Full-time $728; part-time $728 per semester. *Required fees:* $1218. Tuition and fees vary according to degree level, campus/location and program.

Wayne State University, College of Liberal Arts and Sciences, Tracy Neumann, Detroit, MI 48202. Offers history (MA, PhD); public history (MA), including African American history and culture, cultural resource management, gender, sexuality, and women's studies, labor and urban history, museum studies, public policy; world history (Graduate Certificate); JD/MA; M Ed/MA; MLIS/MA. *Program availability:* Evening/weekend. *Faculty:* 23 full-time (11 women). *Students:* 18 full-time (7 women), 16 part-time (7 women); includes 4 minority (2 Black or African American, non-Hispanic/Latino; 2 Two or more races, non-Hispanic/Latino). Average age 37. 38 applicants, 34% accepted, 13 enrolled. In 2019, 7 master's, 3 doctorates awarded. *Degree requirements:* For master's, thesis (for some programs), final oral exam on thesis or essay and seminar; internship and project (for public history); for doctorate, variable foreign language requirement, comprehensive exam, thesis/dissertation, qualifying exam in 4 fields of history. *Entrance requirements:* For master's, GRE General Test, minimum undergraduate GPA of 3.25 in history, 3.0 overall; at least 18 credits in history and related subjects at the advanced undergraduate level; foreign language; letter of intent; research paper; at least two letters of recommendation from former instructors; for doctorate, GRE General Test, minimum GPA of 3.0, 3.25 in minimum of 18 semester credits in history and related subjects; letter of intent; research paper; at least three letters of recommendation from former professors; for Graduate Certificate, baccalaureate degree from accredited college or university; minimum GPA of 3.0, 3.25 in a minimum of eighteen semester credits in history and related subjects at the advanced undergraduate level. Additional exam requirements/recommendations for international students: required—TOEFL (minimum score 550 paper-based; 79 iBT), TWE (minimum score 5.5), Michigan English Language Assessment Battery (minimum score 85); recommended—IELTS (minimum score 6.5). *Application deadline:* For fall admission, 1/15 priority date for domestic and international students; for winter admission, 4/15 for domestic students, 4/15 priority date for international students; for spring admission, 10/15 for domestic students, 10/15 priority date for international students. Application fee: $50. Electronic applications accepted. *Expenses: Tuition:* Full-time $34,567. *Financial support:* In 2019–20, 18 students received support, including 2 fellowships with tuition reimbursements available (averaging $20,797 per year), 2 research assistantships with tuition reimbursements available (averaging $23,960 per year), 7 teaching assistantships with tuition reimbursements available (averaging $19,967 per year); scholarships/grants, health care benefits, and unspecified assistantships also available. Financial award applicants required to submit FAFSA. *Unit head:* Dr. Elizabeth V. Faue, Professor/Chair, 313-577-2525, E-mail: evfaue@wayne.edu. *Application contact:* Dr. Tracy Neumann, Associate Professor and Director of Graduate Studies, 313-577-2525, E-mail: tracyneumann@wayne.edu.
Website: http://clas.wayne.edu/history/

Western Carolina University, Graduate School, College of Arts and Sciences, Department of History, Cullowhee, NC 28723. Offers MA. *Program availability:* Part-time, evening/weekend. *Degree requirements:* For master's, comprehensive exam, thesis or alternative. *Entrance requirements:* For master's, GRE General Test, appropriate undergraduate degree, 3 letters of recommendation, statement of purpose. Additional exam requirements/recommendations for international students: required—TOEFL (minimum score 550 paper-based, 79 iBT) or IELTS (6.5). *Expenses:* Contact institution.

Western Connecticut State University, Division of Graduate Studies, Maricostas School of Arts and Sciences, Department of History and Non-Western Cultures, Danbury, CT 06810-6885. Offers MA. *Program availability:* Part-time. *Entrance requirements:* For master's, minimum GPA of 2.5. Additional exam requirements/recommendations for international students: recommended—TOEFL (minimum score 550 paper-based; 79 iBT), IELTS (minimum score 6).

Western Illinois University, School of Graduate Studies, College of Arts and Sciences, Department of History, Macomb, IL 61455-1390. Offers MA. *Program availability:* Part-time. *Entrance requirements:* Additional exam requirements/recommendations for international students: required—TOEFL (minimum score 550 paper-based; 80 iBT). Electronic applications accepted.

Western Kentucky University, Graduate School, Potter College of Arts and Letters, Department of History, Bowling Green, KY 42101. Offers MA, MA Ed. *Program availability:* Part-time, evening/weekend, online learning. *Degree requirements:* For master's, comprehensive exam, thesis optional, final exam. *Entrance requirements:* For master's, GRE General Test, minimum GPA of 2.75. Additional exam requirements/recommendations for international students: required—TOEFL (minimum score 555 paper-based; 79 iBT).

Western Michigan University, Graduate College, College of Arts and Sciences, Department of History, Kalamazoo, MI 49008. Offers MA, PhD. *Degree requirements:* For master's, thesis optional; for doctorate, thesis/dissertation.

Western Washington University, Graduate School, College of Humanities and Social Sciences, Department of History, Bellingham, WA 98225-5996. Offers MA. *Program availability:* Part-time. *Degree requirements:* For master's, one foreign language, comprehensive exam, thesis (for some programs). *Entrance requirements:* For master's, GRE General Test, minimum GPA of 3.0 in last 60 semester hours or last 90 quarter hours. Additional exam requirements/recommendations for international students: required—TOEFL (minimum score 567 paper-based). Electronic applications accepted.

West Texas A&M University, College of Fine Arts and Humanities, Department of History, Canyon, TX 79015. Offers MA. *Program availability:* Part-time, evening/weekend. *Degree requirements:* For master's, comprehensive exam, thesis optional. *Entrance requirements:* For master's, GRE General Test. Additional exam requirements/recommendations for international students: required—TOEFL (minimum score 550 paper-based). Electronic applications accepted.

West Virginia University, Eberly College of Arts and Sciences, Morgantown, WV 26506. Offers biology (MS, PhD); chemistry (MS, PhD); communication studies (MA, PhD); computational statistics (PhD); creative writing (MFA); English (MA, PhD); forensic and investigative science (MS); forensic science (PhD); geography (MA); geology (MA, PhD); history (MA, PhD); legal studies (MLS); mathematics (MS); physics (MS, PhD); political science (MA, PhD); professional writing and editing (MA); psychology (MA); public administration (MPA); social work (MSW); sociology (MA, PhD); statistics (MS). *Program availability:* Part-time, evening/weekend, online learning. Terminal master's awarded for partial completion of doctoral program. *Degree requirements:* For master's, thesis (for some programs); for doctorate, comprehensive exam, thesis/dissertation. *Entrance requirements:* For master's and doctorate, GRE. Additional exam requirements/recommendations for international students: required—TOEFL (minimum score 600 paper-based); recommended—TWE. Electronic applications accepted.

Wichita State University, Graduate School, Fairmount College of Liberal Arts and Sciences, Department of History, Wichita, KS 67260. Offers MA. *Program availability:* Part-time.

Wilfrid Laurier University, Faculty of Graduate and Postdoctoral Studies, Faculty of Arts, Department of History, Waterloo, ON N2L 3C5, Canada. Offers MA, PhD. *Program availability:* Part-time. *Degree requirements:* For master's, thesis optional; for doctorate, thesis/dissertation. *Entrance requirements:* For master's, honors BA or the equivalent in history; minimum B+ average in undergraduate course work, exclusive of first year level courses; for doctorate, MA in history, minimum A- average. Additional exam requirements/recommendations for international students: required—TOEFL (minimum score 89 iBT). Electronic applications accepted.

Winthrop University, College of Arts and Sciences, Department of History, Rock Hill, SC 29733. Offers MA. *Program availability:* Part-time. *Degree requirements:* For master's, one foreign language. *Entrance requirements:* For master's, GRE General Test or PRAXIS, 24 hours of history at the undergraduate level. Additional exam requirements/recommendations for international students: required—TOEFL (minimum score 550 paper-based; 79 iBT), IELTS (minimum score 6). Electronic applications accepted. *Expenses: Tuition, area resident:* Full-time $7659; part-time $641 per credit hour. Tuition, state resident: full-time $7659; part-time $641 per credit hour. Tuition, nonresident: full-time $14,753; part-time $1234 per credit hour.

Worcester State University, Graduate School, Program in History, Worcester, MA 01602-2597. Offers MA. *Program availability:* Part-time. *Faculty:* 4 full-time (2 women), 1 part-time/adjunct (0 women). *Students:* 3 full-time, 12 part-time (4 women); includes 1 minority (Black or African American, non-Hispanic/Latino). Average age 41. 4 applicants, 100% accepted, 4 enrolled. In 2019, 6 master's awarded. *Degree requirements:* For master's, comprehensive exam (for some programs), thesis, portfolio. For a detail list in Degree Completion requirements please see the graduate catalog at catalog.worcester.edu. *Entrance requirements:* For master's, GRE General Test or MAT, For a detail list of entrance requirements please see the graduate catalog at catalog.worcester.edu. Additional exam requirements/recommendations for international students: required—TOEFL (minimum score 550 paper-based; 79 iBT), IELTS (minimum score 6). *Application deadline:* For fall admission, 3/1 for domestic and international students; for spring admission, 11/1 for domestic and international students; for summer admission, 3/1 for domestic and international students. Applications are processed on a rolling basis. Application fee: $50. Electronic applications accepted. *Expenses: Tuition, area resident:* Full-time $3042; part-time $169 per credit hour. Tuition, state resident: full-time $3042; part-time $169 per credit hour. Tuition, nonresident: full-time $3042; part-time $169 per credit hour. *International tuition:* $3042 full-time. *Required fees:* $2754; $153 per credit hour. *Financial support:* Career-related internships or fieldwork, scholarships/grants, and unspecified assistantships available. Financial award application deadline: 3/1; financial award applicants required to submit FAFSA. *Unit head:* Dr. Tona Hangen, Graduate Coordinator, 508-929-8688, Fax: 508-929-8155, E-mail: thangen@worcester.edu. *Application contact:* Sara Grady, Associate Dean, Graduate Studies and Professional Development, 508-929-8130, Fax: 508-929-8100, E-mail: sara.grady@worcester.edu.

Wright State University, Graduate School, College of Liberal Arts, Department of History, Dayton, OH 45435. Offers MA. *Degree requirements:* For master's, thesis optional. *Entrance requirements:* For master's, GRE General Test, minimum GPA of 3.0 in history, 2.7 overall. Additional exam requirements/recommendations for international students: required—TOEFL.

Yale University, Graduate School of Arts and Sciences, Department of History, New Haven, CT 06520. Offers history (M Phil, MA, PhD); history of science and medicine (MA, PhD). Terminal master's awarded for partial completion of doctoral program. *Degree requirements:* For master's, one foreign language; for doctorate, 2 foreign languages, thesis/dissertation. *Entrance requirements:* For doctorate, GRE General Test.

York University, Faculty of Graduate Studies, Faculty of Liberal Arts and Professional Studies, Program in History, Toronto, ON M3J 1P3, Canada. Offers MA, PhD. *Program availability:* Part-time. *Degree requirements:* For master's, thesis or alternative; for doctorate, one foreign language, comprehensive exam, thesis/dissertation, qualifying exam. Electronic applications accepted.

Youngstown State University, College of Graduate Studies, College of Liberal Arts and Social Sciences, Department of History, Youngstown, OH 44555-0001. Offers MA. *Program availability:* Part-time. *Degree requirements:* For master's, thesis optional, oral and written exams. *Entrance requirements:* For master's, minimum GPA of 2.75. Additional exam requirements/recommendations for international students: required—TOEFL.

History of Medicine

Indiana University Bloomington, University Graduate School, College of Arts and Sciences, Department of History and Philosophy of Science and Medicine, Bloomington, IN 47405-7000. Offers history and philosophy of science and medicine (MA, PhD); studies in science literacy and responsible research (MA); MLS/MA. *Program availability:* Part-time. Terminal master's awarded for partial completion of doctoral program. *Degree requirements:* For master's, one foreign language, thesis optional; for doctorate, 2 foreign languages, thesis/dissertation. *Entrance requirements:* For master's and doctorate, GRE General Test. Additional exam requirements/recommendations for international students: required—TOEFL. Electronic applications accepted.

McGill University, Faculty of Graduate and Postdoctoral Studies, Faculty of Arts, Department of History and Classical Studies, Montréal, QC H3A 2T5, Canada. Offers history (MA, PhD); history of medicine (MA).

McGill University, Faculty of Graduate and Postdoctoral Studies, Faculty of Medicine, Department of Social Studies of Medicine, Montréal, QC H3A 2T5, Canada. Offers medical anthropology (MA, PhD); medical history (MA, PhD); medical sociology (MA, PhD).

Rutgers University - New Brunswick, Graduate School-New Brunswick, Program in History, Piscataway, NJ 08854-8097. Offers African-American history (PhD); early American history (PhD); early modern European history (PhD); east Asian history (PhD); global and comparative history (PhD); history (PhD); history of diplomacy and foreign relations (PhD); history of technology, environment and health (PhD); history of the Atlantic cultures and African diaspora (PhD); Latin American history (PhD); medieval history (PhD); modern European history (PhD); nineteenth and twentieth century American history (PhD); women's and gender history (PhD). *Degree requirements:* For doctorate, thesis/dissertation. *Entrance requirements:* For doctorate, GRE General Test, sample of written work. Electronic applications accepted.

SUNY Brockport, School of Education, Health, and Human Services, Department of Education and Human Development, Brockport, NY 14420-2997. Offers adolescence education (MS Ed), including adolescence biology education, adolescence chemistry education, adolescence English, adolescence mathematics, adolescence physics, adolescence physics education, adolescence social studies education; bilingual education (MS Ed, AGC); childhood curriculum specialist (MS Ed); inclusive generalist education (MS Ed, AGC, Advanced Certificate), including biology (MS Ed, AGC); chemistry (MS Ed), English (MS Ed, Advanced Certificate), mathematics (MS Ed, Advanced Certificate), science (MS Ed, Advanced Certificate), social studies (MS Ed, Advanced Certificate); literacy education B-12 (MS Ed). *Accreditation:* NCATE. *Faculty:* 15 full-time (11 women), 7 part-time/adjunct (4 women). *Students:* 68 full-time (38 women), 262 part-time (196 women); includes 9 minority (2 Black or African American, non-Hispanic/Latino; 1 American Indian or Alaska Native, non-Hispanic/Latino; 2 Asian, non-Hispanic/Latino; 4 Hispanic/Latino). 130 applicants, 77% accepted, 82 enrolled. In 2019, 107 master's, 13 AGCs awarded. *Entrance requirements:* For master's, minimum GPA of 3.0, letters of recommendation, interview (for some programs); statement of objectives, current resume. Additional exam requirements/recommendations for international students: required—TOEFL (minimum score 550 paper-based; 79 iBT), IELTS (minimum score 6.5). *Application deadline:* For fall admission, 3/15 priority date

for domestic and international students; for spring admission, 10/15 priority date for domestic and international students; for summer admission, 3/15 priority date for domestic and international students. Application fee: $80. Electronic applications accepted. *Expenses: Tuition, area resident:* Part-time $471 per credit hour. Tuition, nonresident: part-time $963 per credit hour. *Financial support:* In 2019–20, 1 fellowship with full tuition reimbursement (averaging $7,500 per year), 1 teaching assistantship with full tuition reimbursement (averaging $6,000 per year) were awarded; Federal Work-Study, scholarships/grants, and unspecified assistantships also available. Support available to part-time students. Financial award application deadline: 3/15; financial award applicants required to submit FAFSA. *Unit head:* Dr. Janka Szilagyi, Chairperson, 585-395-5945, Fax: 585-395-2172, E-mail: jszilagy@brockport.edu. *Application contact:* Buffie Edick, Graduate Program Director, 585-395-2326, Fax: 585-395-2172, E-mail: bedick@brockport.edu.
Website: https://www.brockport.edu/academics/education_human_development/department.html

The University of Manchester, School of Biological Sciences, Manchester, United Kingdom. Offers adaptive organismal biology (M Phil, PhD); animal biology (M Phil, PhD); biochemistry (M Phil, PhD); bioinformatics (M Phil, PhD); biomolecular sciences (M Phil, PhD); biotechnology (M Phil, PhD); cell biology (M Phil, PhD); cell matrix research (M Phil, PhD); channels and transporters (M Phil, PhD); developmental biology (M Phil, PhD); environmental biology (M Phil, PhD); evolutionary biology (M Phil, PhD); gene expression (M Phil, PhD); genetics (M Phil, PhD); history of science, technology and medicine (M Phil, PhD); immunology (M Phil, PhD); integrative neurobiology and behavior (M Phil, PhD); membrane trafficking (M Phil, PhD); microbiology (M Phil, PhD); molecular and cellular neuroscience (M Phil, PhD); molecular biology (M Phil, PhD); molecular cancer studies (M Phil, PhD); neuroscience (M Phil, PhD); ophthalmology (M Phil, PhD); optometry (M Phil, PhD); organelle function (M Phil, PhD); pharmacology (M Phil, PhD); physiology (M Phil, PhD); plant sciences (M Phil, PhD); stem cell research (M Phil, PhD); structural biology (M Phil, PhD); systems neuroscience (M Phil, PhD); toxicology (M Phil, PhD).

University of Minnesota, Twin Cities Campus, Graduate School, Program in the History of Science, Technology and Medicine, Minneapolis, MN 55455-0213. Offers MA, PhD. *Program availability:* Part-time. *Degree requirements:* For master's, one foreign language, thesis or alternative; for doctorate, 2 foreign languages, thesis/dissertation. *Entrance requirements:* For master's and doctorate, GRE General Test.

University of Wisconsin–Madison, Graduate School, College of Letters and Science, Program in History of Science, Medicine, and Technology, Madison, WI 53706-1380. Offers MA, PhD. Terminal master's awarded for partial completion of doctoral program. *Degree requirements:* For master's, thesis; for doctorate, 2 foreign languages, thesis/dissertation. *Entrance requirements:* For master's and doctorate, GRE General Test. Electronic applications accepted.

Yale University, Graduate School of Arts and Sciences, Department of History, Program in the History of Science and Medicine, New Haven, CT 06520. Offers MS, PhD. *Degree requirements:* For doctorate, 2 foreign languages, thesis/dissertation. *Entrance requirements:* For doctorate, GRE General Test.

History of Science and Technology

Arizona State University at Tempe, College of Liberal Arts and Sciences, School of Life Sciences, Tempe, AZ 85287-4601. Offers animal behavior (PhD); applied ethics (biomedical and health ethics) (MA); biology (MS, PhD), including biology, biology and society, complex adaptive systems science (PhD), plant biology and conservation (MS); environmental life sciences (PhD); evolutionary biology (PhD); history and philosophy of science (PhD); human and social dimensions of science and technology (PhD); microbiology (PhD); molecular and cellular biology (PhD); neuroscience (PhD). Terminal master's awarded for partial completion of doctoral program. *Degree requirements:* For master's, thesis (for some programs), interactive Program of Study (iPOS) submitted before completing 50 percent of required credit hours; for doctorate, variable foreign language requirement, comprehensive exam, thesis/dissertation, interactive Program of Study (iPOS) submitted before completing 50 percent of required credit hours. *Entrance requirements:* For master's and doctorate, GRE, minimum GPA of 3.0 or equivalent in last 2 years of work leading to bachelor's degree. Additional exam requirements/recommendations for international students: required—TOEFL (minimum score 600 paper-based; 100 iBT). Electronic applications accepted.

Arizona State University at Tempe, Graduate College, Program in Human and Social Dimensions of Science and Technology, Tempe, AZ 85287-5603. Offers PhD. *Degree requirements:* For doctorate, comprehensive exam, thesis/dissertation, interactive Program of Study (iPOS) submitted before completing 50 percent of required credit hours. *Entrance requirements:* For doctorate, GRE, minimum GPA of 3.0 in the last 2 years of work leading to the bachelor's degree, 3 letters of recommendation, statement of research interests and goals, curriculum vitae or resume, completed academic record form, 10-25 page writing sample. Additional exam requirements/recommendations for international students: required—TOEFL (minimum score 550 paper-based; 80 iBT), IELTS (minimum score 6.5). Electronic applications accepted.

Brown University, Graduate School, Department of Egyptology and Assyriology, Providence, RI 02912. Offers ancient western Asian studies (PhD); Egyptology (PhD); history of the exact sciences in antiquity (PhD). *Degree requirements:* For doctorate, 2 foreign languages, comprehensive exam, thesis/dissertation. *Entrance requirements:* For doctorate, GRE General Test.

Carnegie Mellon University, Dietrich College of Humanities and Social Sciences, Department of History, Pittsburgh, PA 15213-3891. Offers African and African-American diaspora (PhD); culture and power (PhD); labor, politics and social movements (PhD); technology, environment, science and health (PhD); women, gender and the family (PhD). *Program availability:* Part-time. *Degree requirements:* For doctorate, oral and written comprehensive exams, dissertation defense. *Entrance requirements:* For doctorate, GRE General Test. Additional exam requirements/recommendations for international students: required—TOEFL. Electronic applications accepted.

Cornell University, Graduate School, Graduate Fields of Arts and Sciences, Field of History, Ithaca, NY 14853. Offers African history (MA, PhD); American history (MA, PhD); ancient Greek history (PhD); ancient history (MA, PhD); ancient Roman history (PhD); early modern European history (MA, PhD); English history (MA, PhD); French history (MA, PhD); German history (MA, PhD); history of science (MA, PhD); Korean history (PhD); Latin American history (MA, PhD); medieval Chinese history (MA, PhD); medieval history (MA, PhD); modern Chinese history (MA, PhD); modern European history (MA, PhD); modern Japanese history (MA, PhD); modern Middle Eastern history (PhD); premodern Islamic history (MA, PhD); premodern Japanese history (MA, PhD); Renaissance history (MA, PhD); Russian history (MA, PhD); South Asian history (PhD); Southeast Asian history (MA, PhD). Terminal master's awarded for partial completion of doctoral program. *Degree requirements:* For master's, thesis; for doctorate, 2 foreign languages, comprehensive exam, thesis/dissertation, 1 year of teaching experience. *Entrance requirements:* For master's and doctorate, GRE General Test, writing sample, 3 letters of recommendation. Additional exam requirements/recommendations for international students: required—TOEFL (minimum score 550 paper-based; 77 iBT). Electronic applications accepted.

Cornell University, Graduate School, Graduate Fields of Arts and Sciences, Field of Science and Technology Studies, Ithaca, NY 14853. Offers history and philosophy of science and technology (MA, PhD); social studies of science and technology (MA, PhD). Terminal master's awarded for partial completion of doctoral program. *Degree requirements:* For master's, one foreign language, thesis; for doctorate, one foreign language, comprehensive exam, thesis/dissertation. *Entrance requirements:* For master's and doctorate, GRE General Test, writing sample, 3 letters of recommendation. Additional exam requirements/recommendations for international students: required—TOEFL (minimum score 550 paper-based; 77 iBT). Electronic applications accepted.

Drexel University, College of Arts and Sciences, Department of History and Politics, Philadelphia, PA 19104-2875. Offers science, technology and society (MS). *Program availability:* Part-time. *Entrance requirements:* For master's, GRE. Additional exam requirements/recommendations for international students: required—TOEFL. Electronic applications accepted.

Georgia Institute of Technology, Graduate Studies, Ivan Allen College of Liberal Arts, School of History and Sociology, Atlanta, GA 30332. Offers history and sociology of technology and science (MS, PhD). *Program availability:* Part-time. *Faculty:* 12 full-time (5 women). *Students:* 12 full-time (6 women), 9 part-time (all women); includes 3 minority (all Black or African American, non-Hispanic/Latino), 3 international. Average age 40. 24 applicants, 46% accepted, 4 enrolled. In 2019, 5 master's, 2 doctorates awarded. Terminal master's awarded for partial completion of doctoral program. *Degree requirements:* For master's, research paper; for doctorate, one foreign language, comprehensive exam, thesis/dissertation. *Entrance requirements:* For master's and doctorate, GRE, college transcripts, three letters of recommendation, biographical

statement. Additional exam requirements/recommendations for international students: required—TOEFL (minimum score 577 paper-based; 90 iBT), IELTS (minimum score 7), TOEFL is the preferred method with the requirements shown on the programs. *Application deadline:* For fall admission, 3/1 priority date for domestic students, 3/1 for international students. Applications are processed on a rolling basis. Application fee: $75 ($85 for international students). Electronic applications accepted. *Expenses: Tuition, area resident:* Full-time $14,064; part-time $586 per credit hour. Tuition, state resident: full-time $14,064; part-time $586 per credit hour. Tuition, nonresident: full-time $29,140; part-time $1215 per credit hour. *International tuition:* $29,140 full-time. *Required fees:* $2024; $840 per semester. $2096. Tuition and fees vary according to course load. *Financial support:* In 2019–20, 3 research assistantships, 6 teaching assistantships were awarded; fellowships, career-related internships or fieldwork, Federal Work-Study, institutionally sponsored loans, tuition waivers (full and partial), and unspecified assistantships also available. Support available to part-time students. Financial award application deadline: 7/1; financial award applicants required to submit FAFSA. *Unit head:* Eric Schatzberg, School Chair, 404-894.1122, Fax: 404-894.0535, E-mail: eschatzberg3@gatech.edu. *Application contact:* Marla Bruner, Director of Graduate Studies, 404-894-1610, Fax: 404-894-1609, E-mail: gradinfo@mail.gatech.edu.
Website: https://hsoc.gatech.edu/

Harvard University, Graduate School of Arts and Sciences, Department of the History of Science, Cambridge, MA 02138. Offers AM, PhD. Terminal master's awarded for partial completion of doctoral program. *Degree requirements:* For master's, one foreign language; for doctorate, 2 foreign languages, thesis/dissertation. *Entrance requirements:* For master's and doctorate, GRE General Test. Additional exam requirements/recommendations for international students: required—TOEFL.

Indiana University Bloomington, University Graduate School, College of Arts and Sciences, Department of History and Philosophy of Science and Medicine, Bloomington, IN 47405-7000. Offers history and philosophy of science and medicine (MA, PhD); studies in science literacy and responsible research (MA); MLS/MA. *Program availability:* Part-time. Terminal master's awarded for partial completion of doctoral program. *Degree requirements:* For master's, one foreign language, thesis optional; for doctorate, 2 foreign languages, thesis/dissertation. *Entrance requirements:* For master's and doctorate, GRE General Test. Additional exam requirements/recommendations for international students: required—TOEFL. Electronic applications accepted.

Johns Hopkins University, Zanvyl Krieger School of Arts and Sciences, Department of the History of Science and Technology, Baltimore, MD 21218. Offers MA, PhD. Terminal master's awarded for partial completion of doctoral program. *Degree requirements:* For master's, one foreign language, thesis; for doctorate, 2 foreign languages, thesis/dissertation. *Entrance requirements:* For doctorate, GRE General Test. Additional exam requirements/recommendations for international students: required—TOEFL (minimum score 600 paper-based; 100 iBT), IELTS. Electronic applications accepted.

Massachusetts Institute of Technology, School of Humanities, Arts, and Social Sciences, Program in Science, Technology, and Society, Cambridge, MA 02139. Offers history, anthropology, and science, technology and society (PhD). *Degree requirements:* For doctorate, one foreign language, comprehensive exam, thesis/dissertation. *Entrance requirements:* For doctorate, GRE General Test. Additional exam requirements/recommendations for international students: required—TOEFL, IELTS. Electronic applications accepted.

Oregon State University, College of Liberal Arts, Program in History of Science, Corvallis, OR 97331. Offers development of the physical, biological, and environmental sciences (MA, MS, PhD). *Program availability:* Part-time. *Degree requirements:* For master's, variable foreign language requirement, thesis optional; for doctorate, one foreign language, thesis/dissertation. *Entrance requirements:* For master's and doctorate, GRE. Additional exam requirements/recommendations for international students: required—TOEFL (minimum score 80 iBT), IELTS (minimum score 6.5).

Princeton University, Graduate School, Department of History, Program in History of Science, Princeton, NJ 08544-1019. Offers PhD. *Degree requirements:* For doctorate, 2 foreign languages, thesis/dissertation. *Entrance requirements:* For doctorate, GRE General Test, sample of written work, 3 letters of recommendation. Additional exam requirements/recommendations for international students: required—TOEFL (minimum score 600 paper-based). Electronic applications accepted.

Rensselaer Polytechnic Institute, Graduate School, School of Humanities, Arts, and Social Sciences, Program in Science and Technology Studies, Troy, NY 12180-3590. Offers MS, PhD. *Faculty:* 15 full-time (5 women), 1 part-time/adjunct (0 women). *Students:* 18 full-time (9 women), 1 (woman) part-time; includes 3 minority (1 Asian, non-Hispanic/Latino; 1 Hispanic/Latino; 1 Two or more races, non-Hispanic/Latino), 5 international. Average age 29. 19 applicants, 63% accepted, 4 enrolled. In 2019, 2 master's, 5 doctorates awarded. Terminal master's awarded for partial completion of doctoral program. *Degree requirements:* For master's, thesis (for some programs); for doctorate, comprehensive exam, thesis/dissertation. *Entrance requirements:* For master's and doctorate, GRE, writing sample. Additional exam requirements/recommendations for international students: required—TOEFL (minimum score 600 paper-based; 100 iBT), IELTS (minimum score 7), PTE (minimum score 68). *Application deadline:* For fall admission, 1/1 priority date for domestic and international students; for spring admission, 8/15 priority date for domestic and international students. Applications are processed on a rolling basis. Application fee: $75. Electronic applications accepted. *Financial support:* In 2019–20, research assistantships (averaging $23,000 per year), teaching assistantships (averaging $23,000 per year) were awarded; fellowships also available. Financial award application deadline: 1/1. *Unit head:* Dr. Atsushi Akera, Graduate Program Director, 518-276-2314, E-mail: akeraa@rpi.edu. *Application contact:* Jarron Decker, Director of Graduate Admissions, 518-276-6216, Fax: 518-276-4072, E-mail: gradadmissions@rpi.edu.
Website: http://www.sts.rpi.edu/pl/graduate-programs-sts

Rutgers University - New Brunswick, Graduate School-New Brunswick, Program in History, Piscataway, NJ 08854-8097. Offers African-American history (PhD); early American history (PhD); early modern European history (PhD); east Asian history (PhD); global and comparative history (PhD); history (PhD); history of diplomacy and foreign relations (PhD); history of technology, environment and health (PhD); history of the Atlantic cultures and African diaspora (PhD); Latin American history (PhD); medieval history (PhD); modern European history (PhD); nineteenth and twentieth century American history (PhD); women's and gender history (PhD). *Degree requirements:* For doctorate, thesis/dissertation. *Entrance requirements:* For doctorate, GRE General Test, sample of written work. Electronic applications accepted.

University of California, Berkeley, Graduate Division, College of Letters and Science, Group in Logic and the Methodology of Science, Berkeley, CA 94720. Offers PhD. *Degree requirements:* For doctorate, qualifying exam, oral defense of dissertation. *Entrance requirements:* For doctorate, GRE General Test, minimum GPA of 3.5, 3 letters of recommendation. Electronic applications accepted.

University of California, San Diego, Graduate Division, Program in Science Studies, La Jolla, CA 92093. Offers communication of science (PhD); history of science (PhD); philosophy of science (PhD); sociology of science (PhD). *Students:* 6 full-time (2 women). In 2019, 3 doctorates awarded. *Degree requirements:* For doctorate, one foreign language, comprehensive exam, thesis/dissertation, internship. *Entrance requirements:* For doctorate, GRE General Test, 3 letters of recommendation. Additional exam requirements/recommendations for international students: required—TOEFL (minimum score 550 paper-based; 80 iBT), IELTS (minimum score 7). Electronic applications accepted. *Financial support:* Fellowships, research assistantships, teaching assistantships, and scholarships/grants available. Financial award applicants required to submit FAFSA. *Unit head:* Cathy Gere, Director, 858-534-6051, E-mail: cgere@ucsd.edu. *Application contact:* Jennifer Dieli, Program Coordinator, 858-534-0491, E-mail: ssadmin@ucsd.edu.
Website: http://sciencestudies.ucsd.edu/

University of California, San Francisco, Graduate Division, Program in History of Health Sciences, San Francisco, CA 94143. Offers MA, PhD, MD/PhD. Terminal master's awarded for partial completion of doctoral program. *Degree requirements:* For master's, 2 foreign languages, thesis; for doctorate, 2 foreign languages, thesis/dissertation. *Entrance requirements:* For master's and doctorate, GRE General Test.

University of Delaware, College of Arts and Sciences, Department of History, Hagley Program in the History of Technology and Industrialization, Newark, DE 19716. Offers MA, PhD. *Degree requirements:* For master's, thesis optional; for doctorate, comprehensive exam, thesis/dissertation. *Entrance requirements:* For master's and doctorate, interview. Electronic applications accepted.

The University of Manchester, School of Biological Sciences, Manchester, United Kingdom. Offers adaptive organismal biology (M Phil, PhD); animal biology (M Phil, PhD); biochemistry (M Phil, PhD); bioinformatics (M Phil, PhD); biomolecular sciences (M Phil, PhD); biotechnology (M Phil, PhD); cell biology (M Phil, PhD); cell matrix research (M Phil, PhD); channels and transporters (M Phil, PhD); developmental biology (M Phil, PhD); environmental biology (M Phil, PhD); evolutionary biology (M Phil, PhD); gene expression (M Phil, PhD); genetics (M Phil, PhD); history of science, technology and medicine (M Phil, PhD); immunology (M Phil, PhD); integrative neurobiology and behavior (M Phil, PhD); membrane trafficking (M Phil, PhD); microbiology (M Phil, PhD); molecular and cellular neuroscience (M Phil, PhD); molecular biology (M Phil, PhD); molecular cancer studies (M Phil, PhD); neuroscience (M Phil, PhD); ophthalmology (M Phil, PhD); optometry (M Phil, PhD); organelle function (M Phil, PhD); pharmacology (M Phil, PhD); physiology (M Phil, PhD); plant sciences (M Phil, PhD); stem cell research (M Phil, PhD); structural biology (M Phil, PhD); systems neuroscience (M Phil, PhD); toxicology (M Phil, PhD).

University of Minnesota, Twin Cities Campus, College of Science and Engineering, Program in History of Science, Technology and Medicine, Minneapolis, MN 55455-0213. Offers MA, PhD. Terminal master's awarded for partial completion of doctoral program. *Degree requirements:* For master's, one foreign language; for doctorate, 2 foreign languages, thesis/dissertation. *Entrance requirements:* For master's and doctorate, GRE General Test. Additional exam requirements/recommendations for international students: required—TOEFL. Electronic applications accepted.

University of Notre Dame, The Graduate School, College of Arts and Letters, Division of Humanities, Program in History and Philosophy of Science, Notre Dame, IN 46556. Offers history and philosophy of science (MA, PhD); theology and science (PhD). *Degree requirements:* For doctorate, 2 foreign languages, comprehensive exam, thesis/dissertation, candidacy exam. *Entrance requirements:* For doctorate, GRE General Test. Additional exam requirements/recommendations for international students: required—TOEFL (minimum score 600 paper-based; 80 iBT). Electronic applications accepted.

University of Oklahoma, College of Arts and Sciences, Department of History of Science, Norman, OK 73019. Offers history of science, technology and medicine (MA, PhD); MLIS/MA. *Program availability:* Part-time. Terminal master's awarded for partial completion of doctoral program. *Degree requirements:* For master's, one foreign language, comprehensive exam (for some programs), thesis (for some programs); for doctorate, 2 foreign languages, comprehensive exam, thesis/dissertation. *Entrance requirements:* For master's, GRE General Test, transcripts, statement of purpose, 3 letters of recommendation, writing sample; for doctorate, GRE General Test, MA in the history of science or related field, transcripts, statement of purpose, 3 letters of recommendation, writing sample. Additional exam requirements/recommendations for international students: required—TOEFL (minimum score 79 iBT) or IELTS (minimum score 6.5). Electronic applications accepted. *Expenses:* Tuition, state resident: full-time $6583.20; part-time $274.30 per credit hour. Tuition, nonresident: full-time $21,242; part-time $885.10 per credit hour. *International tuition:* $21,242.40 full-time. *Required fees:* $1994.20; $72.55 per credit hour. $126.50 per semester. Tuition and fees vary according to course load and degree level.

University of Pennsylvania, School of Arts and Sciences, Graduate Group in the History and Sociology of Science, Philadelphia, PA 19104. Offers AM, PhD. *Faculty:* 25 full-time (13 women), 8 part-time/adjunct (6 women). *Students:* 25 full-time (14 women); includes 2 minority (1 Asian, non-Hispanic/Latino; 1 Hispanic/Latino), 10 international. Average age 31. 55 applicants, 24% accepted, 3 enrolled. In 2019, 3 doctorates awarded. Application fee: $90. *Financial support:* Application deadline: 12/1.
Website: http://hss.sas.upenn.edu/hssc

University of Pittsburgh, Kenneth P. Dietrich School of Arts and Sciences, Department of History and Philosophy of Science, Pittsburgh, PA 15260. Offers PhD. *Faculty:* 11 full-time (3 women). *Students:* 34 full-time (13 women); includes 7 minority (1 Black or African American, non-Hispanic/Latino; 1 American Indian or Alaska Native, non-Hispanic/Latino; 3 Asian, non-Hispanic/Latino; 2 Native Hawaiian or other Pacific Islander, non-Hispanic/Latino), 9 international. 54 applicants, 17% accepted, 7 enrolled. In 2019, 4 doctorates awarded. Terminal master's awarded for partial completion of doctoral program. *Degree requirements:* For doctorate, one foreign language, comprehensive exam, thesis/dissertation, min 72 credit hours, proficiency in logic. *Entrance requirements:* For doctorate, CV, statement of career objectives, writing sample, 3 letters of recommendation. Additional exam requirements/recommendations for international students: required—TOEFL (minimum score 577 paper-based; 90 iBT), IELTS (minimum score 7). *Application deadline:* For fall admission, 1/10 for domestic and international students. Application fee: $75. Electronic applications accepted. *Financial support:* In 2019–20, 16 fellowships with full tuition reimbursements (averaging $31,000 per year), 11 teaching assistantships with full tuition reimbursements (averaging $27,257 per year) were awarded; health care benefits also available. Financial award application deadline: 1/10. *Unit head:* Dr. Michael Dietrich, Department Chair, 412-624-5892, E-mail: mdietrich@pitt.edu. *Application contact:* David Wallace, Co-Director of Admissions, 412-624-5774, Fax: 412-624-5377, E-mail: dmw121@pitt.edu.
Website: http://www.hps.pitt.edu/

University of Toronto, School of Graduate Studies, Faculty of Arts and Science, Institute for the History and Philosophy of Science and Technology, Toronto, ON M5S 1A1, Canada. Offers MA, PhD. *Program availability:* Part-time. *Degree requirements:* For master's, one foreign language, thesis optional, reading ability in French or German; for doctorate, 2 foreign languages, thesis/dissertation, reading knowledge examinations, thesis defense. *Entrance requirements:* For master's, 2 letters of reference, B+ in the final two years of undergraduate work; for doctorate, 2 letters of reference, MA in history and philosophy of science and technology, minimum A- average. Additional exam requirements/recommendations for international students: required—TOEFL (minimum score 580 paper-based; 93 iBT), TWE (minimum score 5). Electronic applications accepted.

University of Wisconsin–Madison, Graduate School, College of Letters and Science, Program in History of Science, Medicine, and Technology, Madison, WI 53706-1380. Offers MA, PhD. Terminal master's awarded for partial completion of doctoral program. *Degree requirements:* For master's, thesis; for doctorate, 2 foreign languages, thesis/dissertation. *Entrance requirements:* For master's and doctorate, GRE General Test. Electronic applications accepted.

Yale University, Graduate School of Arts and Sciences, Department of History, Program in the History of Science and Medicine, New Haven, CT 06520. Offers MS, PhD. *Degree requirements:* For doctorate, 2 foreign languages, thesis/dissertation. *Entrance requirements:* For doctorate, GRE General Test.

Medieval and Renaissance Studies

Arizona State University at Tempe, College of Liberal Arts and Sciences, Department of English, Tempe, AZ 85287-0302. Offers applied linguistics (PhD); creative writing (MFA); English (MA, PhD), including comparative literature (MA), linguistics (MA), literature, rhetoric and composition (MA), rhetoric, composition, and linguistics (PhD); film and media studies (MAS), including American media and popular culture; linguistics (Graduate Certificate); teaching English to speakers of other languages (MTESOL); translation studies (Graduate Certificate). Terminal master's awarded for partial completion of doctoral program. *Degree requirements:* For master's, variable foreign language requirement, comprehensive exam (for some programs), thesis (for some programs), interactive Program of Study (iPOS) submitted before completing 50 percent of required credit hours; for doctorate, variable foreign language requirement, comprehensive exam, thesis/dissertation, interactive Program of Study (iPOS) submitted before completing 50 percent of required credit hours. *Entrance requirements:* For master's and doctorate, GRE, minimum GPA of 3.0 or equivalent in last 2 years of work leading to bachelor's degree. Additional exam requirements/recommendations for international students: required—TOEFL, IELTS, or PTE. Electronic applications accepted.

Arizona State University at Tempe, College of Liberal Arts and Sciences, School of Historical, Philosophical and Religious Studies, Tempe, AZ 85287-4301. Offers European history (MA, PhD); medieval studies (Graduate Certificate); North American history (MA, PhD); philosophy (MA, PhD); public history (MA); religious studies (MA, PhD); Renaissance studies (Graduate Certificate); scholarly publishing (Graduate Certificate). *Program availability:* Part-time. Terminal master's awarded for partial completion of doctoral program. *Degree requirements:* For master's, thesis or alternative, interactive Program of Study (iPOS) submitted before completing 50 percent of required credit hours; for doctorate, variable foreign language requirement, comprehensive exam, thesis/dissertation, interactive Program of Study (iPOS) submitted before completing 50 percent of required credit hours. *Entrance requirements:* For master's and doctorate, GRE, minimum GPA of 3.0 or equivalent in last 2 years of work leading to bachelor's degree. Additional exam requirements/recommendations for international students: required—TOEFL, IELTS, or PTE. Electronic applications accepted.

The Catholic University of America, School of Arts and Sciences, Department of History, Washington, DC 20064. Offers history (MA, PhD), including early modern European history, medieval history, modern European history, U.S. history; religion and society in the late medieval and early modern world (MA); MA/JD; MSLS/MA. *Program availability:* Part-time. *Faculty:* 14 full-time (6 women). *Students:* 5 full-time (4 women), 17 part-time (6 women); includes 3 minority (all Two or more races, non-Hispanic/Latino), 2 international. Average age 30. 14 applicants, 57% accepted, 3 enrolled. In 2019, 3 master's, 1 doctorate awarded. Terminal master's awarded for partial completion of doctoral program. *Degree requirements:* For master's, one foreign language, comprehensive exam, thesis optional, 2 languages (for medievalists), one of which must be Latin; for doctorate, 2 foreign languages, comprehensive exam, thesis/dissertation, 3 languages (for medievalists), one of which must be Latin. *Entrance requirements:* For master's and doctorate, GRE General Test, statement of purpose, official copies of academic transcripts, three letters of recommendation, writing sample. Additional exam requirements/recommendations for international students: required—TOEFL (minimum score 550 paper-based; 80 iBT). *Application deadline:* For fall admission, 7/15 priority date for domestic students, 7/1 for international students; for spring admission, 11/15 priority date for domestic students, 11/1 for international students. Applications are processed on a rolling basis. Application fee: $55. Electronic applications accepted. *Expenses:* Contact institution. *Financial support:* Fellowships, research assistantships, teaching assistantships, Federal Work-Study, scholarships/grants, tuition waivers (full and partial), and unspecified assistantships available. Financial award application deadline: 2/1; financial award applicants required to submit FAFSA. *Unit head:* Dr. Michael Kimmage, Chair, 202-319-5484, Fax: 202-319-5569, E-mail: kimmage@cua.edu. *Application contact:* Dr. Steven Brown, Director of Graduate Admissions, 202-319-5057, Fax: 202-319-6533, E-mail: cua-admissions@cua.edu.
Website: http://history.cua.edu/

The Catholic University of America, School of Arts and Sciences, Program in Medieval and Byzantine Studies, Washington, DC 20064. Offers Byzantine and Orthodox studies (MA); Medieval and Byzantine studies (PhD, Certificate); the Islamic world (MA); the Medieval West (MA). *Program availability:* Part-time. *Students:* 1 (woman) full-time, 5 part-time (2 women). Average age 43. 10 applicants, 30% accepted. *Degree requirements:* For master's, one foreign language, comprehensive exam, thesis or alternative; for doctorate, 2 foreign languages, comprehensive exam, thesis/dissertation. *Entrance requirements:* For master's and doctorate, GRE General Test, statement of purpose, official copies of academic transcripts, three letters of recommendation, writing sample; for Certificate, bachelor's degree. Additional exam requirements/recommendations for international students: required—TOEFL (minimum score 550 paper-based; 80 iBT). *Application deadline:* For fall admission, 7/15 priority date for domestic students, 7/1 for international students; for spring admission, 11/15 priority date for domestic students, 11/1 for international students. Applications are processed on a rolling basis. Application fee: $55. Electronic applications accepted. *Expenses:* Contact institution. *Financial support:* Fellowships, research assistantships, teaching assistantships, Federal Work-Study, scholarships/grants, tuition waivers (full and partial), and unspecified assistantships available. Financial award application deadline: 2/1; financial award applicants required to submit FAFSA. *Unit head:* Dr. Lilla Kopar, Director, 202-319-5794, Fax: 202-319-6609, E-mail: kopar@cua.edu. *Application contact:* Director of Graduate Admissions, 202-319-5057, Fax: 202-319-6533, E-mail: cua-admissions@cua.edu.
Website: http://mbs.cua.edu/

Central European University, Department of Medieval Studies, Budapest, Hungary. Offers comparative history: interdisciplinary Medieval studies (MA); cultural heritage studies (MA); Medieval studies (MA, PhD). *Degree requirements:* For master's, one foreign language, thesis; for doctorate, variable foreign language requirement, comprehensive exam, thesis/dissertation. *Entrance requirements:* For master's and doctorate, interview. Additional exam requirements/recommendations for international students: required—TOEFL (minimum score 570 paper-based); recommended—IELTS (minimum score 6.5). Electronic applications accepted.

Columbia University, Graduate School of Arts and Sciences, New York, NY 10027. Offers African-American studies (MA); American studies (MA); anthropology (MA, PhD); art history and archaeology (MA, PhD); astronomy (PhD); biological sciences (PhD); biotechnology (MA); chemical physics (PhD); chemistry (PhD); classical studies (MA, PhD); classics (MA, PhD); climate and society (MA); conservation biology (MA); earth and environmental sciences (PhD); East Asia: regional studies (MA); East Asian languages and cultures (MA, PhD); ecology, evolution and environmental biology (MA), including conservation biology; ecology, evolution, and environmental biology (PhD), including ecology and evolutionary biology, evolutionary primatology; economics (MA, PhD); English and comparative literature (MA, PhD); French and Romance philology (MA, PhD); Germanic languages (MA, PhD); global French studies (MA); global thought (MA); Hispanic cultural studies (MA); history (PhD); history and literature (MA); human rights studies (MA); Islamic studies (MA); Italian (MA, PhD); Japanese pedagogy (MA); Jewish studies (MA); Latin America and the Caribbean: regional studies (MA); Latin American and Iberian cultures (PhD); mathematics (MA, PhD), including finance (MA); medieval and Renaissance studies (MA); Middle Eastern, South Asian, and African studies (MA, PhD); modern art: critical and curatorial studies (MA); modern European studies (MA); museum anthropology (MA); music (DMA, PhD); oral history (MA); philosophical foundations of physics (MA); philosophy (MA, PhD); physics (PhD); political science (MA, PhD); psychology (PhD); quantitative methods in the social sciences (MA); religion (MA, PhD); Russia, Eurasia and East Europe: regional studies (MA); Russian translation (MA); Slavic cultures (MA); Slavic languages (MA, PhD); sociology (MA, PhD); South Asian studies (MA); statistics (MA, PhD); theatre (PhD). *Program availability:* Part-time. *Students:* 3,506 full-time (1,844 women), 208 part-time (121 women); includes 864 minority (110 Black or African American, non-Hispanic/Latino; 5 American Indian or Alaska Native, non-Hispanic/Latino; 416 Asian, non-Hispanic/Latino; 147 Hispanic/Latino; 6 Native Hawaiian or other Pacific Islander, non-Hispanic/Latino; 180 Two or more races, non-Hispanic/Latino), 2,065 international. 14,545 applicants, 25% accepted, 1,429 enrolled. In 2019, 1,262 master's, 363 doctorates awarded. Terminal master's awarded for partial completion of doctoral program. *Degree requirements:* For master's, variable foreign language requirement, comprehensive exam (for some programs), thesis (for some programs); for doctorate, variable foreign language requirement, comprehensive exam (for some programs), thesis/dissertation. *Entrance requirements:* For master's and doctorate, GRE General Test, GRE Subject Test (for some programs). Additional exam requirements/recommendations for international students: required—TOEFL (minimum score 600 paper-based; 100 iBT), IELTS (minimum score 7.5). Application fee: $115. Electronic applications accepted. *Expenses: Tuition:* Full-time $47,600; part-time $1880 per credit. One-time fee: $105. *Financial support:* Fellowships, research assistantships, teaching assistantships, career-related internships or fieldwork, Federal Work-Study, institutionally sponsored loans, scholarships/grants, traineeships, health care benefits, tuition waivers, and unspecified assistantships available. Support available to part-time students. Financial award application deadline: 12/15. *Unit head:* Dr. Carlos J. Alonso, Dean of the Graduate School of Arts and Sciences and Vice President for Graduate Education, 212-854-2861, E-mail: gsas-dean@columbia.edu. *Application contact:* GSAS Office of Admissions, 212-854-6729, E-mail: gsas-admissions@columbia.edu.
Website: http://gsas.columbia.edu/

Cornell University, Graduate School, Graduate Fields of Arts and Sciences, Field of Archaeology, Ithaca, NY 14853. Offers environmental archaeology (MA); historical archaeology (MA); Latin American archaeology (MA); medieval archaeology (MA); Mediterranean and Near Eastern archaeology (MA); Stone Age archaeology (MA). *Degree requirements:* For master's, one foreign language, thesis. *Entrance requirements:* For master's, GRE General Test, 3 letters of recommendation, sample of written work. Additional exam requirements/recommendations for international students: required—TOEFL (minimum score 550 paper-based; 77 iBT). Electronic applications accepted.

Cornell University, Graduate School, Graduate Fields of Arts and Sciences, Field of English Language and Literature, Ithaca, NY 14853. Offers African-American literature (PhD); American literature after 1865 (PhD); American literature to 1865 (PhD); American studies (PhD); colonial and postcolonial literatures (PhD); creative writing (MFA); cultural studies (PhD); dramatic literature (PhD); English poetry (PhD); English Renaissance to 1660 (PhD); lesbian, bisexual, and gay literary studies (PhD); literary criticism and theory (PhD); Old and Middle English (PhD); prose fiction (PhD); Restoration and the eighteenth-century (PhD); the nineteenth century (PhD); the twentieth century (PhD); women's literature (PhD); MFA/PhD. Terminal master's awarded for partial completion of doctoral program. *Degree requirements:* For master's, one foreign language, thesis; for doctorate, one foreign language, comprehensive exam, thesis/dissertation, teaching experience. *Entrance requirements:* For master's, GRE General Test, 3 letters of recommendation, creative writing sample; for doctorate, 3 letters of recommendation, writing sample. Additional exam requirements/recommendations for international students: required—TOEFL (minimum score 600 paper-based; 77 iBT). Electronic applications accepted.

Cornell University, Graduate School, Graduate Fields of Arts and Sciences, Field of History, Ithaca, NY 14853. Offers African history (MA, PhD); American history (MA, PhD); ancient Greek history (PhD); ancient history (MA, PhD); ancient Roman history (PhD); early modern European history (MA, PhD); English history (MA, PhD); French history (MA, PhD); German history (MA, PhD); history of science (MA, PhD); Korean history (PhD); Latin American history (MA, PhD); medieval Chinese history (MA, PhD); medieval history (MA, PhD); modern Chinese history (MA, PhD); modern European history (MA, PhD); modern Japanese history (MA, PhD); modern Middle Eastern history

(PhD); premodern Islamic history (MA, PhD); premodern Japanese history (MA, PhD); Renaissance history (MA, PhD); Russian history (MA, PhD); South Asian history (PhD); Southeast Asian history (MA, PhD). Terminal master's awarded for partial completion of doctoral program. *Degree requirements:* For master's, thesis; for doctorate, 2 foreign languages, comprehensive exam, thesis/dissertation, 1 year of teaching experience. *Entrance requirements:* For master's and doctorate, GRE General Test, writing sample, 3 letters of recommendation. Additional exam requirements/recommendations for international students: required—TOEFL (minimum score 550 paper-based; 77 iBT). Electronic applications accepted.

Cornell University, Graduate School, Graduate Fields of Arts and Sciences, Field of History of Art, Archaeology and Visual Studies, Ithaca, NY 14853. Offers 19th century art (PhD); African, African American and African diaspora (PhD); American art (PhD); ancient art and archaeology (PhD); Asian American art (PhD); Baroque art (PhD); Comparative Modernities (PhD); digital art (PhD); East Asian art (PhD); history of photography (PhD); Islamic art (PhD); Latin American art (PhD); medieval art (PhD); modern art (PhD); Renaissance art (PhD); Southeast Asian art (PhD); theory and criticism (PhD); visual studies (PhD). *Degree requirements:* For doctorate, one foreign language, comprehensive exam, thesis/dissertation, general exams in 3 areas. *Entrance requirements:* For doctorate, GRE General Test, sample of written work, 3 letters of recommendation. Additional exam requirements/recommendations for international students: required—TOEFL (minimum score 550 paper-based; 77 iBT). Electronic applications accepted.

Cornell University, Graduate School, Graduate Fields of Arts and Sciences, Field of Medieval Studies, Ithaca, NY 14853. Offers medieval archaeology (PhD); medieval art (PhD); medieval history (PhD); medieval literature (PhD); medieval music (PhD); medieval philology and linguistics (PhD); medieval philosophy (PhD). *Degree requirements:* For doctorate, 3 foreign languages, comprehensive exam, thesis/dissertation, teaching experience. *Entrance requirements:* For doctorate, GRE General Test, 3 letters of recommendation, proficiency in Latin (recommended), 20-page writing sample on a Medieval topic. Additional exam requirements/recommendations for international students: required—TOEFL (minimum score 600 paper-based; 77 iBT). Electronic applications accepted.

Fordham University, Graduate School of Arts and Sciences, Program in Medieval Studies, New York, NY 10458. Offers MA, Certificate. *Program availability:* Part-time, evening/weekend. *Students:* Average age 27. 17 applicants, 82% accepted, 3 enrolled. In 2019, 6 master's awarded. *Entrance requirements:* For master's, GRE General Test. Additional exam requirements/recommendations for international students: required—TOEFL (minimum score 650 paper-based). *Application deadline:* For fall admission, 1/4 priority date for domestic students; for spring admission, 11/1 for domestic students. Applications are processed on a rolling basis. Application fee: $70. Electronic applications accepted. *Financial support:* In 2019–20, 4 students received support. Institutionally sponsored loans, tuition waivers (full and partial), and unspecified assistantships available. Financial award application deadline: 1/4; financial award applicants required to submit FAFSA. *Unit head:* Dr. Susanne Hafner, Director, 718-817-4655, E-mail: hafner@fordham.edu. *Application contact:* Garrett Marino, Director of Graduate Admissions, 718-817-4419, Fax: 718-817-3566, E-mail: gmarino10@fordham.edu.

Georgetown University, Graduate School of Arts and Sciences, School of Continuing Studies, Washington, DC 20057. Offers American studies (MALS); applied intelligence (MPS); Catholic studies (MALS); classical civilizations (MALS); emergency and disaster management (MPS); ethics and the professions (MALS); global strategic communications (MPS); hospitality management (MPS); human resources management (MPS); humanities (MALS); individualized study (MALS); integrated marketing communications (MPS); international affairs (MALS); Islam and Muslim-Christian relations (MALS); journalism (MPS); liberal studies (DLS); literature and society (MALS); medieval and early modern European studies (MALS); public relations and corporate communications (MPS); real estate (MPS); religious studies (MALS); social and public policy (MALS); sports industry management (MPS); systems engineering management (MPS); technology management (MPS); the theory and practice of American democracy (MALS); urban and regional planning (MPS); visual culture (MALS). *Entrance requirements:* Additional exam requirements/recommendations for international students: required—TOEFL.

Harvard University, Graduate School of Arts and Sciences, Department of English and American Literature and Language, Cambridge, MA 02138. Offers critical theory (PhD); eighteenth-century literature (PhD); literature: nineteenth-century to the present (PhD); medieval literature and language (PhD); modern British and American literature (PhD); Renaissance literature (PhD). Terminal master's awarded for partial completion of doctoral program. *Degree requirements:* For doctorate, 2 foreign languages, thesis/dissertation, oral exam. *Entrance requirements:* For doctorate, writing sample. Additional exam requirements/recommendations for international students: required—TOEFL.

Indiana University Bloomington, University Graduate School, College of Arts and Sciences, Department of Germanic Studies, Bloomington, IN 47405-7000. Offers German philology and linguistics (PhD); German studies (MA, PhD), including German (MA), German literature and culture (MA), German literature and linguistics (MA); medieval German studies (PhD); teaching German (MAT). *Degree requirements:* For master's, one foreign language, project; for doctorate, one foreign language, comprehensive exam, thesis/dissertation. *Entrance requirements:* For master's, GRE General Test, BA in German or equivalent; for doctorate, GRE General Test, MA in German or equivalent. Additional exam requirements/recommendations for international students: required—TOEFL. Electronic applications accepted.

Loyola University Chicago, Graduate School, Department of English, Chicago, IL 60660. Offers 19th century studies (PhD); English (MA); Medieval and Renaissance literature (PhD); modern literature and culture (PhD); textual studies and digital humanities (PhD). *Program availability:* Part-time, evening/weekend. *Faculty:* 24 full-time (11 women). *Students:* 37 full-time (24 women), 2 part-time (both women); includes 8 minority (1 Black or African American, non-Hispanic/Latino; 1 Asian, non-Hispanic/Latino; 4 Hispanic/Latino; 2 Two or more races, non-Hispanic/Latino). Average age 30. 68 applicants, 40% accepted, 10 enrolled. In 2019, 7 master's, 2 doctorates awarded. Terminal master's awarded for partial completion of doctoral program. *Degree requirements:* For master's, comprehensive exam, thesis or alternative; for doctorate, one foreign language, comprehensive exam, thesis/dissertation. *Entrance requirements:* For master's and doctorate, GRE General Test. Additional exam requirements/recommendations for international students: required—TOEFL, IELTS. *Application deadline:* For fall admission, 6/1 for domestic students. Applications are processed on a rolling basis. Application fee: $0. Electronic applications accepted. *Expenses: Tuition:* Full-time $18,540; part-time $1033 per credit hour. *Required fees:* $904; $230 per credit hour. *Financial support:* In 2019–20, 22 students received support, including 3 fellowships with full tuition reimbursements available (averaging $19,000 per year), research assistantships with full tuition reimbursements available (averaging $10,000 per year), 18 teaching assistantships with full tuition reimbursements available (averaging $19,000 per year); institutionally sponsored loans, tuition waivers (full and partial), and unspecified assistantships also available. Financial award application deadline: 1/15; financial award applicants required to submit FAFSA. *Unit head:* Dr. James Knapp, Graduate Program Director, 773-508-2241, Fax: 773-508-8696, E-mail: jknapp3@luc.edu. *Application contact:* Dr. James Knapp, Graduate Program Director, 773-508-2241, Fax: 773-508-8696, E-mail: jknapp3@luc.edu.
Website: http://www.luc.edu/english/

Rutgers University - New Brunswick, Graduate School-New Brunswick, Program in History, Piscataway, NJ 08854-8097. Offers African-American history (PhD); early American history (PhD); early modern European history (PhD); east Asian history (PhD); global and comparative history (PhD); history (PhD); history of diplomacy and foreign relations (PhD); history of technology, environment and health (PhD); history of the Atlantic cultures and African diaspora (PhD); Latin American history (PhD); medieval history (PhD); modern European history (PhD); nineteenth and twentieth century American history (PhD); women's and gender history (PhD). *Degree requirements:* For doctorate, thesis/dissertation. *Entrance requirements:* For doctorate, GRE General Test, sample of written work. Electronic applications accepted.

Southern Methodist University, Dedman College of Humanities and Sciences, Program in Medieval Studies, Dallas, TX 75275. Offers MA. *Program availability:* Part-time. *Degree requirements:* For master's, 2 foreign languages, thesis. *Entrance requirements:* For master's, GRE General Test, minimum GPA of 3.0. Electronic applications accepted.

University of California, Santa Barbara, Graduate Division, College of Letters and Sciences, Division of Humanities and Fine Arts, Department of English, Santa Barbara, CA 93106-3170. Offers English (PhD), including environment and society, European medieval studies, feminist studies, global studies, technology and society, translation studies, writing studies; MA/PhD. Terminal master's awarded for partial completion of doctoral program. *Degree requirements:* For doctorate, one foreign language, comprehensive exam, thesis/dissertation. *Entrance requirements:* For doctorate, GRE General Test, GRE Subject Test (English literature). Additional exam requirements/recommendations for international students: required—TOEFL (minimum score 550 paper-based; 80 iBT), IELTS (minimum score 7). Electronic applications accepted.

University of California, Santa Barbara, Graduate Division, College of Letters and Sciences, Division of Humanities and Fine Arts, Department of History, Santa Barbara, CA 93106-9410. Offers European medieval studies (PhD); global studies (PhD); public historical studies (PhD); technology and society (PhD); women's studies (PhD); MA/PhD. *Degree requirements:* For doctorate, variable foreign language requirement, comprehensive exam, thesis/dissertation. *Entrance requirements:* For doctorate, GRE. Additional exam requirements/recommendations for international students: required—TOEFL (minimum score 550 paper-based; 80 iBT), IELTS (minimum score 7). Electronic applications accepted.

University of California, Santa Barbara, Graduate Division, College of Letters and Sciences, Division of Humanities and Fine Arts, Department of History of Art and Architecture, Santa Barbara, CA 93106-2014. Offers art history (PhD), including art history, European medieval studies, feminist studies; MA/PhD. Terminal master's awarded for partial completion of doctoral program. *Degree requirements:* For doctorate, 2 foreign languages, comprehensive exam, thesis/dissertation. *Entrance requirements:* For doctorate, GRE. Additional exam requirements/recommendations for international students: required—TOEFL (minimum score 550 paper-based; 80 iBT), IELTS (minimum score 7). Electronic applications accepted.

University of California, Santa Barbara, Graduate Division, College of Letters and Sciences, Division of Humanities and Fine Arts, Department of Religious Studies, Santa Barbara, CA 93106-3130. Offers ancient Mediterranean studies (PhD); cognitive science (PhD); European medieval studies (PhD); feminist studies (PhD); global studies (PhD); religious studies (MA, PhD); translation studies (PhD); MA/PhD. Terminal master's awarded for partial completion of doctoral program. *Degree requirements:* For master's, one foreign language, comprehensive exam (for some programs), thesis (for some programs); for doctorate, 2 foreign languages, thesis/dissertation, methodology. *Entrance requirements:* For master's and doctorate, GRE General Test. Additional exam requirements/recommendations for international students: required—TOEFL (minimum score 550 paper-based; 80 iBT), IELTS (minimum score 7). Electronic applications accepted.

University of California, Santa Barbara, Graduate Division, College of Letters and Sciences, Division of Humanities and Fine Arts, Department of Spanish and Portuguese, Santa Barbara, CA 93106-4150. Offers Hispanic languages and literatures (PhD), including European medieval studies, feminist studies, Hispanic linguistics, Hispanic literature, Luso-Brazilian literature; Hispanic linguistics (MA); Luso-Brazilian literature (MA); Spanish or Spanish-American literature (MA); MA/PhD. Terminal master's awarded for partial completion of doctoral program. *Degree requirements:* For master's, 2 foreign languages, comprehensive exam (for some programs), thesis optional; for doctorate, 3 foreign languages, comprehensive exam, thesis/dissertation. *Entrance requirements:* For master's and doctorate, GRE. Additional exam requirements/recommendations for international students: required—TOEFL (minimum score 550 paper-based; 80 iBT), IELTS (minimum score 7). Electronic applications accepted.

University of California, Santa Barbara, Graduate Division, College of Letters and Sciences, Division of Humanities and Fine Arts, Department of Theater and Dance, Santa Barbara, CA 93106-7060. Offers theater studies (MA, PhD), including European medieval studies (PhD), feminist studies (PhD), theatre studies (PhD); MA/PhD. Terminal master's awarded for partial completion of doctoral program. *Degree requirements:* For master's, comprehensive exam, thesis; for doctorate, one foreign language, comprehensive exam, thesis/dissertation. *Entrance requirements:* For master's and doctorate, GRE. Additional exam requirements/recommendations for international students: required—TOEFL (minimum score 550 paper-based; 80 iBT), IELTS (minimum score 7). Electronic applications accepted.

University of Chicago, Division of the Humanities, Department of Romance Languages and Literatures, Chicago, IL 60637. Offers French and Francophone studies (PhD); Hispanic and Luso-Brazilian studies (PhD); Italian studies (PhD); Renaissance and early modern studies (PhD). Terminal master's awarded for partial completion of doctoral program. *Degree requirements:* For doctorate, 3 foreign languages, comprehensive exam, thesis/dissertation. *Entrance requirements:* For doctorate, GRE General Test, 15-20 page writing sample, statement of purpose, 3 letters of recommendation, transcripts for all previous degrees and institutions attended. Additional exam requirements/recommendations for international students: required—TOEFL (minimum score 104 iBT), IELTS (minimum score 7). Electronic applications accepted.

University of Connecticut, Graduate School, College of Liberal Arts and Sciences, Program in Medieval Studies, Storrs, CT 06269. Offers MA, PhD. Terminal master's awarded for partial completion of doctoral program. *Degree requirements:* For master's, comprehensive exam; for doctorate, 3 foreign languages, thesis/dissertation. *Entrance requirements:* For master's and doctorate, GRE General Test, GRE Subject Test. Additional exam requirements/recommendations for international students: required—TOEFL (minimum score 550 paper-based). Electronic applications accepted.

University of Guelph, Office of Graduate and Postdoctoral Studies, College of Arts, School of English and Theatre Studies, Joint Program in Literary Studies/Theatre

Studies in English, Guelph, ON N1G 2W1, Canada. Offers PhD. *Program availability:* Part-time. *Degree requirements:* For doctorate, one foreign language, comprehensive exam, thesis/dissertation. *Entrance requirements:* For doctorate, MA, 3 letters of reference, writing samples, resume, minimum A- average in graduate course work. Additional exam requirements/recommendations for international students: required—TOEFL. Electronic applications accepted.

University of Minnesota, Twin Cities Campus, Graduate School, College of Liberal Arts, Department of German, Scandinavian, and Dutch, Minneapolis, MN 55455. Offers Germanic studies (MA, PhD), including German, Germanic medieval studies, Scandinavian studies (MA). *Program availability:* Part-time. Terminal master's awarded for partial completion of doctoral program. *Degree requirements:* For doctorate, 2 foreign languages, thesis/dissertation. *Entrance requirements:* For master's, GRE General Test, BA in German, Scandinavian, or equivalent; for doctorate, MA in German, Scandinavian, or equivalent. Additional exam requirements/recommendations for international students: required—TOEFL (minimum score 550 paper-based; 79 iBT). Electronic applications accepted.

University of Notre Dame, The Graduate School, College of Arts and Letters, Division of Humanities, Medieval Institute, Notre Dame, IN 46556. Offers MMS, PhD. Terminal master's awarded for partial completion of doctoral program. *Degree requirements:* For master's, 3 foreign languages, comprehensive exam; for doctorate, 3 foreign languages, thesis/dissertation, candidacy exam. *Entrance requirements:* For master's and doctorate, GRE General Test. Additional exam requirements/recommendations for international students: required—TOEFL (minimum score 600 paper-based; 80 iBT). Electronic applications accepted.

University of Pittsburgh, Kenneth P. Dietrich School of Arts and Sciences, Program in Medieval and Renaissance Studies, Pittsburgh, PA 15260. Offers Doctoral Certificate, Master's Certificate. *Faculty:* 25 full-time (10 women). *Students:* 4 full-time (3 women); includes 1 minority (Asian, non-Hispanic/Latino). Average age 30. *Entrance requirements:* For degree, Good academic standing in a degree granting Univ of Pgh grad program. Additional exam requirements/recommendations for international students: required—TOEFL. *Application deadline:* Applications are processed on a rolling basis. Electronic applications accepted. Application fee is waived when completed online. *Financial support:* Fellowships, research assistantships, teaching assistantships, scholarships/grants, and tuition waivers available. *Unit head:* Christopher Nygren, Director, 412-624-6564, Fax: 412-383-6999, E-mail: cnygren@pitt.edu. *Application contact:* Lorri Keeling-Oliver, Graduate Administrator, 412-624-6564, E-mail: ljk59@pitt.edu. Website: http://www.medren.pitt.edu/

University of Toronto, School of Graduate Studies, Faculty of Arts and Science, Centre for Medieval Studies, Toronto, ON M5S 1A1, Canada. Offers MA, PhD. *Program availability:* Part-time. *Degree requirements:* For master's, one foreign language, 4 courses or 3 courses and thesis; for doctorate, 3 foreign languages, thesis/dissertation, proficiency in Latin, German and French. *Entrance requirements:* For master's, letters of reference, minimum B+ average, course work in the Medieval period; for doctorate, letters of reference. Additional exam requirements/recommendations for international students: required—TOEFL (minimum score 580 paper-based; 93 iBT), TWE (minimum score 5). Electronic applications accepted.

Yale University, Graduate School of Arts and Sciences, Interdisciplinary Program in Medieval Studies, New Haven, CT 06520. Offers M Phil, PhD. *Entrance requirements:* For doctorate, GRE General Test.

Yale University, Graduate School of Arts and Sciences, Program in Renaissance Studies, New Haven, CT 06520. Offers PhD. *Degree requirements:* For doctorate, 3 foreign languages. *Entrance requirements:* For doctorate, GRE General Test.

Public History

Arizona State University at Tempe, College of Liberal Arts and Sciences, School of Historical, Philosophical and Religious Studies, Tempe, AZ 85287-4301. Offers European history (MA, PhD); medieval studies (Graduate Certificate); North American history (MA, PhD); philosophy (MA, PhD); public history (MA); religious studies (MA, PhD); Renaissance studies (Graduate Certificate); scholarly publishing (Graduate Certificate). *Program availability:* Part-time. Terminal master's awarded for partial completion of doctoral program. *Degree requirements:* For master's, thesis or alternative, interactive Program of Study (iPOS) submitted before completing 50 percent of required credit hours; for doctorate, variable foreign language requirement, comprehensive exam, thesis/dissertation, interactive Program of Study (iPOS) submitted before completing 50 percent of required credit hours. *Entrance requirements:* For master's and doctorate, GRE, minimum GPA of 3.0 or equivalent in last 2 years of work leading to bachelor's degree. Additional exam requirements/recommendations for international students: required—TOEFL, IELTS, or PTE. Electronic applications accepted.

California State University, East Bay, Office of Graduate Studies, College of Letters, Arts, and Social Sciences, Department of History, Hayward, CA 94542-3000. Offers history (MA); public history (MA); teaching (MA). *Program availability:* Part-time, evening/weekend. *Degree requirements:* For master's, one foreign language, comprehensive exam, project, thesis, or exam. *Entrance requirements:* For master's, GRE (strongly recommended), minimum GPA of 3.0 in field, 3.3 in history; 2 letters of recommendation; writing sample. Additional exam requirements/recommendations for international students: required—TOEFL (minimum score 550 paper-based). Electronic applications accepted.

California State University, Sacramento, College of Arts and Letters, Department of History, Sacramento, CA 95819. Offers history (MA); public historical studies (PhD); public history (MA). *Program availability:* Part-time. *Students:* 26 full-time (16 women), 45 part-time (18 women); includes 15 minority (2 Black or African American, non-Hispanic/Latino; 1 American Indian or Alaska Native, non-Hispanic/Latino; 1 Asian, non-Hispanic/Latino; 11 Hispanic/Latino). Average age 29. 38 applicants, 71% accepted, 14 enrolled. In 2019, 14 master's awarded. *Degree requirements:* For master's, comprehensive exam (for some programs), thesis, thesis, project or comprehensive exam; writing proficiency exam; for doctorate, thesis/dissertation, qualifying exam. *Entrance requirements:* For master's, minimum GPA of 3.25 in history, 3.0 overall during previous 2 years; BA in history or equivalent. Additional exam requirements/recommendations for international students: required—TOEFL (minimum score 550 paper-based; 80 iBT); recommended—IELTS. *Application deadline:* For fall admission, 2/3 for domestic students, 1/3 for international students; for spring admission, 9/15 for domestic students, 8/15 for international students. Applications are processed on a rolling basis. Application fee: $70. Electronic applications accepted. *Expenses:* Contact institution. *Financial support:* Career-related internships or fieldwork, Federal Work-Study, and scholarships/grants available. Support available to part-time students. Financial award application deadline: 3/1; financial award applicants required to submit FAFSA. *Unit head:* Dr. Jeffrey Wilson, Chair, 916-278-6136, Fax: 916-278-7476, E-mail: jkwilson@saclink.csus.edu. *Application contact:* Jose Martinez, Outreach and Graduate Diversity Coordinator, 916-278-6470, Fax: 916-278-5669, E-mail: martinj@skymail.csus.edu. Website: http://www.csus.edu/hist

Colorado State University, College of Liberal Arts, Department of History, Fort Collins, CO 80523-1776. Offers liberal arts (MA); public history (MA). *Program availability:* Part-time. *Faculty:* 6 full-time (3 women), 1 (woman) part-time/adjunct. *Students:* 22 full-time (13 women), 1 part-time (0 women); includes 2 minority (1 Hispanic/Latino; 1 Two or more races, non-Hispanic/Latino). Average age 26. 28 applicants, 57% accepted, 12 enrolled. In 2019, 15 master's awarded. *Degree requirements:* For master's, variable foreign language requirement, comprehensive exam, thesis (for some programs). *Entrance requirements:* For master's, GRE, 21 undergraduate credits in history; minimum undergraduate GPA of 3.0; personal statement; 3 letters of reference. Additional exam requirements/recommendations for international students: required—TOEFL, IELTS. *Application deadline:* For winter admission, 2/1 for domestic and international students. Application fee: $60 ($70 for international students). Electronic applications accepted. *Expenses:* Tuition, state resident: full-time $10,520; part-time $5844 per credit hour. Tuition, nonresident: full-time $25,791; part-time $14,328 per credit hour. International tuition: $25,791 full-time. *Required fees:* $2512.80. Part-time tuition and fees vary according to course level, course load, degree level, program and student level. *Financial support:* In 2019–20, 22 students received support, including 22 teaching assistantships (averaging $15,210 per year); health care benefits also available. Financial award application deadline: 2/1; financial award applicants required to submit FAFSA. *Unit head:* Dr. Robert Gudmestad, Department Chair, 970-491-6050, Fax: 970-491-2941, E-mail: doug.yarrington@colostate.edu. *Application contact:* Nancy Rehe, Administrative Assistant, 970-491-6334, E-mail: nancy.rehe@colostate.edu. Website: http://history.colostate.edu/

Drew University, Caspersen School of Graduate Studies, Madison, NJ 07940-1493. Offers conflict resolution and leadership (Certificate), including community leadership, moderation, peace building; education (M Ed); finance (MA); history and culture (MA, PhD), including American history, book history, British history, European history, intellectual history, Irish history, print culture, public history; K-12 education (MAT), including art, biology, chemistry, elementary education, English, French, Italian, math, secondary education, special education, teacher of students with disabilities; liberal studies (M Litt, D Litt), including history, Irish/Irish-American studies, literature (M Litt, MMH, D Litt, DMH, CMH), religion, spirituality, teaching in the two-year college, writing; medical humanities (MMH, DMH, CMH), including arts, health, healthcare, literature (M Litt, MMH, D Litt, DMH, CMH), scientific research; poetry (MFA). *Program availability:* Part-time, evening/weekend. Terminal master's awarded for partial completion of doctoral program. *Degree requirements:* For master's and other advanced degree, thesis (for some programs); for doctorate, one foreign language, comprehensive exam (for some programs), thesis/dissertation. *Entrance requirements:* For master's, PRAXIS Core and Subject Area tests (for MAT), GRE/GMAT (for MFin MS in Data Analytics), resume, transcripts, writing sample, personal statement, letters of recommendation; for doctorate, GRE (PhD in history and culture), resume, transcripts, writing sample, personal statement, letters of recommendation; for other advanced degree, resume, transcripts, personal statement. Additional exam requirements/recommendations for international students: required—TOEFL (minimum score 587 paper-based; 80 iBT), IELTS (minimum score 6), TWE (minimum score 4). Electronic applications accepted.

Duquesne University, Graduate School of Liberal Arts, Department of History, Pittsburgh, PA 15282-0001. Offers historical studies (MA); public history (MA). *Program availability:* Part-time, evening/weekend. *Degree requirements:* For master's, comprehensive exam (for some programs), thesis optional. *Entrance requirements:* For master's, GRE General Test, writing sample. Additional exam requirements/recommendations for international students: required—TOEFL. Electronic applications accepted.

East Carolina University, Graduate School, Thomas Harriot College of Arts and Sciences, Department of History, Greenville, NC 27858-4353. Offers American history (MA); Atlantic world (MA); European history (MA); maritime studies (MA); military history (MA); public history (MA). *Program availability:* Part-time. *Application deadline:* For fall admission, 4/1 priority date for domestic and international students; for spring admission, 10/15 priority date for domestic and international students. *Expenses: Tuition, area resident:* Full-time $4749; part-time $185 per credit hour. *Tuition, state resident:* full-time $4749; part-time $185 per credit hour. *Tuition, nonresident:* full-time $17,898; part-time $864 per credit hour. *International tuition:* $17,898 full-time. *Required fees:* $2787. *Financial support:* Application deadline: 1/15. *Unit head:* Dr. Christopher Oakley, Chair, 252-328-1025, E-mail: oakleyc@ecu.edu. *Application contact:* Graduate School Admissions, 252-328-6012, E-mail: gradschool@ecu.edu. Website: https://history.ecu.edu/

Florida State University, The Graduate School, Department of Anthropology, Department of History, Tallahassee, FL 32306. Offers history (MA, MS, PhD); public history (MA). *Program availability:* Part-time. *Faculty:* 27 full-time (10 women), 3 part-time/adjunct (2 women). *Students:* 43 full-time (16 women), 28 part-time (9 women); includes 12 minority (2 Black or African American, non-Hispanic/Latino; 2 Asian, non-Hispanic/Latino; 8 Two or more races, non-Hispanic/Latino). Average age 30. 39 applicants, 87% accepted, 22 enrolled. In 2019, 23 master's, 15 doctorates awarded. *Degree requirements:* For master's, one foreign language, comprehensive exam (for some programs), thesis (for some programs), internships; for doctorate, one foreign language, comprehensive exam, thesis/dissertation. *Entrance requirements:* For master's, GRE General Test, minimum GPA of 3.3, minimum 18 hours of course work in history; for doctorate, GRE General Test, master's degree, minimum graduate GPA of 3.65. Additional exam requirements/recommendations for international students: required—TOEFL (minimum score 550 paper-based; 80 iBT). *Application deadline:* For fall admission, 12/1 for domestic and international students. Applications are processed on a rolling basis. Application fee: $30. Electronic applications accepted. *Financial support:* In 2019–20, 49 students received support, including 7 fellowships with full tuition reimbursements available (averaging $19,000 per year), 5 research

assistantships with full tuition reimbursements available (averaging $15,500 per year), 5 teaching assistantships with full tuition reimbursements available (averaging $18,000 per year); Federal Work-Study, institutionally sponsored loans, scholarships/grants, tuition waivers (full and partial), and unspecified assistantships also available. Financial award application deadline: 12/1; financial award applicants required to submit FAFSA. *Unit head:* Dr. Edward Gray, Chair, 850-644-5888, Fax: 850-644-6402, E-mail: egray@fsu.edu. *Application contact:* Anne Kozar, Academic Program Specialist, 850-644-4494, E-mail: mkozar@fsu.edu.
Website: http://history.fsu.edu/

Georgia Southern University, Jack N. Averitt College of Graduate Studies, College of Arts and Humanities, Program in History, Statesboro, GA 30460. Offers history (MA); public history (Graduate Certificate). *Program availability:* Part-time. *Faculty:* 36 full-time (11 women), 5 part-time/adjunct (0 women). *Students:* 21 full-time (14 women), 5 part-time (1 woman); includes 3 minority (1 Black or African American, non-Hispanic/Latino; 1 Hispanic/Latino; 1 Two or more races, non-Hispanic/Latino). Average age 34. 20 applicants, 85% accepted, 8 enrolled. In 2019, 12 master's awarded. *Degree requirements:* For master's, one foreign language, thesis optional, terminal exams. *Entrance requirements:* For master's, GRE General Test, minimum GPA of 3.0, undergraduate major in history or equivalent, letters of reference. Additional exam requirements/recommendations for international students: required—TOEFL (minimum score 550 paper-based; 80 iBT), IELTS (minimum score 6). *Application deadline:* For fall admission, 3/1 priority date for domestic and international students; for spring admission, 10/1 priority date for domestic students, 10/1 for international students. Applications are processed on a rolling basis. Application fee: $50. Electronic applications accepted. *Expenses: Tuition, area resident:* Full-time $4986; part-time $277 per credit hour. Tuition, nonresident: full-time $19,890; part-time $1105 per credit hour. *International tuition:* $19,890 full-time. *Required fees:* $2114; $1057 per semester. $1057 per semester. Tuition and fees vary according to course load, campus/location and program. *Financial support:* In 2019–20, 21 students received support, including 14 fellowships with full tuition reimbursements available (averaging $7,750 per year), 1 teaching assistantship with full tuition reimbursement available (averaging $7,750 per year); career-related internships or fieldwork, Federal Work-Study, scholarships/grants, tuition waivers (full), and unspecified assistantships also available. Support available to part-time students. Financial award application deadline: 4/15; financial award applicants required to submit FAFSA. *Unit head:* Dr. Timothy Teeter, Graduate Program Director, 912-478-0239, Fax: 912-478-0377, E-mail: tmteeter@georgiasouthern.edu.
Website: http://class.georgiasouthern.edu/history/

Georgia State University, College of Arts and Sciences, Department of History, Atlanta, GA 30302-3083. Offers heritage preservation (MHP); history (MA, PhD), including historic preservation (MA), history (PhD), public history (MA), world history (MA). *Program availability:* Part-time, evening/weekend. *Faculty:* 13 full-time (3 women), 5 part-time/adjunct (2 women). *Students:* 65 full-time (37 women), 61 part-time (35 women); includes 32 minority (15 Black or African American, non-Hispanic/Latino; 4 Asian, non-Hispanic/Latino; 9 Hispanic/Latino; 4 Two or more races, non-Hispanic/Latino), 4 international. Average age 41. 55 applicants, 82% accepted, 25 enrolled. In 2019, 14 master's, 6 doctorates awarded. Terminal master's awarded for partial completion of doctoral program. *Entrance requirements:* For master's, GRE, BA in history; statement of purpose; writing sample; three letters of recommendation; official transcripts; for doctorate, GRE, MA in history; master's thesis; statement of purpose; writing sample; three letters of recommendation; official transcripts; appropriate language skills. Additional exam requirements/recommendations for international students: required—TOEFL (minimum score 550 paper-based; 80 iBT). *Application deadline:* For fall admission, 3/15 for domestic and international students; for spring admission, 10/15 for domestic and international students. Applications are processed on a rolling basis. Application fee: $50. Electronic applications accepted. *Expenses: Tuition, area resident:* Full-time $7164; part-time $398 per credit hour. Tuition, state resident: full-time $7164; part-time $398 per credit hour. Tuition, nonresident: full-time $22,662; part-time $1259 per credit hour. *International tuition:* $22,662 full-time. *Required fees:* $2128; $312 per credit hour. Tuition and fees vary according to course load and program. *Financial support:* In 2019–20, research assistantships with tuition reimbursements (averaging $6,240 per year), teaching assistantships with tuition reimbursements (averaging $14,700 per year) were awarded; scholarships/grants also available. Financial award application deadline: 2/15. *Unit head:* Dr. Michelle Brattain, Chair, 404-413-6374, Fax: 404-413-6384, E-mail: mbrattain@gsu.edu. *Application contact:* Dr. Joe Perry, Director of Graduate Studies, 404-413-6374, Fax: 404-413-6384, E-mail: jbperry@gsu.edu.
Website: https://history.gsu.edu/

Indiana University of Pennsylvania, School of Graduate Studies and Research, College of Humanities and Social Sciences, Department of History, Indiana, PA 15705. Offers history (MA); public history (MA). *Program availability:* Part-time. In 2019, 2 master's awarded. *Degree requirements:* For master's, thesis optional. *Entrance requirements:* For master's, GRE, 2 letters of recommendation. Additional exam requirements/recommendations for international students: required—TOEFL (minimum score 540 paper-based). *Application deadline:* Applications are processed on a rolling basis. Application fee: $50. Electronic applications accepted. *Expenses: Tuition, area resident:* Full-time $9288; part-time $516 per credit. Tuition, nonresident: full-time $13,932; part-time $774 per credit. *Required fees:* $4454. One-time fee: $115 full-time. Tuition and fees vary according to course load and program. *Financial support:* Fellowships with partial tuition reimbursements, research assistantships with tuition reimbursements, career-related internships or fieldwork, Federal Work-Study, scholarships/grants, and unspecified assistantships available. Support available to part-time students. Financial award application deadline: 4/15; financial award applicants required to submit FAFSA. *Unit head:* Dr. R. Scott Moore, Chairperson, 724-357-2573, E-mail: rsmoore@iup.edu. *Application contact:* Dr. Jeanine Mazak-Kahne, Graduate Coordinator, 724-357-2436, E-mail: jmkahne@iup.edu.
Website: http://www.iup.edu/history

Indiana University-Purdue University Indianapolis, School of Liberal Arts, Department of History, Indianapolis, IN 46202. Offers European history (MA); public history (MA); United States history (MA); MA/MA; MA/MLS. *Program availability:* Part-time, evening/weekend. *Degree requirements:* For master's, one foreign language, thesis. *Entrance requirements:* For master's, GRE General Test, minimum GPA of 3.0. Electronic applications accepted.

James Madison University, The Graduate School, College of Arts and Letters, Program in History, Harrisonburg, VA 22807. Offers public history (MA); U.S. history (MA); world history (MA). *Program availability:* Part-time. *Students:* 20 full-time (11 women), 6 part-time (3 women); includes 2 minority (1 Asian, non-Hispanic/Latino; 1 Two or more races, non-Hispanic/Latino). Average age 30. In 2019, 6 master's awarded. *Degree requirements:* For master's, one foreign language, comprehensive exam, thesis. Application fee: $60. Electronic applications accepted. *Financial support:* In 2019–20, 10 students received support, including 3 teaching assistantships with full tuition reimbursements available (averaging $9,284 per year); fellowships, Federal Work-Study, and assistantships (averaging $7911) also available. Financial award application deadline: 3/1; financial award applicants required to submit FAFSA. *Unit head:* Dr. Gabrielle Lanier, Department Head, 540-568-6132, E-mail: laniergm@jmu.edu. *Application contact:* Lynette D. Michael, Director of Graduate Admissions, 540-568-6131 Ext. 6395, Fax: 540-568-7860, E-mail: michaeld@jmu.edu.
Website: http://www.jmu.edu/history

Lehigh University, College of Arts and Sciences, Department of History, Bethlehem, PA 18015. Offers Atlantic world (PhD); British history (PhD); history (MA); industrial and modern America (PhD); public history (MA). *Program availability:* Part-time. *Faculty:* 11 full-time (5 women), 1 (woman) part-time/adjunct. *Students:* 15 full-time (6 women), 16 part-time (4 women); includes 2 minority (1 Black or African American, non-Hispanic/Latino; 1 Two or more races, non-Hispanic/Latino), 2 international. Average age 35. 11 applicants, 45% accepted, 3 enrolled. In 2019, 1 master's, 1 doctorate awarded. Terminal master's awarded for partial completion of doctoral program. *Degree requirements:* For master's, comprehensive exam (for some programs), thesis (for some programs), comprehensive exam or thesis; for doctorate, comprehensive exam, thesis/dissertation. *Entrance requirements:* For master's, GRE General Test, recommendations, writing sample; for doctorate, GRE General Test, recommendations, writing samples. Additional exam requirements/recommendations for international students: required—TOEFL. *Application deadline:* For fall admission, 2/15 for domestic and international students. Applications are processed on a rolling basis. Application fee: $75. *Financial support:* In 2019–20, 1 fellowship with full tuition reimbursement (averaging $22,500 per year) was awarded; research assistantships, teaching assistantships with full tuition reimbursements, scholarships/grants, health care benefits, tuition waivers (full and partial), and unspecified assistantships also available. Financial award application deadline: 1/15. *Unit head:* Prof. Rick Matthews, Chairman, 610-758-3360, Fax: 610-758-6554, E-mail: rm02@lehigh.edu. *Application contact:* Ellen Zimmer Lewis, Graduate Coordinator, 610-758-3360, Fax: 610-758-3360, E-mail: ell414@lehigh.edu.
Website: http://history.cas2.lehigh.edu/

Loyola University Chicago, Graduate School, Department of History, Chicago, IL 60660. Offers history (MA, PhD); public history (MA). *Program availability:* Part-time. *Faculty:* 38 full-time (21 women), 9 part-time/adjunct (6 women). *Students:* 42 full-time (25 women), 10 part-time (6 women); includes 4 minority (1 Black or African American, non-Hispanic/Latino; 3 Hispanic/Latino), 1 international. Average age 30. 67 applicants, 63% accepted, 16 enrolled. In 2019, 12 master's, 6 doctorates awarded. Terminal master's awarded for partial completion of doctoral program. *Degree requirements:* For master's, one foreign language, comprehensive exam, thesis optional, portfolio (for public history program); for doctorate, 2 foreign languages, comprehensive exam, thesis/dissertation. *Entrance requirements:* For master's, research paper/writing sample; for doctorate, seminar paper or master's thesis. Additional exam requirements/recommendations for international students: required—TOEFL (minimum score 550 paper-based), IELTS. *Application deadline:* For fall admission, 5/1 for domestic students; for spring admission, 10/1 for domestic students. Applications are processed on a rolling basis. Electronic applications accepted. Application fee is waived when completed online. *Expenses:* 1033 per credit hour, student development 85-125, technology 30-125, dissertation supervision 1935. *Financial support:* In 2019–20, 20 students received support, including 1 fellowship with full tuition reimbursement available (averaging $20,000 per year), 3 research assistantships with full tuition reimbursements available (averaging $18,000 per year), 14 teaching assistantships with full tuition reimbursements available (averaging $18,000 per year); Federal Work-Study, scholarships/grants, health care benefits, and unspecified assistantships also available. Financial award application deadline: 1/1; financial award applicants required to submit FAFSA. *Unit head:* Dr. Paticia Mooney-Melvin, Director, Graduate Programs, 773-508-2228, Fax: 773-508-3693, E-mail: pmooney@luc.edu. *Application contact:* Dr. Patricia Mooney-Melvin, Director, Graduate Programs, 773-508-2228, Fax: 773-508-3693, E-mail: pmooney@luc.edu.
Website: http://www.luc.edu/history/

Middle Tennessee State University, College of Graduate Studies, College of Liberal Arts, Department of History, Program in Public History, Murfreesboro, TN 37132. Offers PhD. *Program availability:* Part-time, evening/weekend, online learning. *Degree requirements:* For doctorate, one foreign language, comprehensive exam, thesis/dissertation. *Entrance requirements:* For doctorate, GRE. Additional exam requirements/recommendations for international students: required—TOEFL (minimum score 525 paper-based; 71 iBT) or IELTS (minimum score 6).

New York University, Graduate School of Arts and Science, Department of History, New York, NY 10012-1019. Offers African diaspora (PhD); African history (PhD); archival management (Advanced Certificate); Atlantic history (PhD); French studies/history (PhD); Hebrew and Judaic studies/history (PhD); history (MA, PhD), including Europe (PhD), Latin America and the Caribbean (PhD), United States (PhD), women's history (MA); Middle Eastern history (MA); Middle Eastern studies/history (PhD); public history (Advanced Certificate); world history (MA); JD/MA; MA/Advanced Certificate. *Program availability:* Part-time. Terminal master's awarded for partial completion of doctoral program. *Degree requirements:* For master's, seminar paper; for doctorate, one foreign language, thesis/dissertation, oral and written exams; for Advanced Certificate, internship. *Entrance requirements:* For master's, GRE General Test, minimum GPA of 3.0, writing sample; for doctorate, GRE. Additional exam requirements/recommendations for international students: required—TOEFL.

North Carolina State University, Graduate School, College of Humanities and Social Sciences, Department of History, Program in Public History, Raleigh, NC 27695. Offers MA. *Degree requirements:* For master's, thesis optional. *Entrance requirements:* For master's, GRE General Test. Electronic applications accepted.

Northern Kentucky University, Office of Graduate Programs, College of Arts and Sciences, Program in Public History, Highland Heights, KY 41099. Offers MA. *Program availability:* Part-time, evening/weekend. *Degree requirements:* For master's, comprehensive exam, final capstone project. *Entrance requirements:* Additional exam requirements/recommendations for international students: required—TOEFL (minimum score 550 paper-based; 79 iBT); recommended—IELTS (minimum score 6.5). Electronic applications accepted.

Rutgers University - Camden, Graduate School of Arts and Sciences, Program in American and Public History, Camden, NJ 08102. Offers MA. *Program availability:* Part-time, evening/weekend. *Degree requirements:* For master's, comprehensive exam, thesis optional, 30 credits. *Entrance requirements:* For master's, GRE General Test (for full-time applicants), 3 letters of recommendation; history or related undergraduate degree (preferred). Additional exam requirements/recommendations for international students: required—TOEFL, IELTS. Electronic applications accepted.

St. John's University, St. John's College of Liberal Arts and Sciences, Department of History, Queens, NY 11439. Offers history (MA, PhD); public history (MA). *Program availability:* Part-time, evening/weekend. Terminal master's awarded for partial completion of doctoral program. *Degree requirements:* For master's, variable foreign language requirement, comprehensive exam, thesis optional; for doctorate, variable foreign language requirement, thesis/dissertation, annual portfolio, internships. *Entrance requirements:* For master's, letters of recommendation, transcripts, resume, personal statement; for doctorate, GRE General Test, letters of recommendation, transcripts, resume, personal statement. Additional exam requirements/recommendations for international students: required—TOEFL (minimum score 80 iBT), IELTS (minimum score 6.5). Electronic applications accepted.

Shippensburg University of Pennsylvania, School of Graduate Studies, College of Arts and Sciences, Department of History and Philosophy, Shippensburg, PA 17257-2299. Offers applied history (MA). *Program availability:* Part-time, evening/weekend. *Faculty:* 5 full-time (1 woman). *Students:* 10 full-time (7 women), 6 part-time (4 women); includes 2 minority (1 Black or African American, non-Hispanic/Latino; 1 Two or more races, non-Hispanic/Latino). Average age 33. 23 applicants, 78% accepted, 9 enrolled. In 2019, 12 master's awarded. *Degree requirements:* For master's, thesis, thesis, internship, or student teaching and professional practicum. *Entrance requirements:* For master's, 500-word statement of purpose; interview or minimum GPA of 2.75. Additional exam requirements/recommendations for international students: required—TOEFL (minimum score 550 paper-based; 68 iBT), IELTS (minimum score 6), TOEFL (minimum score 550 paper-based, 68 iBT) or IELTS (minimum score 6). *Application deadline:* For fall admission, 2/15 for domestic and international students; for spring admission, 9/15 for domestic and international students; for summer admission, 2/15 for domestic and international students. Applications are processed on a rolling basis. Application fee: $45. Electronic applications accepted. *Expenses:* Tuition, state resident: part-time $516 per credit. Tuition, nonresident: part-time $774 per credit. *Required fees:* $149 per credit. *Financial support:* In 2019–20, 11 students received support. Career-related internships or fieldwork, scholarships/grants, unspecified assistantships, and resident hall director and student payroll positions available. Support available to part-time students. Financial award application deadline: 3/1; financial award applicants required to submit FAFSA. *Unit head:* Dr. John D. Bloom, Professor and Program Coordinator, 717-477-1621, Fax: 717-477-4062, E-mail: jdbloo@ship.edu. *Application contact:* Maya T. Mapp, Director of Admissions, 717-477-1231, Fax: 717-477-4016, E-mail: mtmapp@ship.edu.
Website: http://www.ship.edu/history/

Sonoma State University, School of Social Sciences, Program in Cultural Resources Management, Rohnert Park, CA 94928. Offers MA. *Program availability:* Part-time. *Entrance requirements:* For master's, minimum GPA of 3.0. Additional exam requirements/recommendations for international students: required—TOEFL (minimum score 500 paper-based).

SUNY Brockport, School of Arts and Sciences, Department of History, Brockport, NY 14420-2997. Offers history (MA), including American and world history, American history, American public history, world history. *Program availability:* Part-time, evening/weekend. *Faculty:* 9 full-time (4 women), 1 part-time/adjunct (0 women). *Students:* 6 full-time (2 women), 33 part-time (17 women); includes 2 minority (both Black or African American, non-Hispanic/Latino). 11 applicants, 91% accepted, 5 enrolled. In 2019, 17 master's awarded. *Entrance requirements:* For master's, minimum GPA of 3.0, writing sample, letters of recommendation, statement of objectives. Additional exam requirements/recommendations for international students: required—TOEFL (minimum score 550 paper-based; 79 iBT), IELTS (minimum score 6.5). *Application deadline:* For fall admission, 7/1 priority date for domestic and international students; for spring admission, 11/15 priority date for domestic and international students; for summer admission, 4/15 for domestic and international students. Application fee: $50. Electronic applications accepted. *Expenses:* Tuition, area resident: Part-time $471 per credit hour. Tuition, nonresident: part-time $963 per credit hour. *Financial support:* In 2019–20, 1 fellowship with tuition reimbursement (averaging $3,750 per year), 2 teaching assistantships with full tuition reimbursements (averaging $6,000 per year) were awarded; Federal Work-Study, scholarships/grants, and unspecified assistantships also available. Support available to part-time students. Financial award application deadline: 3/15; financial award applicants required to submit FAFSA. *Unit head:* Dr. Jose Torre, Chairperson, 585-395-5698, Fax: 585-395-2620, E-mail: jrtorre@brockport.edu. *Application contact:* Dr. Carl Davila, Graduate Director, 585-395-5699, Fax: 585-395-2620, E-mail: cdavila@brockport.edu.
Website: https://www.brockport.edu/academics/history/graduate/masters.html

Texas A&M University–Commerce, College of Humanities, Social Sciences and Arts, Commerce, TX 75429. Offers applied criminology (MS); applied linguistics (MA, MS); art (MA, MFA); christianity in history (Graduate Certificate); computational linguistics (Graduate Certificate); creative writing (Graduate Certificate); criminal justice management (Graduate Certificate); criminal justice studies (Graduate Certificate); English (MA, MS, PhD); film studies (Graduate Certificate); history (MA, MS); Holocaust studies (Graduate Certificate); homeland security (Graduate Certificate); music (MM); music performance (MM); political science (MA, MS); public history (Graduate Certificate); sociology (MS); Spanish (MA); studies in children's and adolescent literature and culture (Graduate Certificate); teaching English to speakers of other languages (Graduate Certificate); theater (MA, MS); world history (Graduate Certificate). *Program availability:* Part-time. *Faculty:* 49 full-time (28 women), 8 part-time/adjunct (2 women). *Students:* 34 full-time (21 women), 427 part-time (302 women); includes 175 minority (66 Black or African American, non-Hispanic/Latino; 1 American Indian or Alaska Native, non-Hispanic/Latino; 13 Asian, non-Hispanic/Latino; 79 Hispanic/Latino; 16 Two or more races, non-Hispanic/Latino), 15 international. Average age 38. 193 applicants, 49% accepted, 78 enrolled. In 2019, 122 master's, 6 doctorates awarded. *Degree requirements:* For master's, one foreign language, comprehensive exam, thesis (for some programs); for doctorate, one foreign language, comprehensive exam, thesis/dissertation, departmental qualifying exam. *Entrance requirements:* For master's, GRE General Test, official transcripts, letters of recommendation, resume, statement of goals; for doctorate, GRE General Test, official transcripts, letters of recommendation, statement of goals, writing samples, writing sessions, resumes. Additional exam requirements/recommendations for international students: required—TOEFL (minimum score 550 paper-based; 79 iBT), IELTS (minimum score 6), PTE (minimum score 53). *Application deadline:* For fall admission, 6/1 priority date for international students; for spring admission, 10/15 priority date for international students; for summer admission, 3/15 priority date for international students. Applications are processed on a rolling basis. Application fee: $50 ($75 for international students). Electronic applications accepted. *Expenses:* Tuition, area resident: Full-time $3630; part-time $202 per credit hour. Tuition, state resident: full-time $3630; part-time $202 per credit hour. Tuition, nonresident: full-time $11,232; part-time $624 per credit hour. International tuition: $11,232 full-time. *Required fees:* $2948. *Financial support:* In 2019–20, 30 students received support, including 18 research assistantships with partial tuition reimbursements available (averaging $3,231 per year), 136 teaching assistantships with partial tuition reimbursements available (averaging $4,053 per year); Federal Work-Study, institutionally sponsored loans, scholarships/grants, health care benefits, and unspecified assistantships also available. Financial award application deadline: 5/1; financial award applicants required to submit FAFSA. *Unit head:* Dr. William F. Kuracina, Interim Dean, 903-886-5166, Fax: 903-886-5774, E-mail: william.kuracina@tamuc.edu. *Application contact:* Rebecca Stevens, Graduate Student Services Coordinator, 903-468-6049, E-mail: rebecca.stevens@tamuc.edu.
Website: http://www.tamuc.edu/academics/colleges/humanitiesSocialSciencesArts/

University at Albany, State University of New York, College of Arts and Sciences, Department of History, Albany, NY 12222-0001. Offers history (MA, PhD); public history (Certificate). *Program availability:* Part-time, blended/hybrid learning. *Faculty:* 21 full-time (7 women), 14 part-time/adjunct (11 women). *Students:* 24 full-time (11 women), 50 part-time (19 women); includes 7 minority (2 Black or African American, non-Hispanic/Latino; 1 Asian, non-Hispanic/Latino; 2 Hispanic/Latino; 2 Two or more races, non-Hispanic/Latino), 3 international. 30 applicants, 70% accepted, 15 enrolled. In 2019, 7 master's, 4 doctorates awarded. *Degree requirements:* For master's, variable foreign language requirement, exam, research paper or thesis; for doctorate, thesis/dissertation. *Entrance requirements:* For master's, minimum GPA of 3.0, transcripts of all schools attended, statement of background and goals, departmental questionnaire, resume, names and contact information for 3 recommenders; for doctorate, GRE General Test, minimum GPA of 3.0, transcripts of all schools attended, statement of background and goals, departmental questionnaire, resume, names and contact information for 3 recommenders. Additional exam requirements/recommendations for international students: required—TOEFL (minimum score 550 paper-based). *Application deadline:* For fall admission, 7/15 for domestic students, 5/1 for international students; for spring admission, 11/15 for domestic students, 11/1 for international students. Applications are processed on a rolling basis. Application fee: $75. Electronic applications accepted. *Expenses:* Tuition, area resident: Full-time $11,530; part-time $480 per credit hour. Tuition, nonresident: full-time $23,530; part-time $980 per credit hour. International tuition: $23,530 full-time. *Required fees:* $2185; $96 per credit hour. Part-time tuition and fees vary according to course load and program. *Financial support:* Teaching assistantships and career-related internships or fieldwork available. Financial award application deadline: 3/1. *Unit head:* Patrick Nold, Chair, 518-442-5300, Fax: 518-442-5301, E-mail: rhamm@albany.edu. *Application contact:* Michael DeRensis, Director, Graduate Admissions, 518-442-3980, Fax: 518-442-3922, E-mail: graduate@albany.edu.
Website: https://www.albany.edu/history/

University at Buffalo, the State University of New York, Graduate School, College of Arts and Sciences, Department of History, Buffalo, NY 14260. Offers history (MA, PhD, Advanced Certificate); public history (MA). *Program availability:* Part-time. Terminal master's awarded for partial completion of doctoral program. *Degree requirements:* For master's, project; for doctorate, one foreign language, comprehensive exam, thesis/dissertation. *Entrance requirements:* For doctorate, GRE General Test. Additional exam requirements/recommendations for international students: required—TOEFL (minimum score 550 paper-based; 79 iBT). Electronic applications accepted. *Expenses:* Contact institution.

University of Arkansas at Little Rock, Graduate School, College of Arts, Letters, and Sciences, Department of History, Little Rock, AR 72204-1099. Offers public history (MA). *Program availability:* Part-time. *Degree requirements:* For master's, oral exam. *Entrance requirements:* For master's, GRE General Test, minimum GPA of 3.25 in history, 2.7 overall; 15 hours of undergraduate history; two letters of recommendation.

University of California, Santa Barbara, Graduate Division, College of Letters and Sciences, Division of Humanities and Fine Arts, Department of History, Santa Barbara, CA 93106-9410. Offers European medieval studies (PhD); global studies (PhD); public historical studies (PhD); technology and society (PhD); women's studies (PhD); MA/PhD. *Degree requirements:* For doctorate, variable foreign language requirement, comprehensive exam, thesis/dissertation. *Entrance requirements:* For doctorate, GRE. Additional exam requirements/recommendations for international students: required—TOEFL (minimum score 550 paper-based; 80 iBT), IELTS (minimum score 7). Electronic applications accepted.

University of Colorado Denver, College of Liberal Arts and Sciences, Department of History, Denver, CO 80217. Offers European history (MA); global history (MA); public history (MA); U.S. history (MA). *Program availability:* Part-time, evening/weekend. *Degree requirements:* For master's, comprehensive exam, thesis optional, 36 semester hours (12 courses). *Entrance requirements:* For master's, GRE General Test, writing sample, minimum undergraduate GPA of 3.25, three letters of recommendation, statement of purpose addressing any weaknesses in academic record. Additional exam requirements/recommendations for international students: required—TOEFL (minimum score 537 paper-based; 75 iBT); recommended—IELTS (minimum score 6.5). Electronic applications accepted. Tuition and fees vary according to course load, program and reciprocity agreements.

University of Illinois at Springfield, Graduate Programs, College of Liberal Arts and Sciences, Program in History, Springfield, IL 62703-5407. Offers MA. *Program availability:* Part-time. *Faculty:* 9 full-time (4 women). *Students:* 6 full-time (4 women), 14 part-time (9 women); includes 1 minority (Black or African American, non-Hispanic/Latino), 1 international. Average age 31. 14 applicants, 71% accepted, 5 enrolled. In 2019, 10 master's awarded. *Degree requirements:* For master's, internship; closure exercise; position paper and historiography; thesis or project. *Entrance requirements:* For master's, BA in history or related field, minimum undergraduate cumulative GPA of 2.50 from an accredited college or university, writing sample, statement of purpose. Additional exam requirements/recommendations for international students: required—TOEFL (minimum score 500 paper-based; 61 iBT). *Application deadline:* Applications are processed on a rolling basis. Application fee: $60 ($75 for international students). Electronic applications accepted. *Expenses:* Tuition, area resident: Full-time $7896; part-time $329 per credit hour. Tuition, nonresident: full-time $16,200; part-time $675 per credit hour. *Required fees:* $2735.60; $130.65 per credit hour. *Financial support:* In 2019–20, research assistantships with full tuition reimbursements (averaging $10,562 per year), teaching assistantships with full tuition reimbursements (averaging $10,652 per year) were awarded; fellowships, career-related internships or fieldwork, Federal Work-Study, scholarships/grants, health care benefits, and unspecified assistantships also available. Support available to part-time students. Financial award application deadline: 11/15; financial award applicants required to submit FAFSA. *Unit head:* Dr. John Barker, Program Administrator, 217-206-6512, Fax: 217-206-6217, E-mail: jbark3@uis.edu. *Application contact:* Dr. John Barker, Program Administrator, 217-206-6512, Fax: 217-206-6217, E-mail: jbark3@uis.edu.
Website: his@uis.edu

University of Louisiana at Lafayette, College of Liberal Arts, Department of History, Geography and Philosophy, Lafayette, LA 70504. Offers history (MA), including American history, European history, Latin American history, public history. *Program availability:* Part-time. *Degree requirements:* For master's, one foreign language, thesis or alternative. *Entrance requirements:* For master's, GRE General Test, minimum GPA of 2.75. Additional exam requirements/recommendations for international students: required—TOEFL (minimum score 550 paper-based). Electronic applications accepted. *Expenses:* Tuition, area resident: Full-time $5511; part-time $1630 per credit hour. Tuition, state resident: full-time $5511; part-time $1630 per credit hour. Tuition, nonresident: full-time $19,239; part-time $2409 per credit hour. *Required fees:* $46,637.

University of Louisville, Graduate School, College of Arts and Sciences, Department of History, Louisville, KY 40292-0001. Offers history (MA); public history (Certificate). *Program availability:* Part-time. *Faculty:* 17 full-time (8 women), 4 part-time/adjunct (2 women). *Students:* 11 full-time (5 women), 10 part-time (3 women); includes 4 minority (3 Black or African American, non-Hispanic/Latino; 1 Two or more races, non-Hispanic/Latino). Average age 32. 9 applicants, 100% accepted, 7 enrolled. In 2019, 6 master's, 2 other advanced degrees awarded. *Degree requirements:* For master's, comprehensive exam (for some programs), thesis. *Entrance requirements:* For master's, GRE General Test, 2 letters of reference, official transcripts, statement of purpose, not to exceed 500 words, which describes in reasonably specific terms, academic and career objectives and how they can be advanced through work in program. Additional exam requirements/recommendations for international students: required—TOEFL (minimum score 550 paper-based; 79 iBT), IELTS can be used in place of the TOEFL; recommended—IELTS (minimum score 6.5). *Application deadline:* For fall admission, 2/15 for domestic and international students; for spring admission, 12/1 for domestic and international students. Applications are processed on a rolling basis. Application fee: $65. Electronic applications accepted. *Expenses: Tuition, area resident:* Full-time $13,000; part-time $723 per credit hour. Tuition, state resident: full-time $13,000; part-time $723 per credit hour. Tuition, nonresident: full-time $27,114; part-time $1507 per credit hour. *International tuition:* $27,114 full-time. *Required fees:* $196. Tuition and fees vary according to program and reciprocity agreements. *Financial support:* In 2019–20, 6 students received support. Fellowships, research assistantships, teaching assistantships, health care benefits, and unspecified assistantships available. Financial award application deadline: 2/15. *Unit head:* Dr. Blake Beattie, Chairperson/Associate Professor, 502-852-6818, Fax: 502-852-0770, E-mail: history@louisville.edu. *Application contact:* Dr. Jennifer T. Westerfeld, Director of Graduate Studies/Assoc. Prof, 502-852-3756, E-mail: histgrad@louisville.edu. Website: http://louisville.edu/history/

University of Maryland, Baltimore County, The Graduate School, College of Arts, Humanities and Social Sciences, School of Public Policy, Baltimore, MD 21250. Offers public policy (MPP, PhD), including economics (PhD), educational policy, emergency services (PhD), environmental policy (MPP), evaluation and analytical methods, health policy, policy history (PhD), public management, urban policy. *Program availability:* Part-time, evening/weekend. *Faculty:* 10 full-time (5 women). *Students:* 49 full-time (29 women), 63 part-time (31 women); includes 39 minority (18 Black or African American, non-Hispanic/Latino; 1 American Indian or Alaska Native, non-Hispanic/Latino; 9 Asian, non-Hispanic/Latino; 9 Hispanic/Latino; 2 Two or more races, non-Hispanic/Latino), 10 international. Average age 36. 73 applicants, 74% accepted, 31 enrolled. In 2019, 17 master's, 8 doctorates awarded. Terminal master's awarded for partial completion of doctoral program. *Degree requirements:* For master's, thesis, policy analysis paper, internship for pre-service; for doctorate, comprehensive exam, thesis/dissertation, comprehensive and field qualifying exams. *Entrance requirements:* For master's, GRE General Test, 3 academic letters of reference, resume, official transcripts; for doctorate, GRE General Test, 3 academic letters of reference, resume, research paper, official transcripts. Additional exam requirements/recommendations for international students: required—TOEFL (minimum score 550 paper-based; 80 iBT), IELTS (minimum score 6.5). *Application deadline:* For fall admission, 1/15 priority date for domestic students, 1/1 priority date for international students; for spring admission, 11/1 priority date for domestic students, 5/1 priority date for international students. Applications are processed on a rolling basis. Application fee: $50. Electronic applications accepted. *Expenses:* $14,382 per year. *Financial support:* In 2019–20, 26 students received support, including 23 research assistantships with full tuition reimbursements available (averaging $20,000 per year), 3 teaching assistantships; Federal Work-Study, scholarships/grants, health care benefits, and unspecified assistantships also available. Financial award application deadline: 1/1; financial award applicants required to submit FAFSA. *Unit head:* Dr. Susan Sterett, Director, 410-455-2140, Fax: 410-455-1172, E-mail: ssterett@umbc.edu. *Application contact:* Shelley Morris, Administrator of Academic Affairs, 410-455-3202, Fax: 410-455-1172, E-mail: shelleym@umbc.edu. Website: http://publicpolicy.umbc.edu/

University of North Alabama, College of Arts and Sciences, Department of History, Program in Public History, Florence, AL 35632-0001. Offers historic preservation (MA); historical administration (MA). *Program availability:* Part-time. *Degree requirements:* For master's, comprehensive exam (for some programs), thesis optional. *Entrance requirements:* For master's, GRE, three letters of recommendation; essay; writing sample. Additional exam requirements/recommendations for international students: required—TOEFL (minimum score 79 iBT), IELTS (minimum score 6), TWE, PTE (minimum score 54). Electronic applications accepted.

University of Northern Iowa, Graduate College, College of Social and Behavioral Sciences, Department of History, Cedar Falls, IA 50614. Offers history (MA); public history (MA). *Program availability:* Part-time. *Degree requirements:* For master's, comprehensive exam (for some programs), thesis or alternative. *Entrance requirements:* For master's, minimum GPA of 3.2. Additional exam requirements/recommendations for international students: required—TOEFL (minimum score 500 paper-based; 61 iBT). Electronic applications accepted.

University of South Carolina, The Graduate School, College of Arts and Sciences, Department of History, Program in Public History, Columbia, SC 29208. Offers archive management (MA); historic preservation (MA); museum administration (MA); museum management (Certificate); MLIS/MA. *Degree requirements:* For master's, one foreign language, thesis, internship. *Entrance requirements:* For master's, GRE General Test, writing sample. Additional exam requirements/recommendations for international students: required—TOEFL. Electronic applications accepted.

The University of Texas at Austin, Graduate School, College of Liberal Arts, Department of Anthropology, Austin, TX 78712-1111. Offers archaeology (MA, PhD); cultural forms (MA, PhD); linguistic anthropology (MA, PhD); physical anthropology (MA, PhD); social anthropology (MA, PhD). *Program availability:* Part-time. Terminal master's awarded for partial completion of doctoral program. *Degree requirements:* For master's, thesis; for doctorate, one foreign language, thesis/dissertation. *Entrance requirements:* For master's and doctorate, GRE General Test. Additional exam requirements/recommendations for international students: required—TOEFL. Electronic applications accepted.

University of West Florida, College of Arts, Social Sciences, and Humanities, Department of History, Pensacola, FL 32514-5750. Offers early American studies (MA); public history (MA); traditional history (MA). *Program availability:* Part-time, evening/weekend. *Degree requirements:* For master's, thesis or alternative. *Entrance requirements:* For master's, GRE (minimum score: verbal 500, writing 3.5) or MAT (minimum score 415), minimum GPA of 3.0; minimum 15 hours of upper-level history courses; official transcripts; letter of intent; writing sample (undergraduate research paper preferred). Additional exam requirements/recommendations for international students: required—TOEFL (minimum score 550 paper-based).

Wayne State University, College of Liberal Arts and Sciences, Tracy Neumann, Detroit, MI 48202. Offers history (MA, PhD); public history (MA), including African American history and culture, cultural resource management, gender, sexuality, and women's studies, labor and urban history, museum studies, public policy; world history (Graduate Certificate); JD/MA; M Ed/MA; MLIS/MA. *Program availability:* Evening/weekend. *Faculty:* 23 full-time (11 women). *Students:* 18 full-time (7 women), 16 part-time (7 women); includes 4 minority (2 Black or African American, non-Hispanic/Latino; 2 Two or more races, non-Hispanic/Latino). Average age 37. 38 applicants, 34% accepted, 13 enrolled. In 2019, 7 master's, 3 doctorates awarded. *Degree requirements:* For master's, thesis (for some programs), final oral exam on thesis or essay and seminar; internship and project (for public history); for doctorate, variable foreign language requirement, comprehensive exam, thesis/dissertation, qualifying exam in 4 fields of history. *Entrance requirements:* For master's, GRE General Test, minimum undergraduate GPA of 3.25 in history, 3.0 overall; at least 18 credits in history and related subjects at the advanced undergraduate level; foreign language; letter of intent; research paper; at least two letters of recommendation from former instructors; for doctorate, GRE General Test, minimum GPA of 3.0, 3.25 in minimum of 18 semester credits in history and related subjects; letter of intent; research paper; at least three letters of recommendation from former professors; for Graduate Certificate, baccalaureate degree from accredited college or university; minimum GPA of 3.0, 3.25 in a minimum of eighteen semester credits in history and related subjects at the advanced undergraduate level. Additional exam requirements/recommendations for international students: required—TOEFL (minimum score 550 paper-based; 79 iBT), TWE (minimum score 5.5), Michigan English Language Assessment Battery (minimum score 85); recommended—IELTS (minimum score 6.5). *Application deadline:* For fall admission, 1/15 priority date for domestic and international students; for winter admission, 4/15 for domestic students, 4/15 priority date for international students; for spring admission, 10/15 for domestic students, 10/15 priority date for international students. Application fee: $50. Electronic applications accepted. *Expenses: Tuition:* Full-time $34,567. *Financial support:* In 2019–20, 18 students received support, including 2 fellowships with tuition reimbursements available (averaging $20,797 per year), 2 research assistantships with tuition reimbursements available (averaging $23,960 per year), 7 teaching assistantships with tuition reimbursements available (averaging $19,967 per year); scholarships/grants, health care benefits, and unspecified assistantships also available. Financial award applicants required to submit FAFSA. *Unit head:* Dr. Elizabeth V. Faue, Professor/Chair, 313-577-2525, E-mail: evfaue@wayne.edu. *Application contact:* Dr. Tracy Neumann, Associate Professor and Director of Graduate Studies, 313-577-2525, E-mail: tracyneumann@wayne.edu. Website: http://clas.wayne.edu/history/

Section 8
Humanities

This section contains a directory of institutions offering graduate work in humanities. Additional information about programs listed in the directory may be obtained by writing directly to the dean of a graduate school or chair of a department at the address given in the directory.

For programs offering related work, see also in this book *Area and Cultural Studies, Geography, Interdisciplinary Studies, Philosophy, Political Science and International Affairs, Religious Studies,* and *Sociology, Anthropology, and Archaeology.*

CONTENTS

Program Directories

Humanities

Adams State University, Office of Graduate Studies, Department of History, Government and Philosophy, Alamosa, CO 81101. Offers humanities (MA), including cultural resource management, public administration, U.S. history. *Degree requirements:* For master's, thesis. Application fee: $30. *Unit head:* Chair, 719-587-7771, Fax: 719-587-7176. *Application contact:* Chair, 719-587-7771, Fax: 719-587-7176.
Website: https://www.adams.edu/academics/graduate/humanities/

The American University in Cairo, School of Humanities and Social Sciences, Cairo, Egypt. Offers Arab and Islamic civilizations (Graduate Diploma); Arabic studies (MA); comparative literary studies (Graduate Diploma); Egyptology and Coptology (MA); English and comparative literature (MA); humanities and social sciences (Graduate Diploma); philosophy (MA); psychology (MA); sociology and anthropology (MA); teaching Arabic as a foreign language (MA); teaching English to speakers of other languages (MA). *Program availability:* Part-time, evening/weekend. *Degree requirements:* For master's, comprehensive exam (for some programs), thesis (for some programs). *Entrance requirements:* Additional exam requirements/recommendations for international students: required—TOEFL (minimum score 450 paper-based; 45 iBT), IELTS (minimum score 5). Electronic applications accepted.

Brigham Young University, Graduate Studies, College of Humanities, Department of Comparative Arts and Letters, Provo, UT 84602-1001. Offers comparative studies (MA). *Program availability:* Part-time. *Faculty:* 29 full-time (7 women), 4 part-time/adjunct (2 women). *Students:* 15 full-time (10 women), 1 (woman) part-time; includes 1 minority (Asian, non-Hispanic/Latino). Average age 29. 15 applicants, 60% accepted, 8 enrolled. In 2019, 8 master's awarded. *Degree requirements:* For master's, 2 foreign languages, comprehensive exam, thesis, Coursework â?33 credit hours in seminars at graduate level and other courses by approval. *Entrance requirements:* For master's, GRE, minimum GPA of 3.0 in last 60 hours, writing sample, foreign language experience, undergraduate degree or experience in a humanities discipline, Proficiency in a language of scholarship or other spoken language. Additional exam requirements/recommendations for international students: required—TOEFL (minimum score 580 paper-based; 85 iBT), E3PT (to obtain the required minimum English language proficieny scores for the E3PT, IELTS, or TOEFL tests; or to obtain waiver "f".) *Application deadline:* For fall admission, 3/1 for domestic and international students. Application fee: $50. Electronic applications accepted. *Financial support:* In 2019–20, 15 students received support, including 1 research assistantship, 15 teaching assistantships (averaging $5,000 per year); scholarships/grants, tuition waivers (partial), unspecified assistantships, and student instructorships also available. Support available to part-time students. Financial award application deadline: 9/1. *Unit head:* Dr. Julie Allen, Graduate Coordinator/Professor of Classical Studies, 801-422-7891, Fax: 801-422-0305, E-mail: julie_allen@byu.edu. *Application contact:* Andrea Kristensen, Graduate Program Manager, 801-422-2996, Fax: 801-422-0305, E-mail: andrea_kristensen@byu.edu.
Website: http://cal.byu.edu/

California State University, Dominguez Hills, College of Arts and Humanities, Program in Arts and Humanities, Carson, CA 90747-0001. Offers MA. *Program availability:* Part-time, evening/weekend. *Degree requirements:* For master's, thesis or alternative. *Entrance requirements:* For master's, minimum GPA of 3.0. Additional exam requirements/recommendations for international students: required—TOEFL (minimum score 550 paper-based; 80 iBT).

California State University, Dominguez Hills, College of Extended and International Education, Humanities Program, Carson, CA 90747-0001. Offers MA. *Program availability:* Part-time, evening/weekend, 100% online. *Degree requirements:* For master's, thesis, advancement to candidacy essays. *Entrance requirements:* For master's, minimum GPA of 3.0 in last 60 undergraduate units. Additional exam requirements/recommendations for international students: required—TOEFL. Electronic applications accepted. *Expenses:* Contact institution.

Central Michigan University, College of Graduate Studies, College of Liberal Arts and Social Sciences, Program in Humanities, Mount Pleasant, MI 48859. Offers humanities (MA), including contemporary issues in the humanities: race, class, and gender, images and ideas of self, Native American issues in modern culture, popular culture studies, the rise of industrial society. *Program availability:* Part-time, evening/weekend. *Degree requirements:* For master's, thesis or alternative. Electronic applications accepted. *Expenses: Tuition, area resident:* Full-time $12,267; part-time $8178 per year. Tuition, state resident: full-time $12,267; part-time $8178 per year. Tuition, nonresident: full-time $12,267; part-time $8178 per year. *International tuition:* $16,110 full-time. *Required fees:* $225 per semester. Tuition and fees vary according to degree level and program.

Claremont Graduate University, Graduate Programs, School of Arts and Humanities, Claremont, CA 91711-6160. Offers M Phil, MA, MFA, DCM, DMA, PhD, Certificate, MA/PhD, MBA/MA, MBA/PhD. *Program availability:* Part-time. *Degree requirements:* For doctorate, 2 foreign languages, comprehensive exam, thesis/dissertation, oral and written qualifying exams, oral defense of dissertation, recitals. *Entrance requirements:* For master's and doctorate, GRE General Test. Additional exam requirements/recommendations for international students: required—TOEFL (minimum score 75 iBT). Electronic applications accepted.

The Colorado College, Education Department, Experienced Teacher Program, Colorado Springs, CO 80903-3294. Offers arts and humanities (MAT); integrated natural sciences (MAT); liberal arts (MAT); Southwest studies (MAT). *Program availability:* Part-time. *Degree requirements:* For master's, thesis, oral exam, 50-page paper. *Expenses:* Contact institution.

Colorado School of Mines, Office of Graduate Studies, Division of Humanities, Arts and Social Sciences, Golden, CO 80401. Offers international political economy (Graduate Certificate); science and technology policy (Graduate Certificate). *Program availability:* Part-time. *Entrance requirements:* Additional exam requirements/recommendations for international students: required—TOEFL (minimum score 550 paper-based; 79 iBT). Electronic applications accepted. *Expenses:* Tuition, state resident: full-time $16,650; part-time $925 per credit hour. Tuition, nonresident: full-time $37,350; part-time $2075 per credit hour. *International tuition:* $37,350 full-time. *Required fees:* $2412.

Concordia University, School of Graduate Studies, Faculty of Arts and Science, Program in Humanities, Montréal, QC H3G 1M8, Canada. Offers PhD. *Degree requirements:* For doctorate, one foreign language, comprehensive exam, thesis/dissertation.

Duke University, Graduate School, Program in Humanities, Durham, NC 27708. Offers AM, JD/AM. *Program availability:* Part-time. *Entrance requirements:* For master's, GRE General Test. Additional exam requirements/recommendations for international students: required—TOEFL (minimum score 577 paper-based; 90 iBT) or IELTS (minimum score 7). Electronic applications accepted.

Faulkner University, Alabama Christian College of Arts and Sciences, Department of Humanities, Montgomery, AL 36109-3398. Offers MA, PhD. *Program availability:* Part-time, evening/weekend, online only, 100% online. *Degree requirements:* For master's, thesis; for doctorate, thesis/dissertation. *Entrance requirements:* For master's, MAT with minimum score of 400 (if taken within last five years) or GRE with minimum revised score of 297 (if taken within last five years), bachelor's degree from regionally-accredited college or university, minimum cumulative GPA of 3.0, official transcripts from all colleges and universities attended, three recommendation letters or emails, goal statement (300-word minimum), approval by director; for doctorate, MAT with minimum score of 400 (if taken within last five years), GRE with minimum revised score of 297 (if taken within last five years), or master's degree in related field, minimum cumulative GPA of 3.0, master's degree from regionally-accredited college or university, official transcripts from all colleges and universities attended, three recommendation letters or emails, goal statement (400-500 words), scholarly postgraduate writing sample, approval by director. Additional exam requirements/recommendations for international students: required—TOEFL (minimum score 500 paper-based). Electronic applications accepted. *Expenses:* Contact institution.

Georgetown University, Graduate School of Arts and Sciences, School of Continuing Studies, Washington, DC 20057. Offers American studies (MALS); applied intelligence (MPS); Catholic studies (MALS); classical civilizations (MALS); emergency and disaster management (MPS); ethics and the professions (MALS); global strategic communications (MPS); hospitality management (MPS); human resources management (MPS); humanities (MALS); individualized study (MALS); integrated marketing communications (MPS); international affairs (MALS); Islam and Muslim-Christian relations (MALS); journalism (MPS); liberal studies (DLS); literature and society (MALS); medieval and early modern European studies (MALS); public relations and corporate communications (MPS); real estate (MPS); religious studies (MALS); social and public policy (MALS); sports industry management (MPS); systems engineering management (MPS); technology management (MPS); the theory and practice of American democracy (MALS); urban and regional planning (MPS); visual culture (MALS). *Entrance requirements:* Additional exam requirements/recommendations for international students: required—TOEFL.

The Graduate Center, City University of New York, Graduate Studies, Program in Digital Humanities, New York, NY 10016-4039. Offers data visualization and mapping (MA); digital pedagogy (MA); textual analysis (MA).

Harrison Middleton University, Graduate Program, Tempe, AZ 85282. Offers education (MA, Ed D); humanities (MA); imaginative literature (MA); interdisciplinary studies (DA); jurisprudence (MA); natural science (MA); philosophy and religion (MA); social science (MA). *Program availability:* Part-time, evening/weekend, online learning. *Degree requirements:* For master's and doctorate, capstone project. *Entrance requirements:* For master's, interview; for doctorate, 2 academic letters of reference, interview, essay. Additional exam requirements/recommendations for international students: required—TOEFL (minimum score 550 paper-based; 80 iBT). Electronic applications accepted.

Hollins University, Graduate Programs, Program in Liberal Studies, Roanoke, VA 24020. Offers humanities (MALS); interdisciplinary studies (MALS); leadership (MALS); social sciences (MALS); visual and performing arts (MALS). *Program availability:* Part-time, evening/weekend, 100% online, blended/hybrid learning. *Degree requirements:* For master's, thesis. *Entrance requirements:* For master's, three letters of recommendation, interview, bachelor's degree, undergraduate transcripts, statement of educational objectives. Additional exam requirements/recommendations for international students: required—TOEFL (minimum score 550 paper-based; 80 iBT), IELTS (minimum score 6.5). Electronic applications accepted. *Expenses:* Contact institution.

Hood College, Graduate School, Program in Humanities, Frederick, MD 21701-8575. Offers MA. *Program availability:* Part-time, evening/weekend. *Degree requirements:* For master's, thesis or alternative, portfolio (A). *Entrance requirements:* For master's, minimum GPA of 2.75, essay. Additional exam requirements/recommendations for international students: required—TOEFL (minimum score 575 paper-based; 89 iBT), IELTS (minimum score 6.5). Electronic applications accepted.

Illinois Institute of Technology, Graduate College, Lewis College of Human Sciences, Department of Humanities, Chicago, IL 60616. Offers information architecture (MS); technical communication (PhD); technical communication and information design (MS). *Program availability:* Part-time. *Degree requirements:* For master's, comprehensive exam, thesis or alternative; for doctorate, comprehensive exam, thesis/dissertation. *Entrance requirements:* For master's, GRE General Test (minimum score 144 Quantitative, 153 Verbal, and 4.0 Analytical Writing), minimum undergraduate GPA of 3.0; 2 letters of recommendation from faculty or supervisors; professional statement discussing academic goals; for doctorate, GRE General Test (minimum score 144 Quantitative, 153 Verbal, and 4.0 Analytical Writing), bachelor's or master's degree in a field that, in combination with the 27-credit hour technical core, would provide a solid basis for advanced academic work leading to original research in the field; 3 letters of recommendation from faculty or supervisors; professional statement discussing academic goals. Additional exam requirements/recommendations for international students: required—TOEFL (minimum score 95 iBT); recommended—IELTS (minimum score 7). Electronic applications accepted.

Instituto Tecnologico de Santo Domingo, Graduate School, Area of Humanities and Social Sciences, Santo Domingo, Dominican Republic. Offers accounting (Certificate); adult education (Certificate); applied linguistics (MA); economics (MA); education (M Ed); educational psychology (MA, Certificate); gender and development (MA, Certificate); humanistic studies (MA); international marketing management (Certificate); international relations in the Caribbean basin (Certificate); intervention systems in family therapy (MA); linguistic and literary communication (Certificate); pedagogical support (MA); social science education (M Ed); sustainable human development (MA); terminal illness and death psychology (Certificate); youth and adult education (M Ed).

Instituto Tecnológico y de Estudios Superiores de Monterrey, Campus Central de Veracruz, Graduate Programs, Córdoba, Mexico. Offers administration (MA); administration of information technologies (MTI); computer sciences (MCC); education (MEE); educational institution administration (MAD); educational technology (MTE); electronic commerce (MCE); finance (MAF); humanistic studies (MEH); international business for Latin America (MNL); marketing (MMT); science (MCP). *Program availability:* Part-time, evening/weekend, online learning. *Degree requirements:* For master's, thesis (for some programs). *Entrance requirements:* For master's, PAEP College Board. Electronic applications accepted.

Instituto Tecnológico y de Estudios Superiores de Monterrey, Campus Ciudad de México, Virtual University Division, Ciudad de Mexico, Mexico. Offers administration of information technologies (MA); computer sciences (MA); education (MA, PhD); educational technology (MA); environmental engineering (MA); environmental systems (MA); humanistic studies (MA); industrial engineering (MA); international business for Latin America (MA); quality systems (MA); quality systems and productivity (MA). *Program availability:* Part-time, evening/weekend, online learning. *Entrance requirements:* For master's and doctorate, Instituto entrance exam. Additional exam requirements/recommendations for international students: required—TOEFL.

Instituto Tecnológico y de Estudios Superiores de Monterrey, Campus Ciudad Juárez, Program in Humanistic Studies, Ciudad Juárez, Mexico. Offers MEH.

Instituto Tecnológico y de Estudios Superiores de Monterrey, Campus Estado de México, Professional and Graduate Division, Estado de Mexico, Mexico. Offers administration of information technologies (MITA); architecture (M Arch); business administration (GMBA, MBA); computer sciences (MCS, PhD); education (M Ed); educational institution administration (MAD); educational technology and innovation (PhD); electronic commerce (MEC); environmental systems (MS); finance (MAF); humanistic studies (MHS); information sciences and knowledge management (MISKM); information systems (MS); manufacturing systems (MS); marketing (MEM); quality systems and productivity (MS); science and materials engineering (PhD); telecommunications management (MTM). *Program availability:* Part-time, online learning. *Degree requirements:* For master's, one foreign language, thesis (for some programs); for doctorate, one foreign language, thesis/dissertation. *Entrance requirements:* For master's, E-PAEP 500, interview; for doctorate, E-PAEP 500, research proposal. Additional exam requirements/recommendations for international students: required—TOEFL (minimum score 550 paper-based).

Instituto Tecnológico y de Estudios Superiores de Monterrey, Campus Irapuato, Graduate Programs, Irapuato, Mexico. Offers administration (MBA); administration of information technology (MAIT); administration of telecommunications (MAT); architecture (M Arch); computer science (MCS); education (M Ed); educational administration (MEA); educational innovation and technology (DEIT); educational technology (MET); electronic commerce (MBA); environmental administration and planning (MEAP); environmental systems (MES); finances (MBA); humanistic studies (MHS); international management for Latin American executives (MIMLAE); library and information science (MLIS); manufacturing quality management (MMQM); marketing research (MBA).

Laurentian University, School of Graduate Studies and Research, Programme in Humanities: Interpretation and Values, Sudbury, ON P3E 2C6, Canada. Offers MA. *Program availability:* Part-time.

Loyola University Chicago, Graduate School, Program in Digital Humanities, Chicago, IL 60660. Offers MA. *Program availability:* Part-time. *Faculty:* 11 full-time (6 women). *Students:* 8 full-time (6 women), 1 part-time (0 women), 3 international. Average age 27. 7 applicants, 43% accepted, 1 enrolled. In 2019, 6 master's awarded. *Degree requirements:* For master's, Capstone project. *Entrance requirements:* For master's, BS or BA, transcripts, 2 letters of recommendation, letter of intent. Additional exam requirements/recommendations for international students: required—TOEFL. *Application deadline:* Applications are processed on a rolling basis. Electronic applications accepted. Application fee is waived when completed online. *Expenses:* Contact institution. *Financial support:* In 2019–20, 4 students received support, including 4 fellowships with partial tuition reimbursements available (averaging $9,000 per year); health care benefits and partial tuition remission also available. Financial award application deadline: 2/1. *Unit head:* Elizabeth Hopwood, Instructor, 773-508-3101, Fax: 773-508-2470, E-mail: ehopwood@luc.edu. *Application contact:* Jill Schur, Director of Graduate Enrollment Management, 312-915-8902, E-mail: gradinfo@luc.edu. Website: http://luc.edu/ctsdh

Marshall University, Academic Affairs Division, College of Liberal Arts, Program in Humanities, Huntington, WV 25755. Offers MA, Certificate. *Program availability:* Part-time, evening/weekend. *Degree requirements:* For master's, thesis, comprehensive assessment. *Entrance requirements:* For master's, GRE General Test, MAT, bachelor's degree in humanities, minimum undergraduate GPA of 3.0.

Memorial University of Newfoundland, School of Graduate Studies, Interdisciplinary Programs in Humanities, St. John's, NL A1C 5S7, Canada. Offers M Phil. *Program availability:* Part-time. *Degree requirements:* For master's, comprehensive exam, journal. *Entrance requirements:* For master's, honors bachelor's degree. Electronic applications accepted.

Mount Saint Mary's University, Graduate Division, Los Angeles, CA 90049. Offers business administration (MBA); counseling psychology (MS); creative writing (MFA); education (MS, Certificate); film and television (MFA); health policy and management (MS); humanities (MA); nursing (MSN, Certificate); physical therapy (DPT); religious studies (MA). *Program availability:* Part-time, evening/weekend. *Entrance requirements:* Additional exam requirements/recommendations for international students: required—TOEFL. Electronic applications accepted. *Expenses:* Tuition: Full-time $18,648; part-time $9324 per year. *Required fees:* $540; $540 per unit.

New York University, Graduate School of Arts and Science, XE: Experimental Humanities & Social Engagement, New York, NY 10012-1019. Offers humanities and social thought (MA); religion (Advanced Certificate); social theory (Advanced Certificate). *Program availability:* Part-time. *Degree requirements:* For master's, thesis, comprehensive exam or essay. *Entrance requirements:* For master's, GRE General Test; for Advanced Certificate, master's degree. Additional exam requirements/recommendations for international students: required—TOEFL, IELTS.

Northeast Ohio Medical University, College of Graduate Studies, Rootstown, OH 44272-0095. Offers health-system pharmacy administration (MS); integrated pharmaceutical medicine (MS, PhD); medical ethics and humanities (MS, Certificate); public health (MPH). *Program availability:* Part-time, evening/weekend, 100% online, blended/hybrid learning. *Faculty:* 126 part-time/adjunct (62 women). *Students:* 24 full-time (12 women), 28 part-time (15 women); includes 21 minority (2 Black or African American, non-Hispanic/Latino; 10 Asian, non-Hispanic/Latino; 5 Hispanic/Latino; 4 Two or more races, non-Hispanic/Latino). Average age 26. 31 applicants, 97% accepted, 21 enrolled. In 2019, 15 master's, 13 other advanced degrees awarded. *Degree requirements:* For master's, thesis (for some programs), thesis (for MS in medical ethics and humanities, integrated pharmaceutical medicine, MS in MAS); for doctorate, thesis/dissertation, For IPM Ph.D Program. *Entrance requirements:* Additional exam requirements/recommendations for international students: recommended—TOEFL (minimum score 550 paper-based). *Application deadline:* For fall admission, 7/17 for domestic students. Applications are processed on a rolling basis. Application fee: $95. Electronic applications accepted. *Expenses:* Student health and fitness, student activities. *Financial support:* In 2019–20, 6 students received support. Scholarships/grants and tuition waivers (full and partial) available. Financial award application deadline: 3/15; financial award applicants required to submit FAFSA. *Unit head:* Dr.

Steven Schmidt, Dean, 330-325-6290. *Application contact:* Dr. Steven Schmidt, Dean, 330-325-6290. Website: https://www.neomed.edu/graduatestudies/

Nova Southeastern University, College of Arts, Humanities, and Social Sciences, Fort Lauderdale, FL 33314-7796. Offers advanced conflict resolution practice (Graduate Certificate); child protection (MHS); college student affairs (MS); conflict analysis and resolution (MS, PhD); criminal justice (MS, PhD); cross-disciplinary studies (MA); developmental disabilities (MS); family studies (Graduate Certificate); family systems health care (Graduate Certificate); family therapy (MS, PhD); marriage and family therapy (DMFT); peace studies (Graduate Certificate); qualitative research (Graduate Certificate); solution focused coaching (Graduate Certificate). *Accreditation:* AAMFT/COAMFTE (one or more programs are accredited). *Program availability:* Part-time, evening/weekend, 100% online, blended/hybrid learning. *Faculty:* 60 full-time (37 women), 88 part-time/adjunct (65 women). *Students:* 201 full-time (157 women), 418 part-time (297 women); includes 365 minority (180 Black or African American, non-Hispanic/Latino; 4 American Indian or Alaska Native, non-Hispanic/Latino; 15 Asian, non-Hispanic/Latino; 141 Hispanic/Latino; 25 Two or more races, non-Hispanic/Latino), 49 international. Average age 37. 303 applicants, 84% accepted, 197 enrolled. In 2019, 125 master's, 63 doctorates, 24 other advanced degrees awarded. *Degree requirements:* For master's, comprehensive exam (for some programs), thesis optional, comprehensive exams, portfolios (for some programs), table-top exams (for some programs); for doctorate, comprehensive exam, thesis/dissertation, qualifying exams, portfolios (for some programs). *Entrance requirements:* For master's, interview, minimum GPA of 3.0, writing sample; for doctorate, interview, minimum GPA of 3.5, master's degree in related field, writing sample; for Graduate Certificate, minimum GPA of 3.0. Additional exam requirements/recommendations for international students: required—TOEFL (minimum score 79 paper-based). *Application deadline:* Applications are processed on a rolling basis. Application fee: $50. Electronic applications accepted. *Expenses:* Contact institution. *Financial support:* In 2019–20, 170 students received support. Career-related internships or fieldwork, Federal Work-Study, scholarships/grants, and unspecified assistantships available. Financial award application deadline: 4/1; financial award applicants required to submit FAFSA. *Unit head:* Dr. Honggang Yang, Dean, 954-262-3016, Fax: 954-262-3968, E-mail: yangh@nova.edu. *Application contact:* Marcia Arango, Student Recruitment Coordinator, 954-262-3006, Fax: 954-262-3968, E-mail: marango@nsu.nova.edu. Website: http://cahss.nova.edu/

Old Dominion University, College of Arts and Letters, Institute for the Humanities, Norfolk, VA 23529. Offers arts and entrepreneurship (Certificate); cultural and human geography (MA); cultural studies (MA); gender and sexuality studies (MA); health, communication and culture (Certificate); media and popular culture studies (MA); philosophy and religious studies (MA); social justice and entrepreneurship (Certificate); visual studies (MA); world cultures (MA). *Program availability:* Part-time, evening/weekend. *Degree requirements:* For master's, thesis optional, project. *Entrance requirements:* For master's, GRE General Test, minimum GPA of 3.25. Electronic applications accepted.

Penn State Harrisburg, Graduate School, School of Humanities, Middletown, PA 17057. Offers American studies (MA, PhD); communications (MA); folklore and ethnography (Certificate); heritage and museum practice (Certificate); humanities (MA). *Program availability:* Evening/weekend.

Pepperdine University, Seaver College, Malibu, CA 90263. Offers business (MS), including accounting; communication (MFA), including cinematic media production; humanities (MA, MFA), including American studies (MA), writing for screen and television (MFA); religion (M Div, MA, MS), including ministry (MS), religion (M Div, MA); JD/M Div. *Entrance requirements:* For master's, GRE General Test. Additional exam requirements/recommendations for international students: required—TOEFL. *Expenses:* Contact institution.

Prescott College, Graduate Programs, Program in Arts and Humanities, Prescott, AZ 86301. Offers humanities (MA); social justice and human rights (MA); student-directed independent study (MA). *Program availability:* Part-time, online learning. *Degree requirements:* For master's, thesis, fieldwork or internship, practicum. *Entrance requirements:* For master's, 2 letters of recommendation, resume, essay. Additional exam requirements/recommendations for international students: required—TOEFL (minimum score 500 paper-based). Electronic applications accepted.

Roosevelt University, Graduate Division, College of Arts and Sciences, Department of Humanities, Chicago, IL 60605. Offers creative writing (MFA). Electronic applications accepted. *Expenses:* Contact institution.

St. Edward's University, School of Education, Master of Liberal Arts Program, Austin, TX 78704. Offers humanities (MLA); liberal arts (MLA, Certificate). *Program availability:* Part-time, evening/weekend. *Entrance requirements:* Additional exam requirements/recommendations for international students: required—TOEFL, IELTS. Electronic applications accepted.

Salve Regina University, Program in Humanities, Newport, RI 02840-4192. Offers humanitarian assistance (MA); humanities (PhD); public humanities (MA); religion, peace and justice (MA). *Program availability:* Part-time, evening/weekend, online learning. *Degree requirements:* For master's, thesis optional; for doctorate, one foreign language, comprehensive exam, thesis/dissertation. *Entrance requirements:* For master's, GMAT, GRE General Test, or MAT; for doctorate, GRE General Test. Additional exam requirements/recommendations for international students: required—TOEFL (minimum score 600 paper-based; 100 iBT) or IELTS. Electronic applications accepted.

Sam Houston State University, College of Humanities and Social Sciences, Huntsville, TX 77341. Offers MA, MFA, MPA, PhD, SSP. *Program availability:* Part-time, online learning. Terminal master's awarded for partial completion of doctoral program. *Degree requirements:* For master's, comprehensive exam (for some programs), thesis optional, internship, portfolio; for doctorate, comprehensive exam, thesis/dissertation. *Entrance requirements:* For master's, GRE General Test, personal essay, letters of recommendation, writing sample; for doctorate, GRE General Test, GRE Subject Test (advanced psychology), personal essay, letters of recommendation, resume. Additional exam requirements/recommendations for international students: required—TOEFL (minimum score 550 paper-based; 79 iBT), IELTS (minimum score 6.5). Electronic applications accepted.

San Francisco State University, Division of Graduate Studies, College of Liberal and Creative Arts, School of Humanities and Liberal Studies, San Francisco, CA 94132-1722. Offers MA. *Program availability:* Part-time, evening/weekend. *Expenses: Tuition, area resident:* Full-time $7176; part-time $4164 per year. *Tuition, state resident:* full-time $7176; part-time $4164 per year. *Tuition, nonresident:* full-time $16,680; part-time $396 per unit. *International tuition:* $16,680 full-time. *Required fees:* $1524; $1524 per unit. $762 per semester. Tuition and fees vary according to degree level and program. *Unit head:* Dr. Cristina Ruotolo, Director, 415-338-1099, Fax: 415-338-6159, E-mail: ruotolo@sfsu.edu. *Application contact:* Dr. Tanya Augsburg, MA Coordinator, 415-405-2673, Fax: 415-338-6159, E-mail: tanya@sfsu.edu. Website: https://humanitiesliberalstudies.sfsu.edu/graduate-program

Humanities

Simon Fraser University, Office of Graduate Studies and Postdoctoral Fellows, Faculty of Arts and Social Sciences, Department of Humanities, Burnaby, BC V5A 1S6, Canada. Offers MA. *Degree requirements:* For master's, thesis. *Entrance requirements:* Additional exam requirements/recommendations for international students: required—TOEFL (minimum score 580 paper-based; 93 iBT), IELTS (minimum score 7), TWE (minimum score 5). Electronic applications accepted.

Tiffin University, Program in Humanities, Tiffin, OH 44883-2161. Offers art and visual media (MH); communication (MH); creative writing (MH); English (MH); film studies (MH); humanities (MH); individualized studies (MH). *Program availability:* Part-time, evening/weekend, online only, 100% online, blended/hybrid learning. *Entrance requirements:* For master's, work experience. Additional exam requirements/ recommendations for international students: required—TOEFL (minimum score 550 paper-based; 79 iBT). Electronic applications accepted. Application fee is waived when completed online. *Expenses:* Contact institution.

Towson University, College of Liberal Arts, Program in Global Humanities, Towson, MD 21252-0001. Offers MA. *Program availability:* Part-time, evening/weekend. *Students:* 3 full-time (1 woman), 7 part-time (2 women); includes 2 minority (1 Black or African American, non-Hispanic/Latino; 1 Asian, non-Hispanic/Latino), 1 international. *Entrance requirements:* For master's, bachelor's degree, 2 letters of recommendation, minimum GPA of 3.0, research paper, statement of intent. *Application deadline:* For fall admission, 1/17 for domestic students, 5/15 for international students; for spring admission, 10/15 for domestic students, 12/1 for international students. Applications are processed on a rolling basis. Application fee: $45. Electronic applications accepted. *Expenses: Tuition, area resident:* Full-time $7920; part-time $439 per credit. Tuition, nonresident: full-time $16,344; part-time $908 per credit. *International tuition:* $16,344 full-time. *Required fees:* $2628; $146 per credit. $876 per term. *Financial support:* Application deadline: 4/1. *Unit head:* Dr. Jennifer Ballengee, Program Director, 410-704-5213, E-mail: jballengee@towson.edu. *Application contact:* Coverley Beidleman, Assistant Director of Graduate Admissions, 410-704-5630, Fax: 410-704-3030, E-mail: grads@towson.edu.
Website: https://www.towson.edu/cla/departments/interdisciplinary/grad/humanities/

Trinity Western University, School of Graduate Studies, Master of Arts in Interdisciplinary Humanities, Langley, BC V2Y 1Y1, Canada. Offers general humanities (MAIH); specialized (MAIH), including English, history, philosophy. *Program availability:* Part-time. *Degree requirements:* For master's, thesis or alternative, 30 semester hours. *Entrance requirements:* For master's, Strong undergraduate degree in humanities or English, history or philosophy. Additional exam requirements/recommendations for international students: required—TOEFL (minimum score 105 iBT), IELTS (minimum score 7.5), DuoLingo. *Application deadline:* Applications are processed on a rolling basis. Electronic applications accepted. *Expenses:* Contact institution. *Financial support:* Fellowships, research assistantships, teaching assistantships, career-related internships or fieldwork, scholarships/grants, and unspecified assistantships available. Support available to part-time students. Financial award application deadline: 4/1. *Unit head:* Dr. Bruce Shelvey, Director, E-mail: bruce.shelvey@twu.ca. *Application contact:* Phil Kay, Director, Graduate Admissions, 604-513-2121 Ext. 3444, E-mail: phil.kay@twu.ca.
Website: http://www.twu.ca/academics/

Union Institute & University, PhD Program in Interdisciplinary Studies, Cincinnati, OH 45206-1925. Offers educational studies (PhD), including Martin Luther King studies; ethical and creative leadership (PhD); humanities and culture (PhD); public policy and social change (PhD). *Program availability:* Part-time, online only, blended/hybrid learning. *Degree requirements:* For doctorate, comprehensive exam, thesis/dissertation. *Entrance requirements:* For doctorate, master's degree, three letters of recommendation, statement of purpose. Additional exam requirements/ recommendations for international students: required—TOEFL. Electronic applications accepted. *Expenses:* Contact institution.

United Theological Seminary of the Twin Cities, Graduate Programs, New Brighton, MN 55112-2598. Offers advanced theological studies (Diploma); justice and peace studies (M Div, MA); leadership toward racial justice (M Div, MA, Certificate); Methodist studies (M Div, MA, Certificate); ministry (D Min); ministry renewal and professional development (Certificate); pastoral care and counseling (M Div, MA, MARL); religion and theology (MA); theological and religious studies (Certificate); theology and the arts (M Div, MA); urban ministry (M Div, MA, MARL); women's studies: religion, theology and ministry (M Div, MA). *Accreditation:* ACIPE; ATS. *Program availability:* Part-time, evening/weekend. *Degree requirements:* For master's, thesis; for doctorate, comprehensive exam, thesis/dissertation. *Entrance requirements:* For master's, minimum GPA of 2.75; strong analytical, reflective thinking and writing skills; vocational and academic goals compatible with those of Seminary; for doctorate, M Div or equivalent, minimum GPA of 3.0, 3 years experience in professional ministry; for other advanced degree, BA or equivalent life experience; strong analytical, reflective thinking and writing skills (Certificate); proficiency in English language, previous study of theology at a theological school, recommendation of student's denomination (Diploma). Additional exam requirements/recommendations for international students: required—TOEFL (minimum score 550 paper-based).

University at Buffalo, the State University of New York, Graduate School, College of Arts and Sciences, Program in Interdisciplinary Studies, Buffalo, NY 14260. Offers humanities (MA); natural sciences (MS); social sciences (MS). *Program availability:* Part-time. *Degree requirements:* For master's, thesis or alternative. *Entrance requirements:* Additional exam requirements/recommendations for international students: required—TOEFL (minimum score 550 paper-based; 79 iBT). Electronic applications accepted. *Expenses: Tuition, area resident:* Full-time $11,310; part-time $471 per credit hour. Tuition, state resident: full-time $11,310; part-time $471 per credit hour. Tuition, nonresident: full-time $23,100; part-time $963 per credit hour. *International tuition:* $23,100 full-time. *Required fees:* $2820.

University of California, Merced, Graduate Division, School of Social Sciences, Humanities and Arts, Merced, CA 95343. Offers cognitive and information sciences (PhD); interdisciplinary humanities (MA, PhD); psychological sciences (MA, PhD); social sciences (MA, PhD); sociology (MA, PhD). *Faculty:* 113 full-time (57 women), 2 part-time/adjunct (0 women). *Students:* 194 full-time (128 women), 1 (woman) part-time; includes 81 minority (5 Black or African American, non-Hispanic/Latino; 18 Asian, non-Hispanic/Latino; 54 Hispanic/Latino; 4 Two or more races, non-Hispanic/Latino), 39 international. Average age 31. 218 applicants, 48% accepted, 36 enrolled. In 2019, 12 master's, 23 doctorates awarded. Terminal master's awarded for partial completion of doctoral program. *Degree requirements:* For master's, variable foreign language requirement, comprehensive exam, thesis or alternative, oral defense; for doctorate, variable foreign language requirement, comprehensive exam, thesis/dissertation, oral defense. *Entrance requirements:* For master's and doctorate, GRE. Additional exam requirements/recommendations for international students: required—TOEFL (minimum score 550 paper-based; 80 iBT); recommended—IELTS (minimum score 6.5). *Application deadline:* For fall admission, 1/15 for domestic and international students. Application fee: $105 ($125 for international students). Electronic applications accepted. *Expenses: Tuition, area resident:* Full-time $11,442; part-time $5721 per semester. Tuition, state resident: full-time $11,442; part-time $5721 per semester. Tuition, nonresident: full-time $26,544; part-time $13,272 per semester. *International tuition:* $26,544 full-time. *Required fees:* $564 per semester. *Financial support:* In 2019–20, 183 students received support, including 7 fellowships with full tuition reimbursements available (averaging $22,005 per year), 5 research assistantships with full tuition reimbursements available (averaging $21,420 per year), 171 teaching assistantships with full tuition reimbursements available (averaging $21,911 per year); scholarships/ grants, traineeships, and health care benefits also available. *Unit head:* Dr. Jeffrey Gilger, Dean, 209-228-4343, E-mail: jgilger@ucmerced.edu. *Application contact:* Tsu Ya, Director of Admissions and Academic Services, 209-228-4521, Fax: 209-228-6906, E-mail: tya@ucmerced.edu.

University of California, Santa Cruz, Division of Graduate Studies, Division of Humanities, Program in the History of Consciousness, Santa Cruz, CA 95064. Offers PhD. *Degree requirements:* For doctorate, one foreign language, thesis/dissertation, qualifying exam. *Entrance requirements:* For doctorate, GRE General Test. Additional exam requirements/recommendations for international students: required—TOEFL (minimum score 550 paper-based; 83 iBT); recommended—IELTS (minimum score 8). Electronic applications accepted.

University of Chicago, Division of the Humanities, Master of Arts Program in the Humanities, Chicago, IL 60637. Offers art history (MA); cinema and media studies (MA); classic languages (MA); comparative literature (MA); creative writing (MA); cultural policy studies (MA); digital humanities (MA); East Asian languages and civilizations (MA); English language and literature (MA); gender and sexuality studies (MA); Germanic studies (MA); linguistics (MA); music (MA); near Eastern languages and civilizations (MA); philosophy (MA); poetics (MA); race, politics and culture (MA); Romance languages and literatures (MA); Slavic languages and literatures (MA); South Asian languages and civilizations (MA); theater and performance studies (MA). *Degree requirements:* For master's, thesis. *Entrance requirements:* For master's, GRE General Test, 10-15 page writing sample, statement of purpose, 3 letters of recommendation, transcripts for all previous degrees and institutions attended. Additional exam requirements/recommendations for international students: required—TOEFL (minimum score 104 iBT), IELTS (minimum score 7). Electronic applications accepted. *Expenses:* Contact institution.

University of Colorado Denver, College of Liberal Arts and Sciences, Program in Humanities, Denver, CO 80217. Offers community health (MSS); ethnic studies (MH, MSS); humanities (MH, Graduate Certificate); international studies (MSS); philosophy and theory (MH); social justice (MH, MSS); society and the environment (MSS); visual studies (MH); women's and gender studies (MH, MSS). *Program availability:* Part-time, evening/weekend. *Degree requirements:* For master's, 36 credit hours, project or thesis. *Entrance requirements:* For master's, writing sample, statement of purpose/letter of intent, three letters of recommendation. Additional exam requirements/ recommendations for international students: required—TOEFL (minimum score 537 paper-based; 75 iBT); recommended—IELTS (minimum score 6.5). Electronic applications accepted. Tuition and fees vary according to course load, program and reciprocity agreements.

University of Houston–Clear Lake, School of Human Sciences and Humanities, Programs in Humanities and Fine Arts, Houston, TX 77058-1002. Offers history (MA); humanities (MA); literature (MA). *Program availability:* Part-time, evening/weekend, online learning. *Degree requirements:* For master's, thesis or alternative. *Entrance requirements:* For master's, GRE General Test. Additional exam requirements/ recommendations for international students: required—TOEFL (minimum score 550 paper-based).

University of Louisville, Graduate School, College of Arts and Sciences, Department of Comparative Humanities, Louisville, KY 40292-0001. Offers civic leadership (MA); culture, criticism, and contemporary thought (PhD); linguistics (MA); public arts and letters (PhD); traditional humanities (MA); MA/JD; MA/MBA. *Program availability:* Part-time. *Faculty:* 15 full-time (6 women), 18 part-time/adjunct (9 women). *Students:* 24 full-time (12 women), 16 part-time (8 women); includes 6 minority (1 Black or African American, non-Hispanic/Latino; 1 Hispanic/Latino; 4 Two or more races, non-Hispanic/ Latino), 2 international. Average age 41. 16 applicants, 81% accepted, 8 enrolled. In 2019, 3 master's, 6 doctorates awarded. *Degree requirements:* For master's, one foreign language, thesis or alternative, directed study culminating project; for doctorate, 2 foreign languages, comprehensive exam, thesis/dissertation, internship. *Entrance requirements:* For master's, GRE General Test, Two letters of reference, official transcripts; for doctorate, GRE General Test, three letters of recommendation, statement of intent, scholarly writing sample, transcripts from all institutions attended. Additional exam requirements/recommendations for international students: required—TOEFL (minimum score 550 paper-based; 79 iBT), IELTS can be used in place of the TOEFL; recommended—IELTS (minimum score 6.5). *Application deadline:* For fall admission, 1/15 for domestic and international students; for spring admission, 7/15 for domestic and international students. Applications are processed on a rolling basis. Application fee: $65. Electronic applications accepted. *Expenses:* Contact institution. *Financial support:* In 2019–20, 25 students received support, including 1 fellowship with full tuition reimbursement available (averaging $18,000 per year), 3 teaching assistantships with full tuition reimbursements available (averaging $18,000 per year); research assistantships, scholarships/grants, health care benefits, and unspecified assistantships also available. Financial award application deadline: 1/15. *Unit head:* Dr. Ann Hall, Chair, 502-852-6805, Fax: 502-852-0078, E-mail: ann.hall@louisville.edu. *Application contact:* Dr. Simona Bertacco, Professor and Director of Graduate Studies, 502-852-7161, E-mail: simona.bertacco@louisville.edu.
Website: http://louisville.edu/humanities/

University of Louisville, Graduate School, College of Arts and Sciences, Department of Philosophy, Louisville, KY 40292-0001. Offers humanities (MA, PhD). *Program availability:* Part-time. *Faculty:* 12 full-time (2 women), 9 part-time/adjunct (5 women). *Degree requirements:* For master's, one foreign language, thesis or alternative. *Entrance requirements:* For master's, GRE General Test, Two letters of reference, official transcripts. Additional exam requirements/recommendations for international students: required—TOEFL (minimum score 550 paper-based; 79 iBT), IELTS can be used in place of the TOEFL; recommended—IELTS (minimum score 6.5). *Application deadline:* Applications are processed on a rolling basis. Application fee: $65. Electronic applications accepted. *Expenses: Tuition, area resident:* Full-time $13,000; part-time $723 per credit hour. Tuition, state resident: full-time $13,000; part-time $723 per credit hour. Tuition, nonresident: full-time $27,114; part-time $1507 per credit hour. *International tuition:* $27,114 full-time. *Required fees:* $196. Tuition and fees vary according to program and reciprocity agreements. *Financial support:* In 2019–20, 1 fellowship with full tuition reimbursement (averaging $12,000 per year), 1 teaching assistantship with full tuition reimbursement (averaging $12,000 per year) were awarded; research assistantships, health care benefits, and unspecified assistantships also available. *Unit head:* Dr. Avery Kolers, Chairperson, 502-852-0453, E-mail: avery.kolers@louisville.edu. *Application contact:* Dr. Stephen Hanson, Director of Graduate Studies, 502-852-0451, E-mail: stephen.hanson@louisville.edu.
Website: http://louisville.edu/philosophy

University of South Florida, College of Arts and Sciences, Department of Humanities and Cultural Studies, Tampa, FL 33620-9951. Offers liberal arts (MA), including

American studies, film studies, humanities. *Program availability:* Part-time, evening/weekend. *Faculty:* 8 full-time (3 women). *Students:* 19 full-time (7 women), 6 part-time (4 women); includes 7 minority (2 Black or African American, non-Hispanic/Latino; 2 Asian, non-Hispanic/Latino; 3 Hispanic/Latino), 1 international. Average age 29. 21 applicants, 71% accepted, 15 enrolled. In 2019, 8 master's awarded. *Degree requirements:* For master's, comprehensive exam, thesis, language (for humanities subconcentration). *Entrance requirements:* For master's, GRE Recommended. Contact department for advising, minimum GPA of 3.0, writing sample. Personal statement, letters of recommendation are recommended. Students must select a concentration at the time of application. Additional exam requirements/recommendations for international students: required—TOEFL, TOEFL (minimum score 550 paper-based; 79 iBT) or IELTS (minimum score 6.5). *Application deadline:* For fall admission, 2/15 priority date for domestic students, 2/15 for international students; for spring admission, 10/15 priority date for domestic students, 9/15 for international students; for summer admission, 2/15 for domestic students, 1/15 for international students. Application fee: $30. Electronic applications accepted. *Financial support:* In 2019–20, 5 students received support, including 15 teaching assistantships with tuition reimbursements available (averaging $12,437 per year); scholarships/grants also available. Financial award application deadline: 4/1. *Unit head:* Dr. Andrew Berish, Associate Professor and Chair, 813-974-9380, E-mail: aberish@usf.edu. *Application contact:* Dr. Maria Cizmic, Associate Professor and Graduate Program Director, 813-974-9380, E-mail: mcizmic@usf.edu. Website: http://humanities.usf.edu/

The University of Texas at Dallas, School of Arts and Humanities, Richardson, TX 75080. Offers art history (MA); history (MA); humanities (MA, PhD), including aesthetic studies, history of ideas, studies in literature; Latin American studies (MA). *Program availability:* Part-time, evening/weekend. *Faculty:* 48 full-time (19 women), 11 part-time/adjunct (6 women). *Students:* 123 full-time (76 women), 116 part-time (71 women); includes 62 minority (14 Black or African American, non-Hispanic/Latino; 3 American Indian or Alaska Native, non-Hispanic/Latino; 9 Asian, non-Hispanic/Latino; 25 Hispanic/Latino; 11 Two or more races, non-Hispanic/Latino), 27 international. Average age 40. 130 applicants, 60% accepted, 59 enrolled. In 2019, 30 master's, 16 doctorates awarded. *Degree requirements:* For master's, one foreign language, portfolio; for doctorate, one foreign language, thesis/dissertation. *Entrance requirements:* For master's and doctorate, minimum GPA of 3.0 in undergraduate course work in field. Additional exam requirements/recommendations for international students: required—TOEFL (minimum score 550 paper-based). *Application deadline:* For fall admission, 7/15 for domestic students, 5/1 priority date for international students; for spring admission, 11/15 for domestic students, 9/1 priority date for international students. Applications are processed on a rolling basis. Application fee: $50 ($100 for international students). Electronic applications accepted. *Expenses:* Tuition, area resident: Full-time $16,504. Tuition, state resident: full-time $16,504. Tuition, nonresident: full-time $34,266. Tuition and fees vary according to course load. *Financial support:* In 2019–20, 87 students received support, including 9 fellowships (averaging $5,074 per year), 14 research assistantships with partial tuition reimbursements available (averaging $26,575 per year), 69 teaching assistantships with partial tuition reimbursements available (averaging $14,961 per year); Federal Work-Study, institutionally sponsored loans, scholarships/grants, and unspecified assistantships also available. Support available to part-time students. Financial award application deadline: 4/30; financial award applicants required to submit FAFSA. *Unit head:* Dr. Nils Roemer, Interim Dean, 972-883-2984, Fax: 972-883-2989, E-mail: nroemer@utdallas.edu. *Application contact:* Dr. John Gooch, Associate Dean of Graduate Studies, 972-883-2756, Fax: 972-883-2989, E-mail: john.gooch@utdallas.edu. Website: http://www.utdallas.edu/ah/

The University of Texas Medical Branch, Graduate School of Biomedical Sciences, Program in Medical Humanities, Galveston, TX 77555. Offers MA, PhD. *Degree requirements:* For master's, thesis; for doctorate, thesis/dissertation. *Entrance requirements:* For master's and doctorate, GRE General Test, writing sample. Additional exam requirements/recommendations for international students: required—TOEFL (minimum score 550 paper-based). Electronic applications accepted.

University of Utah, Graduate School, College of Humanities, Department of Environmental Humanities, Salt Lake City, UT 84112-1107. Offers MA, MS. *Faculty:* 5 full-time (3 women). *Students:* 16 full-time (10 women), 1 (woman) part-time; includes 4 minority (1 Asian, non-Hispanic/Latino; 1 Hispanic/Latino; 2 Native Hawaiian or other Pacific Islander, non-Hispanic/Latino). Average age 26. 28 applicants, 43% accepted, 8 enrolled. In 2019, 8 master's awarded. *Degree requirements:* For master's, one foreign language, comprehensive exam (for some programs), thesis or alternative. *Entrance requirements:* For master's, minimum GPA of 3.0; undergraduate degree. Additional exam requirements/recommendations for international students: required—TOEFL (minimum score 500 paper-based; 80 iBT), IELTS. *Application deadline:* For fall admission, 1/15 priority date for domestic and international students. Application fee: $55 ($65 for international students). Electronic applications accepted. *Expenses:* Tuition, state resident: full-time $7085; part-time $272.51 per credit hour. Tuition, nonresident: full-time $24,937; part-time $959.12 per credit hour. *Required fees:*

$880.52; $880.52 per semester. Tuition and fees vary according to degree level, program and student level. *Financial support:* In 2019–20, 15 students received support, including 1 fellowship with full tuition reimbursement available (averaging $17,500 per year), 15 teaching assistantships with full tuition reimbursements available (averaging $17,666 per year). *Unit head:* Jeffrey McCarthy, Director, 801-585-7052, Fax: 801-587-6162, E-mail: jeff.mccarthy@utah.edu. *Application contact:* Cory Pike, Graduate Advisor, 801-581-6156, E-mail: cory.pike@utah.edu. Website: http://environmental-humanities.utah.edu/

Virginia Polytechnic Institute and State University, Graduate School, College of Liberal Arts and Human Sciences, Blacksburg, VA 24061. Offers career and technical education (MS Ed, Ed S); communication (MA); counselor education (MA); creative writing (MFA); curriculum and instruction (MA Ed, Ed S); educational leadership and policy studies (Ed S); educational research and evaluation (PhD); English (MA); social, political, ethical, and cultural thought (PhD); Ed D/PhD. *Faculty:* 452 full-time (241 women), 1 (woman) part-time/adjunct. *Students:* 571 full-time (405 women), 351 part-time (223 women); includes 176 minority (103 Black or African American, non-Hispanic/Latino; 3 American Indian or Alaska Native, non-Hispanic/Latino; 18 Asian, non-Hispanic/Latino; 31 Hispanic/Latino; 1 Native Hawaiian or other Pacific Islander, non-Hispanic/Latino; 20 Two or more races, non-Hispanic/Latino), 93 international. Average age 34. 865 applicants, 55% accepted, 336 enrolled. In 2019, 270 master's, 63 doctorates awarded. *Degree requirements:* For master's, comprehensive exam (for some programs), thesis (for some programs); for doctorate, comprehensive exam (for some programs), thesis/dissertation (for some programs). *Entrance requirements:* For master's and doctorate, GRE/GMAT. Additional exam requirements/recommendations for international students: required—TOEFL (minimum score 90 iBT). *Application deadline:* For fall admission, 8/1 for domestic students, 4/1 for international students; for spring admission, 1/1 for domestic students, 9/1 for international students. Applications are processed on a rolling basis. Application fee: $75. Electronic applications accepted. *Expenses:* Tuition, state resident: full-time $13,700; part-time $761.25 per credit hour. Tuition, nonresident: full-time $27,614; part-time $1534 per credit hour. *Required fees:* $886.50 per term. Tuition and fees vary according to campus/location and program. *Financial support:* In 2019–20, 3 fellowships with full tuition reimbursements (averaging $7,621 per year), 34 research assistantships with full tuition reimbursements (averaging $15,645 per year), 370 teaching assistantships with full tuition reimbursements (averaging $18,225 per year) were awarded; scholarships/grants and unspecified assistantships also available. Financial award application deadline: 3/1; financial award applicants required to submit FAFSA. *Unit head:* Dr. Laura Belmonte, Dean, 540-231-6779, Fax: 540-231-7157, E-mail: belmonte@vt.edu. *Application contact:* Chelsea Blanchet, Executive Assistant, 540-231-6779, Fax: 540-231-7157, E-mail: bchels1@vt.edu. Website: http://www.liberalarts.vt.edu/

Wayland Baptist University, Graduate Programs, Programs in Behavioral and Social Sciences, Plainview, TX 79072-6998. Offers counseling (MA); criminal justice (MACJ); government administration (MPA); history (MA); homeland security (MPA); humanities (MAH); justice administration (MPA). *Program availability:* Part-time, evening/weekend, 100% online, blended/hybrid learning. *Degree requirements:* For master's, comprehensive exam. *Entrance requirements:* For master's, GRE, MAT. Additional exam requirements/recommendations for international students: required—TOEFL (minimum score 500 paper-based; 61 iBT). Electronic applications accepted. *Expenses:* Tuition: Full-time $728; part-time $728 per semester. *Required fees:* $1218. Tuition and fees vary according to degree level, campus/location and program.

Wilson College, Graduate Programs, Chambersburg, PA 17201-1285. Offers accounting (M Acc); choreography and visual art (MFA); education (M Ed); educational technology (MET); healthcare administration (MHA); humanities (MA), including art and culture, critical/cultural theory, English language and literature, women's studies; management (MSM); nursing (MSN), including nursing education, nursing leadership and management; special education (MSE). *Program availability:* Evening/weekend. *Degree requirements:* For master's, project. *Entrance requirements:* For master's, PRAXIS, minimum undergraduate cumulative GPA of 3.0, 2 letters of recommendation, current certification for eligibility to teach in grades K-12, resume, personal interview. Electronic applications accepted.

Wright State University, Graduate School, College of Liberal Arts, Interdisciplinary Program in Humanities, Dayton, OH 45435. Offers M Hum. *Degree requirements:* For master's, thesis or alternative. *Entrance requirements:* Additional exam requirements/recommendations for international students: required—TOEFL.

York University, Faculty of Graduate Studies, Faculty of Liberal Arts and Professional Studies, Program in Humanities, Toronto, ON M3J 1P3, Canada. Offers MA, PhD. *Program availability:* Part-time. *Degree requirements:* For master's, thesis or alternative; for doctorate, comprehensive exam, thesis/dissertation. *Entrance requirements:* Additional exam requirements/recommendations for international students: required—TOEFL (minimum score 600 paper-based). Electronic applications accepted.

Liberal Studies

Abilene Christian University, Office of Graduate Programs, College of Arts and Sciences, Master of Liberal Arts Program, Abilene, TX 79699. Offers MLA. *Program availability:* Part-time. *Students:* 2 part-time (both women); includes 1 minority (Two or more races, non-Hispanic/Latino). 7 applicants, 14% accepted, 1 enrolled. *Degree requirements:* For master's, comprehensive exam, thesis or alternative. *Entrance requirements:* For master's, GRE General Test, official transcripts, recommendations, purpose statement, interview. Additional exam requirements/recommendations for international students: required—TOEFL (minimum score 80 iBT), IELTS (minimum score 6), PTE (minimum score 51). *Application deadline:* For fall admission, 8/10 for domestic students; for spring admission, 11/1 for domestic students. Applications are processed on a rolling basis. Application fee: $65. Electronic applications accepted. *Expenses: Tuition:* Full-time $22,356; part-time $1242 per credit hour. Tuition and fees vary according to program. *Financial support:* Federal Work-Study available. Support available to part-time students. Financial award application deadline: 4/1; financial award applicants required to submit FAFSA. *Unit head:* Dr. Joe Cardot, Graduate Advisor, 325-674-2136, Fax: 325-674-6966, E-mail: cardotj@acu.edu. *Application contact:* Graduate Admissions, 325-674-6911, E-mail: gradinfo@acu.edu. Website: http://www.acu.edu/on-campus/graduate/college-of-arts-and-sciences/liberal-arts.html

Alaska Pacific University, Graduate Programs, Liberal Studies Department, Anchorage, AK 99508-4672. Offers self-designed study (MA).

Albertus Magnus College, Master of Arts in Liberal Studies Program, New Haven, CT 06511-1189. Offers MALS. *Program availability:* Part-time, evening/weekend, 100% online, blended/hybrid learning. *Faculty:* 1 full-time (0 women), 2 part-time/adjunct (0 women). *Students:* 5 full-time (4 women), 1 (woman) part-time; includes 3 minority (all Black or African American, non-Hispanic/Latino). Average age 40. *Degree requirements:* For master's, comprehensive exam, thesis optional, Credits must be completed within 6 years, six months prior to anticipated date of commencement, candidates must request in writing an official audit of credits and pay degree completion fee. All degree requirements must have been completed by the last day of class. *Entrance requirements:* For master's, A bachelor's degree, min. cumulative GPA of 2.8, two letters of recommendations from former professors or professional associates, written 500-600 words essay, proficiency in the use of personal computers. Additional exam requirements/recommendations for international students: required—TOEFL (minimum score 550 paper-based; 80 iBT), One of the following: SAT or ACT, TOEFL, IELTS, DUO Lingo English Proficiency Test, 3+ years at a university/college with English as primary language. *Application deadline:* For fall admission, 7/15 for international students; for spring admission, 11/15 for international students. Applications are processed on a rolling basis. Application fee: $50. Electronic applications accepted.

Liberal Studies

Expenses: Contact institution. *Financial support:* Unspecified assistantships available. Financial award applicants required to submit FAFSA. *Unit head:* Prof. Erik Shoeck, 203-672-6775, E-mail: eschoeck@albertus.edu. *Application contact:* Annette Bosley-Boyce, Dean of the Division of Professional and Graduate Studies, 203-672-6687, E-mail: abosleyboyce@albertus.edu.
Website: https://www.albertus.edu/liberal-studies/ma/

Alvernia University, School of Graduate Studies, Program in Liberal Studies, Reading, PA 19607-1799. Offers MALS. *Program availability:* Part-time, evening/weekend. *Degree requirements:* For master's, thesis optional. *Entrance requirements:* For master's, MAT or GRE (alumni excluded). Electronic applications accepted.

Arizona State University at Tempe, College of Liberal Arts and Sciences, Program in Liberal Studies, Tempe, AZ 85287-6505. Offers MLS. *Program availability:* Part-time, evening/weekend. *Degree requirements:* For master's, thesis or alternative, integrated capstone project, interactive Program of Study (iPOS) submitted before completing 50 percent of required credit hours. *Entrance requirements:* For master's, minimum GPA of 3.0 or equivalent in last 2 years of work leading to bachelor's degree, resume or biographical statement, personal letter expressing liberal studies concentration interest, official college transcripts, 2 letters of recommendation, interview with program director (recommended). Additional exam requirements/recommendations for international students: required—TOEFL, IELTS, or PTE. Electronic applications accepted. *Expenses:* Contact institution.

Arkansas Tech University, College of Arts and Humanities, Russellville, AR 72801. Offers applied sociology (MS); English (M Ed, MA); history (MA); liberal arts (MLA); multi-media journalism (MA); psychology (MS); teaching English as a second language (MA). *Program availability:* Part-time, 100% online, blended/hybrid learning. *Students:* 32 full-time (19 women), 102 part-time (70 women); includes 22 minority (5 Black or African American, non-Hispanic/Latino; 1 American Indian or Alaska Native, non-Hispanic/Latino; 1 Asian, non-Hispanic/Latino; 12 Hispanic/Latino; 3 Two or more races, non-Hispanic/Latino), 9 international. Average age 32. In 2019, 89 master's awarded. *Degree requirements:* For master's, comprehensive exam (for some programs), thesis (for some programs), project. *Entrance requirements:* Additional exam requirements/recommendations for international students: required—TOEFL (minimum score 550 paper-based; 79 iBT), IELTS (minimum score 6.5), PTE (minimum score 58). *Application deadline:* For fall admission, 3/1 priority date for domestic students, 5/1 priority date for international students; for spring admission, 10/1 priority date for domestic and international students. Applications are processed on a rolling basis. Application fee: $40 ($90 for international students). Electronic applications accepted. *Expenses: Tuition, area resident:* Full-time $7008; part-time $292 per credit hour. Tuition, state resident: full-time $7008; part-time $292 per credit hour. Tuition, nonresident: full-time $14,016; part-time $584 per credit hour. *International tuition:* $14,016 full-time. *Required fees:* $343 per term. *Financial support:* In 2019–20, research assistantships with full and partial tuition reimbursements (averaging $4,800 per year), teaching assistantships with full and partial tuition reimbursements (averaging $4,800 per year) were awarded; career-related internships or fieldwork, Federal Work-Study, scholarships/grants, health care benefits, and unspecified assistantships also available. Support available to part-time students. Financial award application deadline: 4/15; financial award applicants required to submit FAFSA. *Unit head:* Dr. Jeffrey Cass, Dean of College of Arts and Humanities, 479-968-0274, Fax: 479-964-0812, E-mail: jcass@atu.edu. *Application contact:* Dr. Richard Schoephoerster, Dean of Graduate College and Research, 479-968-0398, Fax: 479-964-0542, E-mail: gradcollege@atu.edu.
Website: http://www.atu.edu/humanities/

Baker University, School of Professional and Graduate Studies, Program in Liberal Arts, Baldwin City, KS 66006-0065. Offers MLA. *Program availability:* Part-time, evening/weekend, online learning. *Degree requirements:* For master's, portfolio of learning. *Entrance requirements:* Additional exam requirements/recommendations for international students: required—TOEFL (minimum score 600 paper-based; 100 iBT). Electronic applications accepted.

Barry University, College of Arts and Sciences, Interdisciplinary Program, Miami Shores, FL 33161-6695. Offers MA.

Binghamton University, State University of New York, Graduate School, Harpur College of Arts and Sciences, Program in Applied Liberal Studies, Binghamton, NY 13902-6000. Offers MA.

Brooklyn College of the City University of New York, School of Education, Program in Childhood Education, Brooklyn, NY 11210-2889. Offers bilingual education (MS Ed); liberal arts (MS Ed); mathematics (MS Ed); science and environmental education (MS Ed). *Program availability:* Part-time, evening/weekend. *Entrance requirements:* For master's, LAST, interview, previous course work in education, writing sample, resume, 2 letters of recommendation. Additional exam requirements/recommendations for international students: required—TOEFL (minimum score 500 paper-based; 61 iBT). Electronic applications accepted.

Cardinal Stritch University, College of Arts and Sciences, Milwaukee, WI 53217-3985. Offers MA, MS. *Program availability:* Part-time, evening/weekend. *Degree requirements:* For master's, thesis. *Entrance requirements:* Additional exam requirements/recommendations for international students: required—TOEFL (minimum score 79 iBT), IELTS (minimum score 6.5). Electronic applications accepted. *Expenses:* Contact institution.

Clayton State University, School of Graduate Studies, College of Arts and Sciences, Program in Liberal Studies, Morrow, GA 30260-0285. Offers MA. *Program availability:* Part-time. *Degree requirements:* For master's, thesis optional. *Entrance requirements:* For master's, official transcripts, 3 letters of recommendation, statement of purpose, on-campus interview. Additional exam requirements/recommendations for international students: required—TOEFL (minimum score 550 paper-based; 80 iBT). Electronic applications accepted.

Coastal Carolina University, Thomas W. and Robin W. Edwards College of Humanities and Fine Arts, Conway, SC 29528-6054. Offers liberal studies (MA); writing (MA). *Program availability:* Part-time, evening/weekend. *Faculty:* 28 full-time (14 women), 2 part-time/adjunct (both women). *Students:* 42 full-time (22 women), 21 part-time (13 women); includes 16 minority (9 Black or African American, non-Hispanic/Latino; 2 Asian, non-Hispanic/Latino; 2 Hispanic/Latino; 3 Two or more races, non-Hispanic/Latino), 1 international. Average age 31. 55 applicants, 85% accepted, 30 enrolled. In 2019, 18 master's awarded. *Entrance requirements:* For master's, GRE, MAT, personal statement of interest, official transcripts, 2 letters of recommendation, writing sample; for writing program: minimum GPA of 3.3 in 18 hours of undergraduate and graduate coursework in English or related discipline. Additional exam requirements/recommendations for international students: required—TOEFL (minimum score 550 paper-based; 79 iBT). *Application deadline:* For fall admission, 5/1 priority date for domestic and international students; for spring admission, 11/15 priority date for domestic and international students. Applications are processed on a rolling basis. Application fee: $45. Electronic applications accepted. *Expenses: Tuition, area resident:* Full-time $10,764; part-time $598 per credit hour. Tuition, state resident: full-time $10,764; part-time $598 per credit hour. Tuition, nonresident: full-time $19,836; part-

time $1102 per credit hour. *International tuition:* $19,836 full-time. *Required fees:* $90; $5 per credit hour. *Financial support:* Fellowships, research assistantships, teaching assistantships, and tuition waivers available. Financial award application deadline: 3/1; financial award applicants required to submit FAFSA. *Unit head:* Dr. Daniel J. Ennis, Dean, 843-349-2691, E-mail: bornholdt@coastal.edu. *Application contact:* Dr. James O. Luken, Interim Dean, College of Graduate Studies and Research, 843-349-2277, Fax: 843-349-6444, E-mail: ryoung@coastal.edu.
Website: https://www.coastal.edu/humanities/

College of Staten Island of the City University of New York, Graduate Programs, Division of Humanities and Social Sciences, Program in Liberal Studies, Staten Island, NY 10314-6600. Offers MA. *Program availability:* Part-time, evening/weekend. *Faculty:* 4. *Students:* 19. 12 applicants, 58% accepted, 4 enrolled. In 2019, 6 master's awarded. *Degree requirements:* For master's, comprehensive exam, 30 credits; essay that will be extended reflection on problem of contemporary social and/or cultural interest drawing on the intellectual tradition of the liberal arts and on student's own values and analysis. *Entrance requirements:* For master's, BA or BS with minimum cumulative GPA of 3.0, students of other degrees or GPAs of less than 3.0 may be considered following an interview. Additional exam requirements/recommendations for international students: required—TOEFL (minimum score 550 paper-based; 79 iBT), IELTS (minimum score 6.5). *Application deadline:* For fall admission, 8/15 for domestic students, 6/30 for international students; for spring admission, 1/15 for domestic students, 11/25 for international students. Applications are processed on a rolling basis. Application fee: $75. Electronic applications accepted. *Expenses: Tuition, area resident:* Full-time $11,090; part-time $470 per credit. Tuition, state resident: full-time $11,090; part-time $470 per credit. Tuition, nonresident: full-time $20,520; part-time $855 per credit. *International tuition:* $20,520 full-time. *Required fees:* $559; $181 per semester. Tuition and fees vary according to program. *Unit head:* Dr. Don Selby, Graduate Program Coordinator, 718-982-3633, E-mail: don.selby@csi.cuny.edu. *Application contact:* Sasha Spence, Associate Director for Graduate Admissions, 718-982-2019, Fax: 718-982-2500, E-mail: sasha.spence@csi.cuny.edu.
Website: http://csicuny.smartcatalogiq.com/current/Graduate-Catalog/Graduate-Programs-Disciplines-and-Offerings-in-Selected-Disciplines/Liberal-Studies-MA

The Colorado College, Education Department, Experienced Teacher Program, Colorado Springs, CO 80903-3294. Offers arts and humanities (MAT); integrated natural sciences (MAT); liberal arts (MAT); Southwest studies (MAT). *Program availability:* Part-time. *Degree requirements:* For master's, thesis, oral exam, 50-page paper. *Expenses:* Contact institution.

Colorado State University, College of Liberal Arts, Department of History, Fort Collins, CO 80523-1776. Offers liberal arts (MA); public history (MA). *Program availability:* Part-time. *Faculty:* 6 full-time (3 women), 1 (woman) part-time/adjunct. *Students:* 22 full-time (13 women), 1 part-time (0 women); includes 2 minority (1 Hispanic/Latino; 1 Two or more races, non-Hispanic/Latino). Average age 26. 28 applicants, 57% accepted, 12 enrolled. In 2019, 15 master's awarded. *Degree requirements:* For master's, variable foreign language requirement, comprehensive exam, thesis (for some programs). *Entrance requirements:* For master's, GRE, 21 undergraduate credits in history; minimum undergraduate GPA of 3.0; personal statement; 3 letters of reference. Additional exam requirements/recommendations for international students: required—TOEFL, IELTS. *Application deadline:* For winter admission, 2/1 for domestic and international students. Application fee: $60 ($70 for international students). Electronic applications accepted. *Expenses:* Tuition, state resident: full-time $10,520; part-time $5844 per credit hour. Tuition, nonresident: full-time $25,791; part-time $14,328 per credit hour. *International tuition:* $25,791 full-time. *Required fees:* $2512.80. Part-time tuition and fees vary according to course level, course load, degree level, program and student level. *Financial support:* In 2019–20, 22 students received support, including 22 teaching assistantships (averaging $15,210 per year); health care benefits also available. Financial award application deadline: 2/1; financial award applicants required to submit FAFSA. *Unit head:* Dr. Robert Gudmestad, Department Chair, 970-491-6050, Fax: 970-491-2941, E-mail: doug.yarrington@colostate.edu. *Application contact:* Nancy Rehe, Administrative Assistant, 970-491-6334, E-mail: nancy.rehe@colostate.edu.
Website: http://history.colostate.edu/

Converse College, Program in Liberal Arts, Spartanburg, SC 29302. Offers English (MLA); history (MLA); political science (MLA). *Degree requirements:* For master's, capstone paper. *Entrance requirements:* For master's, minimum GPA of 3.0, 2 recommendations.

Dallas Baptist University, Liberal Arts Program, Dallas, TX 75211-9299. Offers art (MLA); Christian studies (MLA); commercial art (MLA); East Asian studies (MLA); English (MLA); English as a second language (MLA); history (MLA); missions (MLA); political science (MLA). *Program availability:* Part-time, evening/weekend, online learning. *Application deadline:* Applications are processed on a rolling basis. Application fee: $25. Electronic applications accepted. Application fee is waived when completed online. *Expenses: Tuition:* Full-time $18,072; part-time $1004 per credit hour. *Required fees:* $1100; $550 per semester. Tuition and fees vary according to course level and degree level. *Unit head:* Jared Ingram, Director, 214-333-5584, E-mail: jaredi@dbu.edu. *Application contact:* Jared Ingram, Director, 214-333-5584, E-mail: jaredi@dbu.edu.
Website: https://www.dbu.edu/graduate/degree-programs/mla

Dartmouth College, Guarini School of Graduate and Advanced Studies, Master of Arts in Liberal Studies Program, Hanover, NH 03755. Offers creative writing (MALS). *Program availability:* Part-time. *Degree requirements:* For master's, thesis. *Entrance requirements:* Additional exam requirements/recommendations for international students: required—TOEFL. Electronic applications accepted.

Delta State University, Graduate Programs, College of Arts and Sciences, Program in Liberal Studies, Cleveland, MS 38733-0001. Offers evolving human voices (MALS); gender and diversity studies (MALS); globalization studies (MALS); Mississippi Delta studies (MALS); philosophy (MALS); religious studies (MALS). *Degree requirements:* For master's, oral and/or written comprehensive exam. *Expenses: Tuition, area resident:* Full-time $7501; part-time $417 per credit hour. Tuition, state resident: full-time $7501; part-time $417 per credit hour. Tuition, nonresident: full-time $7501; part-time $417 per credit hour. *International tuition:* $7501 full-time. *Required fees:* $170; $9.45 per credit hour. $9.45 per semester.

DePaul University, College of Liberal Arts and Social Sciences, Chicago, IL 60614. Offers Arabic (MA); Chinese (MA); critical ethnic studies (MA); English (MA); French (MA); German (MA); history (MA); interdisciplinary studies (MA, MS); international public service (MS); international studies (MA); Italian (MA); Japanese (MA); liberal studies (MA); nonprofit management (MNM); public administration (MPA); public health (MPH); public policy (MPP); public service management (MS); refugee and forced migration studies (MS); social work (MSW); sociology (MA); Spanish (MA); sustainable urban development (MA); women's and gender studies (MA); writing and publishing (MA); writing, rhetoric and discourse (MA); MA/PhD. *Accreditation:* CEPH. *Program availability:* Part-time, evening/weekend, online learning. Terminal master's awarded for partial completion of doctoral program. *Degree requirements:* For master's, variable foreign language requirement, comprehensive exam (for some programs), thesis (for some programs). Electronic applications accepted.

Dominican University of California, School of Liberal Arts and Education, San Rafael, CA 94901-2298. Offers MA. *Program availability:* Part-time, evening/weekend. *Faculty:* 4 full-time (2 women), 1 (woman) part-time/adjunct. *Students:* 25 full-time (19 women), 47 part-time (37 women); includes 19 minority (1 Black or African American, non-Hispanic/Latino; 6 Asian, non-Hispanic/Latino; 6 Hispanic/Latino; 6 Two or more races, non-Hispanic/Latino). Average age 37. 35 applicants, 57% accepted, 15 enrolled. In 2019, 39 master's awarded. *Degree requirements:* For master's, comprehensive exam (for some programs), thesis (for some programs). *Entrance requirements:* For master's, minimum GPA of 3.0. Additional exam requirements/recommendations for international students: required—TOEFL (minimum score 550 paper-based; 80 iBT), IELTS (minimum score 6.5). *Application deadline:* For fall admission, 5/15 for domestic and international students; for spring admission, 11/15 for domestic and international students. Applications are processed on a rolling basis. Application fee: $0. Electronic applications accepted. *Expenses: Required fees:* $360 per semester. Tuition and fees vary according to course load and program. *Financial support:* Scholarships/grants available. Support available to part-time students. Financial award application deadline: 3/2; financial award applicants required to submit FAFSA. *Unit head:* Gigi Gokcek, Dean, 415-482-2427, E-mail: gigi.gokcek@dominican.edu. *Application contact:* Allyse Rudolph, Associate Director of Graduate Admissions, 415-585-3221, E-mail: graduate@dominican.edu.
Website: https://www.dominican.edu/academics/schools/school-liberal-arts-and-education

Drew University, Caspersen School of Graduate Studies, Madison, NJ 07940-1493. Offers conflict resolution and leadership (Certificate), including community leadership, moderation, peace building; education (M Ed); finance (MA); history and culture (MA, PhD), including American history, book history, British history, European history, intellectual history, Irish history, print culture, public history; K-12 education (MAT), including art, biology, chemistry, elementary education, English, French, Italian, math, secondary education, special education, teacher of students with disabilities; liberal studies (M Litt, D Litt), including history, Irish/Irish-American studies, literature (M Litt, MMH, D Litt, DMH, CMH), religion, spirituality, teaching in the two-year college, writing; medical humanities (MMH, DMH, CMH), including arts, health, healthcare, literature (M Litt, MMH, D Litt, DMH, CMH), scientific research; poetry (MFA). *Program availability:* Part-time, evening/weekend. Terminal master's awarded for partial completion of doctoral program. *Degree requirements:* For master's and other advanced degree, thesis (for some programs); for doctorate, one foreign language, comprehensive exam (for some programs), thesis/dissertation. *Entrance requirements:* For master's, PRAXIS Core and Subject Area tests (for MAT), GRE/GMAT (for MFin MS in Data Analytics), resume, transcripts, writing sample, personal statement, letters of recommendation; for doctorate, GRE (PhD in history and culture), resume, transcripts, writing sample, personal statement, letters of recommendation; for other advanced degree, resume, transcripts, personal statement. Additional exam requirements/recommendations for international students: required—TOEFL (minimum score 587 paper-based; 80 iBT), IELTS (minimum score 6), TWE (minimum score 4). Electronic applications accepted.

Duke University, Graduate School, Program in Liberal Studies, Durham, NC 27708. Offers AM. *Program availability:* Part-time, evening/weekend. *Degree requirements:* For master's, thesis or alternative, final project. *Entrance requirements:* For master's, interview. Additional exam requirements/recommendations for international students: required—IELTS (preferred) or TOEFL. Electronic applications accepted.

Eastern Washington University, Graduate Studies, College of Arts, Letters and Education, Department of Music, Cheney, WA 99004-2431. Offers composition (MA); instrumental/vocal performance (MA); jazz pedagogy (MA); liberal arts (MA); music education (MA). *Accreditation:* NASM. *Program availability:* Part-time. *Faculty:* 16 full-time (10 women). *Students:* 8 full-time (4 women), 4 part-time (1 woman); includes 1 minority (Hispanic/Latino), 1 international. Average age 29. 9 applicants, 89% accepted, 4 enrolled. In 2019, 5 master's awarded. *Degree requirements:* For master's, comprehensive exam, thesis or alternative. *Entrance requirements:* For master's, GRE General Test, minimum GPA of 3.0. Additional exam requirements/recommendations for international students: required—TOEFL (minimum score 580 paper-based; 92 iBT), IELTS (minimum score 7), TWE, PTE (minimum score 63). *Application deadline:* For fall admission, 4/1 priority date for domestic students; for spring admission, 1/15 for domestic students. Applications are processed on a rolling basis. Application fee: $75. Electronic applications accepted. *Financial support:* In 2019–20, 8 students received support, including teaching assistantships with partial tuition reimbursements available (averaging $10,000 per year); career-related internships or fieldwork, Federal Work-Study, institutionally sponsored loans, scholarships/grants, health care benefits, tuition waivers (partial), and unspecified assistantships also available. Support available to part-time students. Financial award application deadline: 2/1; financial award applicants required to submit FAFSA. *Unit head:* Dr. Jody Graves, Director of Keyboard Studies, 509-359-6119, E-mail: jgraves@ewu.edu. *Application contact:* Dr. Jody Graves, Director of Keyboard Studies, 509-359-6119, E-mail: jgraves@ewu.edu.
Website: http://www.ewu.edu/cale/programs/music.xml

East Tennessee State University, College of Graduate and Continuing Studies, School of Continuing Studies and Academic Outreach, Johnson City, TN 37614. Offers archival studies (Postbaccalaureate Certificate); liberal studies (MALS); reinforcing education through artistic learning (Postbaccalaureate Certificate); strategic leadership (MPS); training and development (MPS). *Program availability:* Part-time, online learning. *Degree requirements:* For master's, comprehensive exam, thesis (for some programs), professional project. *Entrance requirements:* For master's, GRE General Test, minimum GPA of 2.75, professional portfolio, three letters of recommendation, interview, writing sample; for Postbaccalaureate Certificate, minimum GPA of 2.5, three letters of recommendation, interview. Additional exam requirements/recommendations for international students: required—TOEFL (minimum score 550 paper-based; 79 iBT). Electronic applications accepted.

Fort Hays State University, Graduate School, College of Arts, Humanities, and Social Sciences, Program in Liberal Studies, Hays, KS 67601-4099. Offers MLS. *Program availability:* Online learning. *Degree requirements:* For master's, comprehensive exam, thesis or alternative. *Entrance requirements:* Additional exam requirements/recommendations for international students: required—TOEFL (minimum score 550 paper-based). Electronic applications accepted.

Georgetown University, Graduate School of Arts and Sciences, School of Continuing Studies, Washington, DC 20057. Offers American studies (MALS); applied intelligence (MPS); Catholic studies (MALS); classical civilizations (MALS); emergency and disaster management (MPS); ethics and the professions (MALS); global strategic communications (MPS); hospitality management (MPS); human resources management (MPS); humanities (MALS); individualized study (MALS); integrated marketing communications (MPS); international affairs (MALS); Islam and Muslim-Christian relations (MALS); journalism (MPS); liberal studies (DLS); literature and society (MALS); medieval and early modern European studies (MALS); public relations and corporate communications (MPS); real estate (MPS); religious studies (MALS); social and public policy (MALS); sports industry management (MPS); systems engineering management (MPS); technology management (MPS); the theory and practice of American democracy (MALS); urban and regional planning (MPS); visual culture (MALS). *Entrance*

requirements: Additional exam requirements/recommendations for international students: required—TOEFL.

The Graduate Center, City University of New York, Graduate Studies, Program in Liberal Studies, New York, NY 10016-4039. Offers MA. *Degree requirements:* For master's, thesis. *Entrance requirements:* For master's, GRE General Test. Additional exam requirements/recommendations for international students: required—TOEFL. Electronic applications accepted.

Hampton University, School of Liberal Arts and Education, Hampton, VA 23668. Offers MA, MS, MT, PhD, Ed S. *Accreditation:* NCATE. *Program availability:* Part-time, evening/weekend. *Students:* 91 full-time (53 women), 51 part-time (37 women); includes 133 minority (131 Black or African American, non-Hispanic/Latino; 1 Asian, non-Hispanic/Latino; 1 Native Hawaiian or other Pacific Islander, non-Hispanic/Latino), 2 international. Average age 35. 73 applicants, 56% accepted, 34 enrolled. In 2019, 31 master's, 4 doctorates, 5 other advanced degrees awarded. *Degree requirements:* For master's, comprehensive exam, thesis (for some programs); for doctorate, comprehensive exam, thesis/dissertation. *Entrance requirements:* For master's, GRE General Test, PRAXIS; for doctorate, GRE General Test, GMAT. *Application deadline:* For fall admission, 6/1 priority date for domestic students, 4/1 priority date for international students; for winter admission, 9/1 priority date for international students; for spring admission, 11/1 for domestic students; for summer admission, 4/15 for domestic students, 2/1 priority date for international students. Applications are processed on a rolling basis. Application fee: $35. Electronic applications accepted. *Financial support:* Fellowships, research assistantships, teaching assistantships, career-related internships or fieldwork, Federal Work-Study, institutionally sponsored loans, and scholarships/grants available. Support available to part-time students. Financial award application deadline: 5/1; financial award applicants required to submit FAFSA. *Unit head:* Dr. Linda Malone-Colon, Dean, 757-727-5400. *Application contact:* Dr. Michelle Penn-Marshall, Dean, Graduate College, 757-727-5454, E-mail: hugrad@hamptonu.edu.
Website: http://edhd.hamptonu.edu/

Harvard University, Extension School, Cambridge, MA 02138-3722. Offers applied sciences (CAS); biotechnology (ALM); educational technologies (ALM); educational technology (CET); English for graduate and professional studies (DGP); environmental management (ALM, CEM); information technology (ALM); journalism (ALM); liberal arts (ALM); management (ALM, CM); mathematics for teaching (ALM); museum studies (ALM); premedical studies (Diploma); publication and communication (CPC). *Program availability:* Part-time, evening/weekend. *Degree requirements:* For master's, thesis. *Entrance requirements:* For master's, 3 completed graduate courses with grade of B or higher. Additional exam requirements/recommendations for international students: required—TOEFL (minimum score 600 paper-based), TWE (minimum score 5). *Expenses:* Contact institution.

Hawaii Pacific University, College of Liberal Arts, Honolulu, HI 96813. Offers MA. *Program availability:* Part-time, evening/weekend. *Entrance requirements:* Additional exam requirements/recommendations for international students: recommended—TOEFL (minimum score 550 paper-based; 80 iBT), IELTS (minimum score 6), TWE (minimum score 5). Electronic applications accepted. *Expenses: Tuition:* Full-time $18,000; part-time $1125 per credit. *Required fees:* $213; $38 per semester.

Henderson State University, Graduate Studies, Ellis College of Arts and Sciences, Arkadelphia, AR 71999-0001. Offers MLA. *Program availability:* Part-time. *Degree requirements:* For master's, thesis. *Entrance requirements:* For master's, MAT or GRE, minimum GPA of 2.7, interview, essay. Additional exam requirements/recommendations for international students: required—TOEFL (minimum score 600 paper-based); recommended—IELTS (minimum score 6.5).

Hollins University, Graduate Programs, Program in Liberal Studies, Roanoke, VA 24020. Offers humanities (MALS); interdisciplinary studies (MALS); leadership (MALS); social sciences (MALS); visual and performing arts (MALS). *Program availability:* Part-time, evening/weekend, 100% online, blended/hybrid learning. *Degree requirements:* For master's, thesis. *Entrance requirements:* For master's, three letters of recommendation, interview, bachelor's degree, undergraduate transcripts, statement of educational objectives. Additional exam requirements/recommendations for international students: required—TOEFL (minimum score 550 paper-based; 80 iBT), IELTS (minimum score 6.5). Electronic applications accepted. *Expenses:* Contact institution.

Houston Baptist University, School of Humanities, Program in Liberal Arts, Houston, TX 77074-3298. Offers education (EC-12 art, music, physical education, or Spanish) (MLA); education (EC-6 generalist) (MLA); general liberal arts (MLA); specialization in education (4-8 or 7-12) (MLA). *Program availability:* Part-time, evening/weekend. *Entrance requirements:* For master's, minimum GPA of 2.5, essay/personal statement, resume, bachelor's degree transcript. Additional exam requirements/recommendations for international students: required—TOEFL (minimum score 80 iBT), IELTS (minimum score 6.5). Electronic applications accepted. Application fee is waived when completed online. *Expenses:* Contact institution.

Indiana University Northwest, College of Arts and Sciences, Gary, IN 46408. Offers clinical counseling (MS), including drug and alcohol counseling; community development/urban studies (Graduate Certificate); computer information systems (Graduate Certificate); liberal studies (MLS); race-ethnic studies (Graduate Certificate); women's and gender studies (Graduate Certificate). *Program availability:* Part-time, evening/weekend. *Entrance requirements:* For master's, GRE (recommended for MS), minimum undergraduate GPA of 3.0, bachelor's degree from accredited university (for MS). Electronic applications accepted. *Expenses:* Contact institution.

Indiana University-Purdue University Indianapolis, School of Liberal Arts, Indianapolis, IN 46202. Offers MA, MS, PhD, Certificate, JD/MA, MA/MA, MA/MLS, MD/MA.

Indiana University South Bend, College of Liberal Arts and Sciences, South Bend, IN 46615. Offers advanced computer programming (Graduate Certificate); applied informatics (Graduate Certificate); applied mathematics and computer science (MS); behavior modification (Graduate Certificate); computer applications (Graduate Certificate); computer programming (Graduate Certificate); correctional management and supervision (Graduate Certificate); English (MA); health systems management (Graduate Certificate); international studies (Graduate Certificate); liberal studies (MLS); nonprofit management (Graduate Certificate); paralegal studies (Graduate Certificate); professional writing (Graduate Certificate); public affairs (MPA); public management (Graduate Certificate); social and cultural diversity (Graduate Certificate); strategic sustainability leadership (Graduate Certificate); technology for administration (Graduate Certificate). *Program availability:* Part-time, evening/weekend. *Degree requirements:* For master's, variable foreign language requirement, thesis (for some programs). *Entrance requirements:* For master's, minimum GPA of 3.0. Additional exam requirements/recommendations for international students: required—TOEFL (minimum score 550 paper-based; 80 iBT). *Expenses:* Contact institution.

Jacksonville State University, Graduate Studies, School of Arts and Humanities, Program in Liberal Studies, Jacksonville, AL 36265-1602. Offers MA. *Program* *availability:* Part-time, evening/weekend. *Degree requirements:* For master's, comprehensive exam, thesis (for some programs). *Entrance requirements:* Additional exam requirements/recommendations for international students: required—TOEFL (minimum score 500 paper-based; 61 iBT). Electronic applications accepted.

Johns Hopkins University, Advanced Academic Programs, Program in Liberal Arts, Washington, DC 21218. Offers MA, Certificate. *Program availability:* Part-time, evening/weekend, online learning. *Degree requirements:* For master's, thesis. *Entrance requirements:* For master's, minimum GPA of 3.0. Additional exam requirements/recommendations for international students: required—TOEFL (minimum score 100 iBT). Electronic applications accepted.

Kean University, College of Liberal Arts, Union, NJ 07083. Offers MA. *Program availability:* Part-time. *Faculty:* 91 full-time (52 women). *Students:* 171 full-time (147 women), 115 part-time (89 women); includes 162 minority (71 Black or African American, non-Hispanic/Latino; 13 Asian, non-Hispanic/Latino; 76 Hispanic/Latino; 2 Two or more races, non-Hispanic/Latino), 7 international. Average age 29. 190 applicants, 80% accepted, 108 enrolled. In 2019, 97 master's awarded. *Degree requirements:* For master's, comprehensive exam, thesis, exhibition, practicum, internship. *Entrance requirements:* Additional exam requirements/recommendations for international students: required—TOEFL (minimum score 550 paper-based; 79 iBT), IELTS (minimum score 6.5). *Application deadline:* For fall admission, 6/30 for domestic and international students; for spring admission, 12/1 for domestic and international students. Applications are processed on a rolling basis. Application fee: $75. Electronic applications accepted. *Expenses:* Tuition, state resident: full-time $15,326; part-time $748 per credit. Tuition, nonresident: full-time $20,288; part-time $902 per credit. *Required fees:* $2149.50; $91.25 per credit. Tuition and fees vary according to course level, course load, degree level and program. *Financial support:* Scholarships/grants and unspecified assistantships available. Financial award applicants required to submit FAFSA. *Unit head:* Dr. Jonathan Mercantini, Acting Dean, 908-737-0430, Fax: 908-737-0435, E-mail: jmercant@kean.edu. *Application contact:* Amy Clark, Program Assistant, 908-737-7100, E-mail: gradadmissions@kean.edu.
Website: http://www.kean.edu/academics/college-liberal-arts

Lake Forest College, Graduate Program in Liberal Studies, Lake Forest, IL 60045. Offers American studies (MLS); cinema in East Asia (MLS); environmental studies (MLS); history (MLS); Medieval and Renaissance art (MLS); philosophy (MLS); Spanish (MLS); writing (MLS). *Program availability:* Part-time, evening/weekend. *Faculty:* 10 full-time (4 women). *Students:* 24 part-time (14 women). Average age 45. 10 applicants, 80% accepted, 3 enrolled. In 2019, 5 master's awarded. *Degree requirements:* For master's, thesis optional, 8 courses, including at least 3 interdisciplinary seminars. *Entrance requirements:* For master's, transcript, essay, interview. Additional exam requirements/recommendations for international students: required—TOEFL (minimum score 550 paper-based; 83 iBT); recommended—IELTS (minimum score 6.5). *Application deadline:* For fall admission, 8/15 priority date for domestic students, 7/15 priority date for international students; for spring admission, 12/15 priority date for domestic students, 11/15 priority date for international students. Applications are processed on a rolling basis. Application fee: $30. Electronic applications accepted. Application fee is waived when completed online. *Expenses:* Application fee = $30 — no other fees; tuition = $2,700/course. *Financial support:* In 2019–20, 2 students received support. Partial tuition grants (for full-time teachers) available. *Unit head:* Prof. D. L. LeMahieu, Director, 847-735-5133, Fax: 847-735-6291, E-mail: lemahieu@lakeforest.edu. *Application contact:* Prof. Carol Gayle, Associate Director, 847-735-5083, Fax: 847-735-6291, E-mail: gayle@lakeforest.edu.
Website: http://www.lakeforest.edu/academics/programs/mls/

Louisiana State University and Agricultural & Mechanical College, Graduate School, College of Humanities and Social Sciences, Interdepartmental Program in the Liberal Arts, Baton Rouge, LA 70803. Offers MALA.

Louisiana State University in Shreveport, College of Arts and Sciences, Program in Liberal Arts, Shreveport, LA 71115-2399. Offers MA. *Program availability:* Part-time, evening/weekend. *Degree requirements:* For master's, comprehensive exam, thesis or alternative. *Entrance requirements:* For master's, interview, minimum GPA of 3.0 during final 2 years of course work, statement of purpose. Additional exam requirements/recommendations for international students: required—TOEFL (minimum score 550 paper-based; 61 iBT). Electronic applications accepted.

Madonna University, Program in Liberal Studies, Livonia, MI 48150-1173. Offers MALS. *Expenses:* Tuition: Full-time $15,930; part-time $885 per credit hour. Tuition and fees vary according to degree level and program.

McDaniel College, Graduate and Professional Studies, Program in Liberal Arts, Westminster, MD 21157-4390. Offers liberal arts (MLA); writing for children and young adults (Postbaccalaureate Certificate). *Program availability:* Part-time, evening/weekend, 100% online. *Degree requirements:* For master's, final project. *Entrance requirements:* For master's, 3 recommendations. Additional exam requirements/recommendations for international students: required—TOEFL (minimum score 79 iBT), IELTS (minimum score 6). Electronic applications accepted.

Metropolitan State University, College of Liberal Arts, St. Paul, MN 55106-5000. Offers liberal studies (MA); technical communication (MS). *Program availability:* Part-time, evening/weekend. *Entrance requirements:* For master's, minimum GPA of 2.75, resume. Additional exam requirements/recommendations for international students: required—TOEFL (minimum score 550 paper-based). Electronic applications accepted.

Mississippi College, Graduate School, Program in Liberal Studies, Clinton, MS 39058. Offers MLS. *Program availability:* Part-time. *Degree requirements:* For master's, comprehensive exam, thesis optional. *Entrance requirements:* For master's, GRE, minimum GPA of 2.5. Additional exam requirements/recommendations for international students: recommended—TOEFL, IELTS.

The New School, The New School for Social Research, Department of Liberal Studies, New York, NY 10003. Offers MA. *Program availability:* Part-time. *Faculty:* 15 full-time (8 women), 2 part-time/adjunct (1 woman). *Students:* 23 full-time (10 women), 7 part-time (4 women); includes 7 minority (1 Black or African American, non-Hispanic/Latino; 2 Asian, non-Hispanic/Latino; 2 Hispanic/Latino; 2 Two or more races, non-Hispanic/Latino), 10 international. Average age 28. 34 applicants, 91% accepted, 16 enrolled. In 2019, 9 master's awarded. *Degree requirements:* For master's, thesis. *Entrance requirements:* For master's, GRE, letters of recommendation, writing sample, essays, transcript. Additional exam requirements/recommendations for international students: required—TOEFL (minimum score 100 iBT), IELTS (minimum score 7), PTE (minimum score 68). *Application deadline:* For fall admission, 1/5 priority date for domestic students, 1/1 priority date for international students; for spring admission, 10/15 priority date for domestic and international students. Applications are processed on a rolling basis. Application fee: $50. Electronic applications accepted. *Expenses:* 2260 per credit. *Financial support:* In 2019–20, 25 students received support, including 1 fellowship (averaging $6,243 per year), 6 research assistantships (averaging $4,041 per year), 2 teaching assistantships (averaging $5,618 per year); career-related internships or fieldwork, Federal Work-Study, and scholarships/grants also available. Support available to part-time students. Financial award application deadline: 2/1; financial award applicants required to submit FAFSA. *Unit head:* Dr. Paul Kottman, Department

Chair, 212-229-5777, E-mail: milbergw@newschool.edu. *Application contact:* Merida Gasbaro, Director of Graduate Admissions, 212-229-5600 Ext. 1108, E-mail: escandom@newschool.edu.
Website: http://www.newschool.edu/nssr/liberal-studies/

North Central College, School of Graduate and Professional Studies, Program in Liberal Studies, Naperville, IL 60566-7063. Offers culture and society (MALS). *Program availability:* Part-time, evening/weekend. *Degree requirements:* For master's, thesis optional, project. *Entrance requirements:* For master's, interview. Additional exam requirements/recommendations for international students: required—TOEFL (minimum score 550 paper-based; 80 iBT), IELTS (minimum score 6.5). Electronic applications accepted. Application fee is waived when completed online. *Expenses:* Contact institution.

Northern Arizona University, College of Social and Behavioral Sciences, Sustainable Communities Program, Flagstaff, AZ 86011. Offers MA. *Program availability:* Part-time. *Degree requirements:* For master's, variable foreign language requirement, comprehensive exam (for some programs), thesis, fieldwork experience/internship, oral defense. *Entrance requirements:* Additional exam requirements/recommendations for international students: required—TOEFL (minimum score 80 iBT), IELTS (minimum score 6.5). Electronic applications accepted.

Northern Kentucky University, Office of Graduate Programs, College of Arts and Sciences, Program in Integrative Studies, Highland Heights, KY 41099. Offers MA. *Program availability:* Part-time, evening/weekend. *Degree requirements:* For master's, thesis or capstone. *Entrance requirements:* For master's, statement of purpose, three letters of reference, resume, minimum GPA of 3.0. Additional exam requirements/recommendations for international students: required—TOEFL (minimum score 79 iBT); recommended—IELTS (minimum score 6.5). Electronic applications accepted.

Northwestern University, School of Professional Studies, Program in Liberal Studies, Evanston, IL 60208. Offers American studies (MA); history (MA); religious and ethical studies (MA). *Program availability:* Part-time, evening/weekend.

Notre Dame of Maryland University, Graduate Studies, Program in Liberal Studies, Baltimore, MD 21210-2476. Offers MA. *Program availability:* Part-time, evening/weekend. *Degree requirements:* For master's, thesis or alternative. *Entrance requirements:* For master's, minimum GPA of 3.0. Additional exam requirements/recommendations for international students: required—TOEFL (minimum score 500 paper-based; 61 iBT). Electronic applications accepted.

Oakland University, Graduate Study and Lifelong Learning, College of Arts and Sciences, Program in Liberal Studies, Rochester, MI 48309-4401. Offers MA. *Program availability:* Part-time. *Degree requirements:* For master's, 4-credit final project. *Entrance requirements:* For master's, Personal goal statement, A minimum of a 3.0 grade-point on a 4.0 scale in undergraduate study, At least two strong letters of recommendation that directly address the applicant's intellectual interests. Additional exam requirements/recommendations for international students: required—TOEFL (minimum score 550 paper-based; 79 iBT), IELTS (minimum score 6.5). Electronic applications accepted. *Expenses:* Tuition, area resident: Full-time $12,328; part-time $770.50 per credit hour. Tuition, state resident: full-time $12,328; part-time $770.50 per credit hour. Tuition, nonresident: full-time $16,432; part-time $1027 per credit hour. *International tuition:* $16,432 full-time. Tuition and fees vary according to degree level and program.

Queens College of the City University of New York, School of Social Sciences, Program in Liberal Studies, Queens, NY 11367-1597. Offers MA. *Program availability:* Part-time, evening/weekend. *Entrance requirements:* For master's, minimum GPA of 3.0. Additional exam requirements/recommendations for international students: required—TOEFL (minimum score 61 iBT), IELTS (minimum score 5). Electronic applications accepted.

Reed College, Graduate Program in Liberal Studies, Portland, OR 97202-8199. Offers MALS. *Program availability:* Part-time-only, evening/weekend. *Faculty:* 9 part-time/adjunct (3 women). *Students:* 28 part-time (15 women); includes 2 minority (1 Black or African American, non-Hispanic/Latino; 1 American Indian or Alaska Native, non-Hispanic/Latino). Average age 49. 5 applicants, 80% accepted, 4 enrolled. In 2019, 4 master's awarded. Terminal master's awarded for partial completion of doctoral program. *Degree requirements:* For master's, thesis, oral defense of thesis. *Entrance requirements:* For master's, interview, letters of recommendation, critical essay. Additional exam requirements/recommendations for international students: recommended—TOEFL. *Application deadline:* For fall admission, 7/1 priority date for domestic students, 5/1 for international students; for spring admission, 12/1 priority date for domestic students, 9/1 for international students; for summer admission, 4/1 for domestic students, 2/1 for international students. Applications are processed on a rolling basis. Application fee: $75. Electronic applications accepted. *Expenses:* One unit (4 semester hours) is $4,860. Students pay by the number of units enrolled in a given term. *Financial support:* In 2019–20, 2 students received support. Scholarships/grants and health care benefits available. Support available to part-time students. Financial award application deadline: 5/1; financial award applicants required to submit CSS PROFILE or FAFSA. *Unit head:* Barbara A. Amen, Director, Graduate Studies, 503-777-7259, Fax: 503-517-7345, E-mail: bamen@reed.edu. *Application contact:* Barbara A. Amen, Director, Graduate Studies, 503-777-7259, Fax: 503-517-7345, E-mail: bamen@reed.edu.
Website: http://www.reed.edu/mals

Rice University, Graduate Programs, Susanne M. Glasscock School of Continuing Studies, Houston, TX 77251-1892. Offers MLS. *Program availability:* Part-time, evening/weekend. *Degree requirements:* For master's, thesis or alternative, capstone paper/project. *Entrance requirements:* For master's, bachelor's degree from accredited institution; minimum GPA of 3.0; two letters of recommendation; personal statement; 3 writing samples; current resume. Additional exam requirements/recommendations for international students: required—TOEFL (minimum score 600 paper-based; 90 iBT). *Expenses:* Contact institution.

Rollins College, Hamilton Holt School, Master of Liberal Studies Program, Winter Park, FL 32789. Offers MLS. *Program availability:* Part-time, evening/weekend. *Faculty:* 5 full-time (1 woman), 1 (woman) part-time/adjunct. *Students:* 5 full-time (2 women), 35 part-time (22 women); includes 6 minority (2 Black or African American, non-Hispanic/Latino; 3 Hispanic/Latino; 1 Two or more races, non-Hispanic/Latino). Average age 40. In 2019, 5 master's awarded. *Degree requirements:* For master's, thesis. *Entrance requirements:* For master's, official transcripts, two letters of recommendation, essay. Additional exam requirements/recommendations for international students: required—TOEFL (minimum score 550 paper-based; 80 iBT). *Application deadline:* For fall admission, 4/1 for domestic students; for spring admission, 12/1 for domestic students. Application fee: $50. *Expenses:* $2,031 per credit hour; typical course is 4 credits. *Financial support:* Scholarships/grants and unspecified assistantships available. Support available to part-time students. Financial award applicants required to submit FAFSA. *Unit head:* Dr. Thomas Cook, Faculty Director, 407-646-2037, Fax: 407-646-2363. *Application contact:* Graduate Coordinator, 407-646-2653, Fax: 407-646-1551, E-mail: eveningadmission@rollins.edu.
Website: http://www.rollins.edu/holt/graduate/mls.html

Rutgers University - Camden, Graduate School of Arts and Sciences, Program in Liberal Studies, Camden, NJ 08102. Offers MALS. *Program availability:* Part-time, evening/weekend. *Degree requirements:* For master's, thesis, 30 credits. *Entrance requirements:* For master's, 2 letters of recommendation, writing sample, statement of personal, professional and academic goals. Additional exam requirements/recommendations for international students: required—TOEFL, IELTS. Electronic applications accepted.

St. Edward's University, School of Education, Master of Liberal Arts Program, Austin, TX 78704. Offers humanities (MLA); liberal arts (MLA, Certificate). *Program availability:* Part-time, evening/weekend. *Entrance requirements:* Additional exam requirements/recommendations for international students: required—TOEFL, IELTS. Electronic applications accepted.

St. John's College, Graduate Institute, Annapolis, MD 21401. Offers MALA. *Program availability:* Evening/weekend. *Degree requirements:* For master's, thesis optional. *Entrance requirements:* For master's, bachelor's degree. Additional exam requirements/recommendations for international students: required—TOEFL (minimum score 650 paper-based; 112 iBT), TWE (minimum score 5). Electronic applications accepted.

St. John's College, Graduate Institute in Liberal Education, Program in Liberal Arts, Santa Fe, NM 87505. Offers MA. *Program availability:* Evening/weekend. *Entrance requirements:* For master's, 2 letters of recommendation. Additional exam requirements/recommendations for international students: required—TOEFL, TWE.

St. John's University, St. John's College of Liberal Arts and Sciences, Program in Liberal Studies, Queens, NY 11439. Offers MA. *Program availability:* Part-time, evening/weekend. *Degree requirements:* For master's, capstone project. *Entrance requirements:* For master's, letters of recommendation, transcripts, resume, personal statement. Additional exam requirements/recommendations for international students: required—TOEFL (minimum score 80 iBT), IELTS (minimum score 6.5). Electronic applications accepted.

St. Norbert College, Master of Arts in Liberal Studies Program, De Pere, WI 54115-2099. Offers MA. *Program availability:* Part-time-only, evening/weekend. *Faculty:* 3 full-time (2 women), 2 part-time/adjunct (1 woman). *Students:* 7 part-time (5 women); includes 1 minority (Hispanic/Latino). Average age 41. 1 applicant, 100% accepted, 1 enrolled. *Degree requirements:* For master's, thesis. *Application deadline:* Applications are processed on a rolling basis. Application fee: $50. Electronic applications accepted. *Financial support:* Scholarships/grants available. *Unit head:* Dr. Howard Ebert, Director, 920-403-3956, E-mail: howard.ebert@snc.edu. *Application contact:* Danielle Wahlen, Program Coordinator, 920-403-3957, E-mail: danielle.wahlen@snc.edu. Website: http://www.snc.edu/mls/

San Diego State University, Graduate and Research Affairs, College of Arts and Letters, Program in Liberal Arts and Sciences, San Diego, CA 92182. Offers MA. *Program availability:* Part-time, evening/weekend. *Degree requirements:* For master's, thesis. *Entrance requirements:* For master's, GRE General Test. Additional exam requirements/recommendations for international students: required—TOEFL. Electronic applications accepted.

San Francisco State University, Division of Graduate Studies, College of Liberal and Creative Arts, School of Humanities and Liberal Studies, San Francisco, CA 94132-1722. Offers MA. *Program availability:* Part-time, evening/weekend. *Expenses:* Tuition, area resident: Full-time $7176; part-time $4164 per year. Tuition, state resident: full-time $7176; part-time $4164 per year. Tuition, nonresident: full-time $16,680; part-time $396 per unit. *International tuition:* $16,680 full-time. *Required fees:* $1524; $1524 per unit. $762 per semester. Tuition and fees vary according to degree level and program. *Unit head:* Dr. Cristina Ruotolo, Director, 415-338-1099, Fax: 415-338-6159, E-mail: ruotolo@sfsu.edu. *Application contact:* Dr. Tanya Augsburg, MA Coordinator, 415-405-2673, Fax: 415-338-6159, E-mail: tanya@sfsu.edu. Website: https://humanitiesliberalstudies.sfsu.edu/graduate-program

Simon Fraser University, Office of Graduate Studies and Postdoctoral Fellows, Faculty of Arts and Social Sciences, Program in Liberal Studies, Vancouver, BC V6B 5K3, Canada. Offers MALS. *Program availability:* Part-time, evening/weekend, online learning. *Degree requirements:* For master's, thesis or alternative. *Entrance requirements:* For master's, minimum GPA of 3.0 (on scale of 4.33) or 3.33 based on last 60 credits of undergraduate courses. Additional exam requirements/recommendations for international students: recommended—TOEFL (minimum score 580 paper-based; 93 iBT), IELTS (minimum score 7), TWE (minimum score 5). Electronic applications accepted.

Southern Methodist University, Simmons School of Education and Human Development, Program in Liberal Studies, Dallas, TX 75275. Offers MLS, DLS.

Spring Hill College, Graduate Programs, Program in Liberal Arts, Mobile, AL 36608-1791. Offers fine arts (MLA); leadership and ethics (MLA, Postbaccalaureate Certificate); literature (MLA). *Program availability:* Part-time, evening/weekend. *Faculty:* 3 full-time (0 women), 2 part-time/adjunct (both women). *Students:* 3 full-time (2 women), 12 part-time (5 women); includes 1 minority (Hispanic/Latino), 4 international. Average age 35. In 2019, 9 master's awarded. *Degree requirements:* For master's, capstone course, completion of program within 6 years of initial admittance. *Entrance requirements:* For master's, bachelor's degree with minimum undergraduate GPA of 3.0 or graduate/professional degree. Additional exam requirements/recommendations for international students: required—TOEFL (minimum score 550 paper-based; 80 iBT), IELTS (minimum score 6.5), CPE or CAE (minimum score C), Michigan English Language Assessment Battery (minimum score 90). *Application deadline:* For fall admission, 8/1 priority date for domestic and international students; for spring admission, 12/1 priority date for domestic and international students. Applications are processed on a rolling basis. Application fee: $25 ($35 for international students). Electronic applications accepted. *Expenses:* Contact institution. *Financial support:* Fellowships, research assistantships, teaching assistantships, and tuition waivers available. Financial award applicants required to submit FAFSA. *Unit head:* Dr. Thomas J. Hoffman, Director, 251-380-4184, Fax: 251-460-2115, E-mail: thoffman@shc.edu. *Application contact:* Gary Bracken, Vice President of Enrollment Management, 251-380-3038, Fax: 251-460-2186, E-mail: gbracken@shc.edu. Website: http://ug.shc.edu/graduate-degrees/master-liberal-arts/

State University of New York College at Old Westbury, Program in Liberal Studies, Old Westbury, NY 11568-0210. Offers MA. *Program availability:* Part-time, evening/weekend. *Faculty:* 2 full-time (both women). *Students:* 5 full-time (1 woman), 4 part-time (3 women); includes 4 minority (1 Black or African American, non-Hispanic/Latino; 1 Asian, non-Hispanic/Latino; 2 Hispanic/Latino). Average age 38. 10 applicants, 80% accepted, 5 enrolled. In 2019, 1 master's awarded. *Degree requirements:* For master's, thesis project or internship. *Application deadline:* Applications are processed on a rolling basis. Application fee: $50. Electronic applications accepted. *Financial support:* Applicants required to submit FAFSA. *Unit head:* Dr. Amanda Frisken, Associate Professor, American Studies, 516-876-4853, E-mail: friskena@oldwestbury.edu. *Application contact:* Philip D'Angelo, Graduate Admissions Office, 516-876-3073, E-mail: enroll@oldwestbury.edu.

State University of New York Empire State College, School for Graduate Studies, Program in Liberal Studies, Saratoga Springs, NY 12866-4391. Offers MA. *Program availability:* Part-time, evening/weekend, online learning. *Degree requirements:* For master's, thesis, final project. *Entrance requirements:* Additional exam requirements/recommendations for international students: required—TOEFL (minimum score 600 paper-based). Electronic applications accepted.

Stony Brook University, State University of New York, School of Professional Development, Stony Brook, NY 11794. Offers coaching (Graduate Certificate); environmental management (MPS); German (MAT); higher education administration (MA, Certificate); human resource management (MS, Graduate Certificate); Italian (MAT); liberal studies (MA); mathematics (MAT); school district business leadership (Advanced Certificate); social studies (MAT); Spanish (MAT). *Program availability:* Part-time, evening/weekend, online learning. *Faculty:* 3 full-time (2 women), 104 part-time/adjunct (44 women). *Students:* 226 full-time (148 women), 1,203 part-time (891 women); includes 324 minority (101 Black or African American, non-Hispanic/Latino; 1 American Indian or Alaska Native, non-Hispanic/Latino; 40 Asian, non-Hispanic/Latino; 159 Hispanic/Latino; 2 Native Hawaiian or other Pacific Islander, non-Hispanic/Latino; 21 Two or more races, non-Hispanic/Latino), 5 international. Average age 33. 686 applicants, 88% accepted, 402 enrolled. In 2019, 332 master's, 177 other advanced degrees awarded. *Entrance requirements:* Additional exam requirements/recommendations for international students: required—TOEFL (minimum score 85 iBT). *Application deadline:* For fall admission, 1/15 for domestic students, 6/1 for international students; for spring admission, 10/1 for domestic and international students. Applications are processed on a rolling basis. Application fee: $100. *Expenses:* Contact institution. *Financial support:* Fellowships, research assistantships, teaching assistantships, and career-related internships or fieldwork available. Support available to part-time students. *Unit head:* Patricia Malone, Associate Vice President for Professional Education and Assistant Provost for Engaged Learning, 631-632-7512, Fax: 631-632-9046, E-mail: patricia.malone@stonybrook.edu. *Application contact:* Linda Varga, Office Manager, 631-632-7050, E-mail: Linda.Varga@stonybrook.edu. Website: http://www.stonybrook.edu/spd/

SUNY Brockport, School of Arts and Sciences, Program in Liberal Studies, Brockport, NY 14420-2997. Offers MA. *Program availability:* Part-time, 100% online, blended/hybrid learning. *Students:* 8 full-time (5 women), 38 part-time (27 women); includes 5 minority (3 Black or African American, non-Hispanic/Latino; 2 Hispanic/Latino). 22 applicants, 64% accepted, 12 enrolled. In 2019, 11 master's awarded. *Entrance requirements:* Additional exam requirements/recommendations for international students: required—TOEFL (minimum score 550 paper-based; 79 iBT), IELTS (minimum score 6.5). *Application deadline:* For fall admission, 6/15 for domestic and international students; for spring admission, 10/15 for domestic and international students; for summer admission, 3/15 for domestic and international students. Application fee: $50. Electronic applications accepted. *Expenses:* Tuition, area resident: Part-time $471 per credit hour. Tuition, nonresident: part-time $963 per credit hour. *Financial support:* Fellowships, research assistantships, teaching assistantships, scholarships/grants, and unspecified assistantships available. Financial award applicants required to submit FAFSA. *Unit head:* Dr. Jose Maliekal, Dean, School of Arts and Sciences, 585-395-5806. *Application contact:* Kulathur Rajasethupathy, Graduate Director, 585-395-5760, E-mail: kraja@brockport.edu.

Texas A&M University–Central Texas, Graduate Studies and Research, Killeen, TX 76549. Offers accounting (MS); business administration (MBA); clinical mental health counseling (MS); criminal justice (MCJ); curriculum and instruction (M Ed); educational administration (M Ed); educational psychology - experimental psychology (MS); history (MA); human resource management (MS); information systems (MS); liberal studies (MS); management and leadership (MS); marriage and family therapy (MS); mathematics (MS); political science (MA); school counseling (M Ed); school psychology (Ed S).

Texas Christian University, Master of Liberal Arts Program, Fort Worth, TX 76129-0002. Offers MLA. *Program availability:* Part-time, evening/weekend, 100% online. *Faculty:* 5 part-time/adjunct (0 women). *Students:* 81 full-time (33 women), 30 part-time (22 women); includes 37 minority (21 Black or African American, non-Hispanic/Latino; 2 American Indian or Alaska Native, non-Hispanic/Latino; 8 Hispanic/Latino; 1 Native Hawaiian or other Pacific Islander, non-Hispanic/Latino; 5 Two or more races, non-Hispanic/Latino), 3 international. Average age 32. 85 applicants, 93% accepted, 57 enrolled. In 2019, 33 master's awarded. *Entrance requirements:* Additional exam requirements/recommendations for international students: required—TOEFL (minimum score 550 paper-based; 80 iBT), IELTS (minimum score 6.5). *Application deadline:* For fall admission, 8/15 for domestic students, 6/1 for international students; for spring admission, 1/15 for domestic students, 11/1 for international students. Applications are processed on a rolling basis. Application fee: $60. Electronic applications accepted. *Expenses:* Tuition was $980 per semester hour with online fees of $130 per course. Full time students pay $24 per semester for Graduate Student Senate fees. *Financial support:* In 2019–20, 55 students received support. Scholarships/grants, unspecified assistantships, and employee tuition benefits available. Financial award applicants required to submit FAFSA. *Unit head:* Dr. Peter Worthing, Associate Dean, AddRan College of Liberal Arts, 817-257-6656, E-mail: p.worthing@tcu.edu. *Application contact:* Ellen Irwin, Administrative Assistant, 817-257-7160, Fax: 817-257-7709, E-mail: e.irwin@tcu.edu. Website: https://addran.tcu.edu/academics/graduate-programs/mla/index.php

Thomas Edison State University, Heavin School of Arts and Sciences, Program in Liberal Studies, Trenton, NJ 08608. Offers digital humanities (MALS, Graduate Certificate); geropsychology (MALS, Graduate Certificate); industrial-organizational psychology (MALS, Graduate Certificate); learner-designed area of study (MALS); professional communications (MALS, Graduate Certificate). *Program availability:* Part-time, online learning. *Degree requirements:* For master's, final project. *Entrance requirements:* For master's, bachelor's degree from a regionally-accredited college or university; minimum 2 letters of recommendation; 3-5 years of related working experience; current resume. Additional exam requirements/recommendations for international students: required—TOEFL (minimum score 550 paper-based; 79 iBT). Electronic applications accepted.

Towson University, College of Liberal Arts, Program in Professional Studies, Towson, MD 21252-0001. Offers art history (MA); individualized plan of study (MA). *Program availability:* Part-time, evening/weekend. *Students:* 10 full-time (8 women), 13 part-time (7 women); includes 10 minority (8 Black or African American, non-Hispanic/Latino; 1 Hispanic/Latino; 1 Two or more races, non-Hispanic/Latino), 1 international. *Entrance requirements:* For master's, minimum GPA of 3.0, essay. *Application deadline:* For fall admission, 1/17 for domestic students, 5/15 for international students; for spring admission, 10/15 for domestic students, 12/1 for international students. Applications are processed on a rolling basis. Application fee: $45. Electronic applications accepted. *Expenses:* Tuition, area resident: Full-time $7920; part-time $439 per credit. Tuition, nonresident: full-time $16,344; part-time $908 per credit. *International tuition:* $16,344 full-time. *Required fees:* $2628; $146 per credit. $876 per term. *Financial support:* Application deadline: 4/1. *Unit head:* Dr. Karen Eskow, Program Director, 410-704-2128, E-mail: keskow@towson.edu. *Application contact:* Coverley Beidleman, Assistant

Director of Graduate Admissions, 410-704-5630, Fax: 410-704-3030, E-mail: grads@towson.edu. Website: https://www.towson.edu/cla/departments/interdisciplinary/grad/professional/

Tulane University, School of Professional Advancement, New Orleans, LA 70118-5669. Offers health and wellness management (MPS); homeland security studies (MPS); information technology management (MPS); liberal arts (MLA). *Program availability:* Part-time. *Degree requirements:* For master's, thesis. *Entrance requirements:* For master's, GRE General Test, minimum B average in undergraduate course work. Additional exam requirements/recommendations for international students: required—TOEFL. *Expenses: Tuition:* Full-time $57,004; part-time $3167 per credit hour. *Required fees:* $2086; $44.50 per credit hour. $80 per term. Tuition and fees vary according to course load, degree level and program.

University of Central Oklahoma, The Jackson College of Graduate Studies, College of Liberal Arts, Department of Humanities and Philosophy, Edmond, OK 73034-5209. Offers liberal studies (MA). *Degree requirements:* For master's, comprehensive exam (for some programs), thesis (for some programs). *Entrance requirements:* Additional exam requirements/recommendations for international students: required—TOEFL (minimum score 550 paper-based; 79 iBT), IELTS (minimum score 6.5). Electronic applications accepted.

University of Chicago, Graham School of Continuing Liberal and Professional Studies, Program in Liberal Arts, Chicago, IL 60637. Offers MLA. *Program availability:* Part-time, evening/weekend. *Entrance requirements:* For master's, writing sample, transcripts, 2 letters of recommendation, resume or curriculum vitae. Additional exam requirements/recommendations for international students: required—TOEFL (minimum score 104 iBT), IELTS (minimum score 7). Electronic applications accepted.

University of Delaware, College of Arts and Sciences, Program in Liberal Studies, Newark, DE 19716. Offers MALS. *Program availability:* Part-time, evening/weekend. *Degree requirements:* For master's, thesis. Electronic applications accepted.

University of Detroit Mercy, College of Liberal Arts and Education, Detroit, MI 48221. Offers addiction counseling (MA); addiction studies (Certificate); clinical mental health counseling (MA); clinical psychology (MA, PhD); computer and information systems (MS); criminal justice (MA); curriculum and instruction (MA); economics (MA); educational administration (MA); financial economics (MA); industrial/organizational psychology (MA); information assurance (MS); intelligence analysis (MA); liberal studies (MALS); religious studies (MA); school counseling (MA, Certificate); school psychology (Spec); security administration (MS); special education: emotionally impaired/behaviorally disordered (MA); special education: learning disabilities (MA). *Program availability:* Part-time, evening/weekend. *Degree requirements:* For doctorate, departmental qualifying exam.

University of Memphis, Graduate School, College of Professional and Liberal Studies, Memphis, TN 38152. Offers human resources leadership (MPS); liberal studies (MALS, Graduate Certificate); strategic leadership (MPS, Graduate Certificate); training and development (MPS). *Program availability:* Part-time, evening/weekend, online learning. *Faculty:* 1 full-time, 1 (woman) part-time/adjunct. *Students:* 17 full-time (9 women), 123 part-time (86 women); includes 89 minority (80 Black or African American, non-Hispanic/Latino; 1 Asian, non-Hispanic/Latino; 5 Hispanic/Latino; 3 Two or more races, non-Hispanic/Latino), 1 international. Average age 41. 89 applicants, 80% accepted, 49 enrolled. In 2019, 25 master's, 5 other advanced degrees awarded. *Degree requirements:* For master's, comprehensive exam, thesis (for some programs). *Entrance requirements:* For master's, GRE (for MPS), resume, letters of recommendation, personal essay, interview, minimum undergraduate GPA of 2.75 (for MALS); portfolio in lieu of GRE (for MPS applicants with substantial professional work experience); for Graduate Certificate, essay, letter of recommendation. Additional exam requirements/recommendations for international students: required—TOEFL (minimum score 550 paper-based; 79 iBT). *Application deadline:* For fall admission, 7/1 for domestic students, 5/1 for international students; for spring admission, 11/1 for domestic students, 9/15 for international students. Applications are processed on a rolling basis. Application fee: $35 ($60 for international students). Electronic applications accepted. *Expenses: Tuition, area resident:* Full-time $9216; part-time $512 per credit hour. Tuition, state resident: full-time $9216; part-time $512 per credit hour. Tuition, nonresident: full-time $12,672; part-time $704 per credit hour. *International tuition:* $16,128 full-time. *Required fees:* $1530; $85 per credit hour. Tuition and fees vary according to program. *Financial support:* Research assistantships with full tuition reimbursements, teaching assistantships with tuition reimbursements, Federal Work-Study, scholarships/grants, and unspecified assistantships available. Financial award application deadline: 2/3; financial award applicants required to submit FAFSA. *Unit head:* Dr. Richard Irwin, Executive Dean, 901-678-2716, E-mail: rirwin@memphis.edu. *Application contact:* Dr. Richard Irwin, Executive Dean, 901-678-2716, E-mail: rirwin@memphis.edu. Website: http://www.memphis.edu/univcoll/

University of Miami, Graduate School, College of Arts and Sciences, Program in Liberal Studies, Coral Gables, FL 33124. Offers MALS. *Program availability:* Part-time, evening/weekend. *Degree requirements:* For master's, thesis or alternative. *Entrance requirements:* For master's, minimum GPA of 3.0. Additional exam requirements/recommendations for international students: required—TOEFL. Electronic applications accepted. *Expenses:* Contact institution.

University of Michigan–Flint, Graduate Programs, Program in Liberal Studies in American Culture, Flint, MI 48502-1950. Offers MA, MLS. *Program availability:* Part-time, evening/weekend, 100% online. *Faculty:* 1 part-time/adjunct (0 women). *Students:* 3 full-time (2 women), 17 part-time (8 women); includes 6 minority (3 Black or African American, non-Hispanic/Latino; 2 American Indian or Alaska Native, non-Hispanic/Latino; 1 Asian, non-Hispanic/Latino). Average age 49. 14 applicants, 79% accepted, 6 enrolled. In 2019, 6 master's awarded. *Entrance requirements:* For master's, bachelor's degree from accredited institution; minimum overall undergraduate GPA of 3.0 on 4.0 scale; undergraduate course work totaling 24 credit hours, primarily in the humanities and social sciences. Additional exam requirements/recommendations for international students: required—TOEFL (minimum score 84 iBT), IELTS (minimum score 6.5). *Application deadline:* For fall admission, 8/1 for domestic students, 5/1 for international students; for winter admission, 11/15 for domestic students, 10/1 for international students; for spring admission, 3/15 for domestic students, 1/1 for international students; for summer admission, 5/15 for domestic students. Applications are processed on a rolling basis. Application fee: $55. Electronic applications accepted. *Expenses:* Contact institution. *Financial support:* Federal Work-Study, scholarships/grants, and unspecified assistantships available. Support available to part-time students. Financial award application deadline: 3/1; financial award applicants required to submit FAFSA. *Unit head:* Dr. Jan Furman, Director, 810-762-3285, E-mail: jfurman@umflint.edu. *Application contact:* Matt Bohlen, Associate Director of Graduate Admissions, 810-762-3171, Fax: 810-766-6789, E-mail: mbohlen@umflint.edu. Website: https://www.umflint.edu/graduateprograms/liberal-studies-american-culture-ma

University of Minnesota, Duluth, Graduate School, College of Liberal Arts, Department of Sociology/Anthropology, Liberal Studies Program, Duluth, MN 55812-2496. Offers MLS. *Program availability:* Part-time, evening/weekend.

University of New Hampshire, Graduate School, College of Liberal Arts, Program in Liberal Studies, Durham, NH 03824. Offers MALS. *Students:* 8 part-time (3 women); includes 2 minority (1 Asian, non-Hispanic/Latino; 1 Hispanic/Latino). Average age 50. 1 applicant, 100% accepted. In 2019, 1 master's awarded. *Entrance requirements:* Additional exam requirements/recommendations for international students: required—TOEFL (minimum score 550 paper-based; 80 iBT), IELTS, PTE. *Application deadline:* For fall admission, 7/1 for domestic students; for spring admission, 12/1 for domestic students; for summer admission, 4/1 for domestic students. Application fee: $65. Electronic applications accepted. *Financial support:* Fellowships, research assistantships, and teaching assistantships available. Financial award application deadline: 2/15. *Unit head:* Brigitte Bailey, Director, 603-862-3052, E-mail: liberal.studies@unh.edu. *Application contact:* Brigitte Bailey, Chair, 603-862-3052, E-mail: liberal.studies@unh.edu. Website: http://www.cola.unh.edu/liberal-studies

University of North Carolina Asheville, Master of Liberal Arts and Sciences Program, Asheville, NC 28804-3299. Offers MLAS, Graduate Certificate. *Program availability:* Part-time. *Faculty:* 4 full-time (1 woman), 2 part-time/adjunct (0 women). *Students:* 1 full-time (0 women), 11 part-time (7 women); includes 1 minority (Two or more races, non-Hispanic/Latino). Average age 42. In 2019, 8 master's, 5 Graduate Certificates awarded. *Degree requirements:* For master's, thesis or alternative, minimum 30 credit hours, 3.0 gpa; for Graduate Certificate, minimum 12-15 credit hours, 3.0 gpa. *Entrance requirements:* For master's and Graduate Certificate, essay, 3 letters of recommendation, transcript. Additional exam requirements/recommendations for international students: required—TOEFL (minimum score 85 iBT), IELTS (minimum score 6.5), TOEFL or IELTS. Application fee: $60. *Expenses: Tuition, area resident:* Full-time $4914. Tuition, state resident: full-time $4914. Tuition, nonresident: full-time $21,236. *International tuition:* $21,236 full-time. *Required fees:* $3108.50. *Financial support:* In 2019–20, 3 students received support. Scholarships/grants and tuition waivers for UNC faculty/staff available. Financial award applicants required to submit FAFSA. *Unit head:* Dr. Michael Neelon, Graduate Council Chair, 828-250-2359, E-mail: mneelon@unca.edu. *Application contact:* Lilly Augspurger, Administrative Assistant, 828-251-6099, E-mail: laugspur@unca.edu. Website: https://mlas.unca.edu/

The University of North Carolina at Charlotte, College of Liberal Arts and Sciences, Interdisciplinary Liberal Arts and Sciences Programs, Charlotte, NC 28223-0001. Offers gender, sexuality and women's studies (Graduate Certificate); gerontology (MA, Graduate Certificate); Latin American studies (MA); liberal studies (MA); organizational science (PhD); public policy (PhD). *Program availability:* Part-time, evening/weekend. *Students:* 74 full-time (50 women), 56 part-time (43 women); includes 41 minority (16 Black or African American, non-Hispanic/Latino; 3 Asian, non-Hispanic/Latino; 16 Hispanic/Latino; 6 Two or more races, non-Hispanic/Latino), 16 international. Average age 33. 101 applicants, 51% accepted, 37 enrolled. In 2019, 21 master's, 5 doctorates, 8 other advanced degrees awarded. *Entrance requirements:* For master's, GRE General Test or MAT, bachelor's degree from accredited college or university; official transcripts of all previous academic work attempted beyond high school with minimum overall GPA of 3.0; statement of purpose; recommendation letters; for doctorate, GRE or GMAT, statement of purpose discussing interest in program and objectives for pursuing degree, current resume or curriculum vitae, unofficial transcripts; for Graduate Certificate, bachelor's degree from accredited university and either enrolled and in good standing in a graduate degree program at UNC Charlotte or have a minimum undergraduate GPA of 3.0. Additional exam requirements/recommendations for international students: required—TOEFL (minimum score 557 paper-based; 83 iBT), IELTS (minimum score 6.5), TOEFL (minimum score 557 paper-based, 83 iBT) or IELTS (6.5). *Application deadline:* Applications are processed on a rolling basis. Application fee: $75. Electronic applications accepted. *Expenses:* Tuition, state resident: full-time $4337. Tuition, nonresident: full-time $17,771. *Required fees:* $3093. Tuition and fees vary according to course load, degree level and program. *Financial support:* In 2019–20, 3 students received support, including 2 research assistantships (averaging $6,750 per year), 1 teaching assistantship (averaging $21,000 per year); career-related internships or fieldwork, institutionally sponsored loans, scholarships/grants, unspecified assistantships, and administrative assistantships also available. Support available to part-time students. Financial award applicants required to submit FAFSA. *Unit head:* Dr. Nancy A. Gutierrez, Dean, 704-687-0081, E-mail: ngutierr@uncc.edu. *Application contact:* Kathy B. Giddings, Director of Graduate Admissions, 704-687-5503, Fax: 704-687-3279, E-mail: gradadm@uncc.edu. Website: http://clas.uncc.edu/academics

The University of North Carolina at Greensboro, Graduate School, Program in Liberal Studies, Greensboro, NC 27412-5001. Offers MALS. Electronic applications accepted.

The University of North Carolina Wilmington, College of Arts and Sciences, Graduate Liberal Studies Program, Wilmington, NC 28403-3297. Offers MA. *Program availability:* Part-time, 100% online. *Faculty:* 2 full-time (both women). *Students:* 4 full-time (2 women), 16 part-time (14 women); includes 5 minority (2 Black or African American, non-Hispanic/Latino; 2 Hispanic/Latino; 1 Two or more races, non-Hispanic/Latino). Average age 40. 4 applicants, 100% accepted, 4 enrolled. In 2019, 7 master's awarded. *Degree requirements:* For master's, final project. *Entrance requirements:* For master's, essay, 3 letters of recommendation. Additional exam requirements/recommendations for international students: required—TOEFL (minimum score 79 iBT), IELTS (minimum score 6.5). *Application deadline:* For fall admission, 7/1 for domestic students; for spring admission, 10/15 for domestic students; for summer admission, 4/15 for domestic students. Applications are processed on a rolling basis. Application fee: $75. Electronic applications accepted. *Expenses:* $259.01 per credit hour for in-state students; $936.91 per credit hour for out-of-state students. *Financial support:* Scholarships/grants and unspecified assistantships available. Financial award application deadline: 1/1; financial award applicants required to submit FAFSA. *Unit head:* Dr. Patricia Turrisi, Director, 910-962-3299, Fax: 910-962-3542, E-mail: turrisip@uncw.edu. *Application contact:* Dr. Ashley Hudson, Assistant Director, 910-962-2427, Fax: 910-962-3542, E-mail: hudsona@uncw.edu. Website: http://www.uncw.edu/gls/

University of Pennsylvania, School of Arts and Sciences, College of Liberal and Professional Studies, Philadelphia, PA 19104. Offers applied geosciences (MSAG); applied positive psychology (MAP); chemical sciences (MCS); environmental studies (MES); individualized study (MLA); liberal arts (M Phil); medical physics (MMP); organization dynamics (M Phil). *Students:* 240 full-time (161 women), 290 part-time (180 women); includes 91 minority (31 Black or African American, non-Hispanic/Latino; 31 Asian, non-Hispanic/Latino; 14 Hispanic/Latino; 15 Two or more races, non-Hispanic/Latino), 136 international. Average age 33. 955 applicants, 44% accepted, 272 enrolled. In 2019, 203 master's awarded. *Unit head:* Nora Lewis, Vice Dean, Professional and Liberal Education, 215-898-7326, E-mail: nlewis@sas.upenn.edu. *Application contact:* Nora Lewis, Vice Dean, Professional and Liberal Education, 215-898-7326, E-mail: nlewis@sas.upenn.edu. Website: http://www.sas.upenn.edu/lps/graduate

University of St. Thomas, Program in Liberal Arts, Houston, TX 77006-4696. Offers MLA. *Program availability:* Part-time, evening/weekend. *Faculty:* 29 full-time (12 women), 23 part-time/adjunct (16 women). *Students:* 12 full-time (6 women), 28 part-time (18 women); includes 19 minority (5 Black or African American, non-Hispanic/Latino; 2 Asian, non-Hispanic/Latino; 11 Hispanic/Latino; 1 Two or more races, non-Hispanic/Latino), 1 international. Average age 36. 14 applicants, 93% accepted, 11 enrolled. In 2019, 23 master's awarded. *Degree requirements:* For master's, one foreign language, thesis optional. *Entrance requirements:* For master's, interview, transcripts. Additional exam requirements/recommendations for international students: recommended—TOEFL, IELTS. *Application deadline:* Applications are processed on a rolling basis. Application fee: $35. Electronic applications accepted. *Expenses:* $470/credit hour. *Financial support:* Applicants required to submit FAFSA. *Unit head:* Dr. Thomas Behr, Director, 713-525-6951, E-mail: behrt@stthom.edu. *Application contact:* Kate Henderson, Program Coordinator, 713-525-3556, Fax: 713-525-6924, E-mail: mla@stthom.edu.
Website: http://www.stthom.edu/Academics/School_of_Arts_and_Sciences/Graduate/Master_of_Liberal_Arts/Index.aqf

University of Southern Indiana, Graduate Studies, College of Liberal Arts, Program in Liberal Studies, Evansville, IN 47712-3590. Offers MALS. *Program availability:* Part-time, evening/weekend. *Entrance requirements:* For master's, minimum GPA of 2.5, resume, interview, written statement of interest, three professional references. Additional exam requirements/recommendations for international students: required—TOEFL (minimum score 550 paper-based; 79 iBT), IELTS (minimum score 6). Electronic applications accepted.

University of South Florida, College of Arts and Sciences, Department of Humanities and Cultural Studies, Tampa, FL 33620-9951. Offers liberal arts (MA), including American studies, film studies, humanities. *Program availability:* Part-time, evening/weekend. *Faculty:* 8 full-time (3 women). *Students:* 19 full-time (7 women), 6 part-time (4 women); includes 7 minority (2 Black or African American, non-Hispanic/Latino; 2 Asian, non-Hispanic/Latino; 3 Hispanic/Latino), 1 international. Average age 29. 21 applicants, 71% accepted, 15 enrolled. In 2019, 8 master's awarded. *Degree requirements:* For master's, comprehensive exam, thesis, language (for humanities subconcentration). *Entrance requirements:* For master's, GRE Recommended. Contact department for advising, minimum GPA of 3.0, writing sample. Personal statement, letters of recommendation are recommended. Students must select a concentration at the time of application. Additional exam requirements/recommendations for international students: required—TOEFL, TOEFL (minimum score 550 paper-based; 79 iBT) or IELTS (minimum score 6.5). *Application deadline:* For fall admission, 2/15 priority date for domestic students, 2/15 for international students; for spring admission, 10/15 priority date for domestic students, 9/15 for international students; for summer admission, 2/15 for domestic students, 1/15 for international students. Application fee: $30. Electronic applications accepted. *Financial support:* In 2019–20, 5 students received support, including 15 teaching assistantships with tuition reimbursements available (averaging $12,437 per year); scholarships/grants also available. Financial award application deadline: 4/1. *Unit head:* Dr. Andrew Berish, Associate Professor and Chair, 813-974-9380, E-mail: aberish@usf.edu. *Application contact:* Dr. Maria Cizmic, Associate Professor and Graduate Program Director, 813-974-9380, E-mail: mcizmic@usf.edu.
Website: http://humanities.usf.edu/

University of South Florida, College of Arts and Sciences, Department of Philosophy, Tampa, FL 33620-9951. Offers liberal arts (MA), including social and political thought; philosophy (PhD), including philosophy and religion. *Program availability:* Part-time, evening/weekend. *Faculty:* 15 full-time (4 women). *Students:* 42 full-time (6 women), 10 part-time (4 women); includes 10 minority (3 Black or African American, non-Hispanic/Latino; 3 Asian, non-Hispanic/Latino; 3 Hispanic/Latino; 1 Two or more races, non-Hispanic/Latino). Average age 33. 24 applicants, 75% accepted, 11 enrolled. In 2019, 2 master's, 10 doctorates awarded. Terminal master's awarded for partial completion of doctoral program. *Degree requirements:* For master's, comprehensive exam, thesis; for doctorate, comprehensive exam, thesis/dissertation. *Entrance requirements:* For master's and doctorate, GRE General Test Scores, minimum GPA of 3.0, three letters of recommendation, 10-page philosophy writing sample, statement of philosophical interests. Additional exam requirements/recommendations for international students: required—TOEFL, TOEFL (minimum score 550 paper-based; 79 iBT) or IELTS (minimum score 6.5). *Application deadline:* For fall admission, 1/2 priority date for domestic students, 2/15 for international students; for spring admission, 10/15 priority date for domestic students, 8/1 for international students. Application fee: $30. Electronic applications accepted. *Financial support:* In 2019–20, 15 students received support, including 32 teaching assistantships with tuition reimbursements available (averaging $11,025 per year); unspecified assistantships also available. Financial award application deadline: 1/1. *Unit head:* Dr. William Goodwin, Associate Professor and Chair, 813-974-5670, E-mail: wgoodwin@usf.edu. *Application contact:* Dr. William Goodwin, Associate Professor, 813-974-5670, E-mail: wgoodwin@usf.edu.
Website: http://philosophy.usf.edu/

University of South Florida, St. Petersburg, College of Arts and Sciences, St. Petersburg, FL 33701. Offers digital journalism and design (MA); environmental science and policy (MA, MS); Florida studies (MLA); journalism and media studies (MA); liberal studies (MLA); psychology (MA). *Program availability:* Part-time, online learning. *Degree requirements:* For master's, comprehensive exam, thesis or project. *Entrance requirements:* For master's, GRE, LSAT, MCAT (varies by program), letter of intent, 3 letters of recommendation, writing samples, bachelor's degree from regionally-accredited institution with minimum GPA of 3.0 overall or in upper two years. Additional exam requirements/recommendations for international students: required—TOEFL (minimum score 550 paper-based; 79 iBT); recommended—IELTS. Electronic applications accepted.

University of South Florida Sarasota-Manatee, College of Liberal Arts and Social Sciences, Sarasota, FL 34243. Offers criminal justice (MA); education (MA); educational leadership (M Ed), including curriculum leadership, K-12 public school leadership, non-public/charter school leadership; elementary education (MAT); English education (MA); social work (MSW). *Program availability:* Part-time, 100% online, blended/hybrid learning. *Degree requirements:* For master's, comprehensive exam (for some programs). *Entrance requirements:* For master's, GRE. Additional exam requirements/recommendations for international students: required—TOEFL (minimum score 550 paper-based; 79 iBT), IELTS (minimum score 6.5). Electronic applications accepted.

The University of Texas at El Paso, Graduate School, College of Liberal Arts, Master of Arts in Interdisciplinary Studies Program, El Paso, TX 79968-0001. Offers MAIS. *Program availability:* Part-time, evening/weekend. *Entrance requirements:* For master's, GRE, minimum GPA of 3.0, letters of recommendation. Additional exam requirements/recommendations for international students: required—TOEFL; recommended—IELTS. Electronic applications accepted.

University of the Virgin Islands, College of Liberal Arts and Social Sciences, St. Thomas, VI 00802. Offers M Psych, MPA. *Program availability:* Part-time, evening/weekend. *Degree requirements:* For master's, comprehensive exam, thesis or

alternative. *Entrance requirements:* For master's, GRE, minimum GPA of 2.5. Additional exam requirements/recommendations for international students: required—TOEFL (minimum score 550 paper-based). Electronic applications accepted. *Expenses:* Contact institution.

The University of Toledo, College of Graduate Studies, College of Languages, Literature and Social Sciences, Master of Liberal Studies Program, Toledo, OH 43606-3390. Offers MLS. *Program availability:* Part-time, evening/weekend. *Degree requirements:* For master's, thesis. *Entrance requirements:* For master's, GRE if cumulative GPA is less than 3.0, minimum cumulative point-hour ratio of 2.7 for all previous academic work, three letters of recommendation, statement of purpose, transcripts from all prior institutions attended. Additional exam requirements/recommendations for international students: required—TOEFL (minimum score 550 paper-based; 80 iBT). Electronic applications accepted.

University of Wisconsin–Milwaukee, Graduate School, College of Letters and Science, Program in Liberal Studies, Milwaukee, WI 53201-0413. Offers MLS. *Entrance requirements:* For master's, interview, bachelor's degree. Additional exam requirements/recommendations for international students: required—TOEFL (minimum score 600 paper-based; 79 iBT), IELTS (minimum score 7). Electronic applications accepted.

Vanderbilt University, Program in Liberal Arts and Science, Nashville, TN 37240-1001. Offers MLAS. *Program availability:* Part-time. *Students:* 1 full-time (0 women), 27 part-time (19 women); includes 5 minority (3 Black or African American, non-Hispanic/Latino; 2 Two or more races, non-Hispanic/Latino). Average age 41. 8 applicants, 88% accepted, 4 enrolled. In 2019, 9 master's awarded. *Entrance requirements:* For master's, GRE General Test. Additional exam requirements/recommendations for international students: required—TOEFL (minimum score 570 paper-based; 88 iBT). *Application deadline:* For fall admission, 1/15 priority date for domestic students, 1/15 for international students; for spring admission, 11/15 for domestic and international students. Applications are processed on a rolling basis. *Expenses:* Tuition: Full-time $51,018; part-time $2087 per hour. *Required fees:* $542. Tuition and fees vary according to program. *Financial support:* Institutionally sponsored loans and tuition waivers (partial) available. *Unit head:* Andrea Hearn, Director, 615-875-5831, Fax: 615-343-8702, E-mail: andrea.l.hearn@vanderbilt.edu. *Application contact:* Andrea Hearn, Director, 615-875-5831, Fax: 615-343-8702, E-mail: andrea.l.hearn@vanderbilt.edu.
Website: http://www.vanderbilt.edu/mlas/

Villanova University, Graduate School of Liberal Arts and Sciences, Graduate Liberal Studies Program, Villanova, PA 19085-1699. Offers MA. *Program availability:* Part-time, evening/weekend. *Degree requirements:* For master's, comprehensive exam. *Entrance requirements:* For master's, GRE, statement of objectives, 2 letters of recommendation, writing sample. Additional exam requirements/recommendations for international students: required—TOEFL. Electronic applications accepted.

Virginia Polytechnic Institute and State University, VT Online, Blacksburg, VA 24061. Offers advanced transportation systems (Certificate); aerospace engineering (MS); agricultural and life sciences (MSLFS); business information systems (Graduate Certificate); career and technical education (MS); civil engineering (MS); computer engineering (M Eng, MS); decision support systems (Graduate Certificate); eLearning leadership (MA); electrical engineering (M Eng, MS); engineering administration (MEA); environmental engineering (Certificate); environmental politics and policy (Graduate Certificate); environmental sciences and engineering (MS); foundations of political analysis (Graduate Certificate); health product risk management (Graduate Certificate); industrial and systems engineering (MS); information policy and society (Graduate Certificate); information security (Graduate Certificate); information technology (MIT); instructional technology (MA); integrative STEM education (MA Ed); liberal arts (Graduate Certificate); life sciences: health product risk management (MS); natural resources (MNR, Graduate Certificate); networking (Graduate Certificate); nonprofit and nongovernmental organization management (Graduate Certificate); ocean engineering (MS); political science (MA); security studies (Graduate Certificate); software development (Graduate Certificate). *Expenses:* Tuition, state resident: full-time $13,700; part-time $761.25 per credit hour. Tuition, nonresident: full-time $27,614; part-time $1534 per credit hour. *Required fees:* $886.50 per term. Tuition and fees vary according to campus/location and program.

Wake Forest University, Graduate School of Arts and Sciences, Liberal Studies Program, Winston-Salem, NC 27109. Offers MALS. *Program availability:* Part-time. *Degree requirements:* For master's, thesis. *Entrance requirements:* Additional exam requirements/recommendations for international students: required—TOEFL (minimum score 79 iBT). Electronic applications accepted.

Washburn University, College of Arts and Sciences, Program in Liberal Studies, Topeka, KS 66621. Offers MLS. *Program availability:* Part-time, evening/weekend. *Degree requirements:* For master's, thesis, 15 seminar hours. *Entrance requirements:* For master's, minimum GPA of 3.0 in the last 60 hours of undergraduate coursework. Additional exam requirements/recommendations for international students: required—TOEFL (minimum score 80 iBT).

Wesleyan University, Graduate Liberal Studies Program, Middletown, CT 06459. Offers liberal arts (M Phil); liberal studies (MALS); writing (Graduate Certificate). *Program availability:* Part-time, evening/weekend. *Degree requirements:* For master's, thesis optional; for Graduate Certificate, thesis. *Entrance requirements:* For master's, statement of intent, essay, undergraduate transcripts, two academic letters of recommendation. Additional exam requirements/recommendations for international students: required—TOEFL (minimum score 100 iBT), IELTS (minimum score 7). Electronic applications accepted. *Expenses:* Contact institution.

Western Illinois University, School of Graduate Studies, College of Arts and Sciences, Program in Liberal Arts and Sciences, Macomb, IL 61455-1390. Offers MLAS. *Program availability:* Part-time. *Entrance requirements:* For master's, minimum GPA of 2.75, official transcripts, 1- to 2-page personal statement, academic paper, 3 letters of recommendation. Additional exam requirements/recommendations for international students: required—TOEFL (minimum score 580 paper-based; 92 iBT). Electronic applications accepted.

Wichita State University, Graduate School, Fairmount College of Liberal Arts and Sciences, Interdisciplinary Program in Liberal Studies, Wichita, KS 67260. Offers liberal studies (MA). *Program availability:* Part-time.

Winthrop University, College of Arts and Sciences, Program in Liberal Arts, Rock Hill, SC 29733. Offers MLA. *Program availability:* Part-time. *Entrance requirements:* For master's, interview, minimum GPA of 3.0. Additional exam requirements/recommendations for international students: required—TOEFL (minimum score 550 paper-based; 79 iBT), IELTS (minimum score 6). Electronic applications accepted. *Expenses: Tuition, area resident:* Full-time $7659; part-time $641 per credit hour. Tuition, state resident: full-time $7659; part-time $641 per credit hour. Tuition, nonresident: full-time $14,753; part-time $1234 per credit hour.

Section 9
Language and Literature

This section contains a directory of institutions offering graduate work in language and literature. Additional information about programs listed in the directory may be obtained by writing directly to the dean of a graduate school or chair of a department at the address given in the directory.

For programs offering related work, see also in this book *Area and Cultural Studies, Communication and Media, Political Science and International Affairs,* and *Sociology, Anthropology, and Archaeology.* In another guide in this series:

Graduate Programs in Business, Education, Information Studies, Law & Social Work

See *Special Focus* and *Subject Areas*

CONTENTS
Program Directories

Asian Languages

Cornell University, Graduate School, Graduate Fields of Arts and Sciences, Field of Linguistics, Ithaca, NY 14853. Offers applied linguistics (MA, PhD); East Asian linguistics (MA, PhD); English linguistics (MA, PhD); general linguistics (MA, PhD); Germanic linguistics (MA, PhD); Indo-European linguistics (MA, PhD); phonetics (MA, PhD); phonological theory (MA, PhD); Romance linguistics (MA, PhD); second language acquisition (MA, PhD); semantics (MA, PhD); Slavic linguistics (MA, PhD); sociolinguistics (MA, PhD); South Asian linguistics (MA, PhD); Southeast Asian linguistics (MA, PhD); syntactic theory (MA, PhD). Terminal master's awarded for partial completion of doctoral program. *Degree requirements:* For master's, one foreign language, thesis; for doctorate, one foreign language, comprehensive exam, thesis/dissertation. *Entrance requirements:* For master's and doctorate, GRE General Test, 2 letters of recommendation. Additional exam requirements/recommendations for international students: required—TOEFL (minimum score 600 paper-based; 77 iBT). Electronic applications accepted.

Harvard University, Graduate School of Arts and Sciences, Department of East Asian Languages and Civilizations, Cambridge, MA 02138. Offers Chinese (PhD); Japanese (PhD); Korean (PhD); Mongolian (PhD); Vietnamese (PhD). Terminal master's awarded for partial completion of doctoral program. *Degree requirements:* For doctorate, 3 foreign languages, thesis/dissertation, general exams. *Entrance requirements:* For doctorate, GRE General Test. Additional exam requirements/recommendations for international students: required—TOEFL.

Harvard University, Graduate School of Arts and Sciences, Department of Sanskrit and Indian Studies, Cambridge, MA 02138. Offers Indian philosophy (AM, PhD); Pali (AM, PhD); Sanskrit (AM, PhD); Tibetan (AM, PhD); Urdu (AM, PhD). Terminal master's awarded for partial completion of doctoral program. *Degree requirements:* For master's, 3 foreign languages; for doctorate, 3 foreign languages, thesis/dissertation. *Entrance requirements:* For master's, GRE General Test; for doctorate, GRE General Test, proficiency in French and German. Additional exam requirements/recommendations for international students: required—TOEFL.

Indiana University Bloomington, University Graduate School, College of Arts and Sciences, School of Global and International Studies, Department of East Asian Languages and Cultures, Bloomington, IN 47408. Offers Chinese (MA, PhD); Chinese language pedagogy (MA); East Asian studies (MA); Japanese (MA, PhD); Japanese language pedagogy (MA). *Program availability:* Part-time. *Degree requirements:* For master's, one foreign language, thesis; for doctorate, 2 foreign languages, comprehensive exam, thesis/dissertation. *Entrance requirements:* Additional exam requirements/recommendations for international students: required—TOEFL (minimum score 93 iBT). Electronic applications accepted.

The Ohio State University, Graduate School, College of Arts and Sciences, Division of Arts and Humanities, Department of East Asian Languages and Literatures, Columbus, OH 43210. Offers Chinese (MA, PhD); Japanese (MA, PhD). Terminal master's awarded for partial completion of doctoral program. *Entrance requirements:* For master's and doctorate, GRE General Test (if applying for financial aid). Additional exam requirements/recommendations for international students: required—TOEFL (minimum score 577 paper-based; 90 iBT); recommended—IELTS (minimum score 7.5). Electronic applications accepted.

St. John's College, Graduate Institute in Liberal Education, Program in Eastern Classics, Santa Fe, NM 87505. Offers MA. *Program availability:* Part-time, evening/weekend. *Entrance requirements:* For master's, 2 letters of recommendation. Additional exam requirements/recommendations for international students: required—TOEFL, TWE. *Expenses:* Contact institution.

Stanford University, School of Humanities and Sciences, Department of East Asian Languages and Cultures, Stanford, CA 94305-2004. Offers Chinese (MA, PhD); Japanese (PhD). *Expenses: Tuition:* Full-time $52,479; part-time $34,110 per unit. *Required fees:* $672; $224 per quarter. Tuition and fees vary according to program and student level.
Website: http://www.stanford.edu/dept/asianlang/

University of California, Berkeley, Graduate Division, College of Letters and Science, Department of South and Southeast Asian Studies, Berkeley, CA 94720. Offers Hindi (MA, PhD); Indonesian (MA, PhD); Sanskrit (MA, PhD); Tamil (MA, PhD). Terminal master's awarded for partial completion of doctoral program. *Degree requirements:* For master's, 2 foreign languages, thesis; for doctorate, 2 foreign languages, thesis/dissertation, oral qualifying exam. *Entrance requirements:* For master's and doctorate, GRE General Test, minimum GPA of 3.0, 3 letters of recommendation. Electronic applications accepted.

University of California, Irvine, School of Humanities, East Asian Studies, Irvine, CA 92697. Offers Chinese (MA, PhD); East Asian languages and literatures (MA, PhD); Japanese (MA, PhD). *Students:* 10 full-time (8 women); includes 3 minority (1 American Indian or Alaska Native, non-Hispanic/Latino; 2 Asian, non-Hispanic/Latino), 1 international. Average age 32. 38 applicants, 11% accepted, 2 enrolled. In 2019, 3 doctorates awarded. *Entrance requirements:* For master's and doctorate, GRE General Test, minimum GPA of 3.0. Additional exam requirements/recommendations for international students: required—TOEFL (minimum score 550 paper-based). *Application deadline:* For fall admission, 1/15 priority date for domestic students, 1/15 for international students. Application fee: $120 ($140 for international students). Electronic applications accepted. *Financial support:* Fellowships, research assistantships with full tuition reimbursements, teaching assistantships with partial tuition reimbursements, institutionally sponsored loans, traineeships, health care benefits, and unspecified assistantships available. Financial award application deadline: 3/1; financial award applicants required to submit FAFSA. *Unit head:* Hu Ying, Chair, 949-824-3248, E-mail: huying@uci.edu. *Application contact:* Stephanie Wijetilleke, Graduate Program Administrator, 949-824-1601, E-mail: sisnali@uci.edu.
Website: http://www.hnet.uci.edu/eastasian/

University of California, Los Angeles, Graduate Division, College of Letters and Science, Department of Asian Languages and Cultures, Los Angeles, CA 90095. Offers MA, PhD. Terminal master's awarded for partial completion of doctoral program. *Degree requirements:* For master's, one foreign language, comprehensive exam or thesis; for doctorate, 2 foreign languages, thesis/dissertation, oral and written qualifying exams. *Entrance requirements:* For master's, GRE General Test, bachelor's degree; minimum undergraduate GPA of 3.0 (or its equivalent if letter grade system not used); writing sample; for doctorate, GRE General Test, master's degree; minimum undergraduate GPA of 3.0 (or its equivalent if letter grade system not used); writing sample. Additional exam requirements/recommendations for international students: required—TOEFL. Electronic applications accepted.

University of California, Santa Barbara, Graduate Division, College of Letters and Sciences, Division of Humanities and Fine Arts, Department of East Asian Languages and Cultural Studies, Santa Barbara, CA 93106-7075. Offers applied linguistics (PhD); East Asian languages and cultural studies (MA); translation studies (PhD). *Degree requirements:* For master's, one foreign language, comprehensive exam (for some programs), thesis (for some programs); for doctorate, 2 foreign languages, thesis/dissertation, methodology. *Entrance requirements:* For master's and doctorate, GRE General Test. Additional exam requirements/recommendations for international students: required—TOEFL (minimum score 550 paper-based; 80 iBT), IELTS (minimum score 7). Electronic applications accepted.

University of California, Santa Barbara, Graduate Division, College of Letters and Sciences, Division of Humanities and Fine Arts, Program in Comparative Literature, Santa Barbara, CA 93106-4130. Offers comparative literature (PhD); East Asian literatures (PhD); feminist studies (PhD); French (PhD); global studies (PhD); translation studies (PhD); MA/PhD. *Degree requirements:* For doctorate, 2 foreign languages, comprehensive exam, thesis/dissertation. *Entrance requirements:* For doctorate, GRE. Additional exam requirements/recommendations for international students: required—TOEFL (minimum score 550 paper-based; 80 iBT), IELTS (minimum score 7). Electronic applications accepted.

University of Chicago, Division of the Humanities, Department of East Asian Languages and Civilizations, Chicago, IL 60637. Offers PhD. Terminal master's awarded for partial completion of doctoral program. *Degree requirements:* For doctorate, 2 foreign languages, comprehensive exam, thesis/dissertation, qualifying exam. *Entrance requirements:* For doctorate, GRE General Test, 15-20 page writing sample, statement of purpose, 3 letters of recommendation, transcripts for all previous degrees and institutions attended. Additional exam requirements/recommendations for international students: required—TOEFL (minimum score 104 iBT), IELTS (minimum score 7). Electronic applications accepted.

University of Chicago, Division of the Humanities, Department of South Asian Languages and Civilizations, Chicago, IL 60637. Offers South Asian languages and civilizations (PhD), including Bengali, Hindi, Sanskrit, Tamil, Urdu. Terminal master's awarded for partial completion of doctoral program. *Degree requirements:* For doctorate, 3 foreign languages, comprehensive exam, thesis/dissertation. *Entrance requirements:* For doctorate, GRE General Test, 15-20 page writing sample, statement of purpose, 3 letters of recommendation, transcripts for all previous degrees and institutions attended. Additional exam requirements/recommendations for international students: required—TOEFL (minimum score 104 iBT), IELTS (minimum score 7). Electronic applications accepted.

University of Hawaii at Manoa, Office of Graduate Education, College of Languages, Linguistics and Literature, Department of East Asian Languages and Literatures, Program in Korean, Honolulu, HI 96822. Offers MA, PhD. *Program availability:* Part-time. *Degree requirements:* For master's, 2 foreign languages, thesis optional; for doctorate, 2 foreign languages, comprehensive exam, thesis/dissertation. *Entrance requirements:* For master's and doctorate, GRE General Test. Additional exam requirements/recommendations for international students: required—TOEFL (minimum score 560 paper-based; 83 iBT), IELTS (minimum score 5).

University of Illinois at Urbana-Champaign, Graduate College, College of Liberal Arts and Sciences, School of Literatures, Cultures and Linguistics, Department of East Asian Languages and Cultures, Champaign, IL 61820. Offers East Asian languages and cultures (PhD); East Asian studies (MA).

The University of Iowa, Graduate College, College of Liberal Arts and Sciences, Program in Asian Civilizations, Iowa City, IA 52242-1316. Offers Chinese (MA); Hindi (MA); Sanskrit (MA); South Asian studies (MA). *Degree requirements:* For master's, thesis optional, exam. *Entrance requirements:* For master's, GRE General Test, minimum GPA of 3.0. Additional exam requirements/recommendations for international students: required—TOEFL (minimum score 590 paper-based; 96 iBT). Electronic applications accepted.

The University of Kansas, Graduate Studies, College of Liberal Arts and Sciences, Department of East Asian Languages and Cultures, Lawrence, KS 66045. Offers MA, Graduate Certificate. *Program availability:* Part-time. *Students:* 3 full-time (2 women), 1 international. Average age 27. 6 applicants, 67% accepted. In 2019, 2 master's awarded. *Entrance requirements:* For master's, GRE, current curriculum vitae, statement of purpose explaining academic objectives, writing sample that demonstrates writing skills and basic research capacity, three letters of recommendation, transcripts. Additional exam requirements/recommendations for international students: required—TOEFL, IELTS. *Application deadline:* For fall admission, 2/1 priority date for domestic and international students. Application fee: $65 ($85 for international students). Electronic applications accepted. *Expenses:* Tuition, state resident: full-time $9989. Tuition, nonresident: full-time $23,950. *International tuition:* $23,950 full-time. *Required fees:* $984; $81.99 per credit hour. Tuition and fees vary according to course load, campus/location and program. *Financial support:* Fellowships, teaching assistantships, and unspecified assistantships available. *Unit head:* Dr. Hui Xiao, Chair, 785-864-9079, E-mail: hxiao@ku.edu. *Application contact:* Jared Nietfeld, Graduate Admissions Contact, 785-864-0482, E-mail: nietfeld@ku.edu.
Website: http://ealc.ku.edu/

University of Michigan, Rackham Graduate School, College of Literature, Science, and the Arts, Department of Asian Languages and Cultures, Ann Arbor, MI 48104. Offers PhD. Terminal master's awarded for partial completion of doctoral program. *Degree requirements:* For doctorate, 2 foreign languages, comprehensive exam, thesis/dissertation, preliminary exams, oral defense of dissertation. *Entrance requirements:* Additional exam requirements/recommendations for international students: required—TOEFL (minimum score 560 paper-based; 84 iBT), IELTS (minimum score 6.5). Electronic applications accepted.

University of Minnesota, Twin Cities Campus, Graduate School, College of Liberal Arts, Department of Asian Languages and Literatures, Minneapolis, MN 55455-0213. Offers Asian literatures, cultures, and media (PhD). *Degree requirements:* For doctorate, comprehensive exam, thesis/dissertation. *Entrance requirements:* For doctorate, GRE, 3 letters of recommendation. Additional exam requirements/recommendations for international students: required—TOEFL (minimum score 550 paper-based), IELTS (minimum score 6.5). Electronic applications accepted.

University of Oregon, Graduate School, College of Arts and Sciences, Department of East Asian Languages and Literature, Eugene, OR 97403. Offers Chinese (MA, PhD); Japanese (MA, PhD). *Entrance requirements:* Additional exam requirements/recommendations for international students: required—TOEFL.

University of Southern California, Graduate School, Dana and David Dornsife College of Letters, Arts and Sciences, Department of East Asian Languages and Cultures, Los Angeles, CA 90089. Offers classical Chinese literature (MA, PhD); classical Japanese literature (MA, PhD); linguistics (MA, PhD); modern Chinese literature (MA, PhD); modern Japanese literature (MA, PhD); modern Korean literature (MA, PhD). *Degree requirements:* For master's, thesis; for doctorate, 2 foreign languages, comprehensive exam, thesis/dissertation. *Entrance requirements:* For master's and doctorate, GRE, BA in relevant field. Additional exam requirements/recommendations for international students: required—TOEFL. Electronic applications accepted.

University of Southern California, Graduate School, Dana and David Dornsife College of Letters, Arts and Sciences, Department of Linguistics, Los Angeles, CA 90089. Offers East Asian linguistics (PhD); Hispanic linguistics (PhD); linguistics (PhD); Slavic linguistics (PhD). *Degree requirements:* For doctorate, comprehensive exam, thesis/dissertation. *Entrance requirements:* For doctorate, GRE. Additional exam requirements/recommendations for international students: required—TOEFL (minimum score 100 iBT). Electronic applications accepted.

The University of Texas at Austin, Graduate School, College of Liberal Arts, Department of Asian Studies, Austin, TX 78712-1111. Offers Asian cultures and languages (MA, PhD); Asian studies (MA). *Program availability:* Part-time. *Degree requirements:* For master's, thesis; for doctorate, 3 foreign languages, thesis/dissertation. *Entrance requirements:* For master's and doctorate, GRE General Test. Electronic applications accepted.

University of Washington, Graduate School, College of Arts and Sciences, Department of Asian Languages and Literature, Seattle, WA 98195. Offers Buddhist studies (MA, PhD); Chinese language and literature (MA, PhD); Japanese language and literature (MA, PhD); Korean language and literature (MA, PhD); South Asian language and literature (MA, PhD). *Degree requirements:* For master's, 2 foreign languages,

general exam, thesis or 2 research papers; for doctorate, 3 foreign languages, thesis/dissertation, general exam. *Entrance requirements:* For master's, GRE, minimum GPA of 3.0; for doctorate, GRE, master's degree in related field, minimum GPA of 3.0. Additional exam requirements/recommendations for international students: required—TOEFL. Electronic applications accepted.

University of Wisconsin–Madison, Graduate School, College of Letters and Science, Department of Languages and Cultures of Asia, Madison, WI 53706-1380. Offers civilizations and cultures (PhD); languages and cultures of Asia (MA); languages and literatures (PhD); religions of Asia (PhD). *Program availability:* Part-time. Terminal master's awarded for partial completion of doctoral program. *Degree requirements:* For master's, one foreign language, thesis or alternative; for doctorate, 2 foreign languages, thesis/dissertation. *Entrance requirements:* For master's, minimum GPA of 3.0; for doctorate, minimum GPA of 3.25, master's degree. Electronic applications accepted.

Washington University in St. Louis, The Graduate School, Department of East Asian Languages and Cultures, St. Louis, MO 63130-4899. Offers Chinese (MA); Chinese and comparative literature (PhD); Chinese language and literature (PhD); East Asian studies (MA); Japanese (MA); Japanese and comparative literature (PhD); Japanese language and literature (PhD). Terminal master's awarded for partial completion of doctoral program. *Degree requirements:* For master's, thesis optional; for doctorate, thesis/dissertation. *Entrance requirements:* For master's and doctorate, GRE General Test. Additional exam requirements/recommendations for international students: required—TOEFL. Electronic applications accepted.

Yale University, Graduate School of Arts and Sciences, Department of East Asian Languages and Literatures, New Haven, CT 06520. Offers East Asian languages and literatures (PhD); East Asian languages and literatures and film studies (PhD). *Degree requirements:* For doctorate, 2 foreign languages, thesis/dissertation. *Entrance requirements:* For doctorate, GRE General Test.

Celtic Languages

Harvard University, Graduate School of Arts and Sciences, Department of Celtic Languages and Literatures, Cambridge, MA 02138. Offers Irish (PhD); Welsh (PhD). *Degree requirements:* For doctorate, thesis/dissertation, proficiency in 2 Celtic languages; reading knowledge of French, German, and Latin. *Entrance requirements:* For doctorate, GRE General Test. Additional exam requirements/recommendations for international students: required—TOEFL.

Chinese

Arizona State University at Tempe, College of Liberal Arts and Sciences, School of International Letters and Cultures, Program in Chinese, Tempe, AZ 85287-0202. Offers Asian languages and civilizations: Chinese (MA); Chinese (PhD). *Program availability:* Part-time, evening/weekend. Terminal master's awarded for partial completion of doctoral program. *Degree requirements:* For master's, thesis, oral defense, interactive Program of Study (iPOS) submitted no later than beginning of third semester of study; for doctorate, comprehensive exam, thesis/dissertation, interactive Program of Study (iPOS) submitted before completing 50 percent of required credit hours. *Entrance requirements:* For master's, GRE, minimum GPA of 3.0 in the last two years of work leading to the bachelor's degree, BA in Chinese studies (preferred), personal statement, writing sample, 3 letters of recommendation; for doctorate, GRE, minimum GPA of 3.5 in the last two years of work leading to the bachelor's degree, completion of 3 years of modern Chinese and 1 year of classical Chinese, personal statement, writing sample, 3 letters of recommendation. Additional exam requirements/recommendations for international students: required—TOEFL (minimum score 550 paper-based; 83 iBT), IELTS (minimum score 6.5). Electronic applications accepted.

Brandeis University, Graduate School of Arts and Sciences, Teaching Chinese at the College Level, Waltham, MA 02454-9110. Offers MA. *Faculty:* 4 full-time (2 women), 1 (woman) part-time/adjunct. *Students:* 7 full-time (all women); includes 1 minority (Asian, non-Hispanic/Latino), 6 international. Average age 28. 10 applicants, 90% accepted, 7 enrolled. In 2019, 7 master's awarded. *Degree requirements:* For master's, one foreign language. *Entrance requirements:* For master's, transcripts, letters of recommendation, resume, portfolio, and statement of purpose. Additional exam requirements/recommendations for international students: required—TOEFL, IELTS, PTE. *Application deadline:* For fall admission, 1/15 for domestic and international students. Applications are processed on a rolling basis. Application fee: $75. Electronic applications accepted. *Financial support:* Scholarships/grants available. *Unit head:* Dr. Yu Feng, Director of Graduate Studies, 781-736-2961, E-mail: yfeng@brandeis.edu. *Application contact:* Dr. Yu Feng, Director of Graduate Studies, 781-736-2961, E-mail: yfeng@brandeis.edu. Website: http://www.brandeis.edu/gsas/programs/chinese.html

DePaul University, College of Liberal Arts and Social Sciences, Chicago, IL 60614. Offers Arabic (MA); Chinese (MA); critical ethnic studies (MA); English (MA); French (MA); German (MA); history (MA); interdisciplinary studies (MA, MS); international public service (MS); international studies (MA); Italian (MA); Japanese (MA); liberal studies (MA); nonprofit management (MNM); public administration (MPA); public health (MPH); public policy (MPP); public service management (MS); refugee and forced migration studies (MS); social work (MSW); sociology (MA); Spanish (MA); sustainable urban development (MA); women's and gender studies (MA); writing and publishing (MA); writing, rhetoric and discourse (MA); MA/PhD. *Accreditation:* CEPH. *Program availability:* Part-time, evening/weekend, online learning. Terminal master's awarded for partial completion of doctoral program. *Degree requirements:* For master's, variable foreign language requirement, comprehensive exam (for some programs), thesis (for some programs). Electronic applications accepted.

Harvard University, Graduate School of Arts and Sciences, Department of East Asian Languages and Civilizations, Cambridge, MA 02138. Offers Chinese (PhD); Japanese (PhD); Korean (PhD); Mongolian (PhD); Vietnamese (PhD). Terminal master's awarded for partial completion of doctoral program. *Degree requirements:* For doctorate, 3 foreign languages, thesis/dissertation, general exams. *Entrance requirements:* For doctorate, GRE General Test. Additional exam requirements/recommendations for international students: required—TOEFL.

Hunter College of the City University of New York, Graduate School, School of Arts and Sciences, Department of Classical and Oriental Studies, Program in Teaching Chinese, New York, NY 10065-5085. Offers MA.

Indiana University Bloomington, University Graduate School, College of Arts and Sciences, School of Global and International Studies, Department of East Asian Languages and Cultures, Bloomington, IN 47408. Offers Chinese (MA, PhD); Chinese language pedagogy (MA); East Asian studies (MA); Japanese (MA, PhD); Japanese language pedagogy (MA). *Program availability:* Part-time. *Degree requirements:* For master's, one foreign language, thesis; for doctorate, 2 foreign languages, comprehensive exam, thesis/dissertation. *Entrance requirements:* Additional exam requirements/recommendations for international students: required—TOEFL (minimum score 93 iBT). Electronic applications accepted.

Middlebury College, Language Schools, Chinese School, Middlebury, VT 05753-6002. Offers MA. In 2019, 7 master's awarded. *Degree requirements:* For master's, one foreign language, teaching practicum. *Entrance requirements:* For master's, placement test, 3 letters of recommendation, writing sample, curriculum vitae, official transcripts of undergraduate coursework. Additional exam requirements/recommendations for international students: required—TOEFL (minimum score 600 paper-based; 100 iBT), IELTS (minimum score 7.5). *Application deadline:* Applications are processed on a rolling basis. Application fee: $75. Electronic applications accepted. *Expenses:* Contact institution. *Financial support:* Fellowships and scholarships/grants available. Financial award application deadline: 3/15; financial award applicants required to submit FAFSA. *Unit head:* Cecilia Chang, Director, 802-443-5520, Fax: 802-443-3510, E-mail: cchang@middlebury.edu. *Application contact:* Mimi Clark, Coordinator, 802-443-5520, Fax: 802-443-2075, E-mail: chineseschool@middlebury.edu. Website: http://www.middlebury.edu/ls/grad_programs/chinese

New York University, Steinhardt School of Culture, Education, and Human Development, Department of Teaching and Learning, Program in Multilingual/Multicultural Studies, New York, NY 10012. Offers bilingual education (MA, PhD, Advanced Certificate); foreign language education (MA); teaching English to speakers of other languages (MA, PhD); teaching foreign languages, 7-12 (MA), including Chinese, French, Italian, Japanese, Spanish; teaching French as a foreign language (MA), including teaching English to speakers of other languages; teaching Spanish as a foreign language (MA), including teaching English to speakers of other languages. *Accreditation:* TEAC. *Program availability:* Part-time, evening/weekend. *Entrance requirements:* For doctorate, GRE General Test, interview; for Advanced Certificate, master's degree. Additional exam requirements/recommendations for international students: required—TOEFL (minimum score 100 iBT). Electronic applications accepted.

The Ohio State University, Graduate School, College of Arts and Sciences, Division of Arts and Humanities, Department of East Asian Languages and Literatures, Columbus, OH 43210. Offers Chinese (MA, PhD); Japanese (MA, PhD). Terminal master's awarded for partial completion of doctoral program. *Entrance requirements:* For master's and doctorate, GRE General Test (if applying for financial aid). Additional exam requirements/recommendations for international students: required—TOEFL (minimum score 577 paper-based; 90 iBT); recommended—IELTS (minimum score 7.5). Electronic applications accepted.

Saginaw Valley State University, College of Education, Program in Teaching Chinese as a Foreign Language, University Center, MI 48710. Offers MAT. *Program availability:* Part-time, evening/weekend. *Students:* 12 full-time (7 women), all international. Average age 27. 9 applicants, 100% accepted, 6 enrolled. In 2019, 5 master's awarded. *Entrance requirements:* For master's, minimum GPA of 3.0. Additional exam requirements/recommendations for international students: required—TOEFL (minimum score 550 paper-based; 79 iBT). *Application deadline:* For fall admission, 7/15 for international students; for winter admission, 11/15 for international students; for spring admission, 4/15 for international students. Applications are processed on a rolling basis. Application fee: $30 ($90 for international students). Electronic applications accepted. *Expenses: Tuition, area resident:* Full-time $11,212; part-time $622.90 per credit hour. Tuition, state resident: full-time $11,212; part-time $622.90 per credit hour. Tuition, nonresident: full-time $11,212; part-time $1253 per credit hour. *Required fees:* $263; $14.60 per credit hour. Tuition and fees vary according to course load, degree level and program. *Financial support:* Federal Work-Study and scholarships/grants available. Support available to part-time students. Financial award application deadline: 4/1; financial award applicants required to submit FAFSA. *Unit head:* Dr. Craig Douglas, Dean, 989-964-4057, Fax: 989-964-4563, E-mail: coeconnect@svsu.edu. *Application contact:* Jenna Briggs, Director, Graduate and International Admissions, 989-964-6096, Fax: 989-964-2788, E-mail: gradadm@svsu.edu.

San Francisco State University, Division of Graduate Studies, College of Liberal and Creative Arts, Department of Modern Languages and Literatures, Program in Chinese, San Francisco, CA 94132-1722. Offers MA. *Application deadline:* Applications are processed on a rolling basis. *Expenses: Tuition, area resident:* Full-time $7176; part-time $4164 per year. Tuition, state resident: full-time $7176; part-time $4164 per year. Tuition, nonresident: full-time $16,680; part-time $396 per unit. *International tuition:* $16,680 full-time. *Required fees:* $1524; $1524 per unit. $762 per semester. Tuition and fees vary according to degree level and program. *Unit head:* Dr. Frederik Green, Program Coordinator, 415-338-3120, Fax: 415-338-6159, E-mail: fgreen@sfsu.edu. *Application contact:* Dr. Chris Wen-Chao Li, Program Coordinator and Graduate Advisor, 415-338-1034, Fax: 415-338-6159, E-mail: wenchao@sfsu.edu.
Website: http://chinese.sfsu.edu/

Stanford University, School of Humanities and Sciences, Department of East Asian Languages and Cultures, Stanford, CA 94305-2004. Offers Chinese (MA, PhD); Japanese (PhD). *Expenses: Tuition:* Full-time $52,479; part-time $34,110 per unit. *Required fees:* $672; $224 per quarter. Tuition and fees vary according to program and student level.
Website: http://www.stanford.edu/dept/asianlang/

University of Alberta, Faculty of Graduate Studies and Research, Department of East Asian Studies, Edmonton, AB T6G 2E1, Canada. Offers Chinese literature (MA); East Asian interdisciplinary studies (MA); Japanese literature (MA). *Program availability:* Part-time. *Degree requirements:* For master's, one foreign language, thesis. *Entrance requirements:* Additional exam requirements/recommendations for international students: required—TOEFL. Electronic applications accepted.

University of California, Berkeley, Graduate Division, College of Letters and Science, Department of East Asian Languages and Cultures, Berkeley, CA 94720. Offers Chinese language (PhD); Japanese language (PhD). *Degree requirements:* For doctorate, one foreign language, thesis/dissertation, oral qualifying exam. *Entrance requirements:* For doctorate, GRE General Test, minimum GPA of 3.0, MA thesis, 3 letters of recommendation. Electronic applications accepted.

University of California, Irvine, School of Humanities, East Asian Studies, Irvine, CA 92697. Offers Chinese (MA, PhD); East Asian languages and literatures (MA, PhD); Japanese (MA, PhD). *Students:* 10 full-time (8 women); includes 3 minority (1 American Indian or Alaska Native, non-Hispanic/Latino; 2 Asian, non-Hispanic/Latino), 1 international. Average age 32. 38 applicants, 11% accepted, 2 enrolled. In 2019, 3 doctorates awarded. *Entrance requirements:* For master's and doctorate, GRE General Test, minimum GPA of 3.0. Additional exam requirements/recommendations for international students: required—TOEFL (minimum score 550 paper-based). *Application deadline:* For fall admission, 1/15 priority date for domestic students, 1/15 for international students. Application fee: $120 ($140 for international students). Electronic applications accepted. *Financial support:* Fellowships, research assistantships with full tuition reimbursements, teaching assistantships with partial tuition reimbursements, institutionally sponsored loans, traineeships, health care benefits, and unspecified assistantships available. Financial award application deadline: 3/1; financial award applicants required to submit FAFSA. *Unit head:* Hu Ying, Chair, 949-824-3248, E-mail: huying@uci.edu. *Application contact:* Stephanie Wijetilleke, Graduate Program Administrator, 949-824-1601, E-mail: sisnali@uci.edu.
Website: http://www.hnet.uci.edu/eastasian/

University of Colorado Boulder, Graduate School, College of Arts and Sciences, Department of Asian Languages and Civilizations, Boulder, CO 80309. Offers MA, PhD. Terminal master's awarded for partial completion of doctoral program. *Degree requirements:* For master's, comprehensive exam. *Entrance requirements:* For master's, BA in Chinese or Japanese, minimum undergraduate GPA of 3.0. Additional exam requirements/recommendations for international students: required—TOEFL. Electronic applications accepted. Application fee is waived when completed online.

University of Delaware, College of Arts and Sciences, Department of Foreign Languages and Literatures, Newark, DE 19716. Offers foreign languages and literatures (MA), including French, German, Spanish; foreign languages pedagogy (MA), including French, German, Spanish; technical Chinese translation (MA). *Degree requirements:* For master's, one foreign language, comprehensive exam, thesis optional. *Entrance requirements:* For master's, GRE General Test, letters of recommendation, writing sample. Additional exam requirements/recommendations for international students: required—TOEFL. Electronic applications accepted.

University of Hawaii at Manoa, Office of Graduate Education, College of Languages, Linguistics and Literature, Department of East Asian Languages and Literatures, Program in Chinese, Honolulu, HI 96822. Offers MA, PhD. *Program availability:* Part-time. *Degree requirements:* For master's, 2 foreign languages, thesis optional; for doctorate, 2 foreign languages, comprehensive exam, thesis/dissertation. *Entrance requirements:* For master's and doctorate, GRE General Test. Additional exam requirements/recommendations for international students: required—TOEFL (minimum score 560 paper-based; 83 iBT), IELTS (minimum score 5).

University of Hawaii at Manoa, Office of Graduate Education, School of Pacific and Asian Studies, Program in Asian Studies, Concentration in Chinese Studies, Honolulu, HI 96822. Offers Graduate Certificate. *Program availability:* Part-time. *Degree requirements:* For Graduate Certificate, one foreign language. *Entrance requirements:* For degree, GRE. Additional exam requirements/recommendations for international students: required—TOEFL (minimum score 560 paper-based; 83 iBT), IELTS (minimum score 5).

The University of Iowa, Graduate College, College of Liberal Arts and Sciences, Program in Asian Civilizations, Iowa City, IA 52242-1316. Offers Chinese (MA); Hindi (MA); Sanskrit (MA); South Asian studies (MA). *Degree requirements:* For master's, thesis optional, exam. *Entrance requirements:* For master's, GRE General Test, minimum GPA of 3.0. Additional exam requirements/recommendations for international students: required—TOEFL (minimum score 590 paper-based; 96 iBT). Electronic applications accepted.

The University of Manchester, School of Arts, Languages and Cultures, Manchester, United Kingdom. Offers anthropology, media and performance (PhD); applied theatre (PhD); Arab world studies (PhD); archaeology (PhD); art history and visual studies (PhD); arts and cultural management (PhD); arts management and cultural policy (PhD); Chinese studies (PhD); classics and ancient history (PhD); composition (PhD); creative writing (PhD); drama (PhD); East Asian studies (PhD); electroacoustic composition (PhD); English and American studies (PhD); English language (PhD); French studies (PhD); German studies (PhD); history (PhD); humanitarianism and conflict response (PhD); interpreting studies (PhD); Japanese studies (PhD); Latin American cultural studies (PhD); linguistics (PhD); Middle Eastern studies (PhD); museology (PhD); museum practice (PhD); music (PhD); musicology (PhD); Polish studies (PhD); Portuguese studies (PhD); religions and theology (PhD); Russian studies (PhD); Spanish studies (PhD); translation and intercultural studies (PhD).

University of Massachusetts Amherst, Graduate School, College of Humanities and Fine Arts, Department of Languages, Literatures, and Cultures, Programs in Asian Languages and Literatures, Amherst, MA 01003. Offers Chinese (MA); Japanese (MA). *Program availability:* Part-time. *Degree requirements:* For master's, thesis, general exam. *Entrance requirements:* For master's, GRE General Test. Additional exam requirements/recommendations for international students: required—TOEFL (minimum score 550 paper-based; 80 iBT), IELTS (minimum score 6.5). Electronic applications accepted.

University of Oregon, Graduate School, College of Arts and Sciences, Department of East Asian Languages and Literature, Eugene, OR 97403. Offers Chinese (MA, PhD); Japanese (MA, PhD). *Entrance requirements:* Additional exam requirements/recommendations for international students: required—TOEFL.

University of Pittsburgh, Kenneth P. Dietrich School of Arts and Sciences, Department of East Asian Languages and Literatures, Pittsburgh, PA 15260. Offers Chinese (MA); Japanese (MA). *Program availability:* Part-time. *Faculty:* 6 full-time (4 women), 13 part-time/adjunct (10 women). *Students:* 3 full-time (2 women); includes 2 minority (1 Black or African American, non-Hispanic/Latino; 1 Asian, non-Hispanic/Latino). Average age 27. 13 applicants, 62% accepted, 2 enrolled. *Degree requirements:* For master's, one foreign language, comprehensive exam, thesis. *Entrance requirements:* For master's, personal statement, transcript copies, 3 letters of recommendation (online submissions), writing sample (in English). Additional exam requirements/recommendations for international students: required—TOEFL (minimum score 90 iBT), IELTS (minimum score 7). *Application deadline:* For fall admission, 1/15 for domestic and international students. Application fee: $50. Electronic applications accepted. *Expenses:* $24,480 in-state, $40,848 out-of-state. *Financial support:* Scholarships/grants, health care benefits, tuition waivers (full and partial), and unspecified assistantships available. Financial award application deadline: 1/15. *Unit head:* Dr. Hiroshi Nara, Chair, 412-624-5579, Fax: 412-624-3458, E-mail: hnara@pitt.edu. *Application contact:* Keanna Cash, Graduate Administrator, 412-624-5227, E-mail: kec176@pitt.edu.
Website: http://deall.pitt.edu/

University of Washington, Graduate School, College of Arts and Sciences, Department of Asian Languages and Literature, Seattle, WA 98195. Offers Buddhist studies (MA, PhD); Chinese language and literature (MA, PhD); Japanese language and literature (MA, PhD); Korean language and literature (MA, PhD); South Asian language and literature (MA, PhD). *Degree requirements:* For master's, 2 foreign languages, general exam, thesis or 2 research papers; for doctorate, 3 foreign languages, thesis/dissertation, general exam. *Entrance requirements:* For master's, GRE, minimum GPA of 3.0; for doctorate, GRE, master's degree in related field, minimum GPA of 3.0. Additional exam requirements/recommendations for international students: required—TOEFL. Electronic applications accepted.

University of Wisconsin–Madison, Graduate School, College of Letters and Science, Department of East Asian Languages and Literature, Program in Chinese Literature, Madison, WI 53706-1380. Offers MA, PhD. *Program availability:* Part-time. Terminal master's awarded for partial completion of doctoral program. *Degree requirements:* For master's, one foreign language, seminars, written exam; for doctorate, 3 foreign languages, thesis/dissertation, seminars, preliminary exams, oral exam. *Entrance requirements:* For master's, bachelor's degree or equivalent in Chinese; for doctorate, master's degree or equivalent in Chinese. Electronic applications accepted.

Washington University in St. Louis, The Graduate School, Department of East Asian Languages and Cultures, St. Louis, MO 63130-4899. Offers Chinese (MA); Chinese and comparative literature (PhD); Chinese language and literature (PhD); East Asian studies (MA); Japanese (MA); Japanese and comparative literature (PhD); Japanese language and literature (PhD). Terminal master's awarded for partial completion of doctoral program. *Degree requirements:* For master's, thesis optional; for doctorate, thesis/dissertation. *Entrance requirements:* For master's and doctorate, GRE General Test. Additional exam requirements/recommendations for international students: required—TOEFL. Electronic applications accepted.

Classics

Asbury University, School of Graduate and Professional Studies, Wilmore, KY 40390-1198. Offers biology: alternative certificate (MA Ed); chemistry: alternative certificate (MA Ed); English (MA Ed); English as a second language (MA Ed); ESL (MA Ed); French (MA Ed); Latin: alternative certificate (MA Ed); mathematics: alternative certificate (MA Ed); reading/writing endorsement (MA Ed); social studies (MA Ed); social work (MSW), including child and family services; Spanish (MA Ed); special education (MA Ed); special education: alternative certificate (MA Ed); teacher as leader endorsement (MA Ed). *Accreditation:* NCATE. *Program availability:* Part-time. *Degree requirements:* For master's, action research project, portfolio. *Entrance requirements:* For master's, PRAXIS/NTE, minimum GPA of 2.75, letters of recommendation. Additional exam requirements/recommendations for international students: required—TOEFL (minimum score 550 paper-based). Electronic applications accepted.

Bethel Seminary, Graduate and Professional Programs, St. Paul, MN 55112-6998. Offers Anglican studies (Certificate); children's and family ministry (MA); Christian studies (Certificate); Christian thought (MA); church planting (Certificate); Greek and Hebrew language (M Div); Greek language (M Div); Hebrew language (M Div); marriage and family therapy (MA, Certificate); mental health counseling (MA); ministry (MA, D Min); ministry practice (Certificate); theological studies (MA, Certificate); transformational leadership (MA); young life youth ministry (Certificate). *Accreditation:* ACIPE. *Program availability:* Part-time, evening/weekend, 100% online, blended/hybrid learning. *Degree requirements:* For master's, variable foreign language requirement, thesis (for some programs); for doctorate, thesis/dissertation. *Entrance requirements:* For master's, letters of reference, transcripts, personal statement; for doctorate, M Div, letters of reference, organizational support; for Certificate, letters of reference, family essay, personal statement, and family of origin paper (for marriage and family therapy). Additional exam requirements/recommendations for international students: required—TOEFL (minimum score 550 paper-based; 87 iBT). Electronic applications accepted. *Expenses:* Contact institution.

Boston College, Morrissey Graduate School of Arts and Sciences, Department of Classics, Chestnut Hill, MA 02467-3800. Offers classics (MA); Greek (MA); Latin (MA). *Degree requirements:* For master's, one foreign language, thesis optional. *Entrance requirements:* For master's, GRE. Additional exam requirements/recommendations for international students: required—TOEFL (minimum score 600 paper-based; 100 iBT), IELTS (minimum score 8). Electronic applications accepted.

Boston University, Graduate School of Arts and Sciences, Department of Classical Studies, Boston, MA 02215. Offers MA, PhD, MA/PhD. *Students:* 19 full-time (8 women); includes 3 minority (1 Asian, non-Hispanic/Latino; 1 Hispanic/Latino; 1 Two or more races, non-Hispanic/Latino), 1 international. Average age 26. 22 applicants, 41% accepted, 2 enrolled. In 2019, 2 doctorates awarded. Terminal master's awarded for partial completion of doctoral program. *Degree requirements:* For master's, one foreign language, comprehensive exam; for doctorate, 2 foreign languages, comprehensive exam, thesis/dissertation. *Entrance requirements:* For master's and doctorate, GRE General Test, 3 letters of recommendation, transcripts, scholarly writing sample, personal statement. Additional exam requirements/recommendations for international students: required—TOEFL (minimum score 550 paper-based; 84 iBT). *Application deadline:* For fall admission, 1/15 for domestic and international students; for spring admission, 10/15 for domestic and international students. Application fee: $95. Electronic applications accepted. *Financial support:* In 2019–20, 21 students received support, including 7 fellowships with full tuition reimbursements available (averaging $23,340 per year), 12 teaching assistantships with full tuition reimbursements available (averaging $23,340 per year); career-related internships or fieldwork, Federal Work-Study, institutionally sponsored loans, and health care benefits also available. Financial award application deadline: 1/15. *Unit head:* Stephen Scully, Chair, 617-353-4572, Fax: 617-353-1610, E-mail: sscully@bu.edu. *Application contact:* Arthur Peterson, Department Administrator, 617-353-2426, Fax: 617-353-1610, E-mail: apeter@bu.edu. Website: http://www.bu.edu/classics/

Brandeis University, Graduate School of Arts and Sciences, Department of Ancient Greek and Roman Studies (Classical Studies), Waltham, MA 02454-9110. Offers MA. *Program availability:* Part-time. *Faculty:* 381 full-time (173 women), 171 part-time/adjunct (80 women). *Students:* 12 full-time (9 women), 3 part-time (2 women); includes 2 minority (1 Hispanic/Latino; 1 Two or more races, non-Hispanic/Latino). Average age 26. 36 applicants, 83% accepted, 7 enrolled. In 2019, 11 master's awarded. *Degree requirements:* For master's, variable foreign language requirement, thesis or alternative, paper or thesis. *Entrance requirements:* For master's, transcripts, letters of recommendation, resume, and statement of purpose. Additional exam requirements/recommendations for international students: required—TOEFL, IELTS, PTE. *Application deadline:* For fall admission, 2/15 for domestic and international students; for spring admission, 10/15 for domestic and international students. Application fee: $75. Electronic applications accepted. *Financial support:* In 2019–20, 6 teaching assistantships (averaging $3,200 per year) were awarded; fellowships, scholarships/grants, health care benefits, and tuition waivers (partial) also available. *Unit head:* Dr. Ann Koloski-Ostrow, Director of Graduate Studies, 781-736-2183, E-mail: aoko@brandeis.edu. *Application contact:* David DeVore, Administrator, 781-736-2180, E-mail: classics@brandeis.edu.
Website: http://www.brandeis.edu/gsas/programs/greek_roman.html

Brigham Young University, Graduate Studies, College of Humanities, Department of Comparative Arts and Letters, Provo, UT 84602-1001. Offers comparative studies (MA). *Program availability:* Part-time. *Faculty:* 29 full-time (7 women), 4 part-time/adjunct (2 women). *Students:* 15 full-time (10 women), 1 (woman) part-time; includes 1 minority (Asian, non-Hispanic/Latino). Average age 29. 15 applicants, 60% accepted, 8 enrolled. In 2019, 8 master's awarded. *Degree requirements:* For master's, 2 foreign languages, comprehensive exam, thesis, Coursework - 33 credit hours in seminars at graduate level and other courses by approval. *Entrance requirements:* For master's, GRE, minimum GPA of 3.0 in last 60 hours, writing sample, foreign language experience, undergraduate degree or experience in a humanities discipline, Proficiency in a language of scholarship or other spoken language. Additional exam requirements/recommendations for international students: required—TOEFL (minimum score 580 paper-based; 85 iBT), E3PT (to obtain the required minimum English language proficieny scores for the E3PT, IELTS, or TOEFL tests; or to obtain waiver "f".) *Application deadline:* For fall admission, 3/1 for domestic and international students. Application fee: $50. Electronic applications accepted. *Financial support:* In 2019–20, 15 students received support, including 1 research assistantship, 15 teaching assistantships (averaging $5,000 per year); scholarships/grants, tuition waivers (partial), unspecified assistantships, and student instructorships also available. Support available to part-time students. Financial award application deadline: 9/1. *Unit head:* Dr. Julie Allen, Graduate Coordinator/Professor of Classical Studies, 801-422-7891, Fax: 801-422-0305, E-mail: julie_allen@byu.edu. *Application contact:* Andrea Kristensen, Graduate Program Manager, 801-422-2996, Fax: 801-422-0305, E-mail: andrea_kristensen@byu.edu.
Website: http://cal.byu.edu/

Brock University, Faculty of Graduate Studies, Faculty of Humanities, Program in Classics, St. Catharines, ON L2S 3A1, Canada. Offers MA. *Program availability:* Part-time. *Degree requirements:* For master's, one foreign language, major research paper or thesis. *Entrance requirements:* For master's, honors degree, 3 letters of reference, written work (no more than 20 pages). Additional exam requirements/recommendations for international students: required—TOEFL (minimum score 550 paper-based; 80 iBT), IELTS (minimum score 6.5), TWE (minimum score 4). Electronic applications accepted.

Brown University, Graduate School, Classics Department, Providence, RI 02912. Offers MA, PhD. Terminal master's awarded for partial completion of doctoral program. *Degree requirements:* For master's, one foreign language, thesis; for doctorate, 2 foreign languages, thesis/dissertation. *Entrance requirements:* For master's and doctorate, GRE General Test.

Bryn Mawr College, Graduate School of Arts and Sciences, Department of Greek, Latin, and Classical Studies, Bryn Mawr, PA 19010-2899. Offers MA, PhD. *Program availability:* Part-time. Terminal master's awarded for partial completion of doctoral program. *Degree requirements:* For master's, 2 foreign languages, thesis; for doctorate, 4 foreign languages, comprehensive exam, thesis/dissertation. *Entrance requirements:* For master's and doctorate, GRE General Test, transcripts, three letters of recommendation, statement of interest, resume or curriculum vitae, writing sample. Additional exam requirements/recommendations for international students: required—TOEFL (minimum score 600 paper-based; 100 iBT), IELTS (minimum score 7). Electronic applications accepted.

The Catholic University of America, School of Arts and Sciences, Department of Greek and Latin, Washington, DC 20064. Offers Greek (MA, Certificate); Greek and Latin (MA, PhD, Certificate); Latin (MA, Certificate). *Program availability:* Part-time. *Faculty:* 4 full-time (0 women), 5 part-time/adjunct (4 women). *Students:* 4 full-time (2 women), 15 part-time (9 women); includes 3 minority (all Two or more races, non-Hispanic/Latino), 2 international. Average age 38. 11 applicants, 91% accepted, 1 enrolled. In 2019, 5 master's, 3 doctorates awarded. *Degree requirements:* For master's, one foreign language, comprehensive exam; for doctorate, 2 foreign languages, comprehensive exam, thesis/dissertation. *Entrance requirements:* For master's and doctorate, GRE General Test, statement of purpose, official copies of academic transcripts, three letters of recommendation; for Certificate, bachelor's degree. Additional exam requirements/recommendations for international students: required—TOEFL (minimum score 550 paper-based; 80 iBT). *Application deadline:* For fall admission, 7/15 priority date for domestic students, 7/1 for international students; for spring admission, 11/15 priority date for domestic students, 11/1 for international students. Applications are processed on a rolling basis. Application fee: $55. Electronic applications accepted. *Expenses:* Contact institution. *Financial support:* Fellowships, research assistantships, teaching assistantships, Federal Work-Study, scholarships/grants, tuition waivers (full and partial), and unspecified assistantships available. Financial award application deadline: 2/1; financial award applicants required to submit FAFSA. *Unit head:* Dr. Sarah Ferrario, Chair, 202-319-5216, Fax: 202-319-5297, E-mail: ferrario@cua.edu. *Application contact:* Dr. Steven Brown, Director of Graduate Admissions, 202-319-5057, Fax: 202-319-6533, E-mail: cua-admissions@cua.edu.
Website: http://greeklatin.cua.edu/

Columbia University, Graduate School of Arts and Sciences, New York, NY 10027. Offers African-American studies (MA); American studies (MA); anthropology (MA, PhD); art history and archaeology (MA, PhD); astronomy (PhD); biological sciences (PhD); biotechnology (MA); chemical physics (PhD); chemistry (PhD); classical studies (MA, PhD); classics (MA, PhD); climate and society (MA); conservation biology (MA); earth and environmental sciences (PhD); East Asia: regional studies (MA); East Asian languages and cultures (MA, PhD); ecology, evolution and environmental biology (MA), including conservation biology; ecology, evolution, and environmental biology (PhD), including ecology and evolutionary biology, evolutionary primatology; economics (MA, PhD); English and comparative literature (MA, PhD); French and Romance philology (MA, PhD); Germanic languages (MA, PhD); global French studies (MA); global thought (MA); Hispanic cultural studies (MA); history (PhD); history and literature (MA); human rights studies (MA); Islamic studies (MA); Italian (MA, PhD); Japanese pedagogy (MA); Jewish studies (MA); Latin America and the Caribbean: regional studies (MA); Latin American and Iberian cultures (PhD); mathematics (MA, PhD), including finance (MA); medieval and Renaissance studies (MA); Middle Eastern, South Asian, and African studies (MA, PhD); modern art: critical and curatorial studies (MA); modern European studies (MA); museum anthropology (MA); music (DMA, PhD); oral history (MA); philosophical foundations of physics (MA); philosophy (MA, PhD); physics (PhD); political science (MA, PhD); psychology (PhD); quantitative methods in the social sciences (MA); religion (MA, PhD); Russia, Eurasia and East Europe: regional studies (MA); Russian translation (MA); Slavic cultures (MA); Slavic languages (MA, PhD); sociology (MA, PhD); South Asian studies (MA); statistics (MA, PhD); theatre (PhD). *Program availability:* Part-time. *Students:* 3,506 full-time (1,844 women), 208 part-time (121 women); includes 864 minority (110 Black or African American, non-Hispanic/Latino; 5 American Indian or Alaska Native, non-Hispanic/Latino; 416 Asian, non-Hispanic/Latino; 147 Hispanic/Latino; 6 Native Hawaiian or other Pacific Islander, non-Hispanic/Latino; 180 Two or more races, non-Hispanic/Latino), 2,065 international. 14,545 applicants, 25% accepted, 1,429 enrolled. In 2019, 1,262 master's, 363 doctorates awarded. Terminal master's awarded for partial completion of doctoral program. *Degree requirements:* For master's, variable foreign language requirement, comprehensive exam (for some programs), thesis (for some programs); for doctorate, variable foreign language requirement, comprehensive exam (for some programs), thesis/dissertation. *Entrance requirements:* For master's and doctorate, GRE General Test, GRE Subject Test (for some programs). Additional exam requirements/recommendations for international students: required—TOEFL (minimum score 600 paper-based; 100 iBT), IELTS (minimum score 7.5). Application fee: $115. Electronic applications accepted. *Expenses: Tuition:* Full-time $47,600; part-time $1880 per credit. One-time fee: $105. *Financial support:* Fellowships, research assistantships, teaching assistantships, career-related internships or fieldwork, Federal Work-Study, institutionally sponsored loans, scholarships/grants, traineeships, health care benefits, tuition waivers, and unspecified assistantships available. Support available to part-time students. Financial award application deadline: 12/15. *Unit head:* Dr. Carlos J. Alonso, Dean of the Graduate School of Arts and Sciences and Vice President for Graduate Education, 212-854-2861, E-mail: gsas-dean@columbia.edu. *Application contact:* GSAS Office of Admissions, 212-854-6729, E-mail: gsas-admissions@columbia.edu.
Website: http://gsas.columbia.edu/

Cornell University, Graduate School, Graduate Fields of Arts and Sciences, Field of Classics, Ithaca, NY 14853. Offers ancient history (PhD); ancient philosophy (PhD); classical archaeology (PhD); classical literature and philology (PhD); classical myth (PhD); classical rhetoric (PhD); Greek and Latin language and linguistics (PhD); Indo-European linguistics (PhD); medieval and Renaissance Latin literature (PhD). *Degree requirements:* For doctorate, 2 foreign languages, comprehensive exam, thesis/dissertation. *Entrance requirements:* For doctorate, GRE General Test, 3 letters of recommendation, sample of written work. Additional exam requirements/recommendations for international students: required—TOEFL (minimum score 550 paper-based; 77 iBT). Electronic applications accepted.

Dalhousie University, Faculty of Arts and Social Sciences, Department of Classics, Halifax, NS B3H 4R2, Canada. Offers MA, PhD. *Entrance requirements:* Additional exam requirements/recommendations for international students: required—TOEFL, IELTS, CANTEST, CAEL, or Michigan English Language Assessment Battery. Electronic applications accepted.

Duke University, Graduate School, Department of Classical Studies, Durham, NC 27708-0103. Offers PhD. *Degree requirements:* For doctorate, 2 foreign languages, thesis/dissertation. *Entrance requirements:* For doctorate, GRE General Test. Additional exam requirements/recommendations for international students: required—TOEFL (minimum score 577 paper-based; 90 iBT) or IELTS (minimum score 7). Electronic applications accepted.

Duquesne University, School of Education, Department of Instruction and Leadership, Program in Secondary Education, Pittsburgh, PA 15282-0001. Offers biology (MS Ed); chemistry (MS Ed); English (MS Ed); K-12 education (MS Ed), including Latin; mathematics (MS Ed); physics (MS Ed); social studies (MS Ed). *Program availability:* Part-time, evening/weekend. *Entrance requirements:* For master's, two letters of recommendation, letter of intent, interview, bachelor's degree. Additional exam requirements/recommendations for international students: required—TOEFL (minimum score 550 paper-based), IELTS (minimum score 7). Electronic applications accepted.

Florida State University, The Graduate School, Department of Anthropology, Department of Classics, Tallahassee, FL 32306-1510. Offers ancient history (MA); classical archaeology (MA); classical civilization (MA); classics (PhD), including classical archaeology, classics; Greek (MA); Greek and Latin (MA); Latin (MA). *Faculty:* 18 full-time (8 women), 1 (woman) part-time/adjunct. *Students:* 31 full-time (22 women); includes 4 minority (1 Asian, non-Hispanic/Latino; 3 Two or more races, non-Hispanic/Latino). Average age 27. 41 applicants, 32% accepted, 13 enrolled. In 2019, 16 master's, 4 doctorates awarded. Terminal master's awarded for partial completion of doctoral program. *Degree requirements:* For master's, 2 foreign languages, comprehensive exam, thesis or alternative; for doctorate, 4 foreign languages, comprehensive exam, thesis/dissertation. *Entrance requirements:* For master's and doctorate, GRE General Test, minimum GPA of 3.0, official transcripts, resume/CV, statement of purpose, writing sample. Additional exam requirements/recommendations for international students: required—TOEFL (minimum score 550 paper-based; 80 iBT). *Application deadline:* For fall admission, 12/15 priority date for domestic students, 12/15 for international students. Applications are processed on a rolling basis. Application fee: $30. Electronic applications accepted. *Financial support:* In 2019–20, 39 students received support, including 1 fellowship with full tuition reimbursement available (averaging $18,000 per year), 2 research assistantships with full tuition reimbursements available (averaging $12,000 per year), 24 teaching assistantships with full tuition reimbursements available (averaging $12,400 per year); Federal Work-Study, scholarships/grants, tuition waivers (full), and unspecified assistantships also available. Financial award application deadline: 1/15; financial award applicants required to submit FAFSA. *Unit head:* Dr. John Marincola, Chair, 850-644-0304, Fax: 850-644-4073, E-mail: jmarinco@fsu.edu. *Application contact:* Dr. Jessica Clark, Admissions Director, 850-644-4259, Fax: 850-644-4073, E-mail: jhclark@fsu.edu.
Website: http://classics.fsu.edu/

Fordham University, Graduate School of Arts and Sciences, Department of Classical Languages and Literatures, New York, NY 10458. Offers MA, PhD. *Program availability:* Part-time, evening/weekend. *Students:* Average age 31. 11 applicants, 45% accepted, 2 enrolled. In 2019, 3 master's, 1 doctorate awarded. Terminal master's awarded for partial completion of doctoral program. *Degree requirements:* For master's, one foreign language, comprehensive exam; for doctorate, 2 foreign languages, comprehensive exam, thesis/dissertation. *Entrance requirements:* For master's and doctorate, GRE General Test. Additional exam requirements/recommendations for international students: required—TOEFL (minimum score 650 paper-based). *Application deadline:* For fall admission, 1/4 priority date for domestic students; for spring admission, 11/1 for domestic students. Application fee: $70. Electronic applications accepted. *Financial support:* In 2019–20, 11 students received support, including 2 fellowships with tuition reimbursements available (averaging $27,000 per year), 4 teaching assistantships with tuition reimbursements available (averaging $21,000 per year); Federal Work-Study, institutionally sponsored loans, scholarships/grants, tuition waivers (full and partial), and unspecified assistantships also available. Support available to part-time students. Financial award application deadline: 1/4; financial award applicants required to submit FAFSA. *Unit head:* Dr. Matthew McGowan, Chair, 718-817-3140, Fax: 718-817-3134, E-mail: mamcgowan@fordham.edu. *Application contact:* Garrett Marino, Director of Graduate Admissions, 718-817-4419, Fax: 718-817-3566, E-mail: gmarino10@fordham.edu.

The Graduate Center, City University of New York, Graduate Studies, Program in Classics, New York, NY 10016-4039. Offers MA, PhD. *Degree requirements:* For master's, 2 foreign languages, thesis; for doctorate, 2 foreign languages, thesis/dissertation. *Entrance requirements:* For master's and doctorate, GRE General Test. Additional exam requirements/recommendations for international students: required—TOEFL. Electronic applications accepted.

Harvard University, Graduate School of Arts and Sciences, Department of the Classics, Cambridge, MA 02138. Offers Byzantine Greek (PhD); classical archaeology (PhD); classical philology (PhD); classical philosophy (PhD); medieval Latin (PhD). *Degree requirements:* For doctorate, 4 foreign languages, thesis/dissertation, preliminary and special exams. *Entrance requirements:* For doctorate, GRE General Test. Additional exam requirements/recommendations for international students: required—TOEFL.

Heritage Christian University, Graduate Programs, Florence, AL 35630. Offers counseling (MM); Greek (MA); ministry (MM); New Testament (MA). *Degree requirements:* For master's, practicum (MM), major research paper (MA). *Entrance requirements:* For master's, MAT or GRE, bachelor's degree in Bible from an accredited college or university, minimum GPA of 2.75, 3 letters of recommendation.

Hunter College of the City University of New York, Graduate School, School of Arts and Sciences, Department of Classical and Oriental Studies, Program in Teaching Latin, New York, NY 10065-5085. Offers MA. *Program availability:* Part-time, evening/weekend. *Degree requirements:* For master's, one foreign language. *Entrance requirements:* For master's, undergraduate major in Latin or equivalent with minimum GPA of 3.0; 2 letters of recommendation; personal statement. Additional exam requirements/recommendations for international students: required—TOEFL.

Indiana University Bloomington, University Graduate School, College of Arts and Sciences, Department of Classical Studies, Bloomington, IN 47405. Offers MA, MAT, PhD. *Program availability:* Part-time. *Degree requirements:* For master's, 2 foreign languages, comprehensive exam; for doctorate, 3 foreign languages, thesis/dissertation. *Entrance requirements:* For master's and doctorate, GRE, minimum GPA of 3.0. Additional exam requirements/recommendations for international students: required—TOEFL. Electronic applications accepted.

Johns Hopkins University, Zanvyl Krieger School of Arts and Sciences, Department of Classics, Baltimore, MD 21218. Offers PhD. Terminal master's awarded for partial completion of doctoral program. *Degree requirements:* For doctorate, 4 foreign languages, thesis/dissertation. *Entrance requirements:* For doctorate, GRE General Test. Additional exam requirements/recommendations for international students: required—TOEFL (minimum score 600 paper-based), IELTS (minimum score 7). Electronic applications accepted. *Expenses:* Contact institution.

Knox Theological Seminary, Graduate Programs, Master of Arts Programs, Fort Lauderdale, FL 33308. Offers Biblical and theological studies (MA); Christian and classical studies (MA). *Accreditation:* ATS. *Program availability:* Part-time, evening/weekend. *Entrance requirements:* Additional exam requirements/recommendations for international students: required—TOEFL (minimum score 520 paper-based; 83 iBT), TWE (minimum score 5).

McMaster University, School of Graduate Studies, Faculty of Humanities, Department of Classics, Hamilton, ON L8S 4M2, Canada. Offers MA, PhD. *Degree requirements:* For master's, one foreign language, thesis or alternative; for doctorate, 2 foreign languages, comprehensive exam, thesis/dissertation. *Entrance requirements:* For master's, honors degree, minimum B+ average. Additional exam requirements/recommendations for international students: required—TOEFL (minimum score 580 paper-based).

Memorial University of Newfoundland, School of Graduate Studies, Department of Classics, St. John's, NL A1C 5S7, Canada. Offers MA. *Program availability:* Part-time. *Degree requirements:* For master's, one foreign language, thesis, language exam, translation exam, research essay. *Entrance requirements:* For master's, honors degree in related field, course work in Greek and Latin. Electronic applications accepted.

New York University, Graduate School of Arts and Science, Department of Classics, New York, NY 10012-1019. Offers classics (MA, PhD); poetics and theory (Advanced Certificate). *Program availability:* Part-time. *Degree requirements:* For master's, 4 foreign languages, exam or specialized project; for doctorate, 4 foreign languages, thesis/dissertation, exams. *Entrance requirements:* For master's, GRE General Test, knowledge of Greek and Latin history and literature, proficiency in Greek and Latin translation; for doctorate, GRE General Test. Additional exam requirements/recommendations for international students: required—TOEFL, IELTS.

The Ohio State University, Graduate School, College of Arts and Sciences, Division of Arts and Humanities, Department of Classics, Columbus, OH 43210. Offers ancient Greek and Latin (MA, PhD); Greek studies (MA); Latin studies (MA, PhD); modern Greek (MA, PhD). *Degree requirements:* For master's, 2 foreign languages, thesis or alternative; for doctorate, 2 foreign languages, thesis/dissertation. *Entrance requirements:* For master's and doctorate, GRE General Test. Additional exam requirements/recommendations for international students: required—TOEFL (minimum score 550 paper-based; 79 iBT), Michigan English Language Assessment Battery (minimum score 82); recommended—IELTS (minimum score 7). Electronic applications accepted.

Princeton University, Graduate School, Department of Classics, Princeton, NJ 08544-1019. Offers classical and Hellenic studies (PhD); classical philosophy (PhD); history (the ancient world) (PhD); literature and philology (PhD). *Degree requirements:* For doctorate, thesis/dissertation. *Entrance requirements:* For doctorate, GRE General Test, sample of written work. Additional exam requirements/recommendations for international students: required—TOEFL (minimum score 600 paper-based). Electronic applications accepted.

Queen's University at Kingston, School of Graduate Studies, Faculty of Arts and Science, Department of Classics, Kingston, ON K7L 3N6, Canada. Offers MA. *Program availability:* Part-time. *Degree requirements:* For master's, one foreign language, thesis (for some programs). *Entrance requirements:* For master's, 3 years of Latin, 2 years of Greek. Additional exam requirements/recommendations for international students: required—TOEFL. Electronic applications accepted.

Rutgers University - New Brunswick, Graduate School-New Brunswick, Department of Classics, Piscataway, NJ 08854-8097. Offers classics (MA, MAT, PhD); interdisciplinary classical studies and ancient history (MA, PhD). *Program availability:* Part-time, evening/weekend. Terminal master's awarded for partial completion of doctoral program. *Degree requirements:* For master's, 3 foreign languages, comprehensive exam, thesis or alternative; for doctorate, 3 foreign languages, comprehensive exam, thesis/dissertation. *Entrance requirements:* For master's and doctorate, GRE General Test.

San Francisco State University, Division of Graduate Studies, College of Liberal and Creative Arts, Department of Classics, San Francisco, CA 94132-1722. Offers MA. *Program availability:* Part-time. *Application deadline:* Applications are processed on a rolling basis. *Expenses: Tuition, area resident:* Full-time $7176; part-time $4164 per year. Tuition, state resident: full-time $7176; part-time $4164 per year. Tuition, nonresident: full-time $16,680; part-time $396 per unit. *International tuition:* $16,680 full-time. *Required fees:* $1524; $1524 per unit. $762 per semester. Tuition and fees vary according to degree level and program. *Unit head:* Dr. David Leitao, Chair, 415-338-2068, Fax: 415-338-2664, E-mail: dleitao@sfsu.edu. *Application contact:* Dr. Gillian McIntosh, Graduate Coordinator, 415-338-1537, Fax: 415-338-2664, E-mail: gillianm@sfsu.edu.
Website: http://classics.sfsu.edu/

Stanford University, School of Humanities and Sciences, Department of Classics, Stanford, CA 94305-2004. Offers MA, PhD. *Expenses: Tuition:* Full-time $52,479; part-time $34,110 per unit. *Required fees:* $672; $224 per quarter. Tuition and fees vary according to program and student level. *Unit head:* Walter Scheidel, Chair, 650-723-0479, Fax: 650-725-3801, E-mail: scheidel@stanford.edu. *Application contact:* Graduate Admissions, 866-432-7472, Fax: 650-723-8371, E-mail: gradadmissions@stanford.edu.
Website: http://www.stanford.edu/dept/classics/

Tufts University, Graduate School of Arts and Sciences, Department of Classics, Medford, MA 02155. Offers classics (MA); classics with teaching licensure (MA); digital tools for premodern studies (MA). *Program availability:* Part-time. *Degree requirements:* For master's, 2 foreign languages, comprehensive exam, thesis or alternative. *Entrance requirements:* For master's, GRE General Test, writing sample. Additional exam requirements/recommendations for international students: required—TOEFL (minimum score 550 paper-based; 80 iBT), IELTS (minimum score 6.5). Electronic applications accepted. *Expenses:* Contact institution.

Tulane University, School of Liberal Arts, Department of Classical Studies, New Orleans, LA 70118-5669. Offers MA. *Degree requirements:* For master's, 2 foreign languages, thesis or alternative. *Entrance requirements:* For master's, GRE General Test, minimum B average in undergraduate course work. Additional exam requirements/recommendations for international students: required—TOEFL. Electronic applications accepted. *Expenses: Tuition:* Full-time $57,004; part-time $3167 per credit hour. *Required fees:* $2086; $44.50 per credit hour. $80 per term. Tuition and fees vary according to course load, degree level and program.

UNB Fredericton, School of Graduate Studies, Faculty of Arts - Saint John, Department of Classics and Ancient History, Fredericton, NB E3B 5A3, Canada. Offers classics (MA). *Program availability:* Part-time. *Faculty:* 5 full-time (2 women). *Students:* 1 full-time (0 women), 1 (woman) part-time. Average age 25. 2 applicants, 100% accepted. *Degree requirements:* For master's, thesis. *Entrance requirements:* For master's, minimum GPA of 3.0, minimum of 18 credit hours or equivalent in either Greek or Latin. Additional exam requirements/recommendations for international students: required—TOEFL, TWE. *Application deadline:* For fall admission, 1/31 for domestic and international students; for winter admission, 1/15 priority date for domestic and international students; for spring admission, 1/31 for domestic and international students. Applications are processed on a rolling basis. Application fee: $50 Canadian dollars. Electronic applications accepted. *Expenses: Tuition, area resident:* Full-time $6975 Canadian dollars; part-time $3423 Canadian dollars per year. Tuition, state resident: full-time $6975 Canadian dollars; part-time $3423 Canadian dollars per year. Tuition, Canadian resident: full-time $6975 Canadian dollars; part-time $3423 Canadian dollars per year. *International tuition:* $12,435 Canadian dollars full-time. *Required fees:* $92.25 Canadian dollars per term. Full-time tuition and fees vary according to degree level, campus/location, program, reciprocity agreements and student level. *Financial support:* Teaching assistantships available. Financial award application deadline: 1/31. *Unit head:* Prof. Sears Matthew, Director of Graduate Studies, 506-458-7399, Fax: 506-447-3072, E-mail: matthew.sears@unb.ca. *Application contact:* Angela Peters, Graduate Secretary, 506-

453-4762, Fax: 506-447-3072, E-mail: angela.peters@unb.ca.
Website: http://go.unb.ca/gradprograms

Université de Montréal, Faculty of Arts and Sciences, Program in Classical Studies, Montréal, QC H3C 3J7, Canada. Offers MA. Electronic applications accepted.

University at Buffalo, the State University of New York, Graduate School, College of Arts and Sciences, Department of Classics, Buffalo, NY 14261. Offers classics (MA, PhD); Latin (MA). Terminal master's awarded for partial completion of doctoral program. *Degree requirements:* For master's, 3 foreign languages, project; for doctorate, 4 foreign languages, comprehensive exam, thesis/dissertation, general and 2 special exams. *Entrance requirements:* For master's and doctorate, GRE General Test. Additional exam requirements/recommendations for international students: required—TOEFL, IELTS. Electronic applications accepted. *Expenses:* Contact institution.

University at Buffalo, the State University of New York, Graduate School, Graduate School of Education, Department of Learning and Instruction, Buffalo, NY 14260. Offers biology education (Ed M, Certificate); chemistry education (Ed M, Certificate); childhood education (Ed M); childhood education with bilingual extension (Ed M); college teaching (Advanced Certificate); curriculum, instruction and the science of learning (PhD); early childhood education (Ed M); early childhood education with bilingual extension (Ed M); earth science education (Ed M, Certificate); education and technology (Ed M); education studies (Ed M); educational technology and new literacies (Certificate); educational technology and new literacies (Advanced Certificate); elementary education (Ed D); English education (Ed M, Certificate); English education studies (Ed M); English for speakers of other languages (Ed M); foreign and second language education (PhD); French education (Ed M, Certificate); German education (Ed M, Certificate); gifted education (Certificate); Latin education (Ed M, Certificate); literacy education studies (Ed M); literacy specialist (Ed M); literacy teaching and learning (Certificate); mathematics education (Ed M, Certificate); music education (Ed M, Certificate); music education studies (Ed M); music learning theory (Advanced Certificate); online education (Advanced Certificate); physics education (Ed M, Certificate); science and the public (Ed M); social studies education (Ed M, Certificate); Spanish education (Ed M, Certificate); special education (PhD); teaching English to speakers of other languages (Ed M). *Program availability:* Part-time, evening/weekend, 100% online, blended/hybrid learning. *Faculty:* 26 full-time (19 women), 42 part-time/adjunct (29 women). *Students:* 227 full-time (158 women), 322 part-time (228 women); includes 85 minority (34 Black or African American, non-Hispanic/Latino; 3 American Indian or Alaska Native, non-Hispanic/Latino; 17 Asian, non-Hispanic/Latino; 23 Hispanic/Latino; 8 Two or more races, non-Hispanic/Latino), 42 international. Average age 33. 385 applicants, 61% accepted, 158 enrolled. In 2019, 100 master's, 23 doctorates, 16 other advanced degrees awarded. *Degree requirements:* For master's, comprehensive exam; for doctorate, thesis/dissertation, research analysis exam, research experience; for other advanced degree, thesis (for some programs). *Entrance requirements:* For master's, GRE or MAT for teacher preparation programs only, letters of reference; for doctorate, GRE General Test or MAT, interview, writing sample, letters of recommendation, resume. Additional exam requirements/recommendations for international students: required—TOEFL (minimum score 600 paper-based; 96 iBT), IELTS (minimum score 6.5), PTE (minimum score 55), The Graduate School of Education requires international students to submit test scores for at least one of the exams (TOEFL, IELTS, PTE). *Application deadline:* For fall admission, 2/1 priority date for domestic and international students. Applications are processed on a rolling basis. Application fee: $50. Electronic applications accepted. *Expenses: Tuition, area resident:* Full-time $11,310; part-time $471 per credit hour. Tuition, state resident: full-time $11,310; part-time $471 per credit hour. Tuition, nonresident: full-time $23,100; part-time $963 per credit hour. *International tuition:* $23,100 full-time. *Required fees:* $2820. *Financial support:* In 2019–20, 16 fellowships (averaging $20,000 per year), 5 research assistantships with tuition reimbursements (averaging $26,917 per year) were awarded; teaching assistantships, career-related internships or fieldwork, Federal Work-Study, institutionally sponsored loans, scholarships/grants, tuition waivers (full and partial), and unspecified assistantships also available. Financial award application deadline: 2/28; financial award applicants required to submit FAFSA. *Unit head:* Dr. Julie Gorlewski, Department Chair, 716-645-2455, Fax: 716-645-3161, E-mail: jgorlews@buffalo.edu. *Application contact:* Renad Aref, Assistant Director of Admission Recruitment, 716-645-2110, Fax: 716-645-7937, E-mail: gseinfo@buffalo.edu.
Website: http://ed.buffalo.edu/teaching.html

University of Alberta, Faculty of Graduate Studies and Research, Department of History and Classics, Edmonton, AB T6G 2E1, Canada. Offers ancient history (PhD); classical archaeology (MA, PhD); classical literature (PhD); classics (MA); history (MA, PhD). *Program availability:* Part-time, evening/weekend. *Degree requirements:* For master's, one foreign language, thesis (for some programs); for doctorate, one foreign language, thesis/dissertation. *Entrance requirements:* For master's, minimum B+ average; for doctorate, minimum A- average. Additional exam requirements/recommendations for international students: required—TOEFL (minimum score 580 paper-based). Electronic applications accepted.

The University of Arizona, College of Humanities, Department of Classics, Tucson, AZ 85721. Offers MA. *Program availability:* Part-time. *Degree requirements:* For master's, one foreign language, comprehensive exam, thesis. *Entrance requirements:* For master's, GRE General Test (minimum combined score of 1000 verbal and quantitative), 2 letters of recommendation. Additional exam requirements/recommendations for international students: required—TOEFL (minimum score 550 paper-based; 79 iBT). Electronic applications accepted.

The University of British Columbia, Faculty of Arts, Department of Classical, Near Eastern and Religious Studies, Program in Classics, Vancouver, BC V6T 1Z1, Canada. Offers classics (MA, PhD). *Program availability:* Part-time. *Degree requirements:* For master's, one foreign language, thesis or comprehensive exam; for doctorate, 2 foreign languages, comprehensive exam, thesis/dissertation. *Entrance requirements:* For doctorate, MA. Additional exam requirements/recommendations for international students: required—TOEFL, IELTS. Electronic applications accepted. *Expenses:* Contact institution.

University of Calgary, Faculty of Graduate Studies, Faculty of Arts, Program in Greek and Roman Studies, Calgary, AB T2N 1N4, Canada. Offers MA, PhD. *Program availability:* Part-time. *Degree requirements:* For master's, one foreign language; for doctorate, 2 foreign languages, comprehensive exam, thesis/dissertation. *Entrance requirements:* For master's, BA in classics or related field, knowledge of Latin and/or Greek, minimum GPA of 3.7; for doctorate, MA in classics or related field, knowledge of Latin and Greek, GPA 3.7. Additional exam requirements/recommendations for international students: required—TOEFL. Electronic applications accepted.

University of California, Berkeley, Graduate Division, College of Letters and Science, Department of Classics, Berkeley, CA 94720. Offers classical archaeology (MA, PhD); classics (MA, PhD); Greek (MA); Latin (MA). Terminal master's awarded for partial completion of doctoral program. *Degree requirements:* For master's, one foreign language, exams; for doctorate, 2 foreign languages, thesis/dissertation, qualifying exam. *Entrance requirements:* For master's and doctorate, GRE General Test, minimum GPA of 3.0, 3 letters of recommendation. Additional exam requirements/recommendations for international students: required—TOEFL (minimum score 570 paper-based; 90 iBT), TWE. Electronic applications accepted.

University of California, Irvine, School of Humanities, Department of Classics, Irvine, CA 92697. Offers MA, PhD. *Students:* 2 full-time (1 woman); includes 1 minority (Two or more races, non-Hispanic/Latino). Average age 37. Terminal master's awarded for partial completion of doctoral program. *Degree requirements:* For master's, one foreign language, thesis or alternative; for doctorate, 2 foreign languages, thesis/dissertation. *Entrance requirements:* For master's and doctorate, GRE General Test, minimum GPA of 3.0. Additional exam requirements/recommendations for international students: required—TOEFL (minimum score 550 paper-based). *Application deadline:* For fall admission, 1/15 priority date for domestic students, 1/15 for international students. Applications are processed on a rolling basis. Application fee: $120 ($140 for international students). Electronic applications accepted. *Financial support:* Fellowships, research assistantships with full tuition reimbursements, teaching assistantships, institutionally sponsored loans, traineeships, health care benefits, and unspecified assistantships available. Financial award application deadline: 3/1; financial award applicants required to submit FAFSA. *Unit head:* Susan Jarratt, Interim Chair, 949-824-6406, E-mail: sjarratt@uci.edu. *Application contact:* Zina Giannopoulou, Graduate Advisor, 949-824-2641, Fax: 949-824-1966, E-mail: zgiannop@uci.edu.
Website: http://www.humanities.uci.edu/classics/

University of California, Los Angeles, Graduate Division, College of Letters and Science, Department of Classics, Los Angeles, CA 90095. Offers classics (MA, PhD); Greek (MA); Latin (MA). Terminal master's awarded for partial completion of doctoral program. *Degree requirements:* For master's, 2 foreign languages, comprehensive exam; for doctorate, 2 foreign languages, thesis/dissertation, oral and written qualifying exams. *Entrance requirements:* For doctorate, GRE General Test, bachelor's degree; minimum undergraduate GPA of 3.0 (or its equivalent if letter grade system not used); Greek and Latin. Additional exam requirements/recommendations for international students: required—TOEFL. Electronic applications accepted.

University of California, Riverside, Graduate Division, Tri-Campus Program in Classics, Riverside, CA 92521-0102. Offers PhD. *Degree requirements:* For doctorate, 3 foreign languages, comprehensive exam, thesis/dissertation. *Entrance requirements:* For doctorate, GRE, MA in classics. Additional exam requirements/recommendations for international students: required—TOEFL (minimum score 550 paper-based; 80 iBT). Electronic applications accepted.

University of California, Santa Barbara, Graduate Division, College of Letters and Sciences, Division of Humanities and Fine Arts, Department of Classics, Santa Barbara, CA 93106-2014. Offers ancient history (PhD); classics (MA, PhD); literature and theory (MA); MA/PhD. Terminal master's awarded for partial completion of doctoral program. *Degree requirements:* For master's, 3 foreign languages, comprehensive exam; for doctorate, 4 foreign languages, comprehensive exam, thesis/dissertation. *Entrance requirements:* For master's and doctorate, GRE. Additional exam requirements/recommendations for international students: required—TOEFL (minimum score 550 paper-based; 80 iBT), IELTS (minimum score 7). Electronic applications accepted.

University of Chicago, Division of the Humanities, Department of Classics, Chicago, IL 60637. Offers ancient Greek and Roman philosophy (PhD); ancient Mediterranean world (PhD); classical languages and literatures (PhD); transformations in the classical tradition (PhD). Terminal master's awarded for partial completion of doctoral program. *Degree requirements:* For doctorate, 3 foreign languages, comprehensive exam (for some programs), thesis/dissertation. *Entrance requirements:* For doctorate, GRE General Test, 15-20 page writing sample, statement of purpose, 3 letters of recommendation, transcripts for all previous degrees and institutions attended. Additional exam requirements/recommendations for international students: required—TOEFL (minimum score 104 iBT), IELTS (minimum score 7). Electronic applications accepted.

University of Chicago, Division of the Humanities, Master of Arts Program in the Humanities, Chicago, IL 60637. Offers art history (MA); cinema and media studies (MA); classic languages (MA); comparative literature (MA); creative writing (MA); cultural policy studies (MA); digital humanities (MA); East Asian languages and civilizations (MA); English language and literature (MA); gender and sexuality studies (MA); Germanic studies (MA); linguistics (MA); music (MA); near Eastern languages and civilizations (MA); philosophy (MA); poetics (MA); race, politics and culture (MA); Romance languages and literatures (MA); Slavic languages and literatures (MA); South Asian languages and civilizations (MA); theater and performance studies (MA). *Degree requirements:* For master's, thesis. *Entrance requirements:* For master's, GRE General Test, 10-15 page writing sample, statement of purpose, 3 letters of recommendation, transcripts for all previous degrees and institutions attended. Additional exam requirements/recommendations for international students: required—TOEFL (minimum score 104 iBT), IELTS (minimum score 7). Electronic applications accepted. *Expenses:* Contact institution.

University of Cincinnati, Graduate School, McMicken College of Arts and Sciences, Department of Classics, Cincinnati, OH 45221. Offers MA, PhD. *Program availability:* Part-time. Terminal master's awarded for partial completion of doctoral program. *Degree requirements:* For master's, comprehensive exam (for some programs), thesis (for some programs); for doctorate, 2 foreign languages, comprehensive exam, thesis/dissertation. *Entrance requirements:* For master's and doctorate, GRE. Additional exam requirements/recommendations for international students: required—TOEFL. Electronic applications accepted.

University of Colorado Boulder, Graduate School, College of Arts and Sciences, Department of Classics, Boulder, CO 80309. Offers MA, PhD. Terminal master's awarded for partial completion of doctoral program. *Degree requirements:* For master's, one foreign language, comprehensive exam, thesis or alternative, oral exam; for doctorate, 4 foreign languages, comprehensive exam, thesis/dissertation. *Entrance requirements:* For master's, minimum undergraduate GPA of 2.75; for doctorate, master's degree in classics or related field. Electronic applications accepted. Application fee is waived when completed online.

University of Florida, Graduate School, College of Liberal Arts and Sciences, Department of Classics, Gainesville, FL 32611. Offers classical studies (MA, PhD); Latin (MA, MAT, ML). *Program availability:* Part-time, online learning. *Degree requirements:* For master's, one foreign language, thesis (for some programs); for doctorate, 2 foreign languages, comprehensive exam, thesis/dissertation. *Entrance requirements:* For master's, GRE General Test, minimum GPA of 3.0; for doctorate, GRE General Test, minimum GPA of 3.25 in both graduate and undergraduate work; MA in classical studies or equivalent. Additional exam requirements/recommendations for international students: required—TOEFL (minimum score 550 paper-based; 80 iBT), IELTS (minimum score 6). Electronic applications accepted.

University of Georgia, Franklin College of Arts and Sciences, Department of Classics, Athens, GA 30602. Offers classical languages (MA); Greek (MA); Latin (MA). *Degree requirements:* For master's, one foreign language, thesis. *Entrance requirements:* For master's, GRE General Test. Electronic applications accepted.

Classics

University of Illinois at Urbana-Champaign, Graduate College, College of Liberal Arts and Sciences, School of Literatures, Cultures and Linguistics, Department of the Classics, Champaign, IL 61820. Offers classical philology (PhD); classics (MA); teaching of Latin (MA).

The University of Iowa, Graduate College, College of Liberal Arts and Sciences, Department of Classics, Iowa City, IA 52242-1316. Offers classics (MA, PhD); Greek (MA); Latin (MA). *Degree requirements:* For master's, exam; for doctorate, comprehensive exam, thesis/dissertation. *Entrance requirements:* For master's and doctorate, GRE General Test, minimum GPA of 3.0. Additional exam requirements/recommendations for international students: required—TOEFL (minimum score 550 paper-based; 81 iBT). Electronic applications accepted.

The University of Kansas, Graduate Studies, College of Liberal Arts and Sciences, Department of Classics, Lawrence, KS 66045. Offers MA. *Students:* 10 full-time (4 women); includes 2 minority (1 Asian, non-Hispanic/Latino; 1 Hispanic/Latino). Average age 24. 25 applicants, 48% accepted, 5 enrolled. In 2019, 4 master's awarded. *Entrance requirements:* For master's, GRE (recommended), resume (suggested one-page in length), writing sample (25-page maximum), statement of purpose, three letters of reference, official transcripts. Additional exam requirements/recommendations for international students: required—TOEFL, IELTS. *Application deadline:* For fall admission, 1/15 priority date for domestic and international students; for spring admission, 10/25 priority date for domestic and international students. Application fee: $65 ($85 for international students). Electronic applications accepted. *Expenses:* Tuition, state resident: full-time $9989. Tuition, nonresident: full-time $23,950. *International tuition:* $23,950 full-time. *Required fees:* $984; $81.99 per credit hour. Tuition and fees vary according to course load, campus/location and program. *Financial support:* Fellowships, teaching assistantships, career-related internships or fieldwork, Federal Work-Study, scholarships/grants, traineeships, and unspecified assistantships available. Support available to part-time students. Financial award application deadline: 1/15; financial award applicants required to submit FAFSA. *Unit head:* Prof. Tara Welch, Chair, 785-864-2395, E-mail: tswelch@ku.edu. *Application contact:* Jared Nietfeld, Graduate Admissions Contact, 785-864-0482, E-mail: nietfeld@ku.edu.
Website: http://classics.drupal.ku.edu/

University of Kentucky, Graduate School, College of Arts and Sciences, Program in Modern and Classical Languages and Literatures, Lexington, KY 40506-0032. Offers MA. *Program availability:* Part-time. *Degree requirements:* For master's, one foreign language, comprehensive exam, thesis optional. *Entrance requirements:* For master's, GRE General Test, minimum undergraduate GPA of 2.75. Additional exam requirements/recommendations for international students: required—TOEFL (minimum score 550 paper-based). Electronic applications accepted.

The University of Manchester, School of Arts, Languages and Cultures, Manchester, United Kingdom. Offers anthropology, media and performance (PhD); applied theatre (PhD); Arab world studies (PhD); archaeology (PhD); art history and visual studies (PhD); arts and cultural management (PhD); arts management and cultural policy (PhD); Chinese studies (PhD); classics and ancient history (PhD); composition (PhD); creative writing (PhD); drama (PhD); East Asian studies (PhD); electroacoustic composition (PhD); English and American studies (PhD); English language (PhD); French studies (PhD); German studies (PhD); history (PhD); humanitarianism and conflict response (PhD); interpreting studies (PhD); Japanese studies (PhD); Latin American cultural studies (PhD); linguistics (PhD); Middle Eastern studies (PhD); museology (PhD); museum practice (PhD); music (PhD); musicology (PhD); Polish studies (PhD); Portuguese studies (PhD); religions and theology (PhD); Russian studies (PhD); Spanish studies (PhD); translation and intercultural studies (PhD).

University of Manitoba, Faculty of Graduate Studies, Faculty of Arts, Department of Classics, Winnipeg, MB R3T 2N2, Canada. Offers MA. *Degree requirements:* For master's, thesis.

University of Maryland, College Park, Academic Affairs, College of Arts and Humanities, Department of Classics, College Park, MD 20742. Offers MA. *Degree requirements:* For master's, 2 foreign languages, thesis or alternative. *Entrance requirements:* For master's, writing sample, 3 letters of recommendation. Additional exam requirements/recommendations for international students: required—TOEFL. Electronic applications accepted.

University of Massachusetts Amherst, Graduate School, College of Humanities and Fine Arts, Department of Classics, Amherst, MA 01003. Offers Latin and classical humanities (MAT). *Program availability:* Part-time. *Degree requirements:* For master's, thesis or alternative. *Entrance requirements:* For master's, GRE General Test. Additional exam requirements/recommendations for international students: required—TOEFL (minimum score 550 paper-based; 80 iBT), IELTS (minimum score 6.5). Electronic applications accepted.

University of Massachusetts Boston, College of Liberal Arts, Program in Latin and Classical Humanities, Boston, MA 02125-3393. Offers MA.

University of Michigan, Rackham Graduate School, College of Literature, Science, and the Arts, Department of Classical Studies, Ann Arbor, MI 48109. Offers classical studies (MA, PhD); Greek and Roman history (PhD); Latin (MA); Latin with teaching certification (MAT). Terminal master's awarded for partial completion of doctoral program. *Degree requirements:* For master's, one foreign language, comprehensive exam; for doctorate, 4 foreign languages, comprehensive exam, thesis/dissertation, oral defense of dissertation, preliminary exams, qualifying exams. *Entrance requirements:* For master's, 2-3 years of Latin (for the Latin MAT); for doctorate, strict minimum of 3 years of college-level Latin and 2 years of college-level Greek. Additional exam requirements/recommendations for international students: required—TOEFL (minimum score 560 paper-based). Electronic applications accepted.

University of Michigan, Rackham Graduate School, College of Literature, Science, and the Arts, Interdepartmental Program in Greek and Roman History, Ann Arbor, MI 48109. Offers PhD, Certificate. *Degree requirements:* For doctorate, 4 foreign languages, comprehensive exam, thesis/dissertation, oral defense of dissertation, dissertation prospectus, preliminary exams, qualifying exams. *Entrance requirements:* For doctorate, GRE, strict minimum of 2 years each of classical Greek and Latin. Additional exam requirements/recommendations for international students: required—TOEFL (minimum score 560 paper-based). Electronic applications accepted.

University of Minnesota, Twin Cities Campus, Graduate School, College of Liberal Arts, Department of Classical and Near Eastern Studies, Minneapolis, MN 55455-0213. Offers ancient and medieval art and archaeology (MA, PhD); classics (MA, PhD); Greek (MA, PhD); Latin (MA, PhD); religions in antiquity (MA). *Program availability:* Part-time. Terminal master's awarded for partial completion of doctoral program. *Degree requirements:* For master's, 2 foreign languages, comprehensive exam, thesis or alternative; for doctorate, variable foreign language requirement, comprehensive exam, thesis/dissertation. *Entrance requirements:* For master's and doctorate, GRE, 3 letters of recommendation, writing sample, copies of transcripts, personal statement. Additional exam requirements/recommendations for international students: required—TOEFL. Electronic applications accepted.

University of Missouri, Office of Research and Graduate Studies, College of Arts and Science, Department of Ancient Mediterranean Studies, Columbia, MO 65211. Offers classical languages (MA, PhD); classical studies (MA, PhD). Terminal master's awarded for partial completion of doctoral program. *Degree requirements:* For master's, one foreign language; for doctorate, 2 foreign languages, comprehensive exam, thesis/dissertation. *Entrance requirements:* For master's, GRE General Test, minimum GPA of 3.0 during last 2 years; BA from accredited college/university; reading knowledge of Greek and/or Latin; for doctorate, GRE General Test, minimum GPA of 3.0; MA with major in Greek, Latin, or classics, or equivalent minimum of 21 hours of graduate work; reading knowledge of Greek, Latin, German, and French (or Italian). Additional exam requirements/recommendations for international students: required—TOEFL (minimum score 500 paper-based; 61 iBT), IELTS (minimum score 5.5). Electronic applications accepted.

University of Nebraska–Lincoln, Graduate College, College of Arts and Sciences, Department of Classics and Religious Studies, Lincoln, NE 68588. Offers MA. *Degree requirements:* For master's, thesis optional. *Entrance requirements:* For master's, GRE. Additional exam requirements/recommendations for international students: required—TOEFL (minimum score 550 paper-based). Electronic applications accepted.

The University of North Carolina at Chapel Hill, Graduate School, College of Arts and Sciences, Department of Classics, Chapel Hill, NC 27599. Offers classical archaeology (MA, PhD); classics (MA, PhD). Terminal master's awarded for partial completion of doctoral program. *Degree requirements:* For master's, one foreign language, comprehensive exam, thesis; for doctorate, 2 foreign languages, comprehensive exam, thesis/dissertation. *Entrance requirements:* For master's and doctorate, GRE General Test, minimum GPA of 3.0. Electronic applications accepted.

The University of North Carolina at Greensboro, Graduate School, College of Arts and Sciences, Department of Classical Studies, Greensboro, NC 27412-5001. Offers Latin (M Ed). *Entrance requirements:* For master's, GRE General Test, MAT, or PRAXIS. Additional exam requirements/recommendations for international students: required—TOEFL. Electronic applications accepted.

University of Oregon, Graduate School, College of Arts and Sciences, Department of Classics, Eugene, OR 97403. Offers classical civilization (MA); classics (MA), including Greek, Latin; Greek (MA); Latin (MA). *Program availability:* Part-time. *Degree requirements:* For master's, 2 foreign languages, thesis or alternative. *Entrance requirements:* For master's, GRE General Test, minimum GPA of 3.0. Additional exam requirements/recommendations for international students: required—TOEFL.

University of Ottawa, Faculty of Graduate and Postdoctoral Studies, Faculty of Arts, Department of Classics and Religious Studies, Ottawa, ON K1N 6N5, Canada. Offers classical studies (MA); religious studies (PhD). *Degree requirements:* For master's, comprehensive exam, thesis or alternative; for doctorate, comprehensive exam, thesis/dissertation. *Entrance requirements:* For master's, honors degree or equivalent, minimum B average; for doctorate, master's degree, minimum B+ average. Electronic applications accepted.

University of Pennsylvania, School of Arts and Sciences, Graduate Group in Classical Studies, Philadelphia, PA 19104. Offers AM, PhD. *Faculty:* 17 full-time (8 women). *Students:* 23 full-time (14 women); includes 3 minority (all Two or more races, non-Hispanic/Latino), 7 international. Average age 28. 50 applicants, 18% accepted, 5 enrolled. In 2019, 1 master's, 2 doctorates awarded. Terminal master's awarded for partial completion of doctoral program. Application fee: $90.

University of South Africa, College of Human Sciences, Pretoria, South Africa. Offers adult education (M Ed); African languages (MA, PhD); African politics (MA, PhD); Afrikaans (MA, PhD); ancient history (MA, PhD); ancient Near Eastern studies (MA, PhD); anthropology (MA, PhD); applied linguistics (MA); Arabic (MA, PhD); archaeology (MA); art history (MA); Biblical archaeology (MA); Biblical studies (M Th, D Th, PhD); Christian spirituality (M Th, D Th); church history (M Th, D Th); classical studies (MA, PhD); clinical psychology (MA); communication (MA, PhD); comparative education (M Ed, Ed D); consulting psychology (D Admin, D Com, PhD); curriculum studies (M Ed, Ed D); development studies (M Admin, MA, D Admin, PhD); didactics (M Ed, Ed D); education (M Tech); education management (M Ed, Ed D); educational psychology (M Ed); English (MA); environmental education (M Ed); French (MA, PhD); German (MA, PhD); Greek (MA); guidance and counseling (M Ed); health studies (MA, PhD), including health sciences education (MA), health services management (MA), medical and surgical nursing science (critical care general) (MA), midwifery and neonatal nursing science (MA), trauma and emergency care (MA); history (MA, PhD); history of education (Ed D); inclusive education (M Ed, Ed D); information and communications technology policy and regulation (MA); information science (MA, MIS, PhD); international politics (MA, PhD); Islamic studies (MA, PhD); Italian (MA, PhD); Judaica (MA, PhD); linguistics (MA, PhD); mathematical education (M Ed); mathematics education (MA); missiology (M Th, D Th); modern Hebrew (MA, PhD); musicology (MA, MMus, D Mus, PhD); natural science education (M Ed); New Testament (M Th, D Th); Old Testament (D Th); pastoral therapy (M Th, D Th); philosophy (MA); philosophy of education (M Ed, Ed D); politics (MA, PhD); Portuguese (MA, PhD); practical theology (M Th, D Th); psychology (MA, MS, PhD); psychology of education (M Ed, Ed D); public health (MA); religious studies (MA, D Th, PhD); Romance languages (MA); Russian (MA, PhD); Semitic languages (MA, PhD); social behavior studies in HIV/AIDS (MA); social science (mental health) (MA); social science in development studies (MA); social science in psychology (MA); social science in social work (MA); social science in sociology (MA); social work (MSW, DSW, PhD); socio-education (M Ed, Ed D); sociolinguistics (MA); sociology (MA, PhD); Spanish (MA, PhD); systematic theology (M Th, D Th); TESOL (teaching English to speakers of other languages) (MA); theological ethics (M Th, D Th); theory of literature (MA, PhD); urban ministries (D Th); urban ministry (M Th).

University of Southern California, Graduate School, Dana and David Dornsife College of Letters, Arts and Sciences, Department of Classics, Los Angeles, CA 90089. Offers MA, PhD. Terminal master's awarded for partial completion of doctoral program. *Degree requirements:* For master's, 2 foreign languages, comprehensive exam, thesis or alternative, Greek and Latin; for doctorate, 2 foreign languages, comprehensive exam, thesis/dissertation, Greek and Latin. *Entrance requirements:* Additional exam requirements/recommendations for international students: required—TOEFL. Electronic applications accepted.

The University of Texas at Austin, Graduate School, College of Liberal Arts, Department of Classics, Austin, TX 78712-1111. Offers MA, PhD. *Degree requirements:* For master's, 2 foreign languages, comprehensive exam, thesis; for doctorate, 4 foreign languages, comprehensive exam, thesis/dissertation. *Entrance requirements:* For master's, GRE General Test, proficiency in classics; for doctorate, GRE General Test, master's degree in classics. Electronic applications accepted.

University of Toronto, School of Graduate Studies, Faculty of Arts and Science, Department of Classics, Toronto, ON M5S 1A1, Canada. Offers MA, PhD. *Program availability:* Part-time. *Degree requirements:* For master's, qualifying examinations, sight translation exams in Greek and Latin; for doctorate, thesis/dissertation, qualifying examinations, sight translation exams in Greek and Latin. *Entrance requirements:* For master's, minimum B+ average in final year of an undergraduate program in classics, 3-

4 years of course work in Greek and Latin; for doctorate, minimum B+ average with at least one A-; MA in classics. Electronic applications accepted.

University of Vermont, Graduate College, College of Arts and Sciences, Department of Classics, Burlington, VT 05404. Offers Greek and Latin (MA); Greek and Latin languages (Graduate Certificate); Latin (MAT). *Degree requirements:* For master's, one foreign language, thesis. *Entrance requirements:* For master's, GRE General Test, writing sample (for MA). Additional exam requirements/recommendations for international students: required—TOEFL (minimum score 550 paper-based, 90 iBT) or IELTS (6.5). Electronic applications accepted.

University of Victoria, Faculty of Graduate Studies, Faculty of Humanities, Department of Greek and Roman Studies, Victoria, BC V8W 2Y2, Canada. Offers MA, PhD. *Program availability:* Part-time. *Degree requirements:* For master's, 3 foreign languages, thesis. *Entrance requirements:* For master's, knowledge of Greek and Latin. Additional exam requirements/recommendations for international students: required—TOEFL (minimum score 575 paper-based), IELTS (minimum score 7). Electronic applications accepted.

University of Virginia, College and Graduate School of Arts and Sciences, Department of Classics, Charlottesville, VA 22903. Offers MA, PhD. *Degree requirements:* For master's, one foreign language, comprehensive exam, thesis, oral exam; for doctorate, 2 foreign languages, comprehensive exam, thesis/dissertation, oral exam. *Entrance requirements:* For master's and doctorate, GRE General Test, 2 letters of recommendation. Additional exam requirements/recommendations for international students: required—TOEFL (minimum score 600 paper-based; 90 iBT), IELTS (minimum score 7). Electronic applications accepted.

University of Washington, Graduate School, College of Arts and Sciences, Department of Classics, Seattle, WA 98195. Offers classics (MA, PhD), including ancient philosophy (PhD), classics (PhD), textual studies (PhD), theory and criticism (PhD). *Program availability:* Part-time. Terminal master's awarded for partial completion of doctoral program. *Degree requirements:* For master's, one foreign language, thesis or alternative; for doctorate, 2 foreign languages, comprehensive exam, thesis/dissertation. *Entrance requirements:* For master's, GRE, bachelor's degree in classics, Greek, or Latin; minimum GPA of 3.0; for doctorate, GRE, minimum GPA of 3.0. Additional exam requirements/recommendations for international students: required—TOEFL (minimum score 82 iBT). Electronic applications accepted.

University of Washington, Graduate School, College of Arts and Sciences, Department of Philosophy, Seattle, WA 98195. Offers classics and philosophy (PhD); philosophy (MA, PhD). Terminal master's awarded for partial completion of doctoral program. *Degree requirements:* For master's, 3 papers; for doctorate, thesis/dissertation, general exam. *Entrance requirements:* For master's and doctorate, GRE, minimum GPA of 3.0. Additional exam requirements/recommendations for international students: required—TOEFL.

The University of Western Ontario, School of Graduate and Postdoctoral Studies, Faculty of Arts and Humanities, Department of Classical Studies, London, ON N6A 3K7, Canada. Offers MA. *Program availability:* Part-time. *Degree requirements:* For master's, one foreign language. *Entrance requirements:* For master's, honors degree, minimum B+ average. Additional exam requirements/recommendations for international students: required—TOEFL.

University of Wisconsin–Madison, Graduate School, College of Letters and Science, Department of Classics, Madison, WI 53706-1380. Offers classics (MA, PhD); Greek (MA); Latin (MA). *Program availability:* Part-time. Terminal master's awarded for partial completion of doctoral program. *Degree requirements:* For master's, 3 foreign languages, oral and written exams; for doctorate, 4 foreign languages, thesis/dissertation, written exams. *Entrance requirements:* For master's, GRE; for doctorate, master's degree. Electronic applications accepted.

University of Wisconsin–Milwaukee, Graduate School, College of Letters and Science, Department of Foreign Languages and Literature, Milwaukee, WI 53201-0413. Offers foreign languages and literature (MA), including classic Greek, classics, comparative literature, French/Francophone language, literature, and culture, German language, literature, and culture, interpreting, Latin, linguistics, Spanish language, literature, and culture, translation; interpreting (Graduate Certificate); language, literature, and translation (MA, MALLT); translation (Graduate Certificate). *Program availability:* Part-time. *Degree requirements:* For master's, 2 foreign languages, thesis or alternative. *Entrance requirements:* Additional exam requirements/recommendations for international students: required—TOEFL (minimum score 550 paper-based; 79 iBT), IELTS (minimum score 6.5). Electronic applications accepted.

Villanova University, Graduate School of Liberal Arts and Sciences, Program in Classical Studies, Villanova, PA 19085-1699. Offers MA. *Program availability:* Part-time, evening/weekend, blended/hybrid learning. *Degree requirements:* For master's, comprehensive exam, thesis optional. *Entrance requirements:* For master's, minimum GPA of 3.0. Electronic applications accepted.

Washington University in St. Louis, The Graduate School, Department of Classics, St. Louis, MO 63130-4899. Offers MA, PhD. Terminal master's awarded for partial completion of doctoral program. *Degree requirements:* For master's, thesis or alternative. *Entrance requirements:* For master's and doctorate, GRE General Test. Additional exam requirements/recommendations for international students: required—TOEFL. Electronic applications accepted.

Yale University, Graduate School of Arts and Sciences, Department of Classics, New Haven, CT 06520. Offers M Phil, MA, PhD. *Degree requirements:* For doctorate, 2 foreign languages, thesis/dissertation. *Entrance requirements:* For doctorate, GRE General Test.

Comparative Literature

American University, College of Arts and Sciences, Department of Literature, Washington, DC 20016-8047. Offers creative writing (MFA); literature (MA). *Program availability:* Part-time, evening/weekend. *Degree requirements:* For master's, comprehensive exam. *Entrance requirements:* For master's, GRE, please visit website: https://www.american.edu/cas/literature/, writing sample, statement of purpose, transcripts, 2 letters of recommendation, resume. Additional exam requirements/recommendations for international students: required—TOEFL (minimum score 600 paper-based; 100 iBT). *Expenses:* Contact institution.

The American University in Cairo, School of Humanities and Social Sciences, Cairo, Egypt. Offers Arab and Islamic civilizations (Graduate Diploma); Arabic studies (MA); comparative literary studies (Graduate Diploma); Egyptology and Coptology (MA); English and comparative literature (MA); humanities and social sciences (Graduate Diploma); philosophy (MA); psychology (MA); sociology and anthropology (MA); teaching Arabic as a foreign language (MA); teaching English to speakers of other languages (MA). *Program availability:* Part-time, evening/weekend. *Degree requirements:* For master's, comprehensive exam (for some programs), thesis (for some programs). *Entrance requirements:* Additional exam requirements/recommendations for international students: required—TOEFL (minimum score 450 paper-based; 45 iBT), IELTS (minimum score 5). Electronic applications accepted.

Arizona State University at Tempe, College of Liberal Arts and Sciences, Department of English, Tempe, AZ 85287-0302. Offers applied linguistics (PhD); creative writing (MFA); English (MA, PhD), including comparative literature (MA), linguistics (MA), literature, rhetoric and composition (MA), rhetoric, composition, and linguistics (PhD); film and media studies (MAS), including American media and popular culture; linguistics (Graduate Certificate); teaching English to speakers of other languages (MTESOL); translation studies (Graduate Certificate). Terminal master's awarded for partial completion of doctoral program. *Degree requirements:* For master's, variable foreign language requirement, comprehensive exam (for some programs), thesis (for some programs), interactive Program of Study (iPOS) submitted before completing 50 percent of required credit hours; for doctorate, variable foreign language requirement, comprehensive exam, thesis/dissertation, interactive Program of Study (iPOS) submitted before completing 50 percent of required credit hours. *Entrance requirements:* For master's and doctorate, GRE, minimum GPA of 3.0 or equivalent in last 2 years of work leading to bachelor's degree. Additional exam requirements/recommendations for international students: required—TOEFL, IELTS, or PTE. Electronic applications accepted.

Binghamton University, State University of New York, Graduate School, Harpur College of Arts and Sciences, Department of Comparative Literature, Binghamton, NY 13902-6000. Offers MA, PhD. *Program availability:* Part-time. Terminal master's awarded for partial completion of doctoral program. *Degree requirements:* For master's, 2 foreign languages, comprehensive exam, thesis or alternative; for doctorate, 2 foreign languages, comprehensive exam, thesis/dissertation. *Entrance requirements:* For master's and doctorate, GRE General Test, writing sample. Additional exam requirements/recommendations for international students: required—TOEFL (minimum score 550 paper-based; 80 iBT). Electronic applications accepted.

Brigham Young University, Graduate Studies, College of Humanities, Department of Comparative Arts and Letters, Provo, UT 84602-1001. Offers comparative studies (MA). *Program availability:* Part-time. *Faculty:* 29 full-time (7 women), 4 part-time/adjunct (2 women). *Students:* 15 full-time (10 women), 1 (woman) part-time; includes 1 minority (Asian, non-Hispanic/Latino). Average age 29. 15 applicants, 60% accepted, 8 enrolled. In 2019, 8 master's awarded. *Degree requirements:* For master's, 2 foreign languages, comprehensive exam, thesis, Coursework - 33 credit hours in seminars at graduate level and other courses by approval. *Entrance requirements:* For master's, GRE, minimum GPA of 3.0 in last 60 hours, writing sample, foreign language experience, undergraduate degree or experience in a humanities discipline, Proficiency in a language of scholarship or other spoken language. Additional exam requirements/recommendations for international students: required—TOEFL (minimum score 580 paper-based; 85 iBT), E3PT (to obtain the required minimum English language proficieny scores for the E3PT, IELTS, or TOEFL tests; or to obtain waiver "f".) *Application deadline:* For fall admission, 3/1 for domestic and international students. Application fee: $50. Electronic applications accepted. *Financial support:* In 2019–20, 15 students received support, including 1 research assistantship, 15 teaching assistantships (averaging $5,000 per year); scholarships/grants, tuition waivers (partial), unspecified assistantships, and student instructorships also available. Support available to part-time students. Financial award application deadline: 9/1. *Unit head:* Dr. Julie Allen, Graduate Coordinator/Professor of Classical Studies, 801-422-7891, Fax: 801-422-0305, E-mail: julie_allen@byu.edu. *Application contact:* Andrea Kristensen, Graduate Program Manager, 801-422-2996, Fax: 801-422-0305, E-mail: andrea_kristensen@byu.edu.
Website: http://cal.byu.edu/

Brock University, Faculty of Graduate Studies, Faculty of Humanities, Program in Studies in Comparative Literatures and Arts, St. Catharines, ON L2S 3A1, Canada. Offers MA. *Degree requirements:* For master's, thesis optional. *Entrance requirements:* For master's, honors degree. Additional exam requirements/recommendations for international students: required—TOEFL (minimum score 550 paper-based; 80 iBT), IELTS (minimum score 6.5), TWE (minimum score 4). Electronic applications accepted.

Brown University, Graduate School, Department of Comparative Literature, Providence, RI 02912. Offers PhD. *Degree requirements:* For doctorate, 2 foreign languages, thesis/dissertation, preliminary exam. *Entrance requirements:* For doctorate, GRE General Test, GRE Subject Test.

California State University, Northridge, Graduate Studies, College of Humanities, Department of English, Northridge, CA 91330. Offers creative writing (MA); literature (MA); rhetoric and composition theory (MA). *Program availability:* Part-time, evening/weekend. *Degree requirements:* For master's, thesis or alternative. *Entrance requirements:* For master's, writing proficiency test, GRE General Test or minimum GPA of 3.0. Additional exam requirements/recommendations for international students: required—TOEFL.

Carleton University, Faculty of Graduate Studies, Faculty of Arts and Social Sciences, School for Languages, Literatures, and Comparative Literary Studies, Ottawa, ON K1S 5B6, Canada. Offers cultural mediations (PhD). *Entrance requirements:* Additional exam requirements/recommendations for international students: required—TOEFL.

Carnegie Mellon University, Dietrich College of Humanities and Social Sciences, Department of English, Pittsburgh, PA 15213-3891. Offers communication planning and design (M Des); literary and cultural studies (MA, PhD); professional writing (MAPW), including editing and publishing, policy and non-profit communication, public and media relations / corporate communications, science or healthcare communication, technical writing, writing for new media, writing for print media; rhetoric (MA, PhD). *Program availability:* Part-time. Terminal master's awarded for partial completion of doctoral program. *Degree requirements:* For doctorate, 2 foreign languages, comprehensive exam, thesis/dissertation. *Entrance requirements:* For master's and doctorate, GRE General Test. Additional exam requirements/recommendations for international students: required—TOEFL, TWE.

Comparative Literature

Case Western Reserve University, School of Graduate Studies, Department of Modern Languages and Literatures and Department of English, Program in World Literature, Cleveland, OH 44106. Offers MA. *Faculty:* 14 full-time (9 women). *Students:* 1 (woman) full-time. Average age 48. In 2019, 1 master's awarded. *Degree requirements:* For master's, 2 foreign languages, thesis, written exam. *Entrance requirements:* For master's, GRE General Test, sample of written work; project proposal. Additional exam requirements/recommendations for international students: required—TOEFL (minimum score 577 paper-based; 90 iBT); recommended—IELTS (minimum score 7). *Application deadline:* For fall admission, 3/1 priority date for domestic students. Applications are processed on a rolling basis. Application fee: $50. Electronic applications accepted. *Financial support:* Fellowships, career-related internships or fieldwork, institutionally sponsored loans, health care benefits, and tuition waivers (partial) available. Financial award application deadline: 3/1; financial award applicants required to submit CSS PROFILE or FAFSA. *Unit head:* Prof. Cheryl Toman, Professor of French/Chair, 216-368-2233, Fax: 216-368-2216. *Application contact:* Prof. Marie Lathers, Professor of French and Humanities, 216-368-8983, Fax: 216-368-2216, E-mail: marie.lathers@case.edu.
Website: http://artsci.case.edu/world-literature/

Claremont Graduate University, Graduate Programs, School of Arts and Humanities, Department of English, Claremont, CA 91711-6160. Offers American studies (MA, PhD); critical theory (MA, PhD); early modern studies (MA, PhD); English (M Phil, MA, PhD); literary theory (PhD); literature (MA, PhD); literature and creative writing (MA); literature and film (MA); MBA/MA; MBA/PhD. *Program availability:* Part-time. *Entrance requirements:* For master's and doctorate, GRE General Test. Additional exam requirements/recommendations for international students: required—TOEFL (minimum score 75 iBT). Electronic applications accepted.

Columbia University, Graduate School of Arts and Sciences, New York, NY 10027. Offers African-American studies (MA); American studies (MA); anthropology (MA, PhD); art history and archaeology (MA, PhD); astronomy (PhD); biological sciences (PhD); biotechnology (MA); chemical physics (PhD); chemistry (PhD); classical studies (MA, PhD); classics (MA, PhD); climate and society (MA); conservation biology (MA); earth and environmental sciences (PhD); East Asia: regional studies (MA); East Asian languages and cultures (MA, PhD); ecology, evolution and environmental biology (MA), including conservation biology; ecology, evolution, and environmental biology (PhD), including ecology and evolutionary biology, evolutionary primatology; economics (MA, PhD); English and comparative literature (MA, PhD); French and Romance philology (MA, PhD); Germanic languages (MA, PhD); global French studies (MA); global thought (MA); Hispanic cultural studies (MA); history (PhD); history and literature (MA); human rights studies (MA); Islamic studies (MA); Italian (MA, PhD); Japanese pedagogy (MA); Jewish studies (MA); Latin America and the Caribbean: regional studies (MA); Latin American and Iberian cultures (PhD); mathematics (MA, PhD), including finance (MA); medieval and Renaissance studies (MA); Middle Eastern, South Asian, and African studies (MA, PhD); modern art: critical and curatorial studies (MA); modern European studies (MA); museum anthropology (MA); music (DMA, PhD); oral history (MA); philosophical foundations of physics (MA); philosophy (MA, PhD); physics (PhD); political science (MA, PhD); psychology (PhD); quantitative methods in the social sciences (MA); religion (MA, PhD); Russia, Eurasia and East Europe: regional studies (MA); Russian translation (MA); Slavic cultures (MA); Slavic languages (MA, PhD); sociology (MA, PhD); South Asian studies (MA); statistics (MA, PhD); theatre (PhD). *Program availability:* Part-time. *Students:* 3,506 full-time (1,844 women), 208 part-time (121 women); includes 864 minority (110 Black or African American, non-Hispanic/Latino; 5 American Indian or Alaska Native, non-Hispanic/Latino; 416 Asian, non-Hispanic/Latino; 147 Hispanic/Latino; 6 Native Hawaiian or other Pacific Islander, non-Hispanic/Latino; 180 Two or more races, non-Hispanic/Latino), 2,065 international. 14,545 applicants, 25% accepted, 1,429 enrolled. In 2019, 1,262 master's, 363 doctorates awarded. Terminal master's awarded for partial completion of doctoral program. *Degree requirements:* For master's, variable foreign language requirement, comprehensive exam (for some programs), thesis (for some programs); for doctorate, variable foreign language requirement, comprehensive exam (for some programs), thesis/dissertation. *Entrance requirements:* For master's and doctorate, GRE General Test, GRE Subject Test (for some programs). Additional exam requirements/recommendations for international students: required—TOEFL (minimum score 600 paper-based; 100 iBT), IELTS (minimum score 7.5). Application fee: $115. Electronic applications accepted. *Expenses: Tuition:* Full-time $47,600; part-time $1880 per credit. One-time fee: $105. *Financial support:* Fellowships, research assistantships, teaching assistantships, career-related internships or fieldwork, Federal Work-Study, institutionally sponsored loans, scholarships/grants, traineeships, health care benefits, tuition waivers, and unspecified assistantships available. Support available to part-time students. Financial award application deadline: 12/15. *Unit head:* Dr. Carlos J. Alonso, Dean of the Graduate School of Arts and Sciences and Vice President for Graduate Education, 212-854-2861, E-mail: gsas-dean@columbia.edu. *Application contact:* GSAS Office of Admissions, 212-854-6729, E-mail: gsas-admissions@columbia.edu.
Website: http://gsas.columbia.edu/

Cornell University, Graduate School, Graduate Fields of Arts and Sciences, Field of Comparative Literature, Ithaca, NY 14853. Offers PhD. *Degree requirements:* For doctorate, 2 foreign languages, comprehensive exam, thesis/dissertation, teaching experience. *Entrance requirements:* For doctorate, GRE General Test, proficiency in 2 foreign literatures, writing sample, 3 letters of recommendation. Additional exam requirements/recommendations for international students: required—TOEFL (minimum score 550 paper-based; 77 iBT). Electronic applications accepted.

Dartmouth College, Guarini School of Graduate and Advanced Studies, Comparative Literature Program, Hanover, NH 03755. Offers MA. *Entrance requirements:* For master's, proficiency in 2 languages. Additional exam requirements/recommendations for international students: required—TOEFL. Electronic applications accepted.

Duke University, Graduate School, Program in Literature, Durham, NC 27708. Offers PhD, JD/MA. *Degree requirements:* For doctorate, 2 foreign languages, thesis/dissertation. *Entrance requirements:* For doctorate, GRE General Test, writing sample. Additional exam requirements/recommendations for international students: required—TOEFL (minimum score 577 paper-based; 90 iBT) or IELTS (minimum score 7).

East Carolina University, Graduate School, Thomas Harriot College of Arts and Sciences, Department of English, Greenville, NC 27858-4353. Offers creative writing (MA); English studies (MA); linguistics (MA); literature (MA); multicultural and transnational literatures (MA, Certificate); professional communication (Certificate); rhetoric and composition (MA); rhetoric, writing, and professional communication (PhD); teaching English in the two-year college (Certificate); teaching English to speakers of other languages (MA, Certificate); technical and professional communication (MA). *Program availability:* Part-time, evening/weekend, online learning. *Application deadline:* For fall admission, 7/31 priority date for domestic students, 2/1 priority date for international students; for spring admission, 11/30 priority date for domestic students, 10/1 priority date for international students. *Expenses: Tuition, area resident:* Full-time $4749; part-time $185 per credit hour. Tuition, state resident: full-time $4749; part-time $185 per credit hour. Tuition, nonresident: full-time $17,898; part-time $864 per credit hour. *International tuition:* $17,898 full-time. *Required fees:* $2787. *Financial support:* Application deadline: 3/1. *Unit head:* Dr. Marianne Montgomery, Chair, 252-328-6041, E-mail: montgomerym@ecu.edu. *Application contact:* Graduate School Admissions, 252-328-6012, Fax: 252-328-6071, E-mail: gradschool@ecu.edu.
Website: https://english.ecu.edu/

Emory University, Laney Graduate School, Department of Comparative Literature, Atlanta, GA 30322-1100. Offers comparative literature (PhD); philosophy (Certificate); psychoanalytic studies (PhD); women's studies (Certificate). *Degree requirements:* For doctorate, 2 foreign languages, comprehensive exam, thesis/dissertation. *Entrance requirements:* For doctorate, GRE General Test, minimum GPA of 3.0. Additional exam requirements/recommendations for international students: required—TOEFL. Electronic applications accepted.

Emory University, Laney Graduate School, Department of Spanish and Portuguese, Atlanta, GA 30322-1100. Offers comparative literature (Certificate); film studies (Certificate); Spanish (PhD); women's studies (Certificate). *Degree requirements:* For doctorate, 2 foreign languages, comprehensive exam, thesis/dissertation. *Entrance requirements:* For doctorate, GRE General Test. Additional exam requirements/recommendations for international students: required—TOEFL. Electronic applications accepted.

Fairleigh Dickinson University, Metropolitan Campus, University College: Arts, Sciences, and Professional Studies, Department of English, Philosophy, and Humanities, Program in English and Literature, Teaneck, NJ 07666-1914. Offers MA.

Florida Atlantic University, Dorothy F. Schmidt College of Arts and Letters, Department of Languages, Linguistics, and Comparative Literature, Boca Raton, FL 33431-0991. Offers comparative literature (MA); French (MA); linguistics (MA); Spanish (MA). *Program availability:* Part-time. *Faculty:* 20 full-time (13 women). *Students:* 29 full-time (17 women), 11 part-time (9 women); includes 22 minority (7 Black or African American, non-Hispanic/Latino; 1 Asian, non-Hispanic/Latino; 14 Hispanic/Latino), 4 international. Average age 37. 30 applicants, 67% accepted, 16 enrolled. In 2019, 14 master's awarded. *Degree requirements:* For master's, one foreign language, comprehensive exam, thesis optional. *Entrance requirements:* For master's, GRE General Test, minimum GPA of 3.0. Additional exam requirements/recommendations for international students: required—TOEFL (minimum score 500 paper-based; 61 iBT), IELTS (minimum score 6). *Application deadline:* For fall admission, 7/1 priority date for domestic students, 2/15 for international students; for spring admission, 11/1 for domestic students, 7/15 for international students. Applications are processed on a rolling basis. Application fee: $30. *Expenses: Tuition:* Full-time $20,536; part-time $371.82 per credit hour. Tuition and fees vary according to program. *Financial support:* Fellowships, research assistantships, teaching assistantships with partial tuition reimbursements, Federal Work-Study, and tuition waivers (partial) available. Support available to part-time students. Financial award application deadline: 4/1. *Unit head:* Dr. Marcella Munson, Chair, 561-297-2118, Fax: 561-297-2756, E-mail: mmunson@fau.edu. *Application contact:* Dr. Marcella Munson, Chair, 561-297-2118, Fax: 561-297-2756, E-mail: mmunson@fau.edu.
Website: http://www.fau.edu/LLCL/

Georgetown University, Graduate School of Arts and Sciences, School of Continuing Studies, Washington, DC 20057. Offers American studies (MALS); applied intelligence (MPS); Catholic studies (MALS); classical civilizations (MALS); emergency and disaster management (MPS); ethics and the professions (MALS); global strategic communications (MPS); hospitality management (MPS); human resources management (MPS); humanities (MALS); individualized study (MALS); integrated marketing communications (MPS); international affairs (MALS); Islam and Muslim-Christian relations (MALS); journalism (MPS); liberal studies (DLS); literature and society (MALS); medieval and early modern European studies (MALS); public relations and corporate communications (MPS); real estate (MPS); religious studies (MALS); social and public policy (MALS); sports industry management (MPS); systems engineering management (MPS); technology management (MPS); the theory and practice of American democracy (MALS); urban and regional planning (MPS); visual culture (MALS). *Entrance requirements:* Additional exam requirements/recommendations for international students: required—TOEFL.

The Graduate Center, City University of New York, Graduate Studies, Program in Comparative Literature, New York, NY 10016-4039. Offers comparative literature (MA, PhD), including Italian (PhD). Terminal master's awarded for partial completion of doctoral program. *Degree requirements:* For master's, 2 foreign languages, comprehensive exam, thesis; for doctorate, 3 foreign languages, comprehensive exam, thesis/dissertation. *Entrance requirements:* For master's and doctorate, GRE General Test. Additional exam requirements/recommendations for international students: required—TOEFL. Electronic applications accepted.

Harrison Middleton University, Graduate Program, Tempe, AZ 85282. Offers education (MA, Ed D); humanities (MA); imaginative literature (MA); interdisciplinary studies (DA); jurisprudence (MA); natural science (MA); philosophy and religion (MA); social science (MA). *Program availability:* Part-time, evening/weekend, online learning. *Degree requirements:* For master's and doctorate, capstone project. *Entrance requirements:* For master's, interview; for doctorate, 2 academic letters of reference, interview, essay. Additional exam requirements/recommendations for international students: required—TOEFL (minimum score 550 paper-based; 80 iBT). Electronic applications accepted.

Harvard University, Graduate School of Arts and Sciences, Department of Comparative Literature, Cambridge, MA 02138. Offers comparative literature (PhD); oral literature (PhD). *Degree requirements:* For doctorate, 4 foreign languages, thesis/dissertation, written and oral exams. *Entrance requirements:* For doctorate, GRE General Test, GRE Subject Test (recommended), sample of written work. Additional exam requirements/recommendations for international students: required—TOEFL.

Hunter College of the City University of New York, Graduate School, School of Arts and Sciences, Department of English, Program in Literature, Language, and Theory, New York, NY 10065-5085. Offers MA. *Program availability:* Part-time, evening/weekend. *Degree requirements:* For master's, one foreign language, comprehensive exam, thesis. *Entrance requirements:* For master's, GRE General Test, minimum 18 credits of course work in English, excluding journalism and writing; statement of purpose. Additional exam requirements/recommendations for international students: required—TOEFL.

Indiana University Bloomington, University Graduate School, College of Arts and Sciences, Department of Comparative Literature, Bloomington, IN 47405. Offers MA, MAT, PhD. *Program availability:* Part-time. *Degree requirements:* For master's, 2 foreign languages, comprehensive exam (for some programs), thesis (for some programs); for doctorate, 3 foreign languages, comprehensive exam, thesis/dissertation. *Entrance requirements:* For master's, GRE, proficiency in 1 foreign language, 25-page writing sample, 3 letters of recommendation, transcripts, statement of purpose; for doctorate, GRE, proficiency in 2 foreign languages, 25-page writing sample, 3 letters of recommendation, transcripts, statement of purpose. Additional exam requirements/recommendations for international students: required—TOEFL (minimum score 550 paper-based; 79 iBT). Electronic applications accepted.

Johns Hopkins University, Zanvyl Krieger School of Arts and Sciences, Department of Comparative Thought and Literature, Baltimore, MD 21218. Offers comparative literature (PhD); intellectual history (PhD). *Degree requirements:* For doctorate, 2 foreign languages, thesis/dissertation. *Entrance requirements:* For doctorate, samples of written work. Additional exam requirements/recommendations for international students: required—TOEFL (minimum score 600 paper-based; 100 iBT), IELTS (minimum score 7). Electronic applications accepted. *Expenses:* Contact institution.

Louisiana State University and Agricultural & Mechanical College, Graduate School, College of Humanities and Social Sciences, Interdepartmental Program in Comparative Literature, Baton Rouge, LA 70803. Offers MA, PhD.

New York University, Graduate School of Arts and Science, Department of Comparative Literature, New York, NY 10012-1019. Offers MA, PhD. *Program availability:* Part-time. *Degree requirements:* For master's, 2 foreign languages, thesis; for doctorate, 3 foreign languages, thesis/dissertation. *Entrance requirements:* For master's and doctorate, GRE General Test. Additional exam requirements/recommendations for international students: required—TOEFL, IELTS.

Northwestern University, The Graduate School, Judd A. and Marjorie Weinberg College of Arts and Sciences, Program in Comparative Literary Studies, Evanston, IL 60208. Offers PhD. *Program availability:* Part-time. *Degree requirements:* For doctorate, 2 foreign languages, thesis/dissertation, preliminary exams. *Entrance requirements:* For doctorate, GRE General Test, sample of written work. Additional exam requirements/recommendations for international students: required—TOEFL.

Northwestern University, School of Professional Studies, Program in Literature, Evanston, IL 60208. Offers American literature (MA); British literature (MA); comparative and world literature (MA). *Program availability:* Part-time, evening/weekend.

Penn State University Park, Graduate School, College of the Liberal Arts, Department of Comparative Literature, University Park, PA 16802. Offers comparative literature (MA, PhD); Russian and comparative literature (MA).

Princeton University, Graduate School, Department of Comparative Literature, Princeton, NJ 08544. Offers PhD. *Degree requirements:* For doctorate, variable foreign language requirement, thesis/dissertation. *Entrance requirements:* For doctorate, GRE General Test, GRE Subject Test, sample of written work. Additional exam requirements/recommendations for international students: required—TOEFL (minimum score 600 paper-based). Electronic applications accepted.

Purdue University, Graduate School, College of Liberal Arts, Program in Comparative Literature, West Lafayette, IN 47907. Offers MA, PhD. *Program availability:* Part-time. *Students:* 8 full-time (3 women), 5 part-time (3 women), 10 international. Average age 31. 20 applicants, 35% accepted, 3 enrolled. In 2019, 5 doctorates awarded. *Degree requirements:* For master's, comprehensive exam (for some programs), thesis optional; for doctorate, comprehensive exam, thesis/dissertation. *Entrance requirements:* For master's, GRE General Test, minimum undergraduate GPA of 3.0 or equivalent; for doctorate, GRE General Test, minimum undergraduate GPA of 3.0 or equivalent; master's degree with minimum GPA of 3.0 or equivalent. Additional exam requirements/recommendations for international students: required—TOEFL (minimum score 550 paper-based; 77 iBT); recommended—TWE. *Application deadline:* For fall admission, 1/10 priority date for domestic and international students; for spring admission, 10/1 for domestic and international students. Applications are processed on a rolling basis. Application fee: $60 ($75 for international students). Electronic applications accepted. *Financial support:* In 2019–20, teaching assistantships with tuition reimbursements (averaging $12,000 per year) were awarded; fellowships also available. Support available to part-time students. Financial award application deadline: 4/1; financial award applicants required to submit FAFSA. *Unit head:* Venetria Patton, Head, 765-496-9629, E-mail: vpatton@purdue.edu. *Application contact:* Brandi Plantenga Plantenga, Graduate Contact, 765-496-9629, E-mail: bplante@purdue.edu. Website: https://www.cla.purdue.edu/complit/

Rutgers University - New Brunswick, Graduate School-New Brunswick, Program in Comparative Literature, Piscataway, NJ 08854-8097. Offers MA, PhD. *Program availability:* Part-time. Terminal master's awarded for partial completion of doctoral program. *Degree requirements:* For master's, comprehensive exam; for doctorate, 3 foreign languages, thesis/dissertation, written and oral exams. *Entrance requirements:* For doctorate, GRE General Test, GRE Subject Test (recommended). Additional exam requirements/recommendations for international students: required—TOEFL. Electronic applications accepted.

San Francisco State University, Division of Graduate Studies, College of Liberal and Creative Arts, Department of Comparative and World Literature, San Francisco, CA 94132-1722. Offers comparative literature (MA). *Program availability:* Part-time. *Application deadline:* Applications are processed on a rolling basis. *Expenses:* Tuition, area resident: Full-time $7176; part-time $4164 per year. Tuition, state resident: full-time $7176; part-time $4164 per year. Tuition, nonresident: full-time $16,680; part-time $396 per unit. *International tuition:* $16,680 full-time. *Required fees:* $1524; $1524 per unit. $762 per semester. Tuition and fees vary according to degree level and program. *Unit head:* Dr. Dane Johnson, Chair, 415-338-3072, Fax: 415-338-6159, E-mail: danej@sfsu.edu. *Application contact:* Dr. Shirin Khanmohamadi, Graduate Coordinator, 415-338-7035, Fax: 415-338-6159, E-mail: shirin1@sfsu.edu. Website: http://complit.sfsu.edu/

Stanford University, School of Humanities and Sciences, Department of Comparative Literature, Stanford, CA 94305-2004. Offers PhD. *Expenses: Tuition:* Full-time $52,479; part-time $34,110 per unit. *Required fees:* $672; $224 per quarter. Tuition and fees vary according to program and student level. Website: http://www.stanford.edu/dept/complit/

Stanford University, School of Humanities and Sciences, Program in Modern Thought and Literature, Stanford, CA 94305-2004. Offers PhD. *Expenses: Tuition:* Full-time $52,479; part-time $34,110 per unit. *Required fees:* $672; $224 per quarter. Tuition and fees vary according to program and student level. Website: http://www.stanford.edu/dept/MTL/

Stony Brook University, State University of New York, Graduate School, College of Arts and Sciences, Department of Cultural Studies and Comparative Literature, Stony Brook, NY 11794. Offers comparative literature (MA, PhD); cultural studies (PhD, Certificate). *Program availability:* Evening/weekend. *Faculty:* 3 full-time (1 woman). *Students:* 19 full-time (11 women), 3 part-time (all women); includes 4 minority (1 Black or African American, non-Hispanic/Latino; 2 Asian, non-Hispanic/Latino; 1 Hispanic/Latino), 9 international. Average age 38. In 2019, 6 master's, 2 doctorates awarded. Terminal master's awarded for partial completion of doctoral program. *Degree requirements:* For master's, 2 foreign languages, exam; for doctorate, 3 foreign languages, comprehensive exam, thesis/dissertation. *Entrance requirements:* For master's and doctorate, GRE General Test, minimum GPA of 3.5 in major, 3.0 overall. Additional exam requirements/recommendations for international students: required—TOEFL. *Application deadline:* For fall admission, 1/15 for domestic students; for spring admission, 10/1 for domestic students. Application fee: $100. Electronic applications accepted. *Expenses:* Contact institution. *Financial support:* In 2019–20, 8 teaching assistantships were awarded; fellowships and research assistantships also available.

Unit head: Prof. Mary C Rawlinson, 631-632-7464, Fax: 631-632-5707, E-mail: Mary.Rawlinson@stonybrook.edu. *Application contact:* Mary Moran-Luba, Coordinator, 631-632-6935, Fax: 631-632-5707, E-mail: mary.moran-luba@stonybrook.edu. Website: http://www.stonybrook.edu/commcms/cat/index.html

Université de Montréal, Faculty of Arts and Sciences, Department of Comparative Literature, Montréal, QC H3C 3J7, Canada. Offers comparative literature (MA); literature (PhD). *Degree requirements:* For master's, 2 foreign languages, thesis; for doctorate, 3 foreign languages, thesis/dissertation, general exam. *Entrance requirements:* For doctorate, MA with minimum B+ average. Electronic applications accepted.

Université de Sherbrooke, Faculty of Letters and Human Sciences, Department of Letters and Communications, Sherbrooke, QC J1K 2R1, Canada. Offers comparative Canadian literature (MA, PhD); French literature (MA, PhD); linguistics (MA); theatre (MA). *Degree requirements:* For master's, thesis or alternative; for doctorate, thesis/dissertation. *Entrance requirements:* For master's, minimum GPA of 2.8; for doctorate, minimum GPA of 3.0.

Université du Québec à Chicoutimi, Graduate Programs, Program in Literary Studies, Chicoutimi, QC G7H 2B1, Canada. Offers MA. *Program availability:* Part-time. *Degree requirements:* For master's, thesis optional. *Entrance requirements:* For master's, appropriate bachelor's degree, proficiency in French.

Université du Québec à Montréal, Graduate Programs, Program in Literary Studies, Montréal, QC H3C 3P8, Canada. Offers MA, PhD. *Program availability:* Part-time. *Degree requirements:* For master's, thesis; for doctorate, thesis/dissertation. *Entrance requirements:* For master's, appropriate bachelor's degree or equivalent, proficiency in French; for doctorate, appropriate master's degree or equivalent, proficiency in French.

Université du Québec à Montréal, Graduate Programs, Program in Semiology, Montréal, QC H3C 3P8, Canada. Offers PhD. *Program availability:* Part-time. *Degree requirements:* For doctorate, thesis/dissertation. *Entrance requirements:* For doctorate, appropriate master's degree or equivalent, proficiency in French.

Université du Québec à Rimouski, Graduate Programs, Program in Literary Studies, Rimouski, QC G5L 3A1, Canada. Offers MA, PhD. *Program availability:* Part-time. *Degree requirements:* For master's, thesis or alternative. *Entrance requirements:* For master's, appropriate bachelor's degree, proficiency in French.

Université du Québec à Trois-Rivières, Graduate Programs, Program in Literary Studies, Trois-Rivières, QC G9A 5H7, Canada. Offers MA. *Program availability:* Part-time. *Degree requirements:* For master's, thesis optional. *Entrance requirements:* For master's, appropriate bachelor's degree, proficiency in French.

University at Buffalo, the State University of New York, Graduate School, College of Arts and Sciences, Department of Comparative Literature, Amherst, NY 14260. Offers MA, PhD. *Program availability:* Part-time. *Faculty:* 7 full-time (2 women). *Students:* 30 full-time (16 women), 1 (woman) part-time; includes 7 minority (6 Asian, non-Hispanic/Latino; 1 Hispanic/Latino), 10 international. Average age 25. 35 applicants, 46% accepted, 7 enrolled. In 2019, 3 master's, 3 doctorates awarded. Terminal master's awarded for partial completion of doctoral program. *Degree requirements:* For master's, one foreign language, exam or project; for doctorate, 2 foreign languages, comprehensive exam, thesis/dissertation. *Entrance requirements:* For master's, writing sample, 3 letters of recommendation, statement of purpose, undergraduate transcripts; for doctorate, GRE General Test, writing sample, 3 letters of recommendation, statement of purpose, undergraduate transcripts. Additional exam requirements/recommendations for international students: required—TOEFL (minimum score 550 paper-based; 79 iBT), IELTS. *Application deadline:* For fall admission, 1/1 for domestic and international students. Application fee: $75. Electronic applications accepted. *Expenses: Tuition, area resident:* Full-time $11,310; part-time $471 per credit hour. Tuition, state resident: full-time $11,310; part-time $471 per credit hour. Tuition, nonresident: full-time $23,100; part-time $963 per credit hour. *International tuition:* $23,100 full-time. *Required fees:* $2820. *Financial support:* In 2019–20, 9 students received support, including 2 fellowships with full tuition reimbursements available (averaging $4,150 per year), 9 teaching assistantships with full tuition reimbursements available (averaging $20,400 per year); health care benefits and unspecified assistantships also available. Financial award application deadline: 1/1; financial award applicants required to submit FAFSA. *Unit head:* Dr. Krzysztof Ziarek, Chair, 716-645-0858, Fax: 716-645-5979, E-mail: kziarek@buffalo.edu. *Application contact:* Dr. Kalliopi Nikolopoulou, Director of Graduate Studies, 716-645-0857, Fax: 716-645-5979, E-mail: kn34@buffalo.edu. Website: http://www.complit.buffalo.edu/

University of Arkansas, Graduate School, Interdisciplinary Program in Comparative Literature and Cultural Studies, Fayetteville, AR 72701. Offers MA, PhD. *Students:* 22 full-time (10 women), 17 part-time (9 women); includes 6 minority (1 Black or African American, non-Hispanic/Latino; 2 Asian, non-Hispanic/Latino; 3 Hispanic/Latino), 20 international. 6 applicants, 83% accepted. In 2019, 4 master's, 5 doctorates awarded. *Degree requirements:* For doctorate, 2 foreign languages, comprehensive exam, thesis/dissertation optional. *Entrance requirements:* For doctorate, GRE General Test, official transcripts of all undergraduate and graduate work, three letters of recommendation, writing sample, statement of purpose. Additional exam requirements/recommendations for international students: required—TOEFL (minimum score 550 paper-based; 80 iBT) or IELTS (minimum score 6.5). *Application deadline:* For fall admission, 8/1 for domestic students, 4/1 for international students; for spring admission, 12/1 for domestic students, 10/1 for international students; for summer admission, 4/15 for domestic students, 3/1 for international students. Application fee: $60. Electronic applications accepted. *Financial support:* In 2019–20, 1 research assistantship, 13 teaching assistantships were awarded; fellowships, Federal Work-Study, and institutionally sponsored loans also available. *Unit head:* Dr. Luis Fernando Restrepo, Director Comparative Literature and Cultural Studies, 479-575-7580, E-mail: lrestr@uark.edu. *Application contact:* Dr. Luis Fernando Restrepo, Director Comparative Literature and Cultural Studies, 479-575-7580, E-mail: lrestr@uark.edu. Website: https://fulbright.uark.edu/programs/comparative-literature-cultural-studies/index.php

University of California, Berkeley, Graduate Division, College of Letters and Science, Department of Comparative Literature, Berkeley, CA 94720. Offers PhD. *Degree requirements:* For doctorate, 3 foreign languages, thesis/dissertation, qualifying exam. *Entrance requirements:* For doctorate, GRE General Test, fluency in 1 foreign language (2 preferred), minimum GPA of 3.0, writing sample, 3 letters of recommendation. Additional exam requirements/recommendations for international students: recommended—TOEFL (minimum score 570 paper-based; 90 iBT). Electronic applications accepted.

University of California, Davis, Graduate Studies, Graduate Group in Comparative Literature, Davis, CA 95616. Offers PhD. *Degree requirements:* For doctorate, 3 foreign languages, thesis/dissertation. *Entrance requirements:* For doctorate, GRE General Test, minimum GPA of 3.0. Additional exam requirements/recommendations for international students: required—TOEFL (minimum score 550 paper-based). Electronic applications accepted.

Comparative Literature

University of California, Irvine, School of Humanities, Department of Comparative Literature, Irvine, CA 92697. Offers MA, PhD. *Students:* 36 full-time (19 women); includes 9 minority (1 Black or African American, non-Hispanic/Latino; 4 Asian, non-Hispanic/Latino; 1 Hispanic/Latino; 3 Two or more races, non-Hispanic/Latino), 12 international. Average age 32. 57 applicants, 9% accepted, 1 enrolled. In 2019, 6 master's, 3 doctorates awarded. *Degree requirements:* For master's, one foreign language; for doctorate, 2 foreign languages, thesis/dissertation. *Entrance requirements:* For doctorate, GRE General Test, minimum GPA of 3.5, sample of written work, 3 letters of recommendation. Additional exam requirements/recommendations for international students: required—TOEFL (minimum score 550 paper-based). *Application deadline:* For fall admission, 12/15 for domestic and international students. Application fee: $120 ($140 for international students). Electronic applications accepted. *Financial support:* Fellowships with full tuition reimbursements, research assistantships with full tuition reimbursements, teaching assistantships with partial tuition reimbursements, institutionally sponsored loans, and tuition waivers (partial) available. Financial award application deadline: 3/1; financial award applicants required to submit FAFSA. *Unit head:* Gabriele Schwab, Department Chair, 949-824-6406, Fax: 949-824-6416, E-mail: gmschwab@uci.edu. *Application contact:* Bindya Baliga, Graduate Coordinator, 949-824-7968, E-mail: bbaliga@uci.edu.

University of California, Los Angeles, Graduate Division, College of Letters and Science, Department of Comparative Literature, Los Angeles, CA 90095. Offers MA, PhD. Terminal master's awarded for partial completion of doctoral program. *Degree requirements:* For master's, 2 foreign languages; for doctorate, 2 foreign languages, thesis/dissertation, oral and written qualifying exams. *Entrance requirements:* For doctorate, GRE General Test, bachelor's degree; minimum undergraduate GPA of 3.0, 3.4 in upper-division literature courses (or its equivalent if letter grade system not used); literary proficiency in one foreign language and elementary knowledge of another; writing sample. Additional exam requirements/recommendations for international students: required—TOEFL. Electronic applications accepted.

University of California, Riverside, Graduate Division, Department of Comparative Literature and Foreign Languages, Riverside, CA 92521-0102. Offers comparative literature (MA, PhD). Terminal master's awarded for partial completion of doctoral program. *Degree requirements:* For master's, 3 foreign languages, comprehensive exam; for doctorate, 3 foreign languages, thesis/dissertation, qualifying exams. *Entrance requirements:* For master's and doctorate, GRE General Test, minimum GPA of 3.0. Additional exam requirements/recommendations for international students: required—TOEFL (minimum score 550 paper-based; 80 iBT). Electronic applications accepted.

University of California, Santa Barbara, Graduate Division, College of Letters and Sciences, Division of Humanities and Fine Arts, Program in Comparative Literature, Santa Barbara, CA 93106-4130. Offers comparative literature (PhD); East Asian literatures (PhD); feminist studies (PhD); French (PhD); global studies (PhD); translation studies (PhD); MA/PhD. *Degree requirements:* For doctorate, 2 foreign languages, comprehensive exam, thesis/dissertation. *Entrance requirements:* For doctorate, GRE. Additional exam requirements/recommendations for international students: required—TOEFL (minimum score 550 paper-based; 80 iBT), IELTS (minimum score 7). Electronic applications accepted.

University of California, Santa Cruz, Division of Graduate Studies, Division of Humanities, Department of Literature, Santa Cruz, CA 95064. Offers MA, PhD. Terminal master's awarded for partial completion of doctoral program. *Degree requirements:* For master's, thesis; for doctorate, one foreign language, thesis/dissertation, qualifying exam. *Entrance requirements:* For master's, GRE General Test, writing sample, minimum GPA of 3.5; for doctorate, GRE General Test, minimum GPA of 3.5, writing sample. Additional exam requirements/recommendations for international students: required—TOEFL (minimum score 550 paper-based; 83 iBT); recommended—IELTS (minimum score 8). Electronic applications accepted.

University of Chicago, Division of the Humanities, Department of Comparative Literature, Chicago, IL 60637. Offers PhD. Terminal master's awarded for partial completion of doctoral program. *Degree requirements:* For doctorate, 2 foreign languages, comprehensive exam, thesis/dissertation. *Entrance requirements:* For doctorate, GRE General Test, 15-20 page writing sample, statement of purpose, 3 letters of recommendation, transcripts for all previous degrees and institutions attended. Additional exam requirements/recommendations for international students: required—TOEFL (minimum score 104 iBT), IELTS (minimum score 7). Electronic applications accepted.

University of Chicago, Division of the Humanities, Master of Arts Program in the Humanities, Chicago, IL 60637. Offers art history (MA); cinema and media studies (MA); classic languages (MA); comparative literature (MA); creative writing (MA); cultural policy studies (MA); digital humanities (MA); East Asian languages and civilizations (MA); English language and literature (MA); gender and sexuality studies (MA); Germanic studies (MA); linguistics (MA); music (MA); near Eastern languages and civilizations (MA); philosophy (MA); poetics (MA); race, politics and culture (MA); Romance languages and literatures (MA); Slavic languages and literatures (MA); South Asian languages and civilizations (MA); theater and performance studies (MA). *Degree requirements:* For master's, thesis. *Entrance requirements:* For master's, GRE General Test, 10-15 page writing sample, statement of purpose, 3 letters of recommendation, transcripts for all previous degrees and institutions attended. Additional exam requirements/recommendations for international students: required—TOEFL (minimum score 104 iBT), IELTS (minimum score 7). Electronic applications accepted. *Expenses:* Contact institution.

University of Georgia, Franklin College of Arts and Sciences, Department of Comparative Literature, Athens, GA 30602. Offers MA, PhD. *Degree requirements:* For master's, 2 foreign languages, thesis; for doctorate, one foreign language, thesis/dissertation. *Entrance requirements:* For master's and doctorate, GRE General Test. Electronic applications accepted.

University of Guelph, Office of Graduate and Postdoctoral Studies, College of Arts, School of English and Theatre Studies, Joint Program in Literary Studies/Theatre Studies in English, Guelph, ON N1G 2W1, Canada. Offers PhD. *Program availability:* Part-time. *Degree requirements:* For doctorate, one foreign language, comprehensive exam, thesis/dissertation. *Entrance requirements:* For doctorate, MA, 3 letters of reference, writing samples, resume, minimum A- average in graduate course work. Additional exam requirements/recommendations for international students: required—TOEFL. Electronic applications accepted.

University of Houston, College of Liberal Arts and Social Sciences, Department of Modern and Classical Languages, Houston, TX 77204. Offers world cultures and literatures (MA). *Degree requirements:* For master's, one foreign language, thesis optional. *Entrance requirements:* For master's, GRE General Test, minimum GPA of 3.0 in last 60 hours of course work. Additional exam requirements/recommendations for international students: required—TOEFL (minimum score 500 paper-based). Electronic applications accepted.

University of Illinois at Urbana-Champaign, Graduate College, College of Liberal Arts and Sciences, School of Literatures, Cultures and Linguistics, Program in Comparative and World Literature, Champaign, IL 61820. Offers comparative literature (MA, PhD). *Entrance requirements:* For master's, minimum GPA of 3.0; writing sample.

University of Maryland, College Park, Academic Affairs, College of Arts and Humanities, Department of English, Program in Comparative Literature, College Park, MD 20742. Offers MA, PhD. *Degree requirements:* For master's, thesis, oral defense; for doctorate, 3 foreign languages, thesis/dissertation, comprehensive exams in 4 areas. *Entrance requirements:* For master's, GRE General Test, foreign language, writing sample, 3 letters of recommendation; for doctorate, GRE General Test, minimum GPA of 3.0, foreign language, writing sample. Additional exam requirements/recommendations for international students: required—TOEFL. Electronic applications accepted.

University of Massachusetts Amherst, Graduate School, College of Humanities and Fine Arts, Department of Languages, Literatures, and Cultures, Program in Comparative Literature, Amherst, MA 01003. Offers MA, PhD. *Program availability:* Part-time. Terminal master's awarded for partial completion of doctoral program. *Degree requirements:* For master's, thesis or alternative; for doctorate, comprehensive exam, thesis/dissertation. *Entrance requirements:* For master's and doctorate, GRE General Test, writing samples. Additional exam requirements/recommendations for international students: required—TOEFL (minimum score 550 paper-based; 80 iBT), IELTS (minimum score 6.5). Electronic applications accepted.

University of Memphis, Graduate School, College of Arts and Sciences, Department of English, Memphis, TN 38152. Offers African-American literature (Graduate Certificate); applied linguistics (PhD); composition studies (PhD); creative writing (MFA); English as a second language (MA); linguistics (MA); literary and cultural studies (PhD), including African-American literature; literature (MA); professional writing (MA, PhD); teaching English as a second/foreign language (Graduate Certificate). *Program availability:* Part-time, evening/weekend, 100% online. *Students:* 58 full-time (33 women), 76 part-time (52 women); includes 34 minority (24 Black or African American, non-Hispanic/Latino; 4 Asian, non-Hispanic/Latino; 5 Hispanic/Latino; 1 Two or more races, non-Hispanic/Latino), 16 international. Average age 36. 52 applicants, 92% accepted, 23 enrolled. In 2019, 19 master's, 15 doctorates, 8 other advanced degrees awarded. Terminal master's awarded for partial completion of doctoral program. *Degree requirements:* For master's, variable foreign language requirement, comprehensive exam, thesis optional; for doctorate, variable foreign language requirement, comprehensive exam, thesis/dissertation, qualifying exam. *Entrance requirements:* For master's, GRE, minimum undergraduate GPA of 3.0, statement of purpose, two letters of recommendation; for doctorate, GRE, minimum undergraduate and graduate GPA of 3.25, statement of purpose, writing sample, three letters of recommendation. Additional exam requirements/recommendations for international students: required—TOEFL. *Application deadline:* For fall admission, 1/15 for domestic students; for spring admission, 10/15 for domestic students. Applications are processed on a rolling basis. Application fee: $35 ($60 for international students). Electronic applications accepted. *Expenses:* Tuition, area resident: Full-time $9216; part-time $512 per credit hour. Tuition, state resident: full-time $9216; part-time $512 per credit hour. Tuition, nonresident: full-time $12,672; part-time $704 per credit hour. *International tuition:* $16,128 full-time. *Required fees:* $1530; $85 per credit hour. Tuition and fees vary according to program. *Financial support:* Research assistantships with full tuition reimbursements, teaching assistantships with full tuition reimbursements, Federal Work-Study, scholarships/grants, and unspecified assistantships available. Financial award application deadline: 2/1; financial award applicants required to submit FAFSA. *Unit head:* Dr. Joshua Phillips, Chair, 901-678-2651, Fax: 901-678-2226, E-mail: jsphllps@memphis.edu. *Application contact:* Dr. Jeffrey Scraba, Director of Graduate Studies, 901-678-4768, Fax: 901-678-2226, E-mail: jscraba@memphis.edu. Website: http://www.memphis.edu/english

University of Michigan, Rackham Graduate School, College of Literature, Science, and the Arts, Department of Comparative Literature, Ann Arbor, MI 48109. Offers PhD. *Degree requirements:* For doctorate, thesis/dissertation, 2 languages at advanced level in addition to language of instruction, preliminary exam, topics paper, prospectus, oral defense of dissertation. *Entrance requirements:* For doctorate, GRE General Test. Additional exam requirements/recommendations for international students: required—TOEFL (minimum score 560 paper-based; 84 iBT), Michigan English Language Assessment Battery, or IELTS (minimum score 6.5). Electronic applications accepted.

University of Minnesota, Twin Cities Campus, Graduate School, College of Liberal Arts, Department of Cultural Studies and Comparative Literature, Program in Comparative Literature, Minneapolis, MN 55455-0213. Offers PhD. *Degree requirements:* For doctorate, 3 foreign languages, comprehensive exam, thesis/dissertation. *Entrance requirements:* For doctorate, GRE General Test, sample of written work. Additional exam requirements/recommendations for international students: required—TOEFL.

University of Nebraska–Lincoln, Graduate College, College of Arts and Sciences, Department of English, Lincoln, NE 68588-0333. Offers composition and rhetoric (MA, PhD); creative writing (MA, PhD); literature studies (MA, PhD). *Degree requirements:* For master's, thesis optional; for doctorate, one foreign language, comprehensive exam, thesis/dissertation. *Entrance requirements:* For master's, writing sample; for doctorate, GRE General Test, writing sample. Additional exam requirements/recommendations for international students: required—TOEFL (minimum score 600 paper-based). Electronic applications accepted.

University of New Mexico, Graduate Studies, College of Arts and Sciences, Program in Foreign Languages and Literatures, Albuquerque, NM 87131-2039. Offers comparative literature and cultural studies (MA); French (MA); French studies (PhD); German studies (MA). *Program availability:* Part-time. *Degree requirements:* For master's, one foreign language, thesis optional; for doctorate, 2 foreign languages, thesis/dissertation. *Entrance requirements:* For master's and doctorate, transcript, writing sample, 3 letters of recommendation. Additional exam requirements/recommendations for international students: required—TOEFL. Electronic applications accepted. *Expenses:* Tuition, state resident: full-time $7633; part-time $972 per year. Tuition, nonresident: full-time $22,586; part-time $3840 per year. *International tuition:* $23,292 full-time. *Required fees:* $8608. Tuition and fees vary according to course level, course load, degree level, program and student level.

University of Notre Dame, The Graduate School, College of Arts and Letters, Division of Humanities, PhD Program in Literature, Notre Dame, IN 46556. Offers PhD. *Degree requirements:* For doctorate, 3 foreign languages, thesis/dissertation, candidacy exam. *Entrance requirements:* For doctorate, GRE General Test. Additional exam requirements/recommendations for international students: required—TOEFL (minimum score 600 paper-based; 80 iBT). Electronic applications accepted.

University of Oregon, Graduate School, College of Arts and Sciences, Program in Comparative Literature, Eugene, OR 97403. Offers MA, PhD. *Program availability:* Part-time. Terminal master's awarded for partial completion of doctoral program. *Degree requirements:* For master's, 2 foreign languages, field exam; for doctorate, 2 foreign languages, thesis/dissertation, field exam. *Entrance requirements:* For master's, previous course work in English and literature, proficiency in 3 foreign languages, writing sample; for doctorate, previous course work in English and literature, proficiency in 2 foreign languages, writing sample. Additional exam requirements/recommendations for international students: required—TOEFL.

University of Pennsylvania, School of Arts and Sciences, Graduate Group in Comparative Literature and Literary Theory, Philadelphia, PA 19104. Offers comparative literature (AM, PhD); literary theory (AM, PhD). *Faculty:* 65 full-time (29 women), 8 part-time/adjunct (3 women). *Students:* 32 full-time (18 women); includes 5 minority (3 Black or African American, non-Hispanic/Latino; 2 Hispanic/Latino), 13 international. Average age 31. 107 applicants, 5% accepted, 1 enrolled. In 2019, 3 master's, 3 doctorates awarded. *Entrance requirements:* Additional exam requirements/recommendations for international students: required—TOEFL. Application fee: $80. Website: http://ccat.sas.upenn.edu/Complit

University of Puerto Rico at Rio Piedras, College of Humanities, Department of Comparative Literature, San Juan, PR 00931-3300. Offers MA. *Program availability:* Part-time. *Degree requirements:* For master's, comprehensive exam, thesis. *Entrance requirements:* For master's, EXADEP, interview, minimum GPA of 3.0, letter of recommendation.

University of South Carolina, The Graduate School, College of Arts and Sciences, Department of Languages, Literatures, and Cultures, Columbia, SC 29208. Offers comparative literature (MA, PhD); foreign languages (MAT), including French, German, Spanish; French (MA); German (MA); Spanish (MA). *Program availability:* Part-time. *Degree requirements:* For master's, one foreign language, comprehensive exam, thesis optional; for doctorate, 2 foreign languages, comprehensive exam, thesis/dissertation. *Entrance requirements:* For master's and doctorate, GRE General Test, writing sample. Additional exam requirements/recommendations for international students: required—TOEFL (minimum score 75 iBT). Electronic applications accepted.

University of Southern California, Graduate School, Dana and David Dornsife College of Letters, Arts and Sciences, Comparative Studies in Literature and Culture Doctoral Program, Los Angeles, CA 90089. Offers comparative literature (PhD); comparative media and culture (PhD); Spanish and Latin American studies (PhD). *Degree requirements:* For doctorate, 2 foreign languages, comprehensive exam, thesis/dissertation. *Entrance requirements:* For doctorate, GRE, competence in language other than English (highly recommended). Additional exam requirements/recommendations for international students: required—TOEFL. Electronic applications accepted.

University of South Florida, Innovative Education, Tampa, FL 33620-9951. Offers adult, career and higher education (Graduate Certificate), including college teaching, leadership in developing human resources, leadership in higher education; Africana studies (Graduate Certificate), including diasporas and health disparities, genocide and human rights; aging studies (Graduate Certificate), including gerontology; art research (Graduate Certificate), including museum studies; business foundations (Graduate Certificate); chemical and biomedical engineering (Graduate Certificate), including materials science and engineering, water, health and sustainability; child and family studies (Graduate Certificate), including positive behavior support; civil and industrial engineering (Graduate Certificate), including transportation systems analysis; community and family health (Graduate Certificate), including maternal and child health, social marketing and public health, violence and injury: prevention and intervention, women's health; criminology (Graduate Certificate), including criminal justice administration; data science for public administration (Graduate Certificate); digital humanities (Graduate Certificate); educational measurement and research (Graduate Certificate), including evaluation; English (Graduate Certificate), including comparative literary studies, creative writing, professional and technical communication; entrepreneurship (Graduate Certificate); environmental health (Graduate Certificate), including safety management; epidemiology and biostatistics (Graduate Certificate), including applied biostatistics, biostatistics, concepts and tools of epidemiology, epidemiology, epidemiology of infectious diseases; geography, environment and planning (Graduate Certificate), including community development, environmental policy and management, geographical information systems; geology (Graduate Certificate), including hydrogeology; global health (Graduate Certificate), including disaster management, global health and Latin American and Caribbean studies, global health practice, humanitarian assistance, infection control; government and international affairs (Graduate Certificate), including Cuban studies, globalization studies; health policy and management (Graduate Certificate), including health management and leadership, public health policy and programs; hearing specialist: early intervention (Graduate Certificate); industrial and management systems engineering (Graduate Certificate), including systems engineering, technology management; information studies (Graduate Certificate), including school library media specialist; information systems/decision sciences (Graduate Certificate), including analytics and business intelligence; instructional technology (Graduate Certificate), including distance education, Florida digital/virtual educator, instructional design, multimedia design, Web design; internal medicine, bioethics and medical humanities (Graduate Certificate), including biomedical ethics; Latin American and Caribbean studies (Graduate Certificate); leadership for coastal resiliency planning (Graduate Certificate); mass communications (Graduate Certificate), including multimedia journalism; mathematics and statistics (Graduate Certificate), including mathematics; medicine (Graduate Certificate), including aging and neuroscience, bioinformatics, biotechnology, brain fitness and memory management, clinical investigation, hand and upper limb rehabilitation, health informatics, health sciences, integrative weight management, intellectual property, medicine and gender, metabolic and nutritional medicine, metabolic cardiology, pharmacy sciences; national and competitive intelligence (Graduate Certificate); nursing (Graduate Certificate), including simulation based academic fellowship in advanced pain management; psychological and social foundations (Graduate Certificate), including career counseling, college teaching, diversity in education, mental health counseling, school counseling; public affairs (Graduate Certificate), including nonprofit management, public management, research administration; public health (Graduate Certificate), including assessing chemical toxicity and public health risks, health equity, pharmacoepidemiology, public health generalist, toxicology, translational research in adolescent behavioral health; public health practices (Graduate Certificate), including planning for healthy communities; rehabilitation and mental health counseling (Graduate Certificate), including integrative mental health care, marriage and family therapy, rehabilitation technology; secondary education (Graduate Certificate), including ESOL, foreign language education: culture and content, foreign language education: professional; social work (Graduate Certificate), including geriatric social work/clinical gerontology; special education (Graduate Certificate), including autism spectrum disorder, disabilities education: severe/profound; world languages (Graduate Certificate), including teaching English as a second language (TESL) or foreign language. *Unit head:* Dr. Cynthia DeLuca, Associate Vice President and Assistant Vice Provost, 813-974-3077, Fax: 813-974-7061, E-mail: deluca@usf.edu. *Application contact:* Owen Hooper, Director, Summer and Alternative Calendar Programs, 813-974-6917, E-mail: hooper@usf.edu.
Website: http://www.usf.edu/innovative-education/

The University of Texas at Austin, Graduate School, College of Liberal Arts, Program in Comparative Literature, Austin, TX 78712-1111. Offers MA, PhD. *Degree requirements:* For master's, 2 foreign languages, report or thesis; for doctorate, 3 foreign

languages, thesis/dissertation. *Entrance requirements:* For master's and doctorate, GRE General Test. Electronic applications accepted.

The University of Texas at Dallas, School of Arts and Humanities, Richardson, TX 75080. Offers art history (MA); history (MA); humanities (MA, PhD), including aesthetic studies, history of ideas, studies in literature; Latin American studies (MA). *Program availability:* Part-time, evening/weekend. *Faculty:* 48 full-time (19 women), 11 part-time/adjunct (6 women). *Students:* 123 full-time (76 women), 116 part-time (71 women); includes 62 minority (14 Black or African American, non-Hispanic/Latino; 3 American Indian or Alaska Native, non-Hispanic/Latino; 9 Asian, non-Hispanic/Latino; 25 Hispanic/Latino; 11 Two or more races, non-Hispanic/Latino), 27 international. Average age 40. 130 applicants, 60% accepted, 59 enrolled. In 2019, 30 master's, 16 doctorates awarded. *Degree requirements:* For master's, one foreign language, portfolio; for doctorate, one foreign language, thesis/dissertation. *Entrance requirements:* For master's and doctorate, minimum GPA of 3.0 in undergraduate course work in field. Additional exam requirements/recommendations for international students: required—TOEFL (minimum score 550 paper-based). *Application deadline:* For fall admission, 7/15 for domestic students, 5/1 priority date for international students; for spring admission, 11/15 for domestic students, 9/1 priority date for international students. Applications are processed on a rolling basis. Application fee: $50 ($100 for international students). Electronic applications accepted. *Expenses: Tuition,* area resident: Full-time $16,504. Tuition, state resident: full-time $16,504. Tuition, nonresident: full-time $34,266. Tuition and fees vary according to course load. *Financial support:* In 2019–20, 87 students received support, including 9 fellowships (averaging $5,074 per year), 14 research assistantships with partial tuition reimbursements available (averaging $26,575 per year), 69 teaching assistantships with partial tuition reimbursements available (averaging $14,961 per year); Federal Work-Study, institutionally sponsored loans, scholarships/grants, and unspecified assistantships also available. Support available to part-time students. Financial award application deadline: 4/30; financial award applicants required to submit FAFSA. *Unit head:* Dr. Nils Roemer, Interim Dean, 972-883-2984, Fax: 972-883-2989, E-mail: nroemer@utdallas.edu. *Application contact:* Dr. John Gooch, Associate Dean of Graduate Studies, 972-883-2756, Fax: 972-883-2989, E-mail: john.gooch@utdallas.edu.
Website: http://www.utdallas.edu/ah/

University of Toronto, School of Graduate Studies, Faculty of Arts and Science, Centre for Comparative Literature, Toronto, ON M5S 1A1, Canada. Offers MA, PhD. *Program availability:* Part-time. *Degree requirements:* For doctorate, thesis/dissertation. *Entrance requirements:* For master's, 2 letters of recommendation, sample of work (short essay on a literary topic preferred), resume, bachelor's degree with a B+ average; for doctorate, 2 letters of recommendation, sample of work (short essay on a literary topic preferred), resume, master's degree with average grade of at least A-. Additional exam requirements/recommendations for international students: required—TOEFL (minimum score 580 paper-based; 93 iBT), TWE (minimum score 5). Electronic applications accepted.

University of Utah, Graduate School, College of Humanities, Department of World Languages and Cultures, Salt Lake City, UT 84112. Offers comparative literary and cultural studies (MA, PhD); French (MA); Spanish (MA, MALP); world languages (MA). *Program availability:* Part-time. *Faculty:* 22 full-time (14 women), 2 part-time/adjunct (1 woman). *Students:* 20 full-time (13 women), 5 part-time (3 women); includes 4 minority (all Hispanic/Latino), 8 international. Average age 33. 19 applicants, 68% accepted, 11 enrolled. In 2019, 12 master's, 1 doctorate awarded. Terminal master's awarded for partial completion of doctoral program. *Degree requirements:* For master's, one foreign language, comprehensive exam (for some programs), thesis (for some programs); for doctorate, one foreign language, comprehensive exam, thesis/dissertation. *Entrance requirements:* For master's, bachelor's degree from regionally-accredited college or university with minimum undergraduate overall GPA of 3.0; for doctorate, B.A. degree, B.A. degree. Additional exam requirements/recommendations for international students: required—TOEFL (minimum score 80 paper-based; 80 iBT), IELTS (minimum score 6.5). *Application deadline:* For fall admission, 1/15 priority date for domestic students, 12/15 priority date for international students. Application fee: $50 ($65 for international students). Electronic applications accepted. *Expenses:* Tuition, state resident: full-time $7085; part-time $272.51 per credit hour. Tuition, nonresident: full-time $24,937; part-time $959.12 per credit hour. *Required fees:* $880.52; $880.52 per semester. Tuition and fees vary according to degree level, program and student level. *Financial support:* In 2019–20, 21 students received support, including 21 teaching assistantships with full tuition reimbursements available (averaging $16,095 per year). Financial award application deadline: 1/15; financial award applicants required to submit CSS PROFILE or FAFSA. *Unit head:* Margaret Toscano, Associate Professor of Classics, 801-581-4786, E-mail: margaret.toscano@utah.edu. *Application contact:* Olivia Rose Davis, Graduate Academic Advisor, 801-581-7748, Fax: 801-581-7581, E-mail: olivia.davis@utah.edu.
Website: http://languages.utah.edu/

University of Washington, Graduate School, College of Arts and Sciences, Department of Comparative Literature, Seattle, WA 98195. Offers MA, PhD. *Program availability:* Part-time. Terminal master's awarded for partial completion of doctoral program. *Degree requirements:* For master's, 2 foreign languages, thesis optional; for doctorate, 3 foreign languages, thesis/dissertation. *Entrance requirements:* For master's, GRE General Test, BA in comparative literature or equivalent, minimum GPA of 3.0, proficiency in 1 foreign language; for doctorate, GRE General Test, MA in comparative literature or equivalent, minimum GPA of 3.0, proficiency in 2 foreign languages. Additional exam requirements/recommendations for international students: required—TOEFL. Electronic applications accepted.

The University of Western Ontario, School of Graduate and Postdoctoral Studies, Faculty of Arts and Humanities, Department of Modern Languages and Literatures, London, ON N6A 3K7, Canada. Offers comparative literature (MA, PhD); Hispanic studies (MA, PhD). *Program availability:* Part-time. *Degree requirements:* For master's, 2 foreign languages, thesis (for some programs). *Entrance requirements:* For master's, honors degree in Spanish or equivalent, minimum B average. Additional exam requirements/recommendations for international students: required—TOEFL (comparative literature).

University of Wisconsin–Madison, Graduate School, College of Letters and Science, Department of Comparative Literature, Madison, WI 53706-1380. Offers MA, PhD. *Program availability:* Part-time. Terminal master's awarded for partial completion of doctoral program. *Degree requirements:* For master's, one foreign language, second-year exam; for doctorate, 3 foreign languages, thesis/dissertation, 3 preliminary exams. *Entrance requirements:* For master's, GRE General Test, writing sample; for doctorate, GRE General Test. Electronic applications accepted.

University of Wisconsin–Madison, Graduate School, College of Letters and Science, Department of East Asian Languages and Literature, Program in Chinese Literature, Madison, WI 53706-1380. Offers MA, PhD. *Program availability:* Part-time. Terminal master's awarded for partial completion of doctoral program. *Degree requirements:* For master's, one foreign language, seminars, written exam; for doctorate, 3 foreign languages, thesis/dissertation, seminars, preliminary exams, oral exam. *Entrance* *requirements:* For master's, bachelor's degree or equivalent in Chinese; for doctorate, master's degree or equivalent in Chinese. Electronic applications accepted.

University of Wisconsin–Milwaukee, Graduate School, College of Letters and Science, Department of Foreign Languages and Literature, Milwaukee, WI 53201-0413. Offers foreign languages and literature (MA), including classic Greek, classics, comparative literature, French/Francophone language, literature, and culture, German language, literature, and culture, interpreting, Latin, linguistics, Spanish language, literature, and culture, translation; interpreting (Graduate Certificate); language, literature, and translation (MA, MALLT); translation (Graduate Certificate). *Program availability:* Part-time. *Degree requirements:* For master's, 2 foreign languages, thesis or alternative. *Entrance requirements:* Additional exam requirements/recommendations for international students: required—TOEFL (minimum score 550 paper-based; 79 iBT), IELTS (minimum score 6.5). Electronic applications accepted.

Université Laval, Faculty of Letters, Department of Literature, Programs in Literary Studies, Québec, QC G1K 7P4, Canada. Offers MA, PhD. *Program availability:* Part-time. Terminal master's awarded for partial completion of doctoral program. *Degree requirements:* For master's, thesis; for doctorate, comprehensive exam, thesis/dissertation. *Entrance requirements:* For master's and doctorate, linguistics exams, knowledge of French, knowledge of a second language. Electronic applications accepted.

Washington University in St. Louis, The Graduate School, Department of East Asian Languages and Cultures, St. Louis, MO 63130-4899. Offers Chinese (MA); Chinese and comparative literature (PhD); Chinese language and literature (PhD); East Asian studies (MA); Japanese (MA); Japanese and comparative literature (PhD); Japanese language and literature (PhD). Terminal master's awarded for partial completion of doctoral program. *Degree requirements:* For master's, thesis optional; for doctorate, thesis/dissertation. *Entrance requirements:* For master's and doctorate, GRE General Test. Additional exam requirements/recommendations for international students: required—TOEFL. Electronic applications accepted.

Washington University in St. Louis, The Graduate School, Department of Romance Languages and Literatures, Program in French, St. Louis, MO 63130-4899. Offers

French and comparative literature (PhD); French language and literature (PhD). Terminal master's awarded for partial completion of doctoral program. *Degree requirements:* For doctorate, thesis/dissertation. *Entrance requirements:* For doctorate, GRE General Test. Additional exam requirements/recommendations for international students: required—TOEFL. Electronic applications accepted.

Washington University in St. Louis, The Graduate School, Department of Romance Languages and Literatures, Program in Spanish, St. Louis, MO 63130-4899. Offers Hispanic languages and literatures (PhD); Spanish and comparative literature (PhD). Terminal master's awarded for partial completion of doctoral program. *Degree requirements:* For doctorate, thesis/dissertation. *Entrance requirements:* For doctorate, GRE General Test. Additional exam requirements/recommendations for international students: required—TOEFL. Electronic applications accepted.

Washington University in St. Louis, The Graduate School, Program in Comparative Literature, St. Louis, MO 63130-4899. Offers PhD. Terminal master's awarded for partial completion of doctoral program. *Degree requirements:* For doctorate, thesis/dissertation. *Entrance requirements:* For doctorate, GRE General Test. Additional exam requirements/recommendations for international students: required—TOEFL. Electronic applications accepted.

Western Kentucky University, Graduate School, Potter College of Arts and Letters, Department of English, Bowling Green, KY 42101. Offers education (MA); English (MA Ed); literature (MA), including American literature, British literature, literary theory, women writers, world literature; teaching English as a second language (MA); writing (MA). *Program availability:* Part-time, evening/weekend. *Degree requirements:* For master's, comprehensive exam, thesis optional, final exam. *Entrance requirements:* For master's, GRE General Test, minimum GPA of 2.75. Additional exam requirements/recommendations for international students: required—TOEFL (minimum score 555 paper-based; 79 iBT).

Yale University, Graduate School of Arts and Sciences, Department of Comparative Literature, New Haven, CT 06520. Offers PhD. *Degree requirements:* For doctorate, 2 foreign languages, thesis/dissertation. *Entrance requirements:* For doctorate, GRE General Test.

English

Abilene Christian University, Office of Graduate Programs, College of Arts and Sciences, Department of Language and Literature, Abilene, TX 79699. Offers composition/rhetoric (MA); literature (MA); writing (MA). *Program availability:* Part-time. *Faculty:* 9 part-time/adjunct (3 women). *Students:* 6 full-time (4 women), 2 part-time (both women); includes 3 minority (1 Hispanic/Latino; 2 Two or more races, non-Hispanic/Latino), 1 international. 25 applicants, 28% accepted, 4 enrolled. In 2019, 1 master's awarded. *Degree requirements:* For master's, one foreign language, comprehensive exam (for some programs), thesis (for some programs). *Entrance requirements:* For master's, GRE General Test, official transcripts, recommendations, purpose statement, writing sample. Additional exam requirements/recommendations for international students: required—TOEFL (minimum score 80 iBT), IELTS (minimum score 6), PTE (minimum score 51). *Application deadline:* For fall admission, 8/10 for domestic students; for spring admission, 11/1 for domestic students. Applications are processed on a rolling basis. Application fee: $65. Electronic applications accepted. *Expenses:* $1242 per hour. *Financial support:* In 2019–20, 7 students received support, including 2 teaching assistantships with partial tuition reimbursements available; Federal Work-Study and scholarships/grants also available. Support available to part-time students. Financial award application deadline: 4/1; financial award applicants required to submit FAFSA. *Unit head:* Dr. Todd Womble, Graduate Director, 325-674-2663, Fax: 325-674-2408, E-mail: mtw04b@acu.edu. *Application contact:* Graduate Admissions, 325-674-6911, E-mail: gradinfo@acu.edu.
Website: http://www.acu.edu/on-campus/graduate/college-of-arts-and-sciences/language-and-literature/english.html

Acadia University, Faculty of Arts, Department of English, Wolfville, NS B4P 2R6, Canada. Offers MA. *Entrance requirements:* For master's, honors degree in English, minimum A- average. Additional exam requirements/recommendations for international students: required—TOEFL (minimum score 630 paper-based; 93 iBT), IELTS (minimum score 6.5).

The American University in Cairo, School of Humanities and Social Sciences, Cairo, Egypt. Offers Arab and Islamic civilizations (Graduate Diploma); Arabic studies (MA); comparative literary studies (Graduate Diploma); Egyptology and Coptology (MA); English and comparative literature (MA); humanities and social sciences (Graduate Diploma); philosophy (MA); psychology (MA); sociology and anthropology (MA); teaching Arabic as a foreign language (MA); teaching English to speakers of other languages (MA). *Program availability:* Part-time, evening/weekend. *Degree requirements:* For master's, comprehensive exam (for some programs), thesis (for some programs). *Entrance requirements:* Additional exam requirements/recommendations for international students: required—TOEFL (minimum score 450 paper-based; 45 iBT), IELTS (minimum score 5). Electronic applications accepted.

Andrews University, School of Graduate Studies, College of Arts and Sciences, Department of English, Berrien Springs, MI 49104. Offers MA, MAT. *Program availability:* Part-time. *Faculty:* 8 full-time (4 women), 2 part-time/adjunct (1 woman). *Students:* 1 (woman) full-time, 6 part-time (5 women); includes 1 minority (Hispanic/Latino), 2 international. Average age 38. In 2019, 3 master's awarded. *Degree requirements:* For master's, one foreign language, thesis optional. *Entrance requirements:* For master's, GRE Subject Test. Additional exam requirements/recommendations for international students: required—TOEFL (minimum score 550 paper-based). *Application deadline:* For fall admission, 8/15 for domestic students. Applications are processed on a rolling basis. Application fee: $60. Electronic applications accepted. *Financial support:* Fellowships, research assistantships, teaching assistantships, career-related internships or fieldwork, and Federal Work-Study available. *Unit head:* Dr. Meredith Jones-Gray, Chairperson, 269-471-3298. *Application contact:* Jillian Panigot, Director, University Admissions, 800-253-2874, Fax: 269-471-6321, E-mail: graduate@andrews.edu.

Angelo State University, College of Graduate Studies and Research, College of Arts and Humanities, Department of English and Modern Languages, San Angelo, TX 76909. Offers English (MA); TESOL (MA). *Program availability:* Part-time, evening/weekend. *Entrance requirements:* For master's, essay. Additional exam requirements/recommendations for international students: required—TOEFL or IELTS. Electronic applications accepted.

Appalachian State University, Cratis D. Williams School of Graduate Studies, Department of English, Boone, NC 28608. Offers English (MA). *Program availability:* Part-time, online learning. *Degree requirements:* For master's, one foreign language, comprehensive exam, thesis (for some programs). *Entrance requirements:* For master's, GRE General Test, 3 letters of recommendation. Additional exam requirements/recommendations for international students: required—TOEFL (minimum score 570 paper-based; 79 iBT), IELTS (minimum score 6.5). Electronic applications accepted.

Arcadia University, College of Arts and Sciences, Department of English, Glenside, PA 19038-3295. Offers creative writing (MFA); English (MA). *Program availability:* Part-time, evening/weekend. *Faculty:* 10 full-time (4 women). *Students:* 15 full-time (11 women), 35 part-time (25 women); includes 7 minority (4 Black or African American, non-Hispanic/Latino; 1 Asian, non-Hispanic/Latino; 1 Hispanic/Latino; 1 Two or more races, non-Hispanic/Latino), 1 international. In 2019, 23 master's awarded. *Degree requirements:* For master's, thesis optional, Culminating Project or Master's Thesis. *Entrance requirements:* Additional exam requirements/recommendations for international students: required—Official results from the TOEFL or IELTS are required for all students for whom English is a second language. *Application deadline:* For fall admission, 3/1 priority date for domestic students; for spring admission, 12/15 priority date for domestic students. Applications are processed on a rolling basis. Application fee: $25. *Expenses:* Contact institution. *Financial support:* Unspecified assistantships available. *Unit head:* Jo Ann Weiner, Chair, 215-572-2105, E-mail: weinerj@arcadia.edu. *Application contact:* 215-572-2925, Fax: 215-572-2126, E-mail: grad@arcadia.edu.

Arcadia University, College of Arts and Sciences, Department of English, Program in English, Glenside, PA 19038-3295. Offers english (MA). *Students:* 14 full-time (10 women), 5 part-time (3 women); includes 2 minority (1 Black or African American, non-Hispanic/Latino; 1 Hispanic/Latino), 1 international. In 2019, 13 master's awarded. *Degree requirements:* For master's, Culminating Project or Master's Thesis. *Entrance requirements:* For master's, An academic writing sample (15-20 pages). Additional exam requirements/recommendations for international students: required—TOEFL, TOEFL or IELTS required. *Application deadline:* For fall admission, 3/1 priority date for domestic students; for spring admission, 12/15 priority date for domestic students. Applications are processed on a rolling basis. Application fee: $25. *Expenses:* Contact institution. *Financial support:* Unspecified assistantships available. *Unit head:* Jennifer Matisoff, Director of the M.A. in English, E-mail: matisofj@arcadia.edu. *Application contact:* Jennifer Matisoff, Director of the M.A. in English, E-mail: matisofj@arcadia.edu.

Arizona State University at Tempe, College of Liberal Arts and Sciences, Department of English, Tempe, AZ 85287-0302. Offers applied linguistics (PhD); creative writing (MFA); English (MA, PhD), including comparative literature (MA), linguistics (MA), literature, rhetoric and composition (MA), rhetoric, composition, and linguistics (PhD); film and media studies (MAS), including American media and popular culture; linguistics (Graduate Certificate); teaching English to speakers of other languages (MTESOL); translation studies (Graduate Certificate). Terminal master's awarded for partial completion of doctoral program. *Degree requirements:* For master's, variable foreign language requirement, comprehensive exam (for some programs), thesis (for some programs), interactive Program of Study (iPOS) submitted before completing 50 percent of required credit hours; for doctorate, variable foreign language requirement, comprehensive exam, thesis/dissertation, interactive Program of Study (iPOS) submitted before completing 50 percent of required credit hours. *Entrance requirements:* For master's and doctorate, GRE, minimum GPA of 3.0 or equivalent in last 2 years of work leading to bachelor's degree. Additional exam requirements/recommendations for international students: required—TOEFL, IELTS, or PTE. Electronic applications accepted.

Arkansas State University, Graduate School, College of Humanities and Social Sciences, Department of English and Philosophy, State University, AR 72467. Offers English (MA); English education (MSE, SCCT). *Program availability:* Part-time. *Degree requirements:* For master's, variable foreign language requirement, comprehensive exam, thesis or alternative, preliminary exam; for SCCT, comprehensive exam. *Entrance requirements:* For master's, GRE General Test or MAT, appropriate bachelor's degree, official transcript, valid teaching certificate (for MSE), immunization records; for SCCT, GRE General Test or MAT, interview, master's degree, official transcript, immunization records. Additional exam requirements/recommendations for international students: required—TOEFL (minimum score 550 paper-based; 79 iBT), IELTS (minimum score 6), PTE (minimum score 56). Electronic applications accepted.

Arkansas Tech University, College of Arts and Humanities, Russellville, AR 72801. Offers applied sociology (MS); English (M Ed, MA); history (MA); liberal arts (MLA); multi-media journalism (MA); psychology (MS); teaching English as a second language (MA). *Program availability:* Part-time, 100% online, blended/hybrid learning. *Students:* 32 full-time (19 women), 102 part-time (70 women); includes 22 minority (5 Black or African American, non-Hispanic/Latino; 1 American Indian or Alaska Native, non-Hispanic/Latino; 1 Asian, non-Hispanic/Latino; 12 Hispanic/Latino; 3 Two or more races, non-Hispanic/Latino), 9 international. Average age 32. In 2019, 89 master's awarded. *Degree requirements:* For master's, comprehensive exam (for some programs), thesis (for some programs), project. *Entrance requirements:* Additional exam requirements/recommendations for international students: required—TOEFL (minimum score 550 paper-based; 79 iBT), IELTS (minimum score 6.5), PTE (minimum score 58). *Application deadline:* For fall admission, 3/1 priority date for domestic students, 5/1 priority date for international students; for spring admission, 10/1 priority date for domestic and international students. Applications are processed on a rolling basis. Application fee: $40 ($90 for international students). Electronic applications accepted. *Expenses: Tuition, area resident:* Full-time $7008; part-time $292 per credit hour. Tuition, state resident: full-time $7008; part-time $292 per credit hour. Tuition, nonresident: full-time $14,016; part-time $584 per credit hour. *International tuition:* $14,016 full-time. *Required fees:* $343 per term. *Financial support:* In 2019–20, research assistantships with full and partial tuition reimbursements (averaging $4,800 per year), teaching assistantships with full and partial tuition reimbursements (averaging $4,800 per year) were awarded; career-related internships or fieldwork, Federal Work-Study, scholarships/grants, health care benefits, and unspecified assistantships also available. Support available to part-time students. Financial award application deadline: 4/15; financial award applicants required to submit FAFSA. *Unit head:* Dr. Jeffrey Cass, Dean of College of Arts and Humanities, 479-968-0274, Fax: 479-964-0812, E-mail: jcass@atu.edu. *Application contact:* Dr. Richard Schoephoerster, Dean of Graduate College and Research, 479-968-0398, Fax: 479-964-0542, E-mail: gradcollege@atu.edu.
Website: http://www.atu.edu/humanities/

Asbury University, School of Graduate and Professional Studies, Wilmore, KY 40390-1198. Offers biology: alternative certificate (MA Ed); chemistry: alternative certificate (MA Ed); English (MA Ed); English as a second language (MA Ed); ESL (MA Ed); French (MA Ed); Latin: alternative certificate (MA Ed); mathematics: alternative certificate (MA Ed); reading/writing endorsement (MA Ed); social studies (MA Ed); social work (MSW), including child and family services; Spanish (MA Ed); special education (MA Ed); special education: alternative certificate (MA Ed); teacher as leader endorsement (MA Ed). *Accreditation:* NCATE. *Program availability:* Part-time. *Degree requirements:* For master's, action research project, portfolio. *Entrance requirements:* For master's, PRAXIS/NTE, minimum GPA of 2.75, letters of recommendation. Additional exam requirements/recommendations for international students: required—TOEFL (minimum score 550 paper-based). Electronic applications accepted.

Auburn University, Graduate School, College of Liberal Arts, Department of English, Auburn, AL 36849. Offers MA, MTPC, PhD, Graduate Certificate. *Program availability:* Part-time. *Faculty:* 71 full-time (40 women), 7 part-time/adjunct (2 women). *Students:* 22 full-time (13 women), 33 part-time (22 women); includes 9 minority (2 Black or African American, non-Hispanic/Latino; 4 Asian, non-Hispanic/Latino; 1 Hispanic/Latino; 2 Two or more races, non-Hispanic/Latino), 3 international. Average age 32. 53 applicants, 60% accepted, 15 enrolled. In 2019, 16 master's, 2 doctorates, 1 other advanced degree awarded. *Degree requirements:* For master's, one foreign language, thesis optional, written exam; for doctorate, 2 foreign languages, thesis/dissertation, oral and written exams. *Entrance requirements:* For master's, GRE General Test, sample of written work; for doctorate, GRE General Test, GRE Subject Test, sample of written work. Additional exam requirements/recommendations for international students: recommended—TOEFL (minimum score 550 paper-based; 79 iBT), IELTS (minimum score 6.5). *Application deadline:* Applications are processed on a rolling basis. Application fee: $60 ($70 for international students). Electronic applications accepted. *Expenses: Tuition, area resident:* Full-time $9828; part-time $546 per credit hour. Tuition, state resident: full-time $9828; part-time $546 per credit hour. Tuition, nonresident: full-time $29,484; part-time $1638 per credit hour. *International tuition:* $29,744 full-time. Tuition and fees vary according to course load, program and reciprocity agreements. *Financial support:* In 2019–20, 34 fellowships with tuition reimbursements, 1 research assistantship (averaging $21,333 per year), 44 teaching assistantships with tuition reimbursements (averaging $22,830 per year) were awarded; Federal Work-Study also available. Support available to part-time students. Financial award application deadline: 3/15; financial award applicants required to submit FAFSA. *Unit head:* Dr. Jeremy M. Downes, Chair, 334-844-9079. *Application contact:* Dr. George Flowers, Dean of the Graduate School, 334-844-2125.
Website: https://cla.auburn.edu/english/

Austin Peay State University, College of Graduate Studies, College of Arts and Letters, Department of Languages and Literature, Clarksville, TN 37044. Offers English (MA). *Program availability:* Part-time. *Faculty:* 10 full-time (4 women). *Students:* 9 full-time (8 women), 7 part-time (5 women); includes 1 minority (Two or more races, non-Hispanic/Latino), 1 international. Average age 30. 9 applicants, 100% accepted, 8 enrolled. In 2019, 4 master's awarded. *Degree requirements:* For master's, comprehensive exam, thesis optional. *Entrance requirements:* For master's, GRE General Test, 2 letters of recommendation, minimum undergraduate GPA of 2.9. Additional exam requirements/recommendations for international students: required—TOEFL (minimum score 500 paper-based). *Application deadline:* For fall admission, 8/5 priority date for domestic students. Applications are processed on a rolling basis. Application fee: $45 ($55 for international students). Electronic applications accepted. *Financial support:* Research assistantships with full tuition reimbursements, career-related internships or fieldwork, Federal Work-Study, institutionally sponsored loans, scholarships/grants, and unspecified assistantships available. Support available to part-time students. Financial award application deadline: 7/1; financial award applicants required to submit FAFSA. *Unit head:* Dr. Mercy Cannon, Chair, 931-221-7893, E-mail: cannonm@apsu.edu. *Application contact:* Megan Mitchell, Coordinator of Graduate Admissions, 931-221-6189, Fax: 931-221-7641, E-mail: mitchellm@apsu.edu.
Website: http://www.apsu.edu/langlit/index.php

Azusa Pacific University, College of Liberal Arts and Sciences, Department of English, Azusa, CA 91702-7000. Offers MA. *Program availability:* Part-time. *Expenses:* Contact institution.

Ball State University, Graduate School, College of Sciences and Humanities, Department of English, Muncie, IN 47306. Offers English (MA, PhD), including composition (MA), creative writing (MA), literature, rhetoric and composition; linguistics (MA), including linguistics, teaching English to speakers of other languages (TESOL) and linguistics. *Program availability:* Part-time. *Degree requirements:* For doctorate, variable foreign language requirement, thesis/dissertation. *Entrance requirements:* For master's, GRE General Test, minimum baccalaureate GPA of 2.75 or 3.0 in latter half of

baccalaureate, statement of purpose, writing sample, three letters of recommendation; for doctorate, GRE General Test, GRE Subject Test, minimum graduate GPA of 3.2, statement of purpose, writing sample, three letters of recommendation. Additional exam requirements/recommendations for international students: required—TOEFL (minimum score 550 paper-based; 79 iBT), IELTS (minimum score 6.5). Electronic applications accepted. *Expenses: Tuition, area resident:* Full-time $7506; part-time $417 per credit hour. Tuition, nonresident: full-time $20,610; part-time $1145 per credit hour. *Required fees:* $2126. Tuition and fees vary according to course load, campus/location and program.

Bard College, Master of Arts in Teaching Program, Annandale-on-Hudson, NY 12504. Offers secondary education (MAT), including biology, history, literature, mathematics, Spanish; MS/MAT. *Program availability:* Part-time. *Degree requirements:* For master's, year-long teaching residencies in area middle and high schools. *Entrance requirements:* For master's, GRE General Test, resume, 3 letters of recommendation, personal statement, official transcripts. Additional exam requirements/recommendations for international students: required—TOEFL. Electronic applications accepted. Application fee is waived when completed online.

Baylor University, Graduate School, College of Arts and Sciences, Department of English, Waco, TX 76798. Offers english (MA). Terminal master's awarded for partial completion of doctoral program. *Degree requirements:* For master's, one foreign language, thesis or alternative; for doctorate, 2 foreign languages, comprehensive exam, thesis/dissertation, 1 course in Old English language; 1 course concerned with introduction to graduate study, such as the bibliography and research methods course or an equivalent course at another university; 1 upper-level course in linguistics or literary theory or rhetoric and composition. *Entrance requirements:* For master's, GRE (Verbal and Quantitative); GRE Verbal score of at least 160, 18 hours of upper-level course work in English; for doctorate, GRE (Verbal and Quantitative); GRE Verbal score of at least 166 for direct admission to BA applicants; GRE Verbal score of at least 163 for applicants with an MA degree, 18 hours of upper-level course work in English. Additional exam requirements/recommendations for international students: required—TOEFL. Electronic applications accepted.

Bemidji State University, School of Graduate Studies, Bemidji, MN 56601. Offers biology (MS); education (MS); English (MA, MS); environmental studies (MS); mathematics (MS); mathematics (elementary and middle level education) (MS); special education (M Sp Ed). *Program availability:* Part-time, online learning. *Degree requirements:* For master's, comprehensive exam, thesis (for some programs). *Entrance requirements:* For master's, GRE; GMAT, letters of recommendation, letters of interest. Additional exam requirements/recommendations for international students: required—TOEFL (minimum score 550 paper-based; 80 iBT). Electronic applications accepted. *Expenses:* Contact institution.

Binghamton University, State University of New York, Graduate School, Harpur College of Arts and Sciences, Department of English, Binghamton, NY 13902-6000. Offers creative writing (MA); English (PhD); English/American literature (MA). *Program availability:* Part-time. Terminal master's awarded for partial completion of doctoral program. *Degree requirements:* For master's, one foreign language, thesis; for doctorate, one foreign language, comprehensive exam, thesis/dissertation. *Entrance requirements:* For master's and doctorate, GRE General Test, writing sample. Additional exam requirements/recommendations for international students: required—TOEFL (minimum score 550 paper-based; 80 iBT). Electronic applications accepted.

Bob Jones University, Graduate Programs, Greenville, SC 29614. Offers accountancy (MS); Bible (MA); Bible translation (MA); Biblical studies (Certificate); business administration (MBA); church history (MA, PhD); church ministries (MA); church music (MM); cinema and video production (MA); counseling (MS); curriculum and instruction (Ed D); divinity (M Div); dramatic production (MA); educational leadership (MS, Ed D, Ed S); elementary education (M Ed, MAT); English (M Ed, MA, MAT); fine arts (MA); graphic design (MA); history (M Ed, MA); illustration (MA); interpretative speech (MA); mathematics (M Ed, MAT); medical missions (Certificate); ministry (MM, D Min); multi-categorical special education (M Ed, MAT); music (M Ed); New Testament interpretation (PhD); Old Testament interpretation (PhD); orchestral instrument performance (MM); organ performance (MM); pastoral studies (MA); personnel services (MS, Ed S); piano pedagogy (MM); piano performance (MM); platform arts (MA); rhetoric and public address (MA); secondary education (M Ed); studio art (MA); teaching Bible (MA); theology (MA, PhD); voice performance (MM); youth ministries (MA); M Div/MM.

Boston College, Morrissey Graduate School of Arts and Sciences, Department of English, Chestnut Hill, MA 02467-3800. Offers English (MA, PhD); Irish studies (MA, PhD). Terminal master's awarded for partial completion of doctoral program. *Degree requirements:* For master's, one foreign language, thesis optional; for doctorate, 2 foreign languages, thesis/dissertation. *Entrance requirements:* For master's and doctorate, GRE General Test, GRE Subject Test. Additional exam requirements/recommendations for international students: required—TOEFL (minimum score 600 paper-based; 100 iBT), IELTS (minimum score 8). Electronic applications accepted.

Boston University, Graduate School of Arts and Sciences, Department of English, Boston, MA 02215. Offers MA, PhD, JD/MA. *Students:* 38 full-time (19 women), 1 (woman) part-time; includes 4 minority (1 Black or African American, non-Hispanic/Latino; 3 Hispanic/Latino). Average age 26. 162 applicants, 38% accepted, 9 enrolled. In 2019, 19 master's, 7 doctorates awarded. Terminal master's awarded for partial completion of doctoral program. *Degree requirements:* For master's, one foreign language; for doctorate, 2 foreign languages, comprehensive exam, thesis/dissertation. *Entrance requirements:* For master's and doctorate, GRE General Test (optional), 3 letters of recommendation, transcripts, personal statement, scholarly writing sample, curriculum vitae. Additional exam requirements/recommendations for international students: required—TOEFL (minimum score 550 paper-based; 84 iBT). *Application deadline:* For fall admission, 1/4 for domestic and international students. Application fee: $95. Electronic applications accepted. *Financial support:* In 2019–20, 38 students received support, including 8 fellowships with full tuition reimbursements available (averaging $23,340 per year), 22 teaching assistantships with full tuition reimbursements available (averaging $23,340 per year); Federal Work-Study, scholarships/grants, health care benefits, and unspecified assistantships also available. Financial award application deadline: 1/4. *Unit head:* Robert Chodat, Chair, 617-353-2509, Fax: 617-353-3653, E-mail: rchodat@bu.edu. *Application contact:* Anne Austin, Administrative Assistant, 617-353-2509, Fax: 617-353-3653, E-mail: akaustin@bu.edu.
Website: http://www.bu.edu/english/

Bowie State University, Graduate Programs, Program in English, Bowie, MD 20715-9465. Offers MA. *Program availability:* Part-time, evening/weekend. *Entrance requirements:* For master's, minimum GPA of 2.5, English degree. Electronic applications accepted. *Expenses: Tuition, area resident:* Full-time $11,942; part-time $423 per credit hour. Tuition, state resident: full-time $11,942; part-time $423 per credit hour. Tuition, nonresident: full-time $18,806; part-time $709 per credit hour. *International tuition:* $18,806 full-time. *Required fees:* $1106; $1106 per semester. $553 per semester.

Bowling Green State University, Graduate College, College of Arts and Sciences, Department of English, Program in English, Bowling Green, OH 43403. Offers English

(MA, PhD); literature (MA); rhetoric and writing (PhD); scientific and technical communication (MA). *Program availability:* Part-time. *Degree requirements:* For master's, thesis or alternative; for doctorate, comprehensive exam, thesis/dissertation, foreign language or proficiency in Old English. *Entrance requirements:* For master's and doctorate, GRE General Test. Additional exam requirements/recommendations for international students: required—TOEFL. Electronic applications accepted.

Bradley University, The Graduate School, College of Liberal Arts and Sciences, Department of English, Peoria, IL 61625-0002. Offers MA. *Program availability:* Part-time. *Faculty:* 15 full-time (8 women). *Students:* 11 part-time (8 women); includes 1 minority (Black or African American, non-Hispanic/Latino). Average age 34. 5 applicants, 80% accepted, 3 enrolled. In 2019, 1 master's awarded. *Degree requirements:* For master's, comprehensive exam, thesis optional. *Entrance requirements:* For master's, writing sample, 2 letters of recommendation. Additional exam requirements/recommendations for international students: required—TOEFL (minimum score 550 paper-based; 79 iBT), IELTS (minimum score 6.5), PTE (minimum score 58). *Application deadline:* For fall admission, 5/15 priority date for domestic and international students; for spring admission, 10/15 priority date for domestic and international students. Applications are processed on a rolling basis. Application fee: $40 ($50 for international students). Electronic applications accepted. *Expenses: Tuition:* Part-time $930 per credit hour. *Financial support:* Research assistantships, teaching assistantships, scholarships/grants, tuition waivers (partial), and unspecified assistantships available. Support available to part-time students. Financial award application deadline: 4/1. *Unit head:* Lee Newton, Chair, 309-677-2471, E-mail: lnewton@bradley.edu. *Application contact:* Rachel Webb, Director of On-Campus Graduate Admissions and International Student and Scholar Services, 309-677-2375, E-mail: rkwebb@bradley.edu.
Website: http://www.bradley.edu/academic/departments/english/

Brandeis University, Graduate School of Arts and Sciences, Department of English, Waltham, MA 02454-9110. Offers English (MA, PhD); English/women's, gender, and sexuality studies (MA). *Program availability:* Part-time. *Faculty:* 13 full-time (6 women), 6 part-time/adjunct (3 women). *Students:* 39 full-time (24 women); includes 7 minority (3 Black or African American, non-Hispanic/Latino; 2 Asian, non-Hispanic/Latino; 1 Hispanic/Latino; 1 Two or more races, non-Hispanic/Latino), 7 international. Average age 31. 194 applicants, 12% accepted, 8 enrolled. In 2019, 5 master's, 4 doctorates awarded. Terminal master's awarded for partial completion of doctoral program. *Degree requirements:* For master's, one foreign language, thesis or alternative, paper; for doctorate, 2 foreign languages, thesis/dissertation. *Entrance requirements:* For master's and doctorate, General GRE, transcripts, letters of recommendation, resume, writing sample, and statement of purpose. Additional exam requirements/recommendations for international students: required—TOEFL, IELTS, PTE. *Application deadline:* For fall admission, 1/5 for domestic and international students. Application fee: $75. Electronic applications accepted. *Financial support:* In 2019–20, 30 fellowships with full tuition reimbursements (averaging $25,000 per year), 15 teaching assistantships (averaging $3,550 per year) were awarded; scholarships/grants, health care benefits, and tuition waivers also available. Support available to part-time students. *Unit head:* Dr. Ulka Anjaria, Director of Graduate Studies, 781-736-2162, E-mail: uanjaria@brandeis.edu. *Application contact:* Lisa Pannella, Administrator, 781-736-2130, E-mail: chaucer@brandeis.edu.
Website: http://www.brandeis.edu/gsas/programs/english.html

Bridgewater State University, College of Graduate Studies, College of Humanities and Social Sciences, Department of English, Bridgewater, MA 02325. Offers MA, MAT. *Program availability:* Part-time, evening/weekend. *Degree requirements:* For master's, one foreign language, comprehensive exam, thesis optional. *Entrance requirements:* For master's, GRE General Test.

Brigham Young University, Graduate Studies, College of Humanities, Department of English, Provo, UT 84602-1001. Offers creative writing (MFA); literature (MA); rhetoric/composition (MA). *Faculty:* 55 full-time (18 women). *Students:* 66 full-time (52 women), 1 part-time (0 women); includes 5 minority (1 Asian, non-Hispanic/Latino; 4 Hispanic/Latino). Average age 28. 52 applicants, 63% accepted, 26 enrolled. In 2019, 23 master's awarded. *Degree requirements:* For master's, variable foreign language requirement, comprehensive exam, thesis. *Entrance requirements:* For master's, GRE General Test, creative portfolio (for MFA). Additional exam requirements/recommendations for international students: required—E3PT; recommended—TOEFL (minimum score 580 paper-based; 85 iBT), IELTS (minimum score 7), TSE. *Application deadline:* For fall admission, 1/15 for domestic and international students. Application fee: $50. Electronic applications accepted. *Financial support:* In 2019–20, 67 students received support, including 12 research assistantships (averaging $4,000 per year), 62 teaching assistantships (averaging $6,700 per year); career-related internships or fieldwork, institutionally sponsored loans, scholarships/grants, and unspecified assistantships also available. Support available to part-time students. Financial award application deadline: 2/15. *Unit head:* Prof. Lance Larsen, Chair, 801-4228104, Fax: 801-422-0221, E-mail: lance_larsen@byu.edu. *Application contact:* Tessa Hauglid, English Graduate Program Manager, 801-422-4939, Fax: 801-422-0221, E-mail: tessa_hauglid@byu.edu.
Website: http://english.byu.edu/

Brock University, Faculty of Graduate Studies, Faculty of Humanities, Program in English, St. Catharines, ON L2S 3A1, Canada. Offers MA. *Program availability:* Part-time. *Degree requirements:* For master's, thesis optional. *Entrance requirements:* For master's, honours in English. Additional exam requirements/recommendations for international students: required—TOEFL (minimum score 550 paper-based; 80 iBT), IELTS (minimum score 6.5), TWE (minimum score 4). Electronic applications accepted.

Brooklyn College of the City University of New York, School of Humanities and Social Sciences, Department of English, Brooklyn, NY 11210-2889. Offers creative writing (MFA), including fiction, playwriting, poetry; English (MA). *Program availability:* Part-time, evening/weekend. *Degree requirements:* For master's, one foreign language, comprehensive exam (for some programs), thesis (for some programs). *Entrance requirements:* For master's, advanced undergraduate courses in English, 2 letters of recommendation, writing sample, statement of purpose. Additional exam requirements/recommendations for international students: required—TOEFL. Electronic applications accepted.

Brown University, Graduate School, Department of English, Providence, RI 02912. Offers English (PhD); literary arts (MFA). *Degree requirements:* For doctorate, thesis/dissertation. *Entrance requirements:* For master's and doctorate, GRE General Test, GRE Subject Test.

Bucknell University, Graduate Studies, College of Arts and Sciences, Department of English, Lewisburg, PA 17837. Offers MA. *Program availability:* Part-time. *Degree requirements:* For master's, one foreign language, thesis. *Entrance requirements:* For master's, GRE General Test, GRE Subject Test, minimum GPA of 3.0. Additional exam requirements/recommendations for international students: required—TOEFL (minimum score 600 paper-based).

Buffalo State College, State University of New York, The Graduate School, School of Arts and Humanities, Department of English, Buffalo, NY 14222-1095. Offers English (MA); secondary education (MS Ed), including English. *Program availability:* Part-time, evening/weekend. *Degree requirements:* For master's, thesis or project, 1 foreign language (MS Ed). *Entrance requirements:* For master's, minimum GPA of 2.75, 36 hours in English, New York teaching certificate (MS Ed). Additional exam requirements/recommendations for international students: required—TOEFL (minimum score 550 paper-based).

Cabrini University, Academic Affairs, Radnor, PA 19087. Offers accounting (M Acc); autism spectrum disorder (M Ed); biological sciences (MS), including civic leadership; criminology and criminal justice (MA); curriculum, instruction, and assessment (M Ed); educational leadership (M Ed, Ed D), including curriculum and instructional leadership (Ed D), preK-12 leadership (Ed D); English as a second language (M Ed); organizational leadership (DBA, PhD); preK to 4 (M Ed); reading specialist (M Ed); secondary education (M Ed), including biology, chemistry, English, English/communication, mathematics, social studies; special education grades 7-12 (M Ed); special education preK-8 (M Ed); teaching and learning (M Ed). *Program availability:* Part-time, evening/weekend. *Degree requirements:* For master's, comprehensive exam (for some programs), thesis (for some programs); for doctorate, comprehensive exam (for some programs), thesis/dissertation. *Entrance requirements:* For master's, professional resume, personal statement, two recommendations, official transcripts; for doctorate, official transcripts, minimum master's GPA of 3.0, two recommendations, interview with admissions committee. Additional exam requirements/recommendations for international students: required—TOEFL (minimum score 80 iBT). Electronic applications accepted. Application fee is waived when completed online. *Expenses:* Contact institution.

California Baptist University, Program in English, Riverside, CA 92504-3206. Offers English pedagogy (MA); literature (MA); teaching English to speakers of other languages (TESOL) (MA). *Program availability:* Part-time. *Degree requirements:* For master's, comprehensive exam, project, or thesis. *Entrance requirements:* For master's, GRE (for applicants with a GPA below 2.75) or CSET, minimum undergraduate GPA of 2.75; 18 semester hours of course work in English beyond freshman level; three recommendations; essay; demonstration of writing; interview. Additional exam requirements/recommendations for international students: required—TOEFL (minimum score 80 iBT). Electronic applications accepted. *Expenses:* Contact institution.

California Polytechnic State University, San Luis Obispo, College of Liberal Arts, Department of English, San Luis Obispo, CA 93407. Offers MA. *Program availability:* Part-time. *Faculty:* 3 full-time (2 women). *Students:* 1 (woman) full-time, 14 part-time (12 women); includes 2 minority (both Hispanic/Latino). Average age 30. 13 applicants, 77% accepted, 1 enrolled. In 2019, 5 master's awarded. *Entrance requirements:* Additional exam requirements/recommendations for international students: required—TOEFL (minimum score 80 iBT). *Application deadline:* For fall admission, 4/1 for domestic and international students; for spring admission, 2/1 for domestic students. Applications are processed on a rolling basis. Application fee: $55. *Expenses:* Tuition, state resident: full-time $7176; part-time $4164 per year. Tuition, nonresident: full-time $18,690; part-time $8916 per year. *Required fees:* $4206; $3185 per unit. $1061 per term. *Financial support:* Fellowships, teaching assistantships, career-related internships or fieldwork, Federal Work-Study, institutionally sponsored loans, and tutorships, writing laboratory assistantships available. Support available to part-time students. Financial award application deadline: 3/2; financial award applicants required to submit FAFSA. *Unit head:* Dr. Ryan Hatch, Graduate Coordinator, 805-756-2238, E-mail: rahatch@calpoly.edu. *Application contact:* Dr. Ryan Hatch, Graduate Coordinator, 805-756-2238, E-mail: rahatch@calpoly.edu.
Website: http://cla.calpoly.edu/engl.html

California State Polytechnic University, Pomona, Program in English, Pomona, CA 91768-2557. Offers English (MA), including rhetoric and composition, teaching English to speakers of other languages. *Program availability:* Part-time, evening/weekend. *Degree requirements:* For master's, thesis or alternative. *Entrance requirements:* Additional exam requirements/recommendations for international students: required—TOEFL (minimum score 585 paper-based). Electronic applications accepted. *Expenses:* Contact institution.

California State University, Chico, Office of Graduate Studies, College of Humanities and Fine Arts, English Department, Chico, CA 95929-0722. Offers MA. *Degree requirements:* For master's, thesis, project, or comprehensive exam. *Entrance requirements:* For master's, GRE, two letters of recommendation, statement of purpose, writing sample. Additional exam requirements/recommendations for international students: required—TOEFL (minimum score 550 paper-based; 80 iBT), IELTS (minimum score 6.5), PTE (minimum score 59). Electronic applications accepted.

California State University, Dominguez Hills, College of Arts and Humanities, Department of English, Carson, CA 90747-0001. Offers English literature (MA); rhetoric and composition (Certificate); teaching English as a second language (MA, Certificate). *Program availability:* Part-time, evening/weekend. *Degree requirements:* For master's, comprehensive exam (for some programs), thesis or alternative. *Entrance requirements:* For master's, minimum GPA of 3.0 in last 60 units. Additional exam requirements/recommendations for international students: required—TOEFL (minimum score 550 paper-based). Electronic applications accepted.

California State University, East Bay, Office of Graduate Studies, College of Letters, Arts, and Social Sciences, Department of English, Hayward, CA 94542-3000. Offers English (MA); teaching English to speaker of other languages (MA). *Program availability:* Part-time. *Degree requirements:* For master's, one foreign language, comprehensive exam, thesis optional. *Entrance requirements:* For master's, minimum GPA of 3.0 in field; 2 letters of recommendation; academic or professional writing sample; teaching experience and some degree of bilingualism (preferred for TESOL). Additional exam requirements/recommendations for international students: required—TOEFL (minimum score 550 paper-based); recommended—IELTS (minimum score 6.5). Electronic applications accepted.

California State University, Fresno, Division of Research and Graduate Studies, College of Arts and Humanities, Department of English, Fresno, CA 93740-8027. Offers creative writing (MFA); literature (MA); rhetoric and writing studies (MA). *Program availability:* Part-time, evening/weekend. *Degree requirements:* For master's, one foreign language, thesis. *Entrance requirements:* For master's, GRE General Test, minimum GPA of 3.0, writing sample. Additional exam requirements/recommendations for international students: required—TOEFL. Electronic applications accepted. *Expenses:* Tuition, state resident: full-time $4012; part-time $2506 per semester.

California State University, Fullerton, Graduate Studies, College of Humanities and Social Sciences, Department of English, Comparative Literature, and Linguistics, Fullerton, CA 92831-3599. Offers English (MA); linguistics (MA). *Program availability:* Part-time. *Degree requirements:* For master's, one foreign language, thesis or alternative, project. *Entrance requirements:* For master's, minimum GPA of 3.0, undergraduate major in linguistics or related field.

California State University, Long Beach, Graduate Studies, College of Liberal Arts, Department of English, Long Beach, CA 90840. Offers creative writing (MFA); English (MA). *Program availability:* Part-time. *Degree requirements:* For master's, one foreign language, comprehensive exam or thesis. *Entrance requirements:* For master's, GRE Subject Test, minimum GPA of 3.0 in English. Electronic applications accepted.

California State University, Los Angeles, Graduate Studies, College of Arts and Letters, Department of English, Los Angeles, CA 90032-8530. Offers MA, Certificate. *Program availability:* Part-time, evening/weekend. *Degree requirements:* For master's, comprehensive exam or thesis. *Entrance requirements:* Additional exam requirements/recommendations for international students: required—TOEFL (minimum score 500 paper-based). Electronic applications accepted. *Expenses: Tuition, area resident:* Full-time $7176; part-time $4164 per year. Tuition, state resident: full-time $7176; part-time $4164 per year. Tuition, nonresident: full-time $14,304; part-time $8916 per year. *International tuition:* $14,304 full-time. *Required fees:* $1037.76; $1037.76 per unit. Tuition and fees vary according to degree level and program.

California State University, Northridge, Graduate Studies, College of Humanities, Department of English, Northridge, CA 91330. Offers creative writing (MA); literature (MA); rhetoric and composition theory (MA). *Program availability:* Part-time, evening/weekend. *Degree requirements:* For master's, thesis or alternative. *Entrance requirements:* For master's, writing proficiency test, GRE General Test or minimum GPA of 3.0. Additional exam requirements/recommendations for international students: required—TOEFL.

California State University, Sacramento, College of Arts and Letters, Department of English, Sacramento, CA 95819. Offers composition (MA); creative writing (MA); literature (MA); teaching English to speakers of other languages (MA). *Program availability:* Part-time. *Students:* 39 full-time (27 women), 54 part-time (30 women); includes 26 minority (6 Black or African American, non-Hispanic/Latino; 4 Asian, non-Hispanic/Latino; 16 Hispanic/Latino), 2 international. Average age 30. 42 applicants, 76% accepted, 29 enrolled. In 2019, 23 master's awarded. *Degree requirements:* For master's, comprehensive exam, thesis optional, thesis, project, or comprehensive exam; TESOL exam; writing proficiency exam. *Entrance requirements:* For master's, portfolio (creative writing); minimum GPA of 3.0 in English and overall during previous 2 years. Additional exam requirements/recommendations for international students: required—TOEFL (minimum score 600 paper-based; 100 iBT). *Application deadline:* For fall admission, 2/15 for domestic students, 1/15 for international students; for spring admission, 9/15 for domestic students, 8/30 for international students. Applications are processed on a rolling basis. Application fee: $70. Electronic applications accepted. *Expenses:* Contact institution. *Financial support:* Teaching assistantships, career-related internships or fieldwork, Federal Work-Study, and scholarships/grants available. Support available to part-time students. Financial award application deadline: 3/1; financial award applicants required to submit FAFSA. *Unit head:* Dr. David Toise, Chair, 916-278-6586, E-mail: dwtoise@csus.edu. *Application contact:* Jose Martinez, Graduate Admissions Supervisor, 916-278-7871, E-mail: martinj@skymail.csus.edu.
Website: http://www.csus.edu/engl

California State University, San Bernardino, Graduate Studies, College of Arts and Letters, Program in English, San Bernardino, CA 92407. Offers creative writing (MFA), including fiction; English composition (MA), including composition. *Program availability:* Part-time, evening/weekend. *Faculty:* 7 full-time (all women). *Students:* 14 full-time (9 women), 45 part-time (29 women); includes 37 minority (7 Black or African American, non-Hispanic/Latino; 2 Asian, non-Hispanic/Latino; 26 Hispanic/Latino; 2 Two or more races, non-Hispanic/Latino), 1 international. Average age 31. 22 applicants, 82% accepted, 18 enrolled. In 2019, 21 master's awarded. *Degree requirements:* For master's, one foreign language, thesis. *Entrance requirements:* Additional exam requirements/recommendations for international students: required—TOEFL. *Application deadline:* For fall admission, 7/16 for domestic students. Application fee: $55. *Financial support:* Application deadline: 3/1. *Unit head:* Dr. David Carlson, Chair, 909-537-5834, Fax: 909-537-7086, E-mail: dajcarls@csusb.edu. *Application contact:* Dr. Dorota Huizinga, Dean of Graduate Studies, 909-537-3064, Fax: 909-537-5078, E-mail: dorota.huizinga@csusb.edu.

California State University, San Marcos, College of Humanities, Arts, Behavioral and Social Sciences, Program in Literature and Writing Studies, San Marcos, CA 92096-0001. Offers MA. *Program availability:* Part-time, evening/weekend. *Degree requirements:* For master's, one foreign language, thesis. *Entrance requirements:* For master's, GRE General Test, minimum GPA of 3.0, writing sample. *Expenses: Tuition, area resident:* Full-time $7176. Tuition, state resident: full-time $7176. Tuition, nonresident: full-time $18,640. *International tuition:* $18,640 full-time. *Required fees:* $1960.

California State University, Stanislaus, College of the Arts, Humanities and Social Sciences, MA Program in English, Turlock, CA 95382. Offers literature (Certificate); rhetoric and teaching writing (MA); teaching English to speakers of other languages (MA). *Program availability:* Part-time. *Degree requirements:* For master's, comprehensive exam, thesis or alternative. *Entrance requirements:* For master's, GRE, minimum GPA of 3.0, 2 letters of reference, personal statement. Additional exam requirements/recommendations for international students: required—TOEFL (minimum score 575 paper-based), TWE (minimum score 4). Electronic applications accepted.

Carleton University, Faculty of Graduate Studies, Faculty of Arts and Social Sciences, Department of English Language and Literature, Ottawa, ON K1S 5B6, Canada. Offers MA, PhD. *Degree requirements:* For master's, thesis optional. *Entrance requirements:* For master's, honors degree. Additional exam requirements/recommendations for international students: required—TOEFL.

Carnegie Mellon University, Dietrich College of Humanities and Social Sciences, Department of English, Pittsburgh, PA 15213-3891. Offers communication planning and design (M Des); literary and cultural studies (MA, PhD); professional writing (MAPW), including editing and publishing, policy and non-profit communication, public and media relations / corporate communications, science or healthcare communication, technical writing, writing for new media, writing for print media; rhetoric (MA, PhD). *Program availability:* Part-time. Terminal master's awarded for partial completion of doctoral program. *Degree requirements:* For doctorate, 2 foreign languages, comprehensive exam, thesis/dissertation. *Entrance requirements:* For master's and doctorate, GRE General Test. Additional exam requirements/recommendations for international students: required—TOEFL, TWE.

Case Western Reserve University, School of Graduate Studies, Department of English, Cleveland, OH 44106. Offers MA, PhD. *Program availability:* Part-time. *Degree requirements:* For master's, one foreign language, comprehensive exam, thesis or alternative, written exam; for doctorate, one foreign language, thesis/dissertation, oral and written exams. *Entrance requirements:* For master's and doctorate, GRE General Test, sample of written work, three letters of recommendation. Additional exam requirements/recommendations for international students: required—TOEFL (minimum score 577 paper-based; 90 iBT); recommended—IELTS (minimum score 7). Electronic applications accepted.

The Catholic University of America, School of Arts and Sciences, Department of English Language and Literature, Washington, DC 20064. Offers English (MA, PhD); rhetoric (Certificate). *Program availability:* Part-time. *Faculty:* 9 full-time (3 women), 3 part-time/adjunct (all women). *Students:* 10 full-time (7 women), 22 part-time (14 women); includes 6 minority (3 Hispanic/Latino; 3 Two or more races, non-Hispanic/Latino). Average age 30. 27 applicants, 59% accepted, 8 enrolled. In 2019, 1 master's, 6 doctorates awarded. *Degree requirements:* For master's, one foreign language, comprehensive exam; for doctorate, 2 foreign languages, comprehensive exam, thesis/dissertation. *Entrance requirements:* For master's and doctorate, GRE General Test, statement of purpose, official copies of academic transcripts, three letters of recommendation, writing sample. Additional exam requirements/recommendations for international students: required—TOEFL (minimum score 550 paper-based; 80 iBT). *Application deadline:* For fall admission, 7/15 priority date for domestic students, 7/1 for international students; for spring admission, 11/15 priority date for domestic students, 11/1 for international students. Applications are processed on a rolling basis. Application fee: $55. Electronic applications accepted. *Expenses:* Contact institution. *Financial support:* Fellowships, research assistantships, teaching assistantships, Federal Work-Study, scholarships/grants, tuition waivers (full and partial), and unspecified assistantships available. Financial award application deadline: 2/1; financial award applicants required to submit FAFSA. *Unit head:* Dr. Ernest Suarez, Chair, 202-319-5488, Fax: 202-319-4188, E-mail: johnsong@cua.edu. *Application contact:* Dr. Steven Brown, Director of Graduate Admissions, 202-319-5057, Fax: 202-319-6533, E-mail: cua-admissions@cua.edu.
Website: http://english.cua.edu/

Central Connecticut State University, School of Graduate Studies, College of Liberal Arts and Social Sciences, Department of English, New Britain, CT 06050-4010. Offers English (MA); English education (MAT). *Program availability:* Part-time, evening/weekend. *Degree requirements:* For master's, comprehensive exam, thesis or alternative; for Certificate, qualifying exam. *Entrance requirements:* For master's, minimum undergraduate GPA of 3.0, writing sample, letters of recommendation, essay. Additional exam requirements/recommendations for international students: required—TOEFL (minimum score 550 paper-based; 79 iBT); recommended—IELTS (minimum score 6.5). Electronic applications accepted.

Central Michigan University, College of Graduate Studies, College of Liberal Arts and Social Sciences, Department of English Language and Literature, Mount Pleasant, MI 48859. Offers English composition and communication (MA); English language and literature (MA), including children's and young adult literature, creative writing, English language and literature; TESOL: teaching English to speakers of other languages (MA). *Program availability:* Part-time, evening/weekend. *Degree requirements:* For master's, thesis or alternative. Electronic applications accepted. *Expenses: Tuition, area resident:* Full-time $12,267; part-time $8178 per year. Tuition, state resident: full-time $12,267; part-time $8178 per year. Tuition, nonresident: full-time $12,267; part-time $8178 per year. *International tuition:* $16,110 full-time. *Required fees:* $225 per semester. Tuition and fees vary according to degree level and program.

Central Washington University, School of Graduate Studies and Research, College of Arts and Humanities, Department of English, Ellensburg, WA 98926. Offers literature (MA); professional and creative writing (MA); teaching English to speakers of other languages (MA). *Program availability:* Part-time. *Entrance requirements:* For master's, GRE General Test, minimum GPA of 3.0, writing sample. Additional exam requirements/recommendations for international students: required—TOEFL (minimum score 550 paper-based; 79 iBT) or IELTS (minimum score 6.5). Electronic applications accepted.

Chapman University, Wilkinson College of Arts, Humanities, and Social Sciences, Department of English, Orange, CA 92866. Offers creative writing (MFA); English (MA). *Program availability:* Part-time, evening/weekend. *Faculty:* 24 full-time (11 women), 40 part-time/adjunct (23 women). *Students:* 46 full-time (35 women), 17 part-time (8 women); includes 24 minority (3 Black or African American, non-Hispanic/Latino; 1 American Indian or Alaska Native, non-Hispanic/Latino; 5 Asian, non-Hispanic/Latino; 11 Hispanic/Latino; 4 Two or more races, non-Hispanic/Latino), 5 international. Average age 28. 106 applicants, 76% accepted, 22 enrolled. In 2019, 32 master's awarded. *Degree requirements:* For master's, thesis. *Entrance requirements:* For master's, GRE (if undergraduate GPA less than 3.0), minimum undergraduate GPA of 2.5. Additional exam requirements/recommendations for international students: required—TOEFL (minimum score 80 iBT), IELTS (minimum score 6.5), PTE (minimum score 53). *Application deadline:* For fall admission, 2/1 priority date for domestic students. Applications are processed on a rolling basis. Application fee: $60. Electronic applications accepted. *Expenses:* $1,035 per unit. *Financial support:* Fellowships, teaching assistantships, Federal Work-Study, and scholarships/grants available. Financial award applicants required to submit FAFSA. *Unit head:* Dr. Joanna Levin, Chair, 714-997-6534, E-mail: jlevin@chapman.edu. *Application contact:* Sharnique Dow, Graduate Admission Counselor, 714-997-6770, E-mail: sdow@chapman.edu.
Website: https://www.chapman.edu/wilkinson/english/index.aspx

Chicago State University, School of Graduate and Professional Studies, College of Arts and Sciences, Department of English, Foreign Languages and Literatures, Chicago, IL 60628. Offers creative writing (MFA); English (MA). *Degree requirements:* For master's, comprehensive exam (for some programs), thesis (for some programs). *Entrance requirements:* For master's, minimum GPA of 3.0.

The Citadel, The Military College of South Carolina, Citadel Graduate College, School of Humanities and Social Sciences, Department of English, Fine Arts and Communications, Charleston, SC 29409. Offers English (MA). *Program availability:* Part-time, evening/weekend. *Degree requirements:* For master's, one foreign language, comprehensive exam, thesis optional. *Entrance requirements:* For master's, GRE (minimum combined verbal and quantitative score of 300, 4 on writing assessment section) or MAT (minimum score of 400); GRE Subject Test (for applicants without undergraduate degree in English), minimum undergraduate GPA of 2.5 (3.0 in major); 2 letters of recommendation preferably from former professors; writing sample that demonstrates ability to perform literary analysis and to conduct research; 2-page statement about educational goals and interest in a graduate program in English. Additional exam requirements/recommendations for international students: required—TOEFL (minimum score 550 paper-based). Electronic applications accepted.

City College of the City University of New York, Graduate School, Division of Humanities and the Arts, Department of English, Program in Literature, New York, NY 10031-9198. Offers MA. *Degree requirements:* For master's, one foreign language, comprehensive exam, thesis. *Entrance requirements:* For master's, minimum GPA of 3.0. Additional exam requirements/recommendations for international students: required—TOEFL (minimum score 600 paper-based; 100 iBT). Electronic applications accepted.

Claremont Graduate University, Graduate Programs, School of Arts and Humanities, Department of English, Claremont, CA 91711-6160. Offers American studies (MA, PhD); critical theory (MA, PhD); early modern studies (MA, PhD); English (M Phil, MA, PhD); literary theory (PhD); literature (MA, PhD); literature and creative writing (MA); literature and film (MA); MBA/MA; MBA/PhD. *Program availability:* Part-time. *Entrance requirements:* For master's and doctorate, GRE General Test. Additional exam requirements/recommendations for international students: required—TOEFL (minimum score 75 iBT). Electronic applications accepted.

Clark Atlanta University, School of Arts and Sciences, Department of English and Modern Languages, Atlanta, GA 30314. Offers MA, PhD. *Program availability:* Part-time. *Degree requirements:* For master's, one foreign language, comprehensive exam, thesis; for doctorate, 2 foreign languages, comprehensive exam, thesis/dissertation. *Entrance requirements:* For master's, GRE General Test, minimum GPA of 2.5. Additional exam requirements/recommendations for international students: required—TOEFL (minimum score 500 paper-based; 61 iBT).

Clarks Summit University, Online Master's Programs, South Abington Township, PA 18411. Offers Bible (MA); counseling (MA, MS); curriculum and instruction (M Ed); educational administration (M Ed); literature (MA); organizational leadership (MA). *Program availability:* Part-time, evening/weekend, online learning. *Entrance requirements:* Additional exam requirements/recommendations for international students: required—TOEFL (minimum score 500 paper-based).

Clark University, Graduate School, Department of English, Worcester, MA 01610-1477. Offers MA. *Program availability:* Part-time. *Faculty:* 8 full-time (4 women), 16 part-time/adjunct (10 women). *Students:* 5 full-time (4 women), 5 part-time (all women), 3 international. Average age 27. 33 applicants, 30% accepted, 6 enrolled. In 2019, 12 master's awarded. *Degree requirements:* For master's, thesis, oral exam. *Entrance requirements:* For master's, GRE Subject Test, 2 references, resume or curriculum vitae, personal statement. Additional exam requirements/recommendations for international students: required—TOEFL (minimum score 575 paper-based; 90 iBT), IELTS (minimum score 6.5). *Application deadline:* For fall admission, 1/15 priority date for domestic students. Application fee: $75. Electronic applications accepted. *Expenses:* Contact institution. *Financial support:* Fellowships, research assistantships, teaching assistantships, career-related internships or fieldwork, and tuition waivers (partial) available. Support available to part-time students. *Unit head:* Dr. Lisa Kasmer, Chair, 508-793-7136, E-mail: lkasmer@clarku.edu. *Application contact:* Dr. Lisa Kasmer, Chair, 508-793-7136, E-mail: lkasmer@clarku.edu.
Website: http://www.clarku.edu/departments/english/

Cleveland State University, College of Graduate Studies, College of Liberal Arts and Social Sciences, Department of English, Cleveland, OH 44115. Offers creative writing (MFA), including fiction, non-fiction, playwriting, poetry. *Program availability:* Part-time, evening/weekend. *Faculty:* 14 full-time (8 women), 14 part-time/adjunct (4 women). *Students:* 28 full-time (18 women), 20 part-time (12 women); includes 6 minority (5 Black or African American, non-Hispanic/Latino; 1 Hispanic/Latino). Average age 34. 38 applicants, 68% accepted, 9 enrolled. In 2019, 13 master's awarded. *Entrance requirements:* For master's, minimum GPA of 2.75, undergraduate concentration in English, writing sample, portfolio. Additional exam requirements/recommendations for international students: required—TOEFL (minimum score 550 paper-based; 78 iBT). *Application deadline:* Applications are processed on a rolling basis. Application fee: $40. Electronic applications accepted. *Expenses:* Tuition, state resident: full-time $10,215; part-time $6810 per credit hour. Tuition, nonresident: full-time $17,496; part-time $11,664 per credit hour. *International tuition:* $19,316 full-time. Tuition and fees vary according to degree level and program. *Financial support:* In 2019–20, 8 students received support. Teaching assistantships, tuition waivers (full and partial), and unspecified assistantships available. Financial award application deadline: 2/1; financial award applicants required to submit FAFSA. *Application contact:* Dr. James J. Marino, Associate Professor/Director of Graduate Studies, 216-687-6874, Fax: 216-687-6943, E-mail: j.marino22@csuohio.edu.
Website: http://www.csuohio.edu/class/english/english

College of Charleston, Graduate School, School of Humanities and Social Sciences, Program in English, Charleston, SC 29424-0001. Offers MA. *Program availability:* Part-time, evening/weekend. *Degree requirements:* For master's, one foreign language, comprehensive exam, thesis optional. *Entrance requirements:* For master's, GRE General Test or MAT, minimum GPA of 2.5 overall, 3.0 in major; 2 letters of recommendation; writing sample. Additional exam requirements/recommendations for international students: required—TOEFL (minimum score 81 iBT). Electronic applications accepted.

The College of New Jersey, Office of Graduate and Advancing Education, School of Humanities and Social Sciences, Department of English, Program in English, Ewing, NJ 08628. Offers MA. *Program availability:* Part-time. *Degree requirements:* For master's, comprehensive exam. *Entrance requirements:* For master's, GRE, minimum GPA of 3.0 in field or 2.75 overall. Additional exam requirements/recommendations for international students: required—TOEFL. Electronic applications accepted.

College of Staten Island of the City University of New York, Graduate Programs, Division of Humanities and Social Sciences, Program in English, Staten Island, NY 10314-6600. Offers English (MA), including literature, rhetoric. *Program availability:* Part-time, evening/weekend. *Faculty:* 9. *Students:* 41. 28 applicants, 43% accepted, 9 enrolled. In 2019, 17 master's awarded. *Degree requirements:* For master's, comprehensive exam, Of the 34 credits required for students who have initial certification and desire professional certification as high school teachers of English, 7 four-credit courses are chosen from either the Literature or Rhetoric, three required courses, and a 28-32 page thesis. *Entrance requirements:* For master's, BA with minimum GPA of 3.0 in English courses, 32 undergraduate credits in English, two letters of recommendation, one- to two-page personal statement (500-700 words), minimum 8-10 page paper written for an English course. Additional exam requirements/recommendations for international students: required—TOEFL (minimum score 550 paper-based; 79 iBT), IELTS (minimum score 6.5). *Application deadline:* For fall admission, 4/30 priority date for domestic students, 4/30 for international students; for spring admission, 10/31 priority date for domestic students, 10/31 for international students. Applications are processed on a rolling basis. Application fee: $75. Electronic applications accepted. *Expenses: Tuition, area resident:* Full-time $11,090; part-time $470 per credit. Tuition, state resident: full-time $11,090; part-time $470 per credit. Tuition, nonresident: full-time $20,520; part-time $855 per credit. *International tuition:* $20,520 full-time. *Required fees:* $559; $181 per semester. Tuition and fees vary according to program. *Unit head:* Dr. Katharine Goodland, Graduate Program Coordinator, 718-982-3639, E-mail: katharine.goodland@csi.cuny.edu. *Application contact:* Sasha Spence, Associate Director for Graduate Admissions, 718-982-2019, Fax: 718-982-2500, E-mail: sasha.spence@csi.cuny.edu.
Website: http://csicuny.smartcatalogiq.com/en/current/Graduate-Catalog/Graduate-Programs-Disciplines-and-Offerings-in-Selected-Disciplines/English-MA

Colorado State University, College of Liberal Arts, Department of English, Fort Collins, CO 80523-1773. Offers creative writing (MFA); rhetoric and composition (MA). *Faculty:* 24 full-time (12 women), 6 part-time/adjunct (5 women). *Students:* 72 full-time (54 women), 23 part-time (20 women); includes 13 minority (2 Black or African American, non-Hispanic/Latino; 1 Asian, non-Hispanic/Latino; 5 Hispanic/Latino; 5 Two or more races, non-Hispanic/Latino), 13 international. Average age 30. 170 applicants, 51% accepted, 32 enrolled. In 2019, 32 master's awarded. *Degree requirements:* For master's, thesis (for some programs), portfolio, project or thesis. *Entrance requirements:* For master's, BA/BS or equivalent with minimum cumulative undergraduate GPA of 3.0, transcripts, writing sample, statement of purpose, 3 letters of recommendation. Additional exam requirements/recommendations for international students: recommended—TOEFL (minimum score 550 paper-based; 80 iBT), IELTS (minimum score 6.5). Application fee: $60 ($70 for international students). Electronic applications accepted. *Expenses:* Tuition, state resident: full-time $10,520; part-time $5844 per credit hour. Tuition, nonresident: full-time $25,791; part-time $14,328 per credit hour. *International tuition:* $25,791 full-time. *Required fees:* $2512.80. Part-time tuition and fees vary according to course level, course load, degree level, program and student level. *Financial support:* In 2019–20, 1 fellowship with full and partial tuition reimbursement (averaging $15,210 per year), 1 research assistantship (averaging $7,605 per year), 39 teaching assistantships with full and partial tuition reimbursements (averaging $15,593 per year) were awarded; Federal Work-Study, scholarships/grants, and unspecified assistantships also available. *Unit head:* Dr. Louann Reid, Professor, 970-491-6428, E-mail: louann.reid@colostate.edu. *Application contact:* Marnie Leonard, Administrative Assistant, 970-491-2403, E-mail: marnie.leonard@colostate.edu.
Website: http://english.colostate.edu/

Columbia College Chicago, School of Graduate Studies, English and Creative Writing Department, Chicago, IL 60605-1996. Offers fiction (MFA); nonfiction (MFA); poetry (MFA). *Program availability:* Part-time, evening/weekend. *Degree requirements:* For master's, thesis. *Entrance requirements:* For master's, self-assessment essay, work samples, letters of recommendation, transcripts. Additional exam requirements/recommendations for international students: required—TOEFL, IELTS. Electronic applications accepted.

Columbia University, Graduate School of Arts and Sciences, New York, NY 10027. Offers African-American studies (MA); American studies (MA); anthropology (MA, PhD); art history and archaeology (MA, PhD); astronomy (PhD); biological sciences (PhD); biotechnology (MA); chemical physics (PhD); chemistry (PhD); classical studies (MA, PhD); classics (MA, PhD); climate and society (MA); conservation biology (MA); earth and environmental sciences (PhD); East Asia: regional studies (MA); East Asian languages and cultures (MA, PhD); ecology, evolution and environmental biology (MA), including conservation biology; ecology, evolution, and environmental biology (PhD), including ecology and evolutionary biology, evolutionary primatology; economics (MA, PhD); English and comparative literature (MA, PhD); French and Romance philology (MA, PhD); Germanic languages (MA, PhD); global French studies (MA); global thought (MA); Hispanic cultural studies (MA); history (PhD); history and literature (MA); human rights studies (MA); Islamic studies (MA); Italian (MA, PhD); Japanese pedagogy (MA); Jewish studies (MA); Latin America and the Caribbean: regional studies (MA); Latin American and Iberian cultures (PhD); mathematics (MA, PhD), including finance (MA); medieval and Renaissance studies (MA); Middle Eastern, South Asian, and African studies (MA, PhD); modern art: critical and curatorial studies (MA); modern European studies (MA); museum anthropology (MA); music (DMA, PhD); oral history (MA); philosophical foundations of physics (MA); philosophy (MA, PhD); physics (PhD); political science (MA, PhD); psychology (PhD); quantitative methods in the social sciences (MA); religion (MA, PhD); Russia, Eurasia and East Europe: regional studies (MA); Russian translation (MA); Slavic cultures (MA); Slavic languages (MA, PhD); sociology (MA, PhD); South Asian studies (MA); statistics (MA, PhD); theatre (PhD). *Program availability:* Part-time. *Students:* 3,506 full-time (1,844 women), 208 part-time (121 women); includes 864 minority (110 Black or African American, non-Hispanic/Latino; 5 American Indian or Alaska Native, non-Hispanic/Latino; 416 Asian, non-Hispanic/Latino; 147 Hispanic/Latino; 6 Native Hawaiian or other Pacific Islander, non-Hispanic/Latino; 180 Two or more races, non-Hispanic/Latino), 2,065 international. 14,545 applicants, 25% accepted, 1,429 enrolled. In 2019, 1,262 master's, 363 doctorates awarded. Terminal master's awarded for partial completion of doctoral program. *Degree requirements:* For master's, variable foreign language requirement, comprehensive exam (for some programs), thesis (for some programs); for doctorate, variable foreign language requirement, comprehensive exam (for some programs), thesis/dissertation. *Entrance requirements:* For master's and doctorate, GRE General Test, GRE Subject Test (for some programs). Additional exam requirements/recommendations for international students: required—TOEFL (minimum score 600 paper-based; 100 iBT), IELTS (minimum score 7.5). Application fee: $115. Electronic applications accepted. *Expenses: Tuition:* Full-time $47,600; part-time $1880 per credit. One-time fee: $105. *Financial support:* Fellowships, research assistantships, teaching assistantships, career-related internships or fieldwork, Federal Work-Study, institutionally sponsored loans, scholarships/grants, traineeships, health care benefits, tuition waivers, and unspecified assistantships available. Support available to part-time students. Financial award application deadline: 12/15. *Unit head:* Dr. Carlos J. Alonso, Dean of the Graduate School of Arts and Sciences and Vice President for Graduate Education, 212-854-2861, E-mail: gsas-dean@columbia.edu. *Application contact:* GSAS Office of Admissions, 212-854-6729, E-mail: gsas-admissions@columbia.edu.
Website: http://gsas.columbia.edu/

Concordia University, School of Graduate Studies, Faculty of Arts and Science, Department of English, Program in English Literature, Montréal, QC H3G 1M8, Canada. Offers MA, PhD. *Degree requirements:* For master's, one foreign language, thesis optional. *Entrance requirements:* For master's, honors degree in English, minimum GPA of 3.3 in English literature.

Converse College, Program in Liberal Arts, Spartanburg, SC 29302. Offers English (MLA); history (MLA); political science (MLA). *Degree requirements:* For master's, capstone paper. *Entrance requirements:* For master's, minimum GPA of 3.0, 2 recommendations.

Converse College, Program in Middle Level Education, Spartanburg, SC 29302. Offers language arts/English (MAT); mathematics (MAT); middle level education (M Ed); science (MAT); social studies (MAT).

Cornell University, Graduate School, Graduate Fields of Arts and Sciences, Field of English Language and Literature, Ithaca, NY 14853. Offers African-American literature (PhD); American literature after 1865 (PhD); American literature to 1865 (PhD); American studies (PhD); colonial and postcolonial literatures (PhD); creative writing (MFA); cultural studies (PhD); dramatic literature (PhD); English poetry (PhD); English Renaissance to 1660 (PhD); lesbian, bisexual, and gay literary studies (PhD); literary criticism and theory (PhD); Old and Middle English (PhD); prose fiction (PhD); Restoration and the eighteenth-century (PhD); the nineteenth century (PhD); the twentieth century (PhD); women's literature (PhD); MFA/PhD. Terminal master's awarded for partial completion of doctoral program. *Degree requirements:* For master's, one foreign language, thesis; for doctorate, one foreign language, comprehensive exam, thesis/dissertation, teaching experience. *Entrance requirements:* For master's, GRE General Test, 3 letters of recommendation, creative writing sample; for doctorate, 3 letters of recommendation, writing sample. Additional exam requirements/recommendations for international students: required—TOEFL (minimum score 600 paper-based; 77 iBT). Electronic applications accepted.

Cornell University, Graduate School, Graduate Fields of Arts and Sciences, Field of Linguistics, Ithaca, NY 14853. Offers applied linguistics (MA, PhD); East Asian linguistics (MA, PhD); English linguistics (MA, PhD); general linguistics (MA, PhD); Germanic linguistics (MA, PhD); Indo-European linguistics (MA, PhD); phonetics (MA, PhD); phonological theory (MA, PhD); Romance linguistics (MA, PhD); second language acquisition (MA, PhD); semantics (MA, PhD); Slavic linguistics (MA, PhD); sociolinguistics (MA, PhD); South Asian linguistics (MA, PhD); Southeast Asian linguistics (MA, PhD); syntactic theory (MA, PhD). Terminal master's awarded for partial completion of doctoral program. *Degree requirements:* For master's, one foreign language, thesis; for doctorate, one foreign language, comprehensive exam, thesis/dissertation. *Entrance requirements:* For master's and doctorate, GRE General Test, 2 letters of recommendation. Additional exam requirements/recommendations for international students: required—TOEFL (minimum score 600 paper-based; 77 iBT). Electronic applications accepted.

Creighton University, Graduate School, College of Arts and Sciences, Department of English, Omaha, NE 68178-0001. Offers creative writing (MA, MFA). *Program availability:* Part-time. *Degree requirements:* For master's, thesis optional. *Entrance requirements:* For master's, 10-15 page writing sample, 3 letters of recommendation. Additional exam requirements/recommendations for international students: required—TOEFL (minimum score 90 iBT). Electronic applications accepted.

Dalhousie University, Faculty of Arts and Social Sciences, Department of English, Halifax, NS B3H 4R2, Canada. Offers MA, PhD. *Entrance requirements:* Additional exam requirements/recommendations for international students: required—TOEFL, IELTS, CANTEST, CAEL, or Michigan English Language Assessment Battery. Electronic applications accepted.

DePaul University, College of Liberal Arts and Social Sciences, Chicago, IL 60614. Offers Arabic (MA); Chinese (MA); critical ethnic studies (MA); English (MA); French (MA); German (MA); history (MA); interdisciplinary studies (MA, MS); international public service (MS); international studies (MA); Italian (MA); Japanese (MA); liberal studies (MA); nonprofit management (MNM); public administration (MPA); public health (MPH); public policy (MPP); public service management (MS); refugee and forced migration studies (MS); social work (MSW); sociology (MA); Spanish (MA); sustainable urban development (MA); women's and gender studies (MA); writing and publishing (MA); writing, rhetoric and discourse (MA); MA/PhD. *Accreditation:* CEPH. *Program availability:* Part-time, evening/weekend, online learning. Terminal master's awarded for partial completion of doctoral program. *Degree requirements:* For master's, variable foreign language requirement, comprehensive exam (for some programs), thesis (for some programs). Electronic applications accepted.

Drew University, Caspersen School of Graduate Studies, Madison, NJ 07940-1493. Offers conflict resolution and leadership (Certificate), including community leadership, moderation, peace building; education (M Ed); finance (MA); history and culture (MA, PhD), including American history, book history, British history, European history, intellectual history, Irish history, print culture, public history; K-12 education (MAT), including art, biology, chemistry, elementary education, English, French, Italian, math, secondary education, special education, teacher of students with disabilities; liberal studies (M Litt, D Litt), including history, Irish/Irish-American studies, literature (M Litt, MMH, D Litt, DMH, CMH), religion, spirituality, teaching in the two-year college, writing; medical humanities (MMH, DMH, CMH), including arts, health, healthcare, literature (M Litt, MMH, D Litt, DMH, CMH), scientific research; poetry (MFA). *Program availability:* Part-time, evening/weekend. Terminal master's awarded for partial completion of doctoral program. *Degree requirements:* For master's and other advanced degree, thesis (for some programs); for doctorate, one foreign language, comprehensive exam (for some programs), thesis/dissertation. *Entrance requirements:* For master's, PRAXIS Core and Subject Area tests (for MAT), GRE/GMAT (for MFin MS in Data Analytics), resume, transcripts, writing sample, personal statement, letters of recommendation; for doctorate, GRE (PhD in history and culture), resume, transcripts, writing sample, personal statement, letters of recommendation; for other advanced degree, resume, transcripts, personal statement. Additional exam requirements/recommendations for international students: required—TOEFL (minimum score 587 paper-based; 80 iBT), IELTS (minimum score 6), TWE (minimum score 4). Electronic applications accepted.

Duke University, Graduate School, Department of English, Durham, NC 27708. Offers PhD, JD/AM. *Degree requirements:* For doctorate, 2 foreign languages, thesis/dissertation. *Entrance requirements:* For doctorate, GRE General Test, writing sample. Additional exam requirements/recommendations for international students: required—TOEFL (minimum score 577 paper-based; 90 iBT) or IELTS (minimum score 7). Electronic applications accepted.

Duquesne University, Graduate School of Liberal Arts, Department of English, Pittsburgh, PA 15282-0001. Offers MA, PhD. *Program availability:* Part-time, evening/weekend. Terminal master's awarded for partial completion of doctoral program. *Degree requirements:* For master's, Capstone; for doctorate, 2 foreign languages, comprehensive exam, thesis/dissertation. *Entrance requirements:* For master's and doctorate, GRE General Test, bachelor's degree in English, writing sample. Additional exam requirements/recommendations for international students: required—TOEFL. Electronic applications accepted.

East Carolina University, Graduate School, Thomas Harriot College of Arts and Sciences, Department of English, Greenville, NC 27858-4353. Offers creative writing (MA); English studies (MA); linguistics (MA); literature (MA); multicultural and transnational literatures (MA, Certificate); professional communication (Certificate); rhetoric and composition (MA); rhetoric, writing, and professional communication (PhD); teaching English in the two-year college (Certificate); teaching English to speakers of other languages (MA, Certificate); technical and professional communication (MA). *Program availability:* Part-time, evening/weekend, online learning. *Application deadline:* For fall admission, 7/31 priority date for domestic students, 2/1 priority date for international students; for spring admission, 11/30 priority date for domestic students, 10/1 priority date for international students. *Expenses: Tuition, area resident:* Full-time $4749; part-time $185 per credit hour. Tuition, state resident: full-time $4749; part-time $185 per credit hour. Tuition, nonresident: full-time $17,898; part-time $864 per credit hour. *International tuition:* $17,898 full-time. *Required fees:* $2787. *Financial support:* Application deadline: 3/1. *Unit head:* Dr. Marianne Montgomery, Chair, 252-328-6041, E-mail: montgomerym@ecu.edu. *Application contact:* Graduate School Admissions, 252-328-6012, Fax: 252-328-6071, E-mail: gradschool@ecu.edu. Website: https://english.ecu.edu/

Eastern Illinois University, Graduate School, College of Liberal Arts and Sciences, Department of English, Charleston, IL 61920. Offers MA. *Program availability:* Part-time, evening/weekend. *Degree requirements:* For master's, comprehensive exam (for some programs), thesis (for some programs). *Entrance requirements:* For master's, GMAT or GRE. Additional exam requirements/recommendations for international students: required—TOEFL (minimum score 500 paper-based; 61 iBT), IELTS (minimum score 6). Electronic applications accepted.

Eastern Kentucky University, The Graduate School, College of Arts and Sciences, Department of English and Theatre, Richmond, KY 40475-3102. Offers creative writing (MFA); English (MA). *Program availability:* Part-time, evening/weekend. *Degree requirements:* For master's, thesis optional. *Entrance requirements:* For master's, GRE General Test, minimum GPA of 2.5, minor in English with 3.0 GPA.

Eastern Michigan University, Graduate School, College of Arts and Sciences, Department of English Language and Literature, Program in Children's Literature, Ypsilanti, MI 48197. Offers MA. *Program availability:* Part-time, evening/weekend, online learning. *Students:* 5 full-time (4 women), 5 part-time (3 women); includes 4 minority (3 Hispanic/Latino; 1 Two or more races, non-Hispanic/Latino). Average age 30. 4 applicants, 100% accepted, 1 enrolled. In 2019, 2 master's awarded. *Entrance requirements:* Additional exam requirements/recommendations for international students: required—TOEFL. *Application deadline:* Applications are processed on a rolling basis. Application fee: $45. *Financial support:* Fellowships, research assistantships with full tuition reimbursements, teaching assistantships with full tuition

reimbursements, and tuition waivers (partial) available. Financial award applicants required to submit FAFSA. *Application contact:* Dr. Amanda Allen, Program Coordinator, 734-487-0958, Fax: 734-483-9744, E-mail: aallen36@emich.edu.

Eastern Michigan University, Graduate School, College of Arts and Sciences, Department of English Language and Literature, Program in Literature, Ypsilanti, MI 48197. Offers MA. *Program availability:* Part-time, evening/weekend, online learning. *Students:* 3 full-time (2 women), 10 part-time (7 women); includes 3 minority (1 Hispanic/Latino; 2 Two or more races, non-Hispanic/Latino). Average age 31. 11 applicants, 73% accepted, 5 enrolled. In 2019, 6 master's awarded. *Entrance requirements:* Additional exam requirements/recommendations for international students: required—TOEFL. *Application deadline:* Applications are processed on a rolling basis. Application fee: $45. *Financial support:* Fellowships, research assistantships with full tuition reimbursements, teaching assistantships with full tuition reimbursements, career-related internships or fieldwork, Federal Work-Study, institutionally sponsored loans, scholarships/grants, tuition waivers (partial), and unspecified assistantships available. Support available to part-time students. Financial award applicants required to submit FAFSA. *Application contact:* Dr. Laura J. George, Program Coordinator, 734-487-2425, Fax: 734-483-9744, E-mail: lgeorge@emich.edu.

Eastern New Mexico University, Graduate School, College of Liberal Arts and Sciences, Department of Languages and Literature, Portales, NM 88130. Offers English (MA), including English. *Program availability:* Part-time. *Degree requirements:* For master's, one foreign language, thesis, oral and written comprehensive exams. *Entrance requirements:* For master's, minimum GPA of 3.0, foreign language proficiency, interview. Additional exam requirements/recommendations for international students: required—TOEFL (minimum score 550 paper-based; 79 iBT), IELTS (minimum score 6). Electronic applications accepted. *Expenses: Tuition, area resident:* Full-time $5283; part-time $389.25 per credit hour. Tuition, state resident: full-time $5283; part-time $389.25 per credit hour. Tuition, nonresident: full-time $7007; part-time $389.25 per credit hour. *International tuition:* $7007 full-time. *Required fees:* $36; $35 per semester. One-time fee: $25.

Eastern Washington University, Graduate Studies, College of Arts, Letters and Education, Department of English, Cheney, WA 99004-2431. Offers literature (MA); rhetoric, composition, and technical communication (MA); teaching English as a second language (MA). *Faculty:* 13 full-time (8 women). *Students:* 59 full-time (40 women), 4 part-time (3 women); includes 1 minority (Asian; non-Hispanic/Latino). Average age 33. 100 applicants, 58% accepted, 33 enrolled. In 2019, 32 master's awarded. *Degree requirements:* For master's, comprehensive exam, thesis or alternative. *Entrance requirements:* For master's, GRE General Test, minimum GPA of 3.0. Additional exam requirements/recommendations for international students: required—TOEFL (minimum score 92 paper-based; 92 iBT), IELTS (minimum score 7), PTE (minimum score 63). *Application deadline:* For fall admission, 4/1 priority date for domestic students; for spring admission, 1/15 for domestic students. Applications are processed on a rolling basis. Application fee: $75. *Financial support:* Teaching assistantships with partial tuition reimbursements, career-related internships or fieldwork, Federal Work-Study, institutionally sponsored loans, scholarships/grants, health care benefits, tuition waivers (partial), and unspecified assistantships available. Support available to part-time students. Financial award application deadline: 2/1; financial award applicants required to submit FAFSA. *Application contact:* Kathy White, Advisor/Recruiter for Graduate Studies, 509-359-2491, E-mail: gradprograms@ewu.edu. Website: http://www.ewu.edu/CALE/Programs/English.xml

East Tennessee State University, College of Graduate and Continuing Studies, College of Arts and Sciences, Department of Literature and Language, Johnson City, TN 37614. Offers healthcare translation and interpreting (Postbaccalaureate Certificate); literature (MA); teaching English to speakers of other languages (Postbaccalaureate Certificate). *Program availability:* Part-time, evening/weekend. *Degree requirements:* For master's, comprehensive exam, thesis optional; for Postbaccalaureate Certificate, one foreign language. *Entrance requirements:* For master's, GRE General Test, minimum undergraduate GPA of 3.0 in English, writing sample, three letters of recommendation; for Postbaccalaureate Certificate, GRE General Test, speaking and listening assessment, resume, three letters of recommendation, two years of coursework or basic proficiency in a foreign language. Additional exam requirements/recommendations for international students: required—TOEFL (minimum score 550 paper-based; 79 iBT). Electronic applications accepted.

Emory University, Laney Graduate School, Department of English, Atlanta, GA 30322-1100. Offers PhD, Graduate Certificate. *Degree requirements:* For doctorate, one foreign language, comprehensive exam, thesis/dissertation. *Entrance requirements:* For doctorate, GRE General Test, minimum GPA of 3.0. Additional exam requirements/recommendations for international students: required—TOEFL. Electronic applications accepted.

Emporia State University, Program in English, Emporia, KS 66801-5415. Offers MA. *Program availability:* Part-time. *Degree requirements:* For master's, comprehensive exam, thesis optional. *Entrance requirements:* For master's, minimum undergraduate GPA of 2.75 in last 60 hours. Additional exam requirements/recommendations for international students: required—TOEFL (minimum score 550 paper-based; 68 iBT). *Expenses: Tuition, area resident:* Full-time $6394; part-time $266.41 per credit hour. Tuition, state resident: full-time $6394; part-time $266.41 per credit hour. Tuition, nonresident: full-time $20,128; part-time $828.66 per credit hour. *International tuition:* $20,128 full-time. *Required fees:* $2183; $90.95 per credit hour. Tuition and fees vary according to campus/location and program.

Fairleigh Dickinson University, Metropolitan Campus, University College: Arts, Sciences, and Professional Studies, Department of English, Philosophy, and Humanities, Program in English and Literature, Teaneck, NJ 07666-1914. Offers MA.

Fitchburg State University, Division of Graduate and Continuing Education, Program in Middle School Education, Fitchburg, MA 01420-2697. Offers English (M Ed); general science (M Ed); history (M Ed); math (M Ed). *Accreditation:* NCATE. *Program availability:* Part-time, evening/weekend. *Entrance requirements:* Additional exam requirements/recommendations for international students: required—TOEFL (minimum score 550 paper-based; 79 iBT). Electronic applications accepted. *Expenses:* Contact institution.

Fitchburg State University, Division of Graduate and Continuing Education, Programs in English and Teaching English (Secondary Level), Fitchburg, MA 01420-2697. Offers MA, MAT, Certificate. *Accreditation:* NCATE. *Program availability:* Part-time, evening/weekend. *Entrance requirements:* Additional exam requirements/recommendations for international students: required—TOEFL (minimum score 550 paper-based; 79 iBT). Electronic applications accepted. *Expenses:* Contact institution.

Florida Atlantic University, Dorothy F. Schmidt College of Arts and Letters, Department of English, Boca Raton, FL 33431-0991. Offers American literature (MA). *Program availability:* Part-time. *Faculty:* 22 full-time (12 women). *Students:* 35 full-time (21 women), 20 part-time (13 women); includes 17 minority (1 Black or African American, non-Hispanic/Latino; 12 Hispanic/Latino; 4 Two or more races, non-Hispanic/Latino), 4 international. Average age 31. 108 applicants, 27% accepted, 13 enrolled. In 2019, 16 master's awarded. *Degree requirements:* For master's, one foreign language,

thesis. *Entrance requirements:* For master's, GRE General Test, minimum GPA of 3.0, writing samples, 2 letters of recommendation. Additional exam requirements/recommendations for international students: required—TOEFL (minimum score 500 paper-based; 61 iBT), IELTS (minimum score 6). *Application deadline:* For fall admission, 3/1 for domestic students, 2/15 for international students; for spring admission, 11/1 for domestic students, 7/15 for international students. Applications are processed on a rolling basis. Application fee: $30. Electronic applications accepted. *Expenses: Tuition:* Full-time $20,536; part-time $371.82 per credit hour. Tuition and fees vary according to program. *Financial support:* Fellowships, teaching assistantships with partial tuition reimbursements, Federal Work-Study, and tuition waivers available. Support available to part-time students. Financial award application deadline: 3/1. *Unit head:* Oliver Buckton, Chair, 561-297-3836, E-mail: obuckton@fau.edu. *Application contact:* Oliver Buckton, Chair, 561-297-3836, E-mail: obuckton@fau.edu.
Website: http://www.fau.edu/english/

Florida Gulf Coast University, College of Arts and Sciences, Program in English, Fort Myers, FL 33965-6565. Offers MA. *Program availability:* Part-time. *Entrance requirements:* For master's, GRE General Test, minimum GPA of 3.0. Additional exam requirements/recommendations for international students: required—TOEFL (minimum score 550 paper-based). Electronic applications accepted. *Expenses: Tuition, area resident:* Full-time $6974; part-time $4350 per credit hour. Tuition, state resident: full-time $6974; part-time $4350 per credit hour. Tuition, nonresident: full-time $28,169; part-time $17,595 per credit hour. *International tuition:* $28,169 full-time. *Required fees:* $2027; $1267 per credit hour. $507 per semester. Tuition and fees vary according to course load.

Florida International University, College of Arts, Sciences, and Education, Department of English, Miami, FL 33199. Offers creative writing (MFA); English (MA), including literature; linguistics (MA). *Program availability:* Part-time, evening/weekend. *Faculty:* 64 full-time (30 women), 31 part-time/adjunct (20 women). *Students:* 48 full-time (32 women), 34 part-time (17 women); includes 52 minority (6 Black or African American, non-Hispanic/Latino; 2 Asian, non-Hispanic/Latino; 43 Hispanic/Latino; 1 Two or more races, non-Hispanic/Latino), 2 international. Average age 30. 48 applicants, 56% accepted, 25 enrolled. In 2019, 21 master's awarded. *Entrance requirements:* For master's, GRE General Test, minimum undergraduate GPA of 3.0 (upper-level coursework), letter of intent, two letters of recommendation. Additional exam requirements/recommendations for international students: required—TOEFL (minimum score 550 paper-based; 80 iBT). *Application deadline:* For fall admission, 2/1 for domestic and international students; for spring admission, 10/1 for domestic students, 9/1 for international students. Applications are processed on a rolling basis. Application fee: $30. Electronic applications accepted. *Expenses: Tuition, area resident:* Full-time $8912; part-time $446 per credit hour. Tuition, state resident: full-time $8912; part-time $446 per credit hour. Tuition, nonresident: full-time $21,393; part-time $992 per credit hour. *Required fees:* $2194. *Financial support:* Institutionally sponsored loans and scholarships/grants available. Financial award application deadline: 3/1; financial award applicants required to submit FAFSA. *Unit head:* Dr. Anna Luszczynska, Chair, 305-348-2203, Fax: 305-348-3878, E-mail: Ana.Luszczynska@fiu.edu. *Application contact:* Nanett Rojas, Manager, Admissions Operations, 305-348-7464, Fax: 305-348-7441, E-mail: gradadm@fiu.edu.

Florida State University, The Graduate School, Department of Anthropology, Department of English, Tallahassee, FL 32312. Offers English (MA, MFA, PhD), including creative writing (MFA, PhD), literature (MA, PhD), rhetoric and composition (MA, PhD). *Program availability:* Part-time. *Degree requirements:* For master's, one foreign language, thesis, 33 hours of coursework including capstone essay, thesis or portfolio (MA); 45 hours of coursework including 9-12 thesis hours (MFA); for doctorate, one foreign language, comprehensive exam, thesis/dissertation, 27 hours of coursework, 24 hours of dissertation work. *Entrance requirements:* For master's, GRE General Test, sample of written work, 3 letters of recommendation, resume, statement of purpose; for doctorate, GRE General Test, sample of written work, 3 letters of recommendation, resume. statement of purpose. Additional exam requirements/recommendations for international students: required—TOEFL. Electronic applications accepted.

Fordham University, Graduate School of Arts and Sciences, Department of English Language and Literature, New York, NY 10458. Offers MA, PhD. *Program availability:* Part-time, evening/weekend. *Students:* Average age 31. 185 applicants, 30% accepted, 14 enrolled. In 2019, 9 master's, 10 doctorates awarded. Terminal master's awarded for partial completion of doctoral program. *Degree requirements:* For master's, one foreign language, comprehensive exam, thesis optional; for doctorate, 2 foreign languages, comprehensive exam, thesis/dissertation. *Entrance requirements:* For master's, GRE General Test; for doctorate, GRE General Test, GRE Subject Test. Additional exam requirements/recommendations for international students: required—TOEFL (minimum score 650 paper-based). *Application deadline:* For fall admission, 1/4 priority date for domestic students; for spring admission, 11/1 for domestic students. Application fee: $70. Electronic applications accepted. *Financial support:* In 2019–20, 63 students received support, including 1 fellowship with tuition reimbursement available (averaging $25,390 per year), 49 teaching assistantships with tuition reimbursements available (averaging $19,311 per year); institutionally sponsored loans, tuition waivers (full and partial), and unspecified assistantships also available. Financial award application deadline: 1/4; financial award applicants required to submit FAFSA. *Unit head:* Dr. Julie Chun Kim, Director, Graduate Studies, 718-817-4017, Fax: 718-817-4013, E-mail: jukim@fordham.edu. *Application contact:* Garrett Marino, Director of Graduate Admissions, 718-817-4419, Fax: 718-817-3566, E-mail: gmarino10@fordham.edu.

Fort Hays State University, Graduate School, College of Arts, Humanities, and Social Sciences, Department of English, Hays, KS 67601-4099. Offers MA. *Degree requirements:* For master's, comprehensive exam, thesis or alternative. *Entrance requirements:* Additional exam requirements/recommendations for international students: required—TOEFL (minimum score 550 paper-based). Electronic applications accepted.

Framingham State University, Graduate Studies, Program in English, Framingham, MA 01701-9101. Offers MA.

Gannon University, School of Graduate Studies, College of Humanities, Education, and Social Sciences, School of Humanities, Program in English, Erie, PA 16541-0001. Offers MA. *Program availability:* Part-time, evening/weekend. *Degree requirements:* For master's, thesis. *Entrance requirements:* For master's, undergraduate degree in English. Additional exam requirements/recommendations for international students: required—TOEFL (minimum score 79 iBT). Electronic applications accepted. Application fee is waived when completed online.

Gardner-Webb University, Graduate School, Department of English, Boiling Springs, NC 28017. Offers English (MA); English education (MA). *Program availability:* Part-time, evening/weekend. *Degree requirements:* For master's, comprehensive exam. *Entrance requirements:* For master's, GRE General Test, MAT, or NTE; PRAXIS, minimum GPA of 2.5. Electronic applications accepted. *Expenses:* Contact institution.

George Mason University, College of Humanities and Social Sciences, Department of English, Fairfax, VA 22030. Offers college teaching (Certificate), including higher education pedagogy; creative writing (MFA), including fiction, nonfiction writing, poetry; English (MA), including cultural studies, linguistics, literature, professional writing and rhetoric, teaching of writing and literature; English pedagogy (Certificate); folklore studies (Certificate); linguistics (PhD); writing and rhetoric (PhD). *Program availability:* Part-time. *Degree requirements:* For master's, thesis (for some programs), proficiency in a foreign language by course work or translation test; for doctorate, comprehensive exam, thesis/dissertation, 2 papers. *Entrance requirements:* For master's, official transcripts; expanded goals statement; writing sample; portfolio; 2 letters of recommendation; resume; for doctorate, GRE (for linguistics), expanded goals statement; 2 letters of recommendation (writing and rhetoric); 3 letters of recommendation (linguistics); writing sample; introductory course in linguistics; official transcripts; master's degree in relevant field; for Certificate, official transcripts; expanded goals statement; 2 letters of recommendation; writing sample; resume. Additional exam requirements/recommendations for international students: required—TOEFL (minimum score 575 paper-based; 88 iBT), IELTS (minimum score 6.5), PTE (minimum score 59). Electronic applications accepted.

Georgetown University, Graduate School of Arts and Sciences, Department of English, Washington, DC 20057. Offers British and American literature (MA). *Degree requirements:* For master's, thesis or alternative, independent study, oral exam. *Entrance requirements:* For master's, GRE General Test. Additional exam requirements/recommendations for international students: required—TOEFL.

The George Washington University, Columbian College of Arts and Sciences, Department of English, Washington, DC 20052. Offers MA, PhD. *Program availability:* Part-time, evening/weekend. Terminal master's awarded for partial completion of doctoral program. *Degree requirements:* For master's, one foreign language, comprehensive exam, thesis or alternative; for doctorate, 2 foreign languages, thesis/dissertation, general exam. *Entrance requirements:* For master's and doctorate, GRE General Test, GRE Subject Test, minimum GPA of 3.0, writing sample. Additional exam requirements/recommendations for international students: required—TOEFL (minimum score 550 paper-based; 80 iBT). Electronic applications accepted.

Georgia College & State University, The Graduate School, College of Arts and Sciences, Department of English, Program in English, Milledgeville, GA 31061. Offers MA. *Program availability:* Part-time. *Students:* 10 full-time (7 women), 5 part-time (3 women); includes 1 minority (Black or African American, non-Hispanic/Latino), 2 international. Average age 28. 10 applicants, 100% accepted, 8 enrolled. In 2019, 4 master's awarded. *Degree requirements:* For master's, variable foreign language requirement, comprehensive exam, thesis or alternative, All credit applied to the Master of Arts degree in English must be earned within the prescribed period of five years before graduation. *Entrance requirements:* For master's, bachelor's degree with undergraduate major in English, cumulative gpa of 3.0 or higher, writing sample, letters of recommendation. *Application deadline:* For fall admission, 7/1 priority date for domestic students, 4/1 priority date for international students; for spring admission, 11/1 priority date for domestic students, 9/1 priority date for international students; for summer admission, 4/1 priority date for domestic students. Applications are processed on a rolling basis. Application fee: $40. Electronic applications accepted. *Expenses:* For full time instate students: $2646 matriculation and $1011 fees per semester. *Financial support:* In 2019–20, 9 students received support. Unspecified assistantships available. Support available to part-time students. Financial award applicants required to submit FAFSA. *Unit head:* Dr. Matthew Pangborn, English Department Chair and Professor, 478-445-5574, E-mail: michael.pangborn@gcsu.edu. *Application contact:* Kate Marshall, Graduate Admissions Coordinator, 478-445-1184, Fax: 478-445-1336, E-mail: grad-admit@gcsu.edu.
Website: http://gcsu.edu/artsandsciences/english/english-ma

Georgia Southern University, Jack N. Averitt College of Graduate Studies, College of Arts and Humanities, Program in English, Statesboro, GA 30460. Offers MA. *Program availability:* Part-time. *Students:* 10 full-time (all women), 8 part-time (4 women); includes 1 minority (Black or African American, non-Hispanic/Latino), 1 international. Average age 28. 11 applicants, 91% accepted, 7 enrolled. In 2019, 6 master's awarded. *Degree requirements:* For master's, one foreign language, thesis optional, terminal exams. *Entrance requirements:* For master's, GRE General Test, minimum GPA of 3.0, letters of reference. Additional exam requirements/recommendations for international students: required—TOEFL (minimum score 550 paper-based; 80 iBT), IELTS (minimum score 6). *Application deadline:* For fall admission, 3/1 priority date for domestic and international students; for spring admission, 10/1 priority date for domestic students, 10/1 for international students. Applications are processed on a rolling basis. Application fee: $50. Electronic applications accepted. *Expenses: Tuition, area resident:* Full-time $4986; part-time $277 per credit hour. Tuition, nonresident: full-time $19,890; part-time $1105 per credit hour. *International tuition:* $19,890 full-time. *Required fees:* $2114; $1057 per semester. $1057 per semester. Tuition and fees vary according to course load, campus/location and program. *Financial support:* In 2019–20, 10 students received support, including 4 fellowships with full tuition reimbursements available (averaging $7,750 per year); career-related internships or fieldwork, Federal Work-Study, scholarships/grants, tuition waivers (full), and unspecified assistantships also available. Support available to part-time students. Financial award application deadline: 4/15; financial award applicants required to submit FAFSA. *Unit head:* Dr. Dustin Anderson, Graduate Program Director, 912-478-1354, E-mail: danderson@georgiasouthern.edu.
Website: http://class.georgiasouthern.edu/litphi/

Georgia State University, College of Arts and Sciences, Department of English, Atlanta, GA 30302-3083. Offers creative writing (MA, MFA, PhD), including creative writing (PhD), fiction (MA, MFA), poetry (MA, MFA); English (MA, PhD); literary studies (MA, PhD); rhetoric and composition (MA, PhD). *Program availability:* Part-time. *Faculty:* 17 full-time (7 women). *Students:* 102 full-time (65 women), 58 part-time (39 women); includes 33 minority (24 Black or African American, non-Hispanic/Latino; 4 Asian, non-Hispanic/Latino; 3 Hispanic/Latino; 2 Two or more races, non-Hispanic/Latino), 6 international. Average age 37. 137 applicants, 50% accepted, 29 enrolled. In 2019, 10 master's, 21 doctorates awarded. *Entrance requirements:* For master's and doctorate, GRE. Additional exam requirements/recommendations for international students: required—TOEFL (minimum score 550 paper-based; 80 iBT). *Application deadline:* For fall admission, 1/15 for domestic and international students. Application fee: $50. Electronic applications accepted. *Expenses: Tuition, area resident:* Full-time $7164; part-time $398 per credit hour. Tuition, state resident: full-time $7164; part-time $398 per credit hour. Tuition, nonresident: full-time $22,662; part-time $1259 per credit hour. *International tuition:* $22,662 full-time. *Required fees:* $2128; $312 per credit hour. Tuition and fees vary according to course load and program. *Financial support:* In 2019–20, research assistantships with full tuition reimbursements (averaging $6,000 per year), teaching assistantships with full tuition reimbursements (averaging $15,000 per year) were awarded; career-related internships or fieldwork, traineeships, and health care benefits also available. Financial award application deadline: 2/15. *Unit head:* Dr. Lynnee Lewis Gaillet, Chair, 404-413-5842, Fax: 404-413-5830, E-mail: lgaillet@gsu.edu. *Application contact:* Dr. Lynnee Lewis Gaillet, Chair, 404-413-5842, Fax: 404-413-5830, E-mail: lgaillet@gsu.edu.
Website: http://www.english.gsu.edu

Governors State University, College of Arts and Sciences, Program in English, University Park, IL 60484. Offers MA. *Program availability:* Part-time. *Faculty:* 57 full-time (33 women), 72 part-time/adjunct (40 women). *Students:* 3 full-time (2 women), 7 part-time (5 women); includes 3 minority (1 Black or African American, non-Hispanic/Latino; 2 Hispanic/Latino). Average age 35. 4 applicants, 25% accepted, 1 enrolled. In 2019, 8 master's awarded. *Application deadline:* For fall admission, 4/1 for domestic students. Applications are processed on a rolling basis. Application fee: $50. Electronic applications accepted. *Expenses: Tuition, area resident:* Full-time $8472; part-time $353 per credit hour. Tuition, state resident: full-time $8472; part-time $353 per credit hour. Tuition, nonresident: full-time $16,944; part-time $706 per credit hour. *International tuition:* $16,944 full-time. *Required fees:* $2520; $105 per credit hour. $38 per term. Tuition and fees vary according to course load, degree level and program. *Financial support:* Application deadline: 5/1; applicants required to submit FAFSA. *Unit head:* Jason Zingsheim, Chair, Division of Arts and Letters, 708-534-5000 Ext. 7493, E-mail: jzingsheim@govst.edu. *Application contact:* Jason Zingsheim, Chair, Division of Arts and Letters, 708-534-5000 Ext. 7493, E-mail: jzingsheim@govst.edu.

The Graduate Center, City University of New York, Graduate Studies, Program in English, New York, NY 10016-4039. Offers PhD. *Degree requirements:* For doctorate, 2 foreign languages, thesis/dissertation. *Entrance requirements:* For doctorate, GRE General Test, GRE Subject Test, writing sample, curriculum vitae. Additional exam requirements/recommendations for international students: required—TOEFL. Electronic applications accepted.

Grambling State University, School of Graduate Studies and Research, College of Education, Department of Educational Leadership, Grambling, LA 71245. Offers developmental education (MS, Ed D, PMC), including curriculum and instructional design (Ed D); English (MS); guidance and counseling (MS); higher education administration and management (Ed D); mathematics (MS); reading (MS); science (MS); student development and personnel services (Ed D); educational leadership (M Ed). *Program availability:* Part-time, evening/weekend. *Degree requirements:* For master's, comprehensive exam, thesis (for some programs); for doctorate, comprehensive exam, thesis/dissertation. *Entrance requirements:* For master's, GRE, minimum GPA of 2.5 on last degree; for doctorate, GRE (minimum score 1000, 500 on Verbal), master's degree, minimum GPA of 3.0 on last degree. Additional exam requirements/recommendations for international students: required—TOEFL (minimum score 500 paper-based; 62 iBT). Electronic applications accepted.

Grand Valley State University, College of Liberal Arts and Sciences, English Department, Allendale, MI 49401-9403. Offers MA. *Program availability:* Part-time, evening/weekend. *Faculty:* 19 full-time (10 women), 2 part-time/adjunct (1 woman). *Students:* 1 (woman) full-time, 19 part-time (15 women); includes 2 minority (1 Black or African American, non-Hispanic/Latino; 1 Hispanic/Latino). Average age 33. 14 applicants, 79% accepted, 4 enrolled. In 2019, 10 master's awarded. *Degree requirements:* For master's, comprehensive exam (for some programs), thesis (for some programs), thesis or project. *Entrance requirements:* For master's, GRE General Test, brief statement of purpose, original essay (writing sample). Additional exam requirements/recommendations for international students: required—TOEFL (minimum iBT score of 80), IELTS (6.5), or Michigan English Language Assessment Battery (77). *Application deadline:* Applications are processed on a rolling basis. Application fee: $30. Electronic applications accepted. *Expenses:* $671 per credit hour, 33 credit hours. *Financial support:* In 2019–20, 6 students received support, including 2 fellowships, 4 research assistantships with partial tuition reimbursements available (averaging $4,000 per year); unspecified assistantships also available. *Unit head:* Dr. Ashley Shannon, Chair, 616-331-3400, Fax: 616-331-3430, E-mail: shannoas@gvsu.edu. *Application contact:* Dr. Sherry Johnson, Graduate Program Director, 616-331-3400, Fax: 616-331-3430, E-mail: johnsshe@gvsu.edu.

Harvard University, Extension School, Cambridge, MA 02138-3722. Offers applied sciences (CAS); biotechnology (ALM); educational technologies (ALM); educational technology (CET); English for graduate and professional studies (DGP); environmental management (ALM, CEM); information technology (ALM); journalism (ALM); liberal arts (ALM); management (ALM, CM); mathematics for teaching (ALM); museum studies (ALM); premedical studies (Diploma); publication and communication (CPC). *Program availability:* Part-time, evening/weekend. *Degree requirements:* For master's, thesis. *Entrance requirements:* For master's, 3 completed graduate courses with grade of B or higher. Additional exam requirements/recommendations for international students: required—TOEFL (minimum score 600 paper-based), TWE (minimum score 5). *Expenses:* Contact institution.

Harvard University, Graduate School of Arts and Sciences, Department of English and American Literature and Language, Cambridge, MA 02138. Offers critical theory (PhD); eighteenth-century literature (PhD); literature: nineteenth-century to the present (PhD); medieval literature and language (PhD); modern British and American literature (PhD); Renaissance literature (PhD). Terminal master's awarded for partial completion of doctoral program. *Degree requirements:* For doctorate, 2 foreign languages, thesis/dissertation, oral exam. *Entrance requirements:* For doctorate, writing sample. Additional exam requirements/recommendations for international students: required—TOEFL.

Heritage University, Graduate Programs in Education, Program in Professional Studies, Toppenish, WA 98948-9599. Offers bilingual education/ESL (M Ed); biology (M Ed); English and literature (M Ed); reading/literacy (M Ed); special education (M Ed). *Program availability:* Part-time, evening/weekend. *Degree requirements:* For master's, comprehensive exam (for some programs), thesis (for some programs).

Hofstra University, College of Liberal Arts and Sciences, Programs in Creative Writing, Hempstead, NY 11549. Offers creative writing (MFA). *Program availability:* Part-time, evening/weekend. *Students:* 15 full-time (10 women), 5 part-time (2 women); includes 6 minority (4 Black or African American, non-Hispanic/Latino; 1 Hispanic/Latino; 1 Two or more races, non-Hispanic/Latino), 3 international. Average age 29. 25 applicants, 96% accepted, 9 enrolled. In 2019, 7 master's awarded. *Degree requirements:* For master's, thesis optional, minimum GPA of 3.0. *Entrance requirements:* For master's, writing sample, essay, minimum GPA of 3.0 in literature courses. Additional exam requirements/recommendations for international students: required—TOEFL (minimum score 550 paper-based; 80 iBT); recommended—IELTS (minimum score 6.5). *Application deadline:* Applications are processed on a rolling basis. Application fee: $75. Electronic applications accepted. *Expenses: Tuition:* Full-time $25,164; part-time $1398 per credit. *Required fees:* $580; $165 per semester. Tuition and fees vary according to course load, degree level and program. *Financial support:* In 2019–20, 11 students received support, including 10 fellowships with full and partial tuition reimbursements available (averaging $2,824 per year); research assistantships with full and partial tuition reimbursements available, career-related internships or fieldwork, Federal Work-Study, institutionally sponsored loans, scholarships/grants, tuition waivers (full and partial), unspecified assistantships, and scholarships and endowed scholarships also available. Support available to part-time students. Financial award applicants required to submit FAFSA. *Unit head:* Dr. Kayrn Valerius, Chairperson, 516-463-5455, E-mail: Karyn.Valerius@hofstra.edu. *Application contact:* Sunil Samuel, Assistant Vice President of Admissions, 516-463-4723, Fax: 516-463-4664, E-mail: graduateadmission@hofstra.edu. Website: http://www.hofstra.edu/hclas

Hollins University, Graduate Programs, Graduate Programs in Children's Literature, Roanoke, VA 24020. Offers children's book illustration (Certificate); children's book writing and illustrating (MFA); children's literature (MA, MFA). *Program availability:* Part-time. *Degree requirements:* For master's, one foreign language, thesis. *Entrance requirements:* For master's, transcripts, letters of recommendation, portfolio, personal statement of educational objectives. Additional exam requirements/recommendations for international students: required—TOEFL (minimum score 550 paper-based; 79 iBT), IELTS (minimum score 6.5). Electronic applications accepted. *Expenses:* Contact institution.

Houston Baptist University, College of Education and Behavioral Sciences, Programs in Education, Houston, TX 77074-3298. Offers bilingual education (M Ed); counselor education (M Ed); curriculum and instruction (M Ed); curriculum and instruction (EC-6 bilingual) (M Ed); curriculum and instruction in all-level art, Spanish, music, or physical education (M Ed); curriculum and instruction in EC-6 and special education (EC-12) (M Ed); curriculum and instruction in instructional technology (M Ed); curriculum and instruction in mathematics, science, or social studies (4-8) (M Ed); curriculum and instruction with EC-6 generalist (M Ed); curriculum and instruction with English language arts and reading (4-8) (M Ed); educational administration (M Ed); educational diagnostician (M Ed); executive educational leadership (Ed D); higher education in business management (M Ed); higher education in Christian studies (M Ed); higher education in counseling (M Ed); higher education in educational technology (M Ed); reading (M Ed); special educational leadership (Ed D). *Program availability:* Part-time, evening/weekend, 100% online, blended/hybrid learning. *Degree requirements:* For master's, comprehensive exam; for doctorate, thesis/dissertation. *Entrance requirements:* For master's, minimum GPA of 2.75, two recommendations, resume, bachelor's degree conferred transcript; interview (for non-certified teachers); for doctorate, GRE, 5 letters of recommendation. Additional exam requirements/recommendations for international students: required—TOEFL (minimum score 80 iBT), IELTS (minimum score 6.5). Electronic applications accepted. Application fee is waived when completed online. *Expenses:* Contact institution.

Howard University, Graduate School, Department of English, Washington, DC 20059-0002. Offers MA, PhD. *Program availability:* Part-time. *Degree requirements:* For master's, one foreign language, comprehensive exam, thesis; for doctorate, 2 foreign languages, comprehensive exam, thesis/dissertation, qualifying exam. *Entrance requirements:* For master's, GRE General Test, minimum GPA of 3.0; for doctorate, GRE General Test.

Humboldt State University, Academic Programs, College of Arts, Humanities, and Social Sciences, Department of English, Arcata, CA 95521-8299. Offers English (MA), including composition studies and pedagogy, literary and cultural studies, teaching English as a second language. *Program availability:* Part-time. *Faculty:* 9 full-time (8 women), 14 part-time/adjunct (all women). *Students:* 4 full-time (2 women), 8 part-time (2 women); includes 1 minority (Hispanic/Latino). Average age 28. 13 applicants, 85% accepted, 3 enrolled. In 2019, 7 master's awarded. *Degree requirements:* For master's, variable foreign language requirement, thesis or alternative, qualifying exam. *Entrance requirements:* For master's, GRE, minimum GPA of 3.0, 3 letters of recommendation, sample of writing. Additional exam requirements/recommendations for international students: required—TOEFL (minimum score 500 paper-based). *Application deadline:* For fall admission, 3/1 for domestic students; for spring admission, 11/1 for domestic students. Applications are processed on a rolling basis. Application fee: $55. *Expenses:* Tuition, state resident: full-time $7176; part-time $4164 per term. *Required fees:* $2120; $1672 per term. *Financial support:* Teaching assistantships, career-related internships or fieldwork, Federal Work-Study, and institutionally sponsored loans available. Financial award application deadline: 3/1; financial award applicants required to submit FAFSA. *Unit head:* Dr. Janet Winston, English Graduate Program Coordinator, 707-826-3913, E-mail: winston@humboldt.edu. *Application contact:* Dr. Janet Winston, English Graduate Program Coordinator, 707-826-3913, E-mail: winston@humboldt.edu. Website: http://www.humboldt.edu/english/

Idaho State University, Graduate School, College of Arts and Letters, Department of English and Philosophy, Pocatello, ID 83209-8056. Offers English (MA); English and the teaching of English (PhD); TESOL (Post-Master's Certificate). *Program availability:* Part-time. *Degree requirements:* For master's, one foreign language, comprehensive exam, thesis optional; for doctorate, one foreign language, comprehensive exam, thesis/dissertation, 2 papers, 2 teaching internships; for Post-Master's Certificate, 6 credits of elective linguistics, practicum. *Entrance requirements:* For master's, GRE General Test (minimum 50th percentile verbal), general literature exam, minimum GPA of 3.0, 3 letters of recommendation, 5-page writing sample; for doctorate, GRE General Test, GRE Subject Test, minimum GPA of 3.5, writing examples, 3 letters of recommendation, master's degree in English; for Post-Master's Certificate, GRE (minimum 35th percentile on verbal section), bachelor's degree, minimum undergraduate GPA of 3.0 in last 2 years, 3 letters of recommendation, knowledge of second language. Additional exam requirements/recommendations for international students: required—TOEFL (minimum score 550 paper-based; 80 iBT). Electronic applications accepted.

Illinois State University, Graduate School, College of Arts and Sciences, Department of English, Normal, IL 61790. Offers English (MA, MS, PhD), including English (MA, MS), English studies (PhD); writing (MA, MS). *Faculty:* 43 full-time (29 women), 12 part-time/adjunct (11 women). *Students:* 71 full-time (50 women), 31 part-time (21 women). Average age 31. 61 applicants, 59% accepted, 23 enrolled. In 2019, 11 master's, 9 doctorates awarded. *Degree requirements:* For master's, thesis or alternative; for doctorate, thesis/dissertation, 2 terms of residency. *Entrance requirements:* For master's, GRE General Test, minimum GPA of 3.0 in last 60 hours of course work, writing sample; for doctorate, GRE General Test, writing sample. *Application deadline:* Applications are processed on a rolling basis. Application fee: $50. *Expenses: Tuition, area resident:* Full-time $7956; part-time $9767 per year. Tuition, nonresident: full-time $9233; part-time $17,592 per year. *Required fees:* $1797. *Financial support:* In 2019–20, 70 teaching assistantships were awarded; tuition waivers (full) and unspecified assistantships also available. Financial award application deadline: 4/1. *Unit head:* Dr. Christopher De Santis, Department Chair, 309-438-3650, E-mail: ccdesan@IllinoisState.edu. *Application contact:* Dr. Angela Haas, Graduate Coordinator, 309-438-3651, E-mail: ahaas@IllinoisState.edu. Website: http://www.english.ilstu.edu/

Indiana State University, College of Graduate and Professional Studies, College of Arts and Sciences, Department of English, Terre Haute, IN 47809. Offers British and American literature (MA); English (MA); writing (MA). *Program availability:* Part-time, evening/weekend. *Degree requirements:* For master's, one foreign language, thesis optional. *Entrance requirements:* For master's, minimum GPA of 2.75 in all English courses above freshman level. Additional exam requirements/recommendations for international students: required—TOEFL (minimum score 550 paper-based). Electronic applications accepted.

Indiana University Bloomington, University Graduate School, College of Arts and Sciences, Department of English, Bloomington, IN 47405. Offers creative writing (MA,

MFA), including fiction (MFA), poetry (MFA); literature (PhD); rhetoric (PhD). *Degree requirements:* For master's, 30-36 credit hours plus one language proficiency (for MA); 60 credit hours plus thesis (for MFA); for doctorate, thesis/dissertation, qualifying exam; 90 credit hours; 2nd language proficiency or one language only if acquired at in-depth level. *Entrance requirements:* For master's, GRE General Test, GRE Subject Test (for all but MFA and MA in creative writing), minimum GPA of 3.5; for doctorate, GRE General Test, GRE Subject Test, minimum GPA of 3.7. Additional exam requirements/recommendations for international students: required—TOEFL (minimum score 550 paper-based; 79 iBT), IELTS (minimum score 6.5). Electronic applications accepted.

Indiana University of Pennsylvania, School of Graduate Studies and Research, College of Humanities and Social Sciences, Department of English, English Composition and Applied Linguistics, Indiana, PA 15705. Offers PhD. *Program availability:* Part-time. *Faculty:* 18 full-time (9 women), 1 part-time/adjunct (0 women). *Students:* 16 full-time (11 women), 76 part-time (46 women); includes 12 minority (3 Black or African American, non-Hispanic/Latino; 5 Asian, non-Hispanic/Latino; 4 Hispanic/Latino), 38 international. Average age 37. 118 applicants, 54% accepted, 21 enrolled. In 2019, 16 doctorates awarded. *Degree requirements:* For doctorate, one foreign language, comprehensive exam, thesis/dissertation. *Entrance requirements:* For doctorate, 2 letters of recommendation, official transcripts, goal statement. Additional exam requirements/recommendations for international students: required—TOEFL (minimum score 600 paper-based; 100 iBT), IELTS (minimum score 6.5), TOEFL or IELTS. *Application deadline:* For fall admission, 2/1 priority date for domestic students; for summer admission, 11/1 priority date for domestic students. Applications are processed on a rolling basis. Application fee: $50. Electronic applications accepted. *Expenses:* Contact institution. *Financial support:* In 2019–20, 7 fellowships with full tuition reimbursements (averaging $1,093 per year), 12 research assistantships with tuition reimbursements (averaging $5,236 per year), 7 teaching assistantships with partial tuition reimbursements (averaging $12,518 per year) were awarded; career-related internships or fieldwork, Federal Work-Study, scholarships/grants, and unspecified assistantships also available. Support available to part-time students. Financial award application deadline: 4/15; financial award applicants required to submit FAFSA. *Unit head:* Dr. Gloria Park, Graduate Coordinator, 724-357-3095, E-mail: gloria.park@iup.edu. *Application contact:* Dr. Gloria Park, Graduate Coordinator, 724-357-3095, E-mail: gloria.park@iup.edu.
Website: https://www.iup.edu/english/grad/composition-applied-linguistics-phd/

Indiana University of Pennsylvania, School of Graduate Studies and Research, College of Humanities and Social Sciences, Department of English, Program in Composition and Literature, Indiana, PA 15705. Offers MA. *Program availability:* Part-time, evening/weekend. *Faculty:* 18 full-time (9 women), 1 part-time/adjunct (0 women). *Students:* 13 full-time (9 women), 6 part-time (4 women); includes 1 minority (Hispanic/Latino). Average age 28. 16 applicants, 100% accepted, 10 enrolled. In 2019, 3 master's awarded. *Degree requirements:* For master's, thesis optional. *Entrance requirements:* For master's, official transcripts, goal statement, letters of recommenation. Additional exam requirements/recommendations for international students: required—TOEFL (minimum score 540 paper-based; 76 iBT), IELTS (minimum score 6), TOEFL or IELTS. *Application deadline:* Applications are processed on a rolling basis. Application fee: $50. Electronic applications accepted. *Expenses: Tuition, area resident:* Full-time $9288; part-time $516 per credit. Tuition, nonresident: full-time $13,932; part-time $774 per credit. *Required fees:* $4454. One-time fee: $115 full-time. Tuition and fees vary according to course load and program. *Financial support:* In 2019–20, 1 fellowship (averaging $1,000 per year), 12 research assistantships with tuition reimbursements (averaging $1,250 per year) were awarded; career-related internships or fieldwork, Federal Work-Study, scholarships/grants, and unspecified assistantships also available. Financial award application deadline: 4/15; financial award applicants required to submit FAFSA. *Unit head:* Dr. Michael T. Williamson, Coordinator, 724-357-5913, E-mail: Michael.Williamson2@iup.edu. *Application contact:* Dr. Michael T. Williamson, Coordinator, 724-357-5913, E-mail: Michael.Williamson2@iup.edu.
Website: http://www.iup.edu/english/grad/composition-literature-ma/

Indiana University of Pennsylvania, School of Graduate Studies and Research, College of Humanities and Social Sciences, Department of English, Program in English: Literature, Indiana, PA 15705. Offers MA. *Program availability:* Part-time. *Faculty:* 18 full-time (9 women), 1 part-time/adjunct (0 women). *Students:* 7 full-time (2 women), 4 part-time (all women); includes 1 minority (Black or African American, non-Hispanic/Latino), 1 international. Average age 31. 8 applicants, 100% accepted, 4 enrolled. In 2019, 6 master's awarded. *Degree requirements:* For master's, thesis optional. *Entrance requirements:* For master's, two letters of recommendation, goal statement, official transcripts. Additional exam requirements/recommendations for international students: required—TOEFL (minimum score 540 paper-based; 76 iBT), IELTS (minimum score 6), TOEFL or IELTS. *Application deadline:* Applications are processed on a rolling basis. Application fee: $50. Electronic applications accepted. *Expenses: Tuition, area resident:* Full-time $9288; part-time $516 per credit. Tuition, nonresident: full-time $13,932; part-time $774 per credit. *Required fees:* $4454. One-time fee: $115 full-time. Tuition and fees vary according to course load and program. *Financial support:* In 2019–20, 7 research assistantships with tuition reimbursements (averaging $1,107 per year) were awarded; fellowships, teaching assistantships with tuition reimbursements, Federal Work-Study, scholarships/grants, and unspecified assistantships also available. Financial award application deadline: 4/15; financial award applicants required to submit FAFSA. *Unit head:* Dr. Micheal T. Williamson, Coordinator, 724-357-5913, E-mail: Michael.Williamson2@iup.edu. *Application contact:* Dr. Micheal T. Williamson, Coordinator, 724-357-5913, E-mail: Michael.Williamson2@iup.edu.
Website: http://www.iup.edu/grad/literature/default.aspx

Indiana University of Pennsylvania, School of Graduate Studies and Research, College of Humanities and Social Sciences, Department of English, Program in Literature and Criticism, Indiana, PA 15705. Offers PhD. *Program availability:* Part-time. *Faculty:* 18 full-time (9 women), 1 part-time/adjunct (0 women). *Students:* 18 full-time (9 women), 103 part-time (66 women); includes 21 minority (8 Black or African American, non-Hispanic/Latino; 1 American Indian or Alaska Native, non-Hispanic/Latino; 3 Asian, non-Hispanic/Latino; 5 Hispanic/Latino; 4 Two or more races, non-Hispanic/Latino), 28 international. Average age 39. 44 applicants, 80% accepted, 15 enrolled. In 2019, 22 doctorates awarded. *Degree requirements:* For doctorate, one foreign language, comprehensive exam, thesis/dissertation. *Entrance requirements:* For doctorate, 2 letters of recommendation, official transcripts, goal statement. Additional exam requirements/recommendations for international students: required—TOEFL (minimum score 540 paper-based; 76 iBT), IELTS (minimum score 6), TOEFL or IELTS. *Application deadline:* Applications are processed on a rolling basis. Application fee: $50. Electronic applications accepted. *Expenses:* Contact institution. *Financial support:* In 2019–20, 1 fellowship (averaging $6,700 per year), 14 research assistantships with tuition reimbursements (averaging $7,673 per year), 2 teaching assistantships with partial tuition reimbursements (averaging $12,518 per year) were awarded; career-related internships or fieldwork, Federal Work-Study, scholarships/grants, and unspecified assistantships also available. Support available to part-time students. Financial award application deadline: 4/15; financial award applicants required to submit FAFSA. *Unit head:* Dr. Veronica Watson, Graduate Coordinator, 724-357-4072, E-mail: Veronica.Watson@iup.edu. *Application contact:* Dr. Veronica Watson, Graduate Coordinator, 724-357-4072, E-mail: Veronica.Watson@iup.edu.
Website: http://www.iup.edu/english/grad/literature-criticism-phd/default.aspx

Indiana University-Purdue University Indianapolis, School of Liberal Arts, Department of English, Indianapolis, IN 46202. Offers English (MA); teaching English to speakers of other languages (TESOL) (MA, Certificate); teaching literature (Certificate); teaching writing (Certificate). *Entrance requirements:* For master's, GRE. Additional exam requirements/recommendations for international students: required—TOEFL.

Indiana University South Bend, College of Liberal Arts and Sciences, South Bend, IN 46615. Offers advanced computer programming (Graduate Certificate); applied informatics (Graduate Certificate); applied mathematics and computer science (MS); behavior modification (Graduate Certificate); computer applications (Graduate Certificate); computer programming (Graduate Certificate); correctional management and supervision (Graduate Certificate); English (MA); health systems management (Graduate Certificate); international studies (Graduate Certificate); liberal studies (MLS); nonprofit management (Graduate Certificate); paralegal studies (Graduate Certificate); professional writing (Graduate Certificate); public affairs (MPA); public management (Graduate Certificate); social and cultural diversity (Graduate Certificate); strategic sustainability leadership (Graduate Certificate); technology for administration (Graduate Certificate). *Program availability:* Part-time, evening/weekend. *Degree requirements:* For master's, variable foreign language requirement, thesis (for some programs). *Entrance requirements:* For master's, minimum GPA of 3.0. Additional exam requirements/recommendations for international students: required—TOEFL (minimum score 550 paper-based; 80 iBT). *Expenses:* Contact institution.

Inter American University of Puerto Rico, Metropolitan Campus, Graduate Programs, Program in English, San Juan, PR 00919-1293. Offers MA.

Iona College, School of Arts and Science, Department of English, New Rochelle, NY 10801-1890. Offers MA. *Program availability:* Part-time. *Faculty:* 10 full-time (4 women). *Students:* 2 part-time (both women); both minorities (1 Black or African American, non-Hispanic/Latino; 1 Hispanic/Latino). Average age 25. In 2019, 1 master's awarded. *Degree requirements:* For master's, one foreign language, thesis optional, foreign language competency for use in research. *Entrance requirements:* For master's, minimum GPA of 3.0. Additional exam requirements/recommendations for international students: required—TOEFL (minimum score 550 paper-based; 80 iBT), IELTS (minimum score 6.5). *Application deadline:* For fall admission, 8/1 priority date for domestic students, 5/1 priority date for international students; for spring admission, 1/1 priority date for domestic students, 9/1 priority date for international students. Applications are processed on a rolling basis. Electronic applications accepted. *Financial support:* In 2019–20, 2 students received support. Scholarships/grants, tuition waivers (full and partial), and unspecified assistantships available. Support available to part-time students. Financial award application deadline: 4/15; financial award applicants required to submit FAFSA. *Unit head:* Dean DeFino, PhD, Chair, 914-637-2160, E-mail: ddefino@iona.edu. *Application contact:* RoseDeline Martinez, Director of Graduate Admissions, School of Arts and Science, 914-633-2427, Fax: 914-633-2451, E-mail: rmartinez@iona.edu.
Website: http://www.iona.edu/Academics/School-of-Arts-Science/Departments/English/Graduate-Programs.aspx

Iowa State University of Science and Technology, Department of English, Ames, IA 50011. Offers creative writing (MFA); English (MA); rhetoric and professional communication (PhD). *Degree requirements:* For master's, thesis or alternative; for doctorate, thesis/dissertation. *Entrance requirements:* For master's, GRE General Test, sample of written work, resume, portfolio in creative writing; for doctorate, GRE General Test, sample of written work, resume. Additional exam requirements/recommendations for international students: required—TOEFL (minimum score 600 paper-based; 100 iBT), IELTS (minimum score 7). Electronic applications accepted.

Jackson State University, Graduate School, College of Liberal Arts, Department of English and Modern Foreign Languages, Jackson, MS 39217. Offers English (MA); teaching English (MAT). *Program availability:* Part-time, evening/weekend. *Degree requirements:* For master's, comprehensive exam, thesis or alternative. *Entrance requirements:* For master's, GRE General Test. Additional exam requirements/recommendations for international students: required—TOEFL (minimum score 520 paper-based; 67 iBT). Electronic applications accepted. *Expenses:* Contact institution.

Jacksonville State University, Graduate Studies, School of Arts and Humanities, Department of English, Jacksonville, AL 36265-1602. Offers MA. *Program availability:* Part-time, evening/weekend. *Degree requirements:* For master's, comprehensive exam, thesis (for some programs). *Entrance requirements:* For master's, GRE General Test or MAT. Additional exam requirements/recommendations for international students: required—TOEFL (minimum score 500 paper-based; 61 iBT). Electronic applications accepted.

James Madison University, The Graduate School, College of Arts and Letters, Program in English, Harrisonburg, VA 22807. Offers MA. *Program availability:* Part-time. *Students:* 13 full-time (10 women). Average age 30. In 2019, 4 master's awarded. *Degree requirements:* For master's, one foreign language, thesis. Application fee: $60. Electronic applications accepted. *Financial support:* In 2019–20, 11 students received support, including 7 teaching assistantships with full tuition reimbursements available (averaging $9,284 per year); fellowships, Federal Work-Study, and assistantships (averaging $7911) also available. Financial award application deadline: 3/1; financial award applicants required to submit FAFSA. *Unit head:* Dr. Dabney A. Bankert, Department Head, 540-568-6797, E-mail: bankerda@jmu.edu. *Application contact:* Lynette D. Michael, Director of Graduate Admissions, 540-568-6131 Ext. 6395, Fax: 540-568-7860, E-mail: michaeld@jmu.edu.
Website: http://www.jmu.edu/english

John Carroll University, Graduate School, Department of English, University Heights, OH 44118. Offers MA. *Program availability:* Part-time, evening/weekend. *Degree requirements:* For master's, research essay or thesis. *Entrance requirements:* Additional exam requirements/recommendations for international students: required—TOEFL. *Application deadline:* Applications are processed on a rolling basis. Electronic applications accepted. *Financial support:* Scholarships/grants and unspecified assistantships available. Financial award applicants required to submit FAFSA. *Unit head:* Dr. Maryclaire Moroney, Chair, 216-397-6674, Fax: 216-397-1723, E-mail: mmoroney@jcu.edu. *Application contact:* Dr. Jean Feerick, Graduate Program Coordinator, 216-397-4778, Fax: 216-397-1723, E-mail: jfeerick@jcu.edu.
Website: https://jcu.edu/academics/english/graduate/programs/master-in-english

Johns Hopkins University, Zanvyl Krieger School of Arts and Sciences, Department of English, Baltimore, MD 21218. Offers English and American literature (PhD). *Degree requirements:* For doctorate, 2 foreign languages, comprehensive exam, thesis/dissertation, 10 seminars, 2 oral exams. *Entrance requirements:* For doctorate, GRE General and Subject Tests. Additional exam requirements/recommendations for international students: required—TOEFL (minimum score 600 paper-based; 100 iBT), IELTS. Electronic applications accepted.

Kansas State University, Graduate School, College of Arts and Sciences, Department of English, Manhattan, KS 66506. Offers English (MA); technical writing and professional communication (Graduate Certificate). *Program availability:* Part-time. *Degree requirements:* For master's, one foreign language, thesis optional. *Entrance requirements:* For master's, GRE, minimum B average in English. Additional exam requirements/recommendations for international students: required—TOEFL. Electronic applications accepted.

Kent State University, College of Arts and Sciences, Department of English, Kent, OH 44242-0001. Offers creative writing (MFA); English (MA, PhD); English for teachers (MA); literature and writing (MA); rhetoric and composition (PhD); teaching English as a second language (MA). *Program availability:* Part-time. *Faculty:* 19 full-time (9 women), 2 part-time/adjunct (1 woman). *Students:* 101 full-time (64 women), 12 part-time (8 women); includes 5 minority (3 Black or African American, non-Hispanic/Latino; 1 Asian, non-Hispanic/Latino; 1 Hispanic/Latino), 24 international. Average age 34. 69 applicants, 77% accepted, 18 enrolled. In 2019, 19 master's, 3 doctorates awarded. *Degree requirements:* For master's, thesis (for some programs), final portfolio, final exam, practicum or thesis (for MA in teaching English as a second language); for doctorate, one foreign language, comprehensive exam, thesis/dissertation. *Entrance requirements:* For master's, GRE General Test, goal statement, 3 letters of recommendation, 8-15 page writing sample relevant to the field of study (waived for MA in English for teachers concentration), transcripts, for MA - TESL Int'l English proficiency scores: TOEFL (ibT): 79, MELAB 77, IELTS 6.5, PTE 58; for the M.A. - English, TOEFL (ibT): 94, MELAB 82, IELTS 7.0, PTE 65; for doctorate, GRE General Test, statement of purpose, 3 letters of recommendation, 8-15 page writing sample relevant to field of study, transcripts, Master's degree, 3.0 GPA on 4.0 scale; Ph.D Rhetoric & Comp - English proficiency for Int'l: TOEFL (ibT) 102, MELAB 86, IELTS 7.5, PTE 73; Ph.D - English: TOEFL (ibT) 94, MELAB 82, IELTS 7.5, PTE 73. Additional exam requirements/recommendations for international students: required—See below for scores specific to Masters or Doctorate level. *Application deadline:* Applications are processed on a rolling basis. Application fee: $45 ($70 for international students). Electronic applications accepted. *Financial support:* Fellowships with full tuition reimbursements, teaching assistantships with full tuition reimbursements, and unspecified assistantships available. Financial award application deadline: 1/15. *Unit head:* Dr. Robert Trogdon, Chair, 330-672-2676, E-mail: rtrogdon@kent.edu. *Application contact:* Wesley Raabe, Graduate Studies Coordinator, 330-672-1723, E-mail: wraabe@kent.edu.
Website: http://www.kent.edu/english/

Kutztown University of Pennsylvania, College of Liberal Arts and Sciences, Program in English, Kutztown, PA 19530-0730. Offers MA. *Program availability:* Part-time, evening/weekend. *Faculty:* 7 full-time (4 women). *Students:* 11 full-time (6 women), 8 part-time (4 women); includes 3 minority (1 Asian, non-Hispanic/Latino; 2 Two or more races, non-Hispanic/Latino). Average age 26. 6 applicants, 100% accepted, 4 enrolled. In 2019, 4 master's awarded. *Degree requirements:* For master's, comprehensive exam, thesis optional. *Entrance requirements:* For master's, brief statement of purpose, short writing example, 3 letters of recommendation. Additional exam requirements/recommendations for international students: required—TOEFL (minimum score 550 paper-based, 79 iBT), IELTS (minimum score 6.5), or PTE (minimum score 53). *Application deadline:* For fall admission, 8/1 for domestic and international students; for spring admission, 12/1 for domestic and international students. Application fee: $35. Electronic applications accepted. *Expenses: Tuition, area resident:* Full-time $9288; part-time $515 per credit. Tuition, state resident: full-time $9288. Tuition, nonresident: full-time $13,932; part-time $774 per credit. *Required fees:* $1688; $94 per credit. *Financial support:* Career-related internships or fieldwork, Federal Work-Study, and unspecified assistantships available. Financial award application deadline: 3/1; financial award applicants required to submit FAFSA. *Unit head:* Dr. Andrew Vogel, Department Chair, 610-683-4353, Fax: 610-683-4355, E-mail: vogel@kutztown.edu. *Application contact:* Dr. Andrew Vogel, Department Chair, 610-683-4353, Fax: 610-683-4355, E-mail: vogel@kutztown.edu.
Website: https://www.kutztown.edu/academics/graduate-programs/english.htm

Lakehead University, Graduate Studies, Faculty of Social Sciences and Humanities, Department of English, Thunder Bay, ON P7B 5E1, Canada. Offers English (MA); women's studies (MA). *Program availability:* Part-time, evening/weekend. *Degree requirements:* For master's, one foreign language, thesis optional. *Entrance requirements:* For master's, minimum B average. Additional exam requirements/recommendations for international students: required—TOEFL.

Lamar University, College of Graduate Studies, College of Arts and Sciences, Department of English and Modern Languages, Beaumont, TX 77710. Offers English (MA); teaching Spanish (MA). *Program availability:* Part-time, evening/weekend. *Faculty:* 40 full-time (19 women), 4 part-time/adjunct (all women). *Students:* 10 full-time (7 women), 29 part-time (28 women); includes 20 minority (2 Black or African American, non-Hispanic/Latino; 17 Hispanic/Latino; 1 Two or more races, non-Hispanic/Latino), 12 international. Average age 37. 19 applicants, 84% accepted, 14 enrolled. In 2019, 6 master's awarded. *Degree requirements:* For master's, one foreign language, thesis optional, practicum. *Entrance requirements:* For master's, GRE General Test, minimum GPA of 2.5 in last 60 hours of undergraduate course work. Additional exam requirements/recommendations for international students: required—TOEFL (minimum score 550 paper-based; 79 iBT), IELTS (minimum score 6.5). *Application deadline:* Applications are processed on a rolling basis. Application fee: $25 ($50 for international students). Electronic applications accepted. *Expenses: Tuition, area resident:* Full-time $6324; part-time $351 per credit. Tuition, state resident: full-time $6324; part-time $351 per credit. Tuition, nonresident: full-time $13,920; part-time $773 per credit. *International tuition:* $13,920 full-time. *Required fees:* $2462; $327 per credit. Tuition and fees vary according to course load, campus/location and reciprocity agreements. *Financial support:* In 2019–20, 31 students received support, including 4 teaching assistantships (averaging $8,000 per year); career-related internships or fieldwork, Federal Work-Study, and institutionally sponsored loans also available. Support available to part-time students. Financial award applicants required to submit FAFSA. *Unit head:* Dr. Jim Sanderson, Chair, 409-880-8558, Fax: 409-880-8591. *Application contact:* Celeste Contreas, Director, Admissions and Academic Services, 409-880-8888, Fax: 409-880-7419, E-mail: gradmissions@lamar.edu.
Website: http://artssciences.lamar.edu/english-and-modern-languages

La Salle University, School of Arts and Sciences, Program in Education, Philadelphia, PA 19141-1199. Offers autism spectrum disorders (MA, Certificate); bilingual/bicultural studies (MA); classroom management (MA); dual early childhood and special education (MA); dual middle-level science and math and special education (MA); education (MA); English (MA); English as a second language (Certificate); history (MA); instructional coach (Certificate); instructional leadership (MA); reading specialist (MA, Certificate); secondary education (MA); special education (MA, Certificate). *Program availability:* Part-time, evening/weekend. *Degree requirements:* For master's, comprehensive exam. *Entrance requirements:* For master's, MAT or GRE, 2 letters of recommendation; for Certificate, GMAT or GRE, 2 letters of recommendation. Additional exam requirements/recommendations for international students: required—TOEFL. Electronic applications accepted. Application fee is waived when completed online. *Expenses:* Contact institution.

La Sierra University, College of Arts and Sciences, Department of English and Communication, Riverside, CA 92505. Offers communication (MA), including public relations/advertising, theory emphasis; English (MA), including literary emphasis, writing emphasis. *Program availability:* Part-time. *Degree requirements:* For master's, one foreign language. *Entrance requirements:* For master's, GRE General Test.

Lee University, Program in Education, Cleveland, TN 37320-3450. Offers art (MAT); curriculum and instruction (M Ed, Ed S); early childhood (MAT); educational leadership (M Ed, Ed S); elementary education (MAT); English and math (MAT); English and science (MAT); English and social studies (MAT); higher education administration (MS); history (MAT); history and economics (MAT); math and science (MAT); math and social studies (MAT); middle grades (MAT); science and social studies (MASW); secondary education (MAT); Spanish (MAT); special education (M Ed, MAT); TESOL (MAT). *Accreditation:* NCATE. *Program availability:* Part-time. *Faculty:* 13 full-time (5 women), 9 part-time/adjunct (6 women). *Students:* 24 full-time (15 women), 72 part-time (46 women); includes 14 minority (8 Black or African American, non-Hispanic/Latino; 1 Hispanic/Latino; 5 Two or more races, non-Hispanic/Latino), 1 international. Average age 29. 44 applicants, 86% accepted, 33 enrolled. In 2019, 60 master's, 3 other advanced degrees awarded. *Degree requirements:* For master's, variable foreign language requirement, thesis optional, internship. *Entrance requirements:* For master's, MAT or GRE General Test, minimum undergraduate GPA of 2.75, 3 letters of recommendation, interview, writing sample, official transcripts, background check; for Ed S, minimum undergraduate and master's GPA of 2.75, official transcripts for undergraduate and master's degrees. Additional exam requirements/recommendations for international students: required—TOEFL (minimum score 61 iBT). *Application deadline:* For fall admission, 6/1 priority date for domestic and international students; for spring admission, 11/1 priority date for domestic and international students; for summer admission, 4/1 priority date for domestic and international students. Applications are processed on a rolling basis. Application fee: $25. Electronic applications accepted. *Expenses: Tuition:* Full-time $13,590; part-time $755 per credit hour. *Required fees:* $25. Tuition and fees vary according to program. *Financial support:* In 2019–20, 40 students received support. Career-related internships or fieldwork, Federal Work-Study, institutionally sponsored loans, scholarships/grants, and unspecified assistantships available. Financial award application deadline: 3/1; financial award applicants required to submit FAFSA. *Unit head:* Dr. William Kamm, Director, 423-614-8544, E-mail: wkamm@leeuniversity.edu. *Application contact:* Jeffery McGirt, Director of Graduate Enrollment, 423-614-8691, Fax: 423-614-8317, E-mail: jmcgirt@leeuniversity.edu.
Website: http://www.leeuniversity.edu/academics/graduate/education

Lehigh University, College of Arts and Sciences, Department of English, Bethlehem, PA 18015. Offers MA, PhD. *Program availability:* Part-time. *Faculty:* 11 full-time (4 women). *Students:* 32 full-time (26 women), 5 part-time (3 women); includes 2 minority (1 Black or African American, non-Hispanic/Latino; 1 Asian, non-Hispanic/Latino), 3 international. Average age 29. 46 applicants, 35% accepted, 9 enrolled. In 2019, 5 master's, 5 doctorates awarded. Terminal master's awarded for partial completion of doctoral program. *Degree requirements:* For master's, thesis optional; for doctorate, one foreign language, comprehensive exam, thesis/dissertation. *Entrance requirements:* For master's, minimum GPA of 3.0 in undergraduate English courses; for doctorate, minimum GPA of 3.5 in MA coursework. Additional exam requirements/recommendations for international students: required—TOEFL (minimum score 620 paper-based; 96 iBT). *Application deadline:* For fall admission, 1/1 for domestic and international students. Application fee: $75. Electronic applications accepted. *Financial support:* In 2019–20, 34 students received support, including 1 fellowship with full tuition reimbursement available (averaging $21,750 per year), 25 teaching assistantships with full tuition reimbursements available (averaging $22,290 per year); scholarships/grants, tuition waivers (full and partial), and unspecified assistantships also available. Support available to part-time students. Financial award application deadline: 1/1. *Unit head:* Dr. Dawn Keetley, Chairperson, 610-758-3311, Fax: 610-758-6616, E-mail: dek7@lehigh.edu. *Application contact:* Dr. Amardeep Singh, Director of Graduate Studies, 610-758-4385, Fax: 610-758-6616, E-mail: amsp@lehigh.edu.
Website: http://cas.lehigh.edu/casweb/English

Lehman College of the City University of New York, School of Arts and Humanities, Department of English, Bronx, NY 10468-1589. Offers MA. *Degree requirements:* For master's, thesis. *Entrance requirements:* For master's, GRE, 18 upper-level credits in U.S. or English literature. *Expenses: Tuition, area resident:* Full-time $5545; part-time $470 per credit. Tuition, nonresident: part-time $855 per credit. *Required fees:* $240.

Liberty University, College of Arts and Sciences, Lynchburg, VA 24515. Offers English (MA); history (MA); professional writing (MA). *Accreditation:* AACN. *Program availability:* Part-time, online learning. *Students:* 382 full-time (203 women), 499 part-time (272 women); includes 161 minority (82 Black or African American, non-Hispanic/Latino; 4 American Indian or Alaska Native, non-Hispanic/Latino; 4 Asian, non-Hispanic/Latino; 43 Hispanic/Latino; 1 Native Hawaiian or other Pacific Islander, non-Hispanic/Latino; 27 Two or more races, non-Hispanic/Latino), 9 international. Average age 38. 1,716 applicants, 32% accepted, 320 enrolled. In 2019, 253 master's awarded. *Degree requirements:* For master's, comprehensive exam (for some programs), thesis (for some programs). *Entrance requirements:* For master's, GRE, minimum undergraduate GPA of 3.0, letters of recommendation, statement of purpose. Additional exam requirements/recommendations for international students: required—TOEFL (minimum score 600 paper-based; 100 iBT). *Application deadline:* For fall admission, 6/1 for domestic students; for spring admission, 11/1 for domestic students. Applications are processed on a rolling basis. Application fee: $50. Electronic applications accepted. *Expenses: Tuition:* Full-time $545; part-time $410 per credit hour. One-time fee: $50. *Financial support:* In 2019–20, 659 students received support. Teaching assistantships with tuition reimbursements available and Federal Work-Study available. *Unit head:* Dr. Roger Schultz, Dean, 434-592-4031, Fax: 434-522-0430, E-mail: rschultz@liberty.edu. *Application contact:* Chris Jones, Director of Admissions, 434-592-3966, Fax: 434-522-0430, E-mail: gradadmissions@liberty.edu.
Website: https://www.liberty.edu/arts-sciences/

Lipscomb University, College of Education, Nashville, TN 37204-3951. Offers applied behavior analysis (MS, Certificate); coaching for learning (M Ed, Certificate, Ed S); educational leadership (M Ed, Ed S); English language learning (M Ed, Ed S); instructional coaching (M Ed, Certificate, Ed S); instructional practice (M Ed); learning organizations and strategic change (Ed D); literacy coaching (Certificate, Ed S); reading specialty (M Ed, Ed S); school counseling (M Ed, Ed S); special education (M Ed); teaching, learning, and leading (M Ed); technology integration (M Ed, Ed S); technology integration specialist (Certificate). *Accreditation:* NCATE. *Program availability:* Part-time, evening/weekend, 100% online. *Degree requirements:* For master's, comprehensive exam, portfolio, research project and presentation; for doctorate, practical capstone project in experiential setting. *Entrance requirements:* For master's, MAT (minimum score 31) or GRE General Test (minimum score 294), 2 reference letters, goals statement, writing sample, interview; for doctorate, MAT or GRE General Test, 3 reference letters, artifact of demonstrated academic excellence, written personal statements, interview. Additional exam requirements/recommendations for international students: required—TOEFL (minimum score 570 paper-based; 80 iBT). Electronic applications accepted. *Expenses:* Contact institution.

Long Island University - Brooklyn, Richard L. Conolly College of Liberal Arts and Sciences, Brooklyn, NY 11201-8423. Offers biology (MS); chemistry (MS); clinical psychology (PhD); creative writing (MFA); English (MA); media arts (MA, MFA); political science (MA); psychology (MA); social science (MS); United Nations (Advanced Certificate); urban studies (MA); writing and production for television (MFA). *Program availability:* Part-time. Terminal master's awarded for partial completion of doctoral program. *Degree requirements:* For master's, comprehensive exam (for some programs), thesis (for some programs); for doctorate, thesis/dissertation. *Entrance requirements:* For doctorate, GRE. Additional exam requirements/recommendations for international students: required—TOEFL (minimum score 550 paper-based, 79 iBT) or IELTS. Electronic applications accepted.

Long Island University - Post, College of Liberal Arts and Sciences, Brookville, NY 11548-1300. Offers applied mathematics (MS); behavior analysis (MA); biology (MS); criminal justice (MS); earth science (MS); English (MA); environmental sustainability (MS); genetic counseling (MS); history (MA); interdisciplinary studies (MA, MS); political science (MA); psychology (MA). *Program availability:* Part-time, evening/weekend, blended/hybrid learning. Terminal master's awarded for partial completion of doctoral program. *Degree requirements:* For master's, comprehensive exam (for some programs), thesis (for some programs). *Entrance requirements:* Additional exam requirements/recommendations for international students: required—TOEFL, IELTS, or PTE. Electronic applications accepted.

Louisiana State University and Agricultural & Mechanical College, Graduate School, College of Humanities and Social Sciences, Department of English, Baton Rouge, LA 70803. Offers creative writing (MFA); English (MA, PhD).

Louisiana Tech University, Graduate School, College of Education, Ruston, LA 71272. Offers counseling and guidance (MA), including clinical mental health counseling, human services, orientation and mobility; counseling psychology (PhD); curriculum and instruction (M Ed); cyber education (Graduate Certificate); dynamics of domestic and family violence (Graduate Certificate); early childhood education - PreK-3 (MAT); educational leadership (M Ed, Ed D); elementary education and special education mild/moderate grades 1-5 (MAT); higher education administration (Graduate Certificate); industrial/organizational psychology (MA, PhD); kinesiology (MS); middle school education (MAT), including mathematics; orientation and mobility (Graduate Certificate); rehabilitation teaching for the blind (Graduate Certificate); secondary education (MAT), including agriculture, biology, business, chemistry, English; special education: visually impaired (MAT); teacher leader education (Graduate Certificate); visual impairments - blind education (Graduate Certificate). *Accreditation:* NCATE. *Program availability:* Part-time. *Degree requirements:* For master's, thesis; for doctorate, thesis/dissertation. *Entrance requirements:* For master's and doctorate, GRE General Test. Additional exam requirements/recommendations for international students: required—TOEFL (minimum score 550 paper-based; 80 iBT), IELTS (minimum score 6.5). Electronic applications accepted. *Expenses: Tuition, area resident:* Full-time $6592; part-time $400 per credit. Tuition, state resident: full-time $6592; part-time $400 per credit. Tuition, nonresident: full-time $13,333; part-time $681 per credit. *International tuition:* $13,333 full-time. *Required fees:* $3011; $3011 per unit.

Louisiana Tech University, Graduate School, College of Liberal Arts, Ruston, LA 71272. Offers architecture (M Arch); art (MFA), including graphic design, photography, studio; audiology (Au D); communication (MA), including speech communication, theatre; English (MA), including literature, technical writing; history (MA); speech pathology (MA); technical writing and communication (Graduate Certificate). *Accreditation:* ASHA. *Program availability:* Part-time. *Degree requirements:* For master's, thesis (for some programs); for doctorate, thesis/dissertation. *Entrance requirements:* For master's, GRE General Test; for doctorate, GRE General Test, bachelor's degree, minimum GPA of 3.0 or 3.2 on last 60 hours attempted. Additional exam requirements/recommendations for international students: required—TOEFL (minimum score 550 paper-based; 80 iBT), IELTS (minimum score 6.5). Electronic applications accepted. *Expenses: Tuition, area resident:* Full-time $6592; part-time $400 per credit. Tuition, state resident: full-time $6592; part-time $400 per credit. Tuition, nonresident: full-time $13,333; part-time $681 per credit. *International tuition:* $13,333 full-time. *Required fees:* $3011; $3011 per unit.

Loyola Marymount University, Bellarmine College of Liberal Arts, Program in English, Los Angeles, CA 90045-2659. Offers MA. *Program availability:* Part-time. *Students:* 30 full-time (18 women); includes 11 minority (2 Black or African American, non-Hispanic/Latino; 1 Asian, non-Hispanic/Latino; 7 Hispanic/Latino; 1 Two or more races, non-Hispanic/Latino), 1 international. Average age 29. 69 applicants, 42% accepted. In 2019, 7 master's awarded. *Entrance requirements:* For master's, completed bachelor degree; 5 upper level English courses; graduate admissions application; undergrad GPA of at least 3.0; 2 letters of recommendation; writing sample; personal statement; offical transcripts. Additional exam requirements/recommendations for international students: required—TOEFL, IELTS. *Application deadline:* Applications are processed on a rolling basis. Application fee: $50. Electronic applications accepted. *Financial support:* Fellowships, teaching assistantships, scholarships/grants, and unspecified assistantships available. Financial award application deadline: 3/20; financial award applicants required to submit FAFSA. *Unit head:* Robin Miskolcze, Director, English Program, 310-338-3721, E-mail: robin.miskolcze@lmu.edu. *Application contact:* Ammar Dalal, Vice Provost of Graduate Admission, 310-338-2721, Fax: 310-338-6086, E-mail: graduateadmission@lmu.edu.
Website: http://bellarmine.lmu.edu/english/graduateprogram

Loyola University Chicago, Graduate School, Department of English, Chicago, IL 60660. Offers 19th century studies (PhD); English (MA); Medieval and Renaissance literature (PhD); modern literature and culture (PhD); textual studies and digital humanities (PhD). *Program availability:* Part-time, evening/weekend. *Faculty:* 24 full-time (11 women). *Students:* 37 full-time (24 women), 2 part-time (both women); includes 8 minority (1 Black or African American, non-Hispanic/Latino; 1 Asian, non-Hispanic/Latino; 4 Hispanic/Latino; 2 Two or more races, non-Hispanic/Latino). Average age 30. 68 applicants, 40% accepted, 10 enrolled. In 2019, 7 master's, 2 doctorates awarded. Terminal master's awarded for partial completion of doctoral program. *Degree requirements:* For master's, comprehensive exam, thesis or alternative; for doctorate, one foreign language, comprehensive exam, thesis/dissertation. *Entrance requirements:* For master's and doctorate, GRE General Test. Additional exam requirements/recommendations for international students: required—TOEFL, IELTS. *Application deadline:* For fall admission, 6/1 for domestic students. Applications are processed on a rolling basis. Application fee: $0. Electronic applications accepted. *Expenses: Tuition:* Full-time $18,540; part-time $1033 per credit hour. *Required fees:* $904; $230 per credit hour. *Financial support:* In 2019–20, 22 students received support, including 3 fellowships with full tuition reimbursements available (averaging $19,000 per year), research assistantships with full tuition reimbursements available (averaging $10,000 per year), 18 teaching assistantships with full tuition reimbursements available (averaging $19,000 per year); institutionally sponsored loans, tuition waivers (full and partial), and unspecified assistantships also available. Financial award application deadline: 1/15; financial award applicants required to submit FAFSA. *Unit head:* Dr. James Knapp, Graduate Program Director, 773-508-2241, Fax: 773-508-8696, E-mail: jknapp3@luc.edu. *Application contact:* Dr. James Knapp, Graduate Program Director, 773-508-2241, Fax: 773-508-8696, E-mail: jknapp3@luc.edu.
Website: http://www.luc.edu/english/

Manhattan College, Graduate Programs, School of Education and Health, Program in Special Education, Riverdale, NY 10471. Offers adolescence education students with disabilities generalist extension in English or math or social studies - grades 7-12 (MS Ed); bilingual education (Advanced Certificate); dual childhood/students with disabilities - grades 1-6 (MS Ed); students with disabilities - grades 1-6 (MS Ed). *Program availability:* Part-time, evening/weekend. *Faculty:* 4 full-time (2 women), 9 part-time/adjunct (6 women). *Students:* 62 full-time (58 women). Average age 24. 34 applicants, 79% accepted, 24 enrolled. In 2019, 27 master's awarded. *Degree requirements:* For master's, thesis, internship (if not certified). *Entrance requirements:* For master's, GRE, minimum GPA of 3.0. Additional exam requirements/recommendations for international students: required—TOEFL (minimum score 550 paper-based; 80 iBT), IELTS (minimum score 6). *Application deadline:* For fall admission, 8/10 priority date for domestic students; for spring admission, 1/7 priority date for domestic students. Applications are processed on a rolling basis. Application fee: $75. Electronic applications accepted. *Expenses:* Tuition: $975 per credit; Registration Fee: $110; Informational Service Fee (5 or more credits) $200. *Financial support:* In 2019–20, 52 students received support. Federal Work-Study, scholarships/grants, and unspecified assistantships available. Financial award application deadline: 2/1; financial award applicants required to submit FAFSA. *Unit head:* Dr. Elizabeth Mary Kosky, Director of Childhood and Adolescent Special Education Programs, 718-862-7969, Fax: 718-862-7816, E-mail: elizabeth.kosky@manhattan.edu. *Application contact:* Dr. Colette Geary, Vice President for Enrollment Management, 718-862-7199, E-mail: cgeary01@manhattan.edu.
Website: manhattan.edu

Manhattanville College, School of Education, Jump Start Program, Purchase, NY 10577-2132. Offers childhood education and special education (grades 1-6) (MPS); early childhood education (birth-grade 2) (MAT); education (Advanced Certificate); English and special education (grades 5-12) (MPS); mathematics and special education (grades 5-12) (MPS); science and special education (grades 5-12) (MPS); social studies and special education (grades 5-12) (MPS); Spanish (grades 7-12) (MAT); tesol - teaching English as a second language (all grades) (MPS). *Program availability:* Part-time, evening/weekend. *Faculty:* 5 full-time (all women), 12 part-time/adjunct (9 women). *Students:* 6 full-time (3 women), 37 part-time (28 women); includes 7 minority (2 Black or African American, non-Hispanic/Latino; 1 Asian, non-Hispanic/Latino; 3 Hispanic/Latino; 1 Native Hawaiian or other Pacific Islander, non-Hispanic/Latino). Average age 33. 23 applicants, 74% accepted, 14 enrolled. In 2019, 17 master's, 1 other advanced degree awarded. *Degree requirements:* For master's, comprehensive exam (for some programs), thesis (for some programs), student teaching, research seminars, portfolios, internships, writing assessment; for Advanced Certificate, comprehensive exam (for some programs). *Entrance requirements:* For master's, for programs leading to certification, candidates must submit scores from GRE or MAT(miller analogies test), minimum undergraduate GPA of 3.0, all transcripts from all colleges and universities attended, 2 letters of recommendation, interview, essay (2-3 page personal statement that describes reasons for choosing education as profession and personal philosophy of education), proof of immunization (for those born after 1957). Additional exam requirements/recommendations for international students: required—TOEFL or IELTS are required. Manhattanville College now accepts the Duolingo English Test with a required score of 105; recommended—TOEFL (minimum score 600 paper-based; 110 iBT), IELTS (minimum score 8). *Application deadline:* Applications are processed on a rolling basis. Application fee: $75. Electronic applications accepted. *Expenses:* $935 per credit, $45 technology fee, and $60 registration fee. *Financial support:* In 2019–20, 23 students received support. Teaching assistantships, institutionally sponsored loans, scholarships/grants, tuition waivers, and unspecified assistantships available. Financial award application deadline: 3/15; financial award applicants required to submit FAFSA. *Unit head:* Dr. Shelley Wepner, Dean, 914-323-3153, E-mail: Shelly.Wepner@mville.edu. *Application contact:* Alissa Wilson, Director, SOE Graduate Enrollment Management, 914-323-3150, Fax: 914-694-1732, E-mail: Alissa.Wilson@mville.edu.
Website: http://www.mville.edu/programs/jump-start

Manhattanville College, School of Education, Program in Middle Childhood/Adolescence Education (Grades 5-12), Purchase, NY 10577-2132. Offers biology and special education (MPS); chemistry and special education (MPS); education for sustainability (Advanced Certificate); English and special education (MPS); literacy and special education (MPS); literacy specialist (MPS); math and special education (MPS); mathematics (Advanced Certificate); middle childhood/adolescence ed science (biology or chemistry grades 5-12) or (physics grades 7-12) (MAT); middle childhood/adolescence education (grades 5-12) English (MAT, Advanced Certificate); middle childhood/adolescence education (grades 5-12) mathematics (MAT, Advanced Certificate); middle childhood/adolescence education (grades 5-12) science (biology chemistry, physics, earth science) (Advanced Certificate); middle childhood/adolescence education (grades 5-12) social studies (MAT, Advanced Certificate); physics (MAT, Advanced Certificate); social studies (MAT); social studies and special education (MPS); special education generalist (MPS). *Program availability:* Part-time, evening/weekend. *Faculty:* 3 full-time (2 women), 17 part-time/adjunct (11 women). *Students:* 21 full-time (13 women), 25 part-time (16 women); includes 9 minority (4 Black or African American, non-Hispanic/Latino; 1 Asian, non-Hispanic/Latino; 4 Hispanic/Latino). Average age 29. 10 applicants, 80% accepted, 5 enrolled. In 2019, 15 master's, 4 other advanced degrees awarded. *Degree requirements:* For master's, comprehensive exam (for some programs), thesis (for some programs), student teaching, research seminars, portfolios, internships, writing assessment; for Advanced Certificate, comprehensive exam (for some programs). *Entrance requirements:* For master's, for programs leading to certification, candidates must submit scores from GRE or MAT(Miller Analogies Test), minimum undergraduate GPA of 3.0, all transcripts from all colleges and universities attended, 2 letters of recommendation, interview, essay (2-3 page personal statement that describes reasons for choosing education as profession and personal philosophy of education), proof of immunization (for those born after 1957). Additional exam requirements/recommendations for international students: required—TOEFL or IELTS are required. Manhattanville College now accepts the Duolingo English Test with a required score of 105; recommended—TOEFL (minimum score 600 paper-based; 110 iBT), IELTS (minimum score 8). *Application deadline:* Applications are processed on a rolling basis. Application fee: $75. Electronic applications accepted. *Expenses:* $935 per credit, $45 technology fee, and $60 registration fee. *Financial support:* In 2019–20, 18 students received support. Teaching assistantships, scholarships/grants, tuition waivers, and unspecified assistantships available. Support available to part-time students. Financial award application deadline: 3/15; financial award applicants required to submit FAFSA. *Unit head:* Dr. Shelley Wepner, Dean, 914-323-3153, Fax: 914-323-5493, E-mail: Shelley.Wepner@mville.edu. *Application contact:* Alissa Wilson, Director, Graduate Admissions, 914-323-3150, Fax: 914-694-1732, E-mail: Alissa.Wilson@mville.edu.
Website: http://www.mville.edu/programs#/search/19

Marquette University, Graduate School, College of Arts and Sciences, Department of English, Milwaukee, WI 53201-1881. Offers American literature (PhD); British and American literature (MA); British literature (PhD). *Program availability:* Part-time. Terminal master's awarded for partial completion of doctoral program. *Degree* *requirements:* For master's, comprehensive exam, thesis or alternative; for doctorate, one foreign language, thesis/dissertation, qualifying exam. *Entrance requirements:* For master's and doctorate, GRE General Test, GRE Subject Test, official transcripts from all current and previous colleges/universities except Marquette, three letters of recommendation, statement of purpose, one or two writing samples. Additional exam requirements/recommendations for international students: required—TOEFL. Electronic applications accepted.

Marshall University, Academic Affairs Division, College of Liberal Arts, Department of English, Huntington, WV 25755. Offers MA, Graduate Certificate. *Degree requirements:* For master's, one foreign language, thesis optional. *Entrance requirements:* For master's, GRE General Test.

Mary Baldwin University, Graduate Studies, Program in Shakespeare and Performance, Staunton, VA 24401-3610. Offers acting (M Litt); directing (M Litt); dramaturgy (M Litt); Shakespeare and performance (MFA); teaching (M Litt). *Entrance requirements:* For master's, GRE (M Litt).

Marymount University, School of Design, Arts, and Humanities, Program in English and Humanities, Arlington, VA 22207-4299. Offers English and humanities (MA); teaching English at the community college (Certificate). *Program availability:* Part-time, evening/weekend. *Faculty:* 8 full-time (6 women). *Students:* 1 (woman) full-time, 14 part-time (9 women); includes 4 minority (3 Black or African American, non-Hispanic/Latino; 1 Hispanic/Latino), 3 international. Average age 35. 6 applicants, 100% accepted, 3 enrolled. In 2019, 7 master's awarded. *Degree requirements:* For master's, thesis optional, capstone thesis or practicum project and presentation. *Entrance requirements:* For master's, 2 letters of recommendation, resume, bachelor's degree in English or other humanities discipline, writing sample of 8-10 pages, personal statement. Additional exam requirements/recommendations for international students: required—TOEFL (minimum score 600 paper-based; 96 iBT), IELTS (minimum score 6.5), PTE (minimum score 58). *Application deadline:* For fall admission, 7/16 priority date for domestic and international students; for spring admission, 11/16 priority date for domestic and international students; for summer admission, 4/16 priority date for domestic and international students. Applications are processed on a rolling basis. Application fee: $40. Electronic applications accepted. *Expenses: Tuition:* Part-time $1050 per credit. *Required fees:* $22 per credit. One-time fee: $270 part-time. Tuition and fees vary according to program. *Financial support:* In 2019–20, 5 students received support. Research assistantships, teaching assistantships, career-related internships or fieldwork, scholarships/grants, and unspecified assistantships available. Support available to part-time students. Financial award application deadline: 3/1; financial award applicants required to submit FAFSA. *Unit head:* Dr. Tonya-Marie Howe, Chair, Literature and Languages, 703-284-5762, E-mail: thowe@marymount.edu. *Application contact:* Fiona McDonnell, Administrative Assistant, 703-284-5901, E-mail: gadmissi@marymount.edu.
Website: https://www.marymount.edu/English-Humanities

McGill University, Faculty of Graduate and Postdoctoral Studies, Faculty of Arts, Department of English, Montréal, QC H3A 2T5, Canada. Offers MA, PhD. Electronic applications accepted.

McMaster University, School of Graduate Studies, Faculty of Humanities, Department of English and Cultural Studies, Hamilton, ON L8S 4M2, Canada. Offers cultural studies and critical theory (MA); English (MA, PhD). *Program availability:* Part-time. *Degree requirements:* For master's, one foreign language, thesis; for doctorate, one foreign language, comprehensive exam, thesis/dissertation. *Entrance requirements:* For master's, honors degree, minimum B+ average in at least 6 full courses of English beyond year 1; for doctorate, MA; minimum A- average in two of three courses. Additional exam requirements/recommendations for international students: required—TOEFL (minimum score 580 paper-based).

McNeese State University, Doré School of Graduate Studies, College of Liberal Arts, Department of English and Foreign Languages, Program in Literature, Lake Charles, LA 70609. Offers MA. *Program availability:* Evening/weekend. *Degree requirements:* For master's, one foreign language, thesis or alternative. *Entrance requirements:* For master's, GRE.

Memorial University of Newfoundland, School of Graduate Studies, Department of English, St. John's, NL A1C 5S7, Canada. Offers MA, PhD. *Program availability:* Part-time. *Degree requirements:* For master's, thesis optional; for doctorate, one foreign language, comprehensive exam, thesis/dissertation, oral thesis defense, minimum 3 semesters of full-time study. *Entrance requirements:* For master's, honors degree. Electronic applications accepted.

Mercy College, School of Liberal Arts, Program in English Literature, Dobbs Ferry, NY 10522-1189. Offers MA. *Program availability:* Part-time, evening/weekend, 100% online, blended/hybrid learning. *Students:* 3 full-time (all women), 53 part-time (39 women); includes 20 minority (8 Black or African American, non-Hispanic/Latino; 2 Asian, non-Hispanic/Latino; 8 Hispanic/Latino; 2 Two or more races, non-Hispanic/Latino). Average age 36. 20 applicants, 60% accepted, 8 enrolled. In 2019, 19 master's awarded. *Degree requirements:* For master's, comprehensive exam, thesis. *Entrance requirements:* For master's, transcript(s); two letters of reference; essay or scholarly paper. Additional exam requirements/recommendations for international students: required—TOEFL (minimum score 80 iBT), IELTS (minimum score 6.5). *Application deadline:* Applications are processed on a rolling basis. Application fee: $40. Electronic applications accepted. *Expenses: Tuition:* Full-time $16,146; part-time $897 per credit. *Required fees:* $332; $166 per semester. Tuition and fees vary according to course load and program. *Financial support:* Career-related internships or fieldwork, Federal Work-Study, scholarships/grants, and unspecified assistantships available. Support available to part-time students. Financial award applicants required to submit FAFSA. *Unit head:* Dr. Peter West, Dean, School of Liberal Arts, 914-674-3033, Fax: 914-674-7518, E-mail: pwest@mercy.edu. *Application contact:* Allison Gurdineer, Executive Director of Admissions, 877-637-2946, Fax: 914-674-7382, E-mail: admissions@mercy.edu.
Website: https://www.mercy.edu/degrees-programs/ma-english-literature

Miami University, College of Arts and Science, Department of English, Oxford, OH 45056. Offers MA, MAT, PhD.

Michigan State University, The Graduate School, College of Arts and Letters, Department of English, East Lansing, MI 48824. Offers English (PhD); literature in English (MA). *Entrance requirements:* For master's, GRE General Test, minimum GPA of 3.25, 2 years of foreign language or American Sign Language study, 3 letters of recommendation; for doctorate, GRE General Test, master's degree in English, 2 years of foreign language study, 3 letters of recommendation. Additional exam requirements/recommendations for international students: required—TOEFL. Electronic applications accepted.

Middlebury College, Middlebury Bread Loaf School of English, Middlebury, VT 05753. Offers M Litt, MA. *Program availability:* Part-time. *Entrance requirements:* For master's, 2 letters of recommendation; statement of purpose; official transcripts (both undergraduate and graduate); 3-to 10-page writing sample. Electronic applications accepted. *Expenses:* Contact institution.

Middle Tennessee State University, College of Graduate Studies, College of Liberal Arts, Department of English, Murfreesboro, TN 37132. Offers MA, PhD. *Program availability:* Part-time, evening/weekend, online learning. *Degree requirements:* For master's, one foreign language, comprehensive exam, thesis optional; for doctorate, one foreign language, comprehensive exam, thesis/dissertation. *Entrance requirements:* For master's and doctorate, GRE. Additional exam requirements/recommendations for international students: required—TOEFL (minimum score 525 paper-based; 71 iBT) or IELTS (minimum score 6). Electronic applications accepted.

Midwestern State University, Billie Doris McAda Graduate School, Prothro-Yeager College of Humanities and Social Sciences, Department of English, Humanities, and Philosophy, Wichita Falls, TX 76308. Offers English (MA); philosophy (PhD). *Program availability:* Part-time, evening/weekend. *Degree requirements:* For master's, one foreign language, thesis optional. *Entrance requirements:* For master's, GRE General Test, MAT or GMAT. Additional exam requirements/recommendations for international students: required—TOEFL (minimum score 550 paper-based). Electronic applications accepted.

Millersville University of Pennsylvania, College of Graduate Studies and Adult Learning, College of Arts, Humanities and Social Sciences, Department of English, Millersville, PA 17551-0302. Offers English (M Ed, MA); writing (Postbaccalaureate Certificate). *Program availability:* Part-time, 100% online, blended/hybrid learning. The MA, MED, and Graduate Certificate in Writing can be completed online, blended, and a combination of online and face-to-face courses. Program includes Winter and Summer course options. *Faculty:* 9 full-time (6 women). *Students:* 5 full-time (3 women), 15 part-time (11 women); includes 3 minority (1 Asian, non-Hispanic/Latino; 2 Hispanic/Latino). Average age 33. 10 applicants, 100% accepted, 5 enrolled. In 2019, 10 master's awarded. *Degree requirements:* For master's, thesis (for some programs), Literary Theory, English studies, courses selected in coordination with advisory. *Entrance requirements:* For master's, Sample scholarly work (an 8-15 page critical or research paper recently prepared). Additional exam requirements/recommendations for international students: required—TOEFL, IELTS (minimum score 6), PTE (minimum score 60). *Application deadline:* Applications are processed on a rolling basis. Application fee: $40. Electronic applications accepted. *Expenses: Tuition, area resident:* Part-time $516 per credit. Tuition, state resident: part-time $516 per credit. Tuition, nonresident: part-time $774 per credit. *Required fees:* $118.75 per credit. Tuition and fees vary according to course load, degree level and program. *Financial support:* In 2019–20, 6 students received support. Scholarships/grants and unspecified assistantships available. Financial award application deadline: 3/15; financial award applicants required to submit FAFSA. *Unit head:* Dr. Kim McCollum-Clark, Chair, 717-871-4280, Fax: 717-871-7933, E-mail: Kimbery.McCollum-Clark@millersville.edu. *Application contact:* Dr. James A. Delle, Acting Dean of College of Graduate Studies and Adult Learning/Associate Provost, Academic Administration, 717-871-7462, E-mail: James.Delle@millersville.edu.
Website: http://www.millersville.edu/english/graduate/index.php

Mills College, Graduate Studies, Department of English, Oakland, CA 94613-1000. Offers book art and creative writing (MFA); literature (MA); poetry (MFA); prose (MFA); Spanish creative writing (Certificate); translation (MFA). *Program availability:* Part-time. *Degree requirements:* For master's, comprehensive exam, thesis. *Entrance requirements:* For master's, 15-20 page writing sample. Additional exam requirements/recommendations for international students: required—TOEFL (minimum score 600 paper-based; 100 iBT), IELTS (minimum score 7). Electronic applications accepted. *Expenses:* Contact institution.

Minnesota State University Mankato, College of Graduate Studies and Research, College of Arts and Humanities, Department of English, Mankato, MN 56001. Offers communication and composition (MA); creative writing (MFA); English studies (MA); teaching English as a second language (MA, Certificate); technical communication (MA, Certificate). *Program availability:* Part-time. *Degree requirements:* For master's, one foreign language, comprehensive exam, thesis or alternative. *Entrance requirements:* For master's, minimum GPA of 3.0 during previous 2 years, writing sample (MFA). Additional exam requirements/recommendations for international students: required—TOEFL (minimum score 500 paper-based; 61 iBT). Electronic applications accepted.

Mississippi College, Graduate School, College of Arts and Sciences, School of Humanities and Social Sciences, Department of English, Clinton, MS 39058. Offers M Ed, MA. *Program availability:* Part-time, evening/weekend. *Degree requirements:* For master's, one foreign language, comprehensive exam, thesis or alternative. *Entrance requirements:* For master's, GRE or NTE, minimum GPA of 2.5. Additional exam requirements/recommendations for international students: recommended—TOEFL, IELTS. Electronic applications accepted.

Mississippi State University, College of Arts and Sciences, Department of English, Mississippi State, MS 39762. Offers MA. *Program availability:* Part-time. *Faculty:* 24 full-time (14 women), 1 part-time/adjunct (0 women). *Students:* 22 full-time (16 women), 3 part-time (1 woman); includes 3 minority (2 Black or African American, non-Hispanic/Latino; 1 Hispanic/Latino), 2 international. Average age 26. 20 applicants, 75% accepted, 13 enrolled. In 2019, 7 master's awarded. *Degree requirements:* For master's, thesis optional, comprehensive oral or written exam. *Entrance requirements:* For master's, GRE General Test, minimum GPA of 2.75 on last two years of undergraduate courses. Additional exam requirements/recommendations for international students: required—TOEFL (minimum score 625 paper-based; 106 iBT); recommended—IELTS (minimum score 8). *Application deadline:* For fall admission, 7/1 for domestic students, 5/1 for international students; for spring admission, 11/1 for domestic students, 9/1 for international students. Applications are processed on a rolling basis. Application fee: $60 ($80 for international students). Electronic applications accepted. *Expenses: Tuition, area resident:* Full-time $8880; part-time $456 per credit hour. Tuition, state resident: full-time $8880. Tuition, nonresident: full-time $23,840; part-time $1236 per credit hour. *Required fees:* $110; $11.12 per credit hour. Tuition and fees vary according to course load. *Financial support:* In 2019–20, 19 teaching assistantships with partial tuition reimbursements (averaging $10,000 per year) were awarded; Federal Work-Study, institutionally sponsored loans, scholarships/grants, and unspecified assistantships also available. Financial award application deadline: 4/1; financial award applicants required to submit FAFSA. *Unit head:* Dr. Daniel Punday, Professor and Head, 662-325-3644, Fax: 662-325-3645, E-mail: dp1525@msstate.edu. *Application contact:* Robbie Salters, Admissions and Enrollment Management Assistant and Coordinator, 662-325-5188, E-mail: rsalters@grad.msstate.edu.
Website: http://www.english.msstate.edu

Missouri State University, Graduate College, College of Arts and Letters, Department of English, Springfield, MO 65897. Offers applied second language acquisition (MASLA); English (MA); English education (MS Ed); teaching English to speakers of other languages (Certificate); writing (MA). *Program availability:* Part-time, evening/weekend. *Degree requirements:* For master's, one foreign language, comprehensive exam, thesis or alternative. *Entrance requirements:* For master's, GRE (for MA), 9-12 teacher certification (MS Ed); minimum GPA of 3.0 (MA); personal statement (200- to 250-word description of reasons and goals behind interest in English graduate studies); at least two letters of recommendation from individuals able to speak of the applicant's academic achievements and potential; writing sample. Additional exam requirements/

recommendations for international students: required—TOEFL (minimum score 550 paper-based; 79 iBT), IELTS (minimum score 6). Electronic applications accepted. *Expenses: Tuition, area resident:* Full-time $2600; part-time $1735 per credit hour. Tuition, nonresident: full-time $5240; part-time $3495 per credit hour. *International tuition:* $5240 full-time. *Required fees:* $530; $438 per credit hour. Tuition and fees vary according to class time, course level, course load, degree level, campus/location and program.

Monmouth University, Graduate Studies, Department of English, West Long Branch, NJ 07764-1898. Offers creative writing (MA); literature (MA); rhetoric and writing (MA). *Program availability:* Part-time, evening/weekend. *Faculty:* 7 full-time (5 women). *Students:* 7 full-time (4 women), 34 part-time (22 women); includes 3 minority (2 Hispanic/Latino; 1 Two or more races, non-Hispanic/Latino). Average age 32. In 2019, 14 master's awarded. *Degree requirements:* For master's, comprehensive exam (for some programs), thesis. *Entrance requirements:* For master's, minimum overall GPA of 2.75, fifteen or more credits in literature or related field, essay of 1000 words describing interest and goals, two letters of recommendation, creative writing sample. Additional exam requirements/recommendations for international students: required—TOEFL (minimum score 550 paper-based, 79 iBT), IELTS (minimum score 6), Michigan English Language Assessment Battery (minimum score 77) or Certificate of Advanced English (minimum score of 160). *Application deadline:* For fall admission, 7/15 for domestic students, 6/1 for international students; for spring admission, 12/1 for domestic students, 11/1 for international students; for summer admission, 5/1 for domestic students. Applications are processed on a rolling basis. Application fee: $50. Electronic applications accepted. *Expenses: Tuition:* Full-time $22,194; part-time $14,796 per credit. *Required fees:* $712; $178 per semester. $178 per semester. Tuition and fees vary according to course load. *Financial support:* In 2019–20, 37 students received support. Research assistantships, teaching assistantships, scholarships/grants, and unspecified assistantships available. Support available to part-time students. Financial award applicants required to submit FAFSA. *Unit head:* Dr. Mary Kate Azcuy, Program Director, 732-571-3439, Fax: 732-263-5242, E-mail: mazcuy@monmouth.edu. *Application contact:* Kevin New, Graduate Admission Counselor, 732-571-3452, Fax: 732-263-5123, E-mail: gradadm@monmouth.edu.
Website: https://www.monmouth.edu/graduate/ma-english/

Montana State University, The Graduate School, College of Letters and Science, Department of English, Bozeman, MT 59717. Offers MA. *Program availability:* Part-time. *Degree requirements:* For master's, comprehensive exam. *Entrance requirements:* For master's, GRE General Test, minimum GPA of 3.0, 3 recommendations. Additional exam requirements/recommendations for international students: required—TOEFL (minimum score 550 paper-based). Electronic applications accepted.

Montclair State University, The Graduate School, College of Humanities and Social Sciences, Program in English, Montclair, NJ 07043-1624. Offers MA. *Program availability:* Part-time, evening/weekend. *Degree requirements:* For master's, thesis. *Entrance requirements:* For master's, GRE General Test, 2 letters of recommendation, essay. Additional exam requirements/recommendations for international students: required—TOEFL (minimum score 83 iBT), IELTS (minimum score 6.5). Electronic applications accepted.

Morgan State University, School of Graduate Studies, James H. Gilliam Jr College of Liberal Arts, Department of English, Baltimore, MD 21251. Offers MA, PhD. *Program availability:* Part-time, evening/weekend. *Faculty:* 34 full-time (18 women), 4 part-time/adjunct (2 women). *Students:* 29 full-time (22 women), 5 part-time (all women); includes 23 minority (19 Black or African American, non-Hispanic/Latino; 1 Hispanic/Latino; 3 Two or more races, non-Hispanic/Latino), 4 international. Average age 41. 11 applicants, 64% accepted, 2 enrolled. In 2019, 1 master's awarded. *Degree requirements:* For master's, comprehensive exam, thesis; for doctorate, comprehensive exam, thesis/dissertation. *Entrance requirements:* For master's, GRE, minimum GPA of 2.5; for doctorate, GRE, minimum GPA of 3.0. Additional exam requirements/recommendations for international students: required—TOEFL (minimum score 550 paper-based), IELTS (minimum score 6). *Application deadline:* For fall admission, 2/1 priority date for domestic students, 4/1 for international students; for spring admission, 11/15 for domestic students, 10/1 for international students. Applications are processed on a rolling basis. Application fee: $50 ($70 for international students). Electronic applications accepted. *Expenses:* Tuition, state resident: full-time $455; part-time $455 per credit hour. Tuition, nonresident: full-time $894; part-time $894 per credit hour. *Required fees:* $82; $82 per credit hour. *Financial support:* In 2019–20, 13 students received support. Fellowships with full and partial tuition reimbursements available, research assistantships with full and partial tuition reimbursements available, teaching assistantships with full and partial tuition reimbursements available, career-related internships or fieldwork, Federal Work-Study, scholarships/grants, tuition waivers (full and partial), and unspecified assistantships available. Support available to part-time students. Financial award application deadline: 2/1. *Unit head:* Dr. Jules White, Chair, 443-885-3165, Fax: 443-885-8225, E-mail: judy.white@morgan.edu. *Application contact:* Dr. Jahmaine Smith, Director of Admissions, 443-885-3185, Fax: 443-885-8226, E-mail: gradapply@morgan.edu.
Website: https://morgan.edu/cla/english

Mount Mary University, Graduate Programs, Program in English, Milwaukee, WI 53222-4597. Offers creative writing (MA); professional and new media writing (MA). *Program availability:* Part-time, evening/weekend. *Degree requirements:* For master's, comprehensive exam, thesis or alternative. *Entrance requirements:* For master's, minimum GPA of 2.75. Additional exam requirements/recommendations for international students: required—TOEFL (minimum score 550 paper-based; 80 iBT); recommended—IELTS (minimum score 6.5). Electronic applications accepted. *Expenses:* Contact institution.

Mount Saint Mary's University, Graduate Division, Los Angeles, CA 90049. Offers business administration (MBA); counseling psychology (MS); creative writing (MFA); education (MS, Certificate); film and television (MFA); health policy and management (MS); humanities (MA); nursing (MSN, Certificate); physical therapy (DPT); religious studies (MA). *Program availability:* Part-time, evening/weekend. *Entrance requirements:* Additional exam requirements/recommendations for international students: required—TOEFL. Electronic applications accepted. *Expenses: Tuition:* Full-time $18,648; part-time $9324 per year. *Required fees:* $540; $540 per unit.

Murray State University, College of Humanities and Fine Arts, Department of English and Philosophy, Murray, KY 42071. Offers creative writing (MFA); English (MA); English pedagogy and technology (DA); gender studies (Certificate); teaching English to speakers of other languages (TESOL) (MA). *Program availability:* Part-time, 100% online, blended/hybrid learning. *Entrance requirements:* For master's, doctorate, and Certificate, GRE or GMAT, minimum university GPA of 2.75. Additional exam requirements/recommendations for international students: required—TOEFL (minimum score 527 paper-based; 71 iBT). Electronic applications accepted.

National University, College of Letters and Sciences, La Jolla, CA 92037-1011. Offers biology (MS); counseling psychology (MA), including licensed professional clinical counseling, marriage and family therapy; creative writing (MFA); English (MA); film studies (MA); forensic and crime scene investigations (Certificate); forensic sciences (MFS); human behavior (MA); mathematics for educators (MS); performance psychology (MA); strategic communications (MA). *Program availability:* Part-time, evening/weekend, 100% online, blended/hybrid learning. *Degree requirements:* For master's, thesis (for some programs). *Entrance requirements:* For master's, interview, minimum GPA of 2.5. Additional exam requirements/recommendations for international students: required—TOEFL (minimum score 550 paper-based; 79 iBT), IELTS (minimum score 6). Electronic applications accepted. *Expenses: Tuition:* Full-time $442; part-time $442 per unit.

New Mexico Highlands University, Graduate Studies, College of Arts and Sciences, Department of English, Las Vegas, NM 87701. Offers English (MA), including creative writing, language, rhetoric and composition, literature. *Degree requirements:* For master's, comprehensive exam, thesis. *Entrance requirements:* For master's, minimum undergraduate GPA of 3.0. Additional exam requirements/recommendations for international students: required—TOEFL (minimum score 540 paper-based).

New Mexico State University, College of Arts and Sciences, Department of English, Las Cruces, NM 88003-8001. Offers creative writing (MFA); English (MA), including creative writing, English studies for teachers, literature, rhetoric and professional communication; rhetoric and professional communication (PhD). *Program availability:* Part-time. *Faculty:* 17 full-time (7 women), 1 (woman) part-time/adjunct. *Students:* 43 full-time (28 women), 16 part-time (10 women); includes 25 minority (3 Black or African American, non-Hispanic/Latino; 1 Asian, non-Hispanic/Latino; 20 Hispanic/Latino; 1 Two or more races, non-Hispanic/Latino), 6 international. Average age 35. 46 applicants, 57% accepted, 14 enrolled. In 2019, 16 master's, 4 doctorates awarded. *Degree requirements:* For master's, one foreign language, thesis (for some programs); for doctorate, comprehensive exam, thesis/dissertation, internship. *Entrance requirements:* For master's and doctorate, sample of written work. Additional exam requirements/recommendations for international students: required—TOEFL (minimum score 550 paper-based; 79 iBT), IELTS (minimum score 6.5). *Application deadline:* For fall admission, 2/1 for domestic and international students. Application fee: $40 ($50 for international students). Electronic applications accepted. *Financial support:* In 2019–20, 46 students received support, including 5 fellowships (averaging $4,844 per year), 40 teaching assistantships (averaging $18,521 per year); career-related internships or fieldwork, Federal Work-Study, scholarships/grants, traineeships, health care benefits, and unspecified assistantships also available. Support available to part-time students. Financial award application deadline: 3/1. *Unit head:* Dr. Elizabeth Schirmer, Interim Department Head, 575-646-3931, Fax: 575-646-7725, E-mail: eschirme@nmsu.edu. *Application contact:* Dr. Tracey Eileen Miller-Tomlinson, Director of Graduate Studies, 575-646-2213, Fax: 575-646-7725, E-mail: tomlin@nmsu.edu.
Website: http://english.nmsu.edu

New York University, Graduate School of Arts and Science, Program in English and American Literature, New York, NY 10012-1019. Offers MA, PhD. *Degree requirements:* For master's, one foreign language, thesis or alternative, qualifying exams, special project; for doctorate, one foreign language, thesis/dissertation. *Entrance requirements:* For master's, GRE General Test; GRE Subject Test in English (recommended). Additional exam requirements/recommendations for international students: required—TOEFL, IELTS.

North Carolina Agricultural and Technical State University, The Graduate College, College of Arts, Humanities, and Social Sciences, Department of English, Greensboro, NC 27411. Offers English and African-American literature (MA); English education (MAT). *Program availability:* Part-time, evening/weekend. *Degree requirements:* For master's, comprehensive exam, qualifying exam. *Entrance requirements:* For master's, GRE General Test, minimum GPA of 3.0.

North Carolina Central University, College of Arts and Sciences, Department of Language and Literature, Durham, NC 27707-3129. Offers English (MA). *Program availability:* Part-time, evening/weekend. *Degree requirements:* For master's, one foreign language, comprehensive exam, thesis. *Entrance requirements:* For master's, GRE, minimum GPA of 3.0 in major, 2.5 overall. Additional exam requirements/recommendations for international students: required—TOEFL.

North Carolina State University, Graduate School, College of Humanities and Social Sciences, Department of English, Program in English, Raleigh, NC 27695. Offers MA. *Entrance requirements:* For master's, GRE General Test. Electronic applications accepted.

North Dakota State University, College of Graduate and Interdisciplinary Studies, College of Arts, Humanities and Social Sciences, Department of English, Fargo, ND 58102. Offers composition (MA); rhetoric, writing and culture (PhD). *Program availability:* Part-time. *Degree requirements:* For master's, one foreign language, thesis. *Entrance requirements:* Additional exam requirements/recommendations for international students: required—TOEFL (minimum score 600 paper-based; 100 iBT), IELTS (minimum score 7). Electronic applications accepted. Tuition and fees vary according to program and reciprocity agreements.

Northeastern Illinois University, College of Graduate Studies and Research, College of Arts and Sciences, Programs in English, Chicago, IL 60625. Offers English (MA), including composition, literature. *Program availability:* Part-time, evening/weekend. *Degree requirements:* For master's, comprehensive exam, thesis optional. *Entrance requirements:* For master's, 30 hours of undergraduate course work in literature and composition (literature), BA in English or approval (composition/writing), minimum GPA of 2.75. Additional exam requirements/recommendations for international students: required—TOEFL (minimum score 550 paper-based; 79 iBT). Electronic applications accepted.

Northeastern State University, College of Liberal Arts, Department of Languages and Literature, Tahlequah, OK 74464-2399. Offers English (MA), including literature. *Faculty:* 8 full-time (3 women). *Students:* 5 full-time (4 women), 18 part-time (12 women); includes 6 minority (3 American Indian or Alaska Native, non-Hispanic/Latino; 3 Two or more races, non-Hispanic/Latino). Average age 37. In 2019, 9 master's awarded. *Degree requirements:* For master's, thesis. *Entrance requirements:* For master's, GRE or MAT, minimum GPA of 2.5. Additional exam requirements/recommendations for international students: required—TOEFL. *Application deadline:* For fall admission, 6/1 priority date for domestic students. Applications are processed on a rolling basis. Application fee: $25. Electronic applications accepted. *Expenses: Tuition, area resident:* Full-time $250; part-time $250 per credit hour. Tuition, state resident: full-time $250; part-time $250 per credit hour. Tuition, nonresident: full-time $556; part-time $555.50 per credit hour. *Required fees:* $33.40 per credit hour. *Financial support:* Application deadline: 3/1. *Unit head:* Dr. Christopher Flavin, Department Chair, 918-444-3626, E-mail: flavin@nsuok.edu. *Application contact:* Josh McCollum, Graduate Coordinator, 918-444-2093, E-mail: mccolluj@nsuok.edu.
Website: http://academics.nsuok.edu/languagesliterature/DegreePrograms/English,MA.aspx

Northeastern University, College of Social Sciences and Humanities, Boston, MA 02115. Offers criminology and criminal justice (MSCJ); criminology and justice policy (PhD); economics (MA, PhD); English (MA, PhD); international affairs (MA); law and public policy (PhD); political science (MA, PhD); public administration (MPA); public policy (MPP); security and resilience studies (MS); sociology (MA, PhD); urban and regional policy (MS); urban informatics (MS); world history (MA, PhD). *Program availability:* Online learning. *Degree requirements:* For doctorate, variable foreign language requirement, comprehensive exam, thesis/dissertation. *Entrance requirements:* For master's and doctorate, GRE. Additional exam requirements/recommendations for international students: required—TOEFL, IELTS. Electronic applications accepted. *Expenses:* Contact institution.

Northern Arizona University, College of Arts and Letters, Department of English, Flagstaff, AZ 86011. Offers applied linguistics (PhD); creative writing (MFA), including creative writing; English (MA), including literature, professional writing, rhetoric, writing, and digital media studies, secondary education; professional writing (Graduate Certificate); rhetoric, writing and digital media studies (Graduate Certificate); teaching English as a second language (MA, Graduate Certificate). *Program availability:* Part-time, 100% online, blended/hybrid learning. *Degree requirements:* For master's, variable foreign language requirement, comprehensive exam (for some programs), thesis (for some programs); for doctorate, variable foreign language requirement, comprehensive exam (for some programs), thesis/dissertation (for some programs); for Graduate Certificate, comprehensive exam (for some programs). *Entrance requirements:* Additional exam requirements/recommendations for international students: required—TOEFL (minimum score 80 iBT), IELTS (minimum score 6.5). Electronic applications accepted.

Northern Illinois University, Graduate School, College of Liberal Arts and Sciences, Department of English, De Kalb, IL 60115-2854. Offers MA, PhD. *Program availability:* Part-time. *Faculty:* 32 full-time (13 women), 2 part-time/adjunct (both women). *Students:* 21 full-time (15 women), 61 part-time (40 women); includes 12 minority (3 Black or African American, non-Hispanic/Latino; 5 Hispanic/Latino; 4 Two or more races, non-Hispanic/Latino), 2 international. Average age 36. 21 applicants, 76% accepted, 10 enrolled. In 2019, 14 master's, 3 doctorates awarded. Terminal master's awarded for partial completion of doctoral program. *Degree requirements:* For master's, variable foreign language requirement, comprehensive exam, thesis optional; for doctorate, variable foreign language requirement, thesis/dissertation, candidacy exam, dissertation defense. *Entrance requirements:* For master's, GRE General Test, minimum GPA of 2.75; for doctorate, GRE General Test, minimum GPA of 2.75 (undergraduate), 3.2 (graduate). Additional exam requirements/recommendations for international students: required—TOEFL (minimum score 550 paper-based). *Application deadline:* For fall admission, 6/1 for domestic students, 5/1 for international students; for spring admission, 11/1 for domestic students, 10/1 for international students. Applications are processed on a rolling basis. Application fee: $40. Electronic applications accepted. *Financial support:* In 2019–20, 3 research assistantships with full tuition reimbursements, 45 teaching assistantships with full tuition reimbursements were awarded; fellowships with full tuition reimbursements, career-related internships or fieldwork, Federal Work-Study, scholarships/grants, tuition waivers (full), and unspecified assistantships also available. Support available to part-time students. Financial award applicants required to submit FAFSA. *Unit head:* Dr. Lara Crowley, Chair, 815-753-0615, Fax: 815-753-0606. *Application contact:* Graduate School Office, 815-753-0395, E-mail: gradsch@niu.edu. Website: http://www.engl.niu.edu/

Northern Kentucky University, Office of Graduate Programs, College of Arts and Sciences, Program in English, Highland Heights, KY 41099. Offers composition and rhetoric (Certificate); creative writing (Certificate); cultural studies and discourses (Certificate); English (MA); professional writing (Certificate). *Program availability:* Part-time, evening/weekend. *Degree requirements:* For master's, comprehensive exam (for some programs), capstone (thesis, portfolio, project, or exams); 30 hours of credit; for Certificate, 18 hours of credit. *Entrance requirements:* For master's, bachelor's degree in English or related field from regionally-accredited institution with minimum GPA of 3.0 in major or cognate area coursework; official transcripts for all undergraduate and graduate work; two letters of reference; for Certificate, official transcripts for all undergraduate and graduate work; bachelor's degree from regionally-accredited institution; minimum undergraduate GPA of 2.5. Additional exam requirements/recommendations for international students: required—TOEFL (minimum score 79 iBT); recommended—IELTS (minimum score 6.5). Electronic applications accepted.

Northern Michigan University, Office of Graduate Education and Research, College of Arts and Sciences, Department of English, Marquette, MI 49855-5301. Offers creative writing (MFA); literature (MA); pedagogy (MA); teaching English to speakers of other languages (Graduate Certificate); theater (MA); writing (MA). *Program availability:* Part-time. *Degree requirements:* For master's, thesis (for some programs), capstone project: thesis, practicum or portfolio (for MA); thesis (for MFA). *Entrance requirements:* For master's, minimum GPA of 3.0; bachelor's degree in English or minimum of 30 credit hours in undergraduate English; statement of purpose; resume; critical essay; creative writing sample (for MFA); 3 letters of recommendation; for Graduate Certificate, bachelor's degree. Additional exam requirements/recommendations for international students: required—TOEFL (minimum score 500 paper-based; 61 iBT), IELTS (minimum score 6). *Application deadline:* For fall admission, 2/1 for domestic students; for winter admission, 2/1 for domestic students; for summer admission, 3/17 for domestic students. Applications are processed on a rolling basis. Application fee: $50. Electronic applications accepted. *Financial support:* Teaching assistantships, career-related internships or fieldwork, scholarships/grants, and unspecified assistantships available. Financial award application deadline: 3/1; financial award applicants required to submit FAFSA. *Unit head:* Dr. Lynn Domina, Department Head and Professor, 906-227-1759, E-mail: ldomina@nmu.edu. *Application contact:* Dr. Lesley Larkin, Director of MA Program and Professor, 906-227-1794, E-mail: llarkin@nmu.edu. Website: http://www.nmu.edu/english/

Northwestern State University of Louisiana, Graduate Studies and Research, Department of Language and Communication, Natchitoches, LA 71497. Offers English (MA). *Degree requirements:* For master's, one foreign language, comprehensive exam, thesis or alternative. *Entrance requirements:* For master's, GRE General Test, minimum undergraduate GPA of 2.5. Additional exam requirements/recommendations for international students: required—TOEFL. Electronic applications accepted.

Northwestern University, The Graduate School, Judd A. and Marjorie Weinberg College of Arts and Sciences, Department of English, Evanston, IL 60208. Offers MA, PhD. Terminal master's awarded for partial completion of doctoral program. *Degree requirements:* For master's, thesis; for doctorate, one foreign language, thesis/dissertation, oral and written qualifying exam. *Entrance requirements:* For master's and doctorate, GRE General Test, sample of written work. Additional exam requirements/recommendations for international students: required—TOEFL. Electronic applications accepted.

Northwestern University, School of Professional Studies, Program in Literature, Evanston, IL 60208. Offers American literature (MA); British literature (MA); comparative and world literature (MA). *Program availability:* Part-time, evening/weekend.

Northwest Missouri State University, Graduate School, College of Arts and Sciences, Maryville, MO 64468-6001. Offers biology (MS); elementary mathematics specialist (MS Ed); English (MA); English education (MS Ed); English pedagogy (MA); geographic information science (MS, Certificate); history (MS Ed); mathematics (MS); mathematics

education (MS Ed); teaching: science (MS Ed). *Program availability:* Part-time. *Faculty:* 18 full-time (8 women). *Students:* 10 full-time (5 women), 47 part-time (23 women); includes 6 minority (2 American Indian or Alaska Native, non-Hispanic/Latino; 1 Asian, non-Hispanic/Latino; 1 Hispanic/Latino; 1 Native Hawaiian or other Pacific Islander, non-Hispanic/Latino; 1 Two or more races, non-Hispanic/Latino), 1 international. Average age 31. 17 applicants, 65% accepted, 9 enrolled. In 2019, 25 master's, 6 other advanced degrees awarded. *Degree requirements:* For master's, comprehensive exam. *Entrance requirements:* For master's, GRE General Test, writing sample. Additional exam requirements/recommendations for international students: required—TOEFL (minimum score 550 paper-based; 79 iBT). *Application deadline:* For fall admission, 7/1 for domestic and international students; for spring admission, 11/15 for domestic and international students. Applications are processed on a rolling basis. Application fee: $0 ($75 for international students). Electronic applications accepted. *Expenses:* Contact institution. *Financial support:* Research assistantships with full tuition reimbursements, teaching assistantships with full tuition reimbursements, and administrative assistantships, tutorial assistantships available. Financial award application deadline: 4/1; financial award applicants required to submit FAFSA. *Unit head:* Dr. Michael Steiner, Associate Provost-UG Studies & Dean, 660-562-1197. *Application contact:* Dr. Michael Steiner, Associate Provost-UG Studies & Dean, 660-562-1197. Website: https://www.nwmissouri.edu/academics/departments.htm

Oakland University, Graduate Study and Lifelong Learning, College of Arts and Sciences, Department of English, Rochester, MI 48309-4401. Offers MA. *Program availability:* Part-time. *Entrance requirements:* For master's, minimum GPA of 3.0. Additional exam requirements/recommendations for international students: required—TOEFL (minimum score 550 paper-based; 79 iBT), IELTS (minimum score 6.5). Electronic applications accepted. *Expenses: Tuition, area resident:* Full-time $12,328; part-time $770.50 per credit hour. *Tuition, state resident:* Full-time $12,328; part-time $770.50 per credit hour. *Tuition, nonresident:* full-time $16,432; part-time $1027 per credit hour. *International tuition:* $16,432 full-time. Tuition and fees vary according to degree level and program.

Ohio Dominican University, Division of Arts and Letters, Program in English, Columbus, OH 43219-2099. Offers MA. *Program availability:* Part-time, evening/weekend, online only, 100% online. *Faculty:* 4 full-time (2 women). *Students:* 1 full-time (0 women), 38 part-time (28 women). Average age 38. 8 applicants, 100% accepted, 7 enrolled. In 2019, 11 master's awarded. *Degree requirements:* For master's, thesis or alternative. *Entrance requirements:* For master's, minimum undergraduate GPA of 3.0, 3 letters of recommendation, transcripts. Additional exam requirements/recommendations for international students: required—TOEFL (minimum score 550 paper-based), IELTS (minimum score 6.5). *Application deadline:* For fall admission, 8/15 for domestic students, 6/10 for international students; for spring admission, 1/4 for domestic students, 11/2 for international students; for summer admission, 5/30 for domestic students. Applications are processed on a rolling basis. Application fee: $25. Electronic applications accepted. *Expenses: Tuition:* Full-time $10,800; part-time $600 per credit hour. *Required fees:* $225 per semester. Tuition and fees vary according to program. *Financial support:* Applicants required to submit FAFSA. *Unit head:* Dr. Martin Brick, Director, 614-251-4519, E-mail: brickm@ohiodominican.edu. *Application contact:* John W. Naughton, Vice President for Enrollment and Student Success, 614-251-4721, Fax: 614-251-6654, E-mail: grad@ohiodominican.edu. Website: http://www.ohiodominican.edu/academics/graduate/ma-in-english

The Ohio State University, Graduate School, College of Arts and Sciences, Division of Arts and Humanities, Department of English, Columbus, OH 43210. Offers MA, MFA, PhD. *Degree requirements:* For master's, one foreign language, thesis or written exam; for doctorate, one foreign language, thesis/dissertation. *Entrance requirements:* For master's and doctorate, GRE General Test. Additional exam requirements/recommendations for international students: required—TOEFL (minimum score 600 paper-based; 100 iBT), IELTS (minimum score 8), Michigan English Language Assessment Battery (minimum score 86). Electronic applications accepted.

Ohio University, Graduate College, College of Arts and Sciences, Department of English Language and Literature, Athens, OH 45701-2979. Offers MA, PhD. *Program availability:* Part-time. *Degree requirements:* For master's, one foreign language, thesis or alternative; for doctorate, one foreign language, comprehensive exam, thesis/dissertation, oral exam, public lecture. *Entrance requirements:* For master's, GRE General Test, minimum GPA of 3.0, writing sample; for doctorate, GRE General Test, minimum GPA of 3.0, master's degree in English, writing sample. Additional exam requirements/recommendations for international students: required—TOEFL (minimum score 550 paper-based; 80 iBT) or IELTS (minimum score 6.5). Electronic applications accepted.

Oklahoma State University, College of Arts and Sciences, Department of English, Stillwater, OK 74078. Offers creative writing (MFA); English (MA, PhD). *Faculty:* 31 full-time (18 women), 4 part-time/adjunct (all women). *Students:* 6 full-time (5 women), 108 part-time (59 women); includes 12 minority (2 Black or African American, non-Hispanic/Latino; 1 American Indian or Alaska Native, non-Hispanic/Latino; 2 Asian, non-Hispanic/Latino; 2 Hispanic/Latino; 5 Two or more races, non-Hispanic/Latino), 21 international. Average age 33. 79 applicants, 51% accepted, 21 enrolled. In 2019, 11 master's, 9 doctorates awarded. *Entrance requirements:* For master's, GRE General Test, minimum GPA of 3.0, writing sample; for doctorate, GRE General Test, minimum GPA of 3.5, writing sample. Additional exam requirements/recommendations for international students: required—TOEFL (minimum score 550 paper-based; 79 iBT). *Application deadline:* For fall admission, 3/1 priority date for international students; for spring admission, 8/1 priority date for international students. Applications are processed on a rolling basis. Application fee: $50 ($75 for international students). Electronic applications accepted. *Expenses: Tuition, area resident:* Full-time $4148.10; part-time $2765.40 per credit hour. *Tuition, state resident:* full-time $4148.10; part-time $2765.40 per credit hour. *Tuition, nonresident:* full-time $15,775; part-time $10,516.80 per credit hour. *International tuition:* $15,775.20 full-time. *Required fees:* $2196.90; $122.05 per credit hour. Tuition and fees vary according to course load, campus/location and program. *Financial support:* In 2019–20, 3 research assistantships (averaging $1,055 per year), 97 teaching assistantships (averaging $1,603 per year) were awarded; career-related internships or fieldwork, Federal Work-Study, scholarships/grants, health care benefits, tuition waivers (partial), and unspecified assistantships also available. Support available to part-time students. Financial award application deadline: 3/1; financial award applicants required to submit FAFSA. *Unit head:* Dr. An Cheng, Department Head, 405-744-9474, Fax: 405-744-6326, E-mail: an.cheng@okstate.edu. *Application contact:* Dr. Sheryl Tucker, Dean, 405-744-6368, Fax: 405-744-0355, E-mail: gradi@okstate.edu. Website: http://english.okstate.edu/

Old Dominion University, College of Arts and Letters, Doctoral Program in English, Norfolk, VA 23529. Offers PhD. *Program availability:* Part-time, evening/weekend, online learning. *Degree requirements:* For doctorate, comprehensive exam, thesis/dissertation, research competency in foreign language, statistics, or new media. *Entrance requirements:* For doctorate, GRE General Test, MA in English or related field with minimum GPA of 3.5, writing sample, resume, goals statement, letter of recommendation. Additional exam requirements/recommendations for international students: required—TOEFL; recommended—IELTS. Electronic applications accepted.

English

Old Dominion University, College of Arts and Letters, Master of Arts in English Program, Norfolk, VA 23529. Offers literature (MA); professional writing (MA); rhetoric and composition (MA). *Program availability:* Part-time, evening/weekend. Terminal master's awarded for partial completion of doctoral program. *Degree requirements:* For master's, comprehensive exam, thesis optional. *Entrance requirements:* For master's, GRE General Test, 24 hours in English, sample of written work, BA. Additional exam requirements/recommendations for international students: required—TOEFL. Electronic applications accepted.

Old Dominion University, Darden College of Education, Programs in Secondary Education, Norfolk, VA 23529. Offers chemistry (MS Ed); English (MS Ed); secondary education (MS Ed). *Accreditation:* NCATE. *Program availability:* Part-time, evening/weekend, online learning. *Degree requirements:* For master's, comprehensive exam, thesis. *Entrance requirements:* For master's, GRE General Test or MAT, PRAXIS I (for licensure), minimum GPA of 2.8, teaching certificate. Additional exam requirements/recommendations for international students: required—TOEFL. Electronic applications accepted.

Oregon State University, College of Liberal Arts, Program in English, Corvallis, OR 97331. Offers film and visual studies (MA); literature and culture (MA); rhetoric, writing and composition (MA). *Program availability:* Part-time. *Entrance requirements:* For master's, GRE (recommended). Additional exam requirements/recommendations for international students: required—TOEFL (minimum score 80 iBT), IELTS (minimum score 6.5).

Our Lady of the Lake University, College of Arts and Sciences, Programs in English, San Antonio, TX 78207-4689. Offers literature, creative writing, and social justice (MA); MA/MFA. *Program availability:* Part-time, evening/weekend. *Degree requirements:* For master's, comprehensive exam, thesis optional. *Entrance requirements:* For master's, GRE General Test or MAT taken within the last 5 years, bachelor's degree with at least 18 hours of advanced course work in English and/or communication arts with minimum cumulative GPA of 2.5; 2 letters of recommendation; samples of creative and scholarly writing (25 pages total); personal statement. Additional exam requirements/recommendations for international students: required—TOEFL. Electronic applications accepted. Application fee is waived when completed online.

Pace University, School of Education, New York, NY 10038. Offers adolescent education (MST), including biology, chemistry, earth science, English, foreign languages, mathematics, physics, social studies; childhood education (MST); early childhood development, learning and intervention (MST); educational technology studies (MS); inclusive adolescent education (MST), including biology, chemistry, earth science, English, foreign languages, mathematics, physics, social studies; integrated instruction for educational technology (Certificate); integrated instruction for literacy and technology (Certificate); literacy (MS Ed); special education (MS Ed). *Accreditation:* NCATE. *Program availability:* Part-time, evening/weekend, 100% online, blended/hybrid learning. *Degree requirements:* For master's and Certificate, certification exams. *Entrance requirements:* For master's, GRE (for initial certification programs only), teaching certificate (for MS Ed in literacy and special education programs only). Additional exam requirements/recommendations for international students: required—TOEFL (minimum score 88 iBT), IELTS or PTE. Electronic applications accepted. *Expenses:* Contact institution.

Penn State University Park, Graduate School, College of the Liberal Arts, Department of English, University Park, PA 16802. Offers MA, MFA, PhD.

Pittsburg State University, Graduate School, College of Arts and Sciences, Department of English and Modern Languages, Pittsburg, KS 66762. Offers English (MA), including creative writing, literature, professional writing. *Program availability:* Part-time. *Degree requirements:* For master's, thesis or alternative. *Entrance requirements:* Additional exam requirements/recommendations for international students: required—TOEFL (minimum score 550 paper-based; 79 iBT), IELTS (minimum score 6.5), PTE (minimum score 53). Electronic applications accepted. *Expenses:* Contact institution.

Portland State University, Graduate Studies, College of Liberal Arts and Sciences, Department of English, Portland, OR 97207-0751. Offers creative writing (MFA); English (MA); MA/MS. *Program availability:* Part-time, evening/weekend. *Faculty:* 33 full-time (19 women), 31 part-time/adjunct (14 women). *Students:* 82 full-time (55 women), 42 part-time (20 women); includes 22 minority (1 Black or African American, non-Hispanic/Latino; 3 Asian, non-Hispanic/Latino; 12 Hispanic/Latino; 6 Two or more races, non-Hispanic/Latino), 3 international. Average age 32. 230 applicants, 50% accepted, 48 enrolled. In 2019, 60 master's awarded. *Degree requirements:* For master's, variable foreign language requirement, comprehensive exam (for some programs), thesis (for some programs), oral and written exams. *Entrance requirements:* For master's, GRE (for some programs), statement of purpose, 2 letters of recommendation, transcripts, critical writing sample. Additional exam requirements/recommendations for international students: required—TOEFL (minimum score 600 paper-based; 100 iBT). *Application deadline:* For fall admission, 1/15 for domestic and international students; for winter admission, 9/1 for domestic and international students; for spring admission, 11/1 for domestic and international students. Application fee: $65. Electronic applications accepted. *Expenses: Tuition, area resident:* Full-time $13,020; part-time $6510 per year. Tuition, state resident: Full-time $13,020; part-time $6510 per year. Tuition, nonresident: full-time $19,830; part-time $9915 per year. *International tuition:* $19,830 full-time. *Required fees:* $1226. One-time fee: $350. Tuition and fees vary according to course load, program and reciprocity agreements. *Financial support:* In 2019–20, 15 teaching assistantships with full and partial tuition reimbursements (averaging $10,653 per year) were awarded; career-related internships or fieldwork, Federal Work-Study, scholarships/grants, tuition waivers (full and partial), and unspecified assistantships also available. Support available to part-time students. Financial award application deadline: 3/1; financial award applicants required to submit FAFSA. *Unit head:* Dr. Paul Collins, Chair, 503-725-9777, Fax: 503-725-3561, E-mail: pcollins@pdx.edu. *Application contact:* Chloe Bobar, Academic and Program Coordinator, 503-725-3623, E-mail: cbobar@pdx.edu.
Website: http://www.pdx.edu/english/

Princeton University, Graduate School, Department of English, Princeton, NJ 08544-1019. Offers PhD. *Degree requirements:* For doctorate, 2 foreign languages, thesis/dissertation. *Entrance requirements:* For doctorate, GRE General Test, GRE Subject Test, sample of written work. Additional exam requirements/recommendations for international students: required—TOEFL (minimum score 600 paper-based). Electronic applications accepted.

Purdue University, Graduate School, College of Liberal Arts, Department of English, West Lafayette, IN 47907. Offers creative writing (MFA); literature (MA, PhD), including linguistics, literature and philosophy (PhD), rhetoric and composition, theory and cultural studies (PhD). *Program availability:* Part-time. *Faculty:* 42 full-time (17 women), 9 part-time/adjunct (6 women). *Students:* 85 full-time (58 women), 52 part-time (29 women); includes 23 minority (6 Black or African American, non-Hispanic/Latino; 1 American Indian or Alaska Native, non-Hispanic/Latino; 5 Asian, non-Hispanic/Latino; 7 Hispanic/Latino; 4 Two or more races, non-Hispanic/Latino), 24 international. Average age 31. 245 applicants, 22% accepted, 23 enrolled. In 2019, 11 master's, 22 doctorates awarded. *Degree requirements:* For master's, one foreign language, comprehensive exam (for some programs), thesis (for some programs); for doctorate, one foreign language, comprehensive exam, thesis/dissertation. *Entrance requirements:* For master's, GRE General Test; GRE Subject Test in English literature (recommended for students applying to literary studies), minimum undergraduate GPA of 3.0 or equivalent; for doctorate, GRE General Test; GRE Subject Test in English literature (recommended for students applying to literary studies), master's degree. Additional exam requirements/recommendations for international students: required—TOEFL (minimum score 620 paper-based; 77 iBT). *Application deadline:* For fall admission, 1/15 for domestic and international students. Applications are processed on a rolling basis. Application fee: $60 ($75 for international students). Electronic applications accepted. *Financial support:* Fellowships with tuition reimbursements and teaching assistantships with tuition reimbursements available. Support available to part-time students. Financial award application deadline: 1/15; financial award applicants required to submit FAFSA. *Unit head:* Dorsey Armstrong, Head, 765-494-6478, E-mail: darmstrong@purdue.edu. *Application contact:* Jill M. Quirk, Graduate Contact, 765-494-3748, Fax: 765-494-1700, E-mail: griff@purdue.edu.
Website: https://www.cla.purdue.edu/english/

Purdue University, Graduate School, Program in Philosophy and Literature, West Lafayette, IN 47907. Offers PhD. *Students:* 1 full-time (0 women), 2 part-time (1 woman). Average age 32. 3 applicants. *Degree requirements:* For doctorate, one foreign language, comprehensive exam, thesis/dissertation. *Entrance requirements:* For doctorate, GRE, master's degree in either English, philosophy or foreign languages. Additional exam requirements/recommendations for international students: required—TOEFL. *Application deadline:* For fall admission, 1/10 priority date for domestic students, 1/10 for international students. Application fee: $60 ($75 for international students). Electronic applications accepted. *Financial support:* In 2019–20, teaching assistantships (averaging $1,415 per year) were awarded; fellowships and research assistantships also available. *Unit head:* Venetria K. Patton, Head of the Graduate Program, 765-496-9629, E-mail: vpatton@purdue.edu. *Application contact:* Brandi Plantenga, Graduate Contact, 765-496-9629, E-mail: bplante@purdue.edu.
Website: http://www.cla.purdue.edu/phil-lit/graduate/

Purdue University Fort Wayne, College of Arts and Sciences, Department of English and Linguistics, Fort Wayne, IN 46805-1499. Offers English (MA, MAT); TENL (teaching English as a new language) (Certificate). *Program availability:* Part-time. *Degree requirements:* For master's, one foreign language, thesis (for some programs), teaching certificate (for MAT). *Entrance requirements:* For master's, GRE General Test, minimum GPA of 3.0, major or minor in English, 3 letters of recommendation; for Certificate, bachelor's degree with minimum GPA of 2.5. Additional exam requirements/recommendations for international students: required—TOEFL (minimum score 600 paper-based; 79 iBT).

Purdue University Northwest, Graduate Studies Office, School of Liberal Arts and Social Sciences, Department of English and Philosophy, Hammond, IN 46323-2094. Offers English (MA). *Program availability:* Part-time, evening/weekend, online learning. *Degree requirements:* For master's, comprehensive exam, thesis optional. *Entrance requirements:* Additional exam requirements/recommendations for international students: required—TOEFL. Electronic applications accepted.

Queens College of the City University of New York, Arts and Humanities Division, Department of English, Queens, NY 11367-1597. Offers creative writing and literary translation (MFA); English (MA). *Program availability:* Part-time, evening/weekend. *Faculty:* 47 full-time (25 women), 81 part-time/adjunct (50 women). *Students:* 10 full-time (4 women), 71 part-time (49 women); includes 33 minority (6 Black or African American, non-Hispanic/Latino; 10 Asian, non-Hispanic/Latino; 16 Hispanic/Latino; 1 Two or more races, non-Hispanic/Latino), 1 international. Average age 30. 188 applicants, 35% accepted, 32 enrolled. In 2019, 24 master's awarded. *Degree requirements:* For master's, thesis, oral exam/final essay defense. *Entrance requirements:* For master's, minimum GPA of 3.0; minimum 24 undergraduate credits in English or related field and 10-15 page writing sample (for MA); manuscript (for MFA). Additional exam requirements/recommendations for international students: required—TOEFL (minimum score 100 iBT), IELTS (minimum score 7). *Application deadline:* For fall admission, 4/1 for domestic students; for spring admission, 11/1 for domestic students. Applications are processed on a rolling basis. Application fee: $125. Electronic applications accepted. *Financial support:* In 2019–20, 6 students received support, including 2 fellowships (averaging $20,801 per year), 1 research assistantship (averaging $988 per year); career-related internships or fieldwork and scholarships/grants also available. Financial award application deadline: 4/1; financial award applicants required to submit FAFSA. *Unit head:* Glenn Burger, Chair, 718-997-4661, E-mail: glenn.burger@qc.cuny.edu. *Application contact:* Cassandra Winter, Assistant Director of Graduate Admissions, 718-997-5203, E-mail: cassandra.winter@qc.cuny.edu.
Website: http://english.qc.cuny.edu/

Queen's University at Kingston, School of Graduate Studies, Faculty of Arts and Science, Department of English Language and Literature, Kingston, ON K7L 3N6, Canada. Offers M Phil, MA, PhD. *Degree requirements:* For master's, one foreign language, thesis optional; for doctorate, 2 foreign languages, comprehensive exam, thesis/dissertation. *Entrance requirements:* For master's, 10 full courses in English. Additional exam requirements/recommendations for international students: required—TOEFL, TWE.

Radford University, College of Graduate Studies and Research, English, MA/MS, Radford, VA 24142. Offers MA, MS. *Program availability:* Part-time. *Degree requirements:* For master's, comprehensive exam, thesis (for some programs). *Entrance requirements:* For master's, GRE, minimum GPA of 2.75, 2 letters of reference, sample of expository writing, resume, official transcripts. Additional exam requirements/recommendations for international students: required—TOEFL (minimum score 550 paper-based; 79 iBT), IELTS (minimum score 6.5). Electronic applications accepted.

Rhode Island College, School of Graduate Studies, Faculty of Arts and Sciences, Department of English, Providence, RI 02908-1991. Offers creative writing (MA, CGS); English (MA); literature (CGS). *Program availability:* Part-time, evening/weekend. *Faculty:* 8 full-time (3 women). *Students:* 2 full-time (both women), 11 part-time (7 women). Average age 31. In 2019, 5 master's awarded. *Degree requirements:* For master's, thesis (for some programs). *Entrance requirements:* For master's, GRE General Test, 3 letters of recommendation, interview. Additional exam requirements/recommendations for international students: required—TOEFL (minimum score 550 paper-based; 80 iBT). *Application deadline:* For fall admission, 3/1 for domestic students; for spring admission, 11/1 for domestic students. Applications are processed on a rolling basis. Application fee: $50. Electronic applications accepted. *Expenses: Tuition, area resident:* Part-time $462 per credit hour. Tuition, state resident: part-time $462 per credit hour. *Required fees:* $720. One-time fee: $140. *Financial support:* Teaching assistantships, career-related internships or fieldwork, Federal Work-Study, scholarships/grants, health care benefits, and unspecified assistantships available. Support available to part-time students. Financial award application deadline: 5/15; financial award applicants required to submit FAFSA. *Unit head:* Dr. Alison Shonkwiler, Chair, 401-456-8028. *Application contact:* Dr. Alison Shonkwiler, Chair, 401-456-8028.
Website: http://www.ric.edu/english/Pages/default.aspx

Rice University, Graduate Programs, School of Humanities, Department of English, Houston, TX 77251-1892. Offers MA, PhD. Terminal master's awarded for partial completion of doctoral program. *Degree requirements:* For master's, comprehensive exam, thesis (for some programs); for doctorate, comprehensive exam, thesis/dissertation. *Entrance requirements:* For master's and doctorate, GRE General Test, minimum GPA of 3.0. Additional exam requirements/recommendations for international students: required—TOEFL (minimum score 600 paper-based; 90 iBT). Electronic applications accepted.

Rivier University, School of Graduate Studies, Department of English, Nashua, NH 03060. Offers English (MAT); writing and literature (MA). *Program availability:* Part-time, evening/weekend. *Degree requirements:* For master's, comprehensive exam (for some programs). *Entrance requirements:* For master's, GRE Subject Test.

Rutgers University - Camden, Graduate School of Arts and Sciences, Program in English, Camden, NJ 08102. Offers MA. *Program availability:* Part-time, evening/weekend. *Degree requirements:* For master's, comprehensive exam, thesis optional, 30 credits. *Entrance requirements:* For master's, GRE General Test, 3 letters of recommendation, writing sample, statement of personal, professional, and academic goals. Additional exam requirements/recommendations for international students: required—TOEFL, IELTS. Electronic applications accepted.

Rutgers University - Newark, Graduate School, Program in English, Newark, NJ 07102. Offers MA. *Program availability:* Part-time, evening/weekend. *Degree requirements:* For master's, one foreign language, comprehensive exam, thesis optional. *Entrance requirements:* For master's, GRE, minimum undergraduate B average. Electronic applications accepted.

Rutgers University - New Brunswick, Graduate School-New Brunswick, Program of Literatures in English, Piscataway, NJ 08854-8097. Offers PhD. *Degree requirements:* For doctorate, one foreign language, thesis/dissertation, qualifying exam. *Entrance requirements:* For doctorate, GRE General Test, GRE Subject Test, writing sample, 3 letters of recommendation. Additional exam requirements/recommendations for international students: required—TOEFL. Electronic applications accepted.

St. Cloud State University, School of Graduate Studies, College of Liberal Arts, Department of English, St. Cloud, MN 56301-4498. Offers English (MS); English studies (MA); rhetoric and writing (MA). *Program availability:* Part-time. *Degree requirements:* For master's, thesis or alternative. *Entrance requirements:* For master's, GRE General Test, minimum GPA of 2.75. Additional exam requirements/recommendations for international students: required—Michigan English Language Assessment Battery; recommended—TOEFL (minimum score 550 paper-based), IELTS (minimum score 6.5). Electronic applications accepted.

St. John's University, St. John's College of Liberal Arts and Sciences, Department of English, Queens, NY 11439. Offers MA, PhD. *Program availability:* Part-time, evening/weekend. *Degree requirements:* For master's, comprehensive exam, thesis optional, portfolio; for doctorate, comprehensive exam, thesis/dissertation. *Entrance requirements:* For master's and doctorate, GRE, letters of recommendation, transcripts, resume, personal statement. Additional exam requirements/recommendations for international students: required—TOEFL (minimum score 80 iBT), IELTS (minimum score 6.5). Electronic applications accepted.

Saint Louis University, Graduate Programs, College of Arts and Sciences, Department of English, St. Louis, MO 63103. Offers MA, MA-R, PhD. *Program availability:* Part-time. *Degree requirements:* For master's, one foreign language, comprehensive exam, thesis optional, comprehensive oral exam; for doctorate, 2 foreign languages, comprehensive exam, thesis/dissertation, preliminary oral and written exams. *Entrance requirements:* For master's, GRE General Test, GRE Subject Test, letters of recommendation, resume, writing sample, interview; for doctorate, GRE General Test, GRE Subject Test, letters of recommendation, resumé, writing sample, interview, goal statement, writing sample. Additional exam requirements/recommendations for international students: required—TOEFL (minimum score 550 paper-based).

Saint Louis University–Madrid Campus, Graduate Programs, Master of Arts in English Program, Madrid, Spain. Offers MA. *Program availability:* Part-time. *Degree requirements:* For master's, one foreign language, comprehensive exam, thesis optional. *Entrance requirements:* For master's, GRE General Test, transcripts, 3 letters of recommendation, writing sample, personal statement, curriculum vitae. Additional exam requirements/recommendations for international students: required—TOEFL (minimum score 550 paper-based; 80 iBT). Electronic applications accepted.

St. Mary's University, Graduate Studies, Program in English Literature and Language, San Antonio, TX 78228. Offers MA, JD/MA. *Program availability:* Part-time, evening/weekend. *Degree requirements:* For master's, thesis (for some programs). *Entrance requirements:* For master's, GRE (minimum score within top 35% of verbal section and top 35% of analytical section), minimum GPA of 3.0. Additional exam requirements/recommendations for international students: required—TOEFL (minimum score 550 paper-based; 80 iBT), IELTS (minimum score 6). Electronic applications accepted.

Salem State University, School of Graduate Studies, Program in English, Salem, MA 01970-5353. Offers MA, MAT, MA/MAT. *Program availability:* Part-time, evening/weekend. *Entrance requirements:* For master's, GRE or MAT. Additional exam requirements/recommendations for international students: required—TOEFL (minimum score 550 paper-based; 80 iBT) or IELTS (minimum score 5.5).

Salisbury University, Department of English, Salisbury, MD 21801-6837. Offers English (MA). *Program availability:* Part-time, evening/weekend. *Faculty:* 11 full-time (5 women). *Students:* 9 full-time (7 women), 12 part-time (11 women); includes 2 minority (1 Asian, non-Hispanic/Latino; 1 Hispanic/Latino), 2 international. Average age 34. 13 applicants, 92% accepted, 6 enrolled. In 2019, 14 master's awarded. *Degree requirements:* For master's, variable foreign language requirement, comprehensive exam (for some programs), thesis (for some programs). *Entrance requirements:* For master's, Applicants who wish to be considered for Teaching Assistantships are required to have acceptable score on the GRE General Test. All other applicants - GRE General Test, MAT or Praxis I scores are acceptable, transcripts; personal statement; minimum GPA of 3.0; two letters of recommendation; undergraduate degree in English or related field. *Application deadline:* For fall admission, 8/1 for domestic and international students; for spring admission, 1/1 for domestic and international students. Application fee: $65. Electronic applications accepted. *Expenses:* Contact institution. *Financial support:* In 2019–20, 3 students received support, including 8 teaching assistantships with full tuition reimbursements available (averaging $10,250 per year); career-related internships or fieldwork and scholarships/grants also available. Support available to part-time students. Financial award application deadline: 3/1; financial award applicants required to submit FAFSA. *Unit head:* Dr. John Nieves, Graduate Program Director, 410-677-6511, E-mail: janieves@salisbury.edu. *Application contact:* Dr. John Nieves, Graduate Program Director, 410-677-6511, E-mail: janieves@salisbury.edu.
Website: https://www.salisbury.edu/explore-academics/programs/graduate-degree-programs/english-masters/

Sam Houston State University, College of Humanities and Social Sciences, Department of English, Huntsville, TX 77341. Offers creative writing, editing, and publishing (MFA); English (MA). *Program availability:* Part-time. *Degree requirements:* For master's, comprehensive exam, thesis optional. *Entrance requirements:* For master's, GRE General Test, creative writing sample, letters of recommendation. Additional exam requirements/recommendations for international students: required—TOEFL (minimum score 550 paper-based; 79 iBT), IELTS (minimum score 6.5). Electronic applications accepted.

San Diego State University, Graduate and Research Affairs, College of Arts and Letters, Department of English and Comparative Literature, San Diego, CA 92182. Offers creative writing (MFA); English (MA). *Degree requirements:* For master's, one foreign language, comprehensive exam (for some programs), thesis (for some programs). *Entrance requirements:* For master's, GRE General Test, minimum GPA of 2.85, writing sample, 3 letters of recommendation. Additional exam requirements/recommendations for international students: required—TOEFL. Electronic applications accepted.

San Francisco State University, Division of Graduate Studies, College of Liberal and Creative Arts, Department of English Language and Literature, Program in Composition, San Francisco, CA 94132-1722. Offers teaching composition (Certificate). *Program availability:* Part-time. *Entrance requirements:* Additional exam requirements/recommendations for international students: required—TOEFL, TWE. *Application deadline:* Applications are processed on a rolling basis. *Expenses: Tuition, area resident:* Full-time $7176; part-time $4164 per year. Tuition, state resident: full-time $7176; part-time $4164 per year. Tuition, nonresident: full-time $16,680; part-time $396 per unit. *International tuition:* $16,680 full-time. *Required fees:* $1524; $1524 per unit. $762 per semester. Tuition and fees vary according to degree level and program. *Unit head:* Dr. Gitanjali Shahani, Chair, 415- 338-2264, Fax: 415-338-6159, E-mail: gshahani@sfsu.edu. *Application contact:* Prof. Mark Roberge, Graduate Coordinator, 415-338-7457, Fax: 415-338-6159, E-mail: roberge@sfsu.edu.
Website: http://english.sfsu.edu/graduate-composition

San Francisco State University, Division of Graduate Studies, College of Liberal and Creative Arts, Department of English Language and Literature, Program in English Literatures, San Francisco, CA 94132-1722. Offers MA. *Program availability:* Part-time. *Application deadline:* Applications are processed on a rolling basis. *Expenses: Tuition, area resident:* Full-time $7176; part-time $4164 per year. Tuition, state resident: full-time $7176; part-time $4164 per year. Tuition, nonresident: full-time $16,680; part-time $396 per unit. *International tuition:* $16,680 full-time. *Required fees:* $1524; $1524 per unit. $762 per semester. Tuition and fees vary according to degree level and program. *Unit head:* Dr. Gitanjali Shahani, Chair, 415-338-2264, Fax: 415-338-6159, E-mail: gshahani@sfsu.edu. *Application contact:* Dr. Sara Hackenberg, Program Coordinator, 415-338-7453, Fax: 415-338-6159, E-mail: shackenb@sfsu.edu.
Website: http://english.sfsu.edu/graduate-literature

Seton Hall University, College of Arts and Sciences, Department of English, South Orange, NJ 07079-2697. Offers literature (MA). *Program availability:* Part-time, evening/weekend. *Degree requirements:* For master's, one foreign language, comprehensive exam, thesis (for some programs). *Entrance requirements:* For master's, GRE, minimum of 21 undergraduate credits in English. Additional exam requirements/recommendations for international students: required—TOEFL. Electronic applications accepted.

Simmons University, Gwen Ifill College of Media, Arts, and Humanities, Boston, MA 02115. Offers behavior analysis (MS, PhD, Ed S); children's literature (MA); dietetics (Certificate); elementary education (MAT); English (MA); gender/cultural studies (MA); history (MA); nutrition and health promotion (MS); physical therapy (DPT); public health (MPH); public policy (MPP); special education: moderate and severe disabilities (MS Ed); sports nutrition (Certificate); writing for children (MFA). *Program availability:* Part-time. *Faculty:* 10 full-time (9 women), 7 part-time/adjunct (6 women). *Students:* 2 full-time (both women), 67 part-time (57 women); includes 13 minority (3 Black or African American, non-Hispanic/Latino; 4 Asian, non-Hispanic/Latino; 3 Hispanic/Latino; 3 Two or more races, non-Hispanic/Latino), 1 international. Average age 31. 42 applicants, 62% accepted, 23 enrolled. In 2019, 24 master's awarded. *Degree requirements:* For master's, thesis optional. *Entrance requirements:* For master's, GRE, bachelor's degree from accredited college or university; minimum B average (preferred). Additional exam requirements/recommendations for international students: required—TOEFL (minimum score 600 paper-based; 100 iBT). *Application deadline:* For fall admission, 8/1 for domestic and international students; for spring admission, 12/15 for domestic and international students; for summer admission, 5/1 for domestic and international students. Applications are processed on a rolling basis. Application fee: $35. Electronic applications accepted. *Expenses:* Contact institution. *Financial support:* In 2019–20, 14 students received support, including 1 fellowship (averaging $15,360 per year), 13 teaching assistantships (averaging $2,000 per year); scholarships/grants also available. Financial award applicants required to submit FAFSA. *Unit head:* Dr. Brian Norman, Dean, 617-521-2472, E-mail: brian.norman@simmons.edu. *Application contact:* Patricia Flaherty, Director, Graduate Studies Admission, 617-521-3902, Fax: 617-521-3058, E-mail: gsa@simmons.edu.
Website: https://www.simmons.edu/academics/colleges-schools-departments/ifill

Simon Fraser University, Office of Graduate Studies and Postdoctoral Fellows, Faculty of Arts and Social Sciences, Department of English, Burnaby, BC V5A 1S6, Canada. Offers English (MA, PhD); teachers of English (MA). *Program availability:* Part-time. *Degree requirements:* For master's, one foreign language, thesis or alternative; for doctorate, one foreign language, thesis/dissertation, field exams. *Entrance requirements:* For master's, minimum GPA of 3.0 (on scale of 4.33) or 3.33 based on last 60 credits of undergraduate courses; for doctorate, minimum GPA of 3.5 (on scale of 4.33). Additional exam requirements/recommendations for international students: recommended—TOEFL (minimum score 580 paper-based; 93 iBT), IELTS (minimum score 7), TWE (minimum score 5). Electronic applications accepted.

Slippery Rock University of Pennsylvania, Graduate Studies (Recruitment), College of Liberal Arts, Department of English, Slippery Rock, PA 16057-1383. Offers MA. *Program availability:* Part-time, evening/weekend, online only, 100% online. *Faculty:* 5 full-time (1 woman). *Students:* 24 part-time (20 women); includes 1 minority (Hispanic/Latino). Average age 34. 15 applicants, 73% accepted, 10 enrolled. In 2019, 8 master's awarded. *Degree requirements:* For master's, comprehensive exam (for some programs), thesis (for some programs). *Entrance requirements:* For master's, official transcripts, essay, two letters of recommendation. Additional exam requirements/recommendations for international students: required—TOEFL (minimum score 550 paper-based; 80 iBT). *Application deadline:* For fall admission, 3/1 for domestic students, 5/1 for international students; for spring admission, 11/1 for domestic students, 9/1 for international students. Applications are processed on a rolling basis. Application fee: $25 ($30 for international students). Electronic applications accepted. *Expenses:* $516 per credit in-state tuition, $173.61 per credit in-state fees; $774 per credit out-of-state tuition, $224.31 per credit out-of-state fees; $516 per credit in-state tuition, $105.40 per credit in-state fees (for distance education); $526 per credit out-of-state tuition, $118.90 per credit out-of-state fees (for distance education). *Financial support:* Career-related internships or fieldwork, Federal Work-Study, institutionally sponsored loans, scholarships/grants, tuition waivers (partial), and unspecified assistantships available. Support available to part-time students. Financial award application deadline: 5/1; financial award applicants required to submit FAFSA. *Unit head:* Dr. Jason Stuart,

English

Graduate Coordinator, 724-738-4360, Fax: 724-738-2043, E-mail: jason.stuart@sru.edu. *Application contact:* Brandi Weber-Mortimer, Director of Graduate Admissions, 724-738-2051, Fax: 724-738-2146, E-mail: graduate.admissions@sru.edu. Website: http://www.sru.edu/academics/colleges-and-departments/cola/departments/english

Sonoma State University, Department of English, Rohnert Park, CA 94928. Offers American literature (MA); creative writing (MA); English literature (MA); world literature (MA). *Program availability:* Part-time, evening/weekend. *Degree requirements:* For master's, one foreign language, thesis or alternative. *Entrance requirements:* For master's, minimum GPA of 2.5. Additional exam requirements/recommendations for international students: required—TOEFL (minimum score 500 paper-based).

South Carolina State University, College of Graduate and Professional Studies, Department of Education, Orangeburg, SC 29117-0001. Offers early childhood education (MAT); education (M Ed); elementary education (M Ed, MAT); English (MAT); general science/biology (MAT); mathematics (MAT); secondary education (M Ed), including biology education, business education, counselor education, English education, home economics education, industrial education, mathematics education, science education, social studies education; special education (M Ed), including emotionally handicapped, learning disabilities, mentally handicapped. *Accreditation:* NCATE. *Program availability:* Part-time, evening/weekend. *Degree requirements:* For master's, thesis optional, departmental qualifying exam. *Entrance requirements:* For master's, GRE General Test, NTE, interview, teaching certificate. Electronic applications accepted.

South Dakota State University, Graduate School, College of Arts, Humanities and Social Sciences, Department of English, Brookings, SD 57007. Offers MA. *Program availability:* Part-time. *Degree requirements:* For master's, comprehensive exam (for some programs), thesis (for some programs), oral and written exams. *Entrance requirements:* For master's, minimum GPA of 2.75. Additional exam requirements/recommendations for international students: required—TOEFL (minimum score 600 paper-based; 100 iBT).

Southeastern Louisiana University, College of Arts, Humanities and Social Sciences, Department of English, Hammond, LA 70402. Offers creative writing (MA); language and literacy (MA); professional writing (MA); publishing studies (MA). *Program availability:* Part-time. *Faculty:* 19 full-time (9 women). *Students:* 19 full-time (15 women), 11 part-time (8 women); includes 8 minority (2 Black or African American, non-Hispanic/Latino; 1 American Indian or Alaska Native, non-Hispanic/Latino; 5 Two or more races, non-Hispanic/Latino). Average age 30. 10 applicants, 100% accepted, 9 enrolled. In 2019, 10 master's awarded. *Degree requirements:* For master's, comprehensive exam, thesis optional. *Entrance requirements:* For master's, GRE verbal score of 150 or greater required, 24 semester hours of undergraduate English courses, at least 12 of which must be at the Jr./Sr. level, 2.50 GPA undergraduate degree. Additional exam requirements/recommendations for international students: required—TOEFL (minimum score 500 paper-based; 61 iBT). *Application deadline:* For fall admission, 7/15 priority date for domestic students, 5/1 priority date for international students; for spring admission, 12/1 priority date for domestic students, 9/1 priority date for international students. Applications are processed on a rolling basis. Application fee: $20 ($30 for international students). Electronic applications accepted. *Expenses: Tuition, area resident:* Full-time $6684; part-time $489 per credit hour. Tuition, state resident: full-time $6684; part-time $489 per credit hour. Tuition, nonresident: full-time $19,162; part-time $1183 per credit hour. *International tuition:* $19,162 full-time. *Required fees:* $2124. *Financial support:* In 2019–20, 21 students received support, including 8 research assistantships with tuition reimbursements available (averaging $9,688 per year), 2 teaching assistantships with tuition reimbursements available (averaging $11,000 per year); career-related internships or fieldwork, institutionally sponsored loans, traineeships, and unspecified assistantships also available. Financial award application deadline: 5/1; financial award applicants required to submit FAFSA. *Unit head:* Dr. David Hanson, Department Head, 985-549-2100, Fax: 985-549-5049, E-mail: dhanson@southeastern.edu. *Application contact:* Office of Admissions, 985-549-5637, Fax: 985-549-5632, E-mail: admissions@southeastern.edu.
Website: http://www.southeastern.edu/acad_research/depts/engl

Southeast Missouri State University, School of Graduate Studies, Department of English, Cape Girardeau, MO 63701-4799. Offers teaching English to speakers of other languages (MA). *Program availability:* Part-time, evening/weekend, online learning. *Degree requirements:* For master's, comprehensive exam (for some programs), thesis optional. *Entrance requirements:* Additional exam requirements/recommendations for international students: required—TOEFL (minimum score 550 paper-based; 79 iBT), IELTS (minimum score 6), PTE (minimum score 53). Electronic applications accepted. *Expenses:* Contact institution.

Southern Connecticut State University, School of Graduate Studies, School of Arts and Sciences, Department of English, New Haven, CT 06515-1355. Offers MA, MS, MLS/MS. *Program availability:* Part-time, evening/weekend. *Degree requirements:* For master's, one foreign language, thesis or alternative. *Entrance requirements:* For master's, interview. Electronic applications accepted.

Southern Illinois University Carbondale, Graduate School, College of Liberal Arts, Department of English, Carbondale, IL 62901-4701. Offers composition (MA, PhD), including composition, literature, rhetoric; creative writing (MFA). *Degree requirements:* For master's, one foreign language, thesis; for doctorate, 2 foreign languages, thesis/dissertation. *Entrance requirements:* For master's, GRE General Test, GRE Subject Test, minimum GPA of 2.7; for doctorate, GRE General Test, GRE Subject Test, minimum GPA of 3.25. Additional exam requirements/recommendations for international students: required—TOEFL.

Southern Illinois University Edwardsville, Graduate School, College of Arts and Sciences, Department of English Language and Literature, Program in Literature, Edwardsville, IL 62026. Offers MA, Postbaccalaureate Certificate. *Program availability:* Part-time. *Degree requirements:* For master's, one foreign language, thesis (for some programs), written papers, oral examination. *Entrance requirements:* Additional exam requirements/recommendations for international students: required—TOEFL (minimum score 550 paper-based, 79 iBT), IELTS (minimum score 6.5), Michigan Test of English Language Proficiency or PTE. Electronic applications accepted.

Southern Methodist University, Dedman College of Humanities and Sciences, Department of English, Dallas, TX 75275. Offers MA, PhD. Terminal master's awarded for partial completion of doctoral program. *Degree requirements:* For master's, one foreign language, comprehensive exam, thesis optional, oral exam; for doctorate, one foreign language, comprehensive exam, thesis/dissertation. *Entrance requirements:* For master's, GRE General Test, minimum GPA of 3.0; for doctorate, GRE General Test, minimum GPA of 3.5, BA in English or other appropriate field. Additional exam requirements/recommendations for international students: required—TOEFL (minimum score 550 paper-based). Electronic applications accepted.

Southern New Hampshire University, School of Arts and Sciences, Manchester, NH 03106-1045. Offers clinical mental health counseling (MS); creative writing (MA); criminal justice (MS); cyber security (MS); English (MA); fiction and nonfiction (MFA); history (MA); political science (MS); psychology (MS). *Program availability:* Part-time, evening/weekend. *Degree requirements:* For master's, one foreign language, thesis. *Entrance requirements:* For master's, minimum GPA of 3.0 (for MFA). Additional exam requirements/recommendations for international students: required—TOEFL (minimum score 550 paper-based; 79 iBT), IELTS (minimum score 6.5), TWE (minimum score 5). Electronic applications accepted. *Expenses:* Contact institution.

Spring Hill College, Graduate Programs, Program in Liberal Arts, Mobile, AL 36608-1791. Offers fine arts (MLA); leadership and ethics (MLA, Postbaccalaureate Certificate); literature (MLA). *Program availability:* Part-time, evening/weekend. *Faculty:* 3 full-time (0 women), 2 part-time/adjunct (both women). *Students:* 3 full-time (2 women), 12 part-time (5 women); includes 1 minority (Hispanic/Latino), 4 international. Average age 35. In 2019, 9 master's awarded. *Degree requirements:* For master's, capstone course, completion of program within 6 years of initial admittance. *Entrance requirements:* For master's, bachelor's degree with minimum undergraduate GPA of 3.0 or graduate/professional degree. Additional exam requirements/recommendations for international students: required—TOEFL (minimum score 550 paper-based; 80 iBT), IELTS (minimum score 6.5), CPE or CAE (minimum score C), Michigan English Language Assessment Battery (minimum score 90). *Application deadline:* For fall admission, 8/1 priority date for domestic and international students; for spring admission, 12/1 priority date for domestic and international students. Applications are processed on a rolling basis. Application fee: $25 ($35 for international students). Electronic applications accepted. *Expenses:* Contact institution. *Financial support:* Fellowships, research assistantships, teaching assistantships, and tuition waivers available. Financial award applicants required to submit FAFSA. *Unit head:* Dr. Thomas J. Hoffman, Director, 251-380-4184, Fax: 251-460-2115, E-mail: thoffman@shc.edu. *Application contact:* Gary Bracken, Vice President of Enrollment Management, 251-380-3038, Fax: 251-460-2186, E-mail: gbracken@shc.edu.
Website: http://ug.shc.edu/graduate-degrees/master-liberal-arts/

Stanford University, School of Humanities and Sciences, Department of English, Stanford, CA 94305-2004. Offers MA, PhD. *Expenses: Tuition:* Full-time $52,479; part-time $34,110 per unit. *Required fees:* $672; $224 per quarter. Tuition and fees vary according to program and student level.
Website: http://www.stanford.edu/dept/english/

State University of New York at Fredonia, College of Liberal Arts and Sciences, Fredonia, NY 14063-1136. Offers biology (MS); English (MA); English education 7-12 (MA); interdisciplinary studies (MA, MS); math education (MS Ed); professional writing (CAS); speech pathology (MS); MA/MS. *Program availability:* Part-time, evening/weekend. *Degree requirements:* For master's, comprehensive exam (for some programs), thesis (for some programs). *Entrance requirements:* For master's, GRE. Additional exam requirements/recommendations for international students: required—TOEFL (minimum score 79 iBT), IELTS (minimum score 6.5). Electronic applications accepted.

State University of New York at New Paltz, Graduate and Extended Learning School, School of Liberal Arts and Sciences, Department of English, New Paltz, NY 12561. Offers English (MA). *Program availability:* Part-time, evening/weekend. *Faculty:* 12 full-time (8 women). *Students:* 6 full-time (all women), 35 part-time (23 women); includes 8 minority (2 Black or African American, non-Hispanic/Latino; 3 Hispanic/Latino; 3 Two or more races, non-Hispanic/Latino). 37 applicants, 54% accepted, 16 enrolled. In 2019, 16 master's awarded. *Degree requirements:* For master's, comprehensive exam, thesis (for some programs), foreign language proficiency exam. *Entrance requirements:* For master's, minimum GPA of 3.0, 10-15 page writing sample. Additional exam requirements/recommendations for international students: required—TOEFL (minimum score 563 paper-based; 85 iBT), IELTS (minimum score 7). *Application deadline:* For fall admission, 3/15 priority date for domestic students, 3/15 for international students; for spring admission, 10/15 for domestic and international students. Application fee: $50. Electronic applications accepted. *Expenses: Tuition, area resident:* Full-time $11,310; part-time $471 per credit. Tuition, state resident: full-time $11,310; part-time $471 per credit. Tuition, nonresident: full-time $23,100; part-time $963 per credit. *International tuition:* $23,100 full-time. *Required fees:* $1432; $41.83 per credit. *Financial support:* In 2019–20, 1 research assistantship with partial tuition reimbursement (averaging $5,000 per year), 17 teaching assistantships with partial tuition reimbursements (averaging $5,000 per year) were awarded. Financial award application deadline: 8/1. *Unit head:* Dr. Cyrus Mulready, Chair, 845-257-2739, E-mail: english@newpaltz.edu. *Application contact:* Vika Shock, Director of Graduate Admissions, 845-257-3286, E-mail: gradstudies@newpaltz.edu.
Website: http://www.newpaltz.edu/english/

State University of New York College at Cortland, Graduate Studies, School of Arts and Sciences, Department of English, Cortland, NY 13045. Offers MA. *Program availability:* Part-time, evening/weekend. *Degree requirements:* For master's, one foreign language, comprehensive exam, thesis. *Entrance requirements:* For master's, GRE General Test.

Stephen F. Austin State University, Graduate School, College of Liberal and Applied Arts, Department of English, Nacogdoches, TX 75962. Offers English (MA). *Degree requirements:* For master's, comprehensive exam. *Entrance requirements:* For master's, GRE General Test. Additional exam requirements/recommendations for international students: required—TOEFL.

Stony Brook University, State University of New York, Graduate School, College of Arts and Sciences, Department of Cultural Studies and Comparative Literature, Stony Brook, NY 11794. Offers comparative literature (MA, PhD); cultural studies (PhD, Certificate). *Program availability:* Evening/weekend. *Faculty:* 3 full-time (1 woman). *Students:* 19 full-time (11 women), 3 part-time (all women); includes 4 minority (1 Black or African American, non-Hispanic/Latino; 2 Asian, non-Hispanic/Latino; 1 Hispanic/Latino), 9 international. Average age 38. In 2019, 6 master's, 2 doctorates awarded. Terminal master's awarded for partial completion of doctoral program. *Degree requirements:* For master's, 2 foreign languages, exam; for doctorate, 3 foreign languages, comprehensive exam, thesis/dissertation. *Entrance requirements:* For master's and doctorate, GRE General Test, minimum GPA of 3.5 in major, 3.0 overall. Additional exam requirements/recommendations for international students: required—TOEFL. *Application deadline:* For fall admission, 1/15 for domestic students; for spring admission, 10/1 for domestic students. Application fee: $100. Electronic applications accepted. *Expenses:* Contact institution. *Financial support:* In 2019–20, 8 teaching assistantships were awarded; fellowships and research assistantships also available. *Unit head:* Prof. Mary C Rawlinson, 631-632-7464, Fax: 631-632-5707, E-mail: Mary.Rawlinson@stonybrook.edu. *Application contact:* Mary Moran-Luba, Coordinator, 631-632-6935, Fax: 631-632-5707, E-mail: mary.moran-luba@stonybrook.edu.
Website: http://www.stonybrook.edu/commcms/cat/index.html

Stony Brook University, State University of New York, Graduate School, College of Arts and Sciences, Department of English, Stony Brook, NY 11794. Offers MA, MAT, PhD. *Faculty:* 27 full-time (10 women), 3 part-time/adjunct (1 woman). *Students:* 39 full-time (21 women), 7 part-time (6 women); includes 8 minority (1 Black or African American, non-Hispanic/Latino; 2 Asian, non-Hispanic/Latino; 3 Hispanic/Latino; 2 Two or more races, non-Hispanic/Latino), 4 international. Average age 28. 66 applicants, 38% accepted, 6 enrolled. In 2019, 11 master's, 7 doctorates awarded. Terminal

master's awarded for partial completion of doctoral program. *Entrance requirements:* For master's and doctorate, GRE General Test. Additional exam requirements/recommendations for international students: required—TOEFL. *Application deadline:* For fall admission, 1/15 for domestic students; for spring admission, 10/1 for domestic students. Application fee: $100. Electronic applications accepted. *Expenses:* Contact institution. *Financial support:* In 2019–20, 27 teaching assistantships were awarded; fellowships and research assistantships also available. *Unit head:* Dr. Celia Marshik, Chair, 631-632-7413, E-mail: celia.marshik@stonybrook.edu. *Application contact:* Theresa Spadola, Coordinator, 631-632-7373, E-mail: theresa.spadola@stonybrook.edu.
Website: http://www.stonybrook.edu/english/

Sul Ross State University, College of Arts and Sciences, Department of Languages and Literature, Alpine, TX 79832. Offers English (MA). *Program availability:* Part-time, evening/weekend. *Degree requirements:* For master's, thesis optional. *Entrance requirements:* For master's, GRE General Test, minimum GPA of 2.5 in last 60 hours of undergraduate work.

SUNY Brockport, School of Arts and Sciences, Department of English, Brockport, NY 14420-2997. Offers creative writing (AGC); English (MA), including creative writing, literature. *Program availability:* Part-time. *Faculty:* 8 full-time (4 women). *Students:* 16 full-time (10 women), 15 part-time (8 women); includes 2 minority (both Hispanic/Latino). 13 applicants, 77% accepted, 8 enrolled. In 2019, 18 master's, 1 other advanced degree awarded. *Entrance requirements:* For master's, minimum GPA of 3.0, letters of recommendation, writing sample. Additional exam requirements/recommendations for international students: required—TOEFL (minimum score 550 paper-based; 79 iBT), IELTS (minimum score 6.5). *Application deadline:* For fall admission, 4/15 priority date for domestic and international students; for spring admission, 11/15 priority date for domestic and international students; for summer admission, 4/15 priority date for domestic and international students. Application fee: $50. Electronic applications accepted. *Expenses: Tuition, area resident:* Part-time $471 per credit hour. Tuition, nonresident: part-time $963 per credit hour. *Financial support:* In 2019–20, 3 teaching assistantships with full tuition reimbursements (averaging $6,000 per year) were awarded; Federal Work-Study, scholarships/grants, and unspecified assistantships also available. Support available to part-time students. Financial award application deadline: 3/15; financial award applicants required to submit FAFSA. *Unit head:* Dr. Jennifer Haytock, Chairperson, 585-395-5832, Fax: 585-395-2391, E-mail: jhaytock@brockport.edu. *Application contact:* Dr. Alissa Karl, Graduate Program Director, 585-395-2342, Fax: 585-395-5487, E-mail: akarl@brockport.edu.
Website: https://www.brockport.edu/academics/english/

SUNY Brockport, School of Education, Health, and Human Services, Department of Education and Human Development, Brockport, NY 14420-2997. Offers adolescence education (MS Ed), including adolescence biology education, adolescence chemistry education, adolescence English, adolescence mathematics, adolescence physics, adolescence physics education, adolescence social studies education; bilingual education (MS Ed, AGC); childhood curriculum specialist (MS Ed); inclusive generalist education (MS Ed, AGC, Advanced Certificate), including biology (MS Ed, AGC), chemistry (MS Ed), English (MS Ed, Advanced Certificate), mathematics (MS Ed, Advanced Certificate), science (MS Ed, Advanced Certificate), social studies (MS Ed, Advanced Certificate); literacy education B-12 (MS Ed). *Accreditation:* NCATE. *Faculty:* 15 full-time (11 women), 7 part-time/adjunct (4 women). *Students:* 68 full-time (38 women), 262 part-time (196 women); includes 9 minority (2 Black or African American, non-Hispanic/Latino; 1 American Indian or Alaska Native, non-Hispanic/Latino; 2 Asian, non-Hispanic/Latino; 4 Hispanic/Latino). 130 applicants, 77% accepted, 82 enrolled. In 2019, 107 master's, 13 AGCs awarded. *Entrance requirements:* For master's, minimum GPA of 3.0, letters of recommendation, interview (for some programs); statement of objectives, current resume. Additional exam requirements/recommendations for international students: required—TOEFL (minimum score 550 paper-based; 79 iBT), IELTS (minimum score 6.5). *Application deadline:* For fall admission, 3/15 priority date for domestic and international students; for spring admission, 10/15 priority date for domestic and international students; for summer admission, 3/15 priority date for domestic and international students. Application fee: $80. Electronic applications accepted. *Expenses: Tuition, area resident:* Part-time $471 per credit hour. Tuition, nonresident: part-time $963 per credit hour. *Financial support:* In 2019–20, 1 fellowship with full tuition reimbursement (averaging $7,500 per year), 1 teaching assistantship with full tuition reimbursement (averaging $6,000 per year) were awarded; Federal Work-Study, scholarships/grants, and unspecified assistantships also available. Support available to part-time students. Financial award application deadline: 3/15; financial award applicants required to submit FAFSA. *Unit head:* Dr. Janka Szilagyi, Chairperson, 585-395-5945, Fax: 585-395-2172, E-mail: jszilagy@brockport.edu. *Application contact:* Buffie Edick, Graduate Program Director, 585-395-2326, Fax: 585-395-2172, E-mail: bedick@brockport.edu.
Website: https://www.brockport.edu/academics/education_human_development/department.html

Syracuse University, College of Arts and Sciences, English Department, Syracuse, NY 13244. Offers MA, PhD. *Degree requirements:* For master's, thesis; for doctorate, comprehensive exam, thesis/dissertation. *Entrance requirements:* For master's and doctorate, GRE General Test, transcript from undergraduate/graduate institution, intellectual statement, three letters of recommendation, writing sample, teaching statement. Additional exam requirements/recommendations for international students: required—TOEFL (minimum score 100 iBT). Electronic applications accepted.

Tarleton State University, College of Graduate Studies, College of Liberal and Fine Arts, Department of English and Languages, Stephenville, TX 76402. Offers English (MA). *Program availability:* Part-time, evening/weekend, 100% online, blended/hybrid learning. *Faculty:* 7 full-time (5 women). *Students:* 5 full-time (all women), 18 part-time (11 women); includes 3 minority (2 Hispanic/Latino; 1 Two or more races, non-Hispanic/Latino). Average age 38. 17 applicants, 76% accepted, 8 enrolled. In 2019, 2 master's awarded. *Degree requirements:* For master's, comprehensive exam, thesis (for some programs). *Entrance requirements:* For master's, GRE General Test, minimum GPA of 2.5. Additional exam requirements/recommendations for international students: required—TOEFL (minimum score 520 paper-based; 69 iBT); recommended—IELTS (minimum score 6), TSE (minimum score 50). *Application deadline:* For fall admission, 8/15 priority date for domestic students; for spring admission, 1/7 for domestic students. Applications are processed on a rolling basis. Application fee: $50 ($130 for international students). Electronic applications accepted. *Expenses:* Tuition, state resident: part-time $221.73 per credit hour. Tuition, nonresident: part-time $636.73 per credit hour. *Required fees:* $198 per credit hour. $100 per semester. Tuition and fees vary according to degree level. *Financial support:* Research assistantships, teaching assistantships, career-related internships or fieldwork, and Federal Work-Study available. Support available to part-time students. Financial award application deadline: 5/1; financial award applicants required to submit FAFSA. *Unit head:* TBD, Department Head, 254-968-9039, Fax: 254-968-1931. *Application contact:* Wendy Weiss, Graduate Admissions Coordinator, 254-968-9104, Fax: 254-968-9670, E-mail: weiss@tarleton.edu.
Website: https://www.tarleton.edu/english/index.html

Temple University, College of Liberal Arts, Department of English, Philadelphia, PA 19122-6096. Offers creative writing (MFA); English (MA, PhD). *Program availability:* Part-time. *Faculty:* 24 full-time (12 women), 21 part-time/adjunct (9 women). *Students:* 75 full-time (44 women), 10 part-time (7 women); includes 18 minority (3 Black or African American, non-Hispanic/Latino; 1 American Indian or Alaska Native, non-Hispanic/Latino; 6 Asian, non-Hispanic/Latino; 7 Hispanic/Latino; 1 Two or more races, non-Hispanic/Latino), 2 international. 142 applicants, 62% accepted, 26 enrolled. In 2019, 10 master's, 4 doctorates awarded. *Entrance requirements:* For master's, statement of goals, 3 letters of recommendation, writing sample; for doctorate, GRE, 3 letters of recommendation, writing sample, statement of goals. Additional exam requirements/recommendations for international students: required—TOEFL, IELTS, PTE, one of three is required. *Application deadline:* For fall admission, 2/15 for domestic students. Application fee: $60. Electronic applications accepted. *Financial support:* Fellowships, teaching assistantships, and Federal Work-Study available. Financial award application deadline: 12/15; financial award applicants required to submit FAFSA. *Unit head:* Katherine Henry, Chairperson, 215-204-1756, E-mail: khenry@temple.edu. *Application contact:* Sharon Logan, Coordinator, 215-204-1796, Fax: 215-204-9620, E-mail: logansd@temple.edu.
Website: http://www.cla.temple.edu/english/

Tennessee Technological University, College of Graduate Studies, College of Arts and Sciences, Department of English, Cookeville, TN 38505. Offers MA. *Program availability:* Part-time. *Faculty:* 23 full-time (8 women). *Students:* 7 full-time (5 women), 6 part-time (5 women). 9 applicants, 67% accepted, 5 enrolled. In 2019, 4 master's awarded. *Degree requirements:* For master's, comprehensive exam, thesis or alternative. *Entrance requirements:* For master's, GRE General Test. Additional exam requirements/recommendations for international students: required—TOEFL (minimum score 527 paper-based; 71 iBT), IELTS (minimum score 5.5), PTE (minimum score 48), or TOEIC (Test of English as an International Communication). *Application deadline:* For fall admission, 8/1 for domestic students, 5/1 for international students; for spring admission, 12/1 for domestic students, 10/1 for international students; for summer admission, 5/1 for domestic students, 2/1 for international students. Applications are processed on a rolling basis. Application fee: $35 ($40 for international students). Electronic applications accepted. *Expenses: Tuition, area resident:* Part-time $597 per credit hour. Tuition, state resident: part-time $597 per credit hour. Tuition, nonresident: part-time $1323 per credit hour. *Financial support:* In 2019–20, 8 teaching assistantships (averaging $8,000 per year) were awarded; fellowships and research assistantships also available. Financial award application deadline: 4/1. *Unit head:* Dr. Linda Null, Interim Chairperson, 931-372-3343, Fax: 931-372-6142, E-mail: lnull@tntech.edu. *Application contact:* Shelia K. Kendrick, Coordinator of Graduate Studies, 931-372-3808, Fax: 931-372-3497, E-mail: skendrick@tntech.edu.

Texas A&M International University, Office of Graduate Studies and Research, College of Arts and Sciences, Department of Humanities, Laredo, TX 78041. Offers English (MA); history and political thought (MA); language, literature and translation (MA). *Degree requirements:* For master's, comprehensive exam (for some programs), thesis (for some programs). *Entrance requirements:* For master's, GRE General Test. Additional exam requirements/recommendations for international students: required—TOEFL (minimum score 550 paper-based; 79 iBT).

Texas A&M University, College of Liberal Arts, Department of English, College Station, TX 77843. Offers English (PhD). *Faculty:* 36. *Students:* 62 full-time (50 women), 23 part-time (19 women); includes 21 minority (2 Black or African American, non-Hispanic/Latino; 5 Asian, non-Hispanic/Latino; 12 Hispanic/Latino; 2 Two or more races, non-Hispanic/Latino), 24 international. Average age 32. 63 applicants, 49% accepted, 16 enrolled. In 2019, 10 master's, 13 doctorates awarded. Terminal master's awarded for partial completion of doctoral program. *Degree requirements:* For master's, one foreign language, thesis optional; for doctorate, 2 foreign languages, comprehensive exam, thesis/dissertation. *Entrance requirements:* For master's and doctorate, GRE General Test, sample of written work. Additional exam requirements/recommendations for international students: required—TOEFL (minimum score 550 paper-based; 80 iBT), IELTS (minimum score 6), PTE (minimum score 53). *Application deadline:* For fall admission, 12/14 for domestic students. Application fee: $65 ($90 for international students). Electronic applications accepted. *Expenses:* Contact institution. *Financial support:* In 2019–20, 64 students received support, including 5 fellowships with tuition reimbursements available (averaging $15,899 per year), 9 research assistantships with partial tuition reimbursements available (averaging $7,525 per year), 59 teaching assistantships with partial tuition reimbursements available (averaging $14,268 per year); career-related internships or fieldwork, institutionally sponsored loans, scholarships/grants, traineeships, health care benefits, tuition waivers (full and partial), and unspecified assistantships also available. Support available to part-time students. Financial award application deadline: 3/15; financial award applicants required to submit FAFSA. *Unit head:* Dr. Maura Ives, Department Head, 979-845-8319, E-mail: m-ives@tamu.edu. *Application contact:* Director of Graduate Studies, 979-845-9836, Fax: 979-862-2292, E-mail: engl-graduate-office@lists.tamu.edu.
Website: https://liberalarts.tamu.edu/english/

Texas A&M University–Commerce, College of Humanities, Social Sciences and Arts, Commerce, TX 75429. Offers applied criminology (MS); applied linguistics (MA, MS); art (MA, MFA); christianity in history (Graduate Certificate); computational linguistics (Graduate Certificate); creative writing (Graduate Certificate); criminal justice management (Graduate Certificate); criminal justice studies (Graduate Certificate); English (MA, MS, PhD); film studies (Graduate Certificate); history (MA, MS); Holocaust studies (Graduate Certificate); homeland security (Graduate Certificate); music (MM); music performance (MM); political science (MA, MS); public history (Graduate Certificate); sociology (MS); Spanish (MA); studies in children's and adolescent literature and culture (Graduate Certificate); teaching English to speakers of other languages (Graduate Certificate); theater (MA, MS); world history (Graduate Certificate). *Program availability:* Part-time. *Faculty:* 49 full-time (28 women), 8 part-time/adjunct (2 women). *Students:* 34 full-time (21 women), 427 part-time (302 women); includes 175 minority (66 Black or African American, non-Hispanic/Latino; 1 American Indian or Alaska Native, non-Hispanic/Latino; 13 Asian, non-Hispanic/Latino; 79 Hispanic/Latino; 16 Two or more races, non-Hispanic/Latino), 15 international. Average age 38. 193 applicants, 49% accepted, 78 enrolled. In 2019, 122 master's, 6 doctorates awarded. *Degree requirements:* For master's, one foreign language, comprehensive exam, thesis (for some programs); for doctorate, one foreign language, comprehensive exam, thesis/dissertation, departmental qualifying exam. *Entrance requirements:* For master's, GRE General Test, official transcripts, letters of recommendation, resume, statement of goals; for doctorate, GRE General Test, official transcripts, letters of recommendation, statement of goals, writing samples, writing sessions, resumes. Additional exam requirements/recommendations for international students: required—TOEFL (minimum score 550 paper-based; 79 iBT), IELTS (minimum score 6), PTE (minimum score 53). *Application deadline:* For fall admission, 6/1 priority date for international students; for spring admission, 10/15 priority date for international students; for summer admission, 3/15 priority date for international students. Applications are processed on a rolling basis. Application fee: $50 ($75 for international students). Electronic applications accepted. *Expenses: Tuition, area resident:* Full-time $3630; part-time $202 per credit hour. Tuition, state resident: full-time $3630; part-time $202 per credit hour. Tuition,

nonresident: full-time $11,232; part-time $624 per credit hour. *International tuition:* $11,232 full-time. *Required fees:* $2948. *Financial support:* In 2019–20, 30 students received support, including 18 research assistantships with partial tuition reimbursements available (averaging $3,231 per year), 136 teaching assistantships with partial tuition reimbursements available (averaging $4,053 per year); Federal Work-Study, institutionally sponsored loans, scholarships/grants, health care benefits, and unspecified assistantships also available. Financial award application deadline: 5/1; financial award applicants required to submit FAFSA. *Unit head:* Dr. William F. Kuracina, Interim Dean, 903-886-5166, Fax: 903-886-5774, E-mail: william.kuracina@tamuc.edu. *Application contact:* Rebecca Stevens, Graduate Student Services Coordinator, 903-468-6049, E-mail: rebecca.stevens@tamuc.edu.
Website: http://www.tamuc.edu/academics/colleges/humanitiesSocialSciencesArts/

Texas A&M University–Corpus Christi, College of Graduate Studies, College of Liberal Arts, Program in English, Corpus Christi, TX 78412. Offers MA. *Program availability:* Part-time, evening/weekend. *Degree requirements:* For master's, comprehensive exam, thesis optional, capstone experience. *Entrance requirements:* For master's, essay (500-1,000 words), writing sample (minimum of 2,000 words), 3 letters of recommendation. Additional exam requirements/recommendations for international students: required—TOEFL (minimum score 550 paper-based; 79 iBT), IELTS (minimum score 6.5). Electronic applications accepted.

Texas A&M University–Kingsville, College of Graduate Studies, College of Arts and Sciences, Department of Language and Literature, Kingsville, TX 78363. Offers cultural studies (MA); English (MA, MS); Spanish (MA). *Entrance requirements:* Additional exam requirements/recommendations for international students: required—TOEFL (minimum score 550 paper-based; 79 iBT); recommended—IELTS. Electronic applications accepted.

Texas A&M University–San Antonio, School of Arts and Sciences, San Antonio, TX 78224. Offers English (MA). *Program availability:* Part-time, evening/weekend, online learning. *Degree requirements:* For master's, comprehensive exam, thesis. *Entrance requirements:* For master's, GRE (Verbal and Writing), analytical writing sample of 6-10 pages; two letters of recommendation, at least one from former professor. Additional exam requirements/recommendations for international students: required—TOEFL (minimum score 550 paper-based; 79 iBT), IELTS (minimum score 6). Electronic applications accepted. *Expenses: Tuition, area resident:* Full-time $3822; part-time $1068 per semester. *Required fees:* $2146; $1412 per unit. $706 per semester.

Texas A&M University–Texarkana, Graduate Studies and Research, College of Education and Liberal Arts, Texarkana, TX 75503. Offers adult education (MS); curriculum and instruction (M Ed); education (MS); educational administration (M Ed); English (MA); instructional technology (MS); interdisciplinary studies (MA, MS); special education (MS). *Program availability:* Part-time, evening/weekend. *Degree requirements:* For master's, comprehensive exam (for some programs), thesis optional. *Entrance requirements:* For master's, minimum GPA of 2.5 on last 60 hours of bachelor's degree. Additional exam requirements/recommendations for international students: required—TOEFL. Electronic applications accepted.

Texas Christian University, AddRan College of Liberal Arts, Department of English, Fort Worth, TX 76129-0002. Offers English (MA, PhD); rhetoric and composition (PhD). *Faculty:* 18 full-time (11 women), 1 (woman) part-time/adjunct. *Students:* 54 full-time (38 women); includes 12 minority (3 Black or African American, non-Hispanic/Latino; 7 Hispanic/Latino; 2 Two or more races, non-Hispanic/Latino), 5 international. Average age 29. 33 applicants, 70% accepted, 12 enrolled. In 2019, 5 master's, 6 doctorates awarded. *Degree requirements:* For master's, one foreign language, thesis; for doctorate, one foreign language, comprehensive exam, thesis/dissertation. *Entrance requirements:* For master's and doctorate, GRE General Test. Additional exam requirements/recommendations for international students: required—TOEFL. *Application deadline:* 1/10 for domestic and international students. Application fee: $60. Electronic applications accepted. *Expenses:* Contact institution. *Financial support:* In 2019–20, 47 students received support, including 4 fellowships with full tuition reimbursements available (averaging $21,000 per year), 7 research assistantships with full tuition reimbursements available, 24 teaching assistantships with full tuition reimbursements available (averaging $18,660 per year); career-related internships or fieldwork, health care benefits, tuition waivers (full), and unspecified assistantships also available. Financial award application deadline: 1/10; financial award applicants required to submit FAFSA. *Unit head:* Dr. Brad E. Lucas, Director of Graduate Studies, 817-257-6981, Fax: 817-257-6238, E-mail: b.e.lucas2@tcu.edu. *Application contact:* Merry Roberts, English Department Office Manager, 817-257-6890, Fax: 817-257-6238, E-mail: m.roberts@tcu.edu.
Website: http://www.eng.tcu.edu/

Texas Southern University, College of Liberal Arts and Behavioral Sciences, Department of English, Houston, TX 77004-4584. Offers MA. *Program availability:* Part-time. *Degree requirements:* For master's, one foreign language, comprehensive exam, thesis. *Entrance requirements:* For master's, GRE General Test, minimum GPA of 2.5. Additional exam requirements/recommendations for international students: required—TOEFL. Electronic applications accepted.

Texas State University, The Graduate College, College of Liberal Arts, Program in Literature, San Marcos, TX 78666. Offers MA. *Program availability:* Part-time, evening/weekend. *Degree requirements:* For master's, comprehensive exam, thesis optional. *Entrance requirements:* For master's, baccalaureate degree from regionally-accredited university with minimum GPA of 2.75 on last 60 undergraduate semester hours, 3.25 in minimum of 24 hours of undergraduate English including at least 12 advanced hours; minimum of 6 hours in a foreign language; 2 letters of recommendation; writing sample of non-fiction prose. Additional exam requirements/recommendations for international students: required—TOEFL (minimum score 550 paper-based; 78 iBT), IELTS (minimum score 6.5). Electronic applications accepted.

Texas Tech University, Graduate School, College of Arts and Sciences, Department of English, Lubbock, TX 79409-3091. Offers English (MA, PhD); technical communication (MA); technical communication and rhetoric (PhD). *Program availability:* Part-time, evening/weekend, 100% online, blended/hybrid learning. *Faculty:* 67 full-time (34 women), 4 part-time/adjunct (3 women). *Students:* 105 full-time (67 women), 102 part-time (74 women); includes 44 minority (8 Black or African American, non-Hispanic/Latino; 1 American Indian or Alaska Native, non-Hispanic/Latino; 2 Asian, non-Hispanic/Latino; 24 Hispanic/Latino; 9 Two or more races, non-Hispanic/Latino), 11 international. Average age 33. 201 applicants, 54% accepted, 58 enrolled. In 2019, 16 master's, 28 doctorates awarded. Terminal master's awarded for partial completion of doctoral program. *Degree requirements:* For master's, variable foreign language requirement, comprehensive exam, thesis optional; for doctorate, variable foreign language requirement, comprehensive exam, thesis/dissertation. *Entrance requirements:* For master's and doctorate, GRE General Test. Additional exam requirements/recommendations for international students: required—TOEFL (minimum score 550 paper-based; 79 iBT), IELTS (minimum score 6.5). *Application deadline:* For fall admission, 6/1 priority date for domestic students, 1/15 priority date for international students; for spring admission, 9/1 priority date for domestic students, 6/15 priority date for international students. Applications are processed on a rolling basis. Application fee: $65. Electronic applications accepted. *Expenses:* Contact institution. *Financial support:* In 2019–20, 127 students received support, including 103 fellowships (averaging $2,361 per year), 5 research assistantships (averaging $18,968 per year), 101 teaching assistantships (averaging $17,254 per year); career-related internships or fieldwork, Federal Work-Study, scholarships/grants, and unspecified assistantships also available. Financial award application deadline: 1/8; financial award applicants required to submit FAFSA. *Unit head:* Dr. Brian Still, Department Chair, 806-834-6439, Fax: 806-742-0989, E-mail: brian.still@ttu.edu. *Application contact:* Dr. Julie Nelson Couch, Director of Graduate Studies, 806-834-1742, Fax: 806-742-0989, E-mail: english.gradadvisor@ttu.edu.
Website: www.english.ttu.edu/

Texas Woman's University, Graduate School, College of Arts and Sciences, Department of English, Speech, and Foreign Languages, Denton, TX 76204. Offers English (MA, MAT); rhetoric (PhD). *Program availability:* Part-time. *Faculty:* 7 full-time (5 women), 1 (woman) part-time/adjunct. *Students:* 6 full-time (5 women), 47 part-time (43 women); includes 18 minority (5 Black or African American, non-Hispanic/Latino; 2 Asian, non-Hispanic/Latino; 8 Hispanic/Latino; 3 Two or more races, non-Hispanic/Latino), 1 international. Average age 37. 25 applicants, 88% accepted, 14 enrolled. In 2019, 8 master's, 3 doctorates awarded. *Degree requirements:* For master's, comprehensive exam, thesis or alternative, professional paper, thesis or coursework; for doctorate, comprehensive exam, thesis/dissertation, residency for at least 2 consecutive semesters (strongly encouraged), oral defense of dissertation. *Entrance requirements:* For master's, 3 letters of reference, minimum GPA of 3.0 on previous upper-division undergraduate and graduate work, writing sample, statement of purpose; for doctorate, writing sample, 3 letters of reference, interview (for graduate assistants), minimum GPA of 3.0 on previous upper-division and graduate work, statement of purpose, masters's degree (bachelor's or masters must be in English). Additional exam requirements/recommendations for international students: required—TOEFL (minimum score 600 paper-based; 79 iBT); recommended—IELTS (minimum score 6.5). *Application deadline:* For fall admission, 7/1 priority date for domestic students, 3/1 priority date for international students; for spring admission, 11/1 priority date for domestic students, 7/1 priority date for international students; for summer admission, 4/1 priority date for domestic students, 2/1 priority date for international students. Applications are processed on a rolling basis. Application fee: $50 ($75 for international students). Electronic applications accepted. *Expenses: Tuition, area resident:* Full-time $4973.40; part-time $276.30 per semester hour. Tuition, state resident: full-time $4973.40; part-time $276.30 per semester hour. Tuition, nonresident: full-time $12,569; part-time $698.30 per semester hour. *International tuition:* $12,569.40 full-time. *Required fees:* $2524.30. Tuition and fees vary according to course level, course load, degree level and program. *Financial support:* In 2019–20, 25 students received support, including 16 teaching assistantships (averaging $10,412 per year); career-related internships or fieldwork, scholarships/grants, health care benefits, and unspecified assistantships also available. Support available to part-time students. Financial award application deadline: 3/1; financial award applicants required to submit FAFSA. *Unit head:* Dr. Genevieve West, Chair, 940-898-2324, Fax: 940-898-2297, E-mail: engspfl@twu.edu. *Application contact:* Korie Hawkins, Associate Director of Admissions, Graduate Recruitment, 940-898-3188, Fax: 940-898-3081, E-mail: admissions@twu.edu.
Website: http://www.twu.edu/english-speech-foreign-languages/

Tiffin University, Program in Humanities, Tiffin, OH 44883-2161. Offers art and visual media (MH); communication (MH); creative writing (MH); English (MH); film studies (MH); humanities (MH); individualized studies (MH). *Program availability:* Part-time, evening/weekend, online only, 100% online, blended/hybrid learning. *Entrance requirements:* For master's, work experience. Additional exam requirements/recommendations for international students: required—TOEFL (minimum score 550 paper-based; 79 iBT). Electronic applications accepted. Application fee is waived when completed online. *Expenses:* Contact institution.

Trinity College, Graduate Programs, Program in English, Hartford, CT 06106-3100. Offers literary studies (MA); writing, rhetoric, and media arts (MA). *Program availability:* Part-time, evening/weekend. *Degree requirements:* For master's, thesis (for some programs). *Entrance requirements:* For master's, minimum GPA of 3.0.

Trinity Western University, School of Graduate Studies, Master of Arts in Interdisciplinary Humanities, Langley, BC V2Y 1Y1, Canada. Offers general humanities (MAIH); specialized (MAIH), including English, history, philosophy. *Program availability:* Part-time. *Degree requirements:* For master's, thesis or alternative, 30 semester hours. *Entrance requirements:* For master's, Strong undergraduate degree in humanities or English, history or philosophy. Additional exam requirements/recommendations for international students: required—TOEFL (minimum score 105 iBT), IELTS (minimum score 7.5), DuoLingo. *Application deadline:* Applications are processed on a rolling basis. Electronic applications accepted. *Expenses:* Contact institution. *Financial support:* Fellowships, research assistantships, teaching assistantships, career-related internships or fieldwork, scholarships/grants, and unspecified assistantships available. Support available to part-time students. Financial award application deadline: 4/1. *Unit head:* Dr. Bruce Shelvey, Director, E-mail: bruce.shelvey@twu.ca. *Application contact:* Phil Kay, Director, Graduate Admissions, 604-513-2121 Ext. 3444, E-mail: phil.kay@twu.ca.
Website: http://www.twu.ca/academics/

Truman State University, Office of Graduate Studies, School of Arts and Letters, Program in English, Kirksville, MO 63501-4221. Offers MA. *Degree requirements:* For master's, comprehensive exam, thesis. *Entrance requirements:* For master's, GRE General Test, minimum GPA of 3.0. Additional exam requirements/recommendations for international students: required—TOEFL (minimum score 550 paper-based). Electronic applications accepted. Application fee is waived when completed online. *Expenses:* Tuition, state resident: full-time $4630; part-time $385.50 per credit hour. Tuition, nonresident: full-time $8018; part-time $668 per credit hour. *International tuition:* $8018 full-time. *Required fees:* $324. Full-time tuition and fees vary according to course level, course load, program and reciprocity agreements.

Tufts University, Graduate School of Arts and Sciences, Department of English, Medford, MA 02155. Offers MA, PhD. Terminal master's awarded for partial completion of doctoral program. *Degree requirements:* For master's, one foreign language, thesis; for doctorate, 2 foreign languages, thesis/dissertation. *Entrance requirements:* For master's and doctorate, GRE General Test, GRE Subject Test, writing sample. Additional exam requirements/recommendations for international students: required—TOEFL (minimum score 550 paper-based; 80 iBT), IELTS (minimum score 6.5). Electronic applications accepted. *Expenses:* Contact institution.

Tulane University, School of Liberal Arts, Department of English, New Orleans, LA 70118-5669. Offers MA. *Degree requirements:* For master's, one foreign language, thesis or alternative. *Entrance requirements:* For master's, GRE General Test, minimum B average in undergraduate course work. Additional exam requirements/recommendations for international students: required—TOEFL. Electronic applications accepted. *Expenses: Tuition:* Full-time $57,004; part-time $3167 per credit hour. *Required fees:* $2086; $44.50 per credit hour. $80 per term. Tuition and fees vary according to course load, degree level and program.

UNB Fredericton, School of Graduate Studies, Faculty of Arts - Saint John, Department of English, Fredericton, NB E3B 5A3, Canada. Offers MA, PhD. *Program availability:* Part-time. *Faculty:* 13 full-time (6 women), 2 part-time/adjunct (0 women). *Students:* 31 full-time (14 women), 2 part-time (0 women), 6 international. Average age 35. In 2019, 6 master's, 1 doctorate awarded. *Degree requirements:* For master's, thesis, 18 credit hours; for doctorate, one foreign language, comprehensive exam, thesis/dissertation. *Entrance requirements:* For master's, BA with minimum GPA of 3.5, honors English (preferred); for doctorate, minimum GPA of 3.7; MA in English. Additional exam requirements/recommendations for international students: required—TWE (minimum score 4), TOEFL (minimum paper-based score 600) or IELTS (minimum score 7). *Application deadline:* For winter admission, 1/15 priority date for domestic and international students. Applications are processed on a rolling basis. Application fee: $50 Canadian dollars. Electronic applications accepted. *Expenses: Tuition, area resident:* Full-time $6975 Canadian dollars; part-time $3423 Canadian dollars per year. Tuition, state resident: full-time $6975 Canadian dollars; part-time $3423 Canadian dollars per year. Tuition, Canadian resident: full-time $6975 Canadian dollars; part-time $3423 Canadian dollars per year. *International tuition:* $12,435 Canadian dollars full-time. *Required fees:* $92.25 Canadian dollars per term. Full-time tuition and fees vary according to degree level, campus/location, program, reciprocity agreements and student level. *Financial support:* Fellowships, research assistantships with full tuition reimbursements, teaching assistantships with full tuition reimbursements, and health care benefits available. Financial award application deadline: 1/31. *Unit head:* Dr. Rendall Martin, Director of Graduate Studies, 506-458-7407, Fax: 506-453-5069, E-mail: rmartin@unb.ca. *Application contact:* Theresa Keenan, Graduate Secretary, 506-451-6809, Fax: 506-453-5069, E-mail: tkeenan@unb.ca. Website: http://go.unb.ca/gradprograms

Universidad de las Américas Puebla, Division of Graduate Studies, School of Humanities, Program in Literature, Puebla, Mexico. Offers MA. *Program availability:* Part-time, evening/weekend. *Degree requirements:* For master's, one foreign language, thesis. *Entrance requirements:* Additional exam requirements/recommendations for international students: required—TOEFL.

Université de Montréal, Faculty of Arts and Sciences, Department of English Studies, Montréal, QC H3C 3J7, Canada. Offers MA, PhD. *Degree requirements:* For doctorate, thesis/dissertation, general exam. *Entrance requirements:* For master's, BA in English with minimum B+ average; for doctorate, MA in English with minimum B+ average. Electronic applications accepted.

University at Albany, State University of New York, College of Arts and Sciences, Department of English, Albany, NY 12222-0001. Offers MA, PhD. *Program availability:* Part-time, blended/hybrid learning. *Faculty:* 24 full-time (10 women), 28 part-time/adjunct (14 women). *Students:* 37 full-time (24 women), 66 part-time (39 women); includes 14 minority (4 Black or African American, non-Hispanic/Latino; 2 Asian, non-Hispanic/Latino; 5 Hispanic/Latino; 3 Two or more races, non-Hispanic/Latino), 19 international. 82 applicants, 35% accepted, 21 enrolled. In 2019, 18 master's, 4 doctorates awarded. *Degree requirements:* For master's, one foreign language; for doctorate, one foreign language, comprehensive exam, thesis/dissertation, residency. *Entrance requirements:* For master's, GRE General Test, GRE Subject Test, transcripts of all schools attended, statement of background and goals, departmental questionnaire, resume, names and contact information for 3 recommenders; for doctorate, GRE General Test, GRE Subject Test. Additional exam requirements/recommendations for international students: required—TOEFL (minimum score 550 paper-based). *Application deadline:* For fall admission, 1/15 for domestic and international students; for spring admission, 11/15 for domestic and international students. Applications are processed on a rolling basis. Application fee: $75. Electronic applications accepted. *Expenses: Tuition, area resident:* Full-time $11,530; part-time $480 per credit hour. Tuition, nonresident: full-time $23,530; part-time $980 per credit hour. *International tuition:* $23,530 full-time. *Required fees:* $2185; $96 per credit hour. Part-time tuition and fees vary according to course load and program. *Financial support:* Fellowships and career-related internships or fieldwork available. Financial award application deadline: 2/15. *Unit head:* Glyne Griffith, Chair, 518-442-4056, Fax: 518-442-4599. *Application contact:* Michael DeRensis, Director, Graduate Admissions, 518-442-3980, Fax: 518-442-3922, E-mail: graduate@albany.edu. Website: https://www.albany.edu/english/

University at Buffalo, the State University of New York, Graduate School, College of Arts and Sciences, Department of English, Buffalo, NY 14260. Offers MA, PhD. *Program availability:* Part-time. Terminal master's awarded for partial completion of doctoral program. *Degree requirements:* For master's, thesis or alternative; for doctorate, thesis/dissertation, departmental qualifying exam. *Entrance requirements:* For master's and doctorate, GRE General Test, sample of written work. Additional exam requirements/recommendations for international students: required—TOEFL (minimum score 79 iBT). Electronic applications accepted. *Expenses: Tuition, area resident:* Full-time $11,310; part-time $471 per credit hour. Tuition, state resident: full-time $11,310; part-time $471 per credit hour. Tuition, nonresident: full-time $23,100; part-time $963 per credit hour. *International tuition:* $23,100 full-time. *Required fees:* $2820.

University at Buffalo, the State University of New York, Graduate School, Graduate School of Education, Department of Learning and Instruction, Buffalo, NY 14260. Offers biology education (Ed M, Certificate); chemistry education (Ed M, Certificate); childhood education (Ed M); childhood education with bilingual extension (Ed M); college teaching (Advanced Certificate); curriculum, instruction and the science of learning (PhD); early childhood education (Ed M); early childhood education with bilingual extension (Ed M); earth science education (Ed M, Certificate); education and technology (Ed M); education studies (Ed M); educational technology and new literacies (Certificate); educational technology and new literacies (Advanced Certificate); elementary education (Ed D); English education (Ed M, Certificate); English education studies (Ed M); English for speakers of other languages (Ed M); foreign and second language education (PhD); French education (Ed M, Certificate); German education (Ed M, Certificate); gifted education (Certificate); Latin education (Ed M, Certificate); literacy education studies (Ed M); literacy specialist (Ed M); literacy teaching and learning (Certificate); mathematics education (Ed M, Certificate); music education (Ed M, Certificate); music education studies (Ed M); music learning theory (Advanced Certificate); online education (Advanced Certificate); physics education (Ed M, Certificate); science and the public (Ed M); social studies education (Ed M, Certificate); Spanish education (Ed M, Certificate); special education (PhD); teaching English to speakers of other languages (Ed M). *Program availability:* Part-time, evening/weekend, 100% online, blended/hybrid learning. *Faculty:* 26 full-time (19 women), 42 part-time/adjunct (29 women). *Students:* 227 full-time (158 women), 322 part-time (228 women); includes 85 minority (34 Black or African American, non-Hispanic/Latino; 3 American Indian or Alaska Native, non-Hispanic/Latino; 17 Asian, non-Hispanic/Latino; 23 Hispanic/Latino; 8 Two or more races, non-Hispanic/Latino), 42 international. Average age 33. 385 applicants, 61% accepted, 158 enrolled. In 2019, 100 master's, 23 doctorates, 16 other advanced degrees awarded. *Degree requirements:* For master's, comprehensive exam; for doctorate, thesis/dissertation, research analysis exam, research experience; for other advanced degree, thesis (for some programs). *Entrance requirements:* For master's, GRE or MAT for teacher preparation programs only, letters of reference; for doctorate,

GRE General Test or MAT, interview, writing sample, letters of recommendation, resume. Additional exam requirements/recommendations for international students: required—TOEFL (minimum score 600 paper-based; 96 iBT), IELTS (minimum score 6.5), PTE (minimum score 55), The Graduate School of Education requires international students to submit test scores for at least one of the exams (TOEFL, IELTS, PTE). *Application deadline:* For fall admission, 2/1 priority date for domestic and international students. Applications are processed on a rolling basis. Application fee: $50. Electronic applications accepted. *Expenses: Tuition, area resident:* Full-time $11,310; part-time $471 per credit hour. Tuition, state resident: full-time $11,310; part-time $471 per credit hour. Tuition, nonresident: full-time $23,100; part-time $963 per credit hour. *International tuition:* $23,100 full-time. *Required fees:* $2820. *Financial support:* In 2019–20, 16 fellowships (averaging $20,000 per year), 5 research assistantships with tuition reimbursements (averaging $26,917 per year) were awarded; teaching assistantships, career-related internships or fieldwork, Federal Work-Study, institutionally sponsored loans, scholarships/grants, tuition waivers (full and partial), and unspecified assistantships also available. Financial award application deadline: 2/28; financial award applicants required to submit FAFSA. *Unit head:* Dr. Julie Gorlewski, Department Chair, 716-645-2455, Fax: 716-645-3161, E-mail: jgorlews@buffalo.edu. *Application contact:* Renad Aref, Assistant Director of Admission Recruitment, 716-645-2110, Fax: 716-645-7937, E-mail: gseinfo@buffalo.edu. Website: http://ed.buffalo.edu/teaching.html

The University of Akron, Graduate School, Buchtel College of Arts and Sciences, Department of English, Program in Literature, Akron, OH 44325. Offers MA. *Degree requirements:* For master's, thesis optional. *Entrance requirements:* For master's, statement of purpose. Additional exam requirements/recommendations for international students: required—TOEFL (minimum score 92 iBT).

The University of Alabama, Graduate School, College of Arts and Sciences, Department of English, Tuscaloosa, AL 35487. Offers composition and rhetoric (PhD); creative writing (MFA), including fiction, poetry; literature (MA, PhD); rhetoric and composition (MA); teaching English as a second language (MATESOL). *Faculty:* 21 full-time (14 women). *Students:* 122 full-time (82 women), 8 part-time (5 women); includes 29 minority (11 Black or African American, non-Hispanic/Latino; 2 American Indian or Alaska Native, non-Hispanic/Latino; 5 Asian, non-Hispanic/Latino; 3 Hispanic/Latino; 8 Two or more races, non-Hispanic/Latino), 8 international. Average age 29. 230 applicants, 25% accepted, 35 enrolled. In 2019, 32 master's awarded. *Degree requirements:* For master's, one foreign language, comprehensive exam, thesis; for doctorate, 2 foreign languages, comprehensive exam, thesis/dissertation. *Entrance requirements:* For master's, GRE (minimum score of 300, except for MFA), minimum GPA of 3.0, critical writing sample; for doctorate, GRE (minimum score of 300), minimum GPA of 3.5 on master's or equivalent graduate work, critical writing sample. Additional exam requirements/recommendations for international students: recommended—TOEFL (minimum score 550 paper-based; 79 iBT). *Application deadline:* For fall admission, 12/31 for domestic and international students. Application fee: $50 ($60 for international students). Electronic applications accepted. *Expenses: Tuition, area resident:* Full-time $10,780; part-time $440 per credit hour. Tuition, nonresident: full-time $30,250; part-time $1550 per credit hour. *Financial support:* In 2019–20, 113 students received support, including fellowships with full tuition reimbursements available (averaging $15,000 per year), research assistantships with full tuition reimbursements available (averaging $13,500 per year), teaching assistantships with full tuition reimbursements available (averaging $13,500 per year); career-related internships or fieldwork, scholarships/grants, health care benefits, and unspecified assistantships also available. Financial award application deadline: 12/31. *Unit head:* Dr. David Ainsworth, Associate Professor and Interim Chair, 205-348-9524, Fax: 205-348-1388, E-mail: dainsworth@ua.edu. *Application contact:* Jennifer Fuqua, Graduate Coordinator, 205-348-0766, Fax: 205-348-1388, E-mail: jfuqua@ua.edu.

The University of Alabama at Birmingham, College of Arts and Sciences, Program in English, Birmingham, AL 35294. Offers creative writing (MA); literature (MA); rhetoric and composition (MA). *Program availability:* Part-time. *Faculty:* 35 full-time (18 women). *Students:* 6 full-time (5 women), 21 part-time (16 women); includes 5 minority (3 Black or African American, non-Hispanic/Latino; 1 American Indian or Alaska Native, non-Hispanic/Latino; 1 Two or more races, non-Hispanic/Latino). Average age 32. 13 applicants, 69% accepted, 5 enrolled. In 2019, 11 master's awarded. *Degree requirements:* For master's, one foreign language, comprehensive exam, thesis or alternative. *Entrance requirements:* For master's, GRE General Test or MAT, minimum GPA of 2.75. *Application deadline:* For fall admission, 7/1 for domestic students; for spring admission, 11/1 for domestic students. Applications are processed on a rolling basis. Application fee: $45 ($60 for international students). Electronic applications accepted. *Financial support:* Teaching assistantships and career-related internships or fieldwork available. *Unit head:* Dr. Gale Temple, Program Director, 205-934-8593, Fax: 205-975-6610, E-mail: gtemple@uab.edu. *Application contact:* Susan Noblitt Banks, Director of Graduate School Operations, 205-934-8227, Fax: 205-934-8413, E-mail: gradschool@uab.edu. Website: http://www.uab.edu/cas/english/academic-programs

The University of Alabama in Huntsville, School of Graduate Studies, College of Arts, Humanities, and Social Sciences, Department of English, Huntsville, AL 35899. Offers education (MA); English (MA); technical writing (Certificate); TESOL (Certificate). *Program availability:* Part-time. *Degree requirements:* For master's, one foreign language, comprehensive exam, thesis or alternative, oral and written exams. *Entrance requirements:* For master's and Certificate, GRE General Test, minimum GPA of 3.0. Additional exam requirements/recommendations for international students: required—TOEFL (minimum score 500 paper-based; 80 iBT), IELTS (minimum score 6.5). Electronic applications accepted.

University of Alaska Anchorage, College of Arts and Sciences, Department of English, Anchorage, AK 99508. Offers MA. *Program availability:* Part-time. *Degree requirements:* For master's, comprehensive exam, thesis or alternative. *Entrance requirements:* For master's, GRE General Test, GRE Subject Test, portfolio, minimum GPA of 3.5, writing sample. Additional exam requirements/recommendations for international students: required—TOEFL (minimum score 550 paper-based).

University of Alaska Fairbanks, College of Liberal Arts, Department of English, Fairbanks, AK 99775-5720. Offers creative writing (MFA); literature (MA); MA/MFA. *Program availability:* Part-time. *Degree requirements:* For master's, comprehensive exam, oral defense of project or thesis. *Entrance requirements:* For master's, bachelor's degree from accredited institution with minimum cumulative undergraduate and major GPA of 3.0, creative writing sample (MFA), scholarly to critical writing sample (MA), creative writing sample and scholarly writing sample (MFA/MA). Additional exam requirements/recommendations for international students: required—TOEFL (minimum score 550 paper-based; 79 iBT), IELTS (minimum score 6.5). Electronic applications accepted.

University of Alberta, Faculty of Graduate Studies and Research, Department of English and Film Studies, Edmonton, AB T6G 2E1, Canada. Offers English (MA, PhD). *Program availability:* Part-time, evening/weekend. *Degree requirements:* For master's, one foreign language, thesis optional; for doctorate, 2 foreign languages, thesis/dissertation. *Entrance requirements:* For master's, honors BA or equivalent; for doctorate, honors BA and MA. Additional exam requirements/recommendations for international students: required—TOEFL (minimum score 600 paper-based). Electronic applications accepted.

The University of Arizona, College of Humanities, Department of English, English Language/Linguistics Program, Tucson, AZ 85721. Offers English (MA, PhD); ESL (MA). *Entrance requirements:* Additional exam requirements/recommendations for international students: required—TOEFL (minimum score 550 paper-based; 79 iBT); recommended—IELTS (minimum score 7). Electronic applications accepted.

University of Arkansas, Graduate School, J. William Fulbright College of Arts and Sciences, Department of English, Program in English, Fayetteville, AR 72701. Offers MA, PhD. *Students:* 32 full-time (21 women), 12 part-time (7 women); includes 3 minority (1 American Indian or Alaska Native, non-Hispanic/Latino; 1 Hispanic/Latino; 1 Two or more races, non-Hispanic/Latino), 3 international. 33 applicants, 61% accepted. In 2019, 13 master's, 2 doctorates awarded. *Entrance requirements:* For master's, GRE General Test; for doctorate, GRE General Test, GRE Subject Test. *Application deadline:* For fall admission, 8/1 for domestic students, 4/1 for international students; for spring admission, 12/1 for domestic students, 10/1 for international students; for summer admission, 4/15 for domestic students, 3/1 for international students. Applications are processed on a rolling basis. Application fee: $60. Electronic applications accepted. *Financial support:* In 2019–20, 3 research assistantships, 44 teaching assistantships were awarded; fellowships with tuition reimbursements, career-related internships or fieldwork, and Federal Work-Study also available. Support available to part-time students. Financial award application deadline: 4/1; financial award applicants required to submit FAFSA. *Unit head:* Dr. William Quinn, Department Chair, 479-575-4301, Fax: 479-575-5919, E-mail: wquinn@uark.edu. *Application contact:* Dr. Joshua Smith, 479-575-4694, Fax: 479-575-5919, E-mail: jbs016@uark.edu.
Website: https://fulbright.uark.edu/departments/english/

The University of British Columbia, Faculty of Arts, Department of English, Vancouver, BC V6T 1Z1, Canada. Offers MA, PhD. *Degree requirements:* For master's, thesis or alternative; for doctorate, one foreign language, comprehensive exam, thesis/dissertation. *Entrance requirements:* For master's, BA or equivalent; for doctorate, MA. Additional exam requirements/recommendations for international students: required—TOEFL, IELTS. Electronic applications accepted. *Expenses:* Contact institution.

The University of British Columbia, Faculty of Arts, School of Library, Archival and Information Studies, Master of Arts Program in Children's Literature, Vancouver, BC V6T 1Z1, Canada. Offers MA. *Program availability:* Part-time. *Degree requirements:* For master's, thesis. *Entrance requirements:* For master's, minimum GPA of 3.3 in undergraduate upper-division courses. Additional exam requirements/recommendations for international students: required—TOEFL. Electronic applications accepted. *Expenses:* Contact institution.

University of California, Berkeley, Graduate Division, College of Letters and Science, Department of English, Berkeley, CA 94720. Offers PhD. *Degree requirements:* For doctorate, 2 foreign languages, thesis/dissertation, qualifying exam. *Entrance requirements:* For doctorate, GRE General Test, GRE Subject Test, minimum GPA of 3.0, writing sample, 3 letters of recommendation. Electronic applications accepted.

University of California, Davis, Graduate Studies, Program in English, Davis, CA 95616. Offers creative writing (MA); English (MA, PhD). Terminal master's awarded for partial completion of doctoral program. *Degree requirements:* For master's, one foreign language, thesis optional; for doctorate, 2 foreign languages, thesis/dissertation. *Entrance requirements:* For master's and doctorate, GRE General Test, GRE Subject Test, minimum GPA of 3.0, writing sample. Additional exam requirements/recommendations for international students: required—TOEFL (minimum score 550 paper-based). Electronic applications accepted.

University of California, Irvine, School of Humanities, Department of English, Program in English, Irvine, CA 92697. Offers English (MA); English and American literature (PhD). *Students:* 59 full-time (34 women); includes 15 minority (2 Black or African American, non-Hispanic/Latino; 4 Asian, non-Hispanic/Latino; 5 Hispanic/Latino; 4 Two or more races, non-Hispanic/Latino), 4 international. Average age 31. 166 applicants, 16% accepted, 13 enrolled. In 2019, 23 master's, 8 doctorates awarded. Terminal master's awarded for partial completion of doctoral program. *Degree requirements:* For master's, one foreign language, comprehensive exam; for doctorate, 2 foreign languages, comprehensive exam, thesis/dissertation. *Entrance requirements:* For doctorate, GRE General Test, GRE Subject Test, minimum GPA of 3.5, sample of written work, 3 letters of recommendation. Additional exam requirements/recommendations for international students: required—TOEFL (minimum score 550 paper-based). *Application deadline:* For fall admission, 12/1 for domestic and international students. Application fee: $120 ($140 for international students). Electronic applications accepted. *Financial support:* In 2019–20, 59 students received support. Fellowships with full tuition reimbursements available, research assistantships, teaching assistantships with partial tuition reimbursements available, institutionally sponsored loans, health care benefits, tuition waivers (full and partial), and unspecified assistantships available. Financial award application deadline: 3/1; financial award applicants required to submit FAFSA. *Unit head:* Martin Harries, Department Chair, 949-824-6715, Fax: 949-824-2916, E-mail: martin.harries@uci.edu. *Application contact:* Jerome Christensen, Graduate Faculty Advisor, 949-824-9046, Fax: 949-824-2916, E-mail: jchris@uci.edu.

University of California, Los Angeles, Graduate Division, College of Letters and Science, Department of English, Los Angeles, CA 90095. Offers MA, PhD. Terminal master's awarded for partial completion of doctoral program. *Degree requirements:* For master's, one foreign language, comprehensive exam, thesis; for doctorate, 2 foreign languages, thesis/dissertation, oral and written qualifying exams. *Entrance requirements:* For doctorate, GRE General Test, GRE Subject Test (literature), bachelor's degree; minimum undergraduate GPA of 3.0, 3.5 in upper-division English courses (or its equivalent if letter grade system not used), 3.7 in graduate courses for applicant with master's degree; writing sample. Additional exam requirements/recommendations for international students: required—TOEFL. Electronic applications accepted.

University of California, Riverside, Graduate Division, Department of English, Riverside, CA 92521-0102. Offers MA, PhD. *Degree requirements:* For master's, one foreign language, comprehensive exam; for doctorate, 2 foreign languages, thesis/dissertation, qualifying exams. *Entrance requirements:* For doctorate, GRE General Test, minimum GPA of 3.5. Additional exam requirements/recommendations for international students: required—TOEFL (minimum score 550 paper-based; 80 iBT). Electronic applications accepted.

University of California, San Diego, Graduate Division, Department of Literature, La Jolla, CA 92093. Offers literature (PhD); writing (MFA). *Students:* 77 full-time (54 women). 244 applicants, 20% accepted, 20 enrolled. In 2019, 8 master's, 6 doctorates awarded. *Degree requirements:* For master's, thesis; for doctorate, one foreign language, comprehensive exam, thesis/dissertation, 3 quarters of teaching assistantship. *Entrance requirements:* For master's, writing sample; for doctorate, GRE General Test, writing sample. Additional exam requirements/recommendations for international students: required—TOEFL (minimum score 550 paper-based; 80 iBT), IELTS (minimum score 7); recommended—TSE. *Application deadline:* For fall admission, 12/3 for domestic students. Application fee: $105 ($125 for international students). Electronic applications accepted. *Financial support:* Fellowships, research assistantships, teaching assistantships, scholarships/grants, and readerships available. Financial award applicants required to submit FAFSA. *Unit head:* Yingjin Zhang, Chair, 858-534-5991, E-mail: litchair@ucsd.edu. *Application contact:* Alyssa Simons, Graduate Coordinator, 858-534-2739, E-mail: litgrad@ucsd.edu.
Website: http://literature.ucsd.edu

University of California, Santa Barbara, Graduate Division, College of Letters and Sciences, Division of Humanities and Fine Arts, Department of English, Santa Barbara, CA 93106-3170. Offers English (PhD), including environment and society, European medieval studies, feminist studies, global studies, technology and society, translation studies, writing studies; MA/PhD. Terminal master's awarded for partial completion of doctoral program. *Degree requirements:* For doctorate, one foreign language, comprehensive exam, thesis/dissertation. *Entrance requirements:* For doctorate, GRE General Test, GRE Subject Test (English literature). Additional exam requirements/recommendations for international students: required—TOEFL (minimum score 550 paper-based; 80 iBT), IELTS (minimum score 7). Electronic applications accepted.

University of California, Santa Cruz, Division of Graduate Studies, Division of Humanities, Department of Literature, Santa Cruz, CA 95064. Offers MA, PhD. Terminal master's awarded for partial completion of doctoral program. *Degree requirements:* For master's, thesis; for doctorate, one foreign language, thesis/dissertation, qualifying exam. *Entrance requirements:* For master's, GRE General Test, writing sample, minimum GPA of 3.5; for doctorate, GRE General Test, minimum GPA of 3.5, writing sample. Additional exam requirements/recommendations for international students: required—TOEFL (minimum score 550 paper-based; 83 iBT); recommended—IELTS (minimum score 8). Electronic applications accepted.

University of Central Arkansas, Graduate School, College of Liberal Arts, Department of English, Conway, AR 72035-0001. Offers MA. *Program availability:* Part-time. *Degree requirements:* For master's, comprehensive exam, thesis optional. *Entrance requirements:* For master's, GRE General Test, minimum GPA of 2.7. Additional exam requirements/recommendations for international students: required—TOEFL (minimum score 550 paper-based). Electronic applications accepted.

University of Central Florida, College of Arts and Humanities, Department of English, Orlando, FL 32816. Offers MA, MFA, PhD, Certificate. *Program availability:* Part-time, evening/weekend. *Students:* 37 full-time (26 women), 46 part-time (28 women); includes 18 minority (4 Black or African American, non-Hispanic/Latino; 1 Asian, non-Hispanic/Latino; 13 Hispanic/Latino), 1 international. Average age 30. 59 applicants, 66% accepted, 26 enrolled. In 2019, 24 master's awarded. *Degree requirements:* For master's, one foreign language, thesis or alternative; for doctorate, thesis/dissertation. *Entrance requirements:* For master's, GRE General Test, letters of recommendation, goal statement. Additional exam requirements/recommendations for international students: required—TOEFL. *Application deadline:* For fall admission, 3/30 for domestic students; for spring admission, 11/1 for domestic students. Application fee: $30. Electronic applications accepted. *Financial support:* In 2019–20, 19 students received support, including 6 fellowships with partial tuition reimbursements available (averaging $9,167 per year), 3 research assistantships with partial tuition reimbursements available (averaging $4,105 per year), 13 teaching assistantships with partial tuition reimbursements available (averaging $5,478 per year); career-related internships or fieldwork, Federal Work-Study, institutionally sponsored loans, tuition waivers (partial), and unspecified assistantships also available. Financial award application deadline: 3/1; financial award applicants required to submit FAFSA. *Unit head:* Dr. Trey Philpotts, Chair, 407-823-1159, E-mail: trey.philpotts@ucf.edu. *Application contact:* Associate Director, Graduate Admissions, 407-823-2766, Fax: 407-823-6442, E-mail: gradadmissions@ucf.edu.
Website: http://www.english.cah.ucf.edu/

University of Central Missouri, The Graduate School, Warrensburg, MO 64093. Offers accountancy (MA); accounting (MBA); applied mathematics (MS); aviation safety (MA); biology (MS); business administration (MBA); career and technology education (MS); college student personnel administration (MS); communication (MA); computer information systems and information technology (MS); computer science (MS); counseling (MS); criminal justice and criminology (MS); educational leadership (Ed S); educational leadership and policy analysis (Ed D); educational technology (MS, Ed S); elementary and early childhood education (MSE); English (MA); english language learners - teaching english as a second language (MA); environmental studies (MA); finance (MBA); history (MA); industrial hygiene (MS); industrial management (MS); information systems (MBA); kinesiology (MS); library science and information services (MS); literacy education (MSE); marketing (MBA); mathematics (MS); music (MA); occupational safety management (MS); professional leadership - adult, career, and technical education (Ed S); professional leadership - counseling (Ed S); psychology (MS); rural family nursing (MS); school administration (MSE); social gerontology (MS); sociology (MA); special education (MSE); speech language pathology (MS); teaching (MAT); technology (MS); technology management (PhD); theatre (MA). *Accreditation:* ASHA. *Program availability:* Part-time, 100% online, blended/hybrid learning. *Faculty:* 236 full-time (113 women), 97 part-time/adjunct (61 women). *Students:* 787 full-time (448 women), 1,459 part-time (997 women); includes 213 minority (72 Black or African American, non-Hispanic/Latino; 5 American Indian or Alaska Native, non-Hispanic/Latino; 27 Asian, non-Hispanic/Latino; 59 Hispanic/Latino; 50 Two or more races, non-Hispanic/Latino), 574 international. Average age 30. 1,477 applicants, 68% accepted, 664 enrolled. In 2019, 831 master's, 93 other advanced degrees awarded. *Degree requirements:* For master's and Ed S, comprehensive exam (for some programs), thesis (for some programs). *Entrance requirements:* For master's, A GRE or GMAT test score may be required by some of the programs, A minimum GPA, letters of recommendation, a statement of purpose may be required by some of the programs; for Ed S, A master's degree is required for the application of an Education Specialist's degree program. Additional exam requirements/recommendations for international students: required—TOEFL (minimum score 550 paper-based; 79 iBT). *Application deadline:* For fall admission, 6/1 priority date for domestic and international students; for spring admission, 10/15 priority date for domestic and international students; for summer admission, 4/1 priority date for domestic and international students. Applications are processed on a rolling basis. Application fee: $30 ($75 for international students). Electronic applications accepted. *Expenses: Tuition, area resident:* Full-time $7524; part-time $313.50 per credit hour. Tuition, state resident: full-time $7524; part-time $313.50 per credit hour. Tuition, nonresident: full-time $15,048; part-time $627 per credit hour. *International tuition:* $15,048 full-time. *Required fees:* $915; $30.50 per credit hour. *Financial support:* In 2019–20, 89 students received support. Research assistantships, teaching assistantships, career-related internships or fieldwork, Federal Work-Study, scholarships/grants, unspecified assistantships, and administrative and laboratory assistantships available. Support available to part-time students. Financial award application deadline: 4/1; financial award applicants required to submit FAFSA. *Unit head:* Shellie Hewitt, Director of Graduate and International Student Services, 660-543-4621, Fax: 660-543-4778, E-mail: hewitt@ucmo.edu. *Application contact:* Shellie Hewitt, Director of Graduate and International Student Services, 660-543-4621, Fax:

660-543-4778, E-mail: hewitt@ucmo.edu.
Website: http://www.ucmo.edu/graduate/

University of Central Oklahoma, The Jackson College of Graduate Studies, College of Liberal Arts, Department of English, Edmond, OK 73034-5209. Offers composition and rhetoric (MA); creative writing (MA); literature (MA); teaching English as a second language (MA). *Program availability:* Part-time. *Degree requirements:* For master's, variable foreign language requirement, comprehensive exam (for some programs), thesis (for some programs), portfolio. *Entrance requirements:* For master's, 18-24 hours of course work in English language and literature; writing sample; essay. Additional exam requirements/recommendations for international students: required—TOEFL (minimum score 550 paper-based; 79 iBT), IELTS (minimum score 6.5). Electronic applications accepted.

University of Chicago, Division of the Humanities, Department of English Language and Literature, Chicago, IL 60637. Offers PhD. Terminal master's awarded for partial completion of doctoral program. *Degree requirements:* For doctorate, 2 foreign languages, comprehensive exam, thesis/dissertation. *Entrance requirements:* For doctorate, GRE General Test, 15-20 page writing sample, statement of purpose, 3 letters of recommendation, transcripts for all previous degrees and institutions attended. Additional exam requirements/recommendations for international students: required—TOEFL (minimum score 104 iBT), IELTS (minimum score 7). Electronic applications accepted.

University of Chicago, Division of the Humanities, Master of Arts Program in the Humanities, Chicago, IL 60637. Offers art history (MA); cinema and media studies (MA); classic languages (MA); comparative literature (MA); creative writing (MA); cultural policy studies (MA); digital humanities (MA); East Asian languages and civilizations (MA); English language and literature (MA); gender and sexuality studies (MA); Germanic studies (MA); linguistics (MA); music (MA); near Eastern languages and civilizations (MA); philosophy (MA); poetics (MA); race, politics and culture (MA); Romance languages and literatures (MA); Slavic languages and literatures (MA); South Asian languages and civilizations (MA); theater and performance studies (MA). *Degree requirements:* For master's, thesis. *Entrance requirements:* For master's, GRE General Test, 10-15 page writing sample, statement of purpose, 3 letters of recommendation, transcripts for all previous degrees and institutions attended. Additional exam requirements/recommendations for international students: required—TOEFL (minimum score 104 iBT), IELTS (minimum score 7). Electronic applications accepted. *Expenses:* Contact institution.

University of Cincinnati, Graduate School, McMicken College of Arts and Sciences, Department of English and Comparative Literature, Cincinnati, OH 45221. Offers MA, MAT, PhD. *Program availability:* Part-time. Terminal master's awarded for partial completion of doctoral program. *Degree requirements:* For master's, one foreign language, thesis (for some programs); for doctorate, 2 foreign languages, thesis/ dissertation. *Entrance requirements:* For master's, GRE General Test, letters of recommendation (3), writing samples; for doctorate, GRE General Test, GRE Subject Test, letters of recommendation (3), writing samples. Additional exam requirements/ recommendations for international students: required—TOEFL. Electronic applications accepted.

University of Colorado Boulder, Graduate School, College of Arts and Sciences, Department of English, Boulder, CO 80309. Offers literature (MA, PhD), including creative writing (MA). Terminal master's awarded for partial completion of doctoral program. *Degree requirements:* For master's, one foreign language, comprehensive exam, thesis or alternative; for doctorate, 2 foreign languages, comprehensive exam, thesis/dissertation. *Entrance requirements:* For master's, GRE General Test, GRE Subject Test, minimum undergraduate GPA of 3.0; for doctorate, GRE General Test, GRE Subject Test. Electronic applications accepted. Application fee is waived when completed online.

University of Colorado Boulder, Graduate School, College of Arts and Sciences, Department of Spanish and Portuguese, Boulder, CO 80309. Offers Hispanic linguistics (MA); medieval and early modern Hispanic literatures (PhD); peninsular and Latin American literature (MA). Terminal master's awarded for partial completion of doctoral program. *Degree requirements:* For master's, one foreign language, comprehensive exam, thesis or alternative; for doctorate, 2 foreign languages, thesis/dissertation. *Entrance requirements:* For master's, minimum undergraduate GPA of 2.75. Electronic applications accepted. Application fee is waived when completed online.

University of Colorado Denver, College of Liberal Arts and Sciences, Department of English, Denver, CO 80217. Offers applied linguistics (MA). *Program availability:* Part-time, evening/weekend. *Degree requirements:* For master's, variable foreign language requirement, comprehensive exam (for some programs), thesis (for some programs), minimum of 33 credit hours (for literature program), 30 (for rhetoric and teaching of writing and applied linguistics programs). *Entrance requirements:* For master's, GRE General Test, minimum GPA of 3.0 in undergraduate courses, critical writing sample, letters of recommendation, completion of 24 semester hours in English courses (at least 16 at the upper-division level), statement of purpose. Additional exam requirements/ recommendations for international students: required—TOEFL (minimum score 537 paper-based; 75 iBT); recommended—IELTS (minimum score 6.5). Tuition and fees vary according to course load, program and reciprocity agreements.

University of Connecticut, Graduate School, College of Liberal Arts and Sciences, Department of English, Storrs, CT 06269. Offers MA, PhD. Terminal master's awarded for partial completion of doctoral program. *Degree requirements:* For master's, comprehensive exam; for doctorate, thesis/dissertation. *Entrance requirements:* For master's and doctorate, GRE General Test, GRE Subject Test. Additional exam requirements/recommendations for international students: required—TOEFL (minimum score 550 paper-based). Electronic applications accepted.

University of Dayton, Department of English, Dayton, OH 45469. Offers literary and cultural studies (MA); teaching English to speakers of other languages (TESOL) (MA); writing and rhetoric (MA). *Program availability:* Part-time. *Degree requirements:* For master's, thesis optional. *Entrance requirements:* For master's, 24 undergraduate-level semester hours in literature and/or writing; minimum GPA of 3.0; transcripts; personal statement; 8-10 page writing sample; three professional letters of recommendation. Additional exam requirements/recommendations for international students: required—TOEFL (minimum score 550 paper-based, 80 iBT) or IELTS. Electronic applications accepted.

University of Delaware, College of Arts and Sciences, Department of English, Newark, DE 19716. Offers English and American literature (MA, PhD); MA/PhD. Terminal master's awarded for partial completion of doctoral program. *Degree requirements:* For master's, one foreign language, thesis optional; for doctorate, 2 foreign languages, comprehensive exam, thesis/dissertation, specialty exam. *Entrance requirements:* For master's and doctorate, GRE General Test, GRE Subject Test. Additional exam requirements/recommendations for international students: required—TOEFL (minimum score 550 paper-based). Electronic applications accepted.

University of Denver, Division of Arts, Humanities and Social Sciences, Department of English, Denver, CO 80208. Offers creative writing (PhD); literary studies (MA, PhD).

Program availability: Part-time. *Faculty:* 30 full-time (17 women), 1 part-time/adjunct (0 women). *Students:* 29 full-time (20 women), 8 part-time (7 women); includes 9 minority (1 American Indian or Alaska Native, non-Hispanic/Latino; 1 Asian, non-Hispanic/Latino; 4 Hispanic/Latino; 3 Two or more races, non-Hispanic/Latino). Average age 30. 220 applicants, 16% accepted, 15 enrolled. In 2019, 3 master's, 11 doctorates awarded. *Degree requirements:* For master's, thesis; for doctorate, one foreign language, comprehensive exam, thesis/dissertation. *Entrance requirements:* For master's, GRE General Test, bachelor's degree, transcripts, academic essay, personal statement, three letters of recommendation, writing sample; for doctorate, GRE General Test, master's degree, transcripts, personal statement, three letters of recommendation, resume, writing sample. Additional exam requirements/recommendations for international students: required—TOEFL (minimum score 550 paper-based; 80 iBT). *Application deadline:* For fall admission, 12/14 for domestic and international students. Applications are processed on a rolling basis. Application fee: $65. Electronic applications accepted. *Expenses:* Contact institution. *Financial support:* In 2019–20, 37 students received support, including 1 research assistantship with tuition reimbursement available (averaging $300 per year), 19 teaching assistantships with tuition reimbursements available (averaging $11,495 per year); Federal Work-Study, institutionally sponsored loans, scholarships/grants, and unspecified assistantships also available. Support available to part-time students. Financial award application deadline: 2/15; financial award applicants required to submit FAFSA. *Unit head:* Dr. Maik Nwosu, Professor and Chair, 303-871-2879, E-mail: mnwosu@du.edu. *Application contact:* Joel Lewis, Assistant to the Chair II, 303-871-2742, E-mail: Joel.Lewis@du.edu. Website: http://www.du.edu/ahss/english

University of Florida, Graduate School, College of Liberal Arts and Sciences, Department of English, Gainesville, FL 32611. Offers creative writing (MFA); English (MA, PhD). *Degree requirements:* For master's, one foreign language, comprehensive exam, thesis or alternative; for doctorate, one foreign language, comprehensive exam, thesis/dissertation. *Entrance requirements:* For master's and doctorate, GRE General Test, minimum GPA of 3.0. Additional exam requirements/recommendations for international students: required—TOEFL (minimum score 550 paper-based; 80 iBT), IELTS (minimum score 6). Electronic applications accepted.

University of Georgia, Franklin College of Arts and Sciences, Department of English, Athens, GA 30602. Offers English (MA, MAT, PhD). *Degree requirements:* For master's, one foreign language, thesis (MA); for doctorate, 2 foreign languages, thesis/ dissertation. *Entrance requirements:* For master's and doctorate, GRE General Test. Additional exam requirements/recommendations for international students: required— TWE. Electronic applications accepted.

University of Guam, Office of Graduate Studies, College of Liberal Arts and Social Sciences, Department of English, Mangilao, GU 96923. Offers MA. *Entrance requirements:* For master's, GRE. Additional exam requirements/recommendations for international students: required—TOEFL.

University of Guelph, Office of Graduate and Postdoctoral Studies, College of Arts, School of English and Theatre Studies, Program in English, Guelph, ON N1G 2W1, Canada. Offers MA. *Program availability:* Part-time. *Degree requirements:* For master's, thesis (for some programs). *Entrance requirements:* For master's, letters of reference, 4-year honours undergraduate degree in English or drama. Additional exam requirements/ recommendations for international students: required—TOEFL. Electronic applications accepted.

University of Hawaii at Manoa, Office of Graduate Education, College of Languages, Linguistics and Literature, Department of English, Honolulu, HI 96822. Offers MA, PhD. *Program availability:* Part-time. *Degree requirements:* For master's, 2 foreign languages, thesis optional; for doctorate, 2 foreign languages, comprehensive exam, thesis/ dissertation. *Entrance requirements:* For master's, GRE General Test; for doctorate, GRE General Test, GRE Subject Test. Additional exam requirements/recommendations for international students: required—TOEFL (minimum score 600 paper-based; 100 iBT), IELTS (minimum score 7).

University of Houston–Clear Lake, School of Human Sciences and Humanities, Programs in Humanities and Fine Arts, Houston, TX 77058-1002. Offers history (MA); humanities (MA); literature (MA). *Program availability:* Part-time, evening/weekend, online learning. *Degree requirements:* For master's, thesis or alternative. *Entrance requirements:* For master's, GRE General Test. Additional exam requirements/ recommendations for international students: required—TOEFL (minimum score 550 paper-based).

University of Houston - Downtown, College of Humanities and Social Sciences, Department of English, Houston, TX 77002. Offers rhetoric and composition (MA); technical communication (MS). *Program availability:* Part-time, evening/weekend. *Faculty:* 10 full-time (3 women). *Students:* 8 full-time (7 women), 29 part-time (19 women); includes 23 minority (11 Black or African American, non-Hispanic/Latino; 1 American Indian or Alaska Native, non-Hispanic/Latino; 1 Asian, non-Hispanic/Latino; 7 Hispanic/Latino; 3 Two or more races, non-Hispanic/Latino), 2 international. Average age 38. 25 applicants, 80% accepted, 13 enrolled. In 2019, 18 master's awarded. *Entrance requirements:* Additional exam requirements/recommendations for international students: required—TOEFL (minimum score 550 paper-based; 50 iBT). *Application deadline:* For fall admission, 8/9 for domestic students; for spring admission, 12/2 for domestic students; for summer admission, 5/17 for domestic students. Application fee: $35 ($80 for international students). Electronic applications accepted. *Expenses:* $386 in-state resident; $758 non-resident, per credit. *Financial support:* Federal Work-Study and scholarships/grants available. Financial award application deadline: 4/1; financial award applicants required to submit FAFSA. *Unit head:* Dr. Paul Kintzele, Department Chair, English, 713-221-8254, Fax: 713-221-8090, E-mail: kintzelep@uhd.edu. *Application contact:* Ceshia Love, Director of Admissions, 713-221-8093, Fax: 713-223-7408, E-mail: gradadmissions@uhd.edu. Website: https://www.uhd.edu/academics/humanities/undergraduate-programs/english/Pages/english-english.aspx

University of Illinois at Chicago, College of Liberal Arts and Sciences, Department of English, Chicago, IL 60607-7128. Offers MA, PhD. *Program availability:* Part-time, evening/weekend. *Degree requirements:* For doctorate, variable foreign language requirement, thesis/dissertation, written and oral exams. *Entrance requirements:* For master's, GRE General Test, GRE Subject Test; for doctorate, GRE General Test, GRE Subject Test, minimum GPA of 2.0. Additional exam requirements/recommendations for international students: required—TOEFL. Electronic applications accepted.

University of Illinois at Springfield, Graduate Programs, College of Liberal Arts and Sciences, Department of English and Modern Languages, Springfield, IL 62703-5407. Offers MA, Graduate Certificate. *Program availability:* Part-time. *Faculty:* 11 full-time (8 women). *Students:* 1 (woman) full-time, 11 part-time (8 women); includes 2 minority (both Black or African American, non-Hispanic/Latino). Average age 36. 4 applicants, 75% accepted, 1 enrolled. In 2019, 3 master's awarded. *Degree requirements:* For master's, thesis, critical project, or creative project. *Entrance requirements:* For master's, GRE General Test, minimum overall undergraduate GPA of 3.0; analytical writing sample or sample of creative work; curriculum vitae/academic resume; three references, two of which must be academic references. Additional exam requirements/

recommendations for international students: required—TOEFL (minimum score 580 paper-based; 61 iBT). *Application deadline:* Applications are processed on a rolling basis. Application fee: $60 ($75 for international students). Electronic applications accepted. *Expenses: Tuition, area resident:* Full-time $7896; part-time $329 per credit hour. Tuition, nonresident: full-time $16,200; part-time $675 per credit hour. *Required fees:* $2735.60; $130.65 per credit hour. *Financial support:* In 2019–20, research assistantships with full tuition reimbursements (averaging $10,562 per year), teaching assistantships with full tuition reimbursements (averaging $10,652 per year) were awarded; fellowships, career-related internships or fieldwork, Federal Work-Study, scholarships/grants, health care benefits, and unspecified assistantships also available. Support available to part-time students. Financial award application deadline: 11/15; financial award applicants required to submit FAFSA. *Unit head:* Dr. John Barker, Program Administrator, 217-206-6512, Fax: 217-206-6217, E-mail: jbark3@uis.edu. *Application contact:* Dr. John Barker, Program Administrator, 217-206-6512, Fax: 217-206-6217, E-mail: jbark3@uis.edu.
Website: eng-ga@uis.edu

University of Illinois at Urbana-Champaign, Graduate College, College of Liberal Arts and Sciences, Department of English, Champaign, IL 61820. Offers creative writing (MFA); English (MA, PhD).

University of Indianapolis, Graduate Programs, Shaheen College of Arts and Sciences, Department of English Language and Literature, Indianapolis, IN 46227-3697. Offers English (MA). *Program availability:* Part-time, evening/weekend. *Entrance requirements:* For master's, GRE Subject Test, minimum GPA of 2.5. Additional exam requirements/recommendations for international students: required—TOEFL (minimum score 550 paper-based). Electronic applications accepted.

The University of Iowa, Graduate College, College of Liberal Arts and Sciences, Department of English, Iowa City, IA 52242-1316. Offers English (PhD); literary studies (MA); nonfiction writing (MFA). *Degree requirements:* For master's, thesis (for some programs), exam; for doctorate, comprehensive exam, thesis/dissertation. *Entrance requirements:* For master's and doctorate, GRE General Test, minimum GPA of 3.0. Additional exam requirements/recommendations for international students: required—TOEFL (minimum score 640 paper-based; 111 iBT). Electronic applications accepted.

The University of Kansas, Graduate Studies, College of Liberal Arts and Sciences, Department of English, Lawrence, KS 66045. Offers creative writing (MFA), including fine arts/creative writing; English (MA, PhD). *Program availability:* Part-time. *Students:* 80 full-time (54 women), 2 part-time (1 woman); includes 21 minority (7 Black or African American, non-Hispanic/Latino; 4 Asian, non-Hispanic/Latino; 6 Hispanic/Latino; 4 Two or more races, non-Hispanic/Latino), 9 international. Average age 31. 186 applicants, 10% accepted, 12 enrolled. In 2019, 13 master's, 12 doctorates awarded. *Entrance requirements:* For master's and doctorate, GRE General Test, two examples of academic writing; resume; statement of approximately 500 words describing interests, training, experience (including teaching experience), academic ability, and goals; three letters of recommendation; official transcripts. Additional exam requirements/recommendations for international students: required—TOEFL, IELTS, TOEFL or IELTS. *Application deadline:* For fall admission, 12/31 for domestic and international students. Application fee: $65 ($85 for international students). Electronic applications accepted. *Expenses:* Tuition, state resident: full-time $9989. Tuition, nonresident: full-time $23,950. *International tuition:* $23,950 full-time. *Required fees:* $984; $81.99 per credit hour. Tuition and fees vary according to course load, campus/location and program. *Financial support:* Fellowships, research assistantships, teaching assistantships, and unspecified assistantships available. *Unit head:* Kathryn Conrad, Chair, 785-864-2572, E-mail: kconrad@ku.edu. *Application contact:* Mary Strickell, Graduate Admissions Contact, 785-864-9438, E-mail: maryj@ku.edu.
Website: http://www.english.ku.edu

University of Kentucky, Graduate School, College of Arts and Sciences, Program in English, Lexington, KY 40506-0032. Offers MA, PhD. *Degree requirements:* For master's, one foreign language, comprehensive exam, thesis optional; for doctorate, one foreign language, comprehensive exam, thesis/dissertation. *Entrance requirements:* For master's, GRE General Test, minimum undergraduate GPA of 2.75; for doctorate, GRE General Test, minimum graduate GPA of 3.0. Additional exam requirements/recommendations for international students: required—TOEFL (minimum score 550 paper-based). Electronic applications accepted.

University of La Verne, Regional and Online Campuses, Graduate Credential Program in Education, California Statewide Campus, La Verne, CA 91750-4443. Offers administration services (preliminary) (Credential); education specialist: mild/moderate (Credential); English (Certificate); multiple subject teaching (Credential); pupil personnel services: school counseling (Credential); single subject teaching (Credential); special education (MS); special emphasis (M Ed). *Accreditation:* NCATE. *Program availability:* Part-time. *Entrance requirements:* For degree, California Basic Educational Skills Test, minimum undergraduate GPA of 2.75, 3 letters of recommendation, interview. *Expenses:* Contact institution.

University of Lethbridge, School of Graduate Studies, Lethbridge, AB T1K 3M4, Canada. Offers addictions counseling (M Sc); agricultural biotechnology (M Sc); agricultural studies (M Sc, MA); anthropology (MA); archaeology (M Sc, MA); art (MA, MFA); biochemistry (M Sc); biological sciences (M Sc); biomolecular science (PhD); biosystems and biodiversity (PhD); Canadian studies (MA); chemistry (M Sc); computer science (M Sc); computer science and geographical information science (M Sc); counseling (MC); counseling psychology (M Ed); dramatic arts (MA); earth, space, and physical science (PhD); economics (MA); education (MA, PhD); educational leadership (M Ed); English (MA); environmental science (M Sc); evolution and behavior (PhD); exercise science (M Sc); French (MA); French/German (MA); French/Spanish (MA); general education (M Ed); geography (M Sc, MA); German (MA); health sciences (M Sc); individualized multidisciplinary (M Sc, MA); kinesiology (M Sc, MA); management (M Sc), including accounting, finance, human resource management and labor relations, information systems, international management, marketing, policy and strategy; mathematics (M Sc); music (M Mus, MA); Native American studies (MA); neuroscience (M Sc, PhD); new media (MA, MFA); nursing (M Sc, MN); philosophy (MA); physics (M Sc); political science (MA); psychology (M Sc, MA); religious studies (MA); sociology (MA); theatre and dramatic arts (MFA); theoretical and computational science (PhD); urban and regional studies (MA); women and gender studies (MA). *Program availability:* Part-time, evening/weekend. *Degree requirements:* For master's, thesis (for some programs); for doctorate, comprehensive exam, thesis/dissertation. *Entrance requirements:* For master's, GMAT (for M Sc in management), bachelor's degree in related field, minimum GPA of 3.0 during previous 20 graded semester courses, 2 years' teaching or related experience (M Ed); for doctorate, master's degree, minimum graduate GPA of 3.5. Additional exam requirements/recommendations for international students: required—TOEFL (minimum score 580 paper-based; 93 iBT). Electronic applications accepted.

University of Louisiana at Lafayette, College of Liberal Arts, Department of English, Lafayette, LA 70504. Offers American culture (MA, PhD), including history, sociology; American literature and language (PhD); creative writing (MA, PhD), including creative writing (MA), folklore (MA), rhetoric (MA); folklore (MA, PhD); linguistic studies (MA, PhD); professional writing (PhD); rhetoric (MA, PhD); TESOL studies (MA, PhD). *Program availability:* Part-time. Terminal master's awarded for partial completion of doctoral program. *Degree requirements:* For master's, one foreign language, thesis or alternative; for doctorate, 2 foreign languages, comprehensive exam, thesis/dissertation. *Entrance requirements:* For master's, GRE General Test, minimum GPA of 2.75; for doctorate, GRE General Test, minimum GPA of 3.0. Additional exam requirements/recommendations for international students: required—TOEFL (minimum score 550 paper-based). Electronic applications accepted. *Expenses: Tuition, area resident:* Full-time $5511; part-time $1630 per credit hour. Tuition, state resident: full-time $5511; part-time $1630 per credit hour. Tuition, nonresident: full-time $19,239; part-time $2409 per credit hour. *Required fees:* $46,637.

University of Louisiana at Monroe, Graduate School, College of Arts, Education, and Sciences, Department of English, Monroe, LA 71209-0001. Offers MA. *Program availability:* Part-time, evening/weekend, online learning. *Faculty:* 3 full-time (2 women). *Students:* 10 full-time (5 women), 4 part-time (all women); includes 4 minority (3 Black or African American, non-Hispanic/Latino; 1 Two or more races, non-Hispanic/Latino), 1 international. Average age 26. 12 applicants, 58% accepted, 4 enrolled. In 2019, 7 master's awarded. *Degree requirements:* For master's, one foreign language, thesis optional. *Entrance requirements:* For master's, GRE General Test (verbal and quantitative), minimum GPA of 3.0 in English, 2.5 overall. Additional exam requirements/recommendations for international students: required—TOEFL (minimum score 500 paper-based; 61 iBT); recommended—IELTS (minimum score 5.5). *Application deadline:* For fall admission, 8/1 for domestic students, 6/1 for international students; for spring admission, 1/1 for domestic students, 11/1 for international students; for summer admission, 6/1 for domestic students, 3/1 for international students. Applications are processed on a rolling basis. Application fee: $40. Electronic applications accepted. *Expenses: Tuition, area resident:* Full-time $6489. Tuition, state resident: full-time $6489. Tuition, nonresident: full-time $18,989. *Required fees:* $2748. Tuition and fees vary according to course load and program. *Financial support:* In 2019–20, 11 students received support. Teaching assistantships with full tuition reimbursements available, career-related internships or fieldwork, Federal Work-Study, scholarships/grants, and unspecified assistantships available. Financial award application deadline: 2/15; financial award applicants required to submit FAFSA. *Unit head:* Dr. Mary Adams, Program Coordinator, 318-342-1500, Fax: 318-342-1755, E-mail: madams@ulm.edu. *Application contact:* Dr. Jack Heflin, Graduate Coordinator, 318-342-1521, E-mail: heflin@ulm.edu.
Website: http://www.ulm.edu/english

University of Louisville, Graduate School, College of Arts and Sciences, Department of English, Louisville, KY 40292. Offers English (MA), including creative writing, literature, rhetoric and composition (MA, PhD); rhetoric and composition (PhD), including rhetoric and composition (MA, PhD). *Program availability:* Part-time, evening/weekend. *Faculty:* 34 full-time (16 women), 29 part-time/adjunct (15 women). *Students:* 39 full-time (22 women), 19 part-time (12 women); includes 6 minority (3 Black or African American, non-Hispanic/Latino; 1 Hispanic/Latino; 2 Two or more races, non-Hispanic/Latino), 3 international. Average age 31. 42 applicants, 71% accepted, 20 enrolled. In 2019, 12 master's, 5 doctorates awarded. *Degree requirements:* For master's, one foreign language, thesis optional, culminating project of 25-30 pages; for doctorate, comprehensive exam, thesis/dissertation, Year long program; Student teacher program. *Entrance requirements:* For master's, GRE General Test, Two letters of reference, official transcripts; for doctorate, GRE General Test, Three letters of reference, official transcripts. Additional exam requirements/recommendations for international students: required—TOEFL (minimum score 550 paper-based; 79 iBT), IELTS can be used in place of the TOEFL; recommended—IELTS (minimum score 6.5). *Application deadline:* For fall admission, 7/15 priority date for domestic and international students; for spring admission, 12/1 priority date for domestic and international students; for summer admission, 5/15 priority date for domestic and international students. Applications are processed on a rolling basis. Application fee: $65. Electronic applications accepted. *Expenses:* Contact institution. *Financial support:* In 2019–20, 38 students received support, including 3 fellowships with full tuition reimbursements available (averaging $19,992 per year), 13 teaching assistantships with full tuition reimbursements available (averaging $19,992 per year); research assistantships, health care benefits, and unspecified assistantships also available. Financial award application deadline: 1/5. *Unit head:* Dr. Glynis Ridley, Chair, 502-852-6803, E-mail: glynis.ridley@louisville.edu. *Application contact:* Dr. Steven Matthew Biberman, Acting Director of Graduate Studies, 502-852-3052, E-mail: steven.biberman@louisville.edu.
Website: http://www.louisville.edu/english

University of Maine, Graduate School, College of Liberal Arts and Sciences, Department of English, Orono, ME 04469. Offers MA. *Program availability:* Part-time, evening/weekend. *Faculty:* 17 full-time (11 women). *Students:* 22 full-time (10 women); includes 1 minority (Two or more races, non-Hispanic/Latino). Average age 26. 21 applicants, 86% accepted, 9 enrolled. In 2019, 7 master's awarded. *Degree requirements:* For master's, one foreign language, thesis optional. *Entrance requirements:* For master's, GRE General Test, minimum GPA of 3.0. *Application deadline:* For fall admission, 1/15 priority date for domestic and international students. Applications are processed on a rolling basis. Application fee: $65. Electronic applications accepted. *Expenses: Tuition, area resident:* Full-time $8100; part-time $450 per credit hour. Tuition, state resident: full-time $8100; part-time $450 per credit hour. Tuition, nonresident: full-time $26,388; part-time $1466 per credit hour. *International tuition:* $26,388 full-time. *Required fees:* $1257; $278 per semester. Tuition and fees vary according to course load. *Financial support:* In 2019–20, 24 students received support, including 22 teaching assistantships with full tuition reimbursements available (averaging $15,825 per year); Federal Work-Study, scholarships/grants, tuition waivers (full and partial), and unspecified assistantships also available. Financial award application deadline: 3/1; financial award applicants required to submit FAFSA. *Unit head:* Dr. Steve Evans, Chair, 207-581-3823, Fax: 207-581-1604, E-mail: steven.evans@maine.edu. *Application contact:* Scott G. Delcourt, Assistant Vice President for Graduate Studies and Senior Associate Dean, 207-581-3291, Fax: 207-581-3232, E-mail: graduate@maine.edu.
Website: https://english.umaine.edu/graduate-program/

The University of Manchester, School of Arts, Languages and Cultures, Manchester, United Kingdom. Offers anthropology, media and performance (PhD); applied theatre (PhD); Arab world studies (PhD); archaeology (PhD); art history and visual studies (PhD); arts and cultural management (PhD); arts management and cultural policy (PhD); Chinese studies (PhD); classics and ancient history (PhD); composition (PhD); creative writing (PhD); drama (PhD); East Asian studies (PhD); electroacoustic composition (PhD); English and American studies (PhD); English language (PhD); French studies (PhD); German studies (PhD); history (PhD); humanitarianism and conflict response (PhD); interpreting studies (PhD); Japanese studies (PhD); Latin American cultural studies (PhD); linguistics (PhD); Middle Eastern studies (PhD); museology (PhD); museum practice (PhD); music (PhD); musicology (PhD); Polish studies (PhD); Portuguese studies (PhD); religions and theology (PhD); Russian studies (PhD); Spanish studies (PhD); translation and intercultural studies (PhD).

University of Manitoba, Faculty of Graduate Studies, Faculty of Arts, Department of English, Film, and Theatre, Winnipeg, MB R3T 2N2, Canada. Offers English (MA, PhD). *Degree requirements:* For master's, one foreign language, thesis; for doctorate, one foreign language, thesis/dissertation.

University of Maryland, Baltimore County, The Graduate School, College of Arts, Humanities and Social Sciences, Program in English: Texts, Technologies, and Literature, Baltimore, MD 21250. Offers MA. *Program availability:* Part-time, evening/weekend. *Faculty:* 14 full-time (11 women). *Students:* 5 full-time (4 women), 9 part-time (6 women); includes 7 minority (4 Black or African American, non-Hispanic/Latino; 1 American Indian or Alaska Native, non-Hispanic/Latino; 1 Asian, non-Hispanic/Latino; 1 Hispanic/Latino). Average age 29. 25 applicants, 84% accepted, 8 enrolled. In 2019, 5 master's awarded. *Degree requirements:* For master's, thesis or portfolio. *Entrance requirements:* For master's, GRE. Additional exam requirements/recommendations for international students: required—TOEFL. *Application deadline:* For fall admission, 5/1 for domestic students; for spring admission, 5/1 for domestic students. Applications are processed on a rolling basis. Electronic applications accepted. *Expenses: Tuition, area resident:* Full-time $659. Tuition, state resident: full-time $659. Tuition, nonresident: full-time $1132. *International tuition:* $1132 full-time. *Required fees:* $140; $140 per credit hour. *Financial support:* In 2019–20, 4 students received support, including 4 teaching assistantships; unspecified assistantships also available. Financial award application deadline: 5/1. *Unit head:* Dr. Orianne Smith, English Department Chair, 410-455-2384, Fax: 410-455-3010, E-mail: osmith@umbc.edu. *Application contact:* Dr. Lucille McCarthy, Graduate Program Director, 410-455-2384, Fax: 410-455-3010, E-mail: mccarthy@umbc.edu.
Website: http://www.umbc.edu/english/ma.html

University of Maryland, College Park, Academic Affairs, College of Arts and Humanities, Department of English, Program in English Language and Literature, College Park, MD 20742. Offers MA, PhD. *Degree requirements:* For master's, thesis optional; for doctorate, one foreign language, thesis/dissertation, oral and written exams. *Entrance requirements:* For master's, GRE General Test, minimum GPA of 3.5, writing sample, 3 letters of recommendation; for doctorate, GRE General Test, minimum GPA of 3.7, writing sample. Additional exam requirements/recommendations for international students: required—TOEFL. Electronic applications accepted.

University of Massachusetts Amherst, Graduate School, College of Humanities and Fine Arts, Department of English, Amherst, MA 01003. Offers American studies (PhD); composition and rhetoric (PhD); creative writing (MFA); English and American literature (MA, PhD). *Program availability:* Part-time. Terminal master's awarded for partial completion of doctoral program. *Degree requirements:* For master's, one foreign language, thesis optional; for doctorate, one foreign language, comprehensive exam, thesis/dissertation. *Entrance requirements:* For master's, manuscript; for doctorate, GRE General Test, manuscript. Additional exam requirements/recommendations for international students: required—TOEFL (minimum score 550 paper-based; 80 iBT), IELTS (minimum score 6.5). Electronic applications accepted.

University of Massachusetts Boston, College of Liberal Arts, Program in English, Boston, MA 02125-3393. Offers MA. *Program availability:* Part-time, evening/weekend. *Entrance requirements:* For master's, minimum GPA of 2.75. Electronic applications accepted.

University of Memphis, Graduate School, College of Arts and Sciences, Department of English, Memphis, TN 38152. Offers African-American literature (Graduate Certificate); applied linguistics (PhD); composition studies (PhD); creative writing (MFA); English as a second language (MA); linguistics (MA); literary and cultural studies (PhD), including African-American literature; literature (MA); professional writing (MA, PhD); teaching English as a second/foreign language (Graduate Certificate). *Program availability:* Part-time, evening/weekend, 100% online. *Students:* 58 full-time (33 women), 76 part-time (52 women); includes 34 minority (24 Black or African American, non-Hispanic/Latino; 4 Asian, non-Hispanic/Latino; 5 Hispanic/Latino; 1 Two or more races, non-Hispanic/Latino), 16 international. Average age 36. 52 applicants, 92% accepted, 23 enrolled. In 2019, 19 master's, 15 doctorates, 8 other advanced degrees awarded. Terminal master's awarded for partial completion of doctoral program. *Degree requirements:* For master's, variable foreign language requirement, comprehensive exam, thesis optional; for doctorate, variable foreign language requirement, comprehensive exam, thesis/dissertation, qualifying exam. *Entrance requirements:* For master's, GRE, minimum undergraduate GPA of 3.0, statement of purpose, two letters of recommendation; for doctorate, GRE, minimum undergraduate and graduate GPA of 3.25, statement of purpose, writing sample, three letters of recommendation. Additional exam requirements/recommendations for international students: required—TOEFL. *Application deadline:* For fall admission, 1/15 for domestic students; for spring admission, 10/15 for domestic students. Applications are processed on a rolling basis. Application fee: $35 ($60 for international students). Electronic applications accepted. *Expenses: Tuition, area resident:* Full-time $9216; part-time $512 per credit hour. Tuition, state resident: full-time $9216; part-time $512 per credit hour. Tuition, nonresident: full-time $12,672; part-time $704 per credit hour. *International tuition:* $16,128 full-time. *Required fees:* $1530; $85 per credit hour. Tuition and fees vary according to program. *Financial support:* Research assistantships with full tuition reimbursements, teaching assistantships with full tuition reimbursements, Federal Work-Study, scholarships/grants, and unspecified assistantships available. Financial award application deadline: 2/1; financial award applicants required to submit FAFSA. *Unit head:* Dr. Joshua Phillips, Chair, 901-678-2651, Fax: 901-678-2226, E-mail: jsphllps@memphis.edu. *Application contact:* Dr. Jeffrey Scraba, Director of Graduate Studies, 901-678-4768, Fax: 901-678-2226, E-mail: jscraba@memphis.edu.
Website: http://www.memphis.edu/english

University of Miami, Graduate School, College of Arts and Sciences, Department of English, Coral Gables, FL 33124. Offers creative writing (MFA); English (MA, PhD). *Program availability:* Part-time. Terminal master's awarded for partial completion of doctoral program. *Degree requirements:* For master's, one foreign language, thesis optional; for doctorate, one foreign language, thesis/dissertation. *Entrance requirements:* For master's and doctorate, GRE General Test. Electronic applications accepted.

University of Michigan, Rackham Graduate School, College of Literature, Science, and the Arts, Department of English Language and Literature, Ann Arbor, MI 48109. Offers creative writing (MFA); English and education (PhD); English and women's studies (PhD); English language and literature (PhD). *Degree requirements:* For doctorate, 2 foreign languages, comprehensive exam, thesis/dissertation, oral defense of dissertation, preliminary exam. *Entrance requirements:* For doctorate, writing sample. Additional exam requirements/recommendations for international students: required—TOEFL (minimum score 620 paper-based; 106 iBT). Electronic applications accepted.

University of Michigan, Rackham Graduate School, College of Literature, Science, and the Arts, Department of Women's Studies, Ann Arbor, MI 48109. Offers English and women's studies (PhD); history and women's studies (PhD); LGBTQ studies (Certificate); psychology and women's studies (PhD); women's studies (Certificate). *Degree requirements:* For doctorate, variable foreign language requirement, comprehensive exam (for some programs), thesis/dissertation. *Entrance requirements:* For doctorate, previous undergraduate coursework in women's studies. Electronic applications accepted.

University of Michigan–Flint, College of Arts and Sciences, Program in English Language and Literature, Flint, MI 48502-1950. Offers literature (MA); writing and rhetoric (MA). *Program availability:* Part-time. *Faculty:* 25 full-time (16 women), 5 part-time/adjunct (4 women). *Students:* 11 full-time (6 women), 10 part-time (8 women); includes 2 minority (1 Black or African American, non-Hispanic/Latino; 1 Hispanic/Latino), 2 international. Average age 34. 14 applicants, 93% accepted, 2 enrolled. In 2019, 11 master's awarded. *Entrance requirements:* For master's, bachelor's degree with major or significant coursework in English or related fields from regionally-accredited institution; minimum overall undergraduate GPA of 3.0. Additional exam requirements/recommendations for international students: required—TOEFL (minimum score 84 iBT), IELTS (minimum score 6.5). *Application deadline:* For fall admission, 8/1 for domestic students, 5/1 for international students; for winter admission, 11/15 for domestic students, 10/1 for international students; for spring admission, 3/15 for domestic students, 1/1 for international students; for summer admission, 5/15 for domestic students. Applications are processed on a rolling basis. Application fee: $55. Electronic applications accepted. *Expenses:* Contact institution. *Financial support:* Career-related internships or fieldwork, Federal Work-Study, scholarships/grants, and unspecified assistantships available. Support available to part-time students. Financial award application deadline: 3/1; financial award applicants required to submit FAFSA. *Unit head:* Dr. James Schirmer, Department Chair, 810-762-3285, E-mail: jschirm@umich.edu. *Application contact:* Matt Bohlen, Associate Director of Graduate Programs, 810-762-3171, Fax: 810-766-6789, E-mail: mbohlen@umflint.edu.
Website: http://www.umflint.edu/graduateprograms/english-language-and-literature-ma

University of Minnesota, Duluth, Graduate School, College of Liberal Arts, Department of English, Duluth, MN 55812-2496. Offers MA. *Program availability:* Part-time. *Degree requirements:* For master's, one foreign language, comprehensive exam, 2 extended papers or projects. *Entrance requirements:* For master's, GRE General Test, minimum GPA of 3.0. Additional exam requirements/recommendations for international students: required—TOEFL.

University of Minnesota, Twin Cities Campus, Graduate School, College of Liberal Arts, Department of English, Minneapolis, MN 55455. Offers MA, PhD. Terminal master's awarded for partial completion of doctoral program. *Degree requirements:* For master's, one foreign language, thesis or alternative; for doctorate, 2 foreign languages, thesis/dissertation. *Entrance requirements:* For master's and doctorate, GRE General Test. Additional exam requirements/recommendations for international students: required—TOEFL (minimum score 620 paper-based, 105 iBT) or IELTS (minimum score 7.5). Electronic applications accepted.

University of Mississippi, Graduate School, College of Liberal Arts, University, MS 38677. Offers anthropology (MA); biology (MS, PhD); chemistry (MS, DA, PhD); creative writing (MFA); documentary expression (MFA); economics (MA, PhD); English (MA, PhD); experimental psychology (PhD); history (MA, PhD); mathematics (MS, PhD); modern languages (MA); music (MM); philosophy (MA); physics (MA, MS, PhD); political science (MA, PhD); Southern studies (MA); studio art (MFA). *Program availability:* Part-time. *Faculty:* 481 full-time (215 women), 71 part-time/adjunct (40 women). *Students:* 509 full-time (258 women), 55 part-time (21 women); includes 89 minority (40 Black or African American, non-Hispanic/Latino; 13 Asian, non-Hispanic/Latino; 25 Hispanic/Latino; 11 Two or more races, non-Hispanic/Latino), 157 international. Average age 29. In 2019, 119 master's, 51 doctorates awarded. *Degree requirements:* For doctorate, thesis/dissertation. *Entrance requirements:* For master's, GRE General Test, minimum GPA of 3.0; for doctorate, GRE General Test. Additional exam requirements/recommendations for international students: required—TOEFL. *Application deadline:* Applications are processed on a rolling basis. Application fee: $50. Electronic applications accepted. *Expenses:* Tuition, state resident: full-time $8718; part-time $484.25 per credit hour. Tuition, nonresident: full-time $24,990; part-time $1388.25 per credit hour. *Required fees:* $100; $4.16 per credit hour. *Financial support:* Fellowships, research assistantships, teaching assistantships, career-related internships or fieldwork, Federal Work-Study, institutionally sponsored loans, scholarships/grants, and unspecified assistantships available. Financial award application deadline: 3/1; financial award applicants required to submit FAFSA. *Unit head:* Dr. Lee Michael Cohen, Dean, 662-915-7177, Fax: 662-915-5792, E-mail: libarts@olemiss.edu. *Application contact:* Tameka Smith, Graduate Activities Specialist for Admissions, 662-915-7474, Fax: 662-915-7577, E-mail: gschool@olemiss.edu.
Website: ventress@olemiss.edu

University of Missouri, Office of Research and Graduate Studies, College of Arts and Science, Department of English, Columbia, MO 65211. Offers MA, PhD. Terminal master's awarded for partial completion of doctoral program. *Entrance requirements:* For master's, GRE General Test, minimum GPA of 3.0; for doctorate, GRE General Test, minimum GPA of 3.0; MA in English or equivalent.

University of Missouri–Kansas City, College of Arts and Sciences, Department of English Language and Literature, Kansas City, MO 64110-2499. Offers English (MA, PhD). *Program availability:* Part-time, evening/weekend. *Degree requirements:* For master's, one foreign language; for doctorate, 2 foreign languages, comprehensive exam, thesis/dissertation. *Entrance requirements:* For master's, GRE General Test, 3 letters of recommendation. Additional exam requirements/recommendations for international students: required—TOEFL (minimum score 550 paper-based; 80 iBT). Electronic applications accepted.

University of Missouri–St. Louis, College of Arts and Sciences, Department of English, St. Louis, MO 63121. Offers creative writing (MFA); English (MA). *Program availability:* Part-time, evening/weekend. *Degree requirements:* For master's, thesis optional. *Entrance requirements:* For master's, two letters of recommendation; writing sample (MFA). Additional exam requirements/recommendations for international students: required—TOEFL (minimum score 550 paper-based; 79 iBT), IELTS (minimum score 6.5). Electronic applications accepted. *Expenses: Tuition, area resident:* Full-time $9005.40; part-time $6003.60 per credit hour. Tuition, state resident: full-time $9005.40; part-time $6003.60 per credit hour. Tuition, nonresident: full-time $22,108; part-time $14,738.40 per credit hour. *International tuition:* $22,108 full-time. Tuition and fees vary according to course load.

University of Montana, Graduate School, College of Humanities and Sciences, Department of English, Program in Literature, Missoula, MT 59812. Offers MA. *Degree requirements:* For master's, thesis optional. *Entrance requirements:* For master's, GRE General Test, sample of written work. Additional exam requirements/recommendations for international students: required—TOEFL.

University of Montevallo, College of Arts and Sciences, Department of English, Montevallo, AL 35115. Offers MA. *Program availability:* Part-time. *Students:* 2 full-time (both women), 2 part-time (1 woman); includes 1 minority (American Indian or Alaska Native, non-Hispanic/Latino). In 2019, 3 master's awarded. *Degree requirements:* For master's, comprehensive exam, thesis optional. *Entrance requirements:* For master's, GRE General Test, MAT, minimum undergraduate GPA of 2.75 in last 60 hours or 2.5 overall, bachelor's degree in English or equivalent. Additional exam requirements/recommendations for international students: required—TOEFL (minimum score 550 paper-based). *Application deadline:* For fall admission, 7/15 for domestic students; for spring admission, 11/15 for domestic students. Application fee: $30. *Expenses: Tuition, area resident:* Full-time $10,512; part-time $438 per contact hour. Tuition, state resident: full-time $10,512; part-time $438 per credit hour. Tuition, nonresident: full-time $22,464; part-time $936 per credit hour. *International tuition:* $22,464 full-time. *Financial support:* Federal Work-Study, scholarships/grants, and unspecified assistantships available. *Unit head:* Dr. Paul Mahaffey, Chair, 205-665-6420, E-mail: mahaffey@montevallo.edu. *Application contact:* Alexander Beringer, Associate Professor, 205-665-6420, E-mail: aberinger@montevallo.edu. Website: http://www.montevallo.edu/english/

University of Nebraska at Kearney, College of Arts and Sciences, College of Arts and Sciences, Kearney, NE 68849. Offers creative writing (MA); literature (MA); writing (MA). *Program availability:* Part-time, evening/weekend, 100% online, blended/hybrid learning. *Faculty:* 14 full-time (10 women). *Students:* 2 full-time (1 woman), 27 part-time (24 women); includes 2 minority (both Two or more races, non-Hispanic/Latino). Average age 31. 7 applicants, 71% accepted, 5 enrolled. In 2019, 6 master's awarded. *Degree requirements:* For master's, comprehensive exam (for some programs), thesis optional, thesis or exam. *Entrance requirements:* For master's, writing sample, three letters of recommendation, letter of interest. Additional exam requirements/recommendations for international students: required—TOEFL (minimum score 550 paper-based; 79 iBT), IELTS (minimum score 6.5). *Application deadline:* For fall admission, 7/10 for domestic students, 5/10 for international students; for spring admission, 10/10 for domestic students, 9/10 for international students; for summer admission, 4/10 for domestic students, 1/10 for international students. Applications are processed on a rolling basis. Application fee: $45. Electronic applications accepted. *Expenses: Tuition, area resident:* Full-time $4662; part-time $259 per credit hour. Tuition, nonresident: full-time $10,242; part-time $569 per credit hour. *International tuition:* $10,242 full-time. *Required fees:* $1222; $381.50 per term. Full-time tuition and fees vary according to course load, campus/location and program. *Financial support:* In 2019–20, 2 students received support, including 2 teaching assistantships with full tuition reimbursements available (averaging $10,980 per year); career-related internships or fieldwork, scholarships/grants, and unspecified assistantships also available. Support available to part-time students. Financial award application deadline: 2/28; financial award applicants required to submit FAFSA. *Unit head:* Dr. Michelle Beissel-Heath, Graduate Program Director, 308-865-8109, E-mail: beisselheamp@unk.edu. *Application contact:* Linda Johnson, Director, Graduate Admissions and Programs, 308-717-7881, E-mail: gradstudies@unk.edu. Website: https://www.unk.edu/academics/english/index.php

University of Nebraska at Omaha, Graduate Studies, College of Arts and Sciences, Department of English, Omaha, NE 68182. Offers advanced writing (Certificate); English (MA); teaching English to speakers of other languages (Certificate); technical communication (Certificate). *Program availability:* Part-time, evening/weekend. *Degree requirements:* For master's, comprehensive exam, thesis (for some programs). *Entrance requirements:* For master's, GRE or MAT, minimum GPA of 3.0, transcripts, 3 letters of recommendation, statement of purpose, writing sample; for Certificate, minimum GPA of 3.0, transcripts, statement of purpose. Additional exam requirements/recommendations for international students: required—TOEFL, IELTS, PTE. Electronic applications accepted.

University of Nebraska–Lincoln, Graduate College, College of Arts and Sciences, Department of English, Lincoln, NE 68588-0333. Offers composition and rhetoric (MA, PhD); creative writing (MA, PhD); literature studies (MA, PhD). *Degree requirements:* For master's, thesis optional; for doctorate, one foreign language, comprehensive exam, thesis/dissertation. *Entrance requirements:* For master's, writing sample; for doctorate, GRE General Test, writing sample. Additional exam requirements/recommendations for international students: required—TOEFL (minimum score 600 paper-based). Electronic applications accepted.

University of Nevada, Las Vegas, Graduate College, College of Liberal Arts, Department of English, Las Vegas, NV 89154-5011. Offers creative writing (MFA); English (MA, PhD). *Program availability:* Part-time. *Faculty:* 22 full-time (8 women). *Students:* 71 full-time (44 women), 11 part-time (3 women); includes 25 minority (3 Black or African American, non-Hispanic/Latino; 2 Asian, non-Hispanic/Latino; 14 Hispanic/Latino; 1 Native Hawaiian or other Pacific Islander, non-Hispanic/Latino; 5 Two or more races, non-Hispanic/Latino), 4 international. Average age 33. 207 applicants, 16% accepted, 24 enrolled. In 2019, 15 master's, 7 doctorates awarded. *Degree requirements:* For master's, one foreign language, comprehensive exam (for some programs), thesis, creative thesis; for doctorate, one foreign language, comprehensive exam, thesis/dissertation. *Entrance requirements:* For master's, GRE General Test, GRE Subject Test, writing sample; statement of purpose; 2 letters of recommendation; transcripts from all colleges; for doctorate, GRE General Test, GRE Subject Test, MA in English with minimum GPA of 3.5; writing sample; 3 letters of recommendation; statement of purpose. Additional exam requirements/recommendations for international students: required—TOEFL (minimum score 550 paper-based; 80 iBT), IELTS (minimum score 7). *Application deadline:* For fall admission, 1/15 for domestic and international students; for spring admission, 11/1 for domestic students, 10/1 for international students. Application fee: $60 ($95 for international students). Electronic applications accepted. *Expenses:* Contact institution. *Financial support:* In 2019–20, 75 students received support, including 1 fellowship with full tuition reimbursement available (averaging $15,000 per year), 2 research assistantships with full tuition reimbursements available (averaging $16,250 per year), 72 teaching assistantships with full tuition reimbursements available (averaging $14,826 per year); institutionally sponsored loans, scholarships/grants, health care benefits, and unspecified assistantships also available. Financial award application deadline: 3/15; financial award applicants required to submit FAFSA. *Unit head:* Dr. Gary Totten, Chair/Professor, 702-895-1258, Fax: 702-895-4801, E-mail: english.chair@unlv.edu. *Application contact:* Dr. Kelly J. Mays, Graduate Coordinator, 702-895-3589, Fax: 702-895-4801, E-mail: english.gradcoord@unlv.edu. Website: http://english.unlv.edu/

University of Nevada, Reno, Graduate School, College of Liberal Arts, Department of English, Reno, NV 89557. Offers MA, MATE, PhD. Terminal master's awarded for partial completion of doctoral program. *Degree requirements:* For master's, variable foreign language requirement, thesis optional; for doctorate, variable foreign language requirement, thesis/dissertation. *Entrance requirements:* For master's, GRE General Test, minimum GPA of 2.75; for doctorate, GRE General Test, minimum GPA of 3.0. Additional exam requirements/recommendations for international students: required—TOEFL (minimum score 500 paper-based; 61 iBT), IELTS (minimum score 6). Electronic applications accepted.

University of New Hampshire, Graduate School, College of Liberal Arts, Department of English, Durham, NH 03824. Offers English (MST, PhD); language and linguistics (MA); literature (MA); writing (MFA). *Program availability:* Part-time. *Students:* 65 full-time (43 women), 29 part-time (25 women); includes 6 minority (3 Black or African American, non-Hispanic/Latino; 1 Asian, non-Hispanic/Latino; 1 Hispanic/Latino; 1 Two or more races, non-Hispanic/Latino), 5 international. Average age 33. 91 applicants, 74% accepted, 27 enrolled. In 2019, 27 master's, 5 doctorates awarded. *Entrance*

requirements: Additional exam requirements/recommendations for international students: required—TOEFL (minimum score 550 paper-based; 80 iBT), IELTS, PTE. *Application deadline:* For fall admission, 7/1 for domestic students; for spring admission, 12/1 for domestic students; for summer admission, 4/1 for domestic students. Application fee: $65. Electronic applications accepted. *Financial support:* In 2019–20, 69 students received support, including 1 fellowship, 38 teaching assistantships; research assistantships, career-related internships or fieldwork, Federal Work-Study, scholarships/grants, and tuition waivers (full and partial) also available. Support available to part-time students. Financial award application deadline: 2/15. *Unit head:* Dr. Rachel Trubowitz, Chair, 603-862-0254. *Application contact:* Janine Wilks, Administrative Assistant, 603-862-3963, E-mail: engl.grad@unh.edu. Website: http://cola.unh.edu/english

University of New Mexico, Graduate Studies, College of Arts and Sciences, Program in English, Albuquerque, NM 87131-2039. Offers MA, PhD. *Degree requirements:* For master's, one foreign language, comprehensive exam (for some programs), thesis or alternative, portfolio; for doctorate, 2 foreign languages, comprehensive exam, thesis/dissertation. *Entrance requirements:* For master's, GRE General Test; for doctorate, GRE General Test, GRE Subject Test (literature). Electronic applications accepted. *Expenses:* Tuition, state resident: full-time $7633; part-time $972 per year. Tuition, nonresident: full-time $22,586; part-time $3840 per year. *International tuition:* $23,292 full-time. *Required fees:* $8608. Tuition and fees vary according to course level, course load, degree level, program and student level.

University of New Orleans, Graduate School, College of Liberal Arts, Education and Human Development, Department of English, Program in English, New Orleans, LA 70148. Offers MA. *Program availability:* Part-time, evening/weekend. *Entrance requirements:* For master's, GRE General Test. Additional exam requirements/recommendations for international students: required—TOEFL (minimum score 550 paper-based; 79 iBT), IELTS (minimum score 6.5). Electronic applications accepted.

University of North Alabama, College of Arts and Sciences, Department of English, Program in English, Florence, AL 35632-0001. Offers MA. *Program availability:* Part-time. *Degree requirements:* For master's, comprehensive exam (for some programs), thesis optional. *Entrance requirements:* For master's, GRE, MAT. Additional exam requirements/recommendations for international students: required—TOEFL (minimum score 79 iBT), IELTS (minimum score 6), PTE (minimum score 54). Electronic applications accepted.

The University of North Carolina at Chapel Hill, Graduate School, College of Arts and Sciences, Department of English, Chapel Hill, NC 27599. Offers MA, PhD. *Degree requirements:* For master's, one foreign language, comprehensive exam, thesis; for doctorate, 2 foreign languages, comprehensive exam, thesis/dissertation. *Entrance requirements:* For master's and doctorate, GRE General Test, GRE Subject Test, minimum GPA of 3.0 for last 2 undergraduate years, writing sample. Additional exam requirements/recommendations for international students: required—TOEFL. Electronic applications accepted.

The University of North Carolina at Charlotte, College of Liberal Arts and Sciences, Department of English, Charlotte, NC 28223-0001. Offers applied linguistics (Graduate Certificate); english (MA), including applied linguistics, children's lit., composition/rhetoric, creative writing, english ed., english for specific purposes, literature, tech/prof w; technical and professional writing (Graduate Certificate). *Program availability:* Part-time, evening/weekend. *Faculty:* 31 full-time (16 women), 1 (woman) part-time/adjunct. *Students:* 26 full-time (19 women), 32 part-time (23 women); includes 18 minority (9 Black or African American, non-Hispanic/Latino; 3 Asian, non-Hispanic/Latino; 1 Hispanic/Latino; 5 Two or more races, non-Hispanic/Latino), 1 international. Average age 30. 26 applicants, 96% accepted, 17 enrolled. In 2019, 16 master's, 3 other advanced degrees awarded. *Degree requirements:* For master's, comprehensive exam (for some programs), thesis, project. *Entrance requirements:* For master's, minimum undergraduate GPA of 3.0, statement of purpose, recommendation letters; unofficial transcript; for Graduate Certificate, statement of purpose, three letters of recommendation, writing sample, minimum GPA of 2.75, current GRE score/current MAT score/portfolio of professional-level documents (technical/professional writing). Additional exam requirements/recommendations for international students: required—TOEFL (minimum score 557 paper-based; 83 iBT), IELTS (minimum score 6.5), TOEFL (minimum score 557 paper-based, 83 iBT) or IELTS (6.5). *Application deadline:* For fall admission, 3/1 priority date for domestic students. Applications are processed on a rolling basis. Application fee: $75. Electronic applications accepted. *Expenses:* Tuition, state resident: full-time $4337. Tuition, nonresident: full-time $17,771. *Required fees:* $3093. Tuition and fees vary according to course load, degree level and program. *Financial support:* In 2019–20, 15 students received support, including 15 teaching assistantships (averaging $8,015 per year); career-related internships or fieldwork, institutionally sponsored loans, scholarships/grants, and unspecified assistantships also available. Support available to part-time students. Financial award application deadline: 3/1; financial award applicants required to submit FAFSA. *Unit head:* Dr. Mark West, Professor and Chair, 704-687-0618, E-mail: miwest@uncc.edu. *Application contact:* Kathy B. Giddings, Director of Graduate Admissions, 704-687-5503, Fax: 704-687-1668, E-mail: gradadm@uncc.edu. Website: http://english.uncc.edu/

The University of North Carolina at Greensboro, Graduate School, College of Arts and Sciences, Department of English, Program in English, Greensboro, NC 27412-5001. Offers American literature (PhD); English (M Ed, MA); English literature (PhD); rhetoric and composition (PhD). *Degree requirements:* For master's, comprehensive exam, thesis or alternative; for doctorate, variable foreign language requirement, thesis/dissertation, preliminary exam. *Entrance requirements:* For master's, GRE General Test, GRE Subject Test, minimum GPA of 3.0; for doctorate, GRE General Test, GRE Subject Test, critical writing sample, minimum GPA of 3.0. Additional exam requirements/recommendations for international students: required—TOEFL. Electronic applications accepted.

The University of North Carolina Wilmington, College of Arts and Sciences, Department of English, Wilmington, NC 28403-3297. Offers MA. *Program availability:* Part-time. *Faculty:* 18 full-time (9 women). *Students:* 23 full-time (19 women), 3 part-time (2 women); includes 5 minority (1 Black or African American, non-Hispanic/Latino; 2 American Indian or Alaska Native, non-Hispanic/Latino; 1 Hispanic/Latino; 1 Two or more races, non-Hispanic/Latino). Average age 26. 18 applicants, 83% accepted, 12 enrolled. In 2019, 8 master's awarded. *Degree requirements:* For master's, comprehensive exam, thesis or alternative. *Entrance requirements:* For master's, 3 recommendations, statement of interest, writing sample. Additional exam requirements/recommendations for international students: required—TOEFL (minimum score 79 iBT), IELTS (minimum score 6.5). *Application deadline:* For fall admission, 7/1 for domestic students; for spring admission, 11/1 for domestic students; for summer admission, 5/1 for domestic students. Applications are processed on a rolling basis. Application fee: $75. Electronic applications accepted. *Expenses: Tuition, area resident:* Full-time $4719; part-time $326 per credit hour. Tuition, state resident: full-time $4719; part-time $326 per credit hour. Tuition, nonresident: full-time $18,548; part-time $1099 per credit hour. *Required fees:* $2738. Tuition and fees vary according to program. *Financial support:* Teaching assistantships and scholarships/grants available. Financial award

application deadline: 1/1; financial award applicants required to submit FAFSA. *Unit head:* Dr. Tiffany Gilbert, Chair, 910-962-7746, Fax: 910-962-7186, E-mail: gilbertt@uncw.edu. *Application contact:* Dr. Meghan Sweeney, Graduate Coordinator, 910-962-3054, Fax: 910-962-7186, E-mail: sweeneym@uncw.edu.
Website: http://www.uncw.edu/english/graduate/index.html

University of North Dakota, Graduate School, College of Arts and Sciences, Department of English, Grand Forks, ND 58202. Offers MA, PhD. *Degree requirements:* For master's, one foreign language, comprehensive exam, thesis or alternative; for doctorate, one foreign language, comprehensive exam, thesis/dissertation. *Entrance requirements:* For master's and doctorate, GRE General Test, minimum GPA of 3.0. Additional exam requirements/recommendations for international students: required—TOEFL (minimum score 550 paper-based; 79 iBT), IELTS (minimum score 6.5). Electronic applications accepted.

University of Northern Colorado, Graduate School, College of Humanities and Social Sciences, Department of English, Greeley, CO 80639. Offers MA. *Program availability:* Part-time. *Degree requirements:* For master's, comprehensive exam. *Entrance requirements:* For master's, GRE General Test, 2 letters of recommendation. Electronic applications accepted.

University of Northern Iowa, Graduate College, College of Humanities, Arts and Sciences, Department of Languages and Literatures, MA Program in English, Cedar Falls, IA 50614. Offers creative writing (MA); English (MA); literature (MA). *Program availability:* Part-time, evening/weekend. *Degree requirements:* For master's, one foreign language, comprehensive exam, thesis or alternative, portfolio. *Entrance requirements:* Additional exam requirements/recommendations for international students: required—TOEFL (minimum score 600 paper-based; 100 iBT). Electronic applications accepted.

University of North Florida, College of Arts and Sciences, Department of English, Jacksonville, FL 32224. Offers MA. *Program availability:* Part-time, evening/weekend. *Degree requirements:* For master's, comprehensive exam, thesis optional. *Entrance requirements:* For master's, GRE General Test, minimum GPA of 3.0 in last 60 hours, writing sample. Additional exam requirements/recommendations for international students: required—TOEFL (minimum score 500 paper-based; 61 iBT). Electronic applications accepted.

University of North Texas, Toulouse Graduate School, Denton, TX 76203-5459. Offers accounting (MS); applied anthropology (MA, MS); applied behavior analysis (Certificate); applied geography (MA); applied technology and performance improvement (M Ed, MS); art education (MA); art history (MA); arts leadership (Certificate); audiology (Au D); behavior analysis (MS); behavioral science (PhD); biochemistry and molecular biology (MS); biology (MA, MS); biomedical engineering (MS); business analysis (MS); chemistry (MS); clinical health psychology (PhD); communication studies (MA, MS); computer engineering (MS); computer science (MS); counseling (M Ed, MS), including clinical mental health counseling (MS), college and university counseling, elementary school counseling, secondary school counseling; creative writing (MA); criminal justice (MS); curriculum and instruction (M Ed); decision sciences (MBA); design (MA, MFA), including fashion design (MFA), innovation studies, interior design (MFA); early childhood studies (MS); economics (MS); educational leadership (M Ed, Ed D); educational psychology (MS, PhD), including family studies (MS), gifted and talented (MS), human development (MS), learning and cognition (MS), research, measurement and evaluation (MS); electrical engineering (MS); emergency management (MPA); engineering technology (MS); English (MA); English as a second language (MA); environmental science (MS); finance (MBA, MS); financial management (MPA); French (MA); health services management (MBA); higher education (M Ed, Ed D); history (MA, MS); hospitality management (MS); human resources management (MPA); information science (MS); information systems (PhD); information technologies (MBA); interdisciplinary studies (MA, MS); international studies (MA); international sustainable tourism (MS); jazz studies (MM); journalism (MA, MJ, Graduate Certificate), including interactive and virtual digital communication (Graduate Certificate), narrative journalism (Graduate Certificate), public relations (Graduate Certificate); kinesiology (MS); linguistics (MA); local government management (MPA); logistics (PhD); logistics and supply chain management (MBA); long-term care, senior housing, and aging services (MA); management (PhD); marketing (MBA); mathematics (MA, MS); mechanical and energy engineering (MS, PhD); music (MA), including ethnomusicology, music theory, musicology, performance; music composition (PhD); music education (MM Ed, PhD); nonprofit management (MPA); operations and supply chain management (MBA); performance (MM, DMA); philosophy (MA); political science (MA); professional and technical communication (MA); radio, television and film (MA, MFA); rehabilitation counseling (Certificate); sociology (MA); Spanish (MA); special education (M Ed); speech-language pathology (MA); strategic management (MBA); studio art (MFA); teaching (M Ed); MBA/MS. *Program availability:* Part-time, evening/weekend, online learning. Terminal master's awarded for partial completion of doctoral program. *Degree requirements:* For master's, variable foreign language requirement, comprehensive exam (for some programs), thesis (for some programs); for doctorate, variable foreign language requirement, comprehensive exam (for some programs), thesis/dissertation; for other advanced degree, variable foreign language requirement, comprehensive exam (for some programs). *Entrance requirements:* For master's and doctorate, GRE, GMAT. Additional exam requirements/recommendations for international students: required—TOEFL (minimum score 550 paper-based; 79 iBT). Electronic applications accepted.

University of Notre Dame, The Graduate School, College of Arts and Letters, Division of Humanities, Department of English, Notre Dame, IN 46556. Offers creative writing (MFA); English (MA, PhD). *Degree requirements:* For doctorate, one foreign language, thesis/dissertation, candidacy exam. *Entrance requirements:* For master's, GRE General Test, minimum GPA of 3.0; for doctorate, GRE General Test, GRE Subject Test, minimum GPA of 3.0. Additional exam requirements/recommendations for international students: required—TOEFL (minimum score 600 paper-based; 80 iBT). Electronic applications accepted.

University of Oklahoma, College of Arts and Sciences, Department of English, Norman, OK 73019. Offers literary and cultural studies (MA, PhD); writing and rhetoric studies (MA, PhD). *Program availability:* Part-time. *Degree requirements:* For master's, one foreign language, comprehensive exam (for some programs), thesis (for some programs), exam or thesis; for doctorate, one foreign language, comprehensive exam, thesis/dissertation. *Entrance requirements:* For master's, GRE, BA in English or related field; for doctorate, GRE, MA in English or related field. Additional exam requirements/recommendations for international students: required—TOEFL (minimum score 79 iBT) or IELTS (minimum score 6.5). Electronic applications accepted. *Expenses:* Tuition, state resident: full-time $6583.20; part-time $274.30 per credit hour. Tuition, nonresident: full-time $21,242; part-time $885.10 per credit hour. *International tuition:* $21,242.40 full-time. *Required fees:* $1994.20; $72.55 per credit hour. $126.50 per semester. Tuition and fees vary according to course load and degree level.

University of Oregon, Graduate School, College of Arts and Sciences, Department of English, Eugene, OR 97403. Offers MA, PhD. Terminal master's awarded for partial completion of doctoral program. *Degree requirements:* For master's, one foreign language; for doctorate, 2 foreign languages, thesis/dissertation. *Entrance requirements:* For master's, GRE General Test; for doctorate, GRE Subject Test (English literature), minimum GPA of 3.5. Additional exam requirements/recommendations for international students: required—TOEFL.

University of Ottawa, Faculty of Graduate and Postdoctoral Studies, Faculty of Arts, Department of English, Ottawa, ON K1N 6N5, Canada. Offers MA, PhD. *Program availability:* Part-time, evening/weekend. *Degree requirements:* For master's, one foreign language, thesis optional; for doctorate, 2 foreign languages, comprehensive exam, thesis/dissertation. *Entrance requirements:* For master's, honors degree or equivalent, minimum B average; for doctorate, master's degree, minimum B+ average. Electronic applications accepted.

University of Pennsylvania, School of Arts and Sciences, Graduate Group in English, Philadelphia, PA 19104. Offers AM, PhD. *Faculty:* 47 full-time (22 women), 9 part-time/adjunct (4 women). *Students:* 68 full-time (31 women); includes 23 minority (7 Black or African American, non-Hispanic/Latino; 10 Asian, non-Hispanic/Latino; 3 Hispanic/Latino; 3 Two or more races, non-Hispanic/Latino), 11 international. Average age 26. 504 applicants, 3% accepted, 12 enrolled. In 2019, 10 master's, 10 doctorates awarded. Terminal master's awarded for partial completion of doctoral program. Application fee: $90.
Website: http://www.english.upenn.edu

University of Pittsburgh, Kenneth P. Dietrich School of Arts and Sciences, Department of English, Pittsburgh, PA 15260. Offers English (MA, PhD); writing (MFA). *Faculty:* 55 full-time (25 women), 1 part-time/adjunct (0 women). *Students:* 101 full-time (68 women); includes 48 minority (15 Black or African American, non-Hispanic/Latino; 1 American Indian or Alaska Native, non-Hispanic/Latino; 19 Asian, non-Hispanic/Latino; 13 Hispanic/Latino). Average age 31. 354 applicants, 10% accepted, 17 enrolled. In 2019, 16 master's, 5 doctorates awarded. Terminal master's awarded for partial completion of doctoral program. *Degree requirements:* For master's, variable foreign language requirement, thesis; for doctorate, variable foreign language requirement, comprehensive exam, thesis/dissertation. *Entrance requirements:* For master's and doctorate, writing sample. Additional exam requirements/recommendations for international students: required—TOEFL, IELTS, TOEFL or IELTS. *Application deadline:* For fall admission, 12/10 for domestic students. Application fee: $75. Electronic applications accepted. *Financial support:* In 2019–20, 81 students received support, including 25 fellowships with full tuition reimbursements available (averaging $23,790 per year), 6 research assistantships with full and partial tuition reimbursements available (averaging $19,480 per year), 50 teaching assistantships with full and partial tuition reimbursements available (averaging $19,649 per year); Federal Work-Study, institutionally sponsored loans, health care benefits, tuition waivers (full and partial), and unspecified assistantships also available. Support available to part-time students. Financial award application deadline: 12/10. *Unit head:* Dr. Gayle Rogers, Chair; Professor, 412-624-6509, Fax: 412-624-6639, E-mail: grogers@pitt.edu. *Application contact:* Jesse Daugherty, Manager of Graduate Administration - Humanities Division; Graduate Administrator, 412-624-6549, Fax: 412-624-6639, E-mail: jed110@pitt.edu.
Website: http://www.english.pitt.edu

University of Puerto Rico at Mayagüez, Graduate Studies, College of Arts and Sciences, Department of English, Mayagüez, PR 00681-9000. Offers English education (MA). *Program availability:* Part-time. *Degree requirements:* For master's, one foreign language, comprehensive exam, thesis. *Entrance requirements:* For master's, minimum GPA of 3.0; course work in linguistics or language, American literature, British literature, and structure/grammar or syntax. Additional exam requirements/recommendations for international students: required—TOEFL (minimum score 550 paper-based; 79 iBT). Electronic applications accepted.

University of Puerto Rico at Rio Piedras, College of Humanities, Department of English, San Juan, PR 00931-3300. Offers Caribbean linguistics (PhD); Caribbean literature (PhD); English (MA). *Program availability:* Part-time. *Degree requirements:* For master's, one foreign language, comprehensive exam, thesis; for doctorate, residency. *Entrance requirements:* For master's, PAEG or GRE, interview, minimum GPA of 3.0, 2 letters of recommendation; for doctorate, PAEG or GRE, minimum GPA of 3.0, 3 letters of recommendation, interview.

University of Regina, Faculty of Graduate Studies and Research, Faculty of Arts, Department of English, Regina, SK S4S 0A2, Canada. Offers creative writing (MA); English (MA, PhD). *Program availability:* Part-time. *Faculty:* 22 full-time (10 women), 2 part-time/adjunct (1 woman). *Students:* 8 full-time (6 women), 5 part-time (4 women). Average age 30. 16 applicants, 44% accepted. In 2019, 4 master's awarded. *Degree requirements:* For master's, thesis (for some programs); for doctorate, thesis/dissertation. *Entrance requirements:* For master's, overall GPA of 75 percent, writing sample, portfolio of creative material (for creative writing). Applicants must have successfully completed ENGL 399 or an equivalent course in Literary Theory. At the discretion graduate chair students with qualification may be admitted and to pass ENGL 399 in addition to MA courses. Additional exam requirements/recommendations for international students: required—TOEFL (minimum score 600 paper-based; 100 iBT), IELTS (minimum score 7.5), PTE (minimum score 68), Could be one of the test listed above. Other option are CAEL, MELAB, CANTEST and U or R ESL. *Application deadline:* For fall admission, 3/15 for domestic and international students; for winter admission, 10/15 for domestic and international students; for spring admission, 2/15 for domestic and international students. Applications are processed on a rolling basis. Application fee: $100. Electronic applications accepted. *Expenses: Tuition:* Full-time $6684 Canadian dollars. *Required fees:* $100 Canadian dollars; $3351.45 Canadian dollars per trimester. $1117.15 Canadian dollars per semester. Tuition and fees vary according to course level, course load, degree level and program. *Financial support:* Fellowships, research assistantships, teaching assistantships, career-related internships or fieldwork, Federal Work-Study, scholarships/grants, unspecified assistantships, and travel award and Graduate Scholarship Base Funds available. Support available to part-time students. Financial award application deadline: 9/30. *Unit head:* Dr. Marcel DeCoste, Department Head, 306-585-4691, Fax: 306-585-5429, E-mail: marcel.decoste@uregina.ca. *Application contact:* Dr. Michael Trussler, Graduate Chair, 306-585-4315, Fax: 306-585-5429, E-mail: Michael.Trussler@uregina.ca.
Website: http://www.uregina.ca/arts/english

University of Rhode Island, Graduate School, College of Arts and Sciences, Department of English, Kingston, RI 02881. Offers American literature and culture (PhD); British literature and culture (PhD); creative writing (PhD); critical theories (PhD); English (MA); film (PhD); gender studies (PhD); MLIS/MA. *Program availability:* Part-time. *Faculty:* 18 full-time (10 women). *Students:* 29 full-time (19 women), 11 part-time (7 women); includes 2 minority (both Black or African American, non-Hispanic/Latino), 8 international. 15 applicants, 40% accepted, 6 enrolled. In 2019, 2 master's, 9 doctorates awarded. *Entrance requirements:* Additional exam requirements/recommendations for international students: required—TOEFL (minimum score 91 iBT). *Application deadline:* For fall admission, 1/15 for domestic and international students. Application fee: $65. Electronic applications accepted. *Expenses: Tuition, area resident:* Full-time $13,734; part-time $763 per credit. Tuition, state resident: full-time $13,734; part-time $763 per credit. Tuition, nonresident: full-time $26,512; part-time $1473 per credit. *International tuition:* $26,512 full-time. *Required fees:* $1780; $52 per credit. $35 per term. One-time

fee: $165. *Financial support:* In 2019–20, 24 teaching assistantships with tuition reimbursements (averaging $19,520 per year) were awarded. Financial award application deadline: 1/15; financial award applicants required to submit FAFSA. *Unit head:* Dr. Travis Williams, Chair, 401-874-9501, E-mail: tdwilliams@uri.edu. *Application contact:* Dr. David Faflik, Director of Graduate Studies, 401-874-4670, E-mail: faflik@uri.edu.
Website: http://www.uri.edu/artsci/eng/

University of Rochester, School of Arts and Sciences, Department of English, Rochester, NY 14627. Offers MA, PhD. *Faculty:* 24 full-time (8 women). *Students:* 68 full-time (39 women), 2 part-time (1 woman); includes 8 minority (1 Black or African American, non-Hispanic/Latino; 1 Asian, non-Hispanic/Latino; 3 Hispanic/Latino; 3 Two or more races, non-Hispanic/Latino), 8 international. Average age 29. 110 applicants, 35% accepted, 18 enrolled. In 2019, 18 master's, 4 doctorates awarded. Terminal master's awarded for partial completion of doctoral program. *Degree requirements:* For master's, comprehensive exam or comprehensive essay; for doctorate, one foreign language, comprehensive exam, thesis/dissertation, qualifying exam. *Entrance requirements:* For master's and doctorate, GRE, personal statement (two to three pages, double spaced), writing sample, two to three letters of recommendation. *Application deadline:* For fall admission, 1/15 for domestic and international students. Application fee: $60. Electronic applications accepted. *Financial support:* Fellowships with full and partial tuition reimbursements, teaching assistantships with full and partial tuition reimbursements, and health care benefits available. Support available to part-time students. *Unit head:* Katherine Mannheimer, Associate Professor and Chair, 585-275-9257, E-mail: katherine.mannheimer@rochester.edu. *Application contact:* Carrie Morriss, Graduate Coordinator, 585-275-9256, E-mail: carrie.morriss@rochester.edu.
Website: https://www.sas.rochester.edu/eng/graduate/index.html

University of St. Thomas, College of Arts and Sciences, Graduate Program in English, St. Paul, MN 55105-1096. Offers english literature (MA); teaching college english (Certificate). *Program availability:* Part-time, evening/weekend. *Degree requirements:* For master's, thesis, oral review. *Entrance requirements:* For master's, minimum GPA of 3.0, minimum 5 upper-level undergraduate courses in literature, sample of written work, personal statement, BA from accredited university, transcripts. Additional exam requirements/recommendations for international students: required—TOEFL (minimum score 80 iBT), IELTS (minimum score 6.5). Electronic applications accepted. *Expenses:* Contact institution.

University of Saskatchewan, College of Graduate and Postdoctoral Studies, College of Arts and Science, Department of English, Saskatoon, SK S7N 5A2, Canada. Offers MA, PhD. *Degree requirements:* For master's, one foreign language, thesis; for doctorate, one foreign language, comprehensive exam (for some programs), thesis/dissertation. *Entrance requirements:* Additional exam requirements/recommendations for international students: required—TOEFL (minimum score 80 iBT); recommended—IELTS (minimum score 6.5). Electronic applications accepted.

University of South Africa, College of Human Sciences, Pretoria, South Africa. Offers adult education (M Ed); African languages (MA, PhD); African politics (MA, PhD); Afrikaans (MA, PhD); ancient history (MA, PhD); ancient Near Eastern studies (MA, PhD); anthropology (MA, PhD); applied linguistics (MA); Arabic (MA, PhD); archaeology (MA); art history (MA); Biblical archaeology (MA); Biblical studies (M Th, D Th, PhD); Christian spirituality (M Th, D Th); church history (M Th, D Th); classical studies (MA, PhD); clinical psychology (MA); communication (MA, PhD); comparative education (M Ed, Ed D); consulting psychology (D Admin, D Com, PhD); curriculum studies (M Ed, Ed D); development studies (M Admin, MA, D Admin, PhD); didactics (M Ed, Ed D); education (M Tech); education management (M Ed, Ed D); educational psychology (M Ed); English (MA); environmental education (M Ed); French (MA, PhD); German (MA, PhD); Greek (MA); guidance and counseling (M Ed); health studies (MA, PhD), including health sciences education (MA), health services management (MA), medical and surgical nursing science (critical care general) (MA), midwifery and neonatal nursing science (MA), trauma and emergency care (MA); history (MA, PhD); history of education (Ed D); inclusive education (M Ed, Ed D); information and communications technology policy and regulation (MA); information science (MA, MIS, PhD); international politics (MA, PhD); Islamic studies (MA, PhD); Italian (MA, PhD); Judaica (MA, PhD); linguistics (MA, PhD); mathematical education (M Ed); mathematics education (MA); missiology (M Th, D Th); modern Hebrew (MA, PhD); musicology (MA, MMus, D Mus, PhD); natural science education (M Ed); New Testament (M Th, D Th); Old Testament (D Th); pastoral therapy (M Th, D Th); philosophy (MA); philosophy of education (M Ed, Ed D); politics (MA, PhD); Portuguese (MA, PhD); practical theology (M Th, D Th); psychology (MA, MS, PhD); psychology of education (M Ed, Ed D); public health (MA); religious studies (MA, D Th, PhD); Romance languages (MA); Russian (MA, PhD); Semitic languages (MA, PhD); social behavior studies in HIV/AIDS (MA); social science (mental health) (MA); social science in development studies (MA); social science in psychology (MA); social science in social work (MA); social science in sociology (MA); social work (MSW, DSW, PhD); socio-education (M Ed, Ed D); sociolinguistics (MA); sociology (MA, PhD); Spanish (MA, PhD); systematic theology (M Th, D Th); TESOL (teaching English to speakers of other languages) (MA); theological ethics (M Th, D Th); theory of literature (MA, PhD); urban ministries (D Th); urban ministry (M Th).

University of South Alabama, College of Arts and Sciences, Department of English, Mobile, AL 36688. Offers creative writing (MA); literature (MA). *Program availability:* Part-time, evening/weekend. *Faculty:* 10 full-time (3 women), 1 part-time/adjunct (0 women). *Students:* 19 full-time (12 women), 3 part-time (1 woman); includes 4 minority (1 Black or African American, non-Hispanic/Latino; 1 American Indian or Alaska Native, non-Hispanic/Latino; 1 Hispanic/Latino; 1 Two or more races, non-Hispanic/Latino), 1 international. Average age 33. 6 applicants, 100% accepted, 6 enrolled. In 2019, 7 master's awarded. *Degree requirements:* For master's, one foreign language, comprehensive exam, thesis optional. *Entrance requirements:* For master's, GRE. Additional exam requirements/recommendations for international students: required—TOEFL (minimum score 79 iBT), IELTS (minimum score 6.5), TOEFL or IELTS score must be submitted - not both. *Application deadline:* For fall admission, 7/15 priority date for domestic students, 5/15 priority date for international students; for spring admission, 12/1 priority date for domestic students, 11/1 priority date for international students; for summer admission, 5/1 for domestic students, 4/1 for international students. Applications are processed on a rolling basis. Application fee: $35. Electronic applications accepted. *Expenses: Tuition, area resident:* Part-time $442 per credit hour. Tuition, state resident: full-time $10,608; part-time $442 per credit hour. Tuition, nonresident: full-time $21,216; part-time $884 per credit hour. *Financial support:* Fellowships, research assistantships, teaching assistantships, career-related internships or fieldwork, Federal Work-Study, institutionally sponsored loans, scholarships/grants, and unspecified assistantships available. Support available to part-time students. Financial award application deadline: 3/31; financial award applicants required to submit FAFSA. *Unit head:* Dr. Ellen Harrington, Interim Chair, English, 251-460-6146, E-mail: eharrington@southalabama.edu. *Application contact:* Dr. Ellen Harrington, Interim Chair, English, 251-460-6146, E-mail: eharrington@southalabama.edu.
Website: http://www.southalabama.edu/colleges/artsandsci/english/

University of South Carolina, The Graduate School, College of Arts and Sciences, Department of English Language and Literature, Columbia, SC 29208. Offers creative writing (MFA); English (MA, PhD); English education (MAT); MLIS/MA. *Program availability:* Part-time. *Degree requirements:* For master's, one foreign language, comprehensive exam, thesis; for doctorate, 2 foreign languages, comprehensive exam, thesis/dissertation. *Entrance requirements:* For master's, GRE General Test (MFA), GRE Subject Test (MA, MAT), sample of written work; for doctorate, GRE General Test, GRE Subject Test, sample of written work. Additional exam requirements/recommendations for international students: required—TOEFL. Electronic applications accepted.

University of South Dakota, Graduate School, College of Arts and Sciences, Department of English, Vermillion, SD 57069. Offers MA, PhD. *Degree requirements:* For master's, comprehensive exam (for some programs), thesis (for some programs); for doctorate, comprehensive exam, thesis/dissertation. *Entrance requirements:* For master's, minimum GPA of 3.0, writing sample; for doctorate, GRE, minimum GPA of 3.0, writing sample. Additional exam requirements/recommendations for international students: required—TOEFL (minimum score 620 paper-based; 105 iBT). Electronic applications accepted.

University of Southern California, Graduate School, Dana and David Dornsife College of Letters, Arts and Sciences, Department of English, Los Angeles, CA 90089. Offers English (MA, PhD); literature and creative writing (PhD). Terminal master's awarded for partial completion of doctoral program. *Degree requirements:* For doctorate, one foreign language, comprehensive exam, thesis/dissertation. *Entrance requirements:* For doctorate, GRE General Test, GRE Subject Test (English literature). Additional exam requirements/recommendations for international students: required—TOEFL. Electronic applications accepted.

University of Southern Indiana, Graduate Studies, College of Liberal Arts, Program in English, Evansville, IN 47712-3590. Offers MA. *Program availability:* Part-time, evening/weekend. *Entrance requirements:* For master's, writing sample, three letters of recommendation. Additional exam requirements/recommendations for international students: required—TOEFL (minimum score 550 paper-based; 79 iBT), IELTS (minimum score 6). Electronic applications accepted.

University of South Florida, College of Arts and Sciences, Department of English, Tampa, FL 33620-9951. Offers MA, MFA, PhD. *Program availability:* Part-time, evening/weekend. *Faculty:* 26 full-time (15 women). *Students:* 64 full-time (45 women), 27 part-time (19 women); includes 15 minority (6 Black or African American, non-Hispanic/Latino; 3 Asian, non-Hispanic/Latino; 5 Hispanic/Latino; 1 Two or more races, non-Hispanic/Latino), 1 international. Average age 33. 95 applicants, 52% accepted, 24 enrolled. In 2019, 16 master's, 6 doctorates awarded. *Degree requirements:* For master's, comprehensive exam, thesis (for some programs), thesis (for MFA); thesis or portfolio (for MA); for doctorate, one foreign language, comprehensive exam, thesis/dissertation. *Entrance requirements:* For master's, a competitive Verbal aptitude score on the GRE general test, with a target Analytical Writing score of 4.0 (while the Quantitative score is not a determining factor in our admission decisions, both Verbal and Quantitative scores are factors in some university scholarships and fellowships), minimum undergraduate GPA of 3.5 (for MA), 3.2 (for MFA); three letters of recommendation; personal statement; writing sample from 10 to 20 pages (depending on genre); for doctorate, a competitive Verbal aptitude score on the GRE general test, with a target Analytical Writing score of 4.0 (while the Quantitative score is not a determining factor in our admission decisions, both Verbal and Quantitative scores factor in some university scholarships and fellowships), minimum graduate GPA of 3.7; three letters of recommendation; 2-3 page personal statement; 2500-word writing sample from English coursework. Additional exam requirements/recommendations for international students: required—TOEFL, TOEFL minimum score 550 paper-based; 79 iBT or IELTS minimum score 6.5 (for MA and PhD); TOEFL minimum score 600 paper-based (for MFA). *Application deadline:* For fall admission, 1/1 for domestic and international students. Applications are processed on a rolling basis. Application fee: $30. Electronic applications accepted. *Financial support:* In 2019–20, 23 students received support, including 2 research assistantships (averaging $17,221 per year), 79 teaching assistantships with tuition reimbursements available (averaging $11,576 per year); unspecified assistantships also available. Financial award application deadline: 6/30; financial award applicants required to submit FAFSA. *Unit head:* Dr. Laura Runge, Professor and Chairperson, 813-974-9496, E-mail: runge@usf.edu. *Application contact:* Dr. John Lennon, Associate Professor and Graduate Director, 813-974-2663, Fax: 813-974-2270, E-mail: jflennon@usf.edu.
Website: http://english.usf.edu/

University of South Florida, Innovative Education, Tampa, FL 33620-9951. Offers adult, career and higher education (Graduate Certificate), including college teaching, leadership in developing human resources, leadership in higher education; Africana studies (Graduate Certificate), including diasporas and health disparities, genocide and human rights; aging studies (Graduate Certificate), including gerontology; art research (Graduate Certificate), including museum studies; business foundations (Graduate Certificate); chemical and biomedical engineering (Graduate Certificate), including materials science and engineering, water, health and sustainability; child and family studies (Graduate Certificate), including positive behavior support; civil and industrial engineering (Graduate Certificate), including transportation systems analysis; community and family health (Graduate Certificate), including maternal and child health, social marketing and public health, violence and injury: prevention and intervention, women's health; criminology (Graduate Certificate), including criminal justice administration; data science for public administration (Graduate Certificate); digital humanities (Graduate Certificate); educational measurement and research (Graduate Certificate), including evaluation; English (Graduate Certificate), including comparative literary studies, creative writing, professional and technical communication; entrepreneurship (Graduate Certificate); environmental health (Graduate Certificate), including safety management; epidemiology and biostatistics (Graduate Certificate), including applied biostatistics, biostatistics, concepts and tools of epidemiology, epidemiology, epidemiology of infectious diseases; geography, environment and planning (Graduate Certificate), including community development, environmental policy and management, geographical information systems; geology (Graduate Certificate), including hydrogeology; global health (Graduate Certificate), including disaster management, global health and Latin American and Caribbean studies, global health practice, humanitarian assistance, infection control; government and international affairs (Graduate Certificate), including Cuban studies, globalization studies; health policy and management (Graduate Certificate), including health management and leadership, public health policy and programs; hearing specialist: early intervention (Graduate Certificate); industrial and management systems engineering (Graduate Certificate), including systems engineering, technology management; information studies (Graduate Certificate), including school library media specialist; information systems/decision sciences (Graduate Certificate), including analytics and business intelligence; instructional technology (Graduate Certificate), including distance education, Florida digital/virtual educator, instructional design, multimedia design, Web design; internal medicine, bioethics and medical humanities (Graduate Certificate), including biomedical ethics; Latin American and Caribbean studies (Graduate Certificate); leadership for

coastal resiliency planning (Graduate Certificate); mass communications (Graduate Certificate), including multimedia journalism; mathematics and statistics (Graduate Certificate), including mathematics; medicine (Graduate Certificate), including aging and neuroscience, bioinformatics, biotechnology, brain fitness and memory management, clinical investigation, hand and upper limb rehabilitation, health informatics, health sciences, integrative weight management, intellectual property, medicine and gender, metabolic and nutritional medicine, metabolic cardiology, pharmacy sciences; national and competitive intelligence (Graduate Certificate); nursing (Graduate Certificate), including simulation based academic fellowship in advanced pain management; psychological and social foundations (Graduate Certificate), including career counseling, college teaching, diversity in education, mental health counseling, school counseling; public affairs (Graduate Certificate), including nonprofit management, public management, research administration; public health (Graduate Certificate), including assessing chemical toxicity and public health risks, health equity, pharmacoepidemiology, public health generalist, toxicology, translational research in adolescent behavioral health; public health practices (Graduate Certificate), including planning for healthy communities; rehabilitation and mental health counseling (Graduate Certificate), including integrative mental health care, marriage and family therapy, rehabilitation technology; secondary education (Graduate Certificate), including ESOL, foreign language education: culture and content, foreign language education: professional; social work (Graduate Certificate), including geriatric social work/clinical gerontology; special education (Graduate Certificate), including autism spectrum disorder, disabilities education: severe/profound; world languages (Graduate Certificate), including teaching English as a second language (TESL) or foreign language. *Unit head:* Dr. Cynthia DeLuca, Associate Vice President and Assistant Vice Provost, 813-974-3077, Fax: 813-974-7061, E-mail: deluca@usf.edu. *Application contact:* Owen Hooper, Director, Summer and Alternative Calendar Programs, 813-974-6917, E-mail: hooper@usf.edu.
Website: http://www.usf.edu/innovative-education/

The University of Tennessee, Graduate School, College of Arts and Sciences, Department of English, Knoxville, TN 37996. Offers MA, PhD. *Program availability:* Part-time. *Degree requirements:* For master's, one foreign language, thesis or alternative; for doctorate, one foreign language, thesis/dissertation. *Entrance requirements:* For master's, GRE General Test, minimum GPA of 2.7; for doctorate, GRE General Test, GRE Subject Test, minimum GPA of 2.7. Additional exam requirements/recommendations for international students: required—TOEFL. Electronic applications accepted.

The University of Tennessee at Chattanooga, Program in English, Chattanooga, TN 37403. Offers creative writing (MA); literary study (MA); rhetoric and writing (MA). *Program availability:* Part-time. *Faculty:* 51 full-time (27 women), 22 part-time/adjunct (17 women). *Students:* 15 full-time (9 women), 16 part-time (14 women); includes 4 minority (2 Black or African American, non-Hispanic/Latino; 1 Asian, non-Hispanic/Latino; 1 Native Hawaiian or other Pacific Islander, non-Hispanic/Latino). Average age 33. 15 applicants, 100% accepted, 10 enrolled. In 2019, 8 master's awarded. *Degree requirements:* For master's, comprehensive exam, thesis. *Entrance requirements:* For master's, minimum GPA of 3.0 in English, two letters of recommendation. Additional exam requirements/recommendations for international students: required—TOEFL (minimum score 550 paper-based; 79 iBT), IELTS (minimum score 6). *Application deadline:* For fall admission, 6/15 priority date for domestic students, 7/1 for international students; for spring admission, 11/1 priority date for domestic students, 11/1 for international students. Applications are processed on a rolling basis. Application fee: $35 ($40 for international students). Electronic applications accepted. *Financial support:* Research assistantships, teaching assistantships, career-related internships or fieldwork, scholarships/grants, health care benefits, and unspecified assistantships available. Support available to part-time students. Financial award application deadline: 7/1; financial award applicants required to submit FAFSA. *Unit head:* Dr. Andrew McCarthy, Department Head, 423-425-4615, Fax: 423-425-2282, E-mail: andrew-mccarthy@utc.edu. *Application contact:* Dr. Joanne Romagni, Dean of the Graduate School, 423-425-4478, Fax: 423-425-5223, E-mail: joanne-romagni@utc.edu.
Website: http://www.utc.edu/english/

The University of Texas at Arlington, Graduate School, College of Liberal Arts, Department of English, Arlington, TX 76019. Offers English (MA); literature (PhD). *Program availability:* Part-time, evening/weekend. *Degree requirements:* For master's, thesis or comprehensive exam; for doctorate, one foreign language, comprehensive exam, thesis/dissertation. *Entrance requirements:* For master's, GRE General Test, minimum 5-page writing sample, minimum GPA of 3.0, 3 letters of recommendation; for doctorate, GRE General Test, minimum graduate GPA of 3.5, writing sample, 3 letters of recommendation. Additional exam requirements/recommendations for international students: required—TOEFL (minimum score 550 paper-based).

The University of Texas at Austin, Graduate School, College of Liberal Arts, Department of English, Austin, TX 78712-1111. Offers creative writing (MFA); English (MA, PhD). *Program availability:* Part-time. Terminal master's awarded for partial completion of doctoral program. *Degree requirements:* For master's, 2 foreign languages; for doctorate, variable foreign language requirement. *Entrance requirements:* For master's and doctorate, GRE General Test. Electronic applications accepted.

The University of Texas at El Paso, Graduate School, College of Liberal Arts, Department of English, El Paso, TX 79968-0001. Offers bilingual professional writing (Certificate); English and American literature (MA); rhetoric and composition (PhD); rhetoric and writing studies (MA); teaching English (MAT). *Program availability:* Part-time, evening/weekend. *Degree requirements:* For master's, thesis optional. *Entrance requirements:* For master's, GRE General Test, minimum GPA of 3.0. Additional exam requirements/recommendations for international students: required—TOEFL. Electronic applications accepted.

The University of Texas at San Antonio, College of Liberal and Fine Arts, Department of English, San Antonio, TX 78249-0617. Offers MA, PhD. *Program availability:* Part-time, evening/weekend. Terminal master's awarded for partial completion of doctoral program. *Degree requirements:* For master's, comprehensive exam, thesis optional; for doctorate, one foreign language, comprehensive exam, thesis/dissertation. *Entrance requirements:* For master's, GRE General Test, minimum GPA of 3.3 on all upper-division English courses, 18 hours of English of which 12 hours must be upper-division English literature; for doctorate, GRE General Test, GRE Subject Test (English literature), 18 hours of upper-division and/or graduate English, minimum GPA of 3.5, statement of purpose, writing sample, 3 letters of recommendation. Additional exam requirements/recommendations for international students: required—TOEFL (minimum score 550 paper-based; 79 iBT), IELTS (minimum score 6.5). Electronic applications accepted.

The University of Texas at Tyler, College of Arts and Sciences, Department of Literature and Languages, Tyler, TX 75799-0001. Offers English (MA); interdisciplinary studies (MAIS). *Program availability:* Part-time, evening/weekend. *Faculty:* 10 full-time (7 women). *Students:* 14 full-time (10 women), 32 part-time (26 women); includes 4 minority (3 Hispanic/Latino; 1 Two or more races, non-Hispanic/Latino). Average age 33. 23 applicants, 83% accepted, 11 enrolled. In 2019, 18 master's awarded. *Degree requirements:* For master's, one foreign language, comprehensive exam, thesis optional. *Entrance requirements:* For master's, GRE General Test, minimum GPA of 3.0; four semesters or the equivalent of one foreign language. Additional exam requirements/recommendations for international students: required—TOEFL. *Application deadline:* For fall admission, 8/17 priority date for domestic students, 7/1 priority date for international students; for spring admission, 12/21 priority date for domestic students, 11/1 priority date for international students. Applications are processed on a rolling basis. Application fee: $25 ($50 for international students). Electronic applications accepted. *Financial support:* In 2019–20, fellowships with full and partial tuition reimbursements (averaging $1,000 per year), 1 research assistantship with full and partial tuition reimbursement (averaging $6,000 per year) was awarded; teaching assistantships with full and partial tuition reimbursements, Federal Work-Study, institutionally sponsored loans, scholarships/grants, tuition waivers, and unspecified assistantships also available. Financial award application deadline: 7/1; financial award applicants required to submit FAFSA. *Unit head:* Dr. Hui Wu, Chair, 903-566-7289, E-mail: hui_wu@uttyler.edu. *Application contact:* Dr. Hui Wu, Chair, 903-566-7289, E-mail: hui_wu@uttyler.edu.
Website: https://www.uttyler.edu/litlang/

The University of Texas of the Permian Basin, Office of Graduate Studies, College of Arts and Sciences, Department of Literature and Languages, Program in English, Odessa, TX 79762-0001. Offers MA. *Program availability:* Part-time, evening/weekend. *Degree requirements:* For master's, comprehensive exam (for some programs), thesis (for some programs). *Entrance requirements:* For master's, GRE General Test. Additional exam requirements/recommendations for international students: required—TOEFL (minimum score 550 paper-based).

The University of Texas Rio Grande Valley, College of Liberal Arts, Department of Literatures and Cultural Studies, Edinburg, TX 78539. Offers English (MA); Spanish (MA). *Faculty:* 12 full-time (8 women). *Students:* 23 full-time (17 women), 54 part-time (34 women); includes 72 minority (2 Black or African American, non-Hispanic/Latino; 70 Hispanic/Latino), 3 international. Average age 32. 18 applicants, 89% accepted, 12 enrolled. In 2019, 26 master's awarded. *Expenses:* Tuition, area resident: Full-time $5959; part-time $440 per credit hour. Tuition, state resident: full-time $5959. Tuition, nonresident: full-time $5959. *International tuition:* $13,321 full-time. *Required fees:* $1169; $185 per credit hour.
Website: utrgv.edu/literatures/index.htm

The University of the South, Sewanee School of Letters, Sewanee, TN 37383. Offers American and English literature (MA); creative writing (MFA). *Program availability:* Part-time. *Faculty:* 3 full-time (1 woman), 7 part-time/adjunct (4 women). *Students:* 40 part-time (24 women); includes 5 minority (1 Black or African American, non-Hispanic/Latino; 1 Asian, non-Hispanic/Latino; 1 Hispanic/Latino; 2 Two or more races, non-Hispanic/Latino). Average age 42. In 2019, 16 master's awarded. *Degree requirements:* For master's, thesis (for some programs). *Entrance requirements:* For master's, writing sample, two letters of recommendation, official transcripts. *Application deadline:* For summer admission, 4/15 for domestic students. Applications are processed on a rolling basis. Application fee: $0. Electronic applications accepted. *Expenses:* Contact institution. *Financial support:* Institutionally sponsored loans and scholarships/grants available. *Unit head:* Justin Taylor, Director of the School of Letters, 931-598-1636, E-mail: sletters@sewanee.edu. *Application contact:* April R. Alvarez, Associate Director of the School of Letters, 931-598-1636, E-mail: sletters@sewanee.edu.
Website: http://letters.sewanee.edu/

The University of Toledo, College of Graduate Studies, College of Languages, Literature and Social Sciences, Department of English Language and Literature, Toledo, OH 43606-3390. Offers English as a second language (MA); teaching of writing (Certificate). *Program availability:* Part-time. *Degree requirements:* For master's, thesis. *Entrance requirements:* For master's, GRE if GPA is less than 3.0, minimum cumulative point-hour ratio of 2.7 for all previous academic work, three letters of recommendation, transcripts from all prior institutions attended, critical essay; for Certificate, statement of purpose, transcripts from all prior institutions attended, 2 letters of recommendation. Additional exam requirements/recommendations for international students: required—TOEFL (minimum score 550 paper-based; 80 iBT). Electronic applications accepted.

University of Toronto, School of Graduate Studies, Faculty of Arts and Science, Department of English, Toronto, ON M5S 1A1, Canada. Offers creative writing (MA); English (MA, PhD); JD/MA. *Program availability:* Part-time. *Degree requirements:* For master's, thesis optional; for doctorate, 2 foreign languages, thesis/dissertation. *Entrance requirements:* For master's, minimum B+ average, 2 letters of reference, portfolio (creative writing program); for doctorate, minimum A- average, 2 letters of reference, writing sample. Additional exam requirements/recommendations for international students: required—TOEFL (minimum score 580 paper-based; 93 iBT), TWE (minimum score 5). Electronic applications accepted.

The University of Tulsa, Graduate School, Kendall College of Arts and Sciences, Department of English, Tulsa, OK 74104-3189. Offers English language and literature (MA, PhD); JD/MA. *Program availability:* Part-time, evening/weekend. Terminal master's awarded for partial completion of doctoral program. *Degree requirements:* For master's, independent research project; for doctorate, one foreign language, comprehensive exam, thesis/dissertation. *Entrance requirements:* For master's, GRE General Test, writing sample; for doctorate, GRE General Test, writing sample, list of language proficiencies. Additional exam requirements/recommendations for international students: required—TOEFL (minimum score 577 paper-based; 91 iBT), IELTS (minimum score 6.5). Electronic applications accepted. *Expenses: Tuition:* Full-time $22,896; part-time $1272 per credit hour. *Required fees:* $6 per credit hour. Tuition and fees vary according to course load and program.

University of Utah, Graduate School, College of Humanities, Department of English, Salt Lake City, UT 84112. Offers English (MA, MFA, PhD), including creative writing (MFA, PhD), literary and cultural studies (MA, PhD), rhetoric and composition (MA, PhD). *Faculty:* 17 full-time (9 women). *Students:* 51 full-time (28 women), 19 part-time (9 women); includes 11 minority (1 Black or African American, non-Hispanic/Latino; 4 Asian, non-Hispanic/Latino; 3 Hispanic/Latino; 3 Two or more races, non-Hispanic/Latino), 7 international. Average age 33. 248 applicants, 14% accepted, 18 enrolled. In 2019, 5 master's, 8 doctorates awarded. *Degree requirements:* For master's, one foreign language, thesis (for some programs), for MA - essay written & presented; for MFA - thesis; for doctorate, variable foreign language requirement, comprehensive exam, thesis/dissertation. *Entrance requirements:* For master's, exams required to be admitted, students applying to the MA or MFA degree programs must hold a BA or BS degree from an accredited College or University; a cumulative GPA of 3.3; TOEFL/IELTS scores for International applicants; for doctorate, students applying to the PhD degree programs must hold a BA or BS degree from an accredited College or University; successful completion of a previous Master's degree; a cumulative GPA of 3.3; TOEFL/IELTS scores for International applicants, NA. Additional exam requirements/recommendations for international students: required—TOEFL (minimum score 80 paper-based; 80 iBT), IELTS (minimum score 6.5). *Application deadline:* For fall admission, 12/15 for domestic and international students. Application fee: $55 ($65 for international students). Electronic applications accepted. *Expenses:* Tuition, state resident: full-time $7085; part-time $272.51 per credit hour. Tuition, nonresident: full-

time $24,937; part-time $959.12 per credit hour. *Required fees:* $880.52; $880.52 per semester. Tuition and fees vary according to degree level, program and student level. *Financial support:* In 2019–20, 14 students received support, including 14 fellowships with full tuition reimbursements available (averaging $20,000 per year), 34 teaching assistantships with full tuition reimbursements available (averaging $18,000 per year); health care benefits and unspecified assistantships also available. Financial award application deadline: 4/15; financial award applicants required to submit FAFSA. *Unit head:* Prof. Scott Black, Chair, Department of English, 801-581-3393, Fax: 801-585-5167, E-mail: scott.black@utah.edu. *Application contact:* Prof. Gerri Mackey, Graduate Academic Advisor, Department of English, 801-581-7850, Fax: 801-585-5167, E-mail: gerri.mackey@utah.edu.
Website: http://english.utah.edu/

University of Vermont, Graduate College, College of Arts and Sciences, Department of English, Burlington, VT 05405. Offers MA. *Degree requirements:* For master's, one foreign language, thesis. *Entrance requirements:* For master's, GRE General Test, writing sample. Additional exam requirements/recommendations for international students: required—TOEFL (minimum score 550 paper-based, 90 iBT) or IELTS (6.5). Electronic applications accepted.

University of Victoria, Faculty of Graduate Studies, Faculty of Humanities, Department of English, Victoria, BC V8W 2Y2, Canada. Offers MA, PhD. *Program availability:* Part-time. *Degree requirements:* For master's, one foreign language, thesis (for some programs); for doctorate, 2 foreign languages, comprehensive exam, thesis/dissertation, candidacy exam. *Entrance requirements:* For master's, minimum A- average in last 2 years of undergraduate course work, writing sample, resume; for doctorate, minimum A- average in graduate course work, writing sample, resumé. Additional exam requirements/recommendations for international students: required—TOEFL (minimum score 630 paper-based). Electronic applications accepted.

University of Virginia, College and Graduate School of Arts and Sciences, Department of English Language and Literature, Program in English, Charlottesville, VA 22903. Offers MA, PhD, JD/MA. *Degree requirements:* For master's, one foreign language, oral exam or thesis; for doctorate, 2 foreign languages, comprehensive exam, thesis/dissertation. *Entrance requirements:* For master's, GRE General Test, GRE Subject Test, 3 letters of recommendation, 2 writing samples; for doctorate, GRE General Test, GRE Subject Test, 3 letters of recommendation; 2 writing samples. Additional exam requirements/recommendations for international students: required—TOEFL (minimum score 600 paper-based; 90 iBT), IELTS (minimum score 7). Electronic applications accepted.

University of Washington, Graduate School, College of Arts and Sciences, Department of English, Seattle, WA 98195. Offers creative writing (MFA); English as a second language (MAT); English literature and language (MA, MAT, PhD). *Program availability:* Part-time. Terminal master's awarded for partial completion of doctoral program. *Degree requirements:* For master's, one foreign language, thesis (for some programs); for doctorate, one foreign language, thesis/dissertation. *Entrance requirements:* For master's, GRE General Test, GRE Subject Test (MA and MAT in English), minimum GPA of 3.0; for doctorate, GRE General Test, GRE Subject Test. Additional exam requirements/recommendations for international students: required—TOEFL. Electronic applications accepted.

University of Waterloo, Graduate Studies and Postdoctoral Affairs, Faculty of Arts, Department of English Language and Literature, Waterloo, ON N2L 3G1, Canada. Offers English language and literature (PhD); literary studies (MA); rhetoric and communication design (MA). *Program availability:* Part-time. *Degree requirements:* For master's, one foreign language, thesis optional; for doctorate, 2 foreign languages, thesis/dissertation. *Entrance requirements:* For master's, honors degree, minimum B+ average; for doctorate, master's degree, minimum A- average. Additional exam requirements/recommendations for international students: required—TOEFL, IELTS, PTE. Electronic applications accepted.

The University of Western Ontario, School of Graduate and Postdoctoral Studies, Faculty of Arts and Humanities, Department of English, London, ON N6A 3K7, Canada. Offers Canadian literature (MA); English (PhD); English literature (MA). *Degree requirements:* For master's, one foreign language, thesis or alternative; for doctorate, 2 foreign languages, thesis/dissertation, qualifying exam. *Entrance requirements:* For master's, minimum A average in appropriate field; for doctorate, MA or equivalent, minimum A average. Additional exam requirements/recommendations for international students: required—TOEFL (minimum score 630 paper-based).

University of West Florida, College of Arts, Social Sciences, and Humanities, Department of English, Pensacola, FL 32514-5750. Offers creative writing (MA); literature (MA). *Program availability:* Part-time, evening/weekend. *Degree requirements:* For master's, thesis. *Entrance requirements:* For master's, GRE (minimum score: verbal 500, writing 4.5) or MAT (minimum score 413), official transcripts; two-page statement of purpose; writing sample (2500 words of literary analysis for literature track, or 2500 words of fiction/non-fiction prose or 10 poems for creative writing track); three letters of recommendation from instructors; 20 hours' upper-division undergraduate coursework in English. Additional exam requirements/recommendations for international students: required—TOEFL (minimum score 550 paper-based).

University of Windsor, Faculty of Graduate Studies, Faculty of Arts and Social Sciences, Department of English Language, Literature and Creative Writing, Windsor, ON N9B 3P4, Canada. Offers English: creative writing and language and literature (MA); English: language and literature (MA). *Program availability:* Part-time. *Degree requirements:* For master's, thesis. *Entrance requirements:* For master's, minimum B average, portfolio. Additional exam requirements/recommendations for international students: required—TOEFL (minimum score 600 paper-based). Electronic applications accepted.

University of Wisconsin–Eau Claire, College of Arts and Sciences, Program in English, Eau Claire, WI 54702-4004. Offers literature and textual interpretation (MA); writing (MA). *Program availability:* Part-time. *Degree requirements:* For master's, oral defense with thesis. *Entrance requirements:* For master's, minimum GPA of 3.25 in English, 3.0 overall; bachelor's degree with minimum of 24 credits in English. Additional exam requirements/recommendations for international students: required—TOEFL (minimum score 79 iBT).

University of Wisconsin–Madison, Graduate School, College of Letters and Science, Department of English, Madison, WI 53706-1380. Offers applied English linguistics (MA); composition and rhetoric (PhD); creative writing (MFA); English language and linguistics (PhD); literary studies (MA, PhD). *Degree requirements:* For doctorate, thesis/dissertation.

University of Wisconsin–Milwaukee, Graduate School, College of Letters and Science, Department of English, Milwaukee, WI 53201-0413. Offers English (MA, PhD), including creative writing, English language and linguistics, English secondary education, literary and critical studies, literature and cultural theory (PhD), literature and language studies, literature, culture, and media, media, cinema and digital studies, professional and technical communication (MA), professional and technical writing, professional writing (PhD), rhetoric and composition (PhD), rhetoric and writing. *Degree requirements:* For master's, thesis or alternative; for doctorate, one foreign language, thesis/dissertation. *Entrance requirements:* For master's, GRE General Test, GRE Subject Test; for doctorate, GRE. Additional exam requirements/recommendations for international students: required—TOEFL (minimum score 550 paper-based; 79 iBT), IELTS (minimum score 6.5). Electronic applications accepted.

University of Wisconsin–Oshkosh, Graduate Studies, College of Letters and Science, Department of English, Oshkosh, WI 54901. Offers MA. *Program availability:* Part-time. *Degree requirements:* For master's, thesis or alternative. *Entrance requirements:* For master's, GRE. Additional exam requirements/recommendations for international students: required—TOEFL (minimum score 550 paper-based; 79 iBT). Electronic applications accepted.

University of Wyoming, College of Arts and Sciences, Department of English, Laramie, WY 82071. Offers creative writing (MFA); English (MA). *Program availability:* Part-time. *Degree requirements:* For master's, thesis or alternative, internship. *Entrance requirements:* For master's, GRE General Test, minimum GPA of 3.0. Electronic applications accepted.

Université Laval, Faculty of Letters, Department of Literature, Programs in Ancient Civilization, Québec, QC G1K 7P4, Canada. Offers MA, PhD. *Program availability:* Part-time. Terminal master's awarded for partial completion of doctoral program. *Degree requirements:* For master's, thesis; for doctorate, comprehensive exam, thesis/dissertation. *Entrance requirements:* For master's and doctorate, English test (comprehension of written English), knowledge of French, knowledge of an ancient language. Electronic applications accepted.

Université Laval, Faculty of Letters, Department of Literature, Programs in English Literatures, Québec, QC G1K 7P4, Canada. Offers MA, PhD. *Program availability:* Part-time. Terminal master's awarded for partial completion of doctoral program. *Degree requirements:* For master's, thesis (for some programs); for doctorate, comprehensive exam, thesis/dissertation. *Entrance requirements:* For master's, French exam, knowledge of English; for doctorate, French exam, knowledge of English, knowledge of a third language. Electronic applications accepted.

Utah State University, School of Graduate Studies, College of Humanities and Social Sciences, Department of English, Logan, UT 84322. Offers American studies (MA, MS), including folklore, western American literature and culture; English (MA, MS), including literature and writing, technical writing. *Program availability:* Part-time, evening/weekend. *Degree requirements:* For master's, thesis or alternative. *Entrance requirements:* For master's, GRE General Test or MAT, minimum GPA of 3.0, recommendation letters, writing samples. Additional exam requirements/recommendations for international students: required—TOEFL.

Valdosta State University, Department of English, Valdosta, GA 31698. Offers English (MA); English studies for language arts teachers (MA). *Program availability:* Part-time, 100% online, blended/hybrid learning. *Degree requirements:* For master's, one foreign language, thesis, comprehensive written and/or oral exams. *Entrance requirements:* For master's, GRE General Test, minimum GPA of 3.0. Additional exam requirements/recommendations for international students: required—TOEFL (minimum score 523 paper-based); recommended—IELTS. Electronic applications accepted. *Expenses:* Contact institution.

Valparaiso University, Graduate School and Continuing Education, Program in English Studies and Communication, Valparaiso, IN 46383. Offers English studies and communication (MA). *Program availability:* Part-time, evening/weekend. *Entrance requirements:* For master's, minimum GPA of 3.0. Additional exam requirements/recommendations for international students: required—TOEFL (minimum score 550 paper-based; 80 iBT), IELTS (minimum score 6). Electronic applications accepted.

Vanderbilt University, Department of English, Nashville, TN 37240-1001. Offers MA, MAT, PhD. *Faculty:* 30 full-time (21 women). *Students:* 41 full-time (26 women); includes 15 minority (11 Black or African American, non-Hispanic/Latino; 1 Asian, non-Hispanic/Latino; 1 Hispanic/Latino; 2 Two or more races, non-Hispanic/Latino), 4 international. Average age 28. 168 applicants, 11% accepted, 12 enrolled. In 2019, 7 master's, 4 doctorates awarded. *Degree requirements:* For master's, thesis; for doctorate, one foreign language, comprehensive exam, thesis/dissertation, final and qualifying exams. *Entrance requirements:* For master's and doctorate, GRE General Test, sample of written work. Additional exam requirements/recommendations for international students: required—TOEFL (minimum score 570 paper-based; 88 iBT). *Application deadline:* For fall admission, 1/15 for domestic and international students. Electronic applications accepted. *Expenses: Tuition:* Full-time $51,018; part-time $2087 per hour. *Required fees:* $542. Tuition and fees vary according to program. *Financial support:* Fellowships, research assistantships, teaching assistantships with full tuition reimbursements, Federal Work-Study, institutionally sponsored loans, scholarships/grants, and health care benefits available. Financial award application deadline: 1/15; financial award applicants required to submit CSS PROFILE or FAFSA. *Unit head:* Dr. Dana Nelson, Chair, 615-322-2541, Fax: 615-343-8028, E-mail: dana.d.nelson@vanderbilt.edu. *Application contact:* Vera Kutzinski, Director of Graduate Studies, 615-322-2541, Fax: 615-343-8028, E-mail: vera.kutzinski@vanderbilt.edu.
Website: http://as.vanderbilt.edu/english/graduate/

Villanova University, Graduate School of Liberal Arts and Sciences, Department of English, Villanova, PA 19085-1699. Offers MA. *Program availability:* Part-time, evening/weekend. *Degree requirements:* For master's, comprehensive exam, thesis optional. *Entrance requirements:* For master's, GRE General Test, minimum GPA of 3.0, writing sample, 3 recommendation letters. Additional exam requirements/recommendations for international students: required—TOEFL. Electronic applications accepted.

Virginia Commonwealth University, Graduate School, College of Humanities and Sciences, Department of English, Program in English, Richmond, VA 23284-9005. Offers literature (MA). *Program availability:* Part-time. *Entrance requirements:* For master's, GRE General Test. Additional exam requirements/recommendations for international students: required—TWE, TOEFL (minimum score 600 paper-based; 100 iBT) or IELTS (minimum score 6.5). Electronic applications accepted.

Virginia Polytechnic Institute and State University, Graduate School, College of Liberal Arts and Human Sciences, Blacksburg, VA 24061. Offers career and technical education (MS Ed, Ed S); communication (MA); counselor education (MA); creative writing (MFA); curriculum and instruction (MA Ed, Ed S); educational leadership and policy studies (Ed S); educational research and evaluation (PhD); English (MA); social, political, ethical, and cultural thought (PhD); Ed D/PhD. *Faculty:* 452 full-time (241 women), 1 (woman) part-time/adjunct. *Students:* 571 full-time (405 women), 351 part-time (223 women); includes 176 minority (103 Black or African American, non-Hispanic/Latino; 3 American Indian or Alaska Native, non-Hispanic/Latino; 18 Asian, non-Hispanic/Latino; 31 Hispanic/Latino; 1 Native Hawaiian or other Pacific Islander, non-Hispanic/Latino; 20 Two or more races, non-Hispanic/Latino), 93 international. Average age 34. 865 applicants, 55% accepted, 336 enrolled. In 2019, 270 master's, 63 doctorates awarded. *Degree requirements:* For master's, comprehensive exam (for some programs), thesis (for some programs); for doctorate, comprehensive exam (for some programs), thesis/dissertation (for some programs). *Entrance requirements:* For master's and doctorate, GRE/GMAT. Additional exam requirements/recommendations

for international students: required—TOEFL (minimum score 90 iBT). *Application deadline:* For fall admission, 8/1 for domestic students, 4/1 for international students; for spring admission, 1/1 for domestic students, 9/1 for international students. Applications are processed on a rolling basis. Application fee: $75. Electronic applications accepted. *Expenses:* Tuition, state resident: full-time $13,700; part-time $761.25 per credit hour. Tuition, nonresident: full-time $27,614; part-time $1534 per credit hour. *Required fees:* $886.50 per term. Tuition and fees vary according to campus/location and program. *Financial support:* In 2019–20, 3 fellowships with full tuition reimbursements (averaging $7,621 per year), 34 research assistantships with full tuition reimbursements (averaging $15,645 per year), 370 teaching assistantships with full tuition reimbursements (averaging $18,225 per year) were awarded; scholarships/grants and unspecified assistantships also available. Financial award application deadline: 3/1; financial award applicants required to submit FAFSA. *Unit head:* Dr. Laura Belmonte, Dean, 540-231-6779, Fax: 540-231-7157, E-mail: belmonte@vt.edu. *Application contact:* Chelsea Blanchet, Executive Assistant, 540-231-6779, Fax: 540-231-7157, E-mail: bchels1@vt.edu.
Website: http://www.liberalarts.vt.edu/

Wake Forest University, Graduate School of Arts and Sciences, Department of English, Winston-Salem, NC 27109. Offers MA. *Program availability:* Part-time. *Degree requirements:* For master's, one foreign language, thesis. *Entrance requirements:* For master's, GRE General Test, writing sample. Additional exam requirements/recommendations for international students: required—TOEFL (minimum score 79 iBT). Electronic applications accepted.

Washington State University, College of Arts and Sciences, Department of English, Pullman, WA 99164. Offers MA, PhD. *Degree requirements:* For master's, one foreign language, comprehensive exam (for some programs), thesis (for some programs), oral exam; for doctorate, 2 foreign languages, comprehensive exam, thesis/dissertation, oral exam, written exam. *Entrance requirements:* For master's and doctorate, GRE General Test, GRE Subject Test, official transcripts; writing sample (approximately 10 pages); three letters of recommendation; statement of purpose (approximately 500 words); undergraduate major in English or other appropriate discipline. Additional exam requirements/recommendations for international students: required—TOEFL, IELTS. Electronic applications accepted.

Washington University in St. Louis, The Graduate School, Department of English, St. Louis, MO 63130-4899. Offers English and American literature (PhD); writing (MFA). Terminal master's awarded for partial completion of doctoral program. *Degree requirements:* For master's, thesis or written exam; for doctorate, 2 foreign languages, thesis/dissertation. *Entrance requirements:* For master's and doctorate, GRE General Test, sample of written work. Additional exam requirements/recommendations for international students: required—TOEFL. Electronic applications accepted.

Wayne State University, College of Liberal Arts and Sciences, Department of English, Detroit, MI 48202. Offers English (MA); film and media studies (PhD); literary and cultural studies (PhD); rhetoric and composition studies (PhD). *Faculty:* 27. *Students:* 59 full-time (36 women), 31 part-time (24 women); includes 17 minority (4 Black or African American, non-Hispanic/Latino; 4 Asian, non-Hispanic/Latino; 3 Hispanic/Latino; 6 Two or more races, non-Hispanic/Latino), 4 international. Average age 33. 87 applicants, 44% accepted, 17 enrolled. In 2019, 12 master's, 9 doctorates awarded. Terminal master's awarded for partial completion of doctoral program. *Degree requirements:* For master's, variable foreign language requirement, essay, thesis, or portfolio of work approved by Director of Graduate Studies; for doctorate, one foreign language, comprehensive exam, thesis/dissertation. *Entrance requirements:* For master's, statement of purpose; two academic letters of reference; sample essay from previous English course; for doctorate, statement of purpose; two academic letters of reference; sample of scholarly or critical writing. Additional exam requirements/recommendations for international students: required—TOEFL (minimum score 550 paper-based; 79 iBT), TWE (minimum score 5.5), Michigan English Language Assessment Battery (minimum score 85); recommended—IELTS (minimum score 6.5). *Application deadline:* For fall admission, 1/15 for domestic students. Applications are processed on a rolling basis. Application fee: $50. Electronic applications accepted. *Expenses:* Tuition: Full-time $34,567. *Financial support:* In 2019–20, 54 students received support, including 5 fellowships with tuition reimbursements available (averaging $21,500 per year), 1 research assistantship with tuition reimbursement available (averaging $19,967 per year), 28 teaching assistantships with tuition reimbursements available (averaging $19,967 per year); scholarships/grants, health care benefits, and unspecified assistantships also available. Financial award applicants required to submit FAFSA. *Unit head:* Dr. Caroline Maun, Chair and Associate Professor, 313-577-7692, E-mail: av4495@wayne.edu. *Application contact:* Dr. Richard Marback, Director of Graduate Studies, 313-577-7694, E-mail: aa4749@wayne.edu.
Website: http://clas.wayne.edu/english/

Weber State University, Telitha E. Lindquist College of Arts and Humanities, Program in English, Ogden, UT 84408-1001. Offers MA. *Program availability:* Part-time, evening/weekend. *Faculty:* 4 full-time (1 woman). *Students:* 5 full-time (4 women), 34 part-time (24 women); includes 6 minority (1 Asian, non-Hispanic/Latino; 2 Hispanic/Latino; 3 Two or more races, non-Hispanic/Latino), 1 international. Average age 34. In 2019, 13 master's awarded. *Degree requirements:* For master's, one foreign language. *Entrance requirements:* For master's, 3 letters of recommendation, 5- to 8-page writing sample. Additional exam requirements/recommendations for international students: required—TOEFL (minimum score 550 paper-based; 79 iBT). *Application deadline:* For fall admission, 3/15 for domestic students; for spring admission, 3/15 for domestic students; for summer admission, 10/15 for domestic students. Application fee: $60 ($90 for international students). Electronic applications accepted. *Expenses: Tuition, area resident:* Full-time $7197; part-time $4981 per credit. Tuition, state resident: full-time $7197; part-time $4981 per credit. Tuition, nonresident: full-time $16,560; part-time $11,589 per credit. *Required fees:* $643 per semester. One-time fee: $60. Tuition and fees vary according to course load and program. *Financial support:* In 2019–20, 6 students received support. Scholarships/grants available. Financial award application deadline: 4/1; financial award applicants required to submit FAFSA. *Unit head:* Dr. Mali Subbiah, Program Director, 801-626-6335, Fax: 801-626-7760, E-mail: msubbiah@weber.edu. *Application contact:* Rami Collins, Administrative Specialist, 801-626-7179, Fax: 801-626-7760, E-mail: masterofenglish@weber.edu.
Website: http://weber.edu/maenglish

Western Carolina University, Graduate School, College of Arts and Sciences, Department of English, Cullowhee, NC 28723. Offers literature (MA); professional writing (MA); rhetoric and composition (MA); teaching English to speakers of other languages (Certificate); technical and professional writing (Certificate). *Program availability:* Part-time, evening/weekend. *Degree requirements:* For master's, one foreign language, comprehensive exam, thesis (for some programs). *Entrance requirements:* For master's, appropriate undergraduate degree, writing sample, 3 letters of recommendation. Additional exam requirements/recommendations for international students: required—TOEFL (minimum score 550 paper-based, 79 iBT) or IELTS (6.5). Electronic applications accepted. *Expenses:* Contact institution.

Western Connecticut State University, Division of Graduate Studies, Maricostas School of Arts and Sciences, Department of English, Danbury, CT 06810-6885. Offers

literature (MA). *Program availability:* Part-time. *Entrance requirements:* For master's, minimum GPA of 2.5, writing sample. Additional exam requirements/recommendations for international students: recommended—TOEFL (minimum score 550 paper-based; 79 iBT), IELTS (minimum score 6).

Western Illinois University, School of Graduate Studies, College of Arts and Sciences, Department of English and Journalism, Macomb, IL 61455-1390. Offers English (MA); literary studies (Certificate). *Program availability:* Part-time. *Entrance requirements:* Additional exam requirements/recommendations for international students: required—TOEFL (minimum score 575 paper-based; 88 iBT). Electronic applications accepted.

Western Kentucky University, Graduate School, Potter College of Arts and Letters, Department of English, Bowling Green, KY 42101. Offers education (MA); English (MA Ed); literature (MA), including American literature, British literature, literary theory, women writers, world literature; teaching English as a second language (MA); writing (MA). *Program availability:* Part-time, evening/weekend. *Degree requirements:* For master's, comprehensive exam, thesis optional, final exam. *Entrance requirements:* For master's, GRE General Test, minimum GPA of 2.75. Additional exam requirements/recommendations for international students: required—TOEFL (minimum score 555 paper-based; 79 iBT).

Western Michigan University, Graduate College, College of Arts and Sciences, Department of English, Kalamazoo, MI 49008. Offers creative writing (MFA, PhD); English (MA, PhD); English teaching (MA). *Degree requirements:* For doctorate, one foreign language, thesis/dissertation.

Western Washington University, Graduate School, College of Humanities and Social Sciences, Department of English, Bellingham, WA 98225-5996. Offers MA. *Program availability:* Part-time. *Degree requirements:* For master's, one foreign language, comprehensive exam, thesis (for some programs). *Entrance requirements:* For master's, GRE General Test, writing sample, minimum GPA of 3.0 in last 60 semester hours or last 90 quarter hours of course work. Additional exam requirements/recommendations for international students: required—TOEFL (minimum score 567 paper-based). Electronic applications accepted.

Westfield State University, College of Graduate and Continuing Education, Department of English, Westfield, MA 01086. Offers MA. *Program availability:* Part-time, evening/weekend. *Degree requirements:* For master's, one foreign language, thesis. *Entrance requirements:* For master's, GRE General Test, MAT, minimum undergraduate GPA of 2.8, 3.0 in all English classes; undergraduate course work in English. Additional exam requirements/recommendations for international students: recommended—TOEFL (minimum score 550 paper-based; 79 iBT).

West Texas A&M University, College of Fine Arts and Humanities, Department of English, Philosophy and Modern Languages, Canyon, TX 79015. Offers English (MA). *Program availability:* Part-time, evening/weekend. *Degree requirements:* For master's, comprehensive exam, thesis optional. *Entrance requirements:* For master's, GRE General Test. Additional exam requirements/recommendations for international students: required—TOEFL (minimum score 550 paper-based). Electronic applications accepted.

West Virginia University, Eberly College of Arts and Sciences, Morgantown, WV 26506. Offers biology (MS, PhD); chemistry (MS, PhD); communication studies (MA, PhD); computational statistics (PhD); creative writing (MFA); English (MA, PhD); forensic and investigative science (MS); forensic science (PhD); geography (MA); geology (MA, PhD); history (MA, PhD); legal studies (MLS); mathematics (MS); physics (MS, PhD); political science (MA, PhD); professional writing and editing (MA); psychology (MA); public administration (MPA); social work (MSW); sociology (MA, PhD); statistics (MS). *Program availability:* Part-time, evening/weekend, online learning. Terminal master's awarded for partial completion of doctoral program. *Degree requirements:* For master's, thesis (for some programs); for doctorate, comprehensive exam, thesis/dissertation. *Entrance requirements:* For master's and doctorate, GRE. Additional exam requirements/recommendations for international students: required—TOEFL (minimum score 600 paper-based); recommended—TWE. Electronic applications accepted.

Wichita State University, Graduate School, Fairmount College of Liberal Arts and Sciences, Department of English, Wichita, KS 67260. Offers creative writing (MFA); English (MA). *Program availability:* Part-time, evening/weekend. *Entrance requirements:* For master's, writing sample (MFA).

Wilfrid Laurier University, Faculty of Graduate and Postdoctoral Studies, Faculty of Arts, Department of English and Film Studies, Waterloo, ON N2L 3C5, Canada. Offers English (MA); English and film (PhD). *Degree requirements:* For master's, thesis optional; for doctorate, thesis/dissertation. *Entrance requirements:* For master's, honours BA or the equivalent in English, minimum B+ in English courses above first year level; for doctorate, MA in English, minimum A- average in graduate work. Additional exam requirements/recommendations for international students: recommended—TOEFL (minimum score 89 iBT). Electronic applications accepted.

Wilson College, Graduate Programs, Chambersburg, PA 17201-1285. Offers accounting (M Acc); choreography and visual art (MFA); education (M Ed); educational technology (MET); healthcare administration (MHA); humanities (MA), including art and culture, critical/cultural theory, English language and literature, women's studies; management (MSM); nursing (MSN), including nursing education, nursing leadership and management; special education (MSE). *Program availability:* Evening/weekend. *Degree requirements:* For master's, project. *Entrance requirements:* For master's, PRAXIS, minimum undergraduate cumulative GPA of 3.0, 2 letters of recommendation, current certification for eligibility to teach in grades K-12, resume, personal interview. Electronic applications accepted.

Winona State University, College of Liberal Arts, Department of English, Winona, MN 55987. Offers English (MS); literature and language (MA); TESOL (MA). *Program availability:* Part-time. *Degree requirements:* For master's, thesis or alternative.

Winthrop University, College of Arts and Sciences, Department of English, Rock Hill, SC 29733. Offers MA. *Program availability:* Part-time, evening/weekend. *Degree requirements:* For master's, one foreign language, comprehensive exam, thesis optional. *Entrance requirements:* For master's, GRE General Test, MAT or PRAXIS, 24 undergraduate hours of course work in English. Additional exam requirements/recommendations for international students: required—TOEFL (minimum score 550 paper-based; 79 iBT). Electronic applications accepted. *Expenses: Tuition, area resident:* Full-time $7659; part-time $641 per credit hour. Tuition, state resident: full-time $7659; part-time $641 per credit hour. Tuition, nonresident: full-time $14,753; part-time $1234 per credit hour.

Wright State University, Graduate School, College of Liberal Arts, Department of English Language and Literatures, Dayton, OH 45435. Offers English (MA). *Degree requirements:* For master's, thesis optional, portfolio. *Entrance requirements:* For master's, 20 hours in upper-level English. Additional exam requirements/recommendations for international students: required—TOEFL.

Xavier University, College of Arts and Sciences, Department of English, Cincinnati, OH 45207. Offers MA. *Program availability:* Part-time, evening/weekend. *Degree* *requirements:* For master's, one foreign language, comprehensive exam, thesis optional. *Entrance requirements:* For master's, GRE, writing sample; minimum GPA of 3.2 in undergraduate English courses, 3.0 for all undergraduate coursework; official transcript; intent/purpose statement. Additional exam requirements/recommendations for international students: required—TOEFL (minimum score 550 paper-based; 79 iBT). Electronic applications accepted. Application fee is waived when completed online. *Expenses:* Contact institution.

Yale University, Graduate School of Arts and Sciences, Department of English Language and Literature, New Haven, CT 06520. Offers MA, PhD. Terminal master's awarded for partial completion of doctoral program. *Degree requirements:* For master's, 2 foreign languages; for doctorate, 3 foreign languages, thesis/dissertation. *Entrance requirements:* For master's and doctorate, GRE General Test, GRE Subject Test.

York University, Faculty of Graduate Studies, Faculty of Liberal Arts and Professional Studies, Program in English, Toronto, ON M3J 1P3, Canada. Offers MA, PhD. *Program availability:* Part-time. *Degree requirements:* For master's, thesis or alternative; for doctorate, one foreign language, comprehensive exam, thesis/dissertation. Electronic applications accepted.

Youngstown State University, College of Graduate Studies, College of Liberal Arts and Social Sciences, Department of English, Youngstown, OH 44555-0001. Offers MA. *Program availability:* Part-time. *Degree requirements:* For master's, portfolio. *Entrance requirements:* For master's, bachelor's degree in English, minimum GPA of 2.7. Additional exam requirements/recommendations for international students: required—TOEFL.

French

American University, College of Arts and Sciences, Department of World Languages and Cultures, Washington, DC 20016-8045. Offers Spanish: Latin American studies (MA); teaching English as a foreign language (MA); teaching English to speakers of other languages (MA, Certificate); translation: French (Certificate); translation: Russian (Certificate); translation: Spanish (Certificate). *Program availability:* Part-time, evening/weekend. *Degree requirements:* For master's, one foreign language, comprehensive exam, thesis or alternative. *Entrance requirements:* For master's, GRE; Please see website:https://www.american.edu/cas/wlc/, writing sample, statement of purpose, transcripts, 2 letters of recommendation, resume; for Certificate, bachelor's degree, statement of purpose, transcripts, resume. Additional exam requirements/recommendations for international students: required—TOEFL (minimum score 600 paper-based; 100 iBT). *Expenses:* Contact institution.

Arizona State University at Tempe, College of Liberal Arts and Sciences, School of International Letters and Cultures, Program in French, Tempe, AZ 85287-0202. Offers comparative literature (MA); linguistics (MA); literature (MA). *Program availability:* Part-time, evening/weekend. *Degree requirements:* For master's, thesis or applied project, interactive Program of Study (iPOS) submitted no later than beginning of third semester of study or before completing 50 percent of coursework towards completion of degree. *Entrance requirements:* For master's, GRE, minimum GPA of 3.25 in the last two years of work leading to the bachelor's degree in French major, personal statement, writing sample (preferably written in French), 3 letters of recommendation. Additional exam requirements/recommendations for international students: required—TOEFL (minimum score 550 paper-based; 83 iBT), IELTS (minimum score 6.5). Electronic applications accepted.

Asbury University, School of Graduate and Professional Studies, Wilmore, KY 40390-1198. Offers biology: alternative certificate (MA Ed); chemistry: alternative certificate (MA Ed); English (MA Ed); English as a second language (MA Ed); ESL (MA Ed); French (MA Ed); Latin: alternative certificate (MA Ed); mathematics: alternative certificate (MA Ed); reading/writing endorsement (MA Ed); social studies (MA Ed); social work (MSW), including child and family services; Spanish (MA Ed); special education (MA Ed); special education: alternative certificate (MA Ed); teacher as leader endorsement (MA Ed). *Accreditation:* NCATE. *Program availability:* Part-time. *Degree requirements:* For master's, action research project, portfolio. *Entrance requirements:* For master's, PRAXIS/NTE, minimum GPA of 2.75, letters of recommendation. Additional exam requirements/recommendations for international students: required—TOEFL (minimum score 550 paper-based). Electronic applications accepted.

Binghamton University, State University of New York, Graduate School, Harpur College of Arts and Sciences, Department of Romance Languages and Literatures, Program in French, Binghamton, NY 13902-6000. Offers MA. *Program availability:* Part-time. *Degree requirements:* For master's, one foreign language, comprehensive exam, thesis or alternative. *Entrance requirements:* For master's, GRE General Test. Additional exam requirements/recommendations for international students: required—TOEFL (minimum score 550 paper-based; 80 iBT). Electronic applications accepted.

Boston College, Morrissey Graduate School of Arts and Sciences, Department of Romance Languages and Literatures, Chestnut Hill, MA 02467-3800. Offers French (MA); Italian (MA); Spanish (MA). *Program availability:* Part-time. Terminal master's awarded for partial completion of doctoral program. *Degree requirements:* For master's, one foreign language. *Entrance requirements:* Additional exam requirements/recommendations for international students: required—TOEFL (minimum score 600 paper-based; 100 iBT), IELTS (minimum score 8). Electronic applications accepted.

Bowling Green State University, Graduate College, College of Arts and Sciences, Department of Romance and Classical Studies, Program in French, Bowling Green, OH 43403. Offers French (MA). *Program availability:* Part-time. *Degree requirements:* For master's, one foreign language, thesis or alternative. *Entrance requirements:* For master's, GRE General Test. Additional exam requirements/recommendations for international students: required—TOEFL. Electronic applications accepted.

Brooklyn College of the City University of New York, School of Humanities and Social Sciences, Department of Modern Languages and Literatures, Brooklyn, NY 11210-2889. Offers French (MA); Spanish (MA). *Degree requirements:* For master's, comprehensive exam or research paper. *Entrance requirements:* For master's, 18 credits in advanced courses in Spanish, 2 letters of recommendation. Additional exam requirements/recommendations for international students: required—TOEFL (minimum score 500 paper-based; 61 iBT). Electronic applications accepted.

Brown University, Graduate School, Department of French Studies, Providence, RI 02912. Offers PhD. *Degree requirements:* For doctorate, variable foreign language requirement, thesis/dissertation, preliminary exam.

California State University, Long Beach, Graduate Studies, College of Liberal Arts, Department of Romance, German, Russian Languages and Literatures, Program in French and Francophone Studies, Long Beach, CA 90840. Offers MA. *Program availability:* Part-time. *Degree requirements:* For master's, one foreign language, comprehensive exam, thesis optional. *Entrance requirements:* For master's, BA in French. Electronic applications accepted.

California State University, Los Angeles, Graduate Studies, College of Arts and Letters, Department of Modern Languages and Literatures, Los Angeles, CA 90032-8530. Offers French (MA); Spanish (MA). *Program availability:* Part-time, evening/weekend. *Degree requirements:* For master's, comprehensive exam. *Entrance requirements:* Additional exam requirements/recommendations for international students: required—TOEFL (minimum score 500 paper-based). Electronic applications accepted. *Expenses: Tuition, area resident:* Full-time $7176; part-time $4164 per year. Tuition, state resident: full-time $7176; part-time $4164 per year. Tuition, nonresident: full-time $14,304; part-time $8916 per year. *International tuition:* $14,304 full-time. *Required fees:* $1037.76; $1037.76 per unit. Tuition and fees vary according to degree level and program.

Carleton University, Faculty of Graduate Studies, Faculty of Arts and Social Sciences, Department of French, Ottawa, ON K1S 5B6, Canada. Offers MA. *Degree requirements:* For master's, thesis optional. *Entrance requirements:* For master's, honors degree.

Case Western Reserve University, School of Graduate Studies, Department of Modern Languages and Literatures, Program in French, Cleveland, OH 44106. Offers MA. *Program availability:* Part-time. Terminal master's awarded for partial completion of doctoral program. *Degree requirements:* For master's, one foreign language, comprehensive exam. *Entrance requirements:* For master's, GRE General Test, writing sample, three letters of recommendation. Additional exam requirements/recommendations for international students: required—TOEFL (minimum score 577 paper-based; 90 iBT); recommended—IELTS (minimum score 7). Electronic applications accepted.

Central Connecticut State University, School of Graduate Studies, College of Liberal Arts and Social Sciences, Department of Modern Languages, New Britain, CT 06050-4010. Offers modern language (MA, Certificate), including French, German (Certificate), Italian, Spanish (MA); Spanish (MS, Certificate). *Program availability:* Part-time, evening/weekend. *Degree requirements:* For master's, one foreign language, comprehensive exam, thesis or alternative; for Certificate, qualifying exam. *Entrance requirements:* For master's, minimum undergraduate GPA of 2.7, 24 credits of undergraduate courses in each language in which graduate work will be undertaken. Additional exam requirements/recommendations for international students: required—TOEFL (minimum score 550 paper-based; 79 iBT); recommended—IELTS (minimum score 6.5). Electronic applications accepted.

Colorado State University, College of Liberal Arts, Department of Languages, Literatures and Cultures, Fort Collins, CO 80523-1774. Offers French (MA). *Program availability:* Part-time, evening/weekend. *Degree requirements:* For master's, one foreign language, comprehensive exam, thesis, teaching portfolio or additional coursework. *Entrance requirements:* For master's, BA in the language object of study, or having studied in a country in which that language was the language of instruction (French or Spanish). Additional exam requirements/recommendations for international students: required—TOEFL (minimum score 550 paper-based; 79 iBT); recommended—IELTS (minimum score 6.5), TSE (minimum score 58). Electronic applications accepted. *Expenses:* Tuition, state resident: full-time $10,520; part-time $5844 per credit hour. Tuition, nonresident: full-time $25,791; part-time $14,328 per credit hour. *International tuition:* $25,791 full-time. *Required fees:* $2512.80. Part-time tuition and fees vary according to course level, course load, degree level, program and student level.

Columbia University, Graduate School of Arts and Sciences, New York, NY 10027. Offers African-American studies (MA); American studies (MA); anthropology (MA, PhD); art history and archaeology (MA, PhD); astronomy (PhD); biological sciences (PhD); biotechnology (MA); chemical physics (PhD); chemistry (PhD); classical studies (MA, PhD); classics (MA, PhD); climate and society (MA); conservation biology (MA); earth and environmental sciences (PhD); East Asia: regional studies (MA); East Asian languages and cultures (MA, PhD); ecology, evolution and environmental biology (MA), including conservation biology; ecology, evolution, and environmental biology (PhD), including ecology and evolutionary biology, evolutionary primatology; economics (MA, PhD); English and comparative literature (MA, PhD); French and Romance philology (MA, PhD); Germanic languages (MA, PhD); global French studies (MA); global thought (MA); Hispanic cultural studies (MA); history (PhD); history and literature (MA); human rights studies (MA); Islamic studies (MA); Italian (MA, PhD); Japanese pedagogy (MA); Jewish studies (MA); Latin America and the Caribbean: regional studies (MA); Latin American and Iberian cultures (PhD); mathematics (MA, PhD), including finance (MA); medieval and Renaissance studies (MA); Middle Eastern, South Asian, and African studies (MA, PhD); modern art: critical and curatorial studies (MA); modern European studies (MA); museum anthropology (MA); music (DMA, PhD); oral history (MA); philosophical foundations of physics (MA); philosophy (MA, PhD); physics (PhD); political science (MA, PhD); psychology (PhD); quantitative methods in the social sciences (MA); religion (MA, PhD); Russia, Eurasia and East Europe: regional studies (MA); Russian translation (MA); Slavic cultures (MA); Slavic languages (MA, PhD); sociology (MA, PhD); South Asian studies (MA); statistics (MA, PhD); theatre (PhD). *Program availability:* Part-time. *Students:* 3,506 full-time (1,844 women), 208 part-time (121 women); includes 864 minority (110 Black or African American, non-Hispanic/Latino; 5 American Indian or Alaska Native, non-Hispanic/Latino; 416 Asian, non-Hispanic/Latino; 147 Hispanic/Latino; 6 Native Hawaiian or other Pacific Islander, non-Hispanic/Latino; 180 Two or more races, non-Hispanic/Latino), 2,065 international. 14,545 applicants, 25% accepted, 1,429 enrolled. In 2019, 1,262 master's, 363 doctorates awarded. Terminal master's awarded for partial completion of doctoral program. *Degree requirements:* For master's, variable foreign language requirement, comprehensive exam (for some programs), thesis (for some programs); for doctorate, variable foreign language requirement, comprehensive exam (for some programs), thesis/dissertation. *Entrance requirements:* For master's and doctorate, GRE General Test, GRE Subject Test (for some programs). Additional exam requirements/recommendations for international students: required—TOEFL (minimum score 600 paper-based; 100 iBT), IELTS (minimum score 7.5). Application fee: $115. Electronic applications accepted. *Expenses: Tuition:* Full-time $47,600; part-time $1880 per credit. One-time fee: $105. *Financial support:* Fellowships, research assistantships, teaching assistantships, career-related internships or fieldwork, Federal Work-Study, institutionally sponsored loans, scholarships/grants, traineeships, health care benefits, tuition waivers, and unspecified assistantships available. Support available to part-time students. Financial award application deadline: 12/15. *Unit head:* Dr. Carlos J. Alonso, Dean of the Graduate School of Arts and Sciences and Vice President for Graduate Education, 212-854-2861, E-mail: gsas-dean@columbia.edu. *Application contact:* GSAS Office of Admissions, 212-854-6729, E-mail: gsas-admissions@columbia.edu. Website: http://gsas.columbia.edu/

Concordia University, School of Graduate Studies, Faculty of Arts and Science, Department of Études Françaises, Montréal, QC H3G 1M8, Canada. Offers Anglais-Français en langue et techniques de localization (Certificate); littératures Francophones et résonances médiatiques (MA); translation (Diploma); translation studies (MA). *Degree requirements:* For other advanced degree, one foreign language.

Cornell University, Graduate School, Graduate Fields of Arts and Sciences, Field of Romance Studies, Ithaca, NY 14853. Offers French linguistics (PhD); French literature (PhD); Hispanic literature (PhD); Italian linguistics (PhD); Italian literature (PhD); Romance linguistics (PhD); Spanish linguistics (PhD). *Degree requirements:* For doctorate, 2 foreign languages, comprehensive exam, thesis/dissertation. *Entrance requirements:* For doctorate, GRE General Test, sample of written work, 3 letters of recommendation. Additional exam requirements/recommendations for international students: required—TOEFL (minimum score 550 paper-based; 77 iBT). Electronic applications accepted.

Dalhousie University, Faculty of Arts and Social Sciences, Department of French, Halifax, NS B3H 4R2, Canada. Offers MA, PhD. *Entrance requirements:* Additional exam requirements/recommendations for international students: required—TOEFL, IELTS, CANTEST, CAEL, or Michigan English Language Assessment Battery. Electronic applications accepted.

DePaul University, College of Liberal Arts and Social Sciences, Chicago, IL 60614. Offers Arabic (MA); Chinese (MA); critical ethnic studies (MA); English (MA); French (MA); German (MA); history (MA); interdisciplinary studies (MA, MS); international public service (MS); international studies (MA); Italian (MA); Japanese (MA); liberal studies (MA); nonprofit management (MNM); public administration (MPA); public health (MPH); public policy (MPP); public service management (MS); refugee and forced migration studies (MS); social work (MSW); sociology (MA); Spanish (MA); sustainable urban development (MA); women's and gender studies (MA); writing and publishing (MA); writing, rhetoric and discourse (MA); MA/PhD. *Accreditation:* CEPH. *Program availability:* Part-time, evening/weekend, online learning. Terminal master's awarded for partial completion of doctoral program. *Degree requirements:* For master's, variable foreign language requirement, comprehensive exam (for some programs), thesis (for some programs). Electronic applications accepted.

Drew University, Caspersen School of Graduate Studies, Madison, NJ 07940-1493. Offers conflict resolution and leadership (Certificate), including community leadership, moderation, peace building; education (M Ed); finance (MA); history and culture (MA, PhD), including American history, book history, British history, European history, intellectual history, Irish history, print culture, public history; K-12 education (MAT), including art, biology, chemistry, elementary education, English, French, Italian, math, secondary education, special education, teacher of students with disabilities; liberal studies (M Litt, D Litt), including history, Irish/Irish-American studies, literature (M Litt, MMH, D Litt, DMH, CMH), religion, spirituality, teaching in the two-year college, writing; medical humanities (MMH, DMH, CMH), including arts, health, healthcare, literature (M Litt, MMH, D Litt, DMH, CMH), scientific research; poetry (MFA). *Program availability:* Part-time, evening/weekend. Terminal master's awarded for partial completion of doctoral program. *Degree requirements:* For master's and other advanced degree, thesis (for some programs); for doctorate, one foreign language, comprehensive exam (for some programs), thesis/dissertation. *Entrance requirements:* For master's, PRAXIS Core and Subject Area tests (for MAT), GRE/GMAT (for MFin MS in Data Analytics), resume, transcripts, writing sample, personal statement, letters of recommendation; for doctorate, GRE (PhD in history and culture), resume, transcripts, writing sample, personal statement, letters of recommendation; for other advanced degree, resume, transcripts, personal statement. Additional exam requirements/recommendations for international students: required—TOEFL (minimum score 587 paper-based; 80 iBT), IELTS (minimum score 6), TWE (minimum score 4). Electronic applications accepted.

Duke University, Graduate School, Department of Romance Studies, Durham, NC 27708. Offers French (PhD); Italian (PhD); Spanish (PhD); JD/AM. *Degree requirements:* For doctorate, 2 foreign languages, thesis/dissertation. *Entrance requirements:* For doctorate, GRE General Test. Additional exam requirements/recommendations for international students: required—TOEFL (minimum score 577 paper-based; 90 iBT) or IELTS (minimum score 7). Electronic applications accepted.

Emory University, Laney Graduate School, Department of French and Italian, Atlanta, GA 30322-1100. Offers French (PhD); French and educational studies (PhD). *Degree requirements:* For doctorate, one foreign language, comprehensive exam, thesis/dissertation. *Entrance requirements:* For doctorate, GRE General Test. Additional exam requirements/recommendations for international students: recommended—TOEFL. Electronic applications accepted.

Florida Atlantic University, Dorothy F. Schmidt College of Arts and Letters, Department of Languages, Linguistics, and Comparative Literature, Boca Raton, FL 33431-0991. Offers comparative literature (MA); French (MA); linguistics (MA); Spanish (MA). *Program availability:* Part-time. *Faculty:* 20 full-time (13 women). *Students:* 29 full-time (17 women), 11 part-time (9 women); includes 22 minority (7 Black or African American, non-Hispanic/Latino; 1 Asian, non-Hispanic/Latino; 14 Hispanic/Latino), 4 international. Average age 37. 30 applicants, 67% accepted, 16 enrolled. In 2019, 14 master's awarded. *Degree requirements:* For master's, one foreign language, comprehensive exam, thesis optional. *Entrance requirements:* For master's, GRE General Test, minimum GPA of 3.0. Additional exam requirements/recommendations for international students: required—TOEFL (minimum score 500 paper-based; 61 iBT), IELTS (minimum score 6). *Application deadline:* For fall admission, 7/1 priority date for domestic students, 2/15 for international students; for spring admission, 11/1 for domestic students, 7/15 for international students. Applications are processed on a rolling basis. Application fee: $30. *Expenses: Tuition:* Full-time $20,536; part-time $371.82 per credit hour. Tuition and fees vary according to program. *Financial support:* Fellowships, research assistantships, teaching assistantships with partial tuition reimbursements, Federal Work-Study, and tuition waivers (partial) available. Support available to part-time students. Financial award application deadline: 4/1. *Unit head:* Dr. Marcella Munson, Chair, 561-297-2118, Fax: 561-297-2756, E-mail: mmunson@fau.edu. *Application contact:* Dr. Marcella Munson, Chair, 561-297-2118, Fax: 561-297-2756, E-mail: mmunson@fau.edu. Website: http://www.fau.edu/LLCL/

Florida State University, The Graduate School, Department of Anthropology, Department of Modern Languages and Linguistics, Program in French, Tallahassee, FL 32306. Offers MA, PhD. *Faculty:* 7 full-time (5 women), 1 (woman) part-time/adjunct. *Students:* 14 full-time (8 women), 1 part-time (0 women); includes 6 minority (5 Black or African American, non-Hispanic/Latino; 1 American Indian or Alaska Native, non-Hispanic/Latino). In 2019, 1 master's awarded. Terminal master's awarded for partial

completion of doctoral program. *Degree requirements:* For master's, comprehensive exam, thesis optional; for doctorate, 2 foreign languages, thesis/dissertation, reading knowledge of French and 2 other languages. *Entrance requirements:* For master's and doctorate, GRE General Test, minimum GPA of 3.0. Additional exam requirements/recommendations for international students: required—TOEFL (minimum score 550 paper-based; 80 iBT). *Application deadline:* For fall admission, 1/15 priority date for domestic and international students. Application fee: $30. Electronic applications accepted. *Financial support:* In 2019–20, 14 teaching assistantships with partial tuition reimbursements (averaging $14,500 per year) were awarded; fellowships with partial tuition reimbursements and research assistantships with partial tuition reimbursements also available. Financial award application deadline: 1/15; financial award applicants required to submit FAFSA. *Unit head:* Dr. Reinier Leushuis, Chair, Fax: 850-644-0524, E-mail: rleushuis@fsu.edu. *Application contact:* Wendy E. Pigott, Graduate Academic Coordinator, 850-644-8397, Fax: 850-644-0524, E-mail: wpigott@fsu.edu. Website: http://www.modlang.fsu.edu/Programs2/French/Graduate-Programs

George Mason University, College of Humanities and Social Sciences, Department of Modern and Classical Languages, Fairfax, VA 22030. Offers foreign languages (MA), including French, Spanish, Spanish and French, Spanish/bilingual-multicultural education. *Degree requirements:* For master's, one foreign language, thesis optional, take-home exit exam. *Entrance requirements:* For master's, goals statement, language proficiency statement. Additional exam requirements/recommendations for international students: required—TOEFL (minimum score 575 paper-based; 88 iBT), IELTS (minimum score 6.5), PTE (minimum score 59). Electronic applications accepted.

Georgia State University, College of Arts and Sciences, Department of World Languages and Cultures, Program in French, Atlanta, GA 30302-3083. Offers applied linguistics and pedagogy (MA); French studies (MA); literature and culture (MA). *Program availability:* Part-time. *Entrance requirements:* For master's, GRE, statement of purpose, writing sample in the target language, 2 letters of recommendation, official transcripts. Additional exam requirements/recommendations for international students: required—TOEFL (minimum score 79 iBT). Application fee: $50. Electronic applications accepted. *Expenses: Tuition:* area resident: Full-time $7164; part-time $398 per credit hour. Tuition, state resident: full-time $7164; part-time $398 per credit hour. Tuition, nonresident: full-time $22,662; part-time $1259 per credit hour. *International tuition:* $22,662 full-time. *Required fees:* $2128; $312 per credit hour. Tuition and fees vary according to course load and program. *Financial support:* Institutionally sponsored loans available. Financial award applicants required to submit FAFSA. *Unit head:* Dr. William Nichols, Department Chair, 404-413-5980, Fax: 404-413-5982, E-mail: wnichols@gsu.edu. *Application contact:* Vicky Hanning, Administrative Coordinator, 404-413-5990, Fax: 404-413-5036, E-mail: vcasem@gsu.edu. Website: https://wlc.gsu.edu/

Georgia State University, College of Arts and Sciences, Department of World Languages and Cultures, Program in Translation and Interpretation, Atlanta, GA 30302-3083. Offers interpretation (Certificate), including Spanish; translation (Certificate), including French, German, Spanish. *Program availability:* Part-time. *Entrance requirements:* For degree, entrance examination involving translating one passage from English to the target language and one passage from the target language to English, 3 letters of recommendation, resume/curriculum vitae, official transcripts. Additional exam requirements/recommendations for international students: required—TOEFL (minimum score 79 iBT). Application fee: $50. Electronic applications accepted. *Expenses: Tuition,* area resident: Full-time $7164; part-time $398 per credit hour. Tuition, state resident: full-time $7164; part-time $398 per credit hour. Tuition, nonresident: full-time $22,662; part-time $1259 per credit hour. *International tuition:* $22,662 full-time. *Required fees:* $2128; $312 per credit hour. Tuition and fees vary according to course load and program. *Unit head:* Dr. William Nichols, Chair, 404-413-5980, Fax: 404-413-5982, E-mail: wnichols@gsu.edu. *Application contact:* Vicky Hanning, Administrative Coordinator, 404-413-5990, Fax: 404-413-5982, E-mail: vassem@gsu.edu. Website: http://wlc.gsu.edu/home/graduate/graduate-certificate/

The Graduate Center, City University of New York, Graduate Studies, Program in French, New York, NY 10016-4039. Offers PhD. *Degree requirements:* For doctorate, 2 foreign languages, thesis/dissertation. *Entrance requirements:* For doctorate, GRE General Test. Additional exam requirements/recommendations for international students: required—TOEFL. Electronic applications accepted.

Harvard University, Graduate School of Arts and Sciences, Department of Romance Languages and Literatures, Cambridge, MA 02138. Offers French (AM, PhD); Italian (AM, PhD); Portuguese (AM, PhD); Spanish (AM, PhD). Terminal master's awarded for partial completion of doctoral program. *Degree requirements:* For master's, 2 foreign languages; for doctorate, 2 foreign languages, thesis/dissertation. *Entrance requirements:* For master's and doctorate, GRE General Test, sample of written work. Additional exam requirements/recommendations for international students: required—TOEFL.

Howard University, Graduate School, Department of Modern Languages and Literatures, Washington, DC 20059-0002. Offers French (MA); Spanish (MA). *Program availability:* Part-time. *Degree requirements:* For master's, one foreign language, comprehensive exam, thesis. *Entrance requirements:* For master's, GRE General Test, writing samples in English and French or Spanish.

Hunter College of the City University of New York, Graduate School, School of Arts and Sciences, Department of Romance Languages, Program in French, New York, NY 10065-5085. Offers MA. *Program availability:* Part-time, evening/weekend. *Degree requirements:* For master's, 2 foreign languages, comprehensive exam, thesis optional. *Entrance requirements:* For master's, GRE General Test, GRE Subject Test, ability to read, speak, and write French; interview. Additional exam requirements/recommendations for international students: required—TOEFL.

Illinois State University, Graduate School, College of Arts and Sciences, Department of Foreign Languages, Literatures and Cultures, Normal, IL 61790. Offers French (MA); French and German (MA); French and Spanish (MA); German (MA); German and Spanish (MA); Spanish (MA). *Faculty:* 23 full-time (13 women), 7 part-time/adjunct (all women). *Students:* 14 full-time (7 women), 4 part-time (2 women). Average age 30. 12 applicants, 83% accepted, 6 enrolled. In 2019, 7 master's awarded. *Degree requirements:* For master's, variable foreign language requirement, comprehensive exam, 1 term of residency. *Entrance requirements:* For master's, GRE General Test, minimum GPA of 2.8 in last 60 hours of course work. *Application deadline:* Applications are processed on a rolling basis. Application fee: $50. *Expenses: Tuition, area resident:* Full-time $7956; part-time $9767 per year. Tuition, nonresident: full-time $9233; part-time $17,592 per year. *Required fees:* $1797. *Financial support:* In 2019–20, 13 teaching assistantships were awarded; tuition waivers (full) and unspecified assistantships also available. Financial award application deadline: 4/1. *Unit head:* Dr. Bruce Brningham, Department Chair, 309-438-3604. *Application contact:* Dr. Ryan Davis, Graduate Coordinator, 309-438-7759, Fax: 309-438-7912, E-mail: rdavis2@IllinoisState.edu. Website: http://www.foreignlanguages.ilstu.edu/

Indiana University Bloomington, University Graduate School, College of Arts and Sciences, Department of French and Italian, Bloomington, IN 47405. Offers French (MA,

French

PhD), including French and Francophone studies (MA), French instruction (MA), French linguistics; Italian (MA, PhD). *Program availability:* Part-time. Terminal master's awarded for partial completion of doctoral program. *Degree requirements:* For master's, variable foreign language requirement, comprehensive exam (for some programs), thesis or alternative; for doctorate, variable foreign language requirement, comprehensive exam, thesis/dissertation. *Entrance requirements:* For master's, GRE General Test, BA or equivalent undergraduate preparation in French or Italian; for doctorate, GRE General Test, MA from degree program at IU; MA in the specific field. Additional exam requirements/recommendations for international students: required—TOEFL (minimum score 550 paper-based; 79 iBT), GRE General Test (recommended). Electronic applications accepted.

Johns Hopkins University, Zanvyl Krieger School of Arts and Sciences, Department of German and Romance Languages and Literatures, Baltimore, MD 21218. Offers German (MA, PhD); romance languages (PhD), including French, Italian, Spanish. Terminal master's awarded for partial completion of doctoral program. *Degree requirements:* For master's, comprehensive exam; for doctorate, 2 foreign languages, comprehensive exam, thesis/dissertation. *Entrance requirements:* For doctorate, GRE General Test. Additional exam requirements/recommendations for international students: required—TOEFL (minimum score 600 paper-based; 100 iBT), IELTS. Electronic applications accepted. *Expenses:* Contact institution.

Kansas State University, Graduate School, College of Arts and Sciences, Department of Modern Languages, Manhattan, KS 66506. Offers literature (MA), including French, German, Spanish; second language acquisition (MA), including French, German, Spanish, teaching English as a foreign language. *Program availability:* Part-time, evening/weekend, blended/hybrid learning. *Degree requirements:* For master's, thesis optional. *Entrance requirements:* For master's, teaching certificate. Additional exam requirements/recommendations for international students: required—TOEFL (minimum score 550 paper-based; 83 iBT), TOEFL (minimum speaking-portion score of 26). Electronic applications accepted.

Kent State University, College of Arts and Sciences, Department of Modern and Classical Language Studies, Kent, OH 44242-0001. Offers French (MA), including applied linguistics and pedagogy, literature; German (MA), including applied linguistics and pedagogy, literature; Latin (MA), including applied linguistics and pedagogy, literature; Spanish (MA), including applied linguistics and pedagogy, literature; translation (MA), including Arabic, French, German, Japanese, Russian, Spanish; translation studies (PhD); MA/MBA. *Program availability:* Part-time, 100% online. *Faculty:* 18 full-time (11 women), 6 part-time/adjunct (3 women). *Students:* 81 full-time (49 women), 23 part-time (14 women); includes 18 minority (3 Black or African American, non-Hispanic/Latino; 3 Asian, non-Hispanic/Latino; 11 Hispanic/Latino; 1 Two or more races, non-Hispanic/Latino), 45 international. Average age 32. 115 applicants, 73% accepted, 47 enrolled. In 2019, 27 master's, 7 doctorates awarded. *Degree requirements:* For master's, variable foreign language requirement, comprehensive exam (for some programs), thesis (for some programs); for doctorate, variable foreign language requirement, comprehensive exam, thesis/dissertation. *Entrance requirements:* For master's, transcripts, goal statement, 3 letters of recommendation, CD/MP3 with a 5-10 minute oral sample of first and second languages (conversational not read from a script), Writing sample(s) in the applicant's second language, which should be accompanied by a signed declaration that the sample is original work; for doctorate, transcripts, MA in translation, a foreign language, or in any other relevant discipline with prior experience or training in translation; proficiency in a foreign language; minimum GPA of 3.5 from MA; goal statement; 3 letters of recommendation; essay or writing sample (7-10 pages) from a research paper on any aspect of translation. Additional exam requirements/recommendations for international students: required—TOEFL (minimum score 79 iBT), IELTS (minimum score 6.5), PTE (minimum score 58), Michigan English Language Assessment Battery (minimum score 77). *Application deadline:* For fall admission, 2/1 for domestic and international students. Applications are processed on a rolling basis. Application fee: $45 ($70 for international students). Electronic applications accepted. *Financial support:* Fellowships with full tuition reimbursements, teaching assistantships with full tuition reimbursements, and unspecified assistantships available. Financial award application deadline: 2/1. *Unit head:* Dr. Keiran Dunne, Professor of French Translation; Department Chair, 330-672-2150, E-mail: kdunne@kent.edu. *Application contact:* Brian James Baer, Professor of Russian Translation; Graduate Coordinator, 330-672-1813, E-mail: bbaer@kent.edu. Website: http://www.kent.edu/mcls

Lake Forest College, Master of Arts in Teaching Program, Lake Forest, IL 60045. Offers elementary education (MAT); K-12 French (MAT); K-12 music (MAT); K-12 Spanish (MAT); K-12 visual art (MAT); secondary biology (MAT); secondary chemistry (MAT); secondary English (MAT); secondary history (MAT); secondary mathematics (MAT). *Degree requirements:* For master's, comprehensive exam, portfolio. *Entrance requirements:* For master's, GRE. *Expenses:* Tuition: Full-time $29,600; part-time $3200 per course.

Louisiana State University and Agricultural & Mechanical College, Graduate School, College of Humanities and Social Sciences, Department of French Studies, Baton Rouge, LA 70803. Offers French literature and linguistics (MA, PhD).

McGill University, Faculty of Graduate and Postdoctoral Studies, Faculty of Arts, Department of French Language and Literature, Montréal, QC H3A 2T5, Canada. Offers MA, PhD.

McMaster University, School of Graduate Studies, Faculty of Humanities, Department of French, Hamilton, ON L8S 4M2, Canada. Offers MA. *Program availability:* Part-time, evening/weekend. *Degree requirements:* For master's, thesis or alternative. *Entrance requirements:* For master's, honors degree in French, minimum B+ average. Additional exam requirements/recommendations for international students: required—TOEFL (minimum score 580 paper-based).

Memorial University of Newfoundland, School of Graduate Studies, Department of French and Spanish, St. John's, NL A1C 5S7, Canada. Offers French studies (MA). *Program availability:* Part-time. *Degree requirements:* For master's, one foreign language, thesis. *Entrance requirements:* For master's, honors degree (minimum 2nd class standing). Electronic applications accepted.

Miami University, College of Arts and Science, Department of French and Italian, Oxford, OH 45056. Offers French (MA).

Michigan State University, The Graduate School, College of Arts and Letters, Department of Romance and Classical Studies, East Lansing, MI 48824. Offers French (MA); French language and literature (PhD); Hispanic cultural studies (PhD); Hispanic literatures (MA); Spanish as a second or bilingual language (MA). *Entrance requirements:* Additional exam requirements/recommendations for international students: required—TOEFL. Electronic applications accepted.

Middlebury College, Language Schools, French School, Middlebury, VT 05753-6002. Offers MA, DML. In 2019, 27 master's, 4 doctorates awarded. *Degree requirements:* For master's, one foreign language; for doctorate, 2 foreign languages, comprehensive exam, thesis/dissertation, residence abroad, teaching experience. *Entrance requirements:* For master's, online placement test, 3 letters of recommendation, critical

essay, transcripts, personal statement; for doctorate, 1st and 2nd language online placement exam, 3 letters of recommendation, critical essay, transcripts, personal statement, MA in first language, oral interview. *Application deadline:* Applications are processed on a rolling basis. Application fee: $75. Electronic applications accepted. *Expenses:* Contact institution. *Financial support:* Fellowships and scholarships/grants available. Financial award application deadline: 3/10; financial award applicants required to submit FAFSA. *Unit head:* Armelle Crouzieres-Ingenthron, Director, 802-443-2427, Fax: 802-443-2075, E-mail: crouzier@middlebury.edu. *Application contact:* Sheila Schwaneflugel, Coordinator, 802-443-5526, Fax: 802-443-2075, E-mail: sschwaneflugel@middlebury.edu.
Website: http://www.middlebury.edu/ls/grad_programs/french

Middle Tennessee State University, College of Graduate Studies, College of Liberal Arts, Department of Foreign Languages and Literatures, Murfreesboro, TN 37132. Offers foreign languages (MAT), including French, German, Spanish. *Program availability:* Part-time, evening/weekend, online learning. *Degree requirements:* For master's, one foreign language, comprehensive exam, thesis optional. *Entrance requirements:* For master's, GRE. Additional exam requirements/recommendations for international students: required—TOEFL (minimum score 525 paper-based; 71 iBT) or IELTS (minimum score 6). Electronic applications accepted.

Millersville University of Pennsylvania, College of Graduate Studies and Adult Learning, College of Arts, Humanities and Social Sciences, Department of Language and Culture Studies, Millersville, PA 17551-0302. Offers languages and cultures (MA). *Program availability:* Part-time. *Faculty:* 3 full-time (2 women). *Students:* 4 part-time (all women); includes 2 minority (both Hispanic/Latino). Average age 31. 1 applicant. In 2019, 4 master's awarded. *Degree requirements:* For master's, Exit requirement: exam, portfolio, or research project/presentation. *Entrance requirements:* For master's, ACTFL (OPI and WPT), 24 undergraduate credits in selected language. Additional exam requirements/recommendations for international students: required—TOEFL, IELTS (minimum score 6), PTE (minimum score 60). *Application deadline:* Applications are processed on a rolling basis. Application fee: $40. Electronic applications accepted. *Expenses: Tuition, area resident:* Part-time $516 per credit. Tuition, state resident: part-time $516 per credit. Tuition, nonresident: part-time $774 per credit. *Required fees:* $118.75 per credit. Tuition and fees vary according to course load, degree level and program. *Financial support:* Scholarships/grants and unspecified assistantships available. Financial award application deadline: 3/15; financial award applicants required to submit FAFSA. *Unit head:* Dr. Christine M. Gaudry, Chair, 717-871-7152, E-mail: Christine.Gaudry@millersville.edu. *Application contact:* Dr. Susanne Nimmrichter, Graduate Coordinator, 717-871-7153, E-mail: susanne.nimmrichter@millersville.edu.
Website: http://www.millersville.edu/languages

Millersville University of Pennsylvania, College of Graduate Studies and Adult Learning, College of Arts, Humanities and Social Sciences, Department of Language and Culture Studies, Language and Culture Studies: French Option, Millersville, PA 17551-0302. Offers language and cultures (MA). *Program availability:* Part-time. *Degree requirements:* For master's, Exit requirement: exam, portfolio, or research project/presentation. *Entrance requirements:* For master's, ACTFL (OPI and WPT), 24 undergraduate credits in selected language. Additional exam requirements/recommendations for international students: required—TOEFL, IELTS (minimum score 6), PTE (minimum score 60). *Application deadline:* Applications are processed on a rolling basis. Application fee: $40. Electronic applications accepted. *Expenses: Tuition, area resident:* Part-time $516 per credit. Tuition, state resident: part-time $516 per credit. Tuition, nonresident: part-time $774 per credit. *Required fees:* $118.75 per credit. Tuition and fees vary according to course load, degree level and program. *Financial support:* Scholarships/grants and unspecified assistantships available. Financial award application deadline: 3/15; financial award applicants required to submit FAFSA. *Unit head:* Dr. Christine M. Gaudry, Associate Professor/Program Contact, 717-871-7152, E-mail: christine.gaudry@millersville.edu. *Application contact:* Dr. Susanne J. Nimmrichter, Graduate Coordinator, Department of Language and Culture Studies, 717-871-7153, E-mail: susanne.nimmrichter@millersville.edu.
Website: http://www.millersville.edu/languages

Minnesota State University Mankato, College of Graduate Studies and Research, College of Arts and Humanities, Department of World Languages and Cultures, Program in French, Mankato, MN 56001. Offers French (MS); French education (MS). *Degree requirements:* For master's, one foreign language, comprehensive exam, thesis or alternative. *Entrance requirements:* For master's, minimum GPA of 3.0 during previous 2 years. Additional exam requirements/recommendations for international students: required—TOEFL. Electronic applications accepted.

Montclair State University, The Graduate School, College of Education and Human Services, MAT Program in Teaching, Montclair, NJ 07043-1624. Offers art (MAT); biology (MAT); chemistry (MAT); earth science (MAT); English (MAT); French (MAT); health and physical education (MAT); health education (MAT); mathematics (MAT); music (MAT); physical education (MAT); physical science (MAT); social studies (MAT); Spanish (MAT); teacher of English as a second language (MAT). *Degree requirements:* For master's, comprehensive exam, thesis or alternative. *Entrance requirements:* For master's, interview, 2 letters of recommendation. Additional exam requirements/recommendations for international students: required—TOEFL (minimum score 83 iBT), IELTS (minimum score 6.5). Electronic applications accepted.

Montclair State University, The Graduate School, College of Humanities and Social Sciences, Program in French, Montclair, NJ 07043-1624. Offers French literature (MA); French studies (MA). *Program availability:* Part-time, evening/weekend. *Degree requirements:* For master's, comprehensive exam, thesis optional. *Entrance requirements:* Additional exam requirements/recommendations for international students: required—TOEFL (minimum score 83 iBT), IELTS (minimum score 6.5). Electronic applications accepted.

New York University, Graduate School of Arts and Science, Center for French Civilization and Culture, Department of French, New York, NY 10012-1019. Offers French (PhD); French language and civilization (MA); Romance languages and literatures (MA). *Program availability:* Part-time. Terminal master's awarded for partial completion of doctoral program. *Degree requirements:* For master's, one foreign language, thesis (for some programs); for doctorate, one foreign language, thesis/dissertation. *Entrance requirements:* For master's and doctorate, GRE General Test, proficiency in French. Additional exam requirements/recommendations for international students: required—TOEFL, IELTS.

New York University, Graduate School of Arts and Science, Center for French Civilization and Culture, Institute of French Studies, New York, NY 10012-1019. Offers French civilization (PhD); French studies (MA, PhD, Advanced Certificate); French studies and anthropology (PhD); French studies and history (PhD); French studies and journalism (MA); French studies and sociology (PhD); JD/MA; MBA/MA. *Program availability:* Part-time. Terminal master's awarded for partial completion of doctoral program. *Degree requirements:* For master's, one foreign language, comprehensive exam; for doctorate, one foreign language, thesis/dissertation, qualifying exam. *Entrance requirements:* For master's and doctorate, GRE General Test, knowledge of

French. Additional exam requirements/recommendations for international students: required—TOEFL, IELTS.

New York University, Steinhardt School of Culture, Education, and Human Development, Department of Teaching and Learning, Program in Multilingual/Multicultural Studies, New York, NY 10012. Offers bilingual education (MA, PhD, Advanced Certificate); foreign language education (MA); teaching English to speakers of other languages (MA, PhD); teaching foreign languages, 7-12 (MA), including Chinese, French, Italian, Japanese, Spanish; teaching French as a foreign language (MA), including teaching English to speakers of other languages; teaching Spanish as a foreign language (MA), including teaching English to speakers of other languages. *Accreditation:* TEAC. *Program availability:* Part-time, evening/weekend. *Entrance requirements:* For doctorate, GRE General Test, interview; for Advanced Certificate, master's degree. Additional exam requirements/recommendations for international students: required—TOEFL (minimum score 100 iBT). Electronic applications accepted.

North Carolina State University, Graduate School, College of Humanities and Social Sciences, Department of Foreign Languages and Literatures, Program in French Language and Literature, Raleigh, NC 27695. Offers MA. *Degree requirements:* For master's, thesis optional. *Entrance requirements:* For master's, fluency in French. Electronic applications accepted.

Northern Illinois University, Graduate School, College of Liberal Arts and Sciences, World Languages & Cultures, De Kalb, IL 60115-2854. Offers French (MA); Spanish (MA). *Program availability:* Part-time. *Faculty:* 25 full-time (11 women). *Students:* 1 (woman) full-time, 12 part-time (9 women); includes 8 minority (1 Black or African American, non-Hispanic/Latino; 7 Hispanic/Latino), 1 international. Average age 35. 3 applicants, 67% accepted, 1 enrolled. In 2019, 1 master's awarded. *Degree requirements:* For master's, one foreign language, comprehensive exam, thesis or alternative, language proficiency exam. *Entrance requirements:* For master's, GRE General Test, interview, minimum GPA of 2.75, undergraduate major in French or Spanish. Additional exam requirements/recommendations for international students: required—TOEFL (minimum score 550 paper-based). *Application deadline:* For fall admission, 6/1 for domestic students, 5/1 for international students; for spring admission, 11/1 for domestic students, 10/1 for international students. Applications are processed on a rolling basis. Application fee: $40. Electronic applications accepted. *Financial support:* In 2019–20, 7 teaching assistantships with full tuition reimbursements were awarded; fellowships with full tuition reimbursements, research assistantships with full tuition reimbursements, career-related internships or fieldwork, Federal Work-Study, scholarships/grants, tuition waivers (full), and unspecified assistantships also available. Support available to part-time students. Financial award applicants required to submit FAFSA. *Unit head:* Dr. John Bentley, Chair, 815-753-1559, Fax: 815-753-5989. *Application contact:* Graduate School Office, 815-753-0395, E-mail: gradsch@niu.edu. Website: http://www.forlangs.net/

Northwestern University, The Graduate School, Judd A. and Marjorie Weinberg College of Arts and Sciences, Department of French and Italian, Evanston, IL 60208. Offers French/Francophone studies (PhD); Italian studies (Graduate Certificate). *Degree requirements:* For doctorate, one foreign language, thesis/dissertation, written and oral exams. *Entrance requirements:* For doctorate, GRE, writing sample, cassette recording. Additional exam requirements/recommendations for international students: required—TOEFL.

The Ohio State University, Graduate School, College of Arts and Sciences, Division of Arts and Humanities, Department of French and Italian, Columbus, OH 43210. Offers French (MA, PhD); Italian (MA); Italian studies (PhD). Terminal master's awarded for partial completion of doctoral program. *Degree requirements:* For master's, variable foreign language requirement, thesis optional; for doctorate, variable foreign language requirement, thesis/dissertation. *Entrance requirements:* For master's and doctorate, GRE General Test. Additional exam requirements/recommendations for international students: required—TOEFL (minimum score 550 paper-based; 79 iBT), IELTS (minimum score 7), Michigan English Language Assessment Battery (minimum score 82). Electronic applications accepted.

Ohio University, Graduate College, College of Arts and Sciences, Department of Modern Languages, Athens, OH 45701-2979. Offers French (MA); Spanish (MA). *Program availability:* Part-time. *Degree requirements:* For master's, 2 foreign languages, comprehensive exam, thesis optional. *Entrance requirements:* For master's, oral and written samples. Additional exam requirements/recommendations for international students: required—TOEFL (minimum score 550 paper-based; 80 iBT) or IELTS (minimum score 6.5). Electronic applications accepted.

Penn State University Park, Graduate School, College of the Liberal Arts, Department of French and Francophone Studies, University Park, PA 16802. Offers French (MA, PhD).

Portland State University, Graduate Studies, College of Liberal Arts and Sciences, Department of World Languages and Literatures, Portland, OR 97207-0751. Offers French (MA); German (MA); Japanese (MA); Spanish (MA); world literature and language (MA). *Program availability:* Part-time. *Faculty:* 40 full-time (22 women), 39 part-time/adjunct (32 women). *Students:* 16 full-time (11 women), 12 part-time (6 women); includes 9 minority (2 Asian, non-Hispanic/Latino; 6 Hispanic/Latino; 1 Two or more races, non-Hispanic/Latino), 8 international. Average age 34. 14 applicants, 64% accepted, 7 enrolled. In 2019, 14 master's awarded. *Degree requirements:* For master's, variable foreign language requirement, thesis (for some programs). *Entrance requirements:* For master's, ACTFL, BA in the major language, minimum GPA of 3.0 in all coursework. Additional exam requirements/recommendations for international students: required—TOEFL (minimum score 550 paper-based; 80 iBT), IELTS (minimum score 6.5). *Application deadline:* For fall admission, 4/1 for domestic students, 3/1 for international students; for winter admission, 9/1 for domestic students, 7/1 for international students; for spring admission, 11/1 for domestic and international students. Applications are processed on a rolling basis. Application fee: $65. *Expenses: Tuition, area resident:* Full-time $13,020; part-time $6510 per year. *Tuition, state resident:* full-time $13,020; part-time $6510 per year. *Tuition, nonresident:* full-time $19,830; part-time $9915 per year. *International tuition:* $19,830 full-time. *Required fees:* $1226. One-time fee: $350. Tuition and fees vary according to course load, program and reciprocity agreements. *Financial support:* In 2019–20, 16 teaching assistantships with full and partial tuition reimbursements (averaging $16,549 per year) were awarded; research assistantships, Federal Work-Study, scholarships/grants, and unspecified assistantships also available. Support available to part-time students. Financial award application deadline: 3/1; financial award applicants required to submit FAFSA. *Unit head:* Dr. Gina Greco, Chair, 503-725-5287, E-mail: grecog@pdx.edu. *Application contact:* Kelli Martin, Graduate Admissions Specialist, 503-725-3243, E-mail: k.martin@pdx.edu. Website: http://www.pdx.edu/wll/

Princeton University, Graduate School, Department of French and Italian, Princeton, NJ 08544. Offers French language and literature (PhD). *Degree requirements:* For doctorate, 2 foreign languages, thesis/dissertation. *Entrance requirements:* For doctorate, GRE General Test, sample of written work. Additional exam requirements/

recommendations for international students: required—TOEFL (minimum score 600 paper-based). Electronic applications accepted.

Purdue University, Graduate School, College of Liberal Arts, School of Languages and Cultures, West Lafayette, IN 47907. Offers French (MA, MAT), including multiple possible; German (MA, MAT), including multiple possible; Japanese pedagogy (MA), including pedagogy, SLA; Spanish (MA, MAT), including multiple possible. *Faculty:* 32 full-time (16 women), 6 part-time/adjunct (3 women). *Students:* 33 full-time (18 women), 24 part-time (16 women); includes 7 minority (1 Black or African American, non-Hispanic/Latino; 6 Hispanic/Latino), 38 international. Average age 34. 54 applicants, 41% accepted, 14 enrolled. In 2019, 9 master's awarded. Terminal master's awarded for partial completion of doctoral program. *Degree requirements:* For master's, one foreign language. *Entrance requirements:* For master's, Bachelor of Arts (or equivalent); 3 letters of recommendation; statement of purpose; speaking & writing samples. Additional exam requirements/recommendations for international students: required—TOEFL (minimum score 550 paper-based; 77 iBT); recommended—TWE. *Application deadline:* For fall admission, 12/12 for domestic and international students; for spring admission, 10/1 for domestic and international students. Applications are processed on a rolling basis. Application fee: $60 ($75 for international students). Electronic applications accepted. *Financial support:* In 2019–20, fellowships with tuition reimbursements (averaging $15,750 per year), teaching assistantships with tuition reimbursements (averaging $13,463 per year) were awarded. Support available to part-time students. Financial award applicants required to submit FAFSA. *Unit head:* Jennifer M. William, Head, 765-494-3834, E-mail: jmwilliam@purdue.edu. *Application contact:* Joni L. Hipsher, Graduate Contact, 765-494-3841, E-mail: jlhipshe@purdue.edu. Website: http://www.cla.purdue.edu/slc/main/

Queens College of the City University of New York, Arts and Humanities Division, Department of European Languages and Literatures, Queens, NY 11367-1597. Offers French (MA); Italian (MA). *Program availability:* Part-time-only, evening/weekend. *Degree requirements:* For master's, 2 foreign languages, thesis optional, oral exam. *Entrance requirements:* For master's, minimum GPA of 3.0. Additional exam requirements/recommendations for international students: recommended—TOEFL (minimum score 61 iBT), IELTS (minimum score 5). Electronic applications accepted.

Queen's University at Kingston, School of Graduate Studies, Faculty of Arts and Science, Department of French Studies, Kingston, ON K7L 3N6, Canada. Offers MA, PhD. *Program availability:* Part-time. *Degree requirements:* For master's, thesis or 4 credits and oral exam; for doctorate, one foreign language, comprehensive exam, thesis/dissertation. *Entrance requirements:* For master's, minimum B+ average; for doctorate, minimum 80% average. Additional exam requirements/recommendations for international students: required—TOEFL (minimum score 550 paper-based). Electronic applications accepted.

Rutgers University - New Brunswick, Graduate School-New Brunswick, Program in French, Piscataway, NJ 08854-8097. Offers French (MA, PhD); French studies (MAT). *Program availability:* Part-time, evening/weekend. Terminal master's awarded for partial completion of doctoral program. *Degree requirements:* For master's, one foreign language, written and oral exams (MA); for doctorate, 3 foreign languages, thesis/dissertation, qualifying exam. *Entrance requirements:* For master's and doctorate, GRE General Test.

St. John Fisher College, Ralph C. Wilson Jr. School of Education, Program in Adolescence Education and Special Education, Rochester, NY 14618-3597. Offers adolescence education: biology with special education (MS Ed); adolescence education: chemistry with special education (MS Ed); adolescence education: English with special education (MS Ed); adolescence education: French with special education (MS Ed); adolescence education: math with special education (MS Ed); adolescence education: physics with special education (MS Ed); adolescence education: social studies with special education (MS Ed); adolescence education: Spanish with special education (MS Ed). *Program availability:* Part-time, evening/weekend. *Faculty:* 7 full-time (6 women), 3 part-time/adjunct (all women). *Students:* 10 full-time (6 women), 1 part-time (0 women); includes 10 minority (all Black or African American, non-Hispanic/Latino). Average age 25. 17 applicants, 76% accepted, 7 enrolled. In 2019, 18 master's awarded. *Degree requirements:* For master's, field experiences, student teaching. *Entrance requirements:* For master's, LAST, 2 letters of recommendation, personal statement, current resume. Additional exam requirements/recommendations for international students: required—TOEFL (minimum score 575 paper-based; 80 iBT). *Application deadline:* Applications are processed on a rolling basis. Application fee: $30. Electronic applications accepted. *Expenses:* Contact institution. *Financial support:* Scholarships/grants available. Financial award applicants required to submit FAFSA. *Unit head:* Whitney Rapp, Program Director, 585-899-3813, E-mail: wrapp@sjfc.edu. *Application contact:* Michelle Gosier, Director of Transfer and Graduate Admissions, 585-385-8064, E-mail: mgosier@sjfc.edu.

Saint Louis University, Graduate Programs, College of Arts and Sciences, Department of Languages, Literatures, and Cultures, St. Louis, MO 63103. Offers French (MA); Spanish (MA). *Program availability:* Part-time. *Degree requirements:* For master's, one foreign language, comprehensive exam, thesis/dissertation (Spanish). *Entrance requirements:* For master's, GRE General Test or MAT, letters of recommendation, resume, interview. Additional exam requirements/recommendations for international students: required—TOEFL (minimum score 525 paper-based). Electronic applications accepted.

San Francisco State University, Division of Graduate Studies, College of Liberal and Creative Arts, Department of Modern Languages and Literatures, Program in French, San Francisco, CA 94132-1722. Offers MA. *Application deadline:* Applications are processed on a rolling basis. *Expenses: Tuition, area resident:* Full-time $7176; part-time $4164 per year. Tuition, state resident: full-time $7176; part-time $4164 per year. Tuition, nonresident: full-time $16,680; part-time $396 per unit. *International tuition:* $16,680 full-time. *Required fees:* $1524; $1524 per unit. $762 per semester. Tuition and fees vary according to degree level and program. *Unit head:* Dr. Anne Linton, Program Coordinator and Graduate Advisor, 415-338-6061, Fax: 415-338-6159, E-mail: aelinton@sfsu.edu. *Application contact:* Dr. Anne Linton, Program Coordinator and Graduate Advisor, 415-338-6061, Fax: 415-338-6159, E-mail: aelinton@sfsu.edu. Website: http://mll.sfsu.edu/french-program/

Simon Fraser University, Office of Graduate Studies and Postdoctoral Fellows, Faculty of Arts and Social Sciences, Department of French, Burnaby, BC V5A 1S6, Canada. Offers MA. *Degree requirements:* For master's, one foreign language, thesis or alternative. *Entrance requirements:* For master's, minimum GPA of 3.0 (on scale of 4.33) or 3.33 based on last 60 credits of undergraduate courses. Additional exam requirements/recommendations for international students: recommended—TOEFL (minimum score 580 paper-based; 93 iBT), IELTS (minimum score 7), TWE (minimum score 5). Electronic applications accepted.

Southern Oregon University, Graduate Studies, Department of Foreign Languages and Literatures, Ashland, OR 97520. Offers French language teaching (MA); Spanish language teaching (MA). *Program availability:* Part-time, online learning. *Degree requirements:* For master's, thesis (for some programs). *Entrance requirements:* For master's, GRE General Test, minimum cumulative GPA of 3.0 in the last 90 quarter credits (60 semester credits) of undergraduate coursework. Additional exam requirements/recommendations for international students: required—TOEFL (minimum score 540 paper-based; 76 iBT), IELTS (minimum score 6), ELPT (minimum score 964) or ELS (minimum score 112). Electronic applications accepted.

Stanford University, School of Humanities and Sciences, Department of French and Italian, Stanford, CA 94305-2004. Offers French and Italian (PhD). *Expenses: Tuition:* Full-time $52,479; part-time $34,110 per unit. *Required fees:* $672; $224 per quarter. Tuition and fees vary according to program and student level.
Website: http://www.stanford.edu/dept/fren-ital/

State University of New York at New Paltz, Graduate and Extended Learning School, School of Education, Department of Teaching and Learning, New Paltz, NY 12561. Offers adolescence education: biology (MAT, MS Ed); adolescence education: chemistry (MAT, MS Ed); adolescence education: earth science (MAT, MS Ed); adolescence education: English (MAT, MS Ed); adolescence education: French (MAT, MS Ed); adolescence education: social studies (MAT, MS Ed); adolescence education: Spanish (MAT, MS Ed); second language education (MS Ed, AC), including second language education (MS Ed), teaching English language learners (AC). *Accreditation:* NCATE. *Program availability:* Part-time, evening/weekend. *Faculty:* 11 full-time (5 women), 9 part-time/adjunct (5 women). *Students:* 36 full-time (19 women), 22 part-time (6 women); includes 7 minority (1 Black or African American, non-Hispanic/Latino; 5 Hispanic/Latino; 1 Two or more races, non-Hispanic/Latino). 56 applicants, 61% accepted, 19 enrolled. In 2019, 28 master's awarded. *Degree requirements:* For master's, comprehensive exam (for some programs), portfolio. *Entrance requirements:* For master's, minimum GPA of 3.0, New York state teaching certificate (MS Ed). Additional exam requirements/recommendations for international students: required—TOEFL (minimum score 550 paper-based; 80 iBT), IELTS (minimum score 6.5). *Application deadline:* For fall admission, 3/1 priority date for domestic students, 3/1 for international students; for spring admission, 10/1 priority date for domestic students, 10/1 for international students. Application fee: $50. Electronic applications accepted. *Expenses: Tuition, area resident:* Full-time $11,310; part-time $471 per credit. Tuition, state resident: full-time $11,310; part-time $471 per credit. Tuition, nonresident: full-time $23,100; part-time $963 per credit. *International tuition:* $23,100 full-time. *Required fees:* $1432; $41.83 per credit. *Financial support:* Application deadline: 8/1. *Unit head:* Dr. Aaron Isabelle, Associate Dean, 845-257-2837, E-mail: isabella@newpaltz.edu. *Application contact:* Vika Shock, Director of Graduate Admissions, 845-257-3285, Fax: 845-257-3284, E-mail: gradstudies@newpaltz.edu.
Website: http://www.newpaltz.edu/secondaryed/

State University of New York College at Geneseo, Graduate Studies, School of Education, Program in Adolescence Education, Geneseo, NY 14454. Offers English 7-12 (MS Ed); French 7-12 (MS Ed); social studies 7-12 (MS Ed); Spanish 7-12 (MS Ed). *Program availability:* Part-time, evening/weekend. *Faculty:* 7 full-time (5 women), 1 part-time/adjunct (0 women). *Students:* 2 full-time (1 woman), 1 (woman) part-time. Average age 29. 10 applicants, 40% accepted, 2 enrolled. In 2019, 3 master's awarded. *Degree requirements:* For master's, 2 foreign languages, comprehensive examination, thesis or research project. *Entrance requirements:* For master's, GRE, MAT, EAS, edTPA, PRAXIS, or another substantially equivalent test, proof of New York State initial certification or equivalent certification from another state. Additional exam requirements/recommendations for international students: required—TOEFL (minimum score 550 paper-based; 80 iBT), IELTS (minimum score 6.5), PTE. *Application deadline:* For fall admission, 4/1 priority date for domestic students; for spring admission, 11/1 priority date for domestic students; for summer admission, 4/1 priority date for domestic students. Applications are processed on a rolling basis. Application fee: $50. Electronic applications accepted. *Expenses:* Contact institution. *Financial support:* In 2019–20, 3 students received support. Fellowships, research assistantships, scholarships/grants, health care benefits, tuition waivers (full and partial), and unspecified assistantships available. Support available to part-time students. Financial award application deadline: 4/1; financial award applicants required to submit FAFSA. *Unit head:* Dr. Dennis Showers, Interim Dean of School of Education, 585-245-5264, Fax: 585-245-5220, E-mail: showers@geneseo.edu. *Application contact:* Michael R. George, Director of Graduate Admissions, 585-245-5148, Fax: 585-245-5550, E-mail: georgem@geneseo.edu.
Website: https://www.geneseo.edu/education/graduate-programs-education

Stony Brook University, State University of New York, Graduate School, College of Arts and Sciences, Department of European Languages, Literatures, and Cultures, Program in French, Stony Brook, NY 11794. Offers MA. *Program availability:* Evening/weekend. *Students:* 2 part-time (1 woman); includes 1 minority (American Indian or Alaska Native, non-Hispanic/Latino). 2 applicants, 100% accepted, 2 enrolled. In 2019, 1 master's awarded. *Entrance requirements:* For master's, GRE General Test. Additional exam requirements/recommendations for international students: required—TOEFL. *Application deadline:* For fall admission, 1/15 for domestic students; for spring admission, 10/1 for domestic students. Application fee: $100. *Expenses:* Contact institution. *Unit head:* Madeline Turan, Coordinator, 631-632-7445, Fax: 631-632-9612, E-mail: madeline.turan@stonybrook.edu. *Application contact:* Elizabeth Tolson, Coordinator, 631-632-7440, Fax: 631-632-9612, E-mail: Elizabeth-A.Tolson@stonybrook.edu.

Syracuse University, College of Arts and Sciences, MA Program in French and Francophone Studies, Syracuse, NY 13244. Offers MA. *Program availability:* Part-time. *Degree requirements:* For master's, comprehensive exam, thesis or alternative. *Entrance requirements:* For master's, GRE General Test, writing sample of 5 to 15 pages in French (e.g., paper written for undergraduate French course, honors or senior thesis), personal statement, three letters of recommendation, transcripts. Additional exam requirements/recommendations for international students: required—TOEFL (minimum score 100 iBT). Electronic applications accepted.

Tufts University, Graduate School of Arts and Sciences, Program in French, Medford, MA 02155. Offers MA. *Degree requirements:* For master's, one foreign language. *Entrance requirements:* For master's, GRE General Test, writing sample. Additional exam requirements/recommendations for international students: required—TOEFL (minimum score 550 paper-based; 80 iBT), IELTS (minimum score 6.5). Electronic applications accepted. *Expenses:* Contact institution.

Tulane University, School of Liberal Arts, Department of French and Italian, New Orleans, LA 70118-5669. Offers French (MA, PhD). *Degree requirements:* For master's, one foreign language, thesis or alternative; for doctorate, 2 foreign languages, thesis/dissertation. *Entrance requirements:* For master's, GRE General Test, minimum B average in undergraduate course work; for doctorate, GRE General Test. Additional exam requirements/recommendations for international students: required—TOEFL. Electronic applications accepted. *Expenses: Tuition:* Full-time $57,004; part-time $3167 per credit hour. *Required fees:* $2086; $44.50 per credit hour. $80 per term. Tuition and fees vary according to course load, degree level and program.

Université de Moncton, Faculty of Arts and Social Sciences, Department of French Studies, Moncton, NB E1A 3E9, Canada. Offers MA, PhD. *Program availability:* Part-time. Terminal master's awarded for partial completion of doctoral program. *Degree requirements:* For master's, thesis, proficiency in French; for doctorate, thesis/dissertation, proficiency in French. *Entrance requirements:* For master's, honors degree in French; for doctorate, MA in French. Electronic applications accepted.

Université de Montréal, Faculty of Arts and Sciences, Department of French Literature, Montréal, QC H3C 3J7, Canada. Offers MA, PhD. *Degree requirements:* For master's, one foreign language, thesis; for doctorate, one foreign language, thesis/dissertation, general exam. Electronic applications accepted.

Université de Sherbrooke, Faculty of Letters and Human Sciences, Department of Letters and Communications, Sherbrooke, QC J1K 2R1, Canada. Offers comparative Canadian literature (MA, PhD); French literature (MA, PhD); linguistics (MA); theatre (MA). *Degree requirements:* For master's, thesis or alternative; for doctorate, thesis/dissertation. *Entrance requirements:* For master's, minimum GPA of 2.8; for doctorate, minimum GPA of 3.0.

Université du Québec à Chicoutimi, Graduate Programs, Program in Didactics of French-Mother Tongue, Chicoutimi, QC G7H 2B1, Canada. Offers Diploma. *Program availability:* Part-time. *Entrance requirements:* For degree, appropriate bachelor's degree, proficiency in French.

University at Buffalo, the State University of New York, Graduate School, College of Arts and Sciences, Department of Romance Languages and Literatures, Buffalo, NY 14260-4620. Offers French (MA, PhD); Spanish (MA, PhD). *Program availability:* Part-time. Terminal master's awarded for partial completion of doctoral program. *Degree requirements:* For master's, 2 foreign languages, comprehensive exam, thesis (for some programs); for doctorate, 2 foreign languages, comprehensive exam, thesis/dissertation, Preliminary exam one (1) year after Comprehensive exam. *Entrance requirements:* For master's, completed application form, application fee, original official transcripts for all previous college work, 3 letters of recommendation, personal statement, 1 writing sample in the target language, 1 writing sample in English (for international), CV, GPA of 3.0 or above preferred; for doctorate, GRE, TOEFL (if international), completed application form, application fee, original official transcripts for all previous college work, 3 letters of recommendation, personal statement, 1 writing sample in target language, 1 writing sample in English (for international), CV, GPA of 3.0 or above preferred. Additional exam requirements/recommendations for international students: required—TOEFL (minimum score 550 paper-based; 79 iBT), IELTS (minimum score 6.5), PTE (minimum score 55). Electronic applications accepted. *Expenses: Tuition, area resident:* Full-time $11,310; part-time $471 per credit hour. Tuition, state resident: full-time $11,310; part-time $471 per credit hour. Tuition, nonresident: full-time $23,100; part-time $963 per credit hour. *International tuition:* $23,100 full-time. *Required fees:* $2820.

University at Buffalo, the State University of New York, Graduate School, Graduate School of Education, Department of Learning and Instruction, Buffalo, NY 14260. Offers biology education (Ed M, Certificate); chemistry education (Ed M, Certificate); childhood education (Ed M); childhood education with bilingual extension (Ed M); college teaching (Advanced Certificate); curriculum, instruction and the science of learning (PhD); early childhood education (Ed M); early childhood education with bilingual extension (Ed M); earth science education (Ed M, Certificate); education and technology (Ed M); education studies (Ed M); educational technology and new literacies (Certificate); educational technology and new literacies (Advanced Certificate); elementary education (Ed D); English education (Ed M, Certificate); English education studies (Ed M); English for speakers of other languages (Ed M); foreign and second language education (PhD); French education (Ed M, Certificate); German education (Ed M, Certificate); gifted education (Certificate); Latin education (Ed M, Certificate); literacy education studies (Ed M); literacy specialist (Ed M); literacy teaching and learning (Certificate); mathematics education (Ed M, Certificate); music education (Ed M, Certificate); music education studies (Ed M); music learning theory (Advanced Certificate); online education (Advanced Certificate); physics education (Ed M, Certificate); science and the public (Ed M); social studies education (Ed M, Certificate); Spanish education (Ed M, Certificate); special education (PhD); teaching English to speakers of other languages (Ed M). *Program availability:* Part-time, evening/weekend, 100% online, blended/hybrid learning. *Faculty:* 26 full-time (19 women), 42 part-time/adjunct (29 women). *Students:* 227 full-time (158 women), 322 part-time (228 women); includes 85 minority (34 Black or African American, non-Hispanic/Latino; 3 American Indian or Alaska Native, non-Hispanic/Latino; 17 Asian, non-Hispanic/Latino; 23 Hispanic/Latino; 8 Two or more races, non-Hispanic/Latino), 42 international. Average age 33. 385 applicants, 61% accepted, 158 enrolled. In 2019, 100 master's, 23 doctorates, 16 other advanced degrees awarded. *Degree requirements:* For master's, comprehensive exam; for doctorate, thesis/dissertation, research analysis exam, research experience; for other advanced degree, thesis (for some programs). *Entrance requirements:* For master's, GRE or MAT for teacher preparation programs only, letters of reference; for doctorate, GRE General Test or MAT, interview, writing sample, letters of recommendation, resume. Additional exam requirements/recommendations for international students: required—TOEFL (minimum score 600 paper-based; 96 iBT), IELTS (minimum score 6.5), PTE (minimum score 55), The Graduate School of Education requires international students to submit test scores for at least one of the exams (TOEFL, IELTS, PTE). *Application deadline:* For fall admission, 2/1 priority date for domestic and international students. Applications are processed on a rolling basis. Application fee: $50. Electronic applications accepted. *Expenses: Tuition, area resident:* Full-time $11,310; part-time $471 per credit hour. Tuition, state resident: full-time $11,310; part-time $471 per credit hour. Tuition, nonresident: full-time $23,100; part-time $963 per credit hour. *International tuition:* $23,100 full-time. *Required fees:* $2820. *Financial support:* In 2019–20, 16 fellowships (averaging $20,000 per year), 5 research assistantships with tuition reimbursements (averaging $26,917 per year) were awarded; teaching assistantships, career-related internships or fieldwork, Federal Work-Study, institutionally sponsored loans, scholarships/grants, tuition waivers (full and partial), and unspecified assistantships also available. Financial award application deadline: 2/28; financial award applicants required to submit FAFSA. *Unit head:* Dr. Julie Gorlewski, Department Chair, 716-645-2455, Fax: 716-645-3161, E-mail: jgorlews@buffalo.edu. *Application contact:* Renad Aref, Assistant Director of Admission Recruitment, 716-645-2110, Fax: 716-645-7937, E-mail: gseinfo@buffalo.edu.
Website: http://ed.buffalo.edu/teaching.html

The University of Alabama, Graduate School, College of Arts and Sciences, Department of Modern Languages and Classics, Tuscaloosa, AL 35487. Offers French (MA, PhD); French and Spanish (PhD); German (MA); Romance languages (MA, PhD); Spanish (MA, PhD). *Program availability:* Part-time. *Faculty:* 20 full-time (11 women). *Students:* 39 full-time (17 women), 6 part-time (3 women); includes 14 minority (5 Black or African American, non-Hispanic/Latino; 7 Hispanic/Latino; 2 Two or more races, non-Hispanic/Latino), 10 international. Average age 31. 19 applicants, 89% accepted, 11 enrolled. In 2019, 6 master's, 3 doctorates awarded. *Degree requirements:* For master's, comprehensive exam, thesis optional; for doctorate, one foreign language, thesis/dissertation, preliminary exam. *Entrance requirements:* For master's and doctorate, minimum GPA of 3.0, writing sample. Additional exam requirements/recommendations for international students: required—TOEFL or IELTS. *Application deadline:* For fall admission, 7/6 priority date for domestic students, 1/15 priority date for international students; for spring admission, 12/5 priority date for domestic students, 6/1 priority date for international students. Applications are processed on a rolling basis. Application fee: $50 ($60 for international students). Electronic applications accepted. *Expenses:*

Tuition, area resident: Full-time $10,780; part-time $440 per credit hour. Tuition, nonresident: full-time $30,250; part-time $1550 per credit hour. *Financial support:* In 2019–20, 40 students received support. Fellowships, research assistantships with full tuition reimbursements available, teaching assistantships with full tuition reimbursements available, career-related internships or fieldwork, Federal Work-Study, institutionally sponsored loans, and scholarships/grants available. Financial award application deadline: 7/14. *Unit head:* Dr. Douglas Lightfoot, Department Chair, 205-348-5059, E-mail: lightfoot@ua.edu. *Application contact:* Dr. K. Barbara Fischer, Graduate Director/Associate Professor, 205-348-8465, Fax: 205-348-2042, E-mail: bfischer@bama.ua.edu.
Website: http://bama.ua.edu/~mlc

University of Alberta, Faculty of Graduate Studies and Research, Department of Modern Languages and Cultural Studies, Edmonton, AB T6G 2E1, Canada. Offers applied linguistics (Germanic, Romance, Slavic) (MA); French language, literatures and linguistics (PhD); French language, literatures, and linguistics (MA); Germanic languages, literatures and linguistics (PhD); Germanic languages, literatures, and linguistics (MA); Italian studies (MA); Slavic languages and literatures (Russian, Ukrainian) (MA, PhD); Slavic linguistics (Russian, Ukrainian) (MA, PhD); Spanish and Latin American studies (MA, PhD); Ukrainian folklore (MA, PhD). *Program availability:* Part-time. *Degree requirements:* For master's, one foreign language, thesis; for doctorate, 2 foreign languages, comprehensive exam, thesis/dissertation. *Entrance requirements:* For master's and doctorate, 1 language other than English. Additional exam requirements/recommendations for international students: required—Michigan English Language Assessment Battery or TOEFL (minimum score 550 paper-based). Electronic applications accepted.

The University of Arizona, College of Humanities, Department of French and Italian, Tucson, AZ 85721. Offers French (MA). *Program availability:* Part-time. *Entrance requirements:* For master's, 3 letters of reference, writing sample in French, audio recording. Additional exam requirements/recommendations for international students: required—TOEFL (minimum score 550 paper-based; 79 iBT). Electronic applications accepted.

University of Arkansas, Graduate School, J. William Fulbright College of Arts and Sciences, Department of World Languages, Literatures and Cultures, Fayetteville, AR 72701. Offers French (MA); German (MA); Spanish (MA). *Students:* 22 full-time (11 women); includes 3 minority (2 Hispanic/Latino; 1 Two or more races, non-Hispanic/Latino), 10 international. 17 applicants, 100% accepted. In 2019, 11 master's awarded. *Application deadline:* For fall admission, 8/1 for domestic students, 4/1 for international students; for spring admission, 12/1 for domestic students, 10/1 for international students; for summer admission, 4/15 for domestic students, 3/1 for international students. Applications are processed on a rolling basis. Application fee: $60. Electronic applications accepted. *Financial support:* In 2019–20, 1 research assistantship, 26 teaching assistantships were awarded; fellowships with tuition reimbursements, career-related internships or fieldwork, and Federal Work-Study also available. Support available to part-time students. Financial award application deadline: 4/1; financial award applicants required to submit FAFSA. *Unit head:* Dr. Steven Bell, Department Chair, 479-575-2951, E-mail: sbell@uark.edu. *Application contact:* Dr. Steven Bell, Department Chair, 479-575-2951, E-mail: sbell@uark.edu.
Website: https://fulbright.uark.edu/departments/world-languages/

The University of British Columbia, Faculty of Arts, Department of French, Hispanic and Italian Studies, Vancouver, BC V6T 1Z1, Canada. Offers French (MA, PhD); Hispanic studies (MA, PhD). *Program availability:* Part-time. *Degree requirements:* For master's, thesis optional; for doctorate, 2 foreign languages, comprehensive exam, thesis/dissertation. *Entrance requirements:* For doctorate, MA. Additional exam requirements/recommendations for international students: required—TOEFL. Electronic applications accepted. *Expenses:* Contact institution.

University of California, Berkeley, Graduate Division, College of Letters and Science, Department of French, Berkeley, CA 94720. Offers PhD. *Degree requirements:* For doctorate, one foreign language, thesis/dissertation, qualifying exam. *Entrance requirements:* For doctorate, minimum GPA of 3.0, 3 letters of recommendation. Electronic applications accepted.

University of California, Berkeley, Graduate Division, College of Letters and Science, Group in Romance Languages and Literatures, Berkeley, CA 94720. Offers French (PhD); Italian (PhD); Spanish (PhD). *Degree requirements:* For doctorate, thesis/dissertation, qualifying exam. *Entrance requirements:* For doctorate, GRE General Test, minimum GPA of 3.0, 3 letters of recommendation. Additional exam requirements/recommendations for international students: required—TOEFL (minimum score 570 paper-based; 90 iBT). Electronic applications accepted.

University of California, Davis, Graduate Studies, Program in French, Davis, CA 95616. Offers PhD. *Program availability:* Part-time. *Degree requirements:* For doctorate, thesis/dissertation. *Entrance requirements:* For doctorate, GRE General Test, minimum GPA of 3.0. Additional exam requirements/recommendations for international students: required—TOEFL (minimum score 550 paper-based). Electronic applications accepted.

University of California, Irvine, School of Humanities, Department of European Languages and Studies, Irvine, CA 92697. Offers French (MA, PhD); German (MA, PhD). *Students:* 9 full-time (3 women), 1 part-time; includes 1 minority (Hispanic/Latino), 2 international. Average age 28. 12 applicants, 33% accepted, 2 enrolled. In 2019, 3 master's awarded. *Entrance requirements:* For master's and doctorate, GRE General Test, minimum GPA of 3.0. Additional exam requirements/recommendations for international students: required—TOEFL (minimum score 550 paper-based). *Application deadline:* For fall admission, 1/15 for domestic and international students. Applications are processed on a rolling basis. Application fee: $120 ($140 for international students). Electronic applications accepted. *Financial support:* Fellowships, research assistantships with full tuition reimbursements, teaching assistantships, institutionally sponsored loans, traineeships, health care benefits, and unspecified assistantships available. Financial award application deadline: 3/1; financial award applicants required to submit FAFSA. *Unit head:* Prof. John Smith, Chair, 949-824-6406, Fax: 949-824-6416, E-mail: jhsmith@uci.edu. *Application contact:* Bindya Baliga, Graduate Program Coordinator, 949-824-7968, Fax: 949-824-6416, E-mail: bbaliga@uci.edu.
Website: http://www.humanities.uci.edu/els/

University of California, Los Angeles, Graduate Division, College of Letters and Science, Department of French and Francophone Studies, Los Angeles, CA 90095. Offers MA, PhD. Terminal master's awarded for partial completion of doctoral program. *Degree requirements:* For master's, one foreign language, comprehensive exam; for doctorate, 2 foreign languages, thesis/dissertation, oral and written qualifying exams. *Entrance requirements:* For doctorate, GRE General Test, bachelor's degree; minimum undergraduate GPA of 3.0 (or its equivalent if letter grade system not used); writing sample in French. Additional exam requirements/recommendations for international students: required—TOEFL. Electronic applications accepted.

University of California, Santa Barbara, Graduate Division, College of Letters and Sciences, Division of Humanities and Fine Arts, Program in Comparative Literature, Santa Barbara, CA 93106-4130. Offers comparative literature (PhD); East Asian literatures (PhD); feminist studies (PhD); French (PhD); global studies (PhD); translation

studies (PhD); MA/PhD. *Degree requirements:* For doctorate, 2 foreign languages, comprehensive exam, thesis/dissertation. *Entrance requirements:* For doctorate, GRE. Additional exam requirements/recommendations for international students: required—TOEFL (minimum score 550 paper-based; 80 iBT), IELTS (minimum score 7). Electronic applications accepted.

University of Chicago, Division of the Humanities, Department of Romance Languages and Literatures, Chicago, IL 60637. Offers French and Francophone studies (PhD); Hispanic and Luso-Brazilian studies (PhD); Italian studies (PhD); Renaissance and early modern studies (PhD). Terminal master's awarded for partial completion of doctoral program. *Degree requirements:* For doctorate, 3 foreign languages, comprehensive exam, thesis/dissertation. *Entrance requirements:* For doctorate, GRE General Test, 15-20 page writing sample, statement of purpose, 3 letters of recommendation, transcripts for all previous degrees and institutions attended. Additional exam requirements/recommendations for international students: required—TOEFL (minimum score 104 iBT), IELTS (minimum score 7). Electronic applications accepted.

University of Cincinnati, Graduate School, McMicken College of Arts and Sciences, Dept. of Romance and Arabic Languages and Literatures, Program in French, Cincinnati, OH 45221. Offers MA, PhD. Terminal master's awarded for partial completion of doctoral program. *Degree requirements:* For master's, thesis optional; for doctorate, 2 foreign languages, thesis/dissertation. *Entrance requirements:* For master's, minimum GPA of 3.0. Electronic applications accepted.

University of Colorado Boulder, Graduate School, College of Arts and Sciences, Department of French and Italian, Boulder, CO 80309. Offers MA, PhD. Terminal master's awarded for partial completion of doctoral program. *Degree requirements:* For master's, 2 foreign languages, comprehensive exam, thesis or alternative; for doctorate, 3 foreign languages, thesis/dissertation. *Entrance requirements:* For master's, GRE General Test, minimum undergraduate GPA of 3.0; for doctorate, GRE General Test. Electronic applications accepted. Application fee is waived when completed online.

University of Delaware, College of Arts and Sciences, Department of Foreign Languages and Literatures, Newark, DE 19716. Offers foreign languages and literatures (MA), including French, German, Spanish; foreign languages pedagogy (MA), including French, German, Spanish; technical Chinese translation (MA). *Degree requirements:* For master's, one foreign language, comprehensive exam, thesis optional. *Entrance requirements:* For master's, GRE General Test, letters of recommendation, writing sample. Additional exam requirements/recommendations for international students: required—TOEFL. Electronic applications accepted.

University of Florida, Graduate School, College of Liberal Arts and Sciences, Department of Languages, Literatures and Cultures, Gainesville, FL 32611. Offers French and Francophone studies (MA, PhD); German (MA, PhD), including women's and gender studies (PhD). *Degree requirements:* For master's, comprehensive exam, thesis optional; for doctorate, one foreign language, comprehensive exam, thesis/dissertation. *Entrance requirements:* For master's and doctorate, GRE General Test, minimum GPA of 3.0. Additional exam requirements/recommendations for international students: required—TOEFL (minimum score 550 paper-based; 80 iBT), IELTS (minimum score 6). Electronic applications accepted.

University of Georgia, Franklin College of Arts and Sciences, Department of Romance Languages, Athens, GA 30602. Offers French (PhD); Italian (MA, PhD); Portuguese (MA, PhD); romance linguistics (MA); Spanish (PhD). *Degree requirements:* For master's, one foreign language; for doctorate, 2 foreign languages, thesis/dissertation. *Entrance requirements:* For master's and doctorate, GRE General Test. Electronic applications accepted.

University of Guelph, Office of Graduate and Postdoctoral Studies, College of Arts, School of Languages and Literatures, Guelph, ON N1G 2W1, Canada. Offers European studies (MA); French studies (MA). *Entrance requirements:* For master's, honours BA or equivalent. Electronic applications accepted.

University of Hawaii at Manoa, Office of Graduate Education, College of Languages, Linguistics and Literature, Department of Languages and Literatures of Europe and the Americas, Program in French, Honolulu, HI 96822. Offers MA. *Program availability:* Part-time. *Degree requirements:* For master's, one foreign language, thesis optional. *Entrance requirements:* Additional exam requirements/recommendations for international students: required—TOEFL (minimum score 580 paper-based; 92 iBT), IELTS (minimum score 5).

University of Illinois at Chicago, College of Liberal Arts and Sciences, School of Literatures, Cultural Studies and Linguistics, Department of French and Francophone Studies, Chicago, IL 60607-7128. Offers MA. *Program availability:* Part-time. *Degree requirements:* For master's, one foreign language, thesis optional, exam. *Entrance requirements:* For master's, minimum GPA of 2.75. Additional exam requirements/recommendations for international students: required—TOEFL. Electronic applications accepted.

University of Illinois at Urbana-Champaign, Graduate College, College of Liberal Arts and Sciences, School of Literatures, Cultures and Linguistics, Department of French, Champaign, IL 61820. Offers MA, PhD.

The University of Iowa, Graduate College, College of Liberal Arts and Sciences, Department of French and Italian, Iowa City, IA 52242-1316. Offers French (MA, PhD). *Degree requirements:* For master's, thesis optional, exam; for doctorate, comprehensive exam, thesis/dissertation. *Entrance requirements:* For master's and doctorate, GRE General Test, minimum GPA of 3.0. Additional exam requirements/recommendations for international students: required—TOEFL (minimum score 550 paper-based; 81 iBT). Electronic applications accepted.

The University of Kansas, Graduate Studies, College of Liberal Arts and Sciences, Department of French, Francophone & Italian Studies, Lawrence, KS 66045-7590. Offers French (MA, PhD). *Students:* 12 full-time (6 women); includes 1 minority (Black or African American, non-Hispanic/Latino), 5 international. Average age 29. 10 applicants, 50% accepted, 3 enrolled. In 2019, 3 master's, 1 doctorate awarded. *Entrance requirements:* For master's and doctorate, GRE, statement of academic purpose and goals, resume, sample essay, three letters of recommendation, official transcripts. Additional exam requirements/recommendations for international students: required—TOEFL, IELTS. *Application deadline:* For fall admission, 1/15 priority date for domestic and international students; for spring admission, 11/1 for domestic and international students. Application fee: $65 ($85 for international students). Electronic applications accepted. *Expenses:* Tuition, state resident: full-time $9989. Tuition, nonresident: full-time $23,950. International tuition: $23,950 full-time. *Required fees:* $984; $81.99 per credit hour. Tuition and fees vary according to course load, campus/location and program. *Financial support:* Fellowships, teaching assistantships, and unspecified assistantships available. Financial award application deadline: 1/15; financial award applicants required to submit FAFSA. *Unit head:* Dr. Bruce Hayes, Chair, 785-864-9062, E-mail: bhayes@ku.edu. *Application contact:* Jared Nietfeld, Graduate Admissions Contact, 785-864-0482, E-mail: nietfeld@ku.edu.
Website: http://www.frenchitalian.ku.edu

University of Lethbridge, School of Graduate Studies, Lethbridge, AB T1K 3M4, Canada. Offers addictions counseling (M Sc); agricultural biotechnology (M Sc);

agricultural studies (M Sc, MA); anthropology (MA); archaeology (M Sc, MA); art (MA, MFA); biochemistry (M Sc); biological sciences (M Sc); biomolecular science (PhD); biosystems and biodiversity (PhD); Canadian studies (MA); chemistry (M Sc); computer science (M Sc); computer science and geographical information science (M Sc); counseling (MC); counseling psychology (M Ed); dramatic arts (MA); earth, space, and physical science (PhD); economics (MA); education (MA, PhD); educational leadership (M Ed); English (MA); environmental science (M Sc); evolution and behavior (PhD); exercise science (M Sc); French (MA); French/German (MA); French/Spanish (MA); general education (M Ed); geography (M Sc, MA); German (MA); health sciences (M Sc); individualized multidisciplinary (M Sc, MA); kinesiology (M Sc, MA); management (M Sc), including accounting, finance, human resource management and labor relations, information systems, international management, marketing, policy and strategy; mathematics (M Sc); music (M Mus, MA); Native American studies (MA); neuroscience (M Sc, PhD); new media (MA, MFA); nursing (M Sc, MN); philosophy (MA); physics (M Sc); political science (MA); psychology (M Sc, MA); religious studies (MA); sociology (MA); theatre and dramatic arts (MFA); theoretical and computational science (PhD); urban and regional studies (MA); women and gender studies (MA). *Program availability:* Part-time, evening/weekend. *Degree requirements:* For master's, thesis (for some programs); for doctorate, comprehensive exam, thesis/dissertation. *Entrance requirements:* For master's, GMAT (for M Sc in management), bachelor's degree in related field, minimum GPA of 3.0 during previous 20 graded semester courses, 2 years' teaching or related experience (M Ed); for doctorate, master's degree, minimum graduate GPA of 3.5. Additional exam requirements/recommendations for international students: required—TOEFL (minimum score 580 paper-based; 93 iBT). Electronic applications accepted.

University of Louisiana at Lafayette, College of Liberal Arts, Department of Modern Languages, Program in Francophone Studies, Lafayette, LA 70504. Offers PhD. *Degree requirements:* For doctorate, 2 foreign languages, comprehensive exam, thesis/dissertation. *Entrance requirements:* For doctorate, GRE General Test, minimum GPA of 2.75. Additional exam requirements/recommendations for international students: required—TOEFL (minimum score 550 paper-based). Electronic applications accepted. *Expenses: Tuition, area resident:* Full-time $5511; part-time $1630 per credit hour. Tuition, state resident: full-time $5511; part-time $1630 per credit hour. Tuition, nonresident: full-time $19,239; part-time $2409 per credit hour. *Required fees:* $46,637.

University of Louisiana at Lafayette, College of Liberal Arts, Department of Modern Languages, Program in French, Lafayette, LA 70504. Offers MA. *Program availability:* Part-time. *Degree requirements:* For master's, 2 foreign languages, thesis or alternative. *Entrance requirements:* For master's, GRE General Test, minimum GPA of 2.75. Additional exam requirements/recommendations for international students: required—TOEFL (minimum score 550 paper-based). Electronic applications accepted. *Expenses: Tuition, area resident:* Full-time $5511; part-time $1630 per credit hour. Tuition, state resident: full-time $5511; part-time $1630 per credit hour. Tuition, nonresident: full-time $19,239; part-time $2409 per credit hour. *Required fees:* $46,637.

University of Louisville, Graduate School, College of Arts and Sciences, Department of Classical and Modern Languages, Louisville, KY 40292-0001. Offers French (MA); Spanish (MA); translation and interpretation (Certificate). *Program availability:* Part-time, evening/weekend. *Faculty:* 27 full-time (13 women), 25 part-time/adjunct (20 women). *Students:* 7 full-time (6 women), 8 part-time (5 women); includes 10 minority (1 Asian, non-Hispanic/Latino; 8 Hispanic/Latino; 1 Two or more races, non-Hispanic/Latino). Average age 36. 4 applicants, 100% accepted, 4 enrolled. In 2019, 11 master's awarded. *Degree requirements:* For master's, one foreign language, thesis (for some programs). *Entrance requirements:* For master's, Two letters of reference, official transcripts. Additional exam requirements/recommendations for international students: required—TOEFL (minimum score 550 paper-based; 79 iBT), IELTS can be used in place of the TOEFL; recommended—IELTS (minimum score 6.5). *Application deadline:* Applications are processed on a rolling basis. Application fee: $65. Electronic applications accepted. *Expenses: Tuition, area resident:* Full-time $13,000; part-time $723 per credit hour. Tuition, state resident: full-time $13,000; part-time $723 per credit hour. Tuition, nonresident: full-time $27,114; part-time $1507 per credit hour. *International tuition:* $27,114 full-time. *Required fees:* $196. Tuition and fees vary according to program and reciprocity agreements. *Financial support:* In 2019–20, 12 students received support. Fellowships, research assistantships, teaching assistantships, scholarships/grants, health care benefits, and unspecified assistantships available. *Unit head:* Dr. Regina Roebuck, Associate Professor and Chair, 502-852-0483, E-mail: regina.roebuck@louisville.edu. *Application contact:* Dr. Manuel Medina, Professor and Director of Graduate Studies, E-mail: manuel.medina@louisville.edu.
Website: http://louisville.edu/modernlanguages/

University of Maine, Graduate School, College of Liberal Arts and Sciences, Department of Modern Languages and Classics, Orono, ME 04469. Offers French (MA, MAT); Spanish (MAT). *Program availability:* Part-time. *Faculty:* 7 full-time (4 women). *Students:* 3 full-time (2 women), 3 part-time (all women); includes 2 minority (both Hispanic/Latino). Average age 33. 3 applicants, 67% accepted, 2 enrolled. In 2019, 2 master's awarded. *Degree requirements:* For master's, one foreign language, thesis (for some programs). *Entrance requirements:* For master's, GRE General Test; PRAXIS II (for MAT). Additional exam requirements/recommendations for international students: required—TOEFL, PRAXIS II. *Application deadline:* For fall admission, 2/1 priority date for domestic and international students. Applications are processed on a rolling basis. Application fee: $65. Electronic applications accepted. *Expenses: Tuition, area resident:* Full-time $8100; part-time $450 per credit hour. Tuition, state resident: full-time $8100; part-time $450 per credit hour. Tuition, nonresident: full-time $26,388; part-time $1466 per credit hour. *International tuition:* $26,388 full-time. *Required fees:* $1257; $278 per semester. Tuition and fees vary according to course load. *Financial support:* In 2019–20, 3 students received support. Fellowships with full tuition reimbursements available, teaching assistantships with full tuition reimbursements available, Federal Work-Study, and tuition waivers (full and partial) available. Financial award application deadline: 3/1; financial award applicants required to submit FAFSA. *Unit head:* Dr. Jane Smith, Chair, 207-581-2075, Fax: 207-581-1832. *Application contact:* Scott G. Delcourt, Assistant Vice President for Graduate Studies/Senior Associate Dean, 207-581-3291, Fax: 207-581-3232, E-mail: graduate@maine.edu.
Website: https://umaine.edu/mlandc/graduate-programs/

The University of Manchester, School of Arts, Languages and Cultures, Manchester, United Kingdom. Offers anthropology, media and performance (PhD); applied theatre (PhD); Arab world studies (PhD); archaeology (PhD); art history and visual studies (PhD); arts and cultural management (PhD); arts management and cultural policy (PhD); Chinese studies (PhD); classics and ancient history (PhD); composition (PhD); creative writing (PhD); drama (PhD); East Asian studies (PhD); electroacoustic composition (PhD); English and American studies (PhD); English language (PhD); French studies (PhD); German studies (PhD); history (PhD); humanitarianism and conflict response (PhD); interpreting studies (PhD); Japanese studies (PhD); Latin American cultural studies (PhD); linguistics (PhD); Middle Eastern studies (PhD); museology (PhD); museum practice (PhD); music (PhD); musicology (PhD); Polish studies (PhD); Portuguese studies (PhD); religions and theology (PhD); Russian studies (PhD); Spanish studies (PhD); translation and intercultural studies (PhD).

University of Manitoba, Faculty of Graduate Studies, Faculty of Arts, Department of French, Spanish and Italian, Winnipeg, MB R3T 2N2, Canada. Offers French (MA, PhD). *Degree requirements:* For master's, one foreign language, thesis; for doctorate, 2 foreign languages, thesis/dissertation.

University of Maryland, College Park, Academic Affairs, College of Arts and Humanities, School of Languages, Literatures, and Cultures, Modern French Studies Program, College Park, MD 20742. Offers PhD. *Entrance requirements:* For doctorate, GRE, letters of recommendation, writing sample. Additional exam requirements/recommendations for international students: required—TOEFL.

University of Maryland, College Park, Academic Affairs, College of Arts and Humanities, School of Languages, Literatures, and Cultures, Program in French Language and Literature, College Park, MD 20742. Offers MA. *Degree requirements:* For master's, one foreign language, comprehensive exam, thesis or alternative. *Entrance requirements:* For master's, GRE General Test, GRE Subject Test, minimum GPA of 3.0, 3 letters of recommendation. Additional exam requirements/recommendations for international students: required—TOEFL. Electronic applications accepted.

University of Massachusetts Amherst, Graduate School, College of Humanities and Fine Arts, Department of Languages, Literatures, and Cultures, Program in French and Francophone Studies, Amherst, MA 01003. Offers French (MAT); French and Francophone studies (MA). *Program availability:* Part-time. *Degree requirements:* For master's, thesis or alternative. *Entrance requirements:* For master's, GRE General Test. Additional exam requirements/recommendations for international students: required—TOEFL (minimum score 550 paper-based; 80 iBT), IELTS (minimum score 6.5). Electronic applications accepted.

University of Memphis, Graduate School, College of Arts and Sciences, Department of World Languages and Literatures, Memphis, TN 38152. Offers romance languages (MA), including French, Spanish. *Program availability:* Part-time. *Students:* 16 full-time (11 women), 5 part-time (4 women); includes 13 minority (1 Black or African American, non-Hispanic/Latino; 11 Hispanic/Latino; 1 Two or more races, non-Hispanic/Latino), 1 international. Average age 33. 10 applicants, 100% accepted, 5 enrolled. In 2019, 4 master's awarded. *Degree requirements:* For master's, 2 foreign languages, comprehensive exam. *Entrance requirements:* For master's, GRE, interview in language of concentration, writing sample, letter of intent, two letters of recommendation. Additional exam requirements/recommendations for international students: required—TOEFL (minimum score 94 iBT). *Application deadline:* For fall admission, 5/15 for domestic students, 4/5 for international students; for spring admission, 11/30 for domestic students, 10/5 for international students. Applications are processed on a rolling basis. Application fee: $35 ($60 for international students). Electronic applications accepted. *Expenses: Tuition, area resident:* Full-time $9216; part-time $512 per credit hour. Tuition, state resident: full-time $9216; part-time $512 per credit hour. Tuition, nonresident: full-time $12,672; part-time $704 per credit hour. *International tuition:* $16,128 full-time. *Required fees:* $1530; $85 per credit hour. Tuition and fees vary according to program. *Financial support:* Research assistantships with full tuition reimbursements, teaching assistantships with full tuition reimbursements, Federal Work-Study, scholarships/grants, and unspecified assistantships available. Financial award application deadline: 2/1; financial award applicants required to submit FAFSA. *Unit head:* Dr. William Thompson, Chair, 901-678-2507, E-mail: wjthmpsn@memphis.edu. *Application contact:* Dr. Fernando Burgos, Graduate Coordinator, 901-678-3158, E-mail: fburgos@memphis.edu.
Website: http://www.memphis.edu/fl/

University of Miami, Graduate School, College of Arts and Sciences, Department of Modern Languages and Literatures, Coral Gables, FL 33124. Offers romance studies (PhD), including French, Spanish. *Degree requirements:* For doctorate, 2 foreign languages, thesis/dissertation, area exam, qualifying exam. *Entrance requirements:* For doctorate, 1 writing sample in English and 1 writing sample in French or Spanish, minimum GPA of 3.0, oral interview, letters of recommendation. Additional exam requirements/recommendations for international students: required—TOEFL (minimum score 550 paper-based; 59 iBT). Electronic applications accepted.

University of Michigan, Rackham Graduate School, College of Literature, Science, and the Arts, Department of Romance Languages and Literatures, Program in French, Ann Arbor, MI 48109. Offers PhD. *Degree requirements:* For doctorate, 2 foreign languages, thesis/dissertation, oral defense of dissertation, preliminary exams in essay format. *Entrance requirements:* Additional exam requirements/recommendations for international students: required—TOEFL or Michigan English Language Assessment Battery. Electronic applications accepted.

University of Minnesota, Twin Cities Campus, Graduate School, College of Liberal Arts, Department of French and Italian, Minneapolis, MN 55455-0213. Offers French (MA, PhD). *Program availability:* Part-time. *Degree requirements:* For master's, one foreign language, comprehensive exam, thesis optional; for doctorate, one foreign language, thesis/dissertation, individualized exam on topic areas. *Entrance requirements:* For master's and doctorate, GRE, minimum GPA of 3.25 (recommended). Additional exam requirements/recommendations for international students: required—TOEFL (minimum score 550 paper-based). Electronic applications accepted.

University of Missouri, Office of Research and Graduate Studies, College of Arts and Science, Department of Romance Languages and Literatures, Columbia, MO 65211. Offers French (MA, PhD). Terminal master's awarded for partial completion of doctoral program. *Entrance requirements:* For master's, GRE General Test, minimum GPA of 3.0 in field of major; bachelor's degree; for doctorate, GRE General Test, minimum GPA of 3.0 in field of major; master's degree. Additional exam requirements/recommendations for international students: required—TOEFL.

University of Missouri–Kansas City, College of Arts and Sciences, Department of Foreign Languages and Literatures, Kansas City, MO 64110-2499. Offers romance languages and literatures (MA), including French, Spanish. *Program availability:* Part-time. *Degree requirements:* For master's, 2 foreign languages. *Entrance requirements:* For master's, GRE General Test, minimum GPA of 2.75, 2 letters of recommendation. Additional exam requirements/recommendations for international students: required—TOEFL (minimum score 550 paper-based; 80 iBT). Electronic applications accepted.

University of Montana, Graduate School, College of Humanities and Sciences, Department of Modern and Classical Languages and Literatures, Missoula, MT 59812. Offers French (MA); German (MA); Spanish (MA). *Degree requirements:* For master's, one foreign language. *Entrance requirements:* For master's, GRE General Test. Additional exam requirements/recommendations for international students: required—TOEFL.

University of Nebraska–Lincoln, Graduate College, College of Arts and Sciences, Department of Modern Languages and Literatures, Lincoln, NE 68588. Offers French (MA, PhD); German (MA, PhD); Spanish (MA, PhD). *Degree requirements:* For master's, thesis optional; for doctorate, comprehensive exam, thesis/dissertation. *Entrance requirements:* For master's and doctorate, writing sample in target language. Additional exam requirements/recommendations for international students: required—TOEFL (minimum score 550 paper-based). Electronic applications accepted.

University of New Mexico, Graduate Studies, College of Arts and Sciences, Program in Foreign Languages and Literatures, Albuquerque, NM 87131-2039. Offers comparative literature and cultural studies (MA); French (MA); French studies (PhD); German studies (MA). *Program availability:* Part-time. *Degree requirements:* For master's, one foreign language, thesis optional; for doctorate, 2 foreign languages, thesis/dissertation. *Entrance requirements:* For master's and doctorate, transcript, writing sample, 3 letters of recommendation. Additional exam requirements/recommendations for international students: required—TOEFL. Electronic applications accepted. *Expenses:* Tuition, state resident: full-time $7633; part-time $972 per year. Tuition, nonresident: full-time $22,586; part-time $3840 per year. *International tuition:* $23,292 full-time. *Required fees:* $8608. Tuition and fees vary according to course level, course load, degree level, program and student level.

The University of North Carolina at Chapel Hill, Graduate School, College of Arts and Sciences, Department of Romance Languages and Literatures, Chapel Hill, NC 27599. Offers French (MA, PhD); Italian (MA, PhD); Portuguese (MA, PhD); Romance languages (MA, PhD); Romance philology (MA, PhD); Spanish (MA, PhD). *Degree requirements:* For master's, one foreign language, comprehensive exam, thesis; for doctorate, 2 foreign languages, comprehensive exam, thesis/dissertation. *Entrance requirements:* For master's and doctorate, GRE General Test, minimum GPA of 3.0. Additional exam requirements/recommendations for international students: required—TOEFL (minimum score 550 paper-based). Electronic applications accepted.

The University of North Carolina at Greensboro, Graduate School, College of Arts and Sciences, Department of Languages, Literatures, and Cultures, Program in French, Greensboro, NC 27412-5001. Offers MA. *Degree requirements:* For master's, one foreign language, comprehensive exam, thesis or alternative. *Entrance requirements:* For master's, GRE General Test, 3-5 minute tape demonstrating foreign language proficiency, composition in French, sample paper in English. Additional exam requirements/recommendations for international students: required—TOEFL. Electronic applications accepted.

University of North Texas, Toulouse Graduate School, Denton, TX 76203-5459. Offers accounting (MS); applied anthropology (MA, MS); applied behavior analysis (Certificate); applied geography (MA); applied technology and performance improvement (M Ed, MS); art education (MA); art history (MA); arts leadership (Certificate); audiology (Au D); behavior analysis (MS); behavioral science (PhD); biochemistry and molecular biology (MS); biology (MA, MS); biomedical engineering (MS); business analysis (MS); chemistry (MS); clinical health psychology (PhD); communication studies (MA, MS); computer engineering (MS); computer science (MS); counseling (M Ed, MS), including clinical mental health counseling (MS), college and university counseling, elementary school counseling, secondary school counseling; creative writing (MA); criminal justice (MS); curriculum and instruction (M Ed); decision sciences (MBA); design (MA, MFA), including fashion design (MFA), innovation studies, interior design (MFA); early childhood studies (MS); economics (MS); educational leadership (M Ed, Ed D); educational psychology (MS, PhD), including family studies (MS), gifted and talented (MS), human development (MS), learning and cognition (MS), research, measurement and evaluation (MS); electrical engineering (MS); emergency management (MPA); engineering technology (MS); English (MA); English as a second language (MA); environmental science (MS); finance (MBA, MS); financial management (MPA); French (MA); health services management (MBA); higher education (M Ed, Ed D); history (MA, MS); hospitality management (MS); human resources management (MPA); information science (MS); information systems (PhD); information technologies (MBA); interdisciplinary studies (MA, MS); international studies (MA); international sustainable tourism (MS); jazz studies (MM); journalism (MA, MJ, Graduate Certificate), including interactive and virtual digital communication (Graduate Certificate), narrative journalism (Graduate Certificate), public relations (Graduate Certificate); kinesiology (MS); linguistics (MA); local government management (MPA); logistics (PhD); logistics and supply chain management (MBA); long-term care, senior housing, and aging services (MA); management (PhD); marketing (MBA); mathematics (MA, MS); mechanical and energy engineering (MS, PhD); music (MA), including ethnomusicology, music theory, musicology, performance; music composition (PhD); music education (MM Ed, PhD); nonprofit management (MPA); operations and supply chain management (MBA); performance (MM, DMA); philosophy (MA); political science (MA); professional and technical communication (MA); radio, television and film (MA, MFA); rehabilitation counseling (Certificate); sociology (MA); Spanish (MA); special education (M Ed); speech-language pathology (MA); strategic management (MBA); studio art (MFA); teaching (M Ed); MBA/MS. *Program availability:* Part-time, evening/weekend, online learning. Terminal master's awarded for partial completion of doctoral program. *Degree requirements:* For master's, variable foreign language requirement, comprehensive exam (for some programs), thesis (for some programs); for doctorate, variable foreign language requirement, comprehensive exam (for some programs), thesis/dissertation; for other advanced degree, variable foreign language requirement, comprehensive exam (for some programs). *Entrance requirements:* For master's and doctorate, GRE, GMAT. Additional exam requirements/recommendations for international students: required—TOEFL (minimum score 550 paper-based; 79 iBT). Electronic applications accepted.

University of Notre Dame, The Graduate School, College of Arts and Letters, Division of Humanities, Department of Romance Languages and Literatures, Notre Dame, IN 46556. Offers French and Francophone studies (MA); Iberian and Latin American studies (MA); Italian studies (MA); Romance literatures (MA). *Degree requirements:* For master's, 2 foreign languages, comprehensive exam, thesis optional. *Entrance requirements:* For master's, GRE General Test, BA in target language. Additional exam requirements/recommendations for international students: required—TOEFL (minimum score 600 paper-based; 80 iBT). Electronic applications accepted.

University of Oklahoma, College of Arts and Sciences, Department of Modern Languages, Literatures, and Linguistics, Norman, OK 73019. Offers French (MA, PhD, MBA/MA); German (MA); Spanish (MA, PhD); MBA/MA. *Program availability:* Part-time. Terminal master's awarded for partial completion of doctoral program. *Degree requirements:* For master's, one foreign language, comprehensive exam, thesis optional; for doctorate, one foreign language, comprehensive exam, thesis/dissertation. *Entrance requirements:* For master's, BA (or equivalent) in French, German, or Spanish, or equivalent hours in the major; for doctorate, MA (or equivalent) in French or Spanish. Additional exam requirements/recommendations for international students: required—TOEFL (minimum score 79 iBT) or IELTS (minimum score 6.5). Electronic applications accepted. *Expenses:* Tuition, state resident: full-time $6583.20; part-time $274.30 per credit hour. Tuition, nonresident: full-time $21,242; part-time $885.10 per credit hour. *International tuition:* $21,242.40 full-time. *Required fees:* $1994.20; $72.55 per credit hour. $126.50 per semester. Tuition and fees vary according to course load and degree level.

University of Oregon, Graduate School, College of Arts and Sciences, Department of Romance Languages, Program in French, Eugene, OR 97403. Offers MA. *Program availability:* Part-time. *Degree requirements:* For master's, one foreign language. *Entrance requirements:* For master's, GRE General Test, minimum GPA of 3.0. Additional exam requirements/recommendations for international students: required—TOEFL.

University of Ottawa, Faculty of Graduate and Postdoctoral Studies, Faculty of Arts, Department of Lettres Françaises, Ottawa, ON K1N 6N5, Canada. Offers MA, PhD. *Degree requirements:* For master's, thesis or alternative; for doctorate, thesis/dissertation, oral exam. *Entrance requirements:* For master's, honors degree or equivalent, minimum B average; for doctorate, master's degree, minimum B+ average. Electronic applications accepted.

University of Pennsylvania, School of Arts and Sciences, Graduate Group in Romance Languages, Philadelphia, PA 19104. Offers French (AM, PhD); Italian (AM, PhD); Spanish (AM, PhD). *Faculty:* 65 full-time (29 women), 8 part-time/adjunct (3 women). *Students:* 60 full-time (31 women); includes 7 minority (1 Asian, non-Hispanic/Latino; 5 Hispanic/Latino; 1 Two or more races, non-Hispanic/Latino), 37 international. Average age 32. 46 applicants, 37% accepted, 8 enrolled. In 2019, 10 master's, 4 doctorates awarded. Terminal master's awarded for partial completion of doctoral program. Application fee: $90.
Website: http://www.sas.upenn.edu/graduate-division

University of Pittsburgh, Kenneth P. Dietrich School of Arts and Sciences, Department of French and Italian Languages and Literatures, Pittsburgh, PA 15260. Offers French (MA, PhD), including film studies (PhD), French (MA), Romance languages and literatures (PhD); Italian (MA). *Program availability:* Part-time. *Faculty:* 8 full-time (3 women). *Students:* 16 full-time (6 women); includes 3 minority (2 Black or African American, non-Hispanic/Latino; 1 Asian, non-Hispanic/Latino). Average age 29. 18 applicants, 22% accepted, 3 enrolled. In 2019, 2 master's, 1 doctorate awarded. Terminal master's awarded for partial completion of doctoral program. *Degree requirements:* For master's, one foreign language, comprehensive exam; for doctorate, one foreign language, comprehensive exam, thesis/dissertation. *Entrance requirements:* For doctorate, application must be completed through Apply Yourself; 3 letters of recommendation; unofficial transcripts of all post-secondary academic work, and official translations if these are not in English; personal statement (1-3 pages single-spaced) written in English outlining goals and reasons for pursuing graduate education in French. Additional exam requirements/recommendations for international students: required—TOEFL (minimum score 90 iBT) or IELTS (minimum score 7). *Application deadline:* For fall admission, 1/10 priority date for domestic and international students. Application fee: $50. Electronic applications accepted. *Financial support:* In 2019–20, 88 students received support, including 2 fellowships with full tuition reimbursements available (averaging $23,690 per year), 8 teaching assistantships with full tuition reimbursements available (averaging $20,250 per year); scholarships/grants, health care benefits, tuition waivers (full), and unspecified assistantships also available. Financial award application deadline: 1/10. *Unit head:* Dr. Todd Reeser, Department Chair, 412-624-6258, E-mail: reeser@pitt.edu. *Application contact:* Keanna Cash, Graduate Administrator, 412-624-5227, Fax: 412-624-6263, E-mail: kec176@pitt.edu.
Website: http://frenchanditalian.pitt.edu

University of Regina, Faculty of Graduate Studies and Research, Faculty of Arts, Department of French, Regina, SK S4S 0A2, Canada. Offers MA. *Program availability:* Part-time. *Faculty:* 5 full-time (0 women), 4 part-time/adjunct (3 women). *Students:* 13 full-time (9 women), 2 part-time (1 woman). Average age 30. 17 applicants, 82% accepted. In 2019, 1 master's awarded. *Degree requirements:* For master's, thesis (for some programs). *Entrance requirements:* For master's, post secondary transcript, 2 letter of recommendations. Additional exam requirements/recommendations for international students: required—TOEFL (minimum score 580 paper-based; 80 iBT), IELTS (minimum score 6.5), PTE (minimum score 59), CAEL, MELAB, CANTEST and Uof R ESL. Application fee: $100. Electronic applications accepted. *Expenses:* *Tuition:* Full-time $6684 Canadian dollars. *Required fees:* $100 Canadian dollars; $3351.45 Canadian dollars per trimester. $1117.15 Canadian dollars per semester. Tuition and fees vary according to course level, course load, degree level and program. *Financial support:* In 2019–20, 21 students received support, including 7 fellowships, 2 teaching assistantships; research assistantships, career-related internships or fieldwork, Federal Work-Study, scholarships/grants, unspecified assistantships, and travel award and Graduate Scholarship Base funds also available. Support available to part-time students. Financial award application deadline: 9/30. *Unit head:* Dr. Emmanuel Aito, Director, 306-337-2576, Fax: 306-585-4827, E-mail: emmanuel.aito@uregina.ca. *Application contact:* Dr. Andre Magnan, Graduate Coordinator/Advisor, 306-585-4863, E-mail: Andre.Magnan@uregina.ca.
Website: http://www.uregina.ca/arts/french

University of Saskatchewan, College of Graduate and Postdoctoral Studies, College of Arts and Science, Department of Languages, Literatures, and Cultural Studies, Saskatoon, SK S7N 5A2, Canada. Offers French (MA). *Degree requirements:* For master's, 2 foreign languages, thesis. *Entrance requirements:* Additional exam requirements/recommendations for international students: required—TOEFL (minimum score 80 iBT); recommended—IELTS (minimum score 6.5). Electronic applications accepted.

University of South Africa, College of Human Sciences, Pretoria, South Africa. Offers adult education (M Ed); African languages (MA, PhD); African politics (MA, PhD); Afrikaans (MA, PhD); ancient history (MA, PhD); ancient Near Eastern studies (MA, PhD); anthropology (MA, PhD); applied linguistics (MA); Arabic (MA, PhD); archaeology (MA); art history (MA); Biblical archaeology (MA); Biblical studies (M Th, D Th, PhD); Christian spirituality (M Th, D Th); church history (M Th, D Th); classical studies (MA, PhD); clinical psychology (MA); communication (MA, PhD); comparative education (M Ed, Ed D); consulting psychology (D Admin, D Com, PhD); curriculum studies (M Ed, Ed D); development studies (M Admin, MA, D Admin, PhD); didactics (M Ed, Ed D); education (M Tech); education management (M Ed, Ed D); educational psychology (M Ed); English (MA); environmental education (M Ed); French (MA, PhD); German (MA, PhD); Greek (MA); guidance and counseling (M Ed); health studies (MA, PhD), including health sciences education (MA), health services management (MA), medical and surgical nursing science (critical care general) (MA), midwifery and neonatal nursing science (MA), trauma and emergency care (MA); history (MA, PhD); history of education (Ed D); inclusive education (M Ed, Ed D); information and communications technology policy and regulation (MA); information science (MA, MIS, PhD); international politics (MA, PhD); Islamic studies (MA, PhD); Italian (MA, PhD); Judaica (MA, PhD); linguistics (MA, PhD); mathematical education (M Ed); mathematics education (MA); missiology (M Th, D Th); modern Hebrew (MA, PhD); musicology (MA, MMus, D Mus, PhD); natural science education (M Ed); New Testament (M Th, D Th); Old Testament (D Th); pastoral therapy (M Th, D Th); philosophy (MA); philosophy of education (M Ed, Ed D); politics (MA, PhD); Portuguese (MA, PhD); practical theology (M Th, D Th); psychology (MA, MS, PhD); psychology of education (M Ed, Ed D); public health (MA); religious studies (MA, D Th, PhD); Romance languages (MA); Russian (MA, PhD); Semitic languages (MA, PhD); social behavior studies in HIV/AIDS (MA); social science (mental health) (MA); social science in development studies (MA); social science in psychology (MA); social science in social work (MA); social science in sociology (MA); social work (MSW, DSW, PhD); socio-education (M Ed, Ed D); sociolinguistics (MA); sociology (MA, PhD); Spanish (MA, PhD); systematic theology (M Th, D Th); TESOL (teaching English to speakers of other languages) (MA); theological ethics (M Th, D Th); theory of literature (MA, PhD); urban ministries (D Th); urban ministry (M Th).

French

University of South Carolina, The Graduate School, College of Arts and Sciences, Department of Languages, Literatures, and Cultures, Columbia, SC 29208. Offers comparative literature (MA, PhD); foreign languages (MAT), including French, German, Spanish; French (MA); German (MA); Spanish (MA). *Program availability:* Part-time. *Degree requirements:* For master's, one foreign language, comprehensive exam, thesis optional; for doctorate, 2 foreign languages, comprehensive exam, thesis/dissertation. *Entrance requirements:* For master's and doctorate, GRE General Test, writing sample. Additional exam requirements/recommendations for international students: required—TOEFL (minimum score 75 iBT). Electronic applications accepted.

The University of Tennessee, Graduate School, College of Arts and Sciences, Department of Modern Foreign Languages and Literatures, Program in French, Knoxville, TN 37996. Offers MA. *Degree requirements:* For master's, one foreign language, thesis or alternative. *Entrance requirements:* For master's, minimum GPA of 2.7. Additional exam requirements/recommendations for international students: required—TOEFL. Electronic applications accepted.

The University of Tennessee, Graduate School, College of Arts and Sciences, Department of Modern Foreign Languages and Literatures, Program in Modern Foreign Languages, Knoxville, TN 37996. Offers applied linguistics (PhD); French (PhD); German (PhD); Italian (PhD); Portuguese (PhD); Russian (PhD); Spanish (PhD). *Degree requirements:* For doctorate, 2 foreign languages, thesis/dissertation. *Entrance requirements:* For doctorate, minimum GPA of 2.7. Additional exam requirements/recommendations for international students: required—TOEFL. Electronic applications accepted.

The University of Texas at Arlington, Graduate School, College of Liberal Arts, Department of Modern Languages, Arlington, TX 76019. Offers French (MA); Spanish (MA). *Program availability:* Part-time, evening/weekend. *Degree requirements:* For master's, 2 foreign languages, comprehensive exam, thesis optional. *Entrance requirements:* For master's, GRE General Test, minimum GPA of 3.0, 3 letters of recommendation. Additional exam requirements/recommendations for international students: required—TOEFL (minimum score 550 paper-based).

The University of Texas at Austin, Graduate School, College of Liberal Arts, Department of French and Italian, Austin, TX 78712-1111. Offers French linguistics (MA, PhD); French studies (MA, PhD); Italian studies (MA, PhD); Romance linguistics (PhD). *Program availability:* Part-time. *Degree requirements:* For master's, one foreign language, thesis; for doctorate, 2 foreign languages, thesis/dissertation. *Entrance requirements:* For master's, GRE General Test, minimum GPA of 3.0, bachelor's degree in French or equivalent; for doctorate, GRE General Test, minimum GPA of 3.0, master's degree in French. Additional exam requirements/recommendations for international students: required—TOEFL. Electronic applications accepted.

The University of Toledo, College of Graduate Studies, College of Languages, Literature and Social Sciences, Department of Foreign Languages, Toledo, OH 43606-3390. Offers French (MA); German (MA); Spanish (MA). *Program availability:* Part-time. *Degree requirements:* For master's, one foreign language, comprehensive exam, comprehensive reading exam in 1 additional foreign language. *Entrance requirements:* For master's, minimum cumulative point-hour ratio of 2.7 for all previous academic work. Additional exam requirements/recommendations for international students: required—TOEFL (minimum score 550 paper-based; 80 iBT). Electronic applications accepted.

University of Toronto, School of Graduate Studies, Faculty of Arts and Science, Department of French, Toronto, ON M5S 1A1, Canada. Offers French language and literature (MA, PhD). *Program availability:* Part-time. *Degree requirements:* For master's, research essay; for doctorate, one foreign language, thesis/dissertation, field exam. *Entrance requirements:* For master's, 2 letters of reference, writing sample, minimum B+ average overall and in French, undergraduate major in French; for doctorate, 7 courses in French language and literature, minimum A- average, writing sample. Additional exam requirements/recommendations for international students: required—TOEFL (minimum score 580 paper-based; 93 iBT), TWE (minimum score 5). Electronic applications accepted.

University of Utah, Graduate School, College of Humanities, Department of World Languages and Cultures, Salt Lake City, UT 84112. Offers comparative literary and cultural studies (MA, PhD); French (MA); Spanish (MA, MALP); world languages (MA). *Program availability:* Part-time. *Faculty:* 22 full-time (14 women), 2 part-time/adjunct (1 woman). *Students:* 20 full-time (13 women), 5 part-time (3 women); includes 4 minority (all Hispanic/Latino), 8 international. Average age 33. 19 applicants, 68% accepted, 11 enrolled. In 2019, 12 master's, 1 doctorate awarded. Terminal master's awarded for partial completion of doctoral program. *Degree requirements:* For master's, one foreign language, comprehensive exam (for some programs), thesis (for some programs); for doctorate, one foreign language, comprehensive exam, thesis/dissertation. *Entrance requirements:* For master's, bachelor's degree from regionally-accredited college or university with minimum undergraduate overall GPA of 3.0; for doctorate, B.A. degree, B.A. degree. Additional exam requirements/recommendations for international students: required—TOEFL (minimum score 80 paper-based; 80 iBT), IELTS (minimum score 6.5). *Application deadline:* For fall admission, 1/15 priority date for domestic students, 12/15 priority date for international students. Application fee: $50 ($65 for international students). Electronic applications accepted. *Expenses:* Tuition, state resident: full-time $7085; part-time $272.51 per credit hour. Tuition, nonresident: full-time $24,937; part-time $959.12 per credit hour. *Required fees:* $880.52; $880.52 per semester. Tuition and fees vary according to degree level, program and student level. *Financial support:* In 2019–20, 21 students received support, including 21 teaching assistantships with full tuition reimbursements available (averaging $16,095 per year). Financial award application deadline: 1/15; financial award applicants required to submit CSS PROFILE or FAFSA. *Unit head:* Margaret Toscano, Associate Professor of Classics, 801-581-4786, E-mail: margaret.toscano@utah.edu. *Application contact:* Olivia Rose Davis, Graduate Academic Advisor, 801-581-7748, Fax: 801-581-7581, E-mail: olivia.davis@utah.edu.
Website: http://languages.utah.edu/

University of Victoria, Faculty of Graduate Studies, Faculty of Humanities, Department of French, Victoria, BC V8W 2Y2, Canada. Offers literature (MA); teaching emphasis (MA). *Program availability:* Part-time, evening/weekend. *Degree requirements:* For master's, 2 foreign languages, thesis optional. *Entrance requirements:* For master's, BA in French. Additional exam requirements/recommendations for international students: required—TOEFL (minimum score 575 paper-based), IELTS (minimum score 7). Electronic applications accepted.

University of Virginia, College and Graduate School of Arts and Sciences, Department of French, Charlottesville, VA 22903. Offers MA, PhD. *Degree requirements:* For master's, one foreign language, comprehensive exam; for doctorate, one foreign language, comprehensive exam, thesis/dissertation. *Entrance requirements:* For master's and doctorate, GRE General Test, minimum GPA of 3.0 in major and overall; 2 letters of recommendation; writing sample. Additional exam requirements/recommendations for international students: required—TOEFL (minimum score 600 paper-based; 90 iBT), IELTS (minimum score 7). Electronic applications accepted.

University of Washington, Graduate School, College of Arts and Sciences, Division of French and Italian Studies, Seattle, WA 98195. Offers French (MA, PhD); Italian (MA). Terminal master's awarded for partial completion of doctoral program. *Degree requirements:* For master's, 2 foreign languages, exam; for doctorate, 3 foreign languages, thesis/dissertation, exam. *Entrance requirements:* For master's and doctorate, GRE General Test, minimum GPA of 3.0. Additional exam requirements/recommendations for international students: required—TOEFL. Electronic applications accepted.

University of Waterloo, Graduate Studies and Postdoctoral Affairs, Faculty of Arts, Department of French Studies, Waterloo, ON N2L 3G1, Canada. Offers French (MA, PhD). *Program availability:* Part-time. *Entrance requirements:* For master's, honors degree, minimum B average, course work and assignments in French, resume. Additional exam requirements/recommendations for international students: required—TOEFL, IELTS. Electronic applications accepted.

The University of Western Ontario, School of Graduate and Postdoctoral Studies, Faculty of Arts and Humanities, Department of French Studies, London, ON N6A 3K7, Canada. Offers MA, PhD. *Degree requirements:* For master's, thesis or alternative; for doctorate, one foreign language, thesis/dissertation. *Entrance requirements:* For master's, minimum B average, honors degree, 2 years of teaching experience (MAT); for doctorate, MA or equivalent, minimum B average in French. Additional exam requirements/recommendations for international students: required—TOEFL. Electronic applications accepted.

University of Wisconsin–Madison, Graduate School, College of Letters and Science, Department of French and Italian, Program in French, Madison, WI 53706-1380. Offers MA, PhD. *Program availability:* Part-time. *Degree requirements:* For master's, one foreign language; for doctorate, one foreign language, thesis/dissertation. *Entrance requirements:* For master's and doctorate, GRE. Electronic applications accepted.

University of Wisconsin–Madison, Graduate School, College of Letters and Science, Department of French and Italian, Program in French Studies, Madison, WI 53706-1380. Offers MFS, Certificate. *Program availability:* Part-time. *Degree requirements:* For master's, one foreign language, thesis, internship; for Certificate, one foreign language, internship. *Entrance requirements:* For master's, GRE. Electronic applications accepted.

University of Wisconsin–Milwaukee, Graduate School, College of Letters and Science, Department of Foreign Languages and Literature, Milwaukee, WI 53201-0413. Offers foreign languages and literature (MA), including classic Greek, classics, comparative literature, French/Francophone language, literature, and culture, German language, literature, and culture, interpreting, Latin, linguistics, Spanish language, literature, and culture, translation; interpreting (Graduate Certificate); language, literature, and translation (MA, MALLT); translation (Graduate Certificate). *Program availability:* Part-time. *Degree requirements:* For master's, 2 foreign languages, thesis or alternative. *Entrance requirements:* Additional exam requirements/recommendations for international students: required—TOEFL (minimum score 550 paper-based; 79 iBT), IELTS (minimum score 6.5). Electronic applications accepted.

University of Wyoming, College of Arts and Sciences, Department of Modern and Classical Languages, Program in French, Laramie, WY 82071. Offers MA. *Program availability:* Part-time. *Degree requirements:* For master's, one foreign language, thesis or alternative. *Entrance requirements:* For master's, GRE General Test, minimum GPA of 3.0.

Vanderbilt University, Department of Frech, Nashville, TN 37240-1001. Offers French (MA, MAT, PhD). *Faculty:* 14 full-time (9 women). *Students:* 12 full-time (7 women); includes 2 minority (1 Hispanic/Latino; 1 Two or more races, non-Hispanic/Latino), 1 international. Average age 29. 15 applicants, 13% accepted, 1 enrolled. In 2019, 2 master's, 1 doctorate awarded. Terminal master's awarded for partial completion of doctoral program. *Degree requirements:* For master's, one foreign language, comprehensive exam; for doctorate, 2 foreign languages, comprehensive exam, thesis/dissertation, final and qualifying exams. *Entrance requirements:* For master's and doctorate, GRE General Test. Additional exam requirements/recommendations for international students: required—TOEFL (minimum score 570 paper-based; 88 iBT). *Application deadline:* For fall admission, 1/15 for domestic and international students. Electronic applications accepted. *Expenses: Tuition:* Full-time $51,018; part-time $2087 per hour. *Required fees:* $542. Tuition and fees vary according to program. *Financial support:* Fellowships, teaching assistantships, career-related internships or fieldwork, Federal Work-Study, institutionally sponsored loans, scholarships/grants, and health care benefits available. Financial award application deadline: 1/15; financial award applicants required to submit CSS PROFILE or FAFSA. *Unit head:* Dr. Lynn Ramey, Chair, 615-322-6900, Fax: 615-343-6909, E-mail: lynn.ramey@vanderbilt.edu. *Application contact:* Nathalie Debrauwere-Miller, Director of Graduate Studies, 615-322-6900, Fax: 615-343-6909, E-mail: n.debrau@vanderbilt.edu.
Website: http://as.vanderbilt.edu/french-italian/

Washington University in St. Louis, The Graduate School, Department of Romance Languages and Literatures, Program in French, St. Louis, MO 63130-4899. Offers French and comparative literature (PhD); French language and literature (PhD). Terminal master's awarded for partial completion of doctoral program. *Degree requirements:* For doctorate, thesis/dissertation. *Entrance requirements:* For doctorate, GRE General Test. Additional exam requirements/recommendations for international students: required—TOEFL. Electronic applications accepted.

Wayne State University, College of Liberal Arts and Sciences, Department of Classical and Modern Languages, Literatures, and Cultures, Detroit, MI 48202. Offers classics (MA), including ancient Greek and Latin, ancient studies, classics, Latin; German (MA); language learning (MALL), including Arabic (MA, MALL), French (MA, MALL, PhD), German (MALL, PhD), Italian (MA, MALL), Spanish (MA, MALL, PhD); modern languages (PhD), including French (MA, MALL, PhD), German (MALL, PhD), Spanish (MA, MALL, PhD); Near Eastern languages (MA), including Arabic (MA, MALL), Hebrew; Romance languages (MA), including French (MA, MALL, PhD), Italian (MA, MALL), Spanish (MA, MALL, PhD). *Faculty:* 20. *Students:* 30 full-time (22 women), 15 part-time (9 women); includes 11 minority (4 Black or African American, non-Hispanic/Latino; 1 American Indian or Alaska Native, non-Hispanic/Latino; 2 Asian, non-Hispanic/Latino; 3 Hispanic/Latino; 1 Two or more races, non-Hispanic/Latino), 2 international. Average age 40. 32 applicants, 34% accepted, 9 enrolled. In 2019, 8 master's, 1 doctorate awarded. *Degree requirements:* For master's, variable foreign language requirement, comprehensive exam (for some programs), thesis (for some programs); for doctorate, one foreign language, comprehensive exam, thesis/dissertation. *Entrance requirements:* Additional exam requirements/recommendations for international students: required—TOEFL (minimum score 550 paper-based; 79 iBT), TWE (minimum score 5.5), Michigan English Language Assessment Battery (minimum score 85); recommended—IELTS (minimum score 6.5). Application fee: $50. Electronic applications accepted. *Expenses: Tuition:* Full-time $34,567. *Financial support:* In 2019–20, 22 students received support, including 1 fellowship with tuition reimbursement available (averaging $20,000 per year), 15 teaching assistantships with tuition reimbursements available (averaging $20,015 per year); research assistantships, scholarships/grants, health care benefits, and unspecified assistantships also available. Financial award applicants required to submit FAFSA. *Unit head:* Dr. Vanessa DEGifis, DR., Department Chair, 313-577-6244, Fax: 313-577-6243, E-mail: vdegifis@wayne.edu. *Application contact:* Terrie Pickering,

Academic Services Officer, 313 577 3003, E-mail: t.pickering@wayne.edu.
Website: http://clas.wayne.edu/languages/

Western Kentucky University, Graduate School, Potter College of Arts and Letters, Department of Modern Languages, Bowling Green, KY 42101. Offers French (MA Ed); German (MA Ed); Spanish (MA Ed).

Yale University, Graduate School of Arts and Sciences, Department of French, New Haven, CT 06520. Offers M Phil, MA, PhD. *Degree requirements:* For doctorate, 3 foreign languages, thesis/dissertation. *Entrance requirements:* For doctorate, GRE General Test.

York University, Faculty of Graduate Studies, Glendon Campus, Program in French Studies, Toronto, ON M3J 1P3, Canada. Offers MA, PhD. *Degree requirements:* For master's, thesis or alternative. Electronic applications accepted.

German

Arizona State University at Tempe, College of Liberal Arts and Sciences, School of International Letters and Cultures, Program in German, Tempe, AZ 85287-0202. Offers comparative literature (MA); language and culture (MA); literature (MA). *Degree requirements:* For master's, thesis, applied pedagogical project, or paper portfolio consisting of 2 seminar papers; interactive Program of Study (iPOS) submitted no later than beginning of third semester of study or before completing 50 percent of coursework. *Entrance requirements:* For master's, minimum GPA of 3.0 in the last two years of work leading to the bachelor's degree, personal statement, writing sample (preferably written in German), 3 letters of recommendation. Additional exam requirements/recommendations for international students: required—TOEFL (minimum score 550 paper-based; 83 iBT), IELTS (minimum score 6.5). Electronic applications accepted.

Bowling Green State University, Graduate College, College of Arts and Sciences, Department of German, Russian, and East Asian Languages, Bowling Green, OH 43403. Offers German (MA); MA/MA. *Program availability:* Part-time. *Degree requirements:* For master's, one foreign language, thesis or alternative. *Entrance requirements:* For master's, GRE General Test. Additional exam requirements/recommendations for international students: required—TOEFL. Electronic applications accepted.

Brown University, Graduate School, Department of German Studies, Providence, RI 02912. Offers PhD. *Degree requirements:* For doctorate, 2 foreign languages, thesis/dissertation, preliminary exam. *Entrance requirements:* For doctorate, GRE General Test.

California State University, Long Beach, Graduate Studies, College of Liberal Arts, Department of Romance, German, Russian Languages and Literatures, Program in German, Long Beach, CA 90840. Offers MA. *Program availability:* Part-time. *Degree requirements:* For master's, one foreign language, comprehensive exam or thesis. Electronic applications accepted.

Central Connecticut State University, School of Graduate Studies, College of Liberal Arts and Social Sciences, Department of Modern Languages, New Britain, CT 06050-4010. Offers modern language (MA, Certificate), including French, German (Certificate), Italian, Spanish (MA); Spanish (MS, Certificate). *Program availability:* Part-time, evening/weekend. *Degree requirements:* For master's, one foreign language, comprehensive exam, thesis or alternative; for Certificate, qualifying exam. *Entrance requirements:* For master's, minimum undergraduate GPA of 2.7, 24 credits of undergraduate courses in each language in which graduate work will be undertaken. Additional exam requirements/recommendations for international students: required—TOEFL (minimum score 550 paper-based; 79 iBT); recommended—IELTS (minimum score 6.5). Electronic applications accepted.

Columbia University, Graduate School of Arts and Sciences, New York, NY 10027. Offers African-American studies (MA); American studies (MA); anthropology (MA, PhD); art history and archaeology (MA, PhD); astronomy (PhD); biological sciences (PhD); biotechnology (MA); chemical physics (PhD); chemistry (PhD); classical studies (MA, PhD); classics (MA, PhD); climate and society (MA); conservation biology (MA); earth and environmental sciences (PhD); East Asia: regional studies (MA); East Asian languages and cultures (MA, PhD); ecology, evolution and environmental biology (MA), including conservation biology; ecology, evolution, and environmental biology (PhD), including ecology and evolutionary biology, evolutionary primatology; economics (MA, PhD); English and comparative literature (MA, PhD); French and Romance philology (MA, PhD); Germanic languages (MA, PhD); global French studies (MA); global thought (MA); Hispanic cultural studies (MA); history (PhD); history and literature (MA); human rights studies (MA); Islamic studies (MA); Italian (MA, PhD); Japanese pedagogy (MA); Jewish studies (MA); Latin America and the Caribbean: regional studies (MA); Latin American and Iberian cultures (PhD); mathematics (MA, PhD), including finance (MA); medieval and Renaissance studies (MA); Middle Eastern, South Asian, and African studies (MA, PhD); modern art: critical and curatorial studies (MA); modern European studies (MA); museum anthropology (MA); music (DMA, PhD); oral history (MA); philosophical foundations of physics (MA); philosophy (MA, PhD); physics (PhD); political science (MA, PhD); psychology (PhD); quantitative methods in the social sciences (MA); religion (MA, PhD); Russia, Eurasia and East Europe: regional studies (MA); Russian translation (MA); Slavic cultures (MA); Slavic languages (MA, PhD); sociology (MA, PhD); South Asian studies (MA); statistics (MA, PhD); theatre (PhD). *Program availability:* Part-time. *Students:* 3,506 full-time (1,844 women), 208 part-time (121 women); includes 864 minority (110 Black or African American, non-Hispanic/Latino; 5 American Indian or Alaska Native, non-Hispanic/Latino; 416 Asian, non-Hispanic/Latino; 147 Hispanic/Latino; 6 Native Hawaiian or other Pacific Islander, non-Hispanic/Latino; 180 Two or more races, non-Hispanic/Latino), 2,065 international. 14,545 applicants, 25% accepted, 1,429 enrolled. In 2019, 1,262 master's, 363 doctorates awarded. Terminal master's awarded for partial completion of doctoral program. *Degree requirements:* For master's, variable foreign language requirement, comprehensive exam (for some programs), thesis (for some programs); for doctorate, variable foreign language requirement, comprehensive exam (for some programs), thesis/dissertation. *Entrance requirements:* For master's and doctorate, GRE General Test, GRE Subject Test (for some programs). Additional exam requirements/recommendations for international students: required—TOEFL (minimum score 600 paper-based; 100 iBT), IELTS (minimum score 7.5). Application fee: $115. Electronic applications accepted. *Expenses: Tuition:* Full-time $47,600; part-time $1880 per credit. One-time fee: $105. *Financial support:* Fellowships, research assistantships, teaching assistantships, career-related internships or fieldwork, Federal Work-Study, institutionally sponsored loans, scholarships/grants, traineeships, health care benefits, tuition waivers, and unspecified assistantships available. Support available to part-time students. Financial award application deadline: 12/15. *Unit head:* Dr. Carlos J. Alonso, Dean of the Graduate School of Arts and Sciences and Vice President for Graduate Education, 212-854-2861, E-mail: gsas-dean@columbia.edu. *Application contact:* GSAS Office of Admissions, 212-854-6729, E-mail: gsas-admissions@columbia.edu.
Website: http://gsas.columbia.edu/

Cornell University, Graduate School, Graduate Fields of Arts and Sciences, Field of Germanic Studies, Ithaca, NY 14853. Offers German area studies (MA, PhD); German intellectual history (MA, PhD); Germanic linguistics (MA, PhD); Germanic literature (MA, PhD); old Norse (MA, PhD). Terminal master's awarded for partial completion of doctoral program. *Degree requirements:* For master's, one foreign language, thesis; for doctorate, 2 foreign languages, comprehensive exam, thesis/dissertation. *Entrance requirements:* For master's and doctorate, GRE General Test, fluency in German, writing sample, 2 letters of recommendation. Additional exam requirements/recommendations for international students: required—TOEFL (minimum score 550 paper-based; 77 iBT). Electronic applications accepted.

Cornell University, Graduate School, Graduate Fields of Arts and Sciences, Field of Linguistics, Ithaca, NY 14853. Offers applied linguistics (MA, PhD); East Asian linguistics (MA, PhD); English linguistics (MA, PhD); general linguistics (MA, PhD); Germanic linguistics (MA, PhD); Indo-European linguistics (MA, PhD); phonetics (MA, PhD); phonological theory (MA, PhD); Romance linguistics (MA, PhD); second language acquisition (MA, PhD); semantics (MA, PhD); Slavic linguistics (MA, PhD); sociolinguistics (MA, PhD); South Asian linguistics (MA, PhD); Southeast Asian linguistics (MA, PhD); syntactic theory (MA, PhD). Terminal master's awarded for partial completion of doctoral program. *Degree requirements:* For master's, one foreign language, thesis; for doctorate, one foreign language, comprehensive exam, thesis/dissertation. *Entrance requirements:* For master's and doctorate, GRE General Test, 2 letters of recommendation. Additional exam requirements/recommendations for international students: required—TOEFL (minimum score 600 paper-based; 77 iBT). Electronic applications accepted.

Dalhousie University, Faculty of Arts and Social Sciences, Department of German, Halifax, NS B3H 4R2, Canada. Offers MA. *Entrance requirements:* Additional exam requirements/recommendations for international students: required—TOEFL, IELTS, CANTEST, CAEL, or Michigan English Language Assessment Battery. Electronic applications accepted.

DePaul University, College of Liberal Arts and Social Sciences, Chicago, IL 60614. Offers Arabic (MA); Chinese (MA); critical ethnic studies (MA); English (MA); French (MA); German (MA); history (MA); interdisciplinary studies (MA, MS); international public service (MS); international studies (MA); Italian (MA); Japanese (MA); liberal studies (MA); nonprofit management (MNM); public administration (MPA); public health (MPH); public policy (MPP); public service management (MS); refugee and forced migration studies (MS); social work (MSW); sociology (MA); Spanish (MA); sustainable urban development (MA); women's and gender studies (MA); writing and publishing (MA); writing, rhetoric and discourse (MA); MA/PhD. *Accreditation:* CEPH. *Program availability:* Part-time, evening/weekend, online learning. Terminal master's awarded for partial completion of doctoral program. *Degree requirements:* For master's, variable foreign language requirement, comprehensive exam (for some programs), thesis (for some programs). Electronic applications accepted.

Duke University, Graduate School, Carolina-Duke Graduate Program in German Studies, Durham, NC 27708-0256. Offers PhD. *Program availability:* Part-time. *Degree requirements:* For doctorate, thesis/dissertation. *Entrance requirements:* For doctorate, GRE General Test, writing sample. Additional exam requirements/recommendations for international students: required—TOEFL (minimum score 577 paper-based; 90 iBT) or IELTS (minimum score 7). Electronic applications accepted.

Florida State University, The Graduate School, Department of Anthropology, Department of Modern Languages and Linguistics, Program in German, Tallahassee, FL 32306. Offers MA. *Faculty:* 4 full-time (3 women), 1 part-time/adjunct. *Students:* 4 full-time (1 woman), 1 (woman) part-time; includes 3 minority (1 Black or African American, non-Hispanic/Latino; 1 Asian, non-Hispanic/Latino; 1 Two or more races, non-Hispanic/Latino). In 2019, 2 master's awarded. *Degree requirements:* For master's, thesis optional. *Entrance requirements:* For master's, GRE General Test, minimum GPA of 3.0. Additional exam requirements/recommendations for international students: required—TOEFL (minimum score 550 paper-based; 80 iBT). *Application deadline:* For fall admission, 1/15 priority date for domestic and international students. Electronic applications accepted. *Financial support:* In 2019–20, 4 teaching assistantships with partial tuition reimbursements (averaging $14,500 per year) were awarded; research assistantships also available. Financial award application deadline: 1/15; financial award applicants required to submit FAFSA. *Unit head:* Dr. Christian Weber, Divisional Coordinator, 850-644-8194, Fax: 850-644-0524, E-mail: cweber@fsu.edu. *Application contact:* Wendy E. Pigott, Graduate Academic Coordinator, 850-644-8397, Fax: 850-644-0524, E-mail: wpigott@fsu.edu.
Website: http://www.modlang.fsu.edu/Programs2/German/Graduate-program

Georgetown University, Graduate School of Arts and Sciences, Department of German, Washington, DC 20057. Offers MA, PhD, MA/PhD. *Degree requirements:* For master's, 2 foreign languages, research project; for doctorate, 3 foreign languages, thesis/dissertation. *Entrance requirements:* For master's, GRE General Test. Additional exam requirements/recommendations for international students: required—TOEFL.

Georgetown University, Graduate School of Arts and Sciences, Walsh School of Foreign Service, BMW Center for German and European Studies, Washington, DC 20057. Offers MA, MA/JD, MA/PhD. *Degree requirements:* For master's, 2 foreign languages, comprehensive exam. *Entrance requirements:* For master's, GRE General Test. Additional exam requirements/recommendations for international students: required—TOEFL. Electronic applications accepted.

Georgia State University, College of Arts and Sciences, Department of World Languages and Cultures, Program in Translation and Interpretation, Atlanta, GA 30302-3083. Offers interpretation (Certificate), including Spanish; translation (Certificate), including French, German, Spanish. *Program availability:* Part-time. *Entrance requirements:* For degree, entrance examination involving translating one passage from English to the target language and one passage from the target language to English, 3 letters of recommendation, resume/curriculum vitae, official transcripts. Additional exam requirements/recommendations for international students: required—TOEFL (minimum

score 79 iBT). Application fee: $50. Electronic applications accepted. *Expenses: Tuition, area resident:* Full-time $7164; part-time $398 per credit hour. Tuition, state resident: full-time $7164; part-time $398 per credit hour. Tuition, nonresident: full-time $22,662; part-time $1259 per credit hour. *International tuition:* $22,662 full-time. *Required fees:* $2128; $312 per credit hour. Tuition and fees vary according to course load and program. *Unit head:* Dr. William Nichols, Chair, 404-413-5980, Fax: 404-413-5982, E-mail: wnichols@gsu.edu. *Application contact:* Vicky Hanning, Administrative Coordinator, 404-413-5990, Fax: 404-413-5982, E-mail: vassem@gsu.edu.
Website: http://wlc.gsu.edu/home/graduate/graduate-certificate/

Harvard University, Graduate School of Arts and Sciences, Department of Germanic Languages and Literatures, Cambridge, MA 02138. Offers German (PhD); Scandinavian (PhD). Terminal master's awarded for partial completion of doctoral program. *Degree requirements:* For doctorate, 2 foreign languages, thesis/dissertation, exams. *Entrance requirements:* For doctorate, GRE General Test, German writing sample. Additional exam requirements/recommendations for international students: required—TOEFL.

Illinois State University, Graduate School, College of Arts and Sciences, Department of Foreign Languages, Literatures and Cultures, Normal, IL 61790. Offers French (MA); French and German (MA); French and Spanish (MA); German (MA); German and Spanish (MA); Spanish (MA). *Faculty:* 23 full-time (13 women), 7 part-time/adjunct (all women). *Students:* 14 full-time (7 women), 4 part-time (2 women). Average age 30. 12 applicants, 83% accepted, 6 enrolled. In 2019, 7 master's awarded. *Degree requirements:* For master's, variable foreign language requirement, comprehensive exam, 1 term of residency. *Entrance requirements:* For master's, GRE General Test, minimum GPA of 2.8 in last 60 hours of course work. *Application deadline:* Applications are processed on a rolling basis. Application fee: $50. *Expenses: Tuition, area resident:* Full-time $7956; part-time $9767 per year. Tuition, nonresident: full-time $9233; part-time $17,592 per year. *Required fees:* $1797. *Financial support:* In 2019–20, 13 teaching assistantships were awarded; tuition waivers (full) and unspecified assistantships also available. Financial award application deadline: 4/1. *Unit head:* Dr. Bruce Brningham, Department Chair, 309-438-3604. *Application contact:* Dr. Ryan Davis, Graduate Coordinator, 309-438-7759, Fax: 309-438-7912, E-mail: rdavis2@IllinoisState.edu.
Website: http://www.foreignlanguages.ilstu.edu/

Indiana University Bloomington, University Graduate School, College of Arts and Sciences, Department of Germanic Studies, Bloomington, IN 47405-7000. Offers German philology and linguistics (PhD); German studies (MA, PhD), including German (MA), German literature and culture (MA), German literature and linguistics (MA); medieval German studies (PhD); teaching German (MAT). *Degree requirements:* For master's, one foreign language, project; for doctorate, one foreign language, comprehensive exam, thesis/dissertation. *Entrance requirements:* For master's, GRE General Test, BA in German or equivalent; for doctorate, GRE General Test, MA in German or equivalent. Additional exam requirements/recommendations for international students: required—TOEFL. Electronic applications accepted.

Johns Hopkins University, Zanvyl Krieger School of Arts and Sciences, Department of German and Romance Languages and Literatures, Baltimore, MD 21218. Offers German (MA, PhD); romance languages (PhD), including French, Italian, Spanish. Terminal master's awarded for partial completion of doctoral program. *Degree requirements:* For master's, comprehensive exam; for doctorate, 2 foreign languages, comprehensive exam, thesis/dissertation. *Entrance requirements:* For doctorate, GRE General Test. Additional exam requirements/recommendations for international students: required—TOEFL (minimum score 600 paper-based; 100 iBT), IELTS. Electronic applications accepted. *Expenses:* Contact institution.

Kansas State University, Graduate School, College of Arts and Sciences, Department of Modern Languages, Manhattan, KS 66506. Offers literature (MA), including French, German, Spanish; second language acquisition (MA), including French, German, Spanish, teaching English as a foreign language. *Program availability:* Part-time, evening/weekend, blended/hybrid learning. *Degree requirements:* For master's, thesis optional. *Entrance requirements:* For master's, teaching certificate. Additional exam requirements/recommendations for international students: required—TOEFL (minimum score 550 paper-based; 83 iBT), TOEFL (minimum speaking-portion score of 26). Electronic applications accepted.

Kent State University, College of Arts and Sciences, Department of Modern and Classical Language Studies, Kent, OH 44242-0001. Offers French (MA), including applied linguistics and pedagogy, literature; German (MA), including applied linguistics and pedagogy, literature; Latin (MA), including applied linguistics and pedagogy, literature; Spanish (MA), including applied linguistics and pedagogy, literature; translation (MA), including Arabic, French, German, Japanese, Russian, Spanish; translation studies (PhD); MA/MBA. *Program availability:* Part-time, 100% online. *Faculty:* 18 full-time (11 women), 6 part-time/adjunct (3 women). *Students:* 81 full-time (49 women), 23 part-time (14 women); includes 18 minority (3 Black or African American, non-Hispanic/Latino; 3 Asian, non-Hispanic/Latino; 11 Hispanic/Latino; 1 Two or more races, non-Hispanic/Latino), 45 international. Average age 32. 115 applicants, 73% accepted, 47 enrolled. In 2019, 27 master's, 7 doctorates awarded. *Degree requirements:* For master's, variable foreign language requirement, comprehensive exam (for some programs), thesis (for some programs); for doctorate, variable foreign language requirement, comprehensive exam, thesis/dissertation. *Entrance requirements:* For master's, transcripts, goal statement, 3 letters of recommendation, CD/MP3 with a 5-10 minute oral sample of first and second languages (conversational not read from a script), Writing sample(s) in the applicant's second language, which should be accompanied by a signed declaration that the sample is original work; for doctorate, transcripts; MA in translation, a foreign language, or in any other relevant discipline with prior experience or training in translation; proficiency in a foreign language; minimum GPA of 3.5 from MA; goal statement; 3 letters of recommendation; essay or writing sample (7-10 pages) from a research paper on any aspect of translation. Additional exam requirements/recommendations for international students: required—TOEFL (minimum score 79 iBT), IELTS (minimum score 6.5), PTE (minimum score 58), Michigan English Language Assessment Battery (minimum score 77). *Application deadline:* For fall admission, 2/1 for domestic and international students. Applications are processed on a rolling basis. Application fee: $45 ($70 for international students). Electronic applications accepted. *Financial support:* Fellowships with full tuition reimbursements, teaching assistantships with full tuition reimbursements, and unspecified assistantships available. Financial award application deadline: 2/1. *Unit head:* Dr. Keiran Dunne, Professor of French Translation; Department Chair, 330-672-2150, E-mail: kdunne@kent.edu. *Application contact:* Brian James Baer, Professor of Russian Translation; Graduate Coordinator, 330-672-1813, E-mail: bbaer@kent.edu.
Website: http://www.kent.edu/mcls/

McGill University, Faculty of Graduate and Postdoctoral Studies, Faculty of Arts, Department of German Studies, Montréal, QC H3A 2T5, Canada. Offers MA, PhD.

Memorial University of Newfoundland, School of Graduate Studies, Department of German and Russian, St. John's, NL A1C 5S7, Canada. Offers German language and literature (M Phil, MA). *Program availability:* Part-time. *Degree requirements:* For master's, one foreign language, thesis (for some programs), comprehensive exam (M Phil). *Entrance requirements:* For master's, honors degree (minimum 2nd class standing). Electronic applications accepted.

Michigan State University, The Graduate School, College of Arts and Letters, Department of Linguistics and Germanic, Slavic, Asian, and African Languages, East Lansing, MI 48824. Offers German studies (MA, PhD); linguistics (MA, PhD); teaching English to speakers of other languages (MA). *Program availability:* Part-time, evening/weekend. *Entrance requirements:* For master's, GRE General Test, minimum GPA of 3.2 in last 2 undergraduate years, 2 years of college-level foreign language, 3 letters of recommendation, portfolio (German studies); for doctorate, GRE General Test, minimum graduate GPA of 3.5, 3 letters of recommendation, master's degree or sufficient graduate course work in linguistics or language of study, master's thesis or major research paper. Additional exam requirements/recommendations for international students: required—TOEFL. Electronic applications accepted.

Middlebury College, Language Schools, German School, Middlebury, VT 05753-6002. Offers MA, DML. In 2019, 4 master's awarded. *Degree requirements:* For master's, one foreign language; for doctorate, 2 foreign languages, comprehensive exam, thesis/dissertation, residence abroad, teaching experience. *Entrance requirements:* For master's, placement exam, 3 letters of recommendation, transcripts, personal statement; for doctorate, 1st and 2nd language placement exams, 3 letters of recommendation, transcripts, personal statement, MA in German. *Application deadline:* Applications are processed on a rolling basis. Application fee: $75. Electronic applications accepted. *Expenses:* Contact institution. *Financial support:* Fellowships and scholarships/grants available. Financial award application deadline: 3/9; financial award applicants required to submit FAFSA. *Unit head:* Dr. Bettina Matthias, Director, 802-443-3527, Fax: 802-443-2075, E-mail: bmatthia@middlebury.edu. *Application contact:* Christina Ellison, Coordinator, 802-443-5203, Fax: 802-443-2075, E-mail: germanschool@middlebury.edu.
Website: http://www.middlebury.edu/ls/grad_programs/german

Middle Tennessee State University, College of Graduate Studies, College of Liberal Arts, Department of Foreign Languages and Literatures, Murfreesboro, TN 37132. Offers foreign languages (MAT), including French, German, Spanish. *Program availability:* Part-time, evening/weekend, online learning. *Degree requirements:* For master's, one foreign language, comprehensive exam, thesis optional. *Entrance requirements:* For master's, GRE. Additional exam requirements/recommendations for international students: required—TOEFL (minimum score 525 paper-based; 71 iBT) or IELTS (minimum score 6). Electronic applications accepted.

Millersville University of Pennsylvania, College of Graduate Studies and Adult Learning, College of Arts, Humanities and Social Sciences, Department of Language and Culture Studies, Millersville, PA 17551-0302. Offers languages and cultures (MA). *Program availability:* Part-time. *Faculty:* 3 full-time (2 women). *Students:* 4 part-time (all women); includes 2 minority (both Hispanic/Latino). Average age 31. 1 applicant. In 2019, 4 master's awarded. *Degree requirements:* For master's, Exit requirement: exam, portfolio, or research project/presentation. *Entrance requirements:* For master's, ACTFL (OPI and WPT), 24 undergraduate credits in selected language. Additional exam requirements/recommendations for international students: required—TOEFL, IELTS (minimum score 6), PTE (minimum score 60). *Application deadline:* Applications are processed on a rolling basis. Application fee: $40. Electronic applications accepted. *Expenses: Tuition, area resident:* Part-time $516 per credit. Tuition, state resident: part-time $516 per credit. Tuition, nonresident: part-time $774 per credit. *Required fees:* $118.75 per credit. Tuition and fees vary according to course load, degree level and program. *Financial support:* Scholarships/grants and unspecified assistantships available. Financial award application deadline: 3/15; financial award applicants required to submit FAFSA. *Unit head:* Dr. Christine M. Gaudry, Chair, 717-871-7152, E-mail: Christine.Gaudry@millersville.edu. *Application contact:* Dr. Susanne Nimmrichter, Graduate Coordinator, 717-871-7153, E-mail: susanne.nimmrichter@millersville.edu.
Website: http://www.millersville.edu/languages

Millersville University of Pennsylvania, College of Graduate Studies and Adult Learning, College of Arts, Humanities and Social Sciences, Department of Language and Culture Studies: Language and Culture Studies: Spanish Option, Millersville, PA 17551-0302. Offers language and cultures (MA). *Program availability:* Part-time-only. *Students:* 4 part-time (all women); includes 2 minority (both Hispanic/Latino). Average age 31. 1 applicant. In 2019, 1 master's awarded. *Degree requirements:* For master's, Exit requirement: exam, portfolio, or research project/presentation. *Entrance requirements:* For master's, ACTFL (OPI and WPT), 24 undergraduate credits in selected language. Additional exam requirements/recommendations for international students: required—TOEFL, IELTS (minimum score 6), PTE (minimum score 60). *Application deadline:* Applications are processed on a rolling basis. Application fee: $40. Electronic applications accepted. *Expenses: Tuition, area resident:* Part-time $516 per credit. Tuition, state resident: part-time $516 per credit. Tuition, nonresident: part-time $774 per credit. *Required fees:* $118.75 per credit. Tuition and fees vary according to course load, degree level and program. *Financial support:* Scholarships/grants and unspecified assistantships available. Financial award application deadline: 3/15; financial award applicants required to submit FAFSA. *Unit head:* Dr. Christine M. Gaudry, Chair, 717-871-7156, E-mail: Christine.Gaudry@millersville.edu. *Application contact:* Dr. Susanne J. Nimmrichter, Graduate Coordinator, 717-871-7153, E-mail: Sussanne.Nimmrichter@millersville.edu.
Website: http://www.millersville.edu/languages

New York University, Graduate School of Arts and Science, Department of German, New York, NY 10012-1019. Offers German studies and critical thought (MA, PhD). *Program availability:* Part-time. Terminal master's awarded for partial completion of doctoral program. *Degree requirements:* For master's, one foreign language, thesis; for doctorate, 2 foreign languages, thesis/dissertation. *Entrance requirements:* For master's, GRE; for doctorate, GRE, sample of written work. Additional exam requirements/recommendations for international students: required—TOEFL, IELTS.

Northwestern University, The Graduate School, Judd A. and Marjorie Weinberg College of Arts and Sciences, Department of German, Evanston, IL 60208. Offers German literature and critical thought (PhD). *Degree requirements:* For doctorate, one foreign language, thesis/dissertation. *Entrance requirements:* For doctorate, GRE General Test. Additional exam requirements/recommendations for international students: required—TOEFL. Electronic applications accepted.

The Ohio State University, Graduate School, College of Arts and Sciences, Division of Arts and Humanities, Department of Germanic Languages and Literatures, Columbus, OH 43210. Offers MA, PhD. *Degree requirements:* For master's, one foreign language, thesis optional; for doctorate, 2 foreign languages, thesis/dissertation. *Entrance requirements:* For master's and doctorate, GRE General Test. Additional exam requirements/recommendations for international students: required—TOEFL (minimum score 550 paper-based; 79 iBT), Michigan English Language Assessment Battery (minimum score 82); recommended—IELTS (minimum score 7). Electronic applications accepted.

Penn State University Park, Graduate School, College of the Liberal Arts, Department of Germanic and Slavic Languages and Literatures, University Park, PA 16802. Offers German (MA, PhD).

Portland State University, Graduate Studies, College of Liberal Arts and Sciences, Department of World Languages and Literatures, Portland, OR 97207-0751. Offers French (MA); German (MA); Japanese (MA); Spanish (MA); world literature and language (MA). *Program availability:* Part-time. *Faculty:* 40 full-time (22 women), 39 part-time/adjunct (32 women). *Students:* 16 full-time (11 women), 12 part-time (6 women); includes 9 minority (2 Asian, non-Hispanic/Latino; 6 Hispanic/Latino; 1 Two or more races, non-Hispanic/Latino), 8 international. Average age 34. 14 applicants, 64% accepted, 7 enrolled. In 2019, 14 master's awarded. *Degree requirements:* For master's, variable foreign language requirement, thesis (for some programs). *Entrance requirements:* For master's, ACTFL, BA in the major language, minimum GPA of 3.0 in all coursework. Additional exam requirements/recommendations for international students: required—TOEFL (minimum score 550 paper-based; 80 iBT), IELTS (minimum score 6.5). *Application deadline:* For fall admission, 4/1 for domestic students, 3/1 for international students; for winter admission, 9/1 for domestic students, 7/1 for international students; for spring admission, 11/1 for domestic and international students. Applications are processed on a rolling basis. Application fee: $65. *Expenses: Tuition, area resident:* Full-time $13,020; part-time $6510 per year. Tuition, state resident: full-time $13,020; part-time $6510 per year. Tuition, nonresident: full-time $19,830; part-time $9915 per year. *International tuition:* $19,830 full-time. *Required fees:* $1226. One-time fee: $350. Tuition and fees vary according to course load, program and reciprocity agreements. *Financial support:* In 2019–20, 16 teaching assistantships with full and partial tuition reimbursements (averaging $16,549 per year) were awarded; research assistantships, Federal Work-Study, scholarships/grants, and unspecified assistantships also available. Support available to part-time students. Financial award application deadline: 3/1; financial award applicants required to submit FAFSA. *Unit head:* Dr. Gina Greco, Chair, 503-725-5287, E-mail: grecog@pdx.edu. *Application contact:* Kelli Martin, Graduate Admissions Specialist, 503-725-3243, E-mail: k.martin@pdx.edu.
Website: http://www.pdx.edu/wll/

Princeton University, Graduate School, Department of German, Princeton, NJ 08544-1019. Offers PhD. *Degree requirements:* For doctorate, 2 foreign languages, thesis/dissertation. *Entrance requirements:* For doctorate, GRE General Test. Additional exam requirements/recommendations for international students: required—TOEFL (minimum score 600 paper-based). Electronic applications accepted.

Purdue University, Graduate School, College of Liberal Arts, School of Languages and Cultures, West Lafayette, IN 47907. Offers French (MA, MAT), including multiple possible; German (MA, MAT), including multiple possible; Japanese pedagogy (MA), including pedagogy, SLA; Spanish (MA, MAT), including multiple possible. *Faculty:* 32 full-time (16 women), 6 part-time/adjunct (3 women). *Students:* 33 full-time (18 women), 24 part-time (16 women); includes 7 minority (1 Black or African American, non-Hispanic/Latino; 6 Hispanic/Latino), 38 international. Average age 34. 54 applicants, 41% accepted, 14 enrolled. In 2019, 9 master's awarded. Terminal master's awarded for partial completion of doctoral program. *Degree requirements:* For master's, one foreign language. *Entrance requirements:* For master's, Bachelor of Arts (or equivalent); 3 letters of recommendation; statement of purpose; speaking & writing samples. Additional exam requirements/recommendations for international students: required—TOEFL (minimum score 550 paper-based; 77 iBT); recommended—TWE. *Application deadline:* For fall admission, 12/12 for domestic and international students; for spring admission, 10/1 for domestic and international students. Applications are processed on a rolling basis. Application fee: $60 ($75 for international students). Electronic applications accepted. *Financial support:* In 2019–20, fellowships with tuition reimbursements (averaging $15,750 per year), teaching assistantships with tuition reimbursements (averaging $13,463 per year) were awarded. Support available to part-time students. Financial award applicants required to submit FAFSA. *Unit head:* Jennifer M. William, Head, 765-494-3834, E-mail: jmwilliam@purdue.edu. *Application contact:* Joni L. Hipsher, Graduate Contact, 765-494-3841, E-mail: jlhipshe@purdue.edu.
Website: http://www.cla.purdue.edu/slc/main/

Rutgers University - New Brunswick, Graduate School-New Brunswick, Program in German, Piscataway, NJ 08854-8097. Offers German (MAT, PhD); German literature (MA, PhD). *Program availability:* Part-time, evening/weekend. Terminal master's awarded for partial completion of doctoral program. *Degree requirements:* For master's, one foreign language, comprehensive exam, thesis or alternative; for doctorate, 2 foreign languages, comprehensive exam, thesis/dissertation. *Entrance requirements:* For master's and doctorate, GRE General Test. Additional exam requirements/recommendations for international students: required—TOEFL. Electronic applications accepted.

San Francisco State University, Division of Graduate Studies, College of Liberal and Creative Arts, Department of Modern Languages and Literatures, Program in German, San Francisco, CA 94132-1722. Offers MA. *Application deadline:* Applications are processed on a rolling basis. *Expenses: Tuition, area resident:* Full-time $7176; part-time $4164 per year. Tuition, state resident: full-time $7176; part-time $4164 per year. Tuition, nonresident: full-time $16,680; part-time $396 per unit. *International tuition:* $16,680 full-time. *Required fees:* $1524; $1524 per unit. $762 per semester. Tuition and fees vary according to degree level and program. *Unit head:* Dr. Llona Vandergriff, Program Coordinator, 415-338-1106, Fax: 415-338-6159, E-mail: vdgriff@sfsu.edu. *Application contact:* Dr. Llona Vandergriff, Program Coordinator, 415-338-1106, Fax: 415-338-6159, E-mail: vdgriff@sfsu.edu.
Website: http://german.sfsu.edu/

Stanford University, School of Humanities and Sciences, Department of German Studies, Stanford, CA 94305-2004. Offers MA, PhD. *Expenses: Tuition:* Full-time $52,479; part-time $34,110 per unit. *Required fees:* $672; $224 per quarter. Tuition and fees vary according to program and student level. *Unit head:* Kathryn Starkey, Chair, 978-604-5635, E-mail: starkey@stanford.edu. *Application contact:* Graduate Admissions, 866-432-7472, Fax: 650-723-8371, E-mail: gradadmissions@stanford.edu.
Website: http://www.stanford.edu/dept/german/

Tufts University, Graduate School of Arts and Sciences, Department of International Literary and Cultural Studies, Medford, MA 02155. Offers German (MA); German with teaching licensure (MA). *Program availability:* Part-time. *Degree requirements:* For master's, one foreign language, oral and written exam. *Entrance requirements:* For master's, GRE General Test. Additional exam requirements/recommendations for international students: required—TOEFL (minimum score 550 paper-based; 80 iBT), IELTS (minimum score 6.5). Electronic applications accepted. *Expenses:* Contact institution.

Université de Montréal, Faculty of Arts and Sciences, Department of Literatures and Modern Languages, Program in German Studies, Montréal, QC H3C 3J7, Canada. Offers MA. *Degree requirements:* For master's, 2 foreign languages, thesis. Electronic applications accepted.

University at Buffalo, the State University of New York, Graduate School, Graduate School of Education, Department of Learning and Instruction, Buffalo, NY 14260. Offers biology education (Ed M, Certificate); chemistry education (Ed M, Certificate); childhood education (Ed M); childhood education with bilingual extension (Ed M); college teaching (Advanced Certificate); curriculum, instruction and the science of learning (PhD); early childhood education (Ed M); early childhood education with bilingual extension (Ed M); earth science education (Ed M, Certificate); education and technology (Ed M); education studies (Ed M); educational technology and new literacies (Certificate); educational technology and new literacies (Advanced Certificate); elementary education (Ed D); English education (Ed M, Certificate); English education studies (Ed M); English for speakers of other languages (Ed M); foreign and second language education (PhD); French education (Ed M, Certificate); German education (Ed M, Certificate); gifted education (Certificate); Latin education (Ed M, Certificate); literacy education studies (Ed M); literacy specialist (Ed M); literacy teaching and learning (Certificate); mathematics education (Ed M, Certificate); music education (Ed M, Certificate); music education studies (Ed M); music learning theory (Advanced Certificate); online education (Advanced Certificate); physics education (Ed M, Certificate); science and the public (Ed M); social studies education (Ed M, Certificate); Spanish education (Ed M, Certificate); special education (PhD); teaching English to speakers of other languages (Ed M). *Program availability:* Part-time, evening/weekend, 100% online, blended/hybrid learning. *Faculty:* 26 full-time (19 women), 42 part-time/adjunct (29 women). *Students:* 227 full-time (158 women), 322 part-time (228 women); includes 85 minority (34 Black or African American, non-Hispanic/Latino; 3 American Indian or Alaska Native, non-Hispanic/Latino; 17 Asian, non-Hispanic/Latino; 23 Hispanic/Latino; 8 Two or more races, non-Hispanic/Latino), 42 international. Average age 33. 385 applicants, 61% accepted, 158 enrolled. In 2019, 100 master's, 23 doctorates, 16 other advanced degrees awarded. *Degree requirements:* For master's, comprehensive exam; for doctorate, thesis/dissertation, research analysis exam, research experience; for other advanced degree, thesis (for some programs). *Entrance requirements:* For master's, GRE or MAT for teacher preparation programs only, letters of reference; for doctorate, GRE General Test or MAT, interview, writing sample, letters of recommendation, resume. Additional exam requirements/recommendations for international students: required—TOEFL (minimum score 600 paper-based; 96 iBT), IELTS (minimum score 6.5), PTE (minimum score 55), The Graduate School of Education requires international students to submit test scores for at least one of the exams (TOEFL, IELTS, PTE). *Application deadline:* For fall admission, 2/1 priority date for domestic and international students. Applications are processed on a rolling basis. Application fee: $50. Electronic applications accepted. *Expenses: Tuition, area resident:* Full-time $11,310; part-time $471 per credit hour. Tuition, state resident: full-time $11,310; part-time $471 per credit hour. Tuition, nonresident: full-time $23,100; part-time $963 per credit hour. *International tuition:* $23,100 full-time. *Required fees:* $2820. *Financial support:* In 2019–20, 16 fellowships (averaging $20,000 per year), 5 research assistantships with tuition reimbursements (averaging $26,917 per year) were awarded; teaching assistantships, career-related internships or fieldwork, Federal Work-Study, institutionally sponsored loans, scholarships/grants, tuition waivers (full and partial), and unspecified assistantships also available. Financial award application deadline: 2/28; financial award applicants required to submit FAFSA. *Unit head:* Dr. Julie Gorlewski, Department Chair, 716-645-2455, Fax: 716-645-3161, E-mail: jgorlews@buffalo.edu. *Application contact:* Renad Aref, Assistant Director of Admission Recruitment, 716-645-2110, Fax: 716-645-7937, E-mail: gseinfo@buffalo.edu.
Website: http://ed.buffalo.edu/teaching.html

The University of Alabama, Graduate School, College of Arts and Sciences, Department of Modern Languages and Classics, Tuscaloosa, AL 35487. Offers French (MA, PhD); French and Spanish (PhD); German (MA); Romance languages (MA, PhD); Spanish (MA, PhD). *Program availability:* Part-time. *Faculty:* 20 full-time (11 women). *Students:* 39 full-time (17 women), 6 part-time (3 women); includes 14 minority (5 Black or African American, non-Hispanic/Latino; 7 Hispanic/Latino; 2 Two or more races, non-Hispanic/Latino), 10 international. Average age 31. 19 applicants, 89% accepted, 11 enrolled. In 2019, 6 master's, 3 doctorates awarded. *Degree requirements:* For master's, comprehensive exam, thesis optional; for doctorate, one foreign language, thesis/dissertation, preliminary exam. *Entrance requirements:* For master's and doctorate, minimum GPA of 3.0, writing sample. Additional exam requirements/recommendations for international students: required—TOEFL or IELTS. *Application deadline:* For fall admission, 7/6 priority date for domestic students, 1/15 priority date for international students; for spring admission, 12/5 priority date for domestic students, 6/1 priority date for international students. Applications are processed on a rolling basis. Application fee: $50 ($60 for international students). Electronic applications accepted. *Expenses: Tuition, area resident:* Full-time $10,780; part-time $440 per credit hour. Tuition, nonresident: full-time $30,250; part-time $1550 per credit hour. *Financial support:* In 2019–20, 40 students received support. Fellowships, research assistantships with full tuition reimbursements available, teaching assistantships with full tuition reimbursements available, career-related internships or fieldwork, Federal Work-Study, institutionally sponsored loans, and scholarships/grants available. Financial award application deadline: 7/14. *Unit head:* Dr. Douglas Lightfoot, Department Chair, 205-348-5059, E-mail: lightfoot@ua.edu. *Application contact:* Dr. K. Barbara Fischer, Graduate Director/Associate Professor, 205-348-8465, Fax: 205-348-2042, E-mail: bfischer@bama.ua.edu.
Website: http://bama.ua.edu/~mlc

University of Alberta, Faculty of Graduate Studies and Research, Department of Modern Languages and Cultural Studies, Edmonton, AB T6G 2E1, Canada. Offers applied linguistics (Germanic, Romance, Slavic) (MA); French language, literatures and linguistics (PhD); French language, literatures, and linguistics (MA); Germanic languages, literatures and linguistics (PhD); Germanic languages, literatures, and linguistics (MA); Italian studies (MA); Slavic languages and literatures (Russian, Ukrainian) (MA, PhD); Slavic linguistics (Russian, Ukrainian) (MA, PhD); Spanish and Latin American studies (MA, PhD); Ukrainian folklore (MA, PhD). *Program availability:* Part-time. *Degree requirements:* For master's, one foreign language, thesis; for doctorate, 2 foreign languages, comprehensive exam, thesis/dissertation. *Entrance requirements:* For master's and doctorate, 1 language other than English. Additional exam requirements/recommendations for international students: required—Michigan English Language Assessment Battery or TOEFL (minimum score 550 paper-based). Electronic applications accepted.

The University of Arizona, College of Humanities, Department of German Studies, Tucson, AZ 85721. Offers German (MA); transcultural German (PhD). *Degree requirements:* For master's, one foreign language, comprehensive exam, oral exam; for doctorate, 2 foreign languages, comprehensive exam, thesis/dissertation, oral exam, oral defense. *Entrance requirements:* For master's, minimum major GPA of 3.3, 3 letters of recommendation, audio sample, curriculum vitae. Additional exam requirements/recommendations for international students: required—TOEFL (minimum score 550 paper-based; 79 iBT). Electronic applications accepted.

University of Arkansas, Graduate School, J. William Fulbright College of Arts and Sciences, Department of World Languages, Literatures and Cultures, Fayetteville, AR 72701. Offers French (MA); German (MA); Spanish (MA). *Students:* 22 full-time (11 women); includes 3 minority (2 Hispanic/Latino; 1 Two or more races, non-Hispanic/Latino), 10 international. 17 applicants, 100% accepted. In 2019, 11 master's awarded. *Application deadline:* For fall admission, 8/1 for domestic students, 4/1 for international students; for spring admission, 12/1 for domestic students, 10/1 for international students; for summer admission, 4/15 for domestic students, 3/1 for international students. Applications are processed on a rolling basis. Application fee: $60. Electronic

applications accepted. *Financial support:* In 2019–20, 1 research assistantship, 26 teaching assistantships were awarded; fellowships with tuition reimbursements, career-related internships or fieldwork, and Federal Work-Study also available. Support available to part-time students. Financial award application deadline: 4/1; financial award applicants required to submit FAFSA. *Unit head:* Dr. Steven Bell, Department Chair, 479-575-2951, E-mail: sbell@uark.edu. *Application contact:* Dr. Steven Bell, Department Chair, 479-575-2951, E-mail: sbell@uark.edu.
Website: https://fulbright.uark.edu/departments/world-languages/

The University of British Columbia, Faculty of Arts, Department of Central, Eastern and Northern European Studies, Vancouver, BC V6T 1Z1, Canada. Offers Germanic studies (MA, PhD). *Program availability:* Part-time. *Degree requirements:* For master's, one foreign language, thesis optional, exam; for doctorate, one foreign language, comprehensive exam, thesis/dissertation. *Entrance requirements:* For master's, BA in German; for doctorate, MA in German. Additional exam requirements/recommendations for international students: required—TOEFL. Electronic applications accepted. *Expenses:* Contact institution.

University of Calgary, Faculty of Graduate Studies, Faculty of Arts, Program in Languages, Literature and Culture, Calgary, AB T2N 1N4, Canada. Offers German (MA); linguistics (MA, PhD). *Degree requirements:* For master's, one foreign language, thesis; for doctorate, one foreign language, comprehensive exam, thesis/dissertation. *Entrance requirements:* For doctorate, MA. Additional exam requirements/recommendations for international students: required—TOEFL (minimum score 560 paper-based). Electronic applications accepted.

University of California, Berkeley, Graduate Division, College of Letters and Science, Department of German, Berkeley, CA 94720. Offers PhD. *Degree requirements:* For doctorate, 2 foreign languages, thesis/dissertation, qualifying exam. *Entrance requirements:* For doctorate, GRE General Test, minimum GPA of 3.0, writing sample, 3 letters of recommendation. Electronic applications accepted.

University of California, Davis, Graduate Studies, Program in German, Davis, CA 95616. Offers MA, PhD. Terminal master's awarded for partial completion of doctoral program. *Degree requirements:* For master's, comprehensive exam (for some programs), thesis (for some programs); for doctorate, thesis/dissertation. *Entrance requirements:* For master's, GRE; for doctorate, GRE, master's degree or equivalent. Additional exam requirements/recommendations for international students: required—TOEFL (minimum score 550 paper-based). Electronic applications accepted.

University of California, Irvine, School of Humanities, Department of European Languages and Studies, Irvine, CA 92697. Offers French (MA, PhD); German (MA, PhD). *Students:* 9 full-time (3 women), 1 part-time; includes 1 minority (Hispanic/Latino), 2 international. Average age 28. 12 applicants, 33% accepted, 2 enrolled. In 2019, 3 master's awarded. *Entrance requirements:* For master's and doctorate, GRE General Test, minimum GPA of 3.0. Additional exam requirements/recommendations for international students: required—TOEFL (minimum score 550 paper-based). *Application deadline:* For fall admission, 1/15 for domestic and international students. Applications are processed on a rolling basis. Application fee: $120 ($140 for international students). Electronic applications accepted. *Financial support:* Fellowships, research assistantships with full tuition reimbursements, teaching assistantships, institutionally sponsored loans, traineeships, health care benefits, and unspecified assistantships available. Financial award application deadline: 3/1; financial award applicants required to submit FAFSA. *Unit head:* Prof. John Smith, Chair, 949-824-6406, Fax: 949-824-6416, E-mail: jhsmith@uci.edu. *Application contact:* Bindya Baliga, Graduate Program Coordinator, 949-824-7968, Fax: 949-824-6416, E-mail: bbaliga@uci.edu.
Website: http://www.humanities.uci.edu/els/

University of California, Los Angeles, Graduate Division, College of Letters and Science, Department of Germanic Languages, Program in Germanic Languages, Los Angeles, CA 90095. Offers MA, PhD. Terminal master's awarded for partial completion of doctoral program. *Degree requirements:* For master's, one foreign language, comprehensive exam or thesis; for doctorate, 2 foreign languages, thesis/dissertation, oral and written qualifying exams. *Entrance requirements:* For master's, GRE General Test, bachelor's degree; minimum undergraduate GPA of 3.0 (or its equivalent if letter grade system not used); for doctorate, GRE General Test, master's degree; minimum undergraduate GPA of 3.0 (or its equivalent if letter grade system not used). Additional exam requirements/recommendations for international students: required—TOEFL. Electronic applications accepted.

University of Chicago, Division of the Humanities, Department of Germanic Studies, Chicago, IL 60637. Offers PhD. Terminal master's awarded for partial completion of doctoral program. *Degree requirements:* For doctorate, 2 foreign languages, comprehensive exam, thesis/dissertation. *Entrance requirements:* For doctorate, GRE General Test, 15-20 page writing sample, statement of purpose, 3 letters of recommendation, transcripts for all previous degrees and institutions attended. Additional exam requirements/recommendations for international students: required—TOEFL (minimum score 104 iBT), IELTS (minimum score 7). Electronic applications accepted.

University of Chicago, Division of the Humanities, Master of Arts Program in the Humanities, Chicago, IL 60637. Offers art history (MA); cinema and media studies (MA); classic languages (MA); comparative literature (MA); creative writing (MA); cultural policy studies (MA); digital humanities (MA); East Asian languages and civilizations (MA); English language and literature (MA); gender and sexuality studies (MA); Germanic studies (MA); linguistics (MA); music (MA); near Eastern languages and civilizations (MA); philosophy (MA); poetics (MA); race, politics and culture (MA); Romance languages and literatures (MA); Slavic languages and literatures (MA); South Asian languages and civilizations (MA); theater and performance studies (MA). *Degree requirements:* For master's, thesis. *Entrance requirements:* For master's, GRE General Test, 10-15 page writing sample, statement of purpose, 3 letters of recommendation, transcripts for all previous degrees and institutions attended. Additional exam requirements/recommendations for international students: required—TOEFL (minimum score 104 iBT), IELTS (minimum score 7). Electronic applications accepted. *Expenses:* Contact institution.

University of Cincinnati, Graduate School, McMicken College of Arts and Sciences, Department of German Studies, Cincinnati, OH 45221-0372. Offers MA, PhD. *Program availability:* Part-time. *Faculty:* 6 full-time (4 women), 1 part-time/adjunct. *Students:* 13 full-time; includes 3 minority (1 Black or African American, non-Hispanic/Latino; 1 Hispanic/Latino; 1 Two or more races, non-Hispanic/Latino), 2 international. Average age 25. In 2019, 5 master's awarded. Terminal master's awarded for partial completion of doctoral program. *Degree requirements:* For master's, one foreign language, comprehensive exam, thesis or alternative; for doctorate, one foreign language, comprehensive exam, thesis/dissertation. *Entrance requirements:* For doctorate, MA in German or equivalent. Additional exam requirements/recommendations for international students: required—TOEFL (minimum score 560 paper-based). *Application deadline:* For fall admission, 2/1 for domestic and international students; for winter admission, 1/15 priority date for domestic students, 1/15 for international students. Applications are processed on a rolling basis. Application fee: $40. Electronic applications accepted. *Financial support:* In 2019–20, 11 students received support, including 1 fellowship with full tuition reimbursement available (averaging $17,200 per year), 2 research assistantships with full tuition reimbursements available (averaging $15,000 per year), 8 teaching assistantships with full tuition reimbursements available (averaging $15,000 per year); scholarships/grants, health care benefits, tuition waivers (partial), and unspecified assistantships also available. Financial award application deadline: 1/15. *Unit head:* Dr. Todd Herzog, Head, 513-556-2751, Fax: 513-556-1991, E-mail: herzoghr@ucmail.uc.edu. *Application contact:* Dr. Tanja Nusser, Graduate Program Director, 513-556-0049, Fax: 513-556-1991, E-mail: tanja.nusser@uc.edu.
Website: https://www.artsci.uc.edu/departments/german.html

University of Colorado Boulder, Graduate School, College of Arts and Sciences, Department of Germanic and Slavic Languages and Literatures, Boulder, CO 80309. Offers MA. Terminal master's awarded for partial completion of doctoral program. *Degree requirements:* For master's, 2 foreign languages, comprehensive exam, thesis or alternative. *Entrance requirements:* For master's, minimum undergraduate GPA of 2.75. Electronic applications accepted. Application fee is waived when completed online.

University of Delaware, College of Arts and Sciences, Department of Foreign Languages and Literatures, Newark, DE 19716. Offers foreign languages and literatures (MA), including French, German, Spanish; foreign languages pedagogy (MA), including French, German, Spanish; technical Chinese translation (MA). *Degree requirements:* For master's, one foreign language, comprehensive exam, thesis optional. *Entrance requirements:* For master's, GRE General Test, letters of recommendation, writing sample. Additional exam requirements/recommendations for international students: required—TOEFL. Electronic applications accepted.

University of Florida, Graduate School, College of Liberal Arts and Sciences, Department of Languages, Literatures and Cultures, Gainesville, FL 32611. Offers French and Francophone studies (MA, PhD); German (MA, PhD), including women's and gender studies (PhD). *Degree requirements:* For master's, comprehensive exam, thesis optional; for doctorate, one foreign language, comprehensive exam, thesis/dissertation. *Entrance requirements:* For master's and doctorate, GRE General Test, minimum GPA of 3.0. Additional exam requirements/recommendations for international students: required—TOEFL (minimum score 550 paper-based; 80 iBT), IELTS (minimum score 6). Electronic applications accepted.

University of Georgia, Franklin College of Arts and Sciences, Department of Germanic and Slavic Studies, Athens, GA 30602. Offers German (MA). *Degree requirements:* For master's, one foreign language, thesis. *Entrance requirements:* For master's, GRE General Test. Electronic applications accepted.

University of Illinois at Chicago, College of Liberal Arts and Sciences, School of Literatures, Cultural Studies and Linguistics, Department of Germanic Studies, Chicago, IL 60607-7128. Offers MA, PhD. *Program availability:* Part-time. Terminal master's awarded for partial completion of doctoral program. *Degree requirements:* For master's, thesis optional, exam; for doctorate, 2 foreign languages, thesis/dissertation. *Entrance requirements:* For master's and doctorate, GRE General Test, minimum GPA of 2.75. Additional exam requirements/recommendations for international students: required—TOEFL. Electronic applications accepted.

University of Illinois at Urbana-Champaign, Graduate College, College of Liberal Arts and Sciences, School of Literatures, Cultures and Linguistics, Department of Germanic Languages and Literatures, Champaign, IL 61820. Offers German (MA, PhD).

University of Kentucky, Graduate School, College of Arts and Sciences, Program in German, Lexington, KY 40506-0032. Offers MA. *Degree requirements:* For master's, one foreign language, comprehensive exam, thesis optional. *Entrance requirements:* For master's, GRE General Test, minimum undergraduate GPA of 2.75. Additional exam requirements/recommendations for international students: required—TOEFL (minimum score 550 paper-based). Electronic applications accepted.

University of Lethbridge, School of Graduate Studies, Lethbridge, AB T1K 3M4, Canada. Offers addictions counseling (M Sc); agricultural biotechnology (M Sc); agricultural studies (M Sc, MA); anthropology (MA); archaeology (M Sc, MA); art (MA, MFA); biochemistry (M Sc); biological sciences (M Sc); biomolecular science (PhD); biosystems and biodiversity (PhD); Canadian studies (MA); chemistry (M Sc); computer science (M Sc); computer science and geographical information science (M Sc); counseling (MC); counseling psychology (M Ed); dramatic arts (MA); earth, space, and physical science (PhD); economics (MA); education (MA, PhD); educational leadership (M Ed); English (MA); environmental science (M Sc); evolution and behavior (PhD); exercise science (M Sc); French (MA); French/German (MA); French/Spanish (MA); general education (M Ed); geography (M Sc, MA); German (MA); health sciences (M Sc); individualized multidisciplinary (M Sc, MA); kinesiology (M Sc, MA); management (M Sc), including accounting, finance, human resource management and labor relations, information systems, international management, marketing, policy and strategy; mathematics (M Sc); music (M Mus, MA); Native American studies (MA); neuroscience (M Sc, PhD); new media (MA, MFA); nursing (M Sc, MN); philosophy (MA); physics (M Sc); political science (MA); psychology (M Sc, MA); religious studies (MA); sociology (MA); theatre and dramatic arts (MFA); theoretical and computational science (PhD); urban and regional studies (MA); women and gender studies (MA). *Program availability:* Part-time, evening/weekend. *Degree requirements:* For master's, thesis (for some programs); for doctorate, comprehensive exam, thesis/dissertation. *Entrance requirements:* For master's, GMAT (for M Sc in management), bachelor's degree in related field, minimum GPA of 3.0 during previous 20 graded semester courses, 2 years' teaching or related experience (M Ed); for doctorate, master's degree, minimum graduate GPA of 3.5. Additional exam requirements/recommendations for international students: required—TOEFL (minimum score 580 paper-based; 93 iBT). Electronic applications accepted.

The University of Manchester, School of Arts, Languages and Cultures, Manchester, United Kingdom. Offers anthropology, media and performance (PhD); applied theatre (PhD); Arab world studies (PhD); archaeology (PhD); art history and visual studies (PhD); arts and cultural management (PhD); arts management and cultural policy (PhD); Chinese studies (PhD); classics and ancient history (PhD); composition (PhD); creative writing (PhD); drama (PhD); East Asian studies (PhD); electroacoustic composition (PhD); English and American studies (PhD); English language (PhD); French studies (PhD); German studies (PhD); history (PhD); humanitarianism and conflict response (PhD); interpreting studies (PhD); Japanese studies (PhD); Latin American cultural studies (PhD); linguistics (PhD); Middle Eastern studies (PhD); museology (PhD); museum practice (PhD); music (PhD); musicology (PhD); Polish studies (PhD); Portuguese studies (PhD); religions and theology (PhD); Russian studies (PhD); Spanish studies (PhD); translation and intercultural studies (PhD).

University of Manitoba, Faculty of Graduate Studies, Faculty of Arts, Department of German and Slavic Studies, Winnipeg, MB R3T 2N2, Canada. Offers German language and literature (MA); Slavic languages and literatures (MA). *Degree requirements:* For master's, one foreign language, thesis or alternative.

University of Maryland, College Park, Academic Affairs, College of Arts and Humanities, School of Languages, Literatures, and Cultures, Department of Germanic Studies, College Park, MD 20742. Offers Germanic language and literature (MA, PhD). *Degree requirements:* For master's, one foreign language, thesis optional, exams; for doctorate, 2 foreign languages, comprehensive exam, thesis/dissertation, reading exam, oral defense. *Entrance requirements:* For master's, writing sample, 3 letters of recommendation, interview; for doctorate, MA in German or related discipline. Additional exam requirements/recommendations for international students: required—TOEFL. Electronic applications accepted.

University of Massachusetts Amherst, Graduate School, College of Humanities and Fine Arts, Department of Languages, Literatures, and Cultures, Programs in German and Scandinavian Studies, Amherst, MA 01003. Offers MA, PhD. *Program availability:* Part-time. Terminal master's awarded for partial completion of doctoral program. *Degree requirements:* For master's, thesis or alternative; for doctorate, one foreign language, comprehensive exam, thesis/dissertation. *Entrance requirements:* For master's and doctorate, writing sample in English and German. Additional exam requirements/ recommendations for international students: required—TOEFL (minimum score 550 paper-based; 80 iBT), IELTS (minimum score 6.5). Electronic applications accepted.

University of Michigan, Rackham Graduate School, College of Literature, Science, and the Arts, Department of Germanic Languages and Literatures, Ann Arbor, MI 48109. Offers German (AM, PhD); German studies (Certificate). *Degree requirements:* For doctorate, one foreign language, comprehensive exam, thesis/dissertation, oral defense of dissertation, preliminary exam. *Entrance requirements:* For doctorate, GRE General Test. Additional exam requirements/recommendations for international students: required—TOEFL (minimum score 560 paper-based). Electronic applications accepted.

University of Minnesota, Twin Cities Campus, Graduate School, College of Liberal Arts, Department of German, Scandinavian, and Dutch, Minneapolis, MN 55455. Offers Germanic studies (MA, PhD), including German, Germanic medieval studies, Scandinavian studies (MA). *Program availability:* Part-time. Terminal master's awarded for partial completion of doctoral program. *Degree requirements:* For doctorate, 2 foreign languages, thesis/dissertation. *Entrance requirements:* For master's, GRE General Test, BA in German, Scandinavian, or equivalent; for doctorate, MA in German, Scandinavian, or equivalent. Additional exam requirements/recommendations for international students: required—TOEFL (minimum score 550 paper-based; 79 iBT). Electronic applications accepted.

University of Missouri, Office of Research and Graduate Studies, College of Arts and Science, Department of German and Russian Studies, Columbia, MO 65211. Offers MA. *Entrance requirements:* For master's, GRE General Test, minimum GPA of 3.0.

University of Montana, Graduate School, College of Humanities and Sciences, Department of Modern and Classical Languages and Literatures, Missoula, MT 59812. Offers French (MA); German (MA); Spanish (MA). *Degree requirements:* For master's, one foreign language. *Entrance requirements:* For master's, GRE General Test. Additional exam requirements/recommendations for international students: required— TOEFL.

University of Nebraska–Lincoln, Graduate College, College of Arts and Sciences, Department of Modern Languages and Literatures, Lincoln, NE 68588. Offers French (MA, PhD); German (MA, PhD); Spanish (MA, PhD). *Degree requirements:* For master's, thesis optional; for doctorate, comprehensive exam, thesis/dissertation. *Entrance requirements:* For master's and doctorate, writing sample in target language. Additional exam requirements/recommendations for international students: required— TOEFL (minimum score 550 paper-based). Electronic applications accepted.

University of New Mexico, Graduate Studies, College of Arts and Sciences, Program in Foreign Languages and Literatures, Albuquerque, NM 87131-2039. Offers comparative literature and cultural studies (MA); French (MA); French studies (PhD); German studies (MA). *Program availability:* Part-time. *Degree requirements:* For master's, one foreign language, thesis optional; for doctorate, 2 foreign languages, thesis/dissertation. *Entrance requirements:* For master's and doctorate, transcript, writing sample, 3 letters of recommendation. Additional exam requirements/ recommendations for international students: required—TOEFL. Electronic applications accepted. *Expenses:* Tuition, state resident: full-time $7633; part-time $972 per year. Tuition, nonresident: full-time $22,586; part-time $3840 per year. *International tuition:* $23,292 full-time. *Required fees:* $8608. Tuition and fees vary according to course level, course load, degree level, program and student level.

The University of North Carolina at Chapel Hill, Graduate School, College of Arts and Sciences, Department of Germanic and Slavic Languages and Literatures, Chapel Hill, NC 27599. Offers German studies (PhD). *Program availability:* Part-time. Terminal master's awarded for partial completion of doctoral program. *Degree requirements:* For doctorate, one foreign language, comprehensive exam, thesis/dissertation. *Entrance requirements:* For doctorate, GRE General Test, minimum GPA of 3.0.

University of Oklahoma, College of Arts and Sciences, Department of Modern Languages, Literatures, and Linguistics, Norman, OK 73019. Offers French (MA, PhD, MBA/MA); German (MA); Spanish (MA, PhD); MBA/MA. *Program availability:* Part-time. Terminal master's awarded for partial completion of doctoral program. *Degree requirements:* For master's, one foreign language, comprehensive exam, thesis optional; for doctorate, one foreign language, comprehensive exam, thesis/dissertation. *Entrance requirements:* For master's, BA (or equivalent) in French, German, or Spanish, or equivalent hours in the major; for doctorate, MA (or equivalent) in French or Spanish. Additional exam requirements/recommendations for international students: required— TOEFL (minimum score 79 iBT) or IELTS (minimum score 6.5). Electronic applications accepted. *Expenses:* Tuition, state resident: full-time $6583.20; part-time $274.30 per credit hour. Tuition, nonresident: full-time $21,242; part-time $885.10 per credit hour. *International tuition:* $21,242.40 full-time. *Required fees:* $1994.20; $72.55 per credit hour. $126.50 per semester. Tuition and fees vary according to course load and degree level.

University of Oregon, Graduate School, College of Arts and Sciences, Department of Germanic Languages and Literatures, Eugene, OR 97403. Offers MA, PhD. *Degree requirements:* For master's, 2 foreign languages, thesis or alternative; for doctorate, 3 foreign languages, thesis/dissertation. *Entrance requirements:* For master's and doctorate, minimum GPA of 3.0. Additional exam requirements/recommendations for international students: required—TOEFL.

University of Pennsylvania, School of Arts and Sciences, Graduate Group in Germanic Languages, Philadelphia, PA 19104. Offers AM, PhD. *Faculty:* 16 full-time (6 women), 6 part-time/adjunct (1 woman). *Students:* 10 full-time (5 women), 2 international. Average age 31. 10 applicants, 40% accepted. In 2019, 1 master's, 1 doctorate awarded. Terminal master's awarded for partial completion of doctoral program. Application fee: $90.
Website: http://www.sas.upenn.edu/graduate-division

University of South Africa, College of Human Sciences, Pretoria, South Africa. Offers adult education (M Ed); African languages (MA, PhD); African politics (MA, PhD); Afrikaans (MA, PhD); ancient history (MA, PhD); ancient Near Eastern studies (MA, PhD); anthropology (MA, PhD); applied linguistics (MA); Arabic (MA, PhD); archaeology (MA); art history (MA); Biblical archaeology (MA); Biblical studies (M Th, D Th, PhD); Christian spirituality (M Th, D Th); church history (M Th, D Th); classical studies (MA, PhD); clinical psychology (MA); communication (MA, PhD); comparative education (M Ed, Ed D); consulting psychology (D Admin, D Com, PhD); curriculum studies (M Ed,

Ed D); development studies (M Admin, MA, D Admin, PhD); didactics (M Ed, Ed D); education (M Tech); education management (M Ed, Ed D); educational psychology (M Ed); English (MA); environmental education (M Ed); French (MA, PhD); German (MA, PhD); Greek (MA); guidance and counseling (M Ed); health studies (MA, PhD), including health sciences education (MA), health services management (MA), medical and surgical nursing science (critical care general) (MA), midwifery and neonatal nursing science (MA), trauma and emergency care (MA); history (MA, PhD); history of education (Ed D); inclusive education (M Ed, Ed D); information and communications technology policy and regulation (MA); information science (MA, MIS, PhD); international politics (MA, PhD); Islamic studies (MA, PhD); Italian (MA, PhD); Judaica (MA, PhD); linguistics (MA, PhD); mathematical education (M Ed); mathematics education (MA); missiology (M Th, D Th); modern Hebrew (MA, PhD); musicology (MA, MMus, D Mus, PhD); natural science education (M Ed); New Testament (M Th, D Th); Old Testament (D Th); pastoral therapy (M Th, D Th); philosophy (MA); philosophy of education (M Ed, Ed D); politics (MA, PhD); Portuguese (MA, PhD); practical theology (M Th, D Th); psychology (MA, MS, PhD); psychology of education (M Ed, Ed D); public health (MA); religious studies (MA, D Th, PhD); Romance languages (MA); Russian (MA, PhD); Semitic languages (MA, PhD); social behavior studies in HIV/AIDS (MA); social science (mental health) (MA); social science in development studies (MA); social science in psychology (MA); social science in social work (MA); social science in sociology (MA); social work (MSW, DSW, PhD); socio-education (M Ed, Ed D); sociolinguistics (MA); sociology (MA, PhD); Spanish (MA, PhD); systematic theology (M Th, D Th); TESOL (teaching English to speakers of other languages) (MA); theological ethics (M Th, D Th); theory of literature (MA, PhD); urban ministries (D Th); urban ministry (M Th).

University of South Carolina, The Graduate School, College of Arts and Sciences, Department of Languages, Literatures, and Cultures, Columbia, SC 29208. Offers comparative literature (MA, PhD); foreign languages (MAT), including French, German, Spanish; French (MA); German (MA); Spanish (MA). *Program availability:* Part-time. *Degree requirements:* For master's, one foreign language, comprehensive exam, thesis optional; for doctorate, 2 foreign languages, comprehensive exam, thesis/dissertation. *Entrance requirements:* For master's and doctorate, GRE General Test, writing sample. Additional exam requirements/recommendations for international students: required— TOEFL (minimum score 75 iBT). Electronic applications accepted.

The University of Tennessee, Graduate School, College of Arts and Sciences, Department of Modern Foreign Languages and Literatures, Program in German, Knoxville, TN 37996. Offers MA. *Program availability:* Part-time. *Degree requirements:* For master's, one foreign language, thesis or alternative. *Entrance requirements:* For master's, minimum GPA of 2.7. Additional exam requirements/recommendations for international students: required—TOEFL. Electronic applications accepted.

The University of Tennessee, Graduate School, College of Arts and Sciences, Department of Modern Foreign Languages and Literatures, Program in Modern Foreign Languages, Knoxville, TN 37996. Offers applied linguistics (PhD); French (PhD); German (PhD); Italian (PhD); Portuguese (PhD); Russian (PhD); Spanish (PhD). *Degree requirements:* For doctorate, 2 foreign languages, thesis/dissertation. *Entrance requirements:* For doctorate, minimum GPA of 2.7. Additional exam requirements/ recommendations for international students: required—TOEFL. Electronic applications accepted.

The University of Texas at Austin, Graduate School, College of Liberal Arts, Department of Germanic Studies, Austin, TX 78712-1111. Offers MA, PhD. *Degree requirements:* For master's, one foreign language, thesis or alternative; for doctorate, 2 foreign languages, thesis/dissertation. *Entrance requirements:* For master's and doctorate, GRE General Test.

The University of Toledo, College of Graduate Studies, College of Languages, Literature and Social Sciences, Department of Foreign Languages, Toledo, OH 43606-3390. Offers French (MA); German (MA); Spanish (MA). *Program availability:* Part-time. *Degree requirements:* For master's, one foreign language, comprehensive exam, comprehensive reading exam in 1 additional foreign language. *Entrance requirements:* For master's, minimum cumulative point-hour ratio of 2.7 for all previous academic work. Additional exam requirements/recommendations for international students: required— TOEFL (minimum score 550 paper-based; 80 iBT). Electronic applications accepted.

University of Toronto, School of Graduate Studies, Faculty of Arts and Science, Department of Germanic Languages and Literatures, Toronto, ON M5S 1A1, Canada. Offers MA, PhD. *Program availability:* Part-time. *Degree requirements:* For master's, thesis optional, German language competence exam; for doctorate, thesis/dissertation, qualifying exam, thesis defense. *Entrance requirements:* For master's, 7 two-semester courses in German language and literature, 3 letters of recommendation; for doctorate, MA in German, minimum A- average, 3 letters of recommendation, writing sample, resume. Additional exam requirements/recommendations for international students: required—TOEFL (minimum score 580 paper-based; 93 iBT), TWE (minimum score 5). Electronic applications accepted.

University of Vermont, Graduate College, College of Arts and Sciences, Program in German, Burlington, VT 05405. Offers MA. *Degree requirements:* For master's, one foreign language, thesis. *Entrance requirements:* For master's, GRE General Test. Additional exam requirements/recommendations for international students: required— TOEFL (minimum score 550 paper-based; 90 iBT), IELTS (minimum score 6.5). Electronic applications accepted.

University of Victoria, Faculty of Graduate Studies, Faculty of Humanities, Department of Germanic and Slavic Studies, Victoria, BC V8W 2Y2, Canada. Offers German studies (MA). *Program availability:* Part-time. *Degree requirements:* For master's, 2 foreign languages, oral defense of thesis. *Entrance requirements:* For master's, BA in German, minimum B+ average in undergraduate course work. Additional exam requirements/ recommendations for international students: required—TOEFL (minimum score 575 paper-based), IELTS (minimum score 7). Electronic applications accepted.

University of Virginia, College and Graduate School of Arts and Sciences, Department of Germanic Languages and Literatures, Charlottesville, VA 22903. Offers German (MA). *Degree requirements:* For master's, one foreign language, comprehensive exam, thesis. *Entrance requirements:* For master's, GRE General Test, 3 letters of recommendation, critical writing sample. Additional exam requirements/ recommendations for international students: required—TOEFL (minimum score 600 paper-based; 90 iBT), IELTS (minimum score 7). Electronic applications accepted.

University of Washington, Graduate School, College of Arts and Sciences, Department of Germanics, Seattle, WA 98195. Offers MA, PhD. *Program availability:* Part-time. Terminal master's awarded for partial completion of doctoral program. *Degree requirements:* For master's, one foreign language, 2 research papers; for doctorate, 2 foreign languages, thesis/dissertation, 3 research papers. *Entrance requirements:* For master's and doctorate, GRE, minimum GPA of 3.0. Additional exam requirements/ recommendations for international students: required—TOEFL. Electronic applications accepted.

University of Waterloo, Graduate Studies and Postdoctoral Affairs, Faculty of Arts, Department of Germanic and Slavic Studies, Waterloo, ON N2L 3G1, Canada. Offers German (MA, PhD); Russian (MA). *Program availability:* Part-time, evening/weekend.

Degree requirements: For master's, one foreign language, thesis optional; for doctorate, 2 foreign languages, comprehensive exam, thesis/dissertation. *Entrance requirements:* For master's, honors degree, minimum B average; for doctorate, master's degree, minimum B average. Additional exam requirements/recommendations for international students: required—TOEFL, IELTS, PTE. Electronic applications accepted.

University of Wisconsin–Madison, Graduate School, College of Letters and Science, Department of German, Nordic, and Slavic, Madison, WI 53706-1380. Offers German (MA, PhD); Scandinavian studies (MA, PhD), including area studies (MA), folklore (PhD), literature, philology; Slavic languages and literature (MA, PhD). *Program availability:* Part-time. *Degree requirements:* For master's, 2 foreign languages, exam; for doctorate, thesis/dissertation, exam. *Entrance requirements:* For master's, minimum GPA of 3.25; for doctorate, minimum GPA of 3.5. Electronic applications accepted.

University of Wisconsin–Milwaukee, Graduate School, College of Letters and Science, Department of Foreign Languages and Literature, Milwaukee, WI 53201-0413. Offers foreign languages and literature (MA), including classic Greek, classics, comparative literature, French/Francophone language, literature, and culture, German language, literature, and culture, interpreting, Latin, linguistics, Spanish language, literature, and culture, translation; interpreting (Graduate Certificate); language, literature, and translation (MA, MALLT); translation (Graduate Certificate). *Program availability:* Part-time. *Degree requirements:* For master's, 2 foreign languages, thesis or alternative. *Entrance requirements:* Additional exam requirements/recommendations for international students: required—TOEFL (minimum score 550 paper-based; 79 iBT), IELTS (minimum score 6.5). Electronic applications accepted.

University of Wyoming, College of Arts and Sciences, Department of Modern and Classical Languages, Program in German, Laramie, WY 82071. Offers MA. *Program availability:* Part-time. *Degree requirements:* For master's, one foreign language, thesis or alternative. *Entrance requirements:* For master's, GRE General Test, minimum GPA of 3.0.

Vanderbilt University, Department of Germanic and Slavic Languages, Nashville, TN 37240-1001. Offers MA, MAT, PhD. *Faculty:* 7 full-time (4 women). *Students:* 22 full-time (15 women); includes 2 minority (1 Black or African American, non-Hispanic/Latino; 1 Hispanic/Latino), 3 international. Average age 30. 6 applicants, 83% accepted, 3 enrolled. In 2019, 3 doctorates awarded. Terminal master's awarded for partial completion of doctoral program. *Degree requirements:* For master's, one foreign language, comprehensive exam; for doctorate, 2 foreign languages, comprehensive exam, thesis/dissertation, qualifying and final exams. *Entrance requirements:* For master's and doctorate, GRE General Test, sample of written work. Additional exam requirements/recommendations for international students: required—TOEFL (minimum score 570 paper-based; 88 iBT). *Application deadline:* For fall admission, 1/15 for domestic and international students. Electronic applications accepted. *Expenses: Tuition:* Full-time $51,018; part-time $2087 per hour. *Required fees:* $542. Tuition and fees vary according to program. *Financial support:* Fellowships, teaching assistantships, career-related internships or fieldwork, Federal Work-Study, institutionally sponsored loans, scholarships/grants, and health care benefits available. Financial award application deadline: 1/15; financial award applicants required to submit CSS PROFILE or FAFSA. *Unit head:* Dr. Lutz Koepnick, Chair, 615-322-2611, Fax: 615-343-7258, E-mail: lutz.koepnick@vanderbilt.edu. *Application contact:* Meike Werner, Director of Graduate Studies, 615-875-9065, Fax: 615-343-7258, E-mail: meike.werner@Vanderbilt.Edu.
Website: http://www.vanderbilt.edu/german/graduate/

Washington University in St. Louis, The Graduate School, Department of Germanic Languages and Literatures, St. Louis, MO 63130-4899. Offers PhD. Terminal master's awarded for partial completion of doctoral program. *Degree requirements:* For doctorate, thesis/dissertation. *Entrance requirements:* For doctorate, GRE General Test, sample of written work. Additional exam requirements/recommendations for international students: required—TOEFL. Electronic applications accepted.

Wayne State University, College of Liberal Arts and Sciences, Department of Classical and Modern Languages, Literatures, and Cultures, Detroit, MI 48202. Offers classics (MA), including ancient Greek and Latin, ancient studies, classics, Latin; German (MA); language learning (MALL), including Arabic (MA, MALL), French (MA, MALL, PhD), German (MALL, PhD), Italian (MA, MALL), Spanish (MA, MALL, PhD); modern languages (PhD), including French (MA, MALL, PhD), German (MALL, PhD), Spanish (MA, MALL, PhD); Near Eastern languages (MA), including Arabic (MA, MALL), Hebrew; Romance languages (MA), including French (MA, MALL, PhD), Italian (MA, MALL), Spanish (MA, MALL, PhD). *Faculty:* 20. *Students:* 30 full-time (22 women), 15 part-time (9 women); includes 11 minority (4 Black or African American, non-Hispanic/Latino; 1 American Indian or Alaska Native, non-Hispanic/Latino; 2 Asian, non-Hispanic/Latino; 3 Hispanic/Latino; 1 Two or more races, non-Hispanic/Latino), 2 international. Average age 40. 32 applicants, 34% accepted, 9 enrolled. In 2019, 8 master's, 1 doctorate awarded. *Degree requirements:* For master's, variable foreign language requirement, comprehensive exam (for some programs), thesis (for some programs); for doctorate, one foreign language, comprehensive exam, thesis/dissertation. *Entrance requirements:* Additional exam requirements/recommendations for international students: required—TOEFL (minimum score 550 paper-based; 79 iBT), TWE (minimum score 5.5), Michigan English Language Assessment Battery (minimum score 85); recommended—IELTS (minimum score 6.5). Application fee: $50. Electronic applications accepted. *Expenses: Tuition:* Full-time $34,567. *Financial support:* In 2019–20, 22 students received support, including 1 fellowship with tuition reimbursement available (averaging $20,000 per year), 15 teaching assistantships with tuition reimbursements available (averaging $20,015 per year); research assistantships, scholarships/grants, health care benefits, and unspecified assistantships also available. Financial award applicants required to submit FAFSA. *Unit head:* Dr. Vanessa DEGifis, DR., Department Chair, 313-577-6244, Fax: 313-577-6243, E-mail: vdegifis@wayne.edu. *Application contact:* Terrie Pickering, Academic Services Officer, 313 577 3003, E-mail: t.pickering@wayne.edu.
Website: http://clas.wayne.edu/languages/

Western Kentucky University, Graduate School, Potter College of Arts and Letters, Department of Modern Languages, Bowling Green, KY 42101. Offers French (MA Ed); German (MA Ed); Spanish (MA Ed).

Yale University, Graduate School of Arts and Sciences, Department of German, New Haven, CT 06520. Offers PhD. Terminal master's awarded for partial completion of doctoral program. *Degree requirements:* For doctorate, 3 foreign languages, thesis/dissertation. *Entrance requirements:* For doctorate, GRE General Test.

Hispanic and Latin American Languages

Boston University, Graduate School of Arts and Sciences, Department of Romance Studies, Boston, MA 02215. Offers Hispanic language and literature (MA, PhD). *Students:* 35 full-time (24 women), 2 part-time (both women); includes 11 minority (2 Black or African American, non-Hispanic/Latino; 9 Hispanic/Latino), 14 international. Average age 28. 31 applicants, 52% accepted, 6 enrolled. In 2019, 2 master's, 5 doctorates awarded. Terminal master's awarded for partial completion of doctoral program. *Degree requirements:* For master's, one foreign language, comprehensive exam; for doctorate, 2 foreign languages, comprehensive exam, thesis/dissertation. *Entrance requirements:* For master's and doctorate, GRE General Test, sample of written work, 3 letters of recommendation, transcripts, personal statement, summary of related coursework. Additional exam requirements/recommendations for international students: required—TOEFL (minimum score 550 paper-based; 84 iBT). *Application deadline:* For fall admission, 1/15 for domestic and international students. Application fee: $95. Electronic applications accepted. *Financial support:* In 2019–20, 37 students received support, including 11 fellowships with full tuition reimbursements available (averaging $23,340 per year), 22 teaching assistantships with full tuition reimbursements available (averaging $23,340 per year); Federal Work-Study, scholarships/grants, and health care benefits also available. Financial award application deadline: 1/15. *Unit head:* Odile Cazenave, Chair, 617-353-6225, Fax: 617-353-6246, E-mail: cazenave@bu.edu. *Application contact:* Michael Williams, Administrative Assistant, 617-353-2641, Fax: 617-353-6246, E-mail: mawillia@bu.edu.
Website: http://www.bu.edu/rs/

Brigham Young University, Graduate Studies, College of Humanities, Department of Spanish and Portuguese, Provo, UT 84602. Offers Portuguese (MA), including Luso-Brazilian literatures, Portuguese linguistics, Portuguese pedagogy; Spanish (MA), including Hispanic linguistics, Hispanic literatures, Spanish pedagogy. *Faculty:* 33 full-time (8 women). *Students:* 34 full-time (24 women); includes 14 minority (1 Black or African American, non-Hispanic/Latino; 1 American Indian or Alaska Native, non-Hispanic/Latino; 1 Asian, non-Hispanic/Latino; 11 Hispanic/Latino). Average age 33. 17 applicants, 65% accepted, 9 enrolled. In 2019, 11 master's awarded. *Degree requirements:* For master's, 2 foreign languages, comprehensive exam, thesis, 1 semester of teaching. *Entrance requirements:* For master's, GRE, prerequisite second language requirement (can be fulfilled concurrently), prerequisite teaching methods course (can be fulfilled concurrently). Additional exam requirements/recommendations for international students: required—TOEFL (minimum score 580 paper-based; 85 iBT). *Application deadline:* For fall admission, 2/1 for domestic and international students. Application fee: $50. Electronic applications accepted. *Expenses:* $13,515 to complete two-year degree. *Financial support:* In 2019–20, 22 students received support, including 2 teaching assistantships with partial tuition reimbursements available (averaging $8,431 per year); scholarships/grants also available. Financial award application deadline: 2/1. *Unit head:* Dr. Scott Alvord, Interim Chair, Department of Spanish & Portuguese, 801-422-7546, Fax: 801-422-0308, E-mail: scott_alvord@byu.edu. *Application contact:* Brian A Price, Graduate Program Manager, 801-422-3453, Fax: 801-422-0308, E-mail: brian_price@byu.edu.
Website: http://spanport.byu.edu/

California State University, San Marcos, College of Humanities, Arts, Behavioral and Social Sciences, Program in Spanish, San Marcos, CA 92096-0001. Offers Hispanic cultures and society (MA); Hispanic language and linguistics (MA); Hispanic literatures and literary theory (MA). *Program availability:* Part-time, evening/weekend. *Degree requirements:* For master's, 2 foreign languages, exam. *Entrance requirements:* For master's, GRE General Test, minimum GPA of 3.0 overall and in upper-division Spanish courses, official transcripts, three letters of recommendation, 750-word statement of purpose (in English), academic writing sample (in Spanish). Additional exam requirements/recommendations for international students: required—TOEFL (minimum score 500 paper-based), TWE (minimum score 4.5). Electronic applications accepted. *Expenses: Tuition, area resident:* Full-time $7176. Tuition, state resident: full-time $7176. Tuition, nonresident: full-time $18,640. *International tuition:* $18,640 full-time. *Required fees:* $1960.

Cornell University, Graduate School, Graduate Fields of Arts and Sciences, Field of Romance Studies, Ithaca, NY 14853. Offers French linguistics (PhD); French literature (PhD); Hispanic literature (PhD); Italian linguistics (PhD); Italian literature (PhD); Romance linguistics (PhD); Spanish linguistics (PhD). *Degree requirements:* For doctorate, 2 foreign languages, comprehensive exam, thesis/dissertation. *Entrance requirements:* For doctorate, GRE General Test, sample of written work, 3 letters of recommendation. Additional exam requirements/recommendations for international students: required—TOEFL (minimum score 550 paper-based; 77 iBT). Electronic applications accepted.

The Graduate Center, City University of New York, Graduate Studies, Program in Latin American, Iberian and Latino Cultures, New York, NY 10016-4039. Offers PhD. *Degree requirements:* For doctorate, 2 foreign languages, thesis/dissertation. *Entrance requirements:* For doctorate, GRE General Test. Additional exam requirements/recommendations for international students: required—TOEFL. Electronic applications accepted.

Indiana University Bloomington, University Graduate School, College of Arts and Sciences, Department of Spanish and Portuguese, Bloomington, IN 47405. Offers Portuguese (MA, PhD); Spanish (MA, PhD), including Hispanic linguistics, Hispanic literatures. *Degree requirements:* For master's, one foreign language, comprehensive exam, thesis (for Spanish); for doctorate, 2 foreign languages, comprehensive exam, thesis/dissertation. *Entrance requirements:* For master's, GRE General Test, bachelor's degree in Portuguese or Spanish, minimum GPA of 3.0; for doctorate, GRE General Test, master's degree in Portuguese or Spanish, minimum GPA of 3.0. Additional exam requirements/recommendations for international students: required—TOEFL (minimum score 79 iBT). Electronic applications accepted.

Michigan State University, The Graduate School, College of Arts and Letters, Department of Romance and Classical Studies, East Lansing, MI 48824. Offers French (MA); French language and literature (PhD); Hispanic cultural studies (PhD); Hispanic literatures (MA); Spanish as a second or bilingual language (MA). *Entrance requirements:* Additional exam requirements/recommendations for international students: required—TOEFL. Electronic applications accepted.

Queens College of the City University of New York, Arts and Humanities Division, Department of Hispanic Languages and Literatures, Queens, NY 11367-1597. Offers Spanish (MA). *Program availability:* Part-time. *Degree requirements:* For master's, 2 foreign languages, thesis optional. *Entrance requirements:* For master's, minimum GPA of 3.0. Additional exam requirements/recommendations for international students: required—TOEFL (minimum score 61 iBT). Electronic applications accepted.

Stony Brook University, State University of New York, Graduate School, College of Arts and Sciences, Department of Hispanic Languages and Literature, Stony Brook, NY 11794. Offers MA, PhD. *Program availability:* Evening/weekend. *Faculty:* 14 full-time (9 women), 5 part-time/adjunct (2 women). *Students:* 32 full-time (17 women), 3 part-time (2 women); includes 17 minority (2 Black or African American, non-Hispanic/Latino; 15 Hispanic/Latino), 15 international. Average age 35. 19 applicants, 74% accepted, 7 enrolled. In 2019, 2 master's, 1 doctorate awarded. *Degree requirements:* For master's, one foreign language, thesis or alternative; for doctorate, 2 foreign languages, thesis/dissertation. *Entrance requirements:* For master's, GRE General Test, BA in Spanish; for doctorate, GRE General Test, MA in Spanish. Additional exam requirements/recommendations for international students: required—TOEFL. *Application deadline:* For fall admission, 1/15 for domestic students; for spring admission, 10/1 for domestic students. Application fee: $100. Electronic applications accepted. *Expenses:* Contact institution. *Financial support:* In 2019–20, 17 teaching assistantships were awarded; fellowships, research assistantships, tuition waivers, and unspecified assistantships also available. *Unit head:* Dr. Daniela Flesler, Chair, 631-632-9668, Fax: 631-632-9724, E-mail: daniela.flesler@stonybrook.edu. *Application contact:* Mary Moran-Luba, Coordinator, 631-632-6935, Fax: 631-632-9724, E-mail: mary.moran-luba@stonybrook.edu.
Website: https://www.stonybrook.edu/commcms/hispanic/

Université de Montréal, Faculty of Arts and Sciences, Department of Literatures and Modern Languages, Montréal, QC H3C 3J7, Canada. Offers German literature (PhD); German studies (MA); Hispanic literature (PhD); Hispanic studies (MA). Terminal master's awarded for partial completion of doctoral program. *Degree requirements:* For master's, 2 foreign languages, thesis; for doctorate, 2 foreign languages, thesis/dissertation, general exam. Electronic applications accepted.

University of California, Berkeley, Graduate Division, College of Letters and Science, Department of Spanish and Portuguese, Berkeley, CA 94720. Offers Hispanic languages and literatures (PhD). *Degree requirements:* For doctorate, thesis/dissertation, qualifying exam. *Entrance requirements:* For doctorate, GRE General Test, minimum GPA of 3.0, 3 letters of recommendation. Additional exam requirements/recommendations for international students: required—TOEFL (minimum score 570 paper-based; 90 iBT). Electronic applications accepted.

University of California, Los Angeles, Graduate Division, College of Letters and Science, Department of Spanish and Portuguese, Program in Hispanic Languages and Literature, Los Angeles, CA 90095. Offers PhD. *Degree requirements:* For doctorate, 2 foreign languages, thesis/dissertation, oral and written qualifying exams. *Entrance requirements:* For doctorate, GRE General Test, master's degree; minimum undergraduate GPA of 3.0 (or its equivalent if letter grade system not used); writing sample. Additional exam requirements/recommendations for international students: required—TOEFL. Electronic applications accepted.

University of California, Santa Barbara, Graduate Division, College of Letters and Sciences, Division of Humanities and Fine Arts, Department of Spanish and Portuguese, Santa Barbara, CA 93106-4150. Offers Hispanic languages and literatures (PhD), including European medieval studies, feminist studies, Hispanic linguistics, Hispanic literature, Luso-Brazilian literature; Hispanic linguistics (MA); Luso-Brazilian literature (MA); Spanish or Spanish-American literature (MA); MA/PhD. Terminal master's awarded for partial completion of doctoral program. *Degree requirements:* For master's, 2 foreign languages, comprehensive exam (for some programs), thesis optional; for doctorate, 3 foreign languages, comprehensive exam, thesis/dissertation. *Entrance requirements:* For master's and doctorate, GRE. Additional exam requirements/recommendations for international students: required—TOEFL (minimum score 550 paper-based; 80 iBT), IELTS (minimum score 7). Electronic applications accepted.

University of Colorado Boulder, Graduate School, College of Arts and Sciences, Department of Spanish and Portuguese, Boulder, CO 80309. Offers Hispanic linguistics (MA); medieval and early modern Hispanic literatures (PhD); peninsular and Latin American literature (MA). Terminal master's awarded for partial completion of doctoral

program. *Degree requirements:* For master's, one foreign language, comprehensive exam, thesis or alternative; for doctorate, 2 foreign languages, thesis/dissertation. *Entrance requirements:* For master's, minimum undergraduate GPA of 2.75. Electronic applications accepted. Application fee is waived when completed online.

University of Illinois at Chicago, College of Liberal Arts and Sciences, School of Literatures, Cultural Studies and Linguistics, Chicago, IL 60607-7128. Offers French and Francophone studies (MA); Germanic studies (MA); Hispanic and Italian studies (MAT, PhD), including Hispanic linguistics (PhD), Hispanic literary and cultural studies (PhD), teaching of Spanish (MAT); linguistics (MA), including teaching English to speakers of other languages/applied linguistics; Slavic and Baltic languages and literatures (MA), including Slavic studies (MA, PhD); Slavic and Baltic languages and literatures (PhD), including Slavic studies (MA, PhD). *Program availability:* Part-time. Terminal master's awarded for partial completion of doctoral program. *Degree requirements:* For master's, one foreign language, exam. *Entrance requirements:* For master's, minimum GPA of 2.75. Additional exam requirements/recommendations for international students: required—TOEFL. Electronic applications accepted.

University of Massachusetts Amherst, Graduate School, College of Humanities and Fine Arts, Department of Languages, Literatures, and Cultures, Program in Spanish and Portuguese Studies, Amherst, MA 01003. Offers Hispanic literatures, cultures and linguistics (MA, PhD); teaching Spanish (MAT). *Program availability:* Part-time. Terminal master's awarded for partial completion of doctoral program. *Degree requirements:* For master's, one foreign language, thesis or alternative; for doctorate, 2 foreign languages, comprehensive exam, thesis/dissertation. *Entrance requirements:* For master's and doctorate, GRE General Test, sample academic term paper. Additional exam requirements/recommendations for international students: required—TOEFL (minimum score 550 paper-based; 80 iBT), IELTS (minimum score 6.5). Electronic applications accepted.

University of Minnesota, Twin Cities Campus, Graduate School, College of Liberal Arts, Department of Spanish and Portuguese Studies, Minneapolis, MN 55455-0213. Offers Hispanic and Lusophone literatures, cultures and linguistics (PhD); Hispanic linguistics (MA); Hispanic literature (MA); Lusophone literature (MA). *Degree requirements:* For master's, 2 foreign languages, comprehensive exam, thesis or alternative; for doctorate, 2 foreign languages, comprehensive exam, thesis/dissertation. *Entrance requirements:* For master's and doctorate, GRE General Test, samples of written work, 3 letters of recommendation, voice sample, statement of purpose. Additional exam requirements/recommendations for international students: required—TOEFL (minimum score 550 paper-based; 79 iBT). Electronic applications accepted.

The University of North Carolina at Greensboro, Graduate School, College of Arts and Sciences, Department of Languages, Literatures, and Cultures, Program in Spanish, Greensboro, NC 27412-5001. Offers advanced Spanish language and Hispanic cultural studies (Certificate); Spanish (MA). *Degree requirements:* For master's, one foreign language, comprehensive exam, thesis or alternative. *Entrance requirements:* For master's, GRE General Test, 3-5 minute tape demonstrating foreign language proficiency, composition in Spanish, sample paper in English. Additional exam requirements/recommendations for international students: required—TOEFL. Electronic applications accepted.

The University of Texas at Austin, Graduate School, College of Liberal Arts, Department of Spanish and Portuguese, Austin, TX 78712-1111. Offers Hispanic linguistics (MA, PhD); Hispanic literature (MA, PhD); Ibero-romance philology and linguistics (PhD); Luso-Brazilian literature (MA, PhD). *Degree requirements:* For master's, 2 foreign languages, thesis or alternative; for doctorate, 3 foreign languages, thesis/dissertation. *Entrance requirements:* For master's and doctorate, GRE General Test. Electronic applications accepted.

University of Washington, Graduate School, College of Arts and Sciences, Division of Spanish and Portuguese Studies, Seattle, WA 98195. Offers Hispanic literary and cultural studies (MA). *Degree requirements:* For master's, 2 foreign languages, thesis optional, exam. *Entrance requirements:* For master's, GRE General Test, minimum GPA of 3.0. Additional exam requirements/recommendations for international students: required—TOEFL. Electronic applications accepted.

Italian

Binghamton University, State University of New York, Graduate School, Harpur College of Arts and Sciences, Department of Romance Languages and Literatures, Program in Italian, Binghamton, NY 13902-6000. Offers MA. *Program availability:* Part-time. *Degree requirements:* For master's, one foreign language, comprehensive exam, thesis or alternative. *Entrance requirements:* For master's, GRE General Test. Additional exam requirements/recommendations for international students: required—TOEFL (minimum score 550 paper-based; 80 iBT). Electronic applications accepted.

Boston College, Morrissey Graduate School of Arts and Sciences, Department of Romance Languages and Literatures, Chestnut Hill, MA 02467-3800. Offers French (MA); Italian (MA); Spanish (MA). *Program availability:* Part-time. Terminal master's awarded for partial completion of doctoral program. *Degree requirements:* For master's, one foreign language. *Entrance requirements:* Additional exam requirements/recommendations for international students: required—TOEFL (minimum score 600 paper-based; 100 iBT), IELTS (minimum score 8). Electronic applications accepted.

Brown University, Graduate School, Department of Italian Studies, Providence, RI 02912. Offers PhD. Terminal master's awarded for partial completion of doctoral program. *Degree requirements:* For doctorate, 2 foreign languages, thesis/dissertation, preliminary exam.

Central Connecticut State University, School of Graduate Studies, College of Liberal Arts and Social Sciences, Department of Modern Languages, New Britain, CT 06050-4010. Offers modern language (MA, Certificate), including French, German (Certificate), Italian, Spanish (MA); Spanish (MS, Certificate). *Program availability:* Part-time, evening/weekend. *Degree requirements:* For master's, one foreign language, comprehensive exam, thesis or alternative; for Certificate, qualifying exam. *Entrance requirements:* For master's, minimum undergraduate GPA of 2.7, 24 credits of undergraduate courses in each language in which graduate work will be undertaken. Additional exam requirements/recommendations for international students: required—TOEFL (minimum score 550 paper-based; 79 iBT); recommended—IELTS (minimum score 6.5). Electronic applications accepted.

Columbia University, Graduate School of Arts and Sciences, New York, NY 10027. Offers African-American studies (MA); American studies (MA); anthropology (MA, PhD); art history and archaeology (MA, PhD); astronomy (PhD); biological sciences (PhD);

biotechnology (MA); chemical physics (PhD); chemistry (PhD); classical studies (MA, PhD); classics (MA, PhD); climate and society (MA); conservation biology (MA); earth and environmental sciences (PhD); East Asia: regional studies (MA); East Asian languages and cultures (MA, PhD); ecology, evolution and environmental biology (MA), including conservation biology; ecology, evolution, and environmental biology (PhD), including ecology and evolutionary biology, evolutionary primatology; economics (MA, PhD); English and comparative literature (MA, PhD); French and Romance philology (MA, PhD); Germanic languages (MA, PhD); global French studies (MA); global thought (MA); Hispanic cultural studies (MA); history (PhD); history and literature (MA); human rights studies (MA); Islamic studies (MA); Italian (MA, PhD); Japanese pedagogy (MA); Jewish studies (MA); Latin America and the Caribbean: regional studies (MA); Latin American and Iberian cultures (PhD); mathematics (MA, PhD), including finance (MA); medieval and Renaissance studies (MA); Middle Eastern, South Asian, and African studies (MA, PhD); modern art: critical and curatorial studies (MA); modern European studies (MA); museum anthropology (MA); music (DMA, PhD); oral history (MA); philosophical foundations of physics (MA); philosophy (MA, PhD); physics (PhD); political science (MA, PhD); psychology (PhD); quantitative methods in the social sciences (MA); religion (MA, PhD); Russia, Eurasia and East Europe: regional studies (MA); Russian translation (MA); Slavic cultures (MA); Slavic languages (MA, PhD); sociology (MA, PhD); South Asian studies (MA); statistics (MA, PhD); theatre (PhD). *Program availability:* Part-time. *Students:* 3,506 full-time (1,844 women), 208 part-time (121 women); includes 864 minority (110 Black or African American, non-Hispanic/Latino; 5 American Indian or Alaska Native, non-Hispanic/Latino; 416 Asian, non-Hispanic/Latino; 147 Hispanic/Latino; 6 Native Hawaiian or other Pacific Islander, non-Hispanic/Latino; 180 Two or more races, non-Hispanic/Latino), 2,065 international. 14,545 applicants, 25% accepted, 1,429 enrolled. In 2019, 1,262 master's, 363 doctorates awarded. Terminal master's awarded for partial completion of doctoral program. *Degree requirements:* For master's, variable foreign language requirement, comprehensive exam (for some programs), thesis (for some programs); for doctorate, variable foreign language requirement, comprehensive exam (for some programs), thesis/dissertation. *Entrance requirements:* For master's and doctorate, GRE General Test, GRE Subject Test (for some programs). Additional exam requirements/recommendations for international students: required—TOEFL (minimum score 600 paper-based; 100 iBT), IELTS (minimum score 7.5). Application fee: $115. Electronic

applications accepted. *Expenses: Tuition:* Full-time $47,600; part-time $1880 per credit. One-time fee: $105. *Financial support:* Fellowships, research assistantships, teaching assistantships, career-related internships or fieldwork, Federal Work-Study, institutionally sponsored loans, scholarships/grants, traineeships, health care benefits, tuition waivers, and unspecified assistantships available. Support available to part-time students. Financial award application deadline: 12/15. *Unit head:* Dr. Carlos J. Alonso, Dean of the Graduate School of Arts and Sciences and Vice President for Graduate Education, 212-854-2861, E-mail: gsas-dean@columbia.edu. *Application contact:* GSAS Office of Admissions, 212-854-6729, E-mail: gsas-admissions@columbia.edu.
Website: http://gsas.columbia.edu/

Cornell University, Graduate School, Graduate Fields of Arts and Sciences, Field of Romance Studies, Ithaca, NY 14853. Offers French linguistics (PhD); French literature (PhD); Hispanic literature (PhD); Italian linguistics (PhD); Italian literature (PhD); Romance linguistics (PhD); Spanish linguistics (PhD). *Degree requirements:* For doctorate, 2 foreign languages, comprehensive exam, thesis/dissertation. *Entrance requirements:* For doctorate, GRE General Test, sample of written work, 3 letters of recommendation. Additional exam requirements/recommendations for international students: required—TOEFL (minimum score 550 paper-based; 77 iBT). Electronic applications accepted.

DePaul University, College of Liberal Arts and Social Sciences, Chicago, IL 60614. Offers Arabic (MA); Chinese (MA); critical ethnic studies (MA); English (MA); French (MA); German (MA); history (MA); interdisciplinary studies (MA, MS); international public service (MS); international studies (MA); Italian (MA); Japanese (MA); liberal studies (MA); nonprofit management (MNM); public administration (MPA); public health (MPH); public policy (MPP); public service management (MS); refugee and forced migration studies (MS); social work (MSW); sociology (MA); Spanish (MA); sustainable urban development (MA); women's and gender studies (MA); writing and publishing (MA); writing, rhetoric and discourse (MA); MA/PhD. *Accreditation:* CEPH. *Program availability:* Part-time, evening/weekend, online learning. Terminal master's awarded for partial completion of doctoral program. *Degree requirements:* For master's, variable foreign language requirement, comprehensive exam (for some programs), thesis (for some programs). Electronic applications accepted.

Drew University, Caspersen School of Graduate Studies, Madison, NJ 07940-1493. Offers conflict resolution and leadership (Certificate), including community leadership, moderation, peace building; education (M Ed); finance (MA); history and culture (MA, PhD), including American history, book history, British history, European history, intellectual history, Irish history, print culture, public history; K-12 education (MAT), including art, biology, chemistry, elementary education, English, French, Italian, math, secondary education, special education, teacher of students with disabilities; liberal studies (M Litt, D Litt), including history, Irish/Irish-American studies, literature (M Litt, MMH, D Litt, DMH, CMH), religion, spirituality, teaching in the two-year college, writing; medical humanities (MMH, DMH, CMH), including arts, health, healthcare, literature (M Litt, MMH, D Litt, DMH, CMH), scientific research; poetry (MFA). *Program availability:* Part-time, evening/weekend. Terminal master's awarded for partial completion of doctoral program. *Degree requirements:* For master's and other advanced degree, thesis (for some programs); for doctorate, one foreign language, comprehensive exam (for some programs), thesis/dissertation. *Entrance requirements:* For master's, PRAXIS Core and Subject Area tests (for MAT), GRE/GMAT (for MFin MS in Data Analytics), resume, transcripts, writing sample, personal statement, letters of recommendation; for doctorate, GRE (PhD in history and culture), resume, transcripts, writing sample, personal statement, letters of recommendation; for other advanced degree, resume, transcripts, personal statement. Additional exam requirements/recommendations for international students: required—TOEFL (minimum score 587 paper-based; 80 iBT), IELTS (minimum score 6), TWE (minimum score 4). Electronic applications accepted.

Duke University, Graduate School, Department of Romance Studies, Durham, NC 27708. Offers French (PhD); Italian (PhD); Spanish (PhD); JD/AM. *Degree requirements:* For doctorate, 2 foreign languages, thesis/dissertation. *Entrance requirements:* For doctorate, GRE General Test. Additional exam requirements/recommendations for international students: required—TOEFL (minimum score 577 paper-based; 90 iBT) or IELTS (minimum score 7). Electronic applications accepted.

Florida State University, The Graduate School, Department of Anthropology, Department of Modern Languages and Linguistics, Program in Italian Studies, Tallahassee, FL 32306. Offers MA. *Faculty:* 6 full-time (4 women). *Students:* 6 full-time (5 women); includes 2 minority (1 Hispanic/Latino; 1 Two or more races, non-Hispanic/Latino). In 2019, 3 master's awarded. *Degree requirements:* For master's, comprehensive exam. *Entrance requirements:* For master's, GRE General Test, minimum GPA of 3.0. Additional exam requirements/recommendations for international students: required—TOEFL (minimum score 550 paper-based; 80 iBT). *Application deadline:* For fall admission, 1/15 priority date for domestic students, 1/15 for international students. Application fee: $30. Electronic applications accepted. *Financial support:* In 2019–20, 5 teaching assistantships with partial tuition reimbursements were awarded. Financial award application deadline: 1/15. *Unit head:* Dr. Mark Pietralunga, Coordinator, 850-644-8392, Fax: 850-644-0524, E-mail: mpietral@fsu.edu. *Application contact:* Wendy E. Pigott, Graduate Academic Coordinator, 850-644-8397, Fax: 850-644-0524, E-mail: wpigott@fsu.edu.
Website: http://modlang.ez.fsu.edu/Language-divisions-programs/Italian-Division/Graduate-Program

The Graduate Center, City University of New York, Graduate Studies, Program in Comparative Literature, New York, NY 10016-4039. Offers comparative literature (MA, PhD), including Italian (PhD). Terminal master's awarded for partial completion of doctoral program. *Degree requirements:* For master's, 2 foreign languages, comprehensive exam, thesis; for doctorate, 3 foreign languages, comprehensive exam, thesis/dissertation. *Entrance requirements:* For master's and doctorate, GRE General Test. Additional exam requirements/recommendations for international students: required—TOEFL. Electronic applications accepted.

Harvard University, Graduate School of Arts and Sciences, Department of Romance Languages and Literatures, Cambridge, MA 02138. Offers French (AM, PhD); Italian (AM, PhD); Portuguese (AM, PhD); Spanish (AM, PhD). Terminal master's awarded for partial completion of doctoral program. *Degree requirements:* For master's, 2 foreign languages; for doctorate, 2 foreign languages, thesis/dissertation. *Entrance requirements:* For master's and doctorate, GRE General Test, sample of written work. Additional exam requirements/recommendations for international students: required—TOEFL.

Hunter College of the City University of New York, Graduate School, School of Arts and Sciences, Department of Romance Languages, Program in Italian, New York, NY 10065-5085. Offers MA. *Degree requirements:* For master's, 2 foreign languages, comprehensive exam, thesis optional. *Entrance requirements:* For master's, GRE General Test, GRE Subject Test, ability to read, speak, and write Italian; interview. Additional exam requirements/recommendations for international students: required—TOEFL.

Indiana University Bloomington, University Graduate School, College of Arts and Sciences, Department of French and Italian, Bloomington, IN 47405. Offers French (MA, PhD), including French and Francophone studies (MA), French instruction (MA), French linguistics; Italian (MA, PhD). *Program availability:* Part-time. Terminal master's awarded for partial completion of doctoral program. *Degree requirements:* For master's, variable foreign language requirement, comprehensive exam (for some programs), thesis or alternative; for doctorate, variable foreign language requirement, comprehensive exam, thesis/dissertation. *Entrance requirements:* For master's, GRE General Test, BA or equivalent undergraduate preparation in French or Italian; for doctorate, GRE General Test, MA from degree program at IU; MA in the specific field. Additional exam requirements/recommendations for international students: required—TOEFL (minimum score 550 paper-based; 79 iBT), GRE General Test (recommended). Electronic applications accepted.

Johns Hopkins University, Zanvyl Krieger School of Arts and Sciences, Department of German and Romance Languages and Literatures, Baltimore, MD 21218. Offers German (MA, PhD); romance languages (PhD), including French, Italian, Spanish. Terminal master's awarded for partial completion of doctoral program. *Degree requirements:* For master's, comprehensive exam; for doctorate, 2 foreign languages, comprehensive exam, thesis/dissertation. *Entrance requirements:* For doctorate, GRE General Test. Additional exam requirements/recommendations for international students: required—TOEFL (minimum score 600 paper-based; 100 iBT), IELTS. Electronic applications accepted. *Expenses:* Contact institution.

McGill University, Faculty of Graduate and Postdoctoral Studies, Faculty of Arts, Department of Italian Studies, Montréal, QC H3A 2T5, Canada. Offers MA, PhD.

Middlebury College, Language Schools, Italian School, Middlebury, VT 05753-6002. Offers MA, DML. In 2019, 12 master's, 1 doctorate awarded. *Degree requirements:* For master's, one foreign language; for doctorate, 2 foreign languages, comprehensive exam, thesis/dissertation, residence abroad, teaching experience. *Entrance requirements:* For master's, online placement exam, 3 letters of recommendation, writing sample in Italian, transcripts, 200-word essay; for doctorate, 1st and 2nd language online placement exams, 3 letters of recommendation, writing sample in Italian, transcripts, 200-word essay. *Application deadline:* Applications are processed on a rolling basis. Application fee: $75. Electronic applications accepted. *Expenses:* Contact institution. *Financial support:* Fellowships and scholarships/grants available. Financial award application deadline: 3/10; financial award applicants required to submit FAFSA. *Unit head:* Dr. Antonio Vitti, Director, 802-443-5727, Fax: 802-443-2075, E-mail: acvitti@middlebury.edu. *Application contact:* Joseph Tamagni, Coordinator, 802-443-5727, Fax: 802-443-2075, E-mail: italianschool@middlebury.edu.
Website: http://www.middlebury.edu/ls/grad_programs/italian

New York University, Graduate School of Arts and Science, Department of Italian Studies, New York, NY 10012-1019. Offers MA, PhD. *Program availability:* Part-time. Terminal master's awarded for partial completion of doctoral program. *Degree requirements:* For master's, one foreign language, thesis; for doctorate, 3 foreign languages, thesis/dissertation. *Entrance requirements:* For master's and doctorate, GRE General Test. Additional exam requirements/recommendations for international students: required—TOEFL, IELTS.

New York University, Steinhardt School of Culture, Education, and Human Development, Department of Teaching and Learning, Program in Multilingual/Multicultural Studies, New York, NY 10012. Offers bilingual education (MA, PhD, Advanced Certificate); foreign language education (MA); teaching English to speakers of other languages (MA, PhD); teaching foreign languages, 7-12 (MA), including Chinese, French, Italian, Japanese, Spanish; teaching French as a foreign language (MA), including teaching English to speakers of other languages; teaching Spanish as a foreign language (MA), including teaching English to speakers of other languages. *Accreditation:* TEAC. *Program availability:* Part-time, evening/weekend. *Entrance requirements:* For doctorate, GRE General Test, interview; for Advanced Certificate, master's degree. Additional exam requirements/recommendations for international students: required—TOEFL (minimum score 100 iBT). Electronic applications accepted.

Northwestern University, The Graduate School, Judd A. and Marjorie Weinberg College of Arts and Sciences, Department of French and Italian, Evanston, IL 60208. Offers French/Francophone studies (PhD); Italian studies (Graduate Certificate). *Degree requirements:* For doctorate, one foreign language, thesis/dissertation, written and oral exams. *Entrance requirements:* For doctorate, GRE, writing sample, cassette recording. Additional exam requirements/recommendations for international students: required—TOEFL.

The Ohio State University, Graduate School, College of Arts and Sciences, Division of Arts and Humanities, Department of French and Italian, Columbus, OH 43210. Offers French (MA, PhD); Italian (MA); Italian studies (PhD). Terminal master's awarded for partial completion of doctoral program. *Degree requirements:* For master's, variable foreign language requirement, thesis optional; for doctorate, variable foreign language requirement, thesis/dissertation. *Entrance requirements:* For master's and doctorate, GRE General Test. Additional exam requirements/recommendations for international students: required—TOEFL (minimum score 550 paper-based; 79 iBT), IELTS (minimum score 7), Michigan English Language Assessment Battery (minimum score 82). Electronic applications accepted.

Queens College of the City University of New York, Arts and Humanities Division, Department of European Languages and Literatures, Queens, NY 11367-1597. Offers French (MA); Italian (MA). *Program availability:* Part-time-only, evening/weekend. *Degree requirements:* For master's, 2 foreign languages, thesis optional, oral exam. *Entrance requirements:* For master's, minimum GPA of 3.0. Additional exam requirements/recommendations for international students: recommended—TOEFL (minimum score 61 iBT), IELTS (minimum score 5). Electronic applications accepted.

Rutgers University - New Brunswick, Graduate School-New Brunswick, Program in Italian, Piscataway, NJ 08854-8097. Offers Italian (MA, PhD); Italian literature and literary criticism (MA); language, literature and culture (MAT). *Program availability:* Part-time, evening/weekend. Terminal master's awarded for partial completion of doctoral program. *Degree requirements:* For master's, one foreign language, comprehensive exam (for some programs), thesis optional; for doctorate, 2 foreign languages, thesis/dissertation, qualifying exam. *Entrance requirements:* For master's and doctorate, GRE General Test. Additional exam requirements/recommendations for international students: required—TOEFL.

San Francisco State University, Division of Graduate Studies, College of Liberal and Creative Arts, Department of Modern Languages and Literatures, Program in Italian, San Francisco, CA 94132-1722. Offers MA. *Application deadline:* Applications are processed on a rolling basis. *Expenses: Tuition, area resident:* Full-time $7176; part-time $4164 per year. Tuition, state resident: full-time $7176; part-time $4164 per year. Tuition, nonresident: full-time $16,680; part-time $396 per unit. *International tuition:* $16,680 full-time. *Required fees:* $1524; $1524 per unit. $762 per semester. Tuition and fees vary according to degree level and program. *Unit head:* Dr. Olivia Albiero, Program Coordinator, 415-338-7452, Fax: 415-338-6159, E-mail: albiero@sfsu.edu. *Application contact:* Dr. Olivia Albiero, Program Coordinator, 415-338-7452, Fax: 415-338-6159, E-mail: albiero@sfsu.edu.
Website: http://mll.sfsu.edu/italian-program/

Stanford University, School of Humanities and Sciences, Department of French and Italian, Stanford, CA 94305-2004. Offers French and Italian (PhD). *Expenses: Tuition:* Full-time $52,479; part-time $34,110 per unit. *Required fees:* $672; $224 per quarter. Tuition and fees vary according to program and student level. Website: http://www.stanford.edu/dept/fren-ital/

Stony Brook University, State University of New York, Graduate School, College of Arts and Sciences, Department of European Languages, Literatures, and Cultures, Program in Italian, Stony Brook, NY 11794. Offers MA. *Program availability:* Evening/weekend. *Students:* 2 applicants, 100% accepted, 2 enrolled. In 2019, 3 master's awarded. *Entrance requirements:* Additional exam requirements/recommendations for international students: required—TOEFL. *Application deadline:* For fall admission, 1/15 for domestic students; for spring admission, 10/1 for domestic students. Application fee: $100. Electronic applications accepted. *Expenses:* Contact institution. *Unit head:* Prof. Sarah Jourdain, Chair, 631-632-7440, Fax: 631-632-9612, E-mail: sarah.jourdain@stonybrook.edu. *Application contact:* Elizabeth Tolson, Coordinator, 631-632-7440, Fax: 631-632-9612, E-mail: elizabeth-a.tolson@stonybrook.edu.

University of Alberta, Faculty of Graduate Studies and Research, Department of Modern Languages and Cultural Studies, Edmonton, AB T6G 2E1, Canada. Offers applied linguistics (Germanic, Romance, Slavic) (MA); French language, literatures and linguistics (PhD); French language, literatures, and linguistics (MA); Germanic languages, literatures and linguistics (PhD); Germanic languages, literatures, and linguistics (MA); Italian studies (MA); Slavic languages and literatures (Russian, Ukrainian) (MA, PhD); Slavic linguistics (Russian, Ukrainian) (MA, PhD); Spanish and Latin American studies (MA, PhD); Ukrainian folklore (MA, PhD). *Program availability:* Part-time. *Degree requirements:* For master's, one foreign language, thesis; for doctorate, 2 foreign languages, comprehensive exam, thesis/dissertation. *Entrance requirements:* For master's and doctorate, 1 language other than English. Additional exam requirements/recommendations for international students: required—Michigan English Language Assessment Battery or TOEFL (minimum score 550 paper-based). Electronic applications accepted.

University of California, Berkeley, Graduate Division, College of Letters and Science, Department of Italian Studies, Berkeley, CA 94720. Offers PhD. *Degree requirements:* For doctorate, one foreign language, thesis/dissertation, oral and written qualifying exams. *Entrance requirements:* For doctorate, GRE General Test, minimum GPA of 3.0, 3 letters of recommendation. Additional exam requirements/recommendations for international students: required—TOEFL (minimum score 570 paper-based; 90 iBT). Electronic applications accepted.

University of California, Berkeley, Graduate Division, College of Letters and Science, Group in Romance Languages and Literatures, Berkeley, CA 94720. Offers French (PhD); Italian (PhD); Spanish (PhD). *Degree requirements:* For doctorate, thesis/dissertation, qualifying exam. *Entrance requirements:* For doctorate, GRE General Test, minimum GPA of 3.0, 3 letters of recommendation. Additional exam requirements/recommendations for international students: required—TOEFL (minimum score 570 paper-based; 90 iBT). Electronic applications accepted.

University of California, Los Angeles, Graduate Division, College of Letters and Science, Department of Italian, Los Angeles, CA 90095. Offers MA, PhD. Terminal master's awarded for partial completion of doctoral program. *Degree requirements:* For master's, one foreign language, comprehensive exam or thesis; for doctorate, 2 foreign languages, thesis/dissertation, oral and written qualifying exams. *Entrance requirements:* For master's, GRE General Test, bachelor's degree; minimum undergraduate GPA of 3.0 (or its equivalent if letter grade system not used); for doctorate, GRE General Test, master's degree; minimum undergraduate GPA of 3.0 (or its equivalent if letter grade system not used). Additional exam requirements/recommendations for international students: required—TOEFL. Electronic applications accepted.

University of Chicago, Division of the Humanities, Department of Romance Languages and Literatures, Chicago, IL 60637. Offers French and Francophone studies (PhD); Hispanic and Luso-Brazilian studies (PhD); Italian studies (PhD); Renaissance and early modern studies (PhD). Terminal master's awarded for partial completion of doctoral program. *Degree requirements:* For doctorate, 3 foreign languages, comprehensive exam, thesis/dissertation. *Entrance requirements:* For doctorate, GRE General Test, 15-20 page writing sample, statement of purpose, 3 letters of recommendation, transcripts for all previous degrees and institutions attended. Additional exam requirements/recommendations for international students: required—TOEFL (minimum score 104 iBT), IELTS (minimum score 7). Electronic applications accepted.

University of Georgia, Franklin College of Arts and Sciences, Department of Romance Languages, Athens, GA 30602. Offers French (PhD); Italian (MA, PhD); Portuguese (MA, PhD); romance linguistics (MA); Spanish (PhD). *Degree requirements:* For master's, one foreign language; for doctorate, 2 foreign languages, thesis/dissertation. *Entrance requirements:* For master's and doctorate, GRE General Test. Electronic applications accepted.

University of Illinois at Urbana-Champaign, Graduate College, College of Liberal Arts and Sciences, School of Literatures, Cultures and Linguistics, Department of Spanish, Italian and Portuguese, Champaign, IL 61820. Offers Italian (MA, PhD); Portuguese (MA, PhD); Spanish (MA, PhD).

University of Massachusetts Amherst, Graduate School, College of Humanities and Fine Arts, Department of Languages, Literatures, and Cultures, Program in Italian Studies, Amherst, MA 01003. Offers MAT. *Program availability:* Part-time. *Degree requirements:* For master's, comprehensive exam, thesis or alternative. *Entrance requirements:* For master's, GRE General Test. Additional exam requirements/recommendations for international students: required—TOEFL (minimum score 550 paper-based; 80 iBT), IELTS (minimum score 6.5). Electronic applications accepted.

University of Michigan, Rackham Graduate School, College of Literature, Science, and the Arts, Department of Romance Languages and Literatures, Program in Italian, Ann Arbor, MI 48109. Offers PhD. *Degree requirements:* For doctorate, 2 foreign languages, thesis/dissertation, oral defense of dissertation, preliminary exams in essay format. *Entrance requirements:* Additional exam requirements/recommendations for international students: required—TOEFL or Michigan English Language Assessment Battery. Electronic applications accepted.

The University of North Carolina at Chapel Hill, Graduate School, College of Arts and Sciences, Department of Romance Languages and Literatures, Chapel Hill, NC 27599. Offers French (MA, PhD); Italian (MA, PhD); Portuguese (MA, PhD); Romance languages (MA, PhD); Romance philology (MA, PhD); Spanish (MA, PhD). *Degree requirements:* For master's, one foreign language, comprehensive exam, thesis; for doctorate, 2 foreign languages, comprehensive exam, thesis/dissertation. *Entrance requirements:* For master's and doctorate, GRE General Test, minimum GPA of 3.0. Additional exam requirements/recommendations for international students: required—TOEFL (minimum score 550 paper-based). Electronic applications accepted.

University of Notre Dame, The Graduate School, College of Arts and Letters, Division of Humanities, Department of Romance Languages and Literatures, Notre Dame, IN 46556. Offers French and Francophone studies (MA); Iberian and Latin American studies (MA); Italian studies (MA); Romance literatures (MA). *Degree requirements:* For master's, 2 foreign languages, comprehensive exam, thesis optional. *Entrance requirements:* For master's, GRE General Test, BA in target language. Additional exam requirements/recommendations for international students: required—TOEFL (minimum score 600 paper-based; 80 iBT). Electronic applications accepted.

University of Oregon, Graduate School, College of Arts and Sciences, Department of Romance Languages, Program in Italian, Eugene, OR 97403. Offers MA. *Program availability:* Part-time. *Degree requirements:* For master's, variable foreign language requirement. *Entrance requirements:* For master's, GRE General Test, minimum GPA of 3.0. Additional exam requirements/recommendations for international students: required—TOEFL.

University of Pennsylvania, School of Arts and Sciences, Graduate Group in Romance Languages, Philadelphia, PA 19104. Offers French (AM, PhD); Italian (AM, PhD); Spanish (AM, PhD). *Faculty:* 65 full-time (29 women), 8 part-time/adjunct (3 women). *Students:* 60 full-time (31 women); includes 7 minority (1 Asian, non-Hispanic/Latino; 5 Hispanic/Latino; 1 Two or more races, non-Hispanic/Latino), 37 international. Average age 32. 46 applicants, 37% accepted, 8 enrolled. In 2019, 10 master's, 4 doctorates awarded. Terminal master's awarded for partial completion of doctoral program. Application fee: $90. Website: http://www.sas.upenn.edu/graduate-division

University of Pittsburgh, Kenneth P. Dietrich School of Arts and Sciences, Department of French and Italian Languages and Literatures, Pittsburgh, PA 15260. Offers French (MA, PhD), including film studies (PhD), French (MA), Romance languages and literatures (PhD); Italian (MA). *Program availability:* Part-time. *Faculty:* 8 full-time (3 women). *Students:* 16 full-time (6 women); includes 3 minority (2 Black or African American, non-Hispanic/Latino; 1 Asian, non-Hispanic/Latino). Average age 29. 18 applicants, 22% accepted, 3 enrolled. In 2019, 2 master's, 1 doctorate awarded. Terminal master's awarded for partial completion of doctoral program. *Degree requirements:* For master's, one foreign language, comprehensive exam; for doctorate, one foreign language, comprehensive exam, thesis/dissertation. *Entrance requirements:* For doctorate, application must be completed through Apply Yourself; 3 letters of recommendation; unofficial transcripts of all post-secondary academic work, and official translations if these are not in English; personal statement (1-3 pages single-spaced) written in English outlining goals and reasons for pursuing graduate education in French. Additional exam requirements/recommendations for international students: required—TOEFL (minimum score 90 iBT) or IELTS (minimum score 7). *Application deadline:* For fall admission, 1/10 priority date for domestic and international students. Application fee: $50. Electronic applications accepted. *Financial support:* In 2019–20, 88 students received support, including 2 fellowships with full tuition reimbursements available (averaging $23,690 per year), 8 teaching assistantships with full tuition reimbursements available (averaging $20,250 per year); scholarships/grants, health care benefits, tuition waivers (full), and unspecified assistantships also available. Financial award application deadline: 1/10. *Unit head:* Dr. Todd Reeser, Department Chair, 412-624-6258, E-mail: reeser@pitt.edu. *Application contact:* Keanna Cash, Graduate Administrator, 412-624-5227, Fax: 412-624-6263, E-mail: kec176@pitt.edu. Website: http://frenchanditalian.pitt.edu

University of South Africa, College of Human Sciences, Pretoria, South Africa. Offers adult education (M Ed); African languages (MA, PhD); African politics (MA, PhD); Afrikaans (MA, PhD); ancient history (MA, PhD); ancient Near Eastern studies (MA, PhD); anthropology (MA, PhD); applied linguistics (MA); Arabic (MA, PhD); archaeology (MA); art history (MA); Biblical archaeology (MA); Biblical studies (M Th, D Th, PhD); Christian spirituality (M Th, D Th); church history (M Th, D Th); classical studies (MA, PhD); clinical psychology (MA); communication (MA, PhD); comparative education (M Ed, Ed D); consulting psychology (D Admin, D Com, PhD); curriculum studies (M Ed, Ed D); development studies (M Admin, MA, D Admin, PhD); didactics (M Ed, Ed D); education (M Tech); education management (M Ed, Ed D); educational psychology (M Ed); English (MA); environmental education (M Ed); French (MA, PhD); German (MA, PhD); Greek (MA); guidance and counseling (M Ed); health studies (MA, PhD), including health sciences education (MA), health services management (MA), medical and surgical nursing science (critical care general) (MA), midwifery and neonatal nursing science (MA), trauma and emergency care (MA); history (MA, PhD); history of education (Ed D); inclusive education (M Ed, Ed D); information and communications technology policy and regulation (MA); information science (MA, MIS, PhD); international politics (MA, PhD); Islamic studies (MA, PhD); Italian (MA, PhD); Judaica (MA, PhD); linguistics (MA, PhD); mathematical education (M Ed); mathematics education (MA); missiology (M Th, D Th); modern Hebrew (MA, PhD); musicology (MA, MMus, D Mus, PhD); natural science education (M Ed); New Testament (M Th, D Th); Old Testament (D Th); pastoral therapy (M Th, D Th); philosophy (MA); philosophy of education (M Ed, Ed D); politics (MA, PhD); Portuguese (MA, PhD); practical theology (M Th, D Th); psychology (MA, MS, PhD); psychology of education (M Ed, Ed D); public health (MA); religious studies (MA, D Th, PhD); Romance languages (MA); Russian (MA, PhD); Semitic languages (MA, PhD); social behavior studies in HIV/AIDS (MA); social science (mental health) (MA); social science in development studies (MA); social science in psychology (MA); social science in social work (MA); social science in sociology (MA); social work (MSW, DSW, PhD); socio-education (M Ed, Ed D); sociolinguistics (MA); sociology (MA, PhD); Spanish (MA, PhD); systematic theology (M Th, D Th); TESOL (teaching English to speakers of other languages) (MA); theological ethics (M Th, D Th); theory of literature (MA, PhD); urban ministries (D Th); urban ministry (M Th).

The University of Tennessee, Graduate School, College of Arts and Sciences, Department of Modern Foreign Languages and Literatures, Program in Modern Foreign Languages, Knoxville, TN 37996. Offers applied linguistics (PhD); French (PhD); German (PhD); Italian (PhD); Portuguese (PhD); Russian (PhD); Spanish (PhD). *Degree requirements:* For doctorate, 2 foreign languages, thesis/dissertation. *Entrance requirements:* For doctorate, minimum GPA of 2.7. Additional exam requirements/recommendations for international students: required—TOEFL. Electronic applications accepted.

The University of Texas at Austin, Graduate School, College of Liberal Arts, Department of French and Italian, Austin, TX 78712-1111. Offers French linguistics (MA, PhD); French studies (MA, PhD); Italian studies (MA, PhD); Romance linguistics (PhD). *Program availability:* Part-time. *Degree requirements:* For master's, one foreign language, thesis; for doctorate, 2 foreign languages, thesis/dissertation. *Entrance requirements:* For master's, GRE General Test, minimum GPA of 3.0, bachelor's degree in French or equivalent; for doctorate, GRE General Test, minimum GPA of 3.0, master's degree in French. Additional exam requirements/recommendations for international students: required—TOEFL. Electronic applications accepted.

University of Toronto, School of Graduate Studies, Faculty of Arts and Science, Department of Italian Studies, Toronto, ON M5S 1A1, Canada. Offers MA, PhD. *Program availability:* Part-time. *Degree requirements:* For doctorate, 2 foreign languages, comprehensive exam, thesis/dissertation, oral defense, language exam(s). *Entrance requirements:* For master's, minimum B average in last 2 years in Italian and in final year overall; 2 letters of recommendation; for doctorate, MA in Italian, minimum A-average. Electronic applications accepted.

Italian

University of Victoria, Faculty of Graduate Studies, Faculty of Humanities, Department of Hispanic and Italian Studies, Victoria, BC V8W 2Y2, Canada. Offers Hispanic and Italian studies (MA); Hispanic studies (MA). *Degree requirements:* For master's, one foreign language, comprehensive exam, thesis (for some programs). *Entrance requirements:* For master's, undergraduate major in Hispanic studies, minimum B+ average. Additional exam requirements/recommendations for international students: required—TOEFL (minimum score 575 paper-based), IELTS (minimum score 7). Electronic applications accepted.

University of Washington, Graduate School, College of Arts and Sciences, Division of French and Italian Studies, Seattle, WA 98195. Offers French (MA, PhD); Italian (MA). Terminal master's awarded for partial completion of doctoral program. *Degree requirements:* For master's, 2 foreign languages, exam; for doctorate, 3 foreign languages, thesis/dissertation, exam. *Entrance requirements:* For master's and doctorate, GRE General Test, minimum GPA of 3.0. Additional exam requirements/recommendations for international students: required—TOEFL. Electronic applications accepted.

University of Wisconsin–Madison, Graduate School, College of Letters and Science, Department of French and Italian, Program in Italian, Madison, WI 53706-1380. Offers MA, PhD. *Program availability:* Part-time. *Degree requirements:* For master's, one foreign language; for doctorate, 2 foreign languages, thesis/dissertation. *Entrance requirements:* For master's and doctorate, GRE. Electronic applications accepted.

Wayne State University, College of Liberal Arts and Sciences, Department of Classical and Modern Languages, Literatures, and Cultures, Detroit, MI 48202. Offers classics (MA), including ancient Greek and Latin, ancient studies, classics, Latin; German (MA); language learning (MALL), including Arabic (MA, MALL), French (MA, MALL, PhD), German (MALL, PhD), Italian (MA, MALL), Spanish (MA, MALL, PhD); modern languages (PhD), including French (MA, MALL, PhD), German (MALL, PhD), Spanish (MA, MALL, PhD); Near Eastern languages (MA), including Arabic (MA, MALL), Hebrew; Romance languages (MA), including French (MA, MALL, PhD), Italian (MA, MALL), Spanish (MA, MALL, PhD). *Faculty:* 20. *Students:* 30 full-time (22 women), 15 part-time (9 women); includes 11 minority (4 Black or African American, non-Hispanic/Latino; 1 American Indian or Alaska Native, non-Hispanic/Latino; 2 Asian, non-Hispanic/Latino; 3 Hispanic/Latino; 1 Two or more races, non-Hispanic/Latino), 2 international. Average age 40. 32 applicants, 34% accepted, 9 enrolled. In 2019, 8 master's, 1 doctorate awarded. *Degree requirements:* For master's, variable foreign language requirement, comprehensive exam (for some programs), thesis (for some programs); for doctorate, one foreign language, comprehensive exam, thesis/dissertation. *Entrance requirements:* Additional exam requirements/recommendations for international students: required—TOEFL (minimum score 550 paper-based; 79 iBT), TWE (minimum score 5.5), Michigan English Language Assessment Battery (minimum score 85); recommended—IELTS (minimum score 6.5). Application fee: $50. Electronic applications accepted. *Expenses: Tuition:* Full-time $34,567. *Financial support:* In 2019–20, 22 students received support, including 1 fellowship with tuition reimbursement available (averaging $20,000 per year), 15 teaching assistantships with tuition reimbursements available (averaging $20,015 per year); research assistantships, scholarships/grants, health care benefits, and unspecified assistantships also available. Financial award applicants required to submit FAFSA. *Unit head:* Dr. Vanessa DEGifis, DR., Department Chair, 313-577-6244, Fax: 313-577-6243, E-mail: vdegifis@wayne.edu. *Application contact:* Terrie Pickering, Academic Services Officer, 313 577 3003, E-mail: t.pickering@wayne.edu.
Website: http://clas.wayne.edu/languages/

Yale University, Graduate School of Arts and Sciences, Department of Italian Language and Literature, New Haven, CT 06520. Offers PhD. *Degree requirements:* For doctorate, 3 foreign languages, thesis/dissertation. *Entrance requirements:* For doctorate, GRE General Test.

Japanese

Arizona State University at Tempe, College of Liberal Arts and Sciences, School of International Letters and Cultures, Program in Japanese, Tempe, AZ 85287-0202. Offers Asian languages and civilizations: Japanese (MA). *Program availability:* Part-time, evening/weekend. *Degree requirements:* For master's, thesis, oral defense, interactive Program of Study (iPOS) submitted no later than beginning of third semester of study. *Entrance requirements:* For master's, minimum GPA of 3.25 in the last two years of work leading to the bachelor's degree; BA in Japanese or at least 5 semesters of modern Japanese (preferred); personal statement; writing sample; 3 letters of recommendation. Additional exam requirements/recommendations for international students: required—TOEFL (minimum score 550 paper-based; 83 iBT), IELTS (minimum score 6.5). Electronic applications accepted.

Columbia University, Graduate School of Arts and Sciences, New York, NY 10027. Offers African-American studies (MA); American studies (MA); anthropology (MA, PhD); art history and archaeology (MA, PhD); astronomy (PhD); biological sciences (PhD); biotechnology (MA); chemical physics (PhD); chemistry (PhD); classical studies (MA, PhD); classics (MA, PhD); climate and society (MA); conservation biology (MA); earth and environmental sciences (PhD); East Asia: regional studies (MA); East Asian languages and cultures (MA, PhD); ecology, evolution and environmental biology (MA), including conservation biology; ecology, evolution, and environmental biology (PhD), including ecology and evolutionary biology, evolutionary primatology; economics (MA, PhD); English and comparative literature (MA, PhD); French and Romance philology (MA, PhD); Germanic languages (MA, PhD); global French studies (MA); global thought (MA); Hispanic cultural studies (MA); history (PhD); history and literature (MA); human rights studies (MA); Islamic studies (MA); Italian (MA, PhD); Japanese pedagogy (MA); Jewish studies (MA); Latin America and the Caribbean: regional studies (MA); Latin American and Iberian cultures (PhD); mathematics (MA, PhD), including finance (MA); medieval and Renaissance studies (MA); Middle Eastern, South Asian, and African studies (MA, PhD); modern art: critical and curatorial studies (MA); modern European studies (MA); museum anthropology (MA); music (DMA, PhD); oral history (MA); philosophical foundations of physics (MA); philosophy (MA, PhD); physics (PhD); political science (MA, PhD); psychology (PhD); quantitative methods in the social sciences (MA); religion (MA, PhD); Russia, Eurasia and East Europe: regional studies (MA); Russian translation (MA); Slavic cultures (MA); Slavic languages (MA, PhD); sociology (MA, PhD); South Asian studies (MA); statistics (MA, PhD); theatre (PhD). *Program availability:* Part-time. *Students:* 3,506 full-time (1,844 women), 208 part-time (121 women); includes 864 minority (110 Black or African American, non-Hispanic/Latino; 5 American Indian or Alaska Native, non-Hispanic/Latino; 416 Asian, non-Hispanic/Latino; 147 Hispanic/Latino; 6 Native Hawaiian or other Pacific Islander, non-Hispanic/Latino; 180 Two or more races, non-Hispanic/Latino), 2,065 international. 14,545 applicants, 25% accepted, 1,429 enrolled. In 2019, 1,262 master's, 363 doctorates awarded. Terminal master's awarded for partial completion of doctoral program. *Degree requirements:* For master's, variable foreign language requirement, comprehensive exam (for some programs), thesis (for some programs); for doctorate, variable foreign language requirement, comprehensive exam (for some programs), thesis/dissertation. *Entrance requirements:* For master's and doctorate, GRE General Test, GRE Subject Test (for some programs). Additional exam requirements/recommendations for international students: required—TOEFL (minimum score 600 paper-based; 100 iBT), IELTS (minimum score 7.5). Application fee: $115. Electronic applications accepted. *Expenses: Tuition:* Full-time $47,600; part-time $1880 per credit. One-time fee: $105. *Financial support:* Fellowships, research assistantships, teaching assistantships, career-related internships or fieldwork, Federal Work-Study, institutionally sponsored loans, scholarships/grants, traineeships, health care benefits, tuition waivers, and unspecified assistantships available. Support available to part-time students. Financial award application deadline: 12/15. *Unit head:* Dr. Carlos J. Alonso, Dean of the Graduate School of Arts and Sciences and Vice President for Graduate Education, 212-854-2861, E-mail: gsas-dean@columbia.edu. *Application contact:* GSAS Office of Admissions, 212-854-6729, E-mail: gsas-admissions@columbia.edu.
Website: http://gsas.columbia.edu/

DePaul University, College of Liberal Arts and Social Sciences, Chicago, IL 60614. Offers Arabic (MA); Chinese (MA); critical ethnic studies (MA); English (MA); French (MA); German (MA); history (MA); interdisciplinary studies (MA, MS); international public service (MS); international studies (MA); Italian (MA); Japanese (MA); liberal studies (MA); nonprofit management (MNM); public administration (MPA); public health (MPH); public policy (MPP); public service management (MS); refugee and forced migration studies (MS); social work (MSW); sociology (MA); Spanish (MA); sustainable urban development (MA); women's and gender studies (MA); writing and publishing (MA); writing, rhetoric and discourse (MA); MA/PhD. *Accreditation:* CEPH. *Program availability:* Part-time, evening/weekend, online learning. Terminal master's awarded for partial completion of doctoral program. *Degree requirements:* For master's, variable foreign language requirement, comprehensive exam (for some programs), thesis (for some programs). Electronic applications accepted.

Harvard University, Graduate School of Arts and Sciences, Department of East Asian Languages and Civilizations, Cambridge, MA 02138. Offers Chinese (PhD); Japanese (PhD); Korean (PhD); Mongolian (PhD); Vietnamese (PhD). Terminal master's awarded for partial completion of doctoral program. *Degree requirements:* For doctorate, 3 foreign languages, thesis/dissertation, general exams. *Entrance requirements:* For doctorate, GRE General Test. Additional exam requirements/recommendations for international students: required—TOEFL.

Indiana University Bloomington, University Graduate School, College of Arts and Sciences, School of Global and International Studies, Department of East Asian Languages and Cultures, Bloomington, IN 47408. Offers Chinese (MA, PhD); Chinese language pedagogy (MA); East Asian studies (MA); Japanese (MA, PhD); Japanese language pedagogy (MA). *Program availability:* Part-time. *Degree requirements:* For master's, one foreign language, thesis; for doctorate, 2 foreign languages, comprehensive exam, thesis/dissertation. *Entrance requirements:* Additional exam requirements/recommendations for international students: required—TOEFL (minimum score 93 iBT). Electronic applications accepted.

Kent State University, College of Arts and Sciences, Department of Modern and Classical Language Studies, Kent, OH 44242-0001. Offers French (MA), including applied linguistics and pedagogy, literature; German (MA), including applied linguistics and pedagogy, literature; Latin (MA), including applied linguistics and pedagogy, literature; Spanish (MA), including applied linguistics and pedagogy, literature; translation (MA), including Arabic, French, German, Japanese, Russian, Spanish; translation studies (PhD); MA/MBA. *Program availability:* Part-time, 100% online. *Faculty:* 18 full-time (11 women), 6 part-time/adjunct (3 women). *Students:* 81 full-time (49 women), 23 part-time (14 women); includes 18 minority (3 Black or African American, non-Hispanic/Latino; 3 Asian, non-Hispanic/Latino; 11 Hispanic/Latino; 1 Two or more races, non-Hispanic/Latino), 45 international. Average age 32. 115 applicants, 73% accepted, 47 enrolled. In 2019, 27 master's, 7 doctorates awarded. *Degree requirements:* For master's, variable foreign language requirement, comprehensive exam (for some programs), thesis (for some programs); for doctorate, variable foreign language requirement, comprehensive exam, thesis/dissertation. *Entrance requirements:* For master's, transcripts, goal statement, 3 letters of recommendation, CD/MP3 with a 5-10 minute oral sample of first and second languages (conversational not read from a script), Writing sample(s) in the applicant's second language, which should be accompanied by a signed declaration that the sample is original work; for doctorate, transcripts; MA in translation, a foreign language, or in any other relevant discipline with prior experience or training in translation; proficiency in a foreign language; minimum GPA of 3.5 from MA; goal statement; 3 letters of recommendation; essay or writing sample (7-10 pages) from a research paper on any aspect of translation. Additional exam requirements/recommendations for international students: required—TOEFL (minimum score 79 iBT), IELTS (minimum score 6.5), PTE (minimum score 58), Michigan English Language Assessment Battery (minimum score 77). *Application deadline:* For fall admission, 2/1 for domestic and international students. Applications are processed on a rolling basis. Application fee: $45 ($70 for international students). Electronic applications accepted. *Financial support:* Fellowships with full tuition reimbursements, teaching assistantships with full tuition reimbursements, and unspecified assistantships available. Financial award application deadline: 2/1. *Unit head:* Dr. Keiran Dunne, Professor of French Translation; Department Chair, 330-672-2150, E-mail: kdunne@kent.edu. *Application contact:* Brian James Baer, Professor of Russian Translation; Graduate Coordinator, 330-672-1813, E-mail: bbaer@kent.edu.
Website: http://www.kent.edu/mcls/

New York University, Steinhardt School of Culture, Education, and Human Development, Department of Teaching and Learning, Program in Multilingual/Multicultural Studies, New York, NY 10012. Offers bilingual education (MA, PhD, Advanced Certificate); foreign language education (MA); teaching English to speakers of other languages (MA, PhD); teaching foreign languages, 7-12 (MA), including Chinese, French, Italian, Japanese, Spanish; teaching French as a foreign language (MA), including teaching English to speakers of other languages; teaching Spanish as a foreign language (MA), including teaching English to speakers of other languages. *Accreditation:* TEAC. *Program availability:* Part-time, evening/weekend. *Entrance* *requirements:* For doctorate, GRE General Test, interview; for Advanced Certificate, master's degree. Additional exam requirements/recommendations for international students: required—TOEFL (minimum score 100 iBT). Electronic applications accepted.

The Ohio State University, Graduate School, College of Arts and Sciences, Division of Arts and Humanities, Department of East Asian Languages and Literatures, Columbus, OH 43210. Offers Chinese (MA, PhD); Japanese (MA, PhD). Terminal master's awarded for partial completion of doctoral program. *Entrance requirements:* For master's and doctorate, GRE General Test (if applying for financial aid). Additional exam requirements/recommendations for international students: required—TOEFL (minimum score 577 paper-based; 90 iBT); recommended—IELTS (minimum score 7.5). Electronic applications accepted.

Portland State University, Graduate Studies, College of Liberal Arts and Sciences, Department of World Languages and Literatures, Portland, OR 97207-0751. Offers French (MA); German (MA); Japanese (MA); Spanish (MA); world literature and language (MA). *Program availability:* Part-time. *Faculty:* 40 full-time (22 women), 39 part-time/adjunct (32 women). *Students:* 16 full-time (11 women), 12 part-time (6 women); includes 9 minority (2 Asian, non-Hispanic/Latino; 6 Hispanic/Latino; 1 Two or more races, non-Hispanic/Latino), 8 international. Average age 34. 14 applicants, 64% accepted, 7 enrolled. In 2019, 14 master's awarded. *Degree requirements:* For master's, variable foreign language requirement, thesis (for some programs). *Entrance requirements:* For master's, ACTFL, BA in the major language, minimum GPA of 3.0 in all coursework. Additional exam requirements/recommendations for international students: required—TOEFL (minimum score 550 paper-based; 80 iBT), IELTS (minimum score 6.5). *Application deadline:* For fall admission, 4/1 for domestic students, 3/1 for international students; for winter admission, 9/1 for domestic students, 7/1 for international students; for spring admission, 11/1 for domestic and international students. Applications are processed on a rolling basis. Application fee: $65. *Expenses: Tuition, area resident:* Full-time $13,020; part-time $6510 per year. Tuition, state resident: full-time $13,020; part-time $6510 per year. Tuition, nonresident: full-time $19,830; part-time $9915 per year. *International tuition:* $19,830 full-time. *Required fees:* $1226. One-time fee: $350. Tuition and fees vary according to course load, program and reciprocity agreements. *Financial support:* In 2019–20, 16 teaching assistantships with full and partial tuition reimbursements (averaging $16,549 per year) were awarded; research assistantships, Federal Work-Study, scholarships/grants, and unspecified assistantships also available. Support available to part-time students. Financial award application deadline: 3/1; financial award applicants required to submit FAFSA. *Unit head:* Dr. Gina Greco, Chair, 503-725-5287, E-mail: grecog@pdx.edu. *Application contact:* Kelli Martin, Graduate Admissions Specialist, 503-725-3243, E-mail: k.martin@pdx.edu.
Website: http://www.pdx.edu/wll/

Purdue University, Graduate School, College of Liberal Arts, School of Languages and Cultures, West Lafayette, IN 47907. Offers French (MA, MAT), including multiple possible; German (MA, MAT), including multiple possible; Japanese pedagogy (MA), including pedagogy, SLA; Spanish (MA, MAT), including multiple possible. *Faculty:* 32 full-time (16 women), 6 part-time/adjunct (3 women). *Students:* 33 full-time (18 women), 24 part-time (16 women); includes 7 minority (1 Black or African American, non-Hispanic/Latino; 6 Hispanic/Latino), 38 international. Average age 34. 54 applicants, 41% accepted, 14 enrolled. In 2019, 9 master's awarded. Terminal master's awarded for partial completion of doctoral program. *Degree requirements:* For master's, one foreign language. *Entrance requirements:* For master's, Bachelor of Arts (or equivalent); 3 letters of recommendation; statement of purpose; speaking & writing samples. Additional exam requirements/recommendations for international students: required—TOEFL (minimum score 550 paper-based; 77 iBT); recommended—TWE. *Application deadline:* For fall admission, 12/12 for domestic and international students; for spring admission, 10/1 for domestic and international students. Applications are processed on a rolling basis. Application fee: $60 ($75 for international students). Electronic applications accepted. *Financial support:* In 2019–20, fellowships with tuition reimbursements (averaging $15,750 per year), teaching assistantships with tuition reimbursements (averaging $13,463 per year) were awarded. Support available to part-time students. Financial award applicants required to submit FAFSA. *Unit head:* Jennifer M. William, Head, 765-494-3834, E-mail: jmwilliam@purdue.edu. *Application contact:* Joni L. Hipsher, Graduate Contact, 765-494-3841, E-mail: jlhipshe@purdue.edu.
Website: http://www.cla.purdue.edu/slc/main/

San Francisco State University, Division of Graduate Studies, College of Liberal and Creative Arts, Department of Modern Languages and Literatures, Program in Japanese, San Francisco, CA 94132-1722. Offers MA. *Program availability:* Part-time. *Application deadline:* Applications are processed on a rolling basis. *Expenses: Tuition, area resident:* Full-time $7176; part-time $4164 per year. Tuition, state resident: full-time $7176; part-time $4164 per year. Tuition, nonresident: full-time $16,680; part-time $396 per unit. *International tuition:* $16,680 full-time. *Required fees:* $1524; $1524 per unit. $762 per semester. Tuition and fees vary according to degree level and program. *Unit head:* Dr. Masahiko Minami, Program Coordinator, 415-338-7451, Fax: 415-338-6159, E-mail: mminami@sfsu.edu. *Application contact:* Dr. Makiko Asano, Graduate Advisor, 415-338-1131, Fax: 415-338-6159, E-mail: masano@sfsu.edu.
Website: http://mll.sfsu.edu/japanese-program/

Stanford University, School of Humanities and Sciences, Department of East Asian Languages and Cultures, Stanford, CA 94305-2004. Offers Chinese (MA, PhD); Japanese (PhD). *Expenses: Tuition:* Full-time $52,479; part-time $34,110 per unit. *Required fees:* $672; $224 per quarter. Tuition and fees vary according to program and student level.
Website: http://www.stanford.edu/dept/asianlang/

University of Alberta, Faculty of Graduate Studies and Research, Department of East Asian Studies, Edmonton, AB T6G 2E1, Canada. Offers Chinese literature (MA); East Asian interdisciplinary studies (MA); Japanese literature (MA). *Program availability:* Part-time. *Degree requirements:* For master's, one foreign language, thesis. *Entrance requirements:* Additional exam requirements/recommendations for international students: required—TOEFL. Electronic applications accepted.

University of California, Berkeley, Graduate Division, College of Letters and Science, Department of East Asian Languages and Cultures, Berkeley, CA 94720. Offers Chinese language (PhD); Japanese language (PhD). *Degree requirements:* For doctorate, one foreign language, thesis/dissertation, oral qualifying exam. *Entrance requirements:* For doctorate, GRE General Test, minimum GPA of 3.0, MA thesis, 3 letters of recommendation. Electronic applications accepted.

University of California, Irvine, School of Humanities, East Asian Studies, Irvine, CA 92697. Offers Chinese (MA, PhD); East Asian languages and literatures (MA, PhD); Japanese (MA, PhD). *Students:* 10 full-time (8 women); includes 3 minority (1 American Indian or Alaska Native, non-Hispanic/Latino; 2 Asian, non-Hispanic/Latino), 1 international. Average age 32. 38 applicants, 11% accepted, 2 enrolled. In 2019, 3 doctorates awarded. *Entrance requirements:* For master's and doctorate, GRE General Test, minimum GPA of 3.0. Additional exam requirements/recommendations for international students: required—TOEFL (minimum score 550 paper-based). *Application deadline:* For fall admission, 1/15 priority date for domestic students, 1/15 for

international students. Application fee: $120 ($140 for international students). Electronic applications accepted. *Financial support:* Fellowships, research assistantships with full tuition reimbursements, teaching assistantships with partial tuition reimbursements, institutionally sponsored loans, traineeships, health care benefits, and unspecified assistantships available. Financial award application deadline: 3/1; financial award applicants required to submit FAFSA. *Unit head:* Hu Ying, Chair, 949-824-3248, E-mail: huying@uci.edu. *Application contact:* Stephanie Wijetilleke, Graduate Program Administrator, 949-824-1601, E-mail: sisnali@uci.edu.
Website: http://www.hnet.uci.edu/eastasian/

University of Colorado Boulder, Graduate School, College of Arts and Sciences, Department of Asian Languages and Civilizations, Boulder, CO 80309. Offers MA, PhD. Terminal master's awarded for partial completion of doctoral program. *Degree requirements:* For master's, comprehensive exam. *Entrance requirements:* For master's, BA in Chinese or Japanese, minimum undergraduate GPA of 3.0. Additional exam requirements/recommendations for international students: required—TOEFL. Electronic applications accepted. Application fee is waived when completed online.

University of Hawaii at Manoa, Office of Graduate Education, College of Languages, Linguistics and Literature, Department of East Asian Languages and Literatures, Program in Japanese, Honolulu, HI 96822. Offers MA, PhD. *Program availability:* Part-time. *Degree requirements:* For master's, 2 foreign languages, thesis optional; for doctorate, 2 foreign languages, comprehensive exam, thesis/dissertation. *Entrance requirements:* For master's and doctorate, GRE General Test. Additional exam requirements/recommendations for international students: required—TOEFL (minimum score 560 paper-based; 83 iBT), IELTS (minimum score 5).

University of Hawaii at Manoa, Office of Graduate Education, School of Pacific and Asian Studies, Program in Asian Studies, Concentration in Japanese Studies, Honolulu, HI 96822. Offers Graduate Certificate. *Program availability:* Part-time. *Degree requirements:* For Graduate Certificate, one foreign language. *Entrance requirements:* For degree, GRE. Additional exam requirements/recommendations for international students: required—TOEFL (minimum score 560 paper-based; 83 iBT), IELTS (minimum score 5).

The University of Manchester, School of Arts, Languages and Cultures, Manchester, United Kingdom. Offers anthropology, media and performance (PhD); applied theatre (PhD); Arab world studies (PhD); archaeology (PhD); art history and visual studies (PhD); arts and cultural management (PhD); arts management and cultural policy (PhD); Chinese studies (PhD); classics and ancient history (PhD); composition (PhD); creative writing (PhD); drama (PhD); East Asian studies (PhD); electroacoustic composition (PhD); English and American studies (PhD); English language (PhD); French studies (PhD); German studies (PhD); history (PhD); humanitarianism and conflict response (PhD); interpreting studies (PhD); Japanese studies (PhD); Latin American cultural studies (PhD); linguistics (PhD); Middle Eastern studies (PhD); museology (PhD); museum practice (PhD); music (PhD); musicology (PhD); Polish studies (PhD); Portuguese studies (PhD); religions and theology (PhD); Russian studies (PhD); Spanish studies (PhD); translation and intercultural studies (PhD).

University of Massachusetts Amherst, Graduate School, College of Humanities and Fine Arts, Department of Languages, Literatures, and Cultures, Programs in Asian Languages and Literatures, Amherst, MA 01003. Offers Chinese (MA); Japanese (MA). *Program availability:* Part-time. *Degree requirements:* For master's, thesis, general exam. *Entrance requirements:* For master's, GRE General Test. Additional exam requirements/recommendations for international students: required—TOEFL (minimum score 550 paper-based; 80 iBT), IELTS (minimum score 6.5). Electronic applications accepted.

University of Oregon, Graduate School, College of Arts and Sciences, Department of East Asian Languages and Literature, Eugene, OR 97403. Offers Chinese (MA, PhD); Japanese (MA, PhD). *Entrance requirements:* Additional exam requirements/recommendations for international students: required—TOEFL.

University of Pittsburgh, Kenneth P. Dietrich School of Arts and Sciences, Department of East Asian Languages and Literatures, Pittsburgh, PA 15260. Offers Chinese (MA); Japanese (MA). *Program availability:* Part-time. *Faculty:* 6 full-time (4 women), 13 part-time/adjunct (10 women). *Students:* 3 full-time (2 women); includes 2 minority (1 Black or African American, non-Hispanic/Latino; 1 Asian, non-Hispanic/Latino). Average age 27. 13 applicants, 62% accepted, 2 enrolled. *Degree requirements:* For master's, one foreign language, comprehensive exam, thesis. *Entrance requirements:* For master's, personal statement, transcript copies, 3 letters of recommendation (online submissions), writing sample (in English). Additional exam requirements/recommendations for international students: required—TOEFL (minimum score 90 iBT), IELTS (minimum score 7). *Application deadline:* For fall admission, 1/15 for domestic and international students. Application fee: $50. Electronic applications accepted. *Expenses:* $24,480 in-state, $40,848 out-of-state. *Financial support:* Scholarships/grants, health care benefits, tuition waivers (full and partial), and unspecified assistantships available. Financial award application deadline: 1/15. *Unit head:* Dr. Hiroshi Nara, Chair, 412-624-5579, Fax: 412-624-3458, E-mail: hnara@pitt.edu. *Application contact:* Keanna Cash, Graduate Administrator, 412-624-5227, E-mail: kec176@pitt.edu.
Website: http://deall.pitt.edu/

University of Washington, Graduate School, College of Arts and Sciences, Department of Asian Languages and Literature, Seattle, WA 98195. Offers Buddhist studies (MA, PhD); Chinese language and literature (MA, PhD); Japanese language and literature (MA, PhD); Korean language and literature (MA, PhD); South Asian language and literature (MA, PhD). *Degree requirements:* For master's, 2 foreign languages, general exam, thesis or 2 research papers; for doctorate, 3 foreign languages, thesis/dissertation, general exam. *Entrance requirements:* For master's, GRE, minimum GPA of 3.0; for doctorate, GRE, master's degree in related field, minimum GPA of 3.0. Additional exam requirements/recommendations for international students: required—TOEFL. Electronic applications accepted.

University of Wisconsin–Madison, Graduate School, College of Letters and Science, Department of East Asian Languages and Literature, Program in Japanese Linguistics, Madison, WI 53706-1380. Offers MA, PhD. *Program availability:* Part-time. Terminal master's awarded for partial completion of doctoral program. *Degree requirements:* For master's, one foreign language, seminars, written exam; for doctorate, 3 foreign languages, thesis/dissertation, seminars, preliminary exams, oral exam. *Entrance requirements:* For master's, GRE General Test, bachelor's degree or equivalent in Japanese; for doctorate, GRE General Test, master's degree or equivalent in Japanese. Electronic applications accepted.

Washington University in St. Louis, The Graduate School, Department of East Asian Languages and Cultures, St. Louis, MO 63130-4899. Offers Chinese (MA); Chinese and comparative literature (PhD); Chinese language and literature (PhD); East Asian studies (MA); Japanese (MA); Japanese and comparative literature (PhD); Japanese language and literature (PhD). Terminal master's awarded for partial completion of doctoral program. *Degree requirements:* For master's, thesis optional; for doctorate, thesis/dissertation. *Entrance requirements:* For master's and doctorate, GRE General Test. Additional exam requirements/recommendations for international students: required—TOEFL. Electronic applications accepted.

Near and Middle Eastern Languages

The American University in Cairo, School of Humanities and Social Sciences, Cairo, Egypt. Offers Arab and Islamic civilizations (Graduate Diploma); Arabic studies (MA); comparative literary studies (Graduate Diploma); Egyptology and Coptology (MA); English and comparative literature (MA); humanities and social sciences (Graduate Diploma); philosophy (MA); psychology (MA); sociology and anthropology (MA); teaching Arabic as a foreign language (MA); teaching English to speakers of other languages (MA). *Program availability:* Part-time, evening/weekend. *Degree requirements:* For master's, comprehensive exam (for some programs), thesis (for some programs). *Entrance requirements:* Additional exam requirements/recommendations for international students: required—TOEFL (minimum score 450 paper-based; 45 iBT), IELTS (minimum score 5). Electronic applications accepted.

Bethel Seminary, Graduate and Professional Programs, St. Paul, MN 55112-6998. Offers Anglican studies (Certificate); children's and family ministry (MA); Christian studies (Certificate); Christian thought (MA); church planting (Certificate); Greek and Hebrew language (M Div); Greek language (M Div); Hebrew language (M Div); marriage and family therapy (MA, Certificate); mental health counseling (MA); ministry (MA, D Min); ministry practice (Certificate); theological studies (MA, Certificate); transformational leadership (MA); young life youth ministry (Certificate). *Accreditation:* ACIPE. *Program availability:* Part-time, evening/weekend, 100% online, blended/hybrid learning. *Degree requirements:* For master's, variable foreign language requirement, thesis (for some programs); for doctorate, thesis/dissertation. *Entrance requirements:* For master's, letters of reference, transcripts, personal statement; for doctorate, M Div, letters of reference, organizational support; for Certificate, letters of reference, family essay, personal statement, and family of origin paper (for marriage and family therapy). Additional exam requirements/recommendations for international students: required—TOEFL (minimum score 550 paper-based; 87 iBT). Electronic applications accepted. *Expenses:* Contact institution.

Brandeis University, Graduate School of Arts and Sciences, Department of Near Eastern and Judaic Studies, Waltham, MA 02454-9110. Offers Near Eastern and Judaic studies (MA); near Eastern and Judaic studies/conflict resolution and coexistence (MA); near Eastern and Judaic studies/Jewish professional leadership (MA); near Eastern and Judaic studies/women's, gender, and sexuality studies (MA); teaching of Hebrew (MAT); the bible and ancient near east (PhD). *Program availability:* Part-time. *Faculty:* 21 full-time (8 women), 5 part-time/adjunct (3 women). *Students:* 34 full-time (15 women), 2 part-time (1 woman); includes 8 minority (1 Black or African American, non-Hispanic/Latino; 2 Asian, non-Hispanic/Latino; 3 Hispanic/Latino; 2 Two or more races, non-Hispanic/Latino), 7 international. Average age 34. 76 applicants, 53% accepted, 5 enrolled. In 2019, 3 master's, 3 doctorates awarded. Terminal master's awarded for partial completion of doctoral program. *Degree requirements:* For master's, one foreign language, thesis or alternative, capstone, thesis, or internship; for doctorate, variable foreign language requirement, comprehensive exam, thesis/dissertation. *Entrance requirements:* For master's and doctorate, GRE General recommended, transcripts, letters of recommendation, resume, writing sample, and statement of purpose. Additional exam requirements/recommendations for international students: required—TOEFL, IELTS, PTE. *Application deadline:* For fall admission, 1/15 priority date for domestic and international students. Applications are processed on a rolling basis. Application fee: $75. Electronic applications accepted. *Financial support:* In 2019–20, 9 fellowships with full tuition reimbursements (averaging $25,000 per year), 8 teaching assistantships (averaging $3,550 per year) were awarded; scholarships/grants, health care benefits, and tuition waivers also available. Support available to part-time students. *Unit head:* Dr. Ilana Szobel, Director of Graduate Studies, 781-736-5230, E-mail: szobel@brandeis.edu. *Application contact:* Jean Mannion, Administrator, 781-736-2950, E-mail: mannion@brandeis.edu.
Website: http://www.brandeis.edu/gsas/programs/nejs.html

California University of Pennsylvania, School of Graduate Studies and Research, College of Liberal Arts, Program in Arabic Language and Linguistics, California, PA 15419-1394. Offers social science (MA). *Expenses: Tuition, area resident:* Full-time $9288; part-time $516 per credit. Tuition, state resident: full-time $9288; part-time $516 per credit. Tuition, nonresident: full-time $13,932; part-time $774 per credit. *Required fees:* $3631; $291.13 per credit. Part-time tuition and fees vary according to course load.

The Catholic University of America, School of Arts and Sciences, Department of Semitic and Egyptian Languages and Literatures, Washington, DC 20064. Offers ancient Near East (Biblical Hebrew/Aramaic) (MA, PhD); Arabic (PhD); Christian Near East (Biblical Hebrew/Aramaic) (MA); Coptic (MA, PhD); Syriac (MA, PhD). *Program availability:* Part-time. *Faculty:* 4 full-time (0 women), 2 part-time/adjunct (1 woman). *Students:* 7 full-time (3 women), 28 part-time (7 women); includes 3 minority (1 Black or African American, non-Hispanic/Latino; 2 Two or more races, non-Hispanic/Latino), 6 international. Average age 35. 16 applicants, 88% accepted, 5 enrolled. In 2019, 4 master's, 3 doctorates awarded. Terminal master's awarded for partial completion of doctoral program. *Degree requirements:* For master's, one foreign language, comprehensive exam; for doctorate, 2 foreign languages, comprehensive exam, thesis/dissertation. *Entrance requirements:* For master's, GRE General Test, statement of purpose, official copies of academic transcripts, three letters of recommendation; for doctorate, GRE General Test, statement of purpose, official copies of academic transcripts, three letters of recommendation, successful completion of MA field. Additional exam requirements/recommendations for international students: required—TOEFL (minimum score 550 paper-based; 80 iBT). *Application deadline:* For fall admission, 7/15 priority date for domestic students, 7/1 for international students; for spring admission, 11/15 priority date for domestic students, 11/1 for international students. Applications are processed on a rolling basis. Application fee: $55. Electronic applications accepted. *Expenses:* Contact institution. *Financial support:* Fellowships, research assistantships, teaching assistantships, Federal Work-Study, scholarships/grants, tuition waivers (full and partial), and unspecified assistantships available. Financial award application deadline: 2/1; financial award applicants required to submit FAFSA. *Unit head:* Dr. Andrew D. Gross, Chair, 202-319-5083, Fax: 202-319-4735, E-mail: grossa@cua.edu. *Application contact:* Dr. Steven Brown, Director of Graduate Admissions, 202-319-5057, Fax: 202-319-6533, E-mail: cua-admissions@cua.edu.
Website: http://semitics.cua.edu/

DePaul University, College of Liberal Arts and Social Sciences, Chicago, IL 60614. Offers Arabic (MA); Chinese (MA); critical ethnic studies (MA); English (MA); French (MA); German (MA); history (MA); interdisciplinary studies (MA, MS); international public service (MS); international studies (MA); Italian (MA); Japanese (MA); liberal studies (MA); nonprofit management (MNM); public administration (MPA); public health (MPH); public policy (MPP); public service management (MS); refugee and forced migration studies (MS); social work (MSW); sociology (MA); Spanish (MA); sustainable urban development (MA); women's and gender studies (MA); writing and publishing (MA); writing, rhetoric and discourse (MA); MA/PhD. *Accreditation:* CEPH. *Program availability:* Part-time, evening/weekend, online learning. Terminal master's awarded for partial completion of doctoral program. *Degree requirements:* For master's, variable foreign language requirement, comprehensive exam (for some programs), thesis (for some programs). Electronic applications accepted.

Georgetown University, Graduate School of Arts and Sciences, Walsh School of Foreign Service, The Center for Contemporary Arab Studies, Washington, DC 20057. Offers MA, Certificate, MA/JD, MA/PhD. *Degree requirements:* For master's, one foreign language, comprehensive exam, thesis or alternative, proficiency in Arabic. *Entrance requirements:* For master's, GRE, minimum GPA of 3.0. Additional exam requirements/recommendations for international students: required—TOEFL (minimum score 600 paper-based; 100 iBT). Electronic applications accepted.

Harvard University, Graduate School of Arts and Sciences, Department of Near Eastern Languages and Civilizations, Cambridge, MA 02138. Offers Akkadian and Sumerian (AM, PhD); Arabic (AM, PhD); Armenian (AM, PhD); biblical history (AM, PhD); Hebrew (AM, PhD); Indo-Muslim culture (AM, PhD); Iranian (AM, PhD); Jewish history and literature (AM, PhD); Persian (AM, PhD); Semitic philology (AM, PhD); Syro-Palestinian archaeology (AM, PhD); Turkish (AM, PhD). *Degree requirements:* For doctorate, variable foreign language requirement, thesis/dissertation, general exams. *Entrance requirements:* For master's, GRE General Test; for doctorate, GRE General Test, proficiency in a Near Eastern language. Additional exam requirements/recommendations for international students: required—TOEFL.

Hebrew Union College–Jewish Institute of Religion, School of Graduate Studies, Program in Hebrew Letters, New York, NY 10012-1186. Offers DHL. *Degree requirements:* For doctorate, one foreign language, thesis/dissertation. *Entrance requirements:* For doctorate, GRE. Additional exam requirements/recommendations for international students: required—TOEFL. *Expenses:* Contact institution.

Houston Baptist University, School of Christian Thought, Program in Classics and Biblical Languages, Houston, TX 77074-3298. Offers MA. *Entrance requirements:* For master's, bachelor's degree conferred transcript, essay/personal statement, resume. Additional exam requirements/recommendations for international students: required—TOEFL (minimum score 80 iBT), IELTS (minimum score 6.5). Electronic applications accepted. Application fee is waived when completed online. *Expenses:* Contact institution.

Indiana University Bloomington, University Graduate School, College of Arts and Sciences, School of Global and International Studies, Department of Near Eastern Languages and Cultures, Bloomington, IN 47405-7000. Offers MA, PhD. *Program availability:* Part-time. Terminal master's awarded for partial completion of doctoral program. *Degree requirements:* For master's, 2 foreign languages, comprehensive exam, thesis or alternative; for doctorate, 3 foreign languages, comprehensive exam, thesis/dissertation. *Entrance requirements:* For master's and doctorate, GRE General Test. Additional exam requirements/recommendations for international students: required—TOEFL. Electronic applications accepted.

Johns Hopkins University, Zanvyl Krieger School of Arts and Sciences, Department of Near Eastern Studies, Baltimore, MD 21218. Offers archaeology (PhD); Assyriology (PhD); Egyptology (PhD); Hebrew Bible/Northwest Semitics (PhD). *Degree requirements:* For doctorate, 2 foreign languages, comprehensive exam, thesis/dissertation. *Entrance requirements:* For doctorate, GRE. Additional exam requirements/recommendations for international students: required—TOEFL (minimum score 600 paper-based; 100 iBT); recommended—IELTS. Electronic applications accepted. *Expenses:* Contact institution.

Kent State University, College of Arts and Sciences, Department of Modern and Classical Language Studies, Kent, OH 44242-0001. Offers French (MA), including applied linguistics and pedagogy, literature; German (MA), including applied linguistics and pedagogy, literature; Latin (MA), including applied linguistics and pedagogy, literature; Spanish (MA), including applied linguistics and pedagogy, literature; translation (MA), including Arabic, French, German, Japanese, Russian, Spanish; translation studies (PhD); MA/MBA. *Program availability:* Part-time, 100% online. *Faculty:* 18 full-time (11 women), 6 part-time/adjunct (3 women). *Students:* 81 full-time (49 women), 23 part-time (14 women); includes 18 minority (3 Black or African American, non-Hispanic/Latino; 3 Asian, non-Hispanic/Latino; 11 Hispanic/Latino; 1 Two or more races, non-Hispanic/Latino), 45 international. Average age 32. 115 applicants, 73% accepted, 47 enrolled. In 2019, 27 master's, 7 doctorates awarded. *Degree requirements:* For master's, variable foreign language requirement, comprehensive exam (for some programs), thesis (for some programs); for doctorate, variable foreign language requirement, comprehensive exam, thesis/dissertation. *Entrance requirements:* For master's, transcripts, goal statement, 3 letters of recommendation, CD/MP3 with a 5-10 minute oral sample of first and second languages (conversational not read from a script), Writing sample(s) in the applicant's second language, which should be accompanied by a signed declaration that the sample is original work; for doctorate, transcripts; MA in translation, a foreign language, or in any other relevant discipline with prior experience or training in translation; proficiency in a foreign language; minimum GPA of 3.5 from MA; goal statement; 3 letters of recommendation; essay or writing sample (7-10 pages) from a research paper on any aspect of translation. Additional exam requirements/recommendations for international students: required—TOEFL (minimum score 79 iBT), IELTS (minimum score 6.5), PTE (minimum score 58), Michigan English Language Assessment Battery (minimum score 77). *Application deadline:* For fall admission, 2/1 for domestic and international students. Applications are processed on a rolling basis. Application fee: $45 ($70 for international students). Electronic applications accepted. *Financial support:* Fellowships with full tuition reimbursements, teaching assistantships with full tuition reimbursements, and unspecified assistantships available. Financial award application deadline: 2/1. *Unit head:* Dr. Keiran Dunne, Professor of French Translation; Department Chair, 330-672-2150, E-mail: kdunne@kent.edu. *Application contact:* Brian James Baer, Professor of Russian Translation; Graduate Coordinator, 330-672-1813, E-mail: bbaer@kent.edu.
Website: http://www.kent.edu/mcls/

London Metropolitan University, Graduate Programs, London, United Kingdom. Offers applied psychology (M Sc); architecture (MA); biomedical science (M Sc); blood science (M Sc); cancer pharmacology (M Sc); computer networking and cyber security (M Sc); computing and information systems (M Sc); conference interpreting (MA); counter-terrorism studies (M Sc); creative, digital and professional writing (MA); crime, violence and prevention (M Sc); criminology (M Sc); curating contemporary art (MA); data analytics (M Sc); digital media (MA); early childhood studies (MA); education (MA, Ed D); financial services law, regulation and compliance (LL M); food science (M Sc); forensic psychology (M Sc); health and social care management and policy (M Sc); human nutrition (M Sc); human resource management (MA); human rights and international conflict (MA); information technology (M Sc); intelligence and security studies (M Sc); international oil, gas and energy law (LL M); international relations (MA); interpreting (MA); learning and teaching in higher education (MA); legal practice (LL M); media and entertainment law (LL M); organizational and consumer psychology (M Sc); psychological therapy (M Sc); psychology of mental health (M Sc); public health (M Sc); public policy and management (MPA); security studies (M Sc); social work (M Sc); spatial planning and urban design (MA); sports therapy (M Sc); supporting older children and young people with dyslexia (MA); teaching languages (MA), including Arabic, English; translation (MA); woman and child abuse (MA).

Middlebury College, Language Schools, Arabic School, Middlebury, VT 05753-6002. Offers MA. In 2019, 4 master's awarded. *Entrance requirements:* For master's, Arabic language oral and written proficiency tests, 3 letters of recommendation, personal statement, transcripts, writing sample in Arabic, Arabic course history, 4 years or equivalent of Arabic language study. Additional exam requirements/recommendations for international students: required—TOEFL (minimum score 100 iBT). *Application deadline:* For summer admission, 5/1 for domestic and international students. Applications are processed on a rolling basis. Application fee: $75. Electronic applications accepted. *Expenses:* Contact institution. *Financial support:* Fellowships and scholarships/grants available. Financial award application deadline: 3/14; financial award applicants required to submit FAFSA. *Unit head:* Dr. Mahmoud Abdalla, Director, 802-443-5230, Fax: 802-443-2075, E-mail: mabdalla@miis.edu. *Application contact:* Barbara Walter, Coordinator, 802-443-5230, Fax: 802-443-2075, E-mail: bwalter@middlebury.edu.
Website: http://www.middlebury.edu/ls/grad_programs/arabic

Middlebury College, Language Schools, Hebrew School, Middlebury, VT 05753-6002. Offers MA. *Program availability:* Blended/hybrid learning. *Students:* 77 part-time (63 women). In 2019, 15 master's awarded. *Entrance requirements:* For master's, oral interview. *Application deadline:* Applications are processed on a rolling basis. Application fee: $75. Electronic applications accepted. *Expenses:* Contact institution. *Financial support:* Fellowships and scholarships/grants available. Financial award application deadline: 3/28; financial award applicants required to submit FAFSA. *Unit head:* Vardit Ringvald, Director, 802-443-3574, E-mail: vringval@middlebury.edu. *Application contact:* Vardit Ringvald, Director, 802-443-3574, E-mail: vringval@middlebury.edu.
Website: http://www.middlebury.edu/ls/hebrew

The Ohio State University, Graduate School, College of Arts and Sciences, Division of Arts and Humanities, Department of Near Eastern Languages and Cultures, Columbus, OH 43210. Offers MA, PhD. Terminal master's awarded for partial completion of doctoral program. *Entrance requirements:* For master's and doctorate, GRE General Test, writing sample. Additional exam requirements/recommendations for international students: required—TOEFL (minimum score 550 paper-based; 79 iBT), Michigan English Language Assessment Battery (minimum score 82); recommended—IELTS (minimum score 7). Electronic applications accepted.

Oral Roberts University, School of Theology and Missions, Tulsa, OK 74171. Offers biblical literature (MA), including advanced languages, Judaic-Christian studies; church ministries and leadership (D Min); clinical pastoral education (M Div); missions (MA); pastoral care and chaplaincy (M Div, D Min); practical theology (MA), including teaching ministries, urban ministries; professional counseling (MA), including addiction studies, marriage and family therapy; theological/historical studies (MA). *Accreditation:* ATS. *Program availability:* Part-time, online learning. *Faculty:* 17 full-time (2 women). *Students:* 268 full-time (146 women), 96 part-time (52 women); includes 66 minority (48 Black or African American, non-Hispanic/Latino; 9 American Indian or Alaska Native, non-Hispanic/Latino; 8 Asian, non-Hispanic/Latino; 1 Native Hawaiian or other Pacific Islander, non-Hispanic/Latino), 65 international. Average age 40. 661 applicants, 24% accepted, 136 enrolled. In 2019, 113 master's, 19 doctorates awarded. *Degree requirements:* For master's, thesis (for some programs), practicum/internship; for doctorate, thesis/dissertation, applied research project. *Entrance requirements:* For master's, GRE General Test or MAT (waived for those with undergraduate degree from regionally accredited institution and 3.0 or higher GPA), minimum GPA of 2.5 (professional) or 3.0 (academic); for doctorate, M Div, minimum GPA of 3.0, 3 years of full-time ministry experience. Additional exam requirements/recommendations for international students: recommended—TOEFL (minimum score 550 paper-based; 79 iBT), IELTS (minimum score 7). *Application deadline:* Applications are processed on a rolling basis. Application fee: $35. Electronic applications accepted. Application fee is waived when completed online. *Expenses: Tuition:* Full-time $11,052; part-time $5526 per year. *Required fees:* $1230; $615 per unit. Tuition and fees vary according to program. *Financial support:* Fellowships and scholarships/grants available. Financial award application deadline: 6/1. *Unit head:* Dr. Bill Buker, Chair, 918-495-6493, E-mail: bbuker@oru.edu. *Application contact:* Joe Sims, Enrollment Counselor, 918-495-6618, E-mail: jsims@oru.edu.
Website: http://www.gradtheology.oru.edu/

University of California, Los Angeles, Graduate Division, College of Letters and Science, Department of Near Eastern Languages and Cultures, Los Angeles, CA 90034. Offers MA, PhD. *Degree requirements:* For master's, one foreign language, comprehensive exam; for doctorate, 2 foreign languages, thesis/dissertation, oral and written qualifying exams. *Entrance requirements:* For master's, GRE General Test, bachelor's degree; minimum undergraduate GPA of 3.25 (or its equivalent if letter grade system not used); for doctorate, GRE General Test, master's degree; minimum undergraduate GPA of 3.25 (or its equivalent if letter grade system not used). Additional exam requirements/recommendations for international students: required—TOEFL. Electronic applications accepted.

University of Chicago, Division of the Humanities, Department of Near Eastern Languages and Civilizations, Chicago, IL 60637. Offers PhD. Terminal master's awarded for partial completion of doctoral program. *Degree requirements:* For doctorate, 2 foreign languages, comprehensive exam, thesis/dissertation. *Entrance requirements:* For doctorate, GRE General Test, 15-20 page writing sample, statement of purpose, 3 letters of recommendation, transcripts for all previous degrees and institutions attended. Additional exam requirements/recommendations for international students: required—TOEFL (minimum score 104 iBT), IELTS (minimum score 7). Electronic applications accepted.

University of Michigan, Rackham Graduate School, College of Literature, Science, and the Arts, Department of Middle East Studies, Ann Arbor, MI 48109. Offers ancient Near Eastern studies (AM, PhD); Arabic for professional purposes (AM); Arabic language and literature (AM, PhD); Armenian studies (AM, PhD); Christianity in late antiquity (AM, PhD); Egyptology (AM, PhD); Hebrew Bible and ancient Israel (AM, PhD); Hebrew literature (AM, PhD); Islamic studies (AM, PhD); Jewish cultural studies (AM, PhD); Jewish mysticism (AM, PhD); Persian and Iranian studies (AM, PhD); Rabbinic literature (AM, PhD); Second Temple Judaism (AM, PhD); teaching Arabic as a foreign language (AM); Turkish studies (AM, PhD). Terminal master's awarded for partial completion of doctoral program. *Degree requirements:* For master's, 2 foreign languages; for doctorate, 4 foreign languages, comprehensive exam, thesis/dissertation, preliminary exams, oral defense of dissertation. *Entrance requirements:* For master's,

ACTFL (for teaching Arabic as a foreign language MA program). Additional exam requirements/recommendations for international students: required—TOEFL (minimum score 560 paper-based; 84 iBT), IELTS (minimum score 6.5). Electronic applications accepted.

University of South Africa, College of Human Sciences, Pretoria, South Africa. Offers adult education (M Ed); African languages (MA, PhD); African politics (MA, PhD); Afrikaans (MA, PhD); ancient history (MA, PhD); ancient Near Eastern studies (MA, PhD); anthropology (MA, PhD); applied linguistics (MA); Arabic (MA, PhD); archaeology (MA); art history (MA); Biblical archaeology (MA); Biblical studies (M Th, D Th, PhD); Christian spirituality (M Th, D Th); church history (M Th, D Th); classical studies (MA, PhD); clinical psychology (MA); communication (MA, PhD); comparative education (M Ed, Ed D); consulting psychology (D Admin, D Com, PhD); curriculum studies (M Ed, Ed D); development studies (M Admin, MA, D Admin, PhD); didactics (M Ed, Ed D); education (M Tech); education management (M Ed, Ed D); educational psychology (M Ed); English (MA); environmental education (M Ed); French (MA, PhD); German (MA, PhD); Greek (MA); guidance and counseling (M Ed); health studies (MA, PhD), including health sciences education (MA), health services management (MA), medical and surgical nursing science (critical care general) (MA), midwifery and neonatal nursing science (MA), trauma and emergency care (MA); history (MA, PhD); history of education (Ed D); inclusive education (M Ed, Ed D); information and communications technology policy and regulation (MA); information science (MA, MIS, PhD); international politics (MA, PhD); Islamic studies (MA, PhD); Italian (MA, PhD); Judaica (MA, PhD); linguistics (MA, PhD); mathematical education (M Ed); mathematics education (MA); missiology (M Th, D Th); modern Hebrew (MA, PhD); musicology (MA, MMus, D Mus, PhD); natural science education (M Ed); New Testament (M Th, D Th); Old Testament (D Th); pastoral therapy (M Th, D Th); philosophy (MA); philosophy of education (M Ed, Ed D); politics (MA, PhD); Portuguese (MA, PhD); practical theology (M Th, D Th); psychology (MA, MS, PhD); psychology of education (M Ed, Ed D); public health (MA); religious studies (MA, D Th, PhD); Romance languages (MA); Russian (MA, PhD); Semitic languages (MA, PhD); social behavior studies in HIV/AIDS (MA); social science (mental health) (MA); social science in development studies (MA); social science in psychology (MA); social science in social work (MA); social science in sociology (MA); social work (MSW, DSW, PhD); socio-education (M Ed, Ed D); sociolinguistics (MA); sociology (MA, PhD); Spanish (MA, PhD); systematic theology (M Th, D Th); TESOL (teaching English to speakers of other languages) (MA); theological ethics (M Th, D Th); theory of literature (MA, PhD); urban ministries (D Th); urban ministry (M Th).

The University of Texas at Austin, Graduate School, College of Liberal Arts, Department of Middle Eastern Studies, Austin, TX 78712-1111. Offers Middle Eastern languages and cultures (MA, PhD); Middle Eastern studies (MA); JD/MA; MA/M Sc; MA/MA; MBA/MA; MPA/MA. *Degree requirements:* For master's, one foreign language, comprehensive exam, thesis; for doctorate, 2 foreign languages, comprehensive exam, thesis/dissertation. *Entrance requirements:* For master's and doctorate, GRE General Test. Additional exam requirements/recommendations for international students: required—TOEFL. Electronic applications accepted.

University of Utah, Graduate School, College of Humanities, Program in Middle East Studies, Salt Lake City, UT 84112. Offers Arabic (MA, PhD); Hebrew (MA); history (MA, PhD); Persian (MA, PhD); political science (MA, PhD). In 2019, 2 doctorates awarded. *Entrance requirements:* For master's, GRE General Test, minimum GPA of 3.2; for doctorate, GRE General Test, MA in Middle East studies or equivalent, minimum GPA of 3.2. Additional exam requirements/recommendations for international students: required—TOEFL (minimum score 580 paper-based; 92 iBT); recommended—IELTS (minimum score 7). *Application fee:* $55 ($65 for international students). *Expenses:* Tuition, state resident: full-time $7085; part-time $272.51 per credit hour. Tuition, nonresident: full-time $24,937; part-time $959.12 per credit hour. *Required fees:* $880.52; $880.52 per semester. Tuition and fees vary according to degree level, program and student level. *Unit head:* Johanna Watzinger-Tharp, Director, 801-581-7148, Fax: 801-581-6105, E-mail: j.tharp@utah.edu. *Application contact:* Kellie Hubbard, Academic Advisor, 801-581-5362, Fax: 801-581-6105, E-mail: kellie.hubbard@utah.edu.
Website: http://www.mec.utah.edu

University of Wisconsin–Madison, Graduate School, College of Letters and Science, Department of Hebrew and Semitic Studies, Madison, WI 53706-1380. Offers MA, PhD. Terminal master's awarded for partial completion of doctoral program. *Degree requirements:* For master's, 2 foreign languages; for doctorate, thesis/dissertation. *Entrance requirements:* For master's and doctorate, GRE. Electronic applications accepted.

Wayne State University, College of Liberal Arts and Sciences, Department of Classical and Modern Languages, Literatures, and Cultures, Detroit, MI 48202. Offers classics (MA), including ancient Greek and Latin, ancient studies, classics, Latin; German (MA); language learning (MALL), including Arabic (MA, MALL), French (MA, MALL, PhD), German (MALL, PhD), Italian (MA, MALL), Spanish (MA, MALL, PhD); modern languages (PhD), including French (MA, MALL, PhD), German (MALL, PhD), Spanish (MA, MALL, PhD); Near Eastern languages (MA), including Arabic (MA, MALL), Hebrew; Romance languages (MA), including French (MA, MALL, PhD), Italian (MA, MALL), Spanish (MA, MALL, PhD). *Faculty:* 20. *Students:* 30 full-time (22 women), 15 part-time (9 women); includes 11 minority (4 Black or African American, non-Hispanic/Latino; 1 American Indian or Alaska Native, non-Hispanic/Latino; 2 Asian, non-Hispanic/Latino; 3 Hispanic/Latino; 1 Two or more races, non-Hispanic/Latino), 2 international. Average age 40. 32 applicants, 34% accepted, 9 enrolled. In 2019, 8 master's, 1 doctorate awarded. *Degree requirements:* For master's, variable foreign language requirement, comprehensive exam (for some programs), thesis (for some programs); for doctorate, one foreign language, comprehensive exam, thesis/dissertation. *Entrance requirements:* Additional exam requirements/recommendations for international students: required—TOEFL (minimum score 550 paper-based; 79 iBT), TWE (minimum score 5.5), Michigan English Language Assessment Battery (minimum score 85); recommended—IELTS (minimum score 6.5). *Application fee:* $50. Electronic applications accepted. *Expenses: Tuition:* Full-time $34,567. *Financial support:* In 2019–20, 22 students received support, including 1 fellowship with tuition reimbursement available (averaging $20,000 per year), 15 teaching assistantships with tuition reimbursements available (averaging $20,015 per year); research assistantships, scholarships/grants, health care benefits, and unspecified assistantships also available. Financial award applicants required to submit FAFSA. *Unit head:* Dr. Vanessa DEGifis, DR., Department Chair, 313-577-6244, Fax: 313-577-6243, E-mail: vdegifis@wayne.edu. *Application contact:* Terrie Pickering, Academic Services Officer, 313 577 3003, E-mail: t.pickering@wayne.edu.
Website: http://clas.wayne.edu/languages/

Yale University, Graduate School of Arts and Sciences, Department of Near Eastern Languages and Civilizations, New Haven, CT 06520. Offers Arabic humanities (MA, PhD); Assyriology (MA, PhD); Egyptology (MA, PhD); the Classical Near East (MA, PhD). *Degree requirements:* For doctorate, 2 foreign languages, thesis/dissertation. *Entrance requirements:* For doctorate, GRE General Test.

Portuguese

Brigham Young University, Graduate Studies, College of Humanities, Department of Spanish and Portuguese, Provo, UT 84602. Offers Portuguese (MA), including Luso-Brazilian literatures, Portuguese linguistics, Portuguese pedagogy; Spanish (MA), including Hispanic linguistics, Hispanic literatures, Spanish pedagogy. *Faculty:* 33 full-time (8 women). *Students:* 34 full-time (24 women); includes 14 minority (1 Black or African American, non-Hispanic/Latino; 1 American Indian or Alaska Native, non-Hispanic/Latino; 1 Asian, non-Hispanic/Latino; 11 Hispanic/Latino). Average age 33. 17 applicants, 65% accepted, 9 enrolled. In 2019, 11 master's awarded. *Degree requirements:* For master's, 2 foreign languages, comprehensive exam, thesis, 1 semester of teaching. *Entrance requirements:* For master's, GRE, prerequisite second language requirement (can be fulfilled concurrently), prerequisite teaching methods course (can be fulfilled concurrently). Additional exam requirements/recommendations for international students: required—TOEFL (minimum score 580 paper-based; 85 iBT). *Application deadline:* For fall admission, 2/1 for domestic and international students. Application fee: $50. Electronic applications accepted. *Expenses:* $13,515 to complete two-year degree. *Financial support:* In 2019–20, 22 students received support, including 2 teaching assistantships with partial tuition reimbursements available (averaging $8,431 per year); scholarships/grants also available. Financial award application deadline: 2/1. *Unit head:* Dr. Scott Alvord, Interim Chair, Department of Spanish & Portuguese, 801-422-7546, Fax: 801-422-0308, E-mail: scott_alvord@byu.edu. *Application contact:* Brian A Price, Graduate Program Manager, 801-422-3453, Fax: 801-422-0308, E-mail: brian_price@byu.edu.
Website: http://spanport.byu.edu/

Emory University, Laney Graduate School, Department of Spanish and Portuguese, Atlanta, GA 30322-1100. Offers comparative literature (Certificate); film studies (Certificate); Spanish (PhD); women's studies (Certificate). *Degree requirements:* For doctorate, 2 foreign languages, comprehensive exam, thesis/dissertation. *Entrance requirements:* For doctorate, GRE General Test. Additional exam requirements/recommendations for international students: required—TOEFL. Electronic applications accepted.

Harvard University, Graduate School of Arts and Sciences, Department of Romance Languages and Literatures, Cambridge, MA 02138. Offers French (AM, PhD); Italian (AM, PhD); Portuguese (AM, PhD); Spanish (AM, PhD). Terminal master's awarded for partial completion of doctoral program. *Degree requirements:* For master's, 2 foreign languages; for doctorate, 2 foreign languages, thesis/dissertation. *Entrance requirements:* For master's and doctorate, GRE General Test, sample of written work. Additional exam requirements/recommendations for international students: required—TOEFL.

Indiana University Bloomington, University Graduate School, College of Arts and Sciences, Department of Spanish and Portuguese, Bloomington, IN 47405. Offers Portuguese (MA, PhD); Spanish (MA, PhD), including Hispanic linguistics, Hispanic literatures. *Degree requirements:* For master's, one foreign language, comprehensive exam, thesis (for Spanish); for doctorate, 2 foreign languages, comprehensive exam, thesis/dissertation. *Entrance requirements:* For master's, GRE General Test, bachelor's degree in Portuguese or Spanish, minimum GPA of 3.0; for doctorate, GRE General Test, master's degree in Portuguese or Spanish, minimum GPA of 3.0. Additional exam requirements/recommendations for international students: required—TOEFL (minimum score 79 iBT). Electronic applications accepted.

New York University, Graduate School of Arts and Science, Department of Spanish and Portuguese Languages and Literatures, New York, NY 10012-1019. Offers Portuguese (MA, PhD); Spanish (PhD); Spanish and Latin American literatures and cultures (MA); Spanish language and translation (MA). *Program availability:* Part-time. *Degree requirements:* For master's, 2 foreign languages, thesis; for doctorate, 2 foreign languages, thesis/dissertation. *Entrance requirements:* For master's, GRE General Test; for doctorate, GRE General Test, master's degree. Additional exam requirements/recommendations for international students: required—TOEFL, IELTS.

Northwestern University, The Graduate School, Judd A. and Marjorie Weinberg College of Arts and Sciences, Department of Spanish and Portuguese, Evanston, IL 60208. Offers PhD.

The Ohio State University, Graduate School, College of Arts and Sciences, Division of Arts and Humanities, Department of Spanish and Portuguese, Columbus, OH 43210. Offers MA, PhD. Terminal master's awarded for partial completion of doctoral program. *Entrance requirements:* For master's and doctorate, GRE General Test, sample of academic writing. Additional exam requirements/recommendations for international students: required—TOEFL (minimum score 550 paper-based; 79 iBT), Michigan English Language Assessment Battery (minimum score 82); recommended—IELTS (minimum score 7). Electronic applications accepted.

Princeton University, Graduate School, Department of Spanish and Portuguese, Princeton, NJ 08544-1019. Offers PhD. *Degree requirements:* For doctorate, variable foreign language requirement, thesis/dissertation. *Entrance requirements:* For doctorate, GRE General Test, sample of written work. Additional exam requirements/recommendations for international students: required—TOEFL (minimum score 600 paper-based). Electronic applications accepted.

Tulane University, School of Liberal Arts, Department of Spanish and Portuguese, New Orleans, LA 70118-5669. Offers Portuguese (MA); Spanish and Portuguese (PhD). *Degree requirements:* For master's, 2 foreign languages; for doctorate, 2 foreign languages, thesis/dissertation. *Entrance requirements:* For master's, GRE General Test, minimum B average in undergraduate course work; for doctorate, GRE General Test. Additional exam requirements/recommendations for international students: required—TOEFL. Electronic applications accepted. *Expenses:* Tuition: Full-time $57,004; part-time $3167 per credit hour. *Required fees:* $2086; $44.50 per credit hour. $80 per term. Tuition and fees vary according to course load, degree level and program.

University of California, Los Angeles, Graduate Division, College of Letters and Science, Department of Spanish and Portuguese, Program in Portuguese, Los Angeles, CA 90095. Offers MA. *Degree requirements:* For master's, one foreign language, comprehensive exam or thesis. *Entrance requirements:* For master's, GRE General Test, bachelor's degree; minimum undergraduate GPA of 3.0 (or its equivalent if letter grade system not used). Additional exam requirements/recommendations for international students: required—TOEFL. Electronic applications accepted.

University of California, Santa Barbara, Graduate Division, College of Letters and Sciences, Division of Humanities and Fine Arts, Department of Spanish and Portuguese, Santa Barbara, CA 93106-4150. Offers Hispanic languages and literatures (PhD), including European medieval studies, feminist studies, Hispanic linguistics, Hispanic literature, Luso-Brazilian literature; Hispanic linguistics (MA); Luso-Brazilian literature (MA); Spanish or Spanish-American literature (MA); MA/PhD. Terminal master's

awarded for partial completion of doctoral program. *Degree requirements:* For master's, 2 foreign languages, comprehensive exam (for some programs), thesis optional; for doctorate, 3 foreign languages, comprehensive exam, thesis/dissertation. *Entrance requirements:* For master's and doctorate, GRE. Additional exam requirements/recommendations for international students: required—TOEFL (minimum score 550 paper-based; 80 iBT), IELTS (minimum score 7). Electronic applications accepted.

University of Georgia, Franklin College of Arts and Sciences, Department of Romance Languages, Athens, GA 30602. Offers French (PhD); Italian (MA, PhD); Portuguese (MA, PhD); romance linguistics (MA); Spanish (PhD). *Degree requirements:* For master's, one foreign language; for doctorate, 2 foreign languages, thesis/dissertation. *Entrance requirements:* For master's and doctorate, GRE General Test. Electronic applications accepted.

University of Illinois at Urbana-Champaign, Graduate College, College of Liberal Arts and Sciences, School of Literatures, Cultures and Linguistics, Department of Spanish, Italian and Portuguese, Champaign, IL 61820. Offers Italian (MA, PhD); Portuguese (MA, PhD); Spanish (MA, PhD).

The University of Manchester, School of Arts, Languages and Cultures, Manchester, United Kingdom. Offers anthropology, media and performance (PhD); applied theatre (PhD); Arab world studies (PhD); archaeology (PhD); art history and visual studies (PhD); arts and cultural management (PhD); arts management and cultural policy (PhD); Chinese studies (PhD); classics and ancient history (PhD); composition (PhD); creative writing (PhD); drama (PhD); East Asian studies (PhD); electroacoustic composition (PhD); English and American studies (PhD); English language (PhD); French studies (PhD); German studies (PhD); history (PhD); humanitarianism and conflict response (PhD); interpreting studies (PhD); Japanese studies (PhD); Latin American cultural studies (PhD); linguistics (PhD); Middle Eastern studies (PhD); museology (PhD); museum practice (PhD); music (PhD); musicology (PhD); Polish studies (PhD); Portuguese studies (PhD); religions and theology (PhD); Russian studies (PhD); Spanish studies (PhD); translation and intercultural studies (PhD).

University of Maryland, College Park, Academic Affairs, College of Arts and Humanities, School of Languages, Literatures, and Cultures, Spanish Language and Literatures Program, College Park, MD 20742. Offers MA, PhD. *Degree requirements:* For master's, comprehensive exam, thesis optional, scholarly paper; for doctorate, 2 foreign languages, thesis/dissertation. *Entrance requirements:* For master's, minimum GPA of 3.0, interview, sample research paper, minimum of 12 credits in upper-level literature, 3 letters of recommendation; for doctorate, minimum GPA of 3.0, interview, sample research paper, minimum of 12 credits in upper-level literature. Additional exam requirements/recommendations for international students: required—TOEFL. Electronic applications accepted.

University of Massachusetts Amherst, Graduate School, College of Humanities and Fine Arts, Department of Languages, Literatures, and Cultures, Program in Spanish and Portuguese Studies, Amherst, MA 01003. Offers Hispanic literatures, cultures and linguistics (MA, PhD); teaching Spanish (MAT). *Program availability:* Part-time. Terminal master's awarded for partial completion of doctoral program. *Degree requirements:* For master's, one foreign language, thesis or alternative; for doctorate, 2 foreign languages, comprehensive exam, thesis/dissertation. *Entrance requirements:* For master's and doctorate, GRE General Test, sample academic term paper. Additional exam requirements/recommendations for international students: required—TOEFL (minimum score 550 paper-based; 80 iBT), IELTS (minimum score 6.5). Electronic applications accepted.

University of Massachusetts Dartmouth, Graduate School, College of Arts and Sciences, Department of Portuguese, North Dartmouth, MA 02747-2300. Offers Luso-Afro Brazilian studies and theory (PhD); Portuguese studies (MA). *Program availability:* Part-time. *Faculty:* 5 full-time (2 women), 2 part-time/adjunct (1 woman). *Students:* 4 full-time (all women), 5 part-time (4 women); includes 2 minority (both Hispanic/Latino), 1 international. Average age 40. 6 applicants, 100% accepted, 2 enrolled. In 2019, 1 master's, 2 doctorates awarded. Terminal master's awarded for partial completion of doctoral program. *Degree requirements:* For master's, comprehensive exam, thesis, comprehensive written exam or research project; for doctorate, comprehensive exam, thesis/dissertation, Dissertation. *Entrance requirements:* For master's, statement of purpose (300-600 words), resume, 3 letters of recommendation, official transcripts; for doctorate, statement of purpose (300-600 words), resume, 3 letters of recommendation, official transcripts, scholarly writing sample (minimum of 10 pages). Additional exam requirements/recommendations for international students: required—TOEFL (minimum score 72 iBT). *Application deadline:* For fall admission, 8/15 for domestic students, 7/15 for international students; for spring admission, 11/15 for domestic students, 10/15 for international students. Application fee: $60. Electronic applications accepted. *Expenses:* Tuition, area resident: Full-time $16,390; part-time $682.92 per credit. Tuition, state resident: full-time $16,390; part-time $682.92 per credit. Tuition, nonresident: full-time $29,578; part-time $1232.42 per credit. *Required fees:* $575. *Financial support:* In 2019–20, 6 fellowships (averaging $18,167 per year), 1 teaching assistantship (averaging $17,000 per year) were awarded; tuition waivers (full) also available. Financial award application deadline: 3/1; financial award applicants required to submit FAFSA. *Unit head:* Anna Klobucka, Graduate Program Director, Portuguese, 508-999-8241, Fax: 508-910-9272, E-mail: aklobucka@umassd.edu. *Application contact:* Scott Webster, Director of Graduate Studies and Admissions, 508-999-8604, Fax: 508-999-8183, E-mail: graduate@umassd.edu.
Website: http://www.umassd.edu/cas/departmentsanddegreeprograms/portguese

University of Minnesota, Twin Cities Campus, Graduate School, College of Liberal Arts, Department of Spanish and Portuguese Studies, Minneapolis, MN 55455-0213. Offers Hispanic and Lusophone literatures, cultures and linguistics (PhD); Hispanic linguistics (MA); Hispanic literature (MA); Lusophone literature (MA). *Degree requirements:* For master's, 2 foreign languages, comprehensive exam, thesis or alternative; for doctorate, 2 foreign languages, comprehensive exam, thesis/dissertation. *Entrance requirements:* For master's and doctorate, GRE General Test, samples of written work, 3 letters of recommendation, voice sample, statement of purpose. Additional exam requirements/recommendations for international students: required—TOEFL (minimum score 550 paper-based; 79 iBT). Electronic applications accepted.

University of New Mexico, Graduate Studies, College of Arts and Sciences, Program in Spanish and Portuguese, Albuquerque, NM 87131-2039. Offers Portuguese (MA); Spanish (MA); Spanish and Portuguese (PhD). *Program availability:* Part-time. *Degree requirements:* For master's, one foreign language, comprehensive exam, thesis optional; for doctorate, one foreign language, comprehensive exam, thesis/dissertation. *Entrance requirements:* For master's, BA in Spanish or Portuguese, 3 letters of recommendation, letter of intent; for doctorate, GRE, 3 letters of recommendation, letter of intent, sample research paper. Additional exam requirements/recommendations for international students: required—TOEFL (minimum score 550 paper-based). Electronic applications accepted. *Expenses:* Tuition, state resident: full-time $7633; part-time $972 per year. Tuition, nonresident: full-time $22,586; part-time $3840 per year. *International tuition:* $23,292 full-time. *Required fees:* $8608. Tuition and fees vary according to course level, course load, degree level, program and student level.

The University of North Carolina at Chapel Hill, Graduate School, College of Arts and Sciences, Department of Romance Languages and Literatures, Chapel Hill, NC 27599. Offers French (MA, PhD); Italian (MA, PhD); Portuguese (MA, PhD); Romance languages (MA, PhD); Romance philology (MA, PhD); Spanish (MA, PhD). *Degree requirements:* For master's, one foreign language, comprehensive exam, thesis; for doctorate, 2 foreign languages, comprehensive exam, thesis/dissertation. *Entrance requirements:* For master's and doctorate, GRE General Test, minimum GPA of 3.0. Additional exam requirements/recommendations for international students: required—TOEFL (minimum score 550 paper-based). Electronic applications accepted.

University of South Africa, College of Human Sciences, Pretoria, South Africa. Offers adult education (M Ed); African languages (MA, PhD); African politics (MA, PhD); Afrikaans (MA, PhD); ancient history (MA, PhD); ancient Near Eastern studies (MA, PhD); anthropology (MA, PhD); applied linguistics (MA); Arabic (MA, PhD); archaeology (MA); art history (MA); Biblical archaeology (MA); Biblical studies (M Th, D Th, PhD); Christian spirituality (M Th, D Th); church history (M Th, D Th); classical studies (MA, PhD); clinical psychology (MA); communication (MA, PhD); comparative education (M Ed, Ed D); consulting psychology (D Admin, D Com, PhD); curriculum studies (M Ed, Ed D); development studies (M Admin, MA, D Admin, PhD); didactics (M Ed, Ed D); education (M Tech); education management (M Ed, Ed D); educational psychology (M Ed); English (MA); environmental education (M Ed); French (MA, PhD); German (MA, PhD); Greek (MA); guidance and counseling (M Ed); health studies (MA, PhD), including health sciences education (MA), health services management (MA), medical and surgical nursing science (critical care general) (MA), midwifery and neonatal nursing science (MA), trauma and emergency care (MA); history (MA, PhD); history of education (Ed D); inclusive education (M Ed, Ed D); information and communications technology policy and regulation (MA); information science (MA, MIS, PhD); international politics (MA, PhD); Islamic studies (MA, PhD); Italian (MA, PhD); Judaica (MA, PhD); linguistics (MA, PhD); mathematical education (M Ed); mathematics education (MA); missiology (M Th, D Th); modern Hebrew (MA, PhD); musicology (MA, MMus, D Mus, PhD); natural science education (M Ed); New Testament (M Th, D Th); Old Testament (D Th); pastoral therapy (M Th, D Th); philosophy (MA); philosophy of education (M Ed, Ed D); politics (MA, PhD); Portuguese (MA, PhD); practical theology (M Th, D Th); psychology (MA, MS, PhD); psychology of education (M Ed, Ed D); public health (MA); religious studies (MA, D Th, PhD); Romance languages (MA); Russian (MA, PhD); Semitic languages (MA, PhD); social behavior studies in HIV/AIDS (MA); social science (mental health) (MA); social science in development studies (MA); social science in psychology (MA); social science in social work (MA); social science in sociology (MA); social work (MSW, DSW, PhD); socio-education (M Ed, Ed D); sociolinguistics (MA); sociology (MA, PhD); Spanish (MA, PhD); systematic theology (M Th, D Th); TESOL (teaching English to speakers of other languages) (MA); theological ethics (M Th, D Th); theory of literature (MA, PhD); urban ministries (D Th); urban ministry (M Th).

The University of Tennessee, Graduate School, College of Arts and Sciences, Department of Modern Foreign Languages and Literatures, Program in Modern Foreign Languages, Knoxville, TN 37996. Offers applied linguistics (PhD); French (PhD); German (PhD); Italian (PhD); Portuguese (PhD); Russian (PhD); Spanish (PhD). *Degree requirements:* For doctorate, 2 foreign languages, thesis/dissertation. *Entrance requirements:* For doctorate, minimum GPA of 2.7. Additional exam requirements/recommendations for international students: required—TOEFL. Electronic applications accepted.

The University of Texas at Austin, Graduate School, College of Liberal Arts, Department of Spanish and Portuguese, Austin, TX 78712-1111. Offers Hispanic linguistics (MA, PhD); Hispanic literature (MA, PhD); Ibero-romance philology and linguistics (PhD); Luso-Brazilian literature (MA, PhD). *Degree requirements:* For master's, 2 foreign languages, thesis or alternative; for doctorate, 3 foreign languages, thesis/dissertation. *Entrance requirements:* For master's and doctorate, GRE General Test. Electronic applications accepted.

University of Toronto, School of Graduate Studies, Faculty of Arts and Science, Department of Spanish and Portuguese, Toronto, ON M5S 1A1, Canada. Offers MA, PhD. *Program availability:* Part-time. *Degree requirements:* For doctorate, thesis/dissertation. *Entrance requirements:* For master's, minimum B average in final year, 2 letters of reference; for doctorate, minimum A- average, 2 letters of reference, writing sample. Additional exam requirements/recommendations for international students: required—TWE (minimum score 5), TOEFL, Michigan English Language Assessment Battery, IELTS, or COPE. Electronic applications accepted.

University of Washington, Graduate School, College of Arts and Sciences, Division of Spanish and Portuguese Studies, Seattle, WA 98195. Offers Hispanic literary and cultural studies (MA). *Degree requirements:* For master's, 2 foreign languages, thesis optional, exam. *Entrance requirements:* For master's, GRE General Test, minimum GPA of 3.0. Additional exam requirements/recommendations for international students: required—TOEFL. Electronic applications accepted.

University of Wisconsin–Madison, Graduate School, College of Letters and Science, Department of Spanish and Portuguese, Program in Portuguese, Madison, WI 53706-1380. Offers MA, PhD. *Degree requirements:* For master's, one foreign language; for doctorate, 2 foreign languages, thesis/dissertation. *Entrance requirements:* For master's, GRE (recommended), minimum GPA of 3.25 in Spanish or Portuguese; for doctorate, GRE (recommended), minimum graduate GPA of 3.4. Additional exam requirements/recommendations for international students: required—TOEFL. Electronic applications accepted.

University of Wisconsin–Milwaukee, Graduate School, College of Letters and Science, Department of Spanish and Portuguese, Milwaukee, WI 53201-0413. Offers MA. *Entrance requirements:* For master's, bachelor's degree. Electronic applications accepted.

Vanderbilt University, Department of Spanish and Portuguese, Nashville, TN 37240-1001. Offers Portuguese (MA); Spanish (PhD). *Faculty:* 11 full-time (4 women). *Students:* 24 full-time (12 women); includes 6 minority (1 Black or African American, non-Hispanic/Latino; 5 Hispanic/Latino), 12 international. Average age 31. 33 applicants, 15% accepted, 4 enrolled. In 2019, 3 master's, 1 doctorate awarded. *Degree requirements:* For master's, one foreign language, thesis; for doctorate, 2 foreign languages, thesis/dissertation, final and qualifying exams. *Entrance requirements:* For master's, GRE General Test; for doctorate, GRE General Test, writing sample in Spanish. Additional exam requirements/recommendations for international students: required—TOEFL (minimum score 570 paper-based; 88 iBT). *Application deadline:* For fall admission, 1/15 for domestic and international students. Electronic applications accepted. *Expenses: Tuition:* Full-time $51,018; part-time $2087 per hour. *Required fees:* $542. Tuition and fees vary according to program. *Financial support:* Fellowships, teaching assistantships with full tuition reimbursements, Federal Work-Study, institutionally sponsored loans, and health care benefits available. Financial award application deadline: 1/15; financial award applicants required to submit CSS PROFILE or FAFSA. *Unit head:* Andres Zamora, Chair, 615-322-6930, Fax: 615-343-7260, E-mail: andres.zamora@vanderbilt.edu. *Application contact:* Jose Cardenas Bunsen, Director of Graduate Studies, 615-322-6930, Fax: 615-343-7260, E-mail: jose.cardenas-bunsen@Vanderbilt.Edu.
Website: http://as.vanderbilt.edu/spanish-portuguese/graduate/index.php

Yale University, Graduate School of Arts and Sciences, Department of Spanish and Portuguese, New Haven, CT 06520. Offers Latin American literature (PhD); Luso-Brazilian and Spanish/Spanish American literatures (PhD); Spanish peninsular literature (PhD). Terminal master's awarded for partial completion of doctoral program. *Degree requirements:* For doctorate, 3 foreign languages, thesis/dissertation. *Entrance requirements:* For doctorate, GRE General Test.

Romance Languages

Boston University, Graduate School of Arts and Sciences, Department of Romance Studies, Boston, MA 02215. Offers Hispanic language and literature (MA, PhD). *Students:* 35 full-time (24 women), 2 part-time (both women); includes 11 minority (2 Black or African American, non-Hispanic/Latino; 9 Hispanic/Latino), 14 international. Average age 28. 31 applicants, 52% accepted, 6 enrolled. In 2019, 2 master's, 5 doctorates awarded. Terminal master's awarded for partial completion of doctoral program. *Degree requirements:* For master's, one foreign language, comprehensive exam; for doctorate, 2 foreign languages, comprehensive exam, thesis/dissertation. *Entrance requirements:* For master's and doctorate, GRE General Test, sample of written work, 3 letters of recommendation, transcripts, personal statement, summary of related coursework. Additional exam requirements/recommendations for international students: required—TOEFL (minimum score 550 paper-based; 84 iBT). *Application deadline:* For fall admission, 1/15 for domestic and international students. Application fee: $95. Electronic applications accepted. *Financial support:* In 2019–20, 37 students received support, including 11 fellowships with full tuition reimbursements available (averaging $23,340 per year), 22 teaching assistantships with full tuition reimbursements available (averaging $23,340 per year); Federal Work-Study, scholarships/grants, and health care benefits also available. Financial award application deadline: 1/15. *Unit head:* Odile Cazenave, Chair, 617-353-6225, Fax: 617-353-6246, E-mail: cazenave@bu.edu. *Application contact:* Michael Williams, Administrative Assistant, 617-353-2641, Fax: 617-353-6246, E-mail: mawillia@bu.edu.
Website: http://www.bu.edu/rs/

Columbia University, Graduate School of Arts and Sciences, New York, NY 10027. Offers African-American studies (MA); American studies (MA); anthropology (MA, PhD); art history and archaeology (MA, PhD); astronomy (PhD); biological sciences (PhD); biotechnology (MA); chemical physics (PhD); chemistry (PhD); classical studies (MA, PhD); classics (MA, PhD); climate and society (MA); conservation biology (MA); earth and environmental sciences (PhD); East Asia: regional studies (MA); East Asian languages and cultures (MA, PhD); ecology, evolution and environmental biology (MA), including conservation biology; ecology, evolution, and environmental biology (PhD), including ecology and evolutionary biology, evolutionary primatology; economics (MA, PhD); English and comparative literature (MA, PhD); French and Romance philology (MA, PhD); Germanic languages (MA, PhD); global French studies (MA); global thought (MA); Hispanic cultural studies (MA); history (PhD); history and literature (MA); human rights studies (MA); Islamic studies (MA); Italian (MA, PhD); Japanese pedagogy (MA); Jewish studies (MA); Latin America and the Caribbean: regional studies (MA); Latin American and Iberian cultures (PhD); mathematics (MA, PhD), including finance (MA); medieval and Renaissance studies (MA); Middle Eastern, South Asian, and African studies (MA, PhD); modern art: critical and curatorial studies (MA); modern European studies (MA); museum anthropology (MA); music (DMA, PhD); oral history (MA); philosophical foundations of physics (MA); philosophy (MA, PhD); physics (PhD); political science (MA, PhD); psychology (PhD); quantitative methods in the social sciences (MA); religion (MA, PhD); Russia, Eurasia and East Europe: regional studies (MA); Russian translation (MA); Slavic cultures (MA); Slavic languages (MA, PhD); sociology (MA, PhD); South Asian studies (MA); statistics (MA, PhD); theatre (PhD). *Program availability:* Part-time. *Students:* 3,506 full-time (1,844 women), 208 part-time (121 women); includes 864 minority (110 Black or African American, non-Hispanic/Latino; 5 American Indian or Alaska Native, non-Hispanic/Latino; 416 Asian, non-Hispanic/Latino; 147 Hispanic/Latino; 6 Native Hawaiian or other Pacific Islander, non-Hispanic/Latino; 180 Two or more races, non-Hispanic/Latino), 2,065 international. 14,545 applicants, 25% accepted, 1,429 enrolled. In 2019, 1,262 master's, 363 doctorates awarded. Terminal master's awarded for partial completion of doctoral program. *Degree requirements:* For master's, variable foreign language requirement, comprehensive exam (for some programs), thesis (for some programs); for doctorate, variable foreign language requirement, comprehensive exam (for some programs), thesis/dissertation. *Entrance requirements:* For master's and doctorate, GRE General Test, GRE Subject Test (for some programs). Additional exam requirements/recommendations for international students: required—TOEFL (minimum score 600 paper-based; 100 iBT), IELTS (minimum score 7.5). Application fee: $115. Electronic applications accepted. *Expenses: Tuition:* Full-time $47,600; part-time $1880 per credit. One-time fee: $105. *Financial support:* Fellowships, research assistantships, teaching assistantships, career-related internships or fieldwork, Federal Work-Study, institutionally sponsored loans, scholarships/grants, traineeships, health care benefits, tuition waivers, and unspecified assistantships available. Support available to part-time students. Financial award application deadline: 12/15. *Unit head:* Dr. Carlos J. Alonso, Dean of the Graduate School of Arts and Sciences and Vice President for Graduate Education, 212-854-2861, E-mail: gsas-dean@columbia.edu. *Application contact:* GSAS Office of Admissions, 212-854-6729, E-mail: gsas-admissions@columbia.edu.
Website: http://gsas.columbia.edu/

Romance Languages

Cornell University, Graduate School, Graduate Fields of Arts and Sciences, Field of Linguistics, Ithaca, NY 14853. Offers applied linguistics (MA, PhD); East Asian linguistics (MA, PhD); English linguistics (MA, PhD); general linguistics (MA, PhD); Germanic linguistics (MA, PhD); Indo-European linguistics (MA, PhD); phonetics (MA, PhD); phonological theory (MA, PhD); Romance linguistics (MA, PhD); second language acquisition (MA, PhD); semantics (MA, PhD); Slavic linguistics (MA, PhD); sociolinguistics (MA, PhD); South Asian linguistics (MA, PhD); Southeast Asian linguistics (MA, PhD); syntactic theory (MA, PhD). Terminal master's awarded for partial completion of doctoral program. *Degree requirements:* For master's, one foreign language, thesis; for doctorate, one foreign language, comprehensive exam, thesis/dissertation. *Entrance requirements:* For master's and doctorate, GRE General Test, 2 letters of recommendation. Additional exam requirements/recommendations for international students: required—TOEFL (minimum score 600 paper-based; 77 iBT). Electronic applications accepted.

Cornell University, Graduate School, Graduate Fields of Arts and Sciences, Field of Romance Studies, Ithaca, NY 14853. Offers French linguistics (PhD); French literature (PhD); Hispanic literature (PhD); Italian linguistics (PhD); Italian literature (PhD); Romance linguistics (PhD); Spanish linguistics (PhD). *Degree requirements:* For doctorate, 2 foreign languages, comprehensive exam, thesis/dissertation. *Entrance requirements:* For doctorate, GRE General Test, sample of written work, 3 letters of recommendation. Additional exam requirements/recommendations for international students: required—TOEFL (minimum score 550 paper-based; 77 iBT). Electronic applications accepted.

Hunter College of the City University of New York, Graduate School, School of Arts and Sciences, Department of Romance Languages, New York, NY 10065-5085. Offers French (MA); Italian (MA); Spanish (MA). *Program availability:* Part-time, evening/weekend. *Degree requirements:* For master's, 2 foreign languages, comprehensive exam, thesis optional. *Entrance requirements:* For master's, GRE General Test, GRE Subject Test, interview, proficiency in chosen language. Additional exam requirements/recommendations for international students: required—TOEFL.

Johns Hopkins University, Zanvyl Krieger School of Arts and Sciences, Department of German and Romance Languages and Literatures, Baltimore, MD 21218. Offers German (MA, PhD); romance languages (PhD), including French, Italian, Spanish. Terminal master's awarded for partial completion of doctoral program. *Degree requirements:* For master's, comprehensive exam; for doctorate, 2 foreign languages, comprehensive exam, thesis/dissertation. *Entrance requirements:* For doctorate, GRE General Test. Additional exam requirements/recommendations for international students: required—TOEFL (minimum score 600 paper-based; 100 iBT), IELTS. Electronic applications accepted. *Expenses:* Contact institution.

Michigan State University, The Graduate School, College of Arts and Letters, Department of Romance and Classical Studies, East Lansing, MI 48824. Offers French (MA); French language and literature (PhD); Hispanic cultural studies (PhD); Hispanic literatures (MA); Spanish as a second or bilingual language (MA). *Entrance requirements:* Additional exam requirements/recommendations for international students: required—TOEFL. Electronic applications accepted.

New York University, Graduate School of Arts and Science, Center for French Civilization and Culture, Department of French, New York, NY 10012-1019. Offers French (PhD); French language and civilization (MA); Romance languages and literatures (MA). *Program availability:* Part-time. Terminal master's awarded for partial completion of doctoral program. *Degree requirements:* For master's, one foreign language, thesis (for some programs); for doctorate, one foreign language, thesis/dissertation. *Entrance requirements:* For master's and doctorate, GRE General Test, proficiency in French. Additional exam requirements/recommendations for international students: required—TOEFL, IELTS.

New York University, Graduate School of Arts and Science, Department of Spanish and Portuguese Languages and Literatures, New York, NY 10012-1019. Offers Portuguese (MA, PhD); Spanish (PhD); Spanish and Latin American literatures and cultures (MA); Spanish language and translation (MA). *Program availability:* Part-time. *Degree requirements:* For master's, 2 foreign languages, thesis; for doctorate, 2 foreign languages, thesis/dissertation. *Entrance requirements:* For master's, GRE General Test; for doctorate, GRE General Test, master's degree. Additional exam requirements/recommendations for international students: required—TOEFL, IELTS.

Northern Illinois University, Graduate School, College of Liberal Arts and Sciences, World Languages & Cultures, De Kalb, IL 60115-2854. Offers French (MA); Spanish (MA). *Program availability:* Part-time. *Faculty:* 25 full-time (11 women). *Students:* 1 (woman) full-time, 12 part-time (9 women); includes 8 minority (1 Black or African American, non-Hispanic/Latino; 7 Hispanic/Latino), 1 international. Average age 35. 3 applicants, 67% accepted, 1 enrolled. In 2019, 1 master's awarded. *Degree requirements:* For master's, one foreign language, comprehensive exam, thesis or alternative, language proficiency exam. *Entrance requirements:* For master's, GRE General Test, interview, minimum GPA of 2.75, undergraduate major in French or Spanish. Additional exam requirements/recommendations for international students: required—TOEFL (minimum score 550 paper-based). *Application deadline:* For fall admission, 6/1 for domestic students, 5/1 for international students; for spring admission, 11/1 for domestic students, 10/1 for international students. Applications are processed on a rolling basis. Application fee: $40. Electronic applications accepted. *Financial support:* In 2019–20, 7 teaching assistantships with full tuition reimbursements were awarded; fellowships with full tuition reimbursements, research assistantships with full tuition reimbursements, career-related internships or fieldwork, Federal Work-Study, scholarships/grants, tuition waivers (full), and unspecified assistantships also available. Support available to part-time students. Financial award applicants required to submit FAFSA. *Unit head:* Dr. John Bentley, Chair, 815-753-1559, Fax: 815-753-5989. *Application contact:* Graduate School Office, 815-753-0395, E-mail: gradsch@niu.edu. Website: http://www.forlangs.net/

Queens College of the City University of New York, Arts and Humanities Division, Department of European Languages and Literatures, Queens, NY 11367-1597. Offers French (MA); Italian (MA). *Program availability:* Part-time-only, evening/weekend. *Degree requirements:* For master's, 2 foreign languages, thesis optional, oral exam. *Entrance requirements:* For master's, minimum GPA of 3.0. Additional exam requirements/recommendations for international students: recommended—TOEFL (minimum score 61 iBT), IELTS (minimum score 5). Electronic applications accepted.

San Diego State University, Graduate and Research Affairs, College of Arts and Letters, Department of European Studies, San Diego, CA 92182. Offers MA. *Degree requirements:* For master's, one foreign language. *Entrance requirements:* For master's, GRE General Test. Additional exam requirements/recommendations for international students: required—TOEFL. Electronic applications accepted.

Stony Brook University, State University of New York, Graduate School, College of Arts and Sciences, Department of European Languages, Literatures, and Cultures, Stony Brook, NY 11794. Offers French (MA), including Romance languages; Italian (MA), including Romance languages. *Program availability:* Evening/weekend. *Faculty:* 9 full-time (4 women), 19 part-time/adjunct (12 women). *Students:* 2 full-time (1 woman), 4 part-time (2 women); includes 2 minority (1 American Indian or Alaska Native, non-Hispanic/Latino; 1 Two or more races, non-Hispanic/Latino), 1 international. Average age 33. 4 applicants, 100% accepted, 4 enrolled. In 2019, 2 master's awarded. *Entrance requirements:* Additional exam requirements/recommendations for international students: required—TOEFL (minimum score 85 iBT). *Application deadline:* For fall admission, 1/15 for domestic students; for spring admission, 10/1 for domestic students. Application fee: $100. *Expenses:* Contact institution. *Financial support:* Fellowships, research assistantships, and teaching assistantships available. *Unit head:* Dr. Sarah Jourdain, Chair, 631-632-7440, E-mail: sarah.jourdain@stonybrook.edu. *Application contact:* Elizabeth Tolson, Coordinator, 631-632-7440, E-mail: elizabeth-a.tolson@stonybrook.edu.
Website: http://www.sunysb.edu/eurolangs/

Texas Tech University, Graduate School, College of Arts and Sciences, Department of Biological Sciences, Lubbock, TX 79409-3131. Offers biology (MS, PhD); environmental sustainability and natural resource management (PSM); microbiology (MS); zoology (MS, PhD). *Program availability:* Part-time, blended/hybrid learning. *Faculty:* 45 full-time (16 women). *Students:* 131 full-time (71 women), 21 part-time (12 women); includes 22 minority (4 Black or African American, non-Hispanic/Latino; 1 Asian, non-Hispanic/Latino; 11 Hispanic/Latino; 6 Two or more races, non-Hispanic/Latino), 66 international. Average age 29. 80 applicants, 48% accepted, 34 enrolled. In 2019, 13 master's, 6 doctorates awarded. *Degree requirements:* For master's, comprehensive exam, thesis or alternative; for doctorate, comprehensive exam, thesis/dissertation. *Entrance requirements:* For master's and doctorate, GRE General Test. Additional exam requirements/recommendations for international students: required—TOEFL (minimum score 550 paper-based; 79 iBT). *Application deadline:* For fall admission, 6/1 priority date for domestic students, 1/15 priority date for international students; for spring admission, 9/1 priority date for domestic students, 6/15 priority date for international students. Applications are processed on a rolling basis. Application fee: $65. Electronic applications accepted. *Expenses:* Contact institution. *Financial support:* In 2019–20, 140 students received support, including 114 fellowships (averaging $1,560 per year), 22 research assistantships (averaging $19,738 per year), 114 teaching assistantships (averaging $17,489 per year); Federal Work-Study and health care benefits also available. Financial award application deadline: 2/15; financial award applicants required to submit FAFSA. *Unit head:* Dr. John Zak, Professor, Chair and Associate Dean, 806-834-2682, Fax: 806-742-2963, E-mail: john.zak@ttu.edu. *Application contact:* Dr. Lou Densmore, Graduate Adviser, 806-834-6479, Fax: 806-742-2963, E-mail: lou.densmore@ttu.edu.
Website: www.depts.ttu.edu/biology/

Texas Tech University, Graduate School, College of Arts and Sciences, Department of Classical and Modern Languages and Literatures, Lubbock, TX 79409-2071. Offers languages and cultures (MA); Romance languages (MA); Spanish (PhD); MBA/MA. *Program availability:* Part-time. *Faculty:* 54 full-time (34 women), 1 (woman) part-time/adjunct. *Students:* 72 full-time (38 women), 15 part-time (12 women); includes 28 minority (1 Asian, non-Hispanic/Latino; 24 Hispanic/Latino; 3 Two or more races, non-Hispanic/Latino), 33 international. Average age 33. 57 applicants, 68% accepted, 28 enrolled. In 2019, 28 master's, 2 doctorates awarded. *Degree requirements:* For master's, comprehensive exam, thesis or alternative; for doctorate, comprehensive exam, thesis/dissertation. *Entrance requirements:* Additional exam requirements/recommendations for international students: required—TOEFL (minimum score 550 paper-based; 79 iBT). *Application deadline:* For fall admission, 6/1 priority date for domestic students, 1/15 priority date for international students; for spring admission, 9/1 priority date for domestic students, 6/15 priority date for international students. Applications are processed on a rolling basis. Application fee: $65. Electronic applications accepted. *Expenses:* Contact institution. *Financial support:* In 2019–20, 83 students received support, including 52 fellowships (averaging $2,880 per year), 76 teaching assistantships (averaging $13,880 per year); research assistantships, Federal Work-Study, scholarships/grants, and unspecified assistantships also available. Financial award application deadline: 4/15; financial award applicants required to submit FAFSA. *Unit head:* Dr. Carmen Pereira-Muro, Department Chair, 806-834-0151, Fax: 806-742-3306, E-mail: carmen.pereira@ttu.edu. *Application contact:* Carla Burrus, Senior Advisor, 806-834-3282, Fax: 806-742-3306, E-mail: carla.burrus@ttu.edu.
Website: www.depts.ttu.edu/classic_modern/

University at Buffalo, the State University of New York, Graduate School, College of Arts and Sciences, Department of Romance Languages and Literatures, Buffalo, NY 14260-4620. Offers French (MA, PhD); Spanish (MA, PhD). *Program availability:* Part-time. Terminal master's awarded for partial completion of doctoral program. *Degree requirements:* For master's, 2 foreign languages, comprehensive exam, thesis (for some programs); for doctorate, 2 foreign languages, comprehensive exam, thesis/dissertation, Preliminary exam one (1) year after Comprehensive exam. *Entrance requirements:* For master's, completed application form, application fee, original official transcripts for all previous college work, 3 letters of recommendation, personal statement, 1 writing sample in the target language, 1 writing sample in English (for international), CV, GPA of 3.0 or above preferred; for doctorate, GRE, TOEFL (if international), completed application form, application fee, original official transcripts for all previous college work, 3 letters of recommendation, personal statement, 1 writing sample in target language, 1 writing sample in English (for international), CV, GPA of 3.0 or above preferred. Additional exam requirements/recommendations for international students: required—TOEFL (minimum score 550 paper-based; 79 iBT), IELTS (minimum score 6.5), PTE (minimum score 55). Electronic applications accepted. *Expenses: Tuition,* area resident: Full-time $11,310; part-time $471 per credit hour. Tuition, state resident: full-time $11,310; part-time $471 per credit hour. Tuition, nonresident: full-time $23,100; part-time $963 per credit hour. *International tuition:* $23,100 full-time. *Required fees:* $2820.

The University of Alabama, Graduate School, College of Arts and Sciences, Department of Modern Languages and Classics, Tuscaloosa, AL 35487. Offers French (MA, PhD); French and Spanish (PhD); German (MA); Romance languages (MA, PhD); Spanish (MA, PhD). *Program availability:* Part-time. *Faculty:* 20 full-time (11 women). *Students:* 39 full-time (17 women), 6 part-time (3 women); includes 14 minority (5 Black or African American, non-Hispanic/Latino; 7 Hispanic/Latino; 2 Two or more races, non-Hispanic/Latino), 10 international. Average age 31. 19 applicants, 89% accepted, 11 enrolled. In 2019, 6 master's, 3 doctorates awarded. *Degree requirements:* For master's, comprehensive exam, thesis optional; for doctorate, one foreign language, thesis/dissertation, preliminary exam. *Entrance requirements:* For master's and doctorate, minimum GPA of 3.0, writing sample. Additional exam requirements/recommendations for international students: required—TOEFL or IELTS. *Application deadline:* For fall admission, 7/6 priority date for domestic students, 1/15 priority date for international students; for spring admission, 12/5 priority date for domestic students, 6/1 priority date for international students. Applications are processed on a rolling basis. Application fee: $50 ($60 for international students). Electronic applications accepted. *Expenses: Tuition,* area resident: Full-time $10,780; part-time $440 per credit hour. Tuition, nonresident: full-time $30,250; part-time $1550 per credit hour. *Financial support:* In 2019–20, 40 students received support. Fellowships, research assistantships with full tuition reimbursements available, teaching assistantships with full tuition reimbursements available, career-related internships or fieldwork, Federal Work-Study, institutionally sponsored loans, and scholarships/grants available. Financial award application deadline: 7/14. *Unit head:* Dr. Douglas Lightfoot, Department Chair, 205-

348-5059, E-mail: lightfoot@ua.edu. *Application contact:* Dr. K. Barbara Fischer, Graduate Director/Associate Professor, 205-348-8465, Fax: 205-348-2042, E-mail: bfischer@bama.ua.edu.
Website: http://bama.ua.edu/~mlc

University of California, Berkeley, Graduate Division, College of Letters and Science, Group in Romance Languages and Literatures, Berkeley, CA 94720. Offers French (PhD); Italian (PhD); Spanish (PhD). *Degree requirements:* For doctorate, thesis/dissertation, qualifying exam. *Entrance requirements:* For doctorate, GRE General Test, minimum GPA of 3.0, 3 letters of recommendation. Additional exam requirements/recommendations for international students: required—TOEFL (minimum score 570 paper-based; 90 iBT). Electronic applications accepted.

University of Chicago, Division of the Humanities, Department of Romance Languages and Literatures, Chicago, IL 60637. Offers French and Francophone studies (PhD); Hispanic and Luso-Brazilian studies (PhD); Italian studies (PhD); Renaissance and early modern studies (PhD). Terminal master's awarded for partial completion of doctoral program. *Degree requirements:* For doctorate, 3 foreign languages, comprehensive exam, thesis/dissertation. *Entrance requirements:* For doctorate, GRE General Test, 15-20 page writing sample, statement of purpose, 3 letters of recommendation, transcripts for all previous degrees and institutions attended. Additional exam requirements/recommendations for international students: required—TOEFL (minimum score 104 iBT), IELTS (minimum score 7). Electronic applications accepted.

University of Chicago, Division of the Humanities, Master of Arts Program in the Humanities, Chicago, IL 60637. Offers art history (MA); cinema and media studies (MA); classic languages (MA); comparative literature (MA); creative writing (MA); cultural policy studies (MA); digital humanities (MA); East Asian languages and civilizations (MA); English language and literature (MA); gender and sexuality studies (MA); Germanic studies (MA); linguistics (MA); music (MA); near Eastern languages and civilizations (MA); philosophy (MA); poetics (MA); race, politics and culture (MA); Romance languages and literatures (MA); Slavic languages and literatures (MA); South Asian languages and civilizations (MA); theater and performance studies (MA). *Degree requirements:* For master's, thesis. *Entrance requirements:* For master's, GRE General Test, 10-15 page writing sample, statement of purpose, 3 letters of recommendation, transcripts for all previous degrees and institutions attended. Additional exam requirements/recommendations for international students: required—TOEFL (minimum score 104 iBT), IELTS (minimum score 7). Electronic applications accepted. *Expenses:* Contact institution.

University of Cincinnati, Graduate School, McMicken College of Arts and Sciences, Dept. of Romance and Arabic Languages and Literatures, Cincinnati, OH 45221. Offers French (MA, PhD); Romance languages and literatures (PhD); Spanish (MA, PhD). *Program availability:* Part-time, evening/weekend. *Faculty:* 18 full-time (11 women). *Students:* 30 full-time (17 women), 6 part-time (4 women); includes 22 minority (1 Black or African American, non-Hispanic/Latino; 16 Hispanic/Latino; 5 Two or more races, non-Hispanic/Latino), 15 international. Average age 30. 32 applicants, 31% accepted, 9 enrolled. In 2019, 3 master's, 3 doctorates awarded. Terminal master's awarded for partial completion of doctoral program. *Degree requirements:* For master's, 2 foreign languages, comprehensive exam, thesis optional; for doctorate, 3 foreign languages, comprehensive exam, thesis/dissertation. *Entrance requirements:* For master's, minimum GPA of 3.0; for doctorate, MA or equivalent in French or Spanish language and literature. Additional exam requirements/recommendations for international students: required—TOEFL (minimum score 80 iBT). *Application deadline:* For fall admission, 2/1 priority date for domestic and international students. Application fee: $65. Electronic applications accepted. *Financial support:* In 2019–20, 21 students received support, including 2 fellowships with full tuition reimbursements available (averaging $200,000 per year), 2 research assistantships (averaging $14,000 per year), 21 teaching assistantships with full tuition reimbursements available (averaging $13,000 per year); unspecified assistantships also available. Financial award application deadline: 2/1. *Unit head:* Dr. Therese Migraine-George, Head, 513-556-1828, E-mail: migrait@uc.edu. *Application contact:* Dr. Nicasio Urbina, Graduate Program Director, 513-556-1838, E-mail: urbinan@uc.edu.
Website: http://asweb.artsci.uc.edu/rll/

University of Illinois at Urbana-Champaign, Graduate College, College of Liberal Arts and Sciences, School of Literatures, Cultures and Linguistics, Program in Romance Linguistics, Champaign, IL 61820. Offers PhD.

University of Miami, Graduate School, College of Arts and Sciences, Department of Modern Languages and Literatures, Coral Gables, FL 33124. Offers romance studies (PhD), including French, Spanish. *Degree requirements:* For doctorate, 2 foreign languages, thesis/dissertation, area exam, qualifying exam. *Entrance requirements:* For doctorate, 1 writing sample in English and 1 writing sample in French or Spanish, minimum GPA of 3.0, oral interview, letters of recommendation. Additional exam requirements/recommendations for international students: required—TOEFL (minimum score 550 paper-based; 59 iBT). Electronic applications accepted.

University of Missouri, Office of Research and Graduate Studies, College of Arts and Science, Department of Romance Languages and Literatures, Columbia, MO 65211. Offers French (MA, PhD). Terminal master's awarded for partial completion of doctoral program. *Entrance requirements:* For master's, GRE General Test, minimum GPA of 3.0 in field of major; bachelor's degree; for doctorate, GRE General Test, minimum GPA of 3.0 in field of major; master's degree. Additional exam requirements/recommendations for international students: required—TOEFL.

University of Missouri–Kansas City, College of Arts and Sciences, Department of Foreign Languages and Literatures, Kansas City, MO 64110-2499. Offers romance languages and literatures (MA), including French, Spanish. *Program availability:* Part-time. *Degree requirements:* For master's, 2 foreign languages. *Entrance requirements:* For master's, GRE General Test, minimum GPA of 2.75, 2 letters of recommendation. Additional exam requirements/recommendations for international students: required—TOEFL (minimum score 550 paper-based; 80 iBT). Electronic applications accepted.

University of New Orleans, Graduate School, College of Liberal Arts, Education and Human Development, Department of Foreign Languages, New Orleans, LA 70148. Offers Romance languages (MA), including language, culture and civilization, literature. *Program availability:* Part-time, evening/weekend. *Entrance requirements:* For master's, GRE General Test, minimum B average. Additional exam requirements/recommendations for international students: required—TOEFL (minimum score 550 paper-based; 79 iBT), IELTS (minimum score 6.5). Electronic applications accepted.

The University of North Carolina at Chapel Hill, Graduate School, College of Arts and Sciences, Department of Romance Languages and Literatures, Chapel Hill, NC 27599. Offers French (MA, PhD); Italian (MA, PhD); Portuguese (MA, PhD); Romance languages (MA, PhD); Romance philology (MA, PhD); Spanish (MA, PhD). *Degree requirements:* For master's, one foreign language, comprehensive exam, thesis; for doctorate, 2 foreign languages, comprehensive exam, thesis/dissertation. *Entrance requirements:* For master's and doctorate, GRE General Test, minimum GPA of 3.0. Additional exam requirements/recommendations for international students: required—TOEFL (minimum score 550 paper-based). Electronic applications accepted.

University of Notre Dame, The Graduate School, College of Arts and Letters, Division of Humanities, Department of Romance Languages and Literatures, Notre Dame, IN 46556. Offers French and Francophone studies (MA); Iberian and Latin American studies (MA); Italian studies (MA); Romance literatures (MA). *Degree requirements:* For master's, 2 foreign languages, comprehensive exam, thesis optional. *Entrance requirements:* For master's, GRE General Test, BA in target language. Additional exam requirements/recommendations for international students: required—TOEFL (minimum score 600 paper-based; 80 iBT). Electronic applications accepted.

University of Oregon, Graduate School, College of Arts and Sciences, Department of Romance Languages, Program in Romance Languages, Eugene, OR 97403. Offers MA, PhD. *Program availability:* Part-time. *Degree requirements:* For master's, 2 foreign languages; for doctorate, 2 foreign languages, thesis/dissertation. *Entrance requirements:* For master's and doctorate, GRE General Test, minimum GPA of 3.0. Additional exam requirements/recommendations for international students: required—TOEFL.

University of Pennsylvania, School of Arts and Sciences, Graduate Group in Romance Languages, Philadelphia, PA 19104. Offers French (AM, PhD); Italian (AM, PhD); Spanish (AM, PhD). *Faculty:* 65 full-time (29 women), 8 part-time/adjunct (3 women). *Students:* 60 full-time (31 women); includes 7 minority (1 Asian, non-Hispanic/Latino; 5 Hispanic/Latino; 1 Two or more races, non-Hispanic/Latino), 37 international. Average age 32. 46 applicants, 37% accepted, 8 enrolled. In 2019, 10 master's, 4 doctorates awarded. Terminal master's awarded for partial completion of doctoral program. Application fee: $90.
Website: http://www.sas.upenn.edu/graduate-division

University of South Africa, College of Human Sciences, Pretoria, South Africa. Offers adult education (M Ed); African languages (MA, PhD); African politics (MA, PhD); Afrikaans (MA, PhD); ancient history (MA, PhD); ancient Near Eastern studies (MA, PhD); anthropology (MA, PhD); applied linguistics (MA); Arabic (MA, PhD); archaeology (MA); art history (MA); Biblical archaeology (MA); Biblical studies (M Th, D Th, PhD); Christian spirituality (M Th, D Th); church history (M Th, D Th); classical studies (MA, PhD); clinical psychology (MA); communication (MA, PhD); comparative education (M Ed, Ed D); consulting psychology (D Admin, D Com, PhD); curriculum studies (M Ed, Ed D); development studies (M Admin, MA, D Admin, PhD); didactics (M Ed, Ed D); education (M Tech); education management (M Ed, Ed D); educational psychology (M Ed); English (MA); environmental education (M Ed); French (MA, PhD); German (MA, PhD); Greek (MA); guidance and counseling (M Ed); health studies (MA, PhD), including health sciences education (MA), health services management (MA), medical and surgical nursing science (critical care general) (MA), midwifery and neonatal nursing science (MA), trauma and emergency care (MA); history (MA, PhD); history of education (Ed D); inclusive education (M Ed, Ed D); information and communications technology policy and regulation (MA); information science (MA, MIS, PhD); international politics (MA, PhD); Islamic studies (MA, PhD); Italian (MA, PhD); Judaica (MA, PhD); linguistics (MA, PhD); mathematical education (M Ed); mathematics education (MA); missiology (M Th, D Th); modern Hebrew (MA, PhD); musicology (MA, MMus, D Mus, PhD); natural science education (M Ed); New Testament (M Th, D Th); Old Testament (D Th); pastoral therapy (M Th, D Th); philosophy (MA); philosophy of education (M Ed, Ed D); politics (MA, PhD); Portuguese (MA, PhD); practical theology (M Th, D Th); psychology (MA, MS, PhD); psychology of education (M Ed, Ed D); public health (MA); religious studies (MA, D Th, PhD); Romance languages (MA); Russian (MA, PhD); Semitic languages (MA, PhD); social behavior studies in HIV/AIDS (MA); social science (mental health) (MA); social science in development studies (MA); social science in psychology (MA); social science in social work (MA); social science in sociology (MA); social work (MSW, DSW, PhD); socio-education (M Ed, Ed D); sociolinguistics (MA); sociology (MA, PhD); Spanish (MA, PhD); systematic theology (M Th, D Th); TESOL (teaching English to speakers of other languages) (MA); theological ethics (M Th, D Th); theory of literature (MA, PhD); urban ministries (D Th); urban ministry (M Th).

The University of Texas at Austin, Graduate School, College of Liberal Arts, Department of French and Italian, Austin, TX 78712-1111. Offers French linguistics (MA, PhD); French studies (MA, PhD); Italian studies (MA, PhD); Romance linguistics (PhD). *Program availability:* Part-time. *Degree requirements:* For master's, one foreign language, thesis; for doctorate, 2 foreign languages, thesis/dissertation. *Entrance requirements:* For master's, GRE General Test, minimum GPA of 3.0, bachelor's degree in French or equivalent; for doctorate, GRE General Test, minimum GPA of 3.0, master's degree in French. Additional exam requirements/recommendations for international students: required—TOEFL. Electronic applications accepted.

Washington University in St. Louis, The Graduate School, Department of Romance Languages and Literatures, St. Louis, MO 63130-4899. Offers French (PhD), including French and comparative literature, French language and literature; Spanish (PhD), including Hispanic languages and literatures, Spanish and comparative literature. Terminal master's awarded for partial completion of doctoral program. *Degree requirements:* For doctorate, thesis/dissertation. *Entrance requirements:* For doctorate, GRE General Test. Additional exam requirements/recommendations for international students: required—TOEFL. Electronic applications accepted.

Wayne State University, College of Liberal Arts and Sciences, Department of Classical and Modern Languages, Literatures, and Cultures, Detroit, MI 48202. Offers classics (MA), including ancient Greek and Latin, ancient studies, classics, Latin; German (MA); language learning (MALL), including Arabic (MA, MALL), French (MA, MALL, PhD), German (MALL, PhD), Italian (MA, MALL), Spanish (MA, MALL, PhD); modern languages (PhD), including French (MA, MALL, PhD), German (MALL, PhD), Spanish (MA, MALL, PhD); Near Eastern languages (MA), including Arabic (MA, MALL), Hebrew; Romance languages (MA), including French (MA, MALL, PhD), Italian (MA, MALL), Spanish (MA, MALL, PhD). *Faculty:* 20. *Students:* 30 full-time (22 women), 15 part-time (9 women); includes 11 minority (4 Black or African American, non-Hispanic/Latino; 1 American Indian or Alaska Native, non-Hispanic/Latino; 2 Asian, non-Hispanic/Latino; 3 Hispanic/Latino; 1 Two or more races, non-Hispanic/Latino), 2 international. Average age 40. 32 applicants, 34% accepted, 9 enrolled. In 2019, 8 master's, 1 doctorate awarded. *Degree requirements:* For master's, variable foreign language requirement, comprehensive exam (for some programs), thesis (for some programs); for doctorate, one foreign language, comprehensive exam, thesis/dissertation. *Entrance requirements:* Additional exam requirements/recommendations for international students: required—TOEFL (minimum score 550 paper-based; 79 iBT), TWE (minimum score 5.5), Michigan English Language Assessment Battery (minimum score 85); recommended—IELTS (minimum score 6.5). Application fee: $50. Electronic applications accepted. *Expenses: Tuition:* Full-time $34,567. *Financial support:* In 2019–20, 22 students received support, including 1 fellowship with tuition reimbursement available (averaging $20,000 per year), 15 teaching assistantships with tuition reimbursements available (averaging $20,015 per year); research assistantships, scholarships/grants, health care benefits, and unspecified assistantships also available. Financial award applicants required to submit FAFSA. *Unit head:* Dr. Vanessa DEGifis, DR., Department Chair, 313-577-6244, Fax: 313-577-6243, E-mail: vdegifis@wayne.edu. *Application contact:* Terrie Pickering, Academic Services Officer, 313 577 3003, E-mail: t.pickering@wayne.edu.
Website: http://clas.wayne.edu/languages/

Russian

American University, College of Arts and Sciences, Department of World Languages and Cultures, Washington, DC 20016-8045. Offers Spanish: Latin American studies (MA); teaching English as a foreign language (MA); teaching English to speakers of other languages (MA, Certificate); translation: French (Certificate); translation: Russian (Certificate); translation: Spanish (Certificate). *Program availability:* Part-time, evening/weekend. *Degree requirements:* For master's, one foreign language, comprehensive exam, thesis or alternative. *Entrance requirements:* For master's, GRE; Please see website:https://www.american.edu/cas/wlc/, writing sample, statement of purpose, transcripts, 2 letters of recommendation, resume; for Certificate, bachelor's degree, statement of purpose, transcripts, resume. Additional exam requirements/recommendations for international students: required—TOEFL (minimum score 600 paper-based; 100 iBT). *Expenses:* Contact institution.

Boston College, Morrissey Graduate School of Arts and Sciences, Department of Slavic and Eastern Languages and Literatures, Program in Russian, Chestnut Hill, MA 02467-3800. Offers MA, MA/JD, MBA/MA. *Degree requirements:* For master's, 3 foreign languages, comprehensive exam, thesis or alternative. *Entrance requirements:* Additional exam requirements/recommendations for international students: required—TOEFL (minimum score 600 paper-based; 100 iBT), IELTS (minimum score 8). Electronic applications accepted.

Brown University, Graduate School, Department of Slavic Studies, Providence, RI 02912. Offers Russian language and literature (AM); Slavic linguistics (AM); Slavic studies (PhD). *Degree requirements:* For master's, one foreign language; for doctorate, 2 foreign languages, thesis/dissertation, preliminary exam.

Columbia University, Graduate School of Arts and Sciences, New York, NY 10027. Offers African-American studies (MA); American studies (MA); anthropology (MA, PhD); art history and archaeology (MA, PhD); astronomy (PhD); biological sciences (PhD); biotechnology (MA); chemical physics (PhD); chemistry (PhD); classical studies (MA, PhD); classics (MA, PhD); climate and society (MA); conservation biology (MA); earth and environmental sciences (PhD); East Asia: regional studies (MA); East Asian languages and cultures (MA, PhD); ecology, evolution and environmental biology (MA), including conservation biology; ecology, evolution, and environmental biology (PhD), including ecology and evolutionary biology, evolutionary primatology; economics (MA, PhD); English and comparative literature (MA, PhD); French and Romance philology (MA, PhD); Germanic languages (MA, PhD); global French studies (MA); global thought (MA); Hispanic cultural studies (MA); history (PhD); history and literature (MA); human rights studies (MA); Islamic studies (MA); Italian (MA, PhD); Japanese pedagogy (MA); Jewish studies (MA); Latin America and the Caribbean: regional studies (MA); Latin American and Iberian cultures (PhD); mathematics (MA, PhD), including finance (MA); medieval and Renaissance studies (MA); Middle Eastern, South Asian, and African studies (MA, PhD); modern art: critical and curatorial studies (MA); modern European studies (MA); museum anthropology (MA); music (DMA, PhD); oral history (MA); philosophical foundations of physics (MA); philosophy (MA, PhD); physics (PhD); political science (MA, PhD); psychology (PhD); quantitative methods in the social sciences (MA); religion (MA, PhD); Russia, Eurasia and East Europe: regional studies (MA); Russian translation (MA); Slavic cultures (MA); Slavic languages (MA, PhD); sociology (MA, PhD); South Asian studies (MA); statistics (MA, PhD); theatre (PhD). *Program availability:* Part-time. *Students:* 3,506 full-time (1,844 women), 208 part-time (121 women); includes 864 minority (110 Black or African American, non-Hispanic/Latino; 5 American Indian or Alaska Native, non-Hispanic/Latino; 416 Asian, non-Hispanic/Latino; 147 Hispanic/Latino; 6 Native Hawaiian or other Pacific Islander, non-Hispanic/Latino; 180 Two or more races, non-Hispanic/Latino), 2,065 international. 14,545 applicants, 25% accepted, 1,429 enrolled. In 2019, 1,262 master's, 363 doctorates awarded. Terminal master's awarded for partial completion of doctoral program. *Degree requirements:* For master's, variable foreign language requirement, comprehensive exam (for some programs), thesis (for some programs); for doctorate, variable foreign language requirement, comprehensive exam (for some programs), thesis/dissertation. *Entrance requirements:* For master's and doctorate, GRE General Test, GRE Subject Test (for some programs). Additional exam requirements/recommendations for international students: required—TOEFL (minimum score 600 paper-based; 100 iBT), IELTS (minimum score 7.5). Application fee: $115. Electronic applications accepted. *Expenses:* Tuition: Full-time $47,600; part-time $1880 per credit. One-time fee: $105. *Financial support:* Fellowships, research assistantships, teaching assistantships, career-related internships or fieldwork, Federal Work-Study, institutionally sponsored loans, scholarships/grants, traineeships, health care benefits, tuition waivers, and unspecified assistantships available. Support available to part-time students. Financial award application deadline: 12/15. *Unit head:* Dr. Carlos J. Alonso, Dean of the Graduate School of Arts and Sciences and Vice President for Graduate Education, 212-854-2861, E-mail: gsas-dean@columbia.edu. *Application contact:* GSAS Office of Admissions, 212-854-6729, E-mail: gsas-admissions@columbia.edu. Website: http://gsas.columbia.edu/

Harvard University, Graduate School of Arts and Sciences, Department of Slavic Languages and Literatures, Cambridge, MA 02138. Offers Polish (PhD); Russian (PhD); Serbo-Croatian (PhD); Slavic philology (PhD); Ukrainian (PhD). *Degree requirements:* For doctorate, 4 foreign languages, thesis/dissertation. *Entrance requirements:* For doctorate, GRE General Test, writing sample. Additional exam requirements/recommendations for international students: required—TOEFL.

Kent State University, College of Arts and Sciences, Department of Modern and Classical Language Studies, Kent, OH 44242-0001. Offers French (MA), including applied linguistics and pedagogy, literature; German (MA), including applied linguistics and pedagogy, literature; Latin (MA), including applied linguistics and pedagogy, literature; Spanish (MA), including applied linguistics and pedagogy, literature; translation (MA), including Arabic, French, German, Japanese, Russian, Spanish; translation studies (PhD); MA/MBA. *Program availability:* Part-time, 100% online. *Faculty:* 18 full-time (11 women), 6 part-time/adjunct (3 women). *Students:* 81 full-time (49 women), 23 part-time (14 women); includes 18 minority (3 Black or African American, non-Hispanic/Latino; 3 Asian, non-Hispanic/Latino; 11 Hispanic/Latino; 1 Two or more races, non-Hispanic/Latino), 45 international. Average age 32. 115 applicants, 73% accepted, 47 enrolled. In 2019, 27 master's, 7 doctorates awarded. *Degree requirements:* For master's, variable foreign language requirement, comprehensive exam (for some programs), thesis (for some programs); for doctorate, variable foreign language requirement, comprehensive exam, thesis/dissertation. *Entrance requirements:* For master's, transcripts, goal statement, 3 letters of recommendation, CD/MP3 with a 5-10 minute oral sample of first and second languages (conversational not read from a script), Writing sample(s) in the applicant's second language, which should be accompanied by a signed declaration that the sample is original work; for doctorate, transcripts, MA in translation, a foreign language, or in any other relevant discipline with prior experience or training in translation; proficiency in a foreign language; minimum GPA of 3.5 from MA; goal statement; 3 letters of recommendation; essay or writing sample (7-10 pages) from a research paper on any aspect of translation. Additional exam requirements/recommendations for international students: required—TOEFL (minimum score 79 iBT), IELTS (minimum score 6.5), PTE (minimum score 58), Michigan English Language Assessment Battery (minimum score 77). *Application deadline:* For fall admission, 2/1 for domestic and international students. Applications are processed on a rolling basis. Application fee: $45 ($70 for international students). Electronic applications accepted. *Financial support:* Fellowships with full tuition reimbursements, teaching assistantships with full tuition reimbursements, and unspecified assistantships available. Financial award application deadline: 2/1. *Unit head:* Dr. Keiran Dunne, Professor of French Translation; Department Chair, 330-672-2150, E-mail: kdunne@kent.edu. *Application contact:* Brian James Baer, Professor of Russian Translation; Graduate Coordinator, 330-672-1813, E-mail: bbaer@kent.edu. Website: http://www.kent.edu/mcls/

McGill University, Faculty of Graduate and Postdoctoral Studies, Faculty of Arts, Department of Russian and Slavic Studies, Montréal, QC H3A 2T5, Canada. Offers Russian literature (MA, PhD).

Middlebury College, Language Schools, Russian School, Middlebury, VT 05753-6002. Offers MA, DML. In 2019, 5 master's awarded. *Degree requirements:* For master's, one foreign language; for doctorate, 2 foreign languages, comprehensive exam, thesis/dissertation. *Entrance requirements:* For master's, language proficiency exam, placement exam, 3 letters of recommendation, writing sample in Russian, personal statement, transcripts; for doctorate, 1st and 2nd language exams, 3 letters of recommendation, writing sample in Russian, personal statement, transcripts. *Application deadline:* Applications are processed on a rolling basis. Application fee: $75. Electronic applications accepted. *Expenses:* Contact institution. *Financial support:* Fellowships and scholarships/grants available. Financial award application deadline: 3/14; financial award applicants required to submit FAFSA. *Unit head:* Dr. Jason Merrill, Director, 802-443-5230, Fax: 802-443-2075, E-mail: jmerrill@middlebury.edu. *Application contact:* Oliver Carling, Coordinator, 802-443-2006, Fax: 802-443-2075, E-mail: ocarling@middlebury.edu. Website: http://www.middlebury.edu/ls/grad_programs/russian

New York University, Graduate School of Arts and Science, Department of Russian and Slavic Studies, New York, NY 10012-1019. Offers Slavic literature (MA). *Program availability:* Part-time. *Degree requirements:* For master's, one foreign language, comprehensive exam, thesis. *Entrance requirements:* For master's, GRE General Test, minimum 3 years of undergraduate Russian or equivalent. Additional exam requirements/recommendations for international students: required—TOEFL, IELTS.

Penn State University Park, Graduate School, College of the Liberal Arts, Department of Comparative Literature, University Park, PA 16802. Offers comparative literature (MA, PhD); Russian and comparative literature (MA).

Princeton University, Graduate School, Department of Slavic Languages and Literatures, Princeton, NJ 08544-1019. Offers Russian and Slavic linguistics (PhD); Russian literature (PhD). *Degree requirements:* For doctorate, variable foreign language requirement, thesis/dissertation. *Entrance requirements:* For doctorate, GRE General Test. Additional exam requirements/recommendations for international students: required—TOEFL (minimum score 600 paper-based). Electronic applications accepted.

The University of Arizona, College of Humanities, Department of Russian and Slavic Studies, Tucson, AZ 85721. Offers Russian (MA). *Program availability:* Part-time. *Degree requirements:* For master's, one foreign language, comprehensive exam (for some programs), thesis (for some programs). *Entrance requirements:* For master's, 3 letters of recommendation, audio sample. Additional exam requirements/recommendations for international students: required—TOEFL (minimum score 550 paper-based; 79 iBT). Electronic applications accepted.

University of California, Berkeley, Graduate Division, College of Letters and Science, Department of Slavic Languages and Literatures, Berkeley, CA 94720. Offers Czech (PhD), including Czech linguistics, Czech literature; Polish (PhD), including Polish linguistics, Polish literature; Russian (PhD), including Russian linguistics, Russian literature; Serbo-Croatian (PhD), including Serbo-Croatian linguistics, Serbo-Croatian literature. Terminal master's awarded for partial completion of doctoral program. *Degree requirements:* For doctorate, thesis/dissertation, oral and written exams. *Entrance requirements:* For doctorate, GRE General Test, minimum GPA of 3.0, 3 letters of recommendation. Additional exam requirements/recommendations for international students: required—TOEFL (minimum score 570 paper-based). Electronic applications accepted.

University of Missouri, Office of Research and Graduate Studies, College of Arts and Science, Department of German and Russian Studies, Columbia, MO 65211. Offers MA. *Entrance requirements:* For master's, GRE General Test, minimum GPA of 3.0.

University of Oregon, Graduate School, College of Arts and Sciences, Program in Russian and East European Studies, Eugene, OR 97403. Offers MA. *Program availability:* Part-time. *Degree requirements:* For master's, 2 foreign languages, thesis. *Entrance requirements:* For master's, GRE General Test (recommended), minimum GPA of 3.0. Additional exam requirements/recommendations for international students: required—TOEFL.

University of South Africa, College of Human Sciences, Pretoria, South Africa. Offers adult education (M Ed); African languages (MA, PhD); African politics (MA, PhD); Afrikaans (MA, PhD); ancient history (MA, PhD); ancient Near Eastern studies (MA, PhD); anthropology (MA, PhD); applied linguistics (MA); Arabic (MA, PhD); archaeology (MA); art history (MA); Biblical archaeology (MA); Biblical studies (M Th, D Th, PhD); Christian spirituality (M Th, D Th); church history (M Th, D Th); classical studies (MA, PhD); clinical psychology (MA); communication (MA, PhD); comparative education (M Ed, Ed D); consulting psychology (D Admin, D Com, PhD); curriculum studies (M Ed, Ed D); development studies (M Admin, MA, D Admin, PhD); didactics (M Ed, Ed D); education (M Tech); education management (M Ed, Ed D); educational psychology (M Ed); English (MA); environmental education (M Ed); French (MA, PhD); German (MA, PhD); Greek (MA); guidance and counseling (M Ed); health studies (MA, PhD), including health sciences education (MA), health services management (MA), medical and surgical nursing science (critical care general) (MA), midwifery and neonatal nursing science (MA), trauma and emergency care (MA); history (MA, PhD); history of education (Ed D); inclusive education (M Ed, Ed D); information and communications technology policy and regulation (MA); information science (MA, MIS, PhD); international politics (MA, PhD); Islamic studies (MA, PhD); Italian (MA, PhD); Judaica (MA, PhD); linguistics (MA, PhD); mathematical education (M Ed); mathematics education (MA); missiology (M Th, D Th); modern Hebrew (MA, PhD); musicology (MA, MMus, D Mus, PhD); natural science education (M Ed); New Testament (M Th, D Th); Old Testament (D Th);

pastoral therapy (M Th, D Th); philosophy (MA); philosophy of education (M Ed, Ed D); politics (MA, PhD); Portuguese (MA, PhD); practical theology (M Th, D Th); psychology (MA, MS, PhD); psychology of education (M Ed, Ed D); public health (MA); religious studies (MA, D Th, PhD); Romance languages (MA); Russian (MA, PhD); Semitic languages (MA, PhD); social behavior studies in HIV/AIDS (MA); social science (mental health) (MA); social science in development studies (MA); social science in psychology (MA); social science in social work (MA); social science in sociology (MA); social work (MSW, DSW, PhD); socio-education (M Ed, Ed D); sociolinguistics (MA); sociology (MA, PhD); Spanish (MA, PhD); systematic theology (M Th, D Th); TESOL (teaching English to speakers of other languages) (MA); theological ethics (M Th, D Th); theory of literature (MA, PhD); urban ministries (D Th); urban ministry (M Th).

The University of Tennessee, Graduate School, College of Arts and Sciences, Department of Modern Foreign Languages and Literatures, Program in Modern Foreign Languages, Knoxville, TN 37996. Offers applied linguistics (PhD); French (PhD); German (PhD); Italian (PhD); Portuguese (PhD); Russian (PhD); Spanish (PhD). *Degree requirements:* For doctorate, 2 foreign languages, thesis/dissertation. *Entrance requirements:* For doctorate, minimum GPA of 2.7. Additional exam requirements/recommendations for international students: required—TOEFL. Electronic applications accepted.

University of Washington, Graduate School, College of Arts and Sciences, Department of Slavic Languages and Literatures, Seattle, WA 98195. Offers Russian literature (MA, PhD); Slavic linguistics (MA, PhD). *Degree requirements:* For master's, 2 foreign languages, thesis optional; for doctorate, 3 foreign languages, thesis/dissertation. *Entrance requirements:* For master's and doctorate, GRE General Test, minimum GPA of 3.0. Additional exam requirements/recommendations for international students: required—TOEFL. Electronic applications accepted.

University of Waterloo, Graduate Studies and Postdoctoral Affairs, Faculty of Arts, Department of Germanic and Slavic Studies, Waterloo, ON N2L 3G1, Canada. Offers German (MA, PhD); Russian (MA). *Program availability:* Part-time, evening/weekend. *Degree requirements:* For master's, one foreign language, thesis optional; for doctorate, 2 foreign languages, comprehensive exam, thesis/dissertation. *Entrance requirements:* For master's, honors degree, minimum B average; for doctorate, master's degree, minimum B average. Additional exam requirements/recommendations for international students: required—TOEFL, IELTS, PTE. Electronic applications accepted.

Yale University, Graduate School of Arts and Sciences, Department of Slavic Languages and Literatures, New Haven, CT 06520. Offers medieval Slavic literature and philology (PhD); Polish literature (PhD); Russian literature (PhD); Slavic languages and literatures and film studies (PhD). *Degree requirements:* For doctorate, 3 foreign languages, thesis/dissertation. *Entrance requirements:* For doctorate, GRE General Test.

Scandinavian Languages

Cornell University, Graduate School, Graduate Fields of Arts and Sciences, Field of Germanic Studies, Ithaca, NY 14853. Offers German area studies (MA, PhD); German intellectual history (MA, PhD); Germanic linguistics (MA, PhD); Germanic literature (MA, PhD); old Norse (MA, PhD). Terminal master's awarded for partial completion of doctoral program. *Degree requirements:* For master's, one foreign language, thesis; for doctorate, 2 foreign languages, comprehensive exam, thesis/dissertation. *Entrance requirements:* For master's and doctorate, GRE General Test, fluency in German, writing sample, 2 letters of recommendation. Additional exam requirements/recommendations for international students: required—TOEFL (minimum score 550 paper-based; 77 iBT). Electronic applications accepted.

Harvard University, Graduate School of Arts and Sciences, Department of Germanic Languages and Literatures, Cambridge, MA 02138. Offers German (PhD); Scandinavian (PhD). Terminal master's awarded for partial completion of doctoral program. *Degree requirements:* For doctorate, 2 foreign languages, thesis/dissertation, exams. *Entrance requirements:* For doctorate, GRE General Test, German writing sample. Additional exam requirements/recommendations for international students: required—TOEFL.

University of California, Berkeley, Graduate Division, College of Letters and Science, Department of Scandinavian Languages and Literatures, Berkeley, CA 94720. Offers PhD. *Degree requirements:* For doctorate, 2 foreign languages, thesis/dissertation, 3 field papers, qualifying exam. *Entrance requirements:* For doctorate, GRE General Test, minimum GPA of 3.0, MA in Scandinavian language or equivalent, 3 letters of recommendation. Additional exam requirements/recommendations for international students: required—TOEFL (minimum score 570 paper-based; 90 iBT). Electronic applications accepted.

University of California, Los Angeles, Graduate Division, College of Letters and Science, Department of Germanic Languages, Program in Scandinavian, Los Angeles, CA 90095. Offers MA. *Degree requirements:* For master's, 3 foreign languages, comprehensive exam. *Entrance requirements:* For master's, GRE General Test, bachelor's degree; minimum undergraduate GPA of 3.0 (or its equivalent if letter grade system not used); writing sample. Additional exam requirements/recommendations for international students: required—TOEFL. Electronic applications accepted.

University of Massachusetts Amherst, Graduate School, College of Humanities and Fine Arts, Department of Languages, Literatures, and Cultures, Programs in German and Scandinavian Studies, Amherst, MA 01003. Offers MA, PhD. *Program availability:* Part-time. Terminal master's awarded for partial completion of doctoral program. *Degree requirements:* For master's, thesis or alternative; for doctorate, one foreign language, comprehensive exam, thesis/dissertation. *Entrance requirements:* For master's and doctorate, writing sample in English and German. Additional exam requirements/recommendations for international students: required—TOEFL (minimum score 550 paper-based; 80 iBT), IELTS (minimum score 6.5). Electronic applications accepted.

University of Minnesota, Twin Cities Campus, Graduate School, College of Liberal Arts, Department of German, Scandinavian, and Dutch, Minneapolis, MN 55455. Offers Germanic studies (MA, PhD), including German, Germanic medieval studies, Scandinavian studies (MA). *Program availability:* Part-time. Terminal master's awarded for partial completion of doctoral program. *Degree requirements:* For doctorate, 2 foreign languages, thesis/dissertation. *Entrance requirements:* For master's, GRE General Test, BA in German, Scandinavian, or equivalent; for doctorate, MA in German, Scandinavian, or equivalent. Additional exam requirements/recommendations for international students: required—TOEFL (minimum score 550 paper-based; 79 iBT). Electronic applications accepted.

University of Washington, Graduate School, College of Arts and Sciences, Department of Scandinavian Studies, Seattle, WA 98195. Offers MA, PhD. *Degree requirements:* For master's, one foreign language, comprehensive exam, thesis optional; for doctorate, 2 foreign languages, comprehensive exam, thesis/dissertation. *Entrance requirements:* For master's, GRE, BA in Scandinavian or equivalent, minimum GPA of 3.0; for doctorate, GRE, master's degree, minimum GPA of 3.0. Additional exam requirements/recommendations for international students: required—TOEFL.

University of Wisconsin–Madison, Graduate School, College of Letters and Science, Department of German, Nordic, and Slavic, Madison, WI 53706-1380. Offers German (MA, PhD); Scandinavian studies (MA, PhD), including area studies (MA), folklore (PhD), literature, philology; Slavic languages and literature (MA, PhD). *Program availability:* Part-time. *Degree requirements:* For master's, 2 foreign languages, exam; for doctorate, thesis/dissertation, exam. *Entrance requirements:* For master's, minimum GPA of 3.25; for doctorate, minimum GPA of 3.5. Electronic applications accepted.

Slavic Languages

Brown University, Graduate School, Department of Slavic Studies, Providence, RI 02912. Offers Russian language and literature (AM); Slavic linguistics (AM); Slavic studies (PhD). *Degree requirements:* For master's, one foreign language; for doctorate, 2 foreign languages, thesis/dissertation, preliminary exam.

Columbia University, Graduate School of Arts and Sciences, New York, NY 10027. Offers African-American studies (MA); American studies (MA); anthropology (MA, PhD); art history and archaeology (MA, PhD); astronomy (PhD); biological sciences (PhD); biotechnology (MA); chemical physics (PhD); chemistry (PhD); classical studies (MA, PhD); classics (MA, PhD); climate and society (MA); conservation biology (MA); earth and environmental sciences (PhD); East Asia: regional studies (MA); East Asian languages and cultures (MA, PhD); ecology, evolution and environmental biology (MA), including conservation biology; ecology, evolution, and environmental biology (PhD), including ecology and evolutionary biology, evolutionary primatology; economics (MA, PhD); English and comparative literature (MA, PhD); French and Romance philology (MA, PhD); Germanic languages (MA, PhD); global French studies (MA); global thought (MA); Hispanic cultural studies (MA); history (PhD); history and literature (MA); human rights studies (MA); Islamic studies (MA); Italian (MA, PhD); Japanese pedagogy (MA); Jewish studies (MA); Latin America and the Caribbean: regional studies (MA); Latin American and Iberian cultures (PhD); mathematics (MA, PhD), including finance (MA); medieval and Renaissance studies (MA); Middle Eastern, South Asian, and African studies (MA, PhD); modern art: critical and curatorial studies (MA); modern European studies (MA); museum anthropology (MA); music (DMA, PhD); oral history (MA); philosophical foundations of physics (MA); philosophy (MA, PhD); physics (PhD); political science (MA, PhD); psychology (PhD); quantitative methods in the social sciences (MA); religion (MA, PhD); Russia, Eurasia and East Europe: regional studies (MA); Russian translation (MA); Slavic cultures (MA); Slavic languages (MA, PhD); sociology (MA, PhD); South Asian studies (MA); statistics (MA, PhD); theatre (PhD). *Program availability:* Part-time. *Students:* 3,506 full-time (1,844 women), 208 part-time (121 women); includes 864 minority (110 Black or African American, non-Hispanic/Latino; 5 American Indian or Alaska Native, non-Hispanic/Latino; 416 Asian, non-Hispanic/Latino; 147 Hispanic/Latino; 6 Native Hawaiian or other Pacific Islander, non-Hispanic/Latino; 180 Two or more races, non-Hispanic/Latino), 2,065 international. 14,545 applicants, 25% accepted, 1,429 enrolled. In 2019, 1,262 master's, 363 doctorates awarded. Terminal master's awarded for partial completion of doctoral program. *Degree requirements:* For master's, variable foreign language requirement, comprehensive exam (for some programs), thesis (for some programs); for doctorate, variable foreign language requirement, comprehensive exam (for some programs), thesis/dissertation. *Entrance requirements:* For master's and doctorate, GRE General Test, GRE Subject Test (for some programs). Additional exam requirements/recommendations for international students: required—TOEFL (minimum score 600 paper-based; 100 iBT), IELTS (minimum score 7.5). Application fee: $115. Electronic applications accepted. *Expenses: Tuition:* Full-time $47,600; part-time $1880 per credit. One-time fee: $105. *Financial support:* Fellowships, research assistantships, teaching assistantships, career-related internships or fieldwork, Federal Work-Study, institutionally sponsored loans, scholarships/grants, traineeships, health care benefits, tuition waivers, and unspecified assistantships available. Support available to part-time students. Financial award application deadline: 12/15. *Unit head:* Dr. Carlos J. Alonso, Dean of the Graduate School of Arts and Sciences and Vice President for Graduate Education, 212-854-2861, E-mail: gsas-dean@columbia.edu. *Application contact:* GSAS Office of Admissions, 212-854-6729, E-mail: gsas-admissions@columbia.edu. Website: http://gsas.columbia.edu/

Cornell University, Graduate School, Graduate Fields of Arts and Sciences, Field of Linguistics, Ithaca, NY 14853. Offers applied linguistics (MA, PhD); East Asian linguistics (MA, PhD); English linguistics (MA, PhD); general linguistics (MA, PhD); Germanic linguistics (MA, PhD); Indo-European linguistics (MA, PhD); phonetics (MA, PhD); phonological theory (MA, PhD); Romance linguistics (MA, PhD); second language acquisition (MA, PhD); semantics (MA, PhD); Slavic linguistics (MA, PhD); sociolinguistics (MA, PhD); South Asian linguistics (MA, PhD); Southeast Asian linguistics (MA, PhD); syntactic theory (MA, PhD). Terminal master's awarded for partial completion of doctoral program. *Degree requirements:* For master's, one foreign language, thesis; for doctorate, one foreign language, comprehensive exam, thesis/dissertation. *Entrance requirements:* For master's and doctorate, GRE General Test, 2 letters of recommendation. Additional exam requirements/recommendations for international students: required—TOEFL (minimum score 600 paper-based; 77 iBT). Electronic applications accepted.

Duke University, Graduate School, Department of Slavic and Eurasian Studies, Durham, NC 27708. Offers AM, Certificate. *Program availability:* Part-time. *Entrance requirements:* For master's, GRE General Test, writing sample. Additional exam requirements/recommendations for international students: required—TOEFL (minimum score 577 paper-based; 90 iBT) or IELTS (minimum score 7). Electronic applications accepted.

Florida State University, The Graduate School, Department of Anthropology, Department of Modern Languages and Linguistics, Program in Slavic Languages/Russian, Tallahassee, FL 32306. Offers Slavic languages and literatures (MA). *Faculty:* 3 full-time (2 women), 1 part-time/adjunct. *Students:* 4 full-time (2 women). In 2019, 2 master's awarded. *Degree requirements:* For master's, comprehensive exam, thesis or alternative. *Entrance requirements:* For master's, GRE General Test, minimum GPA of 3.0. Additional exam requirements/recommendations for international students: required—TOEFL (minimum score 550 paper-based; 80 iBT). *Application deadline:* For fall admission, 1/15 for domestic and international students. Electronic applications accepted. *Financial support:* In 2019–20, 3 students received support, including 4 teaching assistantships with partial tuition reimbursements available; fellowships and institutionally sponsored loans also available. Financial award application deadline: 1/15; financial award applicants required to submit FAFSA. *Unit head:* Dr. Lisa Wakamiya, Divisional Coordinator, Fax: 850-644-0524, E-mail: lwakamiya@fsu.edu. *Application contact:* Wendy E. Pigott, Graduate Academic Coordinator, 850-644-8397, Fax: 850-644-0524, E-mail: wpigott@fsu.edu.

Harvard University, Graduate School of Arts and Sciences, Department of Slavic Languages and Literatures, Cambridge, MA 02138. Offers Polish (PhD); Russian (PhD); Serbo-Croatian (PhD); Slavic philology (PhD); Ukrainian (PhD). *Degree requirements:* For doctorate, 4 foreign languages, thesis/dissertation. *Entrance requirements:* For doctorate, GRE General Test, writing sample. Additional exam requirements/recommendations for international students: required—TOEFL.

Indiana University Bloomington, University Graduate School, College of Arts and Sciences, Department of Slavic and East European Languages and Cultures, Bloomington, IN 47405. Offers MA, MAT, PhD. *Program availability:* Part-time. Terminal master's awarded for partial completion of doctoral program. *Degree requirements:* For master's, variable foreign language requirement; for doctorate, variable foreign language requirement, comprehensive exam, thesis/dissertation. *Entrance requirements:* For master's, GRE General Test. Additional exam requirements/recommendations for international students: required—TOEFL. Electronic applications accepted.

New York University, Graduate School of Arts and Science, Department of Russian and Slavic Studies, New York, NY 10012-1019. Offers Slavic literature (MA). *Program availability:* Part-time. *Degree requirements:* For master's, one foreign language, comprehensive exam, thesis. *Entrance requirements:* For master's, GRE General Test, minimum 3 years of undergraduate Russian or equivalent. Additional exam requirements/recommendations for international students: required—TOEFL, IELTS.

Northwestern University, The Graduate School, Judd A. and Marjorie Weinberg College of Arts and Sciences, Department of Slavic Languages and Literature, Evanston, IL 60208. Offers PhD. *Program availability:* Part-time. *Degree requirements:* For doctorate, 3 foreign languages, thesis/dissertation. *Entrance requirements:* For doctorate, GRE General Test. Additional exam requirements/recommendations for international students: required—TOEFL.

The Ohio State University, Graduate School, College of Arts and Sciences, Division of Arts and Humanities, Department of Slavic and East European Languages and Cultures, Columbus, OH 43210. Offers Slavic linguistics (MA, PhD); Slavic literature, film, and cultural studies (MA, PhD). Terminal master's awarded for partial completion of doctoral program. *Degree requirements:* For master's, variable foreign language requirement, thesis optional; for doctorate, variable foreign language requirement, thesis/dissertation. *Entrance requirements:* For master's and doctorate, GRE General Test, at least 3 years of Russian language study or equivalent. Additional exam requirements/recommendations for international students: required—TOEFL (minimum score 550 paper-based; 79 iBT), Michigan English Language Assessment Battery (minimum score 82); recommended—IELTS (minimum score 7). Electronic applications accepted.

Princeton University, Graduate School, Department of Slavic Languages and Literatures, Princeton, NJ 08544-1019. Offers Russian and Slavic linguistics (PhD); Russian literature (PhD). *Degree requirements:* For doctorate, variable foreign language requirement, thesis/dissertation. *Entrance requirements:* For doctorate, GRE General Test. Additional exam requirements/recommendations for international students: required—TOEFL (minimum score 600 paper-based). Electronic applications accepted.

Stanford University, School of Humanities and Sciences, Department of Slavic Languages and Literatures, Stanford, CA 94305-2004. Offers PhD. *Expenses: Tuition:* Full-time $52,479; part-time $34,110 per unit. *Required fees:* $672; $224 per quarter. Tuition and fees vary according to program and student level.
Website: http://www.stanford.edu/dept/slavic/

University of Alberta, Faculty of Graduate Studies and Research, Department of Modern Languages and Cultural Studies, Edmonton, AB T6G 2E1, Canada. Offers applied linguistics (Germanic, Romance, Slavic) (MA); French language, literatures and linguistics (PhD); French language, literatures, and linguistics (MA); Germanic languages, literatures and linguistics (PhD); Germanic languages, literatures, and linguistics (MA); Italian studies (MA); Slavic languages and literatures (Russian, Ukrainian) (MA, PhD); Slavic linguistics (Russian, Ukrainian) (MA, PhD); Spanish and Latin American studies (MA, PhD); Ukrainian folklore (MA, PhD). *Program availability:* Part-time. *Degree requirements:* For master's, one foreign language, thesis; for doctorate, 2 foreign languages, comprehensive exam, thesis/dissertation. *Entrance requirements:* For master's and doctorate, 1 language other than English. Additional exam requirements/recommendations for international students: required—Michigan English Language Assessment Battery or TOEFL (minimum score 550 paper-based). Electronic applications accepted.

University of California, Berkeley, Graduate Division, College of Letters and Science, Department of Slavic Languages and Literatures, Berkeley, CA 94720. Offers Czech (PhD), including Czech linguistics, Czech literature; Polish (PhD), including Polish linguistics, Polish literature; Russian (PhD), including Russian linguistics, Russian literature; Serbo-Croatian (PhD), including Serbo-Croatian linguistics, Serbo-Croatian literature. Terminal master's awarded for partial completion of doctoral program. *Degree requirements:* For doctorate, thesis/dissertation, oral and written exams. *Entrance requirements:* For doctorate, GRE General Test, minimum GPA of 3.0, 3 letters of recommendation. Additional exam requirements/recommendations for international students: required—TOEFL (minimum score 570 paper-based). Electronic applications accepted.

University of California, Los Angeles, Graduate Division, College of Letters and Science, Department of Slavic Languages and Literatures, Los Angeles, CA 90095. Offers MA, PhD. Terminal master's awarded for partial completion of doctoral program. *Degree requirements:* For master's, 2 foreign languages, comprehensive exam; for doctorate, 2 foreign languages, thesis/dissertation, oral and written qualifying exams. *Entrance requirements:* For master's and doctorate, GRE General Test (not required for applicants whose native language not English), bachelor's degree; minimum undergraduate GPA of 3.0 (or its equivalent if letter grade system not used); writing sample. Additional exam requirements/recommendations for international students: required—TOEFL. Electronic applications accepted.

University of Chicago, Division of the Humanities, Master of Arts Program in the Humanities, Chicago, IL 60637. Offers art history (MA); cinema and media studies (MA); classic languages (MA); comparative literature (MA); creative writing (MA); cultural policy studies (MA); digital humanities (MA); East Asian languages and civilizations (MA); English language and literature (MA); gender and sexuality studies (MA); Germanic studies (MA); linguistics (MA); music (MA); near Eastern languages and civilizations (MA); philosophy (MA); poetics (MA); race, politics and culture (MA); Romance languages and literatures (MA); Slavic languages and literatures (MA); South Asian languages and civilizations (MA); theater and performance studies (MA). *Degree requirements:* For master's, thesis. *Entrance requirements:* For master's, GRE General Test, 10-15 page writing sample, statement of purpose, 3 letters of recommendation, transcripts for all previous degrees and institutions attended. Additional exam requirements/recommendations for international students: required—TOEFL (minimum score 104 iBT), IELTS (minimum score 7). Electronic applications accepted. *Expenses:* Contact institution.

University of Illinois at Chicago, College of Liberal Arts and Sciences, School of Literatures, Cultural Studies and Linguistics, Department of Slavic and Baltic Languages and Literatures, Chicago, IL 60607-7128. Offers Slavic studies (MA, PhD). *Program availability:* Evening/weekend. Terminal master's awarded for partial completion of doctoral program. *Degree requirements:* For doctorate, one foreign language, thesis/dissertation. *Entrance requirements:* For master's and doctorate, GRE General Test, minimum GPA of 3.0. Additional exam requirements/recommendations for international students: required—TOEFL. Electronic applications accepted.

University of Illinois at Urbana-Champaign, Graduate College, College of Liberal Arts and Sciences, School of Literatures, Cultures and Linguistics, Department of Slavic Languages and Literatures, Champaign, IL 61820. Offers MA, PhD.

The University of Kansas, Graduate Studies, College of Liberal Arts and Sciences, Department of Slavic Languages and Literatures, Lawrence, KS 66045. Offers MA, PhD. *Students:* 11 full-time (7 women), 7 international. Average age 30. 6 applicants, 67% accepted, 3 enrolled. In 2019, 2 master's, 1 doctorate awarded. Terminal master's awarded for partial completion of doctoral program. *Entrance requirements:* For master's and doctorate, GRE, curriculum vitae, statement of academic objectives (500 words), Russian language essay (1-2 pages), writing sample (5000-7000 words), official transcripts. Additional exam requirements/recommendations for international students: required—TOEFL, IELTS. *Application deadline:* For fall admission, 1/31 priority date for domestic and international students. Application fee: $65 ($85 for international students). Electronic applications accepted. *Expenses:* Tuition, state resident: full-time $9989. Tuition, nonresident: full-time $23,950. *International tuition:* $23,950 full-time. *Required fees:* $984; $81.99 per credit hour. Tuition and fees vary according to course load, campus/location and program. *Financial support:* Fellowships, teaching assistantships, Federal Work-Study, institutionally sponsored loans, scholarships/grants, and unspecified assistantships available. Financial award application deadline: 1/31. *Unit head:* Ani Kokobobo, Chair, 785-864-2346, E-mail: akokobobo@ku.edu. *Application contact:* Jared Nietfeld, Graduate Admissions Contact, 785-864-0482, E-mail: nietfeld@ku.edu.
Website: https://slavic.ku.edu/

University of Manitoba, Faculty of Graduate Studies, Faculty of Arts, Department of German and Slavic Studies, Winnipeg, MB R3T 2N2, Canada. Offers German language and literature (MA); Slavic languages and literatures (MA). *Degree requirements:* For master's, one foreign language, thesis or alternative.

University of Michigan, Rackham Graduate School, College of Literature, Science, and the Arts, Department of Slavic Languages and Literatures, Ann Arbor, MI 48109-1275. Offers AM, PhD. Terminal master's awarded for partial completion of doctoral program. *Degree requirements:* For doctorate, 3 foreign languages, comprehensive exam, thesis/dissertation, oral defense of dissertation, preliminary exam. *Entrance requirements:* For doctorate, GRE General Test. Additional exam requirements/recommendations for international students: required—TOEFL (minimum score 560 paper-based). Electronic applications accepted.

The University of North Carolina at Chapel Hill, Graduate School, College of Arts and Sciences, Department of Germanic and Slavic Languages and Literatures, Chapel Hill, NC 27599. Offers German studies (PhD). *Program availability:* Part-time. Terminal master's awarded for partial completion of doctoral program. *Degree requirements:* For doctorate, one foreign language, comprehensive exam, thesis/dissertation. *Entrance requirements:* For doctorate, GRE General Test, minimum GPA of 3.0.

University of Pittsburgh, Kenneth P. Dietrich School of Arts and Sciences, Department of Slavic Languages and Literatures, Pittsburgh, PA 15260. Offers film studies (PhD), including Russian literature and culture; Russian literature and culture (MA, PhD). *Faculty:* 5 full-time (2 women), 6 part-time/adjunct (5 women). *Students:* 11 full-time (8 women); includes 1 minority (Asian, non-Hispanic/Latino). Average age 30. 13 applicants, 23% accepted, 2 enrolled. In 2019, 1 master's, 2 doctorates awarded. Terminal master's awarded for partial completion of doctoral program. *Degree requirements:* For master's, 2 foreign languages, comprehensive exam; for doctorate, 3 foreign languages, comprehensive exam, thesis/dissertation. *Entrance requirements:* For doctorate, personal statement, transcript copies, 3 letters of recommendation (online submissions), writing sample (in English); a Russian sample can also be submitted (optional). Additional exam requirements/recommendations for international students: required—either the IELTS or TOEFL are required; recommended—TOEFL (minimum score 90 iBT), IELTS (minimum score 7). *Application deadline:* For fall admission, 1/15 priority date for domestic and international students. Application fee: $50. Electronic applications accepted. *Expenses:* $24,480 in-state, $40,848 out-of-state. *Financial support:* In 2019–20, 100 students received support, including 5 fellowships with full tuition reimbursements available (averaging $22,170 per year), 6 teaching assistantships with full tuition reimbursements available (averaging $20,250 per year); career-related internships or fieldwork, scholarships/grants, health care benefits, tuition waivers (full), and unspecified assistantships also available. Financial award application deadline: 1/15. *Unit head:* Dr. Bella Grigoryan, Department Chair, 412-624-9958, Fax: 412-624-9714, E-mail: grigoryan@pitt.edu. *Application contact:* Keanna Cash, Graduate

Administrator, 412-624-5227, E-mail: kec176@pitt.edu. Website: http://www.slavic.pitt.edu

University of Southern California, Graduate School, Dana and David Dornsife College of Letters, Arts and Sciences, Department of Linguistics, Los Angeles, CA 90089. Offers East Asian linguistics (PhD); Hispanic linguistics (PhD); linguistics (PhD); Slavic linguistics (PhD). *Degree requirements:* For doctorate, comprehensive exam, thesis/dissertation. *Entrance requirements:* For doctorate, GRE. Additional exam requirements/recommendations for international students: required—TOEFL (minimum score 100 iBT). Electronic applications accepted.

University of Southern California, Graduate School, Dana and David Dornsife College of Letters, Arts and Sciences, Department of Slavic Languages and Literatures, Los Angeles, CA 90089. Offers MA, PhD. *Degree requirements:* For master's, one foreign language, comprehensive exam, thesis or alternative, 30 units; for doctorate, 3 foreign languages, comprehensive exam, thesis/dissertation, 60 units. *Entrance requirements:* For doctorate, GRE, BA in Russian literature or equivalent. Additional exam requirements/recommendations for international students: required—TOEFL. Electronic applications accepted.

The University of Texas at Austin, Graduate School, College of Liberal Arts, Department of Slavic and Eurasian Studies, Austin, TX 78712-1111. Offers applied linguistics/pedagogy (PhD); literature and culture (PhD); Slavic languages (MA); Slavic linguistics (PhD). *Degree requirements:* For master's, 2 foreign languages, thesis; for doctorate, 3 foreign languages, thesis/dissertation. *Entrance requirements:* For master's and doctorate, GRE General Test. Electronic applications accepted.

University of Toronto, School of Graduate Studies, Faculty of Arts and Science, Department of Slavic Languages and Literatures, Toronto, ON M5S 1A1, Canada. Offers MA, PhD. *Program availability:* Part-time. *Degree requirements:* For doctorate, comprehensive exam, thesis/dissertation. *Entrance requirements:* For master's, BA in related area; minimum A- average in Slavic courses taken in final year, writing sample, 2 letters of recommendation; for doctorate, MA in Slavic languages and literatures, minimum A- average, writing sample, 2 letters of recommendation. Additional exam requirements/recommendations for international students: required—TOEFL (minimum

score 580 paper-based; 93 iBT), TWE (minimum score 5). Electronic applications accepted.

University of Virginia, College and Graduate School of Arts and Sciences, Department of Slavic Languages and Literatures, Charlottesville, VA 22903. Offers MA, PhD. *Degree requirements:* For master's, one foreign language, comprehensive exam, thesis (for some programs); for doctorate, one foreign language, comprehensive exam, thesis/dissertation. *Entrance requirements:* For master's, GRE General Test, 2 letters of recommendation, writing sample in English; for doctorate, GRE General Test, 2 letters of recommendation; writing sample in English. Additional exam requirements/recommendations for international students: required—TOEFL (minimum score 600 paper-based; 90 iBT), IELTS (minimum score 7). Electronic applications accepted.

University of Washington, Graduate School, College of Arts and Sciences, Department of Slavic Languages and Literatures, Seattle, WA 98195. Offers Russian literature (MA, PhD); Slavic linguistics (MA, PhD). *Degree requirements:* For master's, 2 foreign languages, thesis optional; for doctorate, 3 foreign languages, thesis/dissertation. *Entrance requirements:* For master's and doctorate, GRE General Test, minimum GPA of 3.0. Additional exam requirements/recommendations for international students: required—TOEFL. Electronic applications accepted.

University of Wisconsin–Madison, Graduate School, College of Letters and Science, Department of German, Nordic, and Slavic, Madison, WI 53706-1380. Offers German (MA, PhD); Scandinavian studies (MA, PhD), including area studies (MA), folklore (PhD), literature, philology; Slavic languages and literature (MA, PhD). *Program availability:* Part-time. *Degree requirements:* For master's, 2 foreign languages, exam; for doctorate, thesis/dissertation, exam. *Entrance requirements:* For master's, minimum GPA of 3.25; for doctorate, minimum GPA of 3.5. Electronic applications accepted.

Yale University, Graduate School of Arts and Sciences, Department of Slavic Languages and Literatures, New Haven, CT 06520. Offers medieval Slavic literature and philology (PhD); Polish literature (PhD); Russian literature (PhD); Slavic languages and literatures and film studies (PhD). *Degree requirements:* For doctorate, 3 foreign languages, thesis/dissertation. *Entrance requirements:* For doctorate, GRE General Test.

Spanish

American University, College of Arts and Sciences, Department of World Languages and Cultures, Washington, DC 20016-8045. Offers Spanish: Latin American studies (MA); teaching English as a foreign language (MA); teaching English to speakers of other languages (MA, Certificate); translation: French (Certificate); translation: Russian (Certificate); translation: Spanish (Certificate). *Program availability:* Part-time, evening/weekend. *Degree requirements:* For master's, one foreign language, comprehensive exam, thesis or alternative. *Entrance requirements:* For master's, GRE; Please see website:https://www.american.edu/cas/wlc/, writing sample, statement of purpose, transcripts, 2 letters of recommendation, resume; for Certificate, bachelor's degree, statement of purpose, transcripts, resume. Additional exam requirements/recommendations for international students: required—TOEFL (minimum score 600 paper-based; 100 iBT). *Expenses:* Contact institution.

Arizona State University at Tempe, College of Liberal Arts and Sciences, School of International Letters and Cultures, Program in Spanish, Tempe, AZ 85287-0202. Offers cultural studies (PhD); linguistics (MA), including second language acquisition/applied linguistics, sociolinguistics; literature (PhD); literature and culture (MA). *Program availability:* Part-time. Terminal master's awarded for partial completion of doctoral program. *Degree requirements:* For master's, thesis, oral defense; written comprehensive exam (literature and culture); portfolio review (linguistics); interactive Program of Study (iPOS) submitted before completing 50 percent of required credit hours; for doctorate, comprehensive exam, thesis/dissertation, interactive Program of Study (iPOS) submitted before completing 50 percent of required credit hours. *Entrance requirements:* For master's, GRE (recommended), BA in Spanish or close equivalent from accredited institution with minimum GPA of 3.5, 3 letters of recommendation, personal statement, academic writing sample; for doctorate, GRE (recommended), MA in Spanish or equivalent from accredited institution with minimum GPA of 3.75, 3 letters of recommendation, personal statement, academic writing sample. Additional exam requirements/recommendations for international students: required—TOEFL (minimum score 550 paper-based; 83 iBT), IELTS (minimum score 6.5). Electronic applications accepted.

Asbury University, School of Graduate and Professional Studies, Wilmore, KY 40390-1198. Offers biology: alternative certificate (MA Ed); chemistry: alternative certificate (MA Ed); English (MA Ed); English as a second language (MA Ed); ESL (MA Ed); French (MA Ed); Latin: alternative certificate (MA Ed); mathematics: alternative certificate (MA Ed); reading/writing endorsement (MA Ed); social studies (MA Ed); social work (MSW), including child and family services; Spanish (MA Ed); special education (MA Ed); special education: alternative certificate (MA Ed); teacher as leader endorsement (MA Ed). *Accreditation:* NCATE. *Program availability:* Part-time. *Degree requirements:* For master's, action research project, portfolio. *Entrance requirements:* For master's, PRAXIS/NTE, minimum GPA of 2.75, letters of recommendation. Additional exam requirements/recommendations for international students: required—TOEFL (minimum score 550 paper-based). Electronic applications accepted.

Auburn University, Graduate School, College of Liberal Arts, Department of Foreign Languages and Literatures, Auburn, AL 36849. Offers MA, MHS. *Program availability:* Part-time. *Faculty:* 33 full-time (22 women), 6 part-time/adjunct (3 women). *Students:* 21 full-time (12 women), 6 part-time (3 women); includes 5 minority (1 Black or African American, non-Hispanic/Latino; 4 Hispanic/Latino), 19 international. Average age 28. 18 applicants, 83% accepted, 14 enrolled. In 2019, 5 master's awarded. *Degree requirements:* For master's, one foreign language, comprehensive exam, thesis (for some programs). *Entrance requirements:* For master's, GRE General Test. *Application deadline:* Applications are processed on a rolling basis. Application fee: $60 ($70 for international students). Electronic applications accepted. *Expenses: Tuition, area resident:* Full-time $9828; part-time $546 per credit hour. Tuition, state resident: full-time $9828; part-time $546 per credit hour. Tuition, nonresident: full-time $29,484; part-time $1638 per credit hour. *International tuition:* $29,744 full-time. Tuition and fees vary according to course load, program and reciprocity agreements. *Financial support:* In 2019–20, 3 fellowships with full tuition reimbursements (averaging $29,408 per year), 27 teaching assistantships with partial tuition reimbursements (averaging $19,519 per year) were awarded; Federal Work-Study also available. Support available to part-time students. Financial award application deadline: 3/15; financial award applicants required to submit FAFSA. *Unit head:* Dr. Traci S. O'Brien, Chair, 334-844-6350, Fax: 334-844-

6378, E-mail: tso0001@auburn.edu. *Application contact:* Dr. George Flowers, Dean of the Graduate School, 334-844-2125.
Website: http://www.cla.auburn.edu/forlang/

Bard College, Master of Arts in Teaching Program, Annandale-on-Hudson, NY 12504. Offers secondary education (MAT), including biology, history, literature, mathematics, Spanish; MS/MAT. *Program availability:* Part-time. *Degree requirements:* For master's, year-long teaching residencies in area middle and high schools. *Entrance requirements:* For master's, GRE General Test, resume, 3 letters of recommendation, personal statement, official transcripts. Additional exam requirements/recommendations for international students: required—TOEFL. Electronic applications accepted. Application fee is waived when completed online.

Baylor University, Graduate School, College of Arts and Sciences, Department of Modern Languages and Cultures, Waco, TX 76798. Offers Spanish (MA). *Degree requirements:* For master's, one foreign language, comprehensive exam, thesis optional. *Entrance requirements:* For master's, GRE General Test, 18 hours of undergraduate credit in Spanish, 3 letters of recommendation. Additional exam requirements/recommendations for international students: required—TOEFL. Electronic applications accepted.

Binghamton University, State University of New York, Graduate School, Harpur College of Arts and Sciences, Department of Romance Languages and Literatures, Program in Spanish, Binghamton, NY 13902-6000. Offers MA. *Program availability:* Part-time. *Degree requirements:* For master's, one foreign language, comprehensive exam, thesis or alternative. *Entrance requirements:* For master's, GRE General Test. Additional exam requirements/recommendations for international students: required—TOEFL (minimum score 550 paper-based; 80 iBT). Electronic applications accepted.

Boston College, Morrissey Graduate School of Arts and Sciences, Department of Romance Languages and Literatures, Chestnut Hill, MA 02467-3800. Offers French (MA); Italian (MA); Spanish (MA). *Program availability:* Part-time. Terminal master's awarded for partial completion of doctoral program. *Degree requirements:* For master's, one foreign language. *Entrance requirements:* Additional exam requirements/recommendations for international students: required—TOEFL (minimum score 600 paper-based; 100 iBT), IELTS (minimum score 8). Electronic applications accepted.

Bowling Green State University, Graduate College, College of Arts and Sciences, Department of Romance and Classical Studies, Program in Spanish, Bowling Green, OH 43403. Offers Spanish (MA). *Program availability:* Part-time. *Degree requirements:* For master's, one foreign language, thesis or alternative. *Entrance requirements:* For master's, GRE General Test. Additional exam requirements/recommendations for international students: required—TOEFL. Electronic applications accepted.

Brigham Young University, Graduate Studies, College of Humanities, Department of Spanish and Portuguese, Provo, UT 84602. Offers Portuguese (MA), including Luso-Brazilian literatures, Portuguese linguistics, Portuguese pedagogy; Spanish (MA), including Hispanic linguistics, Hispanic literatures, Spanish pedagogy. *Faculty:* 33 full-time (8 women). *Students:* 34 full-time (24 women); includes 14 minority (1 Black or African American, non-Hispanic/Latino; 1 American Indian or Alaska Native, non-Hispanic/Latino; 1 Asian, non-Hispanic/Latino; 11 Hispanic/Latino). Average age 33. 17 applicants, 65% accepted, 9 enrolled. In 2019, 11 master's awarded. *Degree requirements:* For master's, 2 foreign languages, comprehensive exam, thesis, 1 semester of teaching. *Entrance requirements:* For master's, GRE, prerequisite second language requirement (can be fulfilled concurrently), prerequisite teaching methods course (can be fulfilled concurrently). Additional exam requirements/recommendations for international students: required—TOEFL (minimum score 580 paper-based; 85 iBT). *Application deadline:* For fall admission, 2/1 for domestic and international students. Application fee: $50. Electronic applications accepted. *Expenses:* $13,515 to complete two-year degree. *Financial support:* In 2019–20, 22 students received support, including 2 teaching assistantships with partial tuition reimbursements available (averaging $8,431 per year); scholarships/grants also available. Financial award application deadline: 2/1. *Unit head:* Dr. Scott Alvord, Interim Chair, Department of Spanish & Portuguese, 801-422-7546, Fax: 801-422-0308, E-mail: scott_alvord@byu.edu. *Application contact:* Brian A Price, Graduate Program Manager, 801-422-3453, Fax:

801-422-0308, E-mail: brian_price@byu.edu.
Website: http://spanport.byu.edu/

Brooklyn College of the City University of New York, School of Humanities and Social Sciences, Department of Modern Languages and Literatures, Brooklyn, NY 11210-2889. Offers French (MA); Spanish (MA). *Degree requirements:* For master's, comprehensive exam or research paper. *Entrance requirements:* For master's, 18 credits in advanced courses in Spanish, 2 letters of recommendation. Additional exam requirements/recommendations for international students: required—TOEFL (minimum score 500 paper-based; 61 iBT). Electronic applications accepted.

California State University, Fresno, Division of Research and Graduate Studies, College of Arts and Humanities, Department of Modern and Classical Languages and Literatures, Fresno, CA 93740-8027. Offers Spanish (MA). *Program availability:* Part-time. *Degree requirements:* For master's, one foreign language, thesis or alternative. *Entrance requirements:* For master's, GRE General Test, BA in Spanish, minimum GPA of 3.0. Additional exam requirements/recommendations for international students: required—TOEFL. Electronic applications accepted. *Expenses:* Tuition, state resident: full-time $4012; part-time $2506 per semester.

California State University, Fullerton, Graduate Studies, College of Humanities and Social Sciences, Department of Modern Languages and Literatures, Fullerton, CA 92831-3599. Offers Spanish (MA). *Program availability:* Part-time. *Degree requirements:* For master's, comprehensive exam, thesis or alternative. *Entrance requirements:* For master's, minimum GPA of 2.5 in last 60 hours of course work, undergraduate major in a language.

California State University, Long Beach, Graduate Studies, College of Liberal Arts, Department of Romance, German, Russian Languages and Literatures, Program in Spanish, Long Beach, CA 90840. Offers MA. *Program availability:* Part-time. *Degree requirements:* For master's, one foreign language, thesis or alternative, research paper. *Entrance requirements:* For master's, BA in Spanish. Electronic applications accepted.

California State University, Los Angeles, Graduate Studies, College of Arts and Letters, Department of Modern Languages and Literatures, Los Angeles, CA 90032-8530. Offers French (MA); Spanish (MA). *Program availability:* Part-time, evening/weekend. *Degree requirements:* For master's, comprehensive exam. *Entrance requirements:* Additional exam requirements/recommendations for international students: required—TOEFL (minimum score 500 paper-based). Electronic applications accepted. *Expenses: Tuition, area resident:* Full-time $7176; part-time $4164 per year. Tuition, state resident: full-time $7176; part-time $4164 per year. Tuition, nonresident: full-time $14,304; part-time $8916 per year. *International tuition:* $14,304 full-time. *Required fees:* $1037.76; $1037.76 per unit. Tuition and fees vary according to degree level and program.

California State University, Northridge, Graduate Studies, College of Humanities, Department of Modern and Classical Languages and Literatures, Northridge, CA 91330. Offers Spanish (MA). *Program availability:* Part-time, evening/weekend. *Degree requirements:* For master's, one foreign language. *Entrance requirements:* For master's, GRE General Test or minimum GPA of 3.0. Additional exam requirements/recommendations for international students: required—TOEFL.

California State University, San Bernardino, Graduate Studies, College of Arts and Letters, Program in Spanish, San Bernardino, CA 92407. Offers MA. *Program availability:* Part-time, evening/weekend. *Faculty:* 3 full-time (1 woman). *Students:* 7 full-time (6 women), 16 part-time (13 women); includes 19 minority (all Hispanic/Latino), 1 international. Average age 36. 14 applicants, 86% accepted, 11 enrolled. In 2019, 9 master's awarded. *Degree requirements:* For master's, comprehensive exam, advancement to candidacy. *Entrance requirements:* Additional exam requirements/recommendations for international students: required—TOEFL. *Application deadline:* For fall admission, 7/16 for domestic students. Application fee: $55. *Financial support:* Institutionally sponsored loans available. *Unit head:* Dr. Thomas McGovern, Chair, 909-537-5849, E-mail: mcgovern@csusb.edu. *Application contact:* Dr. Dorota Huizinga, Dean of Graduate Studies, 909-537-3064, E-mail: dorota.huizinga@csusb.edu.

California State University, San Marcos, College of Humanities, Arts, Behavioral and Social Sciences, Program in Spanish, San Marcos, CA 92096-0001. Offers Hispanic cultures and society (MA); Hispanic language and linguistics (MA); Hispanic literatures and literary theory (MA). *Program availability:* Part-time, evening/weekend. *Degree requirements:* For master's, 2 foreign languages, exam. *Entrance requirements:* For master's, GRE General Test, minimum GPA of 3.0 overall and in upper-division Spanish courses, official transcripts, three letters of recommendation, 750-word statement of purpose (in English), academic writing sample (in Spanish). Additional exam requirements/recommendations for international students: required—TOEFL (minimum score 500 paper-based), TWE (minimum score 4.5). Electronic applications accepted. *Expenses: Tuition, area resident:* Full-time $7176. Tuition, state resident: full-time $7176. Tuition, nonresident: full-time $18,640. *International tuition:* $18,640 full-time. *Required fees:* $1960.

The Catholic University of America, School of Arts and Sciences, Department of Modern Languages and Literatures, Washington, DC 20064. Offers Hispanic studies (MA, PhD). *Program availability:* Part-time. *Faculty:* 19 full-time (14 women), 4 part-time/adjunct (all women). *Students:* 2 full-time (0 women), 6 part-time (4 women); includes 1 minority (Two or more races, non-Hispanic/Latino), 5 international. Average age 44. 2 applicants, 50% accepted, 1 enrolled. In 2019, 1 master's awarded. *Degree requirements:* For master's, comprehensive exam; for doctorate, one foreign language, comprehensive exam, thesis/dissertation, annotated bibliography; oral defense of the proposal; oral defense of the dissertation. *Entrance requirements:* For master's, GRE General Test, statement of purpose, official copies of academic transcripts, two letters of recommendation, sample of academic writing; for doctorate, GRE General Test, statement of purpose, official copies of academic transcripts, three letters of recommendation, sample of academic writing (20-25-pages long). Additional exam requirements/recommendations for international students: required—TOEFL (minimum score 550 paper-based; 80 iBT). *Application deadline:* For fall admission, 7/15 priority date for domestic students, 7/1 for international students; for spring admission, 11/15 priority date for domestic students, 11/1 for international students. Applications are processed on a rolling basis. Application fee: $55. Electronic applications accepted. *Expenses:* Contact institution. *Financial support:* Fellowships, research assistantships, teaching assistantships, Federal Work-Study, scholarships/grants, tuition waivers (full and partial), and unspecified assistantships available. Financial award application deadline: 2/1; financial award applicants required to submit FAFSA. *Unit head:* Dr. Claudia Bornholdt, Chair, 202-319-5240, Fax: 202-319-6077, E-mail: kassen@cua.edu. *Application contact:* Dr. Steven Brown, Director of Graduate Admissions, 202-319-5057, Fax: 202-319-6533, E-mail: cua-admissions@cua.edu.
Website: http://modernlanguages.cua.edu/

Central Connecticut State University, School of Graduate Studies, College of Liberal Arts and Social Sciences, Department of Modern Languages, New Britain, CT 06050-4010. Offers modern language (MA, Certificate), including French, German (Certificate), Italian, Spanish (MA); Spanish (MS, Certificate). *Program availability:* Part-time, evening/weekend. *Degree requirements:* For master's, one foreign language, comprehensive exam, thesis or alternative; for Certificate, qualifying exam. *Entrance requirements:* For master's, minimum undergraduate GPA of 2.7, 24 credits of undergraduate courses in each language in which graduate work will be undertaken. Additional exam requirements/recommendations for international students: required—TOEFL (minimum score 550 paper-based; 79 iBT); recommended—IELTS (minimum score 6.5). Electronic applications accepted.

Central Michigan University, College of Graduate Studies, College of Liberal Arts and Social Sciences, Department of World Languages and Cultures, Mount Pleasant, MI 48859. Offers Spanish (MA). *Program availability:* Part-time. *Degree requirements:* For master's, thesis or alternative. Electronic applications accepted. *Expenses: Tuition, area resident:* Full-time $12,267; part-time $8178 per year. Tuition, state resident: full-time $12,267; part-time $8178 per year. Tuition, nonresident: full-time $12,267; part-time $8178 per year. *International tuition:* $16,110 full-time. *Required fees:* $225 per semester. Tuition and fees vary according to degree level and program.

City College of the City University of New York, Graduate School, Division of Humanities and the Arts, Department of Classical and Modern Languages and Literatures, New York, NY 10031-9198. Offers Spanish (MA). *Degree requirements:* For master's, one foreign language, comprehensive exam, thesis or alternative. *Entrance requirements:* For master's, minimum GPA of 3.0. Additional exam requirements/recommendations for international students: required—TOEFL (minimum score 500 paper-based; 61 iBT). Electronic applications accepted.

Cleveland State University, College of Graduate Studies, College of Liberal Arts and Social Sciences, Department of World Languages, Literatures, and Cultures, Cleveland, OH 44115. Offers Spanish (MA). *Program availability:* Part-time, evening/weekend. *Entrance requirements:* For master's, ACTFL oral proficiency rating, undergraduate major in Spanish or equivalent, essay in Spanish, writing sample, 2 letters of reference. Additional exam requirements/recommendations for international students: required—TOEFL (minimum score 550 paper-based; 78 iBT). Electronic applications accepted. *Expenses:* Tuition, state resident: full-time $10,215; part-time $6810 per credit hour. Tuition, nonresident: full-time $17,496; part-time $11,664 per credit hour. *International tuition:* $19,316 full-time. Tuition and fees vary according to degree level and program.

Columbia University, Graduate School of Arts and Sciences, New York, NY 10027. Offers African-American studies (MA); American studies (MA); anthropology (MA, PhD); art history and archaeology (MA, PhD); astronomy (PhD); biological sciences (PhD); biotechnology (MA); chemical physics (PhD); chemistry (PhD); classical studies (MA, PhD); classics (MA, PhD); climate and society (MA); conservation biology (MA); earth and environmental sciences (PhD); East Asia: regional studies (MA); East Asian languages and cultures (MA, PhD); ecology, evolution and environmental biology (MA), including conservation biology; ecology, evolution, and environmental biology (PhD), including ecology and evolutionary biology, evolutionary primatology; economics (MA, PhD); English and comparative literature (MA, PhD); French and Romance philology (MA, PhD); Germanic languages (MA, PhD); global French studies (MA); global thought (MA); Hispanic cultural studies (MA); history (PhD); history and literature (MA); human rights studies (MA); Islamic studies (MA); Italian (MA, PhD); Japanese pedagogy (MA); Jewish studies (MA); Latin America and the Caribbean: regional studies (MA); Latin American and Iberian cultures (PhD); mathematics (MA, PhD), including finance (MA); medieval and Renaissance studies (MA); Middle Eastern, South Asian, and African studies (MA, PhD); modern art: critical and curatorial studies (MA); modern European studies (MA); museum anthropology (MA); music (DMA, PhD); oral history (MA); philosophical foundations of physics (MA); philosophy (MA, PhD); physics (PhD); political science (MA, PhD); psychology (PhD); quantitative methods in the social sciences (MA); religion (MA, PhD); Russia, Eurasia and East Europe: regional studies (MA); Russian translation (MA); Slavic cultures (MA); Slavic languages (MA, PhD); sociology (MA, PhD); South Asian studies (MA); statistics (MA, PhD); theatre (PhD). *Program availability:* Part-time. *Students:* 3,506 full-time (1,844 women), 208 part-time (121 women); includes 864 minority (110 Black or African American, non-Hispanic/Latino; 5 American Indian or Alaska Native, non-Hispanic/Latino; 416 Asian, non-Hispanic/Latino; 147 Hispanic/Latino; 6 Native Hawaiian or other Pacific Islander, non-Hispanic/Latino; 180 Two or more races, non-Hispanic/Latino), 2,065 international. 14,545 applicants, 25% accepted, 1,429 enrolled. In 2019, 1,262 master's, 363 doctorates awarded. Terminal master's awarded for partial completion of doctoral program. *Degree requirements:* For master's, variable foreign language requirement, comprehensive exam (for some programs), thesis (for some programs); for doctorate, variable foreign language requirement, comprehensive exam (for some programs), thesis/dissertation. *Entrance requirements:* For master's and doctorate, GRE General Test, GRE Subject Test (for some programs). Additional exam requirements/recommendations for international students: required—TOEFL (minimum score 600 paper-based; 100 iBT), IELTS (minimum score 7.5). Application fee: $115. Electronic applications accepted. *Expenses: Tuition:* Full-time $47,600; part-time $1880 per credit. One-time fee: $105. *Financial support:* Fellowships, research assistantships, teaching assistantships, career-related internships or fieldwork, Federal Work-Study, institutionally sponsored loans, scholarships/grants, traineeships, health care benefits, tuition waivers, and unspecified assistantships available. Support available to part-time students. Financial award application deadline: 12/15. *Unit head:* Dr. Carlos J. Alonso, Dean of the Graduate School of Arts and Sciences and Vice President for Graduate Education, 212-854-2861, E-mail: gsas-dean@columbia.edu. *Application contact:* GSAS Office of Admissions, 212-854-6729, E-mail: gsas-admissions@columbia.edu.
Website: http://gsas.columbia.edu/

Cornell University, Graduate School, Graduate Fields of Arts and Sciences, Field of Romance Studies, Ithaca, NY 14853. Offers French linguistics (PhD); French literature (PhD); Hispanic literature (PhD); Italian linguistics (PhD); Italian literature (PhD); Romance linguistics (PhD); Spanish linguistics (PhD). *Degree requirements:* For doctorate, 2 foreign languages, comprehensive exam, thesis/dissertation. *Entrance requirements:* For doctorate, GRE General Test, sample of written work, 3 letters of recommendation. Additional exam requirements/recommendations for international students: required—TOEFL (minimum score 550 paper-based; 77 iBT). Electronic applications accepted.

DePaul University, College of Liberal Arts and Social Sciences, Chicago, IL 60614. Offers Arabic (MA); Chinese (MA); critical ethnic studies (MA); English (MA); French (MA); German (MA); history (MA); interdisciplinary studies (MA, MS); international public service (MS); international studies (MA); Italian (MA); Japanese (MA); liberal studies (MA); nonprofit management (MNM); public administration (MPA); public health (MPH); public policy (MPP); public service management (MS); refugee and forced migration studies (MS); social work (MSW); sociology (MA); Spanish (MA); sustainable urban development (MA); women's and gender studies (MA); writing and publishing (MA); writing, rhetoric and discourse (MA); MA/PhD. *Accreditation:* CEPH. *Program availability:* Part-time, evening/weekend, online learning. Terminal master's awarded for partial completion of doctoral program. *Degree requirements:* For master's, variable foreign language requirement, comprehensive exam (for some programs), thesis (for some programs). Electronic applications accepted.

Duke University, Graduate School, Department of Romance Studies, Durham, NC 27708. Offers French (PhD); Italian (PhD); Spanish (PhD); JD/AM. *Degree requirements:* For doctorate, 2 foreign languages, thesis/dissertation. *Entrance requirements:* For doctorate, GRE General Test. Additional exam requirements/

recommendations for international students: required—TOEFL (minimum score 577 paper-based; 90 iBT) or IELTS (minimum score 7). Electronic applications accepted.

Eastern University, Graduate Education Programs, St. Davids, PA 19087-3696. Offers ESL program specialist (K-12) (Certificate); general supervisor (PreK-12) (Certificate); health and physical education (K-12) (Certificate); middle level (4-8) (Certificate); multicultural education (M Ed); music (K-12) (Certificate); Pre K-4 (Certificate); Pre K-4 with special education (Certificate); reading (M Ed); reading specialist (K-12) (Certificate); reading supervisor (K-12) (Certificate); school counseling (MA, CAGS); school principalship (preK-12) (Certificate); school psychology (MS, CAGS); secondary biology education (7-12) (Certificate); secondary chemistry education (7-12) (Certificate); secondary communication education (7-12) (Certificate); secondary English education (7-12) (Certificate); secondary math education (7-12) (Certificate); secondary social studies education (7-12) (Certificate); special education (M Ed); special education (7-12) (Certificate); special education (Pre K-8) (Certificate); special education supervisor (K-12) (Certificate); TESOL (M Ed); world language (Certificate), including Spanish. *Program availability:* Part-time, evening/weekend, online learning. *Students:* 54 full-time (45 women), 149 part-time (134 women); includes 75 minority (54 Black or African American, non-Hispanic/Latino; 3 Asian, non-Hispanic/Latino; 15 Hispanic/Latino; 3 Two or more races, non-Hispanic/Latino). Average age 33. In 2019, 89 master's, 10 other advanced degrees awarded. *Entrance requirements:* Additional exam requirements/recommendations for international students: required—TOEFL. *Application deadline:* Applications are processed on a rolling basis. Application fee: $35. Electronic applications accepted. Application fee is waived when completed online. *Expenses:* Contact institution. *Unit head:* Michael Dziedziak, Executive Director of Enrollment, 800-452-0996, E-mail: gpsadmissions@eastern.edu. *Application contact:* Michael Dziedziak, Executive Director of Enrollment, 800-452-0996, E-mail: gpsadmissions@eastern.edu.
Website: https://www.eastern.edu/academics/programs/education-department-graduate-programs/graduate-programs

Emory University, Laney Graduate School, Department of Spanish and Portuguese, Atlanta, GA 30322-1100. Offers comparative literature (Certificate); film studies (Certificate); Spanish (PhD); women's studies (Certificate). *Degree requirements:* For doctorate, 2 foreign languages, comprehensive exam, thesis/dissertation. *Entrance requirements:* For doctorate, GRE General Test. Additional exam requirements/recommendations for international students: required—TOEFL. Electronic applications accepted.

Florida Atlantic University, Dorothy F. Schmidt College of Arts and Letters, Department of Languages, Linguistics, and Comparative Literature, Boca Raton, FL 33431-0991. Offers comparative literature (MA); French (MA); linguistics (MA); Spanish (MA). *Program availability:* Part-time. *Faculty:* 20 full-time (13 women). *Students:* 29 full-time (17 women), 11 part-time (9 women); includes 22 minority (7 Black or African American, non-Hispanic/Latino; 1 Asian, non-Hispanic/Latino; 14 Hispanic/Latino), 4 international. Average age 37. 30 applicants, 67% accepted, 16 enrolled. In 2019, 14 master's awarded. *Degree requirements:* For master's, one foreign language, comprehensive exam, thesis optional. *Entrance requirements:* For master's, GRE General Test, minimum GPA of 3.0. Additional exam requirements/recommendations for international students: required—TOEFL (minimum score 500 paper-based; 61 iBT), IELTS (minimum score 6). *Application deadline:* For fall admission, 7/1 priority date for domestic students, 2/15 for international students; for spring admission, 11/1 for domestic students, 7/15 for international students. Applications are processed on a rolling basis. Application fee: $30. *Expenses: Tuition:* Full-time $20,536; part-time $371.82 per credit hour. Tuition and fees vary according to program. *Financial support:* Fellowships, research assistantships, teaching assistantships with partial tuition reimbursements, Federal Work-Study, and tuition waivers (partial) available. Support available to part-time students. Financial award application deadline: 4/1. *Unit head:* Dr. Marcella Munson, Chair, 561-297-2118, Fax: 561-297-2756, E-mail: mmunson@fau.edu. *Application contact:* Dr. Marcella Munson, Chair, 561-297-2118, Fax: 561-297-2756, E-mail: mmunson@fau.edu.
Website: http://www.fau.edu/LLCL/

Florida International University, Steven J. Green School of International and Public Affairs, Department of Modern Languages, Miami, FL 33199. Offers Spanish (MA, PhD). *Program availability:* Part-time, evening/weekend. *Faculty:* 25 full-time (16 women), 17 part-time/adjunct (10 women). *Students:* 25 full-time (17 women), 11 part-time (9 women); includes 28 minority (1 Asian, non-Hispanic/Latino; 27 Hispanic/Latino), 7 international. Average age 40. 21 applicants, 57% accepted, 7 enrolled. In 2019, 7 master's, 6 doctorates awarded. *Degree requirements:* For master's, 2 foreign languages, comprehensive exam, thesis or 6 elective credits; for doctorate, 3 foreign languages, comprehensive exam, thesis/dissertation. *Entrance requirements:* For master's, minimum GPA of 3.0, resume, writing sample in Spanish (6-7 pages minimum), 2 letters of recommendation; for doctorate, GRE General Test (minimum score of 1120) or EXADEP (minimum score of 500), minimum GPA of 3.0, letter of intent, resume, writing sample in Spanish (15 pages minimum), 2 letters of recommendation. Additional exam requirements/recommendations for international students: required—TOEFL (minimum score 550 paper-based; 80 iBT). *Application deadline:* For fall admission, 3/15 for domestic and international students. Application fee: $30. Electronic applications accepted. *Expenses: Tuition, area resident:* Full-time $8912; part-time $446 per credit hour. Tuition, state resident: full-time $8912; part-time $446 per credit hour. Tuition, nonresident: full-time $21,393; part-time $992 per credit hour. *Required fees:* $2194. *Financial support:* Institutionally sponsored loans, scholarships/grants, and health care benefits available. Financial award application deadline: 3/1; financial award applicants required to submit FAFSA. *Unit head:* Dr. Pascale Becel, Chair, 305-348-1944, Fax: 305-348-1085, E-mail: Pascale.Becel@fiu.edu. *Application contact:* Nanett Rojas, Manager, Admissions Operations, 305-348-7464, Fax: 305-348-7441, E-mail: gradadm@fiu.edu.

Florida State University, The Graduate School, Department of Anthropology, Department of Modern Languages and Linguistics, Program in Spanish, Tallahassee, FL 32306. Offers MA, PhD. *Faculty:* 13 full-time (7 women), 3 part-time/adjunct (2 women). *Students:* 32 full-time (20 women), 9 part-time (8 women); includes 21 minority (2 Black or African American, non-Hispanic/Latino; 1 Asian, non-Hispanic/Latino; 6 Hispanic/Latino; 12 Two or more races, non-Hispanic/Latino). In 2019, 6 master's, 1 doctorate awarded. Terminal master's awarded for partial completion of doctoral program. *Degree requirements:* For master's, thesis; for doctorate, 2 foreign languages, thesis/dissertation. *Entrance requirements:* For master's and doctorate, GRE General Test, minimum GPA of 3.0. Additional exam requirements/recommendations for international students: required—TOEFL (minimum score 550 paper-based; 80 iBT). *Application deadline:* For fall admission, 1/15 priority date for domestic and international students. Electronic applications accepted. *Financial support:* In 2019–20, fellowships with partial tuition reimbursements (averaging $14,000 per year) were awarded; research assistantships with partial tuition reimbursements and teaching assistantships with partial tuition reimbursements also available. Financial award application deadline: 1/15; financial award applicants required to submit FAFSA. *Unit head:* Dr. Carolina Gonzalez, Divisional Coordinator/Professor, 850-644-3728, Fax: 850-644-0524, E-mail: cgonzalez3@fsu.edu. *Application contact:* Wendy E. Pigott, Graduate Academic Coordinator, 850-644-8397, Fax: 850-644-0524, E-mail: wpigott@fsu.edu.
Website: http://modlang.fsu.edu/Programs2/Spanish/Graduate-program-in-Spanish

George Mason University, College of Humanities and Social Sciences, Department of Modern and Classical Languages, Fairfax, VA 22030. Offers foreign languages (MA), including French, Spanish, Spanish and French, Spanish/bilingual-multicultural education. *Degree requirements:* For master's, one foreign language, thesis optional, take-home exit exam. *Entrance requirements:* For master's, goals statement, language proficiency statement. Additional exam requirements/recommendations for international students: required—TOEFL (minimum score 575 paper-based; 88 iBT), IELTS (minimum score 6.5), PTE (minimum score 59). Electronic applications accepted.

Georgetown University, Graduate School of Arts and Sciences, Department of Spanish and Portuguese, Washington, DC 20057. Offers Spanish (MS, PhD), including Hispanic literature and cultural studies, Spanish linguistics, Spanish literature; MS/PhD. *Degree requirements:* For master's, one foreign language, research project; for doctorate, 3 foreign languages, thesis/dissertation. *Entrance requirements:* Additional exam requirements/recommendations for international students: required—TOEFL.

Georgia Southern University, Jack N. Averitt College of Graduate Studies, College of Arts and Humanities, Program in Spanish, Statesboro, GA 30460. Offers MA. *Program availability:* Part-time, evening/weekend. *Faculty:* 18 full-time (8 women), 1 part-time/adjunct (0 women). *Students:* 12 full-time (9 women), 7 part-time (6 women); includes 12 minority (2 Black or African American, non-Hispanic/Latino; 10 Hispanic/Latino), 1 international. Average age 32. 13 applicants, 100% accepted, 8 enrolled. In 2019, 6 master's awarded. *Degree requirements:* For master's, one foreign language, thesis optional. *Entrance requirements:* For master's, GRE, minimum GPA of 3.0, letters of reference. Additional exam requirements/recommendations for international students: required—TOEFL (minimum score 550 paper-based; 80 iBT), IELTS (minimum score 6). *Application deadline:* For fall admission, 3/1 priority date for domestic and international students; for spring admission, 10/1 priority date for domestic students, 10/1 for international students. Applications are processed on a rolling basis. Application fee: $50. Electronic applications accepted. *Expenses: Tuition, area resident:* Full-time $4986; part-time $277 per credit hour. Tuition, nonresident: full-time $19,890; part-time $1105 per credit hour. *International tuition:* $19,890 full-time. *Required fees:* $2114; $1057 per semester. $1057 per semester. Tuition and fees vary according to course load, campus/location and program. *Financial support:* In 2019–20, 10 students received support, including 7 fellowships with full tuition reimbursements available (averaging $7,750 per year), 3 teaching assistantships with full tuition reimbursements available (averaging $7,750 per year); career-related internships or fieldwork, Federal Work-Study, scholarships/grants, tuition waivers (full), and unspecified assistantships also available. Support available to part-time students. Financial award application deadline: 4/15; financial award applicants required to submit FAFSA. *Unit head:* Dr. Eric Kartchner, Department Chair, 912-478-1381, Fax: 912-478-0652, E-mail: ekartchner@georgiasouthern.edu.
Website: http://class.georgiasouthern.edu/fl

Georgia State University, College of Arts and Sciences, Department of World Languages and Cultures, Program in Spanish, Atlanta, GA 30302-3083. Offers MA. *Entrance requirements:* For master's, GRE, statement of purpose, writing sample in the target language, 2 letters of recommendation, official transcripts. Additional exam requirements/recommendations for international students: required—TOEFL (minimum score 79 iBT). Application fee: $50. Electronic applications accepted. *Expenses: Tuition, area resident:* Full-time $7164; part-time $398 per credit hour. Tuition, state resident: full-time $7164; part-time $398 per credit hour. Tuition, nonresident: full-time $22,662; part-time $1259 per credit hour. *International tuition:* $22,662 full-time. *Required fees:* $2128; $312 per credit hour. Tuition and fees vary according to course load and program. *Financial support:* Institutionally sponsored loans available. *Unit head:* Dr. Fernando Reati, Department Chair, 404-413-5984, Fax: 404-413-5982, E-mail: freati@gsu.edu. *Application contact:* Vicky Hanning, Administrative Coordinator, 404-413-5990, Fax: 404-413-5982, E-mail: vcassem@gsu.edu.
Website: https://wlc.gsu.edu/

Georgia State University, College of Arts and Sciences, Department of World Languages and Cultures, Program in Translation and Interpretation, Atlanta, GA 30302-3083. Offers interpretation (Certificate), including Spanish; translation (Certificate), including French, German, Spanish. *Program availability:* Part-time. *Entrance requirements:* For degree, entrance examination involving translating one passage from English to the target language and one passage from the target language to English, 3 letters of recommendation, resume/curriculum vitae, official transcripts. Additional exam requirements/recommendations for international students: required—TOEFL (minimum score 79 iBT). Application fee: $50. Electronic applications accepted. *Expenses: Tuition, area resident:* Full-time $7164; part-time $398 per credit hour. Tuition, state resident: full-time $7164; part-time $398 per credit hour. Tuition, nonresident: full-time $22,662; part-time $1259 per credit hour. *International tuition:* $22,662 full-time. *Required fees:* $2128; $312 per credit hour. Tuition and fees vary according to course load and program. *Unit head:* Dr. William Nichols, Chair, 404-413-5980, Fax: 404-413-5982, E-mail: wnichols@gsu.edu. *Application contact:* Vicky Hanning, Administrative Coordinator, 404-413-5990, Fax: 404-413-5982, E-mail: vassem@gsu.edu.
Website: http://wlc.gsu.edu/home/graduate/graduate-certificate/

Harvard University, Graduate School of Arts and Sciences, Department of Romance Languages and Literatures, Cambridge, MA 02138. Offers French (AM, PhD); Italian (AM, PhD); Portuguese (AM, PhD); Spanish (AM, PhD). Terminal master's awarded for partial completion of doctoral program. *Degree requirements:* For master's, 2 foreign languages; for doctorate, 2 foreign languages, thesis/dissertation. *Entrance requirements:* For master's and doctorate, GRE General Test, sample of written work. Additional exam requirements/recommendations for international students: required—TOEFL.

Houston Baptist University, School of Humanities, Program in Liberal Arts, Houston, TX 77074-3298. Offers education (EC-12 art, music, physical education, or Spanish) (MLA); education (EC-6 generalist) (MLA); general liberal arts (MLA); specialization in education (4-8 or 7-12) (MLA). *Program availability:* Part-time, evening/weekend. *Entrance requirements:* For master's, minimum GPA of 2.5, essay/personal statement, resume, bachelor's degree transcript. Additional exam requirements/recommendations for international students: required—TOEFL (minimum score 80 iBT), IELTS (minimum score 6.5). Electronic applications accepted. Application fee is waived when completed online. *Expenses:* Contact institution.

Howard University, Graduate School, Department of Modern Languages and Literatures, Washington, DC 20059-0002. Offers French (MA); Spanish (MA). *Program availability:* Part-time. *Degree requirements:* For master's, one foreign language, comprehensive exam, thesis. *Entrance requirements:* For master's, GRE General Test, writing samples in English and French or Spanish.

Hunter College of the City University of New York, Graduate School, School of Arts and Sciences, Department of Romance Languages, Program in Spanish, New York, NY 10065-5085. Offers MA. *Program availability:* Part-time, evening/weekend. *Degree requirements:* For master's, 2 foreign languages, comprehensive exam, thesis optional. *Entrance requirements:* For master's, GRE General Test, GRE Subject Test, ability to read, speak, and write Spanish; interview. Additional exam requirements/ recommendations for international students: required—TOEFL.

Illinois State University, Graduate School, College of Arts and Sciences, Department of Foreign Languages, Literatures and Cultures, Normal, IL 61790. Offers French (MA); French and German (MA); French and Spanish (MA); German (MA); German and Spanish (MA); Spanish (MA). *Faculty:* 23 full-time (13 women), 7 part-time/adjunct (all women). *Students:* 14 full-time (7 women), 4 part-time (2 women). Average age 30. 12 applicants, 83% accepted, 6 enrolled. In 2019, 7 master's awarded. *Degree requirements:* For master's, variable foreign language requirement, comprehensive exam, 1 term of residency. *Entrance requirements:* For master's, GRE General Test, minimum GPA of 2.8 in last 60 hours of course work. *Application deadline:* Applications are processed on a rolling basis. Application fee: $50. *Expenses: Tuition, area resident:* Full-time $7956; part-time $9767 per year. Tuition, nonresident: full-time $9233; part-time $17,592 per year. *Required fees:* $1797. *Financial support:* In 2019–20, 13 teaching assistantships were awarded; tuition waivers (full) and unspecified assistantships also available. Financial award application deadline: 4/1. *Unit head:* Dr. Bruce Brningham, Department Chair, 309-438-3604. *Application contact:* Dr. Ryan Davis, Graduate Coordinator, 309-438-7759, Fax: 309-438-7912, E-mail: rdavis2@IllinoisState.edu.
Website: http://www.foreignlanguages.ilstu.edu/

Indiana State University, College of Graduate and Professional Studies, College of Arts and Sciences, Department of Languages, Literatures, and Linguistics, Terre Haute, IN 47809. Offers applied linguistics/teaching English as a second language (MA); language education (PhD); Spanish/teaching English as a second language (MA); TESL/TEFL (CAS). *Degree requirements:* For master's, comprehensive exam. Electronic applications accepted.

Indiana University Bloomington, University Graduate School, College of Arts and Sciences, Department of Spanish and Portuguese, Bloomington, IN 47405. Offers Portuguese (MA, PhD); Spanish (MA, PhD), including Hispanic linguistics, Hispanic literatures. *Degree requirements:* For master's, one foreign language, comprehensive exam, thesis (for Spanish); for doctorate, 2 foreign languages, comprehensive exam, thesis/dissertation. *Entrance requirements:* For master's, GRE General Test, bachelor's degree in Portuguese or Spanish, minimum GPA of 3.0; for doctorate, GRE General Test, master's degree in Portuguese or Spanish, minimum GPA of 3.0. Additional exam requirements/recommendations for international students: required—TOEFL (minimum score 79 iBT). Electronic applications accepted.

Inter American University of Puerto Rico, Metropolitan Campus, Graduate Programs, Program in Spanish, San Juan, PR 00919-1293. Offers MA. *Program availability:* Part-time, evening/weekend. *Degree requirements:* For master's, one foreign language, comprehensive exam. *Entrance requirements:* For master's, GRE or EXADEP, interview, minimum GPA of 2.5, 6 credits each of Spanish literature and Hispanic-American literature. Electronic applications accepted.

Inter American University of Puerto Rico, Metropolitan Campus, Graduate Programs, Program in Spanish Education, San Juan, PR 00919-1293. Offers MA.

Inter American University of Puerto Rico, Ponce Campus, Graduate School, Mercedita, PR 00715-1602. Offers accounting (MBA); biology (M Ed); chemistry (M Ed); criminal justice (MA); elementary education (M Ed); English as a Second Language (M Ed); finance (MBA); history (M Ed); human resources (MBA); marketing (MBA); mathematics (M Ed); Spanish (M Ed). *Entrance requirements:* For master's, minimum GPA of 2.5.

Iona College, School of Arts and Science, Department of Education, New Rochelle, NY 10801-1890. Offers adolescence education: biology (MS Ed, MST); adolescence education: English (MS Ed); adolescence education: mathematics (MST); adolescence education: social studies (MS Ed, MST); adolescence education: Spanish (MS Ed); adolescence special education 5-12 (MST); childhood and special education (MST); early childhood and childhood (MST); educational leadership (MS Ed). *Accreditation:* NCATE. *Program availability:* Part-time, evening/weekend. *Faculty:* 9 full-time (6 women), 4 part-time/adjunct (2 women). *Students:* 30 full-time (28 women), 28 part-time (20 women); includes 20 minority (3 Black or African American, non-Hispanic/Latino; 4 Asian, non-Hispanic/Latino; 11 Hispanic/Latino; 2 Two or more races, non-Hispanic/ Latino). Average age 26. 39 applicants, 74% accepted, 16 enrolled. In 2019, 15 master's awarded. *Degree requirements:* For master's, thesis or alternative. *Entrance requirements:* For master's, minimum GPA of 3.0, NY State teaching certificate and bachelor's degree (for MS Ed). Additional exam requirements/recommendations for international students: required—TOEFL (minimum score 550 paper-based; 80 iBT), IELTS (minimum score 6.5). *Application deadline:* For fall admission, 8/1 priority date for domestic students, 5/1 priority date for international students; for spring admission, 1/1 priority date for domestic students, 9/1 priority date for international students. Applications are processed on a rolling basis. Electronic applications accepted. *Financial support:* In 2019–20, 46 students received support. Scholarships/grants and unspecified assistantships available. Support available to part-time students. Financial award application deadline: 4/15; financial award applicants required to submit FAFSA. *Unit head:* Malissa Scheuring Leipold, EdD, Chair, 914-633-2210, Fax: 914-633-2281, E-mail: mleipold@iona.edu. *Application contact:* Christopher Kash, Assistant Director of Graduate Admissions, 914-633-2403, E-mail: ckash@iona.edu.
Website: http://www.iona.edu/Academics/School-of-Arts-Science/Departments/ Education/Graduate-Programs.aspx

Johns Hopkins University, Zanvyl Krieger School of Arts and Sciences, Department of German and Romance Languages and Literatures, Baltimore, MD 21218. Offers German (MA, PhD); romance languages (PhD), including French, Italian, Spanish. Terminal master's awarded for partial completion of doctoral program. *Degree requirements:* For master's, comprehensive exam; for doctorate, 2 foreign languages, comprehensive exam, thesis/dissertation. *Entrance requirements:* For doctorate, GRE General Test. Additional exam requirements/recommendations for international students: required—TOEFL (minimum score 600 paper-based; 100 iBT), IELTS. Electronic applications accepted. *Expenses:* Contact institution.

Kansas State University, Graduate School, College of Arts and Sciences, Department of Modern Languages, Manhattan, KS 66506. Offers literature (MA), including French, German, Spanish; second language acquisition (MA), including French, German, Spanish, teaching English as a foreign language. *Program availability:* Part-time, evening/weekend, blended/hybrid learning. *Degree requirements:* For master's, thesis optional. *Entrance requirements:* For master's, teaching certificate. Additional exam requirements/recommendations for international students: required—TOEFL (minimum score 550 paper-based; 83 iBT), TOEFL (minimum speaking-portion score of 26). Electronic applications accepted.

Kent State University, College of Arts and Sciences, Department of Modern and Classical Language Studies, Kent, OH 44242-0001. Offers French (MA), including applied linguistics and pedagogy, literature; German (MA), including applied linguistics and pedagogy, literature; Latin (MA), including applied linguistics and pedagogy, literature; Spanish (MA), including applied linguistics and pedagogy, literature; translation (MA), including Arabic, French, German, Japanese, Russian, Spanish; translation studies (PhD); MA/MBA. *Program availability:* Part-time, 100% online. *Faculty:* 18 full-time (11 women), 6 part-time/adjunct (3 women). *Students:* 81 full-time (49 women), 23 part-time (14 women); includes 18 minority (3 Black or African American, non-Hispanic/Latino; 3 Asian, non-Hispanic/Latino; 11 Hispanic/Latino; 1 Two or more races, non-Hispanic/Latino), 45 international. Average age 32. 115 applicants, 73% accepted, 47 enrolled. In 2019, 27 master's, 7 doctorates awarded. *Degree requirements:* For master's, variable foreign language requirement, comprehensive exam (for some programs), thesis (for some programs); for doctorate, variable foreign language requirement, comprehensive exam, thesis/dissertation. *Entrance requirements:* For master's, transcripts, goal statement, 3 letters of recommendation, CD/MP3 with a 5-10 minute oral sample of first and second languages (conversational not read from a script), Writing sample(s) in the applicant's second language, which should be accompanied by a signed declaration that the sample is original work; for doctorate, transcripts; MA in translation, a foreign language, or in any other relevant discipline with prior experience or training in translation; proficiency in a foreign language; minimum GPA of 3.5 from MA; goal statement; 3 letters of recommendation; essay or writing sample (7-10 pages) from a research paper on any aspect of translation. Additional exam requirements/recommendations for international students: required—TOEFL (minimum score 79 iBT), IELTS (minimum score 6.5), PTE (minimum score 58), Michigan English Language Assessment Battery (minimum score 77). *Application deadline:* For fall admission, 2/1 for domestic and international students. Applications are processed on a rolling basis. Application fee: $45 ($70 for international students). Electronic applications accepted. *Financial support:* Fellowships with full tuition reimbursements, teaching assistantships with full tuition reimbursements, and unspecified assistantships available. Financial award application deadline: 2/1. *Unit head:* Dr. Keiran Dunne, Professor of French Translation; Department Chair, 330-672-2150, E-mail: kdunne@kent.edu. *Application contact:* Brian James Baer, Professor of Russian Translation; Graduate Coordinator, 330-672-1813, E-mail: bbaer@kent.edu.
Website: http://www.kent.edu/mcls/

Lake Forest College, Graduate Program in Liberal Studies, Lake Forest, IL 60045. Offers American studies (MLS); cinema in East Asia (MLS); environmental studies (MLS); history (MLS); Medieval and Renaissance art (MLS); philosophy (MLS); Spanish (MLS); writing (MLS). *Program availability:* Part-time, evening/weekend. *Faculty:* 10 full-time (4 women). *Students:* 24 part-time (14 women). Average age 45. 10 applicants, 80% accepted, 3 enrolled. In 2019, 5 master's awarded. *Degree requirements:* For master's, thesis optional, 8 courses, including at least 3 interdisciplinary seminars. *Entrance requirements:* For master's, transcript, essay, interview. Additional exam requirements/recommendations for international students: required—TOEFL (minimum score 550 paper-based; 83 iBT); recommended—IELTS (minimum score 6.5). *Application deadline:* For fall admission, 8/15 priority date for domestic students, 7/15 priority date for international students; for spring admission, 12/15 priority date for domestic students, 11/15 priority date for international students. Applications are processed on a rolling basis. Application fee: $30. Electronic applications accepted. Application fee is waived when completed online. *Expenses:* Application fee = $30 — no other fees; tuition = $2,700/course. *Financial support:* In 2019–20, 2 students received support. Partial tuition grants (for full-time teachers) available. *Unit head:* Prof. D. L. LeMahieu, Director, 847-735-5133, Fax: 847-735-6291, E-mail: lemahieu@lakeforest.edu. *Application contact:* Prof. Carol Gayle, Associate Director, 847-735-5083, Fax: 847-735-6291, E-mail: gayle@lakeforest.edu.
Website: http://www.lakeforest.edu/academics/programs/mls/

Lake Forest College, Master of Arts in Teaching Program, Lake Forest, IL 60045. Offers elementary education (MAT); K-12 French (MAT); K-12 music (MAT); K-12 Spanish (MAT); K-12 visual art (MAT); secondary biology (MAT); secondary chemistry (MAT); secondary English (MAT); secondary history (MAT); secondary mathematics (MAT). *Degree requirements:* For master's, comprehensive exam, portfolio. *Entrance requirements:* For master's, GRE. *Expenses: Tuition:* Full-time $29,600; part-time $3200 per course.

Lamar University, College of Graduate Studies, College of Arts and Sciences, Department of English and Modern Languages, Beaumont, TX 77710. Offers English (MA); teaching Spanish (MA). *Program availability:* Part-time, evening/weekend. *Faculty:* 40 full-time (19 women), 4 part-time/adjunct (all women). *Students:* 10 full-time (7 women), 29 part-time (28 women); includes 20 minority (2 Black or African American, non-Hispanic/Latino; 17 Hispanic/Latino; 1 Two or more races, non-Hispanic/Latino), 12 international. Average age 37. 19 applicants, 84% accepted, 14 enrolled. In 2019, 6 master's awarded. *Degree requirements:* For master's, one foreign language, thesis optional, practicum. *Entrance requirements:* For master's, GRE General Test, minimum GPA of 2.5 in last 60 hours of undergraduate course work. Additional exam requirements/recommendations for international students: required—TOEFL (minimum score 550 paper-based; 79 iBT), IELTS (minimum score 6.5). *Application deadline:* Applications are processed on a rolling basis. Application fee: $25 ($50 for international students). Electronic applications accepted. *Expenses: Tuition, area resident:* Full-time $6324; part-time $351 per credit. Tuition, state resident: full-time $6324; part-time $351 per credit. Tuition, nonresident: full-time $13,920; part-time $773 per credit. *International tuition:* $13,920 full-time. *Required fees:* $2462; $327 per credit. Tuition and fees vary according to course load, campus/location and reciprocity agreements. *Financial support:* In 2019–20, 31 students received support, including 4 teaching assistantships (averaging $8,000 per year); career-related internships or fieldwork, Federal Work-Study, and institutionally sponsored loans also available. Support available to part-time students. Financial award applicants required to submit FAFSA. *Unit head:* Dr. Jim Sanderson, Chair, 409-880-8558, Fax: 409-880-8591. *Application contact:* Celeste Contreas, Director, Admissions and Academic Services, 409-880-8888, Fax: 409-880-7419, E-mail: gradmissions@lamar.edu.
Website: http://artssciences.lamar.edu/english-and-modern-languages

Lee University, Program in Education, Cleveland, TN 37320-3450. Offers art (MAT); curriculum and instruction (M Ed, Ed S); early childhood (MAT); educational leadership (M Ed, Ed S); elementary education (MAT); English and math (MAT); English and science (MAT); English and social studies (MAT); higher education administration (MS); history (MAT); history and economics (MAT); math and science (MAT); math and social studies (MAT); middle grades (MAT); science and social studies (MASW); secondary education (MAT); Spanish (MAT); special education (M Ed, MAT); TESOL (MAT). *Accreditation:* NCATE. *Program availability:* Part-time. *Faculty:* 13 full-time (5 women), 9 part-time/adjunct (6 women). *Students:* 24 full-time (15 women), 72 part-time (46 women); includes 14 minority (8 Black or African American, non-Hispanic/Latino; 1 Hispanic/Latino; 5 Two or more races, non-Hispanic/Latino), 1 international. Average age 29. 44 applicants, 86% accepted, 33 enrolled. In 2019, 60 master's, 3 other advanced degrees awarded. *Degree requirements:* For master's, variable foreign language requirement, thesis optional, internship. *Entrance requirements:* For master's, MAT or GRE General Test, minimum undergraduate GPA of 2.75, 3 letters of recommendation, interview, writing sample, official transcripts, background check; for Ed S, minimum undergraduate and master's GPA of 2.75, official transcripts for undergraduate and master's degrees. Additional exam requirements/recommendations for international students: required—TOEFL (minimum score 61 iBT). *Application deadline:* For fall admission, 6/1 priority date for domestic and international students; for spring admission, 11/1 priority date for domestic and international students; for summer admission, 4/1 priority date for domestic and international students. Applications are processed on a rolling basis. Application fee: $25. Electronic applications accepted. *Expenses: Tuition:* Full-time $13,590; part-time $755 per credit hour. *Required fees:* $25. Tuition and fees vary according to program. *Financial support:* In 2019–20, 40 students received support. Career-related internships or fieldwork, Federal Work-Study, institutionally sponsored loans, scholarships/grants, and unspecified assistantships available. Financial award application deadline: 3/1; financial award applicants required to submit FAFSA. *Unit head:* Dr. William Kamm, Director, 423-614-8544, E-mail: wkamm@leeuniversity.edu. *Application contact:* Jeffery McGirt, Director of Graduate Enrollment, 423-614-8691, Fax: 423-614-8317, E-mail: jmcgirt@leeuniversity.edu. Website: http://www.leeuniversity.edu/academics/graduate/education

Lehman College of the City University of New York, School of Arts and Humanities, Department of Languages and Literatures, Bronx, NY 10468-1589. Offers Spanish (MA). *Program availability:* Part-time, evening/weekend. *Degree requirements:* For master's, one foreign language. *Expenses: Tuition, area resident:* Full-time $5545; part-time $470 per credit. Tuition, nonresident: part-time $855 per credit. *Required fees:* $240.

Loyola University Chicago, Graduate School, Department of Modern Languages and Literatures, Chicago, IL 60660. Offers Spanish (MA). *Program availability:* Part-time, evening/weekend. *Faculty:* 7 full-time (3 women), 5 part-time/adjunct (3 women). *Students:* 3 full-time (2 women), 3 part-time (all women); includes 2 minority (both Hispanic/Latino). Average age 28. 10 applicants, 80% accepted, 3 enrolled. In 2019, 6 master's awarded. *Degree requirements:* For master's, one foreign language, comprehensive exam (for some programs), thesis or alternative. *Entrance requirements:* Additional exam requirements/recommendations for international students: required—TOEFL (minimum score 67 iBT), Oral Proficiency Interview in Spanish (for non-native speakers of Spanish). *Application deadline:* For fall admission, 2/10 for domestic students; for spring admission, 12/1 for domestic students. Application fee: $50. *Expenses: Tuition:* Full-time $18,540; part-time $1033 per credit hour. *Required fees:* $904; $230 per credit hour. *Financial support:* In 2019–20, 6 students received support, including 3 teaching assistantships (averaging $60,000 per year); tuition waivers (full and partial) also available. Financial award application deadline: 2/1. *Unit head:* Dr. Susan Cavallo, Chair, 773-508-2870, E-mail: scavall@luc.edu. *Application contact:* Dr. Susan Cavallo, Chair, 773-508-2870, E-mail: scavall@luc.edu. Website: http://www.luc.edu/modernlang

Manhattanville College, School of Education, Jump Start Program, Purchase, NY 10577-2132. Offers childhood education and special education (grades 1-6) (MPS); early childhood education (birth-grade 2) (MAT); education (Advanced Certificate); English and special education (grades 5-12) (MPS); mathematics and special education (grades 5-12) (MPS); science and special education (grades 5-12) (MPS); social studies and special education (grades 5-12) (MPS); Spanish (grades 7-12) (MAT); tesol - teaching English as a second language (all grades) (MPS). *Program availability:* Part-time, evening/weekend. *Faculty:* 5 full-time (all women), 12 part-time/adjunct (9 women). *Students:* 6 full-time (3 women), 37 part-time (28 women); includes 7 minority (2 Black or African American, non-Hispanic/Latino; 1 Asian, non-Hispanic/Latino; 3 Hispanic/Latino; 1 Native Hawaiian or other Pacific Islander, non-Hispanic/Latino). Average age 33. 23 applicants, 74% accepted, 14 enrolled. In 2019, 17 master's, 1 other advanced degree awarded. *Degree requirements:* For master's, comprehensive exam (for some programs), thesis (for some programs), student teaching, research seminars, portfolios, internships, writing assessment; for Advanced Certificate, comprehensive exam (for some programs). *Entrance requirements:* For master's, for programs leading to certification, candidates must submit scores from GRE or MAT(miller analogies test), minimum undergraduate GPA of 3.0, all transcripts from all colleges and universities attended, 2 letters of recommendation, interview, essay (2-3 page personal statement that describes reasons for choosing education as profession and personal philosophy of education), proof of immunization (for those born after 1957). Additional exam requirements/recommendations for international students: required—TOEFL or IELTS are required. Manhattanville College now accepts the Duolingo English Test with a required score of 105; recommended—TOEFL (minimum score 600 paper-based; 110 iBT), IELTS (minimum score 8). *Application deadline:* Applications are processed on a rolling basis. Application fee: $75. Electronic applications accepted. *Expenses:* $935 per credit, $45 technology fee, and $60 registration fee. *Financial support:* In 2019–20, 23 students received support. Teaching assistantships, institutionally sponsored loans, scholarships/grants, tuition waivers, and unspecified assistantships available. Financial award application deadline: 3/15; financial award applicants required to submit FAFSA. *Unit head:* Dr. Shelley Wepner, Dean, 914-323-3153, E-mail: Shelly.Wepner@mville.edu. *Application contact:* Alissa Wilson, Director, SOE Graduate Enrollment Management, 914-323-3150, Fax: 914-694-1732, E-mail: Alissa.Wilson@mville.edu.
Website: http://www.mville.edu/programs/jump-start

Manhattanville College, School of Education, Program in Teaching English to Speakers of Other Languages, Purchase, NY 10577-2132. Offers adult and international settings (MPS); bilingual education (childhood/Spanish) (Advanced Certificate); teaching English as a second language (all grades) (MPS, Certificate). *Program availability:* Part-time, evening/weekend. *Faculty:* 1 (woman) full-time, 5 part-time/adjunct (all women). *Students:* 4 full-time (all women), 17 part-time (12 women); includes 8 minority (1 Asian, non-Hispanic/Latino; 7 Hispanic/Latino). Average age 31. 5 applicants, 80% accepted, 4 enrolled. In 2019, 7 master's, 2 Advanced Certificates awarded. *Degree requirements:* For master's, comprehensive exam (for some programs), thesis (for some programs), student teaching, research seminars, portfolios, internships, writing assessment; for other advanced degree, comprehensive exam (for some programs). *Entrance requirements:* For master's, for programs leading to certification, candidates must submit scores from GRE or MAT(Miller Analogies Test), minimum undergraduate GPA of 3.0, all transcripts from all colleges and universities attended, 2 letters of recommendation, interview, essay (2-3 page personal statement that describes reasons for choosing education as profession and personal philosophy of education), proof of immunization (for those born after 1957). Additional exam requirements/ recommendations for international students: required—TOEFL or IELTS are required. Manhattanville College now accepts the Duolingo English Test with a required score of 105; recommended—TOEFL (minimum score 600 paper-based; 110 iBT), IELTS (minimum score 8). *Application deadline:* Applications are processed on a rolling basis. Application fee: $75. Electronic applications accepted. *Expenses:* $935 per credit, $45 technology fee, and $60 registration fee. *Financial support:* In 2019–20, 13 students received support. Teaching assistantships, scholarships/grants, tuition waivers, and unspecified assistantships available. Support available to part-time students. Financial award application deadline: 3/15; financial award applicants required to submit FAFSA. *Unit head:* Dr. Shelly Wepner, Dean, 914-323-3153, Fax: 914-323-5493, E-mail: Shelly.Wepner@mville.edu. *Application contact:* Alissa Wilson, Director, SOE Graduate Enrollment Management, 914-323-3150, Fax: 914-694-1732, E-mail: Alissa.Wilson@mville.edu.
Website: http://www.mville.edu/programs/tesol-teaching-english-speakers-other-languages

Marquette University, Graduate School, College of Arts and Sciences, Department of Foreign Languages and Literatures, Milwaukee, WI 53201-1881. Offers Spanish (MA). *Program availability:* Part-time, evening/weekend. *Degree requirements:* For master's, one foreign language, comprehensive exam. *Entrance requirements:* For master's, official transcripts from all current and previous colleges/universities except Marquette, three letters of recommendation, tape recording of foreign speaking voice. Additional exam requirements/recommendations for international students: required—TOEFL. Electronic applications accepted.

Miami University, College of Arts and Science, Department of Spanish and Portuguese, Oxford, OH 45056. Offers Spanish (MA). *Program availability:* Part-time. *Degree requirements:* For master's, thesis (for some programs), final exam. *Entrance requirements:* For master's, minimum undergraduate GPA of 3.0 during previous 2 years or 2.75 overall. Additional exam requirements/recommendations for international students: required—TOEFL (minimum score 550 paper-based), TWE (minimum score 4). Electronic applications accepted.

Michigan State University, The Graduate School, College of Arts and Letters, Department of Romance and Classical Studies, East Lansing, MI 48824. Offers French (MA); French language and literature (PhD); Hispanic cultural studies (PhD); Hispanic literatures (MA); Spanish as a second or bilingual language (MA). *Entrance requirements:* Additional exam requirements/recommendations for international students: required—TOEFL. Electronic applications accepted.

Middlebury College, Language Schools, Spanish School, Middlebury, VT 05753-6002. Offers MA, DML. In 2019, 40 master's awarded. *Degree requirements:* For master's, one foreign language; for doctorate, 2 foreign languages, comprehensive exam, thesis/ dissertation, residence abroad, teaching experience. *Entrance requirements:* For master's, online placement exam, 3 letters of recommendation, personal statement, transcripts, Spanish essay; for doctorate, 1st and 2nd language placement exams, 3 letters of recommendation, personal statement, transcripts, MA in Spanish. *Application deadline:* Applications are processed on a rolling basis. Application fee: $75. Electronic applications accepted. *Expenses:* Contact institution. *Financial support:* Fellowships and scholarships/grants available. Financial award application deadline: 3/8; financial award applicants required to submit FAFSA. *Unit head:* Dr. Jacobo Sefami, Director, 802-443-5539, Fax: 802-443-2075, E-mail: jsefami@middlebury.edu. *Application contact:* Audrey LaRock, Coordinator, 802-443-5539, Fax: 802-443-2075, E-mail: larock@middlebury.edu.
Website: http://www.middlebury.edu/ls/grad_programs/spanish

Middle Tennessee State University, College of Graduate Studies, College of Liberal Arts, Department of Foreign Languages and Literatures, Murfreesboro, TN 37132. Offers foreign languages (MAT), including French, German, Spanish. *Program availability:* Part-time, evening/weekend, online learning. *Degree requirements:* For master's, one foreign language, comprehensive exam, thesis optional. *Entrance requirements:* For master's, GRE. Additional exam requirements/recommendations for international students: required—TOEFL (minimum score 525 paper-based; 71 iBT) or IELTS (minimum score 6). Electronic applications accepted.

Millersville University of Pennsylvania, College of Graduate Studies and Adult Learning, College of Arts, Humanities and Social Sciences, Department of Language and Culture Studies, Millersville, PA 17551-0302. Offers languages and cultures (MA). *Program availability:* Part-time. *Faculty:* 3 full-time (2 women). *Students:* 4 part-time (all women); includes 2 minority (both Hispanic/Latino). Average age 31. 1 applicant. In 2019, 4 master's awarded. *Degree requirements:* For master's, Exit requirement: exam, portfolio, or research project/presentation. *Entrance requirements:* For master's, ACTFL (OPI and WPT), 24 undergraduate credits in selected language. Additional exam requirements/recommendations for international students: required—TOEFL, IELTS (minimum score 6), PTE (minimum score 60). *Application deadline:* Applications are processed on a rolling basis. Application fee: $40. Electronic applications accepted. *Expenses: Tuition, area resident:* Part-time $516 per credit. Tuition, state resident: part-time $516 per credit. Tuition, nonresident: part-time $774 per credit. *Required fees:* $118.75 per credit. Tuition and fees vary according to course load, degree level and program. *Financial support:* Scholarships/grants and unspecified assistantships available. Financial award application deadline: 3/15; financial award applicants required to submit FAFSA. *Unit head:* Dr. Christine M. Gaudry, Chair, 717-871-7152, E-mail: Christine.Gaudry@millersville.edu. *Application contact:* Dr. Susanne Nimmrichter, Graduate Coordinator, 717-871-7153, E-mail: susanne.nimmrichter@millersville.edu. Website: http://www.millersville.edu/languages

Millersville University of Pennsylvania, College of Graduate Studies and Adult Learning, College of Arts, Humanities and Social Sciences, Department of Language and Culture Studies, Language and Culture Studies: German Option, Millersville, PA 17551-0302. Offers language and cultures (MA). *Program availability:* Part-time-only. In 2019, 3 master's awarded. *Degree requirements:* For master's, Exit requirement: exam, portfolio, or research project/presentation. *Entrance requirements:* For master's, ACTFL (OPI and WPT), 24 undergraduate credits in selected language. Additional exam requirements/recommendations for international students: required—TOEFL, IELTS (minimum score 6), PTE (minimum score 60). *Application deadline:* Applications are processed on a rolling basis. Application fee: $40. Electronic applications accepted. *Expenses: Tuition, area resident:* Part-time $516 per credit. Tuition, state resident: part-time $516 per credit. Tuition, nonresident: part-time $774 per credit. *Required fees:* $118.75 per credit. Tuition and fees vary according to course load, degree level and program. *Financial support:* Scholarships/grants and unspecified assistantships available. Financial award application deadline: 3/15; financial award applicants required to submit FAFSA. *Unit head:* Dr. Christine M. Gaudry, Chair, 717-871-7156, E-mail: Christine.Gaudry@millersville.edu. *Application contact:* Dr. Susanne J. Nimmrichter, Graduate Coordinator, 717-871-7153, E-mail: Susanne.Nimmrichter@millersville.edu. Website: http://www.millersville.edu/languages

Minnesota State University Mankato, College of Graduate Studies and Research, College of Arts and Humanities, Department of World Languages and Cultures, Program in Spanish, Mankato, MN 56001. Offers Spanish (MS); Spanish education (MS); Spanish for the professions (MS). *Degree requirements:* For master's, one foreign language, comprehensive exam, thesis. *Entrance requirements:* For master's, minimum GPA of 3.0 during previous 2 years. Electronic applications accepted.

Montclair State University, The Graduate School, College of Education and Human Services, MAT Program in Teaching, Montclair, NJ 07043-1624. Offers art (MAT); biology (MAT); chemistry (MAT); earth science (MAT); English (MAT); French (MAT); health and physical education (MAT); health education (MAT); mathematics (MAT); music (MAT); physical education (MAT); physical science (MAT); social studies (MAT); Spanish (MAT); teacher of English as a second language (MAT). *Degree requirements:* For master's, comprehensive exam, thesis or alternative. *Entrance requirements:* For master's, interview, 2 letters of recommendation. Additional exam requirements/ recommendations for international students: required—TOEFL (minimum score 83 iBT), IELTS (minimum score 6.5). Electronic applications accepted.

Montclair State University, The Graduate School, College of Humanities and Social Sciences, Program in Spanish, Montclair, NJ 07043-1624. Offers MA. *Program availability:* Part-time, evening/weekend. *Degree requirements:* For master's, comprehensive exam, thesis or alternative. *Entrance requirements:* For master's, GRE General Test, 2 letters of recommendation, essay. Additional exam requirements/

recommendations for international students: required—TOEFL (minimum score 83 iBT), IELTS (minimum score 6.5). Electronic applications accepted.

New Mexico State University, College of Arts and Sciences, Department of Languages and Linguistics, Las Cruces, NM 88003-8001. Offers Spanish (MA). *Program availability:* Part-time, 100% online. *Faculty:* 11 full-time (6 women). *Students:* 11 full-time (7 women), 8 part-time (5 women); includes 12 minority (all Hispanic/Latino), 4 international. Average age 35. 14 applicants, 100% accepted, 6 enrolled. In 2019, 26 master's awarded. *Degree requirements:* For master's, one foreign language, comprehensive exam, thesis optional, oral or written exams. *Entrance requirements:* For master's, sample of written work in Spanish, 3 letters of reference, language evaluation form (or OPI score), letter of intent. Additional exam requirements/recommendations for international students: required—TOEFL (minimum score 550 paper-based; 79 iBT), IELTS (minimum score 6.5). *Application deadline:* For fall admission, 1/15 for domestic students; for spring admission, 9/15 for domestic students. Applications are processed on a rolling basis. Application fee: $40 ($50 for international students). Electronic applications accepted. *Financial support:* In 2019–20, 11 students received support, including 10 teaching assistantships (averaging $15,094 per year); career-related internships or fieldwork, Federal Work-Study, institutionally sponsored loans, scholarships/grants, traineeships, health care benefits, and unspecified assistantships also available. Support available to part-time students. Financial award application deadline: 3/1. *Unit head:* Dr. Glenn Fetzer, Department Head, 575-646-3408, E-mail: gwfetzer@nmsu.edu. *Application contact:* Dr. Jeff Longwell, Graduate Program Director, 575-646-2726, E-mail: jelongwe@nmsu.edu.
Website: http://www.nmsu.edu/~langling/

New York University, Graduate School of Arts and Science, Department of Spanish and Portuguese Languages and Literatures, New York, NY 10012-1019. Offers Portuguese (MA, PhD); Spanish (PhD); Spanish and Latin American literatures and cultures (MA); Spanish language and translation (MA). *Program availability:* Part-time. *Degree requirements:* For master's, 2 foreign languages, thesis; for doctorate, 2 foreign languages, thesis/dissertation. *Entrance requirements:* For master's, GRE General Test; for doctorate, GRE General Test, master's degree. Additional exam requirements/ recommendations for international students: required—TOEFL, IELTS.

New York University, Steinhardt School of Culture, Education, and Human Development, Department of Teaching and Learning, Program in Multilingual/ Multicultural Studies, New York, NY 10012. Offers bilingual education (MA, PhD, Advanced Certificate); foreign language education (MA); teaching English to speakers of other languages (MA, PhD); teaching foreign languages, 7-12 (MA), including Chinese, French, Italian, Japanese, Spanish; teaching French as a foreign language (MA), including teaching English to speakers of other languages; teaching Spanish as a foreign language (MA), including teaching English to speakers of other languages. *Accreditation:* TEAC. *Program availability:* Part-time, evening/weekend. *Entrance requirements:* For doctorate, GRE General Test, interview; for Advanced Certificate, master's degree. Additional exam requirements/recommendations for international students: required—TOEFL (minimum score 100 iBT). Electronic applications accepted.

North Carolina State University, Graduate School, College of Humanities and Social Sciences, Department of Foreign Languages and Literatures, Program in Spanish Language and Literature, Raleigh, NC 27695. Offers MA. *Degree requirements:* For master's, thesis optional. *Entrance requirements:* For master's, fluency in Spanish. Electronic applications accepted.

Northern Arizona University, College of Arts and Letters, Department of Global Languages and Cultures, Flagstaff, AZ 86011. Offers Spanish (MAT); Spanish education (MAT). *Program availability:* Part-time. *Degree requirements:* For master's, variable foreign language requirement, comprehensive exam (for some programs), thesis (for some programs). *Entrance requirements:* Additional exam requirements/ recommendations for international students: required—TOEFL (minimum score 80 iBT), IELTS (minimum score 7). Electronic applications accepted.

Northern Illinois University, Graduate School, College of Liberal Arts and Sciences, World Languages & Cultures, De Kalb, IL 60115-2854. Offers French (MA); Spanish (MA). *Program availability:* Part-time. *Faculty:* 25 full-time (11 women). *Students:* 1 (woman) full-time, 12 part-time (9 women); includes 8 minority (1 Black or African American, non-Hispanic/Latino; 7 Hispanic/Latino), 1 international. Average age 35. 3 applicants, 67% accepted, 1 enrolled. In 2019, 1 master's awarded. *Degree requirements:* For master's, one foreign language, comprehensive exam, thesis or alternative, language proficiency exam. *Entrance requirements:* For master's, GRE General Test, interview, minimum GPA of 2.75, undergraduate major in French or Spanish. Additional exam requirements/recommendations for international students: required—TOEFL (minimum score 550 paper-based). *Application deadline:* For fall admission, 6/1 for domestic students, 5/1 for international students; for spring admission, 11/1 for domestic students, 10/1 for international students. Applications are processed on a rolling basis. Application fee: $40. Electronic applications accepted. *Financial support:* In 2019–20, 7 teaching assistantships with full tuition reimbursements were awarded; fellowships with full tuition reimbursements, research assistantships with full tuition reimbursements, career-related internships or fieldwork, Federal Work-Study, scholarships/grants, tuition waivers (full), and unspecified assistantships also available. Support available to part-time students. Financial award applicants required to submit FAFSA. *Unit head:* Dr. John Bentley, Chair, 815-753-1559, Fax: 815-753-5989. *Application contact:* Graduate School Office, 815-753-0395, E-mail: gradsch@niu.edu.
Website: http://www.forlangs.net/

Northwestern University, The Graduate School, Judd A. and Marjorie Weinberg College of Arts and Sciences, Department of Spanish and Portuguese, Evanston, IL 60208. Offers PhD.

The Ohio State University, Graduate School, College of Arts and Sciences, Division of Arts and Humanities, Department of Spanish and Portuguese, Columbus, OH 43210. Offers MA, PhD. Terminal master's awarded for partial completion of doctoral program. *Entrance requirements:* For master's and doctorate, GRE General Test, sample of academic writing. Additional exam requirements/recommendations for international students: required—TOEFL (minimum score 550 paper-based; 79 iBT), Michigan English Language Assessment Battery (minimum score 82); recommended—IELTS (minimum score 7). Electronic applications accepted.

Ohio University, Graduate College, College of Arts and Sciences, Department of Modern Languages, Athens, OH 45701-2979. Offers French (MA); Spanish (MA). *Program availability:* Part-time. *Degree requirements:* For master's, 2 foreign languages, comprehensive exam, thesis optional. *Entrance requirements:* For master's, oral and written samples. Additional exam requirements/recommendations for international students: required—TOEFL (minimum score 550 paper-based; 80 iBT) or IELTS (minimum score 6.5). Electronic applications accepted.

Penn State University Park, Graduate School, College of the Liberal Arts, Department of Spanish, Italian, and Portuguese, University Park, PA 16802. Offers Spanish (MA, PhD).

Pontifical Catholic University of Puerto Rico, College of Arts and Humanities, Department of Hispanic Studies, Ponce, PR 00717-0777. Offers grammar and writing (Professional Certificate); Hispanic studies (MA). *Program availability:* Part-time, evening/weekend. *Degree requirements:* For master's, variable foreign language requirement, comprehensive exam, thesis or alternative. *Entrance requirements:* For master's, GRE General Test, 2 letters of recommendation, interview, minimum GPA of 2.75. Electronic applications accepted.

Portland State University, Graduate Studies, College of Liberal Arts and Sciences, Department of World Languages and Literatures, Portland, OR 97207-0751. Offers French (MA); German (MA); Japanese (MA); Spanish (MA); world literature and language (MA). *Program availability:* Part-time. *Faculty:* 40 full-time (22 women), 39 part-time/adjunct (32 women). *Students:* 16 full-time (11 women), 12 part-time (6 women); includes 9 minority (2 Asian, non-Hispanic/Latino; 6 Hispanic/Latino; 1 Two or more races, non-Hispanic/Latino), 8 international. Average age 34. 14 applicants, 64% accepted, 7 enrolled. In 2019, 14 master's awarded. *Degree requirements:* For master's, variable foreign language requirement, thesis (for some programs). *Entrance requirements:* For master's, ACTFL, BA in the major language, minimum GPA of 3.0 in all coursework. Additional exam requirements/recommendations for international students: required—TOEFL (minimum score 550 paper-based; 80 iBT), IELTS (minimum score 6.5). *Application deadline:* For fall admission, 4/1 for domestic students, 3/1 for international students; for winter admission, 9/1 for domestic students, 7/1 for international students; for spring admission, 11/1 for domestic and international students. Applications are processed on a rolling basis. Application fee: $65. *Expenses: Tuition, area resident:* Full-time $13,020; part-time $6510 per year. Tuition, state resident: full-time $13,020; part-time $6510 per year. Tuition, nonresident: full-time $19,830; part-time $9915 per year. *International tuition:* $19,830 full-time. *Required fees:* $1226. One-time fee: $350. Tuition and fees vary according to course load, program and reciprocity agreements. *Financial support:* In 2019–20, 16 teaching assistantships with full and partial tuition reimbursements (averaging $16,549 per year) were awarded; research assistantships, Federal Work-Study, scholarships/grants, and unspecified assistantships also available. Support available to part-time students. Financial award application deadline: 3/1; financial award applicants required to submit FAFSA. *Unit head:* Dr. Gina Greco, Chair, 503-725-5287, E-mail: grecog@pdx.edu. *Application contact:* Kelli Martin, Graduate Admissions Specialist, 503-725-3243, E-mail: k.martin@pdx.edu.
Website: http://www.pdx.edu/wll/

Princeton University, Graduate School, Department of Spanish and Portuguese, Princeton, NJ 08544-1019. Offers PhD. *Degree requirements:* For doctorate, variable foreign language requirement, thesis/dissertation. *Entrance requirements:* For doctorate, GRE General Test, sample of written work. Additional exam requirements/ recommendations for international students: required—TOEFL (minimum score 600 paper-based). Electronic applications accepted.

Purdue University, Graduate School, College of Liberal Arts, School of Languages and Cultures, West Lafayette, IN 47907. Offers French (MA, MAT), including multiple possible; German (MA, MAT), including multiple possible; Japanese pedagogy (MA), including pedagogy, SLA; Spanish (MA, MAT), including multiple possible. *Faculty:* 32 full-time (16 women), 6 part-time/adjunct (3 women). *Students:* 33 full-time (18 women), 24 part-time (16 women); includes 7 minority (1 Black or African American, non-Hispanic/Latino; 6 Hispanic/Latino), 38 international. Average age 34. 54 applicants, 41% accepted, 14 enrolled. In 2019, 9 master's awarded. Terminal master's awarded for partial completion of doctoral program. *Degree requirements:* For master's, one foreign language. *Entrance requirements:* For master's, Bachelor of Arts (or equivalent); 3 letters of recommendation; statement of purpose; speaking & writing samples. Additional exam requirements/recommendations for international students: required—TOEFL (minimum score 550 paper-based; 77 iBT); recommended—TWE. *Application deadline:* For fall admission, 12/12 for domestic and international students; for spring admission, 10/1 for domestic and international students. Applications are processed on a rolling basis. Application fee: $60 ($75 for international students). Electronic applications accepted. *Financial support:* In 2019–20, fellowships with tuition reimbursements (averaging $15,750 per year), teaching assistantships with tuition reimbursements (averaging $13,463 per year) were awarded. Support available to part-time students. Financial award applicants required to submit FAFSA. *Unit head:* Jennifer M. William, Head, 765-494-3834, E-mail: jmwilliam@purdue.edu. *Application contact:* Joni L. Hipsher, Graduate Contact, 765-494-3841, E-mail: jlhipshe@purdue.edu.
Website: http://www.cla.purdue.edu/slc/main/

Queens College of the City University of New York, Arts and Humanities Division, Department of Hispanic Languages and Literatures, Queens, NY 11367-1597. Offers Spanish (MA). *Program availability:* Part-time. *Degree requirements:* For master's, 2 foreign languages, thesis optional. *Entrance requirements:* For master's, minimum GPA of 3.0. Additional exam requirements/recommendations for international students: required—TOEFL (minimum score 61 iBT). Electronic applications accepted.

Rutgers University - New Brunswick, Graduate School-New Brunswick, Program in Spanish, Piscataway, NJ 08854-8097. Offers bilingualism and second language acquisition (MA, PhD); Spanish (MA, MAT, PhD); Spanish literature (MA, PhD); translation (MA). *Program availability:* Part-time. *Degree requirements:* For master's, comprehensive exam (for some programs), thesis (for some programs); for doctorate, 2 foreign languages, comprehensive exam, thesis/dissertation. *Entrance requirements:* For master's and doctorate, GRE General Test. Additional exam requirements/ recommendations for international students: required—TOEFL. Electronic applications accepted.

St. John's University, St. John's College of Liberal Arts and Sciences, Department of Languages and Literatures, Queens, NY 11439. Offers Spanish (MA). *Program availability:* Part-time, evening/weekend. *Degree requirements:* For master's, comprehensive exam, thesis optional. *Entrance requirements:* For master's, letters of recommendation, transcripts, resume, personal statement, 24 prerequisite credits in history. Additional exam requirements/recommendations for international students: required—TOEFL (minimum score 80 iBT), IELTS (minimum score 6.5). Electronic applications accepted.

Saint Louis University, Graduate Programs, College of Arts and Sciences, Department of Languages, Literatures, and Cultures, St. Louis, MO 63103. Offers French (MA); Spanish (MA). *Program availability:* Part-time. *Degree requirements:* For master's, one foreign language, comprehensive exam, thesis/dissertation (Spanish). *Entrance requirements:* For master's, GRE General Test or MAT, letters of recommendation, resume, interview. Additional exam requirements/recommendations for international students: required—TOEFL (minimum score 525 paper-based). Electronic applications accepted.

Saint Louis University–Madrid Campus, Graduate Programs, Master of Arts in Spanish Program, Madrid, Spain. Offers MA. *Program availability:* Part-time. *Degree requirements:* For master's, one foreign language, comprehensive exam, thesis optional. *Entrance requirements:* For master's, GRE General Test or MAT, 3 letters of recommendation, curriculum vitae, writing sample, interview. Additional exam requirements/recommendations for international students: required—TOEFL. Electronic applications accepted.

Saint Xavier University, Graduate Studies, School of Education, Chicago, IL 60655-3105. Offers counseling (MA); curriculum and instruction (MA); early childhood education (MA); educational administration (MA); elementary education (MA); individualized studies (MA), including educational technology, English as a second language (ESL), ISTEM (integrative science, technology, engineering, and math), science education; music education (MA); reading (MA); secondary education (MA); Spanish education (MA); special education (MA); teaching and leadership (MA). *Accreditation:* NCATE. *Program availability:* Part-time, evening/weekend. *Degree requirements:* For master's, thesis or project. *Entrance requirements:* For master's, minimum GPA of 3.0. *Expenses:* Contact institution.

Salem State University, School of Graduate Studies, Program in Spanish, Salem, MA 01970-5353. Offers MAT. *Program availability:* Part-time, evening/weekend. *Entrance requirements:* For master's, GRE or MAT. Additional exam requirements/recommendations for international students: required—TOEFL (minimum score 550 paper-based; 80 iBT) or IELTS (minimum score 5.5).

Sam Houston State University, College of Humanities and Social Sciences, Department of Foreign Languages, Huntsville, TX 77341. Offers Spanish (MA). *Program availability:* Part-time. *Degree requirements:* For master's, comprehensive exam, thesis (for some programs). *Entrance requirements:* For master's, GRE General Test, writing sample, letters of recommendation. Additional exam requirements/recommendations for international students: required—TOEFL (minimum score 550 paper-based; 79 iBT), IELTS (minimum score 6.5). Electronic applications accepted.

San Diego State University, Graduate and Research Affairs, College of Arts and Letters, Department of Spanish and Portuguese, San Diego, CA 92182. Offers Spanish (MA). *Degree requirements:* For master's, one foreign language. *Entrance requirements:* For master's, GRE General Test, 3 letters of reference. Additional exam requirements/recommendations for international students: required—TOEFL. Electronic applications accepted.

San Francisco State University, Division of Graduate Studies, College of Liberal and Creative Arts, Department of Modern Languages and Literatures, Program in Spanish, San Francisco, CA 94132-1722. Offers MA. *Program availability:* Part-time. *Application deadline:* Applications are processed on a rolling basis. Electronic applications accepted. *Expenses: Tuition, area resident:* Full-time $7176; part-time $4164 per year. Tuition, state resident: full-time $7176; part-time $4164 per year. Tuition, nonresident: full-time $16,680; part-time $396 per unit. *International tuition:* $16,680 full-time. *Required fees:* $1524; $1524 per unit. $762 per semester. Tuition and fees vary according to degree level and program. *Financial support:* Unspecified assistantships available. *Unit head:* Prof. Michael Hammer, Program Coordinator, 415-338-1658, Fax: 415-338-6159, E-mail: mhammer@sfsu.edu. *Application contact:* Prof. Ana Luengo Palomino, Graduate Advisor, 415-338-7796, Fax: 415-338-6159, E-mail: aluengo@sfsu.edu.
Website: http://mll.sfsu.edu/spanish-program/

Southern Oregon University, Graduate Studies, Department of Foreign Languages and Literatures, Ashland, OR 97520. Offers French language teaching (MA); Spanish language teaching (MA). *Program availability:* Part-time, online learning. *Degree requirements:* For master's, thesis (for some programs). *Entrance requirements:* For master's, GRE General Test, minimum cumulative GPA of 3.0 in the last 90 quarter credits (60 semester credits) of undergraduate coursework. Additional exam requirements/recommendations for international students: required—TOEFL (minimum score 540 paper-based; 76 iBT), IELTS (minimum score 6), ELPT (minimum score 964) or ELS (minimum score 112). Electronic applications accepted.

Stanford University, School of Humanities and Sciences, Department of Iberian and Latin American Cultures, Stanford, CA 94305-2004. Offers Spanish (MA). *Expenses: Tuition:* Full-time $52,479; part-time $34,110 per unit. *Required fees:* $672; $224 per quarter. Tuition and fees vary according to program and student level.
Website: https://dlcl.stanford.edu/departments/iberian-and-latin-american-cultures/about

State University of New York at New Paltz, Graduate and Extended Learning School, School of Education, Department of Teaching and Learning, New Paltz, NY 12561. Offers adolescence education: biology (MAT, MS Ed); adolescence education: chemistry (MAT, MS Ed); adolescence education: earth science (MAT, MS Ed); adolescence education: English (MAT, MS Ed); adolescence education: French (MAT, MS Ed); adolescence education: social studies (MAT, MS Ed); adolescence education: Spanish (MAT, MS Ed); second language education (MS Ed, AC), including second language education (MS Ed), teaching English language learners (AC). *Accreditation:* NCATE. *Program availability:* Part-time, evening/weekend. *Faculty:* 11 full-time (5 women), 9 part-time/adjunct (5 women). *Students:* 36 full-time (19 women), 22 part-time (6 women); includes 7 minority (1 Black or African American, non-Hispanic/Latino; 5 Hispanic/Latino; 1 Two or more races, non-Hispanic/Latino). 56 applicants, 61% accepted, 19 enrolled. In 2019, 28 master's awarded. *Degree requirements:* For master's, comprehensive exam (for some programs), portfolio. *Entrance requirements:* For master's, minimum GPA of 3.0, New York state teaching certificate (MS Ed). Additional exam requirements/recommendations for international students: required—TOEFL (minimum score 550 paper-based; 80 iBT), IELTS (minimum score 6.5). *Application deadline:* For fall admission, 3/1 priority date for domestic students, 3/1 for international students; for spring admission, 10/1 priority date for domestic students, 10/1 for international students. Application fee: $50. Electronic applications accepted. *Expenses: Tuition, area resident:* Full-time $11,310; part-time $471 per credit. Tuition, state resident: full-time $11,310; part-time $471 per credit. Tuition, nonresident: full-time $23,100; part-time $963 per credit. *International tuition:* $23,100 full-time. *Required fees:* $1432; $41.83 per credit. *Financial support:* Application deadline: 8/1. *Unit head:* Dr. Aaron Isabelle, Associate Dean, 845-257-2837, E-mail: isabella@newpaltz.edu. *Application contact:* Vika Shock, Director of Graduate Admissions, 845-257-3285, Fax: 845-257-3284, E-mail: gradstudies@newpaltz.edu.
Website: http://www.newpaltz.edu/secondaryed/

State University of New York College at Geneseo, Graduate Studies, School of Education, Program in Adolescence Education, Geneseo, NY 14454. Offers English 7-12 (MS Ed); French 7-12 (MS Ed); social studies 7-12 (MS Ed); Spanish 7-12 (MS Ed). *Program availability:* Part-time, evening/weekend. *Faculty:* 7 full-time (5 women), 1 part-time/adjunct (0 women). *Students:* 2 full-time (1 woman), 1 (woman) part-time. Average age 29. 10 applicants, 40% accepted, 2 enrolled. In 2019, 3 master's awarded. *Degree requirements:* For master's, 2 foreign languages, comprehensive examination, thesis or research project. *Entrance requirements:* For master's, GRE, MAT, EAS, edTPA, PRAXIS, or another substantially equivalent test, proof of New York State initial certification or equivalent certification from another state. Additional exam requirements/recommendations for international students: required—TOEFL (minimum score 550 paper-based; 80 iBT), IELTS (minimum score 6.5), PTE. *Application deadline:* For fall admission, 4/1 priority date for domestic students; for spring admission, 11/1 priority date for domestic students; for summer admission, 4/1 priority date for domestic students. Applications are processed on a rolling basis. Application fee: $50. Electronic applications accepted. *Expenses:* Contact institution. *Financial support:* In 2019–20, 3 students received support. Fellowships, research assistantships, scholarships/grants,

health care benefits, tuition waivers (full and partial), and unspecified assistantships available. Support available to part-time students. Financial award application deadline: 4/1; financial award applicants required to submit FAFSA. *Unit head:* Dr. Dennis Showers, Interim Dean of School of Education, 585-245-5264, Fax: 585-245-5220, E-mail: showers@geneseo.edu. *Application contact:* Michael R. George, Director of Graduate Admissions, 585-245-5148, Fax: 585-245-5550, E-mail: georgem@geneseo.edu.
Website: https://www.geneseo.edu/education/graduate-programs-education

Syracuse University, College of Arts and Sciences, MA Program in Spanish Literature and Culture, Syracuse, NY 13244. Offers MA. *Program availability:* Part-time. *Degree requirements:* For master's, comprehensive exam, thesis (for some programs). *Entrance requirements:* For master's, GRE General Test, official transcripts, resume, three letters of recommendation. Additional exam requirements/recommendations for international students: required—TOEFL (minimum score 100 iBT). Electronic applications accepted.

Temple University, College of Liberal Arts, Department of Spanish and Portuguese, Philadelphia, PA 19122-6096. Offers Spanish (MA, PhD). *Program availability:* Part-time, evening/weekend, online learning. *Faculty:* 14 full-time (6 women), 12 part-time/adjunct (10 women). *Students:* 34 full-time (22 women), 4 part-time (2 women); includes 11 minority (2 Asian, non-Hispanic/Latino; 9 Hispanic/Latino), 15 international. 37 applicants, 43% accepted, 14 enrolled. In 2019, 5 master's, 7 doctorates awarded. *Degree requirements:* For master's, one foreign language, comprehensive exam; for doctorate, 2 foreign languages, thesis/dissertation. *Entrance requirements:* For master's, GRE (applicants from Spanish-speaking countries may present EXADEP scores instead), writing sample, statement of goals, 3 letters of recommendation; for doctorate, GRE. Applicants from Spanish-speaking countries may present EXADEP scores instead, writing sample, statement of goals, 3 letters of recommendation. Additional exam requirements/recommendations for international students: required—TOEFL, IELTS, PTE. *Application deadline:* For fall admission, 1/15 for domestic students; for spring admission, 9/30 for domestic students. Applications are processed on a rolling basis. Application fee: $60. Electronic applications accepted. *Financial support:* Teaching assistantships, Federal Work-Study, and health care benefits available. Financial award applicants required to submit FAFSA. *Unit head:* Hiram Aldarondo, Chair, 215-204-0134, E-mail: haldaron@temple.edu. *Application contact:* Annette Vega, Coordinator, 215-204-2877, E-mail: avega1@temple.edu.
Website: http://www.cla.temple.edu/spanpor/

Texas A&M University, College of Liberal Arts, Department of Hispanic Studies, College Station, TX 77843. Offers Hispanic studies (PhD). *Faculty:* 13. *Students:* 18 full-time (10 women), 14 part-time (10 women); includes 21 minority (all Hispanic/Latino), 6 international. Average age 39. 5 applicants, 100% accepted, 4 enrolled. In 2019, 5 doctorates awarded. *Degree requirements:* For master's, comprehensive exam (for some programs), thesis optional; for doctorate, comprehensive exam, thesis/dissertation. *Entrance requirements:* For master's and doctorate, letters of recommendation, writing sample, curriculum vitae. Additional exam requirements/recommendations for international students: required—TOEFL (minimum score 550 paper-based; 80 iBT), IELTS (minimum score 6), PTE (minimum score 53). *Application deadline:* For fall admission, 1/31 priority date for domestic students. Application fee: $65 ($90 for international students). Electronic applications accepted. *Expenses:* Contact institution. *Financial support:* In 2019–20, 19 students received support, including 2 fellowships with tuition reimbursements available (averaging $20,500 per year), 17 teaching assistantships with tuition reimbursements available (averaging $17,038 per year); career-related internships or fieldwork, institutionally sponsored loans, scholarships/grants, traineeships, health care benefits, tuition waivers (full and partial), and unspecified assistantships also available. Support available to part-time students. Financial award application deadline: 3/15; financial award applicants required to submit FAFSA. *Unit head:* Dr. Richard Curry, Department Head, 979-845-2109, E-mail: r-curry@tamu.edu. *Application contact:* Dr. Maria Esther Quintana Millamoto, Director of Graduate Studies, E-mail: mequintana@tamu.edu.
Website: https://liberalarts.tamu.edu/hisp/

Texas A&M University–Commerce, College of Humanities, Social Sciences and Arts, Commerce, TX 75429. Offers applied criminology (MS); applied linguistics (MA, MS); art (MA, MFA); christianity in history (Graduate Certificate); computational linguistics (Graduate Certificate); creative writing (Graduate Certificate); criminal justice management (Graduate Certificate); criminal justice studies (Graduate Certificate); English (MA, MS, PhD); film studies (Graduate Certificate); history (MA, MS); Holocaust studies (Graduate Certificate); homeland security (Graduate Certificate); music (MM); music performance (MM); political science (MA, MS); public history (Graduate Certificate); sociology (MS); Spanish (MA); studies in children's and adolescent literature and culture (Graduate Certificate); teaching English to speakers of other languages (Graduate Certificate); theater (MA, MS); world history (Graduate Certificate). *Program availability:* Part-time. *Faculty:* 49 full-time (28 women), 8 part-time/adjunct (2 women). *Students:* 34 full-time (21 women), 427 part-time (302 women); includes 175 minority (66 Black or African American, non-Hispanic/Latino; 1 American Indian or Alaska Native, non-Hispanic/Latino; 13 Asian, non-Hispanic/Latino; 79 Hispanic/Latino; 16 Two or more races, non-Hispanic/Latino), 15 international. Average age 38. 193 applicants, 49% accepted, 78 enrolled. In 2019, 122 master's, 6 doctorates awarded. *Degree requirements:* For master's, one foreign language, comprehensive exam, thesis (for some programs); for doctorate, one foreign language, comprehensive exam, thesis/dissertation, departmental qualifying exam. *Entrance requirements:* For master's, GRE General Test, official transcripts, letters of recommendation, resume, statement of goals; for doctorate, GRE General Test, official transcripts, letters of recommendation, statement of goals, writing samples, writing sessions, resumes. Additional exam requirements/recommendations for international students: required—TOEFL (minimum score 550 paper-based; 79 iBT), IELTS (minimum score 6), PTE (minimum score 53). *Application deadline:* For fall admission, 6/1 priority date for international students; for spring admission, 10/15 priority date for international students; for summer admission, 3/15 priority date for international students. Applications are processed on a rolling basis. Application fee: $50 ($75 for international students). Electronic applications accepted. *Expenses: Tuition, area resident:* Full-time $3630; part-time $202 per credit hour. Tuition, state resident: full-time $3630; part-time $202 per credit hour. Tuition, nonresident: full-time $11,232; part-time $624 per credit hour. *International tuition:* $11,232 full-time. *Required fees:* $2948. *Financial support:* In 2019–20, 30 students received support, including 18 research assistantships with partial tuition reimbursements available (averaging $3,231 per year), 136 teaching assistantships with partial tuition reimbursements available (averaging $4,053 per year); Federal Work-Study, institutionally sponsored loans, scholarships/grants, health care benefits, and unspecified assistantships also available. Financial award application deadline: 5/1; financial award applicants required to submit FAFSA. *Unit head:* Dr. William F. Kuracina, Interim Dean, 903-886-5166, Fax: 903-886-5774, E-mail: william.kuracina@tamuc.edu. *Application contact:* Rebecca Stevens, Graduate Student Services Coordinator, 903-468-6049, E-mail: rebecca.stevens@tamuc.edu.
Website: http://www.tamuc.edu/academics/colleges/humanitiesSocialSciencesArts/

Texas A&M University–Kingsville, College of Graduate Studies, College of Arts and Sciences, Department of Language and Literature, Kingsville, TX 78363. Offers cultural studies (MA); English (MA, MS); Spanish (MA). *Entrance requirements:* Additional exam requirements/recommendations for international students: required—TOEFL (minimum score 550 paper-based; 79 iBT); recommended—IELTS. Electronic applications accepted.

Texas State University, The Graduate College, College of Liberal Arts, Program in Spanish, San Marcos, TX 78666. Offers MA. *Program availability:* Part-time, evening/weekend. *Degree requirements:* For master's, one foreign language, comprehensive exam, thesis optional. *Entrance requirements:* For master's, baccalaureate degree from regionally-accredited university with minimum GPA of 2.75 on last 60 undergraduate semester hours, 3.0 in 12 hours in Spanish; statement of purpose written in Spanish; resume including contact information for 2 references. Additional exam requirements/recommendations for international students: required—TOEFL (minimum score 550 paper-based; 78 iBT), IELTS (minimum score 6.5). Electronic applications accepted.

Texas Tech University, Graduate School, College of Arts and Sciences, Department of Classical and Modern Languages and Literatures, Lubbock, TX 79409-2071. Offers languages and cultures (MA); Romance languages (MA); Spanish (PhD); MBA/MA. *Program availability:* Part-time. *Faculty:* 54 full-time (34 women), 1 (woman) part-time/adjunct. *Students:* 72 full-time (38 women), 15 part-time (12 women); includes 28 minority (1 Asian, non-Hispanic/Latino; 24 Hispanic/Latino; 3 Two or more races, non-Hispanic/Latino), 33 international. Average age 33. 57 applicants, 68% accepted, 28 enrolled. In 2019, 28 master's, 2 doctorates awarded. *Degree requirements:* For master's, comprehensive exam, thesis or alternative; for doctorate, comprehensive exam, thesis/dissertation. *Entrance requirements:* Additional exam requirements/recommendations for international students: required—TOEFL (minimum score 550 paper-based; 79 iBT). *Application deadline:* For fall admission, 6/1 priority date for domestic students, 1/15 priority date for international students; for spring admission, 9/1 priority date for domestic students, 6/15 priority date for international students. Applications are processed on a rolling basis. Application fee: $65. Electronic applications accepted. *Expenses:* Contact institution. *Financial support:* In 2019–20, 83 students received support, including 52 fellowships (averaging $2,880 per year), 76 teaching assistantships (averaging $13,880 per year); research assistantships, Federal Work-Study, scholarships/grants, and unspecified assistantships also available. Financial award application deadline: 4/15; financial award applicants required to submit FAFSA. *Unit head:* Dr. Carmen Pereira-Muro, Department Chair, 806-834-0151, Fax: 806-742-3306, E-mail: carmen.pereira@ttu.edu. *Application contact:* Carla Burrus, Senior Advisor, 806-834-3282, Fax: 806-742-3306, E-mail: carla.burrus@ttu.edu.
Website: www.depts.ttu.edu/classic_modern/

Tulane University, School of Liberal Arts, Department of Spanish and Portuguese, New Orleans, LA 70118-5669. Offers Portuguese (MA); Spanish and Portuguese (PhD). *Degree requirements:* For master's, 2 foreign languages; for doctorate, 2 foreign languages, thesis/dissertation. *Entrance requirements:* For master's, GRE General Test, minimum B average in undergraduate course work; for doctorate, GRE General Test. Additional exam requirements/recommendations for international students: required—TOEFL. Electronic applications accepted. *Expenses: Tuition:* Full-time $57,004; part-time $3167 per credit hour. *Required fees:* $2086; $44.50 per credit hour. $80 per term. Tuition and fees vary according to course load, degree level and program.

Universidad Autonoma de Guadalajara, Graduate Programs, Guadalajara, Mexico. Offers administrative law and justice (LL M); advertising and corporate communications (MA); architecture (M Arch); business (MBA); computational science (MCC); education (Ed M, Ed D); English-Spanish translation (MA); entrepreneurship and management (MBA); integrated management of digital animation (MA); international business (MIB); international corporate law (LL M); Internet technologies (MS); manufacturing systems (MMS); occupational health (MS); philosophy (MA, PhD); power electronics (MS); quality systems (MQS); renewable energy (MS); social evaluation of projects (MBA); strategic market research (MBA); tax law (MA); teaching mathematics (MA).

Université de Montréal, Faculty of Arts and Sciences, Department of Literatures and Modern Languages, Program in Hispanic Studies, Montréal, QC H3C 3J7, Canada. Offers MA. *Degree requirements:* For master's, 2 foreign languages, thesis. Electronic applications accepted.

University at Albany, State University of New York, College of Arts and Sciences, Department of Languages, Literatures, and Cultures, Albany, NY 12222-0001. Offers Spanish (MA, PhD). *Program availability:* Blended/hybrid learning. *Faculty:* 13 full-time (9 women), 13 part-time/adjunct (9 women). *Students:* 24 full-time (12 women), 20 part-time (12 women); includes 18 minority (all Hispanic/Latino), 3 international. 19 applicants, 84% accepted, 8 enrolled. In 2019, 2 master's, 1 doctorate awarded. *Degree requirements:* For doctorate, thesis/dissertation. *Entrance requirements:* For master's and doctorate, transcripts of all schools attended, statement of background and goals, departmental questionnaire, resume, names and contact information for 3 recommenders. Additional exam requirements/recommendations for international students: required—TOEFL (minimum score 550 paper-based). *Application deadline:* For fall admission, 7/15 for domestic students, 5/1 for international students; for spring admission, 11/15 for domestic students. Application fee: $75. Electronic applications accepted. *Expenses: Tuition, area resident:* Full-time $11,530; part-time $480 per credit hour. Tuition, nonresident: full-time $23,530; part-time $980 per credit hour. *International tuition:* $23,530 full-time. *Required fees:* $2185; $96 per credit hour. Part-time tuition and fees vary according to course load and program. *Financial support:* Teaching assistantships available. *Unit head:* Cynthia Fox, Chair, 518-442-4222, Fax: 518-442-4111, E-mail: cfox@albany.edu. *Application contact:* Michael DeRensis, Director, Graduate Admissions, 518-442-3980, Fax: 518-442-3922, E-mail: graduate@albany.edu.
Website: https://www.albany.edu/llc/

University at Buffalo, the State University of New York, Graduate School, College of Arts and Sciences, Department of Romance Languages and Literatures, Buffalo, NY 14260-4620. Offers French (MA, PhD); Spanish (MA, PhD). *Program availability:* Part-time. Terminal master's awarded for partial completion of doctoral program. *Degree requirements:* For master's, 2 foreign languages, comprehensive exam, thesis (for some programs); for doctorate, 2 foreign languages, comprehensive exam, thesis/dissertation, Preliminary exam one (1) year after Comprehensive exam. *Entrance requirements:* For master's, completed application form, application fee, original official transcripts for all previous college work, 3 letters of recommendation, personal statement, 1 writing sample in the target language, 1 writing sample in English (for international), CV, GPA of 3.0 or above preferred; for doctorate, GRE, TOEFL (if international), completed application form, application fee, original official transcripts for all previous college work, 3 letters of recommendation, personal statement, 1 writing sample in target language, 1 writing sample in English (for international), CV, GPA of 3.0 or above preferred. Additional exam requirements/recommendations for international students: required—TOEFL (minimum score 550 paper-based; 79 iBT), IELTS (minimum score 6.5), PTE (minimum score 55). Electronic applications accepted. *Expenses: Tuition, area resident:* Full-time $11,310; part-time $471 per credit hour. Tuition, state resident: full-time $11,310; part-time $471 per credit hour. Tuition, nonresident: full-time $23,100; part-time $963 per credit hour. *International tuition:* $23,100 full-time. *Required fees:* $2820.

University at Buffalo, the State University of New York, Graduate School, Graduate School of Education, Department of Learning and Instruction, Buffalo, NY 14260. Offers biology education (Ed M, Certificate); chemistry education (Ed M, Certificate); childhood education (Ed M); childhood education with bilingual extension (Ed M); college teaching (Advanced Certificate); curriculum, instruction and the science of learning (PhD); early childhood education (Ed M); early childhood education with bilingual extension (Ed M); earth science education (Ed M, Certificate); education and technology (Ed M); education studies (Ed M); educational technology and new literacies (Certificate); educational technology and new literacies (Advanced Certificate); elementary education (Ed D); English education (Ed M, Certificate); English education studies (Ed M); English for speakers of other languages (Ed M); foreign and second language education (PhD); French education (Ed M, Certificate); German education (Ed M, Certificate); gifted education (Certificate); Latin education (Ed M, Certificate); literacy education studies (Ed M); literacy specialist (Ed M); literacy teaching and learning (Certificate); mathematics education (Ed M, Certificate); music education (Ed M, Certificate); music education studies (Ed M); music learning theory (Advanced Certificate); online education (Advanced Certificate); physics education (Ed M, Certificate); science and the public (Ed M); social studies education (Ed M, Certificate); Spanish education (Ed M, Certificate); special education (PhD); teaching English to speakers of other languages (Ed M). *Program availability:* Part-time, evening/weekend, 100% online, blended/hybrid learning. *Faculty:* 26 full-time (19 women), 42 part-time/adjunct (29 women). *Students:* 227 full-time (158 women), 322 part-time (228 women); includes 85 minority (34 Black or African American, non-Hispanic/Latino; 3 American Indian or Alaska Native, non-Hispanic/Latino; 17 Asian, non-Hispanic/Latino; 23 Hispanic/Latino; 8 Two or more races, non-Hispanic/Latino), 42 international. Average age 33. 385 applicants, 61% accepted, 158 enrolled. In 2019, 100 master's, 23 doctorates, 16 other advanced degrees awarded. *Degree requirements:* For master's, comprehensive exam; for doctorate, thesis/dissertation, research analysis exam, research experience; for other advanced degree, thesis (for some programs). *Entrance requirements:* For master's, GRE or MAT for teacher preparation programs only, letters of reference; for doctorate, GRE General Test or MAT, interview, writing sample, letters of recommendation, resume. Additional exam requirements/recommendations for international students: required—TOEFL (minimum score 600 paper-based; 96 iBT), IELTS (minimum score 6.5), PTE (minimum score 55), The Graduate School of Education requires international students to submit test scores for at least one of the exams (TOEFL, IELTS, PTE). *Application deadline:* For fall admission, 2/1 priority date for domestic and international students. Applications are processed on a rolling basis. Application fee: $50. Electronic applications accepted. *Expenses: Tuition, area resident:* Full-time $11,310; part-time $471 per credit hour. Tuition, state resident: full-time $11,310; part-time $471 per credit hour. Tuition, nonresident: full-time $23,100; part-time $963 per credit hour. *International tuition:* $23,100 full-time. *Required fees:* $2820. *Financial support:* In 2019–20, 16 fellowships (averaging $20,000 per year), 5 research assistantships with tuition reimbursements (averaging $26,917 per year) were awarded; teaching assistantships, career-related internships or fieldwork, Federal Work-Study, institutionally sponsored loans, scholarships/grants, tuition waivers (full and partial), and unspecified assistantships also available. Financial award application deadline: 2/28; financial award applicants required to submit FAFSA. *Unit head:* Dr. Julie Gorlewski, Department Chair, 716-645-2455, Fax: 716-645-3161, E-mail: jgorlews@buffalo.edu. *Application contact:* Renad Aref, Assistant Director of Admission Recruitment, 716-645-2110, Fax: 716-645-7937, E-mail: gseinfo@buffalo.edu.
Website: http://ed.buffalo.edu/teaching.html

The University of Alabama, Graduate School, College of Arts and Sciences, Department of Modern Languages and Classics, Tuscaloosa, AL 35487. Offers French (MA, PhD); French and Spanish (PhD); German (MA); Romance languages (MA, PhD); Spanish (MA, PhD). *Program availability:* Part-time. *Faculty:* 20 full-time (11 women). *Students:* 39 full-time (17 women), 6 part-time (3 women); includes 14 minority (5 Black or African American, non-Hispanic/Latino; 7 Hispanic/Latino; 2 Two or more races, non-Hispanic/Latino), 10 international. Average age 31. 19 applicants, 89% accepted, 11 enrolled. In 2019, 6 master's, 3 doctorates awarded. *Degree requirements:* For master's, comprehensive exam, thesis optional; for doctorate, one foreign language, thesis/dissertation, preliminary exam. *Entrance requirements:* For master's and doctorate, minimum GPA of 3.0, writing sample. Additional exam requirements/recommendations for international students: required—TOEFL or IELTS. *Application deadline:* For fall admission, 7/6 priority date for domestic students, 1/15 priority date for international students; for spring admission, 12/5 priority date for domestic students, 6/1 priority date for international students. Applications are processed on a rolling basis. Application fee: $50 ($60 for international students). Electronic applications accepted. *Expenses: Tuition, area resident:* Full-time $10,780; part-time $440 per credit hour. Tuition, nonresident: full-time $30,250; part-time $1550 per credit hour. *Financial support:* In 2019–20, 40 students received support. Fellowships, research assistantships with full tuition reimbursements available, teaching assistantships with full tuition reimbursements available, career-related internships or fieldwork, Federal Work-Study, institutionally sponsored loans, and scholarships/grants available. Financial award application deadline: 7/14. *Unit head:* Dr. Douglas Lightfoot, Department Chair, 205-348-5059, E-mail: lightfoot@ua.edu. *Application contact:* Dr. K. Barbara Fischer, Graduate Director/Associate Professor, 205-348-8465, Fax: 205-348-2042, E-mail: bfischer@bama.ua.edu.
Website: http://bama.ua.edu/~mlc

The University of Arizona, College of Humanities, Department of Spanish and Portuguese, Tucson, AZ 85721. Offers Spanish (MA, PhD). Terminal master's awarded for partial completion of doctoral program. *Degree requirements:* For master's, one foreign language, comprehensive exam, thesis optional; for doctorate, 3 foreign languages, comprehensive exam, thesis/dissertation. *Entrance requirements:* For master's, GRE General Test, minimum GPA of 3.3, writing sample, 3 letters of recommendation, audio sample; for doctorate, GRE General Test, minimum GPA of 3.4, 3 letters of recommendation, statement of purpose, writing sample, audio sample. Additional exam requirements/recommendations for international students: required—TOEFL (minimum score 550 paper-based; 79 iBT). Electronic applications accepted.

University of Arkansas, Graduate School, J. William Fulbright College of Arts and Sciences, Department of World Languages, Literatures and Cultures, Program in Spanish, Fayetteville, AR 72701. Offers MA. *Students:* 9 full-time (4 women); includes 1 minority (Hispanic/Latino), 7 international. 8 applicants, 100% accepted. In 2019, 6 master's awarded. *Degree requirements:* For master's, one foreign language, comprehensive exam, thesis optional. *Entrance requirements:* Additional exam requirements/recommendations for international students: required—TOEFL (minimum score 550 paper-based), IELTS (minimum score 6.5). *Application deadline:* For fall admission, 8/1 priority date for domestic students, 4/1 for international students; for spring admission, 12/1 priority date for domestic students, 10/1 for international students; for summer admission, 4/15 for domestic students, 3/1 for international students. Applications are processed on a rolling basis. Application fee: $60. Electronic applications accepted. *Financial support:* In 2019–20, 1 research assistantship, 14 teaching assistantships (averaging $8,200 per year) were awarded; fellowships with tuition reimbursements, career-related internships or fieldwork, and Federal Work-Study also available. Support available to part-time students. Financial award application

deadline: 1/15; financial award applicants required to submit FAFSA. *Unit head:* Dr. Steven Bell, Department Chair, 479-575-5948, Fax: 479-575-6795, E-mail: sbell@uark.edu. *Application contact:* Dr. Erika Almenara, Graduate Coordinator, 479-575-5940, Fax: 479-575-6795, E-mail: almenar@uark.edu.
Website: https://fulbright.uark.edu/departments/world-languages/

University of California, Berkeley, Graduate Division, College of Letters and Science, Group in Romance Languages and Literatures, Berkeley, CA 94720. Offers French (PhD); Italian (PhD); Spanish (PhD). *Degree requirements:* For doctorate, thesis/dissertation, qualifying exam. *Entrance requirements:* For doctorate, GRE General Test, minimum GPA of 3.0, 3 letters of recommendation. Additional exam requirements/recommendations for international students: required—TOEFL (minimum score 570 paper-based; 90 iBT). Electronic applications accepted.

University of California, Davis, Graduate Studies, Program in Spanish, Davis, CA 95616. Offers MA, PhD. Terminal master's awarded for partial completion of doctoral program. *Degree requirements:* For master's, comprehensive exam (for some programs), thesis (for some programs); for doctorate, 2 foreign languages, thesis/dissertation. *Entrance requirements:* For master's, GRE General Test, minimum GPA of 3.0; for doctorate, GRE General Test, master's degree, minimum GPA of 3.0. Additional exam requirements/recommendations for international students: required—TOEFL (minimum score 550 paper-based).

University of California, Irvine, School of Humanities, Department of Spanish and Portuguese, Irvine, CA 92697. Offers Spanish (MA, MAT, PhD). *Students:* 26 full-time (18 women); includes 14 minority (13 Hispanic/Latino; 1 Two or more races, non-Hispanic/Latino), 7 international. Average age 34. 23 applicants, 26% accepted, 4 enrolled. In 2019, 8 doctorates awarded. *Entrance requirements:* For master's and doctorate, GRE General Test, minimum GPA of 3.0. Additional exam requirements/recommendations for international students: required—TOEFL (minimum score 550 paper-based). *Application deadline:* For fall admission, 1/2 priority date for domestic students, 1/2 for international students. Applications are processed on a rolling basis. Application fee: $120 ($140 for international students). Electronic applications accepted. *Financial support:* Fellowships, teaching assistantships, institutionally sponsored loans, traineeships, health care benefits, and unspecified assistantships available. Financial award application deadline: 3/1; financial award applicants required to submit FAFSA. *Unit head:* Luis Aviles, Department Chair, 949-824-7268, Fax: 949-824-2803, E-mail: laviles@uci.edu. *Application contact:* Evelyn Flores, Graduate Program Coordinator, 949-824-8793, Fax: 949-824-2803, E-mail: evelynf@uci.edu.
Website: http://www.hnet.uci.edu/spanishandportuguese/

University of California, Los Angeles, Graduate Division, College of Letters and Science, Department of Spanish and Portuguese, Program in Spanish, Los Angeles, CA 90095. Offers MA. *Degree requirements:* For master's, one foreign language, comprehensive exam or thesis. *Entrance requirements:* For master's, GRE General Test, bachelor's degree; minimum undergraduate GPA of 3.0 (or its equivalent if letter grade system not used). Additional exam requirements/recommendations for international students: required—TOEFL. Electronic applications accepted.

University of California, Riverside, Graduate Division, Department of Hispanic Studies, Riverside, CA 92521-0102. Offers Spanish (MA, PhD). Terminal master's awarded for partial completion of doctoral program. *Degree requirements:* For master's, one foreign language, comprehensive exam; for doctorate, one foreign language, thesis/dissertation, qualifying exams, 1 quarter of teaching experience. *Entrance requirements:* For master's and doctorate, GRE General Test, minimum GPA of 3.0. Additional exam requirements/recommendations for international students: required—TOEFL (minimum score 550 paper-based; 80 iBT). Electronic applications accepted.

University of California, Santa Barbara, Graduate Division, College of Letters and Sciences, Division of Humanities and Fine Arts, Department of Spanish and Portuguese, Santa Barbara, CA 93106-4150. Offers Hispanic languages and literatures (PhD), including European medieval studies, feminist studies, Hispanic linguistics, Hispanic literature, Luso-Brazilian literature; Hispanic linguistics (MA); Luso-Brazilian literature (MA); Spanish or Spanish-American literature (MA); MA/PhD. Terminal master's awarded for partial completion of doctoral program. *Degree requirements:* For master's, 2 foreign languages, comprehensive exam (for some programs), thesis optional; for doctorate, 3 foreign languages, comprehensive exam, thesis/dissertation. *Entrance requirements:* For master's and doctorate, GRE. Additional exam requirements/recommendations for international students: required—TOEFL (minimum score 550 paper-based; 80 iBT), IELTS (minimum score 7). Electronic applications accepted.

University of Central Arkansas, Graduate School, College of Liberal Arts, Department of Languages, Linguistics, Literatures, and Cultures, Conway, AR 72035-0001. Offers Spanish (MA). *Program availability:* Part-time. *Degree requirements:* For master's, one foreign language, comprehensive exam, thesis optional. *Entrance requirements:* For master's, GRE General Test, minimum GPA of 2.7. Additional exam requirements/recommendations for international students: required—TOEFL (minimum score 550 paper-based). Electronic applications accepted.

University of Central Florida, College of Arts and Humanities, Department of Modern Languages and Literatures, Program in Spanish, Orlando, FL 32816. Offers MA. *Program availability:* Part-time, evening/weekend. *Students:* 5 full-time (4 women), 8 part-time (7 women); includes 12 minority (all Hispanic/Latino). Average age 43. 10 applicants, 80% accepted, 5 enrolled. In 2019, 6 master's awarded. *Degree requirements:* For master's, one foreign language, comprehensive exam, thesis or alternative. *Entrance requirements:* For master's, minimum GPA of 3.0 in last 60 hours, letters of recommendation, writing sample. Additional exam requirements/recommendations for international students: required—TOEFL. *Application deadline:* For fall admission, 7/15 for domestic students; for spring admission, 12/1 for domestic students; for summer admission, 4/15 for domestic students. Application fee: $30. Electronic applications accepted. *Financial support:* In 2019–20, 5 students received support, including 1 fellowship (averaging $5,000 per year), 5 teaching assistantships with partial tuition reimbursements available (averaging $5,592 per year); career-related internships or fieldwork, Federal Work-Study, institutionally sponsored loans, health care benefits, tuition waivers (partial), and unspecified assistantships also available. Financial award application deadline: 3/1; financial award applicants required to submit FAFSA. *Unit head:* Dr. Lisa Nalbone, Director, 407-823-2472, E-mail: lisa.nalbone@ucf.edu. *Application contact:* Associate Director, Graduate Admissions, 407-823-2766, Fax: 407-823-6442, E-mail: gradadmissions@ucf.edu.
Website: http://mll.cah.ucf.edu/graduate/index.php#SpanishMA

University of Chicago, Division of the Humanities, Department of Romance Languages and Literatures, Chicago, IL 60637. Offers French and Francophone studies (PhD); Hispanic and Luso-Brazilian studies (PhD); Italian studies (PhD); Renaissance and early modern studies (PhD). Terminal master's awarded for partial completion of doctoral program. *Degree requirements:* For doctorate, 3 foreign languages, comprehensive exam, thesis/dissertation. *Entrance requirements:* For doctorate, GRE General Test, 15-20 page writing sample, statement of purpose, 3 letters of recommendation, transcripts for all previous degrees and institutions attended. Additional exam requirements/recommendations for international students: required—TOEFL (minimum score 104 iBT), IELTS (minimum score 7). Electronic applications accepted.

University of Cincinnati, Graduate School, McMicken College of Arts and Sciences, Dept. of Romance and Arabic Languages and Literatures, Program in Spanish, Cincinnati, OH 45221. Offers MA, PhD. Terminal master's awarded for partial completion of doctoral program. *Degree requirements:* For master's, thesis optional; for doctorate, 2 foreign languages, thesis/dissertation. *Entrance requirements:* For master's, minimum GPA of 3.0. Electronic applications accepted.

University of Colorado Boulder, Graduate School, College of Arts and Sciences, Department of Spanish and Portuguese, Boulder, CO 80309. Offers Hispanic linguistics (MA); medieval and early modern Hispanic literatures (PhD); peninsular and Latin American literature (MA). Terminal master's awarded for partial completion of doctoral program. *Degree requirements:* For master's, one foreign language, comprehensive exam, thesis or alternative; for doctorate, 2 foreign languages, thesis/dissertation. *Entrance requirements:* For master's, minimum undergraduate GPA of 2.75. Electronic applications accepted. Application fee is waived when completed online.

University of Colorado Denver, College of Liberal Arts and Sciences, Department of Modern Languages, Denver, CO 80217. Offers Spanish (MA). *Program availability:* Part-time. *Degree requirements:* For master's, comprehensive exam, thesis or alternative, 33 credit hours of course work. *Entrance requirements:* For master's, BA in Spanish from accredited institution, or BA in another discipline plus language skills that meet department's standards; minimum GPA of 2.5, 3.0 in all Spanish courses; written statement in Spanish; oral interview; three letters of recommendation. Additional exam requirements/recommendations for international students: required—TOEFL (minimum score 550 paper-based; 80 iBT). Electronic applications accepted. Tuition and fees vary according to course load, program and reciprocity agreements.

University of Delaware, College of Arts and Sciences, Department of Foreign Languages and Literatures, Newark, DE 19716. Offers foreign languages and literatures (MA), including French, German, Spanish; foreign languages pedagogy (MA), including French, German, Spanish; technical Chinese translation (MA). *Degree requirements:* For master's, one foreign language, comprehensive exam, thesis optional. *Entrance requirements:* For master's, GRE General Test, letters of recommendation, writing sample. Additional exam requirements/recommendations for international students: required—TOEFL. Electronic applications accepted.

University of Florida, Graduate School, College of Liberal Arts and Sciences, Department of Spanish and Portuguese Studies, Gainesville, FL 32611. Offers Spanish (MA, MAT, PhD). *Program availability:* Part-time. Terminal master's awarded for partial completion of doctoral program. *Degree requirements:* For master's, one foreign language, comprehensive exam, thesis or extended research paper; for doctorate, 2 foreign languages, comprehensive exam, thesis/dissertation, qualifying exam. *Entrance requirements:* For master's and doctorate, GRE General Test, minimum GPA of 3.0. Additional exam requirements/recommendations for international students: required—TOEFL (minimum score 550 paper-based; 80 iBT), IELTS (minimum score 6). Electronic applications accepted.

University of Georgia, Franklin College of Arts and Sciences, Department of Romance Languages, Athens, GA 30602. Offers French (PhD); Italian (MA, PhD); Portuguese (MA, PhD); romance linguistics (MA); Spanish (PhD). *Degree requirements:* For master's, one foreign language; for doctorate, 2 foreign languages, thesis/dissertation. *Entrance requirements:* For master's and doctorate, GRE General Test. Electronic applications accepted.

University of Hawaii at Manoa, Office of Graduate Education, College of Languages, Linguistics and Literature, Department of Languages and Literatures of Europe and the Americas, Program in Spanish, Honolulu, HI 96822. Offers MA. *Program availability:* Part-time. *Degree requirements:* For master's, one foreign language, thesis optional. *Entrance requirements:* For master's, GRE General Test. Additional exam requirements/recommendations for international students: required—TOEFL (minimum score 580 paper-based; 92 iBT), IELTS (minimum score 5).

University of Houston, College of Liberal Arts and Social Sciences, Department of Hispanic Studies, Houston, TX 77204. Offers Hispanic literature and linguistics (PhD); Spanish (MA, PhD), including creative writing (PhD). *Program availability:* Part-time. *Degree requirements:* For master's, comprehensive exam, thesis optional; for doctorate, 2 foreign languages, comprehensive exam, thesis/dissertation. *Entrance requirements:* For master's and doctorate, GRE. Additional exam requirements/recommendations for international students: required—TOEFL (minimum score 550 paper-based; 79 iBT); recommended—IELTS (minimum score 6.5). Electronic applications accepted.

University of Houston, College of Liberal Arts and Social Sciences, Department of Modern and Classical Languages, Houston, TX 77204. Offers world cultures and literatures (MA). *Degree requirements:* For master's, one foreign language, thesis optional. *Entrance requirements:* For master's, GRE General Test, minimum GPA of 3.0 in last 60 hours of course work. Additional exam requirements/recommendations for international students: required—TOEFL (minimum score 500 paper-based). Electronic applications accepted.

University of Illinois at Chicago, College of Liberal Arts and Sciences, School of Literatures, Cultural Studies and Linguistics, Department of Hispanic and Italian Studies, Chicago, IL 60607-7128. Offers Hispanic linguistics (PhD). *Program availability:* Part-time. Terminal master's awarded for partial completion of doctoral program. *Degree requirements:* For master's, one foreign language, departmental qualifying exam. *Entrance requirements:* For master's, GRE General Test, minimum GPA of 2.75, undergraduate major in Spanish. Additional exam requirements/recommendations for international students: required—TOEFL. Electronic applications accepted.

University of Illinois at Urbana-Champaign, Graduate College, College of Liberal Arts and Sciences, School of Literatures, Cultures and Linguistics, Department of Spanish, Italian and Portuguese, Champaign, IL 61820. Offers Italian (MA, PhD); Portuguese (MA, PhD); Spanish (MA, PhD).

The University of Iowa, Graduate College, College of Liberal Arts and Sciences, Department of Spanish and Portuguese, Iowa City, IA 52242-1316. Offers Spanish (MA, PhD); Spanish creative writing (MFA). *Degree requirements:* For master's, thesis optional, exam; for doctorate, comprehensive exam, thesis/dissertation. *Entrance requirements:* For master's and doctorate, GRE General Test, minimum GPA of 3.0. Additional exam requirements/recommendations for international students: required—TOEFL (minimum score 600 paper-based; 100 iBT). Electronic applications accepted.

The University of Kansas, Graduate Studies, College of Liberal Arts and Sciences, Department of Spanish and Portuguese, Lawrence, KS 66045. Offers MA, PhD. *Students:* 25 full-time (14 women), 1 (woman) part-time; includes 4 minority (all Hispanic/Latino), 14 international. Average age 29. 18 applicants, 56% accepted, 4 enrolled. In 2019, 4 master's, 2 doctorates awarded. *Entrance requirements:* For master's and doctorate, curriculum vitae, three letters of recommendation, writing sample, personal statement (500-750 words), official transcripts. Additional exam requirements/recommendations for international students: required—TOEFL, IELTS. *Application deadline:* For fall admission, 5/15 priority date for domestic and international students; for spring admission, 10/15 priority date for domestic and international students. Application fee: $65 ($85 for international students). Electronic applications accepted. *Expenses:* Tuition, state resident: full-time $9989. Tuition, nonresident: full-time $23,950. *International tuition:* $23,950 full-time. *Required fees:* $984; $81.99 per credit hour. Tuition and fees vary according to course load, campus/location and program. *Financial support:* Fellowships, research assistantships, teaching assistantships, and unspecified assistantships available. Financial award application deadline: 1/15. *Unit head:* Margot Versteeg, Associate Chair, 785-864-0289, E-mail: sarias@ku.edu. *Application contact:* Jared Nietfeld, Graduate Admission Contact, 785-864-0482, E-mail: nietfeld@ku.edu. Website: http://spanport.ku.edu/

University of Lethbridge, School of Graduate Studies, Lethbridge, AB T1K 3M4, Canada. Offers addictions counseling (M Sc); agricultural biotechnology (M Sc); agricultural studies (M Sc, MA); anthropology (MA); archaeology (M Sc, MA); art (MA, MFA); biochemistry (M Sc); biological sciences (M Sc); biomolecular science (PhD); biosystems and biodiversity (PhD); Canadian studies (MA); chemistry (M Sc); computer science (M Sc); computer science and geographical information science (M Sc); counseling (MC); counseling psychology (M Ed); dramatic arts (MA); earth, space, and physical science (PhD); economics (MA); education (MA, PhD); educational leadership (M Ed); English (MA); environmental science (M Sc); evolution and behavior (PhD); exercise science (M Sc); French (MA); French/German (MA); French/Spanish (MA); general education (M Ed); geography (M Sc, MA); German (MA); health sciences (M Sc); individualized multidisciplinary (M Sc, MA); kinesiology (M Sc, MA); management (M Sc), including accounting, finance, human resource management and labor relations, information systems, international management, marketing, policy and strategy; mathematics (M Sc); music (M Mus, MA); Native American studies (MA); neuroscience (M Sc, PhD); new media (MA, MFA); nursing (M Sc, MN); philosophy (MA); physics (M Sc); political science (MA); psychology (M Sc, MA); religious studies (MA); sociology (MA); theatre and dramatic arts (MFA); theoretical and computational science (PhD); urban and regional studies (MA); women and gender studies (MA). *Program availability:* Part-time, evening/weekend. *Degree requirements:* For master's, thesis (for some programs); for doctorate, comprehensive exam, thesis/dissertation. *Entrance requirements:* For master's, GMAT (for M Sc in management), bachelor's degree in related field, minimum GPA of 3.0 during previous 20 graded semester courses, 2 years' teaching or related experience (M Ed); for doctorate, master's degree, minimum graduate GPA of 3.5. Additional exam requirements/recommendations for international students: required—TOEFL (minimum score 580 paper-based; 93 iBT). Electronic applications accepted.

University of Louisville, Graduate School, College of Arts and Sciences, Department of Classical and Modern Languages, Louisville, KY 40292-0001. Offers French (MA); Spanish (MA); translation and interpretation (Certificate). *Program availability:* Part-time, evening/weekend. *Faculty:* 27 full-time (13 women), 25 part-time/adjunct (20 women). *Students:* 7 full-time (6 women), 8 part-time (5 women); includes 10 minority (1 Asian, non-Hispanic/Latino; 8 Hispanic/Latino; 1 Two or more races, non-Hispanic/Latino). Average age 36. 4 applicants, 100% accepted, 4 enrolled. In 2019, 11 master's awarded. *Degree requirements:* For master's, one foreign language, thesis (for some programs). *Entrance requirements:* For master's, Two letters of reference, official transcripts. Additional exam requirements/recommendations for international students: required—TOEFL (minimum score 550 paper-based; 79 iBT), IELTS can be used in place of the TOEFL; recommended—IELTS (minimum score 6.5). *Application deadline:* Applications are processed on a rolling basis. Application fee: $65. Electronic applications accepted. *Expenses: Tuition, area resident:* Full-time $13,000; part-time $723 per credit hour. Tuition, state resident: full-time $13,000; part-time $723 per credit hour. Tuition, nonresident: full-time $27,114; part-time $1507 per credit hour. *International tuition:* $27,114 full-time. *Required fees:* $196. Tuition and fees vary according to program and reciprocity agreements. *Financial support:* In 2019–20, 12 students received support. Fellowships, research assistantships, teaching assistantships, scholarships/grants, health care benefits, and unspecified assistantships available. *Unit head:* Dr. Regina Roebuck, Associate Professor and Chair, 502-852-0483, E-mail: regina.roebuck@louisville.edu. *Application contact:* Dr. Manuel Medina, Professor and Director of Graduate Studies, E-mail: manuel.medina@louisville.edu. Website: http://louisville.edu/modernlanguages/

The University of Manchester, School of Arts, Languages and Cultures, Manchester, United Kingdom. Offers anthropology, media and performance (PhD); applied theatre (PhD); Arab world studies (PhD); archaeology (PhD); art history and visual studies (PhD); arts and cultural management (PhD); arts management and cultural policy (PhD); Chinese studies (PhD); classics and ancient history (PhD); composition (PhD); creative writing (PhD); drama (PhD); East Asian studies (PhD); electroacoustic composition (PhD); English and American studies (PhD); English language (PhD); French studies (PhD); German studies (PhD); history (PhD); humanitarianism and conflict response (PhD); interpreting studies (PhD); Japanese studies (PhD); Latin American cultural studies (PhD); linguistics (PhD); Middle Eastern studies (PhD); museology (PhD); museum practice (PhD); music (PhD); musicology (PhD); Polish studies (PhD); Portuguese studies (PhD); religions and theology (PhD); Russian studies (PhD); Spanish studies (PhD); translation and intercultural studies (PhD).

University of Maryland, College Park, Academic Affairs, College of Arts and Humanities, School of Languages, Literatures, and Cultures, Spanish Language and Literatures Program, College Park, MD 20742. Offers MA, PhD. *Degree requirements:* For master's, comprehensive exam, thesis optional, scholarly paper; for doctorate, 2 foreign languages, thesis/dissertation. *Entrance requirements:* For master's, minimum GPA of 3.0, interview, sample research paper, minimum of 12 credits in upper-level literature, 3 letters of recommendation; for doctorate, minimum GPA of 3.0, interview, sample research paper, minimum of 12 credits in upper-level literature. Additional exam requirements/recommendations for international students: required—TOEFL. Electronic applications accepted.

University of Massachusetts Amherst, Graduate School, College of Humanities and Fine Arts, Department of Languages, Literatures, and Cultures, Program in Spanish and Portuguese Studies, Amherst, MA 01003. Offers Hispanic literatures, cultures and linguistics (MA, PhD); teaching Spanish (MAT). *Program availability:* Part-time. Terminal master's awarded for partial completion of doctoral program. *Degree requirements:* For master's, one foreign language, thesis or alternative; for doctorate, 2 foreign languages, comprehensive exam, thesis/dissertation. *Entrance requirements:* For master's and doctorate, GRE General Test, sample academic term paper. Additional exam requirements/recommendations for international students: required—TOEFL (minimum score 550 paper-based; 80 iBT), IELTS (minimum score 6.5). Electronic applications accepted.

University of Memphis, Graduate School, College of Arts and Sciences, Department of World Languages and Literatures, Memphis, TN 38152. Offers romance languages (MA), including French, Spanish. *Program availability:* Part-time. *Students:* 16 full-time (11 women), 5 part-time (4 women); includes 13 minority (1 Black or African American, non-Hispanic/Latino; 11 Hispanic/Latino; 1 Two or more races, non-Hispanic/Latino). 1 international. Average age 33. 10 applicants, 100% accepted, 5 enrolled. In 2019, 4 master's awarded. *Degree requirements:* For master's, 2 foreign languages, comprehensive exam. *Entrance requirements:* For master's, GRE, interview in language of concentration, writing sample, letter of intent, two letters of recommendation. Additional exam requirements/recommendations for international students: required—

TOEFL (minimum score 94 iBT). *Application deadline:* For fall admission, 5/15 for domestic students, 4/5 for international students; for spring admission, 11/30 for domestic students, 10/5 for international students. Applications are processed on a rolling basis. Application fee: $35 ($60 for international students). Electronic applications accepted. *Expenses: Tuition, area resident:* Full-time $9216; part-time $512 per credit hour. Tuition, state resident: full-time $9216; part-time $512 per credit hour. Tuition, nonresident: full-time $12,672; part-time $704 per credit hour. *International tuition:* $16,128 full-time. *Required fees:* $1530; $85 per credit hour. Tuition and fees vary according to program. *Financial support:* Research assistantships with full tuition reimbursements, teaching assistantships with full tuition reimbursements, Federal Work-Study, scholarships/grants, and unspecified assistantships available. Financial award application deadline: 2/1; financial award applicants required to submit FAFSA. *Unit head:* Dr. William Thompson, Chair, 901-678-2507, E-mail: wjthmpsn@memphis.edu. *Application contact:* Dr. Fernando Burgos, Graduate Coordinator, 901-678-3158, E-mail: fburgos@memphis.edu. Website: http://www.memphis.edu/fl/

University of Miami, Graduate School, College of Arts and Sciences, Department of Modern Languages and Literatures, Coral Gables, FL 33124. Offers romance studies (PhD), including French, Spanish. *Degree requirements:* For doctorate, 2 foreign languages, thesis/dissertation, area exam, qualifying exam. *Entrance requirements:* For doctorate, 1 writing sample in English and 1 writing sample in French or Spanish, minimum GPA of 3.0, oral interview, letters of recommendation. Additional exam requirements/recommendations for international students: required—TOEFL (minimum score 550 paper-based; 59 iBT). Electronic applications accepted.

University of Miami, Graduate School, School of Communication, Coral Gables, FL 33124. Offers communication (PhD); communication studies (MA); film studies (MA, PhD); motion pictures (MFA), including production, producing, and screenwriting; print journalism (MA); public relations (MA); Spanish language journalism (MA); television broadcast journalism (MA). *Program availability:* Part-time. *Degree requirements:* For master's, comprehensive exam (for some programs), thesis (for some programs); for doctorate, comprehensive exam, thesis/dissertation. *Entrance requirements:* For master's, GRE General Test; for doctorate, GRE General Test, master's thesis or scholarly research. Additional exam requirements/recommendations for international students: required—TOEFL (minimum score 600 paper-based; 100 iBT). Electronic applications accepted.

University of Michigan, Rackham Graduate School, College of Literature, Science, and the Arts, Department of Romance Languages and Literatures, Program in Spanish, Ann Arbor, MI 48109-1275. Offers PhD. *Degree requirements:* For doctorate, 2 foreign languages, thesis/dissertation, oral defense of dissertation, preliminary exams in essay format. *Entrance requirements:* Additional exam requirements/recommendations for international students: required—TOEFL or Michigan English Language Assessment Battery. Electronic applications accepted.

University of Minnesota, Twin Cities Campus, Graduate School, College of Liberal Arts, Department of Spanish and Portuguese Studies, Minneapolis, MN 55455-0213. Offers Hispanic and Lusophone literatures, cultures and linguistics (PhD); Hispanic linguistics (MA); Hispanic literature (MA); Lusophone literature (MA). *Degree requirements:* For master's, 2 foreign languages, comprehensive exam, thesis or alternative; for doctorate, 2 foreign languages, comprehensive exam, thesis/dissertation. *Entrance requirements:* For master's and doctorate, GRE General Test, samples of written work, 3 letters of recommendation, voice sample, statement of purpose. Additional exam requirements/recommendations for international students: required—TOEFL (minimum score 550 paper-based; 79 iBT). Electronic applications accepted.

University of Missouri–Kansas City, College of Arts and Sciences, Department of Foreign Languages and Literatures, Kansas City, MO 64110-2499. Offers romance languages and literatures (MA), including French, Spanish. *Program availability:* Part-time. *Degree requirements:* For master's, 2 foreign languages. *Entrance requirements:* For master's, GRE General Test, minimum GPA of 2.75, 2 letters of recommendation. Additional exam requirements/recommendations for international students: required—TOEFL (minimum score 550 paper-based; 80 iBT). Electronic applications accepted.

University of Montana, Graduate School, College of Humanities and Sciences, Department of Modern and Classical Languages and Literatures, Missoula, MT 59812. Offers French (MA); German (MA); Spanish (MA). *Degree requirements:* For master's, one foreign language. *Entrance requirements:* For master's, GRE General Test. Additional exam requirements/recommendations for international students: required—TOEFL.

University of Nebraska–Lincoln, Graduate College, College of Arts and Sciences, Department of Modern Languages and Literatures, Lincoln, NE 68588. Offers French (MA, PhD); German (MA, PhD); Spanish (MA, PhD). *Degree requirements:* For master's, thesis optional; for doctorate, comprehensive exam, thesis/dissertation. *Entrance requirements:* For master's and doctorate, writing sample in target language. Additional exam requirements/recommendations for international students: required—TOEFL (minimum score 550 paper-based). Electronic applications accepted.

University of Nevada, Reno, Graduate School, College of Liberal Arts, Department of World Languages and Literatures, Reno, NV 89557. Offers Spanish (MA). *Degree requirements:* For master's, one foreign language, thesis optional. *Entrance requirements:* For master's, GRE General Test, minimum GPA of 2.75. Additional exam requirements/recommendations for international students: required—TOEFL (minimum score 500 paper-based; 61 iBT), IELTS (minimum score 6).

University of New Hampshire, Graduate School, College of Liberal Arts, Department of Spanish, Durham, NH 03824. Offers MA, Postbaccalaureate Certificate. *Students:* 1 (woman) full-time, 2 part-time (1 woman); includes 1 minority (Black or African American, non-Hispanic/Latino). Average age 35. In 2019, 1 master's awarded. *Entrance requirements:* Additional exam requirements/recommendations for international students: required—TOEFL (minimum score 550 paper-based; 80 iBT), IELTS, PTE. *Application deadline:* For fall admission, 7/1 for domestic students, 4/1 for international students; for spring admission, 12/1 for domestic students; for summer admission, 4/1 for domestic students. Application fee: $65. Electronic applications accepted. *Financial support:* In 2019–20, 1 student received support. Fellowships, research assistantships, teaching assistantships, career-related internships or fieldwork, Federal Work-Study, scholarships/grants, and tuition waivers (full and partial) available. Support available to part-time students. Financial award application deadline: 2/15. *Unit head:* Holly Cashman, Chair, 603-862-3120. *Application contact:* Olivia Babin, Administrative Assistant, 603-862-4005, E-mail: spanish.master@unh.edu. Website: http://cola.unh.edu/llc/program/spanish-ma

University of New Mexico, Graduate Studies, College of Arts and Sciences, Program in Spanish and Portuguese, Albuquerque, NM 87131-2039. Offers Portuguese (MA); Spanish (MA); Spanish and Portuguese (PhD). *Program availability:* Part-time. *Degree requirements:* For master's, one foreign language, comprehensive exam, thesis optional; for doctorate, one foreign language, comprehensive exam, thesis/dissertation. *Entrance requirements:* For master's, BA in Spanish or Portuguese, 3 letters of recommendation, letter of intent; for doctorate, GRE, 3 letters of recommendation, letter of intent, sample research paper. Additional exam requirements/recommendations for international students: required—TOEFL (minimum score 550 paper-based). Electronic applications accepted. *Expenses:* Tuition, state resident: full-time $7633; part-time $972 per year. Tuition, nonresident: full-time $22,586; part-time $3840 per year. *International tuition:* $23,292 full-time. *Required fees:* $8608. Tuition and fees vary according to course level, course load, degree level, program and student level.

The University of North Carolina at Chapel Hill, Graduate School, College of Arts and Sciences, Department of Romance Languages and Literatures, Chapel Hill, NC 27599. Offers French (MA, PhD); Italian (MA, PhD); Portuguese (MA, PhD); Romance languages (MA, PhD); Romance philology (MA, PhD); Spanish (MA, PhD). *Degree requirements:* For master's, one foreign language, comprehensive exam, thesis; for doctorate, 2 foreign languages, comprehensive exam, thesis/dissertation. *Entrance requirements:* For master's and doctorate, GRE General Test, minimum GPA of 3.0. Additional exam requirements/recommendations for international students: required—TOEFL (minimum score 550 paper-based). Electronic applications accepted.

The University of North Carolina at Charlotte, College of Liberal Arts and Sciences, Department of Languages and Culture Studies, Charlotte, NC 28223-0001. Offers language and culture studies: translating (Graduate Certificate), including english/french; english/german; english/japanese; english/russian; english/spanish; spanish (MA), including language, literature and culture (llc); translating and translation studies (its). *Program availability:* Part-time, evening/weekend. *Faculty:* 25 full-time (13 women), 1 (woman) part-time/adjunct. *Students:* 6 full-time (5 women), 17 part-time (14 women); includes 13 minority (2 Black or African American, non-Hispanic/Latino; 1 Asian, non-Hispanic/Latino; 10 Hispanic/Latino). Average age 30. 12 applicants, 100% accepted, 11 enrolled. In 2019, 4 master's, 5 other advanced degrees awarded. *Degree requirements:* For master's, thesis optional. *Entrance requirements:* For master's, baccalaureate degree in Spanish or related field with minimum overall GPA of 2.75; essay that addresses the applicant's motivation for enrolling in program, to include particular areas of research interests and career or professional goals; three letters of reference; oral interview; for Graduate Certificate, essay in English that addresses applicant's motivation for seeking enrollment in program; three letters of recommendation; portfolio of best writing samples in both English and Spanish or of translations into each language; oral interview. Additional exam requirements/recommendations for international students: required—TOEFL (minimum score 557 paper-based; 83 iBT), IELTS (minimum score 6.5), TOEFL (minimum score 557paper-based, 83 iBT) or IELTS (6.5). *Application deadline:* Applications are processed on a rolling basis. Application fee: $75. Electronic applications accepted. *Expenses:* Tuition, state resident: full-time $4337. Tuition, nonresident: full-time $17,771. *Required fees:* $3093. Tuition and fees vary according to course load, degree level and program. *Financial support:* In 2019–20, 8 students received support, including 4 research assistantships (averaging $5,000 per year), 4 teaching assistantships (averaging $4,000 per year); career-related internships or fieldwork, institutionally sponsored loans, scholarships/grants, and unspecified assistantships also available. Support available to part-time students. Financial award applicants required to submit FAFSA. *Unit head:* Dr. Michele Bissiere, Department Chair and Professor of French, 704-687-8754, E-mail: mhbissie@uncc.edu. *Application contact:* Kathy B. Giddings, Director of Graduate Admissions, 704-687-5503, Fax: 704-687-1668, E-mail: gradadm@uncc.edu.
Website: https://languages.uncc.edu/

The University of North Carolina at Greensboro, Graduate School, College of Arts and Sciences, Department of Languages, Literatures, and Cultures, Program in Spanish, Greensboro, NC 27412-5001. Offers advanced Spanish language and Hispanic cultural studies (Certificate); Spanish (MA). *Degree requirements:* For master's, one foreign language, comprehensive exam, thesis or alternative. *Entrance requirements:* For master's, GRE General Test, 3-5 minute tape demonstrating foreign language proficiency, composition in Spanish, sample paper in English. Additional exam requirements/recommendations for international students: required—TOEFL. Electronic applications accepted.

The University of North Carolina Wilmington, College of Arts and Sciences, Department of World Languages and Cultures, Wilmington, NC 28403-3297. Offers Hispanic studies (Postbaccalaureate Certificate); Spanish (MA). *Program availability:* Part-time. *Faculty:* 15 full-time (9 women). *Students:* 11 full-time (7 women), 5 part-time (4 women); includes 6 minority (all Hispanic/Latino), 2 international. Average age 30. 8 applicants, 100% accepted, 8 enrolled. In 2019, 5 master's awarded. *Degree requirements:* For master's, one foreign language, comprehensive exam, thesis or alternative. *Entrance requirements:* For master's, 3 letters of recommendation, 2 three-to five-minute recorded speaking samples (both in English and Spanish), writing sample (both in English and Spanish). Additional exam requirements/recommendations for international students: required—TOEFL (minimum score 79 iBT), IELTS (minimum score 6.5). *Application deadline:* For fall admission, 7/1 for domestic students; for spring admission, 11/1 for domestic students; for summer admission, 3/1 for domestic students. Applications are processed on a rolling basis. Application fee: $75. Electronic applications accepted. *Expenses:* Tuition, area resident: Full-time $4719; part-time $326 per credit hour. Tuition, state resident: full-time $4719; part-time $326 per credit hour. Tuition, nonresident: full-time $18,548; part-time $1099 per credit hour. *Required fees:* $2738. Tuition and fees vary according to program. *Financial support:* Teaching assistantships and scholarships/grants available. Financial award application deadline: 1/1; financial award applicants required to submit FAFSA. *Unit head:* Dr. Derrick Miller, Chair, 910-962-4095, Fax: 910-962-7712, E-mail: millerd@uncw.edu. *Application contact:* Dr. Amanda Boomershine, Graduate Coordinator, 910-962-7922, Fax: 910-962-7712, E-mail: boomershinea@uncw.edu.
Website: http://www.uncw.edu/fll/spanish/spngraduate.html

University of Northern Iowa, Graduate College, College of Humanities, Arts and Sciences, Department of Languages and Literatures, MA Program in Spanish, Cedar Falls, IA 50614. Offers Spanish (MA); Spanish teaching (MA). *Program availability:* Part-time, evening/weekend. *Degree requirements:* For master's, one foreign language, comprehensive exam, thesis or alternative. *Entrance requirements:* For master's, minimum GPA of 3.0, valid teaching license, documentation of successful teaching experience. Additional exam requirements/recommendations for international students: required—TOEFL (minimum score 600 paper-based; 100 iBT). Electronic applications accepted.

University of Northern Iowa, Graduate College, College of Humanities, Arts and Sciences, Department of Languages and Literatures, MA Program in TESOL/Spanish, Cedar Falls, IA 50614. Offers MA.

University of North Texas, Toulouse Graduate School, Denton, TX 76203-5459. Offers accounting (MS); applied anthropology (MA, MS); applied behavior analysis (Certificate); applied geography (MA); applied technology and performance improvement (M Ed, MS); art education (MA); art history (MA); arts leadership (Certificate); audiology (Au D); behavior analysis (MS); behavioral science (PhD); biochemistry and molecular biology (MS); biology (MA, MS); biomedical engineering (MS); business analysis (MS); chemistry (MS); clinical health psychology (PhD); communication studies (MA, MS); computer engineering (MS); computer science (MS); counseling (M Ed, MS), including clinical mental health counseling (MS), college and university counseling, elementary school counseling, secondary school counseling; creative writing (MA); criminal justice (MS); curriculum and instruction (M Ed); decision

sciences (MBA); design (MA, MFA), including fashion design (MFA), innovation studies, interior design (MFA); early childhood studies (MS); economics (MS); educational leadership (M Ed, Ed D); educational psychology (MS, PhD), including family studies (MS), gifted and talented (MS), human development (MS), learning and cognition (MS), research, measurement and evaluation (MS); electrical engineering (MS); emergency management (MPA); engineering technology (MS); English (MA); English as a second language (MA); environmental science (MS); finance (MBA, MS); financial management (MPA); French (MA); health services management (MBA); higher education (M Ed, Ed D); history (MA, MS); hospitality management (MS); human resources management (MPA); information science (MS); information systems (PhD); information technologies (MBA); interdisciplinary studies (MA, MS); international studies (MA); international sustainable tourism (MS); jazz studies (MM); journalism (MA, MJ, Graduate Certificate), including interactive and virtual digital communication (Graduate Certificate), narrative journalism (Graduate Certificate), public relations (Graduate Certificate); kinesiology (MS); linguistics (MA); local government management (MPA); logistics (PhD); logistics and supply chain management (MBA); long-term care, senior housing, and aging services (MA); management (PhD); marketing (MBA); mathematics (MA, MS); mechanical and energy engineering (MS, PhD); music (MA), including ethnomusicology, music theory, musicology, performance; music composition (PhD); music education (MM Ed, PhD); nonprofit management (MPA); operations and supply chain management (MBA); performance (MM, DMA); philosophy (MA); political science (MA); professional and technical communication (MA); radio, television and film (MA, MFA); rehabilitation counseling (Certificate); sociology (MA); Spanish (MA); special education (M Ed); speech-language pathology (MA); strategic management (MBA); studio art (MFA); teaching (M Ed); MBA/MS. *Program availability:* Part-time, evening/weekend, online learning. Terminal master's awarded for partial completion of doctoral program. *Degree requirements:* For master's, variable foreign language requirement, comprehensive exam (for some programs), thesis (for some programs); for doctorate, variable foreign language requirement, comprehensive exam (for some programs), thesis/dissertation; for other advanced degree, variable foreign language requirement, comprehensive exam (for some programs). *Entrance requirements:* For master's and doctorate, GRE, GMAT. Additional exam requirements/recommendations for international students: required—TOEFL (minimum score 550 paper-based; 79 iBT). Electronic applications accepted.

University of Notre Dame, The Graduate School, College of Arts and Letters, Division of Humanities, Department of Romance Languages and Literatures, Notre Dame, IN 46556. Offers French and Francophone studies (MA); Iberian and Latin American studies (MA); Italian studies (MA); Romance literatures (MA). *Degree requirements:* For master's, 2 foreign languages, comprehensive exam, thesis optional. *Entrance requirements:* For master's, GRE General Test, BA in target language. Additional exam requirements/recommendations for international students: required—TOEFL (minimum score 600 paper-based; 80 iBT). Electronic applications accepted.

University of Oklahoma, College of Arts and Sciences, Department of Modern Languages, Literatures, and Linguistics, Norman, OK 73019. Offers French (MA, PhD, MBA/MA); German (MA); Spanish (MA, PhD); MBA/MA. *Program availability:* Part-time. Terminal master's awarded for partial completion of doctoral program. *Degree requirements:* For master's, one foreign language, comprehensive exam, thesis optional; for doctorate, one foreign language, comprehensive exam, thesis/dissertation. *Entrance requirements:* For master's, BA (or equivalent) in French, German, or Spanish, or equivalent hours in the major; for doctorate, MA (or equivalent) in French or Spanish. Additional exam requirements/recommendations for international students: required—TOEFL (minimum score 79 iBT) or IELTS (minimum score 6.5). Electronic applications accepted. *Expenses:* Tuition, state resident: full-time $6583.20; part-time $274.30 per credit hour. Tuition, nonresident: full-time $21,242; part-time $885.10 per credit hour. *International tuition:* $21,242.40 full-time. *Required fees:* $1994.20; $72.55 per credit hour. $126.50 per semester. Tuition and fees vary according to course load and degree level.

University of Oregon, Graduate School, College of Arts and Sciences, Department of Romance Languages, Program in Spanish, Eugene, OR 97403. Offers MA. *Program availability:* Part-time. *Degree requirements:* For master's, one foreign language. *Entrance requirements:* For master's, GRE General Test, minimum GPA of 3.0. Additional exam requirements/recommendations for international students: required—TOEFL.

University of Ottawa, Faculty of Graduate and Postdoctoral Studies, Faculty of Arts, Department of Modern Languages and Literatures, Ottawa, ON K1N 6N5, Canada. Offers Spanish (MA, PhD). *Program availability:* Part-time, evening/weekend. *Degree requirements:* For master's, one foreign language, thesis or alternative; for doctorate, one foreign language, comprehensive exam, thesis/dissertation. *Entrance requirements:* For master's, BA with honors in Spanish, minimum B average; for doctorate, MA in Spanish or equivalent, minimum B average. Electronic applications accepted.

University of Pennsylvania, School of Arts and Sciences, Graduate Group in Romance Languages, Philadelphia, PA 19104. Offers French (AM, PhD); Italian (AM, PhD); Spanish (AM, PhD). *Faculty:* 65 full-time (29 women), 8 part-time/adjunct (3 women). *Students:* 60 full-time (31 women); includes 7 minority (1 Asian, non-Hispanic/Latino; 5 Hispanic/Latino; 1 Two or more races, non-Hispanic/Latino), 37 international. Average age 32. 46 applicants, 37% accepted, 8 enrolled. In 2019, 10 master's, 4 doctorates awarded. Terminal master's awarded for partial completion of doctoral program. Application fee: $90.
Website: http://www.sas.upenn.edu/graduate-division

University of Pittsburgh, Kenneth P. Dietrich School of Arts and Sciences, Department of Hispanic Languages and Literatures, Pittsburgh, PA 15260. Offers TESOL (PhD). *Faculty:* 8 full-time (3 women), 6 part-time/adjunct (all women). *Students:* 40 full-time (16 women), 1 (woman) part-time; includes 38 minority (6 Black or African American, non-Hispanic/Latino; 1 Asian, non-Hispanic/Latino; 28 Hispanic/Latino; 3 Two or more races, non-Hispanic/Latino). Average age 30. 49 applicants, 43% accepted, 8 enrolled. Terminal master's awarded for partial completion of doctoral program. *Degree requirements:* For doctorate, comprehensive exam, thesis/dissertation, upload dissertation or thesis to d.scholarship.pitt.edu. *Entrance requirements:* Additional exam requirements/recommendations for international students: required—TOEFL (minimum score 90 iBT), IELTS (minimum score 7), Either the TOEFL or IELTS are required. *Application deadline:* For fall admission, 1/15 priority date for domestic and international students. Application fee: $50. Electronic applications accepted. *Financial support:* In 2019–20, 75 students received support, including 5 fellowships with full tuition reimbursements available (averaging $23,995 per year), 24 teaching assistantships with full tuition reimbursements available (averaging $20,250 per year); scholarships/grants, health care benefits, tuition waivers (full), and unspecified assistantships also available. Financial award application deadline: 1/15. *Unit head:* Dr. Jerome Branche, Department Chair, 412-624-5468, Fax: 412-624-5520, E-mail: branche@pitt.edu. *Application contact:* Keanna Cash, Graduate Adminstrator, 412-624-5227, Fax: 412-624-5520, E-mail: kec176@pitt.edu.
Website: http://www.linguistics.pitt.edu

University of Rhode Island, Graduate School, College of Arts and Sciences, Department of Modern and Classical Languages and Literatures, Kingston, RI 02881.

Spanish

Offers Spanish (MA). *Program availability:* Part-time. *Faculty:* 33 full-time (20 women). *Students:* 5 part-time (1 woman); includes 3 minority (all Hispanic/Latino). In 2019, 5 master's awarded. *Entrance requirements:* For master's, 2 letters of recommendation. Additional exam requirements/recommendations for international students: required—TOEFL. *Application deadline:* For fall admission, 7/15 for domestic students, 2/1 for international students; for spring admission, 11/15 for domestic students, 7/15 for international students. Application fee: $65. Electronic applications accepted. *Expenses: Tuition, area resident:* Full-time $13,734; part-time $763 per credit. Tuition, state resident: full-time $13,734; part-time $763 per credit. Tuition, nonresident: full-time $26,512; part-time $1473 per credit. *International tuition:* $26,512 full-time. *Required fees:* $1780; $52 per credit. $35 per term. One-time fee: $165. *Financial support:* In 2019–20, 1 teaching assistantship with tuition reimbursement (averaging $19,986 per year) was awarded. Financial award application deadline: 2/1; financial award applicants required to submit FAFSA. *Unit head:* Dr. Karen de Bruin, Department Chair, 401-874-4697, E-mail: debruin@uri.edu. *Application contact:* Dr. Susana de los Heros, Spanish Graduate Admission, 401-874-4707, E-mail: sheros@uri.edu. Website: http://web.uri.edu/languages/

University of South Africa, College of Human Sciences, Pretoria, South Africa. Offers adult education (M Ed); African languages (MA, PhD); African politics (MA, PhD); Afrikaans (MA, PhD); ancient history (MA, PhD); ancient Near Eastern studies (MA, PhD); anthropology (MA, PhD); applied linguistics (MA); Arabic (MA, PhD); archaeology (MA); art history (MA); Biblical archaeology (MA); Biblical studies (M Th, D Th, PhD); Christian spirituality (M Th, D Th); church history (M Th, D Th); classical studies (MA, PhD); clinical psychology (MA); communication (MA, PhD); comparative education (M Ed, Ed D); consulting psychology (D Admin, D Com, PhD); curriculum studies (M Ed, Ed D); development studies (M Admin, MA, D Admin, PhD); didactics (M Ed, Ed D); education (M Tech); education management (M Ed, Ed D); educational psychology (M Ed); English (MA); environmental education (M Ed); French (MA, PhD); German (MA, PhD); Greek (MA); guidance and counseling (M Ed); health studies (MA, PhD), including health sciences education (MA), health services management (MA), medical and surgical nursing science (critical care general) (MA), midwifery and neonatal nursing science (MA), trauma and emergency care (MA); history (MA, PhD); history of education (Ed D); inclusive education (M Ed, Ed D); information and communications technology policy and regulation (MA); information science (MA, MIS, PhD); international politics (MA, PhD); Islamic studies (MA, PhD); Italian (MA, PhD); Judaica (MA, PhD); linguistics (MA, PhD); mathematical education (M Ed); mathematics education (MA); missiology (M Th, D Th); modern Hebrew (MA, PhD); musicology (MA, MMus, D Mus, PhD); natural science education (M Ed); New Testament (M Th, D Th); Old Testament (D Th); pastoral therapy (M Th, D Th); philosophy (MA); philosophy of education (M Ed, Ed D); politics (MA, PhD); Portuguese (MA, PhD); practical theology (M Th, D Th); psychology (MA, MS, PhD); psychology of education (M Ed, Ed D); public health (MA); religious studies (MA, D Th, PhD); Romance languages (MA); Russian (MA, PhD); Semitic languages (MA, PhD); social behavior studies in HIV/AIDS (MA); social science (mental health) (MA); social science in development studies (MA); social science in psychology (MA); social science in social work (MA); social science in sociology (MA); social work (MSW, DSW, PhD); socio-education (M Ed, Ed D); sociolinguistics (MA); sociology (MA, PhD); Spanish (MA, PhD); systematic theology (M Th, D Th); TESOL (teaching English to speakers of other languages) (MA); theological ethics (M Th, D Th); theory of literature (MA, PhD); urban ministries (D Th); urban ministry (M Th).

University of South Carolina, The Graduate School, College of Arts and Sciences, Department of Languages, Literatures, and Cultures, Columbia, SC 29208. Offers comparative literature (MA, PhD); foreign languages (MAT), including French, German, Spanish; French (MA); German (MA); Spanish (MA). *Program availability:* Part-time. *Degree requirements:* For master's, one foreign language, comprehensive exam, thesis optional; for doctorate, 2 foreign languages, comprehensive exam, thesis/dissertation. *Entrance requirements:* For master's and doctorate, GRE General Test, writing sample. Additional exam requirements/recommendations for international students: required—TOEFL (minimum score 75 iBT). Electronic applications accepted.

University of Southern California, Graduate School, Dana and David Dornsife College of Letters, Arts and Sciences, Comparative Studies in Literature and Culture Doctoral Program, Los Angeles, CA 90089. Offers comparative literature (PhD); comparative media and culture (PhD); Spanish and Latin American studies (PhD). *Degree requirements:* For doctorate, 2 foreign languages, comprehensive exam, thesis/dissertation. *Entrance requirements:* For doctorate, GRE, competence in language other than English (highly recommended). Additional exam requirements/recommendations for international students: required—TOEFL. Electronic applications accepted.

The University of Tennessee, Graduate School, College of Arts and Sciences, Department of Modern Foreign Languages and Literatures, Program in Modern Foreign Languages, Knoxville, TN 37996. Offers applied linguistics (PhD); French (PhD); German (PhD); Italian (PhD); Portuguese (PhD); Russian (PhD); Spanish (PhD). *Degree requirements:* For doctorate, 2 foreign languages, thesis/dissertation. *Entrance requirements:* For doctorate, minimum GPA of 2.7. Additional exam requirements/recommendations for international students: required—TOEFL. Electronic applications accepted.

The University of Tennessee, Graduate School, College of Arts and Sciences, Department of Modern Foreign Languages and Literatures, Program in Spanish, Knoxville, TN 37996. Offers MA. *Degree requirements:* For master's, one foreign language, thesis or alternative. *Entrance requirements:* For master's, minimum GPA of 2.7. Additional exam requirements/recommendations for international students: required—TOEFL. Electronic applications accepted.

The University of Texas at Arlington, Graduate School, College of Liberal Arts, Department of Modern Languages, Arlington, TX 76019. Offers French (MA); Spanish (MA). *Program availability:* Part-time, evening/weekend. *Degree requirements:* For master's, 2 foreign languages, comprehensive exam, thesis optional. *Entrance requirements:* For master's, GRE General Test, minimum GPA of 3.0, 3 letters of recommendation. Additional exam requirements/recommendations for international students: required—TOEFL (minimum score 550 paper-based).

The University of Texas at Austin, Graduate School, College of Liberal Arts, Department of Spanish and Portuguese, Austin, TX 78712-1111. Offers Hispanic linguistics (MA, PhD); Hispanic literature (MA, PhD); Ibero-romance philology and linguistics (PhD); Luso-Brazilian literature (MA, PhD). *Degree requirements:* For master's, 2 foreign languages, thesis or alternative; for doctorate, 3 foreign languages, thesis/dissertation. *Entrance requirements:* For master's and doctorate, GRE General Test. Electronic applications accepted.

The University of Texas at El Paso, Graduate School, College of Liberal Arts, Department of Creative Writing, El Paso, TX 79968-0001. Offers creative writing (MFA); creative writing of the Americas (MFA). *Program availability:* Part-time, evening/weekend, online learning. *Degree requirements:* For master's, thesis. *Entrance requirements:* For master's, minimum GPA of 3.0, letters of recommendation, writing sample. Additional exam requirements/recommendations for international students: recommended—TOEFL, IELTS. Electronic applications accepted.

The University of Texas at El Paso, Graduate School, College of Liberal Arts, Department of Languages and Linguistics, El Paso, TX 79968-0001. Offers linguistics (MA); Spanish (MA); teaching English to speakers of other languages (Certificate). *Program availability:* Part-time, evening/weekend. *Degree requirements:* For master's, thesis optional. *Entrance requirements:* For master's, GRE General Test, departmental exam, minimum GPA of 3.0, letters of recommendation. Additional exam requirements/recommendations for international students: required—TOEFL; recommended—IELTS. Electronic applications accepted.

The University of Texas at San Antonio, College of Liberal and Fine Arts, Department of Modern Languages and Literatures, San Antonio, TX 78249-0617. Offers Spanish (MA). *Program availability:* Part-time. *Degree requirements:* For master's, one foreign language, comprehensive exam, thesis optional. *Entrance requirements:* For master's, minimum GPA of 3.0, sample of written and spoken work, letter of recommendation, statement of purpose. Additional exam requirements/recommendations for international students: required—TOEFL (minimum score 550 paper-based; 79 iBT), IELTS (minimum score 6.5). Electronic applications accepted.

The University of Texas of the Permian Basin, Office of Graduate Studies, College of Arts and Sciences, Department of Literature and Languages, Odessa, TX 79762-0001. Offers English (MA); Spanish (MA). *Degree requirements:* For master's, comprehensive exam (for some programs), thesis (for some programs). *Entrance requirements:* For master's, GRE General Test. Additional exam requirements/recommendations for international students: required—TOEFL (minimum score 550 paper-based).

The University of Texas Rio Grande Valley, College of Liberal Arts, Department of Literatures and Cultural Studies, Edinburg, TX 78539. Offers English (MA); Spanish (MA). *Faculty:* 12 full-time (8 women). *Students:* 23 full-time (17 women), 54 part-time (34 women); includes 72 minority (2 Black or African American, non-Hispanic/Latino; 70 Hispanic/Latino), 3 international. Average age 32. 18 applicants, 89% accepted, 12 enrolled. In 2019, 26 master's awarded. *Expenses: Tuition, area resident:* Full-time $5959; part-time $440 per credit hour. Tuition, state resident: full-time $5959. Tuition, nonresident: full-time $5959. *International tuition:* $13,321 full-time. *Required fees:* $1169; $185 per credit hour. Website: utrgv.edu/literatures/index.htm

The University of Texas Rio Grande Valley, College of Liberal Arts, School of Interdisciplinary Programs and Community Engagement, Edinburg, TX 78539. Offers interdisciplinary studies (MAIS, MSIS); Spanish translation and interpreting (MA). *Faculty:* 2 full-time (1 woman). *Students:* 19 full-time (10 women), 38 part-time (26 women); includes 45 minority (1 Black or African American, non-Hispanic/Latino; 44 Hispanic/Latino), 6 international. Average age 35. 17 applicants, 76% accepted, 9 enrolled. In 2019, 27 master's awarded. *Expenses: Tuition, area resident:* Full-time $5959; part-time $440 per credit hour. Tuition, state resident: full-time $5959. Tuition, nonresident: full-time $5959. *International tuition:* $13,321 full-time. *Required fees:* $1169; $185 per credit hour. *Financial support:* Application deadline: 1/15. Website: utrgv.edu/school-of-interdisciplinary-programs-and-community-engagement/index.htm

The University of Toledo, College of Graduate Studies, College of Languages, Literature and Social Sciences, Department of Foreign Languages, Toledo, OH 43606-3390. Offers French (MA); German (MA); Spanish (MA). *Program availability:* Part-time. *Degree requirements:* For master's, one foreign language, comprehensive exam, comprehensive reading exam in 1 additional foreign language. *Entrance requirements:* For master's, minimum cumulative point-hour ratio of 2.7 for all previous academic work. Additional exam requirements/recommendations for international students: required—TOEFL (minimum score 550 paper-based; 80 iBT). Electronic applications accepted.

University of Toronto, School of Graduate Studies, Faculty of Arts and Science, Department of Spanish and Portuguese, Toronto, ON M5S 1A1, Canada. Offers MA, PhD. *Program availability:* Part-time. *Degree requirements:* For doctorate, thesis/dissertation. *Entrance requirements:* For master's, minimum B average in final year, 2 letters of reference; for doctorate, minimum A- average, 2 letters of reference, writing sample. Additional exam requirements/recommendations for international students: required—TWE (minimum score 5), TOEFL, Michigan English Language Assessment Battery, IELTS, or COPE. Electronic applications accepted.

University of Utah, Graduate School, College of Humanities, Department of World Languages and Cultures, Salt Lake City, UT 84112. Offers comparative literary and cultural studies (MA, PhD); French (MA); Spanish (MA, MALP); world languages (MA). *Program availability:* Part-time. *Faculty:* 22 full-time (14 women), 2 part-time/adjunct (1 woman). *Students:* 20 full-time (13 women), 5 part-time (3 women); includes 4 minority (all Hispanic/Latino), 8 international. Average age 33. 19 applicants, 68% accepted, 11 enrolled. In 2019, 12 master's, 1 doctorate awarded. Terminal master's awarded for partial completion of doctoral program. *Degree requirements:* For master's, one foreign language, comprehensive exam (for some programs), thesis (for some programs); for doctorate, one foreign language, comprehensive exam, thesis/dissertation. *Entrance requirements:* For master's, bachelor's degree from regionally-accredited college or university with minimum undergraduate overall GPA of 3.0; for doctorate, B.A. degree, B.A. degree. Additional exam requirements/recommendations for international students: required—TOEFL (minimum score 80 paper-based; 80 iBT), IELTS (minimum score 6.5). *Application deadline:* For fall admission, 1/15 priority date for domestic students, 12/15 priority date for international students. Application fee: $50 ($65 for international students). Electronic applications accepted. *Expenses:* Tuition, state resident: full-time $7085; part-time $272.51 per credit hour. Tuition, nonresident: full-time $24,937; part-time $959.12 per credit hour. *Required fees:* $880.52; $880.52 per semester. Tuition and fees vary according to degree level, program and student level. *Financial support:* In 2019–20, 21 students received support, including 21 teaching assistantships with full tuition reimbursements available (averaging $16,095 per year). Financial award application deadline: 1/15; financial award applicants required to submit CSS PROFILE or FAFSA. *Unit head:* Margaret Toscano, Associate Professor of Classics, 801-581-4786, E-mail: margaret.toscano@utah.edu. *Application contact:* Olivia Rose Davis, Graduate Academic Advisor, 801-581-7748, Fax: 801-581-7581, E-mail: olivia.davis@utah.edu. Website: http://languages.utah.edu/

University of Virginia, College and Graduate School of Arts and Sciences, Department of Spanish, Italian and Portuguese, Charlottesville, VA 22903. Offers Spanish (MA, PhD). *Degree requirements:* For master's, comprehensive exam, thesis; for doctorate, one foreign language, comprehensive exam, thesis/dissertation. *Entrance requirements:* For master's and doctorate, GRE General Test, GRE Subject Test, 2 letters of recommendation. Additional exam requirements/recommendations for international students: required—TOEFL (minimum score 600 paper-based; 90 iBT), IELTS (minimum score 7). Electronic applications accepted.

University of Washington, Graduate School, College of Arts and Sciences, Division of Spanish and Portuguese Studies, Seattle, WA 98195. Offers Hispanic literary and cultural studies (MA). *Degree requirements:* For master's, 2 foreign languages, thesis optional, exam. *Entrance requirements:* For master's, GRE General Test, minimum GPA of 3.0. Additional exam requirements/recommendations for international students: required—TOEFL. Electronic applications accepted.

The University of Western Ontario, School of Graduate and Postdoctoral Studies, Faculty of Arts and Humanities, Department of Modern Languages and Literatures, London, ON N6A 3K7, Canada. Offers comparative literature (MA, PhD); Hispanic studies (MA, PhD). *Program availability:* Part-time. *Degree requirements:* For master's, 2 foreign languages, thesis (for some programs). *Entrance requirements:* For master's, honors degree in Spanish or equivalent, minimum B average. Additional exam requirements/recommendations for international students: required—TOEFL (comparative literature).

University of Wisconsin–Madison, Graduate School, College of Letters and Science, Department of Spanish and Portuguese, Program in Spanish, Madison, WI 53706-1380. Offers MA, PhD. *Degree requirements:* For master's, one foreign language; for doctorate, 2 foreign languages, thesis/dissertation. *Entrance requirements:* For master's, GRE (recommended), minimum GPA of 3.25 in Spanish or Portuguese; for doctorate, GRE (recommended), minimum graduate GPA of 3.4, writing sample. Additional exam requirements/recommendations for international students: required—TOEFL. Electronic applications accepted.

University of Wisconsin–Milwaukee, Graduate School, College of Letters and Science, Department of Foreign Languages and Literature, Milwaukee, WI 53201-0413. Offers foreign languages and literature (MA), including classic Greek, classics, comparative literature, French/Francophone language, literature, and culture, German language, literature, and culture, interpreting, Latin, linguistics, Spanish language, literature, and culture, translation; interpreting (Graduate Certificate); language, literature, and translation (MA, MALLT); translation (Graduate Certificate). *Program availability:* Part-time. *Degree requirements:* For master's, 2 foreign languages, thesis or alternative. *Entrance requirements:* Additional exam requirements/recommendations for international students: required—TOEFL (minimum score 550 paper-based; 79 iBT), IELTS (minimum score 6.5). Electronic applications accepted.

University of Wisconsin–Milwaukee, Graduate School, College of Letters and Science, Department of Spanish and Portuguese, Milwaukee, WI 53201-0413. Offers MA. *Entrance requirements:* For master's, bachelor's degree. Electronic applications accepted.

University of Wyoming, College of Arts and Sciences, Department of Modern and Classical Languages, Program in Spanish, Laramie, WY 82071. Offers MA. *Program availability:* Part-time. *Degree requirements:* For master's, one foreign language, thesis or alternative. *Entrance requirements:* For master's, GRE General Test, minimum GPA of 3.0.

Université Laval, Faculty of Letters, Department of Literature, Programs in Spanish Literatures, Québec, QC G1K 7P4, Canada. Offers MA, PhD. *Program availability:* Part-time. Terminal master's awarded for partial completion of doctoral program. *Degree requirements:* For master's, thesis; for doctorate, comprehensive exam, thesis/dissertation. *Entrance requirements:* For master's and doctorate, linguistics exams, knowledge of French and Spanish. Electronic applications accepted.

Vanderbilt University, Department of Spanish and Portuguese, Nashville, TN 37240-1001. Offers Portuguese (MA); Spanish (PhD). *Faculty:* 11 full-time (4 women). *Students:* 24 full-time (12 women); includes 6 minority (1 Black or African American, non-Hispanic/Latino; 5 Hispanic/Latino),. 12 international. Average age 31. 33 applicants, 15% accepted, 4 enrolled. In 2019, 3 master's, 1 doctorate awarded. *Degree requirements:* For master's, one foreign language, thesis; for doctorate, 2 foreign languages, thesis/dissertation, final and qualifying exams. *Entrance requirements:* For master's, GRE General Test; for doctorate, GRE General Test, writing sample in Spanish. Additional exam requirements/recommendations for international students: required—TOEFL (minimum score 570 paper-based; 88 iBT). *Application deadline:* For fall admission, 1/15 for domestic and international students. Electronic applications accepted. *Expenses: Tuition:* Full-time $51,018; part-time $2087 per hour. *Required fees:* $542. Tuition and fees vary according to program. *Financial support:* Fellowships, teaching assistantships with full tuition reimbursements, Federal Work-Study, institutionally sponsored loans, and health care benefits available. Financial award application deadline: 1/15; financial award applicants required to submit CSS PROFILE or FAFSA. *Unit head:* Andres Zamora, Chair, 615-322-6930, Fax: 615-343-7260, E-mail: andres.zamora@vanderbilt.edu. *Application contact:* Jose Cardenas Bunsen, Director of Graduate Studies, 615-322-6930, Fax: 615-343-7260, E-mail: jose.cardenas-bunsen@Vanderbilt.Edu.
Website: http://as.vanderbilt.edu/spanish-portuguese/graduate/index.php

Washington University in St. Louis, The Graduate School, Department of Romance Languages and Literatures, Program in Spanish, St. Louis, MO 63130-4899. Offers Hispanic languages and literatures (PhD); Spanish and comparative literature (PhD). Terminal master's awarded for partial completion of doctoral program. *Degree requirements:* For doctorate, thesis/dissertation. *Entrance requirements:* For doctorate, GRE General Test. Additional exam requirements/recommendations for international students: required—TOEFL. Electronic applications accepted.

Wayne State University, College of Liberal Arts and Sciences, Department of Classical and Modern Languages, Literatures, and Cultures, Detroit, MI 48202. Offers classics (MA), including ancient Greek and Latin, ancient studies, classics, Latin; German (MA); language learning (MALL), including Arabic (MA, MALL), French (MA, MALL, PhD), German (MALL, PhD), Italian (MA, MALL), Spanish (MA, MALL, PhD); modern languages (PhD), including French (MA, MALL, PhD), German (MALL, PhD), Spanish (MA, MALL, PhD); Near Eastern languages (MA), including Arabic (MA, MALL), Hebrew; Romance languages (MA), including French (MA, MALL, PhD), Italian (MA, MALL), Spanish (MA, MALL, PhD). *Faculty:* 20. *Students:* 30 full-time (22 women), 15 part-time (9 women); includes 11 minority (4 Black or African American, non-Hispanic/Latino; 1 American Indian or Alaska Native, non-Hispanic/Latino; 2 Asian, non-Hispanic/Latino; 3 Hispanic/Latino; 1 Two or more races, non-Hispanic/Latino), 2 international. Average age 40. 32 applicants, 34% accepted, 9 enrolled. In 2019, 8 master's, 1 doctorate awarded. *Degree requirements:* For master's, variable foreign language requirement, comprehensive exam (for some programs), thesis (for some programs); for doctorate, one foreign language, comprehensive exam, thesis/dissertation. *Entrance requirements:* Additional exam requirements/recommendations for international students: required—TOEFL (minimum score 550 paper-based; 79 iBT), TWE (minimum score 5.5), Michigan English Language Assessment Battery (minimum score 85); recommended—IELTS (minimum score 6.5). Application fee: $50. Electronic applications accepted. *Expenses: Tuition:* Full-time $34,567. *Financial support:* In 2019–20, 22 students received support, including 1 fellowship with tuition reimbursement available (averaging $20,000 per year), 15 teaching assistantships with tuition reimbursements available (averaging $20,015 per year); research assistantships, scholarships/grants, health care benefits, and unspecified assistantships also available. Financial award applicants required to submit FAFSA. *Unit head:* Dr. Vanessa DEGifis, DR., Department Chair, 313-577-6244, Fax: 313-577-6243, E-mail: vdegifis@wayne.edu. *Application contact:* Terrie Pickering, Academic Services Officer, 313 577 3003, E-mail: t.pickering@wayne.edu. Website: http://clas.wayne.edu/languages/

Western Kentucky University, Graduate School, Potter College of Arts and Letters, Department of Modern Languages, Bowling Green, KY 42101. Offers French (MA Ed); German (MA Ed); Spanish (MA Ed).

Western Michigan University, Graduate College, College of Arts and Sciences, Department of Spanish, Kalamazoo, MI 49008. Offers MA, PhD.

Wichita State University, Graduate School, Fairmount College of Liberal Arts and Sciences, Department of Modern and Classical Languages and Literatures, Wichita, KS 67260. Offers Spanish (MA). *Program availability:* Part-time.

Worcester State University, Graduate School, Program in Spanish, Worcester, MA 01602-2597. Offers MA. *Program availability:* Part-time. *Faculty:* 2 part-time/adjunct (both women). *Students:* 6 part-time (3 women); includes 3 minority (all Hispanic/Latino). Average age 31. 4 applicants, 100% accepted, 2 enrolled. In 2019, 4 master's awarded. *Degree requirements:* For master's, comprehensive exam, thesis (for some programs), For a detail list in Degree Completion requirements please see the graduate catalog at catalog.worcester.edu. *Entrance requirements:* For master's, GRE, MAT, For a detail list of entrance requirements please see the graduate catalog at catalog.worcester.edu. Additional exam requirements/recommendations for international students: required—TOEFL (minimum score 550 paper-based; 79 iBT), IELTS (minimum score 6). *Application deadline:* For fall admission, 3/1 for domestic and international students; for spring admission, 11/1 for domestic and international students; for summer admission, 3/1 for domestic and international students. Applications are processed on a rolling basis. Application fee: $50. Electronic applications accepted. *Expenses: Tuition, area resident:* Full-time $3042; part-time $169 per credit hour. *Tuition, state resident:* full-time $3042; part-time $169 per credit hour. *Tuition, nonresident:* full-time $3042; part-time $169 per credit hour. *International tuition:* $3042 full-time. *Required fees:* $2754; $153 per credit hour. *Financial support:* Career-related internships or fieldwork, scholarships/grants, and unspecified assistantships available. Financial award application deadline: 3/1; financial award applicants required to submit FAFSA. *Unit head:* Dr. Antonio Guijarro-Donadios, Program Coordinator, 508-929-8619, Fax: 508-929-8174, E-mail: aguijarrodonadios@worcester.edu. *Application contact:* Sara Grady, Associate Dean, Graduate Studies and Professional Development, 508-929-8130, Fax: 508-929-8100, E-mail: sara.grady@worcester.edu.

Yale University, Graduate School of Arts and Sciences, Department of Spanish and Portuguese, New Haven, CT 06520. Offers Latin American literature (PhD); Luso-Brazilian and Spanish/Spanish American literatures (PhD); Spanish peninsular literature (PhD). Terminal master's awarded for partial completion of doctoral program. *Degree requirements:* For doctorate, 3 foreign languages, thesis/dissertation. *Entrance requirements:* For doctorate, GRE General Test.

Section 10
Linguistic Studies

This section contains a directory of institutions offering graduate work in linguistic studies. Additional information about programs listed in the directory may be obtained by writing directly to the dean of a graduate school or chair of a department at the address given in the directory.

For programs offering related work, see also in this book *Area and Cultural Studies, Language and Literature,* and *Sociology, Anthropology, and Archaeology.*

CONTENTS

Program Directories

Linguistics

Arizona State University at Tempe, College of Liberal Arts and Sciences, Department of English, Tempe, AZ 85287-0302. Offers applied linguistics (PhD); creative writing (MFA); English (MA, PhD), including comparative literature (MA), linguistics (MA), literature, rhetoric and composition (MA), rhetoric, composition, and linguistics (PhD); film and media studies (MAS), including American media and popular culture; linguistics (Graduate Certificate); teaching English to speakers of other languages (MTESOL); translation studies (Graduate Certificate). Terminal master's awarded for partial completion of doctoral program. *Degree requirements:* For master's, variable foreign language requirement, comprehensive exam (for some programs), thesis (for some programs), interactive Program of Study (iPOS) submitted before completing 50 percent of required credit hours; for doctorate, variable foreign language requirement, comprehensive exam, thesis/dissertation, interactive Program of Study (iPOS) submitted before completing 50 percent of required credit hours. *Entrance requirements:* For master's and doctorate, GRE, minimum GPA of 3.0 or equivalent in last 2 years of work leading to bachelor's degree. Additional exam requirements/recommendations for international students: required—TOEFL, IELTS, or PTE. Electronic applications accepted.

Ball State University, Graduate School, College of Sciences and Humanities, Department of English, Program in Linguistics, Muncie, IN 47306. Offers linguistics (MA); teaching English to speakers of other languages (TESOL) and linguistics (MA). *Program availability:* Part-time. *Entrance requirements:* For master's, GRE General Test, minimum baccalaureate GPA of 2.75 or 3.0 in latter half of baccalaureate, statement of purpose, writing sample, three letters of recommendation. Additional exam requirements/recommendations for international students: required—TOEFL (minimum score 550 paper-based; 79 iBT), IELTS (minimum score 6.5). Electronic applications accepted. *Expenses: Tuition, area resident:* Full-time $7506; part-time $417 per credit hour. Tuition, nonresident: full-time $20,610; part-time $1145 per credit hour. *Required fees:* $2126. Tuition and fees vary according to course load, campus/location and program.

Biola University, Cook School of Intercultural Studies, La Mirada, CA 90639-0001. Offers anthropology (MA); applied linguistics (MA); intercultural education (PhD); intercultural studies (MA, PhD); linguistics (Certificate); linguistics and Biblical languages (MA); missiology (D Miss); missions (MA); teaching English to speakers of other languages (MA, Certificate). *Program availability:* Part-time, 100% online. *Faculty:* 19. *Students:* 108 full-time (55 women), 154 part-time (86 women); includes 77 minority (11 Black or African American, non-Hispanic/Latino; 1 American Indian or Alaska Native, non-Hispanic/Latino; 43 Asian, non-Hispanic/Latino; 19 Hispanic/Latino; 3 Two or more races, non-Hispanic/Latino), 67 international. Average age 35. 142 applicants, 63% accepted, 52 enrolled. In 2019, 37 master's, 14 doctorates awarded. *Degree requirements:* For master's, comprehensive exam (for some programs), thesis or alternative, All students must successfully complete all required coursework with a minimum GPA of 3.0; for doctorate, thesis/dissertation, All students must present an acceptable dissertation, have satisfactorily passed their qualifying exam and completed all required course work with a minimum 3.3 GPA; for Certificate, All students musts successfully complete all required coursework with a minimum GPA of 3.0. *Entrance requirements:* For master's, minimum undergraduate GPA of 3.0; for doctorate, master's degree or equivalent, 3 years of cross-cultural experience, minimum graduate GPA of 3.3. Additional exam requirements/recommendations for international students: required—TOEFL. *Application deadline:* For fall admission, 7/1 for domestic students, 6/1 for international students; for spring admission, 11/1 for domestic students; for summer admission, 5/1 for domestic students. Applications are processed on a rolling basis. Application fee: $65. Electronic applications accepted. *Financial support:* Scholarships/grants available. Support available to part-time students. Financial award applicants required to submit FAFSA. *Unit head:* Dr. Bulus Y. Galadima, Dean, 562-903-4844. *Application contact:* Graduate Admissions Office, 562-903-4752, E-mail: graduate.admissions@biola.edu.
Website: http://cook.biola.edu

Boston College, Morrissey Graduate School of Arts and Sciences, Department of Slavic and Eastern Languages and Literatures, Program in Linguistics, Chestnut Hill, MA 02467-3800. Offers MA, MA/JD, MBA/MA. *Degree requirements:* For master's, 3 foreign languages, comprehensive exam, thesis or alternative. *Entrance requirements:* Additional exam requirements/recommendations for international students: required—TOEFL (minimum score 600 paper-based; 100 iBT), IELTS (minimum score 8). Electronic applications accepted.

Boston University, Graduate School of Arts and Sciences, Department of Linguistics, Boston, MA 02215. Offers MA, PhD. *Program availability:* Part-time. *Students:* 15 full-time (8 women), 4 part-time (all women); includes 3 minority (1 Asian, non-Hispanic/Latino; 1 Hispanic/Latino; 1 Two or more races, non-Hispanic/Latino), 7 international. Average age 25. 94 applicants, 36% accepted, 9 enrolled. In 2019, 13 master's awarded. Terminal master's awarded for partial completion of doctoral program. *Degree requirements:* For master's, one foreign language; for doctorate, 2 foreign languages, comprehensive exam, thesis/dissertation. *Entrance requirements:* For master's and doctorate, 3 letters of recommendation, transcripts, personal statement, curriculum vitae, writing sample. Additional exam requirements/recommendations for international students: required—TOEFL (minimum score 550 paper-based; 84 iBT). *Application deadline:* For fall admission, 1/6 for domestic and international students. Application fee: $95. Electronic applications accepted. *Financial support:* In 2019–20, 14 students received support, including 5 fellowships with full tuition reimbursements available (averaging $23,340 per year), 1 research assistantship (averaging $23,340 per year), 4 teaching assistantships with full tuition reimbursements available (averaging $23,340 per year); Federal Work-Study, scholarships/grants, and unspecified assistantships also available. Financial award application deadline: 1/6. *Unit head:* Jon Barnes, Director, 617-353-6222, E-mail: carol@bu.edu. *Application contact:* Richard Wong, Department Administrator, 617-358-4640, Fax: 617-358-4641, E-mail: wongr@bu.edu.
Website: http://ling.bu.edu/grad

Brigham Young University, Graduate Studies, College of Humanities, Department of Linguistics, Provo, UT 84602. Offers linguistics (MA); teaching English as a second language (MA). *Program availability:* Part-time. *Faculty:* 24 full-time (3 women). *Students:* 36 full-time (20 women), 17 part-time (12 women); includes 17 minority (1 American Indian or Alaska Native, non-Hispanic/Latino; 8 Asian, non-Hispanic/Latino; 5 Hispanic/Latino; 3 Native Hawaiian or other Pacific Islander, non-Hispanic/Latino). Average age 33. 33 applicants, 91% accepted, 23 enrolled. In 2019, 19 master's awarded. *Degree requirements:* For master's, 2 foreign languages, thesis. *Entrance requirements:* For master's, GRE General Test, minimum GPA of 3.0 in last 60 hours of course work. Additional exam requirements/recommendations for international students: required—TOEFL (minimum score 580 paper-based; 90 iBT), TWE. *Application deadline:* For fall admission, 1/15 for domestic and international students. Application fee: $50. Electronic applications accepted. *Financial support:* In 2019–20, 45 students received support, including 6 research assistantships (averaging $7,200 per year), 23 teaching assistantships (averaging $2,475 per year); career-related internships or fieldwork, scholarships/grants, unspecified assistantships, and travel to conference presentations also available. Financial award application deadline: 7/1. *Unit head:* Dr. Norman Evans, Chair, 801-422-8472, E-mail: norm_evans@byu.edu. *Application contact:* Mary Beth Wald, Graduate Program Manager, 801-422-9010, E-mail: marybeth_wald@byu.edu.
Website: http://linguistics.byu.edu/

Brigham Young University, Graduate Studies, College of Humanities, Department of Spanish and Portuguese, Provo, UT 84602. Offers Portuguese (MA), including Luso-Brazilian literatures, Portuguese linguistics, Portuguese pedagogy; Spanish (MA), including Hispanic linguistics, Hispanic literatures, Spanish pedagogy. *Faculty:* 33 full-time (8 women). *Students:* 34 full-time (24 women); includes 14 minority (1 Black or African American, non-Hispanic/Latino; 1 American Indian or Alaska Native, non-Hispanic/Latino; 1 Asian, non-Hispanic/Latino; 11 Hispanic/Latino). Average age 33. 17 applicants, 65% accepted, 9 enrolled. In 2019, 11 master's awarded. *Degree requirements:* For master's, 2 foreign languages, comprehensive exam, thesis, 1 semester of teaching. *Entrance requirements:* For master's, GRE, prerequisite second language requirement (can be fulfilled concurrently), prerequisite teaching methods course (can be fulfilled concurrently). Additional exam requirements/recommendations for international students: required—TOEFL (minimum score 580 paper-based; 85 iBT). *Application deadline:* For fall admission, 2/1 for domestic and international students. Application fee: $50. Electronic applications accepted. *Expenses:* $13,515 to complete two-year degree. *Financial support:* In 2019–20, 22 students received support, including 2 teaching assistantships with partial tuition reimbursements available (averaging $8,431 per year); scholarships/grants also available. Financial award application deadline: 2/1. *Unit head:* Dr. Scott Alvord, Interim Chair, Department of Spanish & Portuguese, 801-422-7546, Fax: 801-422-0308, E-mail: scott_alvord@byu.edu. *Application contact:* Brian A Price, Graduate Program Manager, 801-422-3453, Fax: 801-422-0308, E-mail: brian_price@byu.edu.
Website: http://spanport.byu.edu/

Brown University, Graduate School, Department of Cognitive, Linguistic and Psychological Sciences, Providence, RI 02912. Offers cognitive science (Sc M, PhD); linguistics (AM, PhD); psychology (PhD). *Degree requirements:* For master's, one foreign language, thesis or alternative; for doctorate, 2 foreign languages, thesis/dissertation.

California State University, Fresno, Division of Research and Graduate Studies, College of Arts and Humanities, Department of Linguistics, Fresno, CA 93740-8027. Offers linguistics (MA), including teaching English as a second language. *Program availability:* Part-time, evening/weekend. *Degree requirements:* For master's, comprehensive exam. *Entrance requirements:* For master's, GRE General Test, minimum GPA of 3.0. Additional exam requirements/recommendations for international students: required—TOEFL. Electronic applications accepted. *Expenses:* Tuition, state resident: full-time $4012; part-time $2506 per semester.

California State University, Fullerton, Graduate Studies, College of Humanities and Social Sciences, Department of English, Comparative Literature, and Linguistics, Fullerton, CA 92831-3599. Offers English (MA); linguistics (MA). *Program availability:* Part-time. *Degree requirements:* For master's, one foreign language, thesis or alternative, project. *Entrance requirements:* For master's, minimum GPA of 3.0, undergraduate major in linguistics or related field.

California State University, Long Beach, Graduate Studies, College of Liberal Arts, Department of Linguistics, Long Beach, CA 90840. Offers general linguistics (MA); language and culture (MA); special concentration (MA); teaching English to speakers of other languages (MA, Graduate Certificate). *Program availability:* Part-time, evening/weekend. *Degree requirements:* For master's, one foreign language, comprehensive exam, thesis optional. Electronic applications accepted.

California State University, Northridge, Graduate Studies, College of Humanities, Linguistics Program, Northridge, CA 91330. Offers MA. *Program availability:* Part-time, evening/weekend. *Degree requirements:* For master's, one foreign language, comprehensive exam, thesis, or project. *Entrance requirements:* For master's, GRE General Test or minimum GPA of 3.0. Additional exam requirements/recommendations for international students: required—TOEFL (minimum score 563 paper-based; 85 iBT).

Carleton University, Faculty of Graduate Studies, Faculty of Arts and Social Sciences, School of Linguistics and Applied Language Studies, Ottawa, ON K1S 5B6, Canada. Offers applied language studies (MA). *Degree requirements:* For master's, thesis optional. *Entrance requirements:* For master's, honors degree. Additional exam requirements/recommendations for international students: required—TOEFL or CAEL.

Carnegie Mellon University, Dietrich College of Humanities and Social Sciences, Department of Modern Languages, Pittsburgh, PA 15213-3891. Offers second language acquisition (MA, PhD). *Degree requirements:* For doctorate, one foreign language, comprehensive exam, thesis/dissertation. *Entrance requirements:* For doctorate, GRE General Test. Additional exam requirements/recommendations for international students: required—TOEFL.

Case Western Reserve University, School of Graduate Studies, Department of Cognitive Science, Cleveland, OH 44106. Offers cognitive linguistics (MA). *Program availability:* Part-time. *Degree requirements:* For master's, thesis. *Entrance requirements:* For master's, GRE, statement of purpose, three letters of recommendation, writing sample. Additional exam requirements/recommendations for international students: required—TOEFL (minimum score 577 paper-based; 90 iBT); recommended—IELTS (minimum score 7). Electronic applications accepted.

Concordia University, School of Graduate Studies, Faculty of Arts and Science, Department of Education, Program in Applied Linguistics, Montréal, QC H3G 1M8, Canada. Offers applied linguistics (MA); teaching English as a second language (Certificate).

Cornell University, Graduate School, Graduate Fields of Arts and Sciences, Field of Asian Studies, Ithaca, NY 14853. Offers East Asian linguistics (MA); East Asian studies (MA); South Asian linguistics (MA); South Asian studies (MA); Southeast Asian linguistics (MA); Southeast Asian studies (MA). *Degree requirements:* For master's, one foreign language, thesis. *Entrance requirements:* For master's, GRE General Test, 3 letters of recommendation. Additional exam requirements/recommendations for international students: required—TOEFL (minimum score 550 paper-based; 77 iBT). Electronic applications accepted.

Cornell University, Graduate School, Graduate Fields of Arts and Sciences, Field of Linguistics, Ithaca, NY 14853. Offers applied linguistics (MA, PhD); East Asian linguistics (MA, PhD); English linguistics (MA, PhD); general linguistics (MA, PhD); Germanic linguistics (MA, PhD); Indo-European linguistics (MA, PhD); phonetics (MA, PhD); phonological theory (MA, PhD); Romance linguistics (MA, PhD); second language acquisition (MA, PhD); semantics (MA, PhD); Slavic linguistics (MA, PhD); sociolinguistics (MA, PhD); South Asian linguistics (MA, PhD); Southeast Asian linguistics (MA, PhD); syntactic theory (MA, PhD). Terminal master's awarded for partial completion of doctoral program. *Degree requirements:* For master's, one foreign language, thesis; for doctorate, one foreign language, comprehensive exam, thesis/dissertation. *Entrance requirements:* For master's and doctorate, GRE General Test, 2 letters of recommendation. Additional exam requirements/recommendations for international students: required—TOEFL (minimum score 600 paper-based; 77 iBT). Electronic applications accepted.

Dallas International University, Graduate Programs, Dallas, TX 75236. Offers applied linguistics (MA, Certificate); language development (MA). *Program availability:* Part-time. *Degree requirements:* For master's, one foreign language, comprehensive exam (for some programs), thesis (for some programs). *Entrance requirements:* For master's, GRE. Additional exam requirements/recommendations for international students: required—TOEFL (minimum score 577 paper-based; 90 iBT). Electronic applications accepted.

East Carolina University, Graduate School, Thomas Harriot College of Arts and Sciences, Department of English, Greenville, NC 27858-4353. Offers creative writing (MA); English studies (MA); linguistics (MA); literature (MA); multicultural and transnational literatures (MA, Certificate); professional communication (Certificate); rhetoric and composition (MA); rhetoric, writing, and professional communication (PhD); teaching English in the two-year college (Certificate); teaching English to speakers of other languages (MA, Certificate); technical and professional communication (MA). *Program availability:* Part-time, evening/weekend, online learning. *Application deadline:* For fall admission, 7/31 priority date for domestic students, 2/1 priority date for international students; for spring admission, 11/30 priority date for domestic students, 10/1 priority date for international students. *Expenses: Tuition, area resident:* Full-time $4749; part-time $185 per credit hour. Tuition, state resident: full-time $4749; part-time $185 per credit hour. Tuition, nonresident: full-time $17,898; part-time $864 per credit hour. *International tuition:* $17,898 full-time. *Required fees:* $2787. *Financial support:* Application deadline: 3/1. *Unit head:* Dr. Marianne Montgomery, Chair, 252-328-6041, E-mail: montgomerym@ecu.edu. *Application contact:* Graduate School Admissions, 252-328-6012, Fax: 252-328-6071, E-mail: gradschool@ecu.edu. Website: https://english.ecu.edu/

Eastern Michigan University, Graduate School, College of Arts and Sciences, Department of English Language and Literature, Program in English Linguistics, Ypsilanti, MI 48197. Offers MA. *Program availability:* Part-time, evening/weekend, online learning. *Students:* 6 full-time (5 women), 4 part-time (3 women); includes 2 minority (1 Asian, non-Hispanic/Latino; 1 Two or more races, non-Hispanic/Latino). Average age 27. 10 applicants, 70% accepted, 4 enrolled. In 2019, 5 master's awarded. *Entrance requirements:* Additional exam requirements/recommendations for international students: required—TOEFL. *Application deadline:* Applications are processed on a rolling basis. Application fee: $45. *Financial support:* Fellowships with tuition reimbursements, research assistantships with full tuition reimbursements, teaching assistantships with full tuition reimbursements, career-related internships or fieldwork, Federal Work-Study, institutionally sponsored loans, scholarships/grants, tuition waivers (partial), and unspecified assistantships available. Support available to part-time students. Financial award applicants required to submit FAFSA. *Application contact:* Dr. T. Daniel Seely, Program Advisor, 734-487-0145, Fax: 734-483-9744, E-mail: tseely@emich.edu.

Florida Atlantic University, Dorothy F. Schmidt College of Arts and Letters, Department of Languages, Linguistics, and Comparative Literature, Boca Raton, FL 33431-0991. Offers comparative literature (MA); French (MA); linguistics (MA); Spanish (MA). *Program availability:* Part-time. *Faculty:* 20 full-time (13 women). *Students:* 29 full-time (17 women), 11 part-time (9 women); includes 22 minority (7 Black or African American, non-Hispanic/Latino; 1 Asian, non-Hispanic/Latino; 14 Hispanic/Latino), 4 international. Average age 37. 30 applicants, 67% accepted, 16 enrolled. In 2019, 14 master's awarded. *Degree requirements:* For master's, one foreign language, comprehensive exam, thesis optional. *Entrance requirements:* For master's, GRE General Test, minimum GPA of 3.0. Additional exam requirements/recommendations for international students: required—TOEFL (minimum score 500 paper-based; 61 iBT), IELTS (minimum score 6). *Application deadline:* For fall admission, 7/1 priority date for domestic students, 2/15 for international students; for spring admission, 11/1 for domestic students, 7/15 for international students. Applications are processed on a rolling basis. Application fee: $30. *Expenses: Tuition:* Full-time $20,536; part-time $371.82 per credit hour. Tuition and fees vary according to program. *Financial support:* Fellowships, research assistantships, teaching assistantships with partial tuition reimbursements, Federal Work-Study, and tuition waivers (partial) available. Support available to part-time students. Financial award application deadline: 4/1. *Unit head:* Dr. Marcella Munson, Chair, 561-297-2118, Fax: 561-297-2756, E-mail: mmunson@fau.edu. *Application contact:* Dr. Marcella Munson, Chair, 561-297-2118, Fax: 561-297-2756, E-mail: mmunson@fau.edu. Website: http://www.fau.edu/LLCL/

Florida International University, College of Arts, Sciences, and Education, Department of English, Miami, FL 33199. Offers creative writing (MFA); English (MA), including literature; linguistics (MA). *Program availability:* Part-time, evening/weekend. *Faculty:* 64 full-time (30 women), 31 part-time/adjunct (20 women). *Students:* 48 full-time (32 women), 34 part-time (17 women); includes 52 minority (6 Black or African American, non-Hispanic/Latino; 2 Asian, non-Hispanic/Latino; 43 Hispanic/Latino; 1 Two or more races, non-Hispanic/Latino), 2 international. Average age 30. 48 applicants, 56% accepted, 25 enrolled. In 2019, 21 master's awarded. *Entrance requirements:* For master's, GRE General Test, minimum undergraduate GPA of 3.0 (upper-level coursework), letter of intent, two letters of recommendation. Additional exam requirements/recommendations for international students: required—TOEFL (minimum score 550 paper-based; 80 iBT). *Application deadline:* For fall admission, 2/1 for domestic and international students; for spring admission, 10/1 for domestic students, 9/1 for international students. Applications are processed on a rolling basis. Application fee: $30. Electronic applications accepted. *Expenses: Tuition, area resident:* Full-time $8912; part-time $446 per credit hour. Tuition, state resident: full-time $8912; part-time $446 per credit hour. Tuition, nonresident: full-time $21,393; part-time $992 per credit hour. *Required fees:* $2194. *Financial support:* Institutionally sponsored loans and scholarships/grants available. Financial award application deadline: 3/1; financial award applicants required to submit FAFSA. *Unit head:* Dr. Anna Luszczynska, Chair, 305-348-2203, Fax: 305-348-3878, E-mail: Ana.Luszczynska@fiu.edu. *Application contact:* Nanett Rojas, Manager, Admissions Operations, 305-348-7464, Fax: 305-348-7441, E-mail: gradadm@fiu.edu.

Gallaudet University, The Graduate School, Washington, DC 20002. Offers American Sign Language/English bilingual early childhood deaf education: birth to 5 (Certificate); audiology (Au D); clinical psychology (PhD); deaf and hard of hearing infants, toddlers, and their families (Certificate); deaf education (MA, Ed S); deaf history (Certificate); deaf studies (Certificate); educating deaf students with disabilities (Certificate); education: teacher preparation (MA), including deaf education, early childhood education and deaf education, elementary education and deaf education, secondary education and deaf education; educational neuroscience (PhD); hearing, speech and language sciences (MS, PhD); international development (MA); interpretation (MA, PhD), including combined interpreting practice and research (MA), interpreting research (MA); linguistics (MA, PhD); mental health counseling (MA); peer mentoring (Certificate); public administration (MPA); school counseling (MA); school psychology (Psy S); sign language teaching (MA); social work (MSW); speech-language pathology (MS). *Program availability:* Part-time. *Faculty:* 101 full-time (70 women). *Students:* 267 full-time (208 women), 139 part-time (95 women); includes 120 minority (38 Black or African American, non-Hispanic/Latino; 20 Asian, non-Hispanic/Latino; 44 Hispanic/Latino; 18 Two or more races, non-Hispanic/Latino), 19 international. Average age 30. 484 applicants, 50% accepted, 162 enrolled. In 2019, 138 master's, 25 doctorates, 14 other advanced degrees awarded. Terminal master's awarded for partial completion of doctoral program. *Degree requirements:* For master's, comprehensive exam (for some programs), thesis optional; for doctorate, comprehensive exam, thesis/dissertation. *Entrance requirements:* For master's and doctorate, GRE General Test or MAT, letters of recommendation, interviews, goals statement, American Sign Language proficiency interview, written English competency. Additional exam requirements/recommendations for international students: required—TOEFL. *Application deadline:* For fall admission, 2/15 for domestic students. Applications are processed on a rolling basis. Application fee: $75. Electronic applications accepted. *Expenses: Tuition:* Full-time $18,180; part-time $688 per credit. *Required fees:* $526; $526. Tuition and fees vary according to course load. *Financial support:* In 2019–20, 50 students received support. Fellowships, research assistantships, teaching assistantships, career-related internships or fieldwork, Federal Work-Study, scholarships/grants, tuition waivers (partial), and unspecified assistantships available. Support available to part-time students. Financial award application deadline: 7/1; financial award applicants required to submit FAFSA. *Unit head:* Dr. Gaurav Mathur, Dean, Graduate School and Continuing Studies, 202-250-2380, Fax: 202-651-5027, E-mail: gaurav.mathur@gallaudet.edu. *Application contact:* Heidi Zornes-Foster, Senior Graduate Admissions Counselor, 202-650-5436, Fax: 202-651-5295, E-mail: graduate.school@gallaudet.edu. Website: www.gallaudet.edu

George Mason University, College of Humanities and Social Sciences, Department of English, Fairfax, VA 22030. Offers college teaching (Certificate), including higher education pedagogy; creative writing (MFA), including fiction, nonfiction writing, poetry; English (MA), including cultural studies, linguistics, literature, professional writing and rhetoric, teaching of writing and literature; English pedagogy (Certificate); folklore studies (Certificate); linguistics (PhD); writing and rhetoric (PhD). *Program availability:* Part-time. *Degree requirements:* For master's, thesis (for some programs), proficiency in a foreign language by course work or translation test; for doctorate, comprehensive exam, thesis/dissertation, 2 papers. *Entrance requirements:* For master's, official transcripts; expanded goals statement; writing sample; portfolio; 2 letters of recommendation; resume; for doctorate, GRE (for linguistics), expanded goals statement; 2 letters of recommendation (writing and rhetoric); 3 letters of recommendation (linguistics); writing sample; introductory course in linguistics; official transcripts; master's degree in relevant field; for Certificate, official transcripts; expanded goals statement; 2 letters of recommendation; writing sample; resume. Additional exam requirements/recommendations for international students: required—TOEFL (minimum score 575 paper-based; 88 iBT), IELTS (minimum score 6.5), PTE (minimum score 59). Electronic applications accepted.

Georgetown University, Graduate School of Arts and Sciences, Department of Linguistics, Washington, DC 20057. Offers language and communication (MA); linguistics (MS, PhD), including applied linguistics, computational linguistics, sociolinguistics, theoretical linguistics. *Faculty:* 21. *Students:* 117. Terminal master's awarded for partial completion of doctoral program. *Degree requirements:* For master's, variable foreign language requirement, comprehensive exam (for some programs), thesis (for some programs); for doctorate, one foreign language, comprehensive exam, thesis/dissertation. *Entrance requirements:* Additional exam requirements/recommendations for international students: required—TOEFL. *Application deadline:* For fall admission, 12/15 for domestic students. Application fee: $80. Electronic applications accepted. *Financial support:* Research assistantships and teaching assistantships available. Financial award application deadline: 12/15. *Unit head:* Dr. Elizabeth Zsiga, Chair, E-mail: linguistics@georgetown.edu. *Application contact:* Graduate School Admissions Office, 202-687-5568. Website: http://linguistics.georgetown.edu/graduate

Georgia State University, College of Arts and Sciences, Department of Applied Linguistics and English as a Second Language, Atlanta, GA 30302-3083. Offers applied linguistics (MA, PhD). *Program availability:* Part-time. *Faculty:* 12 full-time (8 women). *Students:* 60 full-time (43 women), 24 part-time (19 women); includes 23 minority (9 Black or African American, non-Hispanic/Latino; 4 Asian, non-Hispanic/Latino; 7 Hispanic/Latino; 1 Native Hawaiian or other Pacific Islander, non-Hispanic/Latino; 2 Two or more races, non-Hispanic/Latino), 21 international. Average age 33. 91 applicants, 36% accepted, 19 enrolled. In 2019, 23 master's, 3 doctorates awarded. *Degree requirements:* For master's, one foreign language, portfolio; for doctorate, one foreign language, comprehensive exam, thesis/dissertation, qualifying exam. *Entrance requirements:* For master's and doctorate, GRE. Additional exam requirements/recommendations for international students: required—TWE (minimum score 4). *Application deadline:* For fall admission, 1/15 for domestic and international students; for spring admission, 11/15 for domestic and international students. Applications are processed on a rolling basis. Application fee: $50. Electronic applications accepted. *Expenses: Tuition, area resident:* Full-time $7164; part-time $398 per credit hour. Tuition, state resident: full-time $7164; part-time $398 per credit hour. Tuition, nonresident: full-time $22,662; part-time $1259 per credit hour. *International tuition:* $22,662 full-time. *Required fees:* $2128; $312 per credit hour. Tuition and fees vary according to course load and program. *Financial support:* In 2019–20, fellowships with full tuition reimbursements (averaging $23,500 per year), research assistantships with full tuition reimbursements (averaging $5,000 per year), teaching assistantships with full tuition reimbursements (averaging $8,500 per year) were awarded; scholarships/grants and unspecified assistantships also available. Financial award application deadline: 6/1. *Unit head:* Dr. Diane C. Belcher, Chair, Fax: 404-413-5201, E-mail: dbelcher1@gsu.edu. *Application contact:* Dr. Diane C. Belcher, Chair, Fax: 404-413-5201, E-mail: dbelcher1@gsu.edu. Website: https://alsl.gsu.edu/

Georgia State University, College of Arts and Sciences, Department of World Languages and Cultures, Program in French, Atlanta, GA 30302-3083. Offers applied linguistics and pedagogy (MA); French studies (MA); literature and culture (MA). *Program availability:* Part-time. *Entrance requirements:* For master's, GRE, statement of purpose, writing sample in the target language, 2 letters of recommendation, official transcripts. Additional exam requirements/recommendations for international students: required—TOEFL (minimum score 79 iBT). Application fee: $50. Electronic applications

accepted. *Expenses: Tuition, area resident:* Full-time $7164; part-time $398 per credit hour. Tuition, state resident: full-time $7164; part-time $398 per credit hour. Tuition, nonresident: full-time $22,662; part-time $1259 per credit hour. *International tuition:* $22,662 full-time. *Required fees:* $2128; $312 per credit hour. Tuition and fees vary according to course load and program. *Financial support:* Institutionally sponsored loans available. Financial award applicants required to submit FAFSA. *Unit head:* Dr. William Nichols, Department Chair, 404-413-5980, Fax: 404-413-5982, E-mail: wnichols@gsu.edu. *Application contact:* Vicky Hanning, Administrative Coordinator, 404-413-5990, Fax: 404-413-5036, E-mail: vcasem@gsu.edu.
Website: https://wlc.gsu.edu/

The Graduate Center, City University of New York, Graduate Studies, Program in Anthropology, New York, NY 10016-4039. Offers anthropological linguistics (PhD); archaeology (PhD); cultural anthropology (PhD); physical anthropology (PhD). *Degree requirements:* For doctorate, one foreign language, thesis/dissertation. *Entrance requirements:* For doctorate, GRE General Test. Additional exam requirements/recommendations for international students: required—TOEFL. Electronic applications accepted.

The Graduate Center, City University of New York, Graduate Studies, Program in Linguistics, New York, NY 10016-4039. Offers MA, PhD. Terminal master's awarded for partial completion of doctoral program. *Degree requirements:* For master's, one foreign language, thesis; for doctorate, 2 foreign languages, thesis/dissertation. *Entrance requirements:* For master's and doctorate, GRE General Test. Additional exam requirements/recommendations for international students: required—TOEFL. Electronic applications accepted.

Grand Valley State University, College of Liberal Arts and Sciences, Program in Applied Linguistics, Allendale, MI 49401-9403. Offers MA. *Program availability:* Part-time. *Students:* 12 full-time (10 women), 4 part-time (3 women); includes 2 minority (1 Hispanic/Latino; 1 Two or more races, non-Hispanic/Latino), 4 international. Average age 28. 10 applicants, 100% accepted, 5 enrolled. In 2019, 7 master's awarded. *Degree requirements:* For master's, thesis optional, Thesis or project. *Entrance requirements:* For master's, minimum GPA of 3.0 or GRE; personal statement; writing sample; 2 letters of recommendation. Additional exam requirements/recommendations for international students: required—TOEFL (minimum iBT score of 79), IELTS (6.5), or Michigan English Language Assessment Battery (77). *Application deadline:* Applications are processed on a rolling basis. Application fee: $30. Electronic applications accepted. *Expenses:* $671 per credit hour, 36 credit hours. *Financial support:* In 2019–20, 3 students received support, including 1 fellowship with full and partial tuition reimbursement available (averaging $8,000 per year), 2 research assistantships with full and partial tuition reimbursements available (averaging $8,000 per year). *Unit head:* Dr. Ashley Shannon, Department Director, 616-331-3405, Fax: 616-331-3430, E-mail: shannoas@gvsu.edu. *Application contact:* Dr. Shinian Wu, Graduate Program Director, 616-331-3690, Fax: 616-331-3430, E-mail: wus@gvsu.edu.
Website: http://www.gvsu.edu/linguistics/

Harvard University, Graduate School of Arts and Sciences, Department of Linguistics, Cambridge, MA 02138. Offers descriptive linguistics (PhD); historical linguistics (PhD); theoretical linguistics (PhD). *Degree requirements:* For doctorate, 4 foreign languages, thesis/dissertation, field exam, Indo-European language exam, research paper. *Entrance requirements:* For doctorate, GRE General Test. Additional exam requirements/recommendations for international students: required—TOEFL.

Hofstra University, College of Liberal Arts and Sciences, Programs in Forensic Linguistics and Applied Linguistics, Hempstead, NY 11549. Offers applied linguistics (TESOL) (MA); linguistics (MA), including forensic linguistics. *Program availability:* Part-time, evening/weekend. *Students:* 37 full-time (33 women), 8 part-time (5 women); includes 11 minority (2 Black or African American, non-Hispanic/Latino; 3 Asian, non-Hispanic/Latino; 6 Hispanic/Latino), 3 international. Average age 27. 63 applicants, 79% accepted, 23 enrolled. In 2019, 14 master's awarded. *Degree requirements:* For master's, thesis, 36 credits, capstone, minimum GPA of 3.0. *Entrance requirements:* For master's, bachelor's degree in related area, interview, 2 letters of recommendation. Additional exam requirements/recommendations for international students: required—TOEFL (minimum score 550 paper-based; 80 iBT); recommended—IELTS (minimum score 6.5). *Application deadline:* Applications are processed on a rolling basis. Application fee: $75. Electronic applications accepted. *Expenses: Tuition:* Full-time $25,164; part-time $1398 per credit. *Required fees:* $580; $165 per semester. Tuition and fees vary according to course load, degree level and program. *Financial support:* In 2019–20, 34 students received support, including 16 fellowships with full and partial tuition reimbursements available (averaging $3,918 per year); research assistantships with full and partial tuition reimbursements available, career-related internships or fieldwork, Federal Work-Study, institutionally sponsored loans, scholarships/grants, tuition waivers (full and partial), unspecified assistantships, and scholarships and endowed scholarships also available. Support available to part-time students. Financial award applicants required to submit FAFSA. *Unit head:* Dr. John Krapp, Chairperson, 516-463-5843, E-mail: John.J.Krapp@hofstra.edu. *Application contact:* Sunil Samuel, Assistant Vice President of Admissions, 516-463-4723, Fax: 516-463-4664, E-mail: graduateadmission@hofstra.edu.
Website: http://www.hofstra.edu/hclas

Indiana State University, College of Graduate and Professional Studies, College of Arts and Sciences, Department of Languages, Literatures, and Linguistics, Terre Haute, IN 47809. Offers applied linguistics/teaching English as a second language (MA); language education (PhD); Spanish/teaching English as a second language (MA); TESL/TEFL (CAS). *Degree requirements:* For master's, comprehensive exam. Electronic applications accepted.

Indiana University Bloomington, University Graduate School, College of Arts and Sciences, Department of Anthropology, Bloomington, IN 47405. Offers anthropology (MA, PhD), including archaeology (PhD), bioanthropology (PhD), linguistic anthropology (PhD), social-cultural anthropology (PhD). *Degree requirements:* For master's, comprehensive exam (for some programs), thesis or alternative; for doctorate, 2 foreign languages, comprehensive exam, thesis/dissertation. *Entrance requirements:* For master's and doctorate, GRE General Test, minimum GPA of 3.0. Additional exam requirements/recommendations for international students: required—TOEFL (minimum score 550 paper-based, 79 iBT) or IELTS. Electronic applications accepted. *Expenses:* Contact institution.

Indiana University Bloomington, University Graduate School, College of Arts and Sciences, Department of French and Italian, Bloomington, IN 47405. Offers French (MA, PhD), including French and Francophone studies (MA), French instruction (MA), French linguistics; Italian (MA, PhD). *Program availability:* Part-time. Terminal master's awarded for partial completion of doctoral program. *Degree requirements:* For master's, variable foreign language requirement, comprehensive exam (for some programs), thesis or alternative; for doctorate, variable foreign language requirement, comprehensive exam, thesis/dissertation. *Entrance requirements:* For master's, GRE General Test, BA or equivalent undergraduate preparation in French or Italian; for doctorate, GRE General Test, MA from degree program at IU; MA in the specific field. Additional exam requirements/recommendations for international students: required—TOEFL (minimum score 550 paper-based; 79 iBT), GRE General Test (recommended). Electronic applications accepted.

Indiana University Bloomington, University Graduate School, College of Arts and Sciences, Department of Germanic Studies, Bloomington, IN 47405-7000. Offers German philology and linguistics (PhD); German studies (MA, PhD), including German (MA), German literature and culture (MA), German literature and linguistics (MA); medieval German studies (PhD); teaching German (MAT). *Degree requirements:* For master's, one foreign language, project; for doctorate, one foreign language, comprehensive exam, thesis/dissertation. *Entrance requirements:* For master's, GRE General Test, BA in German or equivalent; for doctorate, GRE General Test, MA in German or equivalent. Additional exam requirements/recommendations for international students: required—TOEFL. Electronic applications accepted.

Indiana University Bloomington, University Graduate School, College of Arts and Sciences, Department of Linguistics, Bloomington, IN 47405. Offers African languages and linguistics (PhD); computational linguistics (MA, MS, PhD); linguistics (MA, PhD). Terminal master's awarded for partial completion of doctoral program. *Degree requirements:* For master's, one foreign language, thesis optional; for doctorate, one foreign language, comprehensive exam, thesis/dissertation, proficiency in research tool appropriate to research area. *Entrance requirements:* For master's and doctorate, GRE General Test. Additional exam requirements/recommendations for international students: required—TOEFL (minimum score 580 paper-based; 92 iBT). Electronic applications accepted.

Instituto Tecnologico de Santo Domingo, Graduate School, Area of Humanities and Social Sciences, Santo Domingo, Dominican Republic. Offers accounting (Certificate); adult education (Certificate); applied linguistics (MA); economics (MA); education (M Ed); educational psychology (MA, Certificate); gender and development (MA, Certificate); humanistic studies (MA); international marketing management (Certificate); international relations in the Caribbean basin (Certificate); intervention systems in family therapy (MA); linguistic and literary communication (Certificate); pedagogical support (MA); social science education (M Ed); sustainable human development (MA); terminal illness and death psychology (Certificate); youth and adult education (M Ed).

Iowa State University of Science and Technology, Program in Applied Linguistics and Technology, Ames, IA 50011. Offers PhD. *Entrance requirements:* For doctorate, GRE, official academic transcripts, resume, three letters of recommendation, writing sample. Additional exam requirements/recommendations for international students: required—TOEFL (minimum score 640 paper-based; 111 iBT), IELTS (minimum score 7.5). Electronic applications accepted.

Iowa State University of Science and Technology, Program in Teaching English as a Second Language/Applied Linguistics, Ames, IA 50011. Offers MA. *Entrance requirements:* For master's, GRE, official academic transcripts, resume, three letters of recommendation, statement of personal goals, writing sample. Additional exam requirements/recommendations for international students: required—TOEFL (minimum score 600 paper-based; 100 iBT), IELTS (minimum score 7). Electronic applications accepted.

Kent State University, College of Arts and Sciences, Department of Modern and Classical Language Studies, Kent, OH 44242-0001. Offers French (MA), including applied linguistics and pedagogy, literature; German (MA), including applied linguistics and pedagogy, literature; Latin (MA), including applied linguistics and pedagogy, literature; Spanish (MA), including applied linguistics and pedagogy, literature; translation (MA), including Arabic, French, German, Japanese, Russian, Spanish; translation studies (PhD); MA/MBA. *Program availability:* Part-time, 100% online. *Faculty:* 18 full-time (11 women), 6 part-time/adjunct (3 women). *Students:* 81 full-time (49 women), 23 part-time (14 women); includes 18 minority (3 Black or African American, non-Hispanic/Latino; 3 Asian, non-Hispanic/Latino; 11 Hispanic/Latino; 1 Two or more races, non-Hispanic/Latino), 45 international. Average age 32. 115 applicants, 73% accepted, 47 enrolled. In 2019, 27 master's, 7 doctorates awarded. *Degree requirements:* For master's, variable foreign language requirement, comprehensive exam (for some programs), thesis (for some programs); for doctorate, variable foreign language requirement, comprehensive exam, thesis/dissertation. *Entrance requirements:* For master's, transcripts, goal statement, 3 letters of recommendation, CD/MP3 with a 5-10 minute oral sample of first and second languages (conversational not read from a script), Writing sample(s) in the applicant's second language, which should be accompanied by a signed declaration that the sample is original work; for doctorate, transcripts; MA in translation, a foreign language, or in any other relevant discipline with prior experience or training in translation; proficiency in a foreign language; minimum GPA of 3.5 from MA; goal statement; 3 letters of recommendation; essay or writing sample (7-10 pages) from a research paper on any aspect of translation. Additional exam requirements/recommendations for international students: required—TOEFL (minimum score 79 iBT), IELTS (minimum score 6.5), PTE (minimum score 58), Michigan English Language Assessment Battery (minimum score 77). *Application deadline:* For fall admission, 2/1 for domestic and international students. Applications are processed on a rolling basis. Application fee: $45 ($70 for international students). Electronic applications accepted. *Financial support:* Fellowships with full tuition reimbursements, teaching assistantships with full tuition reimbursements, and unspecified assistantships available. Financial award application deadline: 2/1. *Unit head:* Dr. Keiran Dunne, Professor of French Translation; Department Chair, 330-672-2150, E-mail: kdunne@kent.edu. *Application contact:* Brian James Baer, Professor of Russian Translation; Graduate Coordinator, 330-672-1813, E-mail: bbaer@kent.edu.
Website: http://www.kent.edu/mcls/

Massachusetts Institute of Technology, School of Humanities, Arts, and Social Sciences, Department of Linguistics and Philosophy, Linguistics Section, Cambridge, MA 02139. Offers PhD. *Degree requirements:* For doctorate, comprehensive exam, thesis/dissertation, teaching assistantship during two semesters. *Entrance requirements:* Additional exam requirements/recommendations for international students: required—TOEFL, IELTS. Electronic applications accepted.

McGill University, Faculty of Graduate and Postdoctoral Studies, Faculty of Arts, Department of Linguistics, Montréal, QC H3A 2T5, Canada. Offers language acquisition (PhD); linguistics (MA, PhD).

Memorial University of Newfoundland, School of Graduate Studies, Department of Linguistics, St. John's, NL A1C 5S7, Canada. Offers MA, PhD. *Program availability:* Part-time. *Degree requirements:* For master's, one foreign language, thesis or comprehensive exam; for doctorate, 2 foreign languages, comprehensive exam, thesis/dissertation, oral defense of thesis. *Entrance requirements:* For master's, bachelor's degree in linguistics; for doctorate, master's degree in linguistics. Electronic applications accepted.

Michigan State University, The Graduate School, College of Arts and Letters, Department of Linguistics and Germanic, Slavic, Asian, and African Languages, East Lansing, MI 48824. Offers German studies (MA, PhD); linguistics (MA, PhD); teaching English to speakers of other languages (MA). *Program availability:* Part-time, evening/weekend. *Entrance requirements:* For master's, GRE General Test, minimum GPA of 3.2 in last 2 undergraduate years, 2 years of college-level foreign language, 3 letters of recommendation, portfolio (German studies); for doctorate, GRE General Test, minimum graduate GPA of 3.5, 3 letters of recommendation, master's degree or sufficient graduate course work in linguistics or language of study, master's thesis or major research paper. Additional exam requirements/recommendations for international students: required—TOEFL. Electronic applications accepted.

Montclair State University, The Graduate School, College of Humanities and Social Sciences, Program in Applied Linguistics, Montclair, NJ 07043-1624. Offers MA. *Program availability:* Part-time, evening/weekend. *Degree requirements:* For master's, comprehensive exam. *Entrance requirements:* For master's, GRE General Test, 2 letters of recommendation, essay. Additional exam requirements/recommendations for international students: required—TOEFL (minimum score 83 iBT), IELTS (minimum score 6.5). Electronic applications accepted.

Montclair State University, The Graduate School, College of Humanities and Social Sciences, Program in Computational Linguistics, Montclair, NJ 07043-1624. Offers Certificate. *Program availability:* Part-time, evening/weekend. *Entrance requirements:* For degree, 2 letters of recommendation, essay. Additional exam requirements/recommendations for international students: required—TOEFL (minimum score 83 iBT), IELTS (minimum score 6.5). Electronic applications accepted.

New York University, Graduate School of Arts and Science, Department of Linguistics, New York, NY 10012-1019. Offers MA, PhD. *Program availability:* Part-time. Terminal master's awarded for partial completion of doctoral program. *Degree requirements:* For master's, one foreign language, comprehensive exam, thesis optional; for doctorate, one foreign language, thesis/dissertation, 2 publishable papers. *Entrance requirements:* For master's and doctorate, GRE General Test. Additional exam requirements/recommendations for international students: required—TOEFL, IELTS.

Northeastern Illinois University, College of Graduate Studies and Research, College of Arts and Sciences, Program in Linguistics, Chicago, IL 60625. Offers linguistics (MA). *Program availability:* Part-time, evening/weekend. *Degree requirements:* For master's, one foreign language, comprehensive exam, thesis optional. *Entrance requirements:* For master's, 9 undergraduate hours in a foreign language or equivalent, minimum GPA of 2.75. Additional exam requirements/recommendations for international students: required—TOEFL (minimum score 550 paper-based; 79 iBT). Electronic applications accepted.

Northern Arizona University, College of Arts and Letters, Department of English, Flagstaff, AZ 86011. Offers applied linguistics (PhD); creative writing (MFA), including creative writing; English (MA), including literature, professional writing, rhetoric, writing, and digital media studies, secondary education; professional writing (Graduate Certificate); rhetoric, writing and digital media studies (Graduate Certificate); teaching English as a second language (MA, Graduate Certificate). *Program availability:* Part-time, 100% online, blended/hybrid learning. *Degree requirements:* For master's, variable foreign language requirement, comprehensive exam (for some programs), thesis (for some programs); for doctorate, variable foreign language requirement, comprehensive exam (for some programs), thesis/dissertation (for some programs); for Graduate Certificate, comprehensive exam (for some programs). *Entrance requirements:* Additional exam requirements/recommendations for international students: required—TOEFL (minimum score 80 iBT), IELTS (minimum score 6.5). Electronic applications accepted.

Northwestern University, The Graduate School, Judd A. and Marjorie Weinberg College of Arts and Sciences, Department of Linguistics, Evanston, IL 60208. Offers PhD, JD/PhD. *Program availability:* Part-time. Terminal master's awarded for partial completion of doctoral program. *Degree requirements:* For doctorate, 2 foreign languages, thesis/dissertation, 2 qualifying papers. *Entrance requirements:* For doctorate, GRE General Test. Additional exam requirements/recommendations for international students: required—TOEFL. Electronic applications accepted.

Oakland University, Graduate Study and Lifelong Learning, College of Arts and Sciences, Department of Linguistics, Rochester, MI 48309-4401. Offers linguistics (MA); teaching English as a second language (Certificate). *Program availability:* Part-time. *Degree requirements:* For master's, thesis (for some programs), minimum grade of C+ in each course and an overall minimum GPA of 3.00. *Entrance requirements:* For master's, demonstrated knowledge of the basic principles of linguistics, baccalaureate degree with a minimum GPA of 3.0, statement of purpose their reasons for wishing to pursue graduate studies in linguistics. Additional exam requirements/recommendations for international students: required—TOEFL (minimum score 550 paper-based; 79 iBT), IELTS (minimum score 6.5). Electronic applications accepted. *Expenses: Tuition, area resident:* Full-time $12,328; part-time $770.50 per credit hour. Tuition, state resident: full-time $12,328; part-time $770.50 per credit hour. Tuition, nonresident: full-time $16,432; part-time $1027 per credit hour. *International tuition:* $16,432 full-time. Tuition and fees vary according to degree level and program.

The Ohio State University, Graduate School, College of Arts and Sciences, Division of Arts and Humanities, Department of Linguistics, Columbus, OH 43210. Offers MA, PhD. Terminal master's awarded for partial completion of doctoral program. *Degree requirements:* For master's, one foreign language, exam or thesis; for doctorate, 2 foreign languages, thesis/dissertation, exam. *Entrance requirements:* For master's and doctorate, GRE General Test. Additional exam requirements/recommendations for international students: required—TOEFL (minimum score 600 paper-based; 100 iBT), Michigan English Language Assessment Battery (minimum score 86); recommended—IELTS (minimum score 8). Electronic applications accepted.

The Ohio State University, Graduate School, College of Arts and Sciences, Division of Arts and Humanities, Department of Slavic and East European Languages and Cultures, Columbus, OH 43210. Offers Slavic linguistics (MA, PhD); Slavic literature, film, and cultural studies (MA, PhD). Terminal master's awarded for partial completion of doctoral program. *Degree requirements:* For master's, variable foreign language requirement, thesis optional; for doctorate, variable foreign language requirement, thesis/dissertation. *Entrance requirements:* For master's and doctorate, GRE General Test, at least 3 years of Russian language study or equivalent. Additional exam requirements/recommendations for international students: required—TOEFL (minimum score 550 paper-based; 79 iBT), Michigan English Language Assessment Battery (minimum score 82); recommended—IELTS (minimum score 7). Electronic applications accepted.

Ohio University, Graduate College, College of Arts and Sciences, Department of Linguistics, Athens, OH 45701-2979. Offers applied linguistics (MA). *Program availability:* Part-time. *Degree requirements:* For master's, one foreign language, thesis or alternative. *Entrance requirements:* For master's, minimum GPA of 3.0. Additional exam requirements/recommendations for international students: required—TOEFL (minimum score 600 paper-based; 100 iBT) or IELTS (minimum score 7). Electronic applications accepted.

Old Dominion University, College of Arts and Letters, Program in Applied Linguistics, Norfolk, VA 23529. Offers sociolinguistics (MA); TESOL (MA). *Program availability:* Part-time. *Degree requirements:* For master's, one foreign language, comprehensive exam, thesis optional, program portfolio. *Entrance requirements:* For master's, GRE General Test, sample of written work; 12 hours in English, 9 on the upper-level; minimum B average; letters of recommendation; resume; essay. Additional exam requirements/recommendations for international students: required—TOEFL (minimum score 570 paper-based; 88 iBT). Electronic applications accepted.

Penn State University Park, Graduate School, College of the Liberal Arts, Department of Applied Linguistics, University Park, PA 16802. Offers applied linguistics (PhD); teaching English as a second language (MA).

Purdue University, Graduate School, College of Health and Human Sciences, Department of Speech, Language, and Hearing Sciences, West Lafayette, IN 47907. Offers audiology clinic (MS, Au D, PhD); linguistics (MS, PhD); speech and hearing science (MS, PhD); speech-language pathology (MS, PhD). *Accreditation:* ASHA. *Faculty:* 20 full-time (14 women), 9 part-time/adjunct (5 women). *Students:* 96 full-time (91 women), 12 part-time (10 women); includes 13 minority (3 Black or African American, non-Hispanic/Latino; 5 Asian, non-Hispanic/Latino; 3 Hispanic/Latino; 2 Two or more races, non-Hispanic/Latino), 4 international. Average age 24. 270 applicants, 34% accepted, 38 enrolled. In 2019, 32 master's, 10 doctorates awarded. *Degree requirements:* For master's, comprehensive exam (for some programs), thesis optional; for doctorate, comprehensive exam, thesis/dissertation. *Entrance requirements:* For master's and doctorate, GRE General Test, minimum undergraduate GPA of 3.0 or equivalent. Additional exam requirements/recommendations for international students: required—TOEFL (minimum score 77 iBT). *Application deadline:* For fall admission, 1/1 priority date for domestic and international students; for spring admission, 8/1 priority date for domestic and international students. Applications are processed on a rolling basis. Application fee: $60 ($75 for international students). Electronic applications accepted. *Financial support:* Fellowships with full tuition reimbursements, research assistantships with full tuition reimbursements, teaching assistantships with full tuition reimbursements, career-related internships or fieldwork, and scholarships/grants available. Support available to part-time students. Financial award application deadline: 2/1; financial award applicants required to submit FAFSA. *Unit head:* Preeti Sivasankar, Head, 765-494-3788, E-mail: preeti@purdue.edu. *Application contact:* Vickie L. Parker-Black, Graduate Contact, 765-494-3786, E-mail: vpblack@purdue.edu.
Website: http://www.purdue.edu/hhs/slhs/

Purdue University, Graduate School, College of Liberal Arts, Department of English, West Lafayette, IN 47907. Offers creative writing (MFA); literature (MA, PhD), including linguistics, literature and philosophy (PhD), rhetoric and composition, theory and cultural studies (PhD). *Program availability:* Part-time. *Faculty:* 42 full-time (17 women), 9 part-time/adjunct (6 women). *Students:* 85 full-time (58 women), 52 part-time (29 women); includes 23 minority (6 Black or African American, non-Hispanic/Latino; 1 American Indian or Alaska Native, non-Hispanic/Latino; 5 Asian, non-Hispanic/Latino; 7 Hispanic/Latino; 4 Two or more races, non-Hispanic/Latino), 24 international. Average age 31. 245 applicants, 22% accepted, 23 enrolled. In 2019, 11 master's, 22 doctorates awarded. *Degree requirements:* For master's, one foreign language, comprehensive exam (for some programs), thesis (for some programs); for doctorate, one foreign language, comprehensive exam, thesis/dissertation. *Entrance requirements:* For master's, GRE General Test; GRE Subject Test in English literature (recommended for students applying to literary studies), minimum undergraduate GPA of 3.0 or equivalent; for doctorate, GRE General Test; GRE Subject Test in English literature (recommended for students applying to literary studies), master's degree. Additional exam requirements/recommendations for international students: required—TOEFL (minimum score 620 paper-based; 77 iBT). *Application deadline:* For fall admission, 1/15 for domestic and international students. Applications are processed on a rolling basis. Application fee: $60 ($75 for international students). Electronic applications accepted. *Financial support:* Fellowships with tuition reimbursements and teaching assistantships with tuition reimbursements available. Support available to part-time students. Financial award application deadline: 1/15; financial award applicants required to submit FAFSA. *Unit head:* Dorsey Armstrong, Head, 765-494-6478, E-mail: darmstrong@purdue.edu. *Application contact:* Jill M. Quirk, Graduate Contact, 765-494-3748, Fax: 765-494-1700, E-mail: griff@purdue.edu.
Website: https://www.cla.purdue.edu/english/

Purdue University, Graduate School, College of Liberal Arts, Program in Linguistics, West Lafayette, IN 47907. Offers MS, PhD. *Students:* 18 full-time (11 women), 5 part-time (4 women); includes 4 minority (2 Asian, non-Hispanic/Latino; 2 Hispanic/Latino), 7 international. Average age 29. 47 applicants, 11% accepted, 5 enrolled. In 2019, 2 master's, 2 doctorates awarded. *Degree requirements:* For master's, one foreign language, thesis; for doctorate, 3 foreign languages, comprehensive exam, thesis/dissertation. *Entrance requirements:* For master's and doctorate, GRE General Test (minimum score of 500 for verbal and quantitative respectively), minimum undergraduate GPA of 3.4. Additional exam requirements/recommendations for international students: required—TOEFL (minimum score 620 paper-based; 77 iBT), TWE. *Application deadline:* For fall admission, 1/1 for domestic and international students. Applications are processed on a rolling basis. Application fee: $60 ($75 for international students). Electronic applications accepted. *Financial support:* Fellowships, research assistantships, and teaching assistantships available. Support available to part-time students. Financial award applicants required to submit FAFSA. *Unit head:* Alejandro Cuza-Blanco, Head, 765-496-1685, E-mail: acuza@purdue.edu. *Application contact:* Brani Plantenga, Graduate Contact, 765-496-9629, E-mail: bplante@purdue.edu.
Website: http://www.cla.purdue.edu/linguistics/

Queens College of the City University of New York, Arts and Humanities Division, Department of Linguistics and Communication Disorders, Queens, NY 11367-1597. Offers applied linguistics (MA); speech-language pathology (MA); TESOL (MS Ed, Post-Master's Certificate); TESOL and bilingual education (Post-Master's Certificate). *Accreditation:* ASHA. *Program availability:* Part-time. *Entrance requirements:* For master's, minimum GPA of 3.0. Additional exam requirements/recommendations for international students: required—TOEFL, IELTS. Electronic applications accepted. *Expenses:* Contact institution.

Rice University, Graduate Programs, School of Humanities, Department of Linguistics, Houston, TX 77251-1892. Offers MA, PhD. Terminal master's awarded for partial completion of doctoral program. *Degree requirements:* For master's, one foreign language, thesis; for doctorate, 2 foreign languages, thesis/dissertation, 3 research papers. *Entrance requirements:* For master's and doctorate, GRE General Test, minimum GPA of 3.0. Additional exam requirements/recommendations for international students: required—TOEFL (minimum score 600 paper-based; 90 iBT). Electronic applications accepted.

Rutgers University - New Brunswick, Graduate School-New Brunswick, Department of Linguistics, Piscataway, NJ 08854-8097. Offers PhD. *Degree requirements:* For doctorate, thesis/dissertation, 2 qualifying papers. *Entrance requirements:* For doctorate, GRE General Test, 3 letters of recommendation, writing sample. Additional exam requirements/recommendations for international students: recommended—TOEFL. Electronic applications accepted.

San Diego State University, Graduate and Research Affairs, College of Arts and Letters, Department of Linguistics and Oriental Languages, San Diego, CA 92182. Offers applied linguistics and English as a second language (CAL); computational linguistics (MA); English as a second language/applied linguistics (MA); general

Linguistics

linguistics (MA). *Degree requirements:* For master's, one foreign language, comprehensive exam, thesis optional. *Entrance requirements:* For master's, GRE General Test, 2 letters of recommendation. Additional exam requirements/recommendations for international students: required—TOEFL (minimum score 570 paper-based). Electronic applications accepted.

San Francisco State University, Division of Graduate Studies, College of Liberal and Creative Arts, Department of English Language and Literature, Program in Linguistics, San Francisco, CA 94132-1722. Offers MA. *Program availability:* Part-time. *Degree requirements:* For master's, 2 foreign languages, thesis (for some programs). *Application deadline:* Applications are processed on a rolling basis. *Expenses: Tuition, area resident:* Full-time $7176; part-time $4164 per year. Tuition, state resident: full-time $7176; part-time $4164 per year. Tuition, nonresident: full-time $16,680; part-time $396 per unit. *International tuition:* $16,680 full-time. *Required fees:* $1524; $1524 per unit. $762 per semester. Tuition and fees vary according to degree level and program. *Unit head:* Dr. Gitanjali Shahani, Chair, 415-338-2264, Fax: 415-338-6159, E-mail: gshahani@sfsu.edu. *Application contact:* Dr. Jenny Lederer, Coordinator, 415-388-7406, Fax: 415-338-6159, E-mail: lederer@sfsu.edu.
Website: http://english.sfsu.edu/graduate-linguistics

San Jose State University, Program in Linguistics and Language Development, San Jose, CA 95192-0093. Offers computational linguistics (Certificate); linguistics (MA); teaching English to speakers of other languages (MA, Certificate). *Program availability:* Part-time. *Faculty:* 3 full-time (1 woman), 3 part-time/adjunct (1 woman). *Students:* 18 full-time (14 women), 27 part-time (21 women); includes 19 minority (1 Black or African American, non-Hispanic/Latino; 15 Asian, non-Hispanic/Latino; 3 Hispanic/Latino), 9 international. Average age 35. 26 applicants, 69% accepted, 7 enrolled. In 2019, 18 master's awarded. *Degree requirements:* For master's, comprehensive exam, thesis or alternative. *Entrance requirements:* For master's, statement of purpose, transcripts. Additional exam requirements/recommendations for international students: required—TOEFL (minimum score 577 paper-based; 90 iBT), IELTS (minimum score 7). *Application deadline:* For fall admission, 7/1 for domestic students, 3/1 for international students; for spring admission, 12/1 for domestic students, 11/1 for international students. Applications are processed on a rolling basis. Application fee: $70. Electronic applications accepted. *Expenses: Tuition, area resident:* Full-time $7176; part-time $4164 per credit hour. Tuition, state resident: full-time $7176; part-time $4164 per credit hour. Tuition, nonresident: full-time $7176; part-time $4165 per credit hour. *International tuition:* $7176 full-time. *Required fees:* $2110; $2110. *Financial support:* In 2019–20, 7 students received support. Scholarships/grants available. Financial award application deadline: 5/15; financial award applicants required to submit FAFSA. *Unit head:* Stefan Frazier, Department Chair, 408-924-4443, E-mail: stefan.frazier@sjsu.edu. *Application contact:* Stefan Frazier, Department Chair, 408-924-4443, E-mail: stefan.frazier@sjsu.edu.
Website: http://www.sjsu.edu/linguistics/

Simon Fraser University, Office of Graduate Studies and Postdoctoral Fellows, Faculty of Arts and Social Sciences, Department of Linguistics, Burnaby, BC V5A 1S6, Canada. Offers MA, PhD. *Degree requirements:* For master's, one foreign language, thesis; for doctorate, 2 foreign languages, thesis/dissertation, qualifying papers. *Entrance requirements:* For master's, minimum GPA of 3.0 (on scale of 4.33) or 3.33 based on last 60 credits of undergraduate courses; for doctorate, minimum GPA of 3.5 (on scale of 4.33). Additional exam requirements/recommendations for international students: recommended—TOEFL (minimum score 580 paper-based; 93 iBT), IELTS (minimum score 7), TWE (minimum score 5). Electronic applications accepted.

Southern Illinois University Carbondale, Graduate School, College of Liberal Arts, Department of Linguistics, Carbondale, IL 62901. Offers linguistics (MA); teaching English to speakers of other languages (MA). *Degree requirements:* For master's, one foreign language. *Entrance requirements:* For master's, minimum GPA of 3.0. Additional exam requirements/recommendations for international students: required—TOEFL (minimum score 90 iBT).

Stanford University, School of Humanities and Sciences, Department of Linguistics, Stanford, CA 94305-2004. Offers MA, PhD. *Expenses: Tuition:* Full-time $52,479; part-time $34,110 per unit. *Required fees:* $672; $224 per quarter. Tuition and fees vary according to program and student level.
Website: https://linguistics.stanford.edu/

Stony Brook University, State University of New York, Graduate School, College of Arts and Sciences, Department of Linguistics, Program in Linguistics, Stony Brook, NY 11794. Offers MA, PhD. *Faculty:* 21 full-time (12 women), 5 part-time/adjunct (3 women). *Students:* 44 full-time (23 women), 1 (woman) part-time; includes 2 minority (both Asian, non-Hispanic/Latino), 26 international. Average age 28. 39 applicants, 51% accepted, 10 enrolled. In 2019, 3 master's, 6 doctorates awarded. *Entrance requirements:* For doctorate, GRE. Additional exam requirements/recommendations for international students: required—TOEFL (minimum score 90 iBT). *Application deadline:* For fall admission, 1/15 for domestic students; for spring admission, 10/1 for domestic students. Application fee: $100. Electronic applications accepted. *Expenses:* Contact institution. *Financial support:* In 2019–20, 3 research assistantships, 20 teaching assistantships were awarded; fellowships also available. *Unit head:* Dr. Lori Repetti, Chair, 631-632-7446, E-mail: lori.repetti@stonybrook.edu. *Application contact:* Michelle Carbone, Coordinator, 631-632-7774, Fax: 631-632-9789, E-mail: michelle.carbone@stonybrook.edu.

Syracuse University, College of Arts and Sciences, MA Program in Linguistic Studies, Syracuse, NY 13244. Offers linguistic studies (MA), including information representation and retrieval, language acquisition, language, culture, and society, linguistic theory, logic and language, teaching language (TESOL/TLOTE). *Program availability:* Part-time. *Degree requirements:* For master's, comprehensive exam, thesis or alternative. *Entrance requirements:* For master's, GRE General Test, personal statement detailing interest in field of linguistics and possible concentration areas, transcripts, three recommendation letters. Additional exam requirements/recommendations for international students: required—TOEFL (minimum score 100 iBT). Electronic applications accepted.

Syracuse University, College of Arts and Sciences, MS Program in Computational Linguistics, Syracuse, NY 13244. Offers MS. *Program availability:* Part-time. *Degree requirements:* For master's, thesis or alternative, internship. *Entrance requirements:* For master's, GRE, resume, personal statement, transcripts, three letters of recommendation. Additional exam requirements/recommendations for international students: required—TOEFL (minimum score 100 iBT). Electronic applications accepted.

Teachers College, Columbia University, Department of Arts and Humanities, New York, NY 10027. Offers applied linguistics (MA, Ed D); art and art education (Ed M, MA, Ed D, Ed DCT); arts administration (MA); bilingual and bicultural education (MA); global competence (Certificate); history and education (Ed D, PhD); music and music education (Ed DCT); philosophy and education (MA, Ed D, PhD); social studies education (Ed M, PhD); teaching English to speakers of other languages (Ed M); teaching of English and English education (Ed M, MA, Ed D, PhD), including English education (Ed M, Ed D, PhD), teaching of English (MA); teaching of social studies (MA); TESOL (MA, Ed D). *Faculty:* 26 full-time (17 women). *Students:* 426 full-time (358 women), 390 part-time (259 women); includes 222 minority (44 Black or African American, non-Hispanic/Latino; 2 American Indian or Alaska Native, non-Hispanic/Latino; 94 Asian, non-Hispanic/Latino; 65 Hispanic/Latino; 17 Two or more races, non-Hispanic/Latino), 252 international. 957 applicants, 66% accepted, 375 enrolled. *Unit head:* Dr. ZhaoHong Han, Department Chair, E-mail: zhh2@tc.columbia.edu. *Application contact:* Kelly Sutton-Skinner, Director of Admissions and New Student Enrollment, 212-678-3710, E-mail: kms2237@tc.columbia.edu.

Texas A&M University–Commerce, College of Humanities, Social Sciences and Arts, Commerce, TX 75429. Offers applied criminology (MS); applied linguistics (MA, MS); art (MA, MFA); christianity in history (Graduate Certificate); computational linguistics (Graduate Certificate); creative writing (Graduate Certificate); criminal justice management (Graduate Certificate); criminal justice studies (Graduate Certificate); English (MA, MS, PhD); film studies (Graduate Certificate); history (MA, MS); Holocaust studies (Graduate Certificate); homeland security (Graduate Certificate); music (MM); music performance (MM); political science (MA, MS); public history (Graduate Certificate); sociology (MS); Spanish (MA); studies in children's and adolescent literature and culture (Graduate Certificate); teaching English to speakers of other languages (Graduate Certificate); theater (MA, MS); world history (Graduate Certificate). *Program availability:* Part-time. *Faculty:* 49 full-time (28 women), 8 part-time/adjunct (2 women). *Students:* 34 full-time (21 women), 427 part-time (302 women); includes 175 minority (66 Black or African American, non-Hispanic/Latino; 1 American Indian or Alaska Native, non-Hispanic/Latino; 13 Asian, non-Hispanic/Latino; 79 Hispanic/Latino; 16 Two or more races, non-Hispanic/Latino), 15 international. Average age 38. 193 applicants, 49% accepted, 78 enrolled. In 2019, 122 master's, 6 doctorates awarded. *Degree requirements:* For master's, one foreign language, comprehensive exam, thesis (for some programs); for doctorate, one foreign language, comprehensive exam, thesis/dissertation, departmental qualifying exam. *Entrance requirements:* For master's, GRE General Test, official transcripts, letters of recommendation, resume, statement of goals; for doctorate, GRE General Test, official transcripts, letters of recommendation, statement of goals, writing samples, writing sessions, resumes. Additional exam requirements/recommendations for international students: required—TOEFL (minimum score 550 paper-based; 79 iBT), IELTS (minimum score 6), PTE (minimum score 53). *Application deadline:* For fall admission, 6/1 priority date for international students; for spring admission, 10/15 priority date for international students; for summer admission, 3/15 priority date for international students. Applications are processed on a rolling basis. Application fee: $50 ($75 for international students). Electronic applications accepted. *Expenses: Tuition, area resident:* Full-time $3630; part-time $202 per credit hour. Tuition, state resident: full-time $3630; part-time $202 per credit hour. Tuition, nonresident: full-time $11,232; part-time $624 per credit hour. *International tuition:* $11,232 full-time. *Required fees:* $2948. *Financial support:* In 2019–20, 30 students received support, including 18 research assistantships with partial tuition reimbursements available (averaging $3,231 per year), 136 teaching assistantships with partial tuition reimbursements available (averaging $4,053 per year); Federal Work-Study, institutionally sponsored loans, scholarships/grants, health care benefits, and unspecified assistantships also available. Financial award application deadline: 5/1; financial award applicants required to submit FAFSA. *Unit head:* Dr. William F. Kuracina, Interim Dean, 903-886-5166, Fax: 903-886-5774, E-mail: william.kuracina@tamuc.edu. *Application contact:* Rebecca Stevens, Graduate Student Services Coordinator, 903-468-6049, E-mail: rebecca.stevens@tamuc.edu.
Website: http://www.tamuc.edu/academics/colleges/humanitiesSocialSciencesArts/

Trinity Western University, School of Graduate Studies, Master of Arts in Linguistics, Langley, BC V2Y 1Y1, Canada. Offers linguistics (MA). *Program availability:* Part-time. *Students:* Average age 30. 25 applicants, 60% accepted, 9 enrolled. *Degree requirements:* For master's, writing sample (academic paper). *Entrance requirements:* For master's, minimum GPA of 3.0 in last two years; 12 semester hours; linguistic prerequisites; 1 foreign language. Additional exam requirements/recommendations for international students: required—TOEFL (minimum score 100 iBT), IELTS (minimum score 7), DuoLingo. *Application deadline:* For fall admission, 7/15 priority date for domestic and international students. Applications are processed on a rolling basis. Application fee: $150 Canadian dollars for international students. Electronic applications accepted. *Expenses:* $535 per semester hour x 36 semester hours to complete the degree. Student fees are $28 per sem hour for domestic students, and $38 per sem hour for international students. *Financial support:* Fellowships, teaching assistantships, and scholarships/grants available. *Unit head:* Dr. Sean Allison, Director, MA in Linguistics Program, E-mail: sean.allison@twu.ca. *Application contact:* Tim Macfarlane, Senior Enrolment Advisor, 604-513-2121 Ext. 3046, E-mail: tim.macfarlane@twu.ca.
Website: http://www.twu.ca/academics/graduate/linguistics

Universidad de las Américas Puebla, Division of Graduate Studies, School of Humanities, Program in Applied Linguistics, Puebla, Mexico. Offers linguistics (MA). *Program availability:* Part-time, evening/weekend. *Degree requirements:* For master's, one foreign language, thesis. *Entrance requirements:* Additional exam requirements/recommendations for international students: required—TOEFL.

Université de Montréal, Faculty of Arts and Sciences, Department of Linguistics and Translation, Montréal, QC H3C 3J7, Canada. Offers linguistics (MA, PhD); translation (MA, PhD, DESS). *Degree requirements:* For master's, thesis, general exam; for doctorate, thesis/dissertation, general exam. Electronic applications accepted.

Université de Sherbrooke, Faculty of Letters and Human Sciences, Department of Letters and Communications, Sherbrooke, QC J1K 2R1, Canada. Offers comparative Canadian literature (MA, PhD); French literature (MA, PhD); linguistics (MA); theatre (MA). *Degree requirements:* For master's, thesis or alternative; for doctorate, thesis/dissertation. *Entrance requirements:* For master's, minimum GPA of 2.8; for doctorate, minimum GPA of 3.0.

Université du Québec à Chicoutimi, Graduate Programs, Program in Linguistics, Chicoutimi, QC G7H 2B1, Canada. Offers MA. *Program availability:* Part-time. *Degree requirements:* For master's, thesis. *Entrance requirements:* For master's, appropriate bachelor's degree, proficiency in French.

Université du Québec à Montréal, Graduate Programs, Program in Linguistics, Montréal, QC H3C 3P8, Canada. Offers MA, PhD. *Program availability:* Part-time. *Degree requirements:* For master's, thesis optional; for doctorate, thesis/dissertation. *Entrance requirements:* For master's, appropriate bachelor's degree or equivalent, proficiency in French; for doctorate, appropriate master's degree or equivalent, proficiency in French.

University at Buffalo, the State University of New York, Graduate School, College of Arts and Sciences, Department of Linguistics, Buffalo, NY 14260. Offers interdisciplinary computational linguistics (MS); linguistics (MA, PhD). Terminal master's awarded for partial completion of doctoral program. *Degree requirements:* For master's, exam, project, or thesis; for doctorate, thesis/dissertation, qualifying paper. *Entrance requirements:* For master's and doctorate, GRE General Test. Additional exam requirements/recommendations for international students: required—TOEFL (minimum score 600 paper-based; 100 iBT). Electronic applications accepted. *Expenses:* Contact institution.

University of Alaska Fairbanks, College of Liberal Arts, Program in Linguistics, Fairbanks, AK 99775-6280. Offers applied linguistics (MA), including language documentation, second language acquisition teacher education. *Program availability:* Part-time, 100% online, blended/hybrid learning. Terminal master's awarded for partial completion of doctoral program. *Degree requirements:* For master's, one foreign language, comprehensive exam, oral defense of project or thesis. *Entrance requirements:* For master's, bachelor's degree from accredited institution with minimum cumulative undergraduate and major GPA of 3.0. Additional exam requirements/recommendations for international students: required—TOEFL (minimum score 550 paper-based; 79 iBT), IELTS (minimum score 6.5). Electronic applications accepted.

University of Alberta, Faculty of Graduate Studies and Research, Department of Linguistics, Edmonton, AB T6G 2E1, Canada. Offers experimental linguistics (M Sc, PhD). *Degree requirements:* For master's, thesis (for some programs); for doctorate, thesis/dissertation. *Entrance requirements:* For master's, BA in linguistics; for doctorate, M Sc or MA in linguistics. Additional exam requirements/recommendations for international students: required—TOEFL.

University of Alberta, Faculty of Graduate Studies and Research, Department of Modern Languages and Cultural Studies, Edmonton, AB T6G 2E1, Canada. Offers applied linguistics (Germanic, Romance, Slavic) (MA); French language, literatures and linguistics (PhD); French language, literatures, and linguistics (MA); Germanic languages, literatures and linguistics (PhD); Germanic languages, literatures, and linguistics (MA); Italian studies (MA); Slavic languages and literatures (Russian, Ukrainian) (MA, PhD); Slavic linguistics (Russian, Ukrainian) (MA, PhD); Spanish and Latin American studies (MA, PhD); Ukrainian folklore (MA, PhD). *Program availability:* Part-time. *Degree requirements:* For master's, one foreign language, thesis; for doctorate, 2 foreign languages, comprehensive exam, thesis/dissertation. *Entrance requirements:* For master's and doctorate, 1 language other than English. Additional exam requirements/recommendations for international students: required—Michigan English Language Assessment Battery or TOEFL (minimum score 550 paper-based). Electronic applications accepted.

The University of Arizona, College of Social and Behavioral Sciences, Department of Linguistics, Tucson, AZ 85721. Offers human language technology (MS); linguistics and anthropology (PhD); Native American linguistics (MA). Terminal master's awarded for partial completion of doctoral program. *Degree requirements:* For master's, one foreign language, thesis; for doctorate, one foreign language, comprehensive exam, thesis/dissertation. *Entrance requirements:* For master's, GRE General Test, 3 letters of recommendation, writing sample, resume; for doctorate, GRE General Test, 3 letters of recommendation, statement of purpose, writing sample, resume. Additional exam requirements/recommendations for international students: required—TOEFL (minimum score 550 paper-based; 79 iBT). Electronic applications accepted.

The University of Arizona, College of Social and Behavioral Sciences, Program in Human Language Technology, Tucson, AZ 85721. Offers MS. *Entrance requirements:* Additional exam requirements/recommendations for international students: required—TOEFL (minimum score 550 paper-based; 79 iBT), GRE.

The University of British Columbia, Faculty of Arts, Department of Linguistics, Vancouver, BC V6T 1Z4, Canada. Offers MA, PhD. *Program availability:* Part-time. *Degree requirements:* For master's, one foreign language, thesis optional; for doctorate, 2 foreign languages, thesis/dissertation, 2 qualifying papers. *Entrance requirements:* Additional exam requirements/recommendations for international students: required—TOEFL. Electronic applications accepted. *Expenses:* Contact institution.

University of Calgary, Faculty of Graduate Studies, Faculty of Arts, Program in Languages, Literature and Culture, Calgary, AB T2N 1N4, Canada. Offers German (MA); linguistics (MA, PhD). *Degree requirements:* For master's, one foreign language, thesis; for doctorate, one foreign language, comprehensive exam, thesis/dissertation. *Entrance requirements:* For doctorate, MA. Additional exam requirements/recommendations for international students: required—TOEFL (minimum score 560 paper-based). Electronic applications accepted.

University of California, Berkeley, Graduate Division, College of Letters and Science, Department of Linguistics, Berkeley, CA 94720. Offers PhD. *Degree requirements:* For doctorate, thesis/dissertation, qualifying exam. *Entrance requirements:* For doctorate, GRE General Test, minimum GPA of 3.0, 3 letters of recommendation. Additional exam requirements/recommendations for international students: required—TOEFL (minimum score 570 paper-based; 90 iBT). Electronic applications accepted.

University of California, Davis, Graduate Studies, Graduate Group in Linguistics, Davis, CA 95616. Offers applied linguistics (MA, PhD); linguistics (MA). *Degree requirements:* For master's, one foreign language, comprehensive exam (for some programs), thesis (for some programs); for doctorate, thesis/dissertation. *Entrance requirements:* For master's and doctorate, GRE General Test, minimum GPA of 3.0. Additional exam requirements/recommendations for international students: required—TOEFL (minimum score 550 paper-based). Electronic applications accepted.

University of California, Los Angeles, Graduate Division, College of Letters and Science, Department of Applied Linguistics and Teaching English as a Second Language, Program in Applied Linguistics, Los Angeles, CA 90095. Offers MA, PhD. *Degree requirements:* For master's, one foreign language, thesis; for doctorate, one foreign language, thesis/dissertation, oral and written qualifying exams. *Entrance requirements:* For master's and doctorate, bachelor's degree; minimum undergraduate GPA of 3.0 (or its equivalent if letter grade system not used); research paper. Additional exam requirements/recommendations for international students: required—TOEFL. Electronic applications accepted.

University of California, Los Angeles, Graduate Division, College of Letters and Science, Department of Linguistics, Los Angeles, CA 90095. Offers MA, PhD. Terminal master's awarded for partial completion of doctoral program. *Degree requirements:* For master's, one foreign language, comprehensive exam or thesis; for doctorate, thesis/dissertation, oral and written qualifying exams. *Entrance requirements:* For doctorate, bachelor's degree; minimum undergraduate GPA of 3.0 (or its equivalent if letter grade system not used); writing sample. Additional exam requirements/recommendations for international students: required—TOEFL. Electronic applications accepted.

University of California, San Diego, Graduate Division, Department of Linguistics, La Jolla, CA 92093. Offers PhD. *Students:* 30 full-time (17 women), 1 (woman) part-time. 72 applicants, 22% accepted, 7 enrolled. *Degree requirements:* For doctorate, one foreign language, comprehensive exam, thesis/dissertation, apprentice teaching. *Entrance requirements:* For doctorate, GRE General Test, writing samples, letters of recommendation. Additional exam requirements/recommendations for international students: required—TOEFL (minimum score 550 paper-based; 80 iBT), IELTS (minimum score 7). *Application deadline:* For fall admission, 12/5 for domestic students. Application fee: $105 ($125 for international students). Electronic applications accepted. *Financial support:* Fellowships and teaching assistantships available. Financial award applicants required to submit FAFSA. *Unit head:* Eric Bakovic, Chair, 858-534-1159, E-mail: ebakovic@ucsd.edu. *Application contact:* Alycia Randol, Graduate Coordinator, 858-534-1145, E-mail: arandol@ucsd.edu.
Website: http://ling.ucsd.edu

University of California, Santa Barbara, Graduate Division, College of Letters and Sciences, Division of Humanities and Fine Arts, Department of East Asian Languages and Cultural Studies, Santa Barbara, CA 93106-7075. Offers applied linguistics (PhD); East Asian languages and cultural studies (MA); translation studies (PhD). *Degree requirements:* For master's, one foreign language, comprehensive exam (for some programs), thesis (for some programs); for doctorate, 2 foreign languages, thesis/dissertation, methodology. *Entrance requirements:* For master's and doctorate, GRE General Test. Additional exam requirements/recommendations for international students: required—TOEFL (minimum score 550 paper-based; 80 iBT), IELTS (minimum score 7). Electronic applications accepted.

University of California, Santa Barbara, Graduate Division, College of Letters and Sciences, Division of Humanities and Fine Arts, Department of Linguistics, Santa Barbara, CA 93106-9580. Offers PhD, MA/PhD. Terminal master's awarded for partial completion of doctoral program. *Degree requirements:* For doctorate, one foreign language, comprehensive exam, thesis/dissertation, qualifying paper. *Entrance requirements:* For doctorate, GRE. Additional exam requirements/recommendations for international students: required—TOEFL (minimum score 550 paper-based; 80 iBT), IELTS (minimum score 7). Electronic applications accepted.

University of California, Santa Barbara, Graduate Division, College of Letters and Sciences, Division of Humanities and Fine Arts, Department of Spanish and Portuguese, Santa Barbara, CA 93106-4150. Offers Hispanic languages and literatures (PhD), including European medieval studies, feminist studies, Hispanic linguistics, Hispanic literature, Luso-Brazilian literature; Hispanic linguistics (MA); Luso-Brazilian literature (MA); Spanish or Spanish-American literature (MA); MA/PhD. Terminal master's awarded for partial completion of doctoral program. *Degree requirements:* For master's, 2 foreign languages, comprehensive exam (for some programs), thesis optional; for doctorate, 3 foreign languages, comprehensive exam, thesis/dissertation. *Entrance requirements:* For master's and doctorate, GRE. Additional exam requirements/recommendations for international students: required—TOEFL (minimum score 550 paper-based; 80 iBT), IELTS (minimum score 7). Electronic applications accepted.

University of California, Santa Cruz, Division of Graduate Studies, Division of Humanities, Department of Linguistics, Santa Cruz, CA 95064. Offers MA, PhD. Terminal master's awarded for partial completion of doctoral program. *Degree requirements:* For master's, one foreign language, research paper; for doctorate, one foreign language, thesis/dissertation, qualifying exam. *Entrance requirements:* For master's and doctorate, GRE General Test. Additional exam requirements/recommendations for international students: required—TOEFL (minimum score 550 paper-based; 83 iBT); recommended—IELTS (minimum score 8). Electronic applications accepted.

University of Chicago, Division of the Humanities, Department of Linguistics, Chicago, IL 60637. Offers anthropology and linguistics (PhD); linguistics (PhD). Terminal master's awarded for partial completion of doctoral program. *Degree requirements:* For doctorate, 2 foreign languages, thesis/dissertation. *Entrance requirements:* For doctorate, GRE General Test, 15-20 page writing sample, statement of purpose, 3 letters of recommendation, transcripts for all previous degrees and institutions attended. Additional exam requirements/recommendations for international students: required—TOEFL (minimum score 104 iBT), IELTS (minimum score 7). Electronic applications accepted.

University of Chicago, Division of the Humanities, Master of Arts Program in the Humanities, Chicago, IL 60637. Offers art history (MA); cinema and media studies (MA); classic languages (MA); comparative literature (MA); creative writing (MA); cultural policy studies (MA); digital humanities (MA); East Asian languages and civilizations (MA); English language and literature (MA); gender and sexuality studies (MA); Germanic studies (MA); linguistics (MA); music (MA); near Eastern languages and civilizations (MA); philosophy (MA); poetics (MA); race, politics and culture (MA); Romance languages and literatures (MA); Slavic languages and literatures (MA); South Asian languages and civilizations (MA); theater and performance studies (MA). *Degree requirements:* For master's, thesis. *Entrance requirements:* For master's, GRE General Test, 10-15 page writing sample, statement of purpose, 3 letters of recommendation, transcripts for all previous degrees and institutions attended. Additional exam requirements/recommendations for international students: required—TOEFL (minimum score 104 iBT), IELTS (minimum score 7). Electronic applications accepted. *Expenses:* Contact institution.

University of Colorado Boulder, Graduate School, College of Arts and Sciences, Department of Linguistics, Boulder, CO 80309. Offers MA, PhD. Terminal master's awarded for partial completion of doctoral program. *Degree requirements:* For master's, comprehensive exam, thesis optional; for doctorate, one foreign language, thesis/dissertation. *Entrance requirements:* For master's, GRE General Test, minimum undergraduate GPA of 2.75; for doctorate, GRE General Test. Electronic applications accepted. Application fee is waived when completed online.

University of Colorado Denver, College of Liberal Arts and Sciences, Department of English, Denver, CO 80217. Offers applied linguistics (MA). *Program availability:* Part-time, evening/weekend. *Degree requirements:* For master's, variable foreign language requirement, comprehensive exam (for some programs), thesis (for some programs), minimum of 33 credit hours (for literature program), 30 (for rhetoric and teaching of writing and applied linguistics programs). *Entrance requirements:* For master's, GRE General Test, minimum GPA of 3.0 in undergraduate courses, critical writing sample, letters of recommendation, completion of 24 semester hours in English courses (at least 16 at the upper-division level), statement of purpose. Additional exam requirements/recommendations for international students: required—TOEFL (minimum score 537 paper-based; 75 iBT); recommended—IELTS (minimum score 6.5). Tuition and fees vary according to course load, program and reciprocity agreements.

University of Connecticut, Graduate School, College of Liberal Arts and Sciences, Department of Linguistics, Storrs, CT 06269. Offers MA, PhD. *Degree requirements:* For doctorate, thesis/dissertation. *Entrance requirements:* For doctorate, GRE General Test. Additional exam requirements/recommendations for international students: required—TOEFL (minimum score 550 paper-based). Electronic applications accepted.

University of Delaware, College of Arts and Sciences, Department of Linguistics and Cognitive Science, Newark, DE 19716. Offers linguistics (PhD); linguistics and cognitive science (MA). *Degree requirements:* For doctorate, one foreign language, comprehensive exam, thesis/dissertation, publishable research papers. *Entrance requirements:* For master's, GRE General Test; for doctorate, GRE General Test, writing sample. Additional exam requirements/recommendations for international students: required—TOEFL (minimum score 600 paper-based). Electronic applications accepted.

The University of Findlay, Office of Graduate Admissions, Findlay, OH 45840. Offers applied security and analytics (MSAS); athletic training (MAT); business (MBA), including certified management accountant, certified public accountant, health care management, hospitality management; education (MA Ed, Ed D), including children's literature (MA Ed), curriculum and teaching (MA Ed), education (MA Ed), educational administration (MA Ed), human resource development (MA Ed), mathematics (MA Ed), reading (MA Ed), science education (MA Ed), superintendent (Ed D), teaching (Ed D), technology (MA Ed); environmental, safety, and health management (MSEM); health

informatics (MS); occupational therapy (MOT); pharmacy (Pharm D); physical therapy (DPT); physician assistant (MPA); rhetoric and writing (MA); teaching English to speakers of other languages (TESOL) and applied linguistics (MA). *Program availability:* Part-time, evening/weekend, 100% online, blended/hybrid learning. *Students:* 688 full-time (430 women), 553 part-time (308 women), 170 international. Average age 28. 865 applicants, 31% accepted, 235 enrolled. In 2019, 363 master's, 141 doctorates awarded. *Degree requirements:* For master's, comprehensive exam (for some programs), thesis (for some programs), cumulative project, capstone project; for doctorate, thesis/dissertation (for some programs). *Entrance requirements:* For master's, GRE/GMAT, bachelor's degree from accredited institution, minimum undergraduate GPA of 2.5 in last 64 hours of course work; for doctorate, GRE, MAT, minimum cumulative GPA of 3.0. Additional exam requirements/recommendations for international students: required—TOEFL (minimum score 79 iBT), IELTS (minimum score 7), PTE (minimum score 61). *Application deadline:* Applications are processed on a rolling basis. Electronic applications accepted. *Financial support:* In 2019–20, 10 research assistantships with partial tuition reimbursements (averaging $7,200 per year), 35 teaching assistantships with partial tuition reimbursements (averaging $7,200 per year) were awarded; Federal Work-Study, institutionally sponsored loans, and unspecified assistantships also available. Financial award applicants required to submit FAFSA. *Unit head:* Dave M. Emsweller, Director of Admissions, Interim, 419-434-4578, E-mail: emsweller@findlay.edu. *Application contact:* Amber Feehan, Graduate Admissions Counselor, 419-434-6933, Fax: 419-434-4898, E-mail: feehan@findlay.edu.
Website: http://www.findlay.edu/admissions/graduate/Pages/default.aspx

University of Florida, Graduate School, College of Liberal Arts and Sciences, Department of Linguistics, Gainesville, FL 32611. Offers linguistics (MA, PhD); teaching English as a second language (Certificate). *Program availability:* Part-time. Terminal master's awarded for partial completion of doctoral program. *Degree requirements:* For master's, one foreign language, comprehensive exam, thesis (for some programs); for doctorate, 2 foreign languages, comprehensive exam, thesis/dissertation. *Entrance requirements:* For master's and doctorate, GRE General Test, minimum GPA of 3.0. Additional exam requirements/recommendations for international students: required—TOEFL (minimum score 550 paper-based; 80 iBT), IELTS (minimum score 6). Electronic applications accepted.

University of Georgia, Franklin College of Arts and Sciences, Program in Linguistics, Athens, GA 30602. Offers MA, PhD. *Degree requirements:* For master's, one foreign language, thesis; for doctorate, 2 foreign languages, comprehensive exam, thesis/dissertation. *Entrance requirements:* For master's and doctorate, GRE General Test. Electronic applications accepted. *Expenses:* Contact institution.

University of Hawaii at Manoa, Office of Graduate Education, College of Languages, Linguistics and Literature, Department of Linguistics, Honolulu, HI 96822. Offers MA, PhD. *Program availability:* Part-time. Terminal master's awarded for partial completion of doctoral program. *Degree requirements:* For master's, 2 foreign languages, thesis optional; for doctorate, 2 foreign languages, comprehensive exam, thesis/dissertation. *Entrance requirements:* For master's and doctorate, GRE General Test. Additional exam requirements/recommendations for international students: required—TOEFL (minimum score 600 paper-based; 100 iBT), IELTS (minimum score 7).

University of Houston, College of Liberal Arts and Social Sciences, Department of English, Houston, TX 77204. Offers applied English linguistics (MA); creative writing (MFA); creative writing and literature (MA, PhD); English (MA, PhD). *Degree requirements:* For master's, one foreign language, comprehensive exam (for some programs), thesis (MFA); for doctorate, 2 foreign languages, comprehensive exam, thesis/dissertation. *Entrance requirements:* For master's, GRE General Test, minimum GPA of 3.0 in last 60 hours of course work; for doctorate, GRE General Test, GRE Subject Test (literature), writing sample. Additional exam requirements/recommendations for international students: required—TOEFL (minimum score 550 paper-based; 79 iBT). Electronic applications accepted.

University of Illinois at Chicago, College of Liberal Arts and Sciences, School of Literatures, Cultural Studies and Linguistics, Department of Linguistics, Chicago, IL 60607-7128. Offers MA. *Program availability:* Part-time. *Degree requirements:* For master's, one foreign language, comprehensive exam, thesis (for some programs). *Entrance requirements:* For master's, minimum GPA of 3.0. Additional exam requirements/recommendations for international students: required—TOEFL. Electronic applications accepted.

University of Illinois at Urbana-Champaign, Graduate College, College of Liberal Arts and Sciences, School of Literatures, Cultures and Linguistics, Department of Linguistics, Champaign, IL 61820. Offers linguistics (MA, PhD); teaching of English as a second language (MA).

University of Illinois at Urbana-Champaign, Graduate College, College of Liberal Arts and Sciences, School of Literatures, Cultures and Linguistics, Program in Romance Linguistics, Champaign, IL 61820. Offers PhD.

The University of Iowa, Graduate College, College of Liberal Arts and Sciences, Department of Linguistics, Iowa City, IA 52242-1316. Offers MA, PhD. *Degree requirements:* For master's, thesis optional, exam; for doctorate, comprehensive exam, thesis/dissertation. *Entrance requirements:* For master's and doctorate, GRE General Test, minimum GPA of 3.0. Additional exam requirements/recommendations for international students: required—TOEFL (minimum score 550 paper-based; 81 iBT). Electronic applications accepted.

The University of Kansas, Graduate Studies, College of Liberal Arts and Sciences, Department of Linguistics, Lawrence, KS 66045. Offers MA, PhD. *Students:* 27 full-time (13 women), 1 (woman) part-time; includes 1 minority (Hispanic/Latino), 16 international. Average age 28. 52 applicants, 42% accepted, 6 enrolled. In 2019, 7 master's, 1 doctorate awarded. Terminal master's awarded for partial completion of doctoral program. *Entrance requirements:* For master's and doctorate, GRE General Test, curriculum vitae, statement of purpose, 3 letters of recommendation. Additional exam requirements/recommendations for international students: required—TOEFL, IELTS. *Application deadline:* For fall admission, 12/15 for domestic and international students. Application fee: $65 ($85 for international students). Electronic applications accepted. *Expenses:* Tuition, state resident: full-time $9989. Tuition, nonresident: full-time $23,950. *International tuition:* $23,950 full-time. *Required fees:* $984; $81.99 per credit hour. Tuition and fees vary according to course load, campus/location and program. *Financial support:* Fellowships, research assistantships, teaching assistantships, scholarships/grants, and unspecified assistantships available. Financial award application deadline: 12/15. *Unit head:* Joan A. Sereno, Chair, 785-864-2619, E-mail: sereno@ku.edu. *Application contact:* Corinna Johnson, Office Manager, 785-864-3450, E-mail: cljohns@ku.edu.
Website: http://www.linguistics.ku.edu/

University of Louisville, Graduate School, College of Arts and Sciences, Department of Comparative Humanities, Louisville, KY 40292-0001. Offers civic leadership (MA); culture, criticism, and contemporary thought (PhD); linguistics (MA); public arts and letters (PhD); traditional humanities (MA); MA/JD; MA/MBA. *Program availability:* Part-time. *Faculty:* 15 full-time (6 women), 18 part-time/adjunct (9 women). *Students:* 24 full-time (12 women), 16 part-time (8 women); includes 6 minority (1 Black or African American, non-Hispanic/Latino; 1 Hispanic/Latino; 4 Two or more races, non-Hispanic/Latino), 2 international. Average age 41. 16 applicants, 81% accepted, 8 enrolled. In 2019, 3 master's, 6 doctorates awarded. *Degree requirements:* For master's, one foreign language, thesis or alternative, directed study culminating project; for doctorate, 2 foreign languages, comprehensive exam, thesis/dissertation, internship. *Entrance requirements:* For master's, GRE General Test, Two letters of reference, official transcripts; for doctorate, GRE General Test, three letters of recommendation, statement of intent, scholarly writing sample, transcripts from all institutions attended. Additional exam requirements/recommendations for international students: required—TOEFL (minimum score 550 paper-based; 79 iBT), IELTS can be used in place of the TOEFL; recommended—IELTS (minimum score 6.5). *Application deadline:* For fall admission, 1/15 for domestic and international students; for spring admission, 7/15 for domestic and international students. Applications are processed on a rolling basis. Application fee: $65. Electronic applications accepted. *Expenses:* Contact institution. *Financial support:* In 2019–20, 25 students received support, including 1 fellowship with full tuition reimbursement available (averaging $18,000 per year), 3 teaching assistantships with full tuition reimbursements available (averaging $18,000 per year); research assistantships, scholarships/grants, health care benefits, and unspecified assistantships also available. Financial award application deadline: 1/15. *Unit head:* Dr. Ann Hall, Chair, 502-852-6805, Fax: 502-852-0078, E-mail: ann.hall@louisville.edu. *Application contact:* Dr. Simona Bertacco, Professor and Director of Graduate Studies, 502-852-7161, E-mail: simona.bertacco@louisville.edu.
Website: http://louisville.edu/humanities/

The University of Manchester, School of Arts, Languages and Cultures, Manchester, United Kingdom. Offers anthropology, media and performance (PhD); applied theatre (PhD); Arab world studies (PhD); archaeology (PhD); art history and visual studies (PhD); arts and cultural management (PhD); arts management and cultural policy (PhD); Chinese studies (PhD); classics and ancient history (PhD); composition (PhD); creative writing (PhD); drama (PhD); East Asian studies (PhD); electroacoustic composition (PhD); English and American studies (PhD); English language (PhD); French studies (PhD); German studies (PhD); history (PhD); humanitarianism and conflict response (PhD); interpreting studies (PhD); Japanese studies (PhD); Latin American cultural studies (PhD); linguistics (PhD); Middle Eastern studies (PhD); museology (PhD); museum practice (PhD); music (PhD); musicology (PhD); Polish studies (PhD); Portuguese studies (PhD); religions and theology (PhD); Russian studies (PhD); Spanish studies (PhD); translation and intercultural studies (PhD).

University of Manitoba, Faculty of Graduate Studies, Faculty of Arts, Department of Linguistics, Winnipeg, MB R3T 2N2, Canada. Offers MA, PhD.

University of Maryland, Baltimore County, The Graduate School, College of Arts, Humanities and Social Sciences, Department of Modern Languages, Linguistics and Intercultural Communication, Program in Intercultural Communication, Baltimore, MD 21250. Offers MA. *Program availability:* Part-time, evening/weekend. *Faculty:* 16 full-time (9 women). *Students:* 10 full-time (6 women), 5 part-time (2 women); includes 5 minority (3 Black or African American, non-Hispanic/Latino; 2 Hispanic/Latino), 3 international. Average age 29. 16 applicants, 94% accepted, 8 enrolled. In 2019, 4 master's awarded. *Degree requirements:* For master's, one foreign language, comprehensive exam (for some programs), thesis (for some programs). *Entrance requirements:* For master's, GRE General Test, minimum GPA of 3.0, 3 letters of recommendation, self-evaluation and statement of support, resume, writing sample in modern language. Additional exam requirements/recommendations for international students: required—TOEFL (minimum score 550 paper-based, 80 iBT) or IELTS. *Application deadline:* For fall admission, 1/31 for domestic and international students. Application fee: $50. Electronic applications accepted. *Expenses:* $14,382 per year. *Financial support:* In 2019–20, 8 students received support, including 8 teaching assistantships with full tuition reimbursements available (averaging $12,874 per year); Federal Work-Study, scholarships/grants, health care benefits, and tuition waivers (full) also available. Financial award application deadline: 1/31; financial award applicants required to submit FAFSA. *Unit head:* Dr. Nicoleta Bazgan, Program Director, 410-455-3116, Fax: 410-455-1025, E-mail: nbazgan@umbc.edu. *Application contact:* Dr. Nicoleta Bazgan, Program Director, 410-455-3116, Fax: 410-455-1025, E-mail: nbazgan@umbc.edu.
Website: http://www.umbc.edu/mll/incc/

University of Maryland, College Park, Academic Affairs, College of Arts and Humanities, Department of Linguistics, College Park, MD 20742. Offers MA, PhD. *Degree requirements:* For master's, thesis or alternative; for doctorate, thesis/dissertation. *Entrance requirements:* For master's, GRE General Test, minimum GPA of 3.0, sample of work, 3 letters of recommendation; for doctorate, GRE General Test, minimum GPA of 3.0, sample of work. Additional exam requirements/recommendations for international students: required—TOEFL. Electronic applications accepted.

University of Massachusetts Amherst, Graduate School, College of Humanities and Fine Arts, Department of Linguistics, Amherst, MA 01003. Offers MA, PhD. *Program availability:* Part-time. *Degree requirements:* For master's, thesis or alternative; for doctorate, comprehensive exam, thesis/dissertation. *Entrance requirements:* For doctorate, GRE General Test, writing sample. Additional exam requirements/recommendations for international students: required—TOEFL (minimum score 550 paper-based; 80 iBT), IELTS (minimum score 6.5). Electronic applications accepted.

University of Massachusetts Boston, College of Liberal Arts, Program in Applied Linguistics, Boston, MA 02125-3393. Offers MA, PhD. *Program availability:* Part-time, evening/weekend. *Entrance requirements:* For master's, minimum GPA of 2.75. Electronic applications accepted.

University of Memphis, Graduate School, College of Arts and Sciences, Department of English, Memphis, TN 38152. Offers African-American literature (Graduate Certificate); applied linguistics (PhD); composition studies (PhD); creative writing (MFA); English as a second language (MA); linguistics (MA); literary and cultural studies (PhD), including African-American literature; literature (MA); professional writing (MA, PhD); teaching English as a second/foreign language (Graduate Certificate). *Program availability:* Part-time, evening/weekend, 100% online. *Students:* 58 full-time (33 women), 76 part-time (52 women); includes 34 minority (24 Black or African American, non-Hispanic/Latino; 4 Asian, non-Hispanic/Latino; 5 Hispanic/Latino; 1 Two or more races, non-Hispanic/Latino), 16 international. Average age 36. 52 applicants, 92% accepted, 23 enrolled. In 2019, 19 master's, 15 doctorates, 8 other advanced degrees awarded. Terminal master's awarded for partial completion of doctoral program. *Degree requirements:* For master's, variable foreign language requirement, comprehensive exam, thesis optional; for doctorate, variable foreign language requirement, comprehensive exam, thesis/dissertation, qualifying exam. *Entrance requirements:* For master's, GRE, minimum undergraduate GPA of 3.0, statement of purpose, two letters of recommendation; for doctorate, GRE, minimum undergraduate and graduate GPA of 3.25, statement of purpose, writing sample, three letters of recommendation. Additional exam requirements/recommendations for international students: required—TOEFL. *Application deadline:* For fall admission, 1/15 for domestic students; for spring admission, 10/15 for domestic students. Applications are processed on a rolling basis. Application fee: $35 ($60 for international students). Electronic applications accepted. *Expenses: Tuition, area resident:* Full-time $9216; part-time $512 per credit hour.

Tuition, state resident: full-time $9216; part-time $512 per credit hour. Tuition, nonresident: full-time $12,672; part-time $704 per credit hour. *International tuition:* $16,128 full-time. *Required fees:* $1530; $85 per credit hour. Tuition and fees vary according to program. *Financial support:* Research assistantships with full tuition reimbursements, teaching assistantships with full tuition reimbursements, Federal Work-Study, scholarships/grants, and unspecified assistantships available. Financial award application deadline: 2/1; financial award applicants required to submit FAFSA. *Unit head:* Dr. Joshua Phillips, Chair, 901-678-2651, Fax: 901-678-2226, E-mail: jsphllps@memphis.edu. *Application contact:* Dr. Jeffrey Scraba, Director of Graduate Studies, 901-678-4768, Fax: 901-678-2226, E-mail: jscraba@memphis.edu.
Website: http://www.memphis.edu/english

University of Michigan, Rackham Graduate School, College of Literature, Science, and the Arts, Department of Anthropology, Ann Arbor, MI 48109. Offers anthropological archaeology (PhD); biological anthropology (PhD); linguistic anthropology (PhD); sociocultural anthropology (PhD). *Degree requirements:* For doctorate, one foreign language, comprehensive exam, thesis/dissertation, preliminary examination, oral defense of dissertation. *Entrance requirements:* For doctorate, GRE General Test. Additional exam requirements/recommendations for international students: required—TOEFL (minimum score 560 paper-based; 84 iBT). Electronic applications accepted.

University of Michigan, Rackham Graduate School, College of Literature, Science, and the Arts, Department of Linguistics, Ann Arbor, MI 48109. Offers PhD. *Degree requirements:* For doctorate, one foreign language, thesis/dissertation, oral defense of dissertation. *Entrance requirements:* Additional exam requirements/recommendations for international students: required—TOEFL (minimum score 600 paper-based; 100 iBT), IELTS (minimum score 7.5), Michigan English Language Assessment Battery. Electronic applications accepted.

University of Minnesota, Twin Cities Campus, Graduate School, College of Liberal Arts, Institute of Linguistics, English as a Second Language, and Slavic Languages and Literatures (ILES), Program in Linguistics, Minneapolis, MN 55455-0213. Offers MA, PhD. Terminal master's awarded for partial completion of doctoral program. *Degree requirements:* For master's, one foreign language, comprehensive exam, thesis; for doctorate, 2 foreign languages, comprehensive exam, thesis/dissertation. *Entrance requirements:* For master's and doctorate, GRE General Test, 3 letters of recommendation, unit questionnaire. Additional exam requirements/recommendations for international students: required—TOEFL (minimum score 550 paper-based; 79 iBT). Electronic applications accepted.

University of Montana, Graduate School, College of Humanities and Sciences, Department of Anthropology, Missoula, MT 59812. Offers anthropology (MA, PhD); applied anthropology (PhD); applied medical anthropology (MA); cultural heritage (MA, PhD); forensic anthropology (MA); linguistic anthropology (MA). *Degree requirements:* For master's, thesis (for some programs). *Entrance requirements:* For master's, GRE General Test. Additional exam requirements/recommendations for international students: required—TOEFL.

University of Montana, Graduate School, College of Humanities and Sciences, Program in Linguistics, Missoula, MT 59812. Offers MA. *Entrance requirements:* For master's, GRE General Test. Additional exam requirements/recommendations for international students: required—TOEFL.

University of New Hampshire, Graduate School, College of Liberal Arts, Department of English, Durham, NH 03824. Offers English (MST, PhD); language and linguistics (MA); literature (MA); writing (MFA). *Program availability:* Part-time. *Students:* 65 full-time (43 women), 29 part-time (25 women); includes 6 minority (3 Black or African American, non-Hispanic/Latino; 1 Asian, non-Hispanic/Latino; 1 Hispanic/Latino; 1 Two or more races, non-Hispanic/Latino), 5 international. Average age 33. 91 applicants, 74% accepted, 27 enrolled. In 2019, 27 master's, 5 doctorates awarded. *Entrance requirements:* Additional exam requirements/recommendations for international students: required—TOEFL (minimum score 550 paper-based; 80 iBT), IELTS, PTE. *Application deadline:* For fall admission, 7/1 for domestic students; for spring admission, 12/1 for domestic students; for summer admission, 4/1 for domestic students. Application fee: $65. Electronic applications accepted. *Financial support:* In 2019–20, 69 students received support, including 1 fellowship, 38 teaching assistantships; research assistantships, career-related internships or fieldwork, Federal Work-Study, scholarships/grants, and tuition waivers (full and partial) also available. Support available to part-time students. Financial award application deadline: 2/15. *Unit head:* Dr. Rachel Trubowitz, Chair, 603-862-0254. *Application contact:* Janine Wilks, Administrative Assistant, 603-862-3963, E-mail: engl.grad@unh.edu.
Website: http://cola.unh.edu/english

University of New Mexico, Graduate Studies, College of Arts and Sciences, Program in Linguistics, Albuquerque, NM 87131-2039. Offers MA, PhD. *Program availability:* Part-time. *Degree requirements:* For master's, comprehensive exam, thesis optional; for doctorate, one foreign language, comprehensive exam, thesis/dissertation, statistics through analysis of variance; knowledge of structure of a non-Indo European language. *Entrance requirements:* For master's, minimum GPA of 3.0, 3 letters of recommendation, letter of intent; for doctorate, MA in linguistics or equivalent, paper of publishable quality, 3 letters of recommendation, letter of intent. Additional exam requirements/recommendations for international students: required—TOEFL (minimum score 550 paper-based; 79 iBT), IELTS (minimum score 7). Electronic applications accepted. *Expenses:* Tuition, state resident: full-time $7633; part-time $972 per year. Tuition, nonresident: full-time $22,586; part-time $3840 per year. *International tuition:* $23,292 full-time. *Required fees:* $8608. Tuition and fees vary according to course level, course load, degree level, program and student level.

University of New Mexico, Graduate Studies, College of Education and Human Sciences, Program in Educational Linguistics, Albuquerque, NM 87131-2039. Offers PhD. *Program availability:* Part-time. *Degree requirements:* For doctorate, comprehensive exam, thesis/dissertation. *Entrance requirements:* For doctorate, master's degree in linguistics or complementary field (recommended). Additional exam requirements/recommendations for international students: required—TOEFL (minimum score 550 paper-based; 79 iBT). Electronic applications accepted. *Expenses:* Tuition, state resident: full-time $7633; part-time $972 per year. Tuition, nonresident: full-time $22,586; part-time $3840 per year. *International tuition:* $23,292 full-time. *Required fees:* $8608. Tuition and fees vary according to course level, course load, degree level, program and student level.

The University of North Carolina at Chapel Hill, Graduate School, College of Arts and Sciences, Department of Linguistics, Chapel Hill, NC 27599. Offers MA. *Degree requirements:* For master's, one foreign language, comprehensive exam, thesis. *Entrance requirements:* For master's, GRE General Test, minimum GPA of 3.0. Additional exam requirements/recommendations for international students: required—TOEFL (minimum score 79 iBT). Electronic applications accepted.

The University of North Carolina at Charlotte, College of Liberal Arts and Sciences, Department of English, Charlotte, NC 28223-0001. Offers applied linguistics (Graduate Certificate); english (MA), including applied linguistics, children's lit., composition/rhetoric, creative writing, english ed., english for specific purposes, literature, tech/prof w; technical and professional writing (Graduate Certificate). *Program availability:* Part-time, evening/weekend. *Faculty:* 31 full-time (16 women), 1 (woman) part-time/adjunct. *Students:* 26 full-time (19 women), 32 part-time (23 women); includes 18 minority (9 Black or African American, non-Hispanic/Latino; 3 Asian, non-Hispanic/Latino; 1 Hispanic/Latino; 5 Two or more races, non-Hispanic/Latino), 1 international. Average age 30. 26 applicants, 96% accepted, 17 enrolled. In 2019, 16 master's, 3 other advanced degrees awarded. *Degree requirements:* For master's, comprehensive exam (for some programs), thesis, project. *Entrance requirements:* For master's, minimum undergraduate GPA of 3.0, statement of purpose, recommendation letters; unofficial transcript; for Graduate Certificate, statement of purpose, three letters of recommendation, writing sample, minimum GPA of 2.75, current GRE score/current MAT score/portfolio of professional-level documents (technical/professional writing). Additional exam requirements/recommendations for international students: required—TOEFL (minimum score 557 paper-based; 83 iBT), IELTS (minimum score 6.5), TOEFL (minimum score 557 paper-based, 83 iBT) or IELTS (6.5). *Application deadline:* For fall admission, 3/1 priority date for domestic students. Applications are processed on a rolling basis. Application fee: $75. Electronic applications accepted. *Expenses:* Tuition, state resident: full-time $4337. Tuition, nonresident: full-time $17,771. *Required fees:* $3093. Tuition and fees vary according to course load, degree level and program. *Financial support:* In 2019–20, 15 students received support, including 15 teaching assistantships (averaging $8,015 per year); career-related internships or fieldwork, institutionally sponsored loans, scholarships/grants, and unspecified assistantships also available. Support available to part-time students. Financial award application deadline: 3/1; financial award applicants required to submit FAFSA. *Unit head:* Dr. Mark West, Professor and Chair, 704-687-0618, E-mail: miwest@uncc.edu. *Application contact:* Kathy B. Giddings, Director of Graduate Admissions, 704-687-5503, Fax: 704-687-1668, E-mail: gradadm@uncc.edu.
Website: http://english.uncc.edu/

University of North Dakota, Graduate School, College of Arts and Sciences, Program in Linguistics, Grand Forks, ND 58202. Offers MA. *Degree requirements:* For master's, one foreign language, thesis, final examination. *Entrance requirements:* For master's, minimum GPA of 3.0. Additional exam requirements/recommendations for international students: required—TOEFL (minimum score 550 paper-based; 79 iBT), IELTS (minimum score 6.5). Electronic applications accepted.

University of North Texas, Toulouse Graduate School, Denton, TX 76203-5459. Offers accounting (MS); applied anthropology (MA, MS); applied behavior analysis (Certificate); applied geography (MA); applied technology and performance improvement (M Ed, MS); art education (MA); art history (MA); arts leadership (Certificate); audiology (Au D); behavior analysis (MS); behavioral science (PhD); biochemistry and molecular biology (MS); biology (MA, MS); biomedical engineering (MS); business analysis (MS); chemistry (MS); clinical health psychology (PhD); communication studies (MA, MS); computer engineering (MS); computer science (MS); counseling (M Ed, MS), including clinical mental health counseling (MS), college and university counseling, elementary school counseling, secondary school counseling; creative writing (MA); criminal justice (MS); curriculum and instruction (M Ed); decision sciences (MBA); design (MA, MFA), including fashion design (MFA), innovation studies, interior design (MFA); early childhood studies (MS); economics (MS); educational leadership (M Ed, Ed D); educational psychology (MS, PhD), including family studies (MS), gifted and talented (MS), human development (MS), learning and cognition (MS), research, measurement and evaluation (MS); electrical engineering (MS); emergency management (MPA); engineering technology (MS); English (MA); English as a second language (MA); environmental science (MS); finance (MBA, MS); financial management (MPA); French (MA); health services management (MBA); higher education (M Ed, Ed D); history (MA, MS); hospitality management (MS); human resources management (MPA); information science (MS); information systems (PhD); information technologies (MBA); interdisciplinary studies (MA, MS); international studies (MA); international sustainable tourism (MS); jazz studies (MM); journalism (MA, MJ, Graduate Certificate), including interactive and virtual digital communication (Graduate Certificate), narrative journalism (Graduate Certificate), public relations (Graduate Certificate); kinesiology (MS); linguistics (MA); local government management (MPA); logistics (PhD); logistics and supply chain management (MBA); long-term care, senior housing, and aging services (MA); management (PhD); marketing (MBA); mathematics (MA, MS); mechanical and energy engineering (MS, PhD); music (MA), including ethnomusicology, music theory, musicology, performance; music composition (PhD); music education (MM Ed, PhD); nonprofit management (MPA); operations and supply chain management (MBA); performance (MM, DMA); philosophy (MA); political science (MA); professional and technical communication (MA); radio, television and film (MA, MFA); rehabilitation counseling (Certificate); sociology (MA); Spanish (MA); special education (M Ed); speech-language pathology (MA); strategic management (MBA); studio art (MFA); teaching (M Ed); MBA/MS. *Program availability:* Part-time, evening/weekend, online learning. Terminal master's awarded for partial completion of doctoral program. *Degree requirements:* For master's, variable foreign language requirement, comprehensive exam (for some programs), thesis (for some programs); for doctorate, variable foreign language requirement, comprehensive exam (for some programs), thesis/dissertation; for other advanced degree, variable foreign language requirement, comprehensive exam (for some programs). *Entrance requirements:* For master's and doctorate, GRE, GMAT. Additional exam requirements/recommendations for international students: required—TOEFL (minimum score 550 paper-based; 79 iBT). Electronic applications accepted.

University of Oregon, Graduate School, College of Arts and Sciences, Department of Linguistics, Eugene, OR 97403. Offers language teaching studies (MA); linguistics (MA, PhD). Terminal master's awarded for partial completion of doctoral program. *Degree requirements:* For master's, 2 foreign languages; for doctorate, thesis/dissertation. *Entrance requirements:* For master's and doctorate, GRE General Test, minimum GPA of 3.0. Additional exam requirements/recommendations for international students: required—TOEFL.

University of Ottawa, Faculty of Graduate and Postdoctoral Studies, Faculty of Arts, Department of Linguistics, Ottawa, ON K1N 6N5, Canada. Offers MA, PhD. *Degree requirements:* For master's, one foreign language, thesis or alternative; for doctorate, 2 foreign languages, comprehensive exam, thesis/dissertation. *Entrance requirements:* For master's, honors degree or equivalent, minimum B average; for doctorate, master's degree, minimum B+ average. Electronic applications accepted.

University of Pennsylvania, Graduate School of Education, Division of Educational Linguistics, Program in Educational Linguistics, Philadelphia, PA 19104. Offers PhD. *Program availability:* Part-time-only. *Students:* 15 full-time (9 women), 7 part-time (6 women); includes 9 minority (1 Black or African American, non-Hispanic/Latino; 5 Asian, non-Hispanic/Latino; 2 Hispanic/Latino; 1 Two or more races, non-Hispanic/Latino), 6 international. Average age 34. 91 applicants, 7% accepted, 6 enrolled. *Financial support:* In 2019–20, 55 students received support.

University of Pennsylvania, School of Arts and Sciences, Graduate Group in Linguistics, Philadelphia, PA 19104-6228. Offers AM, PhD. *Faculty:* 23 full-time (5 women), 1 part-time/adjunct (0 women). *Students:* 35 full-time (18 women); includes 1 minority (Asian, non-Hispanic/Latino), 24 international. Average age 28. 142 applicants, 10% accepted, 8 enrolled. In 2019, 6 doctorates awarded. Terminal master's awarded

for partial completion of doctoral program. *Entrance requirements:* For master's, GRE General Test. Application fee: $90.
Website: http://www.ling.upenn.edu/graduate/

University of Pittsburgh, Kenneth P. Dietrich School of Arts and Sciences, Department of Linguistics, Pittsburgh, PA 15260. Offers applied linguistics (MA); applied linguistics with TESOL (MA); sociolinguistics (PhD). *Faculty:* 7 full-time (4 women), 16 part-time/adjunct (10 women). *Students:* 23 full-time (12 women); includes 2 minority (both Black or African American, non-Hispanic/Latino), 8 international. 138 applicants, 30% accepted, 14 enrolled. In 2019, 2 master's, 2 doctorates awarded. Terminal master's awarded for partial completion of doctoral program. *Degree requirements:* For master's, one foreign language, comprehensive exam, thesis or alternative, Language proficiency; for doctorate, 2 foreign languages, comprehensive exam, thesis/dissertation. *Entrance requirements:* For master's, TESOL MA: undergraduate transcripts, 3 letters of recommendation, career/research statement, CV, writing sample, proposed area of specialization, if applying for Hispanic Linguistics you must show proof of Spanish proficiency; for doctorate, PhD: undergraduate transcripts, graduate transcripts, 3 letters of recommendation, career/research statement, CV, writing sample, proposed area of specialization, if applying for Hispanic Linguistics you must show proof of Spanish proficiency. Additional exam requirements/recommendations for international students: required—TOEFL (minimum score 100 iBT), IELTS (minimum score 7). *Application deadline:* For fall admission, 12/16 priority date for domestic and international students; for spring admission, 3/22 for domestic students. Application fee: $75. Electronic applications accepted. *Financial support:* In 2019–20, 6 students received support, including 4 fellowships with full tuition reimbursements available (averaging $20,250 per year), 2 teaching assistantships (averaging $19,480 per year); research assistantships, scholarships/grants, traineeships, health care benefits, unspecified assistantships, and Employee Tuition Benefits also available. Financial award application deadline: 12/16; financial award applicants required to submit FAFSA. *Unit head:* Dr. Scott Kiesling, Department Chair, 412-624-5916, Fax: 412-624-5520, E-mail: kiesling@pitt.edu. *Application contact:* Joshua Oliver, Graduate Student Administrator, 412-624-6568, Fax: 412-624-5520, E-mail: jjo48@pitt.edu.
Website: http://www.linguistics.pitt.edu/

University of Puerto Rico at Río Piedras, College of Humanities, Department of Hispanic Studies, San Juan, PR 00931-3300. Offers Hispanic linguistics (PhD); Hispanic studies (MA); Latin American literature (PhD); Puerto Rican literature (PhD); Spanish literature (PhD). *Program availability:* Part-time. *Degree requirements:* For master's, one foreign language, comprehensive exam, thesis; for doctorate, one foreign language, comprehensive exam, thesis/dissertation. *Entrance requirements:* For master's, PAEG or GRE, interview, minimum GPA of 3.0, letter of recommendation (2); for doctorate, PAEG or GRE, interview, master's degree, minimum GPA of 3.0, letter of recommendation (2).

University of Puerto Rico at Río Piedras, College of Humanities, Department of Linguistics, San Juan, PR 00931-3300. Offers MA. *Program availability:* Part-time. *Degree requirements:* For master's, one foreign language, comprehensive exam, thesis. *Entrance requirements:* For master's, PAEG or GRE, interview, minimum GPA of 3.0, letter of recommendation (2).

University of Rochester, School of Arts and Sciences, Department of Linguistics, Rochester, NY 14627. Offers computational linguistics (MS); language documentation and description (MA); linguistics (MA). *Program availability:* Part-time. *Faculty:* 8 full-time (4 women). *Students:* 7 full-time (5 women); includes 1 minority (Black or African American, non-Hispanic/Latino), 3 international. Average age 25. 64 applicants, 25% accepted, 2 enrolled. In 2019, 6 master's awarded. Terminal master's awarded for partial completion of doctoral program. *Degree requirements:* For master's, final essay/presentation. *Entrance requirements:* For master's, GRE, statement of purpose, three letters of recommendation, official transcripts, writing sample. Additional exam requirements/recommendations for international students: required—TOEFL. *Application deadline:* For fall admission, 1/15 for domestic and international students. Application fee: $60. Electronic applications accepted. *Financial support:* Research assistantships and scholarships/grants available. Financial award application deadline: 1/15. *Unit head:* Joyce McDonough, Professor and Chair, 585-275-2895, E-mail: joyce.mcdonough@rochester.edu. *Application contact:* Amanda Sherry, Administrative Assistant, 585-275-8053, E-mail: amanda.sherry@rochester.edu.
Website: http://www.sas.rochester.edu/lin/graduate/index.html

University of Saskatchewan, College of Graduate and Postdoctoral Studies, College of Arts and Science, Department of Linguistics and Religious Studies, Saskatoon, SK S7N 5A2, Canada. Offers applied linguistics (MA); religion and culture (MA); teaching English to speakers of other languages (MA). *Degree requirements:* For master's, thesis. *Entrance requirements:* Additional exam requirements/recommendations for international students: required—TOEFL (minimum score 80 iBT); recommended—IELTS (minimum score 6.5). Electronic applications accepted.

University of South Africa, College of Human Sciences, Pretoria, South Africa. Offers adult education (M Ed); African languages (MA, PhD); African politics (MA, PhD); Afrikaans (MA, PhD); ancient history (MA, PhD); ancient Near Eastern studies (MA, PhD); anthropology (MA, PhD); applied linguistics (MA); Arabic (MA, PhD); archaeology (MA); art history (MA); Biblical archaeology (MA); Biblical studies (M Th, D Th, PhD); Christian spirituality (M Th, D Th); church history (M Th, D Th); classical studies (MA, PhD); clinical psychology (MA); communication (MA, PhD); comparative education (M Ed, Ed D); consulting psychology (D Admin, D Com, PhD); curriculum studies (M Ed, Ed D); development studies (M Admin, MA, D Admin, PhD); didactics (M Ed, Ed D); education (M Tech); education management (M Ed, Ed D); educational psychology (M Ed); English (MA); environmental education (M Ed); French (MA, PhD); German (MA, PhD); Greek (MA); guidance and counseling (M Ed); health studies (MA, PhD), including health sciences education (MA), health services management (MA), medical and surgical nursing science (critical care general) (MA), midwifery and neonatal nursing science (MA), trauma and emergency care (MA); history (MA, PhD); history of education (Ed D); inclusive education (M Ed, Ed D); information and communications technology policy and regulation (MA); information science (MA, MIS, PhD); international politics (MA, PhD); Islamic studies (MA, PhD); Italian (MA, PhD); Judaica (MA, PhD); linguistics (MA, PhD); mathematical education (M Ed); mathematics education (MA); missiology (M Th, D Th); modern Hebrew (MA, PhD); musicology (MA, MMus, D Mus, PhD); natural science education (M Ed); New Testament (M Th, D Th); Old Testament (D Th); pastoral therapy (M Th, D Th); philosophy (MA); philosophy of education (M Ed, Ed D); politics (MA, PhD); Portuguese (MA, PhD); practical theology (M Th, D Th); psychology (MA, MS, PhD); psychology of education (M Ed, Ed D); public health (MA); religious studies (MA, D Th, PhD); Romance languages (MA); Russian (MA, PhD); Semitic languages (MA, PhD); social behavior studies in HIV/AIDS (MA); social science (mental health) (MA); social science in development studies (MA); social science in psychology (MA); social science in social work (MA); social science in sociology (MA); social work (MSW, DSW, PhD); socio-education (M Ed, Ed D); sociolinguistics (MA); sociology (MA, PhD); Spanish (MA, PhD); systematic theology (M Th, D Th); TESOL (teaching English to speakers of other languages) (MA); theological ethics (M Th, D Th); theory of literature (MA, PhD); urban ministries (D Th); urban ministry (M Th).

University of South Carolina, The Graduate School, College of Arts and Sciences, Linguistics Program, Columbia, SC 29208. Offers linguistics (MA, PhD); teaching English to speakers of other languages (Certificate). *Program availability:* Part-time. Terminal master's awarded for partial completion of doctoral program. *Degree requirements:* For master's, one foreign language, comprehensive exam, thesis optional; for doctorate, 3 foreign languages, comprehensive exam, thesis/dissertation. *Entrance requirements:* For master's and Certificate, GRE General Test, minimum GPA of 3.0; for doctorate, GRE General Test, minimum GPA of 3.5. Additional exam requirements/recommendations for international students: required—TOEFL. Electronic applications accepted.

University of Southern California, Graduate School, Dana and David Dornsife College of Letters, Arts and Sciences, Department of East Asian Languages and Cultures, Los Angeles, CA 90089. Offers classical Chinese literature (MA, PhD); classical Japanese literature (MA, PhD); linguistics (MA, PhD); modern Chinese literature (MA, PhD); modern Japanese literature (MA, PhD); modern Korean literature (MA, PhD). *Degree requirements:* For master's, thesis; for doctorate, 2 foreign languages, comprehensive exam, thesis/dissertation. *Entrance requirements:* For master's and doctorate, GRE, BA in relevant field. Additional exam requirements/recommendations for international students: required—TOEFL. Electronic applications accepted.

University of Southern California, Graduate School, Dana and David Dornsife College of Letters, Arts and Sciences, Department of Linguistics, Los Angeles, CA 90089. Offers East Asian linguistics (PhD); Hispanic linguistics (PhD); linguistics (PhD); Slavic linguistics (PhD). *Degree requirements:* For doctorate, comprehensive exam, thesis/dissertation. *Entrance requirements:* For doctorate, GRE. Additional exam requirements/recommendations for international students: required—TOEFL (minimum score 100 iBT). Electronic applications accepted.

The University of Tennessee, Graduate School, College of Arts and Sciences, Department of Modern Foreign Languages and Literatures, Program in Modern Foreign Languages, Knoxville, TN 37996. Offers applied linguistics (PhD); French (PhD); German (PhD); Italian (PhD); Portuguese (PhD); Russian (PhD); Spanish (PhD). *Degree requirements:* For doctorate, 2 foreign languages, thesis/dissertation. *Entrance requirements:* For doctorate, minimum GPA of 2.7. Additional exam requirements/recommendations for international students: required—TOEFL. Electronic applications accepted.

The University of Texas at Arlington, Graduate School, College of Liberal Arts, Department of Linguistics and TESOL, Program in Linguistics, Arlington, TX 76019. Offers MA, PhD. *Program availability:* Part-time, evening/weekend. Terminal master's awarded for partial completion of doctoral program. *Degree requirements:* For master's, one foreign language, comprehensive exam (for some programs), thesis optional; for doctorate, 2 foreign languages, comprehensive exam, thesis/dissertation, qualifying exam, dissertation proposal defense, professional development. *Entrance requirements:* For master's, GRE General Test, minimum undergraduate GPA of 3.0, 9 credits of undergraduate foundation courses; for doctorate, GRE General Test, 30 hours of graduate work in linguistics or a related discipline, minimum GPA of 3.5. Additional exam requirements/recommendations for international students: required—TOEFL (minimum score 550 paper-based). Electronic applications accepted.

The University of Texas at Austin, Graduate School, College of Liberal Arts, Department of French and Italian, Austin, TX 78712-1111. Offers French linguistics (MA, PhD); French studies (MA, PhD); Italian studies (MA, PhD); Romance linguistics (PhD). *Program availability:* Part-time. *Degree requirements:* For master's, one foreign language, thesis; for doctorate, 2 foreign languages, thesis/dissertation. *Entrance requirements:* For master's, GRE General Test, minimum GPA of 3.0, bachelor's degree in French or equivalent; for doctorate, GRE General Test, minimum GPA of 3.0, master's degree in French. Additional exam requirements/recommendations for international students: required—TOEFL. Electronic applications accepted.

The University of Texas at Austin, Graduate School, College of Liberal Arts, Department of Linguistics, Austin, TX 78712-1111. Offers MA, PhD. *Degree requirements:* For master's, one foreign language, thesis; for doctorate, 2 foreign languages, thesis/dissertation. *Entrance requirements:* For master's and doctorate, GRE General Test. Electronic applications accepted.

The University of Texas at Austin, Graduate School, College of Liberal Arts, Department of Slavic and Eurasian Studies, Austin, TX 78712-1111. Offers applied linguistics/pedagogy (PhD); literature and culture (PhD); Slavic languages (MA); Slavic linguistics (PhD). *Degree requirements:* For master's, 2 foreign languages, thesis; for doctorate, 3 foreign languages, thesis/dissertation. *Entrance requirements:* For master's and doctorate, GRE General Test. Electronic applications accepted.

The University of Texas at Austin, Graduate School, College of Liberal Arts, Department of Spanish and Portuguese, Austin, TX 78712-1111. Offers Hispanic linguistics (MA, PhD); Hispanic literature (MA, PhD); Ibero-romance philology and linguistics (PhD); Luso-Brazilian literature (MA, PhD). *Degree requirements:* For master's, 2 foreign languages, thesis or alternative; for doctorate, 3 foreign languages, thesis/dissertation. *Entrance requirements:* For master's and doctorate, GRE General Test. Electronic applications accepted.

The University of Texas at El Paso, Graduate School, College of Liberal Arts, Department of Languages and Linguistics, El Paso, TX 79968-0001. Offers linguistics (MA); Spanish (MA); teaching English to speakers of other languages (Certificate). *Program availability:* Part-time, evening/weekend. *Degree requirements:* For master's, thesis optional. *Entrance requirements:* For master's, GRE General Test, departmental exam, minimum GPA of 3.0, letters of recommendation. Additional exam requirements/recommendations for international students: required—TOEFL; recommended—IELTS. Electronic applications accepted.

University of Toronto, School of Graduate Studies, Faculty of Arts and Science, Department of Linguistics, Toronto, ON M5S 1A1, Canada. Offers MA, PhD. *Program availability:* Part-time. *Degree requirements:* For master's, 2 foreign languages; for doctorate, thesis/dissertation, oral thesis proposal. *Entrance requirements:* For master's, BA in linguistics; for doctorate, MA in linguistics. Electronic applications accepted.

University of Utah, Graduate School, College of Humanities, Department of Linguistics, Salt Lake City, UT 84112-0492. Offers MA, PhD. *Faculty:* 8 full-time (5 women). *Students:* 13 full-time (7 women), 1 part-time (0 women); includes 2 minority (1 Asian, non-Hispanic/Latino; 1 Hispanic/Latino), 7 international. Average age 31. In 2019, 1 doctorate awarded. Terminal master's awarded for partial completion of doctoral program. *Entrance requirements:* For master's and doctorate, GRE General Test, minimum undergraduate GPA of 3.0. Additional exam requirements/recommendations for international students: required—TOEFL (minimum score 600 paper-based; 100 iBT), IELTS (minimum score 7). Electronic applications accepted. *Expenses:* Contact institution. *Financial support:* In 2019–20, 12 teaching assistantships (averaging $15,917 per year) were awarded; unspecified assistantships also available. *Unit head:* Dr. Scott Jarvis, Chair, 801-581-8047, Fax: 801-585-7351, E-mail: scott.jarvis@utah.edu. *Application contact:* Kacey Campbell, Academic Advisor, 801-581-3929, Fax: 801-585-7351, E-mail: kacey.campbell@utah.edu.
Website: http://www.linguistics.utah.edu

University of Victoria, Faculty of Graduate Studies, Faculty of Humanities, Department of Linguistics, Victoria, BC V8W 2Y2, Canada. Offers applied linguistics (MA); linguistics (MA, PhD). *Program availability:* Part-time. *Degree requirements:* For master's, one foreign language, thesis, colloquium; for doctorate, 2 foreign languages, comprehensive exam, thesis/dissertation, candidacy exam. *Entrance requirements:* For master's, GRE; for doctorate, GRE, sample of written work. Additional exam requirements/recommendations for international students: required—TOEFL. Electronic applications accepted.

University of Virginia, College and Graduate School of Arts and Sciences, Program in Linguistics, Charlottesville, VA 22903. Offers MA. *Degree requirements:* For master's, one foreign language, comprehensive exam, thesis optional, reading knowledge of French or German. *Entrance requirements:* For master's, GRE General Test. Additional exam requirements/recommendations for international students: required—TOEFL (minimum score 600 paper-based; 90 iBT), IELTS (minimum score 7). Electronic applications accepted.

University of Washington, Graduate School, College of Arts and Sciences, Department of Linguistics, Seattle, WA 98195. Offers computational linguistics (MA); linguistics (MA, PhD); Romance linguistics (MA, PhD). *Program availability:* Part-time. Terminal master's awarded for partial completion of doctoral program. *Degree requirements:* For master's, one foreign language, thesis; for doctorate, 2 foreign languages, thesis/dissertation. *Entrance requirements:* For master's, GRE General Test, minimum GPA of 3.0; for doctorate, GRE, minimum GPA of 3.0. Additional exam requirements/recommendations for international students: required—TOEFL. Electronic applications accepted.

University of Washington, Graduate School, College of Arts and Sciences, Department of Slavic Languages and Literatures, Seattle, WA 98195. Offers Russian literature (MA, PhD); Slavic linguistics (MA, PhD). *Degree requirements:* For master's, 2 foreign languages, thesis optional; for doctorate, 3 foreign languages, thesis/dissertation. *Entrance requirements:* For master's and doctorate, GRE General Test, minimum GPA of 3.0. Additional exam requirements/recommendations for international students: required—TOEFL. Electronic applications accepted.

University of Wisconsin–Madison, Graduate School, College of Letters and Science, Department of East Asian Languages and Literature, Program in Japanese Linguistics, Madison, WI 53706-1380. Offers MA, PhD. *Program availability:* Part-time. Terminal master's awarded for partial completion of doctoral program. *Degree requirements:* For master's, one foreign language, seminars, written exam; for doctorate, 3 foreign languages, thesis/dissertation, seminars, preliminary exams, oral exam. *Entrance requirements:* For master's, GRE General Test, bachelor's degree or equivalent in Japanese; for doctorate, GRE General Test, master's degree or equivalent in Japanese. Electronic applications accepted.

University of Wisconsin–Madison, Graduate School, College of Letters and Science, Department of English, Madison, WI 53706-1380. Offers applied English linguistics (MA); composition and rhetoric (PhD); creative writing (MFA); English language and linguistics (PhD); literary studies (MA, PhD). *Degree requirements:* For doctorate, thesis/dissertation.

University of Wisconsin–Madison, Graduate School, College of Letters and Science, Department of Linguistics, Madison, WI 53706-1380. Offers MA, PhD. *Program availability:* Part-time. Terminal master's awarded for partial completion of doctoral program. *Degree requirements:* For master's, 2 foreign languages; for doctorate, 3 foreign languages, thesis/dissertation. Electronic applications accepted.

University of Wisconsin–Milwaukee, Graduate School, College of Letters and Science, Department of Foreign Languages and Literature, Milwaukee, WI 53201-0413. Offers foreign languages and literature (MA), including classic Greek, classics, comparative literature, French/Francophone language, literature, and culture, German language, literature, and culture, interpreting, Latin, linguistics, Spanish language, literature, and culture, translation; interpreting (Graduate Certificate); language, literature, and translation (MA, MALLT); translation (Graduate Certificate). *Program availability:* Part-time. *Degree requirements:* For master's, 2 foreign languages, thesis or alternative. *Entrance requirements:* Additional exam requirements/recommendations for international students: required—TOEFL (minimum score 550 paper-based; 79 iBT), IELTS (minimum score 6.5). Electronic applications accepted.

University of Wisconsin–Milwaukee, Graduate School, College of Letters and Science, Department of Linguistics, Milwaukee, WI 53201-0413. Offers linguistics (MA, PhD), including teaching English to speakers of other languages (MA); teaching English to speakers of other languages, adult- and university-level (Graduate Certificate). Electronic applications accepted.

Université Laval, Faculty of Letters, Department of Languages, Linguistics and Translations, Programs in Linguistics, Québec, QC G1K 7P4, Canada. Offers MA, PhD. Terminal master's awarded for partial completion of doctoral program. *Degree requirements:* For master's, thesis (for some programs); for doctorate, comprehensive exam, thesis/dissertation. *Entrance requirements:* For master's, English test (comprehension of written English), knowledge of French; for doctorate, English exam (comprehension of written English), knowledge of French. Electronic applications accepted.

Virginia International University, School of Education, Fairfax, VA 22030. Offers applied linguistics (MS); education (M Ed); teaching English to speakers of other languages (MA). *Program availability:* Part-time, online learning. *Entrance requirements:* For master's, bachelor's degree. Additional exam requirements/recommendations for international students: required—TOEFL (minimum score 550 paper-based; 80 iBT), IELTS (minimum score 6). Electronic applications accepted.

Wayne State University, College of Liberal Arts and Sciences, Liberal Arts and Sciences Dean, Detroit, MI 48202. Offers MA. *Degree requirements:* For master's, one foreign language, essay. *Entrance requirements:* For master's, minimum one year of foreign language; at least one course in linguistics; statement of purpose. Additional exam requirements/recommendations for international students: required—TOEFL (minimum score 550 paper-based; 79 iBT), TWE (minimum score 5.5), Michigan English Language Assessment Battery (minimum score 85); recommended—IELTS (minimum score 6.5). Electronic applications accepted. *Expenses: Tuition:* Full-time $34,567.

Wesley Biblical Seminary, Graduate Programs, Jackson, MS 39206. Offers apologetics (MA); Biblical languages (M Div); Biblical literature (MA); Christian studies (MA); context and mission (M Div); honors research (M Div); interpretation (M Div); ministry (M Div); spiritual formation (M Div); teaching (M Div); theology (MA). *Accreditation:* ATS. *Program availability:* Part-time. *Degree requirements:* For master's, thesis. *Entrance requirements:* Additional exam requirements/recommendations for international students: required—TOEFL. Electronic applications accepted.

Yale University, Graduate School of Arts and Sciences, Department of Linguistics, New Haven, CT 06520. Offers PhD. *Degree requirements:* For doctorate, 2 foreign languages, thesis/dissertation. *Entrance requirements:* For doctorate, GRE General Test.

York University, Faculty of Graduate Studies, Faculty of Liberal Arts and Professional Studies, Program in Linguistics and Applied Linguistics, Toronto, ON M3J 1P3, Canada. Offers MA, PhD. *Degree requirements:* For master's, thesis.

Translation and Interpretation

American University of Sharjah, Graduate Programs, Sharjah, United Arab Emirates. Offers accounting (MS); biomedical engineering (MSBME); business administration (MBA); chemical engineering (MS Ch E); civil engineering (MSCE); computer engineering (MS); electrical engineering (MSEE); engineering systems management (MS, PhD); mathematics (MS); mechanical engineering (MSME); mechatronics engineering (MS); teaching English to speakers of other languages (MA); translation and interpreting (MA); urban planning (MUP). *Program availability:* Part-time, evening/weekend. *Degree requirements:* For master's, thesis (for some programs). *Entrance requirements:* For master's, GMAT (for MBA). Additional exam requirements/recommendations for international students: required—TOEFL (minimum score 550 paper-based; 80 iBT), TWE (minimum score 5); recommended—IELTS (minimum score 6.5). Electronic applications accepted.

Arizona State University at Tempe, College of Liberal Arts and Sciences, Department of English, Tempe, AZ 85287-0302. Offers applied linguistics (PhD); creative writing (MFA); English (MA, PhD), including comparative literature (MA), linguistics (MA), literature, rhetoric and composition (MA), rhetoric, composition, and linguistics (PhD); film and media studies (MAS), including American media and popular culture; linguistics (Graduate Certificate); teaching English to speakers of other languages (MTESOL); translation studies (Graduate Certificate). Terminal master's awarded for partial completion of doctoral program. *Degree requirements:* For master's, variable foreign language requirement, comprehensive exam (for some programs), thesis (for some programs), interactive Program of Study (iPOS) submitted before completing 50 percent of required credit hours; for doctorate, variable foreign language requirement, comprehensive exam, thesis/dissertation, interactive Program of Study (iPOS) submitted before completing 50 percent of required credit hours. *Entrance requirements:* For master's and doctorate, GRE, minimum GPA of 3.0 or equivalent in last 2 years of work leading to bachelor's degree. Additional exam requirements/recommendations for international students: required—TOEFL, IELTS, or PTE. Electronic applications accepted.

Babel University Professional School of Translation, Program in Translation, Honolulu, HI 96815. Offers MS. *Program availability:* Part-time, evening/weekend, online learning. *Degree requirements:* For master's, comprehensive exam, thesis. *Entrance requirements:* For master's, translation exam. Additional exam requirements/recommendations for international students: recommended—TOEFL (minimum score 550 paper-based).

Binghamton University, State University of New York, Graduate School, Harpur College of Arts and Sciences, Translation Research and Instruction Program, Binghamton, NY 13902-6000. Offers translation (Certificate); translation studies (PhD). *Program availability:* Part-time. *Degree requirements:* For doctorate, one foreign language, comprehensive exam, thesis/dissertation; for Certificate, one foreign language, comprehensive exam. *Entrance requirements:* For doctorate and Certificate, GRE General Test, writing sample. Additional exam requirements/recommendations for international students: required—TOEFL (minimum score 550 paper-based; 80 iBT). Electronic applications accepted.

Columbia University, Graduate School of Arts and Sciences, New York, NY 10027. Offers African-American studies (MA); American studies (MA); anthropology (MA, PhD); art history and archaeology (MA, PhD); astronomy (PhD); biological sciences (PhD); biotechnology (MA); chemical physics (PhD); chemistry (PhD); classical studies (MA, PhD); classics (MA, PhD); climate and society (MA); conservation biology (MA); earth and environmental sciences (PhD); East Asia: regional studies (MA); East Asian languages and cultures (MA, PhD); ecology, evolution and environmental biology (MA), including conservation biology; ecology, evolution, and environmental biology (PhD), including ecology and evolutionary biology, evolutionary primatology; economics (MA, PhD); English and comparative literature (MA, PhD); French and Romance philology (MA, PhD); Germanic languages (MA, PhD); global French studies (MA); global thought (MA); Hispanic cultural studies (MA); history (PhD); history and literature (MA); human rights studies (MA); Islamic studies (MA); Italian (MA, PhD); Japanese pedagogy (MA); Jewish studies (MA); Latin America and the Caribbean: regional studies (MA); Latin American and Iberian cultures (PhD); mathematics (MA, PhD), including finance (MA); medieval and Renaissance studies (MA); Middle Eastern, South Asian, and African studies (MA, PhD); modern art: critical and curatorial studies (MA); modern European studies (MA); museum anthropology (MA); music (DMA, PhD); oral history (MA); philosophical foundations of physics (MA); philosophy (MA, PhD); physics (PhD); political science (MA, PhD); psychology (PhD); quantitative methods in the social sciences (MA); religion (MA, PhD); Russia, Eurasia and East Europe: regional studies (MA); Russian translation (MA); Slavic cultures (MA); Slavic languages (MA, PhD); sociology (MA, PhD); South Asian studies (MA); statistics (MA, PhD); theatre (PhD). *Program availability:* Part-time. *Students:* 3,506 full-time (1,844 women), 208 part-time (121 women); includes 864 minority (110 Black or African American, non-Hispanic/Latino; 5 American Indian or Alaska Native, non-Hispanic/Latino; 416 Asian, non-Hispanic/Latino; 147 Hispanic/Latino; 6 Native Hawaiian or other Pacific Islander, non-Hispanic/Latino; 180 Two or more races, non-Hispanic/Latino), 2,065 international. 14,545 applicants, 25% accepted, 1,429 enrolled. In 2019, 1,262 master's, 363 doctorates awarded. Terminal master's awarded for partial completion of doctoral program. *Degree requirements:* For master's, variable foreign language requirement, comprehensive exam (for some programs), thesis (for some programs); for doctorate, variable foreign language requirement, comprehensive exam (for some programs), thesis/dissertation. *Entrance requirements:* For master's and doctorate, GRE General Test, GRE Subject Test (for some programs). Additional exam requirements/

recommendations for international students: required—TOEFL (minimum score 600 paper-based; 100 iBT), IELTS (minimum score 7.5). Application fee: $115. Electronic applications accepted. *Expenses: Tuition:* Full-time $47,600; part-time $1880 per credit. One-time fee: $105. *Financial support:* Fellowships, research assistantships, teaching assistantships, career-related internships or fieldwork, Federal Work-Study, institutionally sponsored loans, scholarships/grants, traineeships, health care benefits, tuition waivers, and unspecified assistantships available. Support available to part-time students. Financial award application deadline: 12/15. *Unit head:* Dr. Carlos J. Alonso, Dean of the Graduate School of Arts and Sciences and Vice President for Graduate Education, 212-854-2861, E-mail: gsas-dean@columbia.edu. *Application contact:* GSAS Office of Admissions, 212-854-6729, E-mail: gsas-admissions@columbia.edu.
Website: http://gsas.columbia.edu/

Concordia University, School of Graduate Studies, Faculty of Arts and Science, Department of Études Françaises, Montréal, QC H3G 1M8, Canada. Offers Anglais-Français en langue et techniques de localization (Certificate); littératures Francophones et résonances médiatiques (MA); translation (Diploma); translation studies (MA). *Degree requirements:* For other advanced degree, one foreign language.

East Tennessee State University, College of Graduate and Continuing Studies, College of Arts and Sciences, Department of Literature and Language, Johnson City, TN 37614. Offers healthcare translation and interpreting (Postbaccalaureate Certificate); literature (MA); teaching English to speakers of other languages (Postbaccalaureate Certificate). *Program availability:* Part-time, evening/weekend. *Degree requirements:* For master's, comprehensive exam, thesis optional; for Postbaccalaureate Certificate, one foreign language. *Entrance requirements:* For master's, GRE General Test, minimum undergraduate GPA of 3.0 in English, writing sample, three letters of recommendation; for Postbaccalaureate Certificate, GRE General Test, speaking and listening assessment, resume, three letters of recommendation, two years of coursework or basic proficiency in a foreign language. Additional exam requirements/recommendations for international students: required—TOEFL (minimum score 550 paper-based; 79 iBT). Electronic applications accepted.

Gallaudet University, The Graduate School, Washington, DC 20002. Offers American Sign Language/English bilingual early childhood deaf education: birth to 5 (Certificate); audiology (Au D); clinical psychology (PhD); deaf and hard of hearing infants, toddlers, and their families (Certificate); deaf education (MA, Ed S); deaf history (Certificate); deaf studies (Certificate); educating deaf students with disabilities (Certificate); education: teacher preparation (MA), including deaf education, early childhood education and deaf education, elementary education and deaf education, secondary education and deaf education; educational neuroscience (PhD); hearing, speech and language sciences (MS, PhD); international development (MA); interpretation (MA, PhD), including combined interpreting practice and research (MA), interpreting research (MA); linguistics (MA, PhD); mental health counseling (MA); peer mentoring (Certificate); public administration (MPA); school counseling (MA); school psychology (Psy S); sign language teaching (MA); social work (MSW); speech-language pathology (MS). *Program availability:* Part-time. *Faculty:* 101 full-time (70 women). *Students:* 267 full-time (208 women), 139 part-time (95 women); includes 120 minority (38 Black or African American, non-Hispanic/Latino; 20 Asian, non-Hispanic/Latino; 44 Hispanic/Latino; 18 Two or more races, non-Hispanic/Latino), 19 international. Average age 30. 484 applicants, 50% accepted, 162 enrolled. In 2019, 138 master's, 25 doctorates, 14 other advanced degrees awarded. Terminal master's awarded for partial completion of doctoral program. *Degree requirements:* For master's, comprehensive exam (for some programs), thesis optional; for doctorate, comprehensive exam, thesis/dissertation. *Entrance requirements:* For master's and doctorate, GRE General Test or MAT, letters of recommendation, interviews, goals statement, American Sign Language proficiency interview, written English competency. Additional exam requirements/recommendations for international students: required—TOEFL. *Application deadline:* For fall admission, 2/15 for domestic students. Applications are processed on a rolling basis. Application fee: $75. Electronic applications accepted. *Expenses: Tuition:* Full-time $18,180; part-time $688 per credit. *Required fees:* $526; $526. Tuition and fees vary according to course load. *Financial support:* In 2019–20, 50 students received support. Fellowships, research assistantships, teaching assistantships, career-related internships or fieldwork, Federal Work-Study, scholarships/grants, tuition waivers (partial), and unspecified assistantships available. Support available to part-time students. Financial award application deadline: 7/1; financial award applicants required to submit FAFSA. *Unit head:* Dr. Gaurav Mathur, Dean, Graduate School and Continuing Studies, 202-250-2380, Fax: 202-651-5027, E-mail: gaurav.mathur@gallaudet.edu. *Application contact:* Heidi Zornes-Foster, Senior Graduate Admissions Counselor, 202-650-5436, Fax: 202-651-5295, E-mail: graduate.school@gallaudet.edu.
Website: www.gallaudet.edu

Georgia State University, College of Arts and Sciences, Department of World Languages and Cultures, Program in Translation and Interpretation, Atlanta, GA 30302-3083. Offers interpretation (Certificate), including Spanish; translation (Certificate), including French, German, Spanish. *Program availability:* Part-time. *Entrance requirements:* For degree, entrance examination involving translating one passage from English to the target language and one passage from the target language to English, 3 letters of recommendation, resume/curriculum vitae, official transcripts. Additional exam requirements/recommendations for international students: required—TOEFL (minimum score 79 iBT). Application fee: $50. Electronic applications accepted. *Expenses: Tuition, area resident:* Full-time $7164; part-time $398 per credit hour. Tuition, state resident: full-time $7164; part-time $398 per credit hour. Tuition, nonresident: full-time $22,662; part-time $1259 per credit hour. *International tuition:* $22,662 full-time. *Required fees:* $2128; $312 per credit hour. Tuition and fees vary according to course load and program. *Unit head:* Dr. William Nichols, Chair, 404-413-5980, Fax: 404-413-5982, E-mail: wnichols@gsu.edu. *Application contact:* Vicky Hanning, Administrative Coordinator, 404-413-5990, Fax: 404-413-5982, E-mail: vassem@gsu.edu.
Website: http://wlc.gsu.edu/home/graduate/graduate-certificate/

Kent State University, College of Arts and Sciences, Department of Modern and Classical Language Studies, Kent, OH 44242-0001. Offers French (MA), including applied linguistics and pedagogy, literature; German (MA), including applied linguistics and pedagogy, literature; Latin (MA), including applied linguistics and pedagogy, literature; Spanish (MA), including applied linguistics and pedagogy, literature; translation (MA), including Arabic, French, German, Japanese, Russian, Spanish; translation studies (PhD); MA/MBA. *Program availability:* Part-time, 100% online. *Faculty:* 18 full-time (11 women), 6 part-time/adjunct (3 women). *Students:* 81 full-time (49 women), 23 part-time (14 women); includes 18 minority (3 Black or African American, non-Hispanic/Latino; 3 Asian, non-Hispanic/Latino; 11 Hispanic/Latino; 1 Two or more races, non-Hispanic/Latino), 45 international. Average age 32. 115 applicants, 73% accepted, 47 enrolled. In 2019, 27 master's, 7 doctorates awarded. *Degree requirements:* For master's, variable foreign language requirement, comprehensive exam (for some programs), thesis (for some programs); for doctorate, variable foreign language requirement, comprehensive exam, thesis/dissertation. *Entrance requirements:* For master's, transcripts, goal statement, 3 letters of recommendation, CD/MP3 with a 5-10 minute oral sample of first and second languages (conversational not read from a script), Writing sample(s) in the applicant's second language, which should be accompanied by a signed declaration that the sample is original work; for doctorate, transcripts; MA in translation, a foreign language, or in any other relevant discipline with prior experience or training in translation; proficiency in a foreign language; minimum GPA of 3.5 from MA; goal statement; 3 letters of recommendation; essay or writing sample (7-10 pages) from a research paper on any aspect of translation. Additional exam requirements/recommendations for international students: required—TOEFL (minimum score 79 iBT), IELTS (minimum score 6.5), PTE (minimum score 58), Michigan English Language Assessment Battery (minimum score 77). *Application deadline:* For fall admission, 2/1 for domestic and international students. Applications are processed on a rolling basis. Application fee: $45 ($70 for international students). Electronic applications accepted. *Financial support:* Fellowships with full tuition reimbursements, teaching assistantships with full tuition reimbursements, and unspecified assistantships available. Financial award application deadline: 2/1. *Unit head:* Dr. Keiran Dunne, Professor of French Translation; Department Chair, 330-672-2150, E-mail: kdunne@kent.edu. *Application contact:* Brian James Baer, Professor of Russian Translation; Graduate Coordinator, 330-672-1813, E-mail: bbaer@kent.edu.
Website: http://www.kent.edu/mcls/

La Salle University, School of Arts and Sciences, Hispanic Institute, Philadelphia, PA 19141-1199. Offers bilingual/bicultural studies (MA); ESL program specialist (Certificate); interpretation: English/Spanish-Spanish/English (Certificate); teaching English to speakers of other languages (MA); translation and interpretation (MA); translation: English/Spanish-Spanish/English (Certificate). *Program availability:* Part-time, evening/weekend. *Degree requirements:* For master's, one foreign language, project or thesis. *Entrance requirements:* For master's, GRE, MAT, or GMAT, professional resume; two letters of recommendation; for Certificate, GRE, MAT, or GMAT, professional resume; two letters of recommendation; evidence of an advanced level in Spanish. Additional exam requirements/recommendations for international students: required—TOEFL. Electronic applications accepted. Application fee is waived when completed online. *Expenses:* Contact institution.

London Metropolitan University, Graduate Programs, London, United Kingdom. Offers applied psychology (M Sc); architecture (MA); biomedical science (M Sc); blood science (M Sc); cancer pharmacology (M Sc); computer networking and cyber security (M Sc); computing and information systems (M Sc); conference interpreting (MA); counter-terrorism studies (M Sc); creative, digital and professional writing (MA); crime, violence and prevention (M Sc); criminology (M Sc); curating contemporary art (MA); data analytics (M Sc); digital media (MA); early childhood studies (MA); education (MA, Ed D); financial services law, regulation and compliance (LL M); food science (M Sc); forensic psychology (M Sc); health and social care management and policy (M Sc); human nutrition (M Sc); human resource management (MA); human rights and international conflict (MA); information technology (M Sc); intelligence and security studies (M Sc); international oil, gas and energy law (LL M); international relations (MA); interpreting (MA); learning and teaching in higher education (MA); legal practice (LL M); media and entertainment law (LL M); organizational and consumer psychology (M Sc); psychological therapy (M Sc); psychology of mental health (M Sc); public health (M Sc); public policy and management (MPA); security studies (M Sc); social work (M Sc); spatial planning and urban design (MA); sports therapy (M Sc); supporting older children and young people with dyslexia (MA); teaching languages (MA), including Arabic, English; translation (MA); woman and child abuse (MA).

Middlebury Institute of International Studies at Monterey, Graduate School of Translation, Interpretation and Language Education, Program in Translation and Interpretation, Monterey, CA 93940-2691. Offers conference interpretation (MA); translation (MA); translation and interpretation (MA); translation and localization management (MA). *Degree requirements:* For master's, one foreign language, thesis or alternative, exams. *Entrance requirements:* For master's, minimum GPA of 3.0, proficiency in a foreign language. Additional exam requirements/recommendations for international students: required—TOEFL (minimum score 600 paper-based; 100 iBT). Electronic applications accepted.

Mills College, Graduate Studies, Department of English, Oakland, CA 94613-1000. Offers book art and creative writing (MFA); literature (MA); poetry (MFA); prose (MFA); Spanish creative writing (Certificate); translation (MFA). *Program availability:* Part-time. *Degree requirements:* For master's, comprehensive exam, thesis. *Entrance requirements:* For master's, 15-20 page writing sample. Additional exam requirements/recommendations for international students: required—TOEFL (minimum score 600 paper-based; 100 iBT), IELTS (minimum score 7). Electronic applications accepted. *Expenses:* Contact institution.

Montclair State University, The Graduate School, College of Humanities and Social Sciences, Translation and Interpreting in Spanish Certificate Program, Montclair, NJ 07043-1624. Offers Certificate.

New York University, School of Professional Studies, Center for Applied Liberal Arts, Program in Translation, New York, NY 10012-1019. Offers translation (MS), including Chinese to English, English to Spanish, French to English, Spanish to English. *Program availability:* Part-time, evening/weekend, blended/hybrid learning. *Degree requirements:* For master's, thesis. *Entrance requirements:* For master's, GRE or GMAT (only upon request), bachelor's degree, resume with relevant professional work, internship or volunteer experience, 2 letters of recommendation, personal statement. Additional exam requirements/recommendations for international students: required—TOEFL (minimum score 600 paper-based; 100 iBT), IELTS (minimum score 7). Electronic applications accepted. *Expenses:* Contact institution.

Rochester Institute of Technology, Graduate Enrollment Services, National Technical Institute for the Deaf, American Sign Language and Interpreting Education Department, MS Program in Health Care Interpretation, Rochester, NY 14623-5603. Offers MS. *Program availability:* Part-time, blended/hybrid learning. *Entrance requirements:* For master's, ASL interpretation video sample, ASL/English certification or state licensure, two recommendation letters, audio gram (for deaf or hard-of-hearing applicants), personal statement, transcript with minimum GPA of 3.0. Electronic applications accepted.

Rutgers University - New Brunswick, Graduate School-New Brunswick, Program in Spanish, Piscataway, NJ 08854-8097. Offers bilingualism and second language acquisition (MA, PhD); Spanish (MA, MAT, PhD); Spanish literature (MA, PhD); translation (MA). *Program availability:* Part-time. *Degree requirements:* For master's, comprehensive exam (for some programs), thesis (for some programs); for doctorate, 2 foreign languages, comprehensive exam, thesis/dissertation. *Entrance requirements:* For master's and doctorate, GRE General Test. Additional exam requirements/recommendations for international students: required—TOEFL. Electronic applications accepted.

Texas A&M International University, Office of Graduate Studies and Research, College of Arts and Sciences, Department of Humanities, Laredo, TX 78041. Offers English (MA); history and political thought (MA); language, literature and translation (MA). *Degree requirements:* For master's, comprehensive exam (for some programs), thesis (for some programs). *Entrance requirements:* For master's, GRE General Test. Additional exam requirements/recommendations for international students: required—TOEFL (minimum score 550 paper-based; 79 iBT).

Universidad Autonoma de Guadalajara, Graduate Programs, Guadalajara, Mexico. Offers administrative law and justice (LL M); advertising and corporate communications (MA); architecture (M Arch); business (MBA); computational science (MCC); education (Ed M, Ed D); English-Spanish translation (MA); entrepreneurship and management (MBA); integrated management of digital animation (MA); international business (MIB); international corporate law (LL M); Internet technologies (MS); manufacturing systems (MMS); occupational health (MS); philosophy (MA, PhD); power electronics (MS); quality systems (MQS); renewable energy (MS); social evaluation of projects (MBA); strategic market research (MBA); tax law (MA); teaching mathematics (MA).

Université de Montréal, Faculty of Arts and Sciences, Department of Linguistics and Translation, Montréal, QC H3C 3J7, Canada. Offers linguistics (MA, PhD); translation (MA, PhD, DESS). *Degree requirements:* For master's, thesis, general exam; for doctorate, thesis/dissertation, general exam. Electronic applications accepted.

University of California, Santa Barbara, Graduate Division, College of Letters and Sciences, Division of Humanities and Fine Arts, Department of East Asian Languages and Cultural Studies, Santa Barbara, CA 93106-7075. Offers applied linguistics (PhD); East Asian languages and cultural studies (MA); translation studies (PhD). *Degree requirements:* For master's, one foreign language, comprehensive exam (for some programs), thesis (for some programs); for doctorate, 2 foreign languages, thesis/dissertation, methodology. *Entrance requirements:* For master's and doctorate, GRE General Test. Additional exam requirements/recommendations for international students: required—TOEFL (minimum score 550 paper-based; 80 iBT), IELTS (minimum score 7). Electronic applications accepted.

University of California, Santa Barbara, Graduate Division, College of Letters and Sciences, Division of Humanities and Fine Arts, Department of English, Santa Barbara, CA 93106-3170. Offers English (PhD), including environment and society, European medieval studies, feminist studies, global studies, technology and society, translation studies, writing studies; MA/PhD. Terminal master's awarded for partial completion of doctoral program. *Degree requirements:* For doctorate, one foreign language, comprehensive exam, thesis/dissertation. *Entrance requirements:* For doctorate, GRE General Test, GRE Subject Test (English literature). Additional exam requirements/recommendations for international students: required—TOEFL (minimum score 550 paper-based; 80 iBT), IELTS (minimum score 7). Electronic applications accepted.

University of California, Santa Barbara, Graduate Division, College of Letters and Sciences, Division of Humanities and Fine Arts, Department of Religious Studies, Santa Barbara, CA 93106-3130. Offers ancient Mediterranean studies (PhD); cognitive science (PhD); European medieval studies (PhD); feminist studies (PhD); global studies (PhD); religious studies (MA, PhD); translation studies (PhD); MA/PhD. Terminal master's awarded for partial completion of doctoral program. *Degree requirements:* For master's, one foreign language, comprehensive exam (for some programs), thesis (for some programs); for doctorate, 2 foreign languages, thesis/dissertation, methodology. *Entrance requirements:* For master's and doctorate, GRE General Test. Additional exam requirements/recommendations for international students: required—TOEFL (minimum score 550 paper-based; 80 iBT), IELTS (minimum score 7). Electronic applications accepted.

University of California, Santa Barbara, Graduate Division, College of Letters and Sciences, Division of Humanities and Fine Arts, Program in Comparative Literature, Santa Barbara, CA 93106-4130. Offers comparative literature (PhD); East Asian literatures (PhD); feminist studies (PhD); French (PhD); global studies (PhD); translation studies (PhD); MA/PhD. *Degree requirements:* For doctorate, 2 foreign languages, comprehensive exam, thesis/dissertation. *Entrance requirements:* For doctorate, GRE. Additional exam requirements/recommendations for international students: required—TOEFL (minimum score 550 paper-based; 80 iBT), IELTS (minimum score 7). Electronic applications accepted.

University of Delaware, College of Arts and Sciences, Department of Foreign Languages and Literatures, Newark, DE 19716. Offers foreign languages and literatures (MA), including French, German, Spanish; foreign languages pedagogy (MA), including French, German, Spanish; technical Chinese translation (MA). *Degree requirements:* For master's, one foreign language, comprehensive exam, thesis optional. *Entrance requirements:* For master's, GRE General Test, letters of recommendation, writing sample. Additional exam requirements/recommendations for international students: required—TOEFL. Electronic applications accepted.

University of Denver, University College, Denver, CO 80208. Offers arts and culture (MA, Certificate); communication management (MS, Certificate), including translation studies (Certificate), world history and culture (Certificate); environmental policy and management (MS); geographic information systems (MS); global affairs (MA, Certificate), including human capital in organizations (Certificate), philanthropic leadership (Certificate), project management (Certificate), strategic innovation and change (Certificate); healthcare leadership (MS); information communications and technology (MS); leadership and organizations (MS); professional creative writing (MA, Certificate), including emergency planning and response (Certificate), organizational security (Certificate); security management (MS, Certificate); strategic human resources (Certificate). *Program availability:* Part-time, evening/weekend, 100% online, blended/hybrid learning. *Faculty:* 104 part-time/adjunct (52 women). *Students:* 59 full-time (33 women), 1,893 part-time (1,210 women); includes 545 minority (133 Black or African American, non-Hispanic/Latino; 16 American Indian or Alaska Native, non-Hispanic/Latino; 64 Asian, non-Hispanic/Latino; 252 Hispanic/Latino; 4 Native Hawaiian or other Pacific Islander, non-Hispanic/Latino; 76 Two or more races, non-Hispanic/Latino), 78 international. Average age 32. 1,290 applicants, 91% accepted, 752 enrolled. In 2019, 457 master's, 181 other advanced degrees awarded. *Degree requirements:* For master's, capstone project. *Entrance requirements:* For master's, baccalaureate degree, transcripts, two letters of recommendation, personal statement, resume, writing sample (Master of Arts in Professional Creative Writing). Additional exam requirements/recommendations for international students: required—TOEFL (minimum score 550 paper-based; 80 iBT). *Application deadline:* For fall admission, 6/19 priority date for domestic students, 6/14 priority date for international students; for winter admission, 10/25 priority date for domestic students, 9/27 priority date for international students; for spring admission, 2/7 priority date for domestic students, 1/10 priority date for international students; for summer admission, 4/24 priority date for domestic students, 3/27 priority date for international students. Applications are processed on a rolling basis. Application fee: $75. Electronic applications accepted. *Expenses:* Contact institution. *Financial support:* In 2019–20, 56 students received support. Teaching assistantships available. Financial award applicants required to submit FAFSA. *Unit head:* Dr. Michael McGuire, Dean, 303-871-3518, E-mail: michael.mcguire@du.edu. *Application contact:* Admission Team, 303-871-2291, E-mail: ucoladm@du.edu.
Website: http://universitycollege.du.edu/

University of Illinois at Urbana-Champaign, Graduate College, College of Liberal Arts and Sciences, School of Literatures, Cultures and Linguistics, Center for Translation Studies, Champaign, IL 61820. Offers translation and interpreting (MA). *Program availability:* Part-time, online learning. *Entrance requirements:* For master's, BA or BS in languages, linguistics, international studies, area studies, or a related field; three letters of recommendation; resume or curriculum vitae; official transcripts.

The University of Manchester, School of Arts, Languages and Cultures, Manchester, United Kingdom. Offers anthropology, media and performance (PhD); applied theatre (PhD); Arab world studies (PhD); archaeology (PhD); art history and visual studies (PhD); arts and cultural management (PhD); arts management and cultural policy (PhD); Chinese studies (PhD); classics and ancient history (PhD); composition (PhD); creative writing (PhD); drama (PhD); East Asian studies (PhD); electroacoustic composition (PhD); English and American studies (PhD); English language (PhD); French studies (PhD); German studies (PhD); history (PhD); humanitarianism and conflict response (PhD); interpreting studies (PhD); Japanese studies (PhD); Latin American cultural studies (PhD); linguistics (PhD); Middle Eastern studies (PhD); museology (PhD); museum practice (PhD); music (PhD); musicology (PhD); Polish studies (PhD); Portuguese studies (PhD); religions and theology (PhD); Russian studies (PhD); Spanish studies (PhD); translation and intercultural studies (PhD).

University of Nevada, Las Vegas, Graduate College, College of Liberal Arts, Department of World Languages and Cultures, Las Vegas, NV 89154-5047. Offers Hispanic studies (MA); Spanish translation (Certificate). *Program availability:* Part-time. *Faculty:* 5 full-time (4 women). *Students:* 2 full-time (both women), 6 part-time (4 women); includes 5 minority (1 Asian, non-Hispanic/Latino; 4 Hispanic/Latino), 2 international. Average age 37. 9 applicants, 44% accepted, 1 enrolled. In 2019, 5 master's awarded. *Degree requirements:* For master's, one foreign language, comprehensive exam, final research project. *Entrance requirements:* For master's, minimum GPA of 3.0; 2 letters of recommendation. Additional exam requirements/recommendations for international students: required—TOEFL (minimum score 550 paper-based; 80 iBT), IELTS (minimum score 7). *Application deadline:* For fall admission, 5/1 for domestic and international students; for spring admission, 11/15 for domestic students, 10/1 for international students. Application fee: $60 ($95 for international students). Electronic applications accepted. *Expenses:* Contact institution. *Financial support:* In 2019–20, 3 students received support, including 3 teaching assistantships with full tuition reimbursements available (averaging $11,250 per year); institutionally sponsored loans, scholarships/grants, health care benefits, and unspecified assistantships also available. Financial award application deadline: 3/15; financial award applicants required to submit FAFSA. *Unit head:* Dr. Susan Byrne, Chair/Professor, 702-895-3464, Fax: 702-895-1226, E-mail: wlc.chair@unlv.edu. *Application contact:* Dr. Alicia Rico, Graduate Coordinator, 702-895-4874, Fax: 702-895-1226, E-mail: wlc.gradcoord@unlv.edu.
Website: http://liberalarts.unlv.edu/Foreign_Languages/graduates.html

University of Northern Colorado, Graduate School, College of Education and Behavioral Sciences, Department of American Sign Language and Interpreting Studies, Greeley, CO 80639. Offers teaching American Sign Language (MA).

University of North Florida, College of Education and Human Services, Department of Exceptional, Deaf, and Interpreter Education, Jacksonville, FL 32224. Offers American Sign Language (MS); American Sign Language/English interpreting (M Ed); applied behavior analysis (M Ed); autism (M Ed); deaf education (M Ed); disability services (M Ed); exceptional student education (M Ed). *Accreditation:* NCATE. *Program availability:* Part-time, evening/weekend. *Entrance requirements:* For master's, GRE General Test, minimum GPA of 3.0 in last 60 hours, interview, 3 letters of recommendation. Additional exam requirements/recommendations for international students: required—TOEFL (minimum score 500 paper-based). Electronic applications accepted.

University of Ottawa, Faculty of Graduate and Postdoctoral Studies, Faculty of Arts, Institute of Canadian Studies, Ottawa, ON K1N 6N5, Canada. Offers economics (PhD); English (PhD); geography (PhD); history (PhD); lettres Françaises (PhD); linguistics (PhD); philosophy (PhD); political science (PhD); psychology (PhD); religious studies (PhD); translation studies (PhD). *Degree requirements:* For doctorate, comprehensive exam, thesis/dissertation.

University of Ottawa, Faculty of Graduate and Postdoctoral Studies, Faculty of Arts, School of Translation and Interpretation, Ottawa, ON K1N 6N5, Canada. Offers interpreting (MA); Spanish translation (MA); translation (MA); translation studies (PhD). *Degree requirements:* For master's, one foreign language, thesis or alternative, research paper; for doctorate, thesis/dissertation, doctoral exam. *Entrance requirements:* For master's, school-administered exam, honors degree or equivalent, minimum B average; for doctorate, master's degree, minimum B+ average. Electronic applications accepted.

University of Puerto Rico at Rio Piedras, College of Humanities, Program in Translation, San Juan, PR 00931-3300. Offers MA, Certificate. *Program availability:* Part-time, evening/weekend. *Degree requirements:* For master's, 2 foreign languages, comprehensive exam, thesis. *Entrance requirements:* For master's, PAEG, minimum GPA of 3.0, graduate-level knowledge of 2 languages (English, French, or Spanish), letter of recommendation.

University of Rochester, School of Arts and Sciences, Interdisciplinary Program in Literary Translation Studies, Rochester, NY 14627. Offers MA, AC. *Students:* 1 (woman) full-time, 1 part-time (0 women), 1 international. Average age 36. 9 applicants, 67% accepted, 2 enrolled. In 2019, 4 master's awarded. *Degree requirements:* For master's, essay. *Entrance requirements:* For master's, official transcripts, three letters of recommendation, personal statement, translation sample and copies of corresponding pages from source text. Additional exam requirements/recommendations for international students: recommended—TOEFL. *Application deadline:* For fall admission, 2/1 for domestic and international students. Application fee: $60. Electronic applications accepted. *Financial support:* Tuition waivers (partial) and tuition awards available. *Unit head:* Joanna Scott, Director and Professor, 585-275-2784, E-mail: joanna.scott@rochester.edu. *Application contact:* Joanna Scott, Director and Professor, 585-275-2784, E-mail: joanna.scott@rochester.edu.
Website: http://www.sas.rochester.edu/lts/graduate/index.html

The University of Texas Rio Grande Valley, College of Liberal Arts, School of Interdisciplinary Programs and Community Engagement, Edinburg, TX 78539. Offers interdisciplinary studies (MAIS, MSIS); Spanish translation and interpreting (MA). *Faculty:* 2 full-time (1 woman). *Students:* 19 full-time (10 women), 38 part-time (26 women); includes 45 minority (1 Black or African American, non-Hispanic/Latino; 44 Hispanic/Latino), 6 international. Average age 35. 17 applicants, 76% accepted, 9 enrolled. In 2019, 27 master's awarded. *Expenses: Tuition, area resident:* Full-time $5959; part-time $440 per credit hour. Tuition, state resident: full-time $5959. Tuition, nonresident: full-time $5959. *International tuition:* $13,321 full-time. *Required fees:* $1169; $185 per credit hour. *Financial support:* Application deadline: 1/15.
Website: utrgv.edu/school-of-interdisciplinary-programs-and-community-engagement/index.htm

University of Wisconsin–Milwaukee, Graduate School, College of Letters and Science, Department of Foreign Languages and Literature, Milwaukee, WI 53201-0413. Offers foreign languages and literature (MA), including classic Greek, classics, comparative literature, French/Francophone language, literature, and culture, German language, literature, and culture, interpreting, Latin, linguistics, Spanish language, literature, and culture, translation; interpreting (Graduate Certificate); language, literature, and translation (MA, MALLT); translation (Graduate Certificate). *Program* *availability:* Part-time. *Degree requirements:* For master's, 2 foreign languages, thesis or alternative. *Entrance requirements:* Additional exam requirements/recommendations for international students: required—TOEFL (minimum score 550 paper-based; 79 iBT), IELTS (minimum score 6.5). Electronic applications accepted.

Université Laval, Faculty of Letters, Department of Languages, Linguistics and Translations, Programs in Terminology and Translation, Québec, QC G1K 7P4, Canada. Offers MA, Diploma. *Program availability:* Part-time. *Degree requirements:* For master's, thesis (for some programs). *Entrance requirements:* For master's and Diploma, knowledge of French and English. Electronic applications accepted.

Vermont College of Fine Arts, International MFA in Creative Writing and Literary Translation Program, Montpelier, VT 05602. Offers MFA. *Expenses: Tuition:* Full-time $25,864; part-time $880 per credit. *Required fees:* $1322; $661 per term. Tuition and fees vary according to program.

Wesley Biblical Seminary, Graduate Programs, Jackson, MS 39206. Offers apologetics (MA); Biblical languages (M Div); Biblical literature (MA); Christian studies (MA); context and mission (M Div); honors research (M Div); interpretation (M Div); ministry (M Div); spiritual formation (M Div); teaching (M Div); theology (MA). *Accreditation:* ATS. *Program availability:* Part-time. *Degree requirements:* For master's, thesis. *Entrance requirements:* Additional exam requirements/recommendations for international students: required—TOEFL. Electronic applications accepted.

York University, Faculty of Graduate Studies, Glendon Campus, Program in Translation, Toronto, ON M3J 1P3, Canada. Offers MA. *Degree requirements:* For master's, thesis or alternative. *Entrance requirements:* For master's, professional translating experience. Electronic applications accepted.

Section 11
Philosophy and Ethics

This section contains a directory of institutions offering graduate work in philosophy and ethics. Additional information about programs listed in the directory may be obtained by writing directly to the dean of a graduate school or chair of a department at the address given in the directory.

For programs offering related work, see also in this book *Area and Cultural Studies, History, Humanities, Religious Studies*, and *Social Sciences*.

CONTENTS

Program Directories

Ethics

American University, College of Arts and Sciences, Department of Philosophy and Religion, Washington, DC 22016-8056. Offers ethics, peace, and global affairs (MA); philosophy (MA). *Program availability:* Part-time, evening/weekend. *Degree requirements:* For master's, comprehensive exam, thesis (for some programs). *Entrance requirements:* For master's, GRE; Please visit website: https://www.american.edu/cas/philrel/, writing sample, statement of purpose, transcripts, 2 letters of recommendation, resume. Additional exam requirements/recommendations for international students: required—TOEFL. *Expenses:* Contact institution.

American University, School of International Service, Washington, DC 20016-8071. Offers comparative and regional studies (Certificate); cross-cultural communication (Certificate); development management (MS); ethics, peace, and global affairs (MA); European studies (Certificate); global environmental policy (MA, Certificate); global information technology (Certificate); global media (MA); international affairs (MA), including comparative and regional studies, global governance, politics, and security, international economic relations, natural resources and sustainable development, U.S. foreign policy and national security; international arts management (Certificate); international communication (MA, Certificate); international development (MA); international economic policy (Certificate); international economic relations (Certificate); international economics (MA); international peace and conflict resolution (MA, Certificate); international politics (Certificate); international relations (MA, PhD); international service (MIS); peacebuilding (Certificate); social enterprise (MA); the Americas (Certificate); United States foreign policy (Certificate); JD/MA. *Program availability:* Part-time, evening/weekend, 100% online, blended/hybrid learning. Terminal master's awarded for partial completion of doctoral program. *Degree requirements:* For master's, one foreign language, comprehensive exam, thesis or alternative; for doctorate, one foreign language, comprehensive exam, thesis/dissertation. *Entrance requirements:* For master's, transcripts, resume, 2 letters of recommendation, statement of purpose; for doctorate, GRE, transcripts, resume, 3 letters of recommendation, statement of purpose. Additional exam requirements/recommendations for international students: required—TOEFL. Electronic applications accepted. *Expenses:* Contact institution.

Anabaptist Mennonite Biblical Seminary, Graduate and Professional Programs, Elkhart, IN 46517-1999. Offers chaplaincy (M Div); Christian faith formation (M Div); Christian formation (MA); Christian spiritual formation (Certificate); divinity (M Div); pastoral ministry (M Div); pastoral theology for financial professionals (Certificate); peace studies (M Div), including environmental sustainability leadership (M Div, MA), theological studies (M Div, Certificate), including peace studies (M Div), theology and ethics (M Div); theology and peace studies (MA), including conflict transformation, environmental sustainability leadership (M Div, MA), international development administration; United Methodist leadership (M Div). *Accreditation:* ACIPE; ATS. *Program availability:* Part-time, 100% online, blended/hybrid learning. *Degree requirements:* For master's, variable foreign language requirement, comprehensive exam (for some programs), thesis optional, senior interview. *Entrance requirements:* For master's, undergraduate degree transcripts, 3 letters of reference, essay. Additional exam requirements/recommendations for international students: required—TOEFL (minimum score 90 iBT); recommended—IELTS (minimum score 7). Electronic applications accepted.

Arizona State University at Tempe, College of Liberal Arts and Sciences, School of Life Sciences, Tempe, AZ 85287-4601. Offers animal behavior (PhD); applied ethics (biomedical and health ethics) (MA); biology (MS, PhD), including biology, biology and society, complex adaptive systems science (PhD), plant biology and conservation (MS); environmental life sciences (PhD); evolutionary biology (PhD); history and philosophy of science (PhD); human and social dimensions of science and technology (PhD); microbiology (PhD); molecular and cellular biology (PhD); neuroscience (PhD). Terminal master's awarded for partial completion of doctoral program. *Degree requirements:* For master's, thesis (for some programs), interactive Program of Study (iPOS) submitted before completing 50 percent of required credit hours; for doctorate, variable foreign language requirement, comprehensive exam, thesis/dissertation, interactive Program of Study (iPOS) submitted before completing 50 percent of required credit hours. *Entrance requirements:* For master's and doctorate, GRE, minimum GPA of 3.0 or equivalent in last 2 years of work leading to bachelor's degree. Additional exam requirements/recommendations for international students: required—TOEFL (minimum score 600 paper-based; 100 iBT). Electronic applications accepted.

Arizona State University at Tempe, New College of Interdisciplinary Arts and Sciences, Phoenix, AZ 85069-7100. Offers applied ethics and the professions (MA); communication studies (MA); interdisciplinary studies (MA); psychology (MS); social justice and human rights (MA). *Program availability:* Part-time, evening/weekend. *Degree requirements:* For master's, thesis (for some programs), interactive Program of Study (iPOS) submitted before completing 50 percent of required credit hours. *Entrance requirements:* For master's, GRE, minimum GPA of 3.0 or equivalent in last 2 years of work leading to bachelor's degree. Additional exam requirements/recommendations for international students: required—TOEFL, IELTS, or PTE. Electronic applications accepted.

Arizona State University at Tempe, School of Letters and Sciences, Program in Applied Ethics, Tempe, AZ 85287-4503. Offers biomedical and health ethics (MA); ethics and emerging technologies (MA); public administration, policy and ethics (MA); science, technology and ethics (MA). *Program availability:* Part-time, evening/weekend. *Degree requirements:* For master's, thesis or alternative, applied project, interactive Program of Study (iPOS) submitted before completing 50 percent of required credit hours. *Entrance requirements:* For master's, GRE (for ethics and emerging technologies concentration), minimum GPA of 3.0 or equivalent in last 2 years of work leading to bachelor's degree, 2 letters of recommendation, resume, personal statement of interest and qualifications. Additional exam requirements/recommendations for international students: required—TOEFL (minimum score 550 paper-based; 80 iBT). Electronic applications accepted.

Azusa Pacific University, Azusa Pacific Seminary, Program in Theological Studies, Concentration in Theology and Ethics, Azusa, CA 91702-7000. Offers MA. *Accreditation:* ATS.

Chicago Theological Seminary, Graduate and Professional Programs, Chicago, IL 60637-1507. Offers Bible, culture and hermeneutics (PhD); preaching (D Min); religion and health (D Min); religious studies (MA); spirituality and spiritual direction (D Min); theology (M Div); theology, ethics and the human sciences (PhD); M Div/MSW. *Accreditation:* ACIPE; ATS. *Program availability:* Part-time. *Degree requirements:* For master's, thesis; for doctorate, 2 foreign languages, comprehensive exam, thesis/dissertation. *Entrance requirements:* For doctorate, GRE General Test. Additional exam requirements/recommendations for international students: required—TOEFL.

Claremont Graduate University, Graduate Programs, School of Arts and Humanities, Department of Religion, Claremont, CA 91711-6160. Offers Hebrew Bible (MA, PhD); history of Christianity and religions of North America (MA, PhD); New Testament (MA, PhD); philosophy of religion and theology (MA, PhD); theology, ethics and culture (MA, PhD); women's studies in religion (MA, PhD); MA/PhD; MBA/PhD. *Program availability:* Part-time. Terminal master's awarded for partial completion of doctoral program. *Entrance requirements:* For master's and doctorate, GRE General Test. Additional exam requirements/recommendations for international students: required—TOEFL (minimum score 75 iBT). Electronic applications accepted.

Claremont Lincoln University, Graduate Programs, Claremont, CA 91711. Offers ethical leadership (MA); interfaith action (MA); social impact (MA).

Claremont School of Theology, Graduate and Professional Programs, Program in Religion, Claremont, CA 91711-3199. Offers practical theology (PhD), including religious education and formation, spiritual care and counseling; religion (MA, PhD), including comparative theology and philosophy (PhD), Hebrew Bible and Jewish studies (PhD), New Testament and Christian origins (PhD), process studies (PhD), religion, ethics, and society (PhD). *Accreditation:* ACIPE; ATS. Terminal master's awarded for partial completion of doctoral program. *Degree requirements:* For master's, thesis; for doctorate, 2 foreign languages, thesis/dissertation. *Entrance requirements:* For doctorate, GRE General Test. Additional exam requirements/recommendations for international students: required—TOEFL. Electronic applications accepted.

Columbia University, Graduate School of Business, MBA Program, New York, NY 10027. Offers accounting (MBA); decision, risk, and operations (MBA); entrepreneurship (MBA); finance and economics (MBA); healthcare and pharmaceutical management (MBA); human resource management (MBA); international business (MBA); leadership and ethics (MBA); management (MBA); marketing (MBA); media (MBA); private equity (MBA); real estate (MBA); social enterprise (MBA); value investing (MBA); DDS/MBA; JD/MBA; MBA/MIA; MBA/MPH; MBA/MS; MD/MBA. *Entrance requirements:* For master's, GMAT, 2 letters of recommendation. Additional exam requirements/recommendations for international students: required—TOEFL. Electronic applications accepted. *Expenses:* Contact institution.

Emory University, Candler School of Theology, Atlanta, GA 30322. Offers catholic studies (M Div); formation and witness (M Div); history, scripture and tradition (MTS); leadership in church and community (M Div); modern religious thought and experience (MTS); pastoral counseling (Th D); religion and race (M Div); religion, health and science (M Div); scripture and interpretation (M Div); society and personality (M Div); theology (Th M); theology and ethics (M Div); theology and the arts (M Div); traditions of the church (M Div); JD/M Div; JD/MTS; M Div/MBA; M Div/MPH; MBA/MTS; MTS/MPH. *Accreditation:* ACIPE. *Program availability:* Part-time. *Degree requirements:* For master's, thesis optional; for doctorate, comprehensive exam, thesis/dissertation. *Entrance requirements:* For master's, minimum undergraduate GPA of 2.75, completed undergraduate degree from accredited college or university; for doctorate, GRE, DMin: MDiv or other first level theological masters and at least 3 years of professional experience. Additional exam requirements/recommendations for international students: required—TOEFL (minimum score 600 paper-based; 95 iBT). Electronic applications accepted. *Expenses:* Contact institution.

Epic Bible College, Graduate School, Sacramento, CA 95841. Offers Biblical studies (MA); Christian ministry (MA); ethical leadership (MA); ministry (D Min).

Fordham University, Graduate School of Arts and Sciences, Program in Ethics and Society, New York, NY 10458. Offers ethics and society (MA); health care ethics (Certificate). *Program availability:* Part-time. *Students:* Average age 34. 30 applicants, 87% accepted, 10 enrolled. In 2019, 7 master's awarded. *Entrance requirements:* Additional exam requirements/recommendations for international students: required—TOEFL. *Application deadline:* For fall admission, 1/4 priority date for domestic students; for spring admission, 10/31 for domestic students. Applications are processed on a rolling basis. Application fee: $70. Electronic applications accepted. *Financial support:* In 2019–20, 1 student received support. Teaching assistantships, Federal Work-Study, institutionally sponsored loans, scholarships/grants, tuition waivers (partial), and unspecified assistantships available. Financial award application deadline: 1/4. *Unit head:* Rimah Jaber, Interim Director of Academic Programs, Fordham University Center for Ethics Education, 718-817-0927, E-mail: rjaber@fordham.edu. *Application contact:* Garrett Marino, Director of Graduate Admissions, 718-817-4419, Fax: 718-817-3566, E-mail: gmarino10@fordham.edu.

Freed-Hardeman University, Program in Business Administration, Henderson, TN 38340-2399. Offers accounting (MBA); corporate responsibility (MBA); leadership (MBA). *Accreditation:* ACBSP. *Program availability:* Part-time, evening/weekend, online learning. *Entrance requirements:* For master's, GMAT. Additional exam requirements/recommendations for international students: required—TOEFL (minimum score 500 paper-based).

George Mason University, College of Humanities and Social Sciences, Department of Philosophy, Fairfax, VA 22030. Offers ethics and public affairs (MA); philosophy and cultural theory (MA). *Entrance requirements:* For master's, college transcripts, goals statement, 2 letters of recommendation, resume, writing sample; completion of certain undergraduate preparation coursework with grades of B or higher in each course (for philosophy and cultural theory). Additional exam requirements/recommendations for international students: required—TOEFL (minimum score 575 paper-based, 88 iBT), IELTS (6.5), or PTE (59). Electronic applications accepted.

Georgetown University, Graduate School of Arts and Sciences, School of Continuing Studies, Washington, DC 20057. Offers American studies (MALS); applied intelligence (MPS); Catholic studies (MALS); classical civilizations (MALS); emergency and disaster management (MPS); ethics and the professions (MALS); global strategic communications (MPS); hospitality management (MPS); human resources management (MPS); humanities (MALS); individualized study (MALS); integrated marketing communications (MPS); international affairs (MALS); Islam and Muslim-Christian relations (MALS); journalism (MPS); liberal studies (DLS); literature and society (MALS); medieval and early modern European studies (MALS); public relations and corporate communications (MPS); real estate (MPS); religious studies (MALS); social and public policy (MALS); sports industry management (MPS); systems engineering management (MPS); technology management (MPS); the theory and practice of American democracy (MALS); urban and regional planning (MPS); visual culture (MALS). *Entrance requirements:* Additional exam requirements/recommendations for international students: required—TOEFL.

Graduate Theological Union, Graduate Programs, Berkeley, CA 94709-1212. Offers art and religion (MA, PhD, Th D); biblical languages (MA); Biblical studies (PhD, Th D); biblical studies (MA); Buddhist studies (MA); Christian spirituality (MA, PhD, Th D);

cultural and historical studies of religions (MA, PhD, Th D); ethics and social theory (PhD, Th D); history (MA, PhD, Th D); homiletics (MA, PhD, Th D); interdisciplinary studies (PhD, Th D); Jewish studies (MA, PhD, Th D, Certificate); liturgical studies (MA, PhD, Th D); Near Eastern religions (PhD, Th D); Orthodox Christian studies (MA); religion and psychology (MA, PhD, Th D); religion and society/ethics and social theory (MA); systematic and philosophical theology (MA, PhD, Th D). *Accreditation:* ATS. Terminal master's awarded for partial completion of doctoral program. *Degree requirements:* For master's, one foreign language, thesis; for doctorate, one foreign language, comprehensive exam, thesis/dissertation. *Entrance requirements:* For master's, GRE General Test; for doctorate, GRE General Test, MA or M Div. Additional exam requirements/recommendations for international students: required—TOEFL. Electronic applications accepted.

Greensboro College, Program in Theology, Ethics and Culture, Greensboro, NC 27401-1875. Offers MA.

John Brown University, Soderquist College of Business, Siloam Springs, AR 72761-2121. Offers international business (MBA); leadership and ethics (MBA, MS). *Accreditation:* ACBSP. *Program availability:* Part-time, evening/weekend, online only, 100% online, blended/hybrid learning. *Entrance requirements:* For master's, MAT, GMAT or GRE if undergraduate GPA is less than 3.0, recommendation forms from three people, 200-word essay describing professional plans and reason for seeking acceptance. Additional exam requirements/recommendations for international students: required—TOEFL (minimum score 550 paper-based; 79 iBT). Electronic applications accepted.

Lancaster Theological Seminary, Graduate and Professional Programs, Lancaster, PA 17603-2812. Offers biblical studies (MAR); Christian education (MAR); Christianity and the arts (MAR); church history (MAR); congregational life (MAR); lay leadership (Certificate); theological studies (M Div); theology (D Min); theology and ethics (MAR). *Accreditation:* ACIPE; ATS. *Degree requirements:* For doctorate, thesis/dissertation.

Lebanon Valley College, Program in Business Administration, Annville, PA 17003-1400. Offers business administration (MBA); healthcare management (MBA); human resources (MBA); leadership and ethics (MBA); project management (MBA). *Program availability:* Part-time, evening/weekend. *Degree requirements:* For master's, capstone course. *Entrance requirements:* For master's, GMAT, 3 years of work experience, resume, professional statement (application form, resume, personal statement, transcripts). Additional exam requirements/recommendations for international students: required—TOEFL (minimum score 80 iBT), IELTS (minimum score 6.5) or STEP Eiken (grade 1). Electronic applications accepted. *Expenses:* Contact institution.

Lee University, Programs in Religion, Cleveland, TN 37320-3450. Offers biblical studies (MA); ministry studies/leadership (MA); ministry studies/worship (MA); ministry studies/youth and family (MA); theological studies (MA), including ethics, religion. *Program availability:* Part-time, 100% online. *Faculty:* 12 full-time (3 women), 8 part-time/adjunct (0 women). *Students:* 32 full-time (13 women), 104 part-time (33 women); includes 74 minority (10 Black or African American, non-Hispanic/Latino; 60 Hispanic/Latino; 4 Two or more races, non-Hispanic/Latino), 5 international. Average age 38. 43 applicants, 79% accepted, 24 enrolled. In 2019, 15 master's awarded. *Degree requirements:* For master's, variable foreign language requirement, comprehensive exam (for some programs), thesis (for some programs). *Entrance requirements:* For master's, GRE or MAT (for biblical/theological studies only), minimum GPA of 3.0, 3 letters of recommendation, interview, official transcripts, essay. Additional exam requirements/recommendations for international students: required—TOEFL (minimum score 61 iBT). *Application deadline:* For fall admission, 4/1 priority date for domestic and international students; for spring admission, 10/1 priority date for domestic and international students. Applications are processed on a rolling basis. Application fee: $25. Electronic applications accepted. *Expenses:* Contact institution. *Financial support:* In 2019–20, 39 students received support, including 12 teaching assistantships (averaging $2,046 per year); career-related internships or fieldwork, Federal Work-Study, institutionally sponsored loans, scholarships/grants, and unspecified assistantships also available. Financial award application deadline: 3/1; financial award applicants required to submit FAFSA. *Unit head:* Dr. Lisa Long, Director, 423-303-5100, E-mail: llong@leeuniversity.edu. *Application contact:* Jeffery McGirt, Director of Graduate Enrollment, 423-614-8691, Fax: 423-614-8317, E-mail: jmcgirt@leeuniversity.edu.
Website: http://www.leeuniversity.edu/academics/graduate/

Loyola University Chicago, Quinlan School of Business, MBA Programs, Chicago, IL 60611. Offers accounting (MBA); business ethics (MBA); derivative markets (MBA); economics (MBA); entrepreneurship (MBA); finance (MBA); healthcare management (MBA); human resources management (MBA); information systems management (MBA); international business (MBA); management (MBA); marketing (MBA); risk management (MBA); supply chain management (MBA). *Program availability:* Part-time, evening/weekend. *Entrance requirements:* For master's, GMAT or GRE, official transcripts, two letters of recommendation, statement of purpose, resume. Additional exam requirements/recommendations for international students: required—TOEFL (minimum score 90 iBT) or IELTS (minimum score 6.5). Electronic applications accepted. Application fee is waived when completed online. *Expenses:* Contact institution.

Lutheran Theological Seminary Saskatoon, Graduate and Professional Programs, Saskatoon, SK S7N 0X3, Canada. Offers Biblical studies (MTS); church history (MTS); ethics/church and society (MTS); history of Christianity (STM); New Testament (STM); Old Testament (STM); pastoral studies (STM); pastoral theology (MTS); systematic theology (MTS); systematic theology and philosophy of religion (STM); theology (M Div, D Div). *Accreditation:* ATS. *Program availability:* Part-time. *Degree requirements:* For master's, thesis.

Marquette University, Graduate School, College of Arts and Sciences, Department of Philosophy, Milwaukee, WI 53201-1881. Offers ancient philosophy (PhD); British empiricism and analytic philosophy (PhD); Christian philosophy (PhD); early modern European philosophy (PhD); ethics (PhD); German philosophy (PhD); history of philosophy (MA); medieval philosophy (PhD); phenomenology and existentialism (PhD); philosophy of religion (PhD); social and applied philosophy (MA); JD/MA. *Program availability:* Part-time. Terminal master's awarded for partial completion of doctoral program. *Degree requirements:* For master's, variable foreign language requirement, comprehensive exam, thesis or alternative; for doctorate, 2 foreign languages, thesis/dissertation, written and oral qualifying exams. *Entrance requirements:* For master's and doctorate, GRE General Test, official transcripts from all current and previous colleges/universities except Marquette, statement of purpose, at least three letters of recommendation, sample of philosophical writing. Additional exam requirements/recommendations for international students: required—TOEFL (minimum score 530 paper-based). Electronic applications accepted.

New England College of Business and Finance, Program in Business Ethics and Compliance, Boston, MA 02111-2645. Offers MS. *Program availability:* Online learning.

Northwestern University, School of Professional Studies, Program in Liberal Studies, Evanston, IL 60208. Offers American studies (MA); history (MA); religious and ethical studies (MA). *Program availability:* Part-time, evening/weekend.

Oregon State University, College of Liberal Arts, Program in Applied Ethics, Corvallis, OR 97331. Offers biomedical ethics (MA). *Program availability:* Part-time. *Entrance requirements:* For master's, writing sample of 5-7 pages. Additional exam requirements/recommendations for international students: required—TOEFL (minimum score 80 iBT), IELTS (minimum score 6.5).

Phillips Theological Seminary, Programs in Theology, Tulsa, OK 74116. Offers administration of church agencies (M Div); campus ministry (M Div); church-related social work (M Div); college and seminary teaching (M Div); global mission work (M Div); institutional chaplaincy (M Div); ministerial vocations in Christian education (M Div); ministry (D Min), including parish ministry, pastoral counseling, practices of ministry; ministry and culture (MAMC), including Christian education, congregational leadership, history and practice of Christian spirituality, theology, ethics, and culture; ministry of music (M Div); pastoral care and counseling (M Div); pastoral ministry (M Div); theological studies (MTS). *Accreditation:* ATS. *Program availability:* Part-time, online learning. *Degree requirements:* For master's, thesis (for some programs); for doctorate, thesis/dissertation. *Entrance requirements:* For master's, minimum GPA of 2.5; for doctorate, M Div, minimum GPA of 3.0.

Pontifical John Paul II Institute for Studies on Marriage and Family, Graduate Programs, Washington, DC 20064. Offers biotechnology and ethics (MTS); marriage and family (MTS, STD, STL); theology (PhD).

Santa Clara University, Jesuit School of Theology, Berkeley, CA 94709. Offers Biblical studies (MTS); Christian spirituality (MTS); church history (MTS); cultural and historical studies of Catholicism (MTS); divinity (M Div); ethics and social theory/religion and society (MTS); history of art and religion (MTS); liturgical studies (MTS); sacred theology (STD, STB, STL); systematic and philosophical theology (MTS); theology (Th M); M Div/MA. *Program availability:* Part-time, online learning. *Entrance requirements:* For master's and doctorate, Varies based on program. Additional exam requirements/recommendations for international students: required—TOEFL, IELTS, Applicants whose native language is not English are required to submit TOEFL or IELTS scores. Electronic applications accepted.

Schreiner University, MBA Program, Kerrville, TX 78028-5697. Offers ethical leadership (MBA). *Program availability:* Part-time, online only, 100% online. *Faculty:* 2 full-time (0 women), 6 part-time/adjunct (2 women). *Students:* 23 full-time (15 women), 11 part-time (7 women); includes 17 minority (2 Black or African American, non-Hispanic/Latino; 1 Asian, non-Hispanic/Latino; 14 Hispanic/Latino). Average age 30. 45 applicants, 93% accepted, 20 enrolled. In 2019, 30 master's awarded. *Entrance requirements:* For master's, 3 recommendations; personal essay; transcripts; resume. Additional exam requirements/recommendations for international students: required—TOEFL. *Application deadline:* For fall admission, 8/1 priority date for domestic students, 8/1 for international students; for spring admission, 12/1 priority date for domestic students, 12/1 for international students; for summer admission, 5/1 priority date for domestic students, 4/1 for international students. Applications are processed on a rolling basis. Application fee: $25. Electronic applications accepted. *Expenses:* Contact institution. *Financial support:* In 2019–20, 31 students received support. Application deadline: 8/1; applicants required to submit FAFSA. *Unit head:* Dr. Mark Woodhull, Director, 830-792-7479. *Application contact:* Magda Riveros, Graduate Admission Counselor, 800-343-4919, Fax: 830-792-7226, E-mail: MRiveros@schreiner.edu.
Website: http://www.schreiner.edu/online/default.aspx

Southeastern Baptist Theological Seminary, Graduate and Professional Programs, Wake Forest, NC 27587. Offers advanced biblical studies (M Div); Christian education (M Div, MACE); Christian ethics (PhD); Christian ministry (M Div); Christian planting (M Div); church music (MACM); counseling (MACO); evangelism (PhD); language (M Div); ministry (D Min); New Testament (PhD); Old Testament (PhD); philosophy (PhD); theology (Th M, PhD); women's studies (M Div). *Accreditation:* ACIPE; ATS (one or more programs are accredited). *Degree requirements:* For master's, thesis (for some programs), oral exam; for doctorate, thesis/dissertation, fieldwork. *Entrance requirements:* For master's, Cooperative English Test, minimum GPA of 2.0, M Div or equivalent (Th M); for doctorate, GRE General Test or MAT, Cooperative English Test, M Div or equivalent, 3 years of professional experience.

Spring Hill College, Graduate Programs, Program in Liberal Arts, Mobile, AL 36608-1791. Offers fine arts (MLA); leadership and ethics (MLA, Postbaccalaureate Certificate); literature (MLA). *Program availability:* Part-time, evening/weekend. *Faculty:* 3 full-time (0 women), 2 part-time/adjunct (both women). *Students:* 3 full-time (2 women), 12 part-time (5 women); includes 1 minority (Hispanic/Latino), 4 international. Average age 35. In 2019, 9 master's awarded. *Degree requirements:* For master's, capstone course, completion of program within 6 years of initial admittance. *Entrance requirements:* For master's, bachelor's degree with minimum undergraduate GPA of 3.0 or graduate/professional degree. Additional exam requirements/recommendations for international students: required—TOEFL (minimum score 550 paper-based; 80 iBT), IELTS (minimum score 6.5), CPE or CAE (minimum score C), Michigan English Language Assessment Battery (minimum score 90). *Application deadline:* For fall admission, 8/1 priority date for domestic and international students; for spring admission, 12/1 priority date for domestic and international students. Applications are processed on a rolling basis. Application fee: $25 ($35 for international students). Electronic applications accepted. *Expenses:* Contact institution. *Financial support:* Fellowships, research assistantships, teaching assistantships, and tuition waivers available. Financial award applicants required to submit FAFSA. *Unit head:* Dr. Thomas J. Hoffman, Director, 251-380-4184, Fax: 251-460-2115, E-mail: thoffman@shc.edu. *Application contact:* Gary Bracken, Vice President of Enrollment Management, 251-380-3038, Fax: 251-460-2186, E-mail: gbracken@shc.edu.
Website: http://ug.shc.edu/graduate-degrees/master-liberal-arts/

Stevens Institute of Technology, Graduate School, College of Arts and Letters, Program in Policy and Innovation, Hoboken, NJ 07030. Offers MA, Graduate Certificate. *Program availability:* Part-time, evening/weekend. *Faculty:* 34 full-time (18 women), 27 part-time/adjunct (13 women). *Students:* 1 full-time (0 women), 1 (woman) part-time. Average age 31. *Degree requirements:* For master's, thesis optional, minimum B average in major field and overall; for Graduate Certificate, minimum B average. *Entrance requirements:* For master's, International applicants must submit TOEFL/IELTS scores and fulfill the English Language Proficiency Requirement. Applicants to full-time programs who do not qualify for a score waiver are required to submit GRE/GMAT scores. Additional exam requirements/recommendations for international students: required—TOEFL (minimum score 74 iBT), IELTS (minimum score 6). *Application deadline:* For fall admission, 4/15 for domestic and international students; for spring admission, 11/1 for domestic and international students; for summer admission, 5/1 for domestic students. Applications are processed on a rolling basis. Application fee: $60. Electronic applications accepted. *Expenses: Tuition:* Full-time $52,134. *Required fees:* $1880. Tuition and fees vary according to course load. *Financial support:* Fellowships, research assistantships, teaching assistantships, career-related internships or fieldwork, Federal Work-Study, scholarships/grants, and unspecified assistantships available. Financial award application deadline: 2/15; financial award applicants required to submit FAFSA. *Unit head:* Dr. Kelland Thomas, Dean of CAL, 201-216-3728, Fax: 201-216-8245, E-mail: Kelland.Thomas@stevens.edu. *Application contact:* Graduate Admission, 888-783-8367, Fax: 888-511-1306, E-mail:

graduate@stevens.edu.
Website: https://www.stevens.edu/college-arts-and-letters/graduate-programs

Suffolk University, College of Arts and Sciences, Department of Philosophy, Boston, MA 02108-2770. Offers administration of higher education (M Ed, CAGS); disability services (Certificate); ethics and public policy (MS). *Program availability:* Part-time, evening/weekend. *Faculty:* 3 full-time (2 women), 5 part-time/adjunct (0 women). *Students:* 11 full-time (6 women), 23 part-time (20 women); includes 5 minority (2 Black or African American, non-Hispanic/Latino; 2 Hispanic/Latino; 1 Two or more races, non-Hispanic/Latino), 2 international. Average age 31. 35 applicants, 91% accepted, 14 enrolled. In 2019, 24 master's awarded. *Degree requirements:* For master's, internship or thesis; practicum (for M Ed). *Entrance requirements:* For master's, GRE General Test, MAT, GMAT, statement of professional goals, official transcripts, 2 letters of recommendation, resume. Additional exam requirements/recommendations for international students: required—TOEFL (minimum score 550 paper-based; 80 iBT). *Application deadline:* For fall admission, 3/15 priority date for domestic and international students; for spring admission, 10/15 priority date for domestic and international students. Applications are processed on a rolling basis. Application fee: $50. Electronic applications accepted. *Expenses:* Contact institution. *Financial support:* In 2019–20, 10 students received support, including 6 fellowships (averaging $3,600 per year); career-related internships or fieldwork, Federal Work-Study, institutionally sponsored loans, and unspecified assistantships also available. Support available to part-time students. Financial award application deadline: 4/1; financial award applicants required to submit FAFSA. *Unit head:* Dr. Evgenia Cherkasova, Chair of Philosophy Department, 617-573-1970, E-mail: echerkasova@suffolk.edu. *Application contact:* Mara Marzocchi, Associate Director of Graduate Admissions, 617-573-8302, Fax: 617-305-1733, E-mail: grad.admission@suffolk.edu.
Website: http://www.suffolk.edu/college/graduate/69296.php

Texas State University, The Graduate College, College of Liberal Arts, Applied Philosophy and Ethics Program, San Marcos, TX 78666. Offers MA. *Program availability:* Part-time. *Degree requirements:* For master's, comprehensive exam, thesis optional. *Entrance requirements:* For master's, baccalaureate degree from regionally-accredited university with minimum GPA of 3.0 on last 60 undergraduate semester hours, statement of purpose, 2 letters of recommendation, writing sample. Additional exam requirements/recommendations for international students: required—TOEFL (minimum score 550 paper-based; 78 iBT), IELTS (minimum score 6). Electronic applications accepted.

Université de Sherbrooke, Faculty of Theology and Religious Studies, Sherbrooke, QC J1K 2R1, Canada. Offers applied ethics (Diploma); human science of religions (MA); intercultural training (Diploma); philosophy (MA, PhD); spiritual anthropology (Diploma); theology (MA, PhD, Diploma). *Program availability:* Part-time, evening/weekend, online learning. Terminal master's awarded for partial completion of doctoral program. *Entrance requirements:* For master's, bachelor's degree in related discipline; for doctorate, master's degree in related discipline.

Université du Québec à Chicoutimi, Graduate Programs, Program in Ethics, Chicoutimi, QC G7H 2B1, Canada. Offers Diploma. *Entrance requirements:* For degree, appropriate bachelor's degree, proficiency in French.

Université du Québec à Rimouski, Graduate Programs, Program in Ethics, Rimouski, QC G5L 3A1, Canada. Offers MA, Diploma. *Program availability:* Part-time. *Degree requirements:* For master's, thesis. *Entrance requirements:* For master's, appropriate bachelor's degree, proficiency in French.

University of Chicago, Divinity School, PhD Program, Chicago, IL 60637. Offers anthropology and sociology of religions (PhD); Bible (PhD); history of Christianity (PhD); history of Judaism (PhD); history of religions (PhD); Islamic studies (PhD); philosophy of religions (PhD); religion, literature, and visual culture (PhD); religions in America (PhD); religious ethics (PhD); theology (PhD). *Degree requirements:* For doctorate, 2 foreign languages, comprehensive exam, thesis/dissertation. *Entrance requirements:* For doctorate, GRE General Test, 3 letters of recommendation; transcripts; curriculum vitae or resume; writing sample. Additional exam requirements/recommendations for international students: required—TOEFL (minimum score 600 paper-based; 104 iBT), IELTS (minimum score 7). Electronic applications accepted.

University of Detroit Mercy, College of Business Administration, Detroit, MI 48221. Offers business administration (MBA); business fundamentals (Certificate); business turnaround management (Certificate); ethical leadership and change management (Certificate); finance (Certificate); forensic accounting (Certificate); JD/MBA; MBA/MHSA. *Program availability:* Part-time, evening/weekend, 100% online, blended/hybrid learning. *Entrance requirements:* For master's, GMAT, resume, letter of recommendation, transcripts; for Certificate, resume, letter of recommendation, transcripts. Electronic applications accepted. Application fee is waived when completed online. *Expenses:* Contact institution.

University of Maryland, Baltimore, Graduate School, Program in Research Ethics, Baltimore, MD 21201. Offers Certificate. *Program availability:* Part-time, online learning. *Entrance requirements:* For degree, minimum GPA of 3.0, curriculum vitae, essay. Additional exam requirements/recommendations for international students: required—TOEFL (minimum score 80 iBT); recommended—IELTS (minimum score 7). Electronic applications accepted. *Expenses:* Contact institution.

The University of North Carolina at Charlotte, College of Liberal Arts and Sciences, Department of Philosophy, Charlotte, NC 28223-0001. Offers applied ethics (Graduate Certificate); ethics and applied philosophy (MA). *Program availability:* Part-time. *Faculty:* 11 full-time (5 women). *Students:* 8 full-time (5 women), 6 part-time (1 woman); includes 1 minority (Black or African American, non-Hispanic/Latino). Average age 26. 15 applicants, 87% accepted, 10 enrolled. In 2019, 8 master's, 1 other advanced degree awarded. *Degree requirements:* For master's, capstone. *Entrance requirements:* For master's, statement of purpose outlining why applicant seeks admission to program; three recommendations; one official transcript from all colleges or universities attended; philosophical writing sample; for Graduate Certificate, personal statement outlining why the applicant seeks admission to the program; two academic letters of recommendation, in addition to the recommendation forms required by the graduate school, which address the student's philosophical skills and/or ethical reasoning; minimum undergraduate GPA of 2.75. Additional exam requirements/recommendations for international students: required—TOEFL (minimum score 557 paper-based; 83 iBT), IELTS (minimum score 6.5), TOEFL (minimum score 557 paper-based, 83 iBT) or IELTS (6.5). *Application deadline:* For fall admission, 2/1 priority date for domestic students. Applications are processed on a rolling basis. Application fee: $75. Electronic applications accepted. *Expenses:* Tuition, state resident: full-time $4337. Tuition, nonresident: full-time $17,771. *Required fees:* $3093. Tuition and fees vary according to course load, degree level and program. *Financial support:* In 2019–20, 4 students received support, including 4 teaching assistantships (averaging $4,000 per year); career-related internships or fieldwork, institutionally sponsored loans, scholarships/grants, unspecified assistantships, and administrative assistantships also available. Support available to part-time students. Financial award application deadline: 2/1; financial award applicants required to submit FAFSA. *Unit head:* Dr. Shannon Sullivan, Chair, 704-687-5418, E-mail: ssullivan@uncc.edu. *Application contact:* Kathy B. Giddings, Director of Graduate Admissions, 704-687-5503, Fax: 704-687-1668, E-mail: gradadm@uncc.edu.
Website: http://philosophy.uncc.edu/

University of North Florida, College of Arts and Sciences, Department of Philosophy, Jacksonville, FL 32224. Offers applied ethics (Graduate Certificate); practical philosophy and applied ethics (MA). *Program availability:* Part-time, evening/weekend. *Entrance requirements:* For master's, GRE General Test, minimum GPA of 3.0 in last 60 hours, 3 letters of recommendation, writing sample. Additional exam requirements/recommendations for international students: required—TOEFL (minimum score 500 paper-based; 61 iBT). Electronic applications accepted.

University of Pennsylvania, Wharton School, Legal Studies and Business Ethics Department, Philadelphia, PA 19104. Offers MBA, PhD.

University of St. Thomas, School of Law, Minneapolis, MN 55403-2015. Offers law (JD); law/business administration (JD/MBA); law/catholic studies (JD/MA); law/organizational ethics and compliance (JD/LL M); law/social work (JD/MSW); organizational ethics and compliance (LL M, MSL); U.S. law (LL M); JD/LL M; JD/MA; JD/MBA; JD/MSW. *Accreditation:* ABA. *Program availability:* 100% online. *Degree requirements:* For doctorate, mentor externship, public service. *Entrance requirements:* For doctorate, LSAT, 2 letters of recommendation, personal statement. Additional exam requirements/recommendations for international students: recommended—TOEFL (minimum score 80 iBT). Electronic applications accepted. *Expenses:* Contact institution.

University of South Africa, College of Human Sciences, Pretoria, South Africa. Offers adult education (M Ed); African languages (MA, PhD); African politics (MA, PhD); Afrikaans (MA, PhD); ancient history (MA, PhD); ancient Near Eastern studies (MA, PhD); anthropology (MA, PhD); applied linguistics (MA); Arabic (MA, PhD); archaeology (MA); art history (MA); Biblical archaeology (MA); Biblical studies (M Th, D Th, PhD); Christian spirituality (M Th, D Th); church history (M Th, D Th); classical studies (MA, PhD); clinical psychology (MA); communication (MA, PhD); comparative education (M Ed, Ed D); consulting psychology (D Admin, D Com, PhD); curriculum studies (M Ed, Ed D); development studies (M Admin, MA, D Admin, PhD); didactics (M Ed, Ed D); education (M Tech); education management (M Ed, Ed D); educational psychology (M Ed); English (MA); environmental education (M Ed); French (MA, PhD); German (MA, PhD); Greek (MA); guidance and counseling (M Ed); health studies (MA, PhD), including health sciences education (MA), health services management (MA), medical and surgical nursing science (critical care general) (MA), midwifery and neonatal nursing science (MA), trauma and emergency care (MA); history (MA, PhD); history of education (Ed D); inclusive education (M Ed, Ed D); information and communications technology policy and regulation (MA); information science (MA, MIS, PhD); international politics (MA, PhD); Islamic studies (MA, PhD); Italian (MA, PhD); Judaica (MA, PhD); linguistics (MA, PhD); mathematical education (M Ed); mathematics education (MA); missiology (M Th, D Th); modern Hebrew (MA, PhD); musicology (MA, MMus, D Mus, PhD); natural science education (M Ed); New Testament (M Th, D Th); Old Testament (D Th); pastoral therapy (M Th, D Th); philosophy (MA); philosophy of education (M Ed, Ed D); politics (MA, PhD); Portuguese (MA, PhD); practical theology (M Th, D Th); psychology (MA, MS, PhD); psychology of education (M Ed, Ed D); public health (MA); religious studies (MA, D Th, PhD); Romance languages (MA); Russian (MA, PhD); Semitic languages (MA, PhD); social behavior studies in HIV/AIDS (MA); social science (mental health) (MA); social science in development studies (MA); social science in psychology (MA); social science in social work (MA); social science in sociology (MA); social work (MSW, DSW, PhD); socio-education (M Ed, Ed D); sociolinguistics (MA); sociology (MA, PhD); Spanish (MA, PhD); systematic theology (M Th, D Th); TESOL (teaching English to speakers of other languages) (MA); theological ethics (M Th, D Th); theory of literature (MA, PhD); urban ministries (D Th); urban ministry (M Th).

The University of Tennessee at Chattanooga, Engineering Management and Technology Program, Chattanooga, TN 37403. Offers construction management (Graduate Certificate); engineering management (MS); fundamentals of engineering management (Graduate Certificate); leadership and ethics (Graduate Certificate); logistics and supply chain management (Graduate Certificate); power systems management (Graduate Certificate); project and technology management (Graduate Certificate); quality management (Graduate Certificate). *Program availability:* 100% online, blended/hybrid learning. *Students:* 10 full-time (4 women), 44 part-time (6 women); includes 9 minority (4 Black or African American, non-Hispanic/Latino; 1 Asian, non-Hispanic/Latino; 2 Hispanic/Latino; 2 Two or more races, non-Hispanic/Latino), 9 international. Average age 33. 24 applicants, 88% accepted, 8 enrolled. In 2019, 21 master's, 1 other advanced degree awarded. *Degree requirements:* For master's, thesis or alternative, Project as alternative to thesis. *Entrance requirements:* For master's, GRE General Test, letters of recommendation; minimum undergraduate GPA of 2.7 overall or 3.0 in final two years; for Graduate Certificate, baccalaureate degree and professional experience or have already been admitted to engineering/engineering management graduate program. Additional exam requirements/recommendations for international students: required—TOEFL (minimum score 550 paper-based; 79 iBT), IELTS (minimum score 6). *Application deadline:* For fall admission, 6/15 priority date for domestic students, 7/1 for international students; for spring admission, 11/1 priority date for domestic students, 11/1 for international students. Applications are processed on a rolling basis. Application fee: $35 ($40 for international students). Electronic applications accepted. *Financial support:* Research assistantships, teaching assistantships, career-related internships or fieldwork, scholarships/grants, and unspecified assistantships available. Support available to part-time students. Financial award application deadline: 7/1; financial award applicants required to submit FAFSA. *Unit head:* Dr. Ahad Nasab, Department Head, 423-425-4032, Fax: 423-425-5818, E-mail: Ahad-Nasab@utc.edu. *Application contact:* Dr. Joanne Romagni, Dean of the Graduate School, 423-425-4478, Fax: 423-425-5223, E-mail: joanne-romagni@utc.edu.
Website: https://www.utc.edu/college-engineering-computer-science/programs/engineering-management-and-technology/index.php

Université Laval, Faculty of Theology and Religious Sciences, Program in Applied Ethics, Québec, QC G1K 7P4, Canada. Offers DESS. *Program availability:* Part-time. *Entrance requirements:* For degree, knowledge of French. Electronic applications accepted.

Valparaiso University, Graduate School and Continuing Education, Programs in Humane Education, Valparaiso, IN 46383. Offers M Ed, MA, Graduate Certificate. *Program availability:* Part-time, evening/weekend. *Degree requirements:* For master's, thesis, project. *Entrance requirements:* For master's, minimum GPA of 3.0, two letters of reference, official transcripts, personal statement, interview. Additional exam requirements/recommendations for international students: required—TOEFL (minimum score 550 paper-based; 80 iBT), IELTS (minimum score 6). Electronic applications accepted.

Viterbo University, Master of Arts in Servant Leadership Program, La Crosse, WI 54601-4797. Offers ethical leadership in organizations (Certificate); servant leadership (MA). *Program availability:* Part-time, evening/weekend. *Degree requirements:* For master's, 30 credits (15 credits of Servant Leadership core courses and any combination of 15 elective credits). *Entrance requirements:* For master's, letter of reference, statement of goals, baccalaureate degree, transcript, interview. Additional exam requirements/recommendations for international students: required—TOEFL (minimum score 525 paper-based). Electronic applications accepted. *Expenses:* Contact institution.

Xavier University, Williams College of Business, Master of Business Administration Program, Cincinnati, OH 45207. Offers business administration (Exec MBA, MBA); business intelligence (MBA); finance (MBA); health industry (MBA); international business (MBA); marketing (MBA); values-based leadership (MBA); MBA/MHSA; MSN/

MBA. *Accreditation:* AACSB. *Program availability:* Part-time, evening/weekend. *Degree requirements:* For master's, capstone course. *Entrance requirements:* For master's, GMAT or GRE, official transcript; resume. Additional exam requirements/ recommendations for international students: required—TOEFL (minimum score 550 paper-based; 79 iBT). Electronic applications accepted. Application fee is waived when completed online. *Expenses:* Contact institution.

Philosophy

Acadia University, Faculty of Arts, Program in Social and Political Thought, Wolfville, NS B4P 2R6, Canada. Offers MA. *Entrance requirements:* Additional exam requirements/recommendations for international students: required—TOEFL (minimum score 580 paper-based; 93 iBT), IELTS (minimum score 6,5).

American University, College of Arts and Sciences, Department of Philosophy and Religion, Washington, DC 22016-8056. Offers ethics, peace, and global affairs (MA); philosophy (MA). *Program availability:* Part-time, evening/weekend. *Degree requirements:* For master's, comprehensive exam, thesis (for some programs). *Entrance requirements:* For master's, GRE; Please visit website: https://www.american.edu/cas/ philrel/, writing sample, statement of purpose, transcripts, 2 letters of recommendation, resume. Additional exam requirements/recommendations for international students: required—TOEFL. *Expenses:* Contact institution.

The American University in Cairo, School of Humanities and Social Sciences, Cairo, Egypt. Offers Arab and Islamic civilizations (Graduate Diploma); Arabic studies (MA); comparative literary studies (Graduate Diploma); Egyptology and Coptology (MA); English and comparative literature (MA); humanities and social sciences (Graduate Diploma); philosophy (MA); psychology (MA); sociology and anthropology (MA); teaching Arabic as a foreign language (MA); teaching English to speakers of other languages (MA). *Program availability:* Part-time, evening/weekend. *Degree requirements:* For master's, comprehensive exam (for some programs), thesis (for some programs). *Entrance requirements:* Additional exam requirements/recommendations for international students: required—TOEFL (minimum score 450 paper-based; 45 iBT), IELTS (minimum score 5). Electronic applications accepted.

Arizona State University at Tempe, College of Liberal Arts and Sciences, School of Historical, Philosophical and Religious Studies, Tempe, AZ 85287-4301. Offers European history (MA, PhD); medieval studies (Graduate Certificate); North American history (MA, PhD); philosophy (MA, PhD); public history (MA); religious studies (MA, PhD); Renaissance studies (Graduate Certificate); scholarly publishing (Graduate Certificate). *Program availability:* Part-time. Terminal master's awarded for partial completion of doctoral program. *Degree requirements:* For master's, thesis or alternative, interactive Program of Study (iPOS) submitted before completing 50 percent of required credit hours; for doctorate, variable foreign language requirement, comprehensive exam, thesis/dissertation, interactive Program of Study (iPOS) submitted before completing 50 percent of required credit hours. *Entrance requirements:* For master's and doctorate, GRE, minimum GPA of 3.0 or equivalent in last 2 years of work leading to bachelor's degree. Additional exam requirements/recommendations for international students: required—TOEFL, IELTS, or PTE. Electronic applications accepted.

Baylor University, Graduate School, College of Arts and Sciences, Department of Philosophy, Waco, TX 76798. Offers MA, PhD. Terminal master's awarded for partial completion of doctoral program. *Degree requirements:* For master's, comprehensive exam; for doctorate, comprehensive exam, thesis/dissertation, Degree requirements include successful completion of nine hours in contemporary issues in philosophy; six hours in history of philosophy; thirty hours of electives; one to nine hours of prospectus preparation; 9 hours dissertation preparation; at least 18 hours of TA or RA work; and a determined amount of teaching. *Entrance requirements:* For master's and doctorate, GRE General Test. Additional exam requirements/recommendations for international students: required—TOEFL. Electronic applications accepted.

Binghamton University, State University of New York, Graduate School, Harpur College of Arts and Sciences, Department of Philosophy, Binghamton, NY 13902-6000. Offers MA, PhD. *Program availability:* Part-time. Terminal master's awarded for partial completion of doctoral program. *Degree requirements:* For master's, 2 foreign languages, comprehensive exam (for some programs), thesis or alternative; for doctorate, one foreign language, thesis/dissertation. *Entrance requirements:* For master's and doctorate, GRE General Test, writing sample. Additional exam requirements/recommendations for international students: required—TOEFL (minimum score 550 paper-based; 80 iBT). Electronic applications accepted.

Binghamton University, State University of New York, Graduate School, Harpur College of Arts and Sciences, Program in Social, Political, Ethical and Legal Philosophy, Binghamton, NY 13902-6000. Offers MA, PhD. *Program availability:* Part-time. Terminal master's awarded for partial completion of doctoral program. *Degree requirements:* For master's, comprehensive exam, thesis or alternative; for doctorate, one foreign language, thesis/dissertation. *Entrance requirements:* For master's and doctorate, GRE General Test, writing sample. Additional exam requirements/recommendations for international students: required—TOEFL (minimum score 550 paper-based; 80 iBT). Electronic applications accepted.

Boston College, Morrissey Graduate School of Arts and Sciences, Department of Philosophy, Chestnut Hill, MA 02467-3800. Offers MA, PhD. Terminal master's awarded for partial completion of doctoral program. *Degree requirements:* For master's, one foreign language, thesis optional; for doctorate, 2 foreign languages, thesis/dissertation. *Entrance requirements:* For master's and doctorate, GRE General Test. Additional exam requirements/recommendations for international students: required—TOEFL (minimum score 600 paper-based; 100 iBT), IELTS (minimum score 8).

Boston College, Morrissey Graduate School of Arts and Sciences, Department of Theology, Chestnut Hill, MA 02467-3800. Offers philosophy and theology (MA); theology (PhD). *Accreditation:* ATS. Terminal master's awarded for partial completion of doctoral program. *Degree requirements:* For master's, one foreign language, thesis optional; for doctorate, thesis/dissertation. *Entrance requirements:* For master's and doctorate, GRE General Test. Additional exam requirements/recommendations for international students: required—TOEFL (minimum score 600 paper-based; 100 iBT), IELTS (minimum score 8). Electronic applications accepted.

Boston University, Graduate School of Arts and Sciences, Department of Philosophy, Boston, MA 02215. Offers MA, PhD, JD/MA. *Students:* 39 full-time (14 women); includes 6 minority (1 Asian, non-Hispanic/Latino; 2 Hispanic/Latino; 3 Two or more races, non-

Hispanic/Latino), 11 international. Average age 26. 209 applicants, 9% accepted, 6 enrolled. In 2019, 2 master's, 4 doctorates awarded. Terminal master's awarded for partial completion of doctoral program. *Degree requirements:* For master's, one foreign language, thesis; for doctorate, one foreign language, comprehensive exam, thesis/ dissertation. *Entrance requirements:* For master's and doctorate, 3 letters of recommendation, transcripts, personal statement, scholarly writing sample. Additional exam requirements/recommendations for international students: required—TOEFL (minimum score 550 paper-based; 84 iBT). *Application deadline:* For fall admission, 2/1 for domestic and international students. Application fee: $95. Electronic applications accepted. *Financial support:* In 2019–20, 36 students received support, including 10 fellowships with full tuition reimbursements available (averaging $23,340 per year), 22 teaching assistantships with full tuition reimbursements available (averaging $23,340 per year); Federal Work-Study, scholarships/grants, and health care benefits also available. Financial award application deadline: 2/1. *Unit head:* Daniel Dahlstrom, Chair, 617-353-4583, Fax: 617-353-6805, E-mail: dahlstrom@bu.edu. *Application contact:* Laura Hubbard, Senior Program Coordinator, 617-353-2571, Fax: 617-353-6805, E-mail: casphilo@bu.edu.
Website: http://www.bu.edu/philo/

Bowling Green State University, Graduate College, College of Arts and Sciences, Department of Philosophy, Bowling Green, OH 43403. Offers applied philosophy (PhD); institutional theory and history (PhD); philosophy (MA). *Program availability:* Part-time. Terminal master's awarded for partial completion of doctoral program. *Degree requirements:* For master's, thesis or alternative; for doctorate, comprehensive exam, thesis/dissertation, foreign language or research tool. *Entrance requirements:* For master's and doctorate, GRE General Test. Additional exam requirements/ recommendations for international students: required—TOEFL. Electronic applications accepted.

Brandeis University, Graduate School of Arts and Sciences, Department of Philosophy, Waltham, MA 02454-9110. Offers MA. *Program availability:* Part-time. *Faculty:* 11 full-time (4 women). *Students:* 13 full-time (3 women), 4 part-time (0 women); includes 3 minority (1 Black or African American, non-Hispanic/Latino; 2 Hispanic/Latino), 1 international. Average age 25. 124 applicants, 40% accepted, 9 enrolled. In 2019, 11 master's awarded. *Degree requirements:* For master's, thesis or alternative. *Entrance requirements:* For master's, General GRE, transcripts, letters of recommendation, resume, writing sample, and statement of purpose. Additional exam requirements/recommendations for international students: required—TOEFL, IELTS, PTE. *Application deadline:* For fall admission, 2/15 priority date for domestic and international students. Applications are processed on a rolling basis. Application fee: $75. Electronic applications accepted. *Financial support:* In 2019–20, 28 teaching assistantships (averaging $3,200 per year) were awarded; fellowships, scholarships/ grants, health care benefits, and tuition waivers also available. Support available to part-time students. *Unit head:* Dr. Kate Moran, Director of Graduate Study, 781-736-2695, E-mail: gradschool@brandeis.edu. *Application contact:* Julie Seeger, Administrator, 781-736-2789, E-mail: jseeger@brandeis.edu.
Website: http://www.brandeis.edu/gsas/programs/philosophy.html

Brock University, Faculty of Graduate Studies, Faculty of Humanities, Program in Philosophy, St. Catharines, ON L2S 3A1, Canada. Offers MA. *Program availability:* Part-time. *Degree requirements:* For master's, thesis optional. *Entrance requirements:* For master's, honors BA in philosophy. Additional exam requirements/recommendations for international students: required—TOEFL (minimum score 550 paper-based; 80 iBT), IELTS (minimum score 6.5), TWE (minimum score 4). Electronic applications accepted.

Brown University, Graduate School, Department of Philosophy, Providence, RI 02912. Offers PhD. *Faculty:* 16 full-time (5 women), 2 part-time/adjunct (1 woman). *Students:* 29 full-time (8 women); includes 5 minority (4 Asian, non-Hispanic/Latino; 1 Hispanic/ Latino). Average age 26. 240 applicants, 6% accepted, 2 enrolled. In 2019, 4 doctorates awarded. Terminal master's awarded for partial completion of doctoral program. *Degree requirements:* For doctorate, variable foreign language requirement, thesis/dissertation. *Entrance requirements:* For doctorate, GRE General Test. Additional exam requirements/recommendations for international students: required—TOEFL, GRE. *Application deadline:* For fall admission, 1/2 priority date for domestic students. Application fee: $75. Electronic applications accepted. *Financial support:* In 2019–20, 27 students received support, including 5 fellowships with full tuition reimbursements available (averaging $32,000 per year), 17 teaching assistantships with full tuition reimbursements available (averaging $32,000 per year); health care benefits, tuition waivers (full), unspecified assistantships, and proctorships also available. Financial award application deadline: 1/2. *Unit head:* Prof. Bernard Reginster, Chair, 401-863-2718, Fax: 401-863-2719, E-mail: bernard_reginster@brown.edu. *Application contact:* Admission Office, 401-863-2600.
Website: http://www.brown.edu/philosophy

California State University, Long Beach, Graduate Studies, College of Liberal Arts, Department of Philosophy, Long Beach, CA 90840. Offers MA. *Program availability:* Part-time. *Degree requirements:* For master's, comprehensive exam or thesis. Electronic applications accepted.

California State University, Los Angeles, Graduate Studies, College of Arts and Letters, Department of Philosophy, Los Angeles, CA 90032-8530. Offers MA, Graduate Certificate. *Program availability:* Part-time, evening/weekend. *Degree requirements:* For master's, comprehensive exam. *Entrance requirements:* Additional exam requirements/ recommendations for international students: required—TOEFL (minimum score 500 paper-based). Electronic applications accepted. *Expenses:* Tuition, area resident: Full-time $7176; part-time $4164 per year. Tuition, state resident: full-time $7176; part-time $4164 per year. Tuition, nonresident: full-time $14,304; part-time $8916 per year. *International tuition:* $14,304 full-time. *Required fees:* $1037.76; $1037.76 per unit. Tuition and fees vary according to degree level and program.

Carleton University, Faculty of Graduate Studies, Faculty of Arts and Social Sciences, Department of Philosophy, Ottawa, ON K1S 5B6, Canada. Offers MA. *Degree*

requirements: For master's, thesis optional. *Entrance requirements:* For master's, honors degree. Additional exam requirements/recommendations for international students: required—TOEFL.

Carnegie Mellon University, Dietrich College of Humanities and Social Sciences, Department of Philosophy, Pittsburgh, PA 15213-3891. Offers logic, computation and methodology (MS, PhD); philosophy (MA, PhD); pure and applied logic (PhD). *Program availability:* Part-time. *Degree requirements:* For master's, thesis; for doctorate, comprehensive exam, thesis/dissertation. *Entrance requirements:* For master's and doctorate, GRE General Test. Additional exam requirements/recommendations for international students: required—TOEFL. Electronic applications accepted.

The Catholic University of America, School of Philosophy, Washington, DC 20064. Offers MA, PhD, Ph L, MA/JD. *Program availability:* Part-time. *Faculty:* 23 full-time (4 women), 4 part-time/adjunct (3 women). *Students:* 44 full-time (7 women), 53 part-time (19 women); includes 19 minority (2 Black or African American, non-Hispanic/Latino; 6 Asian, non-Hispanic/Latino; 5 Hispanic/Latino; 6 Two or more races, non-Hispanic/Latino), 8 international. Average age 31. 76 applicants, 37% accepted, 22 enrolled. In 2019, 14 master's, 10 doctorates awarded. *Degree requirements:* For master's, one foreign language, thesis, oral exam; for doctorate, 2 foreign languages, comprehensive exam, thesis/dissertation, oral exam. *Entrance requirements:* For master's, GRE General Test, statement of purpose, official copies of academic transcripts, three letters of recommendation, writing sample; for doctorate, GRE General Test, statement of purpose, official copies of academic transcripts, three letters of recommendation. Additional exam requirements/recommendations for international students: required—TOEFL (minimum score 550 paper-based; 80 iBT). *Application deadline:* For fall admission, 7/15 priority date for domestic students, 7/1 for international students; for spring admission, 11/15 priority date for domestic students, 11/1 for international students. Applications are processed on a rolling basis. Application fee: $55. Electronic applications accepted. *Expenses:* Contact institution. *Financial support:* Fellowships, research assistantships, teaching assistantships, Federal Work-Study, scholarships/grants, tuition waivers (full and partial), and unspecified assistantships available. Financial award application deadline: 2/1; financial award applicants required to submit FAFSA. *Unit head:* Dr. John McCarthy, Dean, 202-319-6649, Fax: 202-319-4731, E-mail: mccartjc@cua.edu. *Application contact:* Dr. Steven Brown, Director of Graduate Admissions, 202-319-5057, Fax: 202-319-6533, E-mail: cua-admissions@cua.edu.
Website: http://philosophy.cua.edu/

Central European University, Department of Philosophy, 1051, Hungary. Offers MA, PhD. *Degree requirements:* For master's, one foreign language, thesis; for doctorate, one foreign language, comprehensive exam, thesis/dissertation. *Entrance requirements:* For master's and doctorate, interview. Additional exam requirements/recommendations for international students: required—TOEFL (minimum score 570 paper-based); recommended—IELTS (minimum score 6.5). Electronic applications accepted.

Claremont Graduate University, Graduate Programs, School of Arts and Humanities, Department of Philosophy, Claremont, CA 91711-6160. Offers MA, PhD, MA/PhD, MBA/MA, MBA/PhD. *Program availability:* Part-time. *Degree requirements:* For doctorate, research folio. *Entrance requirements:* For master's and doctorate, GRE General Test. Additional exam requirements/recommendations for international students: required—TOEFL (minimum score 75 iBT). Electronic applications accepted.

Cleveland State University, College of Graduate Studies, College of Liberal Arts and Social Sciences, Department of Philosophy and Comparative Religion, Cleveland, OH 44115. Offers bioethics (MA, Certificate), including bioethics (MA); philosophy (MA), including philosophy. *Program availability:* Part-time, evening/weekend. *Faculty:* 4 full-time (all women), 2 part-time/adjunct (1 woman). *Students:* 2 part-time (1 woman). Average age 39. 11 applicants, 100% accepted, 4 enrolled. In 2019, 1 master's awarded. *Degree requirements:* For master's, comprehensive exam, thesis optional, 32 credit hours of coursework; for Certificate, 12 credit hours of coursework. *Entrance requirements:* For master's and Certificate, BA, BS, or equivalent degree with minimum GPA of 2.75. Additional exam requirements/recommendations for international students: required—TOEFL (minimum score 550 paper-based; 78 iBT). *Application deadline:* For fall admission, 7/1 priority date for domestic students, 5/15 priority date for international students; for spring admission, 11/15 for domestic students, 11/1 for international students; for summer admission, 4/1 for domestic students, 3/15 for international students. Applications are processed on a rolling basis. Application fee: $40. Electronic applications accepted. *Expenses:* Tuition, state resident: full-time $10,215; part-time $6810 per credit hour. Tuition, nonresident: full-time $17,496; part-time $11,664 per credit hour. *International tuition:* $19,316 full-time. Tuition and fees vary according to degree level and program. *Financial support:* In 2019–20, 5 students received support, including 5 teaching assistantships with full tuition reimbursements available (averaging $4,000 per year); health care benefits, tuition waivers (full), and unspecified assistantships also available. Support available to part-time students. *Unit head:* Dr. Mary Ellen Waithe, Chairperson, 216-687-3900, Fax: 216-523-7482, E-mail: m.waithe@csuohio.edu. *Application contact:* Deborah L. Brown, Interim Assistant Director, Graduate Admissions, 216-523-7572, Fax: 216-687-5400, E-mail: d.l.brown@csuohio.edu.
Website: http://www.csuohio.edu/class/philosophy-religion/philosophy-religion

Collège Dominicain de Philosophie et de Théologie, Graduate Programs, Faculty of Philosophy, Ottawa, ON K1R 7G3, Canada. Offers MA Ph, PhD. *Degree requirements:* For master's, thesis; for doctorate, 2 foreign languages, thesis/dissertation, candidacy exam. *Entrance requirements:* For master's, honors degree in philosophy, minimum B average in undergraduate course work; for doctorate, master's degree in philosophy, minimum A average in graduate course work. *Expenses: Tuition, area resident:* Full-time $7032 Canadian dollars; part-time $147 Canadian dollars per credit hour. Tuition, nonresident: part-time $375 Canadian dollars per credit hour. *International tuition:* $19,680 Canadian dollars full-time. One-time fee: $165 Canadian dollars full-time. Full-time tuition and fees vary according to class time, course level, course load, degree level, campus/location, program and student level.

Colorado State University, College of Liberal Arts, Department of Philosophy, Fort Collins, CO 80523-1781. Offers MA. *Program availability:* Part-time. *Students:* Average age 27. 57 applicants, 28% accepted, 8 enrolled. In 2019, 3 master's awarded. *Degree requirements:* For master's, comprehensive exam (for some programs), thesis or alternative, 30-33 credit hours of coursework. *Entrance requirements:* For master's, bachelor's degree; minimum undergraduate GPA of 3.25; statement of purpose; writing sample; letters of recommendation. Additional exam requirements/recommendations for international students: required—TOEFL (minimum score 550 paper-based; 80 iBT), IELTS (minimum score 6.5), PTE (minimum score 58). *Application deadline:* For fall admission, 2/15 for domestic and international students. Application fee: $60 ($70 for international students). Electronic applications accepted. *Expenses:* Tuition, state resident: full-time $10,520; part-time $5844 per credit hour. Tuition, nonresident: full-time $25,791; part-time $14,328 per credit hour. *International tuition:* $25,791 full-time. *Required fees:* $2512.80. Part-time tuition and fees vary according to course level, course load, degree level, program and student level. *Financial support:* In 2019–20, 13 students received support, including 13 teaching assistantships with full tuition reimbursements available (averaging $14,256 per year); fellowships with full tuition reimbursements available, scholarships/grants, and health care benefits also available. Financial award application deadline: 2/15. *Unit head:* Dr. John Didier, Department Chair, 970-491-6315, Fax: 970-491-4900, E-mail: john.didier@colostate.edu. *Application contact:* Gaylene Wolfe, Graduate Coordinator, 970-491-6315, Fax: 970-491-4900, E-mail: gaylene.wolfe@colostate.edu.
Website: http://philosophy.colostate.edu/

Columbia University, Graduate School of Arts and Sciences, New York, NY 10027. Offers African-American studies (MA); American studies (MA); anthropology (MA, PhD); art history and archaeology (MA, PhD); astronomy (PhD); biological sciences (PhD); biotechnology (MA); chemical physics (PhD); chemistry (PhD); classical studies (MA, PhD); classics (MA, PhD); climate and society (MA); conservation biology (MA); earth and environmental sciences (PhD); East Asia: regional studies (MA); East Asian languages and cultures (MA, PhD); ecology, evolution and environmental biology (MA), including conservation biology; ecology, evolution, and environmental biology (PhD), including ecology and evolutionary biology, evolutionary primatology; economics (MA, PhD); English and comparative literature (MA, PhD); French and Romance philology (MA, PhD); Germanic languages (MA, PhD); global French studies (MA); global thought (MA); Hispanic cultural studies (MA); history (PhD); history and literature (MA); human rights studies (MA); Islamic studies (MA); Italian (MA, PhD); Japanese pedagogy (MA); Jewish studies (MA); Latin America and the Caribbean: regional studies (MA); Latin American and Iberian cultures (PhD); mathematics (MA, PhD), including finance (MA); medieval and Renaissance studies (MA); Middle Eastern, South Asian, and African studies (MA, PhD); modern art: critical and curatorial studies (MA); modern European studies (MA); museum anthropology (MA); music (DMA, PhD); oral history (MA); philosophical foundations of physics (MA); philosophy (MA, PhD); physics (PhD); political science (MA, PhD); psychology (PhD); quantitative methods in the social sciences (MA); religion (MA, PhD); Russia, Eurasia and East Europe: regional studies (MA); Russian translation (MA); Slavic cultures (MA); Slavic languages (MA, PhD); sociology (MA, PhD); South Asian studies (MA); statistics (MA, PhD); theatre (PhD). *Program availability:* Part-time. *Students:* 3,506 full-time (1,844 women), 208 part-time (121 women); includes 864 minority (110 Black or African American, non-Hispanic/Latino; 5 American Indian or Alaska Native, non-Hispanic/Latino; 416 Asian, non-Hispanic/Latino; 147 Hispanic/Latino; 6 Native Hawaiian or other Pacific Islander, non-Hispanic/Latino; 180 Two or more races, non-Hispanic/Latino), 2,065 international. 14,545 applicants, 25% accepted, 1,429 enrolled. In 2019, 1,262 master's, 363 doctorates awarded. Terminal master's awarded for partial completion of doctoral program. *Degree requirements:* For master's, variable foreign language requirement, comprehensive exam (for some programs), thesis (for some programs); for doctorate, variable foreign language requirement, comprehensive exam (for some programs), thesis/dissertation. *Entrance requirements:* For master's and doctorate, GRE General Test, GRE Subject Test (for some programs). Additional exam requirements/recommendations for international students: required—TOEFL (minimum score 600 paper-based; 100 iBT), IELTS (minimum score 7.5). Application fee: $115. Electronic applications accepted. *Expenses: Tuition:* Full-time $47,600; part-time $1880 per credit. One-time fee: $105. *Financial support:* Fellowships, research assistantships, teaching assistantships, career-related internships or fieldwork, Federal Work-Study, institutionally sponsored loans, scholarships/grants, traineeships, health care benefits, tuition waivers, and unspecified assistantships available. Support available to part-time students. Financial award application deadline: 12/15. *Unit head:* Dr. Carlos J. Alonso, Dean of the Graduate School of Arts and Sciences and Vice President for Graduate Education, 212-854-2861, E-mail: gsas-dean@columbia.edu. *Application contact:* GSAS Office of Admissions, 212-854-6729, E-mail: gsas-admissions@columbia.edu.
Website: http://gsas.columbia.edu/

Concordia University, School of Graduate Studies, Faculty of Arts and Science, Department of Philosophy, Montréal, QC H3G 1M8, Canada. Offers MA. *Degree requirements:* For master's, comprehensive exam, thesis or alternative. *Entrance requirements:* For master's, honors degree in philosophy or equivalent.

Cornell University, Graduate School, Graduate Fields of Arts and Sciences, Field of Philosophy, Ithaca, NY 14853. Offers PhD. *Degree requirements:* For doctorate, comprehensive exam, thesis/dissertation, teaching experience. *Entrance requirements:* For doctorate, sample of written work in philosophy, 2 letters of recommendation. Additional exam requirements/recommendations for international students: required—TOEFL (minimum score 550 paper-based; 77 iBT). Electronic applications accepted.

Dalhousie University, Faculty of Arts and Social Sciences, Department of Philosophy, Halifax, NS B3H 4R2, Canada. Offers MA, PhD. *Entrance requirements:* For doctorate, MA in philosophy. Additional exam requirements/recommendations for international students: required—TOEFL, IELTS, CANTEST, CAEL, or Michigan English Language Assessment Battery. Electronic applications accepted.

Dallas Theological Seminary, Graduate Programs, Dallas, TX 75204-6499. Offers adult education (Th M); apologetics (Th M); Bible backgrounds (Th M); Bible translation (Th M); Biblical and theological studies (Certificate); biblical counseling (MA); biblical exegesis and linguistics (MA); biblical exposition (PhD); biblical studies (MA); Biblical theology (Th M); children's education (Th M); Christian education (MA, D Min); Christian leadership (MA); cross-cultural ministries (MA); educational administration (Th M); educational leadership (Th M); evangelism and discipleship (Th M); exposition of Biblical books (Th M); family life education (Th M); general studies (Th M); Hebrew and cognate studies (Th M); hermeneutics (Th M); historical theology (Th M); homiletics (Th M); intercultural ministries (Th M); Jesus studies (Th M); leadership studies (Th M); media and communication (MA); media arts (Th M); ministry (D Min); ministry with women (Th M); New Testament studies (Th M, PhD); Old Testament studies (Th M, PhD); parachurch ministries (Th M); pastoral care and counseling (Th M); pastoral theology and practice (Th M); philosophy (Th M); sacred theology (STM); spiritual formation (Th M); systematic theology (Th M); teaching in Christian institutions (Th M); theological studies (PhD); urban ministries (Th M); worship studies (Th M); youth education (Th M). *Program availability:* Part-time, online learning. *Degree requirements:* For master's, variable foreign language requirement, thesis (for some programs); for doctorate, 2 foreign languages, thesis/dissertation. *Entrance requirements:* For master's, GRE or MAT (if minimum undergraduate cumulative GPA is below 2.5 or undergraduate degree is unaccredited). Additional exam requirements/recommendations for international students: required—TOEFL (minimum score 575 paper-based; 85 iBT), TWE. Electronic applications accepted.

Delta State University, Graduate Programs, College of Arts and Sciences, Program in Liberal Studies, Cleveland, MS 38733-0001. Offers evolving human voices (MALS); gender and diversity studies (MALS); globalization studies (MALS); Mississippi Delta studies (MALS); philosophy (MALS); religious studies (MALS). *Degree requirements:* For master's, oral and/or written comprehensive exam. *Expenses: Tuition, area resident:* Full-time $7501; part-time $417 per credit hour. Tuition, state resident: full-time $7501; part-time $417 per credit hour. Tuition, nonresident: full-time $7501; part-time $417 per credit hour. *International tuition:* $7501 full-time. *Required fees:* $170; $9.45 per credit hour. $9.45 per semester.

Dominican School of Philosophy and Theology, Graduate Programs, Berkeley, CA 94708. Offers philosophy (MA); theology (M Div, MA, MTS, Certificate); M Div/MA; MA/MA. *Accreditation:* ATS. *Program availability:* Part-time. *Degree requirements:* For master's, one foreign language, thesis. *Entrance requirements:* For master's, GRE

General Test (for MA), minimum GPA of 3.0 (for MA), 2.3 (for M Div); academic writing sample (for MA); statement of purpose, official transcripts, letters of recommendation. Additional exam requirements/recommendations for international students: required—TOEFL (minimum score 570 paper-based; 80 iBT), IELTS. Electronic applications accepted.

Duke University, Graduate School, Department of Philosophy, Durham, NC 27708. Offers PhD, JD/AM, JD/PhD. *Degree requirements:* For doctorate, one foreign language, thesis/dissertation. *Entrance requirements:* For doctorate, GRE General Test. Additional exam requirements/recommendations for international students: required—TOEFL (minimum score 577 paper-based; 90 iBT) or IELTS (minimum score 7). Electronic applications accepted.

Duquesne University, Graduate School of Liberal Arts, Department of Philosophy, Pittsburgh, PA 15282-0001. Offers MA, PhD. *Program availability:* Part-time, evening/weekend. Terminal master's awarded for partial completion of doctoral program. *Degree requirements:* For master's, one foreign language; for doctorate, 2 foreign languages, comprehensive exam, thesis/dissertation. *Entrance requirements:* For master's, GRE General Test, bachelor's degree in philosophy, minimum GPA of 3.5; for doctorate, GRE General Test, master's degree in philosophy, minimum GPA of 3.75. Additional exam requirements/recommendations for international students: required—TOEFL. Electronic applications accepted.

Eastern Michigan University, Graduate School, College of Arts and Sciences, Department of History and Philosophy, Program in Philosophy, Ypsilanti, MI 48197. Offers MA. *Program availability:* Part-time, evening/weekend, online learning. *Students:* 5 full-time (2 women), 11 part-time (4 women); includes 1 minority (Hispanic/Latino). Average age 33. 16 applicants, 75% accepted, 7 enrolled. In 2019, 3 master's awarded. *Entrance requirements:* Additional exam requirements/recommendations for international students: required—TOEFL. *Application deadline:* Applications are processed on a rolling basis. Application fee: $45. *Financial support:* Fellowships, research assistantships with full tuition reimbursements, teaching assistantships with full tuition reimbursements, career-related internships or fieldwork, Federal Work-Study, institutionally sponsored loans, traineeships, and unspecified assistantships available. Support available to part-time students. Financial award applicants required to submit FAFSA. *Application contact:* Dr. Kate Mehuron, Graduate Coordinator and Advisor, 734-487-3724, Fax: 734-487-6835, E-mail: kmehuron@emich.edu.

Emory University, Laney Graduate School, Department of Comparative Literature, Atlanta, GA 30322-1100. Offers comparative literature (PhD); philosophy (Certificate); psychoanalytic studies (PhD); women's studies (Certificate). *Degree requirements:* For doctorate, 2 foreign languages, comprehensive exam, thesis/dissertation. *Entrance requirements:* For doctorate, GRE General Test, minimum GPA of 3.0. Additional exam requirements/recommendations for international students: required—TOEFL. Electronic applications accepted.

Emory University, Laney Graduate School, Department of Philosophy, Atlanta, GA 30322-1100. Offers PhD. *Degree requirements:* For doctorate, 2 foreign languages, comprehensive exam, thesis/dissertation. *Entrance requirements:* For doctorate, GRE General Test, minimum GPA of 3.0. Additional exam requirements/recommendations for international students: required—TOEFL. Electronic applications accepted.

Florida State University, The Graduate School, Department of Anthropology, Department of Philosophy, Tallahassee, FL 32306-1500. Offers history and philosophy of science (MA); philosophy (MA, PhD). *Faculty:* 20 full-time (6 women), 1 part-time/adjunct. *Students:* 57 full-time (13 women); includes 10 minority (1 Black or African American, non-Hispanic/Latino; 2 Asian, non-Hispanic/Latino; 3 Hispanic/Latino; 4 Two or more races, non-Hispanic/Latino). Average age 25. 88 applicants, 27% accepted, 15 enrolled. In 2019, 12 master's, 3 doctorates awarded. Terminal master's awarded for partial completion of doctoral program. *Degree requirements:* For master's, one foreign language, thesis (for some programs); for doctorate, one foreign language, thesis/dissertation. *Entrance requirements:* For master's and doctorate, GRE General Test. Additional exam requirements/recommendations for international students: required—TOEFL (minimum score 550 paper-based; 80 iBT). *Application deadline:* For fall admission, 3/31 priority date for domestic and international students; for spring admission, 10/19 priority date for domestic and international students. Applications are processed on a rolling basis. Application fee: $30. Electronic applications accepted. *Financial support:* In 2019–20, 54 students received support, including 3 fellowships with full tuition reimbursements available (averaging $30,000 per year), 54 teaching assistantships with full tuition reimbursements available (averaging $16,392 per year); Federal Work-Study, scholarships/grants, health care benefits, and tuition waivers (full and partial) also available. Financial award application deadline: 3/31; financial award applicants required to submit FAFSA. *Unit head:* Dr. John Piers Rawling, Chairman, 850-644-1483, Fax: 850-644-3832, E-mail: prawling@admin.fsu.edu. *Application contact:* Dr. John Piers Rawling, Chairman, 850-644-1483, Fax: 850-644-3832, E-mail: prawling@admin.fsu.edu.
Website: http://philosophy.fsu.edu/

Fordham University, Graduate School of Arts and Sciences, Department of Philosophy, New York, NY 10458. Offers MA, PhD. *Program availability:* Part-time, evening/weekend. *Students:* Average age 30. 131 applicants, 23% accepted, 11 enrolled. In 2019, 8 master's, 4 doctorates awarded. Terminal master's awarded for partial completion of doctoral program. *Degree requirements:* For master's, one foreign language, comprehensive exam; for doctorate, 2 foreign languages, comprehensive exam, thesis/dissertation. *Entrance requirements:* For master's and doctorate, GRE General Test. Additional exam requirements/recommendations for international students: required—TOEFL (minimum score 650 paper-based). *Application deadline:* For fall admission, 1/4 priority date for domestic students; for spring admission, 11/1 for domestic students. Application fee: $70. Electronic applications accepted. *Financial support:* In 2019–20, 45 students received support, including 3 fellowships with tuition reimbursements available (averaging $21,605 per year), 1 research assistantship with tuition reimbursement available (averaging $25,390 per year), 26 teaching assistantships with tuition reimbursements available (averaging $23,644 per year); institutionally sponsored loans, tuition waivers (full and partial), and unspecified assistantships also available. Support available to part-time students. Financial award application deadline: 1/4. *Unit head:* Dr. Giorgio Pini, Department Chair, 718-817-2779, Fax: 718-817-3300, E-mail: pini@fordham.edu. *Application contact:* Garrett Marino, Director of Graduate Admissions, 718-817-4419, Fax: 718-817-3566, E-mail: gmarino10@fordham.edu.

Franciscan University of Steubenville, Graduate Programs, Department of Philosophy, Steubenville, OH 43952-1763. Offers MA. *Program availability:* Part-time. *Degree requirements:* For master's, one foreign language, thesis. *Entrance requirements:* For master's, minimum undergraduate GPA of 3.0. Additional exam requirements/recommendations for international students: required—TOEFL. Electronic applications accepted. Application fee is waived when completed online.

George Mason University, College of Humanities and Social Sciences, Department of Philosophy, Fairfax, VA 22030. Offers ethics and public affairs (MA); philosophy and cultural theory (MA). *Entrance requirements:* For master's, college transcripts, goals statement, 2 letters of recommendation, resume, writing sample; completion of certain undergraduate preparation coursework with grades of B or higher in each course (for philosophy and cultural theory). Additional exam requirements/recommendations for international students: required—TOEFL (minimum score 575 paper-based, 88 iBT), IELTS (6.5), or PTE (59). Electronic applications accepted.

Georgetown University, Graduate School of Arts and Sciences, Department of Philosophy, Washington, DC 20057. Offers bioethics (MA); philosophy (PhD); JD/MA; JD/PhD; MD/PhD. *Degree requirements:* For master's, thesis or alternative; for doctorate, 2 foreign languages, comprehensive exam, thesis/dissertation. *Entrance requirements:* For master's and doctorate, GRE General Test. Additional exam requirements/recommendations for international students: required—TOEFL.

The George Washington University, Columbian College of Arts and Sciences, Department of Philosophy, Washington, DC 20052. Offers philosophy and social policy (MA). *Degree requirements:* For master's, comprehensive exam, thesis or alternative. *Entrance requirements:* For master's, GRE General Test, interview, minimum GPA of 3.0. Additional exam requirements/recommendations for international students: required—TOEFL (minimum score 600 paper-based; 100 iBT). Electronic applications accepted.

Georgia State University, College of Arts and Sciences, Department of Philosophy, Atlanta, GA 30302-4089. Offers MA, MA/JD. *Program availability:* Part-time. *Faculty:* 15 full-time (4 women). *Students:* 48 full-time (15 women); includes 5 minority (1 Black or African American, non-Hispanic/Latino; 3 Hispanic/Latino; 1 Two or more races, non-Hispanic/Latino), 10 international. Average age 25. 133 applicants, 44% accepted, 21 enrolled. In 2019, 25 master's awarded. *Entrance requirements:* For master's, GRE, writing sample, 3 letters of recommendation. Additional exam requirements/recommendations for international students: required—TOEFL (minimum score 550 paper-based; 80 iBT). *Application deadline:* For fall admission, 2/1 priority date for domestic and international students. Applications are processed on a rolling basis. Application fee: $50. Electronic applications accepted. *Expenses: Tuition, area resident:* Full-time $7164; part-time $398 per credit hour. Tuition, state resident: full-time $7164; part-time $398 per credit hour. Tuition, nonresident: full-time $22,662; part-time $1259 per credit hour. *International tuition:* $22,662 full-time. *Required fees:* $2128; $312 per credit hour. Tuition and fees vary according to course load and program. *Financial support:* In 2019–20, fellowships with full tuition reimbursements (averaging $15,000 per year), research assistantships with full tuition reimbursements (averaging $6,000 per year), teaching assistantships with full tuition reimbursements (averaging $10,000 per year) were awarded; health care benefits also available. Financial award application deadline: 8/1; financial award applicants required to submit FAFSA. *Unit head:* Dr. Eddy Nahmias, Chair, 404-413-6109, Fax: 404-413-6124, E-mail: enahmias@gsu.edu. *Application contact:* Dr. Tim O'Keefe, Director of Graduate Studies, 404-413-6108, Fax: 404-413-6124, E-mail: tokeefe@gsu.edu.
Website: https://philosophy.gsu.edu/

Gonzaga University, College of Arts and Sciences, Spokane, WA 99258. Offers philosophy (MA); theology and leadership (MA). *Program availability:* Part-time, blended/hybrid learning. *Degree requirements:* For master's, comprehensive exam. *Entrance requirements:* For master's, GRE or MAT, minimum GPA of 3.0, official transcripts, two to three letters of recommendation, personal statement, writing sample, resume/curriculum vitae. Additional exam requirements/recommendations for international students: required—TOEFL (minimum score 88 iBT) or IELTS (minimum score 6.5). Electronic applications accepted. *Expenses:* Contact institution.

The Graduate Center, City University of New York, Graduate Studies, Program in Philosophy, New York, NY 10016-4039. Offers MA, PhD. Terminal master's awarded for partial completion of doctoral program. *Degree requirements:* For master's, thesis; for doctorate, one foreign language, comprehensive exam, thesis/dissertation. *Entrance requirements:* For master's, GRE General Test; for doctorate, GRE General Test, 3 letters of recommendation, writing sample. Additional exam requirements/recommendations for international students: required—TOEFL. Electronic applications accepted.

Harrison Middleton University, Graduate Program, Tempe, AZ 85282. Offers education (MA, Ed D); humanities (MA); imaginative literature (MA); interdisciplinary studies (DA); jurisprudence (MA); natural science (MA); philosophy and religion (MA); social science (MA). *Program availability:* Part-time, evening/weekend, online learning. *Degree requirements:* For master's and doctorate, capstone project. *Entrance requirements:* For master's, interview; for doctorate, 2 academic letters of reference, interview, essay. Additional exam requirements/recommendations for international students: required—TOEFL (minimum score 550 paper-based; 80 iBT). Electronic applications accepted.

Harvard University, Graduate School of Arts and Sciences, Department of Philosophy, Cambridge, MA 02138. Offers classical philosophy (PhD); philosophy (PhD). *Degree requirements:* For doctorate, 2 foreign languages, thesis/dissertation, final exams. *Entrance requirements:* For doctorate, GRE General Test. Additional exam requirements/recommendations for international students: required—TOEFL.

Harvard University, Graduate School of Arts and Sciences, Department of Sanskrit and Indian Studies, Cambridge, MA 02138. Offers Indian philosophy (AM, PhD); Pali (AM, PhD); Sanskrit (AM, PhD); Tibetan (AM, PhD); Urdu (AM, PhD). Terminal master's awarded for partial completion of doctoral program. *Degree requirements:* For master's, 3 foreign languages; for doctorate, 3 foreign languages, thesis/dissertation. *Entrance requirements:* For master's, GRE General Test; for doctorate, GRE General Test, proficiency in French and German. Additional exam requirements/recommendations for international students: required—TOEFL.

Harvard University, Graduate School of Arts and Sciences, Department of the Classics, Cambridge, MA 02138. Offers Byzantine Greek (PhD); classical archaeology (PhD); classical philology (PhD); classical philosophy (PhD); medieval Latin (PhD). *Degree requirements:* For doctorate, 4 foreign languages, thesis/dissertation, preliminary and special exams. *Entrance requirements:* For doctorate, GRE General Test. Additional exam requirements/recommendations for international students: required—TOEFL.

Houston Baptist University, School of Humanities, Program in Philosophy, Houston, TX 77074-3298. Offers MA. *Entrance requirements:* For master's, bachelor's degree conferred transcript, resume, essay/personal statement. Additional exam requirements/recommendations for international students: required—TOEFL (minimum score 80 iBT), IELTS (minimum score 6.5). Electronic applications accepted. Application fee is waived when completed online. *Expenses:* Contact institution.

Howard University, Graduate School, Department of Philosophy, Washington, DC 20059-0002. Offers MA. *Program availability:* Part-time. *Degree requirements:* For master's, one foreign language, comprehensive exam, thesis. *Entrance requirements:* For master's, GRE General Test. Additional exam requirements/recommendations for international students: required—TOEFL.

Indiana University Bloomington, University Graduate School, College of Arts and Sciences, Department of Philosophy, Bloomington, IN 47405. Offers MA, PhD. Terminal master's awarded for partial completion of doctoral program. *Degree requirements:* For master's, variable foreign language requirement, thesis optional; for doctorate, comprehensive exam, thesis/dissertation, qualifying paper. *Entrance requirements:* For master's and doctorate, GRE General Test, writing sample. Additional exam requirements/recommendations for international students: required—TOEFL. Electronic applications accepted.

Indiana University-Purdue University Indianapolis, School of Liberal Arts, Department of Philosophy, Indianapolis, IN 46202. Offers American philosophy (Certificate); bioethics (Certificate); philosophy (MA); philosophy/bioethics (MA); JD/MA; MD/MA. *Program availability:* Part-time. *Degree requirements:* For master's, thesis optional. *Entrance requirements:* For master's, GRE, writing sample, transcripts, three letters of recommendation, personal statement; for Certificate, letter of recommendation, transcripts, statement of purpose. Additional exam requirements/recommendations for international students: required—TOEFL, PTE, IUPUI ESL Exam. Electronic applications accepted. *Expenses:* Contact institution.

Institute for Christian Studies, Graduate Programs, Toronto, ON M5S 2E6, Canada. Offers education (M Phil F, PhD); history of philosophy (M Phil F, PhD); philosophical aesthetics (M Phil F, PhD); philosophy of religion (M Phil F, PhD); political theory (M Phil F, PhD); systematic philosophy (M Phil F, PhD); theology (M Phil F, PhD); worldview studies (MWS). *Program availability:* Part-time, online learning. *Degree requirements:* For master's, one foreign language, thesis; for doctorate, 2 foreign languages, thesis/dissertation. *Entrance requirements:* For master's and doctorate, philosophy background. Additional exam requirements/recommendations for international students: required—TOEFL (minimum score 600 paper-based).

Institute for Doctoral Studies in the Visual Arts, PhD Program in Visual Art: Philosophy, Aesthetics, and Art Theory, Portland, ME 04102. Offers art theory (PhD); art theory, philosophy and aesthetics (PhD); philosophy (PhD). *Program availability:* Blended/hybrid learning. *Degree requirements:* For doctorate, comprehensive exam, thesis/dissertation, dissertation defense. *Entrance requirements:* For doctorate, curriculum vitae, writing sample, portfolio, interview. Electronic applications accepted. Application fee is waived when completed online. *Expenses: Tuition:* Full-time $42,600.

Johns Hopkins University, Zanvyl Krieger School of Arts and Sciences, Department of Philosophy, Baltimore, MD 21218. Offers MA, PhD. *Degree requirements:* For doctorate, comprehensive exam, thesis/dissertation. *Entrance requirements:* For master's and doctorate, GRE General Test. Additional exam requirements/recommendations for international students: required—TOEFL (minimum score 100 iBT), IELTS (minimum score 7). Electronic applications accepted. *Expenses:* Contact institution.

Kent State University, College of Arts and Sciences, Department of Philosophy, Kent, OH 44242-0001. Offers MA. *Program availability:* Part-time. *Faculty:* 5 full-time (1 woman), 1 part-time/adjunct (0 women). *Students:* 9 full-time (2 women), 3 part-time (all women); includes 2 minority (both Asian, non-Hispanic/Latino). Average age 25. 22 applicants, 73% accepted, 5 enrolled. In 2019, 1 master's awarded. *Degree requirements:* For master's, thesis (for some programs), 2 seminars, logic requirement, thesis or non-thesis project option, graduate proseminar. *Entrance requirements:* For master's, GRE is not required for admission to the graduate program, 3 letters of recommendation, goal statement, transcripts, writing sample. Additional exam requirements/recommendations for international students: required—TOEFL (minimum score 94 iBT), IELTS (minimum score 7), PTE (minimum score 65), Michigan English Language Assessment Battery (minimum score 82). *Application deadline:* For fall admission, 2/1 for domestic and international students. Applications are processed on a rolling basis. Application fee: $45 ($70 for international students). Electronic applications accepted. *Financial support:* Research assistantships, teaching assistantships with full tuition reimbursements, and unspecified assistantships available. Financial award application deadline: 2/1. *Unit head:* Dr. Michael Byron, Professor and Chair, 330-672-2315, E-mail: mbyron@kent.edu. *Application contact:* Dr. Gina Zavota, Associated Professor and Graduate Coordinator, 330-672-0266, E-mail: gzavota@kent.edu.
Website: http://www.kent.edu/philosophy

Lake Forest College, Graduate Program in Liberal Studies, Lake Forest, IL 60045. Offers American studies (MLS); cinema in East Asia (MLS); environmental studies (MLS); history (MLS); Medieval and Renaissance art (MLS); philosophy (MLS); Spanish (MLS); writing (MLS). *Program availability:* Part-time, evening/weekend. *Faculty:* 10 full-time (4 women). *Students:* 24 part-time (14 women). Average age 45. 10 applicants, 80% accepted, 3 enrolled. In 2019, 5 master's awarded. *Degree requirements:* For master's, thesis optional, 8 courses, including at least 3 interdisciplinary seminars. *Entrance requirements:* For master's, transcript, essay, interview. Additional exam requirements/recommendations for international students: required—TOEFL (minimum score 550 paper-based; 83 iBT); recommended—IELTS (minimum score 6.5). *Application deadline:* For fall admission, 8/15 priority date for domestic students, 7/15 priority date for international students; for spring admission, 12/15 priority date for domestic students, 11/15 priority date for international students. Applications are processed on a rolling basis. Application fee: $30. Electronic applications accepted. Application fee is waived when completed online. *Expenses:* Application fee = $30 — no other fees; tuition = $2,700/course. *Financial support:* In 2019–20, 2 students received support. Partial tuition grants (for full-time teachers) available. *Unit head:* Prof. D. L. LeMahieu, Director, 847-735-5133, Fax: 847-735-6291, E-mail: lemahieu@lakeforest.edu. *Application contact:* Prof. Carol Gayle, Associate Director, 847-735-5083, Fax: 847-735-6291, E-mail: gayle@lakeforest.edu.
Website: http://www.lakeforest.edu/academics/programs/mls/

Lincoln Christian University, Graduate Programs, Lincoln, IL 62656-2167. Offers Bible and theology (MA); Biblical studies (MA); church history/historical theology (MA); counseling (MA); formative worship (MA); intercultural studies (MA); ministry (MA); organizational leadership (MA); philosophy and apologetics (MA); spiritual formation (MA); theology (MA). *Program availability:* Online learning. *Entrance requirements:* For master's, minimum cumulative GPA of 2.5 in undergraduate degree studies. Additional exam requirements/recommendations for international students: required—TOEFL (minimum score 550 paper-based); recommended—IELTS (minimum score 6). Application fee is waived when completed online.

Louisiana State University and Agricultural & Mechanical College, Graduate School, College of Humanities and Social Sciences, Department of Philosophy and Religious Studies, Baton Rouge, LA 70803. Offers philosophy (MA).

Loyola Marymount University, Bellarmine College of Liberal Arts, Program in Philosophy, Los Angeles, CA 90045. Offers MA. *Students:* 16 full-time (4 women); includes 4 minority (1 Black or African American, non-Hispanic/Latino; 1 Asian, non-Hispanic/Latino; 2 Hispanic/Latino), 2 international. Average age 30. 26 applicants, 58% accepted. In 2019, 6 master's awarded. *Entrance requirements:* For master's, GRE, bachelor degree; graduate admissions application; undergrad GPA of at least 3.0; 2 letters of recommendation; offical transcripts. Additional exam requirements/recommendations for international students: required—TOEFL. *Application deadline:* For fall admission, 3/15 for domestic students; for spring admission, 11/1 for domestic students. Application fee: $50. Electronic applications accepted. *Financial support:* In 2019–20, 3 teaching assistantships (averaging $13,000 per year) were awarded; fellowships, scholarships/grants, and unspecified assistantships also available. Financial award applicants required to submit FAFSA. *Unit head:* Dr. Brad Stone, Graduate Program Director, Philosophy, 310-338-5807, E-mail: bstone@lmu.edu. *Application contact:* Ammar Dalal, Assistant Vice Provost for Graduate Enrollment, 310-338-2721, Fax: 310-338-6086, E-mail: graduateadmission@lmu.edu.
Website: http://bellarmine.lmu.edu/philosophy/graduateprogram

Loyola University Chicago, Graduate School, Department of Philosophy, Chicago, IL 60660. Offers applied philosophy and philosophy (MA); philosophy (PhD). *Program availability:* Part-time, evening/weekend. *Faculty:* 21 full-time (9 women). *Students:* 52 full-time (8 women), 6 part-time (2 women); includes 18 minority (2 Black or African American, non-Hispanic/Latino; 6 Asian, non-Hispanic/Latino; 9 Hispanic/Latino; 1 Two or more races, non-Hispanic/Latino), 2 international. Average age 32. 135 applicants, 16% accepted, 17 enrolled. In 2019, 9 master's, 2 doctorates awarded. Terminal master's awarded for partial completion of doctoral program. *Degree requirements:* For master's, oral exam paper/thesis; for doctorate, one foreign language, thesis/dissertation, oral exam. *Entrance requirements:* Additional exam requirements/recommendations for international students: required—TOEFL (minimum score 79 iBT). *Application deadline:* For fall admission, 1/15 priority date for domestic and international students. Applications are processed on a rolling basis. Application fee: $50. Electronic applications accepted. Application fee is waived when completed online. *Expenses:* Per Credit Hour, except MA in Medical Sciences $1,033; Thesis Supervision: Course 595 $500; Dissertation Supervision: Course 600 $1,935; Master's Study: Course 605 $565; Doctoral Study: Course 610 $1,350; Student Development Fee, per semester: $172 (for 6 or more hours), $85 (for 1-5 hours); Technology Fee, per semester Registered for 9 or more hours $125; Student Health Insurance Premium, annually $3,095; Graduation and Matriculation Fees (payable at time of registration) $100. *Financial support:* In 2019–20, 19 students received support, including 1 fellowship with full tuition reimbursement available (averaging $20,000 per year), 17 teaching assistantships with full tuition reimbursements available (averaging $19,029 per year); institutionally sponsored loans, health care benefits, unspecified assistantships, and McNair Scholar Merit Funding also available. Financial award application deadline: 1/15; financial award applicants required to submit FAFSA. *Unit head:* Dr. Mark Waymack, Chair, 773-508-2738, Fax: 773-508-2292, E-mail: mwaymac@luc.edu. *Application contact:* Miguel Diaz, Graduate Program Assistant, 773-508-2453, Fax: 773-508-2292, E-mail: mdiaz1@luc.edu.
Website: http://www.luc.edu/philosophy/

Marquette University, Graduate School, College of Arts and Sciences, Department of Philosophy, Milwaukee, WI 53201-1881. Offers ancient philosophy (PhD); British empiricism and analytic philosophy (PhD); Christian philosophy (PhD); early modern European philosophy (PhD); ethics (PhD); German philosophy (PhD); history of philosophy (MA); medieval philosophy (PhD); phenomenology and existentialism (PhD); philosophy of religion (PhD); social and applied philosophy (MA); JD/MA. *Program availability:* Part-time. Terminal master's awarded for partial completion of doctoral program. *Degree requirements:* For master's, variable foreign language requirement, comprehensive exam, thesis or alternative; for doctorate, 2 foreign languages, thesis/dissertation, written and oral qualifying exams. *Entrance requirements:* For master's and doctorate, GRE General Test, official transcripts from all current and previous colleges/universities except Marquette, statement of purpose, at least three letters of recommendation, sample of philosophical writing. Additional exam requirements/recommendations for international students: required—TOEFL (minimum score 530 paper-based). Electronic applications accepted.

Massachusetts Institute of Technology, School of Humanities, Arts, and Social Sciences, Department of Linguistics and Philosophy, Philosophy Section, Cambridge, MA 02139. Offers PhD. *Degree requirements:* For doctorate, comprehensive exam, thesis/dissertation, teaching requirement. *Entrance requirements:* For doctorate, GRE General Test. Additional exam requirements/recommendations for international students: required—TOEFL, IELTS. Electronic applications accepted.

McGill University, Faculty of Graduate and Postdoctoral Studies, Faculty of Arts, Department of Philosophy, Montréal, QC H3A 2T5, Canada. Offers bioethics (MA); philosophy (PhD).

McMaster University, School of Graduate Studies, Faculty of Humanities, Department of Philosophy, Hamilton, ON L8S 4M2, Canada. Offers MA, PhD. *Program availability:* Part-time. *Degree requirements:* For master's, thesis; for doctorate, one foreign language, thesis/dissertation. *Entrance requirements:* For master's, honors degree in philosophy; minimum average B+; for doctorate, master's degree in philosophy. Additional exam requirements/recommendations for international students: required—TOEFL (minimum score 580 paper-based).

Memorial University of Newfoundland, School of Graduate Studies, Department of Philosophy, St. John's, NL A1C 5S7, Canada. Offers MA, PhD. *Program availability:* Part-time. *Degree requirements:* For master's, thesis; for doctorate, comprehensive exam, thesis/dissertation. *Entrance requirements:* For master's, first-class undergraduate degree in philosophy; for doctorate, MA in philosophy or equivalent. Electronic applications accepted.

Miami University, College of Arts and Science, Department of Philosophy, Oxford, OH 45056. Offers MA.

Michigan State University, The Graduate School, College of Arts and Letters, Department of Philosophy, East Lansing, MI 48824. Offers MA, PhD. *Entrance requirements:* Additional exam requirements/recommendations for international students: required—TOEFL. Electronic applications accepted.

Midwestern State University, Billie Doris McAda Graduate School, Prothro-Yeager College of Humanities and Social Sciences, Department of English, Humanities, and Philosophy, Wichita Falls, TX 76308. Offers English (MA); philosophy (PhD). *Program availability:* Part-time, evening/weekend. *Degree requirements:* For master's, one foreign language, thesis optional. *Entrance requirements:* For master's, GRE General Test, MAT or GMAT. Additional exam requirements/recommendations for international students: required—TOEFL (minimum score 550 paper-based). Electronic applications accepted.

Mount St. Mary's University, Program in Philosophical Studies, Emmitsburg, MD 21727-7799. Offers MA. *Program availability:* Part-time. *Students:* 2 part-time (both women); includes 1 minority (Black or African American, non-Hispanic/Latino). In 2019, 3 master's awarded. *Degree requirements:* For master's, one foreign language, thesis. *Entrance requirements:* For master's, undergraduate degree, minimum cumulative undergraduate GPA of 3.0. Additional exam requirements/recommendations for international students: required—TOEFL (minimum score 550 paper-based; 83 iBT). *Application deadline:* For fall admission, 8/1 for domestic students; for spring admission, 12/1 for domestic students. *Expenses:* Contact institution. *Financial support:* Unspecified assistantships available. Financial award applicants required to submit FAFSA.
Website: https://msmary.edu/academics/graduate-programs/master-of-arts-in-philosophical-studies.html

The New School, The New School for Social Research, Department of Philosophy, New York, NY 10003. Offers philosophy (MA); psychoanalysis (PhD). *Program availability:* Part-time. *Faculty:* 12 full-time (4 women), 5 part-time/adjunct (0 women). *Students:* 125 full-time (37 women), 8 part-time (2 women); includes 23 minority (2 Black

or African American, non-Hispanic/Latino; 3 Asian, non-Hispanic/Latino; 12 Hispanic/Latino; 6 Two or more races, non-Hispanic/Latino), 46 international. Average age 33. 146 applicants, 53% accepted, 19 enrolled. In 2019, 37 master's, 5 doctorates awarded. Terminal master's awarded for partial completion of doctoral program. *Degree requirements:* For master's, one foreign language, comprehensive exam, thesis; for doctorate, one foreign language, comprehensive exam, thesis/dissertation. *Entrance requirements:* For master's, GRE, letters of recommendation, writing sample, essays, transcript; for doctorate, letters of recommendation, writing sample, essays, transcript. Additional exam requirements/recommendations for international students: required—TOEFL (minimum score 100 iBT), IELTS (minimum score 7), PTE (minimum score 68). *Application deadline:* For fall admission, 1/5 priority date for domestic and international students; for spring admission, 10/15 priority date for domestic and international students. Applications are processed on a rolling basis. Application fee: $50. Electronic applications accepted. *Expenses:* 2260 per credit. *Financial support:* In 2019–20, 86 students received support, including 14 fellowships (averaging $5,268 per year), 20 research assistantships (averaging $4,088 per year), 25 teaching assistantships with full and partial tuition reimbursements available (averaging $9,914 per year); Federal Work-Study and scholarships/grants also available. Support available to part-time students. Financial award application deadline: 2/1; financial award applicants required to submit FAFSA. *Unit head:* Dr. Zed Adams, Department Chair, 212-229-5777, E-mail: adamsz@newschool.edu. *Application contact:* Merida Gasbarro, Director of Graduate Admission, 212-229-5150 Ext. 2300, E-mail: escandom@newschool.edu.
Website: http://www.newschool.edu/nssr/philosophy/

New York University, Graduate School of Arts and Science, Department of Philosophy, New York, NY 10012-1019. Offers MA, PhD, JD/MA, JD/PhD, MD/MA. *Program availability:* Part-time. *Degree requirements:* For master's, thesis or alternative; for doctorate, one foreign language, thesis/dissertation. *Entrance requirements:* For master's and doctorate, GRE General Test, sample of written work. Additional exam requirements/recommendations for international students: required—TOEFL, IELTS.

Northern Illinois University, Graduate School, College of Liberal Arts and Sciences, Department of Philosophy, De Kalb, IL 60115-2854. Offers MA. *Program availability:* Part-time. *Faculty:* 12 full-time (2 women), 1 part-time/adjunct (0 women). *Students:* 21 full-time (2 women), 13 part-time (2 women); includes 6 minority (2 Hispanic/Latino; 4 Two or more races, non-Hispanic/Latino), 6 international. Average age 27. 101 applicants, 75% accepted, 17 enrolled. In 2019, 8 master's awarded. *Degree requirements:* For master's, comprehensive exam, thesis optional. *Entrance requirements:* For master's, GRE General Test, minimum GPA of 2.75, writing sample, major or minor in philosophy. Additional exam requirements/recommendations for international students: required—TOEFL (minimum score 550 paper-based). *Application deadline:* For fall admission, 3/1 priority date for domestic students, 5/1 for international students; for spring admission, 11/1 for domestic students, 10/1 for international students. Applications are processed on a rolling basis. Application fee: $40. Electronic applications accepted. *Financial support:* In 2019–20, 13 teaching assistantships with full tuition reimbursements were awarded; fellowships with full tuition reimbursements, research assistantships with full tuition reimbursements, Federal Work-Study, scholarships/grants, tuition waivers (full), and unspecified assistantships also available. Support available to part-time students. Financial award applicants required to submit FAFSA. *Unit head:* Dr. Jason Hanna, Chair, 815-753-6299, Fax: 815-753-6302. *Application contact:* Dr. Lenny Clapp, Graduate Advisor, 815-753-6414, E-mail: lclapp@niu.edu.
Website: http://www.niu.edu/phil/

Northwestern University, The Graduate School, Judd A. and Marjorie Weinberg College of Arts and Sciences, Department of Philosophy, Evanston, IL 60208. Offers ancient philosophy (PhD); philosophy (PhD). *Degree requirements:* For doctorate, 2 foreign languages, thesis/dissertation. *Entrance requirements:* For doctorate, GRE General Test, sample of written work. Additional exam requirements/recommendations for international students: required—TOEFL. Electronic applications accepted.

The Ohio State University, Graduate School, College of Arts and Sciences, Division of Arts and Humanities, Department of Philosophy, Columbus, OH 43210. Offers MA, PhD. Terminal master's awarded for partial completion of doctoral program. *Entrance requirements:* For doctorate, GRE General Test, writing sample. Additional exam requirements/recommendations for international students: required—TOEFL (minimum score 600 paper-based; 100 iBT); recommended—IELTS (minimum score 8). Electronic applications accepted.

Ohio University, Graduate College, College of Arts and Sciences, Department of Philosophy, Athens, OH 45701-2979. Offers MA. *Program availability:* Part-time. *Degree requirements:* For master's, thesis. *Entrance requirements:* For master's, 28 hours in philosophy including logic, ancient and modern philosophy; minimum GPA of 3.0; sample of philosophical writing. Additional exam requirements/recommendations for international students: required—TOEFL (minimum score 550 paper-based; 80 iBT) or IELTS (minimum score 6.5). Electronic applications accepted.

Oklahoma State University, College of Arts and Sciences, Department of Philosophy, Stillwater, OK 74078. Offers MA. *Faculty:* 10 full-time (1 woman), 1 part-time/adjunct (0 women). *Students:* 6 full-time (1 woman), 4 part-time (0 women); includes 2 minority (1 Hispanic/Latino; 1 Two or more races, non-Hispanic/Latino), 1 international. Average age 26. 11 applicants, 91% accepted, 6 enrolled. In 2019, 8 master's awarded. *Entrance requirements:* For master's, GRE, 2 letters of recommendation. Additional exam requirements/recommendations for international students: required—TOEFL (minimum score 550 paper-based; 79 iBT). *Application deadline:* For fall admission, 3/1 priority date for international students; for spring admission, 8/1 priority date for international students. Applications are processed on a rolling basis. Application fee: $40 ($75 for international students). Electronic applications accepted. *Expenses: Tuition, area resident:* Full-time $4148.10; part-time $2765.40 per credit hour. Tuition, state resident: full-time $4148.10; part-time $2765.40 per credit hour. Tuition, nonresident: full-time $15,775; part-time $10,516.80 per credit hour. *International tuition:* $15,775.20 full-time. *Required fees:* $2196.90; $122.05 per credit hour. Tuition and fees vary according to course load, campus/location and program. *Financial support:* In 2019–20, 10 teaching assistantships (averaging $1,857 per year) were awarded; research assistantships, career-related internships or fieldwork, Federal Work-Study, scholarships/grants, health care benefits, tuition waivers (partial), and unspecified assistantships also available. Support available to part-time students. Financial award application deadline: 3/1; financial award applicants required to submit FAFSA. *Unit head:* Dr. Scott Gelfand, Department Head, 405-744-9238, Fax: 405-744-4635, E-mail: scott.gelfand@okstate.edu. *Application contact:* Dr. Sheryl Tucker, Vice Prof/Dean/Prof, 405-744-6368, E-mail: gradi@okstate.edu.
Website: http://philosophy.okstate.edu

Old Dominion University, College of Arts and Letters, Institute for the Humanities, Norfolk, VA 23529. Offers arts and entrepreneurship (Certificate); cultural and human geography (MA); cultural studies (MA); gender and sexuality studies (MA); health, communication and culture (Certificate); media and popular culture studies (MA); philosophy and religious studies (MA); social justice and entrepreneurship (Certificate); visual studies (MA); world cultures (MA). *Program availability:* Part-time, evening/weekend. *Degree requirements:* For master's, thesis optional, project. *Entrance requirements:* For master's, GRE General Test, minimum GPA of 3.25. Electronic applications accepted.

Open University, Graduate Programs, Milton Keynes, United Kingdom. Offers business (MBA); education (M Ed); engineering (M Eng); history (MA); music (MA); philosophy (MA).

Penn State University Park, Graduate School, College of the Liberal Arts, Department of Philosophy, University Park, PA 16802. Offers MA, PhD.

Princeton University, Graduate School, Department of Classics, Princeton, NJ 08544-1019. Offers classical and Hellenic studies (PhD); classical philosophy (PhD); history (the ancient world) (PhD); literature and philology (PhD). *Degree requirements:* For doctorate, thesis/dissertation. *Entrance requirements:* For doctorate, GRE General Test, sample of written work. Additional exam requirements/recommendations for international students: required—TOEFL (minimum score 600 paper-based). Electronic applications accepted.

Princeton University, Graduate School, Department of Philosophy, Princeton, NJ 08544-1019. Offers classical philosophy (PhD); philosophy (PhD); philosophy of science (PhD). *Degree requirements:* For doctorate, variable foreign language requirement, thesis/dissertation. *Entrance requirements:* For doctorate, GRE General Test, sample of written work. Additional exam requirements/recommendations for international students: required—TOEFL (minimum score 600 paper-based). Electronic applications accepted.

Princeton University, Graduate School, Department of Politics, Princeton, NJ 08544-1019. Offers political philosophy (PhD); politics (PhD). *Degree requirements:* For doctorate, comprehensive exam, thesis/dissertation, teaching experience. *Entrance requirements:* For doctorate, GRE General Test, sample of written work, letters of recommendation. Additional exam requirements/recommendations for international students: required—TOEFL (minimum score 600 paper-based). Electronic applications accepted.

Purdue University, Graduate School, College of Liberal Arts, Department of Philosophy, West Lafayette, IN 47907. Offers MA, PhD. *Program availability:* Part-time. *Faculty:* 19 full-time (3 women). *Students:* 27 full-time (7 women), 8 part-time (1 woman); includes 2 minority (both Hispanic/Latino), 8 international. Average age 29. 52 applicants, 25% accepted, 6 enrolled. In 2019, 4 master's, 3 doctorates awarded. Terminal master's awarded for partial completion of doctoral program. *Degree requirements:* For master's, thesis optional; for doctorate, comprehensive exam, thesis/dissertation. *Entrance requirements:* For master's and doctorate, GRE General Test, minimum undergraduate GPA of 3.4 or equivalent. Additional exam requirements/recommendations for international students: required—TOEFL (minimum score 550 paper-based; 100 iBT). *Application deadline:* For fall admission, 1/2 for domestic and international students; for spring admission, 12/1 for domestic and international students. Applications are processed on a rolling basis. Application fee: $60 ($75 for international students). Electronic applications accepted. *Financial support:* Fellowships with tuition reimbursements, research assistantships with tuition reimbursements, and teaching assistantships with tuition reimbursements available. Support available to part-time students. Financial award application deadline: 1/15; financial award applicants required to submit FAFSA. *Unit head:* Christopher L. Yeomans, Head, 765-494-4275, E-mail: cyeomans@purdue.edu. *Application contact:* Vickie Sanders, Graduate Contact, 765-494-4275, E-mail: sanders@purdue.edu.
Website: http://www.cla.purdue.edu/philosophy/

Purdue University, Graduate School, Program in Philosophy and Literature, West Lafayette, IN 47907. Offers PhD. *Students:* 1 full-time (0 women), 2 part-time (1 woman). Average age 32. 3 applicants. *Degree requirements:* For doctorate, one foreign language, comprehensive exam, thesis/dissertation. *Entrance requirements:* For doctorate, GRE, master's degree in either English, philosophy or foreign languages. Additional exam requirements/recommendations for international students: required—TOEFL. *Application deadline:* For fall admission, 1/10 priority date for domestic students, 1/10 for international students. Application fee: $60 ($75 for international students). Electronic applications accepted. *Financial support:* In 2019–20, teaching assistantships (averaging $1,415 per year) were awarded; fellowships and research assistantships also available. *Unit head:* Venetria K. Patton, Head of the Graduate Program, 765-496-9629, E-mail: vpatton@purdue.edu. *Application contact:* Brandi Plantenga, Graduate Contact, 765-496-9629, E-mail: bplante@purdue.edu.
Website: http://www.cla.purdue.edu/phil-lit/graduate/

Queen's University at Kingston, School of Graduate Studies, Faculty of Arts and Science, Department of Philosophy, Kingston, ON K7L 3N6, Canada. Offers MA, PhD. *Program availability:* Part-time. *Degree requirements:* For master's, thesis; for doctorate, comprehensive exam, thesis/dissertation. *Entrance requirements:* Additional exam requirements/recommendations for international students: required—TOEFL. Electronic applications accepted.

Regis College, Graduate and Professional Programs, Toronto, ON M5S 2Z5, Canada. Offers eastern Christian studies (Certificate); Ignatian spirituality (Diploma); ministry (D Min); ministry and spirituality (MAMS); philosophical studies (Diploma); retreat direction (Certificate); sacred theology (STM, STD, STB, STL); spiritual direction (Diploma); theological studies (MTS, Diploma); theology (M Div, MA, Th M, PhD, Th D); M Div/MA. *Accreditation:* ATS (one or more programs are accredited). Terminal master's awarded for partial completion of doctoral program. *Degree requirements:* For master's, 2 foreign languages, thesis; for doctorate, 3 foreign languages, comprehensive exam, thesis/dissertation. *Entrance requirements:* For doctorate, minimum GPA of 3.7. Additional exam requirements/recommendations for international students: required—TOEFL (minimum score 580 paper-based; 93 iBT), TWE (minimum score 5).

Rice University, Graduate Programs, School of Humanities, Department of Philosophy, Houston, TX 77251-1892. Offers MA, PhD. Terminal master's awarded for partial completion of doctoral program. *Degree requirements:* For master's, one foreign language; for doctorate, one foreign language, comprehensive exam, thesis/dissertation. *Entrance requirements:* For master's and doctorate, GRE General Test, minimum GPA of 3.0. Additional exam requirements/recommendations for international students: required—TOEFL (minimum score 600 paper-based; 90 iBT). Electronic applications accepted.

Roosevelt University, Graduate Division, College of Arts and Sciences, Department of History and Philosophy, Chicago, IL 60605. Offers history (MA). *Program availability:* Part-time, evening/weekend. Electronic applications accepted.

Rutgers University - New Brunswick, Graduate School-New Brunswick, Program in Philosophy, Piscataway, NJ 08854-8097. Offers PhD. *Degree requirements:* For doctorate, comprehensive exam, thesis/dissertation. *Entrance requirements:* For doctorate, GRE General Test, writing sample. Electronic applications accepted.

Saint Charles Borromeo Seminary, Overbrook, School of Theological Studies, Program in Philosophical Studies, Wynnewood, PA 19096. Offers MA. *Program availability:* Part-time, evening/weekend. *Degree requirements:* For master's, comprehensive exam. *Entrance requirements:* For master's, 18 undergraduate credits in theology and/or philosophy or the equivalent. Additional exam requirements/recommendations for international students: required—TOEFL.

Philosophy

Saint Louis University, Graduate Programs, College of Arts and Sciences, Department of Philosophy, St. Louis, MO 63103. Offers MA, MA-R, PhD. *Program availability:* Part-time. *Degree requirements:* For master's, one foreign language, thesis, comprehensive oral and written exams; for doctorate, 2 foreign languages, thesis/dissertation, preliminary exams, comprehensive oral and written exams. *Entrance requirements:* For master's, GRE General Test, letters of recommendation, resume, writing sample, interview; for doctorate, GRE General Test, letters of recommendation, resumé, writing sample, interview, goal statement, transcripts. Additional exam requirements/ recommendations for international students: required—TOEFL (minimum score 550 paper-based). Electronic applications accepted.

Saint Mary's University, Faculty of Arts, Department of Philosophy, Halifax, NS B3H 3C3, Canada. Offers MA. *Degree requirements:* For master's, thesis. *Entrance requirements:* For master's, 3 letters of recommendation, 2 samples of written work. Additional exam requirements/recommendations for international students: required—TOEFL.

San Diego State University, Graduate and Research Affairs, College of Arts and Letters, Department of Philosophy, San Diego, CA 92182. Offers MA. *Program availability:* Part-time. *Entrance requirements:* For master's, GRE General Test. Additional exam requirements/recommendations for international students: required—TOEFL. Electronic applications accepted.

San Francisco State University, Division of Graduate Studies, College of Liberal and Creative Arts, Department of Philosophy, San Francisco, CA 94132-1722. Offers MA. *Program availability:* Part-time. *Application deadline:* Applications are processed on a rolling basis. *Expenses: Tuition, area resident:* Full-time $7176; part-time $4164 per year. Tuition, state resident: full-time $7176; part-time $4164 per year. Tuition, nonresident: full-time $16,680; part-time $396 per unit. *International tuition:* $16,680 full-time. *Required fees:* $1524; $1524 per unit. $762 per semester. Tuition and fees vary according to degree level and program. *Unit head:* Dr. Asta Sveinsdottir, Chair, 415-338-3136, Fax: 415-338-6159, E-mail: asta@sfsu.edu. *Application contact:* Dr. Alice Sowaal, Graduate Coordinator, 415-338-3136, Fax: 415-338-6159, E-mail: asowaal@sfsu.edu.
Website: http://philosophy.sfsu.edu/

San Jose State University, Program in Philosophy, San Jose, CA 95192-0096. Offers MA. *Faculty:* 4 full-time (2 women), 2 part-time/adjunct (1 woman). *Students:* 4 full-time (1 woman), 13 part-time (1 woman); includes 7 minority (1 Asian, non-Hispanic/Latino; 6 Hispanic/Latino), 2 international. Average age 34. 13 applicants, 77% accepted, 5 enrolled. In 2019, 7 master's awarded. *Application deadline:* For fall admission, 6/1 for domestic students, 5/1 for international students; for spring admission, 11/1 for domestic and international students. Applications are processed on a rolling basis. Application fee: $70. Electronic applications accepted. *Expenses: Tuition, area resident:* Full-time $7176; part-time $4164 per credit hour. Tuition, state resident: full-time $7176; part-time $4164 per credit hour. Tuition, nonresident: full-time $7176; part-time $4165 per credit hour. *International tuition:* $7176 full-time. *Required fees:* $2110; $2110. *Financial support:* In 2019–20, 7 students received support, including 1 fellowship (averaging $3,000 per year); scholarships/grants also available. Financial award application deadline: 5/1; financial award applicants required to submit FAFSA. *Unit head:* Janet D. Stemwedel, Department Chair, 408-924-4470, E-mail: janet.stemwedel@sjsu.edu. *Application contact:* Carlos A. Sanchez, Professor, E-mail: carlos.sanchez@sjsu.edu.
Website: http://www.sjsu.edu/philosophy/

Simon Fraser University, Office of Graduate Studies and Postdoctoral Fellows, Faculty of Arts and Social Sciences, Department of Philosophy, Burnaby, BC V5A 1S6, Canada. Offers MA, PhD. *Degree requirements:* For master's, thesis or alternative; for doctorate, comprehensive exam, thesis/dissertation. *Entrance requirements:* For master's, minimum GPA of 3.0 (on scale of 4.33) or 3.33 based on last 60 credits of undergraduate courses; for doctorate, minimum GPA of 3.5 (on scale of 4.33). Additional exam requirements/recommendations for international students: recommended—TOEFL (minimum score 580 paper-based; 93 iBT), IELTS (minimum score 7), TWE (minimum score 5). Electronic applications accepted.

Southeastern Baptist Theological Seminary, Graduate and Professional Programs, Wake Forest, NC 27587. Offers advanced biblical studies (M Div); Christian education (M Div, MACE); Christian ethics (PhD); Christian ministry (M Div); Christian planting (M Div); church music (MACM); counseling (MACO); evangelism (PhD); language (M Div); ministry (D Min); New Testament (PhD); Old Testament (PhD); philosophy (PhD); theology (Th M, PhD); women's studies (M Div). *Accreditation:* ACIPE; ATS (one or more programs are accredited). *Degree requirements:* For master's, thesis (for some programs), oral exam; for doctorate, thesis/dissertation, fieldwork. *Entrance requirements:* For master's, Cooperative English Test, minimum GPA of 2.0, M Div or equivalent (Th M); for doctorate, GRE General Test or MAT, Cooperative English Test, M Div or equivalent, 3 years of professional experience.

The Southern Baptist Theological Seminary, School of Theology, Louisville, KY 40280-0004. Offers applied theology (D Min); biblical and theological studies (M Div); biblical counseling (M Div, MA, D Min); biblical spirituality (D Min); Christian ministry (M Div); expository preaching (D Min); pastoral studies (M Div); theological studies (MA); theology (Th M, PhD); worldview and apologetics (M Div). *Program availability:* Part-time, evening/weekend, online learning. *Degree requirements:* For master's, 2 foreign languages, thesis; for doctorate, 4 foreign languages, thesis/dissertation. *Entrance requirements:* For master's, GRE General Test, MAT, M Div; for doctorate, GRE General Test, MAT, interview, M Div, field essay. Additional exam requirements/ recommendations for international students: required—TOEFL, TWE.

Southern Evangelical Seminary, Graduate Programs, Matthews, NC 28105. Offers apologetics (MA, D Min, Certificate); Christian education (MA); church ministry (MA, Certificate); divinity (Certificate), including apologetics (M Div, Certificate); Islamic studies (MA, Certificate); Jewish studies (MA); philosophy (MA); philosophy of religion (PhD); religion (MA); theology (M Div), including apologetics (M Div, Certificate), Biblical studies; youth ministry (MA). *Program availability:* Part-time, evening/weekend, online learning. *Degree requirements:* For master's, thesis (for some programs); for doctorate, 2 foreign languages, comprehensive exam (for some programs), thesis/dissertation. *Entrance requirements:* Additional exam requirements/recommendations for international students: required—TOEFL (minimum score 600 paper-based). *Expenses: Tuition:* Full-time $24,000; part-time $12,000 per year. *Required fees:* $600; $300 per semester. $150 per semester.

Southern Illinois University Carbondale, Graduate School, College of Liberal Arts, Department of Philosophy, Carbondale, IL 62901-4701. Offers MA, PhD. *Degree requirements:* For master's, one foreign language, thesis; for doctorate, 2 foreign languages, thesis/dissertation. *Entrance requirements:* For master's, GRE General Test, minimum GPA of 2.7; for doctorate, GRE General Test, minimum GPA of 3.25. Additional exam requirements/recommendations for international students: required—TOEFL.

Stanford University, School of Humanities and Sciences, Department of Philosophy, Stanford, CA 94305-2004. Offers MA, PhD. *Expenses: Tuition:* Full-time $52,479; part-time $34,110 per unit. *Required fees:* $672; $224 per quarter. Tuition and fees vary according to program and student level.
Website: http://philosophy.stanford.edu/

Stony Brook University, State University of New York, Graduate School, College of Arts and Sciences, Department of Philosophy, Stony Brook, NY 11794. Offers MA, PhD, Advanced Certificate. *Program availability:* Evening/weekend. *Faculty:* 15 full-time (3 women), 4 part-time/adjunct (2 women). *Students:* 57 full-time (13 women), 9 part-time (3 women); includes 14 minority (1 Black or African American, non-Hispanic/Latino; 4 Asian, non-Hispanic/Latino; 5 Hispanic/Latino; 4 Two or more races, non-Hispanic/ Latino), 13 international. Average age 32. 137 applicants, 38% accepted, 17 enrolled. In 2019, 6 master's, 3 doctorates awarded. *Degree requirements:* For doctorate, one foreign language, thesis/dissertation. *Entrance requirements:* For master's and doctorate, GRE General Test. Additional exam requirements/recommendations for international students: required—TOEFL (minimum score 90 iBT). *Application deadline:* For fall admission, 1/15 for domestic students; for spring admission, 10/1 for domestic students. Application fee: $100. Electronic applications accepted. *Expenses:* Contact institution. *Financial support:* In 2019–20, 3 fellowships, 22 teaching assistantships were awarded; research assistantships also available. *Unit head:* Dr. Robert Cresae, Chair, 631-632-7570, Fax: 631-632-7522, E-mail: robert.crease@stonybrook.edu. *Application contact:* Dr. Robert Cresae, Chair, 631-632-7570, Fax: 631-632-7522, E-mail: robert.crease@stonybrook.edu.
Website: http://www.sunysb.edu/philosophy/

Syracuse University, College of Arts and Sciences, Department of Philosophy, Syracuse, NY 13244. Offers MA, PhD. *Entrance requirements:* For master's and doctorate, GRE, transcripts from previous institutions, three letters of recommendation, personal statement, writing sample. Additional exam requirements/recommendations for international students: required—TOEFL (minimum score 100 iBT). Electronic applications accepted.

Teachers College, Columbia University, Department of Arts and Humanities, New York, NY 10027. Offers applied linguistics (MA, Ed D); art and art education (Ed M, MA, Ed D, Ed DCT); arts administration (MA); bilingual and bicultural education (MA); global competence (Certificate); history and education (Ed D, PhD); music and music education (Ed DCT); philosophy and education (MA, Ed D, PhD); social studies education (Ed M, PhD); teaching English to speakers of other languages (Ed M); teaching of English and English education (Ed M, MA, Ed D, PhD), including English education (Ed M, Ed D, PhD), teaching of English (MA); teaching of social studies (MA); TESOL (MA, Ed D). *Faculty:* 26 full-time (17 women). *Students:* 426 full-time (358 women), 390 part-time (259 women); includes 222 minority (44 Black or African American, non-Hispanic/Latino; 2 American Indian or Alaska Native, non-Hispanic/ Latino; 94 Asian, non-Hispanic/Latino; 65 Hispanic/Latino; 17 Two or more races, non-Hispanic/Latino), 252 international. 957 applicants, 66% accepted, 375 enrolled. *Unit head:* Dr. ZhaoHong Han, Department Chair, E-mail: zhh2@tc.columbia.edu. *Application contact:* Kelly Sutton-Skinner, Director of Admissions and New Student Enrollment, 212-678-3710, E-mail: kms2237@tc.columbia.edu.

Temple University, College of Liberal Arts, Department of Philosophy, Philadelphia, PA 19122-6096. Offers MA, PhD. *Program availability:* Part-time. *Faculty:* 14 full-time (4 women), 2 part-time/adjunct (0 women). *Students:* 32 full-time (10 women), 2 part-time (0 women); includes 6 minority (1 Asian, non-Hispanic/Latino; 3 Hispanic/Latino; 2 Two or more races, non-Hispanic/Latino), 5 international. 29 applicants, 41% accepted, 7 enrolled. In 2019, 1 master's, 4 doctorates awarded. *Degree requirements:* For master's, thesis optional; for doctorate, one foreign language, thesis/dissertation. *Entrance requirements:* For master's, GRE, statement of goals, resume, writing sample, 3 letters of recommendation; for doctorate, GRE, statement of goals, writing sample, 3 letters of recommendation. Additional exam requirements/recommendations for international students: required—TOEFL, IELTS, PTE, one of three is required. Application fee: $60. Electronic applications accepted. *Financial support:* Fellowships, teaching assistantships, career-related internships or fieldwork, Federal Work-Study, and health care benefits available. Financial award applicants required to submit FAFSA. *Unit head:* Kristin Gjesdal, Chair, 215-204-1742, E-mail: kgjesdal@temple.edu. *Application contact:* Sonia Lawson, Coordinator, 215-204-1742, Fax: 215-204-0200, E-mail: slawson@temple.edu.
Website: http://www.cla.temple.edu/philosophy/

Texas A&M University, College of Liberal Arts, Department of Philosophy and Humanities, College Station, TX 77843. Offers philosophy (MA). *Program availability:* Part-time. *Faculty:* 19. *Students:* 22 full-time (4 women), 7 part-time (3 women); includes 7 minority (2 Black or African American, non-Hispanic/Latino; 1 Asian, non-Hispanic/ Latino; 4 Hispanic/Latino), 4 international. Average age 32. 5 applicants, 100% accepted, 5 enrolled. In 2019, 2 master's, 2 doctorates awarded. Terminal master's awarded for partial completion of doctoral program. *Degree requirements:* For master's, thesis optional; for doctorate, comprehensive exam, thesis/dissertation. *Entrance requirements:* For master's, GRE General Test, letter of recommendation, resume, writing sample; for doctorate, GRE General Test, letters of recommendation, resume, writing sample. Additional exam requirements/recommendations for international students: required—TOEFL (minimum score 550 paper-based; 80 iBT), IELTS (minimum score 6), PTE (minimum score 53). *Application deadline:* For fall admission, 1/15 for domestic and international students. Application fee: $65 ($90 for international students). Electronic applications accepted. *Expenses:* Contact institution. *Financial support:* In 2019–20, 116 students received support, including 18 fellowships with tuition reimbursements available (averaging $21,614 per year), 3 research assistantships with tuition reimbursements available (averaging $13,645 per year), 51 teaching assistantships with tuition reimbursements available (averaging $12,529 per year); career-related internships or fieldwork, institutionally sponsored loans, scholarships/ grants, traineeships, health care benefits, tuition waivers (full and partial), and unspecified assistantships also available. Support available to part-time students. Financial award application deadline: 3/15; financial award applicants required to submit FAFSA. *Unit head:* Dr. Theodore George, Associate Professor and Department Head, 979-845-5605, E-mail: t-george@tamu.edu. *Application contact:* Dr. Kenny Easwaran, Director of Graduate Program, 979-847-6128, E-mail: easwaran@tamu.edu.
Website: http://philosophy.tamu.edu

Texas State University, The Graduate College, College of Liberal Arts, Applied Philosophy and Ethics Program, San Marcos, TX 78666. Offers MA. *Program availability:* Part-time. *Degree requirements:* For master's, comprehensive exam, thesis optional. *Entrance requirements:* For master's, baccalaureate degree from regionally-accredited university with minimum GPA of 3.0 on last 60 undergraduate semester hours, statement of purpose, 2 letters of recommendation, writing sample. Additional exam requirements/recommendations for international students: required—TOEFL (minimum score 550 paper-based; 78 iBT), IELTS (minimum score 6). Electronic applications accepted.

Texas Tech University, Graduate School, College of Arts and Sciences, Department of Philosophy, Lubbock, TX 79409-3092. Offers MA. *Program availability:* Part-time. *Faculty:* 11 full-time (3 women), 1 part-time/adjunct (0 women). *Students:* 16 full-time (1 woman), 2 part-time (both women); includes 4 minority (all Hispanic/Latino), 5 international. Average age 29. 22 applicants, 59% accepted, 5 enrolled. In 2019, 8 master's awarded. *Degree requirements:* For master's, thesis or alternative. *Entrance requirements:* For master's, GRE General Test. Additional exam requirements/ recommendations for international students: required—TOEFL (minimum score 550

paper-based; 79 iBT). *Application deadline:* For fall admission, 6/1 priority date for domestic students, 1/15 priority date for international students; for spring admission, 9/1 priority date for domestic students, 6/15 priority date for international students. Applications are processed on a rolling basis. Application fee: $65. Electronic applications accepted. *Expenses:* Contact institution. *Financial support:* In 2019–20, 18 students received support, including 11 fellowships (averaging $2,652 per year), 18 teaching assistantships (averaging $11,925 per year); research assistantships, Federal Work-Study, and scholarships/grants also available. Financial award application deadline: 4/15; financial award applicants required to submit FAFSA. *Unit head:* Dr. Mark O. Webb, Professor and Chair, 806-742-3275, Fax: 806-742-0730, E-mail: mark.webb@ttu.edu. *Application contact:* Dr. Daniel O. Nathan, Director of Graduate Studies, 806-742-0373 Ext. 340, Fax: 806-742-0730, E-mail: daniel.nathan@ttu.edu.
Website: www.philosophy.ttu.edu/

Trinity Western University, School of Graduate Studies, Master of Arts in Interdisciplinary Humanities, Langley, BC V2Y 1Y1, Canada. Offers general humanities (MAIH); specialized (MAIH), including English, history, philosophy. *Program availability:* Part-time. *Degree requirements:* For master's, thesis or alternative, 30 semester hours. *Entrance requirements:* For master's, Strong undergraduate degree in humanities or English, history or philosophy. Additional exam requirements/recommendations for international students: required—TOEFL (minimum score 105 iBT), IELTS (minimum score 7.5), DuoLingo. *Application deadline:* Applications are processed on a rolling basis. Electronic applications accepted. *Expenses:* Contact institution. *Financial support:* Fellowships, research assistantships, teaching assistantships, career-related internships or fieldwork, scholarships/grants, and unspecified assistantships available. Support available to part-time students. Financial award application deadline: 4/1. *Unit head:* Dr. Bruce Shelvey, Director, E-mail: bruce.shelvey@twu.ca. *Application contact:* Phil Kay, Director, Graduate Admissions, 604-513-2121 Ext. 3444, E-mail: phil.kay@twu.ca.
Website: http://www.twu.ca/academics/

Tufts University, Graduate School of Arts and Sciences, Department of Philosophy, Medford, MA 02155. Offers MA. *Degree requirements:* For master's, comprehensive exam, departmental qualifying exam. *Entrance requirements:* For master's, GRE General Test, writing sample. Additional exam requirements/recommendations for international students: required—TOEFL (minimum score 550 paper-based; 80 iBT), IELTS (minimum score 6.5). Electronic applications accepted. *Expenses:* Contact institution.

Tulane University, School of Liberal Arts, Department of Philosophy, New Orleans, LA 70118-5669. Offers MA, PhD. *Degree requirements:* For master's, thesis or alternative; for doctorate, one foreign language, thesis/dissertation. *Entrance requirements:* For master's, GRE General Test, minimum B average in undergraduate course work; for doctorate, GRE General Test. Additional exam requirements/recommendations for international students: required—TOEFL. Electronic applications accepted. *Expenses: Tuition:* Full-time $57,004; part-time $3167 per credit hour. *Required fees:* $2086; $44.50 per credit hour. $80 per term. Tuition and fees vary according to course load, degree level and program.

Universidad Autonoma de Guadalajara, Graduate Programs, Guadalajara, Mexico. Offers administrative law and justice (LL M); advertising and corporate communications (MA); architecture (M Arch); business (MBA); computational science (MCC); education (Ed M, Ed D); English-Spanish translation (MA); entrepreneurship and management (MBA); integrated management of digital animation (MA); international business (MIB); international corporate law (LL M); Internet technologies (MS); manufacturing systems (MMS); occupational health (MS); philosophy (MA, PhD); power electronics (MS); quality systems (MQS); renewable energy (MS); social evaluation of projects (MBA); strategic market research (MBA); tax law (MA); teaching mathematics (MA).

Université de Montréal, Faculty of Arts and Sciences, Department of Philosophy, Montréal, QC H3C 3J7, Canada. Offers MA, PhD. *Degree requirements:* For master's, 2 foreign languages, thesis; for doctorate, thesis/dissertation, general exam. Electronic applications accepted.

Université de Sherbrooke, Faculty of Letters and Human Sciences, Department of Human Sciences, Sherbrooke, QC J1K 2R1, Canada. Offers history (MA); philosophy (MA). *Degree requirements:* For master's, thesis. *Entrance requirements:* For master's, minimum GPA of 2.75.

Université de Sherbrooke, Faculty of Theology and Religious Studies, Sherbrooke, QC J1K 2R1, Canada. Offers applied ethics (Diploma); human science of religions (MA); intercultural training (Diploma); philosophy (MA, PhD); spiritual anthropology (Diploma); theology (MA, PhD, Diploma). *Program availability:* Part-time, evening/weekend, online learning. Terminal master's awarded for partial completion of doctoral program. *Entrance requirements:* For master's, bachelor's degree in related discipline; for doctorate, master's degree in related discipline.

Université du Québec à Montréal, Graduate Programs, Program in Philosophy, Montréal, QC H3C 3P8, Canada. Offers MA, PhD. *Program availability:* Part-time. *Degree requirements:* For master's, thesis; for doctorate, thesis/dissertation. *Entrance requirements:* For master's, appropriate bachelor's degree or equivalent, proficiency in French; for doctorate, appropriate master's degree or equivalent, proficiency in French.

Université du Québec à Trois-Rivières, Graduate Programs, Program in Philosophy, Trois-Rivières, QC G9A 5H7, Canada. Offers MA, PhD. *Program availability:* Part-time. *Degree requirements:* For master's, thesis; for doctorate, thesis/dissertation. *Entrance requirements:* For master's, appropriate bachelor's degree, proficiency in French; for doctorate, appropriate master's degree, proficiency in French.

University at Albany, State University of New York, College of Arts and Sciences, Department of Philosophy, Albany, NY 12222-0001. Offers MA, PhD. *Program availability:* Blended/hybrid learning. *Faculty:* 11 full-time (3 women), 4 part-time/adjunct (1 woman). *Students:* 10 full-time (2 women), 21 part-time (5 women); includes 5 minority (1 Black or African American, non-Hispanic/Latino; 2 American Indian or Alaska Native, non-Hispanic/Latino; 2 Asian, non-Hispanic/Latino), 2 international. 16 applicants, 88% accepted, 3 enrolled. In 2019, 2 master's awarded. *Degree requirements:* For master's, one foreign language, thesis; for doctorate, thesis/dissertation. *Entrance requirements:* For master's, GRE General Test, transcripts of all schools attended, statement of background and goals, departmental questionnaire, resume, names and contact information for 3 recommenders; for doctorate, GRE General Test. Additional exam requirements/recommendations for international students: required—TOEFL (minimum score 550 paper-based). *Application deadline:* For fall admission, 2/15 for domestic students, 5/1 for international students; for spring admission, 11/15 for domestic students, 11/1 for international students. Applications are processed on a rolling basis. Application fee: $75. Electronic applications accepted. *Expenses: Tuition, area resident:* Full-time $11,530; part-time $480 per credit hour. Tuition, nonresident: full-time $23,530; part-time $980 per credit hour. *International tuition:* $23,530 full-time. *Required fees:* $2185; $96 per credit hour. Part-time tuition and fees vary according to course load and program. *Financial support:* Fellowships available. Financial award application deadline: 3/15. *Unit head:* P. D. Magnus, Chair, 518-442-4250, Fax: 518-442-4259, E-mail: pmagnus@albany.edu. *Application contact:* Michael DeRensis, Director, Graduate Admissions, 518-442-3980, Fax: 518-442-3922, E-mail: graduate@albany.edu.
Website: https://www.albany.edu/philosophy/

University at Buffalo, the State University of New York, Graduate School, College of Arts and Sciences, Department of Philosophy, Buffalo, NY 14260-4150. Offers MA, PhD. *Faculty:* 18 full-time (3 women), 2 part-time/adjunct (1 woman). *Students:* 33 full-time (3 women), 3 part-time (2 women); includes 6 minority (3 Asian, non-Hispanic/Latino; 3 Native Hawaiian or other Pacific Islander, non-Hispanic/Latino), 7 international. Average age 28. 21 applicants, 67% accepted, 8 enrolled. In 2019, 4 master's, 2 doctorates awarded. Terminal master's awarded for partial completion of doctoral program. *Degree requirements:* For master's, variable foreign language requirement, thesis or alternative; for doctorate, variable foreign language requirement, comprehensive exam, thesis/dissertation. *Entrance requirements:* For master's and doctorate, GRE General Test, minimum GPA of 3.0. Additional exam requirements/recommendations for international students: required—TOEFL (minimum score 550 paper-based; 79 iBT). *Application deadline:* For fall admission, 1/4 for domestic and international students. Applications are processed on a rolling basis. Application fee: $75. Electronic applications accepted. *Expenses: Tuition, area resident:* Full-time $11,310; part-time $471 per credit hour. Tuition, state resident: full-time $11,310; part-time $471 per credit hour. Tuition, nonresident: full-time $23,100; part-time $963 per credit hour. *International tuition:* $23,100 full-time. *Required fees:* $2820. *Financial support:* In 2019–20, 19 students received support, including 1 fellowship with full tuition reimbursement available (averaging $7,500 per year), 19 teaching assistantships with full tuition reimbursements available (averaging $20,000 per year); institutionally sponsored loans, tuition waivers (full), and unspecified assistantships also available. Financial award application deadline: 1/15; financial award applicants required to submit FAFSA. *Unit head:* Dr. Neil Williams, Chair, 716-645-0161, Fax: 716-645-6139, E-mail: new@buffalo.edu. *Application contact:* Dr. Lewis Powell, Director of Graduate Studies, 716-645-0148, Fax: 716-645-6139, E-mail: lewispow@buffalo.edu.
Website: www.philosophy@buffalo.edu

University of Alberta, Faculty of Graduate Studies and Research, Department of Philosophy, Edmonton, AB T6G 2E1, Canada. Offers MA, PhD. *Program availability:* Part-time. *Degree requirements:* For master's, thesis; for doctorate, thesis/dissertation. *Entrance requirements:* Additional exam requirements/recommendations for international students: required—TOEFL (minimum score 550 paper-based). Electronic applications accepted.

The University of Arizona, College of Social and Behavioral Sciences, Department of Philosophy, Tucson, AZ 85721. Offers MA, PhD. *Program availability:* Part-time. Terminal master's awarded for partial completion of doctoral program. *Degree requirements:* For master's, exams, qualifying paper; for doctorate, thesis/dissertation, preliminary exams. *Entrance requirements:* For doctorate, GRE General Test, 3 letters of recommendation, writing sample. Additional exam requirements/recommendations for international students: required—TOEFL (minimum score 550 paper-based; 79 iBT). Electronic applications accepted.

University of Arkansas, Graduate School, J. William Fulbright College of Arts and Sciences, Department of Philosophy, Fayetteville, AR 72701. Offers MA, PhD. *Program availability:* Part-time. *Students:* 12 full-time (2 women), 6 part-time (1 woman); includes 1 minority (Black or African American, non-Hispanic/Latino). 14 applicants, 71% accepted. In 2019, 1 master's, 2 doctorates awarded. *Degree requirements:* For master's, thesis; for doctorate, 2 foreign languages, thesis/dissertation. *Application deadline:* For fall admission, 8/1 for domestic students, 4/1 for international students; for spring admission, 12/1 for domestic students, 10/1 for international students; for summer admission, 4/15 for domestic students, 3/1 for international students. Applications are processed on a rolling basis. Application fee: $60. Electronic applications accepted. *Financial support:* In 2019–20, 1 research assistantship, 10 teaching assistantships were awarded; fellowships with tuition reimbursements, career-related internships or fieldwork, and Federal Work-Study also available. Support available to part-time students. Financial award application deadline: 4/1; financial award applicants required to submit FAFSA. *Unit head:* Dr. Edward H. Minar, Department Chair, 479-575-8712, E-mail: eminar@uark.edu. *Application contact:* Dr. Erick Funkhouser, Graduate Coordinator, 479-575-7441, E-mail: efunkho@uark.edu.
Website: https://fulbright.uark.edu/departments/philosophy/

The University of British Columbia, Faculty of Arts, Department of Philosophy, Vancouver, BC V6T 1Z1, Canada. Offers MA, PhD. *Accreditation:* NCATE. *Program availability:* Part-time. *Degree requirements:* For master's, thesis (for some programs); for doctorate, comprehensive exam, thesis/dissertation. *Entrance requirements:* For master's, bachelor's degree with minimum GPA of 3.0 in 3rd- and 4th-year coursework; 3 credits in formal logic; 6 credits at the upper-level in the history of philosophy and in metaphysics, epistemology, or philosophy; 3 credits at the upper-level in ethics or value theory; for doctorate, MA, honors BA with first class standing, or BA with first class standing in philosophy. Additional exam requirements/recommendations for international students: required—TOEFL, IELTS, Michigan English Language Assessment Battery (minimum score 81). Electronic applications accepted. *Expenses:* Contact institution.

University of Calgary, Faculty of Graduate Studies, Faculty of Arts, Program in Philosophy, Calgary, AB T2N 1N4, Canada. Offers MA, PhD. *Program availability:* Part-time. *Degree requirements:* For master's, comprehensive exam (for some programs), thesis (for some programs); for doctorate, thesis/dissertation, candidacy exam. *Entrance requirements:* Additional exam requirements/recommendations for international students: required—TOEFL (minimum score 550 paper-based). Electronic applications accepted.

University of California, Berkeley, Graduate Division, College of Letters and Science, Department of Philosophy, Berkeley, CA 94720. Offers PhD. *Degree requirements:* For doctorate, thesis/dissertation, qualifying exam. *Entrance requirements:* For doctorate, GRE General Test, minimum GPA of 3.0, writing sample, 3 letters of recommendation. Electronic applications accepted.

University of California, Davis, Graduate Studies, Program in Philosophy, Davis, CA 95616. Offers MA, PhD. Terminal master's awarded for partial completion of doctoral program. *Degree requirements:* For doctorate, thesis/dissertation. *Entrance requirements:* For master's and doctorate, GRE General Test, minimum GPA of 3.0. Additional exam requirements/recommendations for international students: required—TOEFL (minimum score 550 paper-based). Electronic applications accepted.

University of California, Irvine, School of Humanities, Department of Philosophy, Irvine, CA 92697. Offers MA, PhD. *Students:* 29 full-time (7 women); includes 6 minority (2 Asian, non-Hispanic/Latino; 2 Hispanic/Latino; 2 Two or more races, non-Hispanic/Latino), 5 international. Average age 29. 82 applicants, 11% accepted, 5 enrolled. In 2019, 1 master's, 5 doctorates awarded. *Entrance requirements:* For master's and doctorate, GRE General Test, minimum GPA of 3.0. Additional exam requirements/recommendations for international students: required—TOEFL (minimum score 550 paper-based). *Application deadline:* For fall admission, 1/15 priority date for domestic students, 1/15 for international students. Applications are processed on a rolling basis. Application fee: $120 ($140 for international students). Electronic applications accepted. *Financial support:* Fellowships, teaching assistantships with partial tuition reimbursements, institutionally sponsored loans, traineeships, health care benefits, and unspecified assistantships available. Financial award application deadline: 3/1; financial award applicants required to submit FAFSA. *Unit head:* Aaron James, Department Chair, E-mail: aaron.james@uci.edu. *Application contact:* Kirsten S. Alonso, Department Coordinator, 949-824-6525, Fax: 949-824-6520, E-mail: kalonso@uci.edu. Website: http://www.hnet.uci.edu/philosophy/

University of California, Irvine, School of Social Sciences, Department of Logic and Philosophy of Science, Irvine, CA 92697. Offers philosophy (PhD). *Students:* 45 full-time (13 women), 1 part-time (0 women); includes 7 minority (1 Asian, non-Hispanic/Latino; 3 Hispanic/Latino; 3 Two or more races, non-Hispanic/Latino), 18 international. Average age 27. 52 applicants, 38% accepted, 12 enrolled. In 2019, 3 doctorates awarded. *Entrance requirements:* For doctorate, GRE, minimum GPA of 3.0. Additional exam requirements/recommendations for international students: required—TOEFL (minimum score 550 paper-based). *Application deadline:* For fall admission, 1/15 for domestic and international students. Application fee: $120 ($140 for international students). *Financial support:* Fellowships, research assistantships with full tuition reimbursements, teaching assistantships, institutionally sponsored loans, traineeships, health care benefits, and unspecified assistantships available. Financial award application deadline: 3/1. *Unit head:* Simon Huttegger, Department Chair, 949-824-3220, E-mail: shuttegg@uci.edu. *Application contact:* James Owen Weatherall, Director of Graduate Studies, 949-824-6656, E-mail: weatherj@uci.edu. Website: http://www.lps.uci.edu/

University of California, Los Angeles, Graduate Division, College of Letters and Science, Department of Philosophy, Los Angeles, CA 90095. Offers MA, PhD. Terminal master's awarded for partial completion of doctoral program. *Degree requirements:* For master's, one foreign language, comprehensive exam; for doctorate, one foreign language, thesis/dissertation, oral and written qualifying exams, 3 quarters of teaching experience. *Entrance requirements:* For doctorate, GRE General Test, bachelor's degree; minimum undergraduate GPA of 3.0 (or its equivalent if letter grade system not used); writing sample. Additional exam requirements/recommendations for international students: required—TOEFL. Electronic applications accepted.

University of California, Riverside, Graduate Division, Department of Philosophy, Riverside, CA 92521-0102. Offers MA, PhD. Terminal master's awarded for partial completion of doctoral program. *Degree requirements:* For master's, logic exam, professional paper; for doctorate, one foreign language, thesis/dissertation, logic exam, proposition papers, qualifying exams. *Entrance requirements:* For master's, GRE General Test, minimum GPA of 3.2; for doctorate, GRE General Test, master's degree in philosophy, minimum GPA of 3.2. Additional exam requirements/recommendations for international students: required—TOEFL (minimum score 550 paper-based; 80 iBT). Electronic applications accepted.

University of California, San Diego, Graduate Division, Department of Philosophy, La Jolla, CA 92093. Offers PhD. *Students:* 49 full-time (16 women), 1 (woman) part-time. 240 applicants, 11% accepted, 8 enrolled. In 2019, 6 doctorates awarded. *Degree requirements:* For doctorate, thesis/dissertation, 3 quarters of teaching assistantship; original essay. *Entrance requirements:* For doctorate, GRE General Test, writing sample. Additional exam requirements/recommendations for international students: required—TOEFL (minimum score 550 paper-based; 80 iBT), IELTS (minimum score 7). *Application deadline:* For fall admission, 1/8 for domestic students. Application fee: $105 ($125 for international students). Electronic applications accepted. *Financial support:* Fellowships, teaching assistantships, and scholarships/grants available. Financial award applicants required to submit FAFSA. *Unit head:* Jonathan Cohen, Chair, 858-534-6812, E-mail: joncohen@aardvark.ucsd.edu. *Application contact:* Becky Burrola, Graduate Coordinator, 858-534-3076, E-mail: rburrola@ucsd.edu. Website: http://philosophy.ucsd.edu/

University of California, Santa Barbara, Graduate Division, College of Letters and Sciences, Division of Humanities and Fine Arts, Department of Philosophy, Santa Barbara, CA 93106-9580. Offers PhD, MA/PhD. Terminal master's awarded for partial completion of doctoral program. *Degree requirements:* For doctorate, thesis/dissertation. *Entrance requirements:* For doctorate, GRE. Additional exam requirements/recommendations for international students: required—TOEFL (minimum score 550 paper-based; 80 iBT), IELTS (minimum score 7). Electronic applications accepted.

University of California, Santa Cruz, Division of Graduate Studies, Division of Humanities, Department of Philosophy, Santa Cruz, CA 95064. Offers MA, PhD. *Degree requirements:* For doctorate, thesis/dissertation, qualifying exam. *Entrance requirements:* For master's, GRE, 3 letters of recommendation; for doctorate, GRE, official transcripts, 3 letters of recommendation. Additional exam requirements/recommendations for international students: required—TOEFL (minimum score 550 paper-based; 83 iBT); recommended—IELTS (minimum score 8). Electronic applications accepted.

University of Chicago, Division of the Humanities, Department of Philosophy, Chicago, IL 60637. Offers ancient philosophy (PhD); philosophy (PhD). Terminal master's awarded for partial completion of doctoral program. *Degree requirements:* For doctorate, variable foreign language requirement, thesis/dissertation. *Entrance requirements:* For doctorate, GRE General Test, 15-20 page writing sample, statement of purpose, 3 letters of recommendation, transcripts for all previous degrees and institutions attended. Additional exam requirements/recommendations for international students: required—TOEFL (minimum score 104 iBT), IELTS (minimum score 7). Electronic applications accepted.

University of Chicago, Division of the Humanities, Master of Arts Program in the Humanities, Chicago, IL 60637. Offers art history (MA); cinema and media studies (MA); classic languages (MA); comparative literature (MA); creative writing (MA); cultural policy studies (MA); digital humanities (MA); East Asian languages and civilizations (MA); English language and literature (MA); gender and sexuality studies (MA); Germanic studies (MA); linguistics (MA); music (MA); near Eastern languages and civilizations (MA); philosophy (MA); poetics (MA); race, politics and culture (MA); Romance languages and literatures (MA); Slavic languages and literatures (MA); South Asian languages and civilizations (MA); theater and performance studies (MA). *Degree requirements:* For master's, thesis. *Entrance requirements:* For master's, GRE General Test, 10-15 page writing sample, statement of purpose, 3 letters of recommendation, transcripts for all previous degrees and institutions attended. Additional exam requirements/recommendations for international students: required—TOEFL (minimum score 104 iBT), IELTS (minimum score 7). Electronic applications accepted. *Expenses:* Contact institution.

University of Cincinnati, Graduate School, McMicken College of Arts and Sciences, Department of Philosophy, Cincinnati, OH 45221. Offers MA, PhD. Terminal master's awarded for partial completion of doctoral program. *Degree requirements:* For master's, thesis; for doctorate, one foreign language, comprehensive exam, thesis/dissertation. *Entrance requirements:* For master's and doctorate, GRE General Test, BA in philosophy or equivalent experience. Additional exam requirements/recommendations for international students: required—TOEFL. Electronic applications accepted.

University of Colorado Boulder, Graduate School, College of Arts and Sciences, Department of Philosophy, Boulder, CO 80309. Offers MA, PhD. Terminal master's awarded for partial completion of doctoral program. *Degree requirements:* For master's, comprehensive exam, thesis; for doctorate, one foreign language, thesis/dissertation, logic and qualifying papers, oral exam. *Entrance requirements:* For master's, GRE General Test, writing sample, minimum undergraduate GPA of 2.75; for doctorate, GRE General Test. Electronic applications accepted. Application fee is waived when completed online.

University of Connecticut, Graduate School, College of Liberal Arts and Sciences, Department of Philosophy, Storrs, CT 06269. Offers MA, PhD. Terminal master's awarded for partial completion of doctoral program. *Degree requirements:* For master's, comprehensive exam; for doctorate, 2 foreign languages, thesis/dissertation. *Entrance requirements:* For master's and doctorate, GRE General Test. Additional exam requirements/recommendations for international students: required—TOEFL (minimum score 550 paper-based). Electronic applications accepted.

University of Florida, Graduate School, College of Liberal Arts and Sciences, Department of Philosophy, Gainesville, FL 32611. Offers MA, PhD. *Program availability:* Part-time. *Degree requirements:* For doctorate, one foreign language, comprehensive exam, thesis/dissertation. *Entrance requirements:* For master's and doctorate, GRE General Test, minimum GPA of 3.0. Additional exam requirements/recommendations for international students: required—TOEFL (minimum score 550 paper-based; 80 iBT), IELTS (minimum score 6). Electronic applications accepted.

University of Georgia, Franklin College of Arts and Sciences, Department of Philosophy, Athens, GA 30602. Offers MA, PhD. *Program availability:* Part-time. *Degree requirements:* For master's, one foreign language, thesis; for doctorate, one foreign language, thesis/dissertation. *Entrance requirements:* For master's and doctorate, GRE General Test. Additional exam requirements/recommendations for international students: required—TOEFL. Electronic applications accepted.

University of Guelph, Office of Graduate and Postdoctoral Studies, College of Arts, Department of Philosophy, Guelph, ON N1G 2W1, Canada. Offers MA, PhD. *Program availability:* Part-time. *Degree requirements:* For master's, thesis (for some programs); for doctorate, one foreign language, thesis/dissertation. *Entrance requirements:* For master's, minimum B- average during previous 2 years of course work; for doctorate, minimum B average. Additional exam requirements/recommendations for international students: required—TOEFL (minimum score 550 paper-based). Electronic applications accepted.

University of Hawaii at Manoa, Office of Graduate Education, College of Arts and Humanities, Department of Philosophy, Honolulu, HI 96822. Offers MA, PhD. *Program availability:* Part-time. *Degree requirements:* For master's, variable foreign language requirement, thesis optional, culminating exam; for doctorate, variable foreign language requirement, comprehensive exam, thesis/dissertation, final oral presentation. *Entrance requirements:* For master's and doctorate, GRE General Test. Additional exam requirements/recommendations for international students: required—TOEFL (minimum score 600 paper-based; 100 iBT), IELTS (minimum score 7).

University of Houston, College of Liberal Arts and Social Sciences, Department of Philosophy, Houston, TX 77204. Offers MA. *Degree requirements:* For master's, thesis (for some programs), thesis or additional course requirements. *Entrance requirements:* For master's, GRE General Test, minimum of 18 hours of course work in philosophy; minimum GPA of 3.3 in last 60 hours. Additional exam requirements/recommendations for international students: required—TOEFL (minimum score 550 paper-based; 79 iBT). Electronic applications accepted.

University of Idaho, College of Graduate Studies, College of Letters, Arts and Social Sciences, Department of Politics and Philosophy, Moscow, ID 83844-2282. Offers political science (MA, PhD); public administration (MPA). *Faculty:* 5 full-time. *Students:* 25 full-time (13 women), 21 part-time (12 women). Average age 32. In 2019, 10 master's awarded. *Entrance requirements:* For master's, minimum GPA of 3.0. Additional exam requirements/recommendations for international students: required—TOEFL (minimum score 96 iBT). *Expenses:* Tuition, state resident: full-time $7753.80; part-time $502 per credit hour. Tuition, nonresident: full-time $26,990; part-time $1571 per credit hour. *Required fees:* $2122.20; $47 per credit hour. *Unit head:* Dr. Graham Hubbs, Chair, 208-885-6328, E-mail: politics-and-philosophy@uidaho.edu. *Application contact:* Dr. Graham Hubbs, Chair, 208-885-6328, E-mail: politics-and-philosophy@uidaho.edu. Website: https://www.uidaho.edu/class/politics-and-philosophy

University of Illinois at Chicago, College of Liberal Arts and Sciences, Department of Philosophy, Chicago, IL 60607-7128. Offers MA, PhD. Terminal master's awarded for partial completion of doctoral program. *Degree requirements:* For doctorate, thesis/dissertation, preliminary exams. *Entrance requirements:* For master's and doctorate, minimum GPA of 2.75. Additional exam requirements/recommendations for international students: required—TOEFL. Electronic applications accepted.

University of Illinois at Urbana-Champaign, Graduate College, College of Liberal Arts and Sciences, Department of Philosophy, Champaign, IL 61820. Offers MA, PhD, PhD/JD.

The University of Iowa, Graduate College, College of Liberal Arts and Sciences, Department of Philosophy, Iowa City, IA 52242-1316. Offers PhD. *Degree requirements:* For doctorate, comprehensive exam, thesis/dissertation. *Entrance requirements:* For doctorate, GRE General Test, minimum GPA of 3.0. Additional exam requirements/recommendations for international students: required—TOEFL (minimum score 550 paper-based; 81 iBT). Electronic applications accepted.

The University of Kansas, Graduate Studies, College of Liberal Arts and Sciences, Department of Philosophy, Lawrence, KS 66045. Offers MA, PhD. *Program availability:* Part-time. *Students:* 30 full-time (6 women), 2 part-time (1 woman); includes 9 minority (4 Asian, non-Hispanic/Latino; 3 Hispanic/Latino; 2 Two or more races, non-Hispanic/Latino), 9 international. Average age 30. 27 applicants, 44% accepted, 4 enrolled. In 2019, 3 master's, 1 doctorate awarded. Terminal master's awarded for partial completion of doctoral program. *Entrance requirements:* For master's and doctorate, GRE, curriculum vitae or resume, statement of purpose, writing sample, three letters of recommendation, official academic transcripts. Additional exam requirements/recommendations for international students: required—TOEFL, IELTS. *Application deadline:* For fall admission, 5/1 for domestic and international students; for spring admission, 12/1 for domestic and international students. Application fee: $65 ($85 for international students). Electronic applications accepted. *Expenses:* Tuition, state resident: full-time $9989. Tuition, nonresident: full-time $23,950. *International tuition:* $23,950 full-time. *Required fees:* $984; $81.99 per credit hour. Tuition and fees vary according to course load, campus/location and program. *Financial support:* Fellowships, teaching assistantships, Federal Work-Study, scholarships/grants, and unspecified assistantships available. Financial award application deadline: 1/1. *Unit head:* Dale Dorsey, Chair, 785-864-2139, E-mail: ddorsey@ku.edu. *Application contact:* Jared Nietfeld, Graduate Program Coordinator, 785-864-0482, E-mail: nietfeld@ku.edu. Website: http://www.philosophy.ku.edu

University of Kentucky, Graduate School, College of Arts and Sciences, Program in Philosophy, Lexington, KY 40506-0032. Offers MA, PhD. *Degree requirements:* For master's, one foreign language, comprehensive exam, thesis; for doctorate, one foreign language, comprehensive exam, thesis/dissertation. *Entrance requirements:* For master's, GRE General Test, minimum undergraduate GPA of 2.75; for doctorate, GRE General Test, minimum graduate GPA of 3.0. Additional exam requirements/recommendations for international students: required—TOEFL (minimum score 550 paper-based). Electronic applications accepted.

University of Lethbridge, School of Graduate Studies, Lethbridge, AB T1K 3M4, Canada. Offers addictions counseling (M Sc); agricultural biotechnology (M Sc); agricultural studies (M Sc, MA); anthropology (MA); archaeology (M Sc, MA); art (MA, MFA); biochemistry (M Sc); biological sciences (M Sc); biomolecular science (PhD); biosystems and biodiversity (PhD); Canadian studies (MA); chemistry (M Sc); computer science (M Sc); computer science and geographical information science (M Sc); counseling (MC); counseling psychology (M Ed); dramatic arts (MA); earth, space, and physical science (PhD); economics (MA); education (MA, PhD); educational leadership (M Ed); English (MA); environmental science (M Sc); evolution and behavior (PhD); exercise science (M Sc); French (MA); French/German (MA); French/Spanish (MA); general education (M Ed); geography (M Sc, MA); German (MA); health sciences (M Sc); individualized multidisciplinary (M Sc, MA); kinesiology (M Sc, MA); management (M Sc), including accounting, finance, human resource management and labor relations, information systems, international management, marketing, policy and strategy; mathematics (M Sc); music (M Mus, MA); Native American studies (MA); neuroscience (M Sc, PhD); new media (MA, MFA); nursing (M Sc, MN); philosophy (MA); physics (M Sc); political science (MA); psychology (M Sc, MA); religious studies (MA); sociology (MA); theatre and dramatic arts (MFA); theoretical and computational science (PhD); urban and regional studies (MA); women and gender studies (MA). *Program availability:* Part-time, evening/weekend. *Degree requirements:* For master's, thesis (for some programs); for doctorate, comprehensive exam, thesis/dissertation. *Entrance requirements:* For master's, GMAT (for M Sc in management), bachelor's degree in related field, minimum GPA of 3.0 during previous 20 graded semester courses, 2 years' teaching or related experience (M Ed); for doctorate, master's degree, minimum graduate GPA of 3.5. Additional exam requirements/recommendations for international students: required—TOEFL (minimum score 580 paper-based; 93 iBT). Electronic applications accepted.

University of Louisville, Graduate School, College of Arts and Sciences, Department of Philosophy, Louisville, KY 40292-0001. Offers humanities (MA, PhD). *Program availability:* Part-time. *Faculty:* 12 full-time (2 women), 9 part-time/adjunct (5 women). *Degree requirements:* For master's, one foreign language, thesis or alternative. *Entrance requirements:* For master's, GRE General Test, Two letters of reference, official transcripts. Additional exam requirements/recommendations for international students: required—TOEFL (minimum score 550 paper-based; 79 iBT), IELTS can be used in place of the TOEFL; recommended—IELTS (minimum score 6.5). *Application deadline:* Applications are processed on a rolling basis. Application fee: $65. Electronic applications accepted. *Expenses: Tuition, area resident:* Full-time $13,000; part-time $723 per credit hour. Tuition, state resident: full-time $13,000; part-time $723 per credit hour. Tuition, nonresident: full-time $27,114; part-time $1507 per credit hour. *International tuition:* $27,114 full-time. *Required fees:* $196. Tuition and fees vary according to program and reciprocity agreements. *Financial support:* In 2019–20, 1 fellowship with full tuition reimbursement (averaging $12,000 per year), 1 teaching assistantship with full tuition reimbursement (averaging $12,000 per year) were awarded; research assistantships, health care benefits, and unspecified assistantships also available. *Unit head:* Dr. Avery Kolers, Chairperson, 502-852-0453, E-mail: avery.kolers@louisville.edu. *Application contact:* Dr. Stephen Hanson, Director of Graduate Studies, 502-852-0451, E-mail: stephen.hanson@louisville.edu.
Website: http://louisville.edu/philosophy

The University of Manchester, School of Social Sciences, Manchester, United Kingdom. Offers ethnographic documentary (M Phil); interdisciplinary study of culture (PhD); philosophy (PhD); politics (PhD); social anthropology (PhD); social anthropology with visual media (PhD); social change (PhD); social statistics (PhD); sociology (PhD); visual anthropology (M Phil).

University of Manitoba, Faculty of Graduate Studies, Faculty of Arts, Department of Philosophy, Winnipeg, MB R3T 2N2, Canada. Offers MA. *Degree requirements:* For master's, variable foreign language requirement, thesis or alternative.

University of Maryland, College Park, Academic Affairs, College of Arts and Humanities, Department of Philosophy, College Park, MD 20742. Offers MA, PhD. *Degree requirements:* For master's, thesis optional; for doctorate, thesis/dissertation, 2 semesters of undergraduate teaching, qualification in symbolic logic. *Entrance requirements:* For master's, GRE General Test, minimum GPA of 3.0, philosophy paper, writing sample, 3 letters of recommendation; for doctorate, GRE General Test, minimum GPA of 3.0, philosophy paper, writing sample. Electronic applications accepted.

University of Massachusetts Amherst, Graduate School, College of Humanities and Fine Arts, Department of Philosophy, Amherst, MA 01003. Offers MA, PhD. *Program availability:* Part-time. Terminal master's awarded for partial completion of doctoral program. *Degree requirements:* For master's, thesis optional; for doctorate, comprehensive exam, thesis/dissertation. *Entrance requirements:* For master's and doctorate, GRE General Test, writing sample, 3 letters of recommendation. Additional exam requirements/recommendations for international students: required—TOEFL (minimum score 550 paper-based; 80 iBT), IELTS (minimum score 6.5). Electronic applications accepted.

University of Memphis, Graduate School, College of Arts and Sciences, Department of Philosophy, Memphis, TN 38152. Offers MA, PhD. *Program availability:* Part-time, evening/weekend. *Students:* 17 full-time (5 women), 14 part-time (7 women); includes 9 minority (5 Black or African American, non-Hispanic/Latino; 3 Hispanic/Latino; 1 Two or more races, non-Hispanic/Latino), 1 international. Average age 32. 15 applicants, 47% accepted, 4 enrolled. In 2019, 2 master's, 3 doctorates awarded. Terminal master's awarded for partial completion of doctoral program. *Degree requirements:* For master's, comprehensive exam, thesis optional, 30-33 hours of class work; for doctorate, variable foreign language requirement, comprehensive exam, thesis/dissertation, 72 hours of class work. *Entrance requirements:* For master's, GRE General Test, minimum GPA of 2.5, 18 hours of undergraduate course work in philosophy, 3 letters of recommendation, writing sample; for doctorate, GRE General Test, minimum GPA of 3.0, bachelor's degree in philosophy, 3 letters of recommendation, writing sample. Additional exam requirements/recommendations for international students: required—TOEFL (minimum score 550 paper-based; 79 iBT). *Application deadline:* For fall admission, 1/5 priority date for domestic students. Applications are processed on a rolling basis. Application fee: $35 ($60 for international students). Electronic applications accepted. *Expenses: Tuition, area resident:* Full-time $9216; part-time $512 per credit hour. Tuition, state resident: full-time $9216; part-time $512 per credit hour. Tuition, nonresident: full-time $12,672; part-time $704 per credit hour. *International tuition:* $16,128 full-time. *Required fees:* $1530; $85 per credit hour. Tuition and fees vary according to program. *Financial support:* Fellowships with full tuition reimbursements, research assistantships with full tuition reimbursements, teaching assistantships with full tuition reimbursements, Federal Work-Study, scholarships/grants, tuition waivers (full), and unspecified assistantships available. Financial award application deadline: 2/1; financial award applicants required to submit FAFSA. *Unit head:* Dr. Remy Debes, Chair, 901-678-3352, Fax: 901-678-4365, E-mail: rdebes@memphis.edu. *Application contact:* Dr. Mary Beth Mader, Director of Graduate Admissions, E-mail: mmader@memphis.edu.
Website: http://www.memphis.edu/philosophy/

University of Miami, Graduate School, College of Arts and Sciences, Department of Philosophy, Coral Gables, FL 33124. Offers MA, PhD. *Program availability:* Part-time. Terminal master's awarded for partial completion of doctoral program. *Degree requirements:* For master's, thesis or alternative; for doctorate, comprehensive exam, thesis/dissertation. *Entrance requirements:* For master's, GRE General Test; for doctorate, GRE General Test, minimum GPA of 3.0, 3 letters of recommendation, writing sample. Additional exam requirements/recommendations for international students: required—TOEFL. Electronic applications accepted.

University of Michigan, Rackham Graduate School, College of Literature, Science, and the Arts, Department of Philosophy, Ann Arbor, MI 48109-1003. Offers AM, PhD. Terminal master's awarded for partial completion of doctoral program. *Degree requirements:* For doctorate, thesis/dissertation, oral defense of dissertation. *Entrance requirements:* For master's and doctorate, 3 letters of recommendation, writing sample. Additional exam requirements/recommendations for international students: required—TOEFL (minimum score 560 paper-based; 84 iBT), MELAB, ECPE. Electronic applications accepted. *Expenses:* Contact institution.

University of Minnesota, Twin Cities Campus, Graduate School, College of Liberal Arts, Department of Philosophy, Minneapolis, MN 55455-0213. Offers MA, PhD. *Program availability:* Part-time. Terminal master's awarded for partial completion of doctoral program. *Degree requirements:* For master's, comprehensive exam, thesis or 3 papers; oral exam; for doctorate, comprehensive exam, thesis/dissertation. *Entrance requirements:* For master's and doctorate, GRE. Additional exam requirements/recommendations for international students: required—TOEFL (minimum score 550 paper-based), IELTS (minimum score 6.5), or Michigan English Language Assessment Battery (minimum score 80). Electronic applications accepted.

University of Mississippi, Graduate School, College of Liberal Arts, University, MS 38677. Offers anthropology (MA); biology (MS, PhD); chemistry (MS, DA, PhD); creative writing (MFA); documentary expression (MFA); economics (MA, PhD); English (MA, PhD); experimental psychology (PhD); history (MA, PhD); mathematics (MS, PhD); modern languages (MA); music (MM); philosophy (MA); physics (MA, MS, PhD); political science (MA, PhD); Southern studies (MA); studio art (MFA). *Program availability:* Part-time. *Faculty:* 481 full-time (215 women), 71 part-time/adjunct (40 women). *Students:* 509 full-time (258 women), 55 part-time (21 women); includes 89 minority (40 Black or African American, non-Hispanic/Latino; 13 Asian, non-Hispanic/Latino; 25 Hispanic/Latino; 11 Two or more races, non-Hispanic/Latino), 157 international. Average age 29. In 2019, 119 master's, 51 doctorates awarded. *Degree requirements:* For doctorate, thesis/dissertation. *Entrance requirements:* For master's, GRE General Test, minimum GPA of 3.0; for doctorate, GRE General Test. Additional exam requirements/recommendations for international students: required—TOEFL. *Application deadline:* Applications are processed on a rolling basis. Application fee: $50. Electronic applications accepted. *Expenses:* Tuition, state resident: full-time $8718; part-time $484.25 per credit hour. Tuition, nonresident: full-time $24,990; part-time $1388.25 per credit hour. *Required fees:* $100; $4.16 per credit hour. *Financial support:* Fellowships, research assistantships, teaching assistantships, career-related internships or fieldwork, Federal Work-Study, institutionally sponsored loans, scholarships/grants, and unspecified assistantships available. Financial award application deadline: 3/1; financial award applicants required to submit FAFSA. *Unit head:* Dr. Lee Michael Cohen, Dean, 662-915-7177, Fax: 662-915-5792, E-mail: libarts@olemiss.edu. *Application contact:* Tameka Smith, Graduate Activities Specialist for Admissions, 662-915-7474, Fax: 662-915-7577, E-mail: gschool@olemiss.edu.
Website: ventress@olemiss.edu

University of Missouri, Office of Research and Graduate Studies, College of Arts and Science, Department of Philosophy, Columbia, MO 65211. Offers MA, PhD. Terminal master's awarded for partial completion of doctoral program. *Entrance requirements:* For master's and doctorate, GRE General Test (minimum score 650 verbal, 700 quantitative), minimum GPA of 3.0, 3.9 in major. Additional exam requirements/recommendations for international students: required—TOEFL.

University of Missouri–St. Louis, College of Arts and Sciences, Department of Philosophy, St. Louis, MO 63121. Offers MA. *Program availability:* Part-time, evening/weekend. *Entrance requirements:* For master's, writing sample, 3 letters of recommendation, personal statement. Additional exam requirements/recommendations for international students: required—TOEFL (minimum score 550 paper-based; 79 iBT), IELTS (minimum score 6.5). Electronic applications accepted. *Expenses: Tuition, area resident:* Full-time $9005.40; part-time $6003.60 per credit hour. Tuition, state resident: full-time $9005.40; part-time $6003.60 per credit hour. Tuition, nonresident: full-time $22,108; part-time $14,738.40 per credit hour. *International tuition:* $22,108 full-time. Tuition and fees vary according to course load.

University of Montana, Graduate School, College of Humanities and Sciences, Department of Philosophy, Missoula, MT 59812. Offers MA. *Degree requirements:* For master's, thesis or additional course work/professional paper. *Entrance requirements:* For master's, GRE General Test. Additional exam requirements/recommendations for international students: required—TOEFL (minimum score 525 paper-based).

University of Nebraska–Lincoln, Graduate College, College of Arts and Sciences, Department of Philosophy, Lincoln, NE 68588. Offers MA, PhD. *Degree requirements:* For master's, thesis optional; for doctorate, comprehensive exam, thesis/dissertation. *Entrance requirements:* For master's and doctorate, GRE General Test, writing sample. Additional exam requirements/recommendations for international students: required—TOEFL (minimum score 600 paper-based). Electronic applications accepted.

University of Nevada, Reno, Graduate School, College of Liberal Arts, Department of Philosophy, Reno, NV 89557. Offers MA. *Degree requirements:* For master's, thesis optional. *Entrance requirements:* For master's, GRE General Test, minimum GPA of 2.75. Additional exam requirements/recommendations for international students: required—TOEFL (minimum score 500 paper-based; 61 iBT), IELTS (minimum score 6). Electronic applications accepted.

University of New Mexico, Graduate Studies, College of Arts and Sciences, Program in Philosophy, Albuquerque, NM 87131-2039. Offers MA, PhD. *Program availability:* Part-time. Terminal master's awarded for partial completion of doctoral program. *Degree requirements:* For master's, thesis (for some programs); for doctorate, one foreign language, comprehensive exam, thesis/dissertation. *Entrance requirements:* For master's and doctorate, GRE. Additional exam requirements/recommendations for international students: required—TOEFL. Electronic applications accepted. *Expenses:* Tuition, state resident: full-time $7633; part-time $972 per year. Tuition, nonresident: full-time $22,586; part-time $3840 per year. *International tuition:* $23,292 full-time. *Required fees:* $8608. Tuition and fees vary according to course level, course load, degree level, program and student level.

The University of North Carolina at Chapel Hill, Graduate School, College of Arts and Sciences, Department of Philosophy, Chapel Hill, NC 27599. Offers MA, PhD. *Degree* *requirements:* For master's, comprehensive exam, thesis; for doctorate, comprehensive exam, thesis/dissertation. *Entrance requirements:* For master's and doctorate, GRE General Test, minimum GPA of 3.0.

The University of North Carolina at Charlotte, College of Liberal Arts and Sciences, Department of Philosophy, Charlotte, NC 28223-0001. Offers applied ethics (Graduate Certificate); ethics and applied philosophy (MA). *Program availability:* Part-time. *Faculty:* 11 full-time (5 women). *Students:* 8 full-time (5 women), 6 part-time (1 woman); includes 1 minority (Black or African American, non-Hispanic/Latino). Average age 26. 15 applicants, 87% accepted, 10 enrolled. In 2019, 8 master's, 1 other advanced degree awarded. *Degree requirements:* For master's, capstone. *Entrance requirements:* For master's, statement of purpose outlining why applicant seeks admission to program; three recommendations; one official transcript from all colleges or universities attended; philosophical writing sample; for Graduate Certificate, personal statement outlining why the applicant seeks admission to the program; two academic letters of recommendation, in addition to the recommendation forms required by the graduate school, which address the student's philosophical skills and/or ethical reasoning; minimum undergraduate GPA of 2.75. Additional exam requirements/recommendations for international students: required—TOEFL (minimum score 557 paper-based; 83 iBT), IELTS (minimum score 6.5), TOEFL (minimum score 557 paper-based, 83 iBT) or IELTS (6.5). *Application deadline:* For fall admission, 2/1 priority date for domestic students. Applications are processed on a rolling basis. Application fee: $75. Electronic applications accepted. *Expenses:* Tuition, state resident: full-time $4337. Tuition, nonresident: full-time $17,771. *Required fees:* $3093. Tuition and fees vary according to course load, degree level and program. *Financial support:* In 2019–20, 4 students received support, including 4 teaching assistantships (averaging $4,000 per year); career-related internships or fieldwork, institutionally sponsored loans, scholarships/grants, unspecified assistantships, and administrative assistantships also available. Support available to part-time students. Financial award application deadline: 2/1; financial award applicants required to submit FAFSA. *Unit head:* Dr. Shannon Sullivan, Chair, 704-687-5418, E-mail: ssullivan@uncc.edu. *Application contact:* Kathy B. Giddings, Director of Graduate Admissions, 704-687-5503, Fax: 704-687-1668, E-mail: gradadm@uncc.edu.
Website: http://philosophy.uncc.edu/

University of North Florida, College of Arts and Sciences, Department of Philosophy, Jacksonville, FL 32224. Offers applied ethics (Graduate Certificate); practical philosophy and applied ethics (MA). *Program availability:* Part-time, evening/weekend. *Entrance requirements:* For master's, GRE General Test, minimum GPA of 3.0 in last 60 hours, 3 letters of recommendation, writing sample. Additional exam requirements/recommendations for international students: required—TOEFL (minimum score 500 paper-based; 61 iBT). Electronic applications accepted.

University of North Georgia, Department of History, Anthropology and Philosophy, Dahlonega, GA 30597. Offers history (MA), including American history, military history, world history. *Unit head:* Dr. Jeff Pardue, Department Head, 678-717-3867. *Application contact:* Cory Thornton, Director of Graduate Admissions, 706-867-2077, E-mail: cory.thornton@ung.edu.
Website: http://ung.edu/history-anthropology-philosophy/

University of North Texas, Toulouse Graduate School, Denton, TX 76203-5459. Offers accounting (MS); applied anthropology (MA, MS); applied behavior analysis (Certificate); applied geography (MA); applied technology and performance improvement (M Ed, MS); art education (MA); art history (MA); arts leadership (Certificate); audiology (Au D); behavior analysis (MS); behavioral science (PhD); biochemistry and molecular biology (MS); biology (MA, MS); biomedical engineering (MS); business analysis (MS); chemistry (MS); clinical health psychology (PhD); communication studies (MA, MS); computer engineering (MS); computer science (MS); counseling (M Ed, MS), including clinical mental health counseling (MS), college and university counseling, elementary school counseling, secondary school counseling; creative writing (MA); criminal justice (MS); curriculum and instruction (M Ed); decision sciences (MBA); design (MA, MFA), including fashion design (MFA), innovation studies, interior design (MFA); early childhood studies (MS); economics (MS); educational leadership (M Ed, Ed D); educational psychology (MS, PhD), including family studies (MS), gifted and talented (MS), human development (MS), learning and cognition (MS), research, measurement and evaluation (MS); electrical engineering (MS); emergency management (MPA); engineering technology (MS); English (MA); English as a second language (MA); environmental science (MS); finance (MBA, MS); financial management (MPA); French (MA); health services management (MBA); higher education (M Ed, Ed D); history (MA, MS); hospitality management (MS); human resources management (MPA); information science (MS); information systems (PhD); information technologies (MBA); interdisciplinary studies (MA, MS); international studies (MA); international sustainable tourism (MS); jazz studies (MM); journalism (MA, MJ, Graduate Certificate), including interactive and virtual digital communication (Graduate Certificate), narrative journalism (Graduate Certificate), public relations (Graduate Certificate); kinesiology (MS); linguistics (MA); local government management (MPA); logistics (PhD); logistics and supply chain management (MBA); long-term care, senior housing, and aging services (MA); management (PhD); marketing (MBA); mathematics (MA, MS); mechanical and energy engineering (MS, PhD); music (MA), including ethnomusicology, music theory, musicology, performance; music composition (PhD); music education (MM Ed, PhD); nonprofit management (MPA); operations and supply chain management (MBA); performance (MM, DMA); philosophy (MA); political science (MA); professional and technical communication (MA); radio, television and film (MA, MFA); rehabilitation counseling (Certificate); sociology (MA); Spanish (MA); special education (M Ed); speech-language pathology (MA); strategic management (MBA); studio art (MFA); teaching (M Ed); MBA/MS. *Program availability:* Part-time, evening/weekend, online learning. Terminal master's awarded for partial completion of doctoral program. *Degree requirements:* For master's, variable foreign language requirement, comprehensive exam (for some programs), thesis (for some programs); for doctorate, variable foreign language requirement, comprehensive exam (for some programs), thesis/dissertation; for other advanced degree, variable foreign language requirement, comprehensive exam (for some programs). *Entrance requirements:* For master's and doctorate, GRE, GMAT. Additional exam requirements/recommendations for international students: required—TOEFL (minimum score 550 paper-based; 79 iBT). Electronic applications accepted.

University of Notre Dame, The Graduate School, College of Arts and Letters, Division of Humanities, Department of Philosophy, Notre Dame, IN 46556. Offers PhD. *Degree requirements:* For doctorate, 2 foreign languages, thesis/dissertation, candidacy exam. *Entrance requirements:* For doctorate, GRE General Test. Additional exam requirements/recommendations for international students: required—TOEFL (minimum score 600 paper-based; 80 iBT). Electronic applications accepted.

University of Oklahoma, College of Arts and Sciences, Department of Philosophy, Norman, OK 73019. Offers MA, PhD. *Program availability:* Part-time. Terminal master's awarded for partial completion of doctoral program. *Degree requirements:* For doctorate, comprehensive exam, thesis/dissertation. *Entrance requirements:* Additional exam requirements/recommendations for international students: required—TOEFL (minimum score 79 iBT) or IELTS (minimum score 6.5). Electronic applications accepted. *Expenses:* Tuition, state resident: full-time $6583.20; part-time $274.30 per credit hour. Tuition, nonresident: full-time $21,242; part-time $885.10 per credit hour. *International tuition:* $21,242.40 full-time. *Required fees:* $1994.20; $72.55 per credit hour. $126.50 per semester. Tuition and fees vary according to course load and degree level.

University of Oregon, Graduate School, College of Arts and Sciences, Department of Philosophy, Eugene, OR 97403. Offers MA, PhD. Terminal master's awarded for partial completion of doctoral program. *Degree requirements:* For master's, one foreign language, thesis or alternative; for doctorate, one foreign language, thesis/dissertation. *Entrance requirements:* For master's and doctorate, GRE General Test. Additional exam requirements/recommendations for international students: required—TOEFL.

University of Ottawa, Faculty of Graduate and Postdoctoral Studies, Faculty of Arts, Department of Philosophy, Ottawa, ON K1N 6N5, Canada. Offers MA, PhD. *Degree requirements:* For master's, thesis or alternative; for doctorate, comprehensive exam, thesis/dissertation. *Entrance requirements:* For master's, honors degree or equivalent, minimum B average; for doctorate, master's degree, minimum B+ average. Electronic applications accepted.

University of Pennsylvania, School of Arts and Sciences, Graduate Group in Philosophy, Philadelphia, PA 19104-6304. Offers AM, PhD, JD/PhD. *Faculty:* 14 full-time (5 women), 2 part-time/adjunct (0 women). *Students:* 38 full-time (12 women); includes 6 minority (2 Black or African American, non-Hispanic/Latino; 1 Asian, non-Hispanic/Latino; 1 Hispanic/Latino; 2 Two or more races, non-Hispanic/Latino), 11 international. Average age 30. 196 applicants, 8% accepted, 12 enrolled. In 2019, 1 master's, 6 doctorates awarded. Terminal master's awarded for partial completion of doctoral program. Application fee: $90. *Financial support:* Application deadline: 12/1.
Website: http://www.sas.upenn.edu/graduate-division

University of Pittsburgh, Kenneth P. Dietrich School of Arts and Sciences, Department of Philosophy, Pittsburgh, PA 15260. Offers PhD. *Faculty:* 20 full-time (6 women). *Students:* 48 full-time (17 women); includes 10 minority (1 Black or African American, non-Hispanic/Latino; 4 Asian, non-Hispanic/Latino; 4 Hispanic/Latino; 1 Two or more races, non-Hispanic/Latino), 22 international. 137 applicants, 12% accepted, 7 enrolled. In 2019, 4 doctorates awarded. Terminal master's awarded for partial completion of doctoral program. *Degree requirements:* For doctorate, comprehensive exam, thesis/dissertation, minimum of 72 credit hours, proficiency in logic. *Entrance requirements:* For doctorate, CV, statement of purpose, 3 letters of recommendation, sample of written work. Additional exam requirements/recommendations for international students: required—TOEFL (minimum score 577 paper-based; 90 iBT), IELTS (minimum score 7). *Application deadline:* For fall admission, 1/10 for domestic and international students. Application fee: $75. Electronic applications accepted. *Financial support:* In 2019–20, 43 students received support, including 19 fellowships with full tuition reimbursements available (averaging $31,000 per year), 1 research assistantship with full tuition reimbursement available (averaging $27,000 per year), 22 teaching assistantships with full tuition reimbursements available (averaging $27,000 per year). Financial award application deadline: 1/10. *Unit head:* Dr. James Shaw, Professor, E-mail: jrs164@pitt.edu. *Application contact:* Kathleen Labuda, Graduate Administrator, 412-624-5774, E-mail: kjd66@pitt.edu.
Website: http://www.philosophy.pitt.edu/

University of Puerto Rico at Rio Piedras, College of Humanities, Department of Philosophy, San Juan, PR 00931-3300. Offers MA. *Program availability:* Part-time. *Degree requirements:* For master's, one foreign language, comprehensive exam, thesis. *Entrance requirements:* For master's, PAEG or GRE, interview, minimum GPA of 3.0, letter of recommendation (2).

University of Regina, Faculty of Graduate Studies and Research, Faculty of Arts, Department of Philosophy, Regina, SK S4S 0A2, Canada. Offers MA. *Program availability:* Part-time. *Faculty:* 9 full-time (2 women), 1 part-time/adjunct. *Students:* 1 full-time (0 women). Average age 30. *Degree requirements:* For master's, thesis. *Entrance requirements:* For master's, offered as Special case program: title of thesis, statement of purpose, list of course and schedule to form the program, list of supervisors and committee members, letter of support, letter of recommendation, post secondary transcripts. Additional exam requirements/recommendations for international students: required—TOEFL (minimum score 580 paper-based; 80 iBT), IELTS (minimum score 6.5), PTE (minimum score 59), other options are CANTEST, MELAB, CAEL and U of R ESL; GRE is required for Psychology. Application fee: $100. *Expenses: Tuition:* Full-time $6684 Canadian dollars. *Required fees:* $100 Canadian dollars; $3351.45 Canadian dollars per trimester. $1117.15 Canadian dollars per semester. Tuition and fees vary according to course level, course load, degree level and program. *Financial support:* Fellowships, research assistantships, teaching assistantships, career-related internships or fieldwork, Federal Work-Study, scholarships/grants, unspecified assistantships, and travel award and Graduate Scholarship Base funds available. Support available to part-time students. Financial award application deadline: 9/30. *Unit head:* Dr. David Elliott, Department Head, 306-585-4324, Fax: 306-585-4827, E-mail: david.elliott@uregina.ca. *Application contact:* Dr. Paul Simard Smith, Graduate coordinator, 306-585-4667, E-mail: paul.simard.smith@uregina.ca.
Website: http://www.uregina.ca/arts/philosophy-classics

University of Rochester, School of Arts and Sciences, Department of Philosophy, Rochester, NY 14627. Offers epistemology (PhD); ethics (PhD); history of ancient philosophy (PhD); history of modern philosophy (PhD); metaphysics (PhD); philosophy of language (PhD); philosophy of mind (PhD). *Faculty:* 11 full-time (5 women). *Students:* 21 full-time (3 women), 1 part-time (0 women); includes 6 minority (1 Asian, non-Hispanic/Latino; 4 Hispanic/Latino; 1 Two or more races, non-Hispanic/Latino), 1 international. Average age 33. 51 applicants, 27% accepted, 5 enrolled. In 2019, 2 doctorates awarded. Terminal master's awarded for partial completion of doctoral program. *Degree requirements:* For doctorate, comprehensive exam, thesis/dissertation, qualifying exam. *Entrance requirements:* For doctorate, GRE General Test, personal statement, transcript, three (or more) confidential letters of recommendation, writing sample in philosophy, list of prior philosophy courses as cover sheet for work sample. Additional exam requirements/recommendations for international students: recommended—TOEFL (minimum score 100 paper-based), IELTS (minimum score 7), TSE (minimum score 68). *Application deadline:* For fall admission, 1/15 for domestic and international students. Application fee: $60. Electronic applications accepted. *Financial support:* In 2019–20, 23 students received support, including 13 fellowships, 10 teaching assistantships; tuition waivers (full and partial) and Mandatory Health Fee provided also available. Financial award application deadline: 1/15. *Unit head:* Randall Curren, Professor and Chair, 585-275-8112, E-mail: randall.curren@rochester.edu. *Application contact:* Cheryl Kingston, Administrative Assistant, 585-275-4105, E-mail: cheryl.kingston@rochester.edu.
Website: https://www.sas.rochester.edu/phl/graduate/index.html

University of St. Thomas, Center for Thomistic Studies, Houston, TX 77006-4696. Offers philosophy (MA, PhD). *Faculty:* 7 full-time (1 woman), 1 part-time/adjunct (0 women). *Students:* 10 full-time (2 women), 29 part-time (4 women); includes 9 minority (2 Asian, non-Hispanic/Latino; 5 Hispanic/Latino; 2 Two or more races, non-Hispanic/Latino), 4 international. Average age 35. 23 applicants, 96% accepted, 6 enrolled. In 2019, 2 master's awarded. *Entrance requirements:* For master's and doctorate, GRE. Additional exam requirements/recommendations for international students: required—

TOEFL (minimum score 80 iBT). *Application deadline:* Applications are processed on a rolling basis. Application fee: $50. Electronic applications accepted. *Expenses:* Contact institution. *Financial support:* In 2019–20, 6 students received support, including 2 fellowships with full and partial tuition reimbursements available (averaging $15,000 per year); research assistantships, teaching assistantships, scholarships/grants, tuition waivers, and unspecified assistantships also available. Financial award application deadline: 2/1; financial award applicants required to submit FAFSA. *Unit head:* Brian T Carl, Assistant Professor, Fax: 713-942-3464, E-mail: carlbt@stthom.edu. *Application contact:* Valerie Hall, Administrative Assistant II, 713-525-3591, Fax: 713-942-3464, E-mail: hallvl@stthom.edu.
Website: http://www.stthom.edu/Academics/School_of_Arts_and_Sciences/Graduate/Philosophy/Philosophy_MA_PhD.aqf

University of Saskatchewan, College of Graduate and Postdoctoral Studies, College of Arts and Science, Department of Philosophy, Saskatoon, SK S7N 5A2, Canada. Offers MA. *Degree requirements:* For master's, thesis. *Entrance requirements:* Additional exam requirements/recommendations for international students: required—TOEFL (minimum score 80 iBT); recommended—IELTS (minimum score 6.5). Electronic applications accepted.

University of South Africa, College of Human Sciences, Pretoria, South Africa. Offers adult education (M Ed); African languages (MA, PhD); African politics (MA, PhD); Afrikaans (MA, PhD); ancient history (MA, PhD); ancient Near Eastern studies (MA, PhD); anthropology (MA, PhD); applied linguistics (MA); Arabic (MA, PhD); archaeology (MA); art history (MA); Biblical archaeology (MA); Biblical studies (M Th, D Th, PhD); Christian spirituality (M Th, D Th); church history (M Th, D Th); classical studies (MA, PhD); clinical psychology (MA); communication (MA, PhD); comparative education (M Ed, Ed D); consulting psychology (D Admin, D Com, PhD); curriculum studies (M Ed, Ed D); development studies (M Admin, MA, D Admin, PhD); didactics (M Ed, Ed D); education (M Tech); education management (M Ed, Ed D); educational psychology (M Ed); English (MA); environmental education (M Ed); French (MA, PhD); German (MA, PhD); Greek (MA); guidance and counseling (M Ed); health studies (MA, PhD), including health sciences education (MA), health services management (MA), medical and surgical nursing science (critical care general) (MA), midwifery and neonatal nursing science (MA), trauma and emergency care (MA); history (MA, PhD); history of education (Ed D); inclusive education (M Ed, Ed D); information and communications technology policy and regulation (MA); information science (MA, MIS, PhD); international politics (MA, PhD); Islamic studies (MA, PhD); Italian (MA, PhD); Judaica (MA, PhD); linguistics (MA, PhD); mathematical education (M Ed); mathematics education (MA); missiology (M Th, D Th); modern Hebrew (MA, PhD); musicology (MA, MMus, D Mus, PhD); natural science education (M Ed); New Testament (M Th, D Th); Old Testament (D Th); pastoral therapy (M Th, D Th); philosophy (MA); philosophy of education (M Ed, Ed D); politics (MA, PhD); Portuguese (MA, PhD); practical theology (M Th, D Th); psychology (MA, MS, PhD); psychology of education (M Ed, Ed D); public health (MA); religious studies (MA, D Th, PhD); Romance languages (MA); Russian (MA, PhD); Semitic languages (MA, PhD); social behavior studies in HIV/AIDS (MA); social science (mental health) (MA); social science in development studies (MA); social science in psychology (MA); social science in social work (MA); social science in sociology (MA); social work (MSW, DSW, PhD); socio-education (M Ed, Ed D); sociolinguistics (MA); sociology (MA, PhD); Spanish (MA, PhD); systematic theology (M Th, D Th); TESOL (teaching English to speakers of other languages) (MA); theological ethics (M Th, D Th); theory of literature (MA, PhD); urban ministries (D Th); urban ministry (M Th).

University of South Carolina, The Graduate School, College of Arts and Sciences, Department of Philosophy, Columbia, SC 29208. Offers MA, PhD. *Program availability:* Part-time. *Degree requirements:* For master's, one foreign language, comprehensive exam, thesis optional; for doctorate, one foreign language, comprehensive exam, thesis/dissertation, candidacy exam. *Entrance requirements:* For master's and doctorate, GRE General Test, 18 hours in philosophy, 3 letters of recommendation, writing sample. Additional exam requirements/recommendations for international students: required—TOEFL (minimum score 590 paper-based). Electronic applications accepted.

University of Southern California, Graduate School, Dana and David Dornsife College of Letters, Arts and Sciences, School of Philosophy, Los Angeles, CA 90089. Offers MA, PhD, MA/JD. *Degree requirements:* For doctorate, one foreign language, thesis/dissertation, area exam, qualifying exam. *Entrance requirements:* For doctorate, GRE General Test. Additional exam requirements/recommendations for international students: required—TOEFL. Electronic applications accepted.

University of South Florida, College of Arts and Sciences, Department of Philosophy, Tampa, FL 33620-9951. Offers liberal arts (MA), including social and political thought; philosophy (PhD), including philosophy and religion. *Program availability:* Part-time, evening/weekend. *Faculty:* 15 full-time (4 women). *Students:* 42 full-time (6 women), 10 part-time (4 women); includes 10 minority (3 Black or African American, non-Hispanic/Latino; 3 Asian, non-Hispanic/Latino; 3 Hispanic/Latino; 1 Two or more races, non-Hispanic/Latino). Average age 33. 24 applicants, 75% accepted, 11 enrolled. In 2019, 2 master's, 10 doctorates awarded. Terminal master's awarded for partial completion of doctoral program. *Degree requirements:* For master's, comprehensive exam, thesis; for doctorate, comprehensive exam, thesis/dissertation. *Entrance requirements:* For master's and doctorate, GRE General Test Scores, minimum GPA of 3.0, three letters of recommendation, 10-page philosophy writing sample, statement of philosophical interests. Additional exam requirements/recommendations for international students: required—TOEFL, TOEFL (minimum score 550 paper-based; 79 iBT) or IELTS (minimum score 6.5). *Application deadline:* For fall admission, 1/2 priority date for domestic students, 2/15 for international students; for spring admission, 10/15 priority date for domestic students, 8/1 for international students. Application fee: $30. Electronic applications accepted. *Financial support:* In 2019–20, 15 students received support, including 32 teaching assistantships with tuition reimbursements available (averaging $11,025 per year); unspecified assistantships also available. Financial award application deadline: 1/1. *Unit head:* Dr. William Goodwin, Associate Professor and Chair, 813-974-5670, E-mail: wgoodwin@usf.edu. *Application contact:* Dr. William Goodwin, Associate Professor, 813-974-5670, E-mail: wgoodwin@usf.edu.
Website: http://philosophy.usf.edu/

The University of Tennessee, Graduate School, College of Arts and Sciences, Department of Philosophy, Knoxville, TN 37996. Offers medical ethics (MA, PhD); philosophy (MA, PhD); religious studies (MA). *Program availability:* Part-time. *Degree requirements:* For master's, thesis or alternative; for doctorate, one foreign language, thesis/dissertation. *Entrance requirements:* For master's and doctorate, GRE General Test, minimum GPA of 2.7. Additional exam requirements/recommendations for international students: required—TOEFL. Electronic applications accepted.

The University of Texas at Austin, Graduate School, College of Liberal Arts, Department of Philosophy, Austin, TX 78712-1111. Offers PhD. *Program availability:* Part-time. Terminal master's awarded for partial completion of doctoral program. *Degree requirements:* For doctorate, one foreign language, thesis/dissertation. *Entrance requirements:* For doctorate, GRE General Test. Electronic applications accepted.

The University of Texas at El Paso, Graduate School, College of Liberal Arts, Department of Philosophy, El Paso, TX 79968-0001. Offers MA. *Degree requirements:* For master's, thesis, oral examination. *Entrance requirements:* For master's, GRE, 2 letters of recommendation.

The University of Texas at San Antonio, College of Liberal and Fine Arts, Department of Philosophy and Classics, San Antonio, TX 78249-0617. Offers MA. *Program availability:* Part-time. *Degree requirements:* For master's, comprehensive exam, thesis. *Entrance requirements:* For master's, GRE. Additional exam requirements/recommendations for international students: required—TOEFL (minimum score 550 paper-based; 79 iBT), IELTS (minimum score 6.5). Electronic applications accepted. *Expenses:* Contact institution.

The University of Toledo, College of Graduate Studies, College of Languages, Literature and Social Sciences, Department of Philosophy, Toledo, OH 43606-3390. Offers MA. *Program availability:* Part-time. *Degree requirements:* For master's, comprehensive exam, thesis, exam. *Entrance requirements:* For master's, minimum cumulative point-hour ratio of 2.7 for all previous academic work, three letters of recommendation. Additional exam requirements/recommendations for international students: required—TOEFL (minimum score 550 paper-based; 80 iBT). Electronic applications accepted.

University of Toronto, School of Graduate Studies, Faculty of Arts and Science, Department of Philosophy, Toronto, ON M5S 1A1, Canada. Offers MA, PhD. *Program availability:* Part-time. *Degree requirements:* For doctorate, one foreign language, thesis/dissertation. *Entrance requirements:* For master's, GRE, 6 courses in philosophy; minimum A- average in philosophy courses, B overall; 2 letters of reference; writing sample; for doctorate, GRE, MA in philosophy, minimum A- average, 2 letters of reference, writing sample. Additional exam requirements/recommendations for international students: required—TOEFL (minimum score 600 paper-based), TWE (minimum score 5). Electronic applications accepted.

University of Utah, Graduate School, College of Humanities, Department of Philosophy, Salt Lake City, UT 84112. Offers MA, MS, PhD. *Faculty:* 11 full-time (4 women), 1 part-time/adjunct (0 women). *Students:* 20 full-time (8 women), 4 part-time (0 women); includes 3 minority (1 Asian, non-Hispanic/Latino; 2 Hispanic/Latino), 6 international. Average age 31. 48 applicants, 15% accepted, 5 enrolled. In 2019, 3 doctorates awarded. Terminal master's awarded for partial completion of doctoral program. *Degree requirements:* For master's, comprehensive exam, thesis optional, option of thesis and non thesis master's degrees; for doctorate, comprehensive exam, thesis/dissertation, Dissertation is required. *Entrance requirements:* Additional exam requirements/recommendations for international students: required—TOEFL (minimum score 500 paper-based; 80 iBT), IELTS (minimum score 6.5). *Application deadline:* For fall admission, 1/15 priority date for domestic and international students. Application fee: $55 ($65 for international students). Electronic applications accepted. Application fee is waived when completed online. *Expenses:* Tuition, state resident: full-time $7085; part-time $272.51 per credit hour. Tuition, nonresident: full-time $24,937; part-time $959.12 per credit hour. *Required fees:* $880.52; $880.52 per semester. Tuition and fees vary according to degree level, program and student level. *Financial support:* In 2019–20, 3 fellowships (averaging $18,700 per year), 2 research assistantships (averaging $25,000 per year), 15 teaching assistantships (averaging $29,067 per year) were awarded; health care benefits also available. *Unit head:* Dr. Matthew Haber, Department Chair, 801-581-8161, Fax: 801-585-5195, E-mail: matt.haber@utah.edu. *Application contact:* Connie Gladden Corbett, Academic Advisor, 801-581-8162, Fax: 801-585-5195, E-mail: c.corbett@utah.edu.
Website: http://www.hum.utah.edu/philosophy/

University of Victoria, Faculty of Graduate Studies, Faculty of Humanities, Department of Philosophy, Victoria, BC V8W 2Y2, Canada. Offers MA. *Program availability:* Part-time, evening/weekend. *Degree requirements:* For master's, thesis. *Entrance requirements:* For master's, writing sample. Additional exam requirements/recommendations for international students: required—TOEFL (minimum score 575 paper-based), IELTS (minimum score 7).

University of Virginia, College and Graduate School of Arts and Sciences, Department of Philosophy, Charlottesville, VA 22903. Offers MA, PhD, JD/MA. *Degree requirements:* For master's, 2 papers; for doctorate, thesis/dissertation, 2 papers. *Entrance requirements:* For master's, GRE General Test, GRE Subject Test, 3 letters of recommendation, writing sample; for doctorate, GRE General Test, GRE Subject Test, 3 letters of recommendation; writing sample. Additional exam requirements/recommendations for international students: required—TOEFL (minimum score 600 paper-based; 90 iBT), IELTS. Electronic applications accepted.

University of Washington, Graduate School, College of Arts and Sciences, Department of Classics, Seattle, WA 98195. Offers classics (MA, PhD), including ancient philosophy (PhD), classics (PhD), textual studies (PhD), theory and criticism (PhD). *Program availability:* Part-time. Terminal master's awarded for partial completion of doctoral program. *Degree requirements:* For master's, one foreign language, thesis or alternative; for doctorate, 2 foreign languages, comprehensive exam, thesis/dissertation. *Entrance requirements:* For master's, GRE, bachelor's degree in classics, Greek, or Latin; minimum GPA of 3.0; for doctorate, GRE, minimum GPA of 3.0. Additional exam requirements/recommendations for international students: required—TOEFL (minimum score 82 iBT). Electronic applications accepted.

University of Washington, Graduate School, College of Arts and Sciences, Department of Philosophy, Seattle, WA 98195. Offers classics and philosophy (PhD); philosophy (MA, PhD). Terminal master's awarded for partial completion of doctoral program. *Degree requirements:* For master's, 3 papers; for doctorate, thesis/dissertation, general exam. *Entrance requirements:* For master's and doctorate, GRE, minimum GPA of 3.0. Additional exam requirements/recommendations for international students: required—TOEFL.

University of Waterloo, Graduate Studies and Postdoctoral Affairs, Faculty of Arts, Department of Philosophy, Waterloo, ON N2L 3G1, Canada. Offers MA, PhD. *Degree requirements:* For master's, thesis or alternative; for doctorate, one foreign language, thesis/dissertation. *Entrance requirements:* For master's, honors degree, minimum B+ average, writing sample, resume; for doctorate, master's degree, minimum A- average, resume. Additional exam requirements/recommendations for international students: required—TOEFL, IELTS, PTE. Electronic applications accepted.

The University of Western Ontario, School of Graduate and Postdoctoral Studies, Faculty of Arts and Humanities, Department of Philosophy, London, ON N6A 3K7, Canada. Offers MA, PhD. *Degree requirements:* For master's, 1 competency exam; for doctorate, comprehensive exam, thesis/dissertation, 2 competency exams. *Entrance requirements:* For master's, honors degree. Additional exam requirements/recommendations for international students: required—TOEFL (minimum score 600 paper-based). Electronic applications accepted.

University of Windsor, Faculty of Graduate Studies, Faculty of Arts and Social Sciences, Department of Philosophy, Windsor, ON N9B 3P4, Canada. Offers MA. *Program availability:* Part-time. *Degree requirements:* For master's, thesis. *Entrance requirements:* For master's, minimum B average. Additional exam requirements/recommendations for international students: required—TOEFL (minimum score 600 paper-based). Electronic applications accepted.

Philosophy

University of Wisconsin–Madison, Graduate School, College of Letters and Science, Department of Philosophy, Madison, WI 53706-1380. Offers MA, PhD. *Program availability:* Part-time. Terminal master's awarded for partial completion of doctoral program. *Degree requirements:* For master's, thesis, preliminary exams; for doctorate, thesis/dissertation, preliminary exams. *Entrance requirements:* For doctorate, GRE, BA in philosophy or related area. Additional exam requirements/recommendations for international students: required—TOEFL. Electronic applications accepted.

University of Wisconsin–Milwaukee, Graduate School, College of Letters and Science, Department of Philosophy, Milwaukee, WI 53201-0413. Offers MA. *Program availability:* Part-time. *Entrance requirements:* For master's, GRE General Test. Additional exam requirements/recommendations for international students: required—TOEFL (minimum score 550 paper-based; 79 iBT), IELTS (minimum score 6.5). Electronic applications accepted.

University of Wyoming, College of Arts and Sciences, Department of Philosophy, Laramie, WY 82071. Offers MA. *Program availability:* Part-time. *Degree requirements:* For master's, thesis, logic proficiency, first-year paper. *Entrance requirements:* For master's, GRE General Test, minimum GPA of 3.0. Additional exam requirements/recommendations for international students: required—TOEFL (minimum score 525 paper-based). Electronic applications accepted.

Université Laval, Faculty of Philosophy, Programs in Philosophy, Québec, QC G1K 7P4, Canada. Offers MA, PhD. Terminal master's awarded for partial completion of doctoral program. *Degree requirements:* For master's, thesis; for doctorate, comprehensive exam, thesis/dissertation. *Entrance requirements:* For master's and doctorate, French exam. Electronic applications accepted.

Vanderbilt University, Department of Philosophy, Nashville, TN 37240-1001. Offers MA, PhD. *Faculty:* 14 full-time (4 women). *Students:* 22 full-time (12 women), 1 (woman) part-time; includes 9 minority (1 Black or African American, non-Hispanic/Latino; 2 Asian, non-Hispanic/Latino; 2 Hispanic/Latino; 4 Two or more races, non-Hispanic/Latino), 3 international. Average age 27. 107 applicants, 10% accepted, 7 enrolled. In 2019, 3 master's, 2 doctorates awarded. Terminal master's awarded for partial completion of doctoral program. *Degree requirements:* For doctorate, one foreign language, comprehensive exam, thesis/dissertation, final and qualifying exams. *Entrance requirements:* For doctorate, GRE General Test, writing sample. Additional exam requirements/recommendations for international students: required—TOEFL (minimum score 570 paper-based; 88 iBT). *Application deadline:* For fall admission, 1/15 for domestic and international students. Electronic applications accepted. *Expenses: Tuition:* Full-time $51,018; part-time $2087 per hour. *Required fees:* $542. Tuition and fees vary according to program. *Financial support:* Fellowships with full tuition reimbursements, teaching assistantships with full tuition reimbursements, Federal Work-Study, institutionally sponsored loans, scholarships/grants, and health care benefits available. Financial award application deadline: 1/15; financial award applicants required to submit CSS PROFILE or FAFSA. *Unit head:* Dr. Robert Talisse, Chair, 615-343-5349, Fax: 615-343-7259, E-mail: robert.talisse@vanderbilt.edu. *Application contact:* Kelly Oliver, Director of Graduate Studies, 615-343-0334, Fax: 615-343-7259, E-mail: kelly.oliver@vanderbilt.edu.
Website: http://www.vanderbilt.edu/AnS/philosophy/

Villanova University, Graduate School of Liberal Arts and Sciences, Department of Philosophy, Villanova, PA 19085-1699. Offers PhD. *Program availability:* Part-time, evening/weekend. *Degree requirements:* For doctorate, 2 foreign languages, comprehensive exam, thesis/dissertation. *Entrance requirements:* For doctorate, GRE, 3 recommendation letters, writing sample, curriculum vitae. Additional exam requirements/recommendations for international students: required—TOEFL.

Washington University in St. Louis, The Graduate School, Department of Philosophy, St. Louis, MO 63130-4899. Offers philosophy (PhD); philosophy-neuroscience-psychology (PhD). *Degree requirements:* For doctorate, thesis/dissertation. *Entrance requirements:* For doctorate, GRE General Test, sample of written work. Additional exam requirements/recommendations for international students: required—TOEFL. Electronic applications accepted.

Wayne State University, College of Liberal Arts and Sciences, Department of Philosophy, Detroit, MI 48202. Offers MA, PhD. Terminal master's awarded for partial completion of doctoral program. *Degree requirements:* For master's, comprehensive exam, thesis (for some programs), essay or thesis; for doctorate, comprehensive exam, thesis/dissertation, oral exam, classroom lectures under supervision of Philosophy Department. *Entrance requirements:* For master's, GRE if upper-division GPA is below 2.75 (or 3.0 if from unaccredited college), writing sample; personal statement; three letters of recommendation; prerequisite courses in logic, value theory, and the history of philosophy; for doctorate, minimum undergraduate upper-division GPA of 3.0, undergraduate major or substantial work in philosophy, writing sample, personal statement, three letters of recommendation. Additional exam requirements/recommendations for international students: required—TOEFL (minimum score 550 paper-based), TWE (minimum score 5.5), Michigan English Language Assessment Battery (minimum score 85); recommended—IELTS (minimum score 6.5). Electronic applications accepted. *Expenses: Tuition:* Full-time $34,567.

Western Michigan University, Graduate College, College of Arts and Sciences, Department of Philosophy, Kalamazoo, MI 49008. Offers MA. *Degree requirements:* For master's, thesis optional.

Wilfrid Laurier University, Faculty of Graduate and Postdoctoral Studies, Faculty of Arts, Department of Philosophy, Waterloo, ON N2L 3C5, Canada. Offers agency (MA); community (MA); self (MA). *Entrance requirements:* For master's, honours BA in philosophy or equivalent with minimum B+ average in philosophy and in final year. Additional exam requirements/recommendations for international students: required—TOEFL (minimum score 89 iBT). Electronic applications accepted.

Yale University, Graduate School of Arts and Sciences, Department of Philosophy, New Haven, CT 06520. Offers PhD. *Degree requirements:* For doctorate, 2 foreign languages, thesis/dissertation. *Entrance requirements:* For doctorate, GRE General Test.

York University, Faculty of Graduate Studies, Faculty of Liberal Arts and Professional Studies, Program in Philosophy, Toronto, ON M3J 1P3, Canada. Offers MA, PhD. *Program availability:* Part-time. *Degree requirements:* For master's, thesis or alternative; for doctorate, one foreign language, thesis/dissertation. Electronic applications accepted.

Section 12
Religious Studies

This section contains a directory of institutions offering graduate work in religious studies. Additional information about programs listed in the directory may be obtained by writing directly to the dean of a graduate school or chair of a department at the address given in the directory.

For programs offering related work, see also in this book *Area and Cultural Studies, History, Humanities,* and *Philosophy.* In another guide in this series:

Graduate Programs in Business, Education, Information Studies, Law & Social Work

See *Subject Areas (Religious Education)*

CONTENTS

Program Directories

Missions and Missiology

Abilene Christian University, Office of Graduate Programs, College of Biblical Studies, Graduate School of Theology, Abilene, TX 79699. Offers ancient and Oriental Christianity (MA); Christian ministry (MACM); divinity (M Div), including ministry, missions; global service (MA); ministry (D Min), including Christian spiritual formation, leadership for missional renewal, preaching for community transformation; modern and American Christianity (MA); New Testament (MA); Old Testament (MA); theology (MA). *Program availability:* Part-time, evening/weekend, online learning. *Faculty:* 12 full-time (2 women), 9 part-time/adjunct (1 woman). *Students:* 116 full-time (24 women), 86 part-time (24 women); includes 61 minority (34 Black or African American, non-Hispanic/Latino; 1 Asian, non-Hispanic/Latino; 21 Hispanic/Latino; 5 Two or more races, non-Hispanic/Latino), 11 international. 185 applicants, 54% accepted, 68 enrolled. In 2019, 17 master's, 2 doctorates awarded. *Degree requirements:* For master's, comprehensive exam (for some programs), thesis (for some programs); for doctorate, one foreign language, thesis/dissertation. *Entrance requirements:* For master's, official transcripts, recommendation, purpose statement, writing assessment; for doctorate, official transcripts, Documentation of Ministry, recommendations, personal statement, Endorsement of Elders or Supervisor. Additional exam requirements/recommendations for international students: required—TOEFL (minimum score 80 iBT), IELTS (minimum score 6), PTE (minimum score 51). *Application deadline:* For fall admission, 8/10 priority date for domestic students; for spring admission, 11/1 for domestic students. Applications are processed on a rolling basis. Application fee: $65. *Expenses:* $676 per hour. *Financial support:* In 2019–20, 39 students received support, including 18 research assistantships with partial tuition reimbursements available; Federal Work-Study also available. Support available to part-time students. Financial award application deadline: 4/1; financial award applicants required to submit FAFSA. *Unit head:* Dr. Tim Sensing, Associate Dean, 325-674-3730, Fax: 325-674-6180, E-mail: sensingt@acu.edu. *Application contact:* Graduate Admissions, 325-674-6911, E-mail: gradinfo@acu.edu.
Website: http://www.acu.edu/gst

Acadia University, Divinity College, Wolfville, NS B4P 2R6, Canada. Offers divinity (M Div); ministry (D Min); theology (MA), including chaplaincy and spiritual care, Christian history, discipleship, evangelism and mission, indigenous community development, leadership and spiritual formation, New Testament, next generation ministry, Old Testament, pastoral care and counseling, prison chaplaincy, Second Temple Judaism, theology. *Accreditation:* ATS. *Program availability:* Part-time. *Degree requirements:* For master's, variable foreign language requirement, thesis (for some programs); for doctorate, one foreign language, comprehensive exam, thesis/dissertation. *Entrance requirements:* For doctorate, minimum GPA of 3.0, 3 years' ministry experience. Additional exam requirements/recommendations for international students: required—TOEFL. *Expenses:* Contact institution.

Anderson University, School of Theology, Anderson, IN 46012. Offers missions (MA); theology (M Div, MTS, D Min). *Accreditation:* ACIPE; ATS. *Program availability:* Part-time. *Degree requirements:* For master's, variable foreign language requirement, thesis (for some programs); for doctorate, thesis/dissertation.

Asbury Theological Seminary, Graduate and Professional Programs, Wilmore, KY 40390-1199. Offers M Div, MA, MAAS, MACE, MACL, MACM, MACP, MAMFC, MAMHC, MAPC, MASF, MAYM, Th M, D Min, PhD, Certificate. *Accreditation:* ATS. *Program availability:* Part-time, online learning. Terminal master's awarded for partial completion of doctoral program. *Degree requirements:* For master's, thesis (for some programs); for doctorate, thesis/dissertation, qualifying exam. *Entrance requirements:* For master's, minimum GPA of 2.75; for doctorate, minimum GPA of 3.0. Additional exam requirements/recommendations for international students: required—TOEFL, IELTS. Electronic applications accepted.

Assemblies of God Theological Seminary, Graduate and Professional Programs, Springfield, MO 65802. Offers Biblical interpretation and theology (PhD); Christian ministries (MA); divinity (M Div); intercultural studies (MA, PhD); leadership and ministry (MLM); ministry (D Min); missiology (DAIS); pastoral studies (MPL); theological studies (MA, Th M). *Accreditation:* ATS. *Program availability:* Part-time, evening/weekend, 100% online. *Faculty:* 12 full-time (3 women), 15 part-time/adjunct (4 women). *Students:* 136 full-time (37 women), 147 part-time (40 women); includes 71 minority (24 Black or African American, non-Hispanic/Latino; 6 American Indian or Alaska Native, non-Hispanic/Latino; 7 Asian, non-Hispanic/Latino; 22 Hispanic/Latino; 7 Native Hawaiian or other Pacific Islander, non-Hispanic/Latino; 5 Two or more races, non-Hispanic/Latino), 14 international. Average age 46. 62 applicants, 100% accepted, 42 enrolled. In 2019, 37 master's, 25 doctorates awarded. *Degree requirements:* For master's, variable foreign language requirement, thesis; for doctorate, variable foreign language requirement, comprehensive exam, thesis/dissertation. *Entrance requirements:* For master's, minimum GPA of 2.5; for doctorate, GRE (for PhD in Bible theology), minimum GPA of 3.0. Additional exam requirements/recommendations for international students: required—TOEFL (minimum score 550 paper-based; 80 iBT). *Application deadline:* For fall admission, 7/1 priority date for domestic students, 6/1 priority date for international students; for spring admission, 12/1 priority date for domestic students, 11/1 priority date for international students. Applications are processed on a rolling basis. Application fee: $75. Electronic applications accepted. *Financial support:* Career-related internships or fieldwork and scholarships/grants available. Support available to part-time students. Financial award application deadline: 7/15; financial award applicants required to submit FAFSA. *Unit head:* Dr. Timothy A. Hager, Dean, 417-268-1000, Fax: 417-268-1001. *Application contact:* Nik White, Seminary Enrollment Coordinator, 417-268-1000, Fax: 417-268-1030, E-mail: info@agts.edu.
Website: http://www.agts.edu

Bethel Seminary, Graduate and Professional Programs, St. Paul, MN 55112-6998. Offers Anglican studies (Certificate); children's and family ministry (MA); Christian studies (Certificate); Christian thought (MA); church planting (Certificate); Greek and Hebrew language (M Div); Greek language (M Div); Hebrew language (M Div); marriage and family therapy (MA, Certificate); mental health counseling (MA); ministry (MA, D Min); ministry practice (Certificate); theological studies (MA, Certificate); transformational leadership (MA); young life youth ministry (Certificate). *Accreditation:* ACIPE. *Program availability:* Part-time, evening/weekend, 100% online, blended/hybrid learning. *Degree requirements:* For master's, variable foreign language requirement, thesis (for some programs); for doctorate, thesis/dissertation. *Entrance requirements:* For master's, letters of reference, transcripts, personal statement; for doctorate, M Div, letters of reference, organizational support; for Certificate, letters of reference, family essay, personal statement, and family of origin paper (for marriage and family therapy). Additional exam requirements/recommendations for international students: required—TOEFL (minimum score 550 paper-based; 87 iBT). Electronic applications accepted. *Expenses:* Contact institution.

Biola University, Cook School of Intercultural Studies, La Mirada, CA 90639-0001. Offers anthropology (MA); applied linguistics (MA); intercultural education (PhD); intercultural studies (MA, PhD); linguistics (Certificate); linguistics and Biblical languages (MA); missiology (D Miss); missions (MA); teaching English to speakers of other languages (MA, Certificate). *Program availability:* Part-time, 100% online. *Faculty:* 19. *Students:* 108 full-time (55 women), 154 part-time (86 women); includes 77 minority (11 Black or African American, non-Hispanic/Latino; 1 American Indian or Alaska Native, non-Hispanic/Latino; 43 Asian, non-Hispanic/Latino; 19 Hispanic/Latino; 3 Two or more races, non-Hispanic/Latino), 67 international. Average age 35. 142 applicants, 63% accepted, 52 enrolled. In 2019, 37 master's, 14 doctorates awarded. *Degree requirements:* For master's, comprehensive exam (for some programs), thesis or alternative, All students must successfully complete all required coursework with a minimum GPA of 3.0; for doctorate, thesis/dissertation, All students must present an acceptable dissertation, have satisfactorily passed their qualifying exam and completed all required course work with a minimum 3.3 GPA; for Certificate, All students musts successfully complete all required coursework with a minimum GPA of 3.0. *Entrance requirements:* For master's, minimum undergraduate GPA of 3.0; for doctorate, master's degree or equivalent, 3 years of cross-cultural experience, minimum graduate GPA of 3.3. Additional exam requirements/recommendations for international students: required—TOEFL. *Application deadline:* For fall admission, 7/1 for domestic students, 6/1 for international students; for spring admission, 11/1 for domestic students; for summer admission, 5/1 for domestic students. Applications are processed on a rolling basis. Application fee: $65. Electronic applications accepted. *Financial support:* Scholarships/grants available. Support available to part-time students. Financial award applicants required to submit FAFSA. *Unit head:* Dr. Bulus Y. Galadima, Dean, 562-903-4844. *Application contact:* Graduate Admissions Office, 562-903-4752, E-mail: graduate.admissions@biola.edu.
Website: http://cook.biola.edu

Biola University, Talbot School of Theology, La Mirada, CA 90639-0001. Offers adult/family ministry (MACE); Bible exposition (MA, Th M); Biblical and theological studies (Certificate); children's ministry (MACE); Christian education (M Div); cross-cultural education ministry (MACE); educational studies (Ed D, PhD); evangelism and discipleship (M Div); general Christian education (MACE); Messianic Jewish studies (M Div, Certificate); missions and intercultural studies (M Div); New Testament (MA, Th M); Old Testament (MA); Old Testament and Semitics (Th M); pastoral and general ministry (M Div); pastoral care and counseling (M Div, MACML); philosophy (MA); preaching and pastoral ministry (MACML); spiritual formation (M Div, Certificate); spiritual formation and soul care (MA); sports ministry (MACML); theology (MA, Th M, D Min, Certificate); youth ministry (MACE). *Program availability:* Part-time, evening/weekend. *Students:* 461 full-time (116 women), 768 part-time (228 women); includes 489 minority (54 Black or African American, non-Hispanic/Latino; 1 American Indian or Alaska Native, non-Hispanic/Latino; 303 Asian, non-Hispanic/Latino; 96 Hispanic/Latino; 3 Native Hawaiian or other Pacific Islander, non-Hispanic/Latino; 32 Two or more races, non-Hispanic/Latino), 162 international. Average age 38. 745 applicants, 70% accepted, 320 enrolled. In 2019, 235 master's, 24 doctorates awarded. *Entrance requirements:* For master's, bachelor's degree from accredited college or university; minimum GPA of 2.6 (for M Div), 3.0 (for MA); for doctorate, M Div or MA. Additional exam requirements/recommendations for international students: required—TOEFL (minimum score 600 paper-based; 88 iBT). *Application deadline:* For fall admission, 7/1 for domestic students, 6/1 for international students; for spring admission, 11/1 for domestic students. Applications are processed on a rolling basis. Application fee: $65. Electronic applications accepted. *Financial support:* Scholarships/grants and unspecified assistantships available. Support available to part-time students. Financial award applicants required to submit FAFSA. *Unit head:* Dr. Clint Arnold, Dean, 562-903-4816, Fax: 562-903-4748. *Application contact:* Graduate Admissions Office, 562-903-4752, E-mail: graduate.admissions@biola.edu.
Website: http://www.talbot.edu/

Briercrest Seminary, Graduate Programs, Program in Christian Ministries, Caronport, SK S0H 0S0, Canada. Offers leadership (MA); marriage and family counseling (MA); missions (MA); pastoral counseling (MA); worship (MA); youth and family ministry (MA). *Program availability:* Part-time. *Degree requirements:* For master's, comprehensive exam, thesis optional. *Entrance requirements:* Additional exam requirements/recommendations for international students: required—TOEFL (minimum score 550 paper-based).

Calvin Theological Seminary, Graduate and Professional Programs, Grand Rapids, MI 49546-4387. Offers Bible and theology (MA); divinity (M Div), including ancient near eastern languages and literature, contextual ministry, evangelism and teaching, history of Christianity, new church development, New Testament, Old Testament, pastoral care and leadership, preaching and worship, theological studies, youth and family ministries; educational ministry (MA); historical theology (PhD); missions and evangelism (MA); pastoral care (MA); philosophical and moral theology (PhD); systematic theology (PhD); theological studies (MTS); theology (Th M); worship (MA); youth and family ministries (MA). *Accreditation:* ACIPE; ATS. *Program availability:* Part-time. *Degree requirements:* For master's, variable foreign language requirement, thesis (for some programs); for doctorate, 4 foreign languages, comprehensive exam, thesis/dissertation. *Entrance requirements:* For doctorate, GRE General Test, Hebrew, Greek, and a modern foreign language. Additional exam requirements/recommendations for international students: required—TOEFL (minimum score 550 paper-based), TWE (minimum score 4). Electronic applications accepted.

Capital University, Trinity Lutheran Seminary, Columbus, OH 43209-2394. Offers African American studies (MTS); Biblical studies (MTS, STM); Christian education (MA); Christian spirituality (STM); church in the world (MTS); church music (MA); divinity (M Div); general theological studies (MTS); mission and evangelism (STM); pastoral leadership and practice (STM); youth and family ministry (MA); MSN/MTS; MTS/JD. *Accreditation:* ACIPE; ATS. *Program availability:* Part-time. *Degree requirements:* For master's, variable foreign language requirement, comprehensive exam (for some programs), thesis (for some programs), field experience (for some programs). *Entrance requirements:* For master's, BA or equivalent (for MA, M Div, MTS); M Div, MTS, or equivalent (for STM); audition (for MACM). Additional exam requirements/recommendations for international students: required—TOEFL. Electronic applications accepted. *Expenses:* Contact institution.

Catholic Theological Union, Graduate and Professional Programs, Chicago, IL 60615-5698. Offers biblical spirituality (Certificate); cross-cultural ministries (D Min); cross-cultural missions (Certificate); divinity (M Div); liturgical studies (Certificate); liturgy (D Min); pastoral studies (MAPS, Certificate); spiritual formation (Certificate); spirituality (D Min); theology (MA); M Div/MA; M Div/MSW; M Div/PhD. *Accreditation:* ACIPE; ATS. *Program availability:* Part-time, evening/weekend. *Degree requirements:* For master's, one foreign language, comprehensive exam (for some programs), thesis (for some programs); for doctorate, thesis/dissertation. *Entrance requirements:* For doctorate, master's degree, 5 years of active ministry.

Cedarville University, Graduate Programs, Cedarville, OH 45314. Offers business administration (MBA); family nurse practitioner (MSN); global ministry (M Div); global public health nursing (MSN); healthcare administration (MBA); ministry (M Min); nurse educator (MSN); operations management (MBA); pharmacy (Pharm D). *Program availability:* Part-time, evening/weekend, 100% online, blended/hybrid learning. *Faculty:* 52 full-time (19 women), 21 part-time/adjunct (13 women). *Students:* 378 full-time (221 women), 45 part-time (23 women); includes 76 minority (46 Black or African American, non-Hispanic/Latino; 2 American Indian or Alaska Native, non-Hispanic/Latino; 22 Asian, non-Hispanic/Latino; 1 Hispanic/Latino; 5 Two or more races, non-Hispanic/Latino), 2 international. Average age 26. 398 applicants, 70% accepted, 172 enrolled. In 2019, 74 master's, 34 doctorates awarded. *Degree requirements:* For master's, portfolio; for doctorate, comprehensive exam. *Entrance requirements:* For master's, GRE may be required, 2 professional recommendations; for doctorate, PCAT, professional recommendation from a practicing pharmacist or current employer/supervisor, resume, essay, interview. Additional exam requirements/recommendations for international students: required—TOEFL (minimum score 550 paper-based; 80 iBT). *Application deadline:* For fall admission, 5/1 priority date for domestic and international students; for spring admission, 11/1 priority date for domestic and international students. Applications are processed on a rolling basis. Application fee: $0. Electronic applications accepted. *Expenses: Tuition:* Full-time $12,594; part-time $566 per credit hour. One-time fee: $100. Tuition and fees vary according to course load and program. *Financial support:* Scholarships/grants and unspecified assistantships available. Support available to part-time students. Financial award application deadline: 1/30; financial award applicants required to submit FAFSA. *Unit head:* Dr. Janice Supplee, Dean of Graduate Studies, 937-766-8000, E-mail: suppleej@cedarville.edu. *Application contact:* Alexis McKay, Graduate Admissions Counselor, 937-766-8000, E-mail: amckay@cedarville.edu.
Website: https://www.cedarville.edu/offices/graduate-school

Central Baptist Theological Seminary, Graduate and Professional Programs, Shawnee, KS 66226. Offers missional church studies (MA); theological studies (MA); theology (M Div, Diploma). *Accreditation:* ACIPE; ATS (one or more programs are accredited). *Program availability:* Part-time. *Degree requirements:* For master's, thesis optional. *Entrance requirements:* Additional exam requirements/recommendations for international students: required—TOEFL (minimum score 547 paper-based; 77 iBT). Electronic applications accepted.

Clarks Summit University, Baptist Bible Seminary, South Abington Township, PA 18411. Offers Biblical apologetics (MA); Biblical studies (MA); church education (M Min); church planting (M Div, M Min); communication (D Min); counseling and spiritual development (D Min); global ministry (M Min, D Min); ministry (PhD); missions (M Min); organizational leadership (M Min); outreach pastor (M Min); pastoral counseling (M Min); pastoral leadership (M Div, M Min); pastoral ministry (D Min); theological studies (D Min); theology (Th M); youth pastor (M Min). *Program availability:* Part-time, evening/weekend, online learning. Terminal master's awarded for partial completion of doctoral program. *Degree requirements:* For master's, 2 foreign languages, thesis, oral exam (for M Div); for doctorate, 2 foreign languages, comprehensive exam (for some programs), thesis/dissertation, oral exam. *Entrance requirements:* For doctorate, Greek and Hebrew entrance exams (for PhD). Electronic applications accepted.

Columbia International University, Seminary and School of Ministry, Columbia, SC 29203. Offers academic ministries (M Div); Bible and theology (Certificate); bible exposition (M Div, MABE); Biblical ministry (Certificate); chaplaincy (M Div); intercultural studies (MAIS); leadership (D Min); member care (D Min); missions (D Min); preaching (D Min); theological studies (MA). *Program availability:* Part-time, evening/weekend. *Degree requirements:* For doctorate, comprehensive exam, thesis/dissertation. *Entrance requirements:* For doctorate, 3 years of ministerial experience, M Div. Additional exam requirements/recommendations for international students: required—TOEFL. Electronic applications accepted.

Dallas Baptist University, Graduate School of Ministry, Program in Global Leadership, Dallas, TX 75211-9299. Offers church planting (MA); East Asian Studies (MA); English as a second language (MA); general studies (MA); global communication (MA); global studies (MA); international business (MA); leading the nonprofit organization (MA); missions (MA); small group ministry (MA); urban ministry (MA). *Program availability:* Part-time, evening/weekend, online learning. *Application deadline:* Applications are processed on a rolling basis. Application fee: $25. Electronic applications accepted. Application fee is waived when completed online. *Expenses: Tuition:* Full-time $18,072; part-time $1004 per credit hour. *Required fees:* $1100; $550 per semester. Tuition and fees vary according to course level and degree level. *Unit head:* Dr. Robert R. Brooks, Dean, 214-333-5494, Fax: 214-333-5673, E-mail: bobb@dbu.edu. *Application contact:* Dr. Brent Thomason, Program Director, 214-333-5236, E-mail: brentt@dbu.edu.
Website: https://www.dbu.edu/ministry/degree-programs/m-a-in-global-leadership

Dallas Baptist University, Liberal Arts Program, Dallas, TX 75211-9299. Offers art (MLA); Christian studies (MLA); commercial art (MLA); East Asian studies (MLA); English (MLA); English as a second language (MLA); history (MLA); missions (MLA); political science (MLA). *Program availability:* Part-time, evening/weekend, online learning. *Application deadline:* Applications are processed on a rolling basis. Application fee: $25. Electronic applications accepted. Application fee is waived when completed online. *Expenses: Tuition:* Full-time $18,072; part-time $1004 per credit hour. *Required fees:* $1100; $550 per semester. Tuition and fees vary according to course level and degree level. *Unit head:* Jared Ingram, Director, 214-333-5584, E-mail: jaredi@dbu.edu. *Application contact:* Jared Ingram, Director, 214-333-5584, E-mail: jaredi@dbu.edu.
Website: https://www.dbu.edu/graduate/degree-programs/mla

Dallas Theological Seminary, Graduate Programs, Dallas, TX 75204-6499. Offers adult education (Th M); apologetics (Th M); Bible backgrounds (Th M); Bible translation (Th M); Biblical and theological studies (Certificate); biblical counseling (MA); biblical exegesis and linguistics (MA); biblical exposition (PhD); biblical studies (MA); Biblical theology (Th M); children's education (Th M); Christian education (MA, D Min); Christian leadership (MA); cross-cultural ministries (MA); educational administration (Th M); educational leadership (Th M); evangelism and discipleship (Th M); exposition of Biblical books (Th M); family life education (Th M); general studies (Th M); Hebrew and cognate studies (Th M); hermeneutics (Th M); historical theology (Th M); homiletics (Th M); intercultural ministries (Th M); Jesus studies (Th M); leadership studies (Th M); media and communication (MA); media arts (Th M); ministry (D Min); ministry with women (Th M); New Testament studies (Th M, PhD); Old Testament studies (Th M, PhD); parachurch ministries (Th M); pastoral care and counseling (Th M); pastoral theology and practice (Th M); philosophy (Th M); sacred theology (STM); spiritual formation (Th M); systematic theology (Th M); teaching in Christian institutions (Th M); theological studies (PhD); urban ministries (Th M); worship studies (Th M); youth education (Th M). *Program availability:* Part-time, online learning. *Degree requirements:* For master's, variable foreign language requirement, thesis (for some programs); for doctorate, 2 foreign languages, thesis/dissertation. *Entrance requirements:* For master's, GRE or MAT (if minimum undergraduate cumulative GPA is below 2.5 or undergraduate degree is unaccredited). Additional exam requirements/recommendations for international students: required—TOEFL (minimum score 575 paper-based; 85 iBT), TWE. Electronic applications accepted.

Ecclesia College, Graduate School, Springdale, AR 72762. Offers Christian leadership (MCL). *Program availability:* Online learning.

Evangelical Seminary, Graduate and Professional Programs, Myerstown, PA 17067-1212. Offers Biblical studies (MAR); congregational ministry (M Div); global and contextual studies (M Div, MAR); historical and theological studies (MAR); interdisciplinary studies (MAR); marriage and family counseling (M Div); marriage and family therapy (MA); New Testament (MAR); Old Testament (MAR); spiritual formation (MAR); teaching ministry (M Div); youth ministry (M Div). *Accreditation:* ATS (one or more programs are accredited). *Program availability:* Part-time, online learning. *Degree requirements:* For master's, 2 foreign languages. *Entrance requirements:* For master's, minimum GPA of 2.5. Additional exam requirements/recommendations for international students: required—TOEFL (minimum score 550 paper-based).

Fresno Pacific University, Biblical Seminary, Program in Urban Mission, Fresno, CA 93702-4709. Offers MA. *Entrance requirements:* For master's, minimum GPA of 2.5.

Fuller Theological Seminary, Graduate Programs, Pasadena, CA 91182. Offers Christian leadership (MACL); clinical psychology (PhD, Psy D); family studies (MA); global leadership (MA); global ministries (D Min); global ministries (Korean language) (D Min); intercultural studies (MA, Th M, PhD); intercultural studies (Korean language) (MA); marital and family therapy (MS); marriage and family enrichment (Certificate); ministry (M Div, D Min); missiology (D Miss); missiology (Korean language) (Th M); theology (MA, Th M, PhD), including evangelism (MA), family life education (MA), pastoral ministry (MA), recovery ministry (MA), worship music ministry (MA), worship, theology, and the arts (MA), youth, family, and culture (MA); theology and ministry (MA).

Gardner-Webb University, School of Divinity, Boiling Springs, NC 28017. Offers biblical studies (M Div); Christian education and formation (M Div); intercultural studies (M Div); ministry (D Min); missiology (M Div); pastoral care and counseling (M Div); pastoral care and counseling/member care for missionaries (D Min); pastoral studies (M Div); M Div/MA; M Div/MBA. *Accreditation:* ACIPE. *Program availability:* Part-time. *Entrance requirements:* For master's, minimum GPA of 2.6; for doctorate, minimum GPA of 2.75. Additional exam requirements/recommendations for international students: required—TOEFL (minimum score 500 paper-based; 61 iBT). Electronic applications accepted. *Expenses:* Contact institution.

Global University, Graduate School of Theology, Springfield, MO 65804. Offers bible and theology (D Min); biblical language (M Div); biblical studies (MA); Christian ministry (M Div, D Min); ministerial studies (MA), including education, leadership, missions, New Testament, Old Testament. *Program availability:* Part-time, evening/weekend, online learning. *Degree requirements:* For master's, thesis (for some programs). *Entrance requirements:* For master's, minimum undergraduate GPA of 3.0. Electronic applications accepted.

Gordon-Conwell Theological Seminary, Graduate and Professional Programs, South Hamilton, MA 01982. Offers Biblical languages (MABL); church history (MACH); counseling (MACO); ministry (D Min); missions/evangelism (MAME); New Testament (MANT); Old Testament (MAOT); religion (MAR); theology (M Div, MATH, Th M, Th D). *Accreditation:* ACIPE; ATS (one or more programs are accredited). *Program availability:* Part-time, evening/weekend. *Degree requirements:* For master's, one foreign language, thesis optional; for doctorate, 2 foreign languages, thesis/dissertation. *Entrance requirements:* For master's, minimum GPA of 2.5; for doctorate, minimum GPA of 3.0.

Grace Mission University, Graduate School, Fullerton, CA 92833. Offers M Div, MACE, MAICS, D Miss.

Grace Theological Seminary, Graduate and Professional Programs, Winona Lake, IN 46590-9907. Offers biblical studies (Certificate); chaplaincy (M Div); exegetical studies (M Div); intercultural studies (M Div, MA, D Min); local church ministry (MA), including camp administration, women's leadership; pastoral counseling (M Div); pastoral studies (M Div, D Min); theology (Diploma). *Accreditation:* ATS. *Program availability:* Part-time, online learning. *Degree requirements:* For master's, thesis optional; for doctorate, 2 foreign languages, thesis/dissertation. *Entrance requirements:* For master's, MAT, minimum GPA of 2.5. Electronic applications accepted.

Hope International University, School of Graduate and Professional Studies, Programs in Ministry, Fullerton, CA 92831-3138. Offers Christian leadership (MCM); church music (MA); church music (Korean track) (MCM); church planting (MCM); intercultural studies (MCM); worship (MCM). *Program availability:* Part-time, evening/weekend, online learning. *Degree requirements:* For master's, thesis (for some programs), project. *Entrance requirements:* For master's, minimum GPA of 3.0, MCM program requires an undergraduate degree in music, 2 references. Additional exam requirements/recommendations for international students: required—TOEFL (minimum score 550 paper-based; 86 iBT); recommended—IELTS (minimum score 6.5). Electronic applications accepted. *Expenses:* Contact institution.

Liberty University, School of Divinity, Lynchburg, VA 24515. Offers Biblical exposition (MA); Biblical languages (M Div); Biblical studies (M Div, MA, MAR, Th M, D Min); chaplaincy (M Div, D Min); Christian apologetics (M Div, MA, MAR, Th M); Christian leadership and church ministries (M Div); Christian ministries (M Div); Christian ministry (MA); Christian thought (M Div); church history (M Div, MAR, Th M); community chaplaincy (M Div, MAR); discipleship (D Min); discipleship and church ministry (M Div, MAR, MCM); evangelism and church planting (MAR, MCM, D Min); expository preaching (D Min); global ministry (MA); global studies (M Div, MAR, MCM, MGS, Th M); healthcare chaplaincy (M Div); homiletics (M Div, MAR, Th M); leadership (M Div, MAR); marketplace chaplaincy (M Div, MCM); ministry leadership (Ed D); pastoral counseling (M Div, MA, MAR, D Min), including addictions and recovery (MA), crisis response and trauma (MA), discipleship and church ministries (MA), leadership (MA), life coaching (MA), marketplace chaplaincy (MA), marriage and family (MA), military resilience (MA), pastoral counseling (MA); pastoral leadership (D Min); pastoral ministries (M Div, M Serv Soc, MCM); religious education (MRE); sports chaplaincy (MA); theology (M Div, MAR, MTS, Th M); theology and apologetics (D Min, PhD); worship (M Div, MAR, MCM, D Min); youth and family ministries (M Div). *Program availability:* Part-time, online learning. *Students:* 2,691 full-time (814 women), 2,570 part-time (732 women); includes 1,484 minority (1,046 Black or African American, non-Hispanic/Latino; 33 American Indian or Alaska Native, non-Hispanic/Latino; 120 Asian, non-Hispanic/Latino; 167 Hispanic/Latino; 8 Native Hawaiian or other Pacific Islander, non-Hispanic/Latino; 110 Two or more races, non-Hispanic/Latino), 101 international. Average age 43. 4,508 applicants, 34% accepted, 952 enrolled. In 2019, 1,251 master's, 71 doctorates awarded. *Degree requirements:* For master's, 2 foreign languages, thesis (for some programs); for doctorate, 2 foreign languages, thesis/dissertation. *Entrance requirements:* For master's, minimum undergraduate GPA of 2.0; for doctorate, GRE General Test or MAT, minimum graduate GPA of 3.0. Additional exam requirements/recommendations for international students: required—TOEFL (minimum score 600 paper-based; 100 iBT). *Application deadline:* For fall admission, 6/1 for domestic students; for spring admission, 11/1 for domestic students. Applications are processed on a rolling basis. Application fee: $50. Electronic applications accepted. *Expenses:*

Missions and Missiology

Contact institution. *Financial support:* Teaching assistantships with tuition reimbursements, career-related internships or fieldwork, and Federal Work-Study available. Financial award applicants required to submit FAFSA. *Unit head:* Dr. Troy Temple, Interim Dean, School of Divinity, E-mail: divinity@liberty.edu. *Application contact:* Jay Bridge, Director of Graduate Admissions, 800-424-9595, Fax: 800-628-7977, E-mail: gradadmissions@liberty.edu.
Website: https://www.liberty.edu/divinity/

Luther Seminary, Graduate and Professional Programs, St. Paul, MN 55108-1445. Offers aging and health (MA); Biblical preaching (D Min); children, youth and family (M Div, MA); congregational mission and leadership (M Th, MA, D Min); history of Christianity (M Th, MA); missions and world religions (M Th); New Testament (M Th, MA); Old Testament (M Th, MA); pastoral care: clinical pastoral theology (M Th); pastoral theology and ministry (M Th); systematic theology (M Th, MA). *Accreditation:* ACIPE; ATS. *Program availability:* Part-time, online learning. *Degree requirements:* For master's, thesis or alternative; for doctorate, 2 foreign languages, thesis/dissertation. *Entrance requirements:* For master's, minimum GPA of 3.0; for doctorate, GRE General Test. Additional exam requirements/recommendations for international students: required—TOEFL, IELTS. Electronic applications accepted.

Mid-America Baptist Theological Seminary, Graduate and Professional Programs, Cordova, TN 38016. Offers biblical counseling (M Div); Christian education (M Div, MACE); ministry (D Min); missiology and intercultural studies (M Div); pastoral ministry (M Div); theology (MA, PhD); worship (MA). *Degree requirements:* For doctorate, 4 foreign languages, thesis/dissertation. *Entrance requirements:* For doctorate, MAT. Additional exam requirements/recommendations for international students: required—TOEFL (minimum score 600 paper-based). Electronic applications accepted.

Midwest University, Graduate Programs, Wentzville, MO 63385. Offers asset management/investment/real estate (MBA); Christian counseling (D Min); Christian education (D Min); counseling (MA), including marriage and family counseling, school counseling; divinity (M Div); education (MA), including brain and gifted education, Christian education; global business management (MBA); global leadership (MBA); leadership (PhD), including brain and gifted educational leadership, entrepreneurial leadership, international aviation leadership, organizational leadership, political leadership; mission studies (D Min); music (MM, DMA); pastoral theology (D Min); public policy/administration (MBA); teaching English to speakers of other languages (MA). *Program availability:* Part-time, online learning. *Degree requirements:* For master's, thesis (for some programs); for doctorate, thesis/dissertation. *Entrance requirements:* Additional exam requirements/recommendations for international students: recommended—TOEFL (minimum score 550 paper-based).

Milligan University, Emmanuel Christian Seminary at Milligan College, Milligan College, TN 37682. Offers Christian care and counseling (M Div); Christian education (M Div); Christian ministries (MACM, Graduate Certificate); Christian ministry (M Div); Christian theology (M Div, MAR); church history (MAR); church history/historical theology (M Div); general studies (M Div); ministry (D Min); New Testament (M Div, MAR); Old Testament (M Div, MAR); urban ministry (M Div); world missions (M Div). *Accreditation:* ACIPE; ATS. *Program availability:* Part-time, blended/hybrid learning. *Faculty:* 12 full-time (1 woman), 5 part-time/adjunct (0 women). *Students:* 70 full-time (28 women), 70 part-time (26 women); includes 19 minority (9 Black or African American, non-Hispanic/Latino; 3 American Indian or Alaska Native, non-Hispanic/Latino; 2 Asian, non-Hispanic/Latino; 5 Hispanic/Latino), 8 international. Average age 34. 109 applicants, 90% accepted, 64 enrolled. In 2019, 21 master's, 3 doctorates awarded. *Degree requirements:* For master's, 2 foreign languages, thesis or alternative, portfolio; for doctorate, thesis/dissertation. *Entrance requirements:* For master's, undergraduate degree and supporting transcripts, essay/personal statement, professional recommendations, interview; for doctorate, M Div or equivalent, essay/personal statement, professional recommendations. Additional exam requirements/recommendations for international students: required—TOEFL (minimum score 550 paper-based, 79 iBT) or IELTS (6.5). *Application deadline:* For fall admission, 8/1 for domestic students, 6/1 for international students; for spring admission, 12/15 for domestic students, 8/1 for international students. Applications are processed on a rolling basis. Application fee: $30. Electronic applications accepted. *Expenses:* 36 - 90 hr programs: $485/hr; $75 one-time records fee; MDIV (90 Hrs)/MAR (58 Hrs) $325/semester (technology and activity fee); MACM (48 Hrs)/DMIN (36 Hrs) $250/semester (technology and activity fees). *Financial support:* Scholarships/grants and unspecified assistantships available. Financial award application deadline: 12/1; financial award applicants required to submit FAFSA. *Unit head:* Dr. Rollin Ramsaran, Academic Dean, Emmanuel Christian Seminary, 423-461-1524, Fax: 423-926-6198, E-mail: raramsaran@milligan.edu. *Application contact:* Lauren Gullett, Director of Admissions and Recruitment for Emmanuel Christian Seminary, 423-461-1535, Fax: 423-926-6198, E-mail: lwgullett@milligan.edu.
Website: http://ecs.milligan.edu/

Missio Seminary, Graduate and Professional Programs, Hatfield, PA 19440-2499. Offers advanced missional leadership (D Min); advanced pastoral studies (Certificate); biblical counseling (Certificate); biblical studies (MA, Certificate); counseling (MA); ministry (M Div, MA); missional theology (MA). *Accreditation:* ATS. *Program availability:* Part-time, evening/weekend. *Degree requirements:* For master's, variable foreign language requirement, thesis optional; for doctorate, thesis/dissertation. *Entrance requirements:* Additional exam requirements/recommendations for international students: required—TOEFL (minimum score 550 paper-based; 80 iBT). Electronic applications accepted.

Nebraska Christian College of Hope International University, Graduate Programs, Papillion, NE 68046. Offers biblical studies (M Div); business as mission/social entrepreneurship (MBA); children, youth, and family (M Div); church planting (M Div); counseling psychology (MS); educational administration (MA); elementary education (M Ed); general management (MBA); gifted and talented education (M Ed); intercultural studies (M Div); international development (MBA); marketing management (MBA); ministry (MA); ministry and leadership (M Div); music education (M Ed); non-profit management (MBA); pastoral care (M Div); secondary education (M Ed); spiritual formation (M Div); worship ministry (M Div).

Northern Seminary, Graduate and Professional Programs, Lombard, IL 60148-5698. Offers Biblical studies (M Div); Christian community development (MA, D Min); Christian ministry (MACM); contextual theology (D Min); missional church ministry (M Div); New Testament (M Div, MANT); New Testament context (D Min); Old Testament (M Div); preaching (D Min); theology (M Div); theology and mission (MA); urban leadership (MA); worship (M Div, MAW). *Program availability:* Part-time, evening/weekend. *Degree requirements:* For master's, thesis (for some programs); for doctorate, thesis/dissertation. *Entrance requirements:* For master's, writing test, all official transcripts, letter of reference from church, 3 letters of reference, autobiographical statement (400 words or more); for doctorate, M Div, 3 years in the ministry post-M Div, 3 letters of reference. Additional exam requirements/recommendations for international students: required—TOEFL (minimum score 550 paper-based). Electronic applications accepted.

Northwest Nazarene University, NNU Graduate School of Theology, Nampa, ID 83686-5897. Offers leadership and formation (MA); missional leadership (M Div); pastoral ministry (MA); spiritual formation (M Div); youth, children, and family ministry (M Div). *Program availability:* Part-time, online only, 100% online. *Degree requirements:* For master's, 2.5 cumulative GPA. *Entrance requirements:* For master's, minimum GPA of 2.5; two recommendations, official transcripts. Additional exam requirements/recommendations for international students: required—TOEFL (minimum score 85 iBT). Electronic applications accepted. *Expenses:* Contact institution.

Northwest University, College of Ministry, Kirkland, WA 98033. Offers ministry (MIM); missional leadership (MA); theology and culture (MA). *Program availability:* Part-time, evening/weekend, online learning. *Degree requirements:* For master's, comprehensive exam (for some programs), thesis (for some programs). *Entrance requirements:* Additional exam requirements/recommendations for international students: required—TOEFL (minimum score 550 paper-based; 75 iBT). Electronic applications accepted.

Nyack College, Alliance Theological Seminary, New York, NY 10004. Offers Biblical literature (MA), including New Testament, Old Testament; Biblical studies (MA); Christian ministry (MPS); intercultural studies (MA); ministry (D Min), including Christian leadership in the global context; theology and missions (M Div); urban ministry (MPS). *Program availability:* Part-time, evening/weekend, 100% online, blended/hybrid learning. *Students:* 203 full-time (89 women), 343 part-time (176 women); includes 418 minority (140 Black or African American, non-Hispanic/Latino; 94 Asian, non-Hispanic/Latino; 172 Hispanic/Latino; 1 Native Hawaiian or other Pacific Islander, non-Hispanic/Latino; 11 Two or more races, non-Hispanic/Latino), 40 international. Average age 43. In 2019, 100 master's, 17 doctorates awarded. *Degree requirements:* For master's, comprehensive exam (for some programs), thesis optional, internship; for doctorate, thesis/dissertation. *Entrance requirements:* For master's, transcripts, Christian experience statement, recommendations; for doctorate, transcripts, documented three years of ministry experience subsequent to 1st graduate theological degree, reference letters, formal academic paper. Additional exam requirements/recommendations for international students: required—TOEFL (minimum score 550 paper-based; 80 iBT). *Application deadline:* Applications are processed on a rolling basis. Application fee: $30. Electronic applications accepted. *Expenses:* $585 per credit. *Financial support:* Career-related internships or fieldwork, Federal Work-Study, and scholarships/grants available. Financial award applicants required to submit FAFSA. *Unit head:* Dr. Ronald Walborn, Dean, 845-770-5715, Fax: 845-358-1663. *Application contact:* Dr. Ronald Walborn, Dean, 845-770-5715, Fax: 845-358-1663.
Website: http://www.nyack.edu/ats

Oral Roberts University, School of Theology and Missions, Tulsa, OK 74171. Offers biblical literature (MA), including advanced languages, Judaic-Christian studies; church ministries and leadership (D Min); clinical pastoral education (M Div); missions (MA); pastoral care and chaplaincy (M Div, D Min); practical theology (MA), including teaching ministries, urban ministries; professional counseling (MA), including addiction studies, marriage and family therapy; theological/historical studies (MA). *Accreditation:* ATS. *Program availability:* Part-time, online learning. *Faculty:* 17 full-time (2 women). *Students:* 268 full-time (146 women), 96 part-time (52 women); includes 66 minority (48 Black or African American, non-Hispanic/Latino; 9 American Indian or Alaska Native, non-Hispanic/Latino; 8 Asian, non-Hispanic/Latino; 1 Native Hawaiian or other Pacific Islander, non-Hispanic/Latino), 65 international. Average age 40. 661 applicants, 24% accepted, 136 enrolled. In 2019, 113 master's, 19 doctorates awarded. *Degree requirements:* For master's, thesis (for some programs), practicum/internship; for doctorate, thesis/dissertation, applied research project. *Entrance requirements:* For master's, GRE General Test or MAT (waived for those with undergraduate degree from regionally accredited institution and 3.0 or higher GPA), minimum GPA of 2.5 (professional) or 3.0 (academic); for doctorate, M Div, minimum GPA of 3.0, 3 years of full-time ministry experience. Additional exam requirements/recommendations for international students: recommended—TOEFL (minimum score 550 paper-based; 79 iBT), IELTS (minimum score 7). *Application deadline:* Applications are processed on a rolling basis. Application fee: $35. Electronic applications accepted. Application fee is waived when completed online. *Expenses: Tuition:* Full-time $11,052; part-time $5526 per year. *Required fees:* $1230; $615 per unit. Tuition and fees vary according to program. *Financial support:* Fellowships and scholarships/grants available. Financial award application deadline: 6/1. *Unit head:* Dr. Bill Buker, Chair, 918-495-6493, E-mail: bbuker@oru.edu. *Application contact:* Joe Sims, Enrollment Counselor, 918-495-6618, E-mail: jsims@oru.edu.
Website: http://www.gradtheology.oru.edu/

Phillips Theological Seminary, Programs in Theology, Tulsa, OK 74116. Offers administration of church agencies (M Div); campus ministry (M Div); church-related social work (M Div); college and seminary teaching (M Div); global mission work (M Div); institutional chaplaincy (M Div); ministerial vocations in Christian education (M Div); ministry (D Min), including parish ministry, pastoral counseling, practices of ministry; ministry and culture (MAMC), including Christian education, congregational leadership, history and practice of Christian spirituality, theology, ethics, and culture; ministry of music (M Div); pastoral care and counseling (M Div); pastoral ministry (M Div); theological studies (MTS). *Accreditation:* ATS. *Program availability:* Part-time, online learning. *Degree requirements:* For master's, thesis (for some programs); for doctorate, thesis/dissertation. *Entrance requirements:* For master's, minimum GPA of 2.5; for doctorate, M Div, minimum GPA of 3.0.

Providence University College & Theological Seminary, Theological Seminary, Otterburne, MB R0A 1G0, Canada. Offers children's ministry (Certificate); Christian studies (MA, Certificate); counseling (MA); cross-cultural discipleship (Certificate); divinity (M Div); educational studies (MA), including counseling psychology, educational ministries, student development, teaching English to speakers of other languages, training teachers of English to speakers of other languages; global studies (MA); lay counseling (Diploma); ministry (D Min); teaching English to speakers of other languages (Certificate); theological studies (MA); training teacher of English to speakers of other languages (Certificate); youth ministry (Certificate). *Accreditation:* ATS. *Program availability:* Part-time. *Degree requirements:* For master's, variable foreign language requirement, thesis (for some programs); for doctorate, thesis/dissertation. *Entrance requirements:* Additional exam requirements/recommendations for international students: recommended—TOEFL (minimum score 550 paper-based).

Reformed Theological Seminary–Jackson Campus, Graduate and Professional Programs, Jackson, MS 39209-3004. Offers Bible, theology, and missions (Certificate); Biblical exegesis (M Div); biblical studies (MA); Christian education (MA); counseling (M Div); marriage and family therapy (MA); ministry (D Min); missions (M Div, MA, D Min); theological studies (MA). *Accreditation:* AAMFT/COAMFTE (one or more programs are accredited); ATS (one or more programs are accredited). *Degree requirements:* For master's, thesis (for some programs), fieldwork; for doctorate, 2 foreign languages, thesis/dissertation. *Entrance requirements:* For master's, minimum GPA of 2.6; for doctorate, minimum GPA of 3.0. Additional exam requirements/recommendations for international students: required—TOEFL.

Regent University, Graduate School, School of Divinity, Virginia Beach, VA 23464. Offers Christian spirituality and formation (MA); divinity (M Div), including Biblical studies (M Div, MTS, Th M, PhD), chaplain ministry, Christian theology (M Div, MTS, Th M, PhD), church and ministry (M Div, MA), history of Christianity (M Div, MTS, Th M, PhD), inter-cultural studies (M Div, MA), interdisciplinary studies (M Div, MA, MTS), marketplace ministry (M Div, MA), missional discipleship, practical healing ministry (M Div, MA), worship and media (M Div, MA); leadership and renewal (D Min), including Christian leadership and renewal, clinical pastoral education, community transformation, military ministry, ministry leadership coaching; practical theology (MA), including church and ministry (M Div, MA), cosmogony, inter-cultural studies (M Div, MA), interdisciplinary studies (M Div, MA, MTS), marketplace ministry (M Div, MA), practical healing ministry (M Div, MA), worship and media (M Div, MA); renewal theology (PhD), including Biblical studies (M Div, MTS, Th M, PhD), Christian theology (M Div, MTS, Th M, PhD), history of Christianity (M Div, MTS, Th M, PhD), practical theology; theological studies (MTS), including Biblical studies (M Div, MTS, Th M, PhD), Christian theology (M Div, MTS, Th M, PhD), history of Christianity (M Div, MTS, Th M, PhD), interdisciplinary studies (M Div, MA, MTS); theology (Th M), including Biblical studies (M Div, MTS, Th M, PhD), Christian theology (M Div, MTS, Th M, PhD), history of Christianity (M Div, MTS, Th M, PhD). *Accreditation:* ACIPE; ATS. *Program availability:* Part-time, evening/weekend, 100% online, blended/hybrid learning. *Faculty:* 15 full-time (3 women), 58 part-time/adjunct (10 women). *Students:* 303 full-time (119 women), 813 part-time (403 women); includes 632 minority (509 Black or African American, non-Hispanic/Latino; 3 American Indian or Alaska Native, non-Hispanic/Latino; 31 Asian, non-Hispanic/Latino; 54 Hispanic/Latino; 2 Native Hawaiian or other Pacific Islander, non-Hispanic/Latino; 33 Two or more races, non-Hispanic/Latino), 16 international. Average age 45. 561 applicants, 66% accepted, 194 enrolled. In 2019, 168 master's, 13 doctorates awarded. *Degree requirements:* For master's, comprehensive exam, thesis or alternative, internship; for doctorate, thesis/dissertation or alternative. *Entrance requirements:* For master's, minimum undergraduate GPA of 2.75, writing sample, personal goal statement, college transcripts; for doctorate, GRE, minimum graduate GPA of 3.5 (PhD), 3.0 (D Min); clergy recommendations; writing sample; transcripts; resume; interview. Additional exam requirements/recommendations for international students: required—TOEFL (minimum score 577 paper-based). *Application deadline:* For fall admission, 5/1 priority date for domestic students. Applications are processed on a rolling basis. Application fee: $50. Electronic applications accepted. *Expenses:* Contact institution. *Financial support:* In 2019–20, 856 students received support. Career-related internships or fieldwork, scholarships/grants, health care benefits, and unspecified assistantships available. Support available to part-time students. Financial award applicants required to submit FAFSA. *Unit head:* Dr. Cornelius Bekker, Dean, 757-352-4258, Fax: 757-352-4597, E-mail: clbekker@regent.edu. *Application contact:* Heidi Cece, Assistant Vice President for Enrollment Management, 800-373-5504, Fax: 757-352-4381, E-mail: admissions@regent.edu. Website: https://www.regent.edu/school-of-divinity/

Rochester University, Center for Missional Leadership, Rochester Hills, MI 48307-2764. Offers MRE.

Saint Paul University, Faculty of Human Sciences, Program in Mission and Interreligious Studies, Ottawa, ON K1S 1C4, Canada. Offers MA. *Degree requirements:* For master's, one foreign language, thesis. *Entrance requirements:* For master's, honors BA in mission, minimum B average.

Simpson University, A.W. Tozer Theological Seminary, Redding, CA 96003-8606. Offers ministry leadership (MA). *Program availability:* Part-time, evening/weekend, 100% online, blended/hybrid learning. *Entrance requirements:* For master's, GRE General Test (if undergraduate GPA less than 2.5), Christian statement, one spiritual recommendation, one academic recommendation. Additional exam requirements/recommendations for international students: required—TOEFL (minimum score 583 paper-based; 94 iBT). Electronic applications accepted. *Expenses:* Contact institution.

Southeastern Baptist Theological Seminary, Graduate and Professional Programs, Wake Forest, NC 27587. Offers advanced biblical studies (M Div); Christian education (M Div, MACE); Christian ethics (PhD); Christian ministry (M Div); Christian planting (M Div); church music (MACM); counseling (MACO); evangelism (PhD); language (M Div); ministry (D Min); New Testament (PhD); Old Testament (PhD); philosophy (PhD); theology (Th M, PhD); women's studies (M Div). *Accreditation:* ACIPE; ATS (one or more programs are accredited). *Degree requirements:* For master's, thesis (for some programs), oral exam; for doctorate, thesis/dissertation, fieldwork. *Entrance requirements:* For master's, Cooperative English Test, minimum GPA of 2.0, M Div or equivalent (Th M); for doctorate, GRE General Test or MAT, Cooperative English Test, M Div or equivalent, 3 years of professional experience.

Southern Adventist University, School of Religion, Collegedale, TN 37315-0370. Offers evangelism and ministry (M Min); old Testament studies (MA); religious studies (MA). *Program availability:* Part-time. *Degree requirements:* For master's, comprehensive exam, thesis (for some programs). *Entrance requirements:* Additional exam requirements/recommendations for international students: required—TOEFL (minimum score 100 iBT).

The Southern Baptist Theological Seminary, Billy Graham School of Missions, Evangelism and Ministry, Louisville, KY 40280-0004. Offers ministry (D Min); missiology (MA, D Miss); missions and evangelism (M Div, Th M, PhD); theological studies (MA). *Accreditation:* ATS. *Program availability:* Part-time, evening/weekend, online learning. *Degree requirements:* For master's, 2 foreign languages; for doctorate, 4 foreign languages, thesis/dissertation. *Entrance requirements:* For doctorate, GRE General Test, MAT, M Div. Additional exam requirements/recommendations for international students: required—TOEFL, TWE.

Southern Evangelical Seminary, Graduate Programs, Matthews, NC 28105. Offers apologetics (MA, D Min, Certificate); Christian education (MA); church ministry (MA, Certificate); divinity (Certificate), including apologetics (M Div, Certificate); Islamic studies (MA, Certificate); Jewish studies (MA); philosophy (MA); philosophy of religion (PhD); religion (MA); theology (M Div), including apologetics (M Div, Certificate), Biblical studies; youth ministry (MA). *Program availability:* Part-time, evening/weekend, online learning. *Degree requirements:* For master's, thesis (for some programs); for doctorate, 2 foreign languages, comprehensive exam (for some programs), thesis/dissertation. *Entrance requirements:* Additional exam requirements/recommendations for international students: required—TOEFL (minimum score 600 paper-based). *Expenses: Tuition:* Full-time $24,000; part-time $12,000 per year. *Required fees:* $600; $300 per semester. $150 per semester.

Southwestern Assemblies of God University, Thomas F. Harrison School of Graduate Studies, Program in Theological Studies, Waxahachie, TX 75165-5735. Offers Bible and theology (MS); Biblical studies (M Div); counseling (M Div); cross cultural missions (M Div); practical theology (M Div); theological studies (M Div). *Program availability:* Online learning. *Degree requirements:* For master's, comprehensive written and oral exams. *Entrance requirements:* For master's, GRE General Test, minimum GPA of 2.5. Electronic applications accepted.

Southwestern Baptist Theological Seminary, Roy Fish School of Evangelism and Missions, Fort Worth, TX 76122-0000. Offers cross-cultural missions (MTS); evangelism (M Div); evangelism and missions (D Min); international church planting (M Div); Islamic studies (M Div, MA Islamic); missiology (MA Miss); missions (M Div); North American church planting (M Div); North American evangelism and international missions (D Min); theology (Th M); world Christian studies (PhD).

Southwestern Christian University, Program in Ministry, Bethany, OK 73008-0340. Offers church planting (M Min); church revitalization and renewal (M Min); intercultural studies (M Min); leadership (M Min); life coaching (M Min); pastoral ministries (M Min); work place ministries (M Min). *Program availability:* Part-time. *Degree requirements:* For master's, thesis. *Entrance requirements:* For master's, minimum GPA of 2.5. Additional exam requirements/recommendations for international students: required—TOEFL (minimum score 500 paper-based). Electronic applications accepted.

Taylor College and Seminary, Graduate and Professional Programs, Edmonton, AB T6J 4T3, Canada. Offers Christian studies (Diploma); intercultural studies (MA, Diploma), including intercultural studies (Diploma), TESOL; theology (M Div, MTS). *Accreditation:* ATS. *Program availability:* Part-time, online learning. *Degree requirements:* For master's, thesis optional. *Entrance requirements:* Additional exam requirements/recommendations for international students: required—TOEFL (minimum score 550 paper-based; 80 iBT), IELTS (minimum score 6.5).

Theological University of the Caribbean, Graduate Programs, Saint Just, PR 00978-0901. Offers childhood and adolescent education (MA); counseling and pastoral care (MA); ministry (D Min); missions (MA).

Trinity Bible College and Graduate School, Graduate School, Ellendale, ND 58436. Offers global theology (MA); missional leadership (MA); rural ministries (MA).

Trinity International University, Trinity Evangelical Divinity School, Deerfield, IL 60015-1284. Offers academic ministry (M Div); Biblical and Near Eastern archaeology and languages (MA); chaplaincy and ministry care (MA); Christian studies (Certificate); church and parachurch ministry (M Div); church history (MA, Th M); counseling (Th M); educational ministries (MA); educational ministry (Th M); educational studies (PhD); intercultural studies (MA, PhD); leadership and management (D Min); mental health counseling (MA); military chaplaincy (D Min); ministry (MA); missions (Th M); missions and evangelism (D Min); New Testament (MA, Th M); Old Testament (Th M); Old Testament and Semitic languages (MA); pastoral ministry and care (D Min); pastoral theology (Th M); preaching and teaching (D Min); spiritual formation and education (D Min); systematic theology (MA, Th M); theological studies (MA, PhD); urban ministry (MA). *Program availability:* Part-time, online learning. *Degree requirements:* For master's, comprehensive exam, thesis, fieldwork; for doctorate, comprehensive exam (for some programs), thesis/dissertation; for Certificate, comprehensive exam, integrative papers. *Entrance requirements:* For master's, GRE, MAT, minimum cumulative undergraduate GPA of 3.0; for doctorate, GRE, minimum cumulative graduate GPA of 3.2; for Certificate, GRE, MAT, minimum undergraduate GPA of 2.5. Additional exam requirements/recommendations for international students: required—TOEFL (minimum score 580 paper-based), TWE (minimum score 4). Electronic applications accepted.

Trinity School for Ministry, Graduate Programs, Ambridge, PA 15003-2397. Offers Anglican studies (Diploma); basic Christian studies (Diploma); divinity (M Div); ministry (D Min); mission and evangelism (MAME, Diploma); religion (MAR); youth ministry (Diploma). *Program availability:* Part-time. *Degree requirements:* For master's, thesis optional; for doctorate, thesis/dissertation. *Entrance requirements:* Additional exam requirements/recommendations for international students: required—TOEFL.

Tyndale University College & Seminary, Graduate Programs, Toronto, ON M2M 3S4, Canada. Offers Biblical studies (M Div); Christian foundations (MTS); Christian studies (Diploma); counseling (M Div); educational ministry (M Div); missions (M Div, Diploma); pastoral and Chinese ministry (M Div); pastoral ministry (M Div); Pentecostal studies (MTS); spiritual formation (M Div, Diploma); theological studies (M Div); theology (Th M); worship and liturgy (M Div, MTS); youth and family ministry (M Div). *Accreditation:* ATS. *Program availability:* Part-time, online learning. *Entrance requirements:* For master's and Diploma, minimum C+ average in undergraduate course work. Additional exam requirements/recommendations for international students: required—TOEFL (minimum score 570 paper-based), TWE (minimum score 5). Electronic applications accepted.

University of South Africa, College of Human Sciences, Pretoria, South Africa. Offers adult education (M Ed); African languages (MA, PhD); African politics (MA, PhD); Afrikaans (MA, PhD); ancient history (MA, PhD); ancient Near Eastern studies (MA, PhD); anthropology (MA, PhD); applied linguistics (MA); Arabic (MA, PhD); archaeology (MA); art history (MA); Biblical archaeology (MA); Biblical studies (M Th, D Th, PhD); Christian spirituality (M Th, D Th); church history (M Th, D Th); classical studies (MA, PhD); clinical psychology (MA); communication (MA, PhD); comparative education (M Ed, Ed D); consulting psychology (D Admin, D Com, PhD); curriculum studies (M Ed, Ed D); development studies (M Admin, MA, D Admin, PhD); didactics (M Ed, Ed D); education (M Tech); education management (M Ed, Ed D); educational psychology (M Ed); English (MA); environmental education (M Ed); French (MA, PhD); German (MA, PhD); Greek (MA); guidance and counseling (M Ed); health studies (MA, PhD), including health sciences education (MA), health services management (MA), medical and surgical nursing science (critical care general) (MA), midwifery and neonatal nursing science (MA), trauma and emergency care (MA); history (MA, PhD); history of education (Ed D); inclusive education (M Ed, Ed D); information and communications technology policy and regulation (MA); information science (MA, MIS, PhD); international politics (MA, PhD); Islamic studies (MA, PhD); Italian (MA, PhD); Judaica (MA, PhD); linguistics (MA, PhD); mathematical education (M Ed); mathematics education (MA); missiology (M Th, D Th); modern Hebrew (MA, PhD); musicology (MA, MMus, D Mus, PhD); natural science education (M Ed); New Testament (M Th, D Th); Old Testament (D Th); pastoral therapy (M Th, D Th); philosophy (MA); philosophy of education (M Ed, Ed D); politics (MA, PhD); Portuguese (MA, PhD); practical theology (M Th, D Th); psychology (MA, MS, PhD); psychology of education (M Ed, Ed D); public health (MA); religious studies (MA, D Th, PhD); Romance languages (MA); Russian (MA, PhD); Semitic languages (MA, PhD); social behavior studies in HIV/AIDS (MA); social science (mental health) (MA); social science in development studies (MA); social science in psychology (MA); social science in social work (MA); social science in sociology (MA); social work (MSW, DSW, PhD); socio-education (M Ed, Ed D); sociolinguistics (MA); sociology (MA, PhD); Spanish (MA, PhD); systematic theology (M Th, D Th); TESOL (teaching English to speakers of other languages) (MA); theological ethics (M Th, D Th); theory of literature (MA, PhD); urban ministries (D Th); urban ministry (M Th).

Villanova University, Villanova School of Business, Master of Science in Church Management Program, Villanova, PA 19085-1699. Offers MSCM. *Program availability:* Part-time-only, online only, 100% online, residence week at beginning of program. *Faculty:* 100 full-time (37 women), 34 part-time/adjunct (5 women). *Students:* 35 part-time (14 women); includes 11 minority (3 Black or African American, non-Hispanic/Latino; 1 Asian, non-Hispanic/Latino; 6 Hispanic/Latino; 1 Two or more races, non-Hispanic/Latino), 4 international. Average age 44. In 2019, 41 master's awarded. *Degree requirements:* For master's, minimum GPA of 3.0. *Entrance requirements:* For master's, Application, official transcripts, 2 letters of recommendation, resume, essay. Additional exam requirements/recommendations for international students: required—TOEFL (minimum score 550 paper-based; 100 iBT). *Application deadline:* For summer admission, 4/30 for domestic and international students. Applications are processed on a rolling basis. Application fee: $65. Electronic applications accepted. *Expenses:* Students who work for the church will receive a 25% tuition discount, allowing their tuition to be $22,050. *Financial support:* Scholarships/grants available. Financial award

application deadline: 6/30; financial award applicants required to submit FAFSA. *Unit head:* Dr. Joyce E. A. Russell, Dean of Villanova School of Business, 610-519-6082, E-mail: joyce.russell@villanova.edu. *Application contact:* Chesley Turner, Director, Center for Church Management, 610-519-6015, E-mail: lauren.turner@villanova.edu.
Website: https://www1.villanova.edu/villanova/business/graduate/specializedprograms/church_mgmt.html

Wesley Biblical Seminary, Graduate Programs, Jackson, MS 39206. Offers apologetics (MA); Biblical languages (M Div); Biblical literature (MA); Christian studies (MA); context and mission (M Div); honors research (M Div); interpretation (M Div); ministry (M Div); spiritual formation (M Div); teaching (M Div); theology (MA). *Accreditation:* ATS. *Program availability:* Part-time. *Degree requirements:* For master's, thesis. *Entrance requirements:* Additional exam requirements/recommendations for international students: required—TOEFL. Electronic applications accepted.

Westminster Theological Seminary, Graduate and Professional Programs, Philadelphia, PA 19118. Offers apologetics (Th M); Biblical and urban studies (Certificate); Biblical counseling (MA); biblical studies (MAR); Christian studies (Certificate); church history (Th M); counseling (M Div); general studies (M Div, MAR); hermeneutics and Bible interpretations (PhD); historical and theological studies (PhD); historical theology (Th M); New Testament (Th M); Old Testament (Th M); pastoral counseling (D Min); pastoral ministry (M Div, D Min); systematic theology (Th M); theological studies (MAR); urban missions (M Div, MA, MAR, D Min). *Accreditation:* ATS. *Program availability:* Part-time. Terminal master's awarded for partial completion of doctoral program. *Degree requirements:* For master's, thesis (for some programs); for doctorate, 4 foreign languages, comprehensive exam (for some programs), thesis/dissertation. *Entrance requirements:* For doctorate, GRE General Test. Additional exam requirements/recommendations for international students: required—TOEFL, TWE.

Wheaton College, Graduate School, Evangelism and Leadership Program, Wheaton, IL 60187-5593. Offers evangelism and leadership (MA); missional church movements (MA). *Program availability:* Part-time. *Degree requirements:* For master's, thesis or alternative. *Entrance requirements:* For master's, GRE or MAT. Additional exam requirements/recommendations for international students: required—TOEFL (minimum score 550 paper-based; 80 iBT), IELTS (minimum score 6.5). Electronic applications accepted. *Expenses: Tuition:* Full-time $16,800; part-time $700 per credit hour. Tuition and fees vary according to degree level and program.

Whitworth University, Graduate Studies in Theology, Spokane, WA 99251-0001. Offers Christian ministry (MA); mission and culture (MA); theology (MA). *Program availability:* Part-time, evening/weekend. Electronic applications accepted. *Expenses: Tuition:* Full-time $11,970; part-time $3990 per credit. Tuition and fees vary according to course load and program.

Pastoral Ministry and Counseling

Abilene Christian University, Office of Graduate Programs, College of Biblical Studies, Graduate School of Theology, Abilene, TX 79699. Offers ancient and Oriental Christianity (MA); Christian ministry (MACM); divinity (M Div), including ministry, missions; global service (MA); ministry (D Min), including Christian spiritual formation, leadership for missional renewal, preaching for community transformation; modern and American Christianity (MA); New Testament (MA); Old Testament (MA); theology (MA). *Program availability:* Part-time, evening/weekend, online learning. *Faculty:* 12 full-time (2 women), 9 part-time/adjunct (1 woman). *Students:* 116 full-time (24 women), 86 part-time (24 women); includes 61 minority (34 Black or African American, non-Hispanic/Latino; 1 Asian, non-Hispanic/Latino; 21 Hispanic/Latino; 5 Two or more races, non-Hispanic/Latino), 11 international. 185 applicants, 54% accepted, 68 enrolled. In 2019, 17 master's, 2 doctorates awarded. *Degree requirements:* For master's, comprehensive exam (for some programs), thesis (for some programs); for doctorate, one foreign language, thesis/dissertation. *Entrance requirements:* For master's, official transcripts, recommendation, purpose statement, writing assessment; for doctorate, official transcripts, Documentation of Ministry, recommendations, personal statement, Endorsement of Elders or Supervisor. Additional exam requirements/recommendations for international students: required—TOEFL (minimum score 80 iBT), IELTS (minimum score 6), PTE (minimum score 51). *Application deadline:* For fall admission, 8/10 priority date for domestic students; for spring admission, 11/1 for domestic students. Applications are processed on a rolling basis. Application fee: $65. *Expenses:* $676 per hour. *Financial support:* In 2019–20, 39 students received support, including 18 research assistantships with partial tuition reimbursements available; Federal Work-Study also available. Support available to part-time students. Financial award application deadline: 4/1; financial award applicants required to submit FAFSA. *Unit head:* Dr. Tim Sensing, Associate Dean, 325-674-3730, Fax: 325-674-6180, E-mail: sensingt@acu.edu. *Application contact:* Graduate Admissions, 325-674-6911, E-mail: gradinfo@acu.edu.
Website: http://www.acu.edu/gst

Acadia University, Divinity College, Wolfville, NS B4P 2R6, Canada. Offers divinity (M Div); ministry (D Min); theology (MA), including chaplaincy and spiritual care, Christian history, discipleship, evangelism and mission, indigenous community development, leadership and spiritual formation, New Testament, next generation ministry, Old Testament, pastoral care and counseling, prison chaplaincy, Second Temple Judaism, theology. *Accreditation:* ATS. *Program availability:* Part-time. *Degree requirements:* For master's, variable foreign language requirement, thesis (for some programs); for doctorate, one foreign language, comprehensive exam, thesis/dissertation. *Entrance requirements:* For doctorate, minimum GPA of 3.0, 3 years' ministry experience. Additional exam requirements/recommendations for international students: required—TOEFL. *Expenses:* Contact institution.

Ambrose University, Ambrose Seminary, Calgary, AB T3H 0L5, Canada. Offers Biblical/theological studies (MA), including New Testament, Old Testament, theology; Christian studies (MCS, Diploma); intercultural ministries (M Div, MA); leadership (Certificate); leadership and ministry (MA), including chaplaincy, poverty studies, preaching; pastoral ministry (M Div). *Accreditation:* ATS (one or more programs are accredited). *Program availability:* Part-time, blended/hybrid learning. *Degree requirements:* For master's, variable foreign language requirement, internship (for M Div, MA in leadership and ministry, MA in intercultural ministries); thesis (for MA in Biblical/theological studies). *Entrance requirements:* For master's, undergraduate degree from other accredited university or bible college, minimum GPA of 2.0. Additional exam requirements/recommendations for international students: required—PTE (minimum score 58), TOEFL (minimum score 560 paper-based, 83 iBT) or IELTS (minimum score 6.5). Electronic applications accepted.

American Baptist Seminary of the West, Graduate and Professional Programs, Berkeley, CA 94704-3029. Offers community leadership (MA); theology (M Div, MA). *Accreditation:* ACIPE; ATS (one or more programs are accredited). *Program availability:* Part-time, evening/weekend, online learning. *Entrance requirements:* Additional exam requirements/recommendations for international students: required—TOEFL (minimum score 550 paper-based). Electronic applications accepted.

Amridge University, Graduate and Professional Programs, Montgomery, AL 36117. Offers Biblical studies (MA, PhD); Christian ministry (MS); family therapy (D Min); human services (MS); leadership and management (MS); marriage and family therapy (M Div, MA, PhD); ministerial leadership (M Div, MS); New Testament studies (MA); Old Testament studies (MA); professional counseling (M Div, MA, PhD); theology (M Div, D Min). *Program availability:* Part-time, evening/weekend, online learning. *Degree requirements:* For master's, one foreign language, comprehensive exam (for some programs), thesis (for some programs); for doctorate, one foreign language, comprehensive exam (for some programs), thesis/dissertation (for some programs). *Entrance requirements:* For master's, official transcript showing an earned 4-year BA or BS from regionally- or nationally-accredited institution; for doctorate, official transcript showing earned graduate degree from regionally- or nationally-accredited institution; writing sample (e.g. career monograph, published journal article, term paper from master's degree or doctoral dissertation); interview. Additional exam requirements/recommendations for international students: required—TOEFL (minimum score 79 iBT). Electronic applications accepted.

Anabaptist Mennonite Biblical Seminary, Graduate and Professional Programs, Elkhart, IN 46517-1999. Offers chaplaincy (M Div); Christian faith formation (M Div); Christian formation (MA); Christian spiritual formation (Certificate); divinity (M Div); pastoral ministry (M Div); pastoral theology for financial professionals (Certificate); peace studies (M Div), including environmental sustainability leadership (M Div, MA); theological studies (M Div, Certificate), including peace studies (M Div), theology and ethics (M Div); theology and peace studies (MA), including conflict transformation, environmental sustainability leadership (M Div, MA), international development administration; United Methodist leadership (M Div). *Accreditation:* ACIPE; ATS. *Program availability:* Part-time, 100% online, blended/hybrid learning. *Degree requirements:* For master's, variable foreign language requirement, comprehensive exam (for some programs), thesis optional, senior interview. *Entrance requirements:* For master's, undergraduate degree transcripts, 3 letters of reference, essay. Additional exam requirements/recommendations for international students: required—TOEFL (minimum score 90 iBT); recommended—IELTS (minimum score 7). Electronic applications accepted.

Anderson University, Clamp Divinity School, Anderson, SC 29621. Offers 21st-century ministry (D Min); ministry (M Min); youth ministry (M Div). *Program availability:* Part-time, online only, 100% online, blended/hybrid learning. *Degree requirements:* For master's, capstone course, ministry project. *Entrance requirements:* For master's, 3 references. *Financial support:* Scholarships/grants and tuition waivers available. Financial award application deadline: 3/1; financial award applicants required to submit FAFSA. *Unit head:* Dr. Michael Duduit, Dean, 864-328-1809, E-mail: ministry@andersonuniversity.edu. *Application contact:* Dr. Ben Brammer, Senior Recruiter, 864-2312039, E-mail: bbrammer@andersonuniversity.edu.
Website: online.andersonuniversity.edu

Andrews University, School of Graduate Studies, Seventh-day Adventist Theological Seminary, Berrien Springs, MI 49104. Offers ministry (M Div, D Min); pastoral ministry (MA); religious education (MA, Ed D, PhD, Ed S); theology (M Th, Th D); youth ministry (MA). *Faculty:* 40 full-time (5 women), 12 part-time/adjunct (2 women). *Students:* 448 full-time (52 women), 456 part-time (84 women); includes 463 minority (193 Black or African American, non-Hispanic/Latino; 3 American Indian or Alaska Native, non-Hispanic/Latino; 49 Asian, non-Hispanic/Latino; 198 Hispanic/Latino; 10 Native Hawaiian or other Pacific Islander, non-Hispanic/Latino; 10 Two or more races, non-Hispanic/Latino), 255 international. Average age 40. In 2019, 171 master's, 41 doctorates, 1 other advanced degree awarded. *Degree requirements:* For master's, thesis optional; for doctorate, variable foreign language requirement, thesis/dissertation. *Entrance requirements:* For master's, GRE Subject Test, minimum GPA of 2.0. Additional exam requirements/recommendations for international students: required—TOEFL (minimum score 550 paper-based). *Application deadline:* Applications are processed on a rolling basis. Application fee: $60. *Financial support:* Fellowships, research assistantships, teaching assistantships, career-related internships or fieldwork, Federal Work-Study, and institutionally sponsored loans available. *Unit head:* Dr. Jiri Moskala, Dean, 269-471-3537. *Application contact:* Jillian Panigot, Director of Graduate Admissions, 800-253-2874, Fax: 269-471-6321.

Appalachian Bible College, Graduate Program, Mount Hope, WV 25880. Offers ministry (MA). *Program availability:* Part-time, online learning. *Entrance requirements:* For master's, ABHE Bible Content Exam, bachelor's degree, 3 references, minimum undergraduate cumulative GPA of 2.5. Additional exam requirements/recommendations for international students: required—TOEFL (minimum score 550 paper-based). Electronic applications accepted.

Aquinas Institute of Theology, Graduate and Professional Programs, St. Louis, MO 63108. Offers biblical studies (Certificate); church music (MM); health care mission (MAHCM); ministry (M Div); pastoral care (Certificate); pastoral ministry (MAPM); pastoral studies (MAPS); preaching (D Min); spiritual direction (Certificate); theology (M Div, MA); Thomistic studies (Certificate); M Div/MA; MA/PhD; MAPS/MSW. *Accreditation:* ATS (one or more programs are accredited). *Program availability:* Part-time, evening/weekend, online learning. *Degree requirements:* For master's, variable foreign language requirement, comprehensive exam (for some programs), thesis (for some programs); for doctorate, thesis/dissertation. *Entrance requirements:* For master's and Certificate, MAT; for doctorate, 3 years of ministerial experience, 6 hours of graduate course work in homiletics, M Div or the equivalent, minimum GPA of 3.0. Additional exam requirements/recommendations for international students: required—TOEFL. *Expenses:* Contact institution.

Asbury Theological Seminary, Graduate and Professional Programs, Wilmore, KY 40390-1199. Offers M Div, MA, MAAS, MACE, MACL, MACM, MACP, MAMFC, MAMHC, MAPC, MASF, MAYM, Th M, D Min, PhD, Certificate. *Accreditation:* ATS. *Program availability:* Part-time, online learning. Terminal master's awarded for partial completion of doctoral program. *Degree requirements:* For master's, thesis (for some programs); for doctorate, thesis/dissertation, qualifying exam. *Entrance requirements:*

For master's, minimum GPA of 2.75; for doctorate, minimum GPA of 3.0. Additional exam requirements/recommendations for international students: required—TOEFL, IELTS. Electronic applications accepted.

Ashland Theological Seminary, Graduate Programs, Ashland, OH 44805. Offers Biblical studies (MA); Christian ministries (MACM), including Black church studies (MACM, D Min), general Christian ministries, leadership, spiritual formation (MACM, D Min); clinical mental health counseling (MA); counseling (MAC); historical and theological studies (MA), including Anabaptism and Pietism, Christian theology, church history, New Testament, Old Testament; ministry (D Min), including Black church studies (MACM, D Min), chaplaincy (M Div, D Min), independent design, spiritual formation (MACM, D Min), transformational leadership; pastoral ministry (M Div), including chaplaincy (M Div, D Min), general ministry. *Accreditation:* ATS. *Program availability:* Part-time. *Degree requirements:* For master's, 2 foreign languages, comprehensive exam (for some programs), thesis (for some programs); for doctorate, thesis/dissertation. *Entrance requirements:* For master's, bachelor's degree from accredited institution with minimum undergraduate GPA of 2.75; for doctorate, M Div, minimum undergraduate GPA of 3.0. Additional exam requirements/recommendations for international students: required—TOEFL (minimum score 500 paper-based; 65 iBT). Electronic applications accepted.

Assemblies of God Theological Seminary, Graduate and Professional Programs, Springfield, MO 65802. Offers Biblical interpretation and theology (PhD); Christian ministries (MA); divinity (M Div); intercultural studies (MA, PhD); leadership and ministry (MLM); ministry (D Min); missiology (DAIS); pastoral studies (MPL); theological studies (MA, Th M). *Accreditation:* ATS. *Program availability:* Part-time, evening/weekend, 100% online. *Faculty:* 12 full-time (3 women), 15 part-time/adjunct (4 women). *Students:* 136 full-time (37 women), 147 part-time (40 women); includes 71 minority (24 Black or African American, non-Hispanic/Latino; 6 American Indian or Alaska Native, non-Hispanic/Latino; 7 Asian, non-Hispanic/Latino; 22 Hispanic/Latino; 7 Native Hawaiian or other Pacific Islander, non-Hispanic/Latino; 5 Two or more races, non-Hispanic/Latino), 14 international. Average age 46. 62 applicants, 100% accepted, 42 enrolled. In 2019, 37 master's, 25 doctorates awarded. *Degree requirements:* For master's, variable foreign language requirement, thesis; for doctorate, variable foreign language requirement, comprehensive exam, thesis/dissertation. *Entrance requirements:* For master's, minimum GPA of 2.5; for doctorate, GRE (for PhD in Bible theology), minimum GPA of 3.0. Additional exam requirements/recommendations for international students: required—TOEFL (minimum score 550 paper-based; 80 iBT). *Application deadline:* For fall admission, 7/1 priority date for domestic students, 6/1 priority date for international students; for spring admission, 12/1 priority date for domestic students, 11/1 priority date for international students. Applications are processed on a rolling basis. Application fee: $75. Electronic applications accepted. *Financial support:* Career-related internships or fieldwork and scholarships/grants available. Support available to part-time students. Financial award application deadline: 7/15; financial award applicants required to submit FAFSA. *Unit head:* Dr. Timothy A. Hager, Dean, 417-268-1000, Fax: 417-268-1001. *Application contact:* Nik White, Seminary Enrollment Coordinator, 417-268-1000, Fax: 417-268-1030, E-mail: info@agts.edu.
Website: http://www.agts.edu

Atlantic School of Theology, Graduate and Professional Programs, Halifax, NS B3H 3B5, Canada. Offers ministry (M Div); theological studies (Graduate Certificate). *Accreditation:* ATS. *Program availability:* Part-time, online learning. *Degree requirements:* For master's, thesis (for some programs). *Entrance requirements:* For master's and Graduate Certificate, minimum B average in undergraduate course work. *Expenses: Required fees:* $7000 Canadian dollars; $700 Canadian dollars per course.

Atlantic University, Spiritual Guidance Mentor Program, Virginia Beach, VA 23451-2061. Offers Certificate. *Program availability:* Online learning. *Degree requirements:* For Certificate, final essay. *Entrance requirements:* For degree, 500-word essay. Electronic applications accepted. *Expenses:* Contact institution.

Austin Presbyterian Theological Seminary, Graduate and Professional Programs, Austin, TX 78705-5797. Offers divinity (M Div); ministry (D Min); ministry practice (MA); theological studies (MA); youth ministry (MA); M Div/MSSW. *Accreditation:* ACIPE; ATS. *Degree requirements:* For master's, Greek, Hebrew (for M Div); for doctorate, thesis/dissertation. *Entrance requirements:* For master's, references (for M Div). Additional exam requirements/recommendations for international students: required—TOEFL (minimum score 550 paper-based; 79 iBT). Electronic applications accepted. *Expenses: Tuition:* Full-time $13,980; part-time $6990 per credit. *Required fees:* $170; $170.

Ave Maria University, Graduate Programs, Ave Maria, FL 34142. Offers pastoral theology (MTS); theology (MA, PhD). Terminal master's awarded for partial completion of doctoral program. *Degree requirements:* For master's, one foreign language, thesis; for doctorate, 3 foreign languages, comprehensive exam, thesis/dissertation. *Entrance requirements:* For master's, GRE; for doctorate, GRE, M Div or equivalent; MA or MTS in religion, theology, or philosophy; bachelor's degree with strong background in religion, theology, and/or philosophy.

Azusa Pacific University, Azusa Pacific Seminary, Program in Divinity, Azusa, CA 91702-7000. Offers Biblical studies (M Div). *Expenses:* Contact institution.

Azusa Pacific University, Azusa Pacific Seminary, Program in Pastoral Studies, Concentration in Church Leadership and Development, Azusa, CA 91702-7000. Offers MAPS. *Degree requirements:* For master's, project.

Bakke Graduate University, Programs in Pastoral Ministry and Business, Dallas, TX 75243-7039. Offers business administration (MBA); church and ministry multiplication (D Min); global urban leadership (MA); leadership (D Min); ministry in complex contexts (D Min); social and civic entrepreneurship (MA); theology of work (D Min); theology reflection (D Min); transformational leadership (DTL); urban youth ministry (D Min). *Program availability:* Part-time, online learning. *Degree requirements:* For master's, thesis; for doctorate, thesis/dissertation. *Entrance requirements:* For master's, 2 years of ministry experience, BA in Biblical studies or theology; for doctorate, 3 years of ministry experience, M Div. Additional exam requirements/recommendations for international students: required—TOEFL. Electronic applications accepted.

Baptist Bible College, Graduate and Professional Programs, Springfield, MO 65803-3498. Offers biblical counseling (MA); church ministry (MA); theology (M Div). *Program availability:* Part-time. *Entrance requirements:* Additional exam requirements/recommendations for international students: required—TOEFL. Electronic applications accepted. *Expenses:* Contact institution.

The Baptist College of Florida, Graduate Programs, Graceville, FL 32440. Offers Christian studies (MA); music and worship leadership (MA). *Program availability:* Part-time, 100% online, blended/hybrid learning. *Faculty:* 13 full-time (2 women). *Students:* 33 full-time (6 women); includes 2 minority (1 Black or African American, non-Hispanic/Latino; 1 Hispanic/Latino). Average age 28. 10 applicants, 100% accepted, 10 enrolled. In 2019, 3 master's awarded. *Degree requirements:* For master's, variable foreign language requirement, comprehensive exam (for some programs), thesis (for some programs). *Entrance requirements:* For master's, regionally-accredited undergraduate degree, undergraduate courses in field, minimum GPA of 2.5. Additional exam requirements/recommendations for international students: required—TOEFL.

Application deadline: For fall admission, 8/10 for domestic and international students; for spring admission, 1/20 for domestic and international students. Applications are processed on a rolling basis. Application fee: $25. Electronic applications accepted. *Expenses: Tuition:* Full-time $4320; part-time $360 per credit hour. *Financial support:* In 2019–20, 2 students received support. Applicants required to submit FAFSA. *Unit head:* Dr. Robin Jumper, Academic Dean, 850-263-3261 Ext. 425, Fax: 850-263-2141, E-mail: grjumper@baptistcollege.edu. *Application contact:* Sandra Richards, Director of Student Life and Marketing, 850-263-3261 Ext. 415, Fax: 850-263-9026, E-mail: skrichards@baptistcollege.edu.
Website: http://www.baptistcollege.edu

Barry University, College of Arts and Sciences, Department of Theology and Philosophy, Miami Shores, FL 33161-6695. Offers ministry (D Min); pastoral ministry for Hispanics (MA); pastoral theology (MA); practical theology (MA). *Accreditation:* ATS. *Program availability:* Part-time, evening/weekend. *Degree requirements:* For master's, comprehensive exam, thesis optional; for doctorate, thesis/dissertation. *Entrance requirements:* For master's, GRE General Test or MAT, minimum GPA of 3.0. Electronic applications accepted.

Bethany Theological Seminary, Graduate and Professional Programs, Richmond, IN 47374-4019. Offers biblical studies (MA Th); ministry studies (M Div); peace studies (M Div, MA Th); theological studies (MA Th, CATS); youth ministry (M Div). *Accreditation:* ACIPE; ATS. *Program availability:* Part-time, online learning. *Degree requirements:* For master's, thesis (for some programs). *Entrance requirements:* For master's, letters of reference. Additional exam requirements/recommendations for international students: required—TOEFL (minimum score 550 paper-based).

Bethel Seminary, Graduate and Professional Programs, St. Paul, MN 55112-6998. Offers Anglican studies (Certificate); children's and family ministry (MA); Christian studies (Certificate); Christian thought (MA); church planting (Certificate); Greek and Hebrew language (M Div); Greek language (M Div); Hebrew language (M Div); marriage and family therapy (MA, Certificate); mental health counseling (MA); ministry (MA, D Min); ministry practice (Certificate); theological studies (MA, Certificate); transformational leadership (MA); young life youth ministry (Certificate). *Accreditation:* ACIPE. *Program availability:* Part-time, evening/weekend, 100% online, blended/hybrid learning. *Degree requirements:* For master's, variable foreign language requirement, thesis (for some programs); for doctorate, thesis/dissertation. *Entrance requirements:* For master's, letters of reference, transcripts, personal statement; for doctorate, M Div, letters of reference, organizational support; for Certificate, letters of reference, family essay, personal statement, and family of origin paper (for marriage and family therapy). Additional exam requirements/recommendations for international students: required—TOEFL (minimum score 550 paper-based; 87 iBT). Electronic applications accepted. *Expenses:* Contact institution.

Bethel University, Adult and Graduate Programs, Program in Ministries, Mishawaka, IN 46545-5591. Offers M Min. *Program availability:* Part-time, evening/weekend, 100% online, blended/hybrid learning. *Degree requirements:* For master's, thesis or alternative. *Entrance requirements:* Additional exam requirements/recommendations for international students: required—TOEFL (minimum score 540 paper-based). Electronic applications accepted.

Biola University, Talbot School of Theology, La Mirada, CA 90639-0001. Offers adult/family ministry (MACE); Bible exposition (MA, Th M); Biblical and theological studies (Certificate); children's ministry (MACE); Christian education (M Div); cross-cultural education ministry (MACE); educational studies (Ed D, PhD); evangelism and discipleship (M Div); general Christian education (MACE); Messianic Jewish studies (M Div, Certificate); missions and intercultural studies (M Div); New Testament (MA, Th M); Old Testament (MA); Old Testament and Semitics (Th M); pastoral and general ministry (M Div); pastoral care and counseling (M Div, MACML); philosophy (MA); preaching and pastoral ministry (MACML); spiritual formation (M Div, Certificate); spiritual formation and soul care (MA); sports ministry (MACML); theology (MA, Th M, D Min, Certificate); youth ministry (MACE). *Program availability:* Part-time, evening/weekend. *Students:* 461 full-time (116 women), 768 part-time (228 women); includes 489 minority (54 Black or African American, non-Hispanic/Latino; 1 American Indian or Alaska Native, non-Hispanic/Latino; 303 Asian, non-Hispanic/Latino; 96 Hispanic/Latino; 3 Native Hawaiian or other Pacific Islander, non-Hispanic/Latino; 32 Two or more races, non-Hispanic/Latino), 162 international. Average age 38. 745 applicants, 70% accepted, 320 enrolled. In 2019, 235 master's, 24 doctorates awarded. *Entrance requirements:* For master's, bachelor's degree from accredited college or university; minimum GPA of 2.6 (for M Div), 3.0 (for MA); for doctorate, M Div or MA. Additional exam requirements/recommendations for international students: required—TOEFL (minimum score 600 paper-based; 88 iBT). *Application deadline:* For fall admission, 7/1 for domestic students, 6/1 for international students; for spring admission, 11/1 for domestic students. Applications are processed on a rolling basis. Application fee: $65. Electronic applications accepted. *Financial support:* Scholarships/grants and unspecified assistantships available. Support available to part-time students. Financial award applicants required to submit FAFSA. *Unit head:* Dr. Clint Arnold, Dean, 562-903-4816, Fax: 562-903-4748. *Application contact:* Graduate Admissions Office, 562-903-4752, E-mail: graduate.admissions@biola.edu.
Website: http://www.talbot.edu/

Bob Jones University, Graduate Programs, Greenville, SC 29614. Offers accountancy (MS); Bible (MA); Bible translation (MA); Biblical studies (Certificate); business administration (MBA); church history (MA, PhD); church ministries (MA); church music (MM); cinema and video production (MA); counseling (MS); curriculum and instruction (Ed D); divinity (M Div); dramatic production (MA); educational leadership (MS, Ed D, Ed S); elementary education (M Ed, MAT); English (M Ed, MA, MAT); fine arts (MA); graphic design (MA); history (M Ed, MA); illustration (MA); interpretative speech (MA); mathematics (M Ed, MAT); medical missions (Certificate); ministry (MM, D Min); multi-categorical special education (M Ed, MAT); music (M Ed); New Testament interpretation (PhD); Old Testament interpretation (PhD); orchestral instrument performance (MM); organ performance (MM); pastoral studies (MA); personnel services (MS, Ed S); piano pedagogy (MM); piano performance (MM); platform arts (MA); rhetoric and public address (MA); secondary education (M Ed); studio art (MA); teaching Bible (MA); theology (MA, PhD); voice performance (MM); youth ministries (MA); M Div/MM.

Boston College, School of Theology and Ministry, Chestnut Hill, MA 02467-3800. Offers church leadership (MA); divinity (M Div); pastoral ministry (MA), including Hispanic ministry, liturgy and worship, pastoral care and counseling, spirituality; religious education (MA, PhD); sacred theology (STD, STL); social justice/social ministry (MA); spiritual direction (MA); theological studies (MTS); theology (Th M, PhD); youth ministry (MA); MA/MA; MS/MA; MSW/MA. *Accreditation:* TEAC. *Program availability:* Part-time. *Degree requirements:* For doctorate, one foreign language, thesis/dissertation. *Entrance requirements:* For doctorate, GRE. Additional exam requirements/recommendations for international students: required—TOEFL (minimum score 550 paper-based). Electronic applications accepted.

Briercrest Seminary, Graduate Programs, Program in Christian Ministries, Caronport, SK S0H 0S0, Canada. Offers leadership (MA); marriage and family counseling (MA); missions (MA); pastoral counseling (MA); worship (MA); youth and family ministry (MA).

Program availability: Part-time. *Degree requirements:* For master's, comprehensive exam, thesis optional. *Entrance requirements:* Additional exam requirements/ recommendations for international students: required—TOEFL (minimum score 550 paper-based).

Briercrest Seminary, Graduate Programs, Program in Theology, Caronport, SK S0H 0S0, Canada. Offers Biblical studies (M Div); leadership and management (M Div); New Testament (MATS); Old Testament (MATS); pastoral counseling (M Div); pastoral ministry (M Div); theological studies (M Div); theology (MATS); worship (M Div); youth and family ministry (M Div). *Accreditation:* ATS. *Program availability:* Part-time. *Degree requirements:* For master's, comprehensive exam, thesis optional. *Entrance requirements:* Additional exam requirements/recommendations for international students: required—TOEFL (minimum score 550 paper-based).

Brite Divinity School, Graduate and Professional Programs, Fort Worth, TX 76109. Offers Biblical interpretation (PhD); divinity (M Div); ministry (D Min); pastoral theology (PhD); theological studies (MTS, CTS); theology (Th M); theology and ministry (MA). *Accreditation:* ACIPE; ATS (one or more programs are accredited); SACS/CC. *Program availability:* Part-time, evening/weekend. *Entrance requirements:* For master's, minimum GPA of 2.5. Additional exam requirements/recommendations for international students: required—TOEFL.

Bryan College, MBA Program, Dayton, TN 37321. Offers business administration (MBA); healthcare administration (MBA); human resources (MBA); marketing (MBA); ministry (MBA); sports management (MBA). *Program availability:* Part-time, evening/ weekend, online only, 100% online. *Faculty:* 1 full-time (0 women), 13 part-time/adjunct (5 women). *Students:* 137 full-time (72 women), 26 part-time (11 women). 70 applicants, 100% accepted, 70 enrolled. In 2019, 28 master's awarded. *Degree requirements:* For master's, minimum gpa of 3.0. *Entrance requirements:* For master's, transcripts showing degree conferral undergrad gpa of 2.75. Additional exam requirements/ recommendations for international students: required—TOEFL (minimum score 70 iBT). *Application deadline:* For fall admission, 9/1 for domestic and international students; for winter admission, 11/15 for domestic and international students; for spring admission, 2/ 1 for domestic and international students; for summer admission, 6/1 for domestic and international students. Applications are processed on a rolling basis. Application fee: $0. Electronic applications accepted. *Expenses:* 595 per credit hour, 36 credit hours required, 250 graduation fee, 65 tech fee per term. *Financial support:* Scholarships/ grants available. Financial award applicants required to submit FAFSA. *Unit head:* Dr. Adina Scruggs, Dean of Adult and Graduate Studies, 423-775-7121, E-mail: adina.scruggs@bryan.edu. *Application contact:* Mandi K Sullivan, Director of Academic Programs, 423-664-9880, E-mail: mandi.sullivan@bryan.edu.
Website: http://www.bryan.edu/academics/adult-education/graduate/online-mba/

Cairn University, Department of Counseling, Langhorne, PA 19047-2990. Offers MS. *Program availability:* Part-time, evening/weekend. *Entrance requirements:* Additional exam requirements/recommendations for international students: required—TOEFL (minimum score 550 paper-based). Electronic applications accepted. Application fee is waived when completed online. *Expenses:* Contact institution.

California Baptist University, Program in Counseling Ministry, Riverside, CA 92504-3206. Offers professional ministry (MA); research in counseling ministry (MA). *Program availability:* Part-time. *Degree requirements:* For master's, comprehensive exam, additional professional ministry practicum or research thesis. *Entrance requirements:* For master's, GRE (minimum score of 300 for applicants with a GPA below 2.75), minimum undergraduate GPA of 2.75; official transcripts; three recommendations; comprehensive essay; interview; three prerequisite classes completed with minimum C grade. Additional exam requirements/recommendations for international students: required—TOEFL (minimum score 80 iBT). Electronic applications accepted. *Expenses:* Contact institution.

California Baptist University, Program in Counseling Ministry and Counseling Psychology (Dual Master's), Riverside, CA 92504-3206. Offers MA/MS. *Program availability:* Part-time. *Entrance requirements:* Additional exam requirements/ recommendations for international students: required—TOEFL (minimum score 80 iBT). Electronic applications accepted. *Expenses:* Contact institution.

Calvary University, Graduate School and Seminary, Kansas City, MO 64147. Offers Bible and theology (MS); Biblical counseling (MA); education (MS), including administration and leadership, Christian education, curriculum and instruction, elementary education; organizational development (MS); pastoral studies (M Div); worship arts (MS). *Program availability:* Part-time, evening/weekend. *Degree requirements:* For master's, variable foreign language requirement, comprehensive exam, thesis or alternative. *Entrance requirements:* For master's, minimum GPA of 2.5, BA or BS, doctrine agreement. Additional exam requirements/recommendations for international students: required—TOEFL (minimum score 550 paper-based). Electronic applications accepted. *Expenses:* Contact institution.

Calvin Theological Seminary, Graduate and Professional Programs, Grand Rapids, MI 49546-4387. Offers Bible and theology (MA); divinity (M Div), including ancient near eastern languages and literature, contextual ministry, evangelism and teaching, history of Christianity, new church development, New Testament, Old Testament, pastoral care and leadership, preaching and worship, theological studies, youth and family ministries; educational ministry (MA); historical theology (PhD); missions and evangelism (MA); pastoral care (MA); philosophical and moral theology (PhD); systematic theology (PhD); theological studies (MTS); theology (Th M); worship (MA); youth and family ministries (MA). *Accreditation:* ACIPE; ATS. *Program availability:* Part-time. *Degree requirements:* For master's, variable foreign language requirement, thesis (for some programs); for doctorate, 4 foreign languages, comprehensive exam, thesis/dissertation. *Entrance requirements:* For doctorate, GRE General Test, Hebrew, Greek, and a modern foreign language. Additional exam requirements/recommendations for international students: required—TOEFL (minimum score 550 paper-based), TWE (minimum score 4). Electronic applications accepted.

Campbell University, Graduate and Professional Programs, Divinity School, Buies Creek, NC 27506. Offers Christian ministry (MA); divinity (M Div); ministry (D Min); JD/ M Div; M Div/MA; M Div/MBA. *Accreditation:* ATS. *Degree requirements:* For doctorate, final project. *Entrance requirements:* For master's, minimum GPA of 2.5; for doctorate, MAT, M Div, minimum graduate GPA of 3.0. Additional exam requirements/ recommendations for international students: required—TOEFL (minimum score 580 paper-based). *Expenses:* Contact institution.

Canadian Southern Baptist Seminary, Graduate Programs, Cochrane, AB T4C 2G1, Canada. Offers Biblical studies (MBS); Christian ministry (MCMin); Christian studies (MCS); ministry (M Div). *Accreditation:* ATS. *Program availability:* Part-time, 100% online, blended/hybrid learning. *Entrance requirements:* Additional exam requirements/ recommendations for international students: required—TOEFL (minimum score 560 paper-based; 83 iBT); recommended—IELTS (minimum score 6.5).

Capital University, Trinity Lutheran Seminary, Columbus, OH 43209-2394. Offers African American studies (MTS); Biblical studies (MTS, STM); Christian education (MA); Christian spirituality (STM); church in the world (MTS); church music (MA); divinity (M Div); general theological studies (MTS); mission and evangelism (STM); pastoral leadership and practice (STM); youth and family ministry (MA); MSN/MTS; MTS/JD. *Accreditation:* ACIPE; ATS. *Program availability:* Part-time. *Degree requirements:* For master's, variable foreign language requirement, comprehensive exam (for some programs), thesis (for some programs), field experience (for some programs). *Entrance requirements:* For master's, BA or equivalent (for MA, M Div, MTS); M Div, MTS, or equivalent (for STM); audition (for MACM). Additional exam requirements/ recommendations for international students: required—TOEFL. Electronic applications accepted. *Expenses:* Contact institution.

Carolina Christian College, Program in Religious Education, Winston-Salem, NC 27102-0777. Offers Christian education (MRE); pastoral care (MRE). *Entrance requirements:* For master's, bachelor's degree from accredited institution, minimum undergraduate "B" average.

Catholic Theological Union, Graduate and Professional Programs, Chicago, IL 60615-5698. Offers biblical spirituality (Certificate); cross-cultural ministries (D Min); cross-cultural missions (Certificate); divinity (M Div); liturgical studies (Certificate); liturgy (D Min); pastoral studies (MAPS, Certificate); spiritual formation (Certificate); spirituality (D Min); theology (MA); M Div/MA; M Div/MSW; M Div/PhD. *Accreditation:* ACIPE; ATS. *Program availability:* Part-time, evening/weekend. *Degree requirements:* For master's, one foreign language, comprehensive exam (for some programs), thesis (for some programs); for doctorate, thesis/dissertation. *Entrance requirements:* For doctorate, master's degree, 5 years of active ministry.

The Catholic University of America, School of Theology and Religious Studies, Washington, DC 20064. Offers M Cat, M Div, MA, D Min, PhD, STD, Certificate, STB, STL, MSLS/MA, STB/M Div. *Program availability:* Part-time. *Faculty:* 39 full-time (5 women), 12 part-time/adjunct (5 women). *Students:* 156 full-time (13 women), 167 part-time (69 women); includes 72 minority (13 Black or African American, non-Hispanic/ Latino; 1 American Indian or Alaska Native, non-Hispanic/Latino; 13 Asian, non-Hispanic/Latino; 22 Hispanic/Latino; 23 Two or more races, non-Hispanic/Latino), 51 international. Average age 36. 178 applicants, 60% accepted, 67 enrolled. In 2019, 56 master's, 27 doctorates awarded. Terminal master's awarded for partial completion of doctoral program. *Degree requirements:* For master's, variable foreign language requirement, comprehensive exam (for some programs), thesis (for some programs); for doctorate, variable foreign language requirement, comprehensive exam, thesis/ dissertation. *Entrance requirements:* For master's and doctorate, GRE General Test, statement of purpose, official copies of academic transcripts, three letters of recommendation. Additional exam requirements/recommendations for international students: required—TOEFL (minimum score 550 paper-based; 80 iBT). *Application deadline:* For fall admission, 7/15 priority date for domestic students, 7/1 for international students; for spring admission, 11/15 priority date for domestic students, 11/1 for international students. Applications are processed on a rolling basis. Application fee: $55. Electronic applications accepted. *Expenses:* Contact institution. *Financial support:* Fellowships, research assistantships, teaching assistantships, Federal Work-Study, scholarships/grants, tuition waivers (full and partial), and unspecified assistantships available. Financial award application deadline: 2/1; financial award applicants required to submit FAFSA. *Unit head:* Very Rev. Mark Morozowich, Dean, 202-319-5684, Fax: 202-319-4967, E-mail: morozowich@cua.edu. *Application contact:* Dr. Steven Brown, Director of Graduate Admissions, 202-319-5057, Fax: 202-319-6533, E-mail: cua-admissions@cua.edu.
Website: https://trs.catholic.edu/

Cedarville University, Graduate Programs, Cedarville, OH 45314. Offers business administration (MBA); family nurse practitioner (MSN); global ministry (M Div); global public health nursing (MSN); healthcare administration (MBA); ministry (M Min); nurse educator (MSN); operations management (MBA); pharmacy (Pharm D). *Program availability:* Part-time, evening/weekend, 100% online, blended/hybrid learning. *Faculty:* 52 full-time (19 women), 21 part-time/adjunct (13 women). *Students:* 378 full-time (221 women), 45 part-time (23 women); includes 76 minority (46 Black or African American, non-Hispanic/Latino; 2 American Indian or Alaska Native, non-Hispanic/Latino; 22 Asian, non-Hispanic/Latino; 1 Hispanic/Latino; 5 Two or more races, non-Hispanic/ Latino), 2 international. Average age 26. 398 applicants, 70% accepted, 172 enrolled. In 2019, 74 master's, 34 doctorates awarded. *Degree requirements:* For master's, portfolio; for doctorate, comprehensive exam. *Entrance requirements:* For master's, GRE may be required, 2 professional recommendations; for doctorate, PCAT, professional recommendation from a practicing pharmacist or current employer/ supervisor, resume, essay, interview. Additional exam requirements/recommendations for international students: required—TOEFL (minimum score 550 paper-based; 80 iBT). *Application deadline:* For fall admission, 5/1 priority date for domestic and international students; for spring admission, 11/1 priority date for domestic and international students. Applications are processed on a rolling basis. Application fee: $0. Electronic applications accepted. *Expenses: Tuition:* Full-time $12,594; part-time $566 per credit hour. One-time fee: $100. Tuition and fees vary according to course load and program. *Financial support:* Scholarships/grants and unspecified assistantships available. Support available to part-time students. Financial award application deadline: 1/30; financial award applicants required to submit FAFSA. *Unit head:* Dr. Janice Supplee, Dean of Graduate Studies, 937-766-8000, E-mail: suppleej@cedarville.edu. *Application contact:* Alexis McKay, Graduate Admissions Counselor, 937-766-8000, E-mail: amckay@cedarville.edu.
Website: https://www.cedarville.edu/offices/graduate-school

Charlotte Christian College and Theological Seminary, Graduate Program, Charlotte, NC 28206. Offers Biblical studies (MA), including New Testament, Old Testament, theology; chaplaincy (M Div); general pastoral studies (M Div); ministry (D Min); pastoral counseling (M Div); urban Christian ministry (MA), including multi-cultural studies, youth ministry. *Program availability:* Part-time, evening/weekend. *Degree requirements:* For master's, variable foreign language requirement, thesis; for doctorate, thesis/dissertation. *Entrance requirements:* For master's, 1000-2000 word essay. Additional exam requirements/recommendations for international students: required—TOEFL, IELTS. Electronic applications accepted. *Expenses:* Contact institution.

Chicago Theological Seminary, Graduate and Professional Programs, Chicago, IL 60637-1507. Offers Bible, culture and hermeneutics (PhD); preaching (D Min); religion and health (D Min); religious studies (MA); spirituality and spiritual direction (D Min); theology (M Div); theology, ethics and the human sciences (PhD); M Div/MSW. *Accreditation:* ACIPE; ATS. *Program availability:* Part-time. *Degree requirements:* For master's, thesis; for doctorate, 2 foreign languages, comprehensive exam, thesis/ dissertation. *Entrance requirements:* For doctorate, GRE General Test. Additional exam requirements/recommendations for international students: required—TOEFL.

Christian Theological Seminary, Graduate and Professional Programs, Indianapolis, IN 46208-3301. Offers educational and arts ministries (MA); marriage and family therapy (MA); pastoral care and counseling (D Min); psychotherapy and faith (MA); theological studies (MTS); theology (M Div). *Accreditation:* AAMFT/COAMFTE (one or more programs are accredited); ACIPE; ATS. *Program availability:* Part-time. Terminal master's awarded for partial completion of doctoral program. *Degree requirements:* For master's, comprehensive exam (for some programs), thesis (for some programs), missionary and cross-cultural experience (for M Div); for doctorate, comprehensive exam, thesis/dissertation. *Entrance requirements:* For doctorate, M Div. Additional exam requirements/recommendations for international students: recommended—TOEFL. Electronic applications accepted.

Christ the King Seminary, Graduate and Professional Programs, East Aurora, NY 14052. Offers divinity (M Div); pastoral ministry (MA); theology (MA). *Accreditation:* ATS. *Program availability:* Part-time, evening/weekend. *Degree requirements:* For master's, comprehensive exam, thesis. *Entrance requirements:* For master's, previous course work in philosophy and religious studies.

Cincinnati Christian University, Graduate School, Program in Counseling, Cincinnati, OH 45204-3200. Offers MAC. *Degree requirements:* For master's, thesis or alternative, integration paper. *Entrance requirements:* For master's, GRE General Test, interview, minimum undergraduate GPA of 3.0. Additional exam requirements/recommendations for international students: required—TOEFL. Electronic applications accepted. *Expenses:* Contact institution.

City Vision University, Program in Technology and Ministry, Kansas City, MO 64109-1845. Offers MS. *Program availability:* Online learning. *Degree requirements:* For master's, capstone project.

Claremont Lincoln University, Graduate Programs, Claremont, CA 91711. Offers ethical leadership (MA); interfaith action (MA); social impact (MA).

Claremont School of Theology, Graduate and Professional Programs, Master of Divinity Program, Claremont, CA 91711-3199. Offers interfaith chaplaincy (M Div); Islamic chaplaincy (M Div); ministerial leadership (M Div). *Accreditation:* ACIPE; ATS. *Program availability:* Part-time, 100% online, blended/hybrid learning. *Entrance requirements:* Additional exam requirements/recommendations for international students: required—TOEFL. Electronic applications accepted.

Claremont School of Theology, Graduate and Professional Programs, Program in Ministry, Claremont, CA 91711-3199. Offers practical theology of conflict, healing and transformation in Korean contexts (D Min); spiritual renewal, contemplative practice, and strategic leadership (D Min). *Accreditation:* ACIPE. *Program availability:* 100% online, blended/hybrid learning. *Degree requirements:* For doctorate, thesis/dissertation. *Entrance requirements:* For doctorate, GRE General Test. Additional exam requirements/recommendations for international students: required—TOEFL. Electronic applications accepted.

Claremont School of Theology, Graduate and Professional Programs, Program in Religion, Claremont, CA 91711-3199. Offers practical theology (PhD), including religious education and formation, spiritual care and counseling; religion (MA, PhD), including comparative theology and philosophy (PhD), Hebrew Bible and Jewish studies (PhD), New Testament and Christian origins (PhD), process studies (PhD), religion, ethics, and society (PhD). *Accreditation:* ACIPE; ATS. Terminal master's awarded for partial completion of doctoral program. *Degree requirements:* For master's, thesis; for doctorate, 2 foreign languages, thesis/dissertation. *Entrance requirements:* For doctorate, GRE General Test. Additional exam requirements/recommendations for international students: required—TOEFL. Electronic applications accepted.

Clarks Summit University, Baptist Bible Seminary, South Abington Township, PA 18411. Offers Biblical apologetics (MA); Biblical studies (MA); church education (M Min); church planting (M Div, M Min); communication (D Min); counseling and spiritual development (D Min); global ministry (M Min, D Min); ministry (PhD); missions (M Min); organizational leadership (M Min); outreach pastor (M Min); pastoral counseling (M Min); pastoral leadership (M Div, M Min); pastoral ministry (D Min); theological studies (D Min); theology (Th M); youth pastor (M Min). *Program availability:* Part-time, evening/weekend, online learning. Terminal master's awarded for partial completion of doctoral program. *Degree requirements:* For master's, 2 foreign languages, thesis, oral exam (for M Div); for doctorate, 2 foreign languages, comprehensive exam (for some programs), thesis/dissertation, oral exam. *Entrance requirements:* For doctorate, Greek and Hebrew entrance exams (for PhD). Electronic applications accepted.

College of Saint Elizabeth, Department of Theology and Philosophy, Morristown, NJ 07960-6989. Offers Catholic studies (Certificate); pastoral care (Certificate); spirituality (Certificate); theology (MA), including Catholic studies, pastoral care, spirituality, theological studies. *Program availability:* Part-time. *Degree requirements:* For master's, thesis. *Entrance requirements:* For master's, baccalaureate degree from accredited institution, personal interview with coordinator and another faculty member, minimum cumulative GPA of 3.0. Additional exam requirements/recommendations for international students: required—TOEFL (minimum score 550 paper-based; 79 iBT), IELTS (minimum score 6.5). Electronic applications accepted. Application fee is waived when completed online.

Columbia International University, Seminary and School of Ministry, Columbia, SC 29203. Offers academic ministries (M Div); Bible and theology (Certificate); bible exposition (M Div, MABE); Biblical ministry (Certificate); chaplaincy (M Div); intercultural studies (MAIS); leadership (D Min); member care (D Min); missions (D Min); preaching (D Min); theological studies (MA). *Program availability:* Part-time, evening/weekend. *Degree requirements:* For doctorate, comprehensive exam, thesis/dissertation. *Entrance requirements:* For doctorate, 3 years of ministerial experience, M Div. Additional exam requirements/recommendations for international students: required—TOEFL. Electronic applications accepted.

Concordia University, Nebraska, Graduate Programs in Education, Program in Family Life Ministry, Seward, NE 68434. Offers MS. *Program availability:* Part-time, evening/weekend. *Degree requirements:* For master's, thesis or alternative. *Entrance requirements:* For master's, GRE, MAT, or NTE, minimum GPA of 3.0, BS in education or equivalent.

Corban University, Graduate School, Program in Counseling, Salem, OR 97301-9392. Offers MA. *Degree requirements:* For master's, internship, practicum.

Corban University, Graduate School, School of Ministry, Salem, OR 97301-9392. Offers Biblical languages (M Div); Biblical leadership (Certificate); Christian leadership (MA); Church ministry (M Div); ministry (D Min). *Program availability:* Part-time, evening/weekend. *Degree requirements:* For master's, thesis. *Entrance requirements:* Additional exam requirements/recommendations for international students: required—TOEFL (minimum score 550 paper-based), IELTS (minimum score 6).

Covenant Theological Seminary, Graduate and Professional Programs, St. Louis, MO 63141-8697. Offers M Div, MA, MAC, MAEM, Th M, D Min, Certificate. *Accreditation:* ATS (one or more programs are accredited). *Program availability:* Part-time, evening/weekend, online learning. *Degree requirements:* For master's, 2 foreign languages, thesis (for some programs); for doctorate, 2 foreign languages, thesis/dissertation; for Certificate, 2 foreign languages. *Entrance requirements:* For doctorate and Certificate, M Div. Additional exam requirements/recommendations for international students: required—TOEFL (minimum score 550 paper-based). Electronic applications accepted.

Criswell College, Graduate School of the Bible, Dallas, TX 75246-1537. Offers biblical studies (M Div); Christian leadership (MA); counseling (MA); Jewish studies (MA); ministry (MA); theological and biblical studies (MA). *Program availability:* Part-time. *Degree requirements:* For master's, 2 foreign languages, thesis optional. *Entrance requirements:* For master's, GRE General Test, minimum GPA of 2.5. Electronic applications accepted.

Dallas Baptist University, Gary Cook School of Leadership, Program in Leadership Studies, Dallas, TX 75211-9299. Offers leadership studies (PhD), including business, general leadership, higher education, ministry. *Program availability:* Part-time, evening/weekend. *Application deadline:* Applications are processed on a rolling basis. Application fee: $25. Electronic applications accepted. Application fee is waived when completed online. *Expenses: Tuition:* Full-time $18,072; part-time $1004 per credit hour. *Required fees:* $1100; $550 per semester. Tuition and fees vary according to course level and degree level. *Unit head:* Dr. Jack Goodyear, Director, 214-333-5595, Fax: 214-333-6809, E-mail: jackg@dbu.edu. *Application contact:* Dr. Mary Nelson, Program Director, 214-333-5396, E-mail: maryn@dbu.edu.
Website: http://www4.dbu.edu/leadership/phdleadership

Dallas Baptist University, Graduate School of Ministry, Program in Children's Ministry, Dallas, TX 75211-9299. Offers general (MA); special needs children ministry (MA). *Program availability:* Part-time, evening/weekend, online learning. *Application deadline:* Applications are processed on a rolling basis. Application fee: $25. Electronic applications accepted. Application fee is waived when completed online. *Expenses: Tuition:* Full-time $18,072; part-time $1004 per credit hour. *Required fees:* $1100; $550 per semester. Tuition and fees vary according to course level and degree level. *Unit head:* Dr. Robert R. Brooks, Dean, 214-333-5494, Fax: 214-333-5673, E-mail: bobb@dbu.edu. *Application contact:* Dr. Shelly Melia, Program Director, 214-333-5943, E-mail: shelly@dbu.edu.
Website: http://www.dbu.edu/ministry/degree-programs/ma-in-childrens-ministry

Dallas Baptist University, Graduate School of Ministry, Program in Christian Counseling, Dallas, TX 75211-9299. Offers MA. *Program availability:* Part-time, evening/weekend. *Application deadline:* Applications are processed on a rolling basis. Application fee: $25. Electronic applications accepted. Application fee is waived when completed online. *Expenses: Tuition:* Full-time $18,072; part-time $1004 per credit hour. *Required fees:* $1100; $550 per semester. Tuition and fees vary according to course level and degree level. *Unit head:* Dr. Robert R. Brooks, Dean, 214-333-5494, Fax: 214-333-5673, E-mail: bobb@dbu.edu. *Application contact:* Dr. Dana Wicker, Program Director, 214-333-5883, Fax: 214-333-5689, E-mail: dana@dbu.edu.
Website: http://www.dbu.edu/ministry/degree-programs/ma-christian-counseling

Dallas Baptist University, Graduate School of Ministry, Program in Christian Ministry, Dallas, TX 75211-9299. Offers chaplaincy (MA); counseling ministry (MA); family ministry (MA); general ministry (MA); leading the nonprofit organization (MA); ministry leadership (MA); professional life coaching (MA); urban ministry (MA). *Program availability:* Part-time, evening/weekend, online learning. *Application deadline:* Applications are processed on a rolling basis. Application fee: $25. Electronic applications accepted. Application fee is waived when completed online. *Expenses: Tuition:* Full-time $18,072; part-time $1004 per credit hour. *Required fees:* $1100; $550 per semester. Tuition and fees vary according to course level and degree level. *Unit head:* Dr. Robert R. Brooks, Dean, 214-333-5494, Fax: 214-333-5673, E-mail: bobb@dbu.edu. *Application contact:* Dr. Jon Choi, Program Director, 214-333-5375, Fax: 214-333-5689, E-mail: jon@dbu.edu.
Website: http://www.dbu.edu/ministry/degree-programs/m-a-in-christian-ministry

Dallas Baptist University, Graduate School of Ministry, Program in Discipleship, Dallas, TX 75211-9299. Offers discipleship for the family (MA); discipleship through communications (MA); local church discipleship (MA). *Program availability:* Part-time-only, evening/weekend, online learning. *Application deadline:* Applications are processed on a rolling basis. Application fee: $25. Electronic applications accepted. Application fee is waived when completed online. *Expenses: Tuition:* Full-time $18,072; part-time $1004 per credit hour. *Required fees:* $1100; $550 per semester. Tuition and fees vary according to course level and degree level. *Unit head:* Dr. Robert R. Brooks, Dean, 214-333-5494, Fax: 214-333-5673, E-mail: bobb@dbu.edu. *Application contact:* Dr. Blanton Feaster, Program Director, 214-333-5256, Fax: 214-333-5689, E-mail: blanton@dbu.edu.
Website: http://www.dbu.edu/ministry/degree-programs/m-a-in-discipleship

Dallas Baptist University, Graduate School of Ministry, Program in Family Ministry, Dallas, TX 75211-9299. Offers Christian counseling (MA); general (MA); leadership (MA); special needs family ministry (MA). *Program availability:* Part-time, evening/weekend, online learning. *Application deadline:* Applications are processed on a rolling basis. Application fee: $25. Electronic applications accepted. Application fee is waived when completed online. *Expenses: Tuition:* Full-time $18,072; part-time $1004 per credit hour. *Required fees:* $1100; $550 per semester. Tuition and fees vary according to course level and degree level. *Unit head:* Dr. Robert R. Brooks, Dean, 214-333-5494, Fax: 214-333-5673, E-mail: bobb@dbu.edu. *Application contact:* Dr. Shelly Melia, Program Director, 214-333-5943, E-mail: shelly@dbu.edu.
Website: https://www.dbu.edu/ministry/degree-programs/m-a-in-family-ministry

Dallas Baptist University, Graduate School of Ministry, Program in Global Leadership, Dallas, TX 75211-9299. Offers church planting (MA); East Asian Studies (MA); English as a second language (MA); general studies (MA); global communication (MA); global studies (MA); international business (MA); leading the nonprofit organization (MA); missions (MA); small group ministry (MA); urban ministry (MA). *Program availability:* Part-time, evening/weekend, online learning. *Application deadline:* Applications are processed on a rolling basis. Application fee: $25. Electronic applications accepted. Application fee is waived when completed online. *Expenses: Tuition:* Full-time $18,072; part-time $1004 per credit hour. *Required fees:* $1100; $550 per semester. Tuition and fees vary according to course level and degree level. *Unit head:* Dr. Robert R. Brooks, Dean, 214-333-5494, Fax: 214-333-5673, E-mail: bobb@dbu.edu. *Application contact:* Dr. Brent Thomason, Program Director, 214-333-5236, E-mail: brentt@dbu.edu.
Website: https://www.dbu.edu/ministry/degree-programs/m-a-in-global-leadership

Dallas Baptist University, Graduate School of Ministry, Program in Student Ministry, Dallas, TX 75211-9299. Offers MA. *Program availability:* Part-time, evening/weekend, online learning. *Application deadline:* Applications are processed on a rolling basis. Application fee: $25. Electronic applications accepted. Application fee is waived when completed online. *Expenses: Tuition:* Full-time $18,072; part-time $1004 per credit hour. *Required fees:* $1100; $550 per semester. Tuition and fees vary according to course level and degree level. *Unit head:* Dr. Robert R. Brooks, Dean, 214-333-5494, Fax: 214-333-5673, E-mail: bobb@dbu.edu. *Application contact:* Dr. Blanton Feaster, Program Director, 214-333-5256, Fax: 214-333-5689, E-mail: blanton@dbu.edu.
Website: https://www.dbu.edu/ministry/degree-programs/m-a-in-student-ministry

Dallas Baptist University, Graduate School of Ministry, Program in Theological Studies, Dallas, TX 75211-9299. Offers Christian heritage (MA); Christian ministry (MA); Christian scriptures (MA). *Program availability:* Part-time, evening/weekend, online learning. *Application deadline:* Applications are processed on a rolling basis. Application fee: $25. Electronic applications accepted. Application fee is waived when completed online. *Expenses: Tuition:* Full-time $18,072; part-time $1004 per credit hour. *Required fees:* $1100; $550 per semester. Tuition and fees vary according to course level and degree level. *Unit head:* Dr. Robert R. Brooks, Dean, 214-333-5494, Fax: 214-333-5673, E-mail: bobb@dbu.edu. *Application contact:* Dr. Jim Lemons, Program Director, 214-

333-5366, Fax: 214-333-5689, E-mail: jiml@dbu.edu.
Website: http://www.dbu.edu/ministry/degree-programs/m-a-in-theological-studies

Dallas Baptist University, Graduate School of Ministry, Worship Studies Program, Dallas, TX 75211-9299. Offers worship leadership (MA); worship theology (MA). *Program availability:* Part-time, evening/weekend. *Application deadline:* Applications are processed on a rolling basis. Application fee: $25. Electronic applications accepted. Application fee is waived when completed online. *Expenses: Tuition:* Full-time $18,072; part-time $1004 per credit hour. *Required fees:* $1100; $550 per semester. Tuition and fees vary according to course level and degree level. *Unit head:* Dr. Robert R. Brooks, Dean, 214-333-5494, Fax: 214-333-5673, E-mail: bobb@dbu.edu. *Application contact:* Dr. Jon Choi, Program Director, 214-333-5375, Fax: 214-333-5375, E-mail: jon@dbu.edu.
Website: http://www.dbu.edu/ministry/degree-programs/m-a-in-worship-studies

Dallas Baptist University, Professional Development Program, Dallas, TX 75211-9299. Offers accounting (MA); church leadership (MA); communication (MA); counseling (MA); criminal justice (MA); English as a second language (MA); finance (MA); higher education (MA); leadership studies (MA); management (MA). *Program availability:* Part-time, evening/weekend, online learning. *Application deadline:* Applications are processed on a rolling basis. Application fee: $25. Electronic applications accepted. Application fee is waived when completed online. *Expenses: Tuition:* Full-time $18,072; part-time $1004 per credit hour. *Required fees:* $1100; $550 per semester. Tuition and fees vary according to course level and degree level. *Unit head:* Jared Ingram, Program Director, 214-333-5584, E-mail: jaredi@dbu.edu. *Application contact:* Jared Ingram, Program Director, 214-333-5584, E-mail: jaredi@dbu.edu.
Website: https://www.dbu.edu/graduate/degree-programs/ma-professional-development

Dallas Theological Seminary, Graduate Programs, Dallas, TX 75204-6499. Offers adult education (Th M); apologetics (Th M); Bible backgrounds (Th M); Bible translation (Th M); Biblical and theological studies (Certificate); biblical counseling (MA); biblical exegesis and linguistics (MA); biblical exposition (PhD); biblical studies (MA); Biblical theology (Th M); children's education (Th M); Christian education (MA, D Min); Christian leadership (MA); cross-cultural ministries (MA); educational administration (Th M); educational leadership (Th M); evangelism and discipleship (Th M); exposition of Biblical books (Th M); family life education (Th M); general studies (Th M); Hebrew and cognate studies (Th M); hermeneutics (Th M); historical theology (Th M); homiletics (Th M); intercultural ministries (Th M); Jesus studies (Th M); leadership studies (Th M); media and communication (MA); media arts (Th M); ministry (D Min); ministry with women (Th M); New Testament studies (Th M, PhD); Old Testament studies (Th M, PhD); parachurch ministries (Th M); pastoral care and counseling (Th M); pastoral theology and practice (Th M); philosophy (Th M); sacred theology (STM); spiritual formation (Th M); systematic theology (Th M); teaching in Christian institutions (Th M); theological studies (PhD); urban ministries (Th M); worship studies (Th M); youth education (Th M). *Program availability:* Part-time, online learning. *Degree requirements:* For master's, variable foreign language requirement, thesis (for some programs); for doctorate, 2 foreign languages, thesis/dissertation. *Entrance requirements:* For master's, GRE or MAT (if minimum undergraduate cumulative GPA is below 2.5 or undergraduate degree is unaccredited). Additional exam requirements/recommendations for international students: required—TOEFL (minimum score 575 paper-based; 85 iBT), TWE. Electronic applications accepted.

Denver Seminary, Graduate and Professional Programs, Littleton, CO 80120. Offers apologetics (Certificate); biblical studies (MA); Christian formation and soul care (MA, Certificate); Christian studies (MA, Certificate); church and parachurch leadership (D Min); counseling licensure (MA); counseling ministry (MA); intercultural ministry (Certificate); leadership (MA, Certificate); marriage and family counseling (D Min); pastoral ministry (D Min); philosophy of religion (MA); spiritual guidance (Certificate); theology (M Div, Certificate); worship (Certificate); youth and family ministry (MA). *Accreditation:* ACA; ACIPE; ATS (one or more programs are accredited). *Program availability:* Part-time, evening/weekend, online learning. *Degree requirements:* For master's, 2 foreign languages, thesis (for some programs); for doctorate, 2 foreign languages, thesis/dissertation. *Entrance requirements:* For doctorate, M Div, 3 years of ministry experience. Additional exam requirements/recommendations for international students: required—TOEFL (minimum score 575 paper-based; 90 iBT). Electronic applications accepted.

Earlham School of Religion, Graduate Programs, Richmond, IN 47374. Offers ministry (M Min); religion (MA); theology (M Div). *Accreditation:* ACIPE; ATS. *Program availability:* Part-time, blended/hybrid learning. *Faculty:* 8 full-time (2 women), 2 part-time/adjunct (1 woman). *Students:* 17 full-time (9 women), 18 part-time (11 women); includes 2 minority (both Black or African American, non-Hispanic/Latino). Average age 38. *Degree requirements:* For master's, variable foreign language requirement, comprehensive exam (for some programs), thesis (for some programs), internship (M Div). *Entrance requirements:* For master's, 3 references, academic writing sample, official college transcripts, background check. Additional exam requirements/recommendations for international students: required—TOEFL (minimum score 550 paper-based; 82 iBT), IELTS (minimum score 7). *Application deadline:* For fall admission, 6/15 priority date for domestic students; for winter admission, 11/15 priority date for domestic students. Applications are processed on a rolling basis. Application fee: $35. Electronic applications accepted. *Financial support:* Scholarships/grants and tuition waivers (full and partial) available. Financial award application deadline: 4/15; financial award applicants required to submit FAFSA. *Unit head:* Matt Hisrich, Dean, 800-432-1377, Fax: 765-983-1688, E-mail: hisrima@earlham.edu. *Application contact:* Julie Dishman, Director of Recruitment and Admissions, 765-983-1523, Fax: 765-983-1688, E-mail: dishmju@earlham.edu.
Website: http://esr.earlham.edu/academic-programs

Eastern Mennonite University, Eastern Mennonite Seminary, Harrisonburg, VA 22802-2462. Offers Christian leadership (MA); divinity (M Div); ministry studies (Certificate); religion (MA); theological studies (Certificate). *Accreditation:* ATS. *Program availability:* Part-time. *Degree requirements:* For master's, thesis (for some programs), supervised field education (for M Div). *Entrance requirements:* For master's, minimum GPA of 2.5. Additional exam requirements/recommendations for international students: required—TOEFL (minimum score 550 paper-based). *Expenses:* Contact institution.

Eastern Mennonite University, Master of Arts in Counseling Program, Harrisonburg, VA 22802-2462. Offers MA, M Div/MA. *Accreditation:* ACA (one or more programs are accredited); ACIPE. *Program availability:* Part-time. *Degree requirements:* For master's, practicum, internship. *Entrance requirements:* For master's, minimum GPA of 3.0. Additional exam requirements/recommendations for international students: required—TOEFL (minimum score 550 paper-based; 79 iBT). Electronic applications accepted. *Expenses:* Contact institution.

Ecumenical Theological Seminary, Program in Ministry, Detroit, MI 48201. Offers D Min. *Accreditation:* ACIPE.

Emory University, Candler School of Theology, Atlanta, GA 30322. Offers catholic studies (M Div); formation and witness (M Div); history, scripture and tradition (MTS); leadership in church and community (M Div); modern religious thought and experience (MTS); pastoral counseling (Th D); religion and race (M Div); religion, health and science (M Div); scripture and interpretation (M Div); society and personality (M Div); theology (Th M); theology and ethics (M Div); theology and the arts (M Div); traditions of the church (M Div); JD/M Div; JD/MTS; M Div/MBA; M Div/MPH; MBA/MTS; MTS/MPH. *Accreditation:* ACIPE. *Program availability:* Part-time. *Degree requirements:* For master's, thesis optional; for doctorate, comprehensive exam, thesis/dissertation. *Entrance requirements:* For master's, minimum undergraduate GPA of 2.75, completed undergraduate degree from accredited college or university; for doctorate, GRE, DMin: MDiv or other first level theological masters and at least 3 years of professional experience. Additional exam requirements/recommendations for international students: required—TOEFL (minimum score 600 paper-based; 95 iBT). Electronic applications accepted. *Expenses:* Contact institution.

Epic Bible College, Graduate School, Sacramento, CA 95841. Offers Biblical studies (MA); Christian ministry (MA); ethical leadership (MA); ministry (D Min).

Evangelical Seminary, Graduate and Professional Programs, Myerstown, PA 17067-1212. Offers Biblical studies (MAR); congregational ministry (M Div); global and contextual studies (M Div, MAR); historical and theological studies (MAR); interdisciplinary studies (MAR); marriage and family counseling (M Div); marriage and family therapy (MA); New Testament (MAR); Old Testament (MAR); spiritual formation (MAR); teaching ministry (M Div); youth ministry (M Div). *Accreditation:* ATS (one or more programs are accredited). *Program availability:* Part-time, online learning. *Degree requirements:* For master's, 2 foreign languages. *Entrance requirements:* For master's, minimum GPA of 2.5. Additional exam requirements/recommendations for international students: required—TOEFL (minimum score 550 paper-based).

Fairfield University, Graduate School of Education and Allied Professions, Fairfield, CT 06824. Offers applied behavior analysis (ATC); applied psychology (MA); clinical mental health counseling (MA, CAS); educational technology (MA); elementary education (MA, CAS); family studies (MA); integration of spirituality and religion in counseling (ATC); marriage and family therapy (MA); reading and language development (Sixth Year Certificate); school counseling (MA, CAS); school psychology (MA, CAS); school-based marriage and family therapy (ATC); secondary education (MA); special education (MA, CAS); substance abuse counseling (ATC); teaching (Certificate); teaching and foundations (MA, CAS); TESOL, world languages, and bilingual education (MA, CAS). *Accreditation:* NCATE. *Program availability:* Part-time, evening/weekend. *Faculty:* 24 full-time (18 women), 28 part-time/adjunct (20 women). *Students:* 169 full-time (149 women), 227 part-time (187 women); includes 96 minority (21 Black or African American, non-Hispanic/Latino; 8 Asian, non-Hispanic/Latino; 60 Hispanic/Latino; 7 Two or more races, non-Hispanic/Latino), 1 international. Average age 31. 194 applicants, 60% accepted, 101 enrolled. In 2019, 136 master's, 28 other advanced degrees awarded. *Degree requirements:* For master's, comprehensive exam. *Entrance requirements:* For master's, One of the following for certification programs: Praxis Core, SAT, ACT, or GRE, minimum GPA of 3.0, 2 recommendations, resume. Additional exam requirements/recommendations for international students: required—TOEFL (minimum score 550 paper-based; 84 iBT), IELTS (minimum score 7.5), TOEFL (minimum score 550 paper-based; 84 iBT) or IELTS (minimum score 7.5). *Application deadline:* For fall admission, 2/15 for international students; for spring admission, 10/1 for international students. Application fee: $60. Electronic applications accepted. *Expenses:* Tuition $815/credit hour; Lab Fee (ED598) $300/semester; Lab Fee (CN457,CN467, PY538, PY540) $70/course; Wilson Reading Course Fee $141/credit hour; Registration Fee $50/semester; Graduate Student Activity Fee (Fall and Spring) $65/semester. *Financial support:* In 2019–20, 34 students received support. Career-related internships or fieldwork and unspecified assistantships available. Support available to part-time students. Financial award applicants required to submit FAFSA. *Unit head:* Dr. Laurie Grupp, Dean, 203-254-4250, Fax: 203-254-4241, E-mail: lgrupp@fairfield.edu. *Application contact:* Melanie Rogers, Director of Graduate Admission, 203-254-4184, Fax: 203-254-4073, E-mail: gradadmis@fairfield.edu.
Website: http://www.fairfield.edu/gseap

Faith Baptist Bible College and Theological Seminary, Graduate Program, Ankeny, IA 50023. Offers Biblical studies (MA); pastoral studies (M Div); pastoral training (MA); religion (MA); theological studies (MA). *Program availability:* Part-time. *Degree requirements:* For master's, thesis or alternative. *Entrance requirements:* Additional exam requirements/recommendations for international students: required—TOEFL (minimum score 550 paper-based; 79 iBT), IELTS (minimum score 6.5). Electronic applications accepted.

Faulkner University, College of Biblical Studies, Montgomery, AL 36109-3398. Offers Biblical studies (MA, PhD); Christian counseling and family ministry (MA); Christian ministry (MA). *Program availability:* Part-time, evening/weekend, 100% online, blended/hybrid learning, synchronous online/on-ground. Terminal master's awarded for partial completion of doctoral program. *Degree requirements:* For master's, comprehensive exam, thesis (for some programs); for doctorate, 3 foreign languages, thesis/dissertation. *Entrance requirements:* Additional exam requirements/recommendations for international students: required—TOEFL (minimum score 500 paper-based). Electronic applications accepted. *Expenses:* Contact institution.

Fordham University, Graduate School of Religion and Religious Education, Bronx, NY 10458. Offers pastoral counseling and spiritual care (MA); pastoral ministry/spirituality/pastoral counseling (D Min); religion and religious education (MA); religious education (MS, PhD, PD); spiritual direction (Certificate). *Program availability:* Part-time, evening/weekend, 100% online, blended/hybrid learning. *Faculty:* 11 full-time (4 women), 16 part-time/adjunct (11 women). *Students:* 126 full-time (66 women), 72 part-time (37 women); includes 51 minority (19 Black or African American, non-Hispanic/Latino; 9 Asian, non-Hispanic/Latino; 20 Hispanic/Latino; 3 Two or more races, non-Hispanic/Latino), 34 international. Average age 41. 85 applicants, 76% accepted, 55 enrolled. In 2019, 48 master's, 12 doctorates, 10 other advanced degrees awarded. Terminal master's awarded for partial completion of doctoral program. *Degree requirements:* For master's, comprehensive exam (for some programs), thesis or alternative, research paper; for doctorate, thesis/dissertation. *Entrance requirements:* For doctorate, MAT or GRE (For Ph.D. only). Additional exam requirements/recommendations for international students: recommended—TOEFL, IELTS. *Application deadline:* For fall admission, 7/1 priority date for domestic students, 5/1 priority date for international students; for spring admission, 12/1 priority date for domestic students, 10/1 priority date for international students. Applications are processed on a rolling basis. Application fee: $100. Electronic applications accepted. *Expenses:* Contact institution. *Financial support:* In 2019–20, 140 students received support, including 8 research assistantships with partial tuition reimbursements available (averaging $10,800 per year); scholarships/grants, tuition waivers (partial), and unspecified assistantships also available. Support available to part-time students. Financial award application deadline: 8/1; financial award applicants required to submit FAFSA. *Unit head:* Faustino M. Cruz, SM, Dean, 718-817-4800, Fax: 718-817-3352, E-mail: fcruz16@fordham.edu. *Application contact:* Dr. Lois D'Amore, Director of Admissions and Student Life, 718-817-4800, Fax: 718-817-3352, E-mail: ldamore@fordham.edu.
Website: http://www.fordham.edu/gre

Freed-Hardeman University, School of Biblical Studies, Program in Ministry, Henderson, TN 38340-2399. Offers M Min. *Program availability:* Part-time. *Degree* *requirements:* For master's, comprehensive exam, internship. *Entrance requirements:* For master's, GRE General Test or MAT. Additional exam requirements/recommendations for international students: required—TOEFL (minimum score 500 paper-based).

Fresno Pacific University, Biblical Seminary, Program in Christian Ministry, Fresno, CA 93702-4709. Offers MA. *Program availability:* Part-time. *Entrance requirements:* For master's, minimum GPA of 2.5. Additional exam requirements/recommendations for international students: required—TOEFL (minimum score 550 paper-based). *Expenses:* Contact institution.

Fuller Theological Seminary, Graduate Programs, Pasadena, CA 91182. Offers Christian leadership (MACL); clinical psychology (PhD, Psy D); family studies (MA); global leadership (MA); global ministries (D Min); global ministries (Korean language) (D Min); intercultural studies (MA, Th M, PhD); intercultural studies (Korean language) (MA); marital and family therapy (MS); marriage and family enrichment (Certificate); ministry (M Div, D Min); missiology (D Miss); missiology (Korean language) (Th M); theology (MA, Th M, PhD), including evangelism (MA), family life education (MA), pastoral ministry (MA), recovery ministry (MA), worship music ministry (MA), worship, theology, and the arts (MA), youth, family, and culture (MA); theology and ministry (MA).

Gannon University, School of Graduate Studies, College of Humanities, Education, and Social Sciences, School of Humanities, Program in Pastoral Studies, Erie, PA 16541-0001. Offers pastoral studies (MA); theological studies (Certificate). *Program availability:* Part-time, evening/weekend. *Degree requirements:* For master's, comprehensive exam, thesis or alternative, research project, internship, written evaluation. *Entrance requirements:* Additional exam requirements/recommendations for international students: required—TOEFL (minimum score 79 iBT). Electronic applications accepted. Application fee is waived when completed online.

Gardner-Webb University, School of Divinity, Boiling Springs, NC 28017. Offers biblical studies (M Div); Christian education and formation (M Div); intercultural studies (M Div); ministry (D Min); missiology (M Div); pastoral care and counseling (M Div); pastoral care and counseling/member care for missionaries (D Min); pastoral studies (M Div); M Div/MA; M Div/MBA. *Accreditation:* ACIPE. *Program availability:* Part-time. *Entrance requirements:* For master's, minimum GPA of 2.6; for doctorate, minimum GPA of 2.75. Additional exam requirements/recommendations for international students: required—TOEFL (minimum score 500 paper-based; 61 iBT). Electronic applications accepted. *Expenses:* Contact institution.

Garrett-Evangelical Theological Seminary, Graduate and Professional Programs, Evanston, IL 60201-3298. Offers Bible and culture (PhD); Christian education (MA); Christian education and congregational studies (PhD); contemporary theology and culture (PhD); divinity (M Div); ethics, church, and society (MA); liturgical studies (PhD); ministry (D Min); music ministry (MA); pastoral care and counseling (MA); pastoral theology, personality, and culture (PhD); spiritual formation and evangelism (MA); theological studies (MTS); M Div/MSW. *Accreditation:* ACIPE; ATS (one or more programs are accredited). *Program availability:* Part-time. *Degree requirements:* For master's, thesis (for some programs); for doctorate, thesis/dissertation. *Entrance requirements:* For doctorate, GRE (PhD). Additional exam requirements/recommendations for international students: required—TOEFL (minimum score 560 paper-based). Electronic applications accepted.

Gateway Seminary, Graduate and Professional Programs, Ontario, CA 91761-8642. Offers divinity (M Div); early childhood education (Certificate); education leadership (MAEL, Diploma); ministry (D Min); theological studies (MTS); theology (Th M); youth ministry (Certificate). *Accreditation:* ACIPE; ATS. *Program availability:* Part-time, evening/weekend. *Degree requirements:* For master's, thesis (for some programs); for doctorate, 2 foreign languages, thesis/dissertation. *Entrance requirements:* For doctorate, MAT. Additional exam requirements/recommendations for international students: required—TOEFL (minimum score 550 paper-based). Electronic applications accepted.

The General Theological Seminary, Graduate and Professional Programs, New York, NY 10011-4977. Offers Anglican studies (STM, Th D, Certificate); ascetical theology (Certificate); biblical studies (Certificate); congregational development (Certificate); divinity (M Div); historical and theological studies (Certificate); spiritual direction (MASD, STM, Certificate); theology (MA). *Accreditation:* ACIPE; ATS. *Program availability:* Part-time, evening/weekend. Terminal master's awarded for partial completion of doctoral program. *Degree requirements:* For master's, thesis; for doctorate, 2 foreign languages, thesis/dissertation. *Entrance requirements:* For master's, GRE General Test; for doctorate, GRE, M Div or MA. Additional exam requirements/recommendations for international students: required—TOEFL.

Geneva College, Program in Leadership Studies, Beaver Falls, PA 15010. Offers business management (MS); ministry leadership (MS); non-profit leadership (MS); organizational management (MS); project management (MS). *Program availability:* Part-time, evening/weekend, online only, 100% online. *Faculty:* 4 part-time/adjunct (3 women). *Students:* 13 full-time (11 women), 2 part-time (both women); includes 7 minority (5 Black or African American, non-Hispanic/Latino; 2 Two or more races, non-Hispanic/Latino). Average age 46. 14 applicants, 57% accepted, 2 enrolled. In 2019, 16 master's awarded. *Degree requirements:* For master's, thesis or alternative, capstone leadership studies project. *Entrance requirements:* For master's, undergraduate degree from regionally-accredited college or university, one to three years of experience in the workplace, minimum GPA of 3.0 (preferred), resume, essay, two recommendations. Additional exam requirements/recommendations for international students: required—TOEFL. *Application deadline:* For fall admission, 9/21 for domestic students; for spring admission, 2/23 for domestic students; for summer admission, 7/22 for domestic students. Applications are processed on a rolling basis. Electronic applications accepted. *Expenses:* $587 per credit + $34 per credit admin fee charge. 36 credits. *Financial support:* Scholarships/grants available. Financial award application deadline: 8/1; financial award applicants required to submit FAFSA. *Unit head:* John D. Gallo, Dean of Graduate, Adult and Online Programs, 800-576-3111, Fax: 724-847-6839, E-mail: msls@geneva.edu. *Application contact:* Graduate Enrollment Representative, 800-576-3111, Fax: 724-847-6839, E-mail: msls@geneva.edu.
Website: https://www.geneva.edu/graduate/leadership-studies/

George Fox University, Portland Seminary, Portland, OR 97223. Offers Biblical studies (M Div, MA); chaplaincy (M Div); Christian history and theology (M Div, MA); creation care (M Div, MA); intercultural studies (M Div, MA); leadership (M Div, MA); leadership and global perspectives (D Min); leadership and spiritual formation (D Min); semiotics and future studies (D Min); spiritual direction (MA, Certificate); spiritual direction supervision (M Div, MA, Certificate); spiritual formation and discipleship (M Div, MA, Certificate). *Accreditation:* ACIPE. *Program availability:* Part-time, evening/weekend, online learning. *Entrance requirements:* For master's, resume, three references (one pastoral, one academic or professional, one personal), one official transcript from each college or university attended; for doctorate, resume, 3 references (1 professional, 1 academic, 1 personal), one official transcript from each college or university attended. Additional exam requirements/recommendations for international students: required—TOEFL (minimum score 577 paper-based; 90 iBT). Electronic applications accepted. *Expenses:* Contact institution.

Global University, Graduate School of Theology, Springfield, MO 65804. Offers bible and theology (D Min); biblical language (M Div); biblical studies (MA); Christian ministry (M Div, D Min); ministerial studies (MA), including education, leadership, missions, New Testament, Old Testament. *Program availability:* Part-time, evening/weekend, online learning. *Degree requirements:* For master's, thesis (for some programs). *Entrance requirements:* For master's, minimum undergraduate GPA of 3.0. Electronic applications accepted.

Gordon-Conwell Theological Seminary, Graduate and Professional Programs, South Hamilton, MA 01982. Offers Biblical languages (MABL); church history (MACH); counseling (MACO); ministry (D Min); missions/evangelism (MAME); New Testament (MANT); Old Testament (MAOT); religion (MAR); theology (M Div, MATH, Th M, Th D). *Accreditation:* ACIPE; ATS (one or more programs are accredited). *Program availability:* Part-time, evening/weekend. *Degree requirements:* For master's, one foreign language, thesis optional; for doctorate, 2 foreign languages, thesis/dissertation. *Entrance requirements:* For master's, minimum GPA of 2.5; for doctorate, minimum GPA of 3.0.

Grace Theological Seminary, Graduate and Professional Programs, Winona Lake, IN 46590-9907. Offers biblical studies (Certificate); chaplaincy (M Div); exegetical studies (M Div); intercultural studies (M Div, MA, D Min); local church ministry (MA), including camp administration, women's leadership; pastoral counseling (M Div); pastoral studies (M Div, D Min); theology (Diploma). *Accreditation:* ATS. *Program availability:* Part-time, online learning. *Degree requirements:* For master's, thesis optional; for doctorate, 2 foreign languages, thesis/dissertation. *Entrance requirements:* For master's, MAT, minimum GPA of 2.5. Electronic applications accepted.

Grand Canyon University, College of Doctoral Studies, Phoenix, AZ 85017-1097. Offers data analytics (DBA); general psychology (PhD), including cognition and instruction, industrial and organizational psychology, integrating technology, learning, and psychology, performance psychology; management (DBA); marketing (DBA); organizational leadership (Ed D), including behavioral health, Christian ministry, health care administration, organizational development. *Degree requirements:* For doctorate, comprehensive exam, thesis/dissertation. *Entrance requirements:* For doctorate, minimum GPA of 3.4 on earned advanced degree from regionally-accredited institution; transcripts; goals statement.

Grand Rapids Theological Seminary of Cornerstone University, Graduate Programs, Grand Rapids, MI 49525-5897. Offers academic (M Div); chaplaincy ministries (M Div); Christian formation (MA); counseling (MA); formation and soul care ministries (M Div); intercultural ministries (M Div); interdisciplinary studies (MA); New Testament (Th M); Old Testament (Th M); pastoral ministries (M Div); small group and discipleship ministries (M Div); student and family ministries (M Div). *Accreditation:* ATS. *Program availability:* Part-time, evening/weekend, 100% online, blended/hybrid learning. *Entrance requirements:* Additional exam requirements/recommendations for international students: required—TOEFL (minimum score 577 paper-based; 90 iBT), IELTS (minimum score 7). Electronic applications accepted.

Greenville University, Program in Leadership and Ministry, Greenville, IL 62246-0159. Offers MA. *Program availability:* Part-time. *Degree requirements:* For master's, 6 hours of research/practicum in applied ministry. *Entrance requirements:* For master's, 1 year of work experience in Christian ministry, interview. Additional exam requirements/recommendations for international students: required—TOEFL (minimum score 525 paper-based). Electronic applications accepted.

Hampton University, School of Liberal Arts and Education, Program in Counseling, Hampton, VA 23668. Offers college student development (MA); community agency counseling (MA); counseling (Ed S); counselor education and supervision (PhD); pastoral counseling (MA); school counseling (MA). *Accreditation:* ACA; NCATE. *Program availability:* Part-time, evening/weekend, online learning. *Students:* 41 full-time (33 women), 16 part-time (11 women); includes 54 minority (52 Black or African American, non-Hispanic/Latino; 1 Asian, non-Hispanic/Latino; 1 Native Hawaiian or other Pacific Islander, non-Hispanic/Latino), 1 international. Average age 33. 24 applicants, 58% accepted, 10 enrolled. In 2019, 9 master's, 1 doctorate, 5 other advanced degrees awarded. *Degree requirements:* For master's, comprehensive exam; for doctorate, comprehensive exam, thesis/dissertation. *Entrance requirements:* For master's, GRE General Test, personal statement, two letters of recommendation; for doctorate, GRE General Test, personal statement, writing sample, three letters of recommendation; for Ed S, personal statement, two letters of recommendation. Additional exam requirements/recommendations for international students: required—TOEFL, TOEFL (minimum score 525 paper-based) or IELTS (6.5). *Application deadline:* For fall admission, 6/1 priority date for domestic students, 4/1 priority date for international students; for winter admission, 9/1 priority date for international students; for spring admission, 11/1 priority date for domestic students, 9/1 for international students; for summer admission, 4/1 priority date for domestic students, 2/1 priority date for international students. Applications are processed on a rolling basis. Application fee: $35. Electronic applications accepted. *Financial support:* Fellowships, research assistantships, teaching assistantships, career-related internships or fieldwork, Federal Work-Study, institutionally sponsored loans, scholarships/grants, tuition waivers, unspecified assistantships, and grant funding provided 10k when students enrolled in the required internships available. Support available to part-time students. Financial award application deadline: 6/30; financial award applicants required to submit FAFSA. *Unit head:* Dr. Richard Mason, Chairperson, 757-728-6160, E-mail: richard.mason@hamptonu.edu. *Application contact:* Dr. Richard Mason, Chairperson, 757-728-6160, E-mail: richard.mason@hamptonu.edu.
Website: http://edhd.hamptonu.edu/counseling/

Harding School of Theology, Graduate Programs, Memphis, TN 38117-5499. Offers Christian ministry (MA); historical theology (MA); ministry (M Div); New Testament (MA); Old Testament (MA); systematic theology (MA); transforming leadership (D Min). *Accreditation:* ATS. *Program availability:* Part-time, online learning. *Degree requirements:* For master's, variable foreign language requirement, thesis (for some programs); for doctorate, one foreign language, thesis/dissertation. *Entrance requirements:* For master's, minimum GPA of 2.7; for doctorate, minimum GPA of 3.0. Additional exam requirements/recommendations for international students: required—TOEFL (minimum score 550 paper-based; 79 iBT). Electronic applications accepted. *Expenses: Tuition:* Full-time $12,240; part-time $8160 per semester hour. *Required fees:* $306; $204 per semester hour. $324 per semester. Tuition and fees vary according to degree level.

Harding University, College of Bible and Ministry, Searcy, AR 72149-0001. Offers M Min. *Program availability:* Part-time, online learning. *Faculty:* 2 full-time (0 women). *Students:* 2 part-time (0 women); includes 1 minority (Black or African American, non-Hispanic/Latino). Average age 48. In 2019, 2 master's awarded. *Entrance requirements:* Additional exam requirements/recommendations for international students: required—TOEFL (minimum score 550 paper-based; 79 iBT). *Financial support:* In 2019–20, 2 students received support. Scholarships/grants and unspecified assistantships available. Financial award applicants required to submit FAFSA. *Unit head:* Dr. Monte Cox, Dean, 501-279-4448, Fax: 501-279-4042, E-mail: mcox@harding.edu. *Application contact:* Dr. Monte Cox, Dean, 501-279-4448, Fax: 501-279-4042, E-mail:

mcox@harding.edu.
Website: http://www.harding.edu/bible

Hardin-Simmons University, Graduate School, Logsdon Seminary, Program in Family Ministry, Abilene, TX 79698-0001. Offers MA. *Program availability:* Part-time. *Degree requirements:* For master's, comprehensive exam, minimum cumulative GPA of 3.0, clinical experience, project. *Entrance requirements:* For master's, letters of recommendation; interview; church endorsement. Additional exam requirements/recommendations for international students: required—TOEFL (minimum score 550 paper-based; 79 iBT). Electronic applications accepted.

Hardin-Simmons University, Graduate School, Logsdon Seminary, Program in Ministry, Abilene, TX 79698-0001. Offers D Min. *Program availability:* Part-time. *Degree requirements:* For doctorate, ministry project. *Entrance requirements:* For doctorate, GRE or MAT, M Div or equivalent, minimum graduate GPA of 3.0, minimum 3 years' ministry experience, active current ministry involvement, interview, 4 letters of recommendation, church endorsement. Additional exam requirements/recommendations for international students: required—TOEFL (minimum score 550 paper-based; 79 iBT).

Hartford Seminary, Graduate Programs, Hartford, CT 06105-2279. Offers Islamic studies (MA); ministry (D Min); religious studies (MA); spirituality (Certificate). *Accreditation:* ATS (one or more programs are accredited). *Program availability:* Part-time, evening/weekend, online learning. *Degree requirements:* For master's, thesis optional, oral exam; for doctorate, thesis/dissertation, oral exam. *Entrance requirements:* For doctorate, experience in ministry, M Div. Additional exam requirements/recommendations for international students: required—TOEFL (minimum score 550 paper-based; 80 iBT).

Heritage Christian University, Graduate Programs, Florence, AL 35630. Offers counseling (MM); Greek (MA); ministry (MM); New Testament (MA). *Degree requirements:* For master's, practicum (MM), major research paper (MA). *Entrance requirements:* For master's, MAT or GRE, bachelor's degree in Bible from an accredited college or university, minimum GPA of 2.75, 3 letters of recommendation.

Holmes Institute, Graduate Program, Golden, CO 80401. Offers consciousness studies (MS). *Program availability:* Online learning. *Degree requirements:* For master's, comprehensive exam, 2 spiritual retreats per year, internship (1 per term), 2 spiritual conferences. *Entrance requirements:* For master's, 2 letters of recommendation, interview, official transcripts of an accredited bachelor's degree. Additional exam requirements/recommendations for international students: required—TOEFL (minimum score 530 paper-based).

Holy Names University, Graduate Division, Department of Counseling Psychology, Oakland, CA 94619-1699. Offers counseling and forensic counseling (MA); counseling psychology (MA); forensic psychology (MA). *Program availability:* Part-time, evening/weekend. *Degree requirements:* For master's, comprehensive paper, seminars. *Entrance requirements:* For master's, minimum undergraduate GPA of 2.6 overall, 3.0 in major. Additional exam requirements/recommendations for international students: required—TOEFL (minimum score 550 paper-based; 79 iBT). Electronic applications accepted. Application fee is waived when completed online. *Expenses:* Contact institution.

Houston Graduate School of Theology, Graduate Programs, Houston, TX 77092. Offers counseling (MA); pastoral ministry (M Div, D Min); theology (MA). *Accreditation:* ATS (one or more programs are accredited). *Program availability:* Part-time, evening/weekend. *Degree requirements:* For master's, thesis (for some programs); for doctorate, thesis/dissertation. *Entrance requirements:* For doctorate, GRE General Test or MAT, M Div or equivalent. Additional exam requirements/recommendations for international students: required—TOEFL (minimum score 550 paper-based).

Howard Payne University, Program in Youth Ministry, Brownwood, TX 76801-2715. Offers MA. *Program availability:* Part-time. *Degree requirements:* For master's, three 2-hour internships/mentorships. *Entrance requirements:* For master's, undergraduate degree from accredited university; leveling courses (for students who do not have undergraduate coursework in Old Testament, New Testament, and youth ministry). Additional exam requirements/recommendations for international students: required—TOEFL (minimum score 79 iBT). Electronic applications accepted.

Huntington University, Graduate School, Huntington, IN 46750-1299. Offers adolescent and young adult education (M Ed); business administration (MBA); counseling (MA), including licensed mental health counselor; early adolescent education (M Ed); elementary education (M Ed); global youth ministry (MA); occupational therapy (OTD); organizational leadership (MA); pastoral leadership (MA); TESOL education (M Ed). *Accreditation:* AOTA. *Program availability:* Part-time, online learning. *Degree requirements:* For master's, comprehensive exam (for some programs), thesis (for some programs). *Entrance requirements:* For master's, GRE (for counseling and education students only); for doctorate, GRE (for occupational therapy students). Additional exam requirements/recommendations for international students: required—TOEFL (minimum score 85 iBT), IELTS (minimum score 6.5). Electronic applications accepted. *Expenses:* Contact institution.

Huntsville Bible College, Program in Ministry, Huntsville, AL 35811-1632. Offers biblical leadership (MM); pastoral studies (MM).

Iliff School of Theology, Graduate and Professional Programs, Denver, CO 80210-4798. Offers biblical studies (MA); church history (MA); religion (MA); religion and social change (MA); specialized ministry (MASM), including justice and peace, pastoral theology and care, religions leadership; theology (M Div, MTS, D Min, PhD), including Biblical studies (PhD), religion and psychological studies (PhD), religion and social change (PhD), theology, philosophy and culture (PhD); theology/ethics (MA). *Accreditation:* ACIPE; ATS. *Program availability:* Part-time, evening/weekend. *Degree requirements:* For master's, one foreign language, thesis (for some programs); for doctorate, 2 foreign languages, comprehensive exam, thesis/dissertation. *Entrance requirements:* For master's, minimum GPA of 3.0, writing sample, references; for doctorate, GRE General Test, minimum GPA of 3.0, writing sample, letters of recommendation. Additional exam requirements/recommendations for international students: required—TOEFL (minimum score 550 paper-based). Electronic applications accepted.

Indiana Wesleyan University, Graduate School, Wesley Seminary, Program in Ministry, Marion, IN 46953-4974. Offers children, youth and family ministry (MA); ministerial leadership (MA). *Accreditation:* ATS. *Program availability:* Part-time, online learning. *Degree requirements:* For master's, one foreign language, capstone practicum and/or project. *Entrance requirements:* Additional exam requirements/recommendations for international students: required—TOEFL. Electronic applications accepted. *Expenses:* Contact institution.

Inter American University of Puerto Rico, Metropolitan Campus, Graduate Programs, Program in Pastoral Theology, San Juan, PR 00919-1293. Offers PhD.

Interdenominational Theological Center, Graduate and Professional Programs, Atlanta, GA 30314-4112. Offers Christian education (MACE); ministry (D Min); pastoral counseling (Th D); theology (M Div); M Div/MACE. *Accreditation:* ACIPE; ATS (one or more programs are accredited). *Program availability:* Part-time, evening/weekend, blended/hybrid learning. *Degree requirements:* For doctorate, thesis/dissertation. *Entrance requirements:* For doctorate, master's degree. Electronic applications accepted.

International Baptist College and Seminary, Program in Ministry, Chandler, AZ 85286. Offers M Min, D Min.

Johnson University, Graduate and Professional Programs, Knoxville, TN 37998. Offers biblical interpretation (Graduate Certificate); business administration (MBA); Christian ministries (Graduate Certificate); clinical mental health counseling (MA); educational technology (MA); intercultural studies (MA); leadership (MBA); leadership studies (PhD); New Testament (MA); nonprofit management (MBA); school counseling (MA); spiritual formation and leadership (Graduate Certificate); strategic ministry (MA); teacher education (MA). *Program availability:* Part-time, 100% online, blended/hybrid learning. *Faculty:* 26 full-time (10 women), 32 part-time/adjunct (9 women). *Students:* 116 full-time (56 women), 196 part-time (91 women); includes 40 minority (23 Black or African American, non-Hispanic/Latino; 1 American Indian or Alaska Native, non-Hispanic/Latino; 4 Asian, non-Hispanic/Latino; 6 Hispanic/Latino; 6 Two or more races, non-Hispanic/Latino), 31 international. Average age 36. In 2019, 87 master's, 6 doctorates, 14 other advanced degrees awarded. *Degree requirements:* For master's, variable foreign language requirement, comprehensive exam, thesis (for some programs), internships; for doctorate, variable foreign language requirement, comprehensive exam, thesis/dissertation, internships. *Entrance requirements:* For master's, PRAXIS (for MA in teacher education); MAT (for counseling); GRE or GMAT (for MBA), interview, 3 references, transcripts, essay, minimum GPA of 2.5 or 3.0 (depending on program); for doctorate, GRE or MAT (taken not less than 5 years prior), interview, 3 references, transcripts, essay, minimum GPA of 3.0; for Graduate Certificate, interview, 3 references, transcripts, essay, minimum GPA of 3.0. Additional exam requirements/recommendations for international students: required—TOEFL (minimum score 527 paper-based; 71 iBT). *Application deadline:* For fall admission, 7/1 for domestic students; for spring admission, 11/1 for domestic students; for summer admission, 4/1 for domestic students. Application fee: $50. Electronic applications accepted. *Expenses:* Contact institution. *Financial support:* Scholarships/grants available. Financial award application deadline: 4/15; financial award applicants required to submit FAFSA. *Unit head:* Lisa Tarwater, Chief Admissions Officer, 865-251-3400, E-mail: ltarwater@johnsonu.edu. *Application contact:* Lisa Tarwater, Chief Admissions Officer, 865-251-3400, E-mail: ltarwater@johnsonu.edu.
Website: www.johnsonu.edu

Johnson University Florida, Program in Strategic Ministry, Kissimmee, FL 34744-5301. Offers children and family (MSM); church administration (MSM); church planting (MSM); intercultural studies (MSM); pastoral ministry (MSM); special needs (MSM); sports ministry (MSM); worship (MSM); youth ministry (MSM). *Program availability:* Online learning. *Degree requirements:* For master's, research trip to Israel, 9-month ministry apprenticeship.

Judson University, Master of Leadership in Ministry Program, Elgin, IL 60123. Offers MLM. *Program availability:* Evening/weekend, online only, blended/hybrid learning. *Faculty:* 1 full-time (0 women), 4 part-time/adjunct (1 woman). *Students:* 6 full-time (4 women), 3 part-time (1 woman). Average age 33. 3 applicants, 100% accepted. In 2019, 6 master's awarded. *Degree requirements:* For master's, thesis or alternative. *Entrance requirements:* For master's, Completed entrance survey ("Am I ready for the Master of Leadership in Ministry Program?"), undergraduate degree in a ministry-related field (preferred). *Application deadline:* Applications are processed on a rolling basis. Application fee: $35. Electronic applications accepted. *Expenses:* Estimated tuition and fees per semester: Tuition ($5,000), Living Expenses ($1,500), Books and Supplies ($500). *Financial support:* In 2019–20, 5 students received support. Scholarships/grants and tuition waivers available. Financial award application deadline: 8/15; financial award applicants required to submit FAFSA. *Unit head:* Dr. David Sanders, Director, 847-628-1052, E-mail: dsanders@judsonu.edu. *Application contact:* Dr. David Sanders, Director, 847-628-1052, E-mail: dsanders@judsonu.edu.
Website: http://www.judsonu.edu/Graduate/Master_of_Leadership_in_Ministry/Overview/

The King's University, Graduate and Professional Programs, Southlake, TX 76092. Offers Biblical studies (Graduate Certificate); Christian ministry (Graduate Certificate); ministry (M Div, MPT, D Min).

Kingswood University, Program in Pastoral Theology, Sussex, NB E4E 5L2, Canada. Offers MA. *Entrance requirements:* For master's, official transcripts, 3 references, statement of purpose. *Expenses: Tuition:* Part-time $370 Canadian dollars per credit hour. One-time fee: $160 Canadian dollars full-time.

Knox Theological Seminary, Graduate Programs, Program in Ministry, Fort Lauderdale, FL 33308. Offers D Min. *Program availability:* Part-time. *Degree requirements:* For doctorate, thesis/dissertation. *Entrance requirements:* For doctorate, M Div or equivalent. Additional exam requirements/recommendations for international students: required—TOEFL, TWE (minimum score 5).

Lancaster Bible College, Capital Bible Seminary, Lancaster, PA 17601. Offers biblical studies (MA, Certificate); Christian counseling and discipleship (MA, Certificate); ministry (MA); theology (M Div). *Program availability:* Part-time, evening/weekend. *Degree requirements:* For master's, 2 foreign languages, comprehensive exam, thesis (for some programs). *Entrance requirements:* For master's, GRE General Test, Greek exam for those with 2 years of Greek, proficiency exam in theology, previous course work in Biblical studies. Additional exam requirements/recommendations for international students: required—TOEFL (minimum score 550 paper-based).

Lancaster Bible College, Graduate School, Lancaster, PA 17601-5036. Offers adult ministries (MA); Bible (MA); children and family ministry (MA); church planting (MA); consulting resource teacher (M Ed); elementary school counseling (M Ed); leadership (PhD); leadership studies (MA); marriage and family counseling (MA); mental health counseling (MA); pastoral studies (MA); secondary school counseling (M Ed); sports ministry (MA); student ministry (MA); town and country ministry (MA). *Program availability:* Part-time, evening/weekend. *Degree requirements:* For master's, comprehensive exam (for some programs), thesis (for some programs). *Entrance requirements:* For master's, bachelor's degree with a minimum of 30 credits of course work in Bible, minimum undergraduate GPA of 3.0, interview. Additional exam requirements/recommendations for international students: required—TOEFL.

La Sierra University, School of Religion, Riverside, CA 92505. Offers pastoral ministry (M Div); religion (MA); religious education (MA); religious studies (MA). *Program availability:* Part-time. *Degree requirements:* For master's, one foreign language, thesis or alternative. *Entrance requirements:* For master's, GRE General Test, minimum GPA of 3.0.

Lee University, Programs in Religion, Cleveland, TN 37320-3450. Offers biblical studies (MA); ministry studies/leadership (MA); ministry studies/worship (MA); ministry studies/youth and family (MA); theological studies (MA), including ethics, religion. *Program availability:* Part-time, 100% online. *Faculty:* 12 full-time (3 women), 8 part-time/adjunct (0 women). *Students:* 32 full-time (13 women), 104 part-time (33 women);

includes 74 minority (10 Black or African American, non-Hispanic/Latino; 60 Hispanic/Latino; 4 Two or more races, non-Hispanic/Latino), 5 international. Average age 38. 43 applicants, 79% accepted, 24 enrolled. In 2019, 15 master's awarded. *Degree requirements:* For master's, variable foreign language requirement, comprehensive exam (for some programs), thesis (for some programs). *Entrance requirements:* For master's, GRE or MAT (for biblical/theological studies only), minimum GPA of 3.0, 3 letters of recommendation, interview, official transcripts, essay. Additional exam requirements/recommendations for international students: required—TOEFL (minimum score 61 iBT). *Application deadline:* For fall admission, 4/1 priority date for domestic and international students; for spring admission, 10/1 priority date for domestic and international students. Applications are processed on a rolling basis. Application fee: $25. Electronic applications accepted. *Expenses:* Contact institution. *Financial support:* In 2019–20, 39 students received support, including 12 teaching assistantships (averaging $2,046 per year); career-related internships or fieldwork, Federal Work-Study, institutionally sponsored loans, scholarships/grants, and unspecified assistantships also available. Financial award application deadline: 3/1; financial award applicants required to submit FAFSA. *Unit head:* Dr. Lisa Long, Director, 423-303-5100, E-mail: llong@leeuniversity.edu. *Application contact:* Jeffery McGirt, Director of Graduate Enrollment, 423-614-8691, Fax: 423-614-8317, E-mail: jmcgirt@leeuniversity.edu.
Website: http://www.leeuniversity.edu/academics/graduate/

Liberty University, School of Behavioral Sciences, Lynchburg, VA 24515. Offers applied psychology (MA), including developmental psychology (MA, MS), industrial/organizational psychology (MA, MS); clinical mental health counseling (MA); community care and counseling (Ed D), including marriage and family counseling, pastoral care and counseling, traumatology; counselor education and supervision (PhD); human services counseling (MA), including addictions and recovery, business, child and family law, Christian ministries, criminal justice, crisis response and trauma, executive leadership, health and wellness, life coaching, marriage and family, military resilience; marriage and family counseling (MA); marriage and family therapy (MA); military resilience (Certificate); pastoral counseling (MA), including addictions and recovery, community chaplaincy, crisis response and trauma, discipleship and church ministry, leadership, life coaching, marriage and family, marriage and family studies, military resilience, parenting and child/adolescent, pastoral counseling, theology; professional counseling (MA); psychology (MS), including developmental psychology (MA, MS), industrial/organizational psychology (MA, MS); school counseling (M Ed). *Program availability:* Part-time, online learning. *Students:* 3,786 full-time (3,065 women), 5,193 part-time (4,081 women); includes 2,733 minority (1,967 Black or African American, non-Hispanic/Latino; 48 American Indian or Alaska Native, non-Hispanic/Latino; 103 Asian, non-Hispanic/Latino; 349 Hispanic/Latino; 19 Native Hawaiian or other Pacific Islander, non-Hispanic/Latino; 247 Two or more races, non-Hispanic/Latino), 133 international. Average age 38. 13,324 applicants, 28% accepted, 2,163 enrolled. In 2019, 2,322 master's, 19 doctorates, 112 other advanced degrees awarded. *Entrance requirements:* For master's, Official bachelor's degree transcripts with a 2.0 GPA or higher. *Application deadline:* Applications are processed on a rolling basis. Application fee: $50. Electronic applications accepted. *Expenses: Tuition:* Full-time $545; part-time $410 per credit hour. One-time fee: $50. *Financial support:* In 2019–20, 1,003 students received support. Teaching assistantships and Federal Work-Study available. Financial award applicants required to submit FAFSA. *Unit head:* Dr. Kenyon Knapp, Dean, School of Behavioral Services, E-mail: kcknapp@liberty.edu. *Application contact:* Jay Bridge, Director of Admissions, 800-424-9595, Fax: 800-628-7977, E-mail: gradadmissions@liberty.edu.
Website: https://www.liberty.edu/behavioral-sciences/

Liberty University, School of Divinity, Lynchburg, VA 24515. Offers Biblical exposition (MA); Biblical languages (M Div); Biblical studies (M Div, MA, MAR, Th M, D Min); chaplaincy (M Div, D Min); Christian apologetics (M Div, MA, MAR, Th M); Christian leadership and church ministries (M Div); Christian ministries (M Div); Christian ministry (MA); Christian thought (M Div); church history (M Div, MAR, Th M); community chaplaincy (M Div, MAR); discipleship (D Min); discipleship and church ministry (M Div, MAR, MCM); evangelism and church planting (MAR, MCM, D Min); expository preaching (D Min); global ministry (MA); global studies (M Div, MAR, MCM, MGS, Th M); healthcare chaplaincy (M Div); homiletics (M Div, MAR, Th M); leadership (M Div, MAR); marketplace chaplaincy (M Div, MCM); ministry leadership (Ed D); pastoral counseling (M Div, MA, MAR, D Min), including addictions and recovery (MA), crisis response and trauma (MA), discipleship and church ministries (MA), leadership (MA), life coaching (MA), marketplace chaplaincy (MA), marriage and family (MA), military resilience (MA), pastoral counseling (MA); pastoral leadership (D Min); pastoral ministries (M Div, M Serv Soc, MCM); religious education (MRE); sports chaplaincy (MA); theology (M Div, MAR, MTS, Th M); theology and apologetics (D Min, PhD); worship (M Div, MAR, MCM, D Min); youth and family ministries (M Div). *Program availability:* Part-time, online learning. *Students:* 2,691 full-time (814 women), 2,570 part-time (732 women); includes 1,484 minority (1,046 Black or African American, non-Hispanic/Latino; 33 American Indian or Alaska Native, non-Hispanic/Latino; 120 Asian, non-Hispanic/Latino; 167 Hispanic/Latino; 8 Native Hawaiian or other Pacific Islander, non-Hispanic/Latino; 110 Two or more races, non-Hispanic/Latino), 101 international. Average age 43. 4,508 applicants, 34% accepted, 952 enrolled. In 2019, 1,251 master's, 71 doctorates awarded. *Degree requirements:* For master's, 2 foreign languages, thesis (for some programs); for doctorate, 2 foreign languages, thesis/dissertation. *Entrance requirements:* For master's, minimum undergraduate GPA of 2.0; for doctorate, GRE General Test or MAT, minimum graduate GPA of 3.0. Additional exam requirements/recommendations for international students: required—TOEFL (minimum score 600 paper-based; 100 iBT). *Application deadline:* For fall admission, 6/1 for domestic students; for spring admission, 11/1 for domestic students. Applications are processed on a rolling basis. Application fee: $50. Electronic applications accepted. *Expenses:* Contact institution. *Financial support:* Teaching assistantships with tuition reimbursements, career-related internships or fieldwork, and Federal Work-Study available. Financial award applicants required to submit FAFSA. *Unit head:* Dr. Troy Temple, Interim Dean, School of Divinity, E-mail: divinity@liberty.edu. *Application contact:* Jay Bridge, Director of Graduate Admissions, 800-424-9595, Fax: 800-628-7977, E-mail: gradadmissions@liberty.edu.
Website: https://www.liberty.edu/divinity/

Liberty University, School of Music, Lynchburg, VA 24515. Offers ethnomusicology (MA); music and worship (MA); music education (MA); worship studies (MA, DWS), including ethnomusicology (MA), leadership (MA), pastoral counseling (MA), worship techniques (MA). *Accreditation:* NASM. *Program availability:* Part-time, online learning. *Students:* 147 full-time (72 women), 220 part-time (103 women); includes 104 minority (61 Black or African American, non-Hispanic/Latino; 1 American Indian or Alaska Native, non-Hispanic/Latino; 15 Asian, non-Hispanic/Latino; 21 Hispanic/Latino; 6 Two or more races, non-Hispanic/Latino), 17 international. Average age 37. 537 applicants, 30% accepted, 89 enrolled. In 2019, 44 master's, 11 doctorates awarded. *Entrance requirements:* For master's, minimum GPA of 3.0; interview; letter of recommendation; statement of purpose; bachelor's/master's degree in music, worship, or related field, or 5 years of experience. Additional exam requirements/recommendations for international students: required—TOEFL (minimum score 600 paper-based; 100 iBT). *Application deadline:* Applications are processed on a rolling basis. Application fee: $50. Electronic

applications accepted. *Expenses: Tuition:* Full-time $545; part-time $410 per credit hour. One-time fee: $50. *Financial support:* In 2019–20, 619 students received support. Federal Work-Study available. Financial award applicants required to submit FAFSA. *Unit head:* Dr. Stephen W. Müller,, Dean, 434-5823459, E-mail: swmuller@liberty.edu. *Application contact:* Jay Bridge, Director of Admissions, 800-424-9595, Fax: 800-628-7977, E-mail: gradadmissions@liberty.edu.
Website: https://www.liberty.edu/music/

Lincoln Christian Seminary, Graduate and Professional Programs, Lincoln, IL 62656-2167. Offers Bible and theology (MA); Christian ministries (MA); counseling (MA); divinity (M Div); leadership ministry (D Min); religious education (MRE). *Accreditation:* ACIPE; ATS. *Program availability:* Part-time. *Degree requirements:* For master's, 2 foreign languages, thesis; for doctorate, thesis/dissertation. *Entrance requirements:* For master's, minimum GPA of 2.5; for doctorate, M Div or equivalent. Additional exam requirements/recommendations for international students: required—TOEFL (minimum score 550 paper-based). Electronic applications accepted.

Lincoln Christian University, Graduate Programs, Lincoln, IL 62656-2167. Offers Bible and theology (MA); Biblical studies (MA); church history/historical theology (MA); counseling (MA); formative worship (MA); intercultural studies (MA); ministry (MA); organizational leadership (MA); philosophy and apologetics (MA); spiritual formation (MA); theology (MA). *Program availability:* Online learning. *Entrance requirements:* For master's, minimum cumulative GPA of 2.5 in undergraduate degree studies. Additional exam requirements/recommendations for international students: required—TOEFL (minimum score 550 paper-based); recommended—IELTS (minimum score 6). Application fee is waived when completed online.

Lipscomb University, Hazelip School of Theology, Nashville, TN 37204-3951. Offers missional and spiritual formation (D Min); theology (M Div). *Program availability:* Part-time, evening/weekend, online learning. *Degree requirements:* For master's, 2 foreign languages, comprehensive exam (for some programs), thesis optional; for doctorate, comprehensive exam, thesis/dissertation. *Entrance requirements:* For master's, 3 references, transcripts, goals statement; for doctorate, 3 references, transcripts, documentation of full-time participation in ministry, writing sample, interview. Additional exam requirements/recommendations for international students: required—TOEFL (minimum score 570 paper-based; 80 iBT). Electronic applications accepted. *Expenses:* Contact institution.

Loras College, Graduate Division, Program in Theology and Ministry, Dubuque, IA 52004-0178. Offers ministry (MA); theology (MA). *Program availability:* Part-time, evening/weekend. *Degree requirements:* For master's, comprehensive exam (for some programs), thesis (for some programs). *Entrance requirements:* For master's, bachelor's degree or undergraduate minor in religious studies or equivalent, minimum undergraduate GPA of 2.75.

Loyola Marymount University, Bellarmine College of Liberal Arts, Program in Pastoral Theology, Los Angeles, CA 90045-8400. Offers MA. *Students:* 50 full-time (23 women); includes 28 minority (1 Black or African American, non-Hispanic/Latino; 1 American Indian or Alaska Native, non-Hispanic/Latino; 5 Asian, non-Hispanic/Latino; 20 Hispanic/Latino; 1 Two or more races, non-Hispanic/Latino), 12 international. Average age 44. 22 applicants, 64% accepted. In 2019, 7 master's awarded. *Entrance requirements:* For master's, GRE or Miller Analogies recommended, BA degree, GPA and submission of written academic work, personal interview, graduate application, official transcripts, statement of intent, letters of recommendation. Additional exam requirements/recommendations for international students: required—TOEFL. Application fee: $50. Electronic applications accepted. *Financial support:* Scholarships/grants available. Financial award applicants required to submit FAFSA. *Unit head:* Dr. Brett Hoover, Director, Pastoral Theology Program, 310-338-1664, E-mail: bhoover@lmu.edu. *Application contact:* Ammar Dalal, Assistant Vice Provost for Graduate Enrollment, 310-338-2721, Fax: 310-338-6086, E-mail: graduateadmission@lmu.edu.
Website: http://bellarmine.lmu.edu/theologicalstudies/graduateprograms/academics/mainpastoraltheology

Loyola University Chicago, Institute of Pastoral Studies, Chicago, IL 60660. Offers Christian spirituality (MA), including spiritual direction; church management (Certificate); counseling for ministry (MA); divinity (M Div); health care ministry leadership (Certificate); health care mission leadership (MA); pastoral counseling (MA, Certificate); pastoral studies (MA); religious education (Certificate); social justice (MA, Certificate); spiritual direction (Certificate); M Div/MA; M Div/MSW; MSW/MA. *Accreditation:* ACIPE. *Program availability:* Part-time, evening/weekend, 100% online, blended/hybrid learning. *Faculty:* 9 full-time (3 women), 20 part-time/adjunct (7 women). *Students:* 72 full-time (45 women), 130 part-time (90 women); includes 55 minority (14 Black or African American, non-Hispanic/Latino; 9 Asian, non-Hispanic/Latino; 28 Hispanic/Latino; 4 Two or more races, non-Hispanic/Latino), 21 international. Average age 45. 90 applicants, 79% accepted, 49 enrolled. In 2019, 48 master's, 8 other advanced degrees awarded. *Degree requirements:* For master's, thesis optional, project. *Entrance requirements:* Additional exam requirements/recommendations for international students: required—TOEFL (minimum score 550 paper-based; 79 iBT), IELTS (minimum score 6.5). *Application deadline:* Applications are processed on a rolling basis. Application fee: $50. Electronic applications accepted. Application fee is waived when completed online. *Expenses:* Contact institution. *Financial support:* In 2019–20, 111 students received support. Career-related internships or fieldwork, Federal Work-Study, scholarships/grants, and unspecified assistantships available. Support available to part-time students. Financial award application deadline: 3/15. *Unit head:* Dr. Peter L Jones, Interim Dean, 312-915-7400, Fax: 312-915-7504, E-mail: pjones5@luc.edu. *Application contact:* Dr. Peter L Jones, Interim Dean, 312-915-7400, Fax: 312-915-7504, E-mail: pjones5@luc.edu.
Website: http://www.luc.edu/ips/

Lutheran School of Theology at Chicago, Graduate and Professional Programs, Chicago, IL 60615-5199. Offers ministry (MAM, D Min); theological studies (MATS, PhD); theology (M Div). *Accreditation:* ACIPE; ATS (one or more programs are accredited). *Program availability:* Part-time. Terminal master's awarded for partial completion of doctoral program. *Degree requirements:* For master's, variable foreign language requirement; for doctorate, variable foreign language requirement, comprehensive exam, thesis/dissertation. *Entrance requirements:* For doctorate, GRE, M Div or equivalent, 3 years of professional experience (D Min).

Lutheran Theological Seminary Saskatoon, Graduate and Professional Programs, Saskatoon, SK S7N 0X3, Canada. Offers Biblical studies (MTS); church history (MTS); ethics/church and society (MTS); history of Christianity (STM); New Testament (STM); Old Testament (STM); pastoral studies (STM); pastoral theology (MTS); systematic theology (MTS); systematic theology and philosophy of religion (STM); theology (M Div, D Div). *Accreditation:* ATS. *Program availability:* Part-time. *Degree requirements:* For master's, thesis.

Luther Rice College & Seminary, Graduate Programs, Lithonia, GA 30038-2454. Offers apologetics (MA); Bible languages (M Div); Biblical counseling (MA); Christian ministry (M Div, D Min); Christian studies (MA); leadership (MA). *Program availability:* Part-time, evening/weekend, online learning. *Degree requirements:* For doctorate, thesis/dissertation. *Entrance requirements:* For master's, bachelor's degree or equivalent; for doctorate, M Div. Additional exam requirements/recommendations for international students: required—TOEFL (minimum score 550 paper-based). Electronic applications accepted.

Luther Seminary, Graduate and Professional Programs, St. Paul, MN 55108-1445. Offers aging and health (MA); Biblical preaching (D Min); children, youth and family (M Div, MA); congregational mission and leadership (M Th, MA, D Min); history of Christianity (M Th, MA); missions and world religions (M Th); New Testament (M Th, MA); Old Testament (M Th, MA); pastoral care: clinical pastoral theology (M Th); pastoral theology and ministry (M Th); systematic theology (M Th, MA). *Accreditation:* ACIPE; ATS. *Program availability:* Part-time, online learning. *Degree requirements:* For master's, thesis or alternative; for doctorate, 2 foreign languages, thesis/dissertation. *Entrance requirements:* For master's, minimum GPA of 3.0; for doctorate, GRE General Test. Additional exam requirements/recommendations for international students: required—TOEFL, IELTS. Electronic applications accepted.

Madonna University, Program in Religious Studies, Livonia, MI 48150-1173. Offers pastoral ministry (MA). *Expenses: Tuition:* Full-time $15,930; part-time $885 per credit hour. Tuition and fees vary according to degree level and program.

Maple Springs Baptist Bible College and Seminary, Graduate and Professional Programs, Capitol Heights, MD 20743. Offers biblical studies (MA, Certificate); Christian counseling (MA); church administration (MA); divinity (M Div); ministry (D Min); religious education (MRE). In 2019, 10 master's, 1 doctorate awarded. Application fee: $40. *Expenses: Tuition:* Part-time $300 per credit. *Application contact:* Anthony E. Broadnax, Registrar and Director of Admissions and Records, 301-736-3631.

Maranatha Baptist University, Doctor of Ministry Program, Watertown, WI 53094. Offers D Min. *Program availability:* Part-time, evening/weekend, online only, 100% online, blended/hybrid learning. *Faculty:* 4 full-time (0 women), 5 part-time/adjunct (0 women). *Students:* 10 part-time (0 women); includes 1 minority (Two or more races, non-Hispanic/Latino), 1 international. Average age 46. In 2019, 1 doctorate awarded. *Degree requirements:* For doctorate, thesis/dissertation, project. *Entrance requirements:* For doctorate, M Div or MA plus sufficient course work to total 60 hours. *Expenses:* Contact institution. *Financial support:* Scholarships/grants available. Financial award applicants required to submit FAFSA. *Unit head:* Mark Herbster, Dean of the Seminary, E-mail: mark.herbster@mbu.edu. *Application contact:* Dr. Jim Harrison, Director of Admissions, 920-206-2327, Fax: 920-261-9109, E-mail: admissions@mbbc.edu.
Website: https://www.mbu.edu/seminary/doctor-of-ministry/

Maranatha Baptist University, Program in Biblical Counseling, Watertown, WI 53094. Offers MA. *Program availability:* Part-time. *Entrance requirements:* For master's, BA or BS. Additional exam requirements/recommendations for international students: recommended—TOEFL. *Expenses: Tuition:* Full-time $5940; part-time $3960 per credit. *Required fees:* $25 per credit. Tuition and fees vary according to degree level and program.

Martin University, Graduate School of Urban Ministry, Indianapolis, IN 46218-3867. Offers urban ministry studies (MA). *Program availability:* Part-time, evening/weekend. *Degree requirements:* For master's, Greek, oral and written comprehensive exam or thesis.

Marymount University, School of Sciences, Mathematics, and Education, Program in Counseling, Arlington, VA 22207-4299. Offers clinical mental health counseling (MA); counseling with forensic and legal studies (MA/MA); pastoral counseling (MA); school counseling (MA); MA/MA. *Accreditation:* ACA (one or more programs are accredited). *Program availability:* Part-time, evening/weekend. *Faculty:* 11 full-time (9 women), 3 part-time/adjunct (all women). *Students:* 119 full-time (100 women), 39 part-time (33 women); includes 54 minority (20 Black or African American, non-Hispanic/Latino; 8 Asian, non-Hispanic/Latino; 20 Hispanic/Latino; 6 Two or more races, non-Hispanic/Latino), 2 international. Average age 28. 122 applicants, 89% accepted, 58 enrolled. In 2019, 41 master's awarded. *Degree requirements:* For master's, thesis or alternative, capstone/internship. *Entrance requirements:* For master's, GRE, 2 letters of recommendation, interview, resume, personal statement. Additional exam requirements/recommendations for international students: required—TOEFL (minimum score 600 paper-based; 96 iBT), IELTS (minimum score 6.5), PTE (minimum score 58). *Application deadline:* For fall admission, 1/15 priority date for domestic and international students. Applications are processed on a rolling basis. Application fee: $40. Electronic applications accepted. *Expenses: Tuition:* Part-time $1050 per credit. *Required fees:* $22 per credit. One-time fee: $270 part-time. Tuition and fees vary according to program. *Financial support:* In 2019–20, 19 students received support. Research assistantships, teaching assistantships, career-related internships or fieldwork, scholarships/grants, and unspecified assistantships available. Support available to part-time students. Financial award application deadline: 3/1; financial award applicants required to submit FAFSA. *Unit head:* Dr. Lisa Jackson-Cherry, Chair, Counseling, 703-284-1633, E-mail: lisa.jackson-cherry@marymount.edu. *Application contact:* Fiona McDonnell, Administrative Assistant, 703-284-5901, E-mail: gadmissi@marymount.edu.
Website: https://www.marymount.edu/Academics/School-of-Sciences-Mathematics-and-Education/Graduate-Programs/Counseling-(M-A-)

The Master's University, The Master's Seminary, Santa Clarita, CA 91321-1200. Offers biblical counseling (MABC); New Testament (Th D); Old Testament (Th D); preaching (D Min); theology (M Div, M Th, Th D). *Program availability:* Part-time. *Degree requirements:* For master's, 2 foreign languages, thesis; for doctorate, 4 foreign languages, thesis/dissertation. *Entrance requirements:* For master's, minimum GPA of 2.75; for doctorate, Th M, minimum GPA of 3.5. Additional exam requirements/recommendations for international students: required—TOEFL (minimum score 550 paper-based).

McCormick Theological Seminary, Graduate and Professional Programs, Chicago, IL 60615. Offers ministry (D Min); theological studies (MATS, Certificate); theology (M Div); M Div/MSW. *Accreditation:* ACIPE; ATS (one or more programs are accredited). *Program availability:* Part-time, evening/weekend. *Degree requirements:* For master's, thesis (for some programs); for doctorate, thesis/dissertation. *Entrance requirements:* For master's, minimum GPA of 3.0; for doctorate, M Div, minimum 3 years in pastorate.

McMaster University, McMaster Divinity College, Hamilton, ON L8S 4M2, Canada. Offers Biblical studies (MA, MTS, Diploma); biblical studies (M Div); Christian interpretation/history (M Div, MA, MTS, Diploma); Christian ministry (M Div, MA, MTS, Diploma); Christian Studies (Certificate); Christian theology (PhD). *Accreditation:* ATS. *Program availability:* Part-time. *Degree requirements:* For master's, one foreign language, thesis optional; for doctorate, 3 foreign languages, comprehensive exam, thesis/dissertation; for other advanced degree, 2 foreign languages, thesis. *Entrance requirements:* For master's, minimum B average in undergraduate course work, 3 letters of reference; for doctorate, minimum B+ average in bachelor's and master's, appropriate modern/ancient language, interview; for other advanced degree, 6 units of related Biblical language, minimum B+ average in undergraduate course work, minimum 15 units of course work in related area of study, 3 letters of recommendation. Additional exam requirements/recommendations for international students: required—TOEFL (minimum score 550 paper-based).

Meadville Lombard Theological School, Graduate and Professional Programs, Chicago, IL 60637-1602. Offers divinity (M Div); ministry (D Min); religion (MA); M Div/MSW. *Accreditation:* ACIPE; ATS. *Program availability:* Part-time, online learning. *Entrance requirements:* For master's, bachelor's degree; for doctorate, bachelor's and masters degrees, 3 years of ministry.

Mercer University, Graduate Studies, Cecil B. Day Campus, James and Carolyn McAfee School of Theology, Atlanta, GA 30341. Offers Christian ministry (MACM); Christian spirituality (D Min); divinity (M Div); preaching (D Min); M Div/MBA; M Div/MS. *Program availability:* Part-time, 100% online. *Faculty:* 9 full-time (4 women), 4 part-time/adjunct (2 women). *Students:* 53 full-time (34 women), 81 part-time (37 women); includes 77 minority (68 Black or African American, non-Hispanic/Latino; 1 Asian, non-Hispanic/Latino; 7 Hispanic/Latino; 1 Two or more races, non-Hispanic/Latino). Average age 41. 107 applicants, 51% accepted, 38 enrolled. In 2019, 43 master's, 7 doctorates awarded. *Degree requirements:* For master's, variable foreign language requirement, thesis (for some programs), minimum GPA; time limits; for doctorate, thesis/dissertation, minimum GPA; time limits. *Entrance requirements:* For master's, Regionally-accredited bachelor's degree with liberal arts core or proof of equivalent degree from foreign university; biographical data; transcripts; letters of recommendation; resume; essays; writing sample; interview; background check; application fee; for doctorate, Regionally-accredited bachelor's degree with liberal arts core or proof of equivalent degree from foreign university; M.Div. or equivalent; biographical data; transcripts; letters of recommendation; resume; essays; writing sample; interview; background check; application fee; Covenant of Support. Additional exam requirements/recommendations for international students: required—TOEFL (minimum score 550 paper-based; 79 iBT). *Application deadline:* For fall admission, 6/15 priority date for domestic and international students; for spring admission, 11/15 priority date for domestic and international students. Applications are processed on a rolling basis. Application fee: $50. Electronic applications accepted. *Expenses:* The M.Div., M.A.C.M., M.T.S. and Non-Degree (for credit) programs are charged at $475 per credit hour. The D.Min. Program is charged at $450 per credit hour. *Financial support:* In 2019–20, 50 students received support, including 2 fellowships with full tuition reimbursements available (averaging $3,000 per year); career-related internships or fieldwork, Federal Work-Study, scholarships/grants, and stipends also available. Support available to part-time students. Financial award application deadline: 1/15; financial award applicants required to submit FAFSA. *Unit head:* Dr. C. Gregory DeLoach, Interim Dean, 678-547-6620, E-mail: deloach_cg@mercer.edu. *Application contact:* Nathan Cost, Director of Admissions, 678-547-6451, E-mail: cost_na@mercer.edu.
Website: http://www.mercer.edu/theology

Mid-America Baptist Theological Seminary, Graduate and Professional Programs, Cordova, TN 38016. Offers biblical counseling (M Div); Christian education (M Div, MACE); ministry (D Min); missiology and intercultural studies (M Div); pastoral ministry (M Div); theology (MA, PhD); worship (MA). *Degree requirements:* For doctorate, 4 foreign languages, thesis/dissertation. *Entrance requirements:* For doctorate, MAT. Additional exam requirements/recommendations for international students: required—TOEFL (minimum score 600 paper-based). Electronic applications accepted.

Mid-America Christian University, Program in Counseling, Oklahoma City, OK 73170-4504. Offers marital and family therapy (MS); pastoral/spiritual direction (MS); professional counselor (MS). *Entrance requirements:* For master's, MAT, bachelor's degree from a regionally accredited college or university, minimum overall cumulative GPA of 2.75 of bachelor course work. Additional exam requirements/recommendations for international students: required—TOEFL (minimum score 550 paper-based).

Midwestern Baptist Theological Seminary, Graduate and Professional Programs, Kansas City, MO 64118-4697. Offers Christian education (MACE); Christian foundations (Graduate Certificate); church music (MCM); counseling (MA); ministry (D Ed Min, D Min); Old or New Testament studies (PhD); theology (M Div). *Accreditation:* ATS. *Program availability:* Part-time, online learning. *Degree requirements:* For doctorate, thesis/dissertation. *Entrance requirements:* For doctorate, MAT. Electronic applications accepted.

Midwest University, Graduate Programs, Wentzville, MO 63385. Offers asset management/investment/real estate (MBA); Christian counseling (D Min); Christian education (D Min); counseling (MA), including marriage and family counseling, school counseling; divinity (M Div); education (MA), including brain and gifted education, Christian education; global business management (MBA); global leadership (MBA); leadership (PhD), including brain and gifted educational leadership, entrepreneurial leadership, international aviation leadership, organizational leadership, political leadership; mission studies (D Min); music (MM, DMA); pastoral theology (D Min); public policy/administration (MBA); teaching English to speakers of other languages (MA). *Program availability:* Part-time, online learning. *Degree requirements:* For master's, thesis (for some programs); for doctorate, thesis/dissertation. *Entrance requirements:* Additional exam requirements/recommendations for international students: recommended—TOEFL (minimum score 550 paper-based).

Milligan University, Area of Counselor Education Programs, Milligan College, TN 37682. Offers clinical mental health counseling (MSC); counseling ministry (Graduate Certificate); school counseling (MSC). *Program availability:* Part-time. *Faculty:* 3 full-time (all women), 2 part-time/adjunct (1 woman). *Students:* 24 full-time (20 women), 4 part-time (3 women); includes 2 minority (1 Black or African American, non-Hispanic/Latino; 1 Two or more races, non-Hispanic/Latino). Average age 30. 33 applicants, 67% accepted, 16 enrolled. In 2019, 15 master's awarded. *Degree requirements:* For master's, thesis or alternative. *Entrance requirements:* For master's, GRE General Test if undergraduate GPA is less than 3.0, undergraduate degree and supporting transcripts, essay/personal statement, professional recommendations, interview. Additional exam requirements/recommendations for international students: required—TOEFL (minimum score 550 paper-based, 79 iBT) or IELTS (6.5). *Application deadline:* For fall admission, 8/1 for domestic students, 6/1 for international students. Applications are processed on a rolling basis. Application fee: $30. Electronic applications accepted. *Expenses:* Up to 60 hr program; $460/hr; $75 one-time records fee; $325/semester (technology and activity fees). *Financial support:* Scholarships/grants available. Financial award application deadline: 12/1; financial award applicants required to submit FAFSA. *Unit head:* Dr. Rebecca Sapp, Director of Master of Science in Counseling Program, 423-461-3071, E-mail: rlsapp@milligan.edu. *Application contact:* Stacy Shankle, Graduate Admissions Recruiter, Healthcare Programs, 423-461-8424, Fax: 423-461-8789, E-mail: srshankle@milligan.edu.

Milligan University, Emmanuel Christian Seminary at Milligan College, Milligan College, TN 37682. Offers Christian care and counseling (M Div); Christian education (M Div); Christian ministries (MACM, Graduate Certificate); Christian ministry (M Div); Christian theology (M Div, MAR); church history (MAR); church history/historical theology (M Div); general studies (M Div); ministry (D Min); New Testament (M Div, MAR); Old Testament (M Div, MAR); urban ministry (M Div); world missions (M Div). *Accreditation:* ACIPE; ATS. *Program availability:* Part-time, blended/hybrid learning. *Faculty:* 12 full-time (1 woman), 5 part-time/adjunct (0 women). *Students:* 70 full-time (28 women), 70 part-time (26 women); includes 19 minority (9 Black or African American, non-Hispanic/Latino; 3 American Indian or Alaska Native, non-Hispanic/Latino; 2 Asian, non-Hispanic/Latino; 5 Hispanic/Latino), 8 international. Average age

34. 109 applicants, 90% accepted, 64 enrolled. In 2019, 21 master's, 3 doctorates awarded. *Degree requirements:* For master's, 2 foreign languages, thesis or alternative, portfolio; for doctorate, thesis/dissertation. *Entrance requirements:* For master's, undergraduate degree and supporting transcripts, essay/personal statement, professional recommendations, interview; for doctorate, M Div or equivalent, essay/personal statement, professional recommendations. Additional exam requirements/recommendations for international students: required—TOEFL (minimum score 550 paper-based, 79 iBT) or IELTS (6.5). *Application deadline:* For fall admission, 8/1 for domestic students, 6/1 for international students; for spring admission, 12/15 for domestic students, 8/1 for international students. Applications are processed on a rolling basis. Application fee: $30. Electronic applications accepted. *Expenses:* 36 - 90 hr programs: $485/hr; $75 one-time records fee; MDIV (90 Hrs)/MAR (58 Hrs) $325/semester (technology and activity fee); MACM (48 Hrs)/DMIN (36 Hrs) $250/semester (technology and activity fees). *Financial support:* Scholarships/grants and unspecified assistantships available. Financial award application deadline: 12/1; financial award applicants required to submit FAFSA. *Unit head:* Dr. Rollin Ramsaran, Academic Dean, Emmanuel Christian Seminary, 423-461-1524, Fax: 423-926-6198, E-mail: raramsaran@milligan.edu. *Application contact:* Lauren Gullett, Director of Admissions and Recruitment for Emmanuel Christian Seminary, 423-461-1535, Fax: 423-926-6198, E-mail: lwgullett@milligan.edu.
Website: http://ecs.milligan.edu/

Missio Seminary, Graduate and Professional Programs, Hatfield, PA 19440-2499. Offers advanced missional leadership (D Min); advanced pastoral studies (Certificate); biblical counseling (Certificate); biblical studies (MA, Certificate); counseling (MA); ministry (M Div, MA); missional theology (MA). *Accreditation:* ATS. *Program availability:* Part-time, evening/weekend. *Degree requirements:* For master's, variable foreign language requirement, thesis optional; for doctorate, thesis/dissertation. *Entrance requirements:* Additional exam requirements/recommendations for international students: required—TOEFL (minimum score 550 paper-based; 80 iBT). Electronic applications accepted.

Missouri Baptist University, Graduate Programs, St. Louis, MO 63141-8660. Offers business administration (MBA); Christian ministries (MACM); counseling (MAC); education (MSE); education administration (MEA); educational leadership (MSE, Ed S); teaching (MAT).

Moody Bible Institute, Graduate School, Chicago, IL 60610-3284. Offers biblical studies (MABS, Graduate Certificate); intercultural studies (MAIS, Graduate Certificate); ministry (M Div, M Min); spiritual formation and discipleship (MASF, Graduate Certificate); urban studies (MA, Graduate Certificate). *Program availability:* Part-time. *Degree requirements:* For master's, 2 foreign languages, fieldwork (MABS); colloquium, field research project (MA Min). *Entrance requirements:* For master's, 30 hours in Bible/theology, 2 years of ministry experience (MA Min).

Mount Marty University, Graduate Studies Division, Yankton, SD 57078-3724. Offers business administration (MBA); nurse anesthesia (MS); nursing (MSN); pastoral ministries (MPM). *Accreditation:* AANA/CANAEP (one or more programs are accredited). *Degree requirements:* For master's, thesis or alternative. *Entrance requirements:* For master's, GRE General Test, minimum GPA of 3.0. Electronic applications accepted.

Mount St. Joseph University, Graduate Program in Religious Studies, Cincinnati, OH 45233-1670. Offers religious studies (MA); spirituality and wellness (Certificate). *Program availability:* Part-time, evening/weekend. *Degree requirements:* For master's, comprehensive exam, 36 hours of credit, pastoral PRAXIS component (3 credit hours), integrating project (3 credit hours). *Entrance requirements:* For master's, undergraduate transcript with minimum overall GPA of 3.0, 3 letters of recommendation from professional colleagues, 3-page essay, interview with the Graduate Admissions Committee, current work resume. Additional exam requirements/recommendations for international students: required—TOEFL (minimum score 560 paper-based; 83 iBT). Electronic applications accepted. *Expenses:* Contact institution.

Nashotah House Theological Seminary, Graduate Programs, Nashotah, WI 53058-9793. Offers Anglican studies (Certificate); Biblical studies (STM); Christian spirituality (STM); church history (STM); liturgy (STM); ministry (M Div, MM); pastoral ministry (MPM); theological studies (MTS); theology (STM, D Min). *Accreditation:* ACIPE; ATS (one or more programs are accredited). *Program availability:* Part-time. *Degree requirements:* For master's, thesis optional. *Entrance requirements:* For master's and Certificate, GRE General Test or MAT, interview, 3 recommendations. Additional exam requirements/recommendations for international students: required—TOEFL. Electronic applications accepted. *Expenses:* Contact institution.

Nebraska Christian College of Hope International University, Graduate Programs, Papillion, NE 68046. Offers biblical studies (M Div); business as mission/social entrepreneurship (MBA); children, youth, and family (M Div); church planting (M Div); counseling psychology (MS); educational administration (MA); elementary education (M Ed); general management (MBA); gifted and talented education (M Ed); intercultural studies (M Div); international development (MBA); marketing management (MBA); ministry (MA); ministry and leadership (M Div); music education (M Ed); non-profit management (MBA); pastoral care (M Div); secondary education (M Ed); spiritual formation (M Div); worship ministry (M Div).

Neumann University, Program in Pastoral Clinical Mental Health Counseling, Aston, PA 19014-1298. Offers pastoral care specialist (Certificate); pastoral clinical mental health counseling (MS); pastoral clinical mental health counseling certificate of advanced study (Certificate); pastoral counseling (PhD); spiritual formation and direction (CSD); spiritual formation and direction supervision certificate of advanced study (Certificate). *Program availability:* Part-time, evening/weekend. *Degree requirements:* For doctorate, comprehensive exam, thesis/dissertation. *Entrance requirements:* For master's and other advanced degree, official transcripts from all institutions attended, letter of intent, three letters of recommendation; for doctorate, MAT, master's degree, official transcripts from all institutions attended, resume or curriculum vitae, letter of intent, two official letters of recommendation. Additional exam requirements/recommendations for international students: required—TOEFL (minimum score 70 iBT). Electronic applications accepted. *Expenses:* Contact institution.

New Brunswick Theological Seminary, Graduate and Professional Programs, New Brunswick, NJ 08901-1196. Offers pastoral care and counseling (D Min). *Accreditation:* ACIPE; ATS. *Program availability:* Part-time, evening/weekend. *Degree requirements:* For master's, variable foreign language requirement, thesis (for some programs); for doctorate, thesis/dissertation. *Entrance requirements:* For master's, BA/BS with minimum GPA of 3.0 (for MA), 2.5 (for M Div); for doctorate, M Div. Additional exam requirements/recommendations for international students: required—TOEFL (minimum score 550 paper-based; 79 iBT); recommended—IELTS (minimum score 6). Electronic applications accepted.

New Orleans Baptist Theological Seminary, Graduate and Professional Programs, Division of Pastoral Ministries, New Orleans, LA 70126-4858. Offers M Div, MAMFC, D Min, PhD. *Accreditation:* ACIPE. *Program availability:* Online learning. *Degree requirements:* For master's, 2 foreign languages, thesis (for some programs); for doctorate, 3 foreign languages, comprehensive exam, thesis/dissertation. *Entrance*

requirements: For master's and doctorate, GRE General Test. Additional exam requirements/recommendations for international students: required—TOEFL.

Northern Seminary, Graduate and Professional Programs, Lombard, IL 60148-5698. Offers Biblical studies (M Div); Christian community development (MA, D Min); Christian ministry (MACM); contextual theology (D Min); missional church ministry (M Div); New Testament (M Div, MANT); New Testament context (D Min); Old Testament (M Div); preaching (D Min); theology (M Div); theology and mission (MA); urban leadership (MA); worship (M Div, MAW). *Program availability:* Part-time, evening/weekend. *Degree requirements:* For master's, thesis (for some programs); for doctorate, thesis/dissertation. *Entrance requirements:* For master's, writing test, all official transcripts, letter of reference from church, 3 letters of reference, autobiographical statement (400 words or more); for doctorate, M Div, 3 years in the ministry post-M Div, 3 letters of reference. Additional exam requirements/recommendations for international students: required—TOEFL (minimum score 550 paper-based). Electronic applications accepted.

North Greenville University, T. Walter Brashier Graduate School, Greer, SC 29651. Offers Christian ministry (MCM, D Min); education (M Ed, MAT); financial planning (MBA); human resources (MBA). *Program availability:* Part-time, evening/weekend, online learning. *Degree requirements:* For master's, comprehensive exam (for some programs), thesis or alternative, capstone course. *Entrance requirements:* For master's, minimum GPA of 2.25 overall, 2.5 in major; for doctorate, MAT. Additional exam requirements/recommendations for international students: required—TOEFL (minimum score 550 paper-based). Electronic applications accepted.

North Park Theological Seminary, Graduate and Professional Programs, Program in Christian Ministry, Chicago, IL 60625-4895. Offers MACM, MA/MBA, MA/MM.

North Park Theological Seminary, Graduate and Professional Programs, Program in Christian Studies, Chicago, IL 60625-4895. Offers adult ministry (Certificate); camping and retreat ministry (Certificate); children and family ministry (Certificate); Christian formation (Certificate); faith and health (Certificate); intercultural studies (Certificate); justice ministry (Certificate); leadership and administration (Certificate); spiritual direction (Certificate); youth ministry (Certificate). *Accreditation:* ACIPE. *Program availability:* Part-time. *Entrance requirements:* For degree, minimum GPA of 2.5. Additional exam requirements/recommendations for international students: required—TOEFL.

Northwest Nazarene University, NNU Graduate School of Theology, Nampa, ID 83686-5897. Offers leadership and formation (MA); missional leadership (M Div); pastoral ministry (MA); spiritual formation (M Div); youth, children, and family ministry (M Div). *Program availability:* Part-time, online only, 100% online. *Degree requirements:* For master's, 2.5 cumulative GPA. *Entrance requirements:* For master's, minimum GPA of 2.5; two recommendations, official transcripts. Additional exam requirements/recommendations for international students: required—TOEFL (minimum score 85 iBT). Electronic applications accepted. *Expenses:* Contact institution.

Northwest University, College of Ministry, Kirkland, WA 98033. Offers ministry (MIM); missional leadership (MA); theology and culture (MA). *Program availability:* Part-time, evening/weekend, online learning. *Degree requirements:* For master's, comprehensive exam (for some programs), thesis (for some programs). *Entrance requirements:* Additional exam requirements/recommendations for international students: required—TOEFL (minimum score 550 paper-based; 75 iBT). Electronic applications accepted.

Nyack College, Alliance Theological Seminary, New York, NY 10004. Offers Biblical literature (MA), including New Testament, Old Testament; Biblical studies (MA); Christian ministry (MPS); intercultural studies (MA); ministry (D Min), including Christian leadership in the global context; theology and missions (M Div); urban ministry (MPS). *Program availability:* Part-time, evening/weekend, 100% online, blended/hybrid learning. *Students:* 203 full-time (89 women), 343 part-time (176 women); includes 418 minority (140 Black or African American, non-Hispanic/Latino; 94 Asian, non-Hispanic/Latino; 172 Hispanic/Latino; 1 Native Hawaiian or other Pacific Islander, non-Hispanic/Latino; 11 Two or more races, non-Hispanic/Latino), 40 international. Average age 43. In 2019, 100 master's, 17 doctorates awarded. *Degree requirements:* For master's, comprehensive exam (for some programs), thesis optional, internship; for doctorate, thesis/dissertation. *Entrance requirements:* For master's, transcripts, Christian experience statement, recommendations; for doctorate, transcripts, documented three years of ministry experience subsequent to 1st graduate theological degree, reference letters, formal academic paper. Additional exam requirements/recommendations for international students: required—TOEFL (minimum score 550 paper-based; 80 iBT). *Application deadline:* Applications are processed on a rolling basis. Application fee: $30. Electronic applications accepted. *Expenses:* $585 per credit. *Financial support:* Career-related internships or fieldwork, Federal Work-Study, and scholarships/grants available. Financial award applicants required to submit FAFSA. *Unit head:* Dr. Ronald Walborn, Dean, 845-770-5715, Fax: 845-358-1663. *Application contact:* Dr. Ronald Walborn, Dean, 845-770-5715, Fax: 845-358-1663.
Website: http://www.nyack.edu/ats

Oakland City University, Chapman Seminary, Oakland City, IN 47660-1099. Offers ministry (M Div); pastoral care (M Div); theology (D Min). *Program availability:* Part-time. *Degree requirements:* For doctorate, thesis/dissertation. *Entrance requirements:* For doctorate, GRE, MAT, letters of recommendation. Additional exam requirements/recommendations for international students: required—TOEFL. *Expenses:* Contact institution.

Oakwood University, Program in Pastoral Studies, Huntsville, AL 35896. Offers MA. *Entrance requirements:* For master's, Biblical Literacy Entrance Test (BLET), minimum cumulative GPA of 2.5, 2 letters of recommendation, current resume, 3 years of pastoral or local church leadership experience. Additional exam requirements/recommendations for international students: required—TOEFL (minimum score 500 paper-based).

Oblate School of Theology, Graduate and Professional Programs, San Antonio, TX 78216-6693. Offers African-American pastoral leadership (D Min); divinity (M Div); pastoral leadership (D Min); pastoral ministry (MAP Min); pastoral studies (Certificate); spiritual formation in the local community (D Min); spirituality (MA Sp, PhD); spirituality and ministry (D Min); theology (MA Th); U.S. Hispanic/Latino ministry (D Min); M Div/MA Th. *Accreditation:* ACIPE; ATS (one or more programs are accredited). *Program availability:* Part-time, 100% online, blended/hybrid learning. *Faculty:* 21 full-time (5 women), 4 part-time/adjunct (0 women). *Students:* 89 full-time (9 women), 54 part-time (31 women); includes 77 minority (11 Black or African American, non-Hispanic/Latino; 8 Asian, non-Hispanic/Latino; 57 Hispanic/Latino; 1 Two or more races, non-Hispanic/Latino), 24 international. Average age 39. In 2019, 24 master's, 1 doctorate awarded. *Degree requirements:* For master's, comprehensive exam (for some programs), thesis (for some programs), practicum; for doctorate, one foreign language, comprehensive exam, thesis/dissertation, paper, practicum. *Entrance requirements:* For master's, MAT, interview, prerequisite course work in theology or religious studies and philosophy, minimum GPA of 2.5; for doctorate, D Min, M Div, MA Th, MA Sp, MA PM. Additional exam requirements/recommendations for international students: required—TOEFL (minimum score 71 iBT). *Application deadline:* For fall admission, 6/30 priority date for domestic and international students; for winter admission, 11/30 for domestic and international students; for spring admission, 11/30 for domestic and international students; for summer admission, 4/30 for domestic and international students.

Applications are processed on a rolling basis. Application fee: $65. Electronic applications accepted. *Expenses:* Contact institution. *Financial support:* In 2019–20, 25 students received support. Scholarships/grants available. Support available to part-time students. Financial award application deadline: 8/15; financial award applicants required to submit FAFSA. *Unit head:* Dr. R. Scott Woodward, Academic Dean, 210-341-1366, Fax: 210-341-4519, E-mail: rsw@ost.edu. *Application contact:* Brenda Reyna, Registrar, 210-341-1366 Ext. 226, Fax: 210-341-4519, E-mail: registrar@ost.edu.

Ohio Christian University, Graduate Programs, Circleville, OH 43113. Offers accounting (MBA); business administration (MBA); digital marketing (MBA); finance (MBA); healthcare management (MBA); human resources (MBA); management (MM); organizational leadership (MBA); pastoral care and counseling (MAM); practical theology (MAM).

Olivet Nazarene University, Graduate School, Department of Practical Ministries, Bourbonnais, IL 60914. Offers MPM. *Program availability:* Part-time. *Degree requirements:* For master's, thesis or alternative.

Oral Roberts University, School of Theology and Missions, Tulsa, OK 74171. Offers biblical literature (MA), including advanced languages, Judaic-Christian studies; church ministries and leadership (D Min); clinical pastoral education (M Div); missions (MA); pastoral care and chaplaincy (M Div, D Min); practical theology (MA), including teaching ministries, urban ministries; professional counseling (MA), including addiction studies, marriage and family therapy; theological/historical studies (MA). *Accreditation:* ATS. *Program availability:* Part-time, online learning. *Faculty:* 17 full-time (2 women). *Students:* 268 full-time (146 women), 96 part-time (52 women); includes 66 minority (48 Black or African American, non-Hispanic/Latino; 9 American Indian or Alaska Native, non-Hispanic/Latino; 8 Asian, non-Hispanic/Latino; 1 Native Hawaiian or other Pacific Islander, non-Hispanic/Latino), 65 international. Average age 40. 661 applicants, 24% accepted, 136 enrolled. In 2019, 113 master's, 19 doctorates awarded. *Degree requirements:* For master's, thesis (for some programs), practicum/internship; for doctorate, thesis/dissertation, applied research project. *Entrance requirements:* For master's, GRE General Test or MAT (waived for those with undergraduate degree from regionally accredited institution and 3.0 or higher GPA), minimum GPA of 2.5 (professional) or 3.0 (academic); for doctorate, M Div, minimum GPA of 3.0, 3 years of full-time ministry experience. Additional exam requirements/recommendations for international students: recommended—TOEFL (minimum score 550 paper-based; 79 iBT), IELTS (minimum score 7). *Application deadline:* Applications are processed on a rolling basis. Application fee: $35. Electronic applications accepted. Application fee is waived when completed online. *Expenses: Tuition:* Full-time $11,052; part-time $5526 per year. *Required fees:* $1230; $615 per unit. Tuition and fees vary according to program. *Financial support:* Fellowships and scholarships/grants available. Financial award application deadline: 6/1. *Unit head:* Dr. Bill Buker, Chair, 918-495-6493, E-mail: bbuker@oru.edu. *Application contact:* Joe Sims, Enrollment Counselor, 918-495-6618, E-mail: jsims@oru.edu.
Website: http://www.gradtheology.oru.edu/

Ottawa University, Graduate Studies-Arizona, Program in Professional Counseling, Ottawa, KS 66067-3399. Offers Christian counseling (MA); expressive arts therapy (MA); marriage and family therapy (MA); treatment of trauma, abuse and deprivation (MA). *Program availability:* Part-time, evening/weekend, online learning. *Degree requirements:* For master's, comprehensive exam, thesis or alternative, field experience, practicum. *Entrance requirements:* For master's, minimum undergraduate GPA of 3.0; course work in theories of personality, abnormal psychology, and human growth and development. Additional exam requirements/recommendations for international students: required—TOEFL (minimum score 550 paper-based).

Pacific Rim Christian University, Program in Christian Ministry, Honolulu, HI 96819. Offers MA.

Pentecostal Theological Seminary, Graduate and Professional Programs, Cleveland, TN 37320-3330. Offers biblical studies (MTS); church ministries (MA); counseling (MA); discipleship and Christian formation (MA); ministry (D Min); Pentecostal theology (MTS); theology (M Div). *Accreditation:* ACIPE; ATS. *Program availability:* Part-time. *Degree requirements:* For master's, variable foreign language requirement, thesis (for some programs), internship.

Pepperdine University, Seaver College, Malibu, CA 90263. Offers business (MS), including accounting; communication (MFA), including cinematic media production; humanities (MA, MFA), including American studies (MA), writing for screen and television (MFA); religion (M Div, MA, MS), including ministry (MS), religion (M Div, MA); JD/M Div. *Entrance requirements:* For master's, GRE General Test. Additional exam requirements/recommendations for international students: required—TOEFL. *Expenses:* Contact institution.

Phillips Theological Seminary, Programs in Theology, Doctor of Ministry Program, Tulsa, OK 74116. Offers parish ministry (D Min); pastoral counseling (D Min); practices of ministry (D Min). *Accreditation:* ATS. *Program availability:* Part-time. *Degree requirements:* For doctorate, thesis/dissertation. *Entrance requirements:* For doctorate, M Div, minimum GPA of 3.0, 3 years of post-M Div pastoral experience. *Expenses:* Contact institution.

Phoenix Seminary, Graduate Programs, Phoenix, AZ 85018. Offers Biblical and theological studies (Graduate Diploma); Biblical communication (M Div); Biblical leadership (MA); Christian counseling (Graduate Diploma); counseling and family (M Div); leadership development (M Div); ministry (D Min); professional counseling (MA). *Accreditation:* ATS (one or more programs are accredited). *Program availability:* Part-time, evening/weekend. *Degree requirements:* For master's, 2 foreign languages, comprehensive exam; for doctorate, 2 foreign languages, thesis/dissertation. *Entrance requirements:* For master's, undergraduate degree with minimum GPA of 2.5; for doctorate, M Div (94 hours) with minimum GPA of 3.0. Additional exam requirements/recommendations for international students: required—TOEFL (minimum score 587 paper-based; 92 iBT), TWE (minimum score 4.5).

Piedmont International University, Graduate School, Winston-Salem, NC 27101-5197. Offers Biblical studies (PhD); curriculum and instruction (M Ed); divinity (M Div); educational leadership (M Ed); leadership (MA, PhD); ministry (MA Min, D Min); non-language track (MABS); PhD preparation track (MABS). *Program availability:* Part-time, online learning. Terminal master's awarded for partial completion of doctoral program. *Degree requirements:* For master's, 2 foreign languages, comprehensive exam, thesis or alternative; for doctorate, 2 foreign languages, comprehensive exam. *Entrance requirements:* For master's, GRE General Test; for doctorate, Hebrew and Greek proficiency, MA. Additional exam requirements/recommendations for international students: required—TOEFL (minimum score 500 paper-based; 60 iBT). Electronic applications accepted. *Expenses: Tuition:* Full-time $3375; part-time $375 per credit. *Required fees:* $400; $200 per semester. Part-time tuition and fees vary according to program.

Pittsburgh Theological Seminary, Graduate and Professional Programs, Pittsburgh, PA 15206-2596. Offers divinity (M Div); theological studies (MA); theology (Th M); theology and ministry (MA, D Min); JD/M Div; M Div/MS; M Div/MSW. *Accreditation:* ATS (one or more programs are accredited). *Program availability:* Part-time, evening/

weekend. *Degree requirements:* For master's, one foreign language, comprehensive exam (for some programs), thesis (for some programs); for doctorate, thesis/dissertation. *Entrance requirements:* For master's, bachelor's degree with minimum GPA of 2.7, interview, references; for doctorate, M Div or equivalent, interview, references. Additional exam requirements/recommendations for international students: required—TOEFL (minimum score 570 paper-based; 89 iBT). Electronic applications accepted.

Point Loma Nazarene University, School of Theology and Christian Ministry, San Diego, CA 92106. Offers M Min. *Program availability:* Part-time, online only, nine-week quads with eight weeks of online coursework and a one-week intensive. *Faculty:* 1 full-time (0 women), 3 part-time/adjunct (0 women). *Students:* 39 part-time (16 women); includes 24 minority (1 Black or African American, non-Hispanic/Latino; 1 Asian, non-Hispanic/Latino; 20 Hispanic/Latino; 2 Two or more races, non-Hispanic/Latino), 5 international. Average age 47. 11 applicants, 82% accepted, 7 enrolled. In 2019, 4 master's awarded. *Degree requirements:* For master's, thesis optional. *Entrance requirements:* For master's, letters of recommendation, essay, transcripts, interview. Additional exam requirements/recommendations for international students: recommended—TOEFL. *Application deadline:* For fall admission, 8/30 priority date for domestic students; for spring admission, 4/4 priority date for domestic students; for summer admission, 6/20 priority date for domestic students. Applications are processed on a rolling basis. Application fee: $0. Electronic applications accepted. *Expenses:* $320 per unit. *Financial support:* In 2019–20, 24 students received support. Scholarships/grants available. Financial award application deadline: 6/5; financial award applicants required to submit FAFSA. *Unit head:* Dr. Mark Maddix, Dean, 619-849-7236, E-mail: MarkMaddix@pointloma.edu. *Application contact:* Dana Barger, Director of Recruitment and Admissions, Graduate and Professional Students, 619-329-6799, E-mail: gradinfo@pointloma.edu.
Website: https://www.pointloma.edu/schools-departments-colleges/school-theology-christian-ministry

Point University, Graduate Programs, West Point, GA 31833. Offers business transformation (MBA); transformative ministry (MTM). *Program availability:* Part-time, online only, 100% online. *Faculty:* 2 full-time (both women), 8 part-time/adjunct (3 women). *Students:* 43 full-time (20 women), 6 part-time (5 women); includes 17 minority (12 Black or African American, non-Hispanic/Latino; 1 American Indian or Alaska Native, non-Hispanic/Latino; 1 Hispanic/Latino; 3 Two or more races, non-Hispanic/Latino), 1 international. Average age 36. *Entrance requirements:* Additional exam requirements/recommendations for international students: required—TOEFL (minimum score 550 paper-based; 80 iBT). *Application deadline:* Applications are processed on a rolling basis. Application fee: $0. Electronic applications accepted. *Application contact:* Rusty Hassell, Dean of Enrollment Management, 706-385-1503, E-mail: rhassell@point.edu.

Providence University College & Theological Seminary, Theological Seminary, Otterburne, MB R0A 1G0, Canada. Offers children's ministry (Certificate); Christian studies (MA, Certificate); counseling (MA); cross-cultural discipleship (Certificate); divinity (M Div); educational studies (MA), including counseling psychology, educational ministries, student development, teaching English to speakers of other languages, training teachers of English to speakers of other languages; global studies (MA); lay counseling (Diploma); ministry (D Min); teaching English to speakers of other languages (Certificate); theological studies (MA); training teacher of English to speakers of other languages (Certificate); youth ministry (Certificate). *Accreditation:* ATS. *Program availability:* Part-time. *Degree requirements:* For master's, variable foreign language requirement, thesis (for some programs); for doctorate, thesis/dissertation. *Entrance requirements:* Additional exam requirements/recommendations for international students: recommended—TOEFL (minimum score 550 paper-based).

Randall University, Department of Bible Studies, Moore, OK 73160-1208. Offers ministry (MA). *Program availability:* Part-time, evening/weekend. *Degree requirements:* For master's, thesis optional. *Entrance requirements:* Additional exam requirements/recommendations for international students: recommended—TOEFL (minimum score 500 paper-based).

Reformed Theological Seminary–Charlotte Campus, Graduate and Professional Programs, Charlotte, NC 28226-6318. Offers biblical studies (MA); ministry (D Min); pastoral ministry (M Div); theological studies (MA). *Program availability:* Part-time. *Degree requirements:* For master's, comprehensive exam; for doctorate, thesis/dissertation. *Entrance requirements:* For master's, minimum GPA of 2.6; for doctorate, minimum GPA of 3.0. Additional exam requirements/recommendations for international students: required—TOEFL (minimum score 550 paper-based). Electronic applications accepted.

Reformed Theological Seminary–Jackson Campus, Graduate and Professional Programs, Jackson, MS 39209-3004. Offers Bible, theology, and missions (Certificate); Biblical exegesis (M Div); biblical studies (MA); Christian education (MA); counseling (M Div); marriage and family therapy (MA); ministry (D Min); missions (M Div, MA, D Min); theological studies (MA). *Accreditation:* AAMFT/COAMFTE (one or more programs are accredited); ATS (one or more programs are accredited). *Degree requirements:* For master's, thesis (for some programs), fieldwork; for doctorate, 2 foreign languages, thesis/dissertation. *Entrance requirements:* For master's, minimum GPA of 2.6; for doctorate, minimum GPA of 3.0. Additional exam requirements/recommendations for international students: required—TOEFL.

Reformed Theological Seminary–Orlando Campus, Graduate Programs, Oviedo, FL 32765. Offers Bible (Certificate); biblical studies (MA); counseling (MA); missions (Certificate); reformed expository preaching (D Min); reformed theology and ministry (D Min); theological studies (MA); theology (M Div, Certificate). *Program availability:* Part-time, online learning. Electronic applications accepted.

Regent University, Graduate School, School of Divinity, Virginia Beach, VA 23464. Offers Christian spirituality and formation (MA); divinity (M Div), including Biblical studies (M Div, MTS, Th M, PhD), chaplain ministry, Christian theology (M Div, MTS, Th M, PhD), church and ministry (M Div, MA), history of Christianity (M Div, MTS, Th M, PhD), inter-cultural studies (M Div, MA), interdisciplinary studies (M Div, MA, MTS), marketplace ministry (M Div, MA), missional discipleship, practical healing ministry (M Div, MA), worship and media (M Div, MA); leadership and renewal (D Min), including Christian leadership and renewal, clinical pastoral education, community transformation, military ministry, ministry leadership coaching; practical theology (MA), including church and ministry (M Div, MA), cosmogony, inter-cultural studies (M Div, MA), interdisciplinary studies (M Div, MA, MTS), marketplace ministry (M Div, MA), practical healing ministry (M Div, MA), worship and media (M Div, MA); renewal theology (PhD), including Biblical studies (M Div, MTS, Th M, PhD), Christian theology (M Div, MTS, Th M, PhD), history of Christianity (M Div, MTS, Th M, PhD), practical theology; theological studies (MTS), including Biblical studies (M Div, MTS, Th M, PhD), Christian theology (M Div, MTS, Th M, PhD), history of Christianity (M Div, MTS, Th M, PhD), interdisciplinary studies (M Div, MA, MTS); theology (Th M), including Biblical studies (M Div, MTS, Th M, PhD), Christian theology (M Div, MTS, Th M, PhD), history of Christianity (M Div, MTS, Th M, PhD). *Accreditation:* ACIPE; ATS. *Program availability:* Part-time, evening/weekend, 100% online, blended/hybrid learning. *Faculty:* 15 full-time (3 women), 58 part-time/adjunct (10 women). *Students:* 303 full-time (119 women), 813

part-time (403 women); includes 632 minority (509 Black or African American, non-Hispanic/Latino; 3 American Indian or Alaska Native, non-Hispanic/Latino; 31 Asian, non-Hispanic/Latino; 54 Hispanic/Latino; 2 Native Hawaiian or other Pacific Islander, non-Hispanic/Latino; 33 Two or more races, non-Hispanic/Latino), 16 international. Average age 45. 561 applicants, 66% accepted, 194 enrolled. In 2019, 168 master's, 13 doctorates awarded. *Degree requirements:* For master's, comprehensive exam, thesis or alternative, internship; for doctorate, thesis/dissertation or alternative. *Entrance requirements:* For master's, minimum undergraduate GPA of 2.75, writing sample, personal goal statement, college transcripts; for doctorate, GRE, minimum graduate GPA of 3.5 (PhD), 3.0 (D Min); clergy recommendations; writing sample; transcripts; resume; interview. Additional exam requirements/recommendations for international students: required—TOEFL (minimum score 577 paper-based). *Application deadline:* For fall admission, 5/1 priority date for domestic students. Applications are processed on a rolling basis. Application fee: $50. Electronic applications accepted. *Expenses:* Contact institution. *Financial support:* In 2019–20, 856 students received support. Career-related internships or fieldwork, scholarships/grants, health care benefits, and unspecified assistantships available. Support available to part-time students. Financial award applicants required to submit FAFSA. *Unit head:* Dr. Cornelius Bekker, Dean, 757-352-4258, Fax: 757-352-4597, E-mail: clbekker@regent.edu. *Application contact:* Heidi Cece, Assistant Vice President for Enrollment Management, 800-373-5504, Fax: 757-352-4381, E-mail: admissions@regent.edu.
Website: https://www.regent.edu/school-of-divinity/

Regent University, Graduate School, School of Psychology and Counseling, Virginia Beach, VA 23464-9800. Offers clinical mental health counseling (MA); clinical psychology (Psy D); counseling and psychological studies - clinical (PhD); counseling and psychological studies - research (PhD); counseling studies (CAGS); counselor education and supervision (PhD); general psychology (MS); human services (MA), including addictions counseling, Biblical counseling, Christian counseling, conflict and mediation ministry, criminal justice and ministry, grief counseling, human services counseling, human services for student affairs, life coaching, marriage and family ministry, trauma and crisis counseling; marriage, couple, and family counseling (MA); pastoral counseling (MA); school counseling (MA); M Div/MA; M Ed/MA; MBA/MA. *Accreditation:* ACA; APA (one or more programs are accredited). *Program availability:* Part-time, evening/weekend, 100% online, blended/hybrid learning. *Degree requirements:* For master's, thesis or alternative, internship, practicum, written competency exam; for doctorate, thesis/dissertation or alternative. *Entrance requirements:* For master's, GRE General Test (including writing exam) or MAT, minimum undergraduate GPA of 3.0, resume, transcripts, writing sample, personal goals statement; for doctorate, GRE General Test (including writing exam), minimum undergraduate GPA of 3.0, graduate 3.5; writing sample; 3 recommendations; resume; college transcripts; personal goals statement. Additional exam requirements/recommendations for international students: required—TOEFL (minimum score 577 paper-based). Electronic applications accepted. *Expenses:* Contact institution.

Regis College, Graduate and Professional Programs, Toronto, ON M5S 2Z5, Canada. Offers eastern Christian studies (Certificate); Ignatian spirituality (Diploma); ministry (D Min); ministry and spirituality (MAMS); philosophical studies (Diploma); retreat direction (Certificate); sacred theology (STM, STD, STB, STL); spiritual direction (Diploma); theological studies (MTS, Diploma); theology (M Div, MA, Th M, PhD, Th D); M Div/MA. *Accreditation:* ATS (one or more programs are accredited). Terminal master's awarded for partial completion of doctoral program. *Degree requirements:* For master's, 2 foreign languages, thesis; for doctorate, 3 foreign languages, comprehensive exam, thesis/dissertation. *Entrance requirements:* For doctorate, minimum GPA of 3.7. Additional exam requirements/recommendations for international students: required—TOEFL (minimum score 580 paper-based; 93 iBT), TWE (minimum score 5).

Richmont Graduate University, School of Ministry, Atlanta, GA 30339. Offers ministry (MA); spiritual direction (Graduate Certificate); spiritual formation and direction (MA). *Program availability:* Part-time, evening/weekend, 100% online, blended/hybrid learning. *Degree requirements:* For master's, thesis optional. *Entrance requirements:* For master's, transcripts, recommendation, personal statement, resume. Electronic applications accepted. *Expenses:* Contact institution.

Sacred Heart Major Seminary, School of Theology, Detroit, MI 48206-1799. Offers pastoral studies (MAPS); theology (M Div, MA). *Accreditation:* ACIPE; ATS. *Program availability:* Part-time, evening/weekend. *Degree requirements:* For master's, one foreign language, thesis optional, integrating project. *Entrance requirements:* For master's, GRE, previous course work in philosophy and theology.

St. Ambrose University, College of Arts and Sciences, Program in Pastoral Theology, Davenport, IA 52803-2898. Offers MP Th. *Program availability:* Part-time. *Degree requirements:* For master's, integration project. *Entrance requirements:* For master's, minimum GPA of 2.6, prior pastoral experience, 9 credits of course work in theology. Additional exam requirements/recommendations for international students: required—TOEFL. Electronic applications accepted. *Expenses:* Contact institution.

St. Augustine's Seminary of Toronto, Graduate and Professional Programs, Scarborough, ON M1M 1M3, Canada. Offers divinity (M Div); lay ministry (Diploma); religious education (MRE); theological studies (MTS, Diploma). *Accreditation:* ATS. *Program availability:* Part-time, evening/weekend. *Entrance requirements:* Additional exam requirements/recommendations for international students: required—TOEFL (minimum score 580 paper-based), TWE (minimum score 5).

St. Bernard's School of Theology and Ministry, Graduate and Professional Programs, Rochester, NY 14618. Offers pastoral studies (MA, Certificate); theological studies (MA); theology (M Div). *Accreditation:* ATS (one or more programs are accredited). *Program availability:* Part-time, evening/weekend. *Degree requirements:* For master's, variable foreign language requirement, thesis (for some programs). *Entrance requirements:* For master's, minimum GPA of 2.5.

St. Catherine University, Graduate Programs, Program in Theology, St. Paul, MN 55105. Offers pastoral ministry (Certificate); spiritual direction (Certificate); theology (MA). *Program availability:* Part-time. *Degree requirements:* For master's, comprehensive exam, thesis (for some programs). *Entrance requirements:* For master's, MAT, minimum GPA of 3.0. Additional exam requirements/recommendations for international students: required—Michigan English Language Assessment Battery or TOEFL (minimum score 600 paper-based; 100 iBT). *Expenses:* Contact institution.

St. John's Seminary, Graduate and Professional Programs, Camarillo, CA 93012-2598. Offers divinity (M Div); pastoral ministry (MAPM); theology (MA). *Accreditation:* ATS. *Program availability:* Part-time. *Degree requirements:* For master's, comprehensive exam (for some programs), thesis optional, comprehensive integration paper (MAPM). *Entrance requirements:* For master's, GRE General Test, minimum GPA of 3.5 (MA), 2.5 (MAPM). Additional exam requirements/recommendations for international students: required—TOEFL (minimum score 550 paper-based; 79 iBT). Electronic applications accepted.

Saint John's University, Saint John's School of Theology and Seminary, Collegeville, MN 56321. Offers divinity (M Div); liturgical music (MA); liturgical studies (MA); pastoral ministry (MA); theology (MA), including church history, liturgy, monastic studies,

scripture, spirituality, systematics; M Div/MA. *Program availability:* Part-time, online learning. *Degree requirements:* For master's, one foreign language, comprehensive exam (for some programs), thesis (for some programs). *Entrance requirements:* For master's, GRE General Test or MAT. Electronic applications accepted.

Saint Joseph's College of Maine, Master of Arts in Pastoral Theology Program, Standish, ME 04084. Offers MA. *Program availability:* Part-time, online learning. *Entrance requirements:* For master's, baccalaureate degree with minimum cumulative GPA of 2.5.

St. Joseph's Seminary, Graduate and Professional Programs, Yonkers, NY 10704. Offers Catholic philosophical studies (MA); divinity (M Div); pastoral studies (MAPS); theology (MA). *Accreditation:* ATS. *Degree requirements:* For master's, one foreign language, thesis. *Entrance requirements:* For master's, 27 credits in philosophy and 9 in theology.

Saint Paul University, Faculty of Canon Law, Ottawa, ON K1S 1C4, Canada. Offers canon law (MCL, JCD, PhD, Graduate Certificate, JCL); canonical practice (Graduate Certificate); ecclesiastical administration (Graduate Certificate). *Program availability:* Part-time. *Degree requirements:* For master's, one foreign language; for doctorate, one foreign language, comprehensive exam, thesis/dissertation; for other advanced degree, one foreign language, comprehensive exam and seminar paper (JCL). *Entrance requirements:* For master's, appropriate bachelor's degree, 18 credits in theology; for doctorate, JCL or MCL; for other advanced degree, B Th or equivalent (JCL), appropriate bachelor's degree, 18 credits in theology.

Saint Paul University, Faculty of Human Sciences, Program in Counseling and Spirituality, Ottawa, ON K1S 1C4, Canada. Offers individual or marital/couple counseling (MA); spiritual care (MA). *Program availability:* Part-time. *Degree requirements:* For master's, research project or thesis. *Entrance requirements:* For master's, honors BA in human sciences, minimum B average, 12 theology credits.

Saints Cyril and Methodius Seminary, Graduate and Professional Programs, Orchard Lake, MI 48324. Offers pastoral ministry (MAPM); religious education (MARE); theology (M Div, MA). *Program availability:* Part-time.

St. Stephen's College, Programs in Theology, Edmonton, AB T6G 2J6, Canada. Offers ministry (D Min); pastoral counseling (MA); social transformation ministry (MA); spirituality and liturgy (MA); theological studies (MTS); theology (M Th). *Program availability:* Part-time, evening/weekend, online learning. Terminal master's awarded for partial completion of doctoral program. *Degree requirements:* For master's, thesis; for doctorate, thesis/dissertation. *Entrance requirements:* Additional exam requirements/recommendations for international students: required—TOEFL. Electronic applications accepted. *Expenses:* Tuition: Full-time $8294 Canadian dollars; part-time $4858 Canadian dollars per course.

St. Thomas University - Florida, School of Theology and Ministry, Institute for Pastoral Ministries, Miami Gardens, FL 33054-6459. Offers pastoral ministries (MA, Certificate); practical theology (PhD). *Program availability:* Part-time, evening/weekend. *Degree requirements:* For master's, comprehensive exam; for doctorate, comprehensive exam, thesis/dissertation. *Entrance requirements:* For master's, interview, minimum GPA of 3.0 or GRE; for doctorate, GRE, MA in theology. Additional exam requirements/recommendations for international students: required—TOEFL (minimum score 550 paper-based; 79 iBT). Electronic applications accepted.

Santa Clara University, College of Arts and Sciences, Santa Clara, CA 95053. Offers pastoral ministries (MA). *Program availability:* Part-time, online learning. *Entrance requirements:* For master's, Two transcripts, two letters of recommendation. Additional exam requirements/recommendations for international students: required—TOEFL (minimum score 90 iBT), IELTS (minimum score 6.5), TOEFL (minimum score 90 iBT) or IELTS (6.5). Electronic applications accepted. *Expenses:* Contact institution.

Seattle University, School of Theology and Ministry, Program in Pastoral Studies, Seattle, WA 98122-1090. Offers MAPS. *Program availability:* Part-time, evening/weekend. *Students:* 9 part-time (6 women); includes 1 minority (Asian, non-Hispanic/Latino), 1 international. Average age 44. 2 applicants, 50% accepted, 1 enrolled. In 2019, 12 master's awarded. *Entrance requirements:* For master's, minimum GPA of 2.75 (3.0 for international students); two years of experience in some form of education, ministry, or service as a profession or volunteer; recommendations; interview with admissions committee. *Application deadline:* For fall admission, 7/1 priority date for domestic students. Application fee: $55. *Financial support:* In 2019–20, 6 students received support. Application deadline: 4/1; applicants required to submit FAFSA. *Unit head:* Dr. Mark Markuly, Director, 206-296-5330, Fax: 206-296-5329, E-mail: markulym@seattleu.edu. *Application contact:* Catherine Kehoe Fallon, Admissions Coordinator, 206-296-5333, Fax: 206-296-5329, E-mail: fallon@seattleu.edu.
Website: https://www.seattleu.edu/stm/degrees/maps/

Seattle University, School of Theology and Ministry, Program in Transformational Leadership, Seattle, WA 98122-1090. Offers MATL. *Faculty:* 22 full-time (12 women), 22 part-time/adjunct (14 women). *Students:* 1 (woman) full-time, 10 part-time (8 women); includes 3 minority (2 Asian, non-Hispanic/Latino; 1 Native Hawaiian or other Pacific Islander, non-Hispanic/Latino), 1 international. Average age 40. 5 applicants, 100% accepted, 4 enrolled. In 2019, 6 master's awarded. *Entrance requirements:* For master's, minimum GPA of 2.75 (3.0 for international students); two years of experience in some form of education, ministry, or service as a profession or volunteer; recommendations; interview with admissions committee. *Application deadline:* For fall admission, 7/1 priority date for domestic students. Application fee: $55. *Financial support:* In 2019–20, 14 students received support. Application deadline: 4/1; applicants required to submit FAFSA. *Unit head:* Dr. Mark Markuly, Dean, 206-296-5330, Fax: 206-296-5329, E-mail: stm@seattleu.edu. *Application contact:* Jean Adler Stean, Assistant Director of Admissions and Student Services, 206-296-5333, Fax: 206-296-5329, E-mail: fallon@seattleu.edu.
Website: http://www.seattleu.edu/stm/degrees/matl/

Selma University, Graduate Programs, Selma, AL 36701-5299. Offers Bible and Christian education (MA); Bible and pastoral ministry (MA).

Seton Hall University, Immaculate Conception Seminary School of Theology, South Orange, NJ 07079-2697. Offers Christian spirituality (Certificate); great spiritual books (Certificate); pastoral ministry (M Div, MA, Certificate); scripture studies (Certificate); Seminary's Theological Education for Parish Services (STEPS) (Certificate); theology (MA). *Program availability:* Part-time, evening/weekend. *Degree requirements:* For master's, comprehensive exam (for some programs), thesis (for some programs), final project (for some programs); 1 foreign language (for MA in theology research option). *Entrance requirements:* For master's, GRE General Test or MAT. Additional exam requirements/recommendations for international students: required—TOEFL (minimum score 600 paper-based; 100 iBT). Electronic applications accepted. *Expenses:* Contact institution.

Shasta Bible College, Program in Biblical Counseling, Redding, CA 96002. Offers biblical counseling and Christian family life education (MA). *Program availability:* Part-time. *Degree requirements:* For master's, comprehensive exam (for some programs), thesis or alternative. *Entrance requirements:* For master's, minimum GPA of 2.5.

Pastoral Ministry and Counseling

Additional exam requirements/recommendations for international students: required—TOEFL (minimum score 550 paper-based).

Shasta Bible College, Program in Christian Ministry, Redding, CA 96002. Offers MA. *Program availability:* Part-time, online learning. *Entrance requirements:* Additional exam requirements/recommendations for international students: required—TOEFL (minimum score 550 paper-based).

Shepherds Theological Seminary, Graduate Programs, Cary, NC 27518. Offers Biblical literature and languages (MA); church ministry (MA); ministry (MTS); New Testament (M Div); Old Testament (M Div); theology (M Div). *Accreditation:* ATS. *Degree requirements:* For master's, thesis.

Shiloh University, Graduate Programs, Kalona, IA 52247. Offers Christian ministries (M Div); leadership of church and spiritual formation (D Min); theological studies (MA). *Program availability:* Part-time, evening/weekend, online only, 100% online. *Degree requirements:* For master's, variable foreign language requirement, thesis optional; for doctorate, comprehensive exam, thesis/dissertation. *Entrance requirements:* For master's, bachelor's degree or educational equivalent from accredited school with minimum GPA of 2.5 on undergraduate work; for doctorate, M Div or equivalent with minimum GPA of 2.5 on graduate work; three years of ministry experience. Additional exam requirements/recommendations for international students: recommended—TOEFL (minimum score 540 paper-based; 76 iBT), IELTS (minimum score 6.5). Electronic applications accepted. *Expenses:* Contact institution.

Simpson University, A.W. Tozer Theological Seminary, Redding, CA 96003-8606. Offers ministry leadership (MA). *Program availability:* Part-time, evening/weekend, 100% online, blended/hybrid learning. *Entrance requirements:* For master's, GRE General Test (if undergraduate GPA less than 2.5), Christian statement, one spiritual recommendation, one academic recommendation. Additional exam requirements/recommendations for international students: required—TOEFL (minimum score 583 paper-based; 94 iBT). Electronic applications accepted. *Expenses:* Contact institution.

Sioux Falls Seminary, Graduate and Professional Programs, Master of Divinity Program, Sioux Falls, SD 57105-1599. Offers marriage and family therapy (M Div); pastoral care and counseling (M Div). *Accreditation:* ACIPE. *Program availability:* Part-time, online learning.

Sioux Falls Seminary, Graduate and Professional Programs, Program in Counseling, Sioux Falls, SD 57105-1599. Offers MA. *Program availability:* Part-time. *Entrance requirements:* For master's, minimum GPA of 2.5.

Southeastern University, Barnett College of Ministry & Theology, Lakeland, FL 33801. Offers family ministry (MA); ministerial leadership (MA, D Min); theological studies (MA); theology (M Div). *Program availability:* Evening/weekend, online learning. *Faculty:* 30 full-time (5 women), 1 part-time/adjunct (0 women). *Students:* 103 full-time (38 women), 195 part-time (77 women); includes 90 minority (28 Black or African American, non-Hispanic/Latino; 1 American Indian or Alaska Native, non-Hispanic/Latino; 16 Asian, non-Hispanic/Latino; 37 Hispanic/Latino; 2 Native Hawaiian or other Pacific Islander, non-Hispanic/Latino; 6 Two or more races, non-Hispanic/Latino), 4 international. Average age 37. In 2019, 73 master's, 5 doctorates awarded. *Degree requirements:* For master's, thesis/project. *Entrance requirements:* Additional exam requirements/recommendations for international students: required—TOEFL (minimum score 76 iBT), IELTS (minimum score 6). Application fee: $50. Electronic applications accepted. *Unit head:* Dr. Alan Ehler, Dean, 863-667-5044, E-mail: ajehler@seu.edu. *Application contact:* Dr. Alan Ehler, Dean, 863-667-5044, E-mail: ajehler@seu.edu.
Website: http://www.seu.edu/ministry/

The Southern Baptist Theological Seminary, Billy Graham School of Missions, Evangelism and Ministry, Louisville, KY 40280-0004. Offers ministry (D Min); missiology (MA, D Miss); missions and evangelism (M Div, Th M, PhD); theological studies (MA). *Accreditation:* ATS. *Program availability:* Part-time, evening/weekend, online learning. *Degree requirements:* For master's, 2 foreign languages; for doctorate, 4 foreign languages, thesis/dissertation. *Entrance requirements:* For doctorate, GRE General Test, MAT, M Div. Additional exam requirements/recommendations for international students: required—TOEFL, TWE.

The Southern Baptist Theological Seminary, School of Theology, Louisville, KY 40280-0004. Offers applied theology (D Min); biblical and theological studies (M Div); biblical counseling (M Div, MA, D Min); biblical spirituality (D Min); Christian ministry (M Div); expository preaching (D Min); pastoral studies (M Div); theological studies (MA); theology (Th M, PhD); worldview and apologetics (M Div). *Program availability:* Part-time, evening/weekend, online learning. *Degree requirements:* For master's, 2 foreign languages, thesis; for doctorate, 4 foreign languages, thesis/dissertation. *Entrance requirements:* For master's, GRE General Test, MAT, M Div; for doctorate, GRE General Test, MAT, interview, M Div, field essay. Additional exam requirements/recommendations for international students: required—TOEFL, TWE.

Southern Evangelical Seminary, Graduate Programs, Matthews, NC 28105. Offers apologetics (MA, D Min, Certificate); Christian education (MA); church ministry (MA, Certificate); divinity (Certificate), including apologetics (M Div, Certificate); Islamic studies (MA, Certificate); Jewish studies (MA); philosophy (MA); philosophy of religion (PhD); religion (MA); theology (M Div), including apologetics (M Div, Certificate), Biblical studies; youth ministry (MA). *Program availability:* Part-time, evening/weekend, online learning. *Degree requirements:* For master's, thesis (for some programs); for doctorate, 2 foreign languages, comprehensive exam (for some programs), thesis/dissertation. *Entrance requirements:* Additional exam requirements/recommendations for international students: required—TOEFL (minimum score 600 paper-based). *Expenses: Tuition:* Full-time $24,000; part-time $12,000 per year. *Required fees:* $600; $300 per semester. $150 per semester.

Southern Methodist University, Perkins School of Theology, Dallas, TX 75275. Offers ministry (M Div, D Min); sacred music (MSM); theological studies (MTS). *Accreditation:* ACIPE. *Program availability:* Part-time. *Degree requirements:* For master's, thesis (for some programs), internship; for doctorate, internship, oral exam, professional project. *Entrance requirements:* For master's, minimum GPA of 2.75; for doctorate, minimum graduate GPA of 3.0, M Div or equivalent, 3 years of ministry experience. Additional exam requirements/recommendations for international students: required—TOEFL (minimum score 600 paper-based; 100 iBT), TWE. *Expenses:* Contact institution.

Southern Wesleyan University, Program in Christian Ministries, Central, SC 29630-1020. Offers M Min. *Program availability:* Part-time, evening/weekend. *Entrance requirements:* For master's, GRE General Test or MAT, biographical paper; 12 semester credit hours of undergraduate work in religion, Bible, or ethics; 2 years of full-time Christian ministry experience. Additional exam requirements/recommendations for international students: required—TOEFL (minimum score 500 paper-based).

South University - Savannah, Graduate Programs, Doctor of Ministry Program, Savannah, GA 31406. Offers D Min.

Southwestern Assemblies of God University, Thomas F. Harrison School of Graduate Studies, Program in Theological Studies, Waxahachie, TX 75165-5735. Offers Bible and theology (MS); Biblical studies (M Div); counseling (M Div); cross cultural missions (M Div); practical theology (M Div); theological studies (M Div). *Program availability:* Online learning. *Degree requirements:* For master's, comprehensive written and oral exams. *Entrance requirements:* For master's, GRE General Test, minimum GPA of 2.5. Electronic applications accepted.

Southwestern Baptist Theological Seminary, School of Preaching, Fort Worth, TX 76122-0000. Offers Th M, D Min, PhD, Certificate.

Southwestern Baptist Theological Seminary, School of Theology, Fort Worth, TX 76122-0000. Offers ministry (D Min); theology (PhD). *Accreditation:* ACIPE; ATS (one or more programs are accredited). *Program availability:* Part-time, evening/weekend. Terminal master's awarded for partial completion of doctoral program. *Degree requirements:* For master's, 2 foreign languages, thesis (for some programs); for doctorate, 2 foreign languages, comprehensive exam, thesis/dissertation, oral exams. *Entrance requirements:* For doctorate, GRE, M Div or equivalent. Additional exam requirements/recommendations for international students: required—TOEFL. Electronic applications accepted.

Southwestern Christian University, Program in Ministry, Bethany, OK 73008-0340. Offers church planting (M Min); church revitalization and renewal (M Min); intercultural studies (M Min); leadership (M Min); life coaching (M Min); pastoral ministries (M Min); work place ministries (M Min). *Program availability:* Part-time. *Degree requirements:* For master's, thesis. *Entrance requirements:* For master's, minimum GPA of 2.5. Additional exam requirements/recommendations for international students: required—TOEFL (minimum score 500 paper-based). Electronic applications accepted.

Spring Arbor University, School of Arts and Sciences, Spring Arbor, MI 49283-9799. Offers communication (MA); spiritual formation and leadership (MA). *Program availability:* Part-time, online learning. *Degree requirements:* For master's, thesis (for some programs). *Entrance requirements:* For master's, GRE (minimum score of 40th percentile and taken within last 5 years), bachelor's degree from regionally-accredited college or university, minimum GPA of 3.0 for at least the last two years of the bachelor's degree, at least two recommendations from professional/academic individuals. Additional exam requirements/recommendations for international students: required—TOEFL (minimum score 600 paper-based). *Expenses:* Contact institution.

SUM Bible College & Theological Seminary, Graduate Programs, Oakland, CA 94603. Offers biblical studies (MA); Christian leadership (MA); theology (M Div). *Entrance requirements:* For master's, minimum GPA of 2.5, currently active in ministry.

Theological University of the Caribbean, Graduate Programs, Saint Just, PR 00978-0901. Offers childhood and adolescent education (MA); counseling and pastoral care (MA); ministry (D Min); missions (MA).

Trevecca Nazarene University, Graduate Religion Programs, Nashville, TN 37210-2877. Offers biblical and theological studies (MA); Christian ministry (MA); pastoral counseling (MA). *Program availability:* Part-time, online learning. *Degree requirements:* For master's, research project. *Entrance requirements:* For master's, minimum GPA of 2.7, official transcript from regionally accredited institution, letter of recommendation. Additional exam requirements/recommendations for international students: required—TOEFL (minimum score 550 paper-based; 80 iBT). Electronic applications accepted. *Expenses:* Contact institution.

Trinity Bible College and Graduate School, Graduate School, Ellendale, ND 58436. Offers global theology (MA); missional leadership (MA); rural ministries (MA).

Trinity College, Faculty of Divinity, Toronto, ON M5S 1H8, Canada. Offers ministry (Diploma); ministry for church musicians (Diploma); theology (M Div, MA, MTS, Th M, D Min, PhD, Th D, Diploma, L Th); M Div/MA. *Accreditation:* ATS. *Program availability:* Part-time. *Degree requirements:* For master's, 2 foreign languages, thesis (for some programs); for doctorate, 3 foreign languages, comprehensive exam, thesis/dissertation; for other advanced degree, thesis (for some programs). *Entrance requirements:* For master's, 1 language (modern or ancient), interview; for doctorate, 2 languages (modern and ancient). Additional exam requirements/recommendations for international students: required—TOEFL, TWE.

Trinity International University, Trinity Evangelical Divinity School, Deerfield, IL 60015-1284. Offers academic ministry (M Div); Biblical and Near Eastern archaeology and languages (MA); chaplaincy and ministry care (MA); Christian studies (Certificate); church and parachurch ministry (M Div); church history (MA, Th M); counseling (Th M); educational ministries (MA); educational ministry (Th M); educational studies (PhD); intercultural studies (MA, PhD); leadership and management (D Min); mental health counseling (MA); military chaplaincy (D Min); ministry (MA); missions (Th M); missions and evangelism (D Min); New Testament (MA, Th M); Old Testament (Th M); Old Testament and Semitic languages (MA); pastoral ministry and care (D Min); pastoral theology (Th M); preaching and teaching (D Min); spiritual formation and education (D Min); systematic theology (MA, Th M); theological studies (MA, PhD); urban ministry (MA). *Program availability:* Part-time, online learning. *Degree requirements:* For master's, comprehensive exam, thesis, fieldwork; for doctorate, comprehensive exam (for some programs), thesis/dissertation; for Certificate, comprehensive exam, integrative papers. *Entrance requirements:* For master's, GRE, MAT, minimum cumulative undergraduate GPA of 3.0; for doctorate, GRE, minimum cumulative graduate GPA of 3.2; for Certificate, GRE, MAT, minimum undergraduate GPA of 2.5. Additional exam requirements/recommendations for international students: required—TOEFL (minimum score 580 paper-based), TWE (minimum score 4). Electronic applications accepted.

Trinity School for Ministry, Graduate Programs, Ambridge, PA 15003-2397. Offers Anglican studies (Diploma); basic Christian studies (Diploma); divinity (M Div); ministry (D Min); mission and evangelism (MAME, Diploma); religion (MAR); youth ministry (Diploma). *Program availability:* Part-time. *Degree requirements:* For master's, thesis optional; for doctorate, thesis/dissertation. *Entrance requirements:* Additional exam requirements/recommendations for international students: required—TOEFL.

Trinity Western University, ACTS Seminaries, Langley, BC V2Y 1Y1, Canada. Offers Christian studies (MA); cross cultural ministry (MA); theology (M Div, M Th, MAMFT, MLE, MTS, D Min). *Program availability:* Part-time. *Faculty:* 13 full-time (0 women), 20 part-time/adjunct (3 women). *Students:* 202 full-time (88 women), 184 part-time (79 women). Average age 35. In 2019, 73 master's awarded. *Degree requirements:* For master's, thesis (for some programs), internship. *Entrance requirements:* For doctorate, M Div or equivalent. Additional exam requirements/recommendations for international students: required—TOEFL (minimum score 100 iBT), IELTS (minimum score 7). *Application deadline:* Applications are processed on a rolling basis. Application fee: $150 Canadian dollars for international students. Electronic applications accepted. Application fee is waived when completed online. *Expenses:* Average of $520 per semester hour for tuition; $15 per semester hour for student fees. Average total tuition cost of $28,300. *Financial support:* Research assistantships, career-related internships or fieldwork, Federal Work-Study, institutionally sponsored loans, and scholarships/grants available. Financial award application deadline: 3/1; financial award applicants required to submit FAFSA. *Unit head:* Ryan Klassen, ACTS Executive Director, E-mail: ryan.klassen@twu.ca. *Application contact:* Liisa Polkki, Director of Admissions, 604-513-2019, Fax: 604-513-2045, E-mail: acts@twu.ca.
Website: http://acts.twu.ca/

Tyndale University College & Seminary, Graduate Programs, Toronto, ON M2M 3S4, Canada. Offers Biblical studies (M Div); Christian foundations (MTS); Christian studies (Diploma); counseling (M Div); educational ministry (M Div); missions (M Div, Diploma); pastoral and Chinese ministry (M Div); pastoral ministry (M Div); Pentecostal studies (MTS); spiritual formation (M Div, Diploma); theological studies (M Div); theology (Th M); worship and liturgy (M Div, MTS); youth and family ministry (M Div). *Accreditation:* ATS. *Program availability:* Part-time, online learning. *Entrance requirements:* For master's and Diploma, minimum C+ average in undergraduate course work. Additional exam requirements/recommendations for international students: required—TOEFL (minimum score 570 paper-based), TWE (minimum score 5). Electronic applications accepted.

Union University, School of Theology and Missions, Jackson, TN 38305-3697. Offers Christian studies (MCS); expository preaching (D Min). *Program availability:* Part-time, evening/weekend, online learning. Electronic applications accepted.

United Lutheran Seminary, Graduate and Professional Programs, Gettysburg, PA 17325-1795. Offers divinity (M Div); ministerial studies (MAMS); outdoor ministry (MAR); parish ministry (D Min); theology (STM). *Accreditation:* ACIPE; ATS (one or more programs are accredited). *Program availability:* Part-time, online learning. *Degree requirements:* For master's, thesis (for some programs). Electronic applications accepted. *Expenses: Tuition:* Full-time $19,500; part-time $1950 per credit. Tuition and fees vary according to course load.

United Lutheran Seminary, Graduate School, Philadelphia, PA 19119-1794. Offers divinity (M Div); ministry (D Min); public leadership (MA); religion (MAR); social ministry and church (Certificate); theology (STM, PhD). *Accreditation:* ACIPE. *Program availability:* Part-time, evening/weekend. *Degree requirements:* For master's, one foreign language, comprehensive exam (for some programs), thesis (for some programs); for doctorate, thesis/dissertation. *Entrance requirements:* For master's, minimum undergraduate GPA of 2.8; for doctorate, minimum GPA of 3.0. Additional exam requirements/recommendations for international students: required—TOEFL (minimum score 550 paper-based; 89 iBT), TWE. Electronic applications accepted.

United Theological Seminary, Graduate and Professional Programs, Dayton, OH 45426. Offers Christian ministries (MA); ministry (M Div, D Min); theological studies (MTS). *Accreditation:* ATS. *Program availability:* Part-time, evening/weekend, online learning. *Degree requirements:* For master's, thesis (for some programs); for doctorate, thesis/dissertation, final exam. *Entrance requirements:* For master's, minimum GPA of 2.5, interview, 5 letters of recommendation; for doctorate, minimum GPA of 3.0, 2 letters of recommendation, interview. Additional exam requirements/recommendations for international students: required—TOEFL (minimum score 550 paper-based). Electronic applications accepted.

United Theological Seminary of the Twin Cities, Graduate Programs, New Brighton, MN 55112-2598. Offers advanced theological studies (Diploma); justice and peace studies (M Div, MA); leadership toward racial justice (M Div, MA, Certificate); Methodist studies (M Div, MA, Certificate); ministry (D Min); ministry renewal and professional development (Certificate); pastoral care and counseling (M Div, MA, MARL); religion and theology (MA); theological and religious studies (Certificate); theology and the arts (M Div, MA); urban ministry (M Div, MA, MARL); women's studies: religion, theology and ministry (M Div, MA). *Accreditation:* ACIPE; ATS. *Program availability:* Part-time, evening/weekend. *Degree requirements:* For master's, thesis; for doctorate, comprehensive exam, thesis/dissertation. *Entrance requirements:* For master's, minimum GPA of 2.75; strong analytical, reflective thinking and writing skills; vocational and academic goals compatible with those of Seminary; for doctorate, M Div or equivalent, minimum GPA of 3.0, 3 years experience in professional ministry; for other advanced degree, BA or equivalent life experience; strong analytical, reflective thinking and writing skills (Certificate); proficiency in English language, previous study of theology at a theological school, recommendation of student's denomination (Diploma). Additional exam requirements/recommendations for international students: required—TOEFL (minimum score 550 paper-based).

University of Chicago, Divinity School, Program in Ministry, Chicago, IL 60637. Offers M Div. *Degree requirements:* For master's, one foreign language, thesis, field education. *Entrance requirements:* For master's, GRE General Test, 3 letters of recommendation; transcripts; curriculum vitae or resume. Additional exam requirements/recommendations for international students: required—TOEFL (minimum score 600 paper-based; 104 iBT), IELTS (minimum score 7). Electronic applications accepted. *Expenses:* Contact institution.

University of Dallas, Ann and Joe O. Neuhoff School of Ministry, Irving, TX 75062. Offers MCSL. *Accreditation:* ACIPE. *Program availability:* Part-time. *Faculty:* 5 full-time (2 women), 2 part-time/adjunct (1 woman). *Students:* 3 full-time (1 woman), 66 part-time (33 women); includes 17 minority (2 Asian, non-Hispanic/Latino; 15 Hispanic/Latino). Average age 47. 24 applicants, 75% accepted, 13 enrolled. In 2019, 15 master's awarded. *Degree requirements:* For master's, comprehensive exam (for some programs), Annotated Bibliography; Capstone Presentation/Case study. *Entrance requirements:* Additional exam requirements/recommendations for international students: required—TOEFL (minimum score 80 paper-based; 80 iBT). *Application deadline:* For fall admission, 8/1 priority date for domestic and international students; for spring admission, 1/1 priority date for domestic and international students; for summer admission, 5/1 priority date for domestic and international students. Applications are processed on a rolling basis. Application fee: $25. Electronic applications accepted. *Expenses: Tuition:* Part-time $1250 per credit hour. *Financial support:* In 2019–20, 12 students received support. Scholarships/grants and unspecified assistantships available. Financial award application deadline: 7/1; financial award applicants required to submit FAFSA. *Unit head:* Dr. Theodore J. Whapham, Dean, 972-721-4068, E-mail: twhapham@udallas.edu. *Application contact:* Dr. Jodi Hunt, Director of Graduate Programs, 972-721-5810, E-mail: jhunt@udallas.edu. Website: https://udallas.edu/ministry/

University of Dayton, Department of Religious Studies, Dayton, OH 45469. Offers pastoral ministry (MA); theological studies (MA); theology (PhD). *Program availability:* Part-time. *Degree requirements:* For master's, thesis or alternative; for doctorate, 2 foreign languages, comprehensive exam, thesis/dissertation. *Entrance requirements:* For master's, 3 letters of recommendation, personal statement, all previous official transcript(s); for doctorate, GRE General Test (minimum score 600 verbal previous scale, 160 current scale), academic writing sample, 3 letters of recommendation, official transcript(s). Additional exam requirements/recommendations for international students: required—TOEFL (minimum score 550 paper-based; 80 iBT). Electronic applications accepted. *Expenses:* Contact institution.

University of Fort Lauderdale, Graduate Program, Lauderhill, FL 33313. Offers MS. *Degree requirements:* For master's, thesis.

University of Northwestern–St. Paul, Master of Divinity Program, St. Paul, MN 55113-1598. Offers M Div. *Program availability:* Part-time, evening/weekend, online learning. Electronic applications accepted.

University of Saint Mary of the Lake–Mundelein Seminary, Graduate and Professional Programs, Mundelein, IL 60060. Offers liturgical studies (MA); ministry (D Min); pastoral studies (MA); theology (M Div). *Accreditation:* ATS (one or more

programs are accredited). *Degree requirements:* For doctorate, 2 foreign languages, comprehensive exam, thesis/dissertation. *Entrance requirements:* For master's and doctorate, bachelor's degree. Additional exam requirements/recommendations for international students: required—TOEFL (minimum score 550 paper-based). Electronic applications accepted.

University of St. Michael's College, Faculty of Theology, Toronto, ON M5S 1J4, Canada. Offers Catholic leadership (MA); eastern Christian studies (Diploma); religious education (Diploma); theological studies (Diploma); theology (M Div, MA, MRE, MTS, D Min, PhD, Th D); theology and Jewish studies (MA). *Accreditation:* ATS (one or more programs are accredited). *Program availability:* Part-time. *Degree requirements:* For master's, thesis (for some programs), 1 foreign language (MA), 2 foreign languages (Th M); for doctorate, 3 foreign languages, comprehensive exam, thesis/dissertation; for other advanced degree, thesis optional. *Entrance requirements:* For master's, M Div or BA, course work in an ancient or modern language, minimum GPA of 3.3; for doctorate, MA in theology, Th M, or M Div with thesis, minimum GPA of 3.7; for other advanced degree, minimum GPA of 2.7. Additional exam requirements/recommendations for international students: required—TOEFL (minimum score 600 paper-based). Electronic applications accepted. *Expenses:* Contact institution.

University of St. Thomas, The Saint Paul Seminary School of Divinity, St. Paul, MN 55105. Offers pastoral ministry (MAPM); religious education (MARE); theology (MA). *Accreditation:* ACIPE; ATS. *Program availability:* Part-time, evening/weekend. *Degree requirements:* For master's, one foreign language, comprehensive exam (for some programs), thesis (for some programs). *Entrance requirements:* For master's, GRE, 3 letters of recommendation, interview. Additional exam requirements/recommendations for international students: required—TOEFL (minimum score 550 paper-based). Electronic applications accepted. *Expenses:* Contact institution.

University of St. Thomas, School of Theology, Houston, TX 77006-4696. Offers divinity (M Div); pastoral studies (MAPS); theological studies (MA). *Accreditation:* ATS. *Program availability:* Part-time-only, online learning. *Faculty:* 7 full-time (2 women), 7 part-time/adjunct (1 woman). *Students:* 80 full-time (3 women), 78 part-time (29 women); includes 64 minority (5 Black or African American, non-Hispanic/Latino; 24 Asian, non-Hispanic/Latino; 34 Hispanic/Latino; 1 Two or more races, non-Hispanic/Latino), 25 international. Average age 38. 20 applicants, 100% accepted, 20 enrolled. In 2019, 15 master's awarded. *Degree requirements:* For master's, comprehensive exam (for some programs). *Entrance requirements:* For master's, Prerequisite Philosophy and Theology completed minimum hours. *Application deadline:* For fall admission, 7/30 for domestic students, 7/15 for international students; for spring admission, 12/15 for domestic students, 12/1 for international students; for summer admission, 5/1 for domestic students, 4/15 for international students. Applications are processed on a rolling basis. Application fee: $25. Electronic applications accepted. Application fee is waived when completed online. *Expenses:* $43,590 (for MDiv), $14,652 (for MAPS). *Financial support:* In 2019–20, 9 students received support. Applicants required to submit FAFSA. *Unit head:* Fr. Paul E. Lockey, Division Dean, 713-654-5760, E-mail: lockeyp@stthom.edu. *Application contact:* Beth Puayu, Assistant to the Dean, 713-654-5706, E-mail: puyaum@stthom.edu.
Website: http://www.stthom.edu/Academics/School_of_Theology_at_St_Marys_Seminary/Index.aqf

University of South Africa, College of Human Sciences, Pretoria, South Africa. Offers adult education (M Ed); African languages (MA, PhD); African politics (MA, PhD); Afrikaans (MA, PhD); ancient history (MA, PhD); ancient Near Eastern studies (MA, PhD); anthropology (MA, PhD); applied linguistics (MA); Arabic (MA, PhD); archaeology (MA); art history (MA); Biblical archaeology (MA); Biblical studies (M Th, D Th, PhD); Christian spirituality (M Th, D Th); church history (M Th, D Th); classical studies (MA, PhD); clinical psychology (MA); communication (MA, PhD); comparative education (M Ed, Ed D); consulting psychology (D Admin, D Com, PhD); curriculum studies (M Ed, Ed D); development studies (M Admin, MA, D Admin, PhD); didactics (M Ed, Ed D); education (M Tech); education management (M Ed, Ed D); educational psychology (M Ed); English (MA); environmental education (M Ed); French (MA, PhD); German (MA, PhD); Greek (MA); guidance and counseling (M Ed); health studies (MA, PhD), including health sciences education (MA), health services management (MA), medical and surgical nursing science (critical care general) (MA), midwifery and neonatal nursing science (MA), trauma and emergency care (MA); history (MA, PhD); history of education (Ed D); inclusive education (M Ed, Ed D); information and communications technology policy and regulation (MA); information science (MA, MIS, PhD); international politics (MA, PhD); Islamic studies (MA, PhD); Italian (MA, PhD); Judaica (MA, PhD); linguistics (MA, PhD); mathematical education (M Ed); mathematics education (MA); missiology (M Th, D Th); modern Hebrew (MA, PhD); musicology (MA, MMus, D Mus, PhD); natural science education (M Ed); New Testament (M Th, D Th); Old Testament (D Th); pastoral therapy (M Th, D Th); philosophy (MA); philosophy of education (M Ed, Ed D); politics (MA, PhD); Portuguese (MA, PhD); practical theology (M Th, D Th); psychology (MA, MS, PhD); psychology of education (M Ed, Ed D); public health (MA); religious studies (MA, D Th, PhD); Romance languages (MA); Russian (MA, PhD); Semitic languages (MA, PhD); social behavior studies in HIV/AIDS (MA); social science (mental health) (MA); social science in development studies (MA); social science in psychology (MA); social science in social work (MA); social science in sociology (MA); social work (MSW, DSW, PhD); socio-education (M Ed, Ed D); sociolinguistics (MA); sociology (MA, PhD); Spanish (MA, PhD); systematic theology (M Th, D Th); TESOL (teaching English to speakers of other languages) (MA); theological ethics (M Th, D Th); theory of literature (MA, PhD); urban ministries (D Th); urban ministry (M Th).

University of the Incarnate Word, College of Humanities, Arts, and Social Sciences, San Antonio, TX 78209-6397. Offers multidisciplinary studies (MA); pastoral ministry (MA). *Program availability:* Part-time, evening/weekend. *Faculty:* 1 full-time (0 women), 6 part-time/adjunct (1 woman). *Students:* 10 full-time (7 women), 7 part-time (5 women); includes 13 minority (all Hispanic/Latino), 1 international. 9 applicants, 100% accepted, 8 enrolled. *Degree requirements:* For master's, thesis or alternative. *Entrance requirements:* For master's, GRE/MAT or three letters of recommendation and personal statement of ministerial and educational goals. Additional exam requirements/recommendations for international students: required—TOEFL (minimum score 560 paper-based; 83 iBT). *Application deadline:* Applications are processed on a rolling basis. Application fee: $20. Electronic applications accepted. *Expenses: Tuition:* Full-time $11,520; part-time $960 per credit hour. *Required fees:* $1128; $94 per credit hour. Tuition and fees vary according to degree level, campus/location, program and student level. *Financial support:* Research assistantships, scholarships/grants, tuition waivers (full and partial), and unspecified assistantships available. Financial award applicants required to submit FAFSA. *Unit head:* Dr. Kevin Vichcales, Dean, 210-829-2759, Fax: 210-829-3830, E-mail: vichcale@uiwtx.edu. *Application contact:* Jessica Delarosa, Director of Admissions, 210-829-6005, Fax: 210-829-3921, E-mail: admis@uiwtx.edu. Website: https://www.uiw.edu/chass/index.html

Ursuline College, School of Graduate and Professional Studies, Theological and Pastoral Studies Program, Pepper Pike, OH 44124-4398. Offers MA. *Program availability:* Part-time. *Faculty:* 2 full-time (both women). *Students:* 3 full-time (all women), 6 part-time (3 women); includes 4 minority (3 Black or African American, non-Hispanic/Latino; 1 Two or more races, non-Hispanic/Latino). Average age 52. 3

applicants, 100% accepted, 1 enrolled. In 2019, 3 master's awarded. *Degree requirements:* For master's, thesis. *Entrance requirements:* For master's, GRE when GPA under 3.0, minimum undergraduate GPA of 3.0, interview. Additional exam requirements/recommendations for international students: required—TOEFL (minimum score 550 paper-based; 80 iBT). *Application deadline:* For fall admission, 8/1 priority date for domestic students. Applications are processed on a rolling basis. Application fee: $25. Electronic applications accepted. *Expenses:* 36 credit hours at $702 per. *Financial support:* In 2019–20, 1 student received support. Federal Work-Study and scholarships/grants available. Financial award application deadline: 3/1; financial award applicants required to submit FAFSA. *Unit head:* Dr. Linda Martin, Director, 440-646-8191, Fax: 440-684-6088, E-mail: lmartin@ursuline.edu. *Application contact:* Melanie Steele, Director, Graduate Admissions, 440-646-8146, Fax: 440-684-6138, E-mail: graduateadmissions@ursuline.edu.

Virginia Beach Theological Seminary, Graduate Programs, Virginia Beach, VA 23464. Offers Biblical studies (MBS, Th M); chaplaincy (MBS); ministry (M Div). *Program availability:* Online learning. *Entrance requirements:* For master's, GRE, interview, minimum cumulative GPA of 2.4, church endorsement, 3 recommendations. Electronic applications accepted.

Virginia University of Lynchburg, Graduate Programs, Lynchburg, VA 24501-6417. Offers Christian ministry (M Div); ministry (D Min). *Program availability:* Online learning.

Viterbo University, Master of Arts in Servant Leadership Program, La Crosse, WI 54601-4797. Offers ethical leadership in organizations (Certificate); servant leadership (MA). *Program availability:* Part-time, evening/weekend. *Degree requirements:* For master's, 30 credits (15 credits of Servant Leadership core courses and any combination of 15 elective credits). *Entrance requirements:* For master's, letter of reference, statement of goals, baccalaureate degree, transcript, interview. Additional exam requirements/recommendations for international students: required—TOEFL (minimum score 525 paper-based). Electronic applications accepted. *Expenses:* Contact institution.

Walla Walla University, Graduate Studies, Center for Cinema, Religion, and Worldview, College Place, WA 99324. Offers Web and interactive media (MA). *Entrance requirements:* For master's, three professional references, transcripts, personal statement.

Walsh University, Master of Arts in Theology Program, North Canton, OH 44720-3396. Offers parish administration (MA); pastoral ministry (MA); religious education (MA). *Program availability:* Part-time, evening/weekend, 100% online. *Faculty:* 2 full-time (0 women), 1 part-time/adjunct (0 women). *Students:* 2 full-time (1 woman), 11 part-time (5 women); includes 1 minority (Black or African American, non-Hispanic/Latino). Average age 45. In 2019, 4 master's awarded. *Degree requirements:* For master's, thesis or alternative, culminating assignment. *Entrance requirements:* For master's, minimum GPA of 3.0, Writing sample. Additional exam requirements/recommendations for international students: required—TOEFL (minimum score 500 paper-based; 61 iBT). *Application deadline:* For fall admission, 7/15 for domestic students. Applications are processed on a rolling basis. Application fee: $0. Electronic applications accepted. *Expenses:* Tuition: $372/credit hour; $50 technology fee. *Financial support:* Unspecified assistantships available. Financial award application deadline: 12/31; financial award applicants required to submit FAFSA. *Unit head:* Dr. Chris Seeman, Graduate Program Director, 330-244-4665, E-mail: cseeman@walsh.edu. *Application contact:* Dr. Chris Seeman, Graduate Program Director, 330-244-4665, E-mail: cseeman@walsh.edu. Website: http://www.walsh.edu/

Wayland Baptist University, Graduate Programs, Programs in Religion, Plainview, TX 79072-6998. Offers Christian ministry (MCM); divinity (M Div); religion (MA). *Program availability:* Part-time, evening/weekend, online learning. *Degree requirements:* For master's, comprehensive exam. *Entrance requirements:* For master's, GRE or MAT, minimum GPA of 3.0; letter of endorsement from Christian congregation, one academic and one personal letter of recommendation (for M Div). Additional exam requirements/recommendations for international students: required—TOEFL (minimum score 500 paper-based; 61 iBT). Electronic applications accepted. *Expenses: Tuition:* Full-time $728; part-time $728 per semester. *Required fees:* $1218. Tuition and fees vary according to degree level, campus/location and program.

Welch College, Program in Theology and Ministry, Gallatin, TN 37066. Offers MA. *Program availability:* Online learning.

Wesley Biblical Seminary, Graduate Programs, Jackson, MS 39206. Offers apologetics (MA); Biblical languages (M Div); Biblical literature (MA); Christian studies (MA); context and mission (M Div); honors research (M Div); interpretation (M Div); ministry (M Div); spiritual formation (M Div); teaching (M Div); theology (MA). *Accreditation:* ATS. *Program availability:* Part-time. *Degree requirements:* For master's, thesis. *Entrance requirements:* Additional exam requirements/recommendations for international students: required—TOEFL. Electronic applications accepted.

Western Seminary - Portland, Graduate Programs, Program in Counseling, Portland, OR 97215-3367. Offers counseling (MA, Certificate); pastoral counseling (M Div); M Div/MA. *Program availability:* Part-time, evening/weekend. *Degree requirements:* For master's, practicum. *Entrance requirements:* Additional exam requirements/recommendations for international students: required—TOEFL. *Expenses:* Contact institution.

Western Seminary - Portland, Graduate Programs, Program in Intercultural Studies, Portland, OR 97215-3367. Offers MA, D Miss, Certificate, G Dip. *Program availability:* Part-time, evening/weekend. *Degree requirements:* For master's, practicum; for doctorate, 2 foreign languages, thesis/dissertation. *Entrance requirements:* Additional exam requirements/recommendations for international students: required—TOEFL.

Western Seminary - Portland, Graduate Programs, Program in Ministry and Leadership, Portland, OR 97215-3367. Offers chaplaincy (MA); coaching (MA); Jewish ministry (MA); pastoral care to women (MA); youth ministry (MA). *Degree requirements:* For master's, practicum. *Entrance requirements:* Additional exam requirements/recommendations for international students: required—TOEFL.

Western Seminary–Sacramento Campus, Graduate Certificate Programs, Rocklin, CA 95765. Offers Bible (Graduate Certificate); coaching (Graduate Certificate); pastoral care to women (Graduate Certificate); theology (Graduate Certificate); youth and family (Graduate Certificate). *Program availability:* Online learning. *Entrance requirements:* For degree, essays, undergraduate transcripts, 4 recommendations. Additional exam requirements/recommendations for international students: required—TOEFL.

Western Seminary–Sacramento Campus, Graduate Diploma Programs, Rocklin, CA 95765. Offers Bible and theology (Graduate Diploma); ministry (Graduate Diploma); pastoral care to women (Graduate Diploma). *Entrance requirements:* For degree, essays, undergraduate transcripts, 4 recommendations. Additional exam requirements/recommendations for international students: required—TOEFL.

Western Seminary–Sacramento Campus, Program in Ministry and Leadership, Rocklin, CA 95765. Offers MA. *Entrance requirements:* For master's, essays, undergraduate transcripts, 4 recommendations. Additional exam requirements/recommendations for international students: required—TOEFL.

Western Seminary - San Jose Campus, Graduate Programs, Milpitas, CA 95035. Offers Bible and theology (Graduate Diploma); Bible, camp and conference ministry (CGS); Biblical and theological studies (MA), including exegetical track, theological track; coaching (CGS); expositional ministry (M Div); marital and family therapy (MA); ministry (Graduate Diploma); ministry and leadership (MA), including camp and conference ministry, coaching, pastoral care to women, youth ministry; pastoral care to women (CGS, Graduate Diploma); pastoral ministry (M Div); theology (CGS); youth and family (CGS). *Program availability:* Part-time, evening/weekend, online learning. *Entrance requirements:* For master's, minimum GPA of 3.0. Electronic applications accepted.

Western Theological Seminary, Graduate and Professional Programs, Holland, MI 49423-3622. Offers divinity (M Div); ministry (D Min); theology (M Th, MA); urban pastoral ministry (Graduate Certificate); M Div/MSW. *Accreditation:* ACIPE; ATS. *Program availability:* Part-time, 100% online, blended/hybrid learning. *Degree requirements:* For doctorate, thesis/dissertation. *Entrance requirements:* Additional exam requirements/recommendations for international students: required—TOEFL. Electronic applications accepted. *Expenses: Tuition:* Full-time $1580; part-time $8910 per credit hour. *Required fees:* $100; $100 per semester.

Westminster Theological Seminary, Graduate and Professional Programs, Philadelphia, PA 19118. Offers apologetics (Th M); Biblical and urban studies (Certificate); Biblical counseling (MA); biblical studies (MAR); Christian studies (Certificate); church history (Th M); counseling (M Div); general studies (M Div, MAR); hermeneutics and Bible interpretations (PhD); historical and theological studies (PhD); historical theology (Th M); New Testament (Th M); Old Testament (Th M); pastoral counseling (D Min); pastoral ministry (M Div, D Min); systematic theology (Th M); theological studies (MAR); urban missions (M Div, MA, MAR, D Min). *Accreditation:* ATS. *Program availability:* Part-time. Terminal master's awarded for partial completion of doctoral program. *Degree requirements:* For master's, thesis (for some programs); for doctorate, 4 foreign languages, comprehensive exam (for some programs), thesis/dissertation. *Entrance requirements:* For doctorate, GRE General Test. Additional exam requirements/recommendations for international students: required—TOEFL, TWE.

Whitworth University, Graduate Studies in Theology, Spokane, WA 99251-0001. Offers Christian ministry (MA); mission and culture (MA); theology (MA). *Program availability:* Part-time, evening/weekend. Electronic applications accepted. *Expenses: Tuition:* Full-time $11,970; part-time $3990 per credit. Tuition and fees vary according to course load and program.

Wilfrid Laurier University, Waterloo Lutheran Seminary, Waterloo, ON N2L 3C5, Canada. Offers divinity (M Div); multifaith spiritual care and counseling (Diploma); pastoral leadership (D Min); spiritual care and counseling (D Min); theology (M Th, MTS); M Div/MTS/MSW. *Accreditation:* ATS. *Program availability:* Part-time. *Degree requirements:* For master's, one foreign language, thesis (for some programs); for doctorate, thesis/dissertation. *Entrance requirements:* For master's, two letters of reference; for doctorate, M Div, two letters of reference. Additional exam requirements/recommendations for international students: required—TOEFL (minimum score 573 paper-based; 89 iBT), IELTS (minimum score 7). Electronic applications accepted. *Expenses:* Contact institution.

World Mission University, Graduate Programs, Los Angeles, CA 90020. Offers biblical preaching (M Div); Christian counseling (M Div, MACC); church ministry (M Div); church music (M Div, DCM); ministry (D Min); music (MA); theology (MAT). *Program availability:* Online learning.

Xavier University, College of Arts and Sciences, Department of Theology, Cincinnati, OH 45207. Offers health care mission integration (MA); theology (MA), including religious education, social and pastoral ministry, theology. *Program availability:* Part-time, evening/weekend. *Degree requirements:* For master's, final paper (or thesis) and defense or comprehension exam. *Entrance requirements:* For master's, MAT or GRE, 2 letters of recommendation; statement of reasons and goals for enrolling in program (1,000-2,000 words); resume; transcript. Additional exam requirements/recommendations for international students: required—TOEFL (minimum score 550 paper-based; 79 iBT). Electronic applications accepted. Application fee is waived when completed online. *Expenses:* Contact institution.

Xavier University of Louisiana, Graduate School, Institute for Black Catholic Studies, New Orleans, LA 70125. Offers pastoral theology (Th M). *Program availability:* Part-time. *Degree requirements:* For master's, comprehensive exam, practicum. *Entrance requirements:* For master's, GRE General Test, MAT, minimum GPA of 2.5. Additional exam requirements/recommendations for international students: required—TOEFL. Electronic applications accepted.

Religion

Abilene Christian University, Office of Graduate Programs, College of Biblical Studies, Graduate School of Theology, Abilene, TX 79699. Offers ancient and Oriental Christianity (MA); Christian ministry (MACM); divinity (M Div), including ministry, missions; global service (MA); ministry (D Min), including Christian spiritual formation, leadership for missional renewal, preaching for community transformation; modern and American Christianity (MA); New Testament (MA); Old Testament (MA); theology (MA). *Program availability:* Part-time, evening/weekend, online learning. *Faculty:* 12 full-time (2 women), 9 part-time/adjunct (1 woman). *Students:* 116 full-time (24 women), 86 part-time (24 women); includes 61 minority (34 Black or African American, non-Hispanic/Latino; 1 Asian, non-Hispanic/Latino; 21 Hispanic/Latino; 5 Two or more races, non-Hispanic/Latino), 11 international. 185 applicants, 54% accepted, 68 enrolled. In 2019, 17 master's, 2 doctorates awarded. *Degree requirements:* For master's, comprehensive exam (for some programs), thesis (for some programs); for doctorate, one foreign language, thesis/dissertation. *Entrance requirements:* For master's, official transcripts, recommendation, purpose statement, writing assessment; for doctorate, official transcripts, Documentation of Ministry, recommendations, personal statement,

Endorsement of Elders or Supervisor. Additional exam requirements/recommendations for international students: required—TOEFL (minimum score 80 iBT), IELTS (minimum score 6), PTE (minimum score 51). *Application deadline:* For fall admission, 8/10 priority date for domestic students; for spring admission, 11/1 for domestic students. Applications are processed on a rolling basis. Application fee: $65. *Expenses:* $676 per hour. *Financial support:* In 2019–20, 39 students received support, including 18 research assistantships with partial tuition reimbursements available; Federal Work-Study also available. Support available to part-time students. Financial award application deadline: 4/1; financial award applicants required to submit FAFSA. *Unit head:* Dr. Tim Sensing, Associate Dean, 325-674-3730, Fax: 325-674-6180, E-mail: sensingt@acu.edu. *Application contact:* Graduate Admissions, 325-674-6911, E-mail: gradinfo@acu.edu.
Website: http://www.acu.edu/gst

Ambrose University, Ambrose Seminary, Calgary, AB T3H 0L5, Canada. Offers Biblical/theological studies (MA), including New Testament, Old Testament, theology; Christian studies (MCS, Diploma); intercultural ministries (M Div, MA); leadership (Certificate); leadership and ministry (MA), including chaplaincy, poverty studies, preaching; pastoral ministry (M Div). *Accreditation:* ATS (one or more programs are accredited). *Program availability:* Part-time, blended/hybrid learning. *Degree requirements:* For master's, variable foreign language requirement, internship (for M Div, MA in leadership and ministry, MA in intercultural ministries); thesis (for MA in Biblical/theological studies). *Entrance requirements:* For master's, undergraduate degree from other accredited university or bible college, minimum GPA of 2.0. Additional exam requirements/recommendations for international students: required—PTE (minimum score 58), TOEFL (minimum score 560 paper-based, 83 iBT) or IELTS (minimum score 6.5). Electronic applications accepted.

The American University of Rome, Graduate School, Rome, Italy. Offers arts management (MA); food studies (MA); peace studies (MA); sustainable cultural heritage (MA). *Degree requirements:* For master's, thesis, internship. *Entrance requirements:* For master's, bachelor's degree in the liberal arts, humanities or social sciences; minimum GPA of 2.75. Additional exam requirements/recommendations for international students: required—TOEFL (minimum score 550 paper-based; 80 iBT), IELTS (minimum score 6.5). Electronic applications accepted.

Amridge University, Graduate and Professional Programs, Montgomery, AL 36117. Offers Biblical studies (MA, PhD); Christian ministry (MS); family therapy (D Min); human services (MS); leadership and management (MS); marriage and family therapy (M Div, MA, PhD); ministerial leadership (M Div, MS); New Testament studies (MA); Old Testament studies (MA); professional counseling (M Div, MA, PhD); theology (M Div, D Min). *Program availability:* Part-time, evening/weekend, online learning. *Degree requirements:* For master's, one foreign language, comprehensive exam (for some programs), thesis (for some programs); for doctorate, one foreign language, comprehensive exam (for some programs), thesis/dissertation (for some programs). *Entrance requirements:* For master's, official transcript showing an earned 4-year BA or BS from regionally- or nationally-accredited institution; for doctorate, official transcript showing earned graduate degree from regionally- or nationally-accredited institution; writing sample (e.g. career monograph, published journal article, term paper from master's degree or doctoral dissertation); interview. Additional exam requirements/recommendations for international students: required—TOEFL (minimum score 79 iBT). Electronic applications accepted.

Arizona State University at Tempe, College of Liberal Arts and Sciences, School of Historical, Philosophical and Religious Studies, Tempe, AZ 85287-4301. Offers European history (MA, PhD); medieval studies (Graduate Certificate); North American history (MA, PhD); philosophy (MA, PhD); public history (MA); religious studies (MA, PhD); Renaissance studies (Graduate Certificate); scholarly publishing (Graduate Certificate). *Program availability:* Part-time. Terminal master's awarded for partial completion of doctoral program. *Degree requirements:* For master's, thesis or alternative, interactive Program of Study (iPOS) submitted before completing 50 percent of required credit hours; for doctorate, variable foreign language requirement, comprehensive exam, thesis/dissertation, interactive Program of Study (iPOS) submitted before completing 50 percent of required credit hours. *Entrance requirements:* For master's and doctorate, GRE, minimum GPA of 3.0 or equivalent in last 2 years of work leading to bachelor's degree. Additional exam requirements/recommendations for international students: required—TOEFL, IELTS, or PTE. Electronic applications accepted.

Athens State University, Graduate Programs, Athens, AL 35611. Offers career and technical education (M Ed); global logistics and supply chain management (MS); religious studies (MA).

Baylor University, Graduate School, College of Arts and Sciences, Department of Religion, Waco, TX 76798. Offers MA, PhD. *Faculty:* 19 full-time (5 women). *Students:* 47 full-time (11 women), 6 part-time (2 women); includes 9 minority (2 Black or African American, non-Hispanic/Latino; 1 American Indian or Alaska Native, non-Hispanic/Latino; 2 Asian, non-Hispanic/Latino; 1 Hispanic/Latino; 3 Two or more races, non-Hispanic/Latino), 2 international. 46 applicants, 17% accepted, 8 enrolled. In 2019, 2 master's, 4 doctorates awarded. Terminal master's awarded for partial completion of doctoral program. *Degree requirements:* For doctorate, 2 foreign languages, comprehensive exam, thesis/dissertation. *Entrance requirements:* Additional exam requirements/recommendations for international students: required—TOEFL. *Application deadline:* For fall admission, 12/15 for domestic students. Application fee: $50. Electronic applications accepted. Application fee is waived when completed online. *Financial support:* In 2019–20, 40 students received support, including 8 fellowships with full tuition reimbursements available (averaging $4,000 per year), 8 teaching assistantships with full tuition reimbursements available (averaging $20,000 per year); tuition waivers (full), unspecified assistantships, and All accepted students receive 100% tuition coverage and graduate assistantship for 5 years. also available. Financial award application deadline: 12/15. *Unit head:* Dr. James D. Nogalski, Graduate Program Director, 254-710-1592, Fax: 254-710-3740, E-mail: james_nogalski@baylor.edu. *Application contact:* Dr. James D. Nogalski, Graduate Program Director, 254-710-1592, Fax: 254-710-3740, E-mail: james_nogalski@baylor.edu.
Website: http://www.baylor.edu/religion/

Bethany Theological Seminary, Graduate and Professional Programs, Richmond, IN 47374-4019. Offers biblical studies (MA Th); ministry studies (M Div); peace studies (M Div, MA Th); theological studies (MA Th, CATS); youth ministry (M Div). *Accreditation:* ACIPE; ATS. *Program availability:* Part-time, online learning. *Degree requirements:* For master's, thesis (for some programs). *Entrance requirements:* For master's, letters of reference. Additional exam requirements/recommendations for international students: required—TOEFL (minimum score 550 paper-based).

Bethel Seminary, Graduate and Professional Programs, St. Paul, MN 55112-6998. Offers Anglican studies (Certificate); children's and family ministry (MA); Christian studies (Certificate); Christian thought (MA); church planting (Certificate); Greek and Hebrew language (M Div); Greek language (M Div); Hebrew language (M Div); marriage and family therapy (MA, Certificate); mental health counseling (MA); ministry (MA, D Min); ministry practice (Certificate); theological studies (MA, Certificate);

transformational leadership (MA); young life youth ministry (Certificate). *Accreditation:* ACIPE. *Program availability:* Part-time, evening/weekend, 100% online, blended/hybrid learning. *Degree requirements:* For master's, variable foreign language requirement, thesis (for some programs); for doctorate, thesis/dissertation. *Entrance requirements:* For master's, letters of reference, transcripts, personal statement; for doctorate, M Div, letters of reference, organizational support; for Certificate, letters of reference, family essay, personal statement, and family of origin paper (for marriage and family therapy). Additional exam requirements/recommendations for international students: required—TOEFL (minimum score 550 paper-based; 87 iBT). Electronic applications accepted. *Expenses:* Contact institution.

Bethesda University, Graduate and Professional Programs, Anaheim, CA 92801. Offers biblical studies (MA); music (MA); theology (M Div). *Entrance requirements:* For master's, interview. Additional exam requirements/recommendations for international students: recommended—TOEFL.

Beulah Heights University, Graduate School, Atlanta, GA 30316. Offers biblical studies (MA); leadership studies (MA). *Entrance requirements:* Additional exam requirements/recommendations for international students: required—TOEFL (minimum score 500 paper-based). Electronic applications accepted.

Biola University, Talbot School of Theology, La Mirada, CA 90639-0001. Offers adult/family ministry (MACE); Bible exposition (MA, Th M); Biblical and theological studies (Certificate); children's ministry (MACE); Christian education (M Div); cross-cultural education ministry (MACE); educational studies (Ed D, PhD); evangelism and discipleship (M Div); general Christian education (MACE); Messianic Jewish studies (M Div, Certificate); missions and intercultural studies (M Div); New Testament (MA, Th M); Old Testament (MA); Old Testament and Semitics (Th M); pastoral and general ministry (M Div); pastoral care and counseling (M Div, MACML); philosophy (MA); preaching and pastoral ministry (MACML); spiritual formation (M Div, Certificate); spiritual formation and soul care (MA); sports ministry (MACML); theology (MA, Th M, D Min, Certificate); youth ministry (MACE). *Program availability:* Part-time, evening/weekend. *Students:* 461 full-time (116 women); 768 part-time (228 women); includes 489 minority (54 Black or African American, non-Hispanic/Latino; 1 American Indian or Alaska Native, non-Hispanic/Latino; 303 Asian, non-Hispanic/Latino; 96 Hispanic/Latino; 3 Native Hawaiian or other Pacific Islander, non-Hispanic/Latino; 32 Two or more races, non-Hispanic/Latino), 162 international. Average age 38. 745 applicants, 70% accepted, 320 enrolled. In 2019, 235 master's, 24 doctorates awarded. *Entrance requirements:* For master's, bachelor's degree from accredited college or university; minimum GPA of 2.6 (for M Div), 3.0 (for MA); for doctorate, M Div or MA. Additional exam requirements/recommendations for international students: required—TOEFL (minimum score 600 paper-based; 88 iBT). *Application deadline:* For fall admission, 7/1 for domestic students, 6/1 for international students; for spring admission, 11/1 for domestic students. Applications are processed on a rolling basis. Application fee: $65. Electronic applications accepted. *Financial support:* Scholarships/grants and unspecified assistantships available. Support available to part-time students. Financial award applicants required to submit FAFSA. *Unit head:* Dr. Clint Arnold, Dean, 562-903-4816, Fax: 562-903-4748. *Application contact:* Graduate Admissions Office, 562-903-4752, E-mail: graduate.admissions@biola.edu.
Website: http://www.talbot.edu/

Bob Jones University, Graduate Programs, Greenville, SC 29614. Offers accountancy (MS); Bible (MA); Bible translation (MA); Biblical studies (Certificate); business administration (MBA); church history (MA, PhD); church ministries (MA); church music (MM); cinema and video production (MA); counseling (MS); curriculum and instruction (Ed D); divinity (M Div); dramatic production (MA); educational leadership (MS, Ed D, Ed S); elementary education (M Ed, MAT); English (M Ed, MA, MAT); fine arts (MA); graphic design (MA); history (M Ed, MA); illustration (MA); interpretative speech (MA); mathematics (M Ed, MAT); medical missions (Certificate); ministry (MM, D Min); multi-categorical special education (M Ed, MAT); music (M Ed); New Testament interpretation (PhD); Old Testament interpretation (PhD); orchestral instrument performance (MM); organ performance (MM); pastoral studies (MA); personnel services (MS, Ed S); piano pedagogy (MM); piano performance (MM); platform arts (MA); rhetoric and public address (MA); secondary education (M Ed); studio art (MA); teaching Bible (MA); theology (MA, PhD); voice performance (MM); youth ministries (MA); M Div/MM.

Boston University, Graduate School of Arts and Sciences, Graduate Program in Religion, Boston, MA 02215. Offers MA, PhD. *Students:* 37 full-time (16 women), 2 part-time (0 women); includes 7 minority (3 Black or African American, non-Hispanic/Latino; 2 Asian, non-Hispanic/Latino; 2 Hispanic/Latino), 2 international. Average age 29. 45 applicants, 22% accepted, 6 enrolled. In 2019, 1 master's, 10 doctorates awarded. Terminal master's awarded for partial completion of doctoral program. *Degree requirements:* For doctorate, 2 foreign languages, comprehensive exam, thesis/dissertation. *Entrance requirements:* For doctorate, 3 letters of recommendation, transcripts, personal statement, academic writing sample. Additional exam requirements/recommendations for international students: required—TOEFL (minimum score 550 paper-based; 84 iBT). *Application deadline:* For fall admission, 1/15 for domestic and international students. Application fee: $95. Electronic applications accepted. *Financial support:* In 2019–20, 38 students received support, including 16 fellowships with full tuition reimbursements available (averaging $23,340 per year), 1 research assistantship with full tuition reimbursement available (averaging $23,340 per year), 9 teaching assistantships with full tuition reimbursements available (averaging $23,340 per year); career-related internships or fieldwork, Federal Work-Study, scholarships/grants, health care benefits, and unspecified assistantships also available. Financial award application deadline: 1/15. *Unit head:* Kecia Ali, Chair, 617-353-4465, Fax: 617-358-3087, E-mail: ka@bu.edu. *Application contact:* Wendy Czik, Department Administrator, 617-353-2635, Fax: 617-358-3087, E-mail: wlczik@bu.edu.
Website: http://www.bu.edu/gpr/

Briercrest Seminary, Graduate Programs, Program in Christian Ministries, Caronport, SK S0H 0S0, Canada. Offers leadership (MA); marriage and family counseling (MA); missions (MA); pastoral counseling (MA); worship (MA); youth and family ministry (MA). *Program availability:* Part-time. *Degree requirements:* For master's, comprehensive exam, thesis optional. *Entrance requirements:* Additional exam requirements/recommendations for international students: required—TOEFL (minimum score 550 paper-based).

Briercrest Seminary, Graduate Programs, Program in Theology, Caronport, SK S0H 0S0, Canada. Offers Biblical studies (M Div); leadership and management (M Div); New Testament (MATS); Old Testament (MATS); pastoral counseling (M Div); pastoral ministry (M Div); theological studies (M Div); theology (MATS); worship (M Div); youth and family ministry (M Div). *Accreditation:* ATS. *Program availability:* Part-time. *Degree requirements:* For master's, comprehensive exam, thesis optional. *Entrance requirements:* Additional exam requirements/recommendations for international students: required—TOEFL (minimum score 550 paper-based).

Brown University, Graduate School, Department of Religious Studies, Providence, RI 02912. Offers Asian religious traditions (PhD); Islam, society and culture (PhD); religion and critical thought (PhD); religions of the ancient Mediterranean (PhD). *Degree requirements:* For doctorate, variable foreign language requirement, thesis/dissertation.

Entrance requirements: For doctorate, GRE General Test. Additional exam requirements/recommendations for international students: required—TOEFL. Electronic applications accepted.

Bryn Athyn College of the New Church, Academy of the New Church Theological School, ViktorTest, PA 19009-0717. Offers divinity (M Div); religious studies (MA). *Program availability:* Part-time, online learning. *Faculty:* 12. *Students:* 7 full-time (0 women), 19 part-time (13 women), 10 international. Average age 37. 26 applicants, 100% accepted, 9 enrolled. In 2019, 6 master's awarded. *Degree requirements:* For master's, variable foreign language requirement, thesis. *Entrance requirements:* Additional exam requirements/recommendations for international students: required—TOEFL. *Application deadline:* For fall admission, 1/31 for domestic students. Applications are processed on a rolling basis. *Financial support:* In 2019–20, 7 students received support. Career-related internships or fieldwork, Federal Work-Study, and institutionally sponsored loans available. Financial award application deadline: 1/31. *Unit head:* Andrew Dibb, Dean, 267-502-2640, E-mail: andrew.dibb@ancts.org. *Application contact:* Andrew Dibb, Dean, 267-502-2640, E-mail: andrew.dibb@ancts.org.
Website: http://www.ancts.org

Cairn University, School of Divinity, Langhorne, PA 19047-2990. Offers divinity (M Div); religion (MA); theology (Th M). *Program availability:* Part-time, evening/weekend, 100% online, blended/hybrid learning. *Entrance requirements:* Additional exam requirements/recommendations for international students: required—TOEFL (minimum score 550 paper-based). Electronic applications accepted. Application fee is waived when completed online. *Expenses:* Contact institution.

California State University, Long Beach, Graduate Studies, College of Liberal Arts, Department of Religious Studies, Long Beach, CA 90840. Offers MA. *Program availability:* Part-time, evening/weekend. *Entrance requirements:* Additional exam requirements/recommendations for international students: required—TOEFL. Electronic applications accepted.

Calvin Theological Seminary, Graduate and Professional Programs, Grand Rapids, MI 49546-4387. Offers Bible and theology (MA); divinity (M Div), including ancient near eastern languages and literature, contextual ministry, evangelism and teaching, history of Christianity, new church development, New Testament, Old Testament, pastoral care and leadership, preaching and worship, theological studies, youth and family ministries; educational ministry (MA); historical theology (PhD); missions and evangelism (MA); pastoral care (MA); philosophical and moral theology (PhD); systematic theology (PhD); theological studies (MTS); theology (Th M); worship (MA); youth and family ministries (MA). *Accreditation:* ACIPE; ATS. *Program availability:* Part-time. *Degree requirements:* For master's, variable foreign language requirement, thesis (for some programs); for doctorate, 4 foreign languages, comprehensive exam, thesis/dissertation. *Entrance requirements:* For doctorate, GRE General Test, Hebrew, Greek, and a modern foreign language. Additional exam requirements/recommendations for international students: required—TOEFL (minimum score 550 paper-based), TWE (minimum score 4). Electronic applications accepted.

Canadian Southern Baptist Seminary, Graduate Programs, Cochrane, AB T4C 2G1, Canada. Offers Biblical studies (MBS); Christian ministry (MCMin); Christian studies (MCS); ministry (M Div). *Accreditation:* ATS. *Program availability:* Part-time, 100% online, blended/hybrid learning. *Entrance requirements:* Additional exam requirements/recommendations for international students: required—TOEFL (minimum score 560 paper-based; 83 iBT); recommended—IELTS (minimum score 6.5).

The Catholic University of America, School of Arts and Sciences, Program in Early Christian Studies, Washington, DC 20064. Offers MA, PhD. *Program availability:* Part-time. *Faculty:* 1 full-time (0 women). *Students:* 3 full-time (1 woman), 1 (woman) part-time, 1 international. Average age 26. 4 applicants, 50% accepted, 1 enrolled. *Degree requirements:* For master's, one foreign language, comprehensive exam; for doctorate, 2 foreign languages, comprehensive exam, thesis/dissertation. *Entrance requirements:* For master's and doctorate, GRE General Test, statement of purpose, official copies of academic transcripts, three letters of recommendation, writing sample. Additional exam requirements/recommendations for international students: required—TOEFL (minimum score 550 paper-based; 80 iBT). *Application deadline:* For fall admission, 7/15 priority date for domestic students, 7/1 for international students; for spring admission, 11/15 priority date for domestic students, 11/1 for international students. Applications are processed on a rolling basis. Application fee: $55. Electronic applications accepted. *Financial support:* Fellowships, research assistantships, teaching assistantships, Federal Work-Study, scholarships/grants, tuition waivers (full and partial), and unspecified assistantships available. Financial award application deadline: 2/1; financial award applicants required to submit FAFSA. *Unit head:* Dr. William E. Klingshirn, Director, 202-319-5795, Fax: 202-319-6609, E-mail: klingshirn@cua.edu. *Application contact:* Dr. Steven Brown, Director of Graduate Admissions, 202-319-5057, Fax: 202-319-6533, E-mail: cua-admissions@cua.edu.
Website: http://earlychristianity.cua.edu/

The Catholic University of America, School of Theology and Religious Studies, Washington, DC 20064. Offers M Cat, M Div, MA, D Min, PhD, STD, Certificate, STB, STL, MSLS/MA, STB/M Div. *Program availability:* Part-time. *Faculty:* 39 full-time (5 women), 12 part-time/adjunct (5 women). *Students:* 156 full-time (13 women), 167 part-time (69 women); includes 72 minority (13 Black or African American, non-Hispanic/Latino; 1 American Indian or Alaska Native, non-Hispanic/Latino; 13 Asian, non-Hispanic/Latino; 22 Hispanic/Latino; 23 Two or more races, non-Hispanic/Latino), 51 international. Average age 36. 178 applicants, 60% accepted, 67 enrolled. In 2019, 56 master's, 27 doctorates awarded. Terminal master's awarded for partial completion of doctoral program. *Degree requirements:* For master's, variable foreign language requirement, comprehensive exam (for some programs), thesis (for some programs); for doctorate, variable foreign language requirement, comprehensive exam, thesis/dissertation. *Entrance requirements:* For master's and doctorate, GRE General Test, statement of purpose, official copies of academic transcripts, three letters of recommendation. Additional exam requirements/recommendations for international students: required—TOEFL (minimum score 550 paper-based; 80 iBT). *Application deadline:* For fall admission, 7/15 priority date for domestic students, 7/1 for international students; for spring admission, 11/15 priority date for domestic students, 11/1 for international students. Applications are processed on a rolling basis. Application fee: $55. Electronic applications accepted. *Expenses:* Contact institution. *Financial support:* Fellowships, research assistantships, teaching assistantships, Federal Work-Study, scholarships/grants, tuition waivers (full and partial), and unspecified assistantships available. Financial award application deadline: 2/1; financial award applicants required to submit FAFSA. *Unit head:* Very Rev. Mark Morozowich, Dean, 202-319-5684, Fax: 202-319-4967, E-mail: morozowich@cua.edu. *Application contact:* Dr. Steven Brown, Director of Graduate Admissions, 202-319-5057, Fax: 202-319-6533, E-mail: cua-admissions@cua.edu.
Website: https://trs.catholic.edu/

Charlotte Christian College and Theological Seminary, Graduate Program, Charlotte, NC 28206. Offers Biblical studies (MA), including New Testament, Old Testament, theology; chaplaincy (M Div); general pastoral studies (M Div); ministry (D Min); pastoral counseling (M Div); urban Christian ministry (MA), including multi-cultural studies, youth ministry. *Program availability:* Part-time, evening/weekend. *Degree requirements:* For master's, variable foreign language requirement, thesis; for doctorate, thesis/dissertation. *Entrance requirements:* For master's, 1000-2000 word essay. Additional exam requirements/recommendations for international students: required—TOEFL, IELTS. Electronic applications accepted. *Expenses:* Contact institution.

Chicago Theological Seminary, Graduate and Professional Programs, Chicago, IL 60637-1507. Offers Bible, culture and hermeneutics (PhD); preaching (D Min); religion and health (D Min); religious studies (MA); spirituality and spiritual direction (D Min); theology (M Div); theology, ethics and the human sciences (PhD); M Div/MSW. *Accreditation:* ACIPE; ATS. *Program availability:* Part-time. *Degree requirements:* For master's, thesis; for doctorate, 2 foreign languages, comprehensive exam, thesis/dissertation. *Entrance requirements:* For doctorate, GRE General Test. Additional exam requirements/recommendations for international students: required—TOEFL.

Christian Brothers University, School of Arts, Memphis, TN 38104-5581. Offers Catholic studies (MACS); educational leadership (MSEL); teacher-leadership (M Ed); teaching (MAT). *Program availability:* Part-time, evening/weekend. *Entrance requirements:* For master's, GRE, GMAT, PRAXIS II. *Expenses:* Contact institution.

Christian Theological Seminary, Graduate and Professional Programs, Indianapolis, IN 46208-3301. Offers educational and arts ministries (MA); marriage and family therapy (MA); pastoral care and counseling (D Min); psychotherapy and faith (MA); theological studies (MTS); theology (M Div). *Accreditation:* AAMFT/COAMFTE (one or more programs are accredited); ACIPE; ATS. *Program availability:* Part-time. Terminal master's awarded for partial completion of doctoral program. *Degree requirements:* For master's, comprehensive exam (for some programs), thesis (for some programs), missionary and cross-cultural experience (for M Div); for doctorate, comprehensive exam, thesis/dissertation. *Entrance requirements:* For doctorate, M Div. Additional exam requirements/recommendations for international students: recommended—TOEFL. Electronic applications accepted.

Cincinnati Christian University, Graduate School, Cincinnati, OH 45204-3200. Offers biblical studies (MA); church history (MA); counseling (MAC); divinity (M Div); ministry (M Min); practical ministries (MA); theological studies (MA). *Program availability:* Part-time. *Degree requirements:* For master's, variable foreign language requirement, thesis (for some programs), oral exam (for M Div). *Entrance requirements:* Additional exam requirements/recommendations for international students: required—TOEFL. Electronic applications accepted.

Claremont Graduate University, Graduate Programs, School of Arts and Humanities, Department of Religion, Claremont, CA 91711-6160. Offers Hebrew Bible (MA, PhD); history of Christianity and religions of North America (MA, PhD); New Testament (MA, PhD); philosophy of religion and theology (MA, PhD); theology, ethics and culture (MA, PhD); women's studies in religion (MA, PhD); MA/PhD; MBA/PhD. *Program availability:* Part-time. Terminal master's awarded for partial completion of doctoral program. *Entrance requirements:* For master's and doctorate, GRE General Test. Additional exam requirements/recommendations for international students: required—TOEFL (minimum score 75 iBT). Electronic applications accepted.

Claremont Lincoln University, Graduate Programs, Claremont, CA 91711. Offers ethical leadership (MA); interfaith action (MA); social impact (MA).

Claremont School of Theology, Graduate and Professional Programs, Program in Religion, Claremont, CA 91711-3199. Offers practical theology (PhD), including religious education and formation, spiritual care and counseling; religion (MA, PhD), including comparative theology and philosophy (PhD), Hebrew Bible and Jewish studies (PhD), New Testament and Christian origins (PhD), process studies (PhD), religion, ethics, and society (PhD). *Accreditation:* ACIPE; ATS. Terminal master's awarded for partial completion of doctoral program. *Degree requirements:* For master's, thesis; for doctorate, 2 foreign languages, thesis/dissertation. *Entrance requirements:* For doctorate, GRE General Test. Additional exam requirements/recommendations for international students: required—TOEFL. Electronic applications accepted.

Clarks Summit University, Baptist Bible Seminary, South Abington Township, PA 18411. Offers Biblical apologetics (MA); Biblical studies (MA); church education (M Min); church planting (M Div, M Min); communication (D Min); counseling and spiritual development (D Min); global ministry (M Min, D Min); ministry (PhD); missions (M Min); organizational leadership (M Min); outreach pastor (M Min); pastoral counseling (M Min); pastoral leadership (M Div, M Min); pastoral ministry (D Min); theological studies (D Min); theology (Th M); youth pastor (M Min). *Program availability:* Part-time, evening/weekend, online learning. Terminal master's awarded for partial completion of doctoral program. *Degree requirements:* For master's, 2 foreign languages, thesis, oral exam (for M Div); for doctorate, 2 foreign languages, comprehensive exam (for some programs), thesis/dissertation, oral exam. *Entrance requirements:* For doctorate, Greek and Hebrew entrance exams (for PhD). Electronic applications accepted.

Columbia University, Graduate School of Arts and Sciences, New York, NY 10027. Offers African-American studies (MA); American studies (MA); anthropology (MA, PhD); art history and archaeology (MA, PhD); astronomy (PhD); biological sciences (PhD); biotechnology (MA); chemical physics (PhD); chemistry (PhD); classical studies (MA, PhD); classics (MA, PhD); climate and society (MA); conservation biology (MA); earth and environmental sciences (PhD); East Asia: regional studies (MA); East Asian languages and cultures (MA, PhD); ecology, evolution and environmental biology (MA), including conservation biology; ecology, evolution, and environmental biology (PhD), including ecology and evolutionary biology, evolutionary primatology; economics (MA, PhD); English and comparative literature (MA, PhD); French and Romance philology (MA, PhD); Germanic languages (MA, PhD); global French studies (MA); global thought (MA); Hispanic cultural studies (MA); history (PhD); history and literature (MA); human rights studies (MA); Islamic studies (MA); Italian (MA, PhD); Japanese pedagogy (MA); Jewish studies (MA); Latin America and the Caribbean: regional studies (MA); Latin American and Iberian cultures (PhD); mathematics (MA, PhD), including finance (MA); medieval and Renaissance studies (MA); Middle Eastern, South Asian, and African studies (MA, PhD); modern art: critical and curatorial studies (MA); modern European studies (MA); museum anthropology (MA); music (DMA, PhD); oral history (MA); philosophical foundations of physics (MA); philosophy (MA, PhD); physics (PhD); political science (MA, PhD); psychology (PhD); quantitative methods in the social sciences (MA); religion (MA, PhD); Russia, Eurasia and East Europe: regional studies (MA); Russian translation (MA); Slavic cultures (MA); Slavic languages (MA, PhD); sociology (MA, PhD); South Asian studies (MA); statistics (MA, PhD); theatre (PhD). *Program availability:* Part-time. *Students:* 3,506 full-time (1,844 women), 208 part-time (121 women); includes 864 minority (110 Black or African American, non-Hispanic/Latino; 5 American Indian or Alaska Native, non-Hispanic/Latino; 416 Asian, non-Hispanic/Latino; 147 Hispanic/Latino; 6 Native Hawaiian or other Pacific Islander, non-Hispanic/Latino; 180 Two or more races, non-Hispanic/Latino), 2,065 international. 14,545 applicants, 25% accepted, 1,429 enrolled. In 2019, 1,262 master's, 363 doctorates awarded. Terminal master's awarded for partial completion of doctoral program. *Degree requirements:* For master's, variable foreign language requirement, comprehensive exam (for some programs), thesis (for some programs); for doctorate, variable foreign language requirement, comprehensive exam (for some programs), thesis/dissertation. *Entrance requirements:* For master's and doctorate, GRE General Test, GRE Subject Test (for some programs). Additional exam requirements/recommendations for international students: required—TOEFL (minimum score 600 paper-based; 100 iBT), IELTS (minimum score 7.5). Application fee: $115. Electronic applications accepted. *Expenses: Tuition:* Full-time $47,600; part-time $1880 per credit. One-time fee: $105. *Financial support:* Fellowships, research assistantships, teaching assistantships, career-related internships or fieldwork, Federal Work-Study, institutionally sponsored loans, scholarships/grants, traineeships, health care benefits, tuition waivers, and unspecified assistantships available. Support available to part-time students. Financial award application deadline: 12/15. *Unit head:* Dr. Carlos J. Alonso, Dean of the Graduate School of Arts and Sciences and Vice President for Graduate Education, 212-854-2861, E-mail: gsas-dean@columbia.edu. *Application contact:* GSAS Office of Admissions, 212-854-6729, E-mail: gsas-admissions@columbia.edu. Website: http://gsas.columbia.edu/

Concordia University, School of Graduate Studies, Faculty of Arts and Science, Department of Religions and Cultures, MA Program in Religion, Montréal, QC H3G 1M8, Canada. Offers MA. *Degree requirements:* For master's, comprehensive exam, thesis optional.

Concordia University, School of Graduate Studies, Faculty of Arts and Science, Department of Religions and Cultures, PhD Program in Religion, Montréal, QC H3G 1M8, Canada. Offers PhD. *Degree requirements:* For doctorate, one foreign language, comprehensive exam, thesis/dissertation.

Concordia University Chicago, College of Graduate Studies, Program in Religion, River Forest, IL 60305-1499. Offers MA. *Program availability:* Part-time, evening/weekend. *Degree requirements:* For master's, comprehensive exam, thesis. *Entrance requirements:* For master's, minimum GPA of 2.9. Additional exam requirements/recommendations for international students: required—TOEFL (minimum score 550 paper-based). Electronic applications accepted.

Concordia University Irvine, School of Theology, Irvine, CA 92612-3299. Offers Christian leadership (MA); research in theology (MA); theology and culture (MA). *Program availability:* Part-time, evening/weekend. *Degree requirements:* For master's, project/thesis or vicarage. *Entrance requirements:* For master's, official college transcript(s), statement of intent, 2 references, interview. Additional exam requirements/recommendations for international students: required—TOEFL. Electronic applications accepted. *Expenses:* Contact institution.

Concordia University of Edmonton, Program in Biblical and Christian Studies, Edmonton, AB T5B 4E4, Canada. Offers MA.

Cornell University, Graduate School, Graduate Fields of Arts and Sciences, Field of Asian Literature, Religion and Culture, Ithaca, NY 14853. Offers Asian religions (MA, PhD); Chinese philosophy (PhD); classical Chinese literature (PhD); classical Japanese literature (PhD); East Asian literature and culture (PhD); Korean literature (PhD); modern Chinese literature (PhD); modern Japanese literature (PhD); South Asian literature and culture (PhD); Southeast Asian literature and culture (PhD). *Degree requirements:* For doctorate, comprehensive exam, thesis/dissertation. *Entrance requirements:* For doctorate, GRE General Test, academic writing sample, 3 letters of recommendation. Additional exam requirements/recommendations for international students: required—TOEFL (minimum score 600 paper-based; 77 iBT). Electronic applications accepted.

Dallas Baptist University, Liberal Arts Program, Dallas, TX 75211-9299. Offers art (MLA); Christian studies (MLA); commercial art (MLA); East Asian studies (MLA); English (MLA); English as a second language (MLA); history (MLA); missions (MLA); political science (MLA). *Program availability:* Part-time, evening/weekend, online learning. *Application deadline:* Applications are processed on a rolling basis. Application fee: $25. Electronic applications accepted. Application fee is waived when completed online. *Expenses: Tuition:* Full-time $18,072; part-time $1004 per credit hour. *Required fees:* $1100; $550 per semester. Tuition and fees vary according to course level and degree level. *Unit head:* Jared Ingram, Director, 214-333-5584, E-mail: jaredi@dbu.edu. *Application contact:* Jared Ingram, Director, 214-333-5584, E-mail: jaredi@dbu.edu. Website: https://www.dbu.edu/graduate/degree-programs/mla

Dallas Theological Seminary, Graduate Programs, Dallas, TX 75204-6499. Offers adult education (Th M); apologetics (Th M); Bible backgrounds (Th M); Bible translation (Th M); Biblical and theological studies (Certificate); biblical counseling (MA); biblical exegesis and linguistics (MA); biblical exposition (PhD); biblical studies (MA); Biblical theology (Th M); children's education (Th M); Christian education (MA, D Min); Christian leadership (MA); cross-cultural ministries (MA); educational administration (Th M); educational leadership (Th M); evangelism and discipleship (Th M); exposition of Biblical books (Th M); family life education (Th M); general studies (Th M); Hebrew and cognate studies (Th M); hermeneutics (Th M); historical theology (Th M); homiletics (Th M); intercultural ministries (Th M); Jesus studies (Th M); leadership studies (Th M); media and communication (MA); media arts (Th M); ministry (D Min); ministry with women (Th M); New Testament studies (Th M, PhD); Old Testament studies (Th M, PhD); parachurch ministries (Th M); pastoral care and counseling (Th M); pastoral theology and practice (Th M); philosophy (Th M); sacred theology (STM); spiritual formation (Th M); systematic theology (Th M); teaching in Christian institutions (Th M); theological studies (PhD); urban ministries (Th M); worship studies (Th M); youth education (Th M). *Program availability:* Part-time, online learning. *Degree requirements:* For master's, variable foreign language requirement, thesis (for some programs); for doctorate, 2 foreign languages, thesis/dissertation. *Entrance requirements:* For master's, GRE or MAT (if minimum undergraduate cumulative GPA is below 2.5 or undergraduate degree is unaccredited). Additional exam requirements/recommendations for international students: required—TOEFL (minimum score 575 paper-based; 85 iBT), TWE. Electronic applications accepted.

Delta State University, Graduate Programs, College of Arts and Sciences, Program in Liberal Studies, Cleveland, MS 38733-0001. Offers evolving human voices (MALS); gender and diversity studies (MALS); globalization studies (MALS); Mississippi Delta studies (MALS); philosophy (MALS); religious studies (MALS). *Degree requirements:* For master's, oral and/or written comprehensive exam. *Expenses: Tuition, area resident:* Full-time $7501; part-time $417 per credit hour. *Tuition, state resident:* full-time $7501; part-time $417 per credit hour. *Tuition, nonresident:* full-time $7501; part-time $417 per credit hour. *International tuition:* $7501 full-time. *Required fees:* $170; $9.45 per credit hour. $9.45 per semester.

Denver Seminary, Graduate and Professional Programs, Littleton, CO 80120. Offers apologetics (Certificate); biblical studies (MA); Christian formation and soul care (MA, Certificate); Christian studies (MA, Certificate); church and parachurch leadership (D Min); counseling licensure (MA); counseling ministry (MA); intercultural ministry (Certificate); leadership (MA, Certificate); marriage and family counseling (D Min); pastoral ministry (D Min); philosophy of religion (MA); spiritual guidance (Certificate); theology (M Div, Certificate); worship (Certificate); youth and family ministry (MA). *Accreditation:* ACA; ACIPE; ATS (one or more programs are accredited). *Program availability:* Part-time, evening/weekend, online learning. *Degree requirements:* For master's, 2 foreign languages, thesis (for some programs); for doctorate, 2 foreign languages, thesis/dissertation. *Entrance requirements:* For doctorate, M Div, 3 years of ministry experience. Additional exam requirements/recommendations for international students: required—TOEFL (minimum score 575 paper-based; 90 iBT). Electronic applications accepted.

Drew University, Caspersen School of Graduate Studies, Madison, NJ 07940-1493. Offers conflict resolution and leadership (Certificate), including community leadership, moderation, peace building; education (M Ed); finance (MA); history and culture (MA, PhD), including American history, book history, British history, European history, intellectual history, Irish history, print culture, public history; K-12 education (MAT), including art, biology, chemistry, elementary education, English, French, Italian, math, secondary education, special education, teacher of students with disabilities; liberal studies (M Litt, D Litt), including history, Irish/Irish-American studies, literature (M Litt, MMH, D Litt, DMH, CMH), religion, spirituality, teaching in the two-year college, writing; medical humanities (MMH, DMH, CMH), including arts, health, healthcare, literature (M Litt, MMH, D Litt, DMH, CMH), scientific research; poetry (MFA). *Program availability:* Part-time, evening/weekend. Terminal master's awarded for partial completion of doctoral program. *Degree requirements:* For master's and other advanced degree, thesis (for some programs); for doctorate, one foreign language, comprehensive exam (for some programs), thesis/dissertation. *Entrance requirements:* For master's, PRAXIS Core and Subject Area tests (for MAT), GRE/GMAT (for MFin MS in Data Analytics), resume, transcripts, writing sample, personal statement, letters of recommendation; for doctorate, GRE (PhD in history and culture), resume, transcripts, writing sample, personal statement, letters of recommendation; for other advanced degree, resume, transcripts, personal statement. Additional exam requirements/recommendations for international students: required—TOEFL (minimum score 587 paper-based; 80 iBT), IELTS (minimum score 6), TWE (minimum score 4). Electronic applications accepted.

Duke University, Graduate School, Department of Religion, Durham, NC 27708. Offers MA, PhD, JD/MA. *Program availability:* Part-time. Terminal master's awarded for partial completion of doctoral program. *Degree requirements:* For master's, one foreign language, thesis or alternative; for doctorate, 2 foreign languages, thesis/dissertation. *Entrance requirements:* For master's and doctorate, GRE General Test. Additional exam requirements/recommendations for international students: required—TOEFL (minimum score 577 paper-based; 90 iBT) or IELTS (minimum score 7). Electronic applications accepted.

Earlham School of Religion, Graduate Programs, Richmond, IN 47374. Offers ministry (M Min); religion (MA); theology (M Div). *Accreditation:* ACIPE; ATS. *Program availability:* Part-time, blended/hybrid learning. *Faculty:* 8 full-time (2 women), 2 part-time/adjunct (1 woman). *Students:* 17 full-time (9 women), 18 part-time (11 women); includes 2 minority (both Black or African American, non-Hispanic/Latino). Average age 38. *Degree requirements:* For master's, variable foreign language requirement, comprehensive exam (for some programs), thesis (for some programs), internship (M Div). *Entrance requirements:* For master's, 3 references, academic writing sample, official college transcripts, background check. Additional exam requirements/recommendations for international students: required—TOEFL (minimum score 550 paper-based; 82 iBT), IELTS (minimum score 7). *Application deadline:* For fall admission, 6/15 priority date for domestic students; for winter admission, 11/15 priority date for domestic students. Applications are processed on a rolling basis. Application fee: $35. Electronic applications accepted. *Financial support:* Scholarships/grants and tuition waivers (full and partial) available. Financial award application deadline: 4/15; financial award applicants required to submit FAFSA. *Unit head:* Matt Hisrich, Dean, 800-432-1377, Fax: 765-983-1688, E-mail: hisrima@earlham.edu. *Application contact:* Julie Dishman, Director of Recruitment and Admissions, 765-983-1523, Fax: 765-983-1688, E-mail: dishmju@earlham.edu. Website: http://esr.earlham.edu/academic-programs

Eastern Mennonite University, Eastern Mennonite Seminary, Harrisonburg, VA 22802-2462. Offers Christian leadership (MA); divinity (M Div); ministry studies (Certificate); religion (MA); theological studies (Certificate). *Accreditation:* ATS. *Program availability:* Part-time. *Degree requirements:* For master's, thesis (for some programs), supervised field education (for M Div). *Entrance requirements:* For master's, minimum GPA of 2.5. Additional exam requirements/recommendations for international students: required—TOEFL (minimum score 550 paper-based). *Expenses:* Contact institution.

East Texas Baptist University, School of Christian Studies, Marshall, TX 75670-1498. Offers MA, MACM. *Program availability:* Part-time, evening/weekend, online only, 100% online. *Faculty:* 2 full-time (0 women), 4 part-time/adjunct (2 women). *Students:* 10 full-time (5 women), 15 part-time (3 women); includes 5 minority (4 Black or African American, non-Hispanic/Latino; 1 Hispanic/Latino). Average age 26. 9 applicants, 89% accepted, 8 enrolled. In 2019, 4 master's awarded. *Entrance requirements:* Additional exam requirements/recommendations for international students: recommended—TOEFL (minimum score 550 paper-based; 79 iBT). *Application deadline:* For fall admission, 8/13 for domestic students; for spring admission, 1/7 for domestic students; for summer admission, 5/5 for domestic students. Applications are processed on a rolling basis. Application fee: $50. Electronic applications accepted. *Expenses:* $725 per credit hour tuition; $155 per semester fees (6 or more hours enrolled); $77 per semester fees (1-5 hours enrolled). *Financial support:* In 2019–20, 24 students received support. Federal Work-Study, scholarships/grants, unspecified assistantships, and staff grants available. Financial award applicants required to submit FAFSA. *Unit head:* Dr. Scott Stevens, Director, 903-923-2178, Fax: 903-923-2077, E-mail: sstevens@etbu.edu. *Application contact:* Den Murley, Director of Graduate Admissions, 903-923-2079, Fax: 903-934-8115, E-mail: gradadmissions@etbu.edu. Website: https://www.etbu.edu/academics/academic-schools/school-christian-studies/department-religion/programs

Elms College, Religious Studies Department, Chicopee, MA 01013-2839. Offers MAAT. *Program availability:* Part-time, evening/weekend. *Faculty:* 5 full-time (1 woman), 3 part-time/adjunct (1 woman). *Students:* 2 full-time (both women), 4 part-time (2 women). Average age 51. 2 applicants, 100% accepted, 2 enrolled. In 2019, 4 master's awarded. *Degree requirements:* For master's, thesis. *Entrance requirements:* For master's, minimum GPA of 3.0. Additional exam requirements/recommendations for international students: required—TOEFL (minimum score 80 iBT). *Application deadline:* For fall admission, 7/1 priority date for domestic students; for spring admission, 11/1 priority date for domestic students. Applications are processed on a rolling basis. Application fee: $0. Electronic applications accepted. *Financial support:* Applicants required to submit FAFSA. *Unit head:* Dr. Tom Cerasulo, Chair, Division of Humanities and Fine Arts, 413-265-2345, E-mail: cerasulot@elms.edu. *Application contact:* Nancy Davis, Director, Office of Graduate and Continuing Education Admissions, 413-265-2456, E-mail: grad@elms.edu.

Emory University, Laney Graduate School, Division of Religion, Atlanta, GA 30322-1100. Offers PhD. *Degree requirements:* For doctorate, 2 foreign languages, comprehensive exam, thesis/dissertation. *Entrance requirements:* For doctorate, GRE General Test, minimum GPA of 3.0. Additional exam requirements/recommendations for international students: required—TOEFL. Electronic applications accepted.

Faith Baptist Bible College and Theological Seminary, Graduate Program, Ankeny, IA 50023. Offers Biblical studies (MA); pastoral studies (M Div); pastoral training (MA); religion (MA); theological studies (MA). *Program availability:* Part-time. *Degree*

requirements: For master's, thesis or alternative. *Entrance requirements:* Additional exam requirements/recommendations for international students: required—TOEFL (minimum score 550 paper-based; 79 iBT), IELTS (minimum score 6.5). Electronic applications accepted.

Florida International University, Steven J. Green School of International and Public Affairs, Department of Religious Studies, Miami, FL 33199. Offers MA, MA/PhD. *Program availability:* Part-time, evening/weekend. *Faculty:* 12 full-time (2 women), 21 part-time/adjunct (9 women). *Students:* 9 full-time (5 women), 6 part-time (2 women); includes 9 minority (1 Black or African American, non-Hispanic/Latino; 1 Asian, non-Hispanic/Latino; 6 Hispanic/Latino; 1 Two or more races, non-Hispanic/Latino), 5 international. Average age 31. 18 applicants, 56% accepted, 8 enrolled. In 2019, 11 master's awarded. *Entrance requirements:* For master's, minimum GPA of 3.0, 2 letters of recommendation. Additional exam requirements/recommendations for international students: required—TOEFL (minimum score 550 paper-based; 80 iBT). *Application deadline:* For fall admission, 2/15 for domestic and international students; for spring admission, 10/1 for domestic students, 9/1 for international students. Application fee: $30. Electronic applications accepted. *Expenses: Tuition, area resident:* Full-time $8912; part-time $446 per credit hour. Tuition, state resident: full-time $8912; part-time $446 per credit hour. Tuition, nonresident: full-time $21,393; part-time $992 per credit hour. *Required fees:* $2194. *Financial support:* Institutionally sponsored loans and scholarships/grants available. Financial award application deadline: 3/1; financial award applicants required to submit FAFSA. *Unit head:* Dr. Erik Larson, Chair, 305-348-3518, Fax: 305-348-1879, E-mail: larsone@fiu.edu. *Application contact:* Nanett Rojas, Manager, Admissions Operations, 305-348-7464, Fax: 305-348-7441, E-mail: gradadm@fiu.edu.

Florida State University, The Graduate School, Department of Anthropology, Department of Physics, Department of Religion, Tallahassee, FL 32306-1520. Offers humanities (PhD), including religion; religion (MA, PhD). *Faculty:* 21 full-time (6 women), 6 part-time/adjunct (4 women). *Students:* 54 full-time (18 women), 5 part-time (2 women); includes 12 minority (2 Black or African American, non-Hispanic/Latino; 3 Asian, non-Hispanic/Latino; 7 Two or more races, non-Hispanic/Latino). Average age 26. 52 applicants, 42% accepted, 14 enrolled. In 2019, 7 master's, 5 doctorates awarded. Terminal master's awarded for partial completion of doctoral program. *Degree requirements:* For master's, one foreign language, comprehensive exam (for some programs), thesis (for some programs); for doctorate, 2 foreign languages, thesis/dissertation. *Entrance requirements:* For master's, GRE General Test, minimum GPA of 3.0; for doctorate, GRE General Test, MA in religion. Additional exam requirements/recommendations for international students: required—TOEFL (minimum score 550 paper-based; 80 iBT). *Application deadline:* For fall admission, 1/15 for domestic and international students. Application fee: $30. Electronic applications accepted. *Financial support:* In 2019–20, 52 students received support, including 5 fellowships with partial tuition reimbursements available (averaging $15,000 per year), 20 research assistantships with partial tuition reimbursements available (averaging $16,500 per year), 32 teaching assistantships with partial tuition reimbursements available (averaging $16,500 per year); institutionally sponsored loans, tuition waivers (partial), and unspecified assistantships also available. Financial award application deadline: 12/15; financial award applicants required to submit FAFSA. *Unit head:* Dr. Aline Kalbian, Chair, 850-644-1020, Fax: 850-644-7225, E-mail: akalbian@fsu.edu. *Application contact:* Dr. Matthew Goff, Director of Graduate Studies, 850-644-1020, Fax: 850-644-7225, E-mail: mgoff@fsu.edu.
Website: http://www.religion.fsu.edu

Fordham University, Graduate School of Religion and Religious Education, Bronx, NY 10458. Offers pastoral counseling and spiritual care (MA); pastoral ministry/spirituality/pastoral counseling (D Min); religion and religious education (MA); religious education (MS, PhD, PD); spiritual direction (Certificate). *Program availability:* Part-time, evening/weekend, 100% online, blended/hybrid learning. *Faculty:* 11 full-time (4 women), 16 part-time/adjunct (11 women). *Students:* 126 full-time (66 women), 72 part-time (37 women); includes 51 minority (19 Black or African American, non-Hispanic/Latino; 9 Asian, non-Hispanic/Latino; 20 Hispanic/Latino; 3 Two or more races, non-Hispanic/Latino), 34 international. Average age 41. 85 applicants, 76% accepted, 55 enrolled. In 2019, 48 master's, 12 doctorates, 10 other advanced degrees awarded. Terminal master's awarded for partial completion of doctoral program. *Degree requirements:* For master's, comprehensive exam (for some programs), thesis or alternative, research paper; for doctorate, thesis/dissertation. *Entrance requirements:* For doctorate, MAT or GRE (For Ph.D. only). Additional exam requirements/recommendations for international students: recommended—TOEFL, IELTS. *Application deadline:* For fall admission, 7/1 priority date for domestic students, 5/1 priority date for international students; for spring admission, 12/1 priority date for domestic students, 10/1 priority date for international students. Applications are processed on a rolling basis. Application fee: $100. Electronic applications accepted. *Expenses:* Contact institution. *Financial support:* In 2019–20, 140 students received support, including 8 research assistantships with partial tuition reimbursements available (averaging $10,800 per year); scholarships/grants, tuition waivers (partial), and unspecified assistantships also available. Support available to part-time students. Financial award application deadline: 8/1; financial award applicants required to submit FAFSA. *Unit head:* Faustino M. Cruz, SM, Dean, 718-817-4800, Fax: 718-817-3352, E-mail: fcruz16@fordham.edu. *Application contact:* Dr. Lois D'Amore, Director of Admissions and Student Life, 718-817-4800, Fax: 718-817-3352, E-mail: ldamore@fordham.edu.
Website: http://www.fordham.edu/gre

The General Theological Seminary, Graduate and Professional Programs, New York, NY 10011-4977. Offers Anglican studies (STM, Th D, Certificate); ascetical theology (Certificate); biblical studies (Certificate); congregational development (Certificate); divinity (M Div); historical and theological studies (Certificate); spiritual direction (MASD, STM, Certificate); theology (MA). *Accreditation:* ACIPE; ATS. *Program availability:* Part-time, evening/weekend. Terminal master's awarded for partial completion of doctoral program. *Degree requirements:* For master's, thesis; for doctorate, 2 foreign languages, thesis/dissertation. *Entrance requirements:* For master's, GRE General Test; for doctorate, GRE, M Div or MA. Additional exam requirements/recommendations for international students: required—TOEFL.

George Mason University, College of Humanities and Social Sciences, Interdisciplinary Studies Program, Fairfax, VA 22030. Offers computational social science (MAIS); energy and sustainability (MAIS); folklore studies (MAIS); higher education (MAIS); individualized studies (MAIS); religion, culture, and values (MAIS); social entrepreneurship (MAIS); social justice and human rights (MAIS); war and the military in society (MAIS); women and gender studies (MAIS). *Degree requirements:* For master's, thesis or alternative, experiential learning (for some programs). *Entrance requirements:* Additional exam requirements/recommendations for international students: required—TOEFL (minimum score 575 paper-based; 88 iBT), IELTS (minimum score 6.5), PTE (minimum score 59). Electronic applications accepted.

Georgetown University, Graduate School of Arts and Sciences, School of Continuing Studies, Washington, DC 20057. Offers American studies (MALS); applied intelligence (MPS); Catholic studies (MALS); classical civilizations (MALS); emergency and disaster management (MPS); ethics and the professions (MALS); global strategic communications (MPS); hospitality management (MPS); human resources management (MPS); humanities (MALS); individualized study (MALS); integrated marketing communications (MPS); international affairs (MALS); Islam and Muslim-Christian relations (MALS); journalism (MPS); liberal studies (DLS); literature and society (MALS); medieval and early modern European studies (MALS); public relations and corporate communications (MPS); real estate (MPS); religious studies (MALS); social and public policy (MALS); sports industry management (MPS); systems engineering management (MPS); technology management (MPS); the theory and practice of American democracy (MALS); urban and regional planning (MPS); visual culture (MALS). *Entrance requirements:* Additional exam requirements/recommendations for international students: required—TOEFL.

The George Washington University, Columbian College of Arts and Sciences, Department of Religion, Washington, DC 20052. Offers Islam (MA), including Hinduism and Islam. *Program availability:* Part-time, evening/weekend. *Degree requirements:* For master's, one foreign language, comprehensive exam, thesis. *Entrance requirements:* For master's, GRE General Test, interview, minimum GPA of 3.0. Additional exam requirements/recommendations for international students: required—TOEFL (minimum score 550 paper-based; 80 iBT). Electronic applications accepted.

Georgia State University, College of Arts and Sciences, Department of Religious Studies, Atlanta, GA 30302-4089. Offers MA. *Program availability:* Part-time. *Faculty:* 6 full-time (2 women), 1 part-time/adjunct (0 women). *Students:* 12 full-time (7 women), 4 part-time (2 women); includes 9 minority (8 Black or African American, non-Hispanic/Latino; 1 Hispanic/Latino). Average age 42. 15 applicants, 87% accepted, 9 enrolled. In 2019, 4 master's awarded. *Entrance requirements:* For master's, GRE. Additional exam requirements/recommendations for international students: required—TOEFL (minimum score 79 iBT). *Application deadline:* For fall admission, 2/1 priority date for domestic and international students. Application fee: $50. Electronic applications accepted. *Expenses: Tuition, area resident:* Full-time $7164; part-time $398 per credit hour. Tuition, state resident: full-time $7164; part-time $398 per credit hour. Tuition, nonresident: full-time $22,662; part-time $1259 per credit hour. *International tuition:* $22,662 full-time. *Required fees:* $2128; $312 per credit hour. Tuition and fees vary according to course load and program. *Financial support:* In 2019–20, research assistantships with full tuition reimbursements (averaging $5,000 per year), teaching assistantships with full tuition reimbursements (averaging $6,000 per year) were awarded; career-related internships or fieldwork, health care benefits, and unspecified assistantships also available. Financial award application deadline: 2/1; financial award applicants required to submit FAFSA. *Unit head:* Dr. Molly Basset, Chair, 404-413-6134, Fax: 404-413-6124, E-mail: mbassett@gsu.edu. *Application contact:* Dr. Molly Basset, Chair, 404-413-6134, Fax: 404-413-6124, E-mail: mbassett@gsu.edu.
Website: http://religiousstudies.gsu.edu/graduate/

Gordon-Conwell Theological Seminary, Graduate and Professional Programs, South Hamilton, MA 01982. Offers Biblical languages (MABL); church history (MACH); counseling (MACO); ministry (D Min); missions/evangelism (MAME); New Testament (MANT); Old Testament (MAOT); religion (MAR); theology (M Div, MATH, Th M, Th D). *Accreditation:* ACIPE; ATS (one or more programs are accredited). *Program availability:* Part-time, evening/weekend. *Degree requirements:* For master's, one foreign language, thesis optional; for doctorate, 2 foreign languages, thesis/dissertation. *Entrance requirements:* For master's, minimum GPA of 2.5; for doctorate, minimum GPA of 3.0.

Grace College of Divinity, Graduate Program, Fayetteville, NC 28314. Offers MCL. *Expenses: Tuition:* Full-time $5040; part-time $280 per credit hour. *Required fees:* $110; $110 per unit. $50 per semester. One-time fee: $10. Tuition and fees vary according to degree level.

Graceland University, Community of Christ Seminary, Independence, MO 64050. Offers MAR. *Program availability:* Evening/weekend. *Entrance requirements:* For master's, minimum cumulative GPA of 3.0. Additional exam requirements/recommendations for international students: required—TOEFL (minimum score 550 paper-based; 80 iBT), WES evaluation of transcripts. Electronic applications accepted. *Expenses:* Contact institution.

Graduate Theological Union, Graduate Programs, Berkeley, CA 94709-1212. Offers art and religion (MA, PhD, Th D); biblical languages (MA); Biblical studies (PhD, Th D); biblical studies (MA); Buddhist studies (MA); Christian spirituality (MA, PhD, Th D); cultural and historical studies of religions (MA, PhD, Th D); ethics and social theory (PhD, Th D); history (MA, PhD, Th D); homiletics (MA, PhD, Th D); interdisciplinary studies (PhD, Th D); Jewish studies (MA, PhD, Th D, Certificate); liturgical studies (MA, PhD, Th D); Near Eastern religions (PhD, Th D); Orthodox Christian studies (MA); religion and psychology (MA, PhD, Th D); religion and society/ethics and social theory (MA); systematic and philosophical theology (MA, PhD, Th D). *Accreditation:* ATS. Terminal master's awarded for partial completion of doctoral program. *Degree requirements:* For master's, one foreign language, thesis; for doctorate, one foreign language, comprehensive exam, thesis/dissertation. *Entrance requirements:* For master's, GRE General Test; for doctorate, GRE General Test, MA or M Div. Additional exam requirements/recommendations for international students: required—TOEFL. Electronic applications accepted.

Grand Rapids Theological Seminary of Cornerstone University, Graduate Programs, Grand Rapids, MI 49525-5897. Offers academic (M Div); chaplaincy ministries (M Div); Christian formation (MA); counseling (MA); formation and soul care ministries (M Div); intercultural ministries (M Div); interdisciplinary studies (MA); New Testament (Th M); Old Testament (Th M); pastoral ministries (M Div); small group and discipleship ministries (M Div); student and family ministries (M Div). *Accreditation:* ATS. *Program availability:* Part-time, evening/weekend, 100% online, blended/hybrid learning. *Entrance requirements:* Additional exam requirements/recommendations for international students: required—TOEFL (minimum score 577 paper-based; 90 iBT), IELTS (minimum score 7). Electronic applications accepted.

Hardin-Simmons University, Graduate School, Logsdon Seminary, Program in Religion, Abilene, TX 79698-0001. Offers MA. *Program availability:* Part-time. *Degree requirements:* For master's, one foreign language, comprehensive exam, thesis or alternative. *Entrance requirements:* For master's, minimum undergraduate GPA of 3.0 in major, 2.7 overall; 18 hours of course work in religious studies; interview. Additional exam requirements/recommendations for international students: required—TOEFL (minimum score 550 paper-based; 79 iBT). Electronic applications accepted. *Expenses:* Contact institution.

Harrison Middleton University, Graduate Program, Tempe, AZ 85282. Offers education (MA, Ed D); humanities (MA); imaginative literature (MA); interdisciplinary studies (DA); jurisprudence (MA); natural science (MA); philosophy and religion (MA); social science (MA). *Program availability:* Part-time, evening/weekend, online learning. *Degree requirements:* For master's and doctorate, capstone project. *Entrance requirements:* For master's, interview; for doctorate, 2 academic letters of reference, interview, essay. Additional exam requirements/recommendations for international students: required—TOEFL (minimum score 550 paper-based; 80 iBT). Electronic applications accepted.

Hartford Seminary, Graduate Programs, Hartford, CT 06105-2279. Offers Islamic studies (MA); ministry (D Min); religious studies (MA); spirituality (Certificate).

Accreditation: ATS (one or more programs are accredited). *Program availability:* Part-time, evening/weekend, online learning. *Degree requirements:* For master's, thesis optional, oral exam; for doctorate, thesis/dissertation, oral exam. *Entrance requirements:* For doctorate, experience in ministry, M Div. Additional exam requirements/recommendations for international students: required—TOEFL (minimum score 550 paper-based; 80 iBT).

Harvard University, Graduate School of Arts and Sciences, Committee on the Study of Religion, Cambridge, MA 02138. Offers PhD. *Degree requirements:* For doctorate, 2 foreign languages, thesis/dissertation. *Entrance requirements:* For doctorate, GRE General Test. Additional exam requirements/recommendations for international students: required—TOEFL.

Heritage Christian University, Graduate Programs, Florence, AL 35630. Offers counseling (MM); Greek (MA); ministry (MM); New Testament (MA). *Degree requirements:* For master's, practicum (MM), major research paper (MA). *Entrance requirements:* For master's, MAT or GRE, bachelor's degree in Bible from an accredited college or university, minimum GPA of 2.75, 3 letters of recommendation.

Hope International University, School of Graduate and Professional Studies, Programs in Ministry, Fullerton, CA 92831-3138. Offers Christian leadership (MCM); church music (MA); church music (Korean track) (MCM); church planting (MCM); intercultural studies (MCM); worship (MCM). *Program availability:* Part-time, evening/weekend, online learning. *Degree requirements:* For master's, thesis (for some programs), project. *Entrance requirements:* For master's, minimum GPA of 3.0, MCM program requires an undergraduate degree in music, 2 references. Additional exam requirements/recommendations for international students: required—TOEFL (minimum score 550 paper-based; 86 iBT); recommended—IELTS (minimum score 6.5). Electronic applications accepted. *Expenses:* Contact institution.

Iliff School of Theology, Graduate and Professional Programs, Denver, CO 80210-4798. Offers biblical studies (MA); church history (MA); religion (MA); religion and social change (MA); specialized ministry (MASM), including justice and peace, pastoral theology and care, religions leadership; theology (M Div, MTS, D Min, PhD), including Biblical studies (PhD), religion and psychological studies (PhD), religion and social change (PhD), theology, philosophy and culture (PhD); theology/ethics (MA). *Accreditation:* ACIPE; ATS. *Program availability:* Part-time, evening/weekend. *Degree requirements:* For master's, one foreign language, thesis (for some programs); for doctorate, 2 foreign languages, comprehensive exam, thesis/dissertation. *Entrance requirements:* For master's, minimum GPA of 3.0, writing sample, references; for doctorate, GRE General Test, minimum GPA of 3.0, writing sample, letters of recommendation. Additional exam requirements/recommendations for international students: required—TOEFL (minimum score 550 paper-based). Electronic applications accepted.

Indiana University Bloomington, University Graduate School, College of Arts and Sciences, Department of Religious Studies, Bloomington, IN 47405-7005. Offers MA, PhD. *Program availability:* Part-time. Terminal master's awarded for partial completion of doctoral program. *Degree requirements:* For master's, one foreign language, thesis or alternative; for doctorate, 2 foreign languages, thesis/dissertation. *Entrance requirements:* For master's, GRE General Test; for doctorate, GRE, MA, writing sample. Additional exam requirements/recommendations for international students: required—TOEFL. Electronic applications accepted.

The Jewish Theological Seminary, The Graduate School, New York, NY 10027-4649. Offers ancient Judaism (MA, DHL, PhD); Bible and ancient Semitic languages (MA, DHL, PhD); interdepartmental studies (MA); Jewish art and visual culture (MA); Jewish gender and women's studies (MA); Jewish history (MA, DHL, PhD); Jewish literature (MA, DHL, PhD); Jewish philosophy (DHL); Jewish thought (MA, PhD); liturgy (MA, DHL, PhD); medieval Jewish studies (MA, DHL, PhD); Midrash (DHL); Midrash and scriptural interpretation (MA, PhD); modern Jewish studies (MA, DHL, PhD); Talmud and rabbinics (MA, DHL, PhD); MA/MSW. *Accreditation:* ACIPE. *Program availability:* Part-time. Terminal master's awarded for partial completion of doctoral program. *Degree requirements:* For master's, one foreign language, comprehensive exam (for some programs), thesis (for some programs); for doctorate, 3 foreign languages, comprehensive exam (for some programs), thesis/dissertation. *Entrance requirements:* For master's, GRE or MAT, 3 letters of recommendation, writing sample; for doctorate, GRE or MAT, 3 letters of recommendation, writing research sample. Additional exam requirements/recommendations for international students: required—TOEFL.

John Carroll University, Graduate School, Department of Theology and Religious Studies, University Heights, OH 44118. Offers MA. *Program availability:* Part-time, evening/weekend. *Degree requirements:* For master's, research essay or thesis, foreign language proficiency. *Entrance requirements:* Additional exam requirements/recommendations for international students: required—TOEFL. *Application deadline:* Applications are processed on a rolling basis. Application fee: $0. Electronic applications accepted. *Financial support:* Scholarships/grants and unspecified assistantships available. Financial award applicants required to submit FAFSA. *Unit head:* Dr. Edward P. Hahnenberg, Chair, 216-397-1674, Fax: 216-397-4518, E-mail: ehahnenberg@jcu.edu. *Application contact:* Dr. Sheila E. McGinn, Program Coordinator, 216-397-4703, Fax: 216-397-4518, E-mail: smcginn@jcu.edu.
Website: https://jcu.edu/academics/trs/degree-programs/trs-ma-degree

Kentucky Christian University, Graduate School, Grayson, KY 41143-2205. Offers Biblical studies (MA); Christian leadership (MA). *Program availability:* Part-time. *Degree requirements:* For master's, comprehensive exam (for some programs), thesis optional. *Entrance requirements:* For master's, minimum cumulative GPA of 2.75 in major or 2.5 overall; 6 additional hours in Bible (for non-Biblical undergraduate majors). Additional exam requirements/recommendations for international students: required—TOEFL (minimum score 550 paper-based). Electronic applications accepted.

Knox Theological Seminary, Graduate Programs, Master of Arts Programs, Fort Lauderdale, FL 33308. Offers Biblical and theological studies (MA); Christian and classical studies (MA). *Accreditation:* ATS. *Program availability:* Part-time, evening/weekend. *Entrance requirements:* Additional exam requirements/recommendations for international students: required—TOEFL (minimum score 520 paper-based; 83 iBT), TWE (minimum score 5).

Lancaster Theological Seminary, Graduate and Professional Programs, Lancaster, PA 17603-2812. Offers biblical studies (MAR); Christian education (MAR); Christianity and the arts (MAR); church history (MAR); congregational life (MAR); lay leadership (Certificate); theological studies (M Div); theology (D Min); theology and ethics (MAR). *Accreditation:* ACIPE; ATS. *Degree requirements:* For doctorate, thesis/dissertation.

La Sierra University, School of Religion, Riverside, CA 92505. Offers pastoral ministry (M Div); religion (MA); religious education (MA); religious studies (MA). *Program availability:* Part-time. *Degree requirements:* For master's, one foreign language, thesis or alternative. *Entrance requirements:* For master's, GRE General Test, minimum GPA of 3.0.

Lee University, Programs in Religion, Cleveland, TN 37320-3450. Offers biblical studies (MA); ministry studies/leadership (MA); ministry studies/worship (MA); ministry studies/youth and family (MA); theological studies (MA), including ethics, religion. *Program availability:* Part-time, 100% online. *Faculty:* 12 full-time (3 women), 8 part-time/adjunct (0 women). *Students:* 32 full-time (13 women), 104 part-time (33 women); includes 74 minority (10 Black or African American, non-Hispanic/Latino; 60 Hispanic/Latino; 4 Two or more races, non-Hispanic/Latino), 5 international. Average age 38. 43 applicants, 79% accepted, 24 enrolled. In 2019, 15 master's awarded. *Degree requirements:* For master's, variable foreign language requirement, comprehensive exam (for some programs), thesis (for some programs). *Entrance requirements:* For master's, GRE or MAT (for biblical/theological studies only), minimum GPA of 3.0, 3 letters of recommendation, interview, official transcripts, essay. Additional exam requirements/recommendations for international students: required—TOEFL (minimum score 61 iBT). *Application deadline:* For fall admission, 4/1 priority date for domestic and international students; for spring admission, 10/1 priority date for domestic and international students. Applications are processed on a rolling basis. Application fee: $25. Electronic applications accepted. *Expenses:* Contact institution. *Financial support:* In 2019–20, 39 students received support, including 12 teaching assistantships (averaging $2,046 per year); career-related internships or fieldwork, Federal Work-Study, institutionally sponsored loans, scholarships/grants, and unspecified assistantships also available. Financial award application deadline: 3/1; financial award applicants required to submit FAFSA. *Unit head:* Dr. Lisa Long, Director, 423-303-5100, E-mail: llong@leeuniversity.edu. *Application contact:* Jeffery McGirt, Director of Graduate Enrollment, 423-614-8691, Fax: 423-614-8317, E-mail: jmcgirt@leeuniversity.edu.
Website: http://www.leeuniversity.edu/academics/graduate/

Liberty University, School of Divinity, Lynchburg, VA 24515. Offers Biblical exposition (MA); Biblical languages (M Div); Biblical studies (M Div, MA, MAR, Th M, D Min); chaplaincy (M Div, D Min); Christian apologetics (M Div, MA, MAR, Th M); Christian leadership and church ministries (M Div); Christian ministries (M Div); Christian ministry (MA); Christian thought (M Div); church history (M Div, MAR, Th M); community chaplaincy (M Div, MAR); discipleship (D Min); discipleship and church ministry (M Div, MAR, MCM); evangelism and church planting (MAR, MCM, D Min); expository preaching (D Min); global ministry (MA); global studies (M Div, MAR, MCM, MGS, Th M); healthcare chaplaincy (M Div); homiletics (M Div, MAR, Th M); leadership (M Div, MAR); marketplace chaplaincy (M Div, MCM); ministry leadership (Ed D); pastoral counseling (M Div, MA, MAR, D Min), including addictions and recovery (MA), crisis response and trauma (MA), discipleship and church ministries (MA), leadership (MA), life coaching (MA), marketplace chaplaincy (MA), marriage and family (MA), military resilience (MA), pastoral counseling (MA); pastoral leadership (D Min); pastoral ministries (M Div, M Serv Soc, MCM); religious education (MRE); sports chaplaincy (MA); theology (M Div, MAR, MTS, Th M); theology and apologetics (D Min, PhD); worship (M Div, MAR, MCM, D Min); youth and family ministries (M Div). *Program availability:* Part-time, online learning. *Students:* 2,691 full-time (814 women), 2,570 part-time (732 women); includes 1,484 minority (1,046 Black or African American, non-Hispanic/Latino; 33 American Indian or Alaska Native, non-Hispanic/Latino; 120 Asian, non-Hispanic/Latino; 167 Hispanic/Latino; 8 Native Hawaiian or other Pacific Islander, non-Hispanic/Latino; 110 Two or more races, non-Hispanic/Latino), 101 international. Average age 43. 4,508 applicants, 34% accepted, 952 enrolled. In 2019, 1,251 master's, 71 doctorates awarded. *Degree requirements:* For master's, 2 foreign languages, thesis (for some programs); for doctorate, 2 foreign languages, thesis/dissertation. *Entrance requirements:* For master's, minimum undergraduate GPA of 2.0; for doctorate, GRE General Test or MAT, minimum graduate GPA of 3.0. Additional exam requirements/recommendations for international students: required—TOEFL (minimum score 600 paper-based; 100 iBT). *Application deadline:* For fall admission, 6/1 for domestic students; for spring admission, 11/1 for domestic students. Applications are processed on a rolling basis. Application fee: $50. Electronic applications accepted. *Expenses:* Contact institution. *Financial support:* Teaching assistantships with tuition reimbursements, career-related internships or fieldwork, and Federal Work-Study available. Financial award applicants required to submit FAFSA. *Unit head:* Dr. Troy Temple, Interim Dean, School of Divinity, E-mail: divinity@liberty.edu. *Application contact:* Jay Bridge, Director of Graduate Admissions, 800-424-9595, Fax: 800-628-7977, E-mail: gradadmissions@liberty.edu.
Website: https://www.liberty.edu/divinity/

Lincoln Christian University, Graduate Programs, Lincoln, IL 62656-2167. Offers Bible and theology (MA); Biblical studies (MA); church history/historical theology (MA); counseling (MA); formative worship (MA); intercultural studies (MA); ministry (MA); organizational leadership (MA); philosophy and apologetics (MA); spiritual formation (MA); theology (MA). *Program availability:* Online learning. *Entrance requirements:* For master's, minimum cumulative GPA of 2.5 in undergraduate degree studies. Additional exam requirements/recommendations for international students: required—TOEFL (minimum score 550 paper-based); recommended—IELTS (minimum score 6). Application fee is waived when completed online.

Loma Linda University, School of Religion, Program in Religion and Society, Loma Linda, CA 92350. Offers MA. *Degree requirements:* For master's, comprehensive exam, thesis optional. *Entrance requirements:* Additional exam requirements/recommendations for international students: required—TOEFL. Electronic applications accepted.

Louisville Presbyterian Theological Seminary, Graduate and Professional Programs, Louisville, KY 40205-1798. Offers Bible (MAR); divinity (M Div); ministry (D Min); religious thought (MAR); JD/M Div; M Div/MBA; M Div/MSSW. *Accreditation:* AAMFT/COAMFTE (one or more programs are accredited); ACIPE; ATS (one or more programs are accredited). *Program availability:* Part-time. *Faculty:* 17 full-time (8 women), 12 part-time/adjunct (6 women). *Students:* 94 full-time (58 women), 58 part-time (37 women); includes 58 minority (44 Black or African American, non-Hispanic/Latino; 4 Asian, non-Hispanic/Latino; 6 Hispanic/Latino; 1 Native Hawaiian or other Pacific Islander, non-Hispanic/Latino; 3 Two or more races, non-Hispanic/Latino), 2 international. Average age 41. In 2019, 25 master's, 10 doctorates awarded. *Degree requirements:* For master's, thesis (for some programs); for doctorate, thesis/dissertation. *Entrance requirements:* For master's, Accredited BA; for doctorate, MDiv or equivalent, M Div. Additional exam requirements/recommendations for international students: required—TOEFL (minimum score 550 paper-based). *Application deadline:* For fall admission, 6/1 priority date for domestic students, 2/1 priority date for international students; for spring admission, 3/4 priority date for domestic students. Applications are processed on a rolling basis. Application fee: $50. Electronic applications accepted. *Expenses: Tuition:* Full-time $11,502; part-time $426 per credit hour. *Required fees:* $336; $336 per semester. $168 per semester. *Financial support:* Career-related internships or fieldwork, Federal Work-Study, institutionally sponsored loans, and scholarships/grants available. Financial award application deadline: 2/1. *Unit head:* Dr. Debra Mumford, Dean, 502-895-3411, Fax: 502-895-1096, E-mail: dmumford@lpts.edu. *Application contact:* Rev. Sandra Moon, Director of Admissions, 502-895-3411, Fax: 502-895-1096, E-mail: smoon@lpts.edu.
Website: http://www.lpts.edu/

Lutheran Theological Seminary Saskatoon, Graduate and Professional Programs, Saskatoon, SK S7N 0X3, Canada. Offers Biblical studies (MTS); church history (MTS); ethics/church and society (MTS); history of Christianity (STM); New Testament (STM);

Religion

Old Testament (STM); pastoral studies (STM); pastoral theology (MTS); systematic theology (MTS); systematic theology and philosophy of religion (STM); theology (M Div, D Div). *Accreditation:* ATS. *Program availability:* Part-time. *Degree requirements:* For master's, thesis.

Luther Rice College & Seminary, Graduate Programs, Lithonia, GA 30038-2454. Offers apologetics (MA); Bible languages (M Div); Biblical counseling (MA); Christian ministry (M Div, D Min); Christian studies (MA); leadership (MA). *Program availability:* Part-time, evening/weekend, online learning. *Degree requirements:* For doctorate, thesis/dissertation. *Entrance requirements:* For master's, bachelor's degree or equivalent; for doctorate, M Div. Additional exam requirements/recommendations for international students: required—TOEFL (minimum score 550 paper-based). Electronic applications accepted.

Maranatha Baptist University, Master of Arts in English Bible Program, Watertown, WI 53094. Offers MA. *Program availability:* Part-time, 100% online. *Entrance requirements:* For master's, BA or BS. *Expenses: Tuition:* Full-time $5940; part-time $3960 per credit. *Required fees:* $25 per credit. Tuition and fees vary according to degree level and program.

McGill University, Faculty of Graduate and Postdoctoral Studies, Faculty of Religious Studies, Montréal, QC H3A 2T5, Canada. Offers MA, STM, PhD. *Accreditation:* ATS.

McMaster University, School of Graduate Studies, Faculty of Social Sciences, Department of Religious Studies, Hamilton, ON L8S 4M2, Canada. Offers MA, PhD. *Program availability:* Part-time. *Degree requirements:* For master's, one foreign language, thesis; for doctorate, 2 foreign languages, comprehensive exam, thesis/dissertation. *Entrance requirements:* For master's, minimum B+ average. Additional exam requirements/recommendations for international students: required—TOEFL (minimum score 580 paper-based).

Memorial University of Newfoundland, School of Graduate Studies, Department of Religious Studies, St. John's, NL A1C 5S7, Canada. Offers MA. *Program availability:* Part-time. *Degree requirements:* For master's, one foreign language, thesis. *Entrance requirements:* For master's, honors degree in religious studies or equivalent. Electronic applications accepted.

Milligan University, Emmanuel Christian Seminary at Milligan College, Milligan College, TN 37682. Offers Christian care and counseling (M Div); Christian education (M Div); Christian ministries (MACM, Graduate Certificate); Christian ministry (M Div); Christian theology (M Div, MAR); church history (MAR); church history/historical theology (M Div); general studies (M Div); ministry (D Min); New Testament (M Div, MAR); Old Testament (M Div, MAR); urban ministry (M Div); world missions (M Div). *Accreditation:* ACIPE; ATS. *Program availability:* Part-time, blended/hybrid learning. *Faculty:* 12 full-time (1 woman), 5 part-time/adjunct (0 women). *Students:* 70 full-time (28 women), 70 part-time (26 women); includes 19 minority (9 Black or African American, non-Hispanic/Latino; 3 American Indian or Alaska Native, non-Hispanic/Latino; 2 Asian, non-Hispanic/Latino; 5 Hispanic/Latino), 8 international. Average age 34. 109 applicants, 90% accepted, 64 enrolled. In 2019, 21 master's, 3 doctorates awarded. *Degree requirements:* For master's, 2 foreign languages, thesis or alternative, portfolio; for doctorate, thesis/dissertation. *Entrance requirements:* For master's, undergraduate degree and supporting transcripts, essay/personal statement, professional recommendations, interview; for doctorate, M Div or equivalent, essay/personal statement, professional recommendations. Additional exam requirements/recommendations for international students: required—TOEFL (minimum score 550 paper-based, 79 iBT) or IELTS (6.5). *Application deadline:* For fall admission, 8/1 for domestic students, 6/1 for international students; for spring admission, 12/15 for domestic students, 8/1 for international students. Applications are processed on a rolling basis. Application fee: $30. Electronic applications accepted. *Expenses:* 36 - 90 hr programs: $485/hr; $75 one-time records fee; MDIV (90 Hrs)/MAR (58 Hrs) $325/semester (technology and activity fee); MACM (48 Hrs)/DMIN (36 Hrs) $250/semester (technology and activity fees). *Financial support:* Scholarships/grants and unspecified assistantships available. Financial award application deadline: 12/1; financial award applicants required to submit FAFSA. *Unit head:* Dr. Rollin Ramsaran, Academic Dean, Emmanuel Christian Seminary, 423-461-1524, Fax: 423-926-6198, E-mail: raramsaran@milligan.edu. *Application contact:* Lauren Gullett, Director of Admissions and Recruitment for Emmanuel Christian Seminary, 423-461-1535, Fax: 423-926-6198, E-mail: lwgullett@milligan.edu.
Website: http://ecs.milligan.edu/

Missouri State University, Graduate College, College of Humanities and Public Affairs, Department of Religious Studies, Springfield, MO 65897. Offers MA, Certificate. *Program availability:* Part-time. *Degree requirements:* For master's, one foreign language, comprehensive exam, thesis or alternative. *Entrance requirements:* For master's, GRE, minimum GPA of 3.2. Additional exam requirements/recommendations for international students: required—TOEFL (minimum score 550 paper-based; 79 iBT), IELTS (minimum score 6). Electronic applications accepted. *Expenses: Tuition, area resident:* Full-time $2600; part-time $1735 per credit hour. Tuition, nonresident: full-time $5240; part-time $3495 per credit hour. *International tuition:* $5240 full-time. *Required fees:* $530; $438 per credit hour. Tuition and fees vary according to class time, course level, course load, degree level, campus/location and program.

Moody Theological Seminary–Michigan, Graduate Programs, Plymouth, MI 48170. Offers Bible (Graduate Certificate); Christian education (MA); counseling psychology (MA); divinity (M Div); theological studies (MA). *Accreditation:* ATS. *Program availability:* Part-time, evening/weekend. *Degree requirements:* For master's, one foreign language, thesis.

Mount St. Joseph University, Graduate Program in Religious Studies, Cincinnati, OH 45233-1670. Offers religious studies (MA); spirituality and wellness (Certificate). *Program availability:* Part-time, evening/weekend. *Degree requirements:* For master's, comprehensive exam, 36 hours of credit, pastoral PRAXIS component (3 credit hours), integrating project (3 credit hours). *Entrance requirements:* For master's, undergraduate transcript with minimum overall GPA of 3.0, 3 letters of recommendation from professional colleagues, 3-page essay, interview with the Graduate Admissions Committee, current work resume. Additional exam requirements/recommendations for international students: required—TOEFL (minimum score 560 paper-based; 83 iBT). Electronic applications accepted. *Expenses:* Contact institution.

Mount Saint Mary's University, Graduate Division, Los Angeles, CA 90049. Offers business administration (MBA); counseling psychology (MS); creative writing (MFA); education (MS, Certificate); film and television (MFA); health policy and management (MS); humanities (MA); nursing (MSN, Certificate); physical therapy (DPT); religious studies (MA). *Program availability:* Part-time, evening/weekend. *Entrance requirements:* Additional exam requirements/recommendations for international students: required—TOEFL. Electronic applications accepted. *Expenses: Tuition:* Full-time $18,648; part-time $9324 per year. *Required fees:* $540; $540 per unit.

Naropa University, Graduate Programs, Program in Religious Studies, Boulder, CO 80302-6697. Offers MA. *Degree requirements:* For master's, comprehensive exam, thesis. *Entrance requirements:* For master's, interview; transcripts; letter of interest; resume/curriculum vitae with pertinent academic, employment and volunteer activity; 2

letters of recommendation. Additional exam requirements/recommendations for international students: required—TOEFL (minimum score 550 paper-based; 80 iBT). Electronic applications accepted. *Expenses:* Contact institution.

Naropa University, Graduate Programs, Program in Religious Studies with Language, Boulder, CO 80302-6697. Offers MA. *Degree requirements:* For master's, comprehensive exam, thesis. *Entrance requirements:* For master's, interview; transcripts; resume/curriculum vitae with pertinent academic, employment and volunteer activity; 2 letters of recommendation; letter of interest. Additional exam requirements/recommendations for international students: required—TOEFL (minimum score 550 paper-based; 80 iBT). Electronic applications accepted. *Expenses:* Contact institution.

Nashotah House Theological Seminary, Graduate Programs, Nashotah, WI 53058-9793. Offers Anglican studies (Certificate); Biblical studies (STM); Christian spirituality (STM); church history (STM); liturgy (STM); ministry (M Div, MM); pastoral ministry (MPM); theological studies (MTS); theology (STM, D Min). *Accreditation:* ACIPE; ATS (one or more programs are accredited). *Program availability:* Part-time. *Degree requirements:* For master's, thesis optional. *Entrance requirements:* For master's and Certificate, GRE General Test or MAT, interview, 3 recommendations. Additional exam requirements/recommendations for international students: required—TOEFL. Electronic applications accepted. *Expenses:* Contact institution.

New Saint Andrews College, Graduate School, Moscow, ID 83843. Offers classical Christian studies (Graduate Certificate); creative writing (MFA); theology and letters (MA). *Program availability:* Part-time, blended/hybrid learning. *Degree requirements:* For master's, comprehensive exam (for some programs), thesis (for some programs), final oral exam. *Entrance requirements:* For master's, GRE, 2 letters of recommendation; for Graduate Certificate, GRE, bachelor's degree, essays, 2 letters of recommendation. Electronic applications accepted. *Expenses: Tuition:* Full-time $8800; part-time $550 per credit.

New York University, Graduate School of Arts and Science, Program in Religious Studies, New York, NY 10012-1019. Offers MA. *Program availability:* Part-time. *Degree requirements:* For master's, one foreign language, thesis. *Entrance requirements:* For master's, GRE General Test. Additional exam requirements/recommendations for international students: required—TOEFL, IELTS.

New York University, Graduate School of Arts and Science, XE: Experimental Humanities & Social Engagement, New York, NY 10012-1019. Offers humanities and social thought (MA); religion (Advanced Certificate); social theory (Advanced Certificate). *Program availability:* Part-time. *Degree requirements:* For master's, thesis, comprehensive exam or essay. *Entrance requirements:* For master's, GRE General Test; for Advanced Certificate, master's degree. Additional exam requirements/recommendations for international students: required—TOEFL, IELTS.

Northern Seminary, Graduate and Professional Programs, Lombard, IL 60148-5698. Offers Biblical studies (M Div); Christian community development (MA, D Min); Christian ministry (MACM); contextual theology (D Min); missional church ministry (M Div); New Testament (M Div, MANT); New Testament context (D Min); Old Testament (M Div); preaching (D Min); theology (M Div); theology and mission (MA); urban leadership (MA); worship (M Div, MAW). *Program availability:* Part-time, evening/weekend. *Degree requirements:* For master's, thesis (for some programs); for doctorate, thesis/dissertation. *Entrance requirements:* For master's, writing test, all official transcripts, letter of reference from church, 3 letters of reference, autobiographical statement (400 words or more); for doctorate, M Div, 3 years in the ministry post-M Div, 3 letters of reference. Additional exam requirements/recommendations for international students: required—TOEFL (minimum score 550 paper-based). Electronic applications accepted.

Northwestern University, The Graduate School, Judd A. and Marjorie Weinberg College of Arts and Sciences, Department of Religious Studies, Evanston, IL 60208. Offers PhD.

Northwestern University, School of Professional Studies, Program in Liberal Studies, Evanston, IL 60208. Offers American studies (MA); history (MA); religious and ethical studies (MA). *Program availability:* Part-time, evening/weekend.

Northwest Nazarene University, NNU Graduate School of Theology, Nampa, ID 83686-5897. Offers leadership and formation (MA); missional leadership (M Div); pastoral ministry (MA); spiritual formation (M Div); youth, children, and family ministry (M Div). *Program availability:* Part-time, online only, 100% online. *Degree requirements:* For master's, 2.5 cumulative GPA. *Entrance requirements:* For master's, minimum GPA of 2.5; two recommendations, official transcripts. Additional exam requirements/recommendations for international students: required—TOEFL (minimum score 85 iBT). Electronic applications accepted. *Expenses:* Contact institution.

Nyack College, College of Bible and Christian Ministry, New York, NY 10004. Offers ancient Judaism and Christian origins (MA). *Program availability:* Part-time, evening/weekend, 100% online, blended/hybrid learning. In 2019, 1 master's awarded. *Degree requirements:* For master's, 2 foreign languages, comprehensive exam. *Entrance requirements:* For master's, GRE, proficiency exam in Biblical Hebrew, essay, Christian experience statement, pastoral reference, academic references, writing sample. Additional exam requirements/recommendations for international students: required—TOEFL (minimum score 550 paper-based; 80 iBT). *Application deadline:* Applications are processed on a rolling basis. Application fee: $30. Electronic applications accepted. *Expenses:* $585 per credit. *Financial support:* Applicants required to submit FAFSA. *Unit head:* Dr. Steven Notley, Director, 646-378-6148, E-mail: steven.notley@nyack.edu. *Application contact:* Dr. Steven Notley, Director, 646-378-6148, E-mail: steven.notley@nyack.edu.

Oblate School of Theology, Graduate and Professional Programs, San Antonio, TX 78216-6693. Offers African-American pastoral leadership (D Min); divinity (M Div); pastoral leadership (D Min); pastoral ministry (MAP Min); pastoral studies (Certificate); spiritual formation in the local community (D Min); spirituality (MA Sp, PhD); spirituality and ministry (D Min); theology (MA Th); U.S. Hispanic/Latino ministry (D Min); M Div/MA Th. *Accreditation:* ACIPE; ATS (one or more programs are accredited). *Program availability:* Part-time, 100% online, blended/hybrid learning. *Faculty:* 21 full-time (5 women), 4 part-time/adjunct (0 women). *Students:* 89 full-time (9 women), 54 part-time (31 women); includes 77 minority (11 Black or African American, non-Hispanic/Latino; 8 Asian, non-Hispanic/Latino; 57 Hispanic/Latino; 1 Two or more races, non-Hispanic/Latino), 24 international. Average age 39. In 2019, 24 master's, 1 doctorate awarded. *Degree requirements:* For master's, comprehensive exam (for some programs), thesis (for some programs), practicum; for doctorate, one foreign language, comprehensive exam, thesis/dissertation, paper, practicum. *Entrance requirements:* For master's, MAT, interview, prerequisite course work in theology or religious studies and philosophy, minimum GPA of 2.5; for doctorate, D Min, M Div, MA Th, MA Sp, MA PM. Additional exam requirements/recommendations for international students: required—TOEFL (minimum score 71 iBT). *Application deadline:* For fall admission, 6/30 priority date for domestic and international students; for winter admission, 11/30 for domestic and international students; for spring admission, 11/30 for domestic and international students; for summer admission, 4/30 for domestic and international students. Applications are processed on a rolling basis. Application fee: $65. Electronic applications accepted. *Expenses:* Contact institution. *Financial support:* In 2019–20, 25 students received support. Scholarships/grants available. Support available to part-time students. Financial award application deadline: 8/15; financial award applicants required to submit FAFSA. *Unit head:* Dr. R. Scott Woodward, Academic Dean, 210-341-1366, Fax: 210-341-4519, E-mail: rsw@ost.edu. *Application contact:* Brenda Reyna, Registrar, 210-341-1366 Ext. 226, Fax: 210-341-4519, E-mail: registrar@ost.edu.

Olivet Nazarene University, Graduate School, Division of Religion, Bourbonnais, IL 60914. Offers biblical literature (MA); religion (MA); theology (MA). *Program availability:* Part-time. *Degree requirements:* For master's, thesis or alternative.

Omega Graduate School, Graduate Programs, Dayton, TN 37321-6736. Offers family life education (M Litt); integration of religion and society (D Phil); organizational leadership (M Litt). *Entrance requirements:* For master's, official transcripts, three letters of recommendation, bachelor's degree or its equivalent, minimum undergraduate GPA of 3.0, minimum of 3 years of professional experience; for doctorate, official transcripts, three letters of recommendation, master's degree with minimum GPA of 3.0, minimum of 5 years of professional experience. *Expenses:* Contact institution.

Pacific School of Religion, Graduate and Professional Programs, Berkeley, CA 94709-1323. Offers M Div, MA, MTS, D Min, PhD, Th D, CAPS, CMS, CSS, CTS. *Accreditation:* ACIPE; ATS (one or more programs are accredited). *Program availability:* Part-time. *Degree requirements:* For master's, one foreign language, thesis (for some programs); for doctorate, thesis/dissertation. *Entrance requirements:* For master's, minimum GPA of 3.0; for doctorate, M Div, minimum GPA of 3.0 (D Min); for other advanced degree, M Div, minimum GPA of 3.0 (CAPS). Additional exam requirements/recommendations for international students: required—TOEFL (minimum score 550 paper-based). Electronic applications accepted.

Pepperdine University, Seaver College, Malibu, CA 90263. Offers business (MS), including accounting; communication (MFA), including cinematic media production; humanities (MA, MFA), including American studies (MA), writing for screen and television (MFA); religion (M Div, MA, MS), including ministry (MS), religion (M Div, MA); JD/M Div. *Entrance requirements:* For master's, GRE General Test. Additional exam requirements/recommendations for international students: required—TOEFL. *Expenses:* Contact institution.

Princeton Theological Seminary, Graduate and Professional Programs, Princeton, NJ 08542-0803. Offers M Div, MA, Th M, D Min, PhD. *Accreditation:* ACIPE; ATS. *Program availability:* Part-time. Terminal master's awarded for partial completion of doctoral program. *Degree requirements:* For doctorate, 2 foreign languages, thesis/dissertation, comprehensive exam (PhD), French and German. *Entrance requirements:* For doctorate, GRE General Test. Additional exam requirements/recommendations for international students: required—TOEFL. Electronic applications accepted.

Princeton University, Graduate School, Department of Religion, Princeton, NJ 08544-1019. Offers PhD. *Degree requirements:* For doctorate, variable foreign language requirement, comprehensive exam, thesis/dissertation. *Entrance requirements:* For doctorate, GRE General Test. Additional exam requirements/recommendations for international students: required—TOEFL (minimum score 600 paper-based). Electronic applications accepted.

Queen's University at Kingston, School of Graduate Studies, Faculty of Arts and Science, School of Religion, Kingston, ON K7L 3N6, Canada. Offers MA. *Degree requirements:* For master's, one foreign language, essay. *Entrance requirements:* For master's, honors BA in religious studies or equivalent. Additional exam requirements/recommendations for international students: required—TOEFL (minimum score 600 paper-based).

Reformed Theological Seminary–Charlotte Campus, Graduate and Professional Programs, Charlotte, NC 28226-6318. Offers biblical studies (MA); ministry (D Min); pastoral ministry (M Div); theological studies (MA). *Program availability:* Part-time. *Degree requirements:* For master's, comprehensive exam; for doctorate, thesis/dissertation. *Entrance requirements:* For master's, minimum GPA of 2.6; for doctorate, minimum GPA of 3.0. Additional exam requirements/recommendations for international students: required—TOEFL (minimum score 550 paper-based). Electronic applications accepted.

Reformed Theological Seminary–Houston Campus, Graduate Program, Houston, TX 77024. Offers MA. Electronic applications accepted.

Reformed Theological Seminary–Jackson Campus, Graduate and Professional Programs, Jackson, MS 39209-3004. Offers Bible, theology, and missions (Certificate); Biblical exegesis (M Div); biblical studies (MA); Christian education (MA); counseling (M Div); marriage and family therapy (MA); ministry (D Min); missions (M Div, MA, D Min); theological studies (MA). *Accreditation:* AAMFT/COAMFTE (one or more programs are accredited); ATS (one or more programs are accredited). *Degree requirements:* For master's, thesis (for some programs), fieldwork; for doctorate, 2 foreign languages, thesis/dissertation. *Entrance requirements:* For master's, minimum GPA of 2.6; for doctorate, minimum GPA of 3.0. Additional exam requirements/recommendations for international students: required—TOEFL.

Reformed Theological Seminary–Washington D.C., Graduate and Professional Programs, McLean, VA 22102. Offers Bible (M Div); biblical studies (MA); practical theology (M Div); religion (MA); theology (M Div). *Program availability:* Part-time, evening/weekend. *Degree requirements:* For master's, variable foreign language requirement, comprehensive exam (for some programs), integrative paper. *Entrance requirements:* For master's, minimum undergraduate GPA of 2.6. Additional exam requirements/recommendations for international students: required—TOEFL (minimum score 550 paper-based), TWE. Electronic applications accepted. *Expenses:* Contact institution.

Regent University, Graduate School, Robertson School of Government, Virginia Beach, VA 23464. Offers government (MA), including American government, healthcare policy and ethics (MA, MPA), international relations, law and public policy, national security studies, political communication, political theory, religion and politics; national security studies (MA), including cybersecurity, homeland security, international security, Middle East politics; public administration (MPA), including emergency management and homeland security, federal government, general public administration, healthcare policy and ethics (MA, MPA), law, nonprofit administration and faith-based organizations, public leadership and management, servant leadership. *Program availability:* Part-time, evening/weekend, 100% online, blended/hybrid learning. *Faculty:* 5 full-time (1 woman), 19 part-time/adjunct (2 women). *Students:* 36 full-time (22 women), 159 part-time (89 women); includes 82 minority (52 Black or African American, non-Hispanic/Latino; 2 American Indian or Alaska Native, non-Hispanic/Latino; 2 Asian, non-Hispanic/Latino; 23 Hispanic/Latino; 3 Two or more races, non-Hispanic/Latino), 4 international. Average age 36. 181 applicants, 70% accepted, 75 enrolled. In 2019, 58 master's awarded. *Degree requirements:* For master's, thesis optional, internship. *Entrance requirements:* For master's, GRE General Test or LSAT, personal essay, writing sample, resume, college transcripts. Additional exam requirements/recommendations for international students: required—TOEFL (minimum score 577 paper-based). *Application deadline:* For fall admission, 5/1 priority date for domestic students; for spring admission, 11/1 priority date for domestic students. Applications are processed on a rolling basis. Application fee: $50. Electronic applications accepted. *Expenses:* Contact institution. *Financial support:* In 2019–20, 132 students received support. Career-related internships or fieldwork, scholarships/grants, and unspecified assistantships available. Support available to part-time students. Financial award applicants required to submit FAFSA. *Unit head:* Dr. Stephen Perry, Interim Dean, 757-352-4082, E-mail: sperry@regent.edu. *Application contact:* Heidi Cece, Assistant Vice President for Enrollment Management, 800-373-5504, Fax: 757-352-4381, E-mail: admissions@regent.edu.
Website: https://www.regent.edu/robertson-school-of-government/

Regent University, Graduate School, School of Divinity, Virginia Beach, VA 23464. Offers Christian spirituality and formation (MA); divinity (M Div), including Biblical studies (M Div, MTS, Th M, PhD), chaplain ministry, Christian theology (M Div, MTS, Th M, PhD), church and ministry (M Div, MA), history of Christianity (M Div, MTS, Th M, PhD), inter-cultural studies (M Div, MA), interdisciplinary studies (M Div, MA, MTS), marketplace ministry (M Div, MA), missional discipleship, practical healing ministry (M Div, MA), worship and media (M Div, MA); leadership and renewal (D Min), including Christian leadership and renewal, clinical pastoral education, community transformation, military ministry, ministry leadership coaching; practical theology (MA), including church and ministry (M Div, MA), cosmogony, inter-cultural studies (M Div, MA), interdisciplinary studies (M Div, MA, MTS), marketplace ministry (M Div, MA), practical healing ministry (M Div, MA), worship and media (M Div, MA); renewal theology (PhD), including Biblical studies (M Div, MTS, Th M, PhD), Christian theology (M Div, MTS, Th M, PhD), history of Christianity (M Div, MTS, Th M, PhD), practical theology; theological studies (MTS), including Biblical studies (M Div, MTS, Th M, PhD), Christian theology (M Div, MTS, Th M, PhD), history of Christianity (M Div, MTS, Th M, PhD), interdisciplinary studies (M Div, MA, MTS); theology (Th M), including Biblical studies (M Div, MTS, Th M, PhD), Christian theology (M Div, MTS, Th M, PhD), history of Christianity (M Div, MTS, Th M, PhD). *Accreditation:* ACIPE; ATS. *Program availability:* Part-time, evening/weekend, 100% online, blended/hybrid learning. *Faculty:* 15 full-time (3 women), 58 part-time/adjunct (10 women). *Students:* 303 full-time (119 women), 813 part-time (403 women); includes 632 minority (509 Black or African American, non-Hispanic/Latino; 3 American Indian or Alaska Native, non-Hispanic/Latino; 31 Asian, non-Hispanic/Latino; 54 Hispanic/Latino; 2 Native Hawaiian or other Pacific Islander, non-Hispanic/Latino; 33 Two or more races, non-Hispanic/Latino), 16 international. Average age 45. 561 applicants, 66% accepted, 194 enrolled. In 2019, 168 master's, 13 doctorates awarded. *Degree requirements:* For master's, comprehensive exam, thesis or alternative, internship; for doctorate, thesis/dissertation or alternative. *Entrance requirements:* For master's, minimum undergraduate GPA of 2.75, writing sample, personal goal statement, college transcripts; for doctorate, GRE, minimum graduate GPA of 3.5 (PhD), 3.0 (D Min); clergy recommendations; writing sample; transcripts; resume; interview. Additional exam requirements/recommendations for international students: required—TOEFL (minimum score 577 paper-based). *Application deadline:* For fall admission, 5/1 priority date for domestic students. Applications are processed on a rolling basis. Application fee: $50. Electronic applications accepted. *Expenses:* Contact institution. *Financial support:* In 2019–20, 856 students received support. Career-related internships or fieldwork, scholarships/grants, health care benefits, and unspecified assistantships available. Support available to part-time students. Financial award applicants required to submit FAFSA. *Unit head:* Dr. Cornelius Bekker, Dean, 757-352-4258, Fax: 757-352-4597, E-mail: clbekker@regent.edu. *Application contact:* Heidi Cece, Assistant Vice President for Enrollment Management, 800-373-5504, Fax: 757-352-4381, E-mail: admissions@regent.edu.
Website: https://www.regent.edu/school-of-divinity/

Rice University, Graduate Programs, School of Humanities, Department of Religious Studies, Houston, TX 77251-1892. Offers African religions (PhD); African-American religions (PhD); contemplative studies (PhD); ghosticism, esotericism, mysticism (PhD); Islam (PhD); Jewish thought and philosophy (PhD); modern Christianity in thought and popular culture (PhD); psychology of religion (PhD); the Bible and beyond (PhD). *Degree requirements:* For doctorate, 2 foreign languages, comprehensive exam, thesis/dissertation. *Entrance requirements:* For doctorate, GRE, letters of recommendation, writing sample. Additional exam requirements/recommendations for international students: required—TOEFL (minimum score 600 paper-based; 90 iBT). Electronic applications accepted.

The Robert E. Webber Institute for Worship Studies, Doctor of Worship Studies Program, Jacksonville, FL 32207. Offers DWS. *Degree requirements:* For doctorate, thesis/dissertation, practicum.

The Robert E. Webber Institute for Worship Studies, Master of Worship Studies Program, Jacksonville, FL 32207. Offers MWS. *Degree requirements:* For master's, internship.

Rutgers University - New Brunswick, Graduate School-New Brunswick, Department of Religion, Piscataway, NJ 08854-8097. Offers religious studies (MA, Graduate Certificate). *Entrance requirements:* For master's and Graduate Certificate, GRE, personal statement, two letters of recommendation, official transcripts. Electronic applications accepted.

Saint John's Seminary, Graduate Programs, Brighton, MA 02135. Offers M Div, MA Th, MAM.

St. Joseph's Seminary, Graduate and Professional Programs, Yonkers, NY 10704. Offers Catholic philosophical studies (MA); divinity (M Div); pastoral studies (MAPS); theology (MA). *Accreditation:* ATS. *Degree requirements:* For master's, one foreign language, thesis. *Entrance requirements:* For master's, 27 credits in philosophy and 9 in theology.

Saint Mary's University, Faculty of Arts, Department of Religious Studies, Halifax, NS B3H 3C3, Canada. Offers theology and religious studies (MA).

Salve Regina University, Program in Humanities, Newport, RI 02840-4192. Offers humanitarian assistance (MA); humanities (PhD); public humanities (MA); religion, peace and justice (MA). *Program availability:* Part-time, evening/weekend, online learning. *Degree requirements:* For master's, thesis optional; for doctorate, one foreign language, comprehensive exam, thesis/dissertation. *Entrance requirements:* For master's, GMAT, GRE General Test, or MAT; for doctorate, GRE General Test. Additional exam requirements/recommendations for international students: required—TOEFL (minimum score 600 paper-based; 100 iBT) or IELTS. Electronic applications accepted.

Santa Clara University, Jesuit School of Theology, Berkeley, CA 94709. Offers Biblical studies (MTS); Christian spirituality (MTS); church history (MTS); cultural and historical studies of Catholicism (MTS); divinity (M Div); ethics and social theory/religion and society (MTS); history of art and religion (MTS); liturgical studies (MTS); sacred theology (STD, STB, STL); systematic and philosophical theology (MTS); theology (Th M); M Div/MA. *Program availability:* Part-time, online learning. *Entrance requirements:* For master's and doctorate, Varies based on program. Additional exam requirements/recommendations for international students: required—TOEFL, IELTS, Applicants whose native language is not English are required to submit TOEFL or IELTS scores. Electronic applications accepted.

Religion

Seattle Pacific University, Master of Arts in Theology Program, Seattle, WA 98119-1997. Offers Asian American ministry (MA); business and applied theology (MA); Christian leadership (MA); Christian scripture (MA); Christian studies (Graduate Certificate); reconciliation and intercultural studies (MA); theology (MA). *Students:* 22 full-time (14 women), 30 part-time (13 women); includes 20 minority (10 Black or African American, non-Hispanic/Latino; 6 Asian, non-Hispanic/Latino; 3 Hispanic/Latino; 1 Native Hawaiian or other Pacific Islander, non-Hispanic/Latino), 3 international. Average age 34. 21 applicants, 52% accepted, 11 enrolled. In 2019, 15 master's awarded. *Degree requirements:* For master's, internship or thesis. *Entrance requirements:* For master's, two letters of recommendation; personal statement; bachelor's degree from regionally-accredited college or university or its equivalent; official copy of transcripts from college or university that granted the bachelor's degree and any institution attended since that time; minimum GPA of 3.0. Additional exam requirements/recommendations for international students: required—TOEFL (minimum score 600 paper-based; 100 iBT). *Application deadline:* For fall admission, 7/31 for domestic students, 6/15 for international students; for winter admission, 11/15 for domestic students; for spring admission, 2/15 for domestic students; for summer admission, 5/1 for domestic students. Applications are processed on a rolling basis. Application fee: $50. Electronic applications accepted. *Financial support:* Application deadline: 4/1; applicants required to submit FAFSA. *Unit head:* Dr. Doug Strong, Dean, 206-281-2473, E-mail: dstrong@spu.edu. *Application contact:* Dr. Doug Strong, Dean, 206-281-2473, E-mail: dstrong@spu.edu.
Website: https://spu.edu/academics/school-of-theology

The Seattle School of Theology and Psychology, Graduate Programs, Seattle, WA 98121. Offers Christian studies (MA); counseling psychology (MA); divinity (M Div). *Program availability:* Part-time. *Entrance requirements:* For master's, MAT.

Selma University, Graduate Programs, Selma, AL 36701-5299. Offers Bible and Christian education (MA); Bible and pastoral ministry (MA).

Seton Hall University, College of Arts and Sciences, Department of Religion, South Orange, NJ 07079-2697. Offers Jewish-Christian studies (MA). *Program availability:* Part-time, evening/weekend. *Degree requirements:* For master's, thesis optional. *Entrance requirements:* For master's, interview or suitable correspondence with department chair. Additional exam requirements/recommendations for international students: required—TOEFL. Electronic applications accepted.

Seton Hall University, Immaculate Conception Seminary School of Theology, South Orange, NJ 07079-2697. Offers Christian spirituality (Certificate); great spiritual books (Certificate); pastoral ministry (M Div, MA, Certificate); scripture studies (Certificate); Seminary's Theological Education for Parish Services (STEPS) (Certificate); theology (MA). *Program availability:* Part-time, evening/weekend. *Degree requirements:* For master's, comprehensive exam (for some programs), thesis (for some programs), final project (for some programs); 1 foreign language (for MA in theology research option). *Entrance requirements:* For master's, GRE General Test or MAT. Additional exam requirements/recommendations for international students: required—TOEFL (minimum score 600 paper-based; 100 iBT). Electronic applications accepted. *Expenses:* Contact institution.

Sioux Falls Seminary, Graduate and Professional Programs, Program in Christian Leadership, Sioux Falls, SD 57105-1599. Offers MA. *Program availability:* Online learning.

Southern Adventist University, School of Religion, Collegedale, TN 37315-0370. Offers evangelism and ministry (M Min); old Testament studies (MA); religious studies (MA). *Program availability:* Part-time. *Degree requirements:* For master's, comprehensive exam, thesis (for some programs). *Entrance requirements:* Additional exam requirements/recommendations for international students: required—TOEFL (minimum score 100 iBT).

The Southern Baptist Theological Seminary, School of Theology, Louisville, KY 40280-0004. Offers applied theology (D Min); biblical and theological studies (M Div); biblical counseling (M Div, MA, D Min); biblical spirituality (D Min); Christian ministry (M Div); expository preaching (D Min); pastoral studies (M Div); theological studies (MA); theology (Th M, PhD); worldview and apologetics (M Div). *Program availability:* Part-time, evening/weekend, online learning. *Degree requirements:* For master's, 2 foreign languages, thesis; for doctorate, 4 foreign languages, thesis/dissertation. *Entrance requirements:* For master's, GRE General Test, MAT, M Div; for doctorate, GRE General Test, MAT, interview, M Div, field essay. Additional exam requirements/recommendations for international students: required—TOEFL, TWE.

Southern California Seminary, Graduate and Professional Programs, El Cajon, CA 92019. Offers Biblical studies (MABS); counseling psychology (MACP); marriage and family therapy (MAMFT); psychology (Psy D); religious studies (MRS); theology (M Div). *Program availability:* Part-time, evening/weekend, online learning. *Degree requirements:* For master's, thesis (for some programs); for doctorate, thesis/dissertation. *Entrance requirements:* For doctorate, master's degree in psychology. Additional exam requirements/recommendations for international students: required—TOEFL (minimum score 550 paper-based). Electronic applications accepted.

Southern Evangelical Seminary, Graduate Programs, Matthews, NC 28105. Offers apologetics (MA, D Min, Certificate); Christian education (MA); church ministry (MA, Certificate); divinity (Certificate), including apologetics (M Div, Certificate); Islamic studies (MA, Certificate); Jewish studies (MA); philosophy (MA); philosophy of religion (PhD); religion (MA); theology (M Div), including apologetics (M Div, Certificate), Biblical studies; youth ministry (MA). *Program availability:* Part-time, evening/weekend, online learning. *Degree requirements:* For master's, thesis (for some programs); for doctorate, 2 foreign languages, comprehensive exam (for some programs), thesis/dissertation. *Entrance requirements:* Additional exam requirements/recommendations for international students: required—TOEFL (minimum score 600 paper-based). *Expenses:* Tuition: Full-time $24,000; part-time $12,000 per year. *Required fees:* $600; $300 per semester. $150 per semester.

Southern Methodist University, Dedman College of Humanities and Sciences, Graduate Program in Religious Studies, Dallas, TX 75275-0133. Offers Hebrew Bible/Old Testament (PhD); religious studies (MA). Terminal master's awarded for partial completion of doctoral program. *Degree requirements:* For master's, one foreign language, thesis, oral and written exams; for doctorate, variable foreign language requirement, thesis/dissertation, oral and written exams. *Entrance requirements:* For master's and doctorate, GRE General Test, minimum GPA of 3.0, course work in religion. Additional exam requirements/recommendations for international students: required—TOEFL (minimum score 550 paper-based; 79 iBT). Electronic applications accepted.

Southwestern Assemblies of God University, Thomas F. Harrison School of Graduate Studies, Program in Theological Studies, Waxahachie, TX 75165-5735. Offers Bible and theology (MS); Biblical studies (M Div); counseling (M Div); cross cultural missions (M Div); practical theology (M Div); theological studies (M Div). *Program availability:* Online learning. *Degree requirements:* For master's, comprehensive written and oral exams. *Entrance requirements:* For master's, GRE General Test, minimum GPA of 2.5. Electronic applications accepted.

Stanford University, School of Humanities and Sciences, Department of Religious Studies, Stanford, CA 94305-2004. Offers PhD. *Expenses: Tuition:* Full-time $52,479; part-time $34,110 per unit. *Required fees:* $672; $224 per quarter. Tuition and fees vary according to program and student level.
Website: http://religiousstudies.stanford.edu/

SUM Bible College & Theological Seminary, Graduate Programs, Oakland, CA 94603. Offers biblical studies (MA); Christian leadership (MA); theology (M Div). *Entrance requirements:* For master's, minimum GPA of 2.5, currently active in ministry.

Syracuse University, College of Arts and Sciences, Department of Religion, Syracuse, NY 13244. Offers MA, PhD. Terminal master's awarded for partial completion of doctoral program. *Degree requirements:* For master's, one foreign language, comprehensive exam, thesis optional; for doctorate, 2 foreign languages, comprehensive exam, thesis/dissertation. *Entrance requirements:* For master's and doctorate, GRE General Test, transcripts from all previous institutions; three letters of recommendation; personal statement of not more than 1000 words, including choice of concentration and religious culture to study at SU. Additional exam requirements/recommendations for international students: required—TOEFL (minimum score 100 iBT). Electronic applications accepted.

Temple University, College of Liberal Arts, Department of Religion, Philadelphia, PA 19122-6096. Offers MA, PhD. *Program availability:* Part-time. *Faculty:* 15 full-time (5 women), 4 part-time/adjunct (1 woman). *Students:* 37 full-time (15 women), 2 part-time (both women); includes 10 minority (7 Black or African American, non-Hispanic/Latino; 2 Asian, non-Hispanic/Latino; 1 Hispanic/Latino), 8 international. 20 applicants, 50% accepted, 9 enrolled. In 2019, 2 master's, 3 doctorates awarded. *Degree requirements:* For master's, variable foreign language requirement, thesis optional; for doctorate, 2 foreign languages, thesis/dissertation. *Entrance requirements:* For master's, GRE, writing sample, statement of goals; for doctorate, GRE General Test, 3 letters of recommendation, writing sample, statement of goals. Additional exam requirements/recommendations for international students: required—TOEFL (minimum score 100 iBT), IELTS (minimum score 7), PTE (minimum score 68), one of three is required. *Application deadline:* For fall admission, 1/15 for domestic students. Application fee: $60. Electronic applications accepted. *Financial support:* Fellowships, teaching assistantships, Federal Work-Study, and health care benefits available. Financial award applicants required to submit FAFSA. *Unit head:* Terry Rey, Chair, 215-204-8755, E-mail: jeremy.schipper@temple.edu. *Application contact:* Jemina Quarles, Coordinator, 215-204-3663, E-mail: jemi@temple.edu.
Website: http://www.cla.temple.edu/religion/

Trevecca Nazarene University, Graduate Religion Programs, Nashville, TN 37210-2877. Offers biblical and theological studies (MA); Christian ministry (MA); pastoral counseling (MA). *Program availability:* Part-time, online learning. *Degree requirements:* For master's, research project. *Entrance requirements:* For master's, minimum GPA of 2.7, official transcript from regionally accredited institution, letter of recommendation. Additional exam requirements/recommendations for international students: required—TOEFL (minimum score 550 paper-based; 80 iBT). Electronic applications accepted. *Expenses:* Contact institution.

Trinity Baptist College, Graduate Programs, Jacksonville, FL 32221. Offers Bible (MA); curriculum and instruction (M Ed); educational leadership (M Ed); special education (M Ed). *Program availability:* Online learning. *Entrance requirements:* For master's, GRE (for M Ed), 2 letters of recommendation; minimum GPA of 2.5 (for M Min), 3.0 (for M Ed); goals essay; official transcripts. *Expenses: Tuition:* Part-time $320 per credit hour. *Required fees:* $65 per term.

Trinity International University Florida, Divinity School, Davie, FL 33324. Offers MA, Certificate. *Expenses: Tuition:* Full-time $5040; part-time $720 per credit hour. *Required fees:* $900; $300 per semester.

Trinity School for Ministry, Graduate Programs, Ambridge, PA 15003-2397. Offers Anglican studies (Diploma); basic Christian studies (Diploma); divinity (M Div); ministry (D Min); mission and evangelism (MAME, Diploma); religion (MAR); youth ministry (Diploma). *Program availability:* Part-time. *Degree requirements:* For master's, thesis optional; for doctorate, thesis/dissertation. *Entrance requirements:* Additional exam requirements/recommendations for international students: required—TOEFL.

Union University, School of Theology and Missions, Jackson, TN 38305-3697. Offers Christian studies (MCS); expository preaching (D Min). *Program availability:* Part-time, evening/weekend, online learning. Electronic applications accepted.

United Lutheran Seminary, Graduate and Professional Programs, Gettysburg, PA 17325-1795. Offers divinity (M Div); ministerial studies (MAMS); outdoor ministry (MAR); parish ministry (D Min); theology (STM). *Accreditation:* ACIPE; ATS (one or more programs are accredited). *Program availability:* Part-time, online learning. *Degree requirements:* For master's, thesis (for some programs). Electronic applications accepted. *Expenses: Tuition:* Full-time $19,500; part-time $1950 per credit. Tuition and fees vary according to course load.

United Lutheran Seminary, Graduate School, Philadelphia, PA 19119-1794. Offers divinity (M Div); ministry (D Min); public leadership (MA); religion (MAR); social ministry and church (Certificate); theology (STM, PhD). *Accreditation:* ACIPE. *Program availability:* Part-time, evening/weekend. *Degree requirements:* For master's, one foreign language, comprehensive exam (for some programs), thesis (for some programs); for doctorate, thesis/dissertation. *Entrance requirements:* For master's, minimum undergraduate GPA of 2.8; for doctorate, minimum GPA of 3.0. Additional exam requirements/recommendations for international students: required—TOEFL (minimum score 550 paper-based; 89 iBT), TWE. Electronic applications accepted.

United Theological Seminary of the Twin Cities, Graduate Programs, New Brighton, MN 55112-2598. Offers advanced theological studies (Diploma); justice and peace studies (M Div, MA); leadership toward racial justice (M Div, MA, Certificate); Methodist studies (M Div, MA, Certificate); ministry (D Min); ministry renewal and professional development (Certificate); pastoral care and counseling (M Div, MA, MARL); religion and theology (MA); theological and religious studies (Certificate); theology and the arts (M Div, MA); urban ministry (M Div, MA, MARL); women's studies: religion, theology and ministry (M Div, MA). *Accreditation:* ACIPE; ATS. *Program availability:* Part-time, evening/weekend. *Degree requirements:* For master's, thesis; for doctorate, comprehensive exam, thesis/dissertation. *Entrance requirements:* For master's, minimum GPA of 2.75; strong analytical, reflective thinking and writing skills; vocational and academic goals compatible with those of Seminary; for doctorate, M Div or equivalent, minimum GPA of 3.0, 3 years experience in professional ministry; for other advanced degree, BA or equivalent life experience; strong analytical, reflective thinking and writing skills (Certificate); proficiency in English language, previous study of theology at a theological school, recommendation of student's denomination (Diploma). Additional exam requirements/recommendations for international students: required—TOEFL (minimum score 550 paper-based).

Université de Montréal, Faculty of Theology and Sciences of Religions, Montréal, QC H3C 3J7, Canada. Offers health, spirituality and bioethics (DESS); practical theology (MA, PhD); religious sciences (MA, PhD); theology (MA, D Th, PhD, L Th); theology-Biblical studies (PhD). *Degree requirements:* For master's, one foreign language; for doctorate, 2 foreign languages, thesis/dissertation, general exam. Electronic applications accepted.

Université de Sherbrooke, Faculty of Theology and Religious Studies, Sherbrooke, QC J1K 2R1, Canada. Offers applied ethics (Diploma); human science of religions (MA); intercultural training (Diploma); philosophy (MA, PhD); spiritual anthropology (Diploma); theology (MA, PhD, Diploma). *Program availability:* Part-time, evening/weekend, online learning. Terminal master's awarded for partial completion of doctoral program. *Entrance requirements:* For master's, bachelor's degree in related discipline; for doctorate, master's degree in related discipline.

Université du Québec à Montréal, Graduate Programs, Program in Religious Sciences, Montréal, QC H3C 3P8, Canada. Offers MA, PhD. *Program availability:* Part-time. *Degree requirements:* For master's, thesis; for doctorate, thesis/dissertation. *Entrance requirements:* For master's, appropriate bachelor's degree or equivalent, proficiency in French; for doctorate, appropriate master's degree or equivalent, proficiency in French.

The University of British Columbia, Faculty of Arts, Department of Classical, Near Eastern and Religious Studies, Program in Ancient Culture, Religion and Ethnicity, Vancouver, BC V6T 1Z1, Canada. Offers MA. *Degree requirements:* For master's, thesis.

The University of British Columbia, Faculty of Arts, Department of Classical, Near Eastern and Religious Studies, Program in Religious Studies, Vancouver, BC V6T 1Z1, Canada. Offers MA, PhD. *Program availability:* Part-time. *Degree requirements:* For master's, 2 foreign languages, comprehensive exam, thesis optional; for doctorate, 2 foreign languages, comprehensive exam, thesis/dissertation. *Entrance requirements:* For doctorate, MA. Additional exam requirements/recommendations for international students: required—TOEFL, IELTS. Electronic applications accepted. *Expenses:* Contact institution.

University of Calgary, Faculty of Graduate Studies, Faculty of Arts, Program in Religious Studies, Calgary, AB T2N 1N4, Canada. Offers MA, PhD. *Program availability:* Part-time. *Degree requirements:* For master's, one foreign language, thesis; for doctorate, 2 foreign languages, thesis/dissertation, candidacy exam. *Entrance requirements:* For master's, minimum GPA of 3.3; for doctorate, minimum GPA of 3.5. Additional exam requirements/recommendations for international students: required—TOEFL (minimum score 550 paper-based).

University of California, Berkeley, Graduate Division, College of Letters and Science, Group in Buddhist Studies, Berkeley, CA 94720. Offers PhD. *Degree requirements:* For doctorate, 4 foreign languages, thesis/dissertation, dissertation defense, qualifying exam. *Entrance requirements:* For doctorate, GRE General Test, MA in Japanese, Chinese, or Sanskrit; minimum GPA of 3.0; 3 letters of recommendation. Electronic applications accepted.

University of California, Riverside, Graduate Division, Department of Religious Studies, Riverside, CA 92521. Offers MA, PhD. Terminal master's awarded for partial completion of doctoral program. *Degree requirements:* For master's, one foreign language, comprehensive exam; for doctorate, 2 foreign languages, comprehensive exam. *Entrance requirements:* For master's, GRE, 3 letters of recommendation from academic references, statement of purpose, personal history, scholarly acuity and interest in the critical questions of the discipline of religious studies; for doctorate, GRE General Test, 3 letters of recommendation from academic references; statement of purpose; personal history; basic and advanced courses in religious studies, beginning work in foreign language and ability to work across methods, traditions, and disciplines. Additional exam requirements/recommendations for international students: required—TOEFL (minimum score 550 paper-based; 80 iBT); recommended—IELTS (minimum score 7). Electronic applications accepted.

University of California, Santa Barbara, Graduate Division, College of Letters and Sciences, Division of Humanities and Fine Arts, Department of Religious Studies, Santa Barbara, CA 93106-3130. Offers ancient Mediterranean studies (PhD); cognitive science (PhD); European medieval studies (PhD); feminist studies (PhD); global studies (PhD); religious studies (MA, PhD); translation studies (PhD); MA/PhD. Terminal master's awarded for partial completion of doctoral program. *Degree requirements:* For master's, one foreign language, comprehensive exam (for some programs), thesis (for some programs); for doctorate, 2 foreign languages, thesis/dissertation, methodology. *Entrance requirements:* For master's and doctorate, GRE General Test. Additional exam requirements/recommendations for international students: required—TOEFL (minimum score 550 paper-based; 80 iBT), IELTS (minimum score 7). Electronic applications accepted.

University of California, Santa Barbara, Graduate Division, College of Letters and Sciences, Division of Social Sciences, Department of Global Studies, Santa Barbara, CA 93106-7065. Offers global culture, ideology, and religion (MA, PhD); global government, human rights, and civil society (MA, PhD); political economy, sustainable development, and the environment (MA, PhD). *Degree requirements:* For master's, one foreign language, thesis, 2 years of a second language; for doctorate, one foreign language, thesis/dissertation, reading proficiency in at least one language other than English. *Entrance requirements:* For master's, GRE, 2 years of a second language with minimum B grade in the final term, statement of purpose, resume or curriculum vitae, 3 letters of recommendation, transcripts (from all post-secondary institutions attended), writing sample (15-20 pages); for doctorate, GRE, statement of purpose, personal achievements/contributions statement, resume or curriculum vitae, 3 letters of recommendation, transcripts from all post-secondary institutions attended, writing sample (15-20 pages). Additional exam requirements/recommendations for international students: required—TOEFL (minimum score 600 paper-based; 94 iBT), IELTS (minimum score 7). Electronic applications accepted.

University of Chicago, Divinity School, Master of Arts in Religious Studies Program, Chicago, IL 60637. Offers MA. *Program availability:* Part-time. *Degree requirements:* For master's, oral examination. *Entrance requirements:* For master's, GRE General Test, 3 letters of recommendation; transcripts; curriculum vitae or resume. Additional exam requirements/recommendations for international students: required—TOEFL (minimum score 600 paper-based; 104 iBT), IELTS (minimum score 7). Electronic applications accepted. *Expenses:* Contact institution.

University of Chicago, Divinity School, Master of Arts Program, Chicago, IL 60637. Offers MA. *Degree requirements:* For master's, one foreign language, 15 courses with minimum B- grade. *Entrance requirements:* For master's, GRE General Test, 3 letters of recommendation; transcripts; curriculum vitae or resume. Additional exam requirements/ recommendations for international students: required—TOEFL (minimum score 600 paper-based; 104 iBT), IELTS (minimum score 7). Electronic applications accepted.

University of Chicago, Divinity School, PhD Program, Chicago, IL 60637. Offers anthropology and sociology of religions (PhD); Bible (PhD); history of Christianity (PhD); history of Judaism (PhD); history of religions (PhD); Islamic studies (PhD); philosophy of religions (PhD); religion, literature, and visual culture (PhD); religions in America (PhD); religious ethics (PhD); theology (PhD). *Degree requirements:* For doctorate, 2 foreign languages, comprehensive exam, thesis/dissertation. *Entrance requirements:* For doctorate, GRE General Test, 3 letters of recommendation; transcripts; curriculum vitae

or resume; writing sample. Additional exam requirements/recommendations for international students: required—TOEFL (minimum score 600 paper-based; 104 iBT), IELTS (minimum score 7). Electronic applications accepted.

University of Colorado Boulder, Graduate School, College of Arts and Sciences, Department of Religious Studies, Boulder, CO 80309. Offers MA. Terminal master's awarded for partial completion of doctoral program. *Degree requirements:* For master's, one foreign language, comprehensive exam, thesis. *Entrance requirements:* For master's, minimum undergraduate GPA of 2.75. Electronic applications accepted. Application fee is waived when completed online.

University of Denver, Division of Arts, Humanities and Social Sciences, Department of Religious Studies, Denver, CO 80208. Offers critical theory and religion (MA); lived religions (MA); philosophy of religion (MA); religion and international studies (MA); sacred texts (MA). *Faculty:* 7 full-time (3 women). *Students:* 11 part-time (6 women); includes 1 minority (Two or more races, non-Hispanic/Latino). Average age 26. 14 applicants, 79% accepted, 4 enrolled. In 2019, 7 master's awarded. *Degree requirements:* For master's, variable foreign language requirement, comprehensive exam (for some programs), thesis (for some programs). *Entrance requirements:* For master's, GRE General Test, bachelor's degree, transcripts, personal statement, writing sample, three letters of recommendation, some prior coursework in the academic study of religion is expected. Additional exam requirements/recommendations for international students: required—TOEFL (minimum score 550 paper-based; 80 iBT). *Application deadline:* For fall admission, 2/1 priority date for domestic and international students. Applications are processed on a rolling basis. Application fee: $65. Electronic applications accepted. *Expenses:* Contact institution. *Financial support:* In 2019–20, 10 students received support. Federal Work-Study, scholarships/grants, and unspecified assistantships available. Financial award application deadline: 2/15; financial award applicants required to submit FAFSA. *Unit head:* Dr. Andrea Stanton, Professor and Department Chair, 303-871-3503, E-mail: andrea.stanton@du.edu. *Application contact:* Dr. Carl Raschke, Professor and Graduate Advisor, 303-871-3117, E-mail: rlgs@du.edu.
Website: http://www.du.edu/ahss/religiousstudies

University of Denver, DU/Iliff Joint PhD Program in the Study of Religion, Denver, CO 80208. Offers future faculty in religion (Certificate); Latinx studies (Certificate); study of religion (PhD). *Program availability:* Part-time. *Faculty:* 7 part-time/adjunct (3 women). *Students:* 19 full-time (7 women), 20 part-time (9 women); includes 5 minority (2 Black or African American, non-Hispanic/Latino; 1 Asian, non-Hispanic/Latino; 2 Hispanic/Latino), 4 international. Average age 38. 41 applicants, 46% accepted, 8 enrolled. In 2019, 9 doctorates, 1 other advanced degree awarded. *Degree requirements:* For doctorate, one foreign language, comprehensive exam, thesis/dissertation. *Entrance requirements:* For doctorate, GRE General Test, two-year master's degree relevant to the student's proposed research interests, transcripts, three letters of recommendation, personal statement, research paper. Additional exam requirements/recommendations for international students: required—TOEFL (minimum score 600 paper-based; 100 iBT). *Application deadline:* For fall admission, 1/15 priority date for domestic and international students. Applications are processed on a rolling basis. Application fee: $65. Electronic applications accepted. *Expenses:* Contact institution. *Financial support:* In 2019–20, 26 students received support, including 10 teaching assistantships (averaging $4,000 per year); scholarships/grants and unspecified assistantships also available. Financial award application deadline: 1/15. *Unit head:* Rhonda Eaker, Manager, DU/Iliff Joint PhD Program, 303- 765-3136, E-mail: Rhonda.Eaker@du.edu. *Application contact:* Information Contact, 303-765-3136, E-mail: jointphd@iliff.edu.
Website: http://www.du.edu/duiliffjoint

University of Denver, Josef Korbel School of International Studies, Denver, CO 80208. Offers conflict resolution (MA); global business and corporate social responsibility (Certificate); global finance, trade and economic integration (MA); global health affairs (Certificate); homeland security (Certificate); humanitarian assistance (Certificate); international administration (MA); international development (MA); international human rights (MA); international security (MA); international studies (MA, PhD); public policy studies (MPP); religion and international affairs (Certificate). *Program availability:* Part-time. *Faculty:* 41 full-time (15 women), 14 part-time/adjunct (2 women). *Students:* 208 full-time (112 women), 24 part-time (13 women); includes 50 minority (11 Black or African American, non-Hispanic/Latino; 10 Asian, non-Hispanic/Latino; 15 Hispanic/Latino; 14 Two or more races, non-Hispanic/Latino), 20 international. Average age 27. 718 applicants, 70% accepted, 88 enrolled. In 2019, 134 master's, 2 doctorates, 26 other advanced degrees awarded. *Degree requirements:* For master's, variable foreign language requirement, thesis (for some programs); for doctorate, one foreign language, comprehensive exam, thesis/dissertation, one extended research paper. *Entrance requirements:* For master's, GRE General Test, bachelor's degree, transcripts, two letters of recommendation, personal statement, resume or curriculum vitae; for doctorate, GRE General Test, bachelor's degree (most have a master's degree), transcripts, personal statement, resume or curriculum vitae, writing sample. Additional exam requirements/recommendations for international students: required—TOEFL (minimum score 587 paper-based; 95 iBT). *Application deadline:* For fall admission, 1/23 priority date for domestic and international students; for winter admission, 11/1 for domestic and international students. Applications are processed on a rolling basis. Application fee: $65. Electronic applications accepted. *Expenses:* Contact institution. *Financial support:* In 2019–20, 161 students received support, including 4 teaching assistantships with tuition reimbursements available (averaging $16,875 per year); research assistantships with tuition reimbursements available, career-related internships or fieldwork, Federal Work-Study, institutionally sponsored loans, scholarships/grants, and unspecified assistantships also available. Support available to part-time students. Financial award application deadline: 2/15; financial award applicants required to submit FAFSA. *Unit head:* Dr. Fritz Mayer, Dean, 303-871-6338, E-mail: frederick.mayer@du.edu. *Application contact:* Admissions Contact, 303-871-2324, E-mail: korbeladm@du.edu.
Website: http://www.du.edu/korbel

University of Florida, Graduate School, College of Liberal Arts and Sciences, Department of Religion, Gainesville, FL 32611. Offers Jewish studies (MA); religion (MA, PhD); tropical conservation and development (MA, PhD); women's and gender studies (MA, PhD). *Program availability:* Part-time. *Degree requirements:* For master's, one foreign language, thesis optional; for doctorate, one foreign language, comprehensive exam, thesis/dissertation. *Entrance requirements:* For master's, GRE General Test, minimum GPA of 3.0. Additional exam requirements/recommendations for international students: required—TOEFL (minimum score 550 paper-based; 80 iBT), IELTS (minimum score 6). Electronic applications accepted.

University of Georgia, Franklin College of Arts and Sciences, Department of Religion, Athens, GA 30602. Offers MA. *Degree requirements:* For master's, one foreign language, thesis. *Entrance requirements:* For master's, GRE General Test. Electronic applications accepted.

University of Hawaii at Manoa, Office of Graduate Education, College of Arts and Humanities, Department of Religion, Honolulu, HI 96822. Offers MA. *Program availability:* Part-time. *Degree requirements:* For master's, one foreign language, thesis optional. *Entrance requirements:* For master's, GRE General Test. Additional exam requirements/recommendations for international students: required—TOEFL (minimum score 600 paper-based; 100 iBT), IELTS (minimum score 7).

University of Illinois at Urbana-Champaign, Graduate College, College of Liberal Arts and Sciences, School of Literatures, Cultures and Linguistics, Department of Religion, Champaign, IL 61820. Offers religious studies (MA). *Degree requirements:* For master's, one foreign language, comprehensive exam, thesis optional.

The University of Iowa, Graduate College, College of Liberal Arts and Sciences, Department of Religious Studies, Iowa City, IA 52242-1316. Offers MA, PhD. Terminal master's awarded for partial completion of doctoral program. *Degree requirements:* For master's, thesis optional, exam; for doctorate, comprehensive exam, thesis/dissertation. *Entrance requirements:* For master's and doctorate, GRE General Test, minimum GPA of 3.0. Additional exam requirements/recommendations for international students: required—TOEFL (minimum score 550 paper-based; 81 iBT). Electronic applications accepted.

The University of Kansas, Graduate Studies, College of Liberal Arts and Sciences, Department of Religious Studies, Lawrence, KS 66045. Offers MA, Graduate Certificate. *Program availability:* Part-time. *Students:* 7 full-time (4 women); includes 1 minority (Two or more races, non-Hispanic/Latino), 3 international. Average age 28. 9 applicants, 67% accepted, 2 enrolled. In 2019, 3 master's awarded. *Entrance requirements:* For master's, GRE, official transcripts, three letters of recommendation, essay of interest and purpose, resume, writing sample. Additional exam requirements/recommendations for international students: required—TOEFL, IELTS. *Application deadline:* For fall admission, 2/1 for domestic and international students. Applications are processed on a rolling basis. Application fee: $65 ($85 for international students). Electronic applications accepted. *Expenses:* Tuition, state resident: full-time $9989. Tuition, nonresident: full-time $23,950. *International tuition:* $23,950 full-time. *Required fees:* $984; $81.99 per credit hour. Tuition and fees vary according to course load, campus/location and program. *Financial support:* Fellowships, teaching assistantships, scholarships/grants, and unspecified assistantships available. Financial award application deadline: 1/1. *Unit head:* Michael Zogry, Chair, 785-864-7257, E-mail: mzogry@ku.edu. *Application contact:* Clare Thoman, Graduate Admission Contact, 785-864-9814, E-mail: clarethoman@ku.edu.
Website: https://religiousstudies.ku.edu/

University of Lethbridge, School of Graduate Studies, Lethbridge, AB T1K 3M4, Canada. Offers addictions counseling (M Sc); agricultural biotechnology (M Sc); agricultural studies (M Sc, MA); anthropology (MA); archaeology (M Sc, MA); art (MA, MFA); biochemistry (M Sc); biological sciences (M Sc); biomolecular science (PhD); biosystems and biodiversity (PhD); Canadian studies (MA); chemistry (M Sc); computer science (M Sc); computer science and geographical information science (M Sc); counseling (MC); counseling psychology (M Ed); dramatic arts (MA); earth, space, and physical science (PhD); economics (MA); education (MA, PhD); educational leadership (M Ed); English (MA); environmental science (M Sc); evolution and behavior (PhD); exercise science (M Sc); French (MA); French/German (MA); French/Spanish (MA); general education (M Ed); geography (M Sc, MA); German (MA); health sciences (M Sc); individualized multidisciplinary (M Sc, MA); kinesiology (M Sc, MA); management (M Sc), including accounting, finance, human resource management and labor relations, information systems, international management, marketing, policy and strategy; mathematics (M Sc); music (M Mus, MA); Native American studies (MA); neuroscience (M Sc, PhD); new media (MA, MFA); nursing (M Sc, MN); philosophy (MA); physics (M Sc); political science (MA); psychology (M Sc, MA); religious studies (MA); sociology (MA); theatre and dramatic arts (MFA); theoretical and computational science (PhD); urban and regional studies (MA); women and gender studies (MA). *Program availability:* Part-time, evening/weekend. *Degree requirements:* For master's, thesis (for some programs); for doctorate, comprehensive exam, thesis/dissertation. *Entrance requirements:* For master's, GMAT (for M Sc in management), bachelor's degree in related field, minimum GPA of 3.0 during previous 20 graded semester courses, 2 years' teaching or related experience (M Ed); for doctorate, master's degree, minimum graduate GPA of 3.5. Additional exam requirements/recommendations for international students: required—TOEFL (minimum score 580 paper-based; 93 iBT). Electronic applications accepted.

The University of Manchester, School of Arts, Languages and Cultures, Manchester, United Kingdom. Offers anthropology, media and performance (PhD); applied theatre (PhD); Arab world studies (PhD); archaeology (PhD); art history and visual studies (PhD); arts and cultural management (PhD); arts management and cultural policy (PhD); Chinese studies (PhD); classics and ancient history (PhD); composition (PhD); creative writing (PhD); drama (PhD); East Asian studies (PhD); electroacoustic composition (PhD); English and American studies (PhD); English language (PhD); French studies (PhD); German studies (PhD); history (PhD); humanitarianism and conflict response (PhD); interpreting studies (PhD); Japanese studies (PhD); Latin American cultural studies (PhD); linguistics (PhD); Middle Eastern studies (PhD); museology (PhD); museum practice (PhD); music (PhD); musicology (PhD); Polish studies (PhD); Portuguese studies (PhD); religions and theology (PhD); Russian studies (PhD); Spanish studies (PhD); translation and intercultural studies (PhD).

University of Manitoba, Faculty of Graduate Studies, Faculty of Arts, Department of Religion, Winnipeg, MB R3T 2N2, Canada. Offers MA, PhD. *Degree requirements:* For master's, one foreign language, thesis or alternative.

University of Michigan, Rackham Graduate School, College of Literature, Science, and the Arts, Department of Middle East Studies, Ann Arbor, MI 48109. Offers ancient Near Eastern studies (AM, PhD); Arabic for professional purposes (AM); Arabic language and literature (AM, PhD); Armenian studies (AM, PhD); Christianity in late antiquity (AM, PhD); Egyptology (AM, PhD); Hebrew Bible and ancient Israel (AM, PhD); Hebrew literature (AM, PhD); Islamic studies (AM, PhD); Jewish cultural studies (AM, PhD); Jewish mysticism (AM, PhD); Persian and Iranian studies (AM, PhD); Rabbinic literature (AM, PhD); Second Temple Judaism (AM, PhD); teaching Arabic as a foreign language (AM); Turkish studies (AM, PhD). Terminal master's awarded for partial completion of doctoral program. *Degree requirements:* For master's, 2 foreign languages; for doctorate, 4 foreign languages, comprehensive exam, thesis/dissertation, preliminary exams, oral defense of dissertation. *Entrance requirements:* For master's, ACTFL (for teaching Arabic as a foreign language MA program). Additional exam requirements/recommendations for international students: required—TOEFL (minimum score 560 paper-based; 84 iBT), IELTS (minimum score 6.5). Electronic applications accepted.

University of Minnesota, Twin Cities Campus, Graduate School, College of Liberal Arts, Department of Classical and Near Eastern Studies, Minneapolis, MN 55455-0213. Offers ancient and medieval art and archaeology (MA, PhD); classics (MA, PhD); Greek (MA, PhD); Latin (MA, PhD); religions in antiquity (MA). *Program availability:* Part-time. Terminal master's awarded for partial completion of doctoral program. *Degree requirements:* For master's, 2 foreign languages, comprehensive exam, thesis or alternative; for doctorate, variable foreign language requirement, comprehensive exam, thesis/dissertation. *Entrance requirements:* For master's and doctorate, GRE, 3 letters of recommendation, writing sample, copies of transcripts, personal statement. Additional exam requirements/recommendations for international students: required—TOEFL. Electronic applications accepted.

The University of North Carolina at Chapel Hill, Graduate School, College of Arts and Sciences, Department of Religious Studies, Chapel Hill, NC 27599. Offers MA, PhD. Terminal master's awarded for partial completion of doctoral program. *Degree requirements:* For master's, one foreign language, comprehensive exam, thesis; for doctorate, 2 foreign languages, comprehensive exam, thesis/dissertation. *Entrance requirements:* For master's and doctorate, GRE General Test, minimum GPA of 3.0. Additional exam requirements/recommendations for international students: required—TOEFL. Electronic applications accepted.

The University of North Carolina at Charlotte, College of Liberal Arts and Sciences, Department of Religious Studies, Charlotte, NC 28223-0001. Offers religious studies (MA). *Program availability:* Part-time. *Faculty:* 12 full-time (6 women). *Students:* 4 full-time (1 woman), 9 part-time (3 women); includes 2 minority (both Hispanic/Latino). Average age 33. 9 applicants, 89% accepted, 7 enrolled. In 2019, 1 master's awarded. *Degree requirements:* For master's, variable foreign language requirement, comprehensive exam (for some programs), thesis (for some programs). *Entrance requirements:* For master's, GRE or MAT, official transcripts of all previous academic work attempted beyond high school; at least three letters of reference from persons familiar with the applicant's academic qualifications; essay (statement of purpose). Additional exam requirements/recommendations for international students: required—TOEFL (minimum score 557 paper-based; 83 iBT), IELTS (minimum score 6.5), TOEFL (minimum score 557 paper-based, 83 iBT) or IELTS (6.5). *Application deadline:* For fall admission, 5/1 priority date for domestic students; for spring admission, 10/1 priority date for domestic students. Applications are processed on a rolling basis. Application fee: $75. Electronic applications accepted. *Expenses:* Tuition, state resident: full-time $4337. Tuition, nonresident: full-time $17,771. *Required fees:* $3093. Tuition and fees vary according to course load, degree level and program. *Financial support:* In 2019–20, 2 students received support, including 2 teaching assistantships (averaging $6,000 per year); career-related internships or fieldwork, institutionally sponsored loans, scholarships/grants, and unspecified assistantships also available. Support available to part-time students. Financial award application deadline: 4/1; financial award applicants required to submit FAFSA. *Unit head:* Dr. Joanne Maguire, Professor and Department Chair, 704-687-5198, E-mail: jmrobin2@uncc.edu. *Application contact:* Kathy B. Giddings, Director of Graduate Admissions, 704-687-5503, Fax: 704-687-1668, E-mail: gradadm@uncc.edu.
Website: http://religiousstudies.uncc.edu/

University of Notre Dame, The Graduate School, College of Arts and Letters, Division of Humanities, Program in Early Christian Studies, Notre Dame, IN 46556. Offers MA. *Degree requirements:* For master's, 3 foreign languages, comprehensive exam. *Entrance requirements:* For master's, GRE General Test. Additional exam requirements/recommendations for international students: required—TOEFL (minimum score 600 paper-based; 80 iBT). Electronic applications accepted.

University of Ottawa, Faculty of Graduate and Postdoctoral Studies, Faculty of Arts, Department of Classics and Religious Studies, Ottawa, ON K1N 6N5, Canada. Offers classical studies (MA); religious studies (PhD). *Degree requirements:* For master's, comprehensive exam, thesis or alternative; for doctorate, comprehensive exam, thesis/dissertation. *Entrance requirements:* For master's, honors degree or equivalent, minimum B average; for doctorate, master's degree, minimum B+ average. Electronic applications accepted.

University of Pennsylvania, School of Arts and Sciences, Graduate Group in Religious Studies, Philadelphia, PA 19104. Offers PhD. *Students:* Average age 29. 24 applicants, 13% accepted, 2 enrolled. In 2019, 5 doctorates awarded. Application fee: $80. *Financial support:* In 2019–20, 10 students received support.
Website: http://www.sas.upenn.edu/religious_studies/graduate

University of Regina, Faculty of Graduate Studies and Research, Faculty of Arts, Department of Religious Studies, Regina, SK S4S 0A2, Canada. Offers MA. *Program availability:* Part-time. *Faculty:* 7 full-time (2 women), 1 part-time/adjunct (0 women). *Students:* 1 (woman) full-time, 1 part-time (0 women). Average age 30. 1 applicant. In 2019, 2 master's awarded. *Degree requirements:* For master's, thesis. *Entrance requirements:* For master's, post secondary transcripts and two letter of recommendations. Additional exam requirements/recommendations for international students: required—TOEFL (minimum score 580 paper-based; 80 iBT), IELTS (minimum score 6.5), PTE (minimum score 59), Could be any of the test listed above and either in CAEL, MELAB, Cantest nad ESl at U of Regina. *Application deadline:* Applications are processed on a rolling basis. Application fee: $100. Electronic applications accepted. *Expenses: Tuition:* Full-time $6684 Canadian dollars. *Required fees:* $100 Canadian dollars; $3351.45 Canadian dollars per trimester. $1117.15 Canadian dollars per semester. Tuition and fees vary according to course level, course load, degree level and program. *Financial support:* Fellowships, research assistantships, teaching assistantships, Federal Work-Study, scholarships/grants, unspecified assistantships, and Travel Award and Graduate Scholarship Base Funds available. Support available to part-time students. Financial award application deadline: 9/30. *Unit head:* Dr. William Arnal, Department Head, 306-585-5680, Fax: 306-585-4815, E-mail: william.arnal@uregina.ca. *Application contact:* Dr. Kevin Bond, Program Chair, 306-585-4335, Fax: 306-585-4815, E-mail: kevin.bond@uregina.ca.
Website: http://www.uregina.ca/arts/religious-studies

University of St. Thomas, Center for Faith and Culture, Houston, TX 77006-4696. Offers MA. *Faculty:* 2 full-time (0 women), 1 part-time/adjunct (0 women). *Students:* 9 part-time (5 women); includes 3 minority (1 Asian, non-Hispanic/Latino; 1 Hispanic/Latino; 1 Two or more races, non-Hispanic/Latino). Average age 49. In 2019, 1 master's awarded. Application fee is waived when completed online. *Expenses:* $407 per credit hour. *Financial support:* Applicants required to submit FAFSA. *Unit head:* Fr. Binh Quach, Director of the Center for Faith and Culture, E-mail: quach@stthom.edu. *Application contact:* Dr. Stuart Squires, Associate Director, E-mail: Squires@stthom.edu.
Website: http://www.stthom.edu/Academics/Centers_of_Excellence/Center_for_Faith_Culture/Index.aqf

University of St. Thomas, College of Arts and Sciences, Catholic Studies Graduate Programs, St. Paul, MN 55105-1096. Offers MA. *Program availability:* Part-time, evening/weekend, 100% online, blended/hybrid learning. *Degree requirements:* For master's, thesis. *Entrance requirements:* For master's, bachelor's degree with minimum GPA of 3.0, writing sample, personal essay, 3 letters of recommendation. Additional exam requirements/recommendations for international students: required—TOEFL. Electronic applications accepted.

University of Saskatchewan, College of Graduate and Postdoctoral Studies, College of Arts and Science, Department of Linguistics and Religious Studies, Saskatoon, SK S7N 5A2, Canada. Offers applied linguistics (MA); religion and culture (MA); teaching English to speakers of other languages (MA). *Degree requirements:* For master's, thesis. *Entrance requirements:* Additional exam requirements/recommendations for international students: required—TOEFL (minimum score 80 iBT); recommended—IELTS (minimum score 6.5). Electronic applications accepted.

University of South Africa, College of Human Sciences, Pretoria, South Africa. Offers adult education (M Ed); African languages (MA, PhD); African politics (MA, PhD); Afrikaans (MA, PhD); ancient history (MA, PhD); ancient Near Eastern studies (MA, PhD); anthropology (MA, PhD); applied linguistics (MA); Arabic (MA, PhD); archaeology (MA); art history (MA); Biblical archaeology (MA); Biblical studies (M Th, D Th, PhD); Christian spirituality (M Th, D Th); church history (M Th, D Th); classical studies (MA, PhD); clinical psychology (MA); communication (MA, PhD); comparative education (M Ed, Ed D); consulting psychology (D Admin, D Com, PhD); curriculum studies (M Ed, Ed D); development studies (M Admin, MA, D Admin, PhD); didactics (M Ed, Ed D); education (M Tech); education management (M Ed, Ed D); educational psychology (M Ed); English (MA); environmental education (M Ed); French (MA, PhD); German (MA, PhD); Greek (MA); guidance and counseling (M Ed); health studies (MA, PhD), including health sciences education (MA), health services management (MA), medical and surgical nursing science (critical care general) (MA), midwifery and neonatal nursing science (MA), trauma and emergency care (MA); history (MA, PhD); history of education (Ed D); inclusive education (M Ed, Ed D); information and communications technology policy and regulation (MA); information science (MA, MIS, PhD); international politics (MA, PhD); Islamic studies (MA, PhD); Italian (MA, PhD); Judaica (MA, PhD); linguistics (MA, PhD); mathematical education (M Ed); mathematics education (MA); missiology (M Th, D Th); modern Hebrew (MA, PhD); musicology (MA, MMus, D Mus, PhD); natural science education (M Ed); New Testament (M Th, D Th); Old Testament (D Th); pastoral therapy (M Th, D Th); philosophy (MA); philosophy of education (M Ed, Ed D); politics (MA, PhD); Portuguese (MA, PhD); practical theology (M Th, D Th); psychology (MA, MS, PhD); psychology of education (M Ed, Ed D); public health (MA); religious studies (MA, D Th, PhD); Romance languages (MA); Russian (MA, PhD); Semitic languages (MA, PhD); social behavior studies in HIV/AIDS (MA); social science (mental health) (MA); social science in development studies (MA); social science in psychology (MA); social science in social work (MA); social science in sociology (MA); social work (MSW, DSW, PhD); socio-education (M Ed, Ed D); sociolinguistics (MA); sociology (MA, PhD); Spanish (MA, PhD); systematic theology (M Th, D Th); TESOL (teaching English to speakers of other languages) (MA); theological ethics (M Th, D Th); theory of literature (MA, PhD); urban ministries (D Th); urban ministry (M Th).

University of South Carolina, The Graduate School, College of Arts and Sciences, Department of Religious Studies, Columbia, SC 29208. Offers MA. *Program availability:* Part-time. *Degree requirements:* For master's, one foreign language, comprehensive exam, thesis. *Entrance requirements:* For master's, GRE General Test or MAT. Additional exam requirements/recommendations for international students: required—TOEFL. Electronic applications accepted.

University of South Florida, College of Arts and Sciences, Department of Philosophy, Tampa, FL 33620-9951. Offers liberal arts (MA), including social and political thought; philosophy (PhD), including philosophy and religion. *Program availability:* Part-time, evening/weekend. *Faculty:* 15 full-time (4 women). *Students:* 42 full-time (6 women), 10 part-time (4 women); includes 10 minority (3 Black or African American, non-Hispanic/Latino; 3 Asian, non-Hispanic/Latino; 3 Hispanic/Latino; 1 Two or more races, non-Hispanic/Latino). Average age 33. 24 applicants, 75% accepted, 11 enrolled. In 2019, 2 master's, 10 doctorates awarded. Terminal master's awarded for partial completion of doctoral program. *Degree requirements:* For master's, comprehensive exam, thesis; for doctorate, comprehensive exam, thesis/dissertation. *Entrance requirements:* For master's and doctorate, GRE General Test Scores, minimum GPA of 3.0, three letters of recommendation, 10-page philosophy writing sample, statement of philosophical interests. Additional exam requirements/recommendations for international students: required—TOEFL, TOEFL (minimum score 550 paper-based; 79 iBT) or IELTS (minimum score 6.5). *Application deadline:* For fall admission, 1/2 priority date for domestic students, 2/15 for international students; for spring admission, 10/15 priority date for domestic students, 8/1 for international students. Application fee: $30. Electronic applications accepted. *Financial support:* In 2019–20, 15 students received support, including 32 teaching assistantships with tuition reimbursements available (averaging $11,025 per year); unspecified assistantships also available. Financial award application deadline: 1/1. *Unit head:* Dr. William Goodwin, Associate Professor and Chair, 813-974-5670, E-mail: wgoodwin@usf.edu. *Application contact:* Dr. William Goodwin, Associate Professor, 813-974-5670, E-mail: wgoodwin@usf.edu.
Website: http://philosophy.usf.edu/

University of South Florida, College of Arts and Sciences, Department of Religious Studies, Tampa, FL 33620-9951. Offers MA. *Program availability:* Part-time, evening/weekend. *Faculty:* 6 full-time (1 woman). *Students:* 11 full-time (4 women); includes 2 minority (both Hispanic/Latino), 3 international. Average age 35. 7 applicants, 43% accepted, 2 enrolled. In 2019, 7 master's awarded. *Degree requirements:* For master's, comprehensive exam, thesis optional. *Entrance requirements:* For master's, GRE required, but no minimum specified, minimum GPA of 3.0, three letters of recommendation, 1-3 page personal statement of intellectual interest, writing sample. Additional exam requirements/recommendations for international students: required—TOEFL, c. *Application deadline:* For fall admission, 2/15 priority date for domestic and international students; for spring admission, 10/15 priority date for domestic students, 9/15 priority date for international students. Applications are processed on a rolling basis. Application fee: $30. Electronic applications accepted. *Financial support:* In 2019–20, 1 student received support, including 7 teaching assistantships with tuition reimbursements available (averaging $9,751 per year); unspecified assistantships also available. Financial award applicants required to submit FAFSA. *Unit head:* Dr. Michael DeJonge, Professor and Chair, 813-974-1848, E-mail: mdejonge@usf.edu. *Application contact:* Dr. Gil Ben-Herut, Associate Professor and Graduate Program Director, 813-974-1852, E-mail: gilb@usf.edu.
Website: http://religious-studies.usf.edu/

The University of Tennessee, Graduate School, College of Arts and Sciences, Department of Philosophy, Knoxville, TN 37996. Offers medical ethics (MA, PhD); philosophy (MA, PhD); religious studies (MA). *Program availability:* Part-time. *Degree requirements:* For master's, thesis or alternative; for doctorate, one foreign language, thesis/dissertation. *Entrance requirements:* For master's and doctorate, GRE General Test, minimum GPA of 2.7. Additional exam requirements/recommendations for international students: required—TOEFL. Electronic applications accepted.

University of the Cumberlands, Program in Christian Studies, Williamsburg, KY 40769-1372. Offers MA. *Program availability:* Part-time, evening/weekend, online learning. *Entrance requirements:* For master's, GRE or MAT. Additional exam requirements/recommendations for international students: required—TOEFL. Electronic applications accepted.

University of the West, Department of Psychology, Rosemead, CA 91770. Offers Buddhist psychology (MA); multicultural counseling (MA). *Program availability:* Part-time, evening/weekend. *Degree requirements:* For master's, fieldwork; comprehensive exam or thesis.

University of the West, Department of Religious Studies, Rosemead, CA 91770. Offers religious studies (MA, PhD), including Buddhism (PhD), Buddhist studies (MA), comparative religions (PhD), comparative religious studies (MA). *Program availability:* Part-time, evening/weekend. *Degree requirements:* For master's, thesis or comprehensive exam, competency in language associated with Buddhist Canon literature; for doctorate, 2 foreign languages, comprehensive exam, thesis/dissertation. *Entrance requirements:* For master's and doctorate, BA in religious studies, theology, philosophy or equivalent from an accredited university; official transcript; three letters of recommendation; essay. Additional exam requirements/recommendations for international students: required—TOEFL, IELTS.

University of Toronto, School of Graduate Studies, Faculty of Arts and Science, Centre for the Study of Religion, Toronto, ON M5S 1A1, Canada. Offers MA, PhD. *Program availability:* Part-time. *Degree requirements:* For master's, one foreign language, research paper, language examination; for doctorate, 2 foreign languages, thesis/dissertation, language examinations, general examinations, oral examination. *Entrance requirements:* For master's, BA in religion or a related field; minimum A-average in final year, 3 letters of recommendation, resume; for doctorate, MA in religion, minimum average of A- in MA courses with no individual grade below a B, 3 letters of recommendation, resume, brief writing sample. Additional exam requirements/recommendations for international students: required—TOEFL (minimum score 580 paper-based; 93 iBT), TWE (minimum score 5). Electronic applications accepted.

University of Valley Forge, Program in Christian Leadership, Phoenixville, PA 19460. Offers MA. *Degree requirements:* For master's, project.

University of Valley Forge, Program in Worship Studies, Phoenixville, PA 19460. Offers MA.

University of Virginia, College and Graduate School of Arts and Sciences, Department of Religious Studies, Charlottesville, VA 22903. Offers religion, politics and global society (MA); religious studies (MA, PhD). *Degree requirements:* For master's, one foreign language, thesis optional; for doctorate, 2 foreign languages, comprehensive exam, thesis/dissertation. *Entrance requirements:* For master's and doctorate, GRE General Test, 3 letters of recommendation. Additional exam requirements/recommendations for international students: required—TOEFL (minimum score 600 paper-based; 90 iBT), IELTS (minimum score 7). Electronic applications accepted.

University of Washington, Graduate School, College of Arts and Sciences, Department of Asian Languages and Literature, Seattle, WA 98195. Offers Buddhist studies (MA, PhD); Chinese language and literature (MA, PhD); Japanese language and literature (MA, PhD); Korean language and literature (MA, PhD); South Asian language and literature (MA, PhD). *Degree requirements:* For master's, 2 foreign languages, general exam, thesis or 2 research papers; for doctorate, 3 foreign languages, thesis/dissertation, general exam. *Entrance requirements:* For master's, GRE, minimum GPA of 3.0; for doctorate, GRE, master's degree in related field, minimum GPA of 3.0. Additional exam requirements/recommendations for international students: required—TOEFL. Electronic applications accepted.

University of Washington, Graduate School, College of Arts and Sciences, Henry M. Jackson School of International Studies, Comparative Religion Program, Seattle, WA 98195. Offers MAIS. *Degree requirements:* For master's, 2 foreign languages. *Entrance requirements:* For master's, GRE General Test, minimum GPA of 3.0 in last two years. Additional exam requirements/recommendations for international students: required—TOEFL (minimum score 500 paper-based; 92 iBT), IELTS (minimum score 7). Electronic applications accepted.

University of Waterloo, Graduate Studies and Postdoctoral Affairs, Faculty of Arts, Department of Religious Studies, Waterloo, ON N2L 3G1, Canada. Offers religious diversity in North America (PhD). *Degree requirements:* For doctorate, thesis/dissertation. *Entrance requirements:* Additional exam requirements/recommendations for international students: required—TOEFL, IELTS, PTE. Electronic applications accepted.

The University of Winnipeg, Faculty of Graduate Studies, Department of Religious Studies, Winnipeg, MB R3B 2E9, Canada. Offers MA. *Program availability:* Part-time.

Université Laval, Faculty of Theology and Religious Sciences, Programs in Human Sciences of Religion, Québec, QC G1K 7P4, Canada. Offers MA, PhD. Terminal master's awarded for partial completion of doctoral program. *Degree requirements:* For master's, thesis (for some programs); for doctorate, comprehensive exam, thesis/dissertation. *Entrance requirements:* For master's, knowledge of French, comprehension of a second language; for doctorate, knowledge of French and English. Electronic applications accepted.

Vancouver School of Theology, Graduate and Professional Programs, Vancouver, BC V6T 1Z1, Canada. Offers denominational studies (Diploma); indigenous and inter-religious studies (MA, Diploma); public and pastoral leadership (MA); public and pastoral leadership in spiritual care (MA); theological studies (MATS, Diploma, Graduate Diploma); theology (M Div, Th M). *Accreditation:* ATS. *Program availability:* Part-time, online learning. *Degree requirements:* For master's, comprehensive exam (for some programs), thesis (for some programs); for other advanced degree, one foreign language, thesis. *Entrance requirements:* Additional exam requirements/recommendations for international students: required—TOEFL (minimum score 80 iBT); recommended—IELTS (minimum score 6.5). Electronic applications accepted.

Vanderbilt University, Department of Religion, Nashville, TN 37240-1001. Offers MA, PhD. *Faculty:* 26 full-time (10 women). *Students:* 54 full-time (37 women); includes 18 minority (11 Black or African American, non-Hispanic/Latino; 2 Asian, non-Hispanic/Latino; 4 Hispanic/Latino; 1 Two or more races, non-Hispanic/Latino), 8 international. Average age 34. 113 applicants, 13% accepted, 6 enrolled. In 2019, 7 master's, 6 doctorates awarded. *Degree requirements:* For master's, one foreign language, thesis; for doctorate, 2 foreign languages, thesis/dissertation, final and qualifying exams. *Entrance requirements:* For master's and doctorate, GRE General Test. Additional exam requirements/recommendations for international students: required—TOEFL (minimum score 570 paper-based; 88 iBT). *Application deadline:* For fall admission, 12/15 for domestic and international students. Electronic applications accepted. *Expenses: Tuition:* Full-time $51,018; part-time $2087 per hour. *Required fees:* $542. Tuition and fees vary according to program. *Financial support:* Fellowships, teaching assistantships, Federal Work-Study, institutionally sponsored loans, health care benefits, and tuition waivers (full and partial) available. Support available to part-time students. Financial award application deadline: 1/15; financial award applicants required to submit CSS PROFILE or FAFSA. *Unit head:* Dr. James Byrd, Jr., Chair and Director of Graduate Studies, 615-343-9977, Fax: 615-343-9957, E-mail: james.p.byrd@vanderbilt.edu. *Application contact:* Karen Eardley, Administrative Assistant, 615-343-3977, Fax: 615-343-9957, E-mail: karen.eardley@vanderbilt.edu.
Website: http://divinity.vanderbilt.edu/degrees/graduate/index.php

Vanguard University of Southern California, Graduate Programs in Religion, Costa Mesa, CA 92626. Offers leadership studies (MA); theology (MA). *Program availability:* Part-time, evening/weekend, 100% online, blended/hybrid learning. *Degree requirements:* For master's, comprehensive exam (for some programs), thesis (for some programs). *Entrance requirements:* For master's, minimum GPA of 3.0 (MA), 2.5 (MTS). Additional exam requirements/recommendations for international students: required—TOEFL (minimum score 550 paper-based; 79 iBT). Electronic applications accepted. *Expenses:* Contact institution.

Virginia University of Lynchburg, Graduate Programs, Lynchburg, VA 24501-6417. Offers Christian ministry (M Div); ministry (D Min). *Program availability:* Online learning.

Wake Forest University, Graduate School of Arts and Sciences, Department for the Study of Religions, Winston-Salem, NC 27109. Offers religious studies (MA). *Accreditation:* ACIPE. *Program availability:* Part-time. *Degree requirements:* For master's, one foreign language, thesis. *Entrance requirements:* For master's, GRE General Test. Additional exam requirements/recommendations for international students: required—TOEFL (minimum score 79 iBT). Electronic applications accepted.

Walla Walla University, Graduate Studies, Center for Cinema, Religion, and Worldview, College Place, WA 99324. Offers Web and interactive media (MA). *Entrance requirements:* For master's, three professional references, transcripts, personal statement.

Washington Adventist University, Program in Religion, Takoma Park, MD 20912. Offers MAR. *Program availability:* Part-time. *Entrance requirements:* Additional exam requirements/recommendations for international students: required—TOEFL (minimum score 550 paper-based), IELTS (minimum score 5).

Washington University in St. Louis, The Graduate School, Department of Jewish, Islamic, and Near Eastern Languages and Cultures, St. Louis, MO 63130-4899. Offers Islamic and Near Eastern studies (MA); Jewish studies (MA). *Degree requirements:* For master's, one foreign language, thesis (for some programs). *Entrance requirements:* For master's, GRE General Test. Additional exam requirements/recommendations for international students: required—TOEFL. Electronic applications accepted.

Wayland Baptist University, Graduate Programs, Programs in Religion, Plainview, TX 79072-6998. Offers Christian ministry (MCM); divinity (M Div); religion (MA). *Program availability:* Part-time, evening/weekend, online learning. *Degree requirements:* For master's, comprehensive exam. *Entrance requirements:* For master's, GRE or MAT, minimum GPA of 3.0; letter of endorsement from Christian congregation, one academic and one personal letter of recommendation (for M Div). Additional exam requirements/recommendations for international students: required—TOEFL (minimum score 500 paper-based; 61 iBT). Electronic applications accepted. *Expenses: Tuition:* Full-time $728; part-time $728 per semester. *Required fees:* $1218. Tuition and fees vary according to degree level, campus/location and program.

Wesley Biblical Seminary, Graduate Programs, Jackson, MS 39206. Offers apologetics (MA); Biblical languages (M Div); Biblical literature (MA); Christian studies (MA); context and mission (M Div); honors research (M Div); interpretation (M Div); ministry (M Div); spiritual formation (M Div); teaching (M Div); theology (MA). *Accreditation:* ATS. *Program availability:* Part-time. *Degree requirements:* For master's, thesis. *Entrance requirements:* Additional exam requirements/recommendations for international students: required—TOEFL. Electronic applications accepted.

Western Michigan University, Graduate College, College of Arts and Sciences, Department of Comparative Religion, Kalamazoo, MI 49008. Offers MA, Graduate Certificate. *Degree requirements:* For master's, one foreign language, thesis optional.

Western Seminary - Portland, Graduate Programs, Program in Biblical and Theological Studies, Portland, OR 97215-3367. Offers biblical and theological studies (MA, G Dip); biblical studies (Certificate); theology (Th M). *Accreditation:* ATS. *Program availability:* Part-time, evening/weekend. *Degree requirements:* For master's, thesis or alternative, practicum. *Entrance requirements:* Additional exam requirements/recommendations for international students: required—TOEFL.

Westminster Seminary California, Programs in Theology, Escondido, CA 92027-4128. Offers Biblical studies (MA); historical theology (MA); theological studies (M Div, MA). *Program availability:* Part-time, evening/weekend. *Degree requirements:* For master's, 2 foreign languages, thesis (for some programs). *Entrance requirements:* For master's, 2 letters of reference. Additional exam requirements/recommendations for international students: required—TOEFL (minimum score 570 paper-based; 89 iBT), TWE (minimum score 4.5).

Westminster Theological Seminary, Graduate and Professional Programs, Philadelphia, PA 19118. Offers apologetics (Th M); Biblical and urban studies (Certificate); Biblical counseling (MA); biblical studies (MAR); Christian studies (Certificate); church history (Th M); counseling (M Div); general studies (M Div, MAR); hermeneutics and Bible interpretations (PhD); historical and theological studies (PhD); historical theology (Th M); New Testament (Th M); Old Testament (Th M); pastoral counseling (D Min); pastoral ministry (M Div, D Min); systematic theology (Th M); theological studies (MAR); urban missions (M Div, MA, MAR, D Min). *Accreditation:* ATS. *Program availability:* Part-time. Terminal master's awarded for partial completion of doctoral program. *Degree requirements:* For master's, thesis (for some programs); for doctorate, 4 foreign languages, comprehensive exam (for some programs), thesis/dissertation. *Entrance requirements:* For doctorate, GRE General Test. Additional exam requirements/recommendations for international students: required—TOEFL, TWE.

Wilfrid Laurier University, Faculty of Graduate and Postdoctoral Studies, Faculty of Arts, Department of Religion and Culture, Waterloo, ON N2L 3C5, Canada. Offers religion and culture (MA); religious diversity of North America (PhD). *Program availability:* Part-time. *Degree requirements:* For master's, thesis optional; for doctorate, thesis/dissertation. *Entrance requirements:* For master's, honors BA or the equivalent in religious studies or other interdisciplinary social science or humanities program, minimum B average in overall undergraduate course work, B+ average in the undergraduate major; for doctorate, MA in religious studies, minimum A- average. Additional exam requirements/recommendations for international students: required—TOEFL (minimum score 89 iBT). Electronic applications accepted.

Won Institute of Graduate Studies, Won Buddhist Studies Program, Glenside, PA 19038. Offers MWBS. *Program availability:* Part-time. *Degree requirements:* For master's, comprehensive exam, comprehensive ordination exam or thesis. *Entrance requirements:* For master's, bachelor's degree or one-year preparatory course in Won Buddhist studies. Additional exam requirements/recommendations for international students: required—TOEFL (minimum score 550 paper-based; 79 iBT). *Expenses:* Contact institution.

Wycliffe College, Division of Advanced Degree Studies, Toronto, ON M5S 1H7, Canada. Offers MA, Th M, D Min, PhD, Th D. *Accreditation:* ATS (one or more programs are accredited). *Program availability:* Part-time. Terminal master's awarded for partial completion of doctoral program. *Degree requirements:* For master's, 2 foreign languages, thesis (for some programs); for doctorate, 3 foreign languages, thesis/dissertation. *Entrance requirements:* Additional exam requirements/recommendations for international students: required—TOEFL (minimum score 600 paper-based). *Expenses:* Contact institution.

Wycliffe College, Division of Basic Degree Studies, Toronto, ON M5S 1H7, Canada. Offers Christian Studies (Diploma); theology (M Div, M Rel, MTS). *Accreditation:* ATS. *Program availability:* Part-time. *Degree requirements:* For master's, one foreign language, thesis. *Entrance requirements:* Additional exam requirements/recommendations for international students: required—TOEFL (minimum score 580 paper-based).

Yale University, Graduate School of Arts and Sciences, Department of Religious Studies, New Haven, CT 06520. Offers PhD. *Degree requirements:* For doctorate, 2 foreign languages, thesis/dissertation. *Entrance requirements:* For doctorate, GRE General Test.

Yeshiva Derech Chaim, Graduate Program, Brooklyn, NY 11218. Offers PhD. *Accreditation:* AARTS.

Theology

Abilene Christian University, Office of Graduate Programs, College of Biblical Studies, Graduate School of Theology, Abilene, TX 79699. Offers ancient and Oriental Christianity (MA); Christian ministry (MACM); divinity (M Div), including ministry, missions; global service (MA); ministry (D Min), including Christian spiritual formation, leadership for missional renewal, preaching for community transformation; modern and American Christianity (MA); New Testament (MA); Old Testament (MA); theology (MA). *Program availability:* Part-time, evening/weekend, online learning. *Faculty:* 12 full-time (2 women), 9 part-time/adjunct (1 woman). *Students:* 116 full-time (24 women), 86 part-time (24 women); includes 61 minority (34 Black or African American, non-Hispanic/Latino; 1 Asian, non-Hispanic/Latino; 21 Hispanic/Latino; 5 Two or more races, non-Hispanic/Latino), 11 international. 185 applicants, 54% accepted, 68 enrolled. In 2019, 17 master's, 2 doctorates awarded. *Degree requirements:* For master's, comprehensive exam (for some programs), thesis (for some programs); for doctorate, one foreign language, thesis/dissertation. *Entrance requirements:* For master's, official transcripts, Recommendation, purpose statement, writing assessment; for doctorate, official transcripts, Documentation of Ministry, Recommendations, personal statement, Endorsement of Elders or Supervisor. Additional exam requirements/recommendations for international students: required—TOEFL (minimum score 80 iBT), IELTS (minimum score 6), PTE (minimum score 51). *Application deadline:* For fall admission, 8/10 priority date for domestic students; for spring admission, 11/1 for domestic students. Applications are processed on a rolling basis. Application fee: $65. *Expenses:* $676 per hour. *Financial support:* In 2019–20, 39 students received support, including 18 research assistantships with partial tuition reimbursements available; Federal Work-Study also available. Support available to part-time students. Financial award application deadline: 4/1; financial award applicants required to submit FAFSA. *Unit head:* Dr. Tim Sensing, Associate Dean, 325-674-3730, Fax: 325-674-6180, E-mail: sensingt@acu.edu. *Application contact:* Graduate Admissions, 325-674-6911, E-mail: gradinfo@acu.edu.
Website: http://www.acu.edu/gst

Acadia University, Divinity College, Wolfville, NS B4P 2R6, Canada. Offers divinity (M Div); ministry (D Min); theology (MA), including chaplaincy and spiritual care, Christian history, discipleship, evangelism and mission, indigenous community development, leadership and spiritual formation, New Testament, next generation ministry, Old Testament, pastoral care and counseling, prison chaplaincy, Second Temple Judaism, theology. *Accreditation:* ATS. *Program availability:* Part-time. *Degree requirements:* For master's, variable foreign language requirement, thesis (for some programs); for doctorate, one foreign language, comprehensive exam, thesis/dissertation. *Entrance requirements:* For doctorate, minimum GPA of 3.0, 3 years' ministry experience. Additional exam requirements/recommendations for international students: required—TOEFL. *Expenses:* Contact institution.

Ambrose University, Ambrose Seminary, Calgary, AB T3H 0L5, Canada. Offers Biblical/theological studies (MA), including New Testament, Old Testament, theology; Christian studies (MCS, Diploma); intercultural ministries (M Div, MA); leadership (Certificate); leadership and ministry (MA), including chaplaincy, poverty studies, preaching; pastoral ministry (M Div). *Accreditation:* ATS (one or more programs are accredited). *Program availability:* Part-time, blended/hybrid learning. *Degree requirements:* For master's, variable foreign language requirement, internship (for M Div, MA in leadership and ministry, MA in intercultural ministries); thesis (for MA in Biblical/theological studies). *Entrance requirements:* For master's, undergraduate degree from other accredited university or bible college, minimum GPA of 2.0. Additional exam requirements/recommendations for international students: required—PTE (minimum score 58), TOEFL (minimum score 560 paper-based, 83 iBT) or IELTS (minimum score 6.5). Electronic applications accepted.

American Baptist Seminary of the West, Graduate and Professional Programs, Berkeley, CA 94704-3029. Offers community leadership (MA); theology (M Div, MA). *Accreditation:* ACIPE; ATS (one or more programs are accredited). *Program availability:* Part-time, evening/weekend, online learning. *Entrance requirements:* Additional exam requirements/recommendations for international students: required—TOEFL (minimum score 550 paper-based). Electronic applications accepted.

American Jewish University, Ziegler School of Rabbinic Studies, Bel Air, CA 90077-1599. Offers MARS. *Degree requirements:* For master's, one foreign language. *Entrance requirements:* For master's, GRE General Test, interview. Additional exam requirements/recommendations for international students: required—TOEFL.

Amridge University, Graduate and Professional Programs, Montgomery, AL 36117. Offers Biblical studies (MA, PhD); Christian ministry (MS); family therapy (D Min); human services (MS); leadership and management (MS); marriage and family therapy (M Div, MA, PhD); ministerial leadership (M Div, MS); New Testament studies (MA); Old Testament studies (MA); professional counseling (M Div, MA, PhD); theology (M Div, D Min). *Program availability:* Part-time, evening/weekend, online learning. *Degree requirements:* For master's, one foreign language, comprehensive exam (for some programs), thesis (for some programs); for doctorate, one foreign language, comprehensive exam (for some programs), thesis/dissertation (for some programs). *Entrance requirements:* For master's, official transcript showing an earned 4-year BA or BS from regionally- or nationally-accredited institution; for doctorate, official transcript showing earned graduate degree from regionally- or nationally-accredited institution; writing sample (e.g. career monograph, published journal article, term paper from master's degree or doctoral dissertation); interview. Additional exam requirements/recommendations for international students: required—TOEFL (minimum score 79 iBT). Electronic applications accepted.

Anabaptist Mennonite Biblical Seminary, Graduate and Professional Programs, Elkhart, IN 46517-1999. Offers chaplaincy (M Div); Christian faith formation (M Div); Christian formation (MA); Christian spiritual formation (Certificate); divinity (M Div); pastoral ministry (M Div); pastoral theology for financial professionals (Certificate); peace studies (M Div), including environmental sustainability leadership (M Div, MA); theological studies (M Div, Certificate), including peace studies (M Div), theology and ethics (M Div); theology and peace studies (MA), including conflict transformation, environmental sustainability leadership (M Div, MA), international development administration; United Methodist leadership (M Div). *Accreditation:* ACIPE; ATS. *Program availability:* Part-time, 100% online, blended/hybrid learning. *Degree requirements:* For master's, variable foreign language requirement, comprehensive exam (for some programs), thesis optional, senior interview. *Entrance requirements:* For master's, undergraduate degree transcripts, 3 letters of reference, essay. Additional exam requirements/recommendations for international students: required—TOEFL (minimum score 90 iBT); recommended—IELTS (minimum score 7). Electronic applications accepted.

Anderson University, School of Theology, Anderson, IN 46012. Offers missions (MA); theology (M Div, MTS, D Min). *Accreditation:* ACIPE; ATS. *Program availability:* Part-time. *Degree requirements:* For master's, variable foreign language requirement, thesis (for some programs); for doctorate, thesis/dissertation.

Andrews University, School of Graduate Studies, Seventh-day Adventist Theological Seminary, Berrien Springs, MI 49104. Offers ministry (M Div, D Min); pastoral ministry (MA); religious education (MA, Ed D, PhD, Ed S); theology (M Th, Th D); youth ministry (MA). *Faculty:* 40 full-time (5 women), 12 part-time/adjunct (2 women). *Students:* 448 full-time (52 women), 456 part-time (84 women); includes 463 minority (193 Black or African American, non-Hispanic/Latino; 3 American Indian or Alaska Native, non-Hispanic/Latino; 49 Asian, non-Hispanic/Latino; 198 Hispanic/Latino; 10 Native Hawaiian or other Pacific Islander, non-Hispanic/Latino; 10 Two or more races, non-Hispanic/Latino), 255 international. Average age 40. In 2019, 171 master's, 41 doctorates, 1 other advanced degree awarded. *Degree requirements:* For master's, thesis optional; for doctorate, variable foreign language requirement, thesis/dissertation. *Entrance requirements:* For master's, GRE Subject Test, minimum GPA of 2.0. Additional exam requirements/recommendations for international students: required—TOEFL (minimum score 550 paper-based). *Application deadline:* Applications are processed on a rolling basis. Application fee: $60. *Financial support:* Fellowships, research assistantships, teaching assistantships, career-related internships or fieldwork, Federal Work-Study, and institutionally sponsored loans available. *Unit head:* Dr. Jiri Moskala, Dean, 269-471-3537. *Application contact:* Jillian Panigot, Director of Graduate Admissions, 800-253-2874, Fax: 269-471-6321.

Apex School of Theology, Graduate Programs, Durham, NC 27703. Offers M Div, MACC, MCE, D Min.

Aquinas Institute of Theology, Graduate and Professional Programs, St. Louis, MO 63108. Offers biblical studies (Certificate); church music (MM); health care mission (MAHCM); ministry (M Div); pastoral care (Certificate); pastoral ministry (MAPM); pastoral studies (MAPS); preaching (D Min); spiritual direction (Certificate); theology (M Div, MA); Thomistic studies (Certificate); M Div/MA; MA/PhD; MAPS/MSW. *Accreditation:* ATS (one or more programs are accredited). *Program availability:* Part-time, evening/weekend, online learning. *Degree requirements:* For master's, variable foreign language requirement, comprehensive exam (for some programs), thesis (for some programs); for doctorate, thesis/dissertation. *Entrance requirements:* For master's and Certificate, MAT; for doctorate, 3 years of ministerial experience, 6 hours of graduate course work in homiletics, M Div or the equivalent, minimum GPA of 3.0. Additional exam requirements/recommendations for international students: required—TOEFL. *Expenses:* Contact institution.

Arlington Baptist University, Program in Biblical and Theological Studies, Arlington, TX 76012-3425. Offers MA. *Entrance requirements:* For master's, official transcript, letter of reference from pastor, two letters of recommendation, essay. Additional exam requirements/recommendations for international students: required—TOEFL. Electronic applications accepted.

Asbury Theological Seminary, Graduate and Professional Programs, Wilmore, KY 40390-1199. Offers M Div, MA, MAAS, MACE, MACL, MACM, MACP, MAMFC, MAMHC, MAPC, MASF, MAYM, Th M, D Min, PhD, Certificate. *Accreditation:* ATS. *Program availability:* Part-time, online learning. Terminal master's awarded for partial completion of doctoral program. *Degree requirements:* For master's, thesis (for some programs); for doctorate, thesis/dissertation, qualifying exam. *Entrance requirements:* For master's, minimum GPA of 2.75; for doctorate, minimum GPA of 3.0. Additional exam requirements/recommendations for international students: required—TOEFL, IELTS. Electronic applications accepted.

Ashland Theological Seminary, Graduate Programs, Ashland, OH 44805. Offers Biblical studies (MA); Christian ministries (MACM), including Black church studies (MACM, D Min), general Christian ministries, leadership, spiritual formation (MACM, D Min); clinical mental health counseling (MA); counseling (MAC); historical and theological studies (MA), including Anabaptism and Pietism, Christian theology, church history, New Testament, Old Testament; ministry (D Min), including Black church studies (MACM, D Min), chaplaincy (M Div, D Min), independent design, spiritual formation (MACM, D Min), transformational leadership; pastoral ministry (M Div), including chaplaincy (M Div, D Min), general ministry. *Accreditation:* ATS. *Program availability:* Part-time. *Degree requirements:* For master's, 2 foreign languages, comprehensive exam (for some programs), thesis (for some programs); for doctorate, thesis/dissertation. *Entrance requirements:* For master's, bachelor's degree from accredited institution with minimum undergraduate GPA of 2.75; for doctorate, M Div, minimum undergraduate GPA of 3.0. Additional exam requirements/recommendations for international students: required—TOEFL (minimum score 500 paper-based; 65 iBT). Electronic applications accepted.

Assemblies of God Theological Seminary, Graduate and Professional Programs, Springfield, MO 65802. Offers Biblical interpretation and theology (PhD); Christian ministries (MA); divinity (M Div); intercultural studies (MA, PhD); leadership and ministry (MLM); ministry (D Min); missiology (DAIS); pastoral studies (MPL); theological studies (MA, Th M). *Accreditation:* ATS. *Program availability:* Part-time, evening/weekend, 100% online. *Faculty:* 12 full-time (3 women), 15 part-time/adjunct (4 women). *Students:* 136 full-time (37 women), 147 part-time (40 women); includes 71 minority (24 Black or African American, non-Hispanic/Latino; 6 American Indian or Alaska Native, non-Hispanic/Latino; 7 Asian, non-Hispanic/Latino; 22 Hispanic/Latino; 7 Native Hawaiian or other Pacific Islander, non-Hispanic/Latino; 5 Two or more races, non-Hispanic/Latino), 14 international. Average age 46. 62 applicants, 100% accepted, 42 enrolled. In 2019, 37 master's, 25 doctorates awarded. *Degree requirements:* For master's, variable foreign language requirement, thesis; for doctorate, variable foreign language requirement, comprehensive exam, thesis/dissertation. *Entrance requirements:* For master's, minimum GPA of 2.5; for doctorate, GRE (for PhD in Bible theology), minimum GPA of 3.0. Additional exam requirements/recommendations for international students: required—TOEFL (minimum score 550 paper-based; 80 iBT). *Application deadline:* For fall admission, 7/1 priority date for domestic students, 6/1 priority date for international students; for spring admission, 12/1 priority date for domestic students, 11/1 priority date for international students. Applications are processed on a rolling basis. Application fee: $75. Electronic applications accepted. *Financial support:* Career-related internships or fieldwork and scholarships/grants available. Support available to part-time students. Financial award application deadline: 7/15; financial award applicants required to submit FAFSA. *Unit head:* Dr. Timothy A. Hager, Dean, 417-268-1000, Fax: 417-268-1001. *Application contact:* Nik White, Seminary Enrollment Coordinator, 417-268-1000, Fax: 417-268-1030, E-mail: info@agts.edu.
Website: http://www.agts.edu

The Athenaeum of Ohio, Graduate Programs, Cincinnati, OH 45230-5900. Offers M Div, MA, MA Th, MABS, Certificate, M Div/MA Th, M Div/MABS. *Program availability:* Part-time, evening/weekend. *Degree requirements:* For master's, variable foreign language requirement, comprehensive exam (for some programs), thesis or alternative. *Entrance requirements:* For master's, bachelor's degree, minimum GPA of 3.0.

Atlantic School of Theology, Graduate and Professional Programs, Halifax, NS B3H 3B5, Canada. Offers ministry (M Div); theological studies (Graduate Certificate). *Accreditation:* ATS. *Program availability:* Part-time, online learning. *Degree requirements:* For master's, thesis (for some programs). *Entrance requirements:* For master's and Graduate Certificate, minimum B average in undergraduate course work. *Expenses: Required fees:* $7000 Canadian dollars; $700 Canadian dollars per course.

Austin Presbyterian Theological Seminary, Graduate and Professional Programs, Austin, TX 78705-5797. Offers divinity (M Div); ministry (D Min); ministry practice (MA); theological studies (MA); youth ministry (MA); M Div/MSSW. *Accreditation:* ACIPE; ATS. *Degree requirements:* For master's, Greek, Hebrew (for M Div); for doctorate, thesis/dissertation. *Entrance requirements:* For master's, references (for M Div). Additional exam requirements/recommendations for international students: required—TOEFL (minimum score 550 paper-based; 79 iBT). Electronic applications accepted. *Expenses: Tuition:* Full-time $13,980; part-time $6990 per credit. *Required fees:* $170; $170.

Ave Maria University, Graduate Programs, Ave Maria, FL 34142. Offers pastoral theology (MTS); theology (MA, PhD). Terminal master's awarded for partial completion of doctoral program. *Degree requirements:* For master's, one foreign language, thesis; for doctorate, 3 foreign languages, comprehensive exam, thesis/dissertation. *Entrance requirements:* For master's, GRE; for doctorate, GRE, M Div or equivalent; MA or MTS in religion, theology, or philosophy; bachelor's degree with strong background in religion, theology, and/or philosophy.

Azusa Pacific University, Azusa Pacific Seminary, Program in Divinity, Azusa, CA 91702-7000. Offers Biblical studies (M Div). *Expenses:* Contact institution.

Azusa Pacific University, Azusa Pacific Seminary, Program in Ministry, Azusa, CA 91702-7000. Offers D Min. *Accreditation:* ATS. *Expenses:* Contact institution.

Azusa Pacific University, Azusa Pacific Seminary, Program in Theological Studies, Concentration in Biblical Studies, Azusa, CA 91702-7000. Offers MA. *Accreditation:* ATS.

Azusa Pacific University, Azusa Pacific Seminary, Program in Theological Studies, Concentration in Theology and Ethics, Azusa, CA 91702-7000. Offers MA. *Accreditation:* ATS.

Azusa Pacific University, College of Liberal Arts and Sciences, Haggard Graduate School of Theology, Azusa, CA 91702-7000. Offers MA. *Expenses:* Contact institution.

Bakke Graduate University, Programs in Pastoral Ministry and Business, Dallas, TX 75243-7039. Offers business administration (MBA); church and ministry multiplication (D Min); global urban leadership (MA); leadership (D Min); ministry in complex contexts (D Min); social and civic entrepreneurship (MA); theology of work (D Min); theology reflection (D Min); transformational leadership (DTL); urban youth ministry (D Min). *Program availability:* Part-time, online learning. *Degree requirements:* For master's, thesis; for doctorate, thesis/dissertation. *Entrance requirements:* For master's, 2 years of ministry experience, BA in Biblical studies or theology; for doctorate, 3 years of ministry experience, M Div. Additional exam requirements/recommendations for international students: required—TOEFL. Electronic applications accepted.

Baptist Bible College, Graduate and Professional Programs, Springfield, MO 65803-3498. Offers biblical counseling (MA); church ministry (MA); theology (M Div). *Program availability:* Part-time. *Entrance requirements:* Additional exam requirements/recommendations for international students: required—TOEFL. Electronic applications accepted. *Expenses:* Contact institution.

The Baptist College of Florida, Graduate Programs, Graceville, FL 32440. Offers Christian studies (MA); music and worship leadership (MA). *Program availability:* Part-time, 100% online, blended/hybrid learning. *Faculty:* 13 full-time (2 women). *Students:* 33 full-time (6 women); includes 2 minority (1 Black or African American, non-Hispanic/Latino; 1 Hispanic/Latino). Average age 28. 10 applicants, 100% accepted, 10 enrolled. In 2019, 3 master's awarded. *Degree requirements:* For master's, variable foreign language requirement, comprehensive exam (for some programs), thesis (for some programs). *Entrance requirements:* For master's, regionally-accredited undergraduate degree, undergraduate courses in field, minimum GPA of 2.5. Additional exam requirements/recommendations for international students: required—TOEFL. *Application deadline:* For fall admission, 8/10 for domestic and international students; for spring admission, 1/20 for domestic and international students. Applications are processed on a rolling basis. Application fee: $25. Electronic applications accepted. *Expenses: Tuition:* Full-time $4320; part-time $360 per credit hour. *Financial support:* In 2019–20, 2 students received support. Applicants required to submit FAFSA. *Unit head:* Dr. Robin Jumper, Academic Dean, 850-263-3261 Ext. 425, Fax: 850-263-2141, E-mail: grjumper@baptistcollege.edu. *Application contact:* Sandra Richards, Director of Student Life and Marketing, 850-263-3261 Ext. 415, Fax: 850-263-9026, E-mail: skrichards@baptistcollege.edu.
Website: http://www.baptistcollege.edu

Baptist Missionary Association Theological Seminary, Graduate and Professional Programs, Jacksonville, TX 75766-5407. Offers M Div, MAR. *Accreditation:* ATS. *Program availability:* Part-time. *Degree requirements:* For master's, variable foreign language requirement, thesis optional. *Entrance requirements:* Additional exam requirements/recommendations for international students: required—TOEFL (minimum score 550 paper-based). Electronic applications accepted.

Barclay College, Master of Arts Program, Haviland, KS 67059-0288. Offers MA. *Program availability:* Online learning. *Degree requirements:* For master's, comprehensive exam, capstone project. *Entrance requirements:* Additional exam requirements/recommendations for international students: required—TOEFL. Electronic applications accepted.

Barry University, College of Arts and Sciences, Department of Theology and Philosophy, Miami Shores, FL 33161-6695. Offers ministry (D Min); pastoral ministry for Hispanics (MA); pastoral theology (MA); practical theology (MA). *Accreditation:* ATS. *Program availability:* Part-time, evening/weekend. *Degree requirements:* For master's, comprehensive exam, thesis optional; for doctorate, thesis/dissertation. *Entrance requirements:* For master's, GRE General Test or MAT, minimum GPA of 3.0. Electronic applications accepted.

Theology

Baylor University, George W. Truett Theological Seminary, Waco, TX 76798. Offers M Div, MACM, MTS, D Min, JD/M Div, M Div/MBA, M Div/MM, M Div/MS Ed, M Div/MSW, MTS/MSW. *Program availability:* Part-time. *Degree requirements:* For master's, 2 foreign languages, thesis or alternative; for doctorate, comprehensive exam, thesis/dissertation, 12 hours of seminars, 12 hours of directed study (including 2 annotated bibliographies reflecting at least 4800 pages of reading, 10 meetings with a field supervisor, 20 meetings with a faculty supervisor, and 3 major learning events). *Entrance requirements:* For master's, 4 recommendations, 2 essays, transcripts from all colleges/universities attended to include conferred undergraduate degree or equivalent, minimum GPA of 2.7, evidence of Christian commitment and leadership; for doctorate, 4 recommendations, 3 essays, writing sample, church recommendation, interview, transcripts from all colleges/universities attended to include conferred M Div or equivalent, minimum GPA of 3.0, 3 years of ministry experience subsequent to M Div. Additional exam requirements/recommendations for international students: required—TOEFL (minimum score 550 paper-based; 80 iBT), IELTS (minimum score 6.5). Electronic applications accepted. Application fee is waived when completed online. *Expenses:* Contact institution.

Bethany Theological Seminary, Graduate and Professional Programs, Richmond, IN 47374-4019. Offers biblical studies (MA Th); ministry studies (M Div); peace studies (M Div, MA Th); theological studies (MA Th, CATS); youth ministry (M Div). *Accreditation:* ACIPE; ATS. *Program availability:* Part-time, online learning. *Degree requirements:* For master's, thesis (for some programs). *Entrance requirements:* For master's, letters of reference. Additional exam requirements/recommendations for international students: required—TOEFL (minimum score 550 paper-based).

Bethel Seminary, Graduate and Professional Programs, St. Paul, MN 55112-6998. Offers Anglican studies (Certificate); children's and family ministry (MA); Christian studies (Certificate); Christian thought (MA); church planting (Certificate); Greek and Hebrew language (M Div); Greek language (M Div); Hebrew language (M Div); marriage and family therapy (MA, Certificate); mental health counseling (MA); ministry (MA, D Min); ministry practice (Certificate); theological studies (MA, Certificate); transformational leadership (MA); young life youth ministry (Certificate). *Accreditation:* ACIPE. *Program availability:* Part-time, evening/weekend, 100% online, blended/hybrid learning. *Degree requirements:* For master's, variable foreign language requirement, thesis (for some programs); for doctorate, thesis/dissertation. *Entrance requirements:* For master's, letters of reference, transcripts, personal statement; for doctorate, M Div, letters of reference, organizational support; for Certificate, letters of reference, family essay, personal statement, and family of origin paper (for marriage and family therapy). Additional exam requirements/recommendations for international students: required—TOEFL (minimum score 550 paper-based; 87 iBT). Electronic applications accepted. *Expenses:* Contact institution.

Bethel University, Adult and Graduate Programs, Program in Theological Studies, Mishawaka, IN 46545-5591. Offers MATS. *Program availability:* Part-time, evening/weekend, 100% online, blended/hybrid learning. *Entrance requirements:* Additional exam requirements/recommendations for international students: required—TOEFL (minimum score 540 paper-based). Electronic applications accepted.

Bethesda University, Graduate and Professional Programs, Anaheim, CA 92801. Offers biblical studies (MA); music (MA); theology (M Div). *Entrance requirements:* For master's, interview. Additional exam requirements/recommendations for international students: recommended—TOEFL.

Beth HaMedrash Shaarei Yosher Institute, Graduate Programs, Brooklyn, NY 11204. *Accreditation:* AARTS.

Beth Hatalmud Rabbinical College, Graduate Programs, Brooklyn, NY 11214. *Accreditation:* AARTS.

Bethlehem College & Seminary, Graduate and Professional Programs, Minneapolis, MN 55415. Offers church planting and revitalization (M Div); exegesis and theology (MA); theology (Th M); worship pastor (M Div). *Degree requirements:* For master's, thesis (for some programs).

Beth Medrash Govoha, Graduate Programs, Lakewood, NJ 08701-2797. *Accreditation:* AARTS.

Bethune-Cookman University, School of Graduate Studies, Daytona Beach, FL 32114-3099. Offers transformative leadership (MS). *Program availability:* Online learning. *Degree requirements:* For master's, thesis. *Entrance requirements:* For master's, GRE or MAT, minimum GPA of 2.75 in the last 60 semester hours; 3 letters of recommendation. Additional exam requirements/recommendations for international students: required—TOEFL (minimum score 550 paper-based). Electronic applications accepted.

Bexley Seabury Seminary, Graduate Programs, Chicago, IL 60637. Offers Anglican studies (Diploma); congregational development (D Min); preaching (D Min); theology (M Div). *Accreditation:* ACIPE. *Program availability:* Part-time. *Degree requirements:* For master's, thesis; for doctorate, thesis/dissertation; for Diploma, thesis (for some programs). *Entrance requirements:* For master's, interview, sample of written work.

Biola University, Talbot School of Theology, La Mirada, CA 90639-0001. Offers adult/family ministry (MACE); Bible exposition (MA, Th M); Biblical and theological studies (Certificate); children's ministry (MACE); Christian education (M Div); cross-cultural education ministry (MACE); educational studies (Ed D, PhD); evangelism and discipleship (M Div); general Christian education (MACE); Messianic Jewish studies (M Div, Certificate); missions and intercultural studies (M Div); New Testament (MA, Th M); Old Testament (MA); Old Testament and Semitics (Th M); pastoral and general ministry (M Div); pastoral care and counseling (M Div, MACML); philosophy (MA); preaching and pastoral ministry (MACML); spiritual formation (M Div, Certificate); spiritual formation and soul care (MA); sports ministry (MACML); theology (MA, Th M, D Min, Certificate); youth ministry (MACE). *Program availability:* Part-time, evening/weekend. *Students:* 461 full-time (116 women), 768 part-time (228 women); includes 489 minority (54 Black or African American, non-Hispanic/Latino; 1 American Indian or Alaska Native, non-Hispanic/Latino; 303 Asian, non-Hispanic/Latino; 96 Hispanic/Latino; 3 Native Hawaiian or other Pacific Islander, non-Hispanic/Latino; 32 Two or more races, non-Hispanic/Latino), 162 international. Average age 38. 745 applicants, 70% accepted, 320 enrolled. In 2019, 235 master's, 24 doctorates awarded. *Entrance requirements:* For master's, bachelor's degree from accredited college or university; minimum GPA of 2.6 (for M Div), 3.0 (for MA); for doctorate, M Div or MA. Additional exam requirements/recommendations for international students: required—TOEFL (minimum score 600 paper-based; 88 iBT). *Application deadline:* For fall admission, 7/1 for domestic students, 6/1 for international students; for spring admission, 11/1 for domestic students. Applications are processed on a rolling basis. Application fee: $65. Electronic applications accepted. *Financial support:* Scholarships/grants and unspecified assistantships available. Support available to part-time students. Financial award applicants required to submit FAFSA. *Unit head:* Dr. Clint Arnold, Dean, 562-903-4816, Fax: 562-903-4748. *Application contact:* Graduate Admissions Office, 562-903-4752, E-mail: graduate.admissions@biola.edu. Website: http://www.talbot.edu/

Bob Jones University, Graduate Programs, Greenville, SC 29614. Offers accountancy (MS); Bible (MA); Bible translation (MA); Biblical studies (Certificate); business administration (MBA); church history (MA, PhD); church ministries (MA); church music (MM); cinema and video production (MA); counseling (MS); curriculum and instruction (Ed D); divinity (M Div); dramatic production (MA); educational leadership (MS, Ed D, Ed S); elementary education (M Ed, MAT); English (M Ed, MA, MAT); fine arts (MA); graphic design (MA); history (M Ed, MA); illustration (MA); interpretative speech (MA); mathematics (M Ed, MAT); medical missions (Certificate); ministry (MM, D Min); multi-categorical special education (M Ed, MAT); music (M Ed); New Testament interpretation (PhD); Old Testament interpretation (PhD); orchestral instrument performance (MM); organ performance (MM); pastoral studies (MA); personnel services (MS, Ed S); piano pedagogy (MM); piano performance (MM); platform arts (MA); rhetoric and public address (MA); secondary education (M Ed); studio art (MA); teaching Bible (MA); theology (MA, PhD); voice performance (MM); youth ministries (MA); M Div/MM.

Boston College, Morrissey Graduate School of Arts and Sciences, Department of Theology, Chestnut Hill, MA 02467-3800. Offers philosophy and theology (MA); theology (PhD). *Accreditation:* ATS. Terminal master's awarded for partial completion of doctoral program. *Degree requirements:* For master's, one foreign language, thesis optional; for doctorate, thesis/dissertation. *Entrance requirements:* For master's and doctorate, GRE General Test. Additional exam requirements/recommendations for international students: required—TOEFL (minimum score 600 paper-based; 100 iBT), IELTS (minimum score 8). Electronic applications accepted.

Boston College, School of Theology and Ministry, Chestnut Hill, MA 02467-3800. Offers church leadership (MA); divinity (M Div); pastoral ministry (MA), including Hispanic ministry, liturgy and worship, pastoral care and counseling, spirituality; religious education (MA, PhD); sacred theology (STD, STL); social justice/social ministry (MA); spiritual direction (MA); theological studies (MTS); theology (Th M, PhD); youth ministry (MA); MA/MA; MS/MA; MSW/MA. *Accreditation:* TEAC. *Program availability:* Part-time. *Degree requirements:* For doctorate, one foreign language, thesis/dissertation. *Entrance requirements:* For doctorate, GRE. Additional exam requirements/recommendations for international students: required—TOEFL (minimum score 550 paper-based). Electronic applications accepted.

Briercrest Seminary, Graduate Programs, Program in Theology, Caronport, SK S0H 0S0, Canada. Offers Biblical studies (M Div); leadership and management (M Div); New Testament (MATS); Old Testament (MATS); pastoral counseling (M Div); pastoral ministry (M Div); theological studies (M Div); theology (MATS); worship (M Div); youth and family ministry (M Div). *Accreditation:* ATS. *Program availability:* Part-time. *Degree requirements:* For master's, comprehensive exam, thesis optional. *Entrance requirements:* Additional exam requirements/recommendations for international students: required—TOEFL (minimum score 550 paper-based).

Brite Divinity School, Graduate and Professional Programs, Fort Worth, TX 76109. Offers Biblical interpretation (PhD); divinity (M Div); ministry (D Min); pastoral theology (PhD); theological studies (MTS, CTS); theology (Th M); theology and ministry (MA). *Accreditation:* ACIPE; ATS (one or more programs are accredited); SACS/CC. *Program availability:* Part-time, evening/weekend. *Entrance requirements:* For master's, minimum GPA of 2.5. Additional exam requirements/recommendations for international students: required—TOEFL.

Bryn Athyn College of the New Church, Academy of the New Church Theological School, ViktorTest, PA 19009-0717. Offers divinity (M Div); religious studies (MA). *Program availability:* Part-time, online learning. *Faculty:* 12. *Students:* 7 full-time (0 women), 19 part-time (13 women), 10 international. Average age 37. 26 applicants, 100% accepted, 9 enrolled. In 2019, 6 master's awarded. *Degree requirements:* For master's, variable foreign language requirement, thesis. *Entrance requirements:* Additional exam requirements/recommendations for international students: required—TOEFL. *Application deadline:* For fall admission, 1/31 for domestic students. Applications are processed on a rolling basis. *Financial support:* In 2019–20, 7 students received support. Career-related internships or fieldwork, Federal Work-Study, and institutionally sponsored loans available. Financial award application deadline: 1/31. *Unit head:* Andrew Dibb, Dean, 267-502-2640, E-mail: andrew.dibb@ancts.org. *Application contact:* Andrew Dibb, Dean, 267-502-2640, E-mail: andrew.dibb@ancts.org. Website: http://www.ancts.org

Byzantine Catholic Seminary of Saints Cyril and Methodius, Graduate and Professional Programs, Pittsburgh, PA 15214. Offers M Div, MAT. *Accreditation:* ATS.

Cairn University, School of Divinity, Langhorne, PA 19047-2990. Offers divinity (M Div); religion (MA); theology (Th M). *Program availability:* Part-time, evening/weekend, 100% online, blended/hybrid learning. *Entrance requirements:* Additional exam requirements/recommendations for international students: required—TOEFL (minimum score 550 paper-based). Electronic applications accepted. Application fee is waived when completed online. *Expenses:* Contact institution.

California Lutheran University, Graduate Studies, Pacific Lutheran Theological Seminary, Thousand Oaks, CA 91360-2787. Offers M Div, MA, MCM, MTS, PhD, Th D, Certificate, M Div/MA. *Accreditation:* ACIPE. *Program availability:* Part-time. *Degree requirements:* For master's, variable foreign language requirement, thesis or alternative. Electronic applications accepted.

Calvary University, Graduate School and Seminary, Kansas City, MO 64147. Offers Bible and theology (MS); Biblical counseling (MA); education (MS), including administration and leadership, Christian education, curriculum and instruction, elementary education; organizational development (MS); pastoral studies (M Div); worship arts (MS). *Program availability:* Part-time, evening/weekend. *Degree requirements:* For master's, variable foreign language requirement, comprehensive exam, thesis or alternative. *Entrance requirements:* For master's, minimum GPA of 2.5, BA or BS, doctrine agreement. Additional exam requirements/recommendations for international students: required—TOEFL (minimum score 550 paper-based). Electronic applications accepted. *Expenses:* Contact institution.

Calvin Theological Seminary, Graduate and Professional Programs, Grand Rapids, MI 49546-4387. Offers Bible and theology (MA); divinity (M Div), including ancient near eastern languages and literature, contextual ministry, evangelism and teaching, history of Christianity, new church development, New Testament, Old Testament, pastoral care and leadership, preaching and worship, theological studies, youth and family ministries; educational ministry (MA); historical theology (PhD); missions and evangelism (MA); pastoral care (MA); philosophical and moral theology (PhD); systematic theology (PhD); theological studies (MTS); theology (Th M); worship (MA); youth and family ministries (MA). *Accreditation:* ACIPE; ATS. *Program availability:* Part-time. *Degree requirements:* For master's, variable foreign language requirement, thesis (for some programs); for doctorate, 4 foreign languages, comprehensive exam, thesis/dissertation. *Entrance requirements:* For doctorate, GRE General Test, Hebrew, Greek, and a modern foreign language. Additional exam requirements/recommendations for international students: required—TOEFL (minimum score 550 paper-based), TWE (minimum score 4). Electronic applications accepted.

Campbellsville University, School of Theology, Campbellsville, KY 42718-2799. Offers marriage and family therapy (MMFT); theology (M Th). *Program availability:* Part-time, evening/weekend, 100% online, blended/hybrid learning. *Degree requirements:* For master's, comprehensive exam, thesis optional. *Entrance requirements:* For master's, GRE General Test, minimum GPA of 3.0 in major, 2.75 overall; 18 hours of undergraduate coursework in Christian studies; college transcripts; letters of recommendation. Additional exam requirements/recommendations for international students: recommended—TOEFL (minimum score 550 paper-based; 79 iBT), IELTS (minimum score 6). Electronic applications accepted. Application fee is waived when completed online. *Expenses:* Contact institution.

Campbell University, Graduate and Professional Programs, Divinity School, Buies Creek, NC 27506. Offers Christian ministry (MA); divinity (M Div); ministry (D Min); JD/M Div; M Div/MA; M Div/MBA. *Accreditation:* ATS. *Degree requirements:* For doctorate, final project. *Entrance requirements:* For master's, minimum GPA of 2.5; for doctorate, MAT, M Div, minimum graduate GPA of 3.0. Additional exam requirements/recommendations for international students: required—TOEFL (minimum score 580 paper-based). *Expenses:* Contact institution.

Canadian Southern Baptist Seminary, Graduate Programs, Cochrane, AB T4C 2G1, Canada. Offers Biblical studies (MBS); Christian ministry (MCMin); Christian studies (MCS); ministry (M Div). *Accreditation:* ATS. *Program availability:* Part-time, 100% online, blended/hybrid learning. *Entrance requirements:* Additional exam requirements/recommendations for international students: required—TOEFL (minimum score 560 paper-based; 83 iBT); recommended—IELTS (minimum score 6.5).

Capital University, Trinity Lutheran Seminary, Columbus, OH 43209-2394. Offers African American studies (MTS); Biblical studies (MTS, STM); Christian education (MA); Christian spirituality (STM); church in the world (MTS); church music (MA); divinity (M Div); general theological studies (MTS); mission and evangelism (STM); pastoral leadership and practice (STM); youth and family ministry (MA); MSN/MTS; MTS/JD. *Accreditation:* ACIPE; ATS. *Program availability:* Part-time. *Degree requirements:* For master's, variable foreign language requirement, comprehensive exam (for some programs), thesis (for some programs), field experience (for some programs). *Entrance requirements:* For master's, BA or equivalent (for MA, M Div, MTS); M Div, MTS, or equivalent (for STM); audition (for MACM). Additional exam requirements/recommendations for international students: required—TOEFL. Electronic applications accepted. *Expenses:* Contact institution.

Carey Theological College, Graduate Programs, Vancouver, BC V6T 1J6, Canada. Offers M Div, MASF, D Min. *Accreditation:* ATS. *Program availability:* Part-time. *Degree requirements:* For doctorate, thesis/dissertation. *Entrance requirements:* For master's, undergraduate degree with minimum GPA of 2.7; for doctorate, M Div with minimum GPA of 3.5. Additional exam requirements/recommendations for international students: required—TOEFL (minimum score 577 paper-based; 90 iBT). Electronic applications accepted.

Carson-Newman University, Program in Applied Theology, Jefferson City, TN 37760. Offers MAAT. *Program availability:* Part-time, evening/weekend. *Faculty:* 1 full-time (0 women), 1 (woman) part-time/adjunct. *Students:* 8 part-time (3 women); includes 1 minority (Black or African American, non-Hispanic/Latino). Average age 42. 2 applicants, 100% accepted, 2 enrolled. In 2019, 3 master's awarded. *Degree requirements:* For master's, thesis optional, completion of degree within five years of admission into program. *Entrance requirements:* For master's, GRE (minimum score of 290), minimum GPA of 3.0. Additional exam requirements/recommendations for international students: recommended—TOEFL (minimum score 79 iBT), IELTS (minimum score 6.5), TSE (minimum score 53). *Application deadline:* For fall admission, 7/15 priority date for domestic students. Applications are processed on a rolling basis. Application fee: $50. *Expenses: Tuition:* Full-time $500. *Required fees:* $675; $375 per credit hour. $125 per term. Tuition and fees vary according to class time, course level, course load, degree level, campus/location and program. *Financial support:* Federal Work-Study and tuition waivers (full and partial) available. Financial award applicants required to submit FAFSA. *Unit head:* Dr. David E. Crutchley, Dean, School of Religion, 865-471-3277, E-mail: dcruthley@cn.edu. *Application contact:* Nilma Stewart, Graduate Admissions and Services Adviser, 865-473-3468, Fax: 865-471-3875, E-mail: adults@cn.edu.
Website: http://www.cn.edu/graduate-adult-studies/programs/religion-graduate

Catholic Distance University, Graduate Programs, Charles Town, WV 25414. Offers religious studies (MRS); theology (MA). *Program availability:* Part-time, evening/weekend, online learning. *Degree requirements:* For master's, comprehensive exam, capstone paper or project.

Catholic Theological Union, Graduate and Professional Programs, Chicago, IL 60615-5698. Offers biblical spirituality (Certificate); cross-cultural ministries (D Min); cross-cultural missions (Certificate); divinity (M Div); liturgical studies (Certificate); liturgy (D Min); pastoral studies (MAPS, Certificate); spiritual formation (Certificate); spirituality (D Min); theology (MA); M Div/MA; M Div/MSW; M Div/PhD. *Accreditation:* ACIPE; ATS. *Program availability:* Part-time, evening/weekend. *Degree requirements:* For master's, one foreign language, comprehensive exam (for some programs), thesis (for some programs); for doctorate, thesis/dissertation. *Entrance requirements:* For doctorate, master's degree, 5 years of active ministry.

The Catholic University of America, School of Canon Law, Washington, DC 20064. Offers Canon law (JCD, JCL); church administration (MCA); JD/JCL. *Program availability:* Part-time. *Faculty:* 5 full-time (1 woman), 2 part-time/adjunct (0 women). *Students:* 26 full-time (3 women), 63 part-time (9 women); includes 19 minority (5 Black or African American, non-Hispanic/Latino; 7 Asian, non-Hispanic/Latino; 3 Hispanic/Latino; 4 Two or more races, non-Hispanic/Latino), 10 international. Average age 40. 57 applicants, 88% accepted, 41 enrolled. In 2019, 19 master's, 1 doctorate awarded. *Degree requirements:* For master's, one foreign language, comprehensive exam, thesis, fluency in canonical Latin; for doctorate, 2 foreign languages, thesis/dissertation, fluency in canonical Latin. *Entrance requirements:* For master's, GRE General Test, statement of purpose, official copies of academic transcripts, two letters of recommendation; for doctorate, GRE General Test, minimum A- average, JCL. Additional exam requirements/recommendations for international students: required—TOEFL (minimum score 550 paper-based; 80 iBT). *Application deadline:* For fall admission, 7/15 priority date for domestic students, 7/1 for international students; for spring admission, 11/15 priority date for domestic students, 11/1 for international students. Applications are processed on a rolling basis. Application fee: $55. Electronic applications accepted. *Expenses:* Contact institution. *Financial support:* Fellowships, research assistantships, teaching assistantships, Federal Work-Study, scholarships/grants, tuition waivers (full and partial), and unspecified assistantships available. Financial award application deadline: 2/1; financial award applicants required to submit FAFSA. *Unit head:* Msgr. Ronny Jenkins, Dean, 202-319-5492, Fax: 202-319-4187, E-mail: cua-canonlaw@cua.edu. *Application contact:* Dr. Steven Brown, Director of Graduate Admissions, 202-319-5057, Fax: 202-319-6533, E-mail: cua-admissions@cua.edu.
Website: https://canonlaw.catholic.edu/

The Catholic University of America, School of Theology and Religious Studies, Washington, DC 20064. Offers M Cat, M Div, MA, D Min, PhD, STD, Certificate, STB, STL, MSLS/MA, STB/M Div. *Program availability:* Part-time. *Faculty:* 39 full-time (5 women), 12 part-time/adjunct (5 women). *Students:* 156 full-time (13 women), 167 part-time (69 women); includes 72 minority (13 Black or African American, non-Hispanic/Latino; 1 American Indian or Alaska Native, non-Hispanic/Latino; 13 Asian, non-Hispanic/Latino; 22 Hispanic/Latino; 23 Two or more races, non-Hispanic/Latino), 51 international. Average age 36. 178 applicants, 60% accepted, 67 enrolled. In 2019, 56 master's, 27 doctorates awarded. Terminal master's awarded for partial completion of doctoral program. *Degree requirements:* For master's, variable foreign language requirement, comprehensive exam (for some programs), thesis (for some programs); for doctorate, variable foreign language requirement, comprehensive exam, thesis/dissertation. *Entrance requirements:* For master's and doctorate, GRE General Test, statement of purpose, official copies of academic transcripts, three letters of recommendation. Additional exam requirements/recommendations for international students: required—TOEFL (minimum score 550 paper-based; 80 iBT). *Application deadline:* For fall admission, 7/15 priority date for domestic students, 7/1 for international students; for spring admission, 11/15 priority date for domestic students, 11/1 for international students. Applications are processed on a rolling basis. Application fee: $55. Electronic applications accepted. *Expenses:* Contact institution. *Financial support:* Fellowships, research assistantships, teaching assistantships, Federal Work-Study, scholarships/grants, tuition waivers (full and partial), and unspecified assistantships available. Financial award application deadline: 2/1; financial award applicants required to submit FAFSA. *Unit head:* Very Rev. Mark Morozowich, Dean, 202-319-5684, Fax: 202-319-4967, E-mail: morozowich@cua.edu. *Application contact:* Dr. Steven Brown, Director of Graduate Admissions, 202-319-5057, Fax: 202-319-6533, E-mail: cua-admissions@cua.edu.
Website: https://trs.catholic.edu/

Central Baptist Theological Seminary, Graduate and Professional Programs, Shawnee, KS 66226. Offers missional church studies (MA); theological studies (MA); theology (M Div, Diploma). *Accreditation:* ACIPE; ATS (one or more programs are accredited). *Program availability:* Part-time. *Degree requirements:* For master's, thesis optional. *Entrance requirements:* Additional exam requirements/recommendations for international students: required—TOEFL (minimum score 547 paper-based; 77 iBT). Electronic applications accepted.

Central Yeshiva Tomchei Tmimim-Lubavitch, Graduate Programs, Brooklyn, NY 11230. Offers Jewish/Judaic studies (MA); Talmudic studies (MA). *Accreditation:* AARTS. *Application contact:* Information Contact, 718-434-0784.

Charlotte Christian College and Theological Seminary, Graduate Program, Charlotte, NC 28206. Offers Biblical studies (MA), including New Testament, Old Testament, theology; chaplaincy (M Div); general pastoral studies (M Div); ministry (D Min); pastoral counseling (M Div); urban Christian ministry (MA), including multi-cultural studies, youth ministry. *Program availability:* Part-time, evening/weekend. *Degree requirements:* For master's, variable foreign language requirement, thesis; for doctorate, thesis/dissertation. *Entrance requirements:* For master's, 1000-2000 word essay. Additional exam requirements/recommendations for international students: required—TOEFL, IELTS. Electronic applications accepted. *Expenses:* Contact institution.

Chicago Theological Seminary, Graduate and Professional Programs, Chicago, IL 60637-1507. Offers Bible, culture and hermeneutics (PhD); preaching (D Min); religion and health (D Min); religious studies (MA); spirituality and spiritual direction (D Min); theology (M Div); theology, ethics and the human sciences (PhD); M Div/MSW. *Accreditation:* ACIPE; ATS. *Program availability:* Part-time. *Degree requirements:* For master's, thesis; for doctorate, 2 foreign languages, comprehensive exam, thesis/dissertation. *Entrance requirements:* For doctorate, GRE General Test. Additional exam requirements/recommendations for international students: required—TOEFL.

Christendom College, Graduate School of Theology, Alexandria, VA 22312. Offers theological studies (MA), including consecrated life, evangelization and catechesis, moral theology, spirituality, systematic theology. *Program availability:* Part-time, evening/weekend, 100% online, blended/hybrid learning. *Degree requirements:* For master's, one foreign language, comprehensive exam, thesis or alternative. Electronic applications accepted.

Christian Theological Seminary, Graduate and Professional Programs, Indianapolis, IN 46208-3301. Offers educational and arts ministries (MA); marriage and family therapy (MA); pastoral care and counseling (D Min); psychotherapy and faith (MA); theological studies (MTS); theology (M Div). *Accreditation:* AAMFT/COAMFTE (one or more programs are accredited); ACIPE; ATS. *Program availability:* Part-time. Terminal master's awarded for partial completion of doctoral program. *Degree requirements:* For master's, comprehensive exam (for some programs), thesis (for some programs), missionary and cross-cultural experience (for M Div); for doctorate, comprehensive exam, thesis/dissertation. *Entrance requirements:* For doctorate, M Div. Additional exam requirements/recommendations for international students: recommended—TOEFL. Electronic applications accepted.

Christ the King Seminary, Graduate and Professional Programs, East Aurora, NY 14052. Offers divinity (M Div); pastoral ministry (MA); theology (MA). *Accreditation:* ATS. *Program availability:* Part-time, evening/weekend. *Degree requirements:* For master's, comprehensive exam, thesis. *Entrance requirements:* For master's, previous course work in philosophy and religious studies.

Church Divinity School of the Pacific, Graduate and Professional Programs, Berkeley, CA 94709-1217. Offers M Div, MA, MTS, D Min, Certificate. *Accreditation:* ACIPE; ATS (one or more programs are accredited). *Program availability:* Part-time. *Degree requirements:* For master's, one foreign language, thesis (for some programs); for doctorate, thesis/dissertation. *Entrance requirements:* For master's and Certificate, GRE General Test, letters of reference; for doctorate, letters of reference. Additional exam requirements/recommendations for international students: required—TOEFL. Electronic applications accepted.

Cincinnati Christian University, Graduate School, Cincinnati, OH 45204-3200. Offers biblical studies (MA); church history (MA); counseling (MAC); divinity (M Div); ministry (M Min); practical ministries (MA); theological studies (MA). *Program availability:* Part-time. *Degree requirements:* For master's, variable foreign language requirement, thesis (for some programs), oral exam (for M Div). *Entrance requirements:* Additional exam requirements/recommendations for international students: required—TOEFL. Electronic applications accepted.

Claremont Graduate University, Graduate Programs, School of Arts and Humanities, Department of Religion, Claremont, CA 91711-6160. Offers Hebrew Bible (MA, PhD); history of Christianity and religions of North America (MA, PhD); New Testament (MA, PhD); philosophy of religion and theology (MA, PhD); theology, ethics and culture (MA, PhD); women's studies in religion (MA, PhD); MA/PhD; MBA/PhD. *Program availability:* Part-time. Terminal master's awarded for partial completion of doctoral program. *Entrance requirements:* For master's and doctorate, GRE General Test. Additional exam requirements/recommendations for international students: required—TOEFL (minimum score 75 iBT). Electronic applications accepted.

Claremont School of Theology, Graduate and Professional Programs, Master of Divinity Program, Claremont, CA 91711-3199. Offers interfaith chaplaincy (M Div); Islamic chaplaincy (M Div); ministerial leadership (M Div). *Accreditation:* ACIPE; ATS.

Theology

Program availability: Part-time, 100% online, blended/hybrid learning. *Entrance requirements:* Additional exam requirements/recommendations for international students: required—TOEFL. Electronic applications accepted.

Claremont School of Theology, Graduate and Professional Programs, Program in Religion, Claremont, CA 91711-3199. Offers practical theology (PhD), including religious education and formation, spiritual care and counseling; religion (MA, PhD), including comparative theology and philosophy (PhD), Hebrew Bible and Jewish studies (PhD), New Testament and Christian origins (PhD), process studies (PhD), religion, ethics, and society (PhD). *Accreditation:* ACIPE; ATS. Terminal master's awarded for partial completion of doctoral program. *Degree requirements:* For master's, thesis; for doctorate, 2 foreign languages, thesis/dissertation. *Entrance requirements:* For doctorate, GRE General Test. Additional exam requirements/recommendations for international students: required—TOEFL. Electronic applications accepted.

Clarks Summit University, Baptist Bible Seminary, South Abington Township, PA 18411. Offers Biblical apologetics (MA); Biblical studies (MA); church education (M Min); church planting (M Div, M Min); communication (D Min); counseling and spiritual development (D Min); global ministry (M Min, D Min); ministry (PhD); missions (M Min); organizational leadership (M Min); outreach pastor (M Min); pastoral counseling (M Min); pastoral leadership (M Div, M Min); pastoral ministry (D Min); theological studies (D Min); theology (Th M); youth pastor (M Min). *Program availability:* Part-time, evening/weekend, online learning. Terminal master's awarded for partial completion of doctoral program. *Degree requirements:* For master's, 2 foreign languages, thesis, oral exam (for M Div); for doctorate, 2 foreign languages, comprehensive exam (for some programs), thesis/dissertation, oral exam. *Entrance requirements:* For doctorate, Greek and Hebrew entrance exams (for PhD). Electronic applications accepted.

Clarks Summit University, Online Master's Programs, South Abington Township, PA 18411. Offers Bible (MA); counseling (MA, MS); curriculum and instruction (M Ed); educational administration (M Ed); literature (MA); organizational leadership (MA). *Program availability:* Part-time, evening/weekend, online learning. *Entrance requirements:* Additional exam requirements/recommendations for international students: required—TOEFL (minimum score 500 paper-based).

Colgate Rochester Crozer Divinity School, Graduate and Professional Programs, Rochester, NY 14620-2530. Offers divinity (M Div, MA, Certificate); peace building and interfaith dialogue (D Min); prophetic preaching (D Min); transformative leadership (D Min). *Accreditation:* ACIPE; ATS (one or more programs are accredited). *Program availability:* Part-time, evening/weekend. *Degree requirements:* For master's, thesis (for some programs), supervised ministry year (for M Div); for doctorate, thesis/dissertation. *Entrance requirements:* For master's, BA/BS, personal statement, 4 recommendations; for doctorate, M Div, 3 years' professional experience, writing sample, personal statement, curriculum vitae, 4 recommendations. Additional exam requirements/recommendations for international students: required—TOEFL (minimum score 600 paper-based; 93 iBT). Electronic applications accepted. *Expenses:* Contact institution.

Collège Dominicain de Philosophie et de Thêologie, Graduate Programs, Faculty of Theology, Ottawa, ON K1R 7G3, Canada. Offers M Th, MA Th, PhD, Th D, L Th. *Program availability:* Part-time, evening/weekend. *Degree requirements:* For master's, 2 foreign languages, research paper; for doctorate, 2 foreign languages, thesis/dissertation, candidacy exam. *Entrance requirements:* For master's, B Th or equivalent, minimum A- average in undergraduate course work; for doctorate, MA Th or equivalent, minimum A- average in graduate course work. *Expenses: Tuition, area resident:* Full-time $7032 Canadian dollars; part-time $147 Canadian dollars per credit hour. Tuition, nonresident: part-time $375 Canadian dollars per credit hour. *International tuition:* $19,680 Canadian dollars full-time. One-time fee: $165 Canadian dollars full-time. Full-time tuition and fees vary according to class time, course level, course load, degree level, campus/location, program and student level.

College of Emmanuel and St. Chad, Bachelor of Theology Program, Saskatoon, SK S7N 0W6, Canada. Offers B Th. *Program availability:* Part-time, online learning. *Degree requirements:* For B Th, internship. *Entrance requirements:* For degree, 1 year of university-level work or equivalent. Additional exam requirements/recommendations for international students: required—TOEFL.

College of Emmanuel and St. Chad, Graduate Programs, Saskatoon, SK S7N 0W6, Canada. Offers M Div, MTS, STM, D Min, L Th. *Program availability:* Part-time. *Degree requirements:* For master's, thesis optional. *Entrance requirements:* For master's, M Div or MTS (for STM). Additional exam requirements/recommendations for international students: required—TOEFL.

College of Saint Elizabeth, Department of Theology and Philosophy, Morristown, NJ 07960-6989. Offers Catholic studies (Certificate); pastoral care (Certificate); spirituality (Certificate); theology (MA), including Catholic studies, pastoral care, spirituality, theological studies. *Program availability:* Part-time. *Degree requirements:* For master's, thesis. *Entrance requirements:* For master's, baccalaureate degree from accredited institution, personal interview with coordinator and another faculty member, minimum cumulative GPA of 3.0. Additional exam requirements/recommendations for international students: required—TOEFL (minimum score 550 paper-based; 79 iBT), IELTS (minimum score 6.5). Electronic applications accepted. Application fee is waived when completed online.

Columbia International University, Seminary and School of Ministry, Columbia, SC 29203. Offers academic ministries (M Div); Bible and theology (Certificate); bible exposition (M Div, MABE); Biblical ministry (Certificate); chaplaincy (M Div); intercultural studies (MAIS); leadership (D Min); member care (D Min); missions (D Min); preaching (D Min); theological studies (MA). *Program availability:* Part-time, evening/weekend. *Degree requirements:* For doctorate, comprehensive exam, thesis/dissertation. *Entrance requirements:* For doctorate, 3 years of ministerial experience, M Div. Additional exam requirements/recommendations for international students: required—TOEFL. Electronic applications accepted.

Columbia Theological Seminary, Graduate and Professional Programs, Decatur, GA 30031-0520. Offers M Div, MATS, Th M, D Min, Th D. *Accreditation:* ACIPE; ATS (one or more programs are accredited). Terminal master's awarded for partial completion of doctoral program. *Degree requirements:* For master's, variable foreign language requirement, thesis (for some programs); for doctorate, one foreign language, thesis/dissertation. *Entrance requirements:* For doctorate, M Div or equivalent, 3 years practice of ministry. Additional exam requirements/recommendations for international students: required—TOEFL.

Concordia Lutheran Seminary, Graduate and Professional Programs, Edmonton, AB T5B 4E3, Canada. Offers M Div, Graduate Certificate. *Accreditation:* ATS (one or more programs are accredited). *Program availability:* Part-time. *Degree requirements:* For master's, thesis or alternative. *Entrance requirements:* For master's, GRE General Test. Additional exam requirements/recommendations for international students: required—TOEFL.

Concordia Seminary, Graduate Programs, St. Louis, MO 63105-3199. Offers M Div, MA, STM, D Min, PhD, Certificate. *Accreditation:* ACIPE; ATS (one or more programs are accredited). Terminal master's awarded for partial completion of doctoral program. *Degree requirements:* For master's, variable foreign language requirement, comprehensive exam (for some programs), thesis (for some programs); for doctorate, 4 foreign languages, thesis/dissertation. *Entrance requirements:* For master's, GRE General Test, previous course work in public speaking, Greek, Hebrew, Old Testament, New Testament, and Christian Doctrine (for M Div); for doctorate, GRE General Test, theological essay in English (foreign students only). Additional exam requirements/recommendations for international students: required—TOEFL.

Concordia Theological Seminary, Graduate and Professional Programs, Fort Wayne, IN 46825-4996. Offers M Div, MA, STM, D Min, PhD. *Accreditation:* ATS. *Program availability:* Part-time. *Degree requirements:* For master's, variable foreign language requirement, thesis (for some programs); for doctorate, comprehensive exam, thesis/dissertation, oral exam. *Entrance requirements:* For master's, GRE General Test (for M Div), minimum GPA of 2.25 (for M Div).

Concordia University, School of Graduate Studies, Faculty of Arts and Science, Department of Theological Studies, Montréal, QC H3G 1M8, Canada. Offers MA. *Degree requirements:* For master's, one foreign language, research papers or thesis. *Entrance requirements:* For master's, minimum B average in theology.

Concordia University Irvine, School of Theology, Irvine, CA 92612-3299. Offers Christian leadership (MA); research in theology (MA); theology and culture (MA). *Program availability:* Part-time, evening/weekend. *Degree requirements:* For master's, project/thesis or vicarage. *Entrance requirements:* For master's, official college transcript(s), statement of intent, 2 references, interview. Additional exam requirements/recommendations for international students: required—TOEFL. Electronic applications accepted. *Expenses:* Contact institution.

Concordia University of Edmonton, Program in Biblical and Christian Studies, Edmonton, AB T5B 4E4, Canada. Offers MA.

Corban University, Graduate School, School of Ministry, Salem, OR 97301-9392. Offers Biblical languages (M Div); Biblical leadership (Certificate); Christian leadership (MA); Church ministry (M Div); ministry (D Min). *Program availability:* Part-time, evening/weekend. *Degree requirements:* For master's, thesis. *Entrance requirements:* Additional exam requirements/recommendations for international students: required—TOEFL (minimum score 550 paper-based), IELTS (minimum score 6).

Covenant Theological Seminary, Graduate and Professional Programs, St. Louis, MO 63141-8697. Offers M Div, MA, MAC, MAEM, Th M, D Min, Certificate. *Accreditation:* ATS (one or more programs are accredited). *Program availability:* Part-time, evening/weekend, online learning. *Degree requirements:* For master's, 2 foreign languages, thesis (for some programs); for doctorate, 2 foreign languages, thesis/dissertation; for Certificate, 2 foreign languages. *Entrance requirements:* For doctorate and Certificate, M Div. Additional exam requirements/recommendations for international students: required—TOEFL (minimum score 550 paper-based). Electronic applications accepted.

Criswell College, Graduate School of the Bible, Dallas, TX 75246-1537. Offers biblical studies (M Div); Christian leadership (MA); counseling (MA); Jewish studies (MA); ministry (MA); theological and biblical studies (MA). *Program availability:* Part-time. *Degree requirements:* For master's, 2 foreign languages, thesis optional. *Entrance requirements:* For master's, GRE General Test, minimum GPA of 2.5. Electronic applications accepted.

Crown College, Adult and Graduate Studies, St. Bonifacius, MN 55375-9001. Offers Christian studies (MA); instructional leadership (MA); international leadership (MA); ministry leadership (MA); organizational leadership (MA). *Program availability:* Part-time, evening/weekend, online learning. *Degree requirements:* For master's, thesis optional. *Entrance requirements:* For master's, 12 credits in foundational studies, minimum GPA of 2.5 and bachelor's degree from regionally-accredited college. Additional exam requirements/recommendations for international students: required—TOEFL (minimum score 550 paper-based; 80 iBT). Electronic applications accepted.

Dallas Baptist University, Graduate School of Ministry, Program in Theological Studies, Dallas, TX 75211-9299. Offers Christian heritage (MA); Christian ministry (MA); Christian scriptures (MA). *Program availability:* Part-time, evening/weekend, online learning. *Application deadline:* Applications are processed on a rolling basis. Application fee: $25. Electronic applications accepted. Application fee is waived when completed online. *Expenses: Tuition:* Full-time $18,072; part-time $1004 per credit hour. *Required fees:* $1100; $550 per semester. Tuition and fees vary according to course level and degree level. *Unit head:* Dr. Robert R. Brooks, Dean, 214-333-5494, Fax: 214-333-5673, E-mail: bobb@dbu.edu. *Application contact:* Dr. Jim Lemons, Program Director, 214-333-5366, Fax: 214-333-5689, E-mail: jiml@dbu.edu.
Website: http://www.dbu.edu/ministry/degree-programs/m-a-in-theological-studies

Dallas Theological Seminary, Graduate Programs, Dallas, TX 75204-6499. Offers adult education (Th M); apologetics (Th M); Bible backgrounds (Th M); Bible translation (Th M); Biblical and theological studies (Certificate); biblical counseling (MA); biblical exegesis and linguistics (MA); biblical exposition (PhD); biblical studies (MA); Biblical theology (Th M); children's education (Th M); Christian education (MA, D Min); Christian leadership (MA); cross-cultural ministries (MA); educational administration (Th M); educational leadership (Th M); evangelism and discipleship (Th M); exposition of Biblical books (Th M); family life education (Th M); general studies (Th M); Hebrew and cognate studies (Th M); hermeneutics (Th M); historical theology (Th M); homiletics (Th M); intercultural ministries (Th M); Jesus studies (Th M); leadership studies (Th M); media and communication (MA); media arts (Th M); ministry (D Min); ministry with women (Th M); New Testament studies (Th M, PhD); Old Testament studies (Th M, PhD); parachurch ministries (Th M); pastoral care and counseling (Th M); pastoral theology and practice (Th M); philosophy (Th M); sacred theology (STM); spiritual formation (Th M); systematic theology (Th M); teaching in Christian institutions (Th M); theological studies (PhD); urban ministries (Th M); worship studies (Th M); youth education (Th M). *Program availability:* Part-time, online learning. *Degree requirements:* For master's, variable foreign language requirement, thesis (for some programs); for doctorate, 2 foreign languages, thesis/dissertation. *Entrance requirements:* For master's, GRE or MAT (if minimum undergraduate cumulative GPA is below 2.5 or undergraduate degree is unaccredited). Additional exam requirements/recommendations for international students: required—TOEFL (minimum score 575 paper-based; 85 iBT), TWE. Electronic applications accepted.

Denver Seminary, Graduate and Professional Programs, Littleton, CO 80120. Offers apologetics (Certificate); biblical studies (MA); Christian formation and soul care (MA, Certificate); Christian studies (MA, Certificate); church and parachurch leadership (D Min); counseling licensure (MA); counseling ministry (MA); intercultural ministry (Certificate); leadership (MA, Certificate); marriage and family counseling (D Min); pastoral ministry (D Min); philosophy of religion (MA); spiritual guidance (Certificate); theology (M Div, Certificate); worship (Certificate); youth and family ministry (MA). *Accreditation:* ACA; ACIPE; ATS (one or more programs are accredited). *Program availability:* Part-time, evening/weekend, online learning. *Degree requirements:* For master's, 2 foreign languages, thesis (for some programs); for doctorate, 2 foreign languages, thesis/dissertation. *Entrance requirements:* For doctorate, M Div, 3 years of ministry experience. Additional exam requirements/recommendations for international students: required—TOEFL (minimum score 575 paper-based; 90 iBT). Electronic applications accepted.

Dominican House of Studies, Pontifical Faculty of the Immaculate Conception, Graduate and Professional Programs in Theology, Washington, DC 20017-1585. Offers moral theology (STL); sacred scripture (STL); systematic theology (STL); theology (M Div, MA, STB); Thomistic studies (MA, STD, STL). *Accreditation:* ATS (one or more programs are accredited). *Program availability:* Part-time. *Faculty:* 18 full-time (1 woman), 6 part-time/adjunct (3 women). *Students:* 75 full-time (7 women), 9 part-time (3 women); includes 2 minority (both Asian, non-Hispanic/Latino), 13 international. Average age 33. 36 applicants, 100% accepted, 33 enrolled. In 2019, 32 master's awarded. *Degree requirements:* For master's, one foreign language, comprehensive exam, thesis, thesis defense; for other advanced degree, 3 foreign languages, comprehensive exam (for some programs), thesis (for some programs), lecture. *Entrance requirements:* For master's, 18 credits of philosophy, reading knowledge of Latin, BA with minimum GPA of 3.0; for other advanced degree, 36 credits of philosophy, BA with minimum GPA of 3.25 (for STB). Additional exam requirements/recommendations for international students: required—TOEFL (minimum score 550 paper-based; 96 iBT). *Application deadline:* For fall admission, 7/1 for domestic and international students; for spring admission, 12/1 for domestic and international students. Applications are processed on a rolling basis. Application fee: $150. Electronic applications accepted. *Financial support:* In 2019–20, 3 students received support. Career-related internships or fieldwork and Federal Work-Study available. Support available to part-time students. Financial award application deadline: 6/30; financial award applicants required to submit FAFSA. *Unit head:* Rev. Thomas Petri, OP, Vice-President/Academic Dean, 202-495-3832, Fax: 202-495-3873, E-mail: dean@dhs.edu. *Application contact:* Audrey Quade, Registrar & Accreditation Liaison, 202-495-3836, Fax: 202-495-3873, E-mail: registrar@dhs.edu.

Dominican School of Philosophy and Theology, Graduate Programs, Berkeley, CA 94708. Offers philosophy (MA); theology (M Div, MA, MTS, Certificate); M Div/MA; MA/MA. *Accreditation:* ATS. *Program availability:* Part-time. *Degree requirements:* For master's, one foreign language, thesis. *Entrance requirements:* For master's, GRE General Test (for MA), minimum GPA of 3.0 (for MA), 2.3 (for M Div); academic writing sample (for MA); statement of purpose, official transcripts, letters of recommendation. Additional exam requirements/recommendations for international students: required—TOEFL (minimum score 570 paper-based; 80 iBT), IELTS. Electronic applications accepted.

Drew University, Caspersen School of Graduate Studies, Madison, NJ 07940-1493. Offers conflict resolution and leadership (Certificate), including community leadership, moderation, peace building; education (M Ed); finance (MA); history and culture (MA, PhD), including American history, book history, British history, European history, intellectual history, Irish history, print culture, public history; K-12 education (MAT), including art, biology, chemistry, elementary education, English, French, Italian, math, secondary education, special education, teacher of students with disabilities; liberal studies (M Litt, D Litt), including history, Irish/Irish-American studies, literature (M Litt, MMH, D Litt, DMH, CMH), religion, spirituality, teaching in the two-year college, writing; medical humanities (MMH, DMH, CMH), including arts, health, healthcare, literature (M Litt, MMH, D Litt, DMH, CMH), scientific research; poetry (MFA). *Program availability:* Part-time, evening/weekend. Terminal master's awarded for partial completion of doctoral program. *Degree requirements:* For master's and other advanced degree, thesis (for some programs); for doctorate, one foreign language, comprehensive exam (for some programs), thesis/dissertation. *Entrance requirements:* For master's, PRAXIS Core and Subject Area tests (for MAT), GRE/GMAT (for MFin MS in Data Analytics), resume, transcripts, writing sample, personal statement, letters of recommendation; for doctorate, GRE (PhD in history and culture), resume, transcripts, writing sample, personal statement, letters of recommendation; for other advanced degree, resume, transcripts, personal statement. Additional exam requirements/recommendations for international students: required—TOEFL (minimum score 587 paper-based; 80 iBT), IELTS (minimum score 6), TWE (minimum score 4). Electronic applications accepted.

Drew University, Theological School, Madison, NJ 07940-1493. Offers M Div, MA, MA Min, STM, D Min, PhD, Certificate. *Accreditation:* ACIPE; ATS. *Program availability:* Part-time, blended/hybrid learning. *Faculty:* 19 full-time (9 women), 20 part-time/adjunct (7 women). *Students:* 204 full-time (100 women), 147 part-time (66 women); includes 137 minority (95 Black or African American, non-Hispanic/Latino; 3 American Indian or Alaska Native, non-Hispanic/Latino; 12 Asian, non-Hispanic/Latino; 16 Hispanic/Latino; 2 Native Hawaiian or other Pacific Islander, non-Hispanic/Latino; 9 Two or more races, non-Hispanic/Latino), 92 international. Average age 42. 226 applicants, 70% accepted, 84 enrolled. In 2019, 29 master's, 27 doctorates awarded. Terminal master's awarded for partial completion of doctoral program. *Degree requirements:* For doctorate, thesis/dissertation. *Entrance requirements:* For master's, resume, transcripts, writing sample, personal statement, letters of recommendation. Additional exam requirements/recommendations for international students: required—TOEFL (minimum score 580 paper-based; 70 iBT), IELTS (minimum score 6), TWE. *Application deadline:* For fall admission, 8/1 for domestic students, 4/1 for international students; for spring admission, 12/1 for domestic students, 10/1 for international students. Applications are processed on a rolling basis. Application fee: $35. Electronic applications accepted. *Expenses:* Contact institution. *Financial support:* Fellowships, career-related internships or fieldwork, Federal Work-Study, institutionally sponsored loans, and scholarships/grants available. Support available to part-time students. Financial award application deadline: 2/15; financial award applicants required to submit FAFSA. *Unit head:* Dr. Melanie Johnson-DeBaufre, Acting Dean of the Theological School, 973-408-3255, E-mail: mjjohnso@drew.edu. *Application contact:* Rev. Dr. Kevin D. Miller, Executive Director of Graduate Admissions, 973-408-3109, E-mail: kmiller@drew.edu.
Website: http://www.drew.edu/theological-school/

Duke University, Divinity School, Durham, NC 27708. Offers M Div, MACP, MACS, MTS, Th M, D Min, Th D, JD/MTS, M Div/MSW. *Accreditation:* ACIPE; ATS. *Program availability:* Part-time, online learning. Terminal master's awarded for partial completion of doctoral program. *Degree requirements:* For master's, thesis (for some programs); for doctorate, 2 foreign languages, comprehensive exam (for some programs), thesis/dissertation. *Entrance requirements:* For master's, 5 letters of reference, bachelor's degree from regionally-accredited college or university prior to intended date of enrollment, minimum GPA of 2.75, commitment to some form of ordained or lay ministry; for doctorate, GRE, M Div, MTS or comparable master's degree from institution accredited by ATS; bachelor's degree from regionally-accredited college or university prior to intended date of enrollment; 4 letters of reference; 2-page statement of purpose; one sample of academic writing. Additional exam requirements/recommendations for international students: required—TOEFL (minimum score 580 paper-based; 93 iBT). Electronic applications accepted. *Expenses:* Contact institution.

Duquesne University, Graduate School of Liberal Arts, Department of Theology, Pittsburgh, PA 15282-0001. Offers pastoral ministry (MA); religious education (MA); systematic theology (PhD); theology (MA). *Program availability:* Part-time, evening/weekend, blended/hybrid learning. Terminal master's awarded for partial completion of doctoral program. *Degree requirements:* For master's, comprehensive exam; for doctorate, 2 foreign languages, comprehensive exam, thesis/dissertation. *Entrance requirements:* For master's and doctorate, GRE General Test. Additional exam requirements/recommendations for international students: required—TOEFL. Electronic applications accepted.

Earlham School of Religion, Graduate Programs, Richmond, IN 47374. Offers ministry (M Min); religion (MA); theology (M Div). *Accreditation:* ACIPE; ATS. *Program availability:* Part-time, blended/hybrid learning. *Faculty:* 8 full-time (2 women), 2 part-time/adjunct (1 woman). *Students:* 17 full-time (9 women), 18 part-time (11 women); includes 2 minority (both Black or African American, non-Hispanic/Latino). Average age 38. *Degree requirements:* For master's, variable foreign language requirement, comprehensive exam (for some programs), thesis (for some programs), internship (M Div). *Entrance requirements:* For master's, 3 references, academic writing sample, official college transcripts, background check. Additional exam requirements/recommendations for international students: required—TOEFL (minimum score 550 paper-based; 82 iBT), IELTS (minimum score 7). *Application deadline:* For fall admission, 6/15 priority date for domestic students; for winter admission, 11/15 priority date for domestic students. Applications are processed on a rolling basis. Application fee: $35. Electronic applications accepted. *Financial support:* Scholarships/grants and tuition waivers (full and partial) available. Financial award application deadline: 4/15; financial award applicants required to submit FAFSA. *Unit head:* Matt Hisrich, Dean, 800-432-1377, Fax: 765-983-1688, E-mail: hisrima@earlham.edu. *Application contact:* Julie Dishman, Director of Recruitment and Admissions, 765-983-1523, Fax: 765-983-1688, E-mail: dishmju@earlham.edu.
Website: http://esr.earlham.edu/academic-programs

Eastern Mennonite University, Eastern Mennonite Seminary, Harrisonburg, VA 22802-2462. Offers Christian leadership (MA); divinity (M Div); ministry studies (Certificate); religion (MA); theological studies (Certificate). *Accreditation:* ATS. *Program availability:* Part-time. *Degree requirements:* For master's, thesis (for some programs), supervised field education (for M Div). *Entrance requirements:* For master's, minimum GPA of 2.5. Additional exam requirements/recommendations for international students: required—TOEFL (minimum score 550 paper-based). *Expenses:* Contact institution.

Eastern University, Palmer Theological Seminary, St. Davids, PA 19096-3430. Offers divinity (M Div); theological studies (MTS); M Div/MA; M Div/MBA. *Accreditation:* ACIPE; MSA/CIHE. *Program availability:* Part-time, online learning. *Students:* 55 full-time (23 women), 169 part-time (69 women); includes 144 minority (61 Black or African American, non-Hispanic/Latino; 2 Asian, non-Hispanic/Latino; 16 Hispanic/Latino; 65 Two or more races, non-Hispanic/Latino), 5 international. Average age 46. In 2019, 68 master's awarded. *Application deadline:* Applications are processed on a rolling basis. Application fee: $30. Electronic applications accepted. Application fee is waived when completed online. *Expenses:* Contact institution. *Unit head:* Michael Dziedziak, Executive Director of Enrollment, 800-452-0996, E-mail: semadmis@eastern.edu. *Application contact:* Michael Dziedziak, Executive Director of Enrollment, 800-452-0996, E-mail: semadmis@eastern.edu.
Website: https://www.palmerseminary.edu/

Ecumenical Theological Seminary, Professional Program, Detroit, MI 48201. Offers M Div. *Accreditation:* ACIPE; ATS.

Eden Theological Seminary, Graduate and Professional Programs, St. Louis, MO 63119-3192. Offers M Div, MAPS, MTS, D Min. *Accreditation:* ACIPE; ATS. *Degree requirements:* For master's, comprehensive exam (for some programs), thesis (for some programs), 2 oral exams; for doctorate, professional essay, supervised in-service projects. *Entrance requirements:* For master's, interview, minimum GPA of 2.7; for doctorate, interview, minimum GPA of 3.0. Additional exam requirements/recommendations for international students: required—TOEFL (minimum score 550 paper-based). Electronic applications accepted.

Emory University, Candler School of Theology, Atlanta, GA 30322. Offers catholic studies (M Div); formation and witness (M Div); history, scripture and tradition (MTS); leadership in church and community (M Div); modern religious thought and experience (MTS); pastoral counseling (Th D); religion and race (M Div); religion, health and science (M Div); scripture and interpretation (M Div); society and personality (M Div); theology (Th M); theology and ethics (M Div); theology and the arts (M Div); traditions of the church (M Div); JD/M Div; JD/MTS; M Div/MBA; M Div/MPH; MBA/MTS; MTS/MPH. *Accreditation:* ACIPE. *Program availability:* Part-time. *Degree requirements:* For master's, thesis optional; for doctorate, comprehensive exam, thesis/dissertation. *Entrance requirements:* For master's, minimum undergraduate GPA of 2.75, completed undergraduate degree from accredited college or university; for doctorate, GRE, DMin: MDiv or other first level theological masters and at least 3 years of professional experience. Additional exam requirements/recommendations for international students: required—TOEFL (minimum score 600 paper-based; 95 iBT). Electronic applications accepted. *Expenses:* Contact institution.

Erskine Theological Seminary, Graduate and Professional Programs, Due West, SC 29639-0668. Offers M Div, MAPM, MATS, Th M, D Min. *Accreditation:* ATS. *Program availability:* Part-time, evening/weekend. *Degree requirements:* For doctorate, thesis/dissertation. *Entrance requirements:* For master's, Myers-Briggs Type Indicator, Taylor Johnson Temperament Analysis, Ministry Specialties Test (MACM), minimum GPA of 3.0, interview with committee (MACM); for doctorate, minimum GPA of 3.0 during M Div. Additional exam requirements/recommendations for international students: required—TOEFL (minimum score 550 paper-based). Electronic applications accepted.

Evangelical Seminary, Graduate and Professional Programs, Myerstown, PA 17067-1212. Offers Biblical studies (MAR); congregational ministry (M Div); global and contextual studies (M Div, MAR); historical and theological studies (MAR); interdisciplinary studies (MAR); marriage and family counseling (M Div); marriage and family therapy (MA); New Testament (MAR); Old Testament (MAR); spiritual formation (MAR); teaching ministry (M Div); youth ministry (M Div). *Accreditation:* ATS (one or more programs are accredited). *Program availability:* Part-time, online learning. *Degree requirements:* For master's, 2 foreign languages. *Entrance requirements:* For master's, minimum GPA of 2.5. Additional exam requirements/recommendations for international students: required—TOEFL (minimum score 550 paper-based).

Evangelical Seminary of Puerto Rico, Graduate and Professional Programs, San Juan, PR 00925-2207. Offers M Div, MAR, D Min. *Accreditation:* ATS. *Program availability:* Part-time. *Degree requirements:* For master's, comprehensive exam. *Entrance requirements:* For doctorate, 3 years experience in ministry service. Additional exam requirements/recommendations for international students: required—TOEFL.

Faith Baptist Bible College and Theological Seminary, Graduate Program, Ankeny, IA 50023. Offers Biblical studies (MA); pastoral studies (M Div); pastoral training (MA); religion (MA); theological studies (MA). *Program availability:* Part-time. *Degree requirements:* For master's, thesis or alternative. *Entrance requirements:* Additional exam requirements/recommendations for international students: required—TOEFL (minimum score 550 paper-based; 79 iBT), IELTS (minimum score 6.5). Electronic applications accepted.

Faith International University, Graduate and Professional Programs, Tacoma, WA 98407. Offers M Div, MACM, MTS, D Min. *Program availability:* Part-time, evening/weekend, online learning. *Degree requirements:* For master's, thesis optional; for doctorate, thesis/dissertation. *Entrance requirements:* For master's, minimum undergraduate GPA of 2.7; for doctorate, minimum graduate GPA of 3.0. Additional exam requirements/recommendations for international students: required—TOEFL (minimum score 550 paper-based). *Expenses: Tuition:* Full-time $7000; part-time $1000 per quarter. *Required fees:* $450; $150 per quarter. Tuition and fees vary according to degree level and student's religious affiliation.

Faith Theological Seminary, Graduate Programs, Baltimore, MD 21212. Offers M Div, D Min, Th D.

Faulkner University, College of Biblical Studies, Montgomery, AL 36109-3398. Offers Biblical studies (MA, PhD); Christian counseling and family ministry (MA); Christian ministry (MA). *Program availability:* Part-time, evening/weekend, 100% online, blended/hybrid learning, synchronous online/on-ground. Terminal master's awarded for partial completion of doctoral program. *Degree requirements:* For master's, comprehensive exam, thesis (for some programs); for doctorate, 3 foreign languages, thesis/dissertation. *Entrance requirements:* Additional exam requirements/recommendations for international students: required—TOEFL (minimum score 500 paper-based). Electronic applications accepted. *Expenses:* Contact institution.

Fordham University, Graduate School of Arts and Sciences, Department of Theology, New York, NY 10458. Offers MA, PhD. *Program availability:* Part-time, evening/weekend. *Students:* Average age 33. 66 applicants, 24% accepted, 10 enrolled. In 2019, 3 master's, 7 doctorates awarded. Terminal master's awarded for partial completion of doctoral program. *Degree requirements:* For master's, one foreign language, comprehensive exam; for doctorate, 2 foreign languages, comprehensive exam, thesis/dissertation. *Entrance requirements:* For master's and doctorate, GRE General Test. Additional exam requirements/recommendations for international students: required—TOEFL (minimum score 650 paper-based). *Application deadline:* For fall admission, 1/4 priority date for domestic students; for spring admission, 11/1 for domestic students. Application fee: $70. Electronic applications accepted. *Financial support:* In 2019–20, 45 students received support, including 2 fellowships with tuition reimbursements available (averaging $25,960 per year), 33 teaching assistantships with tuition reimbursements available (averaging $21,887 per year); institutionally sponsored loans, tuition waivers (full and partial), and unspecified assistantships also available. Support available to part-time students. Financial award application deadline: 1/4. *Unit head:* Dr. Benjamin Dunning, Chair, 212-636-6363, E-mail: dunning@fordham.edu. *Application contact:* Garrett Marino, Director of Graduate Admissions, 718-817-441, Fax: 718-817-3566, E-mail: gmarino10@fordham.edu.

Franciscan School of Theology, Graduate and Professional Programs, Oceanside, CA 92057. Offers M Div, MA, MAMC, MTS. *Accreditation:* ATS (one or more programs are accredited). *Program availability:* Part-time. *Degree requirements:* For master's, one foreign language, thesis. *Entrance requirements:* For master's, GRE General Test (MA). Additional exam requirements/recommendations for international students: required—TOEFL (minimum score 550 paper-based).

Franciscan University of Steubenville, Graduate Programs, Department of Theology, Steubenville, OH 43952-1763. Offers theology and Christian ministry (MA). *Program availability:* Part-time, online learning. *Degree requirements:* For master's, comprehensive exam. *Entrance requirements:* For master's, minimum undergraduate GPA of 3.0. Additional exam requirements/recommendations for international students: required—TOEFL. Electronic applications accepted. Application fee is waived when completed online.

Freed-Hardeman University, School of Biblical Studies, Program in Divinity, Henderson, TN 38340-2399. Offers M Div. *Accreditation:* ATS. *Program availability:* Part-time. *Degree requirements:* For master's, comprehensive exam. *Entrance requirements:* For master's, GRE General Test or MAT. Additional exam requirements/recommendations for international students: required—TOEFL (minimum score 500 paper-based).

Freed-Hardeman University, School of Biblical Studies, Program in New Testament, Henderson, TN 38340-2399. Offers MA. *Program availability:* Part-time. *Degree requirements:* For master's, one foreign language, comprehensive exam, thesis. *Entrance requirements:* For master's, GRE General Test or MAT. Additional exam requirements/recommendations for international students: required—TOEFL (minimum score 500 paper-based).

Fresno Pacific University, Biblical Seminary, Program in Divinity, Fresno, CA 93702-4709. Offers M Div. *Accreditation:* ATS. *Entrance requirements:* For master's, minimum GPA of 2.5. *Expenses:* Contact institution.

Fresno Pacific University, Biblical Seminary, Programs in New Testament, Old Testament, and Theology, Fresno, CA 93702-4709. Offers New Testament (MA); Old Testament (MA); theology (MA). *Accreditation:* ATS. *Program availability:* Part-time. *Entrance requirements:* Additional exam requirements/recommendations for international students: required—TOEFL (minimum score 550 paper-based).

Fuller Theological Seminary, Graduate Programs, Pasadena, CA 91182. Offers Christian leadership (MACL); clinical psychology (PhD, Psy D); family studies (MA); global leadership (MA); global ministries (D Min); global ministries (Korean language) (D Min); intercultural studies (MA, Th M, PhD); intercultural studies (Korean language) (MA); marital and family therapy (MS); marriage and family enrichment (Certificate); ministry (M Div, D Min); missiology (D Miss); missiology (Korean language) (Th M); theology (MA, Th M, PhD), including evangelism (MA), family life education (MA), pastoral ministry (MA), recovery ministry (MA), worship music ministry (MA), worship, theology, and the arts (MA), youth, family, and culture (MA); theology and ministry (MA).

Gannon University, School of Graduate Studies, College of Humanities, Education, and Social Sciences, School of Humanities, Program in Pastoral Studies, Erie, PA 16541-0001. Offers pastoral studies (MA); theological studies (Certificate). *Program availability:* Part-time, evening/weekend. *Degree requirements:* For master's, comprehensive exam, thesis or alternative, research project, internship, written evaluation. *Entrance requirements:* Additional exam requirements/recommendations for international students: required—TOEFL (minimum score 79 iBT). Electronic applications accepted. Application fee is waived when completed online.

Gardner-Webb University, School of Divinity, Boiling Springs, NC 28017. Offers biblical studies (M Div); Christian education and formation (M Div); intercultural studies (M Div); ministry (D Min); missiology (M Div); pastoral care and counseling (M Div); pastoral care and counseling/member care for missionaries (D Min); pastoral studies (M Div); M Div/MA; M Div/MBA. *Accreditation:* ACIPE. *Program availability:* Part-time. *Entrance requirements:* For master's, minimum GPA of 2.6; for doctorate, minimum GPA of 2.75. Additional exam requirements/recommendations for international students: required—TOEFL (minimum score 500 paper-based; 61 iBT). Electronic applications accepted. *Expenses:* Contact institution.

Garrett-Evangelical Theological Seminary, Graduate and Professional Programs, Evanston, IL 60201-3298. Offers Bible and culture (PhD); Christian education (MA); Christian education and congregational studies (PhD); contemporary theology and culture (PhD); divinity (M Div); ethics, church, and society (MA); liturgical studies (PhD); ministry (D Min); music ministry (MA); pastoral care and counseling (MA); pastoral theology, personality, and culture (PhD); spiritual formation and evangelism (MA); theological studies (MTS); M Div/MSW. *Accreditation:* ACIPE; ATS (one or more programs are accredited). *Program availability:* Part-time. *Degree requirements:* For master's, thesis (for some programs); for doctorate, thesis/dissertation. *Entrance requirements:* For doctorate, GRE (PhD). Additional exam requirements/recommendations for international students: required—TOEFL (minimum score 560 paper-based). Electronic applications accepted.

Gateway Seminary, Graduate and Professional Programs, Ontario, CA 91761-8642. Offers divinity (M Div); early childhood education (Certificate); education leadership (MAEL, Diploma); ministry (D Min); theological studies (MTS); theology (Th M); youth ministry (Certificate). *Accreditation:* ACIPE; ATS. *Program availability:* Part-time, evening/weekend. *Degree requirements:* For master's, thesis (for some programs); for doctorate, 2 foreign languages, thesis/dissertation. *Entrance requirements:* For doctorate, MAT. Additional exam requirements/recommendations for international students: required—TOEFL (minimum score 550 paper-based). Electronic applications accepted.

The General Theological Seminary, Graduate and Professional Programs, New York, NY 10011-4977. Offers Anglican studies (STM, Th D, Certificate); ascetical theology (Certificate); biblical studies (Certificate); congregational development (Certificate); divinity (M Div); historical and theological studies (Certificate); spiritual direction (MASD, STM, Certificate); theology (MA). *Accreditation:* ACIPE; ATS. *Program availability:* Part-time, evening/weekend. Terminal master's awarded for partial completion of doctoral program. *Degree requirements:* For master's, thesis; for doctorate, 2 foreign languages, thesis/dissertation. *Entrance requirements:* For master's, GRE General Test; for doctorate, GRE, M Div or MA. Additional exam requirements/recommendations for international students: required—TOEFL.

George Fox University, Portland Seminary, Portland, OR 97223. Offers Biblical studies (M Div, MA); chaplaincy (M Div); Christian history and theology (M Div, MA); creation care (M Div, MA); intercultural studies (M Div, MA); leadership (M Div, MA); leadership and global perspectives (D Min); leadership and spiritual formation (D Min); semiotics and future studies (D Min); spiritual direction (MA, Certificate); spiritual direction supervision (M Div, MA, Certificate); spiritual formation and discipleship (M Div, MA, Certificate). *Accreditation:* ACIPE. *Program availability:* Part-time, evening/weekend, online learning. *Entrance requirements:* For master's, resume, three references (one pastoral, one academic or professional, one personal), one official transcript from each college or university attended; for doctorate, resume, 3 references (1 professional, 1 academic, 1 personal), one official transcript from each college or university attended. Additional exam requirements/recommendations for international students: required—TOEFL (minimum score 577 paper-based; 90 iBT). Electronic applications accepted. *Expenses:* Contact institution.

Georgetown University, Graduate School of Arts and Sciences, Department of Theology, Washington, DC 20057. Offers PhD.

Georgian Court University, School of Arts and Sciences, Lakewood, NJ 08701. Offers applied behavior analysis (MA); autism spectrum disorders (Certificate); clinical mental health counseling (MA); criminal justice and human rights (MS); holistic health studies (MA); homeland security (Certificate); instructional technology (CPC); integrative health (Certificate); mercy spirituality (Certificate); parish business management (Certificate); professional counselor (Certificate); school psychology (MA, Certificate); theology (MA, Certificate). *Program availability:* Part-time, evening/weekend. *Faculty:* 19 full-time (11 women), 7 part-time/adjunct (3 women). *Students:* 90 full-time (80 women), 71 part-time (59 women); includes 26 minority (8 Black or African American, non-Hispanic/Latino; 2 Asian, non-Hispanic/Latino; 14 Hispanic/Latino; 2 Two or more races, non-Hispanic/Latino), 1 international. Average age 32. 138 applicants, 58% accepted, 57 enrolled. In 2019, 68 master's, 19 other advanced degrees awarded. *Degree requirements:* For master's, comprehensive exam (for some programs), thesis (for some programs); for other advanced degree, comprehensive exam (for some programs). *Entrance requirements:* Additional exam requirements/recommendations for international students: required—TOEFL (minimum score 550 paper-based; 79 iBT). *Application deadline:* For fall admission, 8/15 for domestic students, 5/1 for international students; for spring admission, 1/15 for domestic students, 10/1 for international students. Applications are processed on a rolling basis. Application fee: $40. Electronic applications accepted. *Financial support:* Scholarships/grants, health care benefits, and unspecified assistantships available. Financial award application deadline: 4/15; financial award applicants required to submit FAFSA. *Unit head:* Dr. Mary Chinery, Dean, 732-987-2493, Fax: 732-987-2007, E-mail: mchinery@georgian.edu. *Application contact:* Dr. Mary Chinery, Dean, 732-987-2493, Fax: 732-987-2007, E-mail: mchinery@georgian.edu.
Website: https://georgian.edu/academics/school-of-arts-sciences/

Global University, Graduate School of Theology, Springfield, MO 65804. Offers bible and theology (D Min); biblical language (M Div); biblical studies (MA); Christian ministry (M Div, D Min); ministerial studies (MA), including education, leadership, missions, New Testament, Old Testament. *Program availability:* Part-time, evening/weekend, online learning. *Degree requirements:* For master's, thesis (for some programs). *Entrance requirements:* For master's, minimum undergraduate GPA of 3.0. Electronic applications accepted.

Gonzaga University, College of Arts and Sciences, Spokane, WA 99258. Offers philosophy (MA); theology and leadership (MA). *Program availability:* Part-time, blended/hybrid learning. *Degree requirements:* For master's, comprehensive exam. *Entrance requirements:* For master's, GRE or MAT, minimum GPA of 3.0, official transcripts, two to three letters of recommendation, personal statement, writing sample, resume/curriculum vitae. Additional exam requirements/recommendations for international students: required—TOEFL (minimum score 88 iBT) or IELTS (minimum score 6.5). Electronic applications accepted. *Expenses:* Contact institution.

Gordon-Conwell Theological Seminary, Graduate and Professional Programs, South Hamilton, MA 01982. Offers Biblical languages (MABL); church history (MACH); counseling (MACO); ministry (D Min); missions/evangelism (MAME); New Testament (MANT); Old Testament (MAOT); religion (MAR); theology (M Div, MATH, Th M, Th D). *Accreditation:* ACIPE; ATS (one or more programs are accredited). *Program availability:* Part-time, evening/weekend. *Degree requirements:* For master's, one foreign language, thesis optional; for doctorate, 2 foreign languages, thesis/dissertation. *Entrance requirements:* For master's, minimum GPA of 2.5; for doctorate, minimum GPA of 3.0.

Graceland University, Community of Christ Seminary, Independence, MO 64050. Offers MAR. *Program availability:* Evening/weekend. *Entrance requirements:* For master's, minimum cumulative GPA of 3.0. Additional exam requirements/recommendations for international students: required—TOEFL (minimum score 550 paper-based; 80 iBT), WES evaluation of transcripts. Electronic applications accepted. *Expenses:* Contact institution.

Grace School of Theology, Graduate Programs, Conroe, TX 77384-4894. Offers M Div, MABS, MM, Th M.

Grace Theological Seminary, Graduate and Professional Programs, Winona Lake, IN 46590-9907. Offers biblical studies (Certificate); chaplaincy (M Div); exegetical studies (M Div); intercultural studies (M Div, MA, D Min); local church ministry (MA), including camp administration, women's leadership; pastoral counseling (M Div); pastoral studies

(M Div, D Min); theology (Diploma). *Accreditation:* ATS. *Program availability:* Part-time, online learning. *Degree requirements:* For master's, thesis optional; for doctorate, 2 foreign languages, thesis/dissertation. *Entrance requirements:* For master's, MAT, minimum GPA of 2.5. Electronic applications accepted.

Graduate Theological Union, Graduate Programs, Berkeley, CA 94709-1212. Offers art and religion (MA, PhD, Th D); biblical languages (MA); Biblical studies (PhD, Th D); biblical studies (MA); Buddhist studies (MA); Christian spirituality (MA, PhD, Th D); cultural and historical studies of religions (MA, PhD, Th D); ethics and social theory (PhD, Th D); history (MA, PhD, Th D); homiletics (MA, PhD, Th D); interdisciplinary studies (PhD, Th D); Jewish studies (MA, PhD, Th D, Certificate); liturgical studies (MA, PhD, Th D); Near Eastern religions (PhD, Th D); Orthodox Christian studies (MA); religion and psychology (MA, PhD, Th D); religion and society/ethics and social theory (MA); systematic and philosophical theology (MA, PhD, Th D). *Accreditation:* ATS. Terminal master's awarded for partial completion of doctoral program. *Degree requirements:* For master's, one foreign language, thesis; for doctorate, one foreign language, comprehensive exam, thesis/dissertation. *Entrance requirements:* For master's, GRE General Test; for doctorate, GRE General Test, MA or M Div. Additional exam requirements/recommendations for international students: required—TOEFL. Electronic applications accepted.

Grand Rapids Theological Seminary of Cornerstone University, Graduate Programs, Grand Rapids, MI 49525-5897. Offers academic (M Div); chaplaincy ministries (M Div); Christian formation (MA); counseling (MA); formation and soul care ministries (M Div); intercultural ministries (M Div); interdisciplinary studies (MA); New Testament (Th M); Old Testament (Th M); pastoral ministries (M Div); small group and discipleship ministries (M Div); student and family ministries (M Div). *Accreditation:* ATS. *Program availability:* Part-time, evening/weekend, 100% online, blended/hybrid learning. *Entrance requirements:* Additional exam requirements/recommendations for international students: required—TOEFL (minimum score 577 paper-based; 90 iBT), IELTS (minimum score 7). Electronic applications accepted.

Greensboro College, Program in Theology, Ethics and Culture, Greensboro, NC 27401-1875. Offers MA.

Harding School of Theology, Graduate Programs, Memphis, TN 38117-5499. Offers Christian ministry (MA); historical theology (MA); ministry (M Div); New Testament (MA); Old Testament (MA); systematic theology (MA); transforming leadership (D Min). *Accreditation:* ATS. *Program availability:* Part-time, online learning. *Degree requirements:* For master's, variable foreign language requirement, thesis (for some programs); for doctorate, one foreign language, thesis/dissertation. *Entrance requirements:* For master's, minimum GPA of 2.7; for doctorate, minimum GPA of 3.0. Additional exam requirements/recommendations for international students: required—TOEFL (minimum score 550 paper-based; 79 iBT). Electronic applications accepted. *Expenses: Tuition:* Full-time $12,240; part-time $8160 per semester hour. *Required fees:* $306; $204 per semester hour. $324 per semester. Tuition and fees vary according to degree level.

Hardin-Simmons University, Graduate School, Logsdon Seminary, Program in Theology, Abilene, TX 79698-0001. Offers M Div. *Program availability:* Part-time. *Degree requirements:* For master's, ministry formation. *Entrance requirements:* Additional exam requirements/recommendations for international students: required—TOEFL (minimum score 550 paper-based; 79 iBT). Electronic applications accepted. *Expenses:* Contact institution.

Hartford Seminary, Graduate Programs, Hartford, CT 06105-2279. Offers Islamic studies (MA); ministry (D Min); religious studies (MA); spirituality (Certificate). *Accreditation:* ATS (one or more programs are accredited). *Program availability:* Part-time, evening/weekend, online learning. *Degree requirements:* For master's, thesis optional, oral exam; for doctorate, thesis/dissertation, oral exam. *Entrance requirements:* For doctorate, experience in ministry, M Div. Additional exam requirements/recommendations for international students: required—TOEFL (minimum score 550 paper-based; 80 iBT).

Harvard University, Harvard Divinity School, Cambridge, MA 02138. Offers M Div, MTS, Th M. *Accreditation:* ACIPE; ATS. *Degree requirements:* For master's, one foreign language, thesis (for some programs). *Entrance requirements:* For master's, GRE General Test. Additional exam requirements/recommendations for international students: required—TOEFL. Electronic applications accepted. *Expenses:* Contact institution.

Hebrew College, Rabbinical School, Newton Centre, MA 02459. Offers MA. *Entrance requirements:* For master's, interview. Additional exam requirements/recommendations for international students: required—TOEFL.

Hebrew Union College–Jewish Institute of Religion, Rabbinical School, New York, NY 10012-1186. Offers MAHL. *Degree requirements:* For master's, one foreign language. *Entrance requirements:* For master's, GRE, language exam, minimum GPA of 3.0, minimum 2 years of college-level Hebrew. Additional exam requirements/recommendations for international students: required—TOEFL.

Hebrew Union College–Jewish Institute of Religion, School of Graduate Studies, Program in Pastoral Counseling, New York, NY 10012-1186. Offers D Min. *Accreditation:* ACIPE. *Degree requirements:* For doctorate, thesis/dissertation. *Entrance requirements:* For doctorate, M Div (or higher), ordination/certification for ministry. Additional exam requirements/recommendations for international students: required—TOEFL. *Expenses:* Contact institution.

Heritage College and Seminary, Graduate and Professional Programs, Cambridge, ON N3C 3T2, Canada. Offers general (M Div); intercultural studies (M Div); pastoral (M Div); research (M Div); theological studies (MTS, CTS).

Holy Apostles College and Seminary, Department of Theology, Cromwell, CT 06416-2005. Offers bioethics (MA, Certificate, Post Master's Certificate); church history (MA, Certificate, Post Master's Certificate); dogmatic theology (MA, Certificate, Post Master's Certificate); liturgical music (MA, Certificate, Post Master's Certificate); liturgy (MA, Certificate, Post Master's Certificate); moral theology (MA, Certificate, Post Master's Certificate); philosophical theology (MA, Certificate, Post Master's Certificate); religious education (MA, Certificate, Post Master's Certificate); sacred scripture (MA, Post Master's Certificate); sacred scriptures (Certificate); theology (M Div). *Accreditation:* ATS. *Program availability:* Part-time, evening/weekend, online learning. *Degree requirements:* For master's, one foreign language, comprehensive exam, thesis optional; for other advanced degree, culminating paper. *Entrance requirements:* For master's, minimum undergraduate GPA of 3.0; for other advanced degree, minimum graduate GPA of 3.0. Electronic applications accepted. *Expenses: Tuition:* Full-time $4320; part-time $2160 per credit. *Required fees:* $80; $80 per credit. $40 per semester. One-time fee: $150.

Holy Cross Greek Orthodox School of Theology, Theological Programs, Brookline, MA 02445-7496. Offers M Div, MTS, Th M. *Accreditation:* ATS. *Program availability:* Part-time. *Degree requirements:* For master's, 2 foreign languages, thesis (for some programs). *Entrance requirements:* For master's, GRE General Test, interview, official transcripts, letters of recommendation, health report and immunization verification. Additional exam requirements/recommendations for international students: required—TOEFL (minimum score 550 paper-based; 80 iBT).

Hood Theological Seminary, Graduate and Professional Programs, Salisbury, NC 28144. Offers M Div, MTS, D Min. *Accreditation:* ATS. *Program availability:* Part-time, evening/weekend, online learning. *Degree requirements:* For master's, thesis optional; for doctorate, thesis/dissertation. *Expenses: Tuition:* Full-time $17,160; part-time $7920 per credit hour. *Required fees:* $700; $520 per credit hour. $260 per semester. Full-time tuition and fees vary according to course level, course load and program.

Houston Baptist University, School of Christian Thought, Program in Apologetics, Houston, TX 77074-3298. Offers cultural apologetics (MA); philosophical apologetics (MA). *Program availability:* 100% online. *Entrance requirements:* For master's, bachelor's degree conferred transcript, essay/personal statement, resume. Additional exam requirements/recommendations for international students: required—TOEFL (minimum score 80 iBT), IELTS (minimum score 6.5). Electronic applications accepted. Application fee is waived when completed online. *Expenses:* Contact institution.

Houston Graduate School of Theology, Graduate Programs, Houston, TX 77092. Offers counseling (MA); pastoral ministry (M Div, D Min); theology (MA). *Accreditation:* ATS (one or more programs are accredited). *Program availability:* Part-time, evening/weekend. *Degree requirements:* For master's, thesis (for some programs); for doctorate, thesis/dissertation. *Entrance requirements:* For doctorate, GRE General Test or MAT, M Div or equivalent. Additional exam requirements/recommendations for international students: required—TOEFL (minimum score 550 paper-based).

Howard Payne University, Program in Theology and Ministry, Brownwood, TX 76801-2715. Offers MA. *Program availability:* Part-time. *Degree requirements:* For master's, three 2-hour internships/mentorships. *Entrance requirements:* For master's, undergraduate degree from accredited university; leveling courses (for students without undergraduate coursework in Old Testament, New Testament, and theology). Additional exam requirements/recommendations for international students: required—TOEFL (minimum score 79 iBT). Electronic applications accepted.

Howard University, School of Divinity, Washington, DC 20017. Offers M Div, MARS, D Min. *Accreditation:* ACIPE; ATS. *Program availability:* Part-time, evening/weekend. *Degree requirements:* For master's, thesis; for doctorate, thesis/dissertation. *Entrance requirements:* For master's and doctorate, minimum GPA of 3.0. Electronic applications accepted.

Iliff School of Theology, Graduate and Professional Programs, Denver, CO 80210-4798. Offers biblical studies (MA); church history (MA); religion (MA); religion and social change (MA); specialized ministry (MASM), including justice and peace, pastoral theology and care, religions leadership; theology (M Div, MTS, D Min, PhD), including Biblical studies (PhD), religion and psychological studies (PhD), religion and social change (PhD), theology, philosophy and culture (PhD); theology/ethics (MA). *Accreditation:* ACIPE; ATS. *Program availability:* Part-time, evening/weekend. *Degree requirements:* For master's, one foreign language, thesis (for some programs); for doctorate, 2 foreign languages, comprehensive exam, thesis/dissertation. *Entrance requirements:* For master's, minimum GPA of 3.0, writing sample, references; for doctorate, GRE General Test, minimum GPA of 3.0, writing sample, letters of recommendation. Additional exam requirements/recommendations for international students: required—TOEFL (minimum score 550 paper-based). Electronic applications accepted.

Indiana Wesleyan University, Graduate School, Wesley Seminary, Master of Divinity Program, Marion, IN 46953-4974. Offers M Div. *Program availability:* Online learning.

Institute for Christian Studies, Graduate Programs, Toronto, ON M5S 2E6, Canada. Offers education (M Phil F, PhD); history of philosophy (M Phil F, PhD); philosophical aesthetics (M Phil F, PhD); philosophy of religion (M Phil F, PhD); political theory (M Phil F, PhD); systematic philosophy (M Phil F, PhD); theology (M Phil F, PhD); worldview studies (MWS). *Program availability:* Part-time, online learning. *Degree requirements:* For master's, one foreign language, thesis; for doctorate, 2 foreign languages, thesis/dissertation. *Entrance requirements:* For master's and doctorate, philosophy background. Additional exam requirements/recommendations for international students: required—TOEFL (minimum score 600 paper-based).

Inter American University of Puerto Rico, Metropolitan Campus, Graduate Programs, Program in Theological Studies, San Juan, PR 00919-1293. Offers PhD.

Interdenominational Theological Center, Graduate and Professional Programs, Atlanta, GA 30314-4112. Offers Christian education (MACE); ministry (D Min); pastoral counseling (Th D); theology (M Div); M Div/MACE. *Accreditation:* ACIPE; ATS (one or more programs are accredited). *Program availability:* Part-time, evening/weekend, blended/hybrid learning. *Degree requirements:* For doctorate, thesis/dissertation. *Entrance requirements:* For doctorate, master's degree. Electronic applications accepted.

International Baptist College and Seminary, Program in Biblical Studies, Chandler, AZ 85286. Offers MA.

The Jewish Theological Seminary, The Graduate School, New York, NY 10027-4649. Offers ancient Judaism (MA, DHL, PhD); Bible and ancient Semitic languages (MA, DHL, PhD); interdepartmental studies (MA); Jewish art and visual culture (MA); Jewish gender and women's studies (MA); Jewish history (MA, DHL, PhD); Jewish literature (MA, DHL, PhD); Jewish philosophy (DHL); Jewish thought (MA, PhD); liturgy (MA, DHL, PhD); medieval Jewish studies (MA, DHL, PhD); Midrash (DHL); Midrash and scriptural interpretation (MA, PhD); modern Jewish studies (MA, DHL, PhD); Talmud and rabbinics (MA, DHL, PhD); MA/MSW. *Accreditation:* ACIPE. *Program availability:* Part-time. Terminal master's awarded for partial completion of doctoral program. *Degree requirements:* For master's, one foreign language, comprehensive exam (for some programs), thesis (for some programs); for doctorate, 3 foreign languages, comprehensive exam (for some programs), thesis/dissertation. *Entrance requirements:* For master's, GRE or MAT, 3 letters of recommendation, writing sample; for doctorate, GRE or MAT, 3 letters of recommendation, writing research sample. Additional exam requirements/recommendations for international students: required—TOEFL.

The Jewish Theological Seminary, The Rabbinical School, New York, NY 10027-4649. Offers MA, Rabbi. *Accreditation:* ACIPE. *Degree requirements:* For master's and Rabbi, one foreign language, competency exams. *Entrance requirements:* For master's and Rabbi, GRE, interview, writing sample. Additional exam requirements/recommendations for international students: required—TOEFL. *Expenses:* Contact institution.

John Carroll University, Graduate School, Department of Theology and Religious Studies, University Heights, OH 44118. Offers MA. *Program availability:* Part-time, evening/weekend. *Degree requirements:* For master's, research essay or thesis, foreign language proficiency. *Entrance requirements:* Additional exam requirements/recommendations for international students: required—TOEFL. *Application deadline:* Applications are processed on a rolling basis. Application fee: $0. Electronic applications accepted. *Financial support:* Scholarships/grants and unspecified assistantships available. Financial award applicants required to submit FAFSA. *Unit head:* Dr. Edward P. Hahnenberg, Chair, 216-397-1674, Fax: 216-397-4518, E-mail:

ehahnenberg@jcu.edu. *Application contact:* Dr. Sheila E. McGinn, Program Coordinator, 216-397-4703, Fax: 216-397-4518, E-mail: smcginn@jcu.edu.
Website: https://jcu.edu/academics/trs/degree-programs/trs-ma-degree

John Paul the Great Catholic University, School of Theology, Escondido, CA 92025. Offers biblical theology (MA).

Johnson University, Graduate and Professional Programs, Knoxville, TN 37998. Offers biblical interpretation (Graduate Certificate); business administration (MBA); Christian ministries (Graduate Certificate); clinical mental health counseling (MA); educational technology (MA); intercultural studies (MA); leadership (MBA); leadership studies (PhD); New Testament (MA); nonprofit management (MBA); school counseling (MA); spiritual formation and leadership (Graduate Certificate); strategic ministry (MA); teacher education (MA). *Program availability:* Part-time, 100% online, blended/hybrid learning. *Faculty:* 26 full-time (10 women), 32 part-time/adjunct (9 women). *Students:* 116 full-time (56 women), 196 part-time (91 women); includes 40 minority (23 Black or African American, non-Hispanic/Latino; 1 American Indian or Alaska Native, non-Hispanic/Latino; 4 Asian, non-Hispanic/Latino; 6 Hispanic/Latino; 6 Two or more races, non-Hispanic/Latino), 31 international. Average age 36. In 2019, 87 master's, 6 doctorates, 14 other advanced degrees awarded. *Degree requirements:* For master's, variable foreign language requirement, comprehensive exam, thesis (for some programs), internships; for doctorate, variable foreign language requirement, comprehensive exam, thesis/dissertation, internships. *Entrance requirements:* For master's, PRAXIS (for MA in teacher education); MAT (for counseling); GRE or GMAT (for MBA), interview, 3 references, transcripts, essay, minimum GPA of 2.5 or 3.0 (depending on program); for doctorate, GRE or MAT (taken not less than 5 years prior), interview, 3 references, transcripts, essay, minimum GPA of 3.0; for Graduate Certificate, interview, 3 references, transcripts, essay, minimum GPA of 3.0. Additional exam requirements/recommendations for international students: required—TOEFL (minimum score 527 paper-based; 71 iBT). *Application deadline:* For fall admission, 7/1 for domestic students; for spring admission, 11/1 for domestic students; for summer admission, 4/1 for domestic students. Application fee: $50. Electronic applications accepted. *Expenses:* Contact institution. *Financial support:* Scholarships/grants available. Financial award application deadline: 4/15; financial award applicants required to submit FAFSA. *Unit head:* Lisa Tarwater, Chief Admissions Officer, 865-251-3400, E-mail: ltarwater@johnsonu.edu. *Application contact:* Lisa Tarwater, Chief Admissions Officer, 865-251-3400, E-mail: ltarwater@johnsonu.edu.
Website: www.johnsonu.edu

Kehilath Yakov Rabbinical Seminary, Graduate Programs, Ossining, NY 10562. *Accreditation:* AARTS.

Kenrick-Glennon Seminary, Graduate and Professional Programs, St. Louis, MO 63119-4330. Offers M Div, MA. *Accreditation:* ATS. *Degree requirements:* For master's, thesis optional.

Kentucky Christian University, Graduate School, Grayson, KY 41143-2205. Offers Biblical studies (MA); Christian leadership (MA). *Program availability:* Part-time. *Degree requirements:* For master's, comprehensive exam (for some programs), thesis optional. *Entrance requirements:* For master's, minimum cumulative GPA of 2.75 in major or 2.5 overall; 6 additional hours in Bible (for non-Biblical undergraduate majors). Additional exam requirements/recommendations for international students: required—TOEFL (minimum score 550 paper-based). Electronic applications accepted.

The King's University, Graduate and Professional Programs, Southlake, TX 76092. Offers Biblical studies (Graduate Certificate); Christian ministry (Graduate Certificate); ministry (M Div, MPT, D Min).

Kingswood University, Program in Pastoral Theology, Sussex, NB E4E 5L2, Canada. Offers MA. *Entrance requirements:* For master's, official transcripts, 3 references, statement of purpose. *Expenses: Tuition:* Part-time $370 Canadian dollars per credit hour. One-time fee: $160 Canadian dollars full-time.

Knox College, College of Theology, Toronto, ON M5S 2E6, Canada. Offers M Div, MRE, MTS, Th M, D Min, Th D. *Accreditation:* ATS. *Program availability:* Part-time. *Degree requirements:* For master's, one foreign language, thesis (for some programs); for doctorate, 2 foreign languages, thesis/dissertation. *Entrance requirements:* For doctorate, M Div. Additional exam requirements/recommendations for international students: required—TOEFL (minimum score 580 paper-based), TWE (minimum score 5).

Knox Theological Seminary, Graduate Programs, Master of Arts Programs, Fort Lauderdale, FL 33308. Offers Biblical and theological studies (MA); Christian and classical studies (MA). *Accreditation:* ATS. *Program availability:* Part-time, evening/weekend. *Entrance requirements:* Additional exam requirements/recommendations for international students: required—TOEFL (minimum score 520 paper-based; 83 iBT), TWE (minimum score 5).

Knox Theological Seminary, Graduate Programs, Program in Divinity, Fort Lauderdale, FL 33308. Offers M Div. *Accreditation:* ATS. *Program availability:* Part-time, evening/weekend, online only, blended/hybrid learning. *Entrance requirements:* Additional exam requirements/recommendations for international students: required—TOEFL (minimum score 520 paper-based; 83 iBT), TWE (minimum score 5).

Lakeland University, Graduate Studies Division, Program in Theology, Plymouth, WI 53073. Offers MAT. *Faculty:* 4 part-time/adjunct (0 women). *Students:* 12 part-time (6 women). *Degree requirements:* For master's, comprehensive exam. *Entrance requirements:* Additional exam requirements/recommendations for international students: required—TOEFL (minimum score 577 paper-based). *Application deadline:* Applications are processed on a rolling basis. Application fee: $25. *Expenses:* Contact institution. *Financial support:* Scholarships/grants and health care benefits available. Support available to part-time students. Financial award application deadline: 7/9; financial award applicants required to submit FAFSA. *Unit head:* Suzanne Sellars, Head, 920-565-1256. *Application contact:* Rebecca Hagan, Graduate Program Coordinator, 920-565-1256, Fax: 920-565-1206.

Lancaster Bible College, Capital Bible Seminary, Lancaster, PA 17601. Offers biblical studies (MA, Certificate); Christian counseling and discipleship (MA, Certificate); ministry (MA); theology (M Div). *Program availability:* Part-time, evening/weekend. *Degree requirements:* For master's, 2 foreign languages, comprehensive exam, thesis (for some programs). *Entrance requirements:* For master's, GRE General Test, Greek exam for those with 2 years of Greek, proficiency exam in theology, previous course work in Biblical studies. Additional exam requirements/recommendations for international students: required—TOEFL (minimum score 550 paper-based).

Lancaster Bible College, Graduate School, Lancaster, PA 17601-5036. Offers adult ministries (MA); Bible (MA); children and family ministry (MA); church planting (MA); consulting resource teacher (M Ed); elementary school counseling (M Ed); leadership (PhD); leadership studies (MA); marriage and family counseling (MA); mental health counseling (MA); pastoral studies (MA); secondary school counseling (M Ed); sports ministry (MA); student ministry (MA); town and country ministry (MA). *Program availability:* Part-time, evening/weekend. *Degree requirements:* For master's, comprehensive exam (for some programs), thesis (for some programs). *Entrance requirements:* For master's, bachelor's degree with a minimum of 30 credits of course work in Bible, minimum undergraduate GPA of 3.0, interview. Additional exam requirements/recommendations for international students: required—TOEFL.

Lancaster Theological Seminary, Graduate and Professional Programs, Lancaster, PA 17603-2812. Offers biblical studies (MAR); Christian education (MAR); Christianity and the arts (MAR); church history (MAR); congregational life (MAR); lay leadership (Certificate); theological studies (M Div); theology (D Min); theology and ethics (MAR). *Accreditation:* ACIPE; ATS. *Degree requirements:* For doctorate, thesis/dissertation.

Lee University, Programs in Religion, Cleveland, TN 37320-3450. Offers biblical studies (MA); ministry studies/leadership (MA); ministry studies/worship (MA); ministry studies/youth and family (MA); theological studies (MA), including ethics, religion. *Program availability:* Part-time, 100% online. *Faculty:* 12 full-time (3 women), 8 part-time/adjunct (0 women). *Students:* 32 full-time (13 women), 104 part-time (33 women); includes 74 minority (10 Black or African American, non-Hispanic/Latino; 60 Hispanic/Latino; 4 Two or more races, non-Hispanic/Latino), 5 international. Average age 38. 43 applicants, 79% accepted, 24 enrolled. In 2019, 15 master's awarded. *Degree requirements:* For master's, variable foreign language requirement, comprehensive exam (for some programs), thesis (for some programs). *Entrance requirements:* For master's, GRE or MAT (for biblical/theological studies only), minimum GPA of 3.0, 3 letters of recommendation, interview, official transcripts, essay. Additional exam requirements/recommendations for international students: required—TOEFL (minimum score 61 iBT). *Application deadline:* For fall admission, 4/1 priority date for domestic and international students; for spring admission, 10/1 priority date for domestic and international students. Applications are processed on a rolling basis. Application fee: $25. Electronic applications accepted. *Expenses:* Contact institution. *Financial support:* In 2019–20, 39 students received support, including 12 teaching assistantships (averaging $2,046 per year); career-related internships or fieldwork, Federal Work-Study, institutionally sponsored loans, scholarships/grants, and unspecified assistantships also available. Financial award application deadline: 3/1; financial award applicants required to submit FAFSA. *Unit head:* Dr. Lisa Long, Director, 423-303-5100, E-mail: llong@leeuniversity.edu. *Application contact:* Jeffery McGirt, Director of Graduate Enrollment, 423-614-8691, Fax: 423-614-8317, E-mail: jmcgirt@leeuniversity.edu.
Website: http://www.leeuniversity.edu/academics/graduate/

Lenoir-Rhyne University, Graduate Programs, Lutheran Theological Southern Seminary, Hickory, NC 28601. Offers M Div, MACM, MAR, STM. *Accreditation:* ACIPE. *Program availability:* Part-time. *Degree requirements:* For master's, comprehensive exam (for some programs), thesis (for some programs). *Entrance requirements:* Additional exam requirements/recommendations for international students: recommended—TOEFL. *Expenses:* Contact institution.

Lexington Theological Seminary, Graduate and Professional Programs, Lexington, KY 40508-3218. Offers M Div, MA, MAPS, D Min, M Div/MSW. *Accreditation:* ACIPE; ATS. *Program availability:* Part-time, evening/weekend. *Degree requirements:* For master's, thesis; for doctorate, thesis/dissertation. *Entrance requirements:* Additional exam requirements/recommendations for international students: required—TOEFL (minimum score 600 paper-based). *Expenses: Tuition:* Full-time $480. *Required fees:* $360. Tuition and fees vary according to program.

Liberty University, School of Behavioral Sciences, Lynchburg, VA 24515. Offers applied psychology (MA), including developmental psychology (MA, MS), industrial/organizational psychology (MA, MS); clinical mental health counseling (MA); community care and counseling (Ed D), including marriage and family counseling, pastoral care and counseling, traumatology; counselor education and supervision (PhD); human services counseling (MA), including addictions and recovery, business, child and family law, Christian ministries, criminal justice, crisis response and trauma, executive leadership, health and wellness, life coaching, marriage and family, military resilience; marriage and family counseling (MA); marriage and family therapy (MA); military resilience (Certificate); pastoral counseling (MA), including addictions and recovery, community chaplaincy, crisis response and trauma, discipleship and church ministry, leadership, life coaching, marriage and family, marriage and family studies, military resilience, parenting and child/adolescent, pastoral counseling, theology; professional counseling (MA); psychology (MS), including developmental psychology (MA, MS), industrial/organizational psychology (MA, MS); school counseling (M Ed). *Program availability:* Part-time, online learning. *Students:* 3,786 full-time (3,065 women), 5,193 part-time (4,081 women); includes 2,733 minority (1,967 Black or African American, non-Hispanic/Latino; 48 American Indian or Alaska Native, non-Hispanic/Latino; 103 Asian, non-Hispanic/Latino; 349 Hispanic/Latino; 19 Native Hawaiian or other Pacific Islander, non-Hispanic/Latino; 247 Two or more races, non-Hispanic/Latino), 133 international. Average age 38. 13,324 applicants, 28% accepted, 2,163 enrolled. In 2019, 2,322 master's, 19 doctorates, 112 other advanced degrees awarded. *Entrance requirements:* For master's, Official bachelor's degree transcripts with a 2.0 GPA or higher. *Application deadline:* Applications are processed on a rolling basis. Application fee: $50. Electronic applications accepted. *Expenses: Tuition:* Full-time $545; part-time $410 per credit hour. One-time fee: $50. *Financial support:* In 2019–20, 1,003 students received support. Teaching assistantships and Federal Work-Study available. Financial award applicants required to submit FAFSA. *Unit head:* Dr. Kenyon Knapp, Dean, School of Behavioral Services, E-mail: kcknapp@liberty.edu. *Application contact:* Jay Bridge, Director of Admissions, 800-424-9595, Fax: 800-628-7977, E-mail: gradadmissions@liberty.edu.
Website: https://www.liberty.edu/behavioral-sciences/

Liberty University, School of Divinity, Lynchburg, VA 24515. Offers Biblical exposition (MA); Biblical languages (M Div); Biblical studies (M Div, MA, MAR, Th M, D Min); chaplaincy (M Div, D Min); Christian apologetics (M Div, MA, MAR, Th M); Christian leadership and church ministries (M Div); Christian ministries (M Div); Christian ministry (MA); Christian thought (M Div); church history (M Div, MAR, Th M); community chaplaincy (M Div, MAR); discipleship (D Min); discipleship and church ministry (M Div, MAR, MCM); evangelism and church planting (MAR, MCM, D Min); expository preaching (D Min); global ministry (MA); global studies (M Div, MAR, MCM, MGS, Th M); healthcare chaplaincy (M Div); homiletics (M Div, MAR, Th M); leadership (M Div, MAR); marketplace chaplaincy (M Div, MCM); ministry leadership (Ed D); pastoral counseling (M Div, MA, MAR, D Min), including addictions and recovery (MA), crisis response and trauma (MA), discipleship and church ministries (MA), leadership (MA), life coaching (MA), marketplace chaplaincy (MA), marriage and family (MA), military resilience (MA), pastoral counseling (MA); pastoral leadership (D Min); pastoral ministries (M Div, M Serv Soc, MCM); religious education (MRE); sports chaplaincy (MA); theology (M Div, MAR, MTS, Th M); theology and apologetics (D Min, PhD); worship (M Div, MAR, MCM, D Min); youth and family ministries (M Div). *Program availability:* Part-time, online learning. *Students:* 2,691 full-time (814 women), 2,570 part-time (732 women); includes 1,484 minority (1,046 Black or African American, non-Hispanic/Latino; 33 American Indian or Alaska Native, non-Hispanic/Latino; 120 Asian, non-Hispanic/Latino; 167 Hispanic/Latino; 8 Native Hawaiian or other Pacific Islander, non-Hispanic/Latino; 110 Two or more races, non-Hispanic/Latino), 101 international. Average age 43. 4,508 applicants, 34% accepted, 952 enrolled. In 2019, 1,251 master's, 71 doctorates awarded. *Degree requirements:* For master's, 2 foreign languages, thesis (for some programs); for doctorate, 2 foreign languages, thesis/dissertation. *Entrance requirements:* For master's, minimum undergraduate GPA of 2.0; for doctorate, GRE

General Test or MAT, minimum graduate GPA of 3.0. Additional exam requirements/recommendations for international students: required—TOEFL (minimum score 600 paper-based; 100 iBT). *Application deadline:* For fall admission, 6/1 for domestic students; for spring admission, 11/1 for domestic students. Applications are processed on a rolling basis. Application fee: $50. Electronic applications accepted. *Expenses:* Contact institution. *Financial support:* Teaching assistantships with tuition reimbursements, career-related internships or fieldwork, and Federal Work-Study available. Financial award applicants required to submit FAFSA. *Unit head:* Dr. Troy Temple, Interim Dean, School of Divinity, E-mail: divinity@liberty.edu. *Application contact:* Jay Bridge, Director of Graduate Admissions, 800-424-9595, Fax: 800-628-7977, E-mail: gradadmissions@liberty.edu.
Website: https://www.liberty.edu/divinity/

Lincoln Christian Seminary, Graduate and Professional Programs, Lincoln, IL 62656-2167. Offers Bible and theology (MA); Christian ministries (MA); counseling (MA); divinity (M Div); leadership ministry (D Min); religious education (MRE). *Accreditation:* ACIPE; ATS. *Program availability:* Part-time. *Degree requirements:* For master's, 2 foreign languages, thesis; for doctorate, thesis/dissertation. *Entrance requirements:* For master's, minimum GPA of 2.5; for doctorate, M Div or equivalent. Additional exam requirements/recommendations for international students: required—TOEFL (minimum score 550 paper-based). Electronic applications accepted.

Lincoln Christian University, Graduate Programs, Lincoln, IL 62656-2167. Offers Bible and theology (MA); Biblical studies (MA); church history/historical theology (MA); counseling (MA); formative worship (MA); intercultural studies (MA); ministry (MA); organizational leadership (MA); philosophy and apologetics (MA); spiritual formation (MA); theology (MA). *Program availability:* Online learning. *Entrance requirements:* For master's, minimum cumulative GPA of 2.5 in undergraduate degree studies. Additional exam requirements/recommendations for international students: required—TOEFL (minimum score 550 paper-based); recommended—IELTS (minimum score 6). Application fee is waived when completed online.

Lipscomb University, Hazelip School of Theology, Nashville, TN 37204-3951. Offers missional and spiritual formation (D Min); theology (M Div). *Program availability:* Part-time, evening/weekend, online learning. *Degree requirements:* For master's, 2 foreign languages, comprehensive exam (for some programs), thesis optional; for doctorate, comprehensive exam, thesis/dissertation. *Entrance requirements:* For master's, 3 references, transcripts, goals statement; for doctorate, 3 references, transcripts, documentation of full-time participation in ministry, writing sample, interview. Additional exam requirements/recommendations for international students: required—TOEFL (minimum score 570 paper-based; 80 iBT). Electronic applications accepted. *Expenses:* Contact institution.

Logos Evangelical Seminary, Graduate Programs, El Monte, CA 91731. Offers M Div, MA, MAFM, MAICS, Th M, D Min, PhD, Diploma. *Accreditation:* ATS (one or more programs are accredited). *Program availability:* Part-time, 100% online, blended/hybrid learning. *Degree requirements:* For master's, variable foreign language requirement, comprehensive exam (for some programs), thesis (for some programs); for doctorate, variable foreign language requirement, comprehensive exam (for some programs), thesis/dissertation. *Entrance requirements:* For master's, Biblical Language proficiency exam (for Th M), MA in Biblical studies with minimum GPA of 3.33, 1.5 years of Biblical language studies, 2 recommendations, and 1 research paper (for Th M); for doctorate, Biblical Language proficiency exam and research language exam (for PhD), M Div or its equivalent with minimum GPA of 3.0, at least three years of experience in full-time ministry after receiving M Div, and recommendations by two church leaders (for D Min). Additional exam requirements/recommendations for international students: required—TOEFL (minimum score 470 paper-based; 52 iBT); recommended—IELTS. Electronic applications accepted. *Expenses: Tuition:* Full-time $10,410; part-time $4364 per unit. *Required fees:* $100 per semester.

Loras College, Graduate Division, Program in Theology and Ministry, Dubuque, IA 52004-0178. Offers ministry (MA); theology (MA). *Program availability:* Part-time, evening/weekend. *Degree requirements:* For master's, comprehensive exam (for some programs), thesis (for some programs). *Entrance requirements:* For master's, bachelor's degree or undergraduate minor in religious studies or equivalent, minimum undergraduate GPA of 2.75.

Louisville Presbyterian Theological Seminary, Graduate and Professional Programs, Louisville, KY 40205-1798. Offers Bible (MAR); divinity (M Div); ministry (D Min); religious thought (MAR); JD/M Div; M Div/MBA; M Div/MSSW. *Accreditation:* AAMFT/COAMFTE (one or more programs are accredited); ACIPE; ATS (one or more programs are accredited). *Program availability:* Part-time. *Faculty:* 17 full-time (8 women), 12 part-time/adjunct (6 women). *Students:* 94 full-time (58 women), 58 part-time (37 women); includes 58 minority (44 Black or African American, non-Hispanic/Latino; 4 Asian, non-Hispanic/Latino; 6 Hispanic/Latino; 1 Native Hawaiian or other Pacific Islander, non-Hispanic/Latino; 3 Two or more races, non-Hispanic/Latino), 2 international. Average age 41. In 2019, 25 master's, 10 doctorates awarded. *Degree requirements:* For master's, thesis (for some programs); for doctorate, thesis/dissertation. *Entrance requirements:* For master's, Accredited BA; for doctorate, MDiv or equivalent, M Div. Additional exam requirements/recommendations for international students: required—TOEFL (minimum score 550 paper-based). *Application deadline:* For fall admission, 6/1 priority date for domestic students, 2/1 priority date for international students; for spring admission, 3/4 priority date for domestic students. Applications are processed on a rolling basis. Application fee: $50. Electronic applications accepted. *Expenses: Tuition:* Full-time $11,502; part-time $426 per credit hour. *Required fees:* $336; $336 per semester. $168 per semester. *Financial support:* Career-related internships or fieldwork, Federal Work-Study, institutionally sponsored loans, and scholarships/grants available. Financial award application deadline: 2/1. *Unit head:* Dr. Debra Mumford, Dean, 502-895-3411, Fax: 502-895-1096, E-mail: dmumford@lpts.edu. *Application contact:* Rev. Sandra Moon, Director of Admissions, 502-895-3411, Fax: 502-895-1096, E-mail: smoon@lpts.edu.
Website: http://www.lpts.edu/

Lourdes University, Graduate School, Sylvania, OH 43560-2898. Offers business (MBA); leadership (M Ed); nurse anesthesia (MSN); nurse educator (MSN); nurse leader (MSN); organizational leadership (MOL); reading (M Ed); teaching and curriculum (M Ed); theology (MA). *Accreditation:* AANA/CANAEP. *Program availability:* Evening/weekend. *Entrance requirements:* Additional exam requirements/recommendations for international students: required—TOEFL.

Loyola Marymount University, Bellarmine College of Liberal Arts, Program in Theology, Los Angeles, CA 90045-8400. Offers MA. *Accreditation:* ATS. *Students:* 33 full-time (16 women); includes 17 minority (2 Black or African American, non-Hispanic/Latino; 2 Asian, non-Hispanic/Latino; 12 Hispanic/Latino; 1 Native Hawaiian or other Pacific Islander, non-Hispanic/Latino), 2 international. Average age 48. 32 applicants, 50% accepted. In 2019, 6 master's awarded. *Entrance requirements:* For master's, GRE recommended, completed bachelor degree, graduate admissions application, submission of GPA (minimum not listed), writing sample, GRE or standardized test (recommended), personal interview, indication of PATH or THEO program. Additional exam requirements/recommendations for international students: required—TOEFL. Application fee: $50. Electronic applications accepted. *Financial support:* Scholarships/grants available. Financial award applicants required to submit FAFSA. *Unit head:* Dr. Brett Hoover, Director, Theology Program, 310-338-1664, E-mail: bhoover@lmu.edu. *Application contact:* Ammar Dalal, Assistant Vice Provost for Graduate Enrollment, 310-338-2721, Fax: 310-338-6086, E-mail: graduateadmission@lmu.edu.
Website: http://bellarmine.lmu.edu/theologicalstudies/graduateprograms/academics/maintheologyprogram

Loyola University Chicago, Graduate School, Department of Theology, Chicago, IL 60660. Offers theology (PhD). *Program availability:* Part-time, evening/weekend. *Faculty:* 24 full-time (10 women). *Students:* 40 full-time (13 women), 3 part-time (2 women); includes 4 minority (1 Black or African American, non-Hispanic/Latino; 1 Asian, non-Hispanic/Latino; 1 Native Hawaiian or other Pacific Islander, non-Hispanic/Latino; 1 Two or more races, non-Hispanic/Latino), 7 international. Average age 34. 28 applicants, 54% accepted, 6 enrolled. In 2019, 6 master's, 4 doctorates awarded. Terminal master's awarded for partial completion of doctoral program. *Degree requirements:* For master's, comprehensive exam; for doctorate, 2 foreign languages, comprehensive exam, thesis/dissertation. *Entrance requirements:* For master's, GRE General Test, minimum GPA of 3.0, 9 hours of course work in theology; for doctorate, GRE General Test, minimum GPA of 3.0, master's degree or equivalent. Additional exam requirements/recommendations for international students: required—TOEFL (minimum score 550 paper-based), IELTS. *Application deadline:* For fall admission, 1/15 for domestic and international students; for spring admission, 12/1 for domestic and international students. Application fee: $50. Electronic applications accepted. Application fee is waived when completed online. *Expenses:* Contact institution. *Financial support:* In 2019–20, 12 students received support, including 12 research assistantships (averaging $18,000 per year); fellowships, teaching assistantships, and institutionally sponsored loans also available. Financial award application deadline: 1/15; financial award applicants required to submit FAFSA. *Unit head:* Dr. Christopher W Skinner, Chair, 773-5082350, Fax: 773-508-2346, E-mail: cskinner1@luc.edu. *Application contact:* Dr. Christopher W Skinner, Graduate Program Director, 773-5082350, Fax: 773-5082346, E-mail: cskinner1@luc.edu.
Website: http://luc.edu/theology/

Loyola University Chicago, Institute of Pastoral Studies, Chicago, IL 60660. Offers Christian spirituality (MA), including spiritual direction; church management (Certificate); counseling for ministry (MA); divinity (M Div); health care ministry leadership (Certificate); health care mission leadership (MA); pastoral counseling (MA, Certificate); pastoral studies (MA); religious education (Certificate); social justice (MA, Certificate); spiritual direction (Certificate); M Div/MA; M Div/MSW; MSW/MA. *Accreditation:* ACIPE. *Program availability:* Part-time, evening/weekend, 100% online, blended/hybrid learning. *Faculty:* 9 full-time (3 women), 20 part-time/adjunct (7 women). *Students:* 72 full-time (45 women), 130 part-time (90 women); includes 55 minority (14 Black or African American, non-Hispanic/Latino; 9 Asian, non-Hispanic/Latino; 28 Hispanic/Latino; 4 Two or more races, non-Hispanic/Latino), 21 international. Average age 45. 90 applicants, 79% accepted, 49 enrolled. In 2019, 48 master's, 8 other advanced degrees awarded. *Degree requirements:* For master's, thesis optional, project. *Entrance requirements:* Additional exam requirements/recommendations for international students: required—TOEFL (minimum score 550 paper-based; 79 iBT), IELTS (minimum score 6.5). *Application deadline:* Applications are processed on a rolling basis. Application fee: $50. Electronic applications accepted. Application fee is waived when completed online. *Expenses:* Contact institution. *Financial support:* In 2019–20, 111 students received support. Career-related internships or fieldwork, Federal Work-Study, scholarships/grants, and unspecified assistantships available. Support available to part-time students. Financial award application deadline: 3/15. *Unit head:* Dr. Peter L Jones, Interim Dean, 312-915-7400, Fax: 312-915-7504, E-mail: pjones5@luc.edu. *Application contact:* Dr. Peter L Jones, Interim Dean, 312-915-7400, Fax: 312-915-7504, E-mail: pjones5@luc.edu.
Website: http://www.luc.edu/ips/

Loyola University Maryland, Graduate Programs, Loyola College of Arts and Sciences, Department of Theology, Baltimore, MD 21210-2699. Offers MTS. *Program availability:* Evening/weekend. *Students:* 8 full-time (5 women), 11 part-time (6 women); includes 8 minority (3 Black or African American, non-Hispanic/Latino; 2 Asian, non-Hispanic/Latino; 3 Hispanic/Latino). Average age 37. 25 applicants, 60% accepted, 6 enrolled. In 2019, 4 master's awarded. *Degree requirements:* For master's, one foreign language, thesis. *Entrance requirements:* For master's, GRE (optional), online application, application fee, essay, official transcripts, 2 letters of recommendation, writing sample (optional), supplemental form if international. Additional exam requirements/recommendations for international students: required—TOEFL (minimum score 550 paper-based; 80 iBT), IELTS (minimum score 7), TOEFL (minimum score 550 paper-based, 80iBT) or ILETS (minimum score 7). *Application deadline:* For fall admission, 3/1 priority date for domestic students, 3/1 for international students. Applications are processed on a rolling basis. Application fee: $60. Electronic applications accepted. Application fee is waived when completed online. *Expenses:* Contact institution. *Financial support:* Scholarships/grants available. Financial award application deadline: 4/15; financial award applicants required to submit FAFSA. *Unit head:* Nicole Reibe, Director of Program Operations, 410-617-5138, E-mail: nlreibe@loyola.edu. *Application contact:* Office of Graduate Admission, 410-617-5020, E-mail: graduate@loyola.edu.
Website: https://www.loyola.edu/academics/theology/graduate

Loyola University New Orleans, College of Nursing and Health, Loyola Institute for Ministry, New Orleans, LA 70118-6195. Offers pastoral studies (MPS); religious education (MRE); theology and ministry (Certificate). *Program availability:* Part-time, evening/weekend, online learning. *Faculty:* 2 full-time (1 woman), 4 part-time/adjunct (3 women). *Students:* 6 full-time (all women), 85 part-time (67 women); includes 22 minority (7 Black or African American, non-Hispanic/Latino; 1 American Indian or Alaska Native, non-Hispanic/Latino; 4 Asian, non-Hispanic/Latino; 9 Hispanic/Latino; 1 Two or more races, non-Hispanic/Latino), 1 international. Average age 47. 50 applicants, 86% accepted, 10 enrolled. In 2019, 26 master's awarded. *Entrance requirements:* For master's, minimum GPA of 2.5, resume, 2 letters of recommendation, work experience, 3-page statement of purpose, transcripts from an accredited university. Additional exam requirements/recommendations for international students: required—TOEFL (minimum score 550 paper-based; 79 iBT). *Application deadline:* For fall admission, 8/15 for domestic and international students; for spring admission, 1/1 for domestic and international students. Applications are processed on a rolling basis. Application fee: $20. Electronic applications accepted. Application fee is waived when completed online. *Expenses:* Contact institution. *Financial support:* In 2019–20, 37 students received support. Career-related internships or fieldwork, scholarships/grants, health care benefits, and tuition waivers (partial) available. Support available to part-time students. Financial award application deadline: 5/1; financial award applicants required to submit FAFSA. *Unit head:* Dr. Tom Ryan, Director, 504-865-2069, Fax: 504-865-2066, E-mail: tfryan@loyno.edu. *Application contact:* Diane Blair, Manager of Admissions, 504-865-3728, Fax: 504-865-2066, E-mail: lim@loyno.edu.
Website: http://lim.loyno.edu/

Theology

Lubbock Christian University, Graduate Biblical Studies, Lubbock, TX 79407-2099. Offers Bible and ministry (MS); biblical interpretation (MA). *Program availability:* Part-time. *Degree requirements:* For master's, one foreign language, thesis (for some programs). *Entrance requirements:* For master's, GRE General Test or MAT.

Lutheran School of Theology at Chicago, Graduate and Professional Programs, Chicago, IL 60615-5199. Offers ministry (MAM, D Min); theological studies (MATS, PhD); theology (M Div). *Accreditation:* ACIPE; ATS (one or more programs are accredited). *Program availability:* Part-time. Terminal master's awarded for partial completion of doctoral program. *Degree requirements:* For master's, variable foreign language requirement; for doctorate, variable foreign language requirement, comprehensive exam, thesis/dissertation. *Entrance requirements:* For doctorate, GRE, M Div or equivalent, 3 years of professional experience (D Min).

Lutheran Theological Seminary Saskatoon, Graduate and Professional Programs, Saskatoon, SK S7N 0X3, Canada. Offers Biblical studies (MTS); church history (MTS); ethics/church and society (MTS); history of Christianity (STM); New Testament (STM); Old Testament (STM); pastoral studies (STM); pastoral theology (MTS); systematic theology (MTS); systematic theology and philosophy of religion (STM); theology (M Div, D Div). *Accreditation:* ATS. *Program availability:* Part-time. *Degree requirements:* For master's, thesis.

Luther Rice College & Seminary, Graduate Programs, Lithonia, GA 30038-2454. Offers apologetics (MA); Bible languages (M Div); Biblical counseling (MA); Christian ministry (M Div, D Min); Christian studies (MA); leadership (MA). *Program availability:* Part-time, evening/weekend, online learning. *Degree requirements:* For doctorate, thesis/dissertation. *Entrance requirements:* For master's, bachelor's degree or equivalent; for doctorate, M Div. Additional exam requirements/recommendations for international students: required—TOEFL (minimum score 550 paper-based). Electronic applications accepted.

Luther Seminary, Graduate and Professional Programs, St. Paul, MN 55108-1445. Offers aging and health (MA); Biblical preaching (D Min); children, youth and family (M Div, MA); congregational mission and leadership (M Th, MA, D Min); history of Christianity (M Th, MA); missions and world religions (M Th); New Testament (M Th, MA); Old Testament (M Th, MA); pastoral care: clinical pastoral theology (M Th); pastoral theology and ministry (M Th); systematic theology (M Th, MA). *Accreditation:* ACIPE; ATS. *Program availability:* Part-time, online learning. *Degree requirements:* For master's, thesis or alternative; for doctorate, 2 foreign languages, thesis/dissertation. *Entrance requirements:* For master's, minimum GPA of 3.0; for doctorate, GRE General Test. Additional exam requirements/recommendations for international students: required—TOEFL, IELTS. Electronic applications accepted.

Machzikei Hadath Rabbinical College, Graduate Programs, Brooklyn, NY 11204-1805. Offers First Talmudic Degree. *Accreditation:* AARTS.

Madonna University, Program in Religious Studies, Livonia, MI 48150-1173. Offers pastoral ministry (MA). *Expenses:* Tuition: Full-time $15,930; part-time $885 per credit hour. Tuition and fees vary according to degree level and program.

Maple Springs Baptist Bible College and Seminary, Graduate and Professional Programs, Capitol Heights, MD 20743. Offers biblical studies (MA, Certificate); Christian counseling (MA); church administration (MA); divinity (M Div); ministry (D Min); religious education (MRE). In 2019, 10 master's, 1 doctorate awarded. *Application fee:* $40. *Expenses:* Tuition: Part-time $300 per credit. *Application contact:* Anthony E. Broadnax, Registrar and Director of Admissions and Records, 301-736-3631.

Maranatha Baptist University, Master of Divinity Program, Watertown, WI 53094. Offers M Div. *Program availability:* Part-time. *Degree requirements:* For master's, 2 foreign languages. *Entrance requirements:* Additional exam requirements/recommendations for international students: required—TOEFL. *Expenses:* Tuition: Full-time $5940; part-time $3960 per credit. *Required fees:* $25 per credit. Tuition and fees vary according to degree level and program.

Maranatha Baptist University, Program in Biblical Studies, Watertown, WI 53094. Offers MA. *Program availability:* Part-time. *Degree requirements:* For master's, one foreign language. *Entrance requirements:* For master's, BA or BS. *Expenses:* Tuition: Full-time $5940; part-time $3960 per credit. *Required fees:* $25 per credit. Tuition and fees vary according to degree level and program.

Marquette University, Graduate School, College of Arts and Sciences, Department of Theology, Milwaukee, WI 53201-1881. Offers MA, PhD. *Program availability:* Part-time, evening/weekend. Terminal master's awarded for partial completion of doctoral program. *Degree requirements:* For master's, one foreign language, comprehensive exam, thesis or alternative; for doctorate, 2 foreign languages, comprehensive exam, thesis/dissertation. *Entrance requirements:* For master's, GRE General Test, official transcripts from all current and previous colleges/universities except Marquette, three letters of recommendation, short personal statement; for doctorate, GRE General Test, official transcripts from all current and previous colleges/universities except Marquette, three letters of recommendation, short personal statement, academic writing sample. Additional exam requirements/recommendations for international students: required—TOEFL (minimum score 530 paper-based). Electronic applications accepted.

The Master's University, The Master's Seminary, Santa Clarita, CA 91321-1200. Offers biblical counseling (MABC); New Testament (Th D); Old Testament (Th D); preaching (D Min); theology (M Div, M Th, Th D). *Program availability:* Part-time. *Degree requirements:* For master's, 2 foreign languages, thesis; for doctorate, 4 foreign languages, thesis/dissertation. *Entrance requirements:* For master's, minimum GPA of 2.75; for doctorate, Th M, minimum GPA of 3.5. Additional exam requirements/recommendations for international students: required—TOEFL (minimum score 550 paper-based).

McCormick Theological Seminary, Graduate and Professional Programs, Chicago, IL 60615. Offers ministry (D Min); theological studies (MATS, Certificate); theology (M Div); M Div/MSW. *Accreditation:* ACIPE; ATS (one or more programs are accredited). *Program availability:* Part-time, evening/weekend. *Degree requirements:* For master's, thesis (for some programs); for doctorate, thesis/dissertation. *Entrance requirements:* For master's, minimum GPA of 3.0; for doctorate, M Div, minimum 3 years in pastorate.

McGill University, Faculty of Graduate and Postdoctoral Studies, Faculty of Religious Studies, Montréal, QC H3A 2T5, Canada. Offers MA, STM, PhD. *Accreditation:* ATS.

McMaster University, McMaster Divinity College, Hamilton, ON L8S 4M2, Canada. Offers Biblical studies (MA, MTS, Diploma); biblical studies (M Div); Christian interpretation/history (M Div, MA, MTS, Diploma); Christian ministry (M Div, MA, MTS, Diploma); Christian Studies (Certificate); Christian theology (PhD). *Accreditation:* ATS. *Program availability:* Part-time. *Degree requirements:* For master's, one foreign language, thesis optional; for doctorate, 3 foreign languages, comprehensive exam, thesis/dissertation; for other advanced degree, 2 foreign languages, thesis. *Entrance requirements:* For master's, minimum B average in undergraduate course work, 3 letters of reference; for doctorate, minimum B+ average in bachelor's and master's, appropriate modern/ancient language, interview; for other advanced degree, 6 units of related Biblical language, minimum B+ average in undergraduate course work, minimum 15 units of course work in related area of study, 3 letters of recommendation. Additional

exam requirements/recommendations for international students: required—TOEFL (minimum score 550 paper-based).

Meadville Lombard Theological School, Graduate and Professional Programs, Chicago, IL 60637-1602. Offers divinity (M Div); ministry (D Min); religion (MA); M Div/MSW. *Accreditation:* ACIPE; ATS. *Program availability:* Part-time, online learning. *Entrance requirements:* For master's, bachelor's degree; for doctorate, bachelor's and masters degrees, 3 years of ministry.

Memphis Theological Seminary, Graduate and Professional Programs, Memphis, TN 38104-4395. Offers M Div, MAR, D Min. *Accreditation:* ATS. *Program availability:* Part-time. *Degree requirements:* For doctorate, thesis/dissertation. *Entrance requirements:* For doctorate, M Div, 3 years in ministry.

Mercer University, Graduate Studies, Cecil B. Day Campus, James and Carolyn McAfee School of Theology, Atlanta, GA 30341. Offers Christian ministry (MACM); Christian spirituality (D Min); divinity (M Div); preaching (D Min); M Div/MBA; M Div/MS. *Program availability:* Part-time, 100% online. *Faculty:* 9 full-time (4 women), 4 part-time/adjunct (2 women). *Students:* 53 full-time (34 women), 81 part-time (37 women); includes 77 minority (68 Black or African American, non-Hispanic/Latino; 1 Asian, non-Hispanic/Latino; 7 Hispanic/Latino; 1 Two or more races, non-Hispanic/Latino). Average age 41. 107 applicants, 51% accepted, 38 enrolled. In 2019, 43 master's, 7 doctorates awarded. *Degree requirements:* For master's, variable foreign language requirement, thesis (for some programs), minimum GPA; time limits; for doctorate, thesis/dissertation, minimum GPA; time limits. *Entrance requirements:* For master's, Regionally-accredited bachelor's degree with liberal arts core or proof of equivalent degree from foreign university; biographical data; transcripts; letters of recommendation; resume; essays; writing sample; interview; background check; application fee; for doctorate, Regionally-accredited bachelor's degree with liberal arts core or proof of equivalent degree from foreign university; M.Div. or equivalent; biographical data; transcripts; letters of recommendation; resume; essays; writing sample; interview; background check; application fee; Covenant of Support. Additional exam requirements/recommendations for international students: required—TOEFL (minimum score 550 paper-based; 79 iBT). *Application deadline:* For fall admission, 6/15 priority date for domestic and international students; for spring admission, 11/15 priority date for domestic and international students. Applications are processed on a rolling basis. Application fee: $50. Electronic applications accepted. *Expenses:* The M.Div., M.A.C.M., M.T.S. and Non-Degree (for credit) programs are charged at $475 per credit hour. The D.Min. Program is charged at $450 per credit hour. *Financial support:* In 2019–20, 50 students received support, including 2 fellowships with full tuition reimbursements available (averaging $3,000 per year); career-related internships or fieldwork, Federal Work-Study, scholarships/grants, and stipends also available. Support available to part-time students. Financial award application deadline: 1/15; financial award applicants required to submit FAFSA. *Unit head:* Dr. C. Gregory DeLoach, Interim Dean, 678-547-6620, E-mail: deloach_cg@mercer.edu. *Application contact:* Nathan Cost, Director of Admissions, 678-547-6451, E-mail: cost_na@mercer.edu. Website: http://www.mercer.edu/theology

Merrimack College, School of Liberal Arts, North Andover, MA 01845-5800. Offers clinical mental health counseling (MS); interfaith spirituality (Certificate); public affairs (MPA); spiritual direction (MA, Certificate); spirituality (MA). *Program availability:* Part-time, evening/weekend. *Degree requirements:* For master's, internship/strategic capstone (for MPA); 700-hour fieldwork placement (for MS); practicum (for MA in spiritual direction); for Certificate, practicum (for spiritual direction). *Entrance requirements:* For master's, official college transcripts, resume, personal statement, 2 recommendations (3 for MS in clinical mental health counseling); interview (for MA in spirituality). Additional exam requirements/recommendations for international students: required—TOEFL (minimum score 84 iBT), IELTS (minimum score 6.5), PTE (minimum score 56). Electronic applications accepted. Application fee is waived when completed online. *Expenses:* Contact institution.

Mesivta of Eastern Parkway–Yeshiva Zichron Meilech, Graduate Programs, Brooklyn, NY 11218-5559. *Accreditation:* AARTS. *Faculty:* 5,165 full-time (5,132 women), 5 part-time/adjunct (1 woman). *Students:* 398 full-time (55 women), 70 part-time (4 women); includes 729 minority (54 Black or African American, non-Hispanic/Latino; 77 American Indian or Alaska Native, non-Hispanic/Latino; 542 Asian, non-Hispanic/Latino; 53 Hispanic/Latino; 3 Native Hawaiian or other Pacific Islander, non-Hispanic/Latino), 2 international. Average age 44. 3,324 applicants, 2% accepted, 3 enrolled. *Entrance requirements:* Additional exam requirements/recommendations for international students: required—IELTS. *Application deadline:* For fall admission, 1/16 for domestic students; for spring admission, 3/19 for domestic students. Applications are processed on a rolling basis. Application fee: $21. Electronic applications accepted. Application fee is waived when completed online. *Expenses:* Contact institution. *Financial support:* Fellowships and research assistantships available. Financial award application deadline: 12/17; financial award applicants required to submit CSS PROFILE or FAFSA. *Unit head:* Dr. Jane Douglas, Director, 551-4948843, E-mail: jdoug@yomama.com. *Application contact:* Information Contact, 718-438-1002.

Mesivtha Tifereth Jerusalem of America, Graduate Programs, New York, NY 10002-6301. *Accreditation:* AARTS. *Program availability:* Part-time-only. *Faculty:* 6 full-time (2 women), 17 part-time/adjunct (12 women). *Students:* 6 full-time (2 women), 546 part-time (12 women); includes 3,914 minority (54 Black or African American, non-Hispanic/Latino; 6 American Indian or Alaska Native, non-Hispanic/Latino; 425 Asian, non-Hispanic/Latino; 4 Hispanic/Latino; 3,423 Native Hawaiian or other Pacific Islander, non-Hispanic/Latino; 2 Two or more races, non-Hispanic/Latino), 2 international. Average age 22. 14 applicants, 14% accepted, 1 enrolled. *Entrance requirements:* Additional exam requirements/recommendations for international students: required—TOEFL, IELTS, TWE. *Application deadline:* Applications are processed on a rolling basis. Application fee: $55. Electronic applications accepted. Application fee is waived when completed online. *Expenses:* Contact institution. *Financial support:* Fellowships available. Financial award application deadline: 2/2; financial award applicants required to submit CSS PROFILE. *Unit head:* James Charles, Director, 510-4456678, E-mail: jc@yomama.com. *Application contact:* Information Contact, 212-964-2830.

Methodist Theological School in Ohio, Graduate and Professional Programs, Delaware, OH 43015-8004. Offers M Div, MACE, MACM, MTS, D Min. *Accreditation:* ACIPE; ATS. *Program availability:* Part-time. *Entrance requirements:* For master's, 3 letters of recommendation. Additional exam requirements/recommendations for international students: required—TOEFL (minimum score 577 paper-based; 90 iBT).

Mid-America Baptist Theological Seminary, Graduate and Professional Programs, Cordova, TN 38016. Offers biblical counseling (M Div); Christian education (M Div, MACE); ministry (D Min); missiology and intercultural studies (M Div); pastoral ministry (M Div); theology (MA, PhD); worship (MA). *Degree requirements:* For doctorate, 4 foreign languages, thesis/dissertation. *Entrance requirements:* For doctorate, MAT. Additional exam requirements/recommendations for international students: required—TOEFL (minimum score 600 paper-based). Electronic applications accepted.

Mid-America Baptist Theological Seminary Northeast Branch, Program in Theology, Schenectady, NY 12303-3463. Offers M Div. *Program availability:* Part-time, evening/weekend. *Entrance requirements:* Additional exam requirements/

recommendations for international students: required—TOEFL. Electronic applications accepted.

Mid-America Reformed Seminary, Graduate Programs, Dyer, IN 46311. Offers M Div, MTS. *Accreditation:* ATS. *Entrance requirements:* Additional exam requirements/recommendations for international students: required—TOEFL (minimum score 550 paper-based).

Midwestern Baptist Theological Seminary, Graduate and Professional Programs, Kansas City, MO 64118-4697. Offers Christian education (MACE); Christian foundations (Graduate Certificate); church music (MCM); counseling (MA); ministry (D Ed Min, D Min); Old or New Testament studies (PhD); theology (M Div). *Accreditation:* ATS. *Program availability:* Part-time, online learning. *Degree requirements:* For doctorate, thesis/dissertation. *Entrance requirements:* For doctorate, MAT. Electronic applications accepted.

Midwest University, Graduate Programs, Wentzville, MO 63385. Offers asset management/investment/real estate (MBA); Christian counseling (D Min); Christian education (D Min); counseling (MA), including marriage and family counseling, school counseling; divinity (M Div); education (MA), including brain and gifted education, Christian education; global business management (MBA); global leadership (MBA); leadership (PhD), including brain and gifted educational leadership, entrepreneurial leadership, international aviation leadership, organizational leadership, political leadership; mission studies (D Min); music (MM, DMA); pastoral theology (D Min); public policy/administration (MBA); teaching English to speakers of other languages (MA). *Program availability:* Part-time, online learning. *Degree requirements:* For master's, thesis (for some programs); for doctorate, thesis/dissertation. *Entrance requirements:* Additional exam requirements/recommendations for international students: recommended—TOEFL (minimum score 550 paper-based).

Milligan University, Emmanuel Christian Seminary at Milligan College, Milligan College, TN 37682. Offers Christian care and counseling (M Div); Christian education (M Div); Christian ministries (MACM, Graduate Certificate); Christian ministry (M Div); Christian theology (M Div, MAR); church history (MAR); church history/historical theology (M Div); general studies (M Div); ministry (D Min); New Testament (M Div, MAR); Old Testament (M Div, MAR); urban ministry (M Div); world missions (M Div). *Accreditation:* ACIPE; ATS. *Program availability:* Part-time, blended/hybrid learning. *Faculty:* 12 full-time (1 woman), 5 part-time/adjunct (0 women). *Students:* 70 full-time (28 women), 70 part-time (26 women); includes 19 minority (9 Black or African American, non-Hispanic/Latino; 3 American Indian or Alaska Native, non-Hispanic/Latino; 2 Asian, non-Hispanic/Latino; 5 Hispanic/Latino), 8 international. Average age 34. 109 applicants, 90% accepted, 64 enrolled. In 2019, 21 master's, 3 doctorates awarded. *Degree requirements:* For master's, 2 foreign languages, thesis or alternative, portfolio; for doctorate, thesis/dissertation. *Entrance requirements:* For master's, undergraduate degree and supporting transcripts, essay/personal statement, professional recommendations, interview; for doctorate, M Div or equivalent, essay/personal statement, professional recommendations. Additional exam requirements/recommendations for international students: required—TOEFL (minimum score 550 paper-based, 79 iBT) or IELTS (6.5). *Application deadline:* For fall admission, 8/1 for domestic students, 6/1 for international students; for spring admission, 12/15 for domestic students, 8/1 for international students. Applications are processed on a rolling basis. Application fee: $30. Electronic applications accepted. *Expenses:* 36 - 90 hr programs: $485/hr; $75 one-time records fee; MDIV (90 Hrs)/MAR (58 Hrs) $325/semester (technology and activity fee); MACM (48 Hrs)/DMIN (36 Hrs) $250/semester (technology and activity fees). *Financial support:* Scholarships/grants and unspecified assistantships available. Financial award application deadline: 12/1; financial award applicants required to submit FAFSA. *Unit head:* Dr. Rollin Ramsaran, Academic Dean, Emmanuel Christian Seminary, 423-461-1524, Fax: 423-926-6198, E-mail: raramsaran@milligan.edu. *Application contact:* Lauren Gullett, Director of Admissions and Recruitment for Emmanuel Christian Seminary, 423-461-1535, Fax: 423-926-6198, E-mail: lwgullett@milligan.edu.
Website: http://ecs.milligan.edu/

Mirrer Yeshiva Central Institute, Graduate Programs, Brooklyn, NY 11223-2010. *Accreditation:* AARTS.

Missio Seminary, Graduate and Professional Programs, Hatfield, PA 19440-2499. Offers advanced missional leadership (D Min); advanced pastoral studies (Certificate); biblical counseling (Certificate); biblical studies (MA, Certificate); counseling (MA); ministry (M Div, MA); missional theology (MA). *Accreditation:* ATS. *Program availability:* Part-time, evening/weekend. *Degree requirements:* For master's, variable foreign language requirement, thesis optional; for doctorate, thesis/dissertation. *Entrance requirements:* Additional exam requirements/recommendations for international students: required—TOEFL (minimum score 550 paper-based; 80 iBT). Electronic applications accepted.

Moody Bible Institute, Graduate School, Chicago, IL 60610-3284. Offers biblical studies (MABS, Graduate Certificate); intercultural studies (MAIS, Graduate Certificate); ministry (M Div, M Min); spiritual formation and discipleship (MASF, Graduate Certificate); urban studies (MA, Graduate Certificate). *Program availability:* Part-time. *Degree requirements:* For master's, 2 foreign languages, fieldwork (MABS); colloquium, field research project (MA Min). *Entrance requirements:* For master's, 30 hours in Bible/theology, 2 years of ministry experience (MA Min).

Moody Theological Seminary–Michigan, Graduate Programs, Plymouth, MI 48170. Offers Bible (Graduate Certificate); Christian education (MA); counseling psychology (MA); divinity (M Div); theological studies (MA). *Accreditation:* ATS. *Program availability:* Part-time, evening/weekend. *Degree requirements:* For master's, one foreign language, thesis.

Moravian Theological Seminary, Graduate and Certificate Programs, Bethlehem, PA 18018-6614. Offers Biblical studies (Graduate Certificate); formative spirituality (M Div, Graduate Certificate); spiritual direction (MATS, Graduate Certificate); M Div/MACC; M Div/MATS. *Accreditation:* ACIPE; ATS (one or more programs are accredited). *Program availability:* Part-time. *Faculty:* 9 full-time (4 women), 1 (woman) part-time/adjunct. *Students:* 14 full-time (8 women), 62 part-time (45 women); includes 14 minority (2 Black or African American, non-Hispanic/Latino; 11 Hispanic/Latino; 1 Two or more races, non-Hispanic/Latino), 2 international. Average age 44. 124 applicants, 14% accepted, 16 enrolled. In 2019, 13 master's, 1 other advanced degree awarded. *Degree requirements:* For master's, thesis (for some programs). *Entrance requirements:* For master's, transcripts, references, essay(s), denominational endorsement (M Div); for Graduate Certificate, transcripts, references, essay(s), Spiritual Direction experience (for spiritual direction). Additional exam requirements/recommendations for international students: required—TOEFL (minimum score 550 paper-based; 79 iBT), IELTS (minimum score 6.5). *Application deadline:* For fall admission, 7/15 for domestic students, 4/1 priority date for international students; for spring admission, 11/15 for domestic students, 9/1 priority date for international students. Applications are processed on a rolling basis. Application fee: $50. Electronic applications accepted. *Expenses:* Contact institution. *Financial support:* In 2019–20, 46 students received support. Career-related internships or fieldwork, Federal Work-Study, and scholarships/grants available. Support available to part-time students. Financial award application

deadline: 7/15; financial award applicants required to submit FAFSA. *Unit head:* Rev. Dr. Frank L. Crouch, Dean and Vice President, 610-861-1516, E-mail: crouchf@moravian.edu. *Application contact:* Rev. Randy L. D'Angelo, Director of Seminary Enrollment, 610-861-1512, Fax: 610-861-1569, E-mail: dangelor@moravian.edu.
Website: http://moravianseminary.edu

Mount Angel Seminary, Program in Theology, Saint Benedict, OR 97373. Offers M Div, MA. *Accreditation:* ACIPE; ATS. *Program availability:* Part-time. *Students:* Average age 54. 86 applicants, 100% accepted. *Degree requirements:* For master's, thesis optional. *Application deadline:* For fall admission, 7/15 for domestic students. Applications are processed on a rolling basis. Application fee: $25. *Financial support:* Career-related internships or fieldwork available. *Unit head:* Rev. Ernest Skublics, Dean, 503-845-3951. *Application contact:* Very Rev. Patrick Brennan, President-Rector, 503-845-3951.

Mount St. Joseph University, Graduate Program in Religious Studies, Cincinnati, OH 45233-1670. Offers religious studies (MA); spirituality and wellness (Certificate). *Program availability:* Part-time, evening/weekend. *Degree requirements:* For master's, comprehensive exam, 36 hours of credit, pastoral PRAXIS component (3 credit hours), integrating project (3 credit hours). *Entrance requirements:* For master's, undergraduate transcript with minimum overall GPA of 3.0, 3 letters of recommendation from professional colleagues, 3-page essay, interview with the Graduate Admissions Committee, current work resume. Additional exam requirements/recommendations for international students: required—TOEFL (minimum score 560 paper-based; 83 iBT). Electronic applications accepted. *Expenses:* Contact institution.

Mount St. Mary's University, Graduate Seminary, Emmitsburg, MD 21727-7799. Offers M Div, MA. *Accreditation:* ATS. *Students:* 150 full-time, 2 part-time (0 women); includes 11 minority (3 Black or African American, non-Hispanic/Latino; 1 American Indian or Alaska Native, non-Hispanic/Latino; 3 Asian, non-Hispanic/Latino; 4 Hispanic/Latino), 19 international. In 2019, 22 master's awarded. *Degree requirements:* For master's, one foreign language, comprehensive exam, thesis, language proficiency exams. *Entrance requirements:* For master's, 18 credits of course work in philosophy. Additional exam requirements/recommendations for international students: required—TOEFL (minimum score 550 paper-based; 83 iBT). *Application deadline:* For fall admission, 8/1 for domestic and international students. Application fee: $0. *Expenses:* Contact institution. *Financial support:* Applicants required to submit FAFSA. *Unit head:* Rev. Andrew R. Baker, Vice President/Rector, 301-447-5295, Fax: 301-447-5636, E-mail: baker@msmary.edu. *Application contact:* Susan Nield, Seminary Admissions, 301-447-7423, Fax: 301-447-7402, E-mail: nield@msmary.edu.
Website: https://seminary.msmary.edu/index.html

Mount Vernon Nazarene University, Program in Ministry, Mount Vernon, OH 43050-9500. Offers M Min. *Program availability:* Part-time, evening/weekend. *Degree requirements:* For master's, project.

Multnomah University, Multnomah Biblical Seminary, Portland, OR 97220-5898. Offers M Div, MABS, MACL, MATS, Th M, D Min. *Accreditation:* ATS. *Program availability:* Part-time. *Degree requirements:* For master's, variable foreign language requirement, thesis (for some programs). *Entrance requirements:* For master's, interview; for doctorate, interview, M Div equivalency. Additional exam requirements/recommendations for international students: required—TOEFL (minimum score 550 paper-based).

Naropa University, Graduate Programs, Program in Divinity, Boulder, CO 80302-6697. Offers M Div. *Degree requirements:* For master's, comprehensive exam, thesis, clinical pastoral education or fieldwork placement. *Entrance requirements:* For master's, resume/curriculum vitae with pertinent academic, employment and volunteer activity; 2 letters of recommendation; letter of interest; transcripts; phone interview. Additional exam requirements/recommendations for international students: required—TOEFL (minimum score 550 paper-based; 80 iBT). Electronic applications accepted. *Expenses:* Contact institution.

Nashotah House Theological Seminary, Graduate Programs, Nashotah, WI 53058-9793. Offers Anglican studies (Certificate); Biblical studies (STM); Christian spirituality (STM); church history (STM); liturgy (STM); ministry (M Div, MM); pastoral ministry (MPM); theological studies (MTS); theology (STM, D Min). *Accreditation:* ACIPE; ATS (one or more programs are accredited). *Program availability:* Part-time. *Degree requirements:* For master's, thesis optional. *Entrance requirements:* For master's and Certificate, GRE General Test or MAT, interview, 3 recommendations. Additional exam requirements/recommendations for international students: required—TOEFL. Electronic applications accepted. *Expenses:* Contact institution.

Nazarene Theological Seminary, Graduate and Professional Programs, Kansas City, MO 64131-1263. Offers Christian formation and discipleship (MA); intercultural studies (MA); pastoral theology (Graduate Certificate); theological studies (MA); theology (M Div, D Min). *Accreditation:* ACIPE; ATS. *Program availability:* Part-time. *Degree requirements:* For master's, comprehensive exam (for some programs), thesis (for some programs); for doctorate, thesis/dissertation. *Entrance requirements:* For master's and Graduate Certificate, three references; for doctorate, three references, interview. Additional exam requirements/recommendations for international students: required—TOEFL (minimum score 550 paper-based; 80 iBT). Electronic applications accepted.

Nebraska Christian College of Hope International University, Graduate Programs, Papillion, NE 68046. Offers biblical studies (M Div); business as mission/social entrepreneurship (MBA); children, youth, and family (M Div); church planting (M Div); counseling psychology (MS); educational administration (MA); elementary education (M Ed); general management (MBA); gifted and talented education (M Ed); intercultural studies (M Div); international development (MBA); marketing management (MBA); ministry (MA); ministry and leadership (M Div); music education (M Ed); non-profit management (MBA); pastoral care (M Div); secondary education (M Ed); spiritual formation (M Div); worship ministry (M Div).

Ner Israel Rabbinical College, Graduate Programs, Baltimore, MD 21208. Offers MTL, DTL, Professional Certificate. *Accreditation:* AARTS.

Ner Israel Yeshiva College of Toronto, Graduate Programs, Thornhill, ON L4J 8A7, Canada. *Accreditation:* AARTS.

New Brunswick Theological Seminary, Graduate and Professional Programs, New Brunswick, NJ 08901-1196. Offers pastoral care and counseling (D Min). *Accreditation:* ACIPE; ATS. *Program availability:* Part-time, evening/weekend. *Degree requirements:* For master's, variable foreign language requirement, thesis (for some programs); for doctorate, thesis/dissertation. *Entrance requirements:* For master's, BA/BS with minimum GPA of 3.0 (for MA), 2.5 (for M Div); for doctorate, M Div. Additional exam requirements/recommendations for international students: required—TOEFL (minimum score 550 paper-based; 79 iBT); recommended—IELTS (minimum score 6). Electronic applications accepted.

Newman Theological College, Theology Programs, Edmonton, AB T6A 0B2, Canada. Offers M Div, M Th, MTS. *Accreditation:* ATS. *Program availability:* Part-time, 100% online. *Faculty:* 14 full-time (3 women), 5 part-time/adjunct (1 woman). *Students:* 27 full-time (4 women), 9 part-time (5 women). Average age 30. 19 applicants, 100% accepted,

18 enrolled. In 2019, 7 master's awarded. *Degree requirements:* For master's, comprehensive exam, thesis. *Entrance requirements:* For master's, bachelor's degree, 12 undergraduate credits in philosophy. Additional exam requirements/recommendations for international students: required—TOEFL (minimum score 560 paper-based; 86 iBT), IELTS (minimum score 6.5), CAEL. *Application deadline:* For fall admission, 8/19 priority date for domestic students, 2/19 priority date for international students; for winter admission, 11/20 priority date for domestic students; for spring admission, 2/19 priority date for domestic students. Applications are processed on a rolling basis. Application fee: $45 ($250 for international students). *Expenses: Tuition:* Full-time $6900 Canadian dollars; part-time $690 Canadian dollars per course. *Required fees:* $310 Canadian dollars; $190 Canadian dollars per unit. $95 Canadian dollars per semester. One-time fee: $45 Canadian dollars. Tuition and fees vary according to course load. *Financial support:* In 2019–20, 6 students received support. Tuition bursaries available. Support available to part-time students. Financial award application deadline: 5/31. *Unit head:* Dr. Ryan Topping, Academic Dean/Vice President, 780-392-2450 Ext. 2444, Fax: 780-462-4013, E-mail: ryan.topping@newman.edu. *Application contact:* Maria Saulnier, Registrar, 780-392-2451, Fax: 780-462-4013, E-mail: registrar@newman.edu.
Website: http://www.newman.edu/

Newman University, Graduate Theology Program, Wichita, KS 67213-2097. Offers theological studies (MTS); theology (MA). *Program availability:* Part-time, online learning. *Degree requirements:* For master's, 2 foreign languages, comprehensive exam (for some programs), thesis (for some programs). *Entrance requirements:* For master's, letter of recommendation from pastor; bachelor's degree in theology or related field (MA), in any field (MTS). Additional exam requirements/recommendations for international students: required—TOEFL (minimum score 600 paper-based; 100 iBT). *Expenses:* Contact institution.

New Orleans Baptist Theological Seminary, Graduate and Professional Programs, Division of Biblical Studies, New Orleans, LA 70126-4858. Offers M Div, MA, PhD. *Accreditation:* ACIPE; ATS (one or more programs are accredited). *Degree requirements:* For master's, 2 foreign languages, comprehensive exam (for some programs), thesis (for some programs); for doctorate, 4 foreign languages, comprehensive exam, thesis/dissertation. *Entrance requirements:* For doctorate, GRE General Test.

New Orleans Baptist Theological Seminary, Graduate and Professional Programs, Division of Theological and Historical Studies, New Orleans, LA 70126-4858. Offers M Div, MA, D Min, PhD. *Accreditation:* ACIPE; ATS (one or more programs are accredited). *Program availability:* Online learning. *Degree requirements:* For master's, 2 foreign languages, comprehensive exam (for some programs), thesis (for some programs); for doctorate, 3 foreign languages, comprehensive exam, thesis/dissertation. *Entrance requirements:* For doctorate, GRE General Test. Additional exam requirements/recommendations for international students: required—TOEFL.

New Saint Andrews College, Graduate School, Moscow, ID 83843. Offers classical Christian studies (Graduate Certificate); creative writing (MFA); theology and letters (MA). *Program availability:* Part-time, blended/hybrid learning. *Degree requirements:* For master's, comprehensive exam (for some programs), thesis (for some programs), final oral exam. *Entrance requirements:* For master's, GRE, 2 letters of recommendation; for Graduate Certificate, GRE, bachelor's degree, essays, 2 letters of recommendation. Electronic applications accepted. *Expenses: Tuition:* Full-time $8800; part-time $550 per credit.

New York Theological Seminary, Graduate and Professional Programs, New York, NY 10115. Offers M Div, MPS, MSW, D Min. *Accreditation:* ACIPE; ATS (one or more programs are accredited). *Program availability:* Part-time. *Degree requirements:* For doctorate, thesis/dissertation. *Entrance requirements:* For doctorate, M Div, 3 years of ministry experience, interview. Additional exam requirements/recommendations for international students: required—TOEFL.

Northeastern Seminary at Roberts Wesleyan College, Graduate and Professional Programs, Rochester, NY 14624. Offers ministry (D Min), including scripture, spirituality, leadership; theological studies (MA); theology (M Div), including social justice, spiritual formation, biblical studies, transformational leadership; theology and social justice (MA); transformational leadership (MA); M Div/MSW. *Accreditation:* ATS. *Program availability:* Part-time, evening/weekend, 100% online, blended/hybrid learning. *Degree requirements:* For master's, thesis (for some programs); for doctorate, one foreign language, thesis/dissertation. *Entrance requirements:* For doctorate, M Div, 3 years of full-time ministry experience. Additional exam requirements/recommendations for international students: required—TOEFL (minimum score 79 paper-based), IELTS (minimum score 6.5). Electronic applications accepted.

Northern Seminary, Graduate and Professional Programs, Lombard, IL 60148-5698. Offers Biblical studies (M Div); Christian community development (MA, D Min); Christian ministry (MACM); contextual theology (D Min); missional church ministry (M Div); New Testament (M Div, MANT); New Testament context (D Min); Old Testament (M Div); preaching (D Min); theology (M Div); theology and mission (MA); urban leadership (MA); worship (M Div, MAW). *Program availability:* Part-time, evening/weekend. *Degree requirements:* For master's, thesis (for some programs); for doctorate, thesis/dissertation. *Entrance requirements:* For master's, writing test, all official transcripts, letter of reference from church, 3 letters of reference, autobiographical statement (400 words or more); for doctorate, M Div, 3 years in the ministry post-M Div, 3 letters of reference. Additional exam requirements/recommendations for international students: required—TOEFL (minimum score 550 paper-based). Electronic applications accepted.

North Park Theological Seminary, Graduate and Professional Programs, Professional Program, Chicago, IL 60625-4895. Offers M Div, M Div/MBA, M Div/MM. *Accreditation:* ACIPE; ATS. *Program availability:* Part-time. *Entrance requirements:* Additional exam requirements/recommendations for international students: required—TOEFL.

North Park Theological Seminary, Graduate and Professional Programs, Program in Christian Formation, Chicago, IL 60625-4895. Offers MA, MA/MM. *Accreditation:* ATS.

North Park Theological Seminary, Graduate and Professional Programs, Program in Preaching, Chicago, IL 60625-4895. Offers D Min. *Accreditation:* ACIPE; ATS. *Degree requirements:* For doctorate, thesis/dissertation. *Entrance requirements:* For doctorate, 3 years of preaching experience.

North Park Theological Seminary, Graduate and Professional Programs, Program in Theological Studies, Chicago, IL 60625-4895. Offers MATS, MATS/MBA, MATS/MM. *Accreditation:* ACIPE; ATS. *Program availability:* Part-time. *Degree requirements:* For master's, comprehensive exam or thesis. *Entrance requirements:* For master's, minimum GPA of 2.5. Additional exam requirements/recommendations for international students: required—TOEFL.

Northwest Nazarene University, NNU Graduate School of Theology, Nampa, ID 83686-5897. Offers leadership and formation (MA); missional leadership (M Div); pastoral ministry (MA); spiritual formation (M Div); youth, children, and family ministry (M Div). *Program availability:* Part-time, online only, 100% online. *Degree requirements:* For master's, 2.5 cumulative GPA. *Entrance requirements:* For master's, minimum GPA of 2.5; two recommendations, official transcripts. Additional exam requirements/recommendations for international students: required—TOEFL (minimum score 85 iBT). Electronic applications accepted. *Expenses:* Contact institution.

Northwest University, College of Ministry, Kirkland, WA 98033. Offers ministry (MIM); missional leadership (MA); theology and culture (MA). *Program availability:* Part-time, evening/weekend, online learning. *Degree requirements:* For master's, comprehensive exam (for some programs), thesis (for some programs). *Entrance requirements:* Additional exam requirements/recommendations for international students: required—TOEFL (minimum score 550 paper-based; 75 iBT). Electronic applications accepted.

Notre Dame Seminary, Graduate School of Theology, New Orleans, LA 70118-4391. Offers M Div, MA. *Accreditation:* ACIPE; ATS. *Program availability:* Part-time. *Degree requirements:* For master's, one foreign language, comprehensive exam, thesis. *Entrance requirements:* For master's, GRE. Additional exam requirements/recommendations for international students: required—TOEFL.

Nyack College, Alliance Theological Seminary, New York, NY 10004. Offers Biblical literature (MA), including New Testament, Old Testament; Biblical studies (MA); Christian ministry (MPS); intercultural studies (MA); ministry (D Min), including Christian leadership in the global context; theology and missions (M Div); urban ministry (MPS). *Program availability:* Part-time, evening/weekend, 100% online, blended/hybrid learning. *Students:* 203 full-time (89 women), 343 part-time (176 women); includes 418 minority (140 Black or African American, non-Hispanic/Latino; 94 Asian, non-Hispanic/Latino; 172 Hispanic/Latino; 1 Native Hawaiian or other Pacific Islander, non-Hispanic/Latino; 11 Two or more races, non-Hispanic/Latino), 40 international. Average age 43. In 2019, 100 master's, 17 doctorates awarded. *Degree requirements:* For master's, comprehensive exam (for some programs), thesis optional, internship; for doctorate, thesis/dissertation. *Entrance requirements:* For master's, transcripts, Christian experience statement, recommendations; for doctorate, transcripts, documented three years of ministry experience subsequent to 1st graduate theological degree, reference letters, formal academic paper. Additional exam requirements/recommendations for international students: required—TOEFL (minimum score 550 paper-based; 80 iBT). *Application deadline:* Applications are processed on a rolling basis. Application fee: $30. Electronic applications accepted. *Expenses:* $585 per credit. *Financial support:* Career-related internships or fieldwork, Federal Work-Study, and scholarships/grants available. Financial award applicants required to submit FAFSA. *Unit head:* Dr. Ronald Walborn, Dean, 845-770-5715, Fax: 845-358-1663. *Application contact:* Dr. Ronald Walborn, Dean, 845-770-5715, Fax: 845-358-1663.
Website: http://www.nyack.edu/ats

Oakland City University, Chapman Seminary, Oakland City, IN 47660-1099. Offers ministry (M Div); pastoral care (M Div); theology (D Min). *Program availability:* Part-time. *Degree requirements:* For doctorate, thesis/dissertation. *Entrance requirements:* For doctorate, GRE, MAT, letters of recommendation. Additional exam requirements/recommendations for international students: required—TOEFL. *Expenses:* Contact institution.

Oblate School of Theology, Graduate and Professional Programs, San Antonio, TX 78216-6693. Offers African-American pastoral leadership (D Min); divinity (M Div); pastoral leadership (D Min); pastoral ministry (MAP Min); pastoral studies (Certificate); spiritual formation in the local community (D Min); spirituality (MA Sp, PhD); spirituality and ministry (D Min); theology (MA Th); U.S. Hispanic/Latino ministry (D Min); M Div/MA Th. *Accreditation:* ACIPE; ATS (one or more programs are accredited). *Program availability:* Part-time, 100% online, blended/hybrid learning. *Faculty:* 21 full-time (5 women), 4 part-time/adjunct (0 women). *Students:* 89 full-time (9 women), 54 part-time (31 women); includes 77 minority (11 Black or African American, non-Hispanic/Latino; 8 Asian, non-Hispanic/Latino; 57 Hispanic/Latino; 1 Two or more races, non-Hispanic/Latino), 24 international. Average age 39. In 2019, 24 master's, 1 doctorate awarded. *Degree requirements:* For master's, comprehensive exam (for some programs), thesis (for some programs), practicum; for doctorate, one foreign language, comprehensive exam, thesis/dissertation, paper, practicum. *Entrance requirements:* For master's, MAT, interview, prerequisite course work in theology or religious studies and philosophy, minimum GPA of 2.5; for doctorate, D Min, M Div, MA Th, MA Sp, MA PM. Additional exam requirements/recommendations for international students: required—TOEFL (minimum score 71 iBT). *Application deadline:* For fall admission, 6/30 priority date for domestic and international students; for winter admission, 11/30 for domestic and international students; for spring admission, 11/30 for domestic and international students; for summer admission, 4/30 for domestic and international students. Applications are processed on a rolling basis. Application fee: $65. Electronic applications accepted. *Expenses:* Contact institution. *Financial support:* In 2019–20, 25 students received support. Scholarships/grants available. Support available to part-time students. Financial award application deadline: 8/15; financial award applicants required to submit FAFSA. *Unit head:* Dr. R. Scott Woodward, Academic Dean, 210-341-1366, Fax: 210-341-4519, E-mail: rsw@ost.edu. *Application contact:* Brenda Reyna, Registrar, 210-341-1366 Ext. 226, Fax: 210-341-4519, E-mail: registrar@ost.edu.

Ohio Christian University, Graduate Programs, Circleville, OH 43113. Offers accounting (MBA); business administration (MBA); digital marketing (MBA); finance (MBA); healthcare management (MBA); human resources (MBA); management (MM); organizational leadership (MBA); pastoral care and counseling (MAM); practical theology (MAM).

Ohio Dominican University, Division of Arts and Letters, Program in Theology, Columbus, OH 43219-2099. Offers MA. *Program availability:* Part-time, evening/weekend. *Faculty:* 2 full-time (1 woman). *Students:* 12 part-time (6 women); includes 3 minority (1 Black or African American, non-Hispanic/Latino; 1 Hispanic/Latino; 1 Two or more races, non-Hispanic/Latino). Average age 48. 4 applicants, 100% accepted, 4 enrolled. In 2019, 2 master's awarded. *Degree requirements:* For master's, thesis or alternative. *Entrance requirements:* For master's, 3 letters of recommendation, interview, essay. Additional exam requirements/recommendations for international students: required—TOEFL (minimum score 550 paper-based), IELTS (minimum score 6.5). *Application deadline:* For fall admission, 8/15 for domestic students, 6/10 for international students; for spring admission, 1/4 for domestic students, 11/2 for international students; for summer admission, 5/30 for domestic students. Applications are processed on a rolling basis. Application fee: $25. Electronic applications accepted. *Expenses: Tuition:* Full-time $10,800; part-time $600 per credit hour. *Required fees:* $225 per semester. Tuition and fees vary according to program. *Unit head:* Mary Filice, Program Director, 614-251-4578, E-mail: filicem2@ohiodominican.edu. *Application contact:* John W. Naughton, Vice President for Enrollment and Student Success, 614-251-4615, Fax: 614-251-6654, E-mail: grad@ohiodominican.edu.
Website: http://www.ohiodominican.edu/academics/graduate/ma-theology

Ohr Hameir Theological Seminary, Graduate Programs, Cortlandt Manor, NY 10567. *Accreditation:* AARTS.

Oklahoma Christian University, Graduate School of Theology, Oklahoma City, OK 73136-1100. Offers ministry (MACM), including theology (MACM, MTS); scripture (MTS), including theology (MACM, MTS); theology (M Div, MTS), including ministry (M Div), scripture (MTS). *Program availability:* Part-time, 100% online, blended/hybrid learning. *Degree requirements:* For master's, variable foreign language requirement, comprehensive exam, thesis (for some programs). *Entrance requirements:* For master's, bachelor's degree, minimum GPA of 3.0. Additional exam requirements/recommendations for international students: recommended—TOEFL (minimum score 550 paper-based; 79 iBT), IELTS (minimum score 6.5). Electronic applications accepted. *Expenses:* Contact institution.

Oklahoma Wesleyan University, Professional Studies Division, Bartlesville, OK 74006-6299. Offers nursing administration (MSN); nursing education (MSN); strategic leadership (MS); theology and apologetics (MA).

Olivet Nazarene University, Graduate School, Division of Religion, Bourbonnais, IL 60914. Offers biblical literature (MA); religion (MA); theology (MA). *Program availability:* Part-time. *Degree requirements:* For master's, thesis or alternative.

Oral Roberts University, School of Theology and Missions, Tulsa, OK 74171. Offers biblical literature (MA), including advanced languages, Judaic-Christian studies; church ministries and leadership (D Min); clinical pastoral education (M Div); missions (MA); pastoral care and chaplaincy (M Div, D Min); practical theology (MA), including teaching ministries, urban ministries; professional counseling (MA), including addiction studies, marriage and family therapy; theological/historical studies (MA). *Accreditation:* ATS. *Program availability:* Part-time, online learning. *Faculty:* 17 full-time (2 women). *Students:* 268 full-time (146 women), 96 part-time (52 women); includes 66 minority (48 Black or African American, non-Hispanic/Latino; 9 American Indian or Alaska Native, non-Hispanic/Latino; 8 Asian, non-Hispanic/Latino; 1 Native Hawaiian or other Pacific Islander, non-Hispanic/Latino), 65 international. Average age 40. 661 applicants, 24% accepted, 136 enrolled. In 2019, 113 master's, 19 doctorates awarded. *Degree requirements:* For master's, thesis (for some programs), practicum/internship; for doctorate, thesis/dissertation, applied research project. *Entrance requirements:* For master's, GRE General Test or MAT (waived for those with undergraduate degree from regionally accredited institution and 3.0 or higher GPA), minimum GPA of 2.5 (professional) or 3.0 (academic); for doctorate, M Div, minimum GPA of 3.0, 3 years of full-time ministry experience. Additional exam requirements/recommendations for international students: recommended—TOEFL (minimum score 550 paper-based; 79 iBT), IELTS (minimum score 7). *Application deadline:* Applications are processed on a rolling basis. Application fee: $35. Electronic applications accepted. Application fee is waived when completed online. *Expenses: Tuition:* Full-time $11,052; part-time $5526 per year. *Required fees:* $1230; $615 per unit. Tuition and fees vary according to program. *Financial support:* Fellowships and scholarships/grants available. Financial award application deadline: 6/1. *Unit head:* Dr. Bill Buker, Chair, 918-495-6493, E-mail: bbuker@oru.edu. *Application contact:* Joe Sims, Enrollment Counselor, 918-495-6618, E-mail: jsims@oru.edu.
Website: http://www.gradtheology.oru.edu/

Pacific School of Religion, Graduate and Professional Programs, Berkeley, CA 94709-1323. Offers M Div, MA, MTS, D Min, PhD, Th D, CAPS, CMS, CSS, CTS. *Accreditation:* ACIPE; ATS (one or more programs are accredited). *Program availability:* Part-time. *Degree requirements:* For master's, one foreign language, thesis (for some programs); for doctorate, thesis/dissertation. *Entrance requirements:* For master's, minimum GPA of 3.0; for doctorate, M Div, minimum GPA of 3.0 (D Min); for other advanced degree, M Div, minimum GPA of 3.0 (CAPS). Additional exam requirements/recommendations for international students: required—TOEFL (minimum score 550 paper-based). Electronic applications accepted.

Palm Beach Atlantic University, School of Ministry, West Palm Beach, FL 33416-4708. Offers Christian studies (MA); ministry (M Div). *Program availability:* Part-time. *Degree requirements:* For master's, one foreign language, comprehensive exam (for some programs), thesis optional, 8 credits of biblical language (for MDiv). *Entrance requirements:* For master's, minimum GPA of 2.75; writing samples. Additional exam requirements/recommendations for international students: required—TOEFL (minimum score 550 paper-based; 79 iBT). Electronic applications accepted. *Expenses: Tuition:* Part-time $570 per credit hour. *Required fees:* $580 per unit. Tuition and fees vary according to degree level, campus/location and program.

Payne Theological Seminary, Program in Theology, Wilberforce, OH 45384-3474. Offers M Div. *Accreditation:* ACIPE; ATS. *Program availability:* Part-time, evening/weekend, online learning.

Pentecostal Theological Seminary, Graduate and Professional Programs, Cleveland, TN 37320-3330. Offers biblical studies (MTS); church ministries (MA); counseling (MA); discipleship and Christian formation (MA); ministry (D Min); Pentecostal theology (MTS); theology (M Div). *Accreditation:* ACIPE; ATS. *Program availability:* Part-time. *Degree requirements:* For master's, variable foreign language requirement, thesis (for some programs), internship.

Pfeiffer University, Program in Practical Theology, Misenheimer, NC 28109-0960. Offers MA. *Program availability:* Part-time, evening/weekend. *Entrance requirements:* For master's, minimum GPA of 2.75.

Phillips Theological Seminary, Programs in Theology, Tulsa, OK 74116. Offers administration of church agencies (M Div); campus ministry (M Div); church-related social work (M Div); college and seminary teaching (M Div); global mission work (M Div); institutional chaplaincy (M Div); ministerial vocations in Christian education (M Div); ministry (D Min), including parish ministry, pastoral counseling, practices of ministry; ministry and culture (MAMC), including Christian education, congregational leadership, history and practice of Christian spirituality, theology, ethics, and culture; ministry of music (M Div); pastoral care and counseling (M Div); pastoral ministry (M Div); theological studies (MTS). *Accreditation:* ATS. *Program availability:* Part-time, online learning. *Degree requirements:* For master's, thesis (for some programs); for doctorate, thesis/dissertation. *Entrance requirements:* For master's, minimum GPA of 2.5; for doctorate, M Div, minimum GPA of 3.0.

Phoenix Seminary, Graduate Programs, Phoenix, AZ 85018. Offers Biblical and theological studies (Graduate Diploma); Biblical communication (M Div); Biblical leadership (MA); Christian counseling (Graduate Diploma); counseling and family (M Div); leadership development (M Div); ministry (D Min); professional counseling (MA). *Accreditation:* ATS (one or more programs are accredited). *Program availability:* Part-time, evening/weekend. *Degree requirements:* For master's, 2 foreign languages, comprehensive exam; for doctorate, 2 foreign languages, thesis/dissertation. *Entrance requirements:* For master's, undergraduate degree with minimum GPA of 2.5; for doctorate, M Div (94 hours) with minimum GPA of 3.0. Additional exam requirements/recommendations for international students: required—TOEFL (minimum score 587 paper-based; 92 iBT), TWE (minimum score 4.5).

Piedmont International University, Graduate School, Winston-Salem, NC 27101-5197. Offers Biblical studies (PhD); curriculum and instruction (M Ed); divinity (M Div); educational leadership (M Ed); leadership (MA, PhD); ministry (MA Min, D Min); non-language track (MABS); PhD preparation track (MABS). *Program availability:* Part-time, online learning. Terminal master's awarded for partial completion of doctoral program. *Degree requirements:* For master's, 2 foreign languages, comprehensive exam, thesis or alternative; for doctorate, 2 foreign languages, comprehensive exam. *Entrance requirements:* For master's, GRE General Test; for doctorate, Hebrew and Greek proficiency, MA. Additional exam requirements/recommendations for international students: required—TOEFL (minimum score 500 paper-based; 60 iBT). Electronic applications accepted. *Expenses: Tuition:* Full-time $3375; part-time $375 per credit. *Required fees:* $400; $200 per semester. Part-time tuition and fees vary according to program.

Piedmont International University, Temple Baptist Seminary, Winston-Salem, NC 27101-5197. Offers M Div, D Min. *Program availability:* Part-time, evening/weekend, online learning. *Degree requirements:* For master's, comprehensive exam; for doctorate, comprehensive exam, thesis/dissertation. *Entrance requirements:* For master's, bachelor's degree or equivalent from accredited or recognized college or university with minimum GPA of 2.75 and one of the following: aptitude for graduate studies evidenced by the transcript record, the GRE, or ministry achievement; for doctorate, appropriate master's degree with minimum GPA of 3.0 including 6 semester hours each of Greek, Hebrew, and Biblical introduction (Old Testament and New Testament) and 12 semester hours of systematic theology. Additional exam requirements/recommendations for international students: required—TOEFL (minimum score 500 paper-based; 60 iBT). *Expenses: Tuition:* Full-time $3375; part-time $375 per credit. *Required fees:* $400; $200 per semester. Part-time tuition and fees vary according to program.

Pittsburgh Theological Seminary, Graduate and Professional Programs, Pittsburgh, PA 15206-2596. Offers divinity (M Div); theological studies (MA); theology (Th M); theology and ministry (MA, D Min); JD/M Div; M Div/MS; M Div/MSW. *Accreditation:* ATS (one or more programs are accredited). *Program availability:* Part-time, evening/weekend. *Degree requirements:* For master's, one foreign language, comprehensive exam (for some programs), thesis (for some programs); for doctorate, thesis/dissertation. *Entrance requirements:* For master's, bachelor's degree with minimum GPA of 2.7, interview, references; for doctorate, M Div or equivalent, interview, references. Additional exam requirements/recommendations for international students: required—TOEFL (minimum score 570 paper-based; 89 iBT). Electronic applications accepted.

Point Loma Nazarene University, School of Theology and Christian Ministry, San Diego, CA 92106. Offers M Min. *Program availability:* Part-time, online only, nine-week quads with eight weeks of online coursework and a one-week intensive. *Faculty:* 1 full-time (0 women), 3 part-time/adjunct (0 women). *Students:* 39 part-time (16 women); includes 24 minority (1 Black or African American, non-Hispanic/Latino; 1 Asian, non-Hispanic/Latino; 20 Hispanic/Latino; 2 Two or more races, non-Hispanic/Latino), 5 international. Average age 47. 11 applicants, 82% accepted, 7 enrolled. In 2019, 4 master's awarded. *Degree requirements:* For master's, thesis optional. *Entrance requirements:* For master's, letters of recommendation, essay, transcripts, interview. Additional exam requirements/recommendations for international students: recommended—TOEFL. *Application deadline:* For fall admission, 8/30 priority date for domestic students; for spring admission, 4/4 priority date for domestic students; for summer admission, 6/20 priority date for domestic students. Applications are processed on a rolling basis. Application fee: $0. Electronic applications accepted. *Expenses:* $320 per unit. *Financial support:* In 2019–20, 24 students received support. Scholarships/grants available. Financial award application deadline: 6/5; financial award applicants required to submit FAFSA. *Unit head:* Dr. Mark Maddix, Dean, 619-849-7236, E-mail: MarkMaddix@pointloma.edu. *Application contact:* Dana Barger, Director of Recruitment and Admissions, Graduate and Professional Students, 619-329-6799, E-mail: gradinfo@pointloma.edu.
Website: https://www.pointloma.edu/schools-departments-colleges/school-theology-christian-ministry

Pontifical Catholic University of Puerto Rico, College of Arts and Humanities, Department of Theology and Philosophy, Ponce, PR 00717-0777. Offers M Div.

Pontifical College Josephinum, School of Theology, Columbus, OH 43235. Offers M Div, MA. *Accreditation:* ATS. *Program availability:* Part-time. *Degree requirements:* For master's, 3 foreign languages, comprehensive exam, thesis. *Entrance requirements:* For master's, GRE General Test, 15 credit hours of course work in philosophy, 6 credit hours of course work in scripture. Additional exam requirements/recommendations for international students: required—TOEFL (minimum score 600 paper-based).

Pontifical John Paul II Institute for Studies on Marriage and Family, Graduate Programs, Washington, DC 20064. Offers biotechnology and ethics (MTS); marriage and family (MTS, STD, STL); theology (PhD).

Pope St. John XXIII National Seminary, Graduate Program, Weston, MA 02493-2618. Offers M Div. *Accreditation:* ATS.

Princeton Theological Seminary, Graduate and Professional Programs, Princeton, NJ 08542-0803. Offers M Div, MA, Th M, D Min, PhD. *Accreditation:* ACIPE; ATS. *Program availability:* Part-time. Terminal master's awarded for partial completion of doctoral program. *Degree requirements:* For doctorate, 2 foreign languages, thesis/dissertation, comprehensive exam (PhD), French and German. *Entrance requirements:* For doctorate, GRE General Test. Additional exam requirements/recommendations for international students: required—TOEFL. Electronic applications accepted.

Providence College, Department of Theology, Providence, RI 02918. Offers Biblical studies (MA); theology (MA, MTS). *Program availability:* Part-time, evening/weekend. *Degree requirements:* For master's, comprehensive exam, thesis. *Entrance requirements:* For master's, GRE (for MA). Additional exam requirements/recommendations for international students: required—TOEFL (minimum score 577 paper-based; 90 iBT). *Expenses:* Contact institution.

Providence University College & Theological Seminary, Theological Seminary, Otterburne, MB R0A 1G0, Canada. Offers children's ministry (Certificate); Christian studies (MA, Certificate); counseling (MA); cross-cultural discipleship (Certificate); divinity (M Div); educational studies (MA), including counseling psychology, educational ministries, student development, teaching English to speakers of other languages, training teachers of English to speakers of other languages; global studies (MA); lay counseling (Diploma); ministry (D Min); teaching English to speakers of other languages (Certificate); theological studies (MA); training teacher of English to speakers of other languages (Certificate); youth ministry (Certificate). *Accreditation:* ATS. *Program availability:* Part-time. *Degree requirements:* For master's, variable foreign language requirement, thesis (for some programs); for doctorate, thesis/dissertation. *Entrance requirements:* Additional exam requirements/recommendations for international students: recommended—TOEFL (minimum score 550 paper-based).

Rabbinical Academy Mesivta Rabbi Chaim Berlin, Graduate Program, Brooklyn, NY 11230-4715. Offers Advanced Talmudic Degree, Second Talmudic Degree. *Accreditation:* AARTS. *Degree requirements:* For other advanced degree, 2 foreign languages. *Entrance requirements:* For degree, must be a graduate of a rabbinical school.

Rabbinical College Beth Shraga, Graduate Programs, Monsey, NY 10952-3035. *Accreditation:* AARTS.

Rabbinical College Bobover Yeshiva B'nei Zion, Graduate Programs, Brooklyn, NY 11219. Offers First Talmudic Degree, Rabbi. *Accreditation:* AARTS.

Rabbinical College of Long Island, Graduate Programs, Long Beach, NY 11561-3305. *Accreditation:* AARTS.

Theology

Rabbinical Seminary of America, Graduate Programs, Flushing, NY 11367. *Accreditation:* AARTS.

Reconstructionist Rabbinical College, Graduate Programs, Wyncote, PA 19095-1898. Offers Jewish studies (MAJS); rabbinics (MAHL, DHL); women's studies (Certificate). *Program availability:* Part-time. *Degree requirements:* For master's, one foreign language, thesis (MAJS), completion of rabbinical program (MAHL); for doctorate, one foreign language. *Entrance requirements:* For master's, GRE General Test; placement examinations in Hebrew and Judaism (MAHL); for doctorate, GRE General Test, placement examinations in Hebrew and Judaism. *Expenses: Tuition:* Full-time $26,000.

Reformed Episcopal Seminary, Graduate Program, Blue Bell, PA 19422. Offers M Div. *Accreditation:* ATS. *Entrance requirements:* For master's, personal reference letter, pastor's reference letter, transcript.

Reformed Presbyterian Theological Seminary, Graduate and Professional Programs, Pittsburgh, PA 15208-2594. Offers M Div, MTS, D Min. *Accreditation:* ATS. *Program availability:* Part-time, evening/weekend. Electronic applications accepted.

Reformed Theological Seminary–Atlanta Campus, Graduate Programs, Marietta, GA 30067. Offers M Div, MABS, MAR, D Min, Certificate.

Reformed Theological Seminary–Charlotte Campus, Graduate and Professional Programs, Charlotte, NC 28226-6318. Offers biblical studies (MA); ministry (D Min); pastoral ministry (M Div); theological studies (MA). *Program availability:* Part-time. *Degree requirements:* For master's, comprehensive exam; for doctorate, thesis/dissertation. *Entrance requirements:* For master's, minimum GPA of 2.6; for doctorate, minimum GPA of 3.0. Additional exam requirements/recommendations for international students: required—TOEFL (minimum score 550 paper-based). Electronic applications accepted.

Reformed Theological Seminary–Dallas Campus, Graduate and Professional Programs, Dallas, TX 75207. Offers theological studies (MA); theology (M Div).

Reformed Theological Seminary–Jackson Campus, Graduate and Professional Programs, Jackson, MS 39209-3004. Offers Bible, theology, and missions (Certificate); Biblical exegesis (M Div); biblical studies (MA); Christian education (MA); counseling (M Div); marriage and family therapy (MA); ministry (D Min); missions (M Div, MA, D Min); theological studies (MA). *Accreditation:* AAMFT/COAMFTE (one or more programs are accredited); ATS (one or more programs are accredited). *Degree requirements:* For master's, thesis (for some programs), fieldwork; for doctorate, 2 foreign languages, thesis/dissertation. *Entrance requirements:* For master's, minimum GPA of 2.6; for doctorate, minimum GPA of 3.0. Additional exam requirements/recommendations for international students: required—TOEFL.

Reformed Theological Seminary–Orlando Campus, Graduate Programs, Oviedo, FL 32765. Offers Bible (Certificate); biblical studies (MA); counseling (MA); missions (Certificate); reformed expository preaching (D Min); reformed theology and ministry (D Min); theological studies (MA); theology (M Div, Certificate). *Program availability:* Part-time, online learning. Electronic applications accepted.

Reformed Theological Seminary–Washington D.C., Graduate and Professional Programs, McLean, VA 22102. Offers Bible (M Div); biblical studies (MA); practical theology (M Div); religion (MA); theology (M Div). *Program availability:* Part-time, evening/weekend. *Degree requirements:* For master's, variable foreign language requirement, comprehensive exam (for some programs), integrative paper. *Entrance requirements:* For master's, minimum undergraduate GPA of 2.6. Additional exam requirements/recommendations for international students: required—TOEFL (minimum score 550 paper-based), TWE. Electronic applications accepted. *Expenses:* Contact institution.

Reformed University, Graduate Programs, Lawrenceville, GA 30043. Offers management (MBA); theology (M Div).

Regent College, Program in Theology, Vancouver, BC V6T 2E4, Canada. Offers Christian history and theology (M Div, MATS); Christian studies (MATS, G Dip); Christianity, church and culture (M Div, MATS); scripture (M Div, MATS); theology (Th M). *Accreditation:* ATS (one or more programs are accredited). *Program availability:* Part-time. *Degree requirements:* For master's, one foreign language, comprehensive exam (for some programs), thesis (for some programs). *Entrance requirements:* For master's, minimum GPA of 2.8 (MATS, M Div), 3.3 (Th M); for G Dip, minimum GPA of 2.8. Additional exam requirements/recommendations for international students: required—TOEFL (minimum score 575 paper-based; 90 iBT), IELTS (minimum score 6.5). Electronic applications accepted. *Expenses:* Contact institution.

Regent University, Graduate School, School of Divinity, Virginia Beach, VA 23464. Offers Christian spirituality and formation (MA); divinity (M Div), including Biblical studies (M Div, MTS, Th M, PhD), chaplain ministry, Christian theology (M Div, MTS, Th M, PhD), church and ministry (M Div, MA), history of Christianity (M Div, MTS, Th M, PhD), inter-cultural studies (M Div, MA), interdisciplinary studies (M Div, MA, MTS), marketplace ministry (M Div, MA), missional discipleship, practical healing ministry (M Div, MA), worship and media (M Div, MA); leadership and renewal (D Min), including Christian leadership and renewal, clinical pastoral education, community transformation, military ministry, ministry leadership coaching; practical theology (MA), including church and ministry (M Div, MA), cosmogony, inter-cultural studies (M Div, MA), interdisciplinary studies (M Div, MA, MTS), marketplace ministry (M Div, MA), practical healing ministry (M Div, MA), worship and media (M Div, MA); renewal theology (PhD), including Biblical studies (M Div, MTS, Th M, PhD), Christian theology (M Div, MTS, Th M, PhD), history of Christianity (M Div, MTS, Th M, PhD), practical theology; theological studies (MTS), including Biblical studies (M Div, MTS, Th M, PhD), Christian theology (M Div, MTS, Th M, PhD), history of Christianity (M Div, MTS, Th M, PhD), interdisciplinary studies (M Div, MA, MTS); theology (Th M), including Biblical studies (M Div, MTS, Th M, PhD), Christian theology (M Div, MTS, Th M, PhD), history of Christianity (M Div, MTS, Th M, PhD). *Accreditation:* ACIPE; ATS. *Program availability:* Part-time, evening/weekend, 100% online, blended/hybrid learning. *Faculty:* 15 full-time (3 women), 58 part-time/adjunct (10 women). *Students:* 303 full-time (119 women), 813 part-time (403 women); includes 632 minority (509 Black or African American, non-Hispanic/Latino; 3 American Indian or Alaska Native, non-Hispanic/Latino; 31 Asian, non-Hispanic/Latino; 54 Hispanic/Latino; 2 Native Hawaiian or other Pacific Islander, non-Hispanic/Latino; 33 Two or more races, non-Hispanic/Latino), 16 international. Average age 45. 561 applicants, 66% accepted, 194 enrolled. In 2019, 168 master's, 13 doctorates awarded. *Degree requirements:* For master's, comprehensive exam, thesis or alternative, internship; for doctorate, thesis/dissertation or alternative. *Entrance requirements:* For master's, minimum undergraduate GPA of 2.75, writing sample, personal goal statement, college transcripts; for doctorate, GRE, minimum graduate GPA of 3.5 (PhD), 3.0 (D Min); clergy recommendations; writing sample; transcripts; resume; interview. Additional exam requirements/recommendations for international students: required—TOEFL (minimum score 577 paper-based). *Application deadline:* For fall admission, 5/1 priority date for domestic students. Applications are processed on a rolling basis. Application fee: $50. Electronic applications accepted. *Expenses:* Contact institution. *Financial support:* In 2019–20, 856 students received support. Career-related internships or fieldwork, scholarships/grants, health care benefits, and unspecified assistantships available. Support available to part-time students. Financial award applicants required to submit FAFSA. *Unit head:* Dr. Cornelius Bekker, Dean, 757-352-4258, Fax: 757-352-4597, E-mail: clbekker@regent.edu. *Application contact:* Heidi Cece, Assistant Vice President for Enrollment Management, 800-373-5504, Fax: 757-352-4381, E-mail: admissions@regent.edu.
Website: https://www.regent.edu/school-of-divinity/

Regis College, Graduate and Professional Programs, Toronto, ON M5S 2Z5, Canada. Offers eastern Christian studies (Certificate); Ignatian spirituality (Diploma); ministry (D Min); ministry and spirituality (MAMS); philosophical studies (Diploma); retreat direction (Certificate); sacred theology (STM, STD, STB, STL); spiritual direction (Diploma); theological studies (MTS, Diploma); theology (M Div, MA, Th M, PhD, Th D); M Div/MA. *Accreditation:* ATS (one or more programs are accredited). Terminal master's awarded for partial completion of doctoral program. *Degree requirements:* For master's, 2 foreign languages, thesis; for doctorate, 3 foreign languages, comprehensive exam, thesis/dissertation. *Entrance requirements:* For doctorate, minimum GPA of 3.7. Additional exam requirements/recommendations for international students: required—TOEFL (minimum score 580 paper-based; 93 iBT), TWE (minimum score 5).

Sacred Heart Major Seminary, School of Theology, Detroit, MI 48206-1799. Offers pastoral studies (MAPS); theology (M Div, MA). *Accreditation:* ACIPE; ATS. *Program availability:* Part-time, evening/weekend. *Degree requirements:* For master's, one foreign language, thesis optional, integrating project. *Entrance requirements:* For master's, GRE, previous course work in philosophy and theology.

Sacred Heart Seminary and School of Theology, Graduate and Professional Programs, Hales Corners, WI 53130-0429. Offers priestly formation (Certificate); theology (M Div, MA). *Accreditation:* ACIPE; ATS. *Program availability:* Part-time. *Degree requirements:* For master's, essay or comprehensive exam. *Entrance requirements:* For master's, MAT, 6 hours of course work each in philosophy and theology, letter of recommendation. Additional exam requirements/recommendations for international students: required—TOEFL.

St. Andrew's College, Graduate Programs in Theology, Saskatoon, SK S7N 0W3, Canada. Offers M Div, MTS, STM, D Min, Diploma. *Accreditation:* ATS. *Entrance requirements:* Additional exam requirements/recommendations for international students: required—TOEFL.

St. Andrew's College in Winnipeg, Graduate Programs, Winnipeg, MB R3T 2M7, Canada. Offers M Div. *Students:* 1 part-time (0 women). *Application deadline:* For fall admission, 7/31 for domestic students. Application fee: $15. *Financial support:* Fellowships, career-related internships or fieldwork, Federal Work-Study, and institutionally sponsored loans available. Support available to part-time students. Financial award application deadline: 7/31. *Unit head:* Rev. S. Jarmus, Dean TEST, 204-474-8898. *Application contact:* Rev. Roman Bozyk TEST, Registrar, 204-474-6514, Fax: 204-474-7629, E-mail: bozykr@ms.umanitoba.ca.

St. Augustine's Seminary of Toronto, Graduate and Professional Programs, Scarborough, ON M1M 1M3, Canada. Offers divinity (M Div); lay ministry (Diploma); religious education (MRE); theological studies (MTS, Diploma). *Accreditation:* ATS. *Program availability:* Part-time, evening/weekend. *Entrance requirements:* Additional exam requirements/recommendations for international students: required—TOEFL (minimum score 580 paper-based), TWE (minimum score 5).

St. Bernard's School of Theology and Ministry, Graduate and Professional Programs, Rochester, NY 14618. Offers pastoral studies (MA, Certificate); theological studies (MA); theology (M Div). *Accreditation:* ATS (one or more programs are accredited). *Program availability:* Part-time, evening/weekend. *Degree requirements:* For master's, variable foreign language requirement, thesis (for some programs). *Entrance requirements:* For master's, minimum GPA of 2.5.

St. Catherine University, Graduate Programs, Program in Theology, St. Paul, MN 55105. Offers pastoral ministry (Certificate); spiritual direction (Certificate); theology (MA). *Program availability:* Part-time. *Degree requirements:* For master's, comprehensive exam, thesis (for some programs). *Entrance requirements:* For master's, MAT, minimum GPA of 3.0. Additional exam requirements/recommendations for international students: required—Michigan English Language Assessment Battery or TOEFL (minimum score 600 paper-based; 100 iBT). *Expenses:* Contact institution.

Saint Charles Borromeo Seminary, Overbrook, School of Theological Studies, Program in Theology, Wynnewood, PA 19096. Offers MA. *Degree requirements:* For master's, comprehensive exam, research papers. *Entrance requirements:* For master's, M Div. Additional exam requirements/recommendations for international students: required—TOEFL.

St. John's Seminary, Graduate and Professional Programs, Camarillo, CA 93012-2598. Offers divinity (M Div); pastoral ministry (MAPM); theology (MA). *Accreditation:* ATS. *Program availability:* Part-time. *Degree requirements:* For master's, comprehensive exam (for some programs), thesis optional, comprehensive integration paper (MAPM). *Entrance requirements:* For master's, GRE General Test, minimum GPA of 3.5 (MA), 2.5 (MAPM). Additional exam requirements/recommendations for international students: required—TOEFL (minimum score 550 paper-based; 79 iBT). Electronic applications accepted.

Saint John's Seminary, Graduate Programs, Brighton, MA 02135. Offers M Div, MA Th, MAM.

St. John's University, St. John's College of Liberal Arts and Sciences, Department of Theology and Religious Studies, Queens, NY 11439. Offers theology (MA). *Accreditation:* ACIPE. *Program availability:* Part-time, evening/weekend, 100% online, blended/hybrid learning. *Degree requirements:* For master's, comprehensive exam, thesis optional, portfolio. *Entrance requirements:* For master's, letters of recommendation, transcripts, resume, personal statement. Additional exam requirements/recommendations for international students: required—TOEFL (minimum score 80 iBT), IELTS (minimum score 6.5). Electronic applications accepted.

Saint John's University, Saint John's School of Theology and Seminary, Collegeville, MN 56321. Offers divinity (M Div); liturgical music (MA); liturgical studies (MA); pastoral ministry (MA); theology (MA), including church history, liturgy, monastic studies, scripture, spirituality, systematics; M Div/MA. *Program availability:* Part-time, online learning. *Degree requirements:* For master's, one foreign language, comprehensive exam (for some programs), thesis (for some programs). *Entrance requirements:* For master's, GRE General Test or MAT. Electronic applications accepted.

St. Joseph's Seminary, Graduate and Professional Programs, Yonkers, NY 10704. Offers Catholic philosophical studies (MA); divinity (M Div); pastoral studies (MAPS); theology (MA). *Accreditation:* ATS. *Degree requirements:* For master's, one foreign language, thesis. *Entrance requirements:* For master's, 27 credits in philosophy and 9 in theology.

Saint Leo University, Graduate Studies in Theology, Saint Leo, FL 33574-6665. Offers MA, Certificate. *Program availability:* Part-time, evening/weekend, 100% online, blended/hybrid learning. *Faculty:* 9 full-time (0 women), 9 part-time/adjunct (3 women). *Students:* 3 full-time (1 woman), 239 part-time (78 women); includes 180 minority (22

Black or African American, non-Hispanic/Latino; 1 Asian, non-Hispanic/Latino; 13 Hispanic/Latino; 1 Native Hawaiian or other Pacific Islander, non-Hispanic/Latino; 143 Two or more races, non-Hispanic/Latino). Average age 51. 92 applicants, 93% accepted, 66 enrolled. In 2019, 46 master's, 2 other advanced degrees awarded. *Entrance requirements:* For master's, official transcripts, letter of recommendation, bachelor's degree from regionally-accredited university with minimum GPA of 3.0. Additional exam requirements/recommendations for international students: required— TOEFL (minimum score 550 paper-based; 78 iBT). *Application deadline:* For fall admission, 7/1 priority date for domestic and international students; for spring admission, 11/1 priority date for domestic and international students. Applications are processed on a rolling basis. Electronic applications accepted. *Expenses:* MA in Theology $9,060 per FT yr. *Financial support:* In 2019–20, 11 students received support. Fellowships, scholarships/grants, and tuition remission for Saint Leo employees and their dependents available. Financial award application deadline: 3/1; financial award applicants required to submit FAFSA. *Unit head:* Dr. Randall Woodard, Director, Graduate Theology, 352-588-8239, Fax: 352-588-8404, E-mail: randall.woodard@saintleo.edu. *Application contact:* Saint Leo University Office of Graduate Admissions, 800-707-8846, Fax: 352-588-7873, E-mail: grad.admissions@saintleo.edu.
Website: https://www.saintleo.edu/theology-master-degree

Saint Louis University, Graduate Programs, College of Arts and Sciences, Department of Theological Studies, St. Louis, MO 63103. Offers historical theology (MA, PhD); theology (MA). *Program availability:* Part-time. *Degree requirements:* For master's, comprehensive exam; for doctorate, 4 foreign languages, comprehensive exam, thesis/ dissertation, preliminary exams. *Entrance requirements:* For master's, GRE General Test, letters of recommendation, resume; for doctorate, GRE General Test, letters of recommendation, resumé, interview, transcripts, goal statement. Additional exam requirements/recommendations for international students: required—TOEFL (minimum score 550 paper-based). Electronic applications accepted.

Saint Mary Seminary and Graduate School of Theology, Graduate and Professional Programs, Wickliffe, OH 44092-2527. Offers M Div, MA, D Min. *Accreditation:* ATS. *Program availability:* Part-time. *Degree requirements:* For master's, comprehensive exam, symposium; for doctorate, thesis/dissertation, final project, symposium. *Entrance requirements:* For master's, GRE General Test, previous course work in religion; for doctorate, M Div or equivalent, 3 years in full-time ministry, interviews, ministry profile report.

St. Mary's Seminary and University, Ecumenical Institute of Theology, Baltimore, MD 21210-1994. Offers church ministries (MA); theology (MA Th, Certificate). *Accreditation:* ATS. *Program availability:* Part-time, evening/weekend. *Degree requirements:* For master's, thesis or alternative, comprehensive exam or colloquium. *Expenses:* Contact institution.

St. Mary's Seminary and University, School of Theology, Baltimore, MD 21210-1994. Offers M Div, MA Th, STD, STB, STL. *Accreditation:* ATS (one or more programs are accredited). *Program availability:* Part-time. Terminal master's awarded for partial completion of doctoral program. *Degree requirements:* For master's, comprehensive exam; for other advanced degree, one foreign language, thesis. *Entrance requirements:* For master's, Computerized Adaptive Placement Assessment and Support System.

Saint Mary's University, Faculty of Arts, Department of Religious Studies, Halifax, NS B3H 3C3, Canada. Offers theology and religious studies (MA).

St. Mary's University, Graduate Studies, Program in Theology, San Antonio, TX 78228. Offers MA. *Program availability:* Part-time, evening/weekend. *Degree requirements:* For master's, comprehensive exam, thesis optional, 10 clock hours (Graduate Learning Community Experience). *Entrance requirements:* For master's, undergraduate transcripts, writing sample. Additional exam requirements/ recommendations for international students: required—TOEFL (minimum score 550 paper-based; 80 iBT), IELTS (minimum score 6). Electronic applications accepted.

Saint Meinrad School of Theology, Master of Arts (Catholic Philosophical Studies) Program, Saint Meinrad, IN 47577. Offers MA. *Accreditation:* ATS. *Faculty:* 5 full-time, 4 part-time/adjunct (1 woman). *Students:* 32 full-time (0 women); includes 1 minority (Black or African American, non-Hispanic/Latino), 3 international. Average age 28. In 2019, 11 master's awarded. *Degree requirements:* For master's, comprehensive exam. *Entrance requirements:* Additional exam requirements/recommendations for international students: required—TOEFL (minimum score 550 paper-based; 80 iBT). *Application deadline:* For fall admission, 7/1 priority date for domestic and international students; for winter admission, 11/15 for domestic and international students. Applications are processed on a rolling basis. Application fee: $30. *Expenses: Tuition:* Full-time $27,714; part-time $520 per credit hour. *Required fees:* $34 per course. One-time fee: $200. Tuition and fees vary according to program. *Financial support:* Federal Work-Study and scholarships/grants available. Financial award applicants required to submit FAFSA. *Unit head:* Dr. Robert Alvis, Academic Dean, 812-357-6543, Fax: 812-357-6816, E-mail: ralvis@saintmeinrad.edu. *Application contact:* Dr. John Schlachter, Director of Admissions, 812-357-6142, Fax: 812-357-6816, E-mail: jschlachter@saintmeinrad.edu.
Website: https://www.saintmeinrad.edu/priesthood-formation/academic-formation/pre-theologymaster-of-arts/

Saint Meinrad School of Theology, Master of Arts (Theology) Program, Saint Meinrad, IN 47577. Offers MA. *Accreditation:* ATS. *Program availability:* Part-time, evening/ weekend. *Faculty:* 16 full-time (1 woman), 14 part-time/adjunct (6 women). *Students:* 6 full-time (2 women), 52 part-time (22 women); includes 6 minority (2 Black or African American, non-Hispanic/Latino; 4 Hispanic/Latino), 3 international. Average age 49. In 2019, 20 master's awarded. *Degree requirements:* For master's, comprehensive exam, three capstone essays or one research paper. *Entrance requirements:* Additional exam requirements/recommendations for international students: required—TOEFL (minimum score 550 paper-based; 80 iBT). *Application deadline:* For fall admission, 7/1 for domestic and international students; for winter admission, 11/15 for domestic and international students. Applications are processed on a rolling basis. Application fee: $30. Electronic applications accepted. *Expenses: Tuition:* Full-time $27,714; part-time $520 per credit hour. *Required fees:* $34 per course. One-time fee: $200. Tuition and fees vary according to program. *Financial support:* Federal Work-Study, institutionally sponsored loans, and scholarships/grants available. Support available to part-time students. Financial award application deadline: 7/1; financial award applicants required to submit FAFSA. *Unit head:* Sr. Jeana Visel, OSB, Director of Graduate Theology Programs, 812-357-6721, Fax: 812-357-6816. *Application contact:* Dr. John Schlachter, Director of Admissions, 812-357-6142, Fax: 812-357-6816, E-mail: apply@saintmeinrad.edu.

Saint Meinrad School of Theology, Master of Divinity Program, Saint Meinrad, IN 47577. Offers M Div. *Accreditation:* ATS. *Faculty:* 17 full-time (1 woman), 5 part-time/ adjunct (1 woman). *Students:* 91 full-time (0 women); includes 5 minority (1 Black or African American, non-Hispanic/Latino; 4 Hispanic/Latino), 34 international. Average age 30. In 2019, 18 master's awarded. *Entrance requirements:* Additional exam requirements/recommendations for international students: required—TOEFL (minimum score 550 paper-based; 80 iBT). *Application deadline:* For fall admission, 7/1 priority

date for domestic students, 7/1 for international students; for winter admission, 11/15 for domestic and international students. Applications are processed on a rolling basis. Application fee: $0. *Expenses: Tuition:* Full-time $27,714; part-time $520 per credit hour. *Required fees:* $34 per course. One-time fee: $200. Tuition and fees vary according to program. *Financial support:* Federal Work-Study, institutionally sponsored loans, and scholarships/grants available. Financial award application deadline: 7/31; financial award applicants required to submit FAFSA. *Unit head:* Dr. Robert Alvis, Academic Dean, 812-357-6543, Fax: 812-357-6816, E-mail: ralvis@saintmeinrad.edu. *Application contact:* Dr. John Schlachter, Director of Admissions, 812-357-6142, Fax: 812-357-6816, E-mail: apply@saintmeinrad.edu.
Website: https://www.saintmeinrad.edu/priesthood-formation/academic-formation/master-of-divinity/

St. Norbert College, Master of Theological Studies Program, De Pere, WI 54115-2099. Offers MTS. *Program availability:* Part-time-only, evening/weekend. *Faculty:* 6 full-time (3 women), 4 part-time/adjunct (0 women). *Students:* 22 (12 women); includes 3 minority (2 Hispanic/Latino; 1 Two or more races, non-Hispanic/Latino). Average age 53. 2 applicants, 100% accepted, 2 enrolled. In 2019, 3 master's awarded. *Degree requirements:* For master's, comprehensive exam, thesis. *Application deadline:* Applications are processed on a rolling basis. Application fee: $50. Electronic applications accepted. *Financial support:* In 2019–20, 6 students received support. Scholarships/grants available. *Unit head:* Dr. Howard Ebert, Director, 920-403-3956, E-mail: howard.ebert@snc.edu. *Application contact:* Danielle Wahlen, Program Coordinator, 920-403-3957, E-mail: danielle.wahlen@snc.edu.
Website: http://www.snc.edu/mts/

St. Patrick's Seminary & University, School of Theology, Menlo Park, CA 94025-3596. Offers M Div, MA, STB. *Accreditation:* ATS (one or more programs are accredited). *Program availability:* Part-time. *Degree requirements:* For master's, comprehensive exam, thesis or alternative. *Entrance requirements:* For master's, GRE General Test, minimum GPA of 3.0, interview. Additional exam requirements/ recommendations for international students: required—TOEFL (minimum score 550 paper-based; 80 iBT), TWE.

Saint Paul School of Theology, Graduate and Professional Programs, Overland Park, KS 66211. Offers M Div, MA, MTS, D Min. *Accreditation:* ACIPE; ATS. *Program availability:* Part-time. *Degree requirements:* For doctorate, thesis/dissertation. *Entrance requirements:* For master's, minimum GPA of 2.75; for doctorate, minimum GPA of 3.0. Additional exam requirements/recommendations for international students: required— TOEFL.

Saint Paul University, Faculty of Canon Law, Ottawa, ON K1S 1C4, Canada. Offers canon law (MCL, JCD, PhD, Graduate Certificate, JCL); canonical practice (Graduate Certificate); ecclesiastical administration (Graduate Certificate). *Program availability:* Part-time. *Degree requirements:* For master's, one foreign language; for doctorate, one foreign language, comprehensive exam, thesis/dissertation; for other advanced degree, one foreign language, comprehensive exam and seminar paper (JCL). *Entrance requirements:* For master's, appropriate bachelor's degree, 18 credits in theology; for doctorate, JCL or MCL; for other advanced degree, B Th or equivalent (JCL), appropriate bachelor's degree, 18 credits in theology.

Saint Paul University, Faculty of Human Sciences, Program in Counseling and Spirituality, Ottawa, ON K1S 1C4, Canada. Offers individual or marital/couple counseling (MA); spiritual care (MA). *Program availability:* Part-time. *Degree requirements:* For master's, research project or thesis. *Entrance requirements:* For master's, honors BA in human sciences, minimum B average, 12 theology credits.

Saint Paul University, Faculty of Theology, Ottawa, ON K1S 1C4, Canada. Offers MA Th, MP Th, MRE, D Min, D Th, PhD, L Th. *Accreditation:* ATS. *Degree requirements:* For master's and L Th, one foreign language; for doctorate, one foreign language, comprehensive exam, thesis/dissertation. *Entrance requirements:* For master's, B Th; for doctorate, MA Th, L Th, MP Th, M Div.

St. Peter's Seminary, Department of Theology, London, ON N6A 3Y1, Canada. Offers M Div, MTS. *Accreditation:* ATS.

Saints Cyril and Methodius Seminary, Graduate and Professional Programs, Orchard Lake, MI 48324. Offers pastoral ministry (MAPM); religious education (MARE); theology (M Div, MA). *Program availability:* Part-time.

St. Stephen's College, Programs in Theology, Edmonton, AB T6G 2J6, Canada. Offers ministry (D Min); pastoral counseling (MA); social transformation ministry (MA); spirituality and liturgy (MA); theological studies (MTS); theology (M Th). *Program availability:* Part-time, evening/weekend, online learning. Terminal master's awarded for partial completion of doctoral program. *Degree requirements:* For master's, thesis; for doctorate, thesis/dissertation. *Entrance requirements:* Additional exam requirements/ recommendations for international students: required—TOEFL. Electronic applications accepted. *Expenses: Tuition:* Full-time $8294 Canadian dollars; part-time $4858 Canadian dollars per course.

St. Thomas University - Florida, School of Theology and Ministry, Institute for Pastoral Ministries, Miami Gardens, FL 33054-6459. Offers pastoral ministries (MA, Certificate); practical theology (PhD). *Program availability:* Part-time, evening/weekend. *Degree requirements:* For master's, comprehensive exam; for doctorate, comprehensive exam, thesis/dissertation. *Entrance requirements:* For master's, interview, minimum GPA of 3.0 or GRE; for doctorate, GRE, MA in theology. Additional exam requirements/ recommendations for international students: required—TOEFL (minimum score 550 paper-based; 79 iBT). Electronic applications accepted.

St. Tikhon's Orthodox Theological Seminary, Divinity Program, South Canaan, PA 18459. Offers M Div. *Accreditation:* ATS. *Program availability:* Part-time. *Degree requirements:* For master's, thesis optional. *Entrance requirements:* For master's, reference letters, official transcripts. Additional exam requirements/recommendations for international students: required—TOEFL (minimum score 560 paper-based; 87 iBT), IELTS (minimum score 5.5). *Expenses:* Contact institution.

St. Vincent de Paul Regional Seminary, Graduate and Professional Programs, Boynton Beach, FL 33436-4899. Offers theology (M Div, MA Th). *Accreditation:* ATS. *Program availability:* Part-time. *Degree requirements:* For master's, comprehensive exam (for some programs), thesis optional. *Entrance requirements:* For master's, GRE General Test, MAT. Additional exam requirements/recommendations for international students: required—TOEFL.

Saint Vincent Seminary, School of Theology, Latrobe, PA 15650-2690. Offers M Div, MA. *Accreditation:* ATS. *Program availability:* Part-time, evening/weekend. *Faculty:* 7 full-time (1 woman), 12 part-time/adjunct (2 women). *Students:* 45 full-time (0 women), 4 part-time (0 women); includes 2 minority (both Asian, non-Hispanic/Latino), 13 international. Average age 34. 13 applicants, 100% accepted, 13 enrolled. In 2019, 9 master's awarded. *Degree requirements:* For master's, one foreign language, comprehensive exam, thesis optional, public presentation. *Entrance requirements:* For master's, minimum GPA of 2.5. Additional exam requirements/recommendations for international students: required—TOEFL (minimum score 550 paper-based; 79 iBT). *Application deadline:* For fall admission, 8/15 priority date for domestic and international students. Applications are processed on a rolling basis. Application fee: $45. *Expenses:*

Tuition: Full-time $30,178; part-time $1003 per credit. *Financial support:* In 2019–20, 49 students received support. Scholarships/grants available. Support available to part-time students. *Unit head:* Very Rev. Edward M. Mazich, OSB, President/Rector, 724-805-2845, Fax: 724-532-5052, E-mail: edward.mazich@stvincent.edu. *Application contact:* Rev. Patrick T. Cronauer, OSB, Academic Dean, 724-805-2324, Fax: 724-805-2880, E-mail: patrick.cronauer@stvincent.edu.
Website: http://www.saintvincentseminary.edu

St. Vladimir's Orthodox Theological Seminary, Graduate School of Theology, Crestwood, NY 10707-1699. Offers general theological studies (MA); theology (M Div, M Th, D Min). *Accreditation:* ATS. *Program availability:* Part-time. *Faculty:* 7 full-time (1 woman), 23 part-time/adjunct (3 women). *Students:* 75 full-time (6 women), 2 part-time (0 women); includes 11 minority (1 Black or African American, non-Hispanic/Latino; 9 Asian, non-Hispanic/Latino; 1 Two or more races, non-Hispanic/Latino), 13 international. Average age 29. 41 applicants, 95% accepted, 37 enrolled. In 2019, 16 master's, 3 doctorates awarded. *Degree requirements:* For master's, one foreign language, comprehensive exam (for some programs), thesis (for some programs), fieldwork; for doctorate, thesis/dissertation, fieldwork. *Entrance requirements:* For doctorate, M Div, minimum GPA of 3.0. Additional exam requirements/recommendations for international students: required—TOEFL (minimum score 96 iBT). *Application deadline:* For fall admission, 5/1 priority date for domestic and international students. Applications are processed on a rolling basis. Application fee: $75. Electronic applications accepted. *Expenses: Tuition:* Full-time $12,000; part-time $1500 per course. *Required fees:* $150 per semester. Part-time tuition and fees vary according to course load and program. *Financial support:* In 2019–20, 74 students received support. Fellowships, research assistantships, teaching assistantships, and scholarships/grants available. Financial award application deadline: 4/1; financial award applicants required to submit FAFSA. *Unit head:* Rev. Dr. Chad Hatfield, President, 914-961-8313 Ext. 323, Fax: 914-961-4507, E-mail: hatfield@svots.edu. *Application contact:* Gabrielle Russin, Student Affairs Administrator, 914-961-8313 Ext. 348, Fax: 914-961-4507, E-mail: grussin@svots.edu.

Samford University, Beeson School of Divinity, Birmingham, AL 35229. Offers M Div, MATS, D Min, JD/M Div, JD/MATS, M Div/M Ed, M Div/MBA, M Div/MM, M Div/MSW, MATS/MSW. *Program availability:* Part-time. *Faculty:* 14 full-time (2 women), 2 part-time/adjunct (0 women). *Students:* 138 full-time (31 women), 15 part-time (8 women); includes 26 minority (24 Black or African American, non-Hispanic/Latino; 1 Asian, non-Hispanic/Latino; 1 Hispanic/Latino), 5 international. Average age 31. 56 applicants, 98% accepted, 27 enrolled. In 2019, 39 master's, 7 doctorates awarded. *Degree requirements:* For master's, 2 foreign languages, thesis optional; for doctorate, thesis/dissertation. *Entrance requirements:* For master's, Earned undergraduate degree in any discipline, Minimum 2.5 G.P.A; for doctorate, Earned Mast of Divinity Degree (or equivalent) with a minimum 3.0 G.P.A. Additional exam requirements/recommendations for international students: required—TOEFL (minimum score 550 paper-based; 80 iBT). *Application deadline:* For fall admission, 2/15 for domestic and international students; for spring admission, 10/1 for domestic and international students. Application fee: $35. Electronic applications accepted. *Expenses:* $15,790 per year. *Financial support:* In 2019–20, 127 students received support, including 6 teaching assistantships (averaging $1,200 per year); Federal Work-Study and scholarships/grants also available. Financial award application deadline: 2/15; financial award applicants required to submit FAFSA. *Unit head:* Dr. Douglas A Sweeney, Dean, Professor of Divinity, 205-726-2632, E-mail: dsweeney@samford.edu. *Application contact:* Sherri S. Brown, Director of Admission, 205-726-2066, E-mail: sbrown5@samford.edu.
Website: http://www.beesondivinity.com/

San Francisco Theological Seminary, Graduate and Professional Programs, San Anselmo, CA 94960. Offers M Div, MA, MATS, D Min, PhD, Th D, M Div/MA. *Accreditation:* ACIPE; ATS (one or more programs are accredited). *Program availability:* Part-time. *Degree requirements:* For master's, one foreign language, thesis (for some programs); for doctorate, thesis/dissertation. *Entrance requirements:* For master's, minimum GPA of 3.0; for doctorate, M Div. Additional exam requirements/recommendations for international students: required—TOEFL.

Santa Clara University, Jesuit School of Theology, Berkeley, CA 94709. Offers Biblical studies (MTS); Christian spirituality (MTS); church history (MTS); cultural and historical studies of Catholicism (MTS); divinity (M Div); ethics and social theory/religion and society (MTS); history of art and religion (MTS); liturgical studies (MTS); sacred theology (STD, STB, STL); systematic and philosophical theology (MTS); theology (Th M); M Div/MA. *Program availability:* Part-time, online learning. *Entrance requirements:* For master's and doctorate, Varies based on program. Additional exam requirements/recommendations for international students: required—TOEFL, IELTS, Applicants whose native language is not English are required to submit TOEFL or IELTS scores. Electronic applications accepted.

Seattle Pacific University, Master of Arts in Theology Program, Seattle, WA 98119-1997. Offers Asian American ministry (MA); business and applied theology (MA); Christian leadership (MA); Christian scripture (MA); Christian studies (Graduate Certificate); reconciliation and intercultural studies (MA); theology (MA). *Students:* 22 full-time (14 women), 30 part-time (13 women); includes 20 minority (10 Black or African American, non-Hispanic/Latino; 6 Asian, non-Hispanic/Latino; 3 Hispanic/Latino; 1 Native Hawaiian or other Pacific Islander, non-Hispanic/Latino), 3 international. Average age 34. 21 applicants, 52% accepted, 11 enrolled. In 2019, 15 master's awarded. *Degree requirements:* For master's, internship or thesis. *Entrance requirements:* For master's, two letters of recommendation; personal statement; bachelor's degree from regionally-accredited college or university or its equivalent; official copy of transcripts from college or university that granted the bachelor's degree and any institution attended since that time; minimum GPA of 3.0. Additional exam requirements/recommendations for international students: required—TOEFL (minimum score 600 paper-based; 100 iBT). *Application deadline:* For fall admission, 7/31 for domestic students, 6/15 for international students; for winter admission, 11/15 for domestic students; for spring admission, 2/15 for domestic students; for summer admission, 5/1 for domestic students. Applications are processed on a rolling basis. Application fee: $50. Electronic applications accepted. *Financial support:* Application deadline: 4/1; applicants required to submit FAFSA. *Unit head:* Dr. Doug Strong, Dean, 206-281-2473, E-mail: dstrong@spu.edu. *Application contact:* Dr. Doug Strong, Dean, 206-281-2473, E-mail: dstrong@spu.edu.
Website: https://spu.edu/academics/school-of-theology

Seattle Pacific University, Master of Divinity Program, Seattle, WA 98119-1997. Offers M Div. *Students:* 2 full-time (1 woman), 1 part-time (0 women). Average age 32. 19 applicants, 53% accepted, 10 enrolled. *Entrance requirements:* For master's, two letters of recommendation; personal statement; BA; official transcript; minimum GPA of 3.0. Additional exam requirements/recommendations for international students: required—TOEFL (minimum score 600 paper-based; 100 iBT). *Application deadline:* For fall admission, 7/31 for domestic students; for winter admission, 11/15 for domestic students; for spring admission, 2/15 for domestic students; for summer admission, 5/1 for domestic students. Application fee: $50. *Financial support:* Scholarships/grants available. Financial award applicants required to submit FAFSA. *Unit head:* Dr. Doug Strong, Dean, 206-281-2473, E-mail: dstrong@spu.edu. *Application contact:* Dr. Doug Strong, Dean, 206-281-2473, E-mail: dstrong@spu.edu.
Website: http://spu.edu/academics/seattle-pacific-seminary/programs/ma-divinity

The Seattle School of Theology and Psychology, Graduate Programs, Seattle, WA 98121. Offers Christian studies (MA); counseling psychology (MA); divinity (M Div). *Program availability:* Part-time. *Entrance requirements:* For master's, MAT.

Seattle University, School of Theology and Ministry, Program in Divinity, Seattle, WA 98122-1090. Offers M Div, D Min. *Accreditation:* ATS. *Program availability:* Part-time, evening/weekend. *Faculty:* 22 full-time (12 women), 22 part-time/adjunct (14 women). *Students:* 8 full-time (6 women), 49 part-time (28 women); includes 25 minority (16 Black or African American, non-Hispanic/Latino; 3 Asian, non-Hispanic/Latino; 4 Hispanic/Latino; 2 Two or more races, non-Hispanic/Latino), 1 international. Average age 44. 4 applicants, 100% accepted, 2 enrolled. In 2019, 7 master's, 5 doctorates awarded. *Entrance requirements:* For master's, minimum GPA of 2.75 (3.0 for international students); two years of experience in some form of education, ministry, or service as a profession or volunteer; recommendations; interview with admissions committee. *Application deadline:* For fall admission, 7/1 priority date for domestic students. *Financial support:* In 2019–20, 32 students received support. Career-related internships or fieldwork and Federal Work-Study available. Support available to part-time students. Financial award applicants required to submit FAFSA. *Unit head:* Dr. Mark Markuly, Dean, 206-296-5330, Fax: 206-296-5329, E-mail: markulym@seattleu.edu. *Application contact:* Catherine Kehoe Fallon, Admissions Coordinator, 206-296-5333, Fax: 206-296-5329, E-mail: fallon@seattleu.edu.
Website: https://www.seattleu.edu/stm/degrees/mdiv/

Seattle University, School of Theology and Ministry, Program in Transforming Spirituality, Seattle, WA 98122-1090. Offers MATS, Certificate. *Accreditation:* ATS. *Program availability:* Part-time, evening/weekend. *Faculty:* 22 full-time (12 women), 22 part-time/adjunct (14 women). *Students:* 1 full-time (0 women), 6 part-time (3 women); includes 1 minority (Black or African American, non-Hispanic/Latino), 1 international. Average age 46. 4 applicants, 100% accepted, 1 enrolled. In 2019, 2 master's, 1 Certificate awarded. *Entrance requirements:* For master's, minimum GPA of 2.75 (3.0 for international students); two years of experience in some form of education, ministry, or service as a profession or volunteer; recommendations; interview with admissions committee. *Application deadline:* For fall admission, 7/1 for domestic students. Application fee: $55. *Financial support:* In 2019–20, 8 students received support. Career-related internships or fieldwork and Federal Work-Study available. Support available to part-time students. Financial award application deadline: 4/1; financial award applicants required to submit FAFSA. *Unit head:* Dr. Mark Markuly, Director, 206-296-5330, Fax: 206-296-5329, E-mail: markulym@seattleu.edu. *Application contact:* Jean Adler Stean, Assistant Director of Admissions and Student Services, 206-296-5333, Fax: 206-296-5329, E-mail: steanj@seattleu.edu.
Website: http://www.seattleu.edu/stm/degrees/mats/

Seton Hall University, Immaculate Conception Seminary School of Theology, South Orange, NJ 07079-2697. Offers Christian spirituality (Certificate); great spiritual books (Certificate); pastoral ministry (M Div, MA, Certificate); scripture studies (Certificate); Seminary's Theological Education for Parish Services (STEPS) (Certificate); theology (MA). *Program availability:* Part-time, evening/weekend. *Degree requirements:* For master's, comprehensive exam (for some programs), thesis (for some programs), final project (for some programs); 1 foreign language (for MA in theology research option). *Entrance requirements:* For master's, GRE General Test or MAT. Additional exam requirements/recommendations for international students: required—TOEFL (minimum score 600 paper-based; 100 iBT). Electronic applications accepted. *Expenses:* Contact institution.

Shaw University, Divinity School, Raleigh, NC 27601-2399. Offers M Div, MACE. *Accreditation:* ATS. *Program availability:* Part-time, evening/weekend. *Degree requirements:* For master's, thesis. *Entrance requirements:* For master's, official undergraduate transcripts, letters of reference, essay, interview. Electronic applications accepted.

Shepherds Theological Seminary, Graduate Programs, Cary, NC 27518. Offers Biblical literature and languages (MA); church ministry (MA); ministry (MTS); New Testament (M Div); Old Testament (M Div); theology (M Div). *Accreditation:* ATS. *Degree requirements:* For master's, thesis.

Shiloh University, Graduate Programs, Kalona, IA 52247. Offers Christian ministries (M Div); leadership of church and spiritual formation (D Min); theological studies (MA). *Program availability:* Part-time, evening/weekend, online only, 100% online. *Degree requirements:* For master's, variable foreign language requirement, thesis optional; for doctorate, comprehensive exam, thesis/dissertation. *Entrance requirements:* For master's, bachelor's degree or educational equivalent from accredited school with minimum GPA of 2.5 on undergraduate work; for doctorate, M Div or equivalent with minimum GPA of 2.5 on graduate work; three years of ministry experience. Additional exam requirements/recommendations for international students: recommended—TOEFL (minimum score 540 paper-based; 76 iBT), IELTS (minimum score 6.5). Electronic applications accepted. *Expenses:* Contact institution.

Sh'or Yoshuv Rabbinical College, Graduate Programs, Far Rockaway, NY 11691-4002. *Accreditation:* AARTS.

Sioux Falls Seminary, Graduate and Professional Programs, Master of Divinity Program, Sioux Falls, SD 57105-1599. Offers marriage and family therapy (M Div); pastoral care and counseling (M Div). *Accreditation:* ACIPE. *Program availability:* Part-time, online learning.

Sioux Falls Seminary, Graduate and Professional Programs, Program in Bible and Theology, Sioux Falls, SD 57105-1599. Offers MA. *Accreditation:* ACIPE; ATS. *Program availability:* Part-time, online learning. *Degree requirements:* For master's, 2 foreign languages, thesis or alternative. *Entrance requirements:* For master's, minimum GPA of 2.5.

Sioux Falls Seminary, Graduate and Professional Programs, Program in Ministry, Sioux Falls, SD 57105-1599. Offers D Min. *Accreditation:* ACIPE. *Program availability:* Part-time. *Degree requirements:* For doctorate, thesis/dissertation. *Entrance requirements:* For doctorate, M Div, 3 years of ministry.

Sioux Falls Seminary, Graduate and Professional Programs, Program in Theological Studies, Sioux Falls, SD 57105-1599. Offers Certificate.

Southeastern Baptist Theological Seminary, Graduate and Professional Programs, Wake Forest, NC 27587. Offers advanced biblical studies (M Div); Christian education (M Div, MACE); Christian ethics (PhD); Christian ministry (M Div); Christian planting (M Div); church music (MACM); counseling (MACO); evangelism (PhD); language (M Div); ministry (D Min); New Testament (PhD); Old Testament (PhD); philosophy (PhD); theology (Th M, PhD); women's studies (M Div). *Accreditation:* ACIPE; ATS (one or more programs are accredited). *Degree requirements:* For master's, thesis (for some programs), oral exam; for doctorate, thesis/dissertation, fieldwork. *Entrance requirements:* For master's, Cooperative English Test, minimum GPA of 2.0, M Div or equivalent (Th M); for doctorate, GRE General Test or MAT, Cooperative English Test, M Div or equivalent, 3 years of professional experience.

Southeastern University, Barnett College of Ministry & Theology, Lakeland, FL 33801. Offers family ministry (MA); ministerial leadership (MA, D Min); theological studies (MA); theology (M Div). *Program availability:* Evening/weekend, online learning. *Faculty:* 30 full-time (5 women), 1 part-time/adjunct (0 women). *Students:* 103 full-time (38 women), 195 part-time (77 women); includes 90 minority (28 Black or African American, non-Hispanic/Latino; 1 American Indian or Alaska Native, non-Hispanic/Latino; 16 Asian, non-Hispanic/Latino; 37 Hispanic/Latino; 2 Native Hawaiian or other Pacific Islander, non-Hispanic/Latino; 6 Two or more races, non-Hispanic/Latino), 4 international. Average age 37. In 2019, 73 master's, 5 doctorates awarded. *Degree requirements:* For master's, thesis/project. *Entrance requirements:* Additional exam requirements/recommendations for international students: required—TOEFL (minimum score 76 iBT), IELTS (minimum score 6). Application fee: $50. Electronic applications accepted. *Unit head:* Dr. Alan Ehler, Dean, 863-667-5044, E-mail: ajehler@seu.edu. *Application contact:* Dr. Alan Ehler, Dean, 863-667-5044, E-mail: ajehler@seu.edu.
Website: http://www.seu.edu/ministry/

Southern Adventist University, School of Religion, Collegedale, TN 37315-0370. Offers evangelism and ministry (M Min); old Testament studies (MA); religious studies (MA). *Program availability:* Part-time. *Degree requirements:* For master's, comprehensive exam, thesis (for some programs). *Entrance requirements:* Additional exam requirements/recommendations for international students: required—TOEFL (minimum score 100 iBT).

The Southern Baptist Theological Seminary, Billy Graham School of Missions, Evangelism and Ministry, Louisville, KY 40280-0004. Offers ministry (D Min); missiology (MA, D Miss); missions and evangelism (M Div, Th M, PhD); theological studies (MA). *Accreditation:* ATS. *Program availability:* Part-time, evening/weekend, online learning. *Degree requirements:* For master's, 2 foreign languages; for doctorate, 4 foreign languages, thesis/dissertation. *Entrance requirements:* For doctorate, GRE General Test, MAT, M Div. Additional exam requirements/recommendations for international students: required—TOEFL, TWE.

The Southern Baptist Theological Seminary, School of Theology, Louisville, KY 40280-0004. Offers applied theology (D Min); biblical and theological studies (M Div); biblical counseling (M Div, MA, D Min); biblical spirituality (D Min); Christian ministry (M Div); expository preaching (D Min); pastoral studies (M Div); theological studies (MA); theology (Th M, PhD); worldview and apologetics (M Div). *Program availability:* Part-time, evening/weekend, online learning. *Degree requirements:* For master's, 2 foreign languages, thesis; for doctorate, 4 foreign languages, thesis/dissertation. *Entrance requirements:* For master's, GRE General Test, MAT, M Div; for doctorate, GRE General Test, MAT, interview, M Div, field essay. Additional exam requirements/recommendations for international students: required—TOEFL, TWE.

Southern California Seminary, Graduate and Professional Programs, El Cajon, CA 92019. Offers Biblical studies (MABS); counseling psychology (MACP); marriage and family therapy (MAMFT); psychology (Psy D); religious studies (MRS); theology (M Div). *Program availability:* Part-time, evening/weekend, online learning. *Degree requirements:* For master's, thesis (for some programs); for doctorate, thesis/dissertation. *Entrance requirements:* For doctorate, master's degree in psychology. Additional exam requirements/recommendations for international students: required—TOEFL (minimum score 550 paper-based). Electronic applications accepted.

Southern Evangelical Seminary, Graduate Programs, Matthews, NC 28105. Offers apologetics (MA, D Min, Certificate); Christian education (MA); church ministry (MA, Certificate); divinity (Certificate), including apologetics (M Div, Certificate); Islamic studies (MA, Certificate); Jewish studies (MA); philosophy (MA); philosophy of religion (PhD); religion (MA); theology (M Div), including apologetics (M Div, Certificate), Biblical studies; youth ministry (MA). *Program availability:* Part-time, evening/weekend, online learning. *Degree requirements:* For master's, thesis (for some programs); for doctorate, 2 foreign languages, comprehensive exam (for some programs), thesis/dissertation. *Entrance requirements:* Additional exam requirements/recommendations for international students: required—TOEFL (minimum score 600 paper-based). *Expenses: Tuition:* Full-time $24,000; part-time $12,000 per year. *Required fees:* $600; $300 per semester. $150 per semester.

Southern Methodist University, Perkins School of Theology, Dallas, TX 75275. Offers ministry (M Div, D Min); sacred music (MSM); theological studies (MTS). *Accreditation:* ACIPE. *Program availability:* Part-time. *Degree requirements:* For master's, thesis (for some programs), internship; for doctorate, internship, oral exam, professional project. *Entrance requirements:* For master's, minimum GPA of 2.75; for doctorate, minimum graduate GPA of 3.0, M Div or equivalent, 3 years of ministry experience. Additional exam requirements/recommendations for international students: required—TOEFL (minimum score 600 paper-based; 100 iBT), TWE. *Expenses:* Contact institution.

South Florida Bible College and Theological Seminary, Graduate Programs, Deerfield Beach, FL 33442. Offers biblical studies (MA); theology (M Div). *Degree requirements:* For master's, thesis.

Southwestern Assemblies of God University, Thomas F. Harrison School of Graduate Studies, Program in Theological Studies, Waxahachie, TX 75165-5735. Offers Bible and theology (MS); Biblical studies (M Div); counseling (M Div); cross cultural missions (M Div); practical theology (M Div); theological studies (M Div). *Program availability:* Online learning. *Degree requirements:* For master's, comprehensive written and oral exams. *Entrance requirements:* For master's, GRE General Test, minimum GPA of 2.5. Electronic applications accepted.

Southwestern Baptist Theological Seminary, Roy Fish School of Evangelism and Missions, Fort Worth, TX 76122-0000. Offers cross-cultural missions (MTS); evangelism (M Div); evangelism and missions (D Min); international church planting (M Div); Islamic studies (M Div, MA Islamic); missiology (MA Miss); missions (M Div); North American church planting (M Div); North American evangelism and international missions (D Min); theology (Th M); world Christian studies (PhD).

Southwestern Baptist Theological Seminary, School of Theology, Fort Worth, TX 76122-0000. Offers ministry (D Min); theology (PhD). *Accreditation:* ACIPE; ATS (one or more programs are accredited). *Program availability:* Part-time, evening/weekend. Terminal master's awarded for partial completion of doctoral program. *Degree requirements:* For master's, 2 foreign languages, thesis (for some programs); for doctorate, 2 foreign languages, comprehensive exam, thesis/dissertation, oral exams. *Entrance requirements:* For doctorate, GRE, M Div or equivalent. Additional exam requirements/recommendations for international students: required—TOEFL. Electronic applications accepted.

Spring Arbor University, School of Arts and Sciences, Spring Arbor, MI 49283-9799. Offers communication (MA); spiritual formation and leadership (MA). *Program availability:* Part-time, online learning. *Degree requirements:* For master's, thesis (for some programs). *Entrance requirements:* For master's, GRE (minimum score of 40th percentile and taken within last 5 years), bachelor's degree from regionally-accredited college or university, minimum GPA of 3.0 for at least the last two years of the bachelor's degree, at least two recommendations from professional/academic individuals. Additional exam requirements/recommendations for international students: required—TOEFL (minimum score 600 paper-based). *Expenses:* Contact institution.

Spring Hill College, Graduate Programs, Program in Theology, Mobile, AL 36608-1791. Offers MA, MPS, MTS, Postbaccalaureate Certificate. *Program availability:* Part-time, evening/weekend. *Students:* Average age 46. In 2019, 9 master's, 7 other advanced degrees awarded. *Degree requirements:* For master's, variable foreign language requirement, comprehensive exam, thesis (for some programs), completion of program within 6 calendar years of initial enrollment (MTS, MPS); completion of program within 4 1/2 calendar years of formal acceptance (MA). *Entrance requirements:* For master's, bachelor's degree with minimum undergraduate GPA of 3.0; six hours of undergraduate theology, religious studies, or unquestioned equivalency. Additional exam requirements/recommendations for international students: required—TOEFL (minimum score 550 paper-based; 80 iBT), IELTS (minimum score 6.5), CPE or CAE (minimum score C), Michigan English Language Assessment Battery (minimum score 90). *Application deadline:* For fall admission, 8/1 priority date for domestic and international students; for spring admission, 12/1 priority date for domestic and international students. Applications are processed on a rolling basis. Application fee: $25 ($35 for international students). Electronic applications accepted. *Expenses:* Contact institution. *Financial support:* Fellowships, research assistantships, teaching assistantships, and tuition waivers available. Financial award applicants required to submit FAFSA. *Unit head:* Dr. Timothy R. Carmody, Director, 251-380-4665, Fax: 251-460-2194, E-mail: carmody@shc.edu. *Application contact:* Gary Bracken, Vice President of Enrollment Management, 251-380-3038, Fax: 251-460-2186, E-mail: gbracken@shc.edu.
Website: http://ug.shc.edu/graduate-degrees/master-arts-theological-studies/

Starr King School for the Ministry, Professional Program, Berkeley, CA 94709-1209. Offers M Div. *Accreditation:* ACIPE; ATS.

SUM Bible College & Theological Seminary, Graduate Programs, Oakland, CA 94603. Offers biblical studies (MA); Christian leadership (MA); theology (M Div). *Entrance requirements:* For master's, minimum GPA of 2.5, currently active in ministry.

Talmudic University, Program in Talmudic Law, Miami Beach, FL 33140. Offers MRE. *Accreditation:* AARTS. *Degree requirements:* For master's, 2 foreign languages. *Entrance requirements:* For master's, oral exam, undergraduate Judaic studies degree.

Taylor College and Seminary, Graduate and Professional Programs, Edmonton, AB T6J 4T3, Canada. Offers Christian studies (Diploma); intercultural studies (MA, Diploma), including intercultural studies (Diploma), TESOL; theology (M Div, MTS). *Accreditation:* ATS. *Program availability:* Part-time, online learning. *Degree requirements:* For master's, thesis optional. *Entrance requirements:* Additional exam requirements/recommendations for international students: required—TOEFL (minimum score 550 paper-based; 80 iBT), IELTS (minimum score 6.5).

Toronto School of Theology, Graduate Centre for Theological Studies, Toronto, ON M5S 2C3, Canada. Offers M Div, MA, MAMS, MPS, MRE, MSM, MTS, Th M, D Min, PhD, Th D. Terminal master's awarded for partial completion of doctoral program. *Degree requirements:* For master's, thesis or alternative; for doctorate, 3 foreign languages, comprehensive exam, thesis/dissertation. *Entrance requirements:* Additional exam requirements/recommendations for international students: required—TOEFL, IELTS. *Application deadline:* For fall admission, 12/15 priority date for domestic and international students. Applications are processed on a rolling basis. Application fee: $120 Canadian dollars. Electronic applications accepted. *Unit head:* Pamela Couture, Director, 416-978-7822, Fax: 416-978-7821, E-mail: pamela.couture@utoronto.ca. *Application contact:* David Wagschal, Administrator, Graduate Centre for Theological Studies, 416-978-4050, Fax: 416-978-7821, E-mail: inquiries@tst.edu.
Website: http://www.tst.edu/

Trinity Bible College and Graduate School, Graduate School, Ellendale, ND 58436. Offers global theology (MA); missional leadership (MA); rural ministries (MA).

Trinity College, Faculty of Divinity, Toronto, ON M5S 1H8, Canada. Offers ministry (Diploma); ministry for church musicians (Diploma); theology (M Div, MA, MTS, Th M, D Min, PhD, Th D, Diploma, L Th); M Div/MA. *Accreditation:* ATS. *Program availability:* Part-time. *Degree requirements:* For master's, 2 foreign languages, thesis (for some programs); for doctorate, 3 foreign languages, comprehensive exam, thesis/dissertation; for other advanced degree, thesis (for some programs). *Entrance requirements:* For master's, 1 language (modern or ancient), interview; for doctorate, 2 languages (modern and ancient). Additional exam requirements/recommendations for international students: required—TOEFL, TWE.

Trinity International University, Trinity Evangelical Divinity School, Deerfield, IL 60015-1284. Offers academic ministry (M Div); Biblical and Near Eastern archaeology and languages (MA); chaplaincy and ministry care (MA); Christian studies (Certificate); church and parachurch ministry (M Div); church history (MA, Th M); counseling (Th M); educational ministries (MA); educational ministry (Th M); educational studies (PhD); intercultural studies (MA, PhD); leadership and management (D Min); mental health counseling (MA); military chaplaincy (D Min); ministry (MA); missions (Th M); missions and evangelism (D Min); New Testament (MA, Th M); Old Testament (Th M); Old Testament and Semitic languages (MA); pastoral ministry and care (D Min); pastoral theology (Th M); preaching and teaching (D Min); spiritual formation and education (D Min); systematic theology (MA, Th M); theological studies (MA, PhD); urban ministry (MA). *Program availability:* Part-time, online learning. *Degree requirements:* For master's, comprehensive exam, thesis, fieldwork; for doctorate, comprehensive exam (for some programs), thesis/dissertation; for Certificate, comprehensive exam, integrative papers. *Entrance requirements:* For master's, GRE, MAT, minimum cumulative undergraduate GPA of 3.0; for doctorate, GRE, minimum cumulative graduate GPA of 3.2; for Certificate, GRE, MAT, minimum undergraduate GPA of 2.5. Additional exam requirements/recommendations for international students: required—TOEFL (minimum score 580 paper-based), TWE (minimum score 4). Electronic applications accepted.

Trinity School for Ministry, Graduate Programs, Ambridge, PA 15003-2397. Offers Anglican studies (Diploma); basic Christian studies (Diploma); divinity (M Div); ministry (D Min); mission and evangelism (MAME, Diploma); religion (MAR); youth ministry (Diploma). *Program availability:* Part-time. *Degree requirements:* For master's, thesis optional; for doctorate, thesis/dissertation. *Entrance requirements:* Additional exam requirements/recommendations for international students: required—TOEFL.

Trinity Western University, ACTS Seminaries, Langley, BC V2Y 1Y1, Canada. Offers Christian studies (MA); cross cultural ministry (MA); theology (M Div, M Th, MAMFT, MLE, MTS, D Min). *Program availability:* Part-time. *Faculty:* 13 full-time (0 women), 20 part-time/adjunct (3 women). *Students:* 202 full-time (88 women), 184 part-time (79 women). Average age 35. In 2019, 73 master's awarded. *Degree requirements:* For master's, thesis (for some programs), internship. *Entrance requirements:* For doctorate, M Div or equivalent. Additional exam requirements/recommendations for international students: required—TOEFL (minimum score 100 iBT), IELTS (minimum score 7). *Application deadline:* Applications are processed on a rolling basis. Application fee: $150 Canadian dollars for international students. Electronic applications accepted. Application fee is waived when completed online. *Expenses:* Average of $520 per semester hour for tuition; $15 per semester hour for student fees. Average total tuition cost of $28,300. *Financial support:* Research assistantships, career-related internships or fieldwork, Federal Work-Study, institutionally sponsored loans, and scholarships/

grants available. Financial award application deadline: 3/1; financial award applicants required to submit FAFSA. *Unit head:* Ryan Klassen, ACTS Executive Director, E-mail: ryan.klassen@twu.ca. *Application contact:* Liisa Polkki, Director of Admissions, 604-513-2019, Fax: 604-513-2045, E-mail: acts@twu.ca.
Website: http://acts.twu.ca/

Trinity Western University, School of Graduate Studies, MA Biblical Studies and Christian Thought, Langley, BC V2Y 1Y1, Canada. Offers MA. *Accreditation:* ATS. *Program availability:* Part-time. In 2019, 2 master's awarded. *Degree requirements:* For master's, 2 foreign languages, thesis, 2 years Greek, 2 years Hebrew. *Entrance requirements:* For master's, minimum GPA of 3.0, degree in biblical studies, master of divinity or 42 hours Biblical Study credit. *Application deadline:* For fall admission, 6/15 priority date for domestic and international students; for spring admission, 11/1 priority date for domestic and international students. Applications are processed on a rolling basis. Electronic applications accepted. *Expenses: Tuition:* Full-time $13,000 Canadian dollars; part-time $8700 Canadian dollars per semester hour. *Required fees:* $504 Canadian dollars; $336 Canadian dollars per semester hour. $168 Canadian dollars per semester. Tuition and fees vary according to course load, campus/location, program, reciprocity agreements and student level. *Financial support:* Research assistantships, teaching assistantships, institutionally sponsored loans, scholarships/grants, and unspecified assistantships available. *Application contact:* Phil Kay, Director of Graduate and International Admissions, 604-513-2121 Ext. 3444, E-mail: phil.kay@twu.edu.
Website: http://www.twu.ca/biblical

Tri-State Bible College, Graduate Program, South Point, OH 45680-8402. Offers MA. *Entrance requirements:* For master's, bachelor's degree, minimum undergraduate GPA of 2.75, autobiographical statement, two letters of recommendation. Electronic applications accepted.

Truett McConnell University, Balthasar Hubmaier School of Theology and Missions, Cleveland, GA 30528. Offers theology (MA). *Program availability:* Part-time, 100% online. *Students:* 8 full-time (2 women), 12 part-time (2 women); includes 1 minority (Hispanic/Latino), 2 international. Average age 36. 17 applicants, 29% accepted, 2 enrolled. In 2019, 4 master's awarded. *Entrance requirements:* For master's, bachelor's degree from accredited institution, minimum cumulative GPA of 2.5. *Application deadline:* Applications are processed on a rolling basis. Electronic applications accepted. *Expenses: Tuition:* Full-time $6300; part-time $350 per credit hour. *Required fees:* $1010; $1010. Tuition and fees vary according to course load. *Financial support:* Application deadline: 8/1; applicants required to submit FAFSA. *Unit head:* Dr. Mael Disseau, Dean, 706-865-2134 Ext. 6606, E-mail: mdisseau@truett.edu. *Application contact:* Timothy Agee, Graduate Admissions Coordinator, 706-865-2134 Ext. 4305, E-mail: tagee@truett.edu.

Tyndale University College & Seminary, Graduate Programs, Toronto, ON M2M 3S4, Canada. Offers Biblical studies (M Div); Christian foundations (MTS); Christian studies (Diploma); counseling (M Div); educational ministry (M Div); missions (M Div, Diploma); pastoral and Chinese ministry (M Div); pastoral ministry (M Div); Pentecostal studies (MTS); spiritual formation (M Div, Diploma); theological studies (M Div); theology (Th M); worship and liturgy (M Div, MTS); youth and family ministry (M Div). *Accreditation:* ATS. *Program availability:* Part-time, online learning. *Entrance requirements:* For master's and Diploma, minimum C+ average in undergraduate course work. Additional exam requirements/recommendations for international students: required—TOEFL (minimum score 570 paper-based), TWE (minimum score 5). Electronic applications accepted.

Unification Theological Seminary, Graduate Programs, Barrytown, NY 12507. Offers family and educational ministry (D Min); interfaith peacebuilding (MRE); peace and justice ministry (D Min); religious education (MRE), including interfaith peacebuilding; religious studies (MA); theology (M Div). *Program availability:* Part-time, evening/weekend, 100% online, blended/hybrid learning. *Faculty:* 4 full-time (1 woman), 9 part-time/adjunct (1 woman). *Students:* 46 full-time (19 women), 62 part-time (24 women); includes 52 minority (27 Black or African American, non-Hispanic/Latino; 16 Asian, non-Hispanic/Latino; 4 Hispanic/Latino; 5 Two or more races, non-Hispanic/Latino), 34 international. Average age 44. In 2019, 3 master's, 7 doctorates awarded. *Degree requirements:* For master's, variable foreign language requirement, thesis (for some programs); for doctorate, thesis/dissertation. *Entrance requirements:* For master's, bachelor's degree; for doctorate, M Div or equivalency. Additional exam requirements/recommendations for international students: required—TOEFL (minimum score 550 paper-based; 83 iBT). *Application deadline:* For fall admission, 3/15 priority date for domestic and international students; for spring admission, 9/15 priority date for domestic and international students. Applications are processed on a rolling basis. Application fee: $30. Electronic applications accepted. *Expenses: Tuition:* Full-time $9720; part-time $540 per credit. *Required fees:* $270; $15 per credit. $90 per semester. *Financial support:* In 2019–20, 108 students received support. Scholarships/grants available. Financial award application deadline: 6/15; financial award applicants required to submit FAFSA. *Unit head:* Dr. Keisuke Noda, Academic Dean, 212-563-6647 Ext. 101, Fax: 212-563-6431, E-mail: k.noda@uts.edu. *Application contact:* Henry Christopher, Director of Admissions and Financial Aid, 212-563-6647 Ext. 105, Fax: 212-563-6431, E-mail: h.christopher@uts.edu.
Website: http://www.uts.edu/academics/academic-programs

Union Theological Seminary in the City of New York, Graduate and Professional Programs, New York, NY 10027-5710. Offers M Div, MA, STM, D Min, PhD, M Div/MSSW. *Accreditation:* ACIPE; ATS (one or more programs are accredited). *Program availability:* Part-time. *Degree requirements:* For master's, one foreign language, thesis; for doctorate, 2 foreign languages, thesis/dissertation. *Entrance requirements:* For doctorate, GRE General Test, sample of written work.

United Lutheran Seminary, Graduate and Professional Programs, Gettysburg, PA 17325-1795. Offers divinity (M Div); ministerial studies (MAMS); outdoor ministry (MAR); parish ministry (D Min); theology (STM). *Accreditation:* ACIPE; ATS (one or more programs are accredited). *Program availability:* Part-time, online learning. *Degree requirements:* For master's, thesis (for some programs). Electronic applications accepted. *Expenses: Tuition:* Full-time $19,500; part-time $1950 per credit. Tuition and fees vary according to course load.

United Lutheran Seminary, Graduate School, Philadelphia, PA 19119-1794. Offers divinity (M Div); ministry (D Min); public leadership (MA); religion (MAR); social ministry and church (Certificate); theology (STM, PhD). *Accreditation:* ACIPE. *Program availability:* Part-time, evening/weekend. *Degree requirements:* For master's, one foreign language, comprehensive exam (for some programs), thesis (for some programs); for doctorate, thesis/dissertation. *Entrance requirements:* For master's, minimum undergraduate GPA of 2.8; for doctorate, minimum GPA of 3.0. Additional exam requirements/recommendations for international students: required—TOEFL (minimum score 550 paper-based; 89 iBT), TWE. Electronic applications accepted.

United Talmudical Seminary, Graduate Programs, Brooklyn, NY 11211. *Accreditation:* AARTS.

United Theological Seminary, Graduate and Professional Programs, Dayton, OH 45426. Offers Christian ministries (MA); ministry (M Div, D Min); theological studies (MTS). *Accreditation:* ATS. *Program availability:* Part-time, evening/weekend, online learning. *Degree requirements:* For master's, thesis (for some programs); for doctorate, thesis/dissertation, final exam. *Entrance requirements:* For master's, minimum GPA of 2.5, interview, 5 letters of recommendation; for doctorate, minimum GPA of 3.0, 2 letters of recommendation, interview. Additional exam requirements/recommendations for international students: required—TOEFL (minimum score 550 paper-based). Electronic applications accepted.

United Theological Seminary of the Twin Cities, Graduate Programs, New Brighton, MN 55112-2598. Offers advanced theological studies (Diploma); justice and peace studies (M Div, MA); leadership toward racial justice (M Div, MA, Certificate); Methodist studies (M Div, MA, Certificate); ministry (D Min); ministry renewal and professional development (Certificate); pastoral care and counseling (M Div, MA, MARL); religion and theology (MA); theological and religious studies (Certificate); theology and the arts (M Div, MA); urban ministry (M Div, MA, MARL); women's studies: religion, theology and ministry (M Div, MA). *Accreditation:* ACIPE; ATS. *Program availability:* Part-time, evening/weekend. *Degree requirements:* For master's, thesis; for doctorate, comprehensive exam, thesis/dissertation. *Entrance requirements:* For master's, minimum GPA of 2.75; strong analytical, reflective thinking and writing skills; vocational and academic goals compatible with those of Seminary; for doctorate, M Div or equivalent, minimum GPA of 3.0, 3 years experience in professional ministry; for other advanced degree, BA or equivalent life experience; strong analytical, reflective thinking and writing skills (Certificate); proficiency in English language, previous study of theology at a theological school, recommendation of student's denomination (Diploma). Additional exam requirements/recommendations for international students: required—TOEFL (minimum score 550 paper-based).

Université de Montréal, Faculty of Theology and Sciences of Religions, Montréal, QC H3C 3J7, Canada. Offers health, spirituality and bioethics (DESS); practical theology (MA, PhD); religious sciences (MA, PhD); theology (MA, D Th, PhD, L Th); theology-Biblical studies (PhD). *Degree requirements:* For master's, one foreign language; for doctorate, 2 foreign languages, thesis/dissertation, general exam. Electronic applications accepted.

Université de Sherbrooke, Faculty of Theology and Religious Studies, Sherbrooke, QC J1K 2R1, Canada. Offers applied ethics (Diploma); human science of religions (MA); intercultural training (Diploma); philosophy (MA, PhD); spiritual anthropology (Diploma); theology (MA, PhD, Diploma). *Program availability:* Part-time, evening/weekend, online learning. Terminal master's awarded for partial completion of doctoral program. *Entrance requirements:* For master's, bachelor's degree in related discipline; for doctorate, master's degree in related discipline.

Université du Québec à Chicoutimi, Graduate Programs, Program in Theology (Pastoral Studies), Chicoutimi, QC G7H 2B1, Canada. Offers MA, PhD. *Program availability:* Part-time. *Degree requirements:* For doctorate, thesis/dissertation. *Entrance requirements:* For master's, appropriate bachelor's degree, proficiency in French; for doctorate, appropriate master's degree, proficiency in French.

University of Chicago, Divinity School, PhD Program, Chicago, IL 60637. Offers anthropology and sociology of religions (PhD); Bible (PhD); history of Christianity (PhD); history of Judaism (PhD); history of religions (PhD); Islamic studies (PhD); philosophy of religions (PhD); religion, literature, and visual culture (PhD); religions in America (PhD); religious ethics (PhD); theology (PhD). *Degree requirements:* For doctorate, 2 foreign languages, comprehensive exam, thesis/dissertation. *Entrance requirements:* For doctorate, GRE General Test, 3 letters of recommendation; transcripts; curriculum vitae or resume; writing sample. Additional exam requirements/recommendations for international students: required—TOEFL (minimum score 600 paper-based; 104 iBT), IELTS (minimum score 7). Electronic applications accepted.

University of Dayton, Department of Religious Studies, Dayton, OH 45469. Offers pastoral ministry (MA); theological studies (MA); theology (PhD). *Program availability:* Part-time. *Degree requirements:* For master's, thesis or alternative; for doctorate, 2 foreign languages, comprehensive exam, thesis/dissertation. *Entrance requirements:* For master's, 3 letters of recommendation, personal statement, all previous official transcript(s); for doctorate, GRE General Test (minimum score 600 verbal previous scale, 160 current scale), academic writing sample, 3 letters of recommendation, official transcript(s). Additional exam requirements/recommendations for international students: required—TOEFL (minimum score 550 paper-based; 80 iBT). Electronic applications accepted. *Expenses:* Contact institution.

University of Denver, DU/Iliff Joint PhD Program in the Study of Religion, Denver, CO 80208. Offers future faculty in religion (Certificate); Latinx studies (Certificate); study of religion (PhD). *Program availability:* Part-time. *Faculty:* 7 part-time/adjunct (3 women). *Students:* 19 full-time (7 women), 20 part-time (9 women); includes 5 minority (2 Black or African American, non-Hispanic/Latino; 1 Asian, non-Hispanic/Latino; 2 Hispanic/Latino), 4 international. Average age 38. 41 applicants, 46% accepted, 8 enrolled. In 2019, 9 doctorates, 1 other advanced degree awarded. *Degree requirements:* For doctorate, one foreign language, comprehensive exam, thesis/dissertation. *Entrance requirements:* For doctorate, GRE General Test, two-year master's degree relevant to the student's proposed research interests, transcripts, three letters of recommendation, personal statement, research paper. Additional exam requirements/recommendations for international students: required—TOEFL (minimum score 600 paper-based; 100 iBT). *Application deadline:* For fall admission, 1/15 priority date for domestic and international students. Applications are processed on a rolling basis. Application fee: $65. Electronic applications accepted. *Expenses:* Contact institution. *Financial support:* In 2019–20, 26 students received support, including 10 teaching assistantships (averaging $4,000 per year); scholarships/grants and unspecified assistantships also available. Financial award application deadline: 1/15. *Unit head:* Rhonda Eaker, Manager, DU/Iliff Joint PhD Program, 303- 765-3136, E-mail: Rhonda.Eaker@du.edu. *Application contact:* Information Contact, 303-765-3136, E-mail: jointphd@iliff.edu.
Website: http://www.du.edu/duiliffjoint

University of Dubuque, University of Dubuque Theological Seminary, Dubuque, IA 52001. Offers M Div, D Min. *Accreditation:* ACIPE; ATS. *Program availability:* Part-time, 100% online, blended/hybrid learning. *Degree requirements:* For doctorate, thesis/dissertation. *Entrance requirements:* Additional exam requirements/recommendations for international students: recommended—TOEFL (minimum score 550 paper-based; 80 iBT). Electronic applications accepted.

University of Holy Cross, Graduate Programs, New Orleans, LA 70131-7399. Offers biomedical sciences (MS); Catholic theology (MA); counseling (MA, PhD), including community counseling (MA), marriage and family counseling (MA), school counseling (MA); educational leadership (M Ed); executive leadership (Ed D); management (MS), including healthcare management, operations management; teaching and learning (M Ed). *Accreditation:* ACA; NCATE. *Program availability:* Part-time, evening/weekend, online learning. *Degree requirements:* For master's, thesis. *Entrance requirements:* For master's, GRE General Test, minimum GPA of 2.7.

The University of Manchester, School of Arts, Languages and Cultures, Manchester, United Kingdom. Offers anthropology, media and performance (PhD); applied theatre (PhD); Arab world studies (PhD); archaeology (PhD); art history and visual studies (PhD); arts and cultural management (PhD); arts management and cultural policy (PhD); Chinese studies (PhD); classics and ancient history (PhD); composition (PhD); creative writing (PhD); drama (PhD); East Asian studies (PhD); electroacoustic composition

(PhD); English and American studies (PhD); English language (PhD); French studies (PhD); German studies (PhD); history (PhD); humanitarianism and conflict response (PhD); interpreting studies (PhD); Japanese studies (PhD); Latin American cultural studies (PhD); linguistics (PhD); Middle Eastern studies (PhD); museology (PhD); museum practice (PhD); music (PhD); musicology (PhD); Polish studies (PhD); Portuguese studies (PhD); religions and theology (PhD); Russian studies (PhD); Spanish studies (PhD); translation and intercultural studies (PhD).

University of Mobile, Graduate Studies, Programs in Theology, Mobile, AL 36613. Offers biblical and theological studies (MA); worship leadership and theology (MA). *Program availability:* Part-time, evening/weekend. *Degree requirements:* For master's, 2 foreign languages, comprehensive exam, thesis optional. *Entrance requirements:* For master's, See catalog. Additional exam requirements/recommendations for international students: required—TOEFL (minimum score 550 paper-based; 80 iBT).

University of Northwestern–St. Paul, Master of Arts in Theological Studies Program, St. Paul, MN 55113-1598. Offers MATS. *Program availability:* Part-time, evening/weekend, online learning. Electronic applications accepted.

University of Northwestern–St. Paul, Master of Divinity Program, St. Paul, MN 55113-1598. Offers M Div. *Program availability:* Part-time, evening/weekend, online learning. Electronic applications accepted.

University of Notre Dame, The Graduate School, College of Arts and Letters, Division of Humanities, Department of Theology, Notre Dame, IN 46556. Offers M Div, MA, MSM, MTS, PhD. *Accreditation:* ACIPE; ATS. Terminal master's awarded for partial completion of doctoral program. *Degree requirements:* For master's, one foreign language, comprehensive exam, thesis or alternative; for doctorate, 3 foreign languages, comprehensive exam, thesis/dissertation, candidacy exam. *Entrance requirements:* For master's and doctorate, GRE General Test. Additional exam requirements/recommendations for international students: required—TOEFL (minimum score 600 paper-based; 80 iBT). Electronic applications accepted.

University of Notre Dame, The Graduate School, College of Arts and Letters, Division of Humanities, Program in History and Philosophy of Science, Notre Dame, IN 46556. Offers history and philosophy of science (MA, PhD); theology and science (PhD). *Degree requirements:* For doctorate, 2 foreign languages, comprehensive exam, thesis/dissertation, candidacy exam. *Entrance requirements:* For doctorate, GRE General Test. Additional exam requirements/recommendations for international students: required—TOEFL (minimum score 600 paper-based; 80 iBT). Electronic applications accepted.

University of Philosophical Research, Master's in Consciousness Studies Program, Los Angeles, CA 90027. Offers MA. *Degree requirements:* For master's, thesis. Electronic applications accepted.

University of Philosophical Research, Master's in Transformational Psychology Program, Los Angeles, CA 90027. Offers MA. *Degree requirements:* For master's, thesis. Electronic applications accepted.

University of Saint Mary of the Lake–Mundelein Seminary, Graduate and Professional Programs, Mundelein, IL 60060. Offers liturgical studies (MA); ministry (D Min); pastoral studies (MA); theology (M Div). *Accreditation:* ATS (one or more programs are accredited). *Degree requirements:* For doctorate, 2 foreign languages, comprehensive exam, thesis/dissertation. *Entrance requirements:* For master's and doctorate, bachelor's degree. Additional exam requirements/recommendations for international students: required—TOEFL (minimum score 550 paper-based). Electronic applications accepted.

University of St. Michael's College, Faculty of Theology, Toronto, ON M5S 1J4, Canada. Offers Catholic leadership (MA); eastern Christian studies (Diploma); religious education (Diploma); theological studies (Diploma); theology (M Div, MA, MRE, MTS, D Min, PhD, Th D); theology and Jewish studies (MA). *Accreditation:* ATS (one or more programs are accredited). *Program availability:* Part-time. *Degree requirements:* For master's, thesis (for some programs), 1 foreign language (MA), 2 foreign languages (Th M); for doctorate, 3 foreign languages, comprehensive exam, thesis/dissertation; for other advanced degree, thesis optional. *Entrance requirements:* For master's, M Div or BA, course work in an ancient or modern language, minimum GPA of 3.3; for doctorate, MA in theology, Th M, or M Div with thesis, minimum GPA of 3.7; for other advanced degree, minimum GPA of 2.7. Additional exam requirements/recommendations for international students: required—TOEFL (minimum score 600 paper-based). Electronic applications accepted. *Expenses:* Contact institution.

University of St. Thomas, The Saint Paul Seminary School of Divinity, St. Paul, MN 55105. Offers pastoral ministry (MAPM); religious education (MARE); theology (MA). *Accreditation:* ACIPE; ATS. *Program availability:* Part-time, evening/weekend. *Degree requirements:* For master's, one foreign language, comprehensive exam (for some programs), thesis (for some programs). *Entrance requirements:* For master's, GRE, 3 letters of recommendation, interview. Additional exam requirements/recommendations for international students: required—TOEFL (minimum score 550 paper-based). Electronic applications accepted. *Expenses:* Contact institution.

University of St. Thomas, School of Theology, Houston, TX 77006-4696. Offers divinity (M Div); pastoral studies (MAPS); theological studies (MA). *Accreditation:* ATS. *Program availability:* Part-time-only, online learning. *Faculty:* 7 full-time (2 women), 7 part-time/adjunct (1 woman). *Students:* 80 full-time (3 women), 78 part-time (29 women); includes 64 minority (5 Black or African American, non-Hispanic/Latino; 24 Asian, non-Hispanic/Latino; 34 Hispanic/Latino; 1 Two or more races, non-Hispanic/Latino), 25 international. Average age 38. 20 applicants, 100% accepted, 20 enrolled. In 2019, 15 master's awarded. *Degree requirements:* For master's, comprehensive exam (for some programs). *Entrance requirements:* For master's, Prerequisite Philosophy and Theology completed minimum hours. *Application deadline:* For fall admission, 7/30 for domestic students, 7/15 for international students; for spring admission, 12/15 for domestic students, 12/1 for international students; for summer admission, 5/1 for domestic students, 4/15 for international students. Applications are processed on a rolling basis. Application fee: $25. Electronic applications accepted. Application fee is waived when completed online. *Expenses:* $43,590 (for MDiv), $14,652 (for MAPS). *Financial support:* In 2019–20, 9 students received support. Applicants required to submit FAFSA. *Unit head:* Fr. Paul E. Lockey, Division Dean, 713-654-5760, E-mail: lockeyp@stthom.edu. *Application contact:* Beth Puayu, Assistant to the Dean, 713-654-5706, E-mail: puyaum@stthom.edu.
Website: http://www.stthom.edu/Academics/School_of_Theology_at_St_Marys_Seminary/Index.aqf

The University of Scranton, College of Arts and Sciences, Program in Theology, Scranton, PA 18510. Offers MA. *Program availability:* Part-time, evening/weekend. *Degree requirements:* For master's, comprehensive exam (for some programs), thesis (for some programs), capstone experience. *Entrance requirements:* For master's, minimum GPA of 3.0, three letters of reference. Additional exam requirements/recommendations for international students: required—TOEFL (minimum score 500 paper-based; 80 iBT), IELTS (minimum score 6.5). Electronic applications accepted.

University of South Africa, College of Human Sciences, Pretoria, South Africa. Offers adult education (M Ed); African languages (MA, PhD); African politics (MA, PhD); Afrikaans (MA, PhD); ancient history (MA, PhD); ancient Near Eastern studies (MA, PhD); anthropology (MA, PhD); applied linguistics (MA); Arabic (MA, PhD); archaeology (MA); art history (MA); Biblical archaeology (MA); Biblical studies (M Th, D Th, PhD); Christian spirituality (M Th, D Th); church history (M Th, D Th); classical studies (MA, PhD); clinical psychology (MA); communication (MA, PhD); comparative education (M Ed, Ed D); consulting psychology (D Admin, D Com, PhD); curriculum studies (M Ed, Ed D); development studies (M Admin, MA, D Admin, PhD); didactics (M Ed, Ed D); education (M Tech); education management (M Ed, Ed D); educational psychology (M Ed); English (MA); environmental education (M Ed); French (MA, PhD); German (MA, PhD); Greek (MA); guidance and counseling (M Ed); health studies (MA, PhD), including health sciences education (MA), health services management (MA), medical and surgical nursing science (critical care general) (MA), midwifery and neonatal nursing science (MA), trauma and emergency care (MA); history (MA, PhD); history of education (Ed D); inclusive education (M Ed, Ed D); information and communications technology policy and regulation (MA); information science (MA, MIS, PhD); international politics (MA, PhD); Islamic studies (MA, PhD); Italian (MA, PhD); Judaica (MA, PhD); linguistics (MA, PhD); mathematical education (M Ed); mathematics education (MA); missiology (M Th, D Th); modern Hebrew (MA, PhD); musicology (MA, MMus, D Mus, PhD); natural science education (M Ed); New Testament (M Th, D Th); Old Testament (D Th); pastoral therapy (M Th, D Th); philosophy (MA); philosophy of education (M Ed, Ed D); politics (MA, PhD); Portuguese (MA, PhD); practical theology (M Th, D Th); psychology (MA, MS, PhD); psychology of education (M Ed, Ed D); public health (MA); religious studies (MA, D Th, PhD); Romance languages (MA); Russian (MA, PhD); Semitic languages (MA, PhD); social behavior studies in HIV/AIDS (MA); social science (mental health) (MA); social science in development studies (MA); social science in psychology (MA); social science in social work (MA); social science in sociology (MA); social work (MSW, DSW, PhD); socio-education (M Ed, Ed D); sociolinguistics (MA); sociology (MA, PhD); Spanish (MA, PhD); systematic theology (M Th, D Th); TESOL (teaching English to speakers of other languages) (MA); theological ethics (M Th, D Th); theory of literature (MA, PhD); urban ministries (D Th); urban ministry (M Th).

The University of the South, School of Theology, Sewanee, TN 37383. Offers M Div, MA, STM, D Min. *Accreditation:* ACIPE. *Program availability:* Part-time. *Faculty:* 11 full-time (4 women), 8 part-time/adjunct (3 women). *Students:* 59 full-time (21 women), 6 part-time (3 women); includes 3 minority (1 Black or African American, non-Hispanic/Latino; 2 Hispanic/Latino), 6 international. Average age 40. In 2019, 24 master's, 5 doctorates awarded. *Degree requirements:* For master's, thesis (for some programs); for doctorate, thesis/dissertation. *Entrance requirements:* For master's, M Div (for STM); for doctorate, M Div. Additional exam requirements/recommendations for international students: required—TOEFL, IELTS. *Application deadline:* For fall admission, 7/1 for domestic students, 2/1 for international students. Applications are processed on a rolling basis. Application fee: $0. Electronic applications accepted. *Expenses:* Contact institution. *Financial support:* Institutionally sponsored loans and scholarships/grants available. Support available to part-time students. Financial award application deadline: 4/30. *Unit head:* James F. Turrell, Dean, 931-598-1288, Fax: 931-598-1412, E-mail: deansot@sewanee.edu. *Application contact:* Walker Adams, Director of Recruitment and Admission, 931-598-1283, E-mail: theologyadmissions@sewanee.edu.
Website: http://theology.sewanee.edu/

University of the West, Program in Buddhist Chaplaincy, Rosemead, CA 91770. Offers M Div. *Entrance requirements:* Additional exam requirements/recommendations for international students: required—TOEFL (minimum score 550 paper-based; 79 iBT); recommended—IELTS.

University of Valley Forge, Program in Theology, Phoenixville, PA 19460. Offers MA. *Degree requirements:* For master's, project.

The University of Winnipeg, Faculty of Theology, Winnipeg, MB R3B 2E9, Canada. Offers marriage and family therapy (MMFT, Certificate); sacred theology (STM); theology (M Div). *Accreditation:* AAMFT/COAMFTE. *Program availability:* Part-time.

Université Laval, Faculty of Theology and Religious Sciences, Program in Practical Theology, Québec, QC G1K 7P4, Canada. Offers D Th P. *Program availability:* Part-time. *Degree requirements:* For doctorate, comprehensive exam, thesis/dissertation. *Entrance requirements:* For doctorate, knowledge of French and English. Electronic applications accepted.

Université Laval, Faculty of Theology and Religious Sciences, Programs in Theology, Québec, QC G1K 7P4, Canada. Offers MA, PhD. Terminal master's awarded for partial completion of doctoral program. *Degree requirements:* For master's, thesis (for some programs); for doctorate, comprehensive exam, thesis/dissertation. *Entrance requirements:* For master's and doctorate, knowledge of French, comprehension of written English. Electronic applications accepted.

Urshan Graduate School of Theology, Graduate Programs, Florissant, MO 63031. Offers M Div, MACM, MTS. *Accreditation:* ATS. *Program availability:* Online learning. *Degree requirements:* For master's, capstone project (for MACM and MTS); portfolio (for M Div).

Ursuline College, School of Graduate and Professional Studies, Theological and Pastoral Studies Program, Pepper Pike, OH 44124-4398. Offers MA. *Program availability:* Part-time. *Faculty:* 2 full-time (both women). *Students:* 3 full-time (all women), 6 part-time (3 women); includes 4 minority (3 Black or African American, non-Hispanic/Latino; 1 Two or more races, non-Hispanic/Latino). Average age 52. 3 applicants, 100% accepted, 1 enrolled. In 2019, 3 master's awarded. *Degree requirements:* For master's, thesis. *Entrance requirements:* For master's, GRE when GPA under 3.0, minimum undergraduate GPA of 3.0, interview. Additional exam requirements/recommendations for international students: required—TOEFL (minimum score 550 paper-based; 80 iBT). *Application deadline:* For fall admission, 8/1 priority date for domestic students. Applications are processed on a rolling basis. Application fee: $25. Electronic applications accepted. *Expenses:* 36 credit hours at $702 per. *Financial support:* In 2019–20, 1 student received support. Federal Work-Study and scholarships/grants available. Financial award application deadline: 3/1; financial award applicants required to submit FAFSA. *Unit head:* Dr. Linda Martin, Director, 440-646-8191, Fax: 440-684-6088, E-mail: lmartin@ursuline.edu. *Application contact:* Melanie Steele, Director, Graduate Admissions, 440-646-8146, Fax: 440-684-6138, E-mail: graduateadmissions@ursuline.edu.

Vancouver School of Theology, Graduate and Professional Programs, Vancouver, BC V6T 1Z1, Canada. Offers denominational studies (Diploma); indigenous and inter-religious studies (MA, Diploma); public and pastoral leadership (MA); public and pastoral leadership in spiritual care (MA); theological studies (MATS, Diploma, Graduate Diploma); theology (M Div, Th M). *Accreditation:* ATS. *Program availability:* Part-time, online learning. *Degree requirements:* For master's, comprehensive exam (for some programs), thesis (for some programs); for other advanced degree, one foreign language, thesis. *Entrance requirements:* Additional exam requirements/recommendations for international students: required—TOEFL (minimum score 80 iBT); recommended—IELTS (minimum score 6.5). Electronic applications accepted.

Vanderbilt University, Divinity School, Nashville, TN 37240. Offers M Div, MTS, JD/M Div, JD/MTS, M Div/M Ed, MBA/M Div, MBA/MTS, MD/M Div, MD/MTS, MSN/M Div, MSN/MTS. *Accreditation:* ACIPE; ATS. *Program availability:* Part-time. *Entrance* *requirements:* Additional exam requirements/recommendations for international students: required—TOEFL (minimum score 600 paper-based; 95 iBT), IELTS (minimum score 7). Electronic applications accepted. *Expenses: Tuition:* Full-time $51,018; part-time $2087 per hour. *Required fees:* $542. Tuition and fees vary according to program.

Vanguard University of Southern California, Graduate Programs in Religion, Costa Mesa, CA 92626. Offers leadership studies (MA); theology (MA). *Program availability:* Part-time, evening/weekend, 100% online, blended/hybrid learning. *Degree requirements:* For master's, comprehensive exam (for some programs), thesis (for some programs). *Entrance requirements:* For master's, minimum GPA of 3.0 (MA), 2.5 (MTS). Additional exam requirements/recommendations for international students: required—TOEFL (minimum score 550 paper-based; 79 iBT). Electronic applications accepted. *Expenses:* Contact institution.

Victoria University, Emmanuel College, Toronto, ON M5S 1K7, Canada. Offers M Div, MA, MPS, MRE, MSMus, MTS, Th M, D Min, PhD, Th D, Certificate, Diploma, L Th, M Div/MA, M Div/MPS, M Div/MRE. Terminal master's awarded for partial completion of doctoral program. *Degree requirements:* For master's, variable foreign language requirement, thesis (for some programs); for doctorate, 2 foreign languages, thesis/dissertation. *Entrance requirements:* For master's and other advanced degree, BA, BSc; for doctorate, M Div, MA, MTS, Th M. Additional exam requirements/recommendations for international students: required—TOEFL (minimum score 600 paper-based; 100 iBT), IELTS (minimum score 7), TWE (minimum score 5). Electronic applications accepted.

Villanova University, Graduate School of Liberal Arts and Sciences, Department of Theology, Villanova, PA 19085-1699. Offers MA, PhD. *Program availability:* Part-time, evening/weekend. *Degree requirements:* For master's, variable foreign language requirement, comprehensive exam (for some programs), thesis optional; for doctorate, variable foreign language requirement, comprehensive exam (for some programs), thesis/dissertation. *Entrance requirements:* For master's, minimum GPA of 3.0, statement of goals, 3 recommendation letters; for doctorate, transcripts, 3 recommendation letters, essay, curriculum vitae or resume. Additional exam requirements/recommendations for international students: required—TOEFL. Electronic applications accepted.

Virginia Baptist College, Graduate Programs, Fredericksburg, VA 22407. Offers MBS, MCE, MM.

Virginia Beach Theological Seminary, Graduate Programs, Virginia Beach, VA 23464. Offers Biblical studies (MBS, Th M); chaplaincy (MBS); ministry (M Div). *Program availability:* Online learning. *Entrance requirements:* For master's, GRE, interview, minimum cumulative GPA of 2.4, church endorsement, 3 recommendations. Electronic applications accepted.

Virginia Theological Seminary, Graduate and Professional Programs, Alexandria, VA 22304. Offers Christian spirituality (D Min); educational leadership (D Ed Min, D Min); ministry development (D Min); theology (M Div, MA). *Accreditation:* ATS. *Program availability:* Part-time. *Degree requirements:* For master's, 2 foreign languages, thesis; for doctorate, thesis/dissertation. *Entrance requirements:* For master's and doctorate, GRE General Test.

Virginia Union University, Samuel DeWitt Proctor School of Theology, Richmond, VA 23220-1170. Offers M Div, D Min. *Accreditation:* ACIPE. *Program availability:* Part-time, evening/weekend. *Entrance requirements:* Additional exam requirements/recommendations for international students: required—TOEFL.

Walsh University, Master of Arts in Theology Program, North Canton, OH 44720-3396. Offers parish administration (MA); pastoral ministry (MA); religious education (MA). *Program availability:* Part-time, evening/weekend, 100% online. *Faculty:* 2 full-time (0 women), 1 part-time/adjunct (0 women). *Students:* 2 full-time (1 woman), 11 part-time (5 women); includes 1 minority (Black or African American, non-Hispanic/Latino). Average age 45. In 2019, 4 master's awarded. *Degree requirements:* For master's, thesis or alternative, culminating assignment. *Entrance requirements:* For master's, minimum GPA of 3.0, Writing sample. Additional exam requirements/recommendations for international students: required—TOEFL (minimum score 500 paper-based; 61 iBT). *Application deadline:* For fall admission, 7/15 for domestic students. Applications are processed on a rolling basis. Application fee: $0. Electronic applications accepted. *Expenses:* Tuition: $372/credit hour; $50 technology fee. *Financial support:* Unspecified assistantships available. Financial award application deadline: 12/31; financial award applicants required to submit FAFSA. *Unit head:* Dr. Chris Seeman, Graduate Program Director, 330-244-4665, E-mail: cseeman@walsh.edu. *Application contact:* Dr. Chris Seeman, Graduate Program Director, 330-244-4665, E-mail: cseeman@walsh.edu. Website: http://www.walsh.edu/

Wartburg Theological Seminary, Graduate and Professional Programs, Dubuque, IA 52004-5004. Offers diaconal ministry (MA); ministry (M Div); theology (MA). *Accreditation:* ACIPE; ATS. *Program availability:* Online learning. *Degree requirements:* For master's, thesis (for some programs). *Entrance requirements:* For master's, minimum GPA of 3.0 (STM). Additional exam requirements/recommendations for international students: required—TOEFL (minimum score 500 paper-based; 80 iBT). Electronic applications accepted.

Wayland Baptist University, Graduate Programs, Programs in Religion, Plainview, TX 79072-6998. Offers Christian ministry (MCM); divinity (M Div); religion (MA). *Program availability:* Part-time, evening/weekend, online learning. *Degree requirements:* For master's, comprehensive exam. *Entrance requirements:* For master's, GRE or MAT, minimum GPA of 3.0; letter of endorsement from Christian congregation, one academic and one personal letter of recommendation (for M Div). Additional exam requirements/recommendations for international students: required—TOEFL (minimum score 500 paper-based; 61 iBT). Electronic applications accepted. *Expenses: Tuition:* Full-time $728; part-time $728 per semester. *Required fees:* $1218. Tuition and fees vary according to degree level, campus/location and program.

Welch College, Program in Theology and Ministry, Gallatin, TN 37066. Offers MA. *Program availability:* Online learning.

Wesley Biblical Seminary, Graduate Programs, Jackson, MS 39206. Offers apologetics (MA); Biblical languages (M Div); Biblical literature (MA); Christian studies (MA); context and mission (M Div); honors research (M Div); interpretation (M Div); ministry (M Div); spiritual formation (M Div); teaching (M Div); theology (MA). *Accreditation:* ATS. *Program availability:* Part-time. *Degree requirements:* For master's, thesis. *Entrance requirements:* Additional exam requirements/recommendations for international students: required—TOEFL. Electronic applications accepted.

Wesley Theological Seminary, Graduate and Professional Programs, Washington, DC 20016-5690. Offers M Div, MA, MTS, D Min, M Div/MA, M Div/MTS. *Accreditation:* ACIPE; ATS. *Program availability:* Part-time. *Degree requirements:* For master's, thesis; for doctorate, thesis/dissertation. *Entrance requirements:* For master's, minimum GPA of 2.7; for doctorate, minimum GPA of 3.0.

Western Seminary - Portland, Graduate Programs, Master of Divinity Program, Portland, OR 97215-3367. Offers M Div. *Entrance requirements:* Additional exam requirements/recommendations for international students: required—TOEFL.

Western Seminary - Portland, Graduate Programs, Program in Biblical and Theological Studies, Portland, OR 97215-3367. Offers biblical and theological studies (MA, G Dip); biblical studies (Certificate); theology (Th M). *Accreditation:* ATS. *Program availability:* Part-time, evening/weekend. *Degree requirements:* For master's, thesis or alternative, practicum. *Entrance requirements:* Additional exam requirements/recommendations for international students: required—TOEFL.

Western Seminary–Sacramento Campus, Graduate Certificate Programs, Rocklin, CA 95765. Offers Bible (Graduate Certificate); coaching (Graduate Certificate); pastoral care to women (Graduate Certificate); theology (Graduate Certificate); youth and family (Graduate Certificate). *Program availability:* Online learning. *Entrance requirements:* For degree, essays, undergraduate transcripts, 4 recommendations. Additional exam requirements/recommendations for international students: required—TOEFL.

Western Seminary–Sacramento Campus, Graduate Diploma Programs, Rocklin, CA 95765. Offers Bible and theology (Graduate Diploma); ministry (Graduate Diploma); pastoral care to women (Graduate Diploma). *Entrance requirements:* For degree, essays, undergraduate transcripts, 4 recommendations. Additional exam requirements/recommendations for international students: required—TOEFL.

Western Seminary–Sacramento Campus, Master of Divinity Program, Rocklin, CA 95765. Offers M Div. *Entrance requirements:* Additional exam requirements/recommendations for international students: required—TOEFL.

Western Seminary–Sacramento Campus, Program in Biblical and Theological Studies, Rocklin, CA 95765. Offers MA. *Entrance requirements:* For master's, essays, undergraduate transcripts, 4 recommendations. Additional exam requirements/recommendations for international students: required—TOEFL.

Western Seminary - San Jose Campus, Graduate Programs, Milpitas, CA 95035. Offers Bible and theology (Graduate Diploma); Bible, camp and conference ministry (CGS); Biblical and theological studies (MA), including exegetical track, theological track; coaching (CGS); expositional ministry (M Div); marital and family therapy (MA); ministry (Graduate Diploma); ministry and leadership (MA), including camp and conference ministry, coaching, pastoral care to women, youth ministry; pastoral care to women (CGS, Graduate Diploma); pastoral ministry (M Div); theology (CGS); youth and family (CGS). *Program availability:* Part-time, evening/weekend, online learning. *Entrance requirements:* For master's, minimum GPA of 3.0. Electronic applications accepted.

Western Theological Seminary, Graduate and Professional Programs, Holland, MI 49423-3622. Offers divinity (M Div); ministry (D Min); theology (M Th, MA); urban pastoral ministry (Graduate Certificate); M Div/MSW. *Accreditation:* ACIPE; ATS. *Program availability:* Part-time, 100% online, blended/hybrid learning. *Degree requirements:* For doctorate, thesis/dissertation. *Entrance requirements:* Additional exam requirements/recommendations for international students: required—TOEFL. Electronic applications accepted. *Expenses: Tuition:* Full-time $1580; part-time $8910 per credit hour. *Required fees:* $100; $100 per semester.

Westminster Seminary California, Programs in Theology, Escondido, CA 92027-4128. Offers Biblical studies (MA); historical theology (MA); theological studies (M Div, MA). *Program availability:* Part-time, evening/weekend. *Degree requirements:* For master's, 2 foreign languages, thesis (for some programs). *Entrance requirements:* For master's, 2 letters of reference. Additional exam requirements/recommendations for international students: required—TOEFL (minimum score 570 paper-based; 89 iBT), TWE (minimum score 4.5).

Westminster Theological Seminary, Graduate and Professional Programs, Philadelphia, PA 19118. Offers apologetics (Th M); Biblical and urban studies (Certificate); Biblical counseling (MA); biblical studies (MAR); Christian studies (Certificate); church history (Th M); counseling (M Div); general studies (M Div, MAR); hermeneutics and Bible interpretations (PhD); historical and theological studies (PhD); historical theology (Th M); New Testament (Th M); Old Testament (Th M); pastoral counseling (D Min); pastoral ministry (M Div, D Min); systematic theology (Th M); theological studies (MAR); urban missions (M Div, MA, MAR, D Min). *Accreditation:* ATS. *Program availability:* Part-time. Terminal master's awarded for partial completion of doctoral program. *Degree requirements:* For master's, thesis (for some programs); for doctorate, 4 foreign languages, comprehensive exam (for some programs), thesis/dissertation. *Entrance requirements:* For doctorate, GRE General Test. Additional exam requirements/recommendations for international students: required—TOEFL, TWE.

Wheaton College, Graduate School, Evangelism and Leadership Program, Wheaton, IL 60187-5593. Offers evangelism and leadership (MA); missional church movements (MA). *Program availability:* Part-time. *Degree requirements:* For master's, thesis or alternative. *Entrance requirements:* For master's, GRE or MAT. Additional exam requirements/recommendations for international students: required—TOEFL (minimum score 550 paper-based; 80 iBT), IELTS (minimum score 6.5). Electronic applications accepted. *Expenses: Tuition:* Full-time $16,800; part-time $700 per credit hour. Tuition and fees vary according to degree level and program.

Wheaton College, Graduate School, School of Biblical and Theological Studies, Wheaton, IL 60187-5593. Offers Biblical and theological studies (PhD); Biblical archaeology (MA); Biblical exegesis (MA); Biblical studies (MA); general theological studies (MA); historical and systematic theology (MA), including Biblical and theological studies; history of Christianity (MA), including Biblical and theological studies. *Program availability:* Part-time. *Degree requirements:* For doctorate, thesis/dissertation. *Entrance requirements:* For master's, GRE General Test. Additional exam requirements/recommendations for international students: required—TOEFL (minimum score 550 paper-based; 80 iBT), IELTS (minimum score 6.5). Electronic applications accepted. *Expenses: Tuition:* Full-time $16,800; part-time $700 per credit hour. Tuition and fees vary according to degree level and program.

Whitworth University, Graduate Studies in Theology, Spokane, WA 99251-0001. Offers Christian ministry (MA); mission and culture (MA); theology (MA). *Program availability:* Part-time, evening/weekend. Electronic applications accepted. *Expenses: Tuition:* Full-time $11,970; part-time $3990 per credit. Tuition and fees vary according to course load and program.

Wilfrid Laurier University, Waterloo Lutheran Seminary, Waterloo, ON N2L 3C5, Canada. Offers divinity (M Div); multifaith spiritual care and counseling (Diploma); pastoral leadership (D Min); spiritual care and counseling (D Min); theology (M Th, MTS); M Div/MTS/MSW. *Accreditation:* ATS. *Program availability:* Part-time. *Degree requirements:* For master's, one foreign language, thesis (for some programs); for doctorate, thesis/dissertation. *Entrance requirements:* For master's, two letters of reference; for doctorate, M Div, two letters of reference. Additional exam requirements/recommendations for international students: required—TOEFL (minimum score 573 paper-based; 89 iBT), IELTS (minimum score 7). Electronic applications accepted. *Expenses:* Contact institution.

Winebrenner Theological Seminary, Graduate Programs, Findlay, OH 45840. Offers clinical counseling (MA); family ministry (MA); practical theology (MA); theological and ministerial studies (M Div, D Min); theological studies (MA). *Accreditation:* ATS (one or more programs are accredited). *Program availability:* Part-time, 100% online, blended/ hybrid learning. *Degree requirements:* For master's, variable foreign language requirement, thesis (for some programs); for doctorate, thesis/dissertation. *Entrance requirements:* For doctorate, 3 years of post-M Div full-time ministry. Additional exam requirements/recommendations for international students: required—TOEFL (minimum score 550 paper-based; 80 iBT). Electronic applications accepted. *Expenses:* Tuition: Full-time $9450; part-time $525 per credit. Tuition and fees vary according to course load, degree level and program.

World Mission University, Graduate Programs, Los Angeles, CA 90020. Offers biblical preaching (M Div); Christian counseling (M Div, MACC); church ministry (M Div); church music (M Div, DCM); ministry (D Min); music (MA); theology (MAT). *Program availability:* Online learning.

Wycliffe College, Division of Advanced Degree Studies, Toronto, ON M5S 1H7, Canada. Offers MA, Th M, D Min, PhD, Th D. *Accreditation:* ATS (one or more programs are accredited). *Program availability:* Part-time. Terminal master's awarded for partial completion of doctoral program. *Degree requirements:* For master's, 2 foreign languages, thesis (for some programs); for doctorate, 3 foreign languages, thesis/ dissertation. *Entrance requirements:* Additional exam requirements/recommendations for international students: required—TOEFL (minimum score 600 paper-based). *Expenses:* Contact institution.

Wycliffe College, Division of Basic Degree Studies, Toronto, ON M5S 1H7, Canada. Offers Christian Studies (Diploma); theology (M Div, M Rel, MTS). *Accreditation:* ATS. *Program availability:* Part-time. *Degree requirements:* For master's, one foreign language, thesis. *Entrance requirements:* Additional exam requirements/ recommendations for international students: required—TOEFL (minimum score 580 paper-based).

Xavier University, College of Arts and Sciences, Department of Theology, Cincinnati, OH 45207. Offers health care mission integration (MA); theology (MA), including religious education, social and pastoral ministry, theology. *Program availability:* Part-time, evening/weekend. *Degree requirements:* For master's, final paper (or thesis) and defense or comprehension exam. *Entrance requirements:* For master's, MAT or GRE, 2 letters of recommendation; statement of reasons and goals for enrolling in program (1,000-2,000 words); resume; transcript. Additional exam requirements/ recommendations for international students: required—TOEFL (minimum score 550 paper-based; 79 iBT). Electronic applications accepted. Application fee is waived when completed online. *Expenses:* Contact institution.

Xavier University of Louisiana, Graduate School, Institute for Black Catholic Studies, New Orleans, LA 70125. Offers pastoral theology (Th M). *Program availability:* Part-time. *Degree requirements:* For master's, comprehensive exam, practicum. *Entrance requirements:* For master's, GRE General Test, MAT, minimum GPA of 2.5. Additional exam requirements/recommendations for international students: required—TOEFL. Electronic applications accepted.

Yale University, Yale Divinity School, New Haven, CT 06511. Offers M Div, MAR, STM, JD/M Div, JD/MAR, M Div/MBA, M Div/MF, M Div/MSN, M Div/MSW, MAR/MSN, MAR/ MSW, MD/M Div, MD/MAR. *Accreditation:* ACIPE; ATS. *Program availability:* Part-time. *Entrance requirements:* Additional exam requirements/recommendations for international students: required—IELTS (minimum score 7). Electronic applications accepted. *Expenses:* Contact institution.

Yeshiva Beth Moshe, Graduate Programs, Scranton, PA 18505-2124. Offers Second Talmudical Degree, Talmudic Fellow Degree. *Accreditation:* AARTS.

Yeshiva Karlin Stolin, Graduate Programs, Brooklyn, NY 11204. Offers Advanced Rabbinical Degree. *Accreditation:* AARTS.

Yeshiva of Nitra Rabbinical College, Graduate Programs, Mount Kisco, NY 10549. Offers First Talmudic Degree, Second Talmudic Degree. *Accreditation:* AARTS.

Yeshiva Shaar Hatorah Talmudic Research Institute, Graduate Programs, Kew Gardens, NY 11418-1469. *Accreditation:* AARTS.

Yeshivath Zichron Moshe, Graduate Programs, South Fallsburg, NY 12779. Offers Advanced Talmudic Degree, Talmudic Scholar Degree. *Accreditation:* AARTS. *Program availability:* Part-time.

Section 13
Writing

This section contains a directory of institutions offering graduate work in writing, followed by an in-depth entry submitted by an institution that chose to prepare a detailed program description. Additional information about programs listed in the directory but not augmented by an in-depth entry may be obtained by writing directly to the dean of a graduate school or chair of a department at the address given in the directory.

For programs offering related work, see also in this book *Communication and Media* and *Language and Literature*.

CONTENTS

Program Directories

Technical Writing

Carnegie Mellon University, Dietrich College of Humanities and Social Sciences, Department of English, Program in Professional Writing, Pittsburgh, PA 15213-3891. Offers editing and publishing (MAPW); policy and non-profit communication (MAPW); public and media relations/corporate communications (MAPW); science or healthcare communication (MAPW); technical writing (MAPW); writing for new media (MAPW); writing for print media (MAPW). *Program availability:* Part-time. *Entrance requirements:* For master's, GRE General Test. Additional exam requirements/recommendations for international students: required—TOEFL, TWE.

Drexel University, College of Arts and Sciences, Department of Communication, Culture and Media, Philadelphia, PA 19104-2875. Offers communication (MS), including public communication, science communication, technical communication. *Program availability:* Part-time, evening/weekend. *Degree requirements:* For master's, internship, professional portfolio. *Entrance requirements:* Additional exam requirements/recommendations for international students: required—TOEFL. Electronic applications accepted.

Illinois Institute of Technology, Graduate College, Lewis College of Human Sciences, Department of Humanities, Chicago, IL 60616. Offers information architecture (MS); technical communication (PhD); technical communication and information design (MS). *Program availability:* Part-time. *Degree requirements:* For master's, comprehensive exam, thesis or alternative; for doctorate, comprehensive exam, thesis/dissertation. *Entrance requirements:* For master's, GRE General Test (minimum score 144 Quantitative, 153 Verbal, and 4.0 Analytical Writing), minimum undergraduate GPA of 3.0; 2 letters of recommendation from faculty or supervisors; professional statement discussing academic goals; for doctorate, GRE General Test (minimum score 144 Quantitative, 153 Verbal, and 4.0 Analytical Writing), bachelor's or master's degree in a field that, in combination with the 27-credit hour technical core, would provide a solid basis for advanced academic work leading to original research in the field; 3 letters of recommendation from faculty or supervisors; professional statement discussing academic goals. Additional exam requirements/recommendations for international students: required—TOEFL (minimum score 95 iBT); recommended—IELTS (minimum score 7). Electronic applications accepted.

James Madison University, The Graduate School, College of Arts and Letters, Program in Writing, Rhetoric, and Technical Communication, Harrisonburg, VA 22807. Offers MA, MS. *Program availability:* Part-time. *Students:* 10 full-time (6 women), 4 part-time (all women); includes 2 minority (1 Black or African American, non-Hispanic/Latino; 1 Asian, non-Hispanic/Latino). Average age 30. In 2019, 9 master's awarded. Application fee: $60. Electronic applications accepted. *Financial support:* In 2019–20, 10 students received support, including 2 teaching assistantships with full tuition reimbursements available (averaging $9,284 per year); fellowships, career-related internships or fieldwork, Federal Work-Study, and assistantships (averaging $7911) also available. Financial award application deadline: 3/1; financial award applicants required to submit FAFSA. *Unit head:* Dr. Traci A. Zimmerman, Director of the School of Writing, Rhetoric and Technical Communication, 540-568-2334, E-mail: zimmerta@jmu.edu. *Application contact:* Lynette D. Michael, Director of Graduate Admissions, 540-568-6131 Ext. 6395, Fax: 540-568-7860, E-mail: michaeld@jmu.edu. Website: http://www.jmu.edu/wrtc/

Johns Hopkins University, Advanced Academic Programs, Program in Writing, Washington, DC 21218. Offers science writing (MA, Certificate); writing (MA). *Program availability:* Part-time, evening/weekend. *Entrance requirements:* For master's, minimum GPA of 3.0, writing samples. Additional exam requirements/recommendations for international students: required—TOEFL (minimum score 600 paper-based; 100 iBT). Electronic applications accepted.

Laurentian University, School of Graduate Studies and Research, Programme in Science Communication, Sudbury, ON P3E 2C6, Canada. Offers G Dip.

Louisiana Tech University, Graduate School, College of Liberal Arts, Ruston, LA 71272. Offers architecture (M Arch); art (MFA), including graphic design, photography, studio; audiology (Au D); communication (MA), including speech communication, theatre; English (MA), including literature, technical writing; history (MA); speech pathology (MA); technical writing and communication (Graduate Certificate). *Accreditation:* ASHA. *Program availability:* Part-time. *Degree requirements:* For master's, thesis (for some programs); for doctorate, thesis/dissertation. *Entrance requirements:* For master's, GRE General Test; for doctorate, GRE General Test, bachelor's degree, minimum GPA of 3.0 or 3.2 on last 60 hours attempted. Additional exam requirements/recommendations for international students: required—TOEFL (minimum score 550 paper-based; 80 iBT), IELTS (minimum score 6.5). Electronic applications accepted. *Expenses: Tuition, area resident:* Full-time $6592; part-time $400 per credit. Tuition, state resident: full-time $6592; part-time $400 per credit. Tuition, nonresident: full-time $13,333; part-time $681 per credit. *International tuition:* $13,333 full-time. *Required fees:* $3011; $3011 per unit.

Massachusetts Institute of Technology, School of Humanities, Arts, and Social Sciences, Program in Comparative Media Studies/Writing, Graduate Program in Science Writing, Cambridge, MA 02139. Offers SM. *Degree requirements:* For master's, thesis. *Entrance requirements:* For master's, GRE General Test. Additional exam requirements/recommendations for international students: required—TOEFL, IELTS. Electronic applications accepted.

Metropolitan State University, College of Liberal Arts, St. Paul, MN 55106-5000. Offers liberal studies (MA); technical communication (MS). *Program availability:* Part-time, evening/weekend. *Entrance requirements:* For master's, minimum GPA of 2.75, resume. Additional exam requirements/recommendations for international students: required—TOEFL (minimum score 550 paper-based). Electronic applications accepted.

Texas Tech University, Graduate School, College of Arts and Sciences, Department of English, Lubbock, TX 79409-3091. Offers English (MA, PhD); technical communication (MA); technical communication and rhetoric (PhD). *Program availability:* Part-time, evening/weekend, 100% online, blended/hybrid learning. *Faculty:* 67 full-time (34 women), 4 part-time/adjunct (3 women). *Students:* 105 full-time (67 women), 102 part-time (74 women); includes 44 minority (8 Black or African American, non-Hispanic/Latino; 1 American Indian or Alaska Native, non-Hispanic/Latino; 2 Asian, non-Hispanic/Latino; 24 Hispanic/Latino; 9 Two or more races, non-Hispanic/Latino), 11 international. Average age 33. 201 applicants, 54% accepted, 58 enrolled. In 2019, 16 master's, 28 doctorates awarded. Terminal master's awarded for partial completion of doctoral program. *Degree requirements:* For master's, variable foreign language requirement, comprehensive exam, thesis optional; for doctorate, variable foreign language requirement, comprehensive exam, thesis/dissertation. *Entrance requirements:* For master's and doctorate, GRE General Test. Additional exam requirements/recommendations for international students: required—TOEFL (minimum score 550

paper-based; 79 iBT), IELTS (minimum score 6.5). *Application deadline:* For fall admission, 6/1 priority date for domestic students, 1/15 priority date for international students; for spring admission, 9/1 priority date for domestic students, 6/15 priority date for international students. Applications are processed on a rolling basis. Application fee: $65. Electronic applications accepted. *Expenses:* Contact institution. *Financial support:* In 2019–20, 127 students received support, including 103 fellowships (averaging $2,361 per year), 5 research assistantships (averaging $18,968 per year), 101 teaching assistantships (averaging $17,254 per year); career-related internships or fieldwork, Federal Work-Study, scholarships/grants, and unspecified assistantships also available. Financial award application deadline: 1/8; financial award applicants required to submit FAFSA. *Unit head:* Dr. Brian Still, Department Chair, 806-834-6439, Fax: 806-742-0989, E-mail: brian.still@ttu.edu. *Application contact:* Dr. Julie Nelson Couch, Director of Graduate Studies, 806-834-1742, Fax: 806-742-0989, E-mail: english.gradadvisor@ttu.edu. Website: www.english.ttu.edu/

The University of Alabama in Huntsville, School of Graduate Studies, College of Arts, Humanities, and Social Sciences, Department of English, Huntsville, AL 35899. Offers education (MA); English (MA); technical writing (Certificate); TESOL (Certificate). *Program availability:* Part-time. *Degree requirements:* For master's, one foreign language, comprehensive exam, thesis or alternative, oral and written exams. *Entrance requirements:* For master's and Certificate, GRE General Test, minimum GPA of 3.0. Additional exam requirements/recommendations for international students: required—TOEFL (minimum score 500 paper-based; 80 iBT), IELTS (minimum score 6.5). Electronic applications accepted.

University of Arkansas at Little Rock, Graduate School, College of Social Sciences and Communication, Department of Rhetoric and Writing, Little Rock, AR 72204-1099. Offers professional and technical writing (MA). *Program availability:* Part-time, evening/weekend. *Degree requirements:* For master's, thesis or alternative, oral defense of final project. *Entrance requirements:* For master's, GRE, minimum GPA of 3.0, writing portfolio.

University of North Alabama, College of Arts and Sciences, Department of English, Program in Writing, Florence, AL 35632-0001. Offers creative writing (MA); rhetoric and composition (MA); technical writing (MA). *Program availability:* Part-time, 100% online. *Degree requirements:* For master's, comprehensive exam (for some programs), thesis (for some programs). *Entrance requirements:* For master's, GRE, MAT, three letters of recommendation; writing sample. Additional exam requirements/recommendations for international students: required—TOEFL (minimum score 79 iBT), IELTS (minimum score 6), PTE (minimum score 54). Electronic applications accepted.

The University of North Carolina at Charlotte, College of Liberal Arts and Sciences, Department of English, Charlotte, NC 28223-0001. Offers applied linguistics (Graduate Certificate); english (MA), including applied linguistics, children's lit., composition/rhetoric, creative writing, english ed., english for specific purposes, literature, tech/prof w; technical and professional writing (Graduate Certificate). *Program availability:* Part-time, evening/weekend. *Faculty:* 31 full-time (16 women), 1 (woman) part-time/adjunct. *Students:* 26 full-time (19 women), 32 part-time (23 women); includes 18 minority (9 Black or African American, non-Hispanic/Latino; 3 Asian, non-Hispanic/Latino; 1 Hispanic/Latino; 5 Two or more races, non-Hispanic/Latino), 1 international. Average age 30. 26 applicants, 96% accepted, 17 enrolled. In 2019, 16 master's, 3 other advanced degrees awarded. *Degree requirements:* For master's, comprehensive exam (for some programs), thesis, project. *Entrance requirements:* For master's, minimum undergraduate GPA of 3.0, statement of purpose, recommendation letters; unofficial transcript; for Graduate Certificate, statement of purpose, three letters of recommendation, writing sample, minimum GPA of 2.75, current GRE score/current MAT score/portfolio of professional-level documents (technical/professional writing). Additional exam requirements/recommendations for international students: required—TOEFL (minimum score 557 paper-based; 83 iBT), IELTS (minimum score 6.5), TOEFL (minimum score 557 paper-based, 83 iBT) or IELTS (6.5). *Application deadline:* For fall admission, 3/1 priority date for domestic students. Applications are processed on a rolling basis. Application fee: $75. Electronic applications accepted. *Expenses:* Tuition, state resident: full-time $4337. Tuition, nonresident: full-time $17,771. *Required fees:* $3093. Tuition and fees vary according to course load, degree level and program. *Financial support:* In 2019–20, 15 students received support, including 15 teaching assistantships (averaging $8,015 per year); career-related internships or fieldwork, institutionally sponsored loans, scholarships/grants, and unspecified assistantships also available. Support available to part-time students. Financial award application deadline: 3/1; financial award applicants required to submit FAFSA. *Unit head:* Dr. Mark West, Professor and Chair, 704-687-0618, E-mail: miwest@uncc.edu. *Application contact:* Kathy B. Giddings, Director of Graduate Admissions, 704-687-5503, Fax: 704-687-1668, E-mail: gradadm@uncc.edu. Website: http://english.uncc.edu/

The University of North Carolina at Greensboro, Graduate School, College of Arts and Sciences, Department of English, Greensboro, NC 27412-5001. Offers creative writing (MFA); English (M Ed, MA, PhD, Certificate), including American literature (PhD), English (M Ed, MA), English literature (PhD), rhetoric and composition (PhD), technical writing (Certificate), women's studies (Certificate). *Degree requirements:* For master's, comprehensive exam; for doctorate, variable foreign language requirement, thesis/dissertation, preliminary exam. *Entrance requirements:* For master's, GRE General Test, minimum GPA of 3.0; for doctorate, GRE General Test, GRE Subject Test, critical writing sample, minimum GPA of 3.0. Additional exam requirements/recommendations for international students: required—TOEFL. Electronic applications accepted.

University of the Sciences, Program in Biomedical Writing, Philadelphia, PA 19104-4495. Offers biomedical writing (MS); medical marketing writing (Certificate); regulatory affairs writing (Certificate). *Program availability:* Part-time, evening/weekend, online learning. *Entrance requirements:* For master's, GRE General Test. Additional exam requirements/recommendations for international students: required—TOEFL, TWE. *Expenses:* Contact institution.

University of Waterloo, Graduate Studies and Postdoctoral Affairs, Faculty of Arts, Department of English Language and Literature, Waterloo, ON N2L 3G1, Canada. Offers English language and literature (PhD); literary studies (MA); rhetoric and communication design (MA). *Program availability:* Part-time. *Degree requirements:* For master's, one foreign language, thesis optional; for doctorate, 2 foreign languages, thesis/dissertation. *Entrance requirements:* For master's, honors degree, minimum B+ average; for doctorate, master's degree, minimum A- average. Additional exam requirements/recommendations for international students: required—TOEFL, IELTS, PTE. Electronic applications accepted.

Western Carolina University, Graduate School, College of Arts and Sciences, Department of English, Cullowhee, NC 28723. Offers literature (MA); professional writing (MA); rhetoric and composition (MA); teaching English to speakers of other languages (Certificate); technical and professional writing (Certificate). *Program availability:* Part-time, evening/weekend. *Degree requirements:* For master's, one foreign language, comprehensive exam, thesis (for some programs). *Entrance requirements:* For master's, appropriate undergraduate degree, writing sample, 3 letters of recommendation. Additional exam requirements/recommendations for international students: required—TOEFL (minimum score 550 paper-based, 79 iBT) or IELTS (6.5). Electronic applications accepted. *Expenses:* Contact institution.

Writing

Abilene Christian University, Office of Graduate Programs, College of Arts and Sciences, Department of Language and Literature, Abilene, TX 79699. Offers composition/rhetoric (MA); literature (MA); writing (MA). *Program availability:* Part-time. *Faculty:* 9 part-time/adjunct (3 women). *Students:* 6 full-time (4 women), 2 part-time (both women); includes 3 minority (1 Hispanic/Latino; 2 Two or more races, non-Hispanic/Latino), 1 international. 25 applicants, 28% accepted, 4 enrolled. In 2019, 1 master's awarded. *Degree requirements:* For master's, one foreign language, comprehensive exam (for some programs), thesis (for some programs). *Entrance requirements:* For master's, GRE General Test, official transcripts, Recommendations, purpose statement, writing sample. Additional exam requirements/recommendations for international students: required—TOEFL (minimum score 80 iBT), IELTS (minimum score 6), PTE (minimum score 51). *Application deadline:* For fall admission, 8/10 for domestic students; for spring admission, 11/1 for domestic students. Applications are processed on a rolling basis. Application fee: $65. Electronic applications accepted. *Expenses:* $1242 per hour. *Financial support:* In 2019–20, 7 students received support, including 2 teaching assistantships with partial tuition reimbursements available; Federal Work-Study and scholarships/grants also available. Support available to part-time students. Financial award application deadline: 4/1; financial award applicants required to submit FAFSA. *Unit head:* Dr. Todd Womble, Graduate Director, 325-674-2663, Fax: 325-674-2408, E-mail: mtw04b@acu.edu. *Application contact:* Graduate Admissions, 325-674-6911, E-mail: gradinfo@acu.edu.
Website: http://www.acu.edu/on-campus/graduate/college-of-arts-and-sciences/language-and-literature/english.html

Academy of Art University, Graduate Programs, School of Motion Pictures and Television, San Francisco, CA 94105-3410. Offers motion pictures and television (MFA); writing and directing for film (MA). *Program availability:* Part-time, 100% online. *Faculty:* 8 full-time (3 women), 37 part-time/adjunct (13 women). *Students:* 88 full-time (40 women), 38 part-time (15 women); includes 22 minority (9 Black or African American, non-Hispanic/Latino; 1 American Indian or Alaska Native, non-Hispanic/Latino; 3 Asian, non-Hispanic/Latino; 8 Hispanic/Latino; 1 Two or more races, non-Hispanic/Latino), 71 international. Average age 32. 55 applicants, 100% accepted, 23 enrolled. In 2019, 73 master's awarded. *Degree requirements:* For master's, final review. *Entrance requirements:* For master's, statement of intent; resume; portfolio/reel; official college transcripts. *Application deadline:* Applications are processed on a rolling basis. Application fee: $50. Electronic applications accepted. *Expenses: Tuition:* Full-time $1083; part-time $1083 per credit hour. *Required fees:* $860; $860 per unit. $430 per term. One-time fee: $145. Tuition and fees vary according to program. *Financial support:* Career-related internships or fieldwork, Federal Work-Study, and scholarships/grants available. Financial award application deadline: 8/10; financial award applicants required to submit FAFSA. *Application contact:* 800-544-ARTS, E-mail: info@academyart.edu.
Website: http://www.academyart.edu/film-school/index.html

Academy of Art University, Graduate Programs, School of Writing for Film, Television and Digital Media, San Francisco, CA 94105-3410. Offers MFA. *Program availability:* Part-time, 100% online. *Faculty:* 8 full-time (3 women), 37 part-time/adjunct (13 women). *Students:* 21 full-time (15 women), 27 part-time (18 women); includes 15 minority (10 Black or African American, non-Hispanic/Latino; 3 Hispanic/Latino; 2 Two or more races, non-Hispanic/Latino), 6 international. Average age 36. 13 applicants, 100% accepted, 12 enrolled. In 2019, 3 master's awarded. *Degree requirements:* For master's, final review. *Entrance requirements:* For master's, statement of intent; resume; portfolio/reel; official college transcripts. *Application deadline:* Applications are processed on a rolling basis. Application fee: $50. Electronic applications accepted. *Expenses: Tuition:* Full-time $1083; part-time $1083 per credit hour. *Required fees:* $860; $860 per unit. $430 per term. One-time fee: $145. Tuition and fees vary according to program. *Financial support:* Career-related internships or fieldwork, Federal Work-Study, and scholarships/grants available. Financial award application deadline: 8/10; financial award applicants required to submit FAFSA.
Website: http://www.academyart.edu/academics/writing-film-television-digital-media

Adelphi University, College of Arts and Sciences, Program in Creative Writing, Garden City, NY 11530-0701. Offers MFA. *Program availability:* Part-time, evening/weekend. *Degree requirements:* For master's, thesis. *Entrance requirements:* For master's, 2 letters of reference, manuscript in chosen genre (poetry, fiction, playwriting), personal statement essay, college transcript. Additional exam requirements/recommendations for international students: required—TOEFL (minimum score 550 paper-based; 80 iBT), IELTS (minimum score 6.5). Electronic applications accepted. *Expenses:* Contact institution.

Agnes Scott College, Program in Writing and Digital Communication, Decatur, GA 30030-3797. Offers MA.

Albertus Magnus College, Master of Fine Arts in Writing Program, New Haven, CT 06511-1189. Offers MFA. *Program availability:* Part-time, evening/weekend, 100% online, blended/hybrid learning. *Faculty:* 2 full-time (1 woman), 1 part-time/adjunct (0 women). *Students:* 3 full-time (2 women), 1 part-time (0 women); includes 2 minority (1 Black or African American, non-Hispanic/Latino; 1 Hispanic/Latino). Average age 35. 8 applicants, 50% accepted, 1 enrolled. In 2019, 3 master's awarded. *Degree requirements:* For master's, comprehensive exam, thesis optional, satisfactory completion of the Master Prokect, minimum. cumulatie GPA of 3.0, completion within 7 years, payment of all tuition and fees. *Entrance requirements:* For master's, A bachelo's degree with a minimum GPA of 3.0, two letters of recommendation specifically addressing suitability for the program, written essay of 750-1000 words, a sample of written work (in one genre as follows: nonfiction, fiction, poetry). Additional exam requirements/recommendations for international students: required—One of the following: SAT or ACT, TOEFL, IELTS, DUO Lingo English Proficiency Test, 3+ years at a university/college with English as primary language. *Application deadline:* For fall admission, 7/15 for international students; for spring admission, 11/15 for international students. Applications are processed on a rolling basis. Application fee: $50. Electronic applications accepted. *Financial support:* In 2019–20, 5 students received support. Unspecified assistantships available. Financial award applicants required to submit FAFSA. *Unit head:* Charles Rafferty, Co-Director MFA Program, 203-773-4473, E-mail: swallman@albertus.edu. *Application contact:* Prof. Sarah Wallman, Dean of the Division of Professional and Graduate Studies, 203-672-6689, E-mail: abosleyboyce@albertus.edu.
Website: https://www.albertus.edu/fine-arts/mfa/

American College Dublin, Graduate Programs, Dublin, Ireland. Offers business administration (MBA); creative writing (MFA); international business (MBA); oil and gas management (MBA); performance (MFA).

American University, College of Arts and Sciences, Department of Literature, Washington, DC 20016-8047. Offers creative writing (MFA); literature (MA). *Program availability:* Part-time, evening/weekend. *Degree requirements:* For master's, comprehensive exam. *Entrance requirements:* For master's, GRE, please visit website: https://www.american.edu/cas/literature/, writing sample, statement of purpose, transcripts, 2 letters of recommendation, resume. Additional exam requirements/recommendations for international students: required—TOEFL (minimum score 600 paper-based; 100 iBT). *Expenses:* Contact institution.

Antioch University Santa Barbara, Program in Writing and Contemporary Media, Santa Barbara, CA 93101-1581. Offers MFA. *Program availability:* Part-time. *Faculty:* 1 full-time, 5 part-time/adjunct (4 women). *Students:* 13 full-time (8 women), 1 (woman) part-time; includes 4 minority (2 Black or African American, non-Hispanic/Latino; 1 American Indian or Alaska Native, non-Hispanic/Latino; 1 Native Hawaiian or other Pacific Islander, non-Hispanic/Latino). Average age 35. In 2019, 22 master's awarded. *Degree requirements:* For master's, thesis project. *Expenses: Tuition:* Full-time $15,936. *Required fees:* $100. *Unit head:* Ross Brown, Program Director, E-mail: rbrown@antioch.edu. *Application contact:* Ross Brown, Program Director, E-mail: rbrown@antioch.edu.
Website: https://www.antioch.edu/santa-barbara/degrees-programs/creative-writing-communications/writing-contemporary-media-mfa/

Arcadia University, College of Arts and Sciences, Department of English, Program in Creative Writing, Glenside, PA 19038-3295. Offers MFA. *Faculty:* 2 full-time (1 woman). *Students:* 1 (woman) full-time, 28 part-time (20 women); includes 5 minority (3 Black or African American, non-Hispanic/Latino; 1 Asian, non-Hispanic/Latino; 1 Two or more races, non-Hispanic/Latino). In 2019, 9 master's awarded. *Entrance requirements:* Additional exam requirements/recommendations for international students: required—Official results from the TOEFL or IELTS are required. *Application deadline:* Applications are processed on a rolling basis. Application fee: $25. *Expenses:* Contact institution. *Financial support:* Teaching assistantships, unspecified assistantships, and funding packages of between $1,000 and $3,000 are available available. *Unit head:* Joshua Isard, Director, 267-620-4886, E-mail: isardj@arcadia.edu. *Application contact:* Joshua Isard, Director, 267-620-4886, E-mail: isardj@arcadia.edu.
Website: https://www.arcadia.edu/academics/programs/creative-writing-mfa

Arizona State University at Tempe, College of Liberal Arts and Sciences, Department of English, Interdisciplinary Program in Creative Writing, Tempe, AZ 85287-0302. Offers MFA. *Degree requirements:* For master's, thesis, practicum (9 hours). *Entrance requirements:* For master's, undergraduate major in English or creative writing (preferred), minimum GPA of 3.0, 3 letters of recommendation, resume or curriculum vitae, personal statement, official transcripts, 3 copies of manuscript sample (20 pages of poetry, 30 pages of prose, or both). Additional exam requirements/recommendations for international students: required—TOEFL, IELTS, or PTE. Electronic applications accepted.

Arizona State University at Tempe, Herberger Institute for Design and the Arts, School of Film, Dance and Theatre, Tempe, AZ 85287-2002. Offers dance (MFA), including dance, interdisciplinary digital media and performance; theatre (MA, MFA, PhD), including arts entrepreneurship and management (MFA), directing (MFA), dramatic writing (MFA), interdisciplinary digital media and performance (MFA), performance (MFA), performance design (MFA), theatre (MFA), theatre and performance of the Americas (PhD), theatre for youth (MFA, PhD). Terminal master's awarded for partial completion of doctoral program. *Degree requirements:* For master's, comprehensive exam (for some programs), thesis (for some programs), applied project (for some programs); interactive Program of Study (iPOS) submitted before completing 50 percent of required credit hours; for doctorate, comprehensive exam, thesis/dissertation, interactive Program of Study (iPOS) submitted before completing 50 percent of required credit hours. *Entrance requirements:* For master's, GRE or MAT, minimum GPA of 3.0 in last 2 years of work leading to bachelor's degree (depending on program); for doctorate, GRE, minimum GPA of 3.0 or equivalent in last 2 years of work leading to bachelor's degree, 3 letters of recommendation, resume, scholarly writing sample, statement of purpose. Additional exam requirements/recommendations for international students: required—TOEFL, IELTS, or PTE. Electronic applications accepted.

Asbury University, School of Graduate and Professional Studies, Wilmore, KY 40390-1198. Offers biology: alternative certificate (MA Ed); chemistry: alternative certificate (MA Ed); English (MA Ed); English as a second language (MA Ed); ESL (MA Ed); French (MA Ed); Latin: alternative certificate (MA Ed); mathematics: alternative certificate (MA Ed); reading/writing endorsement (MA Ed); social studies (MA Ed); social work (MSW), including child and family services; Spanish (MA Ed); special education (MA Ed); special education: alternative certificate (MA Ed); teacher as leader endorsement (MA Ed). *Accreditation:* NCATE. *Program availability:* Part-time. *Degree requirements:* For master's, action research project, portfolio. *Entrance requirements:* For master's, PRAXIS/NTE, minimum GPA of 2.75, letters of recommendation. Additional exam requirements/recommendations for international students: required—TOEFL (minimum score 550 paper-based). Electronic applications accepted.

Ashland University, College of Arts and Sciences, Program in Creative Writing, Ashland, OH 44805-3702. Offers MFA. *Program availability:* Online learning. *Degree requirements:* For master's, thesis. *Entrance requirements:* For master's, writing sample, minimum GPA of 2.75. Electronic applications accepted. *Expenses:* Contact institution.

Auburn University at Montgomery, College of Liberal Arts & Social Sciences, Department of English and Philosophy, Montgomery, AL 36124. Offers teaching writing (MTW). *Program availability:* Part-time, 100% online, blended/hybrid learning. *Faculty:* 12 full-time (5 women). *Students:* 7 part-time (5 women); includes 1 minority (Black or

African American, non-Hispanic/Latino). Average age 30. 5 applicants, 80% accepted, 2 enrolled. In 2019, 25 master's awarded. *Degree requirements:* For master's, thesis. *Entrance requirements:* For master's, GRE General Test or MAT. Additional exam requirements/recommendations for international students: required—TOEFL (minimum score 500 paper-based; 61 iBT), IELTS (minimum score 5.5), PTE (minimum score 44). *Application deadline:* For fall admission, 7/15 for international students; for spring admission, 11/15 for international students; for summer admission, 4/15 for international students. Applications are processed on a rolling basis. Application fee: $25. Electronic applications accepted. *Expenses: Tuition, area resident:* Full-time $7578; part-time $421 per credit hour. Tuition, state resident: full-time $7578; part-time $421 per credit hour. Tuition, nonresident: full-time $17,046; part-time $947 per credit hour. *International tuition:* $17,046 full-time. *Required fees:* $868. *Financial support:* Teaching assistantships, scholarships/grants, and unspecified assistantships available. Financial award application deadline: 3/1; financial award applicants required to submit FAFSA. *Unit head:* Dr. John Havard, Chair, 334-244-3228, E-mail: jhavard@aum.edu. *Application contact:* Tara Woods, Administrative Associate, 334-244-3376, E-mail: twoods11@aum.edu.
Website: http://www.cas.aum.edu/departments/english-and-philosophy

Ball State University, Graduate School, College of Sciences and Humanities, Department of English, Muncie, IN 47306. Offers English (MA, PhD), including composition (MA), creative writing (MA), literature, rhetoric and composition; linguistics (MA), including linguistics, teaching English to speakers of other languages (TESOL) and linguistics. *Program availability:* Part-time. *Degree requirements:* For doctorate, variable foreign language requirement, thesis/dissertation. *Entrance requirements:* For master's, GRE General Test, minimum baccalaureate GPA of 2.75 or 3.0 in latter half of baccalaureate, statement of purpose, writing sample, three letters of recommendation; for doctorate, GRE General Test, GRE Subject Test, minimum graduate GPA of 3.2, statement of purpose, writing sample, three letters of recommendation. Additional exam requirements/recommendations for international students: required—TOEFL (minimum score 550 paper-based; 79 iBT), IELTS (minimum score 6.5). Electronic applications accepted. *Expenses: Tuition, area resident:* Full-time $7506; part-time $417 per credit hour. Tuition, nonresident: full-time $20,610; part-time $1145 per credit hour. *Required fees:* $2126. Tuition and fees vary according to course load, campus/location and program.

Bard College, Milton Avery Graduate School of the Arts, Annandale-on-Hudson, NY 12504. Offers film/video (MFA); music/sound (MFA); painting (MFA); photography (MFA); sculpture (MFA); writing (MFA). *Degree requirements:* For master's, thesis, project, 8-week summer residency, independent study. *Entrance requirements:* For master's, interview, portfolio, 2 letters of recommendation, history of work in the arts. Additional exam requirements/recommendations for international students: required—TOEFL (minimum score 550 paper-based). Electronic applications accepted. *Expenses:* Contact institution.

Bay Path University, Program in Creative Nonfiction, Longmeadow, MA 01106-2292. Offers MFA. *Program availability:* Part-time, evening/weekend, online only, 100% online. Electronic applications accepted. Application fee is waived when completed online. *Expenses:* Contact institution.

Bennington College, Graduate Programs, MFA Program in Writing, Bennington, VT 05201. Offers MFA. *Program availability:* Online learning. *Degree requirements:* For master's, thesis, collection of essays or poems, or collection of short stories and/or a novel. *Entrance requirements:* For master's, manuscript. *Expenses:* Contact institution.

Binghamton University, State University of New York, Graduate School, Harpur College of Arts and Sciences, Department of English, Binghamton, NY 13902-6000. Offers creative writing (MA); English (PhD); English/American literature (MA). *Program availability:* Part-time. Terminal master's awarded for partial completion of doctoral program. *Degree requirements:* For master's, one foreign language, thesis; for doctorate, one foreign language, comprehensive exam, thesis/dissertation. *Entrance requirements:* For master's and doctorate, GRE General Test, writing sample. Additional exam requirements/recommendations for international students: required—TOEFL (minimum score 550 paper-based; 80 iBT). Electronic applications accepted.

Boston University, Graduate School of Arts and Sciences, Creative Writing Program, Boston, MA 02215. Offers MFA. *Students:* 23 full-time (11 women), 4 part-time (1 woman); includes 7 minority (4 Asian, non-Hispanic/Latino; 1 Hispanic/Latino; 2 Two or more races, non-Hispanic/Latino), 9 international. Average age 32. 730 applicants, 3% accepted, 18 enrolled. In 2019, 18 master's awarded. *Degree requirements:* For master's, one foreign language, thesis. *Entrance requirements:* Additional exam requirements/recommendations for international students: required—TOEFL (minimum score 550 paper-based; 84 iBT). *Application deadline:* For fall admission, 2/1 for domestic and international students. Application fee: $95. Electronic applications accepted. *Financial support:* In 2019–20, 18 students received support, including teaching assistantships with full tuition reimbursements available (averaging $15,500 per year); Federal Work-Study, scholarships/grants, health care benefits, and unspecified assistantships also available. Financial award application deadline: 2/1. *Unit head:* Robert Pinsky, Director, 617-353-2510, Fax: 617-353-3653, E-mail: rpinsky@bu.edu. *Application contact:* Catherine Con, Administrative Coordinator, 617-353-2510, Fax: 617-353-3653, E-mail: crwr@bu.edu.
Website: http://www.bu.edu/creativewriting/

Boston University, Graduate School of Arts and Sciences, Editorial Institute, Boston, MA 02215. Offers MA. *Students:* 5 full-time (4 women), 4 part-time (2 women); includes 2 minority (1 Hispanic/Latino; 1 Two or more races, non-Hispanic/Latino). Average age 34. *Degree requirements:* For master's, thesis. *Entrance requirements:* For master's, GRE General Test, thesis proposal, 3 letters of recommendation, transcripts, personal statement. Additional exam requirements/recommendations for international students: required—TOEFL (minimum score 550 paper-based; 84 iBT). Application fee: $95. *Financial support:* In 2019–20, 7 students received support, including 1 fellowship with full tuition reimbursement available (averaging $6,000 per year), 1 research assistantship with full tuition reimbursement available (averaging $23,340 per year), 2 teaching assistantships with full tuition reimbursements available (averaging $23,340 per year); Federal Work-Study, scholarships/grants, and health care benefits also available. *Unit head:* Archie Burnett, Director, 617-353-6631, E-mail: burnetta@bu.edu. *Application contact:* Ellen Wrigley, Administrative Assistant, 617-353-6631, Fax: 617-353-6917, E-mail: ellen@bu.edu.
Website: http://www.bu.edu/editinst/

Boston University, Graduate School of Arts and Sciences, Playwriting Program, Boston, MA 02215. Offers MFA. *Students:* 5 full-time (4 women); includes 2 minority (both Hispanic/Latino). Average age 27. In 2019, 1 master's awarded. *Degree requirements:* For master's, one foreign language, thesis. *Entrance requirements:* For master's, 3 letters of recommendation, one original full-length play or two one-act plays, transcripts, personal statement, curriculum vitae, ability to read or speak a foreign language. Additional exam requirements/recommendations for international students: required—TOEFL (minimum score 550 paper-based; 84 iBT). *Application deadline:* For fall admission, 1/15 for domestic and international students. Application fee: $95. Electronic applications accepted. *Financial support:* In 2019–20, 5 students received support, including 5 fellowships with full tuition reimbursements available (averaging $16,000 per year), 2 teaching assistantships with full tuition reimbursements available (averaging $11,670 per year); Federal Work-Study, scholarships/grants, health care benefits, and unspecified assistantships also available. Financial award application deadline: 1/15. *Unit head:* Katherine Snodgrass, Artistic Director, 617-353-5104, Fax: 617-353-6196, E-mail: ksnodgra@bu.edu. *Application contact:* Martin Gastmann, Assistant Director of Admissions and Financial Aid, 617-353-2696, Fax: 617-358-5492, E-mail: grs@bu.edu.
Website: http://www.bu.edu/playwriting

Bowling Green State University, Graduate College, College of Arts and Sciences, Department of English, Program in Creative Writing, Bowling Green, OH 43403. Offers fiction (MFA); poetry (MFA). *Program availability:* Part-time. *Degree requirements:* For master's, thesis or alternative. *Entrance requirements:* For master's, GRE General Test. Additional exam requirements/recommendations for international students: required—TOEFL. Electronic applications accepted.

Bowling Green State University, Graduate College, College of Arts and Sciences, Department of English, Program in English, Bowling Green, OH 43403. Offers English (MA, PhD); literature (MA); rhetoric and writing (PhD); scientific and technical communication (MA). *Program availability:* Part-time. *Degree requirements:* For master's, thesis or alternative; for doctorate, comprehensive exam, thesis/dissertation, foreign language or proficiency in Old English. *Entrance requirements:* For master's and doctorate, GRE General Test. Additional exam requirements/recommendations for international students: required—TOEFL. Electronic applications accepted.

Brigham Young University, Graduate Studies, College of Humanities, Department of English, Provo, UT 84602-1001. Offers creative writing (MFA); literature (MA); rhetoric/composition (MA). *Faculty:* 55 full-time (18 women). *Students:* 66 full-time (52 women), 1 part-time (0 women); includes 5 minority (1 Asian, non-Hispanic/Latino; 4 Hispanic/Latino). Average age 28. 52 applicants, 63% accepted, 26 enrolled. In 2019, 23 master's awarded. *Degree requirements:* For master's, variable foreign language requirement, comprehensive exam, thesis. *Entrance requirements:* For master's, GRE General Test, creative portfolio (for MFA). Additional exam requirements/recommendations for international students: required—E3PT; recommended—TOEFL (minimum score 580 paper-based; 85 iBT), IELTS (minimum score 7), TSE. *Application deadline:* For fall admission, 1/15 for domestic and international students. Application fee: $50. Electronic applications accepted. *Financial support:* In 2019–20, 67 students received support, including 12 research assistantships (averaging $4,000 per year), 62 teaching assistantships (averaging $6,700 per year); career-related internships or fieldwork, institutionally sponsored loans, scholarships/grants, and unspecified assistantships also available. Support available to part-time students. Financial award application deadline: 2/15. *Unit head:* Prof. Lance Larsen, Chair, 801-4228104, Fax: 801-422-0221, E-mail: lance_larsen@byu.edu. *Application contact:* Tessa Hauglid, English Graduate Program Manager, 801-422-4939, Fax: 801-422-0221, E-mail: tessa_hauglid@byu.edu.
Website: http://english.byu.edu/

Brooklyn College of the City University of New York, School of Humanities and Social Sciences, Department of English, Brooklyn, NY 11210-2889. Offers creative writing (MFA), including fiction, playwriting, poetry; English (MA). *Program availability:* Part-time, evening/weekend. *Degree requirements:* For master's, one foreign language, comprehensive exam (for some programs), thesis (for some programs). *Entrance requirements:* For master's, advanced undergraduate courses in English, 2 letters of recommendation, writing sample, statement of purpose. Additional exam requirements/recommendations for international students: required—TOEFL. Electronic applications accepted.

Brown University, Graduate School, Department of English, Providence, RI 02912. Offers English (PhD); literary arts (MFA). *Degree requirements:* For doctorate, thesis/dissertation. *Entrance requirements:* For master's and doctorate, GRE General Test, GRE Subject Test.

California College of the Arts, Graduate Programs, MFA in Writing Program, San Francisco, CA 94107. Offers creative non-fiction (MFA); fiction (MFA); poetry (MFA). *Program availability:* Part-time. *Degree requirements:* For master's, thesis. *Entrance requirements:* For master's, appropriate bachelor's degree, portfolio, transcripts, letters of recommendation. Additional exam requirements/recommendations for international students: required—TOEFL, IELTS, or PTE. Electronic applications accepted. *Expenses:* Contact institution.

California Institute of the Arts, School of Critical Studies, Valencia, CA 91355-2340. Offers writing (MFA, Adv C). *Entrance requirements:* For master's, portfolio. Additional exam requirements/recommendations for international students: required—TOEFL.

California State University, Fresno, Division of Research and Graduate Studies, College of Arts and Humanities, Department of English, Fresno, CA 93740-8027. Offers creative writing (MFA); literature (MA); rhetoric and writing studies (MA). *Program availability:* Part-time, evening/weekend. *Degree requirements:* For master's, one foreign language, thesis. *Entrance requirements:* For master's, GRE General Test, minimum GPA of 3.0, writing sample. Additional exam requirements/recommendations for international students: required—TOEFL. Electronic applications accepted. *Expenses:* Tuition, state resident: full-time $4012; part-time $2506 per semester.

California State University, Long Beach, Graduate Studies, College of Liberal Arts, Department of English, Long Beach, CA 90840. Offers creative writing (MFA); English (MA). *Program availability:* Part-time. *Degree requirements:* For master's, one foreign language, comprehensive exam or thesis. *Entrance requirements:* For master's, GRE Subject Test, minimum GPA of 3.0 in English. Electronic applications accepted.

California State University, Northridge, Graduate Studies, College of Humanities, Department of English, Northridge, CA 91330. Offers creative writing (MA); literature (MA); rhetoric and composition theory (MA). *Program availability:* Part-time, evening/weekend. *Degree requirements:* For master's, thesis or alternative. *Entrance requirements:* For master's, writing proficiency test, GRE General Test or minimum GPA of 3.0. Additional exam requirements/recommendations for international students: required—TOEFL.

California State University, Sacramento, College of Arts and Letters, Department of English, Sacramento, CA 95819. Offers composition (MA); creative writing (MA); literature (MA); teaching English to speakers of other languages (MA). *Program availability:* Part-time. *Students:* 39 full-time (27 women), 54 part-time (30 women); includes 26 minority (6 Black or African American, non-Hispanic/Latino; 4 Asian, non-Hispanic/Latino; 16 Hispanic/Latino), 2 international. Average age 30. 42 applicants, 76% accepted, 29 enrolled. In 2019, 23 master's awarded. *Degree requirements:* For master's, comprehensive exam, thesis optional, thesis, project, or comprehensive exam; TESOL exam; writing proficiency exam. *Entrance requirements:* For master's, portfolio (creative writing); minimum GPA of 3.0 in English and overall during previous 2 years. Additional exam requirements/recommendations for international students: required—TOEFL (minimum score 600 paper-based; 100 iBT). *Application deadline:* For fall admission, 2/15 for domestic students, 1/15 for international students; for spring admission, 9/15 for domestic students, 8/30 for international students. Applications are processed on a rolling basis. Application fee: $70. Electronic applications accepted.

Expenses: Contact institution. *Financial support:* Teaching assistantships, career-related internships or fieldwork, Federal Work-Study, and scholarships/grants available. Support available to part-time students. Financial award application deadline: 3/1; financial award applicants required to submit FAFSA. *Unit head:* Dr. David Toise, Chair, 916-278-6586, E-mail: dwtoise@csus.edu. *Application contact:* Jose Martinez, Graduate Admissions Supervisor, 916-278-7871, E-mail: martinj@skymail.csus.edu. Website: http://www.csus.edu/engl

California State University, San Bernardino, Graduate Studies, College of Arts and Letters, Program in English, San Bernardino, CA 92407. Offers creative writing (MFA), including fiction; English composition (MA), including composition. *Program availability:* Part-time, evening/weekend. *Faculty:* 7 full-time (all women). *Students:* 14 full-time (9 women), 45 part-time (29 women); includes 37 minority (7 Black or African American, non-Hispanic/Latino; 2 Asian, non-Hispanic/Latino; 26 Hispanic/Latino; 2 Two or more races, non-Hispanic/Latino), 1 international. Average age 31. 22 applicants, 82% accepted, 18 enrolled. In 2019, 21 master's awarded. *Degree requirements:* For master's, one foreign language, thesis. *Entrance requirements:* Additional exam requirements/recommendations for international students: required—TOEFL. *Application deadline:* For fall admission, 7/16 for domestic students. Application fee: $55. *Financial support:* Application deadline: 3/1. *Unit head:* Dr. David Carlson, Chair, 909-537-5834, Fax: 909-537-7086, E-mail: dajcarls@csusb.edu. *Application contact:* Dr. Dorota Huizinga, Dean of Graduate Studies, 909-537-3064, Fax: 909-537-5078, E-mail: dorota.huizinga@csusb.edu.

California State University, San Marcos, College of Humanities, Arts, Behavioral and Social Sciences, Program in Literature and Writing Studies, San Marcos, CA 92096-0001. Offers MA. *Program availability:* Part-time, evening/weekend. *Degree requirements:* For master's, one foreign language, thesis. *Entrance requirements:* For master's, GRE General Test, minimum GPA of 3.0, writing sample. *Expenses: Tuition, area resident:* Full-time $7176. Tuition, state resident: full-time $7176. Tuition, nonresident: full-time $18,640. *International tuition:* $18,640 full-time. *Required fees:* $1960.

California State University, Stanislaus, College of the Arts, Humanities and Social Sciences, MA Program in English, Turlock, CA 95382. Offers literature (Certificate); rhetoric and teaching writing (MA); teaching English to speakers of other languages (MA). *Program availability:* Part-time. *Degree requirements:* For master's, comprehensive exam, thesis or alternative. *Entrance requirements:* For master's, GRE, minimum GPA of 3.0, 2 letters of reference, personal statement. Additional exam requirements/recommendations for international students: required—TOEFL (minimum score 575 paper-based), TWE (minimum score 4). Electronic applications accepted.

Carlow University, College of Learning and Innovation, Program in Creative Writing, Pittsburgh, PA 15213-3165. Offers fiction (MFA); non-fiction (MFA); poetry (MFA). *Program availability:* Part-time, evening/weekend, low-residency. *Students:* 29 part-time (26 women); includes 2 minority (both Two or more races, non-Hispanic/Latino), 1 international. Average age 45. In 2019, 7 master's awarded. *Degree requirements:* For master's, thesis, manuscript. *Entrance requirements:* For master's, two essays, sample of writing, two letters of recommendation, resume/curriculum vitae. Additional exam requirements/recommendations for international students: required—TOEFL (minimum score 550 paper-based). *Application deadline:* Applications are processed on a rolling basis. Electronic applications accepted. *Expenses:* Contact institution. *Financial support:* Application deadline: 4/1; applicants required to submit FAFSA. *Unit head:* Janet Beatty, Program Director, MFA in Creative Writing, 412-578-6081, Fax: 412-578-8722, E-mail: jpbeatty@carlow.edu. *Application contact:* Janet Beatty, Program Director, MFA in Creative Writing, 412-578-6081, Fax: 412-578-8722, E-mail: jpbeatty@carlow.edu.
Website: http://www.carlow.edu/Master_of_Fine_Arts_in_Creative_Writing.aspx

Carnegie Mellon University, Dietrich College of Humanities and Social Sciences, Department of English, Program in Professional Writing, Pittsburgh, PA 15213-3891. Offers editing and publishing (MAPW); policy and non-profit communication (MAPW); public and media relations/corporate communications (MAPW); science or healthcare communication (MAPW); technical writing (MAPW); writing for new media (MAPW); writing for print media (MAPW). *Program availability:* Part-time. *Entrance requirements:* For master's, GRE General Test. Additional exam requirements/recommendations for international students: required—TOEFL, TWE.

Cedar Crest College, Program in Creative Writing, Allentown, PA 18104-6196. Offers MFA. *Program availability:* Part-time, evening/weekend, blended/hybrid learning. *Degree requirements:* For master's, final book-length creative thesis. Electronic applications accepted. *Expenses:* Contact institution.

Central Michigan University, College of Graduate Studies, College of Liberal Arts and Social Sciences, Department of English Language and Literature, Mount Pleasant, MI 48859. Offers English composition and communication (MA); English language and literature (MA), including children's and young adult literature, creative writing, English language and literature; TESOL: teaching English to speakers of other languages (MA). *Program availability:* Part-time, evening/weekend. *Degree requirements:* For master's, thesis or alternative. Electronic applications accepted. *Expenses: Tuition, area resident:* Full-time $12,267; part-time $8178 per year. Tuition, state resident: full-time $12,267; part-time $8178 per year. Tuition, nonresident: full-time $12,267; part-time $8178 per year. *International tuition:* $16,110 full-time. *Required fees:* $225 per semester. Tuition and fees vary according to degree level and program.

Central Washington University, School of Graduate Studies and Research, College of Arts and Humanities, Department of English, Ellensburg, WA 98926. Offers literature (MA); professional and creative writing (MA); teaching English to speakers of other languages (MA). *Program availability:* Part-time. *Entrance requirements:* For master's, GRE General Test, minimum GPA of 3.0, writing sample. Additional exam requirements/recommendations for international students: required—TOEFL (minimum score 550 paper-based; 79 iBT) or IELTS (minimum score 6.5). Electronic applications accepted.

Chapman University, Wilkinson College of Arts, Humanities, and Social Sciences, Department of English, Orange, CA 92866. Offers creative writing (MFA); English (MA). *Program availability:* Part-time, evening/weekend. *Faculty:* 24 full-time (11 women), 40 part-time/adjunct (23 women). *Students:* 46 full-time (35 women), 17 part-time (8 women); includes 24 minority (3 Black or African American, non-Hispanic/Latino; 1 American Indian or Alaska Native, non-Hispanic/Latino; 5 Asian, non-Hispanic/Latino; 11 Hispanic/Latino; 4 Two or more races, non-Hispanic/Latino), 5 international. Average age 28. 106 applicants, 76% accepted, 22 enrolled. In 2019, 32 master's awarded. *Degree requirements:* For master's, thesis. *Entrance requirements:* For master's, GRE (if undergraduate GPA less than 3.0), minimum undergraduate GPA of 2.5. Additional exam requirements/recommendations for international students: required—TOEFL (minimum score 80 iBT), IELTS (minimum score 6.5), PTE (minimum score 53). *Application deadline:* For fall admission, 2/1 priority date for domestic students. Applications are processed on a rolling basis. Application fee: $60. Electronic applications accepted. *Expenses:* $1,035 per unit. *Financial support:* Fellowships, teaching assistantships, Federal Work-Study, and scholarships/grants available. Financial award applicants required to submit FAFSA. *Unit head:* Dr. Joanna Levin, Chair, 714-997-6534, E-mail: jlevin@chapman.edu. *Application contact:* Sharnique

Dow, Graduate Admission Counselor, 714-997-6770, E-mail: sdow@chapman.edu. Website: https://www.chapman.edu/wilkinson/english/index.aspx

Chatham University, Program in Writing, Pittsburgh, PA 15232-2826. Offers children's writing (MFA); fiction (MFA); non-fiction (MFA); poetry (MFA); professional writing (MPW); screenwriting (MFA). *Program availability:* Part-time, evening/weekend, online learning. *Entrance requirements:* For master's, minimum GPA of 3.0, writing sample, recommendation letters. Additional exam requirements/recommendations for international students: required—TOEFL (minimum score 600 paper-based; 100 iBT), IELTS (minimum score 7), TWE. Electronic applications accepted. Application fee is waived when completed online. *Expenses: Tuition:* Part-time $1017 per credit. *Required fees:* $30 per credit. Tuition and fees vary according to program.

Chicago State University, School of Graduate and Professional Studies, College of Arts and Sciences, Department of English, Foreign Languages and Literatures, Chicago, IL 60628. Offers creative writing (MFA); English (MA). *Degree requirements:* For master's, comprehensive exam (for some programs), thesis (for some programs). *Entrance requirements:* For master's, minimum GPA of 3.0.

City College of the City University of New York, Graduate School, Division of Humanities and the Arts, Department of English, Program in Creative Writing, New York, NY 10031-9198. Offers MFA. *Degree requirements:* For master's, one foreign language, comprehensive exam, thesis. *Entrance requirements:* For master's, minimum GPA of 3.0, 10-15 poems or 30-50 pages of fiction (short stories or novel excerpt). Additional exam requirements/recommendations for international students: required—TOEFL (minimum score 600 paper-based; 100 iBT). Electronic applications accepted.

Claremont Graduate University, Graduate Programs, School of Arts and Humanities, Department of English, Claremont, CA 91711-6160. Offers American studies (MA, PhD); critical theory (MA, PhD); early modern studies (MA, PhD); English (M Phil, MA, PhD); literary theory (PhD); literature (MA, PhD); literature and creative writing (MA); literature and film (MA); MBA/MA; MBA/PhD. *Program availability:* Part-time. *Entrance requirements:* For master's and doctorate, GRE General Test. Additional exam requirements/recommendations for international students: required—TOEFL (minimum score 75 iBT). Electronic applications accepted.

Clemson University, Graduate School, College of Architecture, Arts, and Humanities, Department of English, Clemson, SC 29634. Offers English (MA); rhetoric, communication and information design (PhD); writing, rhetoric and media (MA). *Program availability:* Part-time. *Students:* Average age 32. 52 applicants, 77% accepted, 30 enrolled. In 2019, 21 master's, 7 doctorates awarded. *Degree requirements:* For master's, variable foreign language requirement, thesis (for some programs); for doctorate, comprehensive exam, thesis/dissertation. *Entrance requirements:* For master's, GRE General Test, unofficial transcripts, personal statement, writing sample, letters of recommendation. Additional exam requirements/recommendations for international students: required—TOEFL (minimum score 80 paper-based; 80 iBT); recommended—IELTS (minimum score 6.5), TSE (minimum score 54). *Application deadline:* For fall admission, 4/15 priority date for international students; for spring admission, 10/15 for international students. Applications are processed on a rolling basis. Application fee: $80 ($90 for international students). Electronic applications accepted. *Expenses: Tuition, area resident:* Full-time $10,600; part-time $8688 per semester. Tuition, state resident: full-time $10,600; part-time $8688 per semester. Tuition, nonresident: full-time $22,050; part-time $17,412 per semester. *International tuition:* $22,050 full-time. *Required fees:* $1196; $617 per semester. $617 per semester. Tuition and fees vary according to course load, degree level, campus/location and program. *Financial support:* In 2019–20, 59 students received support, including 6 fellowships with full and partial tuition reimbursements available (averaging $1,667 per year), 43 teaching assistantships with full and partial tuition reimbursements available (averaging $17,154 per year); unspecified assistantships also available. *Unit head:* Dr. Susanna Ashton, Department Chair, 864-656-3151, E-mail: sashton@clemson.edu. *Application contact:* Dr. William Stockton, Graduate Program Coordinator, 864-656-3151, E-mail: wstockt@clemson.edu.
Website: https://www.clemson.edu/caah/departments/english/

Cleveland State University, College of Graduate Studies, College of Liberal Arts and Social Sciences, Department of English, Cleveland, OH 44115. Offers creative writing (MFA), including fiction, non-fiction, playwriting, poetry. *Program availability:* Part-time, evening/weekend. *Faculty:* 14 full-time (8 women), 14 part-time/adjunct (4 women). *Students:* 28 full-time (18 women), 20 part-time (12 women); includes 6 minority (5 Black or African American, non-Hispanic/Latino; 1 Hispanic/Latino). Average age 34. 38 applicants, 68% accepted, 9 enrolled. In 2019, 13 master's awarded. *Entrance requirements:* For master's, minimum GPA of 2.75, undergraduate concentration in English, writing sample, portfolio. Additional exam requirements/recommendations for international students: required—TOEFL (minimum score 550 paper-based; 78 iBT). *Application deadline:* Applications are processed on a rolling basis. Application fee: $40. Electronic applications accepted. *Expenses:* Tuition, state resident: full-time $10,215; part-time $6810 per credit hour. Tuition, nonresident: full-time $17,496; part-time $11,664 per credit hour. *International tuition:* $19,316 full-time. Tuition and fees vary according to degree level and program. *Financial support:* In 2019–20, 8 students received support. Teaching assistantships, tuition waivers (full and partial), and unspecified assistantships available. Financial award application deadline: 2/1; financial award applicants required to submit FAFSA. *Application contact:* Dr. James J. Marino, Associate Professor/Director of Graduate Studies, 216-687-6874, Fax: 216-687-6943, E-mail: j.marino22@csuohio.edu.
Website: http://www.csuohio.edu/class/english/english

Coastal Carolina University, Thomas W. and Robin W. Edwards College of Humanities and Fine Arts, Conway, SC 29528-6054. Offers liberal studies (MA); writing (MA). *Program availability:* Part-time, evening/weekend. *Faculty:* 28 full-time (14 women), 2 part-time/adjunct (both women). *Students:* 42 full-time (22 women), 21 part-time (13 women); includes 16 minority (9 Black or African American, non-Hispanic/Latino; 2 Asian, non-Hispanic/Latino; 2 Hispanic/Latino; 3 Two or more races, non-Hispanic/Latino), 1 international. Average age 31. 55 applicants, 85% accepted, 30 enrolled. In 2019, 18 master's awarded. *Entrance requirements:* For master's, GRE, MAT, personal statement of interest, official transcripts, 2 letters of recommendation, writing sample; for writing program: minimum GPA of 3.3 in 18 hours of undergraduate and graduate coursework in English or related discipline. Additional exam requirements/recommendations for international students: required—TOEFL (minimum score 550 paper-based; 79 iBT). *Application deadline:* For fall admission, 5/1 priority date for domestic and international students; for spring admission, 11/15 priority date for domestic and international students. Applications are processed on a rolling basis. Application fee: $45. Electronic applications accepted. *Expenses: Tuition, area resident:* Full-time $10,764; part-time $598 per credit hour. Tuition, state resident: full-time $10,764; part-time $598 per credit hour. Tuition, nonresident: full-time $19,836; part-time $1102 per credit hour. *International tuition:* $19,836 full-time. *Required fees:* $90; $5 per credit hour. *Financial support:* Fellowships, research assistantships, teaching assistantships, and tuition waivers available. Financial award application deadline: 3/1; financial award applicants required to submit FAFSA. *Unit head:* Dr. Daniel J. Ennis, Dean, 843-349-2691, E-mail: bornholdt@coastal.edu. *Application contact:* Dr. James O. Luken, Interim Dean, College of Graduate Studies and Research, 843-349-2277, Fax:

Writing

843-349-6444, E-mail: ryoung@coastal.edu.
Website: https://www.coastal.edu/humanities/

College of Charleston, Graduate School, School of Humanities and Social Sciences, Program in Creative Writing, Charleston, SC 29424-0001. Offers MFA.

Colorado State University, College of Liberal Arts, Department of English, Fort Collins, CO 80523-1773. Offers creative writing (MFA); rhetoric and composition (MA). *Faculty:* 24 full-time (12 women), 6 part-time/adjunct (5 women). *Students:* 72 full-time (54 women), 23 part-time (20 women); includes 13 minority (2 Black or African American, non-Hispanic/Latino; 1 Asian, non-Hispanic/Latino; 5 Hispanic/Latino; 5 Two or more races, non-Hispanic/Latino), 13 international. Average age 30. 170 applicants, 51% accepted, 32 enrolled. In 2019, 32 master's awarded. *Degree requirements:* For master's, thesis (for some programs), portfolio, project or thesis. *Entrance requirements:* For master's, BA/BS or equivalent with minimum cumulative undergraduate GPA of 3.0, transcripts, writing sample, statement of purpose, 3 letters of recommendation. Additional exam requirements/recommendations for international students: recommended—TOEFL (minimum score 550 paper-based; 80 iBT), IELTS (minimum score 6.5). Application fee: $60 ($70 for international students). Electronic applications accepted. *Expenses:* Tuition, state resident: full-time $10,520; part-time $5844 per credit hour. Tuition, nonresident: full-time $25,791; part-time $14,328 per credit hour. *International tuition:* $25,791 full-time. *Required fees:* $2512.80. Part-time tuition and fees vary according to course level, course load, degree level, program and student level. *Financial support:* In 2019–20, 1 fellowship with full and partial tuition reimbursement (averaging $15,210 per year), 1 research assistantship (averaging $7,605 per year), 39 teaching assistantships with full and partial tuition reimbursements (averaging $15,593 per year) were awarded; Federal Work-Study, scholarships/grants, and unspecified assistantships also available. *Unit head:* Dr. Louann Reid, Professor, 970-491-6428, E-mail: louann.reid@colostate.edu. *Application contact:* Marnie Leonard, Administrative Assistant, 970-491-2403, E-mail: marnie.leonard@colostate.edu. Website: http://english.colostate.edu/

Columbia College Chicago, School of Graduate Studies, English and Creative Writing Department, Chicago, IL 60605-1996. Offers fiction (MFA); nonfiction (MFA); poetry (MFA). *Program availability:* Part-time, evening/weekend. *Degree requirements:* For master's, thesis. *Entrance requirements:* For master's, self-assessment essay, work samples, letters of recommendation, transcripts. Additional exam requirements/recommendations for international students: required—TOEFL, IELTS. Electronic applications accepted.

Columbia University, School of the Arts, Writing Program, New York, NY 10027. Offers writing (MFA), including fiction, nonfiction, poetry. *Degree requirements:* For master's, thesis. *Entrance requirements:* For master's, undergraduate transcript, 3 letters of recommendation, writing sample, essay response to a contemporary work of literature, personal statement. Additional exam requirements/recommendations for international students: required—Either the TOEFL or the IELTS is required. Electronic applications accepted. *Expenses:* Contact institution.

Concordia University, School of Graduate Studies, Faculty of Arts and Science, Department of English, Program in Creative Writing, Montréal, QC H3G 1M8, Canada. Offers MA. *Degree requirements:* For master's, one foreign language, thesis. *Entrance requirements:* For master's, honors degree in English, minimum GPA of 3.3 in English literature, portfolio.

Concordia University, St. Paul, College of Humanities and Social Sciences, St. Paul, MN 55104-5494. Offers creative writing (MFA); criminal justice leadership (MA); family science (MA); human services (MA), including forensic behavioral health. *Accreditation:* NCATE. *Program availability:* Part-time, evening/weekend, 100% online, blended/hybrid learning. *Degree requirements:* For master's, thesis (for some programs), capstone project. *Entrance requirements:* For master's, official transcripts stating the conferral of a Bachelor's degree with a minimum cumulative GPA of 3.0 based on a 4.0 system; personal statement; writing sample in fiction or non-fiction (MFA students only); resume (MA students only). Additional exam requirements/recommendations for international students: required—TOEFL (minimum score 547 paper-based; 78 iBT), IELTS (minimum score 6), PTE (minimum score 78). Electronic applications accepted. *Expenses:* Contact institution.

Converse College, Program in Creative Writing, Spartanburg, SC 29302. Offers MFA.

Cornell University, Graduate School, Graduate Fields of Arts and Sciences, Field of English Language and Literature, Ithaca, NY 14853. Offers African-American literature (PhD); American literature after 1865 (PhD); American literature to 1865 (PhD); American studies (PhD); colonial and postcolonial literatures (PhD); creative writing (MFA); cultural studies (PhD); dramatic literature (PhD); English poetry (PhD); English Renaissance to 1660 (PhD); lesbian, bisexual, and gay literary studies (PhD); literary criticism and theory (PhD); Old and Middle English (PhD); prose fiction (PhD); Restoration and the eighteenth-century (PhD); the nineteenth century (PhD); the twentieth century (PhD); women's literature (PhD); MFA/PhD. Terminal master's awarded for partial completion of doctoral program. *Degree requirements:* For master's, one foreign language, thesis; for doctorate, one foreign language, comprehensive exam, thesis/dissertation, teaching experience. *Entrance requirements:* For master's, GRE General Test, 3 letters of recommendation, creative writing sample; for doctorate, 3 letters of recommendation, writing sample. Additional exam requirements/recommendations for international students: required—TOEFL (minimum score 600 paper-based; 77 iBT). Electronic applications accepted.

Creighton University, Graduate School, College of Arts and Sciences, Department of English, Omaha, NE 68178-0001. Offers creative writing (MA, MFA). *Program availability:* Part-time. *Degree requirements:* For master's, thesis optional. *Entrance requirements:* For master's, 10-15 page writing sample, 3 letters of recommendation. Additional exam requirements/recommendations for international students: required—TOEFL (minimum score 90 iBT). Electronic applications accepted.

DePaul University, College of Liberal Arts and Social Sciences, Chicago, IL 60614. Offers Arabic (MA); Chinese (MA); critical ethnic studies (MA); English (MA); French (MA); German (MA); history (MA); interdisciplinary studies (MA, MS); international public service (MS); international studies (MA); Italian (MA); Japanese (MA); liberal studies (MA); nonprofit management (MNM); public administration (MPA); public health (MPH); public policy (MPP); public service management (MS); refugee and forced migration studies (MS); social work (MSW); sociology (MA); Spanish (MA); sustainable urban development (MA); women's and gender studies (MA); writing and publishing (MA); writing, rhetoric and discourse (MA); MA/PhD. *Accreditation:* CEPH. *Program availability:* Part-time, evening/weekend, online learning. Terminal master's awarded for partial completion of doctoral program. *Degree requirements:* For master's, variable foreign language requirement, comprehensive exam (for some programs), thesis (for some programs). Electronic applications accepted.

Drew University, Caspersen School of Graduate Studies, Madison, NJ 07940-1493. Offers conflict resolution and leadership (Certificate), including community leadership, moderation, peace building; education (M Ed); finance (MA); history and culture (MA, PhD), including American history, book history, British history, European history, intellectual history, Irish history, print culture, public history; K-12 education (MAT),

including art, biology, chemistry, elementary education, English, French, Italian, math, secondary education, special education, teacher of students with disabilities; liberal studies (M Litt, D Litt), including history, Irish/Irish-American studies, literature (M Litt, MMH, D Litt, DMH, CMH), religion, spirituality, teaching in the two-year college, writing; medical humanities (MMH, DMH, CMH), including arts, health, healthcare, literature (M Litt, MMH, D Litt, DMH, CMH), scientific research; poetry (MFA). *Program availability:* Part-time, evening/weekend. Terminal master's awarded for partial completion of doctoral program. *Degree requirements:* For master's and other advanced degree, thesis (for some programs); for doctorate, one foreign language, comprehensive exam (for some programs), thesis/dissertation. *Entrance requirements:* For master's, PRAXIS Core and Subject Area tests (for MAT), GRE/GMAT (for MFin MS in Data Analytics), resume, transcripts, writing sample, personal statement, letters of recommendation; for doctorate, GRE (PhD in history and culture), resume, transcripts, writing sample, personal statement, letters of recommendation; for other advanced degree, resume, transcripts, personal statement. Additional exam requirements/recommendations for international students: required—TOEFL (minimum score 587 paper-based; 80 iBT), IELTS (minimum score 6), TWE (minimum score 4). Electronic applications accepted.

East Carolina University, Graduate School, Thomas Harriot College of Arts and Sciences, Department of English, Greenville, NC 27858-4353. Offers creative writing (MA); English studies (MA); linguistics (MA); literature (MA); multicultural and transnational literatures (MA, Certificate); professional communication (Certificate); rhetoric and composition (MA); rhetoric, writing, and professional communication (PhD); teaching English in the two-year college (Certificate); teaching English to speakers of other languages (MA, Certificate); technical and professional communication (MA). *Program availability:* Part-time, evening/weekend, online learning. *Application deadline:* For fall admission, 7/31 priority date for domestic students, 2/1 priority date for international students; for spring admission, 11/30 priority date for domestic students, 10/1 priority date for international students. *Expenses: Tuition, area resident:* Full-time $4749; part-time $185 per credit hour. Tuition, state resident: full-time $4749; part-time $185 per credit hour. Tuition, nonresident: full-time $17,898; part-time $864 per credit hour. *International tuition:* $17,898 full-time. *Required fees:* $2787. *Financial support:* Application deadline: 3/1. *Unit head:* Dr. Marianne Montgomery, Chair, 252-328-6041, E-mail: montgomerym@ecu.edu. *Application contact:* Graduate School Admissions, 252-328-6012, Fax: 252-328-6071, E-mail: gradschool@ecu.edu. Website: https://english.ecu.edu/

Eastern Kentucky University, The Graduate School, College of Arts and Sciences, Department of English and Theatre, Richmond, KY 40475-3102. Offers creative writing (MFA); English (MA). *Program availability:* Part-time, evening/weekend. *Degree requirements:* For master's, thesis optional. *Entrance requirements:* For master's, GRE General Test, minimum GPA of 2.5, minor in English with 3.0 GPA.

Eastern Michigan University, Graduate School, College of Arts and Sciences, Department of English Language and Literature, Program in Creative Writing, Ypsilanti, MI 48197. Offers MA. *Program availability:* Part-time, evening/weekend, online learning. *Students:* 3 full-time (all women), 9 part-time (2 women); includes 3 minority (all Black or African American, non-Hispanic/Latino). Average age 35. 7 applicants, 71% accepted, 5 enrolled. In 2019, 6 master's awarded. *Entrance requirements:* Additional exam requirements/recommendations for international students: required—TOEFL. *Application deadline:* Applications are processed on a rolling basis. Application fee: $45. *Financial support:* Fellowships, research assistantships with full tuition reimbursements, teaching assistantships with full tuition reimbursements, career-related internships or fieldwork, Federal Work-Study, institutionally sponsored loans, scholarships/grants, tuition waivers (partial), and unspecified assistantships available. Support available to part-time students. Financial award applicants required to submit FAFSA. *Application contact:* Carla Harryman, Program Coordinator, 734-487-3173, Fax: 734-483-9744, E-mail: charryma@emich.edu.

Eastern Michigan University, Graduate School, College of Arts and Sciences, Department of English Language and Literature, Programs in Written Communication, Ypsilanti, MI 48197. Offers technical communication (Graduate Certificate); written communication (MA). *Program availability:* Part-time, evening/weekend, online learning. *Students:* 1 full-time (0 women), 11 part-time (10 women); includes 3 minority (2 Black or African American, non-Hispanic/Latino; 1 Hispanic/Latino). Average age 34. 5 applicants, 100% accepted, 4 enrolled. In 2019, 8 master's awarded. *Entrance requirements:* Additional exam requirements/recommendations for international students: required—TOEFL. *Application deadline:* Applications are processed on a rolling basis. Application fee: $45. *Financial support:* Fellowships, research assistantships with full tuition reimbursements, teaching assistantships with full tuition reimbursements, career-related internships or fieldwork, Federal Work-Study, institutionally sponsored loans, scholarships/grants, tuition waivers (partial), and unspecified assistantships available. Support available to part-time students. Financial award applicants required to submit FAFSA. *Application contact:* Dr. Chalice Randazzo, Program Coordinator, 734-487-4220, Fax: 734-483-9744, E-mail: crandaz1@emich.edu.

Fairfield University, College of Arts and Sciences, Fairfield, CT 06824. Offers American studies (MA); communication (MA); creative writing (MFA); mathematics (MS); public administration (MPA). *Program availability:* Part-time, evening/weekend, online learning. *Faculty:* 35 full-time (19 women), 19 part-time/adjunct (10 women). *Students:* 64 full-time (44 women), 84 part-time (48 women); includes 35 minority (9 Black or African American, non-Hispanic/Latino; 1 American Indian or Alaska Native, non-Hispanic/Latino; 1 Asian, non-Hispanic/Latino; 21 Hispanic/Latino; 3 Two or more races, non-Hispanic/Latino), 7 international. Average age 36. 98 applicants, 68% accepted, 64 enrolled. In 2019, 38 master's awarded. *Degree requirements:* For master's, capstone research course. *Entrance requirements:* For master's, minimum GPA of 3.0, 2 letters of recommendation, resume, personal statement. Additional exam requirements/recommendations for international students: required—TOEFL (minimum score 550 paper-based; 80 iBT) or IELTS (minimum score 6.5). *Application deadline:* For fall admission, 5/15 for international students; for spring admission, 10/15 for international students. Applications are processed on a rolling basis. Application fee: $60. Electronic applications accepted. *Expenses:* Tuition $850/credit hour; Registration Fee $50/semester; Graduate Student Activity Fee (Fall and Spring) $65/semester. *Financial support:* In 2019–20, 11 students received support. Scholarships/grants and unspecified assistantships available. Financial award applicants required to submit FAFSA. *Unit head:* Dr. Richard Greenwald, Dean, 203-254-4000 Ext. 2221, Fax: 203-254-4119, E-mail: rgreenwald@fairfield.edu. *Application contact:* Melanie Rogers, Director of Graduate Admission, 203-254-4184, Fax: 203-254-4073, E-mail: gradadmis@fairfield.edu. Website: http://www.fairfield.edu/cas

Fairleigh Dickinson University, Florham Campus, Maxwell Becton College of Arts and Sciences, Department of English, Communication and Philosophy, Program in Creative Writing, Madison, NJ 07940-1099. Offers creative nonfiction (MFA); fiction (MFA); literary translation (MFA); poetry (MFA); writing for young adults (MFA).

Fairleigh Dickinson University, Florham Campus, Maxwell Becton College of Arts and Sciences, Department of English, Communication and Philosophy, Program in Creative Writing and Literature for Educators, Madison, NJ 07940-1099. Offers MA.

Fitchburg State University, Division of Graduate and Continuing Education, Program in Applied Communications, Fitchburg, MA 01420-2697. Offers applied communication studies (MS); technical and professional writing (MS). *Program availability:* Part-time, evening/weekend. *Entrance requirements:* Additional exam requirements/recommendations for international students: required—TOEFL (minimum score 550 paper-based; 79 iBT). Electronic applications accepted. *Expenses:* Contact institution.

Florida International University, College of Arts, Sciences, and Education, Department of English, Miami, FL 33199. Offers creative writing (MFA); English (MA), including literature; linguistics (MA). *Program availability:* Part-time, evening/weekend. *Faculty:* 64 full-time (30 women), 31 part-time/adjunct (20 women). *Students:* 48 full-time (32 women), 34 part-time (17 women); includes 52 minority (6 Black or African American, non-Hispanic/Latino; 2 Asian, non-Hispanic/Latino; 43 Hispanic/Latino; 1 Two or more races, non-Hispanic/Latino), 2 international. Average age 30. 48 applicants, 56% accepted, 25 enrolled. In 2019, 21 master's awarded. *Entrance requirements:* For master's, GRE General Test, minimum undergraduate GPA of 3.0 (upper-level coursework), letter of intent, two letters of recommendation. Additional exam requirements/recommendations for international students: required—TOEFL (minimum score 550 paper-based; 80 iBT). *Application deadline:* For fall admission, 2/1 for domestic and international students; for spring admission, 10/1 for domestic students, 9/1 for international students. Applications are processed on a rolling basis. Application fee: $30. Electronic applications accepted. *Expenses: Tuition, area resident:* Full-time $8912; part-time $446 per credit hour. Tuition, state resident: full-time $8912; part-time $446 per credit hour. Tuition, nonresident: full-time $21,393; part-time $992 per credit hour. *Required fees:* $2194. *Financial support:* Institutionally sponsored loans and scholarships/grants available. Financial award application deadline: 3/1; financial award applicants required to submit FAFSA. *Unit head:* Dr. Anna Luszczynska, Chair, 305-348-2203, Fax: 305-348-3878, E-mail: Ana.Luszczynska@fiu.edu. *Application contact:* Nanett Rojas, Manager, Admissions Operations, 305-348-7464, Fax: 305-348-7441, E-mail: gradadm@fiu.edu.

Florida State University, The Graduate School, College of Motion Picture Arts, Tallahassee, FL 32306-2350. Offers film production (MFA); screenwriting (MFA). *Faculty:* 28 full-time (8 women), 3 part-time/adjunct (1 woman). *Students:* 64 full-time (33 women); includes 20 minority (10 Black or African American, non-Hispanic/Latino; 1 American Indian or Alaska Native, non-Hispanic/Latino; 4 Asian, non-Hispanic/Latino; 3 Hispanic/Latino; 2 Two or more races, non-Hispanic/Latino), 14 international. Average age 25. 217 applicants, 15% accepted, 32 enrolled. In 2019, 30 master's awarded. *Degree requirements:* For master's, thesis, Thesis film project. *Entrance requirements:* For master's, minimum GPA of 3.0, resume, statement of purpose, writing sample, 3 letters of recommendation, creative portfolio, video pitch. Additional exam requirements/recommendations for international students: required—TOEFL (minimum score 550 paper-based; 80 iBT). *Application deadline:* For fall admission, 12/1 for domestic and international students. Application fee: $30. Electronic applications accepted. *Expenses:* Contact institution. *Financial support:* In 2019–20, 20 students received support, including 20 teaching assistantships with partial tuition reimbursements available (averaging $5,500 per year); institutionally sponsored loans, tuition waivers, and unspecified assistantships also available. Financial award application deadline: 7/1; financial award applicants required to submit FAFSA. *Unit head:* Reb Braddock, Dean, 850-644-8712, Fax: 850-644-2626. *Application contact:* Paige Roberts, Head of Admissions, 850-644-8524, Fax: 850-644-2626, E-mail: proberts@fsu.edu. Website: http://film.fsu.edu/

Florida State University, The Graduate School, Department of Anthropology, Department of English, Tallahassee, FL 32312. Offers English (MA, MFA, PhD), including creative writing (MFA, PhD), literature (MA, PhD), rhetoric and composition (MA, PhD). *Program availability:* Part-time. *Degree requirements:* For master's, one foreign language, thesis, 33 hours of coursework including capstone essay, thesis or portfolio (MA); 45 hours of coursework including 9-12 thesis hours (MFA); for doctorate, one foreign language, comprehensive exam, thesis/dissertation, 27 hours of coursework, 24 hours of dissertation work. *Entrance requirements:* For master's, GRE General Test, sample of written work, 3 letters of recommendation, resume, statement of purpose; for doctorate, GRE General Test, sample of written work, 3 letters of recommendation, resume, statement of purpose. Additional exam requirements/recommendations for international students: required—TOEFL. Electronic applications accepted.

Full Sail University, Creative Writing Master of Fine Arts Program - Online, Winter Park, FL 32792-7437. Offers MFA. *Program availability:* Online learning.

George Mason University, College of Humanities and Social Sciences, Department of English, Program in Creative Writing, Fairfax, VA 22030. Offers fiction (MFA); nonfiction writing (MFA); poetry (MFA). *Degree requirements:* For master's, one foreign language, comprehensive exam (for some programs), thesis, written exam (for poetry); written exam or project (for fiction). *Entrance requirements:* For master's, expanded goals statement; 2 letters of recommendation; portfolio; official transcripts; resume; writing sample. Additional exam requirements/recommendations for international students: required—TOEFL (minimum score 575 paper-based; 88 iBT), IELTS (minimum score 6.5), PTE (minimum score 59). Electronic applications accepted.

Georgia College & State University, The Graduate School, College of Arts and Sciences, Department of English, Program in Creative Writing, Milledgeville, GA 31061. Offers MFA. *Program availability:* Part-time, evening/weekend. *Students:* 12 full-time (10 women), 14 part-time (5 women); includes 5 minority (3 Black or African American, non-Hispanic/Latino; 2 Hispanic/Latino). Average age 30. 28 applicants, 54% accepted, 8 enrolled. In 2019, 9 master's awarded. Terminal master's awarded for partial completion of doctoral program. *Degree requirements:* For master's, thesis, complete program in no more than 4 years. *Entrance requirements:* For master's, writing portfolio, 3 letters of recommendation, statement of purpose, official transcript, resume. Additional exam requirements/recommendations for international students: required—English language proficiency through one of the following ways: TOEFL, IELTS, Duolingo English Test, SAT or the ACT. *Application deadline:* For fall admission, 2/1 priority date for domestic students. Applications are processed on a rolling basis. Application fee: $40. Electronic applications accepted. *Expenses:* Full time enrollment per semester—$2646 matriculation and $1011 fees. *Financial support:* In 2019–20, 23 students received support. Unspecified assistantships available. Financial award application deadline: 7/1; financial award applicants required to submit FAFSA. *Unit head:* Dr. Kerry Neville, Coordinator, 478-445-3509, E-mail: mfa@gcsu.edu. *Application contact:* Kate Marshall, Graduate Admissions Coordinator, 478-445-1184, Fax: 478-445-1336, E-mail: grad-admit@gcsu.edu.
Website: http://www.gcsu.edu/artsandsciences/english/mfa

Georgia Southern University, Jack N. Averitt College of Graduate Studies, College of Arts and Humanities, Program in Professional Communication and Leadership, Statesboro, GA 30458. Offers MA, Certificate. *Program availability:* Part-time, evening/weekend. *Faculty:* 26 full-time (13 women). *Students:* 25 full-time (17 women), 29 part-time (25 women); includes 22 minority (16 Black or African American, non-Hispanic/Latino; 1 Asian, non-Hispanic/Latino; 3 Hispanic/Latino; 2 Two or more races, non-Hispanic/Latino), 3 international. Average age 34. 31 applicants, 97% accepted, 21 enrolled. In 2019, 20 master's awarded. *Degree requirements:* For master's, comprehensive exam, project. *Entrance requirements:* For master's, minimum GPA of 2.5, letters of recommendation, letter of intent, resume. Additional exam requirements/recommendations for international students: required—TOEFL (minimum score 523 paper-based; 70 iBT). *Application deadline:* For fall admission, 6/1 priority date for domestic students, 5/1 priority date for international students; for spring admission, 11/15 priority date for domestic students, 9/15 priority date for international students; for summer admission, 4/15 for domestic students, 9/15 priority date for international students. Applications are processed on a rolling basis. Application fee: $30. Electronic applications accepted. *Expenses: Tuition, area resident:* Full-time $4986; part-time $277 per credit hour. Tuition, nonresident: full-time $19,890; part-time $1105 per credit hour. *International tuition:* $19,890 full-time. *Required fees:* $2114; $1057 per semester. $1057 per semester. Tuition and fees vary according to course load, campus/location and program. *Financial support:* In 2019–20, 14 students received support, including research assistantships with full tuition reimbursements available (averaging $5,000 per year); scholarships/grants and unspecified assistantships also available. Financial award application deadline: 3/15; financial award applicants required to submit FAFSA. *Unit head:* Dr. Kimberly Martin, Program Coordinator, 912-344-2698, E-mail: kimberly.martin@armstrong.edu. *Application contact:* McKenzie Peterman, Graduate Admissions Specialist, 912-478-5678, Fax: 912-478-0740, E-mail: mpeterman@georgiasouthern.edu.
Website: http://www.armstrong.edu/Majors/degree/master_professional_communication_leadership

Georgia State University, College of Arts and Sciences, Department of English, Program in Creative Writing, Atlanta, GA 30302-3083. Offers creative writing (PhD); fiction (MA, MFA); poetry (MA, MFA). *Program availability:* Part-time. *Entrance requirements:* For master's and doctorate, GRE. Additional exam requirements/recommendations for international students: required—TOEFL (minimum score 550 paper-based; 80 iBT). Application fee: $50. Electronic applications accepted. *Expenses: Tuition, area resident:* Full-time $7164; part-time $398 per credit hour. Tuition, state resident: full-time $7164; part-time $398 per credit hour. Tuition, nonresident: full-time $22,662; part-time $1259 per credit hour. *International tuition:* $22,662 full-time. *Required fees:* $2128; $312 per credit hour. Tuition and fees vary according to course load and program. *Financial support:* Research assistantships, teaching assistantships, and unspecified assistantships available. *Unit head:* Dr. Josh Russell, Co-Director of the Creative Writing Program, 404-413-5800, Fax: 404-413-5830, E-mail: josh@gsu.edu. *Application contact:* Dr. Josh Russell, Co-Director of the Creative Writing Program, 404-413-5800, Fax: 404-413-5830, E-mail: josh@gsu.edu. Website: http://www.english.gsu.edu

Goddard College, Graduate Division, Master of Fine Arts in Creative Writing Program, Plainfield, VT 05667-9432. Offers MFA. *Program availability:* Online learning. *Degree requirements:* For master's, thesis, completed full-length manuscript, teaching practicum, 3 critical papers, annotations of 45 to 60 literary works. *Entrance requirements:* For master's, statement of purpose, preliminary bibliography, creative portfolio, three letters of recommendation. Electronic applications accepted. *Expenses:* Contact institution.

Goucher College, MA and MFA Programs, Baltimore, MD 21204-2794. Offers art and technology (MFA); arts administration (MA); cultural sustainability (MA); digital arts (MA); historic preservation (MA); nonfiction (MFA). *Program availability:* Part-time, evening/weekend, blended/hybrid learning. *Degree requirements:* For master's, thesis, e-portfolio. *Entrance requirements:* For master's, digital portfolio (for MA, MFA in digital arts); writing sample (for MFA in creative nonfiction). Additional exam requirements/recommendations for international students: required—TOEFL (minimum score 550 paper-based; 80 iBT). Electronic applications accepted. *Expenses:* Contact institution.

Hamline University, College of Liberal Arts, St. Paul, MN 55104-1284. Offers creative writing (MFA); creative writing for children and young adults (MFA); law (MSL). *Program availability:* Part-time, evening/weekend. *Degree requirements:* For master's, thesis. *Entrance requirements:* For master's, letters of recommendation, official transcripts, personal statement, resume. Additional exam requirements/recommendations for international students: required—TOEFL (minimum score 550 paper-based; 80 iBT), IELTS (minimum score 6.5). Electronic applications accepted. Application fee is waived when completed online. *Expenses:* Contact institution.

Hofstra University, College of Liberal Arts and Sciences, Programs in Creative Writing, Hempstead, NY 11549. Offers creative writing (MFA). *Program availability:* Part-time, evening/weekend. *Students:* 15 full-time (10 women), 5 part-time (2 women); includes 6 minority (4 Black or African American, non-Hispanic/Latino; 1 Hispanic/Latino; 1 Two or more races, non-Hispanic/Latino), 3 international. Average age 29. 25 applicants, 96% accepted, 9 enrolled. In 2019, 7 master's awarded. *Degree requirements:* For master's, thesis optional, minimum GPA of 3.0. *Entrance requirements:* For master's, writing sample, essay, minimum GPA of 3.0 in literature courses. Additional exam requirements/recommendations for international students: required—TOEFL (minimum score 550 paper-based; 80 iBT); recommended—IELTS (minimum score 6.5). *Application deadline:* Applications are processed on a rolling basis. Application fee: $75. Electronic applications accepted. *Expenses: Tuition:* Full-time $25,164; part-time $1398 per credit. *Required fees:* $580; $165 per semester. Tuition and fees vary according to course load, degree level and program. *Financial support:* In 2019–20, 11 students received support, including 10 fellowships with full and partial tuition reimbursements available (averaging $2,824 per year); research assistantships with full and partial tuition reimbursements available, career-related internships or fieldwork, Federal Work-Study, institutionally sponsored loans, scholarships/grants, tuition waivers (full and partial), unspecified assistantships, and scholarships and endowed scholarships also available. Support available to part-time students. Financial award applicants required to submit FAFSA. *Unit head:* Dr. Kayrn Valerius, Chairperson, 516-463-5455, E-mail: Karyn.Valerius@hofstra.edu. *Application contact:* Sunil Samuel, Assistant Vice President of Admissions, 516-463-4723, Fax: 516-463-4664, E-mail: graduateadmission@hofstra.edu.
Website: http://www.hofstra.edu/hclas

Hollins University, Graduate Programs, Graduate Programs in Children's Literature, Roanoke, VA 24020. Offers children's book illustration (Certificate); children's book writing and illustrating (MFA); children's literature (MA, MFA). *Program availability:* Part-time. *Degree requirements:* For master's, one foreign language, thesis. *Entrance requirements:* For master's, transcripts, letters of recommendation, portfolio, personal statement of educational objectives. Additional exam requirements/recommendations for international students: required—TOEFL (minimum score 550 paper-based; 79 iBT), IELTS (minimum score 6.5). Electronic applications accepted. *Expenses:* Contact institution.

Hollins University, Graduate Programs, Program in Creative Writing, Roanoke, VA 24020. Offers creative writing (MFA). *Degree requirements:* For master's, comprehensive exam, thesis. *Entrance requirements:* For master's, portfolio of original work, 3 letters of recommendation, undergraduate transcript, statement of educational objectives. Additional exam requirements/recommendations for international students: required—TOEFL (minimum score 550 paper-based; 80 iBT), IELTS (minimum score 6.5). Electronic applications accepted. *Expenses:* Contact institution.

Writing

Hollins University, Graduate Programs, Program in Playwriting, Roanoke, VA 24020. Offers new play directing (Certificate); new play performance (Certificate); playwriting (MFA). *Program availability:* Part-time. *Degree requirements:* For master's, comprehensive exam, thesis. *Entrance requirements:* For master's, letters of recommendation, bachelor's degree, undergraduate transcripts, manuscript. Additional exam requirements/recommendations for international students: required—TOEFL (minimum score 550 paper-based; 80 iBT), IELTS (minimum score 6.5). Electronic applications accepted. *Expenses:* Contact institution.

Hollins University, Graduate Programs, Program in Screenwriting and Film Studies, Roanoke, VA 24020. Offers screenwriting (MFA); screenwriting and film studies (MA). *Program availability:* Part-time. *Degree requirements:* For master's, one foreign language, comprehensive exam, thesis. *Entrance requirements:* For master's, letters of recommendation, manuscript, transcript review, personal statement. Additional exam requirements/recommendations for international students: required—TOEFL (minimum score 550 paper-based; 80 iBT), IELTS (minimum score 6.5). Electronic applications accepted. *Expenses:* Contact institution.

Holy Names University, Graduate Division, Master of Arts in English: The Writer's Craft Program, Oakland, CA 94619-1699. Offers MA. *Entrance requirements:* For master's, two recommendations, writing sample. Additional exam requirements/recommendations for international students: required—TOEFL (minimum score 550 paper-based; 79 iBT). Electronic applications accepted. Application fee is waived when completed online.

Hunter College of the City University of New York, Graduate School, School of Arts and Sciences, Department of English, Program in Creative Writing, New York, NY 10065-5085. Offers fiction (MFA); memoir (MFA); poetry (MFA). *Program availability:* Part-time, evening/weekend. *Degree requirements:* For master's, thesis. *Entrance requirements:* For master's, creative writing manuscript (up to 10 pages of poetry or 25-30 pages of fiction or nonfiction), nonfiction proposal (for nonfiction applicants only), statement of purpose. Electronic applications accepted.

Hunter College of the City University of New York, Graduate School, School of Arts and Sciences, Department of Theatre, Program in Playwriting, New York, NY 10065-5085. Offers MFA. *Entrance requirements:* For master's, GRE, bachelor's degree, two letters of recommendation, full-length or one-act play of at least 40 pages (both hard copy and PDF attachment). Additional exam requirements/recommendations for international students: required—TOEFL (minimum score 550 paper-based; 60 iBT).

Illinois State University, Graduate School, College of Arts and Sciences, Department of English, Normal, IL 61790. Offers English (MA, MS, PhD), including English (MA, MS), English studies (PhD); writing (MA, MS). *Faculty:* 43 full-time (29 women), 12 part-time/adjunct (11 women). *Students:* 71 full-time (50 women), 31 part-time (21 women). Average age 31. 61 applicants, 59% accepted, 23 enrolled. In 2019, 11 master's, 9 doctorates awarded. *Degree requirements:* For master's, thesis or alternative; for doctorate, thesis/dissertation, 2 terms of residency. *Entrance requirements:* For master's, GRE General Test, minimum GPA of 3.0 in last 60 hours of course work, writing sample; for doctorate, GRE General Test, writing sample. *Application deadline:* Applications are processed on a rolling basis. Application fee: $50. *Expenses: Tuition, area resident:* Full-time $7956; part-time $9767 per year. Tuition, nonresident: full-time $9233; part-time $17,592 per year. *Required fees:* $1797. *Financial support:* In 2019-20, 70 teaching assistantships were awarded; tuition waivers (full) and unspecified assistantships also available. Financial award application deadline: 4/1. *Unit head:* Dr. Christopher De Santis, Department Chair, 309-438-3650, E-mail: ccdesan@IllinoisState.edu. *Application contact:* Dr. Angela Haas, Graduate Coordinator, 309-438-3651, E-mail: ahaas@IllinoisState.edu. Website: http://www.english.ilstu.edu/

Indiana State University, College of Graduate and Professional Studies, College of Arts and Sciences, Department of English, Terre Haute, IN 47809. Offers British and American literature (MA); English (MA); writing (MA). *Program availability:* Part-time, evening/weekend. *Degree requirements:* For master's, one foreign language, thesis optional. *Entrance requirements:* For master's, minimum GPA of 2.75 in all English courses above freshman level. Additional exam requirements/recommendations for international students: required—TOEFL (minimum score 550 paper-based). Electronic applications accepted.

Indiana University Bloomington, University Graduate School, College of Arts and Sciences, Department of English, Bloomington, IN 47405. Offers creative writing (MA, MFA), including fiction (MFA), poetry (MFA); literature (PhD); rhetoric (PhD). *Degree requirements:* For master's, 30-36 credit hours plus one language proficiency (for MA); 60 credit hours plus thesis (for MFA); for doctorate, thesis/dissertation, qualifying exam; 90 credit hours; 2nd language proficiency or one language only if acquired at in-depth level. *Entrance requirements:* For master's, GRE General Test, GRE Subject Test (for all but MFA and MA in creative writing), minimum GPA of 3.5; for doctorate, GRE General Test, GRE Subject Test, minimum GPA of 3.7. Additional exam requirements/recommendations for international students: required—TOEFL (minimum score 550 paper-based; 79 iBT), IELTS (minimum score 6.5). Electronic applications accepted.

Indiana University-Purdue University Indianapolis, School of Liberal Arts, Department of English, Indianapolis, IN 46202. Offers English (MA); teaching English to speakers of other languages (TESOL) (MA, Certificate); teaching literature (Certificate); teaching writing (Certificate). *Entrance requirements:* For master's, GRE. Additional exam requirements/recommendations for international students: required—TOEFL.

Indiana University South Bend, College of Liberal Arts and Sciences, South Bend, IN 46615. Offers advanced computer programming (Graduate Certificate); applied informatics (Graduate Certificate); applied mathematics and computer science (MS); behavior modification (Graduate Certificate); computer applications (Graduate Certificate); computer programming (Graduate Certificate); correctional management and supervision (Graduate Certificate); English (MA); health systems management (Graduate Certificate); international studies (Graduate Certificate); liberal studies (MLS); nonprofit management (Graduate Certificate); paralegal studies (Graduate Certificate); professional writing (Graduate Certificate); public affairs (MPA); public management (Graduate Certificate); social and cultural diversity (Graduate Certificate); strategic sustainability leadership (Graduate Certificate); technology for administration (Graduate Certificate). *Program availability:* Part-time, evening/weekend. *Degree requirements:* For master's, variable foreign language requirement, thesis (for some programs). *Entrance requirements:* For master's, minimum GPA of 3.0. Additional exam requirements/recommendations for international students: required—TOEFL (minimum score 550 paper-based; 80 iBT). *Expenses:* Contact institution.

Institute of American Indian Arts, Low Residency MFA in Creative Writing Program, Santa Fe, NM 87508. Offers creative writing (MFA), including poetry. *Program availability:* Low-residency. *Degree requirements:* For master's, thesis. *Entrance requirements:* For master's, sample of creative work, essay, sample of craft or scholarly essay, two letters of recommendation, all official college transcripts. Electronic applications accepted. Application fee is waived when completed online.

Iowa State University of Science and Technology, Department of English, Ames, IA 50011. Offers creative writing (MFA); English (MA); rhetoric and professional communication (PhD). *Degree requirements:* For master's, thesis or alternative; for doctorate, thesis/dissertation. *Entrance requirements:* For master's, GRE General Test, sample of written work, resume, portfolio in creative writing; for doctorate, GRE General Test, sample of written work, resume. Additional exam requirements/recommendations for international students: required—TOEFL (minimum score 600 paper-based; 100 iBT), IELTS (minimum score 7). Electronic applications accepted.

Iowa State University of Science and Technology, Program in Creative Writing and Environment, Ames, IA 50011. Offers MFA. *Entrance requirements:* For master's, GRE, official academic transcripts, resume, three letters of recommendation, statement of personal goals, writing samples. Additional exam requirements/recommendations for international students: required—TOEFL (minimum score 600 paper-based; 100 iBT), IELTS (minimum score 7). Electronic applications accepted.

Ithaca College, Roy H. Park School of Communications, Program in Image Text, Ithaca, NY 14850. Offers MFA. *Program availability:* Part-time-only. *Faculty:* 12 full-time (3 women). *Students:* 7 part-time (4 women); includes 2 minority (1 Black or African American, non-Hispanic/Latino; 1 Two or more races, non-Hispanic/Latino; 1 international. Average age 37. 22 applicants, 91% accepted, 5 enrolled. In 2019, 8 master's awarded. *Entrance requirements:* Additional exam requirements/recommendations for international students: required—TOEFL (minimum score 550 paper-based; 80 iBT). *Application deadline:* For fall admission, 2/1 for domestic and international students. Applications are processed on a rolling basis. Application fee: $40. Electronic applications accepted. *Expenses:* Contact institution. *Financial support:* In 2019–20, 7 students received support, including 7 fellowships (averaging $6,490 per year); Federal Work-Study and scholarships/grants also available. Support available to part-time students. Financial award application deadline: 3/1; financial award applicants required to submit FAFSA. *Unit head:* Nicholas Muellner, Co-Director, Image Text Program, 607-274-1984, E-mail: nmuellner@ithaca.edu. *Application contact:* Nicole Eversley Bradwell, Director, Office of Admission, 800-429-4274, Fax: 607-274-1263, E-mail: admission@ithaca.edu. Website: https://www.ithaca.edu/admission/graduate-admission/graduate-study-image-text

James Madison University, The Graduate School, College of Arts and Letters, Program in Writing, Rhetoric, and Technical Communication, Harrisonburg, VA 22807. Offers MA, MS. *Program availability:* Part-time. *Students:* 10 full-time (6 women), 4 part-time (all women); includes 2 minority (1 Black or African American, non-Hispanic/Latino; 1 Asian, non-Hispanic/Latino). Average age 30. In 2019, 9 master's awarded. Application fee: $60. Electronic applications accepted. *Financial support:* In 2019–20, 10 students received support, including 2 teaching assistantships with full tuition reimbursements available (averaging $9,284 per year); fellowships, career-related internships or fieldwork, Federal Work-Study, and assistantships (averaging $7911) also available. Financial award application deadline: 3/1; financial award applicants required to submit FAFSA. *Unit head:* Dr. Traci A. Zimmerman, Director of the School of Writing, Rhetoric and Technical Communication, 540-568-2334, E-mail: zimmerta@jmu.edu. *Application contact:* Lynette D. Michael, Director of Graduate Admissions, 540-568-6131 Ext. 6395, Fax: 540-568-7860, E-mail: michaeld@jmu.edu. Website: http://www.jmu.edu/wrtc

Johns Hopkins University, Advanced Academic Programs, Program in Writing, Washington, DC 21218. Offers science writing (MA, Certificate); writing (MA). *Program availability:* Part-time, evening/weekend. *Entrance requirements:* For master's, minimum GPA of 3.0, writing samples. Additional exam requirements/recommendations for international students: required—TOEFL (minimum score 600 paper-based; 100 iBT). Electronic applications accepted.

Johns Hopkins University, Zanvyl Krieger School of Arts and Sciences, The Writing Seminars, Baltimore, MD 21218. Offers fiction writing (MFA); poetry (MFA). *Degree requirements:* For master's, one foreign language, thesis, foreign language exam (MFA). *Entrance requirements:* For master's, GRE General Test (recommended), GRE Subject Test (recommended), foreign language exam, sample of written work, 3 letters of recommendation, transcripts of all college/university course work. Additional exam requirements/recommendations for international students: required—TOEFL (minimum score 600 paper-based; 100 iBT). Electronic applications accepted. *Expenses:* Contact institution.

Kean University, College of Liberal Arts, Program in English Writing Studies, Union, NJ 07083. Offers MA. *Program availability:* Part-time. *Faculty:* 16 full-time (11 women). *Students:* 6 full-time (all women), 11 part-time (7 women); includes 9 minority (6 Black or African American, non-Hispanic/Latino; 2 Asian, non-Hispanic/Latino; 1 Hispanic/Latino). Average age 32. 14 applicants, 93% accepted, 11 enrolled. In 2019, 4 master's awarded. *Degree requirements:* For master's, thesis. *Entrance requirements:* For master's, GRE General Test, minimum GPA of 3.0, official transcripts from all institutions attended, two letters of recommendation, personal statement, professional resume/curriculum vitae. Additional exam requirements/recommendations for international students: required—TOEFL (minimum score 550 paper-based; 79 iBT), IELTS (minimum score 6.5). *Application deadline:* For fall admission, 6/30 for domestic and international students; for spring admission, 12/8 for domestic and international students. Applications are processed on a rolling basis. Application fee: $75. Electronic applications accepted. *Expenses:* Tuition, state resident: full-time $15,326; part-time $748 per credit. Tuition, nonresident: full-time $20,288; part-time $902 per credit. *Required fees:* $2149.50; $91.25 per credit. Tuition and fees vary according to course level, course load, degree level and program. *Financial support:* Scholarships/grants and unspecified assistantships available. Financial award applicants required to submit FAFSA. *Unit head:* Dr. Mia Zamora, Program Coordinator, 908-737-0385, E-mail: schandler@kean.edu. *Application contact:* Amy Clark, Program Assistant, 908-737-7100, E-mail: grad-adm@kean.edu. Website: http://grad.kean.edu/masters-programs/english-writing-studies

Kennesaw State University, College of Humanities and Social Sciences, Program in Professional Writing, Kennesaw, GA 30144. Offers MAPW. *Program availability:* Part-time, evening/weekend. *Students:* 22 full-time (12 women), 37 part-time (23 women); includes 19 minority (13 Black or African American, non-Hispanic/Latino; 1 Asian, non-Hispanic/Latino; 4 Hispanic/Latino; 1 Two or more races, non-Hispanic/Latino), 2 international. Average age 35. 29 applicants, 97% accepted, 22 enrolled. In 2019, 16 master's awarded. *Degree requirements:* For master's, thesis optional. *Entrance requirements:* For master's, GRE General Test, minimum GPA of 2.5, writing sample. Additional exam requirements/recommendations for international students: required—TOEFL (minimum score 80 iBT), IELTS (minimum score 6.5). *Application deadline:* For fall admission, 2/1 priority date for domestic and international students; for spring admission, 10/1 for domestic and international students. Application fee: $60. Electronic applications accepted. *Expenses: Tuition, area resident:* Full-time $7104; part-time $296 per credit hour. Tuition, state resident: full-time $7104; part-time $296 per credit hour. Tuition, nonresident: full-time $25,584; part-time $1066 per credit hour. *International tuition:* $25,584 full-time. *Required fees:* $2006; $1706 per unit. $853 per semester. *Financial support:* Applicants required to submit FAFSA. *Unit head:* Dr. Tony Grooms, Director, 470-578-6440, E-mail: tgrooms@kennesaw.edu. *Application contact:* Terri Brennen, Coordinator, 470-578-3335, Fax: 470-578-9172, E-mail: tbrennen@kennesaw.edu. Website: http://chss.kennesaw.edu/mapw/

Kent State University, College of Arts and Sciences, Department of English, Kent, OH 44242-0001. Offers creative writing (MFA); English (MA, PhD); English for teachers (MA); literature and writing (MA); rhetoric and composition (PhD); teaching English as a second language (MA). *Program availability:* Part-time. *Faculty:* 19 full-time (9 women), 2 part-time/adjunct (1 woman). *Students:* 101 full-time (64 women), 12 part-time (8 women); includes 5 minority (3 Black or African American, non-Hispanic/Latino; 1 Asian, non-Hispanic/Latino; 1 Hispanic/Latino), 24 international. Average age 34. 69 applicants, 77% accepted, 18 enrolled. In 2019, 19 master's, 3 doctorates awarded. *Degree requirements:* For master's, thesis (for some programs), final portfolio, final exam, practicum or thesis (for MA in teaching English as a second language); for doctorate, one foreign language, comprehensive exam, thesis/dissertation. *Entrance requirements:* For master's, GRE General Test, goal statement, 3 letters of recommendation, 8-15 page writing sample relevant to the field of study (waived for MA in English for teachers concentration), transcripts, for MA - TESL Int'l English proficiency scores: TOEFL (ibT): 79, MELAB 77, IELTS 6.5, PTE 58; for the M.A. - English, TOEFL (ibT): 94, MELAB 82, IELTS 7.0, PTE 65; for doctorate, GRE General Test, statement of purpose, 3 letters of recommendation, 8-15 page writing sample relevant to field of study, transcripts, Master's degree, 3.0 GPA on 4.0 scale; Ph.D Rhetoric & Comp - English proficiency for Int'l: TOEFL (ibT) 102, MELAB 86, IELTS 7.5, PTE 73; Ph.D - English: TOEFL (ibT) 94, MELAB 82, IELTS 7.5, PTE 73. Additional exam requirements/recommendations for international students: required—See below for scores specific to Masters or Doctorate level. *Application deadline:* Applications are processed on a rolling basis. Application fee: $45 ($70 for international students). Electronic applications accepted. *Financial support:* Fellowships with full tuition reimbursements, teaching assistantships with full tuition reimbursements, and unspecified assistantships available. Financial award application deadline: 1/15. *Unit head:* Dr. Robert Trogdon, Chair, 330-672-2676, E-mail: rtrogdon@kent.edu. *Application contact:* Wesley Raabe, Graduate Studies Coordinator, 330-672-1723, E-mail: wraabe@kent.edu.
Website: http://www.kent.edu/english/

Lake Forest College, Graduate Program in Liberal Studies, Lake Forest, IL 60045. Offers American studies (MLS); cinema in East Asia (MLS); environmental studies (MLS); history (MLS); Medieval and Renaissance art (MLS); philosophy (MLS); Spanish (MLS); writing (MLS). *Program availability:* Part-time, evening/weekend. *Faculty:* 10 full-time (4 women). *Students:* 24 part-time (14 women). Average age 45. 10 applicants, 80% accepted, 3 enrolled. In 2019, 5 master's awarded. *Degree requirements:* For master's, thesis optional, 8 courses, including at least 3 interdisciplinary seminars. *Entrance requirements:* For master's, transcript, essay, interview. Additional exam requirements/recommendations for international students: required—TOEFL (minimum score 550 paper-based; 83 iBT); recommended—IELTS (minimum score 6.5). *Application deadline:* For fall admission, 8/15 priority date for domestic students, 7/15 priority date for international students; for spring admission, 12/15 priority date for domestic students, 11/15 priority date for international students. Applications are processed on a rolling basis. Application fee: $30. Electronic applications accepted. Application fee is waived when completed online. *Expenses:* Application fee = $30 — no other fees; tuition = $2,700/course. *Financial support:* In 2019–20, 2 students received support. Partial tuition grants (for full-time teachers) available. *Unit head:* Prof. D. L. LeMahieu, Director, 847-735-5133, Fax: 847-735-6291, E-mail: lemahieu@lakeforest.edu. *Application contact:* Prof. Carol Gayle, Associate Director, 847-735-5083, Fax: 847-735-6291, E-mail: gayle@lakeforest.edu.
Website: http://www.lakeforest.edu/academics/programs/mls/

La Sierra University, College of Arts and Sciences, Department of English and Communication, Riverside, CA 92505. Offers communication (MA), including public relations/advertising, theory emphasis; English (MA), including literary emphasis, writing emphasis. *Program availability:* Part-time. *Degree requirements:* For master's, one foreign language. *Entrance requirements:* For master's, GRE General Test.

Lenoir-Rhyne University, Graduate Programs, School of Arts and Letters, Program in Writing, Hickory, NC 28601. Offers MA. *Entrance requirements:* For master's, GRE General Test or MAT, essay; resume; minimum GPA of 2.7 undergraduate, 3.0 graduate. Additional exam requirements/recommendations for international students: required—TOEFL (minimum score 600 paper-based). Electronic applications accepted. *Expenses:* Contact institution.

Lesley University, Graduate School of Arts and Social Sciences, Cambridge, MA 02138-2790. Offers clinical mental health counseling (MA), including holistic counseling, school and community counseling, trauma studies; counseling psychology (MA, CAGS), including professional counseling (MA), school counseling (MA); creative writing (MFA); expressive therapies (MA, PhD, CAGS), including art (MA), clinical mental health counseling (MA), dance (MA), expressive therapies (MA), music (MA); independent studies (CAGS); independent study (MA); intercultural relations (MA, CAGS); interdisciplinary studies (MA), including individualized studies, integrative holistic health, mindfulness studies, peace and conflict transformation, trauma sensitive assessment, intervention, and consultation, women's studies; urban environmental leadership (MA). *Program availability:* Part-time, online learning. *Degree requirements:* For master's, internship, practicum, thesis (for expressive therapies); for doctorate, thesis/dissertation, arts apprenticeship, field placement; for CAGS, thesis, internship (for counseling psychology, expressive therapies). *Entrance requirements:* For master's, MAT (counseling psychology), interview, writing samples, art portfolio; for doctorate, GRE or MAT, interview, master's degree; for CAGS, interview, master's degree. Additional exam requirements/recommendations for international students: required—TOEFL (minimum score 550 paper-based; 80 iBT). Electronic applications accepted.

Lindenwood University, Graduate Programs, School of Accelerated Degree Programs, St. Charles, MO 63301-1695. Offers administration (MSA), including management, marketing, project management; business administration (MBA); communications (MA), including digital and multimedia, media management, promotions, training and development; criminal justice and administration (MS); healthcare administration (MS); human resource management (MS); information technology (Certificate); managing information security (MS); managing information technology (MS); managing virtualization and cloud computing (MS); writing (MFA). *Program availability:* Part-time, evening/weekend, 100% online. *Faculty:* 11 full-time (6 women), 66 part-time/adjunct (23 women). *Students:* 408 full-time (262 women), 60 part-time (40 women); includes 149 minority (111 Black or African American, non-Hispanic/Latino; 2 American Indian or Alaska Native, non-Hispanic/Latino; 2 Asian, non-Hispanic/Latino; 18 Hispanic/Latino; 1 Native Hawaiian or other Pacific Islander, non-Hispanic/Latino; 15 Two or more races, non-Hispanic/Latino), 33 international. Average age 39. 268 applicants, 46% accepted, 99 enrolled. In 2019, 347 master's awarded. *Degree requirements:* For master's, thesis (for some programs), minimum cumulative GPA of 3.0; for Certificate, minimum cumulative GPA of 3.0. *Entrance requirements:* For master's, resume, personal statement, official undergraduate transcript, minimum undergraduate cumulative GPA of 3.0. Additional exam requirements/recommendations for international students: required—TOEFL (minimum score 553 paper-based; 81 iBT); recommended—IELTS (minimum score 6.5). *Application deadline:* For fall admission, 9/30 priority date for domestic and international students; for winter admission, 1/6 priority date for domestic and international students; for spring admission, 4/6 priority date for domestic and international students; for summer admission, 7/8 priority date for domestic and international students. Applications are processed on a rolling basis. Application fee: $0 ($100 for international students). Electronic applications accepted. *Expenses:* Contact institution. *Financial support:* In 2019–20, 145 students received support. Career-related internships or fieldwork, institutionally sponsored loans, scholarships/grants, tuition waivers (partial), and unspecified assistantships available. Financial award application deadline: 6/30; financial award applicants required to submit FAFSA. *Unit head:* Dr. Gina Ganahl, Dean, Accelerated Degree Programs, 636-949-4501, Fax: 636-949-4505, E-mail: gganahl@lindenwood.edu. *Application contact:* Kara Schilli, Assistant Vice President, University Admissions, 636-949-4349, Fax: 636-949-4109, E-mail: adultadmissions@lindenwood.edu.
Website: https://www.lindenwood.edu/academics/academic-schools/school-of-accelerated-degree-programs/

Lipscomb University, Program in Film and Creative Media, Nashville, TN 37204-3951. Offers writer/director (MFA); MFA/MBA. *Program availability:* Part-time, evening/weekend. *Degree requirements:* For master's, professional practicum, portfolio. *Entrance requirements:* For master's, GRE or MAT, 2 references, resume, video portfolio. Additional exam requirements/recommendations for international students: required—TOEFL (minimum score 570 paper-based; 80 iBT). Electronic applications accepted. *Expenses:* Contact institution.

London Metropolitan University, Graduate Programs, London, United Kingdom. Offers applied psychology (M Sc); architecture (MA); biomedical science (M Sc); blood science (M Sc); cancer pharmacology (M Sc); computer networking and cyber security (M Sc); computing and information systems (M Sc); conference interpreting (MA); counter-terrorism studies (M Sc); creative, digital and professional writing (MA); crime, violence and prevention (M Sc); criminology (M Sc); curating contemporary art (MA); data analytics (M Sc); digital media (MA); early childhood studies (MA); education (MA, Ed D); financial services law, regulation and compliance (LL M); food science (M Sc); forensic psychology (M Sc); health and social care management and policy (M Sc); human nutrition (M Sc); human resource management (MA); human rights and international conflict (MA); information technology (M Sc); intelligence and security studies (M Sc); international oil, gas and energy law (LL M); international relations (MA); interpreting (MA); learning and teaching in higher education (MA); legal practice (LL M); media and entertainment law (LL M); organizational and consumer psychology (M Sc); psychological therapy (M Sc); psychology of mental health (M Sc); public health (M Sc); public policy and management (MPA); security studies (M Sc); social work (M Sc); spatial planning and urban design (MA); sports therapy (M Sc); supporting older children and young people with dyslexia (MA); teaching languages (MA), including Arabic, English; translation (MA); woman and child abuse (MA).

Long Island University - Brooklyn, Richard L. Conolly College of Liberal Arts and Sciences, Brooklyn, NY 11201-8423. Offers biology (MS); chemistry (MS); clinical psychology (PhD); creative writing (MFA); English (MA); media arts (MA, MFA); political science (MA); psychology (MA); social science (MS); United Nations (Advanced Certificate); urban studies (MA); writing and production for television (MFA). *Program availability:* Part-time. Terminal master's awarded for partial completion of doctoral program. *Degree requirements:* For master's, comprehensive exam (for some programs), thesis (for some programs); for doctorate, thesis/dissertation. *Entrance requirements:* For doctorate, GRE. Additional exam requirements/recommendations for international students: required—TOEFL (minimum score 550 paper-based, 79 iBT) or IELTS. Electronic applications accepted.

Louisiana State University and Agricultural & Mechanical College, Graduate School, College of Humanities and Social Sciences, Department of English, Baton Rouge, LA 70803. Offers creative writing (MFA); English (MA, PhD).

Loyola Marymount University, School of Film and Television, Writing for the Screen Program, Los Angeles, CA 90094. Offers MFA. *Students:* 46 full-time (19 women); includes 24 minority (14 Black or African American, non-Hispanic/Latino; 2 Asian, non-Hispanic/Latino; 6 Hispanic/Latino; 2 Two or more races, non-Hispanic/Latino), 2 international. Average age 26. 92 applicants, 40% accepted. In 2019, 15 master's awarded. *Entrance requirements:* For master's, GRE Score (waived with GPA 3.0+), graduate application, personal statement, 2 letters of recommendation (one from current employer), official transcripts, visual samples, creative samples, video recording, portfolio list, 1-page resume, $500 deposit. Additional exam requirements/recommendations for international students: required—TOEFL, IELTS. *Application deadline:* For fall admission, 12/4 for domestic students. Application fee: $50. Electronic applications accepted. *Financial support:* Career-related internships or fieldwork, Federal Work-Study, scholarships/grants, and unspecified assistantships available. Financial award applicants required to submit FAFSA. *Unit head:* Patricia Meyer, Director, Writing for the Screen, E-mail: Patricia.Meyer@lmu.edu. *Application contact:* Ammar Dalal, Associate Dean of Graduate Studies, 310-338-2721, Fax: 310-338-6086, E-mail: graduateadmission@lmu.edu.
Website: http://sftv.lmu.edu/academics/graduateprograms/writingforthescreen

Maharishi International University, Graduate Studies, Program in Screenwriting, Fairfield, IA 52557. Offers MFA.

Manhattanville College, Master of Fine Arts in Creative Writing Program, Purchase, NY 10577-2132. Offers creative writing (MFA). *Program availability:* Part-time, evening/weekend. *Faculty:* 5 part-time/adjunct (3 women). *Students:* 10 full-time (6 women), 14 part-time (8 women); includes 3 minority (1 Black or African American, non-Hispanic/Latino; 1 Asian, non-Hispanic/Latino; 1 Hispanic/Latino). Average age 37. 18 applicants, 89% accepted, 12 enrolled. In 2019, 6 master's awarded. *Degree requirements:* For master's, thesis. *Entrance requirements:* For master's, 2 letters of recommendation, 2-3 page autobiographical essay, 10-12 page writing sample, official transcripts of all undergraduate work. Additional exam requirements/recommendations for international students: required—TOEFL or IELTS are required. Manhattanville College now accepts the Duolingo English Test with a required score of 105; recommended—TOEFL (minimum score 550 paper-based; 80 iBT), IELTS (minimum score 6.5). *Application deadline:* Applications are processed on a rolling basis. Application fee: $40. Electronic applications accepted. *Expenses:* $790 per credit. *Financial support:* In 2019–20, 19 students received support, including 4 fellowships with partial tuition reimbursements available (averaging $14,220 per year); scholarships/grants, tuition waivers (partial), and unspecified assistantships also available. Financial award application deadline: 3/15; financial award applicants required to submit FAFSA. *Unit head:* Lori Soderlind, Program Director, 914-323-5239, E-mail: Lori.Soderlind@mville.edu. *Application contact:* Brian Sondey, Director of Graduate Admissions, 914-323-1490, Fax: 914-694-1732, E-mail: Brian.Sondey@mville.edu.
Website: http://mvillemfa.com

Massachusetts Institute of Technology, School of Humanities, Arts, and Social Sciences, Program in Comparative Media Studies/Writing, Graduate Program in Science Writing, Cambridge, MA 02139. Offers SM. *Degree requirements:* For master's, thesis. *Entrance requirements:* For master's, GRE General Test. Additional exam requirements/recommendations for international students: required—TOEFL, IELTS. Electronic applications accepted.

McDaniel College, Graduate and Professional Studies, Program in Liberal Arts, Westminster, MD 21157-4390. Offers liberal arts (MLA); writing for children and young adults (Postbaccalaureate Certificate). *Program availability:* Part-time, evening/weekend, 100% online. *Degree requirements:* For master's, final project. *Entrance requirements:* For master's, 3 recommendations. Additional exam requirements/recommendations for international students: required—TOEFL (minimum score 79 iBT), IELTS (minimum score 6). Electronic applications accepted.

McNeese State University, Doré School of Graduate Studies, College of Liberal Arts, Department of English and Foreign Languages, Program in Creative Writing, Lake Charles, LA 70609. Offers MFA. *Program availability:* Evening/weekend. *Degree requirements:* For master's, thesis, public reading. *Entrance requirements:* For master's, GRE, writing sample.

Michigan State University, The Graduate School, College of Arts and Letters, Program in Rhetoric and Writing, East Lansing, MI 48824. Offers critical studies in literacy and pedagogy (MA); digital rhetoric and professional writing (MA); rhetoric and writing (PhD). *Entrance requirements:* Additional exam requirements/recommendations for international students: required—TOEFL. Electronic applications accepted.

Millersville University of Pennsylvania, College of Graduate Studies and Adult Learning, College of Arts, Humanities and Social Sciences, Department of English, Millersville, PA 17551-0302. Offers English (M Ed, MA); writing (Postbaccalaureate Certificate). *Program availability:* Part-time, 100% online, blended/hybrid learning, The MA, MED, and Graduate Certificate in Writing can be completed online, blended, and a combination of online and face-to-face courses. Program includes Winter and Summer course options. *Faculty:* 9 full-time (6 women). *Students:* 5 full-time (3 women), 15 part-time (11 women); includes 3 minority (1 Asian, non-Hispanic/Latino; 2 Hispanic/Latino). Average age 33. 10 applicants, 100% accepted, 5 enrolled. In 2019, 10 master's awarded. *Degree requirements:* For master's, thesis (for some programs), Literary Theory, English studies, courses selected in coordination with advisory. *Entrance requirements:* For master's, Sample scholarly work (an 8-15 page critical or research paper recently prepared). Additional exam requirements/recommendations for international students: required—TOEFL, IELTS (minimum score 6), PTE (minimum score 60). *Application deadline:* Applications are processed on a rolling basis. Application fee: $40. Electronic applications accepted. *Expenses: Tuition, area resident:* Part-time $516 per credit. Tuition, state resident: part-time $516 per credit. Tuition, nonresident: part-time $774 per credit. *Required fees:* $118.75 per credit. Tuition and fees vary according to course load, degree level and program. *Financial support:* In 2019–20, 6 students received support. Scholarships/grants and unspecified assistantships available. Financial award application deadline: 3/15; financial award applicants required to submit FAFSA. *Unit head:* Dr. Kim McCollom-Clark, Chair, 717-871-4280, Fax: 717-871-7933, E-mail: Kimbery.McCollum-Clark@millersville.edu. *Application contact:* Dr. James A. Delle, Acting Dean of College of Graduate Studies and Adult Learning/Associate Provost, Academic Administration, 717-871-7462, E-mail: James.Delle@millersville.edu.
Website: http://www.millersville.edu/english/graduate/index.php

Mills College, Graduate Studies, Department of English, Oakland, CA 94613-1000. Offers book art and creative writing (MFA); literature (MA); poetry (MFA); prose (MFA); Spanish creative writing (Certificate); translation (MFA). *Program availability:* Part-time. *Degree requirements:* For master's, comprehensive exam, thesis. *Entrance requirements:* For master's, 15-20 page writing sample. Additional exam requirements/recommendations for international students: required—TOEFL (minimum score 600 paper-based; 100 iBT), IELTS (minimum score 7). Electronic applications accepted. *Expenses:* Contact institution.

Mills College, Graduate Studies, Program in Book Art and Creative Writing, Oakland, CA 94613-1000. Offers MFA. *Program availability:* Part-time. *Degree requirements:* For master's, thesis project. *Entrance requirements:* For master's, visual portfolio of 15-25 images, written portfolio sample (for creative writing program). Additional exam requirements/recommendations for international students: required—TOEFL (minimum score 600 paper-based; 100 iBT), IELTS (minimum score 7). Electronic applications accepted.

Minnesota State University Mankato, College of Graduate Studies and Research, College of Arts and Humanities, Department of English, Mankato, MN 56001. Offers communication and composition (MA); creative writing (MFA); English studies (MA); teaching English as a second language (MA, Certificate); technical communication (MA, Certificate). *Program availability:* Part-time. *Degree requirements:* For master's, one foreign language, comprehensive exam, thesis or alternative. *Entrance requirements:* For master's, minimum GPA of 3.0 during previous 2 years, writing sample (MFA). Additional exam requirements/recommendations for international students: required—TOEFL (minimum score 500 paper-based; 61 iBT). Electronic applications accepted.

Missouri State University, Graduate College, College of Arts and Letters, Department of English, Springfield, MO 65897. Offers applied second language acquisition (MASLA); English (MA); English education (MS Ed); teaching English to speakers of other languages (Certificate); writing (MA). *Program availability:* Part-time, evening/weekend. *Degree requirements:* For master's, one foreign language, comprehensive exam, thesis or alternative. *Entrance requirements:* For master's, GRE (for MA), 9-12 teacher certification (MS Ed); minimum GPA of 3.0 (MA); personal statement (200- to 250-word description of reasons and goals behind interest in English graduate studies); at least two letters of recommendation from individuals able to speak of the applicant's academic achievements and potential; writing sample. Additional exam requirements/recommendations for international students: required—TOEFL (minimum score 550 paper-based; 79 iBT), IELTS (minimum score 6). Electronic applications accepted. *Expenses: Tuition, area resident:* Full-time $2600; part-time $1735 per credit hour. Tuition, nonresident: full-time $5240; part-time $3495 per credit hour. *International tuition:* $5240 full-time. *Required fees:* $530; $438 per credit hour. Tuition and fees vary according to class time, course level, course load, degree level, campus/location and program.

Monmouth University, Graduate Studies, Department of English, West Long Branch, NJ 07764-1898. Offers creative writing (MA); literature (MA); rhetoric and writing (MA). *Program availability:* Part-time, evening/weekend. *Faculty:* 7 full-time (5 women). *Students:* 7 full-time (4 women), 34 part-time (22 women); includes 3 minority (2 Hispanic/Latino; 1 Two or more races, non-Hispanic/Latino). Average age 32. In 2019, 14 master's awarded. *Degree requirements:* For master's, comprehensive exam (for some programs), thesis. *Entrance requirements:* For master's, minimum overall GPA of 2.75, fifteen or more credits in literature or related field, essay of 1000 words describing interest and goals, two letters of recommendation, creative writing sample. Additional exam requirements/recommendations for international students: required—TOEFL (minimum score 550 paper-based, 79 iBT), IELTS (minimum score 6), Michigan English Language Assessment Battery (minimum score 77) or Certificate of Advanced English (minimum score of 160). *Application deadline:* For fall admission, 7/15 for domestic students, 6/1 for international students; for spring admission, 12/1 for domestic students, 11/1 for international students; for summer admission, 5/1 for domestic students. Applications are processed on a rolling basis. Application fee: $50. Electronic applications accepted. *Expenses: Tuition:* Full-time $22,194; part-time $14,796 per credit. *Required fees:* $712; $178 per semester. $178 per semester. Tuition and fees vary according to course load. *Financial support:* In 2019–20, 37 students received support. Research assistantships, teaching assistantships, scholarships/grants, and unspecified assistantships available. Support available to part-time students. Financial award applicants required to submit FAFSA. *Unit head:* Dr. Mary Kate Azcuy, Program Director, 732-571-3439, Fax: 732-263-5242, E-mail: mazcuy@monmouth.edu. *Application contact:* Kevin New, Graduate Admission Counselor, 732-571-3452, Fax: 732-263-5123, E-mail: gradadm@monmouth.edu.
Website: https://www.monmouth.edu/graduate/ma-english/

Montclair State University, The Graduate School, College of Humanities and Social Sciences, Teaching Writing Certificate Program, Montclair, NJ 07043-1624. Offers Certificate. *Program availability:* Part-time, evening/weekend. *Entrance requirements:* For degree, 2 letters of recommendation, essay. Additional exam requirements/recommendations for international students: required—TOEFL (minimum score 83 iBT), IELTS (minimum score 6.5). Electronic applications accepted.

Mount Mary University, Graduate Programs, Program in English, Milwaukee, WI 53222-4597. Offers creative writing (MA); professional and new media writing (MA). *Program availability:* Part-time, evening/weekend. *Degree requirements:* For master's, comprehensive exam, thesis or alternative. *Entrance requirements:* For master's, minimum GPA of 2.75. Additional exam requirements/recommendations for international students: required—TOEFL (minimum score 550 paper-based; 80 iBT); recommended—IELTS (minimum score 6.5). Electronic applications accepted. *Expenses:* Contact institution.

Mount Saint Mary's University, Graduate Division, Los Angeles, CA 90049. Offers business administration (MBA); counseling psychology (MS); creative writing (MFA); education (MS, Certificate); film and television (MFA); health policy and management (MS); humanities (MA); nursing (MSN, Certificate); physical therapy (DPT); religious studies (MA). *Program availability:* Part-time, evening/weekend. *Entrance requirements:* Additional exam requirements/recommendations for international students: required—TOEFL. Electronic applications accepted. *Expenses: Tuition:* Full-time $18,648; part-time $9324 per year. *Required fees:* $540; $540 per unit.

Murray State University, College of Humanities and Fine Arts, Department of English and Philosophy, Murray, KY 42071. Offers creative writing (MFA); English (MA); English pedagogy and technology (DA); gender studies (Certificate); teaching English to speakers of other languages (TESOL) (MA). *Program availability:* Part-time, 100% online, blended/hybrid learning. *Entrance requirements:* For master's, doctorate, and Certificate, GRE or GMAT, minimum university GPA of 2.75. Additional exam requirements/recommendations for international students: required—TOEFL (minimum score 527 paper-based; 71 iBT). Electronic applications accepted.

Naropa University, Graduate Programs, Program in Creative Writing, Boulder, CO 80302-6697. Offers MFA. *Program availability:* Part-time, blended/hybrid learning. *Degree requirements:* For master's, thesis. *Entrance requirements:* For master's, creative writing sample; resume/curriculum vitae with pertinent academic, employment and volunteer activities; transcripts; 2 letters of recommendation; letter of interest. Additional exam requirements/recommendations for international students: required—TOEFL (minimum score 550 paper-based; 80 iBT). Electronic applications accepted. *Expenses:* Contact institution.

Naropa University, Graduate Programs, Program in Creative Writing and Poetics, Boulder, CO 80302-6697. Offers MFA. *Program availability:* Part-time. *Degree requirements:* For master's, thesis. *Entrance requirements:* For master's, resume/curriculum vitae with pertinent academic, employment and volunteer activity; 2 letters of recommendation; transcripts; statement of interest; 10-15 page creative writing sample; phone interview. Additional exam requirements/recommendations for international students: required—TOEFL (minimum score 550 paper-based; 80 iBT). Electronic applications accepted. *Expenses:* Contact institution.

National Louis University, College of Arts and Sciences, Chicago, IL 60603. Offers adult education (Ed D); counseling and human services (MS); language and academic development (M Ed, Certificate); psychology (MA, PhD, Certificate); public policy (MA); written communication (MS, Certificate). *Program availability:* Part-time, evening/weekend, online learning. *Degree requirements:* For master's and Certificate, comprehensive exam (for some programs), thesis (for some programs); for doctorate, thesis/dissertation. *Entrance requirements:* For master's, MAT or GRE, 3 professional or academic references, interview, minimum GPA of 3.0; for doctorate, GRE General Test, MAT, or Watson-Glaser Critical Thinking Appraisal, three professional or academic references, statement of academic and professional goals, 3 years of experience in field, interview, master's degree, resume, writing sample; for Certificate, GRE, MAT, or Watson-Glaser Critical Thinking Appraisal, three professional or academic references, statement of academic and professional goals, interview, minimum GPA of 3.0. Additional exam requirements/recommendations for international students: required—Department of Language Studies Assessment or TOEFL (minimum score 550 paper-based; 79 iBT). Electronic applications accepted.

National University, College of Letters and Sciences, La Jolla, CA 92037-1011. Offers biology (MS); counseling psychology (MA), including licensed professional clinical counseling, marriage and family therapy; creative writing (MFA); English (MA); film studies (MA); forensic and crime scene investigations (Certificate); forensic sciences (MFS); human behavior (MA); mathematics for educators (MS); performance psychology (MA); strategic communications (MA). *Program availability:* Part-time, evening/weekend, 100% online, blended/hybrid learning. *Degree requirements:* For master's, thesis (for some programs). *Entrance requirements:* For master's, interview, minimum GPA of 2.5. Additional exam requirements/recommendations for international students: required—TOEFL (minimum score 550 paper-based; 79 iBT), IELTS (minimum score 6). Electronic applications accepted. *Expenses: Tuition:* Full-time $442; part-time $442 per unit.

National University, School of Professional Studies, La Jolla, CA 92037-1011. Offers criminal justice (MCJ); digital cinema production (MFA); digital journalism (MA); homeland security and emergency management (MS); juvenile justice (MS); professional screenwriting (MFA); public administration (MPA), including human resource management, organizational leadership. *Program availability:* Part-time, evening/weekend, 100% online, blended/hybrid learning. *Degree requirements:* For master's, thesis (for some programs). *Entrance requirements:* For master's, interview, minimum GPA of 2.5. Additional exam requirements/recommendations for international students: required—TOEFL (minimum score 550 paper-based; 79 iBT), IELTS (minimum score 6). Electronic applications accepted. *Expenses: Tuition:* Full-time $442; part-time $442 per unit.

New England College, Programs in Writing, Henniker, NH 03242-3293. Offers poetry (MFA); professional writing (MA). *Program availability:* Part-time, evening/weekend. Electronic applications accepted.

New Hampshire Institute of Art, Graduate Studies, Manchester, NH 03104. Offers art education (MA); creative writing (MFA); photography (MFA); teaching visual arts (MAT); visual arts (MFA). *Accreditation:* NASAD. *Degree requirements:* For master's, thesis, corresponding exhibition and artist talk. *Entrance requirements:* For master's, writing sample or visual art portfolio; curriculum vitae; transcripts; letters of recommendation. Additional exam requirements/recommendations for international students: required—

TOEFL (minimum score 550 paper-based; 80 iBT), IELTS (minimum score 6.5). Electronic applications accepted. *Expenses:* Contact institution.

New Mexico Highlands University, Graduate Studies, College of Arts and Sciences, Department of English, Las Vegas, NM 87701. Offers English (MA), including creative writing, language, rhetoric and composition, literature. *Degree requirements:* For master's, comprehensive exam, thesis. *Entrance requirements:* For master's, minimum undergraduate GPA of 3.0. Additional exam requirements/recommendations for international students: required—TOEFL (minimum score 540 paper-based).

New Mexico State University, College of Arts and Sciences, Department of English, Las Cruces, NM 88003-8001. Offers creative writing (MFA); English (MA), including creative writing, English studies for teachers, literature, rhetoric and professional communication; rhetoric and professional communication (PhD). *Program availability:* Part-time. *Faculty:* 17 full-time (7 women), 1 (woman) part-time/adjunct. *Students:* 43 full-time (28 women), 16 part-time (10 women); includes 25 minority (3 Black or African American, non-Hispanic/Latino; 1 Asian, non-Hispanic/Latino; 20 Hispanic/Latino; 1 Two or more races, non-Hispanic/Latino), 6 international. Average age 35. 46 applicants, 57% accepted, 14 enrolled. In 2019, 16 master's, 4 doctorates awarded. *Degree requirements:* For master's, one foreign language, thesis (for some programs); for doctorate, comprehensive exam, thesis/dissertation, internship. *Entrance requirements:* For master's and doctorate, sample of written work. Additional exam requirements/recommendations for international students: required—TOEFL (minimum score 550 paper-based; 79 iBT), IELTS (minimum score 6.5). *Application deadline:* For fall admission, 2/1 for domestic and international students. Application fee: $40 ($50 for international students). Electronic applications accepted. *Financial support:* In 2019–20, 46 students received support, including 5 fellowships (averaging $4,844 per year), 40 teaching assistantships (averaging $18,521 per year); career-related internships or fieldwork, Federal Work-Study, scholarships/grants, traineeships, health care benefits, and unspecified assistantships also available. Support available to part-time students. Financial award application deadline: 3/1. *Unit head:* Dr. Elizabeth Schirmer, Interim Department Head, 575-646-3931, Fax: 575-646-7725, E-mail: eschirme@nmsu.edu. *Application contact:* Dr. Tracey Eileen Miller-Tomlinson, Director of Graduate Studies, 575-646-2213, Fax: 575-646-7725, E-mail: tomlin@nmsu.edu. Website: http://english.nmsu.edu

New Saint Andrews College, Graduate School, Moscow, ID 83843. Offers classical Christian studies (Graduate Certificate); creative writing (MFA); theology and letters (MA). *Program availability:* Part-time, blended/hybrid learning. *Degree requirements:* For master's, comprehensive exam (for some programs), thesis (for some programs), final oral exam. *Entrance requirements:* For master's, GRE, 2 letters of recommendation; for Graduate Certificate, GRE, bachelor's degree, essays, 2 letters of recommendation. Electronic applications accepted. *Expenses: Tuition:* Full-time $8800; part-time $550 per credit.

The New School, Schools of Public Engagement, Creative Writing Program, New York, NY 10011. Offers MFA. *Program availability:* Part-time. *Faculty:* 6 full-time (2 women), 20 part-time/adjunct. *Students:* 194 full-time (142 women), 1 part-time (0 women); includes 51 minority (16 Black or African American, non-Hispanic/Latino; 11 Asian, non-Hispanic/Latino; 19 Hispanic/Latino; 5 Two or more races, non-Hispanic/Latino), 20 international. Average age 29. 321 applicants, 82% accepted, 101 enrolled. In 2019, 98 master's awarded. *Degree requirements:* For master's, thesis. *Entrance requirements:* For master's, transcripts, recommendation letters, statement of purpose, writing portfolio, resume. Additional exam requirements/recommendations for international students: required—TOEFL (minimum score 92 iBT), IELTS (minimum score 7), PTE (minimum score 68). *Application deadline:* For fall admission, 1/15 priority date for domestic and international students. Applications are processed on a rolling basis. Application fee: $50. Electronic applications accepted. *Expenses:* 1810 per credit. *Financial support:* In 2019–20, 176 students received support, including 3 fellowships (averaging $10,405 per year), 9 teaching assistantships (averaging $3,919 per year); career-related internships or fieldwork, scholarships/grants, and unspecified assistantships also available. Financial award application deadline: 2/1; financial award applicants required to submit FAFSA. *Unit head:* Luis Jaramillo, Chair, 212-229-5611 Ext. 2346, E-mail: jaramillo@newschool.edu. *Application contact:* Merida Gasbarro, 212-229-5600 Ext. 1108, E-mail: escandom@newschool.edu. Website: https://www.newschool.edu/public-engagement/mfa-creative-writing/

New York University, Graduate School of Arts and Science, Program in Creative Writing, New York, NY 10012-1019. Offers MA, MFA. *Program availability:* Part-time, evening/weekend. *Degree requirements:* For master's, one foreign language, thesis or alternative. *Entrance requirements:* For master's, GRE General Test, sample of written work. Additional exam requirements/recommendations for international students: required—TOEFL, IELTS.

New York University, School of Professional Studies, Center for Applied Liberal Arts, Program in Professional Writing, New York, NY 10012-1019. Offers professional writing (MS). *Program availability:* Part-time, evening/weekend, 100% online. *Degree requirements:* For master's, thesis. *Entrance requirements:* For master's, GRE or GMAT (only upon request), bachelor's degree, resume with relevant professional work, internship or volunteer experience, two letters of recommendation, personal statement. Additional exam requirements/recommendations for international students: required—TOEFL (minimum score 600 paper-based; 100 iBT), IELTS (minimum score 7). Electronic applications accepted. *Expenses:* Contact institution.

New York University, Tisch School of the Arts, Rita and Burton Goldberg Department of Dramatic Writing, New York, NY 10012-1019. Offers MFA. *Entrance requirements:* For master's, writing sample. Electronic applications accepted.

North Carolina State University, Graduate School, College of Humanities and Social Sciences, Department of English, Program in Creative Writing, Raleigh, NC 27695. Offers MFA. *Entrance requirements:* For master's, GRE. Electronic applications accepted.

North Dakota State University, College of Graduate and Interdisciplinary Studies, College of Arts, Humanities and Social Sciences, Department of English, Fargo, ND 58102. Offers composition (MA); rhetoric, writing and culture (PhD). *Program availability:* Part-time. *Degree requirements:* For master's, one foreign language, thesis. *Entrance requirements:* Additional exam requirements/recommendations for international students: required—TOEFL (minimum score 600 paper-based; 100 iBT), IELTS (minimum score 7). Electronic applications accepted. Tuition and fees vary according to program and reciprocity agreements.

Northern Arizona University, College of Arts and Letters, Department of English, Flagstaff, AZ 86011. Offers applied linguistics (PhD); creative writing (MFA), including creative writing; English (MA), including literature, professional writing, rhetoric, writing, and digital media studies, secondary education; professional writing (Graduate Certificate); rhetoric, writing and digital media studies (Graduate Certificate); teaching English as a second language (MA, Graduate Certificate). *Program availability:* Part-time, 100% online, blended/hybrid learning. *Degree requirements:* For master's, variable foreign language requirement, comprehensive exam (for some programs), thesis (for some programs); for doctorate, variable foreign language requirement, comprehensive exam (for some programs), thesis/dissertation (for some programs); for Graduate Certificate, comprehensive exam (for some programs). *Entrance requirements:* Additional exam requirements/recommendations for international students: required—TOEFL (minimum score 80 iBT), IELTS (minimum score 6.5). Electronic applications accepted.

Northern Kentucky University, Office of Graduate Programs, College of Arts and Sciences, Program in English, Highland Heights, KY 41099. Offers composition and rhetoric (Certificate); creative writing (Certificate); cultural studies and discourses (Certificate); English (MA); professional writing (Certificate). *Program availability:* Part-time, evening/weekend. *Degree requirements:* For master's, comprehensive exam (for some programs), capstone (thesis, portfolio, project, or exams); 30 hours of credit; for Certificate, 18 hours of credit. *Entrance requirements:* For master's, bachelor's degree in English or related field from regionally-accredited institution with minimum GPA of 3.0 in major or cognate area coursework; official transcripts for all undergraduate and graduate work; two letters of reference; for Certificate, official transcripts for all undergraduate and graduate work; bachelor's degree from regionally-accredited institution; minimum undergraduate GPA of 2.5. Additional exam requirements/recommendations for international students: required—TOEFL (minimum score 79 iBT); recommended—IELTS (minimum score 6.5). Electronic applications accepted.

Northern Michigan University, Office of Graduate Education and Research, College of Arts and Sciences, Department of English, Marquette, MI 49855-5301. Offers creative writing (MFA); literature (MA); pedagogy (MA); teaching English to speakers of other languages (Graduate Certificate); theater (MA); writing (MA). *Program availability:* Part-time. *Degree requirements:* For master's, thesis (for some programs), capstone project: thesis, practicum or portfolio (for MA); thesis (for MFA). *Entrance requirements:* For master's, minimum GPA of 3.0; bachelor's degree in English or minimum of 30 credit hours in undergraduate English; statement of purpose; resume; critical essay; creative writing sample (for MFA); 3 letters of recommendation; for Graduate Certificate, bachelor's degree. Additional exam requirements/recommendations for international students: required—TOEFL (minimum score 500 paper-based; 61 iBT), IELTS (minimum score 6). *Application deadline:* For fall admission, 2/1 for domestic students; for winter admission, 2/1 for domestic students; for summer admission, 3/17 for domestic students. Applications are processed on a rolling basis. Application fee: $50. Electronic applications accepted. *Financial support:* Teaching assistantships, career-related internships or fieldwork, scholarships/grants, and unspecified assistantships available. Financial award application deadline: 3/1; financial award applicants required to submit FAFSA. *Unit head:* Dr. Lynn Domina, Department Head and Professor, 906-227-1759, E-mail: ldomina@nmu.edu. *Application contact:* Dr. Lesley Larkin, Director of MA Program and Professor, 906-227-1794, E-mail: llarkin@nmu.edu. Website: http://www.nmu.edu/english/

Northwestern University, Medill School of Journalism, Media, and Integrated Marketing Communications, Evanston, IL 60208. Offers integrated marketing communications (MSIMC), including brand strategy, content marketing, direct and interactive marketing, marketing analytics, strategic communications; interactive publishing (MSJ); magazine writing/editing (MSJ); reporting (MSJ); video/broadcast (MSJ). *Entrance requirements:* For master's, GRE General Test, GMAT or LSAT (for MSJ). Additional exam requirements/recommendations for international students: required—TOEFL. Electronic applications accepted. *Expenses:* Contact institution.

Northwestern University, School of Professional Studies, Program in Creative Writing, Evanston, IL 60208. Offers MA, MFA.

Oklahoma City University, Petree College of Arts and Sciences, Oklahoma City, OK 73106-1402. Offers applied behavioral studies (M Ed); applied sociology: nonprofit leadership (MA); creative writing (MFA); criminology (MS); early childhood education (M Ed); elementary education (M Ed); general studies (MLA); leadership/management (MLA); moving image arts (MFA); professional counseling (M Ed); teaching (MA); teaching English to speakers of other languages (MA). *Program availability:* Part-time, evening/weekend. *Degree requirements:* For master's, capstone/practicum. *Entrance requirements:* For master's, bachelor's degree from accredited institution with minimum GPA of 3.0, essay, recommendation letters. Additional exam requirements/recommendations for international students: required—TOEFL (minimum score 550 paper-based; 80 iBT). Electronic applications accepted. *Expenses:* Contact institution.

Oklahoma State University, College of Arts and Sciences, Department of English, Stillwater, OK 74078. Offers creative writing (MFA); English (MA, PhD). *Faculty:* 31 full-time (18 women), 4 part-time/adjunct (all women). *Students:* 6 full-time (5 women), 108 part-time (59 women); includes 12 minority (2 Black or African American, non-Hispanic/Latino; 1 American Indian or Alaska Native, non-Hispanic/Latino; 2 Asian, non-Hispanic/Latino; 2 Hispanic/Latino; 5 Two or more races, non-Hispanic/Latino), 21 international. Average age 33. 79 applicants, 51% accepted, 21 enrolled. In 2019, 11 master's, 9 doctorates awarded. *Entrance requirements:* For master's, GRE General Test, minimum GPA of 3.0, writing sample; for doctorate, GRE General Test, minimum GPA of 3.5, writing sample. Additional exam requirements/recommendations for international students: required—TOEFL (minimum score 550 paper-based; 79 iBT). *Application deadline:* For fall admission, 3/1 priority date for international students; for spring admission, 8/1 priority date for international students. Applications are processed on a rolling basis. Application fee: $50 ($75 for international students). Electronic applications accepted. *Expenses: Tuition, area resident:* Full-time $4148.10; part-time $2765.40 per credit hour. *Tuition, state resident:* full-time $4148.10; part-time $2765.40 per credit hour. *Tuition, nonresident:* full-time $15,775; part-time $10,516.80 per credit hour. *International tuition:* $15,775.20 full-time. *Required fees:* $2196.90; $122.05 per credit hour. Tuition and fees vary according to course load, campus/location and program. *Financial support:* In 2019–20, 3 research assistantships (averaging $1,055 per year), 97 teaching assistantships (averaging $1,603 per year) were awarded; career-related internships or fieldwork, Federal Work-Study, scholarships/grants, health care benefits, tuition waivers (partial), and unspecified assistantships also available. Support available to part-time students. Financial award application deadline: 3/1; financial award applicants required to submit FAFSA. *Unit head:* Dr. An Cheng, Department Head, 405-744-9474, Fax: 405-744-6326, E-mail: an.cheng@okstate.edu. *Application contact:* Dr. Sheryl Tucker, Dean, 405-744-6368, Fax: 405-744-0355, E-mail: gradi@okstate.edu. Website: http://english.okstate.edu/

Old Dominion University, College of Arts and Letters, Master of Arts in English Program, Norfolk, VA 23529. Offers literature (MA); professional writing (MA); rhetoric and composition (MA). *Program availability:* Part-time, evening/weekend. Terminal master's awarded for partial completion of doctoral program. *Degree requirements:* For master's, comprehensive exam, thesis optional. *Entrance requirements:* For master's, GRE General Test, 24 hours in English, sample of written work, BA. Additional exam requirements/recommendations for international students: required—TOEFL. Electronic applications accepted.

Old Dominion University, College of Arts and Letters, MFA Program in Creative Writing, Norfolk, VA 23529. Offers MFA. *Program availability:* Part-time. *Degree requirements:* For master's, comprehensive exam, thesis. *Entrance requirements:* For master's, sample of written work. Additional exam requirements/recommendations for international students: required—TOEFL. Electronic applications accepted.

Writing

Oregon State University, College of Liberal Arts, Program in Creative Writing, Corvallis, OR 97331. Offers fiction (MFA). *Program availability:* Part-time. *Entrance requirements:* Additional exam requirements/recommendations for international students: required—TOEFL (minimum score 80 iBT), IELTS (minimum score 6.5).

Oregon State University, College of Liberal Arts, Program in English, Corvallis, OR 97331. Offers film and visual studies (MA); literature and culture (MA); rhetoric, writing and composition (MA). *Program availability:* Part-time. *Entrance requirements:* For master's, GRE (recommended). Additional exam requirements/recommendations for international students: required—TOEFL (minimum score 80 iBT), IELTS (minimum score 6.5).

Otis College of Art and Design, Program in Writing, Los Angeles, CA 90045-9785. Offers MFA. *Degree requirements:* For master's, thesis. *Entrance requirements:* For master's, writing sample. Electronic applications accepted.

Our Lady of the Lake University, College of Arts and Sciences, Programs in English, San Antonio, TX 78207-4689. Offers literature, creative writing, and social justice (MA); MA/MFA. *Program availability:* Part-time, evening/weekend. *Degree requirements:* For master's, comprehensive exam, thesis optional. *Entrance requirements:* For master's, GRE General Test or MAT taken within the last 5 years, bachelor's degree with at least 18 hours of advanced course work in English and/or communication arts with minimum cumulative GPA of 2.5; 2 letters of recommendation; samples of creative and scholarly writing (25 pages total); personal statement. Additional exam requirements/recommendations for international students: required—TOEFL. Electronic applications accepted. Application fee is waived when completed online.

Pacific Lutheran University, Division of Humanities, Tacoma, WA 98447. Offers creative writing (MFA). *Program availability:* Part-time, blended/hybrid learning. *Degree requirements:* For master's, thesis, final residency including teaching class. *Entrance requirements:* For master's, portfolio, book review. Additional exam requirements/recommendations for international students: required—TOEFL. Electronic applications accepted. *Expenses:* Contact institution.

Pacific University, Program in Writing, Forest Grove, OR 97116-1797. Offers MFA. *Program availability:* Part-time.

Park University, School of Graduate and Professional Studies, Kansas City, MO 54105. Offers adult education (M Ed); business and government leadership (Graduate Certificate); business, government, and global society (MPA); communication and leadership (MA); creative and life writing (Graduate Certificate); disaster and emergency management (MPA, Graduate Certificate); educational leadership (M Ed); finance (MBA, Graduate Certificate); general business (MBA); global business (Graduate Certificate); healthcare administration (MHA); healthcare services management and leadership (Graduate Certificate); international business (MBA); language and literacy (M Ed), including English for speakers of other languages, special reading teacher/literacy coach; leadership of international healthcare organizations (Graduate Certificate); management information systems (MBA, Graduate Certificate); music performance (ADP, Graduate Certificate), including cello (MM, ADP), piano (MM, ADP), viola (MM, ADP), violin (MM, ADP); nonprofit and community services management (MPA); nonprofit leadership (Graduate Certificate); performance (MM), including cello (MM, ADP), piano (MM, ADP), viola (MM, ADP), violin (MM, ADP); public management (MPA); social work (MSW); teacher leadership (M Ed), including curriculum and assessment, instructional leader. *Program availability:* Part-time, evening/weekend, online learning. *Degree requirements:* For master's, comprehensive exam (for some programs), thesis (for some programs), internship (for some programs); exam (for some programs). *Entrance requirements:* For master's, GRE or GMAT (for some programs), teacher certification (for some M Ed programs), letters of recommendation, essay, resume (for some programs). Additional exam requirements/recommendations for international students: required—TOEFL (minimum score 550 paper-based; 79 iBT), IELTS (minimum score 6). Electronic applications accepted.

Pepperdine University, Seaver College, Malibu, CA 90263. Offers business (MS), including accounting; communication (MFA), including cinematic media production; humanities (MA, MFA), including American studies (MA), writing for screen and television (MFA); religion (M Div, MA, MS), including ministry (MS), religion (M Div, MA); JD/M Div. *Entrance requirements:* For master's, GRE General Test. Additional exam requirements/recommendations for international students: required—TOEFL. *Expenses:* Contact institution.

Pittsburg State University, Graduate School, College of Arts and Sciences, Department of English and Modern Languages, Pittsburg, KS 66762. Offers English (MA), including creative writing, literature, professional writing. *Program availability:* Part-time. *Degree requirements:* For master's, thesis or alternative. *Entrance requirements:* Additional exam requirements/recommendations for international students: required—TOEFL (minimum score 550 paper-based; 79 iBT), IELTS (minimum score 6.5), PTE (minimum score 53). Electronic applications accepted. *Expenses:* Contact institution.

Portland State University, Graduate Studies, College of Liberal Arts and Sciences, Department of English, Portland, OR 97207-0751. Offers creative writing (MFA); English (MA); MA/MS. *Program availability:* Part-time, evening/weekend. *Faculty:* 33 full-time (19 women), 31 part-time/adjunct (14 women). *Students:* 82 full-time (55 women), 42 part-time (20 women); includes 22 minority (1 Black or African American, non-Hispanic/Latino; 3 Asian, non-Hispanic/Latino; 12 Hispanic/Latino; 6 Two or more races, non-Hispanic/Latino), 3 international. Average age 32. 230 applicants, 50% accepted, 48 enrolled. In 2019, 60 master's awarded. *Degree requirements:* For master's, variable foreign language requirement, comprehensive exam (for some programs), thesis (for some programs), oral and written exams. *Entrance requirements:* For master's, GRE (for some programs), statement of purpose, 2 letters of recommendation, transcripts, critical writing sample. Additional exam requirements/recommendations for international students: required—TOEFL (minimum score 600 paper-based; 100 iBT). *Application deadline:* For fall admission, 1/15 for domestic and international students; for winter admission, 9/1 for domestic and international students; for spring admission, 11/1 for domestic and international students. Application fee: $65. Electronic applications accepted. *Expenses: Tuition, area resident:* Full-time $13,020; part-time $6510 per year. Tuition, state resident: full-time $13,020; part-time $6510 per year. Tuition, nonresident: full-time $19,830; part-time $9915 per year. *International tuition:* $19,830 full-time. *Required fees:* $1226. One-time fee: $350. Tuition and fees vary according to course load, program and reciprocity agreements. *Financial support:* In 2019–20, 15 teaching assistantships with full and partial tuition reimbursements (averaging $10,653 per year) were awarded; career-related internships or fieldwork, Federal Work-Study, scholarships/grants, tuition waivers (full and partial), and unspecified assistantships also available. Support available to part-time students. Financial award application deadline: 3/1; financial award applicants required to submit FAFSA. *Unit head:* Dr. Paul Collins, Chair, 503-725-9777, Fax: 503-725-3561, E-mail: pcollins@pdx.edu. *Application contact:* Chloe Bobar, Academic and Program Coordinator, 503-725-3623, E-mail: cbobar@pdx.edu.
Website: http://www.pdx.edu/english/

Pratt Institute, School of Liberal Arts and Sciences, Program in Writing, Brooklyn, NY 11205-3899. Offers MFA. *Students:* 14 full-time (12 women); includes 9 minority (4

Black or African American, non-Hispanic/Latino; 1 Asian, non-Hispanic/Latino; 3 Hispanic/Latino; 1 Two or more races, non-Hispanic/Latino), 2 international. Average age 27. 66 applicants, 35% accepted, 6 enrolled. In 2019, 9 master's awarded. *Degree requirements:* For master's, thesis. *Entrance requirements:* For master's, writing sample. Additional exam requirements/recommendations for international students: required—TOEFL (minimum score 600 paper-based; 100 iBT). *Application deadline:* For fall admission, 1/5 for domestic and international students; for spring admission, 10/1 for domestic and international students. Application fee: $50 ($90 for international students). Electronic applications accepted. *Expenses: Tuition:* Full-time $33,246; part-time $1847 per credit. *Required fees:* $1980. *Financial support:* Career-related internships or fieldwork, Federal Work-Study, institutionally sponsored loans, scholarships/grants, health care benefits, and unspecified assistantships available. Support available to part-time students. Financial award application deadline: 2/1; financial award applicants required to submit FAFSA. *Unit head:* Beth Loffreda, Chairperson, 718-687-5770, E-mail: bloffred@pratt.edu. *Application contact:* Natalie Capannelli, Director of Graduate Admissions, 718-636-3551, Fax: 718-399-4242, E-mail: ncapanne@pratt.edu.
Website: https://www.pratt.edu/academics/liberal-arts-and-sciences/graduate-writing/

Purdue University, Graduate School, College of Liberal Arts, Department of English, West Lafayette, IN 47907. Offers creative writing (MFA); literature (MA, PhD), including linguistics, literature and philosophy (PhD), rhetoric and composition, theory and cultural studies (PhD). *Program availability:* Part-time. *Faculty:* 42 full-time (17 women), 9 part-time/adjunct (6 women). *Students:* 85 full-time (58 women), 52 part-time (29 women); includes 23 minority (6 Black or African American, non-Hispanic/Latino; 1 American Indian or Alaska Native, non-Hispanic/Latino; 5 Asian, non-Hispanic/Latino; 7 Hispanic/Latino; 4 Two or more races, non-Hispanic/Latino), 24 international. Average age 31. 245 applicants, 22% accepted, 23 enrolled. In 2019, 11 master's, 22 doctorates awarded. *Degree requirements:* For master's, one foreign language, comprehensive exam (for some programs), thesis (for some programs); for doctorate, one foreign language, comprehensive exam, thesis/dissertation. *Entrance requirements:* For master's, GRE General Test; GRE Subject Test in English literature (recommended for students applying to literary studies), minimum undergraduate GPA of 3.0 or equivalent; for doctorate, GRE General Test; GRE Subject Test in English literature (recommended for students applying to literary studies), master's degree. Additional exam requirements/recommendations for international students: required—TOEFL (minimum score 620 paper-based; 77 iBT). *Application deadline:* For fall admission, 1/15 for domestic and international students. Applications are processed on a rolling basis. Application fee: $60 ($75 for international students). Electronic applications accepted. *Financial support:* Fellowships with tuition reimbursements and teaching assistantships with tuition reimbursements available. Support available to part-time students. Financial award application deadline: 1/15; financial award applicants required to submit FAFSA. *Unit head:* Dorsey Armstrong, Head, 765-494-6478, E-mail: darmstrong@purdue.edu. *Application contact:* Jill M. Quirk, Graduate Contact, 765-494-3748, Fax: 765-494-1700, E-mail: griff@purdue.edu.
Website: https://www.cla.purdue.edu/english/

Queens College of the City University of New York, Arts and Humanities Division, Department of English, Queens, NY 11367-1597. Offers creative writing and literary translation (MFA); English (MA). *Program availability:* Part-time, evening/weekend. *Faculty:* 47 full-time (25 women), 81 part-time/adjunct (50 women). *Students:* 10 full-time (4 women), 71 part-time (49 women); includes 33 minority (6 Black or African American, non-Hispanic/Latino; 10 Asian, non-Hispanic/Latino; 16 Hispanic/Latino; 1 Two or more races, non-Hispanic/Latino), 1 international. Average age 30. 188 applicants, 35% accepted, 32 enrolled. In 2019, 24 master's awarded. *Degree requirements:* For master's, thesis, oral exam/final essay defense. *Entrance requirements:* For master's, minimum GPA of 3.0; minimum 24 undergraduate credits in English or related field and 10-15 page writing sample (for MA); manuscript (for MFA). Additional exam requirements/recommendations for international students: required—TOEFL (minimum score 100 iBT), IELTS (minimum score 7). *Application deadline:* For fall admission, 4/1 for domestic students; for spring admission, 11/1 for domestic students. Applications are processed on a rolling basis. Application fee: $125. Electronic applications accepted. *Financial support:* In 2019–20, 6 students received support, including 2 fellowships (averaging $20,801 per year), 1 research assistantship (averaging $988 per year); career-related internships or fieldwork and scholarships/grants also available. Financial award application deadline: 4/1; financial award applicants required to submit FAFSA. *Unit head:* Glenn Burger, Chair, 718-997-4661, E-mail: glenn.burger@qc.cuny.edu. *Application contact:* Cassandra Winter, Assistant Director of Graduate Admissions, 718-997-5203, E-mail: cassandra.winter@qc.cuny.edu.
Website: http://english.qc.cuny.edu/

Queens University of Charlotte, College of Arts and Sciences, Charlotte, NC 28274-0002. Offers creative writing (MFA); interior design (MA). *Program availability:* Part-time, online learning. Electronic applications accepted.

Randolph College, Program in Creative Writing, Lynchburg, VA 24503. Offers MFA.

Regent University, Graduate School, School of Communication and the Arts, Virginia Beach, VA 23464-9800. Offers acting (MFA); communication (MA, PhD), including media and arts management and promotion (MA), political communication (MA), strategic communication (MA), technical communication (MA); film and TV (MA), including producing (MA, MFA), production, script writing; film-television (MFA), including directing, producing (MA, MFA), script and screenwriting; journalism (MA); theatre (MA). *Program availability:* Part-time, evening/weekend, 100% online, blended/hybrid learning. *Degree requirements:* For master's, thesis or alternative; for doctorate, thesis/dissertation. *Entrance requirements:* For master's, transcripts, writing sample, resume, audition (for MFA programs); for doctorate, GRE General Test, resume, writing sample, recommendations, interview, transcripts, personal goals statement. Additional exam requirements/recommendations for international students: required—TOEFL (minimum score 577 paper-based). Electronic applications accepted. *Expenses:* Contact institution.

Regis University, College of Contemporary Liberal Studies, Denver, CO 80221-1099. Offers creative writing (MFA); criminology (M Sc); curriculum, instruction and assessment (M Ed); education - teacher leadership (M Ed); educational leadership (M Ed); elementary education (M Ed); literacy (Certificate); reading (M Ed); secondary education (M Ed); special education (M Ed); teacher academic leadership (Certificate); teacher leadership (MA); teacher/educational leadership (M Ed); teaching the linguistically diverse (M Ed). *Program availability:* Part-time, evening/weekend, 100% online, blended/hybrid learning. *Degree requirements:* For master's, thesis (for some programs). *Entrance requirements:* For master's, official transcript reflecting baccalaureate degree awarded from regionally-accredited college or university, work experience, resume, letters of recommendation. Additional exam requirements/recommendations for international students: required—TOEFL (minimum score 550 paper-based; 82 iBT). Electronic applications accepted. *Expenses:* Contact institution.

Reinhardt University, School of Arts & Humanities, Waleska, GA 30183-2981. Offers MFA. *Program availability:* Blended/hybrid learning. *Entrance requirements:* Additional exam requirements/recommendations for international students: required—TOEFL (minimum score 500 paper-based). Application fee is waived when completed online.

Rhode Island College, School of Graduate Studies, Faculty of Arts and Sciences, Department of English, Providence, RI 02908-1991. Offers creative writing (MA, CGS); English (MA); literature (CGS). *Program availability:* Part-time, evening/weekend. *Faculty:* 8 full-time (3 women). *Students:* 2 full-time (both women), 11 part-time (7 women). Average age 31. In 2019, 5 master's awarded. *Degree requirements:* For master's, thesis (for some programs). *Entrance requirements:* For master's, GRE General Test, 3 letters of recommendation, interview. Additional exam requirements/ recommendations for international students: required—TOEFL (minimum score 550 paper-based; 80 iBT). *Application deadline:* For fall admission, 3/1 for domestic students; for spring admission, 11/1 for domestic students. Applications are processed on a rolling basis. Application fee: $50. Electronic applications accepted. *Expenses: Tuition, area resident:* Part-time $462 per credit hour. Tuition, state resident: part-time $462 per credit hour. *Required fees:* $720. One-time fee: $140. *Financial support:* Teaching assistantships, career-related internships or fieldwork, Federal Work-Study, scholarships/grants, health care benefits, and unspecified assistantships available. Support available to part-time students. Financial award application deadline: 5/15; financial award applicants required to submit FAFSA. *Unit head:* Dr. Alison Shonkwiler, Chair, 401-456-8028. *Application contact:* Dr. Alison Shonkwiler, Chair, 401-456-8028. Website: http://www.ric.edu/english/Pages/default.aspx

Rivier University, School of Graduate Studies, Department of English, Nashua, NH 03060. Offers English (MAT); writing and literature (MA). *Program availability:* Part-time, evening/weekend. *Degree requirements:* For master's, comprehensive exam (for some programs). *Entrance requirements:* For master's, GRE Subject Test.

Roosevelt University, Graduate Division, College of Arts and Sciences, Department of Humanities, Chicago, IL 60605. Offers creative writing (MFA). Electronic applications accepted. *Expenses:* Contact institution.

Rosemont College, Schools of Graduate and Professional Studies, Creative Writing Program, Rosemont, PA 19010-1699. Offers MFA. *Program availability:* Part-time, evening/weekend. *Degree requirements:* For master's, comprehensive exam, thesis. *Entrance requirements:* For master's, 3 letters of recommendation, baccalaureate degree with minimum GPA of 3.0, writing sample. Additional exam requirements/ recommendations for international students: required—TOEFL. Electronic applications accepted. Application fee is waived when completed online.

Rowan University, Graduate School, College of Communication and Creative Arts, Program in Writing, Glassboro, NJ 08028-1701. Offers MA. *Program availability:* Part-time, evening/weekend. *Degree requirements:* For master's, thesis. *Entrance requirements:* For master's, GRE General Test. Additional exam requirements/ recommendations for international students: required—TOEFL. Electronic applications accepted. *Expenses: Tuition, area resident:* Part-time $715.50 per semester hour. Tuition, state resident: part-time $715.50 per semester hour. Tuition, nonresident: part-time $715.50 per semester hour. *Required fees:* $161.55 per semester hour.

Rowan University, Graduate School, College of Communication and Creative Arts, Writing, Composition, and Rhetoric Certificate of Graduate Study Program, Glassboro, NJ 08028-1701. Offers CGS. *Expenses: Tuition, area resident:* Part-time $715.50 per semester hour. Tuition, state resident: part-time $715.50 per semester hour. Tuition, nonresident: part-time $715.50 per semester hour. *Required fees:* $161.55 per semester hour.

Rutgers University - Camden, Graduate School of Arts and Sciences, Program in Creative Writing, Camden, NJ 08102. Offers MFA. *Program availability:* Part-time, evening/weekend. *Degree requirements:* For master's, thesis, 42 credits. *Entrance requirements:* For master's, GRE (for assistantships), 2 letters of recommendation, writing sample, statement of personal, professional, and academic goals. Additional exam requirements/recommendations for international students: required—TOEFL, IELTS. Electronic applications accepted.

Rutgers University - Newark, Graduate School, Program in Creative Writing, Newark, NJ 07102. Offers MFA. *Entrance requirements:* For master's, GRE, minimum undergraduate B average.

Rutgers University - New Brunswick, Mason Gross School of the Arts, Theater Department, New Brunswick, NJ 08901. Offers acting (MFA); design (MFA); playwriting (MFA); stage management (MFA); technical direction (MFA). *Degree requirements:* For master's, thesis (for some programs), performance project. *Entrance requirements:* For master's, audition, interview, portfolio. Additional exam requirements/recommendations for international students: required—TOEFL (minimum score 550 paper-based), IELTS (minimum score 7). Electronic applications accepted.

St. Cloud State University, School of Graduate Studies, College of Liberal Arts, Department of English, St. Cloud, MN 56301-4498. Offers English (MS); English studies (MA); rhetoric and writing (MA). *Program availability:* Part-time. *Degree requirements:* For master's, thesis or alternative. *Entrance requirements:* For master's, GRE General Test, minimum GPA of 2.75. Additional exam requirements/recommendations for international students: required—Michigan English Language Assessment Battery; recommended—TOEFL (minimum score 550 paper-based), IELTS (minimum score 6.5). Electronic applications accepted.

St. Joseph's College, New York, Program in Creative Writing, Brooklyn, NY 11205-3688. Offers MFA. *Program availability:* Part-time, evening/weekend. *Faculty:* 2 full-time (0 women), 4 part-time/adjunct (2 women). *Students:* 24 full-time (5 women); includes 9 minority (1 Black or African American, non-Hispanic/Latino; 1 Asian, non-Hispanic/ Latino; 4 Hispanic/Latino; 3 Two or more races, non-Hispanic/Latino), 2 international. Average age 30. 49 applicants, 90% accepted, 20 enrolled. In 2019, 2 master's awarded. *Entrance requirements:* For master's, application, official transcripts, 10 pages of poetry, 20 pages of prose, or a 20-page excerpt from a play, current resume, 500-word personal statement, two letters of recommendation. Additional exam requirements/ recommendations for international students: required—TOEFL (minimum score 80 iBT). *Application deadline:* Applications are processed on a rolling basis. Application fee: $25. Electronic applications accepted. *Expenses:* $28,680 per year. *Financial support:* In 2019–20, 24 students received support. *Unit head:* Lee Clay Johnson, E-mail: ljohnson6@sjcny.edu. *Application contact:* Lee Clay Johnson, E-mail: ljohnson6@sjcny.edu. Website: https://www.sjcny.edu/brooklyn/academics/graduate/graduate-degrees/ creative-writing

Saint Joseph's University, College of Arts and Sciences, Program in Writing Studies, Philadelphia, PA 19131-1395. Offers MA. *Program availability:* Part-time, evening/ weekend. *Entrance requirements:* For master's, 2 letters of recommendation, resume, 2 writing samples. Additional exam requirements/recommendations for international students: required—TOEFL (minimum score 550 paper-based; 80 iBT). Electronic applications accepted. *Expenses:* Contact institution.

Saint Leo University, Graduate Studies in Creative Writing, Saint Leo, FL 33574-6665. Offers creative writing (MA); war literature and writing for veterans (MA). *Program availability:* Part-time, online only, blended/hybrid learning. *Faculty:* 4 full-time (2 women), 1 (woman) part-time/adjunct. *Students:* 1 (woman) full-time, 27 part-time (22 women); includes 15 minority (5 Black or African American, non-Hispanic/Latino; 6 Hispanic/Latino; 4 Two or more races, non-Hispanic/Latino). Average age 42. 21

applicants, 71% accepted, 10 enrolled. In 2019, 14 master's awarded. *Degree requirements:* For master's, thesis. *Entrance requirements:* For master's, official transcripts, 2 professional recommendations, personal statement, bachelor's degree from regionally-accredited university with minimum GPA of 3.25, writing sample. *Application deadline:* For fall admission, 7/1 priority date for domestic and international students; for spring admission, 11/1 priority date for domestic and international students. Applications are processed on a rolling basis. Electronic applications accepted. Application fee is waived when completed online. *Expenses:* MA in Creative Writing $11,490 per FT yr. *Financial support:* In 2019–20, 12 students received support. Tuition remission for Saint Leo employees and their dependents available. Financial award application deadline: 3/1; financial award applicants required to submit FAFSA. *Unit head:* Dr. Steve Kistulentz, Director, 352-588-7218, Fax: 352-588-8300, E-mail: creativewriting@saintleo.edu. *Application contact:* Saint Leo University Office of Graduate Admissions, 800-707-8846, Fax: 352-588-7873, E-mail: grad.admissions@saintleo.edu.
Website: http://www.saintleo.edu/academics/graduate/creative-writing.aspx

Saint Mary's College of California, School of Liberal Arts, MFA Program in Creative Writing, Moraga, CA 94575. Offers MFA. *Degree requirements:* For master's, thesis. *Entrance requirements:* For master's, sample of written work. Electronic applications accepted.

Salve Regina University, The Newport MFA in Creative Writing Program, Newport, RI 02840-4192. Offers MFA. *Application contact:* Laurie Reilly, Graduate Admissions Manager, 401-341-2153, Fax: 401-341-2973, E-mail: laurie.reilly@salve.edu. Website: http://www.salve.edu/newport-mfa-creative-writing

Sam Houston State University, College of Humanities and Social Sciences, Department of English, Huntsville, TX 77341. Offers creative writing, editing, and publishing (MFA); English (MA). *Program availability:* Part-time. *Degree requirements:* For master's, comprehensive exam, thesis optional. *Entrance requirements:* For master's, GRE General Test, creative writing sample, letters of recommendation. Additional exam requirements/recommendations for international students: required— TOEFL (minimum score 550 paper-based; 79 iBT), IELTS (minimum score 6.5). Electronic applications accepted.

San Diego State University, Graduate and Research Affairs, College of Arts and Letters, Department of English and Comparative Literature, San Diego, CA 92182. Offers creative writing (MFA); English (MA). *Degree requirements:* For master's, one foreign language, comprehensive exam (for some programs), thesis (for some programs). *Entrance requirements:* For master's, GRE General Test, minimum GPA of 2.85, writing sample, 3 letters of recommendation. Additional exam requirements/ recommendations for international students: required—TOEFL. Electronic applications accepted.

San Diego State University, Graduate and Research Affairs, College of Arts and Letters, Department of Rhetoric and Writing Studies, San Diego, CA 92182. Offers MA. *Program availability:* Part-time. *Degree requirements:* For master's, thesis. *Entrance requirements:* For master's, GRE General Test, writing sample, 3 letters of reference. Additional exam requirements/recommendations for international students: required— TOEFL. Electronic applications accepted.

San Francisco State University, Division of Graduate Studies, College of Liberal and Creative Arts, Department of Creative Writing, San Francisco, CA 94132-1722. Offers MA, MFA. *Program availability:* Part-time. *Expenses: Tuition, area resident:* Full-time $7176; part-time $4164 per year. Tuition, state resident: full-time $7176; part-time $4164 per year. Tuition, nonresident: full-time $16,680; part-time $396 per unit. *International tuition:* $16,680 full-time. *Required fees:* $1524; $1524 per unit. $762 per semester. Tuition and fees vary according to degree level and program. *Financial support:* Career-related internships or fieldwork and Federal Work-Study available. *Unit head:* Prof. Nona Caspers, Chair, 415-338-1891, Fax: 415-338-6159, E-mail: ncaspers@sfsu.edu. *Application contact:* Prof. May-lee Chai, Graduate Coordinator, 415-338-1118, Fax: 415-338-6159, E-mail: chai@sfsu.edu.
Website: http://creativewriting.sfsu.edu/

Sarah Lawrence College, Graduate Studies, Program in Writing, Bronxville, NY 10708-5999. Offers creative non-fiction (MFA); fiction (MFA); poetry (MFA). *Program availability:* Part-time. *Degree requirements:* For master's, thesis. *Entrance requirements:* For master's, sample of creative writing, minimum B average in undergraduate course work. Additional exam requirements/recommendations for international students: required—TOEFL (minimum score 600 paper-based).

Savannah College of Art and Design, Program in Dramatic Writing, Savannah, GA 31402-3146. Offers MFA. *Program availability:* Part-time. *Degree requirements:* For master's, thesis. *Entrance requirements:* For master's, GRE (recommended), portfolio (submitted in digital format), audition or writing submission, resume, statement of purpose, two letters of recommendation. Additional exam requirements/ recommendations for international students: recommended—TOEFL (minimum score 550 paper-based; 85 iBT), IELTS (minimum score 6.5). Electronic applications accepted.

Savannah College of Art and Design, Program in Writing, Savannah, GA 31402-3146. Offers MFA. *Program availability:* Part-time, 100% online. *Degree requirements:* For master's, thesis. *Entrance requirements:* For master's, GRE (recommended), portfolio (submitted in digital format), audition or writing submission, resume, statement of purpose, two letters of recommendation. Additional exam requirements/ recommendations for international students: recommended—TOEFL (minimum score 550 paper-based; 85 iBT), IELTS (minimum score 6.5). Electronic applications accepted.

School of the Art Institute of Chicago, Graduate Division, Program in Writing, Chicago, IL 60603-3103. Offers MFA, Certificate. *Entrance requirements:* Additional exam requirements/recommendations for international students: required—TOEFL.

School of Visual Arts, Graduate Programs, Program in Visual Narrative, New York, NY 10010-3994. Offers MFA. *Degree requirements:* For master's, thesis, 60 credits. *Entrance requirements:* For master's, portfolio; statement of purpose; unique and complete short story/visual narrative (minimum 2-5 pages/images, or 2-5 minutes for video or animation submissions). Additional exam requirements/recommendations for international students: required—TOEFL (minimum score 550 paper-based; 79 iBT). Electronic applications accepted.

Seattle Pacific University, Master of Fine Arts in Creative Writing Program, Seattle, WA 98119-1997. Offers MFA. *Program availability:* Part-time. *Students:* 1 (woman) full-time, 35 part-time (27 women); includes 4 minority (1 Asian, non-Hispanic/Latino; 2 Hispanic/Latino; 1 Two or more races, non-Hispanic/Latino). Average age 33. 23 applicants, 35% accepted, 8 enrolled. In 2019, 11 master's awarded. *Degree requirements:* For master's, thesis. *Entrance requirements:* For master's, 10 pages of poetry or 25 to 30 double-spaced pages of prose, whether of fiction or creative nonfiction, in the student's chosen genre; three- to four-page (double-spaced) personal essay describing development as writer and as person of faith; three recommendations; bachelor's degree; official transcripts from previous schools attended. *Application deadline:* For winter admission, 11/1 for domestic students; for summer admission, 5/1

for domestic students. Application fee: $50. Electronic applications accepted. *Financial support:* Applicants required to submit FAFSA. *Unit head:* Dr. Scott Cairns, Director, 206-281-2109, E-mail: gwolfe@spu.edu. *Application contact:* The Graduate Center, 206-281-2091.
Website: http://spu.edu/academics/college-of-arts-sciences/mfa

Seton Hill University, MFA Program in Writing Popular Fiction, Greensburg, PA 15601. Offers MFA. *Program availability:* Part-time. *Students:* 64. *Entrance requirements:* For master's, 10-page writing sample, 3 letters of recommendation, resume, letter of intent, official transcripts. Additional exam requirements/recommendations for international students: required—TOEFL (minimum score 650 paper-based; 114 iBT), IELTS (minimum score 7). *Application deadline:* For fall admission, 10/1 priority date for domestic students; for spring admission, 3/1 priority date for domestic students. Applications are processed on a rolling basis. Application fee: $0. Electronic applications accepted. Application fee is waived when completed online. *Expenses:* Contact institution. *Financial support:* Scholarships/grants and tuition discounts available. Support available to part-time students. Financial award application deadline: 8/15; financial award applicants required to submit FAFSA. *Unit head:* Dr. Nicole Peeler, Associate Professor, English/Program Director, Writing Popular Fiction, E-mail: peeler@setonhill.edu. *Application contact:* Ellen Monnich, Assistant Director Graduate & Adult Studies, 724-838-4208, E-mail: monnich@setonhill.edu.
Website: http://www.setonhill.edu/academics/graduate_programs/fiction

Shenandoah University, School of Education and Leadership, Winchester, VA 22601-5195. Offers early childhood literacy (MS); reading licensure (MS); writing (MS). *Accreditation:* TEAC. *Program availability:* Part-time, evening/weekend. *Faculty:* 9 full-time (7 women), 48 part-time/adjunct (28 women). *Students:* 14 full-time (7 women), 200 part-time (152 women); includes 37 minority (20 Black or African American, non-Hispanic/Latino; 1 American Indian or Alaska Native, non-Hispanic/Latino; 5 Asian, non-Hispanic/Latino; 7 Hispanic/Latino; 4 Two or more races, non-Hispanic/Latino), 3 international. Average age 38. 119 applicants, 100% accepted, 81 enrolled. In 2019, 64 master's, 5 doctorates, 25 other advanced degrees awarded. *Degree requirements:* For master's, comprehensive exam (for some programs), thesis (for some programs), internship; for doctorate, comprehensive exam, thesis/dissertation; for Certificate, full-time teaching in area for one year. *Entrance requirements:* For master's, Minimum of 3.0 or satisfactory GRE, 3 letters of recommendation, valid teaching license, writing sample; for doctorate, Minimum graduate GPA of 3.5, 3 years of teaching experience, 3 letters of recommendation, writing samples, interview, resume; for Certificate, 3 letters of recommendation, writing sample, undergraduate degree with GPA of 3.0; essay, 3 letters of recommendation https://www.su.edu/admissions/graduate-students/education-application-information/. Additional exam requirements/recommendations for international students: required—TOEFL (minimum score 550 paper-based; 79 iBT), TOEFL (minimum score 550 paper-based, 79 iBT) OR IELTS (6.5). *Application deadline:* For fall admission, 4/1 for domestic and international students. Application fee: $30. Electronic applications accepted. *Expenses:* $425 per credit hour, $165 per term full-time student services fee, $175 per term full-time (9 credits or more) technology fee, $95 per term part-time (3 to 8.5 credits) technology fee. *Financial support:* In 2019–20, 34 students received support. Scholarships/grants and unspecified assistantships available. Financial award application deadline: 3/1; financial award applicants required to submit FAFSA. *Unit head:* Jill Lindsey, PhD, Director, School of Education and Leadership, 540-545-7324, Fax: 540-665-4726, E-mail: jlindsey@su.edu. *Application contact:* Andrew Woodall, Assistant Vice President for Admissions and Recruitment, 540-665-4581, Fax: 540-665-4627, E-mail: admit@su.edu.
Website: http://www.su.edu/education/

Simmons University, Gwen Ifill College of Media, Arts, and Humanities, Boston, MA 02115. Offers behavior analysis (MS, PhD, Ed S); children's literature (MA); dietetics (Certificate); elementary education (MAT); English (MA); gender/cultural studies (MA); history (MA); nutrition and health promotion (MS); physical therapy (DPT); public health (MPH); public policy (MPP); special education: moderate and severe disabilities (MS Ed); sports nutrition (Certificate); writing for children (MFA). *Program availability:* Part-time. *Faculty:* 10 full-time (9 women), 7 part-time/adjunct (6 women). *Students:* 2 full-time (both women), 67 part-time (57 women); includes 13 minority (3 Black or African American, non-Hispanic/Latino; 4 Asian, non-Hispanic/Latino; 3 Hispanic/Latino; 3 Two or more races, non-Hispanic/Latino), 1 international. Average age 31. 42 applicants, 62% accepted, 23 enrolled. In 2019, 24 master's awarded. *Degree requirements:* For master's, thesis optional. *Entrance requirements:* For master's, GRE, bachelor's degree from accredited college or university; minimum B average (preferred). Additional exam requirements/recommendations for international students: required—TOEFL (minimum score 600 paper-based; 100 iBT). *Application deadline:* For fall admission, 8/1 for domestic and international students; for spring admission, 12/15 for domestic and international students; for summer admission, 5/1 for domestic and international students. Applications are processed on a rolling basis. Application fee: $35. Electronic applications accepted. *Expenses:* Contact institution. *Financial support:* In 2019–20, 14 students received support, including 1 fellowship (averaging $15,360 per year), 13 teaching assistantships (averaging $2,000 per year); scholarships/grants also available. Financial award applicants required to submit FAFSA. *Unit head:* Dr. Brian Norman, Dean, 617-521-2472, E-mail: brian.norman@simmons.edu. *Application contact:* Patricia Flaherty, Director, Graduate Studies Admission, 617-521-3902, Fax: 617-521-3058, E-mail: gsa@simmons.edu.
Website: https://www.simmons.edu/academics/colleges-schools-departments/ifill

Sonoma State University, Department of English, Rohnert Park, CA 94928. Offers American literature (MA); creative writing (MA); English literature (MA); world literature (MA). *Program availability:* Part-time, evening/weekend. *Degree requirements:* For master's, one foreign language, thesis or alternative. *Entrance requirements:* For master's, minimum GPA of 2.5. Additional exam requirements/recommendations for international students: required—TOEFL (minimum score 500 paper-based).

Southeastern Louisiana University, College of Arts, Humanities and Social Sciences, Department of English, Hammond, LA 70402. Offers creative writing (MA); language and literacy (MA); professional writing (MA); publishing studies (MA). *Program availability:* Part-time. *Faculty:* 19 full-time (9 women). *Students:* 19 full-time (15 women), 11 part-time (8 women); includes 8 minority (2 Black or African American, non-Hispanic/Latino; 1 American Indian or Alaska Native, non-Hispanic/Latino; 5 Two or more races, non-Hispanic/Latino). Average age 30. 10 applicants, 100% accepted, 9 enrolled. In 2019, 10 master's awarded. *Degree requirements:* For master's, comprehensive exam, thesis optional. *Entrance requirements:* For master's, GRE verbal score of 150 or greater required, 24 semester hours of undergraduate English courses, at least 12 of which must be at the Jr./Sr. level, 2.50 GPA undergraduate degree. Additional exam requirements/recommendations for international students: required—TOEFL (minimum score 500 paper-based; 61 iBT). *Application deadline:* For fall admission, 7/15 priority date for domestic students, 5/1 priority date for international students; for spring admission, 12/1 priority date for domestic students, 9/1 priority date for international students. Applications are processed on a rolling basis. Application fee: $20 ($30 for international students). Electronic applications accepted. *Expenses: Tuition, area resident:* Full-time $6684; part-time $489 per credit hour. Tuition, state resident: full-time $6684; part-time $489 per credit hour. Tuition, nonresident: full-time $19,162; part-time $1183 per credit hour. *International tuition:* $19,162 full-time. *Required fees:* $2124. *Financial support:* In 2019–20, 21 students received support, including 8 research assistantships with tuition reimbursements available (averaging $9,688 per year), 2 teaching assistantships with tuition reimbursements available (averaging $11,000 per year); career-related internships or fieldwork, institutionally sponsored loans, traineeships, and unspecified assistantships also available. Financial award application deadline: 5/1; financial award applicants required to submit FAFSA. *Unit head:* Dr. David Hanson, Department Head, 985-549-2100, Fax: 985-549-5049, E-mail: dhanson@southeastern.edu. *Application contact:* Office of Admissions, 985-549-5637, Fax: 985-549-5632, E-mail: admissions@southeastern.edu.
Website: http://www.southeastern.edu/acad_research/depts/engl

Southern Illinois University Carbondale, Graduate School, College of Liberal Arts, Department of English, Program in Creative Writing, Carbondale, IL 62901-4701. Offers MFA. *Degree requirements:* For master's, one foreign language, thesis. *Entrance requirements:* For master's, GRE General Test, GRE Subject Test, minimum GPA of 2.7. Additional exam requirements/recommendations for international students: required—TOEFL.

Southern Illinois University Edwardsville, Graduate School, College of Arts and Sciences, Department of English Language and Literature, Program in Creative Writing, Edwardsville, IL 62026. Offers MA. *Program availability:* Part-time. *Degree requirements:* For master's, one foreign language, thesis. *Entrance requirements:* Additional exam requirements/recommendations for international students: required—TOEFL (minimum score 550 paper-based, 79 iBT), IELTS (minimum score 6.5), Michigan Test of English Language Proficiency or PTE. Electronic applications accepted.

Southern New Hampshire University, School of Arts and Sciences, Manchester, NH 03106-1045. Offers clinical mental health counseling (MS); creative writing (MA); criminal justice (MS); cyber security (MS); English (MA); fiction and nonfiction (MFA); history (MA); political science (MS); psychology (MS). *Program availability:* Part-time, evening/weekend. *Degree requirements:* For master's, one foreign language, thesis. *Entrance requirements:* For master's, minimum GPA of 3.0 (for MFA). Additional exam requirements/recommendations for international students: required—TOEFL (minimum score 550 paper-based; 79 iBT), IELTS (minimum score 6.5), TWE (minimum score 5). Electronic applications accepted. *Expenses:* Contact institution.

Spalding University, Graduate Studies, College of Social Sciences and Humanities, Master of Fine Arts in Writing Program, Louisville, KY 40203-2188. Offers MFA. *Program availability:* Online learning. *Degree requirements:* For master's, thesis. *Entrance requirements:* For master's, writing sample, letters of recommendation, personal essays. Additional exam requirements/recommendations for international students: required—TOEFL (minimum score 535 paper-based). Electronic applications accepted.

State University of New York at Fredonia, College of Liberal Arts and Sciences, Fredonia, NY 14063-1136. Offers biology (MS); English (MA); English education 7-12 (MA); interdisciplinary studies (MA, MS); math education (MS Ed); professional writing (CAS); speech pathology (MS); MA/MS. *Program availability:* Part-time, evening/weekend. *Degree requirements:* For master's, comprehensive exam (for some programs), thesis (for some programs). *Entrance requirements:* For master's, GRE. Additional exam requirements/recommendations for international students: required—TOEFL (minimum score 79 iBT), IELTS (minimum score 6.5). Electronic applications accepted.

Stephens College, Division of Graduate and Continuing Studies, Columbia, MO 65215-0002. Offers counseling (M Ed), including addictions counseling, clinical mental health counseling, school counseling; health information administration (Postbaccalaureate Certificate); physician assistant studies (MPAS); TV and screenwriting (MFA). *Program availability:* Part-time, evening/weekend, online learning. *Entrance requirements:* For master's, minimum GPA of 3.0 in last 60 hours. Additional exam requirements/recommendations for international students: required—TOEFL (minimum score 79 iBT). Electronic applications accepted.

Stetson University, College of Arts and Sciences, Department of English, DeLand, FL 32723. Offers MFA. *Program availability:* Blended/hybrid learning. *Faculty:* 2 full-time (both women), 4 part-time/adjunct (2 women). *Students:* 18 full-time (12 women); includes 8 minority (1 Black or African American, non-Hispanic/Latino; 2 Hispanic/Latino; 5 Two or more races, non-Hispanic/Latino). Average age 39. 11 applicants, 82% accepted, 5 enrolled. In 2019, 10 master's awarded. *Degree requirements:* For master's, book-length project. *Entrance requirements:* For master's, GRE General Test, writing sample. Additional exam requirements/recommendations for international students: required—TOEFL (minimum score 90 iBT), IELTS (minimum score 7). *Application deadline:* For fall admission, 8/1 priority date for domestic students; for spring admission, 1/1 priority date for domestic students; for summer admission, 5/1 priority date for domestic students. Applications are processed on a rolling basis. Application fee: $50. Electronic applications accepted. *Expenses:* $913 per credit hour. *Financial support:* In 2019–20, 10 students received support. Federal Work-Study, scholarships/grants, unspecified assistantships, and tuition waivers (for staff and dependents) available. Support available to part-time students. Financial award applicants required to submit FAFSA. *Unit head:* Teresa Carmody, Director, MFA of the Americas Creative Writing Program, 386-822-7741, E-mail: tcarmody@stetson.edu. *Application contact:* Jamie Vanderlip, Director of Admissions for Graduate, Transfer and Adult Populations, 386-822-7100, Fax: 386-822-7112, E-mail: jlvander@stetson.edu.

Stony Brook University, State University of New York, Graduate School, College of Arts and Sciences, Program in Writing and Rhetoric, Stony Brook, NY 11794. Offers teaching writing (Graduate Certificate). *Faculty:* 29 full-time (17 women), 7 part-time/adjunct (5 women). *Students:* 1 (woman) part-time. In 2019, 5 Graduate Certificates awarded. *Entrance requirements:* For degree, two letters of recommendation, statement of purpose. Additional exam requirements/recommendations for international students: required—TOEFL. *Application deadline:* For fall admission, 1/15 for domestic students; for spring admission, 10/1 for domestic students. *Expenses:* Contact institution. *Financial support:* Teaching assistantships available. *Unit head:* Dr. Roger Thompson, Director, 631-632-7390, E-mail: Roger.Thompson@stonybrook.edu. *Application contact:* Adam Schultheiss, Coordinator, 631-632-7390, E-mail: adam.schultheiss@stonybrook.edu.
Website: http://www.stonybrook.edu/commcms/writrhet//

Stony Brook University, State University of New York, Stony Brook Southampton, Program in Creative Writing and Literature, Stony Brook, NY 11794. Offers fiction (MFA); poetry (MFA); scientific writing (MFA), including environmental, medical, technological; scriptwriting (MFA). *Faculty:* 10 full-time (6 women), 20 part-time/adjunct (11 women). *Students:* 32 full-time (22 women), 28 part-time (23 women); includes 9 minority (3 Black or African American, non-Hispanic/Latino; 3 Asian, non-Hispanic/Latino; 2 Hispanic/Latino; 1 Two or more races, non-Hispanic/Latino), 1 international. 54 applicants, 80% accepted, 20 enrolled. In 2019, 23 master's awarded. *Entrance requirements:* Additional exam requirements/recommendations for international students: required—TOEFL (minimum score 85 iBT), IELTS (minimum score 6.5). *Application deadline:* For fall admission, 1/15 for domestic students; for spring

admission, 10/1 for domestic students. Applications are processed on a rolling basis. Application fee: $100. *Expenses:* Contact institution. *Financial support:* In 2019–20, 12 teaching assistantships were awarded. *Unit head:* Carla Caglioti, Executive Director, 631-632-5031, Fax: 631-982-7318, E-mail: carla.caglioti@stonybrook.edu. *Application contact:* Margaret S. Grigonis, Coordinator, 631-632-5028, Fax: 631-982-7318, E-mail: margaret.grigonis@stonybrook.edu.
Website: http://www.stonybrook.edu/southampton/mfa/cwl/index.html

SUNY Brockport, School of Arts and Sciences, Department of English, Brockport, NY 14420-2997. Offers creative writing (AGC); English (MA), including creative writing, literature. *Program availability:* Part-time. *Faculty:* 8 full-time (4 women). *Students:* 16 full-time (10 women), 15 part-time (8 women); includes 2 minority (both Hispanic/Latino). 13 applicants, 77% accepted, 8 enrolled. In 2019, 18 master's, 1 other advanced degree awarded. *Entrance requirements:* For master's, minimum GPA of 3.0, letters of recommendation, writing sample. Additional exam requirements/recommendations for international students: required—TOEFL (minimum score 550 paper-based; 79 iBT), IELTS (minimum score 6.5). *Application deadline:* For fall admission, 4/15 priority date for domestic and international students; for spring admission, 11/15 priority date for domestic and international students; for summer admission, 4/15 priority date for domestic and international students. Application fee: $50. Electronic applications accepted. *Expenses: Tuition, area resident:* Part-time $471 per credit hour. Tuition, nonresident: part-time $963 per credit hour. *Financial support:* In 2019–20, 3 teaching assistantships with full tuition reimbursements (averaging $6,000 per year) were awarded; Federal Work-Study, scholarships/grants, and unspecified assistantships also available. Support available to part-time students. Financial award application deadline: 3/15; financial award applicants required to submit FAFSA. *Unit head:* Dr. Jennifer Haytock, Chairperson, 585-395-5832, Fax: 585-395-2391, E-mail: jhaytock@brockport.edu. *Application contact:* Dr. Alissa Karl, Graduate Program Director, 585-395-2342, Fax: 585-395-5487, E-mail: akarl@brockport.edu.
Website: https://www.brockport.edu/academics/english/

Syracuse University, College of Arts and Sciences, MFA Program in Creative Writing, Syracuse, NY 13244. Offers MFA. *Entrance requirements:* For master's, writing sample, statement of purpose, teaching statement, transcript(s) from undergraduate/graduate institution, three letters of recommendation. Additional exam requirements/recommendations for international students: required—TOEFL (minimum score 100 iBT). Electronic applications accepted.

Syracuse University, College of Arts and Sciences, PhD Program in Composition and Cultural Rhetoric, Syracuse, NY 13244. Offers PhD. *Degree requirements:* For doctorate, comprehensive exam, thesis/dissertation. *Entrance requirements:* For doctorate, GRE, three letters of recommendation, essay on intellectual history and academic interests, statement about teaching interests and practical experience, resume, transcripts. Additional exam requirements/recommendations for international students: required—TOEFL (minimum score 100 iBT). Electronic applications accepted.

Temple University, Center for the Performing and Cinematic Arts, School of Theater, Film and Media Arts, Department of Theater, Philadelphia, PA 19122-6096. Offers acting (MFA); design (MFA); directing (MFA); musical theater collaboration (MFA); musical theater studies (MA); playwriting (MFA). *Accreditation:* NAST. *Program availability:* Part-time. *Faculty:* 14 full-time (5 women), 26 part-time/adjunct (14 women). *Students:* 25 full-time (13 women); includes 6 minority (2 Black or African American, non-Hispanic/Latino; 1 American Indian or Alaska Native, non-Hispanic/Latino; 3 Hispanic/Latino), 3 international. 21 applicants, 71% accepted, 9 enrolled. In 2019, 6 master's awarded. *Entrance requirements:* For master's, audition/interview, portfolio, or samples of written work. Additional exam requirements/recommendations for international students: required—TOEFL, IELTS, PTE, one of three is required. Application fee: $60. Electronic applications accepted. *Expenses:* Contact institution. *Financial support:* Fellowships, teaching assistantships with full tuition reimbursements, Federal Work-Study, scholarships/grants, health care benefits, and unspecified assistantships available. Financial award application deadline: 3/1; financial award applicants required to submit FAFSA. *Unit head:* Fred M. Duer, Chair, Department of Theater; Head of Design and Professor (Scenic Design), 215-204-2804, E-mail: fred.duer@temple.edu. *Application contact:* Paury Flowers, Recruitment Coordinator, CPCA: Admin. Office, 215-777-9135, E-mail: pflowers@temple.edu.
Website: https://tfma.temple.edu/theater

Temple University, College of Liberal Arts, Department of English, Philadelphia, PA 19122-6096. Offers creative writing (MFA); English (MA, PhD). *Program availability:* Part-time. *Faculty:* 24 full-time (12 women), 21 part-time/adjunct (9 women). *Students:* 75 full-time (44 women), 10 part-time (7 women); includes 18 minority (3 Black or African American, non-Hispanic/Latino; 1 American Indian or Alaska Native, non-Hispanic/Latino; 6 Asian, non-Hispanic/Latino; 7 Hispanic/Latino; 1 Two or more races, non-Hispanic/Latino), 2 international. 142 applicants, 62% accepted, 26 enrolled. In 2019, 10 master's, 4 doctorates awarded. *Entrance requirements:* For master's, statement of goals, 3 letters of recommendation, writing sample; for doctorate, GRE, 3 letters of recommendation, writing sample, statement of goals. Additional exam requirements/recommendations for international students: required—TOEFL, IELTS, PTE, one of three is required. *Application deadline:* For fall admission, 2/15 for domestic students. Application fee: $60. Electronic applications accepted. *Financial support:* Fellowships, teaching assistantships, and Federal Work-Study available. Financial award application deadline: 12/15; financial award applicants required to submit FAFSA. *Unit head:* Katherine Henry, Chairperson, 215-204-1756, E-mail: khenry@temple.edu. *Application contact:* Sharon Logan, Coordinator, 215-204-1796, Fax: 215-204-9620, E-mail: logansd@temple.edu.
Website: http://www.cla.temple.edu/english/

Texas A&M University–Commerce, College of Humanities, Social Sciences and Arts, Commerce, TX 75429. Offers applied criminology (MS); applied linguistics (MA, MS); art (MA, MFA); christianity in history (Graduate Certificate); computational linguistics (Graduate Certificate); creative writing (Graduate Certificate); criminal justice management (Graduate Certificate); criminal justice studies (Graduate Certificate); English (MA, MS, PhD); film studies (Graduate Certificate); history (MA, MS); Holocaust studies (Graduate Certificate); homeland security (Graduate Certificate); music (MM); music performance (MM); political science (MA, MS); public history (Graduate Certificate); sociology (MS); Spanish (MA); studies in children's and adolescent literature and culture (Graduate Certificate); teaching English to speakers of other languages (Graduate Certificate); theater (MA, MS); world history (Graduate Certificate). *Program availability:* Part-time. *Faculty:* 49 full-time (28 women), 8 part-time/adjunct (2 women). *Students:* 34 full-time (21 women), 427 part-time (302 women); includes 175 minority (66 Black or African American, non-Hispanic/Latino; 1 American Indian or Alaska Native, non-Hispanic/Latino; 13 Asian, non-Hispanic/Latino; 79 Hispanic/Latino; 16 Two or more races, non-Hispanic/Latino), 15 international. Average age 38. 193 applicants, 49% accepted, 78 enrolled. In 2019, 122 master's, 6 doctorates awarded. *Degree requirements:* For master's, one foreign language, comprehensive exam, thesis (for some programs); for doctorate, one foreign language, comprehensive exam, thesis/dissertation, departmental qualifying exam. *Entrance requirements:* For master's, GRE General Test, official transcripts, letters of recommendation, resume, statement of goals; for doctorate, GRE General Test, official transcripts, letters of recommendation,

statement of goals, writing samples, writing sessions, resumes. Additional exam requirements/recommendations for international students: required—TOEFL (minimum score 550 paper-based; 79 iBT), IELTS (minimum score 6), PTE (minimum score 53). *Application deadline:* For fall admission, 6/1 priority date for international students; for spring admission, 10/15 priority date for international students; for summer admission, 3/15 priority date for international students. Applications are processed on a rolling basis. Application fee: $50 ($75 for international students). Electronic applications accepted. *Expenses: Tuition, area resident:* Full-time $3630; part-time $202 per credit hour. Tuition, state resident: full-time $3630; part-time $202 per credit hour. Tuition, nonresident: full-time $11,232; part-time $624 per credit hour. *International tuition:* $11,232 full-time. *Required fees:* $2948. *Financial support:* In 2019–20, 30 students received support, including 18 research assistantships with partial tuition reimbursements available (averaging $3,231 per year), 136 teaching assistantships with partial tuition reimbursements available (averaging $4,053 per year); Federal Work-Study, institutionally sponsored loans, scholarships/grants, health care benefits, and unspecified assistantships also available. Financial award application deadline: 5/1; financial award applicants required to submit FAFSA. *Unit head:* Dr. William F. Kuracina, Interim Dean, 903-886-5166, Fax: 903-886-5774, E-mail: william.kuracina@tamuc.edu. *Application contact:* Rebecca Stevens, Graduate Student Services Coordinator, 903-468-6049, E-mail: rebecca.stevens@tamuc.edu.
Website: http://www.tamuc.edu/academics/colleges/humanitiesSocialSciencesArts/

Texas State University, The Graduate College, College of Fine Arts and Communication, Program in Theatre Arts, San Marcos, TX 78666. Offers design (MFA); directing (MFA); dramatic writing (MFA); theatre history, dramatic criticism and dramaturgy (MA). *Program availability:* Part-time, evening/weekend. *Degree requirements:* For master's, comprehensive exam, thesis (for some programs). *Entrance requirements:* For master's, official GRE (general test only) required with competitive scores in the verbal reasoning and quantitative reasoning sections, baccalaureate degree from regionally-accredited institution with minimum GPA of 2.75 in last 60 hours of undergraduate course work, 2 letters of recommendation, statement of purpose, curriculum vitae/resume; writing sample (for playwriting applicants only); interview (for directing applicants only). Additional exam requirements/recommendations for international students: required—TOEFL (minimum score 550 paper-based; 78 iBT), IELTS (minimum score 6). Electronic applications accepted.

Texas State University, The Graduate College, College of Liberal Arts, Program in Creative Writing, San Marcos, TX 78666. Offers MFA. *Program availability:* Part-time, evening/weekend. *Degree requirements:* For master's, comprehensive exam, thesis. *Entrance requirements:* For master's, baccalaureate degree from regionally-accredited university with minimum GPA of 2.75 on last 60 undergraduate semester hours, portfolio; 2-3 short stories or up to 30 pages of novel (for fiction); 12 to 15 poems (for poetry). Additional exam requirements/recommendations for international students: required—TOEFL (minimum score 550 paper-based; 78 iBT), IELTS (minimum score 6.5). Electronic applications accepted.

Tiffin University, Program in Humanities, Tiffin, OH 44883-2161. Offers art and visual media (MH); communication (MH); creative writing (MH); English (MH); film studies (MH); humanities (MH); individualized studies (MH). *Program availability:* Part-time, evening/weekend, online only, 100% online, blended/hybrid learning. *Entrance requirements:* For master's, work experience. Additional exam requirements/recommendations for international students: required—TOEFL (minimum score 550 paper-based; 79 iBT). Electronic applications accepted. Application fee is waived when completed online. *Expenses:* Contact institution.

Towson University, College of Liberal Arts, Program in Professional Writing, Towson, MD 21252-0001. Offers MS. *Program availability:* Part-time, evening/weekend. *Students:* 14 full-time (11 women), 28 part-time (17 women); includes 12 minority (5 Black or African American, non-Hispanic/Latino; 3 Asian, non-Hispanic/Latino; 2 Hispanic/Latino; 2 Two or more races, non-Hispanic/Latino). *Entrance requirements:* For master's, sample of written work, minimum GPA of 3.0, 2 letters of recommendation, essay. *Application deadline:* For fall admission, 1/17 for domestic students, 5/15 for international students; for spring admission, 10/15 for domestic students, 12/1 for international students. Applications are processed on a rolling basis. Application fee: $45. Electronic applications accepted. *Expenses: Tuition, area resident:* Full-time $7920; part-time $439 per credit. Tuition, nonresident: full-time $16,344; part-time $908 per credit. *International tuition:* $16,344 full-time. *Required fees:* $2628; $146 per credit. $876 per term. *Financial support:* Application deadline: 4/1. *Unit head:* Prof. Michael Downs, Program Director, 410-704-3695, E-mail: mdowns@towson.edu. *Application contact:* Coverley Beidleman, Assistant Director of Graduate Admissions, 410-704-5630, Fax: 410-704-3030, E-mail: grads@towson.edu.
Website: https://www.towson.edu/cla/departments/english/gradwriting/

Trinity College, Graduate Programs, Program in English, Hartford, CT 06106-3100. Offers literary studies (MA); writing, rhetoric, and media arts (MA). *Program availability:* Part-time, evening/weekend. *Degree requirements:* For master's, thesis (for some programs). *Entrance requirements:* For master's, minimum GPA of 3.0.

Union Institute & University, Master of Arts Program, Cincinnati, OH 45206-1925. Offers creativity studies (MA); health and wellness (MA); history and culture (MA); leadership, public policy, and social issues (MA); literature and writing (MA). *Program availability:* Part-time, online only, 100% online. *Degree requirements:* For master's, thesis. *Entrance requirements:* For master's, transcript, essay, 3 letters of recommendation, resume. Additional exam requirements/recommendations for international students: recommended—TOEFL. Electronic applications accepted. *Expenses:* Contact institution.

The University of Akron, Graduate School, Buchtel College of Arts and Sciences, Department of English, Northeast Ohio MFA Program in Creative Writing, Akron, OH 44325. Offers MFA. *Entrance requirements:* For master's, three letters of recommendation; writing portfolio. Additional exam requirements/recommendations for international students: required—TOEFL (minimum score 92 iBT).

The University of Akron, Graduate School, Buchtel College of Arts and Sciences, Department of English, Program in Composition, Akron, OH 44325. Offers MA. *Degree requirements:* For master's, one foreign language, thesis optional. *Entrance requirements:* For master's, statement of purpose. Additional exam requirements/recommendations for international students: required—TOEFL (minimum score 92 iBT).

The University of Alabama, Graduate School, College of Arts and Sciences, Department of English, Tuscaloosa, AL 35487. Offers composition and rhetoric (PhD); creative writing (MFA), including fiction, poetry; literature (MA, PhD); rhetoric and composition (MA); teaching English as a second language (MATESOL). *Faculty:* 21 full-time (14 women). *Students:* 122 full-time (82 women), 8 part-time (5 women); includes 29 minority (11 Black or African American, non-Hispanic/Latino; 2 American Indian or Alaska Native, non-Hispanic/Latino; 5 Asian, non-Hispanic/Latino; 3 Hispanic/Latino; 8 Two or more races, non-Hispanic/Latino), 8 international. Average age 29. 230 applicants, 25% accepted, 35 enrolled. In 2019, 32 master's awarded. *Degree requirements:* For master's, one foreign language, comprehensive exam, thesis; for doctorate, 2 foreign languages, comprehensive exam, thesis/dissertation. *Entrance requirements:* For master's, GRE (minimum score of 300, except for MFA), minimum

Writing

GPA of 3.0, critical writing sample; for doctorate, GRE (minimum score of 300), minimum GPA of 3.5 on master's or equivalent graduate work, critical writing sample. Additional exam requirements/recommendations for international students: recommended—TOEFL (minimum score 550 paper-based; 79 iBT). *Application deadline:* For fall admission, 12/31 for domestic and international students. Application fee: $50 ($60 for international students). Electronic applications accepted. *Expenses: Tuition, area resident:* Full-time $10,780; part-time $440 per credit hour. Tuition, nonresident: full-time $30,250; part-time $1550 per credit hour. *Financial support:* In 2019–20, 113 students received support, including fellowships with full tuition reimbursements available (averaging $15,000 per year), research assistantships with full tuition reimbursements available (averaging $13,500 per year), teaching assistantships with full tuition reimbursements available (averaging $13,500 per year); career-related internships or fieldwork, scholarships/grants, health care benefits, and unspecified assistantships also available. Financial award application deadline: 12/31. *Unit head:* Dr. David Ainsworth, Associate Professor and Interim Chair, 205-348-9524, Fax: 205-348-1388, E-mail: dainsworth@ua.edu. *Application contact:* Jennifer Fuqua, Graduate Coordinator, 205-348-0766, Fax: 205-348-1388, E-mail: jfuqua@ua.edu.

The University of Alabama at Birmingham, College of Arts and Sciences, Program in English, Birmingham, AL 35294. Offers creative writing (MA); literature (MA); rhetoric and composition (MA). *Program availability:* Part-time. *Faculty:* 35 full-time (18 women). *Students:* 6 full-time (5 women), 21 part-time (16 women); includes 5 minority (3 Black or African American, non-Hispanic/Latino; 1 American Indian or Alaska Native, non-Hispanic/Latino; 1 Two or more races, non-Hispanic/Latino). Average age 32. 13 applicants, 69% accepted, 5 enrolled. In 2019, 11 master's awarded. *Degree requirements:* For master's, one foreign language, comprehensive exam, thesis or alternative. *Entrance requirements:* For master's, GRE General Test or MAT, minimum GPA of 2.75. *Application deadline:* For fall admission, 7/1 for domestic students; for spring admission, 11/1 for domestic students. Applications are processed on a rolling basis. Application fee: $45 ($60 for international students). Electronic applications accepted. *Financial support:* Teaching assistantships and career-related internships or fieldwork available. *Unit head:* Dr. Gale Temple, Program Director, 205-934-8593, Fax: 205-975-6610, E-mail: gtemple@uab.edu. *Application contact:* Susan Noblitt Banks, Director of Graduate School Operations, 205-934-8227, Fax: 205-934-8413, E-mail: gradschool@uab.edu.
Website: http://www.uab.edu/cas/english/academic-programs

University of Alaska Anchorage, College of Arts and Sciences, Program in Creative Writing and Literary Arts, Anchorage, AK 99508. Offers MFA. *Program availability:* Part-time. *Degree requirements:* For master's, comprehensive exam, thesis or alternative. *Entrance requirements:* For master's, portfolio, minimum GPA of 3.0. Additional exam requirements/recommendations for international students: required—TOEFL (minimum score 550 paper-based).

University of Alaska Fairbanks, College of Liberal Arts, Department of English, Fairbanks, AK 99775-5720. Offers creative writing (MFA); literature (MA); MA/MFA. *Program availability:* Part-time. *Degree requirements:* For master's, comprehensive exam, oral defense of project or thesis. *Entrance requirements:* For master's, bachelor's degree from accredited institution with minimum cumulative undergraduate and major GPA of 3.0, creative writing sample (MFA), scholarly to critical writing sample (MA), creative writing sample and scholarly writing sample (MFA/MA). Additional exam requirements/recommendations for international students: required—TOEFL (minimum score 550 paper-based; 79 iBT), IELTS (minimum score 6.5). Electronic applications accepted.

The University of Arizona, College of Humanities, Department of English, Program in Creative Writing, Tucson, AZ 85721. Offers MFA. *Entrance requirements:* Additional exam requirements/recommendations for international students: required—TOEFL (minimum score 550 paper-based; 79 iBT). Electronic applications accepted.

University of Arkansas, Graduate School, J. William Fulbright College of Arts and Sciences, Department of English, Program in Creative Writing, Fayetteville, AR 72701. Offers MFA. *Students:* 38 full-time (28 women), 3 part-time (1 woman); includes 8 minority (1 Black or African American, non-Hispanic/Latino; 2 Asian, non-Hispanic/Latino; 3 Hispanic/Latino; 2 Two or more races, non-Hispanic/Latino). 18 applicants, 67% accepted. In 2019, 14 master's awarded. *Application deadline:* For fall admission, 8/1 for domestic students, 4/1 for international students; for spring admission, 12/1 for domestic students, 10/1 for international students; for summer admission, 4/15 for domestic students, 3/1 for international students. Applications are processed on a rolling basis. Application fee: $60. Electronic applications accepted. *Financial support:* In 2019–20, 1 research assistantship, 29 teaching assistantships were awarded; fellowships with tuition reimbursements, career-related internships or fieldwork, and Federal Work-Study also available. Support available to part-time students. Financial award application deadline: 4/1; financial award applicants required to submit FAFSA. *Unit head:* Dr. Davis McCombs, Program Director, 479-575-4301, E-mail: dmccomb@uark.edu. *Application contact:* Dr. William A. Quinn, Graduate Coordinator, 479-575-5988, Fax: 479-575-5919, E-mail: wquinn@uark.edu.
Website: https://fulbright.uark.edu/departments/english/

University of Arkansas at Little Rock, Graduate School, College of Social Sciences and Communication, Department of Rhetoric and Writing, Little Rock, AR 72204-1099. Offers professional and technical writing (MA). *Program availability:* Part-time, evening/weekend. *Degree requirements:* For master's, thesis or alternative, oral defense of final project. *Entrance requirements:* For master's, GRE, minimum GPA of 3.0, writing portfolio.

University of Baltimore, Graduate School, Yale Gordon College of Arts and Sciences, Program in Creative Writing and Publishing Arts, Baltimore, MD 21201-5779. Offers MFA. *Program availability:* Part-time, evening/weekend. *Entrance requirements:* Additional exam requirements/recommendations for international students: required—TOEFL.

The University of British Columbia, Faculty of Arts, Creative Writing Program, Vancouver, BC V6T 1Z1, Canada. Offers creative writing (MFA); creative writing and theatre (MFA); film production and creative writing (MFA). *Program availability:* Part-time, online learning. *Degree requirements:* For master's, thesis. *Entrance requirements:* For master's, sample of written work. Additional exam requirements/recommendations for international students: required—TOEFL. Electronic applications accepted. *Expenses:* Contact institution.

The University of British Columbia, Faculty of Arts, Department of Theatre and Film, Vancouver, BC V6T 1Z2, Canada. Offers film (MA, MFA), including creative writing and film production (MFA), film production (MFA), film studies (MA); theatre (MA, MFA, PhD), including theatre (MA, PhD), theatre design (MFA), theatre directing (MFA). Terminal master's awarded for partial completion of doctoral program. *Degree requirements:* For master's, variable foreign language requirement, comprehensive exam, thesis; for doctorate, one foreign language, comprehensive exam, thesis/dissertation. *Entrance requirements:* For master's, BA or equivalent; portfolio (for MFA). Additional exam requirements/recommendations for international students: required—TOEFL. *Expenses:* Contact institution.

University of California, Berkeley, UC Berkeley Extension, Certificate Programs in Writing, Editing and Technical Communication, Berkeley, CA 94720. Offers writing (Postbaccalaureate Certificate). *Program availability:* Online learning.

University of California, Davis, Graduate Studies, Program in English, Davis, CA 95616. Offers creative writing (MA); English (MA, PhD). Terminal master's awarded for partial completion of doctoral program. *Degree requirements:* For master's, one foreign language, thesis optional; for doctorate, 2 foreign languages, thesis/dissertation. *Entrance requirements:* For master's and doctorate, GRE General Test, GRE Subject Test, minimum GPA of 3.0, writing sample. Additional exam requirements/recommendations for international students: required—TOEFL (minimum score 550 paper-based). Electronic applications accepted.

University of California, Irvine, School of Humanities, Department of English, Program in Writing, Irvine, CA 92697. Offers creative writing (MFA), including fiction, poetry. *Students:* 32 full-time (13 women); includes 8 minority (2 Black or African American, non-Hispanic/Latino; 2 Asian, non-Hispanic/Latino; 3 Hispanic/Latino; 1 Two or more races, non-Hispanic/Latino). Average age 28. 349 applicants, 3% accepted, 11 enrolled. In 2019, 11 master's awarded. *Entrance requirements:* For master's, minimum GPA of 3.0, sample of written work. *Application deadline:* For fall admission, 1/15 for domestic and international students. Application fee: $120 ($140 for international students). Electronic applications accepted. *Financial support:* Fellowships, research assistantships, teaching assistantships with partial tuition reimbursements, institutionally sponsored loans, and tuition waivers (full and partial) available. Financial award application deadline: 3/1; financial award applicants required to submit FAFSA. *Unit head:* Michael Ryan, Director, 949-824-8773, Fax: 949-824-2916, E-mail: mryan@uci.edu. *Application contact:* Sandy Mueller, Graduate Administrator, 949-824-6718, Fax: 949-824-2916, E-mail: slmuelle@uci.edu.

University of California, Riverside, Graduate Division, Program in Creative Writing and Writing for the Performing Arts, Riverside, CA 92211. Offers MFA. *Degree requirements:* For master's, thesis. *Entrance requirements:* For master's, writing sample. Additional exam requirements/recommendations for international students: required—TOEFL (minimum score 550 paper-based; 80 iBT). Electronic applications accepted.

University of California, San Diego, Graduate Division, Department of Literature, La Jolla, CA 92093. Offers literature (PhD); writing (MFA). *Students:* 77 full-time (54 women). 244 applicants, 20% accepted, 20 enrolled. In 2019, 8 master's, 6 doctorates awarded. *Degree requirements:* For master's, thesis; for doctorate, one foreign language, comprehensive exam, thesis/dissertation, 3 quarters of teaching assistantship. *Entrance requirements:* For master's, writing sample; for doctorate, GRE General Test, writing sample. Additional exam requirements/recommendations for international students: required—TOEFL (minimum score 550 paper-based; 80 iBT), IELTS (minimum score 7); recommended—TSE. *Application deadline:* For fall admission, 12/3 for domestic students. Application fee: $105 ($125 for international students). Electronic applications accepted. *Financial support:* Fellowships, research assistantships, teaching assistantships, scholarships/grants, and readerships available. Financial award applicants required to submit FAFSA. *Unit head:* Yingjin Zhang, Chair, 858-534-5991, E-mail: litchair@ucsd.edu. *Application contact:* Alyssa Simons, Graduate Coordinator, 858-534-2739, E-mail: litgrad@ucsd.edu.
Website: http://literature.ucsd.edu

University of California, Santa Barbara, Graduate Division, College of Letters and Sciences, Division of Humanities and Fine Arts, Department of English, Santa Barbara, CA 93106-3170. Offers English (PhD), including environment and society, European medieval studies, feminist studies, global studies, technology and society, translation studies, writing studies; MA/PhD. Terminal master's awarded for partial completion of doctoral program. *Degree requirements:* For doctorate, one foreign language, comprehensive exam, thesis/dissertation. *Entrance requirements:* For doctorate, GRE General Test, GRE Subject Test (English literature). Additional exam requirements/recommendations for international students: required—TOEFL (minimum score 550 paper-based; 80 iBT), IELTS (minimum score 7). Electronic applications accepted.

University of California, Santa Cruz, Division of Graduate Studies, Division of Social Sciences, Program in Social Documentation, Santa Cruz, CA 95064. Offers MA. *Entrance requirements:* For master's, resume or curriculum vitae, sample of documentary production work. Additional exam requirements/recommendations for international students: required—TOEFL (minimum score 550 paper-based; 83 iBT); recommended—IELTS (minimum score 8). Electronic applications accepted.

University of Central Arkansas, Graduate School, College of Fine Arts and Communication, Program in Creative Writing, Conway, AR 72035-0001. Offers MFA. *Degree requirements:* For master's, thesis project. *Entrance requirements:* For master's, GRE. Electronic applications accepted.

University of Central Oklahoma, The Jackson College of Graduate Studies, College of Liberal Arts, Department of English, Edmond, OK 73034-5209. Offers composition and rhetoric (MA); creative writing (MA); literature (MA); teaching English as a second language (MA). *Program availability:* Part-time. *Degree requirements:* For master's, variable foreign language requirement, comprehensive exam (for some programs), thesis (for some programs), portfolio. *Entrance requirements:* For master's, 18-24 hours of course work in English language and literature; writing sample; essay. Additional exam requirements/recommendations for international students: required—TOEFL (minimum score 550 paper-based; 79 iBT), IELTS (minimum score 6.5). Electronic applications accepted.

University of Chicago, Division of the Humanities, Master of Arts Program in the Humanities, Chicago, IL 60637. Offers art history (MA); cinema and media studies (MA); classic languages (MA); comparative literature (MA); creative writing (MA); cultural policy studies (MA); digital humanities (MA); East Asian languages and civilizations (MA); English language and literature (MA); gender and sexuality studies (MA); Germanic studies (MA); linguistics (MA); music (MA); near Eastern languages and civilizations (MA); philosophy (MA); poetics (MA); race, politics and culture (MA); Romance languages and literatures (MA); Slavic languages and literatures (MA); South Asian languages and civilizations (MA); theater and performance studies (MA). *Degree requirements:* For master's, thesis. *Entrance requirements:* For master's, GRE General Test, 10-15 page writing sample, statement of purpose, 3 letters of recommendation, transcripts for all previous degrees and institutions attended. Additional exam requirements/recommendations for international students: required—TOEFL (minimum score 104 iBT), IELTS (minimum score 7). Electronic applications accepted. *Expenses:* Contact institution.

University of Colorado Boulder, Graduate School, College of Arts and Sciences, Department of English, Boulder, CO 80309. Offers literature (MA, PhD), including creative writing (MA). Terminal master's awarded for partial completion of doctoral program. *Degree requirements:* For master's, one foreign language, comprehensive exam, thesis or alternative; for doctorate, 2 foreign languages, comprehensive exam, thesis/dissertation. *Entrance requirements:* For master's, GRE General Test, GRE Subject Test, minimum undergraduate GPA of 3.0; for doctorate, GRE General Test, GRE Subject Test. Electronic applications accepted. Application fee is waived when completed online.

University of Colorado Denver, School of Education and Human Development, Teacher Education Programs, Denver, CO 80217. Offers elementary linguistically diverse education (MA); elementary math and science education (MA); elementary math education (MA); elementary reading and writing (MA); elementary science education (MA); secondary English education (MA); secondary linguistically diverse education (MA); secondary math education (MA); secondary reading and writing (MA); secondary science education (MA); special education (MA). *Accreditation:* NCATE. *Program availability:* Part-time, evening/weekend. *Degree requirements:* For master's, comprehensive exam. *Entrance requirements:* For master's, GRE or MAT (for those with GPA below 2.75), transcripts, resume, letters of recommendation. Additional exam requirements/recommendations for international students: required—TOEFL (minimum score 537 paper-based; 75 iBT); recommended—IELTS (minimum score 6.5). Electronic applications accepted. Tuition and fees vary according to course load, program and reciprocity agreements.

University of Dayton, Department of English, Dayton, OH 45469. Offers literary and cultural studies (MA); teaching English to speakers of other languages (TESOL) (MA); writing and rhetoric (MA). *Program availability:* Part-time. *Degree requirements:* For master's, thesis optional. *Entrance requirements:* For master's, 24 undergraduate-level semester hours in literature and/or writing; minimum GPA of 3.0; transcripts; personal statement; 8-10 page writing sample; three professional letters of recommendation. Additional exam requirements/recommendations for international students: required—TOEFL (minimum score 550 paper-based, 80 iBT) or IELTS. Electronic applications accepted.

University of Denver, Division of Arts, Humanities and Social Sciences, Department of English, Denver, CO 80208. Offers creative writing (PhD); literary studies (MA, PhD). *Program availability:* Part-time. *Faculty:* 30 full-time (17 women), 1 part-time/adjunct (0 women). *Students:* 29 full-time (20 women), 8 part-time (7 women); includes 9 minority (1 American Indian or Alaska Native, non-Hispanic/Latino; 1 Asian, non-Hispanic/Latino; 4 Hispanic/Latino; 3 Two or more races, non-Hispanic/Latino). Average age 30. 220 applicants, 16% accepted, 15 enrolled. In 2019, 3 master's, 11 doctorates awarded. *Degree requirements:* For master's, thesis; for doctorate, one foreign language, comprehensive exam, thesis/dissertation. *Entrance requirements:* For master's, GRE General Test, bachelor's degree, transcripts, academic essay, personal statement, three letters of recommendation, writing sample; for doctorate, GRE General Test, master's degree, transcripts, personal statement, three letters of recommendation, resume, writing sample. Additional exam requirements/recommendations for international students: required—TOEFL (minimum score 550 paper-based; 80 iBT). *Application deadline:* For fall admission, 12/14 for domestic and international students. Applications are processed on a rolling basis. Application fee: $65. Electronic applications accepted. *Expenses:* Contact institution. *Financial support:* In 2019–20, 37 students received support, including 1 research assistantship with tuition reimbursement available (averaging $300 per year), 19 teaching assistantships with tuition reimbursements available (averaging $11,495 per year); Federal Work-Study, institutionally sponsored loans, scholarships/grants, and unspecified assistantships also available. Support available to part-time students. Financial award application deadline: 2/15; financial award applicants required to submit FAFSA. *Unit head:* Dr. Maik Nwosu, Professor and Chair, 303-871-2879, E-mail: mnwosu@du.edu. *Application contact:* Joel Lewis, Assistant to the Chair II, 303-871-2742, E-mail: Joel.Lewis@du.edu.
Website: http://www.du.edu/ahss/english

University of Denver, University College, Denver, CO 80208. Offers arts and culture (MA, Certificate); communication management (MS, Certificate), including translation studies (Certificate), world history and culture (Certificate); environmental policy and management (MS); geographic information systems (MS); global affairs (MA, Certificate), including human capital in organizations (Certificate), philanthropic leadership (Certificate), project management (Certificate), strategic innovation and change (Certificate); healthcare leadership (MS); information communications and technology (MS); leadership and organizations (MS); professional creative writing (MA, Certificate), including emergency planning and response (Certificate), organizational security (Certificate); security management (MS, Certificate); strategic human resources (Certificate). *Program availability:* Part-time, evening/weekend, 100% online, blended/hybrid learning. *Faculty:* 104 part-time/adjunct (52 women). *Students:* 59 full-time (33 women), 1,893 part-time (1,210 women); includes 545 minority (133 Black or African American, non-Hispanic/Latino; 16 American Indian or Alaska Native, non-Hispanic/Latino; 64 Asian, non-Hispanic/Latino; 252 Hispanic/Latino; 4 Native Hawaiian or other Pacific Islander, non-Hispanic/Latino; 76 Two or more races, non-Hispanic/Latino), 78 international. Average age 32. 1,290 applicants, 91% accepted, 752 enrolled. In 2019, 457 master's, 181 other advanced degrees awarded. *Degree requirements:* For master's, capstone project. *Entrance requirements:* For master's, baccalaureate degree, transcripts, two letters of recommendation, personal statement, resume, writing sample (Master of Arts in Professional Creative Writing). Additional exam requirements/recommendations for international students: required—TOEFL (minimum score 550 paper-based; 80 iBT). *Application deadline:* For fall admission, 6/19 priority date for domestic students, 6/14 priority date for international students; for winter admission, 10/25 priority date for domestic students, 9/27 priority date for international students; for spring admission, 2/7 priority date for domestic students, 1/10 priority date for international students; for summer admission, 4/24 priority date for domestic students, 3/27 priority date for international students. Applications are processed on a rolling basis. Application fee: $75. Electronic applications accepted. *Expenses:* Contact institution. *Financial support:* In 2019–20, 56 students received support. Teaching assistantships available. Financial award applicants required to submit FAFSA. *Unit head:* Dr. Michael McGuire, Dean, 303-871-3518, E-mail: michael.mcguire@du.edu. *Application contact:* Admission Team, 303-871-2291, E-mail: ucoladm@du.edu.
Website: http://universitycollege.du.edu/

The University of Findlay, Office of Graduate Admissions, Findlay, OH 45840. Offers applied security and analytics (MSAS); athletic training (MAT); business (MBA), including certified management accountant, certified public accountant, health care management, hospitality management; education (MA Ed, Ed D), including children's literature (MA Ed), curriculum and teaching (MA Ed), education (MA Ed), educational administration (MA Ed), human resource development (MA Ed), mathematics (MA Ed), reading (MA Ed), science education (MA Ed), superintendent (Ed D), teaching (Ed D), technology (MA Ed); environmental, safety, and health management (MSEM); health informatics (MS); occupational therapy (MOT); pharmacy (Pharm D); physical therapy (DPT); physician assistant (MPA); rhetoric and writing (MA); teaching English to speakers of other languages (TESOL) and applied linguistics (MA). *Program availability:* Part-time, evening/weekend, 100% online, blended/hybrid learning. *Students:* 688 full-time (430 women), 553 part-time (308 women), 170 international. Average age 28. 865 applicants, 31% accepted, 235 enrolled. In 2019, 363 master's, 141 doctorates awarded. *Degree requirements:* For master's, comprehensive exam (for some programs), thesis (for some programs), cumulative project, capstone project; for doctorate, thesis/dissertation (for some programs). *Entrance requirements:* For master's, GRE/GMAT, bachelor's degree from accredited institution, minimum undergraduate GPA of 2.5 in last 64 hours of course work; for doctorate, GRE, MAT, minimum cumulative GPA of 3.0. Additional exam requirements/recommendations for international students: required—TOEFL (minimum score 79 iBT), IELTS (minimum score 7), PTE (minimum score 61). *Application deadline:* Applications are processed on a rolling basis. Electronic applications accepted. *Financial support:* In 2019–20, 10 research assistantships with partial tuition reimbursements (averaging $7,200 per year), 35 teaching assistantships with partial tuition reimbursements (averaging $7,200 per year) were awarded; Federal Work-Study, institutionally sponsored loans, and unspecified assistantships also available. Financial award applicants required to submit FAFSA. *Unit head:* Dave M. Emsweller, Director of Admissions, Interim, 419-434-4578, E-mail: emsweller@findlay.edu. *Application contact:* Amber Feehan, Graduate Admissions Counselor, 419-434-6933, Fax: 419-434-4898, E-mail: feehan@findlay.edu.
Website: http://www.findlay.edu/admissions/graduate/Pages/default.aspx

University of Florida, Graduate School, College of Liberal Arts and Sciences, Department of English, Gainesville, FL 32611. Offers creative writing (MFA); English (MA, PhD). *Degree requirements:* For master's, one foreign language, comprehensive exam, thesis or alternative; for doctorate, one foreign language, comprehensive exam, thesis/dissertation. *Entrance requirements:* For master's and doctorate, GRE General Test, minimum GPA of 3.0. Additional exam requirements/recommendations for international students: required—TOEFL (minimum score 550 paper-based; 80 iBT), IELTS (minimum score 6). Electronic applications accepted.

University of Houston, College of Liberal Arts and Social Sciences, Department of English, Houston, TX 77204. Offers applied English linguistics (MA); creative writing (MFA); creative writing and literature (MA, PhD); English (MA, PhD). *Degree requirements:* For master's, one foreign language, comprehensive exam (for some programs), thesis (MFA); for doctorate, 2 foreign languages, comprehensive exam, thesis/dissertation. *Entrance requirements:* For master's, GRE General Test, minimum GPA of 3.0 in last 60 hours of course work; for doctorate, GRE General Test, GRE Subject Test (literature), writing sample. Additional exam requirements/recommendations for international students: required—TOEFL (minimum score 550 paper-based; 79 iBT). Electronic applications accepted.

University of Houston, College of Liberal Arts and Social Sciences, Department of Hispanic Studies, Houston, TX 77204. Offers Hispanic literature and linguistics (PhD); Spanish (MA, PhD), including creative writing (PhD). *Program availability:* Part-time. *Degree requirements:* For master's, comprehensive exam, thesis optional; for doctorate, 2 foreign languages, comprehensive exam, thesis/dissertation. *Entrance requirements:* For master's and doctorate, GRE. Additional exam requirements/recommendations for international students: required—TOEFL (minimum score 550 paper-based; 79 iBT); recommended—IELTS (minimum score 6.5). Electronic applications accepted.

University of Houston–Victoria, School of Arts and Sciences, Program in Creative Writing, Victoria, TX 77901-4450. Offers MFA. *Degree requirements:* For master's, thesis. *Entrance requirements:* For master's, GRE, two letters of recommendation, twenty- to thirty-page creative writing sample.

University of Idaho, College of Graduate Studies, College of Letters, Arts and Social Sciences, Department of English, Moscow, ID 83844-2282. Offers creative writing (MFA); English (MA, MAT). *Faculty:* 11 full-time. *Students:* 42. Average age 29. In 2019, 23 master's awarded. *Entrance requirements:* For master's, minimum GPA of 3.0. Additional exam requirements/recommendations for international students: required—TOEFL (minimum score 83 iBT). *Application deadline:* For fall admission, 7/30 for domestic students; for spring admission, 12/1 for domestic students. Applications are processed on a rolling basis. Application fee: $60. Electronic applications accepted. *Expenses:* Tuition, state resident: full-time $7753.80; part-time $502 per credit hour. Tuition, nonresident: full-time $26,990; part-time $1571 per credit hour. *Required fees:* $2122.20; $47 per credit hour. *Financial support:* Research assistantships and teaching assistantships available. Financial award applicants required to submit FAFSA. *Unit head:* Dr. Jodie Nicotra, Chair, 208-885-6156, E-mail: englishdept@uidaho.edu. *Application contact:* Dr. Jodie Nicotra, Chair, 208-885-6156, E-mail: englishdept@uidaho.edu.
Website: https://www.uidaho.edu/class/english

University of Illinois at Urbana-Champaign, Graduate College, College of Liberal Arts and Sciences, Department of English, Champaign, IL 61820. Offers creative writing (MFA); English (MA, PhD).

The University of Iowa, Graduate College, College of Liberal Arts and Sciences, Department of English, Iowa City, IA 52242-1316. Offers English (PhD); literary studies (MA); nonfiction writing (MFA). *Degree requirements:* For master's, thesis (for some programs), exam; for doctorate, comprehensive exam, thesis/dissertation. *Entrance requirements:* For master's and doctorate, GRE General Test, minimum GPA of 3.0. Additional exam requirements/recommendations for international students: required—TOEFL (minimum score 640 paper-based; 111 iBT). Electronic applications accepted.

The University of Iowa, Graduate College, College of Liberal Arts and Sciences, Department of Spanish and Portuguese, Iowa City, IA 52242-1316. Offers Spanish (MA, PhD); Spanish creative writing (MFA). *Degree requirements:* For master's, thesis optional, exam; for doctorate, comprehensive exam, thesis/dissertation. *Entrance requirements:* For master's and doctorate, GRE General Test, minimum GPA of 3.0. Additional exam requirements/recommendations for international students: required—TOEFL (minimum score 600 paper-based; 100 iBT). Electronic applications accepted.

The University of Kansas, Graduate Studies, College of Liberal Arts and Sciences, Department of English, Lawrence, KS 66045. Offers creative writing (MFA), including fine arts/creative writing; English (MA, PhD). *Program availability:* Part-time. *Students:* 80 full-time (54 women), 2 part-time (1 woman); includes 21 minority (7 Black or African American, non-Hispanic/Latino; 4 Asian, non-Hispanic/Latino; 6 Hispanic/Latino; 4 Two or more races, non-Hispanic/Latino), 9 international. Average age 31. 186 applicants, 10% accepted, 12 enrolled. In 2019, 13 master's, 12 doctorates awarded. *Entrance requirements:* For master's and doctorate, GRE General Test, two examples of academic writing; resume; statement of approximately 500 words describing interests, training, experience (including teaching experience), academic ability, and goals; three letters of recommendation; official transcripts. Additional exam requirements/recommendations for international students: required—TOEFL, IELTS, TOEFL or IELTS. *Application deadline:* For fall admission, 12/31 for domestic and international students. Application fee: $65 ($85 for international students). Electronic applications accepted. *Expenses:* Tuition, state resident: full-time $9989. Tuition, nonresident: full-time $23,950. *International tuition:* $23,950 full-time. *Required fees:* $984; $81.99 per credit hour. Tuition and fees vary according to course load, campus/location and program. *Financial support:* Fellowships, research assistantships, teaching assistantships, and unspecified assistantships available. *Unit head:* Kathryn Conrad, Chair, 785-864-2572, E-mail: kconrad@ku.edu. *Application contact:* Mary Strickell, Graduate Admissions Contact, 785-864-9438, E-mail: maryj@ku.edu.
Website: http://www.english.ku.edu

University of King's College, Graduate and Advanced Programs, Halifax, NS B3H 2A1, Canada. Offers creative nonfiction (MFA); journalism (MJ).

University of Louisiana at Lafayette, College of Liberal Arts, Department of English, Lafayette, LA 70504. Offers American culture (MA, PhD), including history, sociology; American literature and language (PhD); creative writing (MA, PhD), including creative writing (MA), folklore (MA), rhetoric (MA); folklore (MA, PhD); linguistic studies (MA,

PhD); professional writing (PhD); rhetoric (MA, PhD); TESOL studies (MA, PhD). *Program availability:* Part-time. Terminal master's awarded for partial completion of doctoral program. *Degree requirements:* For master's, one foreign language, thesis or alternative; for doctorate, 2 foreign languages, comprehensive exam, thesis/dissertation. *Entrance requirements:* For master's, GRE General Test, minimum GPA of 2.75; for doctorate, GRE General Test, minimum GPA of 3.0. Additional exam requirements/ recommendations for international students: required—TOEFL (minimum score 550 paper-based). Electronic applications accepted. *Expenses: Tuition, area resident:* Full-time $5511; part-time $1630 per credit hour. Tuition, state resident: full-time $5511; part-time $1630 per credit hour. Tuition, nonresident: full-time $19,239; part-time $2409 per credit hour. *Required fees:* $46,637.

University of Louisville, Graduate School, College of Arts and Sciences, Department of English, Louisville, KY 40292. Offers English (MA), including creative writing, literature, rhetoric and composition (MA, PhD); rhetoric and composition (PhD), including rhetoric and composition (MA, PhD). *Program availability:* Part-time, evening/ weekend. *Faculty:* 34 full-time (16 women), 29 part-time/adjunct (15 women). *Students:* 39 full-time (22 women), 19 part-time (12 women); includes 6 minority (3 Black or African American, non-Hispanic/Latino; 1 Hispanic/Latino; 2 Two or more races, non-Hispanic/ Latino), 3 international. Average age 31. 42 applicants, 71% accepted, 20 enrolled. In 2019, 12 master's, 5 doctorates awarded. *Degree requirements:* For master's, one foreign language, thesis optional, culminating project of 25-30 pages; for doctorate, comprehensive exam, thesis/dissertation, Year long program; Student teacher program. *Entrance requirements:* For master's, GRE General Test, Two letters of reference, official transcripts; for doctorate, GRE General Test, Three letters of reference, official transcripts. Additional exam requirements/recommendations for international students: required—TOEFL (minimum score 550 paper-based; 79 iBT), IELTS can be used in place of the TOEFL; recommended—IELTS (minimum score 6.5). *Application deadline:* For fall admission, 7/15 priority date for domestic and international students; for spring admission, 12/1 priority date for domestic and international students; for summer admission, 5/15 priority date for domestic and international students. Applications are processed on a rolling basis. Application fee: $65. Electronic applications accepted. *Expenses:* Contact institution. *Financial support:* In 2019–20, 38 students received support, including 3 fellowships with full tuition reimbursements available (averaging $19,992 per year), 13 teaching assistantships with full tuition reimbursements available (averaging $19,992 per year); research assistantships, health care benefits, and unspecified assistantships also available. Financial award application deadline: 1/5. *Unit head:* Dr. Glynis Ridley, Chair, 502-852-6803, E-mail: glynis.ridley@louisville.edu. *Application contact:* Dr. Steven Matthew Biberman, Acting Director of Graduate Studies, 502-852-3052, E-mail: steven.biberman@louisville.edu.
Website: http://www.louisville.edu/english

The University of Manchester, School of Arts, Languages and Cultures, Manchester, United Kingdom. Offers anthropology, media and performance (PhD); applied theatre (PhD); Arab world studies (PhD); archaeology (PhD); art history and visual studies (PhD); arts and cultural management (PhD); arts management and cultural policy (PhD); Chinese studies (PhD); classics and ancient history (PhD); composition (PhD); creative writing (PhD); drama (PhD); East Asian studies (PhD); electroacoustic composition (PhD); English and American studies (PhD); English language (PhD); French studies (PhD); German studies (PhD); history (PhD); humanitarianism and conflict response (PhD); interpreting studies (PhD); Japanese studies (PhD); Latin American cultural studies (PhD); linguistics (PhD); Middle Eastern studies (PhD); museology (PhD); museum practice (PhD); music (PhD); musicology (PhD); Polish studies (PhD); Portuguese studies (PhD); religions and theology (PhD); Russian studies (PhD); Spanish studies (PhD); translation and intercultural studies (PhD).

University of Maryland, College Park, Academic Affairs, College of Arts and Humanities, Department of English, Creative Writing Program, College Park, MD 20742. Offers MA, MFA, PhD. *Degree requirements:* For master's, thesis optional, written exam; for doctorate, one foreign language, oral and written exams. *Entrance requirements:* For master's, GRE General Test, writing sample, 3 letters of recommendation. Additional exam requirements/recommendations for international students: required—TOEFL. Electronic applications accepted.

University of Massachusetts Amherst, Graduate School, College of Humanities and Fine Arts, Department of English, Amherst, MA 01003. Offers American studies (PhD); composition and rhetoric (PhD); creative writing (MFA); English and American literature (MA, PhD). *Program availability:* Part-time. Terminal master's awarded for partial completion of doctoral program. *Degree requirements:* For master's, one foreign language, thesis optional; for doctorate, one foreign language, comprehensive exam, thesis/dissertation. *Entrance requirements:* For master's, manuscript; for doctorate, GRE General Test, manuscript. Additional exam requirements/recommendations for international students: required—TOEFL (minimum score 550 paper-based; 80 iBT), IELTS (minimum score 6.5). Electronic applications accepted.

University of Massachusetts Boston, College of Liberal Arts, Program in Creative Writing, Boston, MA 02125-3393. Offers MFA. Electronic applications accepted.

University of Massachusetts Dartmouth, Graduate School, College of Arts and Sciences, Program in Professional Writing and Communication, North Dartmouth, MA 02747-2300. Offers MA, Postbaccalaureate Certificate. *Program availability:* Part-time. *Faculty:* 33 full-time (19 women), 16 part-time/adjunct (12 women). *Students:* 11 full-time (10 women), 8 part-time (5 women); includes 3 minority (2 Black or African American, non-Hispanic/Latino; 1 Two or more races, non-Hispanic/Latino). Average age 36. 12 applicants, 100% accepted, 9 enrolled. In 2019, 10 master's awarded. *Degree requirements:* For master's, thesis, thesis. *Entrance requirements:* For master's, statement of purpose (300-600 words), resume, 3 letters of recommendation, official transcripts, writing sample (10-15 pages); for Postbaccalaureate Certificate, 3-page statement of purpose and official transcripts. Additional exam requirements/ recommendations for international students: required—TOEFL (minimum score 80 iBT). *Application deadline:* Applications are processed on a rolling basis. Application fee: $60. Electronic applications accepted. *Expenses: Tuition, area resident:* Full-time $16,390; part-time $682.92 per credit. Tuition, state resident: full-time $16,390; part-time $682.92 per credit. Tuition, nonresident: full-time $29,578; part-time $1232.42 per credit. *Required fees:* $575. *Financial support:* In 2019–20, 8 fellowships (averaging $13,125 per year), 4 teaching assistantships (averaging $11,475 per year) were awarded; tuition waivers (full) and unspecified assistantships also available. Financial award application deadline: 3/1; financial award applicants required to submit FAFSA. *Unit head:* Karen Gulbrandsen, Graduate Program Director, Professional Writing, 508-910-6932, E-mail: kgulbrandsen@umassd.edu. *Application contact:* Scott Webster, Director of Graduate Studies and Admissions, 508-999-8604, Fax: 508-999-8183, E-mail: graduate@umassd.edu.
Website: http://www.umassd.edu/cas/english/graduate-programs

University of Memphis, Graduate School, College of Arts and Sciences, Department of English, Memphis, TN 38152. Offers African-American literature (Graduate Certificate); applied linguistics (PhD); composition studies (PhD); creative writing (MFA); English as a second language (MA); linguistics (MA); literary and cultural studies (PhD), including African-American literature; literature (MA); professional writing (MA, PhD); teaching English as a second/foreign language (Graduate Certificate). *Program availability:* Part-time, evening/weekend, 100% online. *Students:* 58 full-time (33 women), 76 part-time (52 women); includes 34 minority (24 Black or African American, non-Hispanic/Latino; 4 Asian, non-Hispanic/Latino; 5 Hispanic/Latino; 1 Two or more races, non-Hispanic/ Latino), 16 international. Average age 36. 52 applicants, 92% accepted, 23 enrolled. In 2019, 19 master's, 15 doctorates, 8 other advanced degrees awarded. Terminal master's awarded for partial completion of doctoral program. *Degree requirements:* For master's, variable foreign language requirement, comprehensive exam, thesis optional; for doctorate, variable foreign language requirement, comprehensive exam, thesis/ dissertation, qualifying exam. *Entrance requirements:* For master's, GRE, minimum undergraduate GPA of 3.0, statement of purpose, two letters of recommendation; for doctorate, GRE, minimum undergraduate and graduate GPA of 3.25, statement of purpose, writing sample, three letters of recommendation. Additional exam requirements/recommendations for international students: required—TOEFL. *Application deadline:* For fall admission, 1/15 for domestic students; for spring admission, 10/15 for domestic students. Applications are processed on a rolling basis. Application fee: $35 ($60 for international students). Electronic applications accepted. *Expenses: Tuition, area resident:* Full-time $9216; part-time $512 per credit hour. Tuition, state resident: full-time $9216; part-time $512 per credit hour. Tuition, nonresident: full-time $12,672; part-time $704 per credit hour. *International tuition:* $16,128 full-time. *Required fees:* $1530; $85 per credit hour. Tuition and fees vary according to program. *Financial support:* Research assistantships with full tuition reimbursements, teaching assistantships with full tuition reimbursements, Federal Work-Study, scholarships/grants, and unspecified assistantships available. Financial award application deadline: 2/1; financial award applicants required to submit FAFSA. *Unit head:* Dr. Joshua Phillips, Chair, 901-678-2651, Fax: 901-678-2226, E-mail: jsphllps@memphis.edu. *Application contact:* Dr. Jeffrey Scraba, Director of Graduate Studies, 901-678-4768, Fax: 901-678-2226, E-mail: jscraba@memphis.edu.
Website: http://www.memphis.edu/english

University of Miami, Graduate School, College of Arts and Sciences, Department of English, Coral Gables, FL 33124. Offers creative writing (MFA); English (MA, PhD). *Program availability:* Part-time. Terminal master's awarded for partial completion of doctoral program. *Degree requirements:* For master's, one foreign language, thesis optional; for doctorate, one foreign language, thesis/dissertation. *Entrance requirements:* For master's and doctorate, GRE General Test. Electronic applications accepted.

University of Michigan, Rackham Graduate School, College of Literature, Science, and the Arts, Department of English Language and Literature, Helen Zell Writer's Program, Ann Arbor, MI 48109. Offers MFA. *Degree requirements:* For master's, comprehensive exam, thesis. *Entrance requirements:* For master's, writing sample. Additional exam requirements/recommendations for international students: required—TOEFL (minimum score 620 paper-based; 106 iBT). Electronic applications accepted.

University of Michigan–Flint, College of Arts and Sciences, Program in English Language and Literature, Flint, MI 48502-1950. Offers literature (MA); writing and rhetoric (MA). *Program availability:* Part-time. *Faculty:* 25 full-time (16 women), 5 part-time/adjunct (4 women). *Students:* 11 full-time (6 women), 10 part-time (8 women); includes 2 minority (1 Black or African American, non-Hispanic/Latino; 1 Hispanic/ Latino), 2 international. Average age 34. 14 applicants, 93% accepted, 2 enrolled. In 2019, 11 master's awarded. *Entrance requirements:* For master's, bachelor's degree with major or significant coursework in English or related fields from regionally-accredited institution; minimum overall undergraduate GPA of 3.0. Additional exam requirements/recommendations for international students: required—TOEFL (minimum score 84 iBT), IELTS (minimum score 6.5). *Application deadline:* For fall admission, 8/1 for domestic students, 5/1 for international students; for winter admission, 11/15 for domestic students, 10/1 for international students; for spring admission, 3/15 for domestic students, 1/1 for international students; for summer admission, 5/15 for domestic students. Applications are processed on a rolling basis. Application fee: $55. Electronic applications accepted. *Expenses:* Contact institution. *Financial support:* Career-related internships or fieldwork, Federal Work-Study, scholarships/grants, and unspecified assistantships available. Support available to part-time students. Financial award application deadline: 3/1; financial award applicants required to submit FAFSA. *Unit head:* Dr. James Schirmer, Department Chair, 810-762-3285, E-mail: jschirm@umich.edu. *Application contact:* Matt Bohlen, Associate Director of Graduate Programs, 810-762-3171, Fax: 810-766-6789, E-mail: mbohlen@umflint.edu.
Website: http://www.umflint.edu/graduateprograms/english-language-and-literature-ma

University of Mississippi, Graduate School, College of Liberal Arts, University, MS 38677. Offers anthropology (MA); biology (MS, PhD); chemistry (MS, DA, PhD); creative writing (MFA); documentary expression (MFA); economics (MA, PhD); English (MA, PhD); experimental psychology (PhD); history (MA, PhD); mathematics (MS, PhD); modern languages (MA); music (MM); philosophy (MA); physics (MA, MS, PhD); political science (MA, PhD); Southern studies (MA); studio art (MFA). *Program availability:* Part-time. *Faculty:* 481 full-time (215 women), 71 part-time/adjunct (40 women). *Students:* 509 full-time (258 women), 55 part-time (21 women); includes 89 minority (40 Black or African American, non-Hispanic/Latino; 13 Asian, non-Hispanic/Latino; 25 Hispanic/ Latino; 11 Two or more races, non-Hispanic/Latino), 157 international. Average age 29. In 2019, 119 master's, 51 doctorates awarded. *Degree requirements:* For doctorate, thesis/dissertation. *Entrance requirements:* For master's, GRE General Test, minimum GPA of 3.0; for doctorate, GRE General Test. Additional exam requirements/ recommendations for international students: required—TOEFL. *Application deadline:* Applications are processed on a rolling basis. Application fee: $50. Electronic applications accepted. *Expenses:* Tuition, state resident: full-time $8718; part-time $484.25 per credit hour. Tuition, nonresident: full-time $24,990; part-time $1388.25 per credit hour. *Required fees:* $100; $4.16 per credit hour. *Financial support:* Fellowships, research assistantships, teaching assistantships, career-related internships or fieldwork, Federal Work-Study, institutionally sponsored loans, scholarships/grants, and unspecified assistantships available. Financial award application deadline: 3/1; financial award applicants required to submit FAFSA. *Unit head:* Dr. Lee Michael Cohen, Dean, 662-915-7177, Fax: 662-915-5792, E-mail: libarts@olemiss.edu. *Application contact:* Tameka Smith, Graduate Activities Specialist for Admissions, 662-915-7474, Fax: 662-915-7577, E-mail: gschool@olemiss.edu.
Website: ventress@olemiss.edu

University of Missouri–St. Louis, College of Arts and Sciences, Department of English, St. Louis, MO 63121. Offers creative writing (MFA); English (MA). *Program availability:* Part-time, evening/weekend. *Degree requirements:* For master's, thesis optional. *Entrance requirements:* For master's, two letters of recommendation; writing sample (MFA). Additional exam requirements/recommendations for international students: required—TOEFL (minimum score 550 paper-based; 79 iBT), IELTS (minimum score 6.5). Electronic applications accepted. *Expenses: Tuition, area resident:* Full-time $9005.40; part-time $6003.60 per credit hour. Tuition, state resident: full-time $9005.40; part-time $6003.60 per credit hour. Tuition, nonresident: full-time $22,108; part-time $14,738.40 per credit hour. *International tuition:* $22,108 full-time. Tuition and fees vary according to course load.

University of Montana, Graduate School, College of Humanities and Sciences, Department of English, Program in Creative Writing, Missoula, MT 59812. Offers fiction

(MFA); non-fiction (MFA); poetry (MFA). *Degree requirements:* For master's, final creative paper. *Entrance requirements:* For master's, GRE General Test, sample of written work. Additional exam requirements/recommendations for international students: required—TOEFL.

University of Nebraska at Kearney, College of Arts and Sciences, College of Arts and Sciences, Kearney, NE 68849. Offers creative writing (MA); literature (MA); writing (MA). *Program availability:* Part-time, evening/weekend, 100% online, blended/hybrid learning. *Faculty:* 14 full-time (10 women). *Students:* 2 full-time (1 woman), 27 part-time (24 women); includes 2 minority (both Two or more races, non-Hispanic/Latino). Average age 31. 7 applicants, 71% accepted, 5 enrolled. In 2019, 6 master's awarded. *Degree requirements:* For master's, comprehensive exam (for some programs), thesis optional, thesis or exam. *Entrance requirements:* For master's, writing sample, three letters of recommendation, letter of interest. Additional exam requirements/recommendations for international students: required—TOEFL (minimum score 550 paper-based; 79 iBT), IELTS (minimum score 6.5). *Application deadline:* For fall admission, 7/10 for domestic students, 5/10 for international students; for spring admission, 10/10 for domestic students, 9/10 for international students; for summer admission, 4/10 for domestic students, 1/10 for international students. Applications are processed on a rolling basis. Application fee: $45. Electronic applications accepted. *Expenses: Tuition, area resident:* Full-time $4662; part-time $259 per credit hour. Tuition, nonresident: full-time $10,242; part-time $569 per credit hour. *International tuition:* $10,242 full-time. *Required fees:* $1222; $381.50 per term. Full-time tuition and fees vary according to course load, campus/location and program. *Financial support:* In 2019–20, 2 students received support, including 2 teaching assistantships with full tuition reimbursements available (averaging $10,980 per year); career-related internships or fieldwork, scholarships/grants, and unspecified assistantships also available. Support available to part-time students. Financial award application deadline: 2/28; financial award applicants required to submit FAFSA. *Unit head:* Dr. Michelle Beissel-Heath, Graduate Program Director, 308-865-8109, E-mail: beisselheamp@unk.edu. *Application contact:* Linda Johnson, Director, Graduate Admissions and Programs, 308-717-7881, E-mail: gradstudies@unk.edu. Website: https://www.unk.edu/academics/english/index.php

University of Nebraska at Omaha, Graduate Studies, College of Arts and Sciences, Department of English, Omaha, NE 68182. Offers advanced writing (Certificate); English (MA); teaching English to speakers of other languages (Certificate); technical communication (Certificate). *Program availability:* Part-time, evening/weekend. *Degree requirements:* For master's, comprehensive exam, thesis (for some programs). *Entrance requirements:* For master's, GRE or MAT, minimum GPA of 3.0, transcripts, 3 letters of recommendation, statement of purpose, writing sample; for Certificate, minimum GPA of 3.0, transcripts, statement of purpose. Additional exam requirements/recommendations for international students: required—TOEFL, IELTS, PTE. Electronic applications accepted.

University of Nebraska at Omaha, Graduate Studies, College of Communication, Fine Arts and Media, Writer's Workshop, Omaha, NE 68182. Offers MFA. *Program availability:* Online learning. *Entrance requirements:* For master's, 3 letters of recommendation, statement of purpose, writing sample, minimum GPA of 3.0, official transcripts. Additional exam requirements/recommendations for international students: required—TOEFL, IELTS, PTE. Electronic applications accepted.

University of Nebraska–Lincoln, Graduate College, College of Arts and Sciences, Department of English, Lincoln, NE 68588-0333. Offers composition and rhetoric (MA, PhD); creative writing (MA, PhD); literature studies (MA, PhD). *Degree requirements:* For master's, thesis optional; for doctorate, one foreign language, comprehensive exam, thesis/dissertation. *Entrance requirements:* For master's, writing sample; for doctorate, GRE General Test, writing sample. Additional exam requirements/recommendations for international students: required—TOEFL (minimum score 600 paper-based). Electronic applications accepted.

University of Nevada, Las Vegas, Graduate College, College of Fine Arts, Department of Film, Las Vegas, NV 89154-5015. Offers film/writing for dramatic media (MFA); writing for dramatic media (Certificate). *Program availability:* Part-time. *Faculty:* 3 full-time (0 women). *Students:* 7 full-time (4 women); includes 1 minority (Two or more races, non-Hispanic/Latino), 1 international. Average age 34. 13 applicants, 15% accepted, 2 enrolled. In 2019, 2 master's awarded. *Degree requirements:* For master's, thesis, creative project and defense; for Certificate, creative project and defense. *Entrance requirements:* For master's, writing sample. Additional exam requirements/recommendations for international students: required—TOEFL (minimum score 550 paper-based; 80 iBT), IELTS (minimum score 7). *Application deadline:* For fall admission, 1/15 for domestic and international students. Application fee: $60 ($95 for international students). Electronic applications accepted. *Expenses:* Contact institution. *Financial support:* In 2019–20, 8 students received support, including 8 teaching assistantships with full tuition reimbursements available (averaging $15,250 per year); institutionally sponsored loans, scholarships/grants, health care benefits, and unspecified assistantships also available. Financial award application deadline: 3/15; financial award applicants required to submit FAFSA. *Unit head:* Dr. Heather Addison, Chair/Professor, 702-895-3547, Fax: 702-895-4395, E-mail: film.chair@unlv.edu. *Application contact:* Sean Clark, Graduate Coordinator, 702-895-4210, Fax: 702-895-4194, E-mail: film.gradcoord@unlv.edu. Website: http://film.unlv.edu/

University of Nevada, Las Vegas, Graduate College, College of Liberal Arts, Department of English, Las Vegas, NV 89154-5011. Offers creative writing (MFA); English (MA, PhD). *Program availability:* Part-time. *Faculty:* 22 full-time (8 women). *Students:* 71 full-time (44 women), 11 part-time (3 women); includes 25 minority (3 Black or African American, non-Hispanic/Latino; 2 Asian, non-Hispanic/Latino; 14 Hispanic/Latino; 1 Native Hawaiian or other Pacific Islander, non-Hispanic/Latino; 5 Two or more races, non-Hispanic/Latino), 4 international. Average age 33. 207 applicants, 16% accepted, 24 enrolled. In 2019, 15 master's, 7 doctorates awarded. *Degree requirements:* For master's, one foreign language, comprehensive exam (for some programs), thesis, creative thesis; for doctorate, one foreign language, comprehensive exam, thesis/dissertation. *Entrance requirements:* For master's, GRE General Test, GRE Subject Test, writing sample; statement of purpose; 2 letters of recommendation; transcripts from all colleges; for doctorate, GRE General Test, GRE Subject Test, MA in English with minimum GPA of 3.5; writing sample; 3 letters of recommendation; statement of purpose. Additional exam requirements/recommendations for international students: required—TOEFL (minimum score 550 paper-based; 80 iBT), IELTS (minimum score 7). *Application deadline:* For fall admission, 1/15 for domestic and international students; for spring admission, 11/1 for domestic students, 10/1 for international students. Application fee: $60 ($95 for international students). Electronic applications accepted. *Expenses:* Contact institution. *Financial support:* In 2019–20, 75 students received support, including 1 fellowship with full tuition reimbursement available (averaging $15,000 per year), 2 research assistantships with full tuition reimbursements available (averaging $16,250 per year), 72 teaching assistantships with full tuition reimbursements available (averaging $14,826 per year); institutionally sponsored loans, scholarships/grants, health care benefits, and unspecified assistantships also available. Financial award application deadline: 3/15; financial award

applicants required to submit FAFSA. *Unit head:* Dr. Gary Totten, Chair/Professor, 702-895-1258, Fax: 702-895-4801, E-mail: english.chair@unlv.edu. *Application contact:* Dr. Kelly J. Mays, Graduate Coordinator, 702-895-3589, Fax: 702-895-4801, E-mail: english.gradcoord@unlv.edu. Website: http://english.unlv.edu/

University of New Hampshire, Graduate School, College of Liberal Arts, Department of English, Durham, NH 03824. Offers English (MST, PhD); language and linguistics (MA); literature (MA); writing (MFA). *Program availability:* Part-time. *Students:* 65 full-time (43 women), 29 part-time (25 women); includes 6 minority (3 Black or African American, non-Hispanic/Latino; 1 Asian, non-Hispanic/Latino; 1 Hispanic/Latino; 1 Two or more races, non-Hispanic/Latino), 5 international. Average age 33. 91 applicants, 74% accepted, 27 enrolled. In 2019, 27 master's, 5 doctorates awarded. *Entrance requirements:* Additional exam requirements/recommendations for international students: required—TOEFL (minimum score 550 paper-based; 80 iBT), IELTS, PTE. *Application deadline:* For fall admission, 7/1 for domestic students; for spring admission, 12/1 for domestic students; for summer admission, 4/1 for domestic students. Application fee: $65. Electronic applications accepted. *Financial support:* In 2019–20, 69 students received support, including 1 fellowship, 38 teaching assistantships; research assistantships, career-related internships or fieldwork, Federal Work-Study, scholarships/grants, and tuition waivers (full and partial) also available. Support available to part-time students. Financial award application deadline: 2/15. *Unit head:* Dr. Rachel Trubowitz, Chair, 603-862-0254. *Application contact:* Janine Wilks, Administrative Assistant, 603-862-3963, E-mail: engl.grad@unh.edu. Website: http://cola.unh.edu/english

University of New Mexico, Graduate Studies, College of Arts and Sciences, Program in Creative Writing, Albuquerque, NM 87131-2039. Offers MFA. *Degree requirements:* For master's, comprehensive exam, thesis. *Entrance requirements:* For master's, writing sample. Electronic applications accepted. *Expenses:* Tuition, state resident: full-time $7633; part-time $972 per year. Tuition, nonresident: full-time $22,586; part-time $3840 per year. *International tuition:* $23,292 full-time. *Required fees:* $8608. Tuition and fees vary according to course level, course load, degree level, program and student level.

University of New Mexico, Graduate Studies, College of Fine Arts, Department of Theatre and Dance, Albuquerque, NM 87131-2039. Offers dance (MFA); dance history (MA); dramatic writing (MFA); theatre education and outreach (MA). *Accreditation:* NASD; NAST. *Degree requirements:* For master's, comprehensive exam (for some programs), thesis (for some programs). *Entrance requirements:* For master's, minimum GPA of 3.0; undergraduate major in theatre, dance or closely-related field; 3 letters of recommendation; letter of intent; BA, BFA, BS, or MA in dance movement science or related field, or equivalent experience (for MFA in dance). Electronic applications accepted. *Expenses:* Tuition, state resident: full-time $7633; part-time $972 per year. Tuition, nonresident: full-time $22,586; part-time $3840 per year. *International tuition:* $23,292 full-time. *Required fees:* $8608. Tuition and fees vary according to course level, course load, degree level, program and student level.

University of New Orleans, Graduate School, College of Liberal Arts, Education and Human Development, Department of English, Creative Writing Workshop, New Orleans, LA 70148. Offers MFA. *Degree requirements:* For master's, comprehensive exam, thesis, oral exams. *Entrance requirements:* For master's, GRE General Test. Additional exam requirements/recommendations for international students: required—TOEFL (minimum score 550 paper-based). Electronic applications accepted.

University of North Alabama, College of Arts and Sciences, Department of English, Program in Writing, Florence, AL 35632-0001. Offers creative writing (MA); rhetoric and composition (MA); technical writing (MA). *Program availability:* Part-time, 100% online. *Degree requirements:* For master's, comprehensive exam (for some programs), thesis (for some programs). *Entrance requirements:* For master's, GRE, MAT, three letters of recommendation; writing sample. Additional exam requirements/recommendations for international students: required—TOEFL (minimum score 79 iBT), IELTS (minimum score 6), PTE (minimum score 54). Electronic applications accepted.

The University of North Carolina at Charlotte, College of Liberal Arts and Sciences, Department of English, Charlotte, NC 28223-0001. Offers applied linguistics (Graduate Certificate); english (MA), including applied linguistics, children's lit., composition/rhetoric, creative writing, english ed., english for specific purposes, literature, tech/prof w; technical and professional writing (Graduate Certificate). *Program availability:* Part-time, evening/weekend. *Faculty:* 31 full-time (16 women), 1 (woman) part-time/adjunct. *Students:* 26 full-time (19 women), 32 part-time (23 women); includes 18 minority (9 Black or African American, non-Hispanic/Latino; 3 Asian, non-Hispanic/Latino; 1 Hispanic/Latino; 5 Two or more races, non-Hispanic/Latino), 1 international. Average age 30. 26 applicants, 96% accepted, 17 enrolled. In 2019, 16 master's, 3 other advanced degrees awarded. *Degree requirements:* For master's, comprehensive exam (for some programs), thesis, project. *Entrance requirements:* For master's, minimum undergraduate GPA of 3.0, statement of purpose, recommendation letters; unofficial transcript; for Graduate Certificate, statement of purpose, three letters of recommendation, writing sample, minimum GPA of 2.75, current GRE score/current MAT score/portfolio of professional-level documents (technical/professional writing). Additional exam requirements/recommendations for international students: required—TOEFL (minimum score 557 paper-based; 83 iBT), IELTS (minimum score 6.5), TOEFL (minimum score 557 paper-based, 83 iBT) or IELTS (6.5). *Application deadline:* For fall admission, 3/1 priority date for domestic students. Applications are processed on a rolling basis. Application fee: $75. Electronic applications accepted. *Expenses:* Tuition, state resident: full-time $4337. Tuition, nonresident: full-time $17,771. *Required fees:* $3093. Tuition and fees vary according to course load, degree level and program. *Financial support:* In 2019–20, 15 students received support, including 15 teaching assistantships (averaging $8,015 per year); career-related internships or fieldwork, institutionally sponsored loans, scholarships/grants, and unspecified assistantships also available. Support available to part-time students. Financial award application deadline: 3/1; financial award applicants required to submit FAFSA. *Unit head:* Dr. Mark West, Professor and Chair, 704-687-0618, E-mail: miwest@uncc.edu. *Application contact:* Kathy B. Giddings, Director of Graduate Admissions, 704-687-5503, Fax: 704-687-1668, E-mail: gradadm@uncc.edu. Website: http://english.uncc.edu/

The University of North Carolina at Greensboro, Graduate School, College of Arts and Sciences, Department of English, Program in Creative Writing, Greensboro, NC 27412-5001. Offers MFA. *Degree requirements:* For master's, comprehensive exam, thesis. *Entrance requirements:* For master's, GRE General Test, minimum GPA of 3.0, writing sample. Additional exam requirements/recommendations for international students: required—TOEFL. Electronic applications accepted.

The University of North Carolina Wilmington, College of Arts and Sciences, Department of Creative Writing, Wilmington, NC 28403-3297. Offers MFA. *Faculty:* 11 full-time (5 women). *Students:* 49 full-time (34 women), 15 part-time (9 women); includes 9 minority (2 Black or African American, non-Hispanic/Latino; 4 Hispanic/Latino; 3 Two or more races, non-Hispanic/Latino). Average age 28. 103 applicants, 51% accepted, 23 enrolled. In 2019, 16 master's awarded. *Degree requirements:* For master's, comprehensive exam, thesis. *Entrance requirements:* For master's, writing sample, 3

letters of recommendation, statement of interest. Additional exam requirements/recommendations for international students: required—TOEFL (minimum score 79 iBT), IELTS (minimum score 6.5). *Application deadline:* For fall admission, 1/7 for domestic students. Applications are processed on a rolling basis. Application fee: $75. Electronic applications accepted. *Expenses: Tuition, area resident:* Full-time $4719; part-time $326 per credit hour. Tuition, state resident: full-time $4719; part-time $326 per credit hour. Tuition, nonresident: full-time $18,548; part-time $1099 per credit hour. *Required fees:* $2738. Tuition and fees vary according to program. *Financial support:* Teaching assistantships, scholarships/grants, and unspecified assistantships available. Financial award application deadline: 1/1; financial award applicants required to submit FAFSA. *Unit head:* Dr. David Gessner, Chair, 910-962-7489, Fax: 910-962-7461, E-mail: gessnerdm@uncw.edu. *Application contact:* Melissa Crowe, MFA Coordinator, 910-962-3436, Fax: 910-962-7461, E-mail: crowem@uncw.edu.
Website: http://uncw.edu/writers/mfa/index.html

University of Northern Iowa, Graduate College, College of Humanities, Arts and Sciences, Department of Languages and Literatures, MA Program in English, Cedar Falls, IA 50614. Offers creative writing (MA); English (MA); literature (MA). *Program availability:* Part-time, evening/weekend. *Degree requirements:* For master's, one foreign language, comprehensive exam, thesis or alternative, portfolio. *Entrance requirements:* Additional exam requirements/recommendations for international students: required—TOEFL (minimum score 600 paper-based; 100 iBT). Electronic applications accepted.

University of North Florida, College of Arts and Sciences, Department of English, Jacksonville, FL 32224. Offers MA. *Program availability:* Part-time, evening/weekend. *Degree requirements:* For master's, comprehensive exam, thesis optional. *Entrance requirements:* For master's, GRE General Test, minimum GPA of 3.0 in last 60 hours, writing sample. Additional exam requirements/recommendations for international students: required—TOEFL (minimum score 500 paper-based; 61 iBT). Electronic applications accepted.

University of North Texas, Toulouse Graduate School, Denton, TX 76203-5459. Offers accounting (MS); applied anthropology (MA, MS); applied behavior analysis (Certificate); applied geography (MA); applied technology and performance improvement (M Ed, MS); art education (MA); art history (MA); arts leadership (Certificate); audiology (Au D); behavior analysis (MS); behavioral science (PhD); biochemistry and molecular biology (MS); biology (MA, MS); biomedical engineering (MS); business analysis (MS); chemistry (MS); clinical health psychology (PhD); communication studies (MA, MS); computer engineering (MS); computer science (MS); counseling (M Ed, MS), including clinical mental health counseling (MS), college and university counseling, elementary school counseling, secondary school counseling; creative writing (MA); criminal justice (MS); curriculum and instruction (M Ed); decision sciences (MBA); design (MA, MFA), including fashion design (MFA), innovation studies, interior design (MFA); early childhood studies (MS); economics (MS); educational leadership (M Ed, Ed D); educational psychology (MS, PhD), including family studies (MS), gifted and talented (MS), human development (MS), learning and cognition (MS), research, measurement and evaluation (MS); electrical engineering (MS); emergency management (MPA); engineering technology (MS); English (MA); English as a second language (MA); environmental science (MS); finance (MBA, MS); financial management (MPA); French (MA); health services management (MBA); higher education (M Ed, Ed D); history (MA, MS); hospitality management (MS); human resources management (MPA); information science (MS); information systems (PhD); information technologies (MBA); interdisciplinary studies (MA, MS); international studies (MA); international sustainable tourism (MS); jazz studies (MM); journalism (MA, MJ, Graduate Certificate), including interactive and virtual digital communication (Graduate Certificate), narrative journalism (Graduate Certificate), public relations (Graduate Certificate); kinesiology (MS); linguistics (MA); local government management (MPA); logistics (PhD); logistics and supply chain management (MBA); long-term care, senior housing, and aging services (MA); management (PhD); marketing (MBA); mathematics (MA, MS); mechanical and energy engineering (MS, PhD); music (MA), including ethnomusicology, music theory, musicology, performance; music composition (PhD); music education (MM Ed, PhD); nonprofit management (MPA); operations and supply chain management (MBA); performance (MM, DMA); philosophy (MA); political science (MA); professional and technical communication (MA); radio, television and film (MA, MFA); rehabilitation counseling (Certificate); sociology (MA); Spanish (MA); special education (M Ed); speech-language pathology (MA); strategic management (MBA); studio art (MFA); teaching (M Ed); MBA/MS. *Program availability:* Part-time, evening/weekend, online learning. Terminal master's awarded for partial completion of doctoral program. *Degree requirements:* For master's, variable foreign language requirement, comprehensive exam (for some programs), thesis (for some programs); for doctorate, variable foreign language requirement, comprehensive exam (for some programs), thesis/dissertation; for other advanced degree, variable foreign language requirement, comprehensive exam (for some programs). *Entrance requirements:* For master's and doctorate, GRE, GMAT. Additional exam requirements/recommendations for international students: required—TOEFL (minimum score 550 paper-based; 79 iBT). Electronic applications accepted.

University of Notre Dame, The Graduate School, College of Arts and Letters, Division of Humanities, Department of English, Creative Writing Program, Notre Dame, IN 46556. Offers MFA. *Degree requirements:* For master's, thesis. *Entrance requirements:* For master's, GRE General Test, minimum GPA of 3.0. Additional exam requirements/recommendations for international students: required—TOEFL (minimum score 600 paper-based; 80 iBT). Electronic applications accepted.

University of Oklahoma, College of Arts and Sciences, Department of English, Norman, OK 73019. Offers literary and cultural studies (MA, PhD); writing and rhetoric studies (MA, PhD). *Program availability:* Part-time. *Degree requirements:* For master's, one foreign language, comprehensive exam (for some programs), thesis (for some programs), exam or thesis; for doctorate, one foreign language, comprehensive exam, thesis/dissertation. *Entrance requirements:* For master's, GRE, BA in English or related field; for doctorate, GRE, MA in English or related field. Additional exam requirements/recommendations for international students: required—TOEFL (minimum score 79 iBT) or IELTS (minimum score 6.5). Electronic applications accepted. *Expenses:* Tuition, state resident: full-time $6583.20; part-time $274.30 per credit hour. Tuition, nonresident: full-time $21,242; part-time $885.10 per credit hour. *International tuition:* $21,242.40 full-time. *Required fees:* $1994.20; $72.55 per credit hour. $126.50 per semester. Tuition and fees vary according to course load and degree level.

University of Oregon, Graduate School, College of Arts and Sciences, Department of Creative Writing, Eugene, OR 97403. Offers MFA. *Degree requirements:* For master's, thesis, exam. *Entrance requirements:* For master's, minimum GPA of 3.0. Additional exam requirements/recommendations for international students: required—TOEFL.

University of Pittsburgh, Kenneth P. Dietrich School of Arts and Sciences, Department of English, Pittsburgh, PA 15260. Offers English (MA, PhD); writing (MFA). *Faculty:* 55 full-time (25 women), 1 part-time/adjunct (0 women). *Students:* 101 full-time (68 women); includes 48 minority (15 Black or African American, non-Hispanic/Latino; 1 American Indian or Alaska Native, non-Hispanic/Latino; 19 Asian, non-Hispanic/Latino; 13 Hispanic/Latino). Average age 31. 354 applicants, 10% accepted, 17 enrolled. In 2019, 16 master's, 5 doctorates awarded. Terminal master's awarded for partial completion of doctoral program. *Degree requirements:* For master's, variable foreign language requirement, thesis; for doctorate, variable foreign language requirement, comprehensive exam, thesis/dissertation. *Entrance requirements:* For master's and doctorate, writing sample. Additional exam requirements/recommendations for international students: required—TOEFL, IELTS, TOEFL or IELTS. *Application deadline:* For fall admission, 12/10 for domestic students. Application fee: $75. Electronic applications accepted. *Financial support:* In 2019–20, 81 students received support, including 25 fellowships with full tuition reimbursements available (averaging $23,790 per year), 6 research assistantships with full and partial tuition reimbursements available (averaging $19,480 per year), 50 teaching assistantships with full and partial tuition reimbursements available (averaging $19,649 per year); Federal Work-Study, institutionally sponsored loans, health care benefits, tuition waivers (full and partial), and unspecified assistantships also available. Support available to part-time students. Financial award application deadline: 12/10. *Unit head:* Dr. Gayle Rogers, Chair; Professor, 412-624-6509, Fax: 412-624-6639, E-mail: grogers@pitt.edu. *Application contact:* Jesse Daugherty, Manager of Graduate Administration - Humanities Division; Graduate Administrator, 412-624-6549, Fax: 412-624-6639, E-mail: jed110@pitt.edu.
Website: http://www.english.pitt.edu

University of Regina, Faculty of Graduate Studies and Research, Faculty of Arts, Department of English, Regina, SK S4S 0A2, Canada. Offers creative writing (MA); English (MA, PhD). *Program availability:* Part-time. *Faculty:* 22 full-time (10 women), 2 part-time/adjunct (1 woman). *Students:* 8 full-time (6 women), 5 part-time (4 women). Average age 30. 16 applicants, 44% accepted. In 2019, 4 master's awarded. *Degree requirements:* For master's, thesis (for some programs); for doctorate, thesis/dissertation. *Entrance requirements:* For master's, overall GPA of 75 percent, writing sample, portfolio of creative material (for creative writing). Applicants must have successfully completed ENGL 399 or an equivalent course in Literary Theory. At the discretion graduate chair students with qualification may be admitted and to pass ENGL 399 in addition to MA courses. Additional exam requirements/recommendations for international students: required—TOEFL (minimum score 600 paper-based; 100 iBT), IELTS (minimum score 7.5), PTE (minimum score 68), Could be one of the test listed above. Other option are CAEL, MELAB, CANTEST and U or R ESL. *Application deadline:* For fall admission, 3/15 for domestic and international students; for winter admission, 10/15 for domestic and international students; for spring admission, 2/15 for domestic and international students. Applications are processed on a rolling basis. Application fee: $100. Electronic applications accepted. *Expenses: Tuition:* Full-time $6684 Canadian dollars. *Required fees:* $100 Canadian dollars; $3351.45 Canadian dollars per trimester. $1117.15 Canadian dollars per semester. Tuition and fees vary according to course level, course load, degree level and program. *Financial support:* Fellowships, research assistantships, teaching assistantships, career-related internships or fieldwork, Federal Work-Study, scholarships/grants, unspecified assistantships, and travel award and Graduate Scholarship Base Funds available. Support available to part-time students. Financial award application deadline: 9/30. *Unit head:* Dr. Marcel DeCoste, Department Head, 306-585-4691, Fax: 306-585-5429, E-mail: marcel.decoste@uregina.ca. *Application contact:* Dr. Michael Trussler, Graduate Chair, 306-585-4315, Fax: 306-585-5429, E-mail: Michael.Trussler@uregina.ca.
Website: http://www.uregina.ca/arts/english

University of Rhode Island, Graduate School, College of Arts and Sciences, Department of English, Kingston, RI 02881. Offers American literature and culture (PhD); British literature and culture (PhD); creative writing (PhD); critical theories (PhD); English (MA); film (PhD); gender studies (PhD); MLIS/MA. *Program availability:* Part-time. *Faculty:* 18 full-time (10 women). *Students:* 29 full-time (19 women), 11 part-time (7 women); includes 2 minority (both Black or African American, non-Hispanic/Latino), 8 international. 15 applicants, 40% accepted, 6 enrolled. In 2019, 2 master's, 9 doctorates awarded. *Entrance requirements:* Additional exam requirements/recommendations for international students: required—TOEFL (minimum score 91 iBT). *Application deadline:* For fall admission, 1/15 for domestic and international students. Application fee: $65. Electronic applications accepted. *Expenses: Tuition, area resident:* Full-time $13,734; part-time $763 per credit. Tuition, state resident: full-time $13,734; part-time $763 per credit. Tuition, nonresident: full-time $26,512; part-time $1473 per credit. *International tuition:* $26,512 full-time. *Required fees:* $1780; $52 per credit. $35 per term. One-time fee: $165. *Financial support:* In 2019–20, 24 teaching assistantships with tuition reimbursements (averaging $19,520 per year) were awarded. Financial award application deadline: 1/15; financial award applicants required to submit FAFSA. *Unit head:* Dr. Travis Williams, Chair, 401-874-9501, E-mail: tdwilliams@uri.edu. *Application contact:* Dr. David Faflik, Director of Graduate Studies, 401-874-4670, E-mail: faflik@uri.edu.
Website: http://www.uri.edu/artsci/eng/

University of San Francisco, College of Arts and Sciences, Program in Writing, San Francisco, CA 94117. Offers MFA. *Program availability:* Part-time, evening/weekend. *Faculty:* 2 full-time (1 woman), 14 part-time/adjunct (9 women). *Students:* 92 full-time (57 women), 1 (woman) part-time; includes 42 minority (6 Black or African American, non-Hispanic/Latino; 2 American Indian or Alaska Native, non-Hispanic/Latino; 9 Asian, non-Hispanic/Latino; 18 Hispanic/Latino; 7 Two or more races, non-Hispanic/Latino), 3 international. Average age 34. 133 applicants, 83% accepted, 33 enrolled. In 2019, 27 master's awarded. *Degree requirements:* For master's, thesis. *Entrance requirements:* For master's, minimum overall GPA of 2.7, writing sample, 2 letters of recommendation, resume, interview. Additional exam requirements/recommendations for international students: required—TOEFL (minimum score 100 iBT), IELTS (minimum score 7), PTE (minimum score 65). *Application deadline:* For fall admission, 1/15 for domestic and international students. Applications are processed on a rolling basis. Application fee: $55. Electronic applications accepted. Application fee is waived when completed online. *Financial support:* Fellowships with partial tuition reimbursements, teaching assistantships with partial tuition reimbursements, and scholarships/grants available. Financial award applicants required to submit FAFSA. *Unit head:* Dr. Micah Ballard, Graduate Director, 415-422-6066, E-mail: mfa@usfca.edu. *Application contact:* Dr. Micah Ballard, Graduate Director, 415-422-6066, E-mail: mfa@usfca.edu.
Website: https://www.usfca.edu/arts-sciences/graduate-programs/writing

University of South Alabama, College of Arts and Sciences, Department of English, Mobile, AL 36688. Offers creative writing (MA); literature (MA). *Program availability:* Part-time, evening/weekend. *Faculty:* 10 full-time (3 women), 1 part-time/adjunct (0 women). *Students:* 19 full-time (12 women), 3 part-time (1 woman); includes 4 minority (1 Black or African American, non-Hispanic/Latino; 1 American Indian or Alaska Native, non-Hispanic/Latino; 1 Hispanic/Latino; 1 Two or more races, non-Hispanic/Latino), 1 international. Average age 33. 6 applicants, 100% accepted, 6 enrolled. In 2019, 7 master's awarded. *Degree requirements:* For master's, one foreign language, comprehensive exam, thesis optional. *Entrance requirements:* For master's, GRE. Additional exam requirements/recommendations for international students: required—TOEFL (minimum score 79 iBT), IELTS (minimum score 6.5), TOEFL or IELTS score must be submitted - not both. *Application deadline:* For fall admission, 7/15 priority date for domestic students, 5/15 priority date for international students; for spring admission, 12/1 priority date for domestic students, 11/1 priority date for international students; for summer admission, 5/1 for domestic students, 4/1 for international students.

Applications are processed on a rolling basis. Application fee: $35. Electronic applications accepted. *Expenses: Tuition, area resident:* Part-time $442 per credit hour. Tuition, state resident: full-time $10,608; part-time $442 per credit hour. Tuition, nonresident: full-time $21,216; part-time $884 per credit hour. *Financial support:* Fellowships, research assistantships, teaching assistantships, career-related internships or fieldwork, Federal Work-Study, institutionally sponsored loans, scholarships/grants, and unspecified assistantships available. Support available to part-time students. Financial award application deadline: 3/31; financial award applicants required to submit FAFSA. *Unit head:* Dr. Ellen Harrington, Interim Chair, English, 251-460-6146, E-mail: eharrington@southalabama.edu. *Application contact:* Dr. Ellen Harrington, Interim Chair, English, 251-460-6146, E-mail: eharrington@southalabama.edu.
Website: http://www.southalabama.edu/colleges/artsandsci/english/

University of South Carolina, The Graduate School, College of Arts and Sciences, Department of English Language and Literature, Columbia, SC 29208. Offers creative writing (MFA); English (MA, PhD); English education (MAT); MLIS/MA. *Program availability:* Part-time. *Degree requirements:* For master's, one foreign language, comprehensive exam, thesis; for doctorate, 2 foreign languages, comprehensive exam, thesis/dissertation. *Entrance requirements:* For master's, GRE General Test (MFA), GRE Subject Test (MA, MAT), sample of written work; for doctorate, GRE General Test, GRE Subject Test, sample of written work. Additional exam requirements/recommendations for international students: required—TOEFL. Electronic applications accepted.

University of Southern California, Graduate School, Dana and David Dornsife College of Letters, Arts and Sciences, Department of English, Los Angeles, CA 90089. Offers English (MA, PhD); literature and creative writing (PhD). Terminal master's awarded for partial completion of doctoral program. *Degree requirements:* For doctorate, one foreign language, comprehensive exam, thesis/dissertation. *Entrance requirements:* For doctorate, GRE General Test, GRE Subject Test (English literature). Additional exam requirements/recommendations for international students: required—TOEFL. Electronic applications accepted.

University of Southern Maine, College of Arts, Humanities, and Social Sciences, Program in Creative Writing, Portland, ME 04104. Offers MFA. *Expenses: Tuition, area resident:* Full-time $864; part-time $432 per credit hour. Tuition, state resident: full-time $864; part-time $432 per credit hour. Tuition, nonresident: full-time $2372; part-time $1186 per credit hour. *Required fees:* $141; $108 per credit hour. Tuition and fees vary according to course load.

University of South Florida, Innovative Education, Tampa, FL 33620-9951. Offers adult, career and higher education (Graduate Certificate), including college teaching, leadership in developing human resources, leadership in higher education; Africana studies (Graduate Certificate), including diasporas and health disparities, genocide and human rights; aging studies (Graduate Certificate), including gerontology; art research (Graduate Certificate), including museum studies; business foundations (Graduate Certificate); chemical and biomedical engineering (Graduate Certificate), including materials science and engineering, water, health and sustainability; child and family studies (Graduate Certificate), including positive behavior support; civil and industrial engineering (Graduate Certificate), including transportation systems analysis; community and family health (Graduate Certificate), including maternal and child health, social marketing and public health, violence and injury: prevention and intervention, women's health; criminology (Graduate Certificate), including criminal justice administration; data science for public administration (Graduate Certificate); digital humanities (Graduate Certificate); educational measurement and research (Graduate Certificate), including evaluation; English (Graduate Certificate), including comparative literary studies, creative writing, professional and technical communication; entrepreneurship (Graduate Certificate); environmental health (Graduate Certificate), including safety management; epidemiology and biostatistics (Graduate Certificate), including applied biostatistics, biostatistics, concepts and tools of epidemiology, epidemiology, epidemiology of infectious diseases; geography, environment and planning (Graduate Certificate), including community development, environmental policy and management, geographical information systems; geology (Graduate Certificate), including hydrogeology; global health (Graduate Certificate), including disaster management, global health and Latin American and Caribbean studies, global health practice, humanitarian assistance, infection control; government and international affairs (Graduate Certificate), including Cuban studies, globalization studies; health policy and management (Graduate Certificate), including health management and leadership, public health policy and programs; hearing specialist: early intervention (Graduate Certificate); industrial and management systems engineering (Graduate Certificate), including systems engineering, technology management; information studies (Graduate Certificate), including school library media specialist; information systems/decision sciences (Graduate Certificate), including analytics and business intelligence; instructional technology (Graduate Certificate), including distance education, Florida digital/virtual educator, instructional design, multimedia design, Web design; internal medicine, bioethics and medical humanities (Graduate Certificate), including biomedical ethics; Latin American and Caribbean studies (Graduate Certificate); leadership for coastal resiliency planning (Graduate Certificate); mass communications (Graduate Certificate), including multimedia journalism; mathematics and statistics (Graduate Certificate), including mathematics; medicine (Graduate Certificate), including aging and neuroscience, bioinformatics, biotechnology, brain fitness and memory management, clinical investigation, hand and upper limb rehabilitation, health informatics, health sciences, integrative weight management, intellectual property, medicine and gender, metabolic and nutritional medicine, metabolic cardiology, pharmacy sciences; national and competitive intelligence (Graduate Certificate); nursing (Graduate Certificate), including simulation based academic fellowship in advanced pain management; psychological and social foundations (Graduate Certificate), including career counseling, college teaching, diversity in education, mental health counseling, school counseling; public affairs (Graduate Certificate), including nonprofit management, public management, research administration; public health (Graduate Certificate), including assessing chemical toxicity and public health risks, health equity, pharmacoepidemiology, public health generalist, toxicology, translational research in adolescent behavioral health; public health practices (Graduate Certificate), including planning for healthy communities; rehabilitation and mental health counseling (Graduate Certificate), including integrative mental health care, marriage and family therapy, rehabilitation technology; secondary education (Graduate Certificate), including ESOL, foreign language education: culture and content, foreign language education: professional; social work (Graduate Certificate), including geriatric social work/clinical gerontology; special education (Graduate Certificate), including autism spectrum disorder, disabilities education: severe/profound; world languages (Graduate Certificate), including teaching English as a second language (TESL) or foreign language. *Unit head:* Dr. Cynthia DeLuca, Associate Vice President and Assistant Vice Provost, 813-974-3077, Fax: 813-974-7061, E-mail: deluca@usf.edu. *Application contact:* Owen Hooper, Director, Summer and Alternative Calendar Programs, 813-974-6917, E-mail: hooper@usf.edu.
Website: http://www.usf.edu/innovative-education/

The University of Tampa, Program in Creative Writing, Tampa, FL 33606-1490. Offers MFA. *Program availability:* Part-time. *Degree requirements:* For master's, capstone. *Entrance requirements:* For master's, official transcripts from all colleges and/or universities previously attended, resume, personal statement, letters of recommendation, creative writing sample in genre. Additional exam requirements/recommendations for international students: required—TOEFL (minimum score 577 paper-based; 90 iBT), IELTS (minimum score 7.5). Electronic applications accepted. *Expenses:* Contact institution.

The University of Tennessee at Chattanooga, Program in English, Chattanooga, TN 37403. Offers creative writing (MA); literary study (MA); rhetoric and writing (MA). *Program availability:* Part-time. *Faculty:* 51 full-time (27 women), 22 part-time/adjunct (17 women). *Students:* 15 full-time (9 women), 16 part-time (14 women); includes 4 minority (2 Black or African American, non-Hispanic/Latino; 1 Asian, non-Hispanic/Latino; 1 Native Hawaiian or other Pacific Islander, non-Hispanic/Latino). Average age 33. 15 applicants, 100% accepted, 10 enrolled. In 2019, 8 master's awarded. *Degree requirements:* For master's, comprehensive exam, thesis. *Entrance requirements:* For master's, minimum GPA of 3.0 in English, two letters of recommendation. Additional exam requirements/recommendations for international students: required—TOEFL (minimum score 550 paper-based; 79 iBT), IELTS (minimum score 6). *Application deadline:* For fall admission, 6/15 priority date for domestic students, 7/1 for international students; for spring admission, 11/1 priority date for domestic students, 11/1 for international students. Applications are processed on a rolling basis. Application fee: $35 ($40 for international students). Electronic applications accepted. *Financial support:* Research assistantships, teaching assistantships, career-related internships or fieldwork, scholarships/grants, health care benefits, and unspecified assistantships available. Support available to part-time students. Financial award application deadline: 7/1; financial award applicants required to submit FAFSA. *Unit head:* Dr. Andrew McCarthy, Department Head, 423-425-4615, Fax: 423-425-2282, E-mail: andrew-mccarthy@utc.edu. *Application contact:* Dr. Joanne Romagni, Dean of the Graduate School, 423-425-4478, Fax: 423-425-5223, E-mail: joanne-romagni@utc.edu.
Website: http://www.utc.edu/english/

The University of Texas at Austin, Graduate School, College of Liberal Arts, Department of English, Austin, TX 78712-1111. Offers creative writing (MFA); English (MA, PhD). *Program availability:* Part-time. Terminal master's awarded for partial completion of doctoral program. *Degree requirements:* For master's, 2 foreign languages; for doctorate, variable foreign language requirement. *Entrance requirements:* For master's and doctorate, GRE General Test. Electronic applications accepted.

The University of Texas at Austin, Graduate School, Michener Center for Writers, Austin, TX 78712-1111. Offers fiction (MFA); playwriting (MFA); poetry (MFA); screenwriting (MFA). Electronic applications accepted.

The University of Texas at El Paso, Graduate School, College of Liberal Arts, Department of Creative Writing, El Paso, TX 79968-0001. Offers creative writing (MFA); creative writing of the Americas (MFA). *Program availability:* Part-time, evening/weekend, online learning. *Degree requirements:* For master's, thesis. *Entrance requirements:* For master's, minimum GPA of 3.0, letters of recommendation, writing sample. Additional exam requirements/recommendations for international students: recommended—TOEFL, IELTS. Electronic applications accepted.

The University of Texas at El Paso, Graduate School, College of Liberal Arts, Department of English, El Paso, TX 79968-0001. Offers bilingual professional writing (Certificate); English and American literature (MA); rhetoric and composition (PhD); rhetoric and writing studies (MA); teaching English (MAT). *Program availability:* Part-time, evening/weekend. *Degree requirements:* For master's, thesis optional. *Entrance requirements:* For master's, GRE General Test, minimum GPA of 3.0. Additional exam requirements/recommendations for international students: required—TOEFL. Electronic applications accepted.

The University of Texas Rio Grande Valley, College of Fine Arts, Program in Creative Writing, Edinburg, TX 78539. Offers MFA. *Faculty:* 7 full-time (2 women). *Students:* 13 full-time (6 women), 28 part-time (15 women); includes 40 minority (all Hispanic/Latino). Average age 32. 10 applicants, 50% accepted, 5 enrolled. In 2019, 7 master's awarded. *Expenses: Tuition, area resident:* Full-time $5959; part-time $440 per credit hour. Tuition, state resident: full-time $5959. Tuition, nonresident: full-time $5959. *International tuition:* $13,321 full-time. *Required fees:* $1169; $185 per credit hour.

University of the Sacred Heart, Graduate Programs, Department of Communication, San Juan, PR 00914-0383. Offers contemporary culture and media (MA); digital journalism (MA, Certificate); editing for media (MA, Certificate); public relations (MA, Certificate); publicity (MA, Certificate); scriptwriting (MA, Certificate). *Program availability:* Part-time, evening/weekend. *Degree requirements:* For master's, thesis.

University of the Sacred Heart, Graduate Programs, Program in Creative Writing, San Juan, PR 00914-0383. Offers MFA, Certificate.

The University of the South, Sewanee School of Letters, Sewanee, TN 37383. Offers American and English literature (MA); creative writing (MFA). *Program availability:* Part-time. *Faculty:* 3 full-time (1 woman), 7 part-time/adjunct (4 women). *Students:* 40 part-time (24 women); includes 5 minority (1 Black or African American, non-Hispanic/Latino; 1 Asian, non-Hispanic/Latino; 1 Hispanic/Latino; 2 Two or more races, non-Hispanic/Latino). Average age 42. In 2019, 16 master's awarded. *Degree requirements:* For master's, thesis (for some programs). *Entrance requirements:* For master's, writing sample, two letters of recommendation, official transcripts. *Application deadline:* For summer admission, 4/15 for domestic students. Applications are processed on a rolling basis. Application fee: $0. Electronic applications accepted. *Expenses:* Contact institution. *Financial support:* Institutionally sponsored loans and scholarships/grants available. *Unit head:* Justin Taylor, Director of the School of Letters, 931-598-1636, E-mail: sletters@sewanee.edu. *Application contact:* April R. Alvarez, Associate Director of the School of Letters, 931-598-1636, E-mail: sletters@sewanee.edu.
Website: http://letters.sewanee.edu/

The University of Toledo, College of Graduate Studies, College of Languages, Literature and Social Sciences, Department of English Language and Literature, Toledo, OH 43606-3390. Offers English as a second language (MA); teaching of writing (Certificate). *Program availability:* Part-time. *Degree requirements:* For master's, thesis. *Entrance requirements:* For master's, GRE if GPA is less than 3.0, minimum cumulative point-hour ratio of 2.7 for all previous academic work, three letters of recommendation, transcripts from all prior institutions attended, critical essay; for Certificate, statement of purpose, transcripts from all prior institutions attended, 2 letters of recommendation. Additional exam requirements/recommendations for international students: required—TOEFL (minimum score 550 paper-based; 80 iBT). Electronic applications accepted.

University of Toronto, School of Graduate Studies, Faculty of Arts and Science, Department of English, Toronto, ON M5S 1A1, Canada. Offers creative writing (MA); English (MA, PhD); JD/MA. *Program availability:* Part-time. *Degree requirements:* For master's, thesis optional; for doctorate, 2 foreign languages, thesis/dissertation. *Entrance requirements:* For master's, minimum B+ average, 2 letters of reference, portfolio (creative writing program); for doctorate, minimum A- average, 2 letters of reference, writing sample. Additional exam requirements/recommendations for international students: required—TOEFL (minimum score 580 paper-based; 93 iBT), TWE (minimum score 5). Electronic applications accepted.

University of Utah, Graduate School, College of Humanities, Department of English, Salt Lake City, UT 84112. Offers English (MA, MFA, PhD), including creative writing (MFA, PhD), literary and cultural studies (MA, PhD), rhetoric and composition (MA, PhD). *Faculty:* 17 full-time (9 women). *Students:* 51 full-time (28 women), 19 part-time (9 women); includes 11 minority (1 Black or African American, non-Hispanic/Latino; 4 Asian, non-Hispanic/Latino; 3 Hispanic/Latino; 3 Two or more races, non-Hispanic/Latino), 7 international. Average age 33. 248 applicants, 14% accepted, 18 enrolled. In 2019, 5 master's, 8 doctorates awarded. *Degree requirements:* For master's, one foreign language, thesis (for some programs), for MA - essay written & presented; for MFA - thesis; for doctorate, variable foreign language requirement, comprehensive exam, thesis/dissertation. *Entrance requirements:* For master's, exams required to be admitted, students applying to the MA or MFA degree programs must hold a BA or BS degree from an accredited College or University; a cumulative GPA of 3.3; TOEFL/IELTS scores for International applicants; for doctorate, students applying to the PhD degree programs must hold a BA or BS degree from an accredited College or University; successful completion of a previous Master's degree; a cumulative GPA of 3.3; TOEFL/IELTS scores for International applicants, NA. Additional exam requirements/recommendations for international students: required—TOEFL (minimum score 80 paper-based; 80 iBT), IELTS (minimum score 6.5). *Application deadline:* For fall admission, 12/15 for domestic and international students. Application fee: $55 ($65 for international students). Electronic applications accepted. *Expenses:* Tuition, state resident: full-time $7085; part-time $272.51 per credit hour. Tuition, nonresident: full-time $24,937; part-time $959.12 per credit hour. *Required fees:* $880.52; $880.52 per semester. Tuition and fees vary according to degree level, program and student level. *Financial support:* In 2019–20, 14 students received support, including 14 fellowships with full tuition reimbursements available (averaging $20,000 per year), 34 teaching assistantships with full tuition reimbursements available (averaging $18,000 per year); health care benefits and unspecified assistantships also available. Financial award application deadline: 4/15; financial award applicants required to submit FAFSA. *Unit head:* Prof. Scott Black, Chair, Department of English, 801-581-3393, Fax: 801-585-5167, E-mail: scott.black@utah.edu. *Application contact:* Prof. Gerri Mackey, Graduate Academic Advisor, Department of English, 801-581-7850, Fax: 801-585-5167, E-mail: gerri.mackey@utah.edu.
Website: http://english.utah.edu/

University of Victoria, Faculty of Graduate Studies, Faculty of Fine Arts, Department of Writing, Victoria, BC V8W 2Y2, Canada. Offers MFA. *Entrance requirements:* For master's, portfolio, 2 letters of reference.

University of Virginia, College and Graduate School of Arts and Sciences, Department of English Language and Literature, Program in Creative Writing, Charlottesville, VA 22903. Offers MFA. *Degree requirements:* For master's, comprehensive exam, thesis. *Entrance requirements:* For master's, GRE General Test, writing sample. Additional exam requirements/recommendations for international students: required—TOEFL (minimum score 600 paper-based; 90 iBT), IELTS (minimum score 7). Electronic applications accepted.

University of Washington, Graduate School, College of Arts and Sciences, Department of English, Program in Creative Writing, Seattle, WA 98195. Offers MFA. *Entrance requirements:* For master's, GRE, GMAT. Additional exam requirements/recommendations for international students: required—TOEFL (minimum score 550 paper-based). Electronic applications accepted.

University of Washington, Bothell, Program in Creative Writing and Poetics, Bothell, WA 98011. Offers MFA.

University of West Florida, College of Arts, Social Sciences, and Humanities, Department of English, Pensacola, FL 32514-5750. Offers creative writing (MA); literature (MA). *Program availability:* Part-time, evening/weekend. *Degree requirements:* For master's, thesis. *Entrance requirements:* For master's, GRE (minimum score: verbal 500, writing 4.5) or MAT (minimum score 413), official transcripts; two-page statement of purpose; writing sample (2500 words of literary analysis for literature track, or 2500 words of fiction/non-fiction prose or 10 poems for creative writing track); three letters of recommendation from instructors; 20 hours' upper-division undergraduate coursework in English. Additional exam requirements/recommendations for international students: required—TOEFL (minimum score 550 paper-based).

University of Windsor, Faculty of Graduate Studies, Faculty of Arts and Social Sciences, Department of English Language, Literature and Creative Writing, Windsor, ON N9B 3P4, Canada. Offers English: creative writing and language and literature (MA); English: language and literature (MA). *Program availability:* Part-time. *Degree requirements:* For master's, thesis. *Entrance requirements:* For master's, minimum B average, portfolio. Additional exam requirements/recommendations for international students: required—TOEFL (minimum score 600 paper-based). Electronic applications accepted.

University of Wisconsin–Eau Claire, College of Arts and Sciences, Program in English, Eau Claire, WI 54702-4004. Offers literature and textual interpretation (MA); writing (MA). *Program availability:* Part-time. *Degree requirements:* For master's, oral defense with thesis. *Entrance requirements:* For master's, minimum GPA of 3.25 in English, 3.0 overall; bachelor's degree with minimum of 24 credits in English. Additional exam requirements/recommendations for international students: required—TOEFL (minimum score 79 iBT).

University of Wisconsin–Madison, Graduate School, College of Letters and Science, Department of English, Madison, WI 53706-1380. Offers applied English linguistics (MA); composition and rhetoric (PhD); creative writing (MFA); English language and linguistics (PhD); literary studies (MA, PhD). *Degree requirements:* For doctorate, thesis/dissertation.

University of Wisconsin–Milwaukee, Graduate School, College of Letters and Science, Department of English, Milwaukee, WI 53201-0413. Offers English (MA, PhD), including creative writing, English language and linguistics, English secondary education, literary and critical studies, literature and cultural theory (PhD), literature and language studies, literature, culture, and media, media, cinema and digital studies, professional and technical communication (MA), professional and technical writing, professional writing (PhD), rhetoric and composition (PhD), rhetoric and writing. *Degree requirements:* For master's, thesis or alternative; for doctorate, one foreign language, thesis/dissertation. *Entrance requirements:* For master's, GRE General Test, GRE Subject Test; for doctorate, GRE. Additional exam requirements/recommendations for international students: required—TOEFL (minimum score 550 paper-based; 79 iBT), IELTS (minimum score 6.5). Electronic applications accepted.

University of Wyoming, College of Arts and Sciences, Department of English, Laramie, WY 82071. Offers creative writing (MFA); English (MA). *Program availability:* Part-time. *Degree requirements:* For master's, thesis or alternative, internship. *Entrance requirements:* For master's, GRE General Test, minimum GPA of 3.0. Electronic applications accepted.

Utah State University, School of Graduate Studies, College of Humanities and Social Sciences, Department of English, Logan, UT 84322. Offers American studies (MA, MS), including folklore, western American literature and culture; English (MA, MS), including literature and writing, technical writing. *Program availability:* Part-time, evening/weekend. *Degree requirements:* For master's, thesis or alternative. *Entrance requirements:* For master's, GRE General Test or MAT, minimum GPA of 3.0, recommendation letters, writing samples. Additional exam requirements/recommendations for international students: required—TOEFL.

Vanderbilt University, Program in Creative Writing, Nashville, TN 37240-1001. Offers MFA. *Faculty:* 29 full-time (20 women). *Students:* 16 full-time (11 women); includes 8 minority (1 Black or African American, non-Hispanic/Latino; 3 Asian, non-Hispanic/Latino; 3 Hispanic/Latino; 1 Two or more races, non-Hispanic/Latino), 1 international. Average age 27. 331 applicants, 3% accepted, 6 enrolled. In 2019, 2 master's awarded. *Degree requirements:* For master's, comprehensive exam, thesis. *Entrance requirements:* For master's, GRE General Test, sample of written work. Additional exam requirements/recommendations for international students: required—TOEFL (minimum score 570 paper-based; 88 iBT). *Application deadline:* For fall admission, 1/15 for domestic and international students. Electronic applications accepted. *Expenses: Tuition:* Full-time $51,018; part-time $2087 per hour. *Required fees:* $542. Tuition and fees vary according to program. *Financial support:* Fellowships, teaching assistantships, Federal Work-Study, institutionally sponsored loans, and health care benefits available. Financial award application deadline: 1/15; financial award applicants required to submit CSS PROFILE or FAFSA. *Unit head:* Dr. Dana Nelson, Chair, 615-322-2541, E-mail: dana.d.nelson@vanderbilt.edu. *Application contact:* Katherine Daniels, Director of Graduate Studies, 615-322-2541, E-mail: kate.daniels@vanderbilt.edu.
Website: http://www.vanderbilt.edu/creativewriting/

Vermont College of Fine Arts, International MFA in Creative Writing and Literary Translation Program, Montpelier, VT 05602. Offers MFA. *Expenses: Tuition:* Full-time $25,864; part-time $880 per credit. *Required fees:* $1322; $661 per term. Tuition and fees vary according to program.

Vermont College of Fine Arts, MFA in Writing and Publishing Program, Montpelier, VT 05602. Offers MFA. *Expenses:* Contact institution.

Vermont College of Fine Arts, MFA in Writing for Children and Young Adults Program, Montpelier, VT 05602. Offers MFA. *Entrance requirements:* For master's, original work, bachelor's degree. Electronic applications accepted. *Expenses:* Contact institution.

Vermont College of Fine Arts, MFA in Writing Program, Montpelier, VT 05602. Offers MFA. *Entrance requirements:* For master's, original work; bachelor's degree; evidence of exceptional academic, literary and/or publishing background. *Expenses:* Contact institution.

Virginia Commonwealth University, Graduate School, College of Humanities and Sciences, Department of English, Program in Creative Writing, Richmond, VA 23284-9005. Offers dual genre (MFA); fiction (MFA); poetry (MFA). *Program availability:* Part-time. *Entrance requirements:* For master's, GRE General Test, portfolio. Additional exam requirements/recommendations for international students: required—TOEFL (minimum score 600 paper-based; 100 iBT) or IELTS (minimum score 6.5). Electronic applications accepted.

Virginia Polytechnic Institute and State University, Graduate School, College of Liberal Arts and Human Sciences, Blacksburg, VA 24061. Offers career and technical education (MS Ed, Ed S); communication (MA); counselor education (MA); creative writing (MFA); curriculum and instruction (MA Ed, Ed S); educational leadership and policy studies (Ed S); educational research and evaluation (PhD); English (MA); social, political, ethical, and cultural thought (PhD); Ed D/PhD. *Faculty:* 452 full-time (241 women), 1 (woman) part-time/adjunct. *Students:* 571 full-time (405 women), 351 part-time (223 women); includes 176 minority (103 Black or African American, non-Hispanic/Latino; 3 American Indian or Alaska Native, non-Hispanic/Latino; 18 Asian, non-Hispanic/Latino; 31 Hispanic/Latino; 1 Native Hawaiian or other Pacific Islander, non-Hispanic/Latino; 20 Two or more races, non-Hispanic/Latino), 93 international. Average age 34. 865 applicants, 55% accepted, 336 enrolled. In 2019, 270 master's, 63 doctorates awarded. *Degree requirements:* For master's, comprehensive exam (for some programs), thesis (for some programs); for doctorate, comprehensive exam (for some programs), thesis/dissertation (for some programs). *Entrance requirements:* For master's and doctorate, GRE/GMAT. Additional exam requirements/recommendations for international students: required—TOEFL (minimum score 90 iBT). *Application deadline:* For fall admission, 8/1 for domestic students, 4/1 for international students; for spring admission, 1/1 for domestic students, 9/1 for international students. Applications are processed on a rolling basis. Application fee: $75. Electronic applications accepted. *Expenses:* Tuition, state resident: full-time $13,700; part-time $761.25 per credit hour. Tuition, nonresident: full-time $27,614; part-time $1534 per credit hour. *Required fees:* $886.50 per term. Tuition and fees vary according to campus/location and program. *Financial support:* In 2019–20, 3 fellowships with full tuition reimbursements (averaging $7,621 per year), 34 research assistantships with full tuition reimbursements (averaging $15,645 per year), 370 teaching assistantships with full tuition reimbursements (averaging $18,225 per year) were awarded; scholarships/grants and unspecified assistantships also available. Financial award application deadline: 3/1; financial award applicants required to submit FAFSA. *Unit head:* Dr. Laura Belmonte, Dean, 540-231-6779, Fax: 540-231-7157, E-mail: belmonte@vt.edu. *Application contact:* Chelsea Blanchet, Executive Assistant, 540-231-6779, Fax: 540-231-7157, E-mail: bchels1@vt.edu.
Website: http://www.liberalarts.vt.edu/

Warren Wilson College, MFA Program for Writers, Asheville, NC 28815-9000. Offers MFA. *Degree requirements:* For master's, thesis, public reading, critical essay in 3rd semester. *Entrance requirements:* For master's, manuscript of creative work; personal essay; critical essay. Electronic applications accepted. *Expenses:* Contact institution.

Washington & Jefferson College, Graduate and Continuing Studies, Washington, PA 15301. Offers applied health care economics and outcomes management (MS); professional accounting (MAC); professional writing (Graduate Certificate); thanatology (Graduate Certificate).

Washington University in St. Louis, The Graduate School, Department of English, Writing Program, St. Louis, MO 63130-4899. Offers MFA. *Degree requirements:* For master's, thesis or written exam. *Entrance requirements:* For master's, GRE General Test, sample of written work. Additional exam requirements/recommendations for international students: required—TOEFL. Electronic applications accepted.

Wayne State University, College of Liberal Arts and Sciences, Department of English, Detroit, MI 48202. Offers English (MA); film and media studies (PhD); literary and cultural studies (PhD); rhetoric and composition studies (PhD). *Faculty:* 27. *Students:* 59 full-time (36 women), 31 part-time (24 women); includes 17 minority (4 Black or African American, non-Hispanic/Latino; 4 Asian, non-Hispanic/Latino; 3 Hispanic/Latino; 6 Two or more races, non-Hispanic/Latino), 4 international. Average age 33. 87 applicants, 44% accepted, 17 enrolled. In 2019, 12 master's, 9 doctorates awarded. Terminal master's awarded for partial completion of doctoral program. *Degree requirements:* For master's, variable foreign language requirement, essay, thesis, or portfolio of work approved by Director of Graduate Studies; for doctorate, one foreign language, comprehensive exam, thesis/dissertation. *Entrance requirements:* For master's, statement of purpose; two academic letters of reference; sample essay from previous English course; for doctorate, statement of purpose; two academic letters of reference; sample of scholarly or critical writing. Additional exam requirements/recommendations for international students: required—TOEFL (minimum score 550 paper-based; 79 iBT), TWE (minimum score 5.5), Michigan English Language Assessment Battery (minimum score 85); recommended—IELTS (minimum score 6.5). *Application deadline:* For fall admission, 1/15 for domestic students. Applications are processed on a rolling basis. Application fee: $50. Electronic applications accepted. *Expenses: Tuition:* Full-time $34,567. *Financial support:* In 2019–20, 54 students received support, including 5 fellowships with tuition reimbursements available (averaging $21,500 per year), 1 research assistantship with tuition reimbursement available (averaging $19,967 per year), 28 teaching assistantships with tuition reimbursements available (averaging $19,967 per year); scholarships/grants, health care benefits, and unspecified assistantships also available. Financial award applicants required to submit FAFSA. *Unit head:* Dr. Caroline Maun, Chair and Associate Professor, 313-577-7692, E-mail: av4495@wayne.edu. *Application contact:* Dr. Richard Marback, Director of Graduate Studies, 313-577-7694, E-mail: aa4749@wayne.edu. Website: http://clas.wayne.edu/english/

Wesleyan University, Graduate Liberal Studies Program, Middletown, CT 06459. Offers liberal arts (M Phil); liberal studies (MALS); writing (Graduate Certificate). *Program availability:* Part-time, evening/weekend. *Degree requirements:* For master's, thesis optional; for Graduate Certificate, thesis. *Entrance requirements:* For master's, statement of intent, essay, undergraduate transcripts, two academic letters of recommendation. Additional exam requirements/recommendations for international students: required—TOEFL (minimum score 100 iBT), IELTS (minimum score 7). Electronic applications accepted. *Expenses:* Contact institution.

Western Carolina University, Graduate School, College of Arts and Sciences, Department of English, Cullowhee, NC 28723. Offers literature (MA); professional writing (MA); rhetoric and composition (MA); teaching English to speakers of other languages (Certificate); technical and professional writing (Certificate). *Program availability:* Part-time, evening/weekend. *Degree requirements:* For master's, one foreign language, comprehensive exam, thesis (for some programs). *Entrance requirements:* For master's, appropriate undergraduate degree, writing sample, 3 letters of recommendation. Additional exam requirements/recommendations for international students: required—TOEFL (minimum score 550 paper-based, 79 iBT) or IELTS (6.5). Electronic applications accepted. *Expenses:* Contact institution.

Western Colorado University, Program in Creative Writing, Gunnison, CO 81231. Offers mainstream genre fiction (MFA); poetry (MFA); screenwriting (MFA). *Program availability:* Online learning. *Degree requirements:* For master's, thesis.

Western Connecticut State University, Division of Graduate Studies, Maricostas School of Arts and Sciences, Department of Writing, Linguistics, and Creative Process, Danbury, CT 06810-6885. Offers creative and professional writing (MFA). *Program availability:* Part-time. *Degree requirements:* For master's, thesis, completion of program within 4 years, enrichment project that compliments course of study. *Entrance requirements:* For master's, 2 writing samples: a 20-50 page portfolio of previous writing and a brief essay. Additional exam requirements/recommendations for international students: recommended—TOEFL (minimum score 550 paper-based; 79 iBT), IELTS (minimum score 6). *Expenses:* Contact institution.

Western Kentucky University, Graduate School, Potter College of Arts and Letters, Department of English, Bowling Green, KY 42101. Offers education (MA); English

(MA Ed); literature (MA), including American literature, British literature, literary theory, women writers, world literature; teaching English as a second language (MA); writing (MA). *Program availability:* Part-time, evening/weekend. *Degree requirements:* For master's, comprehensive exam, thesis optional, final exam. *Entrance requirements:* For master's, GRE General Test, minimum GPA of 2.75. Additional exam requirements/recommendations for international students: required—TOEFL (minimum score 555 paper-based; 79 iBT).

Western Michigan University, Graduate College, College of Arts and Sciences, Department of English, Kalamazoo, MI 49008. Offers creative writing (MFA, PhD); English (MA, PhD); English teaching (MA). *Degree requirements:* For doctorate, one foreign language, thesis/dissertation.

Western New England University, College of Arts and Sciences, Program in Creative Writing, Springfield, MA 01119. Offers MFA. *Program availability:* Part-time, evening/weekend. *Entrance requirements:* For master's, official transcripts, two letters of recommendation, writing sample, personal narrative, resume. Additional exam requirements/recommendations for international students: required—TOEFL (minimum score 79 iBT). Electronic applications accepted. *Expenses:* Contact institution.

West Virginia University, Eberly College of Arts and Sciences, Morgantown, WV 26506. Offers biology (MS, PhD); chemistry (MS, PhD); communication studies (MA, PhD); computational statistics (PhD); creative writing (MFA); English (MA, PhD); forensic and investigative science (MS); forensic science (PhD); geography (MA); geology (MA, PhD); history (MA, PhD); legal studies (MLS); mathematics (MS); physics (MS, PhD); political science (MA, PhD); professional writing and editing (MA); psychology (MA); public administration (MPA); social work (MSW); sociology (MA, PhD); statistics (MS). *Program availability:* Part-time, evening/weekend, online learning. Terminal master's awarded for partial completion of doctoral program. *Degree requirements:* For master's, thesis (for some programs); for doctorate, comprehensive exam, thesis/dissertation. *Entrance requirements:* For master's and doctorate, GRE. Additional exam requirements/recommendations for international students: required—TOEFL (minimum score 600 paper-based); recommended—TWE. Electronic applications accepted.

West Virginia Wesleyan College, Program in Creative Writing, Buckhannon, WV 26201. Offers MFA.

Wichita State University, Graduate School, Fairmount College of Liberal Arts and Sciences, Department of English, Wichita, KS 67260. Offers creative writing (MFA); English (MA). *Program availability:* Part-time, evening/weekend. *Entrance requirements:* For master's, writing sample (MFA).

Yale University, School of Drama, New Haven, CT 06520. Offers acting (MFA, Certificate); design (MFA, Certificate), including costume design, lighting design, projection design, set design; directing (MFA, Certificate); dramaturgy and dramatic criticism (MFA, DFA); playwriting (MFA, Certificate); sound design (MFA, Certificate); stage management (MFA, Certificate); technical design and production (MFA, Certificate); theater management (MFA); MFA/MBA. *Degree requirements:* For master's, comprehensive exam (for some programs), thesis (for some programs); for doctorate, thesis/dissertation, oral and written comprehensive exams. *Entrance requirements:* For master's, GRE (verbal, quantitative, and analytical), in-person audition (for acting); portfolio review (for design). Additional exam requirements/recommendations for international students: required—TOEFL. Electronic applications accepted.

ACADEMIC AND PROFESSIONAL PROGRAMS IN INTERDISCIPLINARY STUDIES

Section 14
Interdisciplinary Studies

This section contains a directory of institutions offering graduate work in interdisciplinary studies. Additional information about programs listed in the directory may be obtained by writing directly to the dean of a graduate school or chair of a department at the address given in the directory.

For programs offering related work, see also in this book *Comparative and Interdisciplinary Arts, Humanities,* and *Social Sciences.*

CONTENTS

Interdisciplinary Studies

Alaska Pacific University, Graduate Programs, Liberal Studies Department, Self-Designed Programs, Anchorage, AK 99508-4672. Offers MA. *Program availability:* Part-time, evening/weekend. *Degree requirements:* For master's, thesis or project. *Entrance requirements:* For master's, MAT (preferred), GRE General Test or GMAT. *Expenses:* Contact institution.

Amberton University, Graduate School, Program in Professional Development, Garland, TX 75041-5595. Offers MA. *Program availability:* Part-time, evening/weekend, online learning. *Entrance requirements:* For master's, minimum GPA of 3.0.

Antioch University New England, Graduate School, Department of Environmental Studies, Keene, NH 03431-3552. Offers advocacy for social justice and sustainability (MS); conservation biology (MS); environmental education (MS); environmental studies (PhD); resource management and conservation (MS); science teacher certification (MS); self-designed studies (MS); sustainable development and climate change (MS). *Faculty:* 3 full-time (1 woman), 6 part-time/adjunct (3 women). *Students:* 120 full-time (88 women), 75 part-time (49 women); includes 21 minority (3 Black or African American, non-Hispanic/Latino; 6 Asian, non-Hispanic/Latino; 10 Hispanic/Latino; 1 Native Hawaiian or other Pacific Islander, non-Hispanic/Latino; 1 Two or more races, non-Hispanic/Latino), 7 international. Average age 36. 81 applicants, 98% accepted, 54 enrolled. In 2019, 108 master's, 10 doctorates awarded. *Degree requirements:* For master's, practicum; for doctorate, thesis/dissertation, practicum. *Entrance requirements:* Additional exam requirements/recommendations for international students: required—TOEFL (minimum score 550 paper-based). *Application deadline:* For fall admission, 7/1 for domestic students, 6/1 for international students; for spring admission, 12/1 for domestic and international students. Applications are processed on a rolling basis. Application fee: $50. Electronic applications accepted. *Expenses:* Contact institution. *Financial support:* Applicants required to submit FAFSA. *Unit head:* Dr. Michael Simpson, Chairperson, 603-283-2331, Fax: 603-357-0718, E-mail: msimpson@antioch.edu. *Application contact:* Jennifer Fritz, Director of Admissions, 800-552-8380, Fax: 603-357-0718, E-mail: admissions.ane@antioch.edu. Website: http://www.antiochne.edu/environmental-studies/

Arizona State University at Tempe, New College of Interdisciplinary Arts and Sciences, Program in Interdisciplinary Studies, Phoenix, AZ 85069-7100. Offers MA. *Program availability:* Part-time, evening/weekend. *Degree requirements:* For master's, thesis or alternative, research paper or applied project; interactive Program of Study (iPOS) submitted before completing 50 percent of required credit hours. *Entrance requirements:* For master's, GRE (if GPA less than 3.0 in last 60 hours of undergraduate study), minimum GPA of 3.0 or equivalent in last 2 years of work leading to bachelor's degree, 3 letters of recommendation, official transcripts, personal statement, writing sample of scholarly work or example of professional activities. Additional exam requirements/recommendations for international students: required—TOEFL, IELTS, or PTE. Electronic applications accepted.

Athabasca University, Centre for Interdisciplinary Studies, Athabasca, AB T9S 3A3, Canada. Offers adult education (MA); community studies (MA); cultural studies (MA); educational studies (MA); global change (MA); heritage resource management (Postbaccalaureate Certificate); legislative drafting (Postbaccalaureate Certificate); work, organization, and leadership (MA). *Program availability:* Part-time, evening/weekend, online learning. *Degree requirements:* For master's, project. *Entrance requirements:* Additional exam requirements/recommendations for international students: required—TOEFL (minimum score 560 paper-based). Electronic applications accepted.

Baylor University, Graduate School, College of Arts and Sciences, The Institute of Ecological, Earth and Environmental Sciences, Waco, TX 76798. Offers PhD. *Degree requirements:* For doctorate, comprehensive exam, thesis/dissertation. *Entrance requirements:* For doctorate, GRE. Additional exam requirements/recommendations for international students: required—TOEFL (minimum score 550 paper-based; 80 iBT), recommended—IELTS (minimum score 6.5). Electronic applications accepted. *Expenses:* Contact institution.

Boise State University, College of Arts and Sciences, Program in Interdisciplinary Studies, Boise, ID 83725-0399. Offers MA, MS. *Program availability:* Part-time. *Students:* Average age 37. 7 applicants, 71% accepted, 3 enrolled. In 2019, 2 master's awarded. *Entrance requirements:* For master's, minimum GPA of 3.0. Additional exam requirements/recommendations for international students: required—TOEFL (minimum score 550 paper-based; 80 iBT), IELTS (minimum score 6). *Application deadline:* For fall admission, 3/1 for domestic students; for spring admission, 10/1 for domestic students. Application fee: $65 ($95 for international students). Electronic applications accepted. *Expenses:* Tuition, area resident: Full-time $7110; part-time $470 per credit hour. Tuition, state resident: full-time $7110; part-time $470 per credit hour. Tuition, nonresident: full-time $24,030; part-time $827 per credit hour. International tuition: $24,030 full-time. *Required fees:* $2536. Tuition and fees vary according to course load and program. *Financial support:* Scholarships/grants and unspecified assistantships available. Financial award applicants required to submit FAFSA. *Unit head:* Dr. Nicole Molumby, Director, 208-426-1414, Fax: 208-426-3006, E-mail: nicolemolumby@boisestate.edu. *Application contact:* Dr. Nicole Molumby, Director, 208-426-1414, Fax: 208-426-3006, E-mail: nicolemolumby@boisestate.edu. Website: http://coas.boisestate.edu/interdisciplinary-studies-program/

Bowling Green State University, Graduate College, Interdisciplinary Studies, Bowling Green, OH 43403. Offers M Ed, MA, MS, PhD. *Program availability:* Part-time. *Degree requirements:* For master's, thesis or alternative; for doctorate, comprehensive exam, thesis/dissertation. *Entrance requirements:* For master's and doctorate, GRE General Test. Additional exam requirements/recommendations for international students: required—TOEFL. Electronic applications accepted.

Buffalo State College, State University of New York, The Graduate School, Program in Multidisciplinary Studies, Buffalo, NY 14222-1095. Offers data science and analytics (MS); individualized studies (MA, MS); nutrition (MS). *Program availability:* Part-time, evening/weekend. *Degree requirements:* For master's, thesis or project. *Entrance requirements:* For master's, minimum GPA of 2.5. Additional exam requirements/recommendations for international students: required—TOEFL (minimum score 550 paper-based).

California State University, East Bay, Office of Graduate Studies, Interdisciplinary Programs, Hayward, CA 94542-3000. Offers MA, MS. *Program availability:* Part-time. *Degree requirements:* For master's, comprehensive exam, project or thesis. *Entrance requirements:* Additional exam requirements/recommendations for international students: required—TOEFL (minimum score 550 paper-based). Electronic applications accepted.

California State University, San Bernardino, Graduate Studies, Interdisciplinary Programs, San Bernardino, CA 92407. Offers integrative studies (MA). *Program availability:* Part-time, evening/weekend. *Students:* 6 full-time (3 women); includes 4 minority (1 Black or African American, non-Hispanic/Latino; 1 American Indian or Alaska Native, non-Hispanic/Latino; 2 Hispanic/Latino). Average age 43. 1 applicant. *Degree requirements:* For master's, thesis or alternative. *Entrance requirements:* Additional exam requirements/recommendations for international students: required—TOEFL. *Application deadline:* For fall admission, 7/16 for domestic students; for winter admission, 10/16 for domestic students; for spring admission, 1/22 for domestic students. Application fee: $55. *Financial support:* Application deadline: 3/1. *Unit head:* Dr. Dorota Huizinga, Dean of Graduate Studies, 909-537-3064, Fax: 909-537-7034, E-mail: dorota.huizinga@csusb.edu. *Application contact:* Olivia Rosas, Associate Vice President for Enrollment Services, 909-537-7577, Fax: 909-537-7034, E-mail: orosas@csusb.edu.

California State University, Stanislaus, College of the Arts, Humanities and Social Sciences, Programs in Interdisciplinary Studies, Turlock, CA 95382. Offers MA, MS. *Program availability:* Part-time, evening/weekend. *Degree requirements:* For master's, thesis. *Entrance requirements:* For master's, GRE, minimum GPA of 3.0, personal statement. Additional exam requirements/recommendations for international students: required—TOEFL (minimum score 550 paper-based). Electronic applications accepted.

Cambridge College, School of Education, Boston, MA 02129. Offers autism specialist (M Ed); autism/behavior analyst (M Ed); behavior analyst (Post-Master's Certificate); curriculum and instruction (CAGS); early childhood teacher (M Ed); educational leadership (M Ed, Ed D); elementary teacher (M Ed); English as a second language (M Ed, Certificate); general science (M Ed); health education (Post-Master's Certificate); interdisciplinary studies (M Ed); library teacher (M Ed); mathematics education (M Ed); mathematics specialist (Certificate); school administration (M Ed, CAGS); school nurse education (M Ed); teacher of students with moderate disabilities (M Ed); teaching skills and methodologies (M Ed). *Program availability:* Part-time, evening/weekend, online learning. *Degree requirements:* For master's, thesis, internship/practicum (licensure program only); for doctorate, thesis/dissertation; for other advanced degree, thesis. *Entrance requirements:* For master's, interview, resume, documentation of licensure, 2 professional references; for doctorate, official transcripts, interview, resume, written personal statement/essay, portfolio of scholarly and professional work, 2 professional references, health insurance, immunizations form; for other advanced degree, official transcripts, interview, resume, written personal statement/essay, 2 professional references, health insurance, immunizations form. Additional exam requirements/recommendations for international students: required—TOEFL (minimum score 550 paper-based; 79 iBT), Michigan English Language Assessment Battery (minimum score 85); recommended—IELTS (minimum score 6). Electronic applications accepted. *Expenses:* Contact institution.

Campbell University, Graduate and Professional Programs, School of Education, Buies Creek, NC 27506. Offers elementary education (M Ed); interdisciplinary studies (M Ed); middle grades education (M Ed); physical education (M Ed); school administration (MSA); school counseling (M Ed); secondary education (M Ed). *Accreditation:* NCATE. *Program availability:* Part-time, evening/weekend. *Degree requirements:* For master's, comprehensive exam. *Entrance requirements:* For master's, GRE General Test, minimum GPA of 2.7.

Central Washington University, School of Graduate Studies and Research, Individual Studies Program, Ellensburg, WA 98926. Offers M Ed, MA, MFA, MS. *Program availability:* Part-time. *Entrance requirements:* For master's, GRE General Test, minimum GPA of 3.0. Additional exam requirements/recommendations for international students: required—TOEFL (minimum score 550 paper-based; 79 iBT). Electronic applications accepted.

The Citadel, The Military College of South Carolina, Citadel Graduate College, Zucker Family School of Education, Charleston, SC 29409. Offers elementary/secondary school administration and supervision (M Ed); elementary/secondary school counseling (M Ed); interdisciplinary STEM education (M Ed); literacy education (M Ed, Graduate Certificate); middle grades (MAT, including English, mathematics, science, social studies; physical education (grades K-12) (MAT); school superintendency (Ed S); secondary education (MAT), including biology, English, mathematics, social studies; student affairs (Graduate Certificate); student affairs and college counseling (M Ed). *Accreditation:* NCATE. *Program availability:* Part-time, evening/weekend, 100% online, blended/hybrid learning. *Faculty:* 16 full-time (10 women), 10 part-time/adjunct (7 women). *Students:* 37 full-time (27 women), 166 part-time (128 women); includes 55 minority (42 Black or African American, non-Hispanic/Latino; 1 Asian, non-Hispanic/Latino; 8 Hispanic/Latino; 4 Two or more races, non-Hispanic/Latino). In 2019, 120 master's, 27 other advanced degrees awarded. *Entrance requirements:* For master's, GRE or MAT for MAT Secondary Education, MAT Middle Grades, MAT Physical Education, MEd Counselor Education- Elementary and Secondary, MEd Counselor Education - Student Affairs and College and MEd Higher Education Leadership, MAT Secondary Education: Submission of an official transcript of the baccalaureate degree and all other undergraduate or graduate work directly from each regionally accredited college and university. 3.0 cum GPA. MAT Middle Grades: Submission of official transcript of the baccalaureate degree and all other undergraduate or graduate work directly fr; for other advanced degree, Certificate Higher Education Leadership: Submission of an official transcript reflecting the highest degree earned from a regionally accredited college or university. Certificate Literacy Education: Submission of an official transcript directly from each regionally accredited college or university from which a degree has been conferred, 2.5 cum GPA. Additional exam requirements/recommendations for international students: required—TOEFL (minimum score 550 paper-based; 79 iBT). *Application deadline:* Applications are processed on a rolling basis. Application fee: $40. Electronic applications accepted. *Expenses:* MEd Higher Education Leadership, MEd Interdisciplinary STEM Education, MS Instructional Systems Design and Performance Improvement, Certificate Higher Education Leadership: $695 per credit hour. $165 per semester in fees ($75 Technology Fee + $75 Infrastructure Fee + $15 Registration Fee). *Financial support:* In 2019–20, 21,283 students received support. Federal Work-Study, scholarships/grants, tuition waivers (partial), and Athletics available. Financial award applicants required to submit FAFSA. *Unit head:* Evan Ortlieb, Zucker Family School of Education Dean, 843-953-5097, Fax: 843-953-7258, E-mail: eortlieb@citadel.edu. *Application contact:* Carl Hill, Assistant Director of Enrollment Management, 843-953-6808, Fax: 843-953-7630, E-mail: chill9@citadel.edu. Website: http://www.citadel.edu/root/education-graduate-programs

Clarkson University, Wallace H. Coulter School of Engineering, Program in Interdisciplinary Engineering Science, Potsdam, NY 13699. Offers MS, PhD. *Students:* 2

full-time (0 women), 1 part-time (0 women). 5 applicants, 20% accepted. In 2019, 2 master's, 1 doctorate awarded. *Degree requirements:* For master's, thesis; for doctorate, comprehensive exam, thesis/dissertation. *Entrance requirements:* For master's and doctorate, GRE. Additional exam requirements/recommendations for international students: required—TOEFL (minimum score 550 paper-based, 80 iBT) or IELTS (6.5). *Application deadline:* Applications are processed on a rolling basis. Application fee: $50. Electronic applications accepted. *Expenses: Tuition:* Full-time $24,984; part-time $1388 per credit hour. *Required fees:* $225. Tuition and fees vary according to campus/location and program. *Financial support:* Scholarships/grants and unspecified assistantships available. *Unit head:* Dr. William Jemison, Dean of Engineering, 315-268-6446, E-mail: wjemison@clarkson.edu. *Application contact:* Daniel Capogna, Director of Graduate Admissions & Recruitment, 518-631-9910, E-mail: graduate@clarkson.edu.
Website: https://www.clarkson.edu/academics/graduate

Colorado State University, Interdisciplinary College, Interdisciplinary Programs, Fort Collins, CO 80523-1617. Offers MS, PhD. *Degree requirements:* For master's, comprehensive exam (for some programs), thesis (for some programs); for doctorate, comprehensive exam (for some programs), thesis/dissertation. *Entrance requirements:* For master's, GRE (for some programs), minimum GPA of 3.0; for doctorate, GRE, minimum GPA of 3.0. Additional exam requirements/recommendations for international students: required—TOEFL, IELTS. Electronic applications accepted. *Expenses:* Tuition, state resident: full-time $10,520; part-time $5844 per credit hour. Tuition, nonresident: full-time $25,791; part-time $14,328 per credit hour. *International tuition:* $25,791 full-time. *Required fees:* $2512.80. Part-time tuition and fees vary according to course level, course load, degree level, program and student level.

Concordia University, School of Graduate Studies, Special Individualized Programs, Montréal, QC H3G 1M8, Canada. Offers M Sc, MA, PhD. *Degree requirements:* For master's, comprehensive exam, thesis; for doctorate, one foreign language, comprehensive exam, thesis/dissertation.

Dalhousie University, Faculty of Graduate Studies, Interdisciplinary PhD Program, Halifax, NS B3H 4H6, Canada. Offers PhD. *Degree requirements:* For doctorate, thesis/dissertation. *Entrance requirements:* Additional exam requirements/recommendations for international students: required—TOEFL, IELTS, CANTEST, CAEL or Michigan English Language Assessment Battery. Electronic applications accepted. *Expenses:* Contact institution.

Dallas Baptist University, Gary Cook School of Leadership, Program in Higher Education, Dallas, TX 75211-9299. Offers leadership studies (M Ed); student affairs leadership (M Ed), including community college leadership, distance learning, interdisciplinary studies, student affairs leadership. *Program availability:* Part-time, evening/weekend, online learning. *Application deadline:* Applications are processed on a rolling basis. Application fee: $25. Electronic applications accepted. Application fee is waived when completed online. *Expenses: Tuition:* Full-time $18,072; part-time $1004 per credit hour. *Required fees:* $1100; $550 per semester. Tuition and fees vary according to course level and degree level. *Unit head:* Dr. Jack Goodyear, Dean, 214-333-5595, Fax: 214-333-6809, E-mail: jackg@dbu.edu. *Application contact:* Tish Hearne, Program Director, 214-333-5896, E-mail: tish@dbu.edu.
Website: https://www.dbu.edu/graduate/degree-programs/med-higher-education/

Dallas Baptist University, Professional Development Program, Dallas, TX 75211-9299. Offers accounting (MA); church leadership (MA); communication (MA); counseling (MA); criminal justice (MA); English as a second language (MA); finance (MA); higher education (MA); leadership studies (MA); management (MA). *Program availability:* Part-time, evening/weekend, online learning. *Application deadline:* Applications are processed on a rolling basis. Application fee: $25. Electronic applications accepted. Application fee is waived when completed online. *Expenses: Tuition:* Full-time $18,072; part-time $1004 per credit hour. *Required fees:* $1100; $550 per semester. Tuition and fees vary according to course level and degree level. *Unit head:* Jared Ingram, Program Director, 214-333-5584, E-mail: jaredi@dbu.edu. *Application contact:* Jared Ingram, Program Director, 214-333-5584, E-mail: jaredi@dbu.edu.
Website: https://www.dbu.edu/graduate/degree-programs/ma-professional-development

DePaul University, College of Liberal Arts and Social Sciences, Chicago, IL 60614. Offers Arabic (MA); Chinese (MA); critical ethnic studies (MA); English (MA); French (MA); German (MA); history (MA); interdisciplinary studies (MA, MS); international public service (MS); international studies (MA); Italian (MA); Japanese (MA); liberal studies (MA); nonprofit management (MNM); public administration (MPA); public health (MPH); public policy (MPP); public service management (MS); refugee and forced migration studies (MS); social work (MSW); sociology (MA); Spanish (MA); sustainable urban development (MA); women's and gender studies (MA); writing and publishing (MA); writing, rhetoric and discourse (MA); MA/PhD. *Accreditation:* CEPH. *Program availability:* Part-time, evening/weekend, online learning. Terminal master's awarded for partial completion of doctoral program. *Degree requirements:* For master's, variable foreign language requirement, comprehensive exam (for some programs), thesis (for some programs). Electronic applications accepted.

Eastern Washington University, Graduate Studies, Interdisciplinary Studies, Cheney, WA 99004-2431. Offers MA, MS. *Students:* Average age 20. *Degree requirements:* For master's, comprehensive exam, thesis or alternative. *Entrance requirements:* For master's, minimum GPA of 3.0. Additional exam requirements/recommendations for international students: required—TOEFL (minimum score 580 paper-based; 90 iBT), IELTS (minimum score 7), PTE (minimum score 63). *Application deadline:* For fall admission, 4/1 priority date for domestic students; for spring admission, 1/15 for domestic students. Applications are processed on a rolling basis. Application fee: $75. Electronic applications accepted. *Financial support:* Teaching assistantships with partial tuition reimbursements, career-related internships or fieldwork, Federal Work-Study, institutionally sponsored loans, scholarships/grants, health care benefits, tuition waivers (partial), and unspecified assistantships available. Support available to part-time students. Financial award application deadline: 2/1; financial award applicants required to submit FAFSA. *Application contact:* Kathy White, Advisor/Recruiter for Graduate Studies, 509-359-6297, Fax: 509-359-6044, E-mail: gradprograms@ewu.edu.

Emory University, Laney Graduate School, Graduate Institute of the Liberal Arts, Atlanta, GA 30322-1100. Offers PhD. *Degree requirements:* For doctorate, one foreign language, comprehensive exam, thesis/dissertation. *Entrance requirements:* For doctorate, GRE General Test. Additional exam requirements/recommendations for international students: recommended—TOEFL. Electronic applications accepted.

Fitchburg State University, Division of Graduate and Continuing Education, Program in Interdisciplinary Studies, Fitchburg, MA 01420-2697. Offers applied communications (CAGS); counseling/psychology (CAGS); individualized track (CAGS); reading specialist (CAGS). *Program availability:* Part-time, evening/weekend. *Entrance requirements:* Additional exam requirements/recommendations for international students: required—TOEFL (minimum score 550 paper-based; 79 iBT). Electronic applications accepted. *Expenses:* Contact institution.

Florida Gulf Coast University, Elaine Nicpon Marieb College of Health and Human Services, Program in Health Science, Fort Myers, FL 33965-6565. Offers MS. *Program*

availability: Part-time, evening/weekend, online learning. *Degree requirements:* For master's, final project or thesis. *Entrance requirements:* For master's, GRE General Test or MAT, minimum GPA of 3.0. Additional exam requirements/recommendations for international students: required—TOEFL (minimum score 550 paper-based). Electronic applications accepted. *Expenses: Tuition, area resident:* Full-time $6974; part-time $4350 per credit hour. Tuition, state resident: full-time $6974; part-time $4350 per credit hour. Tuition, nonresident: full-time $28,169; part-time $17,595 per credit hour. *International tuition:* $28,169 full-time. *Required fees:* $2027; $1267 per credit hour. $507 per semester. Tuition and fees vary according to course load.

Florida Institute of Technology, College of Engineering and Science, Program in Interdisciplinary Science, Melbourne, FL 32901-6975. Offers MS. *Program availability:* Part-time. *Degree requirements:* For master's, comprehensive exam (for some programs), thesis optional, minimum of 31 credit hours. *Entrance requirements:* For master's, undergraduate STEM degree, 2 letters of recommendations, resume, statement of objectives. Additional exam requirements/recommendations for international students: required—TOEFL (minimum score 550 paper-based; 79 iBT). Electronic applications accepted.

Fresno Pacific University, Graduate Programs, Individualized Study Program, Fresno, CA 93702-4709. Offers MA. *Program availability:* Part-time, evening/weekend. *Degree requirements:* For master's, thesis. *Entrance requirements:* For master's, GMAT, GRE General Test, or MAT, interview. Additional exam requirements/recommendations for international students: required—TOEFL (minimum score 550 paper-based). Electronic applications accepted. *Expenses:* Contact institution.

Frostburg State University, College of Education, Department of Educational Professions, Program in Interdisciplinary Education, Frostburg, MD 21532-1099. Offers M Ed, Ed D. *Program availability:* Part-time, evening/weekend. *Degree requirements:* For master's, thesis or alternative. *Entrance requirements:* Additional exam requirements/recommendations for international students: required—TOEFL. Electronic applications accepted.

George Mason University, College of Humanities and Social Sciences, Interdisciplinary Studies Program, Fairfax, VA 22030. Offers computational social science (MAIS); energy and sustainability (MAIS); folklore studies (MAIS); higher education (MAIS); individualized studies (MAIS); religion, culture, and values (MAIS); social entrepreneurship (MAIS); social justice and human rights (MAIS); war and the military in society (MAIS); women and gender studies (MAIS). *Degree requirements:* For master's, thesis or alternative, experiential learning (for some programs). *Entrance requirements:* Additional exam requirements/recommendations for international students: required—TOEFL (minimum score 575 paper-based; 88 iBT), IELTS (minimum score 6.5), PTE (minimum score 59). Electronic applications accepted.

Georgetown University, Graduate School of Arts and Sciences, School of Continuing Studies, Washington, DC 20057. Offers American studies (MALS); applied intelligence (MPS); Catholic studies (MALS); classical civilizations (MALS); emergency and disaster management (MPS); ethics and the professions (MALS); global strategic communications (MPS); hospitality management (MPS); human resources management (MPS); humanities (MALS); individualized study (MALS); integrated marketing communications (MPS); international affairs (MALS); Islam and Muslim-Christian relations (MALS); journalism (MPS); liberal studies (DLS); literature and society (MALS); medieval and early modern European studies (MALS); public relations and corporate communications (MPS); real estate (MPS); religious studies (MALS); social and public policy (MALS); sports industry management (MPS); systems engineering management (MPS); technology management (MPS); the theory and practice of American democracy (MALS); urban and regional planning (MPS); visual culture (MALS). *Entrance requirements:* Additional exam requirements/recommendations for international students: required—TOEFL.

Goddard College, Graduate Division, Individualized Master of Arts Program, Plainfield, VT 05667-9432. Offers consciousness studies (MA); embodiment studies (MA); transformative language arts (MA). *Program availability:* Part-time. *Degree requirements:* For master's, thesis. *Entrance requirements:* For master's, 3 letters of recommendation, interview. Electronic applications accepted. *Expenses:* Contact institution.

Grand Rapids Theological Seminary of Cornerstone University, Graduate Programs, Grand Rapids, MI 49525-5897. Offers academic (M Div); chaplaincy ministries (M Div); Christian formation (MA); counseling (MA); formation and soul care ministries (M Div); intercultural ministries (M Div); interdisciplinary studies (MA); New Testament (Th M); Old Testament (Th M); pastoral ministries (M Div); small group and discipleship ministries (M Div); student and family ministries (M Div). *Accreditation:* ATS. *Program availability:* Part-time, evening/weekend, 100% online, blended/hybrid learning. *Entrance requirements:* Additional exam requirements/recommendations for international students: required—TOEFL (minimum score 577 paper-based; 90 iBT), IELTS (minimum score 7). Electronic applications accepted.

Harrison Middleton University, Graduate Program, Tempe, AZ 85282. Offers education (MA, Ed D); humanities (MA); imaginative literature (MA); interdisciplinary studies (DA); jurisprudence (MA); natural science (MA); philosophy and religion (MA); social science (MA). *Program availability:* Part-time, evening/weekend, online learning. *Degree requirements:* For master's and doctorate, capstone project. *Entrance requirements:* For master's, interview; for doctorate, 2 academic letters of reference, interview, essay. Additional exam requirements/recommendations for international students: required—TOEFL (minimum score 550 paper-based; 80 iBT). Electronic applications accepted.

Hiram College, Graduate Studies, Hiram, OH 44234. Offers MAIS. *Program availability:* Part-time, evening/weekend. *Degree requirements:* For master's, two seminars, capstone research project. *Entrance requirements:* For master's, bachelor's degree from an accredited institution, 2 letters of recommendation, writing sample, interview.

Hollins University, Graduate Programs, Program in Liberal Studies, Roanoke, VA 24020. Offers humanities (MALS); interdisciplinary studies (MALS); leadership (MALS); social sciences (MALS); visual and performing arts (MALS). *Program availability:* Part-time, evening/weekend, 100% online, blended/hybrid learning. *Degree requirements:* For master's, thesis. *Entrance requirements:* For master's, three letters of recommendation, interview, bachelor's degree, undergraduate transcripts, statement of educational objectives. Additional exam requirements/recommendations for international students: required—TOEFL (minimum score 550 paper-based; 80 iBT), IELTS (minimum score 6.5). Electronic applications accepted. *Expenses:* Contact institution.

Indiana University Southeast, Master of Interdisciplinary Studies Program, New Albany, IN 47150-6405. Offers MIS, Graduate Certificate. *Program availability:* Part-time. *Degree requirements:* For master's, thesis or alternative. *Entrance requirements:* For master's, GRE, 3 letters of recommendation, interview. Electronic applications accepted. *Expenses:* Contact institution.

Iowa State University of Science and Technology, Program in Interdisciplinary Graduate Studies, Ames, IA 50011. Offers MA, MS. *Entrance requirements:* For master's, GRE. Additional exam requirements/recommendations for international students: recommended—TOEFL (minimum score 550 paper-based; 79 iBT), IELTS (minimum score 6.5). Electronic applications accepted.

Kansas State University, Graduate School, School of Applied and Interdisciplinary Studies, Olathe, KS 66061. Offers applied science and technology (PSM); professional interdisciplinary sciences (Graduate Certificate); professional skills for STEM practitioners (Graduate Certificate). *Program availability:* Part-time, 100% online, blended/hybrid learning. *Degree requirements:* For master's, capstone experience and/or internship. *Entrance requirements:* Additional exam requirements/recommendations for international students: required—TOEFL (minimum score 550 paper-based; 79 iBT), IELTS (minimum score 6.5), PTE (minimum score 58). Electronic applications accepted.

Lehigh University, P.C. Rossin College of Engineering and Applied Science, Center for Polymer Science and Engineering, Bethlehem, PA 18015. Offers M Eng, MS, PhD. *Program availability:* Part-time, evening/weekend, 100% online, blended/hybrid learning. *Faculty:* 5 full-time (3 women). *Students:* 6 full-time (4 women), 32 part-time (13 women); includes 13 minority (4 Black or African American, non-Hispanic/Latino; 5 Asian, non-Hispanic/Latino; 4 Hispanic/Latino), 3 international. Average age 31. 28 applicants, 43% accepted, 7 enrolled. In 2019, 9 master's awarded. Terminal master's awarded for partial completion of doctoral program. *Degree requirements:* For master's, thesis (for some programs); for doctorate, thesis/dissertation. *Entrance requirements:* For master's and doctorate, GRE General Test. Additional exam requirements/recommendations for international students: required—TOEFL (minimum score 487 paper-based; 85 iBT), IELTS (minimum score 6.5), TOEFL or IELTS required. *Application deadline:* For fall admission, 7/15 for domestic students, 1/15 for international students; for spring admission, 12/1 for domestic and international students; for summer admission, 4/30 for domestic and international students. Applications are processed on a rolling basis. Application fee: $75. Electronic applications accepted. *Financial support:* In 2019–20, 1 research assistantship with full tuition reimbursement (averaging $11,025 per year), 1 teaching assistantship with full tuition reimbursement (averaging $11,025 per year) were awarded; health care benefits also available. Financial award application deadline: 1/15. *Unit head:* Dr. Raymond A. Pearson, Director, 610-758-3857, Fax: 610-758-3526, E-mail: rp02@lehigh.edu. *Application contact:* James E. Roberts, Chair, Polymer Education Committee, 610-758-4841, Fax: 610-758-6536, E-mail: jer1@lehigh.edu.
Website: http://www.lehihttps://engineering.lehigh.edu/academics/graduate/research-based/polymer-science-gh.edu/~inpcreng/academics/graduate/polymerscieng.html

Lesley University, Graduate School of Arts and Social Sciences, Cambridge, MA 02138-2790. Offers clinical mental health counseling (MA), including holistic counseling, school and community counseling, trauma studies; counseling psychology (MA, CAGS), including professional counseling (MA), school counseling (MA); creative writing (MFA); expressive therapies (MA, PhD, CAGS), including art (MA), clinical mental health counseling (MA), dance (MA), expressive therapies (MA), music (MA); independent studies (CAGS); independent study (MA); intercultural relations (MA, CAGS); interdisciplinary studies (MA), including individualized studies, integrative holistic health, mindfulness studies, peace and conflict transformation, trauma sensitive assessment, intervention, and consultation, women's studies; urban environmental leadership (MA). *Program availability:* Part-time, online learning. *Degree requirements:* For master's, internship, practicum, thesis (for expressive therapies); for doctorate, thesis/dissertation, arts apprenticeship, field placement; for CAGS, thesis, internship (for counseling psychology, expressive therapies). *Entrance requirements:* For master's, MAT (counseling psychology), interview, writing samples, art portfolio; for doctorate, GRE or MAT, interview, master's degree; for CAGS, interview, master's degree. Additional exam requirements/recommendations for international students: required—TOEFL (minimum score 550 paper-based; 80 iBT). Electronic applications accepted.

Long Island University - Post, College of Education, Information and Technology, Brookville, NY 11548-1300. Offers adolescence education (MS); adolescence education 7-12 (MS); archives and records management (AC); art education (MS); childhood education (MS); childhood education/literacy B-6 (MS); childhood education/special education (MS); clinical mental health counseling (MS, AC); early childhood education (MS); early childhood education/childhood education (MS); educational leadership (AC); educational technology (MS); information studies (PhD); interdisciplinary educational studies (Ed D); middle childhood education (MS); music education (MS); public library administration (AC); school counselor (MS); special education (MS Ed); speech-language pathology (MA); students with disabilities, 7-12 generalist (AC); TESOL (MA). *Accreditation:* ASHA; TEAC. *Program availability:* Part-time, 100% online, blended/hybrid learning. Terminal master's awarded for partial completion of doctoral program. *Degree requirements:* For master's, variable foreign language requirement, comprehensive exam (for some programs), thesis optional; for doctorate, comprehensive exam, thesis/dissertation. *Entrance requirements:* For master's and AC, GRE (for some programs). Additional exam requirements/recommendations for international students: required—TOEFL (minimum score 550 paper-based, 75 iBT), IELTS, or PTE. Electronic applications accepted.

Long Island University - Post, College of Liberal Arts and Sciences, Brookville, NY 11548-1300. Offers applied mathematics (MS); behavior analysis (MA); biology (MS); criminal justice (MS); earth science (MS); English (MA); environmental sustainability (MS); genetic counseling (MS); history (MA); interdisciplinary studies (MA, MS); political science (MA); psychology (MA). *Program availability:* Part-time, evening/weekend, blended/hybrid learning. Terminal master's awarded for partial completion of doctoral program. *Degree requirements:* For master's, comprehensive exam (for some programs), thesis (for some programs). *Entrance requirements:* Additional exam requirements/recommendations for international students: required—TOEFL, IELTS, or PTE. Electronic applications accepted.

Marquette University, Graduate School, Interdisciplinary PhD Program, Milwaukee, WI 53201-1881. Offers PhD. *Program availability:* Part-time. *Degree requirements:* For doctorate, thesis/dissertation. *Entrance requirements:* For doctorate, GRE General Test. Additional exam requirements/recommendations for international students: required—TOEFL (minimum score 630 paper-based). Electronic applications accepted.

Marywood University, Academic Affairs, Center for Interdisciplinary Studies, Scranton, PA 18509-1598. Offers human development (PhD), including educational administration, health promotion, higher education administration, instructional leadership, social work. *Program availability:* Part-time. Electronic applications accepted. *Expenses:* Contact institution.

Massachusetts College of Art and Design, Graduate Programs, MFA Program, Boston, MA 02115-5882. Offers 2D fine arts (MFA), including painting, printmaking; 3D fine arts (MFA), including ceramics, fibers, glass, jewelry and metalsmithing, sculpture; design (MFA, Postbaccalaureate Certificate), including dynamic media; fine arts (MFA), including interdisciplinary; media arts (MFA, Postbaccalaureate Certificate), including film/video (MFA), photography. *Accreditation:* NASAD. *Faculty:* 1 (woman) full-time, 29 part-time/adjunct (14 women). *Students:* 44 full-time (26 women), 28 part-time (17 women); includes 8 minority (5 Asian, non-Hispanic/Latino; 3 Hispanic/Latino), 18 international. 202 applicants, 44% accepted, 35 enrolled. In 2019, 30 master's, 8 other advanced degrees awarded. *Degree requirements:* For master's, thesis, thesis exhibition (for fine arts programs); thesis project and document (for design/dynamic media program). *Entrance requirements:* For master's, portfolio, college transcripts, resume, statement of purpose, letters of reference, interview, 6 credits of art history taken prior to or during MFA program; for Postbaccalaureate Certificate, portfolio, college transcripts, resume, statement of purpose, letters of reference, interview. Additional exam requirements/recommendations for international students: required—TOEFL (minimum score 550 paper-based, 85 iBT) or IELTS (6). *Application deadline:* For fall admission, 1/20 priority date for domestic and international students; for summer admission, 1/20 priority date for domestic and international students. Applications are processed on a rolling basis. Application fee: $90. Electronic applications accepted. *Expenses:* Contact institution. *Financial support:* Research assistantships, teaching assistantships, career-related internships or fieldwork, scholarships/grants, tuition waivers (partial), unspecified assistantships, and adjunct co-teaching positions available. Support available to part-time students. Financial award application deadline: 1/20; financial award applicants required to submit FAFSA. *Unit head:* Lucinda Bliss, Dean of Graduate Studies, 617-879-7157, E-mail: gradadmissions@massart.edu. *Application contact:* Stacy Petersen, Associate Director, Graduate Admissions and Operations, 617-879-7238, E-mail: gradadmissions@massart.edu.
Website: http://www.massart.edu/Admissions/Graduate_Programs.html

Michigan Technological University, Graduate School, Interdisciplinary Programs, Houghton, MI 49931. Offers automotive systems and controls (Graduate Certificate); biochemistry and molecular biology (PhD); computational science and engineering (PhD); data science (Graduate Certificate); sustainability (Graduate Certificate). *Program availability:* Part-time. *Faculty:* 132 full-time, 6 part-time/adjunct. *Students:* 57 full-time (20 women), 19 part-time; includes 7 minority (3 Black or African American, non-Hispanic/Latino; 1 American Indian or Alaska Native, non-Hispanic/Latino; 1 Asian, non-Hispanic/Latino; 2 Two or more races, non-Hispanic/Latino), 42 international. Average age 30. 475 applicants, 29% accepted, 25 enrolled. In 2019, 23 master's, 10 doctorates, 36 other advanced degrees awarded. Terminal master's awarded for partial completion of doctoral program. *Degree requirements:* For master's, comprehensive exam (for some programs), thesis (for some programs); for doctorate, comprehensive exam, thesis/dissertation. *Entrance requirements:* For master's, doctorate, and Graduate Certificate, GRE, statement of purpose, personal statement, official transcripts, 2-3 letters of recommendation. Additional exam requirements/recommendations for international students: required—TOEFL or IELTS. *Application deadline:* Applications are processed on a rolling basis. Application fee: $0. Electronic applications accepted. *Expenses: Tuition, area resident:* Full-time $19,206; part-time $1067 per credit. Tuition, state resident: full-time $19,206; part-time $1067 per credit. Tuition, nonresident: full-time $19,206; part-time $1067 per credit. *International tuition:* $19,206 full-time. *Required fees:* $248; $248 per unit. $124 per semester. Tuition and fees vary according to course load and program. *Financial support:* In 2019–20, 54 students received support, including 9 fellowships with tuition reimbursements available (averaging $16,590 per year), 14 research assistantships with tuition reimbursements available (averaging $16,590 per year), 10 teaching assistantships with tuition reimbursements available (averaging $16,590 per year); career-related internships or fieldwork, Federal Work-Study, scholarships/grants, health care benefits, unspecified assistantships, and cooperative program also available. Financial award applicants required to submit FAFSA. *Unit head:* Dr. Will H Cantrell, Dean of the Graduate School, 906-487-3007, Fax: 906-487-2284, E-mail: cantrell@mtu.edu. *Application contact:* Ashli Wells, Assistant Director of Graduate Enrollment Services, 906-487-3513, Fax: 906-487-2284, E-mail: aesniego@mtu.edu.

Mills College, Graduate Studies, Program in Computer Science, Oakland, CA 94613-1000. Offers computer science (Certificate); interdisciplinary computer science (MA). *Program availability:* Part-time. *Degree requirements:* For master's, thesis. *Entrance requirements:* For master's, three letters of recommendation. Additional exam requirements/recommendations for international students: required—TOEFL (minimum score 600 paper-based; 100 iBT) or IELTS (minimum score 7). Electronic applications accepted. *Expenses:* Contact institution.

Minnesota State University Mankato, College of Graduate Studies and Research, Program in Cross-disciplinary Studies, Mankato, MN 56001. Offers MS. *Program availability:* Part-time, evening/weekend. *Degree requirements:* For master's, comprehensive exam, thesis or alternative. *Entrance requirements:* For master's, GRE General Test, minimum GPA of 3.0 during previous 2 years. Additional exam requirements/recommendations for international students: required—TOEFL. Electronic applications accepted.

Montana State University Billings, College of Education, Department of Educational Theory and Practice, Option in Interdisciplinary Studies, Billings, MT 59101. Offers M Ed. *Program availability:* Part-time, 100% online, blended/hybrid learning. *Degree requirements:* For master's, thesis or alternative. *Entrance requirements:* For master's, GRE General Test or MAT, minimum GPA of 3.0. Additional exam requirements/recommendations for international students: required—TOEFL (minimum score 79 iBT), IELTS (minimum score 6.5). Electronic applications accepted.

Montana Technological University, Interdisciplinary Program, Butte, MT 59701-8997. Offers MS. *Program availability:* Part-time. *Faculty:* 9 full-time (5 women), 4 part-time/adjunct (2 women). *Students:* 5 full-time (4 women), 2 part-time (1 woman); includes 2 minority (1 Black or African American, non-Hispanic/Latino; 1 American Indian or Alaska Native, non-Hispanic/Latino), 1 international. Average age 28. 5 applicants, 80% accepted, 3 enrolled. In 2019, 3 master's awarded. *Degree requirements:* For master's, comprehensive exam (for some programs), thesis optional. *Entrance requirements:* For master's, GRE General Test, minimum GPA of 3.0. Additional exam requirements/recommendations for international students: required—TOEFL (minimum score 545 paper-based; 78 iBT), IELTS (minimum score 6.5). *Application deadline:* For fall admission, 4/1 for domestic students, 3/1 priority date for international students; for spring admission, 10/1 for domestic students, 6/1 priority date for international students. Application fee: $50. *Financial support:* In 2019–20, 3 students received support. Research assistantships, teaching assistantships, career-related internships or fieldwork, tuition waivers (full and partial), and unspecified assistantships available. *Unit head:* Dr. Beverly Hartline, Vice Chancellor of Research/Dean of the Graduate School, 406-496-4456, E-mail: graduatedean@mtech.edu. *Application contact:* Daniel Stirling, Administrator, Graduate School, 406-496-4304, Fax: 406-496-4710, E-mail: gradschool@mtech.edu.
Website: http://www.mtech.edu/academics/gradschool/degreeprograms/degrees-interdisciplinary-ms.htm

Murray State University, College of Education and Human Services, Department of Early Childhood and Elementary Education, Murray, KY 42071. Offers elementary teacher leader (MA Ed); interdisciplinary early childhood education (MA Ed), including elementary education (MA Ed, Ed S), reading and writing; teacher education and professional development (Ed S), including elementary education (MA Ed, Ed S). *Accreditation:* NCATE. *Program availability:* Part-time. *Entrance requirements:* For master's and Ed S, GRE or GMAT, minimum university GPA of 2.75. Additional exam requirements/recommendations for international students: required—TOEFL (minimum score 527 paper-based; 71 iBT). Electronic applications accepted.

New Mexico State University, Graduate School, Interdisciplinary Program, Las Cruces, NM 88003-8001. Offers MA, MS, PhD. *Program availability:* Part-time, blended/

hybrid learning. *Students:* 2 full-time (both women), 6 part-time (3 women); includes 5 minority (1 Asian, non-Hispanic/Latino; 4 Hispanic/Latino). Average age 46. In 2019, 1 master's, 1 doctorate awarded. *Degree requirements:* For master's, comprehensive exam, thesis; for doctorate, comprehensive exam, thesis/dissertation. *Entrance requirements:* For master's, GRE General Test, minimum GPA of 2.5; for doctorate, GRE General Test, minimum GPA of 3.0. Additional exam requirements/recommendations for international students: required—TOEFL (minimum score 550 paper-based; 79 iBT), IELTS (minimum score 6.5). *Application deadline:* Applications are processed on a rolling basis. Application fee: $40 ($50 for international students). Electronic applications accepted. *Financial support:* In 2019–20, 3 students received support, including 1 fellowship (averaging $4,844 per year); career-related internships or fieldwork, Federal Work-Study, scholarships/grants, traineeships, health care benefits, and unspecified assistantships also available. Support available to part-time students. Financial award application deadline: 3/1. *Unit head:* Dr. Luis Cifuentes, Dean of Graduate School, 575-646-5746, Fax: 575-646-7758, E-mail: gradinfo@nmsu.edu. *Application contact:* Graduate Admissions, 575-646-3121, E-mail: admissions@nmsu.edu.
Website: http://idsas.nmsu.edu

New York University, Gallatin School of Individualized Study, New York, NY 10003. Offers MA. *Program availability:* Part-time, evening/weekend. *Degree requirements:* For master's, thesis. *Entrance requirements:* Additional exam requirements/recommendations for international students: required—TOEFL (minimum score 100 paper-based), TOEFL or IELTS are accepted. Electronic applications accepted. *Expenses:* Contact institution.

Niagara University, Graduate Division of Arts and Sciences, Program in Interdisciplinary Studies, Niagara University, NY 14109. Offers MA. *Program availability:* Part-time. *Entrance requirements:* Additional exam requirements/recommendations for international students: required—TOEFL (minimum score 550 paper-based; 79 iBT), IELTS (minimum score 6). Electronic applications accepted. *Expenses:* Contact institution.

Northeastern University, Bouvé College of Health Sciences, Boston, MA 02115-5096. Offers applied behavior analysis (MS); audiology (Au D); counseling psychology (MS, PhD, CAGS); exercise science (MS); nursing (MS, PhD, CAGS), including administration (MS); adult-gerontology acute care nurse practitioner (MS, CAGS), adult-gerontology primary care nurse practitioner (MS, CAGS), anesthesia (MS); family nurse practitioner (MS, CAGS), neonatal nurse practitioner (MS, CAGS), pediatric nurse practitioner (MS, CAGS), psychiatric mental health nurse practitioner (MS, CAGS); nursing practice (DNP); pharmaceutical sciences (MS, PhD), including interdisciplinary concentration, pharmaceutics and drug delivery systems; pharmacology (MS); pharmacy (Pharm D); school psychology (PhD); speech-language pathology (MS); urban health (MPH); MS/MBA. *Accreditation:* AANA/CANAEP; ACPE (one or more programs are accredited); ASHA; CEPH. *Program availability:* Part-time, evening/weekend, online learning. *Degree requirements:* For doctorate, thesis/dissertation (for some programs); for CAGS, comprehensive exam. Electronic applications accepted. *Expenses:* Contact institution.

Northeastern University, College of Engineering, Boston, MA 02115-5096. Offers bioengineering (MS, PhD); chemical engineering (MS, PhD); civil engineering (MS, PhD); computer engineering (PhD); computer systems engineering (MS); electrical and computer engineering (MS); electrical and computer engineering leadership (MS); electrical engineering (PhD); energy systems (MS); engineering and public policy (MS); engineering management (MS, Certificate); environmental engineering (MS); industrial engineering (MS, PhD); information assurance (PhD); information systems (MS); interdisciplinary engineering (PhD); mechanical engineering (PhD); operations research (MS); telecommunication systems management (MS). *Program availability:* Part-time, online learning. Electronic applications accepted. *Expenses:* Contact institution.

Nova Southeastern University, College of Arts, Humanities, and Social Sciences, Fort Lauderdale, FL 33314-7796. Offers advanced conflict resolution practice (Graduate Certificate); child protection (MHS); college student affairs (MS); conflict analysis and resolution (MS, PhD); criminal justice (MS, PhD); cross-disciplinary studies (MA); developmental disabilities (MS); family studies (Graduate Certificate); family systems health care (Graduate Certificate); family therapy (MS, PhD); marriage and family therapy (DMFT); peace studies (Graduate Certificate); qualitative research (Graduate Certificate); solution focused coaching (Graduate Certificate). *Accreditation:* AAMFT/COAMFTE (one or more programs are accredited). *Program availability:* Part-time, evening/weekend, 100% online, blended/hybrid learning. *Faculty:* 60 full-time (37 women), 88 part-time/adjunct (65 women). *Students:* 201 full-time (157 women), 418 part-time (297 women); includes 365 minority (180 Black or African American, non-Hispanic/Latino; 4 American Indian or Alaska Native, non-Hispanic/Latino; 15 Asian, non-Hispanic/Latino; 141 Hispanic/Latino; 25 Two or more races, non-Hispanic/Latino), 49 international. Average age 37. 303 applicants, 84% accepted, 197 enrolled. In 2019, 125 master's, 63 doctorates, 24 other advanced degrees awarded. *Degree requirements:* For master's, comprehensive exam (for some programs), thesis optional, comprehensive exams, portfolios (for some programs), table-top exams (for some programs); for doctorate, comprehensive exam, thesis/dissertation, qualifying exams, portfolios (for some programs). *Entrance requirements:* For master's, interview, minimum GPA of 3.0, writing sample; for doctorate, interview, minimum GPA of 3.5, master's degree in related field, writing sample; for Graduate Certificate, minimum GPA of 3.0. Additional exam requirements/recommendations for international students: required—TOEFL (minimum score 79 paper-based). *Application deadline:* Applications are processed on a rolling basis. Application fee: $50. Electronic applications accepted. *Expenses:* Contact institution. *Financial support:* In 2019–20, 170 students received support. Career-related internships or fieldwork, Federal Work-Study, scholarships/grants, and unspecified assistantships available. Financial award application deadline: 4/1; financial award applicants required to submit FAFSA. *Unit head:* Dr. Honggang Yang, Dean, 954-262-3016, Fax: 954-262-3968, E-mail: yangh@nova.edu. *Application contact:* Marcia Arango, Student Recruitment Coordinator, 954-262-3006, Fax: 954-262-3968, E-mail: marango@nsu.nova.edu.
Website: http://cahss.nova.edu/

The Ohio State University, Graduate School, College of Arts and Sciences, Division of Arts and Humanities, Department of Comparative Studies, Columbus, OH 43210. Offers MA, PhD. Terminal master's awarded for partial completion of doctoral program. *Degree requirements:* For doctorate, thesis/dissertation. *Entrance requirements:* For master's and doctorate, GRE General Test. Additional exam requirements/recommendations for international students: required—TOEFL (minimum score 550 paper-based; 79 iBT), Michigan English Language Assessment Battery (minimum score 82); recommended—IELTS (minimum score 7). Electronic applications accepted.

Oregon State University, Interdisciplinary/Institutional Programs, Program in Interdisciplinary Studies, Corvallis, OR 97331. Offers MAIS. *Program availability:* Part-time. *Entrance requirements:* Additional exam requirements/recommendations for international students: required—TOEFL (minimum score 80 iBT), IELTS (minimum score 6.5).

Regent University, Graduate School, School of Business and Leadership, Virginia Beach, VA 23464. Offers business administration (MBA), including accounting, economics, entrepreneurship, finance and investing, general management, healthcare management (MA, MBA), human resource management (MA, MBA), innovation management, leadership, marketing, not-for-profit management (MA, MBA); business analytics (MS); business and design management (MA); church leadership (MA); leadership (Certificate); organizational leadership (MA, PhD), including ecclesial leadership (DSL, PhD), entrepreneurial leadership (PhD), healthcare management (MA, MBA), human resource development (PhD), human resource management (MA, MBA), individualized studies (DSL, PhD), interdisciplinary studies (MA), leadership coaching and mentoring (MA), not-for-profit management (MA, MBA), organizational development consulting (MA), servant leadership (MA, DSL); strategic leadership (DSL), including ecclesial leadership (DSL, PhD), global consulting, healthcare leadership, individualized studies (DSL, PhD), leadership coaching, servant leadership (MA, DSL), strategic foresight. *Program availability:* Part-time, evening/weekend, 100% online, blended/hybrid learning. *Faculty:* 9 full-time (2 women), 39 part-time/adjunct (14 women). *Students:* 397 full-time (229 women), 828 part-time (474 women); includes 698 minority (531 Black or African American, non-Hispanic/Latino; 5 American Indian or Alaska Native, non-Hispanic/Latino; 35 Asian, non-Hispanic/Latino; 87 Hispanic/Latino; 5 Native Hawaiian or other Pacific Islander, non-Hispanic/Latino; 35 Two or more races, non-Hispanic/Latino), 45 international. Average age 41. 615 applicants, 76% accepted, 275 enrolled. In 2019, 218 master's, 91 doctorates, 1 other advanced degree awarded. *Degree requirements:* For master's, thesis or alternative, 3-credit hour culminating experience; for doctorate, thesis/dissertation. *Entrance requirements:* For master's, college transcripts, resume, essay; for doctorate, college transcripts, resume, essay, writing sample; for Certificate, writing sample, resume, transcripts. Additional exam requirements/recommendations for international students: required—TOEFL (minimum score 577 paper-based). *Application deadline:* For fall admission, 5/1 priority date for domestic students; for spring admission, 10/1 priority date for domestic students. Applications are processed on a rolling basis. Application fee: $50. Electronic applications accepted. *Expenses:* Contact institution. *Financial support:* In 2019–20, 959 students received support. Career-related internships or fieldwork, scholarships/grants, health care benefits, and unspecified assistantships available. Support available to part-time students. Financial award applicants required to submit FAFSA. *Unit head:* Dr. Doris Gomez, Dean, 757-352-4686, Fax: 757-352-4634, E-mail: dorigom@regent.edu. *Application contact:* Heidi Cece, Assistant Vice President for Enrollment Management, 800-373-5504, Fax: 757-352-4381, E-mail: admissions@regent.edu.
Website: https://www.regent.edu/school-of-business-and-leadership/

Regent University, Graduate School, School of Divinity, Virginia Beach, VA 23464. Offers Christian spirituality and formation (MA); divinity (M Div), including Biblical studies (M Div, MTS, Th M, PhD), chaplain ministry, Christian theology (M Div, MTS, Th M, PhD), church and ministry (M Div, MA), history of Christianity (M Div, MTS, Th M, PhD), inter-cultural studies (M Div, MA), interdisciplinary studies (M Div, MA, MTS), marketplace ministry (M Div, MA), missional discipleship, practical healing ministry (M Div, MA), worship and media (M Div, MA); leadership and renewal (D Min), including Christian leadership and renewal, clinical pastoral education, community transformation, military ministry, ministry leadership coaching; practical theology (MA), including church and ministry (M Div, MA), cosmogony, inter-cultural studies (M Div, MA), interdisciplinary studies (M Div, MA, MTS), marketplace ministry (M Div, MA), practical healing ministry (M Div, MA), worship and media (M Div, MA); renewal theology (PhD), including Biblical studies (M Div, MTS, Th M, PhD), Christian theology (M Div, MTS, Th M, PhD), history of Christianity (M Div, MTS, Th M, PhD), practical theology; theological studies (MTS), including Biblical studies (M Div, MTS, Th M, PhD), Christian theology (M Div, MTS, Th M, PhD), history of Christianity (M Div, MTS, Th M, PhD), interdisciplinary studies (M Div, MA, MTS); theology (Th M), including Biblical studies (M Div, MTS, Th M, PhD), Christian theology (M Div, MTS, Th M, PhD), history of Christianity (M Div, MTS, Th M, PhD). *Accreditation:* ACIPE; ATS. *Program availability:* Part-time, evening/weekend, 100% online, blended/hybrid learning. *Faculty:* 15 full-time (3 women), 58 part-time/adjunct (10 women). *Students:* 303 full-time (119 women), 813 part-time (403 women); includes 632 minority (509 Black or African American, non-Hispanic/Latino; 3 American Indian or Alaska Native, non-Hispanic/Latino; 31 Asian, non-Hispanic/Latino; 54 Hispanic/Latino; 2 Native Hawaiian or other Pacific Islander, non-Hispanic/Latino; 33 Two or more races, non-Hispanic/Latino), 16 international. Average age 45. 561 applicants, 66% accepted, 194 enrolled. In 2019, 168 master's, 13 doctorates awarded. *Degree requirements:* For master's, comprehensive exam, thesis or alternative, internship; for doctorate, thesis/dissertation or alternative. *Entrance requirements:* For master's, minimum undergraduate GPA of 2.75, writing sample, personal goal statement, college transcripts; for doctorate, GRE, minimum graduate GPA of 3.5 (PhD), 3.0 (D Min); clergy recommendations; writing sample; transcripts; resume; interview. Additional exam requirements/recommendations for international students: required—TOEFL (minimum score 577 paper-based). *Application deadline:* For fall admission, 5/1 priority date for domestic students. Applications are processed on a rolling basis. Application fee: $50. Electronic applications accepted. *Expenses:* Contact institution. *Financial support:* In 2019–20, 856 students received support. Career-related internships or fieldwork, scholarships/grants, health care benefits, and unspecified assistantships available. Support available to part-time students. Financial award applicants required to submit FAFSA. *Unit head:* Dr. Cornelius Bekker, Dean, 757-352-4258, Fax: 757-352-4597, E-mail: clbekker@regent.edu. *Application contact:* Heidi Cece, Assistant Vice President for Enrollment Management, 800-373-5504, Fax: 757-352-4381, E-mail: admissions@regent.edu.
Website: https://www.regent.edu/school-of-divinity/

Rensselaer Polytechnic Institute, Graduate School, School of Science, Program in Multi-Disciplinary Science, Troy, NY 12180-3590. Offers MS, PhD. *Faculty:* 127 full-time (33 women), 9 part-time/adjunct (4 women). *Students:* 4 full-time (2 women), 1 part-time (0 women), 3 international. Average age 38. 4 applicants, 25% accepted, 1 enrolled. In 2019, 1 master's awarded. Terminal master's awarded for partial completion of doctoral program. *Degree requirements:* For master's, comprehensive exam (for some programs), thesis optional; for doctorate, comprehensive exam, thesis/dissertation. *Entrance requirements:* For master's and doctorate, GRE. Additional exam requirements/recommendations for international students: required—TOEFL (minimum score 600 paper-based; 100 iBT), IELTS (minimum score 7), PTE (minimum score 68). *Application deadline:* For fall admission, 1/1 priority date for domestic and international students; for spring admission, 8/15 priority date for domestic and international students. Applications are processed on a rolling basis. Application fee: $75. Electronic applications accepted. *Financial support:* In 2019–20, research assistantships (averaging $23,000 per year), teaching assistantships (averaging $23,000 per year) were awarded; fellowships also available. Financial award application deadline: 1/1. *Unit head:* Dr. Sibel Adali, Graduate Program Director, 518-276-6455, E-mail: sibel@cs.rpi.edu. *Application contact:* Jarron Decker, Director of Graduate Admissions, 518-276-6216, Fax: 518-276-4072, E-mail: gradadmissions@rpi.edu.
Website: https://science.rpi.edu/itws/programs/graduate/ms/phd-multidisciplinary-science

Rochester Institute of Technology, Graduate Enrollment Services, School of Individualized Study, Graduate Programs Department, MS Program in Professional

Studies, Rochester, NY 14623-5603. Offers MS. *Program availability:* Part-time, evening/weekend, 100% online, blended/hybrid learning. *Degree requirements:* For master's, Capstone Project. *Entrance requirements:* For master's, minimum GPA of 3.0, personal statement, resume, two letters of recommendation. Additional exam requirements/recommendations for international students: required—TOEFL (minimum score 550 paper-based; 79 iBT), IELTS (minimum score 6.5), PTE (minimum score 58). Electronic applications accepted.

Rosalind Franklin University of Medicine and Science, College of Health Professions, Department of Interprofessional Healthcare Studies, Interprofessional Studies Program, North Chicago, IL 60064-3095. Offers interprofessional studies (D Sc). *Program availability:* Part-time, online learning. *Degree requirements:* For doctorate, comprehensive exam, thesis/dissertation. *Entrance requirements:* For doctorate, GRE. Additional exam requirements/recommendations for international students: required—TOEFL.

Rutgers University - New Brunswick, Graduate School-New Brunswick, BioMaPS Institute for Quantitative Biology, Piscataway, NJ 08854-8097. Offers computational biology and molecular biophysics (PhD). *Degree requirements:* For doctorate, comprehensive exam, thesis/dissertation. *Entrance requirements:* For doctorate, GRE. Additional exam requirements/recommendations for international students: required—TOEFL. Electronic applications accepted.

San Diego State University, Graduate and Research Affairs, Interdisciplinary Studies, San Diego, CA 92182. Offers MA, MS. *Program availability:* Part-time. *Degree requirements:* For master's, thesis. *Entrance requirements:* For master's, GRE General Test. Additional exam requirements/recommendations for international students: required—TOEFL. Electronic applications accepted.

Sonoma State University, School of Science and Technology, Department of Kinesiology, Rohnert Park, CA 94928. Offers exercise science/pre-physical therapy (MA); interdisciplinary (MA); interdisciplinary pre-occupational therapy (MA); lifetime physical activity (MA), including coach education, fitness and wellness. *Program availability:* Part-time. *Degree requirements:* For master's, thesis, oral exam. *Entrance requirements:* For master's, minimum GPA of 2.8. Additional exam requirements/recommendations for international students: required—TOEFL (minimum score 500 paper-based).

Southern Illinois University Edwardsville, Graduate School, Program in Integrative Studies, Edwardsville, IL 62026. Offers cultural heritage and resources management (MA, MS); diversity training (MA, MS); organizational design thinking (MS); sustainability (MS). *Program availability:* Part-time, evening/weekend. *Degree requirements:* For master's, variable foreign language requirement, comprehensive exam (for some programs), thesis (for some programs). *Entrance requirements:* Additional exam requirements/recommendations for international students: required—TOEFL (minimum score 550 paper-based; 79 iBT), IELTS (minimum score 6.5). Electronic applications accepted.

Southern Oregon University, Graduate Studies, Program in Interdisciplinary Studies, Ashland, OR 97520. Offers MIS. *Program availability:* Part-time, online learning. *Degree requirements:* For master's, thesis (for some programs). *Entrance requirements:* For master's, GRE General Test, minimum cumulative GPA of 3.0 in the last 90 quarter credits (60 semester credits) of undergraduate coursework. Additional exam requirements/recommendations for international students: required—TOEFL (minimum score 540 paper-based; 76 iBT), IELTS (minimum score 6), ELPT (minimum score 964) or ELS (minimum score 112). Electronic applications accepted.

Southern Utah University, Program in Interdisciplinary Studies, Cedar City, UT 84720-2498. Offers MIS. *Program availability:* 100% online. *Entrance requirements:* Additional exam requirements/recommendations for international students: required—TOEFL (minimum score 550 paper-based; 79 iBT), IELTS (minimum score 6). *Expenses:* Contact institution.

State University of New York at Fredonia, College of Liberal Arts and Sciences, Fredonia, NY 14063-1136. Offers biology (MS); English (MA); English education 7-12 (MA); interdisciplinary studies (MA, MS); math education (MS Ed); professional writing (CAS); speech pathology (MS); MA/MS. *Program availability:* Part-time, evening/weekend. *Degree requirements:* For master's, comprehensive exam (for some programs), thesis (for some programs). *Entrance requirements:* For master's, GRE. Additional exam requirements/recommendations for international students: required—TOEFL (minimum score 79 iBT), IELTS (minimum score 6.5). Electronic applications accepted.

Stephen F. Austin State University, Graduate School, College of Liberal and Applied Arts, Division of Multidisciplinary Programs, Nacogdoches, TX 75962. Offers cultural heritage (MIS); interdisciplinary studies (MIS); publishing (MA). *Program availability:* Part-time. *Degree requirements:* For master's, comprehensive exam, thesis optional. *Entrance requirements:* For master's, GRE General Test. Additional exam requirements/recommendations for international students: required—TOEFL (minimum score 550 paper-based).

Teachers College, Columbia University, Interdisciplinary Programs, New York, NY 10027-6696. Offers Ed M, MA, ME, Ed D. *Students:* 10 full-time (7 women), 18 part-time (12 women); includes 9 minority (2 Black or African American, non-Hispanic/Latino; 3 Asian, non-Hispanic/Latino; 2 Hispanic/Latino; 1 Native Hawaiian or other Pacific Islander, non-Hispanic/Latino; 1 Two or more races, non-Hispanic/Latino), 6 international. 2 applicants, 50% accepted, 1 enrolled. *Application contact:* Kelly Sutton-Skinner, Director of Admissions and New Student Enrollment, E-mail: kms2237@tc.columbia.edu.

Texas A&M University–Texarkana, Graduate Studies and Research, College of Education and Liberal Arts, Texarkana, TX 75503. Offers adult education (MS); curriculum and instruction (M Ed); education (MS); educational administration (M Ed); English (MA); instructional technology (MS); interdisciplinary studies (MA, MS); special education (MS). *Program availability:* Part-time, evening/weekend. *Degree requirements:* For master's, comprehensive exam (for some programs), thesis optional. *Entrance requirements:* For master's, minimum GPA of 2.5 on last 60 hours of bachelor's degree. Additional exam requirements/recommendations for international students: required—TOEFL. Electronic applications accepted.

Texas State University, The Graduate College, College of Applied Arts, Interdisciplinary Studies Program in Occupational Education, San Marcos, TX 78666. Offers MAIS, MSIS. *Program availability:* Part-time, evening/weekend, blended/hybrid learning. *Degree requirements:* For master's, comprehensive exam, thesis optional. *Entrance requirements:* For master's, baccalaureate degree from regionally-accredited university; minimum GPA of 2.75 for last 60 hours of undergraduate work or GRE General Test; statement of personal goals. Additional exam requirements/recommendations for international students: required—TOEFL (minimum score 550 paper-based; 78 iBT), IELTS (minimum score 6.5). Electronic applications accepted.

Texas Tech University, Graduate School, Interdisciplinary Programs, Lubbock, TX 79409-1030. Offers arid land studies (MS); biotechnology (MS); heritage and museum sciences (MA); interdisciplinary studies (MA, MS); wind science and engineering (PhD); JD/MS. *Program availability:* Part-time, 100% online, blended/hybrid learning. *Faculty:* 5 full-time (3 women). *Students:* 114 full-time (46 women), 94 part-time (59 women); includes 72 minority (30 Black or African American, non-Hispanic/Latino; 3 Asian, non-Hispanic/Latino; 31 Hispanic/Latino; 8 Two or more races, non-Hispanic/Latino), 34 international. Average age 31. 118 applicants, 85% accepted, 66 enrolled. In 2019, 57 master's, 4 doctorates awarded. Terminal master's awarded for partial completion of doctoral program. *Degree requirements:* For master's, comprehensive exam (for some programs), thesis (for some programs); for doctorate, comprehensive exam, thesis/dissertation (for some programs). *Entrance requirements:* Additional exam requirements/recommendations for international students: required—TOEFL (minimum score 550 paper-based; 79 iBT), IELTS (minimum score 6.5), PTE (minimum score 60), Cambridge Advanced (B), Cambridge Proficiency (C), ELS English for Academic Purposes (Level 112), Duolingo English Test (100). *Application deadline:* For fall admission, 6/1 priority date for domestic students, 1/15 priority date for international students; for spring admission, 9/1 priority date for domestic students, 6/15 priority date for international students. Applications are processed on a rolling basis. Application fee: $65. Electronic applications accepted. *Expenses:* Tuition, state resident: full-time $7944; part-time $331 per credit hour. Tuition, nonresident: full-time $17,904; part-time $746 per credit hour. *Required fees:* $2556; $55.50 per credit hour. $612 per semester. Tuition and fees vary according to program. *Financial support:* In 2019–20, 150 students received support, including 138 fellowships (averaging $5,639 per year), 26 research assistantships (averaging $18,634 per year), 16 teaching assistantships (averaging $13,404 per year); scholarships/grants and unspecified assistantships also available. Financial award application deadline: 4/15; financial award applicants required to submit FAFSA. *Unit head:* Dr. Mark A. Sheridan, Vice Provost for Graduate and Postdoctoral Affairs/Dean of the Graduate School, 806-834-5537, Fax: 806-742-1746, E-mail: mark.sheridan@ttu.edu. *Application contact:* Dr. David Doerfert, Associate Dean, 806-834-4477, Fax: 806-742-4038, E-mail: david.doerfert@ttu.edu.
Website: www.gradschool.ttu.edu

Trinity Western University, School of Graduate Studies, Master of Arts in Interdisciplinary Humanities, Langley, BC V2Y 1Y1, Canada. Offers general humanities (MAIH); specialized (MAIH), including English, history, philosophy. *Program availability:* Part-time. *Degree requirements:* For master's, thesis or alternative, 30 semester hours. *Entrance requirements:* For master's, Strong undergraduate degree in humanities or English, history or philosophy. Additional exam requirements/recommendations for international students: required—TOEFL (minimum score 105 iBT), IELTS (minimum score 7.5), DuoLingo. *Application deadline:* Applications are processed on a rolling basis. Electronic applications accepted. *Expenses:* Contact institution. *Financial support:* Fellowships, research assistantships, teaching assistantships, career-related internships or fieldwork, scholarships/grants, and unspecified assistantships available. Support available to part-time students. Financial award application deadline: 4/1. *Unit head:* Dr. Bruce Shelvey, Director, E-mail: bruce.shelvey@twu.ca. *Application contact:* Phil Kay, Director, Graduate Admissions, 604-513-2121 Ext. 3444, E-mail: phil.kay@twu.ca.
Website: http://www.twu.ca/academics/

Tufts University, Graduate School of Arts and Sciences, Interdisciplinary Doctoral Program, Medford, MA 02155. Offers PhD. *Degree requirements:* For doctorate, thesis/dissertation. *Entrance requirements:* Additional exam requirements/recommendations for international students: required—TOEFL (minimum score 550 paper-based; 80 iBT), IELTS (minimum score 6.5). Electronic applications accepted. *Expenses:* Contact institution.

Tulane University, School of Science and Engineering, Interdisciplinary PhD Program, New Orleans, LA 70118-5669. Offers PhD. *Expenses: Tuition:* Full-time $57,004; part-time $3167 per credit hour. *Required fees:* $2086; $44.50 per credit hour. $80 per term. Tuition and fees vary according to course load, degree level and program.

UNB Fredericton, School of Graduate Studies, Faculty of Science, Applied Science, and Engineering, Interdisciplinary Studies, Fredericton, NB E3B 5A3, Canada. Offers M IDST, PhD. *Students:* 41 full-time (20 women), 19 part-time (15 women), 10 international. Average age 41. In 2019, 8 doctorates awarded. *Degree requirements:* For master's, thesis; for doctorate, comprehensive exam, thesis/dissertation. *Entrance requirements:* For master's, BA honors degree, minimum GPA of 3.3; for doctorate, master's degree with thesis; minimum A- average. Additional exam requirements/recommendations for international students: required—TOEFL (minimum score 600 paper-based; 100 iBT), IELTS (minimum score 7), TWE (minimum score 5.5). *Application deadline:* Applications are processed on a rolling basis. Application fee: $50 Canadian dollars. Electronic applications accepted. *Expenses: Tuition, area resident:* Full-time $6975 Canadian dollars; part-time $3423 Canadian dollars per year. Tuition, state resident: full-time $6975 Canadian dollars; part-time $3423 Canadian dollars per year. Tuition, Canadian resident: full-time $6975 Canadian dollars; part-time $3423 Canadian dollars per year. *International tuition:* $12,435 Canadian dollars full-time. *Required fees:* $92.25 Canadian dollars per term. Full-time tuition and fees vary according to degree level, campus/location, program, reciprocity agreements and student level. *Financial support:* Fellowships, research assistantships, and teaching assistantships available. Financial award application deadline: 1/15. *Unit head:* Dr. Mary McKenna, Assistant Dean of Graduate Studies, 506-447 3044, Fax: 506-453-4817, E-mail: gradidst@unb.ca. *Application contact:* Jacqueline Seely, Graduate Secretary, 506-453 4672, Fax: 506-453-4817, E-mail: jseely@unb.ca.
Website: http://go.unb.ca/gradprograms

Union Institute & University, PhD Program in Interdisciplinary Studies, Cincinnati, OH 45206-1925. Offers educational studies (PhD), including Martin Luther King studies; ethical and creative leadership (PhD); humanities and culture (PhD); public policy and social change (PhD). *Program availability:* Part-time, online only, blended/hybrid learning. *Degree requirements:* For doctorate, comprehensive exam, thesis/dissertation. *Entrance requirements:* For doctorate, master's degree, three letters of recommendation, statement of purpose. Additional exam requirements/recommendations for international students: required—TOEFL. Electronic applications accepted. *Expenses:* Contact institution.

University at Buffalo, the State University of New York, Graduate School, College of Arts and Sciences, Program in Interdisciplinary Studies, Buffalo, NY 14260. Offers humanities (MA); natural sciences (MS); social sciences (MS). *Program availability:* Part-time. *Degree requirements:* For master's, thesis or alternative. *Entrance requirements:* Additional exam requirements/recommendations for international students: required—TOEFL (minimum score 550 paper-based; 79 iBT). Electronic applications accepted. *Expenses: Tuition, area resident:* Full-time $11,310; part-time $471 per credit hour. Tuition, state resident: full-time $11,310; part-time $471 per credit hour. Tuition, nonresident: full-time $23,100; part-time $963 per credit hour. *International tuition:* $23,100 full-time. *Required fees:* $2820.

University of Alaska Fairbanks, Graduate School for Interdisciplinary Studies, Fairbanks, AK 99775-7560. Offers indigenous studies (PhD); interdisciplinary studies (MA, MS, PhD). *Program availability:* Part-time. *Degree requirements:* For master's, comprehensive exam (for some programs), oral defense of project or thesis, no GRE entrance exam required; for doctorate, one foreign language, comprehensive exam, thesis/dissertation, oral defense of dissertation, master's degree from accredited institution. *Entrance requirements:* For master's, bachelor's degree from accredited institution with minimum cumulative undergraduate and major GPA of 3.0; for doctorate, GRE General Test, minimum cumulative GPA of 3.0, master's degree from an accredited institution. Additional exam requirements/recommendations for international students: required—TOEFL (minimum score 550 paper-based; 79 iBT), Minimum IELTS 6.5 required. Electronic applications accepted.

The University of Arizona, Graduate Interdisciplinary Programs, Tucson, AZ 85721. Offers American Indian studies (MA, PhD); applied mathematics (MS, PMS, PhD), including applied mathematics (MS, PhD), mathematical sciences (PMS); biomedical engineering (MS, PhD); cancer biology (PhD); entomology (MA); entomology and insect science (MS, PhD); genetics (MS, PhD); neuroscience (PhD); physiological sciences (MS, PhD); second language acquisition and teaching (PhD); statistics (MS, PhD). *Program availability:* Part-time. *Entrance requirements:* Additional exam requirements/recommendations for international students: required—TOEFL (minimum score 550 paper-based; 79 iBT).

University of Arkansas at Little Rock, Graduate School, College of Arts, Letters, and Sciences, Department of Philosophy and Interdisciplinary Studies, Little Rock, AR 72204-1099. Offers MA. *Entrance requirements:* For master's, GRE.

University of California, Santa Barbara, Graduate Division, College of Letters and Sciences, Division of Social Sciences, Department of Sociology, Santa Barbara, CA 93106-9430. Offers interdisciplinary emphasis: Black studies (PhD); interdisciplinary emphasis: environment and society (PhD); interdisciplinary emphasis: feminist studies (PhD); interdisciplinary emphasis: global studies (PhD); interdisciplinary emphasis: language, interaction and social organization (PhD); interdisciplinary emphasis: quantitative methods in the social sciences (PhD); interdisciplinary emphasis: technology and society (PhD); sociology (PhD); MA/PhD. Terminal master's awarded for partial completion of doctoral program. *Degree requirements:* For doctorate, comprehensive exam, thesis/dissertation. *Entrance requirements:* For doctorate, GRE General Test. Additional exam requirements/recommendations for international students: required—TOEFL (minimum score 550 paper-based; 80 iBT), IELTS (minimum score 7). Electronic applications accepted.

University of California, Santa Cruz, Division of Graduate Studies, Division of the Arts, Department of Music, Santa Cruz, CA 95064. Offers ethnomusicology (MA); music (PhD), including cross-cultural and interdisciplinary studies; music composition (MA, DMA), including world music composition (DMA); music composition (DMA), including computer-assisted (algorithmic) composition; performance practice (MA). *Degree requirements:* For master's, one foreign language, thesis, recital; for doctorate, one foreign language, thesis/dissertation, qualifying and final examinations. *Entrance requirements:* For master's, GRE General Test, 3 letters of recommendation, writing or composition sample, 10-20 minute unedited recording; for doctorate, GRE General Test, 3 letters of recommendation, writing sample. Additional exam requirements/recommendations for international students: required—TOEFL (minimum score 550 paper-based; 83 iBT); recommended—IELTS (minimum score 8). Electronic applications accepted.

University of Central Florida, College of Graduate Studies, Program in Interdisciplinary Studies, Orlando, FL 32816. Offers interdisciplinary studies (MA). *Students:* 26 full-time (15 women), 42 part-time (29 women); includes 23 minority (8 Black or African American, non-Hispanic/Latino; 1 Asian, non-Hispanic/Latino; 10 Hispanic/Latino; 4 Two or more races, non-Hispanic/Latino), 5 international. Average age 29. 50 applicants, 64% accepted, 24 enrolled. In 2019, 15 master's, 7 other advanced degrees awarded. *Entrance requirements:* For master's, GRE, minimum GPA of 3.0 in last 60 hours, letters of recommendation, resume, personal statement. Additional exam requirements/recommendations for international students: required—TOEFL. *Application deadline:* For fall admission, 7/15 for domestic students; for spring admission, 12/1 for domestic students. Application fee: $30. Electronic applications accepted. *Financial support:* In 2019–20, 1 student received support, including 1 fellowship (averaging $1,000 per year), 1 research assistantship (averaging $6,069 per year). Financial award application deadline: 3/1; financial award applicants required to submit FAFSA. *Unit head:* Dr. John Weishampel, Associate Dean, 407-823-6634, E-mail: john.weishampel@ucf.edu. *Application contact:* Associate Director, Graduate Admissions, 407-823-2766, Fax: 407-823-6442, E-mail: gradadmissions@ucf.edu.
Website: https://www.graduate.ucf.edu/IDS/

University of Central Oklahoma, The Jackson College of Graduate Studies, College of Education and Professional Studies, Department of Adult Education and Safety Science, Edmond, OK 73034-5209. Offers adult and higher education (M Ed), including interdisciplinary studies, student personnel, training. *Program availability:* Part-time. *Degree requirements:* For master's, comprehensive exam (for some programs), thesis (for some programs). *Entrance requirements:* Additional exam requirements/recommendations for international students: required—TOEFL (minimum score 550 paper-based; 79 iBT), IELTS (minimum score 6.5). Electronic applications accepted.

University of Cincinnati, Graduate School, McMicken College of Arts and Sciences, Interdisciplinary Studies Program, Cincinnati, OH 45221. Offers PhD. *Entrance requirements:* For doctorate, GRE General Test. Electronic applications accepted.

University of Colorado Colorado Springs, College of Letters, Arts and Sciences, Master of Sciences Program, Colorado Springs, CO 80918. Offers interdisciplinary sciences (M Sc). *Program availability:* Part-time. *Students:* 3 full-time (1 woman), 32 part-time (14 women); includes 12 minority (1 Black or African American, non-Hispanic/Latino; 8 Hispanic/Latino; 3 Two or more races, non-Hispanic/Latino). Average age 29. 87 applicants, 38% accepted, 26 enrolled. In 2019, 15 master's awarded. *Degree requirements:* For master's, thesis or alternative. *Entrance requirements:* For master's, A bachelor's degree in biological sciences, mathematics, physics or equivalent from an accredited college or university with a minimum GPA of 2.75. Additional exam requirements/recommendations for international students: required—TOEFL (minimum score 80 iBT); recommended—IELTS (minimum score 6.5). *Application deadline:* For fall admission, 3/1 priority date for domestic and international students; for spring admission, 6/1 priority date for domestic and international students. Applications are processed on a rolling basis. Application fee: $60 ($100 for international students). Electronic applications accepted. *Expenses:* Contact institution. *Financial support:* In 2019–20, 21 students received support. Career-related internships or fieldwork, Federal Work-Study, scholarships/grants, and unspecified assistantships available. Support available to part-time students. Financial award application deadline: 3/1; financial award applicants required to submit FAFSA. *Unit head:* Dr. Kelli Klebe, Dean, 719-255-3779, E-mail: kklebe@uccs.edu. *Application contact:* Sarah Elsey, Graduate School Program Director, 719-255-3072, E-mail: gradinfo@uccs.edu.

University of Dayton, Department of Teacher Education, Dayton, OH 45469. Offers adolescence to young adult education (MS Ed); early childhood leadership and advocacy (MS Ed); interdisciplinary education (MS Ed), including visual arts; interdisciplinary education studies (MS Ed); leadership in educational systems (MS Ed); literacy (MS Ed); mathematics education (MS Ed); middle childhood education (MS Ed); multi-age education (MS Ed), including world languages; music education (MS Ed); teacher as leader (MS Ed); teacher education (MS Ed); technology-enhanced learning (MS Ed); trans-disciplinary early childhood education (MS Ed). *Program availability:* Part-time, 100% online. *Degree requirements:* For master's, variable foreign language requirement, thesis or alternative, internship (for teaching licensure or endorsement). *Entrance requirements:* For master's, GRE (minimum score of 149 verbal, 4 on writing) or MAT (minimum score of 396) if undergraduate GPA was under 2.75, minimum GPA of 2.75, 3 letters of recommendation, personal statement or resume, official transcripts. Additional exam requirements/recommendations for international students: required—TOEFL (minimum score 550 paper-based; 80 iBT); recommended—IELTS (minimum score 6.5). Electronic applications accepted. *Expenses:* Contact institution.

University of Florida, Graduate School, College of Public Health and Health Professions, Department of Environmental and Global Health, Gainesville, FL 32611. Offers environmental health (PhD); one health (MHS, PhD). *Entrance requirements:* For master's and doctorate, GRE, minimum GPA of 3.0. Additional exam requirements/recommendations for international students: required—TOEFL (minimum score 550 paper-based; 80 iBT), IELTS (minimum score 6).

University of Houston–Victoria, School of Arts and Sciences, Program in Interdisciplinary Studies, Victoria, TX 77901-4450. Offers MAIS. *Program availability:* Part-time, evening/weekend, online learning. *Degree requirements:* For master's, comprehensive exam or thesis. *Entrance requirements:* For master's, GRE General Test, official transcript, essay. Additional exam requirements/recommendations for international students: required—TOEFL (minimum score 550 paper-based). Electronic applications accepted.

University of Idaho, College of Graduate Studies, Program in Interdisciplinary Studies, Moscow, ID 83844-2282. Offers MA, MS. In 2019, 1 master's awarded. *Entrance requirements:* For master's, GRE, minimum GPA of 3.0. Additional exam requirements/recommendations for international students: required—TOEFL (minimum score 79 iBT). *Application deadline:* For fall admission, 7/30 for domestic students; for spring admission, 12/1 for domestic students. Applications are processed on a rolling basis. Application fee: $60. Electronic applications accepted. *Expenses:* Tuition, state resident: full-time $7753.80; part-time $502 per credit hour. Tuition, nonresident: full-time $26,990; part-time $1571 per credit hour. *Required fees:* $2122.20; $47 per credit hour. *Financial support:* Applicants required to submit FAFSA. *Unit head:* Dr. Jerry McMurtry, Dean of Graduate Studies, 208-885-2647, E-mail: cogs@uidaho.edu. *Application contact:* Dr. Jerry McMurtry, Dean of Graduate Studies, 208-885-2647, E-mail: cogs@uidaho.edu.
Website: https://www.uidaho.edu/cogs/programs-offered/interdisciplinary-studies

University of Illinois at Chicago, Program in Learning Sciences, Chicago, IL 60607-7128. Offers PhD.

University of Illinois at Springfield, Graduate Programs, College of Liberal Arts and Sciences, Department of Liberal and Integrative Studies, Springfield, IL 62703-5407. Offers MA. *Program availability:* Part-time, 100% online, blended/hybrid learning. *Faculty:* 5 full-time (3 women). *Students:* 1 full-time (0 women), 8 part-time (6 women), 1 international. Average age 46. 1 applicant. *Degree requirements:* For master's, project or thesis. *Entrance requirements:* For master's, Personal statement; 2 letters of reference; conversation with an LNT faculty member at the department's discretion; minimum GPA of 2.5 (for campus-based students), 3.0 (for online students). Additional exam requirements/recommendations for international students: required—TOEFL (minimum score 500 paper-based; 61 iBT). *Application deadline:* Applications are processed on a rolling basis. Application fee: $60 ($75 for international students). Electronic applications accepted. *Expenses:* $33.25 per credit hour (online fee). *Financial support:* In 2019–20, research assistantships with full tuition reimbursements (averaging $10,562 per year), teaching assistantships with full tuition reimbursements (averaging $10,652 per year) were awarded; fellowships, career-related internships or fieldwork, Federal Work-Study, scholarships/grants, health care benefits, and unspecified assistantships also available. Support available to part-time students. Financial award application deadline: 11/15; financial award applicants required to submit FAFSA. *Unit head:* Dr. Kamau Kemayo, Program Administrator, 217-206-8048, Fax: 217-206-6217, E-mail: lnt@uis.edu. *Application contact:* Dr. Kamau Kemayo, Program Administrator, 217-206-8048, Fax: 217-206-6217, E-mail: lnt@uis.edu.
Website: http://www.uis.edu/lno/

University of Illinois at Urbana-Champaign, Graduate College, College of Liberal Arts and Sciences, School of Literatures, Cultures and Linguistics, Program in Romance Linguistics, Champaign, IL 61820. Offers PhD.

The University of Kansas, University of Kansas Medical Center, School of Medicine, Interdisciplinary Graduate Program in Biomedical Sciences (IGPBS), Kansas City, KS 66160. Offers PhD, MD/PhD. *Students:* 17 full-time (11 women); includes 3 minority (1 Asian, non-Hispanic/Latino; 1 Hispanic/Latino; 1 Two or more races, non-Hispanic/Latino), 6 international. Average age 25. 112 applicants, 33% accepted, 17 enrolled. Terminal master's awarded for partial completion of doctoral program. *Degree requirements:* For doctorate, comprehensive exam, thesis/dissertation. *Entrance requirements:* Additional exam requirements/recommendations for international students: required—TOEFL. *Application deadline:* For fall admission, 12/1 priority date for domestic and international students. Applications are processed on a rolling basis. Application fee: $60. Electronic applications accepted. *Expenses:* Tuition, state resident: full-time $9989. Tuition, nonresident: full-time $23,950. *International tuition:* $23,950 full-time. *Required fees:* $984; $81.99 per credit hour. Tuition and fees vary according to course load, campus/location and program. *Financial support:* Research assistantships with full tuition reimbursements, teaching assistantships with full tuition reimbursements, scholarships/grants, and unspecified assistantships available. Financial award application deadline: 3/1; financial award applicants required to submit FAFSA. *Unit head:* Dr. Michael Werle, Director, E-mail: mwerle@kumc.edu. *Application contact:* Martin J. Graham, Coordinator, 913-588-2719, Fax: 913-588-5242, E-mail: mgraham4@kumc.edu.
Website: http://www.kumc.edu/igpbs.html

University of Louisville, School of Interdisciplinary and Graduate Studies, Louisville, KY 40292. Offers interdisciplinary studies (MA, MS, PhD), including bioethics and medical humanities (MA), bioinformatics (PhD), sustainability (MA, MS), translational bioengineering (PhD), translational neuroscience (PhD). *Program availability:* Part-time. *Students:* 36 full-time (21 women), 14 part-time (5 women); includes 5 minority (1 Black or African American, non-Hispanic/Latino; 3 Hispanic/Latino; 1 Two or more races, non-Hispanic/Latino), 10 international. Average age 32. 27 applicants, 70% accepted, 14 enrolled. In 2019, 3 master's, 1 doctorate awarded. *Degree requirements:* For master's, variable foreign language requirement, comprehensive exam (for some programs), thesis (for some programs); for doctorate, variable foreign language requirement, comprehensive exam, thesis/dissertation. *Entrance requirements:* For master's and doctorate, GRE General Test, Application fee, two letters of recommendation, transcripts from previous post-secondary educational institutions. Additional exam requirements/recommendations for international students: required—TOEFL (minimum score 550 paper-based; 79 iBT), IELTS (minimum score 6.5). *Application deadline:* For fall admission, 7/1 priority date for domestic students, 5/1 priority date for international students; for winter admission, 7/1 priority date for domestic students, 5/1 for international students; for spring admission, 12/1 priority date for domestic students, 11/1 for international students; for summer admission, 4/1 priority date for domestic students, 4/1 for international students. Applications are processed on a rolling basis.

Interdisciplinary Studies

Application fee: $65. Electronic applications accepted. *Expenses: Tuition, area resident:* Full-time $13,000; part-time $723 per credit hour. Tuition, state resident: full-time $13,000; part-time $723 per credit hour. Tuition, nonresident: full-time $27,114; part-time $1507 per credit hour. *International tuition:* $27,114 full-time. *Required fees:* $196. Tuition and fees vary according to program and reciprocity agreements. *Financial support:* In 2019–20, 35 students received support, including 120 fellowships with full tuition reimbursements available (averaging $20,000 per year); scholarships/grants, health care benefits, unspecified assistantships, and Diversity scholarships also available. Financial award application deadline: 1/1; financial award applicants required to submit FAFSA. *Unit head:* Dr. Paul J. DeMarco, Acting Vice Provost for Graduate Affairs, Acting Dean of the Graduate School, 502-852-0788, Fax: 502-852-2365, E-mail: paul.demarco@louisville.edu. *Application contact:* Dr. Barbara Clark, Acting Associate Dean of the Graduate School, 502-852-6498, Fax: 502-852-3111, E-mail: gradadm@louisville.edu.
Website: http://www.graduate.louisville.edu

University of Maine, Graduate School, Interdisciplinary Doctoral Program, Orono, ME 04469. Offers PhD. *Program availability:* Part-time, evening/weekend. *Students:* 14 full-time (9 women), 6 part-time (3 women); includes 2 minority (1 American Indian or Alaska Native, non-Hispanic/Latino; 1 Asian, non-Hispanic/Latino), 1 international. Average age 41. 3 applicants, 100% accepted, 2 enrolled. In 2019, 4 doctorates awarded. *Degree requirements:* For doctorate, comprehensive exam, thesis/dissertation. *Entrance requirements:* For doctorate, GRE General Test, master's degree. Additional exam requirements/recommendations for international students: required—TOEFL. *Application deadline:* For fall admission, 4/1 for domestic students; for spring admission, 11/1 for domestic students. Applications are processed on a rolling basis. Application fee: $65. Electronic applications accepted. *Expenses: Tuition, area resident:* Full-time $8100; part-time $450 per credit hour. Tuition, state resident: full-time $8100; part-time $450 per credit hour. Tuition, nonresident: full-time $26,388; part-time $1466 per credit hour. *International tuition:* $26,388 full-time. *Required fees:* $1257; $278 per semester. Tuition and fees vary according to course load. *Financial support:* In 2019–20, 7 students received support, including 1 fellowship with full tuition reimbursement available (averaging $34,000 per year), 9 research assistantships with full tuition reimbursements available (averaging $10,000 per year), 1 teaching assistantship with full tuition reimbursement available (averaging $17,000 per year); scholarships/grants and unspecified assistantships also available. Financial award application deadline: 3/1; financial award applicants required to submit FAFSA. *Unit head:* Scott G. Delcourt, Assistant Vice President for Graduate Studies/Senior Associate Dean, 207-581-3291, Fax: 207-581-3232, E-mail: graduate@maine.edu. *Application contact:* Scott G. Delcourt, Assistant Vice President for Graduate Studies/Senior Associate Dean, 207-581-3291, Fax: 207-581-3232, E-mail: graduate@maine.edu.
Website: http://umaine.edu/graduate/

University of Maine, Graduate School, Master of Arts in Interdisciplinary Studies Program, Orono, ME 04469. Offers MA. *Program availability:* Part-time, evening/weekend. *Faculty:* 3 full-time (1 woman), 6 part-time/adjunct (3 women). *Students:* 6 full-time (5 women), 17 part-time (8 women); includes 1 minority (Hispanic/Latino). Average age 46. 20 applicants, 100% accepted, 14 enrolled. In 2019, 3 master's awarded. *Degree requirements:* For master's, thesis or alternative, project. *Entrance requirements:* Additional exam requirements/recommendations for international students: required—TOEFL. *Application deadline:* For fall admission, 4/1 for domestic students; for spring admission, 11/1 for domestic students; for summer admission, 4/1 for domestic students. Applications are processed on a rolling basis. Application fee: $65. Electronic applications accepted. *Expenses: Tuition, area resident:* Full-time $8100; part-time $450 per credit hour. Tuition, state resident: full-time $8100; part-time $450 per credit hour. Tuition, nonresident: full-time $26,388; part-time $1466 per credit hour. *International tuition:* $26,388 full-time. *Required fees:* $1257; $278 per semester. Tuition and fees vary according to course load. *Financial support:* Federal Work-Study, institutionally sponsored loans, and unspecified assistantships available. Financial award application deadline: 3/1; financial award applicants required to submit FAFSA. *Unit head:* Scott G Delcourt, Assistant Vice President for Graduate Studies and Senior Associate Dean, 207-581-3291, Fax: 207-581-3232, E-mail: graduate@umaine.edu. *Application contact:* Scott G Delcourt, Assistant Vice President for Graduate Studies and Senior Associate Dean, 207-581-3291, Fax: 207-581-3232, E-mail: graduate@umaine.edu.
Website: http://umaine.edu/graduate/

University of Manitoba, Faculty of Graduate Studies, Interdisciplinary Programs, Individual Interdisciplinary Programs, Winnipeg, MB R3T 2N2, Canada. Offers M Sc, MA, PhD.

University of Massachusetts Medical School, Graduate School of Biomedical Sciences, Worcester, MA 01655. Offers biomedical sciences (PhD), including biochemistry and molecular pharmacology, bioinformatics and computational biology, cancer biology, immunology and microbiology, interdisciplinary, neuroscience, translational science; biomedical sciences (millennium program) (PhD); clinical and population health research (PhD); clinical investigation (MS). *Faculty:* 1,258 full-time (525 women), 372 part-time/adjunct (238 women). *Students:* 344 full-time (198 women), 1 (woman) part-time; includes 73 minority (12 Black or African American, non-Hispanic/Latino; 1 American Indian or Alaska Native, non-Hispanic/Latino; 45 Asian, non-Hispanic/Latino; 15 Hispanic/Latino), 120 international. Average age 29. 581 applicants, 23% accepted, 56 enrolled. In 2019, 6 master's, 49 doctorates awarded. Terminal master's awarded for partial completion of doctoral program. *Degree requirements:* For master's, comprehensive exam, thesis; for doctorate, comprehensive exam, thesis/dissertation. *Entrance requirements:* For master's, MD, PhD, DVM, or PharmD; for doctorate, bachelor's degree. Additional exam requirements/recommendations for international students: required—TOEFL, IELTS, TOEFL (minimum score 100 IBT) or IELTS (minimum score 7.0). *Application deadline:* For fall admission, 12/1 for domestic and international students. Applications are processed on a rolling basis. Application fee: $80. Electronic applications accepted. Application fee is waived when completed online. *Expenses:* Contact institution. *Financial support:* In 2019–20, 22 fellowships with full tuition reimbursements (averaging $33,061 per year), 322 research assistantships with full tuition reimbursements (averaging $32,850 per year) were awarded; institutionally sponsored loans and scholarships/grants also available. Financial award application deadline: 5/15. *Unit head:* Dr. Mary Ellen Lane, Dean, 508-856-4018, E-mail: maryellen.lane@umassmed.edu. *Application contact:* Dr. Kendall Knight, Assistant Vice Provost for Admissions, 508-856-5628, Fax: 508-856-3659, E-mail: kendall.knight@umassmed.edu.
Website: http://www.umassmed.edu/gsbs/

University of Memphis, Graduate School, College of Arts and Sciences, Department of Earth Sciences, Memphis, TN 38152. Offers earth sciences (MA, MS, PhD), including archaeology (MS), geography (MS), geology (MS), geophysics (MS), interdisciplinary studies (MS); geographic information systems (Graduate Certificate), including geographic information systems, GIS educator, GIS planning, GIS professional. *Program availability:* Part-time, evening/weekend. *Students:* 40 full-time (17 women), 22 part-time (7 women); includes 12 minority (2 Black or African American, non-Hispanic/Latino; 8 Asian, non-Hispanic/Latino; 2 Hispanic/Latino), 18 international. Average age 31. 23 applicants, 91% accepted, 18 enrolled. In 2019, 13 master's, 5 doctorates, 8 other advanced degrees awarded. Terminal master's awarded for partial completion of doctoral program. *Degree requirements:* For master's, comprehensive exam, thesis, seminar presentation; for doctorate, comprehensive exam, thesis/dissertation, qualifying exam, submission of two manuscripts for publication in peer-reviewed journal or books. *Entrance requirements:* For master's, GRE General Test, 3 letters of recommendation, statement of research interests; for doctorate, GRE General Test, 2 letters of recommendation, resume, personal statement. Additional exam requirements/recommendations for international students: required—TOEFL (minimum score 550 paper-based; 79 iBT). *Application deadline:* For fall admission, 1/15 for domestic students; for spring admission, 11/1 for domestic students. Applications are processed on a rolling basis. Application fee: $35 ($60 for international students). Electronic applications accepted. *Expenses: Tuition, area resident:* Full-time $9216; part-time $512 per credit hour. Tuition, state resident: full-time $9216; part-time $512 per credit hour. Tuition, nonresident: full-time $12,672; part-time $704 per credit hour. *International tuition:* $16,128 full-time. *Required fees:* $1530; $85 per credit hour. Tuition and fees vary according to program. *Financial support:* Fellowships with full tuition reimbursements, research assistantships with full tuition reimbursements, teaching assistantships with full tuition reimbursements, Federal Work-Study, scholarships/grants, and unspecified assistantships available. Financial award application deadline: 2/1; financial award applicants required to submit FAFSA. *Unit head:* Dr. Daniel Larsen, Chair, 901-678-4358, Fax: 901-678-2178, E-mail: dlarsen@memphis.edu. *Application contact:* Dr. Daniel Larsen, Chair, 901-678-4358, Fax: 901-678-2178, E-mail: dlarsen@memphis.edu.
Website: http://www.memphis.edu/earthsciences/

University of Minnesota, Twin Cities Campus, Graduate School, College of Liberal Arts, Department of Cultural Studies and Comparative Literature, Program in Comparative Studies in Discourse and Society, Minneapolis, MN 55455-0213. Offers PhD. *Degree requirements:* For doctorate, 2 foreign languages, thesis/dissertation. *Entrance requirements:* For doctorate, GRE General Test, sample of written work. Additional exam requirements/recommendations for international students: required—TOEFL.

University of Missouri–Kansas City, School of Graduate Studies, Kansas City, MO 64110-2499. Offers interdisciplinary studies (PhD), including art history, cell biology and biophysics, chemistry, computer and electrical engineering, computer science and informatics, economics, education, engineering, English, entrepreneurship and innovation, geosciences, history, mathematics and statistics, molecular biology and biochemistry, music education, oral and craniofacial sciences, pharmaceutical sciences, pharmacology, physics, political science, public affairs and administration, religious studies, social science, telecommunications and computer networking; PMBA/MHA. *Degree requirements:* For doctorate, comprehensive exam, thesis/dissertation, residency. *Entrance requirements:* For doctorate, GRE General Test, minimum GPA of 2.75 (undergraduate), 3.0 (graduate). Additional exam requirements/recommendations for international students: required—TOEFL (minimum score 550 paper-based; 80 iBT), TWE (minimum score 4). Electronic applications accepted.

University of Missouri–St. Louis, College of Arts and Sciences, Interdisciplinary Courses, St. Louis, MO 63121. Offers gender studies (Certificate); international studies (Certificate). *Entrance requirements:* Additional exam requirements/recommendations for international students: required—TOEFL (minimum score 550 paper-based; 79 iBT), IELTS (minimum score 6.5). *Expenses: Tuition, area resident:* Full-time $9005.40; part-time $6003.60 per credit hour. Tuition, state resident: full-time $9005.40; part-time $6003.60 per credit hour. Tuition, nonresident: full-time $22,108; part-time $14,738.40 per credit hour. *International tuition:* $22,108 full-time. Tuition and fees vary according to course load.

University of Montana, Graduate School, College of Humanities and Sciences, Division of Biological Sciences, Interdisciplinary Program in Systems Ecology, Missoula, MT 59812. Offers MS, PhD.

University of Montana, Graduate School, Program in Interdisciplinary Studies, Missoula, MT 59812. Offers individualized interdisciplinary studies (PhD); interdisciplinary studies (MIS). *Degree requirements:* For doctorate, thesis/dissertation. *Entrance requirements:* For master's, GRE General Test. Additional exam requirements/recommendations for international students: required—TOEFL.

University of North Alabama, College of Arts and Sciences, Department of Interdisciplinary and Professional Studies, Florence, AL 35632-0001. Offers professional studies (MPS), including community development, higher education administration, information technology, security and safety leadership. *Program availability:* Part-time, 100% online. *Degree requirements:* For master's, thesis optional. *Entrance requirements:* For master's, ETS PPI, personal statement; three letters of recommendation. Additional exam requirements/recommendations for international students: required—TOEFL (minimum score 79 iBT), IELTS (minimum score 6), PTE (minimum score 54). Electronic applications accepted.

The University of North Carolina at Charlotte, College of Liberal Arts and Sciences, Interdisciplinary Liberal Arts and Sciences Programs, Charlotte, NC 28223-0001. Offers gender, sexuality and women's studies (Graduate Certificate); gerontology (MA, Graduate Certificate); Latin American studies (MA); liberal studies (MA); organizational science (PhD); public policy (PhD). *Program availability:* Part-time, evening/weekend. *Students:* 74 full-time (50 women), 56 part-time (43 women); includes 41 minority (16 Black or African American, non-Hispanic/Latino; 3 Asian, non-Hispanic/Latino; 16 Hispanic/Latino; 6 Two or more races, non-Hispanic/Latino), 16 international. Average age 33. 101 applicants, 51% accepted, 37 enrolled. In 2019, 21 master's, 5 doctorates, 8 other advanced degrees awarded. *Entrance requirements:* For master's, GRE General Test or MAT, bachelor's degree from accredited college or university; official transcripts of all previous academic work attempted beyond high school with minimum overall GPA of 3.0; statement of purpose; recommendation letters; for doctorate, GRE or GMAT, statement of purpose discussing interest in program and objectives for pursuing degree, current resume or curriculum vitae, unofficial transcripts; for Graduate Certificate, bachelor's degree from accredited university and either enrolled and in good standing in a graduate degree program at UNC Charlotte or have a minimum undergraduate GPA of 3.0. Additional exam requirements/recommendations for international students: required—TOEFL (minimum score 557 paper-based; 83 iBT), IELTS (minimum score 6.5), TOEFL (minimum score 557 paper-based, 83 iBT) or IELTS (6.5). *Application deadline:* Applications are processed on a rolling basis. Application fee: $75. Electronic applications accepted. *Expenses:* Tuition, state resident: full-time $4337. Tuition, nonresident: full-time $17,771. *Required fees:* $3093. Tuition and fees vary according to course load, degree level and program. *Financial support:* In 2019–20, 3 students received support, including 2 research assistantships (averaging $6,750 per year), 1 teaching assistantship (averaging $21,000 per year); career-related internships or fieldwork, institutionally sponsored loans, scholarships/grants, unspecified assistantships, and administrative assistantships also available. Support available to part-time students. Financial award applicants required to submit FAFSA. *Unit head:* Dr. Nancy A. Gutierrez, Dean, 704-687-0081, E-mail: ngutierr@uncc.edu. *Application contact:* Kathy B. Giddings, Director of Graduate Admissions, 704-687-5503, Fax: 704-

687-3279, E-mail: gradadm@uncc.edu.
Website: http://clas.uncc.edu/academics

University of Northern British Columbia, Office of Graduate Studies, Prince George, BC V2N 4Z9, Canada. Offers business administration (Diploma); community health science (M Sc); disability management (MA); education (M Ed); first nations studies (MA); gender studies (MA); history (MA); interdisciplinary studies (MA); international studies (MA); mathematical, computer and physical sciences (M Sc); natural resources and environmental studies (M Sc, MA, MNRES, PhD); political science (MA); psychology (M Sc, PhD); social work (MSW). *Program availability:* Part-time, evening/weekend, online learning. *Degree requirements:* For master's, thesis; for doctorate, thesis/dissertation. *Entrance requirements:* For master's, GRE, minimum B average in undergraduate course work; for doctorate, candidacy exam, minimum A average in graduate course work.

University of North Texas, Toulouse Graduate School, Denton, TX 76203-5459. Offers accounting (MS); applied anthropology (MA, MS); applied behavior analysis (Certificate); applied geography (MA); applied technology and performance improvement (M Ed, MS); art education (MA); art history (MA); arts leadership (Certificate); audiology (Au D); behavior analysis (MS); behavioral science (PhD); biochemistry and molecular biology (MS); biology (MA, MS); biomedical engineering (MS); business analysis (MS); chemistry (MS); clinical health psychology (PhD); communication studies (MA, MS); computer engineering (MS); computer science (MS); counseling (M Ed, MS), including clinical mental health counseling (MS), college and university counseling, elementary school counseling, secondary school counseling; creative writing (MA); criminal justice (MS); curriculum and instruction (M Ed); decision sciences (MBA); design (MA, MFA), including fashion design (MFA), innovation studies, interior design (MFA); early childhood studies (MS); economics (MS); educational leadership (M Ed, Ed D); educational psychology (MS, PhD), including family studies (MS), gifted and talented (MS), human development (MS), learning and cognition (MS), research, measurement and evaluation (MS); electrical engineering (MS); emergency management (MPA); engineering technology (MS); English (MA); English as a second language (MA); environmental science (MS); finance (MBA, MS); financial management (MPA); French (MA); health services management (MBA); higher education (M Ed, Ed D); history (MA, MS); hospitality management (MS); human resources management (MPA); information science (MS); information systems (PhD); information technologies (MBA); interdisciplinary studies (MA, MS); international studies (MA); international sustainable tourism (MS); jazz studies (MM); journalism (MA, MJ, Graduate Certificate), including interactive and virtual digital communication (Graduate Certificate), narrative journalism (Graduate Certificate), public relations (Graduate Certificate); kinesiology (MS); linguistics (MA); local government management (MPA); logistics (PhD); logistics and supply chain management (MBA); long-term care, senior housing, and aging services (MA); management (PhD); marketing (MBA); mathematics (MA, MS); mechanical and energy engineering (MS, PhD); music (MA), including ethnomusicology, music theory, musicology, performance; music composition (PhD); music education (MM Ed, PhD); nonprofit management (MPA); operations and supply chain management (MBA); performance (MM, DMA); philosophy (MA); political science (MA); professional and technical communication (MA); radio, television and film (MA, MFA); rehabilitation counseling (Certificate); sociology (MA); Spanish (MA); special education (M Ed); speech-language pathology (MA); strategic management (MBA); studio art (MFA); teaching (M Ed); MBA/MS. *Program availability:* Part-time, evening/weekend, online learning. Terminal master's awarded for partial completion of doctoral program. *Degree requirements:* For master's, variable foreign language requirement, comprehensive exam (for some programs), thesis (for some programs); for doctorate, variable foreign language requirement, comprehensive exam (for some programs), thesis/dissertation; for other advanced degree, variable foreign language requirement, comprehensive exam (for some programs). *Entrance requirements:* For master's and doctorate, GRE, GMAT. Additional exam requirements/recommendations for international students: required—TOEFL (minimum score 550 paper-based; 79 iBT). Electronic applications accepted.

University of Oregon, Graduate School, Interdisciplinary Program in Applied Information Management, Eugene, OR 97403. Offers MS. *Program availability:* Part-time, online learning. *Degree requirements:* For master's, project. *Entrance requirements:* Additional exam requirements/recommendations for international students: required—TOEFL. Electronic applications accepted. *Expenses:* Contact institution.

University of Ottawa, Faculty of Graduate and Postdoctoral Studies, Interdisciplinary Programs, Ottawa, ON K1N 6N5, Canada. Offers e-business (Certificate); e-commerce (Certificate); finance (Certificate); health services and policies research (Diploma); population health (PhD); population health risk assessment and management (Certificate); public management and governance (Certificate); systems science (Certificate).

University of Pittsburgh, School of Medicine, Graduate Programs in Medicine, Interdisciplinary Biomedical Graduate Program, Pittsburgh, PA 15260. Offers PhD. *Degree requirements:* For doctorate, comprehensive exam, thesis/dissertation. *Entrance requirements:* For doctorate, GRE General Test, minimum GPA of 3.2, 3 letters of recommendation, official transcripts, baccalaureate degree. Additional exam requirements/recommendations for international students: required—TOEFL (minimum score 600 paper-based; 100 iBT), IELTS (minimum score 7). Electronic applications accepted. *Expenses:* Contact institution.

University of Regina, Faculty of Graduate Studies and Research, Faculty of Media, Art, and Performance, Department of Visual Arts, Regina, SK S4S 0A2, Canada. Offers ceramics (MFA); drawing (MFA); interdisciplinary studies (MA, MFA); intermedia (MFA); painting (MFA); sculpture (MFA). *Program availability:* Part-time. *Faculty:* 11 full-time (6 women), 3 part-time/adjunct (1 woman). *Students:* 6 full-time (3 women), 3 part-time (2 women). Average age 30. 19 applicants, 11% accepted. In 2019, 2 master's awarded. *Degree requirements:* For master's, exhibition, support paper, oral defense. *Entrance requirements:* For master's, submit documentation (CD, DVD or URL's.) of recent work (20 images or equivalent) accompanied by a corresponding sheet indicating: (a) title of each work; (b) media; (c) date; (d) dimensions (if applicable). Other relevant documentation may be included. Additional exam requirements/recommendations for international students: required—TOEFL (minimum score 600 paper-based; 92 iBT), IELTS (minimum score 6.5), PTE (minimum score 65), other options are CAEL, MELAB, Cantest and U of R ESL. *Application deadline:* For fall admission, 1/15 for domestic and international students. *Application fee:* $100. Electronic applications accepted. *Expenses: Tuition:* Full-time $6684 Canadian dollars. *Required fees:* $100 Canadian dollars; $3351.45 Canadian dollars per trimester; $1117.15 Canadian dollars per semester. Tuition and fees vary according to course level, course load, degree level and program. *Financial support:* Fellowships, research assistantships, teaching assistantships, career-related internships or fieldwork, Federal Work-Study, scholarships/grants, unspecified assistantships, and travel award and Graduate Scholarship Base Funds available. Support available to part-time students. Financial award application deadline: 9/30. *Unit head:* Dr. Risa Horowitz, Department Head, 306-585-5641, Fax: 306-585-5526, E-mail: risa.horowitz@uregina.ca. *Application contact:*

Dr. Ruth Chambers, Graduate Coordinator, Visual Arts, 306-585-5575, Fax: 306-585-5526, E-mail: ruth.chambers@uregina.ca.

University of South Dakota, Graduate School, Interdisciplinary Studies Program, Vermillion, SD 57069. Offers MA. *Program availability:* Part-time, online learning. *Degree requirements:* For master's, thesis or alternative. *Entrance requirements:* For master's, minimum GPA of 2.7. Additional exam requirements/recommendations for international students: required—TOEFL (minimum score 550 paper-based; 79 iBT). Electronic applications accepted.

University of South Florida, College of Arts and Sciences, School of Interdisciplinary Global Studies, Tampa, FL 33620-9951. Offers MA, PhD. *Accreditation:* NASPAA. *Program availability:* Part-time, evening/weekend. *Faculty:* 14 full-time (3 women). *Students:* 37 full-time (10 women), 20 part-time (10 women); includes 12 minority (5 Black or African American, non-Hispanic/Latino; 2 Asian, non-Hispanic/Latino; 4 Hispanic/Latino; 1 Two or more races, non-Hispanic/Latino), 17 international. Average age 34. 48 applicants, 67% accepted, 20 enrolled. In 2019, 7 master's, 2 doctorates awarded. *Degree requirements:* For master's, comprehensive exam, thesis (for some programs); for doctorate, comprehensive exam, thesis/dissertation. *Entrance requirements:* For master's, GRE not required, but suggested for full financial consideration; GRE Required for Political Science, 3 letters of recommendation; 500 word personal statement; resume. For political science- must have a background in political science; for doctorate, GRE required, 3 letters of recommendation; 500 word personal statement; writing sample. Additional exam requirements/recommendations for international students: required—TOEFL, TOEFL (minimum score 550 paper-based; 79 iBT) or IELTS (minimum score 6.5). *Application deadline:* For fall admission, 1/5 for domestic and international students; for spring admission, 10/15 for domestic students, 9/15 for international students. Applications are processed on a rolling basis. Application fee: $30. Electronic applications accepted. *Financial support:* In 2019–20, 9 students received support, including 18 teaching assistantships with tuition reimbursements available (averaging $12,390 per year); unspecified assistantships also available. Financial award application deadline: 4/1. *Unit head:* Dr. Scott Solomon, Associate Professor and SIGS Director, 813-974-6394, E-mail: msolomon@usf.edu. *Application contact:* Dr. Steven Roach, Professor and Director of Graduate Studies, 813-974-9753, E-mail: sroach@usf.edu.
Website: http://gia.usf.edu/

The University of Tennessee at Martin, Graduate Programs, College of Education, Health and Behavioral Sciences, Program in Teaching, Martin, TN 38238. Offers curriculum and instruction (MS Ed), including 7-12, K-6; initial licensure (MS Ed), including elementary education, secondary education; initial licensure k-12 (MS Ed), including library service, special education; interdisciplinary (MS Ed). *Program availability:* Part-time, online only, 100% online. *Students:* 70 full-time (50 women), 96 part-time (75 women); includes 38 minority (30 Black or African American, non-Hispanic/Latino; 1 Asian, non-Hispanic/Latino; 2 Hispanic/Latino; 5 Two or more races, non-Hispanic/Latino). Average age 31. 200 applicants, 75% accepted, 97 enrolled. In 2019, 29 master's awarded. *Degree requirements:* For master's, comprehensive exam. *Entrance requirements:* For master's, minimum GPA of 2.5, teaching license. Additional exam requirements/recommendations for international students: required—TOEFL (minimum score 525 paper-based; 71 iBT). *Application deadline:* For fall admission, 7/28 priority date for domestic and international students; for spring admission, 12/17 priority date for domestic and international students; for summer admission, 5/10 priority date for domestic and international students. Applications are processed on a rolling basis. Application fee: $30 ($130 for international students). Electronic applications accepted. *Expenses: Tuition, area resident:* Full-time $9096; part-time $505 per credit hour. Tuition, state resident: full-time $9096; part-time $505 per credit hour. Tuition, nonresident: full-time $15,136; part-time $841 per credit hour. *International tuition:* $23,040 full-time. *Required fees:* $1520; $85 per credit hour. Part-time tuition and fees vary according to course load. *Financial support:* In 2019–20, 35 students received support, including 2 research assistantships with full tuition reimbursements available (averaging $7,540 per year), 5 teaching assistantships with full tuition reimbursements available (averaging $8,133 per year); scholarships/grants and tuition waivers (full and partial) also available. Financial award application deadline: 2/1; financial award applicants required to submit FAFSA. *Unit head:* Cynthia West, Dean, 731-881-7125, Fax: 731-881-7975, E-mail: cwest@utm.edu. *Application contact:* Jolene L. Cunningham, Student Services Specialist, 731-881-7012, Fax: 731-881-7499, E-mail: jcunningham@utm.edu.

The University of Texas at Dallas, School of Interdisciplinary Studies, Richardson, TX 75080. Offers MA. *Program availability:* Part-time, evening/weekend. *Faculty:* 3 full-time (2 women), 4 part-time/adjunct (2 women). *Students:* 17 full-time (14 women), 16 part-time (10 women); includes 17 minority (5 Black or African American, non-Hispanic/Latino; 5 Asian, non-Hispanic/Latino; 4 Hispanic/Latino; 3 Two or more races, non-Hispanic/Latino), 1 international. Average age 35. 35 applicants, 54% accepted, 12 enrolled. In 2019, 6 master's awarded. *Degree requirements:* For master's, research project, seminar. *Entrance requirements:* For master's, GRE General Test, minimum GPA of 3.0. Additional exam requirements/recommendations for international students: required—TOEFL (minimum score 550 paper-based). *Application deadline:* For fall admission, 7/15 for domestic students, 5/1 priority date for international students; for spring admission, 11/15 for domestic students, 9/1 priority date for international students. Applications are processed on a rolling basis. Application fee: $50 ($100 for international students). Electronic applications accepted. *Expenses: Tuition, area resident:* Full-time $16,504. Tuition, state resident: full-time $16,504. Tuition, nonresident: full-time $34,266. Tuition and fees vary according to course load. *Financial support:* Research assistantships with partial tuition reimbursements, teaching assistantships with partial tuition reimbursements, career-related internships or fieldwork, Federal Work-Study, institutionally sponsored loans, and scholarships/grants available. Support available to part-time students. Financial award application deadline: 4/30; financial award applicants required to submit FAFSA. *Unit head:* Dr. George Fair, Dean, 972-883-2350, Fax: 972-883-2440, E-mail: gwfair@utdallas.edu. *Application contact:* Jillian Duquaine-Watson, Program Head - Interdisciplinary Studies, 972-883-2350, Fax: 972-883-2440, E-mail: jmw087000@utdallas.edu.
Website: https://is.utdallas.edu/

The University of Texas at El Paso, Graduate School, College of Liberal Arts, Master of Arts in Interdisciplinary Studies Program, El Paso, TX 79968-0001. Offers MAIS. *Program availability:* Part-time, evening/weekend. *Entrance requirements:* For master's, GRE, minimum GPA of 3.0, letters of recommendation. Additional exam requirements/recommendations for international students: required—TOEFL; recommended—IELTS. Electronic applications accepted.

The University of Texas at San Antonio, College of Education and Human Development, Department of Interdisciplinary Learning and Teaching, San Antonio, TX 78249-0617. Offers education (MA), including curriculum and instruction, early childhood and elementary education, instructional technology, reading and literacy, special education; interdisciplinary learning and teaching (PhD). *Program availability:* Part-time, evening/weekend. *Degree requirements:* For master's, comprehensive exam, thesis optional, 36 hours of course work without thesis (33 with thesis); for doctorate, comprehensive exam, thesis/dissertation, minimum of 60 semester credit hours.

Interdisciplinary Studies

Entrance requirements: For master's, bachelor's degree with minimum GPA of 3.0 in last 60 hours of coursework; 18 hours of undergraduate coursework in education or related field; for doctorate, GRE, transcripts from all colleges and universities attended, professional vitae demonstrating experience in work environment where education was primary professional emphasis, 3 letters of recommendation, statement of purpose, minimum GPA of 3.5. Additional exam requirements/recommendations for international students: required—TOEFL (minimum score 550 paper-based; 79 iBT), IELTS (minimum score 6.5). Electronic applications accepted.

The University of Texas at Tyler, College of Arts and Sciences, Department of Art and Art History, Tyler, TX 75799-0001. Offers art history (MA); interdisciplinary (MAIS); studio art (MFA). *Faculty:* 5 full-time (4 women), 5 part-time/adjunct (4 women). *Students:* 12 full-time (9 women), 3 part-time (1 woman); includes 2 minority (1 Hispanic/Latino; 1 Two or more races, non-Hispanic/Latino). Average age 38. 3 applicants, 100% accepted, 2 enrolled. In 2019, 5 master's awarded. *Degree requirements:* For master's, thesis, graduate committee review. *Entrance requirements:* For master's, minimum GPA of 3.0. Additional exam requirements/recommendations for international students: required—TOEFL. *Application deadline:* For fall admission, 8/17 priority date for domestic students, 7/1 priority date for international students; for spring admission, 12/21 priority date for domestic students, 11/1 priority date for international students. Applications are processed on a rolling basis. Application fee: $25 ($50 for international students). *Financial support:* Application deadline: 7/1; applicants required to submit FAFSA. *Unit head:* Dr. Merrie Wright, Chair, 903-566-7423, Fax: 903-566-7062, E-mail: mewright@uttyler.edu. *Application contact:* Dr. Merrie Wright, Chair, 903-566-7423, Fax: 903-566-7062, E-mail: mewright@uttyler.edu.
Website: https://www.uttyler.edu/art/

The University of Texas at Tyler, College of Arts and Sciences, Department of Biology, Tyler, TX 75799-0001. Offers biology (MS); interdisciplinary studies (MSIS). *Faculty:* 7 full-time (1 woman). *Students:* 11 full-time (8 women), 7 part-time (6 women); includes 4 minority (1 Asian, non-Hispanic/Latino; 1 Hispanic/Latino; 2 Two or more races, non-Hispanic/Latino). Average age 28. 15 applicants, 60% accepted, 8 enrolled. In 2019, 6 master's awarded. *Degree requirements:* For master's, comprehensive exam, thesis, oral qualifying exam, thesis defense. *Entrance requirements:* For master's, GRE General Test, GRE Subject Test, bachelor's degree in biology or equivalent. Additional exam requirements/recommendations for international students: required—TOEFL. *Application deadline:* For fall admission, 8/17 priority date for domestic students, 7/1 priority date for international students; for spring admission, 12/21 priority date for domestic students, 11/1 priority date for international students. Applications are processed on a rolling basis. Application fee: $25 ($50 for international students). Electronic applications accepted. *Financial support:* In 2019–20, 2 research assistantships (averaging $10,000 per year), 10 teaching assistantships (averaging $10,000 per year) were awarded; scholarships/grants also available. Financial award application deadline: 7/1; financial award applicants required to submit FAFSA. *Unit head:* Dr. Lance Williams, Chair, 903-565-5878, E-mail: lwilliams@uttyler.edu. *Application contact:* Dr. Lance Williams, Chair, 903-565-5878, E-mail: lwilliams@uttyler.edu.
Website: http://www.uttyler.edu/biology/

The University of Texas at Tyler, College of Arts and Sciences, Department of Literature and Languages, Tyler, TX 75799-0001. Offers English (MA); interdisciplinary studies (MAIS). *Program availability:* Part-time, evening/weekend. *Faculty:* 10 full-time (7 women). *Students:* 14 full-time (10 women), 32 part-time (26 women); includes 4 minority (3 Hispanic/Latino; 1 Two or more races, non-Hispanic/Latino). Average age 33. 23 applicants, 83% accepted, 11 enrolled. In 2019, 18 master's awarded. *Degree requirements:* For master's, one foreign language, comprehensive exam, thesis optional. *Entrance requirements:* For master's, GRE General Test, minimum GPA of 3.0; four semesters or the equivalent of one foreign language. Additional exam requirements/recommendations for international students: required—TOEFL. *Application deadline:* For fall admission, 8/17 priority date for domestic students, 7/1 priority date for international students; for spring admission, 12/21 priority date for domestic students, 11/1 priority date for international students. Applications are processed on a rolling basis. Application fee: $25 ($50 for international students). Electronic applications accepted. *Financial support:* In 2019–20, fellowships with full and partial tuition reimbursements (averaging $1,000 per year), 1 research assistantship with full and partial tuition reimbursement (averaging $6,000 per year) was awarded; teaching assistantships with full and partial tuition reimbursements, Federal Work-Study, institutionally sponsored loans, scholarships/grants, tuition waivers, and unspecified assistantships also available. Financial award application deadline: 7/1; financial award applicants required to submit FAFSA. *Unit head:* Dr. Hui Wu, Chair, 903-566-7289, E-mail: hui_wu@uttyler.edu. *Application contact:* Dr. Hui Wu, Chair, 903-566-7289, E-mail: hui_wu@uttyler.edu.
Website: https://www.uttyler.edu/litlang/

The University of Texas at Tyler, College of Education and Psychology, Department of Psychology and Counseling, Tyler, TX 75799-0001. Offers clinical psychology (MS), including neuropsychology, school psychology; counseling psychology (MA), including general, marriage and family; interdisciplinary studies (MSIS); school counseling (MA). *Program availability:* Part-time, evening/weekend. *Faculty:* 12 full-time (5 women), 6 part-time/adjunct (3 women). *Students:* 131 full-time (103 women), 83 part-time (67 women); includes 67 minority (10 Black or African American, non-Hispanic/Latino; 1 American Indian or Alaska Native, non-Hispanic/Latino; 7 Asian, non-Hispanic/Latino; 41 Hispanic/Latino; 8 Two or more races, non-Hispanic/Latino), 8 international. Average age 30. 130 applicants, 65% accepted, 47 enrolled. In 2019, 94 master's awarded. *Degree requirements:* For master's, comprehensive exam, thesis optional. *Entrance requirements:* For master's, GRE General Test, minimum GPA of 3.0. Additional exam requirements/recommendations for international students: required—TOEFL. *Application deadline:* For fall admission, 8/17 priority date for domestic students, 7/1 priority date for international students; for spring admission, 12/21 priority date for domestic students, 11/1 priority date for international students. Application fee: $25 ($50 for international students). Electronic applications accepted. *Financial support:* In 2019–20, fellowships with partial tuition reimbursements (averaging $3,000 per year) were awarded; research assistantships, teaching assistantships, career-related internships or fieldwork, Federal Work-Study, and institutionally sponsored loans also available. Support available to part-time students. Financial award application deadline: 7/1. *Unit head:* Dr. Charles B. Barke, Chair, 903-565-5875, E-mail: cbarke@uttyler.edu. *Application contact:* Dr. Charles B. Barke, Chair, 903-565-5875, E-mail: cbarke@uttyler.edu.
Website: http://www.uttyler.edu/psychology/

The University of Texas Health Science Center at San Antonio, Graduate School of Biomedical Sciences, Integrated Biomedical Sciences Program, San Antonio, TX 78229-3900. Offers PhD. *Degree requirements:* For doctorate, comprehensive exam, thesis/dissertation.

The University of Texas Rio Grande Valley, College of Liberal Arts, School of Interdisciplinary Programs and Community Engagement, Edinburg, TX 78539. Offers interdisciplinary studies (MAIS, MSIS); Spanish translation and interpreting (MA). *Faculty:* 2 full-time (1 woman). *Students:* 19 full-time (10 women), 38 part-time (26 women); includes 45 minority (1 Black or African American, non-Hispanic/Latino; 44 Hispanic/Latino), 6 international. Average age 35. 17 applicants, 76% accepted, 9 enrolled. In 2019, 27 master's awarded. *Expenses:* Tuition, area resident: Full-time $5959; part-time $440 per credit hour. Tuition, state resident: full-time $5959. Tuition, nonresident: full-time $5959. *International tuition:* $13,321 full-time. *Required fees:* $1169; $185 per credit hour. *Financial support:* Application deadline: 1/15.
Website: utrgv.edu/school-of-interdisciplinary-programs-and-community-engagement/index.htm

University of Vermont, Graduate College, College of Education and Social Services, Program in Interdisciplinary Studies, Burlington, VT 05405. Offers M Ed. *Degree requirements:* For master's, thesis or alternative. *Entrance requirements:* For master's, resume, writing sample. Additional exam requirements/recommendations for international students: required—TOEFL (minimum score 550 paper-based, 90 iBT) or IELTS (6.5). Electronic applications accepted.

University of Virginia, College and Graduate School of Arts and Sciences, Program in Art and Architectural History, Charlottesville, VA 22903. Offers MA, PhD. *Degree requirements:* For master's, one foreign language, comprehensive exam, thesis; for doctorate, 2 foreign languages, thesis/dissertation, oral exam. *Entrance requirements:* For master's and doctorate, GRE, 2 letters of recommendation. Electronic applications accepted.

University of Washington, Tacoma, Graduate Programs, Interdisciplinary Studies Program, Tacoma, WA 98402-3100. Offers MA. *Program availability:* Part-time, evening/weekend. *Degree requirements:* For master's, thesis or project. *Entrance requirements:* For master's, GRE, statement of intended area of focus, two official transcripts from every college attended, copy of current resume, three recommendations. Additional exam requirements/recommendations for international students: required—TOEFL. Electronic applications accepted.

The University of Western Ontario, School of Graduate and Postdoctoral Studies, Center for the Study of Theory and Criticism, London, ON N6A 3K7, Canada. Offers MA, PhD. *Degree requirements:* For master's, one foreign language, thesis; for doctorate, one foreign language, comprehensive exam, thesis/dissertation. *Entrance requirements:* For master's, honors degree or equivalent, minimum B+ average, 2 samples of written work; for doctorate, MA in humanities or social sciences.

Virginia Commonwealth University, Graduate School, Program in Interdisciplinary Studies, Richmond, VA 23284-9005. Offers MIS. *Program availability:* Part-time. *Degree requirements:* For master's, thesis optional. *Entrance requirements:* For master's, GRE General Test, minimum GPA of 3.0. Additional exam requirements/recommendations for international students: required—TOEFL (minimum score 600 paper-based; 100 iBT); recommended—IELTS (minimum score 6.5). Electronic applications accepted.

Virginia Polytechnic Institute and State University, Graduate School, Intercollege, Blacksburg, VA 24061. Offers genetics, bioinformatics, and computational biology (PhD); information technology (MIT); macromolecular science and engineering (MS, PhD); translational biology, medicine, and health (PhD). *Students:* 203 full-time (86 women), 745 part-time (218 women); includes 278 minority (64 Black or African American, non-Hispanic/Latino; 119 Asian, non-Hispanic/Latino; 59 Hispanic/Latino; 1 Native Hawaiian or other Pacific Islander, non-Hispanic/Latino; 35 Two or more races, non-Hispanic/Latino), 93 international. Average age 33. 603 applicants, 78% accepted, 327 enrolled. In 2019, 138 master's, 20 doctorates awarded. *Degree requirements:* For master's, comprehensive exam (for some programs), thesis (for some programs); for doctorate, comprehensive exam (for some programs), thesis/dissertation (for some programs). *Entrance requirements:* For master's and doctorate, GRE/GMAT. Additional exam requirements/recommendations for international students: required—TOEFL (minimum score 90 iBT). *Application deadline:* For fall admission, 8/1 for domestic students, 4/1 for international students; for spring admission, 1/1 for domestic students, 9/1 for international students. Applications are processed on a rolling basis. Application fee: $75. Electronic applications accepted. *Expenses:* Tuition, state resident: full-time $13,700; part-time $761.25 per credit hour. Tuition, nonresident: full-time $27,614; part-time $1534 per credit hour. *Required fees:* $886.50 per term. Tuition and fees vary according to campus/location and program. *Financial support:* In 2019–20, 4 fellowships with full and partial tuition reimbursements (averaging $17,088 per year), 153 research assistantships with full tuition reimbursements (averaging $23,076 per year), 27 teaching assistantships with full tuition reimbursements (averaging $19,900 per year) were awarded; scholarships/grants also available. Financial award application deadline: 3/1; financial award applicants required to submit FAFSA. *Unit head:* Dr. Karen P. DePauw, Vice President and Dean for Graduate Education, 540-231-7581, Fax: 540-231-1670, E-mail: kpdepauw@vt.edu. *Application contact:* Dr. Janice Austin, 540-231-6691, E-mail: grads@vt.edu.

Virginia State University, College of Graduate Studies, Program in Interdisciplinary Studies, Petersburg, VA 23806-0001. Offers MIS. *Degree requirements:* For master's, thesis optional.

Walden University, Graduate Programs, School of Nursing, Minneapolis, MN 55401. Offers adult-gerontology acute care nurse practitioner (MSN); adult-gerontology nurse practitioner (MSN); education (MSN); family nurse practitioner (MSN); informatics (MSN); leadership and management (MSN); nursing (PhD, Post-Master's Certificate), including education (PhD), healthcare administration (PhD), interdisciplinary health (PhD), leadership (PhD), nursing education (Post-Master's Certificate), nursing informatics (Post-Master's Certificate), nursing leadership and management (Post-Master's Certificate), public health policy (PhD); nursing practice (DNP); psychiatric mental health (MSN). *Accreditation:* AACN. *Program availability:* Part-time, evening/weekend, online only, 100% online. *Degree requirements:* For doctorate, thesis/dissertation (for some programs), residency (for some programs), field experience (for some programs). *Entrance requirements:* For master's, bachelor's degree or equivalent in related field or RN; minimum GPA of 2.5; official transcripts; goal statement (for some programs); access to computer and Internet; for doctorate, master's degree or higher; RN; three years of related professional or academic experience; goal statement; access to computer and Internet; for Post-Master's Certificate, relevant work experience; access to computer and Internet. Additional exam requirements/recommendations for international students: required—TOEFL (minimum score 550 paper-based, 79 iBT), IELTS (minimum score 6.5), Michigan English Language Assessment Battery (minimum score 82), or PTE (minimum score 53). Electronic applications accepted.

Washington State University, College of Agricultural, Human, and Natural Resource Sciences, Department of Human Development, Pullman, WA 99164-4852. Offers prevention science (PhD). *Program availability:* Part-time. *Degree requirements:* For doctorate, comprehensive exam, thesis/dissertation. *Entrance requirements:* For doctorate, GRE General Test, bachelor's or master's degree in prevention science related field (e.g., communication, educational psychology, human development, nursing, psychology, sociology); written statement specifying qualifications, educational goals, and career objectives; official copies of all college transcripts; three letters of reference. Additional exam requirements/recommendations for international students: required—TOEFL, IELTS. Electronic applications accepted.

Western Kentucky University, Graduate School, College of Education and Behavioral Sciences, School of Teacher Education, Bowling Green, KY 42101. Offers elementary education (MAE, Ed S); exceptional education: learning and behavioral disorders (MAE); instructional design (MS); interdisciplinary early childhood education (MAE); library media education (MS); literacy education (MAE); middle grades education (MAE); secondary education (MAE, Ed S); special education: moderate and severe disabilities (MAE). *Program availability:* Part-time, evening/weekend, online learning. *Degree requirements:* For master's, comprehensive exam. *Entrance requirements:* For master's, GRE General Test. Additional exam requirements/recommendations for international students: required—TOEFL (minimum score 555 paper-based; 79 iBT).

Western New Mexico University, Graduate Division, Interdisciplinary Studies, Silver City, NM 88062-0680. Offers MA. *Program availability:* Part-time, online learning. *Degree requirements:* For master's, comprehensive exam (for some programs), thesis optional. *Entrance requirements:* For master's, GRE General Test, GRE Subject Test, minimum GPA of 3.2 in last 64 hours of undergraduate study. Additional exam requirements/recommendations for international students: required—TOEFL (minimum score 550 paper-based).

West Texas A&M University, Program in Interdisciplinary Studies, Canyon, TX 79015. Offers MA, MS. *Program availability:* Part-time, evening/weekend. *Degree requirements:* For master's, comprehensive exam, thesis or alternative. *Entrance requirements:* Additional exam requirements/recommendations for international students: required—TOEFL. Electronic applications accepted.

Worcester Polytechnic Institute, Graduate Admissions, Department of Social Science and Policy Studies, Worcester, MA 01609-2280. Offers interdisciplinary social science (PhD); system dynamics (MS, Graduate Certificate). *Program availability:* Part-time, evening/weekend, 100% online. *Entrance requirements:* For master's and doctorate, GRE General Test, 3 letters of recommendation, statement of purpose. Additional exam requirements/recommendations for international students: required—TOEFL (minimum score 563 paper-based; 84 iBT), IELTS (minimum score 7). Electronic applications accepted.

Worcester Polytechnic Institute, Graduate Admissions, Programs in Interdisciplinary Studies, Worcester, MA 01609-2280. Offers bioscience administration (MS); nuclear science and engineering (Graduate Certificate); power systems management (MS); social science (PhD); system dynamics and innovation management (MS, Graduate Certificate); systems modeling (MS). *Program availability:* Part-time, evening/weekend, 100% online. Terminal master's awarded for partial completion of doctoral program. *Degree requirements:* For master's, thesis; for doctorate, comprehensive exam, thesis/dissertation. *Entrance requirements:* For master's and doctorate, 3 letters of recommendation. Additional exam requirements/recommendations for international students: required—TOEFL (minimum score 563 paper-based; 84 iBT), IELTS (minimum score 7). Electronic applications accepted.

York University, Faculty of Graduate Studies, Program in Interdisciplinary Studies, Toronto, ON M3J 1P3, Canada. Offers MA. *Program availability:* Part-time. *Degree requirements:* For master's, thesis or alternative. Electronic applications accepted.

ACADEMIC AND PROFESSIONAL PROGRAMS IN THE SOCIAL SCIENCES

Section 15
Area and Cultural Studies

This section contains a directory of institutions offering graduate work in area and cultural studies. Additional information about programs listed in the directory may be obtained by writing directly to the dean of a graduate school or chair of a department at the address given in the directory.

For programs offering related work, see also in this book *Geography, History, Language and Literature, Political Science and International Affairs,* and *Sociology, Anthropology, and Archaeology.*

CONTENTS

Program Directories

African-American Studies

Boston University, Graduate School of Arts and Sciences, Program in African American Studies, Boston, MA 02215. Offers MA. *Students:* 1 (woman) full-time; minority (Black or African American, non-Hispanic/Latino). Average age 23. 4 applicants, 75% accepted, 1 enrolled. *Degree requirements:* For master's, one foreign language, comprehensive exam, two major research papers. *Entrance requirements:* For master's, GRE General Test, 3 letters of recommendation, transcripts, personal statement, curriculum vitae, writing sample. Additional exam requirements/recommendations for international students: required—TOEFL (minimum score 550 paper-based; 84 iBT). *Application deadline:* For fall admission, 1/31 for domestic and international students. Application fee: $95. Electronic applications accepted. *Financial support:* In 2019–20, 1 student received support. Federal Work-Study and scholarships/grants available. Financial award application deadline: 1/31. *Unit head:* Louis Chude-Sokei, Director, 617-358-1420, Fax: 617-353-0455, E-mail: locs@bu.edu. *Application contact:* Deirdre James, Program Administrator, 617-358-1421, Fax: 617-353-0455, E-mail: dejames@bu.edu.
Website: http://www.bu.edu/afam/

Capital University, Trinity Lutheran Seminary, Columbus, OH 43209-2394. Offers African American studies (MTS); Biblical studies (MTS, STM); Christian education (MA); Christian spirituality (STM); church in the world (MTS); church music (MA); divinity (M Div); general theological studies (MTS); mission and evangelism (STM); pastoral leadership and practice (STM); youth and family ministry (MA); MSN/MTS; MTS/JD. *Accreditation:* ACIPE; ATS. *Program availability:* Part-time. *Degree requirements:* For master's, variable foreign language requirement, comprehensive exam (for some programs), thesis (for some programs), field experience (for some programs). *Entrance requirements:* For master's, BA or equivalent (for MA, M Div, MTS); M Div, MTS, or equivalent (for STM); audition (for MACM). Additional exam requirements/recommendations for international students: required—TOEFL. Electronic applications accepted. *Expenses:* Contact institution.

Carnegie Mellon University, Dietrich College of Humanities and Social Sciences, Department of History, Pittsburgh, PA 15213-3891. Offers African and African-American diaspora (PhD); culture and power (PhD); labor, politics and social movements (PhD); technology, environment, science and health (PhD); women, gender and the family (PhD). *Program availability:* Part-time. *Degree requirements:* For doctorate, oral and written comprehensive exams, dissertation defense. *Entrance requirements:* For doctorate, GRE General Test. Additional exam requirements/recommendations for international students: required—TOEFL. Electronic applications accepted.

Clark Atlanta University, School of Arts and Sciences, Department of African American Studies, Africana Women's Studies, and History, Atlanta, GA 30314. Offers MA, PhD. *Program availability:* Part-time. *Degree requirements:* For master's, one foreign language, comprehensive exam, thesis optional; for doctorate, one foreign language, comprehensive exam, thesis/dissertation. *Entrance requirements:* For master's, GRE General Test, minimum GPA of 2.5. Additional exam requirements/recommendations for international students: required—TOEFL (minimum score 500 paper-based; 61 iBT). Electronic applications accepted.

Columbia University, Graduate School of Arts and Sciences, New York, NY 10027. Offers African-American studies (MA); American studies (MA); anthropology (MA, PhD); art history and archaeology (MA, PhD); astronomy (PhD); biological sciences (PhD); biotechnology (MA); chemical physics (PhD); chemistry (PhD); classical studies (MA, PhD); classics (MA, PhD); climate and society (MA); conservation biology (MA); earth and environmental sciences (PhD); East Asia: regional studies (MA); East Asian languages and cultures (MA, PhD); ecology, evolution and environmental biology (MA), including conservation biology; ecology, evolution, and environmental biology (PhD), including ecology and evolutionary biology, evolutionary primatology; economics (MA, PhD); English and comparative literature (MA, PhD); French and Romance philology (MA, PhD); Germanic languages (MA, PhD); global French studies (MA); global thought (MA); Hispanic cultural studies (MA); history (PhD); history and literature (MA); human rights studies (MA); Islamic studies (MA); Italian (MA, PhD); Japanese pedagogy (MA); Jewish studies (MA); Latin America and the Caribbean: regional studies (MA); Latin American and Iberian cultures (PhD); mathematics (MA, PhD), including finance (MA); medieval and Renaissance studies (MA); Middle Eastern, South Asian, and African studies (MA, PhD); modern art: critical and curatorial studies (MA); modern European studies (MA); museum anthropology (MA); music (DMA, PhD); oral history (MA); philosophical foundations of physics (MA); philosophy (MA, PhD); physics (PhD); political science (MA, PhD); psychology (PhD); quantitative methods in the social sciences (MA); religion (MA, PhD); Russia, Eurasia and East Europe: regional studies (MA); Russian translation (MA); Slavic cultures (MA); Slavic languages (MA, PhD); sociology (MA, PhD); South Asian studies (MA); statistics (MA, PhD); theatre (PhD). *Program availability:* Part-time. *Students:* 3,506 full-time (1,844 women), 208 part-time (121 women); includes 864 minority (110 Black or African American, non-Hispanic/Latino; 5 American Indian or Alaska Native, non-Hispanic/Latino; 416 Asian, non-Hispanic/Latino; 147 Hispanic/Latino; 6 Native Hawaiian or other Pacific Islander, non-Hispanic/Latino; 180 Two or more races, non-Hispanic/Latino), 2,065 international. 14,545 applicants, 25% accepted, 1,429 enrolled. In 2019, 1,262 master's, 363 doctorates awarded. Terminal master's awarded for partial completion of doctoral program. *Degree requirements:* For master's, variable foreign language requirement, comprehensive exam (for some programs), thesis (for some programs); for doctorate, variable foreign language requirement, comprehensive exam (for some programs), thesis/dissertation. *Entrance requirements:* For master's and doctorate, GRE General Test, GRE Subject Test (for some programs). Additional exam requirements/recommendations for international students: required—TOEFL (minimum score 600 paper-based; 100 iBT), IELTS (minimum score 7.5). Application fee: $115. Electronic applications accepted. *Expenses: Tuition:* Full-time $47,600; part-time $1880 per credit. One-time fee: $105. *Financial support:* Fellowships, research assistantships, teaching assistantships, career-related internships or fieldwork, Federal Work-Study, institutionally sponsored loans, scholarships/grants, traineeships, health care benefits, tuition waivers, and unspecified assistantships available. Support available to part-time students. Financial award application deadline: 12/15. *Unit head:* Dr. Carlos J. Alonso, Dean of the Graduate School of Arts and Sciences and Vice President for Graduate Education, 212-854-2861, E-mail: gsas-dean@columbia.edu. *Application contact:* GSAS Office of Admissions, 212-854-6729, E-mail: gsas-admissions@columbia.edu.
Website: http://gsas.columbia.edu/

Cornell University, Graduate School, Graduate Fields of Arts and Sciences, Field of African and African-American Studies, Ithaca, NY 14853. Offers African studies (MPS); African-American studies (MPS); Africana studies (PhD). *Degree requirements:* For master's, thesis. *Entrance requirements:* For master's, GRE General Test (recommended), 3 letters of recommendation; for doctorate, GRE General Test (recommended), 3 letters of recommendation, personal statement, writing sample.

Additional exam requirements/recommendations for international students: required—TOEFL (minimum score 550 paper-based; 77 iBT). Electronic applications accepted.

Cornell University, Graduate School, Graduate Fields of Arts and Sciences, Field of English Language and Literature, Ithaca, NY 14853. Offers African-American literature (PhD); American literature after 1865 (PhD); American literature to 1865 (PhD); American studies (PhD); colonial and postcolonial literatures (PhD); creative writing (MFA); cultural studies (PhD); dramatic literature (PhD); English poetry (PhD); English Renaissance to 1660 (PhD); lesbian, bisexual, and gay literary studies (PhD); literary criticism and theory (PhD); Old and Middle English (PhD); prose fiction (PhD); Restoration and the eighteenth-century (PhD); the nineteenth century (PhD); the twentieth century (PhD); women's literature (PhD); MFA/PhD. Terminal master's awarded for partial completion of doctoral program. *Degree requirements:* For master's, one foreign language, thesis; for doctorate, one foreign language, comprehensive exam, thesis/dissertation, teaching experience. *Entrance requirements:* For master's, GRE General Test, 3 letters of recommendation, creative writing sample; for doctorate, 3 letters of recommendation, writing sample. Additional exam requirements/recommendations for international students: required—TOEFL (minimum score 600 paper-based; 77 iBT). Electronic applications accepted.

Eastern Michigan University, Graduate School, College of Arts and Sciences, Department of Africology and African-American Studies, Ypsilanti, MI 48197. Offers Graduate Certificate. *Faculty:* 1 (woman) full-time. *Students:* 2 full-time (0 women), 5 part-time (2 women); all minorities (5 Black or African American, non-Hispanic/Latino; 2 Hispanic/Latino). Average age 41. 8 applicants, 75% accepted, 3 enrolled. In 2019, 1 Graduate Certificate awarded. *Entrance requirements:* For degree, bachelor's degree with minimum GPA of 2.7, two letters of reference. *Application deadline:* Applications are processed on a rolling basis. Application fee: $45. *Unit head:* Dr. Victor Okafor, Department Head, 734-487-3460, Fax: 734-487-6891, E-mail: victor.okafor@emich.edu. *Application contact:* Dr. Victor Okafor, Department Head, 734-487-3460, Fax: 734-487-6891, E-mail: victor.okafor@emich.edu.
Website: http://www.emich.edu/aas/

Georgia State University, College of Arts and Sciences, Department of African-American Studies, Atlanta, GA 30302-3083. Offers MA. *Program availability:* Part-time. *Faculty:* 5 full-time (2 women). *Students:* 25 full-time (19 women), 8 part-time (4 women); all minorities (28 Black or African American, non-Hispanic/Latino; 5 Two or more races, non-Hispanic/Latino). Average age 33. 49 applicants, 41% accepted, 14 enrolled. In 2019, 6 master's awarded. *Entrance requirements:* For master's, GRE. Additional exam requirements/recommendations for international students: required—TOEFL (minimum score 550 paper-based; 80 iBT). *Application deadline:* For fall admission, 3/15 for domestic and international students. Application fee: $50. Electronic applications accepted. *Expenses: Tuition, area resident:* Full-time $7164; part-time $398 per credit hour. Tuition, state resident: full-time $7164; part-time $398 per credit hour. Tuition, nonresident: full-time $22,662; part-time $1259 per credit hour. *International tuition:* $22,662 full-time. *Required fees:* $2128; $312 per credit hour. Tuition and fees vary according to course load and program. *Financial support:* In 2019–20, research assistantships with tuition reimbursements (averaging $4,200 per year), teaching assistantships with tuition reimbursements (averaging $4,000 per year) were awarded; health care benefits and unspecified assistantships also available. Financial award applicants required to submit FAFSA. *Unit head:* Dr. Jonathan Gayles, Chair, Department of African-American Studies, 404-413-5142, Fax: 404-413-5140, E-mail: jgayles@gsu.edu. *Application contact:* Dr. Sarita Kaya Davis, Graduate Program Director, 404-413-5134, Fax: 404-413-5140, E-mail: saritadavis@gsu.edu.
Website: https://aas.gsu.edu/

Harvard University, Graduate School of Arts and Sciences, Department of African and African American Studies, Cambridge, MA 02138. Offers PhD.

Indiana University Bloomington, University Graduate School, College of Arts and Sciences, Department of African American and African Diaspora Studies, Bloomington, IN 47405-7000. Offers MA, PhD. *Entrance requirements:* For master's and doctorate, GRE, minimum GPA of 3.0. Additional exam requirements/recommendations for international students: required—TOEFL. Electronic applications accepted. *Expenses:* Contact institution.

Michigan State University, The Graduate School, College of Arts and Letters, Program in African American and African Studies, East Lansing, MI 48824. Offers MA, PhD. *Entrance requirements:* Additional exam requirements/recommendations for international students: required—TOEFL. Electronic applications accepted.

Morgan State University, School of Graduate Studies, James H. Gilliam Jr College of Liberal Arts, Department of History and Geography, Baltimore, MD 21251. Offers African-American studies (MA); history (MA, PhD); museum studies and historic preservation (MA). *Program availability:* Part-time, evening/weekend. *Faculty:* 20 full-time (5 women), 1 part-time/adjunct (0 women). *Students:* 37 full-time (24 women), 8 part-time (6 women); includes 41 minority (36 Black or African American, non-Hispanic/Latino; 5 Hispanic/Latino), 3 international. Average age 37. 13 applicants, 92% accepted, 4 enrolled. In 2019, 4 master's, 4 doctorates awarded. *Degree requirements:* For master's, comprehensive exam, thesis; for doctorate, comprehensive exam, thesis/dissertation. *Entrance requirements:* For master's, GRE, minimum GPA of 2.5; for doctorate, GRE or MAT, minimum GPA of 3.0. Additional exam requirements/recommendations for international students: required—TOEFL (minimum score 550 paper-based). *Application deadline:* For fall admission, 2/1 priority date for domestic students, 4/1 for international students; for spring admission, 11/15 for domestic students, 10/1 for international students. Applications are processed on a rolling basis. Application fee: $50 ($70 for international students). Electronic applications accepted. *Expenses:* Tuition, state resident: full-time $455; part-time $455 per credit hour. Tuition, nonresident: full-time $894; part-time $894 per credit hour. *Required fees:* $82; $82 per credit hour. *Financial support:* In 2019–20, 5 students received support. Fellowships with full and partial tuition reimbursements available, research assistantships with full and partial tuition reimbursements available, teaching assistantships with full and partial tuition reimbursements available, career-related internships or fieldwork, Federal Work-Study, scholarships/grants, tuition waivers (full and partial), and unspecified assistantships available. Support available to part-time students. Financial award application deadline: 2/1. *Unit head:* Dr. Jeremiah I. Dibua, Interim Chair of Department, 443-885-3190, Fax: 443-885-8227, E-mail: jeremiah.dibua@morgan.edu. *Application contact:* Dr. Jahmaine Smith, Director of Admissions, 443-885-3185, Fax: 443-885-8226, E-mail: gradapply@morgan.edu.
Website: https://morgan.edu/college_of_liberal_arts/departments/history_geography_and_museum_studies/graduate_program_handbook.html

North Carolina Agricultural and Technical State University, The Graduate College, College of Arts, Humanities, and Social Sciences, Department of English, Program in

English and African-American Literature, Greensboro, NC 27411. Offers MA. *Program availability:* Part-time, evening/weekend. *Degree requirements:* For master's, comprehensive exam, qualifying exam. *Entrance requirements:* For master's, GRE General Test, minimum GPA of 3.0.

Northwestern University, The Graduate School, Judd A. and Marjorie Weinberg College of Arts and Sciences, Department of African American Studies, Evanston, IL 60208. Offers PhD.

Oblate School of Theology, Graduate and Professional Programs, San Antonio, TX 78216-6693. Offers African-American pastoral leadership (D Min); divinity (M Div); pastoral leadership (D Min); pastoral ministry (MAP Min); pastoral studies (Certificate); spiritual formation in the local community (D Min); spirituality (MA Sp, PhD); spirituality and ministry (D Min); theology (MA Th); U.S. Hispanic/Latino ministry (D Min); M Div/MA Th. *Accreditation:* ACIPE; ATS (one or more programs are accredited). *Program availability:* Part-time, 100% online, blended/hybrid learning. *Faculty:* 21 full-time (5 women), 4 part-time/adjunct (0 women). *Students:* 89 full-time (9 women), 54 part-time (31 women); includes 77 minority (11 Black or African American, non-Hispanic/Latino; 8 Asian, non-Hispanic/Latino; 57 Hispanic/Latino; 1 Two or more races, non-Hispanic/Latino), 24 international. Average age 39. In 2019, 24 master's, 1 doctorate awarded. *Degree requirements:* For master's, comprehensive exam (for some programs), thesis (for some programs), practicum; for doctorate, one foreign language, comprehensive exam, thesis/dissertation, paper, practicum. *Entrance requirements:* For master's, MAT, interview, prerequisite course work in theology or religious studies and philosophy, minimum GPA of 2.5; for doctorate, D Min, M Div, MA Th, MA Sp, MA PM. Additional exam requirements/recommendations for international students: required—TOEFL (minimum score 71 iBT). *Application deadline:* For fall admission, 6/30 priority date for domestic and international students; for winter admission, 11/30 for domestic and international students; for spring admission, 11/30 for domestic and international students; for summer admission, 4/30 for domestic and international students. Applications are processed on a rolling basis. Application fee: $65. Electronic applications accepted. *Expenses:* Contact institution. *Financial support:* In 2019–20, 25 students received support. Scholarships/grants available. Support available to part-time students. Financial award application deadline: 8/15; financial award applicants required to submit FAFSA. *Unit head:* Dr. R. Scott Woodward, Academic Dean, 210-341-1366, Fax: 210-341-4519, E-mail: rsw@ost.edu. *Application contact:* Brenda Reyna, Registrar, 210-341-1366 Ext. 226, Fax: 210-341-4519, E-mail: registrar@ost.edu.

The Ohio State University, Graduate School, College of Arts and Sciences, Division of Arts and Humanities, Department of African-American and African Studies, Columbus, OH 43210. Offers MA, PhD. *Degree requirements:* For master's, comprehensive exam (for some programs), thesis (for some programs), thesis or comprehensive written examination; for doctorate, thesis/dissertation. *Entrance requirements:* For master's and doctorate, GRE General Test. Additional exam requirements/recommendations for international students: required—TOEFL (minimum score 550 paper-based; 79 iBT), Michigan English Language Assessment Battery (minimum score 82); recommended—IELTS (minimum score 7). Electronic applications accepted.

Rutgers University - New Brunswick, Graduate School-New Brunswick, Program in History, Piscataway, NJ 08854-8097. Offers African-American history (PhD); early American history (PhD); early modern European history (PhD); east Asian history (PhD); global and comparative history (PhD); history (PhD); history of diplomacy and foreign relations (PhD); history of technology, environment and health (PhD); history of the Atlantic cultures and African diaspora (PhD); Latin American history (PhD); medieval history (PhD); modern European history (PhD); nineteenth and twentieth century American history (PhD); women's and gender history (PhD). *Degree requirements:* For doctorate, thesis/dissertation. *Entrance requirements:* For doctorate, GRE General Test, sample of written work. Electronic applications accepted.

Syracuse University, College of Arts and Sciences, MA Program in Pan-African Studies, Syracuse, NY 13244. Offers MA. *Entrance requirements:* For master's, GRE General Test (recommended), personal statement, resume, three letters of recommendation, writing sample (10-12 pages), transcripts. Additional exam requirements/recommendations for international students: required—TOEFL (minimum score 600 paper-based; 100 iBT). Electronic applications accepted.

Temple University, College of Liberal Arts, Department of Africology and African American Studies, Philadelphia, PA 19122-6096. Offers MA, PhD. *Program availability:* Part-time. *Faculty:* 6 full-time (2 women), 3 part-time/adjunct (1 woman). *Students:* 30 full-time (16 women), 11 part-time (5 women); includes 36 minority (34 Black or African American, non-Hispanic/Latino; 1 Hispanic/Latino; 1 Two or more races, non-Hispanic/Latino), 2 international. 32 applicants, 47% accepted, 10 enrolled. In 2019, 4 master's, 1 doctorate awarded. *Degree requirements:* For master's, comprehensive exam, thesis optional; for doctorate, one foreign language, thesis/dissertation. *Entrance requirements:* For master's, GRE, bachelor's degree in related discipline, statement of goals, 3 letters of recommendation, writing sample; for doctorate, GRE, bachelor's and master's degree in discipline/related discipline, statement of goals, writing sample, 3 letters of recommendation. Additional exam requirements/recommendations for international students: required—TOEFL, IELTS, PTE, one of three is required. *Application deadline:* For fall admission, 1/15 for domestic students. Application fee: $60. Electronic applications accepted. *Financial support:* Fellowships, teaching assistantships, Federal Work-Study, and health care benefits available. Financial award application deadline: 1/15; financial award applicants required to submit FAFSA. *Unit head:* Dr. Ama Mazama, Graduate Director, 215-204-1992, Fax: 215-204-5953, E-mail: afam@temple.edu. *Application contact:* Tammey Abner, Graduate Coordinator, 215-204-8491, Fax: 215-204-5953, E-mail: tammy.abner@temple.edu.
Website: https://www.cla.temple.edu/africology-and-african-american-studies/

University at Albany, State University of New York, College of Arts and Sciences, Department of Africana Studies, Albany, NY 12222-0001. Offers African studies (MA); Afro-American studies (MA). *Program availability:* Part-time, evening/weekend, blended/hybrid learning. *Faculty:* 6 full-time (3 women), 6 part-time/adjunct (2 women). *Students:* 8 full-time (all women), 5 part-time (4 women); includes 11 minority (7 Black or African American, non-Hispanic/Latino; 2 Hispanic/Latino; 2 Two or more races, non-Hispanic/Latino), 1 international. 8 applicants, 100% accepted, 4 enrolled. In 2019, 6 master's awarded. *Entrance requirements:* For master's, transcripts of all schools attended, statement of background and goals, departmental questionnaire, resume, names and contact information for 3 recommenders. Additional exam requirements/recommendations for international students: required—TOEFL (minimum score 550 paper-based). *Application deadline:* For fall admission, 1/15 for domestic students, 5/15 for international students; for spring admission, 11/15 for domestic and international students. Application fee: $75. Electronic applications accepted. *Expenses: Tuition, area resident:* Full-time $11,530; part-time $480 per credit hour. Tuition, nonresident: full-time $23,530; part-time $980 per credit hour. *International tuition:* $23,530 full-time. *Required fees:* $2185; $96 per credit hour. Part-time tuition and fees vary according to course load and program. *Financial support:* Fellowships, teaching assistantships, and Federal Work-Study available. Financial award application deadline: 5/1. *Unit head:* Oscar Williams, Chair, 518-442-4730, Fax: 518-442-2569, E-mail: owilliams@albany.edu. *Application contact:* Michael DeRensis, Director, Graduate Admissions, 518-442-3980, Fax: 518-442-3922, E-mail: graduate@albany.edu.
Website: http://www.albany.edu/africana/

University of California, Berkeley, Graduate Division, College of Letters and Science, Department of African American Studies, Berkeley, CA 94720. Offers PhD. *Degree requirements:* For doctorate, one foreign language, thesis/dissertation. *Entrance requirements:* For doctorate, minimum GPA of 3.0, 3 letters of recommendation. Additional exam requirements/recommendations for international students: required—TOEFL (minimum score 570 paper-based, 90 iBT) or IELTS (minimum score 7). Electronic applications accepted.

University of California, Los Angeles, Graduate Division, College of Letters and Science, Interdepartmental Program in Afro-American Studies, Los Angeles, CA 90095. Offers MA, MA/JD. *Degree requirements:* For master's, one foreign language, comprehensive exam or thesis. *Entrance requirements:* For master's, GRE General Test, bachelor's degree; minimum undergraduate GPA of 3.0 (or its equivalent if letter grade system not used); writing sample. Additional exam requirements/recommendations for international students: required—TOEFL. Electronic applications accepted.

University of California, Santa Barbara, Graduate Division, College of Letters and Sciences, Division of Social Sciences, Department of Sociology, Santa Barbara, CA 93106-9430. Offers interdisciplinary emphasis: Black studies (PhD); interdisciplinary emphasis: environment and society (PhD); interdisciplinary emphasis: feminist studies (PhD); interdisciplinary emphasis: global studies (PhD); interdisciplinary emphasis: language, interaction and social organization (PhD); interdisciplinary emphasis: quantitative methods in the social sciences (PhD); interdisciplinary emphasis: technology and society (PhD); sociology (PhD); MA/PhD. Terminal master's awarded for partial completion of doctoral program. *Degree requirements:* For doctorate, comprehensive exam, thesis/dissertation. *Entrance requirements:* For doctorate, GRE General Test. Additional exam requirements/recommendations for international students: required—TOEFL (minimum score 550 paper-based; 80 iBT), IELTS (minimum score 7). Electronic applications accepted.

The University of Kansas, Graduate Studies, College of Liberal Arts and Sciences, Department of African and African-American Studies, Lawrence, KS 66045. Offers African and African-American studies (MA); African studies (Graduate Certificate). *Program availability:* Part-time. *Students:* 7 full-time (4 women), 2 part-time (1 woman); includes 7 minority (5 Black or African American, non-Hispanic/Latino; 2 Two or more races, non-Hispanic/Latino). Average age 31. 3 applicants, 100% accepted, 2 enrolled. In 2019, 2 master's, 2 other advanced degrees awarded. *Entrance requirements:* For master's, GRE, all academic transcripts, 3 letters of recommendation, personal statement of purpose, writing sample. Additional exam requirements/recommendations for international students: required—TOEFL, IELTS. *Application deadline:* For fall admission, 5/1 for domestic and international students; for spring admission, 10/1 for domestic and international students. Application fee: $65 ($85 for international students). Electronic applications accepted. *Expenses:* Tuition, state resident: full-time $9989. Tuition, nonresident: full-time $23,950. *International tuition:* $23,950 full-time. *Required fees:* $984; $81.99 per credit hour. Tuition and fees vary according to course load, campus/location and program. *Financial support:* Application deadline: 4/15. *Unit head:* Dr. Cecile Accilien, Chairperson, 785-864-1853, E-mail: cecileaccilien@ku.edu. *Application contact:* Bethany Harris, Director of Graduate Studies, 785-864-0778, E-mail: bethanyharris@ku.edu.
Website: http://www.afs.ku.edu

University of Louisville, Graduate School, College of Arts and Sciences, Department of Pan-African Studies, Louisville, KY 40292. Offers African and Diaspora studies (MA); African-American studies (MA); MSSW/MA. *Program availability:* Part-time. *Faculty:* 7 full-time (2 women), 9 part-time/adjunct (6 women). *Students:* 14 full-time (10 women), 3 part-time (2 women); includes 15 minority (12 Black or African American, non-Hispanic/Latino; 3 Two or more races, non-Hispanic/Latino). Average age 34. 16 applicants, 63% accepted, 3 enrolled. In 2019, 2 master's awarded. *Degree requirements:* For master's, comprehensive exam, thesis optional. *Entrance requirements:* For master's, GRE General Test, Two letters of reference, official transcripts. Additional exam requirements/recommendations for international students: required—TOEFL (minimum score 550 paper-based; 79 iBT), IELTS can be used in place of the TOEFL; recommended—IELTS (minimum score 6.5). *Application deadline:* For fall admission, 3/15 priority date for domestic students, 5/1 priority date for international students; for spring admission, 10/15 for domestic students, 11/1 for international students. Applications are processed on a rolling basis. Application fee: $65. Electronic applications accepted. *Expenses: Tuition, area resident:* Full-time $13,000; part-time $723 per credit hour. Tuition, state resident: full-time $13,000; part-time $723 per credit hour. Tuition, nonresident: full-time $27,114; part-time $1507 per credit hour. *International tuition:* $27,114 full-time. *Required fees:* $196. Tuition and fees vary according to program and reciprocity agreements. *Financial support:* In 2019–20, 7 students received support, including 7 teaching assistantships with full tuition reimbursements available (averaging $16,300 per year); fellowships, research assistantships, health care benefits, and unspecified assistantships also available. Financial award application deadline: 3/3; financial award applicants required to submit FAFSA. *Unit head:* Dr. Ricky L. Jones, Chair, 502-852-0027, E-mail: ricky.jones@louisville.edu. *Application contact:* W.S. Tkweme, Director of Graduate Studies, 502-852-5386, E-mail: ws.tkweme@louisville.edu.
Website: http://www.louisville.edu/panafricanstudies

University of Massachusetts Amherst, Graduate School, College of Humanities and Fine Arts, Department of Afro-American Studies, Amherst, MA 01003. Offers MA, PhD. *Program availability:* Part-time. Terminal master's awarded for partial completion of doctoral program. *Degree requirements:* For master's, thesis or alternative; for doctorate, comprehensive exam, thesis/dissertation. *Entrance requirements:* For master's and doctorate, writing sample, 3 letters of recommendation. Additional exam requirements/recommendations for international students: required—TOEFL (minimum score 550 paper-based; 80 iBT), IELTS (minimum score 6.5). Electronic applications accepted.

University of Memphis, Graduate School, College of Arts and Sciences, Department of English, Memphis, TN 38152. Offers African-American literature (Graduate Certificate); applied linguistics (PhD); composition studies (PhD); creative writing (MFA); English as a second language (MA); linguistics (MA); literary and cultural studies (PhD), including African-American literature; literature (MA); professional writing (MA, PhD); teaching English as a second/foreign language (Graduate Certificate). *Program availability:* Part-time, evening/weekend, 100% online. *Students:* 58 full-time (33 women), 76 part-time (52 women); includes 34 minority (24 Black or African American, non-Hispanic/Latino; 4 Asian, non-Hispanic/Latino; 5 Hispanic/Latino; 1 Two or more races, non-Hispanic/Latino), 16 international. Average age 36. 52 applicants, 92% accepted, 23 enrolled. In 2019, 19 master's, 15 doctorates, 8 other advanced degrees awarded. Terminal master's awarded for partial completion of doctoral program. *Degree requirements:* For master's, variable foreign language requirement, comprehensive exam, thesis optional; for doctorate, variable foreign language requirement, comprehensive exam, thesis/dissertation, qualifying exam. *Entrance requirements:* For master's, GRE, minimum undergraduate GPA of 3.0, statement of purpose, two letters of recommendation; for

doctorate, GRE, minimum undergraduate and graduate GPA of 3.25, statement of purpose, writing sample, three letters of recommendation. Additional exam requirements/recommendations for international students: required—TOEFL. *Application deadline:* For fall admission, 1/15 for domestic students; for spring admission, 10/15 for domestic students. Applications are processed on a rolling basis. Application fee: $35 ($60 for international students). Electronic applications accepted. *Expenses: Tuition, area resident:* Full-time $9216; part-time $512 per credit hour. Tuition, state resident: full-time $9216; part-time $512 per credit hour. Tuition, nonresident: full-time $12,672; part-time $704 per credit hour. *International tuition:* $16,128 full-time. *Required fees:* $1530; $85 per credit hour. Tuition and fees vary according to program. *Financial support:* Research assistantships with full tuition reimbursements, teaching assistantships with full tuition reimbursements, Federal Work-Study, scholarships/grants, and unspecified assistantships available. Financial award application deadline: 2/1; financial award applicants required to submit FAFSA. *Unit head:* Dr. Joshua Phillips, Chair, 901-678-2651, Fax: 901-678-2226, E-mail: jsphllps@memphis.edu. *Application contact:* Dr. Jeffrey Scraba, Director of Graduate Studies, 901-678-4768, Fax: 901-678-2226, E-mail: jscraba@memphis.edu.
Website: http://www.memphis.edu/english

University of Wisconsin–Madison, Graduate School, College of Letters and Science, Department of Afro-American Studies, Madison, WI 53706-1380. Offers MA. *Degree requirements:* For master's, thesis or alternative. *Entrance requirements:* For master's, bachelor's degree in related field, minimum GPA of 3.0. Additional exam requirements/recommendations for international students: required—TOEFL. Electronic applications accepted.

Wayne State University, College of Liberal Arts and Sciences, Tracy Neumann, Detroit, MI 48202. Offers history (MA, PhD); public history (MA), including African American history and culture, cultural resource management, gender, sexuality, and women's studies, labor and urban history, museum studies, public policy; world history (Graduate Certificate); JD/MA; M Ed/MA; MLIS/MA. *Program availability:* Evening/weekend. *Faculty:* 23 full-time (11 women). *Students:* 18 full-time (7 women), 16 part-time (7 women); includes 4 minority (2 Black or African American, non-Hispanic/Latino; 2 Two or more races, non-Hispanic/Latino). Average age 37. 38 applicants, 34% accepted, 13 enrolled. In 2019, 7 master's, 3 doctorates awarded. *Degree requirements:* For master's, thesis (for some programs), final oral exam on thesis or essay and seminar; internship and project (for public history); for doctorate, variable foreign language requirement, comprehensive exam, thesis/dissertation, qualifying exam in 4 fields of history. *Entrance requirements:* For master's, GRE General Test, minimum undergraduate GPA of 3.25 in history, 3.0 overall; at least 18 credits in history and related subjects at the advanced undergraduate level; foreign language; letter of intent; research paper; at least two letters of recommendation from former instructors; for doctorate, GRE General Test, minimum GPA of 3.0, 3.25 in minimum of 18 semester credits in history and related subjects; letter of intent; research paper; at least three letters of recommendation from former professors; for Graduate Certificate, baccalaureate degree from accredited college or university; minimum GPA of 3.0, 3.25 in a minimum of eighteen semester credits in history and related subjects at the advanced undergraduate level. Additional exam requirements/recommendations for international students: required—TOEFL (minimum score 550 paper-based; 79 iBT), TWE (minimum score 5.5), Michigan English Language Assessment Battery (minimum score 85); recommended—IELTS (minimum score 6.5). *Application deadline:* For fall admission, 1/15 priority date for domestic and international students; for winter admission, 4/15 for domestic students, 4/15 priority date for international students; for spring admission, 10/15 for domestic students, 10/15 priority date for international students. Application fee: $50. Electronic applications accepted. *Expenses: Tuition:* Full-time $34,567. *Financial support:* In 2019–20, 18 students received support, including 2 fellowships with tuition reimbursements available (averaging $20,797 per year), 2 research assistantships with tuition reimbursements available (averaging $23,960 per year), 7 teaching assistantships with tuition reimbursements available (averaging $19,967 per year); scholarships/grants, health care benefits, and unspecified assistantships also available. Financial award applicants required to submit FAFSA. *Unit head:* Dr. Elizabeth V. Faue, Professor/Chair, 313-577-2525, E-mail: evfaue@wayne.edu. *Application contact:* Dr. Tracy Neumann, Associate Professor and Director of Graduate Studies, 313-577-2525, E-mail: tracyneumann@wayne.edu.
Website: http://clas.wayne.edu/history/

Yale University, Graduate School of Arts and Sciences, Interdisciplinary Program in African-American Studies, New Haven, CT 06520. Offers PhD. *Entrance requirements:* For doctorate, GRE General Test.

African Studies

Arizona State University at Tempe, College of Liberal Arts and Sciences, School of Social Transformation, Tempe, AZ 85287-4902. Offers African studies (Graduate Certificate); gender studies (PhD, Graduate Certificate); justice studies (MS, PhD); social and cultural pedagogy (MA); socio-economic justice (Graduate Certificate); PhD/JD. *Program availability:* Part-time. Terminal master's awarded for partial completion of doctoral program. *Degree requirements:* For master's, thesis or alternative, interactive Program of Study (iPOS) submitted before completing 50 percent of required credit hours; for doctorate, comprehensive exam, thesis/dissertation, interactive Program of Study (iPOS) submitted before completing 50 percent of required credit hours. *Entrance requirements:* For master's, GRE or LSAT, minimum GPA of 3.0 or equivalent in last 2 years of work leading to bachelor's degree; for doctorate, GRE or LSAT (for justice studies program), minimum GPA of 3.0 or equivalent in last 2 years of work leading to bachelor's degree. Additional exam requirements/recommendations for international students: required—TOEFL, IELTS, or PTE. Electronic applications accepted.

California State University, Long Beach, Graduate Studies, College of Liberal Arts, Department of History, Long Beach, CA 90840. Offers Africa and the Middle East (MA). *Program availability:* Part-time, evening/weekend. *Degree requirements:* For master's, one foreign language, comprehensive exam or thesis. Electronic applications accepted.

Carnegie Mellon University, Dietrich College of Humanities and Social Sciences, Department of History, Pittsburgh, PA 15213-3891. Offers African and African-American diaspora (PhD); culture and power (PhD); labor, politics and social movements (PhD); technology, environment, science and health (PhD); women, gender and the family (PhD). *Program availability:* Part-time. *Degree requirements:* For doctorate, oral and written comprehensive exams, dissertation defense. *Entrance requirements:* For doctorate, GRE General Test. Additional exam requirements/recommendations for international students: required—TOEFL. Electronic applications accepted.

Claremont Graduate University, Graduate Programs, School of Arts and Humanities, Department of History, Claremont, CA 91711-6160. Offers Africana history (Certificate); American studies and U.S. history (MA, PhD); archival studies (MA); early modern studies (MA, PhD); European studies (MA, PhD); oral history (MA, PhD); MBA/MA; MBA/PhD. Terminal master's awarded for partial completion of doctoral program. *Entrance requirements:* For master's and doctorate, GRE General Test. Additional exam requirements/recommendations for international students: required—TOEFL (minimum score 75 iBT). Electronic applications accepted.

Claremont Graduate University, Graduate Programs, School of Educational Studies, Claremont, CA 91711-6160. Offers Africana education (Certificate); education and policy (MA, PhD); higher education/student affairs (MA, PhD); human development (MA, PhD); public school administration (MA, PhD); quantitative evaluation (MA, PhD); special education (MA, PhD); teacher education (MA); teaching and learning (MA, PhD); urban leadership (PhD); MBA/PhD. *Program availability:* Part-time. Terminal master's awarded for partial completion of doctoral program. *Entrance requirements:* For master's and doctorate, GRE General Test. Additional exam requirements/recommendations for international students: required—TOEFL (minimum score 75 iBT). Electronic applications accepted.

College of Staten Island of the City University of New York, Graduate Programs, Division of Humanities and Social Sciences, Program in History, Staten Island, NY 10314-6600. Offers history (MA), including Africa and the Middle East, Asia, Europe, Latin America and the Caribbean, United States. *Program availability:* Part-time, evening/weekend. *Faculty:* 5. *Students:* 17. 12 applicants, 67% accepted, 8 enrolled. In 2019, 1 master's awarded. *Degree requirements:* For master's, comprehensive exam (for some programs), thesis or alternative, the MA in History requires 32 graduate credits at the 700-level, with all graduate courses designated at four credits, for a total of eight courses. Students must take at least one course in each of four of the program's five areas of concentration, rigorous thesis option or portfolio option. *Entrance requirements:* For master's, bachelor's degree with minimum GPA of 3.0 overall and in undergraduate history courses, two letters of recommendation, letter of interest, research-based writing sample. Additional exam requirements/recommendations for international students: required—TOEFL (minimum score 550 paper-based; 79 iBT), IELTS (minimum score 6.5). *Application deadline:* For fall admission, 5/10 priority date for domestic students, 4/25 for international students; for spring admission, 12/2 priority date for domestic students, 11/23 for international students. Applications are processed on a rolling basis. Application fee: $75. Electronic applications accepted. *Expenses: Tuition, area resident:* Full-time $11,090; part-time $470 per credit. Tuition, state resident: full-time $11,090; part-time $470 per credit. Tuition, nonresident: full-time $20,520; part-time $855 per credit. *International tuition:* $20,520 full-time. *Required fees:* $559; $181 per semester. Tuition and fees vary according to program. *Unit head:* Susan Smith-Peter, Graduate Program Coordinator, 718-982-3290, E-mail: susan.smithpeter@csi.cuny.edu. *Application contact:* Sasha Spence, Associate Director for Graduate Admissions, 718-982-2019, Fax: 718-982-2500, E-mail: sasha.spence@csi.cuny.edu.
Website: https://www.csi.cuny.edu/academics-and-research/departments-programs/history/master-arts-history

Columbia University, Graduate School of Arts and Sciences, New York, NY 10027. Offers African-American studies (MA); American studies (MA); anthropology (MA, PhD); art history and archaeology (MA, PhD); astronomy (PhD); biological sciences (PhD); biotechnology (MA); chemical physics (PhD); chemistry (PhD); classical studies (MA, PhD); classics (MA, PhD); climate and society (MA); conservation biology (MA); earth and environmental sciences (PhD); East Asia: regional studies (MA); East Asian languages and cultures (MA, PhD); ecology, evolution and environmental biology (MA), including conservation biology; ecology, evolution, and environmental biology (PhD), including ecology and evolutionary biology, evolutionary primatology; economics (MA, PhD); English and comparative literature (MA, PhD); French and Romance philology (MA, PhD); Germanic languages (MA, PhD); global French studies (MA); global thought (MA); Hispanic cultural studies (MA); history (PhD); history and literature (MA); human rights studies (MA); Islamic studies (MA); Italian (MA, PhD); Japanese pedagogy (MA); Jewish studies (MA); Latin America and the Caribbean: regional studies (MA); Latin American and Iberian cultures (PhD); mathematics (MA, PhD), including finance (MA); medieval and Renaissance studies (MA); Middle Eastern, South Asian, and African studies (MA, PhD); modern art: critical and curatorial studies (MA); modern European studies (MA); museum anthropology (MA); music (DMA, PhD); oral history (MA); philosophical foundations of physics (MA); philosophy (MA, PhD); physics (PhD); political science (MA, PhD); psychology (PhD); quantitative methods in the social sciences (MA); religion (MA, PhD); Russia, Eurasia and East Europe: regional studies (MA); Russian translation (MA); Slavic cultures (MA); Slavic languages (MA, PhD); sociology (MA, PhD); South Asian studies (MA); statistics (MA, PhD); theatre (PhD). *Program availability:* Part-time. *Students:* 3,506 full-time (1,844 women), 208 part-time (121 women); includes 864 minority (110 Black or African American, non-Hispanic/Latino; 5 American Indian or Alaska Native, non-Hispanic/Latino; 416 Asian, non-Hispanic/Latino; 147 Hispanic/Latino; 6 Native Hawaiian or other Pacific Islander, non-Hispanic/Latino; 180 Two or more races, non-Hispanic/Latino), 2,065 international. 14,545 applicants, 25% accepted, 1,429 enrolled. In 2019, 1,262 master's, 363 doctorates awarded. Terminal master's awarded for partial completion of doctoral program. *Degree requirements:* For master's, variable foreign language requirement, comprehensive exam (for some programs), thesis (for some programs); for doctorate, variable foreign language requirement, comprehensive exam (for some programs), thesis/dissertation. *Entrance requirements:* For master's and doctorate, GRE General Test, GRE Subject Test (for some programs). Additional exam requirements/recommendations for international students: required—TOEFL (minimum score 600 paper-based; 100 iBT), IELTS (minimum score 7.5). Application fee: $115. Electronic applications accepted. *Expenses: Tuition:* Full-time $47,600; part-time $1880 per credit. One-time fee: $105. *Financial support:* Fellowships, research assistantships, teaching assistantships, career-related internships or fieldwork, Federal Work-Study, institutionally sponsored loans, scholarships/grants, traineeships, health care benefits, tuition waivers, and unspecified assistantships available. Support available to part-time students. Financial award application deadline: 12/15. *Unit head:* Dr. Carlos J. Alonso, Dean of the Graduate School of Arts and Sciences and Vice President for Graduate Education, 212-854-2861, E-mail: gsas-dean@columbia.edu. *Application contact:* GSAS Office of Admissions, 212-854-6729, E-mail: gsas-admissions@columbia.edu.
Website: http://gsas.columbia.edu/

Cornell University, Graduate School, Graduate Fields of Arts and Sciences, Field of African and African-American Studies, Ithaca, NY 14853. Offers African studies (MPS); African-American studies (MPS); Africana studies (PhD). *Degree requirements:* For master's, thesis. *Entrance requirements:* For master's, GRE General Test (recommended), 3 letters of recommendation; for doctorate, GRE General Test (recommended), 3 letters of recommendation, personal statement, writing sample. Additional exam requirements/recommendations for international students: required—TOEFL (minimum score 550 paper-based; 77 iBT). Electronic applications accepted.

Cornell University, Graduate School, Graduate Fields of Arts and Sciences, Field of History, Ithaca, NY 14853. Offers African history (MA, PhD); American history (MA, PhD); ancient Greek history (PhD); ancient history (MA, PhD); ancient Roman history (PhD); early modern European history (MA, PhD); English history (MA, PhD); French history (MA, PhD); German history (MA, PhD); history of science (MA, PhD); Korean history (PhD); Latin American history (MA, PhD); medieval Chinese history (MA, PhD); medieval history (MA, PhD); modern Chinese history (MA, PhD); modern European history (MA, PhD); modern Japanese history (MA, PhD); modern Middle Eastern history (PhD); premodern Islamic history (MA, PhD); premodern Japanese history (MA, PhD); Renaissance history (MA, PhD); Russian history (MA, PhD); South Asian history (PhD); Southeast Asian history (MA, PhD). Terminal master's awarded for partial completion of doctoral program. *Degree requirements:* For master's, thesis; for doctorate, 2 foreign languages, comprehensive exam, thesis/dissertation, 1 year of teaching experience. *Entrance requirements:* For master's and doctorate, GRE General Test, writing sample, 3 letters of recommendation. Additional exam requirements/recommendations for international students: required—TOEFL (minimum score 550 paper-based; 77 iBT). Electronic applications accepted.

Florida International University, Steven J. Green School of International and Public Affairs, Program in African and African Diaspora Studies, Miami, FL 33199. Offers MA, MA/PhD. *Program availability:* Part-time, evening/weekend. *Faculty:* 3 part-time/adjunct (all women). *Students:* 4 full-time (2 women), 1 part-time (0 women); includes 4 minority (all Black or African American, non-Hispanic/Latino), 1 international. Average age 34. 14 applicants, 43% accepted, 5 enrolled. In 2019, 6 master's awarded. Terminal master's awarded for partial completion of doctoral program. *Degree requirements:* For master's, one foreign language, thesis optional, minimum GPA of 3.0. *Entrance requirements:* For master's, GRE General Test, BA with minimum GPA of 3.0, 2 letters of recommendation, examples of written work. Additional exam requirements/recommendations for international students: required—TOEFL (minimum score 80 iBT). *Application deadline:* For fall admission, 2/1 for domestic and international students; for spring admission, 10/1 for domestic students, 9/1 for international students. Application fee: $30. Electronic applications accepted. *Expenses: Tuition, area resident:* Full-time $8912; part-time $446 per credit hour. Tuition, state resident: full-time $8912; part-time $446 per credit hour. Tuition, nonresident: full-time $21,393; part-time $992 per credit hour. *Required fees:* $2194. *Financial support:* Institutionally sponsored loans, scholarships/grants, and unspecified assistantships available. Financial award application deadline: 3/1; financial award applicants required to submit FAFSA. *Unit head:* Dr. Percy Hintzen, Director, 305-348-2247, Fax: 305-348-3270, E-mail: percy.hintzen@fiu.edu. *Application contact:* Nanett Rojas, Manager, Admissions Operations, 305-348-7464, Fax: 305-348-7441, E-mail: gradadm@fiu.edu.

Harvard University, Graduate School of Arts and Sciences, Department of African and African American Studies, Cambridge, MA 02138. Offers PhD.

Howard University, Graduate School, Department of African Studies, Washington, DC 20059-0002. Offers MA, PhD. *Program availability:* Part-time. *Degree requirements:* For master's, one foreign language, comprehensive exam, thesis, internship; for doctorate, 2 foreign languages, comprehensive exam, thesis/dissertation, field research for some. *Entrance requirements:* For master's, GRE General Test, minimum GPA of 3.0; for doctorate, GRE General Test, minimum GPA of 3.5. Electronic applications accepted.

Indiana University Bloomington, University Graduate School, College of Arts and Sciences, School of Global and International Studies, African Studies Program, Bloomington, IN 47408. Offers MA. *Entrance requirements:* Additional exam requirements/recommendations for international students: required—TOEFL. Electronic applications accepted.

Michigan State University, The Graduate School, College of Arts and Letters, Program in African American and African Studies, East Lansing, MI 48824. Offers MA, PhD. *Entrance requirements:* Additional exam requirements/recommendations for international students: required—TOEFL. Electronic applications accepted.

New York University, Graduate School of Arts and Science, Department of History, New York, NY 10012-1019. Offers African diaspora (PhD); African history (PhD); archival management (Advanced Certificate); Atlantic history (PhD); French studies/history (PhD); Hebrew and Judaic studies/history (PhD); history (MA, PhD), including Europe (PhD), Latin America and the Caribbean (PhD), United States (PhD), women's history (MA); Middle Eastern history (MA); Middle Eastern studies/history (PhD); public history (Advanced Certificate); world history (MA); JD/MA; MA/Advanced Certificate. *Program availability:* Part-time. Terminal master's awarded for partial completion of doctoral program. *Degree requirements:* For master's, seminar paper; for doctorate, one foreign language, thesis/dissertation, oral and written exams; for Advanced Certificate, internship. *Entrance requirements:* For master's, GRE General Test, minimum GPA of 3.0, writing sample; for doctorate, GRE. Additional exam requirements/recommendations for international students: required—TOEFL.

New York University, Graduate School of Arts and Science, Program in Africana Studies, New York, NY 10012-1019. Offers MA. *Entrance requirements:* For master's, GRE, sample of written work. Additional exam requirements/recommendations for international students: required—TOEFL, IELTS.

Northwestern University, The Graduate School, Judd A. and Marjorie Weinberg College of Arts and Sciences, Program of African Studies, Evanston, IL 60208. Offers Graduate Certificate. *Degree requirements:* For Graduate Certificate, one foreign language.

The Ohio State University, Graduate School, College of Arts and Sciences, Division of Arts and Humanities, Department of African-American and African Studies, Columbus, OH 43210. Offers MA, PhD. *Degree requirements:* For master's, comprehensive exam (for some programs), thesis (for some programs), thesis or comprehensive written examination; for doctorate, thesis/dissertation. *Entrance requirements:* For master's and doctorate, GRE General Test. Additional exam requirements/recommendations for international students: required—TOEFL (minimum score 550 paper-based; 79 iBT), Michigan English Language Assessment Battery (minimum score 82); recommended—IELTS (minimum score 7). Electronic applications accepted.

Ohio University, Graduate College, Center for International Studies, Program in African Studies, Athens, OH 45701. Offers MA. *Program availability:* Part-time. *Degree requirements:* For master's, one foreign language, thesis optional. *Entrance requirements:* For master's, minimum GPA of 3.0. Additional exam requirements/recommendations for international students: required—TOEFL (minimum score 550 paper-based; 80 iBT), IELTS (minimum score 6.5).

Rice University, Graduate Programs, School of Humanities, Department of Religious Studies, Houston, TX 77251-1892. Offers African religions (PhD); African-American religions (PhD); contemplative studies (PhD); ghosticism, esotericism, mysticism (PhD); Islam (PhD); Jewish thought and philosophy (PhD); modern Christianity in thought and popular culture (PhD); psychology of religion (PhD); the Bible and beyond (PhD). *Degree requirements:* For doctorate, 2 foreign languages, comprehensive exam, thesis/dissertation. *Entrance requirements:* For doctorate, GRE, letters of recommendation, writing sample. Additional exam requirements/recommendations for international students: required—TOEFL (minimum score 600 paper-based; 90 iBT). Electronic applications accepted.

Rutgers University - New Brunswick, Graduate School-New Brunswick, Program in History, Piscataway, NJ 08854-8097. Offers African-American history (PhD); early American history (PhD); early modern European history (PhD); east Asian history (PhD); global and comparative history (PhD); history (PhD); history of diplomacy and foreign relations (PhD); history of technology, environment and health (PhD); history of the Atlantic cultures and African diaspora (PhD); Latin American history (PhD); medieval history (PhD); modern European history (PhD); nineteenth and twentieth century American history (PhD); women's and gender history (PhD). *Degree requirements:* For doctorate, thesis/dissertation. *Entrance requirements:* For doctorate, GRE General Test, sample of written work. Electronic applications accepted.

Stony Brook University, State University of New York, Graduate School, College of Arts and Sciences, Department of Africana Studies, Stony Brook, NY 11794. Offers MA, Certificate. *Faculty:* 7 full-time (3 women), 1 part-time/adjunct (0 women). *Students:* 1 full-time (0 women); minority (Black or African American, non-Hispanic/Latino). Average age 64. 4 applicants, 25% accepted, 1 enrolled. In 2019, 1 master's awarded. *Degree requirements:* For master's, research thesis project, research seminar. *Entrance requirements:* For master's, GRE General Test, minimum GPA of 3.0, 3 letters of recommendation, bachelor's degree with minimum GPA of 3.0 in all social science and humanities courses. Additional exam requirements/recommendations for international students: required—TOEFL (minimum score 85 iBT). *Application deadline:* For fall admission, 1/15 for domestic students; for spring admission, 10/1 for domestic students. Application fee: $100. *Expenses:* Contact institution. *Financial support:* Teaching assistantships available. *Unit head:* Dr. Tracey L. Walters, Chair, 631-632-7475, E-mail: tracey.walters@stonybrook.edu. *Application contact:* Ann Berrios, Coordinator, 631-632-7470, Fax: 631-632-7794, E-mail: ann.berrios@stonybrook.edu.

Syracuse University, College of Arts and Sciences, MA Program in Pan-African Studies, Syracuse, NY 13244. Offers MA. *Entrance requirements:* For master's, GRE General Test (recommended), personal statement, resume, three letters of recommendation, writing sample (10-12 pages), transcripts. Additional exam requirements/recommendations for international students: required—TOEFL (minimum score 600 paper-based; 100 iBT). Electronic applications accepted.

University at Albany, State University of New York, College of Arts and Sciences, Department of Africana Studies, Albany, NY 12222-0001. Offers African studies (MA); Afro-American studies (MA). *Program availability:* Part-time, evening/weekend, blended/hybrid learning. *Faculty:* 6 full-time (3 women), 6 part-time/adjunct (2 women). *Students:* 8 full-time (all women), 5 part-time (4 women); includes 11 minority (7 Black or African American, non-Hispanic/Latino; 2 Hispanic/Latino; 2 Two or more races, non-Hispanic/Latino), 1 international. 8 applicants, 100% accepted, 4 enrolled. In 2019, 6 master's awarded. *Entrance requirements:* For master's, transcripts of all schools attended, statement of background and goals, departmental questionnaire, resume, names and contact information for 3 recommenders. Additional exam requirements/recommendations for international students: required—TOEFL (minimum score 550 paper-based). *Application deadline:* For fall admission, 1/15 for domestic students, 5/15 for international students; for spring admission, 11/15 for domestic and international students. Application fee: $75. Electronic applications accepted. *Expenses: Tuition, area resident:* Full-time $11,530; part-time $480 per credit hour. Tuition, nonresident: full-time $23,530; part-time $980 per credit hour. *International tuition:* $23,530 full-time. *Required fees:* $2185; $96 per credit hour. Part-time tuition and fees vary according to course load and program. *Financial support:* Fellowships, teaching assistantships, and Federal Work-Study available. Financial award application deadline: 5/1. *Unit head:* Oscar Williams, Chair, 518-442-4730, Fax: 518-442-2569, E-mail: owilliams@albany.edu. *Application contact:* Michael DeRensis, Director, Graduate Admissions, 518-442-3980, Fax: 518-442-3922, E-mail: graduate@albany.edu.
Website: http://www.albany.edu/africana/

The University of Arizona, College of Social and Behavioral Sciences, School of Middle Eastern and North African Studies, Tucson, AZ 85721. Offers MA, PhD, Graduate Certificate. *Program availability:* Part-time, evening/weekend. Terminal master's awarded for partial completion of doctoral program. *Degree requirements:* For master's, one foreign language; for doctorate, 3 foreign languages, thesis/dissertation. *Entrance requirements:* For master's, GRE General Test, 3 letters of recommendation, statement of purpose, curriculum vitae, writing sample; for doctorate, GRE General Test, 3 letters of recommendation, curriculum vitae, writing sample. Additional exam requirements/recommendations for international students: required—TOEFL (minimum score 550 paper-based; 79 iBT). Electronic applications accepted.

University of California, Los Angeles, Graduate Division, International Institute, Interdepartmental Program in African Studies, Los Angeles, CA 90095. Offers MA, MPH/MA. *Degree requirements:* For master's, one foreign language, comprehensive exam or thesis. *Entrance requirements:* For master's, GRE General Test, bachelor's degree; minimum undergraduate GPA of 3.0 (or its equivalent if letter grade system not used); writing sample. Additional exam requirements/recommendations for international students: required—TOEFL. Electronic applications accepted.

University of Illinois at Urbana-Champaign, Graduate College, College of Liberal Arts and Sciences, Center for African Studies, Champaign, IL 61820. Offers MA, MA/MS.

The University of Kansas, Graduate Studies, College of Liberal Arts and Sciences, Department of African and African-American Studies, Lawrence, KS 66045. Offers African and African-American studies (MA); African studies (Graduate Certificate). *Program availability:* Part-time. *Students:* 7 full-time (4 women), 2 part-time (1 woman); includes 7 minority (5 Black or African American, non-Hispanic/Latino; 2 Two or more races, non-Hispanic/Latino). Average age 31. 3 applicants, 100% accepted, 2 enrolled. In 2019, 2 master's, 2 other advanced degrees awarded. *Entrance requirements:* For master's, GRE, all academic transcripts, 3 letters of recommendation, personal statement of purpose, writing sample. Additional exam requirements/recommendations for international students: required—TOEFL, IELTS. *Application deadline:* For fall admission, 5/1 for domestic and international students; for spring admission, 10/1 for domestic and international students. Application fee: $65 ($85 for international students). Electronic applications accepted. *Expenses:* Tuition, state resident: full-time $9989. Tuition, nonresident: full-time $23,950. *International tuition:* $23,950 full-time. *Required fees:* $984; $81.99 per credit hour. Tuition and fees vary according to course load, campus/location and program. *Financial support:* Application deadline: 4/15. *Unit head:* Dr. Cecile Accilien, Chairperson, 785-864-1853, E-mail: cecileaccilien@ku.edu. *Application contact:* Bethany Harris, Director of Graduate Studies, 785-864-0778,

E-mail: bethanyharris@ku.edu.
Website: http://www.afs.ku.edu

University of Louisville, Graduate School, College of Arts and Sciences, Department of Pan-African Studies, Louisville, KY 40292. Offers African and Diaspora studies (MA); African-American studies (MA); MSSW/MA. *Program availability:* Part-time. *Faculty:* 7 full-time (2 women), 9 part-time/adjunct (6 women). *Students:* 14 full-time (10 women), 3 part-time (2 women); includes 15 minority (12 Black or African American, non-Hispanic/Latino; 3 Two or more races, non-Hispanic/Latino). Average age 34. 16 applicants, 63% accepted, 3 enrolled. In 2019, 2 master's awarded. *Degree requirements:* For master's, comprehensive exam, thesis optional. *Entrance requirements:* For master's, GRE General Test, Two letters of reference, official transcripts. Additional exam requirements/recommendations for international students: required—TOEFL (minimum score 550 paper-based; 79 iBT), IELTS can be used in place of the TOEFL; recommended—IELTS (minimum score 6.5). *Application deadline:* For fall admission, 3/15 priority date for domestic students, 5/1 priority date for international students; for spring admission, 10/15 for domestic students, 11/1 for international students. Applications are processed on a rolling basis. Application fee: $65. Electronic applications accepted. *Expenses: Tuition, area resident:* Full-time $13,000; part-time $723 per credit hour. Tuition, state resident: full-time $13,000; part-time $723 per credit hour. Tuition, nonresident: full-time $27,114; part-time $1507 per credit hour. *International tuition:* $27,114 full-time. *Required fees:* $196. Tuition and fees vary according to program and reciprocity agreements. *Financial support:* In 2019–20, 7 students received support, including 7 teaching assistantships with full tuition reimbursements available (averaging $16,300 per year); fellowships, research assistantships, health care benefits, and unspecified assistantships also available. Financial award application deadline: 3/3; financial award applicants required to submit FAFSA. *Unit head:* Dr. Ricky L. Jones, Chair, 502-852-0027, E-mail: ricky.jones@louisville.edu. *Application contact:* W.S. Tkweme, Director of Graduate Studies, 502-852-5386, E-mail: ws.tkweme@louisville.edu.
Website: http://www.louisville.edu/panafricanstudies

University of Michigan, Rackham Graduate School, College of Literature, Science, and the Arts, Center for Middle Eastern and North African Studies, Ann Arbor, MI 48109-1106. Offers AM, JD/AM, MBA/AM. *Program availability:* Part-time. *Degree requirements:* For master's, one foreign language, thesis or alternative. *Entrance requirements:* For master's, GRE General Test. Additional exam requirements/recommendations for international students: required—TOEFL (minimum score 560 paper-based; 84 iBT). Electronic applications accepted.

The University of North Carolina at Charlotte, College of Liberal Arts and Sciences, Department of Africana Studies, Charlotte, NC 28223-0001. Offers africana studies (Graduate Certificate). *Program availability:* Part-time. *Faculty:* 6 full-time (3 women). *Students:* 1 (woman) full-time; minority (Black or African American, non-Hispanic/Latino). Average age 38. *Entrance requirements:* For degree, bachelor's degree from accredited university with minimum cumulative GPA of 3.0 or enrolled and in good standing in a graduate degree program at UNC Charlotte; official transcripts; two-page statement of purpose explaining applicant's educational and work background, interests, and plans; three letters of recommendation. Additional exam requirements/recommendations for international students: required—TOEFL (minimum score 557 paper-based; 83 iBT), IELTS (minimum score 6.5), TOEFL (minimum score 557 paper-based, 83 iBT) or IELTS (6.5). *Application deadline:* Applications are processed on a rolling basis. Application fee: $75. Electronic applications accepted. *Expenses:* Tuition, state resident: full-time $4337. Tuition, nonresident: full-time $17,771. *Required fees:* $3093. Tuition and fees vary according to course load, degree level and program. *Financial support:* Institutionally sponsored loans, scholarships/grants, and unspecified assistantships available. Support available to part-time students. Financial award applicants required to submit FAFSA. *Unit head:* Dr. Julia Jordan Zachary, Professor and Chair, 704-687-5162, E-mail: jjordanz@uncc.edu. *Application contact:* Kathy B. Giddings, Director of Graduate Admissions, 704-687-5503, Fax: 704-687-1668, E-mail: gradadm@uncc.edu.
Website: http://africana.uncc.edu/

University of Pennsylvania, School of Arts and Sciences, Graduate Group in Africana Studies, Philadelphia, PA 19104. Offers MA, PhD. *Faculty:* 16 full-time (11 women), 2 part-time/adjunct (1 woman). *Students:* 13 full-time (9 women); includes 10 minority (8 Black or African American, non-Hispanic/Latino; 1 Asian, non-Hispanic/Latino; 1 Hispanic/Latino), 3 international. Average age 29. 45 applicants, 11% accepted, 2 enrolled. In 2019, 5 doctorates awarded. Application fee: $90.
Website: https://africana.sas.upenn.edu/

University of Pittsburgh, University Center for International Studies, Pittsburgh, PA 15260. Offers African studies (Certificate); Asian studies (Certificate); European Union studies (Certificate); global studies (Certificate); Latin American studies (Certificate); Russian and East European studies (Certificate); West European studies (Certificate). *Program availability:* Part-time, evening/weekend, online learning. *Degree requirements:* For Certificate, one foreign language, comprehensive exam (for some programs). *Entrance requirements:* Additional exam requirements/recommendations for international students: required—TOEFL. *Expenses:* Contact institution.

University of South Florida, Innovative Education, Tampa, FL 33620-9951. Offers adult, career and higher education (Graduate Certificate), including college teaching, leadership in developing human resources, leadership in higher education; Africana studies (Graduate Certificate), including diasporas and health disparities, genocide and human rights; aging studies (Graduate Certificate), including gerontology; art research (Graduate Certificate), including museum studies; business foundations (Graduate Certificate); chemical and biomedical engineering (Graduate Certificate), including materials science and engineering, water, health and sustainability; child and family studies (Graduate Certificate), including positive behavior support; civil and industrial engineering (Graduate Certificate), including transportation systems analysis; community and family health (Graduate Certificate), including maternal and child health, social marketing and public health, violence and injury: prevention and intervention, women's health; criminology (Graduate Certificate), including criminal justice administration; data science for public administration (Graduate Certificate); digital humanities (Graduate Certificate); educational measurement and research (Graduate Certificate), including evaluation; English (Graduate Certificate), including comparative literary studies, creative writing, professional and technical communication; entrepreneurship (Graduate Certificate); environmental health (Graduate Certificate), including safety management; epidemiology and biostatistics (Graduate Certificate), including applied biostatistics, biostatistics, concepts and tools of epidemiology, epidemiology, epidemiology of infectious diseases; geography, environment and planning (Graduate Certificate), including community development, environmental policy and management, geographical information systems; geology (Graduate Certificate), including hydrogeology; global health (Graduate Certificate), including disaster management, global health and Latin American and Caribbean studies, global health practice, humanitarian assistance, infection control; government and international affairs (Graduate Certificate), including Cuban studies, globalization studies; health policy and management (Graduate Certificate), including health management and leadership, public health policy and programs; hearing specialist: early intervention (Graduate Certificate); industrial and management systems engineering (Graduate Certificate), including systems engineering, technology management; information studies (Graduate Certificate), including school library media specialist; information systems/decision sciences (Graduate Certificate), including analytics and business intelligence; instructional technology (Graduate Certificate), including distance education, Florida digital/virtual educator, instructional design, multimedia design, Web design; internal medicine, bioethics and medical humanities (Graduate Certificate), including biomedical ethics; Latin American and Caribbean studies (Graduate Certificate); leadership for coastal resiliency planning (Graduate Certificate); mass communications (Graduate Certificate), including multimedia journalism; mathematics and statistics (Graduate Certificate), including mathematics; medicine (Graduate Certificate), including aging and neuroscience, bioinformatics, biotechnology, brain fitness and memory management, clinical investigation, hand and upper limb rehabilitation, health informatics, health sciences, integrative weight management, intellectual property, medicine and gender, metabolic and nutritional medicine, metabolic cardiology, pharmacy sciences; national and competitive intelligence (Graduate Certificate); nursing (Graduate Certificate), including simulation based academic fellowship in advanced pain management; psychological and social foundations (Graduate Certificate), including career counseling, college teaching, diversity in education, mental health counseling, school counseling; public affairs (Graduate Certificate), including nonprofit management, public management, research administration; public health (Graduate Certificate), including assessing chemical toxicity and public health risks, health equity, pharmacoepidemiology, public health generalist, toxicology, translational research in adolescent behavioral health; public health practices (Graduate Certificate), including planning for healthy communities; rehabilitation and mental health counseling (Graduate Certificate), including integrative mental health care, marriage and family therapy, rehabilitation technology; secondary education (Graduate Certificate), including ESOL, foreign language education: culture and content, foreign language education: professional; social work (Graduate Certificate), including geriatric social work/clinical gerontology; special education (Graduate Certificate), including autism spectrum disorder, disabilities education: severe/profound; world languages (Graduate Certificate), including teaching English as a second language (TESL) or foreign language. *Unit head:* Dr. Cynthia DeLuca, Associate Vice President and Assistant Vice Provost, 813-974-3077, Fax: 813-974-7061, E-mail: deluca@usf.edu. *Application contact:* Owen Hooper, Director, Summer and Alternative Calendar Programs, 813-974-6917, E-mail: hooper@usf.edu.
Website: http://www.usf.edu/innovative-education/

The University of Texas at Austin, Graduate School, College of Liberal Arts, John L. Warfield Center for African and African American Studies, Austin, TX 78712-1111. Offers African Diaspora studies (MA, PhD). *Program availability:* Part-time. *Degree requirements:* For master's, one foreign language, thesis. *Entrance requirements:* For master's, GRE General Test. Electronic applications accepted.

University of Wisconsin–Madison, Graduate School, College of Letters and Science, Department of African Languages and Literature, Madison, WI 53706-1380. Offers MA, PhD. *Program availability:* Part-time. *Degree requirements:* For master's, one foreign language, thesis; for doctorate, 2 foreign languages, comprehensive exam, thesis/dissertation. *Entrance requirements:* For master's, BA in African language and literature; for doctorate, MA in African language and literature. Electronic applications accepted.

University of Wisconsin–Madison, Graduate School, College of Letters and Science, Department of History, Madison, WI 53706-1380. Offers African history (MA, PhD); Central Asian history (MA, PhD); comparative world history (MA, PhD); East Asian history (MA, PhD); European history (MA, PhD); gender and women's history (MA, PhD); Latin American and Caribbean history (MA, PhD); Middle Eastern history (MA, PhD); South Asian history (MA, PhD); Southeast Asian history (MA, PhD); United States history (MA, PhD). Terminal master's awarded for partial completion of doctoral program. *Degree requirements:* For master's, thesis (for some programs); for doctorate, variable foreign language requirement, thesis/dissertation. *Entrance requirements:* For master's and doctorate, GRE General Test. Additional exam requirements/recommendations for international students: required—Michigan English Language Assessment Battery or TOEFL. Electronic applications accepted.

University of Wisconsin–Milwaukee, Graduate School, College of Letters and Science, Department of African and African Diaspora Studies, Milwaukee, WI 53201-0413. Offers Africology (PhD), including culture and society: Africa and the African diaspora, political economy and public policy. *Program availability:* Part-time. *Entrance requirements:* For doctorate, GRE General Test. Additional exam requirements/recommendations for international students: required—TOEFL (minimum score 550 paper-based; 79 iBT), IELTS (minimum score 6.5). Electronic applications accepted.

Yale University, Graduate School of Arts and Sciences, Interdisciplinary Program in African Studies, New Haven, CT 06520. Offers MA. *Degree requirements:* For master's, one foreign language, thesis. *Entrance requirements:* For master's, GRE General Test.

American Indian/Native American Studies

Central Michigan University, College of Graduate Studies, College of Liberal Arts and Social Sciences, Program in Humanities, Mount Pleasant, MI 48859. Offers humanities (MA), including contemporary issues in the humanities: race, class, and gender, images and ideas of self, Native American issues in modern culture, popular culture studies, the rise of industrial society. *Program availability:* Part-time, evening/weekend. *Degree requirements:* For master's, thesis or alternative. Electronic applications accepted. *Expenses: Tuition, area resident:* Full-time $12,267; part-time $8178 per year. Tuition, state resident: full-time $12,267; part-time $8178 per year. Tuition, nonresident: full-time $12,267; part-time $8178 per year. *International tuition:* $16,110 full-time. *Required fees:* $225 per semester. Tuition and fees vary according to degree level and program.

Montana State University, The Graduate School, College of Letters and Science, Department of Native American Studies, Bozeman, MT 59717. Offers MA. *Program availability:* Part-time, online learning. *Degree requirements:* For master's, comprehensive exam. *Entrance requirements:* For master's, minimum GPA of 3.0; 3 letters of recommendation; 2 academic writing samples; statement of purpose. Additional exam requirements/recommendations for international students: required—TOEFL (minimum score 550 paper-based). Electronic applications accepted.

Navajo Technical University, Program in Dine Studies, Crownpoint, NM 87313. Offers MA. *Entrance requirements:* For master's, bachelor's degree, Certificate of Indian Blood (CIB) for tribal eligibility, three letters of recommendation, 500-word essay.

Northeastern State University, College of Liberal Arts, Department of Cherokee and Indigenous Studies, Tahlequah, OK 74464-2399. Offers American studies (MA). *Program availability:* Part-time, evening/weekend. *Faculty:* 12 full-time (3 women). *Students:* 10 full-time (7 women), 14 part-time (8 women); includes 14 minority (6 American Indian or Alaska Native, non-Hispanic/Latino; 2 Hispanic/Latino; 6 Two or more races, non-Hispanic/Latino). Average age 37. In 2019, 5 master's awarded. *Degree requirements:* For master's, thesis, written and oral examinations. *Entrance requirements:* For master's, GRE, minimum GPA of 2.5. Additional exam requirements/recommendations for international students: required—TOEFL. *Application deadline:* For fall admission, 6/1 priority date for domestic students. Applications are processed on a rolling basis. Application fee: $25. Electronic applications accepted. *Expenses: Tuition, area resident:* Full-time $250; part-time $250 per credit hour. Tuition, state resident: full-time $250; part-time $250 per credit hour. Tuition, nonresident: full-time $556; part-time $555.50 per credit hour. *Required fees:* $33.40 per credit hour. *Financial support:* Teaching assistantships and Federal Work-Study available. Financial award application deadline: 3/1. *Unit head:* Dr. Iain Anderson, Director, 918-444-3519, E-mail: andersoi@nsuok.edu. *Application contact:* Josh McCollum, Graduate Coordinator, 918-444-2093, E-mail: mccolluj@nsuok.edu. Website: http://catalog.nsuok.edu/preview_program.php?catoid-12&amp;amp;poid-947&amp;amp;returnto-333

Northern Arizona University, College of Social and Behavioral Sciences, Department of Applied Indigenous Studies, Flagstaff, AZ 86011. Offers indigenous and tribal nation-building (Graduate Certificate). *Program availability:* Part-time, evening/weekend, online only, 100% online, blended/hybrid learning. *Degree requirements:* For Graduate Certificate, comprehensive exam (for some programs). *Entrance requirements:* For degree, undergraduate degree from regionally-accredited institution with minimum GPA of 3.0, or the equivalent. Additional exam requirements/recommendations for international students: required—TOEFL (minimum score 80 iBT), IELTS (minimum score 6.5). Electronic applications accepted.

Trent University, Graduate Studies, The Frost Centre for Canadian Studies and Indigenous Studies, Peterborough, ON K9J 7B8, Canada. Offers Canadian studies (PhD); Canadian studies and indigenous studies (MA). *Program availability:* Part-time. *Degree requirements:* For master's, thesis. *Entrance requirements:* For master's, honors degree.

Trent University, Graduate Studies, Program in Indigenous Studies, Peterborough, ON K9J 7B8, Canada. Offers PhD. *Program availability:* Part-time. *Degree requirements:* For doctorate, thesis/dissertation. *Entrance requirements:* For doctorate, master's degree.

The University of Arizona, Graduate Interdisciplinary Programs, Graduate Interdisciplinary Program in American Indian Studies, Tucson, AZ 85721. Offers MA, PhD. *Program availability:* Part-time. *Degree requirements:* For master's, thesis; for doctorate, one foreign language, comprehensive exam, thesis/dissertation. *Entrance requirements:* For master's, 3 letters of recommendation, 2 writing samples, resume; for doctorate, statement of purpose, 3 letters of recommendation, 2 writing samples, resume. Additional exam requirements/recommendations for international students: required—TOEFL (minimum score 550 paper-based; 79 iBT). Electronic applications accepted.

University of California, Davis, Graduate Studies, Program in Native American Studies, Davis, CA 95616. Offers MA, PhD. Terminal master's awarded for partial completion of doctoral program. *Degree requirements:* For master's, comprehensive exam (for some programs), thesis (for some programs); for doctorate, thesis/dissertation. *Entrance requirements:* For doctorate, GRE. Additional exam requirements/recommendations for international students: required—TOEFL (minimum score 550 paper-based).

University of California, Los Angeles, Graduate Division, College of Letters and Science, Interdepartmental Program in American Indian Studies, Los Angeles, CA 90095. Offers MA, JD/MA. *Degree requirements:* For master's, comprehensive exam or thesis. *Entrance requirements:* For master's, GRE General Test (recommended), bachelor's degree; minimum undergraduate GPA of 3.0 (or its equivalent if letter grade system not used). Additional exam requirements/recommendations for international students: required—TOEFL. Electronic applications accepted.

The University of Kansas, Graduate Studies, College of Liberal Arts and Sciences, Indigenous Studies Program, Lawrence, KS 66045-7515. Offers MA, Graduate Certificate. *Program availability:* Part-time. *Students:* 10 full-time (8 women), 3 part-time (1 woman); includes 8 minority (6 American Indian or Alaska Native, non-Hispanic/Latino; 2 Hispanic/Latino). Average age 30. 9 applicants, 89% accepted, 5 enrolled. In 2019, 3 master's, 4 other advanced degrees awarded. *Entrance requirements:* For master's, GRE, resume, writing sample, minimum GPA of 3.0 (preferred), 3 recommendations, original transcript, 2-page personal statement. Additional exam requirements/recommendations for international students: required—TOEFL, IELTS, TOEFL or IELTS. *Application deadline:* For fall admission, 1/15 priority date for domestic and international students. Application fee: $65 ($85 for international students). Electronic applications accepted. *Expenses:* Tuition, state resident: full-time $9989. Tuition, nonresident: full-time $23,950. *International tuition:* $23,950 full-time. *Required fees:* $984; $81.99 per credit hour. Tuition and fees vary according to course load, campus/location and program. *Financial support:* Fellowships, research assistantships, teaching assistantships, Federal Work-Study, institutionally sponsored loans, and scholarships/grants available. Support available to part-time students. Financial award application deadline: 1/15; financial award applicants required to submit FAFSA. *Unit head:* Dr. Peter Welsh, Director, 785-864-5702, E-mail: phwelsh@ku.edu. *Application contact:* Bethany Harris, Graduate Admission Contact, 785-864-0778, E-mail: bethanyharris@ku.edu. Website: http://www.indigenous.ku.edu

University of Lethbridge, School of Graduate Studies, Lethbridge, AB T1K 3M4, Canada. Offers addictions counseling (M Sc); agricultural biotechnology (M Sc); agricultural studies (M Sc, MA); anthropology (MA); archaeology (M Sc, MA); art (MA, MFA); biochemistry (M Sc); biological sciences (M Sc); biomolecular science (PhD); biosystems and biodiversity (PhD); Canadian studies (MA); chemistry (M Sc); computer science (M Sc); computer science and geographical information science (M Sc); counseling (MC); counseling psychology (M Ed); dramatic arts (MA); earth, space, and physical science (PhD); economics (MA); education (MA, PhD); educational leadership (M Ed); English (MA); environmental science (M Sc); evolution and behavior (PhD); exercise science (M Sc); French (MA); French/German (MA); French/Spanish (MA); general education (M Ed); geography (M Sc, MA); German (MA); health sciences (M Sc); individualized multidisciplinary (M Sc, MA); kinesiology (M Sc, MA); management (M Sc), including accounting, finance, human resource management and labor relations, information systems, international management, marketing, policy and strategy; mathematics (M Sc); music (M Mus, MA); Native American studies (MA); neuroscience (M Sc, PhD); new media (MA, MFA); nursing (M Sc, MN); philosophy (MA); physics (M Sc); political science (MA); psychology (M Sc, MA); religious studies (MA); sociology (MA); theatre and dramatic arts (MFA); theoretical and computational science (PhD); urban and regional studies (MA); women and gender studies (MA). *Program availability:* Part-time, evening/weekend. *Degree requirements:* For master's, thesis (for some programs); for doctorate, comprehensive exam, thesis/dissertation. *Entrance requirements:* For master's, GMAT (for M Sc in management), bachelor's degree in related field, minimum GPA of 3.0 during previous 20 graded semester courses, 2 years' teaching or related experience (M Ed); for doctorate, master's degree, minimum graduate GPA of 3.5. Additional exam requirements/recommendations for international students: required—TOEFL (minimum score 580 paper-based; 93 iBT). Electronic applications accepted.

University of Manitoba, Faculty of Graduate Studies, Faculty of Arts, Department of Native Studies, Winnipeg, MB R3T 2N2, Canada. Offers MA.

University of New Mexico, Graduate Studies, College of Education and Human Sciences, Program in Language, Literacy and Sociocultural Studies, Albuquerque, NM 87131-2039. Offers American Indian education (MA); bilingual education (MA, PhD); educational linguistics (PhD); educational thought and sociocultural studies (MA, PhD); literacy/language arts (MA, PhD); social studies (MA); TESOL (MA, PhD). *Degree requirements:* For master's, comprehensive exam, thesis optional; for doctorate, comprehensive exam, thesis/dissertation, research skills. *Entrance requirements:* For master's, letter of intent, 3 letters of recommendation, resume, BA/BS, department demographic form, transcripts; for doctorate, writing sample, letter of intent, 3 letters of recommendation, resume, BA/BS, MA, department demographic form, transcripts. Additional exam requirements/recommendations for international students: required—TOEFL. Electronic applications accepted. *Expenses:* Tuition, state resident: full-time $7633; part-time $972 per year. Tuition, nonresident: full-time $22,586; part-time $3840 per year. *International tuition:* $23,292 full-time. *Required fees:* $8608. Tuition and fees vary according to course level, course load, degree level, program and student level.

University of Oklahoma, College of Arts and Sciences, Department of Native American Studies, Norman, OK 73019. Offers MA, JD/MA. *Program availability:* Part-time. *Degree requirements:* For master's, one foreign language, thesis or exam. *Entrance requirements:* For master's, BA or BS in related area. Additional exam requirements/recommendations for international students: required—TOEFL (minimum score 79 iBT) or IELTS (minimum score 6.5). Electronic applications accepted. *Expenses:* Tuition, state resident: full-time $6583.20; part-time $274.30 per credit hour. Tuition, nonresident: full-time $21,242; part-time $885.10 per credit hour. *International tuition:* $21,242.40 full-time. *Required fees:* $1994.20; $72.55 per credit hour. $126.50 per semester. Tuition and fees vary according to course load and degree level.

University of South Dakota, Graduate School, School of Education, Division of Curriculum and Instruction, Vermillion, SD 57069. Offers American Indian education (Certificate); curriculum and instruction (Ed D, Ed S); elementary education (MA), including elementary education; English language learners (Certificate); literacy leadership and coaching (Certificate); reading interventionist (Certificate); science, technology and math pedagogy (Certificate); secondary education (MA), including secondary education; special education (MA), including special education; technology for education and training (MS), including technology for education and training. *Accreditation:* NCATE. *Program availability:* Part-time, online learning. *Degree requirements:* For master's and other advanced degree, comprehensive exam, thesis or alternative; for doctorate, comprehensive exam, thesis/dissertation. *Entrance requirements:* For master's, doctorate, and other advanced degree, GRE General Test, MAT, minimum GPA of 2.7. Additional exam requirements/recommendations for international students: required—TOEFL (minimum score 550 paper-based; 79 iBT). Electronic applications accepted.

The University of Tulsa, College of Law, Tulsa, OK 74104. Offers American Indian and indigenous law (LL M); American law for foreign lawyers (LL M); energy and natural resources law (LL M); energy law (MJ); health law (Certificate); Indian law (MJ); law (JD); Native American law (Certificate); sustainable energy and resources law (Certificate); JD/MA; JD/MBA; JD/MS. *Accreditation:* ABA. *Program availability:* Part-time. *Faculty:* 25 full-time (14 women), 11 part-time/adjunct (3 women). *Students:* 283 full-time (142 women), 24 part-time (11 women); includes 88 minority (13 Black or African American, non-Hispanic/Latino; 15 American Indian or Alaska Native, non-Hispanic/Latino; 4 Asian, non-Hispanic/Latino; 13 Hispanic/Latino; 1 Native Hawaiian or other Pacific Islander, non-Hispanic/Latino; 42 Two or more races, non-Hispanic/Latino), 2 international. Average age 28. 621 applicants, 57% accepted, 118 enrolled. In 2019, 5 master's, 88 doctorates, 27 Certificates awarded. *Entrance requirements:* For doctorate, LSAT, BS or BA from 4-year regionally-accredited college/university. Additional exam requirements/recommendations for international students: required—TOEFL (minimum score 570 paper-based; 90 iBT), TOEFL preferred; recommended—IELTS (minimum score 6.5). *Application deadline:* For fall admission, 7/31 priority date for domestic and international students; for spring admission, 12/1 priority date for domestic students, 12/1 for international students; for summer admission, 4/22 for domestic and international students. Applications are processed on a rolling basis. Application fee: $30. Electronic applications accepted. *Expenses:* Contact institution. *Financial support:* In 2019–20, 251 students received support. Federal Work-Study and scholarships/grants available. Support available to part-time students. Financial award application deadline: 8/1; financial award applicants required to submit FAFSA. *Unit head:* Prof. Lyn Suzanne Entzeroth, Dean, 918-631-2400, Fax: 918-631-3126, E-mail: lyn-entzeroth@utulsa.edu. *Application contact:* April M. Fox, Associate Dean of Admissions and Financial Aid, 918-631-2406, Fax: 918-631-3126, E-mail: april-fox@utulsa.edu. Website: http://www.utulsa.edu/law/

American Studies

American Public University System, AMU/APU Graduate Programs, Charles Town, WV 25414. Offers accounting (MS); applied business analytics (MS); business administration (MBA); criminal justice (MA); cybersecurity studies (MS); educational leadership (M Ed); environmental policy and management (MS); global security (DGS); health information management (MS); history (MA), including American military history, American Revolution, civil war, war since 1945, World War II; information technology (MS); international relations and conflict resolution (MA), including American politics and government, comparative government and development, general, international relations, public policy; national security studies (MA); nursing (MSN); political science (MA); public policy (MPP); reverse logistics management (MA), including comparative and security issues, conflict resolution, international and transnational security issues, peacekeeping; space studies (MS); sports management (MS); strategic intelligence (DSI); teaching (M Ed), including secondary social studies; transportation and logistics management (MA). *Program availability:* Part-time, evening/weekend, online only, 100% online. *Students:* 461 full-time (193 women), 7,322 part-time (3,127 women); includes 3,089 minority (1,404 Black or African American, non-Hispanic/Latino; 30 American Indian or Alaska Native, non-Hispanic/Latino; 210 Asian, non-Hispanic/Latino; 753 Hispanic/Latino; 445 Native Hawaiian or other Pacific Islander, non-Hispanic/Latino; 247 Two or more races, non-Hispanic/Latino), 117 international. Average age 37. In 2019, 2,681 master's awarded. *Degree requirements:* For master's, comprehensive exam or practicum; for doctorate, practicum. *Entrance requirements:* For master's, official transcript showing earned bachelor's degree from institution accredited by recognized accrediting body. Additional exam requirements/recommendations for international students: required—TOEFL (minimum score 550 paper-based), IELTS (minimum score 6.5). *Application deadline:* Applications are processed on a rolling basis. Application fee: $0. Electronic applications accepted. *Financial support:* Scholarships/grants available. Financial award applicants required to submit FAFSA. *Unit head:* Dr. Wallace Boston, President, 877-468-6268, Fax: 304-728-2348, E-mail: president@apus.edu. *Application contact:* Yoci Deal, Associate Vice President, Graduate and International Admissions, 877-468-6268, Fax: 304-724-3764, E-mail: info@apus.edu.
Website: http://www.apus.edu

American University, School of International Service, Washington, DC 20016-8071. Offers comparative and regional studies (Certificate); cross-cultural communication (Certificate); development management (MS); ethics, peace, and global affairs (MA); European studies (Certificate); global environmental policy (MA, Certificate); global information technology (Certificate); global media (MA); international affairs (MA), including comparative and regional studies, global governance, politics, and security, international economic relations, natural resources and sustainable development, U.S. foreign policy and national security; international arts management (Certificate); international communication (MA, Certificate); international development (MA); international economic policy (Certificate); international economic relations (Certificate); international economics (MA); international peace and conflict resolution (MA, Certificate); international politics (Certificate); international relations (MA, PhD); international service (MIS); peacebuilding (Certificate); social enterprise (MA); the Americas (Certificate); United States foreign policy (Certificate); JD/MA. *Program availability:* Part-time, evening/weekend, 100% online, blended/hybrid learning. Terminal master's awarded for partial completion of doctoral program. *Degree requirements:* For master's, one foreign language, comprehensive exam, thesis or alternative; for doctorate, one foreign language, comprehensive exam, thesis/dissertation. *Entrance requirements:* For master's, transcripts, resume, 2 letters of recommendation, statement of purpose; for doctorate, GRE, transcripts, resume, 3 letters of recommendation, statement of purpose. Additional exam requirements/recommendations for international students: required—TOEFL. Electronic applications accepted. *Expenses:* Contact institution.

Appalachian State University, Cratis D. Williams School of Graduate Studies, Center for Appalachian Studies, Boone, NC 28608. Offers culture (MA). *Program availability:* Part-time. *Degree requirements:* For master's, one foreign language, comprehensive exam, thesis optional. *Entrance requirements:* For master's, GRE General Test, 3 letters of recommendation. Additional exam requirements/recommendations for international students: required—TOEFL (minimum score 570 paper-based; 79 iBT), IELTS (minimum score 6.5). Electronic applications accepted.

Baylor University, Graduate School, College of Arts and Sciences, Program in American Studies, Waco, TX 76798. Offers MA. *Program availability:* Part-time. *Faculty:* 8 full-time (4 women). *Students:* 3 full-time (0 women); includes 1 minority (Two or more races, non-Hispanic/Latino), 1 international. 2 applicants, 50% accepted. In 2019, 2 master's awarded. *Degree requirements:* For master's, thesis. *Entrance requirements:* Additional exam requirements/recommendations for international students: required—TOEFL (minimum score 550 paper-based), IELTS (minimum score 6.5). *Application deadline:* For fall admission, 2/15 priority date for domestic and international students; for spring admission, 12/1 priority date for domestic students, 12/1 for international students. Application fee: $50. Electronic applications accepted. *Financial support:* In 2019–20, 2 students received support. Scholarships/grants available. Financial award application deadline: 2/15; financial award applicants required to submit FAFSA. *Unit head:* Dr. Marlene Neill, Associate Professor & Graduate Program Director, 254-710-6322, E-mail: Marlene_Neill@baylor.edu. *Application contact:* Marlene Neill, Associate Professor & Graduate Program Director, 254-710-6322, E-mail: Marlene_Neill@baylor.edu.
Website: https://www.baylor.edu/American_Studies/index.php?id=33668

Boston University, Graduate School of Arts and Sciences, Program in American and New England Studies, Boston, MA 02215. Offers PhD. *Students:* 34 full-time (22 women), 4 part-time (2 women); includes 3 minority (2 Black or African American, non-Hispanic/Latino; 1 Hispanic/Latino), 3 international. Average age 28. 50 applicants, 24% accepted, 4 enrolled. In 2019, 6 doctorates awarded. *Degree requirements:* For doctorate, one foreign language, comprehensive exam, thesis/dissertation. *Entrance requirements:* For doctorate, GRE General Test, scholarly writing sample, 3 letters of recommendation, transcripts, personal statement, curriculum vitae. Additional exam requirements/recommendations for international students: required—TOEFL (minimum score 550 paper-based; 84 iBT). *Application deadline:* For fall admission, 1/15 for domestic and international students. Application fee: $95. Electronic applications accepted. *Financial support:* In 2019–20, 36 students received support, including 11 fellowships with full tuition reimbursements available (averaging $23,340 per year), 2 research assistantships with full tuition reimbursements available (averaging $23,340 per year), 15 teaching assistantships with full tuition reimbursements available (averaging $23,340 per year); career-related internships or fieldwork, Federal Work-Study, scholarships/grants, health care benefits, and unspecified assistantships also available. Financial award application deadline: 1/15. *Unit head:* William Moore, Director, 617-353-9912, Fax: 617-353-2556, E-mail: moorewd@bu.edu. *Application contact:* Julia Kline, Senior Program Coordinator, 617-353-2948, Fax: 617-353-2556, E-mail: jgawle@bu.edu.
Website: http://www.bu.edu/AMNESP/

Bowling Green State University, Graduate College, College of Arts and Sciences, American Culture Studies Program, Bowling Green, OH 43403. Offers MA, PhD. *Program availability:* Part-time. *Degree requirements:* For master's, thesis or alternative; for doctorate, comprehensive exam, thesis/dissertation. *Entrance requirements:* For master's and doctorate, GRE General Test. Additional exam requirements/recommendations for international students: required—TOEFL. Electronic applications accepted.

Bowling Green State University, Graduate College, College of Arts and Sciences, Department of Popular Culture, Bowling Green, OH 43403. Offers MA. *Program availability:* Part-time. *Degree requirements:* For master's, thesis or alternative. *Entrance requirements:* For master's, GRE General Test. Additional exam requirements/recommendations for international students: required—TOEFL. Electronic applications accepted.

Brown University, Graduate School, Department of American Studies, Providence, RI 02912. Offers American studies (PhD); American studies for international students (MA); public humanities (MA). *Faculty:* 18 full-time (9 women). *Students:* 30 full-time (20 women); includes 19 minority (3 Black or African American, non-Hispanic/Latino; 1 American Indian or Alaska Native, non-Hispanic/Latino; 5 Asian, non-Hispanic/Latino; 5 Hispanic/Latino; 1 Native Hawaiian or other Pacific Islander, non-Hispanic/Latino; 4 Two or more races, non-Hispanic/Latino). Average age 25. *Degree requirements:* For doctorate, thesis/dissertation, preliminary exam. *Application deadline:* For fall admission, 12/1 priority date for domestic students. Applications are processed on a rolling basis. Application fee: $60. *Financial support:* Fellowships, research assistantships, teaching assistantships, institutionally sponsored loans, tuition waivers (full and partial), and unspecified assistantships available. Financial award application deadline: 1/2. *Unit head:* Matthew Pratt Guterl, Chairman, 401-863-6103. *Application contact:* Jeff Cabral, Administrative Manager, 401-863-2896, E-mail: Jeffrey_cabral@brown.edu.
Website: https://www.brown.edu/academics/american-studies/

California State University, Fullerton, Graduate Studies, College of Humanities and Social Sciences, Department of American Studies, Fullerton, CA 92831-3599. Offers MA. *Program availability:* Part-time. *Entrance requirements:* For master's, minimum GPA of 3.0 in major, 2.5 in last 60 hours.

The Catholic University of America, School of Arts and Sciences, Department of History, Washington, DC 20064. Offers history (MA, PhD), including early modern European history, medieval history, modern European history, U.S. history; religion and society in the late medieval and early modern world (MA); MA/JD; MSLS/MA. *Program availability:* Part-time. *Faculty:* 14 full-time (6 women). *Students:* 5 full-time (4 women), 17 part-time (6 women); includes 3 minority (all Two or more races, non-Hispanic/Latino), 2 international. Average age 30. 14 applicants, 57% accepted, 3 enrolled. In 2019, 3 master's, 1 doctorate awarded. Terminal master's awarded for partial completion of doctoral program. *Degree requirements:* For master's, one foreign language, comprehensive exam, thesis optional, 2 languages (for medievalists), one of which must be Latin; for doctorate, 2 foreign languages, comprehensive exam, thesis/dissertation, 3 languages (for medievalists), one of which must be Latin. *Entrance requirements:* For master's and doctorate, GRE General Test, statement of purpose, official copies of academic transcripts, three letters of recommendation, writing sample. Additional exam requirements/recommendations for international students: required—TOEFL (minimum score 550 paper-based; 80 iBT). *Application deadline:* For fall admission, 7/15 priority date for domestic students, 7/1 for international students; for spring admission, 11/15 priority date for domestic students, 11/1 for international students. Applications are processed on a rolling basis. Application fee: $55. Electronic applications accepted. *Expenses:* Contact institution. *Financial support:* Fellowships, research assistantships, teaching assistantships, Federal Work-Study, scholarships/grants, tuition waivers (full and partial), and unspecified assistantships available. Financial award application deadline: 2/1; financial award applicants required to submit FAFSA. *Unit head:* Dr. Michael Kimmage, Chair, 202-319-5484, Fax: 202-319-5569, E-mail: kimmage@cua.edu. *Application contact:* Dr. Steven Brown, Director of Graduate Admissions, 202-319-5057, Fax: 202-319-6533, E-mail: cua-admissions@cua.edu.
Website: http://history.cua.edu/

Central Michigan University, College of Graduate Studies, College of Liberal Arts and Social Sciences, Department of History, Mount Pleasant, MI 48859. Offers European history (Graduate Certificate); history (MA); modern history (Graduate Certificate); United States history (Graduate Certificate); MA/PhD. *Program availability:* Part-time. *Degree requirements:* For master's, thesis or alternative. Electronic applications accepted. *Expenses: Tuition, area resident:* Full-time $12,267; part-time $8178 per year. Tuition, state resident: full-time $12,267; part-time $8178 per year. Tuition, nonresident: full-time $12,267; part-time $8178 per year. *International tuition:* $16,110 full-time. *Required fees:* $225 per semester. Tuition and fees vary according to degree level and program.

Claremont Graduate University, Graduate Programs, School of Arts and Humanities, Department of English, Claremont, CA 91711-6160. Offers American studies (MA, PhD); critical theory (MA, PhD); early modern studies (MA, PhD); English (M Phil, MA, PhD); literary theory (PhD); literature (MA, PhD); literature and creative writing (MA); literature and film (MA); MBA/MA; MBA/PhD. *Program availability:* Part-time. *Entrance requirements:* For master's and doctorate, GRE General Test. Additional exam requirements/recommendations for international students: required—TOEFL (minimum score 75 iBT). Electronic applications accepted.

Claremont Graduate University, Graduate Programs, School of Arts and Humanities, Department of History, Claremont, CA 91711-6160. Offers Africana history (Certificate); American studies and U.S. history (MA, PhD); archival studies (MA); early modern studies (MA, PhD); European studies (MA, PhD); oral history (MA, PhD); MBA/MA; MBA/PhD. Terminal master's awarded for partial completion of doctoral program. *Entrance requirements:* For master's and doctorate, GRE General Test. Additional exam requirements/recommendations for international students: required—TOEFL (minimum score 75 iBT). Electronic applications accepted.

Clark University, Graduate School, Department of History, Program in United States and Atlantic History, Worcester, MA 01610-1477. Offers history of the Atlantic world (PhD); history of the United States (PhD). *Expenses: Tuition:* Full-time $47,650; part-time $4765 per course. *Required fees:* $1850.

College of Staten Island of the City University of New York, Graduate Programs, Division of Humanities and Social Sciences, Program in History, Staten Island, NY

10314-6600. Offers history (MA), including Africa and the Middle East, Asia, Europe, Latin America and the Caribbean, United States. *Program availability:* Part-time, evening/weekend. *Faculty:* 5. *Students:* 17. 12 applicants, 67% accepted, 8 enrolled. In 2019, 1 master's awarded. *Degree requirements:* For master's, comprehensive exam (for some programs), thesis or alternative, the MA in History requires 32 graduate credits at the 700-level, with all graduate courses designated at four credits, for a total of eight courses. Students must take at least one course in each of four of the program's five areas of concentration, rigorous thesis option or portfolio option. *Entrance requirements:* For master's, bachelor's degree with minimum GPA of 3.0 overall and in undergraduate history courses, two letters of recommendation, letter of interest, research-based writing sample. Additional exam requirements/recommendations for international students: required—TOEFL (minimum score 550 paper-based; 79 iBT), IELTS (minimum score 6.5). *Application deadline:* For fall admission, 5/10 priority date for domestic students, 4/25 for international students; for spring admission, 12/2 priority date for domestic students, 11/23 for international students. Applications are processed on a rolling basis. Application fee: $75. Electronic applications accepted. *Expenses: Tuition, area resident:* Full-time $11,090; part-time $470 per credit. Tuition, state resident: full-time $11,090; part-time $470 per credit. Tuition, nonresident: full-time $20,520; part-time $855 per credit. *International tuition:* $20,520 full-time. *Required fees:* $559; $181 per semester. Tuition and fees vary according to program. *Unit head:* Susan Smith-Peter, Graduate Program Coordinator, 718-982-3290, E-mail: susan.smithpeter@csi.cuny.edu. *Application contact:* Sasha Spence, Associate Director for Graduate Admissions, 718-982-2019, Fax: 718-982-2500, E-mail: sasha.spence@csi.cuny.edu.
Website: https://www.csi.cuny.edu/academics-and-research/departments-programs/history/master-arts-history

The Colorado College, Education Department, Experienced Teacher Program, Colorado Springs, CO 80903-3294. Offers arts and humanities (MAT); integrated natural sciences (MAT); liberal arts (MAT); Southwest studies (MAT). *Program availability:* Part-time. *Degree requirements:* For master's, thesis, oral exam, 50-page paper. *Expenses:* Contact institution.

Columbia University, Graduate School of Arts and Sciences, New York, NY 10027. Offers African-American studies (MA); American studies (MA); anthropology (MA, PhD); art history and archaeology (MA, PhD); astronomy (PhD); biological sciences (PhD); biotechnology (MA); chemical physics (PhD); chemistry (PhD); classical studies (MA, PhD); classics (MA, PhD); climate and society (MA); conservation biology (MA); earth and environmental sciences (PhD); East Asia: regional studies (MA); East Asian languages and cultures (MA, PhD); ecology, evolution and environmental biology (MA), including conservation biology; ecology, evolution, and environmental biology (PhD), including ecology and evolutionary biology, evolutionary primatology; economics (MA, PhD); English and comparative literature (MA, PhD); French and Romance philology (MA, PhD); Germanic languages (MA, PhD); global French studies (MA); global thought (MA); Hispanic cultural studies (MA); history (PhD); history and literature (MA); human rights studies (MA); Islamic studies (MA); Italian (MA, PhD); Japanese pedagogy (MA); Jewish studies (MA); Latin America and the Caribbean: regional studies (MA); Latin American and Iberian cultures (PhD); mathematics (MA, PhD), including finance (MA); medieval and Renaissance studies (MA); Middle Eastern, South Asian, and African studies (MA, PhD); modern art: critical and curatorial studies (MA); modern European studies (MA); museum anthropology (MA); music (DMA, PhD); oral history (MA); philosophical foundations of physics (MA); philosophy (MA, PhD); physics (PhD); political science (MA, PhD); psychology (PhD); quantitative methods in the social sciences (MA); religion (MA, PhD); Russia, Eurasia and East Europe: regional studies (MA); Russian translation (MA); Slavic cultures (MA); Slavic languages (MA, PhD); sociology (MA, PhD); South Asian studies (MA); statistics (MA, PhD); theatre (PhD). *Program availability:* Part-time. *Students:* 3,506 full-time (1,844 women), 208 part-time (121 women); includes 864 minority (110 Black or African American, non-Hispanic/Latino; 5 American Indian or Alaska Native, non-Hispanic/Latino; 416 Asian, non-Hispanic/Latino; 147 Hispanic/Latino; 6 Native Hawaiian or other Pacific Islander, non-Hispanic/Latino; 180 Two or more races, non-Hispanic/Latino), 2,065 international. 14,545 applicants, 25% accepted, 1,429 enrolled. In 2019, 1,262 master's, 363 doctorates awarded. Terminal master's awarded for partial completion of doctoral program. *Degree requirements:* For master's, variable foreign language requirement, comprehensive exam (for some programs), thesis (for some programs); for doctorate, variable foreign language requirement, comprehensive exam (for some programs), thesis/dissertation. *Entrance requirements:* For master's and doctorate, GRE General Test, GRE Subject Test (for some programs). Additional exam requirements/recommendations for international students: required—TOEFL (minimum score 600 paper-based; 100 iBT), IELTS (minimum score 7.5). Application fee: $115. Electronic applications accepted. *Expenses: Tuition:* Full-time $47,600; part-time $1880 per credit. One-time fee: $105. *Financial support:* Fellowships, research assistantships, teaching assistantships, career-related internships or fieldwork, Federal Work-Study, institutionally sponsored loans, scholarships/grants, traineeships, health care benefits, tuition waivers, and unspecified assistantships available. Support available to part-time students. Financial award application deadline: 12/15. *Unit head:* Dr. Carlos J. Alonso, Dean of the Graduate School of Arts and Sciences and Vice President for Graduate Education, 212-854-2861, E-mail: gsas-dean@columbia.edu. *Application contact:* GSAS Office of Admissions, 212-854-6729, E-mail: gsas-admissions@columbia.edu.
Website: http://gsas.columbia.edu/

Cornell University, Graduate School, Graduate Fields of Arts and Sciences, Field of English Language and Literature, Ithaca, NY 14853. Offers African-American literature (PhD); American literature after 1865 (PhD); American literature to 1865 (PhD); American studies (PhD); colonial and postcolonial literatures (PhD); creative writing (MFA); cultural studies (PhD); dramatic literature (PhD); English poetry (PhD); English Renaissance to 1660 (PhD); lesbian, bisexual, and gay literary studies (PhD); literary criticism and theory (PhD); Old and Middle English (PhD); prose fiction (PhD); Restoration and the eighteenth-century (PhD); the nineteenth century (PhD); the twentieth century (PhD); women's literature (PhD); MFA/PhD. Terminal master's awarded for partial completion of doctoral program. *Degree requirements:* For master's, one foreign language, thesis; for doctorate, one foreign language, comprehensive exam, thesis/dissertation, teaching experience. *Entrance requirements:* For master's, GRE General Test, 3 letters of recommendation, creative writing sample; for doctorate, 3 letters of recommendation, writing sample. Additional exam requirements/recommendations for international students: required—TOEFL (minimum score 600 paper-based; 77 iBT). Electronic applications accepted.

Cornell University, Graduate School, Graduate Fields of Arts and Sciences, Field of History of Art, Archaeology and Visual Studies, Ithaca, NY 14853. Offers 19th century art (PhD); African, African American and African diaspora (PhD); American art (PhD); ancient art and archaeology (PhD); Asian American art (PhD); Baroque art (PhD); Comparative Modernities (PhD); digital art (PhD); East Asian art (PhD); history of photography (PhD); Islamic art (PhD); Latin American art (PhD); medieval art (PhD); modern art (PhD); Renaissance art (PhD); Southeast Asian art (PhD); theory and criticism (PhD); visual studies (PhD). *Degree requirements:* For doctorate, one foreign language, comprehensive exam, thesis/dissertation, general exams in 3 areas. *Entrance requirements:* For doctorate, GRE General Test, sample of written work, 3 letters of recommendation. Additional exam requirements/recommendations for international students: required—TOEFL (minimum score 550 paper-based; 77 iBT). Electronic applications accepted.

Drew University, Caspersen School of Graduate Studies, Madison, NJ 07940-1493. Offers conflict resolution and leadership (Certificate), including community leadership, moderation, peace building; education (M Ed); finance (MA); history and culture (MA, PhD), including American history, book history, British history, European history, intellectual history, Irish history, print culture, public history; K-12 education (MAT), including art, biology, chemistry, elementary education, English, French, Italian, math, secondary education, special education, teacher of students with disabilities; liberal studies (M Litt, D Litt), including history, Irish/Irish-American studies, literature (M Litt, MMH, D Litt, DMH, CMH), religion, spirituality, teaching in the two-year college, writing; medical humanities (MMH, DMH, CMH), including arts, health, healthcare, literature (M Litt, MMH, D Litt, DMH, CMH), scientific research; poetry (MFA). *Program availability:* Part-time, evening/weekend. Terminal master's awarded for partial completion of doctoral program. *Degree requirements:* For master's and other advanced degree, thesis (for some programs); for doctorate, one foreign language, comprehensive exam (for some programs), thesis/dissertation. *Entrance requirements:* For master's, PRAXIS Core and Subject Area tests (for MAT), GRE/GMAT (for MFin MS in Data Analytics), resume, transcripts, writing sample, personal statement, letters of recommendation; for doctorate, GRE (PhD in history and culture), resume, transcripts, writing sample, personal statement, letters of recommendation; for other advanced degree, resume, transcripts, personal statement. Additional exam requirements/recommendations for international students: required—TOEFL (minimum score 587 paper-based; 80 iBT), IELTS (minimum score 6), TWE (minimum score 4). Electronic applications accepted.

East Carolina University, Graduate School, Thomas Harriot College of Arts and Sciences, Department of History, Greenville, NC 27858-4353. Offers American history (MA); Atlantic world (MA); European history (MA); maritime studies (MA); military history (MA); public history (MA). *Program availability:* Part-time. *Application deadline:* For fall admission, 4/1 priority date for domestic and international students; for spring admission, 10/15 priority date for domestic and international students. *Expenses: Tuition, area resident:* Full-time $4749; part-time $185 per credit hour. Tuition, state resident: full-time $4749; part-time $185 per credit hour. Tuition, nonresident: full-time $17,898; part-time $864 per credit hour. *International tuition:* $17,898 full-time. *Required fees:* $2787. *Financial support:* Application deadline: 1/15. *Unit head:* Dr. Christopher Oakley, Chair, 252-328-1025, E-mail: oakleyc@ecu.edu. *Application contact:* Graduate School Admissions, 252-328-6012, E-mail: gradschool@ecu.edu.
Website: https://history.ecu.edu/

Emory & Henry College, Graduate Programs, Emory, VA 24327. Offers American history (MA Ed); education professional studies (M Ed); occupational therapy (MOT); organizational leadership (MCOL); physical therapy (DPT); physician assistant studies (MPAS); reading specialist (MA Ed). *Program availability:* Part-time. *Degree requirements:* For master's, thesis optional; for doctorate, thesis/dissertation optional. *Entrance requirements:* For master's, GRE or PRAXIS I, official transcripts from all colleges previously attended, three professional recommendations, essay. Additional exam requirements/recommendations for international students: recommended—TOEFL, IELTS (minimum score 6). Electronic applications accepted. *Expenses:* Contact institution.

Fairfield University, College of Arts and Sciences, Fairfield, CT 06824. Offers American studies (MA); communication (MA); creative writing (MFA); mathematics (MS); public administration (MPA). *Program availability:* Part-time, evening/weekend, online learning. *Faculty:* 35 full-time (19 women), 19 part-time/adjunct (10 women). *Students:* 64 full-time (44 women), 84 part-time (48 women); includes 35 minority (9 Black or African American, non-Hispanic/Latino; 1 American Indian or Alaska Native, non-Hispanic/Latino; 1 Asian, non-Hispanic/Latino; 21 Hispanic/Latino; 3 Two or more races, non-Hispanic/Latino), 7 international. Average age 36. 98 applicants, 68% accepted, 64 enrolled. In 2019, 38 master's awarded. *Degree requirements:* For master's, capstone research course. *Entrance requirements:* For master's, minimum GPA of 3.0, 2 letters of recommendation, resume, personal statement. Additional exam requirements/recommendations for international students: required—TOEFL (minimum score 550 paper-based; 80 iBT) or IELTS (minimum score 6.5). *Application deadline:* For fall admission, 5/15 for international students; for spring admission, 10/15 for international students. Applications are processed on a rolling basis. Application fee: $60. Electronic applications accepted. *Expenses:* Tuition $850/credit hour; Registration Fee $50/semester; Graduate Student Activity Fee (Fall and Spring) $65/semester. *Financial support:* In 2019–20, 11 students received support. Scholarships/grants and unspecified assistantships available. Financial award applicants required to submit FAFSA. *Unit head:* Dr. Richard Greenwald, Dean, 203-254-4000 Ext. 2221, Fax: 203-254-4119, E-mail: rgreenwald@fairfield.edu. *Application contact:* Melanie Rogers, Director of Graduate Admission, 203-254-4184, Fax: 203-254-4073, E-mail: gradadmis@fairfield.edu.
Website: http://www.fairfield.edu/cas

Florida State University, The Graduate School, College of Fine Arts, School of Dance, Tallahassee, FL 32306-2120. Offers dance (MA, MFA). *Accreditation:* NASD. *Faculty:* 19 full-time (13 women), 3 part-time/adjunct (all women). *Students:* 26 full-time (15 women); includes 12 minority (8 Black or African American, non-Hispanic/Latino; 1 Asian, non-Hispanic/Latino; 2 Hispanic/Latino; 1 Two or more races, non-Hispanic/Latino). Average age 28. 45 applicants, 33% accepted, 12 enrolled. In 2019, 12 master's awarded. *Degree requirements:* For master's, comprehensive exam (for some programs), thesis (for some programs), 1 foreign language (for MA in American dance studies). *Entrance requirements:* For master's, letters of recommendation, statement of purpose, transcripts, writing sample, CV/resume, (an audition is also required for MFA and MA in studio and related studies applicants). Additional exam requirements/recommendations for international students: required—TOEFL (minimum score 550 paper-based, 80 iBT), IELTS (minimum score 6.5) or Michigan English Language Assessment Battery (minimum score 77). *Application deadline:* For fall admission, 1/1 priority date for domestic and international students. Applications are processed on a rolling basis. Application fee: $30. Electronic applications accepted. *Financial support:* In 2019–20, 21 students received support, including 2 fellowships with full tuition reimbursements available (averaging $10,000 per year), 9 research assistantships with full tuition reimbursements available (averaging $6,098 per year), 12 teaching assistantships with full tuition reimbursements available (averaging $6,098 per year); scholarships/grants, health care benefits, tuition waivers (full), and unspecified assistantships also available. Financial award application deadline: 1/1; financial award applicants required to submit FAFSA. *Unit head:* Prof. Anjali Austin, Professor and Chair, 850-644-1024, Fax: 850-644-1277, E-mail: aaustin@fsu.edu. *Application contact:* Dr. Jeff Bray, Academic Program Manager, 850-644-1023, Fax: 850-644-1277, E-mail: jbray@fsu.edu.
Website: http://dance.fsu.edu/

Florida State University, The Graduate School, College of Social Sciences and Public Policy, Department of Political Science, Tallahassee, FL 32306-2230. Offers applied American politics and policy (MS); political science (MS, PhD). *Program availability:* Part-time. *Faculty:* 25 full-time (5 women), 1 part-time/adjunct (0 women). *Students:* 56 full-time (27 women), 18 part-time (9 women); includes 27 minority (8 Black or African

American, non-Hispanic/Latino; 2 Asian, non-Hispanic/Latino; 13 Hispanic/Latino; 4 Two or more races, non-Hispanic/Latino), 4 international. Average age 28. 90 applicants, 44% accepted, 28 enrolled. In 2019, 24 master's, 6 doctorates awarded. Terminal master's awarded for partial completion of doctoral program. *Degree requirements:* For master's, thesis optional; for doctorate, comprehensive exam, thesis/dissertation. *Entrance requirements:* For master's, GRE General Test, minimum undergraduate GPA of 3.0; for doctorate, GRE General Test, minimum graduate GPA of 3.5, undergraduate 3.0. Additional exam requirements/recommendations for international students: required—TOEFL (minimum score 600 paper-based; 100 iBT). *Application deadline:* For fall admission, 1/15 priority date for domestic and international students. Applications are processed on a rolling basis. Application fee: $30. Electronic applications accepted. *Financial support:* In 2019–20, 34 students received support, including 16 research assistantships with full tuition reimbursements available (averaging $17,500 per year), 9 teaching assistantships with full tuition reimbursements available (averaging $17,500 per year); Federal Work-Study, institutionally sponsored loans, scholarships/grants, and unspecified assistantships also available. Financial award application deadline: 1/15; financial award applicants required to submit FAFSA. *Unit head:* Dr. Charles Barrilleaux, Department Chair, 850-644-5727, Fax: 850-644-1367, E-mail: cbarrilleaux@fsu.edu. *Application contact:* Elisa Kuchvalek, Academic Coordinator, 850-644-5727, Fax: 850-644-1367, E-mail: ekuchvalek@fsu.edu.
Website: http://coss.fsu.edu/polisci/

Georgetown University, Graduate School of Arts and Sciences, School of Continuing Studies, Washington, DC 20057. Offers American studies (MALS); applied intelligence (MPS); Catholic studies (MALS); classical civilizations (MALS); emergency and disaster management (MPS); ethics and the professions (MALS); global strategic communications (MPS); hospitality management (MPS); human resources management (MPS); humanities (MALS); individualized study (MALS); integrated marketing communications (MPS); international affairs (MALS); Islam and Muslim-Christian relations (MALS); journalism (MPS); liberal studies (DLS); literature and society (MALS); medieval and early modern European studies (MALS); public relations and corporate communications (MPS); real estate (MPS); religious studies (MALS); social and public policy (MALS); sports industry management (MPS); systems engineering management (MPS); technology management (MPS); the theory and practice of American democracy (MALS); urban and regional planning (MPS); visual culture (MALS). *Entrance requirements:* Additional exam requirements/recommendations for international students: required—TOEFL.

The George Washington University, Columbian College of Arts and Sciences, Department of American Studies, Washington, DC 20052. Offers American studies (PhD); folk life (MA); historic preservation (MA); material culture (MA). *Program availability:* Part-time, evening/weekend. Terminal master's awarded for partial completion of doctoral program. *Degree requirements:* For master's, comprehensive exam; for doctorate, one foreign language, thesis/dissertation, general exam. *Entrance requirements:* For master's and doctorate, GRE General Test, minimum GPA of 3.0. Additional exam requirements/recommendations for international students: required—TOEFL (minimum score 550 paper-based; 80 iBT).

Harvard University, Graduate School of Arts and Sciences, Committee on History of American Civilization, Cambridge, MA 02138. Offers PhD. *Degree requirements:* For doctorate, 2 foreign languages, thesis/dissertation. *Entrance requirements:* For doctorate, GRE General Test, GRE Subject Test (recommended). Additional exam requirements/recommendations for international students: required—TOEFL.

Indiana University-Purdue University Indianapolis, School of Liberal Arts, Department of History, Indianapolis, IN 46202. Offers European history (MA); public history (MA); United States history (MA); MA/MA; MA/MLS. *Program availability:* Part-time, evening/weekend. *Degree requirements:* For master's, one foreign language, thesis. *Entrance requirements:* For master's, GRE General Test, minimum GPA of 3.0. Electronic applications accepted.

Indiana University-Purdue University Indianapolis, School of Liberal Arts, Program in American Studies, Indianapolis, IN 46202. Offers PhD.

Inter American University of Puerto Rico, Metropolitan Campus, Graduate Programs, Program in History, San Juan, PR 00919-1293. Offers American history (PhD); history (MA, PhD).

James Madison University, The Graduate School, College of Arts and Letters, Program in History, Harrisonburg, VA 22807. Offers public history (MA); U.S. history (MA); world history (MA). *Program availability:* Part-time. *Students:* 20 full-time (11 women), 6 part-time (3 women); includes 2 minority (1 Asian, non-Hispanic/Latino; 1 Two or more races, non-Hispanic/Latino). Average age 30. In 2019, 6 master's awarded. *Degree requirements:* For master's, one foreign language, comprehensive exam, thesis. Application fee: $60. Electronic applications accepted. *Financial support:* In 2019–20, 10 students received support, including 3 teaching assistantships with full tuition reimbursements available (averaging $9,284 per year); fellowships, Federal Work-Study, and assistantships (averaging $7911) also available. Financial award application deadline: 3/1; financial award applicants required to submit FAFSA. *Unit head:* Dr. Gabrielle Lanier, Department Head, 540-568-6132, E-mail: laniergm@jmu.edu. *Application contact:* Lynette D. Michael, Director of Graduate Admissions, 540-568-6131 Ext. 6395, Fax: 540-568-7860, E-mail: michaeld@jmu.edu.
Website: http://www.jmu.edu/history

Kennesaw State University, College of Humanities and Social Sciences, Master of Arts in American Studies Program, Kennesaw, GA 30144. Offers MA. *Program availability:* Part-time, evening/weekend. *Students:* 4 full-time (3 women), 7 part-time (5 women); includes 2 minority (both Hispanic/Latino). Average age 46. 6 applicants, 100% accepted, 4 enrolled. In 2019, 6 master's awarded. *Degree requirements:* For master's, one foreign language, thesis optional. *Entrance requirements:* For master's, GRE. Additional exam requirements/recommendations for international students: required—TOEFL (minimum score 80 iBT), IELTS (minimum score 6.5). *Application deadline:* For fall admission, 7/1 for domestic and international students; for spring admission, 11/1 for domestic and international students; for summer admission, 4/1 for domestic and international students. Applications are processed on a rolling basis. Application fee: $60. Electronic applications accepted. *Expenses: Tuition, area resident:* Full-time $7104; part-time $296 per credit hour. Tuition, state resident: full-time $7104; part-time $296 per credit hour. Tuition, nonresident: full-time $25,584; part-time $1066 per credit hour. *International tuition:* $25,584 full-time. *Required fees:* $2006; $1706 per unit. $853 per semester. *Financial support:* Applicants required to submit FAFSA. *Unit head:* Dr. Rebecca Hill, Director, 470-578-7543, E-mail: rhill54@kennesaw.edu. *Application contact:* Admissions Counselor, 470-578-4377, Fax: 470-578-9172, E-mail: ksugrad@kennesaw.edu.
Website: http://chss.kennesaw.edu/mast/

Lake Forest College, Graduate Program in Liberal Studies, Lake Forest, IL 60045. Offers American studies (MLS); cinema in East Asia (MLS); environmental studies (MLS); history (MLS); Medieval and Renaissance art (MLS); philosophy (MLS); Spanish (MLS); writing (MLS). *Program availability:* Part-time, evening/weekend. *Faculty:* 10 full-time (4 women). *Students:* 24 part-time (14 women). Average age 45. 10 applicants, 80% accepted, 3 enrolled. In 2019, 5 master's awarded. *Degree requirements:* For master's, thesis optional, 8 courses, including at least 3 interdisciplinary seminars. *Entrance requirements:* For master's, transcript, essay, interview. Additional exam requirements/recommendations for international students: required—TOEFL (minimum score 550 paper-based; 83 iBT); recommended—IELTS (minimum score 6.5). *Application deadline:* For fall admission, 8/15 priority date for domestic students, 7/15 priority date for international students; for spring admission, 12/15 priority date for domestic students, 11/15 priority date for international students. Applications are processed on a rolling basis. Application fee: $30. Electronic applications accepted. Application fee is waived when completed online. *Expenses:* Application fee = $30 — no other fees; tuition = $2,700/course. *Financial support:* In 2019–20, 2 students received support. Partial tuition grants (for full-time teachers) available. *Unit head:* Prof. D. L. LeMahieu, Director, 847-735-5133, Fax: 847-735-6291, E-mail: lemahieu@lakeforest.edu. *Application contact:* Prof. Carol Gayle, Associate Director, 847-735-5083, Fax: 847-735-6291, E-mail: gayle@lakeforest.edu.
Website: http://www.lakeforest.edu/academics/programs/mls/

Lehigh University, College of Arts and Sciences, Department of History, Bethlehem, PA 18015. Offers Atlantic world (PhD); British history (PhD); history (MA); industrial and modern America (PhD); public history (MA). *Program availability:* Part-time. *Faculty:* 11 full-time (5 women), 1 (woman) part-time/adjunct. *Students:* 15 full-time (6 women), 16 part-time (4 women); includes 2 minority (1 Black or African American, non-Hispanic/Latino; 1 Two or more races, non-Hispanic/Latino), 2 international. Average age 35. 11 applicants, 45% accepted, 3 enrolled. In 2019, 1 master's, 1 doctorate awarded. Terminal master's awarded for partial completion of doctoral program. *Degree requirements:* For master's, comprehensive exam (for some programs), thesis (for some programs), comprehensive exam or thesis; for doctorate, comprehensive exam, thesis/dissertation. *Entrance requirements:* For master's, GRE General Test, recommendations, writing sample; for doctorate, GRE General Test, recommendations, writing samples. Additional exam requirements/recommendations for international students: required—TOEFL. *Application deadline:* For fall admission, 2/15 for domestic and international students. Applications are processed on a rolling basis. Application fee: $75. *Financial support:* In 2019–20, 1 fellowship with full tuition reimbursement (averaging $22,500 per year) was awarded; research assistantships, teaching assistantships with full tuition reimbursements, scholarships/grants, health care benefits, tuition waivers (full and partial), and unspecified assistantships also available. Financial award application deadline: 1/15. *Unit head:* Prof. Rick Matthews, Chairman, 610-758-3360, Fax: 610-758-6554, E-mail: rm02@lehigh.edu. *Application contact:* Ellen Zimmer Lewis, Graduate Coordinator, 610-758-3360, Fax: 610-758-3360, E-mail: ell414@lehigh.edu.
Website: http://history.cas2.lehigh.edu/

Michigan State University, The Graduate School, College of Arts and Letters, Program in American Studies, East Lansing, MI 48824. Offers MA, PhD. *Entrance requirements:* Additional exam requirements/recommendations for international students: required—TOEFL. Electronic applications accepted.

Monmouth University, Graduate Studies, Program in History, West Long Branch, NJ 07764-1898. Offers European history (MA); United States history (MA). *Program availability:* Part-time, evening/weekend. *Faculty:* 9 full-time (2 women). *Students:* 2 full-time (1 woman), 24 part-time (9 women); includes 2 minority (1 Black or African American, non-Hispanic/Latino; 1 Hispanic/Latino). Average age 33. In 2019, 10 master's awarded. *Degree requirements:* For master's, comprehensive exam (for some programs), thesis (for some programs). *Entrance requirements:* For master's, minimum GPA of 3.0 in major, 2.5 overall; two letters of recommendation; statement describing historical areas of interest and how graduate study will contribute to professional and academic goals. Additional exam requirements/recommendations for international students: required—TOEFL (minimum score 550 paper-based; 79 iBT), IELTS (minimum score 6) or Michigan English Language Assessment Battery (minimum score 77). *Application deadline:* For fall admission, 7/15 priority date for domestic students, 6/1 for international students; for spring admission, 12/15 priority date for domestic students, 11/1 for international students. Applications are processed on a rolling basis. Application fee: $50. Electronic applications accepted. *Expenses: Tuition:* Full-time $22,194; part-time $14,796 per credit. *Required fees:* $712; $178 per semester. $178 per semester. Tuition and fees vary according to course load. *Financial support:* In 2019–20, 22 students received support. Research assistantships, teaching assistantships, scholarships/grants, and unspecified assistantships available. Support available to part-time students. Financial award applicants required to submit FAFSA. *Unit head:* Dr. Maryann Rhett, Program Director, 732-263-5768, Fax: 732-263-5112, E-mail: mrhett@monmouth.edu. *Application contact:* Kevin New, Graduate Admission Counselor, 732-571-3452, Fax: 732-263-5123, E-mail: gradadm@monmouth.edu.
Website: https://www.monmouth.edu/graduate/ma-history/

New Mexico Highlands University, Graduate Studies, College of Arts and Sciences, Department of Social and Behavioral Sciences, Las Vegas, NM 87701. Offers psychology (MS), including clinical psychology/counseling, general psychology; public affairs (MA), including applied sociology; Southwest studies (MA), including anthropology. *Program availability:* Part-time. *Degree requirements:* For master's, comprehensive exam, thesis or alternative. *Entrance requirements:* For master's, minimum undergraduate GPA of 3.0. Additional exam requirements/recommendations for international students: required—TOEFL (minimum score 540 paper-based).

New York University, Graduate School of Arts and Science, Program in American Studies, New York, NY 10012-1019. Offers MA, PhD. *Program availability:* Part-time. *Degree requirements:* For master's, one foreign language, thesis; for doctorate, 2 foreign languages, thesis/dissertation. *Entrance requirements:* For master's and doctorate, GRE General Test, writing sample. Additional exam requirements/recommendations for international students: required—TOEFL, IELTS.

New York University, Graduate School of Arts and Science, Program in Irish and Irish American Studies, New York, NY 10012-1019. Offers MA. *Program availability:* Part-time. *Entrance requirements:* For master's, GRE General Test. Additional exam requirements/recommendations for international students: required—TOEFL, IELTS.

Northwestern Oklahoma State University, Program in American Studies, Alva, OK 73717. Offers MA. *Program availability:* Part-time. *Degree requirements:* For master's, comprehensive exam, thesis optional. *Entrance requirements:* For master's, GRE or MAT, at least 12 upper-level undergraduate hours in history and/or literature.

Northwestern University, School of Professional Studies, Program in Liberal Studies, Evanston, IL 60208. Offers American studies (MA); history (MA); religious and ethical studies (MA). *Program availability:* Part-time, evening/weekend.

Penn State Harrisburg, Graduate School, School of Humanities, Middletown, PA 17057. Offers American studies (MA, PhD); communications (MA); folklore and ethnography (Certificate); heritage and museum practice (Certificate); humanities (MA). *Program availability:* Evening/weekend.

Pepperdine University, Seaver College, Malibu, CA 90263. Offers business (MS), including accounting; communication (MFA), including cinematic media production; humanities (MA, MFA), including American studies (MA), writing for screen and television (MFA); religion (M Div, MA, MS), including ministry (MS), religion (M Div, MA); JD/M Div. *Entrance requirements:* For master's, GRE General Test. Additional exam requirements/recommendations for international students: required—TOEFL. *Expenses:* Contact institution.

Portland State University, Graduate Studies, College of Urban and Public Affairs, Hatfield School of Government, Department of Political Science, Portland, OR 97207-0751. Offers political science (MA), including American politics, comparative politics, international relations, political theory. *Program availability:* Part-time. *Faculty:* 12 full-time (4 women), 4 part-time/adjunct (1 woman). *Students:* 6 full-time (2 women), 9 part-time (3 women); includes 1 minority (Two or more races, non-Hispanic/Latino), 2 international. Average age 35. 11 applicants, 73% accepted, 4 enrolled. In 2019, 2 master's awarded. *Degree requirements:* For master's, variable foreign language requirement, comprehensive exam, thesis. *Entrance requirements:* For master's, GRE General Test, minimum undergraduate GPA of 3.0 or 3.1 in graduate-level coursework, 2 letters of recommendation, statement of intent. Additional exam requirements/recommendations for international students: required—TOEFL (minimum score 550 paper-based; 90 iBT). *Application deadline:* For fall admission, 2/1 priority date for domestic and international students. Application fee: $65. Electronic applications accepted. *Expenses: Tuition, area resident:* Full-time $13,020; part-time $6510 per year. Tuition, state resident: full-time $13,020; part-time $6510 per year. Tuition, nonresident: full-time $19,830; part-time $9915 per year. *International tuition:* $19,830 full-time. *Required fees:* $1226. One-time fee: $350. Tuition and fees vary according to course load, program and reciprocity agreements. *Financial support:* In 2019–20, 3 teaching assistantships with full and partial tuition reimbursements (averaging $7,209 per year) were awarded; research assistantships, career-related internships or fieldwork, and Federal Work-Study also available. Support available to part-time students. Financial award application deadline: 3/1; financial award applicants required to submit FAFSA. *Unit head:* Melody Valdini, Chair, 503-725-5139, Fax: 503-725-8444, E-mail: mev@pdx.edu. *Application contact:* Dr. David Kinsella, Graduate Committee Chair, 503-725-3035, E-mail: kinsella@pdx.edu.
Website: https://www.pdx.edu/hatfieldschool/political-science

Providence College, Department of History, Providence, RI 02918. Offers American history (MA); modern European history (MA). *Program availability:* Part-time, evening/weekend. *Degree requirements:* For master's, comprehensive exam, thesis optional. *Entrance requirements:* Additional exam requirements/recommendations for international students: required—TOEFL (minimum score 577 paper-based; 90 iBT). *Expenses:* Contact institution.

Purdue University, Graduate School, College of Liberal Arts, Program in American Studies, West Lafayette, IN 47907. Offers MA, PhD. *Students:* 20 full-time (14 women), 6 part-time (all women); includes 14 minority (9 Black or African American, non-Hispanic/Latino; 3 Asian, non-Hispanic/Latino; 1 Hispanic/Latino; 1 Two or more races, non-Hispanic/Latino), 3 international. Average age 32. 28 applicants, 29% accepted, 4 enrolled. In 2019, 1 master's, 10 doctorates awarded. *Degree requirements:* For master's, essay; for doctorate, one foreign language, thesis/dissertation. *Entrance requirements:* For master's, GRE General Test, minimum undergraduate GPA of 3.0 or equivalent; writing sample; for doctorate, GRE General Test, minimum undergraduate GPA of 3.0 or equivalent; writing sample; master's degree with minimum GPA of 3.0 or equivalent. Additional exam requirements/recommendations for international students: required—TOEFL (minimum score 550 paper-based; 77 iBT), TWE. *Application deadline:* For fall admission, 1/15 priority date for domestic students, 1/15 for international students. Applications are processed on a rolling basis. Application fee: $60 ($75 for international students). Electronic applications accepted. *Financial support:* In 2019–20, 34 students received support, including teaching assistantships with tuition reimbursements available (averaging $14,150 per year); fellowships also available. Support available to part-time students. Financial award application deadline: 1/15; financial award applicants required to submit FAFSA. *Unit head:* Rayvon Fouche Fouche, Director, 765-496-0040, E-mail: rfouche@purdue.edu. *Application contact:* Brandi Plantenga, Graduate Contact, 765-496-9629, E-mail: bplante@purdue.edu.
Website: http://www.cla.purdue.edu/american-studies/

Regent University, Graduate School, Robertson School of Government, Virginia Beach, VA 23464. Offers government (MA), including American government, healthcare policy and ethics (MA, MPA), international relations, law and public policy, national security studies, political communication, political theory, religion and politics; national security studies (MA), including cybersecurity, homeland security, international security, Middle East politics; public administration (MPA), including emergency management and homeland security, federal government, general public administration, healthcare policy and ethics (MA, MPA), law, nonprofit administration and faith-based organizations, public leadership and management, servant leadership. *Program availability:* Part-time, evening/weekend, 100% online, blended/hybrid learning. *Faculty:* 5 full-time (1 woman), 19 part-time/adjunct (2 women). *Students:* 36 full-time (22 women), 159 part-time (89 women); includes 82 minority (52 Black or African American, non-Hispanic/Latino; 2 American Indian or Alaska Native, non-Hispanic/Latino; 2 Asian, non-Hispanic/Latino; 23 Hispanic/Latino; 3 Two or more races, non-Hispanic/Latino), 4 international. Average age 36. 181 applicants, 70% accepted, 75 enrolled. In 2019, 58 master's awarded. *Degree requirements:* For master's, thesis optional, internship. *Entrance requirements:* For master's, GRE General Test or LSAT, personal essay, writing sample, resume, college transcripts. Additional exam requirements/recommendations for international students: required—TOEFL (minimum score 577 paper-based). *Application deadline:* For fall admission, 5/1 priority date for domestic students; for spring admission, 11/1 priority date for domestic students. Applications are processed on a rolling basis. Application fee: $50. Electronic applications accepted. *Expenses:* Contact institution. *Financial support:* In 2019–20, 132 students received support. Career-related internships or fieldwork, scholarships/grants, and unspecified assistantships available. Support available to part-time students. Financial award applicants required to submit FAFSA. *Unit head:* Dr. Stephen Perry, Interim Dean, 757-352-4082, E-mail: sperry@regent.edu. *Application contact:* Heidi Cece, Assistant Vice President for Enrollment Management, 800-373-5504, Fax: 757-352-4381, E-mail: admissions@regent.edu.
Website: https://www.regent.edu/robertson-school-of-government/

Rice University, Graduate Programs, School of Humanities, Department of Religious Studies, Houston, TX 77251-1892. Offers African religions (PhD); African-American religions (PhD); contemplative studies (PhD); gnosticism, esotericism, mysticism (PhD); Islam (PhD); Jewish thought and philosophy (PhD); modern Christianity in thought and popular culture (PhD); psychology of religion (PhD); the Bible and beyond (PhD). *Degree requirements:* For doctorate, 2 foreign languages, comprehensive exam, thesis/dissertation. *Entrance requirements:* For doctorate, GRE, letters of recommendation, writing sample. Additional exam requirements/recommendations for international students: required—TOEFL (minimum score 600 paper-based; 90 iBT). Electronic applications accepted.

Rutgers University - Newark, Graduate School, Program in American Studies, Newark, NJ 07102. Offers MA, PhD. *Entrance requirements:* For master's and doctorate, GRE, minimum undergraduate B average.

Saint Louis University, Graduate Programs, College of Arts and Sciences, Department of American Studies, St. Louis, MO 63103. Offers MA, MA-R, PhD. *Program availability:* Part-time. *Degree requirements:* For master's, thesis optional, comprehensive written and oral exams; for doctorate, one foreign language, comprehensive exam, thesis/dissertation, preliminary exams. *Entrance requirements:* For master's, GRE General Test, letters of recommendation, resume; for doctorate, GRE General Test, letters of recommendation, resumé, goal statement, transcripts. Additional exam requirements/recommendations for international students: required—TOEFL (minimum score 525 paper-based). Electronic applications accepted.

Salisbury University, Department of History, Salisbury, MD 21801-6837. Offers history (MA), including Colonial and Revolutionary American history, history of the Chesapeake Bay region, United States history in the 19th and 20th centuries, world history. *Program availability:* Part-time, evening/weekend. *Faculty:* 5 full-time (1 woman). *Students:* 6 full-time (3 women), 5 part-time (2 women); includes 2 minority (both Two or more races, non-Hispanic/Latino). Average age 33. 9 applicants, 89% accepted, 8 enrolled. In 2019, 5 master's awarded. *Degree requirements:* For master's, comprehensive exam, must take history methods and theory course. *Entrance requirements:* For master's, transcripts; resume or CV; personal statement; writing sample if undergraduate degree is from a different institution; minimum GPA of 3.0; three letters of recommendation; if student does not have a history BA, it is requested they take a history methods course upon admission. Additional exam requirements/recommendations for international students: recommended—TOEFL (minimum score 550 paper-based; 79 iBT). *Application deadline:* For fall admission, 4/15 priority date for domestic and international students; for spring admission, 11/15 priority date for domestic and international students. Applications are processed on a rolling basis. Application fee: $65. Electronic applications accepted. *Expenses:* Contact institution. *Financial support:* In 2019–20, 3 students received support, including 4 research assistantships with full tuition reimbursements available (averaging $8,000 per year); career-related internships or fieldwork and scholarships/grants also available. Support available to part-time students. Financial award application deadline: 3/1; financial award applicants required to submit FAFSA. *Unit head:* Dr. Celine Carayon, Graduate Program Director, 410-677-4601, E-mail: cxcarayon@salisbury.edu. *Application contact:* Dr. Celine Carayon, Graduate Program Director, 410-677-4601, E-mail: cxcarayon@salisbury.edu.
Website: https://www.salisbury.edu/explore-academics/programs/graduate-degree-programs/history-masters/

Stockton University, Office of Graduate Studies, Program in American Studies, Galloway, NJ 08205-9441. Offers MA, Certificate. *Program availability:* Part-time. *Faculty:* 16 full-time (9 women). *Students:* 9 part-time (3 women); includes 2 minority (1 Asian, non-Hispanic/Latino; 1 Hispanic/Latino). Average age 27. 7 applicants, 86% accepted, 3 enrolled. In 2019, 8 master's awarded. *Application deadline:* For fall admission, 7/1 for domestic and international students; for winter admission, 11/1 for international students; for spring admission, 12/1 for domestic students. Applications are processed on a rolling basis. Application fee: $50. Electronic applications accepted. *Expenses: Tuition, area resident:* Full-time $750.92; part-time $78.58 per credit hour. Tuition, state resident: full-time $750.92; part-time $78.58 per credit hour. Tuition, nonresident: full-time $846; part-time $78.58 per credit hour. *International tuition:* $1195.96 full-time. *Required fees:* $1464; $78.58 per credit hour. One-time fee: $50 full-time. *Financial support:* Fellowships, research assistantships, scholarships/grants, and unspecified assistantships available. Financial award application deadline: 3/1. *Unit head:* Dr. Kristin Jacobson, Program Director, 609-626-5581, E-mail: gradschool@stockton.edu. *Application contact:* Tara Williams, Assistant Director of Enrollment Management, 609-626-3640, Fax: 609-626-6050, E-mail: gradschool@stockton.edu.

SUNY Brockport, School of Arts and Sciences, Department of History, Brockport, NY 14420-2997. Offers history (MA), including American and world history, American history, American public history, world history. *Program availability:* Part-time, evening/weekend. *Faculty:* 9 full-time (4 women), 1 part-time/adjunct (0 women). *Students:* 6 full-time (2 women), 33 part-time (17 women); includes 2 minority (both Black or African American, non-Hispanic/Latino). 11 applicants, 91% accepted, 5 enrolled. In 2019, 17 master's awarded. *Entrance requirements:* For master's, minimum GPA of 3.0, writing sample, letters of recommendation, statement of objectives. Additional exam requirements/recommendations for international students: required—TOEFL (minimum score 550 paper-based; 79 iBT), IELTS (minimum score 6.5). *Application deadline:* For fall admission, 7/1 priority date for domestic and international students; for spring admission, 11/15 priority date for domestic and international students; for summer admission, 4/15 for domestic and international students. Application fee: $50. Electronic applications accepted. *Expenses: Tuition, area resident:* Part-time $471 per credit hour. Tuition, nonresident: part-time $963 per credit hour. *Financial support:* In 2019–20, 1 fellowship with tuition reimbursement (averaging $3,750 per year), 2 teaching assistantships with full tuition reimbursements (averaging $6,000 per year) were awarded; Federal Work-Study, scholarships/grants, and unspecified assistantships also available. Support available to part-time students. Financial award application deadline: 3/15; financial award applicants required to submit FAFSA. *Unit head:* Dr. Jose Torre, Chairperson, 585-395-5698, Fax: 585-395-2620, E-mail: jrtorre@brockport.edu. *Application contact:* Dr. Carl Davila, Graduate Director, 585-395-5699, Fax: 585-395-2620, E-mail: cdavila@brockport.edu.
Website: https://www.brockport.edu/academics/history/graduate/masters.html

Texas Christian University, AddRan College of Liberal Arts, Department of History, Fort Worth, TX 76129-0002. Offers Latin America (MA, PhD); United States (MA, PhD). *Faculty:* 16 full-time (6 women). *Students:* 47 full-time (20 women); includes 8 minority (1 Black or African American, non-Hispanic/Latino; 6 Hispanic/Latino; 1 Two or more races, non-Hispanic/Latino), 2 international. Average age 35. 25 applicants, 48% accepted, 8 enrolled. In 2019, 2 master's, 3 doctorates awarded. Terminal master's awarded for partial completion of doctoral program. *Degree requirements:* For master's, comprehensive exam, thesis or alternative; for doctorate, one foreign language, comprehensive exam, thesis/dissertation. *Entrance requirements:* For master's and doctorate, GRE General Test. Additional exam requirements/recommendations for international students: recommended—TOEFL. *Application deadline:* 2/1 for domestic and international students; for summer admission, 2/1 for domestic and international students. Application fee: $60. Electronic applications accepted. Full-time tuition and fees vary according to program. *Financial support:* In 2019–20, 50 students received support, including 3 fellowships with full tuition reimbursements available (averaging $25,000 per year), 15 research assistantships with full tuition reimbursements available (averaging $20,000 per year), 5 teaching assistantships with full tuition reimbursements available (averaging $20,000 per year); tuition waivers (full) also available. Financial award application deadline: 2/1. *Unit head:* Dr. William Meier, Associate Professor, 817-257-5882, Fax: 817-257-5650, E-mail: w.meier@tcu.edu. *Application contact:* Heather Confessore, Administrative Assistant, 817-257-7288, Fax: 817-257-5650, E-mail: h.confessore@tcu.edu.
Website: https://addran.tcu.edu/history/academics/areas-of-study/graduate-programs/

Trinity College, Graduate Programs, Program in American Studies, Hartford, CT 06106-3100. Offers American culture studies (MA); museums and communities (MA). *Program availability:* Part-time, evening/weekend. *Degree requirements:* For master's, thesis or alternative. *Entrance requirements:* For master's, minimum GPA of 3.0.

Universidad de las Américas Puebla, Division of Graduate Studies, School of Social Sciences, Program in American Studies, Puebla, Mexico. Offers MA. *Program* *availability:* Part-time, evening/weekend. *Degree requirements:* For master's, one foreign language, thesis.

University at Buffalo, the State University of New York, Graduate School, College of Arts and Sciences, Department of Transnational Studies, Buffalo, NY 14214. Offers American studies (MA, PhD); Canadian studies (MA); global gender studies (MA, PhD). *Program availability:* Part-time. Terminal master's awarded for partial completion of doctoral program. *Degree requirements:* For master's, comprehensive exam (for some programs), thesis optional; for doctorate, comprehensive exam, thesis/dissertation. *Entrance requirements:* For master's, minimum GPA of 3.0; for doctorate, GRE, minimum GPA of 3.0. Additional exam requirements/recommendations for international students: required—TOEFL (minimum score 550 paper-based; 79 iBT), IELTS (minimum score 6.5). Electronic applications accepted. *Expenses: Tuition, area resident:* Full-time $11,310; part-time $471 per credit hour. Tuition, state resident: full-time $11,310; part-time $471 per credit hour. Tuition, nonresident: full-time $23,100; part-time $963 per credit hour. *International tuition:* $23,100 full-time. *Required fees:* $2820.

The University of Alabama, Graduate School, College of Arts and Sciences, Department of American Studies, Tuscaloosa, AL 35487. Offers MA. *Program availability:* Part-time. *Faculty:* 7 full-time (2 women). *Students:* 6 full-time (4 women); includes 3 minority (2 Hispanic/Latino; 1 Two or more races, non-Hispanic/Latino). Average age 29. 10 applicants, 80% accepted, 3 enrolled. In 2019, 8 master's awarded. *Degree requirements:* For master's, comprehensive exam. *Entrance requirements:* For master's, GRE or MAT. Additional exam requirements/recommendations for international students: required—TOEFL. *Application deadline:* For fall admission, 1/15 priority date for domestic and international students; for spring admission, 11/30 priority date for domestic and international students; for summer admission, 1/15 for domestic and international students. Applications are processed on a rolling basis. Application fee: $50 ($60 for international students). Electronic applications accepted. *Expenses: Tuition, area resident:* Full-time $10,780; part-time $440 per credit hour. Tuition, nonresident: full-time $30,250; part-time $1550 per credit hour. *Financial support:* In 2019–20, teaching assistantships with full tuition reimbursements (averaging $18,300 per year) were awarded; career-related internships or fieldwork, health care benefits, and unspecified assistantships also available. Financial award application deadline: 1/10; financial award applicants required to submit FAFSA. *Unit head:* Dr. Edward Tang, Professor and Department Chair, 205-348-9762, Fax: 205-348-9766, E-mail: etang@ua.edu. *Application contact:* Patrick D. Fuller, Senior Graduate Admissions Counselor, 205-348-5923, Fax: 205-348-0400, E-mail: patrick.d.fuller@ua.edu. Website: http://ams.ua.edu/

University of Colorado Denver, College of Liberal Arts and Sciences, Department of History, Denver, CO 80217. Offers European history (MA); global history (MA); public history (MA); U.S. history (MA). *Program availability:* Part-time, evening/weekend. *Degree requirements:* For master's, comprehensive exam, thesis optional, 36 semester hours (12 courses). *Entrance requirements:* For master's, GRE General Test, writing sample, minimum undergraduate GPA of 3.25, three letters of recommendation, statement of purpose addressing any weaknesses in academic record. Additional exam requirements/recommendations for international students: required—TOEFL (minimum score 537 paper-based; 75 iBT); recommended—IELTS (minimum score 6.5). Electronic applications accepted. Tuition and fees vary according to course load, program and reciprocity agreements.

University of Delaware, College of Arts and Sciences, Winterthur Program in American Material Culture, Newark, DE 19716. Offers MA. *Degree requirements:* For master's, thesis. *Entrance requirements:* For master's, GRE General Test, minimum GPA of 3.0. Electronic applications accepted.

University of Hawaii at Manoa, Office of Graduate Education, College of Arts and Humanities, Department of American Studies, Honolulu, HI 96822. Offers American studies (MA, PhD); historic preservation (Graduate Certificate); museum studies (Graduate Certificate). *Program availability:* Part-time. *Degree requirements:* For master's, comprehensive exam (for some programs), thesis (for some programs); for doctorate, comprehensive exam, thesis/dissertation. *Entrance requirements:* For master's and doctorate, GRE General Test. Additional exam requirements/recommendations for international students: required—TOEFL (minimum score 600 paper-based; 100 iBT), IELTS (minimum score 7).

The University of Iowa, Graduate College, College of Liberal Arts and Sciences, Department of American Studies, Iowa City, IA 52242-1316. Offers MA, PhD. *Degree requirements:* For master's, thesis optional, exam; for doctorate, comprehensive exam, thesis/dissertation. *Entrance requirements:* For master's and doctorate, GRE General Test, minimum GPA of 3.0. Additional exam requirements/recommendations for international students: required—TOEFL (minimum score 550 paper-based; 81 iBT). Electronic applications accepted.

The University of Kansas, Graduate Studies, College of Liberal Arts and Sciences, Department of American Studies, Lawrence, KS 66045. Offers MA, PhD, MUP/MA. *Program availability:* Part-time. *Students:* 33 full-time (22 women), 2 part-time (1 woman); includes 13 minority (4 Black or African American, non-Hispanic/Latino; 1 American Indian or Alaska Native, non-Hispanic/Latino; 7 Hispanic/Latino; 1 Two or more races, non-Hispanic/Latino), 1 international. Average age 33. 31 applicants, 32% accepted, 5 enrolled. In 2019, 1 master's, 3 doctorates awarded. Terminal master's awarded for partial completion of doctoral program. *Entrance requirements:* For master's and doctorate, GRE General Test, resume, statement of purpose, three letters of recommendation, official transcripts of all undergraduate and graduate study completed, writing sample. Additional exam requirements/recommendations for international students: required—TOEFL, IELTS. *Application deadline:* For fall admission, 12/1 priority date for domestic and international students. Applications are processed on a rolling basis. Application fee: $65 ($85 for international students). Electronic applications accepted. *Expenses: Tuition,* state resident: full-time $9989. Tuition, nonresident: full-time $23,950. *International tuition:* $23,950 full-time. *Required fees:* $984; $81.99 per credit hour. Tuition and fees vary according to course load, campus/location and program. *Financial support:* Fellowships, research assistantships, teaching assistantships, Federal Work-Study, scholarships/grants, health care benefits, and unspecified assistantships available. Financial award application deadline: 12/1. *Unit head:* Margaret Kelley, Director of Graduate Studies, 785-864-6927, E-mail: mskelley@ku.edu. *Application contact:* Bethany Harris, Graduate Admissions Contact, 785-864-0778, E-mail: bethanyharris@ku.edu. Website: http://americanstudies.ku.edu

University of Louisiana at Lafayette, College of Liberal Arts, Department of History, Geography and Philosophy, Lafayette, LA 70504. Offers history (MA), including American history, European history, Latin American history, public history. *Program availability:* Part-time. *Degree requirements:* For master's, one foreign language, thesis or alternative. *Entrance requirements:* For master's, GRE General Test, minimum GPA of 2.75. Additional exam requirements/recommendations for international students: required—TOEFL (minimum score 550 paper-based). Electronic applications accepted. *Expenses: Tuition, area resident:* Full-time $5511; part-time $1630 per credit hour.

Tuition, state resident: full-time $5511; part-time $1630 per credit hour. Tuition, nonresident: full-time $19,239; part-time $2409 per credit hour. *Required fees:* $46,637.

University of Maryland, College Park, Academic Affairs, College of Arts and Humanities, Department of American Studies, College Park, MD 20742. Offers MA, PhD. *Degree requirements:* For master's, thesis or scholarly paper and exam; for doctorate, thesis/dissertation, 3 comprehensive exams. *Entrance requirements:* For master's, GRE General Test, minimum GPA of 3.0, writing sample, 3 letters of recommendation; for doctorate, GRE General Test. Additional exam requirements/recommendations for international students: required—TOEFL. Electronic applications accepted.

University of Massachusetts Amherst, Graduate School, College of Humanities and Fine Arts, Department of English, Amherst, MA 01003. Offers American studies (PhD); composition and rhetoric (PhD); creative writing (MFA); English and American literature (MA, PhD). *Program availability:* Part-time. Terminal master's awarded for partial completion of doctoral program. *Degree requirements:* For master's, one foreign language, thesis optional; for doctorate, one foreign language, comprehensive exam, thesis/dissertation. *Entrance requirements:* For master's, manuscript; for doctorate, GRE General Test, manuscript. Additional exam requirements/recommendations for international students: required—TOEFL (minimum score 550 paper-based; 80 iBT), IELTS (minimum score 6.5). Electronic applications accepted.

University of Massachusetts Boston, College of Liberal Arts, Program in American Studies, Boston, MA 02125-3393. Offers MA. *Program availability:* Part-time, evening/weekend. *Entrance requirements:* For master's, minimum GPA of 2.75. Electronic applications accepted.

University of Michigan, Rackham Graduate School, College of Literature, Science, and the Arts, Department of American Culture, Ann Arbor, MI 48109-1045. Offers AM, PhD. Terminal master's awarded for partial completion of doctoral program. *Degree requirements:* For doctorate, comprehensive exam, thesis/dissertation, preliminary exams, field exams, oral defense of dissertation. *Entrance requirements:* For doctorate, sample of written work. Additional exam requirements/recommendations for international students: required—TOEFL. Electronic applications accepted.

University of Michigan–Flint, College of Arts and Sciences, Program in Social Sciences, Flint, MI 48502-1950. Offers gender studies (MA); global studies (MA); U.S. history and politics (MA). *Program availability:* Part-time. *Faculty:* 11 full-time (6 women), 4 part-time/adjunct (all women). *Students:* 3 full-time (2 women), 7 part-time (5 women); includes 4 minority (3 Black or African American, non-Hispanic/Latino; 1 Two or more races, non-Hispanic/Latino). Average age 43. 15 applicants, 60% accepted, 2 enrolled. In 2019, 4 master's awarded. *Entrance requirements:* For master's, bachelor's degree from regionally-accredited institution, minimum overall undergraduate GPA of 3.0 on 4.0 scale. Additional exam requirements/recommendations for international students: required—TOEFL (minimum score 84 iBT), IELTS (minimum score 6.5). *Application deadline:* For fall admission, 8/1 for domestic students, 5/1 for international students; for winter admission, 11/15 for domestic students, 10/1 for international students; for spring admission, 3/15 for domestic students, 1/1 for international students; for summer admission, 5/15 for domestic students. Applications are processed on a rolling basis. Application fee: $55. Electronic applications accepted. *Expenses:* Contact institution. *Financial support:* Federal Work-Study, scholarships/grants, and unspecified assistantships available. Financial award application deadline: 3/1; financial award applicants required to submit FAFSA. *Unit head:* Dr. Adam Lutzker, Director, 810-762-3470, Fax: 810-762-3281, E-mail: alutzker@umflint.edu. *Application contact:* Matt Bohlen, Associate Director of Graduate Programs, 810-762-3171, Fax: 810-766-6789, E-mail: mbohlen@umflint.edu. Website: http://www.umflint.edu/graduateprograms/social-sciences-ma

University of Michigan–Flint, Graduate Programs, Program in Liberal Studies in American Culture, Flint, MI 48502-1950. Offers MA, MLS. *Program availability:* Part-time, evening/weekend, 100% online. *Faculty:* 1 part-time/adjunct (0 women). *Students:* 3 full-time (2 women), 17 part-time (8 women); includes 6 minority (3 Black or African American, non-Hispanic/Latino; 2 American Indian or Alaska Native, non-Hispanic/Latino; 1 Asian, non-Hispanic/Latino). Average age 49. 14 applicants, 79% accepted, 6 enrolled. In 2019, 6 master's awarded. *Entrance requirements:* For master's, bachelor's degree from accredited institution; minimum overall undergraduate GPA of 3.0 on 4.0 scale; undergraduate course work totaling 24 credit hours, primarily in the humanities and social sciences. Additional exam requirements/recommendations for international students: required—TOEFL (minimum score 84 iBT), IELTS (minimum score 6.5). *Application deadline:* For fall admission, 8/1 for domestic students, 5/1 for international students; for winter admission, 11/15 for domestic students, 10/1 for international students; for spring admission, 3/15 for domestic students, 1/1 for international students; for summer admission, 5/15 for domestic students. Applications are processed on a rolling basis. Application fee: $55. Electronic applications accepted. *Expenses:* Contact institution. *Financial support:* Federal Work-Study, scholarships/grants, and unspecified assistantships available. Support available to part-time students. Financial award application deadline: 3/1; financial award applicants required to submit FAFSA. *Unit head:* Dr. Jan Furman, Director, 810-762-3285, E-mail: jfurman@umflint.edu. *Application contact:* Matt Bohlen, Associate Director of Graduate Admissions, 810-762-3171, Fax: 810-766-6789, E-mail: mbohlen@umflint.edu. Website: https://www.umflint.edu/graduateprograms/liberal-studies-american-culture-ma

University of Minnesota, Twin Cities Campus, Graduate School, College of Liberal Arts, Department of American Studies, Minneapolis, MN 55455. Offers PhD. *Degree requirements:* For doctorate, one foreign language, comprehensive exam, thesis/dissertation. *Entrance requirements:* For doctorate, GRE General Test, sample of written work, 3 letters of recommendation. Additional exam requirements/recommendations for international students: required—TOEFL (minimum score 550 paper-based).

University of Missouri–St. Louis, College of Arts and Sciences, Department of Political Science, St. Louis, MO 63121. Offers American politics (MA); comparative politics (MA); international politics (MA); political process and behavior (MA); political science (PhD); public administration and public policy (MA); urban and regional politics (MA). *Program availability:* Part-time, evening/weekend. Terminal master's awarded for partial completion of doctoral program. *Degree requirements:* For master's, thesis optional; for doctorate, thesis/dissertation. *Entrance requirements:* For master's, GRE General Test, 2 letters of recommendation, statement of purpose; for doctorate, GRE General Test, 3 letters of recommendation, statement of purpose. Additional exam requirements/recommendations for international students: required—TOEFL (minimum score 550 paper-based; 79 iBT), IELTS (minimum score 6.5). Electronic applications accepted. *Expenses: Tuition, area resident:* Full-time $9005.40; part-time $6003.60 per credit hour. Tuition, state resident: full-time $9005.40; part-time $6003.60 per credit hour. Tuition, nonresident: full-time $22,108; part-time $14,738.40 per credit hour. *International tuition:* $22,108 full-time. Tuition and fees vary according to course load.

University of New Mexico, Graduate Studies, College of Arts and Sciences, Program in American Studies, Albuquerque, NM 87131-2039. Offers MA, PhD. *Program availability:* Part-time. *Degree requirements:* For master's, comprehensive exam (for some programs), thesis (for some programs); for doctorate, one foreign language, comprehensive exam, thesis/dissertation. *Entrance requirements:* For master's, BA in related field; for doctorate, MA in related field, complete dossier. Additional exam requirements/recommendations for international students: required—TOEFL. Electronic applications accepted. *Expenses:* Tuition, state resident: full-time $7633; part-time $972 per year. Tuition, nonresident: full-time $22,586; part-time $3840 per year. *International tuition:* $23,292 full-time. *Required fees:* $8608. Tuition and fees vary according to course level, course load, degree level, program and student level.

University of New Mexico, Graduate Studies, College of Fine Arts, Program in Art History, Albuquerque, NM 87131-2039. Offers art history (MA); art of the Americas (MA); history of architecture (PhD); history of graphic arts (PhD); history of photography (PhD); modern Latin American art (PhD); Native American art (PhD); Pre-Columbian art and architecture (PhD); Spanish colonial art (PhD). *Program availability:* Part-time. *Degree requirements:* For master's, one foreign language, comprehensive exam (for some programs), thesis, symposium; for doctorate, 2 foreign languages, comprehensive exam, thesis/dissertation, symposium. *Entrance requirements:* Additional exam requirements/recommendations for international students: required—TOEFL (minimum score 550 paper-based), IELTS (minimum score 6). Electronic applications accepted. *Expenses:* Tuition, state resident: full-time $7633; part-time $972 per year. Tuition, nonresident: full-time $22,586; part-time $3840 per year. *International tuition:* $23,292 full-time. *Required fees:* $8608. Tuition and fees vary according to course level, course load, degree level, program and student level.

University of Southern California, Graduate School, Dana and David Dornsife College of Letters, Arts and Sciences, Department of American Studies and Ethnicity, Los Angeles, CA 90089. Offers PhD. *Degree requirements:* For doctorate, one foreign language, thesis/dissertation, qualifying exam. *Entrance requirements:* For doctorate, GRE. Additional exam requirements/recommendations for international students: recommended—TOEFL. Electronic applications accepted.

University of South Florida, College of Arts and Sciences, Department of Humanities and Cultural Studies, Tampa, FL 33620-9951. Offers liberal arts (MA), including American studies, film studies, humanities. *Program availability:* Part-time, evening/weekend. *Faculty:* 8 full-time (3 women). *Students:* 19 full-time (7 women), 6 part-time (4 women); includes 7 minority (2 Black or African American, non-Hispanic/Latino; 2 Asian, non-Hispanic/Latino; 3 Hispanic/Latino), 1 international. Average age 29. 21 applicants, 71% accepted, 15 enrolled. In 2019, 8 master's awarded. *Degree requirements:* For master's, comprehensive exam, thesis, language (for humanities subconcentration). *Entrance requirements:* For master's, GRE Recommended. Contact department for advising, minimum GPA of 3.0, writing sample. Personal statement, letters of recommendation are recommended. Students must select a concentration at the time of application. Additional exam requirements/recommendations for international students: required—TOEFL, TOEFL (minimum score 550 paper-based; 79 iBT) or IELTS (minimum score 6.5). *Application deadline:* For fall admission, 2/15 priority date for domestic students, 2/15 for international students; for spring admission, 10/15 priority date for domestic students, 9/15 for international students; for summer admission, 2/15 for domestic students, 1/15 for international students. Application fee: $30. Electronic applications accepted. *Financial support:* In 2019–20, 5 students received support, including 15 teaching assistantships with tuition reimbursements available (averaging $12,437 per year); scholarships/grants also available. Financial award application deadline: 4/1. *Unit head:* Dr. Andrew Berish, Associate Professor and Chair, 813-974-9380, E-mail: aberish@usf.edu. *Application contact:* Dr. Maria Cizmic, Associate Professor and Graduate Program Director, 813-974-9380, E-mail: mcizmic@usf.edu. Website: http://humanities.usf.edu/

The University of Texas at Austin, Graduate School, College of Liberal Arts, Department of American Studies, Austin, TX 78712-1111. Offers MA, PhD. *Program availability:* Part-time. *Degree requirements:* For master's, thesis; for doctorate, one foreign language, thesis/dissertation, qualifying oral exam. *Entrance requirements:* For master's and doctorate, GRE General Test, minimum GPA of 3.5. Electronic applications accepted.

University of Utah, Graduate School, College of Social and Behavioral Science, Department of Political Science, Program in Political Science, Salt Lake City, UT 84112-1107. Offers American politics (MA, MS, PhD); comparative politics (MA, MS, PhD); international relations (MA, MS, PhD); political theory (MA, MS, PhD); public administration (MA, MS, PhD). *Program availability:* Part-time. *Faculty:* 21 full-time (6 women), 2 part-time/adjunct (0 women). *Students:* 100 full-time (55 women), 97 part-time (52 women); includes 36 minority (2 Black or African American, non-Hispanic/Latino; 4 Asian, non-Hispanic/Latino; 20 Hispanic/Latino; 1 Native Hawaiian or other Pacific Islander, non-Hispanic/Latino; 9 Two or more races, non-Hispanic/Latino), 6 international. Average age 32. 47 applicants, 66% accepted, 14 enrolled. In 2019, 84 master's, 5 doctorates awarded. Terminal master's awarded for partial completion of doctoral program. *Degree requirements:* For master's, final project, defense; for doctorate, comprehensive exam, thesis/dissertation. *Entrance requirements:* For master's and doctorate, GRE General Test, minimum GPA of 3.2. Additional exam requirements/recommendations for international students: required—TOEFL (minimum score 580 paper-based; 80 iBT), IELTS (minimum score 6.5). *Application deadline:* For fall admission, 1/15 priority date for domestic and international students. Application fee: $55 ($65 for international students). Electronic applications accepted. *Expenses:* General graduate tuition charged by the university. *Financial support:* In 2019–20, 2 students received support, including 1 fellowship (averaging $24,000 per year), 23 teaching assistantships (averaging $11,043 per year); research assistantships and unspecified assistantships also available. Financial award application deadline: 4/1; financial award applicants required to submit CSS PROFILE or FAFSA. *Unit head:* Dr. Brent J. Steele, Department Chair and Professor, 801-581-7031, Fax: 801-585-6492, E-mail: brent.steele@utah.edu. *Application contact:* Sandy Hiskey, Graduate Academic Advisor, 801-581-8608, Fax: 801-585-6492, E-mail: sandy.hiskey@utah.edu. Website: http://www.poli-sci.utah.edu/

University of West Florida, College of Arts, Social Sciences, and Humanities, Department of History, Pensacola, FL 32514-5750. Offers early American studies (MA); public history (MA); traditional history (MA). *Program availability:* Part-time, evening/weekend. *Degree requirements:* For master's, thesis or alternative. *Entrance requirements:* For master's, GRE (minimum score: verbal 500, writing 3.5) or MAT (minimum score 415), minimum GPA of 3.0; minimum 15 hours of upper-level history courses; official transcripts; letter of intent; writing sample (undergraduate research paper preferred). Additional exam requirements/recommendations for international students: required—TOEFL (minimum score 550 paper-based).

University of Wisconsin–Madison, Graduate School, College of Letters and Science, Department of History, Madison, WI 53706-1380. Offers African history (MA, PhD); Central Asian history (MA, PhD); comparative world history (MA, PhD); East Asian history (MA, PhD); European history (MA, PhD); gender and women's history (MA, PhD); Latin American and Caribbean history (MA, PhD); Middle Eastern history (MA, PhD); South Asian history (MA, PhD); Southeast Asian history (MA, PhD); United States history (MA, PhD). Terminal master's awarded for partial completion of doctoral program. *Degree requirements:* For master's, thesis (for some programs); for doctorate, variable foreign language requirement, thesis/dissertation. *Entrance requirements:* For master's and doctorate, GRE General Test. Additional exam requirements/recommendations for international students: required—Michigan English Language Assessment Battery or TOEFL. Electronic applications accepted.

University of Wyoming, College of Arts and Sciences, American Studies Program, Laramie, WY 82071. Offers MA. *Program availability:* Part-time. *Degree requirements:* For master's, thesis optional. *Entrance requirements:* For master's, GRE General Test, minimum GPA of 3.0.

Utah State University, School of Graduate Studies, College of Humanities and Social Sciences, Department of English, Program in American Studies, Logan, UT 84322. Offers folklore (MA, MS); western American literature and culture (MA, MS). *Program availability:* Part-time, evening/weekend. *Degree requirements:* For master's, thesis or alternative. *Entrance requirements:* For master's, GRE General Test or MAT, minimum GPA of 3.0, 3 letters of recommendation, writing sample. Additional exam requirements/recommendations for international students: required—TOEFL.

Washington State University, College of Arts and Sciences, Program in American Studies, Pullman, WA 99164-4010. Offers MA, PhD. *Program availability:* Part-time. *Degree requirements:* For master's, one foreign language, comprehensive exam, thesis optional, oral exam; for doctorate, one foreign language, comprehensive exam, thesis/dissertation, oral exam. *Entrance requirements:* For master's and doctorate, official college transcripts sent directly from each institution attended, 3-5 page statement of purpose describing areas of interest, minimum GPA of 3.0, writing sample, 3 letters of recommendation. Additional exam requirements/recommendations for international students: required—TOEFL.

Wilfrid Laurier University, Faculty of Graduate and Postdoctoral Studies, Faculty of Arts, Department of Religion and Culture, Waterloo, ON N2L 3C5, Canada. Offers religion and culture (MA); religious diversity of North America (PhD). *Program availability:* Part-time. *Degree requirements:* For master's, thesis optional; for doctorate, thesis/dissertation. *Entrance requirements:* For master's, honors BA or the equivalent in religious studies or other interdisciplinary social science or humanities program, minimum B average in overall undergraduate course work, B+ average in the undergraduate major; for doctorate, MA in religious studies, minimum A- average. Additional exam requirements/recommendations for international students: required—TOEFL (minimum score 89 iBT). Electronic applications accepted.

Yale University, Graduate School of Arts and Sciences, Interdisciplinary Program in American Studies, New Haven, CT 06520. Offers PhD. *Degree requirements:* For doctorate, one foreign language, thesis/dissertation. *Entrance requirements:* For doctorate, GRE General Test.

Youngstown State University, College of Graduate Studies, College of Liberal Arts and Social Sciences, Program in American Studies, Youngstown, OH 44555-0001. Offers MA.

Asian-American Studies

Binghamton University, State University of New York, Graduate School, Harpur College of Arts and Sciences, Department of Asian and Asian American Studies, Binghamton, NY 13902-6000. Offers MA, Certificate. *Program availability:* Part-time. *Degree requirements:* For master's, variable foreign language requirement, comprehensive exam (for some programs), thesis (for some programs). *Entrance requirements:* For master's, GRE General Test, writing sample. Additional exam requirements/recommendations for international students: required—TOEFL (minimum score 80 iBT). Electronic applications accepted.

California State University, Long Beach, Graduate Studies, College of Liberal Arts, Department of Asian and Asian American Studies, Long Beach, CA 90840. Offers Asian studies (MA). *Program availability:* Part-time. *Degree requirements:* For master's, one foreign language, comprehensive exam or thesis. Electronic applications accepted.

San Francisco State University, Division of Graduate Studies, College of Ethnic Studies, Department of Asian American Studies, San Francisco, CA 94132-1722. Offers MA. *Expenses: Tuition, area resident:* Full-time $7176; part-time $4164 per year. Tuition, state resident: full-time $7176; part-time $4164 per year. Tuition, nonresident: full-time $16,680; part-time $396 per unit. *International tuition:* $16,680 full-time. *Required fees:* $1524; $1524 per unit. $762 per semester. Tuition and fees vary according to degree level and program. *Unit head:* Dr. Russell Jeung, Chair, 415-338-2698, Fax: 415-338-0500, E-mail: aas@sfsu.edu. *Application contact:* Dr. Eric Pido, MA Program Coordinator, 415-338-2698, Fax: 415-338-0500, E-mail: epido@sfsu.edu. Website: http://aas.sfsu.edu/

Stony Brook University, State University of New York, Graduate School, College of Arts and Sciences, Department of Asian and Asian American Studies, Stony Brook, NY 11794. Offers contemporary Asian and Asian American studies (MA). *Faculty:* 16 full-time (11 women), 9 part-time/adjunct (8 women). *Students:* 2 full-time (both women), 3 part-time (all women); includes 1 minority (Asian, non-Hispanic/Latino), 2 international. Average age 33. 4 applicants, 25% accepted, 1 enrolled. In 2019, 4 master's awarded. *Entrance requirements:* For master's, GRE, undergraduate transcript, statement of purpose, three letters of recommendation. Additional exam requirements/recommendations for international students: required—TOEFL (minimum score 85 iBT). *Application deadline:* For fall admission, 1/15 for domestic students; for spring admission, 10/1 for domestic students. Application fee: $100. Electronic applications accepted. *Expenses: Tuition, area resident:* Full-time $11,310; part-time $471 per credit. Tuition, state resident: full-time $11,310; part-time $471 per credit. Tuition, nonresident: full-time $23,100; part-time $963 per credit. *International tuition:* $23,100 full-time. *Required fees:* $2247.50. *Financial support:* Applicants required to submit FAFSA. *Unit head:* Dr. Agnes He, Chair, 631-632-4041, Fax: 631-632-4098, E-mail: agnes.he@stonybrook.edu. *Application contact:* Melissa Jordan, Assistant Dean for Records and Admission, 631-632-9712, Fax: 631-632-7243, E-mail:

melissa.jordan@stonybrook.edu.
Website: http://www.stonybrook.edu/commcms/asianamerican/

University of California, Los Angeles, Graduate Division, College of Letters and Science, Program in Asian-American Studies, Los Angeles, CA 90095. Offers MA, MA/MPH, MA/MSW. *Degree requirements:* For master's, one foreign language, comprehensive exam or thesis. *Entrance requirements:* For master's, bachelor's degree; minimum undergraduate GPA of 3.0 (or its equivalent if letter grade system not used); paper or article preferably on Asian Americans. Additional exam requirements/recommendations for international students: required—TOEFL. Electronic applications accepted.

Asian Studies

American University, College of Arts and Sciences, Critical Race, Gender, and Culture Studies, Washington, DC 20016. Offers Asian studies (Graduate Certificate); women's, gender, and sexuality studies (Graduate Certificate). *Entrance requirements:* Additional exam requirements/recommendations for international students: required—TOEFL.

Binghamton University, State University of New York, Graduate School, Harpur College of Arts and Sciences, Department of Asian and Asian American Studies, Binghamton, NY 13902-6000. Offers MA, Certificate. *Program availability:* Part-time. *Degree requirements:* For master's, variable foreign language requirement, comprehensive exam (for some programs), thesis (for some programs). *Entrance requirements:* For master's, GRE General Test, writing sample. Additional exam requirements/recommendations for international students: required—TOEFL (minimum score 80 iBT). Electronic applications accepted.

Brown University, Graduate School, Department of Egyptology and Assyriology, Providence, RI 02912. Offers ancient western Asian studies (PhD); Egyptology (PhD); history of the exact sciences in antiquity (PhD). *Degree requirements:* For doctorate, 2 foreign languages, comprehensive exam, thesis/dissertation. *Entrance requirements:* For doctorate, GRE General Test.

Brown University, Graduate School, Department of Religious Studies, Providence, RI 02912. Offers Asian religious traditions (PhD); Islam, society and culture (PhD); religion and critical thought (PhD); religions of the ancient Mediterranean (PhD). *Degree requirements:* For doctorate, variable foreign language requirement, thesis/dissertation. *Entrance requirements:* For doctorate, GRE General Test. Additional exam requirements/recommendations for international students: required—TOEFL. Electronic applications accepted.

California State University, Long Beach, Graduate Studies, College of Liberal Arts, Department of Asian and Asian American Studies, Long Beach, CA 90840. Offers Asian studies (MA). *Program availability:* Part-time. *Degree requirements:* For master's, one foreign language, comprehensive exam or thesis. Electronic applications accepted.

College of Staten Island of the City University of New York, Graduate Programs, Division of Humanities and Social Sciences, Program in History, Staten Island, NY 10314-6600. Offers history (MA), including Africa and the Middle East, Asia, Europe, Latin America and the Caribbean, United States. *Program availability:* Part-time, evening/weekend. *Faculty:* 5. *Students:* 17. 12 applicants, 67% accepted, 8 enrolled. In 2019, 1 master's awarded. *Degree requirements:* For master's, comprehensive exam (for some programs), thesis or alternative, the MA in History requires 32 graduate credits at the 700-level, with all graduate courses designated at four credits, for a total of eight courses. Students must take at least one course in each of four of the program's five areas of concentration, rigorous thesis option or portfolio option. *Entrance requirements:* For master's, bachelor's degree with minimum GPA of 3.0 overall and in undergraduate history courses, two letters of recommendation, letter of interest, research-based writing sample. Additional exam requirements/recommendations for international students: required—TOEFL (minimum score 550 paper-based; 79 iBT), IELTS (minimum score 6.5). *Application deadline:* For fall admission, 5/10 priority date for domestic students, 4/25 for international students; for spring admission, 12/2 priority date for domestic students, 11/23 for international students. Applications are processed on a rolling basis. Application fee: $75. Electronic applications accepted. *Expenses: Tuition, area resident:* Full-time $11,090; part-time $470 per credit. Tuition, state resident: full-time $11,090; part-time $470 per credit. Tuition, nonresident: full-time $20,520; part-time $855 per credit. *International tuition:* $20,520 full-time. *Required fees:* $559; $181 per semester. Tuition and fees vary according to program. *Unit head:* Susan Smith-Peter, Graduate Program Coordinator, 718-982-3290, E-mail: susan.smithpeter@csi.cuny.edu. *Application contact:* Sasha Spence, Associate Director for Graduate Admissions, 718-982-2019, Fax: 718-982-2500, E-mail: sasha.spence@csi.cuny.edu.
Website: https://www.csi.cuny.edu/academics-and-research/departments-programs/history/master-arts-history

Columbia University, Graduate School of Arts and Sciences, New York, NY 10027. Offers African-American studies (MA); American studies (MA); anthropology (MA, PhD); art history and archaeology (MA, PhD); astronomy (PhD); biological sciences (PhD); biotechnology (MA); chemical physics (PhD); chemistry (PhD); classical studies (MA, PhD); classics (MA, PhD); climate and society (MA); conservation biology (MA); earth and environmental sciences (PhD); East Asia: regional studies (MA); East Asian languages and cultures (MA, PhD); ecology, evolution and environmental biology (MA), including conservation biology; ecology, evolution, and environmental biology (PhD), including ecology and evolutionary biology, evolutionary primatology; economics (MA, PhD); English and comparative literature (MA, PhD); French and Romance philology (MA, PhD); Germanic languages (MA, PhD); global French studies (MA); global thought (MA); Hispanic cultural studies (MA); history (PhD); history and literature (MA); human rights studies (MA); Islamic studies (MA); Italian (MA, PhD); Japanese pedagogy (MA); Jewish studies (MA); Latin America and the Caribbean: regional studies (MA); Latin American and Iberian cultures (PhD); mathematics (MA, PhD), including finance (MA); medieval and Renaissance studies (MA); Middle Eastern, South Asian, and African studies (MA, PhD); modern art: critical and curatorial studies (MA); modern European studies (MA); museum anthropology (MA); music (DMA, PhD); oral history (MA); philosophical foundations of physics (MA); philosophy (MA, PhD); physics (PhD); political science (MA, PhD); psychology (PhD); quantitative methods in the social sciences (MA); religion (MA, PhD); Russia, Eurasia and East Europe: regional studies (MA); Russian translation (MA); Slavic cultures (MA); Slavic languages (MA, PhD); sociology (MA, PhD); South Asian studies (MA); statistics (MA, PhD); theatre (PhD). *Program availability:* Part-time. *Students:* 3,506 full-time (1,844 women), 208 part-time (121 women); includes 864 minority (110 Black or African American, non-Hispanic/Latino; 5 American Indian or Alaska Native, non-Hispanic/Latino; 416 Asian, non-Hispanic/Latino; 147 Hispanic/Latino; 6 Native Hawaiian or other Pacific Islander, non-Hispanic/Latino; 180 Two or more races, non-Hispanic/Latino), 2,065 international. 14,545 applicants, 25% accepted, 1,429 enrolled. In 2019, 1,262 master's, 363 doctorates awarded. Terminal master's awarded for partial completion of doctoral program. *Degree requirements:* For master's, variable foreign language requirement, comprehensive exam (for some programs), thesis (for some programs); for doctorate, variable foreign language requirement, comprehensive exam (for some programs), thesis/dissertation. *Entrance requirements:* For master's and doctorate, GRE General Test, GRE Subject Test (for some programs). Additional exam requirements/recommendations for international students: required—TOEFL (minimum score 600 paper-based; 100 iBT), IELTS (minimum score 7.5). Application fee: $115. Electronic applications accepted. *Expenses: Tuition:* Full-time $47,600; part-time $1880 per credit. One-time fee: $105. *Financial support:* Fellowships, research assistantships, teaching assistantships, career-related internships or fieldwork, Federal Work-Study, institutionally sponsored loans, scholarships/grants, traineeships, health care benefits, tuition waivers, and unspecified assistantships available. Support available to part-time students. Financial award application deadline: 12/15. *Unit head:* Dr. Carlos J. Alonso, Dean of the Graduate School of Arts and Sciences and Vice President for Graduate Education, 212-854-2861, E-mail: gsas-dean@columbia.edu. *Application contact:* GSAS Office of Admissions, 212-854-6729, E-mail: gsas-admissions@columbia.edu.
Website: http://gsas.columbia.edu/

Columbia University, South Asia Institute, New York, NY 10027. Offers MA, Certificate. *Program availability:* Part-time. *Degree requirements:* For master's, thesis, 30 points of coursework. *Entrance requirements:* For master's, BA, BS or equivalent, in any field of study. Additional exam requirements/recommendations for international students: required—TOEFL. Electronic applications accepted. *Expenses:* Contact institution.

Cornell University, Graduate School, Graduate Fields of Arts and Sciences, Field of Asian Literature, Religion and Culture, Ithaca, NY 14853. Offers Asian religions (MA, PhD); Chinese philosophy (PhD); classical Chinese literature (PhD); classical Japanese literature (PhD); East Asian literature and culture (PhD); Korean literature (PhD); modern Chinese literature (PhD); modern Japanese literature (PhD); South Asian literature and culture (PhD); Southeast Asian literature and culture (PhD). *Degree requirements:* For doctorate, comprehensive exam, thesis/dissertation. *Entrance requirements:* For doctorate, GRE General Test, academic writing sample, 3 letters of recommendation. Additional exam requirements/recommendations for international students: required—TOEFL (minimum score 600 paper-based; 77 iBT). Electronic applications accepted.

Cornell University, Graduate School, Graduate Fields of Arts and Sciences, Field of Asian Studies, Ithaca, NY 14853. Offers East Asian linguistics (MA); East Asian studies (MA); South Asian linguistics (MA); South Asian studies (MA); Southeast Asian linguistics (MA); Southeast Asian studies (MA). *Degree requirements:* For master's, one foreign language, thesis. *Entrance requirements:* For master's, GRE General Test, 3 letters of recommendation. Additional exam requirements/recommendations for international students: required—TOEFL (minimum score 550 paper-based; 77 iBT). Electronic applications accepted.

Cornell University, Graduate School, Graduate Fields of Arts and Sciences, Field of History, Ithaca, NY 14853. Offers African history (MA, PhD); American history (MA, PhD); ancient Greek history (PhD); ancient history (MA, PhD); ancient Roman history (PhD); early modern European history (MA, PhD); English history (MA, PhD); French history (MA, PhD); German history (MA, PhD); history of science (MA, PhD); Korean history (PhD); Latin American history (MA, PhD); medieval Chinese history (MA, PhD); medieval history (MA, PhD); modern Chinese history (MA, PhD); modern European history (MA, PhD); modern Japanese history (MA, PhD); modern Middle Eastern history (PhD); premodern Islamic history (MA, PhD); premodern Japanese history (MA, PhD); Renaissance history (MA, PhD); Russian history (MA, PhD); South Asian history (PhD); Southeast Asian history (MA, PhD). Terminal master's awarded for partial completion of doctoral program. *Degree requirements:* For master's, thesis; for doctorate, 2 foreign languages, comprehensive exam, thesis/dissertation, 1 year of teaching experience. *Entrance requirements:* For master's and doctorate, GRE General Test, writing sample, 3 letters of recommendation. Additional exam requirements/recommendations for international students: required—TOEFL (minimum score 550 paper-based; 77 iBT). Electronic applications accepted.

Cornell University, Graduate School, Graduate Fields of Arts and Sciences, Field of History of Art, Archaeology and Visual Studies, Ithaca, NY 14853. Offers 19th century art (PhD); African, African American and African diaspora (PhD); American art (PhD); ancient art and archaeology (PhD); Asian American art (PhD); Baroque art (PhD); Comparative Modernities (PhD); digital art (PhD); East Asian art (PhD); history of photography (PhD); Islamic art (PhD); Latin American art (PhD); medieval art (PhD); modern art (PhD); Renaissance art (PhD); Southeast Asian art (PhD); theory and criticism (PhD); visual studies (PhD). *Degree requirements:* For doctorate, one foreign language, comprehensive exam, thesis/dissertation, general exams in 3 areas. *Entrance requirements:* For doctorate, GRE General Test, sample of written work, 3 letters of recommendation. Additional exam requirements/recommendations for international students: required—TOEFL (minimum score 550 paper-based; 77 iBT). Electronic applications accepted.

Cornell University, Graduate School, Graduate Fields of Arts and Sciences, Field of Linguistics, Ithaca, NY 14853. Offers applied linguistics (MA, PhD); East Asian linguistics (MA, PhD); English linguistics (MA, PhD); general linguistics (MA, PhD); Germanic linguistics (MA, PhD); Indo-European linguistics (MA, PhD); phonetics (MA, PhD); phonological theory (MA, PhD); Romance linguistics (MA, PhD); second language acquisition (MA, PhD); semantics (MA, PhD); Slavic linguistics (MA, PhD); sociolinguistics (MA, PhD); South Asian linguistics (MA, PhD); Southeast Asian linguistics (MA, PhD); syntactic theory (MA, PhD). Terminal master's awarded for partial completion of doctoral program. *Degree requirements:* For master's, one foreign language, thesis; for doctorate, one foreign language, comprehensive exam, thesis/dissertation. *Entrance requirements:* For master's and doctorate, GRE General Test, 2 letters of recommendation. Additional exam requirements/recommendations for international students: required—TOEFL (minimum score 600 paper-based; 77 iBT). Electronic applications accepted.

Dallas Baptist University, Gary Cook School of Leadership, Program in International Studies, Dallas, TX 75211-9299. Offers East Asian studies (MA); European studies (MA); general international studies (MA); global business (MA); international immersion (MA); international ministry (MA); international relations (MA). *Program availability:* Part-

time, evening/weekend. *Application deadline:* Applications are processed on a rolling basis. Application fee: $25. Electronic applications accepted. Application fee is waived when completed online. *Expenses: Tuition:* Full-time $18,072; part-time $1004 per credit hour. *Required fees:* $1100; $550 per semester. Tuition and fees vary according to course level and degree level. *Unit head:* Dr. Jack Goodyear, Dean, 214-333-5595, Fax: 214-333-6809, E-mail: jackg@dbu.edu. *Application contact:* Lee Bratcher, Program Director, 214-333-5808, E-mail: leeb@dbu.edu.
Website: https://www.dbu.edu/graduate/degree-programs/ma-international-studies

Dallas Baptist University, Graduate School of Ministry, Program in Global Leadership, Dallas, TX 75211-9299. Offers church planting (MA); East Asian Studies (MA); English as a second language (MA); general studies (MA); global communication (MA); global studies (MA); international business (MA); leading the nonprofit organization (MA); missions (MA); small group ministry (MA); urban ministry (MA). *Program availability:* Part-time, evening/weekend, online learning. *Application deadline:* Applications are processed on a rolling basis. Application fee: $25. Electronic applications accepted. Application fee is waived when completed online. *Expenses: Tuition:* Full-time $18,072; part-time $1004 per credit hour. *Required fees:* $1100; $550 per semester. Tuition and fees vary according to course level and degree level. *Unit head:* Dr. Robert R. Brooks, Dean, 214-333-5494, Fax: 214-333-5673, E-mail: bobb@dbu.edu. *Application contact:* Dr. Brent Thomason, Program Director, 214-333-5236, E-mail: brentt@dbu.edu.
Website: https://www.dbu.edu/ministry/degree-programs/m-a-in-global-leadership

Dallas Baptist University, Liberal Arts Program, Dallas, TX 75211-9299. Offers art (MLA); Christian studies (MLA); commercial art (MLA); East Asian studies (MLA); English (MLA); English as a second language (MLA); history (MLA); missions (MLA); political science (MLA). *Program availability:* Part-time, evening/weekend, online learning. *Application deadline:* Applications are processed on a rolling basis. Application fee: $25. Electronic applications accepted. Application fee is waived when completed online. *Expenses: Tuition:* Full-time $18,072; part-time $1004 per credit hour. *Required fees:* $1100; $550 per semester. Tuition and fees vary according to course level and degree level. *Unit head:* Jared Ingram, Director, 214-333-5584, E-mail: jaredi@dbu.edu. *Application contact:* Jared Ingram, Director, 214-333-5584, E-mail: jaredi@dbu.edu.
Website: https://www.dbu.edu/graduate/degree-programs/mla

Duke University, Graduate School, Department of East Asian Studies, Durham, NC 27708. Offers AM, Certificate. *Program availability:* Part-time. *Entrance requirements:* For master's, GRE General Test. Additional exam requirements/recommendations for international students: required—TOEFL (minimum score 577 paper-based; 90 iBT) or IELTS (minimum score 7). Electronic applications accepted.

Florida International University, Steven J. Green School of International and Public Affairs, Program in Asian Studies, Miami, FL 33199. Offers MA, MA/PhD. *Program availability:* Part-time, evening/weekend. *Faculty:* 3 part-time/adjunct (2 women). *Students:* 10 full-time (6 women), 5 part-time (4 women); includes 12 minority (2 Asian, non-Hispanic/Latino; 8 Hispanic/Latino; 2 Two or more races, non-Hispanic/Latino). Average age 29. 9 applicants, 67% accepted, 3 enrolled. In 2019, 7 master's awarded. *Entrance requirements:* For master's, minimum GPA of 3.0, letter of intent, letter of recommendation. Additional exam requirements/recommendations for international students: required—TOEFL (minimum score 550 paper-based; 80 iBT). *Application deadline:* For fall admission, 6/1 for domestic students, 4/1 for international students; for spring admission, 10/1 for domestic students, 9/1 for international students. Applications are processed on a rolling basis. Application fee: $30. Electronic applications accepted. *Expenses: Tuition, area resident:* Full-time $8912; part-time $446 per credit hour. Tuition, state resident: full-time $8912; part-time $446 per credit hour. Tuition, nonresident: full-time $21,393; part-time $992 per credit hour. *Required fees:* $2194. *Financial support:* Institutionally sponsored loans, scholarships/grants, and tuition waivers available. Financial award application deadline: 3/1; financial award applicants required to submit FAFSA. *Unit head:* Dr. Steven Heine, Program Director, 305-348-1788, Fax: 305-348-6586, E-mail: asian@fiu.edu. *Application contact:* Nanett Rojas, Manager, Admissions Operations, 305-348-7464, Fax: 305-348-7441, E-mail: gradadm@fiu.edu.

Florida State University, The Graduate School, College of Social Sciences and Public Policy, Program in Asian Studies, Tallahassee, FL 32306. Offers Asian studies (MA). *Program availability:* Part-time. *Faculty:* 4 full-time (all women), 4 part-time/adjunct (0 women). *Students:* 5 full-time (3 women), 4 international. Average age 25. 4 applicants, 100% accepted, 3 enrolled. In 2019, 1 master's awarded. *Degree requirements:* For master's, one foreign language, comprehensive exam, thesis optional. *Entrance requirements:* For master's, GRE General Test, minimum GPA of 3.0. Additional exam requirements/recommendations for international students: required—TOEFL (minimum score 550 paper-based; 80 iBT), IELTS (minimum score 6.5). *Application deadline:* For fall admission, 7/1 for domestic and international students; for spring admission, 11/1 for domestic and international students; for summer admission, 3/1 for domestic and international students. Applications are processed on a rolling basis. Application fee: $30. Electronic applications accepted. *Financial support:* Research assistantships, teaching assistantships, Federal Work-Study, institutionally sponsored loans, and unspecified assistantships available. Financial award application deadline: 2/1; financial award applicants required to submit FAFSA. *Unit head:* Dr. Lee K. Metcalf, Director, 850-644-4418, Fax: 850-645-4981, E-mail: lmetcalf@fsu.edu. *Application contact:* Sabrina Smith, Program Specialist, 850-644-4418, Fax: 850-644-4981, E-mail: ssmith9@fsu.edu.
Website: http://coss.fsu.edu/inaprog/programs/graduate/g-asian

Georgetown University, Graduate School of Arts and Sciences, Walsh School of Foreign Service, Program in Asian Studies, Washington, DC 20057. Offers MA. *Degree requirements:* For master's, comprehensive exam, research project. *Entrance requirements:* Additional exam requirements/recommendations for international students: required—TOEFL.

The George Washington University, Elliott School of International Affairs, Program in Asian Studies, Washington, DC 20052. Offers MA. *Program availability:* Part-time. *Degree requirements:* For master's, one foreign language, capstone project. *Entrance requirements:* For master's, GRE General Test, 2 years (or the equivalent) of an approved Asian language. Additional exam requirements/recommendations for international students: required—TOEFL (minimum score 100 iBT), IELTS (minimum score 7). Electronic applications accepted.

Harvard University, Graduate School of Arts and Sciences, Committee on Inner Asian and Altaic Studies, Cambridge, MA 02138. Offers PhD. *Degree requirements:* For doctorate, 2 foreign languages, thesis/dissertation, oral general exam. *Entrance requirements:* For doctorate, GRE General Test, proficiency in a related foreign language. Additional exam requirements/recommendations for international students: required—TOEFL.

Harvard University, Graduate School of Arts and Sciences, Committee on Regional Studies—East Asia, Cambridge, MA 02138. Offers Chinese studies (AM); Japanese studies (AM); Korean studies (AM); Mongolian studies (AM); Vietnamese studies (AM). *Degree requirements:* For master's, one foreign language, seminar paper. *Entrance requirements:* For master's, GRE General Test. Additional exam requirements/ recommendations for international students: required—TOEFL.

Harvard University, Graduate School of Arts and Sciences, Department of Sanskrit and Indian Studies, Cambridge, MA 02138. Offers Indian philosophy (AM, PhD); Pali (AM, PhD); Sanskrit (AM, PhD); Tibetan (AM, PhD); Urdu (AM, PhD). Terminal master's awarded for partial completion of doctoral program. *Degree requirements:* For master's, 3 foreign languages; for doctorate, 3 foreign languages, thesis/dissertation. *Entrance requirements:* For master's, GRE General Test; for doctorate, GRE General Test, proficiency in French and German. Additional exam requirements/recommendations for international students: required—TOEFL.

Indiana University Bloomington, University Graduate School, College of Arts and Sciences, School of Global and International Studies, Department of Central Eurasian Studies, Bloomington, IN 47405-7000. Offers MA, PhD. Terminal master's awarded for partial completion of doctoral program. *Degree requirements:* For master's, one foreign language, thesis; for doctorate, 2 foreign languages, thesis/dissertation, qualifying exams. *Entrance requirements:* For master's, minimum GPA of 3.0, 2 years of a foreign language; for doctorate, minimum GPA of 3.5, 1 research language. Additional exam requirements/recommendations for international students: required—TOEFL. Electronic applications accepted.

Indiana University Bloomington, University Graduate School, College of Arts and Sciences, School of Global and International Studies, Department of East Asian Languages and Cultures, Bloomington, IN 47408. Offers Chinese (MA, PhD); Chinese language pedagogy (MA); East Asian studies (MA); Japanese (MA, PhD); Japanese language pedagogy (MA). *Program availability:* Part-time. *Degree requirements:* For master's, one foreign language, thesis; for doctorate, 2 foreign languages, comprehensive exam, thesis/dissertation. *Entrance requirements:* Additional exam requirements/recommendations for international students: required—TOEFL (minimum score 93 iBT). Electronic applications accepted.

Johns Hopkins University, School of Advanced International Studies, Washington, DC 20036. Offers global risk (MA); international development (MA, Certificate), including international economics (MA); international economics (Certificate); international economics and finance (MA); international public policy (MIPP); international relations (PhD); international studies (Certificate); Japan studies (MA), including international economics; Korea studies (MA), including international economics; South Asia studies (MA), including international economics; Southeast Asia studies (MA), including international economics; JD/MA; MBA/MA; MHS/MA. *Program availability:* Evening/weekend. *Degree requirements:* For master's, 4-6 international economics courses, 5-6 functional or regional concentration courses, 2 core examinations, proficiency in language other than native language, capstone project; for doctorate, 2 foreign languages, thesis/dissertation, 3 comprehensive exams, economics, quantitative and qualitative course, dissertation prospectus and defense. *Entrance requirements:* For master's, GMAT or GRE General Test, previous course work in economics, foreign language, undergraduate degree; for doctorate, GRE General Test, Master's degree. Additional exam requirements/recommendations for international students: required—TOEFL (minimum score 600 paper-based; 100 iBT), IELTS (minimum score 7), TOEFL (minimum score 600 paper-based; 100 iBT) or IELTS (minimum score 7). Electronic applications accepted. *Expenses:* Contact institution.

Maharishi International University, Graduate Studies, Program in Maharishi Vedic Science, Fairfield, IA 52557. Offers MA, PhD. *Program availability:* Evening/weekend. *Degree requirements:* For master's, thesis; for doctorate, thesis/dissertation. *Entrance requirements:* For master's, minimum GPA of 3.0; for doctorate, GRE, minimum GPA of 3.0. Additional exam requirements/recommendations for international students: required—TOEFL.

McGill University, Faculty of Graduate and Postdoctoral Studies, Faculty of Arts, Department of East Asian Studies, Montréal, QC H3A 2T5, Canada. Offers MA, PhD.

New York University, Graduate School of Arts and Science, Department of East Asian Studies, New York, NY 10012-1019. Offers MA, PhD. *Program availability:* Part-time. *Entrance requirements:* Additional exam requirements/recommendations for international students: required—TOEFL, IELTS. Electronic applications accepted.

The Ohio State University, Graduate School, East Asian Studies Center, Columbus, OH 43210. Offers MA. *Degree requirements:* For master's, thesis optional. *Entrance requirements:* For master's, GRE General Test. Additional exam requirements/recommendations for international students: required—TOEFL (minimum score 550 paper-based; 79 iBT), IELTS (minimum score 7). Electronic applications accepted.

Ohio University, Graduate College, Center for International Studies, Program in Asian Studies, Athens, OH 45701-2979. Offers MA. *Program availability:* Part-time. *Degree requirements:* For master's, one foreign language, thesis optional. *Entrance requirements:* For master's, minimum GPA of 3.0. Additional exam requirements/recommendations for international students: required—TOEFL (minimum score 550 paper-based; 80 iBT); recommended—IELTS (minimum score 6.5). Electronic applications accepted.

Princeton University, Graduate School, Department of East Asian Studies, Princeton, NJ 08544-1019. Offers PhD. *Degree requirements:* For doctorate, 2 foreign languages, thesis/dissertation. *Entrance requirements:* For doctorate, GRE General Test, fluency in Japanese and/or Chinese. Additional exam requirements/recommendations for international students: required—TOEFL (minimum score 600 paper-based). Electronic applications accepted.

Rutgers University - New Brunswick, Graduate School-New Brunswick, Program in East Asian Languages and Cultures, Piscataway, NJ 08854-8097. Offers MA. *Degree requirements:* For master's, one foreign language, final exam. *Entrance requirements:* For master's, GRE, official transcripts, two letters of recommendation, personal statement, writing sample. Additional exam requirements/recommendations for international students: required—TOEFL or IELTS.

Rutgers University - New Brunswick, Graduate School-New Brunswick, Program in History, Piscataway, NJ 08854-8097. Offers African-American history (PhD); early American history (PhD); early modern European history (PhD); east Asian history (PhD); global and comparative history (PhD); history (PhD); history of diplomacy and foreign relations (PhD); history of technology, environment and health (PhD); history of the Atlantic cultures and African diaspora (PhD); Latin American history (PhD); medieval history (PhD); modern European history (PhD); nineteenth and twentieth century American history (PhD); women's and gender history (PhD). *Degree requirements:* For doctorate, thesis/dissertation. *Entrance requirements:* For doctorate, GRE General Test, sample of written work. Electronic applications accepted.

St. John's College, Graduate Institute in Liberal Education, Program in Eastern Classics, Santa Fe, NM 87505. Offers MA. *Program availability:* Part-time, evening/weekend. *Entrance requirements:* For master's, 2 letters of recommendation. Additional exam requirements/recommendations for international students: required—TOEFL, TWE. *Expenses:* Contact institution.

St. John's University, St. John's College of Liberal Arts and Sciences, Institute of Asian Studies, Queens, NY 11439. Offers Chinese studies (MA); East Asian studies (MA). *Program availability:* Part-time, evening/weekend. *Degree requirements:* For master's, one foreign language, comprehensive exam, thesis optional, 33 major credits including two required courses. *Entrance requirements:* For master's, letters of recommendation, transcripts, resume, personal statement. Additional exam requirements/recommendations for international students: required—TOEFL (minimum score 80 iBT), IELTS (minimum score 6.5). Electronic applications accepted.

San Diego State University, Graduate and Research Affairs, College of Arts and Letters, Center for Asian Studies, San Diego, CA 92182. Offers MA. *Degree requirements:* For master's, one foreign language, thesis. *Entrance requirements:* For master's, GRE General Test, 3 letters of reference, writing sample. Additional exam requirements/recommendations for international students: required—TOEFL. Electronic applications accepted.

Seton Hall University, College of Arts and Sciences, Department of Languages, Literatures and Cultures, South Orange, NJ 07079-2697. Offers Asian studies (MA). *Program availability:* Part-time, evening/weekend. *Degree requirements:* For master's, thesis optional. *Entrance requirements:* For master's, strong background in Asian studies or related discipline. Additional exam requirements/recommendations for international students: required—TOEFL. Electronic applications accepted.

Stanford University, School of Humanities and Sciences, Center for East Asian Studies, Stanford, CA 94305-2004. Offers MA. *Expenses:* Tuition: Full-time $52,479; part-time $34,110 per unit. *Required fees:* $672; $224 per quarter. Tuition and fees vary according to program and student level.
Website: http://www.stanford.edu/dept/ceas/

Stony Brook University, State University of New York, Graduate School, College of Arts and Sciences, Department of Asian and Asian American Studies, Stony Brook, NY 11794. Offers contemporary Asian and Asian American studies (MA). *Faculty:* 16 full-time (11 women), 9 part-time/adjunct (8 women). *Students:* 2 full-time (both women), 3 part-time (all women); includes 1 minority (Asian, non-Hispanic/Latino), 2 international. Average age 33. 4 applicants, 25% accepted, 1 enrolled. In 2019, 4 master's awarded. *Entrance requirements:* For master's, GRE, undergraduate transcript, statement of purpose, three letters of recommendation. Additional exam requirements/recommendations for international students: required—TOEFL (minimum score 85 iBT). *Application deadline:* For fall admission, 1/15 for domestic students; for spring admission, 10/1 for domestic students. Application fee: $100. Electronic applications accepted. *Expenses: Tuition, area resident:* Full-time $11,310; part-time $471 per credit. Tuition, state resident: full-time $11,310; part-time $471 per credit. Tuition, nonresident: full-time $23,100; part-time $963 per credit. *International tuition:* $23,100 full-time. *Required fees:* $2247.50. *Financial support:* Applicants required to submit FAFSA. *Unit head:* Dr. Agnes He, Chair, 631-632-4041, Fax: 631-632-4098, E-mail: agnes.he@stonybrook.edu. *Application contact:* Melissa Jordan, Assistant Dean for Records and Admission, 631-632-9712, Fax: 631-632-7243, E-mail: melissa.jordan@stonybrook.edu.
Website: http://www.stonybrook.edu/commcms/asianamerican/

United Theological Seminary of the Twin Cities, Graduate Programs, New Brighton, MN 55112-2598. Offers advanced theological studies (Diploma); justice and peace studies (M Div, MA); leadership toward racial justice (M Div, MA, Certificate); Methodist studies (M Div, MA, Certificate); ministry (D Min); ministry renewal and professional development (Certificate); pastoral care and counseling (M Div, MA, MARL); religion and theology (MA); theological and religious studies (Certificate); theology and the arts (M Div, MA); urban ministry (M Div, MA, MARL); women's studies: religion, theology and ministry (M Div, MA). *Accreditation:* ACIPE; ATS. *Program availability:* Part-time, evening/weekend. *Degree requirements:* For master's, thesis; for doctorate, comprehensive exam, thesis/dissertation. *Entrance requirements:* For master's, minimum GPA of 2.75; strong analytical, reflective thinking and writing skills; vocational and academic goals compatible with those of Seminary; for doctorate, M Div or equivalent, minimum GPA of 3.0, 3 years experience in professional ministry; for other advanced degree, BA or equivalent life experience; strong analytical, reflective thinking and writing skills (Certificate); proficiency in English language, previous study of theology at a theological school, recommendation of student's denomination (Diploma). Additional exam requirements/recommendations for international students: required—TOEFL (minimum score 550 paper-based).

University of Alberta, Faculty of Graduate Studies and Research, Department of East Asian Studies, Edmonton, AB T6G 2E1, Canada. Offers Chinese literature (MA); East Asian interdisciplinary studies (MA); Japanese literature (MA). *Program availability:* Part-time. *Degree requirements:* For master's, one foreign language, thesis. *Entrance requirements:* Additional exam requirements/recommendations for international students: required—TOEFL. Electronic applications accepted.

The University of Arizona, College of Humanities, Department of East Asian Studies, Tucson, AZ 85721. Offers MA, PhD. *Program availability:* Part-time. Terminal master's awarded for partial completion of doctoral program. *Degree requirements:* For master's, one foreign language; for doctorate, 2 foreign languages. *Entrance requirements:* For master's, GRE General Test, 2 letters of recommendation; for doctorate, GRE General Test, 2 letters of recommendation, statement of purpose, writing sample. Additional exam requirements/recommendations for international students: required—TOEFL (minimum score 550 paper-based; 79 iBT). Electronic applications accepted.

University of Bridgeport, College of Public and International Affairs, Bridgeport, CT 06604. Offers East Asian and Pacific Rim studies (MA); global development and peace (MA); global media and communication studies (MA). *Program availability:* Part-time, evening/weekend. *Degree requirements:* For master's, thesis. *Entrance requirements:* Additional exam requirements/recommendations for international students: recommended—TOEFL (minimum score 550 paper-based; 80 iBT), IELTS (minimum score 6.5).

The University of British Columbia, Faculty of Arts, Department of Asian Studies, Vancouver, BC V6T 1Z2, Canada. Offers MA, PhD. *Degree requirements:* For master's, one foreign language, thesis; for doctorate, 2 foreign languages, thesis/dissertation. *Entrance requirements:* For master's, BA; for doctorate, master's degree in Asian studies or equivalent. Additional exam requirements/recommendations for international students: required—TOEFL. Electronic applications accepted. *Expenses:* Contact institution.

The University of British Columbia, Institute of Asian Research, Vancouver, BC V6T 1Z2, Canada. Offers Asia Pacific policy studies (MAAPPS); public policy and global affairs (MPPGA). *Degree requirements:* For master's, thesis optional. *Entrance requirements:* Additional exam requirements/recommendations for international students: required—TOEFL. Electronic applications accepted. *Expenses:* Contact institution.

University of California, Berkeley, Graduate Division, College of Letters and Science, Department of South and Southeast Asian Studies, Berkeley, CA 94720. Offers Hindi (MA, PhD); Indonesian (MA, PhD); Sanskrit (MA, PhD); Tamil (MA, PhD). Terminal master's awarded for partial completion of doctoral program. *Degree requirements:* For master's, 2 foreign languages, thesis; for doctorate, 2 foreign languages, thesis/dissertation, oral qualifying exam. *Entrance requirements:* For master's and doctorate, GRE General Test, minimum GPA of 3.0, 3 letters of recommendation. Electronic applications accepted.

University of California, Berkeley, Graduate Division, College of Letters and Science, Group in Buddhist Studies, Berkeley, CA 94720. Offers PhD. *Degree requirements:* For doctorate, 4 foreign languages, thesis/dissertation, dissertation defense, qualifying exam. *Entrance requirements:* For doctorate, GRE General Test, MA in Japanese, Chinese, or Sanskrit; minimum GPA of 3.0; 3 letters of recommendation. Electronic applications accepted.

University of California, Berkeley, Graduate Division, Group in Asian Studies, Berkeley, CA 94720. Offers East Asian studies (MA); Northeast Asian studies (MA); South Asian studies (MA); Southeast Asian studies (MA); JD/MA; MBA/MA; MJ/MA. *Degree requirements:* For master's, one foreign language, comprehensive exam or thesis. *Entrance requirements:* For master's, GRE General Test, minimum GPA of 3.0, 3 letters of recommendation. Electronic applications accepted.

University of California, Los Angeles, Graduate Division, College of Letters and Science, Department of Asian Languages and Cultures, Los Angeles, CA 90095. Offers MA, PhD. Terminal master's awarded for partial completion of doctoral program. *Degree requirements:* For master's, one foreign language, comprehensive exam or thesis; for doctorate, 2 foreign languages, thesis/dissertation, oral and written qualifying exams. *Entrance requirements:* For master's, GRE General Test, bachelor's degree; minimum undergraduate GPA of 3.0 (or its equivalent if letter grade system not used); writing sample; for doctorate, GRE General Test, master's degree; minimum undergraduate GPA of 3.0 (or its equivalent if letter grade system not used); writing sample. Additional exam requirements/recommendations for international students: required—TOEFL. Electronic applications accepted.

University of California, Los Angeles, Graduate Division, International Institute, Interdepartmental Program in East Asian Studies, Los Angeles, CA 90095. Offers MA. *Degree requirements:* For master's, one foreign language, comprehensive exam. *Entrance requirements:* For master's, GRE General Test, bachelor's degree; minimum undergraduate GPA of 3.0 (or its equivalent if letter grade system not used). Additional exam requirements/recommendations for international students: required—TOEFL. Electronic applications accepted.

University of California, Riverside, Graduate Division, Program in Southeast Asian Studies, Riverside, CA 92521. Offers MA. *Degree requirements:* For master's, one foreign language, thesis or comprehensive exam. *Entrance requirements:* For master's, GRE, statement of purpose to indicate serious interest in Southeast Asian Studies (or specific country or area in this region), writing sample. Additional exam requirements/recommendations for international students: required—TOEFL; recommended—IELTS (minimum score 7). Electronic applications accepted.

University of California, Santa Barbara, Graduate Division, College of Letters and Sciences, Division of Humanities and Fine Arts, Department of East Asian Languages and Cultural Studies, Santa Barbara, CA 93106-7075. Offers applied linguistics (PhD); East Asian languages and cultural studies (MA); translation studies (PhD). *Degree requirements:* For master's, one foreign language, comprehensive exam (for some programs), thesis (for some programs); for doctorate, 2 foreign languages, thesis/dissertation, methodology. *Entrance requirements:* For master's and doctorate, GRE General Test. Additional exam requirements/recommendations for international students: required—TOEFL (minimum score 550 paper-based; 80 iBT), IELTS (minimum score 7). Electronic applications accepted.

University of Chicago, Division of the Humanities, Department of East Asian Languages and Civilizations, Chicago, IL 60637. Offers PhD. Terminal master's awarded for partial completion of doctoral program. *Degree requirements:* For doctorate, 2 foreign languages, comprehensive exam, thesis/dissertation, qualifying exam. *Entrance requirements:* For doctorate, GRE General Test, 15-20 page writing sample, statement of purpose, 3 letters of recommendation, transcripts for all previous degrees and institutions attended. Additional exam requirements/recommendations for international students: required—TOEFL (minimum score 104 iBT), IELTS (minimum score 7). Electronic applications accepted.

University of Chicago, Division of the Humanities, Department of South Asian Languages and Civilizations, Chicago, IL 60637. Offers South Asian languages and civilizations (PhD), including Bengali, Hindi, Sanskrit, Tamil, Urdu. Terminal master's awarded for partial completion of doctoral program. *Degree requirements:* For doctorate, 3 foreign languages, comprehensive exam, thesis/dissertation. *Entrance requirements:* For doctorate, GRE General Test, 15-20 page writing sample, statement of purpose, 3 letters of recommendation, transcripts for all previous degrees and institutions attended. Additional exam requirements/recommendations for international students: required—TOEFL (minimum score 104 iBT), IELTS (minimum score 7). Electronic applications accepted.

University of Chicago, Division of the Humanities, Master of Arts Program in the Humanities, Chicago, IL 60637. Offers art history (MA); cinema and media studies (MA); classic languages (MA); comparative literature (MA); creative writing (MA); cultural policy studies (MA); digital humanities (MA); East Asian languages and civilizations (MA); English language and literature (MA); gender and sexuality studies (MA); Germanic studies (MA); linguistics (MA); music (MA); near Eastern languages and civilizations (MA); philosophy (MA); poetics (MA); race, politics and culture (MA); Romance languages and literatures (MA); Slavic languages and literatures (MA); South Asian languages and civilizations (MA); theater and performance studies (MA). *Degree requirements:* For master's, thesis. *Entrance requirements:* For master's, GRE General Test, 10-15 page writing sample, statement of purpose, 3 letters of recommendation, transcripts for all previous degrees and institutions attended. Additional exam requirements/recommendations for international students: required—TOEFL (minimum score 104 iBT), IELTS (minimum score 7). Electronic applications accepted. *Expenses:* Contact institution.

University of Colorado Boulder, Graduate School, College of Arts and Sciences, Department of Asian Languages and Civilizations, Boulder, CO 80309. Offers MA, PhD. Terminal master's awarded for partial completion of doctoral program. *Degree requirements:* For master's, comprehensive exam. *Entrance requirements:* For master's, BA in Chinese or Japanese, minimum undergraduate GPA of 3.0. Additional exam requirements/recommendations for international students: required—TOEFL. Electronic applications accepted. Application fee is waived when completed online.

University of Hawaii at Manoa, Office of Graduate Education, School of Pacific and Asian Studies, Program in Asian Studies, Concentration in Korean Studies, Honolulu, HI 96822. Offers Graduate Certificate. *Program availability:* Part-time. *Degree requirements:* For Graduate Certificate, one foreign language. *Entrance requirements:* For degree, GRE. Additional exam requirements/recommendations for international students: required—TOEFL (minimum score 560 paper-based; 83 iBT), IELTS (minimum score 5).

University of Hawaii at Manoa, Office of Graduate Education, School of Pacific and Asian Studies, Program in Asian Studies, Concentration in Southeast Asian Studies, Honolulu, HI 96822. Offers Graduate Certificate. *Program availability:* Part-time. *Degree requirements:* For Graduate Certificate, one foreign language. *Entrance requirements:* For degree, GRE. Additional exam requirements/recommendations for international students: required—TOEFL (minimum score 560 paper-based; 83 iBT), IELTS (minimum score 5).

University of Illinois at Urbana-Champaign, Graduate College, College of Liberal Arts and Sciences, Center for South Asian and Middle Eastern Studies, Champaign, IL 61820. Offers MA. *Degree requirements:* For master's, one foreign language, comprehensive exam, thesis or alternative.

University of Illinois at Urbana-Champaign, Graduate College, College of Liberal Arts and Sciences, School of Literatures, Cultures and Linguistics, Department of East Asian Languages and Cultures, Champaign, IL 61820. Offers East Asian languages and cultures (PhD); East Asian studies (MA).

The University of Iowa, Graduate College, College of Liberal Arts and Sciences, Program in Asian Civilizations, Iowa City, IA 52242-1316. Offers Chinese (MA); Hindi (MA); Sanskrit (MA); South Asian studies (MA). *Degree requirements:* For master's, thesis optional, exam. *Entrance requirements:* For master's, GRE General Test, minimum GPA of 3.0. Additional exam requirements/recommendations for international students: required—TOEFL (minimum score 590 paper-based; 96 iBT). Electronic applications accepted.

The University of Kansas, Graduate Studies, College of Liberal Arts and Sciences, Department of East Asian Languages and Cultures, Lawrence, KS 66045. Offers MA, Graduate Certificate. *Program availability:* Part-time. *Students:* 3 full-time (2 women), 1 international. Average age 27. 6 applicants, 67% accepted. In 2019, 2 master's awarded. *Entrance requirements:* For master's, GRE, current curriculum vitae, statement of purpose explaining academic objectives, writing sample that demonstrates writing skills and basic research capacity, three letters of recommendation, transcripts. Additional exam requirements/recommendations for international students: required—TOEFL, IELTS. *Application deadline:* For fall admission, 2/1 priority date for domestic and international students. Application fee: $65 ($85 for international students). Electronic applications accepted. *Expenses:* Tuition, state resident: full-time $9989. Tuition, nonresident: full-time $23,950. *International tuition:* $23,950 full-time. *Required fees:* $984; $81.99 per credit hour. Tuition and fees vary according to course load, campus/location and program. *Financial support:* Fellowships, teaching assistantships, and unspecified assistantships available. *Unit head:* Dr. Hui Xiao, Chair, 785-864-9079, E-mail: hxiao@ku.edu. *Application contact:* Jared Nietfeld, Graduate Admissions Contact, 785-864-0482, E-mail: nietfeld@ku.edu.
Website: http://ealc.ku.edu/

The University of Manchester, School of Arts, Languages and Cultures, Manchester, United Kingdom. Offers anthropology, media and performance (PhD); applied theatre (PhD); Arab world studies (PhD); archaeology (PhD); art history and visual studies (PhD); arts and cultural management (PhD); arts management and cultural policy (PhD); Chinese studies (PhD); classics and ancient history (PhD); composition (PhD); creative writing (PhD); drama (PhD); East Asian studies (PhD); electroacoustic composition (PhD); English and American studies (PhD); English language (PhD); French studies (PhD); German studies (PhD); history (PhD); humanitarianism and conflict response (PhD); interpreting studies (PhD); Japanese studies (PhD); Latin American cultural studies (PhD); linguistics (PhD); Middle Eastern studies (PhD); museology (PhD); museum practice (PhD); music (PhD); musicology (PhD); Polish studies (PhD); Portuguese studies (PhD); religions and theology (PhD); Russian studies (PhD); Spanish studies (PhD); translation and intercultural studies (PhD).

University of Michigan, Rackham Graduate School, College of Literature, Science, and the Arts, Center for Japanese Studies, Ann Arbor, MI 48109-1106. Offers AM, JD/AM, MBA/AM. *Program availability:* Part-time. *Degree requirements:* For master's, one foreign language, thesis optional, 24 credits; 6th-term proficiency (3 years) in Japanese language; seminars with independent research/writing component. *Entrance requirements:* For master's, GRE General Test, academic statement of purpose; curriculum vitae; official transcripts of postsecondary education; 3 letters of recommendation. Additional exam requirements/recommendations for international students: required—TOEFL (minimum score 560 paper-based; 84 iBT); recommended—IELTS (minimum score 6.5). Electronic applications accepted.

University of Michigan, Rackham Graduate School, College of Literature, Science, and the Arts, Center for South Asian Studies, Ann Arbor, MI 48109. Offers MA, Certificate, MBA/MA. *Program availability:* Part-time. *Degree requirements:* For master's, one foreign language, thesis, 24 credits; for Certificate, one foreign language. *Entrance requirements:* For master's, GRE General Test, academic statement of purpose; curriculum vitae; writing sample; official transcripts of postsecondary education; 3 letters of recommendation; for Certificate, GRE General Test, academic statement of purpose; official transcripts; letter of recommendation from academic advisor. Additional exam requirements/recommendations for international students: required—TOEFL (minimum score 560 paper-based; 84 iBT); recommended—IELTS (minimum score 6.5). Electronic applications accepted.

University of Michigan, Rackham Graduate School, College of Literature, Science, and the Arts, Center for Southeast Asian Studies, Ann Arbor, MI 48109-1106. Offers MA, Graduate Certificate, MBA/MA, MPP/MA. *Program availability:* Part-time. *Degree requirements:* For master's, one foreign language, thesis, 25 credits; for Graduate Certificate, one foreign language. *Entrance requirements:* For master's, GRE General Test, academic statement of purpose; curriculum vitae; writing sample; official transcript of postsecondary education; 3 letters of recommendation; for Graduate Certificate, GRE General Test, academic statement of purpose; official transcripts; letter of recommendation from academic advisor. Additional exam requirements/recommendations for international students: required—TOEFL (minimum score 560 paper-based; 84 iBT); recommended—IELTS (minimum score 6.5). Electronic applications accepted.

University of Michigan, Rackham Graduate School, College of Literature, Science, and the Arts, Department of Asian Languages and Cultures, Ann Arbor, MI 48104. Offers PhD. Terminal master's awarded for partial completion of doctoral program. *Degree requirements:* For doctorate, 2 foreign languages, comprehensive exam, thesis/dissertation, preliminary exams, oral defense of dissertation. *Entrance requirements:* Additional exam requirements/recommendations for international students: required—TOEFL (minimum score 560 paper-based; 84 iBT), IELTS (minimum score 6.5). Electronic applications accepted.

University of Michigan, Rackham Graduate School, College of Literature, Science, and the Arts, Kenneth G. Lieberthal and Richard H. Rogel Center for Chinese Studies, Ann Arbor, MI 48109. Offers MA, Graduate Certificate, JD/AM, MBA/AM, MPP/AM. *Program availability:* Part-time. *Degree requirements:* For master's, one foreign language, thesis or alternative, 24 credits; 6th-term proficiency in Chinese language; for Graduate Certificate, one foreign language. *Entrance requirements:* For master's, GRE General Test, academic statement of purpose; curriculum vitae; official transcript of postsecondary education; 3 letters of recommendation. Additional exam requirements/recommendations for international students: required—TOEFL (minimum score 560 paper-based; 84 iBT); recommended—IELTS (minimum score 6.5). Electronic applications accepted.

University of Minnesota, Twin Cities Campus, Graduate School, College of Liberal Arts, Department of Asian Languages and Literatures, Minneapolis, MN 55455-0213. Offers Asian literatures, cultures, and media (PhD). *Degree requirements:* For doctorate, comprehensive exam, thesis/dissertation. *Entrance requirements:* For doctorate, GRE, 3 letters of recommendation. Additional exam requirements/recommendations for international students: required—TOEFL (minimum score 550 paper-based), IELTS (minimum score 6.5). Electronic applications accepted.

University of Oregon, Graduate School, College of Arts and Sciences, Program in Asian Studies, Eugene, OR 97403. Offers MA. *Program availability:* Part-time. *Degree requirements:* For master's, one foreign language, thesis or alternative. *Entrance requirements:* For master's, GRE General Test. Additional exam requirements/recommendations for international students: required—TOEFL.

University of Pennsylvania, School of Arts and Sciences, Graduate Group in East Asian Languages and Civilizations, Philadelphia, PA 19104. Offers AM, PhD. *Faculty:* 24 full-time (7 women), 4 part-time/adjunct (1 woman). *Students:* 39 full-time (26 women), 12 part-time (10 women); includes 4 minority (all Asian, non-Hispanic/Latino), 38 international. Average age 27. 112 applicants, 45% accepted, 20 enrolled. In 2019, 21 master's, 8 doctorates awarded. Application fee: $90.
Website: http://www.sas.upenn.edu/ealc/graduate-program

University of Pennsylvania, School of Arts and Sciences, Graduate Group in South Asian Regional Studies, Philadelphia, PA 19104. Offers AM, PhD. *Faculty:* 14 full-time (4 women), 3 part-time/adjunct (1 woman). *Students:* 22 full-time (10 women), 1 part-time (0 women); includes 5 minority (4 Asian, non-Hispanic/Latino; 1 Two or more races, non-Hispanic/Latino), 14 international. Average age 32. 36 applicants, 22% accepted, 5 enrolled. In 2019, 4 master's, 1 doctorate awarded. Terminal master's awarded for partial completion of doctoral program. Application fee: $90.
Website: http://www.southasia.upenn.edu/graduate-programs

University of Pittsburgh, Kenneth P. Dietrich School of Arts and Sciences, Department of East Asian Languages and Literatures, Pittsburgh, PA 15260. Offers Chinese (MA); Japanese (MA). *Program availability:* Part-time. *Faculty:* 6 full-time (4 women), 13 part-time/adjunct (10 women). *Students:* 3 full-time (2 women); includes 2 minority (1 Black or African American, non-Hispanic/Latino; 1 Asian, non-Hispanic/Latino). Average age 27. 13 applicants, 62% accepted, 2 enrolled. *Degree requirements:* For master's, one foreign language, comprehensive exam, thesis. *Entrance requirements:* For master's, personal statement, transcript copies, 3 letters of recommendation (online submissions), writing sample (in English). Additional exam requirements/recommendations for international students: required—TOEFL (minimum score 90 iBT), IELTS (minimum score 7). *Application deadline:* For fall admission, 1/15 for domestic and international students. Application fee: $50. Electronic applications accepted. *Expenses:* $24,480 in-state, $40,848 out-of-state. *Financial support:* Scholarships/grants, health care benefits, tuition waivers (full and partial), and unspecified assistantships available. Financial award application deadline: 1/15. *Unit head:* Dr. Hiroshi Nara, Chair, 412-624-5579, Fax: 412-624-3458, E-mail: hnara@pitt.edu. *Application contact:* Keanna Cash, Graduate Administrator, 412-624-5227, E-mail: kec176@pitt.edu.
Website: http://deall.pitt.edu/

University of Pittsburgh, University Center for International Studies, Pittsburgh, PA 15260. Offers African studies (Certificate); Asian studies (Certificate); European Union studies (Certificate); global studies (Certificate); Latin American studies (Certificate); Russian and East European studies (Certificate); West European studies (Certificate). *Program availability:* Part-time, evening/weekend, online learning. *Degree requirements:* For Certificate, one foreign language, comprehensive exam (for some programs). *Entrance requirements:* Additional exam requirements/recommendations for international students: required—TOEFL. *Expenses:* Contact institution.

University of San Francisco, College of Arts and Sciences, Program in Asia Pacific Studies, San Francisco, CA 94117. Offers MA, MA/MBA. *Program availability:* Part-time, evening/weekend. *Faculty:* 3 full-time (1 woman), 6 part-time/adjunct (4 women). *Students:* 40 full-time (29 women), 3 part-time (2 women); includes 12 minority (2 Black or African American, non-Hispanic/Latino; 7 Asian, non-Hispanic/Latino; 1 Hispanic/Latino; 2 Two or more races, non-Hispanic/Latino), 25 international. Average age 27. 42 applicants, 93% accepted, 21 enrolled. In 2019, 15 master's awarded. *Degree requirements:* For master's, variable foreign language requirement, thesis. *Entrance requirements:* For master's, minimum GPA of 3.0. Additional exam requirements/recommendations for international students: required—TOEFL (minimum score 90 iBT), IELTS (minimum score 6.5), PTE (minimum score 61). *Application deadline:* For fall admission, 2/1 for domestic and international students. Applications are processed on a rolling basis. Application fee: $55. Electronic applications accepted. Application fee is waived when completed online. *Financial support:* Teaching assistantships with partial tuition reimbursements, career-related internships or fieldwork, and scholarships/grants available. Financial award applicants required to submit FAFSA. *Unit head:* Dr. Brian Dempster, Graduate Director, 415-422-6357, E-mail: maps@usfca.edu. *Application contact:* Information Contact, 415-422-5101, Fax: 415-422-2217, E-mail: asgraduate@usfca.edu.
Website: https://www.usfca.edu/arts-sciences/graduate-programs/asia-pacific-studies

University of Southern California, Graduate School, Dana and David Dornsife College of Letters, Arts and Sciences, Department of East Asian Languages and Cultures, Los Angeles, CA 90089. Offers classical Chinese literature (MA, PhD); classical Japanese literature (MA, PhD); linguistics (MA, PhD); modern Chinese literature (MA, PhD); modern Japanese literature (MA, PhD); modern Korean literature (MA, PhD). *Degree requirements:* For master's, thesis; for doctorate, 2 foreign languages, comprehensive exam, thesis/dissertation. *Entrance requirements:* For master's and doctorate, GRE, BA in relevant field. Additional exam requirements/recommendations for international students: required—TOEFL. Electronic applications accepted.

University of Southern California, Graduate School, Dana and David Dornsife College of Letters, Arts and Sciences, East Asian Studies Center, Los Angeles, CA 90089. Offers MA, MA/MBA. *Program availability:* Part-time. *Degree requirements:* For master's, one foreign language, thesis, language proficiency in an East Asian language (equivalent to 3 years of study). *Entrance requirements:* For master's, GRE (minimum score 1000). Additional exam requirements/recommendations for international students: required—TOEFL (minimum score 600 paper-based; 100 iBT). Electronic applications accepted.

The University of Texas at Austin, Graduate School, College of Liberal Arts, Department of Asian Studies, Austin, TX 78712-1111. Offers Asian cultures and languages (MA, PhD); Asian studies (MA). *Program availability:* Part-time. *Degree requirements:* For master's, thesis; for doctorate, 3 foreign languages, thesis/dissertation. *Entrance requirements:* For master's and doctorate, GRE General Test. Electronic applications accepted.

University of Toronto, School of Graduate Studies, Faculty of Arts and Science, Department of East Asian Studies, Toronto, ON M5S 1A1, Canada. Offers MA, PhD. *Program availability:* Part-time. *Degree requirements:* For master's, thesis optional; for doctorate, 2 foreign languages, comprehensive exam, thesis/dissertation. *Entrance requirements:* For master's, writing sample, 2 letters of recommendation, BA in a specialist or East Asian studies program, minimum B+ average in final year; for doctorate, writing sample, 3 letters of recommendation, MA in East Asian studies. Additional exam requirements/recommendations for international students: required—TOEFL (minimum score 600 paper-based), TWE (minimum score 5). Electronic applications accepted.

University of Utah, Graduate School, College of Humanities, Asian Studies Program, Salt Lake City, UT 84112. Offers MA. *Faculty:* 55 full-time (30 women). *Students:* 2 full-time (both women). Average age 44. 8 applicants, 25% accepted, 1 enrolled. In 2019, 1 master's awarded. *Degree requirements:* For master's, one foreign language, thesis, 3rd-year proficiency in one Asian language. *Entrance requirements:* For master's, GRE. Additional exam requirements/recommendations for international students: required—TOEFL (minimum score 550 paper-based; 80 iBT), IELTS (minimum score 6.5). *Application deadline:* For fall admission, 2/1 for domestic and international students. Application fee: $55 ($65 for international students). Electronic applications accepted. *Expenses:* Tuition, state resident: full-time $7085; part-time $272.51 per credit hour. Tuition, nonresident: full-time $24,937; part-time $959.12 per credit hour. *Required fees:* $880.52; $880.52 per semester. Tuition and fees vary according to degree level, program and student level. *Financial support:* In 2019–20, 2 students received support, including 2 fellowships with full tuition reimbursements available (averaging $15,000 per year). Financial award application deadline: 2/1; financial award applicants required to submit FAFSA. *Unit head:* Dr. Kim Korinek, Director, 801-581-6101, Fax: 801-581-6105, E-mail: kim.korinek@soc.utah.edu. *Application contact:* Patrick T. Cheney, Scholarship and Graduate Program Coordinator, 801-581-6101, Fax: 801-581-6105, E-mail: patrick.cheney@utah.edu.
Website: http://asia-center.utah.edu/

University of Victoria, Faculty of Graduate Studies, Faculty of Humanities, Department of Pacific and Asian Studies, Victoria, BC V8W 2Y2, Canada. Offers MA. *Degree requirements:* For master's, thesis. *Entrance requirements:* For master's, minimum B+ average, writing sample. Additional exam requirements/recommendations for international students: required—TOEFL (minimum score 575 paper-based), IELTS (minimum score 7). Electronic applications accepted.

University of Virginia, College and Graduate School of Arts and Sciences, Department of East Asian Languages, Literatures, and Cultures, Charlottesville, VA 22903. Offers East Asian studies (MA); MBA/MA. *Degree requirements:* For master's, one foreign language, comprehensive exam, thesis. *Entrance requirements:* For master's, GRE General Test, 2 letters of recommendation. Additional exam requirements/recommendations for international students: required—TOEFL, IELTS. Electronic applications accepted.

University of Virginia, College and Graduate School of Arts and Sciences, Department of Middle Eastern and South Asian Languages and Cultures, Charlottesville, VA 22903. Offers Middle Eastern and South Asian studies (MA).

University of Washington, Graduate School, College of Arts and Sciences, Department of Asian Languages and Literature, Seattle, WA 98195. Offers Buddhist studies (MA, PhD); Chinese language and literature (MA, PhD); Japanese language and literature (MA, PhD); Korean language and literature (MA, PhD); South Asian language and literature (MA, PhD). *Degree requirements:* For master's, 2 foreign languages, general exam, thesis or 2 research papers; for doctorate, 3 foreign languages, thesis/dissertation, general exam. *Entrance requirements:* For master's, GRE, minimum GPA of 3.0; for doctorate, GRE, master's degree in related field, minimum GPA of 3.0. Additional exam requirements/recommendations for international students: required—TOEFL. Electronic applications accepted.

University of Washington, Graduate School, College of Arts and Sciences, Henry M. Jackson School of International Studies, China Studies Program, Seattle, WA 98195. Offers MAIS. *Degree requirements:* For master's, one foreign language, thesis optional. *Entrance requirements:* For master's, GRE General Test, minimum GPA of 3.0 in last 2 years. Additional exam requirements/recommendations for international students: required—TOEFL (minimum score 500 paper-based; 92 iBT), IELTS (minimum score 7). Electronic applications accepted.

University of Washington, Graduate School, College of Arts and Sciences, Henry M. Jackson School of International Studies, Japan Studies Program, Seattle, WA 98195. Offers MAIS. *Degree requirements:* For master's, one foreign language. *Entrance requirements:* For master's, GRE General Test, minimum GPA of 3.0 in last two years. Additional exam requirements/recommendations for international students: required—TOEFL (minimum score 500 paper-based; 92 iBT), IELTS (minimum score 7). Electronic applications accepted.

University of Washington, Graduate School, College of Arts and Sciences, Henry M. Jackson School of International Studies, Korea Studies Program, Seattle, WA 98195. Offers MAIS. *Degree requirements:* For master's, one foreign language. *Entrance requirements:* For master's, GRE General Test, minimum GPA of 3.0 in last two years. Additional exam requirements/recommendations for international students: required—TOEFL (minimum score 500 paper-based; 92 iBT), IELTS (minimum score 7). Electronic applications accepted.

University of Washington, Graduate School, College of Arts and Sciences, Henry M. Jackson School of International Studies, Russian, East European and Central Asian Studies Program, Seattle, WA 98195. Offers Central Asian studies (MAIS); East European studies (MAIS); Russian studies (MAIS). *Degree requirements:* For master's, one foreign language, thesis. *Entrance requirements:* For master's, GRE General Test, 2 years of relevant language, minimum GPA of 3.0 in last two years. Additional exam requirements/recommendations for international students: required—TOEFL (minimum score 500 paper-based; 92 iBT), IELTS (minimum score 7). Electronic applications accepted.

University of Washington, Graduate School, College of Arts and Sciences, Henry M. Jackson School of International Studies, South Asian Studies Program, Seattle, WA 98195. Offers MAIS. *Degree requirements:* For master's, one foreign language, thesis optional. *Entrance requirements:* For master's, GRE General Test, minimum GPA of 3.0 in last two years. Additional exam requirements/recommendations for international students: required—TOEFL (minimum score 500 paper-based; 92 iBT), IELTS (minimum score 7). Electronic applications accepted.

University of Washington, Graduate School, College of Arts and Sciences, Henry M. Jackson School of International Studies, Southeast Asian Studies Program, Seattle, WA 98195. Offers MAIS. *Degree requirements:* For master's, one foreign language, thesis optional. *Entrance requirements:* For master's, GRE General Test, minimum GPA of 3.0 in last two years. Additional exam requirements/recommendations for international students: required—TOEFL (minimum score 500 paper-based; 92 iBT), IELTS (minimum score 7). Electronic applications accepted.

University of Wisconsin–Madison, Graduate School, College of Letters and Science, Center for Southeast Asian Studies, Madison, WI 53706. Offers MA. *Program availability:* Part-time. *Degree requirements:* For master's, one foreign language, oral defense of seminar paper. Electronic applications accepted.

University of Wisconsin–Madison, Graduate School, College of Letters and Science, Department of East Asian Languages and Literature, Madison, WI 53706-1380. Offers Chinese literature (MA, PhD); Chinese thought (MA, PhD); Japanese linguistics (MA, PhD); Japanese literature (MA, PhD). *Program availability:* Part-time. Terminal master's awarded for partial completion of doctoral program. *Degree requirements:* For master's, one foreign language, seminars, written exam; for doctorate, 3 foreign languages, thesis/dissertation, seminars, preliminary exams, oral exams. *Entrance requirements:* For master's, GRE General Test, BA or equivalent in major field; for doctorate, GRE General Test, MA or equivalent in major field. Electronic applications accepted.

University of Wisconsin–Madison, Graduate School, College of Letters and Science, Department of History, Madison, WI 53706-1380. Offers African history (MA, PhD); Central Asian history (MA, PhD); comparative world history (MA, PhD); East Asian history (MA, PhD); European history (MA, PhD); gender and women's history (MA, PhD); Latin American and Caribbean history (MA, PhD); Middle Eastern history (MA, PhD); South Asian history (MA, PhD); Southeast Asian history (MA, PhD); United States history (MA, PhD). Terminal master's awarded for partial completion of doctoral program. *Degree requirements:* For master's, thesis (for some programs); for doctorate, variable foreign language requirement, thesis/dissertation. *Entrance requirements:* For master's and doctorate, GRE General Test. Additional exam requirements/recommendations for international students: required—Michigan English Language Assessment Battery or TOEFL. Electronic applications accepted.

University of Wisconsin–Madison, Graduate School, College of Letters and Science, Department of Languages and Cultures of Asia, Madison, WI 53706-1380. Offers civilizations and cultures (PhD); languages and cultures of Asia (MA); languages and literatures (PhD); religions of Asia (PhD). *Program availability:* Part-time. Terminal master's awarded for partial completion of doctoral program. *Degree requirements:* For master's, one foreign language, thesis or alternative; for doctorate, 2 foreign languages, thesis/dissertation. *Entrance requirements:* For master's, minimum GPA of 3.0; for doctorate, minimum GPA of 3.25, master's degree. Electronic applications accepted.

Washington University in St. Louis, The Graduate School, Department of East Asian Languages and Cultures, St. Louis, MO 63130-4899. Offers Chinese (MA); Chinese and comparative literature (PhD); Chinese language and literature (PhD); East Asian studies (MA); Japanese (MA); Japanese and comparative literature (PhD); Japanese language and literature (PhD). Terminal master's awarded for partial completion of doctoral program. *Degree requirements:* For master's, thesis optional; for doctorate, thesis/dissertation. *Entrance requirements:* For master's and doctorate, GRE General Test. Additional exam requirements/recommendations for international students: required—TOEFL. Electronic applications accepted.

Yale University, Graduate School of Arts and Sciences, Program in East Asian Studies, New Haven, CT 06520. Offers MA. *Degree requirements:* For master's, one foreign language. *Entrance requirements:* For master's, GRE General Test.

Canadian Studies

Carleton University, Faculty of Graduate Studies, Faculty of Arts and Social Sciences, School of Canadian Studies, Ottawa, ON K1S 5B6, Canada. Offers MA, PhD. *Degree requirements:* For master's, one foreign language, thesis optional; for doctorate, one foreign language, thesis/dissertation. *Entrance requirements:* For master's, honors degree. Additional exam requirements/recommendations for international students: required—TOEFL. Electronic applications accepted.

Queen's University at Kingston, School of Graduate Studies, Faculty of Arts and Science, Department of Political Studies, Kingston, ON K7L 3N6, Canada. Offers Canadian politics (MA, PhD); comparative politics (MA, PhD); gender and politics (MA, PhD); international relations (MA, PhD); political theory (MA, PhD). *Degree requirements:* For master's, thesis or alternative; for doctorate, one foreign language, thesis/dissertation, qualifying exams. *Entrance requirements:* Additional exam requirements/recommendations for international students: required—TOEFL (minimum score 600 paper-based).

Saint Mary's University, Faculty of Arts, Program in Atlantic Canada Studies, Halifax, NS B3H 3C3, Canada. Offers MA, Certificate. *Program availability:* Part-time, evening/weekend. *Degree requirements:* For master's, thesis. *Entrance requirements:* For master's, honors degree. Electronic applications accepted. *Expenses:* Contact institution.

Trent University, Graduate Studies, The Frost Centre for Canadian Studies and Indigenous Studies, Peterborough, ON K9J 7B8, Canada. Offers Canadian studies (PhD); Canadian studies and indigenous studies (MA). *Program availability:* Part-time. *Degree requirements:* For master's, thesis. *Entrance requirements:* For master's, honors degree.

Université de Saint-Boniface, Program in Canadian Studies, Saint-Boniface, MB R2H 0H7, Canada. Offers MA.

Université de Sherbrooke, Faculty of Letters and Human Sciences, Department of Letters and Communications, Sherbrooke, QC J1K 2R1, Canada. Offers comparative Canadian literature (MA, PhD); French literature (MA, PhD); linguistics (MA); theatre (MA). *Degree requirements:* For master's, thesis or alternative; for doctorate, thesis/dissertation. *Entrance requirements:* For master's, minimum GPA of 2.8; for doctorate, minimum GPA of 3.0.

Université du Québec à Chicoutimi, Graduate Programs, Program in Regional Studies, Chicoutimi, QC G7H 2B1, Canada. Offers MA. *Program availability:* Part-time. *Degree requirements:* For master's, thesis. *Entrance requirements:* For master's, appropriate bachelor's degree, proficiency in French.

University at Buffalo, the State University of New York, Graduate School, College of Arts and Sciences, Department of Transnational Studies, Buffalo, NY 14214. Offers American studies (MA, PhD); Canadian studies (MA); global gender studies (MA, PhD). *Program availability:* Part-time. Terminal master's awarded for partial completion of doctoral program. *Degree requirements:* For master's, comprehensive exam (for some programs), thesis optional; for doctorate, comprehensive exam, thesis/dissertation. *Entrance requirements:* For master's, minimum GPA of 3.0; for doctorate, GRE, minimum GPA of 3.0. Additional exam requirements/recommendations for international students: required—TOEFL (minimum score 550 paper-based; 79 iBT), IELTS (minimum score 6.5). Electronic applications accepted. *Expenses: Tuition, area resident:* Full-time $11,310; part-time $471 per credit hour. Tuition, state resident: full-time $11,310; part-time $471 per credit hour. Tuition, nonresident: full-time $23,100; part-time $963 per credit hour. *International tuition:* $23,100 full-time. *Required fees:* $2820.

University of Lethbridge, School of Graduate Studies, Lethbridge, AB T1K 3M4, Canada. Offers addictions counseling (M Sc); agricultural biotechnology (M Sc); agricultural studies (M Sc, MA); anthropology (MA); archaeology (M Sc, MA); art (MA, MFA); biochemistry (M Sc); biological sciences (M Sc); biomolecular science (PhD); biosystems and biodiversity (PhD); Canadian studies (MA); chemistry (M Sc); computer science (M Sc); computer science and geographical information science (M Sc); counseling (MC); counseling psychology (M Ed); dramatic arts (MA); earth, space, and physical science (PhD); economics (MA); education (MA, PhD); educational leadership (M Ed); English (MA); environmental science (M Sc); evolution and behavior (PhD); exercise science (M Sc); French (MA); French/German (MA); French/Spanish (MA); general education (M Ed); geography (M Sc, MA); German (MA); health sciences (M Sc); individualized multidisciplinary (M Sc, MA); kinesiology (M Sc, MA); management (M Sc), including accounting, finance, human resource management and labor relations, information systems, international management, marketing, policy and strategy; mathematics (M Sc); music (M Mus, MA); Native American studies (MA); neuroscience (M Sc, PhD); new media (MA, MFA); nursing (M Sc, MN); philosophy (MA); physics (M Sc); political science (MA); psychology (M Sc, MA); religious studies (MA); sociology (MA); theatre and dramatic arts (MFA); theoretical and computational science (PhD); urban and regional studies (MA); women and gender studies (MA). *Program availability:* Part-time, evening/weekend. *Degree requirements:* For master's, thesis (for some programs); for doctorate, comprehensive exam, thesis/dissertation. *Entrance requirements:* For master's, GMAT (for M Sc in management), bachelor's degree in related field, minimum GPA of 3.0 during previous 20 graded semester courses, 2 years' teaching or related experience (M Ed); for doctorate, master's degree, minimum graduate GPA of 3.5. Additional exam requirements/recommendations for international students: required—TOEFL (minimum score 580 paper-based; 93 iBT). Electronic applications accepted.

University of Manitoba, Faculty of Graduate Studies, College Universitaire de Saint Boniface, Program in Canadian Studies, Winnipeg, MB R3T 2N2, Canada. Offers MA.

University of Ottawa, Faculty of Graduate and Postdoctoral Studies, Faculty of Arts, Institute of Canadian Studies, Ottawa, ON K1N 6N5, Canada. Offers economics (PhD); English (PhD); geography (PhD); history (PhD); lettres Françaises (PhD); linguistics (PhD); philosophy (PhD); political science (PhD); psychology (PhD); religious studies (PhD); translation studies (PhD). *Degree requirements:* For doctorate, comprehensive exam, thesis/dissertation.

University of Saskatchewan, College of Graduate and Postdoctoral Studies, College of Arts and Science, Department of Indigenous Studies, Saskatoon, SK S7N 5A2, Canada. Offers MA, PhD. *Degree requirements:* For master's, thesis; for doctorate, comprehensive exam (for some programs), thesis/dissertation. *Entrance requirements:* Additional exam requirements/recommendations for international students: required—TOEFL (minimum score 80 iBT); recommended—IELTS (minimum score 6.5). Electronic applications accepted.

Wilfrid Laurier University, Faculty of Graduate and Postdoctoral Studies, Faculty of Arts, Department of Political Science, Waterloo, ON N2L 3C5, Canada. Offers Canadian political studies (MA); comparative politics/international relations (MA). *Program availability:* Part-time. *Degree requirements:* For master's, thesis optional. *Entrance requirements:* For master's, honors bachelor's degree or the equivalent in political science, minimum B average in undergraduate course work. Additional exam requirements/recommendations for international students: required—TOEFL (minimum score 89 iBT). Electronic applications accepted.

Wilfrid Laurier University, Faculty of Graduate and Postdoctoral Studies, Lyle S. Hallman Faculty of Social Work, Waterloo, ON N2L 3C5, Canada. Offers Aboriginal studies (MSW); community, policy, planning and organizations (MSW); critical social policy and organizational studies (PhD); individuals, families and groups (MSW); social work practice (individuals, families, groups and communities) (PhD); social work practice: individuals, families, groups and communities (PhD). *Program availability:* Part-time. *Degree requirements:* For master's, thesis optional; for doctorate, thesis/dissertation. *Entrance requirements:* For master's, course work in social science, research methodology, and statistics; honors BA with a minimum B average; for doctorate, master's degree in social work, minimum A- average. Additional exam requirements/recommendations for international students: required—TOEFL (minimum score 89 iBT). Electronic applications accepted. *Expenses:* Contact institution.

Cultural Studies

American University, College of Arts and Sciences, Critical Race, Gender, and Culture Studies, Washington, DC 20016. Offers Asian studies (Graduate Certificate); women's, gender, and sexuality studies (Graduate Certificate). *Entrance requirements:* Additional exam requirements/recommendations for international students: required—TOEFL.

American University, School of International Service, Washington, DC 20016-8071. Offers comparative and regional studies (Certificate); cross-cultural communication (Certificate); development management (MS); ethics, peace, and global affairs (MA); European studies (Certificate); global environmental policy (MA, Certificate); global information technology (Certificate); global media (MA); international affairs (MA), including comparative and regional studies, global governance, politics, and security, international economic relations, natural resources and sustainable development, U.S. foreign policy and national security; international arts management (Certificate); international communication (MA, Certificate); international development (MA); international economic policy (Certificate); international economic relations (Certificate); international economics (MA); international peace and conflict resolution (MA, Certificate); international politics (Certificate); international relations (MA, PhD); international service (MIS); peacebuilding (Certificate); social enterprise (MA); the Americas (Certificate); United States foreign policy (Certificate); JD/MA. *Program availability:* Part-time, evening/weekend, 100% online, blended/hybrid learning. Terminal master's awarded for partial completion of doctoral program. *Degree requirements:* For master's, one foreign language, comprehensive exam, thesis or alternative; for doctorate, one foreign language, comprehensive exam, thesis/dissertation. *Entrance requirements:* For master's, transcripts, resume, 2 letters of recommendation, statement of purpose; for doctorate, GRE, transcripts, resume, 3 letters of recommendation, statement of purpose. Additional exam requirements/recommendations for international students: required—TOEFL. Electronic applications accepted. *Expenses:* Contact institution.

The American University of Paris, Graduate Programs, Paris, France. Offers cross-cultural and sustainable business management (MA); cultural translation (MA); global communications (MA); global communications and civil society (MA); international affairs (MA); international affairs, conflict resolution and civil society development (MA); Middle East and Islamic studies (MA); Middle East and Islamic studies and international affairs (MA); public policy and international affairs (MA); public policy and international law (MA). *Degree requirements:* For master's, thesis (for some programs). *Entrance requirements:* For master's, minimum undergraduate GPA of 3.0. Additional exam requirements/recommendations for international students: recommended—TOEFL, IELTS. Electronic applications accepted.

Appalachian State University, Cratis D. Williams School of Graduate Studies, Center for Appalachian Studies, Boone, NC 28608. Offers culture (MA). *Program availability:* Part-time. *Degree requirements:* For master's, one foreign language, comprehensive exam, thesis optional. *Entrance requirements:* For master's, GRE General Test, 3 letters of recommendation. Additional exam requirements/recommendations for international students: required—TOEFL (minimum score 570 paper-based; 79 iBT), IELTS (minimum score 6.5). Electronic applications accepted.

Arizona State University at Tempe, College of Liberal Arts and Sciences, Department of English, Program in Film and Media Studies, Tempe, AZ 85287-0402. Offers American media and popular culture (MAS). *Program availability:* Part-time, evening/weekend, online learning. *Degree requirements:* For master's, integrated project. *Entrance requirements:* For master's, minimum GPA of 3.0 or equivalent in last 2 years of work leading to bachelor's degree. Additional exam requirements/recommendations for international students: required—TOEFL, IELTS, or PTE. Electronic applications accepted. *Expenses:* Contact institution.

Arizona State University at Tempe, College of Liberal Arts and Sciences, School of International Letters and Cultures, Program in Spanish, Tempe, AZ 85287-0202. Offers cultural studies (PhD); linguistics (MA), including second language acquisition/applied linguistics, sociolinguistics; literature (PhD); literature and culture (MA). *Program availability:* Part-time. Terminal master's awarded for partial completion of doctoral program. *Degree requirements:* For master's, thesis, oral defense; written comprehensive exam (literature and culture); portfolio review (linguistics); interactive Program of Study (iPOS) submitted before completing 50 percent of required credit hours; for doctorate, comprehensive exam, thesis/dissertation, interactive Program of Study (iPOS) submitted before completing 50 percent of required credit hours. *Entrance requirements:* For master's, GRE (recommended), BA in Spanish or close equivalent from accredited institution with minimum GPA of 3.5, 3 letters of recommendation, personal statement, academic writing sample; for doctorate, GRE (recommended), MA in Spanish or equivalent from accredited institution with minimum GPA of 3.75, 3 letters of recommendation, personal statement, academic writing sample. Additional exam requirements/recommendations for international students: required—TOEFL (minimum score 550 paper-based; 83 iBT), IELTS (minimum score 6.5). Electronic applications accepted.

Assemblies of God Theological Seminary, Graduate and Professional Programs, Springfield, MO 65802. Offers Biblical interpretation and theology (PhD); Christian ministries (MA); divinity (M Div); intercultural studies (MA, PhD); leadership and ministry (MLM); ministry (D Min); missiology (DAIS); pastoral studies (MPL); theological studies (MA, Th M). *Accreditation:* ATS. *Program availability:* Part-time, evening/weekend, 100% online. *Faculty:* 12 full-time (3 women), 15 part-time/adjunct (4 women). *Students:* 136 full-time (37 women), 147 part-time (40 women); includes 71 minority (24 Black or African American, non-Hispanic/Latino; 6 American Indian or Alaska Native, non-Hispanic/Latino; 7 Asian, non-Hispanic/Latino; 22 Hispanic/Latino; 7 Native Hawaiian or other Pacific Islander, non-Hispanic/Latino; 5 Two or more races, non-Hispanic/Latino), 14 international. Average age 46. 62 applicants, 100% accepted, 42 enrolled. In 2019, 37 master's, 25 doctorates awarded. *Degree requirements:* For master's, variable foreign language requirement, thesis; for doctorate, variable foreign language requirement, comprehensive exam, thesis/dissertation. *Entrance requirements:* For master's, minimum GPA of 2.5; for doctorate, GRE (for PhD in Bible theology), minimum GPA of 3.0. Additional exam requirements/recommendations for international students: required—TOEFL (minimum score 550 paper-based; 80 iBT). *Application deadline:* For fall admission, 7/1 priority date for domestic students, 6/1 priority date for international students; for spring admission, 12/1 priority date for domestic students, 11/1 priority date for international students. Applications are processed on a rolling basis. Application fee: $75. Electronic applications accepted. *Financial support:* Career-related internships or fieldwork and scholarships/grants available. Support available to part-time students. Financial award application deadline: 7/15; financial award applicants required to submit FAFSA. *Unit head:* Dr. Timothy A. Hager, Dean, 417-268-1000, Fax: 417-268-1001. *Application contact:* Nik White, Seminary Enrollment Coordinator, 417-268-1000, Fax: 417-268-1030, E-mail: info@agts.edu.
Website: http://www.agts.edu

Athabasca University, Centre for Interdisciplinary Studies, Athabasca, AB T9S 3A3, Canada. Offers adult education (MA); community studies (MA); cultural studies (MA); educational studies (MA); global change (MA); heritage resource management (Postbaccalaureate Certificate); legislative drafting (Postbaccalaureate Certificate); work, organization, and leadership (MA). *Program availability:* Part-time, evening/weekend, online learning. *Degree requirements:* For master's, project. *Entrance requirements:* Additional exam requirements/recommendations for international students: required—TOEFL (minimum score 560 paper-based). Electronic applications accepted.

Biola University, Cook School of Intercultural Studies, La Mirada, CA 90639-0001. Offers anthropology (MA); applied linguistics (MA); intercultural education (PhD); intercultural studies (MA, PhD); linguistics (Certificate); linguistics and Biblical languages (MA); missiology (D Miss); missions (MA); teaching English to speakers of other languages (MA, Certificate). *Program availability:* Part-time, 100% online. *Faculty:* 19. *Students:* 108 full-time (55 women), 154 part-time (86 women); includes 77 minority (11 Black or African American, non-Hispanic/Latino; 1 American Indian or Alaska Native, non-Hispanic/Latino; 43 Asian, non-Hispanic/Latino; 19 Hispanic/Latino; 3 Two or more

races, non-Hispanic/Latino), 67 international. Average age 35. 142 applicants, 63% accepted, 52 enrolled. In 2019, 37 master's, 14 doctorates awarded. *Degree requirements:* For master's, comprehensive exam (for some programs), thesis or alternative, All students must successfully complete all required coursework with a minimum GPA of 3.0; for doctorate, thesis/dissertation, All students must present an acceptable dissertation, have satisfactorily passed their qualifying exam and completed all required course work with a minimum 3.3 GPA; for Certificate, All students musts successfully complete all required coursework with a minimum GPA of 3.0. *Entrance requirements:* For master's, minimum undergraduate GPA of 3.0; for doctorate, master's degree or equivalent, 3 years of cross-cultural experience, minimum graduate GPA of 3.3. Additional exam requirements/recommendations for international students: required—TOEFL. *Application deadline:* For fall admission, 7/1 for domestic students, 6/1 for international students; for spring admission, 11/1 for domestic students; for summer admission, 5/1 for domestic students. Applications are processed on a rolling basis. Application fee: $65. Electronic applications accepted. *Financial support:* Scholarships/grants available. Support available to part-time students. Financial award applicants required to submit FAFSA. *Unit head:* Dr. Bulus Y. Galadima, Dean, 562-903-4844. *Application contact:* Graduate Admissions Office, 562-903-4752, E-mail: graduate.admissions@biola.edu.
Website: http://cook.biola.edu

Biola University, Talbot School of Theology, La Mirada, CA 90639-0001. Offers adult/family ministry (MACE); Bible exposition (MA, Th M); Biblical and theological studies (Certificate); children's ministry (MACE); Christian education (M Div); cross-cultural education ministry (MACE); educational studies (Ed D, PhD); evangelism and discipleship (M Div); general Christian education (MACE); Messianic Jewish studies (M Div, Certificate); missions and intercultural studies (M Div); New Testament (MA, Th M); Old Testament (MA); Old Testament and Semitics (Th M); pastoral and general ministry (M Div); pastoral care and counseling (M Div, MACML); philosophy (MA); preaching and pastoral ministry (MACML); spiritual formation (M Div, Certificate); spiritual formation and soul care (MA); sports ministry (MACML); theology (MA, Th M, D Min, Certificate); youth ministry (MACE). *Program availability:* Part-time, evening/weekend. *Students:* 461 full-time (116 women), 768 part-time (228 women); includes 489 minority (54 Black or African American, non-Hispanic/Latino; 1 American Indian or Alaska Native, non-Hispanic/Latino; 303 Asian, non-Hispanic/Latino; 96 Hispanic/Latino; 3 Native Hawaiian or other Pacific Islander, non-Hispanic/Latino; 32 Two or more races, non-Hispanic/Latino), 162 international. Average age 38. 745 applicants, 70% accepted, 320 enrolled. In 2019, 235 master's, 24 doctorates awarded. *Entrance requirements:* For master's, bachelor's degree from accredited college or university; minimum GPA of 2.6 (for M Div), 3.0 (for MA); for doctorate, M Div or MA. Additional exam requirements/recommendations for international students: required—TOEFL (minimum score 600 paper-based; 88 iBT). *Application deadline:* For fall admission, 7/1 for domestic students, 6/1 for international students; for spring admission, 11/1 for domestic students. Applications are processed on a rolling basis. Application fee: $65. Electronic applications accepted. *Financial support:* Scholarships/grants and unspecified assistantships available. Support available to part-time students. Financial award applicants required to submit FAFSA. *Unit head:* Dr. Clint Arnold, Dean, 562-903-4816, Fax: 562-903-4748. *Application contact:* Graduate Admissions Office, 562-903-4752, E-mail: graduate.admissions@biola.edu.
Website: http://www.talbot.edu/

Boston University, Metropolitan College, Program in Gastronomy, Boston, MA 02215. Offers communications (MLA); history and culture (MLA). *Program availability:* Part-time, evening/weekend. *Faculty:* 3 full-time (2 women), 6 part-time/adjunct (3 women). *Students:* 6 full-time (4 women), 39 part-time (35 women); includes 7 minority (3 Black or African American, non-Hispanic/Latino; 3 Asian, non-Hispanic/Latino; 1 Hispanic/Latino), 5 international. Average age 34. 31 applicants, 87% accepted, 9 enrolled. In 2019, 27 master's awarded. *Entrance requirements:* Additional exam requirements/recommendations for international students: required—TOEFL. *Application deadline:* Applications are processed on a rolling basis. Application fee: $85. Electronic applications accepted. *Expenses:* Contact institution. *Financial support:* In 2019–20, 5 research assistantships (averaging $4,200 per year) were awarded; career-related internships or fieldwork, scholarships/grants, and unspecified assistantships also available. Support available to part-time students. Financial award applicants required to submit FAFSA. *Unit head:* Dr. Megan Elias, Associate Professor of the Practice and Director, 617-353-6916, Fax: 617-353-4130, E-mail: gastrmla@bu.edu. *Application contact:* Barbara Rotger, Program Manager, 617-353-6916, Fax: 617-353-4130, E-mail: brotger@bu.edu.
Website: http://www.bu.edu/met/gastronomy

Brock University, Faculty of Graduate Studies, Faculty of Social Sciences, Program in Popular Culture, St. Catharines, ON L2S 3A1, Canada. Offers MA. *Program availability:* Part-time. *Degree requirements:* For master's, thesis optional. *Entrance requirements:* For master's, honors BA. Additional exam requirements/recommendations for international students: required—TOEFL (minimum score 550 paper-based; 80 iBT), IELTS (minimum score 6.5), TWE (minimum score 4). Electronic applications accepted.

Carnegie Mellon University, Dietrich College of Humanities and Social Sciences, Department of History, Pittsburgh, PA 15213-3891. Offers African and African-American diaspora (PhD); culture and power (PhD); labor, politics and social movements (PhD); technology, environment, science and health (PhD); women, gender and the family (PhD). *Program availability:* Part-time. *Degree requirements:* For doctorate, oral and written comprehensive exams, dissertation defense. *Entrance requirements:* For doctorate, GRE General Test. Additional exam requirements/recommendations for international students: required—TOEFL. Electronic applications accepted.

Central Michigan University, College of Graduate Studies, College of Liberal Arts and Social Sciences, Program in Humanities, Mount Pleasant, MI 48859. Offers humanities (MA), including contemporary issues in the humanities: race, class, and gender, images and ideas of self, Native American issues in modern culture, popular culture studies, the rise of industrial society. *Program availability:* Part-time, evening/weekend. *Degree requirements:* For master's, thesis or alternative. Electronic applications accepted. *Expenses: Tuition, area resident:* Full-time $12,267; part-time $8178 per year. *Tuition, state resident:* full-time $12,267; part-time $8178 per year. *Tuition, nonresident:* full-time $12,267; part-time $8178 per year. *International tuition:* $16,110 full-time. *Required fees:* $225 per semester. Tuition and fees vary according to degree level and program.

Chapman University, Donna Ford Attallah College of Educational Studies, Orange, CA 92866. Offers counseling (MA), including school counseling (MA, Credential); curriculum and instruction (MA), including elementary education, secondary education; education (PhD), including cultural and curricular studies, disability studies, leadership studies, school psychology (PhD, Credential); educational psychology (MA); leadership development (MA); multiple subjects (Credential), including Spanish/English bilingual; pupil personnel services (Credential), including school counseling (MA, Credential); school psychology (PhD, Credential); school psychology (Ed S); single subject (Credential); special education (MA, Credential), including mild/moderate (Credential), moderate/severe (Credential); teaching (MA), including elementary education, secondary education, secondary music education. *Accreditation:* TEAC. *Program availability:* Part-time, evening/weekend. *Faculty:* 33 full-time (19 women), 49 part-time/adjunct (36 women). *Students:* 145 full-time (127 women), 179 part-time (136 women); includes 178 minority (8 Black or African American, non-Hispanic/Latino; 1 American Indian or Alaska Native, non-Hispanic/Latino; 41 Asian, non-Hispanic/Latino; 117 Hispanic/Latino; 11 Two or more races, non-Hispanic/Latino), 16 international. Average age 28. 333 applicants, 61% accepted, 143 enrolled. In 2019, 153 master's, 11 doctorates awarded. *Entrance requirements:* Additional exam requirements/recommendations for international students: required—TOEFL (minimum score 80 iBT), IELTS (minimum score 6.5), PTE (minimum score 53). *Application deadline:* Applications are processed on a rolling basis. Application fee: $60. Electronic applications accepted. *Expenses:* Contact institution. *Financial support:* Fellowships and scholarships/grants available. Financial award applicants required to submit FAFSA. *Unit head:* Dr. Roxanne Greitz Miller, Interim Dean, 714-997-6781, E-mail: rgmiller@chapman.edu. *Application contact:* Shannon McCance, Graduate Admission Counselor, 714-516-5236, E-mail: smccance@chapman.edu.
Website: http://www.chapman.edu/CES/

Charlotte Christian College and Theological Seminary, Graduate Program, Charlotte, NC 28206. Offers Biblical studies (MA), including New Testament, Old Testament, theology; chaplaincy (M Div); general pastoral studies (M Div); ministry (D Min); pastoral counseling (M Div); urban Christian ministry (MA), including multicultural studies, youth ministry. *Program availability:* Part-time, evening/weekend. *Degree requirements:* For master's, variable foreign language requirement, thesis; for doctorate, thesis/dissertation. *Entrance requirements:* For master's, 1000-2000 word essay. Additional exam requirements/recommendations for international students: required—TOEFL, IELTS. Electronic applications accepted. *Expenses:* Contact institution.

Claremont Graduate University, Graduate Programs, School of Arts and Humanities, Department of Cultural Studies, Claremont, CA 91711-6160. Offers Africana studies (Certificate); cultural studies (MA, PhD); media studies (MA, PhD); museum studies (MA). *Program availability:* Part-time. *Entrance requirements:* For master's and doctorate, GRE General Test. Additional exam requirements/recommendations for international students: required—TOEFL (minimum score 75 iBT). Electronic applications accepted.

Columbia International University, Seminary and School of Ministry, Columbia, SC 29203. Offers academic ministries (M Div); Bible and theology (Certificate); bible exposition (M Div, MABE); Biblical ministry (Certificate); chaplaincy (M Div); intercultural studies (MAIS); leadership (D Min); member care (D Min); missions (D Min); preaching (D Min); theological studies (MA). *Program availability:* Part-time, evening/weekend. *Degree requirements:* For doctorate, comprehensive exam, thesis/dissertation. *Entrance requirements:* For doctorate, 3 years of ministerial experience, M Div. Additional exam requirements/recommendations for international students: required—TOEFL. Electronic applications accepted.

Concordia University Irvine, School of Theology, Irvine, CA 92612-3299. Offers Christian leadership (MA); research in theology (MA); theology and culture (MA). *Program availability:* Part-time, evening/weekend. *Degree requirements:* For master's, project/thesis or vicarage. *Entrance requirements:* For master's, official college transcript(s), statement of intent, 2 references, interview. Additional exam requirements/recommendations for international students: required—TOEFL. Electronic applications accepted. *Expenses:* Contact institution.

Cornell University, Graduate School, Graduate Fields of Arts and Sciences, Field of English Language and Literature, Ithaca, NY 14853. Offers African-American literature (PhD); American literature after 1865 (PhD); American literature to 1865 (PhD); American studies (PhD); colonial and postcolonial literatures (PhD); creative writing (MFA); cultural studies (PhD); dramatic literature (PhD); English poetry (PhD); English Renaissance to 1660 (PhD); lesbian, bisexual, and gay literary studies (PhD); literary criticism and theory (PhD); Old and Middle English (PhD); prose fiction (PhD); Restoration and the eighteenth-century (PhD); the nineteenth century (PhD); the twentieth century (PhD); women's literature (PhD); MFA/PhD. Terminal master's awarded for partial completion of doctoral program. *Degree requirements:* For master's, one foreign language, thesis; for doctorate, one foreign language, comprehensive exam, thesis/dissertation, teaching experience. *Entrance requirements:* For master's, GRE General Test, 3 letters of recommendation, creative writing sample; for doctorate, 3 letters of recommendation, writing sample. Additional exam requirements/recommendations for international students: required—TOEFL (minimum score 600 paper-based; 77 iBT). Electronic applications accepted.

Drew University, Caspersen School of Graduate Studies, Madison, NJ 07940-1493. Offers conflict resolution and leadership (Certificate), including community leadership, moderation, peace building; education (M Ed); finance (MA); history and culture (MA, PhD), including American history, book history, British history, European history, intellectual history, Irish history, print culture, public history; K-12 education (MAT), including art, biology, chemistry, elementary education, English, French, Italian, math, secondary education, special education, teacher of students with disabilities; liberal studies (M Litt, D Litt), including history, Irish/Irish-American studies, literature (M Litt, MMH, D Litt, DMH, CMH), religion, spirituality, teaching in the two-year college, writing; medical humanities (MMH, DMH, CMH), including arts, health, healthcare, literature (M Litt, MMH, D Litt, DMH, CMH), scientific research; poetry (MFA). *Program availability:* Part-time, evening/weekend. Terminal master's awarded for partial completion of doctoral program. *Degree requirements:* For master's and other advanced degree, thesis (for some programs); for doctorate, one foreign language, comprehensive exam (for some programs), thesis/dissertation. *Entrance requirements:* For master's, PRAXIS Core and Subject Area tests (for MAT), GRE/GMAT (for MFin MS in Data Analytics), resume, transcripts, writing sample, personal statement, letters of recommendation; for doctorate, GRE (PhD in history and culture), resume, transcripts, writing sample, personal statement, letters of recommendation; for other advanced degree, resume, transcripts, personal statement. Additional exam requirements/recommendations for international students: required—TOEFL (minimum score 587 paper-based; 80 iBT), IELTS (minimum score 6), TWE (minimum score 4). Electronic applications accepted.

Eastern Michigan University, Graduate School, College of Arts and Sciences, Department of Sociology, Anthropology and Criminology, Program in Cultural Museum Studies, Ypsilanti, MI 48197. Offers Graduate Certificate. *Program availability:* Part-time, evening/weekend, online learning. In 2019, 1 Graduate Certificate awarded. *Entrance requirements:* Additional exam requirements/recommendations for international students: required—TOEFL. *Application deadline:* Applications are processed on a rolling basis. Application fee: $45. *Financial support:* Fellowships, research assistantships with full tuition reimbursements, teaching assistantships with full tuition reimbursements, career-related internships or fieldwork, Federal Work-Study, institutionally sponsored loans, scholarships/grants, tuition waivers (partial), and unspecified assistantships available. Support available to part-time students. Financial award applicants required to submit FAFSA. *Application contact:* Dr. Liza Cerroni-Long, Advisor, 734-487-0012, Fax: 734-487-9666, E-mail: liza.cerroni-long@emich.edu.

Florida State University, The Graduate School, College of Fine Arts, Department of Art History, Tallahassee, FL 32306. Offers history and criticism of art (MA, PhD). *Accreditation:* NASAD. *Program availability:* Part-time. *Faculty:* 13 full-time (6 women),

10 part-time/adjunct (6 women). *Students:* 39 full-time (38 women), 7 part-time (all women); includes 7 minority (2 Black or African American, non-Hispanic/Latino; 1 Asian, non-Hispanic/Latino; 3 Hispanic/Latino; 1 Two or more races, non-Hispanic/Latino). Average age 29. 43 applicants, 81% accepted, 15 enrolled. In 2019, 13 master's awarded. Terminal master's awarded for partial completion of doctoral program. *Degree requirements:* For master's, one foreign language, thesis (for some programs), capstone project (for some programs); for doctorate, 2 foreign languages, comprehensive exam, thesis/dissertation. *Entrance requirements:* For master's, GRE General Test, minimum GPA of 3.0; for doctorate, GRE General Test, minimum GPA of 3.5. Additional exam requirements/recommendations for international students: required—TOEFL (minimum score 550 paper-based; 80 iBT), IELTS (minimum score 6.5). *Application deadline:* For fall admission, 7/1 for domestic and international students. Applications are processed on a rolling basis. Application fee: $35. Electronic applications accepted. *Expenses:* Contact institution. *Financial support:* In 2019–20, 37 students received support, including 16 fellowships with full tuition reimbursements available (averaging $6,200 per year), 14 research assistantships with full tuition reimbursements available (averaging $5,100 per year), 9 teaching assistantships with full tuition reimbursements available (averaging $7,140 per year); career-related internships or fieldwork, Federal Work-Study, institutionally sponsored loans, scholarships/grants, tuition waivers (full), and unspecified assistantships also available. Financial award application deadline: 1/1; financial award applicants required to submit FAFSA. *Unit head:* Dr. Adam Jolles, Associate Professor of Art History/Department Chair, 850-644-7066, E-mail: ajolles@fsu.edu. *Application contact:* Juan Barcelo-Gonzalez, Academic Program Specialist/Graduate Student Advisor, 850-644-8207, Fax: 850-644-7065, E-mail: juan.barcelo@fsu.edu.
Website: http://arthistory.fsu.edu/

Gardner-Webb University, School of Divinity, Boiling Springs, NC 28017. Offers biblical studies (M Div); Christian education and formation (M Div); intercultural studies (M Div); ministry (D Min); missiology (M Div); pastoral care and counseling (M Div); pastoral care and counseling/member care for missionaries (D Min); pastoral studies (M Div); M Div/MA; M Div/MBA. *Accreditation:* ACIPE. *Program availability:* Part-time. *Entrance requirements:* For master's, minimum GPA of 2.6; for doctorate, minimum GPA of 2.75. Additional exam requirements/recommendations for international students: required—TOEFL (minimum score 500 paper-based; 61 iBT). Electronic applications accepted. *Expenses:* Contact institution.

George Fox University, Portland Seminary, Portland, OR 97223. Offers Biblical studies (M Div, MA); chaplaincy (M Div); Christian history and theology (M Div, MA); creation care (M Div, MA); intercultural studies (M Div, MA); leadership (M Div, MA); leadership and global perspectives (D Min); leadership and spiritual formation (D Min); semiotics and future studies (D Min); spiritual direction (MA, Certificate); spiritual direction supervision (M Div, MA, Certificate); spiritual formation and discipleship (M Div, MA, Certificate). *Accreditation:* ACIPE. *Program availability:* Part-time, evening/weekend, online learning. *Entrance requirements:* For master's, resume, three references (one pastoral, one academic or professional, one personal), one official transcript from each college or university attended; for doctorate, resume, 3 references (1 professional, 1 academic, 1 personal), one official transcript from each college or university attended. Additional exam requirements/recommendations for international students: required—TOEFL (minimum score 577 paper-based; 90 iBT). Electronic applications accepted. *Expenses:* Contact institution.

George Mason University, College of Humanities and Social Sciences, Program in Cultural Studies, Fairfax, VA 22030. Offers PhD. *Degree requirements:* For doctorate, one foreign language, comprehensive exam, thesis/dissertation, foreign language exams. *Entrance requirements:* For doctorate, GRE, expanded goals statement; 3 letters of recommendation from academic sources; writing sample; master's degree in relevant field; official transcripts. Additional exam requirements/recommendations for international students: required—TOEFL (minimum score 575 paper-based; 88 iBT), IELTS (minimum score 6.5), PTE (minimum score 59). Electronic applications accepted.

Georgia State University, College of Arts and Sciences, Department of World Languages and Cultures, Atlanta, GA 30302-3083. Offers French (MA), including applied linguistics and pedagogy, French studies, literature and culture; Latin American studies (Certificate); Spanish (MA); translation and interpretation (Certificate), including interpretation, translation. *Program availability:* Part-time. *Faculty:* 15 full-time (8 women), 2 part-time/adjunct (1 woman). *Students:* 28 full-time (22 women), 14 part-time (9 women); includes 26 minority (11 Black or African American, non-Hispanic/Latino; 1 Asian, non-Hispanic/Latino; 11 Hispanic/Latino; 3 Two or more races, non-Hispanic/Latino), 4 international. Average age 35. 13 applicants, 77% accepted, 8 enrolled. In 2019, 14 master's, 7 other advanced degrees awarded. *Entrance requirements:* For master's, GRE, statement of purpose, writing sample in the target language, 2 letters of recommendation, official transcripts; for Certificate, entrance examination involving translating one passage from English to the target language and one passage from the target language to English, 3 letters of recommendation, resume/curriculum vitae, official transcripts. Additional exam requirements/recommendations for international students: required—TOEFL (minimum score 79 iBT). *Application deadline:* For fall admission, 3/15 priority date for domestic and international students; for spring admission, 11/15 priority date for domestic and international students. Application fee: $50. Electronic applications accepted. *Expenses: Tuition, area resident:* Full-time $7164; part-time $398 per credit hour. Tuition, state resident: full-time $7164; part-time $398 per credit hour. Tuition, nonresident: full-time $22,662; part-time $1259 per credit hour. *International tuition:* $22,662 full-time. *Required fees:* $2128; $312 per credit hour. Tuition and fees vary according to course load and program. *Financial support:* Applicants required to submit FAFSA. *Unit head:* Dr. Fernando Reati, Department Chair, 404-413-5984, Fax: 404-413-5982, E-mail: freati@gsu.edu. *Application contact:* Amber Amari, Director, Graduate and Scheduling Services, 404-413-5037, E-mail: aamari@gsu.edu.
Website: http://wlc.gsu.edu/

Goucher College, MA and MFA Programs, Baltimore, MD 21204-2794. Offers art and technology (MFA); arts administration (MA); cultural sustainability (MA); digital arts (MA); historic preservation (MA); nonfiction (MFA). *Program availability:* Part-time, evening/weekend, blended/hybrid learning. *Degree requirements:* For master's, thesis, e-portfolio. *Entrance requirements:* For master's, digital portfolio (for MA, MFA in digital arts); writing sample (for MFA in creative nonfiction). Additional exam requirements/recommendations for international students: required—TOEFL (minimum score 550 paper-based; 80 iBT). Electronic applications accepted. *Expenses:* Contact institution.

Grace Theological Seminary, Graduate and Professional Programs, Winona Lake, IN 46590-9907. Offers biblical studies (Certificate); chaplaincy (M Div); exegetical studies (M Div); intercultural studies (M Div, MA, D Min); local church ministry (MA), including camp administration, women's leadership; pastoral counseling (MA); pastoral studies (M Div, D Min); theology (Diploma). *Accreditation:* ATS. *Program availability:* Part-time, online learning. *Degree requirements:* For master's, thesis optional; for doctorate, 2 foreign languages, thesis/dissertation. *Entrance requirements:* For master's, MAT, minimum GPA of 2.5. Electronic applications accepted.

Graduate Theological Union, Graduate Programs, Berkeley, CA 94709-1212. Offers art and religion (MA, PhD, Th D); biblical languages (MA); Biblical studies (PhD, Th D); biblical studies (MA); Buddhist studies (MA); Christian spirituality (MA, PhD, Th D); cultural and historical studies of religions (MA, PhD, Th D); ethics and social theory (PhD, Th D); history (MA, PhD, Th D); homiletics (MA, PhD, Th D); interdisciplinary studies (PhD, Th D); Jewish studies (MA, PhD, Th D, Certificate); liturgical studies (MA, PhD, Th D); Near Eastern religions (PhD, Th D); Orthodox Christian studies (MA); religion and psychology (MA, PhD, Th D); religion and society/ethics and social theory (MA); systematic and philosophical theology (MA, PhD, Th D). *Accreditation:* ATS. Terminal master's awarded for partial completion of doctoral program. *Degree requirements:* For master's, one foreign language, thesis; for doctorate, one foreign language, comprehensive exam, thesis/dissertation. *Entrance requirements:* For master's, GRE General Test; for doctorate, GRE General Test, MA or M Div. Additional exam requirements/recommendations for international students: required—TOEFL. Electronic applications accepted.

Greensboro College, Program in Theology, Ethics and Culture, Greensboro, NC 27401-1875. Offers MA.

Johnson University, Graduate and Professional Programs, Knoxville, TN 37998. Offers biblical interpretation (Graduate Certificate); business administration (MBA); Christian ministries (Graduate Certificate); clinical mental health counseling (MA); educational technology (MA); intercultural studies (MA); leadership (MBA); leadership studies (PhD); New Testament (MA); nonprofit management (MBA); school counseling (MA); spiritual formation and leadership (Graduate Certificate); strategic ministry (MA); teacher education (MA). *Program availability:* Part-time, 100% online, blended/hybrid learning. *Faculty:* 26 full-time (10 women), 32 part-time/adjunct (9 women). *Students:* 116 full-time (56 women), 196 part-time (91 women); includes 40 minority (23 Black or African American, non-Hispanic/Latino; 1 American Indian or Alaska Native, non-Hispanic/Latino; 4 Asian, non-Hispanic/Latino; 6 Hispanic/Latino; 6 Two or more races, non-Hispanic/Latino), 31 international. Average age 36. In 2019, 87 master's, 6 doctorates, 14 other advanced degrees awarded. *Degree requirements:* For master's, variable foreign language requirement, comprehensive exam, thesis (for some programs), internships; for doctorate, variable foreign language requirement, comprehensive exam, thesis/dissertation, internships. *Entrance requirements:* For master's, PRAXIS (for MA in teacher education); MAT (for counseling); GRE or GMAT (for MBA), interview, 3 references, transcripts, essay, minimum GPA of 2.5 or 3.0 (depending on program); for doctorate, GRE or MAT (taken not less than 5 years prior), interview, 3 references, transcripts, essay, minimum GPA of 3.0; for Graduate Certificate, interview, 3 references, transcripts, essay, minimum GPA of 3.0. Additional exam requirements/recommendations for international students: required—TOEFL (minimum score 527 paper-based; 71 iBT). *Application deadline:* For fall admission, 7/1 for domestic students; for spring admission, 11/1 for domestic students; for summer admission, 4/1 for domestic students. Application fee: $50. Electronic applications accepted. *Expenses:* Contact institution. *Financial support:* Scholarships/grants available. Financial award application deadline: 4/15; financial award applicants required to submit FAFSA. *Unit head:* Lisa Tarwater, Chief Admissions Officer, 865-251-3400, E-mail: ltarwater@johnsonu.edu. *Application contact:* Lisa Tarwater, Chief Admissions Officer, 865-251-3400, E-mail: ltarwater@johnsonu.edu.
Website: www.johnsonu.edu

Lincoln Christian University, Graduate Programs, Lincoln, IL 62656-2167. Offers Bible and theology (MA); Biblical studies (MA); church history/historical theology (MA); counseling (MA); formative worship (MA); intercultural studies (MA); ministry (MA); organizational leadership (MA); philosophy and apologetics (MA); spiritual formation (MA); theology (MA). *Program availability:* Online learning. *Entrance requirements:* For master's, minimum cumulative GPA of 2.5 in undergraduate degree studies. Additional exam requirements/recommendations for international students: required—TOEFL (minimum score 550 paper-based); recommended—IELTS (minimum score 6). Application fee is waived when completed online.

Maranatha Baptist University, Master of Arts in Intercultural Studies Program, Watertown, WI 53094. Offers MA. *Program availability:* Part-time. *Entrance requirements:* For master's, BA or BS. Additional exam requirements/recommendations for international students: required—TOEFL. *Expenses: Tuition:* Full-time $5940; part-time $3960 per credit. *Required fees:* $25 per credit. Tuition and fees vary according to degree level and program.

McMaster University, School of Graduate Studies, Faculty of Humanities, Department of English and Cultural Studies, Hamilton, ON L8S 4M2, Canada. Offers cultural studies and critical theory (MA); English (MA, PhD). *Program availability:* Part-time. *Degree requirements:* For master's, one foreign language, thesis; for doctorate, one foreign language, comprehensive exam, thesis/dissertation. *Entrance requirements:* For master's, honors degree, minimum B+ average in at least 6 full courses of English beyond year 1; for doctorate, MA; minimum A- average in two of three courses. Additional exam requirements/recommendations for international students: required—TOEFL (minimum score 580 paper-based).

Nazarene Theological Seminary, Graduate and Professional Programs, Kansas City, MO 64131-1263. Offers Christian formation and discipleship (MA); intercultural studies (MA); pastoral theology (Graduate Certificate); theological studies (MA); theology (M Div, D Min). *Accreditation:* ACIPE; ATS. *Program availability:* Part-time. *Degree requirements:* For master's, comprehensive exam (for some programs), thesis (for some programs); for doctorate, thesis/dissertation. *Entrance requirements:* For master's and Graduate Certificate, three references; for doctorate, three references, interview. Additional exam requirements/recommendations for international students: required—TOEFL (minimum score 550 paper-based; 80 iBT). Electronic applications accepted.

New Mexico State University, College of Education, Department of Curriculum and Instruction, Las Cruces, NM 88003-8001. Offers bilingual education (MA); curriculum and instruction (Ed D, PhD); early childhood education (MA); educational diagnostics (Ed S); language, literacy and culture (MA); learning design and technologies (MA); teaching (MAT); teaching English to speakers of other languages (MA). *Accreditation:* NCATE. *Program availability:* Part-time, evening/weekend, 100% online. *Faculty:* 20 full-time (15 women), 14 part-time/adjunct (11 women). *Students:* 70 full-time (45 women), 209 part-time (158 women); includes 169 minority (10 Black or African American, non-Hispanic/Latino; 2 American Indian or Alaska Native, non-Hispanic/Latino; 5 Asian, non-Hispanic/Latino; 146 Hispanic/Latino; 1 Native Hawaiian or other Pacific Islander, non-Hispanic/Latino; 5 Two or more races, non-Hispanic/Latino), 16 international. Average age 38. 131 applicants, 79% accepted, 79 enrolled. In 2019, 75 master's, 13 doctorates, 16 other advanced degrees awarded. *Degree requirements:* For master's, comprehensive exam, thesis; for doctorate, comprehensive exam, thesis/dissertation. *Entrance requirements:* For master's, minimum cumulative GPA of 3.0; for doctorate, portfolio, minimum cumulative GPA of 3.0. Additional exam requirements/recommendations for international students: required—TOEFL (minimum score 550 paper-based; 79 iBT), IELTS (minimum score 6.5). *Application deadline:* For fall admission, 12/15 priority date for domestic and international students. Applications are processed on a rolling basis. Application fee: $40 ($50 for international students). Electronic applications accepted. *Financial support:* In 2019–20, 139 students received support, including 1 fellowship (averaging $4,844 per year), 12 research assistantships (averaging $13,110 per year), 7 teaching assistantships (averaging $13,243 per year); career-related internships or fieldwork, Federal Work-Study, scholarships/grants,

traineeships, health care benefits, and unspecified assistantships also available. Support available to part-time students. Financial award application deadline: 3/1. *Unit head:* Dr. David Rutledge, Department Head, 575-646-5411, Fax: 575-646-5436, E-mail: rutledge@nmsu.edu. *Application contact:* Dr. David Rutledge, Associate Department Head for Graduate Programs, 575-646-5411, Fax: 575-646-5436, E-mail: rutledge@nmsu.edu.
Website: http://ci.education.nmsu.edu

New York University, Steinhardt School of Culture, Education, and Human Development, New York, NY 10003. Offers MA, MFA, MM, MPH, MS, DPS, DPT, Ed D, PhD, Advanced Certificate, Post Master's Certificate, Postbaccalaureate Certificate, Advanced Certificate/MPH, MA/Advanced Certificate, MA/MA, MA/MS, MLIS/MA. *Accreditation:* TEAC. *Program availability:* Part-time. *Entrance requirements:* For doctorate, GRE General Test, interview. Additional exam requirements/recommendations for international students: required—TOEFL (minimum score 100 iBT). Electronic applications accepted. *Expenses:* Contact institution.

North Central College, School of Graduate and Professional Studies, Program in Liberal Studies, Naperville, IL 60566-7063. Offers culture and society (MALS). *Program availability:* Part-time, evening/weekend. *Degree requirements:* For master's, thesis optional, project. *Entrance requirements:* For master's, interview. Additional exam requirements/recommendations for international students: required—TOEFL (minimum score 550 paper-based; 80 iBT), IELTS (minimum score 6.5). Electronic applications accepted. Application fee is waived when completed online. *Expenses:* Contact institution.

Northern Kentucky University, Office of Graduate Programs, College of Arts and Sciences, Program in English, Highland Heights, KY 41099. Offers composition and rhetoric (Certificate); creative writing (Certificate); cultural studies and discourses (Certificate); English (MA); professional writing (Certificate). *Program availability:* Part-time, evening/weekend. *Degree requirements:* For master's, comprehensive exam (for some programs), capstone (thesis, portfolio, project, or exams); 30 hours of credit; for Certificate, 18 hours of credit. *Entrance requirements:* For master's, bachelor's degree in English or related field from regionally-accredited institution with minimum GPA of 3.0 in major or cognate area coursework; official transcripts for all undergraduate and graduate work; two letters of reference; for Certificate, official transcripts for all undergraduate and graduate work; bachelor's degree from regionally-accredited institution; minimum undergraduate GPA of 2.5. Additional exam requirements/recommendations for international students: required—TOEFL (minimum score 79 iBT); recommended—IELTS (minimum score 6.5). Electronic applications accepted.

Northwest University, College of Ministry, Kirkland, WA 98033. Offers ministry (MIM); missional leadership (MA); theology and culture (MA). *Program availability:* Part-time, evening/weekend, online learning. *Degree requirements:* For master's, comprehensive exam (for some programs), thesis (for some programs). *Entrance requirements:* Additional exam requirements/recommendations for international students: required—TOEFL (minimum score 550 paper-based; 75 iBT). Electronic applications accepted.

Old Dominion University, College of Arts and Letters, Graduate Program in International Studies, Norfolk, VA 23529. Offers conflict and cooperation (MA, PhD); interdependence and transnationalism (MA, PhD); international cultural studies (MA, PhD); international political economy and development (MA, PhD); modeling and simulation (MA, PhD); U.S. foreign policy and international relations (MA, PhD). *Program availability:* Part-time. Terminal master's awarded for partial completion of doctoral program. *Degree requirements:* For master's, one foreign language, comprehensive exam, thesis optional; for doctorate, one foreign language, comprehensive exam, thesis/dissertation. *Entrance requirements:* For master's, GRE General Test, sample of written work, 2 letters of recommendation; for doctorate, GRE General Test, sample of written work, 3 letters of recommendation. Additional exam requirements/recommendations for international students: required—TOEFL (minimum score 570 paper-based). Electronic applications accepted. *Expenses:* Contact institution.

Old Dominion University, College of Arts and Letters, Institute for the Humanities, Norfolk, VA 23529. Offers arts and entrepreneurship (Certificate); cultural and human geography (MA); cultural studies (MA); gender and sexuality studies (MA); health, communication and culture (Certificate); media and popular culture studies (MA); philosophy and religious studies (MA); social justice and entrepreneurship (Certificate); visual studies (MA); world cultures (MA). *Program availability:* Part-time, evening/weekend. *Degree requirements:* For master's, thesis optional, project. *Entrance requirements:* For master's, GRE General Test, minimum GPA of 3.25. Electronic applications accepted.

Pacific Northwest College of Art, Program in Critical Studies, Portland, OR 97209. Offers MA, MA/MFA.

Plymouth State University, College of Graduate Studies, Graduate Studies in Education, Program in Integrated Arts, Plymouth, NH 03264-1595. Offers M Ed.

Regent University, Graduate School, School of Divinity, Virginia Beach, VA 23464. Offers Christian spirituality and formation (MA); divinity (M Div), including Biblical studies (M Div, MTS, Th M, PhD), chaplain ministry, Christian theology (M Div, MTS, Th M, PhD), church and ministry (M Div, MA), history of Christianity (M Div, MTS, Th M, PhD), inter-cultural studies (M Div, MA), interdisciplinary studies (M Div, MA, MTS), marketplace ministry (M Div, MA), missional discipleship, practical healing ministry (M Div, MA), worship and media (M Div, MA); leadership and renewal (D Min), including Christian leadership and renewal, clinical pastoral education, community transformation, military ministry, ministry leadership coaching; practical theology (MA), including church and ministry (M Div, MA), cosmogony, inter-cultural studies (M Div, MA), interdisciplinary studies (M Div, MA, MTS), marketplace ministry (M Div, MA), practical healing ministry (M Div, MA), worship and media (M Div, MA); renewal theology (PhD), including Biblical studies (M Div, MTS, Th M, PhD), Christian theology (M Div, MTS, Th M, PhD), history of Christianity (M Div, MTS, Th M, PhD), practical theology; theological studies (MTS), including Biblical studies (M Div, MTS, Th M, PhD), Christian theology (M Div, MTS, Th M, PhD), history of Christianity (M Div, MTS, Th M, PhD), interdisciplinary studies (M Div, MA, MTS); theology (Th M), including Biblical studies (M Div, MTS, Th M, PhD), Christian theology (M Div, MTS, Th M, PhD), history of Christianity (M Div, MTS, Th M, PhD). *Accreditation:* ACIPE; ATS. *Program availability:* Part-time, evening/weekend, 100% online, blended/hybrid learning. *Faculty:* 15 full-time (3 women), 58 part-time/adjunct (10 women). *Students:* 303 full-time (119 women), 813 part-time (403 women); includes 632 minority (509 Black or African American, non-Hispanic/Latino; 3 American Indian or Alaska Native, non-Hispanic/Latino; 31 Asian, non-Hispanic/Latino; 54 Hispanic/Latino; 2 Native Hawaiian or other Pacific Islander, non-Hispanic/Latino; 33 Two or more races, non-Hispanic/Latino), 16 international. Average age 45. 561 applicants, 66% accepted, 194 enrolled. In 2019, 168 master's, 13 doctorates awarded. *Degree requirements:* For master's, comprehensive exam, thesis or alternative, internship; for doctorate, thesis/dissertation or alternative. *Entrance requirements:* For master's, minimum undergraduate GPA of 2.75, writing sample, personal goal statement, college transcripts; for doctorate, GRE, minimum graduate GPA of 3.5 (PhD), 3.0 (D Min); clergy recommendations; writing sample; transcripts; resume; interview. Additional exam requirements/recommendations for international students: required—TOEFL (minimum score 577 paper-based). *Application deadline:* For fall admission, 5/1 priority date for domestic students. Applications are processed on a rolling basis. Application fee: $50. Electronic applications accepted. *Expenses:* Contact institution. *Financial support:* In 2019–20, 856 students received support. Career-related internships or fieldwork, scholarships/grants, health care benefits, and unspecified assistantships available. Support available to part-time students. Financial award applicants required to submit FAFSA. *Unit head:* Dr. Cornelius Bekker, Dean, 757-352-4258, Fax: 757-352-4597, E-mail: clbekker@regent.edu. *Application contact:* Heidi Cece, Assistant Vice President for Enrollment Management, 800-373-5504, Fax: 757-352-4381, E-mail: admissions@regent.edu.
Website: https://www.regent.edu/school-of-divinity/

St. Francis Xavier University, Graduate Studies, Department of Celtic Studies, Antigonish, NS B2G 2W5, Canada. Offers MA. *Degree requirements:* For master's, thesis. *Entrance requirements:* Additional exam requirements/recommendations for international students: required—TOEFL (minimum score 580 paper-based). *Expenses: Tuition, area resident:* Part-time $1731 Canadian dollars per course. Tuition, state resident: part-time $1731 Canadian dollars per course. Tuition, nonresident: part-time $1988 Canadian dollars per course. *International tuition:* $3976 Canadian dollars full-time. *Required fees:* $185 Canadian dollars per course. Tuition and fees vary according to course level, course load, degree level and program.

San Francisco State University, Division of Graduate Studies, College of Health and Social Sciences, Department of Sexuality Studies, San Francisco, CA 94132-1722. Offers MA. *Expenses: Tuition, area resident:* Full-time $7176; part-time $4164 per year. Tuition, state resident: full-time $7176; part-time $4164 per year. Tuition, nonresident: full-time $16,680; part-time $396 per unit. *International tuition:* $16,680 full-time. *Required fees:* $1524; $1524 per unit. $762 per semester. Tuition and fees vary according to degree level and program. *Unit head:* Dr. Karen Hossfeld, Interim Chair, 415-338-7059, Fax: 415-338-2653, E-mail: hossfeld@sfsu.edu. *Application contact:* Dr. Alexis Martinez, Graduate Coordinator, 415-338-2269, Fax: 415-338-2653, E-mail: alexisnm@sfsu.edu.
Website: http://sxs.sfsu.edu/

School of Visual Arts, Graduate Programs, Critical Theory and the Arts Department, New York, NY 10010-3994. Offers MA. *Degree requirements:* For master's, thesis, 36 credits with minimum cumulative GPA of 3.0. *Entrance requirements:* For master's, writing statement of approximately 1,000 words explaining the development of interest in pursuing an MA; transcripts for previous colleges/universities attended; three letters of recommendation; current resume/curriculum vitae. Additional exam requirements/recommendations for international students: required—TOEFL (minimum score 600 paper-based; 100 iBT). Electronic applications accepted. *Expenses:* Contact institution.

Simmons University, Gwen Ifill College of Media, Arts, and Humanities, Boston, MA 02115. Offers behavior analysis (MS, PhD, Ed S); children's literature (MA); dietetics (Certificate); elementary education (MAT); English (MA); gender/cultural studies (MA); history (MA); nutrition and health promotion (MS); physical therapy (DPT); public health (MPH); public policy (MPP); special education: moderate and severe disabilities (MS Ed); sports nutrition (Certificate); writing for children (MFA). *Program availability:* Part-time. *Faculty:* 10 full-time (9 women), 7 part-time/adjunct (6 women). *Students:* 2 full-time (both women), 67 part-time (57 women); includes 13 minority (3 Black or African American, non-Hispanic/Latino; 4 Asian, non-Hispanic/Latino; 3 Hispanic/Latino; 3 Two or more races, non-Hispanic/Latino), 1 international. Average age 31. 42 applicants, 62% accepted, 23 enrolled. In 2019, 24 master's awarded. *Degree requirements:* For master's, thesis optional. *Entrance requirements:* For master's, GRE, bachelor's degree from accredited college or university; minimum B average (preferred). Additional exam requirements/recommendations for international students: required—TOEFL (minimum score 600 paper-based; 100 iBT). *Application deadline:* For fall admission, 8/1 for domestic and international students; for spring admission, 12/15 for domestic and international students; for summer admission, 5/1 for domestic and international students. Applications are processed on a rolling basis. Application fee: $35. Electronic applications accepted. *Expenses:* Contact institution. *Financial support:* In 2019–20, 14 students received support, including 1 fellowship (averaging $15,360 per year), 13 teaching assistantships (averaging $2,000 per year); scholarships/grants also available. Financial award applicants required to submit FAFSA. *Unit head:* Dr. Brian Norman, Dean, 617-521-2472, E-mail: brian.norman@simmons.edu. *Application contact:* Patricia Flaherty, Director, Graduate Studies Admission, 617-521-3902, Fax: 617-521-3058, E-mail: gsa@simmons.edu.
Website: https://www.simmons.edu/academics/colleges-schools-departments/ifill

Simon Fraser University, Office of Graduate Studies and Postdoctoral Fellows, Faculty of Education, Program in Languages, Cultures, and Literacies, Burnaby, BC V5A 1S6, Canada. Offers PhD.

Southern Illinois University Carbondale, Graduate School, College of Liberal Arts, Department of Foreign Languages and Literatures, Carbondale, IL 62901-4701. Offers MA. *Program availability:* Part-time. *Degree requirements:* For master's, one foreign language, thesis. *Entrance requirements:* For master's, minimum GPA of 2.7. Additional exam requirements/recommendations for international students: required—TOEFL.

Stanford University, School of Humanities and Sciences, Department of Anthropology, Stanford, CA 94305-2004. Offers anthropology (MA); archaeology (PhD); culture and society (PhD); ecology and environment (PhD). *Expenses: Tuition:* Full-time $52,479; part-time $34,110 per unit. *Required fees:* $672; $224 per quarter. Tuition and fees vary according to program and student level.
Website: http://www.stanford.edu/dept/anthsci/

Stony Brook University, State University of New York, Graduate School, College of Arts and Sciences, Department of Cultural Studies and Comparative Literature, Stony Brook, NY 11794. Offers comparative literature (MA, PhD); cultural studies (PhD, Certificate). *Program availability:* Evening/weekend. *Faculty:* 3 full-time (1 woman). *Students:* 19 full-time (11 women), 3 part-time (all women); includes 4 minority (1 Black or African American, non-Hispanic/Latino; 2 Asian, non-Hispanic/Latino; 1 Hispanic/Latino), 9 international. Average age 38. In 2019, 6 master's, 2 doctorates awarded. Terminal master's awarded for partial completion of doctoral program. *Degree requirements:* For master's, 2 foreign languages, exam; for doctorate, 3 foreign languages, comprehensive exam, thesis/dissertation. *Entrance requirements:* For master's and doctorate, GRE General Test, minimum GPA of 3.5 in major, 3.0 overall. Additional exam requirements/recommendations for international students: required—TOEFL. *Application deadline:* For fall admission, 1/15 for domestic students; for spring admission, 10/1 for domestic students. Application fee: $100. Electronic applications accepted. *Expenses:* Contact institution. *Financial support:* In 2019–20, 8 teaching assistantships were awarded; fellowships and research assistantships also available. *Unit head:* Prof. Mary C Rawlinson, 631-632-7464, Fax: 631-632-5707, E-mail: Mary.Rawlinson@stonybrook.edu. *Application contact:* Mary Moran-Luba, Coordinator, 631-632-6935, Fax: 631-632-5707, E-mail: mary.moran-luba@stonybrook.edu.
Website: http://www.stonybrook.edu/commcms/cat/index.html

Taylor College and Seminary, Graduate and Professional Programs, Edmonton, AB T6J 4T3, Canada. Offers Christian studies (Diploma); intercultural studies (MA, Diploma), including intercultural studies (Diploma), TESOL; theology (M Div, MTS).

Accreditation: ATS. *Program availability:* Part-time, online learning. *Degree requirements:* For master's, thesis optional. *Entrance requirements:* Additional exam requirements/recommendations for international students: required—TOEFL (minimum score 550 paper-based; 80 iBT), IELTS (minimum score 6.5).

Texas A&M University, College of Liberal Arts, Department of Performance Studies, College Station, TX 77843. Offers performance studies (MA). *Faculty:* 12. *Students:* 8 full-time (5 women); includes 2 minority (1 Black or African American, non-Hispanic/Latino; 1 Asian, non-Hispanic/Latino), 4 international. Average age 29. 4 applicants, 100% accepted, 3 enrolled. In 2019, 6 master's awarded. *Degree requirements:* For master's, comprehensive exam (for some programs), thesis optional. *Entrance requirements:* For master's, GRE General Test, letters of recommendation, curriculum vitae. Additional exam requirements/recommendations for international students: required—TOEFL (minimum score 550 paper-based; 80 iBT), IELTS (minimum score 6), PTE (minimum score 53). Application fee: $65 ($90 for international students). Electronic applications accepted. *Expenses:* Contact institution. *Financial support:* In 2019–20, 44 students received support, including 2 fellowships (averaging $18,627 per year), 17 teaching assistantships (averaging $19,558 per year); unspecified assistantships also available. Financial award application deadline: 3/15; financial award applicants required to submit FAFSA. *Unit head:* Dr. Steven Oberhelman, Interim Department Head, 979-847-5816, E-mail: s-oberhelman@tamu.edu. *Application contact:* Dr. Leonardo Cardoso, Director of Graduate Studies, E-mail: cardoso@tamu.edu.
Website: https://liberalarts.tamu.edu/performancestudies/

Texas A&M University–Kingsville, College of Graduate Studies, College of Arts and Sciences, Department of Language and Literature, Program in Cultural Studies, Kingsville, TX 78363. Offers MA. *Entrance requirements:* Additional exam requirements/recommendations for international students: required—TOEFL (minimum score 550 paper-based; 79 iBT); recommended—IELTS. Electronic applications accepted.

Texas Tech University, Graduate School, College of Arts and Sciences, Department of Classical and Modern Languages and Literatures, Lubbock, TX 79409-2071. Offers languages and cultures (MA); Romance languages (MA); Spanish (PhD); MBA/MA. *Program availability:* Part-time. *Faculty:* 54 full-time (34 women), 1 (woman) part-time/adjunct. *Students:* 72 full-time (38 women), 15 part-time (12 women); includes 28 minority (1 Asian, non-Hispanic/Latino; 24 Hispanic/Latino; 3 Two or more races, non-Hispanic/Latino), 33 international. Average age 33. 57 applicants, 68% accepted, 28 enrolled. In 2019, 28 master's, 2 doctorates awarded. *Degree requirements:* For master's, comprehensive exam, thesis or alternative; for doctorate, comprehensive exam, thesis/dissertation. *Entrance requirements:* Additional exam requirements/recommendations for international students: required—TOEFL (minimum score 550 paper-based; 79 iBT). *Application deadline:* For fall admission, 6/1 priority date for domestic students, 1/15 priority date for international students; for spring admission, 9/1 priority date for domestic students, 6/15 priority date for international students. Applications are processed on a rolling basis. Application fee: $65. Electronic applications accepted. *Expenses:* Contact institution. *Financial support:* In 2019–20, 83 students received support, including 52 fellowships (averaging $2,880 per year), 76 teaching assistantships (averaging $13,880 per year); research assistantships, Federal Work-Study, scholarships/grants, and unspecified assistantships also available. Financial award application deadline: 4/15; financial award applicants required to submit FAFSA. *Unit head:* Dr. Carmen Pereira-Muro, Department Chair, 806-834-0151, Fax: 806-742-3306, E-mail: carmen.pereira@ttu.edu. *Application contact:* Carla Burrus, Senior Advisor, 806-834-3282, Fax: 806-742-3306, E-mail: carla.burrus@ttu.edu.
Website: www.depts.ttu.edu/classic_modern/

Trent University, Graduate Studies, Program in Cultural Studies, Peterborough, ON K9J 7B8, Canada. Offers PhD.

Trinity College, Graduate Programs, Program in American Studies, Hartford, CT 06106-3100. Offers American culture studies (MA); museums and communities (MA). *Program availability:* Part-time, evening/weekend. *Degree requirements:* For master's, thesis or alternative. *Entrance requirements:* For master's, minimum GPA of 3.0.

Union Institute & University, Master of Arts Program, Cincinnati, OH 45206-1925. Offers creativity studies (MA); health and wellness (MA); history and culture (MA); leadership, public policy, and social issues (MA); literature and writing (MA). *Program availability:* Part-time, online only, 100% online. *Degree requirements:* For master's, thesis. *Entrance requirements:* For master's, transcript, essay, 3 letters of recommendation, resume. Additional exam requirements/recommendations for international students: recommended—TOEFL. Electronic applications accepted. *Expenses:* Contact institution.

Union Institute & University, PhD Program in Interdisciplinary Studies, Cincinnati, OH 45206-1925. Offers educational studies (PhD), including Martin Luther King studies; ethical and creative leadership (PhD); humanities and culture (PhD); public policy and social change (PhD). *Program availability:* Part-time, online only, blended/hybrid learning. *Degree requirements:* For doctorate, comprehensive exam, thesis/dissertation. *Entrance requirements:* For doctorate, master's degree, three letters of recommendation, statement of purpose. Additional exam requirements/recommendations for international students: required—TOEFL. Electronic applications accepted. *Expenses:* Contact institution.

Union University, Institute for International and Intercultural Studies, Jackson, TN 38305-3697. Offers MAIS. *Program availability:* Part-time, evening/weekend. *Degree requirements:* For master's, capstone course. *Entrance requirements:* For master's, GRE, minimum undergraduate GPA of 3.0, 3 letters of reference. Additional exam requirements/recommendations for international students: required—TOEFL (minimum score 560 paper-based). Electronic applications accepted.

University of Alaska Fairbanks, College of Liberal Arts, Center for Cross-Cultural Studies, Fairbanks, AK 99775-6300. Offers MA. *Program availability:* Part-time. *Degree requirements:* For master's, comprehensive exam, project, oral defense of project. *Entrance requirements:* For master's, bachelor's degree from accredited institution with minimum cumulative undergraduate and major GPA of 3.0. Additional exam requirements/recommendations for international students: required—TOEFL (minimum score 550 paper-based; 79 iBT), IELTS (minimum score 8.5). Electronic applications accepted.

University of Arkansas, Graduate School, Interdisciplinary Program in Comparative Literature and Cultural Studies, Fayetteville, AR 72701. Offers MA, PhD. *Students:* 22 full-time (10 women), 17 part-time (9 women); includes 6 minority (1 Black or African American, non-Hispanic/Latino; 2 Asian, non-Hispanic/Latino; 3 Hispanic/Latino), 20 international. 6 applicants, 83% accepted. In 2019, 4 master's, 5 doctorates awarded. *Degree requirements:* For doctorate, 2 foreign languages, comprehensive exam, thesis/dissertation optional. *Entrance requirements:* For doctorate, GRE General Test, official transcripts of all undergraduate and graduate work, three letters of recommendation, writing sample, statement of purpose. Additional exam requirements/recommendations for international students: required—TOEFL (minimum score 550 paper-based; 80 iBT) or IELTS (minimum score 6.5). *Application deadline:* For fall admission, 8/1 for domestic students, 4/1 for international students; for spring admission, 12/1 for domestic students, 10/1 for international students; for summer admission, 4/15 for domestic students, 3/1

for international students. Application fee: $60. Electronic applications accepted. *Financial support:* In 2019–20, 1 research assistantship, 13 teaching assistantships were awarded; fellowships, Federal Work-Study, and institutionally sponsored loans also available. *Unit head:* Dr. Luis Fernando Restrepo, Director Comparative Literature and Cultural Studies, 479-575-7580, E-mail: lrestr@uark.edu. *Application contact:* Dr. Luis Fernando Restrepo, Director Comparative Literature and Cultural Studies, 479-575-7580, E-mail: lrestr@uark.edu.
Website: https://fulbright.uark.edu/programs/comparative-literature-cultural-studies/index.php

University of California, Davis, Graduate Studies, Graduate Group in Cultural Studies, Davis, CA 95616. Offers MA, PhD. *Degree requirements:* For master's, thesis; for doctorate, thesis/dissertation. *Entrance requirements:* For doctorate, GRE. Additional exam requirements/recommendations for international students: required—TOEFL (minimum score 550 paper-based). Electronic applications accepted.

University of California, Irvine, School of Humanities, Program in Culture and Theory, Irvine, CA 92697. Offers PhD. *Students:* 9 full-time (5 women); includes 5 minority (3 Black or African American, non-Hispanic/Latino; 1 Asian, non-Hispanic/Latino; 1 Two or more races, non-Hispanic/Latino), 2 international. Average age 33. 38 applicants, 11% accepted, 3 enrolled. In 2019, 4 doctorates awarded. Application fee: $120 ($140 for international students). *Unit head:* Nasrin Rahimieh, Interim Director, 949-824-0406, E-mail: nasrin.rahimieh@uci.edu. *Application contact:* Arielle Hinojosa, Graduate Counselor, 949-824-6441, Fax: 949-824-7006, E-mail: hinojosa@uci.edu.
Website: http://www.humanities.uci.edu/cultureandtheory/

University of California, Riverside, Graduate Division, Department of Ethnic Studies, Riverside, CA 92521. Offers cultural politics and production (PhD). Terminal master's awarded for partial completion of doctoral program. *Degree requirements:* For doctorate, variable foreign language requirement, comprehensive exam, thesis/dissertation. *Entrance requirements:* For doctorate, GRE, writing sample, statement of purpose, personal history statement, 3 letters of recommendation. Additional exam requirements/recommendations for international students: required—TOEFL (minimum score 550 paper-based; 80 iBT); recommended—IELTS (minimum score 7). Electronic applications accepted.

University of California, Santa Barbara, Graduate Division, College of Letters and Sciences, Division of Social Sciences, Department of Global Studies, Santa Barbara, CA 93106-7065. Offers global culture, ideology, and religion (MA, PhD); global government, human rights, and civil society (MA, PhD); political economy, sustainable development, and the environment (MA, PhD). *Degree requirements:* For master's, one foreign language, thesis, 2 years of a second language; for doctorate, one foreign language, thesis/dissertation, reading proficiency in at least one language other than English. *Entrance requirements:* For master's, GRE, 2 years of a second language with minimum B grade in the final term, statement of purpose, resume or curriculum vitae, 3 letters of recommendation, transcripts (from all post-secondary institutions attended), writing sample (15-20 pages); for doctorate, GRE, statement of purpose, personal achievements/contributions statement, resume or curriculum vitae, 3 letters of recommendation, transcripts from all post-secondary institutions attended, writing sample (15-20 pages). Additional exam requirements/recommendations for international students: required—TOEFL (minimum score 600 paper-based; 94 iBT), IELTS (minimum score 7). Electronic applications accepted.

University of Dayton, Department of English, Dayton, OH 45469. Offers literary and cultural studies (MA); teaching English to speakers of other languages (TESOL) (MA); writing and rhetoric (MA). *Program availability:* Part-time. *Degree requirements:* For master's, thesis optional. *Entrance requirements:* For master's, 24 undergraduate-level semester hours in literature and/or writing; minimum GPA of 3.0; transcripts; personal statement; 8-10 page writing sample; three professional letters of recommendation. Additional exam requirements/recommendations for international students: required—TOEFL (minimum score 550 paper-based, 80 iBT) or IELTS. Electronic applications accepted.

University of Denver, Division of Arts, Humanities and Social Sciences, Department of Media, Film and Journalism Studies, Denver, CO 80208. Offers international and intercultural communication (MA); media and public communication (MA), including media and globalization, strategic communication. *Program availability:* Part-time. *Faculty:* 18 full-time (8 women), 1 part-time/adjunct (0 women). *Students:* 4 full-time (all women), 23 part-time (19 women); includes 6 minority (1 Black or African American, non-Hispanic/Latino; 1 Asian, non-Hispanic/Latino; 3 Hispanic/Latino; 1 Two or more races, non-Hispanic/Latino), 1 international. Average age 26. 35 applicants, 80% accepted, 13 enrolled. In 2019, 14 master's awarded. *Degree requirements:* For master's, variable foreign language requirement, thesis (for some programs). *Entrance requirements:* For master's, GRE General Test, bachelor's degree, transcripts, personal statement, three letters of recommendation. Additional exam requirements/recommendations for international students: required—TOEFL (minimum score 620 paper-based; 105 iBT). *Application deadline:* For fall admission, 2/1 priority date for domestic and international students; for winter admission, 11/14 for domestic and international students; for spring admission, 1/31 for domestic and international students. Applications are processed on a rolling basis. Application fee: $65. Electronic applications accepted. *Expenses:* Contact institution. *Financial support:* In 2019–20, 24 students received support, including 11 teaching assistantships with tuition reimbursements available (averaging $7,612 per year); career-related internships or fieldwork, Federal Work-Study, institutionally sponsored loans, scholarships/grants, and unspecified assistantships also available. Support available to part-time students. Financial award application deadline: 2/15; financial award applicants required to submit FAFSA. *Unit head:* Dr. Lynn Schofield Clark, Professor and Chair, 303-871-3984, Fax: 303-871-4949, E-mail: lynn.clark@du.edu. *Application contact:* Information Contact, 303-871-2166, E-mail: mfjs@du.edu.
Website: http://www.du.edu/ahss/mfjs

University of Denver, University College, Denver, CO 80208. Offers arts and culture (MA, Certificate); communication management (MS, Certificate), including translation studies (Certificate), world history and culture (Certificate); environmental policy and management (MS); geographic information systems (MS); global affairs (MA, Certificate), including human capital in organizations (Certificate), philanthropic leadership (Certificate); project management (Certificate), strategic innovation and change (Certificate); healthcare leadership (MS); information communications and technology (MS); leadership and organizations (MS); professional creative writing (MA, Certificate), including emergency planning and response (Certificate), organizational security (Certificate); security management (MS, Certificate); strategic human resources (Certificate). *Program availability:* Part-time, evening/weekend, 100% online, blended/hybrid learning. *Faculty:* 104 part-time/adjunct (52 women). *Students:* 59 full-time (33 women), 1,893 part-time (1,210 women); includes 545 minority (133 Black or African American, non-Hispanic/Latino; 16 American Indian or Alaska Native, non-Hispanic/Latino; 64 Asian, non-Hispanic/Latino; 252 Hispanic/Latino; 4 Native Hawaiian or other Pacific Islander, non-Hispanic/Latino; 76 Two or more races, non-Hispanic/Latino), 78 international. Average age 32. 1,290 applicants, 91% accepted, 752 enrolled. In 2019, 457 master's, 181 other advanced degrees awarded. *Degree requirements:* For master's, capstone project. *Entrance requirements:* For master's, baccalaureate degree,

transcripts, two letters of recommendation, personal statement, resume, writing sample (Master of Arts in Professional Creative Writing). Additional exam requirements/recommendations for international students: required—TOEFL (minimum score 550 paper-based; 80 iBT). *Application deadline:* For fall admission, 6/19 priority date for domestic students, 6/14 priority date for international students; for winter admission, 10/25 priority date for domestic students, 9/27 priority date for international students; for spring admission, 2/7 priority date for domestic students, 1/10 priority date for international students; for summer admission, 4/24 priority date for domestic students, 3/27 priority date for international students. Applications are processed on a rolling basis. Application fee: $75. Electronic applications accepted. *Expenses:* Contact institution. *Financial support:* In 2019–20, 56 students received support. Teaching assistantships available. Financial award applicants required to submit FAFSA. *Unit head:* Dr. Michael McGuire, Dean, 303-871-3518, E-mail: michael.mcguire@du.edu. *Application contact:* Admission Team, 303-871-2291, E-mail: ucoladm@du.edu.
Website: http://universitycollege.du.edu/

University of Hawaii at Hilo, Program in Hawaiian and Indigenous Language and Culture Revitalization, Hilo, HI 96720-4091. Offers PhD. *Entrance requirements:* Additional exam requirements/recommendations for international students: required—TOEFL, IELTS. Electronic applications accepted.

University of Hawaii at Hilo, Program in Indigenous Language and Culture Education, Hilo, HI 96720-4091. Offers MA. *Entrance requirements:* Additional exam requirements/recommendations for international students: required—TOEFL, IELTS. Electronic applications accepted.

University of Hawaii at Manoa, Office of Graduate Education, International Cultural Studies Graduate Certificate Program, Honolulu, HI 96822. Offers Graduate Certificate. *Program availability:* Part-time. *Entrance requirements:* For degree, GRE General Test. Additional exam requirements/recommendations for international students: required—TOEFL (minimum score 540 paper-based; 76 iBT), IELTS (minimum score 5).

University of Houston, College of Liberal Arts and Social Sciences, Department of Modern and Classical Languages, Houston, TX 77204. Offers world cultures and literatures (MA). *Degree requirements:* For master's, one foreign language, thesis optional. *Entrance requirements:* For master's, GRE General Test, minimum GPA of 3.0 in last 60 hours of course work. Additional exam requirements/recommendations for international students: required—TOEFL (minimum score 500 paper-based). Electronic applications accepted.

University of Houston–Clear Lake, School of Human Sciences and Humanities, Programs in Human Sciences, Houston, TX 77058-1002. Offers behavioral sciences (MA), including criminology, cross cultural studies, general psychology, sociology; clinical psychology (MA); criminology (MA); cross cultural studies (MA); family therapy (MA); fitness and human performance (MA); school psychology (MA). *Accreditation:* AAMFT/COAMFTE. *Program availability:* Part-time, evening/weekend, online learning. *Degree requirements:* For master's, thesis or alternative. *Entrance requirements:* For master's, GRE General Test. Additional exam requirements/recommendations for international students: required—TOEFL (minimum score 550 paper-based). Electronic applications accepted.

The University of Kansas, Graduate Studies, School of Education, Department of Educational Leadership and Policy Studies, Education Leadership and Policy Program, Lawrence, KS 66045-3101. Offers policy studies (PhD); social and cultural studies in education (MSE, PhD). *Program availability:* Part-time, evening/weekend. *Students:* 124 full-time (72 women), 76 part-time (37 women); includes 44 minority (20 Black or African American, non-Hispanic/Latino; 2 American Indian or Alaska Native, non-Hispanic/Latino; 3 Asian, non-Hispanic/Latino; 9 Hispanic/Latino; 10 Two or more races, non-Hispanic/Latino), 48 international. Average age 39. 67 applicants, 67% accepted, 37 enrolled. In 2019, 29 doctorates awarded. *Entrance requirements:* For master's, minimum GPA of 3.0, resume or curriculum vitae, statement of purpose, official academic transcripts, three letters of recommendation; for doctorate, GRE General Test, minimum graduate GPA of 3.5, resume or curriculum vitae, statement of purpose, official academic transcripts, three letters of recommendation, writing sample. Additional exam requirements/recommendations for international students: required—TOEFL, IELTS. *Application deadline:* For fall admission, 7/1 for domestic and international students; for spring admission, 11/1 for domestic and international students; for summer admission, 4/1 for domestic and international students. Application fee: $65 ($85 for international students). Electronic applications accepted. *Expenses:* Tuition, state resident: full-time $9989. Tuition, nonresident: full-time $23,950. *International tuition:* $23,950 full-time. *Required fees:* $984; $81.99 per credit hour. Tuition and fees vary according to course load, campus/location and program. *Financial support:* Fellowships, research assistantships, teaching assistantships, scholarships/grants, and unspecified assistantships available. Financial award application deadline: 3/15. *Unit head:* Dr. Susan B. Twombly, Chair, 785-864-9721, E-mail: stwombly@ku.edu. *Application contact:* Denise Brubaker, Admissions Coordinator, 785-864-7973, E-mail: brubaker@ku.edu.
Website: http://elps.soe.ku.edu/

University of Louisiana at Lafayette, College of Liberal Arts, Department of English, Lafayette, LA 70504. Offers American culture (MA, PhD), including history, sociology; American literature and language (PhD); creative writing (MA, PhD), including creative writing (MA), folklore (MA), rhetoric (MA); folklore (MA, PhD); linguistic studies (MA, PhD); professional writing (PhD); rhetoric (MA, PhD); TESOL studies (MA, PhD). *Program availability:* Part-time. Terminal master's awarded for partial completion of doctoral program. *Degree requirements:* For master's, one foreign language, thesis or alternative; for doctorate, 2 foreign languages, comprehensive exam, thesis/dissertation. *Entrance requirements:* For master's, GRE General Test, minimum GPA of 2.75; for doctorate, GRE General Test, minimum GPA of 3.0. Additional exam requirements/recommendations for international students: required—TOEFL (minimum score 550 paper-based). Electronic applications accepted. *Expenses: Tuition, area resident:* Full-time $5511; part-time $1630 per credit hour. Tuition, state resident: full-time $5511; part-time $1630 per credit hour. Tuition, nonresident: full-time $19,239; part-time $2409 per credit hour. *Required fees:* $46,637.

University of Louisville, Graduate School, College of Arts and Sciences, Department of Comparative Humanities, Louisville, KY 40292-0001. Offers civic leadership (MA); culture, criticism, and contemporary thought (PhD); linguistics (MA); public arts and letters (PhD); traditional humanities (MA); MA/JD; MA/MBA. *Program availability:* Part-time. *Faculty:* 15 full-time (6 women), 18 part-time/adjunct (9 women). *Students:* 24 full-time (12 women), 16 part-time (8 women); includes 6 minority (1 Black or African American, non-Hispanic/Latino; 1 Hispanic/Latino; 4 Two or more races, non-Hispanic/Latino), 2 international. Average age 41. 16 applicants, 81% accepted, 8 enrolled. In 2019, 3 master's, 6 doctorates awarded. *Degree requirements:* For master's, one foreign language, thesis or alternative, directed study culminating project; for doctorate, 2 foreign languages, comprehensive exam, thesis/dissertation, internship. *Entrance requirements:* For master's, GRE General Test, Two letters of reference, official transcripts; for doctorate, GRE General Test, three letters of recommendation, statement of intent, scholarly writing sample, transcripts from all institutions attended. Additional exam requirements/recommendations for international students: required—TOEFL (minimum score 550 paper-based; 79 iBT), IELTS can be used in place of the TOEFL; recommended—IELTS (minimum score 6.5). *Application deadline:* For fall admission, 1/15 for domestic and international students; for spring admission, 7/15 for domestic and international students. Applications are processed on a rolling basis. Application fee: $65. Electronic applications accepted. *Expenses:* Contact institution. *Financial support:* In 2019–20, 25 students received support, including 1 fellowship with full tuition reimbursement available (averaging $18,000 per year), 3 teaching assistantships with full tuition reimbursements available (averaging $18,000 per year); research assistantships, scholarships/grants, health care benefits, and unspecified assistantships also available. Financial award application deadline: 1/15. *Unit head:* Dr. Ann Hall, Chair, 502-852-6805, Fax: 502-852-0078, E-mail: ann.hall@louisville.edu. *Application contact:* Dr. Simona Bertacco, Professor and Director of Graduate Studies, 502-852-7161, E-mail: simona.bertacco@louisville.edu.
Website: http://louisville.edu/humanities/

The University of Manchester, School of Arts, Languages and Cultures, Manchester, United Kingdom. Offers anthropology, media and performance (PhD); applied theatre (PhD); Arab world studies (PhD); archaeology (PhD); art history and visual studies (PhD); arts and cultural management (PhD); arts management and cultural policy (PhD); Chinese studies (PhD); classics and ancient history (PhD); composition (PhD); creative writing (PhD); drama (PhD); East Asian studies (PhD); electroacoustic composition (PhD); English and American studies (PhD); English language (PhD); French studies (PhD); German studies (PhD); history (PhD); humanitarianism and conflict response (PhD); interpreting studies (PhD); Japanese studies (PhD); Latin American cultural studies (PhD); linguistics (PhD); Middle Eastern studies (PhD); museology (PhD); museum practice (PhD); music (PhD); musicology (PhD); Polish studies (PhD); Portuguese studies (PhD); religions and theology (PhD); Russian studies (PhD); Spanish studies (PhD); translation and intercultural studies (PhD).

The University of Manchester, School of Social Sciences, Manchester, United Kingdom. Offers ethnographic documentary (M Phil); interdisciplinary study of culture (PhD); philosophy (PhD); politics (PhD); social anthropology (PhD); social anthropology with visual media (PhD); social change (PhD); social statistics (PhD); sociology (PhD); visual anthropology (M Phil).

University of Massachusetts Boston, College of Liberal Arts, Program in Transnational, Cultural, and Community Studies, Boston, MA 02125-3393. Offers MS.

University of Minnesota, Twin Cities Campus, Graduate School, College of Liberal Arts, Department of Cultural Studies and Comparative Literature, Program in Comparative Studies in Discourse and Society, Minneapolis, MN 55455-0213. Offers PhD. *Degree requirements:* For doctorate, 2 foreign languages, thesis/dissertation. *Entrance requirements:* For doctorate, GRE General Test, sample of written work. Additional exam requirements/recommendations for international students: required—TOEFL.

University of Missouri–St. Louis, College of Arts and Sciences, Interdisciplinary Courses, St. Louis, MO 63121. Offers gender studies (Certificate); international studies (Certificate). *Entrance requirements:* Additional exam requirements/recommendations for international students: required—TOEFL (minimum score 550 paper-based; 79 iBT), IELTS (minimum score 6.5). *Expenses: Tuition, area resident:* Full-time $9005.40; part-time $6003.60 per credit hour. Tuition, state resident: full-time $9005.40; part-time $6003.60 per credit hour. Tuition, nonresident: full-time $22,108; part-time $14,738.40 per credit hour. *International tuition:* $22,108 full-time. Tuition and fees vary according to course load.

University of Montana, Graduate School, Phyllis J. Washington College of Education and Human Sciences, Department of Counselor Education, Missoula, MT 59812. Offers clinical mental health counseling (MA); counseling and supervision (Ed D); counselor education (Ed S); intercultural youth and family development (MA); school counseling (MA). *Accreditation:* ACA. *Degree requirements:* For doctorate, thesis/dissertation. *Entrance requirements:* For master's, doctorate, and Ed S, GRE General Test. Additional exam requirements/recommendations for international students: required—TOEFL.

University of New Mexico, Graduate Studies, College of Education and Human Sciences, Program in Language, Literacy and Sociocultural Studies, Albuquerque, NM 87131-2039. Offers American Indian education (MA); bilingual education (MA, PhD); educational linguistics (PhD); educational thought and sociocultural studies (MA, PhD); literacy/language arts (MA, PhD); social studies (MA); TESOL (MA, PhD). *Degree requirements:* For master's, comprehensive exam, thesis optional; for doctorate, comprehensive exam, thesis/dissertation, research skills. *Entrance requirements:* For master's, letter of intent, 3 letters of recommendation, resume, BA/BS, department demographic form, transcripts; for doctorate, writing sample, letter of intent, 3 letters of recommendation, resume, BA/BS, MA, department demographic form, transcripts. Additional exam requirements/recommendations for international students: required—TOEFL. Electronic applications accepted. *Expenses:* Tuition, state resident: full-time $7633; part-time $972 per year. Tuition, nonresident: full-time $22,586; part-time $3840 per year. *International tuition:* $23,292 full-time. *Required fees:* $8608. Tuition and fees vary according to course level, course load, degree level, program and student level.

The University of North Carolina at Charlotte, College of Liberal Arts and Sciences, Department of Languages and Culture Studies, Charlotte, NC 28223-0001. Offers language and culture studies: translating (Graduate Certificate), including english/french; english/german; english/japanese; english/russian; english/spanish; spanish (MA), including language, literature and culture (llc); translating and translation studies (its). *Program availability:* Part-time, evening/weekend. *Faculty:* 25 full-time (13 women), 1 (woman) part-time/adjunct. *Students:* 6 full-time (5 women), 17 part-time (14 women); includes 13 minority (2 Black or African American, non-Hispanic/Latino; 1 Asian, non-Hispanic/Latino; 10 Hispanic/Latino). Average age 30. 12 applicants, 100% accepted, 11 enrolled. In 2019, 4 master's, 5 other advanced degrees awarded. *Degree requirements:* For master's, thesis optional. *Entrance requirements:* For master's, baccalaureate degree in Spanish or related field with minimum overall GPA of 2.75; essay that addresses the applicant's motivation for enrolling in program, to include particular areas of research interests and career or professional goals; three letters of reference; oral interview; for Graduate Certificate, essay in English that addresses applicant's motivation for seeking enrollment in program; three letters of recommendation; portfolio of best writing samples in both English and Spanish or of translations into each language; oral interview. Additional exam requirements/recommendations for international students: required—TOEFL (minimum score 557 paper-based; 83 iBT), IELTS (minimum score 6.5), TOEFL (minimum score 557paper-based, 83 iBT) or IELTS (6.5). *Application deadline:* Applications are processed on a rolling basis. Application fee: $75. Electronic applications accepted. *Expenses:* Tuition, state resident: full-time $4337. Tuition, nonresident: full-time $17,771. *Required fees:* $3093. Tuition and fees vary according to course load, degree level and program. *Financial support:* In 2019–20, 8 students received support, including 4 research assistantships (averaging $5,000 per year), 4 teaching assistantships (averaging $4,000 per year); career-related internships or fieldwork, institutionally sponsored loans, scholarships/grants, and unspecified assistantships also available. Support available to part-time students. Financial award applicants required to submit FAFSA. *Unit head:* Dr.

Michele Bissiere, Department Chair and Professor of French, 704-687-8754, E-mail: mhbissie@uncc.edu. *Application contact:* Kathy B. Giddings, Director of Graduate Admissions, 704-687-5503, Fax: 704-687-1668, E-mail: gradadm@uncc.edu. Website: https://languages.uncc.edu/

University of Oklahoma, College of Arts and Sciences, Department of English, Norman, OK 73019. Offers literary and cultural studies (MA, PhD); writing and rhetoric studies (MA, PhD). *Program availability:* Part-time. *Degree requirements:* For master's, one foreign language, comprehensive exam (for some programs), thesis (for some programs), exam or thesis; for doctorate, one foreign language, comprehensive exam, thesis/dissertation. *Entrance requirements:* For master's, GRE, BA in English or related field; for doctorate, GRE, MA in English or related field. Additional exam requirements/recommendations for international students: required—TOEFL (minimum score 79 iBT) or IELTS (minimum score 6.5). Electronic applications accepted. *Expenses:* Tuition, state resident: full-time $6583.20; part-time $274.30 per credit hour. Tuition, nonresident: full-time $21,242; part-time $885.10 per credit hour. *International tuition:* $21,242.40 full-time. *Required fees:* $1994.20; $72.55 per credit hour. $126.50 per semester. Tuition and fees vary according to course load and degree level.

University of Pittsburgh, Kenneth P. Dietrich School of Arts and Sciences, Cultural Studies Program, Pittsburgh, PA 15260. Offers Certificate. *Faculty:* 177 full-time (88 women). *Students:* 81 full-time (46 women); includes 38 minority (4 Black or African American, non-Hispanic/Latino; 1 American Indian or Alaska Native, non-Hispanic/Latino; 12 Asian, non-Hispanic/Latino; 13 Hispanic/Latino; 1 Native Hawaiian or other Pacific Islander, non-Hispanic/Latino; 7 Two or more races, non-Hispanic/Latino), 27 international. *Degree requirements:* For Certificate, thesis. *Entrance requirements:* For degree, good academic standing in a University of Pittsburgh graduate degree-granting department or school. Additional exam requirements/recommendations for international students: required—TOEFL. *Application deadline:* Applications are processed on a rolling basis. Application fee: $0. Electronic applications accepted. Application fee is waived when completed online. *Financial support:* Fellowships, research assistantships, teaching assistantships, scholarships/grants, and tuition waivers available. *Unit head:* Dr. Ronald J. Zboray, Director, 412-624-6969, Fax: 412-624-6492, E-mail: zboray@pitt.edu. *Application contact:* Lorri Keeling-Oliver, Graduate Administrator, 412-624-6564, Fax: 412-383-6999, E-mail: ljk59@pitt.edu. Website: http://www.culturalstudies.pitt.edu

University of Saskatchewan, College of Graduate and Postdoctoral Studies, College of Arts and Science, Department of Linguistics and Religious Studies, Saskatoon, SK S7N 5A2, Canada. Offers applied linguistics (MA); religion and culture (MA); teaching English to speakers of other languages (MA). *Degree requirements:* For master's, thesis. *Entrance requirements:* Additional exam requirements/recommendations for international students: required—TOEFL (minimum score 80 iBT); recommended—IELTS (minimum score 6.5). Electronic applications accepted.

University of Southern California, Graduate School, Dana and David Dornsife College of Letters, Arts and Sciences, Comparative Studies in Literature and Culture Doctoral Program, Los Angeles, CA 90089. Offers comparative literature (PhD); comparative media and culture (PhD); Spanish and Latin American studies (PhD). *Degree requirements:* For doctorate, 2 foreign languages, comprehensive exam, thesis/dissertation. *Entrance requirements:* For doctorate, GRE, competence in language other than English (highly recommended). Additional exam requirements/recommendations for international students: required—TOEFL. Electronic applications accepted.

University of Southern Indiana, Graduate Studies, College of Liberal Arts, Program in Second Language Acquisition, Policy, and Culture, Evansville, IN 47712-3590. Offers MA. *Program availability:* Part-time. *Entrance requirements:* For master's, minimum GPA of 3.0, letter of intent, 3 letters of recommendation. Additional exam requirements/recommendations for international students: required—TOEFL (minimum score 550 paper-based; 79 iBT), IELTS (minimum score 6).

University of Southern Maine, College of Management and Human Service, School of Education and Human Development, Program in Counselor Education, Portland, ME 04103. Offers clinical mental health counseling (MS); counseling (CAS); culturally responsive practices in education and human development (CGS); mental health rehabilitation technician/community (CGS); rehabilitation counseling (MS); school counseling (MS); substance abuse counseling (CGS). *Accreditation:* ACA (one or more programs are accredited); CORE; TEAC. *Program availability:* Part-time, evening/weekend. *Degree requirements:* For master's, comprehensive exam, thesis or alternative; for other advanced degree, thesis or alternative. *Entrance requirements:* For master's, GRE General Test or MAT, interview; for other advanced degree, master's degree. Additional exam requirements/recommendations for international students: required—TOEFL (minimum score 550 paper-based; 79 iBT). Electronic applications accepted. *Expenses:* Tuition, area resident: Full-time $864; part-time $432 per credit hour. Tuition, state resident: full-time $864; part-time $432 per credit hour. Tuition, nonresident: full-time $2372; part-time $1186 per credit hour. *Required fees:* $141; $108 per credit hour. Tuition and fees vary according to course load.

The University of Texas at Austin, Graduate School, College of Education, Department of Curriculum and Instruction, Austin, TX 78712-1111. Offers bilingual/bicultural education (M Ed, MA, PhD); cultural studies in education (M Ed, MA, PhD); early childhood education (M Ed, MA, PhD); language and literacy studies (M Ed, PhD); learning technologies (M Ed, MA, PhD); physical education (M Ed, MA, PhD). Terminal master's awarded for partial completion of doctoral program. *Degree requirements:* For doctorate, thesis/dissertation. *Entrance requirements:* For master's and doctorate, GRE General Test. Electronic applications accepted.

The University of Texas at Austin, Graduate School, College of Liberal Arts, Department of Anthropology, Program in Cultural Forms, Austin, TX 78712-1111. Offers MA, PhD. *Program availability:* Part-time. Terminal master's awarded for partial completion of doctoral program. *Degree requirements:* For master's, one foreign language, thesis, report; for doctorate, one foreign language, thesis/dissertation. *Entrance requirements:* For master's and doctorate, GRE General Test. Electronic applications accepted.

The University of Texas at Austin, Graduate School, College of Liberal Arts, Department of Slavic and Eurasian Studies, Austin, TX 78712-1111. Offers applied linguistics/pedagogy (PhD); literature and culture (PhD); Slavic languages (MA); Slavic linguistics (PhD). *Degree requirements:* For master's, 2 foreign languages, thesis; for doctorate, 3 foreign languages, thesis/dissertation. *Entrance requirements:* For master's and doctorate, GRE General Test. Electronic applications accepted.

The University of Texas at Austin, Graduate School, College of Liberal Arts, Teresa Lozano Long Institute of Latin American Studies, Austin, TX 78712-1111. Offers cultural politics of Afro-Latin and indigenous peoples (MA); development studies (MA); environmental studies (MA); human rights (MA); Latin American and international law (LL M); JD/MA; MA/MA; MBA/MA; MP Aff/MA; MSCRP/MA. *Entrance requirements:* For master's, GRE General Test.

The University of Texas at San Antonio, College of Education and Human Development, Department of Bicultural and Bilingual Studies, San Antonio, TX 78249-0617. Offers bicultural and bilingual studies (MA), including bicultural and bilingual

education, bicultural studies; culture, literacy, and language (PhD); teaching English as a second language (MA). *Program availability:* Part-time, evening/weekend. *Degree requirements:* For master's, one foreign language, comprehensive exam, thesis optional; for doctorate, one foreign language, comprehensive exam, thesis/dissertation. *Entrance requirements:* For master's, bachelor's degree with 18 credit hours in field of study or in another appropriate field of study; for doctorate, GRE General Test, resume or curriculum vitae, 3 letters of recommendation, statement of purpose, master's degree. Additional exam requirements/recommendations for international students: required—TOEFL (minimum score 550 paper-based; 79 iBT), IELTS (minimum score 6.5). Electronic applications accepted. *Expenses:* Contact institution.

University of the Sacred Heart, Graduate Programs, Department of Communication, Program in Contemporary Culture and Media, San Juan, PR 00914-0383. Offers MA. *Degree requirements:* For master's, thesis.

University of Utah, Graduate School, College of Humanities, Department of Communication, Salt Lake City, UT 84112. Offers communicating science, health, environment and risk (MA, MS, PhD); critical cultural studies (MA, MS, PhD); digital media (MA, MS, PhD); rhetoric (MA, MS, PhD). *Program availability:* Part-time, evening/weekend. *Faculty:* 29 full-time (15 women). *Students:* 33 full-time (24 women), 6 part-time (3 women); includes 12 minority (2 Black or African American, non-Hispanic/Latino; 4 Asian, non-Hispanic/Latino; 4 Hispanic/Latino; 1 Native Hawaiian or other Pacific Islander, non-Hispanic/Latino; 1 Two or more races, non-Hispanic/Latino), 3 international. Average age 30. 80 applicants, 19% accepted, 9 enrolled. In 2019, 4 master's, 10 doctorates awarded. Terminal master's awarded for partial completion of doctoral program. *Degree requirements:* For master's, variable foreign language requirement, comprehensive exam (for some programs), thesis (for some programs), Programme of Study; for doctorate, comprehensive exam, thesis/dissertation, Programme of Study; Prospectus. *Entrance requirements:* For master's and doctorate, GRE. Additional exam requirements/recommendations for international students: required—TOEFL (minimum score 80 paper-based), IELTS (minimum score 6.5). *Application deadline:* For fall admission, 12/15 for domestic students, 11/15 for international students. Application fee: $55 ($65 for international students). Electronic applications accepted. *Expenses:* Tuition, state resident: full-time $7085; part-time $272.51 per credit hour. Tuition, nonresident: full-time $24,937; part-time $959.12 per credit hour. *Required fees:* $880.52; $880.52 per semester. Tuition and fees vary according to degree level, program and student level. *Financial support:* In 2019–20, 30 students received support, including 2 fellowships with full tuition reimbursements available (averaging $18,500 per year), 3 research assistantships with tuition reimbursements available (averaging $19,667 per year), 28 teaching assistantships with tuition reimbursements available (averaging $19,929 per year). Financial award application deadline: 12/15. *Unit head:* Kevin Coe, Professor and Chair, 801-581-6888, E-mail: kevin.coe@utah.edu. *Application contact:* Travis Ciaramella, Graduate Advisor, 801-585-6337, E-mail: travis.ciaramella@utah.edu. Website: http://www.communication.utah.edu

University of Washington, Bothell, Master of Arts in Cultural Studies Program, Bothell, WA 98011. Offers MA. *Program availability:* Evening/weekend. *Degree requirements:* For master's, thesis. *Entrance requirements:* Additional exam requirements/recommendations for international students: required—TOEFL. Electronic applications accepted.

Washington State University, College of Education, Department of Teaching and Learning, Pullman, WA 99164-2132. Offers cultural studies and social thought in education (PhD); curriculum and instruction (Ed M, MA); English language learners (Ed M, MA); language, literacy and technology (PhD); literacy education (Ed M, MA); mathematics education (PhD); special education (Ed M, MA, PhD); teacher leadership (Ed D); teaching (MIT), including elementary education, secondary education. *Program availability:* Part-time, online learning. *Degree requirements:* For master's, comprehensive exam, thesis, oral or written exam; for doctorate, comprehensive exam, thesis/dissertation, oral and written exam. *Entrance requirements:* For master's, GRE General Test, minimum GPA of 3.0, 3 letters of recommendation, letter of intent, transcripts, resume/curriculum vitae; for doctorate, GRE General Test, minimum GPA of 3.0, 3 letters of recommendation, letter of intent, transcripts, writing sample, resume/curriculum vitae. Additional exam requirements/recommendations for international students: required—TOEFL (minimum score 550 paper-based; 80 iBT). Electronic applications accepted.

Wayne State University, College of Liberal Arts and Sciences, Department of English, Detroit, MI 48202. Offers English (MA); film and media studies (PhD); literary and cultural studies (PhD); rhetoric and composition studies (PhD). *Faculty:* 27. *Students:* 59 full-time (36 women), 31 part-time (24 women); includes 17 minority (4 Black or African American, non-Hispanic/Latino; 4 Asian, non-Hispanic/Latino; 3 Hispanic/Latino; 6 Two or more races, non-Hispanic/Latino), 4 international. Average age 33. 87 applicants, 44% accepted, 17 enrolled. In 2019, 12 master's, 9 doctorates awarded. Terminal master's awarded for partial completion of doctoral program. *Degree requirements:* For master's, variable foreign language requirement, essay, thesis, or portfolio of work approved by Director of Graduate Studies; for doctorate, one foreign language, comprehensive exam, thesis/dissertation. *Entrance requirements:* For master's, statement of purpose; two academic letters of reference; sample essay from previous English course; for doctorate, statement of purpose; two academic letters of reference; sample of scholarly or critical writing. Additional exam requirements/recommendations for international students: required—TOEFL (minimum score 550 paper-based; 79 iBT), TWE (minimum score 5.5), Michigan English Language Assessment Battery (minimum score 85); recommended—IELTS (minimum score 6.5). *Application deadline:* For fall admission, 1/15 for domestic students. Applications are processed on a rolling basis. Application fee: $50. Electronic applications accepted. *Expenses:* Tuition: Full-time $34,567. *Financial support:* In 2019–20, 54 students received support, including 5 fellowships with tuition reimbursements available (averaging $21,500 per year), 1 research assistantship with tuition reimbursement available (averaging $19,967 per year), 28 teaching assistantships with tuition reimbursements available (averaging $19,967 per year); scholarships/grants, health care benefits, and unspecified assistantships also available. Financial award applicants required to submit FAFSA. *Unit head:* Dr. Caroline Maun, Chair and Associate Professor, 313-577-7692, E-mail: av4495@wayne.edu. *Application contact:* Dr. Richard Marback, Director of Graduate Studies, 313-577-7694, E-mail: aa4749@wayne.edu. Website: http://clas.wayne.edu/english/

Wilfrid Laurier University, Faculty of Graduate and Postdoctoral Studies, Faculty of Arts, Cultural Analysis and Social Theory Program, Waterloo, ON N2L 3C5, Canada. Offers body politics (MA); cultural representation and social theory (MA); gender, sexuality and embodiment (MA); globalization, identity and social movements (MA). *Program availability:* Part-time. *Entrance requirements:* For master's, honours BA in humanities, social science or interdisciplinary program with social theory, minimum B+ in final year of full-time study. Additional exam requirements/recommendations for international students: required—TOEFL (minimum score 89 iBT). Electronic applications accepted.

Wilfrid Laurier University, Faculty of Graduate and Postdoctoral Studies, Faculty of Arts, Department of Communication Studies, Waterloo, ON N2L 3C5, Canada. Offers media, technology and culture (MA); visual communication and culture (MA). *Degree requirements:* For master's, thesis optional. *Entrance requirements:* For master's, honours BA in communication studies or a cognate discipline from an approved university with a minimum B+ overall in last two years of study and in undergraduate major. Additional exam requirements/recommendations for international students: required—TOEFL (minimum score 89 iBT). Electronic applications accepted.

Wilson College, Graduate Programs, Chambersburg, PA 17201-1285. Offers accounting (M Acc); choreography and visual art (MFA); education (M Ed); educational technology (MET); healthcare administration (MHA); humanities (MA), including art and culture, critical/cultural theory, English language and literature, women's studies; management (MSM); nursing (MSN), including nursing education, nursing leadership and management; special education (MSE). *Program availability:* Evening/weekend. *Degree requirements:* For master's, project. *Entrance requirements:* For master's, PRAXIS, minimum undergraduate cumulative GPA of 3.0, 2 letters of recommendation, current certification for eligibility to teach in grades K-12, resume, personal interview. Electronic applications accepted.

East European and Russian Studies

Boston College, Morrissey Graduate School of Arts and Sciences, Department of Slavic and Eastern Languages and Literatures, Program in Slavic Studies, Chestnut Hill, MA 02467-3800. Offers MA, MA/JD, MBA/MA. *Degree requirements:* For master's, 3 foreign languages, comprehensive exam, thesis or alternative. *Entrance requirements:* Additional exam requirements/recommendations for international students: required—TOEFL (minimum score 600 paper-based; 100 iBT), IELTS (minimum score 8). Electronic applications accepted.

Brown University, Graduate School, Department of Slavic Studies, Providence, RI 02912. Offers Russian language and literature (AM); Slavic linguistics (AM); Slavic studies (PhD). *Degree requirements:* For master's, one foreign language; for doctorate, 2 foreign languages, thesis/dissertation, preliminary exam.

Carleton University, Faculty of Graduate Studies, Faculty of Public Affairs and Management, Institute of European and Russian Studies, Ottawa, ON K1S 5B6, Canada. Offers European and European Union studies (MA); European integration studies (Diploma); Russian, EurAsian and transition studies (MA). *Degree requirements:* For master's, one foreign language, thesis optional. *Entrance requirements:* For master's, honors degree or equivalent; 2 years of Russian, German or other central east European language. Additional exam requirements/recommendations for international students: required—TOEFL.

Columbia University, Graduate School of Arts and Sciences, New York, NY 10027. Offers African-American studies (MA); American studies (MA); anthropology (MA, PhD); art history and archaeology (MA, PhD); astronomy (PhD); biological sciences (PhD); biotechnology (MA); chemical physics (PhD); chemistry (PhD); classical studies (MA, PhD); classics (MA, PhD); climate and society (MA); conservation biology (MA); earth and environmental sciences (PhD); East Asia: regional studies (MA); East Asian languages and cultures (MA, PhD); ecology, evolution and environmental biology (MA), including conservation biology; ecology, evolution, and environmental biology (PhD), including ecology and evolutionary biology, evolutionary primatology; economics (MA, PhD); English and comparative literature (MA, PhD); French and Romance philology (MA, PhD); Germanic languages (MA, PhD); global French studies (MA); global thought (MA); Hispanic cultural studies (MA); history (PhD); history and literature (MA); human rights studies (MA); Islamic studies (MA); Italian (MA, PhD); Japanese pedagogy (MA); Jewish studies (MA); Latin America and the Caribbean: regional studies (MA); Latin American and Iberian cultures (PhD); mathematics (MA, PhD), including finance (MA); medieval and Renaissance studies (MA); Middle Eastern, South Asian, and African studies (MA, PhD); modern art: critical and curatorial studies (MA); modern European studies (MA); museum anthropology (MA); music (DMA, PhD); oral history (MA); philosophical foundations of physics (MA); philosophy (MA, PhD); physics (PhD); political science (MA, PhD); psychology (PhD); quantitative methods in the social sciences (MA); religion (MA, PhD); Russia, Eurasia and East Europe: regional studies (MA); Russian translation (MA); Slavic cultures (MA); Slavic languages (MA, PhD); sociology (MA, PhD); South Asian studies (MA); statistics (MA, PhD); theatre (PhD). *Program availability:* Part-time. *Students:* 3,506 full-time (1,844 women), 208 part-time (121 women); includes 864 minority (110 Black or African American, non-Hispanic/Latino; 5 American Indian or Alaska Native, non-Hispanic/Latino; 416 Asian, non-Hispanic/Latino; 147 Hispanic/Latino; 6 Native Hawaiian or other Pacific Islander, non-Hispanic/Latino; 180 Two or more races, non-Hispanic/Latino), 2,065 international. 14,545 applicants, 25% accepted, 1,429 enrolled. In 2019, 1,262 master's, 363 doctorates awarded. Terminal master's awarded for partial completion of doctoral program. *Degree requirements:* For master's, variable foreign language requirement, comprehensive exam (for some programs), thesis (for some programs); for doctorate, variable foreign language requirement, comprehensive exam (for some programs), thesis/dissertation. *Entrance requirements:* For master's and doctorate, GRE General Test, GRE Subject Test (for some programs). Additional exam requirements/recommendations for international students: required—TOEFL (minimum score 600 paper-based; 100 iBT), IELTS (minimum score 7.5). Application fee: $115. Electronic applications accepted. *Expenses: Tuition:* Full-time $47,600; part-time $1880 per credit. One-time fee: $105. *Financial support:* Fellowships, research assistantships, teaching assistantships, career-related internships or fieldwork, Federal Work-Study, institutionally sponsored loans, scholarships/grants, traineeships, health care benefits, tuition waivers, and unspecified assistantships available. Support available to part-time students. Financial award application deadline: 12/15. *Unit head:* Dr. Carlos J. Alonso, Dean of the Graduate School of Arts and Sciences and Vice President for Graduate Education, 212-854-2861, E-mail: gsas-dean@columbia.edu. *Application contact:* GSAS Office of Admissions, 212-854-6729, E-mail: gsas-admissions@columbia.edu.
Website: http://gsas.columbia.edu/

Cornell University, Graduate School, Graduate Fields of Arts and Sciences, Field of History, Ithaca, NY 14853. Offers African history (MA, PhD); American history (MA, PhD); ancient Greek history (PhD); ancient history (MA, PhD); ancient Roman history (PhD); early modern European history (MA, PhD); English history (MA, PhD); French history (MA, PhD); German history (MA, PhD); history of science (MA, PhD); Korean history (PhD); Latin American history (MA, PhD); medieval Chinese history (MA, PhD); medieval history (MA, PhD); modern Chinese history (MA, PhD); modern European history (MA, PhD); modern Japanese history (MA, PhD); modern Middle Eastern history (PhD); premodern Islamic history (MA, PhD); premodern Japanese history (MA, PhD); Renaissance history (MA, PhD); Russian history (MA, PhD); South Asian history (PhD); Southeast Asian history (MA, PhD). Terminal master's awarded for partial completion of doctoral program. *Degree requirements:* For master's, thesis; for doctorate, 2 foreign languages, comprehensive exam, thesis/dissertation, 1 year of teaching experience. *Entrance requirements:* For master's and doctorate, GRE General Test, writing sample, 3 letters of recommendation. Additional exam requirements/recommendations for international students: required—TOEFL (minimum score 550 paper-based; 77 iBT). Electronic applications accepted.

Florida State University, The Graduate School, College of Social Sciences and Public Policy, Program in Russian and East European Studies, Tallahassee, FL 32306. Offers Russian and East European studies (MA). *Program availability:* Part-time. *Faculty:* 4 full-time (all women), 4 part-time/adjunct (0 women). *Students:* 1 full-time (0 women), 2 part-time (0 women); includes 1 minority (Hispanic/Latino). Average age 41. 3 applicants, 33% accepted, 1 enrolled. In 2019, 2 master's awarded. *Degree requirements:* For master's, one foreign language, comprehensive exam, thesis optional. *Entrance requirements:* For master's, GRE General Test, minimum GPA of 3.0. Additional exam requirements/recommendations for international students: required—TOEFL (minimum score 550 paper-based; 80 iBT), IELTS (minimum score 6.5). *Application deadline:* For fall admission, 7/1 for domestic and international students; for spring admission, 11/1 for domestic and international students; for summer admission, 3/1 for domestic and international students. Applications are processed on a rolling basis. Application fee: $30. Electronic applications accepted. *Financial support:* In 2019–20, teaching assistantships with full tuition reimbursements (averaging $6,100 per year) were awarded; fellowships, research assistantships, career-related internships or fieldwork, Federal Work-Study, institutionally sponsored loans, and unspecified assistantships also available. Financial award application deadline: 2/1; financial award applicants required to submit FAFSA. *Unit head:* Dr. Lee K. Metcalf, Director, 850-644-4418, Fax: 850-645-4981, E-mail: lmetcalf@fsu.edu. *Application contact:* Sabrina Smith, Academic Program Specialist, 850-644-4418, Fax: 850-645-4981, E-mail: ssmith9@fsu.edu.
Website: http://coss.fsu.edu/inaprog/programs/graduate/g-european

Georgetown University, Graduate School of Arts and Sciences, Walsh School of Foreign Service, Center for Eurasian, Russian and East European Studies, Washington, DC 20057. Offers MA, MA/JD, MA/PhD. *Degree requirements:* For master's, one foreign language, comprehensive exam, thesis optional. *Entrance requirements:* For master's, GRE General Test. Additional exam requirements/recommendations for international students: required—TOEFL.

The George Washington University, Elliott School of International Affairs, Program in European and Eurasian Studies, Washington, DC 20052. Offers MA. *Program availability:* Part-time. *Degree requirements:* For master's, one foreign language, capstone project. *Entrance requirements:* For master's, GRE General Test, 2 years (or the equivalent) of a modern European language or Russian, 2 semesters of introductory economics (macro or micro). Additional exam requirements/recommendations for international students: required—TOEFL (minimum score 100 iBT), IELTS (minimum score 7). Electronic applications accepted.

Harvard University, Graduate School of Arts and Sciences, Committee on Regional Studies-Russia, Eastern Europe, and Central Asia, Cambridge, MA 02138. Offers AM. *Degree requirements:* For master's, one foreign language. *Entrance requirements:* For master's, GRE General Test. Additional exam requirements/recommendations for international students: required—TOEFL.

Indiana University Bloomington, University Graduate School, College of Arts and Sciences, School of Global and International Studies, Russian and East European Institute, Bloomington, IN 47405. Offers MA, Certificate, JD/MA, MA/MA, MBA/MA, MIS/MA, MLS/MA, MPA/MA, MPH/MA, MSSI/MA. *Degree requirements:* For master's, one foreign language, essay, written exams; for Certificate, one foreign language, oral and proficiency exams. *Entrance requirements:* For master's, GRE General Test, minimum 2 years of college Russian (for Russian area studies); for Certificate, GRE General Test. Additional exam requirements/recommendations for international students: recommended—TOEFL (minimum score 550 paper-based). *Expenses:* Contact institution.

The Ohio State University, Graduate School, Center for Slavic and East European Studies, Columbus, OH 43210. Offers MA. *Degree requirements:* For master's, exam or thesis. *Entrance requirements:* For master's, GRE General Test. Additional exam requirements/recommendations for international students: required—TOEFL (minimum score 550 paper-based; 79 iBT), Michigan English Language Assessment Battery (minimum score 82); recommended—IELTS (minimum score 7). Electronic applications accepted.

The Ohio State University, Graduate School, College of Arts and Sciences, Division of Arts and Humanities, Department of Slavic and East European Languages and Cultures, Columbus, OH 43210. Offers Slavic linguistics (MA, PhD); Slavic literature, film, and cultural studies (MA, PhD). Terminal master's awarded for partial completion of doctoral program. *Degree requirements:* For master's, variable foreign language requirement, thesis optional; for doctorate, variable foreign language requirement, thesis/dissertation. *Entrance requirements:* For master's and doctorate, GRE General Test, at least 3 years of Russian language study or equivalent. Additional exam requirements/recommendations for international students: required—TOEFL (minimum score 550 paper-based; 79 iBT), Michigan English Language Assessment Battery (minimum score 82); recommended—IELTS (minimum score 7). Electronic applications accepted.

Stanford University, School of Humanities and Sciences, Center for Russian, East European and Eurasian Studies, Stanford, CA 94305-2004. Offers MA. *Expenses: Tuition:* Full-time $52,479; part-time $34,110 per unit. *Required fees:* $672; $224 per quarter. Tuition and fees vary according to program and student level.
Website: http://creees.stanford.edu/

University of Alberta, Faculty of Graduate Studies and Research, Department of Modern Languages and Cultural Studies, Edmonton, AB T6G 2E1, Canada. Offers applied linguistics (Germanic, Romance, Slavic) (MA); French language, literatures and linguistics (PhD); French language, literatures, and linguistics (MA); Germanic languages, literatures and linguistics (PhD); Germanic languages, literatures, and linguistics (MA); Italian studies (MA); Slavic languages and literatures (Russian, Ukrainian) (MA, PhD); Slavic linguistics (Russian, Ukrainian) (MA, PhD); Spanish and Latin American studies (MA, PhD); Ukrainian folklore (MA, PhD). *Program availability:* Part-time. *Degree requirements:* For master's, one foreign language, thesis; for doctorate, 2 foreign languages, comprehensive exam, thesis/dissertation. *Entrance requirements:* For master's and doctorate, 1 language other than English. Additional exam requirements/recommendations for international students: required—Michigan

English Language Assessment Battery or TOEFL (minimum score 550 paper-based). Electronic applications accepted.

The University of British Columbia, Faculty of Arts, Department of Central, Eastern and Northern European Studies, Vancouver, BC V6T 1Z1, Canada. Offers Germanic studies (MA, PhD). *Program availability:* Part-time. *Degree requirements:* For master's, one foreign language, thesis optional, exam; for doctorate, one foreign language, comprehensive exam, thesis/dissertation. *Entrance requirements:* For master's, BA in German; for doctorate, MA in German. Additional exam requirements/recommendations for international students: required—TOEFL. Electronic applications accepted. *Expenses:* Contact institution.

University of Colorado Boulder, Graduate School, College of Arts and Sciences, Russian Studies Program, Boulder, CO 80309. Offers MA. Electronic applications accepted.

University of Illinois at Chicago, College of Liberal Arts and Sciences, School of Literatures, Cultural Studies and Linguistics, Department of Slavic and Baltic Languages and Literatures, Chicago, IL 60607-7128. Offers Slavic studies (MA, PhD). *Program availability:* Evening/weekend. Terminal master's awarded for partial completion of doctoral program. *Degree requirements:* For doctorate, one foreign language, thesis/dissertation. *Entrance requirements:* For master's and doctorate, GRE General Test, minimum GPA of 3.0. Additional exam requirements/recommendations for international students: required—TOEFL. Electronic applications accepted.

University of Illinois at Urbana-Champaign, Graduate College, College of Liberal Arts and Sciences, Russian, East European, and Eurasian Center, Champaign, IL 61820. Offers MA.

The University of Kansas, Graduate Studies, College of Liberal Arts and Sciences, Center for Russian, East European and Eurasian Studies, Lawrence, KS 66045. Offers foreign area officer (MA); Russian, East European and EurAsian studies (MA, Graduate Certificate); JD/MA. *Program availability:* Part-time. *Students:* 1 (woman) full-time, 1 part-time (0 women). Average age 45. 4 applicants, 100% accepted, 2 enrolled. In 2019, 2 master's awarded. *Entrance requirements:* For master's, GRE General Test, two-page statement of educational and professional objectives, three letters of recommendation, official transcripts, working knowledge of a REES-area language equivalent to at least 2 years. Additional exam requirements/recommendations for international students: required—TOEFL, IELTS. *Application deadline:* For fall admission, 1/1 priority date for domestic and international students. Applications are processed on a rolling basis. Application fee: $65 ($85 for international students). Electronic applications accepted. *Expenses:* Tuition, state resident: full-time $9989. Tuition, nonresident: full-time $23,950. *International tuition:* $23,950 full-time. *Required fees:* $984; $81.99 per credit hour. Tuition and fees vary according to course load, campus/location and program. *Financial support:* Fellowships, research assistantships, and scholarships/grants available. Financial award application deadline: 1/1; financial award applicants required to submit FAFSA. *Unit head:* Vitaly Chernetsky, Acting Director, 785-864-4236, E-mail: vchernetsky@ku.edu. *Application contact:* Clare Thoman, Graduate Admissions Contact, 785-864-9814, E-mail: clarethoman@ku.edu.
Website: http://www.crees.ku.edu/

The University of Manchester, School of Arts, Languages and Cultures, Manchester, United Kingdom. Offers anthropology, media and performance (PhD); applied theatre (PhD); Arab world studies (PhD); archaeology (PhD); art history and visual studies (PhD); arts and cultural management (PhD); arts management and cultural policy (PhD); Chinese studies (PhD); classics and ancient history (PhD); composition (PhD); creative writing (PhD); drama (PhD); East Asian studies (PhD); electroacoustic composition (PhD); English and American studies (PhD); English language (PhD); French studies (PhD); German studies (PhD); history (PhD); humanitarianism and conflict response (PhD); interpreting studies (PhD); Japanese studies (PhD); Latin American cultural studies (PhD); linguistics (PhD); Middle Eastern studies (PhD); museology (PhD); museum practice (PhD); music (PhD); musicology (PhD); Polish studies (PhD); Portuguese studies (PhD); religions and theology (PhD); Russian studies (PhD); Spanish studies (PhD); translation and intercultural studies (PhD).

University of Michigan, Rackham Graduate School, College of Literature, Science, and the Arts, Center for Russian, East European, and Eurasian Studies, Ann Arbor, MI 48109-1042. Offers AM, Certificate, JD/AM, MBA/AM, MPP/AM. *Program availability:* Part-time. *Degree requirements:* For master's and Certificate, one foreign language, thesis. *Entrance requirements:* For master's, GRE General Test, academic statement of purpose; curriculum vitae; official transcripts of post-secondary education; 3 letters of recommendation; writing sample. Additional exam requirements/recommendations for international students: required—TOEFL (minimum score 560 paper-based; 84 iBT). Electronic applications accepted.

The University of North Carolina at Chapel Hill, Graduate School, College of Arts and Sciences, Center for Slavic, Eurasian and East European Studies, Chapel Hill, NC 27599. Offers global studies (MA). *Program availability:* Part-time. *Degree requirements:* For master's, one foreign language, thesis. *Entrance requirements:* For master's, GRE General Test. Additional exam requirements/recommendations for international students: required—TOEFL. Electronic applications accepted.

University of Pittsburgh, University Center for International Studies, Pittsburgh, PA 15260. Offers African studies (Certificate); Asian studies (Certificate); European Union studies (Certificate); global studies (Certificate); Latin American studies (Certificate); Russian and East European studies (Certificate); West European studies (Certificate). *Program availability:* Part-time, evening/weekend, online learning. *Degree requirements:* For Certificate, one foreign language, comprehensive exam (for some programs). *Entrance requirements:* Additional exam requirements/recommendations for international students: required—TOEFL. *Expenses:* Contact institution.

The University of Texas at Austin, Graduate School, College of Liberal Arts, Center for Russian, East European, and Eurasian Studies, Austin, TX 78712-1111. Offers MA, JD/MA, MA/MA, MBA/MA, MGPS/MA, MP Aff/MA. *Program availability:* Part-time. *Degree requirements:* For master's, one foreign language, report or thesis. *Entrance requirements:* For master's, GRE General Test, 3 years of formal language training or equivalent, minimum GPA of 3.0. Electronic applications accepted.

University of Toronto, School of Graduate Studies, Munk School of Global Affairs, Centre for European, Russian and Eurasian Studies, Toronto, ON M5S 1A1, Canada. Offers MA, JD/MA. *Degree requirements:* For master's, one foreign language, language proficiency test. *Entrance requirements:* For master's, minimum B+ average in final year, coursework in Russian/East European subjects, 2 years of study in a relevant language. Additional exam requirements/recommendations for international students: required—TOEFL (minimum score 580 paper-based; 93 iBT), TWE (minimum score 5). Electronic applications accepted.

University of Washington, Graduate School, College of Arts and Sciences, Henry M. Jackson School of International Studies, Russian, East European and Central Asian Studies Program, Seattle, WA 98195. Offers Central Asian studies (MAIS); East European studies (MAIS); Russian studies (MAIS). *Degree requirements:* For master's, one foreign language, thesis. *Entrance requirements:* For master's, GRE General Test, 2 years of relevant language, minimum GPA of 3.0 in last two years. Additional exam requirements/recommendations for international students: required—TOEFL (minimum score 500 paper-based; 92 iBT), IELTS (minimum score 7). Electronic applications accepted.

Yale University, Graduate School of Arts and Sciences, Department of Slavic Languages and Literatures, New Haven, CT 06520. Offers medieval Slavic literature and philology (PhD); Polish literature (PhD); Russian literature (PhD); Slavic languages and literatures and film studies (PhD). *Degree requirements:* For doctorate, 3 foreign languages, thesis/dissertation. *Entrance requirements:* For doctorate, GRE General Test.

Yale University, Graduate School of Arts and Sciences, Program in Russian and East European Studies, New Haven, CT 06520. Offers MA. *Degree requirements:* For master's, 2 foreign languages. *Entrance requirements:* For master's, GRE General Test.

Ethnic Studies

Colorado State University, College of Liberal Arts, Department of Ethnic Studies, Fort Collins, CO 80523-1790. Offers MA. *Degree requirements:* For master's, thesis (for some programs), professional paper. *Entrance requirements:* For master's, personal statement, resume/curriculum vitae, official transcripts, 3 letters of recommendation, minimum GPA of 3.0. Additional exam requirements/recommendations for international students: required—TOEFL (minimum score 550 paper-based; 80 iBT). Electronic applications accepted. *Expenses:* Tuition, state resident: full-time $10,520; part-time $5844 per credit hour. Tuition, nonresident: full-time $25,791; part-time $14,328 per credit hour. *International tuition:* $25,791 full-time. *Required fees:* $2512.80. Part-time tuition and fees vary according to course level, course load, degree level, program and student level.

Cornell University, Graduate School, Graduate Fields of Arts and Sciences, Field of Sociology, Ithaca, NY 14853. Offers economy and society (MA, PhD); gender and life course (MA, PhD); methodology (MA, PhD); organizations (MA, PhD); policy analysis (MA, PhD); political sociology/social movements (MA, PhD); racial and ethnic relations (MA, PhD); social networks (MA, PhD); social psychology (MA, PhD); social stratification (MA, PhD). Terminal master's awarded for partial completion of doctoral program. *Degree requirements:* For master's, thesis; for doctorate, thesis/dissertation, 1 year of teaching experience. *Entrance requirements:* For master's and doctorate, GRE General Test, 2 letters of recommendation, writing sample. Additional exam requirements/recommendations for international students: required—TOEFL (minimum score 550 paper-based; 77 iBT). Electronic applications accepted.

DePaul University, College of Liberal Arts and Social Sciences, Chicago, IL 60614. Offers Arabic (MA); Chinese (MA); critical ethnic studies (MA); English (MA); French (MA); German (MA); history (MA); interdisciplinary studies (MA, MS); international public service (MS); international studies (MA); Italian (MA); Japanese (MA); liberal studies (MA); nonprofit management (MNM); public administration (MPA); public health (MPH); public policy (MPP); public service management (MS); refugee and forced migration studies (MS); social work (MSW); sociology (MA); Spanish (MA); sustainable urban development (MA); women's and gender studies (MA); writing and publishing (MA); writing, rhetoric and discourse (MA); MA/PhD. *Accreditation:* CEPH. *Program availability:* Part-time, evening/weekend, online learning. Terminal master's awarded for partial completion of doctoral program. *Degree requirements:* For master's, variable foreign language requirement, comprehensive exam (for some programs), thesis (for some programs). Electronic applications accepted.

Minnesota State University Mankato, College of Graduate Studies and Research, College of Social and Behavioral Sciences, Department of Ethnic Studies, Mankato, MN 56001. Offers MS. *Degree requirements:* For master's, thesis optional. *Entrance requirements:* For master's, minimum undergraduate GPA of 3.0, baccalaureate degree, at least 9 undergraduate credits in ethnic and cross-cultural areas, knowledge of or skills in two languages, statement of purpose. Electronic applications accepted.

Northern Arizona University, College of Social and Behavioral Sciences, Ethnic Studies Program, Flagstaff, AZ 86011. Offers Graduate Certificate. *Program availability:* Part-time. *Degree requirements:* For Graduate Certificate, comprehensive exam (for some programs). *Entrance requirements:* For degree, undergraduate degree from regionally-accredited institution with minimum GPA of 3.0, or the equivalent. Additional exam requirements/recommendations for international students: required—TOEFL (minimum score 80 iBT), IELTS (minimum score 6.5). Electronic applications accepted.

San Francisco State University, Division of Graduate Studies, College of Ethnic Studies, Program in Ethnic Studies, San Francisco, CA 94132-1722. Offers MA. *Expenses: Tuition, area resident:* Full-time $7176; part-time $4164 per year. Tuition, state resident: full-time $7176; part-time $4164 per year. Tuition, nonresident: full-time $16,680; part-time $396 per unit. *International tuition:* $16,680 full-time. *Required fees:* $1524; $1524 per unit. $762 per semester. Tuition and fees vary according to degree level and program. *Unit head:* Dr. Amy H. Sueyoshi, Dean, 415-338-1693, Fax: 415-338-1739, E-mail: ethnicst@sfsu.edu. *Application contact:* Dr. Katynka Z. Martinez, Graduate Coordinator, 415-338-3182, Fax: 415-338-1739, E-mail: katynka@sfsu.edu.
Website: http://maethnicstudies.sfsu.edu/

United Theological Seminary of the Twin Cities, Graduate Programs, New Brighton, MN 55112-2598. Offers advanced theological studies (Diploma); justice and peace studies (M Div, MA); leadership toward racial justice (M Div, MA, Certificate); Methodist studies (M Div, MA, Certificate); ministry (D Min); ministry renewal and professional development (Certificate); pastoral care and counseling (M Div, MA, MARL); religion and theology (MA); theological and religious studies (Certificate); theology and the arts (M Div, MA); urban ministry (M Div, MA, MARL); women's studies: religion, theology and ministry (M Div, MA). *Accreditation:* ACIPE; ATS. *Program availability:* Part-time, evening/weekend. *Degree requirements:* For master's, thesis; for doctorate, comprehensive exam, thesis/dissertation. *Entrance requirements:* For master's, minimum GPA of 2.75; strong analytical, reflective thinking and writing skills; vocational and academic goals compatible with those of Seminary; for doctorate, M Div or equivalent, minimum GPA of 3.0, 3 years experience in professional ministry; for other advanced degree, BA or equivalent life experience; strong analytical, reflective thinking and writing skills (Certificate); proficiency in English language, previous study of theology at a theological school, recommendation of student's denomination (Diploma). Additional exam requirements/recommendations for international students: required—TOEFL (minimum score 550 paper-based).

The University of British Columbia, Faculty of Arts, Department of Classical, Near Eastern and Religious Studies, Program in Ancient Culture, Religion and Ethnicity, Vancouver, BC V6T 1Z1, Canada. Offers MA. *Degree requirements:* For master's, thesis.

University of California, Berkeley, Graduate Division, College of Letters and Science, Department of Ethnic Studies, Berkeley, CA 94720. Offers PhD. *Degree requirements:* For doctorate, one foreign language, thesis/dissertation, qualifying exam. *Entrance requirements:* For doctorate, minimum GPA of 3.0, 3 letters of recommendation. Electronic applications accepted.

University of California, Riverside, Graduate Division, Department of Ethnic Studies, Riverside, CA 92521. Offers cultural politics and production (PhD). Terminal master's awarded for partial completion of doctoral program. *Degree requirements:* For doctorate, variable foreign language requirement, comprehensive exam, thesis/dissertation. *Entrance requirements:* For doctorate, GRE, writing sample, statement of purpose, personal history statement, 3 letters of recommendation. Additional exam requirements/recommendations for international students: required—TOEFL (minimum score 550 paper-based; 80 iBT); recommended—IELTS (minimum score 7). Electronic applications accepted.

University of California, San Diego, Graduate Division, Department of Ethnic Studies, La Jolla, CA 92093. Offers PhD. *Students:* 32 full-time (24 women), 1 (woman) part-time. 78 applicants, 18% accepted, 5 enrolled. In 2019, 6 doctorates awarded. *Degree requirements:* For doctorate, one foreign language, comprehensive exam, thesis/dissertation. *Entrance requirements:* For doctorate, GRE General Test, writing sample. Additional exam requirements/recommendations for international students: required—TOEFL (minimum score 550 paper-based; 80 iBT), IELTS (minimum score 7). *Application deadline:* For fall admission, 1/8 for domestic students. Application fee: $105 ($125 for international students). Electronic applications accepted. *Financial support:* Fellowships, teaching assistantships, and scholarships/grants available. Financial award applicants required to submit FAFSA. *Unit head:* Dayo Gore, Chair, 858-534-8194, E-mail: dgore@ucsd.edu. *Application contact:* Christa Ludeking, Graduate Coordinator, 858-534-6040, E-mail: ethnicstudiesphd@ucsd.edu.
Website: http://ethnicstudies.ucsd.edu

University of Colorado Boulder, Graduate School, College of Arts and Sciences, Department of Ethnic Studies, Boulder, CO 80309. Offers PhD. Electronic applications accepted. Application fee is waived when completed online.

University of Colorado Denver, College of Liberal Arts and Sciences, Program in Humanities, Denver, CO 80217. Offers community health (MSS); ethnic studies (MH, MSS); humanities (MH, Graduate Certificate); international studies (MSS); philosophy and theory (MH); social justice (MH, MSS); society and the environment (MSS); visual studies (MH); women's and gender studies (MH, MSS). *Program availability:* Part-time, evening/weekend. *Degree requirements:* For master's, 36 credit hours, project or thesis. *Entrance requirements:* For master's, writing sample, statement of purpose/letter of intent, three letters of recommendation. Additional exam requirements/recommendations for international students: required—TOEFL (minimum score 537 paper-based; 75 iBT); recommended—IELTS (minimum score 6.5). Electronic applications accepted. Tuition and fees vary according to course load, program and reciprocity agreements.

University of New Mexico, Graduate Studies, College of Arts and Sciences, Program in Anthropology, Albuquerque, NM 87131-2039. Offers archaeology (MA, MS, PhD); ethnology (MA, MS, PhD); evolutionary anthropology (PhD); public archaeology (MA, MS, PhD). Terminal master's awarded for partial completion of doctoral program. *Degree requirements:* For master's, comprehensive exam (for some programs), thesis or alternative, 1-2 exams; for doctorate, one foreign language, comprehensive exam, thesis/dissertation, exam, proposal, oral defense, skill and/or second language. *Entrance requirements:* For master's and doctorate, GRE General Test, 3 letters of recommendation, letter of interest, transcripts. Additional exam requirements/recommendations for international students: required—TOEFL (minimum score 550 paper-based), IELTS (minimum score 7). Electronic applications accepted. *Expenses:* Tuition, state resident: full-time $7633; part-time $972 per year. Tuition, nonresident: full-time $22,586; part-time $3840 per year. *International tuition:* $23,292 full-time. *Required fees:* $8608. Tuition and fees vary according to course level, course load, degree level, program and student level.

Université Laval, Faculty of Letters, Department of History, Programs in Ethnology of French-Speaking People in North America, Québec, QC G1K 7P4, Canada. Offers MA, PhD. Terminal master's awarded for partial completion of doctoral program. *Degree requirements:* For master's, thesis; for doctorate, comprehensive exam, thesis/dissertation. *Entrance requirements:* For master's and doctorate, English exam (comprehension of written English), knowledge of French. Electronic applications accepted.

Folklore

The George Washington University, Columbian College of Arts and Sciences, Department of American Studies, Washington, DC 20052. Offers American studies (PhD); folk life (MA); historic preservation (MA); material culture (MA). *Program availability:* Part-time, evening/weekend. Terminal master's awarded for partial completion of doctoral program. *Degree requirements:* For master's, comprehensive exam; for doctorate, one foreign language, thesis/dissertation, general exam. *Entrance requirements:* For master's and doctorate, GRE General Test, minimum GPA of 3.0. Additional exam requirements/recommendations for international students: required—TOEFL (minimum score 550 paper-based; 80 iBT).

Indiana University Bloomington, University Graduate School, College of Arts and Sciences, Department of Folklore and Ethnomusicology, Bloomington, IN 47405. Offers ethnomusicology (MA, PhD), including folklore. Terminal master's awarded for partial completion of doctoral program. *Degree requirements:* For master's, one foreign language, comprehensive exam, project, thesis, or exam; for doctorate, 2 foreign languages, comprehensive exam, thesis/dissertation. *Entrance requirements:* For master's, GRE General Test (minimum scores: 151 for Verbal, 150 for Quantitative, 4.5 for Analytical), minimum GPA of 3.0, writing sample, curriculum vitae, 3 letters of recommendation, personal statement; for doctorate, GRE General Test (minimum scores: 151 for Verbal, 150 for Quantitative, 4.5 for Analytical), minimum GPA of 3.0, writing sample, curriculum vitae, 3 letters of recommendation, personal statement, MA. Additional exam requirements/recommendations for international students: required—TOEFL (minimum score 550 paper-based; 79 iBT). Electronic applications accepted. *Expenses:* Contact institution.

Memorial University of Newfoundland, School of Graduate Studies, Department of Folklore, St. John's, NL A1C 5S7, Canada. Offers MA, PhD. *Program availability:* Part-time. *Degree requirements:* For master's, thesis optional; for doctorate, one foreign language, comprehensive exam, thesis/dissertation, oral thesis defense. *Entrance requirements:* For master's, 36 credit hours of course work in folklore, humanities, or social studies; honors degree; for doctorate, MA in folklore or related field. Electronic applications accepted.

Penn State Harrisburg, Graduate School, School of Humanities, Middletown, PA 17057. Offers American studies (MA, PhD); communications (MA); folklore and ethnography (Certificate); heritage and museum practice (Certificate); humanities (MA). *Program availability:* Evening/weekend.

University of Alberta, Faculty of Graduate Studies and Research, Department of Modern Languages and Cultural Studies, Edmonton, AB T6G 2E1, Canada. Offers applied linguistics (Germanic, Romance, Slavic) (MA); French language, literatures and linguistics (PhD); French language, literatures, and linguistics (MA); Germanic languages, literatures and linguistics (PhD); Germanic languages, literatures, and linguistics (MA); Italian studies (MA); Slavic languages and literatures (Russian, Ukrainian) (MA, PhD); Slavic linguistics (Russian, Ukrainian) (MA, PhD); Spanish and Latin American studies (MA, PhD); Ukrainian folklore (MA, PhD). *Program availability:* Part-time. *Degree requirements:* For master's, one foreign language, thesis; for doctorate, 2 foreign languages, comprehensive exam, thesis/dissertation. *Entrance requirements:* For master's and doctorate, 1 language other than English. Additional exam requirements/recommendations for international students: required—Michigan English Language Assessment Battery or TOEFL (minimum score 550 paper-based). Electronic applications accepted.

University of California, Berkeley, Graduate Division, College of Letters and Science, Department of Anthropology, Group in Folklore, Berkeley, CA 94720. Offers MA. *Entrance requirements:* For master's, GRE General Test, minimum GPA of 3.0, 3 letters of recommendation. Additional exam requirements/recommendations for international students: recommended—TOEFL (minimum score 570 paper-based; 90 iBT). Electronic applications accepted.

University of Louisiana at Lafayette, College of Liberal Arts, Department of English, Lafayette, LA 70504. Offers American culture (MA, PhD), including history, sociology; American literature and language (PhD); creative writing (MA, PhD), including creative writing (MA), folklore (MA), rhetoric (MA); folklore (MA, PhD); linguistic studies (MA, PhD); professional writing (PhD); rhetoric (MA, PhD); TESOL studies (MA, PhD). *Program availability:* Part-time. Terminal master's awarded for partial completion of doctoral program. *Degree requirements:* For master's, one foreign language, thesis or alternative; for doctorate, 2 foreign languages, comprehensive exam, thesis/dissertation. *Entrance requirements:* For master's, GRE General Test, minimum GPA of 2.75; for doctorate, GRE General Test, minimum GPA of 3.0. Additional exam requirements/recommendations for international students: required—TOEFL (minimum score 550 paper-based). Electronic applications accepted. *Expenses: Tuition, area resident:* Full-time $5511; part-time $1630 per credit hour. Tuition, state resident: full-time $5511; part-time $1630 per credit hour. Tuition, nonresident: full-time $19,239; part-time $2409 per credit hour. *Required fees:* $46,637.

The University of North Carolina at Chapel Hill, Graduate School, College of Arts and Sciences, Curriculum in Folklore, Chapel Hill, NC 27599. Offers MA. *Degree requirements:* For master's, one foreign language, comprehensive exam, thesis. *Entrance requirements:* For master's, GRE General Test, minimum GPA of 3.0, writing sample. Electronic applications accepted.

University of Oregon, Graduate School, College of Arts and Sciences, Folklore Program, Eugene, OR 97403. Offers independent study: folklore (MA, MS). *Program availability:* Part-time. *Degree requirements:* For master's, one foreign language, project or thesis. *Entrance requirements:* For master's, GRE General Test, minimum GPA of 3.0. Additional exam requirements/recommendations for international students: required—TOEFL.

The University of Texas at Austin, Graduate School, College of Liberal Arts, Department of Anthropology, Program in Cultural Forms, Austin, TX 78712-1111. Offers MA, PhD. *Program availability:* Part-time. Terminal master's awarded for partial completion of doctoral program. *Degree requirements:* For master's, one foreign language, thesis, report; for doctorate, one foreign language, thesis/dissertation. *Entrance requirements:* For master's and doctorate, GRE General Test. Electronic applications accepted.

University of Wisconsin–Madison, Graduate School, College of Letters and Science, Department of German, Nordic, and Slavic, Madison, WI 53706-1380. Offers German (MA, PhD); Scandinavian studies (MA, PhD), including area studies (MA), folklore (PhD), literature, philology; Slavic languages and literature (MA, PhD). *Program availability:* Part-time. *Degree requirements:* For master's, 2 foreign languages, exam; for doctorate, thesis/dissertation, exam. *Entrance requirements:* For master's, minimum GPA of 3.25; for doctorate, minimum GPA of 3.5. Electronic applications accepted.

Utah State University, School of Graduate Studies, College of Humanities and Social Sciences, Department of English, Program in American Studies, Logan, UT 84322. Offers folklore (MA, MS); western American literature and culture (MA, MS). *Program availability:* Part-time, evening/weekend. *Degree requirements:* For master's, thesis or alternative. *Entrance requirements:* For master's, GRE General Test or MAT, minimum GPA of 3.0, 3 letters of recommendation, writing sample. Additional exam requirements/recommendations for international students: required—TOEFL.

Gender Studies

American University, College of Arts and Sciences, Critical Race, Gender, and Culture Studies, Washington, DC 20016. Offers Asian studies (Graduate Certificate); women's, gender, and sexuality studies (Graduate Certificate). *Entrance requirements:* Additional exam requirements/recommendations for international students: required—TOEFL.

American University, College of Arts and Sciences, Department of Economics, Washington, DC 20016-8029. Offers applied microeconomics (Certificate); economics (MA, PhD); gender analysis in economics (Certificate); international economic relations (Certificate); international economics (MA). *Program availability:* Part-time, evening/weekend, 100% online, blended/hybrid learning. Terminal master's awarded for partial completion of doctoral program. *Degree requirements:* For master's, comprehensive exam, thesis or alternative; for doctorate, comprehensive exam, thesis/dissertation. *Entrance requirements:* For master's, GRE; Please visit website: https://www.american.edu/cas/economics/, statement of purpose, transcripts, 2 letters of recommendation, resume; for doctorate, GRE, statement of purpose, transcripts, 2 letters of recommendation, resume; for Certificate, bachelor's degree, statement of purpose, transcripts, resume. Additional exam requirements/recommendations for international students: required—TOEFL (minimum score 600 paper-based; 100 iBT). Electronic applications accepted. *Expenses:* Contact institution.

The American University in Cairo, School of Global Affairs and Public Policy, Cairo, Egypt. Offers gender and women's studies (MA); global affairs (MGA); international and comparative law (LL M); international human rights law (MA); journalism and mass communication (MA); Middle East studies (MA); migration and refugee studies (MA, Diploma); public administration (MPA); public policy (MPP); television and digital journalism (MA). *Program availability:* Part-time, evening/weekend. *Degree requirements:* For master's, comprehensive exam (for some programs), thesis (for some programs). *Entrance requirements:* Additional exam requirements/recommendations for international students: required—TOEFL (minimum score 450 paper-based; 45 iBT), IELTS (minimum score 5). Electronic applications accepted. *Expenses:* Contact institution.

Arizona State University at Tempe, College of Liberal Arts and Sciences, School of Social Transformation, Tempe, AZ 85287-4902. Offers African studies (Graduate Certificate); gender studies (PhD, Graduate Certificate); justice studies (MS, PhD); social and cultural pedagogy (MA); socio-economic justice (Graduate Certificate); PhD/JD. *Program availability:* Part-time. Terminal master's awarded for partial completion of doctoral program. *Degree requirements:* For master's, thesis or alternative, interactive Program of Study (iPOS) submitted before completing 50 percent of required credit hours; for doctorate, comprehensive exam, thesis/dissertation, interactive Program of Study (iPOS) submitted before completing 50 percent of required credit hours. *Entrance requirements:* For master's, GRE or LSAT, minimum GPA of 3.0 or equivalent in last 2 years of work leading to bachelor's degree; for doctorate, GRE or LSAT (for justice studies program), minimum GPA of 3.0 or equivalent in last 2 years of work leading to bachelor's degree. Additional exam requirements/recommendations for international students: required—TOEFL, IELTS, or PTE. Electronic applications accepted.

Brandeis University, Graduate School of Arts and Sciences, Department of Anthropology, Waltham, MA 02454. Offers anthropology/women's, gender, and sexuality studies (MA); Mesoamerican archaeology (MA, PhD); sociocultural anthropology (MA, PhD). *Program availability:* Part-time. *Faculty:* 13 full-time (6 women), 1 (woman) part-time/adjunct. *Students:* 28 full-time (19 women), 1 (woman) part-time; includes 6 minority (1 Black or African American, non-Hispanic/Latino; 3 Asian, non-Hispanic/Latino; 2 Two or more races, non-Hispanic/Latino), 3 international. Average age 27. 50 applicants, 60% accepted, 9 enrolled. In 2019, 6 master's, 2 doctorates awarded. Terminal master's awarded for partial completion of doctoral program. *Degree requirements:* For master's, thesis or alternative, paper; for doctorate, one foreign language, comprehensive exam, thesis/dissertation. *Entrance requirements:* For master's and doctorate, General GRE, transcripts, letters of recommendation, resume, statement of purpose, and writing sample. Additional exam requirements/recommendations for international students: required—TOEFL, IELTS, PTE. *Application deadline:* For fall admission, 1/15 priority date for domestic and international students. Applications are processed on a rolling basis. Application fee: $75. Electronic applications accepted. *Financial support:* In 2019–20, 8 fellowships with full tuition reimbursements (averaging $25,000 per year), 8 teaching assistantships (averaging $3,550 per year) were awarded; scholarships/grants and health care benefits also available. Support available to part-time students. *Unit head:* Dr. Charles Golden, Director of Graduate Studies, 781-736-2217, E-mail: cgolden@brandeis.edu. *Application contact:* Laurel Woolf, Administrator, 781-736-4873, E-mail: lwoolf@brandeis.edu.
Website: http://www.brandeis.edu/gsas/programs/anthropology.html

Brandeis University, Graduate School of Arts and Sciences, Department of English, Waltham, MA 02454-9110. Offers English (MA, PhD); English/women's, gender, and sexuality studies (MA). *Program availability:* Part-time. *Faculty:* 13 full-time (6 women), 6 part-time/adjunct (3 women). *Students:* 39 full-time (24 women); includes 7 minority (3 Black or African American, non-Hispanic/Latino; 2 Asian, non-Hispanic/Latino; 1 Hispanic/Latino; 1 Two or more races, non-Hispanic/Latino), 7 international. Average age 31. 194 applicants, 12% accepted, 8 enrolled. In 2019, 5 master's, 4 doctorates awarded. Terminal master's awarded for partial completion of doctoral program. *Degree requirements:* For master's, one foreign language, thesis or alternative, paper; for doctorate, 2 foreign languages, thesis/dissertation. *Entrance requirements:* For master's and doctorate, General GRE, transcripts, letters of recommendation, resume, writing sample, and statement of purpose. Additional exam requirements/recommendations for international students: required—TOEFL, IELTS, PTE. *Application deadline:* For fall admission, 1/5 for domestic and international students. Application fee: $75. Electronic applications accepted. *Financial support:* In 2019–20, 30 fellowships with full tuition reimbursements (averaging $25,000 per year), 15 teaching assistantships (averaging $3,550 per year) were awarded; scholarships/grants, health care benefits, and tuition waivers also available. Support available to part-time students. *Unit head:* Dr. Ulka Anjaria, Director of Graduate Studies, 781-736-2162, E-mail: uanjaria@brandeis.edu. *Application contact:* Lisa Pannella, Administrator, 781-736-2130, E-mail: chaucer@brandeis.edu.
Website: http://www.brandeis.edu/gsas/programs/english.html

Brandeis University, Graduate School of Arts and Sciences, Department of Near Eastern and Judaic Studies, Waltham, MA 02454-9110. Offers Near Eastern and Judaic studies (MA); near Eastern and Judaic studies/conflict resolution and coexistence (MA); near Eastern and Judaic studies/Jewish professional leadership (MA); near Eastern and Judaic studies/women's, gender, and sexuality studies (MA); teaching of Hebrew (MAT); the bible and ancient near east (PhD). *Program availability:* Part-time. *Faculty:* 21 full-time (8 women), 5 part-time/adjunct (3 women). *Students:* 34 full-time (15 women), 2 part-time (1 woman); includes 8 minority (1 Black or African American, non-Hispanic/Latino; 2 Asian, non-Hispanic/Latino; 3 Hispanic/Latino; 2 Two or more races, non-Hispanic/Latino), 7 international. Average age 34. 76 applicants, 53% accepted, 5 enrolled. In 2019, 3 master's, 3 doctorates awarded. Terminal master's awarded for partial completion of doctoral program. *Degree requirements:* For master's, one foreign language, thesis or alternative, capstone, thesis, or internship; for doctorate, variable foreign language requirement, comprehensive exam, thesis/dissertation. *Entrance requirements:* For master's and doctorate, GRE General recommended, transcripts, letters of recommendation, resume, writing sample, and statement of purpose. Additional exam requirements/recommendations for international students: required—TOEFL, IELTS, PTE. *Application deadline:* For fall admission, 1/15 priority date for domestic and international students. Applications are processed on a rolling basis. Application fee: $75. Electronic applications accepted. *Financial support:* In 2019–20, 9 fellowships with full tuition reimbursements (averaging $25,000 per year), 8 teaching assistantships (averaging $3,550 per year) were awarded; scholarships/grants, health care benefits, and tuition waivers also available. Support available to part-time students. *Unit head:* Dr. Ilana Szobel, Director of Graduate Studies, 781-736-5230, E-mail: szobel@brandeis.edu. *Application contact:* Jean Mannion, Administrator, 781-736-2950, E-mail: mannion@brandeis.edu.
Website: http://www.brandeis.edu/gsas/programs/nejs.html

Brandeis University, Graduate School of Arts and Sciences, Program in Women's, Gender, and Sexuality Studies, Waltham, MA 02454-9110. Offers anthropology/women's, gender, and sexuality studies (MA); English/women's, gender, and sexuality studies (MA); near Eastern and Judaic studies /women's, gender, and sexuality studies (MA); public policy/women's, gender, and sexuality studies (MA); sociology/women's, gender, and sexuality studies (MA); sustainable international development/women's, gender, and sexuality studies (MA); women's, gender, and sexuality studies (MA). *Program availability:* Part-time. *Faculty:* 19 full-time (16 women), 2 part-time/adjunct (both women). *Students:* 6 full-time (all women); includes 2 minority (both Hispanic/Latino). Average age 27. 41 applicants, 54% accepted, 8 enrolled. In 2019, 4 master's awarded. *Degree requirements:* For master's, thesis or alternative. *Entrance requirements:* For master's, GRE General, transcripts, letters of recommendation, resume, statement of purpose, and writing sample. Additional exam requirements/recommendations for international students: required—TOEFL, IELTS, PTE. *Application deadline:* For fall admission, 1/15 for domestic and international students. Application fee: $75. Electronic applications accepted. *Financial support:* Fellowships, scholarships/grants, health care benefits, and tuition waivers available. Support available to part-time students. *Unit head:* Dr. Ellen Schattschneider, Director of Graduate Studies, 781-736-2219, E-mail: eschatt@brandeis.edu. *Application contact:* Alexandra Brandon, Administrator, 781-736-3045, E-mail: abrandon@brandeis.edu.
Website: http://www.brandeis.edu/gsas/programs/wgs.html

Carnegie Mellon University, Dietrich College of Humanities and Social Sciences, Department of History, Pittsburgh, PA 15213-3891. Offers African and African-American diaspora (PhD); culture and power (PhD); labor, politics and social movements (PhD); technology, environment, science and health (PhD); women, gender and the family (PhD). *Program availability:* Part-time. *Degree requirements:* For doctorate, oral and written comprehensive exams, dissertation defense. *Entrance requirements:* For doctorate, GRE General Test. Additional exam requirements/recommendations for international students: required—TOEFL. Electronic applications accepted.

Central European University, Department of Gender Studies, 1051, Hungary. Offers MA, PhD. *Degree requirements:* For master's, one foreign language, thesis; for doctorate, one foreign language, comprehensive exam, thesis/dissertation. *Entrance requirements:* For master's and doctorate, essay, interview, statement of purpose. Additional exam requirements/recommendations for international students: required—TOEFL (minimum score 570 paper-based); recommended—IELTS (minimum score 6.5). Electronic applications accepted.

Central Michigan University, College of Graduate Studies, College of Liberal Arts and Social Sciences, Program in Humanities, Mount Pleasant, MI 48859. Offers humanities (MA), including contemporary issues in the humanities: race, class, and gender, images and ideas of self, Native American issues in modern culture, popular culture studies, the rise of industrial society. *Program availability:* Part-time, evening/weekend. *Degree requirements:* For master's, thesis or alternative. Electronic applications accepted. *Expenses: Tuition, area resident:* Full-time $12,267; part-time $8178 per year. Tuition, state resident: full-time $12,267; part-time $8178 per year. Tuition, nonresident: full-time $12,267; part-time $8178 per year. *International tuition:* $16,110 full-time. *Required fees:* $225 per semester. Tuition and fees vary according to degree level and program.

The College of New Jersey, Office of Graduate and Advancing Education, School of Humanities and Social Sciences, Department of Women's and Gender Studies, Ewing, NJ 08628. Offers gender studies (Certificate). *Program availability:* Part-time. *Entrance requirements:* For degree, two letters of recommendation, official transcripts, essay. Additional exam requirements/recommendations for international students: required—TOEFL. Electronic applications accepted.

Cornell University, Graduate School, Graduate Fields of Arts and Sciences, Field of Sociology, Ithaca, NY 14853. Offers economy and society (MA, PhD); gender and life course (MA, PhD); methodology (MA, PhD); organizations (MA, PhD); policy analysis (MA, PhD); political sociology/social movements (MA, PhD); racial and ethnic relations (MA, PhD); social networks (MA, PhD); social psychology (MA, PhD); social stratification (MA, PhD). Terminal master's awarded for partial completion of doctoral program. *Degree requirements:* For master's, thesis; for doctorate, thesis/dissertation, 1 year of teaching experience. *Entrance requirements:* For master's and doctorate, GRE General Test, 2 letters of recommendation, writing sample. Additional exam requirements/recommendations for international students: required—TOEFL (minimum score 550 paper-based; 77 iBT). Electronic applications accepted.

Delta State University, Graduate Programs, College of Arts and Sciences, Program in Liberal Studies, Cleveland, MS 38733-0001. Offers evolving human voices (MALS); gender and diversity studies (MALS); globalization studies (MALS); Mississippi Delta studies (MALS); philosophy (MALS); religious studies (MALS). *Degree requirements:* For master's, oral and/or written comprehensive exam. *Expenses: Tuition, area resident:* Full-time $7501; part-time $417 per credit hour. Tuition, state resident: full-time $7501; part-time $417 per credit hour. Tuition, nonresident: full-time $7501; part-time $417 per credit hour. *International tuition:* $7501 full-time. *Required fees:* $170; $9.45 per credit hour. $9.45 per semester.

DePaul University, College of Liberal Arts and Social Sciences, Chicago, IL 60614. Offers Arabic (MA); Chinese (MA); critical ethnic studies (MA); English (MA); French (MA); German (MA); history (MA); interdisciplinary studies (MA, MS); international public service (MS); international studies (MA); Italian (MA); Japanese (MA); liberal studies

(MA); nonprofit management (MNM); public administration (MPA); public health (MPH); public policy (MPP); public service management (MS); refugee and forced migration studies (MS); social work (MSW); sociology (MA); Spanish (MA); sustainable urban development (MA); women's and gender studies (MA); writing and publishing (MA); writing, rhetoric and discourse (MA); MA/PhD. *Accreditation:* CEPH. *Program availability:* Part-time, evening/weekend, online learning. Terminal master's awarded for partial completion of doctoral program. *Degree requirements:* For master's, variable foreign language requirement, comprehensive exam (for some programs), thesis (for some programs). Electronic applications accepted.

Eastern Michigan University, Graduate School, College of Arts and Sciences, Department of Women's and Gender Studies, Ypsilanti, MI 48197. Offers MA, Graduate Certificate. *Program availability:* Part-time, evening/weekend. *Faculty:* 2 full-time (both women). *Students:* 4 full-time (all women), 6 part-time (all women); includes 4 minority (1 American Indian or Alaska Native, non-Hispanic/Latino; 1 Hispanic/Latino; 2 Two or more races, non-Hispanic/Latino), 2 international. Average age 30. 7 applicants, 100% accepted, 4 enrolled. In 2019, 9 master's, 1 other advanced degree awarded. *Entrance requirements:* Additional exam requirements/recommendations for international students: required—TOEFL. *Application deadline:* For fall admission, 6/15 for domestic and international students; for winter admission, 9/15 for domestic and international students; for spring admission, 3/1 for domestic and international students. Applications are processed on a rolling basis. Application fee: $45. *Financial support:* Fellowships, research assistantships with full tuition reimbursements, teaching assistantships with full tuition reimbursements, career-related internships or fieldwork, Federal Work-Study, institutionally sponsored loans, scholarships/grants, tuition waivers (partial), and unspecified assistantships available. Support available to part-time students. Financial award applicants required to submit FAFSA. *Unit head:* Dr. Elizabeth Currans, Interim Department Head, 734-487-1177, Fax: 734-487-5029, E-mail: ecurrans@emich.edu. *Application contact:* Dr. Jackie Goodman, Graduate Coordinator, 734-487-1177, Fax: 734-487-5029, E-mail: jgoodma9@emich.edu.
Website: http://www.emich.edu/wgstudies/

George Mason University, College of Humanities and Social Sciences, Interdisciplinary Studies Program, Fairfax, VA 22030. Offers computational social science (MAIS); energy and sustainability (MAIS); folklore studies (MAIS); higher education (MAIS); individualized studies (MAIS); religion, culture, and values (MAIS); social entrepreneurship (MAIS); social justice and human rights (MAIS); war and the military in society (MAIS); women and gender studies (MAIS). *Degree requirements:* For master's, thesis or alternative, experiential learning (for some programs). *Entrance requirements:* Additional exam requirements/recommendations for international students: required—TOEFL (minimum score 575 paper-based; 88 iBT), IELTS (minimum score 6.5), PTE (minimum score 59). Electronic applications accepted.

The George Washington University, Elliott School of International Affairs, Program in Global Gender Policy, Washington, DC 20052. Offers Graduate Certificate.

Georgia State University, College of Arts and Sciences, Institute for Women's, Gender, and Sexuality Studies, Atlanta, GA 30302-3083. Offers MA, Graduate Certificate. *Program availability:* Part-time. *Faculty:* 6 full-time (all women). *Students:* 15 full-time (all women), 5 part-time (all women); includes 10 minority (8 Black or African American, non-Hispanic/Latino; 2 Hispanic/Latino), 3 international. Average age 31. 31 applicants, 61% accepted, 9 enrolled. In 2019, 4 master's, 3 other advanced degrees awarded. *Entrance requirements:* For master's and Graduate Certificate, GRE, two official transcripts from each college or university attended, three letters of recommendation addressing student's ability to undertake graduate study, 750-1000 word statement of purpose, academic writing sample. Additional exam requirements/recommendations for international students: required—TOEFL (minimum score 550 paper-based; 80 iBT). *Application deadline:* For fall admission, 2/15 for domestic and international students. Application fee: $50. Electronic applications accepted. *Expenses: Tuition, area resident:* Full-time $7164; part-time $398 per credit hour. Tuition, state resident: full-time $7164; part-time $398 per credit hour. Tuition, nonresident: full-time $22,662; part-time $1259 per credit hour. *International tuition:* $22,662 full-time. *Required fees:* $2128; $312 per credit hour. Tuition and fees vary according to course load and program. *Financial support:* In 2019–20, research assistantships with full tuition reimbursements (averaging $7,000 per year), teaching assistantships with full tuition reimbursements (averaging $7,500 per year) were awarded; career-related internships or fieldwork, health care benefits, and unspecified assistantships also available. Financial award application deadline: 2/15. *Unit head:* Dr. Stephanie Evans, Fax: 404-413-6585, E-mail: sevans62@gsu.edu. *Application contact:* Dr. Megan Sinnott, Director of Graduate Studies, Fax: 404-413-6585, E-mail: megansinnott@gsu.edu.
Website: https://wgss.gsu.edu/

Indiana University Bloomington, University Graduate School, College of Arts and Sciences, Department of Gender Studies, Bloomington, IN 47405. Offers PhD. Terminal master's awarded for partial completion of doctoral program. *Degree requirements:* For doctorate, comprehensive exam. *Entrance requirements:* Additional exam requirements/recommendations for international students: required—TOEFL (minimum score 550 paper-based, 79 iBT) or IELTS. Electronic applications accepted.

Indiana University Northwest, College of Arts and Sciences, Gary, IN 46408. Offers clinical counseling (MS), including drug and alcohol counseling; community development/urban studies (Graduate Certificate); computer information systems (Graduate Certificate); liberal studies (MLS); race-ethnic studies (Graduate Certificate); women's and gender studies (Graduate Certificate). *Program availability:* Part-time, evening/weekend. *Entrance requirements:* For master's, GRE (recommended for MS), minimum undergraduate GPA of 3.0, bachelor's degree from accredited university (for MS). Electronic applications accepted. *Expenses:* Contact institution.

Instituto Tecnologico de Santo Domingo, Graduate School, Area of Humanities and Social Sciences, Santo Domingo, Dominican Republic. Offers accounting (Certificate); adult education (Certificate); applied linguistics (MA); economics (MA); education (M Ed); educational psychology (MA, Certificate); gender and development (MA, Certificate); humanistic studies (MA); international marketing management (Certificate); international relations in the Caribbean basin (Certificate); intervention systems in family therapy (MA); linguistic and literary communication (Certificate); pedagogical support (MA); social science education (M Ed); sustainable human development (MA); terminal illness and death psychology (Certificate); youth and adult education (M Ed).

Kansas State University, Graduate School, College of Arts and Sciences, Department of Gender, Women and Sexuality Studies, Manhattan, KS 66506. Offers Graduate Certificate. *Entrance requirements:* For degree, minimum GPA of 3.0, letters of recommendation. Additional exam requirements/recommendations for international students: required—TOEFL, TWE, or IELTS.

Loyola University Chicago, Graduate School, Programs in Women's Studies and Gender Studies, Chicago, IL 60660. Offers MA. *Program availability:* Part-time. *Faculty:* 5 full-time (4 women), 1 (woman) part-time/adjunct. *Students:* 14 full-time (13 women), 2 part-time (both women); includes 5 minority (all Hispanic/Latino). Average age 25. 16 applicants, 44% accepted, 4 enrolled. In 2019, 12 master's awarded. *Degree requirements:* For master's, thesis or alternative, can do practicum or internship instead of thesis. Must also do capstone course. *Entrance requirements:* For master's, No, GPA of 3.0, personal statement, 3 letters of reference and writing sample. Additional exam requirements/recommendations for international students: required—TOEFL (minimum score 550 paper-based; 79 iBT), IELTS (minimum score 6.5). *Application deadline:* For fall admission, 6/1 for domestic and international students; for spring admission, 11/1 for domestic and international students. Applications are processed on a rolling basis. Electronic applications accepted. Application fee is waived when completed online. *Expenses: Tuition:* Full-time $18,540; part-time $1033 per credit hour. *Required fees:* $904; $230 per credit hour. *Financial support:* In 2019–20, 7 students received support. Teaching assistantships, health care benefits, tuition waivers (full and partial), and unspecified assistantships available. Financial award application deadline: 4/1. *Unit head:* Dr. Susan Grossman, Graduate Program Director, WSGS, 312-915-6456, E-mail: sgrossm@luc.edu. *Application contact:* Jill Schur, Director of Graduate Enrollment Management, 312-915-8902, E-mail: gradinfo@luc.edu.
Website: https://www.luc.edu/wsgs/

Memorial University of Newfoundland, School of Graduate Studies, Department of Sociology, St. John's, NL A1C 5S7, Canada. Offers gender (PhD); maritime sociology (PhD); sociology (M Phil, MA); work and development (PhD). *Program availability:* Part-time. *Degree requirements:* For master's, comprehensive exam, thesis optional, program journal (M Phil); for doctorate, one foreign language, comprehensive exam, thesis/dissertation, oral defense of thesis. *Entrance requirements:* For master's, 2nd class degree from university of recognized standing in area of study; for doctorate, MA, M Phil, or equivalent. Electronic applications accepted.

Memorial University of Newfoundland, School of Graduate Studies, Interdisciplinary Program in Gender Studies, St. John's, NL A1C 5S7, Canada. Offers MGS. *Program availability:* Part-time. Electronic applications accepted.

Middle Tennessee State University, College of Graduate Studies, College of Liberal Arts, Program in Women's and Gender Studies, Murfreesboro, TN 37132. Offers Graduate Certificate. *Program availability:* Part-time, evening/weekend, online learning. Electronic applications accepted.

Minnesota State University Mankato, College of Graduate Studies and Research, College of Social and Behavioral Sciences, Department of Gender and Women's Studies, Mankato, MN 56001. Offers MS. *Program availability:* Part-time. *Degree requirements:* For master's, comprehensive exam, thesis or alternative. *Entrance requirements:* For master's, minimum GPA of 3.0, essay. Additional exam requirements/recommendations for international students: required—TOEFL.

Murray State University, College of Humanities and Fine Arts, Department of English and Philosophy, Murray, KY 42071. Offers creative writing (MFA); English (MA); English pedagogy and technology (DA); gender studies (Certificate); teaching English to speakers of other languages (TESOL) (MA). *Program availability:* Part-time, 100% online, blended/hybrid learning. *Entrance requirements:* For master's, doctorate, and Certificate, GRE or GMAT, minimum university GPA of 2.75. Additional exam requirements/recommendations for international students: required—TOEFL (minimum score 527 paper-based; 71 iBT). Electronic applications accepted.

Northern Arizona University, College of Social and Behavioral Sciences, Women's and Gender Studies Program, Flagstaff, AZ 86011. Offers Graduate Certificate. *Program availability:* Part-time. *Degree requirements:* For Graduate Certificate, comprehensive exam (for some programs). *Entrance requirements:* Additional exam requirements/recommendations for international students: required—TOEFL (minimum score 80 iBT), IELTS (minimum score 6.5). Electronic applications accepted.

Northwestern University, The Graduate School, Program in Gender and Sexuality Studies, Evanston, IL 60208. Offers Graduate Certificate.

The Ohio State University, Graduate School, College of Arts and Sciences, Division of Arts and Humanities, Department of Women's, Gender and Sexuality Studies, Columbus, OH 43210. Offers MA, PhD. Terminal master's awarded for partial completion of doctoral program. *Entrance requirements:* For master's and doctorate, GRE (if GPA is less than 3.0 for all work), scholarly writing sample. Additional exam requirements/recommendations for international students: required—TOEFL (minimum score 550 paper-based; 79 iBT), Michigan English Language Assessment Battery (minimum score 82); recommended—IELTS (minimum score 7). Electronic applications accepted.

Old Dominion University, College of Arts and Letters, Institute for the Humanities, Norfolk, VA 23529. Offers arts and entrepreneurship (Certificate); cultural and human geography (MA); cultural studies (MA); gender and sexuality studies (MA); health, communication and culture (Certificate); media and popular culture studies (MA); philosophy and religious studies (MA); social justice and entrepreneurship (Certificate); visual studies (MA); world cultures (MA). *Program availability:* Part-time, evening/weekend. *Degree requirements:* For master's, thesis optional, project. *Entrance requirements:* For master's, GRE General Test, minimum GPA of 3.25. Electronic applications accepted.

Oregon State University, College of Liberal Arts, Program in Women, Gender, and Sexuality Studies, Corvallis, OR 97331. Offers feminist leadership (PhD). *Program availability:* Part-time. *Degree requirements:* For master's, one foreign language; for doctorate, thesis/dissertation. *Entrance requirements:* Additional exam requirements/recommendations for international students: required—TOEFL (minimum score 80 iBT), IELTS (minimum score 6.5).

Queen's University at Kingston, School of Graduate Studies, Faculty of Arts and Science, Department of Political Studies, Kingston, ON K7L 3N6, Canada. Offers Canadian politics (MA, PhD); comparative politics (MA, PhD); gender and politics (MA, PhD); international relations (MA, PhD); political theory (MA, PhD). *Degree requirements:* For master's, thesis or alternative; for doctorate, one foreign language, thesis/dissertation, qualifying exams. *Entrance requirements:* Additional exam requirements/recommendations for international students: required—TOEFL (minimum score 600 paper-based).

Rutgers University - New Brunswick, Graduate School-New Brunswick, Program in Women's and Gender Studies, Piscataway, NJ 08854-8097. Offers MA, PhD. *Program availability:* Part-time. *Degree requirements:* For master's, thesis or alternative; for doctorate, comprehensive exam, thesis/dissertation. *Entrance requirements:* For master's and doctorate, GRE General Test, writing sample, 3 letters of recommendation. Additional exam requirements/recommendations for international students: required—TOEFL.

Saint Mary's University, Faculty of Arts, Program in Women and Gender Studies, Halifax, NS B3H 3C3, Canada. Offers MA. *Program availability:* Part-time. *Degree requirements:* For master's, thesis. *Entrance requirements:* For master's, honors degree.

San Diego State University, Graduate and Research Affairs, College of Arts and Letters, Program in Lesbian, Gay, Bisexual and Transgender Studies, San Diego, CA 92182. Offers Graduate Certificate.

Simmons University, Gwen Ifill College of Media, Arts, and Humanities, Boston, MA 02115. Offers behavior analysis (MS, PhD, Ed S); children's literature (MA); dietetics (Certificate); elementary education (MAT); English (MA); gender/cultural studies (MA);

history (MA); nutrition and health promotion (MS); physical therapy (DPT); public health (MPH); public policy (MPP); special education: moderate and severe disabilities (MS Ed); sports nutrition (Certificate); writing for children (MFA). *Program availability:* Part-time. *Faculty:* 10 full-time (9 women), 7 part-time/adjunct (6 women). *Students:* 2 full-time (both women), 67 part-time (57 women); includes 13 minority (3 Black or African American, non-Hispanic/Latino; 4 Asian, non-Hispanic/Latino; 3 Hispanic/Latino; 3 Two or more races, non-Hispanic/Latino), 1 international. Average age 31. 42 applicants, 62% accepted, 23 enrolled. In 2019, 24 master's awarded. *Degree requirements:* For master's, thesis optional. *Entrance requirements:* For master's, GRE, bachelor's degree from accredited college or university; minimum B average (preferred). Additional exam requirements/recommendations for international students: required—TOEFL (minimum score 600 paper-based; 100 iBT). *Application deadline:* For fall admission, 8/1 for domestic and international students; for spring admission, 12/15 for domestic and international students; for summer admission, 5/1 for domestic and international students. Applications are processed on a rolling basis. Application fee: $35. Electronic applications accepted. *Expenses:* Contact institution. *Financial support:* In 2019–20, 14 students received support, including 1 fellowship (averaging $15,360 per year), 13 teaching assistantships (averaging $2,000 per year); scholarships/grants also available. Financial award applicants required to submit FAFSA. *Unit head:* Dr. Brian Norman, Dean, 617-521-2472, E-mail: brian.norman@simmons.edu. *Application contact:* Patricia Flaherty, Director, Graduate Studies Admission, 617-521-3902, Fax: 617-521-3058, E-mail: gsa@simmons.edu.
Website: https://www.simmons.edu/academics/colleges-schools-departments/ifill

Simon Fraser University, Office of Graduate Studies and Postdoctoral Fellows, Faculty of Arts and Social Sciences, Department of Gender, Sexuality and Women's Studies, Burnaby, BC V5A 1S6, Canada. Offers MA, PhD. *Degree requirements:* For master's, thesis or alternative; for doctorate, comprehensive exam, thesis/dissertation. *Entrance requirements:* For master's, minimum GPA of 3.0 (on scale of 4.33) or 3.33 based on last 60 credits of undergraduate courses; for doctorate, minimum GPA of 3.5 (on scale of 4.33). Additional exam requirements/recommendations for international students: recommended—TOEFL (minimum score 580 paper-based; 93 iBT), IELTS (minimum score 7), TWE (minimum score 5). Electronic applications accepted.

Stony Brook University, State University of New York, Graduate School, College of Arts and Sciences, Department of Women's, Gender, and Sexuality Studies, Stony Brook, NY 11794. Offers Certificate. *Faculty:* 7 full-time (6 women), 1 (woman) part-time/adjunct. *Students:* 19 full-time (16 women); includes 5 minority (1 Black or African American, non-Hispanic/Latino; 3 Hispanic/Latino; 1 Two or more races, non-Hispanic/Latino), 6 international. Average age 33. 24 applicants, 42% accepted, 6 enrolled. In 2019, 6 Certificates awarded. *Entrance requirements:* For degree, GRE, minimum GPA of 2.75, 3 letters of recommendation. Additional exam requirements/recommendations for international students: required—TOEFL, IELTS, IELTS: Overall score of 6.5, with no subsection recommended to be below 6; TOEFL iBT: 80 for master's level, 90 for admission to a doctoral program. *Application deadline:* For fall admission, 1/15 for domestic students; for spring admission, 10/1 for domestic students. *Expenses:* Contact institution. *Financial support:* In 2019–20, 28 teaching assistantships were awarded. *Unit head:* Prof. Lisa Diedrich, Professor and Chair, 631-632-1967, E-mail: lisa.diedrich@stonybrook.edu. *Application contact:* Prof. Victoria Hesford, Associate Professor & Director of Graduate Studies, 631-632-7456, E-mail: victoria.hesford@stonybrook.edu.
Website: http://www.stonybrook.edu/commcms/wgss/

Texas Woman's University, Graduate School, College of Arts and Sciences, Department of Multicultural Women's and Gender Studies, Denton, TX 76204. Offers MA, PhD. *Program availability:* Part-time. *Faculty:* 4 full-time (3 women), 1 (woman) part-time/adjunct. *Students:* 8 full-time (all women), 31 part-time (30 women); includes 20 minority (7 Black or African American, non-Hispanic/Latino; 1 American Indian or Alaska Native, non-Hispanic/Latino; 3 Asian, non-Hispanic/Latino; 6 Hispanic/Latino; 3 Two or more races, non-Hispanic/Latino), 3 international. Average age 36. 7 applicants, 100% accepted, 4 enrolled. In 2019, 4 master's, 5 doctorates awarded. *Degree requirements:* For master's, comprehensive exam, thesis or alternative, thesis or coursework; for doctorate, comprehensive exam, thesis/dissertation, exam is a portfolio; dissertation defense. *Entrance requirements:* For master's, 2 letters of reference, personal essay, minimum GPA of 3.0 in last 60 hours of undergraduate work, writing sample, written statement about interests and goals; for doctorate, statement of purpose, writing sample, curriculum vitae/resume, 2 reference letters, minimum GPA of 3.5 in prior graduate level course work. Additional exam requirements/recommendations for international students: required—TOEFL (minimum score 79 iBT); recommended—IELTS (minimum score 6.5), TSE (minimum score 53). *Application deadline:* For fall admission, 3/1 priority date for domestic and international students; for spring admission, 11/1 priority date for domestic students; 7/1 priority date for international students; for summer admission, 5/1 for domestic students, 2/1 priority date for international students. Applications are processed on a rolling basis. Application fee: $50 ($75 for international students). Electronic applications accepted. *Expenses: Tuition, area resident:* Full-time $4973.40; part-time $276.30 per semester hour. *Tuition, state resident:* full-time $4973.40; part-time $276.30 per semester hour. *Tuition, nonresident:* full-time $12,569; part-time $698.30 per semester hour. *International tuition:* $12,569.40 full-time. *Required fees:* $2524.30. Tuition and fees vary according to course level, course load, degree level and program. *Financial support:* In 2019–20, 17 students received support, including 13 teaching assistantships (averaging $11,469 per year); career-related internships or fieldwork, scholarships/grants, health care benefits, and unspecified assistantships also available. Support available to part-time students. Financial award application deadline: 3/1; financial award applicants required to submit FAFSA. *Unit head:* Dr. Christina Bejarano, Chair, 940-898-2119, Fax: 940-898-2101, E-mail: womenstudies@twu.edu. *Application contact:* Korie Hawkins, Associate Director of Admissions, Graduate Recruitment, 940-898-3188, Fax: 940-898-3081, E-mail: admissions@twu.edu.
Website: http://www.twu.edu/ws/

University at Albany, State University of New York, College of Arts and Sciences, Department of Women's, Gender and Sexuality Studies, Albany, NY 12222-0001. Offers MA. *Program availability:* Evening/weekend, blended/hybrid learning. *Faculty:* 5 full-time (all women), 1 (woman) part-time/adjunct. *Students:* 11 full-time (10 women); includes 5 minority (3 Black or African American, non-Hispanic/Latino; 1 Hispanic/Latino; 1 Two or more races, non-Hispanic/Latino), 3 international. 22 applicants, 86% accepted, 7 enrolled. In 2019, 9 master's awarded. *Entrance requirements:* For master's, transcripts of all schools attended, statement of background and goals, departmental questionnaire, resume, names and contact information for 3 recommenders. Additional exam requirements/recommendations for international students: required—TOEFL (minimum score 550 paper-based). *Application deadline:* For fall admission, 8/1 for domestic students, 5/1 for international students; for spring admission, 11/15 for domestic students. Applications are processed on a rolling basis. Application fee: $75. Electronic applications accepted. *Expenses: Tuition, area resident:* Full-time $11,530; part-time $480 per credit hour. *Tuition, nonresident:* full-time $23,530; part-time $980 per credit hour. *International tuition:* $23,530 full-time. *Required fees:* $2185; $96 per credit hour. Part-time tuition and fees vary according to course load and program. *Unit head:* Janell Hobson, Chair, 518-442-4220, Fax: 518-442-4419, E-mail: jhobson@albany.edu.

Application contact: Michael DeRensis, Director, Graduate Admissions, 518-442-3980, Fax: 518-442-3922, E-mail: graduate@albany.edu.
Website: https://www.albany.edu/ws/

University at Buffalo, the State University of New York, Graduate School, College of Arts and Sciences, Department of Transnational Studies, Buffalo, NY 14214. Offers American studies (MA, PhD); Canadian studies (MA); global gender studies (MA, PhD). *Program availability:* Part-time. Terminal master's awarded for partial completion of doctoral program. *Degree requirements:* For master's, comprehensive exam (for some programs), thesis optional; for doctorate, comprehensive exam, thesis/dissertation. *Entrance requirements:* For master's, minimum GPA of 3.0; for doctorate, GRE, minimum GPA of 3.0. Additional exam requirements/recommendations for international students: required—TOEFL (minimum score 550 paper-based; 79 iBT), IELTS (minimum score 6.5). Electronic applications accepted. *Expenses: Tuition, area resident:* Full-time $11,310; part-time $471 per credit hour. *Tuition, state resident:* full-time $11,310; part-time $471 per credit hour. *Tuition, nonresident:* full-time $23,100; part-time $963 per credit hour. *International tuition:* $23,100 full-time. *Required fees:* $2820.

The University of Arizona, College of Social and Behavioral Sciences, Department of Gender and Women's Studies, Tucson, AZ 85721. Offers MA, PhD, Certificate. *Program availability:* Part-time. *Degree requirements:* For master's, thesis/project. *Entrance requirements:* For master's and doctorate, GRE (minimum score: 500 verbal, 500 quantitative, 4.5 analytical), 3 letters of recommendation. Additional exam requirements/recommendations for international students: required—TOEFL (minimum score 600 paper-based; 100 iBT). Electronic applications accepted.

The University of British Columbia, Faculty of Arts, Institute for Gender, Race, Sexuality, and Social Justice, Vancouver, BC V6T 1Z2, Canada. Offers MA, PhD. *Expenses:* Contact institution.

University of California, Los Angeles, Graduate Division, College of Letters and Science, Program in Gender Studies, Los Angeles, CA 90095. Offers MA, PhD. Terminal master's awarded for partial completion of doctoral program. *Degree requirements:* For master's, comprehensive exam, thesis; for doctorate, one foreign language, thesis/dissertation, written and oral qualifying exams. *Entrance requirements:* For doctorate, GRE General Test, bachelor's degree; minimum undergraduate GPA of 3.0 (or its equivalent if letter grade system not used); writing sample. Additional exam requirements/recommendations for international students: required—TOEFL. Electronic applications accepted.

University of Chicago, Division of the Humanities, Master of Arts Program in the Humanities, Chicago, IL 60637. Offers art history (MA); cinema and media studies (MA); classic languages (MA); comparative literature (MA); creative writing (MA); cultural policy studies (MA); digital humanities (MA); East Asian languages and civilizations (MA); English language and literature (MA); gender and sexuality studies (MA); Germanic studies (MA); linguistics (MA); music (MA); near Eastern languages and civilizations (MA); philosophy (MA); poetics (MA); race, politics and culture (MA); Romance languages and literatures (MA); Slavic languages and literatures (MA); South Asian languages and civilizations (MA); theater and performance studies (MA). *Degree requirements:* For master's, thesis. *Entrance requirements:* For master's, GRE General Test, 10-15 page writing sample, statement of purpose, 3 letters of recommendation, transcripts for all previous degrees and institutions attended. Additional exam requirements/recommendations for international students: required—TOEFL (minimum score 104 iBT), IELTS (minimum score 7). Electronic applications accepted. *Expenses:* Contact institution.

University of Colorado Denver, College of Liberal Arts and Sciences, Program in Humanities, Denver, CO 80217. Offers community health (MSS); ethnic studies (MH, MSS); humanities (MH, Graduate Certificate); international studies (MSS); philosophy and theory (MH); social justice (MH, MSS); society and the environment (MSS); visual studies (MH); women's and gender studies (MH, MSS). *Program availability:* Part-time, evening/weekend. *Degree requirements:* For master's, 36 credit hours, project or thesis. *Entrance requirements:* For master's, writing sample, statement of purpose/letter of intent, three letters of recommendation. Additional exam requirements/recommendations for international students: required—TOEFL (minimum score 537 paper-based; 75 iBT); recommended—IELTS (minimum score 6.5). Electronic applications accepted. Tuition and fees vary according to course load, program and reciprocity agreements.

University of Florida, Graduate School, College of Liberal Arts and Sciences, Center for Women's Studies and Gender Research, Gainesville, FL 32611. Offers gender and development (Graduate Certificate); women's studies (MA, Graduate Certificate); MA/JD; MA/MA. Terminal master's awarded for partial completion of doctoral program. *Degree requirements:* For master's, thesis or project. *Entrance requirements:* For master's, GRE General Test (minimum score 1000), minimum GPA of 3.2. Additional exam requirements/recommendations for international students: required—TOEFL (minimum score 550 paper-based; 80 iBT), IELTS (minimum score 6). Electronic applications accepted.

University of Lethbridge, School of Graduate Studies, Lethbridge, AB T1K 3M4, Canada. Offers addictions counseling (M Sc); agricultural biotechnology (M Sc); agricultural studies (M Sc, MA); anthropology (MA); archaeology (M Sc, MA); art (MA, MFA); biochemistry (M Sc); biological sciences (M Sc); biomolecular science (PhD); biosystems and biodiversity (PhD); Canadian studies (MA); chemistry (M Sc); computer science (M Sc); computer science and geographical information science (M Sc); counseling (MC); counseling psychology (M Ed); dramatic arts (MA); earth, space, and physical science (PhD); economics (MA); education (MA, PhD); educational leadership (M Ed); English (MA); environmental science (M Sc); evolution and behavior (PhD); exercise science (M Sc); French (MA); French/German (MA); French/Spanish (MA); general education (M Ed); geography (M Sc, MA); German (MA); health sciences (M Sc); individualized multidisciplinary (M Sc, MA); kinesiology (M Sc, MA); management (M Sc), including accounting, finance, human resource management and labor relations, information systems, international management, marketing, policy and strategy; mathematics (M Sc); music (M Mus, MA); Native American studies (MA); neuroscience (M Sc, PhD); new media (MA, MFA); nursing (M Sc, MN); philosophy (MA); physics (M Sc); political science (MA); psychology (M Sc, MA); religious studies (MA); sociology (MA); theatre and dramatic arts (MFA); theoretical and computational science (PhD); urban and regional studies (MA); women and gender studies (MA). *Program availability:* Part-time, evening/weekend. *Degree requirements:* For master's, thesis (for some programs); for doctorate, comprehensive exam, thesis/dissertation. *Entrance requirements:* For master's, GMAT (for M Sc in management), bachelor's degree in related field, minimum GPA of 3.0 during previous 20 graded semester courses, 2 years' teaching or related experience (M Ed); for doctorate, master's degree, minimum graduate GPA of 3.5. Additional exam requirements/recommendations for international students: required—TOEFL (minimum score 580 paper-based; 93 iBT). Electronic applications accepted.

University of Maryland, Baltimore County, The Graduate School, College of Arts, Humanities and Social Sciences, Program in Gender and Women's Studies, Baltimore, MD 21250. Offers Postbaccalaureate Certificate. *Program availability:* Part-time,

evening/weekend, online learning. *Students:* 1 applicant. In 2019, 2 Postbaccalaureate Certificates awarded. *Application deadline:* Applications are processed on a rolling basis. Application fee: $0. Electronic applications accepted. *Expenses: Tuition, area resident:* Full-time $659. Tuition, state resident: full-time $659. Tuition, nonresident: full-time $1132. *International tuition:* $1132 full-time. *Required fees:* $140; $140 per credit hour. *Financial support:* In 2019–20, teaching assistantships with partial tuition reimbursements (averaging $7,500 per year) were awarded; health care benefits and unspecified assistantships also available. *Unit head:* Dr. Carole McCann, Director/ Associate Professor, 410-455-2161, E-mail: mccann@umbc.edu. *Application contact:* Kathryn Nee, Coordinator of Domestic Admissions, 410-455-2944, E-mail: nee@umbc.edu.
Website: https://gwst.umbc.edu/gwst-post-bac-certificate/

University of Memphis, Graduate School, College of Arts and Sciences, Program in Interdisciplinary Studies, Memphis, TN 38152. Offers museum studies (Graduate Certificate); women's and gender studies (Graduate Certificate). *Students:* 10 full-time (7 women), 5 part-time (1 woman); includes 6 minority (2 Black or African American, non-Hispanic/Latino; 3 Asian, non-Hispanic/Latino; 1 Two or more races, non-Hispanic/ Latino), 3 international. Average age 31. 4 applicants, 100% accepted, 1 enrolled. In 2019, 2 Graduate Certificates awarded. *Degree requirements:* For Graduate Certificate, minimum GPA of 3.0. *Entrance requirements:* For degree, GRE, letter of interest, undergraduate transcript. Additional exam requirements/recommendations for international students: required—TOEFL (minimum score 550 paper-based). *Application deadline:* For fall admission, 4/3 for domestic students. Application fee: $35 ($60 for international students). *Expenses: Tuition, area resident:* Full-time $9216; part-time $512 per credit hour. Tuition, state resident: full-time $9216; part-time $512 per credit hour. Tuition, nonresident: full-time $12,672; part-time $704 per credit hour. *International tuition:* $16,128 full-time. *Required fees:* $1530; $85 per credit hour. Tuition and fees vary according to program. *Financial support:* Research assistantships with full tuition reimbursements, teaching assistantships with full tuition reimbursements, Federal Work-Study, scholarships/grants, and unspecified assistantships available. Financial award application deadline: 2/1; financial award applicants required to submit FAFSA. *Unit head:* Dr. Robert Marczynski, Director, 901-678-3516, E-mail: marczyns@memphis.edu. *Application contact:* Dr. Robert Marczynski, Director, 901-678-3516, E-mail: marczyns@memphis.edu.
Website: http://www.memphis.edu/isc/

University of Michigan–Flint, College of Arts and Sciences, Program in Social Sciences, Flint, MI 48502-1950. Offers gender studies (MA); global studies (MA); U.S. history and politics (MA). *Program availability:* Part-time. *Faculty:* 11 full-time (6 women), 4 part-time/adjunct (all women). *Students:* 3 full-time (2 women), 7 part-time (5 women); includes 4 minority (3 Black or African American, non-Hispanic/Latino; 1 Two or more races, non-Hispanic/Latino). Average age 43. 15 applicants, 60% accepted, 2 enrolled. In 2019, 4 master's awarded. *Entrance requirements:* For master's, bachelor's degree from regionally-accredited institution, minimum overall undergraduate GPA of 3.0 on 4.0 scale. Additional exam requirements/recommendations for international students: required—TOEFL (minimum score 84 iBT), IELTS (minimum score 6.5). *Application deadline:* For fall admission, 8/1 for domestic students, 5/1 for international students; for winter admission, 11/15 for domestic students, 10/1 for international students; for spring admission, 3/15 for domestic students, 1/1 for international students; for summer admission, 5/15 for domestic students. Applications are processed on a rolling basis. Application fee: $55. Electronic applications accepted. *Expenses:* Contact institution. *Financial support:* Federal Work-Study, scholarships/grants, and unspecified assistantships available. Financial award application deadline: 3/1; financial award applicants required to submit FAFSA. *Unit head:* Dr. Adam Lutzker, Director, 810-762-3470, Fax: 810-762-3281, E-mail: alutzker@umflint.edu. *Application contact:* Matt Bohlen, Associate Director of Graduate Programs, 810-762-3171, Fax: 810-766-6789, E-mail: mbohlen@umflint.edu.
Website: http://www.umflint.edu/graduateprograms/social-sciences-ma

University of Missouri–St. Louis, College of Arts and Sciences, Interdisciplinary Courses, St. Louis, MO 63121. Offers gender studies (Certificate); international studies (Certificate). *Entrance requirements:* Additional exam requirements/recommendations for international students: required—TOEFL (minimum score 550 paper-based; 79 iBT), IELTS (minimum score 6.5). *Expenses: Tuition, area resident:* Full-time $9005.40; part-time $6003.60 per credit hour. Tuition, state resident: full-time $9005.40; part-time $6003.60 per credit hour. Tuition, nonresident: full-time $22,108; part-time $14,738.40 per credit hour. *International tuition:* $22,108 full-time. Tuition and fees vary according to course load.

The University of North Carolina at Charlotte, College of Liberal Arts and Sciences, Interdisciplinary Liberal Arts and Sciences Programs, Charlotte, NC 28223-0001. Offers gender, sexuality and women's studies (Graduate Certificate); gerontology (MA, Graduate Certificate); Latin American studies (MA); liberal studies (MA); organizational science (PhD); public policy (PhD). *Program availability:* Part-time, evening/weekend. *Students:* 74 full-time (50 women), 56 part-time (43 women); includes 41 minority (16 Black or African American, non-Hispanic/Latino; 3 Asian, non-Hispanic/Latino; 16 Hispanic/Latino; 6 Two or more races, non-Hispanic/Latino), 16 international. Average age 33. 101 applicants, 51% accepted, 37 enrolled. In 2019, 21 master's, 5 doctorates, 8 other advanced degrees awarded. *Entrance requirements:* For master's, GRE General Test or MAT, bachelor's degree from accredited college or university; official transcripts of all previous academic work attempted beyond high school with minimum overall GPA of 3.0; statement of purpose; recommendation letters; for doctorate, GRE or GMAT, statement of purpose discussing interest in program and objectives for pursuing degree, current resume or curriculum vitae, unofficial transcripts; for Graduate Certificate, bachelor's degree from accredited university and either enrolled and in good standing in a graduate degree program at UNC Charlotte or have a minimum undergraduate GPA of 3.0. Additional exam requirements/recommendations for international students: required—TOEFL (minimum score 557 paper-based; 83 iBT), IELTS (minimum score 6.5), TOEFL (minimum score 557 paper-based, 83 iBT) or IELTS (6.5). *Application deadline:* Applications are processed on a rolling basis. Application fee: $75. Electronic applications accepted. *Expenses:* Tuition, state resident: full-time $4337. Tuition, nonresident: full-time $17,771. *Required fees:* $3093. Tuition and fees vary according to course load, degree level and program. *Financial support:* In 2019–20, 3 students received support, including 2 research assistantships (averaging $6,750 per year), 1 teaching assistantship (averaging $21,000 per year); career-related internships or fieldwork, institutionally sponsored loans, scholarships/grants, unspecified assistantships, and administrative assistantships also available. Support available to part-time students. Financial award applicants required to submit FAFSA. *Unit head:* Dr. Nancy A. Gutierrez, Dean, 704-687-0081, E-mail: ngutierr@uncc.edu. *Application contact:* Kathy B. Giddings, Director of Graduate Admissions, 704-687-5503, Fax: 704-687-3279, E-mail: gradadm@uncc.edu.
Website: http://clas.uncc.edu/academics

The University of North Carolina at Greensboro, Graduate School, College of Arts and Sciences, Program in Women's and Gender Studies, Greensboro, NC 27412-5001. Offers MA, Certificate. Electronic applications accepted.

University of Northern British Columbia, Office of Graduate Studies, Prince George, BC V2N 4Z9, Canada. Offers business administration (Diploma); community health science (M Sc); disability management (MA); education (M Ed); first nations studies (MA); gender studies (MA); history (MA); interdisciplinary studies (MA); international studies (MA); mathematical, computer and physical sciences (M Sc); natural resources and environmental studies (M Sc, MA, MNRES, PhD); political science (MA); psychology (M Sc, PhD); social work (MSW). *Program availability:* Part-time, evening/ weekend, online learning. *Degree requirements:* For master's, thesis; for doctorate, thesis/dissertation. *Entrance requirements:* For master's, GRE, minimum B average in undergraduate course work; for doctorate, candidacy exam, minimum A average in graduate course work.

University of Northern Iowa, Graduate College, MA Program in Women's and Gender Studies, Cedar Falls, IA 50614. Offers MA. *Degree requirements:* For master's, comprehensive exam (for some programs), thesis or alternative. *Entrance requirements:* For master's, minimum GPA of 3.0. Additional exam requirements/recommendations for international students: required—TOEFL (minimum score 500 paper-based; 61 iBT). Electronic applications accepted.

University of Oklahoma, College of Arts and Sciences, Women's and Gender Studies Department, Norman, OK 73019. Offers Graduate Certificate. *Program availability:* Part-time. *Entrance requirements:* Additional exam requirements/recommendations for international students: required—TOEFL (minimum score 79 iBT) or IELTS (minimum score 6.5). Electronic applications accepted. *Expenses:* Tuition, state resident: full-time $6583.20; part-time $274.30 per credit hour. Tuition, nonresident: full-time $21,242; part-time $885.10 per credit hour. *International tuition:* $21,242.40 full-time. *Required fees:* $1994.20; $72.55 per credit hour. $126.50 per semester. Tuition and fees vary according to course load and degree level.

University of Rhode Island, Graduate School, College of Arts and Sciences, Department of English, Kingston, RI 02881. Offers American literature and culture (PhD); British literature and culture (PhD); creative writing (PhD); critical theories (PhD); English (MA); film (PhD); gender studies (PhD); MLIS/MA. *Program availability:* Part-time. *Faculty:* 18 full-time (10 women). *Students:* 29 full-time (19 women), 11 part-time (7 women); includes 2 minority (both Black or African American, non-Hispanic/Latino), 8 international. 15 applicants, 40% accepted, 6 enrolled. In 2019, 2 master's, 9 doctorates awarded. *Entrance requirements:* Additional exam requirements/recommendations for international students: required—TOEFL (minimum score 91 iBT). *Application deadline:* For fall admission, 1/15 for domestic and international students. Application fee: $65. Electronic applications accepted. *Expenses: Tuition, area resident:* Full-time $13,734; part-time $763 per credit. Tuition, state resident: full-time $13,734; part-time $763 per credit. Tuition, nonresident: full-time $26,512; part-time $1473 per credit. *International tuition:* $26,512 full-time. *Required fees:* $1780; $52 per credit. $35 per term. One-time fee: $165. *Financial support:* In 2019–20, 24 teaching assistantships with tuition reimbursements (averaging $19,520 per year) were awarded. Financial award application deadline: 1/15; financial award applicants required to submit FAFSA. *Unit head:* Dr. Travis Williams, Chair, 401-874-9501, E-mail: tdwilliams@uri.edu. *Application contact:* Dr. David Faflik, Director of Graduate Studies, 401-874-4670, E-mail: faflik@uri.edu.
Website: http://www.uri.edu/artsci/eng/

University of Rhode Island, Graduate School, College of Arts and Sciences, Program in Gender and Women's Studies, Kingston, RI 02881. Offers Graduate Certificate. *Faculty:* 3 full-time (all women). *Students:* 1 applicant. In 2019, 4 Graduate Certificates awarded. Application fee: $65. Electronic applications accepted. *Expenses: Tuition, area resident:* Full-time $13,734; part-time $763 per credit. Tuition, state resident: full-time $13,734; part-time $763 per credit. Tuition, nonresident: full-time $26,512; part-time $1473 per credit. *International tuition:* $26,512 full-time. *Required fees:* $1780; $52 per credit. $35 per term. One-time fee: $165. *Unit head:* Dr. Rosaria Pisa, Director, 401-874-2482, E-mail: rpisa@uri.edu. *Application contact:* Donna Hughes, Graduate Program Director, 401-8742757, E-mail: donnahughes@uri.edu.
Website: http://web.uri.edu/gws/graduate-certificate-program/

University of South Florida, College of Arts and Sciences, Department of Women's and Gender Studies, Tampa, FL 33620-9951. Offers MA. *Program availability:* Part-time. *Faculty:* 4 full-time (3 women). *Students:* 6 full-time (all women), 3 part-time (2 women); includes 13 minority (3 Black or African American, non-Hispanic/Latino; 2 Asian, non-Hispanic/Latino; 4 Hispanic/Latino; 4 Two or more races, non-Hispanic/ Latino). Average age 28. 8 applicants, 88% accepted, 4 enrolled. In 2019, 4 master's awarded. *Degree requirements:* For master's, comprehensive exam, thesis (for some programs), thesis or internship or portfolio. *Entrance requirements:* For master's, GRE scores (preferred percentiles for Verbal Reasoning at 75 or better and Analytical Writing at 70 or better), minimum GPA of 3.0, A personal narrative statement of purpose; A writing sample (appropriate examples include a term paper or research paper); Three letters of recommendation; resume or Curriculum Vita (CV). Additional exam requirements/recommendations for international students: required—TOEFL, TOEFL (minimum score 550 paper-based; 79 iBT) or IELTS (minimum score 6.5). *Application deadline:* For fall admission, 2/15 priority date for domestic and international students; for spring admission, 10/15 priority date for domestic students, 9/15 priority date for international students; for summer admission, 2/15 priority date for domestic students, 1/ 15 priority date for international students. Applications are processed on a rolling basis. Application fee: $30. Electronic applications accepted. *Financial support:* In 2019–20, 3 students received support. Teaching assistantships with tuition reimbursements available available. Financial award application deadline: 3/1. *Unit head:* Dr. Diane Price Herndl, Professor and Chairperson, 813-974-0987, Fax: 813-974-0336, E-mail: priceherndl@usf.edu. *Application contact:* Dr. Kim Golombisky, Associate Professor and Graduate Director, 813-974-0986, Fax: 813-974-0336, E-mail: kgolombi@usf.edu.
Website: http://wgs.usf.edu/

University of South Florida, Innovative Education, Tampa, FL 33620-9951. Offers adult, career and higher education (Graduate Certificate), including college teaching, leadership in developing human resources, leadership in higher education; Africana studies (Graduate Certificate), including diasporas and health disparities, genocide and human rights; aging studies (Graduate Certificate), including gerontology; art research (Graduate Certificate), including museum studies; business foundations (Graduate Certificate); chemical and biomedical engineering (Graduate Certificate), including materials science and engineering, water, health and sustainability; child and family studies (Graduate Certificate), including positive behavior support; civil and industrial engineering (Graduate Certificate), including transportation systems analysis; community and family health (Graduate Certificate), including maternal and child health, social marketing and public health, violence and injury: prevention and intervention, women's health; criminology (Graduate Certificate), including criminal justice administration; data science for public administration (Graduate Certificate); digital humanities (Graduate Certificate); educational measurement and research (Graduate Certificate), including evaluation; English (Graduate Certificate), including comparative literary studies, creative writing, professional and technical communication; entrepreneurship (Graduate Certificate); environmental health (Graduate Certificate), including safety management; epidemiology and biostatistics (Graduate Certificate), including applied biostatistics, biostatistics, concepts and tools of epidemiology,

epidemiology, epidemiology of infectious diseases; geography, environment and planning (Graduate Certificate), including community development, environmental policy and management, geographical information systems; geology (Graduate Certificate), including hydrogeology; global health (Graduate Certificate), including disaster management, global health and Latin American and Caribbean studies, global health practice, humanitarian assistance, infection control; government and international affairs (Graduate Certificate), including Cuban studies, globalization studies; health policy and management (Graduate Certificate), including health management and leadership, public health policy and programs; hearing specialist: early intervention (Graduate Certificate); industrial and management systems engineering (Graduate Certificate), including systems engineering, technology management; information studies (Graduate Certificate), including school library media specialist; information systems/decision sciences (Graduate Certificate), including analytics and business intelligence; instructional technology (Graduate Certificate), including distance education, Florida digital/virtual educator, instructional design, multimedia design, Web design; internal medicine, bioethics and medical humanities (Graduate Certificate), including biomedical ethics; Latin American and Caribbean studies (Graduate Certificate); leadership for coastal resiliency planning (Graduate Certificate); mass communications (Graduate Certificate), including multimedia journalism; mathematics and statistics (Graduate Certificate), including mathematics; medicine (Graduate Certificate), including aging and neuroscience, bioinformatics, biotechnology, brain fitness and memory management, clinical investigation, hand and upper limb rehabilitation, health informatics, health sciences, integrative weight management, intellectual property, medicine and gender, metabolic and nutritional medicine, metabolic cardiology, pharmacy sciences; national and competitive intelligence (Graduate Certificate); nursing (Graduate Certificate), including simulation based academic fellowship in advanced pain management; psychological and social foundations (Graduate Certificate), including career counseling, college teaching, diversity in education, mental health counseling, school counseling; public affairs (Graduate Certificate), including nonprofit management, public management, research administration; public health (Graduate Certificate), including assessing chemical toxicity and public health risks, health equity, pharmacoepidemiology, public health generalist, toxicology, translational research in adolescent behavioral health; public health practices (Graduate Certificate), including planning for healthy communities; rehabilitation and mental health counseling (Graduate Certificate), including integrative mental health care, marriage and family therapy, rehabilitation technology; secondary education (Graduate Certificate), including ESOL, foreign language education: culture and content, foreign language education: professional; social work (Graduate Certificate), including geriatric social work/clinical gerontology; special education (Graduate Certificate), including autism spectrum disorder, disabilities education: severe/profound; world languages (Graduate Certificate), including teaching English as a second language (TESL) or foreign language. *Unit head:* Dr. Cynthia DeLuca, Associate Vice President and Assistant Vice Provost, 813-974-3077, Fax: 813-974-7061, E-mail: deluca@usf.edu. *Application contact:* Owen Hooper, Director, Summer and Alternative Calendar Programs, 813-974-6917, E-mail: hooper@usf.edu.
Website: http://www.usf.edu/innovative-education/

The University of Toledo, College of Graduate Studies, College of Languages, Literature and Social Sciences, Department of Women's and Gender Studies, Toledo, OH 43606-3390. Offers Certificate. *Program availability:* Part-time.

University of Toronto, School of Graduate Studies, Faculty of Arts and Science, Women and Gender Studies Institute, Toronto, ON M5S 1A1, Canada. Offers MA, PhD. *Entrance requirements:* For master's, minimum B+ in final year of undergraduate study. Additional exam requirements/recommendations for international students: required—TOEFL (minimum score 580 paper-based; 93 iBT), TWE (minimum score 5). Electronic applications accepted.

University of Wisconsin–Milwaukee, Graduate School, College of Letters and Science, Department of Women's and Gender Studies, Milwaukee, WI 53201-0413.

Offers MA, Graduate Certificate. *Program availability:* Part-time. *Entrance requirements:* For master's, 3 letters of recommendation, sample of written work, letter of intent. Electronic applications accepted.

Wayne State University, College of Liberal Arts and Sciences, Tracy Neumann, Detroit, MI 48202. Offers history (MA, PhD); public history (MA), including African American history and culture, cultural resource management, gender, sexuality, and women's studies, labor and urban history, museum studies, public policy; world history (Graduate Certificate); JD/MA; M Ed/MA; MLIS/MA. *Program availability:* Evening/weekend. *Faculty:* 23 full-time (11 women). *Students:* 18 full-time (7 women), 16 part-time (7 women); includes 4 minority (2 Black or African American, non-Hispanic/Latino; 2 Two or more races, non-Hispanic/Latino). Average age 37. 38 applicants, 34% accepted, 13 enrolled. In 2019, 7 master's, 3 doctorates awarded. *Degree requirements:* For master's, thesis (for some programs), final oral exam on thesis or essay and seminar; internship and project (for public history); for doctorate, variable foreign language requirement, comprehensive exam, thesis/dissertation, qualifying exam in 4 fields of history. *Entrance requirements:* For master's, GRE General Test, minimum undergraduate GPA of 3.25 in history, 3.0 overall; at least 18 credits in history and related subjects at the advanced undergraduate level; foreign language; letter of intent; research paper; at least two letters of recommendation from former instructors; for doctorate, GRE General Test, minimum GPA of 3.0, 3.25 in minimum of 18 semester credits in history and related subjects; letter of intent; research paper; at least three letters of recommendation from former professors; for Graduate Certificate, baccalaureate degree from accredited college or university; minimum GPA of 3.0, 3.25 in a minimum of eighteen semester credits in history and related subjects at the advanced undergraduate level. Additional exam requirements/recommendations for international students: required—TOEFL (minimum score 550 paper-based; 79 iBT), TWE (minimum score 5.5), Michigan English Language Assessment Battery (minimum score 85); recommended—IELTS (minimum score 6.5). *Application deadline:* For fall admission, 1/15 priority date for domestic and international students; for winter admission, 4/15 for domestic students, 4/15 priority date for international students; for spring admission, 10/15 for domestic students, 10/15 priority date for international students. Application fee: $50. Electronic applications accepted. *Expenses: Tuition:* Full-time $34,567. *Financial support:* In 2019–20, 18 students received support, including 2 fellowships with tuition reimbursements available (averaging $20,797 per year), 2 research assistantships with tuition reimbursements available (averaging $23,960 per year), 7 teaching assistantships with tuition reimbursements available (averaging $19,967 per year); scholarships/grants, health care benefits, and unspecified assistantships also available. Financial award applicants required to submit FAFSA. *Unit head:* Dr. Elizabeth V. Faue, Professor/Chair, 313-577-2525, E-mail: evfaue@wayne.edu. *Application contact:* Dr. Tracy Neumann, Associate Professor and Director of Graduate Studies, 313-577-2525, E-mail: tracyneumann@wayne.edu. Website: http://clas.wayne.edu/history/

Wilfrid Laurier University, Faculty of Graduate and Postdoctoral Studies, Faculty of Arts, Cultural Analysis and Social Theory Program, Waterloo, ON N2L 3C5, Canada. Offers body politics (MA); cultural representation and social theory (MA); gender, sexuality and embodiment (MA); globalization, identity and social movements (MA). *Program availability:* Part-time. *Entrance requirements:* For master's, honours BA in humanities, social science or interdisciplinary program with social theory, minimum B+ in final year of full-time study. Additional exam requirements/recommendations for international students: required—TOEFL (minimum score 89 iBT). Electronic applications accepted.

York University, Faculty of Graduate Studies, Faculty of Liberal Arts and Professional Studies, Program in Gender, Feminist and Women's Studies, Toronto, ON M3J 1P3, Canada. Offers MA, PhD. *Degree requirements:* For master's, thesis or alternative; for doctorate, comprehensive exam, thesis/dissertation. Electronic applications accepted.

Hispanic Studies

Brown University, Graduate School, Department of Hispanic Studies, Providence, RI 02912. Offers PhD. *Faculty:* 8 full-time (6 women). *Students:* 17 full-time (13 women); includes 12 minority (1 Black or African American, non-Hispanic/Latino; 9 Hispanic/Latino; 2 Two or more races, non-Hispanic/Latino), 8 international. 51 applicants, 10% accepted, 3 enrolled. In 2019, 2 doctorates awarded. Terminal master's awarded for partial completion of doctoral program. *Degree requirements:* For doctorate, 2 foreign languages, comprehensive exam, thesis/dissertation. *Entrance requirements:* For doctorate, Preliminary written exams based on a reading list of canonical literature of Latin America and Spain; an oral exam based on a reading list related to the dissertation, A dissertation proposal and dissertation. Additional exam requirements/recommendations for international students: required—TOEFL (minimum score 100 paper-based). *Application deadline:* For fall admission, 1/2 priority date for domestic and international students. Application fee: $60. Electronic applications accepted. *Financial support:* In 2019–20, 17 students received support, including 5 fellowships with full tuition reimbursements available (averaging $31,000 per year), 9 teaching assistantships; tuition waivers (full) also available. Financial award application deadline: 1/2. *Unit head:* Laura R. Bass, Chair, 401-8632569, E-mail: laura_bass@brown.edu. *Application contact:* Michelle Clayton, Director of Graduate Studies, 401-863-2569.

California State University, Los Angeles, Graduate Studies, College of Natural and Social Sciences, Department of Chicano Studies, Los Angeles, CA 90032-8530. Offers Mexican-American studies (MA). *Program availability:* Part-time, evening/weekend. *Degree requirements:* For master's, one foreign language, comprehensive exam or thesis. *Entrance requirements:* For master's, undergraduate major in Mexican-American studies or related area, 20 upper-division units in Chicano studies, minimum GPA of 2.75 in last 90 quarter units. Additional exam requirements/recommendations for international students: required—TOEFL (minimum score 500 paper-based). Electronic applications accepted. *Expenses: Tuition, area resident:* Full-time $7176; part-time $4164 per year. Tuition, state resident: full-time $7176; part-time $4164 per year. Tuition, nonresident: full-time $14,304; part-time $8916 per year. *International tuition:* $14,304 full-time. *Required fees:* $1037.76; $1037.76 per unit. Tuition and fees vary according to degree level and program.

California State University, Northridge, Graduate Studies, College of Humanities, Department of Chicana and Chicano Studies, Northridge, CA 91330. Offers MA. *Degree requirements:* For master's, thesis, project. *Entrance requirements:* Additional exam requirements/recommendations for international students: required—TOEFL.

California State University, San Marcos, College of Humanities, Arts, Behavioral and Social Sciences, Program in Spanish, San Marcos, CA 92096-0001. Offers Hispanic cultures and society (MA); Hispanic language and linguistics (MA); Hispanic literatures and literary theory (MA). *Program availability:* Part-time, evening/weekend. *Degree requirements:* For master's, 2 foreign languages, exam. *Entrance requirements:* For master's, GRE General Test, minimum GPA of 3.0 overall and in upper-division Spanish courses, official transcripts, three letters of recommendation, 750-word statement of purpose (in English), academic writing sample (in Spanish). Additional exam requirements/recommendations for international students: required—TOEFL (minimum score 500 paper-based), TWE (minimum score 4.5). Electronic applications accepted. *Expenses: Tuition, area resident:* Full-time $7176. Tuition, state resident: full-time $7176. Tuition, nonresident: full-time $18,640. *International tuition:* $18,640 full-time. *Required fees:* $1960.

The Catholic University of America, School of Arts and Sciences, Department of Modern Languages and Literatures, Washington, DC 20064. Offers Hispanic studies (MA, PhD). *Program availability:* Part-time. *Faculty:* 19 full-time (14 women), 4 part-time/adjunct (all women). *Students:* 2 full-time (0 women), 6 part-time (4 women); includes 1 minority (Two or more races, non-Hispanic/Latino), 5 international. Average age 44. 2 applicants, 50% accepted, 1 enrolled. In 2019, 1 master's awarded. *Degree requirements:* For master's, comprehensive exam; for doctorate, one foreign language, comprehensive exam, thesis/dissertation, annotated bibliography; oral defense of the proposal; oral defense of the dissertation. *Entrance requirements:* For master's, GRE General Test, statement of purpose, official copies of academic transcripts, two letters of recommendation, sample of academic writing; for doctorate, GRE General Test, statement of purpose, official copies of academic transcripts, three letters of recommendation, sample of academic writing (20-25-pages long). Additional exam requirements/recommendations for international students: required—TOEFL (minimum score 550 paper-based; 80 iBT). *Application deadline:* For fall admission, 7/15 priority date for domestic students, 7/1 for international students; for spring admission, 11/15 priority date for domestic students, 11/1 for international students. Applications are processed on a rolling basis. Application fee: $55. Electronic applications accepted. *Expenses:* Contact institution. *Financial support:* Fellowships, research assistantships, teaching assistantships, Federal Work-Study, scholarships/grants, tuition waivers (full and partial), and unspecified assistantships available. Financial award application deadline: 2/1; financial award applicants required to submit FAFSA. *Unit head:* Dr. Claudia Bornholdt, Chair, 202-319-5240, Fax: 202-319-6077, E-mail: kassen@cua.edu.

Hispanic Studies

Application contact: Dr. Steven Brown, Director of Graduate Admissions, 202-319-5057, Fax: 202-319-6533, E-mail: cua-admissions@cua.edu. Website: http://modernlanguages.cua.edu/

The Citadel, The Military College of South Carolina, Citadel Graduate College, School of Humanities and Social Sciences, Department of Modern Languages, Literatures and Cultures, Charleston, SC 29409. Offers Hispanic studies (Graduate Certificate). *Entrance requirements:* Additional exam requirements/recommendations for international students: required—TOEFL (minimum score 550 paper-based; 79 iBT). Electronic applications accepted.

Columbia University, Graduate School of Arts and Sciences, New York, NY 10027. Offers African-American studies (MA); American studies (MA); anthropology (MA, PhD); art history and archaeology (MA, PhD); astronomy (PhD); biological sciences (PhD); biotechnology (MA); chemical physics (PhD); chemistry (PhD); classical studies (MA, PhD); classics (MA, PhD); climate and society (MA); conservation biology (MA); earth and environmental sciences (PhD); East Asia: regional studies (MA); East Asian languages and cultures (MA, PhD); ecology, evolution and environmental biology (MA), including conservation biology; ecology, evolution, and environmental biology (PhD), including ecology and evolutionary biology, evolutionary primatology; economics (MA, PhD); English and comparative literature (MA, PhD); French and Romance philology (MA, PhD); Germanic languages (MA, PhD); global French studies (MA); global thought (MA); Hispanic cultural studies (MA); history (PhD); history and literature (MA); human rights studies (MA); Islamic studies (MA); Italian (MA, PhD); Japanese pedagogy (MA); Jewish studies (MA); Latin America and the Caribbean: regional studies (MA); Latin American and Iberian cultures (PhD); mathematics (MA, PhD), including finance (MA); medieval and Renaissance studies (MA); Middle Eastern, South Asian, and African studies (MA, PhD); modern art: critical and curatorial studies (MA); modern European studies (MA); museum anthropology (MA); music (DMA, PhD); oral history (MA); philosophical foundations of physics (MA); philosophy (MA, PhD); physics (PhD); political science (MA, PhD); psychology (PhD); quantitative methods in the social sciences (MA); religion (MA, PhD); Russia, Eurasia and East Europe: regional studies (MA); Russian translation (MA); Slavic cultures (MA); Slavic languages (MA, PhD); sociology (MA, PhD); South Asian studies (MA); statistics (MA, PhD); theatre (PhD). *Program availability:* Part-time. *Students:* 3,506 full-time (1,844 women), 208 part-time (121 women); includes 864 minority (110 Black or African American, non-Hispanic/Latino; 5 American Indian or Alaska Native, non-Hispanic/Latino; 416 Asian, non-Hispanic/Latino; 147 Hispanic/Latino; 6 Native Hawaiian or other Pacific Islander, non-Hispanic/Latino; 180 Two or more races, non-Hispanic/Latino), 2,065 international. 14,545 applicants, 25% accepted, 1,429 enrolled. In 2019, 1,262 master's, 363 doctorates awarded. Terminal master's awarded for partial completion of doctoral program. *Degree requirements:* For master's, variable foreign language requirement, comprehensive exam (for some programs), thesis (for some programs); for doctorate, variable foreign language requirement, comprehensive exam (for some programs), thesis/dissertation. *Entrance requirements:* For master's and doctorate, GRE General Test, GRE Subject Test (for some programs). Additional exam requirements/recommendations for international students: required—TOEFL (minimum score 600 paper-based; 100 iBT), IELTS (minimum score 7.5). Application fee: $115. Electronic applications accepted. *Expenses: Tuition:* Full-time $47,600; part-time $1880 per credit. One-time fee: $105. *Financial support:* Fellowships, research assistantships, teaching assistantships, career-related internships or fieldwork, Federal Work-Study, institutionally sponsored loans, scholarships/grants, traineeships, health care benefits, tuition waivers, and unspecified assistantships available. Support available to part-time students. Financial award application deadline: 12/15. *Unit head:* Dr. Carlos J. Alonso, Dean of the Graduate School of Arts and Sciences and Vice President for Graduate Education, 212-854-2861, E-mail: gsas-dean@columbia.edu. *Application contact:* GSAS Office of Admissions, 212-854-6729, E-mail: gsas-admissions@columbia.edu. Website: http://gsas.columbia.edu/

La Salle University, School of Arts and Sciences, Hispanic Institute, Philadelphia, PA 19141-1199. Offers bilingual/bicultural studies (MA); ESL program specialist (Certificate); interpretation: English/Spanish-Spanish/English (Certificate); teaching English to speakers of other languages (MA); translation and interpretation (MA); translation: English/Spanish-Spanish/English (Certificate). *Program availability:* Part-time, evening/weekend. *Degree requirements:* For master's, one foreign language, project or thesis. *Entrance requirements:* For master's, GRE, MAT, or GMAT, professional resume; two letters of recommendation; for Certificate, GRE, MAT, or GMAT, professional resume; two letters of recommendation; evidence of an advanced level in Spanish. Additional exam requirements/recommendations for international students: required—TOEFL. Electronic applications accepted. Application fee is waived when completed online. *Expenses:* Contact institution.

Louisiana State University and Agricultural & Mechanical College, Graduate School, College of Humanities and Social Sciences, Department of Foreign Languages and Literatures, Baton Rouge, LA 70803. Offers Hispanic studies (MA).

McGill University, Faculty of Graduate and Postdoctoral Studies, Faculty of Arts, Department of Hispanic Studies, Montréal, QC H3A 2T5, Canada. Offers MA, PhD.

Michigan State University, The Graduate School, College of Arts and Letters, Department of Romance and Classical Studies, East Lansing, MI 48824. Offers French (MA); French language and literature (PhD); Hispanic cultural studies (PhD); Hispanic literatures (MA); Spanish as a second or bilingual language (MA). *Entrance requirements:* Additional exam requirements/recommendations for international students: required—TOEFL. Electronic applications accepted.

Oregon State University, College of Liberal Arts, Program in Contemporary Hispanic Studies, Corvallis, OR 97331. Offers MA. *Entrance requirements:* For master's, ACTFL OPI (Oral Proficiency Interview).

Pontifical Catholic University of Puerto Rico, College of Arts and Humanities, Department of Hispanic Studies, Ponce, PR 00717-0777. Offers grammar and writing (Professional Certificate); Hispanic studies (MA). *Program availability:* Part-time, evening/weekend. *Degree requirements:* For master's, variable foreign language requirement, comprehensive exam, thesis or alternative. *Entrance requirements:* For master's, GRE General Test, 2 letters of recommendation, interview, minimum GPA of 2.75. Electronic applications accepted.

St. Thomas University - Florida, School of Leadership Studies, Program in Hispanic Media, Miami Gardens, FL 33054-6459. Offers MA, Certificate. *Program availability:* Part-time, evening/weekend. *Degree requirements:* For master's, comprehensive exam. *Entrance requirements:* Additional exam requirements/recommendations for international students: required—TOEFL (minimum score 550 paper-based; 79 iBT). Electronic applications accepted.

Stephen F. Austin State University, Graduate School, College of Liberal and Applied Arts, Department of Languages, Cultures and Communication, Nacogdoches, TX 75962. Offers communication (MA); Hispanic studies (MA). *Program availability:* Part-time. *Degree requirements:* For master's, comprehensive exam, thesis optional. *Entrance requirements:* For master's, GRE General Test. Additional exam requirements/recommendations for international students: required—TOEFL (minimum score 550 paper-based).

Texas A&M University–Kingsville, College of Graduate Studies, College of Arts and Sciences, Department of Language and Literature, Interdisciplinary Program in Hispanic Culture, Kingsville, TX 78363. Offers PhD. *Degree requirements:* For doctorate, variable foreign language requirement, comprehensive exam, thesis/dissertation. *Entrance requirements:* For doctorate, GRE, MAT, GMAT, minimum GPA of 3.2, at least three letters of recommendation, demonstrated oral and written proficiency in Spanish. Additional exam requirements/recommendations for international students: required—TOEFL (minimum score 550 paper-based; 79 iBT). Electronic applications accepted.

University of Alberta, Faculty of Graduate Studies and Research, Department of Modern Languages and Cultural Studies, Edmonton, AB T6G 2E1, Canada. Offers applied linguistics (Germanic, Romance, Slavic) (MA); French language, literatures and linguistics (PhD); French language, literatures, and linguistics (MA); Germanic languages, literatures and linguistics (PhD); Germanic languages, literatures, and linguistics (MA); Italian studies (MA); Slavic languages and literatures (Russian, Ukrainian) (MA, PhD); Slavic linguistics (Russian, Ukrainian) (MA, PhD); Spanish and Latin American studies (MA, PhD); Ukrainian folklore (MA, PhD). *Program availability:* Part-time. *Degree requirements:* For master's, one foreign language, thesis; for doctorate, 2 foreign languages, comprehensive exam, thesis/dissertation. *Entrance requirements:* For master's and doctorate, 1 language other than English. Additional exam requirements/recommendations for international students: required—Michigan English Language Assessment Battery or TOEFL (minimum score 550 paper-based). Electronic applications accepted.

The University of British Columbia, Faculty of Arts, Department of French, Hispanic and Italian Studies, Vancouver, BC V6T 1Z1, Canada. Offers French (MA, PhD); Hispanic studies (MA, PhD). *Program availability:* Part-time. *Degree requirements:* For master's, thesis optional; for doctorate, 2 foreign languages, comprehensive exam, thesis/dissertation. *Entrance requirements:* For doctorate, MA. Additional exam requirements/recommendations for international students: required—TOEFL. Electronic applications accepted. *Expenses:* Contact institution.

University of California, Riverside, Graduate Division, Department of Hispanic Studies, Riverside, CA 92521-0102. Offers Spanish (MA, PhD). Terminal master's awarded for partial completion of doctoral program. *Degree requirements:* For master's, one foreign language, comprehensive exam; for doctorate, one foreign language, thesis/dissertation, qualifying exams, 1 quarter of teaching experience. *Entrance requirements:* For master's and doctorate, GRE General Test, minimum GPA of 3.0. Additional exam requirements/recommendations for international students: required—TOEFL (minimum score 550 paper-based; 80 iBT). Electronic applications accepted.

University of California, Santa Barbara, Graduate Division, College of Letters and Sciences, Division of Humanities and Fine Arts, Department of Spanish and Portuguese, Santa Barbara, CA 93106-4150. Offers Hispanic languages and literatures (PhD), including European medieval studies, feminist studies, Hispanic linguistics, Hispanic literature, Luso-Brazilian literature; Hispanic linguistics (MA); Luso-Brazilian literature (MA); Spanish or Spanish-American literature (MA); MA/PhD. Terminal master's awarded for partial completion of doctoral program. *Degree requirements:* For master's, 2 foreign languages, comprehensive exam (for some programs), thesis optional; for doctorate, 3 foreign languages, comprehensive exam, thesis/dissertation. *Entrance requirements:* For master's and doctorate, GRE. Additional exam requirements/recommendations for international students: required—TOEFL (minimum score 550 paper-based; 80 iBT), IELTS (minimum score 7). Electronic applications accepted.

University of California, Santa Barbara, Graduate Division, College of Letters and Sciences, Division of Social Sciences, Department of Chicana and Chicano Studies, Santa Barbara, CA 93106-4120. Offers MA/PhD. *Entrance requirements:* Additional exam requirements/recommendations for international students: required—TOEFL (minimum score 550 paper-based; 80 iBT), IELTS (minimum score 7). Electronic applications accepted.

University of Houston, College of Liberal Arts and Social Sciences, Department of Hispanic Studies, Houston, TX 77204. Offers Hispanic literature and linguistics (PhD); Spanish (MA, PhD), including creative writing (PhD). *Program availability:* Part-time. *Degree requirements:* For master's, comprehensive exam, thesis optional; for doctorate, 2 foreign languages, comprehensive exam, thesis/dissertation. *Entrance requirements:* For master's and doctorate, GRE. Additional exam requirements/recommendations for international students: required—TOEFL (minimum score 550 paper-based; 79 iBT); recommended—IELTS (minimum score 6.5). Electronic applications accepted.

University of Illinois at Chicago, College of Liberal Arts and Sciences, School of Literatures, Cultural Studies and Linguistics, Department of Hispanic and Italian Studies, Chicago, IL 60607-7128. Offers Hispanic linguistics (PhD). *Program availability:* Part-time. Terminal master's awarded for partial completion of doctoral program. *Degree requirements:* For master's, one foreign language, departmental qualifying exam. *Entrance requirements:* For master's, GRE General Test, minimum GPA of 2.75, undergraduate major in Spanish. Additional exam requirements/recommendations for international students: required—TOEFL. Electronic applications accepted.

University of Kentucky, Graduate School, College of Arts and Sciences, Program in Hispanic Studies, Lexington, KY 40506-0032. Offers MA, PhD. *Degree requirements:* For master's, one foreign language, comprehensive exam, thesis optional; for doctorate, 2 foreign languages, comprehensive exam, thesis/dissertation. *Entrance requirements:* For master's, GRE General Test, minimum undergraduate GPA of 2.75; for doctorate, GRE General Test, minimum graduate GPA of 3.0. Additional exam requirements/recommendations for international students: required—TOEFL (minimum score 550 paper-based). Electronic applications accepted.

University of Nevada, Las Vegas, Graduate College, College of Liberal Arts, Department of World Languages and Cultures, Las Vegas, NV 89154-5047. Offers Hispanic studies (MA); Spanish translation (Certificate). *Program availability:* Part-time. *Faculty:* 5 full-time (4 women). *Students:* 2 full-time (both women), 6 part-time (4 women); includes 5 minority (1 Asian, non-Hispanic/Latino; 4 Hispanic/Latino), 2 international. Average age 37. 9 applicants, 44% accepted, 1 enrolled. In 2019, 5 master's awarded. *Degree requirements:* For master's, one foreign language, comprehensive exam, final research project. *Entrance requirements:* For master's, minimum GPA of 3.0; 2 letters of recommendation. Additional exam requirements/recommendations for international students: required—TOEFL (minimum score 550 paper-based; 80 iBT), IELTS (minimum score 7). *Application deadline:* For fall admission, 5/1 for domestic and international students; for spring admission, 11/15 for domestic students, 10/1 for international students. Application fee: $60 ($95 for international students). Electronic applications accepted. *Expenses:* Contact institution. *Financial support:* In 2019–20, 3 students received support, including 3 teaching assistantships with full tuition reimbursements available (averaging $11,250 per year); institutionally sponsored loans, scholarships/grants, health care benefits, and unspecified assistantships also available. Financial award application deadline: 3/15; financial award applicants required to submit FAFSA. *Unit head:* Dr. Susan Byrne, Chair/Professor, 702-895-3464, Fax: 702-895-1226, E-mail: wlc.chair@unlv.edu. *Application contact:* Dr. Alicia Rico, Graduate Coordinator, 702-895-4874, Fax: 702-895-1226, E-mail: wlc.gradcoord@unlv.edu. Website: http://liberalarts.unlv.edu/Foreign_Languages/graduates.html

The University of North Carolina at Greensboro, Graduate School, College of Arts and Sciences, Department of Languages, Literatures, and Cultures, Program in Spanish, Greensboro, NC 27412-5001. Offers advanced Spanish language and Hispanic cultural studies (Certificate); Spanish (MA). *Degree requirements:* For master's, one foreign language, comprehensive exam, thesis or alternative. *Entrance requirements:* For master's, GRE General Test, 3-5 minute tape demonstrating foreign language proficiency, composition in Spanish, sample paper in English. Additional exam requirements/recommendations for international students: required—TOEFL. Electronic applications accepted.

The University of North Carolina Wilmington, College of Arts and Sciences, Department of World Languages and Cultures, Wilmington, NC 28403-3297. Offers Hispanic studies (Postbaccalaureate Certificate); Spanish (MA). *Program availability:* Part-time. *Faculty:* 15 full-time (9 women). *Students:* 11 full-time (7 women), 5 part-time (4 women); includes 6 minority (all Hispanic/Latino), 2 international. Average age 30. 8 applicants, 100% accepted, 8 enrolled. In 2019, 5 master's awarded. *Degree requirements:* For master's, one foreign language, comprehensive exam, thesis or alternative. *Entrance requirements:* For master's, 3 letters of recommendation, 2 three-to five-minute recorded speaking samples (both in English and Spanish), writing sample (both in English and Spanish). Additional exam requirements/recommendations for international students: required—TOEFL (minimum score 79 iBT), IELTS (minimum score 6.5). *Application deadline:* For fall admission, 7/1 for domestic students; for spring admission, 11/1 for domestic students; for summer admission, 3/1 for domestic students. Applications are processed on a rolling basis. Application fee: $75. Electronic applications accepted. *Expenses: Tuition, area resident:* Full-time $4719; part-time $326 per credit hour. Tuition, state resident: full-time $4719; part-time $326 per credit hour. Tuition, nonresident: full-time $18,548; part-time $1099 per credit hour. *Required fees:* $2738. Tuition and fees vary according to program. *Financial support:* Teaching assistantships and scholarships/grants available. Financial award application deadline: 1/1; financial award applicants required to submit FAFSA. *Unit head:* Dr. Derrick Miller, Chair, 910-962-4095, Fax: 910-962-7712, E-mail: millerd@uncw.edu. *Application contact:* Dr. Amanda Boomershine, Graduate Coordinator, 910-962-7922, Fax: 910-962-7712, E-mail: boomershinea@uncw.edu.
Website: http://www.uncw.edu/fll/spanish/spngraduate.html

University of Puerto Rico at Mayagüez, Graduate Studies, College of Arts and Sciences, Department of Hispanic Studies, Mayagüez, PR 00681-9000. Offers MA. *Program availability:* Part-time. *Degree requirements:* For master's, comprehensive exam, thesis. *Entrance requirements:* For master's, minimum GPA of 2.75, BA in Hispanic studies or its equivalent. Electronic applications accepted.

University of Puerto Rico at Rio Piedras, College of Humanities, Department of Hispanic Studies, San Juan, PR 00931-3300. Offers Hispanic linguistics (PhD); Hispanic studies (MA); Latin American literature (PhD); Puerto Rican literature (PhD); Spanish literature (PhD). *Program availability:* Part-time. *Degree requirements:* For master's, one foreign language, comprehensive exam, thesis; for doctorate, one foreign language, comprehensive exam, thesis/dissertation. *Entrance requirements:* For master's, PAEG or GRE, interview, minimum GPA of 3.0, letter of recommendation (2); for doctorate, PAEG or GRE, interview, master's degree, minimum GPA of 3.0, letter of recommendation (2).

The University of Texas at Austin, Graduate School, College of Liberal Arts, Center for Mexican American Studies, Austin, TX 78712-1111. Offers MA.

University of Victoria, Faculty of Graduate Studies, Faculty of Humanities, Department of Hispanic and Italian Studies, Victoria, BC V8W 2Y2, Canada. Offers Hispanic and Italian studies (MA); Hispanic studies (MA). *Degree requirements:* For master's, one foreign language, comprehensive exam, thesis (for some programs). *Entrance requirements:* For master's, undergraduate major in Hispanic studies, minimum B+ average. Additional exam requirements/recommendations for international students: required—TOEFL (minimum score 575 paper-based), IELTS (minimum score 7). Electronic applications accepted.

Villanova University, Graduate School of Liberal Arts and Sciences, Department of Romance Languages and Literatures, Villanova, PA 19085-1699. Offers Hispanic studies (MA). *Program availability:* Part-time, evening/weekend. *Degree requirements:* For master's, one foreign language, comprehensive exam. *Entrance requirements:* For master's, minimum GPA of 3.0, writing sample in Spanish. Additional exam requirements/recommendations for international students: required—TOEFL. Electronic applications accepted.

Holocaust and Genocide Studies

Chapman University, Wilkinson College of Arts, Humanities, and Social Sciences, War and Society Program, Orange, CA 92866. Offers MA. *Program availability:* Part-time, evening/weekend. *Faculty:* 10 full-time (2 women), 7 part-time/adjunct (3 women). *Students:* 13 full-time (7 women), 11 part-time (6 women); includes 9 minority (2 Black or African American, non-Hispanic/Latino; 2 Asian, non-Hispanic/Latino; 5 Hispanic/Latino), 1 international. Average age 31. 17 applicants, 88% accepted, 10 enrolled. In 2019, 8 master's awarded. *Degree requirements:* For master's, thesis. *Entrance requirements:* For master's, GRE (if undergraduate GPA less than 3.0), minimum 2.5 undergraduate GPA. Additional exam requirements/recommendations for international students: required—TOEFL (minimum score 80 iBT), IELTS (minimum score 6.5), PTE (minimum score 53). *Application deadline:* For fall admission, 2/1 priority date for domestic students. Applications are processed on a rolling basis. Application fee: $60. Electronic applications accepted. *Expenses:* $1,035 per unit. *Financial support:* Fellowships, teaching assistantships, Federal Work-Study, scholarships/grants, and unspecified assistantships available. *Unit head:* Dr. Gregory A. Daddis, Director, 714-997-6834, E-mail: daddis@chapman.edu. *Application contact:* Sharnique Dow, Graduate Admissions Counselor, 714-997-6770, E-mail: sdow@chapman.edu.
Website: https://www.chapman.edu/wilkinson/graduate-studies/ma-warsociety.aspx

Clark University, Graduate School, Department of History, Program in Holocaust History and Genocide Studies, Worcester, MA 01610-1477. Offers genocide studies (PhD); history of the Holocaust (PhD). *Students:* Average age 33. 31 applicants, 13% accepted, 4 enrolled. In 2019, 2 doctorates awarded. *Entrance requirements:* For doctorate, GRE. Additional exam requirements/recommendations for international students: required—TOEFL (minimum score 575 paper-based; 90 iBT), IELTS (minimum score 6.5). *Application deadline:* For fall admission, 1/15 priority date for domestic students. Application fee: $75. Electronic applications accepted. *Expenses: Tuition:* Full-time $47,650; part-time $4765 per course. *Required fees:* $1850. *Financial support:* Fellowships, research assistantships, teaching assistantships, and tuition waivers (partial) available. *Unit head:* Shelly Tenenbaum, Professor, 508-793-7241, E-mail: stenenbaum@clarku.edu. *Application contact:* Mary Jane Rein, Executive Director, 508-793-8897, Fax: 508-793-8827, E-mail: mrein@clarku.edu.

College of Saint Elizabeth, Program in Education, Morristown, NJ 07960-6989. Offers assistive technology (Certificate); education (MA); ESL (Certificate); Holocaust/genocide education (Certificate); middle school science (Certificate); online teaching in the 21st century (Certificate); teaching (Certificate), including K-12, K-6, teacher of students with disabilities. *Program availability:* Part-time. *Degree requirements:* For master's and Certificate, thesis. *Entrance requirements:* For master's, certification. Additional exam requirements/recommendations for international students: required—TOEFL (minimum score 550 paper-based; 79 iBT), IELTS (minimum score 6.5). Electronic applications accepted. Application fee is waived when completed online.

Gratz College, Graduate Programs, Programs in Holocaust and Genocide Studies, Melrose Park, PA 19027. Offers MA, PhD. *Program availability:* Online learning.

Kean University, College of Liberal Arts, Program in Holocaust and Genocide Studies, Union, NJ 07083. Offers MA. *Program availability:* Part-time. *Faculty:* 14 full-time (7 women). *Students:* 6 full-time (2 women), 5 part-time (3 women); includes 4 minority (3 Black or African American, non-Hispanic/Latino; 1 Hispanic/Latino). Average age 37. 12 applicants, 100% accepted, 4 enrolled. In 2019, 3 master's awarded. *Degree requirements:* For master's, thesis. *Entrance requirements:* For master's, minimum cumulative GPA of 3.0, official transcripts from all institutions attended, two letters of recommendation from professional associates, personal statement, professional resume/curriculum vitae. Additional exam requirements/recommendations for international students: required—TOEFL (minimum score 550 paper-based; 79 iBT), IELTS (minimum score 6.5). *Application deadline:* For fall admission, 6/30 for domestic and international students; for spring admission, 12/1 for domestic and international students. Applications are processed on a rolling basis. Application fee: $75. Electronic applications accepted. *Expenses:* Tuition, state resident: full-time $15,326; part-time $748 per credit. Tuition, nonresident: full-time $20,288; part-time $902 per credit. *Required fees:* $2149.50; $91.25 per credit. Tuition and fees vary according to course level, course load, degree level and program. *Financial support:* Scholarships/grants and unspecified assistantships available. Financial award applicants required to submit FAFSA. *Unit head:* Dr. Dennis Klein, Program Coordinator, 908-737-0256, E-mail: dklein@kean.edu. *Application contact:* Amy Clark, Program Assistant, 908-737-7100, E-mail: gradadmissions@kean.edu.
Website: http://grad.kean.edu/mahgs

Stockton University, Office of Graduate Studies, Program in Holocaust and Genocide Studies, Galloway, NJ 08205-9441. Offers MA. *Program availability:* Part-time, evening/weekend, online only, 100% online. *Faculty:* 5 full-time (3 women), 4 part-time/adjunct (all women). *Students:* 31 part-time (24 women); includes 8 minority (1 Asian, non-Hispanic/Latino; 3 Hispanic/Latino; 4 Two or more races, non-Hispanic/Latino). Average age 34. 15 applicants, 80% accepted, 8 enrolled. In 2019, 4 master's awarded. *Entrance requirements:* Additional exam requirements/recommendations for international students: required—TOEFL. *Application deadline:* For fall admission, 7/1 for domestic and international students; for spring admission, 12/1 for domestic students, 11/1 for international students. Applications are processed on a rolling basis. Application fee: $50. Electronic applications accepted. *Expenses: Tuition, area resident:* Full-time $750.92; part-time $78.58 per credit hour. Tuition, state resident: full-time $750.92; part-time $78.58 per credit hour. Tuition, nonresident: full-time $846; part-time $78.58 per credit hour. *International tuition:* $1195.96 full-time. *Required fees:* $1464; $78.58 per credit hour. One-time fee: $50 full-time. *Financial support:* Fellowships, research assistantships, career-related internships or fieldwork, Federal Work-Study, scholarships/grants, and unspecified assistantships available. Financial award application deadline: 3/1; financial award applicants required to submit FAFSA. *Unit head:* Dr. Elisa Forgey, Program Director, 609-626-3640, Fax: 609-626-6050, E-mail: mahg@stockton.edu. *Application contact:* Tara Williams, Assistant Director of Graduate Enrollment Management, 609-626-3640, Fax: 609-626-6050, E-mail: gradschool@stockton.edu.

Texas A&M University–Commerce, College of Humanities, Social Sciences and Arts, Commerce, TX 75429. Offers applied criminology (MS); applied linguistics (MA, MS); art (MA, MFA); christianity in history (Graduate Certificate); computational linguistics (Graduate Certificate); creative writing (Graduate Certificate); criminal justice management (Graduate Certificate); criminal justice studies (Graduate Certificate); English (MA, MS, PhD); film studies (Graduate Certificate); history (MA, MS); Holocaust studies (Graduate Certificate); homeland security (Graduate Certificate); music (MM); music performance (MM); political science (MA, MS); public history (Graduate Certificate); sociology (MS); Spanish (MA); studies in children's and adolescent literature and culture (Graduate Certificate); teaching English to speakers of other languages (Graduate Certificate); theater (MA, MS); world history (Graduate Certificate). *Program availability:* Part-time. *Faculty:* 49 full-time (28 women), 8 part-time/adjunct (2 women). *Students:* 34 full-time (21 women), 427 part-time (302 women); includes 175 minority (66 Black or African American, non-Hispanic/Latino; 1 American Indian or Alaska Native, non-Hispanic/Latino; 13 Asian, non-Hispanic/Latino; 79 Hispanic/Latino; 16 Two or more races, non-Hispanic/Latino), 15 international. Average age 38. 193 applicants, 49% accepted, 78 enrolled. In 2019, 122 master's, 6 doctorates awarded. *Degree requirements:* For master's, one foreign language, comprehensive exam, thesis (for some programs); for doctorate, one foreign language, comprehensive exam, thesis/dissertation, departmental qualifying exam. *Entrance requirements:* For master's, GRE General Test, official transcripts, letters of recommendation, resume, statement of goals; for doctorate, GRE General Test, official transcripts, letters of recommendation, statement of goals, writing samples, writing sessions, resumes. Additional exam requirements/recommendations for international students: required—TOEFL (minimum score 550 paper-based; 79 iBT), IELTS (minimum score 6), PTE (minimum score 53). *Application deadline:* For fall admission, 6/1 priority date for international students; for spring admission, 10/15 priority date for international students; for summer admission, 3/15 priority date for international students. Applications are processed on a rolling basis. Application fee: $50 ($75 for international students). Electronic applications accepted. *Expenses: Tuition, area resident:* Full-time $3630; part-time $202 per credit hour. Tuition, state resident: full-time $3630; part-time $202 per credit hour. Tuition, nonresident: full-time $11,232; part-time $624 per credit hour. *International tuition:* $11,232 full-time. *Required fees:* $2948. *Financial support:* In 2019–20, 30 students received support, including 18 research assistantships with partial tuition reimbursements available (averaging $3,231 per year), 136 teaching assistantships with

partial tuition reimbursements available (averaging $4,053 per year); Federal Work-Study, institutionally sponsored loans, scholarships/grants, health care benefits, and unspecified assistantships also available. Financial award application deadline: 5/1; financial award applicants required to submit FAFSA. *Unit head:* Dr. William F. Kuracina, Interim Dean, 903-886-5166, Fax: 903-886-5774, E-mail: william.kuracina@tamuc.edu. *Application contact:* Rebecca Stevens, Graduate Student Services Coordinator, 903-468-6049, E-mail: rebecca.stevens@tamuc.edu.
Website: http://www.tamuc.edu/academics/colleges/humanitiesSocialSciencesArts/

University of South Florida, Innovative Education, Tampa, FL 33620-9951. Offers adult, career and higher education (Graduate Certificate), including college teaching, leadership in developing human resources, leadership in higher education; Africana studies (Graduate Certificate), including diasporas and health disparities, genocide and human rights; aging studies (Graduate Certificate), including gerontology; art research (Graduate Certificate), including museum studies; business foundations (Graduate Certificate); chemical and biomedical engineering (Graduate Certificate), including materials science and engineering, water, health and sustainability; child and family studies (Graduate Certificate), including positive behavior support; civil and industrial engineering (Graduate Certificate), including transportation systems analysis; community and family health (Graduate Certificate), including maternal and child health, social marketing and public health, violence and injury: prevention and intervention, women's health; criminology (Graduate Certificate), including criminal justice administration; data science for public administration (Graduate Certificate); digital humanities (Graduate Certificate); educational measurement and research (Graduate Certificate), including evaluation; English (Graduate Certificate), including comparative literary studies, creative writing, professional and technical communication; entrepreneurship (Graduate Certificate); environmental health (Graduate Certificate), including safety management; epidemiology and biostatistics (Graduate Certificate), including applied biostatistics, biostatistics, concepts and tools of epidemiology, epidemiology, epidemiology of infectious diseases; geography, environment and planning (Graduate Certificate), including community development, environmental policy and management, geographical information systems; geology (Graduate Certificate), including hydrogeology; global health (Graduate Certificate), including disaster management, global health and Latin American and Caribbean studies, global health practice, humanitarian assistance, infection control; government and international affairs (Graduate Certificate), including Cuban studies, globalization studies; health policy and management (Graduate Certificate), including health management and leadership, public health policy and programs; hearing specialist: early intervention (Graduate Certificate); industrial and management systems engineering (Graduate Certificate), including systems engineering, technology management; information studies (Graduate Certificate), including school library media specialist; information systems/decision sciences (Graduate Certificate), including analytics and business intelligence; instructional technology (Graduate Certificate), including distance education, Florida digital/virtual educator, instructional design, multimedia design, Web design; internal medicine, bioethics and medical humanities (Graduate Certificate), including biomedical ethics; Latin American and Caribbean studies (Graduate Certificate); leadership for coastal resiliency planning (Graduate Certificate); mass communications (Graduate Certificate), including multimedia journalism; mathematics and statistics (Graduate Certificate), including mathematics; medicine (Graduate Certificate), including aging and neuroscience, bioinformatics, biotechnology, brain fitness and memory management, clinical investigation, hand and upper limb rehabilitation, health informatics, health sciences, integrative weight management, intellectual property, medicine and gender, metabolic and nutritional medicine, metabolic cardiology, pharmacy sciences; national and competitive intelligence (Graduate Certificate); nursing (Graduate Certificate), including simulation based academic fellowship in advanced pain management; psychological and social foundations (Graduate Certificate), including career counseling, college teaching, diversity in education, mental health counseling, school counseling; public affairs (Graduate Certificate), including nonprofit management, public management, research administration; public health (Graduate Certificate), including assessing chemical toxicity and public health risks, health equity, pharmacoepidemiology, public health generalist, toxicology, translational research in adolescent behavioral health; public health practices (Graduate Certificate), including planning for healthy communities; rehabilitation and mental health counseling (Graduate Certificate), including integrative mental health care, marriage and family therapy, rehabilitation technology; secondary education (Graduate Certificate), including ESOL, foreign language education: culture and content, foreign language education: professional; social work (Graduate Certificate), including geriatric social work/clinical gerontology; special education (Graduate Certificate), including autism spectrum disorder, disabilities education: severe/profound; world languages (Graduate Certificate), including teaching English as a second language (TESL) or foreign language. *Unit head:* Dr. Cynthia DeLuca, Associate Vice President and Assistant Vice Provost, 813-974-3077, Fax: 813-974-7061, E-mail: deluca@usf.edu. *Application contact:* Owen Hooper, Director, Summer and Alternative Calendar Programs, 813-974-6917, E-mail: hooper@usf.edu.
Website: http://www.usf.edu/innovative-education/

Jewish Studies

Academy for Jewish Religion California, Graduate Programs, Los Angeles, CA 90024. Offers MJS. *Expenses:* Contact institution.

American Jewish University, Graduate School of Nonprofit Management, Program in Jewish Communal Studies, Bel Air, CA 90077-1599. Offers MAJCS. *Degree requirements:* For master's, thesis. *Entrance requirements:* For master's, GMAT or GRE General Test, interview.

Biola University, Talbot School of Theology, La Mirada, CA 90639-0001. Offers adult/family ministry (MACE); Bible exposition (MA, Th M); Biblical and theological studies (Certificate); children's ministry (MACE); Christian education (M Div); cross-cultural education ministry (MACE); educational studies (Ed D, PhD); evangelism and discipleship (M Div); general Christian education (MACE); Messianic Jewish studies (M Div, Certificate); missions and intercultural studies (M Div); New Testament (MA, Th M); Old Testament (MA); Old Testament and Semitics (Th M); pastoral and general ministry (M Div); pastoral care and counseling (M Div, MACML); philosophy (MA); preaching and pastoral ministry (MACML); spiritual formation (M Div, Certificate); spiritual formation and soul care (MA); sports ministry (MACML); theology (MA, Th M, D Min, Certificate); youth ministry (MACE). *Program availability:* Part-time, evening/weekend. *Students:* 461 full-time (116 women), 768 part-time (228 women); includes 489 minority (54 Black or African American, non-Hispanic/Latino; 1 American Indian or Alaska Native, non-Hispanic/Latino; 303 Asian, non-Hispanic/Latino; 96 Hispanic/Latino; 3 Native Hawaiian or other Pacific Islander, non-Hispanic/Latino; 32 Two or more races, non-Hispanic/Latino), 162 international. Average age 38. 745 applicants, 70% accepted, 320 enrolled. In 2019, 235 master's, 24 doctorates awarded. *Entrance requirements:* For master's, bachelor's degree from accredited college or university; minimum GPA of 2.6 (for M Div), 3.0 (for MA); for doctorate, M Div or MA. Additional exam requirements/recommendations for international students: required—TOEFL (minimum score 600 paper-based; 88 iBT). *Application deadline:* For fall admission, 7/1 for domestic students, 6/1 for international students; for spring admission, 11/1 for domestic students. Applications are processed on a rolling basis. Application fee: $65. Electronic applications accepted. *Financial support:* Scholarships/grants and unspecified assistantships available. Support available to part-time students. Financial award applicants required to submit FAFSA. *Unit head:* Dr. Clint Arnold, Dean, 562-903-4816, Fax: 562-903-4748. *Application contact:* Graduate Admissions Office, 562-903-4752, E-mail: graduate.admissions@biola.edu.
Website: http://www.talbot.edu/

Brandeis University, Graduate School of Arts and Sciences, Department of Near Eastern and Judaic Studies, Waltham, MA 02454-9110. Offers Near Eastern and Judaic studies (MA); near Eastern and Judaic studies/conflict resolution and coexistence (MA); near Eastern and Judaic studies/Jewish professional leadership (MA); near Eastern and Judaic studies/women's, gender, and sexuality studies (MA); teaching of Hebrew (MAT); the bible and ancient near east (PhD). *Program availability:* Part-time. *Faculty:* 21 full-time (8 women), 5 part-time/adjunct (3 women). *Students:* 34 full-time (15 women), 2 part-time (1 woman); includes 8 minority (1 Black or African American, non-Hispanic/Latino; 2 Asian, non-Hispanic/Latino; 3 Hispanic/Latino; 2 Two or more races, non-Hispanic/Latino), 7 international. Average age 34. 76 applicants, 53% accepted, 5 enrolled. In 2019, 3 master's, 3 doctorates awarded. Terminal master's awarded for partial completion of doctoral program. *Degree requirements:* For master's, one foreign language, thesis or alternative, capstone, thesis, or internship; for doctorate, variable foreign language requirement, comprehensive exam, thesis/dissertation. *Entrance requirements:* For master's and doctorate, GRE General recommended, transcripts, letters of recommendation, resume, writing sample, and statement of purpose. Additional exam requirements/recommendations for international students: required—TOEFL, IELTS, PTE. *Application deadline:* For fall admission, 1/15 priority date for domestic and international students. Applications are processed on a rolling basis. Application fee: $75. Electronic applications accepted. *Financial support:* In 2019–20, 9 fellowships with full tuition reimbursements (averaging $25,000 per year), 8 teaching assistantships (averaging $3,550 per year) were awarded; scholarships/grants, health care benefits, and tuition waivers also available. Support available to part-time students. *Unit head:* Dr. Ilana Szobel, Director of Graduate Studies, 781-736-5230, E-mail: szobel@brandeis.edu. *Application contact:* Jean Mannion, Administrator, 781-736-2950, E-mail: mannion@brandeis.edu.
Website: http://www.brandeis.edu/gsas/programs/nejs.html

Brandeis University, Graduate School of Arts and Sciences, Hornstein: Jewish Professional Leadership Program, Waltham, MA 02454-9110. Offers jewish professional leadership and business administration (MBA/MA); jewish professional leadership and near eastern and judaic studies (MA/MA); jewish professional leadership and public policy (MPP/MA); MA/MA; MBA/MA; MPP/MA. *Program availability:* Part-time. *Faculty:* 3 full-time (1 woman), 2 part-time/adjunct (1 woman). *Students:* 22 full-time (12 women), 4 international. Average age 30. 29 applicants, 97% accepted, 13 enrolled. *Entrance requirements:* Additional exam requirements/recommendations for international students: required—TOEFL, IELTS, PTE. *Application deadline:* For fall admission, 1/15 for domestic and international students. Applications are processed on a rolling basis. Application fee: $75. Electronic applications accepted. *Financial support:* Scholarships/grants available. *Unit head:* Dr. Ellen Smith, Director of Graduate Studies, 781-736-2998, E-mail: esmith2@brandeis.edu. *Application contact:* Claire Pavlik-Purgus, Administrator, 781-736-2990, Fax: 781-736-2070, E-mail: hornstein@brandeis.edu.
Website: http://www.brandeis.edu/gsas/programs/hornstein.html

Brandeis University, Graduate School of Arts and Sciences, Program in Women's, Gender, and Sexuality Studies, Waltham, MA 02454-9110. Offers anthropology/women's, gender, and sexuality studies (MA); English/women's, gender, and sexuality studies (MA); near Eastern and Judaic studies /women's, gender, and sexuality studies (MA); public policy/women's, gender, and sexuality studies (MA); sociology/women's, gender, and sexuality studies (MA); sustainable international development/women's, gender, and sexuality studies (MA); women's, gender, and sexuality studies (MA). *Program availability:* Part-time. *Faculty:* 19 full-time (16 women), 2 part-time/adjunct (both women). *Students:* 6 full-time (all women); includes 2 minority (both Hispanic/Latino). Average age 27. 41 applicants, 54% accepted, 8 enrolled. In 2019, 4 master's awarded. *Degree requirements:* For master's, thesis or alternative. *Entrance requirements:* For master's, GRE General, transcripts, letters of recommendation, resume, statement of purpose, and writing sample. Additional exam requirements/recommendations for international students: required—TOEFL, IELTS, PTE. *Application deadline:* For fall admission, 1/15 for domestic and international students. Application fee: $75. Electronic applications accepted. *Financial support:* Fellowships, scholarships/grants, health care benefits, and tuition waivers available. Support available to part-time students. *Unit head:* Dr. Ellen Schattschneider, Director of Graduate Studies, 781-736-2219, E-mail: eschatt@brandeis.edu. *Application contact:* Alexandra Brandon, Administrator, 781-736-3045, E-mail: abrandon@brandeis.edu.
Website: http://www.brandeis.edu/gsas/programs/wgs.html

Brooklyn College of the City University of New York, School of Humanities and Social Sciences, Department of Judaic Studies, Brooklyn, NY 11210-2889. Offers MA. *Program availability:* Part-time, evening/weekend. *Degree requirements:* For master's, 2 foreign languages, comprehensive exam or thesis. *Entrance requirements:* For master's, 18 upper-level credits in Judaic studies, interview, 2 letters of recommendation. Additional exam requirements/recommendations for international students: required—TOEFL (minimum score 525 paper-based; 70 iBT). Electronic applications accepted.

Central Yeshiva Tomchei Tmimim-Lubavitch, Graduate Programs, Brooklyn, NY 11230. Offers Jewish/Judaic studies (MA); Talmudic studies (MA). *Accreditation:* AARTS. *Application contact:* Information Contact, 718-434-0784.

Columbia University, Graduate School of Arts and Sciences, New York, NY 10027. Offers African-American studies (MA); American studies (MA); anthropology (MA, PhD); art history and archaeology (MA, PhD); astronomy (PhD); biological sciences (PhD);

biotechnology (MA); chemical physics (PhD); chemistry (PhD); classical studies (MA, PhD); classics (MA, PhD); climate and society (MA); conservation biology (MA); earth and environmental sciences (PhD); East Asia: regional studies (MA); East Asian languages and cultures (MA, PhD); ecology, evolution and environmental biology (MA), including conservation biology; ecology, evolution, and environmental biology (PhD), including ecology and evolutionary biology, evolutionary primatology; economics (MA, PhD); English and comparative literature (MA, PhD); French and Romance philology (MA, PhD); Germanic languages (MA, PhD); global French studies (MA); global thought (MA); Hispanic cultural studies (MA); history (PhD); history and literature (MA); human rights studies (MA); Islamic studies (MA); Italian (MA, PhD); Japanese pedagogy (MA); Jewish studies (MA); Latin America and the Caribbean: regional studies (MA); Latin American and Iberian cultures (PhD); mathematics (MA, PhD), including finance (MA); medieval and Renaissance studies (MA); Middle Eastern, South Asian, and African studies (MA, PhD); modern art: critical and curatorial studies (MA); modern European studies (MA); museum anthropology (MA); music (DMA, PhD); oral history (MA); philosophical foundations of physics (MA); philosophy (MA, PhD); physics (PhD); political science (MA, PhD); psychology (PhD); quantitative methods in the social sciences (MA); religion (MA, PhD); Russia, Eurasia and East Europe: regional studies (MA); Russian translation (MA); Slavic cultures (MA); Slavic languages (MA, PhD); sociology (MA, PhD); South Asian studies (MA); statistics (MA, PhD); theatre (PhD). *Program availability:* Part-time. *Students:* 3,506 full-time (1,844 women), 208 part-time (121 women); includes 864 minority (110 Black or African American, non-Hispanic/Latino; 5 American Indian or Alaska Native, non-Hispanic/Latino; 416 Asian, non-Hispanic/Latino; 147 Hispanic/Latino; 6 Native Hawaiian or other Pacific Islander, non-Hispanic/Latino; 180 Two or more races, non-Hispanic/Latino), 2,065 international. 14,545 applicants, 25% accepted, 1,429 enrolled. In 2019, 1,262 master's, 363 doctorates awarded. Terminal master's awarded for partial completion of doctoral program. *Degree requirements:* For master's, variable foreign language requirement, comprehensive exam (for some programs), thesis (for some programs); for doctorate, variable foreign language requirement, comprehensive exam (for some programs), thesis/dissertation. *Entrance requirements:* For master's and doctorate, GRE General Test, GRE Subject Test (for some programs). Additional exam requirements/recommendations for international students: required—TOEFL (minimum score 600 paper-based; 100 iBT), IELTS (minimum score 7.5). Application fee: $115. Electronic applications accepted. *Expenses: Tuition:* Full-time $47,600; part-time $1880 per credit. One-time fee: $105. *Financial support:* Fellowships, research assistantships, teaching assistantships, career-related internships or fieldwork, Federal Work-Study, institutionally sponsored loans, scholarships/grants, traineeships, health care benefits, tuition waivers, and unspecified assistantships available. Support available to part-time students. Financial award application deadline: 12/15. *Unit head:* Dr. Carlos J. Alonso, Dean of the Graduate School of Arts and Sciences and Vice President for Graduate Education, 212-854-2861, E-mail: gsas-dean@columbia.edu. *Application contact:* GSAS Office of Admissions, 212-854-6729, E-mail: gsas-admissions@columbia.edu. Website: http://gsas.columbia.edu/

Concordia University, School of Graduate Studies, Faculty of Arts and Science, Department of Religions and Cultures, Program in Judaic Studies, Montréal, QC H3G 1M8, Canada. Offers MA. *Degree requirements:* For master's, one foreign language, comprehensive exam, thesis optional. *Entrance requirements:* For master's, Hebrew exam, honors degree in Judaic studies or equivalent. Additional exam requirements/recommendations for international students: required—TOEFL.

Cornell University, Graduate School, Graduate Fields of Arts and Sciences, Field of Near Eastern Studies, Ithaca, NY 14853. Offers ancient Near Eastern studies (MA, PhD); Arabic and Islamic studies (MA, PhD); biblical studies (MA, PhD); Hebrew and Judaic studies (MA, PhD). Terminal master's awarded for partial completion of doctoral program. *Degree requirements:* For master's, one foreign language, thesis; for doctorate, 2 foreign languages, comprehensive exam, thesis/dissertation. *Entrance requirements:* For master's and doctorate, GRE General Test, 2 years of 1 Near Eastern language, 3 letters of recommendation, writing sample. Additional exam requirements/recommendations for international students: required—TOEFL (minimum score 550 paper-based; 77 iBT). Electronic applications accepted.

Criswell College, Graduate School of the Bible, Dallas, TX 75246-1537. Offers biblical studies (M Div); Christian leadership (MA); counseling (MA); Jewish studies (MA); ministry (MA); theological and biblical studies (MA). *Program availability:* Part-time. *Degree requirements:* For master's, 2 foreign languages, thesis optional. *Entrance requirements:* For master's, GRE General Test, minimum GPA of 2.5. Electronic applications accepted.

Dallas Theological Seminary, Graduate Programs, Dallas, TX 75204-6499. Offers adult education (Th M); apologetics (Th M); Bible backgrounds (Th M); Bible translation (Th M); Biblical and theological studies (Certificate); biblical counseling (MA); biblical exegesis and linguistics (MA); biblical exposition (PhD); biblical studies (MA); Biblical theology (Th M); children's education (Th M); Christian education (MA, D Min); Christian leadership (MA); cross-cultural ministries (MA); educational administration (Th M); educational leadership (Th M); evangelism and discipleship (Th M); exposition of Biblical books (Th M); family life education (Th M); general studies (Th M); Hebrew and cognate studies (Th M); hermeneutics (Th M); historical theology (Th M); homiletics (Th M); intercultural ministries (Th M); Jesus studies (Th M); leadership studies (Th M); media and communication (MA); media arts (Th M); ministry (D Min); ministry with women (Th M); New Testament studies (Th M, PhD); Old Testament studies (Th M, PhD); parachurch ministries (Th M); pastoral care and counseling (Th M); pastoral theology and practice (Th M); philosophy (Th M); sacred theology (STM); spiritual formation (Th M); systematic theology (Th M); teaching in Christian institutions (Th M); theological studies (PhD); urban ministries (Th M); worship studies (Th M); youth education (Th M). *Program availability:* Part-time, online learning. *Degree requirements:* For master's, variable foreign language requirement, thesis (for some programs); for doctorate, 2 foreign languages, thesis/dissertation. *Entrance requirements:* For master's, GRE or MAT (if minimum undergraduate cumulative GPA is below 2.5 or undergraduate degree is unaccredited). Additional exam requirements/recommendations for international students: required—TOEFL (minimum score 575 paper-based; 85 iBT), TWE. Electronic applications accepted.

Graduate Theological Union, Graduate Programs, Berkeley, CA 94709-1212. Offers art and religion (MA, PhD, Th D); biblical languages (MA); Biblical studies (PhD, Th D); biblical studies (MA); Buddhist studies (MA); Christian spirituality (MA, PhD, Th D); cultural and historical studies of religions (MA, PhD, Th D); ethics and social theory (PhD, Th D); history (MA, PhD, Th D); homiletics (MA, PhD, Th D); interdisciplinary studies (PhD, Th D); Jewish studies (MA, PhD, Th D, Certificate); liturgical studies (MA, PhD, Th D); Near Eastern religions (PhD, Th D); Orthodox Christian studies (MA); religion and psychology (MA, PhD, Th D); religion and society/ethics and social theory (MA); systematic and philosophical theology (MA, PhD, Th D). *Accreditation:* ATS. Terminal master's awarded for partial completion of doctoral program. *Degree requirements:* For master's, one foreign language, thesis; for doctorate, one foreign language, comprehensive exam, thesis/dissertation. *Entrance requirements:* For master's, GRE General Test; for doctorate, GRE General Test, MA or M Div. Additional exam requirements/recommendations for international students: required—TOEFL. Electronic applications accepted.

Gratz College, Graduate Programs, Program in Jewish Christian Studies, Melrose Park, PA 19027. Offers Graduate Certificate. *Program availability:* Online learning.

Gratz College, Graduate Programs, Program in Jewish Studies, Melrose Park, PA 19027. Offers MA. *Program availability:* Part-time, online learning. *Degree requirements:* For master's, one foreign language, comprehensive exam, thesis optional.

Harvard University, Graduate School of Arts and Sciences, Department of Near Eastern Languages and Civilizations, Cambridge, MA 02138. Offers Akkadian and Sumerian (AM, PhD); Arabic (AM, PhD); Armenian (AM, PhD); biblical history (AM, PhD); Hebrew (AM, PhD); Indo-Muslim culture (AM, PhD); Iranian (AM, PhD); Jewish history and literature (AM, PhD); Persian (AM, PhD); Semitic philology (AM, PhD); Syro-Palestinian archaeology (AM, PhD); Turkish (AM, PhD). *Degree requirements:* For doctorate, variable foreign language requirement, thesis/dissertation, general exams. *Entrance requirements:* For master's, GRE General Test; for doctorate, GRE General Test, proficiency in a Near Eastern language. Additional exam requirements/recommendations for international students: required—TOEFL.

Hebrew College, Cantor Educator Program, Newton Centre, MA 02459. Offers MJ Ed. *Entrance requirements:* For master's, GRE, interview. Additional exam requirements/recommendations for international students: required—TOEFL.

Hebrew College, Program in Jewish Studies, Newton Centre, MA 02459. Offers Jewish liturgical music (Certificate); Jewish music education (Certificate); Jewish studies (MA). *Program availability:* Part-time, evening/weekend, online learning. *Degree requirements:* For master's, one foreign language. *Entrance requirements:* For master's, GRE, interview. Additional exam requirements/recommendations for international students: required—TOEFL.

Hebrew Union College–Jewish Institute of Religion, School of Graduate Studies, Program in Judaic Studies, New York, NY 10012-1186. Offers MAJS. *Program availability:* Part-time. *Degree requirements:* For master's, one foreign language, thesis. *Entrance requirements:* For master's, GRE, minimum 2 years of college-level Hebrew.

Indiana University Bloomington, University Graduate School, College of Arts and Sciences, Robert A. and Sandra S. Borns Jewish Studies Program, Bloomington, IN 47405. Offers Jewish studies (MA), including nonprofit management; Jewish studies and history (MA). *Degree requirements:* For master's, one foreign language, thesis. *Entrance requirements:* Additional exam requirements/recommendations for international students: required—TOEFL. Electronic applications accepted.

The Jewish Theological Seminary, The Graduate School, New York, NY 10027-4649. Offers ancient Judaism (MA, DHL, PhD); Bible and ancient Semitic languages (MA, DHL, PhD); interdepartmental studies (MA); Jewish art and visual culture (MA); Jewish gender and women's studies (MA); Jewish history (MA, DHL, PhD); Jewish literature (MA, DHL, PhD); Jewish philosophy (DHL); Jewish thought (MA, PhD); liturgy (MA, DHL, PhD); medieval Jewish studies (MA, DHL, PhD); Midrash (DHL); Midrash and scriptural interpretation (MA, PhD); modern Jewish studies (MA, DHL, PhD); Talmud and rabbinics (MA, DHL, PhD); MA/MSW. *Accreditation:* ACIPE. *Program availability:* Part-time. Terminal master's awarded for partial completion of doctoral program. *Degree requirements:* For master's, one foreign language, comprehensive exam (for some programs), thesis (for some programs); for doctorate, 3 foreign languages, comprehensive exam (for some programs), thesis/dissertation. *Entrance requirements:* For master's, GRE or MAT, 3 letters of recommendation, writing sample; for doctorate, GRE or MAT, 3 letters of recommendation, writing research sample. Additional exam requirements/recommendations for international students: required—TOEFL.

The Jewish Theological Seminary, William Davidson Graduate School of Jewish Education, New York, NY 10027-4649. Offers MA, Ed D. *Program availability:* Part-time, online learning. *Degree requirements:* For master's, one foreign language, thesis optional; for doctorate, one foreign language, comprehensive exam, thesis/dissertation. *Entrance requirements:* For master's, GRE or MAT, 3 letters of recommendation; for doctorate, GRE or MAT, writing sample, 3 letters of recommendation. Additional exam requirements/recommendations for international students: recommended—TOEFL.

McGill University, Faculty of Graduate and Postdoctoral Studies, Faculty of Arts, Department of Jewish Studies, Montréal, QC H3A 2T5, Canada. Offers MA.

New York University, Graduate School of Arts and Science, Skirball Department of Hebrew and Judaic Studies, New York, NY 10012-1019. Offers Hebrew and Judaic studies (MA, PhD); Hebrew and Judaic studies/museum studies (MA). *Program availability:* Part-time. Terminal master's awarded for partial completion of doctoral program. *Degree requirements:* For master's, 2 foreign languages, comprehensive exam, thesis optional; for doctorate, 4 foreign languages, comprehensive exam, thesis/dissertation. *Entrance requirements:* For master's and doctorate, GRE General Test. Additional exam requirements/recommendations for international students: required—TOEFL, IELTS.

New York University, Steinhardt School of Culture, Education, and Human Development, Applied Statistics, Social Science, and Humanities, Program in Education and Jewish Studies, New York, NY 10012-1019. Offers MA, PhD, MA/MA. *Program availability:* Part-time. *Entrance requirements:* For doctorate, GRE General Test, interview. Additional exam requirements/recommendations for international students: required—TOEFL (minimum score 100 iBT). Electronic applications accepted.

Reconstructionist Rabbinical College, Graduate Programs, Wyncote, PA 19095-1898. Offers Jewish studies (MAJS); rabbinics (MAHL, DHL); women's studies (Certificate). *Program availability:* Part-time. *Degree requirements:* For master's, one foreign language, thesis (MAJS), completion of rabbinical program (MAHL); for doctorate, one foreign language. *Entrance requirements:* For master's, GRE General Test; placement examinations in Hebrew and Judaism (MAHL); for doctorate, GRE General Test, placement examinations in Hebrew and Judaism. *Expenses: Tuition:* Full-time $26,000.

Rice University, Graduate Programs, School of Humanities, Department of Religious Studies, Houston, TX 77251-1892. Offers African religions (PhD); African-American religions (PhD); contemplative studies (PhD); ghosticism, esotericism, mysticism (PhD); Islam (PhD); Jewish thought and philosophy (PhD); modern Christianity in thought and popular culture (PhD); psychology of religion (PhD); the Bible and beyond (PhD). *Degree requirements:* For doctorate, 2 foreign languages, comprehensive exam, thesis/dissertation. *Entrance requirements:* For doctorate, GRE, letters of recommendation, writing sample. Additional exam requirements/recommendations for international students: required—TOEFL (minimum score 600 paper-based; 90 iBT). Electronic applications accepted.

Rutgers University - New Brunswick, Graduate School-New Brunswick, Department of Jewish Studies, New Brunswick, NJ 08901. Offers MA, Certificate. *Program availability:* Part-time.

Seton Hall University, College of Arts and Sciences, Department of Religion, South Orange, NJ 07079-2697. Offers Jewish-Christian studies (MA). *Program availability:* Part-time, evening/weekend. *Degree requirements:* For master's, thesis optional. *Entrance requirements:* For master's, interview or suitable correspondence with department chair. Additional exam requirements/recommendations for international students: required—TOEFL. Electronic applications accepted.

Southern Evangelical Seminary, Graduate Programs, Matthews, NC 28105. Offers apologetics (MA, D Min, Certificate); Christian education (MA); church ministry (MA, Certificate); divinity (Certificate), including apologetics (M Div, Certificate); Islamic studies (MA, Certificate); Jewish studies (MA); philosophy (MA); philosophy of religion (PhD); religion (MA); theology (M Div), including apologetics (M Div, Certificate), Biblical studies; youth ministry (MA). *Program availability:* Part-time, evening/weekend, online learning. *Degree requirements:* For master's, thesis (for some programs); for doctorate, 2 foreign languages, comprehensive exam (for some programs), thesis/dissertation. *Entrance requirements:* Additional exam requirements/recommendations for international students: required—TOEFL (minimum score 600 paper-based). *Expenses: Tuition:* Full-time $24,000; part-time $12,000 per year. *Required fees:* $600; $300 per semester. $150 per semester.

Spertus Institute for Jewish Learning and Leadership, Program in Jewish Studies, Chicago, IL 60605-1901. Offers MAJPS, MAJS, DJS, DSJS. *Program availability:* Part-time, evening/weekend, online learning. *Degree requirements:* For master's, one foreign language, thesis (for some programs); for doctorate, one foreign language, thesis/dissertation. *Entrance requirements:* For master's, interview, BAJS (for MAJS); for doctorate, MAJS.

Telshe Yeshiva - Chicago, Graduate Program, Chicago, IL 60625-5598. Offers Second Talmudic Degree. *Accreditation:* AARTS.

Towson University, College of Liberal Arts, Program in Leadership and Jewish Studies, Towson, MD 21252. Offers Jewish communal service (Postbaccalaureate Certificate). *Students:* 4 full-time (3 women), 12 part-time (5 women); includes 3 minority (2 Black or African American, non-Hispanic/Latino; 1 Hispanic/Latino). *Entrance requirements:* For master's, bachelor's degree, minimum GPA of 3.0, letters of recommendation, statement of intent, sample of work, interview, resume; for Postbaccalaureate Certificate, bachelor's degree, minimum GPA of 3.0, statement of intent, sample of work, interview, 2 letters of recommendation, resume. Additional exam requirements/recommendations for international students: required—TOEFL. *Application deadline:* For fall admission, 1/17 for domestic students, 5/15 for international students; for spring admission, 10/15 for domestic students, 12/1 for international students. Applications are processed on a rolling basis. Application fee: $45. Electronic applications accepted. *Expenses: Tuition, area resident:* Full-time $7920; part-time $439 per credit. Tuition, nonresident: full-time $16,344; part-time $908 per credit. *International tuition:* $16,344 full-time. *Required fees:* $2628; $146 per credit. $876 per term. *Unit head:* Prof. Jill Max, Program Director, 410-704-7120, E-mail: jmax@towson.edu. *Application contact:* Coverley Beidleman, Assistant Director of Graduate Admissions, 410-704-5630, Fax: 410-704-3030, E-mail: grads@towson.edu.
Website: https://www.towson.edu/cla/centers/baltimorehebrewinstitute/programs.html

University of California, San Diego, Graduate Division, Department of History, La Jolla, CA 92093. Offers history (MA, PhD); Judaic studies (MA). *Students:* 74 full-time (32 women), 1 (woman) part-time. 121 applicants, 21% accepted, 7 enrolled. In 2019, 7 master's, 12 doctorates awarded. *Degree requirements:* For master's, one foreign language, comprehensive exam; for doctorate, one foreign language, comprehensive exam, thesis/dissertation. *Entrance requirements:* For master's, GRE General Test, minimum GPA of 3.0; for doctorate, GRE General Test, writing sample (7-15 pages long), preferably in a history course. Additional exam requirements/recommendations for international students: required—TOEFL (minimum score 550 paper-based; 80 iBT), IELTS (minimum score 7). *Application deadline:* For fall admission, 1/4 for domestic students. Application fee: $105 ($125 for international students). Electronic applications accepted. *Financial support:* Fellowships, research assistantships, teaching assistantships, career-related internships or fieldwork, scholarships/grants, and readerships available. Financial award applicants required to submit FAFSA. *Unit head:* Edward Watts, Chair, 858-534-2733, E-mail: ewatts@ucsd.edu. *Application contact:* Sally Hargate, Graduate Coordinator, 858-822-0664, E-mail: shargate@ucsd.edu.
Website: http://history.ucsd.edu

University of Connecticut, Graduate School, College of Liberal Arts and Sciences, Center for Judaic Studies and Contemporary Jewish Life, Storrs, CT 06269. Offers Judaic studies (MA, PhD). *Entrance requirements:* Additional exam requirements/recommendations for international students: required—TOEFL (minimum score 550 paper-based). Electronic applications accepted.

University of Florida, Graduate School, College of Liberal Arts and Sciences, Department of History, Gainesville, FL 32611. Offers historic preservation (MA, PhD); history (MA, PhD); Jewish studies (MA); women's and gender studies (PhD); JD/MA; JD/PhD. *Program availability:* Part-time. Terminal master's awarded for partial completion of doctoral program. *Degree requirements:* For master's, variable foreign language requirement, thesis optional, 30 credit hours; for doctorate, variable foreign language requirement, comprehensive exam, thesis/dissertation, 90 credit hours. *Entrance requirements:* For master's and doctorate, GRE General Test, minimum GPA of 3.0. Additional exam requirements/recommendations for international students: required—TOEFL (minimum score 550 paper-based; 80 iBT), IELTS (minimum score 6). Electronic applications accepted.

University of Florida, Graduate School, College of Liberal Arts and Sciences, Department of Religion, Gainesville, FL 32611. Offers Jewish studies (MA); religion (MA, PhD); tropical conservation and development (MA, PhD); women's and gender studies (MA, PhD). *Program availability:* Part-time. *Degree requirements:* For master's, one foreign language, thesis optional; for doctorate, one foreign language, comprehensive exam, thesis/dissertation. *Entrance requirements:* For master's, GRE General Test, minimum GPA of 3.0. Additional exam requirements/recommendations for international students: required—TOEFL (minimum score 550 paper-based; 80 iBT), IELTS (minimum score 6). Electronic applications accepted.

University of Maryland, College Park, Academic Affairs, College of Arts and Humanities, Meyerhoff Center for Jewish Studies, College Park, MD 20742. Offers MA. *Degree requirements:* For master's, thesis or 2 major research papers. *Entrance requirements:* For master's, GRE General Test, 3 letters of recommendation, writing sample. Additional exam requirements/recommendations for international students: required—TOEFL.

University of Michigan, Rackham Graduate School, College of Literature, Science, and the Arts, Department of Middle East Studies, Ann Arbor, MI 48109. Offers ancient Near Eastern studies (AM, PhD); Arabic for professional purposes (AM); Arabic language and literature (AM, PhD); Armenian studies (AM, PhD); Christianity in late antiquity (AM, PhD); Egyptology (AM, PhD); Hebrew Bible and ancient Israel (AM, PhD); Hebrew literature (AM, PhD); Islamic studies (AM, PhD); Jewish cultural studies (AM, PhD); Jewish mysticism (AM, PhD); Persian and Iranian studies (AM, PhD); Rabbinic literature (AM, PhD); Second Temple Judaism (AM, PhD); teaching Arabic as a foreign language (AM); Turkish studies (AM, PhD). Terminal master's awarded for partial completion of doctoral program. *Degree requirements:* For master's, 2 foreign languages; for doctorate, 4 foreign languages, comprehensive exam, thesis/dissertation, preliminary exams, oral defense of dissertation. *Entrance requirements:* For master's, ACTFL (for teaching Arabic as a foreign language MA program). Additional exam requirements/recommendations for international students: required—TOEFL (minimum score 560 paper-based; 84 iBT), IELTS (minimum score 6.5). Electronic applications accepted.

University of Michigan, Rackham Graduate School, College of Literature, Science, and the Arts, Jean and Samuel Frankel Center for Judaic Studies, Ann Arbor, MI 48178. Offers MA, Graduate Certificate. *Program availability:* Part-time. *Degree requirements:* For master's, thesis; for Graduate Certificate, one foreign language, capstone course (including public lecture), reading knowledge of 1 Jewish language. *Entrance requirements:* For master's, GRE General Test; for Graduate Certificate, currently enrolled in a PhD or professional degree program at the University of Michigan. Additional exam requirements/recommendations for international students: required—TOEFL (minimum score 560 paper-based). Electronic applications accepted.

University of St. Michael's College, Faculty of Theology, Toronto, ON M5S 1J4, Canada. Offers Catholic leadership (MA); eastern Christian studies (Diploma); religious education (Diploma); theological studies (Diploma); theology (M Div, MA, MRE, MTS, D Min, PhD, Th D); theology and Jewish studies (MA). *Accreditation:* ATS (one or more programs are accredited). *Program availability:* Part-time. *Degree requirements:* For master's, thesis (for some programs), 1 foreign language (MA), 2 foreign languages (Th M); for doctorate, 3 foreign languages, comprehensive exam, thesis/dissertation; for other advanced degree, thesis optional. *Entrance requirements:* For master's, M Div or BA, course work in an ancient or modern language, minimum GPA of 3.3; for doctorate, MA in theology, Th M, or M Div with thesis, minimum GPA of 3.7; for other advanced degree, minimum GPA of 2.7. Additional exam requirements/recommendations for international students: required—TOEFL (minimum score 600 paper-based). Electronic applications accepted. *Expenses:* Contact institution.

University of Wisconsin–Madison, Graduate School, College of Letters and Science, Department of Hebrew and Semitic Studies, Madison, WI 53706-1380. Offers MA, PhD. Terminal master's awarded for partial completion of doctoral program. *Degree requirements:* For master's, 2 foreign languages; for doctorate, thesis/dissertation. *Entrance requirements:* For master's and doctorate, GRE. Electronic applications accepted.

Washington University in St. Louis, The Graduate School, Department of Jewish, Islamic, and Near Eastern Languages and Cultures, St. Louis, MO 63130-4899. Offers Islamic and Near Eastern studies (MA); Jewish studies (MA). *Degree requirements:* For master's, one foreign language, thesis (for some programs). *Entrance requirements:* For master's, GRE General Test. Additional exam requirements/recommendations for international students: required—TOEFL. Electronic applications accepted.

Yeshiva University, Bernard Revel Graduate School of Jewish Studies, New York, NY 10033-3201. Offers MA, PhD. *Program availability:* Part-time. Terminal master's awarded for partial completion of doctoral program. *Degree requirements:* For master's, comprehensive exam; for doctorate, 2 foreign languages, comprehensive exam, thesis/dissertation. *Entrance requirements:* For master's and doctorate, GRE General Test (recommended), reading knowledge of Hebrew, minimum GPA of 3.0.

Latin American Studies

American University, College of Arts and Sciences, Department of World Languages and Cultures, Washington, DC 20016-8045. Offers Spanish: Latin American studies (MA); teaching English as a foreign language (MA); teaching English to speakers of other languages (MA, Certificate); translation: French (Certificate); translation: Russian (Certificate); translation: Spanish (Certificate). *Program availability:* Part-time, evening/weekend. *Degree requirements:* For master's, one foreign language, comprehensive exam, thesis or alternative. *Entrance requirements:* For master's, GRE; Please see website:https://www.american.edu/cas/wlc/, writing sample, statement of purpose, transcripts, 2 letters of recommendation, resume; for Certificate, bachelor's degree, statement of purpose, transcripts, resume. Additional exam requirements/recommendations for international students: required—TOEFL (minimum score 600 paper-based; 100 iBT). *Expenses:* Contact institution.

Brown University, Graduate School, Department of Portuguese and Brazilian Studies, Providence, RI 02912. Offers Brazilian studies (AM); English as a second language and cross-cultural studies (AM); Portuguese and Brazilian studies (AM, PhD); Portuguese bilingual education and cross-cultural studies (AM). *Degree requirements:* For doctorate, thesis/dissertation.

California State University, Los Angeles, Graduate Studies, College of Natural and Social Sciences, Department of Latin American Studies, Los Angeles, CA 90032-8530. Offers MA. *Program availability:* Part-time, evening/weekend. *Degree requirements:* For master's, one foreign language, comprehensive exam, thesis. *Entrance requirements:* For master's, minimum GPA of 2.5. Additional exam requirements/recommendations for international students: required—TOEFL (minimum score 500 paper-based). Electronic applications accepted. *Expenses: Tuition, area resident:* Full-time $7176; part-time $4164 per year. Tuition, state resident: full-time $7176; part-time $4164 per year. Tuition, nonresident: full-time $14,304; part-time $8916 per year. *International tuition:* $14,304 full-time. *Required fees:* $1037.76; $1037.76 per unit. Tuition and fees vary according to degree level and program.

Centro de Estudios Avanzados de Puerto Rico y el Caribe, Graduate Program in Puerto Rican and Caribbean Studies, Old San Juan, PR 00902-3970. Offers Puerto Rican and Caribbean history (MA, PhD); Puerto Rican and Caribbean literature (MA, PhD); Puerto Rican studies (MA). *Program availability:* Part-time, evening/weekend. *Degree requirements:* For master's, comprehensive exam, thesis; for doctorate, 2 foreign languages, comprehensive exam, thesis/dissertation. *Entrance requirements:* For master's and doctorate, interview.

College of Staten Island of the City University of New York, Graduate Programs, Division of Humanities and Social Sciences, Program in History, Staten Island, NY 10314-6600. Offers history (MA), including Africa and the Middle East, Asia, Europe, Latin America and the Caribbean, United States. *Program availability:* Part-time, evening/weekend. *Faculty:* 5. *Students:* 17. 12 applicants, 67% accepted, 8 enrolled. In 2019, 1 master's awarded. *Degree requirements:* For master's, comprehensive exam (for some programs), thesis or alternative, the MA in History requires 32 graduate credits at the 700-level, with all graduate courses designated at four credits, for a total of eight courses. Students must take at least one course in each of four of the program's five areas of concentration, rigorous thesis option or portfolio option. *Entrance requirements:* For master's, bachelor's degree with minimum GPA of 3.0 overall and in undergraduate history courses, two letters of recommendation, letter of interest, research-based writing sample. Additional exam requirements/recommendations for international students: required—TOEFL (minimum score 550 paper-based; 79 iBT), IELTS (minimum score 6.5). *Application deadline:* For fall admission, 5/10 priority date for domestic students, 4/25 for international students; for spring admission, 12/2 priority date for domestic students, 11/23 for international students. Applications are processed on a rolling basis. Application fee: $75. Electronic applications accepted. *Expenses: Tuition, area resident:* Full-time $11,090; part-time $470 per credit. Tuition, state resident: full-time $11,090; part-time $470 per credit. Tuition, nonresident: full-time $20,520; part-time $855 per credit. *International tuition:* $20,520 full-time. *Required fees:* $559; $181 per semester. Tuition and fees vary according to program. *Unit head:* Susan Smith-Peter, Graduate Program Coordinator, 718-982-3290, E-mail: susan.smithpeter@csi.cuny.edu. *Application contact:* Sasha Spence, Associate Director for Graduate Admissions, 718-982-2019, Fax: 718-982-2500, E-mail: sasha.spence@csi.cuny.edu. Website: https://www.csi.cuny.edu/academics-and-research/departments-programs/history/master-arts-history

Columbia University, Graduate School of Arts and Sciences, New York, NY 10027. Offers African-American studies (MA); American studies (MA); anthropology (MA, PhD); art history and archaeology (MA, PhD); astronomy (PhD); biological sciences (PhD); biotechnology (MA); chemical physics (PhD); chemistry (PhD); classical studies (MA, PhD); classics (MA, PhD); climate and society (MA); conservation biology (MA); earth and environmental sciences (PhD); East Asia: regional studies (MA); East Asian languages and cultures (MA, PhD); ecology, evolution and environmental biology (MA), including conservation biology; ecology, evolution, and environmental biology (PhD), including ecology and evolutionary biology, evolutionary primatology; economics (MA, PhD); English and comparative literature (MA, PhD); French and Romance philology (MA, PhD); Germanic languages (MA, PhD); global French studies (MA); global thought (MA); Hispanic cultural studies (MA); history (PhD); history and literature (MA); human rights studies (MA); Islamic studies (MA); Italian (MA, PhD); Japanese pedagogy (MA); Jewish studies (MA); Latin America and the Caribbean: regional studies (MA); Latin American and Iberian cultures (PhD); mathematics (MA, PhD), including finance (MA); medieval and Renaissance studies (MA); Middle Eastern, South Asian, and African studies (MA, PhD); modern art: critical and curatorial studies (MA); modern European studies (MA); museum anthropology (MA); music (DMA, PhD); oral history (MA); philosophical foundations of physics (MA); philosophy (MA, PhD); physics (PhD); political science (MA, PhD); psychology (PhD); quantitative methods in the social sciences (MA); religion (MA, PhD); Russia, Eurasia and East Europe: regional studies (MA); Russian translation (MA); Slavic cultures (MA); Slavic languages (MA, PhD); sociology (MA, PhD); South Asian studies (MA); statistics (MA, PhD); theatre (PhD). *Program availability:* Part-time. *Students:* 3,506 full-time (1,844 women), 208 part-time (121 women); includes 864 minority (110 Black or African American, non-Hispanic/Latino; 5 American Indian or Alaska Native, non-Hispanic/Latino; 416 Asian, non-Hispanic/Latino; 147 Hispanic/Latino; 6 Native Hawaiian or other Pacific Islander, non-Hispanic/Latino; 180 Two or more races, non-Hispanic/Latino), 2,065 international. 14,545 applicants, 25% accepted, 1,429 enrolled. In 2019, 1,262 master's, 363 doctorates awarded. Terminal master's awarded for partial completion of doctoral program. *Degree requirements:* For master's, variable foreign language requirement, comprehensive exam (for some programs), thesis (for some programs); for doctorate, variable foreign language requirement, comprehensive exam (for some programs), thesis/dissertation. *Entrance requirements:* For master's and doctorate, GRE General Test, GRE Subject Test (for some programs). Additional exam requirements/recommendations for international students: required—TOEFL (minimum score 600 paper-based; 100 iBT), IELTS (minimum score 7.5). Application fee: $115. Electronic applications accepted. *Expenses: Tuition:* Full-time $47,600; part-time $1880 per credit. One-time fee: $105. *Financial support:* Fellowships, research assistantships, teaching assistantships, career-related internships or fieldwork, Federal Work-Study, institutionally sponsored loans, scholarships/grants, traineeships, health care benefits, tuition waivers, and unspecified assistantships available. Support available to part-time students. Financial award application deadline: 12/15. *Unit head:* Dr. Carlos J. Alonso, Dean of the Graduate School of Arts and Sciences and Vice President for Graduate Education, 212-854-2861, E-mail: gsas-dean@columbia.edu. *Application contact:* GSAS Office of Admissions, 212-854-6729, E-mail: gsas-admissions@columbia.edu. Website: http://gsas.columbia.edu/

Cornell University, Graduate School, Graduate Fields of Arts and Sciences, Field of Archaeology, Ithaca, NY 14853. Offers environmental archaeology (MA); historical archaeology (MA); Latin American archaeology (MA); medieval archaeology (MA); Mediterranean and Near Eastern archaeology (MA); Stone Age archaeology (MA). *Degree requirements:* For master's, one foreign language, thesis. *Entrance requirements:* For master's, GRE General Test, 3 letters of recommendation, sample of written work. Additional exam requirements/recommendations for international students: required—TOEFL (minimum score 550 paper-based; 77 iBT). Electronic applications accepted.

Cornell University, Graduate School, Graduate Fields of Arts and Sciences, Field of History, Ithaca, NY 14853. Offers African history (MA, PhD); American history (MA, PhD); ancient Greek history (PhD); ancient history (MA, PhD); ancient Roman history (PhD); early modern European history (MA, PhD); English history (MA, PhD); French history (MA, PhD); German history (MA, PhD); history of science (MA, PhD); Korean history (PhD); Latin American history (MA, PhD); medieval Chinese history (MA, PhD); medieval history (MA, PhD); modern Chinese history (MA, PhD); modern European history (MA, PhD); modern Japanese history (MA, PhD); modern Middle Eastern history (PhD); premodern Islamic history (MA, PhD); premodern Japanese history (MA, PhD); Renaissance history (MA, PhD); Russian history (MA, PhD); South Asian history (PhD); Southeast Asian history (MA, PhD). Terminal master's awarded for partial completion of doctoral program. *Degree requirements:* For master's, thesis; for doctorate, 2 foreign languages, comprehensive exam, thesis/dissertation, 1 year of teaching experience. *Entrance requirements:* For master's and doctorate, GRE General Test, writing sample, 3 letters of recommendation. Additional exam requirements/recommendations for international students: required—TOEFL (minimum score 550 paper-based; 77 iBT). Electronic applications accepted.

Cornell University, Graduate School, Graduate Fields of Arts and Sciences, Field of History of Art, Archaeology and Visual Studies, Ithaca, NY 14853. Offers 19th century art (PhD); African, African American and African diaspora (PhD); American art (PhD); ancient art and archaeology (PhD); Asian American art (PhD); Baroque art (PhD);

Comparative Modernities (PhD); digital art (PhD); East Asian art (PhD); history of photography (PhD); Islamic art (PhD); Latin American art (PhD); medieval art (PhD); modern art (PhD); Renaissance art (PhD); Southeast Asian art (PhD); theory and criticism (PhD); visual studies (PhD). *Degree requirements:* For doctorate, one foreign language, comprehensive exam, thesis/dissertation, general exams in 3 areas. *Entrance requirements:* For doctorate, GRE General Test, sample of written work, 3 letters of recommendation. Additional exam requirements/recommendations for international students: required—TOEFL (minimum score 550 paper-based; 77 iBT). Electronic applications accepted.

Duke University, Graduate School, Department of History, Durham, NC 27708. Offers history (AM, PhD); Latin American studies (PhD); JD/AM. *Degree requirements:* For doctorate, 2 foreign languages, thesis/dissertation. *Entrance requirements:* For doctorate, GRE General Test. Additional exam requirements/recommendations for international students: required—TOEFL (minimum score 577 paper-based; 90 iBT) or IELTS (minimum score 7). Electronic applications accepted.

Georgetown University, Graduate School of Arts and Sciences, Walsh School of Foreign Service, Center for Latin American Studies, Washington, DC 20057-1026. Offers MA, MA/JD, MA/PhD. *Program availability:* Part-time, evening/weekend. *Degree requirements:* For master's, one foreign language, comprehensive exam, thesis optional. *Entrance requirements:* For master's, GRE General Test, minimum B average. Additional exam requirements/recommendations for international students: required—TOEFL. Electronic applications accepted.

The George Washington University, Elliott School of International Affairs, Program in Latin American and Hemispheric Studies, Washington, DC 20052. Offers MA. *Program availability:* Part-time. *Degree requirements:* For master's, one foreign language, capstone project. *Entrance requirements:* For master's, GRE General Test, 2 years (or the equivalent) of Spanish or Portuguese. Additional exam requirements/recommendations for international students: required—TOEFL (minimum score 100 iBT), IELTS (minimum score 7). Electronic applications accepted.

Georgia State University, College of Arts and Sciences, Department of World Languages and Cultures, Atlanta, GA 30302-3083. Offers French (MA), including applied linguistics and pedagogy, French studies, literature and culture; Latin American studies (Certificate); Spanish (MA); translation and interpretation (Certificate), including interpretation, translation. *Program availability:* Part-time. *Faculty:* 15 full-time (8 women), 2 part-time/adjunct (1 woman). *Students:* 28 full-time (22 women), 14 part-time (9 women); includes 26 minority (11 Black or African American, non-Hispanic/Latino; 1 Asian, non-Hispanic/Latino; 11 Hispanic/Latino; 3 Two or more races, non-Hispanic/Latino), 4 international. Average age 35. 13 applicants, 77% accepted, 8 enrolled. In 2019, 14 master's, 7 other advanced degrees awarded. *Entrance requirements:* For master's, GRE, statement of purpose, writing sample in the target language, 2 letters of recommendation, official transcripts; for Certificate, entrance examination involving translating one passage from English to the target language and one passage from the target language to English, 3 letters of recommendation, resume/curriculum vitae, official transcripts. Additional exam requirements/recommendations for international students: required—TOEFL (minimum score 79 iBT). *Application deadline:* For fall admission, 3/15 priority date for domestic and international students; for spring admission, 11/15 priority date for domestic and international students. Application fee: $50. Electronic applications accepted. *Expenses: Tuition, area resident:* Full-time $7164; part-time $398 per credit hour. Tuition, state resident: full-time $7164; part-time $398 per credit hour. Tuition, nonresident: full-time $22,662; part-time $1259 per credit hour. *International tuition:* $22,662 full-time. *Required fees:* $2128; $312 per credit hour. Tuition and fees vary according to course load and program. *Financial support:* Applicants required to submit FAFSA. *Unit head:* Dr. Fernando Reati, Department Chair, 404-413-5984, Fax: 404-413-5982, E-mail: freati@gsu.edu. *Application contact:* Amber Amari, Director, Graduate and Scheduling Services, 404-413-5037, E-mail: aamari@gsu.edu. Website: http://wlc.gsu.edu/

Indiana University Bloomington, University Graduate School, College of Arts and Sciences, School of Global and International Studies, Center for Latin American and Caribbean Studies, Bloomington, IN 47405. Offers MA, MBA/MA, MIS/MA, MLS/MA, MPA/MA, MPH/MA. *Program availability:* Part-time. *Degree requirements:* For master's, one foreign language, oral and written exam. *Entrance requirements:* For master's, GRE General Test. Additional exam requirements/recommendations for international students: required—TOEFL. Electronic applications accepted.

La Salle University, School of Arts and Sciences, Hispanic Institute, Philadelphia, PA 19141-1199. Offers bilingual/bicultural studies (MA); ESL program specialist (Certificate); interpretation: English/Spanish-Spanish/English (Certificate); teaching English to speakers of other languages (MA); translation and interpretation (MA); translation: English/Spanish-Spanish/English (Certificate). *Program availability:* Part-time, evening/weekend. *Degree requirements:* For master's, one foreign language, project or thesis. *Entrance requirements:* For master's, GRE, MAT, or GMAT, professional resume; two letters of recommendation; for Certificate, GRE, MAT, or GMAT, professional resume; two letters of recommendation; evidence of an advanced level in Spanish. Additional exam requirements/recommendations for international students: required—TOEFL. Electronic applications accepted. Application fee is waived when completed online. *Expenses:* Contact institution.

Michigan State University, The Graduate School, College of Social Science, Program in Chicano/Latino Studies, East Lansing, MI 48824. Offers PhD. *Entrance requirements:* Additional exam requirements/recommendations for international students: required—TOEFL. Electronic applications accepted.

New York University, Graduate School of Arts and Science, Center for Latin American and Caribbean Studies, New York, NY 10012-1019. Offers MA, JD/MA. *Program availability:* Part-time. *Degree requirements:* For master's, one foreign language, thesis or alternative, major project. *Entrance requirements:* For master's, GRE General Test, knowledge of Portuguese or Spanish. Additional exam requirements/recommendations for international students: required—TOEFL, IELTS.

Northeastern Illinois University, College of Graduate Studies and Research, College of Arts and Sciences, Program in Latin American Literatures and Cultures, Chicago, IL 60625. Offers MA.

The Ohio State University, Graduate School, Center for Latin American Studies, Columbus, OH 43210. Offers MA. *Entrance requirements:* For master's, GRE General Test. Additional exam requirements/recommendations for international students: required—TOEFL (minimum score 550 paper-based; 79 iBT), IELTS (minimum score 7). Electronic applications accepted.

Ohio University, Graduate College, Center for International Studies, Program in Latin American Studies, Athens, OH 45701-2979. Offers MA. *Program availability:* Part-time. *Degree requirements:* For master's, one foreign language, thesis optional. *Entrance requirements:* For master's, minimum GPA of 3.0. Additional exam requirements/recommendations for international students: required—TOEFL (minimum score 550 paper-based; 80 iBT), IELTS (minimum score 6.5). Electronic applications accepted.

Latin American Studies

San Diego State University, Graduate and Research Affairs, College of Arts and Letters, Center for Latin American Studies, San Diego, CA 92182. Offers MA, MBA/MA. *Degree requirements:* For master's, 2 foreign languages, thesis or alternative. *Entrance requirements:* For master's, GRE General Test, 3 letters of reference. Additional exam requirements/recommendations for international students: required—TOEFL. Electronic applications accepted.

Simon Fraser University, Office of Graduate Studies and Postdoctoral Fellows, Faculty of Arts and Social Sciences, Latin American Studies Program, Vancouver, BC V6B 5K3, Canada. Offers MA, Graduate Certificate. *Degree requirements:* For master's, one foreign language, thesis; for Graduate Certificate, one foreign language, Spanish or Portuguese language exam. *Entrance requirements:* For master's, minimum GPA of 3.0 (on scale of 4.33) or 3.33 based on last 60 credits of undergraduate courses; for Graduate Certificate, current enrollment in a master's or doctoral program. Additional exam requirements/recommendations for international students: recommended—TOEFL (minimum score 580 paper-based; 93 iBT), IELTS (minimum score 7), TWE (minimum score 5). Electronic applications accepted.

Texas Christian University, AddRan College of Liberal Arts, Department of History, Fort Worth, TX 76129-0002. Offers Latin America (MA, PhD); United States (MA, PhD). *Faculty:* 16 full-time (6 women). *Students:* 47 full-time (20 women); includes 8 minority (1 Black or African American, non-Hispanic/Latino; 6 Hispanic/Latino; 1 Two or more races, non-Hispanic/Latino), 2 international. Average age 35. 25 applicants, 48% accepted, 8 enrolled. In 2019, 2 master's, 3 doctorates awarded. Terminal master's awarded for partial completion of doctoral program. *Degree requirements:* For master's, comprehensive exam, thesis or alternative; for doctorate, one foreign language, comprehensive exam, thesis/dissertation. *Entrance requirements:* For master's and doctorate, GRE General Test. Additional exam requirements/recommendations for international students: recommended—TOEFL. *Application deadline:* 2/1 for domestic and international students; for summer admission, 2/1 for domestic and international students. Application fee: $60. Electronic applications accepted. Full-time tuition and fees vary according to program. *Financial support:* In 2019–20, 50 students received support, including 3 fellowships with full tuition reimbursements available (averaging $25,000 per year), 15 research assistantships with full tuition reimbursements available (averaging $20,000 per year), 5 teaching assistantships with full tuition reimbursements available (averaging $20,000 per year); tuition waivers (full) also available. Financial award application deadline: 2/1. *Unit head:* Dr. William Meier, Associate Professor, 817-257-5882, Fax: 817-257-5650, E-mail: w.meier@tcu.edu. *Application contact:* Heather Confessore, Administrative Assistant, 817-257-7288, Fax: 817-257-5650, E-mail: h.confessore@tcu.edu.
Website: https://addran.tcu.edu/history/academics/areas-of-study/graduate-programs/

Tulane University, School of Liberal Arts, Roger Thayer Stone Center for Latin American Studies, New Orleans, LA 70118-5669. Offers MA, PhD, MBA/MA, MCL/MA. Terminal master's awarded for partial completion of doctoral program. *Degree requirements:* For master's, one foreign language, thesis optional; for doctorate, 2 foreign languages, thesis/dissertation. *Entrance requirements:* For master's, GRE General Test, minimum B average in undergraduate course work; for doctorate, GRE General Test. Additional exam requirements/recommendations for international students: required—TOEFL. Electronic applications accepted. *Expenses:* Tuition: Full-time $57,004; part-time $3167 per credit hour. *Required fees:* $2086; $44.50 per credit hour. $80 per term. Tuition and fees vary according to course load, degree level and program.

University at Albany, State University of New York, College of Arts and Sciences, Department of Latin American, Caribbean, and U.S. Latino Studies, Albany, NY 12222-0001. Offers MA, PhD, Certificate. *Program availability:* Part-time, blended/hybrid learning. *Faculty:* 10 full-time (7 women). *Students:* 7 full-time (2 women), 18 part-time (12 women); includes 18 minority (1 Black or African American, non-Hispanic/Latino; 16 Hispanic/Latino; 1 Two or more races, non-Hispanic/Latino), 1 international. 3 applicants, 100% accepted, 2 enrolled. In 2019, 2 master's awarded. *Degree requirements:* For master's, thesis. *Entrance requirements:* For master's, ability to read and write Spanish, transcripts of all schools attended, statement of background and goals, departmental questionnaire, resume, names and contact information for 3 recommenders. Additional exam requirements/recommendations for international students: required—TOEFL (minimum score 550 paper-based). *Application deadline:* For fall admission, 3/15 for domestic students, 5/1 for international students; for spring admission, 11/15 for domestic students, 11/1 for international students. Applications are processed on a rolling basis. Application fee: $75. Electronic applications accepted. *Expenses: Tuition, area resident:* Full-time $11,530; part-time $480 per credit hour. Tuition, nonresident: full-time $23,530; part-time $980 per credit hour. *International tuition:* $23,530 full-time. *Required fees:* $2185; $96 per credit hour. Part-time tuition and fees vary according to course load and program. *Financial support:* Fellowships, research assistantships, and teaching assistantships available. Financial award application deadline: 3/15. *Unit head:* Pedro Caban, Chair, 518-442-4890, Fax: 518-442-4790, E-mail: pcaban@albany.edu. *Application contact:* Michael DeRensis, Director, Graduate Admissions, 518-442-3980, Fax: 518-442-3922, E-mail: graduate@albany.edu.
Website: https://www.albany.edu/lacs/

The University of Arizona, College of Social and Behavioral Sciences, Center for Latin American Studies, Tucson, AZ 85721. Offers MA. *Program availability:* Part-time. *Degree requirements:* For master's, 2 foreign languages, comprehensive exam, thesis optional. *Entrance requirements:* For master's, GRE, 2 letters of recommendation, resume. Additional exam requirements/recommendations for international students: required—TOEFL (minimum score 550 paper-based; 79 iBT). Electronic applications accepted.

University of California, Los Angeles, Graduate Division, International Institute, Interdepartmental Program in Latin American Studies, Los Angeles, CA 90095. Offers MA, M Ed/MA, MA/MA, MBA/MA, MLIS/MA, MPH/MA. *Degree requirements:* For master's, 2 foreign languages, comprehensive exam or thesis. *Entrance requirements:* For master's, GRE General Test, bachelor's degree; minimum undergraduate GPA of 3.0 (or its equivalent if letter grade system not used); language requirement. Additional exam requirements/recommendations for international students: required—TOEFL. Electronic applications accepted.

University of California, San Diego, Graduate Division, Latin American Studies Program, La Jolla, CA 92093. Offers MA. *Students:* 20 full-time (15 women). 23 applicants, 78% accepted, 5 enrolled. In 2019, 6 master's awarded. *Degree requirements:* For master's, one foreign language, thesis. *Entrance requirements:* For master's, GRE General Test, minimum GPA of 3.0; writing sample; statement of purpose. Additional exam requirements/recommendations for international students: required—TOEFL (minimum score 550 paper-based; 80 iBT), IELTS (minimum score 7). *Application deadline:* For fall admission, 1/16 for domestic students. Application fee: $105 ($125 for international students). Electronic applications accepted. *Financial support:* Fellowships, research assistantships, teaching assistantships, scholarships/grants, unspecified assistantships, and readerships available. Financial award applicants required to submit FAFSA. *Unit head:* Luis Martin-Cabrera, Director, E-mail: las-director@ucsd.edu. *Application contact:* Jessica Cassidy, Graduate Coordinator, 858-534-7967, E-mail: las@ucsd.edu.

University of California, Santa Barbara, Graduate Division, College of Letters and Sciences, Division of Humanities and Fine Arts, Program in Latin American and Iberian Studies, Santa Barbara, CA 93106-4150. Offers MA. *Degree requirements:* For master's, one foreign language, comprehensive exam (for some programs), thesis. *Entrance requirements:* For master's, GRE. Additional exam requirements/recommendations for international students: required—TOEFL (minimum score 550 paper-based; 80 iBT), IELTS (minimum score 7). Electronic applications accepted.

University of Chicago, Division of the Social Sciences and Division of the Humanities, Center for Latin American Studies, Chicago, IL 60637. Offers MA. *Degree requirements:* For master's, one foreign language, thesis. *Entrance requirements:* For master's, GRE General Test, 3 letters of recommendation, writing sample (dependent on program), statement of purpose, resume or curriculum vitae. Additional exam requirements/recommendations for international students: required—TOEFL (minimum score 104 iBT), IELTS (minimum score 7). Electronic applications accepted. *Expenses:* Contact institution.

University of Connecticut, Graduate School, College of Liberal Arts and Sciences, Institute of Latina/o, Caribbean, and Latin American Studies, Storrs, CT 06269. Offers Latino and Latin American studies (MA). *Degree requirements:* For master's, comprehensive exam. *Entrance requirements:* For master's, GRE General Test. Additional exam requirements/recommendations for international students: required—TOEFL (minimum score 550 paper-based). Electronic applications accepted.

University of Florida, Graduate School, College of Liberal Arts and Sciences, Center for Latin American Studies, Gainesville, FL 32611. Offers Latin American studies (MA, Certificate); sustainable development practice (MDP); tropical conservation and development (MA); JD/MA. *Program availability:* Part-time. *Degree requirements:* For master's, thesis. *Entrance requirements:* For master's, GRE General Test, minimum GPA of 3.0. Additional exam requirements/recommendations for international students: required—TOEFL (minimum score 550 paper-based; 80 iBT), IELTS (minimum score 6). Electronic applications accepted.

University of Illinois at Chicago, College of Liberal Arts and Sciences, Latin American and Latino Studies Program, Chicago, IL 60607-7128. Offers MA.

University of Illinois at Urbana-Champaign, Graduate College, College of Liberal Arts and Sciences, Center for Latin American and Caribbean Studies, Champaign, IL 61820. Offers Latin American studies (MA).

The University of Kansas, Graduate Studies, College of Liberal Arts and Sciences, Latin American and Caribbean Studies Program, Lawrence, KS 66045. Offers Brazilian studies (Graduate Certificate); Central American and Mexican studies (Graduate Certificate); Latin American and Caribbean studies (Graduate Certificate); Latin American studies (MA). *Program availability:* Part-time. *Students:* 1 full-time (0 women), 1 part-time (0 women), 1 international. Average age 35. 3 applicants, 100% accepted, 1 enrolled. In 2019, 2 master's, 1 other advanced degree awarded. *Entrance requirements:* For master's, GRE, minimum GPA of 3.0; three letters of recommendation; 10-page writing sample, preferably in one of the social sciences or humanities; resume; language proficiency in either Spanish or Portuguese. Additional exam requirements/recommendations for international students: required—TOEFL, IELTS. *Application deadline:* For fall admission, 4/1 for domestic students, 1/15 for international students; for spring admission, 11/15 for domestic students, 10/1 for international students. Application fee: $65 ($85 for international students). Electronic applications accepted. *Expenses:* Tuition, state resident: full-time $9989. Tuition, nonresident: full-time $23,950. International tuition: $23,950 full-time. *Required fees:* $984; $81.99 per credit hour. Tuition and fees vary according to course load, campus/location and program. *Financial support:* Fellowships, research assistantships, teaching assistantships, scholarships/grants, and unspecified assistantships available. Financial award application deadline: 1/15. *Unit head:* Santa Arias, Chair, 785-864-1131, E-mail: sarias@ku.edu. *Application contact:* Clare Thoman, Graduate Admissions Contact, 785-864-9814, E-mail: clarethoman@ku.edu.
Website: https://latamst.ku.edu/

University of Louisiana at Lafayette, College of Liberal Arts, Department of History, Geography and Philosophy, Lafayette, LA 70504. Offers history (MA), including American history, European history, Latin American history, public history. *Program availability:* Part-time. *Degree requirements:* For master's, one foreign language, thesis or alternative. *Entrance requirements:* For master's, GRE General Test, minimum GPA of 2.75. Additional exam requirements/recommendations for international students: required—TOEFL (minimum score 550 paper-based). Electronic applications accepted. *Expenses: Tuition, area resident:* Full-time $5511; part-time $1630 per credit hour. Tuition, state resident: full-time $5511; part-time $1630 per credit hour. Tuition, nonresident: full-time $19,239; part-time $2409 per credit hour. *Required fees:* $46,637.

The University of Manchester, School of Arts, Languages and Cultures, Manchester, United Kingdom. Offers anthropology, media and performance (PhD); applied theatre (PhD); Arab world studies (PhD); archaeology (PhD); art history and visual studies (PhD); arts and cultural management (PhD); arts management and cultural policy (PhD); Chinese studies (PhD); classics and ancient history (PhD); composition (PhD); creative writing (PhD); drama (PhD); East Asian studies (PhD); electroacoustic composition (PhD); English and American studies (PhD); English language (PhD); French studies (PhD); German studies (PhD); history (PhD); humanitarianism and conflict response (PhD); interpreting studies (PhD); Japanese studies (PhD); Latin American cultural studies (PhD); linguistics (PhD); Middle Eastern studies (PhD); museology (PhD); museum practice (PhD); music (PhD); musicology (PhD); Polish studies (PhD); Portuguese studies (PhD); religions and theology (PhD); Russian studies (PhD); Spanish studies (PhD); translation and intercultural studies (PhD).

University of Massachusetts Dartmouth, Graduate School, College of Arts and Sciences, Department of Portuguese, North Dartmouth, MA 02747-2300. Offers Luso-Afro Brazilian studies and theory (PhD); Portuguese studies (MA). *Program availability:* Part-time. *Faculty:* 5 full-time (2 women), 2 part-time/adjunct (1 woman). *Students:* 4 full-time (all women), 5 part-time (4 women); includes 2 minority (both Hispanic/Latino), 1 international. Average age 40. 6 applicants, 100% accepted, 2 enrolled. In 2019, 1 master's, 2 doctorates awarded. Terminal master's awarded for partial completion of doctoral program. *Degree requirements:* For master's, comprehensive exam, thesis, comprehensive written exam or research project; for doctorate, comprehensive exam, thesis/dissertation, Dissertation. *Entrance requirements:* For master's, statement of purpose (300-600 words), resume, 3 letters of recommendation, official transcripts; for doctorate, statement of purpose (300-600 words), resume, 3 letters of recommendation, official transcripts, scholarly writing sample (minimum of 10 pages). Additional exam requirements/recommendations for international students: required—TOEFL (minimum score 72 iBT). *Application deadline:* For fall admission, 8/15 for domestic students, 7/15 for international students; for spring admission, 11/15 for domestic students, 10/15 for international students. Application fee: $60. Electronic applications accepted. *Expenses: Tuition, area resident:* Full-time $16,390; part-time $682.92 per credit. Tuition, state resident: full-time $16,390; part-time $682.92 per credit. Tuition, nonresident: full-time $29,578; part-time $1232.42 per credit. *Required fees:* $575. *Financial support:* In

2019–20, 6 fellowships (averaging $18,167 per year), 1 teaching assistantship (averaging $17,000 per year) were awarded; tuition waivers (full) also available. Financial award application deadline: 3/1; financial award applicants required to submit FAFSA. *Unit head:* Anna Klobucka, Graduate Program Director, Portuguese, 508-999-8241, Fax: 508-910-9272, E-mail: aklobucka@umassd.edu. *Application contact:* Scott Webster, Director of Graduate Studies and Admissions, 508-999-8604, Fax: 508-999-8183, E-mail: graduate@umassd.edu.
Website: http://www.umassd.edu/cas/departmentsanddegreeprograms/portguese

University of Miami, Graduate School, College of Arts and Sciences, Program in Latin American Studies, Coral Gables, FL 33124. Offers Latin American studies (MA). *Program availability:* Part-time. *Degree requirements:* For master's, comprehensive exam (for some programs), thesis, linguistic competency in Spanish or Portuguese, reading competency in a second Latin American language. *Entrance requirements:* For master's, GRE, 3 letters of recommendation. Additional exam requirements/recommendations for international students: required—TOEFL. Electronic applications accepted.

University of New Mexico, Graduate Studies, College of Arts and Sciences, Program in Latin American Studies, Albuquerque, NM 87131. Offers MA, PhD, JD/MA, MA/MA, MA/MPH, MBA/MA, MCRP/MA. *Program availability:* Part-time. *Degree requirements:* For master's, one foreign language, comprehensive exam (for some programs), thesis (for some programs); for doctorate, 2 foreign languages, comprehensive exam, thesis/dissertation. *Entrance requirements:* For master's, GRE General Test, intermediate competence in Spanish, Portuguese or indigenous Latin American language; for doctorate, GRE General Test, master's degree in related field, one Latin American language. Additional exam requirements/recommendations for international students: required—TOEFL. Electronic applications accepted. *Expenses:* Tuition, state resident: full-time $7633; part-time $972 per year. Tuition, nonresident: full-time $22,586; part-time $3840 per year. *International tuition:* $23,292 full-time. *Required fees:* $8608. Tuition and fees vary according to course level, course load, degree level, program and student level.

University of New Mexico, Graduate Studies, College of Fine Arts, Program in Art History, Albuquerque, NM 87131-2039. Offers art history (MA); art of the Americas (MA); history of architecture (PhD); history of graphic arts (PhD); history of photography (PhD); modern Latin American art (PhD); Native American art (PhD); Pre-Columbian art and architecture (PhD); Spanish colonial art (PhD). *Program availability:* Part-time. *Degree requirements:* For master's, one foreign language, comprehensive exam (for some programs), thesis, symposium; for doctorate, 2 foreign languages, comprehensive exam, thesis/dissertation, symposium. *Entrance requirements:* Additional exam requirements/recommendations for international students: required—TOEFL (minimum score 550 paper-based), IELTS (minimum score 6). Electronic applications accepted. *Expenses:* Tuition, state resident: full-time $7633; part-time $972 per year. Tuition, nonresident: full-time $22,586; part-time $3840 per year. *International tuition:* $23,292 full-time. *Required fees:* $8608. Tuition and fees vary according to course level, course load, degree level, program and student level.

The University of North Carolina at Chapel Hill, Graduate School, College of Arts and Sciences, Department of Political Science, Chapel Hill, NC 27599. Offers Latin American studies (Certificate); political science (MA, PhD); trans-Atlantic studies (MA). *Degree requirements:* For master's, comprehensive exam; for doctorate, one foreign language, comprehensive exam, thesis/dissertation. *Entrance requirements:* For master's and doctorate, GRE General Test, minimum GPA of 3.0 recommended. Electronic applications accepted.

The University of North Carolina at Charlotte, College of Liberal Arts and Sciences, Interdisciplinary Liberal Arts and Sciences Programs, Charlotte, NC 28223-0001. Offers gender, sexuality and women's studies (Graduate Certificate); gerontology (MA, Graduate Certificate); Latin American studies (MA); liberal studies (MA); organizational science (PhD); public policy (PhD). *Program availability:* Part-time, evening/weekend. *Students:* 74 full-time (50 women), 56 part-time (43 women); includes 41 minority (16 Black or African American, non-Hispanic/Latino; 3 Asian, non-Hispanic/Latino; 16 Hispanic/Latino; 6 Two or more races, non-Hispanic/Latino), 16 international. Average age 33. 101 applicants, 51% accepted, 37 enrolled. In 2019, 21 master's, 5 doctorates, 8 other advanced degrees awarded. *Entrance requirements:* For master's, GRE General Test or MAT, bachelor's degree from accredited college or university; official transcripts of all previous academic work attempted beyond high school with minimum overall GPA of 3.0; statement of purpose; recommendation letters; for doctorate, GRE or GMAT, statement of purpose discussing interest in program and objectives for pursuing degree, current resume or curriculum vitae, unofficial transcripts; for Graduate Certificate, bachelor's degree from accredited university and either enrolled and in good standing in a graduate degree program at UNC Charlotte or have a minimum undergraduate GPA of 3.0. Additional exam requirements/recommendations for international students: required—TOEFL (minimum score 557 paper-based; 83 iBT), IELTS (minimum score 6.5), TOEFL (minimum score 557 paper-based, 83 iBT) or IELTS (6.5). *Application deadline:* Applications are processed on a rolling basis. Application fee: $75. Electronic applications accepted. *Expenses:* Tuition, state resident: full-time $4337. Tuition, nonresident: full-time $17,771. *Required fees:* $3093. Tuition and fees vary according to course load, degree level and program. *Financial support:* In 2019–20, 3 students received support, including 2 research assistantships (averaging $6,750 per year), 1 teaching assistantship (averaging $21,000 per year); career-related internships or fieldwork, institutionally sponsored loans, scholarships/grants, unspecified assistantships, and administrative assistantships also available. Support available to part-time students. Financial award applicants required to submit FAFSA. *Unit head:* Dr. Nancy A. Gutierrez, Dean, 704-687-0081, E-mail: ngutierr@uncc.edu. *Application contact:* Kathy B. Giddings, Director of Graduate Admissions, 704-687-5503, Fax: 704-687-3279, E-mail: gradadm@uncc.edu.
Website: http://clas.uncc.edu/academics

University of Notre Dame, The Graduate School, College of Arts and Letters, Division of Humanities, Department of Romance Languages and Literatures, Notre Dame, IN 46556. Offers French and Francophone studies (MA); Iberian and Latin American studies (MA); Italian studies (MA); Romance literatures (MA). *Degree requirements:* For master's, 2 foreign languages, comprehensive exam, thesis optional. *Entrance requirements:* For master's, GRE General Test, BA in target language. Additional exam requirements/recommendations for international students: required—TOEFL (minimum score 600 paper-based; 80 iBT). Electronic applications accepted.

University of Pittsburgh, University Center for International Studies, Pittsburgh, PA 15260. Offers African studies (Certificate); Asian studies (Certificate); European Union studies (Certificate); global studies (Certificate); Latin American studies (Certificate); Russian and East European studies (Certificate); West European studies (Certificate). *Program availability:* Part-time, evening/weekend, online learning. *Degree requirements:* For Certificate, one foreign language, comprehensive exam (for some programs). *Entrance requirements:* Additional exam requirements/recommendations for international students: required—TOEFL. *Expenses:* Contact institution.

University of Southern California, Graduate School, Dana and David Dornsife College of Letters, Arts and Sciences, Comparative Studies in Literature and Culture Doctoral Program, Los Angeles, CA 90089. Offers comparative literature (PhD); comparative media and culture (PhD); Spanish and Latin American studies (PhD). *Degree requirements:* For doctorate, 2 foreign languages, comprehensive exam, thesis/dissertation. *Entrance requirements:* For doctorate, GRE, competence in language other than English (highly recommended). Additional exam requirements/recommendations for international students: required—TOEFL. Electronic applications accepted.

University of South Florida, Innovative Education, Tampa, FL 33620-9951. Offers adult, career and higher education (Graduate Certificate), including college teaching, leadership in developing human resources, leadership in higher education; Africana studies (Graduate Certificate), including diasporas and health disparities, genocide and human rights; aging studies (Graduate Certificate), including gerontology; art research (Graduate Certificate), including museum studies; business foundations (Graduate Certificate); chemical and biomedical engineering (Graduate Certificate), including materials science and engineering, water, health and sustainability; child and family studies (Graduate Certificate), including positive behavior support; civil and industrial engineering (Graduate Certificate), including transportation systems analysis; community and family health (Graduate Certificate), including maternal and child health, social marketing and public health, violence and injury: prevention and intervention, women's health; criminology (Graduate Certificate), including criminal justice administration; data science for public administration (Graduate Certificate); digital humanities (Graduate Certificate); educational measurement and research (Graduate Certificate), including evaluation; English (Graduate Certificate), including comparative literary studies, creative writing, professional and technical communication; entrepreneurship (Graduate Certificate); environmental health (Graduate Certificate), including safety management; epidemiology and biostatistics (Graduate Certificate), including applied biostatistics, biostatistics, concepts and tools of epidemiology, epidemiology, epidemiology of infectious diseases; geography, environment and planning (Graduate Certificate), including community development, environmental policy and management, geographical information systems; geology (Graduate Certificate), including hydrogeology; global health (Graduate Certificate), including disaster management, global health and Latin American and Caribbean studies, global health practice, humanitarian assistance, infection control; government and international affairs (Graduate Certificate), including Cuban studies, globalization studies; health policy and management (Graduate Certificate), including health management and leadership, public health policy and programs; hearing specialist: early intervention (Graduate Certificate); industrial and management systems engineering (Graduate Certificate), including systems engineering, technology management; information studies (Graduate Certificate), including school library media specialist; information systems/decision sciences (Graduate Certificate), including analytics and business intelligence; instructional technology (Graduate Certificate), including distance education, Florida digital/virtual educator, instructional design, multimedia design, Web design; internal medicine, bioethics and medical humanities (Graduate Certificate), including biomedical ethics; Latin American and Caribbean studies (Graduate Certificate); leadership for coastal resiliency planning (Graduate Certificate); mass communications (Graduate Certificate), including multimedia journalism; mathematics and statistics (Graduate Certificate), including mathematics; medicine (Graduate Certificate), including aging and neuroscience, bioinformatics, biotechnology, brain fitness and memory management, clinical investigation, hand and upper limb rehabilitation, health informatics, health sciences, integrative weight management, intellectual property, medicine and gender, metabolic and nutritional medicine, metabolic cardiology, pharmacy sciences; national and competitive intelligence (Graduate Certificate); nursing (Graduate Certificate), including simulation based academic fellowship in advanced pain management; psychological and social foundations (Graduate Certificate), including career counseling, college teaching, diversity in education, mental health counseling, school counseling; public affairs (Graduate Certificate), including nonprofit management, public management, research administration; public health (Graduate Certificate), including assessing chemical toxicity and public health risks, health equity, pharmacoepidemiology, public health generalist, toxicology, translational research in adolescent behavioral health; public health practices (Graduate Certificate), including planning for healthy communities; rehabilitation and mental health counseling (Graduate Certificate), including integrative mental health care, marriage and family therapy, rehabilitation technology; secondary education (Graduate Certificate), including ESOL, foreign language education: culture and content, foreign language education: professional; social work (Graduate Certificate), including geriatric social work/clinical gerontology; special education (Graduate Certificate), including autism spectrum disorder, disabilities education: severe/profound; world languages (Graduate Certificate), including teaching English as a second language (TESL) or foreign language. *Unit head:* Dr. Cynthia DeLuca, Associate Vice President and Assistant Vice Provost, 813-974-3077, Fax: 813-974-7061, E-mail: deluca@usf.edu. *Application contact:* Owen Hooper, Director, Summer and Alternative Calendar Programs, 813-974-6917, E-mail: hooper@usf.edu.
Website: http://www.usf.edu/innovative-education/

The University of Texas at Austin, Graduate School, College of Liberal Arts, Teresa Lozano Long Institute of Latin American Studies, Austin, TX 78712-1111. Offers cultural politics of Afro-Latin and indigenous peoples (MA); development studies (MA); environmental studies (MA); human rights (MA); Latin American and international law (LL M); JD/MA; MA/MA; MBA/MA; MP Aff/MA; MSCRP/MA. *Entrance requirements:* For master's, GRE General Test.

The University of Texas at Dallas, School of Arts and Humanities, Richardson, TX 75080. Offers art history (MA); history (MA); humanities (MA, PhD), including aesthetic studies, history of ideas, studies in literature; Latin American studies (MA). *Program availability:* Part-time, evening/weekend. *Faculty:* 48 full-time (19 women), 11 part-time/adjunct (6 women). *Students:* 123 full-time (76 women), 116 part-time (71 women); includes 62 minority (14 Black or African American, non-Hispanic/Latino; 3 American Indian or Alaska Native, non-Hispanic/Latino; 9 Asian, non-Hispanic/Latino; 25 Hispanic/Latino; 11 Two or more races, non-Hispanic/Latino), 27 international. Average age 40. 130 applicants, 60% accepted, 59 enrolled. In 2019, 30 master's, 16 doctorates awarded. *Degree requirements:* For master's, one foreign language, portfolio; for doctorate, one foreign language, thesis/dissertation. *Entrance requirements:* For master's and doctorate, minimum GPA of 3.0 in undergraduate course work in field. Additional exam requirements/recommendations for international students: required—TOEFL (minimum score 550 paper-based). *Application deadline:* For fall admission, 7/15 for domestic students, 5/1 priority date for international students; for spring admission, 11/15 for domestic students, 9/1 priority date for international students. Applications are processed on a rolling basis. Application fee: $50 ($100 for international students). Electronic applications accepted. *Expenses: Tuition, area resident:* Full-time $16,504. Tuition, state resident: full-time $16,504. Tuition, nonresident: full-time $34,266. Tuition and fees vary according to course load. *Financial support:* In 2019–20, 87 students received support, including 9 fellowships (averaging $5,074 per year), 14 research assistantships with partial tuition reimbursements available (averaging $26,575 per year), 69 teaching assistantships with partial tuition reimbursements available (averaging $14,961 per year); Federal Work-Study, institutionally sponsored loans, scholarships/grants, and unspecified assistantships also available. Support available to part-time students. Financial award application deadline: 4/30; financial award

applicants required to submit FAFSA. *Unit head:* Dr. Nils Roemer, Interim Dean, 972-883-2984, Fax: 972-883-2989, E-mail: nroemer@utdallas.edu. *Application contact:* Dr. John Gooch, Associate Dean of Graduate Studies, 972-883-2756, Fax: 972-883-2989, E-mail: john.gooch@utdallas.edu.
Website: http://www.utdallas.edu/ah/

University of Utah, Graduate School, College of Humanities, Latin American Studies Program, Salt Lake City, UT 84112-1107. Offers MA. *Program availability:* Evening/weekend. *Students:* 3 full-time (2 women); includes 2 minority (both Hispanic/Latino). Average age 30. 1 applicant, 100% accepted. In 2019, 1 master's awarded. *Degree requirements:* For master's, 2 foreign languages, comprehensive exam (for some programs), thesis, Third-year language proficiency in either Spanish or Portuguese, and first-year proficiency in a second language spoken in Latin America. *Entrance requirements:* For master's, GRE, minimum undergraduate GPA of 3.0. Additional exam requirements/recommendations for international students: required—TOEFL (minimum score 550 paper-based; 80 iBT), IELTS (minimum score 6.5). *Application deadline:* For fall admission, 2/1 for domestic and international students. Application fee: $55 ($65 for international students). *Expenses:* Tuition, state resident: full-time $7085; part-time $272.51 per credit hour. Tuition, nonresident: full-time $24,937; part-time $959.12 per credit hour. *Required fees:* $880.52; $880.52 per semester. Tuition and fees vary according to degree level, program and student level. *Financial support:* In 2019–20, 2 students received support, including 1 fellowship with full tuition reimbursement available (averaging $15,000 per year), 1 teaching assistantship with full tuition reimbursement available. Financial award application deadline: 2/1; financial award applicants required to submit FAFSA. *Unit head:* Dr. Claudio Holzner, Director, 801-581-6101, Fax: 801-581-6105, E-mail: claudio.holzner@poli-sci.utah.edu. *Application contact:* Patrick T. Cheney, Scholarship and Graduate Program Coordinator, 801-584-6101, Fax: 801-581-6105, E-mail: patrick.cheney@utah.edu.
Website: http://latin-american-studies.utah.edu/

University of Wisconsin–Madison, Graduate School, College of Letters and Science, Department of History, Madison, WI 53706-1380. Offers African history (MA, PhD); Central Asian history (MA, PhD); comparative world history (MA, PhD); East Asian history (MA, PhD); European history (MA, PhD); gender and women's history (MA, PhD); Latin American and Caribbean history (MA, PhD); Middle Eastern history (MA, PhD); South Asian history (MA, PhD); Southeast Asian history (MA, PhD); United States history (MA, PhD). Terminal master's awarded for partial completion of doctoral program. *Degree requirements:* For master's, thesis (for some programs); for doctorate, variable foreign language requirement, thesis/dissertation. *Entrance requirements:* For master's and doctorate, GRE General Test. Additional exam requirements/recommendations for international students: required—Michigan English Language Assessment Battery or TOEFL. Electronic applications accepted.

University of Wisconsin–Madison, Graduate School, College of Letters and Science, Latin American, Caribbean and Iberian Studies Program, Madison, WI 53706-1380. Offers MA, MA/JD. *Degree requirements:* For master's, 2 foreign languages, thesis. *Entrance requirements:* For master's, minimum GPA of 3.0. Electronic applications accepted.

University of Wisconsin–Milwaukee, Graduate School, College of Letters and Science, Department of Foreign Languages and Literature, Milwaukee, WI 53201-0413. Offers foreign languages and literature (MA), including classic Greek, classics, comparative literature, French/Francophone language, literature, and culture, German language, literature, and culture, interpreting, Latin, linguistics, Spanish language, literature, and culture, translation; interpreting (Graduate Certificate); language, literature, and translation (MA, MALLT); translation (Graduate Certificate). *Program availability:* Part-time. *Degree requirements:* For master's, 2 foreign languages, thesis or alternative. *Entrance requirements:* Additional exam requirements/recommendations for international students: required—TOEFL (minimum score 550 paper-based; 79 iBT), IELTS (minimum score 6.5). Electronic applications accepted.

Vanderbilt University, Program in Latin American Studies, Nashville, TN 37240-1001. Offers MA, LL M/MA, MBA/MA. *Faculty:* 53 full-time (20 women). *Students:* 4 full-time (2 women); includes 1 minority (Hispanic/Latino). Average age 26. 19 applicants, 26% accepted, 3 enrolled. In 2019, 2 master's awarded. *Degree requirements:* For master's, 2 foreign languages, thesis or alternative. *Entrance requirements:* For master's, GRE General Test. Additional exam requirements/recommendations for international students: required—TOEFL (minimum score 570 paper-based; 88 iBT). *Application deadline:* For fall admission, 1/15 for domestic and international students. Application fee: $0. Electronic applications accepted. *Expenses: Tuition:* Full-time $51,018; part-time $2087 per hour. *Required fees:* $542. Tuition and fees vary according to program. *Financial support:* Teaching assistantships with full tuition reimbursements, Federal Work-Study, institutionally sponsored loans, and health care benefits available. Financial award application deadline: 1/15; financial award applicants required to submit CSS PROFILE or FAFSA. *Unit head:* Dr. Edward Fischer, Director, 615-322-2527, Fax: 615-343-6002, E-mail: edward.f.fischer@vanderbilt.edu. *Application contact:* Nicolette M. Kostiw, Assistant Director/Director of Graduate Studies, 615-322-2527, Fax: 615-343-6002, E-mail: nicolette.m.wilhide@vanderbilt.edu.
Website: http://www.vanderbilt.edu/clas/graduate-programs/

Yale University, Graduate School of Arts and Sciences, Department of Spanish and Portuguese, New Haven, CT 06520. Offers Latin American literature (PhD); Luso-Brazilian and Spanish/Spanish American literatures (PhD); Spanish peninsular literature (PhD). Terminal master's awarded for partial completion of doctoral program. *Degree requirements:* For doctorate, 3 foreign languages, thesis/dissertation. *Entrance requirements:* For doctorate, GRE General Test.

Near and Middle Eastern Studies

The American University in Cairo, School of Humanities and Social Sciences, Cairo, Egypt. Offers Arab and Islamic civilizations (Graduate Diploma); Arabic studies (MA); comparative literary studies (Graduate Diploma); Egyptology and Coptology (MA); English and comparative literature (MA); humanities and social sciences (Graduate Diploma); philosophy (MA); psychology (MA); sociology and anthropology (MA); teaching Arabic as a foreign language (MA); teaching English to speakers of other languages (MA). *Program availability:* Part-time, evening/weekend. *Degree requirements:* For master's, comprehensive exam (for some programs), thesis (for some programs). *Entrance requirements:* Additional exam requirements/recommendations for international students: required—TOEFL (minimum score 450 paper-based; 45 iBT), IELTS (minimum score 5). Electronic applications accepted.

The American University of Paris, Graduate Programs, Paris, France. Offers cross-cultural and sustainable business management (MA); cultural translation (MA); global communications (MA); global communications and civil society (MA); international affairs (MA); international affairs, conflict resolution and civil society development (MA); Middle East and Islamic studies (MA); Middle East and Islamic studies and international affairs (MA); public policy and international affairs (MA); public policy and international law (MA). *Degree requirements:* For master's, thesis (for some programs). *Entrance requirements:* For master's, minimum undergraduate GPA of 3.0. Additional exam requirements/recommendations for international students: recommended—TOEFL, IELTS. Electronic applications accepted.

Brandeis University, Graduate School of Arts and Sciences, Department of Near Eastern and Judaic Studies, Waltham, MA 02454-9110. Offers Near Eastern and Judaic studies (MA); near Eastern and Judaic studies/conflict resolution and coexistence (MA); near Eastern and Judaic studies/Jewish professional leadership (MA); near Eastern and Judaic studies/women's, gender, and sexuality studies (MA); teaching of Hebrew (MAT); the bible and ancient near east (PhD). *Program availability:* Part-time. *Faculty:* 21 full-time (8 women), 5 part-time/adjunct (3 women). *Students:* 34 full-time (15 women), 2 part-time (1 woman); includes 8 minority (1 Black or African American, non-Hispanic/Latino; 2 Asian, non-Hispanic/Latino; 3 Hispanic/Latino; 2 Two or more races, non-Hispanic/Latino), 7 international. Average age 34. 76 applicants, 53% accepted, 5 enrolled. In 2019, 3 master's, 3 doctorates awarded. Terminal master's awarded for partial completion of doctoral program. *Degree requirements:* For master's, one foreign language, thesis or alternative, capstone, thesis, or internship; for doctorate, variable foreign language requirement, comprehensive exam, thesis/dissertation. *Entrance requirements:* For master's and doctorate, GRE General recommended, transcripts, letters of recommendation, resume, writing sample, and statement of purpose. Additional exam requirements/recommendations for international students: required—TOEFL, IELTS, PTE. *Application deadline:* For fall admission, 1/15 priority date for domestic and international students. Applications are processed on a rolling basis. Application fee: $75. Electronic applications accepted. *Financial support:* In 2019–20, 9 fellowships with full tuition reimbursements (averaging $25,000 per year), 8 teaching assistantships (averaging $3,550 per year) were awarded; scholarships/grants, health care benefits, and tuition waivers also available. Support available to part-time students. *Unit head:* Dr. Ilana Szobel, Director of Graduate Studies, 781-736-5230, E-mail: szobel@brandeis.edu. *Application contact:* Jean Mannion, Administrator, 781-736-2950, E-mail: mannion@brandeis.edu.
Website: http://www.brandeis.edu/gsas/programs/nejs.html

Brown University, Graduate School, Department of Egyptology and Assyriology, Providence, RI 02912. Offers ancient western Asian studies (PhD); Egyptology (PhD); history of the exact sciences in antiquity (PhD). *Degree requirements:* For doctorate, 2 foreign languages, comprehensive exam, thesis/dissertation. *Entrance requirements:* For doctorate, GRE General Test.

California State University, Long Beach, Graduate Studies, College of Liberal Arts, Department of History, Long Beach, CA 90840. Offers Africa and the Middle East (MA). *Program availability:* Part-time, evening/weekend. *Degree requirements:* For master's, one foreign language, comprehensive exam or thesis. Electronic applications accepted.

The Catholic University of America, School of Arts and Sciences, Department of Semitic and Egyptian Languages and Literatures, Washington, DC 20064. Offers ancient Near East (Biblical Hebrew/Aramaic) (MA, PhD); Arabic (PhD); Christian Near East (Biblical Hebrew/Aramaic) (MA); Coptic (MA, PhD); Syriac (MA, PhD). *Program availability:* Part-time. *Faculty:* 4 full-time (0 women), 2 part-time/adjunct (1 woman). *Students:* 7 full-time (3 women), 28 part-time (7 women); includes 3 minority (1 Black or African American, non-Hispanic/Latino; 2 Two or more races, non-Hispanic/Latino), 6 international. Average age 35. 16 applicants, 88% accepted, 5 enrolled. In 2019, 4 master's, 3 doctorates awarded. Terminal master's awarded for partial completion of doctoral program. *Degree requirements:* For master's, one foreign language, comprehensive exam; for doctorate, 2 foreign languages, comprehensive exam, thesis/dissertation. *Entrance requirements:* For master's, GRE General Test, statement of purpose, official copies of academic transcripts, three letters of recommendation; for doctorate, GRE General Test, statement of purpose, official copies of academic transcripts, three letters of recommendation, successful completion of MA field. Additional exam requirements/recommendations for international students: required—TOEFL (minimum score 550 paper-based; 80 iBT). *Application deadline:* For fall admission, 7/15 priority date for domestic students, 7/1 for international students; for spring admission, 11/15 priority date for domestic students, 11/1 for international students. Applications are processed on a rolling basis. Application fee: $55. Electronic applications accepted. *Expenses:* Contact institution. *Financial support:* Fellowships, research assistantships, teaching assistantships, Federal Work-Study, scholarships/grants, tuition waivers (full and partial), and unspecified assistantships available. Financial award application deadline: 2/1; financial award applicants required to submit FAFSA. *Unit head:* Dr. Andrew D. Gross, Chair, 202-319-5083, Fax: 202-319-4735, E-mail: grossa@cua.edu. *Application contact:* Dr. Steven Brown, Director of Graduate Admissions, 202-319-5057, Fax: 202-319-6533, E-mail: cua-admissions@cua.edu.
Website: http://semitics.cua.edu/

The Catholic University of America, School of Arts and Sciences, Program in Medieval and Byzantine Studies, Washington, DC 20064. Offers Byzantine and Orthodox studies (MA); Medieval and Byzantine studies (PhD, Certificate); the Islamic world (MA); the Medieval West (MA). *Program availability:* Part-time. *Students:* 1 (woman) full-time, 5 part-time (2 women). Average age 43. 10 applicants, 30% accepted. *Degree requirements:* For master's, one foreign language, comprehensive exam, thesis or alternative; for doctorate, 2 foreign languages, comprehensive exam, thesis/dissertation. *Entrance requirements:* For master's and doctorate, GRE General Test, statement of purpose, official copies of academic transcripts, three letters of recommendation, writing sample; for Certificate, bachelor's degree. Additional exam requirements/recommendations for international students: required—TOEFL (minimum score 550 paper-based; 80 iBT). *Application deadline:* For fall admission, 7/15 priority date for domestic students, 7/1 for international students; for spring admission, 11/15 priority date for domestic students, 11/1 for international students. Applications are processed on a rolling basis. Application fee: $55. Electronic applications accepted. *Expenses:* Contact institution. *Financial support:* Fellowships, research assistantships, teaching assistantships, Federal Work-Study, scholarships/grants, tuition waivers (full and partial), and unspecified assistantships available. Financial award application deadline: 2/1; financial award applicants required to submit FAFSA. *Unit head:* Dr. Lilla Kopar, Director, 202-319-5794, Fax: 202-319-6609, E-mail: kopar@cua.edu. *Application contact:* Director of Graduate Admissions, 202-319-5057, Fax: 202-319-6533, E-mail:

cua-admissions@cua.edu.
Website: http://mbs.cua.edu/

College of Staten Island of the City University of New York, Graduate Programs, Division of Humanities and Social Sciences, Program in History, Staten Island, NY 10314-6600. Offers history (MA), including Africa and the Middle East, Asia, Europe, Latin America and the Caribbean, United States. *Program availability:* Part-time, evening/weekend. *Faculty:* 5. *Students:* 17. 12 applicants, 67% accepted, 8 enrolled. In 2019, 1 master's awarded. *Degree requirements:* For master's, comprehensive exam (for some programs), thesis or alternative, the MA in History requires 32 graduate credits at the 700-level, with all graduate courses designated at four credits, for a total of eight courses. Students must take at least one course in each of four of the program's five areas of concentration, rigorous thesis option or portfolio option. *Entrance requirements:* For master's, bachelor's degree with minimum GPA of 3.0 overall and in undergraduate history courses, two letters of recommendation, letter of interest, research-based writing sample. Additional exam requirements/recommendations for international students: required—TOEFL (minimum score 550 paper-based; 79 iBT), IELTS (minimum score 6.5). *Application deadline:* For fall admission, 5/10 priority date for domestic students, 4/25 for international students; for spring admission, 12/2 priority date for domestic students, 11/23 for international students. Applications are processed on a rolling basis. Application fee: $75. Electronic applications accepted. *Expenses: Tuition, area resident:* Full-time $11,090; part-time $470 per credit. Tuition, state resident: full-time $11,090; part-time $470 per credit. Tuition, nonresident: full-time $20,520; part-time $855 per credit. *International tuition:* $20,520 full-time. *Required fees:* $559; $181 per semester. Tuition and fees vary according to program. *Unit head:* Susan Smith-Peter, Graduate Program Coordinator, 718-982-3290, E-mail: susan.smithpeter@csi.cuny.edu. *Application contact:* Sasha Spence, Associate Director for Graduate Admissions, 718-982-2019, Fax: 718-982-2500, E-mail: sasha.spence@csi.cuny.edu.
Website: https://www.csi.cuny.edu/academics-and-research/departments-programs/history/master-arts-history

Columbia University, Graduate School of Arts and Sciences, New York, NY 10027. Offers African-American studies (MA); American studies (MA); anthropology (MA, PhD); art history and archaeology (MA, PhD); astronomy (PhD); biological sciences (PhD); biotechnology (MA); chemical physics (PhD); chemistry (PhD); classical studies (MA, PhD); classics (MA, PhD); climate and society (MA); conservation biology (MA); earth and environmental sciences (PhD); East Asia: regional studies (MA); East Asian languages and cultures (MA, PhD); ecology, evolution and environmental biology (MA), including conservation biology; ecology, evolution, and environmental biology (PhD), including ecology and evolutionary biology, evolutionary primatology; economics (MA, PhD); English and comparative literature (MA, PhD); French and Romance philology (MA, PhD); Germanic languages (MA, PhD); global French studies (MA); global thought (MA); Hispanic cultural studies (MA); history (PhD); history and literature (MA); human rights studies (MA); Islamic studies (MA); Italian (MA, PhD); Japanese pedagogy (MA); Jewish studies (MA); Latin America and the Caribbean: regional studies (MA); Latin American and Iberian cultures (PhD); mathematics (MA, PhD), including finance (MA); medieval and Renaissance studies (MA); Middle Eastern, South Asian, and African studies (MA, PhD); modern art: critical and curatorial studies (MA); modern European studies (MA); museum anthropology (MA); music (DMA, PhD); oral history (MA); philosophical foundations of physics (MA); philosophy (MA, PhD); physics (PhD); political science (MA, PhD); psychology (PhD); quantitative methods in the social sciences (MA); religion (MA, PhD); Russia, Eurasia and East Europe: regional studies (MA); Russian translation (MA); Slavic cultures (MA); Slavic languages (MA, PhD); sociology (MA, PhD); South Asian studies (MA); statistics (MA, PhD); theatre (PhD). *Program availability:* Part-time. *Students:* 3,506 full-time (1,844 women), 208 part-time (121 women); includes 864 minority (110 Black or African American, non-Hispanic/Latino; 5 American Indian or Alaska Native, non-Hispanic/Latino; 416 Asian, non-Hispanic/Latino; 147 Hispanic/Latino; 6 Native Hawaiian or other Pacific Islander, non-Hispanic/Latino; 180 Two or more races, non-Hispanic/Latino), 2,065 international. 14,545 applicants, 25% accepted, 1,429 enrolled. In 2019, 1,262 master's, 363 doctorates awarded. Terminal master's awarded for partial completion of doctoral program. *Degree requirements:* For master's, variable foreign language requirement, comprehensive exam (for some programs), thesis (for some programs); for doctorate, variable foreign language requirement, comprehensive exam (for some programs), thesis/dissertation. *Entrance requirements:* For master's and doctorate, GRE General Test, GRE Subject Test (for some programs). Additional exam requirements/recommendations for international students: required—TOEFL (minimum score 600 paper-based; 100 iBT), IELTS (minimum score 7.5). Application fee: $115. Electronic applications accepted. *Expenses: Tuition:* Full-time $47,600; part-time $1880 per credit. One-time fee: $105. *Financial support:* Fellowships, research assistantships, teaching assistantships, career-related internships or fieldwork, Federal Work-Study, institutionally sponsored loans, scholarships/grants, traineeships, health care benefits, tuition waivers, and unspecified assistantships available. Support available to part-time students. Financial award application deadline: 12/15. *Unit head:* Dr. Carlos J. Alonso, Dean of the Graduate School of Arts and Sciences and Vice President for Graduate Education, 212-854-2861, E-mail: gsas-dean@columbia.edu. *Application contact:* GSAS Office of Admissions, 212-854-6729, E-mail: gsas-admissions@columbia.edu.
Website: http://gsas.columbia.edu/

Cornell University, Graduate School, Graduate Fields of Arts and Sciences, Field of Archaeology, Ithaca, NY 14853. Offers environmental archaeology (MA); historical archaeology (MA); Latin American archaeology (MA); medieval archaeology (MA); Mediterranean and Near Eastern archaeology (MA); Stone Age archaeology (MA). *Degree requirements:* For master's, one foreign language, thesis. *Entrance requirements:* For master's, GRE General Test, 3 letters of recommendation, sample of written work. Additional exam requirements/recommendations for international students: required—TOEFL (minimum score 550 paper-based; 77 iBT). Electronic applications accepted.

Cornell University, Graduate School, Graduate Fields of Arts and Sciences, Field of History, Ithaca, NY 14853. Offers African history (MA, PhD); American history (MA, PhD); ancient Greek history (PhD); ancient history (MA, PhD); ancient Roman history (PhD); early modern European history (MA, PhD); English history (MA, PhD); French history (MA, PhD); German history (MA, PhD); history of science (MA, PhD); Korean history (PhD); Latin American history (MA, PhD); medieval Chinese history (MA, PhD); medieval history (MA, PhD); modern Chinese history (MA, PhD); modern European history (MA, PhD); modern Japanese history (MA, PhD); modern Middle Eastern history (PhD); premodern Islamic history (MA, PhD); premodern Japanese history (MA, PhD); Renaissance history (MA, PhD); Russian history (MA, PhD); South Asian history (PhD); Southeast Asian history (MA, PhD). Terminal master's awarded for partial completion of doctoral program. *Degree requirements:* For master's, thesis; for doctorate, 2 foreign languages, comprehensive exam, thesis/dissertation, 1 year of teaching experience. *Entrance requirements:* For master's and doctorate, GRE General Test, writing sample, 3 letters of recommendation. Additional exam requirements/recommendations for international students: required—TOEFL (minimum score 550 paper-based; 77 iBT). Electronic applications accepted.

Cornell University, Graduate School, Graduate Fields of Arts and Sciences, Field of History of Art, Archaeology and Visual Studies, Ithaca, NY 14853. Offers 19th century art (PhD); African, African American and African diaspora (PhD); American art (PhD); ancient art and archaeology (PhD); Asian American art (PhD); Baroque art (PhD); Comparative Modernities (PhD); digital art (PhD); East Asian art (PhD); history of photography (PhD); Islamic art (PhD); Latin American art (PhD); medieval art (PhD); modern art (PhD); Renaissance art (PhD); Southeast Asian art (PhD); theory and criticism (PhD); visual studies (PhD). *Degree requirements:* For doctorate, one foreign language, comprehensive exam, thesis/dissertation, general exams in 3 areas. *Entrance requirements:* For doctorate, GRE General Test, sample of written work, 3 letters of recommendation. Additional exam requirements/recommendations for international students: required—TOEFL (minimum score 550 paper-based; 77 iBT). Electronic applications accepted.

Cornell University, Graduate School, Graduate Fields of Arts and Sciences, Field of Near Eastern Studies, Ithaca, NY 14853. Offers ancient Near Eastern studies (MA, PhD); Arabic and Islamic studies (MA, PhD); biblical studies (MA, PhD); Hebrew and Judaic studies (MA, PhD). Terminal master's awarded for partial completion of doctoral program. *Degree requirements:* For master's, one foreign language, thesis; for doctorate, 2 foreign languages, comprehensive exam, thesis/dissertation. *Entrance requirements:* For master's and doctorate, GRE General Test, 2 years of 1 Near Eastern language, 3 letters of recommendation, writing sample. Additional exam requirements/recommendations for international students: required—TOEFL (minimum score 550 paper-based; 77 iBT). Electronic applications accepted.

George Mason University, College of Humanities and Social Sciences, Program in Middle East and Islamic Studies, Fairfax, VA 22030. Offers MA, Certificate. *Degree requirements:* For master's, one foreign language, thesis optional. *Entrance requirements:* For master's, GRE, resume, 3 letters of recommendation, goals statement, writing sample, official transcripts. Additional exam requirements/recommendations for international students: required—TOEFL (minimum score 575 paper-based; 88 iBT), IELTS (minimum score 6.5), PTE (minimum score 59). Electronic applications accepted.

Georgetown University, Graduate School of Arts and Sciences, Walsh School of Foreign Service, The Center for Contemporary Arab Studies, Washington, DC 20057. Offers MA, Certificate, MA/JD, MA/PhD. *Degree requirements:* For master's, one foreign language, comprehensive exam, thesis or alternative, proficiency in Arabic. *Entrance requirements:* For master's, GRE, minimum GPA of 3.0. Additional exam requirements/recommendations for international students: required—TOEFL (minimum score 600 paper-based; 100 iBT). Electronic applications accepted.

The George Washington University, Columbian College of Arts and Sciences, Department of Religion, Washington, DC 20052. Offers Islam (MA), including Hinduism and Islam. *Program availability:* Part-time, evening/weekend. *Degree requirements:* For master's, one foreign language, comprehensive exam, thesis. *Entrance requirements:* For master's, GRE General Test, interview, minimum GPA of 3.0. Additional exam requirements/recommendations for international students: required—TOEFL (minimum score 550 paper-based; 80 iBT). Electronic applications accepted.

The George Washington University, Elliott School of International Affairs, Program in Middle East Studies, Washington, DC 20052. Offers MA. *Program availability:* Part-time. *Degree requirements:* For master's, one foreign language, capstone project. *Entrance requirements:* For master's, GRE General Test, 2 years (or equivalent) of an approved regional language. Additional exam requirements/recommendations for international students: required—TOEFL (minimum score 100 iBT), IELTS (minimum score 7). Electronic applications accepted.

Harvard University, Graduate School of Arts and Sciences, Committee on Middle Eastern Studies, Cambridge, MA 02138. Offers anthropology and Middle Eastern studies (PhD); economics and Middle Eastern studies (PhD); fine arts and Middle Eastern studies (PhD); history and Middle Eastern studies (PhD); regional studies–Middle East (AM). Terminal master's awarded for partial completion of doctoral program. *Degree requirements:* For master's, one foreign language; for doctorate, 2 foreign languages, thesis/dissertation. *Entrance requirements:* For master's, GRE General Test; for doctorate, GRE General Test, 1 year of course work in Middle Eastern regional studies, proficiency in a related language. Additional exam requirements/recommendations for international students: required—TOEFL.

Harvard University, Graduate School of Arts and Sciences, Department of Near Eastern Languages and Civilizations, Cambridge, MA 02138. Offers Akkadian and Sumerian (AM, PhD); Arabic (AM, PhD); Armenian (AM, PhD); biblical history (AM, PhD); Hebrew (AM, PhD); Indo-Muslim culture (AM, PhD); Iranian (AM, PhD); Jewish history and literature (AM, PhD); Persian (AM, PhD); Semitic philology (AM, PhD); Syro-Palestinian archaeology (AM, PhD); Turkish (AM, PhD). *Degree requirements:* For doctorate, variable foreign language requirement, thesis/dissertation, general exams. *Entrance requirements:* For master's, GRE General Test; for doctorate, GRE General Test, proficiency in a Near Eastern language. Additional exam requirements/recommendations for international students: required—TOEFL.

Johns Hopkins University, Zanvyl Krieger School of Arts and Sciences, Department of Near Eastern Studies, Baltimore, MD 21218. Offers archaeology (PhD); Assyriology (PhD); Egyptology (PhD); Hebrew Bible/Northwest Semitics (PhD). *Degree requirements:* For doctorate, 2 foreign languages, comprehensive exam, thesis/dissertation. *Entrance requirements:* For doctorate, GRE. Additional exam requirements/recommendations for international students: required—TOEFL (minimum score 600 paper-based; 100 iBT); recommended—IELTS. Electronic applications accepted. *Expenses:* Contact institution.

McGill University, Faculty of Graduate and Postdoctoral Studies, Faculty of Arts, Institute of Islamic Studies, Montréal, QC H3A 2T5, Canada. Offers MA, PhD, Diploma.

New York University, Graduate School of Arts and Science, Hagop Kevorkian Center for Near Eastern Studies, Department of Middle Eastern and Islamic Studies, New York, NY 10012-1019. Offers Middle Eastern and Islamic studies (MA, PhD); Middle Eastern and Islamic studies/history (PhD). *Program availability:* Part-time. Terminal master's awarded for partial completion of doctoral program. *Degree requirements:* For master's, 2 foreign languages, thesis; for doctorate, 4 foreign languages, comprehensive exam, thesis/dissertation. *Entrance requirements:* For doctorate, GRE General Test. Additional exam requirements/recommendations for international students: required—TOEFL, IELTS.

New York University, Graduate School of Arts and Science, Hagop Kevorkian Center for Near Eastern Studies, Program in Near Eastern Studies, New York, NY 10012-1019. Offers Near Eastern studies/museum studies (MA). *Program availability:* Part-time. *Degree requirements:* For master's, one foreign language, thesis. *Entrance requirements:* For master's, GRE General Test. Additional exam requirements/recommendations for international students: required—TOEFL, IELTS.

Princeton University, Graduate School, Department of Near Eastern Studies, Princeton, NJ 08544-1019. Offers MA, PhD. *Degree requirements:* For master's, one foreign language, thesis; for doctorate, 2 foreign languages, thesis/dissertation. *Entrance requirements:* For master's and doctorate, GRE General Test. Additional exam requirements/recommendations for international students: required—TOEFL. Electronic applications accepted.

Rice University, Graduate Programs, School of Humanities, Department of Religious Studies, Houston, TX 77251-1892. Offers African religions (PhD); African-American religions (PhD); contemplative studies (PhD); gnosticism, esotericism, mysticism (PhD); Islam (PhD); Jewish thought and philosophy (PhD); modern Christianity in thought and popular culture (PhD); psychology of religion (PhD); the Bible and beyond (PhD). *Degree requirements:* For doctorate, 2 foreign languages, comprehensive exam, thesis/dissertation. *Entrance requirements:* For doctorate, GRE, letters of recommendation, writing sample. Additional exam requirements/recommendations for international students: required—TOEFL (minimum score 600 paper-based; 90 iBT). Electronic applications accepted.

Southern Evangelical Seminary, Graduate Programs, Matthews, NC 28105. Offers apologetics (MA, D Min, Certificate); Christian education (MA); church ministry (MA, Certificate); divinity (Certificate), including apologetics (M Div, Certificate); Islamic studies (MA, Certificate); Jewish studies (MA); philosophy (MA); philosophy of religion (PhD); religion (MA); theology (M Div), including apologetics (M Div, Certificate), Biblical studies; youth ministry (MA). *Program availability:* Part-time, evening/weekend, online learning. *Degree requirements:* For master's, thesis (for some programs); for doctorate, 2 foreign languages, comprehensive exam (for some programs), thesis/dissertation. *Entrance requirements:* Additional exam requirements/recommendations for international students: required—TOEFL (minimum score 600 paper-based). *Expenses: Tuition:* Full-time $24,000; part-time $12,000 per year. *Required fees:* $600; $300 per semester. $150 per semester.

Southwestern Baptist Theological Seminary, Roy Fish School of Evangelism and Missions, Fort Worth, TX 76122-0000. Offers cross-cultural missions (MTS); evangelism (M Div); evangelism and missions (D Min); international church planting (M Div); Islamic studies (M Div, MA Islamic); missiology (MA Miss); missions (M Div); North American church planting (M Div); North American evangelism and international missions (D Min); theology (Th M); world Christian studies (PhD).

The University of Arizona, College of Social and Behavioral Sciences, School of Middle Eastern and North African Studies, Tucson, AZ 85721. Offers MA, PhD, Graduate Certificate. *Program availability:* Part-time, evening/weekend. Terminal master's awarded for partial completion of doctoral program. *Degree requirements:* For master's, one foreign language; for doctorate, 3 foreign languages, thesis/dissertation. *Entrance requirements:* For master's, GRE General Test, 3 letters of recommendation, statement of purpose, curriculum vitae, writing sample; for doctorate, GRE General Test, 3 letters of recommendation, curriculum vitae, writing sample. Additional exam requirements/recommendations for international students: required—TOEFL (minimum score 550 paper-based; 79 iBT). Electronic applications accepted.

University of California, Berkeley, Graduate Division, College of Letters and Science, Department of Near Eastern Studies, Berkeley, CA 94720. Offers Near Eastern studies (MA, PhD). *Degree requirements:* For doctorate, 2 foreign languages, thesis/dissertation, qualifying exam. *Entrance requirements:* For master's and doctorate, GRE General Test, minimum GPA of 3.0, 3 letters of recommendation. Electronic applications accepted.

University of California, Los Angeles, Graduate Division, College of Letters and Science, Department of Near Eastern Languages and Cultures, Los Angeles, CA 90034. Offers MA, PhD. *Degree requirements:* For master's, one foreign language, comprehensive exam; for doctorate, 2 foreign languages, thesis/dissertation, oral and written qualifying exams. *Entrance requirements:* For master's, GRE General Test, bachelor's degree; minimum undergraduate GPA of 3.25 (or its equivalent if letter grade system not used); for doctorate, GRE General Test, master's degree; minimum undergraduate GPA of 3.25 (or its equivalent if letter grade system not used). Additional exam requirements/recommendations for international students: required—TOEFL. Electronic applications accepted.

University of California, Los Angeles, Graduate Division, College of Letters and Science, Interdepartmental Program in Indo-European Studies, Los Angeles, CA 90095. Offers PhD. *Degree requirements:* For doctorate, 2 foreign languages, thesis/dissertation, oral and written qualifying exams. *Entrance requirements:* For doctorate, bachelor's degree; minimum undergraduate GPA of 3.0 (or its equivalent if letter grade system not used); writing sample; competence in Latin. Additional exam requirements/recommendations for international students: required—TOEFL. Electronic applications accepted.

University of California, Los Angeles, Graduate Division, International Institute, Interdepartmental Program in Islamic Studies, Los Angeles, CA 90095. Offers MA, PhD, MPH/MA. *Degree requirements:* For master's, one foreign language, comprehensive exam; for doctorate, one foreign language, thesis/dissertation, oral and written qualifying exams. *Entrance requirements:* For master's, GRE General Test, bachelor's degree; minimum undergraduate GPA of 3.0 (or its equivalent if letter grade system not used); language requirement; for doctorate, GRE General Test, master's degree; minimum undergraduate GPA of 3.0 (or its equivalent if letter grade system not used); proficiency in Arabic. Additional exam requirements/recommendations for international students: required—TOEFL. Electronic applications accepted.

University of Chicago, Divinity School, PhD Program, Chicago, IL 60637. Offers anthropology and sociology of religions (PhD); Bible (PhD); history of Christianity (PhD); history of Judaism (PhD); history of religions (PhD); Islamic studies (PhD); philosophy of religions (PhD); religion, literature, and visual culture (PhD); religions in America (PhD); religious ethics (PhD); theology (PhD). *Degree requirements:* For doctorate, 2 foreign languages, comprehensive exam, thesis/dissertation. *Entrance requirements:* For doctorate, GRE General Test, 3 letters of recommendation; transcripts; curriculum vitae or resume; writing sample. Additional exam requirements/recommendations for international students: required—TOEFL (minimum score 600 paper-based; 104 iBT), IELTS (minimum score 7). Electronic applications accepted.

University of Chicago, Division of the Humanities, Department of Near Eastern Languages and Civilizations, Chicago, IL 60637. Offers PhD. Terminal master's awarded for partial completion of doctoral program. *Degree requirements:* For doctorate, 2 foreign languages, comprehensive exam, thesis/dissertation. *Entrance requirements:* For doctorate, GRE General Test, 15-20 page writing sample, statement of purpose, 3 letters of recommendation, transcripts for all previous degrees and institutions attended. Additional exam requirements/recommendations for international students: required—TOEFL (minimum score 104 iBT), IELTS (minimum score 7). Electronic applications accepted.

University of Chicago, Division of the Social Sciences and Division of the Humanities, Center for Middle Eastern Studies, Chicago, IL 60637. Offers MA. *Degree requirements:* For master's, one foreign language, thesis. *Entrance requirements:* For master's, GRE General Test, 3 letters of recommendation, statement of purpose, transcripts, resume or curriculum vitae, writing sample (dependent on department). Additional exam requirements/recommendations for international students: required—TOEFL (minimum score 104 iBT), IELTS (minimum score 7). Electronic applications accepted. *Expenses:* Contact institution.

University of Illinois at Urbana-Champaign, Graduate College, College of Liberal Arts and Sciences, Center for South Asian and Middle Eastern Studies, Champaign, IL 61820. Offers MA. *Degree requirements:* For master's, one foreign language, comprehensive exam, thesis or alternative.

The University of Kansas, Graduate Studies, College of Liberal Arts and Sciences, Center for Russian, East European and Eurasian Studies, Lawrence, KS 66045. Offers foreign area officer (MA); Russian, East European and EurAsian studies (MA, Graduate Certificate); JD/MA. *Program availability:* Part-time. *Students:* 1 (woman) full-time, 1 part-time (0 women). Average age 45. 4 applicants, 100% accepted, 2 enrolled. In 2019, 2 master's awarded. *Entrance requirements:* For master's, GRE General Test, two-page statement of educational and professional objectives, three letters of recommendation, official transcripts, working knowledge of a REES-area language equivalent to at least 2 years. Additional exam requirements/recommendations for international students: required—TOEFL, IELTS. *Application deadline:* For fall admission, 1/1 priority date for domestic and international students. Applications are processed on a rolling basis. Application fee: $65 ($85 for international students). Electronic applications accepted. *Expenses:* Tuition, state resident: full-time $9989. Tuition, nonresident: full-time $23,950. *International tuition:* $23,950 full-time. *Required fees:* $984; $81.99 per credit hour. Tuition and fees vary according to course load, campus/location and program. *Financial support:* Fellowships, research assistantships, and scholarships/grants available. Financial award application deadline: 1/1; financial award applicants required to submit FAFSA. *Unit head:* Vitaly Chernetsky, Acting Director, 785-864-4236, E-mail: vchernetsky@ku.edu. *Application contact:* Clare Thoman, Graduate Admissions Contact, 785-864-9814, E-mail: clarethoman@ku.edu.
Website: http://www.crees.ku.edu/

The University of Manchester, School of Arts, Languages and Cultures, Manchester, United Kingdom. Offers anthropology, media and performance (PhD); applied theatre (PhD); Arab world studies (PhD); archaeology (PhD); art history and visual studies (PhD); arts and cultural management (PhD); arts management and cultural policy (PhD); Chinese studies (PhD); classics and ancient history (PhD); composition (PhD); creative writing (PhD); drama (PhD); East Asian studies (PhD); electroacoustic composition (PhD); English and American studies (PhD); English language (PhD); French studies (PhD); German studies (PhD); history (PhD); humanitarianism and conflict response (PhD); interpreting studies (PhD); Japanese studies (PhD); Latin American cultural studies (PhD); linguistics (PhD); Middle Eastern studies (PhD); museology (PhD); museum practice (PhD); music (PhD); musicology (PhD); Polish studies (PhD); Portuguese studies (PhD); religions and theology (PhD); Russian studies (PhD); Spanish studies (PhD); translation and intercultural studies (PhD).

University of Memphis, Graduate School, College of Arts and Sciences, Department of History, Memphis, TN 38152. Offers ancient Egyptian history (MA, PhD). *Program availability:* 100% online. *Students:* 21 full-time (13 women), 41 part-time (29 women); includes 15 minority (12 Black or African American, non-Hispanic/Latino; 1 Asian, non-Hispanic/Latino; 2 Hispanic/Latino), 1 international. Average age 35. 27 applicants, 81% accepted, 9 enrolled. In 2019, 9 master's, 7 doctorates awarded. *Degree requirements:* For master's, comprehensive exam, thesis optional; for doctorate, one foreign language, comprehensive exam, thesis/dissertation, 60 credits plus 12 dissertation credits, 2 research seminars. *Entrance requirements:* For master's, GRE General Test or MAT, 18 undergraduate hours of course work in history with minimum GPA of 3.0, 2 letters of recommendation, writing sample, statement of research interest; for doctorate, GRE General Test, GRE Subject Test, MA in history or related field, three letters of recommendation, writing sample, statement of purpose. Additional exam requirements/recommendations for international students: required—TOEFL (minimum score 550 paper-based; 79 iBT). *Application deadline:* For fall admission, 1/15 for domestic students; for spring admission, 9/15 for domestic students. Applications are processed on a rolling basis. Application fee: $35 ($60 for international students). Electronic applications accepted. *Expenses: Tuition, area resident:* Full-time $9216; part-time $512 per credit hour. Tuition, state resident: full-time $9216; part-time $512 per credit hour. Tuition, nonresident: full-time $12,672; part-time $704 per credit hour. *International tuition:* $16,128 full-time. *Required fees:* $1530; $85 per credit hour. Tuition and fees vary according to program. *Financial support:* Research assistantships with full tuition reimbursements, teaching assistantships with full tuition reimbursements, career-related internships or fieldwork, Federal Work-Study, scholarships/grants, and unspecified assistantships available. Financial award application deadline: 2/1; financial award applicants required to submit FAFSA. *Unit head:* Dr. Daniel Unowsky, Chair, 901-678-3385, Fax: 901-678-2720, E-mail: dunowsky@memphis.edu. *Application contact:* Dr. Andrew Daily, Graduate Coordinator, 901-678-2868, Fax: 901-678-2720, E-mail: amdaily@memphis.edu.
Website: https://www.memphis.edu/history

University of Michigan, Rackham Graduate School, College of Literature, Science, and the Arts, Center for Middle Eastern and North African Studies, Ann Arbor, MI 48109-1106. Offers AM, JD/AM, MBA/AM. *Program availability:* Part-time. *Degree requirements:* For master's, one foreign language, thesis or alternative. *Entrance requirements:* For master's, GRE General Test. Additional exam requirements/recommendations for international students: required—TOEFL (minimum score 560 paper-based; 84 iBT). Electronic applications accepted.

University of Michigan, Rackham Graduate School, College of Literature, Science, and the Arts, Department of Middle East Studies, Ann Arbor, MI 48109. Offers ancient Near Eastern studies (AM, PhD); Arabic for professional purposes (AM); Arabic language and literature (AM, PhD); Armenian studies (AM, PhD); Christianity in late antiquity (AM, PhD); Egyptology (AM, PhD); Hebrew Bible and ancient Israel (AM, PhD); Hebrew literature (AM, PhD); Islamic studies (AM, PhD); Jewish cultural studies (AM, PhD); Jewish mysticism (AM, PhD); Persian and Iranian studies (AM, PhD); Rabbinic literature (AM, PhD); Second Temple Judaism (AM, PhD); teaching Arabic as a foreign language (AM); Turkish studies (AM, PhD). Terminal master's awarded for partial completion of doctoral program. *Degree requirements:* For master's, 2 foreign languages; for doctorate, 4 foreign languages, comprehensive exam, thesis/dissertation, preliminary exams, oral defense of dissertation. *Entrance requirements:* For master's, ACTFL (for teaching Arabic as a foreign language MA program). Additional exam requirements/recommendations for international students: required—TOEFL (minimum score 560 paper-based; 84 iBT), IELTS (minimum score 6.5). Electronic applications accepted.

University of Pennsylvania, School of Arts and Sciences, Graduate Group in Near Eastern Languages and Civilizations, Philadelphia, PA 19104. Offers AM, PhD. *Faculty:* 24 full-time (11 women), 4 part-time/adjunct (0 women). *Students:* 16 full-time (5 women); includes 2 minority (1 Asian, non-Hispanic/Latino; 1 Two or more races, non-Hispanic/Latino), 5 international. Average age 32. 44 applicants, 9% accepted, 1 enrolled. In 2019, 1 master's, 4 doctorates awarded. Application fee: $90.
Website: http://www.sas.upenn.edu/nelc/grad_programs/grad_programs.html

University of South Africa, College of Human Sciences, Pretoria, South Africa. Offers adult education (M Ed); African languages (MA, PhD); African politics (MA, PhD); Afrikaans (MA, PhD); ancient history (MA, PhD); ancient Near Eastern studies (MA, PhD); anthropology (MA, PhD); applied linguistics (MA); Arabic (MA, PhD); archaeology (MA); art history (MA); Biblical archaeology (MA); Biblical studies (M Th, D Th, PhD);

Christian spirituality (M Th, D Th); church history (M Th, D Th); classical studies (MA, PhD); clinical psychology (MA); communication (MA, PhD); comparative education (M Ed, Ed D); consulting psychology (D Admin, D Com, PhD); curriculum studies (M Ed, Ed D); development studies (M Admin, MA, D Admin, PhD); didactics (M Ed, Ed D); education (M Tech); education management (M Ed, Ed D); educational psychology (M Ed); English (MA); environmental education (M Ed); French (MA, PhD); German (MA, PhD); Greek (MA); guidance and counseling (M Ed); health studies (MA, PhD), including health sciences education (MA), health services management (MA), medical and surgical nursing science (critical care general) (MA), midwifery and neonatal nursing science (MA), trauma and emergency care (MA); history (MA, PhD); history of education (Ed D); inclusive education (M Ed, Ed D); information and communications technology policy and regulation (MA); information science (MA, MIS, PhD); international politics (MA, PhD); Islamic studies (MA, PhD); Italian (MA, PhD); Judaica (MA, PhD); linguistics (MA, PhD); mathematical education (M Ed); mathematics education (MA); missiology (M Th, D Th); modern Hebrew (MA, PhD); musicology (MA, MMus, D Mus, PhD); natural science education (M Ed); New Testament (M Th, D Th); Old Testament (D Th); pastoral therapy (M Th, D Th); philosophy (MA); philosophy of education (M Ed, Ed D); politics (MA, PhD); Portuguese (MA, PhD); practical theology (M Th, D Th); psychology (MA, MS, PhD); psychology of education (M Ed, Ed D); public health (MA); religious studies (MA, D Th, PhD); Romance languages (MA); Russian (MA, PhD); Semitic languages (MA, PhD); social behavior studies in HIV/AIDS (MA); social science (mental health) (MA); social science in development studies (MA); social science in psychology (MA); social science in social work (MA); social science in sociology (MA); social work (MSW, DSW, PhD); socio-education (M Ed, Ed D); sociolinguistics (MA); sociology (MA, PhD); Spanish (MA, PhD); systematic theology (M Th, D Th); TESOL (teaching English to speakers of other languages) (MA); theological ethics (M Th, D Th); theory of literature (MA, PhD); urban ministries (D Th); urban ministry (M Th).

The University of Texas at Austin, Graduate School, College of Liberal Arts, Department of Middle Eastern Studies, Austin, TX 78712-1111. Offers Middle Eastern languages and cultures (MA, PhD); Middle Eastern studies (MA); JD/MA; MA/M Sc; MA/MA; MBA/MA; MPA/MA. *Degree requirements:* For master's, one foreign language, comprehensive exam, thesis; for doctorate, 2 foreign languages, comprehensive exam, thesis/dissertation. *Entrance requirements:* For master's and doctorate, GRE General Test. Additional exam requirements/recommendations for international students: required—TOEFL. Electronic applications accepted.

University of Toronto, School of Graduate Studies, Faculty of Arts and Science, Department of Near and Middle Eastern Civilizations, Toronto, ON M5S 1A1, Canada. Offers MA, PhD. *Program availability:* Part-time. *Degree requirements:* For master's, thesis optional; for doctorate, 2 foreign languages, thesis/dissertation, language proficiency exams. *Entrance requirements:* For master's, BA in relevant area, minimum B+ average in final year, prior coursework in ancient Near Eastern or Islamic civilizations, 2 letters of reference; for doctorate, MA in relevant area with a minimum A-average, 2 letters of reference. Additional exam requirements/recommendations for international students: required—TOEFL (minimum score 580 paper-based; 93 iBT), TWE (minimum score 5). Electronic applications accepted.

University of Utah, Graduate School, College of Humanities, Program in Middle East Studies, Salt Lake City, UT 84112. Offers Arabic (MA, PhD); Hebrew (MA); history (MA, PhD); Persian (MA, PhD); political science (MA, PhD). In 2019, 2 doctorates awarded. *Entrance requirements:* For master's, GRE General Test, minimum GPA of 3.2; for doctorate, GRE General Test, MA in Middle East studies or equivalent, minimum GPA of 3.2. Additional exam requirements/recommendations for international students: required—TOEFL (minimum score 580 paper-based; 92 iBT); recommended—IELTS (minimum score 7). Application fee: $55 ($65 for international students). *Expenses:* Tuition, state resident: full-time $7085; part-time $272.51 per credit hour. Tuition, nonresident: full-time $24,937; part-time $959.12 per credit hour. *Required fees:* $880.52; $880.52 per semester. Tuition and fees vary according to degree level, program and student level. *Unit head:* Johanna Watzinger-Tharp, Director, 801-581-7148, Fax: 801-581-6105, E-mail: j.tharp@utah.edu. *Application contact:* Kellie Hubbard, Academic Advisor, 801-581-5362, Fax: 801-581-6105, E-mail: kellie.hubbard@utah.edu.
Website: http://www.mec.utah.edu

University of Virginia, College and Graduate School of Arts and Sciences, Department of Middle Eastern and South Asian Languages and Cultures, Charlottesville, VA 22903. Offers Middle Eastern and South Asian studies (MA).

University of Washington, Graduate School, College of Arts and Sciences, Department of Near Eastern Languages and Civilization, Seattle, WA 98195. Offers MA. *Degree requirements:* For master's, 2 foreign languages, exams. *Entrance requirements:* For master's, GRE, minimum GPA of 3.0. Additional exam requirements/recommendations for international students: required—TOEFL. Electronic applications accepted.

University of Washington, Graduate School, College of Arts and Sciences, Henry M. Jackson School of International Studies, Middle East Studies Program, Seattle, WA 98195. Offers MAIS. *Degree requirements:* For master's, one foreign language, thesis optional. *Entrance requirements:* For master's, GRE General Test, minimum GPA of 3.0 in last two years. Additional exam requirements/recommendations for international students: required—TOEFL (minimum score 500 paper-based; 92 iBT), IELTS (minimum score 7). Electronic applications accepted.

University of Washington, Graduate School, Interdisciplinary Program in Near and Middle Eastern Studies, Seattle, WA 98195. Offers PhD. *Degree requirements:* For doctorate, 3 foreign languages, thesis/dissertation. *Entrance requirements:* For doctorate, GRE General Test, minimum GPA of 3.0. Additional exam requirements/recommendations for international students: required—TOEFL. Electronic applications accepted.

University of Waterloo, Graduate Studies and Postdoctoral Affairs, Faculty of Arts, Department of Classical Studies, Waterloo, ON N2L 3G1, Canada. Offers ancient Mediterranean cultures (MA). *Degree requirements:* For master's, one foreign language.

University of Wisconsin–Madison, Graduate School, College of Letters and Science, Department of History, Madison, WI 53706-1380. Offers African history (MA, PhD); Central Asian history (MA, PhD); comparative world history (MA, PhD); East Asian history (MA, PhD); European history (MA, PhD); gender and women's history (MA, PhD); Latin American and Caribbean history (MA, PhD); Middle Eastern history (MA, PhD); South Asian history (MA, PhD); Southeast Asian history (MA, PhD); United States history (MA, PhD). Terminal master's awarded for partial completion of doctoral program. *Degree requirements:* For master's, thesis (for some programs); for doctorate, variable foreign language requirement, thesis/dissertation. *Entrance requirements:* For master's and doctorate, GRE General Test. Additional exam requirements/recommendations for international students: required—Michigan English Language Assessment Battery or TOEFL. Electronic applications accepted.

Washington University in St. Louis, The Graduate School, Department of Jewish, Islamic, and Near Eastern Languages and Cultures, St. Louis, MO 63130-4899. Offers Islamic and Near Eastern studies (MA); Jewish studies (MA). *Degree requirements:* For master's, one foreign language, thesis (for some programs). *Entrance requirements:* For master's, GRE General Test. Additional exam requirements/recommendations for international students: required—TOEFL. Electronic applications accepted.

Wayne State University, College of Liberal Arts and Sciences, Department of Classical and Modern Languages, Literatures, and Cultures, Detroit, MI 48202. Offers classics (MA), including ancient Greek and Latin, ancient studies, classics, Latin; German (MA); language learning (MALL), including Arabic (MA, MALL), French (MA, MALL, PhD), German (MALL, PhD), Italian (MA, MALL), Spanish (MA, MALL, PhD); modern languages (PhD), including French (MA, MALL, PhD), German (MALL, PhD), Spanish (MA, MALL, PhD); Near Eastern languages (MA), including Arabic (MA, MALL), Hebrew; Romance languages (MA), including French (MA, MALL, PhD), Italian (MA, MALL), Spanish (MA, MALL, PhD). *Faculty:* 20. *Students:* 30 full-time (22 women), 15 part-time (9 women); includes 11 minority (4 Black or African American, non-Hispanic/Latino; 1 American Indian or Alaska Native, non-Hispanic/Latino; 2 Asian, non-Hispanic/Latino; 3 Hispanic/Latino; 1 Two or more races, non-Hispanic/Latino), 2 international. Average age 40. 32 applicants, 34% accepted, 9 enrolled. In 2019, 8 master's, 1 doctorate awarded. *Degree requirements:* For master's, variable foreign language requirement, comprehensive exam (for some programs), thesis (for some programs); for doctorate, one foreign language, comprehensive exam, thesis/dissertation. *Entrance requirements:* Additional exam requirements/recommendations for international students: required—TOEFL (minimum score 550 paper-based; 79 iBT), TWE (minimum score 5.5), Michigan English Language Assessment Battery (minimum score 85); recommended—IELTS (minimum score 6.5). Application fee: $50. Electronic applications accepted. *Expenses: Tuition:* Full-time $34,567. *Financial support:* In 2019–20, 22 students received support, including 1 fellowship with tuition reimbursement available (averaging $20,000 per year), 15 teaching assistantships with tuition reimbursements available (averaging $20,015 per year); research assistantships, scholarships/grants, health care benefits, and unspecified assistantships also available. Financial award applicants required to submit FAFSA. *Unit head:* Dr. Vanessa DEGifis, DR., Department Chair, 313-577-6244, Fax: 313-577-6243, E-mail: vdegifis@wayne.edu. *Application contact:* Terrie Pickering, Academic Services Officer, 313 577 3003, E-mail: t.pickering@wayne.edu.
Website: http://clas.wayne.edu/languages/

Yale University, Graduate School of Arts and Sciences, Department of Near Eastern Languages and Civilizations, New Haven, CT 06520. Offers Arabic humanities (MA, PhD); Assyriology (MA, PhD); Egyptology (MA, PhD); the Classical Near East (MA, PhD). *Degree requirements:* For doctorate, 2 foreign languages, thesis/dissertation. *Entrance requirements:* For doctorate, GRE General Test.

Northern Studies

University of Alaska Fairbanks, College of Liberal Arts, Department of Arctic and Northern Studies, Fairbanks, AK 99775-6460. Offers Arctic policy (MA); environmental politics and policy (MA); Northern history (MA). *Program availability:* Part-time, blended/hybrid learning. *Degree requirements:* For master's, comprehensive exam, oral defense of project or thesis. *Entrance requirements:* For master's, bachelor's degree from accredited institution, preference given to applicants with 3.0 GPA or higher. Additional exam requirements/recommendations for international students: required—TOEFL (minimum score 550 paper-based; 79 iBT), IELTS (minimum score 6.5). Electronic applications accepted.

University of Manitoba, Faculty of Graduate Studies, Faculty of Arts, Department of Icelandic Language and Literature, Winnipeg, MB R3T 2N2, Canada. Offers MA.

Pacific Area/Pacific Rim Studies

Naval Postgraduate School, Departments and Academic Groups, Department of National Security Affairs, Monterey, CA 93943. Offers security studies (MA, PhD), including civil-military relations (MA), combating terrorism: policy and strategy (MA), defense decision-making and planning (MA), Europe and Eurasia (MA), Far East, Southeast Asia, and the Pacific (MA), homeland security and defense (MA), Middle East, South Asia, Sub-Saharan Africa (MA), stabilization and reconstruction (MA), western hemisphere (MA). *Program availability:* Part-time. *Degree requirements:* For master's, thesis (for some programs).

University of Bridgeport, College of Public and International Affairs, Bridgeport, CT 06604. Offers East Asian and Pacific Rim studies (MA); global development and peace (MA); global media and communication studies (MA). *Program availability:* Part-time, evening/weekend. *Degree requirements:* For master's, thesis. *Entrance requirements:*

Pacific Area/Pacific Rim Studies

Additional exam requirements/recommendations for international students: recommended—TOEFL (minimum score 550 paper-based; 80 iBT), IELTS (minimum score 6.5).

The University of British Columbia, Institute of Asian Research, Vancouver, BC V6T 1Z2, Canada. Offers Asia Pacific policy studies (MAAPPS); public policy and global affairs (MPPGA). *Degree requirements:* For master's, thesis optional. *Entrance requirements:* Additional exam requirements/recommendations for international students: required—TOEFL. Electronic applications accepted. *Expenses:* Contact institution.

University of Guam, Office of Graduate Studies, College of Liberal Arts and Social Sciences, Micronesian Studies Program, Mangilao, GU 96923. Offers MA. *Degree requirements:* For master's, thesis. *Entrance requirements:* For master's, GRE General Test. Additional exam requirements/recommendations for international students: required—TOEFL.

University of Hawaii at Manoa, Office of Graduate Education, School of Pacific and Asian Studies, Program in Pacific Island Studies, Honolulu, HI 96822. Offers MA, Graduate Certificate. *Program availability:* Part-time. *Degree requirements:* For master's, thesis optional. *Entrance requirements:* Additional exam requirements/recommendations for international students: required—TOEFL (minimum score 580 paper-based; 92 iBT), IELTS (minimum score 5).

University of San Francisco, College of Arts and Sciences, Program in Asia Pacific Studies, San Francisco, CA 94117. Offers MA, MA/MBA. *Program availability:* Part-time, evening/weekend. *Faculty:* 3 full-time (1 woman), 6 part-time/adjunct (4 women). *Students:* 40 full-time (29 women), 3 part-time (2 women); includes 12 minority (2 Black or African American, non-Hispanic/Latino; 7 Asian, non-Hispanic/Latino; 1 Hispanic/Latino; 2 Two or more races, non-Hispanic/Latino), 25 international. Average age 27. 42 applicants, 93% accepted, 21 enrolled. In 2019, 15 master's awarded. *Degree requirements:* For master's, variable foreign language requirement, thesis. *Entrance requirements:* For master's, minimum GPA of 3.0. Additional exam requirements/recommendations for international students: required—TOEFL (minimum score 90 iBT), IELTS (minimum score 6.5), PTE (minimum score 61). *Application deadline:* For fall admission, 2/1 for domestic and international students. Applications are processed on a rolling basis. Application fee: $55. Electronic applications accepted. Application fee is waived when completed online. *Financial support:* Teaching assistantships with partial tuition reimbursements, career-related internships or fieldwork, and scholarships/grants available. Financial award applicants required to submit FAFSA. *Unit head:* Dr. Brian Dempster, Graduate Director, 415-422-6357, E-mail: maps@usfca.edu. *Application contact:* Information Contact, 415-422-5101, Fax: 415-422-2217, E-mail: asgraduate@usfca.edu.
Website: https://www.usfca.edu/arts-sciences/graduate-programs/asia-pacific-studies

University of Victoria, Faculty of Graduate Studies, Faculty of Humanities, Department of Pacific and Asian Studies, Victoria, BC V8W 2Y2, Canada. Offers MA. *Degree requirements:* For master's, thesis. *Entrance requirements:* For master's, minimum B+ average, writing sample. Additional exam requirements/recommendations for international students: required—TOEFL (minimum score 575 paper-based), IELTS (minimum score 7). Electronic applications accepted.

Western European Studies

American University, School of International Service, Washington, DC 20016-8071. Offers comparative and regional studies (Certificate); cross-cultural communication (Certificate); development management (MS); ethics, peace, and global affairs (MA); European studies (Certificate); global environmental policy (MA, Certificate); global information technology (Certificate); global media (MA); international affairs (MA), including comparative and regional studies, global governance, politics, and security, international economic relations, natural resources and sustainable development, U.S. foreign policy and national security; international arts management (Certificate); international communication (MA, Certificate); international development (MA); international economic policy (Certificate); international economic relations (Certificate); international economics (MA); international peace and conflict resolution (MA, Certificate); international politics (Certificate); international relations (MA, PhD); international service (MIS); peacebuilding (Certificate); social enterprise (MA); the Americas (Certificate); United States foreign policy (Certificate); JD/MA. *Program availability:* Part-time, evening/weekend, 100% online, blended/hybrid learning. Terminal master's awarded for partial completion of doctoral program. *Degree requirements:* For master's, one foreign language, comprehensive exam, thesis or alternative; for doctorate, one foreign language, comprehensive exam, thesis/dissertation. *Entrance requirements:* For master's, transcripts, resume, 2 letters of recommendation, statement of purpose; for doctorate, GRE, transcripts, resume, 3 letters of recommendation, statement of purpose. Additional exam requirements/recommendations for international students: required—TOEFL. Electronic applications accepted. *Expenses:* Contact institution.

Boston College, Morrissey Graduate School of Arts and Sciences, Department of History, Chestnut Hill, MA 02467-3800. Offers European national studies (MA); history (MA, PhD); medieval studies (MA). Terminal master's awarded for partial completion of doctoral program. *Degree requirements:* For master's, one foreign language, comprehensive exam, thesis optional; for doctorate, 2 foreign languages, comprehensive exam, thesis/dissertation. *Entrance requirements:* For master's and doctorate, GRE General Test, writing sample. Additional exam requirements/recommendations for international students: required—TOEFL (minimum score 600 paper-based; 100 iBT), IELTS (minimum score 8). Electronic applications accepted.

Brown University, Graduate School, Department of Portuguese and Brazilian Studies, Providence, RI 02912. Offers Brazilian studies (AM); English as a second language and cross-cultural studies (AM); Portuguese and Brazilian studies (AM, PhD); Portuguese bilingual education and cross-cultural studies (AM). *Degree requirements:* For doctorate, thesis/dissertation.

Carleton University, Faculty of Graduate Studies, Faculty of Public Affairs and Management, Institute of European and Russian Studies, Ottawa, ON K1S 5B6, Canada. Offers European and European Union studies (MA); European integration studies (Diploma); Russian, EurAsian and transition studies (MA). *Degree requirements:* For master's, one foreign language, thesis optional. *Entrance requirements:* For master's, honors degree or equivalent; 2 years of Russian, German or other central east European language. Additional exam requirements/recommendations for international students: required—TOEFL.

The Catholic University of America, School of Arts and Sciences, Department of History, Washington, DC 20064. Offers history (MA, PhD), including early modern European history, medieval history, modern European history, U.S. history; religion and society in the late medieval and early modern world (MA); MA/JD; MSLS/MA. *Program availability:* Part-time. *Faculty:* 14 full-time (6 women). *Students:* 5 full-time (4 women), 17 part-time (6 women); includes 3 minority (all Two or more races, non-Hispanic/Latino), 2 international. Average age 30. 14 applicants, 57% accepted, 3 enrolled. In 2019, 3 master's, 1 doctorate awarded. Terminal master's awarded for partial completion of doctoral program. *Degree requirements:* For master's, one foreign language, comprehensive exam, thesis optional, 2 languages (for medievalists), one of which must be Latin; for doctorate, 2 foreign languages, comprehensive exam, thesis/dissertation, 3 languages (for medievalists), one of which must be Latin. *Entrance requirements:* For master's and doctorate, GRE General Test, statement of purpose, official copies of academic transcripts, three letters of recommendation, writing sample. Additional exam requirements/recommendations for international students: required—TOEFL (minimum score 550 paper-based; 80 iBT). *Application deadline:* For fall admission, 7/15 priority date for domestic students, 7/1 for international students; for spring admission, 11/15 priority date for domestic students, 11/1 for international students. Applications are processed on a rolling basis. Application fee: $55. Electronic applications accepted. *Expenses:* Contact institution. *Financial support:* Fellowships, research assistantships, teaching assistantships, Federal Work-Study, scholarships/grants, tuition waivers (full and partial), and unspecified assistantships available. Financial award application deadline: 2/1; financial award applicants required to submit FAFSA. *Unit head:* Dr. Michael Kimmage, Chair, 202-319-5484, Fax: 202-319-5569, E-mail: kimmage@cua.edu. *Application contact:* Dr. Steven Brown, Director of Graduate Admissions, 202-319-5057, Fax: 202-319-6533, E-mail: cua-admissions@cua.edu.
Website: http://history.cua.edu/

Central Michigan University, College of Graduate Studies, College of Liberal Arts and Social Sciences, Department of History, Mount Pleasant, MI 48859. Offers European history (Graduate Certificate); history (MA); modern history (Graduate Certificate); United States history (Graduate Certificate); MA/PhD. *Program availability:* Part-time. *Degree requirements:* For master's, thesis or alternative. Electronic applications accepted. *Expenses: Tuition, area resident:* Full-time $12,267; part-time $8178 per year. Tuition, state resident: full-time $12,267; part-time $8178 per year. Tuition, nonresident: full-time $12,267; part-time $8178 per year. *International tuition:* $16,110 full-time. *Required fees:* $225 per semester. Tuition and fees vary according to degree level and program.

Claremont Graduate University, Graduate Programs, School of Arts and Humanities, Department of History, Claremont, CA 91711-6160. Offers Africana history (Certificate); American studies and U.S. history (MA, PhD); archival studies (MA); early modern studies (MA, PhD); European studies (MA, PhD); oral history (MA, PhD); MBA/MA; MBA/PhD. Terminal master's awarded for partial completion of doctoral program. *Entrance requirements:* For master's and doctorate, GRE General Test. Additional exam requirements/recommendations for international students: required—TOEFL (minimum score 75 iBT). Electronic applications accepted.

College of Staten Island of the City University of New York, Graduate Programs, Division of Humanities and Social Sciences, Program in History, Staten Island, NY 10314-6600. Offers history (MA), including Africa and the Middle East, Asia, Europe, Latin America and the Caribbean, United States. *Program availability:* Part-time, evening/weekend. *Faculty:* 5. *Students:* 17. 12 applicants, 67% accepted, 8 enrolled. In 2019, 1 master's awarded. *Degree requirements:* For master's, comprehensive exam (for some programs), thesis or alternative, the MA in History requires 32 graduate credits at the 700-level, with all graduate courses designated at four credits, for a total of eight courses. Students must take at least one course in each of four of the program's five areas of concentration, rigorous thesis option or portfolio option. *Entrance requirements:* For master's, bachelor's degree with minimum GPA of 3.0 overall and in undergraduate history courses, two letters of recommendation, letter of interest, research-based writing sample. Additional exam requirements/recommendations for international students: required—TOEFL (minimum score 550 paper-based; 79 iBT), IELTS (minimum score 6.5). *Application deadline:* For fall admission, 5/10 priority date for domestic students, 4/25 for international students; for spring admission, 12/2 priority date for domestic students, 11/23 for international students. Applications are processed on a rolling basis. Application fee: $75. Electronic applications accepted. *Expenses: Tuition, area resident:* Full-time $11,090; part-time $470 per credit. Tuition, state resident: full-time $11,090; part-time $470 per credit. Tuition, nonresident: full-time $20,520; part-time $855 per credit. *International tuition:* $20,520 full-time. *Required fees:* $559; $181 per semester. Tuition and fees vary according to program. *Unit head:* Susan Smith-Peter, Graduate Program Coordinator, 718-982-3290, E-mail: susan.smithpeter@csi.cuny.edu. *Application contact:* Sasha Spence, Associate Director for Graduate Admissions, 718-982-2019, Fax: 718-982-2500, E-mail: sasha.spence@csi.cuny.edu.
Website: https://www.csi.cuny.edu/academics-and-research/departments-programs/history/master-arts-history

Columbia University, Graduate School of Arts and Sciences, New York, NY 10027. Offers African-American studies (MA); American studies (MA); anthropology (MA, PhD); art history and archaeology (MA, PhD); astronomy (PhD); biological sciences (PhD); biotechnology (MA); chemical physics (PhD); chemistry (PhD); classical studies (MA, PhD); classics (MA, PhD); climate and society (MA); conservation biology (MA); earth and environmental sciences (PhD); East Asia: regional studies (MA); East Asian languages and cultures (MA, PhD); ecology, evolution and environmental biology (MA), including conservation biology; ecology, evolution, and environmental biology (PhD), including ecology and evolutionary biology, evolutionary primatology; economics (MA, PhD); English and comparative literature (MA, PhD); French and Romance philology (MA, PhD); Germanic languages (MA, PhD); global French studies (MA); global thought (MA); Hispanic cultural studies (MA); history (PhD); history and literature (MA); human rights studies (MA); Islamic studies (MA); Italian (MA, PhD); Japanese pedagogy (MA); Jewish studies (MA); Latin America and the Caribbean: regional studies (MA); Latin American and Iberian cultures (PhD); mathematics (MA, PhD), including finance (MA); medieval and Renaissance studies (MA); Middle Eastern, South Asian, and African studies (MA, PhD); modern art: critical and curatorial studies (MA); modern European studies (MA); museum anthropology (MA); music (DMA, PhD); oral history (MA); philosophical foundations of physics (MA); philosophy (MA, PhD); physics (PhD); political science (MA, PhD); psychology (PhD); quantitative methods in the social sciences (MA); religion (MA, PhD); Russia, Eurasia and East Europe: regional studies

(MA); Russian translation (MA); Slavic cultures (MA); Slavic languages (MA, PhD); sociology (MA, PhD); South Asian studies (MA, PhD); statistics (MA, PhD); theatre (PhD). *Program availability:* Part-time. *Students:* 3,506 full-time (1,844 women), 208 part-time (121 women); includes 864 minority (110 Black or African American, non-Hispanic/Latino; 5 American Indian or Alaska Native, non-Hispanic/Latino; 416 Asian, non-Hispanic/Latino; 147 Hispanic/Latino; 6 Native Hawaiian or other Pacific Islander, non-Hispanic/Latino; 180 Two or more races, non-Hispanic/Latino), 2,065 international. 14,545 applicants, 25% accepted, 1,429 enrolled. In 2019, 1,262 master's, 363 doctorates awarded. Terminal master's awarded for partial completion of doctoral program. *Degree requirements:* For master's, variable foreign language requirement, comprehensive exam (for some programs), thesis (for some programs); for doctorate, variable foreign language requirement, comprehensive exam (for some programs), thesis/dissertation. *Entrance requirements:* For master's and doctorate, GRE General Test, GRE Subject Test (for some programs). Additional exam requirements/recommendations for international students: required—TOEFL (minimum score 600 paper-based; 100 iBT), IELTS (minimum score 7.5). Application fee: $115. Electronic applications accepted. *Expenses: Tuition:* Full-time $47,600; part-time $1880 per credit. One-time fee: $105. *Financial support:* Fellowships, research assistantships, teaching assistantships, career-related internships or fieldwork, Federal Work-Study, institutionally sponsored loans, scholarships/grants, traineeships, health care benefits, tuition waivers, and unspecified assistantships available. Support available to part-time students. Financial award application deadline: 12/15. *Unit head:* Dr. Carlos J. Alonso, Dean of the Graduate School of Arts and Sciences and Vice President for Graduate Education, 212-854-2861, E-mail: gsas-dean@columbia.edu. *Application contact:* GSAS Office of Admissions, 212-854-6729, E-mail: gsas-admissions@columbia.edu.
Website: http://gsas.columbia.edu/

Cornell University, Graduate School, Graduate Fields of Arts and Sciences, Field of History, Ithaca, NY 14853. Offers African history (MA, PhD); American history (MA, PhD); ancient Greek history (PhD); ancient history (MA, PhD); ancient Roman history (PhD); early modern European history (MA, PhD); English history (MA, PhD); French history (MA, PhD); German history (MA, PhD); history of science (MA, PhD); Korean history (PhD); Latin American history (MA, PhD); medieval Chinese history (MA, PhD); medieval history (MA, PhD); modern Chinese history (MA, PhD); modern European history (MA, PhD); modern Japanese history (MA, PhD); modern Middle Eastern history (PhD); premodern Islamic history (MA, PhD); premodern Japanese history (MA, PhD); Renaissance history (MA, PhD); Russian history (MA, PhD); South Asian history (PhD); Southeast Asian history (MA, PhD). Terminal master's awarded for partial completion of doctoral program. *Degree requirements:* For master's, thesis; for doctorate, 2 foreign languages, comprehensive exam, thesis/dissertation, 1 year of teaching experience. *Entrance requirements:* For master's and doctorate, GRE General Test, writing sample, 3 letters of recommendation. Additional exam requirements/recommendations for international students: required—TOEFL (minimum score 550 paper-based; 77 iBT). Electronic applications accepted.

Dallas Baptist University, Gary Cook School of Leadership, Program in International Studies, Dallas, TX 75211-9299. Offers East Asian studies (MA); European studies (MA); general international studies (MA); global business (MA); international immersion (MA); international ministry (MA); international relations (MA). *Program availability:* Part-time, evening/weekend. *Application deadline:* Applications are processed on a rolling basis. Application fee: $25. Electronic applications accepted. Application fee is waived when completed online. *Expenses: Tuition:* Full-time $18,072; part-time $1004 per credit hour. *Required fees:* $1100; $550 per semester. Tuition and fees vary according to course level and degree level. *Unit head:* Dr. Jack Goodyear, Dean, 214-333-5595, Fax: 214-333-6809, E-mail: jackg@dbu.edu. *Application contact:* Lee Bratcher, Program Director, 214-333-5808, E-mail: leeb@dbu.edu.
Website: https://www.dbu.edu/graduate/degree-programs/ma-international-studies

Drew University, Caspersen School of Graduate Studies, Madison, NJ 07940-1493. Offers conflict resolution and leadership (Certificate), including community leadership, moderation, peace building; education (M Ed); finance (MA); history and culture (MA, PhD), including American history, book history, British history, European history, intellectual history, Irish history, print culture, public history; K-12 education (MAT), including art, biology, chemistry, elementary education, English, French, Italian, math, secondary education, special education, teacher of students with disabilities; liberal studies (M Litt, D Litt), including history, Irish/Irish-American studies, literature (M Litt, MMH, D Litt, DMH, CMH), religion, spirituality, teaching in the two-year college, writing; medical humanities (MMH, DMH, CMH), including arts, health, healthcare, literature (M Litt, MMH, D Litt, DMH, CMH), scientific research; poetry (MFA). *Program availability:* Part-time, evening/weekend. Terminal master's awarded for partial completion of doctoral program. *Degree requirements:* For master's and other advanced degree, thesis (for some programs); for doctorate, one foreign language, comprehensive exam (for some programs), thesis/dissertation. *Entrance requirements:* For master's, PRAXIS Core and Subject Area tests (for MAT), GRE/GMAT (for MFin MS in Data Analytics), resume, transcripts, writing sample, personal statement, letters of recommendation; for doctorate, GRE (PhD in history and culture), resume, transcripts, writing sample, personal statement, letters of recommendation; for other advanced degree, resume, transcripts, personal statement. Additional exam requirements/recommendations for international students: required—TOEFL (minimum score 587 paper-based; 80 iBT), IELTS (minimum score 6), TWE (minimum score 4). Electronic applications accepted.

East Carolina University, Graduate School, Thomas Harriot College of Arts and Sciences, Department of History, Greenville, NC 27858-4353. Offers American history (MA); Atlantic world (MA); European history (MA); maritime studies (MA); military history (MA); public history (MA). *Program availability:* Part-time. *Application deadline:* For fall admission, 4/1 priority date for domestic and international students; for spring admission, 10/15 priority date for domestic and international students. *Expenses: Tuition, area resident:* Full-time $4749; part-time $185 per credit hour. Tuition, state resident: full-time $4749; part-time $185 per credit hour. Tuition, nonresident: full-time $17,898; part-time $864 per credit hour. *International tuition:* $17,898 full-time. *Required fees:* $2787. *Financial support:* Application deadline: 1/15. *Unit head:* Dr. Christopher Oakley, Chair, 252-328-1025, E-mail: oakleyc@ecu.edu. *Application contact:* Graduate School Admissions, 252-328-6012, E-mail: gradschool@ecu.edu.
Website: https://history.ecu.edu/

Georgetown University, Graduate School of Arts and Sciences, Walsh School of Foreign Service, BMW Center for German and European Studies, Washington, DC 20057. Offers MA, MA/JD, MA/PhD. *Degree requirements:* For master's, 2 foreign languages, comprehensive exam. *Entrance requirements:* For master's, GRE General Test. Additional exam requirements/recommendations for international students: required—TOEFL. Electronic applications accepted.

The George Washington University, Elliott School of International Affairs, Program in European and Eurasian Studies, Washington, DC 20052. Offers MA. *Program availability:* Part-time. *Degree requirements:* For master's, one foreign language, capstone project. *Entrance requirements:* For master's, GRE General Test, 2 years (or the equivalent) of a modern European language or Russian, 2 semesters of introductory economics (macro or micro). Additional exam requirements/recommendations for international students: required—TOEFL (minimum score 100 iBT), IELTS (minimum score 7). Electronic applications accepted.

Indiana University Bloomington, University Graduate School, College of Arts and Sciences, School of Global and International Studies, Institute for European Studies, Bloomington, IN 47405. Offers MA, MA/MBA, MPA/MA. *Program availability:* Part-time. *Degree requirements:* For master's, one foreign language, thesis. *Entrance requirements:* For master's, GRE General Test. Additional exam requirements/recommendations for international students: required—TOEFL. Electronic applications accepted.

Indiana University-Purdue University Indianapolis, School of Liberal Arts, Department of History, Indianapolis, IN 46202. Offers European history (MA); public history (MA); United States history (MA); MA/MA; MA/MLS. *Program availability:* Part-time, evening/weekend. *Degree requirements:* For master's, one foreign language, thesis. *Entrance requirements:* For master's, GRE General Test, minimum GPA of 3.0. Electronic applications accepted.

Monmouth University, Graduate Studies, Program in History, West Long Branch, NJ 07764-1898. Offers European history (MA); United States history (MA). *Program availability:* Part-time, evening/weekend. *Faculty:* 9 full-time (2 women). *Students:* 2 full-time (1 woman), 24 part-time (9 women); includes 2 minority (1 Black or African American, non-Hispanic/Latino; 1 Hispanic/Latino). Average age 33. In 2019, 10 master's awarded. *Degree requirements:* For master's, comprehensive exam (for some programs), thesis (for some programs). *Entrance requirements:* For master's, minimum GPA of 3.0 in major, 2.5 overall; two letters of recommendation; statement describing historical areas of interest and how graduate study will contribute to professional and academic goals. Additional exam requirements/recommendations for international students: required—TOEFL (minimum score 550 paper-based; 79 iBT), IELTS (minimum score 6) or Michigan English Language Assessment Battery (minimum score 77). *Application deadline:* For fall admission, 7/15 priority date for domestic students, 6/1 for international students; for spring admission, 12/15 priority date for domestic students, 11/1 for international students. Applications are processed on a rolling basis. Application fee: $50. Electronic applications accepted. *Expenses: Tuition:* Full-time $22,194; part-time $14,796 per credit. *Required fees:* $712; $178 per semester. $178 per semester. Tuition and fees vary according to course load. *Financial support:* In 2019–20, 22 students received support. Research assistantships, teaching assistantships, scholarships/grants, and unspecified assistantships available. Support available to part-time students. Financial award applicants required to submit FAFSA. *Unit head:* Dr. Maryann Rhett, Program Director, 732-263-5768, Fax: 732-263-5112, E-mail: mrhett@monmouth.edu. *Application contact:* Kevin New, Graduate Admission Counselor, 732-571-3452, Fax: 732-263-5123, E-mail: gradadm@monmouth.edu.
Website: https://www.monmouth.edu/graduate/ma-history/

New York University, Graduate School of Arts and Science, Center for European Studies, New York, NY 10012-1019. Offers MA. *Entrance requirements:* For master's, GRE General Test. Additional exam requirements/recommendations for international students: required—TOEFL, IELTS. Electronic applications accepted.

San Diego State University, Graduate and Research Affairs, College of Arts and Letters, Department of European Studies, San Diego, CA 92182. Offers MA. *Degree requirements:* For master's, one foreign language. *Entrance requirements:* For master's, GRE General Test. Additional exam requirements/recommendations for international students: required—TOEFL. Electronic applications accepted.

University of Colorado Denver, College of Liberal Arts and Sciences, Department of History, Denver, CO 80217. Offers European history (MA); global history (MA); public history (MA); U.S. history (MA). *Program availability:* Part-time, evening/weekend. *Degree requirements:* For master's, comprehensive exam, thesis optional, 36 semester hours (12 courses). *Entrance requirements:* For master's, GRE General Test, writing sample, minimum undergraduate GPA of 3.25, three letters of recommendation, statement of purpose addressing any weaknesses in academic record. Additional exam requirements/recommendations for international students: required—TOEFL (minimum score 537 paper-based; 75 iBT); recommended—IELTS (minimum score 6.5). Electronic applications accepted. Tuition and fees vary according to course load, program and reciprocity agreements.

University of Guelph, Office of Graduate and Postdoctoral Studies, College of Arts, School of Languages and Literatures, Program in European Studies, Guelph, ON N1G 2W1, Canada. Offers MA. *Degree requirements:* For master's, research paper. *Entrance requirements:* For master's, curriculum vitae, writing sample, 2 letters of recommendation.

University of Illinois at Urbana-Champaign, Graduate College, College of Liberal Arts and Sciences, European Union Center, Champaign, IL 61820. Offers MA. *Degree requirements:* For master's, one foreign language.

University of Louisiana at Lafayette, College of Liberal Arts, Department of History, Geography and Philosophy, Lafayette, LA 70504. Offers history (MA), including American history, European history, Latin American history, public history. *Program availability:* Part-time. *Degree requirements:* For master's, one foreign language, thesis or alternative. *Entrance requirements:* For master's, GRE General Test, minimum GPA of 2.75. Additional exam requirements/recommendations for international students: required—TOEFL (minimum score 550 paper-based). Electronic applications accepted. *Expenses: Tuition, area resident:* Full-time $5511; part-time $1630 per credit hour. Tuition, state resident: full-time $5511; part-time $1630 per credit hour. Tuition, nonresident: full-time $19,239; part-time $2409 per credit hour. *Required fees:* $46,637.

University of Nevada, Reno, Graduate School, Interdisciplinary Program in Basque Studies, Reno, NV 89557. Offers PhD. *Degree requirements:* For doctorate, thesis/dissertation. *Entrance requirements:* For doctorate, GRE General Test, master's degree in related field, minimum GPA of 3.0. Additional exam requirements/recommendations for international students: required—TOEFL (minimum score 500 paper-based; 61 iBT), IELTS (minimum score 6). Electronic applications accepted.

University of Pittsburgh, University Center for International Studies, Pittsburgh, PA 15260. Offers African studies (Certificate); Asian studies (Certificate); European Union studies (Certificate); global studies (Certificate); Latin American studies (Certificate); Russian and East European studies (Certificate); West European studies (Certificate). *Program availability:* Part-time, evening/weekend, online learning. *Degree requirements:* For Certificate, one foreign language, comprehensive exam (for some programs). *Entrance requirements:* Additional exam requirements/recommendations for international students: required—TOEFL. *Expenses:* Contact institution.

University of Virginia, College and Graduate School of Arts and Sciences, Program in European Studies, Charlottesville, VA 22903. Offers MA.

Women's Studies

American University, College of Arts and Sciences, Critical Race, Gender, and Culture Studies, Washington, DC 20016. Offers Asian studies (Graduate Certificate); women's, gender, and sexuality studies (Graduate Certificate). *Entrance requirements:* Additional exam requirements/recommendations for international students: required—TOEFL.

The American University in Cairo, School of Global Affairs and Public Policy, Cairo, Egypt. Offers gender and women's studies (MA); global affairs (MGA); international and comparative law (LL M); international human rights law (MA); journalism and mass communication (MA); Middle East studies (MA); migration and refugee studies (MA, Diploma); public administration (MPA); public policy (MPP); television and digital journalism (MA). *Program availability:* Part-time, evening/weekend. *Degree requirements:* For master's, comprehensive exam (for some programs), thesis (for some programs). *Entrance requirements:* Additional exam requirements/recommendations for international students: required—TOEFL (minimum score 450 paper-based; 45 iBT), IELTS (minimum score 5). Electronic applications accepted. *Expenses:* Contact institution.

Brandeis University, Graduate School of Arts and Sciences, Department of Anthropology, Waltham, MA 02454. Offers anthropology/women's, gender, and sexuality studies (MA); Mesoamerican archaeology (MA, PhD); sociocultural anthropology (MA, PhD). *Program availability:* Part-time. *Faculty:* 13 full-time (6 women), 1 (woman) part-time/adjunct. *Students:* 28 full-time (19 women), 1 (woman) part-time; includes 6 minority (1 Black or African American, non-Hispanic/Latino; 3 Asian, non-Hispanic/Latino; 2 Two or more races, non-Hispanic/Latino), 3 international. Average age 27. 50 applicants, 60% accepted, 9 enrolled. In 2019, 6 master's, 2 doctorates awarded. Terminal master's awarded for partial completion of doctoral program. *Degree requirements:* For master's, thesis or alternative, paper; for doctorate, one foreign language, comprehensive exam, thesis/dissertation. *Entrance requirements:* For master's and doctorate, General GRE, transcripts, letters of recommendation, resume, statement of purpose, and writing sample. Additional exam requirements/recommendations for international students: required—TOEFL, IELTS, PTE. *Application deadline:* For fall admission, 1/15 priority date for domestic and international students. Applications are processed on a rolling basis. Application fee: $75. Electronic applications accepted. *Financial support:* In 2019–20, 8 fellowships with full tuition reimbursements (averaging $25,000 per year), 8 teaching assistantships (averaging $3,550 per year) were awarded; scholarships/grants and health care benefits also available. Support available to part-time students. *Unit head:* Dr. Charles Golden, Director of Graduate Studies, 781-736-2217, E-mail: cgolden@brandeis.edu. *Application contact:* Laurel Woolf, Administrator, 781-736-4873, E-mail: lwoolf@brandeis.edu. Website: http://www.brandeis.edu/gsas/programs/anthropology.html

Brandeis University, Graduate School of Arts and Sciences, Department of English, Waltham, MA 02454-9110. Offers English (MA, PhD); English/women's, gender, and sexuality studies (MA). *Program availability:* Part-time. *Faculty:* 13 full-time (6 women), 6 part-time/adjunct (3 women). *Students:* 39 full-time (24 women); includes 7 minority (3 Black or African American, non-Hispanic/Latino; 2 Asian, non-Hispanic/Latino; 1 Hispanic/Latino; 1 Two or more races, non-Hispanic/Latino), 7 international. Average age 31. 194 applicants, 12% accepted, 8 enrolled. In 2019, 5 master's, 4 doctorates awarded. Terminal master's awarded for partial completion of doctoral program. *Degree requirements:* For master's, one foreign language, thesis or alternative, paper; for doctorate, 2 foreign languages, thesis/dissertation. *Entrance requirements:* For master's and doctorate, General GRE, transcripts, letters of recommendation, resume, writing sample, and statement of purpose. Additional exam requirements/recommendations for international students: required—TOEFL, IELTS, PTE. *Application deadline:* For fall admission, 1/5 for domestic and international students. Application fee: $75. Electronic applications accepted. *Financial support:* In 2019–20, 30 fellowships with full tuition reimbursements (averaging $25,000 per year), 15 teaching assistantships (averaging $3,550 per year) were awarded; scholarships/grants, health care benefits, and tuition waivers also available. Support available to part-time students. *Unit head:* Dr. Ulka Anjaria, Director of Graduate Studies, 781-736-2162, E-mail: uanjaria@brandeis.edu. *Application contact:* Lisa Pannella, Administrator, 781-736-2130, E-mail: chaucer@brandeis.edu. Website: http://www.brandeis.edu/gsas/programs/english.html

Brandeis University, Graduate School of Arts and Sciences, Department of Near Eastern and Judaic Studies, Waltham, MA 02454-9110. Offers Near Eastern and Judaic studies (MA); near Eastern and Judaic studies/conflict resolution and coexistence (MA); near Eastern and Judaic studies/Jewish professional leadership (MA); near Eastern and Judaic studies/women's, gender, and sexuality studies (MA); teaching of Hebrew (MAT); the bible and ancient near east (PhD). *Program availability:* Part-time. *Faculty:* 21 full-time (8 women), 5 part-time/adjunct (3 women). *Students:* 34 full-time (15 women), 2 part-time (1 woman); includes 8 minority (1 Black or African American, non-Hispanic/Latino; 2 Asian, non-Hispanic/Latino; 3 Hispanic/Latino; 2 Two or more races, non-Hispanic/Latino), 7 international. Average age 34. 76 applicants, 53% accepted, 5 enrolled. In 2019, 3 master's, 3 doctorates awarded. Terminal master's awarded for partial completion of doctoral program. *Degree requirements:* For master's, one foreign language, thesis or alternative, capstone, thesis, or internship; for doctorate, variable foreign language requirement, comprehensive exam, thesis/dissertation. *Entrance requirements:* For master's and doctorate, GRE General recommended, transcripts, letters of recommendation, resume, writing sample, and statement of purpose. Additional exam requirements/recommendations for international students: required—TOEFL, IELTS, PTE. *Application deadline:* For fall admission, 1/15 priority date for domestic and international students. Applications are processed on a rolling basis. Application fee: $75. Electronic applications accepted. *Financial support:* In 2019–20, 9 fellowships with full tuition reimbursements (averaging $25,000 per year), 8 teaching assistantships (averaging $3,550 per year) were awarded; scholarships/grants, health care benefits, and tuition waivers also available. Support available to part-time students. *Unit head:* Dr. Ilana Szobel, Director of Graduate Studies, 781-736-5230, E-mail: szobel@brandeis.edu. *Application contact:* Jean Mannion, Administrator, 781-736-2950, E-mail: mannion@brandeis.edu. Website: http://www.brandeis.edu/gsas/programs/nejs.html

Brandeis University, Graduate School of Arts and Sciences, Department of Sociology, Waltham, MA 02454-9110. Offers social policy and sociology (PhD); sociology (PhD); sociology/women's, gender, and sexuality studies (MA). *Program availability:* Part-time. *Faculty:* 8 full-time (5 women), 1 (woman) part-time/adjunct. *Students:* 20 full-time (17 women); includes 5 minority (1 Black or African American, non-Hispanic/Latino; 3 Asian, non-Hispanic/Latino; 1 Hispanic/Latino), 2 international. Average age 29. 76 applicants, 17% accepted, 8 enrolled. In 2019, 2 master's, 4 doctorates awarded. Terminal master's awarded for partial completion of doctoral program. *Degree requirements:* For master's, thesis or alternative; for doctorate, comprehensive exam, thesis/dissertation. *Entrance*

requirements: For master's and doctorate, GRE General, transcripts, letters of recommendation, resume, writing sample, and statement of purpose. Additional exam requirements/recommendations for international students: required—TOEFL, IELTS, PTE. *Application deadline:* For fall admission, 12/15 for domestic and international students. Application fee: $75. Electronic applications accepted. *Financial support:* In 2019–20, 9 fellowships with full tuition reimbursements (averaging $25,000 per year), 13 teaching assistantships (averaging $3,550 per year) were awarded; scholarships/grants and health care benefits also available. *Unit head:* Dr. Karen Hansen, Director of Graduate Studies, 781-736-2651, E-mail: khansen@brandeis.edu. *Application contact:* Lauren Jordahl, Administrator, 781-736-2644, E-mail: ljordahl@brandeis.edu. Website: http://www.brandeis.edu/gsas/programs/sociology.html

Brandeis University, Graduate School of Arts and Sciences, Program in Women's, Gender, and Sexuality Studies, Waltham, MA 02454-9110. Offers anthropology/women's, gender, and sexuality studies (MA); English/women's, gender, and sexuality studies (MA); near Eastern and Judaic studies /women's, gender, and sexuality studies (MA); public policy/women's, gender, and sexuality studies (MA); sociology/women's, gender, and sexuality studies (MA); sustainable international development/women's, gender, and sexuality studies (MA); women's, gender, and sexuality studies (MA). *Program availability:* Part-time. *Faculty:* 19 full-time (16 women), 2 part-time/adjunct (both women). *Students:* 6 full-time (all women); includes 2 minority (both Hispanic/Latino). Average age 27. 41 applicants, 54% accepted, 8 enrolled. In 2019, 4 master's awarded. *Degree requirements:* For master's, thesis or alternative. *Entrance requirements:* For master's, GRE General, transcripts, letters of recommendation, resume, statement of purpose, and writing sample. Additional exam requirements/recommendations for international students: required—TOEFL, IELTS, PTE. *Application deadline:* For fall admission, 1/15 for domestic and international students. Application fee: $75. Electronic applications accepted. *Financial support:* Fellowships, scholarships/grants, health care benefits, and tuition waivers available. Support available to part-time students. *Unit head:* Dr. Ellen Schattschneider, Director of Graduate Studies, 781-736-2219, E-mail: eschatt@brandeis.edu. *Application contact:* Alexandra Brandon, Administrator, 781-736-3045, E-mail: abrandon@brandeis.edu. Website: http://www.brandeis.edu/gsas/programs/wgs.html

Carnegie Mellon University, Dietrich College of Humanities and Social Sciences, Department of History, Pittsburgh, PA 15213-3891. Offers African and African-American diaspora (PhD); culture and power (PhD); labor, politics and social movements (PhD); technology, environment, science and health (PhD); women, gender and the family (PhD). *Program availability:* Part-time. *Degree requirements:* For doctorate, oral and written comprehensive exams, dissertation defense. *Entrance requirements:* For doctorate, GRE General Test. Additional exam requirements/recommendations for international students: required—TOEFL. Electronic applications accepted.

Chatham University, Program in Business Administration, Pittsburgh, PA 15232-2826. Offers business administration (MBA); healthcare management (MBA); sustainability (MBA); women's leadership (MBA). *Program availability:* Part-time, evening/weekend. *Faculty:* 1 full-time (0 women), 12 part-time/adjunct (3 women). *Students:* 16 full-time (12 women), 24 part-time (17 women); includes 7 minority (2 Black or African American, non-Hispanic/Latino; 1 Asian, non-Hispanic/Latino; 2 Hispanic/Latino; 2 Two or more races, non-Hispanic/Latino), 7 international. Average age 28. 75 applicants, 29% accepted, 10 enrolled. In 2019, 20 master's awarded. *Entrance requirements:* For master's, minimum GPA of 3.0, letters of recommendation. Additional exam requirements/recommendations for international students: required—TOEFL (minimum score 600 paper-based; 100 iBT), IELTS (minimum score 7), TWE. *Application deadline:* For fall admission, 4/1 for domestic and international students; for spring admission, 11/1 for domestic students, 10/1 for international students. Applications are processed on a rolling basis. Application fee: $45. Electronic applications accepted. Application fee is waived when completed online. *Expenses:* Contact institution. *Financial support:* Applicants required to submit FAFSA. *Unit head:* Dr. Rachel Chung, Director of Business and Entrepreneurship Program, 412-365-2433. *Application contact:* Melanie Jo Elmer, Assistant Director of Graduate Admission, 412-365-1394, Fax: 412-365-1609, E-mail: gradadmissions@chatham.edu. Website: http://www.chatham.edu/mba

Claremont Graduate University, Graduate Programs, School of Arts and Humanities, Department of Religion, Claremont, CA 91711-6160. Offers Hebrew Bible (MA, PhD); history of Christianity and religions of North America (MA, PhD); New Testament (MA, PhD); philosophy of religion and theology (MA, PhD); theology, ethics and culture (MA, PhD); women's studies in religion (MA, PhD); MA/PhD; MBA/PhD. *Program availability:* Part-time. Terminal master's awarded for partial completion of doctoral program. *Entrance requirements:* For master's and doctorate, GRE General Test. Additional exam requirements/recommendations for international students: required—TOEFL (minimum score 75 iBT). Electronic applications accepted.

Claremont Graduate University, Graduate Programs, School of Arts and Humanities, Program in Applied Women's Studies, Claremont, CA 91711-6160. Offers MA. *Entrance requirements:* For master's, GRE General Test. Additional exam requirements/recommendations for international students: required—TOEFL (minimum score 75 iBT). Electronic applications accepted.

Cornell University, Graduate School, Graduate Fields of Arts and Sciences, Field of English Language and Literature, Ithaca, NY 14853. Offers African-American literature (PhD); American literature after 1865 (PhD); American literature to 1865 (PhD); American studies (PhD); colonial and postcolonial literatures (PhD); creative writing (MFA); cultural studies (PhD); dramatic literature (PhD); English poetry (PhD); English Renaissance to 1660 (PhD); lesbian, bisexual, and gay literary studies (PhD); literary criticism and theory (PhD); Old and Middle English (PhD); prose fiction (PhD); Restoration and the eighteenth-century (PhD); the nineteenth century (PhD); the twentieth century (PhD); women's literature (PhD); MFA/PhD. Terminal master's awarded for partial completion of doctoral program. *Degree requirements:* For master's, one foreign language, thesis; for doctorate, one foreign language, comprehensive exam, thesis/dissertation, teaching experience. *Entrance requirements:* For master's, GRE General Test, 3 letters of recommendation, creative writing sample; for doctorate, 3 letters of recommendation, writing sample. Additional exam requirements/recommendations for international students: required—TOEFL (minimum score 600 paper-based; 77 iBT). Electronic applications accepted.

DePaul University, College of Liberal Arts and Social Sciences, Chicago, IL 60614. Offers Arabic (MA); Chinese (MA); critical ethnic studies (MA); English (MA); French (MA); German (MA); history (MA); interdisciplinary studies (MA, MS); international public service (MS); international studies (MA); Italian (MA); Japanese (MA); liberal studies (MA); nonprofit management (MNM); public administration (MPA); public health (MPH); public policy (MPP); public service management (MS); refugee and forced migration studies (MS); social work (MSW); sociology (MA); Spanish (MA); sustainable urban development (MA); women's and gender studies (MA); writing and publishing (MA); writing, rhetoric and discourse (MA); MA/PhD. *Accreditation:* CEPH. *Program availability:* Part-time, evening/weekend, online learning. Terminal master's awarded for partial completion of doctoral program. *Degree requirements:* For master's, variable foreign language requirement, comprehensive exam (for some programs), thesis (for some programs). Electronic applications accepted.

Eastern Michigan University, Graduate School, College of Arts and Sciences, Department of Women's and Gender Studies, Ypsilanti, MI 48197. Offers MA, Graduate Certificate. *Program availability:* Part-time, evening/weekend. *Faculty:* 2 full-time (both women). *Students:* 4 full-time (all women), 6 part-time (all women); includes 4 minority (1 American Indian or Alaska Native, non-Hispanic/Latino; 1 Hispanic/Latino; 2 Two or more races, non-Hispanic/Latino), 2 international. Average age 30. 7 applicants, 100% accepted, 4 enrolled. In 2019, 9 master's, 1 other advanced degree awarded. *Entrance requirements:* Additional exam requirements/recommendations for international students: required—TOEFL. *Application deadline:* For fall admission, 6/15 for domestic and international students; for winter admission, 9/15 for domestic and international students; for spring admission, 3/1 for domestic and international students. Applications are processed on a rolling basis. Application fee: $45. *Financial support:* Fellowships, research assistantships with full tuition reimbursements, teaching assistantships with full tuition reimbursements, career-related internships or fieldwork, Federal Work-Study, institutionally sponsored loans, scholarships/grants, tuition waivers (partial), and unspecified assistantships available. Support available to part-time students. Financial award applicants required to submit FAFSA. *Unit head:* Dr. Elizabeth Currans, Interim Department Head, 734-487-1177, Fax: 734-487-5029, E-mail: ecurrans@emich.edu. *Application contact:* Dr. Jackie Goodman, Graduate Coordinator, 734-487-1177, Fax: 734-487-5029, E-mail: jgoodma9@emich.edu.
Website: http://www.emich.edu/wgstudies/

Emory University, Laney Graduate School, Department of Comparative Literature, Atlanta, GA 30322-1100. Offers comparative literature (PhD); philosophy (Certificate); psychoanalytic studies (PhD); women's studies (Certificate). *Degree requirements:* For doctorate, 2 foreign languages, comprehensive exam, thesis/dissertation. *Entrance requirements:* For doctorate, GRE General Test, minimum GPA of 3.0. Additional exam requirements/recommendations for international students: required—TOEFL. Electronic applications accepted.

Emory University, Laney Graduate School, Department of Spanish and Portuguese, Atlanta, GA 30322-1100. Offers comparative literature (Certificate); film studies (Certificate); Spanish (PhD); women's studies (Certificate). *Degree requirements:* For doctorate, 2 foreign languages, comprehensive exam, thesis/dissertation. *Entrance requirements:* For doctorate, GRE General Test. Additional exam requirements/recommendations for international students: required—TOEFL. Electronic applications accepted.

Emory University, Laney Graduate School, Department of Women's, Gender, and Sexuality Studies, Atlanta, GA 30322-1100. Offers PhD. *Degree requirements:* For doctorate, comprehensive exam, thesis/dissertation. *Entrance requirements:* For doctorate, GRE General Test, writing sample. Additional exam requirements/recommendations for international students: required—TOEFL. Electronic applications accepted.

Florida Atlantic University, Dorothy F. Schmidt College of Arts and Letters, Center for Women, Gender and Sexuality Studies, Boca Raton, FL 33431-0991. Offers MA. *Program availability:* Part-time. *Faculty:* 2 full-time (both women). *Students:* 7 full-time (6 women), 1 (woman) part-time; includes 5 minority (1 Black or African American, non-Hispanic/Latino; 4 Hispanic/Latino). Average age 24. 3 applicants, 100% accepted, 3 enrolled. In 2019, 4 master's awarded. *Degree requirements:* For master's, comprehensive exam, thesis or alternative. *Entrance requirements:* For master's, GRE General Test, minimum GPA of 3.0. Additional exam requirements/recommendations for international students: required—TOEFL (minimum score 500 paper-based; 61 iBT), IELTS (minimum score 6). *Application deadline:* For fall admission, 7/1 for domestic students, 2/15 for international students; for spring admission, 11/1 for domestic students, 7/15 for international students. Applications are processed on a rolling basis. Application fee: $30. Electronic applications accepted. *Expenses: Tuition:* Full-time $20,536; part-time $371.82 per credit hour. Tuition and fees vary according to program. *Financial support:* Fellowships, teaching assistantships, career-related internships or fieldwork, Federal Work-Study, institutionally sponsored loans, scholarships/grants, and unspecified assistantships available. Support available to part-time students. Financial award applicants required to submit FAFSA. *Unit head:* William Trapani, Director, 561-297-2051, E-mail: wtrapan1@fau.edu. *Application contact:* William Trapani, Director, 561-297-2051, E-mail: wtrapan1@fau.edu.
Website: http://www.fau.edu/artsandletters/wgss/

George Mason University, College of Humanities and Social Sciences, Interdisciplinary Studies Program, Fairfax, VA 22030. Offers computational social science (MAIS); energy and sustainability (MAIS); folklore studies (MAIS); higher education (MAIS); individualized studies (MAIS); religion, culture, and values (MAIS); social entrepreneurship (MAIS); social justice and human rights (MAIS); war and the military in society (MAIS); women and gender studies (MAIS). *Degree requirements:* For master's, thesis or alternative, experiential learning (for some programs). *Entrance requirements:* Additional exam requirements/recommendations for international students: required—TOEFL (minimum score 575 paper-based; 88 iBT), IELTS (minimum score 6.5), PTE (minimum score 59). Electronic applications accepted.

The George Washington University, Columbian College of Arts and Sciences, Department of Women's Studies, Washington, DC 20052. Offers MA, Certificate. *Program availability:* Part-time, evening/weekend. *Degree requirements:* For master's, comprehensive exam, thesis or alternative. *Entrance requirements:* For master's, GRE General Test, minimum GPA of 3.0. Additional exam requirements/recommendations for international students: required—TOEFL (minimum score 550 paper-based; 80 iBT). Electronic applications accepted.

Georgia State University, College of Arts and Sciences, Institute for Women's, Gender, and Sexuality Studies, Atlanta, GA 30302-3083. Offers MA, Graduate Certificate. *Program availability:* Part-time. *Faculty:* 6 full-time (all women). *Students:* 15 full-time (all women), 5 part-time (all women); includes 10 minority (8 Black or African American, non-Hispanic/Latino; 2 Hispanic/Latino), 3 international. Average age 31. 31 applicants, 61% accepted, 9 enrolled. In 2019, 4 master's, 3 other advanced degrees awarded. *Entrance requirements:* For master's and Graduate Certificate, GRE, two official transcripts from each college or university attended, three letters of recommendation addressing student's ability to undertake graduate study, 750-1000 word statement of purpose, academic writing sample. Additional exam requirements/recommendations for international students: required—TOEFL (minimum score 550 paper-based; 80 iBT). *Application deadline:* For fall admission, 2/15 for domestic and international students. Application fee: $50. Electronic applications accepted. *Expenses: Tuition, area resident:* Full-time $7164; part-time $398 per credit hour. *Tuition, state resident:* full-time $7164; part-time $398 per credit hour. *Tuition, nonresident:* full-time $22,662; part-time $1259 per credit hour. *International tuition:* $22,662 full-time. *Required fees:* $2128; $312 per credit hour. Tuition and fees vary according to course load and program. *Financial support:* In 2019–20, research assistantships with full tuition reimbursements (averaging $7,000 per year), teaching assistantships with full tuition reimbursements (averaging $7,500 per year) were awarded; career-related internships or fieldwork, health care benefits, and unspecified assistantships also available. Financial award application deadline: 2/15. *Unit head:* Dr. Stephanie Evans, Fax: 404-413-6585, E-mail: sevans62@gsu.edu. *Application contact:* Dr. Megan Sinnott, Director of Graduate Studies, Fax: 404-413-6585, E-mail: megansinnott@gsu.edu.
Website: https://wgss.gsu.edu/

Grace Theological Seminary, Graduate and Professional Programs, Winona Lake, IN 46590-9907. Offers biblical studies (Certificate); chaplaincy (M Div); exegetical studies (M Div); intercultural studies (M Div, MA, D Min); local church ministry (MA), including camp administration, women's leadership; pastoral counseling (M Div); pastoral studies (M Div, D Min); theology (Diploma). *Accreditation:* ATS. *Program availability:* Part-time, online learning. *Degree requirements:* For master's, thesis optional; for doctorate, 2 foreign languages, thesis/dissertation. *Entrance requirements:* For master's, MAT, minimum GPA of 2.5. Electronic applications accepted.

Inter American University of Puerto Rico, Metropolitan Campus, Graduate Programs, Program in Women's and Gender Studies, San Juan, PR 00919-1293. Offers MA.

The Jewish Theological Seminary, The Graduate School, New York, NY 10027-4649. Offers ancient Judaism (MA, DHL, PhD); Bible and ancient Semitic languages (MA, DHL, PhD); interdepartmental studies (MA); Jewish art and visual culture (MA); Jewish gender and women's studies (MA); Jewish history (MA, DHL, PhD); Jewish literature (MA, DHL, PhD); Jewish philosophy (DHL); Jewish thought (MA, PhD); liturgy (MA, DHL, PhD); medieval Jewish studies (MA, DHL, PhD); Midrash (DHL); Midrash and scriptural interpretation (MA, PhD); modern Jewish studies (MA, DHL, PhD); Talmud and rabbinics (MA, DHL, PhD); MA/MSW. *Accreditation:* ACIPE. *Program availability:* Part-time. Terminal master's awarded for partial completion of doctoral program. *Degree requirements:* For master's, one foreign language, comprehensive exam (for some programs), thesis (for some programs); for doctorate, 3 foreign languages, comprehensive exam (for some programs), thesis/dissertation. *Entrance requirements:* For master's, GRE or MAT, 3 letters of recommendation, writing sample; for doctorate, GRE or MAT, 3 letters of recommendation, writing research sample. Additional exam requirements/recommendations for international students: required—TOEFL.

Kansas State University, Graduate School, College of Arts and Sciences, Department of Gender, Women and Sexuality Studies, Manhattan, KS 66506. Offers Graduate Certificate. *Entrance requirements:* For degree, minimum GPA of 3.0, letters of recommendation. Additional exam requirements/recommendations for international students: required—TOEFL, TWE, or IELTS.

Lakehead University, Graduate Studies, Faculty of Education, Thunder Bay, ON P7B 5E1, Canada. Offers educational studies (PhD); gerontology (M Ed); women's studies (M Ed). *Program availability:* Part-time, evening/weekend. *Degree requirements:* For master's, project or thesis. *Entrance requirements:* For master's, minimum B average. Additional exam requirements/recommendations for international students: required—TOEFL.

Lakehead University, Graduate Studies, Faculty of Social Sciences and Humanities, Department of English, Thunder Bay, ON P7B 5E1, Canada. Offers English (MA); women's studies (MA). *Program availability:* Part-time, evening/weekend. *Degree requirements:* For master's, one foreign language, thesis optional. *Entrance requirements:* For master's, minimum B average. Additional exam requirements/recommendations for international students: required—TOEFL.

Lakehead University, Graduate Studies, Faculty of Social Sciences and Humanities, Department of History, Thunder Bay, ON P7B 5E1, Canada. Offers gerontology (MA); history (MA); women's studies (MA). *Program availability:* Part-time. *Degree requirements:* For master's, one foreign language, thesis. *Entrance requirements:* For master's, minimum B average. Additional exam requirements/recommendations for international students: required—TOEFL.

Lakehead University, Graduate Studies, Faculty of Social Sciences and Humanities, Department of Sociology, Thunder Bay, ON P7B 5E1, Canada. Offers gerontology (MA); health services and policy research (MA); sociology (MA); women's studies (MA). *Program availability:* Part-time, evening/weekend. *Degree requirements:* For master's, research project or thesis. *Entrance requirements:* For master's, minimum B average. Additional exam requirements/recommendations for international students: required—TOEFL.

Lakehead University, Graduate Studies, School of Social Work, Thunder Bay, ON P7B 5E1, Canada. Offers gerontology (MSW); social work (MSW); women's studies (MSW). *Program availability:* Part-time. *Degree requirements:* For master's, thesis or project. *Entrance requirements:* For master's, minimum B average. Additional exam requirements/recommendations for international students: required—TOEFL.

Lakehead University, Graduate Studies, Women's Studies Collaborative Program, Thunder Bay, ON P7B 5E1, Canada. Offers M Ed, MA, MSW. *Program availability:* Part-time. *Degree requirements:* For master's, thesis (for some programs). *Entrance requirements:* Additional exam requirements/recommendations for international students: required—TOEFL.

Lesley University, Graduate School of Arts and Social Sciences, Cambridge, MA 02138-2790. Offers clinical mental health counseling (MA), including holistic counseling, school and community counseling, trauma studies; counseling psychology (MA, CAGS), including professional counseling (MA), school counseling (MA); creative writing (MFA); expressive therapies (MA, PhD, CAGS), including art (MA), clinical mental health counseling (MA), dance (MA), expressive therapies (MA), music (MA); independent studies (CAGS); independent study (MA); intercultural relations (MA, CAGS); interdisciplinary studies (MA), including individualized studies, integrative holistic health, mindfulness studies, peace and conflict transformation, trauma sensitive assessment, intervention, and consultation, women's studies; urban environmental leadership (MA). *Program availability:* Part-time, online learning. *Degree requirements:* For master's, internship, practicum, thesis (for expressive therapies); for doctorate, thesis/dissertation, arts apprenticeship, field placement; for CAGS, thesis, internship (for counseling psychology, expressive therapies). *Entrance requirements:* For master's, MAT (counseling psychology), interview, writing samples, art portfolio; for doctorate, GRE or MAT, interview, master's degree; for CAGS, interview, master's degree. Additional exam requirements/recommendations for international students: required—TOEFL (minimum score 550 paper-based; 80 iBT). Electronic applications accepted.

London Metropolitan University, Graduate Programs, London, United Kingdom. Offers applied psychology (M Sc); architecture (MA); biomedical science (M Sc); blood science (M Sc); cancer pharmacology (M Sc); computer networking and cyber security (M Sc); computing and information systems (M Sc); conference interpreting (MA); counter-terrorism studies (M Sc); creative, digital and professional writing (MA); crime, violence and prevention (M Sc); criminology (M Sc); curating contemporary art (MA); data analytics (M Sc); digital media (MA); early childhood studies (MA); education (MA, Ed D); financial services law, regulation and compliance (LL M); food science (M Sc);

forensic psychology (M Sc); health and social care management and policy (M Sc); human nutrition (M Sc); human resource management (MA); human rights and international conflict (MA); information technology (M Sc); intelligence and security studies (M Sc); international oil, gas and energy law (LL M); international relations (MA); interpreting (MA); learning and teaching in higher education (MA); legal practice (LL M); media and entertainment law (LL M); organizational and consumer psychology (M Sc); psychological therapy (M Sc); psychology of mental health (M Sc); public health (M Sc); public policy and management (MPA); security studies (M Sc); social work (M Sc); spatial planning and urban design (MA); sports therapy (M Sc); supporting older children and young people with dyslexia (MA); teaching languages (MA), including Arabic, English; translation (MA); woman and child abuse (MA).

Loyola University Chicago, Graduate School, Programs in Women's Studies and Gender Studies, Chicago, IL 60660. Offers MA. *Program availability:* Part-time. *Faculty:* 5 full-time (4 women), 1 (woman) part-time/adjunct. *Students:* 14 full-time (13 women), 2 part-time (both women); includes 5 minority (all Hispanic/Latino). Average age 25. 16 applicants, 44% accepted, 4 enrolled. In 2019, 12 master's awarded. *Degree requirements:* For master's, thesis or alternative, can do practicum or internship instead of thesis. Must also do capstone course. *Entrance requirements:* For master's, No, GPA of 3.0, personal statement, 3 letters of reference and writing sample. Additional exam requirements/recommendations for international students: required—TOEFL (minimum score 550 paper-based; 79 iBT), IELTS (minimum score 6.5). *Application deadline:* For fall admission, 6/1 for domestic and international students; for spring admission, 11/1 for domestic and international students. Applications are processed on a rolling basis. Electronic applications accepted. Application fee is waived when completed online. *Expenses: Tuition:* Full-time $18,540; part-time $1033 per credit hour. *Required fees:* $904; $230 per credit hour. *Financial support:* In 2019–20, 7 students received support. Teaching assistantships, health care benefits, tuition waivers (full and partial), and unspecified assistantships available. Financial award application deadline: 4/1. *Unit head:* Dr. Susan Grossman, Graduate Program Director, WSGS, 312-915-6456, E-mail: sgrossm@luc.edu. *Application contact:* Jill Schur, Director of Graduate Enrollment Management, 312-915-8902, E-mail: gradinfo@luc.edu.
Website: https://www.luc.edu/wsgs/

Middle Tennessee State University, College of Graduate Studies, College of Liberal Arts, Program in Women's and Gender Studies, Murfreesboro, TN 37132. Offers Graduate Certificate. *Program availability:* Part-time, evening/weekend, online learning. Electronic applications accepted.

Minnesota State University Mankato, College of Graduate Studies and Research, College of Social and Behavioral Sciences, Department of Gender and Women's Studies, Mankato, MN 56001. Offers MS. *Program availability:* Part-time. *Degree requirements:* For master's, comprehensive exam, thesis or alternative. *Entrance requirements:* For master's, minimum GPA of 3.0, essay. Additional exam requirements/recommendations for international students: required—TOEFL.

Mount Saint Vincent University, Graduate Programs, Department of Women's Studies, Halifax, NS B3M 2J6, Canada. Offers MA. *Program availability:* Part-time. *Degree requirements:* For master's, thesis. Electronic applications accepted.

Northern Arizona University, College of Social and Behavioral Sciences, Women's and Gender Studies Program, Flagstaff, AZ 86011. Offers Graduate Certificate. *Program availability:* Part-time. *Degree requirements:* For Graduate Certificate, comprehensive exam (for some programs). *Entrance requirements:* Additional exam requirements/recommendations for international students: required—TOEFL (minimum score 80 iBT), IELTS (minimum score 6.5). Electronic applications accepted.

The Ohio State University, Graduate School, College of Arts and Sciences, Division of Arts and Humanities, Department of Women's, Gender and Sexuality Studies, Columbus, OH 43210. Offers MA, PhD. Terminal master's awarded for partial completion of doctoral program. *Entrance requirements:* For master's and doctorate, GRE (if GPA is less than 3.0 for all work), scholarly writing sample. Additional exam requirements/recommendations for international students: required—TOEFL (minimum score 550 paper-based; 79 iBT), Michigan English Language Assessment Battery (minimum score 82); recommended—IELTS (minimum score 7). Electronic applications accepted.

Old Dominion University, College of Arts and Letters, Program in Applied Sociology, Norfolk, VA 23529. Offers criminal justice (MA); general sociology (MA); women's studies (MA). *Program availability:* Part-time, evening/weekend. *Degree requirements:* For master's, thesis. *Entrance requirements:* For master's, GRE General Test, minimum GPA of 3.0; 12 credits in criminal justice, sociology, or women's studies. Additional exam requirements/recommendations for international students: required—TOEFL. Electronic applications accepted. *Expenses:* Contact institution.

Oregon State University, College of Liberal Arts, Program in Women, Gender, and Sexuality Studies, Corvallis, OR 97331. Offers feminist leadership (PhD). *Program availability:* Part-time. *Degree requirements:* For master's, one foreign language; for doctorate, thesis/dissertation. *Entrance requirements:* Additional exam requirements/recommendations for international students: required—TOEFL (minimum score 80 iBT), IELTS (minimum score 6.5).

Queen's University at Kingston, School of Graduate Studies, Faculty of Arts and Science, Department of Sociology, Kingston, ON K7L 3N6, Canada. Offers communication and information technology (MA, PhD); feminist sociology (MA, PhD); socio-legal studies (MA, PhD); sociological theory (MA, PhD). *Program availability:* Part-time. *Degree requirements:* For master's, thesis; for doctorate, comprehensive exam, thesis/dissertation. *Entrance requirements:* For master's, honors bachelor's degree in sociology; for doctorate, honors bachelor's degree, master's degree in sociology. Additional exam requirements/recommendations for international students: required—TOEFL.

Reconstructionist Rabbinical College, Graduate Programs, Wyncote, PA 19095-1898. Offers Jewish studies (MAJS); rabbinics (MAHL, DHL); women's studies (Certificate). *Program availability:* Part-time. *Degree requirements:* For master's, one foreign language, thesis (MAJS), completion of rabbinical program (MAHL); for doctorate, one foreign language. *Entrance requirements:* For master's, GRE General Test; placement examinations in Hebrew and Judaism (MAHL); for doctorate, GRE General Test, placement examinations in Hebrew and Judaism. *Expenses: Tuition:* Full-time $26,000.

Rutgers University - New Brunswick, Graduate School-New Brunswick, Department of Political Science, Piscataway, NJ 08854-8097. Offers American politics (PhD); comparative politics (PhD); international relations (PhD); political theory (PhD); public law (PhD); United Nations and global policy studies (MA); women and politics (PhD). *Degree requirements:* For doctorate, one foreign language, comprehensive exam, thesis/dissertation. *Entrance requirements:* For master's, bachelor's degree from accredited U.S. college or university or a comparable institution in another country; for doctorate, GRE General Test. Additional exam requirements/recommendations for international students: required—TOEFL.

Rutgers University - New Brunswick, Graduate School-New Brunswick, Program in Women's and Gender Studies, Piscataway, NJ 08854-8097. Offers MA, PhD. *Program availability:* Part-time. *Degree requirements:* For master's, thesis or alternative; for doctorate, comprehensive exam, thesis/dissertation. *Entrance requirements:* For master's and doctorate, GRE General Test, writing sample, 3 letters of recommendation. Additional exam requirements/recommendations for international students: required—TOEFL.

Saint Mary's University, Faculty of Arts, Program in Women and Gender Studies, Halifax, NS B3H 3C3, Canada. Offers MA. *Program availability:* Part-time. *Degree requirements:* For master's, thesis. *Entrance requirements:* For master's, honors degree.

San Diego State University, Graduate and Research Affairs, College of Arts and Letters, Department of Women's Studies, San Diego, CA 92182. Offers MA. *Entrance requirements:* For master's, GRE General Test, 2 letters of reference. Additional exam requirements/recommendations for international students: required—TOEFL. Electronic applications accepted.

San Francisco State University, Division of Graduate Studies, College of Liberal and Creative Arts, Department of Women and Gender Studies, San Francisco, CA 94132-1722. Offers MA. *Program availability:* Part-time, evening/weekend. *Expenses: Tuition, area resident:* Full-time $7176; part-time $4164 per year. Tuition, state resident: full-time $7176; part-time $4164 per year. Tuition, nonresident: full-time $16,680; part-time $396 per unit. *International tuition:* $16,680 full-time. *Required fees:* $1524; $1524 per unit. $762 per semester. Tuition and fees vary according to degree level and program. *Unit head:* Dr. Kasturi Ray, Chair, 415-338-3128, Fax: 415-338-6159, E-mail: kasturi@sfsu.edu. *Application contact:* Dr. Deborah Cohler, Graduate Coordinator, 415-338-3150, Fax: 415-338-6159, E-mail: dcohler@sfsu.edu.
Website: http://wgsdept.sfsu.edu/graduate-studies

Sarah Lawrence College, Graduate Studies, Program in Women's History, Bronxville, NY 10708-5999. Offers MA. *Program availability:* Part-time. *Degree requirements:* For master's, thesis. *Entrance requirements:* For master's, previous course work in history, minimum B average in undergraduate course work. Additional exam requirements/recommendations for international students: required—TOEFL (minimum score 600 paper-based). Electronic applications accepted.

Simon Fraser University, Office of Graduate Studies and Postdoctoral Fellows, Faculty of Arts and Social Sciences, Department of Gender, Sexuality and Women's Studies, Burnaby, BC V5A 1S6, Canada. Offers MA, PhD. *Degree requirements:* For master's, thesis or alternative; for doctorate, comprehensive exam, thesis/dissertation. *Entrance requirements:* For master's, minimum GPA of 3.0 (on scale of 4.33) or 3.33 based on last 60 credits of undergraduate courses; for doctorate, minimum GPA of 3.5 (on scale of 4.33). Additional exam requirements/recommendations for international students: recommended—TOEFL (minimum score 580 paper-based; 93 iBT), IELTS (minimum score 7), TWE (minimum score 5). Electronic applications accepted.

Smith College, Graduate and Special Programs, Center for Women in Mathematics Post-Baccalaureate Program, Northampton, MA 01063. Offers Postbaccalaureate Certificate. *Students:* 9 full-time (all women); includes 5 minority (1 Black or African American, non-Hispanic/Latino; 3 Asian, non-Hispanic/Latino; 1 Hispanic/Latino). Average age 25. 17 applicants, 65% accepted, 8 enrolled. In 2019, 8 Postbaccalaureate Certificates awarded. *Entrance requirements:* Additional exam requirements/recommendations for international students: required—TOEFL (minimum score 595 paper-based; 97 iBT), IELTS (minimum score 7.5). *Application deadline:* For fall admission, 3/15 for domestic students; for spring admission, 10/15 for domestic students. Application fee: $60. *Expenses: Tuition:* Full-time $36,940; part-time $1690 per credit. *Required fees:* $90. Full-time tuition and fees vary according to course load, degree level and program. *Financial support:* In 2019–20, 9 students received support. Scholarships/grants and tuition waivers (full) available. Financial award application deadline: 3/15. *Unit head:* Julianna Tymoczko, Director, 413-585-3775, E-mail: jtymoczko@smith.edu. *Application contact:* Ruth Morgan, Program Coordinator, 413-585-3050, Fax: 413-585-3054, E-mail: rmorgan@smith.edu.

Southeastern Baptist Theological Seminary, Graduate and Professional Programs, Wake Forest, NC 27587. Offers advanced biblical studies (M Div); Christian education (M Div, MACE); Christian ethics (PhD); Christian ministry (M Div); Christian planting (M Div); church music (MACM); counseling (MACO); evangelism (PhD); language (M Div); ministry (D Min); New Testament (PhD); Old Testament (PhD); philosophy (PhD); theology (Th M, PhD); women's studies (M Div). *Accreditation:* ACIPE; ATS (one or more programs are accredited). *Degree requirements:* For master's, thesis (for some programs), oral exam; for doctorate, thesis/dissertation, fieldwork. *Entrance requirements:* For master's, Cooperative English Test, minimum GPA of 2.0, M Div or equivalent (Th M); for doctorate, GRE General Test or MAT, Cooperative English Test, M Div or equivalent, 3 years of professional experience.

Southern Connecticut State University, School of Graduate Studies, School of Arts and Sciences, Program in Women's Studies, New Haven, CT 06515-1355. Offers MA. *Program availability:* Part-time, evening/weekend. *Degree requirements:* For master's, thesis or alternative. *Entrance requirements:* For master's, interview. Electronic applications accepted.

Stony Brook University, State University of New York, Graduate School, College of Arts and Sciences, Department of Women's, Gender, and Sexuality Studies, Stony Brook, NY 11794. Offers Certificate. *Faculty:* 7 full-time (6 women), 1 (woman) part-time/adjunct. *Students:* 19 full-time (16 women); includes 5 minority (1 Black or African American, non-Hispanic/Latino; 3 Hispanic/Latino; 1 Two or more races, non-Hispanic/Latino), 6 international. Average age 33. 24 applicants, 42% accepted, 6 enrolled. In 2019, 6 Certificates awarded. *Entrance requirements:* For degree, GRE, minimum GPA of 2.75, 3 letters of recommendation. Additional exam requirements/recommendations for international students: required—TOEFL, IELTS, IELTS: Overall score of 6.5, with no subsection recommended to be below 6; TOEFL iBT: 80 for master's level, 90 for admission to a doctoral program. *Application deadline:* For fall admission, 1/15 for domestic students; for spring admission, 10/1 for domestic students. *Expenses:* Contact institution. *Financial support:* In 2019–20, 28 teaching assistantships were awarded. *Unit head:* Prof. Lisa Diedrich, Professor and Chair, 631-632-1967, E-mail: lisa.diedrich@stonybrook.edu. *Application contact:* Prof. Victoria Hesford, Associate Professor & Director of Graduate Studies, 631-632-7456, E-mail: victoria.hesford@stonybrook.edu.
Website: http://www.stonybrook.edu/commcms/wgss/

Texas Woman's University, Graduate School, College of Arts and Sciences, Department of Multicultural Women's and Gender Studies, Denton, TX 76204. Offers MA, PhD. *Program availability:* Part-time. *Faculty:* 4 full-time (3 women), 1 (woman) part-time/adjunct. *Students:* 8 full-time (all women), 31 part-time (30 women); includes 20 minority (7 Black or African American, non-Hispanic/Latino; 1 American Indian or Alaska Native, non-Hispanic/Latino; 3 Asian, non-Hispanic/Latino; 6 Hispanic/Latino; 3 Two or more races, non-Hispanic/Latino), 3 international. Average age 36. 7 applicants, 100% accepted, 4 enrolled. In 2019, 4 master's, 5 doctorates awarded. *Degree requirements:* For master's, comprehensive exam, thesis or alternative, thesis or coursework; for doctorate, comprehensive exam, thesis/dissertation, exam is a portfolio; dissertation defense. *Entrance requirements:* For master's, 2 letters of reference, personal essay, minimum GPA of 3.0 in last 60 hours of undergraduate work, writing

sample, written statement about interests and goals; for doctorate, statement of purpose, writing sample, curriculum vitae/resume, 2 reference letters, minimum GPA of 3.5 in prior graduate level course work. Additional exam requirements/recommendations for international students: required—TOEFL (minimum score 79 iBT); recommended—IELTS (minimum score 6.5), TSE (minimum score 53). *Application deadline:* For fall admission, 3/1 priority date for domestic and international students; for spring admission, 11/1 priority date for domestic students, 7/1 priority date for international students; for summer admission, 5/1 for domestic students, 2/1 priority date for international students. Applications are processed on a rolling basis. Application fee: $50 ($75 for international students). Electronic applications accepted. *Expenses: Tuition, area resident:* Full-time $4973.40; part-time $276.30 per semester hour. Tuition, state resident: full-time $4973.40; part-time $276.30 per semester hour. Tuition, nonresident: full-time $12,569; part-time $698.30 per semester hour. *International tuition:* $12,569.40 full-time. *Required fees:* $2524.30. Tuition and fees vary according to course level, course load, degree level and program. *Financial support:* In 2019–20, 17 students received support, including 13 teaching assistantships (averaging $11,469 per year); career-related internships or fieldwork, scholarships/grants, health care benefits, and unspecified assistantships also available. Support available to part-time students. Financial award application deadline: 3/1; financial award applicants required to submit FAFSA. *Unit head:* Dr. Christina Bejarano, Chair, 940-898-2119, Fax: 940-898-2101, E-mail: womenstudies@twu.edu. *Application contact:* Korie Hawkins, Associate Director of Admissions, Graduate Recruitment, 940-898-3188, Fax: 940-898-3081, E-mail: admissions@twu.edu.
Website: http://www.twu.edu/ws/

Towson University, College of Liberal Arts, Program in Women's Studies, Towson, MD 21252-0001. Offers MS, Postbaccalaureate Certificate. *Students:* 7 full-time (6 women), 2 part-time (both women); includes 4 minority (all Black or African American, non-Hispanic/Latino), 1 international. *Entrance requirements:* For master's, bachelor's degree with minimum GPA of 3.0, 9 credits of course work in women's studies and/or the social sciences, essay, 2 letters of recommendation; for Postbaccalaureate Certificate, bachelor's degree, 9 units in women's studies and/or the social sciences, 2 letters of recommendation, essay. *Application deadline:* For fall admission, 1/17 for domestic students, 5/15 for international students; for spring admission, 10/15 for domestic students, 12/1 for international students. Applications are processed on a rolling basis. Application fee: $45. Electronic applications accepted. *Expenses: Tuition, area resident:* Full-time $7920; part-time $439 per credit. Tuition, nonresident: full-time $16,344; part-time $908 per credit. *International tuition:* $16,344 full-time. *Required fees:* $2628; $146 per credit. $876 per term. *Financial support:* Application deadline: 4/1. *Unit head:* Dr. Cindy Gissendanner, Department Chair, 410-704-5456, E-mail: cgissendanner@towson.edu. *Application contact:* Coverley Beidleman, Assistant Director of Graduate Admissions, 410-704-5630, Fax: 410-704-3030, E-mail: grads@towson.edu.
Website: https://www.towson.edu/cla/departments/womengender/grad/

United Theological Seminary of the Twin Cities, Graduate Programs, New Brighton, MN 55112-2598. Offers advanced theological studies (Diploma); justice and peace studies (M Div, MA); leadership toward racial justice (M Div, MA, Certificate); Methodist studies (M Div, MA, Certificate); ministry (D Min); ministry renewal and professional development (Certificate); pastoral care and counseling (M Div, MA, MARL); religion and theology (MA); theological and religious studies (Certificate); theology and the arts (M Div, MA); urban ministry (M Div, MA, MARL); women's studies: religion, theology and ministry (M Div, MA). *Accreditation:* ACIPE; ATS. *Program availability:* Part-time, evening/weekend. *Degree requirements:* For master's, thesis; for doctorate, comprehensive exam, thesis/dissertation. *Entrance requirements:* For master's, minimum GPA of 2.75; strong analytical, reflective thinking and writing skills; vocational and academic goals compatible with those of Seminary; for doctorate, M Div or equivalent, minimum GPA of 3.0, 3 years experience in professional ministry; for other advanced degree, BA or equivalent life experience; strong analytical, reflective thinking and writing skills (Certificate); proficiency in English language, previous study of theology at a theological school, recommendation of student's denomination (Diploma). Additional exam requirements/recommendations for international students: required—TOEFL (minimum score 550 paper-based).

University at Albany, State University of New York, College of Arts and Sciences, Department of Women's, Gender and Sexuality Studies, Albany, NY 12222-0001. Offers MA. *Program availability:* Evening/weekend, blended/hybrid learning. *Faculty:* 5 full-time (all women), 1 (woman) part-time/adjunct. *Students:* 11 full-time (10 women); includes 5 minority (3 Black or African American, non-Hispanic/Latino; 1 Hispanic/Latino; 1 Two or more races, non-Hispanic/Latino), 3 international. 22 applicants, 86% accepted, 7 enrolled. In 2019, 9 master's awarded. *Entrance requirements:* For master's, transcripts of all schools attended, statement of background and goals, departmental questionnaire, resume, names and contact information for 3 recommenders. Additional exam requirements/recommendations for international students: required—TOEFL (minimum score 550 paper-based). *Application deadline:* For fall admission, 8/1 for domestic students, 5/1 for international students; for spring admission, 11/15 for domestic students. Applications are processed on a rolling basis. Application fee: $75. Electronic applications accepted. *Expenses: Tuition, area resident:* Full-time $11,530; part-time $480 per credit hour. Tuition, nonresident: full-time $23,530; part-time $980 per credit hour. *International tuition:* $23,530 full-time. *Required fees:* $2185; $96 per credit hour. Part-time tuition and fees vary according to course load and program. *Unit head:* Janell Hobson, Chair, 518-442-4220, Fax: 518-442-4419, E-mail: jhobson@albany.edu. *Application contact:* Michael DeRensis, Director, Graduate Admissions, 518-442-3980, Fax: 518-442-3922, E-mail: graduate@albany.edu.
Website: https://www.albany.edu/ws/

The University of Alabama, Graduate School, College of Arts and Sciences, Department of Gender and Race Studies, Tuscaloosa, AL 35487. Offers women's studies (MA). *Program availability:* Part-time. *Faculty:* 6 full-time (3 women). *Students:* 17 full-time (15 women), 3 part-time (all women); includes 9 minority (6 Black or African American, non-Hispanic/Latino; 1 American Indian or Alaska Native, non-Hispanic/Latino; 1 Hispanic/Latino; 1 Two or more races, non-Hispanic/Latino), 2 international. Average age 27. 20 applicants, 90% accepted, 10 enrolled. In 2019, 10 master's awarded. *Degree requirements:* For master's, comprehensive exam, thesis optional. *Entrance requirements:* For master's, MAT or GRE. Additional exam requirements/recommendations for international students: required—TOEFL. *Application deadline:* For fall admission, 3/7 priority date for domestic students, 3/7 for international students. Applications are processed on a rolling basis. Application fee: $50 ($60 for international students). Electronic applications accepted. *Expenses: Tuition, area resident:* Full-time $10,780; part-time $440 per credit hour. Tuition, nonresident: full-time $30,250; part-time $1550 per credit hour. *Financial support:* In 2019–20, 10 students received support, including research assistantships with tuition reimbursements available (averaging $10,908 per year), teaching assistantships with tuition reimbursements available (averaging $10,908 per year); health care benefits and unspecified assistantships also available. Financial award application deadline: 4/1. *Unit head:* Dr. Utz McKnight, Chair, 205-348-5528, E-mail: umcknigh@bama.ua.edu. *Application contact:* Patrick D. Fuller, Senior Graduate Admissions Counselor, 205-348-5923, Fax: 205-348-0400, E-mail: patrick.d.fuller@ua.edu.
Website: http://www.as.ua.edu/grs/

The University of Arizona, College of Social and Behavioral Sciences, Department of Gender and Women's Studies, Tucson, AZ 85721. Offers MA, PhD, Certificate. *Program availability:* Part-time. *Degree requirements:* For master's, thesis/project. *Entrance requirements:* For master's and doctorate, GRE (minimum score: 500 verbal, 500 quantitative, 4.5 analytical), 3 letters of recommendation. Additional exam requirements/recommendations for international students: required—TOEFL (minimum score 600 paper-based; 100 iBT). Electronic applications accepted.

University of California, Santa Barbara, Graduate Division, College of Letters and Sciences, Division of Humanities and Fine Arts, Department of English, Santa Barbara, CA 93106-3170. Offers English (PhD), including environment and society, European medieval studies, feminist studies, global studies, technology and society, translation studies, writing studies; MA/PhD. Terminal master's awarded for partial completion of doctoral program. *Degree requirements:* For doctorate, one foreign language, comprehensive exam, thesis/dissertation. *Entrance requirements:* For doctorate, GRE General Test, GRE Subject Test (English literature). Additional exam requirements/recommendations for international students: required—TOEFL (minimum score 550 paper-based; 80 iBT), IELTS (minimum score 7). Electronic applications accepted.

University of California, Santa Barbara, Graduate Division, College of Letters and Sciences, Division of Humanities and Fine Arts, Department of History, Santa Barbara, CA 93106-9410. Offers European medieval studies (PhD); global studies (PhD); public historical studies (PhD); technology and society (PhD); women's studies (PhD); MA/PhD. *Degree requirements:* For doctorate, variable foreign language requirement, comprehensive exam, thesis/dissertation. *Entrance requirements:* For doctorate, GRE. Additional exam requirements/recommendations for international students: required—TOEFL (minimum score 550 paper-based; 80 iBT), IELTS (minimum score 7). Electronic applications accepted.

University of California, Santa Barbara, Graduate Division, College of Letters and Sciences, Division of Humanities and Fine Arts, Department of History of Art and Architecture, Santa Barbara, CA 93106-2014. Offers art history (PhD), including art history, European medieval studies, feminist studies; MA/PhD. Terminal master's awarded for partial completion of doctoral program. *Degree requirements:* For doctorate, 2 foreign languages, comprehensive exam, thesis/dissertation. *Entrance requirements:* For doctorate, GRE. Additional exam requirements/recommendations for international students: required—TOEFL (minimum score 550 paper-based; 80 iBT), IELTS (minimum score 7). Electronic applications accepted.

University of California, Santa Barbara, Graduate Division, College of Letters and Sciences, Division of Humanities and Fine Arts, Department of Religious Studies, Santa Barbara, CA 93106-3130. Offers ancient Mediterranean studies (PhD); cognitive science (PhD); European medieval studies (PhD); feminist studies (PhD); global studies (PhD); religious studies (MA, PhD); translation studies (PhD); MA/PhD. Terminal master's awarded for partial completion of doctoral program. *Degree requirements:* For master's, one foreign language, comprehensive exam (for some programs), thesis (for some programs); for doctorate, 2 foreign languages, thesis/dissertation, methodology. *Entrance requirements:* For master's and doctorate, GRE General Test. Additional exam requirements/recommendations for international students: required—TOEFL (minimum score 550 paper-based; 80 iBT), IELTS (minimum score 7). Electronic applications accepted.

University of California, Santa Barbara, Graduate Division, College of Letters and Sciences, Division of Humanities and Fine Arts, Department of Spanish and Portuguese, Santa Barbara, CA 93106-4150. Offers Hispanic languages and literatures (PhD), including European medieval studies, feminist studies, Hispanic linguistics, Hispanic literature, Luso-Brazilian literature; Hispanic linguistics (MA); Luso-Brazilian literature (MA); Spanish or Spanish-American literature (MA); MA/PhD. Terminal master's awarded for partial completion of doctoral program. *Degree requirements:* For master's, 2 foreign languages, comprehensive exam (for some programs), thesis optional; for doctorate, 3 foreign languages, comprehensive exam, thesis/dissertation. *Entrance requirements:* For master's and doctorate, GRE. Additional exam requirements/recommendations for international students: required—TOEFL (minimum score 550 paper-based; 80 iBT), IELTS (minimum score 7). Electronic applications accepted.

University of California, Santa Barbara, Graduate Division, College of Letters and Sciences, Division of Humanities and Fine Arts, Department of Theater and Dance, Santa Barbara, CA 93106-7060. Offers theater studies (MA, PhD), including European medieval studies (PhD), feminist studies (PhD), theatre studies (PhD); MA/PhD. Terminal master's awarded for partial completion of doctoral program. *Degree requirements:* For master's, comprehensive exam, thesis; for doctorate, one foreign language, comprehensive exam, thesis/dissertation. *Entrance requirements:* For master's and doctorate, GRE. Additional exam requirements/recommendations for international students: required—TOEFL (minimum score 550 paper-based; 80 iBT), IELTS (minimum score 7). Electronic applications accepted.

University of California, Santa Barbara, Graduate Division, College of Letters and Sciences, Division of Humanities and Fine Arts, Program in Comparative Literature, Santa Barbara, CA 93106-4130. Offers comparative literature (PhD); East Asian literatures (PhD); feminist studies (PhD); French (PhD); global studies (PhD); translation studies (PhD); MA/PhD. *Degree requirements:* For doctorate, 2 foreign languages, comprehensive exam, thesis/dissertation. *Entrance requirements:* For doctorate, GRE. Additional exam requirements/recommendations for international students: required—TOEFL (minimum score 550 paper-based; 80 iBT), IELTS (minimum score 7). Electronic applications accepted.

University of California, Santa Barbara, Graduate Division, College of Letters and Sciences, Division of Social Sciences, Department of Communication, Santa Barbara, CA 93106-4020. Offers cognitive science (PhD); communication (PhD); feminist studies (PhD); language, interaction and social organization (PhD); quantitative methods in the social sciences (PhD); society and technology (PhD); MA/PhD. Terminal master's awarded for partial completion of doctoral program. *Degree requirements:* For doctorate, comprehensive exam, thesis/dissertation. *Entrance requirements:* For doctorate, GRE. Additional exam requirements/recommendations for international students: required—TOEFL (minimum score 80 iBT), IELTS (minimum score 7). Electronic applications accepted.

University of California, Santa Barbara, Graduate Division, College of Letters and Sciences, Division of Social Sciences, Department of Feminist Studies, Santa Barbara, CA 93106-7110. Offers MA, PhD, MA/PhD. Terminal master's awarded for partial completion of doctoral program. *Degree requirements:* For master's, thesis (for some programs); for doctorate, one foreign language, comprehensive exam, thesis/dissertation. *Entrance requirements:* For master's and doctorate, GRE. Additional exam requirements/recommendations for international students: required—TOEFL (minimum score 550 paper-based; 80 iBT), IELTS (minimum score 7). Electronic applications accepted.

University of California, Santa Barbara, Graduate Division, College of Letters and Sciences, Division of Social Sciences, Department of Sociology, Santa Barbara, CA

93106-9430. Offers interdisciplinary emphasis: Black studies (PhD); interdisciplinary emphasis: environment and society (PhD); interdisciplinary emphasis: feminist studies (PhD); interdisciplinary emphasis: global studies (PhD); interdisciplinary emphasis: language, interaction and social organization (PhD); interdisciplinary emphasis: quantitative methods in the social sciences (PhD); interdisciplinary emphasis: technology and society (PhD); sociology (PhD); MA/PhD. Terminal master's awarded for partial completion of doctoral program. *Degree requirements:* For doctorate, comprehensive exam, thesis/dissertation. *Entrance requirements:* For doctorate, GRE General Test. Additional exam requirements/recommendations for international students: required—TOEFL (minimum score 550 paper-based; 80 iBT), IELTS (minimum score 7). Electronic applications accepted.

University of Cincinnati, Graduate School, McMicken College of Arts and Sciences, Department of Women's, Gender, and Sexuality Studies, Cincinnati, OH 45221-0164. Offers MA, Certificate, MA/JD. *Program availability:* Part-time. Terminal master's awarded for partial completion of doctoral program. *Degree requirements:* For master's, comprehensive exam, final paper/project. *Entrance requirements:* For master's, GRE General Test, 3 letters of recommendation. Additional exam requirements/recommendations for international students: required—TOEFL (minimum score 600 paper-based), IELTS (minimum score 6.5). Electronic applications accepted.

University of Colorado Denver, College of Liberal Arts and Sciences, Program in Humanities, Denver, CO 80217. Offers community health (MSS); ethnic studies (MH, MSS); humanities (MH, Graduate Certificate); international studies (MSS); philosophy and theory (MH); social justice (MH, MSS); society and the environment (MSS); visual studies (MH); women's and gender studies (MH, MSS). *Program availability:* Part-time, evening/weekend. *Degree requirements:* For master's, 36 credit hours, project or thesis. *Entrance requirements:* For master's, writing sample, statement of purpose/letter of intent, three letters of recommendation. Additional exam requirements/recommendations for international students: required—TOEFL (minimum score 537 paper-based; 75 iBT); recommended—IELTS (minimum score 6.5). Electronic applications accepted. Tuition and fees vary according to course load, program and reciprocity agreements.

University of Florida, Graduate School, College of Liberal Arts and Sciences, Center for Women's Studies and Gender Research, Gainesville, FL 32611. Offers gender and development (Graduate Certificate); women's studies (MA, Graduate Certificate); MA/JD; MA/MA. Terminal master's awarded for partial completion of doctoral program. *Degree requirements:* For master's, thesis or project. *Entrance requirements:* For master's, GRE General Test (minimum score 1000), minimum GPA of 3.2. Additional exam requirements/recommendations for international students: required—TOEFL (minimum score 550 paper-based; 80 iBT), IELTS (minimum score 6). Electronic applications accepted.

University of Georgia, Franklin College of Arts and Sciences, Institute for Women's Studies, Athens, GA 30602. Offers Certificate.

University of Hawaii at Manoa, Office of Graduate Education, College of Social Sciences, Advanced Women's Studies Program, Honolulu, HI 96822. Offers Graduate Certificate. *Program availability:* Part-time. *Entrance requirements:* Additional exam requirements/recommendations for international students: required—TOEFL (minimum score 500 paper-based; 61 iBT), IELTS (minimum score 5).

The University of Iowa, Graduate College, College of Liberal Arts and Sciences, Department of Gender, Women's and Sexuality Studies, Iowa City, IA 52242-1316. Offers Certificate. *Entrance requirements:* Additional exam requirements/recommendations for international students: required—TOEFL (minimum score 550 paper-based; 81 iBT).

University of Lethbridge, School of Graduate Studies, Lethbridge, AB T1K 3M4, Canada. Offers addictions counseling (M Sc); agricultural biotechnology (M Sc); agricultural studies (M Sc, MA); anthropology (MA); archaeology (M Sc, MA); art (MA, MFA); biochemistry (M Sc); biological sciences (M Sc); biomolecular science (PhD); biosystems and biodiversity (PhD); Canadian studies (MA); chemistry (M Sc); computer science (M Sc); computer science and geographical information science (M Sc); counseling (MC); counseling psychology (M Ed); dramatic arts (MA); earth, space, and physical science (PhD); economics (MA); education (MA, PhD); educational leadership (M Ed); English (MA); environmental science (M Sc); evolution and behavior (PhD); exercise science (M Sc); French (MA); French/German (MA); French/Spanish (MA); general education (M Ed); geography (M Sc, MA); German (MA); health sciences (M Sc); individualized multidisciplinary (M Sc, MA); kinesiology (M Sc, MA); management (M Sc), including accounting, finance, human resource management and labor relations, information systems, international management, marketing, policy and strategy; mathematics (M Sc); music (M Mus, MA); Native American studies (MA); neuroscience (M Sc, PhD); new media (MA, MFA); nursing (M Sc, MN); philosophy (MA); physics (M Sc); political science (MA); psychology (M Sc, MA); religious studies (MA); sociology (MA); theatre and dramatic arts (MFA); theoretical and computational science (PhD); urban and regional studies (MA); women and gender studies (MA). *Program availability:* Part-time, evening/weekend. *Degree requirements:* For master's, thesis (for some programs); for doctorate, comprehensive exam, thesis/dissertation. *Entrance requirements:* For master's, GMAT (for M Sc in management), bachelor's degree in related field, minimum GPA of 3.0 during previous 20 graded semester courses, 2 years' teaching or related experience (M Ed); for doctorate, master's degree, minimum graduate GPA of 3.5. Additional exam requirements/recommendations for international students: required—TOEFL (minimum score 580 paper-based; 93 iBT). Electronic applications accepted.

University of Louisville, Graduate School, College of Arts and Sciences, Department of Women's, Gender and Sexuality Studies, Louisville, KY 40292. Offers MA, Certificate, MSSW/MA. *Program availability:* Part-time. *Faculty:* 4 full-time (all women), 8 part-time/adjunct (all women). *Students:* 10 full-time (all women), 5 part-time (all women); includes 5 minority (2 Black or African American, non-Hispanic/Latino; 1 Asian, non-Hispanic/Latino; 2 Two or more races, non-Hispanic/Latino). Average age 30. 4 applicants, 75% accepted, 2 enrolled. In 2019, 2 master's, 1 other advanced degree awarded. *Degree requirements:* For master's, thesis or alternative. *Entrance requirements:* For master's, 2 letters of reference, official transcripts, undergraduate degree, writing sample, statement of intent. Additional exam requirements/recommendations for international students: required—TOEFL (minimum score 550 paper-based; 79 iBT), IELTS can be used in place of the TOEFL; recommended—IELTS (minimum score 6.5). *Application deadline:* For fall admission, 7/15 priority date for domestic and international students; for spring admission, 12/5 for domestic students, 11/5 for international students. Applications are processed on a rolling basis. Application fee: $65. Electronic applications accepted. *Expenses: Tuition, area resident:* Full-time $13,000; part-time $723 per credit hour. Tuition, state resident: full-time $13,000; part-time $723 per credit hour. Tuition, nonresident: full-time $27,114; part-time $1507 per credit hour. *International tuition:* $27,114 full-time. *Required fees:* $196. Tuition and fees vary according to program and reciprocity agreements. *Financial support:* In 2019–20, 9 students received support, including 2 teaching assistantships with full tuition reimbursements available (averaging $12,000 per year); fellowships, research assistantships, scholarships/grants, health care benefits, and unspecified assistantships also available. Financial award application deadline: 3/15; financial award applicants required to submit FAFSA. *Unit head:* Dr. Dawn Heinecken, Professor and Chairperson, 502-852-8160, E-mail: dawn.heinecken@louisville.edu. *Application contact:* Dr. Dawn Heinecken, Professor and Chairperson, 502-852-8160, E-mail: dawn.heinecken@louisville.edu.
Website: http://louisville.edu/wgs/

University of Maryland, Baltimore County, The Graduate School, College of Arts, Humanities and Social Sciences, Program in Gender and Women's Studies, Baltimore, MD 21250. Offers Postbaccalaureate Certificate. *Program availability:* Part-time, evening/weekend, online learning. *Students:* 1 applicant. In 2019, 2 Postbaccalaureate Certificates awarded. *Application deadline:* Applications are processed on a rolling basis. Application fee: $0. Electronic applications accepted. *Expenses: Tuition, area resident:* Full-time $659. Tuition, state resident: full-time $659. Tuition, nonresident: full-time $1132. *International tuition:* $1132 full-time. *Required fees:* $140; $140 per credit hour. *Financial support:* In 2019–20, teaching assistantships with partial tuition reimbursements (averaging $7,500 per year) were awarded; health care benefits and unspecified assistantships also available. *Unit head:* Dr. Carole McCann, Director/Associate Professor, 410-455-2161, E-mail: mccann@umbc.edu. *Application contact:* Kathryn Nee, Coordinator of Domestic Admissions, 410-455-2944, E-mail: nee@umbc.edu.
Website: https://gwst.umbc.edu/gwst-post-bac-certificate/

University of Maryland, College Park, Academic Affairs, College of Arts and Humanities, Department of Women's Studies, College Park, MD 20742. Offers MA, PhD. *Degree requirements:* For master's, thesis or alternative; for doctorate, one foreign language, thesis/dissertation or alternative. *Entrance requirements:* For master's, GRE General Test, writing sample, 3 letters of recommendation. Additional exam requirements/recommendations for international students: required—TOEFL.

University of Michigan, Rackham Graduate School, College of Literature, Science, and the Arts, Department of Women's Studies, Ann Arbor, MI 48109. Offers English and women's studies (PhD); history and women's studies (PhD); LGBTQ studies (Certificate); psychology and women's studies (PhD); women's studies (Certificate). *Degree requirements:* For doctorate, variable foreign language requirement, comprehensive exam (for some programs), thesis/dissertation. *Entrance requirements:* For doctorate, previous undergraduate coursework in women's studies. Electronic applications accepted.

University of Minnesota, Twin Cities Campus, Graduate School, College of Liberal Arts, Department of Gender, Women, and Sexuality Studies, Minneapolis, MN 55455-0213. Offers feminist studies (PhD). *Degree requirements:* For doctorate, comprehensive exam, thesis/dissertation. *Entrance requirements:* For doctorate, GRE. Additional exam requirements/recommendations for international students: required—TOEFL (minimum score 550 paper-based). Electronic applications accepted.

University of New Hampshire, Graduate School, Interdisciplinary Programs, Program in Feminist Studies, Durham, NH 03824. Offers Postbaccalaureate Certificate. *Students:* 1 full-time; includes 1 minority (Black or African American, non-Hispanic/Latino). Average age 32. 8 applicants, 100% accepted, 8 enrolled. In 2019, 1 Postbaccalaureate Certificate awarded. *Entrance requirements:* Additional exam requirements/recommendations for international students: required—TOEFL (minimum score 550 paper-based; 80 iBT), IELTS, PTE. *Application deadline:* For fall admission, 7/1 for domestic students; for spring admission, 12/1 for domestic students; for summer admission, 4/1 for domestic students. Application fee: $25. Electronic applications accepted. *Financial support:* In 2019–20, 1 student received support. Application deadline: 2/15. *Unit head:* Siobhan Senier, Coordinator, 603-862-2466, Fax: 603-862-3563, E-mail: siobhan.senier@unh.edu. *Application contact:* Avary Thorne, Administrative Assistant, 603-862-2194, E-mail: avary.thorne@unh.edu.
Website: https://cola.unh.edu/womens-studies/program/feminist-studies-certificate

The University of North Carolina at Charlotte, College of Liberal Arts and Sciences, Interdisciplinary Liberal Arts and Sciences Programs, Charlotte, NC 28223-0001. Offers gender, sexuality and women's studies (Graduate Certificate); gerontology (MA, Graduate Certificate); Latin American studies (MA); liberal studies (MA); organizational science (PhD); public policy (PhD). *Program availability:* Part-time, evening/weekend. *Students:* 74 full-time (50 women), 56 part-time (43 women); includes 41 minority (16 Black or African American, non-Hispanic/Latino; 3 Asian, non-Hispanic/Latino; 16 Hispanic/Latino; 6 Two or more races, non-Hispanic/Latino), 16 international. Average age 33. 101 applicants, 51% accepted, 37 enrolled. In 2019, 21 master's, 5 doctorates, 8 other advanced degrees awarded. *Entrance requirements:* For master's, GRE General Test or MAT, bachelor's degree from accredited college or university; official transcripts of all previous academic work attempted beyond high school with minimum overall GPA of 3.0; statement of purpose; recommendation letters; for doctorate, GRE or GMAT, statement of purpose discussing interest in program and objectives for pursuing degree, current resume or curriculum vitae, unofficial transcripts; for Graduate Certificate, bachelor's degree from accredited university and either enrolled and in good standing in a graduate degree program at UNC Charlotte or have a minimum undergraduate GPA of 3.0. Additional exam requirements/recommendations for international students: required—TOEFL (minimum score 557 paper-based; 83 iBT), IELTS (minimum score 6.5), TOEFL (minimum score 557 paper-based, 83 iBT) or IELTS (6.5). *Application deadline:* Applications are processed on a rolling basis. Application fee: $75. Electronic applications accepted. *Expenses:* Tuition, state resident: full-time $4337. Tuition, nonresident: full-time $17,771. *Required fees:* $3093. Tuition and fees vary according to course load, degree level and program. *Financial support:* In 2019–20, 3 students received support, including 2 research assistantships (averaging $6,750 per year), 1 teaching assistantship (averaging $21,000 per year); career-related internships or fieldwork, institutionally sponsored loans, scholarships/grants, unspecified assistantships, and administrative assistantships also available. Support available to part-time students. Financial award applicants required to submit FAFSA. *Unit head:* Dr. Nancy A. Gutierrez, Dean, 704-687-0081, E-mail: ngutierr@uncc.edu. *Application contact:* Kathy B. Giddings, Director of Graduate Admissions, 704-687-5503, Fax: 704-687-3279, E-mail: gradadm@uncc.edu.
Website: http://clas.uncc.edu/academics

The University of North Carolina at Greensboro, Graduate School, College of Arts and Sciences, Department of English, Greensboro, NC 27412-5001. Offers creative writing (MFA); English (M Ed, MA, PhD, Certificate), including American literature (PhD), English (M Ed, MA), English literature (PhD), rhetoric and composition (PhD), technical writing (Certificate), women's studies (Certificate). *Degree requirements:* For master's, comprehensive exam; for doctorate, variable foreign language requirement, thesis/dissertation, preliminary exam. *Entrance requirements:* For master's, GRE General Test, minimum GPA of 3.0; for doctorate, GRE General Test, GRE Subject Test, critical writing sample, minimum GPA of 3.0. Additional exam requirements/recommendations for international students: required—TOEFL. Electronic applications accepted.

The University of North Carolina at Greensboro, Graduate School, College of Arts and Sciences, Program in Women's and Gender Studies, Greensboro, NC 27412-5001. Offers MA, Certificate. Electronic applications accepted.

University of Northern Iowa, Graduate College, MA Program in Women's and Gender Studies, Cedar Falls, IA 50614. Offers MA. *Degree requirements:* For master's, comprehensive exam (for some programs), thesis or alternative. *Entrance requirements:* For master's, minimum GPA of 3.0. Additional exam requirements/recommendations for international students: required—TOEFL (minimum score 500 paper-based; 61 iBT). Electronic applications accepted.

University of Oklahoma, College of Arts and Sciences, Women's and Gender Studies Department, Norman, OK 73019. Offers Graduate Certificate. *Program availability:* Part-time. *Entrance requirements:* Additional exam requirements/recommendations for international students: required—TOEFL (minimum score 79 iBT) or IELTS (minimum score 6.5). Electronic applications accepted. *Expenses:* Tuition, state resident: full-time $6583.20; part-time $274.30 per credit hour. Tuition, nonresident: full-time $21,242; part-time $885.10 per credit hour. *International tuition:* $21,242.40 full-time. *Required fees:* $1994.20; $72.55 per credit hour. $126.50 per semester. Tuition and fees vary according to course load and degree level.

University of Ottawa, Faculty of Graduate and Postdoctoral Studies, Faculty of Social Sciences, Institute of Women's Studies, Ottawa, ON K1N 6N5, Canada. Offers criminology (MA, MCA); education (MA); English (MA); history (MA); human kinetics (MA); law (LL M); lettres Françaises (MA); nursing (M Sc); pastoral studies (MA); political science (MA); religious studies (MA); sociology (MA). *Degree requirements:* For master's, thesis or alternative.

University of Pittsburgh, Kenneth P. Dietrich School of Arts and Sciences, Gender, Sexuality, and Women's Studies Program, Pittsburgh, PA 15260. Offers Doctoral Certificate, Master's Certificate. *Faculty:* 100 full-time (65 women). *Students:* 73 full-time (50 women); includes 27 minority (7 Black or African American, non-Hispanic/Latino; 7 Asian, non-Hispanic/Latino; 8 Hispanic/Latino; 5 Two or more races, non-Hispanic/Latino). 15 applicants, 100% accepted, 15 enrolled. In 2019, 8 Master's Certificates awarded. *Degree requirements:* For other advanced degree, good standing in a U of Pittsburgh graduate degree-granting department. *Application deadline:* Applications are processed on a rolling basis. Electronic applications accepted. Application fee is waived when completed online. *Unit head:* Dr. Nancy Glazener, Director, 412-624-6486, Fax: 412-624-6492. *Application contact:* Dr. Nancy Glazener, Director, 412-624-6486, Fax: 412-624-6492.
Website: http://www.gsws.pitt.edu/

University of Regina, Faculty of Graduate Studies and Research, Faculty of Arts, Department of Women's and Gender Studies, Regina, SK S4S 0A2, Canada. Offers MA. *Program availability:* Part-time. *Faculty:* 4 full-time (all women), 2 part-time/adjunct (both women). *Students:* 3 full-time (all women). Average age 30. *Degree requirements:* For master's, thesis. *Entrance requirements:* For master's, post secondary transcripts and letter of recommendations. Additional exam requirements/recommendations for international students: required—TOEFL (minimum score 580 paper-based; 80 iBT), IELTS (minimum score 6.5), PTE (minimum score 59), other options are CAEL, MELAB, Cantest and U of R ESL. Application fee: $100 Canadian dollars. *Expenses: Tuition:* Full-time $6684 Canadian dollars. *Required fees:* $100 Canadian dollars; $3351.45 Canadian dollars per trimester. $1117.15 Canadian dollars per semester. Tuition and fees vary according to course level, course load, degree level and program. *Financial support:* Fellowships, research assistantships, teaching assistantships, career-related internships or fieldwork, Federal Work-Study, institutionally sponsored loans, scholarships/grants, and unspecified assistantships available. Support available to part-time students. Financial award application deadline: 9/30. *Application contact:* Claire Carter, Graduate Coordinator, 306-585-4668, Fax: 306-585-4815, E-mail: Claire.Carter@uregina.ca.
Website: http://www.uregina.ca/arts/womens-gender-studies

University of Rhode Island, Graduate School, College of Arts and Sciences, Program in Gender and Women's Studies, Kingston, RI 02881. Offers Graduate Certificate. *Faculty:* 3 full-time (all women). *Students:* 1 applicant. In 2019, 4 Graduate Certificates awarded. Application fee: $65. Electronic applications accepted. *Expenses: Tuition, area resident:* Full-time $13,734; part-time $763 per credit. Tuition, state resident: full-time $13,734; part-time $763 per credit. Tuition, nonresident: full-time $26,512; part-time $1473 per credit. *International tuition:* $26,512 full-time. *Required fees:* $1780; $52 per credit. $35 per term. One-time fee: $165. *Unit head:* Dr. Rosaria Pisa, Director, 401-874-2482, E-mail: rpisa@uri.edu. *Application contact:* Donna Hughes, Graduate Program Director, 401-8742757, E-mail: donnahughes@uri.edu.
Website: http://web.uri.edu/gws/graduate-certificate-program/

University of South Carolina, The Graduate School, College of Arts and Sciences, Program in Women's Studies, Columbia, SC 29208. Offers Certificate. *Program availability:* Part-time. *Entrance requirements:* For degree, GRE General Test or MAT. Additional exam requirements/recommendations for international students: required—TOEFL. Electronic applications accepted.

University of South Florida, College of Arts and Sciences, Department of Women's and Gender Studies, Tampa, FL 33620-9951. Offers MA. *Program availability:* Part-time. *Faculty:* 4 full-time (3 women). *Students:* 6 full-time (all women), 3 part-time (2 women); includes 13 minority (3 Black or African American, non-Hispanic/Latino; 2 Asian, non-Hispanic/Latino; 4 Hispanic/Latino; 4 Two or more races, non-Hispanic/Latino). Average age 28. 8 applicants, 88% accepted, 4 enrolled. In 2019, 4 master's awarded. *Degree requirements:* For master's, comprehensive exam, thesis (for some programs), thesis or internship or portfolio. *Entrance requirements:* For master's, GRE scores (preferred percentiles for Verbal Reasoning at 75 or better and Analytical Writing at 70 or better), minimum GPA of 3.0, A personal narrative statement of purpose; A writing sample (appropriate examples include a term paper or research paper); Three letters of recommendation; resume or Curriculum Vita (CV). Additional exam requirements/recommendations for international students: required—TOEFL, TOEFL (minimum score 550 paper-based; 79 iBT) or IELTS (minimum score 6.5). *Application deadline:* For fall admission, 2/15 priority date for domestic and international students; for spring admission, 10/15 priority date for domestic students, 9/15 priority date for international students; for summer admission, 2/15 priority date for domestic students, 1/15 priority date for international students. Applications are processed on a rolling basis. Application fee: $30. Electronic applications accepted. *Financial support:* In 2019–20, 3 students received support. Teaching assistantships with tuition reimbursements available available. Financial award application deadline: 3/1. *Unit head:* Dr. Diane Price Herndl, Professor and Chairperson, 813-974-0987, Fax: 813-974-0336, E-mail: priceherndl@usf.edu. *Application contact:* Dr. Kim Golombisky, Associate Professor and Graduate Director, 813-974-0986, Fax: 813-974-0336, E-mail: kgolombi@usf.edu.
Website: http://wgs.usf.edu/

The University of Toledo, College of Graduate Studies, College of Languages, Literature and Social Sciences, Department of Women's and Gender Studies, Toledo, OH 43606-3390. Offers Certificate. *Program availability:* Part-time.

University of Toronto, School of Graduate Studies, Faculty of Arts and Science, Women and Gender Studies Institute, Toronto, ON M5S 1A1, Canada. Offers MA, PhD. *Entrance requirements:* For master's, minimum B+ in final year of undergraduate study. Additional exam requirements/recommendations for international students: required—TOEFL (minimum score 580 paper-based; 93 iBT), TWE (minimum score 5). Electronic applications accepted.

University of Washington, Graduate School, College of Arts and Sciences, Department of Gender, Women and Sexuality Studies, Seattle, WA 98195. Offers PhD. Terminal master's awarded for partial completion of doctoral program. *Degree requirements:* For doctorate, one foreign language, thesis/dissertation, exam. *Entrance requirements:* For doctorate, GRE General Test. Additional exam requirements/recommendations for international students: required—TOEFL. Electronic applications accepted.

University of Wisconsin–Madison, Graduate School, College of Letters and Science, Department of History, Madison, WI 53706-1380. Offers African history (MA, PhD); Central Asian history (MA, PhD); comparative world history (MA, PhD); East Asian history (MA, PhD); European history (MA, PhD); gender and women's history (MA, PhD); Latin American and Caribbean history (MA, PhD); Middle Eastern history (MA, PhD); South Asian history (MA, PhD); Southeast Asian history (MA, PhD); United States history (MA, PhD). Terminal master's awarded for partial completion of doctoral program. *Degree requirements:* For master's, thesis (for some programs); for doctorate, variable foreign language requirement, thesis/dissertation. *Entrance requirements:* For master's and doctorate, GRE General Test. Additional exam requirements/recommendations for international students: required—Michigan English Language Assessment Battery or TOEFL. Electronic applications accepted.

University of Wisconsin–Milwaukee, Graduate School, College of Letters and Science, Department of Women's and Gender Studies, Milwaukee, WI 53201-0413. Offers MA, Graduate Certificate. *Program availability:* Part-time. *Entrance requirements:* For master's, three letters of recommendation, sample of written work, letter of intent. Electronic applications accepted.

Université Laval, Faculty of Social Sciences, Program in Feminist Studies, Québec, QC G1K 7P4, Canada. Offers Diploma. *Program availability:* Part-time. *Entrance requirements:* For degree, knowledge of French, comprehension of written English. Electronic applications accepted.

Wayne State University, College of Liberal Arts and Sciences, Tracy Neumann, Detroit, MI 48202. Offers history (MA, PhD); public history (MA), including African American history and culture, cultural resource management, gender, sexuality, and women's studies, labor and urban history, museum studies, public policy; world history (Graduate Certificate); JD/MA; M Ed/MA; MLIS/MA. *Program availability:* Evening/weekend. *Faculty:* 23 full-time (11 women). *Students:* 18 full-time (7 women), 16 part-time (7 women); includes 4 minority (2 Black or African American, non-Hispanic/Latino; 2 Two or more races, non-Hispanic/Latino). Average age 37. 38 applicants, 34% accepted, 13 enrolled. In 2019, 7 master's, 3 doctorates awarded. *Degree requirements:* For master's, thesis (for some programs), final oral exam on thesis or essay and seminar; internship and project (for public history); for doctorate, variable foreign language requirement, comprehensive exam, thesis/dissertation, qualifying exam in 4 fields of history. *Entrance requirements:* For master's, GRE General Test, minimum undergraduate GPA of 3.25 in history, 3.0 overall; at least 18 credits in history and related subjects at the advanced undergraduate level; foreign language; letter of intent; research paper; at least two letters of recommendation from former instructors; for doctorate, GRE General Test, minimum GPA of 3.0, 3.25 in minimum of 18 semester credits in history and related subjects; letter of intent; research paper; at least three letters of recommendation from former professors; for Graduate Certificate, baccalaureate degree from accredited college or university; minimum GPA of 3.0, 3.25 in a minimum of eighteen semester credits in history and related subjects at the advanced undergraduate level. Additional exam requirements/recommendations for international students: required—TOEFL (minimum score 550 paper-based; 79 iBT), TWE (minimum score 5.5), Michigan English Language Assessment Battery (minimum score 85); recommended—IELTS (minimum score 6.5). *Application deadline:* For fall admission, 1/15 priority date for domestic and international students; for winter admission, 4/15 for domestic students, 4/15 priority date for international students; for spring admission, 10/15 for domestic students, 10/15 priority date for international students. Application fee: $50. Electronic applications accepted. *Expenses: Tuition:* Full-time $34,567. *Financial support:* In 2019–20, 18 students received support, including 2 fellowships with tuition reimbursements available (averaging $20,797 per year), 2 research assistantships with tuition reimbursements available (averaging $23,960 per year), 7 teaching assistantships with tuition reimbursements available (averaging $19,967 per year); scholarships/grants, health care benefits, and unspecified assistantships also available. Financial award applicants required to submit FAFSA. *Unit head:* Dr. Elizabeth V. Faue, Professor/Chair, 313-577-2525, E-mail: evfaue@wayne.edu. *Application contact:* Dr. Tracy Neumann, Associate Professor and Director of Graduate Studies, 313-577-2525, E-mail: tracyneumann@wayne.edu.
Website: http://clas.wayne.edu/history/

Western Seminary - Portland, Graduate Programs, Program in Ministry and Leadership, Portland, OR 97215-3367. Offers chaplaincy (MA); coaching (MA); Jewish ministry (MA); pastoral care to women (MA); youth ministry (MA). *Degree requirements:* For master's, practicum. *Entrance requirements:* Additional exam requirements/recommendations for international students: required—TOEFL.

Western Seminary–Sacramento Campus, Graduate Certificate Programs, Rocklin, CA 95765. Offers Bible (Graduate Certificate); coaching (Graduate Certificate); pastoral care to women (Graduate Certificate); theology (Graduate Certificate); youth and family (Graduate Certificate). *Program availability:* Online learning. *Entrance requirements:* For degree, essays, undergraduate transcripts, 4 recommendations. Additional exam requirements/recommendations for international students: required—TOEFL.

Western Seminary–Sacramento Campus, Graduate Diploma Programs, Rocklin, CA 95765. Offers Bible and theology (Graduate Diploma); ministry (Graduate Diploma); pastoral care to women (Graduate Diploma). *Entrance requirements:* For degree, essays, undergraduate transcripts, 4 recommendations. Additional exam requirements/recommendations for international students: required—TOEFL.

Western Seminary - San Jose Campus, Graduate Programs, Milpitas, CA 95035. Offers Bible and theology (Graduate Diploma); Bible, camp and conference ministry (CGS); Biblical and theological studies (MA), including exegetical track, theological track; coaching (CGS); expositional ministry (M Div); marital and family therapy (MA); ministry (Graduate Diploma); ministry and leadership (MA), including camp and conference ministry, coaching, pastoral care to women, youth ministry; pastoral care to women (CGS, Graduate Diploma); pastoral ministry (M Div); theology (CGS); youth and family (CGS). *Program availability:* Part-time, evening/weekend, online learning. *Entrance requirements:* For master's, minimum GPA of 3.0. Electronic applications accepted.

Wilson College, Graduate Programs, Chambersburg, PA 17201-1285. Offers accounting (M Acc); choreography and visual art (MFA); education (M Ed); educational technology (MET); healthcare administration (MHA); humanities (MA), including art and culture, critical/cultural theory, English language and literature, women's studies; management (MSM); nursing (MSN), including nursing education, nursing leadership and management; special education (MSE). *Program availability:* Evening/weekend. *Degree requirements:* For master's, project. *Entrance requirements:* For master's, PRAXIS, minimum undergraduate cumulative GPA of 3.0, 2 letters of recommendation, current certification for eligibility to teach in grades K-12, resume, personal interview. Electronic applications accepted.

York University, Faculty of Graduate Studies, Faculty of Liberal Arts and Professional Studies, Program in Gender, Feminist and Women's Studies, Toronto, ON M3J 1P3,

Canada. Offers MA, PhD. *Degree requirements:* For master's, thesis or alternative; for doctorate, comprehensive exam, thesis/dissertation. Electronic applications accepted.

Section 16
Communication and Media

This section contains a directory of institutions offering graduate work in communication and media, followed by an in-depth entry submitted by an institution that chose to prepare a detailed program description. Additional information about programs listed in the directory but not augmented by an in-depth entry may be obtained by writing directly to the dean of a graduate school or chair of a department at the address given in the directory.

For programs offering related work, see also in this book *Film, Television, and Video; Language and Literature;* and *Psychology and Counseling.* In the other guides in this series:

Graduate Programs in Engineering & Applied Sciences
See *Computer Science and Information Technology* and *Telecommunications*

Graduate Programs in Business, Education, Information Studies, Law & Social Work
See *Advertising and Public Relations*

CONTENTS

Program Directories

Communication—General

Abilene Christian University, Office of Graduate Programs, College of Arts and Sciences, Department of Communication and Sociology, Abilene, TX 79699. Offers corporate communication (MA). *Program availability:* Part-time. *Faculty:* 6 part-time/adjunct (3 women). *Students:* 6 full-time (5 women), 3 part-time (2 women); includes 3 minority (2 Black or African American, non-Hispanic/Latino; 1 Hispanic/Latino), 1 international. 24 applicants, 13% accepted, 1 enrolled. In 2019, 3 master's awarded. *Degree requirements:* For master's, comprehensive exam, thesis. *Entrance requirements:* For master's, GRE General Test, official transcripts, Recommendations, purpose statement, writing sample. Additional exam requirements/recommendations for international students: required—TOEFL (minimum score 80 iBT), IELTS (minimum score 6), PTE (minimum score 51). *Application deadline:* For fall admission, 8/10 for domestic students; for spring admission, 11/1 for domestic students. Applications are processed on a rolling basis. Application fee: $65. Electronic applications accepted. *Expenses:* $1242 per hour. *Financial support:* In 2019–20, 6 students received support, including 4 research assistantships with partial tuition reimbursements available, 6 teaching assistantships with partial tuition reimbursements available; Federal Work-Study also available. Support available to part-time students. Financial award application deadline: 4/1; financial award applicants required to submit FAFSA. *Unit head:* Dr. Lauren Lemley, Graduate Director, 325-674-2136, E-mail: lauren.lemley@acu.edu. *Application contact:* Graduate Admissions, 325-674-6911, E-mail: gradinfo@acu.edu.
Website: http://www.acu.edu/on-campus/graduate/college-of-arts-and-sciences/communication-and-sociology/communication.html

American University, School of Communication, Washington, DC 20016. Offers MA, MFA, PhD. *Accreditation:* ACEJMC (one or more programs are accredited). *Program availability:* Part-time, evening/weekend, 100% online. *Degree requirements:* For master's, comprehensive exam, thesis or alternative; for doctorate, comprehensive exam, thesis/dissertation. *Entrance requirements:* For doctorate, GRE General Test. Additional exam requirements/recommendations for international students: required—TOEFL (minimum score 600 paper-based; 100 iBT), IELTS (minimum score 7). Electronic applications accepted.

The American University in Cairo, School of Sciences and Engineering, Cairo, Egypt. Offers biotechnology (MS); chemistry (MS); computer science (MS); computing (M Comp); construction engineering (M Eng, MS); electronics and communications engineering (M Eng); environmental engineering (MS); environmental system design (M Eng); mechanical engineering (M Eng, MS); nanotechnology (MS); physics (MS); robotics, control and smart systems (MS); sciences and engineering (PhD); sustainable development (MS, Graduate Diploma). *Program availability:* Part-time, evening/weekend. *Degree requirements:* For master's, comprehensive exam (for some programs), thesis (for some programs); for doctorate, comprehensive exam (for some programs), thesis/dissertation. *Entrance requirements:* Additional exam requirements/recommendations for international students: required—TOEFL (minimum score 450 paper-based; 45 iBT), IELTS (minimum score 5). Electronic applications accepted.

The American University of Paris, Graduate Programs, Paris, France. Offers cross-cultural and sustainable business management (MA); cultural translation (MA); global communications (MA); global communications and civil society (MA); international affairs (MA); international affairs, conflict resolution and civil society development (MA); Middle East and Islamic studies (MA); Middle East and Islamic studies and international affairs (MA); public policy and international affairs (MA); public policy and international law (MA). *Degree requirements:* For master's, thesis (for some programs). *Entrance requirements:* For master's, minimum undergraduate GPA of 3.0. Additional exam requirements/recommendations for international students: recommended—TOEFL, IELTS. Electronic applications accepted.

Andrews University, School of Graduate Studies, College of Arts and Sciences, Interdisciplinary Studies in Communication Program, Berrien Springs, MI 49104. Offers MA. *Faculty:* 3 full-time (all women). *Students:* 7 full-time (all women), 3 part-time (2 women); includes 5 minority (3 Black or African American, non-Hispanic/Latino; 1 Asian, non-Hispanic/Latino; 1 Hispanic/Latino), 5 international. Average age 31. *Application deadline:* Applications are processed on a rolling basis. Application fee: $60. Electronic applications accepted. *Financial support:* Research assistantships, teaching assistantships, Federal Work-Study, institutionally sponsored loans and scholarships/grants available. *Unit head:* Desrene Vernon-Brebnor, Graduate Coordinator, 269-471-3126. *Application contact:* Jillian Panigot, Director, University Admissions, 800-253-2874, Fax: 269-471-3228, E-mail: graduate@andrews.edu.
Website: https://www.andrews.edu/wp/comm/graduate-degrees/program-information.html

Angelo State University, College of Graduate Studies and Research, College of Arts and Humanities, Department of Communication and Mass Media, San Angelo, TX 76909. Offers communication (MA). *Program availability:* Part-time, evening/weekend. *Degree requirements:* For master's, comprehensive exam, thesis optional. *Entrance requirements:* Additional exam requirements/recommendations for international students: required—TOEFL or IELTS. Electronic applications accepted.

Arizona State University at Tempe, College of Liberal Arts and Sciences, Hugh Downs School of Human Communication, Tempe, AZ 85287. Offers communication (PhD). *Program availability:* Evening/weekend. *Degree requirements:* For doctorate, comprehensive exam, thesis/dissertation, interactive Program of Study (iPOS) submitted before completing 50 percent of required credit hours. *Entrance requirements:* For doctorate, GRE, minimum GPA of 3.0 or equivalent in last 2 years of work leading to bachelor's degree. Additional exam requirements/recommendations for international students: required—TOEFL, IELTS, or PTE. Electronic applications accepted.

Arizona State University at Tempe, New College of Interdisciplinary Arts and Sciences, Program in Communication Studies, Phoenix, AZ 85069-7100. Offers MA. *Program availability:* Part-time, evening/weekend. *Degree requirements:* For master's, thesis, applied project or written comprehensive exam; interactive Program of Study (iPOS) submitted before completing 50 percent of required credit hours. *Entrance requirements:* For master's, GRE (if GPA less than 3.0 in last 60 hours of undergraduate study), minimum GPA of 3.0 or equivalent in last 2 years of work leading to bachelor's degree, 3 letters of recommendation, official transcripts, writing sample of scholarly work or example of professional activities. Additional exam requirements/recommendations for international students: required—TOEFL, IELTS, or PTE. Electronic applications accepted.

Arkansas State University, Graduate School, College of Media and Communication, Department of Communication, State University, AR 72467. Offers communication studies (MA, SCCT); health communications (Graduate Certificate). *Program availability:* Part-time. *Degree requirements:* For master's, one foreign language, comprehensive exam, thesis or alternative; for other advanced degree, comprehensive

exam. *Entrance requirements:* For master's, GRE General Test or MAT, appropriate bachelor's degree, writing sample, letter of recommendation, official transcripts, immunization records; for other advanced degree, GRE or MAT, appropriate master's degree, interview, official transcript, immunization records. Additional exam requirements/recommendations for international students: required—TOEFL (minimum score 550 paper-based; 79 iBT), IELTS (minimum score 6), PTE (minimum score 56). Electronic applications accepted.

Ashland University, College of Arts and Sciences, Program in Corporate and Strategic Communication, Ashland, OH 44805-3702. Offers communication (MA). *Program availability:* Online learning. Electronic applications accepted. *Expenses: Tuition:* Full-time $10,800; part-time $5400 per credit hour. *Required fees:* $720; $360 per credit hour.

Auburn University, Graduate School, College of Liberal Arts, School of Communication and Journalism, Auburn, AL 36849. Offers MA, Graduate Certificate. *Program availability:* Part-time. *Faculty:* 45 full-time (27 women), 8 part-time/adjunct (6 women). *Students:* 20 full-time (14 women), 3 part-time (2 women); includes 4 minority (3 Black or African American, non-Hispanic/Latino; 1 Two or more races, non-Hispanic/Latino), 2 international. Average age 25. 18 applicants, 78% accepted, 6 enrolled. In 2019, 8 master's awarded. *Degree requirements:* For master's, thesis (for some programs). *Entrance requirements:* For master's, GRE General Test. Additional exam requirements/recommendations for international students: required—iTEP; recommended—TOEFL (minimum score 550 paper-based; 79 iBT), IELTS (minimum score 6.5). *Application deadline:* Applications are processed on a rolling basis. Application fee: $60 ($70 for international students). Electronic applications accepted. *Expenses: Tuition, area resident:* Full-time $9828; part-time $546 per credit hour. Tuition, state resident: full-time $9828; part-time $546 per credit hour. Tuition, nonresident: full-time $29,484; part-time $1638 per credit hour. *International tuition:* $29,744 full-time. Tuition and fees vary according to course load, program and reciprocity agreements. *Financial support:* In 2019–20, 16 teaching assistantships with tuition reimbursements (averaging $14,702 per year) were awarded; Federal Work-Study also available. Support available to part-time students. Financial award application deadline: 3/15; financial award applicants required to submit FAFSA. *Unit head:* Dr. Jennifer Wood Adams, Director, 334-844-2751, E-mail: jennifer.adams@auburn.edu. *Application contact:* Dr. George Flowers, Dean of the Graduate School, 334-844-2125.
Website: http://www.cla.auburn.edu/cmjn/

Austin Peay State University, College of Graduate Studies, College of Arts and Letters, Department of Communication, Clarksville, TN 37044. Offers marketing communication (MA); media management (MA). *Program availability:* Part-time, evening/weekend, online learning. *Faculty:* 7 full-time (4 women), 2 part-time/adjunct (both women). *Students:* 6 full-time (4 women), 50 part-time (32 women); includes 19 minority (13 Black or African American, non-Hispanic/Latino; 1 American Indian or Alaska Native, non-Hispanic/Latino; 5 Two or more races, non-Hispanic/Latino). Average age 32. 24 applicants, 83% accepted, 15 enrolled. In 2019, 21 master's awarded. *Degree requirements:* For master's, comprehensive exam, thesis (for some programs). *Entrance requirements:* For master's, GRE General Test, minimum GPA of 2.5. Additional exam requirements/recommendations for international students: required—TOEFL (minimum score 500 paper-based). *Application deadline:* For fall admission, 8/5 priority date for domestic students. Applications are processed on a rolling basis. Application fee: $45 ($55 for international students). Electronic applications accepted. *Financial support:* Research assistantships with full tuition reimbursements, career-related internships or fieldwork, Federal Work-Study, institutionally sponsored loans, scholarships/grants, and unspecified assistantships available. Support available to part-time students. Financial award application deadline: 7/1; financial award applicants required to submit FAFSA. *Unit head:* Dr. Kathy Heuston, Interim Chair, 931-221-7554, Fax: 931-221-7265, E-mail: leek@apsu.edu. *Application contact:* Megan Mitchell, Coordinator of Graduate Admissions, 931-221-6189, Fax: 931-221-7641, E-mail: mitchellm@apsu.edu.
Website: http://www.apsu.edu/communication/index.php

Ball State University, Graduate School, College of Communication, Information, and Media, Muncie, IN 47306. Offers MA, MS, Certificate. *Program availability:* Part-time, 100% online, blended/hybrid learning. *Degree requirements:* For master's, comprehensive exam (for some programs), thesis (for some programs). *Entrance requirements:* For master's, GRE (for some programs), minimum baccalaureate GPA of 2.75 or 3.0 in latter half of baccalaureate. Additional exam requirements/recommendations for international students: required—TOEFL (minimum score 550 paper-based; 79 iBT), IELTS (minimum score 6.5). Electronic applications accepted. *Expenses: Tuition, area resident:* Full-time $7506; part-time $417 per credit hour. Tuition, nonresident: full-time $20,610; part-time $1145 per credit hour. *Required fees:* $2126. Tuition and fees vary according to course load, campus/location and program.

Baylor University, Graduate School, College of Arts and Sciences, Department of Communication, Waco, TX 76798. Offers MA. *Program availability:* Part-time. *Entrance requirements:* For master's, GRE General Test, transcripts; 3 letters of recommendation; personal statement of intent; scholarly writing sample. Additional exam requirements/recommendations for international students: required—TOEFL, IELTS, PTE. Electronic applications accepted.

Bay Path University, Program in Communications, Longmeadow, MA 01106-2292. Offers MS. *Program availability:* Part-time, evening/weekend, 100% online, blended/hybrid learning. Electronic applications accepted. Application fee is waived when completed online.

Bellarmine University, School of Communication, Louisville, KY 40205. Offers MA, MSDM. *Program availability:* Part-time, evening/weekend. *Faculty:* 5 full-time (2 women). *Students:* 10 full-time (5 women), 14 part-time (11 women); includes 4 minority (3 Black or African American, non-Hispanic/Latino; 1 Two or more races, non-Hispanic/Latino), 5 international. Average age 23. 36 applicants, 53% accepted, 14 enrolled. In 2019, 32 master's awarded. *Degree requirements:* For master's, thesis optional. *Entrance requirements:* For master's, personal statement; professional/academic writing sample; essay; letters of recommendation; resume. Additional exam requirements/recommendations for international students: required—TOEFL (PB - 550, IB - 79, or CB-213) or MELAB (78 or higher) or ILETS (6.0 or higher) or language training at an approved center. *Application deadline:* Applications are processed on a rolling basis. Application fee: $40. Electronic applications accepted. Tuition and fees vary according to degree level and program. *Financial support:* Scholarships/grants available. Financial award applicants required to submit FAFSA. *Unit head:* Dr. Mary O. Huff, Dean, 502-272-8359, E-mail: mhuff@bellarmine.edu. *Application contact:* Dr. Sara Pettingill, Dean of Graduate Admission, 502-272-8401, Fax: 502-272-8002, E-mail:

spettingill@bellarmine.edu.
Website: https://www.bellarmine.edu/communication/

Boise State University, College of Arts and Sciences, Department of Communication and Media, Boise, ID 83725-0399. Offers MA. *Program availability:* Part-time. *Students:* 9 full-time (5 women), 8 part-time (7 women); includes 2 minority (1 Hispanic/Latino; 1 Two or more races, non-Hispanic/Latino). *Entrance requirements:* For master's, GRE General Test, minimum GPA of 3.0, writing sample. Additional exam requirements/recommendations for international students: required—TOEFL, IELTS. Electronic applications accepted. *Expenses: Tuition, area resident:* Full-time $7110; part-time $470 per credit hour. Tuition, state resident: full-time $7110; part-time $470 per credit hour. Tuition, nonresident: full-time $24,030; part-time $827 per credit hour. *International tuition:* $24,030 full-time. *Required fees:* $2536. Tuition and fees vary according to course load and program. *Financial support:* Research assistantships, teaching assistantships, and unspecified assistantships available. Financial award applicants required to submit FAFSA. *Unit head:* Todd Norton, Department Chair, 208-426-1922, E-mail: toddnorton@boisestate.edu. *Application contact:* Dr. John McClellan, Director of Graduate Studies, 208-426-2450, E-mail: johnmcclellan@boisestate.edu.
Website: https://www.boisestate.edu/comm-media/

Boston University, College of Communication, Department of Mass Communication, Advertising, and Public Relations, Boston, MA 02215. Offers advertising (MS); mass communication (MS), including communication studies, marketing communication research; public relations (MS); JD/MS. *Program availability:* Part-time. *Faculty:* 26 full-time, 33 part-time/adjunct. *Students:* 275 full-time (228 women), 29 part-time (24 women); includes 24 minority (11 Black or African American, non-Hispanic/Latino; 5 Asian, non-Hispanic/Latino; 5 Hispanic/Latino; 3 Two or more races, non-Hispanic/Latino), 230 international. Average age 23. 719 applicants, 61% accepted, 188 enrolled. In 2019, 121 master's awarded. *Degree requirements:* For master's, comprehensive exam (for some programs), thesis (for some programs). *Entrance requirements:* For master's, transcript(s), resume/CV, 3 letters of recommendation, personal statement/essay. Additional exam requirements/recommendations for international students: required—TOEFL (minimum score 600 paper-based; 100 iBT), either TOEFL or IELTS; recommended—IELTS (minimum score 7). *Application deadline:* For fall admission, 5/1 for domestic and international students. Applications are processed on a rolling basis. Application fee: $95. Electronic applications accepted. *Financial support:* Research assistantships, teaching assistantships with partial tuition reimbursements, career-related internships or fieldwork, Federal Work-Study, scholarships/grants, and unspecified assistantships available. Support available to part-time students. Financial award application deadline: 5/1; financial award applicants required to submit FAFSA. *Unit head:* Donald Wright, Chairperson, 617-353-3482, E-mail: mcadvpr@bu.edu. *Application contact:* Jackie Cummings, Admission and Financial Aid Counselor, 617-353-3481, E-mail: comgrad@bu.edu.
Website: http://www.bu.edu/com/academics/masscomm-ad-pr/

Bowling Green State University, Graduate College, College of Arts and Sciences, School of Media and Communication, Bowling Green, OH 43403. Offers media and communication (MA, PhD); strategic communication (MA). *Program availability:* Part-time. Terminal master's awarded for partial completion of doctoral program. *Degree requirements:* For master's, thesis or alternative; for doctorate, comprehensive exam, thesis/dissertation. *Entrance requirements:* For master's and doctorate, GRE General Test. Additional exam requirements/recommendations for international students: required—TOEFL. Electronic applications accepted.

Brigham Young University, Graduate Studies, College of Fine Arts and Communications, School of Communications, Provo, UT 84602. Offers mass communications (MA). *Faculty:* 19 full-time (2 women). *Students:* 26 full-time (16 women), 13 part-time (8 women); includes 11 minority (2 Black or African American, non-Hispanic/Latino; 4 Asian, non-Hispanic/Latino; 4 Hispanic/Latino; 1 Native Hawaiian or other Pacific Islander, non-Hispanic/Latino). Average age 31. 19 applicants, 84% accepted, 15 enrolled. In 2019, 11 master's awarded. *Degree requirements:* For master's, thesis. *Entrance requirements:* For master's, GRE, Minimum GPA of 3.0 in last 60 hours of course work. Additional exam requirements/recommendations for international students: required—TOEFL (minimum score 580 paper-based; 85 iBT). *Application deadline:* For fall admission, 3/31 priority date for domestic and international students. Applications are processed on a rolling basis. Application fee: $50. Electronic applications accepted. *Financial support:* In 2019–20, 18 students received support, including 24 research assistantships (averaging $3,339 per year), 3 teaching assistantships (averaging $3,669 per year); scholarships/grants, unspecified assistantships, and supplementary awards also available. Financial award application deadline: 4/30; financial award applicants required to submit FAFSA. *Unit head:* Edward Carter, Director, 801-422-2997, Fax: 801-422-0160, E-mail: ed_carter@byu.edu. *Application contact:* Debby Jackson, Graduate Program Manager, 801-422-2632, Fax: 801-422-0160, E-mail: debby_jackson@byu.edu.
Website: http://cfac.byu.edu/departments/communications

Bryant University, College of Arts and Sciences, Smithfield, RI 02917. Offers communication (MA, Graduate Certificate); organizational communication (Graduate Certificate). *Program availability:* Part-time, evening/weekend. *Degree requirements:* For master's, thesis optional, Culminating Project A (alternate requirement) Comprehensive Exam A (alternate requirement). *Entrance requirements:* For master's and Graduate Certificate, GRE (waived if essay is submitted), resume, official undergraduate transcript(s), essay or GRE scores, 3 letters of recommendation (2 academic, 1 professional). Additional exam requirements/recommendations for international students: required—TOEFL (minimum score 550 paper-based; 80 iBT). Electronic applications accepted. *Expenses:* Contact institution.

Cabrini University, Academic Affairs, Radnor, PA 19087. Offers accounting (M Acc); autism spectrum disorder (M Ed); biological sciences (MS), including civic leadership; criminology and criminal justice (MA); curriculum, instruction, and assessment (M Ed); educational leadership (M Ed, Ed D), including curriculum and instructional leadership (Ed D), preK-12 leadership (Ed D); English as a second language (M Ed); organizational leadership (DBA, PhD); preK to 4 (M Ed); reading specialist (M Ed); secondary education (M Ed), including biology, chemistry, English, English/communication, mathematics, social studies; special education grades 7-12 (M Ed); special education preK-8 (M Ed); teaching and learning (M Ed). *Program availability:* Part-time, evening/weekend. *Degree requirements:* For master's, comprehensive exam (for some programs), thesis (for some programs); for doctorate, comprehensive exam (for some programs), thesis/dissertation. *Entrance requirements:* For master's, professional resume, personal statement, two recommendations, official transcripts; for doctorate, official transcripts, minimum master's GPA of 3.0, two recommendations, interview with admissions committee. Additional exam requirements/recommendations for international students: required—TOEFL (minimum score 80 iBT). Electronic applications accepted. Application fee is waived when completed online. *Expenses:* Contact institution.

California Baptist University, Program in Communication, Riverside, CA 92504-3206. Offers MA. *Program availability:* Part-time, evening/weekend, online only, 100% online, blended/hybrid learning. *Degree requirements:* For master's, thesis or alternative, comprehensive project, defended paper. *Entrance requirements:* For master's, bachelor's degree, official transcripts, 2 recommendations, current resume, 500-word essay, minimum GPA of 2.5. Additional exam requirements/recommendations for international students: required—TOEFL (minimum score 80 iBT). Electronic applications accepted. *Expenses:* Contact institution.

California State University, Chico, Office of Graduate Studies, College of Communication and Education, Department of Communication Arts and Sciences, Program in Communication Studies, Chico, CA 95929-0722. Offers MA. *Degree requirements:* For master's, thesis or project. *Entrance requirements:* For master's, GRE, three letters of recommendation, two writing samples, one-page statement of purpose, minimum GPA of 3.0. Additional exam requirements/recommendations for international students: required—TOEFL (minimum score 550 paper-based; 80 iBT), IELTS (minimum score 6.5), PTE (minimum score 59). Electronic applications accepted.

California State University, East Bay, Office of Graduate Studies, College of Letters, Arts, and Social Sciences, Department of Communication, Hayward, CA 94542-3000. Offers MA. *Program availability:* Part-time. *Degree requirements:* For master's, comprehensive exam, project, thesis, or exam. *Entrance requirements:* For master's, GRE, minimum GPA of 3.0 in field; 3 letters of recommendation; sample of scholarly writing. Additional exam requirements/recommendations for international students: required—TOEFL (minimum score 550 paper-based). Electronic applications accepted.

California State University, Fresno, Division of Research and Graduate Studies, College of Arts and Humanities, Department of Communication, Fresno, CA 93740-8027. Offers MA. *Program availability:* Part-time, evening/weekend. *Degree requirements:* For master's, thesis or alternative. *Entrance requirements:* For master's, GRE General Test, minimum GPA of 3.1. Additional exam requirements/recommendations for international students: required—TOEFL. Electronic applications accepted. *Expenses:* Tuition, state resident: full-time $4012; part-time $2506 per semester.

California State University, Fullerton, Graduate Studies, College of Communications, Department of Communications, Fullerton, CA 92831-3599. Offers communications in tourism and entertainment (MA); mass communications research and theory (MA); professional communications (MA). *Program availability:* Part-time. *Entrance requirements:* For master's, GRE General Test.

California State University, Fullerton, Graduate Studies, College of Communications, Department of Human Communication Studies, Fullerton, CA 92831-3599. Offers communication studies (MA). *Program availability:* Part-time. *Degree requirements:* For master's, comprehensive exam, thesis or alternative. *Entrance requirements:* For master's, minimum GPA of 3.0 in major.

California State University, Long Beach, Graduate Studies, College of Liberal Arts, Department of Communication Studies, Long Beach, CA 90840. Offers MA. *Program availability:* Part-time. *Degree requirements:* For master's, comprehensive exam or thesis. *Entrance requirements:* For master's, GRE. Electronic applications accepted.

California State University, Los Angeles, Graduate Studies, College of Arts and Letters, Department of Communication Studies, Los Angeles, CA 90032-8530. Offers MA, MFA. *Program availability:* Part-time, evening/weekend. *Degree requirements:* For master's, comprehensive exam or thesis. *Entrance requirements:* For master's, minimum GPA of 2.75 in last 90 units of course work. Additional exam requirements/recommendations for international students: required—TOEFL (minimum score 500 paper-based). Electronic applications accepted. *Expenses: Tuition, area resident:* Full-time $7176; part-time $4164 per year. Tuition, state resident: full-time $7176; part-time $4164 per year. Tuition, nonresident: full-time $14,304; part-time $8916 per year. *International tuition:* $14,304 full-time. *Required fees:* $1037.76; $1037.76 per unit. Tuition and fees vary according to degree level and program.

California State University, Northridge, Graduate Studies, Mike Curb College of Arts, Media, and Communication, Northridge, CA 91330. Offers MA, MFA, MM. *Program availability:* Part-time, evening/weekend. *Entrance requirements:* Additional exam requirements/recommendations for international students: required—TOEFL.

California State University, Sacramento, College of Arts and Letters, Department of Communication Studies, Sacramento, CA 95819. Offers MA. *Program availability:* Part-time. *Students:* 25 part-time (16 women); includes 8 minority (1 Black or African American, non-Hispanic/Latino; 1 Asian, non-Hispanic/Latino; 6 Hispanic/Latino), 1 international. Average age 30. 19 applicants, 58% accepted, 10 enrolled. In 2019, 8 master's awarded. *Degree requirements:* For master's, comprehensive exam, thesis, thesis or project; writing proficiency exam. *Entrance requirements:* For master's, GRE, minimum GPA of 3.25 during previous 2 years. Additional exam requirements/recommendations for international students: required—TOEFL (minimum score 550 paper-based; 80 iBT); recommended—IELTS. *Application deadline:* For fall admission, 3/1 for domestic students, 2/1 for international students; for spring admission, 9/15 for domestic students, 8/15 for international students. Applications are processed on a rolling basis. Application fee: $70. Electronic applications accepted. *Expenses:* Contact institution. *Financial support:* Teaching assistantships, career-related internships or fieldwork, Federal Work-Study, and scholarships/grants available. Support available to part-time students. Financial award application deadline: 3/1; financial award applicants required to submit FAFSA. *Unit head:* Dr. Gerri Smith, Chair, 916-278-6688, E-mail: smithg@csus.edu. *Application contact:* Jose Martinez, Outreach and Graduate Diversity Coordinator, 916-278-6470, Fax: 916-278-5669, E-mail: martinj@skymail.csus.edu.
Website: http://www.al.csus.edu/coms

California State University, San Bernardino, Graduate Studies, College of Arts and Letters, Program in Communication Studies, San Bernardino, CA 92407. Offers communication studies (MA); integrated marketing communication (MA). *Faculty:* 6 full-time (5 women), 1 (woman) part-time/adjunct. *Students:* 14 full-time (7 women), 19 part-time (13 women); includes 25 minority (4 Black or African American, non-Hispanic/Latino; 1 Asian, non-Hispanic/Latino; 13 Hispanic/Latino; 7 Two or more races, non-Hispanic/Latino), 2 international. Average age 29. 33 applicants, 70% accepted, 14 enrolled. In 2019, 13 master's awarded. *Degree requirements:* For master's, comprehensive exam. *Entrance requirements:* Additional exam requirements/recommendations for international students: required—TOEFL. *Application deadline:* For fall admission, 5/15 for domestic students. Application fee: $55. *Unit head:* Shafiqur Rahman, Department Chair, 909-537-5820, E-mail: shafiqur.rahman@csusb.edu. *Application contact:* Dr. Dorota Huizinga, Dean of Graduate Studies, 909-537-3064, Fax: 909-537-7034, E-mail: dorota.huizinga@csusb.edu.

Carleton University, Faculty of Graduate Studies, Faculty of Public Affairs and Management, School of Journalism and Communication, Program in Communication, Ottawa, ON K1S 5B6, Canada. Offers MA, PhD. *Degree requirements:* For master's, thesis optional; for doctorate, comprehensive exam, thesis/dissertation. *Entrance requirements:* For master's, honors degree. Additional exam requirements/recommendations for international students: required—TOEFL.

Carnegie Mellon University, Dietrich College of Humanities and Social Sciences, Department of English, Pittsburgh, PA 15213-3891. Offers communication planning and design (M Des); literary and cultural studies (MA, PhD); professional writing (MAPW), including editing and publishing, policy and non-profit communication, public and media relations / corporate communications, science or healthcare communication, technical writing, writing for new media, writing for print media; rhetoric (MA, PhD). *Program availability:* Part-time. Terminal master's awarded for partial completion of doctoral program. *Degree requirements:* For doctorate, 2 foreign languages, comprehensive exam, thesis/dissertation. *Entrance requirements:* For master's and doctorate, GRE General Test. Additional exam requirements/recommendations for international students: required—TOEFL, TWE.

Central Connecticut State University, School of Graduate Studies, College of Liberal Arts and Social Sciences, Department of Communication, New Britain, CT 06050-4010. Offers communication (MS); public relations/promotions (Certificate). *Program availability:* Part-time, evening/weekend. *Degree requirements:* For master's, comprehensive exam, thesis or alternative, special project; for Certificate, qualifying exam. *Entrance requirements:* For master's, minimum undergraduate GPA of 3.0, resume, references, essay. Additional exam requirements/recommendations for international students: required—TOEFL (minimum score 550 paper-based; 79 iBT); recommended—IELTS (minimum score 6.5). Electronic applications accepted.

Central Michigan University, College of Graduate Studies, College of the Arts and Media, Department of Communication and Dramatic Arts, Mount Pleasant, MI 48859. Offers communication (MA), including communication and dramatic arts. *Program availability:* Part-time. *Degree requirements:* For master's, thesis. *Entrance requirements:* Additional exam requirements/recommendations for international students: recommended—TOEFL (minimum score 100 iBT), IELTS. Electronic applications accepted. *Expenses: Tuition, area resident:* Full-time $12,267; part-time $8178 per year. Tuition, state resident: full-time $12,267; part-time $8178 per year. Tuition, nonresident: full-time $12,267; part-time $8178 per year. *International tuition:* $16,110 full-time. *Required fees:* $225 per semester. Tuition and fees vary according to degree level and program.

Chapman University, School of Communication, Orange, CA 92866. Offers MS. *Program availability:* Evening/weekend. *Faculty:* 21 full-time (14 women), 7 part-time/adjunct (1 woman). *Students:* 8 full-time (6 women), 9 part-time (7 women); includes 5 minority (2 Asian, non-Hispanic/Latino; 2 Hispanic/Latino; 1 Two or more races, non-Hispanic/Latino). Average age 28. 24 applicants, 75% accepted, 12 enrolled. In 2019, 6 master's awarded. *Degree requirements:* For master's, capstone research project. *Entrance requirements:* For master's, GRE. Additional exam requirements/recommendations for international students: required—TOEFL (minimum score 80 iBT), IELTS (minimum score 6.5), PTE (minimum score 53). *Application deadline:* For fall admission, 1/15 priority date for domestic students. Application fee: $60. Electronic applications accepted. *Expenses:* $1,185 per unit. *Financial support:* Fellowships, research assistantships, Federal Work-Study, scholarships/grants, and unspecified assistantships available. Financial award applicants required to submit FAFSA. *Unit head:* Dr. Lisa Sparks, Dean, 714-744-7088, E-mail: ditommas@chapman.edu. *Application contact:* Shannon McCance, Admission Counselor, 714-997-6711, E-mail: smccance@chapman.edu.
Website: https://www.chapman.edu/communication/index.aspx

Chatham University, Program in Communication, Pittsburgh, PA 15232-2826. Offers environmental communication (M Comm); health communication (M Comm); strategic communication (M Comm). *Program availability:* Part-time, online learning. *Entrance requirements:* Additional exam requirements/recommendations for international students: required—TOEFL, IELTS. Electronic applications accepted. Application fee is waived when completed online. *Expenses: Tuition:* Part-time $1017 per credit. *Required fees:* $30 per credit. Tuition and fees vary according to program.

Clarks Summit University, Baptist Bible Seminary, South Abington Township, PA 18411. Offers Biblical apologetics (MA); Biblical studies (MA); church education (M Min); church planting (M Div, M Min); communication (D Min); counseling and spiritual development (D Min); global ministry (M Min, D Min); ministry (PhD); missions (M Min); organizational leadership (M Min); outreach pastor (M Min); pastoral counseling (M Min); pastoral leadership (M Div, M Min); pastoral ministry (D Min); theological studies (D Min); theology (Th M); youth pastor (M Min). *Program availability:* Part-time, evening/weekend, online learning. Terminal master's awarded for partial completion of doctoral program. *Degree requirements:* For master's, 2 foreign languages, thesis, oral exam (for M Div); for doctorate, 2 foreign languages, comprehensive exam (for some programs), thesis/dissertation, oral exam. *Entrance requirements:* For doctorate, Greek and Hebrew entrance exams (for PhD). Electronic applications accepted.

Clark University, Graduate School, School of Professional Studies, Program in Professional Communication, Worcester, MA 01610-1477. Offers MSPC. *Program availability:* Part-time, evening/weekend. *Degree requirements:* For master's, thesis optional. *Entrance requirements:* For master's, 2 references, resume or curriculum vitae, personal statement. Additional exam requirements/recommendations for international students: required—TOEFL (minimum score 575 paper-based; 90 iBT), IELTS (minimum score 6.5). Electronic applications accepted. *Expenses:* Contact institution.

Clemson University, Graduate School, College of Behavioral, Social and Health Sciences, Department of Communication, Clemson, SC 29634. Offers communication, technology and society (MA). *Faculty:* 26 full-time (16 women). *Students:* 23 full-time (18 women), 3 part-time (1 woman); includes 4 minority (2 Black or African American, non-Hispanic/Latino; 2 Hispanic/Latino), 2 international. Average age 23. 33 applicants, 67% accepted, 15 enrolled. In 2019, 10 master's awarded. *Expenses:* Full-Time Student per Semester: Tuition: $4600 (in-state), $9525 (out-of-state), Fees: $598; Graduate Assistant Per Semester: $1144; Part-Time Student Per Credit Hour: $556 (in-state), $1106 (out-of-state), Fees: $617. *Financial support:* In 2019–20, 21 students received support, including 20 teaching assistantships with full and partial tuition reimbursements available (averaging $12,000 per year); career-related internships or fieldwork and unspecified assistantships also available. *Unit head:* Dr. Joseph Mazer, Department Chair, 864-656-0599, E-mail: JMAZER@clemson.edu. *Application contact:* Dr. Erin Ash, Director of Graduate Studies, 864-656-1567, E-mail: ASH3@clemson.edu.
Website: http://www.clemson.edu/cbshs/departments/communication/index.html

Clemson University, Graduate School, College of Business, Department of Graphic Communications, Clemson, SC 29634. Offers MS. *Faculty:* 13 full-time (6 women), 5 part-time/adjunct (1 woman). *Students:* 11 full-time (8 women), 5 part-time (all women); includes 3 minority (1 Black or African American, non-Hispanic/Latino; 2 Hispanic/Latino), 1 international. Average age 25. 15 applicants, 73% accepted, 9 enrolled. In 2019, 7 master's awarded. *Expenses:* Full-Time Student per Semester: Tuition: $4600 (in-state), $9525 (out-of-state), Fees: $598; Graduate Assistant Per Semester: $1144; Part-Time Student Per Credit Hour: $556 (in-state), $1106 (out-of-state), Fees: $617. *Financial support:* In 2019–20, 7 students received support. Career-related internships or fieldwork and unspecified assistantships available. *Unit head:* Dr. Chip Tonkin, Department Chair, 864-656-3447, E-mail: tonkin@clemson.edu. *Application contact:* Dr. Nona Woolbright, Graduate Coordinator, 864-656-0105, E-mail: nwoolbr@clemson.edu.
Website: https://www.clemson.edu/business/departments/graphics/

Cleveland State University, College of Graduate Studies, College of Liberal Arts and Social Sciences, School of Communication, Cleveland, OH 44115. Offers applied communication theory and methodology (MA). *Program availability:* Part-time, evening/weekend. *Degree requirements:* For master's, comprehensive exam (for some programs), thesis, project, comprehensive exam, or collaborative project. *Entrance requirements:* For master's, GRE or MAT, minimum undergraduate GPA of 2.75, 2 letters of recommendation, statement of interest. Additional exam requirements/recommendations for international students: required—TOEFL (minimum score 550 paper-based; 78 iBT). Electronic applications accepted. *Expenses:* Contact institution.

Cleveland State University, College of Graduate Studies, Maxine Goodman Levin College of Urban Affairs, Program in Urban Studies and Public Affairs, Cleveland, OH 44115. Offers communication (PhD); public administration (PhD); urban policy and development (PhD). *Program availability:* Part-time, evening/weekend. *Degree requirements:* For doctorate, comprehensive exam, thesis/dissertation. *Entrance requirements:* For doctorate, GRE General Test (minimum score: verbal and quantitative 50th percentile, analytical writing 4.0), minimum GPA of 3.5. Additional exam requirements/recommendations for international students: required—TOEFL (minimum score 550 paper-based; 78 iBT), IELTS (6.0), or International Test of English Proficiency (iTEP). Electronic applications accepted. *Expenses:* Contact institution.

The College of New Rochelle, Graduate School, Division of Art and Communication Studies, Program in Communication Studies, New Rochelle, NY 10805-2308. Offers MS, Certificate. *Program availability:* Part-time, evening/weekend. *Degree requirements:* For master's, thesis or alternative, thesis or comprehensive exam. *Entrance requirements:* For master's, GRE General Test, interview, minimum GPA of 3.0. Additional exam requirements/recommendations for international students: required—TOEFL.

Columbia College Chicago, School of Graduate Studies, Communication Department, Chicago, IL 60605-1996. Offers civic media (MA). *Degree requirements:* For master's, thesis. *Entrance requirements:* For master's, self-assessment essay, work sample, interview, letters of recommendation, transcripts, resume. Additional exam requirements/recommendations for international students: required—TOEFL, IELTS. Electronic applications accepted. *Expenses:* Contact institution.

Columbia University, Graduate School of Business, Doctoral Program in Business, New York, NY 10027. Offers business (PhD), including accounting, decision, risk, and operations, finance and economics, management, marketing. *Accreditation:* AACSB. *Degree requirements:* For doctorate, comprehensive exam, thesis/dissertation, major field exam, research paper, thesis proposal. *Entrance requirements:* For doctorate, GMAT or GRE (finance), 2 letters of reference, resume. Additional exam requirements/recommendations for international students: required—TOEFL. Electronic applications accepted. *Expenses:* Contact institution.

Columbia University, School of Professional Studies, Program in Communications Practice, New York, NY 10027. Offers MS. Electronic applications accepted. *Expenses: Tuition:* Full-time $47,600; part-time $1880 per credit. One-time fee: $105.

Concordia University, School of Graduate Studies, Faculty of Arts and Science, Department of Communication Studies, Montréal, QC H3G 1M8, Canada. Offers communication (PhD); communication studies (Diploma); media studies (MA). *Degree requirements:* For master's, thesis optional; for doctorate, one foreign language, comprehensive exam, thesis/dissertation, research practicum, seminar. *Entrance requirements:* For master's, bachelor's degree in communications, 2 years of media-related experience; for doctorate, MA in communications.

Cornell University, Graduate School, Graduate Fields of Agriculture and Life Sciences, Field of Communication, Ithaca, NY 14853. Offers communication (MS, PhD); human-computer interaction (MS, PhD); language and communication (MS, PhD); media communication and society (MS, PhD); organizational communication (MS, PhD); science, environment and health communication (MS, PhD); social psychology of communication (MS, PhD). *Degree requirements:* For master's, thesis (MS); for doctorate, comprehensive exam, thesis/dissertation. *Entrance requirements:* For master's and doctorate, GRE General Test, 3 letters of recommendation. Additional exam requirements/recommendations for international students: required—TOEFL (minimum score 600 paper-based; 100 iBT). Electronic applications accepted.

Dallas Baptist University, College of Fine Arts, Dallas, TX 75211-9299. Offers communication (MA), including communication for ministry, communication leadership, communication studies, marketing communication, organizational communication management, worship studies. *Program availability:* Part-time, evening/weekend. Application fee: $25. *Expenses: Tuition:* Full-time $18,072; part-time $1004 per credit hour. *Required fees:* $1100; $550 per semester. Tuition and fees vary according to course level and degree level. *Unit head:* Dr. Wes Moore, Dean, 214-333-5316, E-mail: wesm@dbu.edu. *Application contact:* Carter Willis, Program Director, 214-333-5867, E-mail: carterw@dbu.edu.
Website: https://www.dbu.edu/graduate/degree-programs/ma-communication/index.html

Dallas Baptist University, Graduate School of Ministry, Program in Global Leadership, Dallas, TX 75211-9299. Offers church planting (MA); East Asian Studies (MA); English as a second language (MA); general studies (MA); global communication (MA); global studies (MA); international business (MA); leading the nonprofit organization (MA); missions (MA); small group ministry (MA); urban ministry (MA). *Program availability:* Part-time, evening/weekend, online learning. *Application deadline:* Applications are processed on a rolling basis. Application fee: $25. Electronic applications accepted. Application fee is waived when completed online. *Expenses: Tuition:* Full-time $18,072; part-time $1004 per credit hour. *Required fees:* $1100; $550 per semester. Tuition and fees vary according to course level and degree level. *Unit head:* Dr. Robert R. Brooks, Dean, 214-333-5494, Fax: 214-333-5673, E-mail: bobb@dbu.edu. *Application contact:* Dr. Brent Thomason, Program Director, 214-333-5236, E-mail: brentt@dbu.edu.
Website: https://www.dbu.edu/ministry/degree-programs/m-a-in-global-leadership

Dallas Baptist University, Professional Development Program, Dallas, TX 75211-9299. Offers accounting (MA); church leadership (MA); communication (MA); counseling (MA); criminal justice (MA); English as a second language (MA); finance (MA); higher education (MA); leadership studies (MA); management (MA). *Program availability:* Part-time, evening/weekend, online learning. *Application deadline:* Applications are processed on a rolling basis. Application fee: $25. Electronic applications accepted. Application fee is waived when completed online. *Expenses: Tuition:* Full-time $18,072; part-time $1004 per credit hour. *Required fees:* $1100; $550 per semester. Tuition and fees vary according to course level and degree level. *Unit head:* Jared Ingram, Program Director, 214-333-5584, E-mail: jaredi@dbu.edu. *Application contact:* Jared Ingram, Program Director, 214-333-5584, E-mail: jaredi@dbu.edu.
Website: https://www.dbu.edu/graduate/degree-programs/ma-professional-development

DePaul University, College of Communication, Chicago, IL 60604. Offers digital communication and media arts (MA); health communication (MA); journalism (MA); media and cinema studies (MA); multicultural communication (MA); organizational communication (MA); public relations and advertising (MA); relational communication (MA). *Program availability:* Part-time, evening/weekend. *Entrance requirements:* Additional exam requirements/recommendations for international students: required—TOEFL (minimum score 590 paper-based; 96 iBT), IELTS (minimum score 7.5) or PTE. Electronic applications accepted.

DEREE - The American College of Greece, Graduate Programs, Athens, Greece. Offers applied psychology (MS); communication (MA); leadership (MS); marketing (MS).

Drake University, School of Journalism and Mass Communication, Des Moines, IA 50311-4516. Offers brand communication (MCL); communication leadership (MCL); public affairs and advocacy (MCL). *Program availability:* Part-time, evening/weekend, 100% online, blended/hybrid learning. *Expenses: Tuition:* Full-time $19,300; part-time $625 per credit hour. Tuition and fees vary according to degree level, program and student level.

Drexel University, College of Arts and Sciences, Department of Communication, Culture and Media, Philadelphia, PA 19104-2875. Offers communication (MS), including public communication, science communication, technical communication. *Program availability:* Part-time, evening/weekend. *Degree requirements:* For master's, internship, professional portfolio. *Entrance requirements:* Additional exam requirements/recommendations for international students: required—TOEFL. Electronic applications accepted.

Drury University, Master of Arts in Communication Program, Springfield, MO 65802. Offers integrated communication (MAC); organizational leadership and change (MAC). *Program availability:* Part-time, evening/weekend. *Faculty:* 3 full-time (1 woman), 2 part-time/adjunct (0 women). *Students:* 14 full-time (8 women); includes 5 minority (4 Black or African American, non-Hispanic/Latino; 1 Asian, non-Hispanic/Latino). Average age 29. 16 applicants, 94% accepted, 12 enrolled. In 2019, 8 master's awarded. *Entrance requirements:* For master's, bachelor's degree, 3.0 GPA. Additional exam requirements/recommendations for international students: recommended—TOEFL (minimum score 80 iBT), IELTS (minimum score 6.5). *Application deadline:* For fall admission, 8/10 priority date for domestic and international students; for spring admission, 1/8 priority date for domestic and international students; for summer admission, 5/26 priority date for domestic and international students. Applications are processed on a rolling basis. Application fee: $25. Electronic applications accepted. *Expenses:* Contact institution. *Financial support:* Career-related internships or fieldwork, scholarships/grants, and unspecified assistantships available. Financial award application deadline: 6/30; financial award applicants required to submit FAFSA. *Unit head:* Dr. Charles Taylor, Program Director, 417-873-7391, E-mail: ctaylor@drury.edu. *Application contact:* Dr. Charles Taylor, Program Director, 417-873-7391, E-mail: ctaylor@drury.edu.
Website: http://www.drury.edu/communication-masters

Duquesne University, Graduate School of Liberal Arts, Department of Communication and Rhetorical Studies, Pittsburgh, PA 15282-0001. Offers communication (MA); rhetoric (PhD). *Program availability:* Part-time, evening/weekend, 100% online. Terminal master's awarded for partial completion of doctoral program. *Degree requirements:* For master's, thesis optional, practicum; for doctorate, 2 foreign languages, comprehensive exam, thesis/dissertation. *Entrance requirements:* For master's and doctorate, GRE General Test. Additional exam requirements/recommendations for international students: required—TOEFL. Electronic applications accepted.

Eastern Illinois University, Graduate School, College of Liberal Arts and Sciences, Department of Communication Studies, Charleston, IL 61920. Offers communication pedagogy (MA). *Program availability:* Part-time, evening/weekend. *Degree requirements:* For master's, comprehensive exam (for some programs), thesis (for some programs). *Entrance requirements:* For master's, GMAT or GRE. Additional exam requirements/recommendations for international students: required—TOEFL (minimum score 500 paper-based; 61 iBT), IELTS (minimum score 6). Electronic applications accepted.

Eastern Michigan University, Graduate School, College of Arts and Sciences, School of Communication, Media and Theatre Arts, Program in Communication, Ypsilanti, MI 48197. Offers MA. *Program availability:* Part-time, evening/weekend, online learning. *Students:* 6 full-time (2 women), 16 part-time (10 women); includes 11 minority (6 Black or African American, non-Hispanic/Latino; 1 Asian, non-Hispanic/Latino; 2 Hispanic/Latino; 2 Two or more races, non-Hispanic/Latino). Average age 29. 23 applicants, 70% accepted, 5 enrolled. In 2019, 9 master's awarded. *Entrance requirements:* Additional exam requirements/recommendations for international students: required—TOEFL. *Application deadline:* Applications are processed on a rolling basis. Application fee: $45. *Financial support:* Fellowships, research assistantships with full tuition reimbursements, teaching assistantships with full tuition reimbursements, career-related internships or fieldwork, Federal Work-Study, institutionally sponsored loans, scholarships/grants, tuition waivers (partial), and unspecified assistantships available. Support available to part-time students. Financial award applicants required to submit FAFSA. *Application contact:* Dr. Doris Fields, Coordinator, 734-487-4199, Fax: 734-487-3443, E-mail: dfields1@emich.edu.

Eastern New Mexico University, Graduate School, College of Fine Arts, Portales, NM 88130. Offers communication (MA). *Program availability:* Part-time, online learning. *Degree requirements:* For master's, comprehensive exam, thesis optional. *Entrance requirements:* For master's, minimum GPA of 3.0, writing sample. Additional exam requirements/recommendations for international students: required—TOEFL (minimum score 550 paper-based; 79 iBT), IELTS (minimum score 6). Electronic applications accepted. *Expenses: Tuition, area resident:* Full-time $5283; part-time $389.25 per credit hour. Tuition, state resident: full-time $5283; part-time $389.25 per credit hour. Tuition, nonresident: full-time $7007; part-time $389.25 per credit hour. *International tuition:* $7007 full-time. *Required fees:* $36; $35 per semester. One-time fee: $25.

Eastern University, Graduate Education Programs, St. Davids, PA 19087-3696. Offers ESL program specialist (K-12) (Certificate); general supervisor (PreK-12) (Certificate); health and physical education (K-12) (Certificate); middle level (4-8) (Certificate); multicultural education (M Ed); music (K-12) (Certificate); Pre K-4 (Certificate); Pre K-4 with special education (Certificate); reading (M Ed); reading specialist (K-12) (Certificate); reading supervisor (K-12) (Certificate); school counseling (MA, CAGS); school principalship (preK-12) (Certificate); school psychology (MS, CAGS); secondary biology education (7-12) (Certificate); secondary chemistry education (7-12) (Certificate); secondary communication education (7-12) (Certificate); secondary English education (7-12) (Certificate); secondary math education (7-12) (Certificate); secondary social studies education (7-12) (Certificate); special education (M Ed); special education (7-12) (Certificate); special education (Pre K-8) (Certificate); special education supervisor (K-12) (Certificate); TESOL (M Ed); world language (Certificate), including Spanish. *Program availability:* Part-time, evening/weekend, online learning. *Students:* 54 full-time (45 women), 149 part-time (134 women); includes 75 minority (54 Black or African American, non-Hispanic/Latino; 3 Asian, non-Hispanic/Latino; 15 Hispanic/Latino; 3 Two or more races, non-Hispanic/Latino). Average age 33. In 2019, 89 master's, 10 other advanced degrees awarded. *Entrance requirements:* Additional exam requirements/recommendations for international students: required—TOEFL. *Application deadline:* Applications are processed on a rolling basis. Application fee: $35. Electronic applications accepted. Application fee is waived when completed online. *Expenses:* Contact institution. *Unit head:* Michael Dziedziak, Executive Director of Enrollment, 800-452-0996, E-mail: gpsadmissions@eastern.edu. *Application contact:* Michael Dziedziak, Executive Director of Enrollment, 800-452-0996, E-mail: gpsadmissions@eastern.edu.
Website: https://www.eastern.edu/academics/programs/education-department-graduate-programs/graduate-programs

Eastern Washington University, Graduate Studies, College of Social Sciences, Department of Communication Studies, Cheney, WA 99004-2431. Offers MSC. *Program availability:* Part-time, evening/weekend. *Faculty:* 5 full-time (3 women). *Students:* 21 full-time (12 women), 3 part-time (1 woman); includes 3 minority (2 Asian, non-Hispanic/Latino; 1 Hispanic/Latino). Average age 31. 9 applicants, 89% accepted, 6 enrolled. In 2019, 9 master's awarded. *Degree requirements:* For master's, comprehensive exam, thesis or alternative. *Entrance requirements:* For master's, GRE General Test, minimum GPA of 3.0. Additional exam requirements/recommendations for international students: required—TOEFL (minimum score 580 paper-based; 92 iBT), IELTS (minimum score 7), TWE, PTE (minimum score 63). *Application deadline:* For fall admission, 4/1 priority date for domestic students; for spring admission, 1/15 for domestic students. Applications are processed on a rolling basis. Application fee: $75. Electronic applications accepted. *Financial support:* Teaching assistantships with partial tuition reimbursements, career-related internships or fieldwork, Federal Work-Study, institutionally sponsored loans, scholarships/grants, health care benefits, tuition waivers (partial), and unspecified assistantships available. Support available to part-time students. Financial award application deadline: 2/1; financial award applicants required to submit FAFSA. *Unit head:* Dr. Peter Shields, Professor, 509-359-4947. *Application contact:* Kathy White, Advisor/Recruiter for Graduate Studies, 509-359-6297, Fax: 509-359-6044, E-mail: gradprograms@ewu.edu.

East Stroudsburg University of Pennsylvania, Graduate and Extended Studies, College of Arts and Sciences, Department of Communication, East Stroudsburg, PA 18301-2999. Offers MA. *Degree requirements:* For master's, thesis (for some programs). *Entrance requirements:* For master's, resume, 3 letters of recommendation, letter of intent, writing sample (either academic paper or professional writing sample). Additional exam requirements/recommendations for international students: recommended—TOEFL (minimum score 560 paper-based; 83 iBT), IELTS. Electronic applications accepted.

East Tennessee State University, College of Graduate and Continuing Studies, College of Arts and Sciences, Department of Communication and Performance, Johnson City, TN 37614. Offers communication and storytelling studies (MA), including communication studies; storytelling (Postbaccalaureate Certificate). *Program availability:* Part-time. *Degree requirements:* For master's, comprehensive exam, thesis optional, admission to candidacy after completion of core semester hours. *Entrance requirements:* For master's, GRE General Test, minimum GPA of 3.0; three letters of recommendation; for Postbaccalaureate Certificate, essay, official transcript from each undergraduate and graduate institution attended, three letters of recommendation from academic or professional mentors or associates. Additional exam requirements/recommendations for international students: required—TOEFL (minimum score 550 paper-based; 79 iBT). Electronic applications accepted.

Edinboro University of Pennsylvania, Department of Communication, Journalism and Media, Edinboro, PA 16444. Offers MA. *Program availability:* Part-time, evening/weekend. *Faculty:* 4 full-time (2 women). *Students:* 24 full-time (13 women), 6 part-time (all women); includes 7 minority (5 Black or African American, non-Hispanic/Latino; 2 Hispanic/Latino), 3 international. Average age 26. 25 applicants, 64% accepted, 12 enrolled. In 2019, 14 master's awarded. *Degree requirements:* For master's, thesis or alternative, competency exam. *Entrance requirements:* For master's, GRE or MAT, minimum QPA of 2.8. Additional exam requirements/recommendations for international students: required—TOEFL (minimum score 550 paper-based; 213 iBT), IELTS (minimum score 6.5). *Application deadline:* Applications are processed on a rolling basis. Application fee: $30. Electronic applications accepted. *Expenses: Tuition, area resident:* Full-time $11,261; part-time $625.60 per credit. Tuition, state resident: full-time $11,261; part-time $625.60 per credit. Tuition, nonresident: full-time $16,850; part-time $936.10 per credit. *International tuition:* $16,850 full-time. *Required fees:* $57.75 per credit. *Financial support:* In 2019–20, 21 students received support. Research assistantships with tuition reimbursements available, career-related internships or fieldwork, Federal Work-Study, scholarships/grants, and unspecified assistantships available. Support available to part-time students. Financial award application deadline: 2/15; financial award applicants required to submit FAFSA. *Unit head:* Dr. Melissa Gibson, Graduate program Head, 814-732-1592, E-mail: mgibson@edinboro.edu. *Application contact:* Dr. Melissa Gibson, Graduate program Head, 814-732-1592, E-mail: mgibson@edinboro.edu.
Website: http://www.edinboro.edu/departments/communication-studies/

Fairfield University, College of Arts and Sciences, Fairfield, CT 06824. Offers American studies (MA); communication (MA); creative writing (MFA); mathematics (MS); public administration (MPA). *Program availability:* Part-time, evening/weekend, online learning. *Faculty:* 35 full-time (19 women), 19 part-time/adjunct (10 women). *Students:* 64 full-time (44 women), 84 part-time (48 women); includes 35 minority (9 Black or African American, non-Hispanic/Latino; 1 American Indian or Alaska Native, non-Hispanic/Latino; 1 Asian, non-Hispanic/Latino; 21 Hispanic/Latino; 3 Two or more races, non-Hispanic/Latino), 7 international. Average age 36. 98 applicants, 68% accepted, 64 enrolled. In 2019, 38 master's awarded. *Degree requirements:* For master's, capstone research course. *Entrance requirements:* For master's, minimum GPA of 3.0, 2 letters of recommendation, resume, personal statement. Additional exam requirements/recommendations for international students: required—TOEFL (minimum score 550 paper-based; 80 iBT) or IELTS (minimum score 6.5). *Application deadline:* For fall admission, 5/15 for international students; for spring admission, 10/15 for international students. Applications are processed on a rolling basis. Application fee: $60. Electronic applications accepted. *Expenses:* Tuition $850/credit hour; Registration Fee $50/semester; Graduate Student Activity Fee (Fall and Spring) $65/semester. *Financial support:* In 2019–20, 11 students received support. Scholarships/grants and unspecified assistantships available. Financial award applicants required to submit FAFSA. *Unit head:* Dr. Richard Greenwald, Dean, 203-254-4000 Ext. 2221, Fax: 203-254-4119, E-mail: rgreenwald@fairfield.edu. *Application contact:* Melanie Rogers, Director of Graduate Admission, 203-254-4184, Fax: 203-254-4073, E-mail: gradadmis@fairfield.edu.
Website: http://www.fairfield.edu/cas

Fairleigh Dickinson University, Metropolitan Campus, University College: Arts, Sciences, and Professional Studies, School of Art and Media Studies, Program in Media and Communications, Teaneck, NJ 07666-1914. Offers MA.

Fitchburg State University, Division of Graduate and Continuing Education, Program in Applied Communications, Fitchburg, MA 01420-2697. Offers applied communication studies (MS); technical and professional writing (MS). *Program availability:* Part-time, evening/weekend. *Entrance requirements:* Additional exam requirements/recommendations for international students: required—TOEFL (minimum score 550 paper-based; 79 iBT). Electronic applications accepted. *Expenses:* Contact institution.

Fitchburg State University, Division of Graduate and Continuing Education, Program in Interdisciplinary Studies, Fitchburg, MA 01420-2697. Offers applied communications (CAGS); counseling/psychology (CAGS); individualized track (CAGS); reading specialist (CAGS). *Program availability:* Part-time, evening/weekend. *Entrance requirements:*

Additional exam requirements/recommendations for international students: required—TOEFL (minimum score 550 paper-based; 79 iBT). Electronic applications accepted. *Expenses:* Contact institution.

Florida Atlantic University, Dorothy F. Schmidt College of Arts and Letters, School of Communication and Multimedia Studies, Boca Raton, FL 33431-0991. Offers communication studies (MA); film and video (Certificate); media, technology and entertainment (MFA). *Program availability:* Part-time. *Faculty:* 23 full-time (9 women). *Students:* 30 full-time (19 women), 13 part-time (5 women); includes 22 minority (9 Black or African American, non-Hispanic/Latino; 1 Asian, non-Hispanic/Latino; 6 Hispanic/Latino; 6 Two or more races, non-Hispanic/Latino), 7 international. Average age 30. 32 applicants, 66% accepted, 19 enrolled. In 2019, 8 master's awarded. *Degree requirements:* For master's, one foreign language, comprehensive exam (for some programs), thesis (for some programs). *Entrance requirements:* For master's, GRE General Test, minimum GPA of 3.0, essay, letters of recommendation. *Application deadline:* For fall admission, 7/1 priority date for domestic students, 4/1 for international students; for spring admission, 11/1 for domestic students, 10/1 for international students. Applications are processed on a rolling basis. Application fee: $30. Electronic applications accepted. *Expenses: Tuition:* Full-time $20,536; part-time $371.82 per credit hour. Tuition and fees vary according to program. *Financial support:* Teaching assistantships with partial tuition reimbursements, Federal Work-Study, institutionally sponsored loans, scholarships/grants, and unspecified assistantships available. Support available to part-time students. Financial award application deadline: 3/1; financial award applicants required to submit FAFSA. *Unit head:* Dr. Carol Bishop Mills, Director, 561-297-0042, Fax: 561-297-2615, E-mail: millsc@fau.edu. *Application contact:* Dr. Stephen Charbonneau, Graduate Director, 561-297-3856, Fax: 561-297-2615, E-mail: scharbo1@fau.edu.
Website: http://www.fau.edu/scms/

Florida Institute of Technology, College of Psychology and Liberal Arts, Program in Global Strategic Communication, Melbourne, FL 32901-6975. Offers global strategic communication (MS). *Program availability:* Part-time. *Degree requirements:* For master's, comprehensive exam (for some programs), thesis or alternative, minimum of 36 credit hours. *Entrance requirements:* For master's, GRE General Test (recommended), 2 letters of recommendation, statement of objectives, previous work experience, transcripts. Additional exam requirements/recommendations for international students: required—TOEFL (minimum score 550 paper-based; 79 iBT). Electronic applications accepted.

Florida International University, College of Communication, Architecture and The Arts, School of Communication and Journalism, Miami, FL 33199. Offers mass communication (MS), including global strategic communications, Spanish language journalism. *Program availability:* Part-time, evening/weekend. *Faculty:* 30 full-time (22 women), 71 part-time/adjunct (42 women). *Students:* 85 full-time (68 women), 76 part-time (59 women); includes 117 minority (20 Black or African American, non-Hispanic/Latino; 2 Asian, non-Hispanic/Latino; 88 Hispanic/Latino; 7 Two or more races, non-Hispanic/Latino), 22 international. Average age 28. 120 applicants, 75% accepted, 63 enrolled. In 2019, 107 master's awarded. *Entrance requirements:* For master's, 2 letters of recommendation; minimum GPA of 3.0 during last 60 hours of upper-level work; resume. Additional exam requirements/recommendations for international students: required—TOEFL (minimum score 550 paper-based; 80 iBT). *Application deadline:* For fall admission, 6/1 for domestic students, 4/1 for international students; for spring admission, 10/1 for domestic students, 9/1 for international students. Applications are processed on a rolling basis. Application fee: $30. Electronic applications accepted. *Expenses: Tuition, area resident:* Full-time $8912; part-time $446 per credit hour. *Tuition, state resident:* full-time $8912; part-time $446 per credit hour. *Tuition, nonresident:* full-time $21,393; part-time $992 per credit hour. *Required fees:* $2194. *Financial support:* Institutionally sponsored loans and scholarships/grants available. Financial award application deadline: 3/1; financial award applicants required to submit FAFSA. *Unit head:* Dr. Aileen Izquierdo, Chair, 305-919-5795, E-mail: aileen.izquierdo@fiu.edu. *Application contact:* Nanett Rojas, Manager, Admissions Operations, 305-348-7464, Fax: 305-348-7441, E-mail: gradadm@fiu.edu.
Website: https://scj.fiu.edu/

Florida State University, The Graduate School, College of Communication and Information, School of Communication, Tallahassee, FL 32306. Offers communication theory and research (PhD); integrated marketing communication (MA, MS); media and communication studies (MA, MS); public interest media and communication (MA, MS). *Program availability:* Part-time. *Faculty:* 23 full-time (13 women), 1 part-time/adjunct (0 women). *Students:* 19 full-time (16 women), 121 part-time (84 women); includes 73 minority (22 Black or African American, non-Hispanic/Latino; 15 Asian, non-Hispanic/Latino; 27 Hispanic/Latino; 9 Two or more races, non-Hispanic/Latino). Average age 24. 196 applicants, 54% accepted, 48 enrolled. In 2019, 65 master's, 5 doctorates awarded. *Degree requirements:* For master's, thesis (for some programs); for doctorate, comprehensive exam, thesis/dissertation. *Entrance requirements:* For master's, GRE General Test, minimum GPA of 3.0; for doctorate, GRE General Test, minimum GPA of 3.3 in graduate course work. Additional exam requirements/recommendations for international students: required—TOEFL (minimum score 600 paper-based; 100 iBT), IELTS (minimum score 7). *Application deadline:* For fall admission, 7/1 priority date for domestic students, 5/1 priority date for international students; for spring admission, 11/1 priority date for domestic and international students; for summer admission, 3/1 priority date for domestic and international students. Applications are processed on a rolling basis. Application fee: $30. Electronic applications accepted. *Expenses:* $5,748 state resident full-time, $2,874 state resident part-time; $13,320 nonresident full-time, $6,660 nonresident part-time. *Financial support:* In 2019–20, 109 students received support, including 20 research assistantships with full tuition reimbursements available (averaging $12,726 per year), 139 teaching assistantships with full tuition reimbursements available (averaging $10,602 per year); scholarships/grants, tuition waivers (full and partial), and unspecified assistantships also available. Financial award application deadline: 11/1; financial award applicants required to submit FAFSA. *Unit head:* Dr. Jennifer Proffitt, Director, 850-644-5034, Fax: 850-644-8642, E-mail: jennifer.proffitt@cci.fsu.edu. *Application contact:* Natashia Hinson-Turner, Graduate Coordinator, 850-644-5034, Fax: 850-644-8642, E-mail: comgradadvising@cci.fsu.edu.
Website: http://www.cci.fsu.edu

Fordham University, Gabelli School of Business, New York, NY 10023. Offers accounting (MBA, MS); applied statistics and decision-making (MS); business economics (DPS); capital markets (DPS); communications and media management (MBA); electronic business (MBA); entrepreneurship (MBA); finance (MBA, PhD); global finance (MS); global sustainability (MBA); health administration (MS); healthcare management (MBA); information systems (MBA, MS); investor relations (MS); management (EMBA, MBA, MS, PhD); marketing (MBA); marketing intelligence (MS); media management (MS); nonprofit leadership (MS); quantitative finance (MS); strategy and decision-making (DPS); taxation (MS); JD/MBA; MS/MBA. *Accreditation:* AACSB. *Program availability:* Part-time, evening/weekend, 100% online, blended/hybrid learning. *Faculty:* 130 full-time (49 women), 73 part-time/adjunct (12 women). *Students:* 1,038 full-time, 503 part-time; includes 227 minority (57 Black or African American, non-Hispanic/Latino; 1 American Indian or Alaska Native, non-Hispanic/Latino; 65 Asian, non-Hispanic/Latino; 91 Hispanic/Latino; 1 Native Hawaiian or other Pacific Islander, non-Hispanic/Latino; 12 Two or more races, non-Hispanic/Latino), 985 international. Average age 27. 4,250 applicants, 62% accepted, 764 enrolled. In 2019, 899 master's awarded. Terminal master's awarded for partial completion of doctoral program. *Degree requirements:* For master's, internships (for some degrees); for doctorate, comprehensive exam (for some programs), thesis/dissertation. *Entrance requirements:* For master's, GMAT/GRE, 2 letters of recommendation, resume, 2 essays, transcripts, interview. Additional exam requirements/recommendations for international students: required—TOEFL (minimum score 100 iBT), IELTS (minimum score 7). *Application deadline:* For fall admission, 11/15 for domestic and international students; for winter admission, 1/10 for domestic students, 1/1 for international students; for spring admission, 5/15 for domestic students, 3/1 for international students; for summer admission, 7/10 for domestic students, 6/5 for international students. Application fee: $130. Electronic applications accepted. *Expenses:* Contact institution. *Financial support:* Career-related internships or fieldwork, institutionally sponsored loans, scholarships/grants, and unspecified assistantships available. Support available to part-time students. Financial award application deadline: 6/5; financial award applicants required to submit FAFSA. *Unit head:* Dr. Donna Rapaccioli, Dean, 212-636-6165, Fax: 212-307-1779, E-mail: rapaccioli@fordham.edu. *Application contact:* Lawrence Mur'ray, Senior Assistant Dean of Graduate Admissions and Advising, 212-636-6200, Fax: 212-636-7076, E-mail: admissionsgb@fordham.edu.
Website: http://www.fordham.edu/gabelli

Fordham University, Graduate School of Arts and Sciences, Department of Communication and Media Studies, New York, NY 10458. Offers public media (MA). *Program availability:* Part-time, evening/weekend. *Students:* Average age 25. 88 applicants, 52% accepted, 17 enrolled. In 2019, 18 master's awarded. *Degree requirements:* For master's, thesis, internship. *Entrance requirements:* For master's, GRE General Test. Additional exam requirements/recommendations for international students: required—TOEFL (minimum score 600 paper-based). *Application deadline:* For fall admission, 1/4 priority date for domestic students; for spring admission, 11/1 for domestic students. Application fee: $70. Electronic applications accepted. *Financial support:* In 2019–20, 3 students received support, including 2 research assistantships with full and partial tuition reimbursements available (averaging $23,200 per year); career-related internships or fieldwork, Federal Work-Study, institutionally sponsored loans, scholarships/grants, tuition waivers (full and partial), and unspecified assistantships also available. Financial award application deadline: 1/4. *Unit head:* Jacqueline Reich, Chair, 718-817-4850, E-mail: jreich8@fordham.edu. *Application contact:* Garrett Marino, Director of Graduate Admissions, 718-817-4419, Fax: 718-817-3566, E-mail: gmarino10@fordham.edu.

Fort Hays State University, Graduate School, College of Arts, Humanities, and Social Sciences, Department of Communication Studies, Hays, KS 67601-4099. Offers communication (MS). *Program availability:* Part-time. *Degree requirements:* For master's, comprehensive exam, thesis optional. *Entrance requirements:* Additional exam requirements/recommendations for international students: required—TOEFL (minimum score 550 paper-based). Electronic applications accepted.

George Mason University, College of Humanities and Social Sciences, Department of Communication, Fairfax, VA 22030. Offers communication (MA, PhD, Certificate); science communication (Certificate). *Degree requirements:* For master's, comprehensive exam, thesis or project; for doctorate, comprehensive exam, thesis/dissertation; for Certificate, 15-18 credits. *Entrance requirements:* For master's, GRE, expanded goals statement; 2 letters of recommendation; resume; official transcripts; writing sample; for doctorate, GRE, 3 letters of recommendation; expanded goals statement; resume; official transcript; writing sample; for Certificate, GRE, expanded goals statement, resume, 2 letters of recommendation, official transcripts. Additional exam requirements/recommendations for international students: required—TOEFL (minimum score 570 paper-based; 88 iBT), IELTS (minimum score 6.5), PTE (minimum score 59). Electronic applications accepted.

Georgetown University, Graduate School of Arts and Sciences, Communication, Culture & Technology Program, Washington, DC 20057. Offers MA. *Program availability:* Part-time, evening/weekend. *Faculty:* 10 full-time (4 women), 12 part-time/adjunct (7 women). *Students:* 120 full-time (100 women), 10 part-time (6 women). Average age 25. *Degree requirements:* For master's, thesis optional, 36 graduate credits. *Entrance requirements:* For master's, GRE General Test (unless applicant already has a master's or higher), 3 letters of recommendation, writing sample, resume, statement of purpose, video statement (highly recommended). Additional exam requirements/recommendations for international students: required—TOEFL (minimum score 100 iBT), IELTS (minimum score 7.5). *Application deadline:* For fall admission, 4/1 for domestic and international students; for spring admission, 10/1 for domestic and international students. Application fee: $90. Electronic applications accepted. *Financial support:* Fellowships and scholarships/grants available. Financial award application deadline: 1/15. *Unit head:* Prof. Matthew Tinkcom, Director, 202-687-6618, E-mail: Matthew.Tinkcom@georgetown.edu. *Application contact:* Ai-Hui Tan, Director, CCT Academic Affairs, 202-687-6618, E-mail: cctadmissions@georgetown.edu.
Website: http://cct.georgetown.edu/

The George Washington University, Elliott School of International Affairs, Program in Global Communication, Washington, DC 20052. Offers MA. *Program availability:* Part-time. *Degree requirements:* For master's, one foreign language, capstone project. *Entrance requirements:* For master's, GRE General Test, 2 years (or equivalent) of a modern, spoken foreign language; introductory microeconomics/macroeconomics. Additional exam requirements/recommendations for international students: required—TOEFL (minimum score 100 iBT), IELTS (minimum score 7). Electronic applications accepted.

Georgia State University, College of Arts and Sciences, Department of Communication, Atlanta, GA 30302-3083. Offers film, video, and digital imaging (MA), including critical studies, production, screenwriting; human communication and social influence (MA); mass communication (MA); media and society (PhD); moving image studies (PhD); public communication (PhD); rhetoric and politics (PhD). *Program availability:* Part-time. *Faculty:* 22 full-time (16 women), 1 part-time/adjunct (0 women). *Students:* 67 full-time (46 women), 26 part-time (17 women); includes 44 minority (40 Black or African American, non-Hispanic/Latino; 1 Asian, non-Hispanic/Latino; 1 Hispanic/Latino; 1 Native Hawaiian or other Pacific Islander, non-Hispanic/Latino; 1 Two or more races, non-Hispanic/Latino), 12 international. Average age 36. 82 applicants, 49% accepted, 22 enrolled. In 2019, 9 master's, 5 doctorates awarded. *Degree requirements:* For master's, variable foreign language requirement, thesis (for some programs); for doctorate, comprehensive exam, thesis/dissertation. *Entrance requirements:* For master's and doctorate, GRE. Additional exam requirements/recommendations for international students: required—TOEFL (minimum score 550 paper-based; 80 iBT), IELTS (minimum score 6.5). *Application deadline:* For fall admission, 2/10 for domestic and international students; for spring admission, 10/15 for domestic and international students. Application fee: $50. Electronic applications accepted. *Expenses: Tuition, area resident:* Full-time $7164; part-time $398 per credit hour. *Tuition, state resident:* full-time $7164; part-time $398 per credit hour. *Tuition, nonresident:* full-time $22,662; part-time $1259 per credit hour. *International tuition:*

$22,662 full-time. *Required fees:* $2128; $312 per credit hour. Tuition and fees vary according to course load and program. *Financial support:* In 2019–20, fellowships with tuition reimbursements (averaging $15,000 per year), teaching assistantships with tuition reimbursements (averaging $15,000 per year) were awarded; career-related internships or fieldwork and unspecified assistantships also available. Financial award applicants required to submit FAFSA. *Unit head:* Dr. Greg Lisby, Chair, 404-413-5639, Fax: 404-413-5634, E-mail: glisby@gsu.edu. *Application contact:* Dr. Greg Lisby, Chair, 404-413-5639, Fax: 404-413-5634, E-mail: glisby@gsu.edu. Website: http://communication.gsu.edu

Governors State University, College of Arts and Sciences, Program in Communication and Training, University Park, IL 60484. Offers communication studies (MA). *Program availability:* Part-time. *Faculty:* 57 full-time (33 women), 72 part-time/adjunct (40 women). *Students:* 1 (woman) full-time, 9 part-time (8 women); includes 8 minority (7 Black or African American, non-Hispanic/Latino; 1 Hispanic/Latino). Average age 45. 11 applicants, 45% accepted, 5 enrolled. In 2019, 9 master's awarded. *Application deadline:* For fall admission, 4/1 for domestic students. Applications are processed on a rolling basis. Application fee: $50. Electronic applications accepted. *Expenses: Tuition, area resident:* Full-time $8472; part-time $353 per credit hour. Tuition, state resident: full-time $8472; part-time $353 per credit hour. Tuition, nonresident: full-time $16,944; part-time $706 per credit hour. *International tuition:* $16,944 full-time. *Required fees:* $2520; $105 per credit hour. $38 per term. Tuition and fees vary according to course load, degree level and program. *Financial support:* Application deadline: 5/1; applicants required to submit FAFSA. *Unit head:* Jason Zingsheim, Chair, Division of Arts and Letters, 708-534-5000 Ext. 7493, E-mail: jzingsheim@govst.edu. *Application contact:* Jason Zingsheim, Chair, Division of Arts and Letters, 708-534-5000 Ext. 7493, E-mail: jzingsheim@govst.edu.

Grand Valley State University, College of Liberal Arts and Sciences, School of Communications, Allendale, MI 49401-9403. Offers MS. *Program availability:* Part-time, evening/weekend. *Faculty:* 2 full-time (0 women), 1 part-time/adjunct (0 women). *Students:* 15 full-time (9 women), 26 part-time (18 women); includes 14 minority (8 Black or African American, non-Hispanic/Latino; 2 Hispanic/Latino; 4 Two or more races, non-Hispanic/Latino), 4 international. Average age 29. 33 applicants, 100% accepted, 14 enrolled. In 2019, 22 master's awarded. *Degree requirements:* For master's, thesis optional, thesis or project. *Entrance requirements:* For master's, minimum GPA of 3.0 in last 60 hours, 2 letters of recommendation, interview, essay or personal statement. Additional exam requirements/recommendations for international students: required—TOEFL (minimum iBT score of 80), IELTS (6.5), or Michigan English Language Assessment Battery (77). *Application deadline:* For fall admission, 8/15 priority date for domestic students; for winter admission, 12/15 priority date for domestic students; for spring admission, 4/15 priority date for domestic students. Applications are processed on a rolling basis. Application fee: $30. Electronic applications accepted. *Expenses:* $671 per credit hour, 36 credit hours. *Financial support:* In 2019–20, 13 students received support, including 9 fellowships, 1 research assistantship with full and partial tuition reimbursement available (averaging $8,000 per year); career-related internships or fieldwork, Federal Work-Study, and institutionally sponsored loans also available. Support available to part-time students. Financial award application deadline: 4/15. *Unit head:* Dr. Richard Besel, Department Director, 616-331-8045, Fax: 616-331-2700, E-mail: beselri@gvsu.edu. *Application contact:* Dr. Alex Nesterenko, Graduate Program Director, 616-331-3667, Fax: 616-331-2700, E-mail: nesterea@gvsu.edu. Website: https://www.gvsu.edu/grad/communications/

Harvard University, Extension School, Cambridge, MA 02138-3722. Offers applied sciences (CAS); biotechnology (ALM); educational technologies (ALM); educational technology (CET); English for graduate and professional studies (DGP); environmental management (ALM, CEM); information technology (ALM); journalism (ALM); liberal arts (ALM); management (ALM, CM); mathematics for teaching (ALM); museum studies (ALM); premedical studies (Diploma); publication and communication (CPC). *Program availability:* Part-time, evening/weekend. *Degree requirements:* For master's, thesis. *Entrance requirements:* For master's, 3 completed graduate courses with grade of B or higher. Additional exam requirements/recommendations for international students: required—TOEFL (minimum score 600 paper-based), TWE (minimum score 5). *Expenses:* Contact institution.

Hawaii Pacific University, College of Liberal Arts, Program in Communication, Honolulu, HI 96813. Offers MA. *Program availability:* Part-time, evening/weekend. *Entrance requirements:* For master's, transcripts, personal statement, letter of recommendation, resume. Additional exam requirements/recommendations for international students: recommended—TOEFL (minimum score 550 paper-based; 80 iBT), IELTS (minimum score 6), TWE (minimum score 5). Electronic applications accepted. *Expenses: Tuition:* Full-time $18,000; part-time $1125 per credit. *Required fees:* $213; $38 per semester.

Howard University, Cathy Hughes School of Communications, Washington, DC 20059-0002. Offers MA, MFA, MS, PhD. *Program availability:* Part-time, evening/weekend. Terminal master's awarded for partial completion of doctoral program. *Degree requirements:* For master's, comprehensive exam (for some programs), thesis optional; for doctorate, one foreign language, comprehensive exam, thesis/dissertation. *Entrance requirements:* For master's, GRE General Test, minimum GPA of 3.0; for doctorate, GRE General Test, minimum GPA of 3.2. Additional exam requirements/recommendations for international students: required—TOEFL. Electronic applications accepted. *Expenses:* Contact institution.

Idaho State University, Graduate School, College of Arts and Letters, Department of Communication, Media, and Persuasion, Pocatello, ID 83209-8115. Offers communication (MA). *Program availability:* Part-time. *Degree requirements:* For master's, comprehensive exam, paper or thesis. *Entrance requirements:* For master's, GRE General Test, minimum GPA of 3.0 in all upper-level courses. Additional exam requirements/recommendations for international students: required—TOEFL (minimum score 550 paper-based; 80 iBT). Electronic applications accepted.

Illinois Institute of Technology, Graduate College, Lewis College of Human Sciences, Department of Humanities, Chicago, IL 60616. Offers information architecture (MS); technical communication (PhD); technical communication and information design (MS). *Program availability:* Part-time. *Degree requirements:* For master's, comprehensive exam, thesis or alternative; for doctorate, comprehensive exam, thesis/dissertation. *Entrance requirements:* For master's, GRE General Test (minimum score 144 Quantitative, 153 Verbal, and 4.0 Analytical Writing), minimum undergraduate GPA of 3.0; 2 letters of recommendation from faculty or supervisors; professional statement discussing academic goals; for doctorate, GRE General Test (minimum score 144 Quantitative, 153 Verbal, and 4.0 Analytical Writing), bachelor's or master's degree in a field that, in combination with the 27-credit hour technical core, would provide a solid basis for advanced academic work leading to original research in the field; 3 letters of recommendation from faculty or supervisors; professional statement discussing academic goals. Additional exam requirements/recommendations for international students: required—TOEFL (minimum score 95 iBT); recommended—IELTS (minimum score 7). Electronic applications accepted.

Illinois State University, Graduate School, College of Arts and Sciences, School of Communication, Normal, IL 61790. Offers MA, MS. *Faculty:* 40 full-time (20 women), 24 part-time/adjunct (19 women). *Students:* 64 full-time (50 women), 14 part-time (9 women). Average age 24. 71 applicants, 66% accepted, 33 enrolled. In 2019, 35 master's awarded. *Degree requirements:* For master's, thesis or alternative. *Entrance requirements:* For master's, GRE General Test, minimum GPA of 2.8 in last 60 hours of course work. *Application deadline:* Applications are processed on a rolling basis. Application fee: $50. *Expenses: Tuition, area resident:* Full-time $7956; part-time $9767 per year. Tuition, nonresident: full-time $9233; part-time $17,592 per year. *Required fees:* $1797. *Financial support:* In 2019–20, 2 research assistantships, 42 teaching assistantships were awarded; tuition waivers (full) and unspecified assistantships also available. Financial award application deadline: 4/1. *Unit head:* Dr. Stephen Hunt, Executive Director, 309-438-7279, E-mail: skhunt2@IllinoisState.edu. *Application contact:* Dr. Aimee Miller-Ott, Graduate Coordinator, 309-438-3277, E-mail: aeott@IllinoisState.edu. Website: http://www.communication.ilstu.edu/

Indiana State University, College of Graduate and Professional Studies, College of Arts and Sciences, Department of Communication, Terre Haute, IN 47809. Offers communication studies (MA); radio, television and film (MA). *Program availability:* Part-time. *Degree requirements:* For master's, thesis (for some programs), oral and written exam. *Entrance requirements:* For master's, GRE General Test. Additional exam requirements/recommendations for international students: required—TOEFL.

Indiana University of Pennsylvania, School of Graduate Studies and Research, College of Education and Communications, Department of Communications Media, Indiana, PA 15705. Offers communications media and instructional technology (PhD). *Program availability:* Part-time, evening/weekend. *Faculty:* 7 full-time (2 women). *Students:* 18 full-time (10 women), 36 part-time (14 women); includes 12 minority (8 Black or African American, non-Hispanic/Latino; 3 Hispanic/Latino; 1 Two or more races, non-Hispanic/Latino), 8 international. Average age 36. 43 applicants, 72% accepted, 22 enrolled. In 2019, 7 doctorates awarded. Terminal master's awarded for partial completion of doctoral program. *Degree requirements:* For doctorate, comprehensive exam, thesis/dissertation. *Entrance requirements:* For doctorate, GRE or MAT if earned masters less than 5 years ago, Goal statement, 2 letters of recommendation and official transcript. If earned masters degree five or more years prior to application and have five or more years of full time employment: curriculum vitae, writing sample, personal interview and academic portfolio. If earned masters less than five years ago: curriculum vitae and writing sample. Additional exam requirements/recommendations for international students: required—TOEFL (minimum score 540 paper-based; 76 iBT), IELTS (minimum score 6), TOEFL or IELTS. *Application deadline:* Applications are processed on a rolling basis. Application fee: $50. Electronic applications accepted. *Expenses: Tuition, area resident:* Full-time $9288; part-time $516 per credit. Tuition, nonresident: full-time $13,932; part-time $774 per credit. *Required fees:* $4454. One-time fee: $115 full-time. Tuition and fees vary according to course load and program. *Financial support:* In 2019–20, 4 fellowships with full tuition reimbursements (averaging $1,075 per year), 11 research assistantships with tuition reimbursements (averaging $5,353 per year), 3 teaching assistantships with partial tuition reimbursements (averaging $25,035 per year) were awarded; career-related internships or fieldwork, Federal Work-Study, scholarships/grants, tuition waivers (full), and unspecified assistantships also available. Support available to part-time students. Financial award application deadline: 4/15; financial award applicants required to submit FAFSA. *Unit head:* Dr. Gail Wilson, Chairperson, 724-357-2492, Fax: 724-357-5503, E-mail: bgwilson@iup.edu. *Application contact:* Amber Dworek, Director of Graduate Admissions, 724-357-2222, E-mail: a.m.dworek@iup.edu. Website: http://www.iup.edu/commmedia/

Indiana University-Purdue University Indianapolis, School of Liberal Arts, Department of Communication Studies, Indianapolis, IN 46202. Offers applied communication (MA); health communication (PhD). *Program availability:* Part-time. *Degree requirements:* For master's, comprehensive exam, thesis; for doctorate, thesis/dissertation. *Entrance requirements:* For doctorate, master's degree. Additional exam requirements/recommendations for international students: required—TOEFL; recommended—IELTS. Electronic applications accepted.

Indiana University South Bend, Ernestine M. Raclin School of the Arts, South Bend, IN 46615. Offers communication studies (MA); music (MM), including composition, performance; music performance (AD). *Accreditation:* NASM. *Program availability:* Part-time. *Entrance requirements:* For master's, performance audition. Additional exam requirements/recommendations for international students: required—TOEFL (minimum score 600 paper-based; 90 iBT). Electronic applications accepted. *Expenses:* Contact institution.

Instituto Tecnologico de Santo Domingo, Graduate School, Area of Humanities and Social Sciences, Santo Domingo, Dominican Republic. Offers accounting (Certificate); adult education (Certificate); applied linguistics (MA); economics (MA); education (M Ed); educational psychology (MA, Certificate); gender and development (MA, Certificate); humanistic studies (MA); international marketing management (Certificate); international relations in the Caribbean basin (Certificate); intervention systems in family therapy (MA); linguistic and literary communication (Certificate); pedagogical support (MA); social science education (M Ed) sustainable human development (MA); terminal illness and death psychology (Certificate); youth and adult education (M Ed).

Instituto Tecnológico y de Estudios Superiores de Monterrey, Campus Ciudad Obregón, Programs in Education, Program in Communications, Ciudad Obregón, Mexico. Offers ME.

Instituto Tecnológico y de Estudios Superiores de Monterrey, Campus Monterrey, Graduate and Research Division, Program in Natural and Social Sciences, Monterrey, Mexico. Offers biotechnology (MS); chemistry (MS, PhD); communications (MS); education (MA). *Program availability:* Part-time. *Degree requirements:* For master's, one foreign language, thesis; for doctorate, one foreign language, thesis/dissertation. *Entrance requirements:* For master's, EXADEP; for doctorate, EXADEP, master's degree in related field. Additional exam requirements/recommendations for international students: required—TOEFL.

International University in Geneva, Leadership Programs, Geneva, Switzerland. Offers international relations and diplomacy (MIRD); media and communication (MA); public administration (DPA). *Degree requirements:* For master's, comprehensive exam. *Entrance requirements:* Additional exam requirements/recommendations for international students: required—TOEFL. Electronic applications accepted.

James Madison University, The Graduate School, College of Arts and Letters, Program in Communication and Advocacy, Harrisonburg, VA 22807. Offers environmental communication (MA); health communication (MA); strategic communication (MA). *Program availability:* Part-time, evening/weekend. *Students:* 26 full-time (20 women), 7 part-time (all women); includes 8 minority (5 Black or African American, non-Hispanic/Latino; 1 Asian, non-Hispanic/Latino; 2 Two or more races, non-Hispanic/Latino), 6 international. Average age 30. In 2019, 12 master's awarded. Application fee: $60. Electronic applications accepted. *Financial support:* In 2019–20, 23 students received support, including 7 teaching assistantships with full tuition reimbursements available (averaging $9,284 per year); fellowships, Federal Work-Study, and assistantships (averaging $7911) also available. Financial award application deadline: 3/1; financial award applicants required to submit FAFSA. *Unit head:* Dr. Eric M. Fife, Director of the School of Communication Studies, 540-568-6449, E-mail: fifeem@jmu.edu. *Application contact:* Lynette D. Michael, Director of Graduate Admissions, 540-568-6131 Ext. 6395, Fax: 540-568-7860, E-mail: michaeld@jmu.edu. Website: http://www.jmu.edu/commstudies/

Johns Hopkins University, Advanced Academic Programs, Program in Communication, Washington, DC 21218. Offers MA, MA/MBA. *Program availability:* Part-time, evening/weekend, online learning. *Entrance requirements:* For master's, minimum GPA of 3.0, strong writing skills. Additional exam requirements/recommendations for international students: required—TOEFL (minimum score 100 iBT). Electronic applications accepted.

Johns Hopkins University, Engineering Program for Professionals, Part-time Program in Computer Science, Baltimore, MD 21218. Offers communications and networking (MS); computer science (Post-Master's Certificate). *Program availability:* Part-time, evening/weekend, 100% online, blended/hybrid learning. *Entrance requirements:* Additional exam requirements/recommendations for international students: required—TOEFL (minimum score 600 paper-based; 100 iBT). Electronic applications accepted.

Johns Hopkins University, Engineering Program for Professionals, Part-time Program in Electrical and Computer Engineering, Baltimore, MD 21218. Offers communications and networking (MS); electrical and computer engineering (Graduate Certificate, Post-Master's Certificate); photonics (MS). *Program availability:* Part-time, evening/weekend, 100% online, blended/hybrid learning. *Entrance requirements:* Additional exam requirements/recommendations for international students: required—TOEFL (minimum score 600 paper-based; 100 iBT). Electronic applications accepted.

Kansas State University, Graduate School, College of Arts and Sciences, A.Q. Miller School of Journalism and Mass Communications, Manhattan, KS 66506. Offers advertising (MS); community journalism (MS); global communication (MS); health communication (MS); media management (MS); public relations (MS). *Program availability:* Part-time, evening/weekend. *Degree requirements:* For master's, comprehensive exam, thesis. *Entrance requirements:* For master's, GRE General Test, minimum GPA of 3.0. Additional exam requirements/recommendations for international students: required—TOEFL (minimum score 79 iBT). Electronic applications accepted.

Kansas State University, Graduate School, College of Arts and Sciences, Department of Communication Studies, Manhattan, KS 66505. Offers MA. *Degree requirements:* For master's, thesis or alternative. *Entrance requirements:* For master's, GRE General Test (recommended), minimum GPA of 3.0. Additional exam requirements/recommendations for international students: required—TOEFL. Electronic applications accepted.

Kansas State University, Graduate School, College of Arts and Sciences, Department of English, Manhattan, KS 66506. Offers English (MA); technical writing and professional communication (Graduate Certificate). *Program availability:* Part-time. *Degree requirements:* For master's, one foreign language, thesis optional. *Entrance requirements:* For master's, GRE, minimum B average in English. Additional exam requirements/recommendations for international students: required—TOEFL. Electronic applications accepted.

Kansas State University, Graduate School, College of Engineering, Department of Electrical and Computer Engineering, Manhattan, KS 66506. Offers electrical engineering (MS), including bioengineering, communication systems, design of computer systems, electrical engineering, energy and power systems, integrated circuits and devices, real time embedded systems, renewable energy, signal processing. *Program availability:* Part-time, evening/weekend, online learning. *Degree requirements:* For master's, thesis or alternative, final exam; for doctorate, thesis/dissertation, final exam, preliminary exams. *Entrance requirements:* For master's, GRE General Test, bachelor's degree in electrical engineering or computer science, minimum GPA of 3.0; for doctorate, GRE General Test. Additional exam requirements/recommendations for international students: required—TOEFL (minimum score 600 paper-based; 85 iBT). Electronic applications accepted.

Kean University, College of Liberal Arts, Program in Communication Studies, Union, NJ 07083. Offers MA. *Program availability:* Part-time. *Faculty:* 16 full-time (8 women). *Students:* 10 full-time (8 women), 11 part-time (8 women); includes 13 minority (10 Black or African American, non-Hispanic/Latino; 2 Hispanic/Latino; 1 Two or more races, non-Hispanic/Latino), 2 international. Average age 30. 12 applicants, 75% accepted, 6 enrolled. In 2019, 5 master's awarded. *Degree requirements:* For master's, comprehensive exam, thesis optional. *Entrance requirements:* For master's, GRE General Test, minimum cumulative GPA of 3.0, official transcripts from all institutions attended, three letters of recommendation, professional resume/curriculum vitae, personal statement. Additional exam requirements/recommendations for international students: required—TOEFL (minimum score 550 paper-based; 79 iBT), IELTS (minimum score 6.5). *Application deadline:* For fall admission, 6/30 for domestic and international students; for spring admission, 12/1 for domestic and international students. Applications are processed on a rolling basis. Application fee: $75. Electronic applications accepted. *Expenses:* Tuition, state resident: full-time $15,326; part-time $748 per credit. Tuition, nonresident: full-time $20,288; part-time $902 per credit. *Required fees:* $2149.50; $91.25 per credit. Tuition and fees vary according to course level, course load, degree level and program. *Financial support:* Scholarships/grants and unspecified assistantships available. Financial award applicants required to submit FAFSA. *Unit head:* Dr. Wenli Yuan, Program Coordinator, 908-737-0471, E-mail: wyuan@kean.edu. *Application contact:* Amy Clark, Program Assistant, 908-737-7100, E-mail: grad-adm@kean.edu.
Website: http://grad.kean.edu/masters-programs/communication-studies

Kennesaw State University, College of Humanities and Social Sciences, Program in Integrated Global Communication, Kennesaw, GA 30144. Offers MA. *Students:* 6 full-time (5 women), 16 part-time (12 women); includes 8 minority (7 Black or African American, non-Hispanic/Latino; 1 Hispanic/Latino), 1 international. Average age 38. 7 applicants, 86% accepted, 3 enrolled. In 2019, 9 master's awarded. *Entrance requirements:* For master's, GRE, BA or BS in communication or related field from accredited college or university; official transcripts; two-page resume; 500-word personal statement; three letters of recommendation. Additional exam requirements/recommendations for international students: required—TOEFL (minimum score 80 iBT), IELTS (minimum score 6.5). *Application deadline:* For fall admission, 6/1 for domestic and international students. Application fee: $60. Electronic applications accepted. *Expenses: Tuition, area resident:* Full-time $7104; part-time $296 per credit hour. Tuition, state resident: full-time $7104; part-time $296 per credit hour. Tuition, nonresident: full-time $25,584; part-time $1066 per credit hour. *International tuition:* $25,584 full-time. *Required fees:* $2006; $1706 per unit. $853 per semester. *Financial support:* Applicants required to submit FAFSA. *Unit head:* Director, 470-578-3638. *Application contact:* Admissions Counselor, 470-578-4377, Fax: 470-578-9172, E-mail: ksugrad@kennesaw.edu.
Website: http://chss.kennesaw.edu/maigc/

Kent State University, College of Communication and Information, School of Communication Studies, Kent, OH 44242-0001. Offers communication studies (MA);

MBA/MA. *Program availability:* Part-time. *Faculty:* 6 full-time (5 women). *Students:* 8 full-time (7 women), 5 part-time (3 women); includes 3 minority (all Black or African American, non-Hispanic/Latino), 3 international. Average age 29. 18 applicants, 83% accepted, 7 enrolled. In 2019, 9 master's awarded. *Degree requirements:* For master's, thesis, coursework, project, or internship. *Entrance requirements:* For master's, GRE General Test (for applicants seeking assistantship), minimum GPA of 3.0, goal statement, undergraduate major/minor in communication, scholarly writing sample, 3 letters of recommendation, curriculum vitae/resume. Additional exam requirements/recommendations for international students: required—TOEFL (minimum score 94 iBT), IELTS (minimum score 7), PTE (minimum score 65), Michigan English Language Assessment Battery (minimum score 82). *Application deadline:* For fall admission, 1/15 for domestic students, 12/20 for international students; for spring admission, 11/15 for domestic students, 10/20 for international students. Applications are processed on a rolling basis. Application fee: $45 ($70 for international students). Electronic applications accepted. *Financial support:* Research assistantships with full tuition reimbursements, teaching assistantships with full tuition reimbursements, career-related internships or fieldwork, and unspecified assistantships available. Financial award application deadline: 1/15. *Unit head:* Dr. Elizabeth E. Graham, Director & Professor, 330-672-2659, E-mail: egraha18@kent.edu. *Application contact:* Dr. Elizabeth E. Graham, Director & Professor, 330-672-2659, E-mail: egraha18@kent.edu.
Website: http://www.kent.edu/comm/

La Salle University, School of Arts and Sciences, Program in Strategic Communication, Philadelphia, PA 19141-1199. Offers communication consulting and development (MA); communication management (MA); general professional communication (MA); professional and business communication (Certificate); public relations (MA); social and new media (Certificate). *Program availability:* Part-time, evening/weekend, online learning. *Degree requirements:* For master's, practicum. *Entrance requirements:* For master's, writing assessment, professional resume; minimum overall B average; two letters of recommendation (if GPA below 3.25); brief personal statement (about 500 words); interview; for Certificate, writing assessment, minimum GPA of 2.75 in undergraduate studies; brief personal statement (about 500 words); interview. Additional exam requirements/recommendations for international students: required—TOEFL. Electronic applications accepted. Application fee is waived when completed online. *Expenses:* Contact institution.

Lasell College, Graduate and Professional Studies in Communication, Newton, MA 02466-2709. Offers health communication (MSC, Graduate Certificate); integrated marketing communication (MSC, Graduate Certificate); public relations (MSC, Graduate Certificate). *Program availability:* Part-time, evening/weekend, 100% online, blended/hybrid learning. *Faculty:* 3 full-time (2 women), 10 part-time/adjunct (4 women). *Students:* 25 full-time (18 women), 34 part-time (27 women); includes 10 minority (7 Black or African American, non-Hispanic/Latino; 3 Hispanic/Latino), 15 international. Average age 31. 40 applicants, 48% accepted, 14 enrolled. In 2019, 34 master's, 2 other advanced degrees awarded. *Degree requirements:* For master's, comprehensive exam, thesis or alternative, minimum GPA of 3.0; special project or internship. *Entrance requirements:* For master's, one-page personal statement, 2 letters of recommendation, resume, bachelor's degree transcript; for Graduate Certificate, bachelor's degree transcript, 2 letters of recommendation, 1-page personal statement, resume. Additional exam requirements/recommendations for international students: required—TOEFL (minimum score 550 paper-based, 79 iBT) or IELTS (minimum score 6). *Application deadline:* For fall admission, 8/31 priority date for domestic students, 6/30 priority date for international students; for spring admission, 12/31 priority date for domestic students, 10/31 priority date for international students. Applications are processed on a rolling basis. Electronic applications accepted. *Expenses: Tuition:* Part-time $600 per credit. *Required fees:* $40 per semester. *Financial support:* Federal Work-Study, scholarships/grants, and tuition discounts available. Support available to part-time students. Financial award application deadline: 8/31; financial award applicants required to submit FAFSA. *Unit head:* Chrystal Porter, Vice President of Graduate and Professional Studies, 617-243-2083, Fax: 617-243-2450, E-mail: gradinfo@lasell.edu. *Application contact:* Adrienne Franciosi, Assistant Vice President of Graduate and Professional Studies, 617-243-2214, Fax: 617-243-2450, E-mail: gradinfo@lasell.edu.
Website: http://www.lasell.edu/academics/graduate-and-professional-studies/programs-of-study/master-of-science-in-communication.html

La Sierra University, College of Arts and Sciences, Department of English and Communication, Riverside, CA 92505. Offers communication (MA), including public relations/advertising, theory emphasis; English (MA), including literary emphasis, writing emphasis. *Program availability:* Part-time. *Degree requirements:* For master's, one foreign language. *Entrance requirements:* For master's, GRE General Test.

Lawrence Technological University, College of Arts and Sciences, Southfield, MI 48075-1058. Offers bioinformatics (Graduate Certificate); computer science (MS), including data science, big data, and data mining, intelligent systems; educational technology (MA), including robotics; instructional design, communication, and presentation (Graduate Certificate); integrated science (MA); science education (MA); technical and professional communication (MS, Graduate Certificate); writing for the digital age (Graduate Certificate). *Program availability:* Part-time, evening/weekend. *Faculty:* 5 full-time (2 women), 2 part-time/adjunct (1 woman). *Students:* 1 (woman) full-time, 25 part-time (15 women); includes 6 minority (3 Black or African American, non-Hispanic/Latino; 2 Asian, non-Hispanic/Latino; 1 Hispanic/Latino), 6 international. Average age 34. 50 applicants, 68% accepted, 3 enrolled. In 2019, 14 master's, 4 other advanced degrees awarded. *Degree requirements:* For master's, thesis (for some programs). *Entrance requirements:* Additional exam requirements/recommendations for international students: required—TOEFL (minimum score 550 paper-based; 79 iBT), IELTS (minimum score 6.5). *Application deadline:* For fall admission, 5/24 for international students; for spring admission, 10/13 for international students; for summer admission, 2/18 for international students. Applications are processed on a rolling basis. Application fee: $50. Electronic applications accepted. *Expenses: Tuition:* Full-time $16,618; part-time $8309 per year. *Required fees:* $600; $600. *Financial support:* In 2019–20, 4 students received support. Scholarships/grants and tuition reduction available. Financial award application deadline: 4/1; financial award applicants required to submit FAFSA. *Unit head:* Glen Bauer, Interim Dean, 248-204-3532, Fax: 248-204-3518, E-mail: scidean@ltu.edu. *Application contact:* Jane Rohrback, Director of Admissions, 248-204-3160, Fax: 248-204-2228, E-mail: admissions@ltu.edu.

Liberty University, School Of Communication & the Arts, Lynchburg, VA 24515. Offers communication (MA); promotion and video content (MA); social media management (MS); strategic communication (MA). *Program availability:* Part-time. *Students:* 335 full-time (235 women), 331 part-time (204 women); includes 190 minority (114 Black or African American, non-Hispanic/Latino; 2 American Indian or Alaska Native, non-Hispanic/Latino; 18 Asian, non-Hispanic/Latino; 24 Hispanic/Latino; 1 Native Hawaiian or other Pacific Islander, non-Hispanic/Latino; 31 Two or more races, non-Hispanic/Latino), 19 international. Average age 33. 1,223 applicants, 40% accepted, 242 enrolled. In 2019, 146 master's awarded. *Degree requirements:* For master's, thesis (for some programs). *Entrance requirements:* For master's, minimum undergraduate GPA of 3.0, faculty recommendation, written statement of purpose, writing sample. Additional exam requirements/recommendations for international students: required—TOEFL (minimum

score 600 paper-based; 100 iBT). *Application deadline:* For fall admission, 6/1 for domestic students; for spring admission, 11/1 for domestic students. Applications are processed on a rolling basis. Application fee: $50. Electronic applications accepted. *Expenses: Tuition:* Full-time $545; part-time $410 per credit hour. One-time fee: $50. *Financial support:* In 2019–20, 882 students received support. Federal Work-Study and unspecified assistantships available. Financial award applicants required to submit FAFSA. *Unit head:* Dr. Scott Hayes, Residential Dean, E-mail: smhayes@liberty.edu. *Application contact:* Dr. Jay Bridge, Director of OnlineAdmissions, 800-4249505, E-mail: gradadmissions@liberty.edu.
Website: https://www.liberty.edu/communication/

Lindenwood University, Graduate Programs, School of Accelerated Degree Programs, St. Charles, MO 63301-1695. Offers administration (MSA), including management, marketing, project management; business administration (MBA); communications (MA), including digital and multimedia, media management, promotions, training and development; criminal justice and administration (MS); healthcare administration (MS); human resource management (MS); information technology (Certificate); managing information security (MS); managing information technology (MS); managing virtualization and cloud computing (MS); writing (MFA). *Program availability:* Part-time, evening/weekend, 100% online. *Faculty:* 11 full-time (6 women), 66 part-time/adjunct (23 women). *Students:* 408 full-time (262 women), 60 part-time (40 women); includes 149 minority (111 Black or African American, non-Hispanic/Latino; 2 American Indian or Alaska Native, non-Hispanic/Latino; 2 Asian, non-Hispanic/Latino; 18 Hispanic/Latino; 1 Native Hawaiian or other Pacific Islander, non-Hispanic/Latino; 15 Two or more races, non-Hispanic/Latino), 33 international. Average age 39. 268 applicants, 46% accepted, 99 enrolled. In 2019, 347 master's awarded. *Degree requirements:* For master's, thesis (for some programs), minimum cumulative GPA of 3.0; for Certificate, minimum cumulative GPA of 3.0. *Entrance requirements:* For master's, resume, personal statement, official undergraduate transcript, minimum undergraduate cumulative GPA of 3.0. Additional exam requirements/recommendations for international students: required—TOEFL (minimum score 553 paper-based; 81 iBT); recommended—IELTS (minimum score 6.5). *Application deadline:* For fall admission, 9/30 priority date for domestic and international students; for winter admission, 1/6 priority date for domestic and international students; for spring admission, 4/6 priority date for domestic and international students; for summer admission, 7/8 priority date for domestic and international students. Applications are processed on a rolling basis. Application fee: $0 ($100 for international students). Electronic applications accepted. *Expenses:* Contact institution. *Financial support:* In 2019–20, 145 students received support. Career-related internships or fieldwork, institutionally sponsored loans, scholarships/grants, tuition waivers (partial), and unspecified assistantships available. Financial award application deadline: 6/30; financial award applicants required to submit FAFSA. *Unit head:* Dr. Gina Ganahl, Dean, Accelerated Degree Programs, 636-949-4501, Fax: 636-949-4505, E-mail: gganahl@lindenwood.edu. *Application contact:* Kara Schilli, Assistant Vice President, University Admissions, 636-949-4349, Fax: 636-949-4109, E-mail: adultadmissions@lindenwood.edu.
Website: https://www.lindenwood.edu/academics/academic-schools/school-of-accelerated-degree-programs/

Lindenwood University–Belleville, Graduate Programs, Belleville, IL 62226. Offers business administration (MBA); communications (MA), including digital and multimedia, media management, promotions, training and development; counseling (MA); criminal justice administration (MS); education (MA); healthcare administration (MS); human resource management (MS); school administration (MA); teaching (MAT).

Louisiana State University and Agricultural & Mechanical College, Graduate School, College of Humanities and Social Sciences, Department of Communication Studies, Baton Rouge, LA 70803. Offers MA, PhD.

Loyola University Chicago, Graduate School, School of Communication, Chicago, IL 60611. Offers digital storytelling (MC); global strategic communication (MS). *Program availability:* Part-time, evening/weekend. *Students:* 50 full-time (34 women), 13 part-time (11 women); includes 18 minority (9 Black or African American, non-Hispanic/Latino; 2 Asian, non-Hispanic/Latino; 6 Hispanic/Latino; 1 Two or more races, non-Hispanic/Latino), 18 international. Average age 29. 100 applicants, 56% accepted, 29 enrolled. In 2019, 17 master's awarded. *Entrance requirements:* For master's, TOEFL, Bachelor's degree (official, final transcript), 3.0 cumulative GPA preferred, prior experience (academic or professional) preferred, recommendations, statement of purpose, writing sample (for Global Strategic Communication program). If international student, transcript evaluation is required. *Application deadline:* Applications are processed on a rolling basis. Electronic applications accepted. *Expenses:* Contact institution. *Financial support:* Career-related internships or fieldwork and scholarships/grants available. Financial award applicants required to submit FAFSA. *Unit head:* Dr. Hong Cheng, Dean, 312-915-6548, E-mail: hcheng5@luc.edu. *Application contact:* Maria Villanueva, Associate Director of GPEM Operations, E-mail: mvilla2@luc.edu.
Website: http://www.luc.edu/soc/

Lynn University, Eugene M. and Christine E. Lynn College of Communication and Design, Boca Raton, FL 33431-5598. Offers communication and media (MS); digital media (Certificate); digital media and design (MS); graphic and Web design (MFA); visual effects animation (MFA). *Program availability:* Part-time, evening/weekend. *Faculty:* 17 full-time (6 women), 3 part-time/adjunct (2 women). *Students:* 28 full-time (15 women), 32 part-time (16 women); includes 15 minority (8 Black or African American, non-Hispanic/Latino; 6 Hispanic/Latino; 1 Two or more races, non-Hispanic/Latino), 19 international. Average age 28. 36 applicants, 92% accepted, 20 enrolled. In 2019, 30 master's awarded. *Degree requirements:* For master's, thesis (for some programs), completion of degree in four calendar years; minimum cumulative GPA of 3.0 and C grade or higher in each course; orientation seminar (one credit); 36 credits of foundation and specialization or a thesis. *Entrance requirements:* For master's, Bachelor's degree from accredited institution, minimum undergraduate GPA of 3.0, official undergraduate transcripts, letter of recommendation from academic or professional source, writing sample demonstrating capacity to perform at graduate level. Additional exam requirements/recommendations for international students: required—TOEFL (minimum score 550 paper-based; 80 iBT), IELTS (minimum score 6.5). *Application deadline:* For fall admission, 8/10 for domestic students, 7/31 for international students; for spring admission, 12/18 for domestic students, 12/2 for international students; for summer admission, 4/12 for domestic students, 4/2 for international students. Applications are processed on a rolling basis. Application fee: $45. Electronic applications accepted. *Expenses:* $740.00 per hour. *Financial support:* In 2019–20, 15 students received support. Career-related internships or fieldwork, Federal Work-Study, scholarships/grants, tuition waivers (full and partial), and unspecified assistantships available. Support available to part-time students. Financial award application deadline: 3/1; financial award applicants required to submit FAFSA. *Unit head:* Dr. David L. Jaffe, Dean, 561-237-7099, Fax: 561-237-7097, E-mail: djaffe@lynn.edu. *Application contact:* Steven Pruitt, Director of Graduate Admission, 561-237-7834, Fax: 561-237-7100, E-mail: admission@lynn.edu.
Website: https://www.lynn.edu/academics/colleges-schools/communication-and-design

Marist College, Graduate Programs, School of Communication and the Arts, Poughkeepsie, NY 12601-1387. Offers communication (MA); integrated marketing

communication (MA); museum studies (MA). *Program availability:* Part-time, online learning. *Degree requirements:* For master's, thesis or comprehensive exam. *Entrance requirements:* For master's, GRE, minimum undergraduate GPA of 3.0, resume, 3 letters of recommendation. Additional exam requirements/recommendations for international students: required—TOEFL (minimum score 550 paper-based; 80 iBT); recommended—IELTS (minimum score 6.5). Electronic applications accepted.

Marquette University, Graduate School, College of Communication, Milwaukee, WI 53201-1881. Offers advertising and public relations (MA); communication studies (MA); digital storytelling (Certificate); journalism (MA); mass communication (MA); science, health and environmental communication (MA). *Accreditation:* ACEJMC (one or more programs are accredited). *Program availability:* Part-time, evening/weekend. *Degree requirements:* For master's, comprehensive exam, thesis or alternative. *Entrance requirements:* For master's, GRE, official transcripts from all current and previous colleges/universities except Marquette, three letters of recommendation, statement of academic and professional goals. Additional exam requirements/recommendations for international students: required—TOEFL (minimum score 530 paper-based). Electronic applications accepted.

Marshall University, Academic Affairs Division, College of Liberal Arts, Department of Communication Studies, Huntington, WV 25755. Offers MA. *Degree requirements:* For master's, thesis optional. *Entrance requirements:* For master's, GRE General Test.

Marywood University, Academic Affairs, Insalaco College of Creative and Performing Arts, Department of Communication Arts, Scranton, PA 18509-1598. Offers MA. *Program availability:* Part-time. Electronic applications accepted.

McGill University, Faculty of Graduate and Postdoctoral Studies, Faculty of Arts, Department of Art History and Communication Studies, Montréal, QC H3A 2T5, Canada. Offers MA, PhD.

Michigan State University, The Graduate School, College of Communication Arts and Sciences, Department of Communication, East Lansing, MI 48824. Offers MA, PhD. *Entrance requirements:* Additional exam requirements/recommendations for international students: required—TOEFL (minimum score 580 paper-based). Electronic applications accepted.

Minnesota State University Mankato, College of Graduate Studies and Research, College of Arts and Humanities, Department of Communication Studies, Mankato, MN 56001. Offers communication education (Certificate); communication studies (MA, MS); forensics (MFA); professional communication (Certificate). *Degree requirements:* For master's, one foreign language, comprehensive exam, thesis. *Entrance requirements:* For master's, minimum GPA of 3.0 during previous 2 years, writing sample. Electronic applications accepted.

Minnesota State University Mankato, College of Graduate Studies and Research, College of Arts and Humanities, Department of English, Mankato, MN 56001. Offers communication and composition (MA); creative writing (MFA); English studies (MA); teaching English as a second language (MA, Certificate); technical communication (MA, Certificate). *Program availability:* Part-time. *Degree requirements:* For master's, one foreign language, comprehensive exam, thesis or alternative. *Entrance requirements:* For master's, minimum GPA of 3.0 during previous 2 years, writing sample (MFA). Additional exam requirements/recommendations for international students: required—TOEFL (minimum score 500 paper-based; 61 iBT). Electronic applications accepted.

Mississippi College, Graduate School, College of Arts and Sciences, School of Christian Studies and the Arts, Department of Communication, Clinton, MS 39058. Offers applied communication (MSC); public relations and corporate communication (MSC). *Program availability:* Part-time. *Degree requirements:* For master's, comprehensive exam, thesis optional. *Entrance requirements:* For master's, GRE or NTE, minimum GPA of 2.5. Additional exam requirements/recommendations for international students: recommended—TOEFL, IELTS. Electronic applications accepted.

Mississippi State University, College of Agriculture and Life Sciences, School of Human Sciences, Mississippi State, MS 39762. Offers agriculture and extension education (MS), including communication, leadership; agriculture science (PhD), including agriculture and extension education; fashion design and merchandising (MS), including design and product development, merchandising; human development and family studies (MS, PhD). *Accreditation:* NCATE (one or more programs are accredited). *Program availability:* Part-time. *Faculty:* 21 full-time (11 women). *Students:* 26 full-time (21 women), 62 part-time (46 women); includes 16 minority (12 Black or African American, non-Hispanic/Latino; 1 American Indian or Alaska Native, non-Hispanic/Latino; 1 Hispanic/Latino; 2 Two or more races, non-Hispanic/Latino), 4 international. Average age 34. 26 applicants, 69% accepted, 16 enrolled. In 2019, 12 master's, 4 doctorates awarded. *Degree requirements:* For master's, thesis optional, comprehensive oral or written exam. *Entrance requirements:* For master's, GRE, minimum GPA of 2.75 in last 4 semesters of course work; for doctorate, minimum GPA of 3.0 on prior graduate work. Additional exam requirements/recommendations for international students: required—TOEFL (minimum score 477 paper-based; 53 iBT); recommended—IELTS (minimum score 4.5). *Application deadline:* For fall admission, 7/1 for domestic students, 5/1 for international students; for spring admission, 11/1 for domestic students, 9/1 for international students. Applications are processed on a rolling basis. Application fee: $60 ($80 for international students). Electronic applications accepted. *Expenses: Tuition, area resident:* Full-time $8880; part-time $456 per credit hour. Tuition, state resident: full-time $8880. Tuition, nonresident: full-time $23,840; part-time $1236 per credit hour. *Required fees:* $110; $11.12 per credit hour. Tuition and fees vary according to course load. *Financial support:* In 2019–20, 15 research assistantships (averaging $12,541 per year) were awarded; Federal Work-Study, institutionally sponsored loans, and unspecified assistantships also available. Financial award application deadline: 4/1; financial award applicants required to submit FAFSA. *Unit head:* Dr. Michael Newman, Professor and Director, 662-325-2950, E-mail: mnewman@humansci.msstate.edu. *Application contact:* Ryan King, Admissions and Enrollment Assistant, 662-325-8951, E-mail: rjk101@grad.msstate.edu.
Website: http://www.humansci.msstate.edu

Missouri State University, Graduate College, College of Arts and Letters, Department of Communication, Springfield, MO 65897. Offers MA. *Program availability:* Part-time, 100% online, blended/hybrid learning. *Degree requirements:* For master's, comprehensive exam, thesis or alternative. *Entrance requirements:* For master's, GRE General Test or MAT, minimum GPA of 3.0 for last 60 credit hours of academic work. Additional exam requirements/recommendations for international students: required—TOEFL (minimum score 550 paper-based; 79 iBT), IELTS (minimum score 6). Electronic applications accepted. *Expenses: Tuition, area resident:* Full-time $2600; part-time $1735 per credit hour. Tuition, nonresident: full-time $5240; part-time $3495 per credit hour. *International tuition:* $5240 full-time. *Required fees:* $530; $438 per credit hour. Tuition and fees vary according to class time, course level, course load, degree level, campus/location and program.

Missouri State University, Graduate College, Interdisciplinary Program in Professional Studies, Springfield, MO 65897. Offers administrative studies (Certificate); applied communication (MS); criminal justice (MS); environmental management (MS);

homeland security (MS); individualized (MS); professional studies (MS); screenwriting and producing (MS); sports management (MS). *Program availability:* Part-time, evening/weekend, 100% online, blended/hybrid learning. *Degree requirements:* For master's, comprehensive exam, thesis or alternative. *Entrance requirements:* For master's, GRE, GMAT (if GPA less than 3.0). Additional exam requirements/recommendations for international students: required—TOEFL (minimum score 550 paper-based; 79 iBT), IELTS (minimum score 6). Electronic applications accepted. *Expenses: Tuition, area resident:* Full-time $2600; part-time $1735 per credit hour. Tuition, nonresident: full-time $5240; part-time $3495 per credit hour. *International tuition:* $5240 full-time. *Required fees:* $530; $438 per credit hour. Tuition and fees vary according to class time, course level, course load, degree level, campus/location and program.

Monmouth University, Graduate Studies, Department of Communication, West Long Branch, NJ 07764-1898. Offers public service communication specialist (Certificate); strategic public relations and new media (Certificate). *Program availability:* Part-time, evening/weekend, online learning. *Faculty:* 7 full-time (5 women). *Students:* 14 full-time (11 women), 20 part-time (14 women); includes 6 minority (2 Black or African American, non-Hispanic/Latino; 3 Hispanic/Latino; 1 Two or more races, non-Hispanic/Latino), 2 international. Average age 27. In 2019, 10 master's awarded. *Degree requirements:* For master's, comprehensive exam (for some programs), thesis (for some programs), project. *Entrance requirements:* For master's, GRE, baccalaureate degree with minimum GPA of 3.0 in major, 2.75 overall; two letters of recommendation; personal essay (750 words or less describing preparation for study and personal objectives); digital or hard copy portfolio of select samples of work including writing sample; resume. Additional exam requirements/recommendations for international students: required—TOEFL (minimum score 550 paper-based; 79 iBT), IELTS (minimum score 6), Michigan English Language Assessment Battery (minimum score 77). *Application deadline:* For fall admission, 7/15 priority date for domestic students, 6/1 for international students; for spring admission, 12/1 priority date for domestic students, 11/1 for international students; for summer admission, 5/1 for domestic students. Applications are processed on a rolling basis. Application fee: $50. Electronic applications accepted. *Expenses: Tuition:* Full-time $22,194; part-time $14,796 per credit. *Required fees:* $712; $178 per semester. $178 per semester. Tuition and fees vary according to course load. *Financial support:* In 2019–20, 35 students received support. Research assistantships, teaching assistantships, institutionally sponsored loans, scholarships/grants, and unspecified assistantships available. Support available to part-time students. Financial award applicants required to submit FAFSA. *Unit head:* Dr. Deanna Shoemaker, Program Director, 732-571-3449, Fax: 732-571-3609, E-mail: dshoemak@monmouth.edu. *Application contact:* Kevin New, Graduate Admission Counselor, 732-571-3452, Fax: 732-263-5123, E-mail: gradadm@monmouth.edu.
Website: http://www.monmouth.edu/cpc

Montana State University Billings, College of Arts and Sciences, Department of Communication and Theatre, Billings, MT 59101. Offers public relations (MS). *Program availability:* Part-time, 100% online, blended/hybrid learning. *Degree requirements:* For master's, comprehensive exam, thesis optional. *Entrance requirements:* For master's, GRE General Test, minimum undergraduate GPA of 3.0, letters of recommendation, letter of intent, resume. Additional exam requirements/recommendations for international students: required—TOEFL (minimum score 79 iBT), IELTS (minimum score 6.5). Electronic applications accepted.

Moore College of Art & Design, Program in Social Engagement, Philadelphia, PA 19103. Offers MA. *Program availability:* Part-time. *Degree requirements:* For master's, thesis.

Mount Saint Vincent University, Graduate Programs, Department of Communication Studies, Halifax, NS B3M 2J6, Canada. Offers communication (MA); public relations (MPR).

New Mexico State University, College of Arts and Sciences, Department of Communication Studies, Las Cruces, NM 88003-8001. Offers MA. *Program availability:* Part-time. *Faculty:* 6 full-time (4 women). *Students:* 17 full-time (16 women), 7 part-time (3 women); includes 17 minority (1 Black or African American, non-Hispanic/Latino; 1 Asian, non-Hispanic/Latino; 13 Hispanic/Latino; 2 Two or more races, non-Hispanic/Latino), 1 international. Average age 31. 20 applicants, 70% accepted, 8 enrolled. In 2019, 8 master's awarded. *Degree requirements:* For master's, thesis optional, comprehensive exam optional, applied project optional. *Entrance requirements:* For master's, minimum GPA of 3.25. Additional exam requirements/recommendations for international students: required—TOEFL (minimum score 550 paper-based; 79 iBT), IELTS (minimum score 6.5). *Application deadline:* Applications are processed on a rolling basis. Application fee: $40 ($50 for international students). Electronic applications accepted. *Financial support:* In 2019–20, 16 students received support, including 2 fellowships (averaging $500 per year), 11 teaching assistantships (averaging $18,609 per year); career-related internships or fieldwork, Federal Work-Study, scholarships/grants, traineeships, health care benefits, and unspecified assistantships also available. Support available to part-time students. Financial award application deadline: 3/1. *Unit head:* Dr. Eric Morgan, Department Head, 575-646-2801, Fax: 575-646-4642, E-mail: emorgan@nmsu.edu. *Application contact:* Dr. Eric Morgan, Department Head, 575-646-2801, Fax: 575-646-4642, E-mail: emorgan@nmsu.edu.
Website: http://commstudies.nmsu.edu

New York Institute of Technology, College of Arts and Sciences, Department of Communication Arts, Old Westbury, NY 11568. Offers MA. *Program availability:* Part-time. *Faculty:* 9 full-time (4 women), 18 part-time/adjunct (6 women). *Students:* 58 full-time (32 women), 20 part-time (12 women); includes 15 minority (8 Black or African American, non-Hispanic/Latino; 2 Asian, non-Hispanic/Latino; 4 Hispanic/Latino; 1 Two or more races, non-Hispanic/Latino), 43 international. Average age 26. 88 applicants, 74% accepted, 33 enrolled. In 2019, 79 master's awarded. *Degree requirements:* For master's, thesis or alternative, Must complete Portfolio Project or Thesis. *Entrance requirements:* For master's, If undergraduate GPA is below 2.49, applicants are required to take the GRE and achieve a minimum score of 153 in the verbal section, Minimum undergraduate GPA of 2.85 for full matriculation; basic media production competencies, as evidenced by undergraduate transcripts or hands-on professional experience; copies of undergraduate transcripts for all schools attended and proof of degree. Additional exam requirements/recommendations for international students: required—TOEFL (minimum score 79 iBT), IELTS (minimum score 6), PTE (minimum score 53), Duolingo English Test. *Application deadline:* For fall admission, 7/1 for international students; for spring admission, 12/15 for international students. Applications are processed on a rolling basis. Application fee: $50. Electronic applications accepted. *Expenses: Tuition:* Full-time $23,760; part-time $1320 per credit. *Required fees:* $260; $220 per unit. Full-time tuition and fees vary according to degree level and program. Part-time tuition and fees vary according to course load and program. *Financial support:* In 2019–20, 38 students received support. Research assistantships, teaching assistantships, Federal Work-Study, scholarships/grants, and unspecified assistantships available. Support available to part-time students. Financial award application deadline: 2/15; financial award applicants required to submit FAFSA. *Unit head:* Don Fizzinoglia, Department Chair, 516-686-1468, E-mail: dfizzino@nyit.edu. *Application contact:* Alice Dolitsky, Director, Graduate Admissions, 800-345-6948, Fax: 516-686-1116, E-mail: admissions@nyit.edu.
Website: https://www.nyit.edu/degrees/communication_arts_ma

New York University, Steinhardt School of Culture, Education, and Human Development, Department of Media, Culture and Communication, New York, NY 10012. Offers media, culture and communication (MA, PhD); MLIS/MA. *Program availability:* Part-time. Terminal master's awarded for partial completion of doctoral program. *Entrance requirements:* For master's, GRE General Test; for doctorate, GRE General Test, interview. Additional exam requirements/recommendations for international students: required—TOEFL (minimum score 100 iBT). Electronic applications accepted.

Norfolk State University, School of Graduate Studies, School of Liberal Arts, Department of Media and Communication, Norfolk, VA 23504. Offers MA. *Program availability:* Part-time. *Degree requirements:* For master's, thesis. *Entrance requirements:* For master's, GRE, minimum GPA of 2.5, letters of recommendation. Additional exam requirements/recommendations for international students: required—TOEFL.

North Carolina State University, Graduate School, College of Humanities and Social Sciences, Department of Communication, Raleigh, NC 27695. Offers MS. *Program availability:* Part-time. *Entrance requirements:* For master's, GRE, minimum undergraduate GPA of 3.0 during last 60 hours. Electronic applications accepted.

North Dakota State University, College of Graduate and Interdisciplinary Studies, College of Arts, Humanities and Social Sciences, Department of Communication, Fargo, ND 58102. Offers communication (PhD); mass communication (MA); speech communication (MS). *Program availability:* Part-time, online learning. Terminal master's awarded for partial completion of doctoral program. *Degree requirements:* For master's, thesis (for some programs); for doctorate, comprehensive exam, thesis/dissertation, 2-3 publications. *Entrance requirements:* For master's, GRE, minimum undergraduate GPA of 3.25; for doctorate, GRE, minimum undergraduate GPA of 3.5. Additional exam requirements/recommendations for international students: required—TOEFL (minimum score 600 paper-based; 100 iBT), IELTS (minimum score 7). Electronic applications accepted. Tuition and fees vary according to program and reciprocity agreements.

Northeastern State University, College of Liberal Arts, Department of Communication, Art and Theatre, Tahlequah, OK 74464-2399. Offers communication arts (MA). *Program availability:* Part-time, evening/weekend. *Faculty:* 3 full-time (all women). *Students:* 8 full-time (4 women), 9 part-time (7 women); includes 8 minority (2 Black or African American, non-Hispanic/Latino; 4 American Indian or Alaska Native, non-Hispanic/Latino; 2 Two or more races, non-Hispanic/Latino). Average age 29. In 2019, 3 master's awarded. *Degree requirements:* For master's, comprehensive exam. *Entrance requirements:* For master's, GRE, MAT, minimum GPA of 2.5. Additional exam requirements/recommendations for international students: required—TOEFL. *Application deadline:* For fall admission, 6/1 priority date for domestic students. Applications are processed on a rolling basis. Application fee: $25. Electronic applications accepted. *Expenses: Tuition, area resident:* Full-time $250; part-time $250 per credit hour. Tuition, state resident: full-time $250; part-time $250 per credit hour. Tuition, nonresident: full-time $556; part-time $555.50 per credit hour. *Required fees:* $33.40 per credit hour. *Financial support:* Teaching assistantships and Federal Work-Study available. Financial award application deadline: 3/1. *Unit head:* Dr. Dana Eversole, Department Chair, 918-444-2891, Fax: 918-458-2348, E-mail: eversole@nsuok.edu. *Application contact:* Josh McCollum, Graduate Coordinator, 918-444-2093, E-mail: mccolluj@nsuok.edu.
Website: http://academics.nsuok.edu/communicationstudies/MasterofArts.aspx

Northern Arizona University, College of Social and Behavioral Sciences, School of Communication, Flagstaff, AZ 86011. Offers communication (MA); communication studies (Graduate Certificate); science communication (Graduate Certificate). *Program availability:* Part-time, 100% online, blended/hybrid learning. *Degree requirements:* For master's, variable foreign language requirement, comprehensive exam (for some programs), thesis (for some programs); for Graduate Certificate, comprehensive exam (for some programs). *Entrance requirements:* For master's, GRE General Test. Additional exam requirements/recommendations for international students: required—TOEFL (minimum score 80 iBT), IELTS (minimum score 6.5). Electronic applications accepted.

Northern Illinois University, Graduate School, College of Liberal Arts and Sciences, Department of Communication, De Kalb, IL 60115-2854. Offers communication studies (MA). *Program availability:* Part-time. *Faculty:* 24 full-time (11 women), 1 part-time/adjunct (0 women). *Students:* 22 full-time (15 women), 4 part-time (3 women); includes 7 minority (5 Black or African American, non-Hispanic/Latino; 2 Hispanic/Latino), 1 international. Average age 26. 23 applicants, 78% accepted, 11 enrolled. In 2019, 9 master's awarded. *Degree requirements:* For master's, comprehensive exam, thesis optional. *Entrance requirements:* For master's, GRE General Test, minimum GPA of 2.75. Additional exam requirements/recommendations for international students: required—TOEFL (minimum score 550 paper-based). *Application deadline:* For fall admission, 6/1 for domestic students, 5/1 for international students; for spring admission, 11/1 for domestic students, 10/1 for international students. Applications are processed on a rolling basis. Application fee: $40. Electronic applications accepted. *Financial support:* In 2019–20, 22 teaching assistantships with full tuition reimbursements were awarded; fellowships with full tuition reimbursements, research assistantships with full tuition reimbursements, career-related internships or fieldwork, Federal Work-Study, scholarships/grants, tuition waivers (full), and unspecified assistantships also available. Support available to part-time students. Financial award applicants required to submit FAFSA. *Unit head:* Dr. Mehdi Semati, Acting Chair, 815-753-7028, Fax: 815-753-7109, E-mail: msemati@niu.edu. *Application contact:* Dr. Kathleen Valde, Director, Graduate Studies, 815-753-7005, E-mail: kvalde@niu.edu.
Website: http://www.comm.niu.edu/

Northern Kentucky University, Office of Graduate Programs, College of Informatics, Program in Communication, Highland Heights, KY 41099. Offers communication (MA); communication teaching (Certificate); documentary studies (Certificate); public relations (Certificate); relationships (Certificate). *Program availability:* Part-time, evening/weekend. Terminal master's awarded for partial completion of doctoral program. *Degree requirements:* For master's, comprehensive exams, thesis or applied capstone project. *Entrance requirements:* For master's, GRE, minimum GPA of 3.0, 3 letters of recommendation, letter of intent. Additional exam requirements/recommendations for international students: required—TOEFL (minimum score 79 iBT); recommended—IELTS (minimum score 6.5). Electronic applications accepted.

Northwestern University, The Graduate School, School of Communication, Department of Communication Studies, Evanston, IL 60208. Offers communication studies (PhD), including interaction and social influence, rhetoric and public culture; managerial communication (MSC); media, technology and society (PhD); technology and social behavior (PhD). Terminal master's awarded for partial completion of doctoral program. *Degree requirements:* For doctorate, thesis/dissertation. *Entrance requirements:* For master's and doctorate, GRE General Test. Additional exam requirements/recommendations for international students: required—TOEFL. Electronic applications accepted.

Notre Dame of Maryland University, Graduate Studies, Program in Contemporary Communication, Baltimore, MD 21210-2476. Offers MA. *Program availability:* Part-time, evening/weekend. *Degree requirements:* For master's, thesis optional. *Entrance requirements:* For master's, minimum GPA of 3.0. Additional exam requirements/recommendations for international students: required—TOEFL (minimum score 500 paper-based; 61 iBT). Electronic applications accepted.

The Ohio State University, Graduate School, College of Arts and Sciences, Division of Social and Behavioral Sciences, School of Communication, Columbus, OH 43210. Offers MA, PhD. *Entrance requirements:* For master's and doctorate, GRE. Additional exam requirements/recommendations for international students: required—TOEFL (minimum score 640 paper-based; 111 iBT); recommended—IELTS (minimum score 8.5). Electronic applications accepted.

Ohio University, Graduate College, Scripps College of Communication, Athens, OH 45701-2979. Offers MA, MCTP, MFA, MS, PhD. *Program availability:* Part-time. *Degree requirements:* For master's, comprehensive exam (for some programs), thesis or alternative; for doctorate, comprehensive exam, thesis/dissertation. *Entrance requirements:* For master's and doctorate, GRE General Test. Additional exam requirements/recommendations for international students: required—TOEFL or IELTS. Electronic applications accepted. *Expenses:* Contact institution.

Old Dominion University, College of Arts and Letters, Institute for the Humanities, Norfolk, VA 23529. Offers arts and entrepreneurship (Certificate); cultural and human geography (MA); cultural studies (MA); gender and sexuality studies (MA); health, communication and culture (Certificate); media and popular culture studies (MA); philosophy and religious studies (MA); social justice and entrepreneurship (Certificate); visual studies (MA); world cultures (MA). *Program availability:* Part-time, evening/weekend. *Degree requirements:* For master's, thesis optional, project. *Entrance requirements:* For master's, GRE General Test, minimum GPA of 3.25. Electronic applications accepted.

Pace University, Dyson College of Arts and Sciences, MA Program in Media and Communication Arts, New York, NY 10038. Offers MA. *Program availability:* Part-time, evening/weekend. *Degree requirements:* For master's, comprehensive exam, thesis, internship. *Entrance requirements:* For master's, portfolio containing examples of prior work (press releases, advertisements, presentations, writing samples, etc.) and official transcripts. Additional exam requirements/recommendations for international students: required—TOEFL (minimum score 100 iBT). Electronic applications accepted.

Penn State Harrisburg, Graduate School, School of Humanities, Middletown, PA 17057. Offers American studies (MA, PhD); communications (MA); folklore and ethnography (Certificate); heritage and museum practice (Certificate); humanities (MA). *Program availability:* Evening/weekend.

Penn State University Park, Graduate School, College of the Liberal Arts, Department of Communication Arts and Sciences, University Park, PA 16802. Offers MA, PhD.

Pepperdine University, Seaver College, Malibu, CA 90263. Offers business (MS), including accounting; communication (MFA), including cinematic media production; humanities (MA, MFA), including American studies (MA), writing for screen and television (MFA); religion (M Div, MA, MS), including ministry (MS), religion (M Div, MA); JD/M Div. *Entrance requirements:* For master's, GRE General Test. Additional exam requirements/recommendations for international students: required—TOEFL. *Expenses:* Contact institution.

Pittsburg State University, Graduate School, College of Arts and Sciences, Department of Communication, Pittsburg, KS 66762. Offers MA. *Program availability:* Part-time. *Degree requirements:* For master's, thesis or alternative. *Entrance requirements:* Additional exam requirements/recommendations for international students: required—TOEFL (minimum score 550 paper-based; 79 iBT), IELTS (minimum score 6.5), PTE (minimum score 53). Electronic applications accepted. *Expenses:* Contact institution.

Point Park University, School of Communication, Pittsburgh, PA 15222-1984. Offers communication technology (MA); media communication (MA). *Program availability:* Part-time, evening/weekend. *Degree requirements:* For master's, comprehensive exam (for some programs), thesis or alternative. *Entrance requirements:* For master's, GRE (if GPA less than 2.75), minimum GPA of 2.75, 2 letters of recommendation, statement of intent. Additional exam requirements/recommendations for international students: required—TOEFL (minimum score 570 paper-based; 88 iBT), IELTS (minimum score 6.5); recommended—TWE (minimum score 5). Electronic applications accepted.

Purdue University, Graduate School, College of Liberal Arts, Department of Communication, West Lafayette, IN 47907. Offers MA, MS, PhD. *Faculty:* 20 full-time (10 women), 2 part-time/adjunct (0 women). *Students:* 49 full-time (32 women), 354 part-time (271 women); includes 95 minority (35 Black or African American, non-Hispanic/Latino; 11 Asian, non-Hispanic/Latino; 37 Hispanic/Latino; 1 Native Hawaiian or other Pacific Islander, non-Hispanic/Latino; 11 Two or more races, non-Hispanic/Latino), 16 international. Average age 33. 200 applicants, 67% accepted, 113 enrolled. In 2019, 278 master's, 9 doctorates awarded. *Degree requirements:* For master's, comprehensive exams or thesis; for doctorate, thesis/dissertation. *Entrance requirements:* For master's and doctorate, GRE General Test, minimum undergraduate GPA of 3.0 or equivalent. Additional exam requirements/recommendations for international students: required—TOEFL (minimum score 600 paper-based; 77 iBT). *Application deadline:* For fall admission, 1/1 priority date for domestic students, 1/1 for international students; for spring admission, 8/1 for domestic and international students. Applications are processed on a rolling basis. Application fee: $60 ($75 for international students). Electronic applications accepted. *Financial support:* In 2019–20, 70 students received support. Fellowships, research assistantships, teaching assistantships, and scholarships/grants available. Financial award application deadline: 1/1; financial award applicants required to submit FAFSA. *Unit head:* Dr. Marifran Mattson, Head, 765-494-7596, E-mail: mmattson@purdue.edu. *Application contact:* Jill Dyson, Graduate Coordinator, 765-494-3304, E-mail: jdyson@purdue.edu.
Website: http://www.cla.purdue.edu/communication/

Purdue University Fort Wayne, College of Arts and Sciences, Department of Communication, Fort Wayne, IN 46805-1499. Offers professional communication (MA, MS). *Program availability:* Part-time. *Entrance requirements:* For master's, minimum GPA of 3.0. Additional exam requirements/recommendations for international students: required—TOEFL (minimum score 550 paper-based; 79 iBT); recommended—TWE. Electronic applications accepted.

Purdue University Northwest, Graduate Studies Office, School of Liberal Arts and Social Sciences, Department of Communication and Creative Arts, Hammond, IN 46323-2094. Offers communication (MA). *Program availability:* Part-time, evening/weekend. *Degree requirements:* For master's, comprehensive exam, thesis or extended course work. *Entrance requirements:* For master's, minimum GPA of 3.0. Additional exam requirements/recommendations for international students: required—TOEFL. Electronic applications accepted.

Queen's University at Kingston, School of Graduate Studies, Faculty of Arts and Science, Department of Sociology, Kingston, ON K7L 3N6, Canada. Offers communication and information technology (MA, PhD); feminist sociology (MA, PhD); socio-legal studies (MA, PhD); sociological theory (MA, PhD). *Program availability:* Part-time. *Degree requirements:* For master's, thesis; for doctorate, comprehensive exam, thesis/dissertation. *Entrance requirements:* For master's, honors bachelor's degree in sociology; for doctorate, honors bachelor's degree, master's degree in sociology. Additional exam requirements/recommendations for international students: required—TOEFL.

Queens University of Charlotte, Knight School of Communication, Charlotte, NC 28274-0002. Offers organizational and strategic communication (MA). *Program availability:* Part-time, evening/weekend, online learning. *Degree requirements:* For master's, capstone course. *Entrance requirements:* Additional exam requirements/recommendations for international students: required—TOEFL. *Expenses:* Contact institution.

Quinnipiac University, School of Communications, Hamden, CT 06518-1940. Offers MS. *Program availability:* Part-time, evening/weekend, online learning. *Entrance requirements:* Additional exam requirements/recommendations for international students: required—TOEFL (minimum score 575 paper-based; 90 iBT), IELTS (minimum score 6.5). Electronic applications accepted. *Expenses: Tuition:* Part-time $1055 per credit. *Required fees:* $945 per semester. Tuition and fees vary according to course load and program.

Regent University, Graduate School, School of Communication and the Arts, Virginia Beach, VA 23464-9800. Offers acting (MFA); communication (MA, PhD), including media and arts management and promotion (MA), political communication (MA), strategic communication (MA), technical communication (MA); film and TV (MA), including producing (MA, MFA), production, script writing; film-television (MFA), including directing, producing (MA, MFA), script and screenwriting; journalism (MA); theatre (MA). *Program availability:* Part-time, evening/weekend, 100% online, blended/hybrid learning. *Degree requirements:* For master's, thesis or alternative; for doctorate, thesis/dissertation. *Entrance requirements:* For master's, transcripts, writing sample, resume, audition (for MFA programs); for doctorate, GRE General Test, resume, writing sample, recommendations, interview, transcripts, personal goals statement. Additional exam requirements/recommendations for international students: required—TOEFL (minimum score 577 paper-based). Electronic applications accepted. *Expenses:* Contact institution.

Rochester Institute of Technology, Graduate Enrollment Services, College of Imaging Arts and Sciences, School of Media Sciences, Rochester, NY 14623-5603. Offers MS. *Program availability:* Part-time. *Entrance requirements:* For master's, GRE, minimum GPA of 3.0 (recommended). Electronic applications accepted. *Expenses:* Contact institution.

Rochester Institute of Technology, Graduate Enrollment Services, College of Liberal Arts, School of Communication, MS Program in Communication and Media Technologies, Rochester, NY 14623-5603. Offers MS. *Program availability:* Part-time. *Degree requirements:* For master's, thesis or alternative, Thesis or comprehensive exam plus two additional courses. *Entrance requirements:* For master's, minimum GPA of 3.0 (recommended), three writing samples, personal statement, two letters of reference. Additional exam requirements/recommendations for international students: required—TOEFL (minimum score 570 paper-based; 88 iBT), IELTS (minimum score 6.5), PTE (minimum score 61). Electronic applications accepted.

Roosevelt University, Graduate Division, College of Arts and Sciences, Department of Communication, Chicago, IL 60605. Offers integrated marketing communications (MSIMC). *Program availability:* Part-time, evening/weekend. Electronic applications accepted.

Rutgers University - New Brunswick, School of Communication and Information, Ph.D. program in Communication, Information and Media, New Brunswick, NJ 08901. Offers PhD. *Program availability:* Part-time. *Degree requirements:* For doctorate, comprehensive exam, thesis/dissertation, qualifying exams. *Entrance requirements:* For doctorate, GRE General Test, proficiency in statistics. Additional exam requirements/recommendations for international students: required—TOEFL (minimum score 600 paper-based). Electronic applications accepted.

Sacred Heart University, Graduate Programs, College of Arts and Sciences, Department of Communication, Fairfield, CT 06825. Offers corporate communications and public relations (MA Comm); digital multimedia journalism (MA Comm); digital multimedia production (MA Comm); film and television production (MA); media literacy and digital culture (MA), including children, health and media, media and social justice, political action and media production; sports communication and media (MA), including athletic communications and promotions, sports broadcasting. *Program availability:* Part-time, evening/weekend. *Degree requirements:* For master's, thesis or alternative. *Entrance requirements:* For master's, bachelor's degree. Additional exam requirements/recommendations for international students: required—TOEFL (minimum score 570 paper-based, 80 iBT), TWE, or IELTS (6.5). Electronic applications accepted. *Expenses:* Contact institution.

Saginaw Valley State University, College of Arts and Behavioral Sciences, Program in Communication and Media Administration, University Center, MI 48710. Offers MA. *Program availability:* Part-time, evening/weekend. *Faculty:* 7 full-time (3 women), 1 (woman) part-time/adjunct. *Students:* 7 full-time (0 women), 5 part-time (4 women); includes 1 minority (Black or African American, non-Hispanic/Latino), 7 international. Average age 28. 19 applicants, 68% accepted, 6 enrolled. In 2019, 3 master's awarded. *Degree requirements:* For master's, thesis. *Entrance requirements:* For master's, minimum GPA of 3.0. Additional exam requirements/recommendations for international students: required—TOEFL (minimum score 540 paper-based; 76 iBT). *Application deadline:* For fall admission, 7/15 for international students; for winter admission, 11/15 for international students; for spring admission, 4/15 for international students. Applications are processed on a rolling basis. Application fee: $30 ($90 for international students). Electronic applications accepted. *Expenses: Tuition, area resident:* Full-time $11,212; part-time $622.90 per credit hour. Tuition, state resident: full-time $11,212; part-time $622.90 per credit hour. Tuition, nonresident: full-time $11,212; part-time $1253 per credit hour. *Required fees:* $263; $14.60 per credit hour. Tuition and fees vary according to course load, degree level and program. *Financial support:* Federal Work-Study and scholarships/grants available. Support available to part-time students. Financial award application deadline: 4/1; financial award applicants required to submit FAFSA. *Unit head:* Dr. Robert Drew, Professor of Communication, 989-964-7495, E-mail: rdrew@svsu.edu. *Application contact:* Jenna Briggs, Director, Graduate and International Admissions, 989-964-6096, Fax: 989-964-2788, E-mail: gradadm@svsu.edu.

Saint Louis University, Graduate Programs, College of Arts and Sciences, Department of Communication, St. Louis, MO 63103. Offers MA, MA-R. *Program availability:* Part-time. *Degree requirements:* For master's, thesis (for some programs), comprehensive oral and written exams. *Entrance requirements:* For master's, GRE General Test, letters of recommendation, resume, interview. Additional exam requirements/recommendations for international students: required—TOEFL (minimum score 525 paper-based). Electronic applications accepted.

Communication—General

St. Mary's University, Graduate Studies, Program in Communication Studies, San Antonio, TX 78228. Offers communication studies (MA); JD/MA. *Program availability:* Part-time, evening/weekend, online learning. *Degree requirements:* For master's, thesis (for some programs). *Entrance requirements:* For master's, GRE General Test, MAT, minimum GPA of 3.1; professional experience. Additional exam requirements/recommendations for international students: required—TOEFL (minimum score 550 paper-based; 80 iBT), IELTS (minimum score 6). Electronic applications accepted.

St. Thomas University - Florida, School of Leadership Studies, Miami Gardens, FL 33054-6459. Offers MA, MPS, MS, Ed D, Certificate. *Program availability:* Part-time, evening/weekend. *Entrance requirements:* Additional exam requirements/recommendations for international students: required—TOEFL (minimum score 550 paper-based; 79 iBT).

Sam Houston State University, College of Humanities and Social Sciences, Department of Communication Studies, Huntsville, TX 77341. Offers MA. *Program availability:* Part-time, evening/weekend, online learning. *Degree requirements:* For master's, comprehensive exam, thesis optional. *Entrance requirements:* For master's, GRE General Test, three letters of recommendation. Additional exam requirements/recommendations for international students: required—TOEFL (minimum score 550 paper-based; 79 iBT), IELTS (minimum score 6.5). Electronic applications accepted.

San Diego State University, Graduate and Research Affairs, College of Professional Studies and Fine Arts, School of Communication, San Diego, CA 92182. Offers advertising and public relations (MA); critical-cultural studies (MA); interaction studies (MA); intercultural and international studies (MA); new media studies (MA); news and information studies (MA); telecommunications and media management (MA). *Degree requirements:* For master's, thesis. *Entrance requirements:* For master's, GRE General Test, 3 letters of recommendation. Additional exam requirements/recommendations for international students: required—TOEFL. Electronic applications accepted.

San Jose State University, Program in Communication Studies, San Jose, CA 95192-0079. Offers MA. *Faculty:* 6 full-time (3 women), 1 part-time/adjunct (0 women). *Students:* 15 full-time (9 women), 22 part-time (14 women); includes 15 minority (9 Asian, non-Hispanic/Latino; 6 Hispanic/Latino), 3 international. Average age 28. 41 applicants, 59% accepted, 17 enrolled. In 2019, 15 master's awarded. *Application deadline:* For fall admission, 6/1 for domestic students, 3/1 for international students. Applications are processed on a rolling basis. Application fee: $70. Electronic applications accepted. *Expenses: Tuition, area resident:* Full-time $7176; part-time $4164 per credit hour. Tuition, state resident: full-time $7176; part-time $4164 per credit hour. Tuition, nonresident: full-time $7176; part-time $4165 per credit hour. *International tuition:* $7176 full-time. *Required fees:* $2110; $2110. *Financial support:* In 2019–20, 15 students received support, including 1 fellowship (averaging $1,000 per year); scholarships/grants also available. Financial award application deadline: 5/1; financial award applicants required to submit FAFSA. *Unit head:* Anne Marie Todd, Department Chair, 408-924-5391, E-mail: annemarie.todd@sjsu.edu. *Application contact:* Oona Tatton, Graduate Coordinator, E-mail: oona.hatton@sjsu.edu.
Website: http://www.sjsu.edu/comm/

Seton Hall University, College of Communication and the Arts, South Orange, NJ 07079-2697. Offers museum professions (MA), including exhibition development, museum management, museum registration; public relations (MA); strategic communication (MA). *Program availability:* Part-time, evening/weekend, online learning. *Degree requirements:* For master's, thesis (for some programs). *Entrance requirements:* For master's, GRE or MAT, official transcripts, resume, personal statement, 3 letters of recommendation. Additional exam requirements/recommendations for international students: required—TOEFL (minimum iBT score 80) or IELTS (6.5). Electronic applications accepted.

Shippensburg University of Pennsylvania, School of Graduate Studies, College of Arts and Sciences, Department of Communication/Journalism, Shippensburg, PA 17257-2299. Offers communication studies (MS). *Program availability:* Part-time, evening/weekend. *Faculty:* 6 full-time (2 women), 2 part-time/adjunct (both women). *Students:* 4 full-time (3 women), 5 part-time (2 women). Average age 27. 9 applicants, 33% accepted, 1 enrolled. In 2019, 6 master's awarded. *Degree requirements:* For master's, thesis, 6-credit thesis or 3-credit professional project, candidacy. *Entrance requirements:* For master's, GRE or MAT (if GPA less than 2.75), 3 professional references, resume, essay, 500-word statement of purpose. Additional exam requirements/recommendations for international students: required—TOEFL (minimum score 550 paper-based; 80 iBT), IELTS (minimum score 6), TOEFL (minimum score 550 paper-based, 80 iBT) or IELTS (minimum score 6). *Application deadline:* For fall admission, 4/30 for international students; for spring admission, 9/30 for international students. Applications are processed on a rolling basis. Application fee: $45. Electronic applications accepted. *Expenses:* Tuition, state resident: part-time $516 per credit. Tuition, nonresident: part-time $774 per credit. *Required fees:* $149 per credit. *Financial support:* In 2019–20, 7 students received support. Career-related internships or fieldwork, scholarships/grants, unspecified assistantships, and resident hall director and student payroll positions available. Support available to part-time students. Financial award application deadline: 3/1; financial award applicants required to submit FAFSA. *Unit head:* Dr. Kyle R. Heim, Assistant Professor and Program Coordinator, 717-477-1521, Fax: 717-477-4013, E-mail: krheim@ship.edu. *Application contact:* Maya T. Mapp, Director of Admissions, 717-477-1231, Fax: 717-477-4016, E-mail: mtmapp@ship.edu.
Website: http://www.ship.edu/communication_journalism/

Simon Fraser University, Office of Graduate Studies and Postdoctoral Fellows, Faculty of Communication, Art and Technology, School of Communication, Burnaby, BC V5A 1S6, Canada. Offers MA, PhD, MA/MA. *Degree requirements:* For master's, thesis or alternative, annual formal review; for doctorate, comprehensive exam, thesis/dissertation, annual formal review. *Entrance requirements:* For master's, minimum GPA of 3.0 (on scale of 4.33) or 3.33 based on last 60 credits of undergraduate courses; for doctorate, minimum GPA of 3.5 (on scale of 4.33). Additional exam requirements/recommendations for international students: recommended—TOEFL (minimum score 580 paper-based; 93 iBT), IELTS (minimum score 7), TWE (minimum score 5). Electronic applications accepted.

South Dakota State University, Graduate School, College of Arts, Humanities and Social Sciences, School of Communication and Journalism, Brookings, SD 57007. Offers communication studies and journalism (MS). *Accreditation:* ACEJMC. *Program availability:* Part-time, evening/weekend. *Degree requirements:* For master's, thesis, oral exam. *Entrance requirements:* Additional exam requirements/recommendations for international students: required—TOEFL (minimum score 550 paper-based; 79 iBT).

Southeastern Louisiana University, College of Arts, Humanities and Social Sciences, Department of Communication and Media Studies, Hammond, LA 70402. Offers health communications (MA); journalism (MA); marketing (MA); public relations (MA); sociology (MA). *Program availability:* Part-time. *Faculty:* 7 full-time (5 women). *Students:* 10 full-time (6 women), 11 part-time (6 women); includes 7 minority (5 Black or African American, non-Hispanic/Latino; 2 Hispanic/Latino). Average age 30. 9 applicants, 100% accepted, 6 enrolled. In 2019, 3 master's awarded. *Degree requirements:* For master's, comprehensive exam. *Entrance requirements:* For master's, GRE (minimum score 148 on Verbal section, 3.5 Written), Minimum 2.5 undergraduate GPA. Additional exam requirements/recommendations for international students: required—TOEFL (minimum score 525 paper-based; 75 iBT). *Application deadline:* For fall admission, 7/15 priority date for domestic students, 6/1 priority date for international students; for spring admission, 12/1 priority date for domestic students, 10/1 priority date for international students. Applications are processed on a rolling basis. Application fee: $20 ($30 for international students). Electronic applications accepted. *Expenses: Tuition, area resident:* Full-time $6684; part-time $489 per credit hour. Tuition, state resident: full-time $6684; part-time $489 per credit hour. Tuition, nonresident: full-time $19,162; part-time $1183 per credit hour. *International tuition:* $19,162 full-time. *Required fees:* $2124. *Financial support:* In 2019–20, 11 students received support, including 3 research assistantships with tuition reimbursements available (averaging $10,100 per year); career-related internships or fieldwork, institutionally sponsored loans, and unspecified assistantships also available. Financial award application deadline: 5/1; financial award applicants required to submit FAFSA. *Unit head:* Dr. James O'Connor, Department Head, 985-549-5060, Fax: 985-549-3088, E-mail: james.oconnor@selu.edu. *Application contact:* Office of Admissions, 985-549-5637, Fax: 985-549-5632, E-mail: admissions@southeastern.edu.
Website: http://www.southeastern.edu/acad_research/depts/comm/index.html

Southern Illinois University Carbondale, Graduate School, College of Mass Communication and Media Arts, Carbondale, IL 62901-4701. Offers MA, MFA, MS, PhD, MBA/MA. *Program availability:* Part-time. *Degree requirements:* For doctorate, thesis/dissertation. *Entrance requirements:* For doctorate, GRE General Test, minimum GPA of 3.25. Additional exam requirements/recommendations for international students: required—TOEFL.

Southern Utah University, Program in Communication, Cedar City, UT 84720-2498. Offers MA. *Program availability:* Part-time, 100% online. *Entrance requirements:* For master's, GRE. Additional exam requirements/recommendations for international students: required—TOEFL (minimum score 550 paper-based; 79 iBT), IELTS (minimum score 6), TOEFL (minimum score 550 paper-based, 79 iBT) or IELTS (minimum score 6). Electronic applications accepted. *Expenses:* Contact institution.

Spring Arbor University, School of Arts and Sciences, Spring Arbor, MI 49283-9799. Offers communication (MA); spiritual formation and leadership (MA). *Program availability:* Part-time, online learning. *Degree requirements:* For master's, thesis (for some programs). *Entrance requirements:* For master's, GRE (minimum score of 40th percentile and taken within last 5 years), bachelor's degree from regionally-accredited college or university, minimum GPA of 3.0 for at least the last two years of the bachelor's degree, at least two recommendations from professional/academic individuals. Additional exam requirements/recommendations for international students: required—TOEFL (minimum score 600 paper-based). *Expenses:* Contact institution.

Stanford University, School of Humanities and Sciences, Department of Communication, Stanford, CA 94305. Offers MA, PhD. *Faculty:* 16 full-time (7 women), 3 part-time/adjunct (0 women). *Students:* 60 full-time (34 women). Average age 30. 207 applicants, 13% accepted, 14 enrolled. In 2019, 24 master's, 6 doctorates awarded. Terminal master's awarded for partial completion of doctoral program. *Degree requirements:* For master's, thesis, project; for doctorate, thesis/dissertation, qualifying examination, area examination, 2 projects. *Entrance requirements:* For doctorate, GRE General Test. Additional exam requirements/recommendations for international students: required—TOEFL (minimum score 650 paper-based; 115 iBT). *Application deadline:* For fall admission, 12/1 for domestic and international students. Application fee: $125. Electronic applications accepted. *Expenses: Tuition:* Full-time $52,479; part-time $34,110 per unit. *Required fees:* $672; $224 per quarter. Tuition and fees vary according to program and student level. *Financial support:* Fellowships, research assistantships, and teaching assistantships available. *Unit head:* James Hamilton, Chair, 650-723-5448, E-mail: jayth@stanford.edu. *Application contact:* Katrin Wheeler, Student Services Manager, 650-724-8920, Fax: 650-725-2472, E-mail: comm-studentservices@stanford.edu.
Website: http://communication.stanford.edu/

State University of New York at Oswego, Graduate Studies, School of Communication, Media and the Arts, Oswego, NY 13126. Offers strategic communication (MA), including health communication, integrated media and social networks, organizational communication. *Students:* 34. In 2019, 17 master's awarded. *Entrance requirements:* For master's, GRE, official transcript, statement of purpose, resume, two letters of recommendation. *Application deadline:* Applications are processed on a rolling basis. Application fee: $65. Electronic applications accepted. *Financial support:* Fellowships, research assistantships, teaching assistantships, institutionally sponsored loans, scholarships/grants, and unspecified assistantships available. Support available to part-time students. Financial award application deadline: 4/1; financial award applicants required to submit FAFSA. *Unit head:* Dr. Julie Pretzat, Dean, 315-312-6612, E-mail: julie.pretzat@oswego.edu. *Application contact:* Dr. Julie Pretzat, Dean, 315-312-6612, E-mail: julie.pretzat@oswego.edu.

Stephen F. Austin State University, Graduate School, College of Liberal and Applied Arts, Department of Languages, Cultures and Communication, Nacogdoches, TX 75962. Offers communication (MA); Hispanic studies (MA). *Program availability:* Part-time. *Degree requirements:* For master's, comprehensive exam, thesis optional. *Entrance requirements:* For master's, GRE General Test. Additional exam requirements/recommendations for international students: required—TOEFL (minimum score 550 paper-based).

Stevens Institute of Technology, Graduate School, Charles V. Schaefer Jr. School of Engineering and Science, Department of Electrical and Computer Engineering, Program in Electrical Engineering, Hoboken, NJ 07030. Offers autonomous robotics (Certificate); electrical engineering (M Eng, PhD, Certificate), including computer architecture and digital systems (M Eng), microelectronics and photonics science and technology (M Eng), signal processing for communications (M Eng), telecommunications systems engineering (M Eng), wireless communications (M Eng, Certificate). *Program availability:* Part-time, evening/weekend. *Faculty:* 20 full-time (6 women), 2 part-time/adjunct. *Students:* 137 full-time (21 women), 23 part-time (5 women); includes 6 minority (2 Black or African American, non-Hispanic/Latino; 4 Asian, non-Hispanic/Latino), 134 international. Average age 25. In 2019, 82 master's, 5 doctorates, 1 other advanced degree awarded. Terminal master's awarded for partial completion of doctoral program. *Degree requirements:* For master's, thesis optional, minimum B average in major field and overall; for doctorate, comprehensive exam (for some programs), thesis/dissertation; for Certificate, minimum B average. *Entrance requirements:* For master's, International applicants must submit TOEFL/IELTS scores and fulfill the English Language Proficiency Requirement. Applicants to full-time programs who do not qualify for a score waiver are required to submit GRE/GMAT scores. Additional exam requirements/recommendations for international students: required—TOEFL (minimum score 74 iBT), IELTS (minimum score 6). *Application deadline:* For fall admission, 4/15 for domestic and international students; for spring admission, 11/1 for domestic and international students; for summer admission, 5/1 for domestic students. Applications are processed on a rolling basis. Application fee: $60. Electronic applications accepted. *Expenses: Tuition:* Full-time $52,134. *Required fees:* $1880. Tuition and fees vary according to course load. *Financial support:* Fellowships, research assistantships, teaching assistantships, career-related internships or fieldwork, Federal Work-Study, scholarships/grants, and unspecified assistantships available. Financial award application deadline: 2/15; financial award applicants required to submit FAFSA. *Unit head:* Dr. Jean Zu, Dean of SES, 201-216.8233, Fax: 201-216.8372, E-mail: Jean.Zu@stevens.edu. *Application contact:* Graduate Admissions, 888-783-8367, Fax: 888-511-1306, E-mail: graduate@stevens.edu.

Stevenson University, Program in Communication Studies, Stevenson, MD 21153. Offers MS. *Program availability:* Part-time, online only, 100% online, blended/hybrid learning. *Faculty:* 1 full-time (0 women), 3 part-time/adjunct (2 women). *Students:* 5 full-time (4 women), 18 part-time (15 women); includes 14 minority (12 Black or African American, non-Hispanic/Latino; 1 Asian, non-Hispanic/Latino; 1 Two or more races, non-Hispanic/Latino). Average age 27. 18 applicants, 67% accepted, 5 enrolled. In 2019, 11 master's awarded. *Degree requirements:* For master's, project or thesis. *Entrance requirements:* For master's, personal statement (3-5 paragraphs), official college transcript from degree-granting institution; additional transcripts may be required to demonstrate satisfaction of program-specific prerequisites, Bachelor's degree from a regionally accredited institution Minimum cumulative GPA of 3.0 on a 4.0 scale in past academic work. *Application deadline:* For fall admission, 8/9 priority date for domestic students; for spring admission, 1/11 priority date for domestic students; for summer admission, 5/1 priority date for domestic students. Applications are processed on a rolling basis. Application fee: $0. Electronic applications accepted. *Expenses:* $670 per credit. *Financial support:* Unspecified assistantships available. Financial award applicants required to submit FAFSA. *Unit head:* Dr. Lee Krahenbuhl, Interim Dean Stevenson University Online & Program Coordinator, 443-352-5348, E-mail: lkrahenbuhl@stevenson.edu. *Application contact:* Amanda Millar, Director, Admissions, 443-352-4243, Fax: 443-352-4440, E-mail: amillar@stevenson.edu.
Website: http://www.stevenson.edu/online/academics/online-graduate-programs/communication-studies/

Syracuse University, College of Visual and Performing Arts, MA Program in Communication and Rhetorical Studies, Syracuse, NY 13244. Offers MA. *Program availability:* Part-time. *Degree requirements:* For master's, comprehensive exam (for some programs), thesis (for some programs). *Entrance requirements:* For master's, GRE General Test, three letters of recommendation, writing sample, transcripts, personal statement, resume. Additional exam requirements/recommendations for international students: required—TOEFL (minimum score 90 iBT). Electronic applications accepted.

Syracuse University, S. I. Newhouse School of Public Communications, Syracuse, NY 13244. Offers MA, MS, PhD, JD/MA, JD/MS, MS/MA. *Accreditation:* ACEJMC (one or more programs are accredited). *Program availability:* Online learning. *Degree requirements:* For master's, comprehensive exam (for some programs); for doctorate, thesis/dissertation, qualifying exams. *Entrance requirements:* For master's and doctorate, GRE General Test, resume, official transcripts, personal statement, three letters of recommendation. Additional exam requirements/recommendations for international students: required—TOEFL (minimum score 100 iBT), IELTS (minimum score 7). Electronic applications accepted.

Tarleton State University, College of Graduate Studies, College of Liberal and Fine Arts, Department of Communication Studies, Stephenville, TX 76402. Offers MA. *Program availability:* Part-time. *Faculty:* 5 full-time (2 women). *Students:* 6 full-time (all women), 20 part-time (12 women); includes 8 minority (6 Black or African American, non-Hispanic/Latino; 1 Hispanic/Latino; 1 Two or more races, non-Hispanic/Latino). Average age 34. 16 applicants, 88% accepted, 9 enrolled. In 2019, 3 master's awarded. *Degree requirements:* For master's, comprehensive exam, thesis (for some programs). *Entrance requirements:* For master's, GRE, minimum overall GPA of 2.5. Additional exam requirements/recommendations for international students: required—TOEFL (minimum score 520 paper-based; 69 iBT); recommended—IELTS (minimum score 6), TSE (minimum score 50). *Application deadline:* For fall admission, 8/15 for domestic students; for spring admission, 1/5 for domestic students. Applications are processed on a rolling basis. Application fee: $50 ($130 for international students). Electronic applications accepted. *Expenses:* Tuition, state resident: part-time $221.73 per credit hour. Tuition, nonresident: part-time $636.73 per credit hour. *Required fees:* $198 per credit hour. $100 per semester. Tuition and fees vary according to degree level. *Financial support:* Teaching assistantships, career-related internships or fieldwork, Federal Work-Study, scholarships/grants, and unspecified assistantships available. Financial award applicants required to submit FAFSA. *Unit head:* Dr. Christopher Gearhart, Department Head, 254-968-9023, E-mail: gearhart@tarleton.edu. *Application contact:* Wendy Weiss, Graduate Admissions Coordinator, 254-968-9104, Fax: 254-968-9670, E-mail: weiss@tarleton.edu.
Website: https://www.tarleton.edu/communications/index.html

Teachers College, Columbia University, Department of Mathematics, Science and Technology, New York, NY 10027-6696. Offers biology 7-12 (MA); chemistry 7-12 (MA); communication and education (MA, Ed D); computing in education (MA); earth science 7-12 (MA); instructional technology and media (Ed M, MA, Ed D); mathematics education (Ed M, MA, Ed D, Ed DCT, PhD); physics 7-12 (MA); science and dental education (MA); science education (Ed M, MS, Ed DCT, PhD); supervisor/teacher of science education (MA); technology specialist (MA). *Faculty:* 13 full-time (8 women). *Students:* 166 full-time (124 women), 188 part-time (113 women); includes 122 minority (40 Black or African American, non-Hispanic/Latino; 1 American Indian or Alaska Native, non-Hispanic/Latino; 50 Asian, non-Hispanic/Latino; 23 Hispanic/Latino; 8 Two or more races, non-Hispanic/Latino), 120 international. 476 applicants, 51% accepted, 125 enrolled. *Unit head:* Dr. Erica Walker, Chair, 212-678-8246, E-mail: ewalker@tc.edu. *Application contact:* Kelly Sutton Skinner, Director of Admission and New Student Enrollment, 212-678-3710, E-mail: kms2237@tc.columbia.edu.
Website: http://www.tc.columbia.edu/mathematics-science-and-technology/

Temple University, Klein College of Media and Communication, Department of Communication and Social Influence, Philadelphia, PA 19122-6096. Offers communication management (MS); globalization and development communication (MS); media and communication (PhD). *Program availability:* Part-time, evening/weekend, online learning. *Faculty:* 8 full-time (3 women), 3 part-time/adjunct (all women). *Students:* 10 full-time (8 women), 13 part-time (9 women); includes 12 minority (10 Black or African American, non-Hispanic/Latino; 1 Hispanic/Latino; 1 Two or more races, non-Hispanic/Latino), 2 international. 27 applicants, 89% accepted, 13 enrolled. In 2019, 7 master's awarded. *Degree requirements:* For master's, capstone course; for doctorate, thesis/dissertation. *Entrance requirements:* For master's, GRE (required for m.s. in communication for development and social change), 2 letters of recommendation, statement of goals, resume; for doctorate, GRE, writing sample, statement of goals, master's degree in related discipline, 3 letters of recommendation. Additional exam requirements/recommendations for international students: required—TOEFL, IELTS, PTE, one of three is required. *Application deadline:* Applications are processed on a rolling basis. Application fee: $60. Electronic applications accepted. *Expenses:* Contact institution. *Financial support:* Teaching assistantships, Federal Work-Study, and health care benefits available. Financial award applicants required to submit FAFSA. *Unit head:* Jan Fernbeck, Co-Chair, 215-204-1497, E-mail: nmckenna@temple.edu. *Application contact:* Nicole McKenna, Graduate Office Director, 215-204-1497, E-mail: nmckenna@temple.edu.
Website: https://klein.temple.edu/academics/graduate-programs

Texas A&M University, College of Liberal Arts, Department of Communication, College Station, TX 77843. Offers communication (PhD). *Faculty:* 22. *Students:* 37 full-time (24 women), 11 part-time (7 women); includes 11 minority (5 Black or African American, non-Hispanic/Latino; 1 Asian, non-Hispanic/Latino; 5 Hispanic/Latino), 13 international. Average age 31. 61 applicants, 54% accepted, 16 enrolled. In 2019, 1 master's, 7 doctorates awarded. *Degree requirements:* For master's, comprehensive exam (for some programs), thesis optional; for doctorate, comprehensive exam, thesis/dissertation. *Entrance requirements:* For master's and doctorate, letters of recommendation, statement of purpose, writing sample, curriculum vitae. Additional exam requirements/recommendations for international students: required—TOEFL (minimum score 550 paper-based; 80 iBT), IELTS (minimum score 6), PTE (minimum score 53). *Application deadline:* For fall admission, 12/15 for domestic students. Applications are processed on a rolling basis. Application fee: $65 ($90 for international students). Electronic applications accepted. *Expenses:* Contact institution. *Financial support:* In 2019–20, 39 students received support, including 10 fellowships with tuition reimbursements available (averaging $16,201 per year), 4 research assistantships with tuition reimbursements available (averaging $9,481 per year), 31 teaching assistantships with tuition reimbursements available (averaging $18,819 per year); career-related internships or fieldwork, institutionally sponsored loans, scholarships/grants, traineeships, health care benefits, tuition waivers (full and partial), and unspecified assistantships also available. Support available to part-time students. Financial award application deadline: 3/15; financial award applicants required to submit FAFSA. *Unit head:* Dr. J. Kevin Barge, Head, 979-845-5514, E-mail: kbarge@tamu.edu. *Application contact:* Dr. Kristan Poirot, Director of Graduate Studies, 979-845-2842, E-mail: poirot@tamu.edu.
Website: http://comm.tamu.edu/

Texas A&M University–Corpus Christi, College of Graduate Studies, College of Liberal Arts, Corpus Christi, TX 78412. Offers communication (MA); English (MA); history (MA); psychology (MA), including clinical psychology, general psychology; public administration (MPA); studio art (MFA). *Program availability:* Part-time, evening/weekend. *Degree requirements:* For master's, comprehensive exam (for some programs). *Entrance requirements:* For master's, portfolio. Additional exam requirements/recommendations for international students: required—TOEFL (minimum score 550 paper-based; 79 iBT), IELTS (minimum score 6.5). Electronic applications accepted.

Texas Christian University, Bob Schieffer College of Communication, Fort Worth, TX 76129-0002. Offers communication studies (MS); strategic communication (MS). *Program availability:* Part-time. *Faculty:* 27 full-time (13 women). *Students:* 35 full-time (25 women); includes 6 minority (2 Black or African American, non-Hispanic/Latino; 3 Hispanic/Latino; 1 Native Hawaiian or other Pacific Islander, non-Hispanic/Latino), 3 international. Average age 25. 36 applicants, 78% accepted, 21 enrolled. In 2019, 12 master's awarded. *Degree requirements:* For master's, comprehensive exam (for some programs), thesis (for some programs). *Entrance requirements:* For master's, GRE General Test, 2 official transcripts, academic/professional objectives statement, 3 letters of recommendation. Additional exam requirements/recommendations for international students: required—TOEFL (minimum score 550 paper-based; 80 iBT). *Application deadline:* For fall admission, 2/15 for domestic and international students; for spring admission, 10/15 for domestic and international students. Applications are processed on a rolling basis. Application fee: $60. Electronic applications accepted. *Expenses:* Contact institution. *Financial support:* In 2019–20, 23 students received support, including 20 teaching assistantships with full tuition reimbursements available (averaging $12,500 per year); health care benefits, tuition waivers (full and partial), and unspecified assistantships also available. Financial award application deadline: 2/15. *Unit head:* Dr. Julie O'Neil, Associate Dean, 817-257-6966, Fax: 817-257-5921, E-mail: j.oneil@tcu.edu. *Application contact:* Ashley Tully, Coordinator of Degree of Certification, 817-257-4935, Fax: 817-257-5921, E-mail: A.TULLY@tcu.edu.
Website: http://www.schieffercollege.tcu.edu/

Texas Southern University, Tavis Smiley School of Communication, Houston, TX 77004-4584. Offers MA. *Program availability:* Part-time. *Degree requirements:* For master's, comprehensive exam, thesis. *Entrance requirements:* For master's, GRE General Test, minimum GPA of 2.5. Additional exam requirements/recommendations for international students: required—TOEFL. Electronic applications accepted.

Texas State University, The Graduate College, College of Fine Arts and Communication, Program in Communication Studies, San Marcos, TX 78666. Offers MA. *Program availability:* Part-time, evening/weekend. *Degree requirements:* For master's, comprehensive exam, thesis optional. *Entrance requirements:* For master's, baccalaureate degree from regionally-accredited institution with minimum GPA of 3.2 in last 60 hours of undergraduate course work, 3 letters of recommendation, statement of purpose. Additional exam requirements/recommendations for international students: required—TOEFL (minimum score 550 paper-based; 78 iBT), IELTS (minimum score 6), TOEFL (minimum iBT scores: 19 listening, 19 reading, 19 speaking, 18 writing). Electronic applications accepted.

Texas Tech University, Graduate School, College of Media and Communication, Department of Communication Studies, Lubbock, TX 79409-3082. Offers MA. *Program availability:* Part-time, Online courses are being introduced regularly for an online modality of this degree. *Faculty:* 19 full-time (10 women), 5 part-time/adjunct (3 women). *Students:* 27 full-time (22 women), 3 part-time (all women); includes 7 minority (3 Black or African American, non-Hispanic/Latino; 1 Asian, non-Hispanic/Latino; 3 Hispanic/Latino), 3 international. Average age 24. 26 applicants, 65% accepted, 14 enrolled. In 2019, 11 master's awarded. *Degree requirements:* For master's, comprehensive exam (for some programs), thesis or alternative. *Entrance requirements:* For master's, GRE (only if GPA is under 3.0), minimum undergraduate GPA of 3.0. Additional exam requirements/recommendations for international students: required—TOEFL (minimum score 550 paper-based; 79 iBT). *Application deadline:* For fall admission, 6/1 priority date for domestic students, 1/15 priority date for international students; for spring admission, 9/1 priority date for domestic students, 6/15 priority date for international students. Applications are processed on a rolling basis. Application fee: $65. Electronic applications accepted. *Expenses:* Contact institution. *Financial support:* In 2019–20, 29 students received support, including 20 fellowships (averaging $2,982 per year), 27 teaching assistantships (averaging $10,213 per year); scholarships/grants and unspecified assistantships also available. Financial award application deadline: 4/15; financial award applicants required to submit FAFSA. *Unit head:* Dr. Mark A. Gring, Associate Professor and Interim Department Chairperson, 806-843-3913, E-mail: mark.gring@ttu.edu. *Application contact:* Dr. Narissra Punyanunt-Carter, Professor, 806-834-3273, E-mail: n.punyanunt@ttu.edu.
Website: www.depts.ttu.edu/comc/programs/commstudies/

Tiffin University, Program in Humanities, Tiffin, OH 44883-2161. Offers art and visual media (MH); communication (MH); creative writing (MH); English (MH); film studies (MH); humanities (MH); individualized studies (MH). *Program availability:* Part-time, evening/weekend, online only, 100% online, blended/hybrid learning. *Entrance requirements:* For master's, work experience. Additional exam requirements/

recommendations for international students: required—TOEFL (minimum score 550 paper-based; 79 iBT). Electronic applications accepted. Application fee is waived when completed online. *Expenses:* Contact institution.

Towson University, College of Fine Arts and Communication, Program in Communication Management, Towson, MD 21252-0001. Offers MS. *Students:* 11 full-time (10 women), 19 part-time (13 women); includes 19 minority (13 Black or African American, non-Hispanic/Latino; 4 Hispanic/Latino; 2 Two or more races, non-Hispanic/Latino). *Entrance requirements:* For master's, bachelor's degree with 24 credits in mass communications, public relations, advertising or communication studies; advanced writing and basic statistics courses; professional experience; minimum GPA of 3.0; letter of recommendation; resume. Additional exam requirements/recommendations for international students: required—TOEFL. *Application deadline:* For fall admission, 1/17 for domestic students, 5/15 for international students; for spring admission, 10/15 for domestic students, 12/1 for international students. Applications are processed on a rolling basis. Application fee: $45. Electronic applications accepted. *Expenses: Tuition, area resident:* Full-time $7920; part-time $439 per credit. Tuition, nonresident: full-time $16,344; part-time $908 per credit. *International tuition:* $16,344 full-time. *Required fees:* $2628; $146 per credit. $876 per term. *Financial support:* Application deadline: 4/1. *Unit head:* Dr. Lingling Zhang, Program Director, 410-704-3458, E-mail: lizhang@towson.edu. *Application contact:* Coverley Beidleman, Assistant Director of Graduate Admissions, 410-704-5630, Fax: 410-704-3030, E-mail: grads@towson.edu.
Website: https://www.towson.edu/cofac/departments/mass-communication/communication-management/

Trinity Washington University, School of Business and Graduate Studies, Washington, DC 20017-1094. Offers business administration (MBA); communication (MA); international security studies (MA); organizational management (MSA), including federal program management, human resource management, nonprofit management, organizational development, public and community health. *Program availability:* Part-time, evening/weekend. *Degree requirements:* For master's, thesis (for some programs), capstone project (MSA). *Entrance requirements:* For master's, minimum GPA of 2.5. Additional exam requirements/recommendations for international students: required—TOEFL (minimum score 550 paper-based).

Troy University, Graduate School, College of Communication and Fine Arts, Troy, AL 36082. Offers strategic communication (MS). *Program availability:* Part-time, evening/weekend, online learning. *Faculty:* 3 full-time (all women), 2 part-time/adjunct (0 women). *Students:* 34 full-time (25 women), 80 part-time (57 women); includes 40 minority (35 Black or African American, non-Hispanic/Latino; 5 Hispanic/Latino). Average age 31. 69 applicants, 100% accepted, 53 enrolled. In 2019, 61 master's awarded. *Degree requirements:* For master's, comprehensive exam, thesis optional, minimum GPA of 3.0, admission to candidacy. *Entrance requirements:* For master's, GRE (minimum score of 850 on old exam or 290 on new exam), MAT (minimum score of 385) or GMAT (minimum score of 380), bachelor's degree; minimum undergraduate GPA of 2.5 or 3.0 on last 30 semester hours, letter of recommendation; transcript. Additional exam requirements/recommendations for international students: required—TOEFL (minimum score 523 paper-based; 70 iBT), IELTS (minimum score 6). *Application deadline:* For fall admission, 6/1 for international students; for spring admission, 10/15 for international students. Applications are processed on a rolling basis. Application fee: $50. Electronic applications accepted. *Expenses: Tuition, area resident:* Full-time $7650; part-time $2550 per semester hour. Tuition, state resident: full-time $7650; part-time $2550 per semester hour. Tuition, nonresident: full-time $15,300; part-time $5100 per semester hour. *International tuition:* $15,300 full-time. *Required fees:* $856; $352 per semester hour. $176 per semester. *Financial support:* In 2019–20, 36 students received support. Fellowships, research assistantships, teaching assistantships, career-related internships or fieldwork, Federal Work-Study, scholarships/grants, traineeships, tuition waivers, and unspecified assistantships available. Support available to part-time students. Financial award application deadline: 3/1; financial award applicants required to submit FAFSA. *Unit head:* Dr. Larry Blocher, Dean, 334-670-3869, Fax: 334-670-3547, E-mail: lblocher@troy.edu. *Application contact:* Haley McKinnon, Director of Graduate Admissions, 334-670-3178, Fax: 334-670-3733, E-mail: hmckinnon@troy.edu.
Website: https://www.troy.edu/academics/colleges-schools/college-communication-fine-arts/index.html

Université de Montréal, Faculty of Arts and Sciences, Department of Communication, Montréal, QC H3C 3J7, Canada. Offers communication (PhD); communication sciences (M Sc). *Degree requirements:* For master's, thesis; for doctorate, one foreign language, thesis/dissertation, general exam. *Entrance requirements:* For doctorate, proficiency in French. Electronic applications accepted.

Université du Québec à Montréal, Graduate Programs, Program in Communications, Montréal, QC H3C 3P8, Canada. Offers MA, PhD. *Program availability:* Part-time. *Degree requirements:* For master's, thesis; for doctorate, thesis/dissertation. *Entrance requirements:* For master's, appropriate bachelor's degree or equivalent, proficiency in French; for doctorate, appropriate master's degree or equivalent, proficiency in French.

Université du Québec à Trois-Rivières, Graduate Programs, Program in Social Communication, Trois-Rivières, QC G9A 5H7, Canada. Offers MA, DESS.

University at Albany, State University of New York, College of Arts and Sciences, Department of Communication, Albany, NY 12222-0001. Offers communication (MA); sociology and communication (PhD). *Program availability:* Part-time, blended/hybrid learning. *Faculty:* 17 full-time (9 women), 21 part-time/adjunct (13 women). *Students:* 39 full-time (28 women), 36 part-time (32 women); includes 18 minority (9 Black or African American, non-Hispanic/Latino; 4 Asian, non-Hispanic/Latino; 4 Hispanic/Latino; 1 Two or more races, non-Hispanic/Latino), 14 international. 49 applicants, 71% accepted, 19 enrolled. In 2019, 18 master's, 1 doctorate awarded. *Degree requirements:* For master's, comprehensive exam, thesis or alternative; for doctorate, comprehensive exam, thesis/dissertation. *Entrance requirements:* For master's, minimum GPA of 3.0, transcripts of all schools attended, statement of background and goals, departmental questionnaire, resume, names and contact information for 3 recommenders; for doctorate, GRE, minimum GPA of 3.0, transcripts of all schools attended, statement of background and goals, departmental questionnaire, resume, names and contact information for 3 recommenders. Additional exam requirements/recommendations for international students: required—TOEFL (minimum score 550 paper-based). *Application deadline:* For fall admission, 1/15 priority date for domestic students, 5/1 for international students. Applications are processed on a rolling basis. Application fee: $75. Electronic applications accepted. *Expenses: Tuition, area resident:* Full-time $11,530; part-time $480 per credit hour. Tuition, nonresident: full-time $23,530; part-time $980 per credit hour. *International tuition:* $23,530 full-time. *Required fees:* $2185; $96 per credit hour. Part-time tuition and fees vary according to course load and program. *Financial support:* Fellowships, teaching assistantships, career-related internships or fieldwork, and institutionally sponsored loans available. Financial award application deadline: 3/1. *Unit head:* Annis Golden, Chair, 518-442-4871, Fax: 518-442-3884, E-mail: agolden@albany.edu. *Application contact:* Michael DeRensis, Director, Graduate Admissions, 518-442-3980, Fax: 518-442-3922, E-mail: graduate@albany.edu.
Website: https://www.albany.edu/communication/

University at Buffalo, the State University of New York, Graduate School, College of Arts and Sciences, Department of Communication, Buffalo, NY 14260. Offers MA, PhD. *Faculty:* 18 full-time (6 women), 11 part-time/adjunct (7 women). *Students:* 23 full-time (15 women), 6 part-time (4 women); includes 14 minority (2 Black or African American, non-Hispanic/Latino; 12 Asian, non-Hispanic/Latino), 11 international. Average age 30. 78 applicants, 47% accepted, 8 enrolled. In 2019, 9 master's, 4 doctorates awarded. Terminal master's awarded for partial completion of doctoral program. *Degree requirements:* For master's, thesis; for doctorate, comprehensive exam, thesis/dissertation. *Entrance requirements:* For master's, minimum GPA of 3.0; for doctorate, GRE General Test, minimum GPA of 3.0. Additional exam requirements/recommendations for international students: required—TOEFL (minimum score 600 paper-based; 100 iBT), IELTS (minimum score 7), GRE; recommended—TWE. *Application deadline:* For fall admission, 1/1 priority date for domestic students, 4/1 priority date for international students. Applications are processed on a rolling basis. Application fee: $75. Electronic applications accepted. Application fee is waived when completed online. *Expenses: Tuition, area resident:* Full-time $11,310; part-time $471 per credit hour. Tuition, state resident: full-time $11,310; part-time $471 per credit hour. Tuition, nonresident: full-time $23,100; part-time $963 per credit hour. *International tuition:* $23,100 full-time. *Required fees:* $2820. *Financial support:* In 2019–20, 2 students received support, including 1 fellowship with full tuition reimbursement available (averaging $10,000 per year), 2 research assistantships with full tuition reimbursements available (averaging $19,000 per year), 13 teaching assistantships with full tuition reimbursements available (averaging $20,000 per year); career-related internships or fieldwork, institutionally sponsored loans, scholarships/grants, health care benefits, and unspecified assistantships also available. Financial award application deadline: 1/1. *Unit head:* Dr. Mark G. Frank, Chairman, 716-645-1170, Fax: 716-645-2086, E-mail: mfrank83@buffalo.edu. *Application contact:* Rose Gryckiewicz, Graduate Program Coordinator, 716-645-1505, Fax: 716-645-2086, E-mail: rfg@buffalo.edu.
Website: http://www.cas.buffalo.edu/communication

The University of Akron, Graduate School, Buchtel College of Arts and Sciences, School of Communication, Akron, OH 44325. Offers MA. *Program availability:* Part-time, evening/weekend. *Degree requirements:* For master's, thesis, project or written comprehensive exam. *Entrance requirements:* For master's, baccalaureate degree in communication, journalism, or related field; essay of no more than 500 words outlining reasons for choosing graduate program in communication at The University of Akron. Additional exam requirements/recommendations for international students: required—TOEFL (minimum score 79 iBT), IELTS (minimum score 6.5). Electronic applications accepted.

The University of Alabama, Graduate School, College of Communication and Information Sciences, Tuscaloosa, AL 35487-0172. Offers MA, MFA, MLIS, PhD. *Accreditation:* ACEJMC (one or more programs are accredited at the [master's] level). *Faculty:* 88 full-time (36 women), 2 part-time/adjunct (1 woman). *Students:* 201 full-time (141 women), 205 part-time (147 women); includes 74 minority (43 Black or African American, non-Hispanic/Latino; 1 American Indian or Alaska Native, non-Hispanic/Latino; 2 Asian, non-Hispanic/Latino; 18 Hispanic/Latino; 10 Two or more races, non-Hispanic/Latino), 29 international. Average age 32. 322 applicants, 77% accepted, 139 enrolled. In 2019, 155 master's, 8 doctorates awarded. *Degree requirements:* For master's, comprehensive exam, thesis or alternative; for doctorate, comprehensive exam, thesis/dissertation. *Entrance requirements:* For master's, GRE; for doctorate, GRE, minimum graduate GPA of 3.0, master's degree. Additional exam requirements/recommendations for international students: required—TOEFL (minimum score 600 paper-based; 100 iBT). *Application deadline:* For fall admission, 2/15 priority date for domestic and international students; for winter admission, 11/1 priority date for international students; for spring admission, 11/1 priority date for domestic students. Applications are processed on a rolling basis. Application fee: $50 ($60 for international students). Electronic applications accepted. *Expenses: Tuition, area resident:* Full-time $10,780; part-time $440 per credit hour. Tuition, nonresident: full-time $30,250; part-time $1550 per credit hour. *Financial support:* In 2019–20, 70 students received support. Fellowships with tuition reimbursements available, research assistantships with tuition reimbursements available, teaching assistantships with tuition reimbursements available, institutionally sponsored loans, health care benefits, and unspecified assistantships available. Financial award application deadline: 2/15. *Unit head:* Dr. Mark Nelson, Dean, 205-348-4787, E-mail: mnelson@ua.edu. *Application contact:* Allison Payne, Executive Assistant, 205-348-4786, E-mail: allison.s.payne@ua.edu.
Website: http://www.cis.ua.edu

The University of Alabama at Birmingham, College of Arts and Sciences, Program in Communication Management, Birmingham, AL 35294. Offers MA. *Program availability:* Part-time, evening/weekend. *Faculty:* 9 full-time (2 women), 1 (woman) part-time/adjunct. *Students:* 14 full-time (9 women), 13 part-time (12 women); includes 11 minority (all Black or African American, non-Hispanic/Latino), 4 international. Average age 29. 20 applicants, 75% accepted, 8 enrolled. In 2019, 25 master's awarded. *Degree requirements:* For master's, comprehensive exam, thesis or alternative. *Entrance requirements:* For master's, minimum undergraduate GPA of 3.0, letters of reference. Additional exam requirements/recommendations for international students: required—TOEFL (minimum score 550 paper-based; 80 iBT), IELTS (minimum score 6.5). *Application deadline:* For fall admission, 8/1 for domestic and international students; for spring admission, 12/1 for domestic and international students; for summer admission, 5/1 for domestic and international students. Applications are processed on a rolling basis. Application fee: $45 ($60 for international students). Electronic applications accepted. *Financial support:* In 2019–20, 3 students received support, including 3 teaching assistantships (averaging $20,000 per year). *Unit head:* Dr. Jonathan H. Amsbary, Graduate Program Director, 205-934-3877, Fax: 205-934-8916, E-mail: amsbary@uab.edu. *Application contact:* Holly Hebard, Director of Graduate School Operations, 205-934-8227, Fax: 205-934-8413, E-mail: gradschool@uab.edu.
Website: http://www.uab.edu/cas/communication/graduate-program

University of Alaska Fairbanks, College of Liberal Arts, Department of Communication and Journalism, Fairbanks, AK 99775-5680. Offers professional communication (MA). *Program availability:* Part-time. *Degree requirements:* For master's, comprehensive exam, thesis, oral defense of thesis. *Entrance requirements:* For master's, bachelor's degree from accredited institution with minimum cumulative undergraduate and major GPA of 3.0, academic writing sample. Additional exam requirements/recommendations for international students: required—TOEFL (minimum score 550 paper-based; 79 iBT), IELTS (minimum score 6.5). Electronic applications accepted.

University of Alberta, Faculty of Extension, Edmonton, AB T6G 2E1, Canada. Offers communications and technology (MA).

University of Alberta, Faculty of Graduate Studies and Research, Program in Communications and Technology, Edmonton, AB T6G 2E1, Canada. Offers MACT.

The University of Arizona, College of Social and Behavioral Sciences, Department of Communication, Tucson, AZ 85721. Offers MA, PhD. *Program availability:* Part-time. Terminal master's awarded for partial completion of doctoral program. *Degree requirements:* For master's, thesis optional; for doctorate, comprehensive exam, thesis/dissertation. *Entrance requirements:* For master's, GRE General Test, minimum GPA of 3.25, writing sample, 3 letters of recommendation; for doctorate, GRE General Test, minimum GPA of 3.5, writing sample, 3 letters of recommendation, statement of purpose. Additional exam requirements/recommendations for international students: required—TOEFL (minimum score 600 paper-based; 90 iBT). Electronic applications accepted.

University of Arkansas, Graduate School, J. William Fulbright College of Arts and Sciences, Department of Communication, Fayetteville, AR 72701. Offers MA. *Program availability:* Part-time. *Students:* 23 full-time (14 women), 2 part-time (1 woman); includes 6 minority (4 Black or African American, non-Hispanic/Latino; 2 Hispanic/Latino), 1 international. 18 applicants, 89% accepted. In 2019, 14 master's awarded. *Entrance requirements:* For master's, GRE General Test. *Application deadline:* For fall admission, 8/1 for domestic students, 4/1 for international students; for spring admission, 12/1 for domestic students, 10/1 for international students; for summer admission, 4/15 for domestic students, 3/1 for international students. Applications are processed on a rolling basis. Application fee: $60. Electronic applications accepted. *Financial support:* In 2019–20, 21 teaching assistantships were awarded; fellowships, research assistantships, career-related internships or fieldwork, and Federal Work-Study also available. Support available to part-time students. Financial award application deadline: 4/1; financial award applicants required to submit FAFSA. *Unit head:* Dr. Robert Brady, Department Chair, 479-575-3048, Fax: 479-575-6734, E-mail: rbrady@uark.edu. *Application contact:* Dr. Ryan Neville-Shepard, Graduate Coordinator, 479-575-5952, Fax: 479-575-6734, E-mail: rnevshep@uark.edu.
Website: https://fulbright.uark.edu/departments/communication/

University of Bridgeport, College of Public and International Affairs, Bridgeport, CT 06604. Offers East Asian and Pacific Rim studies (MA); global development and peace (MA); global media and communication studies (MA). *Program availability:* Part-time, evening/weekend. *Degree requirements:* For master's, thesis. *Entrance requirements:* Additional exam requirements/recommendations for international students: recommended—TOEFL (minimum score 550 paper-based; 80 iBT), IELTS (minimum score 6.5).

University of California, Davis, Graduate Studies, Program in Communication, Davis, CA 95616. Offers MA. *Degree requirements:* For master's, comprehensive exam (for some programs), thesis (for some programs). *Entrance requirements:* For master's, GRE. Additional exam requirements/recommendations for international students: required—TOEFL (minimum score 550 paper-based).

University of California, San Diego, Graduate Division, Department of Communication, La Jolla, CA 92093. Offers PhD. *Students:* 22 full-time (19 women). 101 applicants, 19% accepted, 10 enrolled. In 2019, 2 doctorates awarded. *Degree requirements:* For doctorate, one foreign language, comprehensive exam, thesis/dissertation, 2 quarters of teaching assistantship. *Entrance requirements:* For doctorate, GRE General Test, demonstrated competence in a natural language other than English, writing samples, letters of recommendation. Additional exam requirements/recommendations for international students: required—TOEFL (minimum score 550 paper-based; 80 iBT), IELTS (minimum score 7), PTE. *Application deadline:* For fall admission, 12/17 for domestic students. Application fee: $105 ($125 for international students). Electronic applications accepted. *Financial support:* Fellowships, research assistantships, teaching assistantships, and scholarships/grants available. Financial award applicants required to submit FAFSA. *Unit head:* Brian Goldfarb, Chair, 858-534-2366, E-mail: bgoldfarb@ucsd.edu. *Application contact:* Melanie Lynn, Graduate Coordinator, 858-534-2379, E-mail: comm-gradadmissions@ucsd.edu.
Website: http://communication.ucsd.edu

University of California, Santa Barbara, Graduate Division, College of Letters and Sciences, Division of Social Sciences, Department of Communication, Santa Barbara, CA 93106-4020. Offers cognitive science (PhD); communication (PhD); feminist studies (PhD); language, interaction and social organization (PhD); quantitative methods in the social sciences (PhD); society and technology (PhD); MA/PhD. Terminal master's awarded for partial completion of doctoral program. *Degree requirements:* For doctorate, comprehensive exam, thesis/dissertation. *Entrance requirements:* For doctorate, GRE. Additional exam requirements/recommendations for international students: required—TOEFL (minimum score 80 iBT), IELTS (minimum score 7). Electronic applications accepted.

University of California, Santa Cruz, Division of Graduate Studies, Division of Physical and Biological Sciences, Program in Science Communication, Santa Cruz, CA 95064. Offers Certificate. *Entrance requirements:* For degree, GRE General Test, GRE Subject Test, bachelor's degree in science. Additional exam requirements/recommendations for international students: required—TOEFL (minimum score 550 paper-based; 83 iBT); recommended—IELTS (minimum score 8). Electronic applications accepted.

University of Central Missouri, The Graduate School, Warrensburg, MO 64093. Offers accountancy (MA); accounting (MBA); applied mathematics (MS); aviation safety (MA); biology (MS); business administration (MBA); career and technology education (MS); college student personnel administration (MS); communication (MA); computer information systems and information technology (MS); computer science (MS); counseling (MS); criminal justice and criminology (MS); educational leadership (Ed S); educational leadership and policy analysis (Ed D); educational technology (MS, Ed S); elementary and early childhood education (MSE); English (MA); english language learners - teaching english as a second language (MA); environmental studies (MA); finance (MBA); history (MA); industrial hygiene (MS); industrial management (MS); information systems (MBA); kinesiology (MS); library science and information services (MS); literacy education (MSE); marketing (MBA); mathematics (MS); music (MA); occupational safety management (MS); professional leadership - adult, career, and technical education (Ed S); professional leadership - counseling (Ed S); psychology (MS); rural family nursing (MS); school administration (MSE); social gerontology (MS); sociology (MA); special education (MSE); speech language pathology (MS); teaching (MAT); technology (MS); technology management (PhD); theatre (MA). *Accreditation:* ASHA. *Program availability:* Part-time, 100% online, blended/hybrid learning. *Faculty:* 236 full-time (113 women), 97 part-time/adjunct (61 women). *Students:* 787 full-time (448 women), 1,459 part-time (997 women); includes 213 minority (72 Black or African American, non-Hispanic/Latino; 5 American Indian or Alaska Native, non-Hispanic/Latino; 27 Asian, non-Hispanic/Latino; 59 Hispanic/Latino; 50 Two or more races, non-Hispanic/Latino), 574 international. Average age 30. 1,477 applicants, 68% accepted, 664 enrolled. In 2019, 831 master's, 93 other advanced degrees awarded. *Degree requirements:* For master's and Ed S, comprehensive exam (for some programs), thesis (for some programs). *Entrance requirements:* For master's, A GRE or GMAT test score may be required by some of the programs, A minimum GPA, letters of recommendation, a statement of purpose may be required by some of the programs; for Ed S, A master's degree is required for the application of an Education Specialist's degree program. Additional exam requirements/recommendations for international students: required—TOEFL (minimum score 550 paper-based; 79 iBT). *Application deadline:* For fall admission, 6/1 priority date for domestic and international students; for spring admission, 10/15 priority date for domestic and international students; for summer admission, 4/1 priority date for domestic and international students. Applications are processed on a rolling basis. Application fee: $30 ($75 for international students). Electronic applications accepted. *Expenses: Tuition, area resident:* Full-time $7524; part-time $313.50 per credit hour. Tuition, state resident: full-time $7524; part-time $313.50 per credit hour. Tuition, nonresident: full-time $15,048; part-time $627 per credit hour. *International tuition:* $15,048 full-time. *Required fees:* $915; $30.50 per credit hour. *Financial support:* In 2019–20, 89 students received support. Research assistantships, teaching assistantships, career-related internships or fieldwork, Federal Work-Study, scholarships/grants, unspecified assistantships, and administrative and laboratory assistantships available. Support available to part-time students. Financial award application deadline: 4/1; financial award applicants required to submit FAFSA. *Unit head:* Shellie Hewitt, Director of Graduate and International Student Services, 660-543-4621, Fax: 660-543-4778, E-mail: hewitt@ucmo.edu. *Application contact:* Shellie Hewitt, Director of Graduate and International Student Services, 660-543-4621, Fax: 660-543-4778, E-mail: hewitt@ucmo.edu.
Website: http://www.ucmo.edu/graduate/

University of Cincinnati, Graduate School, McMicken College of Arts and Sciences, Department of Communication, Cincinnati, OH 45221. Offers MA. *Program availability:* Part-time, evening/weekend. *Degree requirements:* For master's, thesis or alternative, 33 credit hours in COMM; Completion project of either a thesis or praxis. *Entrance requirements:* For master's, GRE General Test, undergraduate course work in communication. Additional exam requirements/recommendations for international students: required—TOEFL. Electronic applications accepted.

University of Colorado Boulder, Graduate School, College of Media, Communication and Information, Program in Communication, Boulder, CO 80309. Offers MA, PhD. Terminal master's awarded for partial completion of doctoral program. *Degree requirements:* For master's, comprehensive exam, thesis optional; for doctorate, comprehensive exam, thesis/dissertation. *Entrance requirements:* For master's and doctorate, GRE General Test, minimum undergraduate GPA of 3.2. Electronic applications accepted. Application fee is waived when completed online.

University of Colorado Colorado Springs, College of Letters, Arts and Sciences, Department of Communication, Colorado Springs, CO 80918. Offers MA. *Program availability:* Part-time, 100% online, blended/hybrid learning. *Faculty:* 17 full-time (14 women), 13 part-time/adjunct (5 women). *Students:* 6 full-time (all women), 12 part-time (all women); includes 8 minority (4 Hispanic/Latino; 4 Two or more races, non-Hispanic/Latino). Average age 30. 15 applicants, 80% accepted, 9 enrolled. In 2019, 14 master's awarded. *Degree requirements:* For master's, thesis optional. *Entrance requirements:* Additional exam requirements/recommendations for international students: recommended—TOEFL (minimum score 80 iBT), IELTS (minimum score 6.5). *Application deadline:* Applications are processed on a rolling basis. Application fee: $60 ($100 for international students). Electronic applications accepted. *Expenses:* Contact institution. *Financial support:* In 2019–20, 3 students received support, including 2 research assistantships (averaging $4,500 per year), 1 teaching assistantship (averaging $2,000 per year); fellowships, career-related internships or fieldwork, Federal Work-Study, scholarships/grants, traineeships, and unspecified assistantships also available. Support available to part-time students. Financial award application deadline: 3/1; financial award applicants required to submit FAFSA. *Unit head:* Dr. Kay Yoon, Director of Graduate Studies, 719-255-4985, Fax: 719-255-4030, E-mail: kyoon@uccs.edu. *Application contact:* Sarah Elsey, Graduate School Program Manager, 719-255-3072, E-mail: gradinfo@uccs.edu.
Website: https://www.uccs.edu/comm/graduate

University of Colorado Denver, College of Liberal Arts and Sciences, Department of Communication, Denver, CO 80217. Offers MA. *Program availability:* Part-time, evening/weekend. *Degree requirements:* For master's, comprehensive exam, 33 credits; thesis or substantial writing project. *Entrance requirements:* For master's, GRE General Test (minimum score of 153) or LSAT (minimum score of 150), minimum undergraduate GPA of 3.25, three letters of recommendation, two official transcripts, resume, academic writing sample. Additional exam requirements/recommendations for international students: required—TOEFL (minimum score 80 iBT); recommended—IELTS (minimum score 6.5). Electronic applications accepted. Tuition and fees vary according to course load, program and reciprocity agreements.

University of Connecticut, Graduate School, College of Liberal Arts and Sciences, Department of Communication, Storrs, CT 06269. Offers MA, Au D, PhD. *Accreditation:* ASHA (one or more programs are accredited). Terminal master's awarded for partial completion of doctoral program. *Degree requirements:* For master's, comprehensive exam; for doctorate, thesis/dissertation. *Entrance requirements:* For master's and doctorate, GRE General Test. Additional exam requirements/recommendations for international students: required—TOEFL (minimum score 550 paper-based). Electronic applications accepted.

University of Dayton, Department of Communication, Dayton, OH 45469. Offers communication (MA); interdisciplinary communication (MA). *Program availability:* Part-time, 100% online. *Degree requirements:* For master's, comprehensive exam (for some programs), thesis optional, 36 credit hours of course work. *Entrance requirements:* For master's, GRE, minimum undergraduate GPA of 3.0, 3 letters of recommendation, personal statement, curriculum vitae/resume, transcripts, writing samples (if applying for a graduate assistantship). Additional exam requirements/recommendations for international students: required—TOEFL (minimum score 550 paper-based; 80 iBT). Electronic applications accepted.

University of Delaware, College of Arts and Sciences, Department of Communication, Newark, DE 19716. Offers MA. *Program availability:* Part-time, evening/weekend. *Degree requirements:* For master's, comprehensive exam (for some programs), thesis (for some programs). *Entrance requirements:* For master's, GRE General Test, minimum GPA of 3.0. Additional exam requirements/recommendations for international students: required—TOEFL (minimum score 600 paper-based). Electronic applications accepted.

University of Denver, University College, Denver, CO 80208. Offers arts and culture (MA, Certificate); communication management (MS, Certificate), including translation studies (Certificate), world history and culture (Certificate); environmental policy and management (MS); geographic information systems (MS); global affairs (MA, Certificate), including human capital in organizations (Certificate), philanthropic leadership (Certificate), project management (Certificate), strategic innovation and change (Certificate); healthcare leadership (MS); information communications and technology (MS); leadership and organizations (MS); professional creative writing (MA, Certificate), including emergency planning and response (Certificate), organizational security (Certificate); security management (MS, Certificate); strategic human resources (Certificate). *Program availability:* Part-time, evening/weekend, 100% online, blended/hybrid learning. *Faculty:* 104 part-time/adjunct (52 women). *Students:* 59 full-time (33 women), 1,893 part-time (1,210 women); includes 545 minority (133 Black or African American, non-Hispanic/Latino; 16 American Indian or Alaska Native, non-Hispanic/Latino; 64 Asian, non-Hispanic/Latino; 252 Hispanic/Latino; 4 Native Hawaiian or other Pacific Islander, non-Hispanic/Latino; 76 Two or more races, non-Hispanic/Latino), 78 international. Average age 32. 1,290 applicants, 91% accepted, 752 enrolled. In 2019, 457 master's, 181 other advanced degrees awarded. *Degree requirements:* For master's, capstone project. *Entrance requirements:* For master's, baccalaureate degree, transcripts, two letters of recommendation, personal statement, resume, writing sample (Master of Arts in Professional Creative Writing). Additional exam requirements/

recommendations for international students: required—TOEFL (minimum score 550 paper-based; 80 iBT). *Application deadline:* For fall admission, 6/19 priority date for domestic students, 6/14 priority date for international students; for winter admission, 10/25 priority date for domestic students, 9/27 priority date for international students; for spring admission, 2/7 priority date for domestic students, 1/10 priority date for international students; for summer admission, 4/24 priority date for domestic students, 3/27 priority date for international students. Applications are processed on a rolling basis. Application fee: $75. Electronic applications accepted. *Expenses:* Contact institution. *Financial support:* In 2019–20, 56 students received support. Teaching assistantships available. Financial award applicants required to submit FAFSA. *Unit head:* Dr. Michael McGuire, Dean, 303-871-3518, E-mail: michael.mcguire@du.edu. *Application contact:* Admission Team, 303-871-2291, E-mail: ucoladm@du.edu. Website: http://universitycollege.du.edu/

University of Dubuque, Program in Communication, Dubuque, IA 52001-5099. Offers information technologies communication (MAC); leadership and management (MAC); strategic and corporate communication (MAC). *Program availability:* Part-time, evening/weekend. *Degree requirements:* For master's, thesis optional. *Entrance requirements:* For master's, GRE, minimum GPA of 2.5, 3 recommendations. Additional exam requirements/recommendations for international students: required—TOEFL (minimum score 550 paper-based). Electronic applications accepted.

University of Florida, Graduate School, College of Journalism and Communications, Gainesville, FL 32611. Offers advertising (M Adv); mass communication (MAMC, PhD), including international/intercultural communication (MAMC), journalism (MAMC), mass communication, public relations (MAMC), science/health communication (MAMC), telecommunication (MAMC); JD/MAMC; JD/PhD. *Accreditation:* ACEJMC (one or more programs are accredited). *Program availability:* Part-time, online learning. *Degree requirements:* For master's, comprehensive exam (for some programs), thesis; for doctorate, comprehensive exam (for some programs), thesis/dissertation. *Entrance requirements:* For master's and doctorate, GRE General Test (minimum scores: 156 Verbal, 146 Quantitative), minimum GPA of 3.0, resume, statement of goals, 3 letters of recommendation. Additional exam requirements/recommendations for international students: required—TOEFL (minimum score 550 paper-based; 80 iBT), IELTS (minimum score 6). Electronic applications accepted.

University of Georgia, Grady College of Journalism and Mass Communication, Athens, GA 30602. Offers journalism and mass communication (MA); mass communication (PhD). *Degree requirements:* For master's, comprehensive exam, thesis (MA); for doctorate, comprehensive exam, thesis/dissertation. *Entrance requirements:* For master's and doctorate, GRE General Test. Additional exam requirements/recommendations for international students: required—TOEFL, TWE for PhD. Electronic applications accepted.

University of Hartford, College of Arts and Sciences, Program in Communication, West Hartford, CT 06117-1599. Offers MA. *Program availability:* Part-time, evening/weekend. *Faculty:* 7 full-time (2 women). *Students:* 22 full-time (11 women), 5 part-time (4 women); includes 14 minority (4 Black or African American, non-Hispanic/Latino; 8 Hispanic/Latino; 2 Two or more races, non-Hispanic/Latino), 4 international. Average age 25. 28 applicants, 75% accepted, 12 enrolled. In 2019, 20 master's awarded. *Degree requirements:* For master's, comprehensive exam, thesis optional. *Entrance requirements:* For master's, GRE, 3 letters of recommendation. Additional exam requirements/recommendations for international students: required—TOEFL (minimum score 550 paper-based). *Application deadline:* For fall admission, 4/15 for domestic students; for spring admission, 11/15 for domestic students. Applications are processed on a rolling basis. Application fee: $45. Electronic applications accepted. *Expenses:* Contact institution. *Financial support:* Teaching assistantships, career-related internships or fieldwork, Federal Work-Study, and unspecified assistantships available. Support available to part-time students. Financial award application deadline: 6/1; financial award applicants required to submit FAFSA. *Unit head:* Dr. Sundeep Muppidi, Graduate Director, 860-768-5054, E-mail: muppidi@hartford.edu. *Application contact:* Renee Murphy, Assistant Director of Graduate Admissions, 860-768-4371, Fax: 860-768-5160, E-mail: rmurphy@hartford.edu. Website: http://uhaweb.hartford.edu/cmm/

University of Hawaii at Manoa, Office of Graduate Education, College of Social Sciences, School of Communications, Honolulu, HI 96822. Offers communication (MA); telecommunication and information resource management (Graduate Certificate). *Program availability:* Part-time. *Degree requirements:* For master's, thesis optional. *Entrance requirements:* Additional exam requirements/recommendations for international students: required—TOEFL (minimum score 600 paper-based; 100 iBT), IELTS (minimum score 7).

University of Houston, College of Liberal Arts and Social Sciences, Jack J. Valenti School of Communication, Houston, TX 77204. Offers health communication (MA); mass communication studies (MA); public relations studies (MA); speech communication (MA). *Program availability:* Part-time. *Degree requirements:* For master's, comprehensive exam (for some programs), thesis (for some programs), 30-33 hours. *Entrance requirements:* For master's, GRE. Additional exam requirements/recommendations for international students: required—TOEFL. Electronic applications accepted.

University of Illinois at Chicago, College of Liberal Arts and Sciences, Department of Communication, Chicago, IL 60607-7128. Offers MA, PhD. *Program availability:* Evening/weekend. *Degree requirements:* For master's, thesis. *Entrance requirements:* For master's, GRE General Test, minimum GPA of 3.0 in last 90 hours. Additional exam requirements/recommendations for international students: required—TOEFL. Electronic applications accepted.

University of Illinois at Springfield, Graduate Programs, College of Liberal Arts and Sciences, Program in Communication, Springfield, IL 62703-5407. Offers MA. *Program availability:* Part-time. *Faculty:* 9 full-time (4 women). *Students:* 10 full-time (all women), 4 part-time (3 women); includes 2 minority (1 Black or African American, non-Hispanic/Latino; 1 Hispanic/Latino), 1 international. Average age 26. 20 applicants, 50% accepted, 7 enrolled. In 2019, 7 master's awarded. *Degree requirements:* For master's, comprehensive exam, thesis, or project. *Entrance requirements:* For master's, Departmental writing proficiency exam, minimum undergraduate GPA of 3.0; two letters of recommendation, including one from an academic source; one- to two-page personal statement of purpose. Additional exam requirements/recommendations for international students: required—TOEFL (minimum score 580 paper-based). *Application deadline:* Applications are processed on a rolling basis. Application fee: $60 ($75 for international students). Electronic applications accepted. *Expenses: Tuition, area resident:* Full-time $7896; part-time $329 per credit hour. Tuition, nonresident: full-time $16,200; part-time $675 per credit hour. *Required fees:* $2735.60; $130.65 per credit hour. *Financial support:* In 2019–20, research assistantships with full tuition reimbursements (averaging $10,562 per year), teaching assistantships with full tuition reimbursements (averaging $10,652 per year) were awarded; fellowships, career-related internships or fieldwork, Federal Work-Study, scholarships/grants, health care benefits, and unspecified assistantships also available. Support available to part-time students. Financial award application deadline: 11/15; financial award applicants required to submit FAFSA. *Unit*

head: Dr. Amie Kincaid, Program Administrator, 217-206-8415, Fax: 217-206-6217, E-mail: akinc2@uis.edu. *Application contact:* Dr. Amie Kincaid, Program Administrator, 217-206-8415, Fax: 217-206-6217, E-mail: akinc2@uis.edu. Website: com@uis.edu

University of Illinois at Urbana-Champaign, Graduate College, College of Liberal Arts and Sciences, Department of Communication, Champaign, IL 61820. Offers MA, PhD. *Program availability:* Part-time, evening/weekend, online learning. Terminal master's awarded for partial completion of doctoral program.

University of Illinois at Urbana-Champaign, Graduate College, College of Media, Institute of Communications Research, Champaign, IL 61820. Offers communications and media (PhD).

The University of Iowa, Graduate College, College of Liberal Arts and Sciences, Department of Communication Studies, Iowa City, IA 52242-1316. Offers interpersonal communication and relationships (MA, PhD); media studies (MA, PhD); rhetoric and public advocacy (MA, PhD). *Degree requirements:* For master's, thesis optional, exam; for doctorate, comprehensive exam, thesis/dissertation. *Entrance requirements:* For master's and doctorate, GRE General Test, minimum GPA of 3.0. Additional exam requirements/recommendations for international students: required—TOEFL (minimum score 550 paper-based; 81 iBT). Electronic applications accepted.

The University of Kansas, Graduate Studies, College of Liberal Arts and Sciences, Department of Communication Studies, Lawrence, KS 66045-7574. Offers communication studies (MA, PhD); professional workplace communication (Graduate Certificate). *Program availability:* Part-time, evening/weekend. *Students:* 57 full-time (33 women), 12 part-time (9 women); includes 11 minority (5 Black or African American, non-Hispanic/Latino; 2 Asian, non-Hispanic/Latino; 1 Hispanic/Latino; 3 Two or more races, non-Hispanic/Latino), 12 international. Average age 32. 65 applicants, 40% accepted, 12 enrolled. In 2019, 4 master's, 4 doctorates, 1 other advanced degree awarded. *Entrance requirements:* For master's and doctorate, GRE General Test, official transcript, three letters of recommendation, two- to three-page statement of purpose, resume, research writing sample. Additional exam requirements/recommendations for international students: required—TOEFL. *Application deadline:* For fall admission, 5/5 for domestic and international students; for spring admission, 11/15 for domestic and international students; for summer admission, 4/15 for domestic and international students. Application fee: $65 ($85 for international students). Electronic applications accepted. *Expenses:* Tuition, state resident: full-time $9989. Tuition, nonresident: full-time $23,950. International tuition: $23,950 full-time. *Required fees:* $984; $81.99 per credit hour. Tuition and fees vary according to course load, campus/location and program. *Financial support:* Fellowships, research assistantships, teaching assistantships, and unspecified assistantships available. Financial award application deadline: 1/3; financial award applicants required to submit FAFSA. *Unit head:* Jay P. Childers, Chair, 785-864-1474, E-mail: jaychilders@ku.edu. *Application contact:* Clare Thoman, Graduate Admission Contact, 785-864-9814, E-mail: claarethoman@ku.edu. Website: http://www.coms.ku.edu

University of Louisiana at Lafayette, College of Liberal Arts, Department of Communication, Lafayette, LA 70504. Offers communication (MS). *Program availability:* Part-time. *Entrance requirements:* For master's, GRE General Test, minimum GPA of 2.75. Additional exam requirements/recommendations for international students: required—TOEFL (minimum score 550 paper-based). Electronic applications accepted. *Expenses: Tuition, area resident:* Full-time $5511; part-time $1630 per credit hour. Tuition, state resident: full-time $5511; part-time $1630 per credit hour. Tuition, nonresident: full-time $19,239; part-time $2409 per credit hour. *Required fees:* $46,637.

University of Louisiana at Monroe, Graduate School, College of Arts, Education, and Sciences, Department of Communication, Monroe, LA 71209-0001. Offers MA. *Program availability:* Part-time, evening/weekend, online learning. *Faculty:* 4 full-time (2 women), 1 (woman) part-time/adjunct. *Students:* 6 full-time (4 women), 10 part-time (8 women); includes 11 minority (9 Black or African American, non-Hispanic/Latino; 1 Asian, non-Hispanic/Latino; 1 Hispanic/Latino). Average age 24. 17 applicants, 65% accepted, 8 enrolled. In 2019, 7 master's awarded. *Degree requirements:* For master's, thesis optional. *Entrance requirements:* For master's, GRE (minimum verbal and quantitative score: 284), 2.5 minimum GPA. Additional exam requirements/recommendations for international students: required—TOEFL (minimum score 500 paper-based; 61 iBT); recommended—IELTS (minimum score 5.5). *Application deadline:* For fall admission, 8/1 for domestic students, 6/1 for international students; for spring admission, 1/1 for domestic students, 11/1 for international students; for summer admission, 6/1 for domestic students, 3/1 for international students. Applications are processed on a rolling basis. Application fee: $40. Electronic applications accepted. *Expenses: Tuition, area resident:* Full-time $6489. Tuition, state resident: full-time $6489. Tuition, nonresident: full-time $18,989. *Required fees:* $2748. Tuition and fees vary according to course load and program. *Financial support:* In 2019–20, 10 students received support. Career-related internships or fieldwork, Federal Work-Study, scholarships/grants, and unspecified assistantships available. Financial award application deadline: 2/15; financial award applicants required to submit FAFSA. *Unit head:* Dr. Lesli Pace, Program Coordinator, 318-342-1165, Fax: 318-342-1422, E-mail: pace@ulm.edu. *Application contact:* Dr. Adaobi Duru, Graduate Coordinator, 318-324-1199, Fax: 318-342-1422, E-mail: duru@ulm.edu. Website: http://www.ulm.edu/communication

University of Louisville, Graduate School, College of Arts and Sciences, Department of Communication, Louisville, KY 40292-0001. Offers MA. *Program availability:* Part-time, evening/weekend, 100% online, blended/hybrid learning. *Faculty:* 22 full-time (13 women), 38 part-time/adjunct (23 women). *Students:* 11 full-time (8 women), 4 part-time (2 women); includes 4 minority (2 Black or African American, non-Hispanic/Latino; 1 Hispanic/Latino; 1 Two or more races, non-Hispanic/Latino), 1 international. Average age 29. 8 applicants, 75% accepted, 6 enrolled. In 2019, 6 master's awarded. *Entrance requirements:* For master's, GRE General Test, Two letters of reference, official transcripts. Additional exam requirements/recommendations for international students: required—TOEFL (minimum score 550 paper-based; 79 iBT), IELTS can be used in place of the TOEFL; recommended—IELTS (minimum score 6.5). *Application deadline:* For fall admission, 7/1 priority date for domestic students, 5/1 priority date for international students; for spring admission, 11/1 for domestic and international students. Applications are processed on a rolling basis. Application fee: $65. Electronic applications accepted. *Expenses: Tuition, area resident:* Full-time $13,000; part-time $723 per credit hour. Tuition, state resident: full-time $13,000; part-time $723 per credit hour. Tuition, nonresident: full-time $27,114; part-time $1507 per credit hour. *International tuition:* $27,114 full-time. *Required fees:* $196. Tuition and fees vary according to program and reciprocity agreements. *Financial support:* In 2019–20, 9 students received support. Fellowships, research assistantships, teaching assistantships, scholarships/grants, health care benefits, and unspecified assistantships available. Financial award applicants required to submit FAFSA. *Unit head:* Dr. Al Futrell, Chair, 502-852-6976, E-mail: al@louisville.edu. *Application contact:* Steve Sohn, Associate Professor and Director of Graduate Studies, 502-852-2929, E-mail: steve.sohn@louisville.edu. Website: http://louisville.edu/communication

University of Maine, Graduate School, College of Liberal Arts and Sciences, Department of Communication and Journalism, Orono, ME 04469. Offers MA, PhD. *Program availability:* Part-time. *Students:* 17 full-time (7 women), 1 (woman) part-time; includes 3 minority (1 Black or African American, non-Hispanic/Latino; 1 Hispanic/Latino; 1 Two or more races, non-Hispanic/Latino), 2 international. Average age 27. 25 applicants, 52% accepted, 7 enrolled. In 2019, 1 master's, 1 doctorate awarded. *Degree requirements:* For master's, thesis (for some programs); for doctorate, comprehensive exam, thesis/dissertation. *Entrance requirements:* For master's, GRE General Test. Additional exam requirements/recommendations for international students: required—TOEFL. *Application deadline:* For fall admission, 2/1 priority date for domestic students. Applications are processed on a rolling basis. Application fee: $65. Electronic applications accepted. *Expenses: Tuition, area resident:* Full-time $8100; part-time $450 per credit hour. Tuition, state resident: full-time $8100; part-time $450 per credit hour. Tuition, nonresident: full-time $26,388; part-time $1466 per credit hour. *International tuition:* $26,388 full-time. *Required fees:* $1257; $278 per semester. Tuition and fees vary according to course load. *Financial support:* In 2019–20, 22 students received support, including 7 research assistantships with full tuition reimbursements available (averaging $21,400 per year), 15 teaching assistantships with full tuition reimbursements available (averaging $15,600 per year); career-related internships or fieldwork, Federal Work-Study, institutionally sponsored loans, tuition waivers (full and partial), and unspecified assistantships also available. Support available to part-time students. Financial award application deadline: 3/1. *Unit head:* Dr. Nathan Stormer, Chair, 207-581-1938, Fax: 207-581-1286, E-mail: nathan@maine.edu. *Application contact:* Scott G. Delcourt, Assistant Vice President for Graduate Studies and Senior Associate Dean, 207-581-3291, Fax: 207-581-3232, E-mail: graduate@maine.edu.
Website: http://cmj.umaine.edu/graduate-program/

University of Maryland, Baltimore County, The Graduate School, College of Arts, Humanities and Social Sciences, Department of Modern Languages, Linguistics and Intercultural Communication, Program in Intercultural Communication, Baltimore, MD 21250. Offers MA. *Program availability:* Part-time, evening/weekend. *Faculty:* 16 full-time (9 women). *Students:* 10 full-time (6 women), 5 part-time (2 women); includes 5 minority (3 Black or African American, non-Hispanic/Latino; 2 Hispanic/Latino), 3 international. Average age 29. 16 applicants, 94% accepted, 8 enrolled. In 2019, 4 master's awarded. *Degree requirements:* For master's, one foreign language, comprehensive exam (for some programs), thesis (for some programs). *Entrance requirements:* For master's, GRE General Test, minimum GPA of 3.0, 3 letters of recommendation, self-evaluation and statement of support, resume, writing sample in modern language. Additional exam requirements/recommendations for international students: required—TOEFL (minimum score 550 paper-based, 80 iBT) or IELTS. *Application deadline:* For fall admission, 1/31 for domestic and international students. Application fee: $50. Electronic applications accepted. *Expenses:* $14,382 per year. *Financial support:* In 2019–20, 8 students received support, including 8 teaching assistantships with full tuition reimbursements available (averaging $12,874 per year); Federal Work-Study, scholarships/grants, health care benefits, and tuition waivers (full) also available. Financial award application deadline: 1/31; financial award applicants required to submit FAFSA. *Unit head:* Dr. Nicoleta Bazgan, Program Director, 410-455-3116, Fax: 410-455-1025, E-mail: nbazgan@umbc.edu. *Application contact:* Dr. Nicoleta Bazgan, Program Director, 410-455-3116, Fax: 410-455-1025, E-mail: nbazgan@umbc.edu.
Website: http://www.umbc.edu/mll/incc/

University of Maryland, College Park, Academic Affairs, College of Arts and Humanities, Department of Communication, College Park, MD 20742. Offers MA, PhD. *Degree requirements:* For master's, thesis optional; for doctorate, comprehensive exam, thesis/dissertation. *Entrance requirements:* For master's, GRE General Test, minimum GPA of 3.0, sample of scholarly writing, 3 letters of recommendation, statement of goals and experiences; for doctorate, GRE General Test. Additional exam requirements/recommendations for international students: required—TOEFL. Electronic applications accepted.

University of Massachusetts Amherst, Graduate School, College of Social and Behavioral Sciences, Department of Communication, Amherst, MA 01003. Offers MA, PhD. *Program availability:* Part-time. Terminal master's awarded for partial completion of doctoral program. *Degree requirements:* For master's, thesis or alternative; for doctorate, comprehensive exam, thesis/dissertation. *Entrance requirements:* For master's and doctorate, GRE General Test, 3 letters of recommendation. Additional exam requirements/recommendations for international students: required—TOEFL (minimum score 550 paper-based; 80 iBT), IELTS (minimum score 6.5). Electronic applications accepted.

University of Memphis, Graduate School, College of Communication and Fine Arts, Department of Communication and Film, Memphis, TN 38152. Offers communication (MA); communication arts (PhD); film and video production (MA). *Program availability:* Part-time. *Students:* 13 full-time (10 women), 31 part-time (18 women); includes 16 minority (13 Black or African American, non-Hispanic/Latino; 1 Asian, non-Hispanic/Latino; 1 Hispanic/Latino; 1 Two or more races, non-Hispanic/Latino), 2 international. Average age 36. 20 applicants, 100% accepted, 11 enrolled. In 2019, 9 master's, 3 doctorates awarded. *Degree requirements:* For master's, comprehensive exam, thesis or alternative, culminating project; for doctorate, comprehensive exam, thesis/dissertation. *Entrance requirements:* For master's and doctorate, GRE General Test, personal goal statement, letters of recommendation, writing sample. Additional exam requirements/recommendations for international students: required—TOEFL (minimum score 600 paper-based). *Application deadline:* For fall admission, 1/13 priority date for domestic students. Applications are processed on a rolling basis. Application fee: $35 ($60 for international students). *Expenses: Tuition, area resident:* Full-time $9216; part-time $512 per credit hour. Tuition, state resident: full-time $9216; part-time $512 per credit hour. Tuition, nonresident: full-time $12,672; part-time $704 per credit hour. *International tuition:* $16,128 full-time. *Required fees:* $1530; $85 per credit hour. Tuition and fees vary according to program. *Financial support:* Research assistantships with full tuition reimbursements, teaching assistantships with full tuition reimbursements, Federal Work-Study, scholarships/grants, and unspecified assistantships available. Financial award application deadline: 2/1; financial award applicants required to submit FAFSA. *Unit head:* Dr. Wendy Atkins-Sayre, Department Chair, 901-678-3012, E-mail: wltknssy@memphis.edu. *Application contact:* Dr. Marina Levina, Director of Graduate Studies, 901-678-3185, Fax: 901-678-4331, E-mail: mlevina@memphis.edu.
Website: https://www.memphis.edu/communication/

University of Miami, Graduate School, School of Communication, Coral Gables, FL 33124. Offers communication (PhD); communication studies (MA); film studies (MA, PhD); motion pictures (MFA), including production, producing, and screenwriting; print journalism (MA); public relations (MA); Spanish language journalism (MA); television broadcast journalism (MA). *Program availability:* Part-time. *Degree requirements:* For master's, comprehensive exam (for some programs), thesis (for some programs); for doctorate, comprehensive exam, thesis/dissertation. *Entrance requirements:* For master's, GRE General Test; for doctorate, GRE General Test, master's thesis or scholarly research. Additional exam requirements/recommendations for international

students: required—TOEFL (minimum score 600 paper-based; 100 iBT). Electronic applications accepted.

University of Michigan, Rackham Graduate School, College of Literature, Science, and the Arts, Department of Communication and Media, Ann Arbor, MI 48109-1285. Offers PhD. *Degree requirements:* For doctorate, comprehensive exam, thesis/dissertation, first-year research project, 2 terms in student instructor position, publications, presentations. *Entrance requirements:* For doctorate, GRE, U.S. bachelor's degree or its equivalent from accredited institution. Additional exam requirements/recommendations for international students: required—TOEFL (minimum score 600 paper-based; 102 iBT). Electronic applications accepted. *Expenses:* Contact institution.

University of Minnesota, Twin Cities Campus, Graduate School, College of Design, Department of Design, Housing, and Apparel, Minneapolis, MN 55455-0213. Offers apparel (MA, MS, PhD); design communication (MA, MS, PhD); housing studies (MA, MS, PhD, Postbaccalaureate Certificate); interactive design (MFA); interior design (MA, MS, PhD). *Program availability:* Part-time. *Degree requirements:* For master's and Postbaccalaureate Certificate, comprehensive exam, thesis (for some programs); for doctorate, comprehensive exam, thesis/dissertation. *Entrance requirements:* For master's, GRE General Test, minimum GPA of 3.0 (preferred), portfolio, 3 letters of recommendation; for doctorate, GRE General Test, minimum GPA of 3.0 (preferred), portfolio, 3 letters of recommendation, writing sample; for Postbaccalaureate Certificate, GRE General Test, minimum GPA of 3.0 (preferred). Additional exam requirements/recommendations for international students: required—TOEFL (minimum score 550 paper-based; 79 iBT). Electronic applications accepted.

University of Minnesota, Twin Cities Campus, Graduate School, College of Liberal Arts, Department of Communication Studies, Minneapolis, MN 55455-0213. Offers MA, PhD. *Degree requirements:* For master's, thesis or alternative; for doctorate, thesis/dissertation. *Entrance requirements:* For master's, GRE General Test, minimum GPA of 3.0; for doctorate, GRE General Test, minimum graduate GPA of 3.5. Additional exam requirements/recommendations for international students: required—TOEFL. Electronic applications accepted.

University of Missouri, Office of Research and Graduate Studies, College of Arts and Science, Department of Communication, Columbia, MO 65211. Offers MA, PhD. Terminal master's awarded for partial completion of doctoral program. *Entrance requirements:* For master's and doctorate, GRE General Test (minimum score 500 verbal, 500 quantitative, 4.0 analytical preferred), minimum GPA of 3.0.

University of Missouri–St. Louis, College of Arts and Sciences, Department of Communication and Media, St. Louis, MO 63121. Offers communication (MA). *Program availability:* Part-time, evening/weekend. *Degree requirements:* For master's, thesis optional. *Entrance requirements:* For master's, 3 letters of recommendation, minimum GPA of 3.25, BA in communication or related discipline. Additional exam requirements/recommendations for international students: required—TOEFL (minimum score 600 paper-based). Electronic applications accepted. *Expenses: Tuition, area resident:* Full-time $9005.40; part-time $6003.60 per credit hour. Tuition, state resident: full-time $9005.40; part-time $6003.60 per credit hour. Tuition, nonresident: full-time $22,108; part-time $14,738.40 per credit hour. *International tuition:* $22,108 full-time. Tuition and fees vary according to course load.

University of Montana, Graduate School, College of Humanities and Sciences, Department of Communication Studies, Missoula, MT 59812. Offers MA. *Degree requirements:* For master's, thesis (for some programs). *Entrance requirements:* For master's, GRE General Test. Additional exam requirements/recommendations for international students: required—TOEFL (minimum score 525 paper-based).

University of Nebraska at Omaha, Graduate Studies, College of Communication, Fine Arts and Media, School of Communication, Omaha, NE 68182. Offers communication (MA); human resources and training (Certificate); technical communication (Certificate). *Program availability:* Part-time, evening/weekend. *Degree requirements:* For master's, comprehensive exam, thesis (for some programs). *Entrance requirements:* For master's, minimum GPA of 3.0, 15 undergraduate communication courses, resume, statement of purpose, 3 letters of recommendation. Additional exam requirements/recommendations for international students: required—TOEFL, IELTS, PTE. Electronic applications accepted.

University of Nebraska–Lincoln, Graduate College, College of Arts and Sciences, Department of Communication Studies, Lincoln, NE 68588. Offers instructional communication (MA, PhD); interpersonal communication (MA, PhD); marketing, communication studies, and advertising (MA, PhD); organizational communication (MA, PhD); rhetoric and culture (MA, PhD). *Degree requirements:* For master's, thesis optional; for doctorate, comprehensive exam, thesis/dissertation. *Entrance requirements:* For master's and doctorate, GRE General Test, writing sample. Additional exam requirements/recommendations for international students: required—TOEFL (minimum score 600 paper-based). Electronic applications accepted.

University of Nevada, Las Vegas, Graduate College, Greenspun College of Urban Affairs, Department of Communication Studies, Las Vegas, NV 89154-4052. Offers MA. *Program availability:* Part-time. *Faculty:* 4 full-time (2 women), 2 part-time/adjunct (0 women). *Students:* 18 full-time (10 women), 3 part-time (all women); includes 10 minority (2 Black or African American, non-Hispanic/Latino; 2 Asian, non-Hispanic/Latino; 5 Hispanic/Latino; 1 Two or more races, non-Hispanic/Latino). Average age 28. 21 applicants, 67% accepted, 10 enrolled. In 2019, 5 master's awarded. *Degree requirements:* For master's, comprehensive exam (for some programs), thesis optional. *Entrance requirements:* For master's, GRE General Test, writing sample; 3 letters of recommendation; statement of purpose. Additional exam requirements/recommendations for international students: required—TOEFL (minimum score 550 paper-based; 80 iBT), IELTS (minimum score 7). *Application deadline:* For fall admission, 1/15 for domestic and international students; for spring admission, 10/15 for domestic students, 10/1 for international students. Application fee: $60 ($95 for international students). Electronic applications accepted. *Expenses:* Contact institution. *Financial support:* In 2019–20, 17 students received support, including 1 research assistantship with full tuition reimbursement available (averaging $11,250 per year), 16 teaching assistantships with full tuition reimbursements available (averaging $11,250 per year); institutionally sponsored loans, scholarships/grants, health care benefits, and unspecified assistantships also available. Financial award application deadline: 3/15; financial award applicants required to submit FAFSA. *Unit head:* Dr. Michael Bruner, Professor/Chair, 702-895-5125, E-mail: commstudies.chair@unlv.edu. *Application contact:* Dr. Michael Bruner, Graduate Coordinator, 702-895-3640, Fax: 702-895-4805, E-mail: commstudies.gradcoord@unlv.edu.
Website: http://communicationstudies.unlv.edu/

University of New Mexico, Graduate Studies, College of Arts and Sciences, Program in Communication, Albuquerque, NM 87131-2039. Offers MA, PhD. *Program availability:* Part-time. *Degree requirements:* For master's, 30 hours of class work and 6-hour thesis or project, or 36 hours of class work and comprehensive exam; for doctorate, 2 foreign languages, comprehensive exam, thesis/dissertation. *Entrance requirements:* For master's, GRE General Test, letters of recommendation, letter of intent, curriculum vitae, transcripts; for doctorate, GRE General Test, letters of recommendation, writing sample, letter of intent, curriculum vitae, transcripts. Additional exam requirements/recommendations for international students: required—TOEFL (minimum score 550 paper-based). Electronic applications accepted. *Expenses:* Tuition, state resident: full-time $7633; part-time $972 per year. Tuition, nonresident: full-time $22,586; part-time $3840 per year. *International tuition:* $23,292 full-time. *Required fees:* $8608. Tuition and fees vary according to course level, course load, degree level, program and student level.

The University of North Carolina at Chapel Hill, Graduate School, College of Arts and Sciences, Department of Communication Studies, Chapel Hill, NC 27599. Offers PhD. *Degree requirements:* For doctorate, comprehensive exam, thesis/dissertation. *Entrance requirements:* For doctorate, GRE General Test, minimum GPA of 3.0. Additional exam requirements/recommendations for international students: required—TOEFL (minimum score 550 paper-based; 79 iBT). Electronic applications accepted.

The University of North Carolina at Chapel Hill, Graduate School, Hussman School of Journalism and Media, Chapel Hill, NC 27599. Offers digital communication (MA, Certificate); media and communication (MA, PhD), including interdisciplinary health communication (MA), journalism (MA), strategic communication (MA), theory and research (MA), visual communication (MA); JD/PhD; MA/JD. *Accreditation:* ACEJMC (one or more programs are accredited). *Program availability:* Part-time, all course instruction online, plus two on-campus experiences totaling seven days. *Faculty:* 30 full-time (15 women), 5 part-time/adjunct (4 women). *Students:* 68 full-time (45 women), 82 part-time (58 women); includes 35 minority (13 Black or African American, non-Hispanic/Latino; 1 American Indian or Alaska Native, non-Hispanic/Latino; 4 Asian, non-Hispanic/Latino; 1 Hispanic/Latino; 16 Two or more races, non-Hispanic/Latino), 9 international. Average age 34. 205 applicants, 49% accepted, 73 enrolled. In 2019, 32 master's, 5 doctorates, 24 other advanced degrees awarded. *Degree requirements:* For master's, comprehensive exam, thesis; for doctorate, comprehensive exam, thesis/dissertation. *Entrance requirements:* For master's, Online master's degree only: GRE General Test (waiver available); Residential master's degree: minimum GPA of 3.0; for doctorate, minimum GPA of 3.0. Additional exam requirements/recommendations for international students: required—TOEFL (minimum iBT score of 105) or IELTS (7.5). Application fee: $95. Electronic applications accepted. *Expenses:* Ph.D.: 7,550 per semester N.C. resident, 15,883 non-res; Residential M.A.: 8,425 per semester N.C., 16,708 non-res; Online M.A./certificate: 2,262 per semester N.C., 4,698 non-res. *Financial support:* In 2019–20, 60 students received support, including 41 fellowships with full tuition reimbursements available (averaging $17,901 per year), 4 research assistantships with full tuition reimbursements available (averaging $17,465 per year); scholarships/grants and health care benefits also available. Financial award application deadline: 12/15; financial award applicants required to submit FAFSA. *Unit head:* Susan King, Dean, 919-962-1204, Fax: 919-962-0620, E-mail: susanking@unc.edu. *Application contact:* Casey Hart, Assistant Director, Graduate Studies, 919-843-9471, Fax: 919-962-0620, E-mail: mjgrad@unc.edu.
Website: http://hussman.unc.edu

The University of North Carolina at Charlotte, College of Liberal Arts and Sciences, Department of Communication Studies, Charlotte, NC 28223-0001. Offers communication studies (MA). *Program availability:* Part-time, evening/weekend. *Faculty:* 18 full-time (10 women). *Students:* 9 full-time (7 women), 14 part-time (13 women); includes 12 minority (7 Black or African American, non-Hispanic/Latino; 3 Hispanic/Latino; 2 Two or more races, non-Hispanic/Latino). Average age 24. 35 applicants, 60% accepted, 12 enrolled. In 2019, 16 master's awarded. Terminal master's awarded for partial completion of doctoral program. *Degree requirements:* For master's, comprehensive exam (for some programs), thesis (for some programs). *Entrance requirements:* For master's, bachelor's degree from accredited institution; transcripts from all post-secondary educational institutions in which the candidate was enrolled; minimum overall GPA of 3.0 as undergraduate and in junior and senior years; three letters of recommendation; personal statement; writing sample. Additional exam requirements/recommendations for international students: required—TOEFL (minimum score 557 paper-based; 83 iBT), IELTS (minimum score 6.5), TOEFL (minimum score 557 paper-based,83 iBT) or IELTS (6.5). *Application deadline:* For fall admission, 1/15 priority date for domestic students. Applications are processed on a rolling basis. Application fee: $75. Electronic applications accepted. *Expenses:* Tuition, state resident: full-time $4337. Tuition, nonresident: full-time $17,771. *Required fees:* $3093. Tuition and fees vary according to course load, degree level and program. *Financial support:* In 2019–20, 13 students received support, including 13 teaching assistantships (averaging $14,083 per year); career-related internships or fieldwork, institutionally sponsored loans, scholarships/grants, and unspecified assistantships also available. Support available to part-time students. Financial award application deadline: 1/15; financial award applicants required to submit FAFSA. *Unit head:* Dr. Jason Black, Chair, 704-687-0783, E-mail: jblac143@uncc.edu. *Application contact:* Kathy B. Giddings, Director of Graduate Admissions, 704-687-5503, Fax: 704-687-1668, E-mail: gradadm@uncc.edu.
Website: http://communication.uncc.edu/

The University of North Carolina at Greensboro, Graduate School, College of Arts and Sciences, Department of Communication Studies, Greensboro, NC 27412-5001. Offers MA. *Program availability:* Part-time. *Degree requirements:* For master's, thesis or alternative. *Entrance requirements:* For master's, GRE General Test, MAT, or PRAXIS. Additional exam requirements/recommendations for international students: required—TOEFL. Electronic applications accepted.

University of North Dakota, Graduate School, College of Arts and Sciences, School of Communication, Grand Forks, ND 58202. Offers communication and public discourse (PhD). *Program availability:* Part-time. *Degree requirements:* For doctorate, thesis/dissertation. *Entrance requirements:* For doctorate, GRE General Test, minimum GPA of 3.0. Additional exam requirements/recommendations for international students: required—TOEFL (minimum score 550 paper-based; 79 iBT), IELTS (minimum score 6.5). Electronic applications accepted.

University of Northern Colorado, Graduate School, College of Humanities and Social Sciences, School of Communication, Greeley, CO 80639. Offers MA. *Program availability:* Part-time. *Degree requirements:* For master's, comprehensive exam, thesis or alternative. *Entrance requirements:* For master's, GRE General Test, 3 letters of recommendation. Electronic applications accepted.

University of Northern Iowa, Graduate College, College of Humanities, Arts and Sciences, Department of Communication Studies, Cedar Falls, IA 50614. Offers MA. *Program availability:* Part-time, evening/weekend. *Degree requirements:* For master's, comprehensive exam, thesis or alternative. *Entrance requirements:* For master's, minimum GPA of 3.0. Additional exam requirements/recommendations for international students: required—TOEFL (minimum score 500 paper-based; 61 iBT). Electronic applications accepted.

University of North Texas, Toulouse Graduate School, Denton, TX 76203-5459. Offers accounting (MS); applied anthropology (MA, MS); applied behavior analysis (Certificate); applied geography (MA); applied technology and performance improvement (M Ed, MS); art education (MA); art history (MA); arts leadership (Certificate); audiology (Au D); behavior analysis (MS); behavioral science (PhD); biochemistry and molecular biology (MS); biology (MA, MS); biomedical engineering (MS); business analysis (MS); chemistry (MS); clinical health psychology (PhD); communication studies (MA, MS); computer engineering (MS); computer science (MS); counseling (M Ed, MS), including clinical mental health counseling (MS), college and university counseling, elementary school counseling, secondary school counseling; creative writing (MA); criminal justice (MS); curriculum and instruction (M Ed); decision sciences (MBA); design (MA, MFA), including fashion design (MFA), innovation studies, interior design (MFA); early childhood studies (MS); economics (MS); educational leadership (M Ed, Ed D); educational psychology (MS, PhD), including family studies (MS), gifted and talented (MS), human development (MS), learning and cognition (MS), research, measurement and evaluation (MS); electrical engineering (MS); emergency management (MPA); engineering technology (MS); English (MA); English as a second language (MA); environmental science (MS); finance (MBA, MS); financial management (MPA); French (MA); health services management (MBA); higher education (M Ed, Ed D); history (MA, MS); hospitality management (MS); human resources management (MPA); information science (MS); information systems (PhD); information technologies (MBA); interdisciplinary studies (MA, MS); international studies (MA); international sustainable tourism (MS); jazz studies (MM); journalism (MA, MJ, Graduate Certificate), including interactive and virtual digital communication (Graduate Certificate), narrative journalism (Graduate Certificate), public relations (Graduate Certificate); kinesiology (MS); linguistics (MA); local government management (MPA); logistics (PhD); logistics and supply chain management (MBA); long-term care, senior housing, and aging services (MA); management (PhD); marketing (MBA); mathematics (MA, MS); mechanical and energy engineering (MS, PhD); music (MA), including ethnomusicology, music theory, musicology, performance; music composition (PhD); music education (MM Ed, PhD); nonprofit management (MPA); operations and supply chain management (MBA); performance (MM, DMA); philosophy (MA); political science (MA); professional and technical communication (MA); radio, television and film (MA, MFA); rehabilitation counseling (Certificate); sociology (MA); Spanish (MA); special education (M Ed); speech-language pathology (MA); strategic management (MBA); studio art (MFA); teaching (M Ed); MBA/MS. *Program availability:* Part-time, evening/weekend, online learning. Terminal master's awarded for partial completion of doctoral program. *Degree requirements:* For master's, variable foreign language requirement, comprehensive exam (for some programs), thesis (for some programs); for doctorate, variable foreign language requirement, comprehensive exam (for some programs), thesis/dissertation; for other advanced degree, variable foreign language requirement, comprehensive exam (for some programs). *Entrance requirements:* For master's and doctorate, GRE, GMAT. Additional exam requirements/recommendations for international students: required—TOEFL (minimum score 550 paper-based; 79 iBT). Electronic applications accepted.

University of Oklahoma, College of Arts and Sciences, Department of Communication, Norman, OK 73019. Offers communication (MA); communication technology (PhD); health communication (PhD); intercultural/international communication (PhD); organizational communication (PhD); political/mass communication (PhD); social influence/interpersonal communication (PhD). *Program availability:* Part-time. *Degree requirements:* For master's, comprehensive exam (for some programs), thesis (for some programs), comprehensive exams or thesis; for doctorate, comprehensive exam, thesis/dissertation. *Entrance requirements:* For master's, GRE (for assistantship), statement of purpose, transcripts, writing sample, letters of recommendation; for doctorate, GRE, statement of purpose, transcripts, writing sample, letters of recommendation. Additional exam requirements/recommendations for international students: required—TOEFL (minimum score 79 iBT) or IELTS (minimum score 6.5). Electronic applications accepted. *Expenses:* Tuition, state resident: full-time $6583.20; part-time $274.30 per credit hour. Tuition, nonresident: full-time $21,242; part-time $885.10 per credit hour. *International tuition:* $21,242.40 full-time. *Required fees:* $1994.20; $72.55 per credit hour. $126.50 per semester. Tuition and fees vary according to course load and degree level.

University of Oregon, Graduate School, School of Journalism and Communication, Eugene, OR 97403. Offers journalism (MA, MS); media studies (MA, MS, PhD); multimedia journalism (MA, MS); strategic communication (MA, MS). *Accreditation:* ASHA. *Program availability:* Part-time. *Degree requirements:* For master's, thesis or alternative. *Entrance requirements:* For master's, GRE General Test; for doctorate, master's degree.

University of Ottawa, Faculty of Graduate and Postdoctoral Studies, Faculty of Arts, Department of Communication, Ottawa, ON K1N 6N5, Canada. Offers MA. Electronic applications accepted.

University of Pennsylvania, Annenberg School for Communication, Philadelphia, PA 19104. Offers PhD. *Faculty:* 18 full-time (7 women), 7 part-time/adjunct (2 women). *Students:* 68 full-time (43 women), 1 (woman) part-time; includes 17 minority (6 Black or African American, non-Hispanic/Latino; 4 Asian, non-Hispanic/Latino; 5 Hispanic/Latino; 2 Two or more races, non-Hispanic/Latino), 18 international. Average age 30. 247 applicants, 6% accepted, 11 enrolled. In 2019, 17 doctorates awarded. *Entrance requirements:* Additional exam requirements/recommendations for international students: required—TOEFL. Application fee: $70. *Financial support:* In 2019–20, 80 students received support. *Unit head:* John L. Jackson, Jr., Dean. *Application contact:* Joanne Murray, Assistant Dean for Graduate Studies, 215-573-6349, Fax: 215-898-2024, E-mail: joanne.murray@asc.upenn.edu.
Website: http://www.asc.upenn.edu/

University of Pittsburgh, Kenneth P. Dietrich School of Arts and Sciences, Department of Communication, Pittsburgh, PA 15260. Offers MA, PhD. *Degree requirements:* For master's, comprehensive exam, thesis optional; for doctorate, comprehensive exam, thesis/dissertation. *Entrance requirements:* For master's and doctorate, GRE General Test, sample of written work, curriculum vitae. Additional exam requirements/recommendations for international students: required—TOEFL (minimum score 577 paper-based; 90 iBT), IELTS (minimum score 7). Electronic applications accepted. *Expenses:* Contact institution.

University of Portland, Department of Communication Studies, Portland, OR 97203-5798. Offers communication (MA); management communication (MS). *Program availability:* Part-time, evening/weekend. *Degree requirements:* For master's, thesis optional. *Entrance requirements:* For master's, GRE General Test, 3 letters of recommendation, resume, statement of goals, official transcripts. Additional exam requirements/recommendations for international students: required—TOEFL (minimum score 100 iBT), IELTS (minimum score 7.5). Electronic applications accepted.

University of Puerto Rico at Rio Piedras, School of Communication, Program in Communication Theory and Research, San Juan, PR 00931-3300. Offers MA.

University of Rhode Island, Graduate School, College of Arts and Sciences, Department of Communication Studies, Kingston, RI 02881. Offers MA. *Program availability:* Part-time. *Faculty:* 36 full-time (20 women). *Students:* 8 full-time (4 women), 10 part-time (4 women); includes 1 minority (Black or African American, non-Hispanic/Latino). 8 applicants, 75% accepted, 6 enrolled. In 2019, 7 master's awarded. *Entrance requirements:* For master's, GRE. Additional exam requirements/recommendations for international students: required—TOEFL. *Application deadline:* Applications are

processed on a rolling basis. Application fee: $65. Electronic applications accepted. *Expenses: Tuition, area resident:* Full-time $13,734; part-time $763 per credit. Tuition, state resident: full-time $13,734; part-time $763 per credit. Tuition, nonresident: full-time $26,512; part-time $1473 per credit. *International tuition:* $26,512 full-time. *Required fees:* $1780; $52 per credit. $35 per term. One-time fee: $165. *Financial support:* In 2019–20, 4 teaching assistantships with tuition reimbursements (averaging $15,189 per year) were awarded. Financial award application deadline: 2/1; financial award applicants required to submit FAFSA. *Unit head:* Dr. Dana Kovarsky, Chair, Fax: 401-874-2735, E-mail: danak@uri.edu. *Application contact:* Dr. Abran Salazar, Director of Graduate Studies, 401-874-9015, E-mail: abran_salazar@uri.edu.
Website: http://www.uri.edu/artsci/com/

University of San Francisco, College of Arts and Sciences, Program in Professional Communication, San Francisco, CA 94117. Offers MA. *Program availability:* Part-time, evening/weekend. *Faculty:* 6 full-time (4 women), 2 part-time/adjunct (1 woman). *Students:* 50 full-time (39 women), 10 part-time (9 women); includes 25 minority (10 Black or African American, non-Hispanic/Latino; 6 Asian, non-Hispanic/Latino; 7 Hispanic/Latino; 2 Two or more races, non-Hispanic/Latino), 20 international. Average age 29. 72 applicants, 83% accepted, 24 enrolled. In 2019, 21 master's awarded. *Entrance requirements:* Additional exam requirements/recommendations for international students: required—TOEFL (minimum score 90 iBT), IELTS (minimum score 6.5), PTE (minimum score 61). *Application deadline:* For fall admission, 2/1 for domestic and international students. Applications are processed on a rolling basis. Application fee: $55. Electronic applications accepted. Application fee is waived when completed online. *Financial support:* Career-related internships or fieldwork and scholarships/grants available. Financial award applicants required to submit FAFSA. *Unit head:* David Ryan, Graduate Director, 415-422-6708, E-mail: mapc@usfca.edu. *Application contact:* David Ryan, Graduate Director, 415-422-6708, E-mail: mapc@usfca.edu.
Website: https://www.usfca.edu/arts-sciences/graduate-programs/professional-communication

University of South Africa, College of Human Sciences, Pretoria, South Africa. Offers adult education (M Ed); African languages (MA, PhD); African politics (MA, PhD); Afrikaans (MA, PhD); ancient history (MA, PhD); ancient Near Eastern studies (MA, PhD); anthropology (MA, PhD); applied linguistics (MA); Arabic (MA, PhD); archaeology (MA); art history (MA); Biblical archaeology (MA); Biblical studies (M Th, D Th, PhD); Christian spirituality (M Th, D Th); church history (M Th, D Th); classical studies (MA, PhD); clinical psychology (MA); communication (MA, PhD); comparative education (M Ed, Ed D); consulting psychology (D Admin, D Com, PhD); curriculum studies (M Ed, Ed D); development studies (M Admin, MA, D Admin, PhD); didactics (M Ed, Ed D); education (M Tech); education management (M Ed, Ed D); educational psychology (M Ed); English (MA); environmental education (M Ed); French (MA, PhD); German (MA, PhD); Greek (MA); guidance and counseling (M Ed); health studies (MA, PhD), including health sciences education (MA), health services management (MA), medical and surgical nursing science (critical care general) (MA), midwifery and neonatal nursing science (MA), trauma and emergency care (MA); history (MA, PhD); history of education (Ed D); inclusive education (M Ed, Ed D); information and communications technology policy and regulation (MA); information science (MA, MIS, PhD); international politics (MA, PhD); Islamic studies (MA, PhD); Italian (MA, PhD); Judaica (MA, PhD); linguistics (MA, PhD); mathematical education (M Ed); mathematics education (MA); missiology (M Th, D Th); modern Hebrew (MA, PhD); musicology (MA, MMus, D Mus, PhD); natural science education (M Ed); New Testament (M Th, D Th); Old Testament (D Th); pastoral therapy (M Th, D Th); philosophy (MA); philosophy of education (M Ed, Ed D); politics (MA, PhD); Portuguese (MA, PhD); practical theology (M Th, D Th); psychology (MA, MS, PhD); psychology of education (M Ed, Ed D); public health (MA); religious studies (MA, D Th, PhD); Romance languages (MA); Russian (MA, PhD); Semitic languages (MA, PhD); social behavior studies in HIV/AIDS (MA); social science (mental health) (MA); social science in development studies (MA); social science in psychology (MA); social science in social work (MA); social science in sociology (MA); social work (MSW, DSW, PhD); socio-education (M Ed, Ed D); sociolinguistics (MA); sociology (MA, PhD); Spanish (MA, PhD); systematic theology (M Th, D Th); TESOL (teaching English to speakers of other languages) (MA); theological ethics (M Th, D Th); theory of literature (MA, PhD); urban ministries (D Th); urban ministry (M Th).

University of South Alabama, College of Arts and Sciences, Department of Communication, Mobile, AL 36688. Offers MA. *Program availability:* Part-time, evening/weekend. *Faculty:* 4 full-time (2 women). *Students:* 7 full-time (3 women), 2 part-time (both women); includes 2 minority (both Black or African American, non-Hispanic/Latino). Average age 25. 2 applicants, 100% accepted, 1 enrolled. In 2019, 9 master's awarded. *Degree requirements:* For master's, comprehensive exam, thesis optional. *Entrance requirements:* For master's, GRE, GMAT. Additional exam requirements/recommendations for international students: required—TOEFL (minimum score 71 iBT), IELTS (minimum score 6), PTE (minimum score 48), One of the above is required for admission - not all. *Application deadline:* For fall admission, 7/1 priority date for domestic students, 6/1 priority date for international students; for spring admission, 12/1 priority date for domestic students, 11/1 priority date for international students; for summer admission, 5/1 for domestic students, 4/1 for international students. Applications are processed on a rolling basis. Application fee: $35. Electronic applications accepted. *Expenses: Tuition, area resident:* Part-time $442 per credit hour. Tuition, state resident: full-time $10,608; part-time $442 per credit hour. Tuition, nonresident: full-time $21,216; part-time $884 per credit hour. *Financial support:* Fellowships, research assistantships, teaching assistantships, career-related internships or fieldwork, Federal Work-Study, institutionally sponsored loans, scholarships/grants, and unspecified assistantships available. Support available to part-time students. Financial award application deadline: 3/31; financial award applicants required to submit FAFSA. *Unit head:* Dr. Richard Ward, Chair, Interim, 251-380-2819, E-mail: rward@southalabama.edu. *Application contact:* Dr. Steve Rockwell, Graduate Studies Chair, 251-380-2801, E-mail: srockwell@southalabama.edu.
Website: http://comm.southalabama.edu/colleges/artsandsci/communication/

University of South Dakota, Graduate School, College of Arts and Sciences, Department of Communication Studies, Vermillion, SD 57069. Offers MA. *Program availability:* Part-time. *Degree requirements:* For master's, comprehensive exam (for some programs), thesis (for some programs). *Entrance requirements:* For master's, minimum GPA of 3.0. Additional exam requirements/recommendations for international students: required—TOEFL (minimum score 575 paper-based; 79 iBT). Electronic applications accepted.

University of Southern California, Graduate School, Annenberg School for Communication and Journalism, School of Communication, Program in Communication, Los Angeles, CA 90089. Offers culture and community (PhD); global and transnational communication (PhD); groups, organizations and networks (PhD); health communication and social dynamics (PhD); information, political economy and entertainment (PhD); new media and technology (PhD); rhetoric, politics and public media (PhD). *Students:* 88 full-time (63 women); includes 28 minority (2 Black or African American, non-Hispanic/Latino; 6 Asian, non-Hispanic/Latino; 10 Hispanic/Latino; 10 Two or more races, non-Hispanic/Latino), 34 international. Average age 29. 161 applicants, 12% accepted, 14 enrolled. In 2019, 13 doctorates awarded. *Degree requirements:* For doctorate, thesis/dissertation. *Entrance requirements:* For doctorate, GRE General Test, resume or curriculum vitae, scholarly writing, 3 letters of recommendation, statement of purpose. Additional exam requirements/recommendations for international students: required—TOEFL (minimum score 114 iBT), IELTS (minimum score 8); recommended—TWE. *Application deadline:* For fall admission, 12/1 for domestic and international students. Application fee: $90. Electronic applications accepted. *Financial support:* In 2019–20, 15 students received support, including 15 fellowships with full tuition reimbursements available (averaging $52,427 per year); research assistantships, teaching assistantships, Federal Work-Study, health care benefits, and unspecified assistantships also available. Financial award application deadline: 12/1. *Unit head:* Dr. Robeson Taj Frazier, Director of the PhD Program, 213-740-6595, E-mail: rfrazier@usc.edu. *Application contact:* Allyson Hill, Associate Dean for Admissions, 213-821-0770, Fax: 213-740-1933, E-mail: ascadm@usc.edu.
Website: http://www.annenberg.usc.edu

University of Southern California, Graduate School, Annenberg School for Communication and Journalism, School of Communication, Program in Global Communication, Los Angeles, CA 90089. Offers MA/M Sc. *Students:* 35 full-time (29 women); includes 5 minority (2 Black or African American, non-Hispanic/Latino; 2 Asian, non-Hispanic/Latino; 1 Hispanic/Latino), 24 international. Average age 24. 322 applicants, 16% accepted, 35 enrolled. *Entrance requirements:* Additional exam requirements/recommendations for international students: required—TOEFL (minimum score 114 iBT), IELTS (minimum score 8). *Application deadline:* For fall admission, 3/1 priority date for domestic and international students. Applications are processed on a rolling basis. Application fee: $0. Electronic applications accepted. Application fee is waived when completed online. *Expenses:* Contact institution. *Financial support:* In 2019–20, 16 students received support, including 16 research assistantships (averaging $10,000 per year); Federal Work-Study, institutionally sponsored loans, and scholarships/grants also available. Support available to part-time students. Financial award application deadline: 1/1; financial award applicants required to submit FAFSA. *Unit head:* Dr. Patricia Riley, Director, 213-740-3949, Fax: 213-740-0013, E-mail: priley@usc.edu. *Application contact:* Allyson Hill, Associate Dean for Admissions, 213-821-0770, Fax: 213-740-1933, E-mail: ascadm@usc.edu.
Website: http://www.annenberg.usc.edu

University of Southern California, Graduate School, Annenberg School for Communication and Journalism, School of Communication, Program in Public Diplomacy, Los Angeles, CA 90089. Offers MPD. *Program availability:* Part-time. *Students:* 25 full-time (22 women); includes 11 minority (1 Black or African American, non-Hispanic/Latino; 2 Asian, non-Hispanic/Latino; 5 Hispanic/Latino; 1 Native Hawaiian or other Pacific Islander, non-Hispanic/Latino; 2 Two or more races, non-Hispanic/Latino), 11 international. Average age 26. 47 applicants, 47% accepted, 13 enrolled. In 2019, 17 master's awarded. *Degree requirements:* For master's, thesis. *Entrance requirements:* For master's, GRE, resume, writing samples, statement of purpose, recommendation letters. Additional exam requirements/recommendations for international students: required—TOEFL (minimum score 114 iBT), IELTS (minimum score 8). *Application deadline:* For fall admission, 1/15 priority date for domestic and international students. Application fee: $90. Electronic applications accepted. *Financial support:* In 2019–20, 6 fellowships (averaging $15,000 per year) were awarded; career-related internships or fieldwork, Federal Work-Study, and scholarships/grants also available. Support available to part-time students. Financial award application deadline: 1/15; financial award applicants required to submit FAFSA. *Unit head:* Dr. Robert David Banks, Faculty Program Co-Director, 213-821-7851, E-mail: robertdb@usc.edu. *Application contact:* Allyson Hill, Associate Dean for Admissions, 213-821-0770, Fax: 213-740-1933, E-mail: ascadm@usc.edu.
Website: http://www.annenberg.usc.edu

University of Southern Indiana, Graduate Studies, College of Liberal Arts, Program in Communication, Evansville, IN 47712-3590. Offers MA. *Program availability:* Part-time, evening/weekend. *Entrance requirements:* For master's, GRE, written letter of intent, three professional letters of recommendation. Additional exam requirements/recommendations for international students: required—TOEFL (minimum score 550 paper-based; 79 iBT), IELTS (minimum score 6). Electronic applications accepted.

University of Southern Mississippi, College of Arts and Sciences, School of Communication, Hattiesburg, MS 39406-0001. Offers communication (MA, MS, PhD); public relations (MS). *Program availability:* Part-time. *Students:* 30 full-time (23 women), 35 part-time (23 women); includes 11 minority (8 Black or African American, non-Hispanic/Latino; 1 American Indian or Alaska Native, non-Hispanic/Latino; 1 Asian, non-Hispanic/Latino; 1 Hispanic/Latino), 15 international. 38 applicants, 45% accepted, 4 enrolled. In 2019, 10 master's, 7 doctorates awarded. *Degree requirements:* For master's, comprehensive exam, thesis optional; for doctorate, comprehensive exam, thesis/dissertation. *Entrance requirements:* For master's, GRE General Test, minimum GPA of 3.0 in last 60 hours and in major; for doctorate, GRE General Test, minimum GPA of 3.5. Additional exam requirements/recommendations for international students: required—TOEFL, IELTS. *Application deadline:* For fall admission, 3/1 priority date for domestic students, 3/1 for international students; for spring admission, 1/10 priority date for domestic and international students. Applications are processed on a rolling basis. Application fee: $60. Electronic applications accepted. *Expenses: Tuition, area resident:* Full-time $4393; part-time $488 per credit hour. Tuition, nonresident: full-time $5393; part-time $600 per credit hour. *Required fees:* $6 per semester. *Financial support:* Fellowships with full tuition reimbursements, research assistantships, teaching assistantships with full tuition reimbursements, Federal Work-Study, institutionally sponsored loans, scholarships/grants, health care benefits, and unspecified assistantships available. Financial award application deadline: 3/15; financial award applicants required to submit FAFSA. *Unit head:* Dr. John Meyer, Director, 601-266-4271, Fax: 601-266-4275, E-mail: John.Meyer@usm.edu. *Application contact:* Dr. John Meyer, Director, 601-266-4271, Fax: 601-266-4275, E-mail: John.Meyer@usm.edu.
Website: https://www.usm.edu/communication-studies

University of South Florida, College of Arts and Sciences, Department of Communication, Tampa, FL 33620-9951. Offers MA, PhD. *Program availability:* Part-time. *Faculty:* 13 full-time (9 women), 1 part-time/adjunct (0 women). *Students:* 33 full-time (20 women), 15 part-time (9 women); includes 18 minority (7 Black or African American, non-Hispanic/Latino; 3 Asian, non-Hispanic/Latino; 6 Hispanic/Latino; 2 Two or more races, non-Hispanic/Latino), 8 international. Average age 35. 56 applicants, 32% accepted, 10 enrolled. In 2019, 3 master's, 5 doctorates awarded. *Degree requirements:* For master's, comprehensive exam, thesis (for some programs); for doctorate, comprehensive exam, thesis/dissertation. *Entrance requirements:* For master's, GRE with preferred scores of at least 153V (61st percentile), 2 letters of recommendation, writing sample, statement of purpose, transcripts, CV or resume; for doctorate, GRE with preferred scores of at least 153V (61st percentile), 3.0 GPA, 3 letters of recommendation, writing sample, statement of purpose, transcripts, CV or resume. Additional exam requirements/recommendations for international students: required—TOEFL (minimum score 550 paper-based; 79 iBT), IELTS. *Application deadline:* For fall admission, 1/15 for domestic and international students; for spring admission, 10/15 for domestic students, 9/15 for international students. Applications are

processed on a rolling basis. Application fee: $30. Electronic applications accepted. *Financial support:* In 2019–20, 10 students received support, including 32 teaching assistantships with full tuition reimbursements available (averaging $9,875 per year); unspecified assistantships also available. Financial award application deadline: 1/15; financial award applicants required to submit FAFSA. *Unit head:* Dr. Patrice Buzzanell, Associate Professor/Interim Chair, 813-974-2145, E-mail: pmbuzzanell@usf.edu. *Application contact:* Dr. Ambar Basu, Associate Professor and Graduate Program Director, 813-974-2145, Fax: 813-974-6817, E-mail: abasu@usf.edu.
Website: http://communication.usf.edu/

The University of Tennessee, Graduate School, College of Communication and Information, Knoxville, TN 37996. Offers advertising (MS, PhD); communications (MS, PhD); information sciences (MS, PhD); journalism and electronic media (MS, PhD); public relations (MS, PhD). *Program availability:* Part-time, evening/weekend, online learning. *Degree requirements:* For master's, thesis or alternative; for doctorate, thesis/dissertation. *Entrance requirements:* For master's and doctorate, GRE General Test, minimum GPA of 2.7. Additional exam requirements/recommendations for international students: required—TOEFL. Electronic applications accepted.

The University of Tennessee at Martin, Graduate Programs, College of Humanities and Fine Arts, Martin, TN 38238. Offers strategic communication (MASC). *Program availability:* Part-time, blended/hybrid learning. *Faculty:* 18 full-time (7 women). *Students:* 22 part-time (16 women); includes 2 minority (both Black or African American, non-Hispanic/Latino). Average age 38. 12 applicants, 67% accepted, 8 enrolled. In 2019, 7 master's awarded. *Degree requirements:* For master's, comprehensive exam. *Entrance requirements:* For master's, GRE, Minimum cumulative 2.5 GPA. Additional exam requirements/recommendations for international students: required—TOEFL (minimum score 525 paper-based; 71 iBT). *Application deadline:* For fall admission, 7/28 priority date for domestic and international students; for spring admission, 12/15 priority date for domestic and international students; for summer admission, 5/10 priority date for domestic and international students. Applications are processed on a rolling basis. Application fee: $30 ($130 for international students). Electronic applications accepted. *Expenses: Tuition, area resident:* Full-time $9096; part-time $505 per credit hour. Tuition, state resident: full-time $9096; part-time $505 per credit hour. Tuition, nonresident: full-time $15,136; part-time $841 per credit hour. *International tuition:* $23,040 full-time. *Required fees:* $1520; $85 per credit hour. Part-time tuition and fees vary according to course load. *Financial support:* In 2019–20, 16 students received support, including 1 research assistantship with full tuition reimbursement available (averaging $9,048 per year); teaching assistantships with full tuition reimbursements available, scholarships/grants, and tuition waivers (full and partial) also available. Financial award application deadline: 2/1; financial award applicants required to submit FAFSA. *Unit head:* Dr. Lynn Alexander, Dean, 731-881-7490, Fax: 731-881-7276, E-mail: lalexand@utm.edu. *Application contact:* Jolene L. Cunningham, Student Services Specialist, 731-881-7012, Fax: 731-881-7499, E-mail: jcunningham@utm.edu.
Website: http://www.utm.edu/departments/chfa/

The University of Texas at Arlington, Graduate School, College of Liberal Arts, Department of Communication, Arlington, TX 76019. Offers MA. *Program availability:* Part-time, evening/weekend. *Degree requirements:* For master's, comprehensive exam (for some programs), thesis or alternative. *Entrance requirements:* For master's, GRE General Test. Additional exam requirements/recommendations for international students: required—TOEFL (minimum score 550 paper-based). Electronic applications accepted.

The University of Texas at Austin, Graduate School, College of Communication, Department of Communication Studies, Austin, TX 78712-1111. Offers MA, PhD. *Entrance requirements:* For master's and doctorate, GRE General Test. Electronic applications accepted.

The University of Texas at Dallas, School of Behavioral and Brain Sciences, Program in Communication Sciences and Disorders, Richardson, TX 75080. Offers audiology (Au D); communication disorders (MS); communication sciences and disorders (PhD). *Program availability:* Part-time, evening/weekend. *Faculty:* 15 full-time (9 women), 19 part-time/adjunct (18 women). *Students:* 289 full-time (279 women), 19 part-time (18 women); includes 68 minority (8 Black or African American, non-Hispanic/Latino; 24 Asian, non-Hispanic/Latino; 24 Hispanic/Latino; 12 Two or more races, non-Hispanic/Latino), 10 international. Average age 25. 519 applicants, 18% accepted, 83 enrolled. In 2019, 117 master's, 18 doctorates awarded. *Degree requirements:* For doctorate, thesis/dissertation. *Entrance requirements:* For master's and doctorate, GRE General Test, minimum GPA of 3.0 in upper-level course work in field. Additional exam requirements/recommendations for international students: required—TOEFL (minimum score 550 paper-based). *Application deadline:* For fall admission, 7/15 for domestic students, 5/1 priority date for international students; for spring admission, 11/15 for domestic students, 9/1 priority date for international students. Applications are processed on a rolling basis. Application fee: $50 ($100 for international students). Electronic applications accepted. *Expenses: Tuition, area resident:* Full-time $16,504. Tuition, state resident: full-time $16,504. Tuition, nonresident: full-time $34,266. Tuition and fees vary according to course load. *Financial support:* In 2019–20, 26 students received support, including 8 research assistantships with partial tuition reimbursements available (averaging $26,122 per year), 18 teaching assistantships with partial tuition reimbursements available (averaging $18,900 per year); fellowships, Federal Work-Study, institutionally sponsored loans, scholarships/grants, and unspecified assistantships also available. Support available to part-time students. Financial award application deadline: 4/30; financial award applicants required to submit FAFSA. *Unit head:* Dr. Robert D. Stillman, Area Head, 214-905-3106, Fax: 972-883-3022, E-mail: stillman@utdallas.edu. *Application contact:* Dr. Robert D. Stillman, Area Head, 214-905-3106, Fax: 972-883-3022, E-mail: stillman@utdallas.edu.
Website: https://bbs.utdallas.edu/degrees/csd-degrees/

The University of Texas at El Paso, Graduate School, College of Liberal Arts, Department of Communication, El Paso, TX 79902. Offers MA. *Program availability:* Part-time, evening/weekend. Terminal master's awarded for partial completion of doctoral program. *Degree requirements:* For master's, thesis optional. *Entrance requirements:* For master's, GRE General Test, minimum GPA of 3.0. Additional exam requirements/recommendations for international students: required—TOEFL. Electronic applications accepted.

The University of Texas at San Antonio, College of Liberal and Fine Arts, Department of Communication, San Antonio, TX 78249-0617. Offers MA. *Program availability:* Part-time, evening/weekend, online learning. *Degree requirements:* For master's, comprehensive exam, thesis optional, 36 course hours. *Entrance requirements:* For master's, GRE, minimum GPA of 3.0 in last 60 hours, statement of purpose, two academic letters of recommendation. Additional exam requirements/recommendations for international students: required—TOEFL (minimum score 550 paper-based; 79 iBT), IELTS (minimum score 6.5). Electronic applications accepted. *Expenses:* Contact institution.

The University of Texas at Tyler, College of Arts and Sciences, Department of Communication, Tyler, TX 75799-0001. Offers communication (MA); interdisciplinary studies (MAIS, MSIS). *Program availability:* Part-time. *Faculty:* 3 full-time (2 women). *Students:* 4 full-time (all women), 3 part-time (1 woman); includes 2 minority (1 Hispanic/Latino; 1 Two or more races, non-Hispanic/Latino). Average age 27. 2 applicants, 100% accepted, 2 enrolled. In 2019, 2 master's awarded. *Entrance requirements:* For master's, GRE General Test, minimum GPA of 2.5. Additional exam requirements/recommendations for international students: required—TOEFL. *Application deadline:* For fall admission, 8/17 priority date for domestic students, 5/31 priority date for international students; for spring admission, 12/21 priority date for domestic students, 11/1 priority date for international students. Applications are processed on a rolling basis. Application fee: $25 ($50 for international students). Electronic applications accepted. *Financial support:* Fellowships, research assistantships, and teaching assistantships available. Financial award application deadline: 7/1; financial award applicants required to submit FAFSA. *Unit head:* Dr. Dennis Robertson, Chair, 903-566-7066, E-mail: dennisrobertson@uttyler.edu. *Application contact:* Dr. Dennis Robertson, Chair, 903-566-7066, E-mail: dennisrobertson@uttyler.edu.
Website: http://www.uttyler.edu/communication/

The University of Texas Rio Grande Valley, College of Liberal Arts, Department of Communication, Edinburg, TX 78539. Offers communication (MA). *Accreditation:* NAST. *Faculty:* 7 full-time (3 women). *Students:* 14 full-time (6 women), 19 part-time (15 women); includes 26 minority (all Hispanic/Latino), 2 international. Average age 32. 8 applicants, 100% accepted, 7 enrolled. In 2019, 9 master's awarded. *Entrance requirements:* Additional exam requirements/recommendations for international students: required—TOEFL or IELTS. *Expenses: Tuition, area resident:* Full-time $5959; part-time $440 per credit hour. Tuition, state resident: full-time $5959. Tuition, nonresident: full-time $5959. *International tuition:* $13,321 full-time. *Required fees:* $1169; $185 per credit hour.
Website: www.utrgv.edu/communication/index.htm

University of the Incarnate Word, School of Media and Design, San Antonio, TX 78209-6397. Offers communication arts (MA); fashion design (MA). *Program availability:* Part-time, evening/weekend. *Faculty:* 6 full-time (3 women), 2 part-time/adjunct (0 women). *Students:* 21 full-time (11 women), 5 part-time (4 women); includes 16 minority (2 Black or African American, non-Hispanic/Latino; 14 Hispanic/Latino), 3 international. 7 applicants, 100% accepted, 6 enrolled. In 2019, 9 master's awarded. *Degree requirements:* For master's, thesis or alternative, capstone. *Entrance requirements:* For master's, GRE, interview, writing sample. Additional exam requirements/recommendations for international students: required—TOEFL (minimum score 560 paper-based; 83 iBT). *Application deadline:* Applications are processed on a rolling basis. Application fee: $20. Electronic applications accepted. *Expenses: Tuition:* Full-time $11,520; part-time $960 per credit hour. *Required fees:* $1128; $94 per credit hour. Tuition and fees vary according to degree level, campus/location, program and student level. *Financial support:* Federal Work-Study, scholarships/grants, tuition waivers (partial), and unspecified assistantships available. Financial award applicants required to submit FAFSA. *Unit head:* Dr. Sharon Welkey, Dean, 210-829-6091, Fax: 210-829-3196, E-mail: welkey@uiwtx.edu. *Application contact:* Jessica Delarosa, Director of Admissions, 210-8296005, Fax: 210-829-3921, E-mail: admis@uiwtx.edu.
Website: https://www.uiw.edu/smd/index.html

University of the Incarnate Word, School of Professional Studies, San Antonio, TX 78209-6397. Offers communication arts (MAA), including applied administration, communication arts, healthcare administration, industrial and organizational psychology, organizational development; organizational development and leadership (MS); professional studies (DBA). *Program availability:* Part-time, evening/weekend, 100% online, blended/hybrid learning. *Faculty:* 16 full-time (12 women), 41 part-time/adjunct (18 women). *Students:* 503 full-time (236 women), 385 part-time (175 women); includes 571 minority (124 Black or African American, non-Hispanic/Latino; 5 American Indian or Alaska Native, non-Hispanic/Latino; 35 Asian, non-Hispanic/Latino; 382 Hispanic/Latino; 3 Native Hawaiian or other Pacific Islander, non-Hispanic/Latino; 22 Two or more races, non-Hispanic/Latino), 1 international. 670 applicants, 99% accepted, 296 enrolled. In 2019, 429 master's, 5 doctorates awarded. *Degree requirements:* For master's, comprehensive exam (for some programs), thesis or alternative. *Entrance requirements:* For master's, GMAT, GRE, official transcripts from all other colleges attended. Additional exam requirements/recommendations for international students: required—TOEFL (minimum score 560 paper-based; 83 iBT). *Application deadline:* Applications are processed on a rolling basis. Electronic applications accepted. *Expenses: Tuition:* Full-time $11,520; part-time $960 per credit hour. *Required fees:* $1128; $94 per credit hour. Tuition and fees vary according to degree level, campus/location, program and student level. *Financial support:* Scholarships/grants and unspecified assistantships available. Financial award applicants required to submit FAFSA. *Unit head:* Vincent Porter, Dean, 210-8292770, E-mail: porterv@uiwtx.edu. *Application contact:* Julie Weber, Director of Marketing and Recruitment, 210-318-1876, Fax: 210-829-2756, E-mail: eapadmission@uiwtx.edu.
Website: https://sps.uiw.edu/

University of the Pacific, College of the Pacific, Department of Communication, Stockton, CA 95211-0197. Offers MA. *Degree requirements:* For master's, thesis. *Entrance requirements:* For master's, GRE General Test. Additional exam requirements/recommendations for international students: required—TOEFL.

University of the Sacred Heart, Graduate Programs, Department of Communication, San Juan, PR 00914-0383. Offers contemporary culture and media (MA); digital journalism (MA, Certificate); editing for media (MA, Certificate); public relations (MA, Certificate); publicity (MA, Certificate); scriptwriting (MA, Certificate). *Program availability:* Part-time, evening/weekend. *Degree requirements:* For master's, thesis.

The University of Toledo, College of Graduate Studies, College of Communication and the Arts, Department of Communication, Toledo, OH 43606-3390. Offers Certificate. *Program availability:* Part-time. *Entrance requirements:* For degree, minimum GPA of 2.7 for all prior academic work, transcripts from all prior institutions attended; statement of purpose. Electronic applications accepted.

University of Utah, Graduate School, College of Humanities, Department of Communication, Salt Lake City, UT 84112. Offers communicating science, health, environment and risk (MA, MS, PhD); critical cultural studies (MA, MS, PhD); digital media (MA, MS, PhD); rhetoric (MA, MS, PhD). *Program availability:* Part-time, evening/weekend. *Faculty:* 29 full-time (15 women). *Students:* 33 full-time (24 women), 6 part-time (3 women); includes 12 minority (2 Black or African American, non-Hispanic/Latino; 4 Asian, non-Hispanic/Latino; 4 Hispanic/Latino; 1 Native Hawaiian or other Pacific Islander, non-Hispanic/Latino; 1 Two or more races, non-Hispanic/Latino), 3 international. Average age 30. 80 applicants, 19% accepted, 9 enrolled. In 2019, 4 master's, 10 doctorates awarded. Terminal master's awarded for partial completion of doctoral program. *Degree requirements:* For master's, variable foreign language requirement, comprehensive exam (for some programs), thesis (for some programs), Programme of Study; for doctorate, comprehensive exam, thesis/dissertation, Programme of Study; Prospectus. *Entrance requirements:* For master's and doctorate, GRE. Additional exam requirements/recommendations for international students: required—TOEFL (minimum score 80 paper-based), IELTS (minimum score 6.5). *Application deadline:* For fall admission, 12/15 for domestic students, 11/15 for international students. Application fee: $55 ($65 for international students). Electronic applications accepted. *Expenses:* Tuition, state resident: full-time $7085; part-time

$272.51 per credit hour. Tuition, nonresident: full-time $24,937; part-time $959.12 per credit hour. *Required fees:* $880.52; $880.52 per semester. Tuition and fees vary according to degree level, program and student level. *Financial support:* In 2019–20, 30 students received support, including 2 fellowships with full tuition reimbursements available (averaging $18,500 per year), 3 research assistantships with tuition reimbursements available (averaging $19,667 per year), 28 teaching assistantships with tuition reimbursements available (averaging $19,929 per year). Financial award application deadline: 12/15. *Unit head:* Kevin Coe, Professor and Chair, 801-581-6888, E-mail: kevin.coe@utah.edu. *Application contact:* Travis Ciaramella, Graduate Advisor, 801-585-6337, E-mail: travis.ciaramella@utah.edu. Website: http://www.communication.utah.edu

University of Washington, Graduate School, College of Arts and Sciences, Department of Communication, Seattle, WA 98195. Offers MA, MC, PhD. *Program availability:* Part-time. Terminal master's awarded for partial completion of doctoral program. *Degree requirements:* For master's, thesis, project (MC); for doctorate, thesis/dissertation. *Entrance requirements:* For master's and doctorate, GRE, minimum GPA of 3.0, writing sample. Additional exam requirements/recommendations for international students: required—TOEFL. Electronic applications accepted.

University of Washington, Graduate School, College of Arts and Sciences, School of Art, Division of Design, Seattle, WA 98195. Offers industrial design (MFA); visual communication design (MFA).

University of West Florida, College of Arts, Social Sciences, and Humanities, Department of Communication, Pensacola, FL 32514-5750. Offers strategic communication and leadership (MA). *Program availability:* Part-time, evening/weekend. *Degree requirements:* For master's, thesis or alternative. *Entrance requirements:* For master's, GRE (minimum score: verbal 470, writing 4.0), MAT (minimum score 413), or GMAT (minimum score of 400), minimum GPA of 3.2; official transcripts; undergraduate degree in related field; three letters of reference; current curriculum vitae/resume. Additional exam requirements/recommendations for international students: required—TOEFL (minimum score 550 paper-based).

University of Windsor, Faculty of Graduate Studies, Faculty of Arts and Social Sciences, Department of Communication Studies, Windsor, ON N9B 3P4, Canada. Offers communication and social justice (MA). *Degree requirements:* For master's, thesis. *Entrance requirements:* For master's, writing sample/media production or multimedia portfolio. Additional exam requirements/recommendations for international students: required—TOEFL (minimum score 600 paper-based). Electronic applications accepted.

University of Wisconsin–Madison, Graduate School, College of Letters and Science, Department of Communication Arts, Madison, WI 53706-1380. Offers communication science (MA, PhD); film (MA, PhD); media and cultural studies (MA, PhD); rhetoric (MA, PhD). Terminal master's awarded for partial completion of doctoral program. *Degree requirements:* For master's, one foreign language, thesis (for some programs); for doctorate, one foreign language, thesis/dissertation. *Entrance requirements:* For master's and doctorate, GRE General Test, minimum GPA of 3.5. Electronic applications accepted.

University of Wisconsin–Milwaukee, Graduate School, College of Letters and Science, Department of Communication, Milwaukee, WI 53201-0413. Offers communication (MA, PhD), including rhetorical leadership; rhetorical leadership (Graduate Certificate). *Program availability:* Part-time. *Degree requirements:* For master's, thesis or alternative; for doctorate, comprehensive exam. *Entrance requirements:* For master's, GRE General Test, minimum GPA of 3.0. Additional exam requirements/recommendations for international students: required—TOEFL (minimum score 550 paper-based; 79 iBT), IELTS (minimum score 6). Electronic applications accepted.

University of Wisconsin–Stevens Point, College of Fine Arts and Communication, Division of Communication, Stevens Point, WI 54481-3897. Offers interpersonal communication (MA); media studies (MA); organizational communication (MA); public relations (MA). *Program availability:* Part-time. *Degree requirements:* For master's, thesis or alternative. *Entrance requirements:* For master's, GRE. Additional exam requirements/recommendations for international students: required—TOEFL (minimum score 575 paper-based).

University of Wisconsin–Superior, Graduate Division, Department of Communicating Arts, Superior, WI 54880-4500. Offers mass communication (MA); speech communication (MA); theater (MA). *Program availability:* Part-time. *Degree requirements:* For master's, comprehensive exam, thesis or alternative, position paper or project. *Entrance requirements:* For master's, minimum GPA of 2.75. Electronic applications accepted.

University of Wisconsin–Whitewater, School of Graduate Studies, College of Arts and Communications, Department of Communication, Whitewater, WI 53190-1790. Offers corporate communication (MS); mass communication (MS). *Program availability:* Part-time, evening/weekend, online learning. *Degree requirements:* For master's, thesis or alternative. *Entrance requirements:* For master's, 2 letters of recommendation, goal statement. Additional exam requirements/recommendations for international students: required—TOEFL (minimum score 550 paper-based; 80 iBT), IELTS (minimum score 6). Electronic applications accepted.

University of Wyoming, College of Arts and Sciences, Department of Communication and Journalism, Laramie, WY 82071. Offers communication (MA). *Program availability:* Part-time. *Degree requirements:* For master's, thesis. *Entrance requirements:* For master's, GRE General Test, minimum GPA of 3.0.

Utah State University, School of Graduate Studies, College of Humanities and Social Sciences, Department of Journalism and Communication, Logan, UT 84322. Offers MA, MS. *Program availability:* Part-time. *Degree requirements:* For master's, comprehensive exam, thesis. *Entrance requirements:* For master's, GRE General Test or MAT, minimum GPA of 3.0. Additional exam requirements/recommendations for international students: required—TOEFL. Electronic applications accepted.

Valparaiso University, Graduate School and Continuing Education, Program in English Studies and Communication, Valparaiso, IN 46383. Offers English studies and communication (MA). *Program availability:* Part-time, evening/weekend. *Entrance requirements:* For master's, minimum GPA of 3.0. Additional exam requirements/recommendations for international students: required—TOEFL (minimum score 550 paper-based; 80 iBT), IELTS (minimum score 6). Electronic applications accepted.

Valparaiso University, Graduate School and Continuing Education, Program in Media and Communication, Valparaiso, IN 46383. Offers digital media (MS, Certificate); sports media (MS, Certificate). *Program availability:* Part-time, evening/weekend. *Entrance requirements:* For master's, minimum GPA of 3.0, undergraduate minor in communication. Additional exam requirements/recommendations for international students: required—TOEFL (minimum score 550 paper-based; 80 iBT), IELTS (minimum score 6). Electronic applications accepted.

Villanova University, Graduate School of Liberal Arts and Sciences, Department of Communication, Villanova, PA 19085-1699. Offers MA. *Program availability:* Part-time,

evening/weekend. *Degree requirements:* For master's, comprehensive exam (for some programs), thesis optional. *Entrance requirements:* For master's, GRE or GMAT, minimum GPA of 3.0, writing sample, statement of goals, 3 letters of recommendation. Additional exam requirements/recommendations for international students: required—TOEFL. Electronic applications accepted.

Virginia Commonwealth University, Graduate School, College of Humanities and Sciences, Richard T. Robertson School of Media and Culture, Program in Media, Art, and Text, Richmond, VA 23284-9005. Offers PhD. *Entrance requirements:* For doctorate, GRE. Additional exam requirements/recommendations for international students: required—TOEFL (minimum score 600 paper-based; 100 iBT); recommended—IELTS (minimum score 6.5). Electronic applications accepted.

Virginia Polytechnic Institute and State University, Graduate School, College of Liberal Arts and Human Sciences, Blacksburg, VA 24061. Offers career and technical education (MS Ed, Ed S); communication (MA); counselor education (MA); creative writing (MFA); curriculum and instruction (MA Ed, Ed S); educational leadership and policy studies (Ed S); educational research and evaluation (PhD); English (MA); social, political, ethical, and cultural thought (PhD); Ed D/PhD. *Faculty:* 452 full-time (241 women), 1 (woman) part-time/adjunct. *Students:* 571 full-time (405 women), 351 part-time (223 women); includes 176 minority (103 Black or African American, non-Hispanic/Latino; 3 American Indian or Alaska Native, non-Hispanic/Latino; 18 Asian, non-Hispanic/Latino; 31 Hispanic/Latino; 1 Native Hawaiian or other Pacific Islander, non-Hispanic/Latino; 20 Two or more races, non-Hispanic/Latino), 93 international. Average age 34. 865 applicants, 55% accepted, 336 enrolled. In 2019, 270 master's, 63 doctorates awarded. *Degree requirements:* For master's, comprehensive exam (for some programs), thesis (for some programs); for doctorate, comprehensive exam (for some programs), thesis/dissertation (for some programs). *Entrance requirements:* For master's and doctorate, GRE/GMAT. Additional exam requirements/recommendations for international students: required—TOEFL (minimum score 90 iBT). *Application deadline:* For fall admission, 8/1 for domestic students, 4/1 for international students; for spring admission, 1/1 for domestic students, 9/1 for international students. Applications are processed on a rolling basis. Application fee: $75. Electronic applications accepted. *Expenses:* Tuition, state resident: full-time $13,700; part-time $761.25 per credit hour. Tuition, nonresident: full-time $27,614; part-time $1534 per credit hour. *Required fees:* $886.50 per term. Tuition and fees vary according to campus/location and program. *Financial support:* In 2019–20, 3 fellowships with full tuition reimbursements (averaging $7,621 per year), 34 research assistantships with full tuition reimbursements (averaging $15,645 per year), 370 teaching assistantships with full tuition reimbursements (averaging $18,225 per year) were awarded; scholarships/grants and unspecified assistantships also available. Financial award application deadline: 3/1; financial award applicants required to submit FAFSA. *Unit head:* Dr. Laura Belmonte, Dean, 540-231-6779, Fax: 540-231-7157, E-mail: belmonte@vt.edu. *Application contact:* Chelsea Blanchet, Executive Assistant, 540-231-6779, Fax: 540-231-7157, E-mail: bchels1@vt.edu.
Website: http://www.liberalarts.vt.edu/

Wake Forest University, Graduate School of Arts and Sciences, Department of Communication, Winston-Salem, NC 27109. Offers speech communication (MA). *Program availability:* Part-time. *Degree requirements:* For master's, one foreign language, thesis. *Entrance requirements:* For master's, GRE General Test, writing sample. Additional exam requirements/recommendations for international students: required—TOEFL (minimum score 79 iBT). Electronic applications accepted.

Walden University, Graduate Programs, School of Management, Minneapolis, MN 55401. Offers accounting (MBA, MS, DBA), including accounting for the professional (MS), accounting with CPA emphasis (MS), self-designed (MS); advanced project management (Graduate Certificate); applied project management (Graduate Certificate); auditing (Graduate Certificate); bridge to business administration (Post-Doctoral Certificate); bridge to management (Post-Doctoral Certificate); business management (Graduate Certificate); communication (MBA); corporate finance (MBA); digital marketing (Graduate Certificate); entrepreneurship (DBA); entrepreneurship and small business (MBA); finance (MS, DBA), including finance for the professional (MS), finance with CFA/investment (MS), finance with CPA emphasis (MS); global supply chain management (DBA); healthcare management (MBA, DBA); human resource management (MBA, MS, Graduate Certificate), including functional human resource management (MS), general program (MS), integrating functional and strategic human resource management (MS), organizational strategy (MS); human resources management (DBA); information systems management (DBA); international business (MBA, DBA); leadership (MBA, MS, DBA, Graduate Certificate), including general program (MS), human resource leadership (MS), leader development (MS), self-designed (MS); management (MS, PhD), including communications (MS), finance (PhD), general program (MS), healthcare management (MS), human resource management (MS), human resources management (PhD), information systems management (PhD), international business (MS), leadership (MS), leadership and organizational change (PhD), marketing (MS), project management (MS), strategy and operations (MS); managerial accounting (Graduate Certificate); marketing (MBA, MS, DBA); project management (MBA, MS, DBA); self-designed (MBA, DBA); social impact management (DBA); technology entrepreneurship (DBA). *Accreditation:* ACBSP. *Program availability:* Part-time, evening/weekend, online only, 100% online. *Degree requirements:* For master's, thesis (for some programs), residency (for EMBA); for doctorate, thesis/dissertation (for some programs), residency. *Entrance requirements:* For master's, bachelor's degree or higher; minimum GPA of 2.5; official transcripts; goal statement (for some programs); access to computer and Internet; for doctorate, master's degree or higher; three years of related professional or academic experience (preferred); minimum GPA of 3.0; goal statement and current resume (for select programs); official transcripts; access to computer and Internet; for other advanced degree, relevant work experience; access to computer and Internet. Additional exam requirements/recommendations for international students: required—TOEFL (minimum score 550 paper-based, 79 iBT), IELTS (minimum score 6.5), Michigan English Language Assessment Battery (minimum score 82), or PTE (minimum score 53). Electronic applications accepted.

Walla Walla University, Graduate Studies, Center for Cinema, Religion, and Worldview, College Place, WA 99324. Offers Web and interactive media (MA). *Entrance requirements:* For master's, three professional references, transcripts, personal statement.

Washington State University, The Edward R. Murrow College of Communication, Pullman, WA 99164-2520. Offers communication (MA, PhD); strategic communication (MA). *Degree requirements:* For master's, comprehensive exam (for some programs), thesis optional, oral exam; for doctorate, comprehensive exam, thesis/dissertation. *Entrance requirements:* For master's, GRE General Test, minimum GPA of 3.25, 3 letters of recommendation; for doctorate, GRE General Test, minimum undergraduate GPA of 3.25, graduate 3.5; MA in communication; 3 letters of recommendation. Additional exam requirements/recommendations for international students: required—TOEFL (minimum score 580 paper-based). Electronic applications accepted.

Wayne State College, School of Education and Counseling, Department of Educational Foundations and Leadership, Program in Curriculum and Instruction, Wayne, NE 68787.

Offers alternative education (MSE); business and information technology education (MSE); communication arts education (MSE); early childhood education (MSE); elementary education (MSE); English as a second language (MSE); English education (MSE); family and consumer sciences education (MSE); industrial technology and vocational education (MSE); learning communities (MSE); mathematics education (MSE); music education (MSE); science education (MSE); social science education (MSE). *Accreditation:* NCATE. *Program availability:* Part-time, evening/weekend. *Degree requirements:* For master's, comprehensive exam, thesis optional. *Entrance requirements:* For master's, GRE General Test. Additional exam requirements/ recommendations for international students: required—TOEFL (minimum score 550 paper-based).

Wayne State University, College of Fine, Performing and Communication Arts, Department of Communication, Detroit, MI 48202. Offers communication (PhD), including democratic participation and culture, identity and representation, media, society and culture, risk, crisis and conflict, wellness, work life and relationships; communication and new media (Graduate Certificate); communication studies (MA); dispute resolution (MADR, Graduate Certificate), including community and urban studies (MADR), conflict area studies (MADR), health and family (MADR), international conflict and cooperation (MADR), professional practice (MADR), theory of conflict (MADR), workplace (MADR); health communication (Graduate Certificate); journalism (MA); media arts (MA); media studies (MA); public relations and organizational communication (MA); JD/MADR. *Program availability:* Online learning. *Degree requirements:* For master's, thesis (for some programs), thesis or essay; for doctorate, thesis/dissertation. *Entrance requirements:* For master's, GRE (for MA if undergraduate GPA less than 3.2), personal statement; BA or BS in communication or related field with minimum upper-division GPA of 3.2 and minimum upper-division undergraduate GPA of 3.0, and sample of academic writing (for MA); undergraduate degree with minimum upper-division GPA of 3.0 and three letters of recommendation (for MADR); for doctorate, GRE, undergraduate degree in communication or related field; master's degree in communication or related field with minimum GPA of 3.5; letters of recommendation; personal statement; sample of written scholarship. Additional exam requirements/ recommendations for international students: required—TOEFL (minimum score 100 iBT), IELTS, TWE. Electronic applications accepted. *Expenses:* Contact institution.

Weber State University, Telitha E. Lindquist College of Arts and Humanities, Department of Communication, Ogden, UT 84408-1001. Offers MPC. *Program availability:* Part-time, evening/weekend. *Faculty:* 9 full-time (5 women), 1 (woman) part-time/adjunct. *Students:* 11 full-time (8 women), 35 part-time (24 women); includes 5 minority (1 Asian, non-Hispanic/Latino; 2 Hispanic/Latino; 2 Two or more races, non-Hispanic/Latino), 2 international. Average age 34. In 2019, 24 master's awarded. *Degree requirements:* For master's, thesis optional. *Entrance requirements:* For master's, GRE. Additional exam requirements/recommendations for international students: required—TOEFL (minimum score 550 paper-based; 85 iBT). *Application deadline:* For fall admission, 4/1 for domestic students. Application fee: $60 ($90 for international students). Electronic applications accepted. *Expenses: Tuition, area resident:* Full-time $7197; part-time $4981 per credit. Tuition, state resident: full-time $7197; part-time $4981 per credit. Tuition, nonresident: full-time $16,560; part-time $11,589 per credit. *Required fees:* $643 per semester. One-time fee: $60. Tuition and fees vary according to course load and program. *Financial support:* In 2019–20, 7 students received support. Scholarships/grants and tuition waivers (full and partial) available. Financial award application deadline: 4/1; financial award applicants required to submit FAFSA. *Unit head:* Dr. Sarah Steimel, Program Director, 801-626-6535, Fax: 801-626-7760, E-mail: sarahsteimel@weber.edu. *Application contact:* Shari Love, Office Specialist, 801-626-7499, Fax: 801-626-7975, E-mail: slove@weber.edu.
Website: http://www.weber.edu/mpc

Webster University, School of Communications, St. Louis, MO 63119-3194. Offers MA. *Program availability:* Part-time, evening/weekend, online learning. *Degree requirements:* For master's, thesis (for some programs). *Entrance requirements:* For master's, 36 hours of graduate course work. Additional exam requirements/recommendations for international students: required—TOEFL.

Webster University, School of Education, Department of Multidisciplinary Studies, St. Louis, MO 63119-3194. Offers applied educational psychology (MA, Ed S); communication arts (MA); early childhood education (MA, MAT); education and innovation (MA); educational technology (MET); elementary education (MAT); mathematics for educators (MA); middle school education (MAT); multidisciplinary studies (MAT); multimodal literacy for global impact (MA); reading (MA); secondary school education (MAT); special education (MA, MAT); teaching English as a second language (MA); transformative learning in the global community (Ed S). *Program availability:* Part-time. *Entrance requirements:* For master's, minimum GPA of 2.5. Additional exam requirements/recommendations for international students: required—TOEFL.

Western Illinois University, School of Graduate Studies, College of Fine Arts and Communication, Department of Communication, Macomb, IL 61455-1390. Offers MA. *Program availability:* Part-time. *Degree requirements:* For master's, comprehensive exam (for some programs), thesis or alternative. *Entrance requirements:* Additional exam requirements/recommendations for international students: required—TOEFL (minimum score 580 paper-based; 92 iBT). Electronic applications accepted.

Western Kentucky University, Graduate School, Potter College of Arts and Letters, Department of Communication, Bowling Green, KY 42101. Offers communication (MA); organizational communication (Graduate Certificate). *Program availability:* Part-time, evening/weekend. *Degree requirements:* For master's, comprehensive exam, thesis optional, final exam. *Entrance requirements:* For master's, GRE General Test, minimum GPA of 2.75. Additional exam requirements/recommendations for international students: required—TOEFL (minimum score 555 paper-based; 79 iBT).

Western Michigan University, Graduate College, College of Arts and Sciences, School of Communication, Kalamazoo, MI 49008. Offers MA.

Western New England University, College of Arts and Sciences, Program in Communication, Springfield, MA 01119. Offers public relations (MA). *Program availability:* Part-time, evening/weekend. *Degree requirements:* For master's, independent study or thesis. *Entrance requirements:* For master's, official transcript, personal statement, resume, three letters of recommendation. Additional exam requirements/recommendations for international students: required—TOEFL (minimum score 79 iBT). Electronic applications accepted. *Expenses:* Contact institution.

West Texas A&M University, College of Fine Arts and Humanities, Department of Communication, Canyon, TX 79015. Offers MA. *Program availability:* Part-time. *Degree requirements:* For master's, comprehensive exam, thesis optional. *Entrance requirements:* For master's, GRE General Test, 24 hours of undergraduate communications courses, letter of recommendation, interview with communication advisor. Additional exam requirements/recommendations for international students: required—TOEFL (minimum score 550 paper-based). Electronic applications accepted.

West Virginia University, Eberly College of Arts and Sciences, Morgantown, WV 26506. Offers biology (MS, PhD); chemistry (MS, PhD); communication studies (MA, PhD); computational statistics (PhD); creative writing (MFA); English (MA, PhD); forensic and investigative science (MS); forensic science (PhD); geography (MA); geology (MA, PhD); history (MA, PhD); legal studies (MLS); mathematics (MS); physics (MS, PhD); political science (MA, PhD); professional writing and editing (MA); psychology (MA); public administration (MPA); social work (MSW); sociology (MA, PhD); statistics (MS). *Program availability:* Part-time, evening/weekend, online learning. Terminal master's awarded for partial completion of doctoral program. *Degree requirements:* For master's, thesis (for some programs); for doctorate, comprehensive exam, thesis/dissertation. *Entrance requirements:* For master's and doctorate, GRE. Additional exam requirements/recommendations for international students: required—TOEFL (minimum score 600 paper-based); recommended—TWE. Electronic applications accepted.

Wichita State University, Graduate School, Fairmount College of Liberal Arts and Sciences, Elliott School of Communication, Wichita, KS 67260. Offers communication (MA). *Program availability:* Part-time.

Wilfrid Laurier University, Faculty of Graduate and Postdoctoral Studies, Faculty of Arts, Department of Communication Studies, Waterloo, ON N2L 3C5, Canada. Offers media, technology and culture (MA); visual communication and culture (MA). *Degree requirements:* For master's, thesis optional. *Entrance requirements:* For master's, honours BA in communication studies or a cognate discipline from an approved university with a minimum B+ overall in last two years of study and in undergraduate major. Additional exam requirements/recommendations for international students: required—TOEFL (minimum score 89 iBT). Electronic applications accepted.

York University, Faculty of Graduate Studies, Program in Communication and Culture, Toronto, ON M3J 1P3, Canada. Offers MA, PhD. *Degree requirements:* For master's, thesis or alternative; for doctorate, comprehensive exam, thesis/dissertation. Electronic applications accepted.

Arts Journalism

Academy of Art University, Graduate Programs, Program in Fashion Journalism, San Francisco, CA 94105-3410. Offers MA. *Program availability:* Part-time, evening/ weekend, 100% online. *Faculty:* 22 full-time (16 women), 54 part-time/adjunct (40 women). *Students:* 14 full-time (13 women), 12 part-time (all women); includes 5 minority (3 Black or African American, non-Hispanic/Latino; 1 American Indian or Alaska Native, non-Hispanic/Latino; 1 Hispanic/Latino), 12 international. Average age 31. 4 applicants, 100% accepted, 2 enrolled. In 2019, 14 master's awarded. *Degree requirements:* For master's, final review. *Entrance requirements:* For master's, statement of intent; resume; portfolio/reel; official college transcripts. *Application deadline:* Applications are processed on a rolling basis. Application fee: $50. Electronic applications accepted. *Expenses: Tuition:* Full-time $1083; part-time $1083 per credit hour. *Required fees:* $860; $860 per unit. $430 per term. One-time fee: $145. Tuition and fees vary according to program. *Financial support:* Career-related internships or fieldwork, Federal Work-Study, and scholarships/grants available. Financial award application deadline: 8/10; financial award applicants required to submit FAFSA.
Website: http://www.academyart.edu/academics/fashion/graduate-degrees

Syracuse University, S. I. Newhouse School of Public Communications, MA Program in Arts Journalism, Syracuse, NY 13244. Offers MA. *Accreditation:* ACEJMC. *Entrance requirements:* For master's, GRE General Test, resume, official transcripts, personal statement, three letters of recommendation. Additional exam requirements/ recommendations for international students: required—TOEFL (minimum score 600 paper-based; 100 iBT). Electronic applications accepted.

Broadcast Journalism

American University, School of Communication, Division of Journalism, Washington, DC 20016-8001. Offers broadcast journalism (MA); international journalism (MA); investigative journalism (MA); journalism and digital storytelling (MA). *Accreditation:* ACEJMC. *Program availability:* Part-time, evening/weekend. *Degree requirements:* For master's, comprehensive exam, thesis or alternative. *Entrance requirements:* Additional exam requirements/recommendations for international students: required—TOEFL (minimum score 600 paper-based; 100 iBT), IELTS (minimum score 7). Electronic applications accepted.

The American University in Cairo, School of Global Affairs and Public Policy, Cairo, Egypt. Offers gender and women's studies (MA); global affairs (MGA); international and comparative law (LL M); international human rights law (MA); journalism and mass communication (MA); Middle East studies (MA); migration and refugee studies (MA,

Diploma); public administration (MPA); public policy (MPP); television and digital journalism (MA). *Program availability:* Part-time, evening/weekend. *Degree requirements:* For master's, comprehensive exam (for some programs), thesis (for some programs). *Entrance requirements:* Additional exam requirements/recommendations for international students: required—TOEFL (minimum score 450 paper-based; 45 iBT), IELTS (minimum score 5). Electronic applications accepted. *Expenses:* Contact institution.

Kent State University, College of Communication and Information, School of Media and Journalism, Kent, OH 44242-0001. Offers journalism and mass communication (MA), including media management, public relations, reporting and editing-broadcast, reporting and editing-convergence, reporting and editing-journalism educators, reporting and editing-magazine, reporting and editing-newspaper. *Program availability:* Part-time, 100% online. *Faculty:* 7 full-time (6 women), 5 part-time/adjunct (2 women). *Students:* 11 full-time (8 women), 35 part-time (22 women); includes 3 minority (all Black or African American, non-Hispanic/Latino), 3 international. Average age 34. 18 applicants, 78% accepted, 10 enrolled. In 2019, 40 master's awarded. *Degree requirements:* For master's, thesis, thesis or project. *Entrance requirements:* For master's, GRE, Bachelor's degree, minimum GPA of 3.0, statement of purpose, 2 letters of recommendation, resume or vitae, official transcript(s), writing sample. Additional exam requirements/recommendations for international students: required—TOEFL (minimum score 100 iBT), IELTS (minimum score 7), PTE (minimum score 65), Michigan English Language Assessment Battery (minimum score 82). *Application deadline:* For fall admission, 7/1 for domestic and international students. Applications are processed on a rolling basis. Application fee: $45 ($70 for international students). Electronic applications accepted. *Financial support:* Research assistantships with full tuition reimbursements, teaching assistantships with full tuition reimbursements, scholarships/grants, and unspecified assistantships available. Financial award application deadline: 3/1. *Unit head:* Jeff Fruit, Interim Director and Professor, 330-672-2572, E-mail: jmc@kent.edu. *Application contact:* Tang Tang, Graduate Coordinator/Professor, 330-672-1132, E-mail: ttang2@kent.edu.
Website: http://www.kent.edu/jmc

Northwestern University, Medill School of Journalism, Media, and Integrated Marketing Communications, Evanston, IL 60208. Offers integrated marketing communications (MSIMC), including brand strategy, content marketing, direct and interactive marketing, marketing analytics, strategic communications; interactive publishing (MSJ); magazine writing/editing (MSJ); reporting (MSJ); video/broadcast (MSJ). *Entrance requirements:* For master's, GRE General Test, GMAT or LSAT (for MSJ). Additional exam requirements/recommendations for international students: required—TOEFL. Electronic applications accepted. *Expenses:* Contact institution.

Quinnipiac University, School of Communications, Program in Journalism, Hamden, CT 06518-1940. Offers journalism (MS), including broadcast/multimedia, writing; sports journalism (MS), including broadcast/multimedia. *Program availability:* Part-time, evening/weekend. *Degree requirements:* For master's, project. *Entrance requirements:* For master's, minimum GPA of 3.0, portfolio or writing sample. Additional exam requirements/recommendations for international students: required—TOEFL (minimum score 575 paper-based; 90 iBT), IELTS (minimum score 6.5). Electronic applications accepted. *Expenses: Tuition:* Part-time $1055 per credit. *Required fees:* $945 per semester. Tuition and fees vary according to course load and program.

Quinnipiac University, School of Communications, Program in Sports Journalism, Hamden, CT 06518-1940. Offers MS. *Program availability:* Part-time, evening/weekend. *Entrance requirements:* For master's, minimum GPA of 3.0, portfolio or writing sample. Additional exam requirements/recommendations for international students: required—TOEFL (minimum score 575 paper-based; 90 iBT), IELTS (minimum score 6.5). Electronic applications accepted. *Expenses: Tuition:* Part-time $1055 per credit. *Required fees:* $945 per semester. Tuition and fees vary according to course load and program.

Syracuse University, S. I. Newhouse School of Public Communications, MS Program in Broadcast and Digital Journalism, Syracuse, NY 13244. Offers MS. *Accreditation:* ACEJMC. *Entrance requirements:* For master's, GRE General Test, resume, official transcripts, personal statement, three letters of recommendation. Additional exam requirements/recommendations for international students: required—TOEFL (minimum score 100 iBT). Electronic applications accepted.

University of Maryland, College Park, Academic Affairs, Philip Merrill College of Journalism, College Park, MD 20742. Offers broadcast journalism (MA); journalism (MA); journalism and media studies (PhD); online news (MA); public affairs reporting (MA). *Accreditation:* ACEJMC (one or more programs are accredited). *Program availability:* Part-time, evening/weekend. *Degree requirements:* For doctorate, thesis/dissertation, preliminary written and oral comprehensive exams. *Entrance requirements:* For master's and doctorate, GRE General Test, minimum GPA of 3.0, 3 letters of recommendation. Additional exam requirements/recommendations for international students: required—TOEFL. Electronic applications accepted.

University of Miami, Graduate School, School of Communication, Coral Gables, FL 33124. Offers communication (PhD); communication studies (MA); film studies (MA, PhD); motion pictures (MFA), including production, producing, and screenwriting; print journalism (MA); public relations (MA); Spanish language journalism (MA); television broadcast journalism (MA). *Program availability:* Part-time. *Degree requirements:* For master's, comprehensive exam (for some programs), thesis (for some programs); for doctorate, comprehensive exam, thesis/dissertation. *Entrance requirements:* For master's, GRE General Test; for doctorate, GRE General Test, master's thesis or scholarly research. Additional exam requirements/recommendations for international students: required—TOEFL (minimum score 600 paper-based; 100 iBT). Electronic applications accepted.

University of the Sacred Heart, Graduate Programs, Department of Communication, San Juan, PR 00914-0383. Offers contemporary culture and media (MA); digital journalism (MA, Certificate); editing for media (MA, Certificate); public relations (MA, Certificate); publicity (MA, Certificate); scriptwriting (MA, Certificate). *Program availability:* Part-time, evening/weekend. *Degree requirements:* For master's, thesis.

Corporate and Organizational Communication

American University, School of Communication, Division of Public Communication, Washington, DC 20016-8001. Offers advocacy and social impact (MA); corporate communication and reputation management (MA); political communication (MA); strategic communication (MA). *Accreditation:* ACEJMC. *Program availability:* Part-time, evening/weekend, 100% online. *Degree requirements:* For master's, comprehensive exam, thesis or alternative. *Entrance requirements:* Additional exam requirements/recommendations for international students: required—TOEFL (minimum score 600 paper-based; 100 iBT), IELTS (minimum score 7). Electronic applications accepted.

Ashland University, College of Arts and Sciences, Program in Corporate and Strategic Communication, Ashland, OH 44805-3702. Offers communication (MA). *Program availability:* Online learning. Electronic applications accepted. *Expenses: Tuition:* Full-time $10,800; part-time $5400 per credit hour. *Required fees:* $720; $360 per credit hour.

Austin Peay State University, College of Graduate Studies, College of Arts and Letters, Department of Communication, Clarksville, TN 37044. Offers marketing communication (MA); media management (MA). *Program availability:* Part-time, evening/weekend, online learning. *Faculty:* 7 full-time (4 women), 2 part-time/adjunct (both women). *Students:* 6 full-time (4 women), 50 part-time (32 women); includes 19 minority (13 Black or African American, non-Hispanic/Latino; 1 American Indian or Alaska Native, non-Hispanic/Latino; 5 Two or more races, non-Hispanic/Latino). Average age 32. 24 applicants, 83% accepted, 15 enrolled. In 2019, 21 master's awarded. *Degree requirements:* For master's, comprehensive exam, thesis (for some programs). *Entrance requirements:* For master's, GRE General Test, minimum GPA of 2.5. Additional exam requirements/recommendations for international students: required—TOEFL (minimum score 500 paper-based). *Application deadline:* For fall admission, 8/5 priority date for domestic students. Applications are processed on a rolling basis. Application fee: $45 ($55 for international students). Electronic applications accepted. *Financial support:* Research assistantships with full tuition reimbursements, career-related internships or fieldwork, Federal Work-Study, institutionally sponsored loans, scholarships/grants, and unspecified assistantships available. Support available to part-time students. Financial award application deadline: 7/1; financial award applicants required to submit FAFSA. *Unit head:* Dr. Kathy Heuston, Interim Chair, 931-221-7554, Fax: 931-221-7265, E-mail: leek@apsu.edu. *Application contact:* Megan Mitchell, Coordinator of Graduate Admissions, 931-221-6189, Fax: 931-221-7641, E-mail: mitchellm@apsu.edu.
Website: http://www.apsu.edu/communication/index.php

Baruch College of the City University of New York, Weissman School of Arts and Sciences, Program in Corporate Communication, New York, NY 10010-5585. Offers MA. *Program availability:* Part-time, evening/weekend. *Degree requirements:* For master's, thesis or alternative. *Entrance requirements:* For master's, GRE/GMAT, 3 letters of recommendation; personal essay; resume; official transcripts. Additional exam requirements/recommendations for international students: required—TOEFL. Electronic applications accepted.

Bellevue University, Graduate School, College of Arts and Sciences, Bellevue, NE 68005-3098. Offers clinical counseling (MS); healthcare administration (MHA); human services (MA); international security and intelligence studies (MS); managerial communication (MA). *Program availability:* Online learning.

Boston University, Metropolitan College, Program in Gastronomy, Boston, MA 02215. Offers communications (MLA); history and culture (MLA). *Program availability:* Part-time, evening/weekend. *Faculty:* 3 full-time (2 women), 6 part-time/adjunct (3 women). *Students:* 6 full-time (4 women), 39 part-time (35 women); includes 7 minority (3 Black or African American, non-Hispanic/Latino; 3 Asian, non-Hispanic/Latino; 1 Hispanic/Latino), 5 international. Average age 34. 31 applicants, 87% accepted, 9 enrolled. In 2019, 27 master's awarded. *Entrance requirements:* Additional exam requirements/recommendations for international students: required—TOEFL. *Application deadline:* Applications are processed on a rolling basis. Application fee: $85. Electronic applications accepted. *Expenses:* Contact institution. *Financial support:* In 2019–20, 5 research assistantships (averaging $4,200 per year) were awarded; career-related internships or fieldwork, scholarships/grants, and unspecified assistantships also available. Support available to part-time students. Financial award applicants required to submit FAFSA. *Unit head:* Dr. Megan Elias, Associate Professor of the Practice and Director, 617-353-6916, Fax: 617-353-4130, E-mail: gastrmla@bu.edu. *Application contact:* Barbara Rotger, Program Manager, 617-353-6916, Fax: 617-353-4130, E-mail: brotger@bu.edu.
Website: http://www.bu.edu/met/gastronomy

Bowie State University, Graduate Programs, Program in Organizational Communication, Bowie, MD 20715-9465. Offers MA, Certificate. *Program availability:* Part-time, evening/weekend. *Degree requirements:* For master's, comprehensive exam, thesis optional, research paper. *Entrance requirements:* For master's, minimum GPA of 2.5. Electronic applications accepted. *Expenses: Tuition, area resident:* Full-time $11,942; part-time $423 per credit hour. Tuition, state resident: full-time $11,942; part-time $423 per credit hour. Tuition, nonresident: full-time $18,806; part-time $709 per credit hour. *International tuition:* $18,806 full-time. *Required fees:* $1106; $1106 per semester. $553 per semester.

Bryant University, College of Arts and Sciences, Smithfield, RI 02917. Offers communication (MA, Graduate Certificate); organizational communication (Graduate Certificate). *Program availability:* Part-time, evening/weekend. *Degree requirements:* For master's, thesis optional, Culminating Project A (alternate requirement) Comprehensive Exam A (alternate requirement). *Entrance requirements:* For master's and Graduate Certificate, GRE (waived if essay is submitted), resume, official undergraduate transcript(s), essay or GRE scores, 3 letters of recommendation (2 academic, 1 professional). Additional exam requirements/recommendations for international students: required—TOEFL (minimum score 550 paper-based; 80 iBT). Electronic applications accepted. *Expenses:* Contact institution.

California State University, San Bernardino, Graduate Studies, College of Arts and Letters, Program in Communication Studies, San Bernardino, CA 92407. Offers communication studies (MA); integrated marketing communication (MA). *Faculty:* 6 full-time (5 women), 1 (woman) part-time/adjunct. *Students:* 14 full-time (7 women), 19 part-time (13 women); includes 25 minority (4 Black or African American, non-Hispanic/Latino; 1 Asian, non-Hispanic/Latino; 13 Hispanic/Latino; 7 Two or more races, non-Hispanic/Latino), 2 international. Average age 29. 33 applicants, 70% accepted, 14 enrolled. In 2019, 13 master's awarded. *Degree requirements:* For master's, comprehensive exam. *Entrance requirements:* Additional exam requirements/recommendations for international students: required—TOEFL. *Application deadline:* For fall admission, 5/15 for domestic students. Application fee: $55. *Unit head:* Shafiqur Rahman, Department Chair, 909-537-5820, E-mail: shafiqur.rahman@csusb.edu.

Corporate and Organizational Communication

Application contact: Dr. Dorota Huizinga, Dean of Graduate Studies, 909-537-3064, Fax: 909-537-7034, E-mail: dorota.huizinga@csusb.edu.

Carnegie Mellon University, Dietrich College of Humanities and Social Sciences, Department of English, Program in Professional Writing, Pittsburgh, PA 15213-3891. Offers editing and publishing (MAPW); policy and non-profit communication (MAPW); public and media relations/corporate communications (MAPW); science or healthcare communication (MAPW); technical writing (MAPW); writing for new media (MAPW); writing for print media (MAPW). *Program availability:* Part-time. *Entrance requirements:* For master's, GRE General Test. Additional exam requirements/recommendations for international students: required—TOEFL, TWE.

City College of the City University of New York, Graduate School, Division of Humanities and the Arts, Department of Media and Communication Arts, Program in Branding and Integrated Communications, New York, NY 10031. Offers MPS. *Entrance requirements:* Additional exam requirements/recommendations for international students: required—TOEFL (minimum score 90 iBT).

Columbia University, Graduate School of Business, MBA Program, New York, NY 10027. Offers accounting (MBA); decision, risk, and operations (MBA); entrepreneurship (MBA); finance and economics (MBA); healthcare and pharmaceutical management (MBA); human resource management (MBA); international business (MBA); leadership and ethics (MBA); management (MBA); marketing (MBA); media (MBA); private equity (MBA); real estate (MBA); social enterprise (MBA); value investing (MBA); DDS/MBA; JD/MBA; MBA/MIA; MBA/MPH; MBA/MS; MD/MBA. *Entrance requirements:* For master's, GMAT, 2 letters of recommendation. Additional exam requirements/recommendations for international students: required—TOEFL. Electronic applications accepted. *Expenses:* Contact institution.

Columbia University, School of Professional Studies, Program in Strategic Communications, New York, NY 10027. Offers MS. *Program availability:* Part-time, evening/weekend. *Entrance requirements:* For master's, minimum undergraduate GPA of 3.0. Additional exam requirements/recommendations for international students: required—American Language Program placement test. Electronic applications accepted. *Expenses: Tuition:* Full-time $47,600; part-time $1880 per credit. One-time fee: $105.

Concordia University, St. Paul, College of Business and Technology, St. Paul, MN 55104-5494. Offers business administration (MBA), including cyber-security leadership; health care management (MBA); human resource management (MA); information technology (MBA); leadership and management (MA); strategic communication management (MA). *Accreditation:* ACBSP. *Program availability:* Part-time, evening/weekend, 100% online, blended/hybrid learning. *Degree requirements:* For master's, thesis (for some programs). *Entrance requirements:* For master's, official transcripts from regionally-accredited institution stating the conferral of a bachelor's degree with minimum cumulative GPA of 3.0; personal statement; professional resume. Additional exam requirements/recommendations for international students: recommended—TOEFL (minimum score 547 paper-based; 78 iBT), IELTS (minimum score 6). Electronic applications accepted. *Expenses:* Contact institution.

Concordia University Wisconsin, Graduate Programs, Batterman School of Business, MBA Program, Mequon, WI 53097-2402. Offers finance (MBA); health care administration (MBA); human resource management (MBA); international business (MBA); international business-bilingual English/Chinese (MBA); management (MBA); management information systems (MBA); managerial communications (MBA); marketing (MBA); public administration (MBA); risk management (MBA). *Program availability:* Online learning. *Degree requirements:* For master's, comprehensive exam, thesis or alternative. *Entrance requirements:* Additional exam requirements/recommendations for international students: required—TOEFL. *Expenses:* Contact institution.

Cornell University, Graduate School, Graduate Fields of Agriculture and Life Sciences, Field of Communication, Ithaca, NY 14853. Offers communication (MS, PhD); human-computer interaction (MS, PhD); language and communication (MS, PhD); media communication and society (MS, PhD); organizational communication (MS, PhD); science, environment and health communication (MS, PhD); social psychology of communication (MS, PhD). *Degree requirements:* For master's, thesis (MS); for doctorate, comprehensive exam, thesis/dissertation. *Entrance requirements:* For master's and doctorate, GRE General Test, 3 letters of recommendation. Additional exam requirements/recommendations for international students: required—TOEFL (minimum score 600 paper-based; 100 iBT). Electronic applications accepted.

DePaul University, College of Communication, Chicago, IL 60604. Offers digital communication and media arts (MA); health communication (MA); journalism (MA); media and cinema studies (MA); multicultural communication (MA); organizational communication (MA); public relations and advertising (MA); relational communication (MA). *Program availability:* Part-time, evening/weekend. *Entrance requirements:* Additional exam requirements/recommendations for international students: required—TOEFL (minimum score 590 paper-based; 96 iBT), IELTS (minimum score 7.5) or PTE. Electronic applications accepted.

Drexel University, College of Arts and Sciences, Department of Communication, Culture and Media, Program in Communication, Philadelphia, PA 19104-2875. Offers public communication (MS); science communication (MS); technical communication (MS). *Program availability:* Part-time, evening/weekend. *Degree requirements:* For master's, internship, professional portfolio. *Entrance requirements:* For master's, GRE or minimum GPA of 3.0. Additional exam requirements/recommendations for international students: required—TOEFL. Electronic applications accepted.

East Carolina University, Graduate School, Thomas Harriot College of Arts and Sciences, Department of English, Greenville, NC 27858-4353. Offers creative writing (MA); English studies (MA); linguistics (MA); literature (MA); multicultural and transnational literatures (MA, Certificate); professional communication (Certificate); rhetoric and composition (MA); rhetoric, writing, and professional communication (PhD); teaching English in the two-year college (Certificate); teaching English to speakers of other languages (MA, Certificate); technical and professional communication (MA). *Program availability:* Part-time, evening/weekend, online learning. *Application deadline:* For fall admission, 7/31 priority date for domestic students, 2/1 priority date for international students; for spring admission, 11/30 priority date for domestic students, 10/1 priority date for international students. *Expenses: Tuition, area resident:* Full-time $4749; part-time $185 per credit hour. Tuition, state resident: full-time $4749; part-time $185 per credit hour. Tuition, nonresident: full-time $17,898; part-time $864 per credit hour. *International tuition:* $17,898 full-time. *Required fees:* $2787. *Financial support:* Application deadline: 3/1. *Unit head:* Dr. Marianne Montgomery, Chair, 252-328-6041, E-mail: montgomerym@ecu.edu. *Application contact:* Graduate School Admissions, 252-328-6012, Fax: 252-328-6071, E-mail: gradschool@ecu.edu.
Website: https://english.ecu.edu/

Eastern Michigan University, Graduate School, Academic and Student Affairs Division, Ypsilanti, MI 48197. Offers individualized studies (MA, MS); integrated marketing communications (MS). *Faculty:* 2 full-time (1 woman). *Students:* 4 full-time (3 women), 25 part-time (20 women); includes 8 minority (3 Black or African American, non-Hispanic/Latino; 1 American Indian or Alaska Native, non-Hispanic/Latino; 2 Asian, non-Hispanic/Latino; 1 Hispanic/Latino; 1 Two or more races, non-Hispanic/Latino), 3 international. Average age 37. 56 applicants, 77% accepted, 19 enrolled. In 2019, 1 master's awarded. *Entrance requirements:* Additional exam requirements/recommendations for international students: required—TOEFL. Application fee: $45. *Unit head:* Dr. Wade Tornquist, Interim Dean, 734-487-0042, Fax: 734-487-0050, E-mail: wade.tornquist@emich.edu. *Application contact:* Graduate Admissions, 734-487-2400, Fax: 734-487-6559, E-mail: graduate.admissions@emich.edu.

Eastern Michigan University, Graduate School, College of Business, Department of Marketing, Program in Integrated Marketing Communications, Ypsilanti, MI 48197. Offers MS, Postbaccalaureate Certificate. *Students:* 18 full-time (16 women), 47 part-time (30 women); includes 30 minority (18 Black or African American, non-Hispanic/Latino; 2 Asian, non-Hispanic/Latino; 8 Hispanic/Latino; 2 Two or more races, non-Hispanic/Latino). Average age 30. 24 applicants, 79% accepted, 14 enrolled. In 2019, 20 master's, 1 other advanced degree awarded. Application fee: $45. *Application contact:* K. Michelle Henry, Director, Graduate Business Programs, 734-487-4444, Fax: 734-478-1316, E-mail: cob.graduate@emich.edu.

Fairleigh Dickinson University, Florham Campus, Maxwell Becton College of Arts and Sciences, Department of English, Communication and Philosophy, Program in Corporate and Organizational Communication, Madison, NJ 07940-1099. Offers MA, MA/MBA. *Entrance requirements:* For master's, GRE General Test.

Florida State University, The Graduate School, College of Communication and Information, School of Communication, Tallahassee, FL 32306. Offers communication theory and research (PhD); integrated marketing communication (MA, MS); media and communication studies (MA, MS); public interest media and communication (MA, MS). *Program availability:* Part-time. *Faculty:* 23 full-time (13 women), 1 part-time/adjunct (0 women). *Students:* 19 full-time (16 women), 121 part-time (84 women); includes 73 minority (22 Black or African American, non-Hispanic/Latino; 15 Asian, non-Hispanic/Latino; 27 Hispanic/Latino; 9 Two or more races, non-Hispanic/Latino). Average age 24. 196 applicants, 54% accepted, 48 enrolled. In 2019, 65 master's, 5 doctorates awarded. *Degree requirements:* For master's, thesis (for some programs); for doctorate, comprehensive exam, thesis/dissertation. *Entrance requirements:* For master's, GRE General Test, minimum GPA of 3.0; for doctorate, GRE General Test, minimum GPA of 3.3 in graduate course work. Additional exam requirements/recommendations for international students: required—TOEFL (minimum score 600 paper-based; 100 iBT), IELTS (minimum score 7). *Application deadline:* For fall admission, 7/1 priority date for domestic students, 5/1 priority date for international students; for spring admission, 11/1 priority date for domestic and international students; for summer admission, 3/1 priority date for domestic and international students. Applications are processed on a rolling basis. Application fee: $30. Electronic applications accepted. *Expenses:* $5,748 state resident full-time, $2,874 state resident part-time; $13,320 nonresident full-time, $6,660 nonresident part-time. *Financial support:* In 2019–20, 109 students received support, including 20 research assistantships with full tuition reimbursements available (averaging $12,726 per year), 139 teaching assistantships with full tuition reimbursements available (averaging $10,602 per year); scholarships/grants, tuition waivers (full and partial), and unspecified assistantships also available. Financial award application deadline: 11/1; financial award applicants required to submit FAFSA. *Unit head:* Dr. Jennifer Proffitt, Director, 850-644-5034, Fax: 850-644-8642, E-mail: jennifer.proffitt@cci.fsu.edu. *Application contact:* Natashia Hinson-Turner, Graduate Coordinator, 850-644-5034, Fax: 850-644-8642, E-mail: comgradadvising@cci.fsu.edu.
Website: http://www.cci.fsu.edu

Franklin University, Marketing and Communication Program, Columbus, OH 43215-5399. Offers MS. *Program availability:* Part-time, evening/weekend. *Entrance requirements:* For master's, minimum undergraduate GPA of 2.75. Additional exam requirements/recommendations for international students: required—TOEFL (minimum score 550 paper-based). Electronic applications accepted.

Georgia Southern University, Jack N. Averitt College of Graduate Studies, College of Arts and Humanities, Program in Professional Communication and Leadership, Statesboro, GA 30458. Offers MA, Certificate. *Program availability:* Part-time, evening/weekend. *Faculty:* 26 full-time (13 women). *Students:* 25 full-time (17 women), 29 part-time (25 women); includes 22 minority (16 Black or African American, non-Hispanic/Latino; 1 Asian, non-Hispanic/Latino; 3 Hispanic/Latino; 2 Two or more races, non-Hispanic/Latino), 3 international. Average age 34. 31 applicants, 97% accepted, 21 enrolled. In 2019, 20 master's awarded. *Degree requirements:* For master's, comprehensive exam, project. *Entrance requirements:* For master's, minimum GPA of 2.5, letters of recommendation, letter of intent, resume. Additional exam requirements/recommendations for international students: required—TOEFL (minimum score 523 paper-based; 70 iBT). *Application deadline:* For fall admission, 6/1 priority date for domestic students, 5/1 priority date for international students; for spring admission, 11/15 priority date for domestic students, 9/15 priority date for international students; for summer admission, 4/15 for domestic students, 9/15 priority date for international students. Applications are processed on a rolling basis. Application fee: $30. Electronic applications accepted. *Expenses: Tuition, area resident:* Full-time $4986; part-time $277 per credit hour. Tuition, nonresident: full-time $19,890; part-time $1105 per credit hour. *International tuition:* $19,890 full-time. *Required fees:* $2114; $1057 per semester. $1057 per semester. Tuition and fees vary according to course load, campus/location and program. *Financial support:* In 2019–20, 14 students received support, including research assistantships with full tuition reimbursements available (averaging $5,000 per year); scholarships/grants and unspecified assistantships also available. Financial award application deadline: 3/15; financial award applicants required to submit FAFSA. *Unit head:* Dr. Kimberly Martin, Program Coordinator, 912-344-2698, E-mail: kimberly.martin@armstrong.edu. *Application contact:* McKenzie Peterman, Graduate Admissions Specialist, 912-478-5678, Fax: 912-478-0740, E-mail: mpeterman@georgiasouthern.edu.
Website: http://www.armstrong.edu/Majors/degree/master_professional_communication_leadership

HEC Montreal, School of Business Administration, Graduate Diploma Programs in Administration, Program in Marketing Communication and Brand option, Montréal, QC H3T 2A7, Canada. Offers Graduate Diploma. *Program availability:* Part-time-only. *Entrance requirements:* For degree, bachelor's degree in administration (marketing option), work experience. Electronic applications accepted.

High Point University, Norcross Graduate School, High Point, NC 27268. Offers athletic training (MSAT); business administration (MBA); educational leadership (M Ed, Ed D); elementary education (M Ed, MAT); pharmacy (Pharm D); physical therapy (DPT); physician assistant studies (MPAS); secondary mathematics (M Ed, MAT); special education (M Ed); strategic communication (MA). *Accreditation:* NCATE. *Program availability:* Part-time, evening/weekend. *Degree requirements:* For master's, comprehensive exam (for some programs), thesis (for some programs). *Entrance requirements:* For master's, GMAT (MBA), GRE, MAT, minimum GPA of 3.0. Additional exam requirements/recommendations for international students: required—TOEFL (minimum score 550 paper-based). Electronic applications accepted.

Howard University, Cathy Hughes School of Communications, Department of Strategic, Legal and Management Communication, Washington, DC 20059-0002. Offers intercultural communication (MA, PhD); organizational communication (MA, PhD). *Program availability:* Part-time. Terminal master's awarded for partial completion of doctoral program. *Degree requirements:* For master's, comprehensive exam or thesis; for doctorate, one foreign language, comprehensive exam, thesis/dissertation. *Entrance requirements:* For master's, English proficiency exam, GRE General Test, minimum GPA of 3.0; for doctorate, English proficiency exam, GRE General Test, master's degree in related field, minimum GPA of 3.5. Additional exam requirements/recommendations for international students: required—TOEFL.

Illinois Institute of Technology, Stuart School of Business, Program in Marketing Analytics and Communication, Chicago, IL 60661. Offers MS, MBA/MS. *Program availability:* Part-time, evening/weekend. *Entrance requirements:* For master's, GRE (minimum score 1000) or GMAT (500). Additional exam requirements/recommendations for international students: required—TOEFL (minimum score 600 paper-based; 85 iBT); recommended—IELTS (minimum score 7). Electronic applications accepted. *Expenses:* Contact institution.

Iowa State University of Science and Technology, Department of English, Ames, IA 50011. Offers creative writing (MFA); English (MA); rhetoric and professional communication (PhD). *Degree requirements:* For master's, thesis or alternative; for doctorate, thesis/dissertation. *Entrance requirements:* For master's, GRE General Test, sample of written work, resume, portfolio in creative writing; for doctorate, GRE General Test, sample of written work, resume. Additional exam requirements/recommendations for international students: required—TOEFL (minimum score 600 paper-based; 100 iBT), IELTS (minimum score 7). Electronic applications accepted.

Iowa State University of Science and Technology, Program in Rhetoric and Professional Communication, Ames, IA 50011. Offers PhD. *Entrance requirements:* For doctorate, GRE, official academic transcripts, resume, three letters of recommendation, writing sample. Additional exam requirements/recommendations for international students: required—TOEFL (minimum score 640 paper-based; 111 iBT), IELTS (minimum score 7.5). Electronic applications accepted.

Iowa State University of Science and Technology, Program in Rhetoric, Composition, and Professional Communication, Ames, IA 50011. Offers MA. *Entrance requirements:* For master's, GRE, official academic transcripts, resume, three letters of recommendation, writing sample. Additional exam requirements/recommendations for international students: required—TOEFL (minimum score 600 paper-based; 100 iBT), IELTS (minimum score 7). Electronic applications accepted.

La Salle University, School of Arts and Sciences, Program in Strategic Communication, Philadelphia, PA 19141-1199. Offers communication consulting and development (MA); communication management (MA); general professional communication (MA); professional and business communication (Certificate); public relations (MA); social and new media (Certificate). *Program availability:* Part-time, evening/weekend, online learning. *Degree requirements:* For master's, practicum. *Entrance requirements:* For master's, writing assessment, professional resume; minimum overall B average; two letters of recommendation (if GPA below 3.25); brief personal statement (about 500 words); interview; for Certificate, writing assessment, minimum GPA of 2.75 in undergraduate studies; brief personal statement (about 500 words); interview. Additional exam requirements/recommendations for international students: required—TOEFL. Electronic applications accepted. Application fee is waived when completed online. *Expenses:* Contact institution.

Lasell College, Graduate and Professional Studies in Communication, Newton, MA 02466-2709. Offers health communication (MSC, Graduate Certificate); integrated marketing communication (MSC, Graduate Certificate); public relations (MSC, Graduate Certificate). *Program availability:* Part-time, evening/weekend, 100% online, blended/hybrid learning. *Faculty:* 3 full-time (2 women), 10 part-time/adjunct (4 women). *Students:* 25 full-time (18 women), 34 part-time (27 women); includes 10 minority (7 Black or African American, non-Hispanic/Latino; 3 Hispanic/Latino), 15 international. Average age 31. 40 applicants, 48% accepted, 14 enrolled. In 2019, 34 master's, 2 other advanced degrees awarded. *Degree requirements:* For master's, comprehensive exam, thesis or alternative, minimum GPA of 3.0; special project or internship. *Entrance requirements:* For master's, one-page personal statement, 2 letters of recommendation, resume, bachelor's degree transcript; for Graduate Certificate, bachelor's degree transcript, 2 letters of recommendation, 1-page personal statement, resume. Additional exam requirements/recommendations for international students: required—TOEFL (minimum score 550 paper-based, 79 iBT) or IELTS (minimum score 6). *Application deadline:* For fall admission, 8/31 priority date for domestic students, 6/30 priority date for international students; for spring admission, 12/31 priority date for domestic students, 10/31 priority date for international students. Applications are processed on a rolling basis. Electronic applications accepted. *Expenses: Tuition:* Part-time $600 per credit. *Required fees:* $40 per semester. *Financial support:* Federal Work-Study, scholarships/grants, and tuition discounts available. Support available to part-time students. Financial award application deadline: 8/31; financial award applicants required to submit FAFSA. *Unit head:* Chrystal Porter, Vice President of Graduate and Professional Studies, 617-243-2083, Fax: 617-243-2450, E-mail: gradinfo@lasell.edu. *Application contact:* Adrienne Franciosi, Assistant Vice President of Graduate and Professional Studies, 617-243-2214, Fax: 617-243-2450, E-mail: gradinfo@lasell.edu. Website: http://www.lasell.edu/academics/graduate-and-professional-studies/programs-of-study/master-of-science-in-communication.html

Loyola University Chicago, Quinlan School of Business, Master of Science in Integrated Marketing Communications Program, Chicago, IL 60611. Offers MS. *Program availability:* Part-time, evening/weekend. *Entrance requirements:* For master's, GMAT or GRE, official transcripts, two letters of recommendation, statement of purpose, resume. Additional exam requirements/recommendations for international students: required—TOEFL (minimum score 90 iBT) or IELTS (minimum score 6.5). Electronic applications accepted. Application fee is waived when completed online. *Expenses:* Contact institution.

Manhattanville College, School of Professional Studies, Master of Science in Marketing Communication Management, Purchase, NY 10577-2132. Offers marketing communication management (MS). *Program availability:* Part-time, evening/weekend. *Faculty:* 6 part-time/adjunct (5 women). *Students:* 19 full-time (13 women), 6 part-time (3 women); includes 9 minority (3 Black or African American, non-Hispanic/Latino; 5 Hispanic/Latino; 1 Two or more races, non-Hispanic/Latino), 2 international. Average age 26. 13 applicants, 77% accepted, 4 enrolled. In 2019, 7 master's, 1 other advanced degree awarded. *Degree requirements:* For master's, thesis (for some programs), final project. *Entrance requirements:* For master's, scores of GRE and GMAT are optional, personal essay, transcripts, 2 letters of recommendation (academic or professional), resume, health form with proof of immunization (for those born after 1957). Additional exam requirements/recommendations for international students: required—TOEFL or IELTS are required. Manhattanville College now accepts the Duolingo English Test with a required score of 105; recommended—TOEFL (minimum score 550 paper-based; 80 iBT), IELTS (minimum score 6.5). *Application deadline:* Applications are processed on a rolling basis. Application fee: $75. Electronic applications accepted. *Expenses:* $935 per credit, $45 technology fee, and $60 registration fee. *Financial support:* In 2019–20, 14 students received support. Scholarships/grants and unspecified assistantships available. Financial award applicants required to submit FAFSA. *Unit head:* Laura Persky, Associate Dean, 914-323-5188, E-mail: Laura.Persky@mville.edu. *Application contact:* Jean Mann, Program Director, 914-323-5419, E-mail: Jean.Mann@mville.edu. Website: https://www.mville.edu/programs/ms-marketing-communication-management

Marist College, Graduate Programs, School of Communication and the Arts, Program in Integrated Marketing Communication, Poughkeepsie, NY 12601-1387. Offers MA. *Entrance requirements:* For master's, GRE or GMAT, official undergraduate/graduate transcripts from all institutions attended; current resume; completed recommendation forms for three references; personal statement.

Minnesota State University Mankato, College of Graduate Studies and Research, College of Arts and Humanities, Department of Communication Studies, Mankato, MN 56001. Offers communication education (Certificate); communication studies (MA, MS); forensics (MFA); professional communication (Certificate). *Degree requirements:* For master's, one foreign language, comprehensive exam, thesis. *Entrance requirements:* For master's, minimum GPA of 3.0 during previous 2 years, writing sample. Electronic applications accepted.

Mississippi College, Graduate School, College of Arts and Sciences, School of Christian Studies and the Arts, Department of Communication, Clinton, MS 39058. Offers applied communication (MSC); public relations and corporate communication (MSC). *Program availability:* Part-time. *Degree requirements:* For master's, comprehensive exam, thesis optional. *Entrance requirements:* For master's, GRE or NTE, minimum GPA of 2.5. Additional exam requirements/recommendations for international students: recommended—TOEFL, IELTS. Electronic applications accepted.

Montclair State University, The Graduate School, College of the Arts, MA Program in Public and Organizational Relations, Montclair, NJ 07043-1624. Offers MA. *Program availability:* Part-time, evening/weekend. *Degree requirements:* For master's, comprehensive exam. *Entrance requirements:* For master's, GRE General Test, 2 letters of recommendation. Additional exam requirements/recommendations for international students: required—TOEFL (minimum score 83 iBT) or IELTS (minimum score 6.5). Electronic applications accepted.

Murray State University, Arthur J. Bauernfeind College of Business, Department of Organizational Communication, Murray, KY 42071. Offers nursing education (MA). *Program availability:* Part-time, evening/weekend, 100% online, blended/hybrid learning. *Entrance requirements:* For master's, GRE or GMAT, minimum university GPA of 2.75. Additional exam requirements/recommendations for international students: required—TOEFL (minimum score 527 paper-based; 71 iBT). Electronic applications accepted.

New Mexico State University, College of Arts and Sciences, Department of English, Las Cruces, NM 88003-8001. Offers creative writing (MFA); English (MA), including creative writing, English studies for teachers, literature, rhetoric and professional communication; rhetoric and professional communication (PhD). *Program availability:* Part-time. *Faculty:* 17 full-time (7 women), 1 (woman) part-time/adjunct. *Students:* 43 full-time (28 women), 16 part-time (10 women); includes 25 minority (3 Black or African American, non-Hispanic/Latino; 1 Asian, non-Hispanic/Latino; 20 Hispanic/Latino; 1 Two or more races, non-Hispanic/Latino), 6 international. Average age 35. 46 applicants, 57% accepted, 14 enrolled. In 2019, 16 master's, 4 doctorates awarded. *Degree requirements:* For master's, one foreign language, thesis (for some programs); for doctorate, comprehensive exam, thesis/dissertation, internship. *Entrance requirements:* For master's and doctorate, sample of written work. Additional exam requirements/recommendations for international students: required—TOEFL (minimum score 550 paper-based; 79 iBT), IELTS (minimum score 6.5). *Application deadline:* For fall admission, 2/1 for domestic and international students. Application fee: $40 ($50 for international students). Electronic applications accepted. *Financial support:* In 2019–20, 46 students received support, including 5 fellowships (averaging $4,844 per year), 40 teaching assistantships (averaging $18,521 per year); career-related internships or fieldwork, Federal Work-Study, scholarships/grants, traineeships, health care benefits, and unspecified assistantships also available. Support available to part-time students. Financial award application deadline: 3/1. *Unit head:* Dr. Elizabeth Schirmer, Interim Department Head, 575-646-3931, Fax: 575-646-7725, E-mail: eschirme@nmsu.edu. *Application contact:* Dr. Tracey Eileen Miller-Tomlinson, Director of Graduate Studies, 575-646-2213, Fax: 575-646-7725, E-mail: tomlin@nmsu.edu. Website: http://english.nmsu.edu

New York University, School of Professional Studies, Division of Programs in Business, Program in Integrated Marketing, New York, NY 10012-1019. Offers integrated marketing (MS), including brand management, digital marketing, marketing analytics. *Program availability:* Part-time, evening/weekend. *Degree requirements:* For master's, thesis, capstone project. *Entrance requirements:* For master's, GRE or GMAT (only upon request), bachelor's degree, resume with relevant professional work, internship or volunteer experience, two letters of recommendation, personal statement. Additional exam requirements/recommendations for international students: required—TOEFL (minimum score 600 paper-based; 100 iBT), IELTS (minimum score 7). Electronic applications accepted. *Expenses:* Contact institution.

New York University, School of Professional Studies, Division of Programs in Business, Programs in Marketing and Public Relations, New York, NY 10012-1019. Offers public relations and corporate communication (MS), including corporate and organizational communication, public relations management. *Program availability:* Part-time, evening/weekend. *Degree requirements:* For master's, thesis. *Entrance requirements:* For master's, GRE or GMAT (only upon request), bachelor's degree, resume with relevant professional work, internship or volunteer experience, 2 letters of recommendation, personal statement. Additional exam requirements/recommendations for international students: required—TOEFL (minimum score 600 paper-based; 100 iBT), IELTS (minimum score 7). Electronic applications accepted. *Expenses:* Contact institution.

Northeastern University, College of Professional Studies, Boston, MA 02115-5096. Offers applied nutrition (MS); college athletics administration (MSL); commerce and economic development (MS); corporate and organizational communication (MS); criminal justice (MS); digital media (MPS); elearning and instructional design (M Ed); elementary education (MAT); geographic information technology (MPS); global studies and international relations (MS); higher education administration (M Ed); homeland security (MA); human services (MS); informatics (MPS); leadership (MS); learning analytics (M Ed); learning and instruction (M Ed); nonprofit management (MS); professional sports administration (MSL); project management (MS); regulatory affairs for drugs, biologics, and medical devices (MS); respiratory care leadership (MS); special education (M Ed); technical communication (MS). *Program availability:* Part-time, evening/weekend, 100% online, blended/hybrid learning. *Faculty:* 85 full-time (53 women), 892 part-time/adjunct (379 women). *Students:* 5,699 part-time (3,305 women). In 2019, 1,787 master's awarded. *Application deadline:* Applications are processed on a rolling basis. Application fee: $0. Electronic applications accepted. *Expenses:* Contact institution. *Financial support:* Applicants required to submit FAFSA. *Unit head:* Dr. Mary Loeffelholz, Dean of the College of Professional Studies, 617-373-6060. *Application*

contact: Dr. Mary Loeffelholz, Dean of the College of Professional Studies, 617-373-6060.
Website: https://cps.northeastern.edu/

Northwestern University, The Graduate School, School of Communication, Department of Communication Studies, Evanston, IL 60208. Offers communication studies (PhD), including interaction and social influence, rhetoric and public culture; managerial communication (MSC); media, technology and society (PhD); technology and social behavior (PhD). Terminal master's awarded for partial completion of doctoral program. *Degree requirements:* For doctorate, thesis/dissertation. *Entrance requirements:* For master's and doctorate, GRE General Test. Additional exam requirements/recommendations for international students: required—TOEFL. Electronic applications accepted.

Northwestern University, Medill School of Journalism, Media, and Integrated Marketing Communications, Integrated Marketing Communications Program, Evanston, IL 60208. Offers brand strategy (MSIMC); content marketing (MSIMC); direct and interactive marketing (MSIMC); marketing analytics (MSIMC); strategic communications (MSIMC). *Program availability:* Part-time. *Entrance requirements:* For master's, GRE General Test or GMAT, full-time work experience (preferred). Additional exam requirements/recommendations for international students: required—TOEFL. Electronic applications accepted.

Ohio University, Graduate College, Scripps College of Communication, School of Communication Studies, Athens, OH 45701-2979. Offers health communication (PhD); organizational communication (MA); relating and organizing (PhD); rhetoric and public culture (PhD). *Program availability:* Part-time, online learning. Terminal master's awarded for partial completion of doctoral program. *Degree requirements:* For master's, capstone; for doctorate, comprehensive exam, thesis/dissertation. *Entrance requirements:* For master's, GRE; for doctorate, GRE General Test, minimum GPA of 3.0. Additional exam requirements/recommendations for international students: required—TOEFL (minimum score 550 paper-based; 80 iBT) or IELTS (minimum score 6.5). Electronic applications accepted.

Radford University, College of Graduate Studies and Research, Strategic Communication, MS, Radford, VA 24142. Offers MS. *Program availability:* Part-time, evening/weekend. *Degree requirements:* For master's, comprehensive exam, thesis optional. *Entrance requirements:* For master's, GRE, minimum GPA of 2.75, short essay, 3 letters of reference, resume, official transcripts. Additional exam requirements/recommendations for international students: required—TOEFL (minimum score 550 paper-based; 79 iBT), IELTS (minimum score 6.5). Electronic applications accepted.

Regent University, Graduate School, School of Communication and the Arts, Virginia Beach, VA 23464-9800. Offers acting (MFA); communication (MA, PhD), including media and arts management and promotion (MA), political communication (MA), strategic communication (MA), technical communication (MA); film and TV (MA), including producing (MA, MFA), production, script writing; film-television (MFA), including directing, producing (MA, MFA), script and screenwriting; journalism (MA); theatre (MA). *Program availability:* Part-time, evening/weekend, 100% online, blended/hybrid learning. *Degree requirements:* For master's, thesis or alternative; for doctorate, thesis/dissertation. *Entrance requirements:* For master's, transcripts, writing sample, resume, audition (for MFA programs); for doctorate, GRE General Test, resume, writing sample, recommendations, interview, transcripts, personal goals statement. Additional exam requirements/recommendations for international students: required—TOEFL (minimum score 577 paper-based). Electronic applications accepted. *Expenses:* Contact institution.

Regis College, Business and Communication, Weston, MA 02493. Offers MA. *Program availability:* Part-time, evening/weekend, 100% online, blended/hybrid learning. *Entrance requirements:* For master's, GRE or MAT, official transcripts, recommendations, personal statement, resume, interview. Additional exam requirements/recommendations for international students: required—TOEFL (minimum score 560 paper-based; 79 iBT); recommended—IELTS (minimum score 6.5). *Application deadline:* Applications are processed on a rolling basis. Application fee: $65. Electronic applications accepted. *Financial support:* Federal Work-Study and unspecified assistantships available. Financial award applicants required to submit FAFSA. *Unit head:* Dr. William Koehler, Dean, 781-768-8326, E-mail: william.koehler@regiscollege.edu. *Application contact:* Hillary Lyons, Assistant Director of Graduate Admission, 781-768-7746, E-mail: hillary.lyons@regiscollege.edu.

Rider University, College of Liberal Arts and Sciences, Program in Business Communication, Lawrenceville, NJ 08648-3001. Offers business communication studies (MA); health communication (MA). *Program availability:* Part-time, 100% online, blended/hybrid learning. *Entrance requirements:* For master's, application fee, 2 letters of recommendation, official transcripts, statement of aims and objectives, interview. Additional exam requirements/recommendations for international students: required—TOEFL (minimum score 540 paper-based; 79 iBT). Electronic applications accepted.

Roosevelt University, Graduate Division, College of Arts and Sciences, Department of Communication, Chicago, IL 60605. Offers integrated marketing communications (MSIMC). *Program availability:* Part-time, evening/weekend. Electronic applications accepted.

Rowan University, Graduate School, College of Communication and Creative Arts, Integrated Marketing Communication and New Media Certificate of Graduate Study Program, Glassboro, NJ 08028-1701. Offers CGS. Electronic applications accepted. *Expenses: Tuition, area resident:* Part-time $715.50 per semester hour. Tuition, state resident: part-time $715.50 per semester hour. Tuition, nonresident: part-time $715.50 per semester hour. *Required fees:* $161.55 per semester hour.

St. Bonaventure University, School of Graduate Studies, Jandoli School of Communication, Integrated Marketing Communication, St. Bonaventure, NY 14778-2284. Offers MA. *Program availability:* Part-time, evening/weekend, online only, 100% online. *Faculty:* 4 full-time (2 women), 5 part-time/adjunct (3 women). *Students:* 9 full-time (7 women), 27 part-time (20 women); includes 8 minority (4 Black or African American, non-Hispanic/Latino; 4 Hispanic/Latino), 1 international. Average age 27. 20 applicants, 100% accepted, 14 enrolled. In 2019, 24 master's awarded. *Degree requirements:* For master's, Integrated Marketing Communications Campaign project. *Entrance requirements:* For master's, official transcripts, personal statement describing desire to pursue the IMC program. Additional exam requirements/recommendations for international students: required—TOEFL (minimum score 550 paper-based; 79 iBT). *Application deadline:* For fall admission, 3/15 for domestic students, 2/1 for international students; for spring admission, 10/15 for domestic students, 7/1 for international students. Applications are processed on a rolling basis. Application fee: $0. Electronic applications accepted. *Expenses:* $770 per credit hour tuition/$35 per credit hour fee. *Financial support:* In 2019–20, 8 students received support. Scholarships/grants, health care benefits, and unspecified assistantships available. Financial award application deadline: 4/15; financial award applicants required to submit FAFSA. *Unit head:* Heather Harris, Director, 716-375-2075, Fax: 716-375-2588, E-mail: hharris@sbu.edu. *Application contact:* Matthew Retchless, Director of Graduate Admissions, 716-375-2021, Fax: 716-375-4015, E-mail: gradsch@sbu.edu.
Website: http://www.sbu.edu/academics/schools/journalism-and-mass-communications/graduate-degrees/ma-integrated-marketing-communications

St. Bonaventure University, School of Graduate Studies, Jandoli School of Communication, Program in Strategic Leadership, St. Bonaventure, NY 14778-2284. Offers MA. *Program availability:* Part-time, evening/weekend, online only, 100% online. *Faculty:* 4 full-time (3 women), 2 part-time/adjunct (1 woman). *Students:* 9 full-time (5 women), 32 part-time (14 women); includes 14 minority (6 Black or African American, non-Hispanic/Latino; 1 American Indian or Alaska Native, non-Hispanic/Latino; 4 Hispanic/Latino; 3 Two or more races, non-Hispanic/Latino), 1 international. Average age 40. 15 applicants, 100% accepted, 9 enrolled. In 2019, 19 master's awarded. *Degree requirements:* For master's, portfolio, capstone project, 360 degree evaluation. *Entrance requirements:* For master's, official transcripts, three years of work experience, current resume, short essay (500 words) on candidate's goals for engaging in such a learning experience. Additional exam requirements/recommendations for international students: required—TOEFL (minimum score 550 paper-based; 79 iBT). *Application deadline:* For fall admission, 3/15 for domestic students, 2/1 for international students; for spring admission, 10/15 for domestic students, 7/1 for international students. Applications are processed on a rolling basis. Application fee: $0. Electronic applications accepted. *Expenses:* 770 per credit hour/$35 per credit hour fee. *Financial support:* Scholarships/grants and health care benefits available. Financial award application deadline: 4/15; financial award applicants required to submit FAFSA. *Unit head:* Dr. Kimberly DeSimone, Program Director, 716-375-2060, Fax: 716-375-2588, E-mail: kdesimon@sbu.edu. *Application contact:* Matthew Retchless, Director of Graduate Admissions, 716-375-2021, Fax: 716-375-4015, E-mail: gradsch@sbu.edu.
Website: https://online.sbu.edu/programs/master/msl?schoolsrc-42787

Seton Hall University, College of Communication and the Arts, Program in Strategic Communication, South Orange, NJ 07079-2697. Offers MA. *Program availability:* Part-time, evening/weekend, online learning. *Degree requirements:* For master's, thesis (for some programs). *Entrance requirements:* For master's, GRE or MAT, official transcripts, resume, personal statement, 3 letters of recommendation. Additional exam requirements/recommendations for international students: required—TOEFL (minimum iBT score 80) or IELTS (6.5). Electronic applications accepted.

Southern Illinois University Edwardsville, Graduate School, College of Arts and Sciences, Department of Applied Communication Studies, Program in Corporate and Organizational Communication, Edwardsville, IL 62026. Offers MA. *Program availability:* Part-time, evening/weekend. *Degree requirements:* For master's, comprehensive exam (for some programs), thesis (for some programs). *Entrance requirements:* Additional exam requirements/recommendations for international students: required—TOEFL (minimum score 550 paper-based, 79 iBT), IELTS (minimum score 6.5), Michigan Test of English Language Proficiency or PTE. Electronic applications accepted.

Spalding University, Graduate Studies, College of Social Sciences and Humanities, Program in Business and Communication, Louisville, KY 40203-2188. Offers MS. *Program availability:* Part-time, evening/weekend. *Degree requirements:* For master's, project. *Entrance requirements:* For master's, GRE or GMAT, personal essay, interview, letters of recommendation, transcripts, resume. Additional exam requirements/recommendations for international students: required—TOEFL (minimum score 535 paper-based).

State University of New York at Oswego, Graduate Studies, School of Communication, Media and the Arts, Oswego, NY 13126. Offers strategic communication (MA), including health communication, integrated media and social networks, organizational communication. *Students:* 34. In 2019, 17 master's awarded. *Entrance requirements:* For master's, GRE, official transcript, statement of purpose, resume, two letters of recommendation. *Application deadline:* Applications are processed on a rolling basis. Application fee: $65. Electronic applications accepted. *Financial support:* Fellowships, research assistantships, teaching assistantships, institutionally sponsored loans, scholarships/grants, and unspecified assistantships available. Support available to part-time students. Financial award application deadline: 4/1; financial award applicants required to submit FAFSA. *Unit head:* Dr. Julie Pretzat, Dean, 315-312-6612, E-mail: julie.pretzat@oswego.edu. *Application contact:* Dr. Julie Pretzat, Dean, 315-312-6612, E-mail: julie.pretzat@oswego.edu.

Suffolk University, College of Arts and Sciences, Advertising and Public Relations Department, Boston, MA 02108-2770. Offers communication studies (MAC); integrated marketing communication (MAC); public relations and advertising (MAC). *Program availability:* Part-time, evening/weekend. *Faculty:* 8 full-time (7 women), 2 part-time/adjunct (1 woman). *Students:* 26 full-time (21 women), 4 part-time (2 women); includes 3 minority (1 Asian, non-Hispanic/Latino; 2 Hispanic/Latino), 17 international. Average age 25. 51 applicants, 65% accepted, 8 enrolled. In 2019, 20 master's awarded. *Degree requirements:* For master's, thesis optional. *Entrance requirements:* For master's, GRE General Test, MAT, or GMAT, 2 letters of recommendation, resume. Additional exam requirements/recommendations for international students: required—TOEFL (minimum score 550 paper-based; 80 iBT). *Application deadline:* For fall admission, 3/15 priority date for domestic and international students; for spring admission, 10/15 priority date for domestic and international students. Applications are processed on a rolling basis. Application fee: $50. Electronic applications accepted. *Expenses:* Contact institution. *Financial support:* In 2019–20, 24 students received support, including 3 fellowships (averaging $3,600 per year); career-related internships or fieldwork, Federal Work-Study, institutionally sponsored loans, and scholarships/grants also available. Support available to part-time students. Financial award application deadline: 4/1; financial award applicants required to submit FAFSA. *Unit head:* Robert Rosenthal, Chair, 617-573-8502, E-mail: rrosenthal@suffolk.edu. *Application contact:* Mara Marzocchi, Associate Director of Graduate Admissions, 617-573-8302, Fax: 617-305-1733, E-mail: grad.admission@suffolk.edu.
Website: http://www.suffolk.edu/college/graduate/69298.php

Temple University, Klein College of Media and Communication, Department of Communication and Social Influence, Philadelphia, PA 19122-6096. Offers communication management (MS); globalization and development communication (MS); media and communication (PhD). *Program availability:* Part-time, evening/weekend, online learning. *Faculty:* 8 full-time (3 women), 3 part-time/adjunct (all women). *Students:* 10 full-time (8 women), 13 part-time (9 women); includes 12 minority (10 Black or African American, non-Hispanic/Latino; 1 Hispanic/Latino; 1 Two or more races, non-Hispanic/Latino), 2 international. 27 applicants, 89% accepted, 13 enrolled. In 2019, 7 master's awarded. *Degree requirements:* For master's, capstone course; for doctorate, thesis/dissertation. *Entrance requirements:* For master's, GRE (required for m.s. in communication for development and social change), 2 letters of recommendation, statement of goals, resume; for doctorate, GRE, writing sample, statement of goals, master's degree in related discipline, 3 letters of recommendation. Additional exam requirements/recommendations for international students: required—TOEFL, IELTS, PTE, one of three is required. *Application deadline:* Applications are processed on a rolling basis. Application fee: $60. Electronic applications accepted. *Expenses:* Contact institution. *Financial support:* Teaching assistantships, Federal Work-Study, and health care benefits available. Financial award applicants required to submit FAFSA. *Unit head:* Jan Fernbeck, Co-Chair, 215-204-1497, E-mail: nmckenna@temple.edu. *Application contact:* Nicole McKenna, Graduate Office Director,

215-204-1497, E-mail: nmckenna@temple.edu.
Website: https://klein.temple.edu/academics/graduate-programs

Texas Christian University, Bob Schieffer College of Communication, Fort Worth, TX 76129-0002. Offers communication studies (MS); strategic communication (MS). *Program availability:* Part-time. *Faculty:* 27 full-time (13 women). *Students:* 35 full-time (25 women); includes 6 minority (2 Black or African American, non-Hispanic/Latino; 3 Hispanic/Latino; 1 Native Hawaiian or other Pacific Islander, non-Hispanic/Latino), 3 international. Average age 25. 36 applicants, 78% accepted, 21 enrolled. In 2019, 12 master's awarded. *Degree requirements:* For master's, comprehensive exam (for some programs), thesis (for some programs). *Entrance requirements:* For master's, GRE General Test, 2 official transcripts, academic/professional objectives statement, 3 letters of recommendation. Additional exam requirements/recommendations for international students: required—TOEFL (minimum score 550 paper-based; 80 iBT). *Application deadline:* For fall admission, 2/15 for domestic and international students; for spring admission, 10/15 for domestic and international students. Applications are processed on a rolling basis. Application fee: $60. Electronic applications accepted. *Expenses:* Contact institution. *Financial support:* In 2019–20, 23 students received support, including 20 teaching assistantships with full tuition reimbursements available (averaging $12,500 per year); health care benefits, tuition waivers (full and partial), and unspecified assistantships also available. Financial award application deadline: 2/15. *Unit head:* Dr. Julie O'Neil, Associate Dean, 817-257-6966, Fax: 817-257-5921, E-mail: j.oneil@tcu.edu. *Application contact:* Ashley Tully, Coordinator of Degree of Certification, 817-257-4935, Fax: 817-257-5921, E-mail: A.TULLY@tcu.edu. Website: http://www.schieffercollege.tcu.edu/

Towson University, College of Fine Arts and Communication, Program in Communication Management, Towson, MD 21252-0001. Offers MS. *Students:* 11 full-time (10 women), 19 part-time (13 women); includes 19 minority (13 Black or African American, non-Hispanic/Latino; 4 Hispanic/Latino; 2 Two or more races, non-Hispanic/Latino). *Entrance requirements:* For master's, bachelor's degree with 24 credits in mass communications, public relations, advertising or communication studies; advanced writing and basic statistics courses; professional experience; minimum GPA of 3.0; letter of recommendation; resume. Additional exam requirements/recommendations for international students: required—TOEFL. *Application deadline:* For fall admission, 1/17 for domestic students, 5/15 for international students; for spring admission, 10/15 for domestic students, 12/1 for international students. Applications are processed on a rolling basis. Application fee: $45. Electronic applications accepted. *Expenses:* Tuition, area resident: Full-time $7920; part-time $439 per credit. Tuition, nonresident: full-time $16,344; part-time $908 per credit. *International tuition:* $16,344 full-time. *Required fees:* $2628; $146 per credit. $876 per term. *Financial support:* Application deadline: 4/1. *Unit head:* Dr. Lingling Zhang, Program Director, 410-704-3458, E-mail: lizhang@towson.edu. *Application contact:* Coverley Beidleman, Assistant Director of Graduate Admissions, 410-704-5630, Fax: 410-704-3030, E-mail: grads@towson.edu. Website: https://www.towson.edu/cofac/departments/mass-communication/communication-management/

Troy University, Graduate School, College of Communication and Fine Arts, Troy, AL 36082. Offers strategic communication (MS). *Program availability:* Part-time, evening/weekend, online learning. *Faculty:* 3 full-time (all women), 2 part-time/adjunct (0 women). *Students:* 34 full-time (25 women), 80 part-time (57 women); includes 40 minority (35 Black or African American, non-Hispanic/Latino; 5 Hispanic/Latino). Average age 31. 69 applicants, 100% accepted, 53 enrolled. In 2019, 61 master's awarded. *Degree requirements:* For master's, comprehensive exam, thesis optional, minimum GPA of 3.0, admission to candidacy. *Entrance requirements:* For master's, GRE (minimum score of 850 on old exam or 290 on new exam), MAT (minimum score of 385) or GMAT (minimum score of 380), bachelor's degree, minimum undergraduate GPA of 2.5 or 3.0 on last 30 semester hours, letter of recommendation; transcript. Additional exam requirements/recommendations for international students: required—TOEFL (minimum score 523 paper-based; 70 iBT), IELTS (minimum score 6). *Application deadline:* For fall admission, 6/1 for international students; for spring admission, 10/15 for international students. Applications are processed on a rolling basis. Application fee: $50. Electronic applications accepted. *Expenses: Tuition, area resident:* Full-time $7650; part-time $2550 per semester hour. Tuition, state resident: full-time $7650; part-time $2550 per semester hour. Tuition, nonresident: full-time $15,300; part-time $5100 per semester hour. *International tuition:* $15,300 full-time. *Required fees:* $856; $352 per semester hour. $176 per semester. *Financial support:* In 2019–20, 36 students received support. Fellowships, research assistantships, teaching assistantships, career-related internships or fieldwork, Federal Work-Study, scholarships/grants, traineeships, tuition waivers, and unspecified assistantships available. Support available to part-time students. Financial award application deadline: 3/1; financial award applicants required to submit FAFSA. *Unit head:* Dr. Larry Blocher, Dean, 334-670-3869, Fax: 334-670-3547, E-mail: lblocher@troy.edu. *Application contact:* Haley McKinnon, Director of Graduate Admissions, 334-670-3178, Fax: 334-670-3733, E-mail: hmckinnon@troy.edu. Website: https://www.troy.edu/academics/colleges-schools/college-communication-fine-arts/index.html

Universidad Autonoma de Guadalajara, Graduate Programs, Guadalajara, Mexico. Offers administrative law and justice (LL M); advertising and corporate communications (MA); architecture (M Arch); business (MBA); computational science (MCC); education (Ed M, Ed D); English-Spanish translation (MA); entrepreneurship and management (MBA); integrated management of digital animation (MA); international business (MIB); international corporate law (LL M); Internet technologies (MS); manufacturing systems (MMS); occupational health (MS); philosophy (MA, PhD); power electronics (MS); quality systems (MQS); renewable energy (MS); social evaluation of projects (MBA); strategic market research (MBA); tax law (MA); teaching mathematics (MA).

Universidad Iberoamericana, Graduate School, Santo Domingo D.N., Dominican Republic. Offers business administration (MBA, PMBA); constitutional law (LL M); dentistry (DMD); educational management (MA); integrated marketing communication (MA); psychopedagogical intervention (M Ed); real estate law (LL M); strategic management of human talent (MM).

Université de Sherbrooke, Faculty of Administration, Program in Marketing Communications, Sherbrooke, QC J1K 2R1, Canada. Offers M Adm. *Degree requirements:* For master's, one foreign language, thesis. *Entrance requirements:* For master's, bachelor's degree in related field, minimum GPA of 3.0 (on 4.3 scale). Electronic applications accepted.

University of Alaska Fairbanks, College of Liberal Arts, Department of Communication and Journalism, Fairbanks, AK 99775-5680. Offers professional communication (MA). *Program availability:* Part-time. *Degree requirements:* For master's, comprehensive exam, thesis, oral defense of thesis. *Entrance requirements:* For master's, bachelor's degree from accredited institution with minimum cumulative undergraduate and major GPA of 3.0, academic writing sample. Additional exam requirements/recommendations for international students: required—TOEFL (minimum score 550 paper-based; 79 iBT), IELTS (minimum score 6.5). Electronic applications accepted.

University of Colorado Denver, Business School, Program in Marketing, Denver, CO 80217. Offers advanced market analytics in a big data world (MS); brand communication in the digital era (MS); global marketing (MS); high-tech and entrepreneurial marketing (MS); marketing and global sustainability (MS); marketing intelligence and strategy in the 21st century (MS); sports and entertainment business (MS). *Program availability:* Part-time, evening/weekend. *Degree requirements:* For master's, 30 semester hours (21 of marketing core courses, 9 of marketing electives). *Entrance requirements:* For master's, GMAT, resume, essay, two letters of recommendation, financial statements (for international applicants). Additional exam requirements/recommendations for international students: required—TOEFL (minimum score 525 paper-based; 71 iBT); recommended—IELTS (minimum score 6.5). Electronic applications accepted. *Expenses:* Contact institution.

University of Illinois at Urbana-Champaign, Graduate College, Program in Strategic Brand Communication, Champaign, IL 61820. Offers MS. *Program availability:* Online learning.

University of Nebraska–Lincoln, Graduate College, College of Arts and Sciences, Department of Communication Studies, Lincoln, NE 68588. Offers instructional communication (MA, PhD); interpersonal communication (MA, PhD); marketing, communication studies, and advertising (MA, PhD); organizational communication (MA, PhD); rhetoric and culture (MA, PhD). *Degree requirements:* For master's, thesis optional; for doctorate, comprehensive exam, thesis/dissertation. *Entrance requirements:* For master's and doctorate, GRE General Test, writing sample. Additional exam requirements/recommendations for international students: required—TOEFL (minimum score 600 paper-based). Electronic applications accepted.

University of Oklahoma, College of Arts and Sciences, Department of Communication, Norman, OK 73019. Offers communication (MA); communication technology (PhD); health communication (PhD); intercultural/international communication (PhD); organizational communication (PhD); political/mass communication (PhD); social influence/interpersonal communication (PhD). *Program availability:* Part-time. *Degree requirements:* For master's, comprehensive exam (for some programs), thesis (for some programs), comprehensive exams or thesis; for doctorate, comprehensive exam, thesis/dissertation. *Entrance requirements:* For master's, GRE (for assistantship), statement of purpose, transcripts, writing sample, letters of recommendation; for doctorate, GRE, statement of purpose, transcripts, writing sample, letters of recommendation. Additional exam requirements/recommendations for international students: required—TOEFL (minimum score 79 iBT) or IELTS (minimum score 6.5). Electronic applications accepted. *Expenses:* Tuition, state resident: full-time $6583.20; part-time $274.30 per credit hour. Tuition, nonresident: full-time $21,242; part-time $885.10 per credit hour. *International tuition:* $21,242.40 full-time. *Required fees:* $1994.20; $72.55 per credit hour. $126.50 per semester. Tuition and fees vary according to course load and degree level.

University of Portland, Department of Communication Studies, Portland, OR 97203-5798. Offers communication (MA); management communication (MS). *Program availability:* Part-time, evening/weekend. *Degree requirements:* For master's, thesis optional. *Entrance requirements:* For master's, GRE General Test, 3 letters of recommendation, resume, statement of goals, official transcripts. Additional exam requirements/recommendations for international students: required—TOEFL (minimum score 100 iBT), IELTS (minimum score 7.5). Electronic applications accepted.

University of Southern California, Graduate School, Annenberg School for Communication and Journalism, School of Communication, Program in Communication Management, Los Angeles, CA 90089. Offers MCM, JD/MCM, MCM/MAJCS. *Program availability:* Part-time, evening/weekend, 100% online. *Students:* 298 full-time, 133 part-time; includes 175 minority (52 Black or African American, non-Hispanic/Latino; 38 Asian, non-Hispanic/Latino; 69 Hispanic/Latino; 3 Native Hawaiian or other Pacific Islander, non-Hispanic/Latino; 13 Two or more races, non-Hispanic/Latino), 132 international. Average age 28. 690 applicants, 45% accepted, 161 enrolled. In 2019, 205 master's awarded. *Degree requirements:* For master's, professional project. *Entrance requirements:* For master's, GRE General Test or GMAT, resume, writing samples, recommendation letters, statement of purpose. Additional exam requirements/recommendations for international students: required—TOEFL (minimum score 114 iBT), IELTS (minimum score 8). *Application deadline:* For fall admission, 3/1 priority date for domestic students, 1/1 priority date for international students. Applications are processed on a rolling basis. Application fee: $90. Electronic applications accepted. *Financial support:* In 2019–20, 10 students received support. Career-related internships or fieldwork, Federal Work-Study, and scholarships/grants available. Support available to part-time students. Financial award application deadline: 1/1; financial award applicants required to submit FAFSA. *Unit head:* Dr. Rebecca Weintraub, Faculty Program Director, 213-821-0764, Fax: 213-740-8036, E-mail: weintrau@usc.edu. *Application contact:* Allyson Hill, Associate Dean for Admissions, 213-821-0770, Fax: 213-740-1933, E-mail: ascadm@usc.edu. Website: http://www.annenberg.usc.edu

University of South Florida, Innovative Education, Tampa, FL 33620-9951. Offers adult, career and higher education (Graduate Certificate), including college teaching, leadership in developing human resources, leadership in higher education; Africana studies (Graduate Certificate), including diasporas and health disparities, genocide and human rights; aging studies (Graduate Certificate), including gerontology; art research (Graduate Certificate), including museum studies; business foundations (Graduate Certificate); chemical and biomedical engineering (Graduate Certificate), including materials science and engineering, water, health and sustainability; child and family studies (Graduate Certificate), including positive behavior support; civil and industrial engineering (Graduate Certificate), including transportation systems analysis; community and family health (Graduate Certificate), including maternal and child health, social marketing and public health, violence and injury: prevention and intervention, women's health; criminology (Graduate Certificate), including criminal justice administration; data science for public administration (Graduate Certificate); digital humanities (Graduate Certificate); educational measurement and research (Graduate Certificate), including evaluation; English (Graduate Certificate), including comparative literary studies, creative writing, professional and technical communication; entrepreneurship (Graduate Certificate); environmental health (Graduate Certificate), including safety management; epidemiology and biostatistics (Graduate Certificate), including applied biostatistics, biostatistics, concepts and tools of epidemiology, epidemiology, epidemiology of infectious diseases; geography, environment and planning (Graduate Certificate), including community development, environmental policy and management, geographical information systems; geology (Graduate Certificate), including hydrogeology; global health (Graduate Certificate), including disaster management, global health and Latin American and Caribbean studies, global health practice, humanitarian assistance, infection control; government and international affairs (Graduate Certificate), including Cuban studies, globalization studies; health policy and management (Graduate Certificate), including health management and leadership, public health policy and programs; hearing specialist: early intervention (Graduate Certificate); industrial and management systems engineering (Graduate Certificate), including systems engineering, technology management; information studies (Graduate Certificate), including school library media specialist; information systems/decision

sciences (Graduate Certificate), including analytics and business intelligence; instructional technology (Graduate Certificate), including distance education, Florida digital/virtual educator, instructional design, multimedia design, Web design; internal medicine, bioethics and medical humanities (Graduate Certificate), including biomedical ethics; Latin American and Caribbean studies (Graduate Certificate); leadership for coastal resiliency planning (Graduate Certificate); mass communications (Graduate Certificate), including multimedia journalism; mathematics and statistics (Graduate Certificate), including mathematics; medicine (Graduate Certificate), including aging and neuroscience, bioinformatics, biotechnology, brain fitness and memory management, clinical investigation, hand and upper limb rehabilitation, health informatics, health sciences, integrative weight management, intellectual property, medicine and gender, metabolic and nutritional medicine, metabolic cardiology, pharmacy sciences; national and competitive intelligence (Graduate Certificate); nursing (Graduate Certificate), including simulation based academic fellowship in advanced pain management; psychological and social foundations (Graduate Certificate), including career counseling, college teaching, diversity in education, mental health counseling, school counseling; public affairs (Graduate Certificate), including nonprofit management, public management, research administration; public health (Graduate Certificate), including assessing chemical toxicity and public health risks, health equity, pharmacoepidemiology, public health generalist, toxicology, translational research in adolescent behavioral health; public health practices (Graduate Certificate), including planning for healthy communities; rehabilitation and mental health counseling (Graduate Certificate), including integrative mental health care, marriage and family therapy, rehabilitation technology; secondary education (Graduate Certificate), including ESOL, foreign language education: culture and content, foreign language education: professional; social work (Graduate Certificate), including geriatric social work/clinical gerontology; special education (Graduate Certificate), including autism spectrum disorder, disabilities education: severe/profound; world languages (Graduate Certificate), including teaching English as a second language (TESL) or foreign language. *Unit head:* Dr. Cynthia DeLuca, Associate Vice President and Assistant Vice Provost, 813-974-3077, Fax: 813-974-7061, E-mail: deluca@usf.edu. *Application contact:* Owen Hooper, Director, Summer and Alternative Calendar Programs, 813-974-6917, E-mail: hooper@usf.edu.
Website: http://www.usf.edu/innovative-education/

University of Wisconsin–Stevens Point, College of Fine Arts and Communication, Division of Communication, Stevens Point, WI 54481-3897. Offers interpersonal communication (MA); media studies (MA); organizational communication (MA); public relations (MA). *Program availability:* Part-time. *Degree requirements:* For master's, thesis or alternative. *Entrance requirements:* For master's, GRE. Additional exam requirements/recommendations for international students: required—TOEFL (minimum score 575 paper-based).

University of Wisconsin–Whitewater, School of Graduate Studies, College of Arts and Communications, Department of Communication, Whitewater, WI 53190-1790. Offers corporate communication (MS); mass communication (MS). *Program availability:* Part-time, evening/weekend, online learning. *Degree requirements:* For master's, thesis or alternative. *Entrance requirements:* For master's, 2 letters of recommendation, goal statement. Additional exam requirements/recommendations for international students: required—TOEFL (minimum score 550 paper-based; 80 iBT), IELTS (minimum score 6). Electronic applications accepted.

Washington State University, The Edward R. Murrow College of Communication, Pullman, WA 99164-2520. Offers communication (MA, PhD); strategic communication (MA). *Degree requirements:* For master's, comprehensive exam (for some programs), thesis optional, oral exam; for doctorate, comprehensive exam, thesis/dissertation. *Entrance requirements:* For master's, GRE General Test, minimum GPA of 3.25, 3 letters of recommendation; for doctorate, GRE General Test, minimum undergraduate GPA of 3.25, graduate 3.5; MA in communication; 3 letters of recommendation. Additional exam requirements/recommendations for international students: required—TOEFL (minimum score 580 paper-based). Electronic applications accepted.

Webster University, School of Communications, Program in Communications Management, St. Louis, MO 63119-3194. Offers MA.

Western Kentucky University, Graduate School, Potter College of Arts and Letters, Department of Communication, Bowling Green, KY 42101. Offers communication (MA); organizational communication (Graduate Certificate). *Program availability:* Part-time, evening/weekend. *Degree requirements:* For master's, comprehensive exam, thesis optional, final exam. *Entrance requirements:* For master's, GRE General Test, minimum GPA of 2.75. Additional exam requirements/recommendations for international students: required—TOEFL (minimum score 555 paper-based; 79 iBT).

West Virginia University, Reed College of Media, Morgantown, WV 26506. Offers data marketing communications (MS); integrated marketing communications (MS, Graduate Certificate); journalism (MSJ); media solutions and innovation (MSJ). *Program availability:* Part-time, online learning. *Degree requirements:* For master's, thesis or alternative. *Entrance requirements:* For master's, GRE General Test, minimum GPA of 3.0, writing samples. Additional exam requirements/recommendations for international students: required—TOEFL (minimum score 550 paper-based). Electronic applications accepted.

Health Communication

Arkansas State University, Graduate School, College of Media and Communication, Department of Communication, State University, AR 72467. Offers communication studies (MA, SCCT); health communications (Graduate Certificate). *Program availability:* Part-time. *Degree requirements:* For master's, one foreign language, comprehensive exam, thesis or alternative; for other advanced degree, comprehensive exam. *Entrance requirements:* For master's, GRE General Test or MAT, appropriate bachelor's degree, writing sample, letter of recommendation, official transcripts, immunization records; for other advanced degree, GRE or MAT, appropriate master's degree, interview, official transcript, immunization records. Additional exam requirements/recommendations for international students: required—TOEFL (minimum score 550 paper-based; 79 iBT), IELTS (minimum score 6), PTE (minimum score 56). Electronic applications accepted.

Boston University, Metropolitan College, Program in Health Communication, Boston, MA 02215. Offers MS. *Program availability:* Part-time, online learning. *Faculty:* 1 (woman) full-time, 12 part-time/adjunct (5 women). *Students:* 37 part-time (34 women); includes 5 minority (2 Black or African American, non-Hispanic/Latino; 2 Asian, non-Hispanic/Latino; 1 Hispanic/Latino), 2 international. Average age 33. In 2019, 26 master's awarded. *Entrance requirements:* For master's, bachelor's degree, minimum GPA of 3.0. Additional exam requirements/recommendations for international students: required—TOEFL (minimum score 100 iBT). *Application deadline:* For fall admission, 8/1 priority date for domestic students, 6/1 priority date for international students; for spring admission, 12/1 priority date for domestic students, 11/15 priority date for international students; for summer admission, 4/1 priority date for domestic students, 3/1 priority date for international students. Applications are processed on a rolling basis. Application fee: $85. Electronic applications accepted. *Expenses:* Contact institution. *Financial support:* Unspecified assistantships available. Support available to part-time students. Financial award applicants required to submit FAFSA. *Unit head:* Leigh Curtin-Wilding, Director, 617-358-5643. *Application contact:* Enrollment Services, 617-353-9185, E-mail: met@bu.edu.
Website: http://www.bu.edu/online/online_programs/graduate_degree/master_health_communication/

Chatham University, Program in Communication, Pittsburgh, PA 15232-2826. Offers environmental communication (M Comm); health communication (M Comm); strategic communication (M Comm). *Program availability:* Part-time, online learning. *Entrance requirements:* Additional exam requirements/recommendations for international students: required—TOEFL, IELTS. Electronic applications accepted. Application fee is waived when completed online. *Expenses: Tuition:* Part-time $1017 per credit. *Required fees:* $30 per credit. Tuition and fees vary according to program.

The College of New Jersey, Office of Graduate and Advancing Education, School of Nursing, Health, and Exercise Science, Program in Public Health, Ewing, NJ 08628. Offers global health (MPH); health communications (MPH); precision health (MPH).

Cornell University, Graduate School, Graduate Fields of Agriculture and Life Sciences, Field of Communication, Ithaca, NY 14853. Offers communication (MS, PhD); human-computer interaction (MS, PhD); language and communication (MS, PhD); media communication and society (MS, PhD); organizational communication (MS, PhD); science, environment and health communication (MS, PhD); social psychology of communication (MS, PhD). *Degree requirements:* For master's, thesis (MS); for doctorate, comprehensive exam, thesis/dissertation. *Entrance requirements:* For master's and doctorate, GRE General Test, 3 letters of recommendation. Additional exam requirements/recommendations for international students: required—TOEFL (minimum score 600 paper-based; 100 iBT). Electronic applications accepted.

DePaul University, College of Communication, Chicago, IL 60604. Offers digital communication and media arts (MA); health communication (MA); journalism (MA); media and cinema studies (MA); multicultural communication (MA); organizational communication (MA); public relations and advertising (MA); relational communication (MA). *Program availability:* Part-time, evening/weekend. *Entrance requirements:* Additional exam requirements/recommendations for international students: required—TOEFL (minimum score 590 paper-based; 96 iBT), IELTS (minimum score 7.5) or PTE. Electronic applications accepted.

East Carolina University, Graduate School, College of Fine Arts and Communication, School of Communication, Greenville, NC 27858-4353. Offers communication (MA); health communication (Certificate). *Application deadline:* For fall admission, 6/1 priority date for domestic students; for spring admission, 10/15 for domestic students. *Expenses: Tuition, area resident:* Full-time $4749; part-time $185 per credit hour. Tuition, state resident: full-time $4749; part-time $185 per credit hour. Tuition, nonresident: full-time $17,898; part-time $864 per credit hour. *International tuition:* $17,898 full-time. *Required fees:* $2787. *Unit head:* Dr. Linda Kean, Director, 252-328-4227, E-mail: keanl@ecu.edu. *Application contact:* Graduate School Admissions, 252-328-6012, Fax: 252-328-6071, E-mail: gradschool@ecu.edu.
Website: https://communication.ecu.edu/

Fontbonne University, Graduate Programs, St. Louis, MO 63105-3098. Offers accounting (MBA, MS); art (MA); art (K-12) (MAT); business (MBA); computer science (MS); deaf education (MA); early intervention in deaf education (MA); education (MA), including autism spectrum disorders, curriculum and instruction, diverse learners, early childhood education, reading, special education; elementary education (MAT); family and consumer sciences (MA), including multidisciplinary health communication studies; fine arts (MFA); instructional design and technology (MS); management and leadership (MM); middle school education (MAT); secondary education (MAT); special education (MAT); speech-language pathology (MS); supply chain management (MS); theatre (MA). *Accreditation:* ASHA. *Program availability:* Part-time, evening/weekend, online learning. *Degree requirements:* For master's, comprehensive exam (for some programs), thesis (for some programs). *Entrance requirements:* Additional exam requirements/recommendations for international students: required—TOEFL (minimum score 500 paper-based; 65 iBT). Electronic applications accepted. *Expenses: Tuition:* Full-time $6975; part-time $775 per credit hour. *Required fees:* $225; $25 per credit hour. Tuition and fees vary according to degree level and program.

Gannon University, School of Graduate Studies, College of Humanities, Education, and Social Sciences, School of Humanities, Program in Health Communication, Erie, PA 16541-0001. Offers MA. *Entrance requirements:* For master's, bachelor's degree from accredited college or university, transcripts, 3 professional letters of recommendation, statement of professional and career goals. Additional exam requirements/recommendations for international students: required—TOEFL (minimum score 79 iBT). Electronic applications accepted. Application fee is waived when completed online.

The George Washington University, Milken Institute School of Public Health, Department of Global Health, Washington, DC 20052. Offers global health (Dr PH); global health communication (MPH). *Entrance requirements:* For master's, GMAT, GRE General Test, or MCAT. Additional exam requirements/recommendations for international students: required—TOEFL.

Indiana University-Purdue University Indianapolis, School of Liberal Arts, Department of Communication Studies, Indianapolis, IN 46202. Offers applied communication (MA); health communication (PhD). *Program availability:* Part-time. *Degree requirements:* For master's, comprehensive exam, thesis; for doctorate, thesis/dissertation. *Entrance requirements:* For doctorate, master's degree. Additional exam requirements/recommendations for international students: required—TOEFL; recommended—IELTS. Electronic applications accepted.

Johns Hopkins University, Bloomberg School of Public Health, Department of Health, Behavior and Society, Baltimore, MD 21218. Offers genetic counseling (Sc M); health education and health communication (MSPH); social and behavioral sciences (PhD); social factors in health (MHS). *Degree requirements:* For master's, comprehensive exam (for some programs), thesis (for some programs); for doctorate, comprehensive exam, thesis/dissertation. *Entrance requirements:* For master's, GRE, curriculum vitae, 3 letters of recommendation; for doctorate, GRE, transcripts, curriculum vitae, 3 recommendation letters. Additional exam requirements/recommendations for international students: required—TOEFL (minimum score 100 iBT), IELTS (minimum score 7). Electronic applications accepted.

Kansas State University, Graduate School, College of Arts and Sciences, A.Q. Miller School of Journalism and Mass Communications, Manhattan, KS 66506. Offers advertising (MS); community journalism (MS); global communication (MS); health communication (MS); media management (MS); public relations (MS). *Program availability:* Part-time, evening/weekend. *Degree requirements:* For master's, comprehensive exam, thesis. *Entrance requirements:* For master's, GRE General Test, minimum GPA of 3.0. Additional exam requirements/recommendations for international students: required—TOEFL (minimum score 79 iBT). Electronic applications accepted.

Lasell College, Graduate and Professional Studies in Communication, Newton, MA 02466-2709. Offers health communication (MSC, Graduate Certificate); integrated marketing communication (MSC, Graduate Certificate); public relations (MSC, Graduate Certificate). *Program availability:* Part-time, evening/weekend, 100% online, blended/hybrid learning. *Faculty:* 3 full-time (2 women), 10 part-time/adjunct (4 women). *Students:* 25 full-time (18 women), 34 part-time (27 women); includes 10 minority (7 Black or African American, non-Hispanic/Latino; 3 Hispanic/Latino), 15 international. Average age 31. 40 applicants, 48% accepted, 14 enrolled. In 2019, 34 master's, 2 other advanced degrees awarded. *Degree requirements:* For master's, comprehensive exam, thesis or alternative, minimum GPA of 3.0; special project or internship. *Entrance requirements:* For master's, one-page personal statement, 2 letters of recommendation, resume, bachelor's degree transcript; for Graduate Certificate, bachelor's degree transcript, 2 letters of recommendation, 1-page personal statement, resume. Additional exam requirements/recommendations for international students: required—TOEFL (minimum score 550 paper-based, 79 iBT) or IELTS (minimum score 6). *Application deadline:* For fall admission, 8/31 priority date for domestic students, 6/30 priority date for international students; for spring admission, 12/31 priority date for domestic students, 10/31 priority date for international students. Applications are processed on a rolling basis. Electronic applications accepted. *Expenses: Tuition:* Part-time $600 per credit. *Required fees:* $40 per semester. *Financial support:* Federal Work-Study, scholarships/grants, and tuition discounts available. Support available to part-time students. Financial award application deadline: 8/31; financial award applicants required to submit FAFSA. *Unit head:* Chrystal Porter, Vice President of Graduate and Professional Studies, 617-243-2083, Fax: 617-243-2450, E-mail: gradinfo@lasell.edu. *Application contact:* Adrienne Franciosi, Assistant Vice President of Graduate and Professional Studies, 617-243-2214, Fax: 617-243-2450, E-mail: gradinfo@lasell.edu.
Website: http://www.lasell.edu/academics/graduate-and-professional-studies/programs-of-study/master-of-science-in-communication.html

Marquette University, Graduate School, College of Communication, Milwaukee, WI 53201-1881. Offers advertising and public relations (MA); communication studies (MA); digital storytelling (Certificate); journalism (MA); mass communication (MA); science, health and environmental communication (MA). *Accreditation:* ACEJMC (one or more programs are accredited). *Program availability:* Part-time, evening/weekend. *Degree requirements:* For master's, comprehensive exam, thesis or alternative. *Entrance requirements:* For master's, GRE, official transcripts from all current and previous colleges/universities except Marquette, three letters of recommendation, statement of academic and professional goals. Additional exam requirements/recommendations for international students: required—TOEFL (minimum score 530 paper-based). Electronic applications accepted.

Michigan State University, The Graduate School, College of Communication Arts and Sciences, Program in Health Communication, East Lansing, MI 48824. Offers MA. *Entrance requirements:* Additional exam requirements/recommendations for international students: required—TOEFL. Electronic applications accepted.

Ohio University, Graduate College, Scripps College of Communication, School of Communication Studies, Athens, OH 45701-2979. Offers health communication (PhD); organizational communication (MA); relating and organizing (PhD); rhetoric and public culture (PhD). *Program availability:* Part-time, online learning. Terminal master's awarded for partial completion of doctoral program. *Degree requirements:* For master's, capstone; for doctorate, comprehensive exam, thesis/dissertation. *Entrance requirements:* For master's, GRE; for doctorate, GRE General Test, minimum GPA of 3.0. Additional exam requirements/recommendations for international students: required—TOEFL (minimum score 550 paper-based; 80 iBT) or IELTS (minimum score 6.5). Electronic applications accepted.

Rider University, College of Liberal Arts and Sciences, Program in Business Communication, Lawrenceville, NJ 08648-3001. Offers business communication studies (MA); health communication (MA). *Program availability:* Part-time, 100% online, blended/hybrid learning. *Entrance requirements:* For master's, application fee, 2 letters of recommendation, official transcripts, statement of aims and objectives, interview. Additional exam requirements/recommendations for international students: required—TOEFL (minimum score 540 paper-based; 79 iBT). Electronic applications accepted.

Southeastern Louisiana University, College of Arts, Humanities and Social Sciences, Department of Communication and Media Studies, Hammond, LA 70402. Offers health communications (MA); journalism (MA); marketing (MA); public relations (MA); sociology (MA). *Program availability:* Part-time. *Faculty:* 7 full-time (5 women). *Students:* 10 full-time (6 women), 11 part-time (6 women); includes 7 minority (5 Black or African American, non-Hispanic/Latino; 2 Hispanic/Latino). Average age 30. 9 applicants, 100% accepted, 6 enrolled. In 2019, 3 master's awarded. *Degree requirements:* For master's, comprehensive exam. *Entrance requirements:* For master's, GRE (minimum score 148 on Verbal section, 3.5 Written), Minimum 2.5 undergraduate GPA. Additional exam requirements/recommendations for international students: required—TOEFL (minimum score 525 paper-based; 75 iBT). *Application deadline:* For fall admission, 7/15 priority date for domestic students, 6/1 priority date for international students; for spring admission, 12/1 priority date for domestic students, 10/1 priority date for international students. Applications are processed on a rolling basis. Application fee: $20 ($30 for international students). Electronic applications accepted. *Expenses: Tuition, area resident:* Full-time $6684; part-time $489 per credit hour. Tuition, state resident: full-time $6684; part-time $489 per credit hour. Tuition, nonresident: full-time $19,162; part-time $1183 per credit hour. *International tuition:* $19,162 full-time. *Required fees:* $2124. *Financial support:* In 2019–20, 11 students received support, including 3 research assistantships with tuition reimbursements available (averaging $10,100 per year); career-related internships or fieldwork, institutionally sponsored loans, and unspecified assistantships also available. Financial award application deadline: 5/1; financial award applicants required to submit FAFSA. *Unit head:* Dr. James O'Connor, Department Head, 985-549-5060, Fax: 985-549-3088, E-mail: james.oconnor@selu.edu. *Application contact:* Office of Admissions, 985-549-5637, Fax: 985-549-5632, E-mail: admissions@southeastern.edu.
Website: http://www.southeastern.edu/acad_research/depts/comm/index.html

Southern Illinois University Edwardsville, Graduate School, College of Arts and Sciences, Department of Applied Communication Studies, Program in Health Communication, Edwardsville, IL 62026. Offers MA. *Program availability:* Part-time, evening/weekend. *Degree requirements:* For master's, comprehensive exam (for some programs), thesis (for some programs). *Entrance requirements:* Additional exam requirements/recommendations for international students: required—TOEFL (minimum score 550 paper-based, 79 iBT), IELTS (minimum score 6.5), Michigan Test of English Language Proficiency or PTE. Electronic applications accepted.

State University of New York at Oswego, Graduate Studies, School of Communication, Media and the Arts, Oswego, NY 13126. Offers strategic communication (MA), including health communication, integrated media and social networks, organizational communication. *Students:* 34. In 2019, 17 master's awarded. *Entrance requirements:* For master's, GRE, official transcript, statement of purpose, resume, two letters of recommendation. *Application deadline:* Applications are processed on a rolling basis. Application fee: $65. Electronic applications accepted. *Financial support:* Fellowships, research assistantships, teaching assistantships, institutionally sponsored loans, scholarships/grants, and unspecified assistantships available. Support available to part-time students. Financial award application deadline: 4/1; financial award applicants required to submit FAFSA. *Unit head:* Dr. Julie Pretzat, Dean, 315-312-6612, E-mail: julie.pretzat@oswego.edu. *Application contact:* Dr. Julie Pretzat, Dean, 315-312-6612, E-mail: julie.pretzat@oswego.edu.

Stony Brook University, State University of New York, School of Journalism, Stony Brook, NY 11794. Offers health communication (Certificate); journalism (MS). *Faculty:* 11 full-time (4 women), 11 part-time/adjunct (3 women). In 2019, 2 master's awarded. *Entrance requirements:* For master's, GRE, MCAT, DAT, or GMAT, bachelor's degree with minimum GPA of 3.0. Additional exam requirements/recommendations for international students: required—TOEFL (minimum score 600 paper-based; 100 iBT). *Application deadline:* For fall admission, 1/15 for domestic students; for spring admission, 10/1 for domestic students. Application fee: $100. *Expenses:* Contact institution. *Financial support:* Teaching assistantships available. *Unit head:* Dr. Laura Lindenfeld, Dean, 631-632-7403, E-mail: laura.lindenfeld@stonybrook.edu. *Application contact:* Maureen Robinson, Coordinator, 631-632-7403, Fax: 631-632-7550, E-mail: maureen.robinson@stonybrook.edu.
Website: https://journalism.cc.stonybrook.edu/

Stony Brook University, State University of New York, Stony Brook Medicine, Renaissance School of Medicine, Program in Public Health, Stony Brook, NY 11794. Offers community health (MPH); evaluation sciences (MPH); family violence (MPH); health communication (Certificate); health economics (MPH); health education and promotion (Certificate); population health (MPH); substance abuse (MPH). *Accreditation:* CEPH. *Program availability:* Part-time, evening/weekend. *Students:* 39 full-time (30 women), 17 part-time (12 women); includes 24 minority (3 Black or African American, non-Hispanic/Latino; 13 Asian, non-Hispanic/Latino; 7 Hispanic/Latino; 1 Two or more races, non-Hispanic/Latino), 2 international. Average age 28. 174 applicants, 67% accepted, 70 enrolled. In 2019, 22 master's awarded. *Entrance requirements:* For master's, GRE, 3 references, bachelor's degree from accredited college or university with minimum GPA of 3.0, essays, interview. Additional exam requirements/recommendations for international students: required—TOEFL (minimum score 90 iBT). *Application deadline:* For fall admission, 7/15 for domestic students. Application fee: $100. Electronic applications accepted. *Expenses:* Contact institution. *Financial support:* In 2019–20, 4 research assistantships were awarded; fellowships also available. *Unit head:* Dr. Lisa A. Benz Scott, Director, 631-444-9396, E-mail: publichealth@stonybrookmedicine.edu. *Application contact:* Joanie Maniaci, Assistant Director for Student Affairs, 631-444-2074, Fax: 631-444-6035, E-mail: joanmarie.maniaci@stonybrook.edu.
Website: https://publichealth.stonybrookmedicine.edu/

Tufts University, School of Medicine, Public Health and Professional Degree Programs, Boston, MA 02111. Offers biomedical sciences (MS); health communication (MS, Certificate); pain research, education and policy (MS, Certificate); physician assistant (MS); public health (MPH, Dr PH), including behavioral science (MPH), biostatistics (MPH), epidemiology (MPH), health communication (MPH), health services (MPH), management and policy (MPH), nutrition (MPH); DMD/MPH; DVM/MPH; JD/MPH; MD/MPH; MMS/MPH; MS/MBA; MS/MPH. *Accreditation:* CEPH (one or more programs are accredited). *Program availability:* Part-time, evening/weekend. *Students:* 450 full-time (291 women), 68 part-time (58 women); includes 201 minority (34 Black or African American, non-Hispanic/Latino; 1 American Indian or Alaska Native, non-Hispanic/Latino; 106 Asian, non-Hispanic/Latino; 41 Hispanic/Latino; 1 Native Hawaiian or other Pacific Islander, non-Hispanic/Latino; 18 Two or more races, non-Hispanic/Latino), 16 international. Average age 27. 1,076 applicants, 70% accepted, 213 enrolled. In 2019, 268 master's, 2 doctorates awarded. Terminal master's awarded for partial completion of doctoral program. *Degree requirements:* For master's, thesis (for some programs); for doctorate, thesis/dissertation. *Entrance requirements:* For master's, GRE General Test, MCAT, or GMAT, LSAT for applicants to the JD/MPH combined degree; for doctorate, GRE General Test or MCAT. Additional exam requirements/recommendations for international students: required—TOEFL (minimum score 100 iBT); recommended—IELTS (minimum score 7), TSE. *Application deadline:* For fall admission, 1/15 priority date for domestic and international students; for spring admission, 10/25 priority date for domestic and international students. Applications are processed on a rolling basis. Application fee: $70. Electronic applications accepted. *Expenses:* Contact institution. *Financial support:* In 2019–20, 13 students received support, including 1 fellowship (averaging $3,000 per year), 50 research assistantships (averaging $1,000 per year), 65 teaching assistantships (averaging $2,000 per year); Federal Work-Study and scholarships/grants also available. Financial award application deadline: 2/23; financial award applicants required to submit FAFSA. *Unit head:* Dr. Aviva Must, Dean, 617-636-0935, Fax: 617-636-0898, E-mail: aviva.must@tufts.edu. *Application contact:* Emily Keily, Director of Admissions, 617-636-0935, Fax: 617-636-0898, E-mail: med-phpd@tufts.edu.
Website: http://publichealth.tufts.edu

University of Florida, Graduate School, College of Health and Human Performance, Department of Health Education and Behavior, Gainesville, FL 32611. Offers health and human performance (PhD), including health behavior; health communication (Graduate Certificate); health education and behavior (MS). *Accreditation:* NCATE (one or more programs are accredited). *Program availability:* Part-time. Terminal master's awarded for partial completion of doctoral program. *Degree requirements:* For master's, comprehensive exam, thesis (for some programs); for doctorate, comprehensive exam, thesis/dissertation. *Entrance requirements:* For master's and doctorate, GRE General Test (minimum score 293), minimum GPA of 3.0. Additional exam requirements/recommendations for international students: required—TOEFL (minimum score 550 paper-based; 80 iBT), IELTS (minimum score 6). Electronic applications accepted.

University of Florida, Graduate School, College of Journalism and Communications, Program in Mass Communication, Gainesville, FL 32611. Offers international/intercultural communication (MAMC); journalism (MAMC); mass communication (MAMC, PhD), including clinical translational science (MAMC); public relations (MAMC);

science/health communication (MAMC); telecommunication (MAMC). *Entrance requirements:* For master's and doctorate, GRE General Test, minimum GPA of 3.0.

University of Houston, College of Liberal Arts and Social Sciences, Jack J. Valenti School of Communication, Houston, TX 77204. Offers health communication (MA); mass communication studies (MA); public relations studies (MA); speech communication (MA). *Program availability:* Part-time. *Degree requirements:* For master's, comprehensive exam (for some programs), thesis (for some programs), 30-33 hours. *Entrance requirements:* For master's, GRE. Additional exam requirements/recommendations for international students: required—TOEFL. Electronic applications accepted.

University of Missouri, Office of Research and Graduate Studies, School of Journalism, Columbia, MO 65211. Offers health communications (MA); journalism (PhD). *Accreditation:* ACEJMC (one or more programs are accredited). *Program availability:* Part-time. Terminal master's awarded for partial completion of doctoral program. *Entrance requirements:* For master's and doctorate, GRE General Test, minimum GPA of 3.0. Additional exam requirements/recommendations for international students: required—TOEFL, IELTS. Electronic applications accepted.

The University of North Carolina at Chapel Hill, Graduate School, Hussman School of Journalism and Media, Chapel Hill, NC 27599. Offers digital communication (MA, Certificate); media and communication (MA, PhD), including interdisciplinary health communication (MA), journalism (MA), strategic communication (MA), theory and research (MA), visual communication (MA); JD/PhD; MA/JD. *Accreditation:* ACEJMC (one or more programs are accredited). *Program availability:* Part-time, all course instruction online, plus two on-campus experiences totaling seven days. *Faculty:* 30 full-time (15 women), 5 part-time/adjunct (4 women). *Students:* 68 full-time (45 women), 82 part-time (58 women); includes 35 minority (13 Black or African American, non-Hispanic/Latino; 1 American Indian or Alaska Native, non-Hispanic/Latino; 4 Asian, non-Hispanic/Latino; 1 Hispanic/Latino; 16 Two or more races, non-Hispanic/Latino), 9 international. Average age 34. 205 applicants, 49% accepted, 73 enrolled. In 2019, 32 master's, 5 doctorates, 24 other advanced degrees awarded. *Degree requirements:* For master's, comprehensive exam, thesis; for doctorate, comprehensive exam, thesis/dissertation. *Entrance requirements:* For master's, Online master's degree only: GRE General Test (waiver available); Residential master's degree: minimum GPA of 3.0; for doctorate, minimum GPA of 3.0. Additional exam requirements/recommendations for international students: required—TOEFL (minimum iBT score of 105) or IELTS (7.5). Application fee: $95. Electronic applications accepted. *Expenses:* Ph.D.: 7,550 per semester N.C. resident, 15,883 non-res; Residential M.A.: 8,425 per semester N.C., 16,708 non-res; Online M.A./certificate: 2,262 per semester N.C., 4,698 non-res. *Financial support:* In 2019–20, 60 students received support, including 41 fellowships with full tuition reimbursements available (averaging $17,901 per year), 4 research assistantships with full tuition reimbursements available (averaging $17,465 per year); scholarships/grants and health care benefits also available. Financial award application deadline: 12/15; financial award applicants required to submit FAFSA. *Unit head:* Susan King, Dean, 919-962-1204, Fax: 919-962-0620, E-mail: susanking@unc.edu. *Application contact:* Casey Hart, Assistant Director, Graduate Studies, 919-843-9471, Fax: 919-962-0620, E-mail: mjgrad@unc.edu.
Website: http://hussman.unc.edu

University of Oklahoma, College of Arts and Sciences, Department of Communication, Norman, OK 73019. Offers communication (MA); communication technology (PhD); health communication (PhD); intercultural/international communication (PhD); organizational communication (PhD); political/mass communication (PhD); social influence/interpersonal communication (PhD). *Program availability:* Part-time. *Degree requirements:* For master's, comprehensive exam (for some programs), thesis (for some programs), comprehensive exams or thesis; for doctorate, comprehensive exam, thesis/dissertation. *Entrance requirements:* For master's, GRE (for assistantship), statement of purpose, transcripts, writing sample, letters of recommendation; for doctorate, GRE, statement of purpose, transcripts, writing sample, letters of recommendation. Additional exam requirements/recommendations for international students: required—TOEFL (minimum score 79 iBT) or IELTS (minimum score 6.5). Electronic applications accepted. *Expenses:* Tuition, state resident: full-time $6583.20; part-time $274.30 per credit hour. Tuition, nonresident: full-time $21,242; part-time $885.10 per credit hour. *International tuition:* $21,242.40 full-time. *Required fees:* $1994.20; $72.55 per credit hour. $126.50 per semester. Tuition and fees vary according to course load and degree level.

University of St. Thomas, Opus College of Business, Master of Science in Health Care Communication Program, Minneapolis, MN 55403. Offers MS. *Program availability:* Part-time, evening/weekend. *Entrance requirements:* For master's, resume, 3 essay questions, bachelor's degree, 1 letter of recommendation. Electronic applications accepted.

University of Southern California, Graduate School, Annenberg School for Communication and Journalism, School of Communication, Program in Communication, Los Angeles, CA 90089. Offers culture and community (PhD); global and transnational communication (PhD); groups, organizations and networks (PhD); health communication and social dynamics (PhD); information, political economy and entertainment (PhD); new media and technology (PhD); rhetoric, politics and public media (PhD). *Students:* 88 full-time (63 women); includes 28 minority (2 Black or African American, non-Hispanic/Latino; 6 Asian, non-Hispanic/Latino; 10 Hispanic/Latino; 10 Two or more races, non-Hispanic/Latino), 34 international. Average age 29. 161 applicants, 12% accepted, 14 enrolled. In 2019, 13 doctorates awarded. *Degree requirements:* For doctorate, thesis/dissertation. *Entrance requirements:* For doctorate, GRE General Test, resume or curriculum vitae, scholarly writing, 3 letters of recommendation, statement of purpose. Additional exam requirements/recommendations for international students: required—TOEFL (minimum score 114 iBT), IELTS (minimum score 8); recommended—TWE. *Application deadline:* For fall admission, 12/1 for domestic and international students. Application fee: $90. Electronic applications accepted. *Financial support:* In 2019–20, 15 students received support, including 15 fellowships with full tuition reimbursements available (averaging $52,427 per year); research assistantships, teaching assistantships, Federal Work-Study, health care benefits, and unspecified assistantships also available. Financial award application deadline: 12/1. *Unit head:* Dr. Robeson Taj Frazier, Director of the PhD Program, 213-740-6595, E-mail: rfrazier@usc.edu. *Application contact:* Allyson Hill, Associate Dean for Admissions, 213-821-0770, Fax: 213-740-1933, E-mail: ascadm@usc.edu.
Website: http://www.annenberg.usc.edu

University of Southern California, Keck School of Medicine and Graduate School, Graduate Programs in Medicine, Department of Preventive Medicine, Master of Public Health Program, Los Angeles, CA 90032. Offers biostatistics and epidemiology (MPH); child and family health (MPH); community health promotion (MPH); environmental health (MPH); geohealth (MPH); global health leadership (MPH); health communication (MPH); health services and policy (MPH). *Accreditation:* CEPH. *Program availability:* Part-time, evening/weekend, 100% online. *Faculty:* 37 full-time (28 women), 8 part-time/adjunct (6 women). *Students:* 261 full-time (201 women), 74 part-time (55 women); includes 224 minority (46 Black or African American, non-Hispanic/Latino; 2 American Indian or Alaska Native, non-Hispanic/Latino; 79 Asian, non-Hispanic/Latino; 56 Hispanic/Latino; 6 Native Hawaiian or other Pacific Islander, non-Hispanic/Latino; 35 Two or more races, non-Hispanic/Latino), 21 international. Average age 28. 420 applicants, 76% accepted, 94 enrolled. In 2019, 123 master's awarded. *Degree requirements:* For master's, practicum, final report, oral presentation. *Entrance requirements:* For master's, GRE General Test, MCAT, GMAT, minimum GPA of 3.0. Additional exam requirements/recommendations for international students: required—TOEFL (minimum score 600 paper-based; 90 iBT). *Application deadline:* For fall admission, 12/1 priority date for domestic students, 5/1 priority date for international students; for spring admission, 9/1 priority date for domestic and international students; for summer admission, 3/1 for domestic and international students. Applications are processed on a rolling basis. Application fee: $135. Electronic applications accepted. *Financial support:* Career-related internships or fieldwork, Federal Work-Study, institutionally sponsored loans, and scholarships/grants available. Support available to part-time students. Financial award application deadline: 5/4; financial award applicants required to submit CSS PROFILE or FAFSA. *Unit head:* Dr. Louise A. Rohrbach, Director, 323-442-8237, Fax: 323-442-8297, E-mail: rohrbac@usc.edu. *Application contact:* Valerie Burris, Admissions Counselor, 323-442-7257, Fax: 323-442-8297, E-mail: valeriem@usc.edu.
Website: https://preventivemedicine.usc.edu/education/graduate-programs/mph/

Wayne State University, College of Fine, Performing and Communication Arts, Department of Communication, Detroit, MI 48202. Offers communication (PhD), including democratic participation and culture, identity and representation, media, society and culture, risk, crisis and conflict, wellness, work life and relationships; communication and new media (Graduate Certificate); communication studies (MA); dispute resolution (MADR, Graduate Certificate), including community and urban studies (MADR), conflict area studies (MADR), health and family (MADR), international conflict and cooperation (MADR), professional practice (MADR), theory of conflict (MADR), workplace (MADR); health communication (Graduate Certificate); journalism (MA); media arts (MA); media studies (MA); public relations and organizational communication (MA); JD/MADR. *Program availability:* Online learning. *Degree requirements:* For master's, thesis (for some programs), thesis or essay; for doctorate, thesis/dissertation. *Entrance requirements:* For master's, GRE (for MA if undergraduate GPA less than 3.2), personal statement; BA or BS in communication or related field with minimum upper-division GPA of 3.2 and minimum upper-division undergraduate GPA of 3.0, and sample of academic writing (for MA); undergraduate degree with minimum upper-division GPA of 3.0 and three letters of recommendation (for MADR); for doctorate, GRE, undergraduate degree in communication or related field; master's degree in communication or related field with minimum GPA of 3.5; letters of recommendation; personal statement; sample of written scholarship. Additional exam requirements/recommendations for international students: required—TOEFL (minimum score 100 iBT), IELTS, TWE. Electronic applications accepted. *Expenses:* Contact institution.

Internet and Interactive Multimedia

Academy of Art University, Graduate Programs, School of Communications and Media Technologies, San Francisco, CA 94105-3410. Offers communications and media technologies (MA). *Program availability:* Part-time, 100% online. *Faculty:* 2 full-time (1 woman), 12 part-time/adjunct (6 women). *Students:* 25 full-time (15 women), 15 part-time (9 women); includes 5 minority (4 Black or African American, non-Hispanic/Latino; 1 Two or more races, non-Hispanic/Latino), 23 international. Average age 31. 14 applicants, 100% accepted, 9 enrolled. In 2019, 17 master's awarded. *Degree requirements:* For master's, final review. *Entrance requirements:* For master's, statement of intent; resume; portfolio/reel; official college transcripts. *Application deadline:* Applications are processed on a rolling basis. Application fee: $50. Electronic applications accepted. *Expenses: Tuition:* Full-time $1083; part-time $1083 per credit hour. *Required fees:* $860; $860 per unit. $430 per term. One-time fee: $145. Tuition and fees vary according to program. *Financial support:* Career-related internships or fieldwork, Federal Work-Study, and scholarships/grants available. Financial award application deadline: 8/10; financial award applicants required to submit FAFSA.
Website: http://www.academyart.edu/multimedia-communications-school/

Agnes Scott College, Program in Writing and Digital Communication, Decatur, GA 30030-3797. Offers MA.

Alfred University, Graduate School, College of Ceramics, School of Art and Design, Alfred, NY 14802-1205. Offers ceramic art (MFA); electronic integrated arts (MFA); painting (MFA); sculpture/dimensional studies (MFA). *Accreditation:* NASAD. *Faculty:* 29 full-time (15 women), 4 part-time/adjunct (0 women). *Students:* 43 full-time (27 women); includes 4 minority (1 Asian, non-Hispanic/Latino; 2 Hispanic/Latino; 1 Two or more races, non-Hispanic/Latino), 12 international. Average age 29. 170 applicants, 24% accepted, 20 enrolled. In 2019, 18 master's awarded. *Degree requirements:* For master's, thesis or alternative, exhibit. *Entrance requirements:* For master's, portfolio. Additional exam requirements/recommendations for international students: required—TOEFL (minimum score 550 paper-based; 80 iBT), IELTS (minimum score 6). *Application deadline:* For fall admission, 1/15 for domestic and international students. Applications are processed on a rolling basis. Application fee: $60. Electronic applications accepted. Application fee is waived when completed online. *Expenses:* $23,530 per year. *Financial support:* In 2019–20, 40 students received support. Teaching assistantships with full tuition reimbursements available and tuition waivers (full) available. Financial award application deadline: 3/15; financial award applicants required to submit FAFSA. *Unit head:* Gerar Edizel, Interim Dean, 607-871-2412, E-mail: fedizel@alfred.edu. *Application contact:* Lindsey Gertin, Assistant Director of Graduate Admissions, 607-871-2017, Fax: 607-871-2198, E-mail: gradinquiry@alfred.edu.
Website: http://art.alfred.edu/graduate/

Ball State University, Graduate School, College of Communication, Information, and Media, Department of Journalism, Program in Emerging Media Design and Development, Muncie, IN 47306. Offers MA. *Program availability:* Part-time, evening/weekend. *Entrance requirements:* For master's, GRE General Test (minimum score 150 verbal), minimum baccalaureate GPA of 2.75 or 3.0 in latter half of baccalaureate, transcripts of all prior course work, three letters of recommendation, current resume, statement of purpose, writing sample, portfolio. Additional exam requirements/recommendations for international students: required—TOEFL (minimum score 550 paper-based; 79 iBT), IELTS (minimum score 6.5). Electronic applications accepted. *Expenses: Tuition, area resident:* Full-time $7506; part-time $417 per credit hour. Tuition, nonresident: full-time $20,610; part-time $1145 per credit hour. *Required fees:* $2126. Tuition and fees vary according to course load, campus/location and program.

Boston University, Metropolitan College, Department of Computer Science, Boston, MA 02215. Offers computer information systems (MS), including computer networks, data analytics, database management and business intelligence, health informatics, IT project management, security, Web application development; computer networks (Certificate); computer science (MS); data analytics (Certificate); digital forensics (Certificate); health informatics (Certificate); information technology project management (Certificate); software development (MS); software engineering in health care systems (Certificate); telecommunications (MS), including security. *Program availability:* Part-time, evening/weekend, online learning. *Faculty:* 16 full-time (3 women), 52 part-time/adjunct (5 women). *Students:* 253 full-time (80 women), 856 part-time (243 women); includes 246 minority (53 Black or African American, non-Hispanic/Latino; 1 American Indian or Alaska Native, non-Hispanic/Latino; 129 Asian, non-Hispanic/Latino; 48 Hispanic/Latino; 15 Two or more races, non-Hispanic/Latino), 418 international. Average age 30. 1,079 applicants, 72% accepted, 297 enrolled. In 2019, 513 master's awarded. *Entrance requirements:* For master's and Certificate, official transcripts from regionally-accredited bachelor's degree program, 3 letters of recommendation, professional resume, personal statement. Additional exam requirements/recommendations for international students: required—TOEFL (minimum score 84 iBT), IELTS. *Application deadline:* For fall admission, 8/1 priority date for domestic students, 6/1 priority date for international students; for spring admission, 12/1 priority date for domestic students, 11/15 priority date for international students; for summer admission, 4/1 priority date for domestic students, 3/1 priority date for international students. Applications are processed on a rolling basis. Application fee: $85. Electronic applications accepted. *Expenses:* Contact institution. *Financial support:* In 2019–20, 11 research assistantships (averaging $8,400 per year), 23 teaching assistantships (averaging $3,400 per year) were awarded; unspecified assistantships also available. Support available to part-time students. Financial award applicants required to submit FAFSA. *Unit head:* Dr. Anatoly Temkin, Chair, 617-353-2566, Fax: 617-353-2367, E-mail: csinfo@bu.edu. *Application contact:* Enrollment Services, 617-353-6004, E-mail: met@bu.edu. Website: http://www.bu.edu/csmet/

Brandeis University, Rabb School of Continuing Studies, Division of Graduate Professional Studies, Master of Science in Digital Marketing and Design Program, Waltham, MA 02454-9110. Offers MS. *Program availability:* Part-time-only. *Entrance requirements:* For master's, undergraduate degree with at least 2 marketing courses and/or 2 years of relevant work experience; four-year bachelor's degree from U.S. accredited institution or equivalent; statement of goals; resume or curriculum vitae; letter of recommendation. Additional exam requirements/recommendations for international students: required—TWE (minimum score 4.5), TOEFL (minimum scores: 600 paper-based, 100 iBT), IELTS (7), or PTE (68). Electronic applications accepted. *Expenses:* Contact institution.

Brooklyn College of the City University of New York, School of Visual, Media and Performing Arts, Program in Performance and Interactive Media Arts, Brooklyn, NY 11210-2889. Offers MFA. *Entrance requirements:* For master's, 2 letters of recommendation, resume, portfolio, interview. Additional exam requirements/recommendations for international students: required—TOEFL (minimum score 550 paper-based; 61 iBT). Electronic applications accepted.

California State University, East Bay, Office of Graduate Studies, College of Letters, Arts, and Social Sciences, Multimedia Graduate Program, Hayward, CA 94542-3000. Offers MA. *Program availability:* Part-time. *Degree requirements:* For master's, multimedia project or thesis. *Entrance requirements:* For master's, minimum GPA of 2.5; resume; 2 letters of recommendation; multimedia portfolio; statement of purpose. Additional exam requirements/recommendations for international students: required—TOEFL (minimum score 550 paper-based). Electronic applications accepted. *Expenses:* Contact institution.

Champlain College, Graduate Studies, Burlington, VT 05402-0670. Offers business (MBA); digital forensic science (MS); early childhood education (M Ed); emergent media (MFA, MS); executive leadership (MS); health care administration (MS); information security operations (MS); law (MS); mediation and applied conflict studies (MS). *Program availability:* Part-time, online learning. *Degree requirements:* For master's, capstone project. *Entrance requirements:* Additional exam requirements/recommendations for international students: required—TOEFL (minimum score 550 paper-based; 80 iBT). Electronic applications accepted.

College of Saint Elizabeth, Program in Social Media Design and Management, Morristown, NJ 07960-6989. Offers MA. *Program availability:* Part-time. *Degree requirements:* For master's, thesis. *Entrance requirements:* Additional exam requirements/recommendations for international students: required—TOEFL (minimum score 550 paper-based; 79 iBT), IELTS (minimum score 6.5). Electronic applications accepted. Application fee is waived when completed online.

Concordia University, School of Graduate Studies, Faculty of Engineering and Computer Science, Concordia Institute for Information Systems Engineering (CIISE), Montréal, QC H3G 1M8, Canada. Offers 3D graphics and game development (Certificate); information and systems engineering (PhD); information systems security (M Eng, MA Sc); quality systems engineering (M Eng, MA Sc); service engineering and network management (Certificate).

Concordia University, School of Graduate Studies, Faculty of Fine Arts, Department of Studio Arts, Montréal, QC H3G 1M8, Canada. Offers studio arts (MFA), including fibers and material practices, film production, intermedia, painting and drawing, photography, print media, sculpture. *Degree requirements:* For master's, thesis or alternative. *Entrance requirements:* For master's, portfolio.

DePaul University, College of Computing and Digital Media, Chicago, IL 60604. Offers animation (MA, MFA); applied technology (MS); business information technology (MS); computational finance (MS); computer and information sciences (PhD); computer science (MS); creative producing (MFA); cybersecurity (MS); data science (MS); digital communication and media arts (MA); documentary (MFA); e-commerce technology (MS); experience design (MA); film and television (MS); film and television directing (MFA); game design (MFA); game programming (MS); health informatics (MS); human centered design (PhD); human-computer interaction (MS); information systems (MS); network engineering and security (MS); product innovation and computing (MS); screenwriting (MFA); software engineering (MS); JD/MS. *Program availability:* Part-time, evening/weekend, online learning. *Degree requirements:* For master's, thesis (for some

programs); for doctorate, comprehensive exam, thesis/dissertation. *Entrance requirements:* For master's, GRE or GMAT (for MS in computational finance only), bachelor's degree, resume (MS in predictive analytics only), IT experience (MS in information technology project management only), portfolio review (all MFA programs and MA in animation); for doctorate, GRE, master's degree in computer science. Additional exam requirements/recommendations for international students: required—TOEFL (minimum score 590 paper-based; 80 iBT), IELTS (minimum score 6.5), PTE (minimum score 53). Electronic applications accepted. *Expenses:* Contact institution.

Elon University, Program in Interactive Media, Elon, NC 27244-2010. Offers interactive media (MA). *Accreditation:* ACEJMC. *Faculty:* 8 full-time (2 women), 1 (woman) part-time/adjunct. *Students:* 32 full-time (22 women); includes 21 minority (19 Black or African American, non-Hispanic/Latino; 1 Asian, non-Hispanic/Latino; 1 Hispanic/Latino). Average age 23. 44 applicants, 91% accepted, 31 enrolled. In 2019, 28 master's awarded. *Degree requirements:* For master's, 6-hour capstone. *Entrance requirements:* For master's, GRE. Additional exam requirements/recommendations for international students: required—TOEFL (minimum score 550 paper-based; 79 iBT). *Application deadline:* For fall admission, 5/1 priority date for domestic students. Applications are processed on a rolling basis. Application fee: $60. Electronic applications accepted. *Financial support:* Applicants required to submit FAFSA. *Unit head:* Dr. Rochelle Ford, Dean of the School of Communications, 336-278-5724, E-mail: rford9@elon.edu. *Application contact:* Art Fadde, Director of Graduate Admissions, 800-334-8448 Ext. 3, Fax: 336-278-7699, E-mail: afadde@elon.edu.
Website: http://www.elon.edu/imedia

Fairfield University, School of Engineering, Fairfield, CT 06824. Offers database management (CAS); electrical and computer engineering (MS); information security (CAS); management of technology (MS); mechanical engineering (MS); network technology (CAS); software engineering (MS); Web application development (CAS). *Program availability:* Part-time, evening/weekend. *Faculty:* 10 full-time (2 women), 15 part-time/adjunct (1 woman). *Students:* 46 full-time (24 women), 57 part-time (10 women); includes 23 minority (5 Black or African American, non-Hispanic/Latino; 9 Asian, non-Hispanic/Latino; 9 Hispanic/Latino), 33 international. Average age 29. 68 applicants, 62% accepted, 30 enrolled. In 2019, 100 master's awarded. *Degree requirements:* For master's, capstone course. *Entrance requirements:* For master's, resume, 2 recommendations. Additional exam requirements/recommendations for international students: required—TOEFL (minimum score 550 paper-based; 80 iBT), IELTS (minimum score 6.5), TOEFL (minimum score 550 paper-based; 80 iBT) or IELTS (minimum score 6.5). *Application deadline:* For fall admission, 5/15 for international students; for spring admission, 10/15 for international students. Applications are processed on a rolling basis. Application fee: $60. Electronic applications accepted. *Expenses:* Tuition $900/credit hour; Registration Fee $50/semester; Graduate Student Activity Fee (Fall and Spring) $65/semester. *Financial support:* In 2019–20, 20 students received support. Scholarships/grants and unspecified assistantships available. Financial award applicants required to submit FAFSA. *Unit head:* Richard Heist, Dean, 203-254-4147, Fax: 203-254-4013, E-mail: rheist@fairfield.edu. *Application contact:* Melanie Rogers, Director of Graduate Admission, 203-254-4184, Fax: 203-254-4073, E-mail: gradadmis@fairfield.edu. Website: http://www.fairfield.edu/soe

Full Sail University, Education Media Design and Technology Master of Science Program - Online, Winter Park, FL 32792-7437. Offers MS. *Program availability:* Online learning. *Entrance requirements:* Additional exam requirements/recommendations for international students: required—TOEFL (minimum score 550 paper-based; 79 iBT).

Full Sail University, Game Design Master of Science Program - Campus, Winter Park, FL 32792-7437. Offers MS.

Full Sail University, Internet Marketing Master of Science Program - Online, Winter Park, FL 32792-7437. Offers MS. *Program availability:* Online learning.

Georgetown University, Graduate School of Arts and Sciences, Communication, Culture & Technology Program, Washington, DC 20057. Offers MA. *Program availability:* Part-time, evening/weekend. *Faculty:* 10 full-time (4 women), 12 part-time/adjunct (7 women). *Students:* 120 full-time (100 women), 10 part-time (6 women). Average age 25. *Degree requirements:* For master's, thesis optional, 36 graduate credits. *Entrance requirements:* For master's, GRE General Test (unless applicant already has a master's or higher), 3 letters of recommendation, writing sample, resume, statement of purpose, video statement (highly recommended). Additional exam requirements/recommendations for international students: required—TOEFL (minimum score 100 iBT), IELTS (minimum score 7.5). *Application deadline:* For fall admission, 4/1 for domestic and international students; for spring admission, 10/1 for domestic and international students. Application fee: $90. Electronic applications accepted. *Financial support:* Fellowships and scholarships/grants available. Financial award application deadline: 1/15. *Unit head:* Prof. Matthew Tinkcom, Director, 202-687-6618, E-mail: Matthew.Tinkcom@georgetown.edu. *Application contact:* Ai-Hui Tan, Director, CCT Academic Affairs, 202-687-6618, E-mail: cctadmissions@georgetown.edu. Website: http://cct.georgetown.edu/

Georgia Institute of Technology, Graduate Studies, Ivan Allen College of Liberal Arts, School of Literature, Media, and Communication, Atlanta, GA 30332. Offers digital media (MS, PhD). *Program availability:* Part-time. *Faculty:* 16 full-time (7 women). *Students:* 67 full-time (43 women), 4 part-time (2 women); includes 19 minority (9 Black or African American, non-Hispanic/Latino; 8 Asian, non-Hispanic/Latino; 2 Two or more races, non-Hispanic/Latino), 29 international. Average age 28. 129 applicants, 43% accepted, 32 enrolled. In 2019, 16 master's, 3 doctorates awarded. Terminal master's awarded for partial completion of doctoral program. *Degree requirements:* For master's, thesis optional, project studio, paid internship, responsible conduct of research training; for doctorate, comprehensive exam, thesis/dissertation, portfolio review, responsible conduct of research training. *Entrance requirements:* For master's and doctorate, GRE, three letters of recommendation, transcripts from each college/university attended, design portfolio, statement of purpose. Additional exam requirements/recommendations for international students: required—TOEFL (minimum score 650 paper-based; 114 iBT), IELTS, TOEFL is the preferred method with the requirements shown on the programs. *Application deadline:* For fall admission, 1/8 priority date for domestic and international students. Applications are processed on a rolling basis. Application fee: $75 ($85 for international students). Electronic applications accepted. *Expenses:* Tuition, area resident: Full-time $14,064; part-time $586 per credit hour. Tuition, state resident: full-time $14,064; part-time $586 per credit hour. Tuition, nonresident: full-time $29,140; part-time $1215 per credit hour. International tuition: $29,140 full-time. *Required fees:* $2024; $840 per semester. $2096. Tuition and fees vary according to course load. *Financial support:* In 2019–20, 6 research assistantships, 2 teaching assistantships were awarded; fellowships, career-related internships or fieldwork, Federal Work-Study, institutionally sponsored loans, tuition waivers (full and partial), and unspecified assistantships also available. Support available to part-time students. Financial award application deadline: 7/1; financial award applicants required to submit FAFSA. *Unit head:* Richard Utz, School Chair, 404-894-2730, Fax: 404-894-1287, E-mail: richard.utz@lmc.gatech.edu. *Application contact:* Marla Bruner, Director of Graduate Studies, 404-894-1610, Fax: 404-894-1609, E-mail:

gradinfo@mail.gatech.edu.
Website: http://lmc.gatech.edu

Ithaca College, Roy H. Park School of Communications, Executive Master's in Communications Innovation Program, Ithaca, NY 14850. Offers MS. *Program availability:* Part-time-only, online only, Majority online with intensive on-site classes held over long weekends at various locations throughout the world. *Faculty:* 12 full-time (3 women). *Students:* 5 part-time (2 women); includes 1 minority (Black or African American, non-Hispanic/Latino). Average age 40. 8 applicants, 75% accepted, 5 enrolled. *Entrance requirements:* Additional exam requirements/recommendations for international students: required—TOEFL (minimum score 550 paper-based; 80 iBT). *Application deadline:* For fall admission, 2/1 for domestic and international students. Applications are processed on a rolling basis. Application fee: $40. Electronic applications accepted. *Expenses:* Contact institution. *Financial support:* In 2019–20, 5 students received support, including 4 fellowships (averaging $11,250 per year); Federal Work-Study and scholarships/grants also available. Support available to part-time students. Financial award application deadline: 3/1; financial award applicants required to submit FAFSA. *Unit head:* Dr. Diane Gayeski, Director, Communications Innovation Program, 607-274-3895, E-mail: gayeski@Ithaca.edu. *Application contact:* Nicole Eversley Bradwell, Director, Office of Admission, 800-429-4274, Fax: 607-274-1263, E-mail: admission@ithaca.edu.
Website: https://www.ithaca.edu/admission/graduate-admission/graduate-study-communications-innovation

Kutztown University of Pennsylvania, College of Visual and Performing Arts, Program in Communication Design, Kutztown, PA 19530-0730. Offers MFA. *Program availability:* Part-time. *Faculty:* 7 full-time (6 women). *Students:* 6 full-time (5 women), 15 part-time (10 women); includes 4 minority (1 Asian, non-Hispanic/Latino; 2 Hispanic/Latino; 1 Two or more races, non-Hispanic/Latino). Average age 34. 15 applicants, 93% accepted, 10 enrolled. In 2019, 2 master's awarded. *Entrance requirements:* For master's, resume documenting a minimum of 3 years professional experience in the field, artist's statement, porfolio. Additional exam requirements/recommendations for international students: required—TOEFL (minimum score 550 paper-based, 79 iBT), IELTS (minimum score 6.5), or PTE (minimum score 53). *Application deadline:* For fall admission, 3/1 priority date for domestic and international students. Application fee: $35. Electronic applications accepted. *Expenses: Tuition, area resident:* Full-time $9288; part-time $515 per credit. Tuition, state resident: full-time $9288. Tuition, nonresident: full-time $13,932; part-time $774 per credit. *Required fees:* $1688; $94 per credit. *Financial support:* Career-related internships or fieldwork, Federal Work-Study, and unspecified assistantships available. Support available to part-time students. Financial award application deadline: 3/1; financial award applicants required to submit FAFSA. *Unit head:* Denise Bosler, Department Chair, 610-683-4531, Fax: 610-683-4619, E-mail: bosler@kutztown.edu. *Application contact:* Kathy Sue Traylor, Department Secretary, 610-683-4530, E-mail: traylor@kutztown.edu.
Website: http://kucd.kutztown.edu

Liberty University, School Of Communication & the Arts, Lynchburg, VA 24515. Offers communication (MA); promotion and video content (MA); social media management (MS); strategic communication (MA). *Program availability:* Part-time. *Students:* 335 full-time (235 women), 331 part-time (204 women); includes 190 minority (114 Black or African American, non-Hispanic/Latino; 2 American Indian or Alaska Native, non-Hispanic/Latino; 18 Asian, non-Hispanic/Latino; 24 Hispanic/Latino; 1 Native Hawaiian or other Pacific Islander, non-Hispanic/Latino; 31 Two or more races, non-Hispanic/Latino), 19 international. Average age 33. 1,223 applicants, 40% accepted, 242 enrolled. In 2019, 146 master's awarded. *Degree requirements:* For master's, thesis (for some programs). *Entrance requirements:* For master's, minimum undergraduate GPA of 3.0, faculty recommendation, written statement of purpose, writing sample. Additional exam requirements/recommendations for international students: required—TOEFL (minimum score 600 paper-based; 100 iBT). *Application deadline:* For fall admission, 6/1 for domestic students; for spring admission, 11/1 for domestic students. Applications are processed on a rolling basis. Application fee: $50. Electronic applications accepted. *Expenses: Tuition:* Full-time $545; part-time $410 per credit hour. One-time fee: $50. *Financial support:* In 2019–20, 882 students received support. Federal Work-Study and unspecified assistantships available. Financial award applicants required to submit FAFSA. *Unit head:* Dr. Scott Hayes, Residential Dean, E-mail: smhayes@liberty.edu. *Application contact:* Dr. Jay Bridge, Director of OnlineAdmissions, 800-4249505, E-mail: gradadmissions@liberty.edu.
Website: https://www.liberty.edu/communication/

Lindenwood University, Graduate Programs, School of Arts, Media, and Communications, St. Charles, MO 63301-1695. Offers advertising (MA); art history (MA); cinema and media arts (MFA); communications (MA); digital and Web design (MA); fashion and business design (MS); journalism (MA); mass communications (MA); social media and digital content (MS). *Program availability:* Part-time, 100% online. *Faculty:* 20 full-time (5 women), 15 part-time/adjunct (6 women). *Students:* 64 full-time (42 women), 76 part-time (57 women); includes 43 minority (20 Black or African American, non-Hispanic/Latino; 13 Hispanic/Latino; 10 Two or more races, non-Hispanic/Latino), 8 international. Average age 33. 145 applicants, 46% accepted, 56 enrolled. In 2019, 11 master's awarded. *Degree requirements:* For master's, thesis (for some programs), minimum cumulative GPA of 3.0. *Entrance requirements:* For master's, audition or interview, minimum GPA of 3.0, portfolio, letter of recommendation. Additional exam requirements/recommendations for international students: required—TOEFL (minimum score 553 paper-based; 81 iBT); recommended—IELTS (minimum score 6.5). *Application deadline:* For fall admission, 8/9 priority date for domestic students, 6/1 priority date for international students; for spring admission, 12/20 for domestic students, 11/1 priority date for international students; for summer admission, 5/15 priority date for domestic students, 3/27 priority date for international students. Applications are processed on a rolling basis. Application fee: $0 ($100 for international students). Electronic applications accepted. *Expenses: Tuition:* Full-time $8910; part-time $495 per credit. Tuition and fees vary according to course load, degree level and program. *Financial support:* In 2019–20, 23 students received support. Career-related internships or fieldwork, institutionally sponsored loans, scholarships/grants, tuition waivers (partial), and unspecified assistantships available. Financial award application deadline: 6/30; financial award applicants required to submit FAFSA. *Unit head:* Dr. Jason Lively, Dean, School of Arts, Media, and Communications, 636-949-4164, Fax: 636-949-4910, E-mail: JLively@lindenwood.edu. *Application contact:* Kara Schilli, Assistant Vice President, University Admissions, 636-949-4349, Fax: 636-949-4109, E-mail: adultadmissions@lindenwood.edu.
Website: https://www.lindenwood.edu/academics/academic-schools/school-of-arts-media-and-communications/

Lindenwood University–Belleville, Graduate Programs, Belleville, IL 62226. Offers business administration (MBA); communications (MA), including digital and multimedia, media management, promotions, training and development; counseling (MA); criminal justice administration (MS); education (MA); healthcare administration (MS); human resource management (MS); school administration (MA); teaching (MAT).

Lindsey Wilson College, Louisville Center for Design, Columbia, KY 42728. Offers interactive design (MA). *Program availability:* Online learning.

London Metropolitan University, Graduate Programs, London, United Kingdom. Offers applied psychology (M Sc); architecture (MA); biomedical science (M Sc); blood science (M Sc); cancer pharmacology (M Sc); computer networking and cyber security (M Sc); computing and information systems (M Sc); conference interpreting (MA); counter-terrorism studies (M Sc); creative, digital and professional writing (MA); crime, violence and prevention (M Sc); criminology (M Sc); curating contemporary art (MA); data analytics (M Sc); digital media (MA); early childhood studies (MA); education (MA, Ed D); financial services law, regulation and compliance (LL M); food science (M Sc); forensic psychology (M Sc); health and social care management and policy (M Sc); human nutrition (M Sc); human resource management (MA); human rights and international conflict (MA); information technology (M Sc); intelligence and security studies (M Sc); international oil, gas and energy law (LL M); international relations (MA); interpreting (MA); learning and teaching in higher education (MA); legal practice (LL M); media and entertainment law (LL M); organizational and consumer psychology (M Sc); psychological therapy (M Sc); psychology of mental health (M Sc); public health (M Sc); public policy and management (MPA); security studies (M Sc); social work (M Sc); spatial planning and urban design (MA); sports therapy (M Sc); supporting older children and young people with dyslexia (MA); teaching languages (MA), including Arabic, English; translation (MA); woman and child abuse (MA).

Long Island University - Post, College of Arts, Communications and Design, Brookville, NY 11548-1300. Offers art (MA); clinical art therapy (MA); clinical art therapy and counseling (MA); digital game design and development (MA); fine arts and design (MFA); interactive multimedia arts (MA); museum studies (MA); music (MA); theatre (MFA). *Degree requirements:* For master's, variable foreign language requirement, comprehensive exam (for some programs), thesis. *Entrance requirements:* For master's, performance audition or portfolio. Additional exam requirements/recommendations for international students: required—TOEFL (minimum score 550 paper-based; 79 iBT). Electronic applications accepted.

Louisiana State University and Agricultural & Mechanical College, Graduate School, College of Engineering, Program in Digital Media Arts and Engineering, Baton Rouge, LA 70803. Offers M Sc. *Entrance requirements:* For master's, GRE, digital portfolio.

Lynn University, Eugene M. and Christine E. Lynn College of Communication and Design, Boca Raton, FL 33431-5598. Offers communication and media (MS); digital media (Certificate); digital media and design (MS); graphic and Web design (MFA); visual effects animation (MFA). *Program availability:* Part-time, evening/weekend. *Faculty:* 17 full-time (6 women), 3 part-time/adjunct (2 women). *Students:* 28 full-time (15 women), 32 part-time (16 women); includes 15 minority (8 Black or African American, non-Hispanic/Latino; 6 Hispanic/Latino; 1 Two or more races, non-Hispanic/Latino), 19 international. Average age 28. 36 applicants, 92% accepted, 20 enrolled. In 2019, 30 master's awarded. *Degree requirements:* For master's, thesis (for some programs), completion of degree in four calendar years; minimum cumulative GPA of 3.0 and C grade or higher in each course; orientation seminar (one credit); 36 credits of foundation and specialization or a thesis. *Entrance requirements:* For master's, Bachelor's degree from accredited institution, minimum undergraduate GPA of 3.0, official undergraduate transcripts, letter of recommendation from academic or professional source, writing sample demonstrating capacity to perform at graduate level. Additional exam requirements/recommendations for international students: required—TOEFL (minimum score 550 paper-based; 80 iBT), IELTS (minimum score 6.5). *Application deadline:* For fall admission, 8/10 for domestic students, 7/31 for international students; for spring admission, 12/18 for domestic students, 12/2 for international students; for summer admission, 4/12 for domestic students, 4/2 for international students. Applications are processed on a rolling basis. Application fee: $45. Electronic applications accepted. *Expenses:* $740.00 per hour. *Financial support:* In 2019–20, 15 students received support. Career-related internships or fieldwork, Federal Work-Study, scholarships/grants, tuition waivers (full and partial), and unspecified assistantships available. Support available to part-time students. Financial award application deadline: 3/1; financial award applicants required to submit FAFSA. *Unit head:* Dr. David L. Jaffe, Dean, 561-237-7099, Fax: 561-237-7097, E-mail: djaffe@lynn.edu. *Application contact:* Steven Pruitt, Director of Graduate Admission, 561-237-7834, Fax: 561-237-7100, E-mail: admission@lynn.edu.
Website: https://www.lynn.edu/academics/colleges-schools/communication-and-design

Minneapolis College of Art and Design, Master of Arts in Graphic and Web Design, Minneapolis, MN 55404-4347. Offers MA. *Program availability:* Part-time, evening/weekend. *Students:* 22 applicants, 82% accepted, 14 enrolled. *Entrance requirements:* For master's, No exams are required for the MA in Graphic and Web Design, MA students must hold an undergraduate degree before enrolling. Other admissions requirements can be found online here: https://mcad.edu/admissions-and-aid/master-of-arts/application-checklist. Additional exam requirements/recommendations for international students: required—TOEFL (minimum score 550 paper-based; 79 iBT), IELTS (minimum score 6.5), MCAD also accepts the Duolingo Exam for English Language requirement. A score of 100 or higher is required. *Application deadline:* For fall admission, 4/1 priority date for domestic and international students; for spring admission, 11/1 priority date for domestic and international students. Applications are processed on a rolling basis. Application fee: $50. Electronic applications accepted. *Expenses: Tuition:* Full-time $41,344. *Required fees:* $450. One-time fee: $300 full-time. *Financial support:* Career-related internships or fieldwork available. Support available to part-time students. Financial award application deadline: 3/15; financial award applicants required to submit FAFSA. *Unit head:* Lafe Smith, Director, Master of Arts in Graphic and Web Design, E-mail: lsmith257@mcad.edu. *Application contact:* Mary Kazura, Director of Admissions, 612-874-3668, E-mail: mkazura@mcad.edu.
Website: https://mcad.edu/academic-programs/graphic-and-web-design

Montclair State University, The Graduate School, Feliciano School of Business, General MBA Program, Montclair, NJ 07043-1624. Offers accounting (MBA); business analytics (MBA); digital marketing (MBA); finance (MBA); general business administration (MBA); human resources management (MBA); management (MBA); management of information and technology (MBA); marketing (MBA); project management (MBA). *Program availability:* Part-time, evening/weekend. *Degree requirements:* For master's, culminating experience. *Entrance requirements:* For master's, GMAT or GRE General Test, 2 letters of recommendation, resume, essay. Additional exam requirements/recommendations for international students: required—TOEFL (minimum score 83 iBT), IELTS (minimum score 6.5). Electronic applications accepted.

Mount Mary University, Graduate Programs, Program in English, Milwaukee, WI 53222-4597. Offers creative writing (MA); professional and new media writing (MA). *Program availability:* Part-time, evening/weekend. *Degree requirements:* For master's, comprehensive exam, thesis or alternative. *Entrance requirements:* For master's, minimum GPA of 2.75. Additional exam requirements/recommendations for international students: required—TOEFL (minimum score 550 paper-based; 80 iBT); recommended—IELTS (minimum score 6.5). Electronic applications accepted. *Expenses:* Contact institution.

National University, School of Professional Studies, La Jolla, CA 92037-1011. Offers criminal justice (MCJ); digital cinema production (MFA); digital journalism (MA);

homeland security and emergency management (MS); juvenile justice (MS); professional screenwriting (MFA); public administration (MPA), including human resource management, organizational leadership. *Program availability:* Part-time, evening/weekend, 100% online, blended/hybrid learning. *Degree requirements:* For master's, thesis (for some programs). *Entrance requirements:* For master's, interview, minimum GPA of 2.5. Additional exam requirements/recommendations for international students: required—TOEFL (minimum score 550 paper-based; 79 iBT), IELTS (minimum score 6). Electronic applications accepted. *Expenses: Tuition:* Full-time $442; part-time $442 per unit.

New Mexico Highlands University, Graduate Studies, College of Arts and Sciences, Department of Computer Sciences, Las Vegas, NM 87701. Offers media arts and computer science (MS), including computer science. *Degree requirements:* For master's, comprehensive exam, thesis. *Entrance requirements:* For master's, minimum undergraduate GPA of 3.0. Additional exam requirements/recommendations for international students: required—TOEFL (minimum score 540 paper-based).

The New School, Parsons School of Design, Program in Communication Design, New York, NY 10011. Offers MPS. *Program availability:* Part-time. *Faculty:* 2 full-time (0 women), 5 part-time/adjunct (3 women). *Students:* 15 full-time (13 women); includes 2 minority (both Asian, non-Hispanic/Latino), 13 international. Average age 25. 129 applicants, 23% accepted, 14 enrolled. In 2019, 14 master's awarded. *Degree requirements:* For master's, thesis or alternative. *Entrance requirements:* For master's, transcripts, resume, statement of purpose, recommendation letters, portfolio. Additional exam requirements/recommendations for international students: required—TOEFL (minimum score 92 iBT), IELTS (minimum score 7), PTE (minimum score 63). *Application deadline:* For fall admission, 1/1 priority date for domestic and international students. Applications are processed on a rolling basis. Application fee: $50. Electronic applications accepted. *Expenses:* 1810 per credit. *Financial support:* In 2019–20, 11 students received support, including 11 research assistantships (averaging $2,541 per year), 1 teaching assistantship (averaging $4,682 per year); career-related internships or fieldwork, Federal Work-Study, and scholarships/grants also available. Support available to part-time students. Financial award application deadline: 2/1; financial award applicants required to submit FAFSA. *Unit head:* Brendan Griffiths, Program Director, 212-229-8900 Ext. 1544, E-mail: brendan@newschool.edu. *Application contact:* Simone Varadian, Senior Director, 212-229-5150 Ext. 4117, E-mail: thinkparsonsgrad@newschool.edu.
Website: https://www.newschool.edu/parsons/mps-communication-design/

New York University, Tandon School of Engineering, Department of Technology, Culture and Society, New York, NY 10012-1019. Offers integrated digital media (MS). *Program availability:* Part-time, evening/weekend. *Degree requirements:* For master's, comprehensive exam (for some programs), thesis (for some programs). *Entrance requirements:* Additional exam requirements/recommendations for international students: required—TOEFL (minimum score 550 paper-based; 90 iBT); recommended—IELTS (minimum score 7). Electronic applications accepted. *Expenses:* Contact institution.

New York University, Tisch School of the Arts, Interactive Telecommunications Program, Brooklyn, NY 11201. Offers MPS. *Program availability:* Part-time, evening/weekend. *Degree requirements:* For master's, thesis, 60 graduate level credits including thesis. *Entrance requirements:* For master's, online application, personal statement, resume, 2 letters of recommendation, official transcripts showing a bachelor's degree, language score TOEFL or IELTS, 1 minute introductory video, optional group interview. Additional exam requirements/recommendations for international students: required—They can waive the language test if they grew up in an English speaking country or completed a 4 year bachelor's degree in an English speaking college/university; recommended—TOEFL (minimum score 100 iBT), IELTS (minimum score 7), TSE. Electronic applications accepted.

Northeastern University, College of Professional Studies, Boston, MA 02115-5096. Offers applied nutrition (MS); college athletics administration (MSL); commerce and economic development (MS); corporate and organizational communication (MS); criminal justice (MS); digital media (MPS); elearning and instructional design (M Ed); elementary education (MAT); geographic information technology (MPS); global studies and international relations (MS); higher education administration (M Ed); homeland security (MA); human services (MS); informatics (MPS); leadership (MS); learning analytics (M Ed); learning and instruction (M Ed); nonprofit management (MS); professional sports administration (MSL); project management (MS); regulatory affairs for drugs, biologics, and medical devices (MS); respiratory care leadership (MS); special education (M Ed); technical communication (MS). *Program availability:* Part-time, evening/weekend, 100% online, blended/hybrid learning. *Faculty:* 85 full-time (53 women), 892 part-time/adjunct (379 women). *Students:* 5,699 part-time (3,305 women). In 2019, 1,787 master's awarded. *Application deadline:* Applications are processed on a rolling basis. Application fee: $0. Electronic applications accepted. *Expenses:* Contact institution. *Financial support:* Applicants required to submit FAFSA. *Unit head:* Dr. Mary Loeffelholz, Dean of the College of Professional Studies, 617-373-6060. *Application contact:* Dr. Mary Loeffelholz, Dean of the College of Professional Studies, 617-373-6060.
Website: https://cps.northeastern.edu/

Northwestern University, School of Professional Studies, Program in Information Systems, Evanston, IL 60208. Offers analytics and business intelligence (MS); database and Internet technologies (MS); information systems (MS); information systems management (MS); information systems security (MS); medical informatics (MS); software project management and development (MS). *Program availability:* Part-time, evening/weekend.

The Ohio State University, Graduate School, College of Arts and Sciences, Division of Arts and Humanities, Department of Design, Columbus, OH 43210. Offers design (MA); design research and development (MFA); digital animation and interactive media (MFA). *Accreditation:* NASAD. *Program availability:* Part-time. *Entrance requirements:* For master's, GRE General Test (for all applicants with cumulative GPA below 3.0), portfolio. Additional exam requirements/recommendations for international students: recommended—TOEFL (minimum score 550 paper-based; 79 iBT). Electronic applications accepted.

Ohio University, Graduate College, Scripps College of Communication, School of Visual Communication, Athens, OH 45701-2979. Offers MA. *Entrance requirements:* For master's, minimum GPA of 2.5, portfolio. Additional exam requirements/recommendations for international students: required—TOEFL (minimum score 600 paper-based; 100 iBT) or IELTS (minimum score 7). Electronic applications accepted.

Pace University, Lubin School of Business, Marketing Program, New York, NY 10038. Offers customer intelligence & analytics (MS); marketing management (MBA); social media and mobile marketing (MS). *Program availability:* Part-time, evening/weekend. *Entrance requirements:* For master's, GMAT, GRE, undergraduate degree, transcripts from all accredited colleges/universities attended, 2 letters of recommendation, resume, personal statement. For 1 year fast track MBA in Marketing Management, must have a cumulative GPA of 3.30 or above, a grade of B or better for all business core courses from an AACSB-accredited U.S. business school. Additional exam requirements/

recommendations for international students: required—TOEFL (minimum score 90 iBT), IELTS (minimum score 7) or PTE (minimum score 61). Electronic applications accepted.

Pratt Institute, School of Art, Program in Digital Arts, Brooklyn, NY 11205-3899. Offers MFA, MS/MFA. *Accreditation:* NASAD. *Students:* 53 full-time (41 women), 10 part-time (5 women); includes 6 minority (3 Asian, non-Hispanic/Latino; 3 Hispanic/Latino), 51 international. Average age 24. 259 applicants, 36% accepted, 25 enrolled. In 2019, 14 master's awarded. *Degree requirements:* For master's, thesis, exhibit. *Entrance requirements:* For master's, portfolio or video, letters of recommendation. Additional exam requirements/recommendations for international students: required—TOEFL (minimum score 550 paper-based; 79 iBT). *Application deadline:* For fall admission, 1/5 for domestic and international students; for spring admission, 10/1 for domestic and international students. Application fee: $50 ($90 for international students). Electronic applications accepted. *Expenses: Tuition:* Full-time $33,246; part-time $1847 per credit. *Required fees:* $1980. *Financial support:* Career-related internships or fieldwork, Federal Work-Study, institutionally sponsored loans, scholarships/grants, health care benefits, and unspecified assistantships available. Support available to part-time students. Financial award application deadline: 2/1; financial award applicants required to submit FAFSA. *Unit head:* Peter Patchen, Chair, 718-636-3693, Fax: 718-399-4494, E-mail: ppatchen@pratt.edu. *Application contact:* Natalie Capannelli, Director of Graduate Admissions, 718-636-3551, Fax: 718-399-4242, E-mail: ncapanne@pratt.edu. Website: https://www.pratt.edu/academics/school-of-art/graduate-school-of-art/digital-arts-grad/

Quinnipiac University, School of Communications, Program in Interactive Media and Communications, Hamden, CT 06518-1940. Offers interactive media (MS); media design (MS); social media (MS); UX design (MS). *Program availability:* Part-time, evening/weekend, online only, 100% online. *Entrance requirements:* For master's, minimum GPA of 3.0, portfolio or writing sample. Additional exam requirements/recommendations for international students: required—TOEFL (minimum score 575 paper-based; 90 iBT), IELTS (minimum score 6.5). Electronic applications accepted. *Expenses:* Contact institution.

Rochester Institute of Technology, Graduate Enrollment Services, College of Imaging Arts and Sciences, School of Design, Advanced Certificate Program in User Experience Design and Development, Rochester, NY 14623-5603. Offers Advanced Certificate. *Program availability:* Part-time, evening/weekend, online only, 100% online. *Entrance requirements:* Additional exam requirements/recommendations for international students: required—TOEFL (minimum score 550 paper-based; 79 iBT), IELTS (minimum score 6.5), PTE (minimum score 58). Electronic applications accepted. *Expenses:* Contact institution.

Rochester Institute of Technology, Graduate Enrollment Services, College of Liberal Arts, School of Communication, Advanced Certificate Program in Communication and Digital Media, Rochester, NY 14623-5603. Offers Advanced Certificate. *Program availability:* Part-time, evening/weekend, online only, 100% online. *Entrance requirements:* For degree, Minimum of 3.0 GPA, personal statement, two letters of reference. Additional exam requirements/recommendations for international students: required—TOEFL (minimum score 570 paper-based; 88 iBT), IELTS (minimum score 6.5), PTE (minimum score 61). Electronic applications accepted. *Expenses:* Contact institution.

Rochester Institute of Technology, Graduate Enrollment Services, Golisano College of Computing and Information Sciences, Information Science and Technologies Department, Advanced Certificate Program in Web Development, Rochester, NY 14623-5603. Offers Advanced Certificate. *Program availability:* Part-time, evening/weekend. *Entrance requirements:* For degree, minimum GPA of 3.0, personal statement, resume, two letters of recommendation. Additional exam requirements/recommendations for international students: required—TOEFL (minimum score 570 paper-based; 88 iBT), IELTS (minimum score 6.5), PTE (minimum score 61). Electronic applications accepted. *Expenses:* Contact institution.

Rocky Mountain College of Art + Design, Program in Education, Leadership + Emerging Technologies, Lakewood, CO 80214. Offers MA. *Accreditation:* NASAD. *Program availability:* Online learning.

Sam Houston State University, College of Fine Arts and Mass Communication, Department of Mass Communication, Huntsville, TX 77341. Offers digital media (MA). *Program availability:* Part-time. *Degree requirements:* For master's, comprehensive exam (for some programs), thesis optional. *Entrance requirements:* For master's, GRE General Test, personal statement, digital media portfolio. Electronic applications accepted.

San Diego State University, Graduate and Research Affairs, College of Professional Studies and Fine Arts, School of Art and Design, San Diego, CA 92182. Offers studio arts (MA, MFA), including applied design, graphic design, interior architecture, multimedia and photography, painting and printmaking, sculpture. *Accreditation:* NASAD (one or more programs are accredited). *Degree requirements:* For master's, variable foreign language requirement, thesis. *Entrance requirements:* For master's, GRE General Test, bachelor's degree in related field, slide portfolio, typed slide information sheet, 2 letters of recommendation. Additional exam requirements/recommendations for international students: required—TOEFL. Electronic applications accepted.

San Diego State University, Graduate and Research Affairs, College of Professional Studies and Fine Arts, School of Communication, San Diego, CA 92182. Offers advertising and public relations (MA); critical-cultural studies (MA); interaction studies (MA); intercultural and international studies (MA); new media studies (MA); news and information studies (MA); telecommunications and media management (MA). *Degree requirements:* For master's, thesis. *Entrance requirements:* For master's, GRE General Test, 3 letters of recommendation. Additional exam requirements/recommendations for international students: required—TOEFL. Electronic applications accepted.

Savannah College of Art and Design, Program in Interactive Design and Game Development, Savannah, GA 31402-3146. Offers MA, MFA. *Program availability:* Part-time, 100% online. *Degree requirements:* For master's, final project (for MA); thesis (for MFA). *Entrance requirements:* For master's, GRE (recommended), portfolio (submitted in digital format), audition or writing submission, resume, statement of purpose, two letters of recommendation. Additional exam requirements/recommendations for international students: recommended—TOEFL (minimum score 550 paper-based; 85 iBT), IELTS (minimum score 6.5). Electronic applications accepted.

School of Visual Arts, Graduate Programs, Interaction Design Department, New York, NY 10010-3994. Offers MFA. *Degree requirements:* For master's, thesis, 60 credits, residency of two academic years, thesis project. *Entrance requirements:* For master's, portfolio, statement of purpose, resume. Additional exam requirements/recommendations for international students: required—TOEFL (minimum score 550 paper-based; 79 iBT). Electronic applications accepted.

School of Visual Arts, Graduate Programs, Program in Photography, Video and Related Media, New York, NY 10010-3994. Offers MFA. *Accreditation:* NASAD. *Degree requirements:* For master's, thesis, 60 credits; minimum GPA of 3.3; thesis project. *Entrance requirements:* For master's, portfolio (still images and/or videos) submitted through SlideRoom. Additional exam requirements/recommendations for international students: required—TOEFL (minimum score 550 paper-based; 79 iBT). Electronic applications accepted.

Southern New Hampshire University, School of Business, Manchester, NH 03106-1045. Offers accounting (MBA, Graduate Certificate); accounting finance (MS); accounting/auditing (MS); accounting/forensic accounting (MS); accounting/management accounting (MS); accounting/taxation (MS); applied economics (MS); athletic administration (MBA, Graduate Certificate); business administration (IMBA, Certificate), including business information systems (Certificate), human resource management (Certificate); business analytics (MBA); business intelligence (MBA); communication (MA), including new media and marketing, public relations; community economic development (MBA); criminal justice (MBA); data analytics (MS); economics (MBA); engineering management (MBA); entrepreneurship (MBA); finance (MBA, MS, Graduate Certificate); finance/corporate finance (MS); finance/investments (MS); forensic accounting (MBA); forensic accounting and fraud examination (Graduate Certificate); healthcare informatics (MBA); healthcare management (MBA); human resource management (MS); human resources (MBA); information technology (MS); information technology management (MBA); international business (PhD); Internet marketing (MBA); leadership (MBA); leadership of nonprofit organizations (Graduate Certificate); management (MS); marketing (MBA, MS, Graduate Certificate); music business (MBA); operations and project management (MS); operations and supply chain management (MBA, Graduate Certificate); organizational leadership (MS); project management (MBA, Graduate Certificate); public administration (MBA, Graduate Certificate); quantitative analysis (MBA); Six Sigma (Graduate Certificate); Six Sigma quality (MBA); social media marketing (MBA, Graduate Certificate); sport management (MBA, MS, Graduate Certificate); sustainability and environmental compliance (MBA); MBA/Certificate. *Accreditation:* ACBSP. *Program availability:* Part-time, evening/weekend, online learning. Terminal master's awarded for partial completion of doctoral program. *Degree requirements:* For master's, one foreign language, comprehensive exam (for some programs), thesis or alternative; for doctorate, one foreign language, comprehensive exam, thesis/dissertation. *Entrance requirements:* For master's, minimum GPA of 2.5; for doctorate, GMAT. Additional exam requirements/recommendations for international students: required—TOEFL (minimum score 500 paper-based). Electronic applications accepted.

State University of New York at Oswego, Graduate Studies, Department of Art, Oswego, NY 13126. Offers art (MA); graphic design and digital media (MA). *Accreditation:* NASAD. *Program availability:* Part-time. *Students:* 4. In 2019, 4 master's awarded. *Degree requirements:* For master's, exhibit, final presentation. *Entrance requirements:* For master's, slides of previous work. Additional exam requirements/recommendations for international students: required—TOEFL (minimum score 560 paper-based). *Application deadline:* For fall admission, 4/1 for domestic students; for spring admission, 10/1 for domestic students. Applications are processed on a rolling basis. Application fee: $65. Electronic applications accepted. *Financial support:* Teaching assistantships with full and partial tuition reimbursements, career-related internships or fieldwork, Federal Work-Study, institutionally sponsored loans, scholarships/grants, health care benefits, tuition waivers (partial), and unspecified assistantships available. Support available to part-time students. Financial award application deadline: 4/1; financial award applicants required to submit FAFSA. *Unit head:* Kelly Roe, Chair, 315-312-2850, E-mail: kelly.roe@oswego.edu. *Application contact:* Juan Perdiguero, Program Coordinator, 315-312-3240, E-mail: juan.perdiguero@oswego.edu.
Website: http://www.oswego.edu/academics/colleges_and_departments/departments/art.html

Stonehill College, Program in Integrated Marketing Communications, Easton, MA 02357. Offers MA.

Texas Woman's University, Graduate School, College of Arts and Sciences, School of the Arts, Department of Visual Arts, Denton, TX 76204. Offers art (MA, MAT, MFA), including art education (MA, MAT), art history (MA), ceramics (MFA), graphic design (MA), intermedia (MFA), painting (MFA), photography (MFA), sculpture (MFA). *Faculty:* 6 full-time (5 women). *Students:* 13 full-time (9 women), 8 part-time (5 women); includes 5 minority (1 Asian, non-Hispanic/Latino; 3 Hispanic/Latino; 1 Two or more races, non-Hispanic/Latino), 1 international. Average age 36. 15 applicants, 80% accepted, 9 enrolled. In 2019, 8 master's awarded. *Degree requirements:* For master's, comprehensive exam, thesis (for some programs), exhibit (MFA), oral exam, thesis or professional paper (MA). *Entrance requirements:* For master's, portfolio, interview, current curriculum vitae, letter of intent, 3 letters of recommendation, artist statement, separate application. Additional exam requirements/recommendations for international students: required—TOEFL (minimum score 79 iBT); recommended—IELTS (minimum score 6.5), TSE (minimum score 53). *Application deadline:* For fall admission, 2/15 for domestic and international students; for spring admission, 11/15 for domestic and international students. Application fee: $50 ($75 for international students). Electronic applications accepted. *Expenses: Tuition, area resident:* Full-time $4973.40; part-time $276.30 per semester hour. Tuition, state resident: full-time $4973.40; part-time $276.30 per semester hour. Tuition, nonresident: full-time $12,569; part-time $698.30 per semester hour. *International tuition:* $12,569.40 full-time. *Required fees:* $2524.30. Tuition and fees vary according to course level, course load, degree level and program. *Financial support:* In 2019–20, 15 students received support, including 12 teaching assistantships (averaging $4,968 per year); career-related internships or fieldwork, scholarships/grants, health care benefits, and unspecified assistantships also available. Support available to part-time students. Financial award application deadline: 3/1; financial award applicants required to submit FAFSA. *Unit head:* Dr. Vagner Whitehead, Chair, 940-898-2530, Fax: 940-898-2496, E-mail: visualarts@twu.edu. *Application contact:* Korie Hawkins, Associate Director of Admissions, Graduate Recruitment, 940-898-3188, Fax: 940-898-3081, E-mail: admissions@twu.edu.
Website: http://www.twu.edu/visual-arts/

Thomas Jefferson University, Kanbar College of Design, Engineering and Commerce, Program in User Experience and Interaction Design, Philadelphia, PA 19107. Offers MS. *Entrance requirements:* For master's, portfolio. Additional exam requirements/recommendations for international students: required—TOEFL (minimum score 550 paper-based; 79 iBT). Electronic applications accepted.

Touro College, Graduate School of Technology, New York, NY 10001. Offers information systems (MS); instructional technology (MS); Web and multimedia design (MA). *Program availability:* Part-time, evening/weekend, 100% online, blended/hybrid learning. *Faculty:* 9 full-time (1 woman), 25 part-time/adjunct (10 women). *Students:* 136 full-time (52 women), 34 part-time (15 women); includes 99 minority (22 Black or African American, non-Hispanic/Latino; 55 Asian, non-Hispanic/Latino; 22 Hispanic/Latino), 61 international. Average age 34. 54 applicants, 93% accepted, 29 enrolled. In 2019, 46 master's awarded. *Degree requirements:* For master's, thesis. *Entrance requirements:* Additional exam requirements/recommendations for international students: required—TOEFL (minimum score 80 paper-based), IELTS (minimum score 6), PTE (minimum score 58). *Application deadline:* For fall admission, 8/15 for domestic students, 7/15 for international students; for spring admission, 1/10 for domestic students, 12/15 for international students; for summer admission, 5/28 for domestic students. Applications are processed on a rolling basis. Application fee: $50. Electronic applications accepted. *Financial support:* Federal Work-Study, scholarships/grants, and unspecified assistantships available. Financial award applicants required to submit FAFSA. *Unit head:* Robert Grosberg, Executive Director of Administration, 202-463-0400 Ext. 55496, E-mail: robert.grosberg@touro.edu. *Application contact:* James David Shafer, Director of Marketing and Recruiting, 212-463-0400 Ext. 55585, E-mail: james.shafer@touro.edu.
Website: http://www.touro.edu/gst/

Towson University, College of Fine Arts and Communication, Program in Interactive Media Design, Towson, MD 21252-0001. Offers Postbaccalaureate Certificate. *Program availability:* Online learning. *Students:* 11 part-time (8 women); includes 4 minority (1 Black or African American, non-Hispanic/Latino; 2 Asian, non-Hispanic/Latino; 1 Two or more races, non-Hispanic/Latino). *Entrance requirements:* For degree, minimum GPA of 3.0; resume; letter of intent; bachelor's degree in art or art education, or a bachelor's degree in another discipline with a minimum of 9 credits of course work in studio art and/or professional experience working in the field of art education or graphic design. *Application deadline:* For fall admission, 1/17 for domestic students, 5/15 for international students; for spring admission, 10/15 for domestic students, 12/1 for international students. Applications are processed on a rolling basis. Application fee: $45. Electronic applications accepted. *Expenses: Tuition, area resident:* Full-time $7920; part-time $439 per credit. Tuition, nonresident: full-time $16,344; part-time $908 per credit. *International tuition:* $16,344 full-time. *Required fees:* $2628; $146 per credit. $876 per term. *Unit head:* Prof. Bridget Sullivan, Program Director, 410-704-2802, E-mail: bsullivan@towson.edu. *Application contact:* Coverley Beidleman, Assistant Director of Graduate Admissions, 410-704-5630, Fax: 410-704-3030, E-mail: grads@towson.edu.
Website: https://www.towson.edu/cofac/departments/art/grad/interactivemediadesign/

Towson University, Jess and Mildred Fisher College of Science and Mathematics, Program in Applied Information Technology, Towson, MD 21252-0001. Offers applied information technology (MS); Internet application development (Postbaccalaureate Certificate). *Students:* 79 full-time (33 women), 126 part-time (43 women); includes 113 minority (77 Black or African American, non-Hispanic/Latino; 23 Asian, non-Hispanic/Latino; 5 Hispanic/Latino; 8 Two or more races, non-Hispanic/Latino), 36 international. *Entrance requirements:* For master's and Postbaccalaureate Certificate, bachelor's degree, minimum GPA of 3.0. Additional exam requirements/recommendations for international students: required—TOEFL. *Application deadline:* For fall admission, 1/17 for domestic students, 5/15 for international students; for spring admission, 10/15 for domestic students, 12/1 for international students. Applications are processed on a rolling basis. Application fee: $45. Electronic applications accepted. *Expenses: Tuition, area resident:* Full-time $7920; part-time $439 per credit. Tuition, nonresident: full-time $16,344; part-time $908 per credit. *International tuition:* $16,344 full-time. *Required fees:* $2628; $146 per credit. $876 per term. *Unit head:* Dr. Suranjan Charkraborty, Graduate Program Director, 410-704-4769, E-mail: ait@towson.edu. *Application contact:* Coverley Beidleman, Assistant Director of Graduate Admissions, 410-704-5630, Fax: 410-704-3030, E-mail: cbeidleman@towson.edu.
Website: https://www.towson.edu/fcsm/departments/emergingtech/

Universidad Autonoma de Guadalajara, Graduate Programs, Guadalajara, Mexico. Offers administrative law and justice (LL M); advertising and corporate communications (MA); architecture (M Arch); business (MBA); computational science (MCC); education (Ed M, Ed D); English-Spanish translation (MA); entrepreneurship and management (MBA); integrated management of digital animation (MA); international business (MIB); international corporate law (LL M); Internet technologies (MS); manufacturing systems (MMS); occupational health (MS); philosophy (MA, PhD); power electronics (MS); quality systems (MQS); renewable energy (MS); social evaluation of projects (MBA); strategic market research (MBA); tax law (MA); teaching mathematics (MA).

University of Advancing Technology, Master of Science Program in Technology, Tempe, AZ 85283-1042. Offers advancing computer science (MS); emerging technologies (MS); game production and management (MS); information assurance (MS); technology leadership (MS). *Degree requirements:* For master's, project or thesis. *Entrance requirements:* Additional exam requirements/recommendations for international students: required—TOEFL (minimum score 550 paper-based). Electronic applications accepted.

The University of British Columbia, Faculty of Arts, Center for Digital Media, Vancouver, BC V6T 1Z1, Canada. Offers MDM.

University of California, Santa Cruz, Jack Baskin School of Engineering, Department of Computational Media, Santa Cruz, CA 95064. Offers computational media (MS, PhD); games and playable media (MS). *Faculty:* 14 full-time (4 women), 5 part-time/adjunct (1 woman). *Students:* 108 full-time (35 women); includes 24 minority (2 Black or African American, non-Hispanic/Latino; 17 Asian, non-Hispanic/Latino; 4 Hispanic/Latino; 1 Native Hawaiian or other Pacific Islander, non-Hispanic/Latino), 57 international. 180 applicants, 67% accepted, 56 enrolled. In 2019, 8 master's, 1 doctorate awarded. Terminal master's awarded for partial completion of doctoral program. *Degree requirements:* For master's, thesis, Capstone project or research project with written report; for doctorate, thesis/dissertation. *Entrance requirements:* Additional exam requirements/recommendations for international students: required—TOEFL (minimum score 570 paper-based; 89 iBT), IELTS (minimum score 8), Non-native speakers must submit either TOEFL or IELTS scores. *Application deadline:* For fall admission, 1/10 for domestic and international students. Application fee: $120 ($140 for international students). Electronic applications accepted. *Financial support:* In 2019–20, 64 students received support, including 23 fellowships (averaging $12,023 per year), 15 research assistantships (averaging $8,092 per year), 47 teaching assistantships (averaging $21,909 per year); institutionally sponsored loans also available. Financial award application deadline: 1/10; financial award applicants required to submit FAFSA. *Unit head:* Dr. Sri Kurniawan, Professor and Department Chair, E-mail: skurnia@ucsc.edu. *Application contact:* Emily Jackson, Graduate Advisor, 831-459-3531, E-mail: bsoe-ga@rt.ucsc.edu.
Website: https://grad.soe.ucsc.edu/computational-media

University of Chicago, Division of the Humanities, Program in Digital Studies of Language, Culture, and History, Chicago, IL 60637-1513. Offers MA. *Entrance requirements:* For master's, BA in the humanities, arts, or history.

University of Colorado Boulder, Graduate School, College of Media, Communication and Information, Program in Intermedia Art, Writing and Performance, Boulder, CO 80309. Offers PhD. Electronic applications accepted. Application fee is waived when completed online.

University of Miami, Graduate School, College of Arts and Sciences, Department of Art and Art History, Coral Gables, FL 33124. Offers art history (MA); ceramics/glass (MFA); graphic design/multimedia (MFA); painting (MFA); photography/digital imaging (MFA); printmaking (MFA); sculpture (MFA). *Program availability:* Part-time. *Degree requirements:* For master's, variable foreign language requirement, thesis, exhibit (MFA), comprehensive exam (MA). *Entrance requirements:* For master's, GRE General Test (MA), research paper (MA), slide portfolio (MFA). Additional exam requirements/recommendations for international students: required—TOEFL. Electronic applications accepted.

University of Montana, Graduate School, College of Visual and Performing Arts, School of Media Arts, Missoula, MT 59812. Offers digital filmmaking (MFA); integrated digital media (MFA).

University of North Texas, Toulouse Graduate School, Denton, TX 76203-5459. Offers accounting (MS); applied anthropology (MA, MS); applied behavior analysis (Certificate); applied geography (MA); applied technology and performance improvement (M Ed, MS); art education (MA); art history (MA); arts leadership (Certificate); audiology (Au D); behavior analysis (MS); behavioral science (PhD); biochemistry and molecular biology (MS); biology (MA, MS); biomedical engineering (MS); business analysis (MS); chemistry (MS); clinical health psychology (PhD); communication studies (MA, MS); computer engineering (MS); computer science (MS); counseling (M Ed, MS), including clinical mental health counseling (MS), college and university counseling, elementary school counseling, secondary school counseling; creative writing (MA); criminal justice (MS); curriculum and instruction (M Ed); decision sciences (MBA); design (MA, MFA), including fashion design (MFA), innovation studies, interior design (MFA); early childhood studies (MS); economics (MS); educational leadership (M Ed, Ed D); educational psychology (MS, PhD), including family studies (MS), gifted and talented (MS), human development (MS), learning and cognition (MS), research, measurement and evaluation (MS); electrical engineering (MS); emergency management (MPA); engineering technology (MS); English (MA); English as a second language (MA); environmental science (MS); finance (MBA, MS); financial management (MPA); French (MA); health services management (MBA); higher education (M Ed, Ed D); history (MA, MS); hospitality management (MS); human resources management (MPA); information science (MS); information systems (PhD); information technologies (MBA); interdisciplinary studies (MA, MS); international studies (MA); international sustainable tourism (MS); jazz studies (MM); journalism (MA, MJ, Graduate Certificate), including interactive and virtual digital communication (Graduate Certificate), narrative journalism (Graduate Certificate), public relations (Graduate Certificate); kinesiology (MS); linguistics (MA); local government management (MPA); logistics (PhD); logistics and supply chain management (MBA); long-term care, senior housing, and aging services (MA); management (PhD); marketing (MBA); mathematics (MA, MS); mechanical and energy engineering (MS, PhD); music (MA), including ethnomusicology, music theory, musicology, performance; music composition (PhD); music education (MM Ed, PhD); nonprofit management (MPA); operations and supply chain management (MBA); performance (MM, DMA); philosophy (MA); political science (MA); professional and technical communication (MA); radio, television and film (MA, MFA); rehabilitation counseling (Certificate); sociology (MA); Spanish (MA); special education (M Ed); speech-language pathology (MA); strategic management (MBA); studio art (MFA); teaching (M Ed); MBA/MS. *Program availability:* Part-time, evening/weekend, online learning. Terminal master's awarded for partial completion of doctoral program. *Degree requirements:* For master's, variable foreign language requirement, comprehensive exam (for some programs), thesis (for some programs); for doctorate, variable foreign language requirement, comprehensive exam (for some programs), thesis/dissertation; for other advanced degree, variable foreign language requirement, comprehensive exam (for some programs). *Entrance requirements:* For master's and doctorate, GRE, GMAT. Additional exam requirements/recommendations for international students: required—TOEFL (minimum score 550 paper-based; 79 iBT). Electronic applications accepted.

University of Pennsylvania, Stuart Weitzman School of Design, Department of Fine Arts, Philadelphia, PA 19104. Offers emerging design and research (Certificate); fine arts (MFA); time-based and interactive media (Certificate). *Faculty:* 7 full-time (3 women), 1 part-time/adjunct (0 women). *Students:* 34 full-time (19 women), 1 (woman) part-time; includes 11 minority (3 Black or African American, non-Hispanic/Latino; 2 Asian, non-Hispanic/Latino; 4 Hispanic/Latino; 2 Two or more races, non-Hispanic/Latino), 10 international. Average age 27. 88 applicants, 48% accepted, 17 enrolled. In 2019, 11 master's, 3 other advanced degrees awarded. *Application deadline:* Applications are processed on a rolling basis. Application fee: $80. Electronic applications accepted. *Financial support:* In 2019–20, 30 students received support, including teaching assistantships (averaging $6,000 per year); fellowships with full tuition reimbursements available, research assistantships, Federal Work-Study, scholarships/grants, health care benefits, and unspecified assistantships also available. Financial award applicants required to submit FAFSA. *Application contact:* Joan Weston, Director of Admissions & Financial Aid, 215-898-6520, E-mail: weston@design.upenn.edu.
Website: http://www.design.upenn.edu/mfa

University of Southern California, Graduate School, School of Cinematic Arts, Interactive Media and Games Division, Los Angeles, CA 90089. Offers interactive media (MFA). *Degree requirements:* For master's, thesis, thesis project. *Entrance requirements:* Additional exam requirements/recommendations for international students: required—TOEFL (minimum score 600 paper-based; 100 iBT). Electronic applications accepted. *Expenses:* Contact institution.

University of Southern California, Graduate School, Viterbi School of Engineering, Department of Computer Science, Los Angeles, CA 90089. Offers computer networks (MS); computer science (MS, PhD); computer security (MS); game development (MS); high performance computing and simulations (MS); human language technology (MS); intelligent robotics (MS); multimedia and creative technologies (MS); software engineering (MS). *Program availability:* Part-time, evening/weekend, online learning. *Entrance requirements:* For master's and doctorate, GRE General Test. Additional exam requirements/recommendations for international students: required—TOEFL. Electronic applications accepted.

University of Southern California, Graduate School, Viterbi School of Engineering, Ming Hsieh Department of Electrical Engineering, Los Angeles, CA 90089. Offers computer engineering (MS, PhD); electric power (MS); electrical engineering (MS, PhD, Engr); engineering technology commercialization (Graduate Certificate); multimedia and creative technologies (MS); telecommunications (MS); VLSI design (MS); wireless health technology (MS). *Program availability:* Part-time, online learning. Terminal master's awarded for partial completion of doctoral program. *Degree requirements:* For master's, thesis optional; for doctorate, thesis/dissertation. *Entrance requirements:* For master's and doctorate, GRE General Test. Additional exam requirements/recommendations for international students: recommended—TOEFL. Electronic applications accepted.

University of South Florida, Innovative Education, Tampa, FL 33620-9951. Offers adult, career and higher education (Graduate Certificate), including college teaching, leadership in developing human resources, leadership in higher education; Africana studies (Graduate Certificate), including diasporas and health disparities, genocide and human rights; aging studies (Graduate Certificate), including gerontology; art research (Graduate Certificate), including museum studies; business foundations (Graduate Certificate); chemical and biomedical engineering (Graduate Certificate), including materials science and engineering, water, health and sustainability; child and family studies (Graduate Certificate), including positive behavior support; civil and industrial engineering (Graduate Certificate), including transportation systems analysis; community and family health (Graduate Certificate), including maternal and child health, social marketing and public health, violence and injury: prevention and intervention, women's health; criminology (Graduate Certificate), including criminal justice administration; data science for public administration (Graduate Certificate); digital humanities (Graduate Certificate); educational measurement and research (Graduate Certificate), including evaluation; English (Graduate Certificate), including comparative literary studies, creative writing, professional and technical communication; entrepreneurship (Graduate Certificate); environmental health (Graduate Certificate), including safety management; epidemiology and biostatistics (Graduate Certificate), including applied biostatistics, biostatistics, concepts and tools of epidemiology, epidemiology, epidemiology of infectious diseases; geography, environment and planning (Graduate Certificate), including community development, environmental policy and management, geographical information systems; geology (Graduate Certificate), including hydrogeology; global health (Graduate Certificate), including disaster management, global health and Latin American and Caribbean studies, global health practice, humanitarian assistance, infection control; government and international affairs (Graduate Certificate), including Cuban studies, globalization studies; health policy and management (Graduate Certificate), including health management and leadership, public health policy and programs; hearing specialist: early intervention (Graduate Certificate); industrial and management systems engineering (Graduate Certificate), including systems engineering, technology management; information studies (Graduate Certificate), including school library media specialist; information systems/decision sciences (Graduate Certificate), including analytics and business intelligence; instructional technology (Graduate Certificate), including distance education, Florida digital/virtual educator, instructional design, multimedia design, Web design; internal medicine, bioethics and medical humanities (Graduate Certificate), including biomedical ethics; Latin American and Caribbean studies (Graduate Certificate); leadership for coastal resiliency planning (Graduate Certificate); mass communications (Graduate Certificate), including multimedia journalism; mathematics and statistics (Graduate Certificate), including mathematics; medicine (Graduate Certificate), including aging and neuroscience, bioinformatics, biotechnology, brain fitness and memory management, clinical investigation, hand and upper limb rehabilitation, health informatics, health sciences, integrative weight management, intellectual property, medicine and gender, metabolic and nutritional medicine, metabolic cardiology, pharmacy sciences; national and competitive intelligence (Graduate Certificate); nursing (Graduate Certificate), including simulation based academic fellowship in advanced pain management; psychological and social foundations (Graduate Certificate), including career counseling, college teaching, diversity in education, mental health counseling, school counseling; public affairs (Graduate Certificate), including nonprofit management, public management, research administration; public health (Graduate Certificate), including assessing chemical toxicity and public health risks, health equity, pharmacoepidemiology, public health generalist, toxicology, translational research in adolescent behavioral health; public health practices (Graduate Certificate), including planning for healthy communities; rehabilitation and mental health counseling (Graduate Certificate), including integrative mental health care, marriage and family therapy, rehabilitation technology; secondary education (Graduate Certificate), including ESOL, foreign language education: culture and content, foreign language education: professional; social work (Graduate Certificate), including geriatric social work/clinical gerontology; special education (Graduate Certificate), including autism spectrum disorder, disabilities education: severe/profound; world languages (Graduate Certificate), including teaching English as a second language (TESL) or foreign language. *Unit head:* Dr. Cynthia DeLuca, Associate Vice President and Assistant Vice Provost, 813-974-3077, Fax: 813-974-7061, E-mail: deluca@usf.edu. *Application contact:* Owen Hooper, Director, Summer and Alternative Calendar Programs, 813-974-6917, E-mail: hooper@usf.edu.
Website: http://www.usf.edu/innovative-education/

The University of Tennessee, Graduate School, College of Communication and Information, Knoxville, TN 37996. Offers advertising (MS, PhD); communications (MS, PhD); information sciences (MS, PhD); journalism and electronic media (MS, PhD); public relations (MS, PhD). *Program availability:* Part-time, evening/weekend, online learning. *Degree requirements:* For master's, thesis or alternative; for doctorate, thesis/dissertation. *Entrance requirements:* For master's and doctorate, GRE General Test, minimum GPA of 2.7. Additional exam requirements/recommendations for international students: required—TOEFL. Electronic applications accepted.

The University of Texas at Dallas, School of Arts, Technology, and Emerging Communication, Richardson, TX 75080. Offers arts and technology (MA, MFA, PhD); emerging media and communication (MA). *Faculty:* 22 full-time (10 women), 2 part-time/adjunct (0 women). *Students:* 40 full-time (20 women), 14 part-time (5 women); includes 11 minority (4 Black or African American, non-Hispanic/Latino; 3 Asian, non-Hispanic/Latino; 3 Hispanic/Latino; 1 Two or more races, non-Hispanic/Latino), 16 international. Average age 34. 85 applicants, 20% accepted, 14 enrolled. In 2019, 8 master's awarded. *Degree requirements:* For master's and doctorate, portfolio, thesis, or capstone project. *Entrance requirements:* For master's and doctorate, minimum GPA of 3.3 in upper-level coursework in field. Additional exam requirements/recommendations for international students: required—TOEFL (minimum score 550 paper-based). *Application deadline:* For fall admission, 7/15 for domestic students, 5/1 priority date for international students; for spring admission, 11/15 for domestic students, 9/1 priority date for international students. Applications are processed on a rolling basis. Application fee: $50 ($100 for international students). Electronic applications accepted. *Expenses: Tuition, area resident:* Full-time $16,504. Tuition, state resident: full-time $16,504. Tuition, nonresident: full-time $34,266. Tuition and fees vary according to course load. *Financial support:* In 2019–20, 36 students received support, including 10 research assistantships with partial tuition reimbursements available (averaging $26,280 per year), 26 teaching assistantships with partial tuition reimbursements available (averaging $15,886 per year); career-related internships or fieldwork, Federal Work-Study, institutionally sponsored loans, scholarships/grants, and unspecified assistantships also available. Support available to part-time students. Financial award application deadline: 4/30; financial award applicants required to submit FAFSA. *Unit head:* Dr. Anne Balsamo, Dean, 972-883-4376, E-mail: atecdean@utdallas.edu. *Application contact:* Dr. Kim Knight, Associate Dean for Graduate Studies, 972-883-4346, E-mail: kak102020@utdallas.edu.
Website: https://atec.utdallas.edu/

University of the Sacred Heart, Graduate Programs, Department of Communication, San Juan, PR 00914-0383. Offers contemporary culture and media (MA); digital journalism (MA, Certificate); editing for media (MA, Certificate); public relations (MA, Certificate); publicity (MA, Certificate); scriptwriting (MA, Certificate). *Program availability:* Part-time, evening/weekend. *Degree requirements:* For master's, thesis.

University of the Sacred Heart, Graduate Programs, Department of Education, San Juan, PR 00914-0383. Offers early childhood education (M Ed); information technology and multimedia (Certificate); instruction systems and education technology (M Ed), including English, information technology and multimedia, instructional design, mathematics, Spanish. *Program availability:* Part-time, evening/weekend. *Degree requirements:* For master's, thesis. *Entrance requirements:* For master's, EXADEP, minimum undergraduate GPA of 2.75, interview.

University of Utah, Graduate School, College of Engineering, Department of Entertainment Arts and Engineering, Salt Lake City, UT 84112. Offers game art (MEAE); game engineering (MEAE); game production (MEAE); technical art (MEAE). *Faculty:* 11 full-time (2 women), 23 part-time/adjunct (3 women). *Students:* 129 full-time (34 women); includes 71 minority (1 Black or African American, non-Hispanic/Latino; 63 Asian, non-Hispanic/Latino; 7 Hispanic/Latino), 57 international. Average age 25. 221 applicants, 49% accepted, 75 enrolled. In 2019, 58 master's awarded. *Degree requirements:* For master's, Thesis Game Project. *Entrance requirements:* For master's, portfolio submission, code sample submission, letters of recommendation. Additional exam requirements/recommendations for international students: required—TOEFL (minimum score 100 iBT), IELTS (minimum score 7), GRE. *Application deadline:* For fall admission, 2/28 for domestic and international students. Application fee: $55. Electronic applications accepted. Application fee is waived when completed online. *Expenses:* Https://fbs.admin.utah.edu/download/income/Graduate/EAEngRes.pdf. *Financial support:* In 2019–20, 83 students received support, including 26 research assistantships with partial tuition reimbursements available (averaging $15,900 per year), 53 teaching assistantships with partial tuition reimbursements available (averaging $15,900 per year); scholarships/grants, health care benefits, and unspecified assistantships also available. Financial award application deadline: 2/28; financial award applicants required to submit FAFSA. *Unit head:* Hallie Huber, Academic Program Manager, 801-581-5460, E-mail: hallie.huber@utah.edu. *Application contact:* CJ Lederman, Graduate Student Advisor, 801-587-1299, E-mail: cj@eae.utah.edu.
Website: http://eae.utah.edu/

University of Utah, Graduate School, College of Humanities, Department of Communication, Salt Lake City, UT 84112. Offers communicating science, health, environment and risk (MA, MS, PhD); critical cultural studies (MA, MS, PhD); digital media (MA, MS, PhD); rhetoric (MA, MS, PhD). *Program availability:* Part-time, evening/weekend. *Faculty:* 29 full-time (15 women). *Students:* 33 full-time (24 women), 6 part-time (3 women); includes 12 minority (2 Black or African American, non-Hispanic/Latino; 4 Asian, non-Hispanic/Latino; 4 Hispanic/Latino; 1 Native Hawaiian or other Pacific Islander, non-Hispanic/Latino; 1 Two or more races, non-Hispanic/Latino), 3 international. Average age 30. 80 applicants, 19% accepted, 9 enrolled. In 2019, 4 master's, 10 doctorates awarded. Terminal master's awarded for partial completion of doctoral program. *Degree requirements:* For master's, variable foreign language requirement, comprehensive exam (for some programs), thesis (for some programs), Programme of Study; for doctorate, comprehensive exam, thesis/dissertation, Programme of Study; Prospectus. *Entrance requirements:* For master's and doctorate, GRE. Additional exam requirements/recommendations for international students: required—TOEFL (minimum score 80 paper-based), IELTS (minimum score 6.5). *Application deadline:* For fall admission, 12/15 for domestic students, 11/15 for international students. Application fee: $55 ($65 for international students). Electronic applications accepted. *Expenses:* Tuition, state resident: full-time $7085; part-time $272.51 per credit hour. Tuition, nonresident: full-time $24,937; part-time $959.12 per credit hour. *Required fees:* $880.52; $880.52 per semester. Tuition and fees vary according to degree level, program and student level. *Financial support:* In 2019–20, 30 students received support, including 2 fellowships with full tuition reimbursements available (averaging $18,500 per year), 3 research assistantships with tuition reimbursements available (averaging $19,667 per year), 28 teaching assistantships with tuition reimbursements available (averaging $19,929 per year). Financial award application deadline: 12/15. *Unit head:* Kevin Coe, Professor and Chair, 801-581-6888, E-mail: kevin.coe@utah.edu. *Application contact:* Travis Ciaramella, Graduate Advisor, 801-585-6337, E-mail: travis.ciaramella@utah.edu.
Website: http://www.communication.utah.edu

Virginia Polytechnic Institute and State University, Graduate School, College of Architecture and Urban Studies, Blacksburg, VA 24061. Offers architecture (M Arch, MS); architecture and design research (PhD); building construction science management (MS); creative technologies (MFA); environmental design and planning (PhD); government and international affairs (MPIA); landscape architecture (MLA, PhD); planning, governance, and globalization (PhD); public administration and public affairs (MPA, PhD); urban and regional planning (MURPL). *Accreditation:* ASLA (one or more programs are accredited). *Faculty:* 145 full-time (58 women), 2 part-time/adjunct (1 woman). *Students:* 304 full-time (156 women), 180 part-time (77 women); includes 90 minority (40 Black or African American, non-Hispanic/Latino; 19 Asian, non-Hispanic/Latino; 24 Hispanic/Latino; 7 Two or more races, non-Hispanic/Latino), 130 international. Average age 33. 475 applicants, 72% accepted, 126 enrolled. In 2019, 130 master's, 23 doctorates awarded. *Degree requirements:* For master's, comprehensive exam (for some programs), thesis (for some programs); for doctorate, comprehensive exam (for some programs), thesis/dissertation (for some programs). *Entrance requirements:* For master's and doctorate, GRE/GMAT. Additional exam requirements/recommendations for international students: required—TOEFL (minimum score 90 iBT). *Application deadline:* For fall admission, 8/1 for domestic students, 4/1 for international students; for spring admission, 1/1 for domestic students, 9/1 for international students. Applications are processed on a rolling basis. Application fee: $75. Electronic applications accepted. *Expenses:* Tuition, state resident: full-time $13,700; part-time $761.25 per credit hour. Tuition, nonresident: full-time $27,614; part-time $1534 per credit hour. *Required fees:* $886.50 per term. Tuition and fees vary according to campus/location and program. *Financial support:* In 2019–20, 2 fellowships with full tuition reimbursements (averaging $24,875 per year), 35 research assistantships with full tuition reimbursements (averaging $16,344 per year), 126 teaching assistantships with full tuition reimbursements (averaging $11,525 per year) were awarded; scholarships/grants and unspecified assistantships also available. Financial award application deadline: 3/1; financial award applicants required to submit FAFSA. *Unit head:* Dr. Richard Blythe, Dean, 540-231-6416, Fax: 540-231-6332, E-mail: richbl1@vt.edu. *Application contact:* Christine Mattsson-Coon, Executive Assistant, 540-231-6416, Fax: 540-231-6332, E-mail: cmattsso@vt.edu.
Website: http://www.caus.vt.edu/

Walla Walla University, Graduate Studies, Center for Cinema, Religion, and Worldview, College Place, WA 99324. Offers Web and interactive media (MA). *Entrance requirements:* For master's, three professional references, transcripts, personal statement.

Webster University, School of Communications, Program in New Media Production, St. Louis, MO 63119-3194. Offers MA.

Wilmington University, College of Technology, New Castle, DE 19720-6491. Offers cybersecurity (MS); information assurance (MS); information systems technologies (MS); management and management information systems (MS); technology project management (MS); Web design (MS). *Program availability:* Part-time, evening/weekend. *Entrance requirements:* Additional exam requirements/recommendations for international students: required—TOEFL (minimum score 500 paper-based). Electronic applications accepted.

Worcester Polytechnic Institute, Graduate Admissions, Program in Interactive Media and Game Development, Worcester, MA 01609-2280. Offers interactive media & game development (MS). *Program availability:* Part-time, evening/weekend. *Entrance requirements:* For master's, GRE (recommended), 3 letters of recommendation, statement of purpose, portfolio (recommended). Additional exam requirements/recommendations for international students: required—TOEFL (minimum score 563 paper-based; 84 iBT), IELTS (minimum score 7). Electronic applications accepted.

Journalism

American University, School of Communication, Division of Journalism, Washington, DC 20016-8001. Offers broadcast journalism (MA); international journalism (MA); investigative journalism (MA); journalism and digital storytelling (MA). *Accreditation:* ACEJMC. *Program availability:* Part-time, evening/weekend. *Degree requirements:* For master's, comprehensive exam, thesis or alternative. *Entrance requirements:* Additional exam requirements/recommendations for international students: required—TOEFL (minimum score 600 paper-based; 100 iBT), IELTS (minimum score 7). Electronic applications accepted.

The American University in Cairo, School of Global Affairs and Public Policy, Cairo, Egypt. Offers gender and women's studies (MA); global affairs (MGA); international and comparative law (LL M); international human rights law (MA); journalism and mass communication (MA); Middle East studies (MA); migration and refugee studies (MA, Diploma); public administration (MPA); public policy (MPP); television and digital journalism (MA). *Program availability:* Part-time, evening/weekend. *Degree requirements:* For master's, comprehensive exam (for some programs), thesis (for some programs). *Entrance requirements:* Additional exam requirements/recommendations for international students: required—TOEFL (minimum score 450 paper-based; 45 iBT), IELTS (minimum score 5). Electronic applications accepted. *Expenses:* Contact institution.

Arizona State University at Tempe, Walter Cronkite School of Journalism and Mass Communication, Phoenix, AZ 85004. Offers journalism and mass communication (PhD); mass communication (MMC). *Accreditation:* ACEJMC. Terminal master's awarded for partial completion of doctoral program. *Degree requirements:* For master's, 9-hour professional capstone experience; interactive Program of Study (iPOS) submitted before completing 50 percent of required credit hours; for doctorate, comprehensive exam, thesis/dissertation, interactive Program of Study (iPOS) submitted before completing 50 percent of required credit hours. *Entrance requirements:* For master's and doctorate, GRE, minimum GPA of 3.0 or equivalent in last 2 years of work leading to bachelor's degree. Additional exam requirements/recommendations for international students: required—TOEFL, IELTS, or PTE. Electronic applications accepted. *Expenses:* Contact institution.

Arkansas State University, Graduate School, College of Media and Communication, Department of Media, State University, AR 72467. Offers mass communications (MSMC). *Program availability:* Part-time. *Degree requirements:* For master's, comprehensive exam, thesis or alternative. *Entrance requirements:* For master's, GRE General Test or MAT, appropriate bachelor's degree, letters of reference, educational experience, professional experience, official transcripts, immunization records. Additional exam requirements/recommendations for international students: required—TOEFL (minimum score 550 paper-based; 79 iBT), IELTS (minimum score 6), PTE (minimum score 56). Electronic applications accepted.

Arkansas Tech University, College of Arts and Humanities, Russellville, AR 72801. Offers applied sociology (MS); English (M Ed, MA); history (MA); liberal arts (MLA); multi-media journalism (MA); psychology (MS); teaching English as a second language (MA). *Program availability:* Part-time, 100% online, blended/hybrid learning. *Students:* 32 full-time (19 women), 102 part-time (70 women); includes 22 minority (5 Black or African American, non-Hispanic/Latino; 1 American Indian or Alaska Native, non-Hispanic/Latino; 1 Asian, non-Hispanic/Latino; 12 Hispanic/Latino; 3 Two or more races, non-Hispanic/Latino), 9 international. Average age 32. In 2019, 89 master's awarded. *Degree requirements:* For master's, comprehensive exam (for some programs), thesis (for some programs), project. *Entrance requirements:* Additional exam requirements/recommendations for international students: required—TOEFL (minimum score 550 paper-based; 79 iBT), IELTS (minimum score 6.5), PTE (minimum score 58). *Application deadline:* For fall admission, 3/1 priority date for domestic students, 5/1 priority date for international students; for spring admission, 10/1 priority date for domestic and international students. Applications are processed on a rolling basis. Application fee: $40 ($90 for international students). Electronic applications accepted. *Expenses: Tuition, area resident:* Full-time $7008; part-time $292 per credit hour. Tuition, state resident: full-time $7008; part-time $292 per credit hour. Tuition, nonresident: full-time $14,016; part-time $584 per credit hour. *International tuition:* $14,016 full-time. *Required fees:* $343 per term. *Financial support:* In 2019–20, research assistantships with full and partial tuition reimbursements (averaging $4,800 per year), teaching assistantships with full and partial tuition reimbursements (averaging $4,800 per year) were awarded; career-related internships or fieldwork, Federal Work-Study, scholarships/grants, health care benefits, and unspecified assistantships also available. Support available to part-time students. Financial award application deadline: 4/15; financial award applicants required to submit FAFSA. *Unit head:* Dr. Jeffrey Cass, Dean of College of Arts and Humanities, 479-968-0274, Fax: 479-964-0812, E-mail: jcass@atu.edu. *Application contact:* Dr. Richard Schoephoerster, Dean of Graduate College and Research, 479-968-0398, Fax: 479-964-0542, E-mail: gradcollege@atu.edu.
Website: http://www.atu.edu/humanities/

Ball State University, Graduate School, College of Communication, Information, and Media, Department of Journalism, Program in Journalism, Muncie, IN 47306. Offers MA. *Program availability:* Online only, 100% online. *Entrance requirements:* For master's, GRE General Test (minimum score 150 verbal), minimum baccalaureate GPA of 2.75 or 3.0 in latter half of baccalaureate, transcripts of all prior course work, current resume or curriculum vitae, 1000-word statement of purpose, writing sample. Additional exam requirements/recommendations for international students: required—TOEFL (minimum score 550 paper-based; 79 iBT), IELTS (minimum score 6.5). Electronic applications accepted. *Expenses: Tuition, area resident:* Full-time $7506; part-time $417 per credit hour. Tuition, nonresident: full-time $20,610; part-time $1145 per credit hour. *Required fees:* $2126. Tuition and fees vary according to course load, campus/location and program.

Baylor University, Graduate School, College of Arts and Sciences, Department of Journalism, Public Relations and New Media, Waco, TX 76798. Offers journalism, public relations, advertising, photography (MIJ); news editorial, public relations, advertising, photography (MA). *Program availability:* 100% online. *Faculty:* 8 full-time (4 women). *Students:* 6 full-time (3 women), 4 part-time (3 women); includes 1 minority (Hispanic/Latino), 1 international. 9 applicants, 56% accepted, 5 enrolled. In 2019, 8 master's awarded. *Degree requirements:* For master's, one foreign language, thesis, internship. *Entrance requirements:* Additional exam requirements/recommendations for international students: required—TOEFL (minimum score 550 paper-based), IELTS (minimum score 6.5). *Application deadline:* For fall admission, 2/15 priority date for domestic students, 2/15 for international students; for spring admission, 12/1 priority date for domestic students, 12/1 for international students; for summer admission, 5/1 priority date for domestic students, 5/1 for international students. Application fee: $50. Electronic applications accepted. *Financial support:* In 2019–20, 6 students received support, including 6 teaching assistantships with partial tuition reimbursements available (averaging $1,800 per year); scholarships/grants also available. Financial award application deadline: 2/15; financial award applicants required to submit FAFSA. *Unit head:* Dr. Marlene Neill, Associate Professor & Graduate Program Director, 254-710-6322, E-mail: Marlene_Neill@baylor.edu. *Application contact:* Dr. Marlene Neill, Associate Professor & Graduate Program Director, 254-710-6322, Fax: 254-710-6322, E-mail: Marlene_Neill@baylor.edu.
Website: https://www.baylor.edu/journalism/index.php?id=859623

Boston University, College of Communication, Department of Journalism, Boston, MA 02215. Offers MS. *Program availability:* Part-time. *Faculty:* 24 full-time, 15 part-time/adjunct. *Students:* 58 full-time (46 women), 3 part-time (2 women); includes 6 minority (2 Black or African American, non-Hispanic/Latino; 1 Asian, non-Hispanic/Latino; 3 Hispanic/Latino), 30 international. Average age 27. 162 applicants, 76% accepted, 36 enrolled. In 2019, 29 master's awarded. *Degree requirements:* For master's, thesis, professional project. *Entrance requirements:* For master's, transcript(s), resume/CV, writing samples, 3 letters of recommendation. Additional exam requirements/recommendations for international students: required—TOEFL (minimum score 600 paper-based; 100 iBT), either TOEFL or IELTS; recommended—IELTS (minimum score 7). *Application deadline:* For fall admission, 5/1 for domestic and international students. Applications are processed on a rolling basis. Application fee: $95. Electronic applications accepted. *Financial support:* Teaching assistantships with partial tuition reimbursements, career-related internships or fieldwork, Federal Work-Study, scholarships/grants, and unspecified assistantships available. Support available to part-time students. Financial award application deadline: 5/1; financial award applicants required to submit FAFSA. *Unit head:* William McKeen, Chairman, 617-353-3484, Fax: 617-353-1086, E-mail: wmckeen@bu.edu. *Application contact:* Jackie Cummings, Admission and Financial Aid Counselor, 617-353-3481, E-mail: comgrad@bu.edu.
Website: http://www.bu.edu/com/academics/journalism/

California State University, Northridge, Graduate Studies, Mike Curb College of Arts, Media, and Communication, Department of Journalism, Northridge, CA 91330. Offers mass communication (MA). *Program availability:* Part-time, evening/weekend. *Degree requirements:* For master's, thesis. *Entrance requirements:* For master's, GRE General Test. Additional exam requirements/recommendations for international students: required—TOEFL.

Carleton University, Faculty of Graduate Studies, Faculty of Public Affairs and Management, School of Journalism and Communication, Ottawa, ON K1S 5B6, Canada. Offers communication (MA, PhD); journalism (MJ). *Degree requirements:* For master's, thesis optional; for doctorate, comprehensive exam, thesis/dissertation. *Entrance requirements:* For master's, honors degree. Additional exam requirements/recommendations for international students: required—TOEFL.

Columbia University, Graduate School of Journalism, New York, NY 10027. Offers MA, MS, PhD, JD/MS, MIA/MS, MS/MBA. *Accreditation:* ACEJMC. *Program availability:* Part-time. *Degree requirements:* For master's, thesis; for doctorate, thesis/dissertation. *Entrance requirements:* For master's, writing test, 2-3 samples of journalistic work, minimum typing speed of 50 words per minute; for doctorate, GRE. Additional exam requirements/recommendations for international students: required—TOEFL. *Expenses:* Contact institution.

Concordia University, School of Graduate Studies, Faculty of Arts and Science, Department of Journalism, Montréal, QC H3G 1M8, Canada. Offers journalism (Graduate Diploma); journalism studies (MA); visual journalism (Diploma). *Degree requirements:* For other advanced degree, one foreign language. *Entrance requirements:* Additional exam requirements/recommendations for international students: required—departmental English test or TOEFL.

CUNY Craig Newmark Graduate School of Journalism, Graduate Program, New York, NY 10018. Offers entrepreneurial journalism (MA); journalism (MA); social journalism (MA). *Accreditation:* ACEJMC. *Degree requirements:* For master's, internship, final or capstone project. *Entrance requirements:* For master's, 3 letters of recommendation, personal statement, resume, interview, 3 writing samples. Additional exam requirements/recommendations for international students: required—TOEFL (minimum score 105 iBT). Electronic applications accepted.

DePaul University, College of Communication, Chicago, IL 60604. Offers digital communication and media arts (MA); health communication (MA); journalism (MA); media and cinema studies (MA); multicultural communication (MA); organizational communication (MA); public relations and advertising (MA); relational communication (MA). *Program availability:* Part-time, evening/weekend. *Entrance requirements:* Additional exam requirements/recommendations for international students: required—TOEFL (minimum score 590 paper-based; 96 iBT), IELTS (minimum score 7.5) or PTE. Electronic applications accepted.

Florida Agricultural and Mechanical University, Division of Graduate Studies, Research, and Continuing Education, School of Journalism and Graphic Communication, Tallahassee, FL 32307-3200. Offers journalism (MS). *Degree requirements:* For master's, comprehensive exam, thesis (for some programs). *Entrance requirements:* For master's, GRE General Test, minimum GPA of 3.0. Additional exam requirements/recommendations for international students: required—TOEFL.

Florida International University, College of Communication, Architecture and The Arts, School of Communication and Journalism, Miami, FL 33199. Offers mass communication (MS), including global strategic communications, Spanish language journalism. *Program availability:* Part-time, evening/weekend. *Faculty:* 30 full-time (22 women), 71 part-time/adjunct (42 women). *Students:* 85 full-time (68 women), 76 part-time (59 women); includes 117 minority (20 Black or African American, non-Hispanic/Latino; 2 Asian, non-Hispanic/Latino; 88 Hispanic/Latino; 7 Two or more races, non-Hispanic/Latino), 22 international. Average age 28. 120 applicants, 75% accepted, 63 enrolled. In 2019, 107 master's awarded. *Entrance requirements:* For master's, 2 letters

of recommendation; minimum GPA of 3.0 during last 60 hours of upper-level work; resume. Additional exam requirements/recommendations for international students: required—TOEFL (minimum score 550 paper-based; 80 iBT). *Application deadline:* For fall admission, 6/1 for domestic students, 4/1 for international students; for spring admission, 10/1 for domestic students, 9/1 for international students. Applications are processed on a rolling basis. Application fee: $30. Electronic applications accepted. *Expenses: Tuition, area resident:* Full-time $8912; part-time $446 per credit hour. Tuition, state resident: full-time $8912; part-time $446 per credit hour. Tuition, nonresident: full-time $21,393; part-time $992 per credit hour. *Required fees:* $2194. *Financial support:* Institutionally sponsored loans and scholarships/grants available. Financial award application deadline: 3/1; financial award applicants required to submit FAFSA. *Unit head:* Dr. Aileen Izquierdo, Chair, 305-919-5795, E-mail: aileen.izquierdo@fiu.edu. *Application contact:* Nanett Rojas, Manager, Admissions Operations, 305-348-7464, Fax: 305-348-7441, E-mail: gradadm@fiu.edu.
Website: https://scj.fiu.edu/

Full Sail University, New Media Journalism Master of Arts Program - Online, Winter Park, FL 32792-7437. Offers MA.

Georgetown University, Graduate School of Arts and Sciences, School of Continuing Studies, Washington, DC 20057. Offers American studies (MALS); applied intelligence (MPS); Catholic studies (MALS); classical civilizations (MALS); emergency and disaster management (MPS); ethics and the professions (MALS); global strategic communications (MPS); hospitality management (MPS); human resources management (MPS); humanities (MALS); individualized study (MALS); integrated marketing communications (MPS); international affairs (MALS); Islam and Muslim-Christian relations (MALS); journalism (MPS); liberal studies (DLS); literature and society (MALS); medieval and early modern European studies (MALS); public relations and corporate communications (MPS); real estate (MPS); religious studies (MALS); social and public policy (MALS); sports industry management (MPS); systems engineering management (MPS); technology management (MPS); the theory and practice of American democracy (MALS); urban and regional planning (MPS); visual culture (MALS). *Entrance requirements:* Additional exam requirements/recommendations for international students: required—TOEFL.

Harvard University, Extension School, Cambridge, MA 02138-3722. Offers applied sciences (CAS); biotechnology (ALM); educational technologies (ALM); educational technology (CET); English for graduate and professional studies (DGP); environmental management (ALM, CEM); information technology (ALM); journalism (ALM); liberal arts (ALM); management (ALM, CM); mathematics for teaching (ALM); museum studies (ALM); premedical studies (Diploma); publication and communication (CPC). *Program availability:* Part-time, evening/weekend. *Degree requirements:* For master's, thesis. *Entrance requirements:* For master's, 3 completed graduate courses with grade of B or higher. Additional exam requirements/recommendations for international students: required—TOEFL (minimum score 600 paper-based), TWE (minimum score 5). *Expenses:* Contact institution.

Hofstra University, Lawrence Herbert School of Communication, Programs in Journalism and Public Relations, Hempstead, NY 11549. Offers journalism (MA); public relations (MA). *Program availability:* Part-time, evening/weekend. *Students:* 47 full-time (27 women), 17 part-time (12 women); includes 35 minority (22 Black or African American, non-Hispanic/Latino; 2 American Indian or Alaska Native, non-Hispanic/Latino; 2 Asian, non-Hispanic/Latino; 9 Hispanic/Latino), 6 international. Average age 28. 73 applicants, 75% accepted, 23 enrolled. In 2019, 28 master's awarded. *Degree requirements:* For master's, thesis. *Entrance requirements:* For master's, bachelor's degree. Additional exam requirements/recommendations for international students: required—TOEFL (minimum score 550 paper-based; 95 iBT); recommended—IELTS (minimum score 6.5). *Application deadline:* Applications are processed on a rolling basis. Application fee: $75. Electronic applications accepted. *Expenses:* Tuition: Full-time $25,164; part-time $1398 per credit. *Required fees:* $580; $165 per semester. Tuition and fees vary according to course load, degree level and program. *Financial support:* In 2019–20, 29 students received support, including 23 fellowships with full and partial tuition reimbursements available (averaging $3,783 per year); research assistantships with full and partial tuition reimbursements available, career-related internships or fieldwork, Federal Work-Study, institutionally sponsored loans, scholarships/grants, tuition waivers (full and partial), unspecified assistantships, and scholarships and endowed scholarships also available. Support available to part-time students. Financial award applicants required to submit FAFSA. *Unit head:* Prof. Jeff Morosoff, Chairperson, 516-463-5248, E-mail: jeffrey.morosoff@hofstra.edu. *Application contact:* Sunil Samuel, Assistant Vice President of Admissions, 516-463-4723, Fax: 516-463-4664, E-mail: graduateadmission@hofstra.edu.
Website: http://www.hofstra.edu/academics/colleges/soc/

Iowa State University of Science and Technology, Greenlee School of Journalism and Communication, Ames, IA 50011. Offers journalism and mass communication (MS). *Entrance requirements:* For master's, GRE General Test. Additional exam requirements/recommendations for international students: required—TOEFL (minimum score 570 paper-based; 88 iBT), IELTS (minimum score 6.5). Electronic applications accepted.

Kansas State University, Graduate School, College of Arts and Sciences, A.Q. Miller School of Journalism and Mass Communications, Manhattan, KS 66506. Offers advertising (MS); community journalism (MS); global communication (MS); health communication (MS); media management (MS); public relations (MS). *Program availability:* Part-time, evening/weekend. *Degree requirements:* For master's, comprehensive exam, thesis. *Entrance requirements:* For master's, GRE General Test, minimum GPA of 3.0. Additional exam requirements/recommendations for international students: required—TOEFL (minimum score 79 iBT). Electronic applications accepted.

Kent State University, College of Communication and Information, School of Media and Journalism, Kent, OH 44242-0001. Offers journalism and mass communication (MA), including media management, public relations, reporting and editing-broadcast, reporting and editing-convergence, reporting and editing-journalism educators, reporting and editing-magazine, reporting and editing-newspaper. *Program availability:* Part-time, 100% online. *Faculty:* 7 full-time (6 women), 5 part-time/adjunct (2 women). *Students:* 11 full-time (8 women), 35 part-time (22 women); includes 3 minority (all Black or African American, non-Hispanic/Latino), 3 international. Average age 34. 18 applicants, 78% accepted, 10 enrolled. In 2019, 40 master's awarded. *Degree requirements:* For master's, thesis, thesis or project. *Entrance requirements:* For master's, GRE, Bachelor's degree, minimum GPA of 3.0, statement of purpose, 2 letters of recommendation, resume or vitae, official transcript(s), writing sample. Additional exam requirements/recommendations for international students: required—TOEFL (minimum score 100 iBT), IELTS (minimum score 7), PTE (minimum score 65), Michigan English Language Assessment Battery (minimum score 82). *Application deadline:* For fall admission, 7/1 for domestic and international students. Applications are processed on a rolling basis. Application fee: $45 ($70 for international students). Electronic applications accepted. *Financial support:* Research assistantships with full tuition reimbursements, teaching assistantships with full tuition reimbursements, scholarships/grants, and unspecified assistantships available. Financial award application deadline: 3/1. *Unit head:* Jeff Fruit, Interim Director and Professor, 330-672-2572, E-mail: jmc@kent.edu. *Application contact:* Tang Tang, Graduate Coordinator/Professor, 330-672-1132, E-mail:

ttang2@kent.edu.
Website: http://www.kent.edu/jmc

Lindenwood University, Graduate Programs, School of Arts, Media, and Communications, St. Charles, MO 63301-1695. Offers advertising (MA); art history (MA); cinema and media arts (MFA); communications (MA); digital and Web design (MA); fashion and business design (MS); journalism (MA); mass communications (MA); social media and digital content (MS). *Program availability:* Part-time, 100% online. *Faculty:* 20 full-time (5 women), 15 part-time/adjunct (6 women). *Students:* 64 full-time (42 women), 76 part-time (57 women); includes 43 minority (20 Black or African American, non-Hispanic/Latino; 13 Hispanic/Latino; 10 Two or more races, non-Hispanic/Latino), 8 international. Average age 33. 145 applicants, 46% accepted, 56 enrolled. In 2019, 11 master's awarded. *Degree requirements:* For master's, thesis (for some programs), minimum cumulative GPA of 3.0. *Entrance requirements:* For master's, audition or interview, minimum GPA of 3.0, portfolio, letter of recommendation. Additional exam requirements/recommendations for international students: required—TOEFL (minimum score 553 paper-based; 81 iBT); recommended—IELTS (minimum score 6.5). *Application deadline:* For fall admission, 8/9 priority date for domestic students, 6/1 priority date for international students; for spring admission, 12/20 for domestic students, 11/1 priority date for international students; for summer admission, 5/15 priority date for domestic students, 3/27 priority date for international students. Applications are processed on a rolling basis. Application fee: $0 ($100 for international students). Electronic applications accepted. *Expenses: Tuition:* Full-time $8910; part-time $495 per credit. Tuition and fees vary according to course load, degree level and program. *Financial support:* In 2019–20, 23 students received support. Career-related internships or fieldwork, institutionally sponsored loans, scholarships/grants, tuition waivers (partial), and unspecified assistantships available. Financial award application deadline: 6/30; financial award applicants required to submit FAFSA. *Unit head:* Dr. Jason Lively, Dean, School of Arts, Media, and Communications, 636-949-4164, Fax: 636-949-4910, E-mail: JLively@lindenwood.edu. *Application contact:* Kara Schilli, Assistant Vice President, University Admissions, 636-949-4349, Fax: 636-949-4109, E-mail: adultadmissions@lindenwood.edu.
Website: https://www.lindenwood.edu/academics/academic-schools/school-of-arts-media-and-communications/

Marquette University, Graduate School, College of Communication, Milwaukee, WI 53201-1881. Offers advertising and public relations (MA); communication studies (MA); digital storytelling (Certificate); journalism (MA); mass communication (MA); science, health and environmental communication (MA). *Accreditation:* ACEJMC (one or more programs are accredited). *Program availability:* Part-time, evening/weekend. *Degree requirements:* For master's, comprehensive exam, thesis or alternative. *Entrance requirements:* For master's, GRE, official transcripts from all current and previous colleges/universities except Marquette, three letters of recommendation, statement of academic and professional goals. Additional exam requirements/recommendations for international students: required—TOEFL (minimum score 530 paper-based). Electronic applications accepted.

Marshall University, Academic Affairs Division, College of Arts and Media, Program in Journalism, Huntington, WV 25755. Offers journalism (MAJ, Certificate), including health care public relations (MAJ). *Degree requirements:* For master's, thesis optional. *Entrance requirements:* For master's, GRE General Test.

Michigan State University, The Graduate School, College of Communication Arts and Sciences, School of Journalism, East Lansing, MI 48824. Offers MA. *Entrance requirements:* Additional exam requirements/recommendations for international students: required—TOEFL. Electronic applications accepted.

Morgan State University, School of Graduate Studies, School of Global Journalism and Communication, Baltimore, MD 21043. Offers journalism (MA). *Program availability:* Part-time, evening/weekend. *Faculty:* 8 full-time (3 women), 3 part-time/adjunct (0 women). *Students:* 12 full-time (7 women), 4 part-time (3 women); includes 15 minority (13 Black or African American, non-Hispanic/Latino; 2 Hispanic/Latino), 1 international. Average age 30. 8 applicants, 75% accepted, 4 enrolled. In 2019, 5 master's awarded. *Entrance requirements:* For master's, GRE, Minimum GPA 3.0. Additional exam requirements/recommendations for international students: required—TOEFL (minimum score 550 paper-based; 70 iBT). *Application deadline:* For fall admission, 2/2 priority date for domestic students, 4/15 for international students. Applications are processed on a rolling basis. Application fee: $50 ($70 for international students). Electronic applications accepted. *Expenses:* Tuition, state resident: full-time $455; part-time $455 per credit hour. Tuition, nonresident: full-time $894; part-time $894 per credit hour. *Required fees:* $82; $82 per credit hour. *Financial support:* In 2019–20, 5 students received support. Fellowships with full and partial tuition reimbursements available, research assistantships with full and partial tuition reimbursements available, teaching assistantships with full and partial tuition reimbursements available, career-related internships or fieldwork, Federal Work-Study, institutionally sponsored loans, scholarships/grants, tuition waivers (full and partial), and unspecified assistantships available. Support available to part-time students. Financial award application deadline: 2/1. *Unit head:* DeWayne Wickham, Dean, 443-885-3330, Fax: 443-885-8322. *Application contact:* Dr. Jahmaine Smith, Director of Admissions, 443-885-3185, Fax: 443-885-8226, E-mail: gradapply@morgan.edu.
Website: https://www.morgan.edu/sgjc

Murray State University, Arthur J. Bauernfeind College of Business, Department of Journalism and Mass Communications, Murray, KY 42071. Offers mass communications (MA, MS), including public relations. *Program availability:* Part-time. *Entrance requirements:* For master's, GRE or GMAT, minimum university GPA of 2.75. Additional exam requirements/recommendations for international students: required—TOEFL (minimum score 527 paper-based; 51 iBT). Electronic applications accepted.

National University, School of Professional Studies, La Jolla, CA 92037-1011. Offers criminal justice (MCJ); digital cinema production (MFA); digital journalism (MA); homeland security and emergency management (MS); juvenile justice (MS); professional screenwriting (MFA); public administration (MPA), including human resource management, organizational leadership. *Program availability:* Part-time, evening/weekend, 100% online, blended/hybrid learning. *Degree requirements:* For master's, thesis (for some programs). *Entrance requirements:* For master's, interview, minimum GPA of 2.5. Additional exam requirements/recommendations for international students: required—TOEFL (minimum score 550 paper-based; 79 iBT), IELTS (minimum score 6). Electronic applications accepted. *Expenses: Tuition:* Full-time $442; part-time $442 per unit.

New York University, Graduate School of Arts and Science, Arthur L. Carter Journalism Institute, New York, NY 10012-1019. Offers biomedical journalism (MS); cultural reporting and criticism (MA); French studies/journalism (MA); journalism (MA); Latin American and Caribbean studies/journalism (MA); Near Eastern studies/journalism (MA); science and environmental reporting (Advanced Certificate); MA/Advanced Certificate. *Accreditation:* ACEJMC. *Program availability:* Part-time. *Entrance requirements:* For master's, GRE General Test, sample of written work. Additional exam requirements/recommendations for international students: required—TOEFL, IELTS.

New York University, Graduate School of Arts and Science, Department of Biology, New York, NY 10012-1019. Offers biology (PhD); biomedical journalism (MS); cancer and molecular biology (PhD); computational biology (PhD); computers in biological research (MS); developmental genetics (PhD); general biology (MS); immunology and microbiology (PhD); molecular genetics (PhD); neurobiology (PhD); oral biology (MS); plant biology (PhD); recombinant DNA technology (MS); MS/MBA. *Program availability:* Part-time. Terminal master's awarded for partial completion of doctoral program. *Degree requirements:* For master's, thesis or alternative, qualifying paper; for doctorate, comprehensive exam, thesis/dissertation. *Entrance requirements:* For master's and doctorate, GRE General Test. Additional exam requirements/recommendations for international students: required—TOEFL, IELTS.

Northeastern University, College of Arts, Media and Design, Boston, MA 02115-5096. Offers architecture (M Arch); arts administration and cultural entrepreneurship (MS); experience design (MFA, MS); game science and design (MS); information design and visualization (MFA); interdisciplinary arts (MFA); journalism (MA); media advocacy (MS); music industry leadership (MS); sustainable building systems (MS); sustainable urban environments (M Des). Electronic applications accepted. *Expenses:* Contact institution.

Northwestern University, Medill School of Journalism, Media, and Integrated Marketing Communications, Evanston, IL 60208. Offers integrated marketing communications (MSIMC), including brand strategy, content marketing, direct and interactive marketing, marketing analytics, strategic communications; interactive publishing (MSJ); magazine writing/editing (MSJ); reporting (MSJ); video/broadcast (MSJ). *Entrance requirements:* For master's, GRE General Test, GMAT or LSAT (for MSJ). Additional exam requirements/recommendations for international students: required—TOEFL. Electronic applications accepted. *Expenses:* Contact institution.

Ohio University, Graduate College, Scripps College of Communication, E.W. Scripps School of Journalism, Athens, OH 45701-2979. Offers journalism (MS); mass communication (PhD). *Program availability:* Part-time. *Degree requirements:* For master's, thesis or alternative; for doctorate, comprehensive exam, thesis/dissertation. *Entrance requirements:* For master's and doctorate, GRE General Test, minimum GPA of 3.0. Additional exam requirements/recommendations for international students: required—TOEFL (minimum score 550 paper-based; 80 iBT) or IELTS (minimum score 6.5). Electronic applications accepted.

Point Park University, School of Communication, Pittsburgh, PA 15222-1984. Offers communication technology (MA); media communication (MA). *Program availability:* Part-time, evening/weekend. *Degree requirements:* For master's, comprehensive exam (for some programs), thesis or alternative. *Entrance requirements:* For master's, GRE (if GPA less than 2.75), minimum GPA of 2.75, 2 letters of recommendation, statement of intent. Additional exam requirements/recommendations for international students: required—TOEFL (minimum score 570 paper-based; 88 iBT), IELTS (minimum score 6.5); recommended—TWE (minimum score 5). Electronic applications accepted.

Quinnipiac University, School of Communications, Program in Journalism, Hamden, CT 06518-1940. Offers journalism (MS), including broadcast/multimedia, writing; sports journalism (MS), including broadcast/multimedia. *Program availability:* Part-time, evening/weekend. *Degree requirements:* For master's, project. *Entrance requirements:* For master's, minimum GPA of 3.0, portfolio or writing sample. Additional exam requirements/recommendations for international students: required—TOEFL (minimum score 575 paper-based; 90 iBT), IELTS (minimum score 6.5). Electronic applications accepted. *Expenses: Tuition:* Part-time $1055 per credit. *Required fees:* $945 per semester. Tuition and fees vary according to course load and program.

Regent University, Graduate School, School of Communication and the Arts, Virginia Beach, VA 23464-9800. Offers acting (MFA); communication (MA, PhD), including media and arts management and promotion (MA), political communication (MA), strategic communication (MA), technical communication (MA); film and TV (MA), including producing (MA, MFA), production, script writing; film-television (MFA), including directing, producing (MA, MFA), script and screenwriting; journalism (MA); theatre (MA). *Program availability:* Part-time, evening/weekend, 100% online, blended/hybrid learning. *Degree requirements:* For master's, thesis or alternative; for doctorate, thesis/dissertation. *Entrance requirements:* For master's, transcripts, writing sample, resume, audition (for MFA programs); for doctorate, GRE General Test, resume, writing sample, recommendations, interview, transcripts, personal goals statement. Additional exam requirements/recommendations for international students: required—TOEFL (minimum score 577 paper-based). Electronic applications accepted. *Expenses:* Contact institution.

Sacred Heart University, Graduate Programs, College of Arts and Sciences, Department of Communication, Fairfield, CT 06825. Offers corporate communications and public relations (MA Comm); digital multimedia journalism (MA Comm); digital multimedia production (MA Comm); film and television production (MA); media literacy and digital culture (MA), including children, health and media, media and social justice, political action and media production; sports communication and media (MA), including athletic communications and promotions, sports broadcasting. *Program availability:* Part-time, evening/weekend. *Degree requirements:* For master's, thesis or alternative. *Entrance requirements:* For master's, bachelor's degree. Additional exam requirements/recommendations for international students: required—TOEFL (minimum score 570 paper-based, 80 iBT), TWE, or IELTS (6.5). Electronic applications accepted. *Expenses:* Contact institution.

South Dakota State University, Graduate School, College of Arts, Humanities and Social Sciences, School of Communication and Journalism, Brookings, SD 57007. Offers communication studies and journalism (MS). *Accreditation:* ACEJMC. *Program availability:* Part-time, evening/weekend. *Degree requirements:* For master's, thesis, oral exam. *Entrance requirements:* Additional exam requirements/recommendations for international students: required—TOEFL (minimum score 550 paper-based; 79 iBT).

Southeastern Louisiana University, College of Arts, Humanities and Social Sciences, Department of Communication and Media Studies, Hammond, LA 70402. Offers health communications (MA); journalism (MA); marketing (MA); public relations (MA); sociology (MA). *Program availability:* Part-time. *Faculty:* 7 full-time (5 women). *Students:* 10 full-time (6 women), 11 part-time (6 women); includes 7 minority (5 Black or African American, non-Hispanic/Latino; 2 Hispanic/Latino). Average age 30. 9 applicants, 100% accepted, 6 enrolled. In 2019, 3 master's awarded. *Degree requirements:* For master's, comprehensive exam. *Entrance requirements:* For master's, GRE (minimum score 148 on Verbal section, 3.5 Written), Minimum 2.5 undergraduate GPA. Additional exam requirements/recommendations for international students: required—TOEFL (minimum score 525 paper-based; 75 iBT). *Application deadline:* For fall admission, 7/15 priority date for domestic students, 6/1 priority date for international students; for spring admission, 12/1 priority date for domestic students, 10/1 priority date for international students. Applications are processed on a rolling basis. Application fee: $20 ($30 for international students). Electronic applications accepted. *Expenses: Tuition, area resident:* Full-time $6684; part-time $489 per credit hour. Tuition, state resident: full-time $6684; part-time $489 per credit hour. Tuition, nonresident: full-time $19,162; part-time $1183 per credit hour. *International tuition:* $19,162 full-time. *Required fees:* $2124. *Financial support:* In 2019–20, 11 students received support, including 3 research assistantships with tuition reimbursements available (averaging $10,100 per year);

career-related internships or fieldwork, institutionally sponsored loans, and unspecified assistantships also available. Financial award application deadline: 5/1; financial award applicants required to submit FAFSA. *Unit head:* Dr. James O'Connor, Department Head, 985-549-5060, Fax: 985-549-3088, E-mail: james.oconnor@selu.edu. *Application contact:* Office of Admissions, 985-549-5637, Fax: 985-549-5632, E-mail: admissions@southeastern.edu.
Website: http://www.southeastern.edu/acad_research/depts/comm/index.html

Stony Brook University, State University of New York, School of Journalism, Stony Brook, NY 11794. Offers health communication (Certificate); journalism (MS). *Faculty:* 11 full-time (4 women), 11 part-time/adjunct (3 women). In 2019, 2 master's awarded. *Entrance requirements:* For master's, GRE, MCAT, DAT, or GMAT, bachelor's degree with minimum GPA of 3.0. Additional exam requirements/recommendations for international students: required—TOEFL (minimum score 600 paper-based; 100 iBT). *Application deadline:* For fall admission, 1/15 for domestic students; for spring admission, 10/1 for domestic students. Application fee: $100. *Expenses:* Contact institution. *Financial support:* Teaching assistantships available. *Unit head:* Dr. Laura Lindenfeld, Dean, 631-632-7403, E-mail: laura.lindenfeld@stonybrook.edu. *Application contact:* Maureen Robinson, Coordinator, 631-632-7403, Fax: 631-632-7550, E-mail: maureen.robinson@stonybrook.edu.
Website: https://journalism.cc.stonybrook.edu/

Syracuse University, S. I. Newhouse School of Public Communications, MA Program in Magazine, Newspaper and Online Journalism, Syracuse, NY 13244. Offers MA. *Accreditation:* ACEJMC. *Entrance requirements:* For master's, GRE General Test, resume, official transcripts, personal statement, three letters of recommendation. Additional exam requirements/recommendations for international students: required—TOEFL (minimum score 600 paper-based; 100 iBT). Electronic applications accepted.

Syracuse University, S. I. Newhouse School of Public Communications, MS Program in Broadcast and Digital Journalism, Syracuse, NY 13244. Offers MS. *Accreditation:* ACEJMC. *Entrance requirements:* For master's, GRE General Test, resume, official transcripts, personal statement, three letters of recommendation. Additional exam requirements/recommendations for international students: required—TOEFL (minimum score 100 iBT). Electronic applications accepted.

Temple University, Klein College of Media and Communication, Department of Journalism, Philadelphia, PA 19122-6096. Offers MJ. *Faculty:* 18 full-time (8 women), 10 part-time/adjunct (5 women). *Students:* 6 full-time (4 women), 2 part-time (1 woman); includes 3 minority (2 Black or African American, non-Hispanic/Latino; 1 Asian, non-Hispanic/Latino), 1 international. 24 applicants, 71% accepted, 7 enrolled. In 2019, 4 master's awarded. *Entrance requirements:* For master's, GRE (optional), writing sample (strongly encouraged), statement of goals, 2 letters of recommendation. Additional exam requirements/recommendations for international students: required—TOEFL (minimum score 105 iBT), IELTS (minimum score 7), PTE (minimum score 72), one of three is required. *Application deadline:* For fall admission, 2/15 for domestic students. Applications are processed on a rolling basis. Application fee: $60. Electronic applications accepted. *Expenses:* Contact institution. *Financial support:* Federal Work-Study and scholarships/grants available. Financial award application deadline: 2/15; financial award applicants required to submit FAFSA. *Unit head:* David Mindich, Chair, 215-204-1788, E-mail: mindich@temple.edu. *Application contact:* Nicole McKenna, Graduate Office Director, 215-204-1497, E-mail: nmckenna@temple.edu.
Website: https://klein.temple.edu/academics/graduate-programs/master-journalism

The University of Alabama, Graduate School, College of Communication and Information Sciences, Department of Journalism and Creative Media, Tuscaloosa, AL 35487-0172. Offers journalism and creative media (MA). *Accreditation:* ACEJMC. *Program availability:* Part-time, evening/weekend, online learning. *Faculty:* 17 full-time (5 women). *Students:* 15 full-time (11 women), 27 part-time (14 women); includes 14 minority (7 Black or African American, non-Hispanic/Latino; 1 Asian, non-Hispanic/Latino; 4 Hispanic/Latino; 2 Two or more races, non-Hispanic/Latino). Average age 34. 41 applicants, 80% accepted, 16 enrolled. In 2019, 13 master's awarded. *Degree requirements:* For master's, comprehensive exam (for some programs), thesis (for some programs). *Entrance requirements:* For master's, TOEFL scores (for international applicants), completed online application form; application fee; resume/cv; statement of purpose; 3 letters of recommendation; transcripts from previous institution. Additional exam requirements/recommendations for international students: required—TOEFL (minimum score 550 paper-based; 79 iBT). *Application deadline:* For fall admission, 3/31 priority date for domestic students, 2/15 priority date for international students; for spring admission, 11/1 priority date for domestic students, 9/15 priority date for international students. Applications are processed on a rolling basis. Application fee: $50 ($60 for international students). Electronic applications accepted. *Expenses: Tuition, area resident:* Full-time $10,780; part-time $440 per credit hour. *Tuition, nonresident:* full-time $30,250; part-time $1550 per credit hour. *Financial support:* In 2019–20, 9 students received support. Application deadline: 1/31; applicants required to submit FAFSA. *Unit head:* Dr. Cory Armstrong, Department Chair, 205-348-9684, Fax: 205-348-9684, E-mail: cory.i.armstrong@ua.edu. *Application contact:* Dr. Bill Evans, Associate Dean for Graduate Studies, 205-348-3176, Fax: 205-348-9684, E-mail: wevans@ua.edu.
Website: http://www.jcm.ua.edu/

The University of Arizona, College of Social and Behavioral Sciences, School of Journalism, Tucson, AZ 85721. Offers international journalism studies (MA); professional journalism (MA). *Program availability:* Part-time. *Degree requirements:* For master's, project. *Entrance requirements:* For master's, GRE, minimum GPA of 3.0. Additional exam requirements/recommendations for international students: required—TOEFL. Electronic applications accepted.

University of Arkansas, Graduate School, J. William Fulbright College of Arts and Sciences, School of Journalism and Strategic Media, Fayetteville, AR 72701. Offers journalism (MA). *Students:* 11 full-time (8 women), 4 part-time (2 women); includes 3 minority (2 Black or African American, non-Hispanic/Latino; 1 Hispanic/Latino), 3 international. 9 applicants, 67% accepted. In 2019, 6 master's awarded. *Application deadline:* For fall admission, 8/1 for domestic students, 4/1 for international students; for spring admission, 12/1 for domestic students, 10/1 for international students; for summer admission, 4/15 for domestic students, 3/1 for international students. Application fee: $60. Electronic applications accepted. *Financial support:* In 2019–20, 4 research assistantships, 3 teaching assistantships were awarded; fellowships with tuition reimbursements, career-related internships or fieldwork, and Federal Work-Study also available. Support available to part-time students. Financial award application deadline: 4/1; financial award applicants required to submit FAFSA. *Unit head:* Dr. Larry Foley, Department Chair, 479-575-6307, E-mail: lfoley@uark.edu. *Application contact:* Dr. Rob Wells, Graduate Coordinator, 479-575-6305, E-mail: rswells@uark.edu.
Website: https://fulbright.uark.edu/departments/journalism/

The University of British Columbia, Faculty of Arts, School of Journalism, Vancouver, BC V6T 1Z2, Canada. Offers MJ. *Degree requirements:* For master's, thesis, 3-month internship. *Entrance requirements:* For master's, portfolio, resume, letters of reference. Additional exam requirements/recommendations for international students: required—TOEFL, IELTS. Electronic applications accepted. *Expenses:* Contact institution.

University of California, Berkeley, Graduate Division, Graduate School of Journalism, Berkeley, CA 94720. Offers MJ, JD/MJ, MJ/MA. *Degree requirements:* For master's, project. *Entrance requirements:* For master's, GRE General Test, 3 work samples, minimum GPA of 3.0, 3 letters of recommendation. Additional exam requirements/recommendations for international students: required—TOEFL (minimum score 600 paper-based). Electronic applications accepted.

University of Colorado Boulder, Graduate School, College of Media, Communication and Information, Program in Journalism, Boulder, CO 80309. Offers journalism (MA); media research and practice (PhD). *Accreditation:* ACEJMC. Electronic applications accepted. Application fee is waived when completed online.

University of Florida, Graduate School, College of Journalism and Communications, Program in Mass Communication, Gainesville, FL 32611. Offers international/intercultural communication (MAMC); journalism (MAMC); mass communication (MAMC, PhD), including clinical translational science (MAMC); public relations (MAMC); science/health communication (MAMC); telecommunication (MAMC). *Entrance requirements:* For master's and doctorate, GRE General Test, minimum GPA of 3.0.

University of Georgia, Grady College of Journalism and Mass Communication, Athens, GA 30602. Offers journalism and mass communication (MA); mass communication (PhD). *Degree requirements:* For master's, comprehensive exam, thesis (MA); for doctorate, comprehensive exam, thesis/dissertation. *Entrance requirements:* For master's and doctorate, GRE General Test. Additional exam requirements/recommendations for international students: required—TOEFL, TWE for PhD. Electronic applications accepted.

University of Illinois at Springfield, Graduate Programs, College of Public Affairs and Administration, Public Affairs Reporting Program, Springfield, IL 62703-5407. Offers MA. *Program availability:* Part-time. *Faculty:* 1 full-time (0 women), 1 part-time/adjunct (0 women). *Students:* 8 full-time (3 women); includes 3 minority (1 Black or African American, non-Hispanic/Latino; 1 Hispanic/Latino; 1 Two or more races, non-Hispanic/Latino). Average age 26. 15 applicants, 73% accepted, 7 enrolled. In 2019, 10 master's awarded. *Degree requirements:* For master's, internship, professional portfolio. *Entrance requirements:* For master's, literacy/competency writing test, interview, written work samples, narrative statement on qualifications and interest in program, 3 letters of reference. Additional exam requirements/recommendations for international students: required—TOEFL (minimum score 500 paper-based; 61 iBT). *Application deadline:* Applications are processed on a rolling basis. Application fee: $60 ($75 for international students). Electronic applications accepted. *Expenses: Tuition, area resident:* Full-time $7896; part-time $329 per credit hour. Tuition, nonresident: full-time $16,200; part-time $675 per credit hour. *Required fees:* $2735.60; $130.65 per credit hour. *Financial support:* In 2019–20, research assistantships with full tuition reimbursements (averaging $10,562 per year), teaching assistantships with full tuition reimbursements (averaging $10,652 per year) were awarded; fellowships, career-related internships or fieldwork, Federal Work-Study, scholarships/grants, health care benefits, and unspecified assistantships also available. Support available to part-time students. Financial award application deadline: 11/15; financial award applicants required to submit FAFSA. *Unit head:* Dr. Jason Piscia, Director, 217-206-7494, Fax: 217-206-7807, E-mail: jason.piscia@uis.edu. *Application contact:* Dr. Jason Piscia, Director, 217-206-7494, Fax: 217-206-7807, E-mail: jason.piscia@uis.edu.
Website: http://www.uis.edu/publicaffairsreporting

University of Illinois at Urbana-Champaign, Graduate College, College of Media, Department of Journalism, Champaign, IL 61820. Offers MS, MS/JD, MS/MBA.

The University of Iowa, Graduate College, College of Liberal Arts and Sciences, School of Journalism and Mass Communication, Iowa City, IA 52242-1316. Offers journalism and media communication (MA); mass communication (PhD); strategic communication (MA); JD/MA; JD/PhD. *Degree requirements:* For master's, thesis optional, exam; for doctorate, comprehensive exam, thesis/dissertation. *Entrance requirements:* For master's and doctorate, GRE General Test, minimum GPA of 3.0. Additional exam requirements/recommendations for international students: required—TOEFL (minimum score 637 paper-based; 110 iBT). Electronic applications accepted.

The University of Kansas, Graduate Studies, William Allen White School of Journalism and Mass Communications, Lawrence, KS 66045. Offers journalism (MS); journalism and mass communications (PhD); JD/MS. *Program availability:* Part-time. *Students:* 23 full-time (14 women), 80 part-time (59 women); includes 18 minority (5 Black or African American, non-Hispanic/Latino; 8 Hispanic/Latino; 5 Two or more races, non-Hispanic/Latino), 10 international. Average age 33. 58 applicants, 71% accepted, 32 enrolled. In 2019, 44 master's, 2 doctorates awarded. Terminal master's awarded for partial completion of doctoral program. *Entrance requirements:* For master's and doctorate, GRE, minimum GPA of 3.0; official transcript; current resume; two writing samples, preferably academic, or samples of professional work that reflect years of experience; statement of academic interests and professional goals; three letters of reference. Additional exam requirements/recommendations for international students: required—TOEFL, IELTS. *Application deadline:* For fall admission, 1/1 priority date for domestic and international students; for spring admission, 8/1 for domestic and international students; for summer admission, 5/15 for domestic and international students. Application fee: $65 ($85 for international students). Electronic applications accepted. *Expenses:* Tuition, state resident: full-time $9989. Tuition, nonresident: full-time $23,950. *International tuition:* $23,950 full-time. *Required fees:* $984; $81.99 per credit hour. Tuition and fees vary according to course load, campus/location and program. *Financial support:* Fellowships, research assistantships, teaching assistantships, career-related internships or fieldwork, scholarships/grants, and unspecified assistantships available. Support available to part-time students. Financial award application deadline: 2/1; financial award applicants required to submit FAFSA. *Unit head:* Ann Brill, Dean, 785-864-4755, E-mail: abrill@ku.edu. *Application contact:* Jammie A. Johnson, Graduate Advisor/Administrative Assistant, 785-864-7649, E-mail: jamjohn@ku.edu.
Website: http://www.journalism.ku.edu/

University of King's College, Graduate and Advanced Programs, Halifax, NS B3H 2A1, Canada. Offers creative nonfiction (MFA); journalism (MJ).

University of Maryland, College Park, Academic Affairs, Philip Merrill College of Journalism, College Park, MD 20742. Offers broadcast journalism (MA); journalism (MA); journalism and media studies (PhD); online news (MA); public affairs reporting (MA). *Accreditation:* ACEJMC (one or more programs are accredited). *Program availability:* Part-time, evening/weekend. *Degree requirements:* For doctorate, thesis/dissertation, preliminary written and oral comprehensive exams. *Entrance requirements:* For master's and doctorate, GRE General Test, minimum GPA of 3.0, 3 letters of recommendation. Additional exam requirements/recommendations for international students: required—TOEFL. Electronic applications accepted.

University of Memphis, Graduate School, College of Communication and Fine Arts, Department of Journalism and Strategic Media, Memphis, TN 38152. Offers entrepreneurial journalism (Graduate Certificate); journalism and strategic media (MA). *Program availability:* Part-time, evening/weekend, online learning. *Students:* 10 full-time (8 women), 17 part-time (12 women); includes 9 minority (8 Black or African American, non-Hispanic/Latino; 1 Two or more races, non-Hispanic/Latino). Average age 31. 23 applicants, 100% accepted, 13 enrolled. In 2019, 8 master's awarded. *Degree*

requirements: For master's, comprehensive exam, thesis (for some programs), culminating experience: project, thesis, or referred paper. *Entrance requirements:* For master's, GRE General Test, MAT, transcripts, resume, goal statement. Additional exam requirements/recommendations for international students: required—TOEFL (minimum score 600 paper-based). *Application deadline:* For fall admission, 6/1 for domestic and international students; for spring admission, 10/1 for domestic and international students; for summer admission, 2/1 for domestic and international students. Applications are processed on a rolling basis. Application fee: $35 ($60 for international students). Electronic applications accepted. *Expenses: Tuition, area resident:* Full-time $9216; part-time $512 per credit hour. Tuition, state resident: full-time $9216; part-time $512 per credit hour. Tuition, nonresident: full-time $12,672; part-time $704 per credit hour. *International tuition:* $16,128 full-time. *Required fees:* $1530; $85 per credit hour. Tuition and fees vary according to program. *Financial support:* Research assistantships with full tuition reimbursements, Federal Work-Study, scholarships/grants, and unspecified assistantships available. Support available to part-time students. Financial award application deadline: 2/1; financial award applicants required to submit FAFSA. *Unit head:* Dr. David Arant, Chair, 901-678-2402, Fax: 901-678-4287, E-mail: darant@memphis.edu. *Application contact:* Dr. David Arant, Chair, 901-678-2402, Fax: 901-678-4287, E-mail: darant@memphis.edu.
Website: http://www.memphis.edu/jrsm/

University of Miami, Graduate School, School of Communication, Coral Gables, FL 33124. Offers communication (PhD); communication studies (MA); film studies (MA, PhD); motion pictures (MFA), including production, producing, and screenwriting; print journalism (MA); public relations (MA); Spanish language journalism (MA); television broadcast journalism (MA). *Program availability:* Part-time. *Degree requirements:* For master's, comprehensive exam (for some programs), thesis (for some programs); for doctorate, comprehensive exam, thesis/dissertation. *Entrance requirements:* For master's, GRE General Test; for doctorate, GRE General Test, master's thesis or scholarly research. Additional exam requirements/recommendations for international students: required—TOEFL (minimum score 600 paper-based; 100 iBT). Electronic applications accepted.

University of Mississippi, Graduate School, School of Journalism and New Media, University, MS 38677. Offers integrated marketing communications (MA); journalism (MA). *Faculty:* 33 full-time (15 women), 19 part-time/adjunct (8 women). *Students:* 42 full-time (26 women), 23 part-time (19 women); includes 13 minority (6 Black or African American, non-Hispanic/Latino; 4 Hispanic/Latino; 3 Two or more races, non-Hispanic/Latino), 4 international. Average age 26. In 2019, 18 master's awarded. *Degree requirements:* For master's, thesis. *Application deadline:* Applications are processed on a rolling basis. Application fee: $50. Electronic applications accepted. *Expenses:* Tuition, state resident: full-time $8718; part-time $484.25 per credit hour. Tuition, nonresident: full-time $24,990; part-time $1388.25 per credit hour. *Required fees:* $100; $4.16 per credit hour. *Unit head:* Dr. Debora Wenger, Interim Dean, 662-915-7146, Fax: 662-915-7765, E-mail: jour-imc@olemiss.edu. *Application contact:* Tameka Smith, Graduate Activities Specialist for Admission, 662-915-7474, Fax: 662-915-7577, E-mail: gschool@olemiss.edu.
Website: https://jnm.olemiss.edu/

University of Missouri, Office of Research and Graduate Studies, School of Journalism, Columbia, MO 65211. Offers health communications (MA); journalism (PhD). *Accreditation:* ACEJMC (one or more programs are accredited). *Program availability:* Part-time. Terminal master's awarded for partial completion of doctoral program. *Entrance requirements:* For master's and doctorate, GRE General Test, minimum GPA of 3.0. Additional exam requirements/recommendations for international students: required—TOEFL, IELTS. Electronic applications accepted.

University of Montana, Graduate School, School of Journalism, Missoula, MT 59812. Offers MA. *Degree requirements:* For master's, thesis or alternative, professional project. *Entrance requirements:* For master's, GRE. Additional exam requirements/recommendations for international students: required—TOEFL (minimum score 580 paper-based). Electronic applications accepted.

University of Nebraska–Lincoln, Graduate College, College of Journalism and Mass Communications, Lincoln, NE 68588. Offers marketing, communication and advertising (MA); professional journalism (MA). *Program availability:* Online learning. *Degree requirements:* For master's, thesis. *Entrance requirements:* For master's, samples of work. Additional exam requirements/recommendations for international students: required—TOEFL (minimum score 600 paper-based). Electronic applications accepted.

University of Nevada, Las Vegas, Graduate College, Greenspun College of Urban Affairs, Hank Greenspun School of Journalism and Media Studies, Las Vegas, NV 89154-5007. Offers MA. *Program availability:* Part-time. *Faculty:* 4 full-time (0 women). *Students:* 12 full-time (7 women), 7 part-time (3 women); includes 11 minority (2 Black or African American, non-Hispanic/Latino; 7 Hispanic/Latino; 1 Native Hawaiian or other Pacific Islander, non-Hispanic/Latino; 1 Two or more races, non-Hispanic/Latino), 2 international. Average age 29. 14 applicants, 79% accepted, 9 enrolled. In 2019, 5 master's awarded. *Degree requirements:* For master's, comprehensive exam, thesis optional, oral exam. *Entrance requirements:* For master's, GRE General Test, bachelor's degree with minimum GPA 3.0; 3 letters of recommendation; statement of purpose; writing sample. Additional exam requirements/recommendations for international students: required—TOEFL (minimum score 550 paper-based; 80 iBT), IELTS (minimum score 7). *Application deadline:* For fall admission, 3/15 for domestic and international students. Application fee: $60 ($95 for international students). Electronic applications accepted. *Expenses:* Contact institution. *Financial support:* In 2019–20, 7 students received support, including 5 research assistantships with full tuition reimbursements available (averaging $11,500 per year), 6 teaching assistantships with full tuition reimbursements available (averaging $11,250 per year); institutionally sponsored loans, scholarships/grants, health care benefits, and unspecified assistantships also available. Financial award application deadline: 3/15; financial award applicants required to submit FAFSA. *Unit head:* Dr. Kevin Stoker, Chair and Professor, 702-895-2619, Fax: 702-895-0252, E-mail: jms.chair@unlv.edu. *Application contact:* Dr. Ben Burroughs, Graduate Coordinator, 702-895-3647, Fax: 702-895-5189, E-mail: jms.gradcoord@unlv.edu.
Website: http://journalism.unlv.edu/

University of Nevada, Reno, Graduate School, Donald W. Reynolds School of Journalism, Reno, NV 89557. Offers MA. *Degree requirements:* For master's, thesis. *Entrance requirements:* For master's, GRE General Test, minimum GPA of 2.75. Additional exam requirements/recommendations for international students: required—TOEFL (minimum score 500 paper-based; 61 iBT), IELTS (minimum score 6). Electronic applications accepted.

The University of North Carolina at Chapel Hill, Graduate School, Hussman School of Journalism and Media, Chapel Hill, NC 27599. Offers digital communication (MA, Certificate); media and communication (MA, PhD), including interdisciplinary health communication (MA), journalism (MA), strategic communication (MA), theory and research (MA), visual communication (MA); JD/PhD; MA/JD. *Accreditation:* ACEJMC (one or more programs are accredited). *Program availability:* Part-time, all course instruction online, plus two on-campus experiences totaling seven days. *Faculty:* 30 full-time (15 women), 5 part-time/adjunct (4 women). *Students:* 68 full-time (45 women), 82 part-time (58 women); includes 35 minority (13 Black or African American, non-Hispanic/Latino; 1 American Indian or Alaska Native, non-Hispanic/Latino; 4 Asian, non-Hispanic/Latino; 1 Hispanic/Latino; 16 Two or more races, non-Hispanic/Latino), 9 international. Average age 34. 205 applicants, 49% accepted, 73 enrolled. In 2019, 32 master's, 5 doctorates, 24 other advanced degrees awarded. *Degree requirements:* For master's, comprehensive exam, thesis; for doctorate, comprehensive exam, thesis/dissertation. *Entrance requirements:* For master's, Online master's degree only: GRE General Test (waiver available). Residential master's degree: minimum GPA of 3.0; for doctorate, minimum GPA of 3.0. Additional exam requirements/recommendations for international students: required—TOEFL (minimum iBT score of 105) or IELTS (7.5). Application fee: $95. Electronic applications accepted. *Expenses:* Ph.D.: 7,550 per semester N.C. resident, 15,883 non-res; Residential M.A.: 8,425 per semester N.C., 16,708 non-res; Online M.A./certificate: 2,262 per semester N.C., 4,698 non-res. *Financial support:* In 2019–20, 60 students received support, including 41 fellowships with full tuition reimbursements available (averaging $17,901 per year), 4 research assistantships with full tuition reimbursements available (averaging $17,465 per year); scholarships/grants and health care benefits also available. Financial award application deadline: 12/15; financial award applicants required to submit FAFSA. *Unit head:* Susan King, Dean, 919-962-1204, Fax: 919-962-0620, E-mail: susanking@unc.edu. *Application contact:* Casey Hart, Assistant Director, Graduate Studies, 919-843-9471, Fax: 919-962-0620, E-mail: mjgrad@unc.edu.
Website: http://hussman.unc.edu

University of North Texas, Toulouse Graduate School, Denton, TX 76203-5459. Offers accounting (MS); applied anthropology (MA, MS); applied behavior analysis (Certificate); applied geography (MA); applied technology and performance improvement (M Ed, MS); art education (MA); art history (MA); arts leadership (Certificate); audiology (Au D); behavior analysis (MS); behavioral science (PhD); biochemistry and molecular biology (MS); biology (MA, MS); biomedical engineering (MS); business analysis (MS); chemistry (MS); clinical health psychology (PhD); communication studies (MA, MS); computer engineering (MS); computer science (MS); counseling (M Ed, MS), including clinical mental health counseling (MS), college and university counseling, elementary school counseling, secondary school counseling; creative writing (MA); criminal justice (MS); curriculum and instruction (M Ed); decision sciences (MBA); design (MA, MFA), including fashion design (MFA), innovation studies, interior design (MFA); early childhood studies (MS); economics (MS); educational leadership (M Ed, Ed D); educational psychology (MS, PhD), including family studies (MS), gifted and talented (MS), human development (MS), learning and cognition (MS), research, measurement and evaluation (MS); electrical engineering (MS); emergency management (MPA); engineering technology (MS); English (MA); English as a second language (MA); environmental science (MS); finance (MBA, MS); financial management (MPA); French (MA); health services management (MBA); higher education (M Ed, Ed D); history (MA, MS); hospitality management (MS); human resources management (MPA); information science (MS); information systems (PhD); information technologies (MBA); interdisciplinary studies (MA, MS); international studies (MA); international sustainable tourism (MS); jazz studies (MM); journalism (MA, MJ, Graduate Certificate), including interactive and virtual digital communication (Graduate Certificate), narrative journalism (Graduate Certificate), public relations (Graduate Certificate); kinesiology (MS); linguistics (MA); local government management (MPA); logistics (PhD); logistics and supply chain management (MBA); long-term care, senior housing, and aging services (MA); management (PhD); marketing (MBA); mathematics (MA, MS); mechanical and energy engineering (MS, PhD); music (MA), including ethnomusicology, music theory, musicology, performance; music composition (PhD); music education (MM Ed, PhD); nonprofit management (MPA); operations and supply chain management (MBA); performance (MM, DMA); philosophy (MA); political science (MA); professional and technical communication (MA); radio, television and film (MA, MFA); rehabilitation counseling (Certificate); sociology (MA); Spanish (MA); special education (M Ed); speech-language pathology (MA); strategic management (MBA); studio art (MFA); teaching (M Ed); MBA/MS. *Program availability:* Part-time, evening/weekend, online learning. Terminal master's awarded for partial completion of doctoral program. *Degree requirements:* For master's, variable foreign language requirement, comprehensive exam (for some programs), thesis (for some programs); for doctorate, variable foreign language requirement, comprehensive exam (for some programs), thesis/dissertation; for other advanced degree, variable foreign language requirement, comprehensive exam (for some programs). *Entrance requirements:* For master's and doctorate, GRE, GMAT. Additional exam requirements/recommendations for international students: required—TOEFL (minimum score 550 paper-based; 79 iBT). Electronic applications accepted.

University of Oregon, Graduate School, School of Journalism and Communication, Eugene, OR 97403. Offers journalism (MA, MS); media studies (MA, MS, PhD); multimedia journalism (MA, MS); strategic communication (MA, MS). *Accreditation:* ASHA. *Program availability:* Part-time. *Degree requirements:* For master's, thesis or alternative. *Entrance requirements:* For master's, GRE General Test; for doctorate, master's degree.

University of Puerto Rico at Rio Piedras, School of Communication, Program in Journalism, San Juan, PR 00931-3300. Offers MA.

University of Regina, Faculty of Graduate Studies and Research, Faculty of Arts, School of Journalism, Regina, SK S4S 0A2, Canada. Offers MJ. *Program availability:* Part-time. *Faculty:* 7 full-time (2 women). *Students:* 8 full-time (3 women). Average age 30. 27 applicants, 7% accepted. In 2019, 5 master's awarded. *Degree requirements:* For master's, project. *Entrance requirements:* For master's, written project concept; statement of interest; statement of ability, post secondary transcripts and 2 letter of recommendations. Additional exam requirements/recommendations for international students: required—TOEFL (minimum score 580 paper-based; 80 iBT), IELTS (minimum score 6.5), PTE (minimum score 59), other options are CAEL, Cantest, MELAB and ESl at U of Regina. *Application deadline:* For fall admission, 6/30 for domestic and international students. Application fee: $100 Canadian dollars. Electronic applications accepted. *Expenses: Tuition:* Full-time $6684 Canadian dollars. *Required fees:* $100 Canadian dollars; $3351.45 Canadian dollars per trimester. $1117.15 Canadian dollars per semester. Tuition and fees vary according to course level, course load, degree level and program. *Financial support:* Fellowships, research assistantships, teaching assistantships, career-related internships or fieldwork, Federal Work-Study, scholarships/grants, unspecified assistantships, and Travel award and Graduate Scholarship Base funds available. Support available to part-time students. Financial award application deadline: 9/30. *Unit head:* Dr. Mark Taylor, Department Head, 306-585-4091, Fax: 306-585-4867, E-mail: mark.taylor@uregina.ca. *Application contact:* Trevor Grant, Graduate Program Coordinator (on leave), 306-585-5051, Fax: 306-585-4867, E-mail: treveor.grant@uregina.ca.
Website: http://www.uregina.ca/arts/journalism/

University of South Carolina, The Graduate School, College of Information and Communications, School of Journalism and Mass Communications, Columbia, SC 29208. Offers MA, MMC, PhD. *Accreditation:* ACEJMC. *Program availability:* Part-time. *Degree requirements:* For master's, comprehensive exam, thesis (for some programs);

for doctorate, one foreign language, comprehensive exam, thesis/dissertation. *Entrance requirements:* For master's and doctorate, GRE General Test, minimum GPA of 3.0. Additional exam requirements/recommendations for international students: required—TOEFL (minimum score 600 paper-based; 75 iBT). Electronic applications accepted.

University of Southern California, Graduate School, Annenberg School for Communication and Journalism, School of Journalism, Program in Journalism, Los Angeles, CA 90089. Offers MS. *Accreditation:* ACEJMC. *Program availability:* Part-time. *Students:* 39 full-time, 1 part-time; includes 17 minority (3 Black or African American, non-Hispanic/Latino; 4 Asian, non-Hispanic/Latino; 8 Hispanic/Latino; 2 Two or more races, non-Hispanic/Latino), 9 international. Average age 25. 124 applicants, 52% accepted, 38 enrolled. In 2019, 42 master's awarded. *Degree requirements:* For master's, professional project. *Entrance requirements:* For master's, GRE General Test, resume, writing samples, letters of recommendation, statement of purpose. Additional exam requirements/recommendations for international students: required—TOEFL (minimum score 114 iBT), IELTS (minimum score 8). *Application deadline:* For summer admission, 1/1 priority date for domestic and international students. Application fee: $90. Electronic applications accepted. *Financial support:* In 2019–20, 25 fellowships with full and partial tuition reimbursements (averaging $30,000 per year), 4 teaching assistantships with full and partial tuition reimbursements (averaging $20,000 per year) were awarded; career-related internships or fieldwork, Federal Work-Study, institutionally sponsored loans, scholarships/grants, health care benefits, and unspecified assistantships also available. Support available to part-time students. Financial award application deadline: 1/1; financial award applicants required to submit FAFSA. *Unit head:* Dr. Lisa Pecot-Herbert, Director, 213-821-1184, E-mail: pecotheb@usc.edu. *Application contact:* Allyson Hill, Associate Dean for Admissions, 213-821-0770, Fax: 213-740-1933, E-mail: ascadm@usc.edu. Website: http://www.annenberg.usc.edu

University of Southern California, Graduate School, Annenberg School for Communication and Journalism, School of Journalism, Program in Specialized Journalism, Los Angeles, CA 90089. Offers specialized journalism (MA); specialized journalism (the arts) (MA). *Accreditation:* ACEJMC. *Program availability:* Part-time. *Students:* 29 full-time, 3 part-time; includes 15 minority (6 Black or African American, non-Hispanic/Latino; 1 Asian, non-Hispanic/Latino; 8 Hispanic/Latino), 5 international. Average age 32. 74 applicants, 61% accepted, 28 enrolled. In 2019, 24 master's awarded. *Degree requirements:* For master's, thesis, professional project. *Entrance requirements:* For master's, GRE General Test, resume, portfolio of professional work, letters of recommendation, statement of purpose. Additional exam requirements/recommendations for international students: required—TOEFL (minimum score 114 iBT), IELTS (minimum score 8). *Application deadline:* For summer admission, 1/15 priority date for domestic and international students. Applications are processed on a rolling basis. Application fee: $90. Electronic applications accepted. *Financial support:* In 2019–20, 6 fellowships with full and partial tuition reimbursements (averaging $40,000 per year) were awarded; research assistantships, Federal Work-Study, scholarships/grants, and health care benefits also available. Support available to part-time students. Financial award application deadline: 1/1; financial award applicants required to submit FAFSA. *Unit head:* Sandy Andrew Tolan, Professor of Journalism and Faculty Program Director, 213-740-2472, E-mail: atolan@usc.edu. *Application contact:* Allyson Hill, Associate Dean for Admissions, 213-821-0770, Fax: 213-740-1933, E-mail: ascadm@usc.edu.

University of South Florida, Innovative Education, Tampa, FL 33620-9951. Offers adult, career and higher education (Graduate Certificate), including college teaching, leadership in developing human resources, leadership in higher education; Africana studies (Graduate Certificate), including diasporas and health disparities, genocide and human rights; aging studies (Graduate Certificate), including gerontology; art research (Graduate Certificate), including museum studies; business foundations (Graduate Certificate); chemical and biomedical engineering (Graduate Certificate), including materials science and engineering, water, health and sustainability; child and family studies (Graduate Certificate), including positive behavior support; civil and industrial engineering (Graduate Certificate), including transportation systems analysis; community and family health (Graduate Certificate), including maternal and child health, social marketing and public health, violence and injury: prevention and intervention, women's health; criminology (Graduate Certificate), including criminal justice administration; data science for public administration (Graduate Certificate); digital humanities (Graduate Certificate); educational measurement and research (Graduate Certificate), including evaluation; English (Graduate Certificate), including comparative literary studies, creative writing, professional and technical communication; entrepreneurship (Graduate Certificate); environmental health (Graduate Certificate), including safety management; epidemiology and biostatistics (Graduate Certificate), including applied biostatistics, biostatistics, concepts and tools of epidemiology, epidemiology, epidemiology of infectious diseases; geography, environment and planning (Graduate Certificate), including community development, environmental policy and management, geographical information systems; geology (Graduate Certificate), including hydrogeology; global health (Graduate Certificate), including disaster management, global health and Latin American and Caribbean studies, global health practice, humanitarian assistance, infection control; government and international affairs (Graduate Certificate), including Cuban studies, globalization studies; health policy and management (Graduate Certificate), including health management and leadership, public health policy and programs; hearing specialist: early intervention (Graduate Certificate); industrial and management systems engineering (Graduate Certificate), including systems engineering, technology management; information studies (Graduate Certificate), including school library media specialist; information systems/decision sciences (Graduate Certificate), including analytics and business intelligence; instructional technology (Graduate Certificate), including distance education, Florida digital/virtual educator, instructional design, multimedia design, Web design; internal medicine, bioethics and medical humanities (Graduate Certificate), including biomedical ethics; Latin American and Caribbean studies (Graduate Certificate); leadership for coastal resiliency planning (Graduate Certificate); mass communications (Graduate Certificate), including multimedia journalism; mathematics and statistics (Graduate Certificate), including mathematics; medicine (Graduate Certificate), including aging and neuroscience, bioinformatics, biotechnology, brain fitness and memory management, clinical investigation, hand and upper limb rehabilitation, health informatics, health sciences, integrative weight management, intellectual property, medicine and gender, metabolic and nutritional medicine, metabolic cardiology, pharmacy sciences; national and competitive intelligence (Graduate Certificate); nursing (Graduate Certificate), including simulation based academic fellowship in advanced pain management; psychological and social foundations (Graduate Certificate), including career counseling, college teaching, diversity in education, mental health counseling, school counseling; public affairs (Graduate Certificate), including nonprofit management, public management, research administration; public health (Graduate Certificate), including assessing chemical toxicity and public health risks, health equity, pharmacoepidemiology, public health generalist, toxicology, translational research in adolescent behavioral health; public health practices (Graduate Certificate), including

planning for healthy communities; rehabilitation and mental health counseling (Graduate Certificate), including integrative mental health care, marriage and family therapy, rehabilitation technology; secondary education (Graduate Certificate), including ESOL, foreign language education: culture and content, foreign language education: professional; social work (Graduate Certificate), including geriatric social work/clinical gerontology; special education (Graduate Certificate), including autism spectrum disorder, disabilities education: severe/profound; world languages (Graduate Certificate), including teaching English as a second language (TESL) or foreign language. *Unit head:* Dr. Cynthia DeLuca, Associate Vice President and Assistant Vice Provost, 813-974-3077, Fax: 813-974-7061, E-mail: deluca@usf.edu. *Application contact:* Owen Hooper, Director, Summer and Alternative Calendar Programs, 813-974-6917, E-mail: hooper@usf.edu.
Website: http://www.usf.edu/innovative-education/

University of South Florida, St. Petersburg, College of Arts and Sciences, St. Petersburg, FL 33701. Offers digital journalism and design (MA); environmental science and policy (MA, MS); Florida studies (MLA); journalism and media studies (MA); liberal studies (MLA); psychology (MA). *Program availability:* Part-time, online learning. *Degree requirements:* For master's, comprehensive exam, thesis or project. *Entrance requirements:* For master's, GRE, LSAT, MCAT (varies by program), letter of intent, 3 letters of recommendation, writing samples, bachelor's degree from regionally-accredited institution with minimum GPA of 3.0 overall or in upper two years. Additional exam requirements/recommendations for international students: required—TOEFL (minimum score 550 paper-based; 79 iBT); recommended—IELTS. Electronic applications accepted.

The University of Tennessee, Graduate School, College of Communication and Information, Knoxville, TN 37996. Offers advertising (MS, PhD); communications (MS, PhD); information sciences (MS, PhD); journalism and electronic media (MS, PhD); public relations (MS, PhD). *Program availability:* Part-time, evening/weekend, online learning. *Degree requirements:* For master's, thesis or alternative; for doctorate, thesis/dissertation. *Entrance requirements:* For master's and doctorate, GRE General Test, minimum GPA of 2.7. Additional exam requirements/recommendations for international students: required—TOEFL. Electronic applications accepted.

The University of Texas at Austin, Graduate School, College of Communication, School of Journalism, Austin, TX 78712-1111. Offers MA, PhD, MA/MA, MBA/MA, MP Aff/MA. *Program availability:* Part-time. *Degree requirements:* For master's, thesis; for doctorate, one foreign language, thesis/dissertation. *Entrance requirements:* For master's and doctorate, GRE General Test. Electronic applications accepted.

The University of Western Ontario, School of Graduate and Postdoctoral Studies, Faculty of Information and Media Studies, Program in Journalism, London, ON N6A 3K7, Canada. Offers MA. *Degree requirements:* For master's, internship. *Entrance requirements:* For master's, honors degree, minimum B average during previous 2 years of course work. Additional exam requirements/recommendations for international students: required—TOEFL (minimum score 640 paper-based), TWE (minimum score 5). Electronic applications accepted.

University of Wisconsin–Madison, Graduate School, College of Agricultural and Life Sciences, Department of Life Sciences Communication, Madison, WI 53706-1380. Offers life sciences communication (MPS, MS); mass communications (PhD). *Program availability:* Part-time. Terminal master's awarded for partial completion of doctoral program. *Degree requirements:* For master's, thesis (for some programs); for doctorate, thesis/dissertation. *Entrance requirements:* For master's, GRE; for doctorate, GRE, master's degree in a communication field or related area of study. Additional exam requirements/recommendations for international students: required—TOEFL. Electronic applications accepted.

University of Wisconsin–Madison, Graduate School, College of Letters and Science, School of Journalism and Mass Communication, Program in Journalism and Mass Communication, Madison, WI 53706-1380. Offers MA.

Université Laval, Faculty of Letters, Department of Information and Communication, Program in International Journalism, Québec, QC G1K 7P4, Canada. Offers Diploma. *Entrance requirements:* For degree, English exam, French exam, test on international current events, interview, knowledge of French, knowledge of English. Electronic applications accepted.

Virginia Commonwealth University, Graduate School, College of Humanities and Sciences, Richard T. Robertson School of Media and Culture, Program in Mass Communications, Richmond, VA 23284-9005. Offers multimedia journalism (MS); strategic public relations (MS). *Degree requirements:* For master's, comprehensive exam, thesis optional. *Entrance requirements:* For master's, GRE General Test. Additional exam requirements/recommendations for international students: required—TOEFL (minimum score 600 paper-based; 100 iBT); recommended—IELTS (minimum score 6.5). Electronic applications accepted.

Wayne State University, College of Fine, Performing and Communication Arts, Department of Communication, Detroit, MI 48202. Offers communication (PhD), including democratic participation and culture, identity and representation, media, society and culture, risk, crisis and conflict, wellness, work life and relationships; communication and new media (Graduate Certificate); communication studies (MA); dispute resolution (MADR, Graduate Certificate), including community and urban studies (MADR), conflict area studies (MADR), health and family (MADR), international conflict and cooperation (MADR), professional practice (MADR), theory of conflict (MADR), workplace (MADR); health communication (Graduate Certificate); journalism (MA); media arts (MA); media studies (MA); public relations and organizational communication (MA); JD/MADR. *Program availability:* Online learning. *Degree requirements:* For master's, thesis (for some programs), thesis or essay; for doctorate, thesis/dissertation. *Entrance requirements:* For master's, GRE (for MA if undergraduate GPA less than 3.2), personal statement; BA or BS in communication or related field with minimum upper-division GPA of 3.2 and minimum upper-division undergraduate GPA of 3.0, and sample of academic writing (for MA); undergraduate degree with minimum upper-division GPA of 3.0 and three letters of recommendation (for MADR); for doctorate, GRE, undergraduate degree in communication or related field; master's degree in communication or related field with minimum GPA of 3.5; letters of recommendation; personal statement; sample of written scholarship. Additional exam requirements/recommendations for international students: required—TOEFL (minimum score 100 iBT), IELTS, TWE. Electronic applications accepted. *Expenses:* Contact institution.

West Virginia University, Reed College of Media, Morgantown, WV 26506. Offers data marketing communications (MS); integrated marketing communications (MS, Graduate Certificate); journalism (MSJ); media solutions and innovation (MSJ). *Program availability:* Part-time, online learning. *Degree requirements:* For master's, thesis or alternative. *Entrance requirements:* For master's, GRE General Test, minimum GPA of 3.0, writing samples. Additional exam requirements/recommendations for international students: required—TOEFL (minimum score 550 paper-based). Electronic applications accepted.

Mass Communication

American University, School of Communication, Division of Public Communication, Washington, DC 20016-8001. Offers advocacy and social impact (MA); corporate communication and reputation management (MA); political communication (MA); strategic communication (MA). *Accreditation:* ACEJMC. *Program availability:* Part-time, evening/weekend, 100% online. *Degree requirements:* For master's, comprehensive exam, thesis or alternative. *Entrance requirements:* Additional exam requirements/recommendations for international students: required—TOEFL (minimum score 600 paper-based; 100 iBT), IELTS (minimum score 7). Electronic applications accepted.

American University, School of International Service, Washington, DC 20016-8071. Offers comparative and regional studies (Certificate); cross-cultural communication (Certificate); development management (MS); ethics, peace, and global affairs (MA); European studies (Certificate); global environmental policy (MA, Certificate); global information technology (Certificate); global media (MA); international affairs (MA), including comparative and regional studies, global governance, politics, and security, international economic relations, natural resources and sustainable development, U.S. foreign policy and national security; international arts management (Certificate); international communication (MA, Certificate); international development (MA); international economic policy (Certificate); international economic relations (Certificate); international economics (MA); international peace and conflict resolution (MA, Certificate); international politics (Certificate); international relations (MA, PhD); international service (MIS); peacebuilding (Certificate); social enterprise (MA); the Americas (Certificate); United States foreign policy (Certificate); JD/MA. *Program availability:* Part-time, evening/weekend, 100% online, blended/hybrid learning. Terminal master's awarded for partial completion of doctoral program. *Degree requirements:* For master's, one foreign language, comprehensive exam, thesis or alternative; for doctorate, one foreign language, comprehensive exam, thesis/dissertation. *Entrance requirements:* For master's, transcripts, resume, 2 letters of recommendation, statement of purpose; for doctorate, GRE, transcripts, resume, 3 letters of recommendation, statement of purpose. Additional exam requirements/recommendations for international students: required—TOEFL. Electronic applications accepted. *Expenses:* Contact institution.

The American University in Cairo, School of Global Affairs and Public Policy, Cairo, Egypt. Offers gender and women's studies (MA); global affairs (MGA); international and comparative law (LL M); international human rights law (MA); journalism and mass communication (MA); Middle East studies (MA); migration and refugee studies (MA, Diploma); public administration (MPA); public policy (MPP); television and digital journalism (MA). *Program availability:* Part-time, evening/weekend. *Degree requirements:* For master's, comprehensive exam (for some programs), thesis (for some programs). *Entrance requirements:* Additional exam requirements/recommendations for international students: required—TOEFL (minimum score 450 paper-based; 45 iBT), IELTS (minimum score 5). Electronic applications accepted. *Expenses:* Contact institution.

Arizona State University at Tempe, Walter Cronkite School of Journalism and Mass Communication, Phoenix, AZ 85004. Offers journalism and mass communication (PhD); mass communication (MMC). *Accreditation:* ACEJMC. Terminal master's awarded for partial completion of doctoral program. *Degree requirements:* For master's, 9-hour professional capstone experience; interactive Program of Study (iPOS) submitted before completing 50 percent of required credit hours; for doctorate, comprehensive exam, thesis/dissertation, interactive Program of Study (iPOS) submitted before completing 50 percent of required credit hours. *Entrance requirements:* For master's and doctorate, GRE, minimum GPA of 3.0 or equivalent in last 2 years of work leading to bachelor's degree. Additional exam requirements/recommendations for international students: required—TOEFL, IELTS, or PTE. Electronic applications accepted. *Expenses:* Contact institution.

Arkansas State University, Graduate School, College of Media and Communication, Department of Media, State University, AR 72467. Offers mass communications (MSMC). *Program availability:* Part-time. *Degree requirements:* For master's, comprehensive exam, thesis or alternative. *Entrance requirements:* For master's, GRE General Test or MAT, appropriate bachelor's degree, letters of reference, educational experience, professional experience, official transcripts, immunization records. Additional exam requirements/recommendations for international students: required—TOEFL (minimum score 550 paper-based; 79 iBT), IELTS (minimum score 6), PTE (minimum score 56). Electronic applications accepted.

Boston University, College of Communication, Department of Mass Communication, Advertising, and Public Relations, Boston, MA 02215. Offers advertising (MS); mass communication (MS), including communication studies, marketing communication research; public relations (MS); JD/MS. *Program availability:* Part-time. *Faculty:* 26 full-time, 33 part-time/adjunct. *Students:* 275 full-time (228 women), 29 part-time (24 women); includes 24 minority (11 Black or African American, non-Hispanic/Latino; 5 Asian, non-Hispanic/Latino; 5 Hispanic/Latino; 3 Two or more races, non-Hispanic/Latino), 230 international. Average age 23. 719 applicants, 61% accepted, 188 enrolled. In 2019, 121 master's awarded. *Degree requirements:* For master's, comprehensive exam (for some programs), thesis (for some programs). *Entrance requirements:* For master's, transcript(s), resume/CV, 3 letters of recommendation, personal statement/essay. Additional exam requirements/recommendations for international students: required—TOEFL (minimum score 600 paper-based; 100 iBT), either TOEFL or IELTS; recommended—IELTS (minimum score 7). *Application deadline:* For fall admission, 5/1 for domestic and international students. Applications are processed on a rolling basis. Application fee: $95. Electronic applications accepted. *Financial support:* Research assistantships, teaching assistantships with partial tuition reimbursements, career-related internships or fieldwork, Federal Work-Study, scholarships/grants, and unspecified assistantships available. Support available to part-time students. Financial award application deadline: 5/1; financial award applicants required to submit FAFSA. *Unit head:* Donald Wright, Chairperson, 617-353-3482, E-mail: mcadvpr@bu.edu. *Application contact:* Jackie Cummings, Admission and Financial Aid Counselor, 617-353-3481, E-mail: comgrad@bu.edu.
Website: http://www.bu.edu/com/academics/masscomm-ad-pr/

Brigham Young University, Graduate Studies, College of Fine Arts and Communications, School of Communications, Provo, UT 84602. Offers mass communications (MA). *Faculty:* 19 full-time (2 women). *Students:* 26 full-time (16 women), 13 part-time (8 women); includes 11 minority (2 Black or African American, non-Hispanic/Latino; 4 Asian, non-Hispanic/Latino; 4 Hispanic/Latino; 1 Native Hawaiian or other Pacific Islander, non-Hispanic/Latino). Average age 31. 19 applicants, 84% accepted, 15 enrolled. In 2019, 11 master's awarded. *Degree requirements:* For master's, thesis. *Entrance requirements:* For master's, GRE, Minimum GPA of 3.0 in last 60 hours of course work. Additional exam requirements/recommendations for international students: required—TOEFL (minimum score 580 paper-based; 85 iBT). *Application deadline:* For fall admission, 3/31 priority date for domestic and international students. Applications are processed on a rolling basis. Application fee: $50. Electronic applications accepted. *Financial support:* In 2019–20, 18 students received support, including 24 research assistantships (averaging $3,339 per year), 3 teaching assistantships (averaging $3,669 per year); scholarships/grants, unspecified assistantships, and supplementary awards also available. Financial award application deadline: 4/30; financial award applicants required to submit FAFSA. *Unit head:* Edward Carter, Director, 801-422-2997, Fax: 801-422-0160, E-mail: ed_carter@byu.edu. *Application contact:* Debby Jackson, Graduate Program Manager, 801-422-2632, Fax: 801-422-0160, E-mail: debby_jackson@byu.edu.
Website: http://cfac.byu.edu/departments/communications

California State University, Fullerton, Graduate Studies, College of Communications, Department of Communications, Fullerton, CA 92831-3599. Offers communications in tourism and entertainment (MA); mass communications research and theory (MA); professional communications (MA). *Program availability:* Part-time. *Entrance requirements:* For master's, GRE General Test.

California State University, Northridge, Graduate Studies, Mike Curb College of Arts, Media, and Communication, Department of Journalism, Northridge, CA 91330. Offers mass communication (MA). *Program availability:* Part-time, evening/weekend. *Degree requirements:* For master's, thesis. *Entrance requirements:* For master's, GRE General Test. Additional exam requirements/recommendations for international students: required—TOEFL.

Drexel University, College of Arts and Sciences, Department of Communication, Culture and Media, Program in Communication, Philadelphia, PA 19104-2875. Offers public communication (MS); science communication (MS); technical communication (MS). *Program availability:* Part-time, evening/weekend. *Degree requirements:* For master's, internship, professional portfolio. *Entrance requirements:* For master's, GRE or minimum GPA of 3.0. Additional exam requirements/recommendations for international students: required—TOEFL. Electronic applications accepted.

Florida International University, College of Communication, Architecture and The Arts, School of Communication and Journalism, Miami, FL 33199. Offers mass communication (MS), including global strategic communications, Spanish language journalism. *Program availability:* Part-time, evening/weekend. *Faculty:* 30 full-time (22 women), 71 part-time/adjunct (42 women). *Students:* 85 full-time (68 women), 76 part-time (59 women); includes 117 minority (20 Black or African American, non-Hispanic/Latino; 2 Asian, non-Hispanic/Latino; 88 Hispanic/Latino; 7 Two or more races, non-Hispanic/Latino), 22 international. Average age 28. 120 applicants, 75% accepted, 63 enrolled. In 2019, 107 master's awarded. *Entrance requirements:* For master's, 2 letters of recommendation; minimum GPA of 3.0 during last 60 hours of upper-level work; resume. Additional exam requirements/recommendations for international students: required—TOEFL (minimum score 550 paper-based; 80 iBT). *Application deadline:* For fall admission, 6/1 for domestic students, 4/1 for international students; for spring admission, 10/1 for domestic students, 9/1 for international students. Applications are processed on a rolling basis. Application fee: $30. Electronic applications accepted. *Expenses: Tuition, area resident:* Full-time $8912; part-time $446 per credit hour. Tuition, state resident: full-time $8912; part-time $446 per credit hour. Tuition, nonresident: full-time $21,393; part-time $992 per credit hour. *Required fees:* $2194. *Financial support:* Institutionally sponsored loans and scholarships/grants available. Financial award application deadline: 3/1; financial award applicants required to submit FAFSA. *Unit head:* Dr. Aileen Izquierdo, Chair, 305-919-5795, E-mail: aileen.izquierdo@fiu.edu. *Application contact:* Nanett Rojas, Manager, Admissions Operations, 305-348-7464, Fax: 305-348-7441, E-mail: gradadm@fiu.edu.
Website: https://scj.fiu.edu/

Fordham University, Graduate School of Arts and Sciences, Department of Communication and Media Studies, New York, NY 10458. Offers public media (MA). *Program availability:* Part-time, evening/weekend. *Students:* Average age 25. 88 applicants, 52% accepted, 17 enrolled. In 2019, 18 master's awarded. *Degree requirements:* For master's, thesis, internship. *Entrance requirements:* For master's, GRE General Test. Additional exam requirements/recommendations for international students: required—TOEFL (minimum score 600 paper-based). *Application deadline:* For fall admission, 1/4 priority date for domestic students; for spring admission, 11/1 for domestic students. Application fee: $70. Electronic applications accepted. *Financial support:* In 2019–20, 3 students received support, including 2 research assistantships with full and partial tuition reimbursements available (averaging $23,200 per year); career-related internships or fieldwork, Federal Work-Study, institutionally sponsored loans, scholarships/grants, tuition waivers (full and partial), and unspecified assistantships also available. Financial award application deadline: 1/4. *Unit head:* Jacqueline Reich, Chair, 718-817-4850, E-mail: jreich8@fordham.edu. *Application contact:* Garrett Marino, Director of Graduate Admissions, 718-817-4419, Fax: 718-817-3566, E-mail: gmarino10@fordham.edu.

The George Washington University, Columbian College of Arts and Sciences, School of Media and Public Affairs, Washington, DC 20052. Offers MA, Graduate Certificate. *Entrance requirements:* For master's, GRE General Test. Additional exam requirements/recommendations for international students: required—TOEFL (minimum score 550 paper-based; 80 iBT). Electronic applications accepted.

Georgia State University, College of Arts and Sciences, Department of Communication, Atlanta, GA 30302-3083. Offers film, video, and digital imaging (MA), including critical studies, production, screenwriting; human communication and social influence (MA); mass communication (MA); media and society (PhD); moving image studies (PhD); public communication (PhD); rhetoric and politics (PhD). *Program availability:* Part-time. *Faculty:* 22 full-time (16 women), 1 part-time/adjunct (0 women). *Students:* 67 full-time (46 women), 26 part-time (17 women); includes 44 minority (40 Black or African American, non-Hispanic/Latino; 1 Asian, non-Hispanic/Latino; 1 Hispanic/Latino; 1 Native Hawaiian or other Pacific Islander, non-Hispanic/Latino; 1 Two or more races, non-Hispanic/Latino), 12 international. Average age 36. 82 applicants, 49% accepted, 22 enrolled. In 2019, 9 master's, 5 doctorates awarded. *Degree requirements:* For master's, variable foreign language requirement, thesis (for some programs); for doctorate, comprehensive exam, thesis/dissertation. *Entrance requirements:* For master's and doctorate, GRE. Additional exam requirements/recommendations for international students: required—TOEFL (minimum score 550 paper-based; 80 iBT), IELTS (minimum score 6.5). *Application deadline:* For fall admission, 2/10 for domestic and international students; for spring admission, 10/15 for domestic and international students. Application fee: $50. Electronic applications accepted. *Expenses: Tuition, area resident:* Full-time $7164; part-time $398 per credit hour. Tuition, state resident: full-time $7164; part-time $398 per credit hour. Tuition, nonresident: full-time $22,662; part-time $1259 per credit hour. *International tuition:* $22,662 full-time. *Required fees:* $2128; $312 per credit hour. Tuition and fees vary according to course load and program. *Financial support:* In 2019–20, fellowships with tuition reimbursements (averaging $15,000 per year), teaching assistantships with tuition reimbursements (averaging $15,000 per year) were awarded; career-related internships or fieldwork and unspecified assistantships also available. Financial award applicants required to submit FAFSA. *Unit head:* Dr. Greg Lisby, Chair, 404-413-5639, Fax: 404-413-5634, E-mail: glisby@gsu.edu. *Application contact:* Dr. Greg Lisby, Chair, 404-413-5639, Fax: 404-413-5634, E-mail: glisby@gsu.edu. Website: http://communication.gsu.edu

Grambling State University, School of Graduate Studies and Research, College of Professional Studies, Department of Mass Communication, Grambling, LA 71245. Offers MA. *Program availability:* Part-time. *Degree requirements:* For master's, comprehensive exam, thesis optional. *Entrance requirements:* For master's, GRE, minimum GPA of 2.5 on last degree. Additional exam requirements/recommendations for international students: required—TOEFL (minimum score 500 paper-based; 62 iBT). Electronic applications accepted.

Howard University, Cathy Hughes School of Communications, Department of Communication, Culture and Media Studies, Washington, DC 20059-0002. Offers mass communication (MA, PhD); media studies (MA, PhD). *Program availability:* Part-time, evening/weekend. *Degree requirements:* For master's, comprehensive exam (for some programs), thesis optional; for doctorate, one foreign language, comprehensive exam, thesis/dissertation. *Entrance requirements:* For master's, GRE, minimum GPA of 3.0; for doctorate, GRE, minimum graduate GPA of 3.5. Additional exam requirements/recommendations for international students: required—TOEFL. Electronic applications accepted.

Iona College, School of Arts and Science, Department of Mass Communication, New Rochelle, NY 10801-1890. Offers public relations (MA); sports communication and media (MA). *Accreditation:* ACEJMC (one or more programs are accredited). *Program availability:* Part-time, evening/weekend. *Students:* Average age 25. 16 applicants, 94% accepted, 11 enrolled. In 2019, 9 master's, 1 other advanced degree awarded. *Degree requirements:* For master's, comprehensive exam (for some programs), thesis or alternative. *Entrance requirements:* For master's, GRE General Test if undergraduate GPA is below 3.0. Additional exam requirements/recommendations for international students: required—TOEFL (minimum score 550 paper-based; 80 iBT), IELTS (minimum score 6). *Application deadline:* For fall admission, 8/1 for domestic students, 5/1 for international students; for spring admission, 1/1 for domestic students, 9/1 for international students. Applications are processed on a rolling basis. Electronic applications accepted. *Expenses:* Contact institution. *Financial support:* In 2019–20, 1 student received support. Scholarships/grants, tuition waivers (partial), and unspecified assistantships available. Support available to part-time students. Financial award application deadline: 4/15; financial award applicants required to submit FAFSA. *Unit head:* Anthony Kelso, PhD, Chair, 914-633-7795, E-mail: akelso@iona.edu. *Application contact:* RoseDeline Martinez, Director of Graduate Admissions, School of Arts and Sciences, 914-633-2427, Fax: 914-633-2277, E-mail: rmartinez@iona.edu. Website: http://www.iona.edu/Academics/School-of-Arts-Science/Departments/Mass-Communication/Graduate-Programs.aspx

Iowa State University of Science and Technology, Greenlee School of Journalism and Communication, Ames, IA 50011. Offers journalism and mass communication (MS). *Entrance requirements:* For master's, GRE General Test. Additional exam requirements/recommendations for international students: required—TOEFL (minimum score 570 paper-based; 88 iBT), IELTS (minimum score 6.5). Electronic applications accepted.

Kansas State University, Graduate School, College of Arts and Sciences, A.Q. Miller School of Journalism and Mass Communications, Manhattan, KS 66506. Offers advertising (MS); community journalism (MS); global communication (MS); health communication (MS); media management (MS); public relations (MS). *Program availability:* Part-time, evening/weekend. *Degree requirements:* For master's, comprehensive exam, thesis. *Entrance requirements:* For master's, GRE General Test, minimum GPA of 3.0. Additional exam requirements/recommendations for international students: required—TOEFL (minimum score 79 iBT). Electronic applications accepted.

Kent State University, College of Communication and Information, School of Media and Journalism, Kent, OH 44242-0001. Offers journalism and mass communication (MA), including media management, public relations, reporting and editing-broadcast, reporting and editing-convergence, reporting and editing-journalism educators, reporting and editing-magazine, reporting and editing-newspaper. *Program availability:* Part-time, 100% online. *Faculty:* 7 full-time (6 women), 5 part-time/adjunct (2 women). *Students:* 11 full-time (8 women), 35 part-time (22 women); includes 3 minority (all Black or African American, non-Hispanic/Latino), 3 international. Average age 34. 18 applicants, 78% accepted, 10 enrolled. In 2019, 40 master's awarded. *Degree requirements:* For master's, thesis, thesis or project. *Entrance requirements:* For master's, GRE, Bachelor's degree, minimum GPA of 3.0, statement of purpose, 2 letters of recommendation, resume or vitae, official transcript(s), writing sample. Additional exam requirements/recommendations for international students: required—TOEFL (minimum score 100 iBT), IELTS (minimum score 7), PTE (minimum score 65), Michigan English Language Assessment Battery (minimum score 82). *Application deadline:* For fall admission, 7/1 for domestic and international students. Applications are processed on a rolling basis. Application fee: $45 ($70 for international students). Electronic applications accepted. *Financial support:* Research assistantships with full tuition reimbursements, teaching assistantships with full tuition reimbursements, scholarships/grants, and unspecified assistantships available. Financial award application deadline: 3/1. *Unit head:* Jeff Fruit, Interim Director and Professor, 330-672-2572, E-mail: jmc@kent.edu. *Application contact:* Tang Tang, Graduate Coordinator/Professor, 330-672-1132, E-mail: ttang2@kent.edu. Website: http://www.kent.edu/jmc

Lindenwood University, Graduate Programs, School of Arts, Media, and Communications, St. Charles, MO 63301-1695. Offers advertising (MA); art history (MA); cinema and media arts (MFA); communications (MA); digital and Web design (MA); fashion and business design (MS); journalism (MA); mass communications (MA); social media and digital content (MS). *Program availability:* Part-time, 100% online. *Faculty:* 20 full-time (5 women), 15 part-time/adjunct (6 women). *Students:* 64 full-time (42 women), 76 part-time (57 women); includes 43 minority (20 Black or African American, non-Hispanic/Latino; 13 Hispanic/Latino; 10 Two or more races, non-Hispanic/Latino), 8 international. Average age 33. 145 applicants, 46% accepted, 56 enrolled. In 2019, 11 master's awarded. *Degree requirements:* For master's, thesis (for some programs), minimum cumulative GPA of 3.0. *Entrance requirements:* For master's, audition or interview, minimum GPA of 3.0, portfolio, letter of recommendation. Additional exam requirements/recommendations for international students: required—TOEFL (minimum score 553 paper-based; 81 iBT); recommended—IELTS (minimum score 6.5). *Application deadline:* For fall admission, 8/9 priority date for domestic students, 6/1 priority date for international students; for spring admission, 12/20 for domestic students, 11/1 priority date for international students; for summer admission, 5/15 priority date for domestic students, 3/27 priority date for international students. Applications are processed on a rolling basis. Application fee: $0 ($100 for international

students). Electronic applications accepted. *Expenses: Tuition:* Full-time $8910; part-time $495 per credit. Tuition and fees vary according to course load, degree level and program. *Financial support:* In 2019–20, 23 students received support. Career-related internships or fieldwork, institutionally sponsored loans, scholarships/grants, tuition waivers (partial), and unspecified assistantships available. Financial award application deadline: 6/30; financial award applicants required to submit FAFSA. *Unit head:* Dr. Jason Lively, Dean, School of Arts, Media, and Communications, 636-949-4164, Fax: 636-949-4910, E-mail: JLively@lindenwood.edu. *Application contact:* Kara Schilli, Assistant Vice President, University Admissions, 636-949-4349, Fax: 636-949-4109, E-mail: adultadmissions@lindenwood.edu. Website: https://www.lindenwood.edu/academics/academic-schools/school-of-arts-media-and-communications/

Louisiana State University and Agricultural & Mechanical College, Graduate School, Manship School of Mass Communication, Baton Rouge, LA 70803. Offers MMC, PhD, JD/MMC. *Accreditation:* ACEJMC.

Lynn University, Eugene M. and Christine E. Lynn College of Communication and Design, Boca Raton, FL 33431-5598. Offers communication and media (MS); digital media (Certificate); digital media and design (MS); graphic and Web design (MFA); visual effects animation (MFA). *Program availability:* Part-time, evening/weekend. *Faculty:* 17 full-time (6 women), 3 part-time/adjunct (2 women). *Students:* 28 full-time (15 women), 32 part-time (16 women); includes 15 minority (8 Black or African American, non-Hispanic/Latino; 6 Hispanic/Latino; 1 Two or more races, non-Hispanic/Latino), 19 international. Average age 28. 36 applicants, 92% accepted, 20 enrolled. In 2019, 30 master's awarded. *Degree requirements:* For master's, thesis (for some programs), completion of degree in four calendar years; minimum cumulative GPA of 3.0 and C grade or higher in each course; orientation seminar (one credit); 36 credits of foundation and specialization or a thesis. *Entrance requirements:* For master's, Bachelor's degree from accredited institution, minimum undergraduate GPA of 3.0, official undergraduate transcripts, letter of recommendation from academic or professional source, writing sample demonstrating capacity to perform at graduate level. Additional exam requirements/recommendations for international students: required—TOEFL (minimum score 550 paper-based; 80 iBT), IELTS (minimum score 6.5). *Application deadline:* For fall admission, 8/10 for domestic students, 7/31 for international students; for spring admission, 12/18 for domestic students, 12/2 for international students; for summer admission, 4/12 for domestic students, 4/2 for international students. Applications are processed on a rolling basis. Application fee: $45. Electronic applications accepted. *Expenses:* $740.00 per hour. *Financial support:* In 2019–20, 15 students received support. Career-related internships or fieldwork, Federal Work-Study, scholarships/grants, tuition waivers (full and partial), and unspecified assistantships available. Support available to part-time students. Financial award application deadline: 3/1; financial award applicants required to submit FAFSA. *Unit head:* Dr. David L. Jaffe, Dean, 561-237-7099, Fax: 561-237-7097, E-mail: djaffe@lynn.edu. *Application contact:* Steven Pruitt, Director of Graduate Admission, 561-237-7834, Fax: 561-237-7100, E-mail: admission@lynn.edu. Website: https://www.lynn.edu/academics/colleges-schools/communication-and-design

Marquette University, Graduate School, College of Communication, Milwaukee, WI 53201-1881. Offers advertising and public relations (MA); communication studies (MA); digital storytelling (Certificate); journalism (MA); mass communication (MA); science, health and environmental communication (MA). *Accreditation:* ACEJMC (one or more programs are accredited). *Program availability:* Part-time, evening/weekend. *Degree requirements:* For master's, comprehensive exam, thesis or alternative. *Entrance requirements:* For master's, GRE, official transcripts from all current and previous colleges/universities except Marquette, three letters of recommendation, statement of academic and professional goals. Additional exam requirements/recommendations for international students: required—TOEFL (minimum score 530 paper-based). Electronic applications accepted.

Middle Tennessee State University, College of Graduate Studies, College of Mass Communication, Program in Mass Communication, Murfreesboro, TN 37132. Offers MS. *Program availability:* Part-time, evening/weekend, online learning. *Degree requirements:* For master's, comprehensive exam, thesis optional. *Entrance requirements:* For master's, GRE. Additional exam requirements/recommendations for international students: required—TOEFL (minimum score 525 paper-based; 71 iBT) or IELTS (minimum score 6).

Murray State University, Arthur J. Bauernfeind College of Business, Department of Journalism and Mass Communications, Murray, KY 42071. Offers mass communications (MA, MS), including public relations. *Program availability:* Part-time. *Entrance requirements:* For master's, GRE or GMAT, minimum university GPA of 2.75. Additional exam requirements/recommendations for international students: required—TOEFL (minimum score 527 paper-based; 51 iBT). Electronic applications accepted.

North Dakota State University, College of Graduate and Interdisciplinary Studies, College of Arts, Humanities and Social Sciences, Department of Communication, Fargo, ND 58102. Offers communication (PhD); mass communication (MA); speech communication (MS). *Program availability:* Part-time, online learning. Terminal master's awarded for partial completion of doctoral program. *Degree requirements:* For master's, thesis (for some programs); for doctorate, comprehensive exam, thesis/dissertation, 2-3 publications. *Entrance requirements:* For master's, GRE, minimum undergraduate GPA of 3.25; for doctorate, GRE, minimum undergraduate GPA of 3.5. Additional exam requirements/recommendations for international students: required—TOEFL (minimum score 600 paper-based; 100 iBT), IELTS (minimum score 7). Electronic applications accepted. Tuition and fees vary according to program and reciprocity agreements.

Oklahoma State University, College of Arts and Sciences, School of Media and Strategic Communications, Stillwater, OK 74078. Offers mass communication (MS). *Faculty:* 12 full-time (3 women). *Students:* 14 full-time (12 women), 18 part-time (12 women); includes 8 minority (1 Black or African American, non-Hispanic/Latino; 2 American Indian or Alaska Native, non-Hispanic/Latino; 1 Asian, non-Hispanic/Latino; 1 Hispanic/Latino; 3 Two or more races, non-Hispanic/Latino), 2 international. Average age 25. 21 applicants, 81% accepted, 13 enrolled. In 2019, 14 master's awarded. *Entrance requirements:* For master's, GRE, minimum GPA of 3.0. Additional exam requirements/recommendations for international students: required—TOEFL (minimum score 550 paper-based; 79 iBT). *Application deadline:* For fall admission, 3/1 priority date for international students; for spring admission, 8/1 priority date for international students. Applications are processed on a rolling basis. Application fee: $50 ($75 for international students). Electronic applications accepted. *Expenses: Tuition, area resident:* Full-time $4148.10; part-time $2765.40 per credit hour. *Tuition, state resident:* full-time $4148.10; part-time $2765.40 per credit hour. *Tuition, nonresident:* full-time $15,775; part-time $10,516.80 per credit hour. *International tuition:* $15,775.20 full-time. *Required fees:* $2196.90; $122.05 per credit hour. Tuition and fees vary according to course load, campus/location and program. *Financial support:* In 2019–20, 9 teaching assistantships (averaging $1,791 per year) were awarded; research assistantships, career-related internships or fieldwork, Federal Work-Study, scholarships/grants, health care benefits, tuition waivers (partial), and unspecified assistantships also available. Support available to part-time students. Financial award application deadline: 3/1; financial award applicants required to submit FAFSA. *Unit head:* Dr. Max Andrews,

Director, 405-744-4207, Fax: 405-744-7104, E-mail: max.andrews@okstate.edu. *Application contact:* Dr. Sheryl Tucker, Dean, 405-744-6368, Fax: 405-744-0355, E-mail: gradi@okstate.edu.
Website: http://media.okstate.edu

Penn State University Park, Graduate School, Donald P. Bellisario College of Communications, Department of Communications, University Park, PA 16802. Offers mass communications (PhD); media studies (MA).

Point Park University, School of Communication, Pittsburgh, PA 15222-1984. Offers communication technology (MA); media communication (MA). *Program availability:* Part-time, evening/weekend. *Degree requirements:* For master's, comprehensive exam (for some programs), thesis or alternative. *Entrance requirements:* For master's, GRE (if GPA less than 2.75), minimum GPA of 2.75, 2 letters of recommendation, statement of intent. Additional exam requirements/recommendations for international students: required—TOEFL (minimum score 570 paper-based; 88 iBT), IELTS (minimum score 6.5); recommended—TWE (minimum score 5). Electronic applications accepted.

St. Cloud State University, School of Graduate Studies, College of Liberal Arts, Department of Mass Communications, St. Cloud, MN 56301-4498. Offers MS. *Degree requirements:* For master's, thesis or alternative. *Entrance requirements:* For master's, minimum GPA of 2.75. Additional exam requirements/recommendations for international students: required—Michigan English Language Assessment Battery; recommended—TOEFL (minimum score 600 paper-based), IELTS (minimum score 6.5). Electronic applications accepted.

St. John's University, College of Professional Studies, Department of Mass Communications, Queens, NY 11439. Offers international communications (MS). *Entrance requirements:* For master's, letters of recommendation, transcripts, resume, personal statement, proficiency in a foreign language. Additional exam requirements/recommendations for international students: required—TOEFL (minimum score 90 iBT), IELTS (minimum score 6.5). Electronic applications accepted.

San Jose State University, Program in Journalism and Mass Communication, San Jose, CA 95192-0055. Offers mass communications (MS). *Accreditation:* ACEJMC. *Program availability:* Part-time, evening/weekend. *Faculty:* 13 full-time (6 women). *Students:* 31 full-time (18 women), 6 part-time (5 women); includes 8 minority (2 Asian, non-Hispanic/Latino; 6 Hispanic/Latino), 7 international. 31 applicants, 55% accepted, 12 enrolled. In 2019, 7 master's awarded. *Degree requirements:* For master's, thesis or alternative. *Entrance requirements:* For master's, GRE. Additional exam requirements/recommendations for international students: required—TOEFL, IELTS, TWE, PTE. *Application deadline:* For fall admission, 6/1 for domestic students, 5/1 for international students; for spring admission, 11/1 for domestic students, 10/1 for international students. Applications are processed on a rolling basis. Application fee: $70. Electronic applications accepted. *Expenses: Tuition, area resident:* Full-time $7176; part-time $4164 per credit hour. Tuition, state resident: full-time $7176; part-time $4164 per credit hour. Tuition, nonresident: full-time $7176; part-time $4165 per credit hour. *International tuition:* $7176 full-time. *Required fees:* $2110; $2110. *Financial support:* In 2019–20, 1 student received support, including 10 teaching assistantships (averaging $9,728 per year); scholarships/grants and unspecified assistantships also available. Financial award application deadline: 5/1; financial award applicants required to submit FAFSA. *Unit head:* Phylis West Johnson, School Director, 408-924-3249, E-mail: phylis.west@sjsu.edu. *Application contact:* Scott Fosdick, PdD, Graduate Coordinator, E-mail: scott.fosdick@sjsu.edu.
Website: http://www.jmc.sjsu.edu/

Southern Illinois University Carbondale, Graduate School, College of Mass Communication and Media Arts, Department of Mass Communication and Media Arts, Carbondale, IL 62901-4701. Offers MFA, PhD. *Degree requirements:* For doctorate, thesis/dissertation. *Entrance requirements:* For master's, minimum GPA of 2.7; for doctorate, GRE, minimum GPA of 3.25. Additional exam requirements/recommendations for international students: required—TOEFL (minimum score 100 iBT).

Southern Illinois University Edwardsville, Graduate School, College of Arts and Sciences, Department of Mass Communications, Program in Mass Communications, Edwardsville, IL 62026. Offers MS. *Program availability:* Part-time, evening/weekend. *Degree requirements:* For master's, comprehensive exam (for some programs), thesis (for some programs). *Entrance requirements:* Additional exam requirements/recommendations for international students: required—TOEFL (minimum score 550 paper-based; 79 iBT), IELTS (minimum score 6.5). Electronic applications accepted.

Southern University and Agricultural and Mechanical College, Graduate School, College of Humanities and Interdisciplinary Studies, Department of Mass Communication, Baton Rouge, LA 70813. Offers MA. *Degree requirements:* For master's, comprehensive exam, thesis. *Entrance requirements:* For master's, GRE General Test. Additional exam requirements/recommendations for international students: required—TOEFL (minimum score 525 paper-based).

Stephen F. Austin State University, Graduate School, College of Liberal and Applied Arts, Department of Mass Communication, Nacogdoches, TX 75962. Offers MA.

Syracuse University, S. I. Newhouse School of Public Communications, MS Program in Communications Management, Syracuse, NY 13244. Offers MS. *Program availability:* Part-time, evening/weekend, online learning. *Degree requirements:* For master's, comprehensive exam, internship. *Entrance requirements:* For master's, GRE General Test, minimum 5 years of experience in public relations or related field; portfolio; 3 letters of recommendation including 1 from current employer, client, or business partner; resume. Additional exam requirements/recommendations for international students: required—TOEFL (minimum score 100 iBT). Electronic applications accepted.

Syracuse University, S. I. Newhouse School of Public Communications, PhD Program in Mass Communications, Syracuse, NY 13244. Offers PhD. *Degree requirements:* For doctorate, comprehensive exam, thesis/dissertation, qualifying exams. *Entrance requirements:* For doctorate, GRE General Test, resume, personal statement, official transcript, three letters of recommendation, writing sample. Additional exam requirements/recommendations for international students: required—TOEFL (minimum score 100 iBT). Electronic applications accepted.

Texas Christian University, Bob Schieffer College of Communication, Department of Strategic Communication, Fort Worth, TX 76129-0002. Offers MS. *Program availability:* Part-time. *Faculty:* 8 full-time (6 women). *Students:* 20 full-time (12 women); includes 4 minority (1 Black or African American, non-Hispanic/Latino; 3 Hispanic/Latino), 3 international. Average age 26. 19 applicants, 79% accepted, 13 enrolled. In 2019, 7 master's awarded. *Degree requirements:* For master's, thesis or alternative, thesis OR capstone project required. *Entrance requirements:* For master's, GRE General Test, 15 semester hours (five courses) in undergraduate journalism, advertising or public relations, or substantial professional experience in a communication discipline as determined by the graduate faculty. Additional exam requirements/recommendations for international students: required—TOEFL (minimum score 550 paper-based; 80 iBT). *Application deadline:* For fall admission, 7/1 for domestic and international students; for spring admission, 10/15 for domestic and international students. Applications are processed on a rolling basis. Application fee: $60. Electronic applications accepted. Full-time tuition and fees vary according to program. *Financial support:* In 2019–20, 13 students received support, including 11 teaching assistantships with full tuition reimbursements available (averaging $12,500 per year); tuition waivers (full) also available. Financial award application deadline: 7/1. *Unit head:* Dr. Jacque Lambiase, Department Chair, 817-257-6552, Fax: 817-257-7322, E-mail: j.lambiase@tcu.edu. *Application contact:* Dr. Catherine Coleman, Director of Graduate Studies, 817-257-7452, Fax: 817-257-7322, E-mail: c.coleman@tcu.edu.
Website: https://schieffercollege.tcu.edu/stratcomm/

Texas State University, The Graduate College, College of Fine Arts and Communication, Program in Mass Communication, San Marcos, TX 78666. Offers MA. *Program availability:* Part-time. *Degree requirements:* For master's, comprehensive exam, thesis optional. *Entrance requirements:* For master's, baccalaureate degree from regionally-accredited institution with minimum GPA of 3.0 in last 60 hours of course work, statement of purpose, 2 letters of recommendation, current resume. Additional exam requirements/recommendations for international students: required—TOEFL (minimum score 100 iBT), IELTS (minimum score 7). Electronic applications accepted.

Texas Tech University, Graduate School, College of Media and Communication, Department of Media and Communication, Lubbock, TX 79409-3082. Offers mass communications (MA); media and communication (PhD); strategic communication and innovation (MA). *Program availability:* Part-time, evening/weekend, 100% online, blended/hybrid learning. *Faculty:* 20 full-time (12 women), 7 part-time/adjunct (3 women). *Students:* 97 full-time (56 women), 167 part-time (102 women); includes 66 minority (17 Black or African American, non-Hispanic/Latino; 5 Asian, non-Hispanic/Latino; 36 Hispanic/Latino; 8 Two or more races, non-Hispanic/Latino), 20 international. Average age 31. 161 applicants, 64% accepted, 84 enrolled. In 2019, 98 master's, 6 doctorates awarded. *Degree requirements:* For master's, thesis optional; for doctorate, comprehensive exam, thesis/dissertation. *Entrance requirements:* For doctorate, GRE. Additional exam requirements/recommendations for international students: required—TOEFL (minimum score 550 paper-based; 79 iBT). *Application deadline:* For fall admission, 6/1 priority date for domestic students, 1/15 priority date for international students; for spring admission, 9/1 priority date for domestic students, 6/15 priority date for international students. Applications are processed on a rolling basis. Application fee: $65. Electronic applications accepted. *Expenses:* Contact institution. *Financial support:* In 2019–20, 148 students received support, including 121 fellowships (averaging $4,201 per year), 16 research assistantships (averaging $13,825 per year), 71 teaching assistantships (averaging $12,545 per year); career-related internships or fieldwork, scholarships/grants, and unspecified assistantships also available. Support available to part-time students. Financial award application deadline: 4/15; financial award applicants required to submit FAFSA. *Unit head:* Dr. Coy Callison, Professor and Associate Dean of Graduate Studies, 806-834-5344, E-mail: coy.callison@ttu.edu. *Application contact:* Elaine Taylor, Graduate Program Administrative, 806-834-7064, Fax: 806-742-1085, E-mail: elaine.taylor@ttu.edu.
Website: www.depts.ttu.edu/comc/

The University of Alabama, Graduate School, College of Communication and Information Sciences, Department of General Communications and Information Sciences, Tuscaloosa, AL 35487-0172. Offers PhD. *Students:* 41 full-time (26 women), 13 part-time (9 women); includes 11 minority (6 Black or African American, non-Hispanic/Latino; 1 American Indian or Alaska Native, non-Hispanic/Latino; 1 Hispanic/Latino; 3 Two or more races, non-Hispanic/Latino), 21 international. Average age 33. 33 applicants, 79% accepted, 11 enrolled. In 2019, 8 doctorates awarded. *Degree requirements:* For doctorate, comprehensive exam, thesis/dissertation. *Entrance requirements:* For doctorate, GRE, master's degree, minimum undergraduate and graduate GPA of 3.0. Additional exam requirements/recommendations for international students: required—TOEFL (minimum score 100 iBT). *Application deadline:* For fall admission, 2/15 priority date for domestic students, 2/15 for international students; for winter admission, 11/1 priority date for domestic students, 11/1 for international students. Applications are processed on a rolling basis. Application fee: $50 ($60 for international students). Electronic applications accepted. *Expenses: Tuition, area resident:* Full-time $10,780; part-time $440 per credit hour. Tuition, nonresident: full-time $30,250; part-time $1550 per credit hour. *Financial support:* In 2019–20, 28 students received support. Fellowships with full tuition reimbursements available, research assistantships with full tuition reimbursements available, teaching assistantships with full tuition reimbursements available, institutionally sponsored loans, health care benefits, and unspecified assistantships available. Financial award application deadline: 3/1. *Unit head:* Dr. William Evans, Associate Dean for Graduate Studies, 205-348-3176, Fax: 205-348-6774, E-mail: wevans@ua.edu. *Application contact:* Dr. William Evans, Associate Dean for Graduate Studies, 205-348-3176, Fax: 205-348-6774, E-mail: wevans@ua.edu.
Website: http://www.cis.ua.edu/graduate

University of Arkansas at Little Rock, Graduate School, College of Social Sciences and Communication, School of Mass Communication, Little Rock, AR 72204-1099. Offers MA. *Program availability:* Part-time, evening/weekend. *Degree requirements:* For master's, comprehensive exam, thesis optional. *Entrance requirements:* For master's, GRE General Test, minimum GPA of 2.7.

University of Colorado Boulder, Graduate School, College of Media, Communication and Information, Boulder, CO 80309. Offers MA, MFA, PhD. Terminal master's awarded for partial completion of doctoral program. *Degree requirements:* For master's, comprehensive exam, thesis or alternative; for doctorate, comprehensive exam, thesis/dissertation. *Entrance requirements:* For master's, GRE General Test, minimum undergraduate GPA of 2.75; for doctorate, GRE General Test, minimum undergraduate GPA of 3.2, graduate 3.5. Electronic applications accepted. Application fee is waived when completed online.

University of Denver, Division of Arts, Humanities and Social Sciences, Department of Media, Film and Journalism Studies, Denver, CO 80208. Offers international and intercultural communication (MA); media and public communication (MA), including media and globalization, strategic communication. *Program availability:* Part-time. *Faculty:* 18 full-time (8 women), 1 part-time/adjunct (0 women). *Students:* 4 full-time (all women), 23 part-time (19 women); includes 6 minority (1 Black or African American, non-Hispanic/Latino; 1 Asian, non-Hispanic/Latino; 3 Hispanic/Latino; 1 Two or more races, non-Hispanic/Latino), 1 international. Average age 26. 35 applicants, 80% accepted, 13 enrolled. In 2019, 14 master's awarded. *Degree requirements:* For master's, variable foreign language requirement, thesis (for some programs). *Entrance requirements:* For master's, GRE General Test, bachelor's degree, transcripts, personal statement, three letters of recommendation. Additional exam requirements/recommendations for international students: required—TOEFL (minimum score 620 paper-based; 105 iBT). *Application deadline:* For fall admission, 2/1 priority date for domestic and international students; for winter admission, 11/14 for domestic and international students; for spring admission, 1/31 for domestic and international students. Applications are processed on a rolling basis. Application fee: $65. Electronic applications accepted. *Expenses:* Contact institution. *Financial support:* In 2019–20, 24 students received support, including 11 teaching assistantships with tuition reimbursements available (averaging $7,612 per year); career-related internships or fieldwork, Federal Work-Study, institutionally sponsored loans, scholarships/grants, and

unspecified assistantships also available. Support available to part-time students. Financial award application deadline: 2/15; financial award applicants required to submit FAFSA. *Unit head:* Dr. Lynn Schofield Clark, Professor and Chair, 303-871-3984, Fax: 303-871-4949, E-mail: lynn.clark@du.edu. *Application contact:* Information Contact, 303-871-2166, E-mail: mfjs@du.edu.
Website: http://www.du.edu/ahss/mfjs

University of Florida, Graduate School, College of Journalism and Communications, Program in Mass Communication, Gainesville, FL 32611. Offers international/intercultural communication (MAMC); journalism (MAMC); mass communication (MAMC, PhD), including clinical translational science (MAMC); public relations (MAMC); science/health communication (MAMC); telecommunication (MAMC). *Entrance requirements:* For master's and doctorate, GRE General Test, minimum GPA of 3.0.

University of Georgia, Grady College of Journalism and Mass Communication, Athens, GA 30602. Offers journalism and mass communication (MA); mass communication (PhD). *Degree requirements:* For master's, comprehensive exam, thesis (MA); for doctorate, comprehensive exam, thesis/dissertation. *Entrance requirements:* For master's and doctorate, GRE General Test. Additional exam requirements/recommendations for international students: required—TOEFL, TWE for PhD. Electronic applications accepted.

University of Houston, College of Liberal Arts and Social Sciences, Jack J. Valenti School of Communication, Houston, TX 77204. Offers health communication (MA); mass communication studies (MA); public relations studies (MA); speech communication (MA). *Program availability:* Part-time. *Degree requirements:* For master's, comprehensive exam (for some programs), thesis (for some programs), 30-33 hours. *Entrance requirements:* For master's, GRE. Additional exam requirements/recommendations for international students: required—TOEFL. Electronic applications accepted.

The University of Iowa, Graduate College, College of Liberal Arts and Sciences, School of Journalism and Mass Communication, Iowa City, IA 52242-1316. Offers journalism and media communication (MA); mass communication (PhD); strategic communication (MA); JD/MA; JD/PhD. *Degree requirements:* For master's, thesis optional, exam; for doctorate, comprehensive exam, thesis/dissertation. *Entrance requirements:* For master's and doctorate, GRE General Test, minimum GPA of 3.0. Additional exam requirements/recommendations for international students: required—TOEFL (minimum score 637 paper-based; 110 iBT). Electronic applications accepted.

University of Minnesota, Twin Cities Campus, Graduate School, College of Liberal Arts, School of Journalism and Mass Communication, Minneapolis, MN 55455-0213. Offers mass communication (MA, PhD); strategic communication (professional program) (MA). *Degree requirements:* For master's, thesis; for doctorate, comprehensive exam, thesis/dissertation. *Entrance requirements:* For master's, GRE; GMAT (for strategic communications program), letters of recommendation, minimum undergraduate GPA of 3.0, writing sample; two years professional experience (for strategic communications program); for doctorate, GRE, letters of recommendation, minimum undergraduate GPA of 3.0, writing sample. Additional exam requirements/recommendations for international students: required—TOEFL (minimum score 79 iBT). Electronic applications accepted.

University of Nebraska–Lincoln, Graduate College, College of Journalism and Mass Communications, Lincoln, NE 68588. Offers marketing, communication and advertising (MA); professional journalism (MA). *Program availability:* Online learning. *Degree requirements:* For master's, thesis. *Entrance requirements:* For master's, samples of work. Additional exam requirements/recommendations for international students: required—TOEFL (minimum score 600 paper-based). Electronic applications accepted.

University of Oklahoma, College of Arts and Sciences, Department of Communication, Norman, OK 73019. Offers communication (MA); communication technology (PhD); health communication (PhD); intercultural/international communication (PhD); organizational communication (PhD); political/mass communication (PhD); social influence/interpersonal communication (PhD). *Program availability:* Part-time. *Degree requirements:* For master's, comprehensive exam (for some programs), thesis (for some programs), comprehensive exams or thesis; for doctorate, comprehensive exam, thesis/dissertation. *Entrance requirements:* For master's, GRE (for assistantship), statement of purpose, transcripts, writing sample, letters of recommendation; for doctorate, GRE, statement of purpose, transcripts, writing sample, letters of recommendation. Additional exam requirements/recommendations for international students: required—TOEFL (minimum score 79 iBT) or IELTS (minimum score 6.5). Electronic applications accepted. *Expenses:* Tuition, state resident: full-time $6583.20; part-time $274.30 per credit hour. Tuition, nonresident: full-time $21,242; part-time $885.10 per credit hour. *International tuition:* $21,242.40 full-time. *Required fees:* $1994.20; $72.55 per credit hour. $126.50 per semester. Tuition and fees vary according to course load and degree level.

University of Puerto Rico at Rio Piedras, School of Communication, San Juan, PR 00931-3300. Offers MA. *Program availability:* Part-time. *Degree requirements:* For master's, comprehensive exam, thesis. *Entrance requirements:* For master's, GRE, PAEG, minimum GPA of 3.0, 2 letters of recommendation, interview.

University of South Florida, College of Arts and Sciences, Zimmerman School of Advertising and Mass Communications, Tampa, FL 33620-9951. Offers MA. *Program availability:* Part-time, evening/weekend. *Faculty:* 11 full-time (6 women). *Students:* 24 full-time (20 women), 20 part-time (17 women); includes 8 minority (4 Black or African American, non-Hispanic/Latino; 4 Hispanic/Latino), 20 international. Average age 26. 28 applicants, 79% accepted, 14 enrolled. In 2019, 12 master's awarded. *Degree requirements:* For master's, comprehensive exam, thesis (for some programs). *Entrance requirements:* For master's, 153V (60th percentile), 144Q (18th percentile) preferred on the GRE, minimum 3.00 GPA; bachelor's degree in appropriate field; resume; 3 letters of recommendation; letter of intent. Students may be required to take additional courses to meet concentration foundation knowledge. Additional exam requirements/recommendations for international students: required—TOEFL, TOEFL (minimum score 550 paper-based; 79 iBT) or IELTS (minimum score 6.5). *Application deadline:* For fall admission, 2/15 priority date for domestic and international students. Application fee: $30. Electronic applications accepted. *Financial support:* In 2019–20, 6 students received support, including 9 teaching assistantships with tuition reimbursements available (averaging $10,513 per year); unspecified assistantships also available. Financial award application deadline: 2/28. *Unit head:* Dr. Wayne Garcia, Director and Senior Instructor, 813-498-1925, Fax: 813-974-2592, E-mail: wgarcia@usf.edu. *Application contact:* Dr. Art Ramirez, Jr., Associate Director, 813-974-2591, Fax: 813-974-2592, E-mail: aramirez2@usf.edu.
Website: http://masscom.usf.edu/grad/

University of South Florida, Innovative Education, Tampa, FL 33620-9951. Offers adult, career and higher education (Graduate Certificate), including college teaching, leadership in developing human resources, leadership in higher education; Africana studies (Graduate Certificate), including diasporas and health disparities, genocide and human rights; aging studies (Graduate Certificate), including gerontology; art research (Graduate Certificate), including museum studies; business foundations (Graduate Certificate); chemical and biomedical engineering (Graduate Certificate), including materials science and engineering, water, health and sustainability; child and family studies (Graduate Certificate), including positive behavior support; civil and industrial engineering (Graduate Certificate), including transportation systems analysis; community and family health (Graduate Certificate), including maternal and child health, social marketing and public health, violence and injury: prevention and intervention, women's health; criminology (Graduate Certificate), including criminal justice administration; data science for public administration (Graduate Certificate); digital humanities (Graduate Certificate); educational measurement and research (Graduate Certificate), including evaluation; English (Graduate Certificate), including comparative literary studies, creative writing, professional and technical communication; entrepreneurship (Graduate Certificate); environmental health (Graduate Certificate), including safety management; epidemiology and biostatistics (Graduate Certificate), including applied biostatistics, biostatistics, concepts and tools of epidemiology, epidemiology, epidemiology of infectious diseases; geography, environment and planning (Graduate Certificate), including community development, environmental policy and management, geographical information systems; geology (Graduate Certificate), including hydrogeology; global health (Graduate Certificate), including disaster management, global health and Latin American and Caribbean studies, global health practice, humanitarian assistance, infection control; government and international affairs (Graduate Certificate), including Cuban studies, globalization studies; health policy and management (Graduate Certificate), including health management and leadership, public health policy and programs; hearing specialist: early intervention (Graduate Certificate); industrial and management systems engineering (Graduate Certificate), including systems engineering, technology management; information studies (Graduate Certificate), including school library media specialist; information systems/decision sciences (Graduate Certificate), including analytics and business intelligence; instructional technology (Graduate Certificate), including distance education, Florida digital/virtual educator, instructional design, multimedia design, Web design; internal medicine, bioethics and medical humanities (Graduate Certificate), including biomedical ethics; Latin American and Caribbean studies (Graduate Certificate); leadership for coastal resiliency planning (Graduate Certificate); mass communications (Graduate Certificate), including multimedia journalism; mathematics and statistics (Graduate Certificate), including mathematics; medicine (Graduate Certificate), including aging and neuroscience, bioinformatics, biotechnology, brain fitness and memory management, clinical investigation, hand and upper limb rehabilitation, health informatics, health sciences, integrative weight management, intellectual property, medicine and gender, metabolic and nutritional medicine, metabolic cardiology, pharmacy sciences; national and competitive intelligence (Graduate Certificate); nursing (Graduate Certificate), including simulation based academic fellowship in advanced pain management; psychological and social foundations (Graduate Certificate), including career counseling, college teaching, diversity in education, mental health counseling, school counseling; public affairs (Graduate Certificate), including nonprofit management, public management, research administration; public health (Graduate Certificate), including assessing chemical toxicity and public health risks, health equity, pharmacoepidemiology, public health generalist, toxicology, translational research in adolescent behavioral health; public health practices (Graduate Certificate), including planning for healthy communities; rehabilitation and mental health counseling (Graduate Certificate), including integrative mental health care, marriage and family therapy, rehabilitation technology; secondary education (Graduate Certificate), including ESOL, foreign language education: culture and content, foreign language education: professional; social work (Graduate Certificate), including geriatric social work/clinical gerontology; special education (Graduate Certificate), including autism spectrum disorder, disabilities education: severe/profound; world languages (Graduate Certificate), including teaching English as a second language (TESL) or foreign language. *Unit head:* Dr. Cynthia DeLuca, Associate Vice President and Assistant Vice Provost, 813-974-3077, Fax: 813-974-7061, E-mail: deluca@usf.edu. *Application contact:* Owen Hooper, Director, Summer and Alternative Calendar Programs, 813-974-6917, E-mail: hooper@usf.edu.
Website: http://www.usf.edu/innovative-education/

University of Wisconsin–Madison, Graduate School, College of Letters and Science, School of Journalism and Mass Communication, Program in Journalism and Mass Communication, Madison, WI 53706-1380. Offers MA.

University of Wisconsin–Madison, Graduate School, College of Letters and Science, School of Journalism and Mass Communication, Program in Mass Communication, Madison, WI 53706-1380. Offers PhD. *Degree requirements:* For doctorate, thesis/dissertation.

University of Wisconsin–Superior, Graduate Division, Department of Communicating Arts, Superior, WI 54880-4500. Offers mass communication (MA); speech communication (MA); theater (MA). *Program availability:* Part-time. *Degree requirements:* For master's, comprehensive exam, thesis or alternative, position paper or project. *Entrance requirements:* For master's, minimum GPA of 2.75. Electronic applications accepted.

University of Wisconsin–Whitewater, School of Graduate Studies, College of Arts and Communications, Department of Communication, Whitewater, WI 53190-1790. Offers corporate communication (MS); mass communication (MS). *Program availability:* Part-time, evening/weekend, online learning. *Degree requirements:* For master's, thesis or alternative. *Entrance requirements:* For master's, 2 letters of recommendation, goal statement. Additional exam requirements/recommendations for international students: required—TOEFL (minimum score 550 paper-based; 80 iBT), IELTS (minimum score 6). Electronic applications accepted.

Université Laval, Faculty of Letters, Department of Information and Communication, Program in Public Communication, Québec, QC G1K 7P4, Canada. Offers MA, PhD. *Program availability:* Part-time. *Degree requirements:* For master's, thesis (for some programs). *Entrance requirements:* For master's, knowledge of French, knowledge of English. Electronic applications accepted.

Virginia Commonwealth University, Graduate School, College of Humanities and Sciences, Richard T. Robertson School of Media and Culture, Program in Mass Communications, Richmond, VA 23284-9005. Offers multimedia journalism (MS); strategic public relations (MS). *Degree requirements:* For master's, comprehensive exam, thesis optional. *Entrance requirements:* For master's, GRE General Test. Additional exam requirements/recommendations for international students: required—TOEFL (minimum score 600 paper-based; 100 iBT); recommended—IELTS (minimum score 6.5). Electronic applications accepted.

Media Studies

American University, School of Communication, Division of Communication Studies, Washington, DC 20016-8001. Offers media industries and institutions (PhD); media, public issues, and engagement (PhD); media, technology, and culture (PhD). *Degree requirements:* For doctorate, comprehensive exam, thesis/dissertation. *Entrance requirements:* For doctorate, GRE General Test. Additional exam requirements/recommendations for international students: required—TOEFL (minimum score 600 paper-based; 100 iBT), IELTS (minimum score 7). Electronic applications accepted.

American University, School of Communication, Film and Media Arts Division, Washington, DC 20016-8001. Offers art in entertainment (MFA); environmental and wildlife filmmaking (MFA); film and media arts (MFA); game design (MA); games and interactive media (MFA); games and interactivity (MFA); political, cultural, and social impact (MFA); producing film, television and video (MA). *Program availability:* Part-time, evening/weekend. *Degree requirements:* For master's, comprehensive exam, thesis or alternative. *Entrance requirements:* Additional exam requirements/recommendations for international students: required—TOEFL (minimum score 600 paper-based; 100 iBT), IELTS (minimum score 7). Electronic applications accepted.

Angelo State University, College of Graduate Studies and Research, College of Arts and Humanities, Department of Communication and Mass Media, San Angelo, TX 76909. Offers communication (MA). *Program availability:* Part-time, evening/weekend. *Degree requirements:* For master's, comprehensive exam, thesis optional. *Entrance requirements:* Additional exam requirements/recommendations for international students: required—TOEFL or IELTS. Electronic applications accepted.

Arizona State University at Tempe, College of Liberal Arts and Sciences, Department of English, Program in Film and Media Studies, Tempe, AZ 85287-0402. Offers American media and popular culture (MAS). *Program availability:* Part-time, evening/weekend, online learning. *Degree requirements:* For master's, integrated project. *Entrance requirements:* For master's, minimum GPA of 3.0 or equivalent in last 2 years of work leading to bachelor's degree. Additional exam requirements/recommendations for international students: required—TOEFL, IELTS, or PTE. Electronic applications accepted. *Expenses:* Contact institution.

Arizona State University at Tempe, Herberger Institute for Design and the Arts, School of Arts, Media and Engineering, Tempe, AZ 85287-8709. Offers media arts and sciences (PhD). *Degree requirements:* For doctorate, comprehensive exam, thesis/dissertation, interactive Program of Study (iPOS) submitted before completing 50 percent of required credit hours. *Entrance requirements:* For doctorate, GRE, minimum GPA of 3.25 in last 2 years of work leading to bachelor's degree, portfolio of supporting material, statement of educational/career goals, 3 letters of recommendation, resume/curriculum vitae. Additional exam requirements/recommendations for international students: required—TOEFL, IELTS, or PTE. Electronic applications accepted.

Arkansas State University, Graduate School, College of Media and Communication, Department of Media, State University, AR 72467. Offers mass communications (MSMC). *Program availability:* Part-time. *Degree requirements:* For master's, comprehensive exam, thesis or alternative. *Entrance requirements:* For master's, GRE General Test or MAT, appropriate bachelor's degree, letters of reference, educational experience, professional experience, official transcripts, immunization records. Additional exam requirements/recommendations for international students: required—TOEFL (minimum score 550 paper-based; 79 iBT), IELTS (minimum score 6), PTE (minimum score 56). Electronic applications accepted.

Austin Peay State University, College of Graduate Studies, College of Arts and Letters, Department of Communication, Clarksville, TN 37044. Offers marketing communication (MA); media management (MA). *Program availability:* Part-time, evening/weekend, online learning. *Faculty:* 7 full-time (4 women), 2 part-time/adjunct (both women). *Students:* 6 full-time (4 women), 50 part-time (32 women); includes 19 minority (13 Black or African American, non-Hispanic/Latino; 1 American Indian or Alaska Native, non-Hispanic/Latino; 5 Two or more races, non-Hispanic/Latino). Average age 32. 24 applicants, 83% accepted, 15 enrolled. In 2019, 21 master's awarded. *Degree requirements:* For master's, comprehensive exam, thesis (for some programs). *Entrance requirements:* For master's, GRE General Test, minimum GPA of 2.5. Additional exam requirements/recommendations for international students: required—TOEFL (minimum score 500 paper-based). *Application deadline:* For fall admission, 8/5 priority date for domestic students. Applications are processed on a rolling basis. Application fee: $45 ($55 for international students). Electronic applications accepted. *Financial support:* Research assistantships with full tuition reimbursements, career-related internships or fieldwork, Federal Work-Study, institutionally sponsored loans, scholarships/grants, and unspecified assistantships available. Support available to part-time students. Financial award application deadline: 7/1; financial award applicants required to submit FAFSA. *Unit head:* Dr. Kathy Heuston, Interim Chair, 931-221-7554, Fax: 931-221-7265, E-mail: leek@apsu.edu. *Application contact:* Megan Mitchell, Coordinator of Graduate Admissions, 931-221-6189, Fax: 931-221-7641, E-mail: mitchellm@apsu.edu.
Website: http://www.apsu.edu/communication/index.php

Boston University, College of Communication, Department of Film and Television, Boston, MA 02215. Offers MFA, MS. *Program availability:* Part-time. *Faculty:* 17 full-time, 25 part-time/adjunct. *Students:* 79 full-time (54 women), 5 part-time (2 women); includes 14 minority (5 Black or African American, non-Hispanic/Latino; 3 Asian, non-Hispanic/Latino; 5 Hispanic/Latino; 1 Two or more races, non-Hispanic/Latino), 21 international. Average age 25. 275 applicants, 46% accepted, 55 enrolled. In 2019, 61 master's awarded. *Degree requirements:* For master's, thesis (for some programs). *Entrance requirements:* For master's, transcript(s), resume/CV, writing and creative samples, letters of recommendation. Additional exam requirements/recommendations for international students: required—TOEFL (minimum score 600 paper-based; 100 iBT), either TOEFL or IELTS; recommended—IELTS (minimum score 7). *Application deadline:* For fall admission, 5/1 for domestic and international students. Applications are processed on a rolling basis. Application fee: $95. Electronic applications accepted. *Financial support:* Research assistantships, teaching assistantships with partial tuition reimbursements, career-related internships or fieldwork, Federal Work-Study, scholarships/grants, and unspecified assistantships available. Support available to part-time students. Financial award application deadline: 5/1; financial award applicants required to submit FAFSA. *Unit head:* Paul Schneider, Chairman, 617-353-3483, Fax: 617-353-1084, E-mail: ftvchair@bu.edu. *Application contact:* Jackie Cummings, Admission and Financial Aid Counselor, 617-353-3481, E-mail: comgrad@bu.edu.
Website: http://www.bu.edu/com/academics/film-tv/

Boston University, College of Communication, Division of Emerging Media Studies, Boston, MA 02215. Offers MA, PhD. *Program availability:* Part-time. *Faculty:* 4 full-time (1 woman). *Students:* 48 full-time (39 women), 2 part-time (both women); includes 4 minority (1 Asian, non-Hispanic/Latino; 2 Hispanic/Latino; 1 Two or more races, non-Hispanic/Latino), 34 international. Average age 25. 180 applicants, 56% accepted, 35 enrolled. In 2019, 24 master's awarded. *Degree requirements:* For master's, thesis optional; for doctorate, comprehensive exam, thesis/dissertation. *Entrance requirements:* For master's, transcript(s), resume/CV, writing samples, 3 letters of recommendation; for doctorate, GRE, transcript(s), resume/CV, writing samples, 3 letters of recommendation. Additional exam requirements/recommendations for international students: required—TOEFL (minimum score 600 paper-based; 100 iBT), either TOEFL or IELTS; recommended—IELTS (minimum score 7). *Application deadline:* For fall admission, 5/1 for domestic and international students. Applications are processed on a rolling basis. Application fee: $95. Electronic applications accepted. *Financial support:* In 2019–20, 3 fellowships with full tuition reimbursements were awarded; research assistantships, teaching assistantships, career-related internships or fieldwork, Federal Work-Study, scholarships/grants, health care benefits, and unspecified assistantships also available. Financial award application deadline: 5/1; financial award applicants required to submit FAFSA. *Unit head:* Dr. James Katz, Professor of Emerging Media/Chair of the Division of Emerging Media Studies, 617-353-7733, E-mail: dems@bu.edu. *Application contact:* Jackie Cummings, Admission and Financial Aid Counselor, 617-353-3481, E-mail: comgrad@bu.edu.
Website: http://www.bu.edu/com/academics/emerging-media/

Bowling Green State University, Graduate College, College of Arts and Sciences, School of Media and Communication, Bowling Green, OH 43403. Offers media and communication (MA, PhD); strategic communication (MA). *Program availability:* Part-time. Terminal master's awarded for partial completion of doctoral program. *Degree requirements:* For master's, thesis or alternative; for doctorate, comprehensive exam, thesis/dissertation. *Entrance requirements:* For master's and doctorate, GRE General Test. Additional exam requirements/recommendations for international students: required—TOEFL. Electronic applications accepted.

Brooklyn College of the City University of New York, School of Visual, Media and Performing Arts, Department of Television and Radio, Brooklyn, NY 11210-2889. Offers media studies (MS); television production (MFA). *Program availability:* Part-time, evening/weekend. *Degree requirements:* For master's, comprehensive exam. *Entrance requirements:* For master's, GRE General Test or MAT, 12 credits in television/radio with a minimum B average, 2 letters of recommendation. Additional exam requirements/recommendations for international students: required—TOEFL (minimum score 580 paper-based; 92 iBT). Electronic applications accepted.

Carnegie Mellon University, School of Computer Science and College of Fine Arts, Program in Entertainment Technology, Pittsburgh, PA 15213-3891. Offers MET.

Central Michigan University, College of Graduate Studies, College of the Arts and Media, School of Broadcast and Cinematic Arts, Mount Pleasant, MI 48859. Offers electronic media management (MA); electronic media production (MA); electronic media studies (MA); film theory and criticism (MA). *Program availability:* Part-time. *Degree requirements:* For master's, thesis or alternative. *Entrance requirements:* For master's, undergraduate degree in broadcasting, film studies, or an associated discipline with minimum GPA of 2.7. Electronic applications accepted. *Expenses: Tuition, area resident:* Full-time $12,267; part-time $8178 per year. *Tuition, state resident:* full-time $12,267; part-time $8178 per year. *Tuition, nonresident:* full-time $12,267; part-time $8178 per year. *International tuition:* $16,110 full-time. *Required fees:* $225 per semester. Tuition and fees vary according to degree level and program.

Champlain College, Graduate Studies, Burlington, VT 05402-0670. Offers business (MBA); digital forensic science (MS); early childhood education (M Ed); emergent media (MFA, MS); executive leadership (MS); health care administration (MS); information security operations (MS); law (MS); mediation and applied conflict studies (MS). *Program availability:* Part-time, online learning. *Degree requirements:* For master's, capstone project. *Entrance requirements:* Additional exam requirements/recommendations for international students: required—TOEFL (minimum score 550 paper-based; 80 iBT). Electronic applications accepted.

City College of the City University of New York, Graduate School, Division of Humanities and the Arts, Department of Media and Communication Arts, Program in Film, New York, NY 10031-9198. Offers MFA. *Entrance requirements:* For master's, BA or BFA with minimum GPA of 3.0, undergraduate training in film and video or equivalent work/industry experience, online video portfolio, 2 letters of recommendation, official transcripts, resume. Additional exam requirements/recommendations for international students: required—TOEFL (minimum score 575 paper-based; 91 iBT), IELTS (minimum score 6.5). Electronic applications accepted.

Claremont Graduate University, Graduate Programs, School of Arts and Humanities, Department of Cultural Studies, Claremont, CA 91711-6160. Offers Africana studies (Certificate); cultural studies (MA, PhD); media studies (MA, PhD); museum studies (MA). *Program availability:* Part-time. *Entrance requirements:* For master's and doctorate, GRE General Test. Additional exam requirements/recommendations for international students: required—TOEFL (minimum score 75 iBT). Electronic applications accepted.

College of Staten Island of the City University of New York, Graduate Programs, Division of Humanities and Social Sciences, Program in Cinema and Media Studies, Staten Island, NY 10314-6600. Offers MA. *Program availability:* Part-time, evening/weekend. *Faculty:* 1. *Students:* 5. 12 applicants. In 2019, 5 master's awarded. *Degree requirements:* For master's, comprehensive exam (for some programs), thesis optional, 36 credits in graduate cinema and media studies courses, remaining credits are to be fulfilled, following advisement, through electives offered in the graduate program in Cinema and Media Studies. A written thesis, or a production thesis, or an examination is to be completed. *Entrance requirements:* For master's, bachelor's degree with minimum B average in undergraduate cinema studies or communications courses; 10-12 page writing sample; three letters of recommendation; 1-2 page statement of intent detailing interest in the field, background in film and media studies, and/or research interests; three letters of recommendation. Additional exam requirements/recommendations for international students: required—TOEFL (minimum score 550 paper-based; 79 iBT), IELTS (minimum score 6.5). *Application deadline:* For fall admission, 6/15 priority date for domestic students, 6/15 for international students; for spring admission, 11/25 priority date for domestic students, 11/25 for international students. Applications are processed on a rolling basis. Application fee: $75. Electronic applications accepted. *Expenses: Tuition, area resident:* Full-time $11,090; part-time $470 per credit. *Tuition, state resident:* full-time $11,090; part-time $470 per credit. *Tuition, nonresident:* full-time $20,520; part-time $855 per credit. *International tuition:* $20,520 full-time. *Required fees:* $559; $181 per semester. Tuition and fees vary according to program. *Unit head:* Bilge Yesil, Graduate Program Coordinator, 718-982-2549, E-mail: cinemamasters@csi.cuny.edu. *Application contact:* Sasha Spence, Associate Director for Graduate Admissions, 718-982-2019, Fax: 718-982-2500, E-mail:

sasha.spence@csi.cuny.edu.
Website: https://www.csi.cuny.edu/academics-and-research/departments-programs/media-culture

Colorado State University, College of Liberal Arts, Department of Journalism and Media Communication, Fort Collins, CO 80523-1785. Offers communications and media management (MCMM); public communication and technology (MS, PhD). *Program availability:* Part-time, blended/hybrid learning. *Faculty:* 13 full-time (8 women), 6 part-time/adjunct (3 women). *Students:* 24 full-time (17 women), 54 part-time (37 women); includes 23 minority (1 Black or African American, non-Hispanic/Latino; 1 American Indian or Alaska Native, non-Hispanic/Latino; 3 Asian, non-Hispanic/Latino; 14 Hispanic/Latino; 4 Two or more races, non-Hispanic/Latino), 10 international. Average age 32. 45 applicants, 58% accepted, 19 enrolled. In 2019, 15 master's, 2 doctorates awarded. Terminal master's awarded for partial completion of doctoral program. *Degree requirements:* For master's, thesis (for some programs), research project; for doctorate, comprehensive exam, thesis/dissertation. *Entrance requirements:* For master's, GRE General Test (for MS program only), minimum GPA of 3.0; transcripts; letters of recommendation; writing sample, curriculum vitae/resume; statement of purpose; for doctorate, GRE General Test, minimum GPA of 3.0; transcripts; letters of recommendation; writing sample, curriculum vitae/resume; statement of purpose. Additional exam requirements/recommendations for international students: required—TOEFL (minimum score 550 paper-based; 80 iBT), IELTS (minimum score 6.5); recommended—TWE. Application fee: $60 ($70 for international students). Electronic applications accepted. *Expenses:* Contact institution. *Financial support:* In 2019–20, 2 research assistantships with full and partial tuition reimbursements (averaging $20,340 per year), 31 teaching assistantships with full and partial tuition reimbursements (averaging $16,537 per year) were awarded; scholarships/grants, health care benefits, and unspecified assistantships also available. *Unit head:* Prof. Greg Luft, Professor and Department Chair, 970-491-1979, Fax: 970-491-2908, E-mail: greg.luft@colostate.edu. *Application contact:* Linda Kidder, Graduate Program Administrator, 970-491-5132, Fax: 970-491-2908, E-mail: linda.kidder@colostate.edu.
Website: http://journalism.colostate.edu/

Columbia University, School of the Arts, Film and Media Studies Program, New York, NY 10027. Offers MA. *Program availability:* Part-time. Terminal master's awarded for partial completion of doctoral program. *Degree requirements:* For master's, thesis. *Entrance requirements:* For master's, undergraduate transcript, 3 letters of recommendation, autobiographical essay, 2 samples of scholarly writing, graduate transcript (if applicable). Additional exam requirements/recommendations for international students: required—Either the TOEFL or the IELTS is required. Electronic applications accepted. *Expenses:* Contact institution.

Concordia University, School of Graduate Studies, Faculty of Arts and Science, Department of Communication Studies, Montréal, QC H3G 1M8, Canada. Offers communication (PhD); communication studies (Diploma); media studies (MA). *Degree requirements:* For master's, thesis optional; for doctorate, one foreign language, comprehensive exam, thesis/dissertation, research practicum, seminar. *Entrance requirements:* For master's, bachelor's degree in communications, 2 years of media-related experience; for doctorate, MA in communications.

Cornell University, Graduate School, Graduate Fields of Agriculture and Life Sciences, Field of Communication, Ithaca, NY 14853. Offers communication (MS, PhD); human-computer interaction (MS, PhD); language and communication (MS, PhD); media communication and society (MS, PhD); organizational communication (MS, PhD); science, environment and health communication (MS, PhD); social psychology of communication (MS, PhD). *Degree requirements:* For master's, thesis (MS); for doctorate, comprehensive exam, thesis/dissertation. *Entrance requirements:* For master's and doctorate, GRE General Test, 3 letters of recommendation. Additional exam requirements/recommendations for international students: required—TOEFL (minimum score 600 paper-based; 100 iBT). Electronic applications accepted.

Dallas Theological Seminary, Graduate Programs, Dallas, TX 75204-6499. Offers adult education (Th M); apologetics (Th M); Bible backgrounds (Th M); Bible translation (Th M); Biblical and theological studies (Certificate); biblical counseling (MA); biblical exegesis and linguistics (MA); biblical exposition (PhD); biblical studies (MA); Biblical theology (Th M); children's education (Th M); Christian education (MA, D Min); Christian leadership (MA); cross-cultural ministries (MA); educational administration (Th M); educational leadership (Th M); evangelism and discipleship (Th M); exposition of Biblical books (Th M); family life education (Th M); general studies (Th M); Hebrew and cognate studies (Th M); hermeneutics (Th M); historical theology (Th M); homiletics (Th M); intercultural ministries (Th M); Jesus studies (Th M); leadership studies (Th M); media and communication (MA); media arts (Th M); ministry (D Min); ministry with women (Th M); New Testament studies (Th M, PhD); Old Testament studies (Th M, PhD); parachurch ministries (Th M); pastoral care and counseling (Th M); pastoral theology and practice (Th M); philosophy (Th M); sacred theology (STM); spiritual formation (Th M); systematic theology (Th M); teaching in Christian institutions (Th M); theological studies (PhD); urban ministries (Th M); worship studies (Th M); youth education (Th M). *Program availability:* Part-time, online learning. *Degree requirements:* For master's, variable foreign language requirement, thesis (for some programs); for doctorate, 2 foreign languages, thesis/dissertation. *Entrance requirements:* For master's, GRE or MAT (if minimum undergraduate cumulative GPA is below 2.5 or undergraduate degree is unaccredited). Additional exam requirements/recommendations for international students: required—TOEFL (minimum score 575 paper-based; 85 iBT), TWE. Electronic applications accepted.

DePaul University, College of Communication, Chicago, IL 60604. Offers digital communication and media arts (MA); health communication (MA); journalism (MA); media and cinema studies (MA); multicultural communication (MA); organizational communication (MA); public relations and advertising (MA); relational communication (MA). *Program availability:* Part-time, evening/weekend. *Entrance requirements:* Additional exam requirements/recommendations for international students: required—TOEFL (minimum score 590 paper-based; 96 iBT), IELTS (minimum score 7.5) or PTE. Electronic applications accepted.

Drexel University, College of Arts and Sciences, Department of Communication, Culture and Media, Philadelphia, PA 19104-2875. Offers communication (MS), including public communication, science communication, technical communication. *Program availability:* Part-time, evening/weekend. *Degree requirements:* For master's, internship, professional portfolio. *Entrance requirements:* Additional exam requirements/recommendations for international students: required—TOEFL. Electronic applications accepted.

Duke University, Graduate School, Master of Fine Arts in Experimental and Documentary Arts Program, Durham, NC 27708. Offers MFA. *Degree requirements:* For master's, thesis, final project. *Entrance requirements:* For master's, portfolio. Additional exam requirements/recommendations for international students: required—TOEFL (minimum score 577 paper-based; 90 iBT) or IELTS (minimum score 7). Electronic applications accepted.

Fairleigh Dickinson University, Metropolitan Campus, University College: Arts, Sciences, and Professional Studies, School of Art and Media Studies, Program in Media and Communications, Teaneck, NJ 07666-1914. Offers MA.

Fielding Graduate University, Graduate Programs, School of Psychology, Programs in Media Psychology, Santa Barbara, CA 93105-3814. Offers MA, PhD, Graduate Certificate. *Program availability:* Part-time, evening/weekend, 100% online, blended/hybrid learning. Terminal master's awarded for partial completion of doctoral program. *Degree requirements:* For master's, thesis or alternative, Capstone project; for doctorate, thesis/dissertation. *Entrance requirements:* For master's, bachelor's degree from regionally-accredited U.S. institution or equivalent, resume, statement of purpose, official transcript; for doctorate, bachelor's or master's degree from regionally-accredited U.S. institution or equivalent, curriculum vitae, statement of purpose, critical thinking writing sample, 2 letters of recommendation, official transcript; for Graduate Certificate, bachelor's degree from regionally-accredited U.S. institution or equivalent. Electronic applications accepted. *Expenses:* Contact institution.

Florida Atlantic University, Dorothy F. Schmidt College of Arts and Letters, School of Communication and Multimedia Studies, Boca Raton, FL 33431-0991. Offers communication studies (MA); film and video (Certificate); media, technology and entertainment (MFA). *Program availability:* Part-time. *Faculty:* 23 full-time (9 women). *Students:* 30 full-time (19 women), 13 part-time (5 women); includes 22 minority (9 Black or African American, non-Hispanic/Latino; 1 Asian, non-Hispanic/Latino; 6 Hispanic/Latino; 6 Two or more races, non-Hispanic/Latino), 7 international. Average age 30. 32 applicants, 66% accepted, 19 enrolled. In 2019, 8 master's awarded. *Degree requirements:* For master's, one foreign language, comprehensive exam (for some programs), thesis (for some programs). *Entrance requirements:* For master's, GRE General Test, minimum GPA of 3.0, essay, letters of recommendation. *Application deadline:* For fall admission, 7/1 priority date for domestic students, 4/1 for international students; for spring admission, 11/1 for domestic students, 10/1 for international students. Applications are processed on a rolling basis. Application fee: $30. Electronic applications accepted. *Expenses: Tuition:* Full-time $20,536; part-time $371.82 per credit hour. Tuition and fees vary according to program. *Financial support:* Teaching assistantships with partial tuition reimbursements, Federal Work-Study, institutionally sponsored loans, scholarships/grants, and unspecified assistantships available. Support available to part-time students. Financial award application deadline: 3/1; financial award applicants required to submit FAFSA. *Unit head:* Dr. Carol Bishop Mills, Director, 561-297-0042, Fax: 561-297-2615, E-mail: millsc@fau.edu. *Application contact:* Dr. Stephen Charbonneau, Graduate Director, 561-297-3856, Fax: 561-297-2615, E-mail: scharbo1@fau.edu.
Website: http://www.fau.edu/scms/

Florida State University, The Graduate School, College of Communication and Information, School of Communication, Tallahassee, FL 32306. Offers communication theory and research (PhD); integrated marketing communication (MA, MS); media and communication studies (MA, MS); public interest media and communication (MA, MS). *Program availability:* Part-time. *Faculty:* 23 full-time (13 women), 1 part-time/adjunct (0 women). *Students:* 19 full-time (16 women), 121 part-time (84 women); includes 73 minority (22 Black or African American, non-Hispanic/Latino; 15 Asian, non-Hispanic/Latino; 27 Hispanic/Latino; 9 Two or more races, non-Hispanic/Latino). Average age 24. 196 applicants, 54% accepted, 48 enrolled. In 2019, 65 master's, 5 doctorates awarded. *Degree requirements:* For master's, thesis (for some programs); for doctorate, comprehensive exam, thesis/dissertation. *Entrance requirements:* For master's, GRE General Test, minimum GPA of 3.0; for doctorate, GRE General Test, minimum GPA of 3.3 in graduate course work. Additional exam requirements/recommendations for international students: required—TOEFL (minimum score 600 paper-based; 100 iBT), IELTS (minimum score 7). *Application deadline:* For fall admission, 7/1 priority date for domestic students, 5/1 priority date for international students; for spring admission, 11/1 priority date for domestic and international students; for summer admission, 3/1 priority date for domestic and international students. Applications are processed on a rolling basis. Application fee: $30. Electronic applications accepted. *Expenses:* $5,748 state resident full-time, $2,874 state resident part-time; $13,320 nonresident full-time, $6,660 nonresident part-time. *Financial support:* In 2019–20, 109 students received support, including 20 research assistantships with full tuition reimbursements available (averaging $12,726 per year), 139 teaching assistantships with full tuition reimbursements available (averaging $10,602 per year); scholarships/grants, tuition waivers (full and partial), and unspecified assistantships also available. Financial award application deadline: 11/1; financial award applicants required to submit FAFSA. *Unit head:* Dr. Jennifer Proffitt, Director, 850-644-5034, Fax: 850-644-8642, E-mail: jennifer.proffitt@cci.fsu.edu. *Application contact:* Natashia Hinson-Turner, Graduate Coordinator, 850-644-5034, Fax: 850-644-8642, E-mail: comgradadvising@cci.fsu.edu.
Website: http://www.cci.fsu.edu

Fordham University, Gabelli School of Business, New York, NY 10023. Offers accounting (MBA, MS); applied statistics and decision-making (MS); business economics (DPS); capital markets (DPS); communications and media management (MBA); electronic business (MBA); entrepreneurship (MBA); finance (MBA, PhD); global finance (MS); global sustainability (MBA); health administration (MS); healthcare management (MBA); information systems (MBA, MS); investor relations (MS); management (EMBA, MBA, MS, PhD); marketing (MBA); marketing intelligence (MS); media management (MS); nonprofit leadership (MS); quantitative finance (MS); strategy and decision-making (DPS); taxation (MS); JD/MBA; MS/MBA. *Accreditation:* AACSB. *Program availability:* Part-time, evening/weekend, 100% online, blended/hybrid learning. *Faculty:* 130 full-time (49 women), 73 part-time/adjunct (12 women). *Students:* 1,038 full-time, 503 part-time; includes 227 minority (57 Black or African American, non-Hispanic/Latino; 1 American Indian or Alaska Native, non-Hispanic/Latino; 65 Asian, non-Hispanic/Latino; 91 Hispanic/Latino; 1 Native Hawaiian or other Pacific Islander, non-Hispanic/Latino; 12 Two or more races, non-Hispanic/Latino), 985 international. Average age 27. 4,250 applicants, 62% accepted, 764 enrolled. In 2019, 899 master's awarded. Terminal master's awarded for partial completion of doctoral program. *Degree requirements:* For master's, internships (for some degrees); for doctorate, comprehensive exam (for some programs), thesis/dissertation. *Entrance requirements:* For master's, GMAT/GRE, 2 letters of recommendation, resume, 2 essays, transcripts, interview. Additional exam requirements/recommendations for international students: required—TOEFL (minimum score 100 iBT), IELTS (minimum score 7). *Application deadline:* For fall admission, 11/15 for domestic and international students; for winter admission, 1/10 for domestic students, 1/1 for international students; for spring admission, 5/15 for domestic students, 3/1 for international students; for summer admission, 7/10 for domestic students, 6/5 for international students. Application fee: $130. Electronic applications accepted. *Expenses:* Contact institution. *Financial support:* Career-related internships or fieldwork, institutionally sponsored loans, scholarships/grants, and unspecified assistantships available. Support available to part-time students. Financial award application deadline: 6/5; financial award applicants required to submit FAFSA. *Unit head:* Dr. Donna Rapaccioli, Dean, 212-636-6165, Fax: 212-307-1779, E-mail: rapaccioli@fordham.edu. *Application contact:* Lawrence Mur'ray, Senior Assistant Dean of Graduate Admissions and Advising, 212-636-6200, Fax: 212-636-7076, E-mail: admissionsgb@fordham.edu.
Website: http://www.fordham.edu/gabelli

Media Studies

Fordham University, Graduate School of Arts and Sciences, Department of Communication and Media Studies, New York, NY 10458. Offers public media (MA). *Program availability:* Part-time, evening/weekend. *Students:* Average age 25. 88 applicants, 52% accepted, 17 enrolled. In 2019, 18 master's awarded. *Degree requirements:* For master's, thesis, internship. *Entrance requirements:* For master's, GRE General Test. Additional exam requirements/recommendations for international students: required—TOEFL (minimum score 600 paper-based). *Application deadline:* For fall admission, 1/4 priority date for domestic students; for spring admission, 11/1 for domestic students. Application fee: $70. Electronic applications accepted. *Financial support:* In 2019–20, 3 students received support, including 2 research assistantships with full and partial tuition reimbursements available (averaging $23,200 per year); career-related internships or fieldwork, Federal Work-Study, institutionally sponsored loans, scholarships/grants, tuition waivers (full and partial), and unspecified assistantships also available. Financial award application deadline: 1/4. *Unit head:* Jacqueline Reich, Chair, 718-817-4850, E-mail: jreich8@fordham.edu. *Application contact:* Garrett Marino, Director of Graduate Admissions, 718-817-4419, Fax: 718-817-3566, E-mail: gmarino10@fordham.edu.

Full Sail University, Media Design Master of Fine Arts Program - Online, Winter Park, FL 32792-7437. Offers MFA. *Program availability:* Online learning.

Georgetown University, Graduate School of Arts and Sciences, School of Continuing Studies, Washington, DC 20057. Offers American studies (MALS); applied intelligence (MPS); Catholic studies (MALS); classical civilizations (MALS); emergency and disaster management (MPS); ethics and the professions (MALS); global strategic communications (MPS); hospitality management (MPS); human resources management (MPS); humanities (MALS); individualized study (MALS); integrated marketing communications (MPS); international affairs (MALS); Islam and Muslim-Christian relations (MALS); journalism (MPS); liberal studies (DLS); literature and society (MALS); medieval and early modern European studies (MALS); public relations and corporate communications (MPS); real estate (MPS); religious studies (MALS); social and public policy (MALS); sports industry management (MPS); systems engineering management (MPS); technology management (MPS); the theory and practice of American democracy (MALS); urban and regional planning (MPS); visual culture (MALS). *Entrance requirements:* Additional exam requirements/recommendations for international students: required—TOEFL.

Georgia State University, College of Arts and Sciences, Department of Communication, Atlanta, GA 30302-3083. Offers film, video, and digital imaging (MA), including critical studies, production, screenwriting; human communication and social influence (MA); mass communication (MA); media and society (PhD); moving image studies (PhD); public communication (PhD); rhetoric and politics (PhD). *Program availability:* Part-time. *Faculty:* 22 full-time (16 women), 1 part-time/adjunct (0 women). *Students:* 67 full-time (46 women), 26 part-time (17 women); includes 44 minority (40 Black or African American, non-Hispanic/Latino; 1 Asian, non-Hispanic/Latino; 1 Hispanic/Latino; 1 Native Hawaiian or other Pacific Islander, non-Hispanic/Latino; 1 Two or more races, non-Hispanic/Latino), 12 international. Average age 36. 82 applicants, 49% accepted, 22 enrolled. In 2019, 9 master's, 5 doctorates awarded. *Degree requirements:* For master's, variable foreign language requirement, thesis (for some programs); for doctorate, comprehensive exam, thesis/dissertation. *Entrance requirements:* For master's and doctorate, GRE. Additional exam requirements/recommendations for international students: required—TOEFL (minimum score 550 paper-based; 80 iBT), IELTS (minimum score 6.5). *Application deadline:* For fall admission, 2/10 for domestic and international students; for spring admission, 10/15 for domestic and international students. Application fee: $50. Electronic applications accepted. *Expenses: Tuition, area resident:* Full-time $7164; part-time $398 per credit hour. Tuition, state resident: full-time $7164; part-time $398 per credit hour. Tuition, nonresident: full-time $22,662; part-time $1259 per credit hour. *International tuition:* $22,662 full-time. *Required fees:* $2128; $312 per credit hour. Tuition and fees vary according to course load and program. *Financial support:* In 2019–20, fellowships with tuition reimbursements (averaging $15,000 per year), teaching assistantships with tuition reimbursements (averaging $15,000 per year) were awarded; career-related internships or fieldwork and unspecified assistantships also available. Financial award applicants required to submit FAFSA. *Unit head:* Dr. Greg Lisby, Chair, 404-413-5639, Fax: 404-413-5634, E-mail: glisby@gsu.edu. *Application contact:* Dr. Greg Lisby, Chair, 404-413-5639, Fax: 404-413-5634, E-mail: glisby@gsu.edu.
Website: http://communication.gsu.edu

Howard University, Cathy Hughes School of Communications, Department of Communication, Culture and Media Studies, Washington, DC 20059-0002. Offers mass communication (MA, PhD); media studies (MA, PhD). *Program availability:* Part-time, evening/weekend. *Degree requirements:* For master's, comprehensive exam (for some programs), thesis optional; for doctorate, one foreign language, comprehensive exam, thesis/dissertation. *Entrance requirements:* For master's, GRE, minimum GPA of 3.0; for doctorate, GRE, minimum graduate GPA of 3.5. Additional exam requirements/recommendations for international students: required—TOEFL. Electronic applications accepted.

Hunter College of the City University of New York, Graduate School, School of Arts and Sciences, Department of Film and Media Studies, Program in Integrated Media Arts, New York, NY 10065-5085. Offers MFA. *Program availability:* Part-time, evening/weekend. *Entrance requirements:* For master's, GRE General Test, 3 letters of recommendation, portfolio of media works, minimum GPA of 3.0. Additional exam requirements/recommendations for international students: required—TOEFL, TWE.

Indiana State University, College of Graduate and Professional Studies, College of Arts and Sciences, Department of Communication, Terre Haute, IN 47809. Offers communication studies (MA); radio, television and film (MA). *Program availability:* Part-time. *Degree requirements:* For master's, thesis (for some programs), oral and written exam. *Entrance requirements:* For master's, GRE General Test. Additional exam requirements/recommendations for international students: required—TOEFL.

Indiana University Bloomington, University Graduate School, College of Arts and Sciences, The Media School, Bloomington, IN 47405-7000. Offers media (MS); media arts and sciences (MA, PhD). *Degree requirements:* For master's, comprehensive exam (for some programs), thesis (for some programs); for doctorate, comprehensive exam, thesis/dissertation. *Entrance requirements:* Additional exam requirements/recommendations for international students: required—TOEFL. Electronic applications accepted.

Indiana University of Pennsylvania, School of Graduate Studies and Research, College of Education and Communications, Department of Communications Media, Program in Communications Media and Instructional Technology, Indiana, PA 15705. Offers PhD. *Program availability:* Part-time, evening/weekend. *Faculty:* 8 full-time (2 women). *Students:* 11 full-time (8 women), 33 part-time (12 women); includes 7 minority (5 Black or African American, non-Hispanic/Latino; 2 Hispanic/Latino), 8 international. Average age 38. 24 applicants, 63% accepted, 13 enrolled. In 2019, 7 doctorates awarded. *Degree requirements:* For doctorate, comprehensive exam, thesis/dissertation. *Entrance requirements:* For doctorate, If did not receive masters degree over five years ago, then must submit: recent official GRE or MAT scores. MAT scores need to meet department minimum requirements, a current curriculum vitae or resume and a writing sample that reflects your ability to do academic work and research, goal statement, 2 letters of recommendation, official transcripts. If earned masters degree over five years ago and have five years or more experience, must submit: -current curriculum vitae,a writing sample, including a written response to a research question or problem a personal interview & an academic portfolio. Additional exam requirements/recommendations for international students: required—TOEFL (minimum score 540 paper-based; 76 iBT), IELTS (minimum score 6), TOEFL or IELTS. *Application deadline:* Applications are processed on a rolling basis. Application fee: $50. Electronic applications accepted. *Expenses:* Contact institution. *Financial support:* In 2019–20, 2 fellowships with tuition reimbursements (averaging $1,550 per year), 4 research assistantships with tuition reimbursements (averaging $7,472 per year), 3 teaching assistantships with partial tuition reimbursements (averaging $25,035 per year) were awarded. Financial award application deadline: 4/15; financial award applicants required to submit FAFSA. *Unit head:* Dr. Zachary Stiegler, Coordinator, 724-357-3219, E-mail: zachary.stiegler@iup.edu. *Application contact:* Dr. Zachary Stiegler, Coordinator, 724-357-3219, E-mail: zachary.stiegler@iup.edu.
Website: http://www.iup.edu/commmedia/programs/phdcmit/

International University in Geneva, Leadership Programs, Geneva, Switzerland. Offers international relations and diplomacy (MIRD); media and communication (MA); public administration (DPA). *Degree requirements:* For master's, comprehensive exam. *Entrance requirements:* Additional exam requirements/recommendations for international students: required—TOEFL. Electronic applications accepted.

Johns Hopkins University, Advanced Academic Programs, Program in Film and Media, Baltimore, MD 21218. Offers MA. *Program availability:* Part-time.

Kent State University, College of Communication and Information, School of Media and Journalism, Kent, OH 44242-0001. Offers journalism and mass communication (MA), including media management, public relations, reporting and editing-broadcast, reporting and editing-convergence, reporting and editing-journalism educators, reporting and editing-magazine, reporting and editing-newspaper. *Program availability:* Part-time, 100% online. *Faculty:* 7 full-time (6 women), 5 part-time/adjunct (2 women). *Students:* 11 full-time (8 women), 35 part-time (22 women); includes 3 minority (all Black or African American, non-Hispanic/Latino), 3 international. Average age 34. 18 applicants, 78% accepted, 10 enrolled. In 2019, 40 master's awarded. *Degree requirements:* For master's, thesis, thesis or project. *Entrance requirements:* For master's, GRE, Bachelor's degree, minimum GPA of 3.0, statement of purpose, 2 letters of recommendation, resume or vitae, official transcript(s), writing sample. Additional exam requirements/recommendations for international students: required—TOEFL (minimum score 100 iBT), IELTS (minimum score 7), PTE (minimum score 65), Michigan English Language Assessment Battery (minimum score 82). *Application deadline:* For fall admission, 7/1 for domestic and international students. Applications are processed on a rolling basis. Application fee: $45 ($70 for international students). Electronic applications accepted. *Financial support:* Research assistantships with full tuition reimbursements, teaching assistantships with full tuition reimbursements, scholarships/grants, and unspecified assistantships available. Financial award application deadline: 3/1. *Unit head:* Jeff Fruit, Interim Director and Professor, 330-672-2572, E-mail: jmc@kent.edu. *Application contact:* Tang Tang, Graduate Coordinator/Professor, 330-672-1132, E-mail: ttang2@kent.edu.
Website: http://www.kent.edu/jmc

La Salle University, School of Arts and Sciences, Program in Strategic Communication, Philadelphia, PA 19141-1199. Offers communication consulting and development (MA); communication management (MA); general professional communication (MA); professional and business communication (Certificate); public relations (MA); social and new media (Certificate). *Program availability:* Part-time, evening/weekend, online learning. *Degree requirements:* For master's, practicum. *Entrance requirements:* For master's, writing assessment, professional resume; minimum overall B average; two letters of recommendation (if GPA below 3.25); brief personal statement (about 500 words); interview; for Certificate, writing assessment, minimum GPA of 2.75 in undergraduate studies; brief personal statement (about 500 words); interview. Additional exam requirements/recommendations for international students: required—TOEFL. Electronic applications accepted. Application fee is waived when completed online. *Expenses:* Contact institution.

Lindenwood University, Graduate Programs, School of Accelerated Degree Programs, St. Charles, MO 63301-1695. Offers administration (MSA), including management, marketing, project management; business administration (MBA); communications (MA), including digital and multimedia, media management, promotions, training and development; criminal justice and administration (MS); healthcare administration (MS); human resource management (MS); information technology (Certificate); managing information security (MS); managing information technology (MS); managing virtualization and cloud computing (MS); writing (MFA). *Program availability:* Part-time, evening/weekend, 100% online. *Faculty:* 11 full-time (6 women), 66 part-time/adjunct (23 women). *Students:* 408 full-time (262 women), 60 part-time (40 women); includes 149 minority (111 Black or African American, non-Hispanic/Latino; 2 American Indian or Alaska Native, non-Hispanic/Latino; 2 Asian, non-Hispanic/Latino; 18 Hispanic/Latino; 1 Native Hawaiian or other Pacific Islander, non-Hispanic/Latino; 15 Two or more races, non-Hispanic/Latino), 33 international. Average age 39. 268 applicants, 46% accepted, 99 enrolled. In 2019, 347 master's awarded. *Degree requirements:* For master's, thesis (for some programs), minimum cumulative GPA of 3.0; for Certificate, minimum cumulative GPA of 3.0. *Entrance requirements:* For master's, resume, personal statement, official undergraduate transcript, minimum undergraduate cumulative GPA of 3.0. Additional exam requirements/recommendations for international students: required—TOEFL (minimum score 553 paper-based; 81 iBT); recommended—IELTS (minimum score 6.5). *Application deadline:* For fall admission, 9/30 priority date for domestic and international students; for winter admission, 1/6 priority date for domestic and international students; for spring admission, 4/6 priority date for domestic and international students; for summer admission, 7/8 priority date for domestic and international students. Applications are processed on a rolling basis. Application fee: $0 ($100 for international students). Electronic applications accepted. *Expenses:* Contact institution. *Financial support:* In 2019–20, 145 students received support. Career-related internships or fieldwork, institutionally sponsored loans, scholarships/grants, tuition waivers (partial), and unspecified assistantships available. Financial award application deadline: 6/30; financial award applicants required to submit FAFSA. *Unit head:* Dr. Gina Ganahl, Dean, Accelerated Degree Programs, 636-949-4501, Fax: 636-949-4505, E-mail: gganahl@lindenwood.edu. *Application contact:* Kara Schilli, Assistant Vice President, University Admissions, 636-949-4349, Fax: 636-949-4109, E-mail: adultadmissions@lindenwood.edu.
Website: https://www.lindenwood.edu/academics/academic-schools/school-of-accelerated-degree-programs/

Lindenwood University, Graduate Programs, School of Arts, Media, and Communications, St. Charles, MO 63301-1695. Offers advertising (MA); art history (MA); cinema and media arts (MFA); communications (MA); digital and Web design (MA); fashion and business design (MS); journalism (MA); mass communications (MA); social media and digital content (MS). *Program availability:* Part-time, 100% online.

Faculty: 20 full-time (5 women), 15 part-time/adjunct (6 women). *Students:* 64 full-time (42 women), 76 part-time (57 women); includes 43 minority (20 Black or African American, non-Hispanic/Latino; 13 Hispanic/Latino; 10 Two or more races, non-Hispanic/Latino), 8 international. Average age 33. 145 applicants, 46% accepted, 56 enrolled. In 2019, 11 master's awarded. *Degree requirements:* For master's, thesis (for some programs), minimum cumulative GPA of 3.0. *Entrance requirements:* For master's, audition or interview, minimum GPA of 3.0, portfolio, letter of recommendation. Additional exam requirements/recommendations for international students: required—TOEFL (minimum score 553 paper-based; 81 iBT); recommended—IELTS (minimum score 6.5). *Application deadline:* For fall admission, 8/9 priority date for domestic students, 6/1 priority date for international students; for spring admission, 12/20 for domestic students, 11/1 priority date for international students; for summer admission, 5/15 priority date for domestic students, 3/27 priority date for international students. Applications are processed on a rolling basis. Application fee: $0 ($100 for international students). Electronic applications accepted. *Expenses: Tuition:* Full-time $8910; part-time $495 per credit. Tuition and fees vary according to course load, degree level and program. *Financial support:* In 2019–20, 23 students received support. Career-related internships or fieldwork, institutionally sponsored loans, scholarships/grants, tuition waivers (partial), and unspecified assistantships available. Financial award application deadline: 6/30; financial award applicants required to submit FAFSA. *Unit head:* Dr. Jason Lively, Dean, School of Arts, Media, and Communications, 636-949-4164, Fax: 636-949-4910, E-mail: JLively@lindenwood.edu. *Application contact:* Kara Schilli, Assistant Vice President, University Admissions, 636-949-4349, Fax: 636-949-4109, E-mail: adultadmissions@lindenwood.edu.
Website: https://www.lindenwood.edu/academics/academic-schools/school-of-arts-media-and-communications/

Lindenwood University–Belleville, Graduate Programs, Belleville, IL 62226. Offers business administration (MBA); communications (MA), including digital and multimedia, media management, promotions, training and development; counseling (MA); criminal justice administration (MS); education (MA); healthcare administration (MS); human resource management (MS); school administration (MA); teaching (MAT).

Long Island University - Brooklyn, Richard L. Conolly College of Liberal Arts and Sciences, Brooklyn, NY 11201-8423. Offers biology (MS); chemistry (MS); clinical psychology (PhD); creative writing (MFA); English (MA); media arts (MA, MFA); political science (MA); psychology (MA); social science (MS); United Nations (Advanced Certificate); urban studies (MA); writing and production for television (MFA). *Program availability:* Part-time. Terminal master's awarded for partial completion of doctoral program. *Degree requirements:* For master's, comprehensive exam (for some programs), thesis (for some programs); for doctorate, thesis/dissertation. *Entrance requirements:* For doctorate, GRE. Additional exam requirements/recommendations for international students: required—TOEFL (minimum score 550 paper-based, 79 iBT) or IELTS. Electronic applications accepted.

Louisiana State University and Agricultural & Mechanical College, Graduate School, Manship School of Mass Communication, Baton Rouge, LA 70803. Offers MMC, PhD, JD/MMC. *Accreditation:* ACEJMC.

Loyola University Maryland, Graduate Programs, Loyola College of Arts and Sciences, Emerging Media Department, Baltimore, MD 21210-2699. Offers emerging media (MA). *Program availability:* Part-time-only, blended/hybrid learning. *Students:* 5 full-time (4 women), 42 part-time (33 women); includes 16 minority (12 Black or African American, non-Hispanic/Latino; 2 Asian, non-Hispanic/Latino; 2 Hispanic/Latino), 1 international. Average age 33. 11 applicants, 82% accepted, 9 enrolled. In 2019, 22 master's awarded. *Degree requirements:* For master's, thesis. *Entrance requirements:* For master's, essay, transcripts, resume, letters of recommendation. Additional exam requirements/recommendations for international students: required—TOEFL (minimum score 550 paper-based; 80 iBT), IELTS (minimum score 7), TOEFL (minimum score 550 paper-based, 80 iBT) or ILETS (minimum score 7). *Application deadline:* For fall admission, 7/1 priority date for domestic and international students; for spring admission, 11/1 priority date for domestic and international students; for summer admission, 4/1 priority date for domestic and international students. Applications are processed on a rolling basis. Application fee: $60. Electronic applications accepted. *Expenses:* Contact institution. *Financial support:* Career-related internships or fieldwork and scholarships/grants available. Financial award application deadline: 4/15; financial award applicants required to submit FAFSA. *Unit head:* Erin Richardson, Director of Program Operations, 410-617-2462, E-mail: erichardson@loyola.edu. *Application contact:* Office of Graduate Admission, 410-617-5020, E-mail: graduate@loyola.edu.
Website: https://www.loyola.edu/academics/emerging-media

Lynn University, Eugene M. and Christine E. Lynn College of Communication and Design, Boca Raton, FL 33431-5598. Offers communication and media (MS); digital media (Certificate); digital media and design (MS); graphic and Web design (MFA); visual effects animation (MFA). *Program availability:* Part-time, evening/weekend. *Faculty:* 17 full-time (6 women), 3 part-time/adjunct (2 women). *Students:* 28 full-time (15 women), 32 part-time (16 women); includes 15 minority (8 Black or African American, non-Hispanic/Latino; 6 Hispanic/Latino; 1 Two or more races, non-Hispanic/Latino), 19 international. Average age 28. 36 applicants, 92% accepted, 20 enrolled. In 2019, 30 master's awarded. *Degree requirements:* For master's, thesis (for some programs), completion of degree in four calendar years; minimum cumulative GPA of 3.0 and C grade or higher in each course; orientation seminar (one credit); 36 credits of foundation and specialization or a thesis. *Entrance requirements:* For master's, Bachelor's degree from accredited institution, minimum undergraduate GPA of 3.0, official undergraduate transcripts, letter of recommendation from academic or professional source, writing sample demonstrating capacity to perform at graduate level. Additional exam requirements/recommendations for international students: required—TOEFL (minimum score 550 paper-based; 80 iBT), IELTS (minimum score 6.5). *Application deadline:* For fall admission, 8/10 for domestic students, 7/31 for international students; for spring admission, 12/18 for domestic students, 12/2 for international students; for summer admission, 4/12 for domestic students, 4/2 for international students. Applications are processed on a rolling basis. Application fee: $45. Electronic applications accepted. *Expenses:* $740.00 per hour. *Financial support:* In 2019–20, 15 students received support. Career-related internships or fieldwork, Federal Work-Study, scholarships/grants, tuition waivers (full and partial), and unspecified assistantships available. Support available to part-time students. Financial award application deadline: 3/1; financial award applicants required to submit FAFSA. *Unit head:* Dr. David L. Jaffe, Dean, 561-237-7099, Fax: 561-237-7097, E-mail: djaffe@lynn.edu. *Application contact:* Steven Pruitt, Director of Graduate Admission, 561-237-7834, Fax: 561-237-7100, E-mail: admission@lynn.edu.
Website: https://www.lynn.edu/academics/colleges-schools/communication-and-design

Massachusetts College of Art and Design, Graduate Programs, MFA Program, Boston, MA 02115-5882. Offers 2D fine arts (MFA), including painting, printmaking; 3D fine arts (MFA), including ceramics, fibers, glass, jewelry and metalsmithing, sculpture; design (MFA, Postbaccalaureate Certificate), including dynamic media; fine arts (MFA), including interdisciplinary; media arts (MFA, Postbaccalaureate Certificate), including film/video (MFA), photography. *Accreditation:* NASAD. *Faculty:* 1 (woman) full-time, 29 part-time/adjunct (14 women). *Students:* 44 full-time (26 women), 28 part-time (17 women); includes 8 minority (5 Asian, non-Hispanic/Latino; 3 Hispanic/Latino), 18 international. 202 applicants, 44% accepted, 35 enrolled. In 2019, 30 master's, 8 other advanced degrees awarded. *Degree requirements:* For master's, thesis, thesis exhibition (for fine arts programs); thesis project and document (for design/dynamic media program). *Entrance requirements:* For master's, portfolio, college transcripts, resume, statement of purpose, letters of reference, interview, 6 credits of art history taken prior to or during MFA program; for Postbaccalaureate Certificate, portfolio, college transcripts, resume, statement of purpose, letters of reference, interview. Additional exam requirements/recommendations for international students: required—TOEFL (minimum score 550 paper-based, 85 iBT) or IELTS (6). *Application deadline:* For fall admission, 1/20 priority date for domestic and international students; for summer admission, 1/20 priority date for domestic and international students. Applications are processed on a rolling basis. Application fee: $90. Electronic applications accepted. *Expenses:* Contact institution. *Financial support:* Research assistantships, teaching assistantships, career-related internships or fieldwork, scholarships/grants, tuition waivers (partial), unspecified assistantships, and adjunct co-teaching positions available. Support available to part-time students. Financial award application deadline: 1/20; financial award applicants required to submit FAFSA. *Unit head:* Lucinda Bliss, Dean of Graduate Studies, 617-879-7157, E-mail: gradadmissions@massart.edu. *Application contact:* Stacy Petersen, Associate Director, Graduate Admissions and Operations, 617-879-7238, E-mail: gradadmissions@massart.edu.
Website: http://www.massart.edu/Admissions/Graduate_Programs.html

Massachusetts Institute of Technology, School of Architecture and Planning, Program in Media Arts and Sciences, Cambridge, MA 02139. Offers media arts and sciences (SM, PhD); media technology (SM). Terminal master's awarded for partial completion of doctoral program. *Degree requirements:* For master's, thesis; for doctorate, comprehensive exam, thesis/dissertation. *Entrance requirements:* Additional exam requirements/recommendations for international students: required—IELTS. Electronic applications accepted.

Massachusetts Institute of Technology, School of Humanities, Arts, and Social Sciences, Program in Comparative Media Studies/Writing, Program in Comparative Media Studies, Cambridge, MA 02139. Offers SM. *Degree requirements:* For master's, thesis. *Entrance requirements:* For master's, GRE General Test. Additional exam requirements/recommendations for international students: required—IELTS. Electronic applications accepted.

Metropolitan College of New York, Program in Business Administration, New York, NY 10006. Offers financial services (MBA); general management (MBA); healthcare systems and risk management (MBA); media management (MBA). *Accreditation:* ACBSP. *Program availability:* Evening/weekend. *Degree requirements:* For master's, thesis, 10-day study abroad. *Entrance requirements:* For master's, GMAT. Additional exam requirements/recommendations for international students: required—TOEFL (minimum score 600 paper-based). Electronic applications accepted. *Expenses:* Contact institution.

Michigan State University, The Graduate School, College of Communication Arts and Sciences, Department of Media and Information, East Lansing, MI 48824. Offers media and information management (MA); serious game design (MA). *Entrance requirements:* Additional exam requirements/recommendations for international students: required—TOEFL. Electronic applications accepted.

Michigan State University, The Graduate School, College of Communication Arts and Sciences, Program in Communication Arts and Sciences–Information and Media, East Lansing, MI 48824. Offers PhD. *Entrance requirements:* Additional exam requirements/recommendations for international students: required—TOEFL. Electronic applications accepted.

Monmouth University, Graduate Studies, Department of Communication, West Long Branch, NJ 07764-1898. Offers public service communication specialist (Certificate); strategic public relations and new media (Certificate). *Program availability:* Part-time, evening/weekend, online learning. *Faculty:* 7 full-time (5 women). *Students:* 14 full-time (11 women), 20 part-time (14 women); includes 6 minority (2 Black or African American, non-Hispanic/Latino; 3 Hispanic/Latino; 1 Two or more races, non-Hispanic/Latino), 2 international. Average age 27. In 2019, 10 master's awarded. *Degree requirements:* For master's, comprehensive exam (for some programs), thesis (for some programs), project. *Entrance requirements:* For master's, GRE, baccalaureate degree with minimum GPA of 3.0 in major, 2.75 overall; two letters of recommendation; personal essay (750 words or less describing preparation for study and personal objectives); digital or hard copy portfolio of select samples of work including writing sample; resume. Additional exam requirements/recommendations for international students: required—TOEFL (minimum score 550 paper-based; 79 iBT), IELTS (minimum score 6), Michigan English Language Assessment Battery (minimum score 77). *Application deadline:* For fall admission, 7/15 priority date for domestic students, 6/1 for international students; for spring admission, 12/1 priority date for domestic students, 11/1 for international students; for summer admission, 5/1 for domestic students. Applications are processed on a rolling basis. Application fee: $50. Electronic applications accepted. *Expenses: Tuition:* Full-time $22,194; part-time $14,796 per credit. *Required fees:* $712; $178 per semester. $178 per semester. Tuition and fees vary according to course load. *Financial support:* In 2019–20, 35 students received support. Research assistantships, teaching assistantships, institutionally sponsored loans, scholarships/grants, and unspecified assistantships available. Support available to part-time students. Financial award applicants required to submit FAFSA. *Unit head:* Dr. Deanna Shoemaker, Program Director, 732-571-3449, Fax: 732-571-3609, E-mail: dshoemak@monmouth.edu. *Application contact:* Kevin New, Graduate Admission Counselor, 732-571-3452, Fax: 732-263-5123, E-mail: gradadm@monmouth.edu.
Website: http://www.monmouth.edu/cpc

New Mexico Highlands University, Graduate Studies, College of Arts and Sciences, Department of Computer Sciences, Las Vegas, NM 87701. Offers media arts and computer science (MS), including computer science. *Degree requirements:* For master's, comprehensive exam, thesis. *Entrance requirements:* For master's, minimum undergraduate GPA of 3.0. Additional exam requirements/recommendations for international students: required—TOEFL (minimum score 540 paper-based).

The New School, Schools of Public Engagement, Program in Media Studies, New York, NY 10011. Offers documentary media studies (Graduate Certificate); media management (MS, Graduate Certificate); media studies (MA). *Program availability:* Part-time, 100% online. *Faculty:* 17 full-time (8 women), 25 part-time/adjunct (8 women). *Students:* 228 full-time (167 women), 98 part-time (74 women); includes 117 minority (61 Black or African American, non-Hispanic/Latino; 9 Asian, non-Hispanic/Latino; 41 Hispanic/Latino; 1 Native Hawaiian or other Pacific Islander, non-Hispanic/Latino; 5 Two or more races, non-Hispanic/Latino), 116 international. Average age 28. 235 applicants, 95% accepted, 120 enrolled. In 2019, 114 master's, 31 other advanced degrees awarded. *Degree requirements:* For master's, thesis, capstone project (for MS); for Graduate Certificate, thesis optional, synthesis paper (for media management). *Entrance requirements:* For master's, two letters of recommendation, statement of purpose, resume, transcripts, writing sample (strongly encouraged). Additional exam requirements/recommendations for international students: required—TOEFL (minimum

score 92 iBT), IELTS (minimum score 7), PTE (minimum score 68). *Application deadline:* For fall admission, 2/5 priority date for domestic and international students; for spring admission, 10/15 priority date for domestic and international students. Applications are processed on a rolling basis. Application fee: $50. Electronic applications accepted. *Expenses:* 1625 per credit. *Financial support:* In 2019–20, 262 students received support, including 4 fellowships (averaging $801 per year), 28 research assistantships (averaging $4,030 per year), 3 teaching assistantships (averaging $5,250 per year); career-related internships or fieldwork, Federal Work-Study, scholarships/grants, and unspecified assistantships also available. Support available to part-time students. Financial award application deadline: 2/1; financial award applicants required to submit FAFSA. *Unit head:* Vladan Nikolic, Dean of the School of Media Studies and Associate Dean of the Schools of Public Engagement, 212-229-8903 Ext. 4054, E-mail: nikolicv@newschool.edu. *Application contact:* Merida Gasbarro, Director of Graduate Admission, 212-229-5600 Ext. 1108, E-mail: escandom@newschool.edu.
Website: https://www.newschool.edu/public-engagement/ma-media-studies/

New York University, Graduate School of Arts and Science, Department of Anthropology, Program in Culture and Media, New York, NY 10012-1019. Offers MA/Advanced Certificate, PhD/Advanced Certificate. *Entrance requirements:* Additional exam requirements/recommendations for international students: required—TOEFL, IELTS.

New York University, School of Professional Studies, Preston Robert Tisch Institute for Global Sport, New York, NY 10012-1019. Offers sports business (MS), including global sports media, professional and collegiate sports operations, sports law, sports marketing and sales. *Program availability:* Part-time, evening/weekend. *Degree requirements:* For master's, thesis. *Entrance requirements:* For master's, GRE or GMAT (only upon request), bachelor's degree, resume with relevant professional work, internship or volunteer experience, 2 letters of recommendation, personal statement. Additional exam requirements/recommendations for international students: required—TOEFL (minimum score 600 paper-based; 100 iBT), IELTS (minimum score 7). Electronic applications accepted. *Expenses:* Contact institution.

New York University, Steinhardt School of Culture, Education, and Human Development, Department of Media, Culture and Communication, New York, NY 10012. Offers media, culture and communication (MA, PhD); MLIS/MA. *Program availability:* Part-time. Terminal master's awarded for partial completion of doctoral program. *Entrance requirements:* For master's, GRE General Test; for doctorate, GRE General Test, interview. Additional exam requirements/recommendations for international students: required—TOEFL (minimum score 100 iBT). Electronic applications accepted.

Norfolk State University, School of Graduate Studies, School of Liberal Arts, Department of Media and Communication, Norfolk, VA 23504. Offers MA. *Program availability:* Part-time. *Degree requirements:* For master's, thesis. *Entrance requirements:* For master's, GRE, minimum GPA of 2.5, letters of recommendation. Additional exam requirements/recommendations for international students: required—TOEFL.

Northeastern University, College of Arts, Media and Design, Boston, MA 02115-5096. Offers architecture (M Arch); arts administration and cultural entrepreneurship (MS); experience design (MFA, MS); game science and design (MS); information design and visualization (MFA); interdisciplinary arts (MFA); journalism (MA); media advocacy (MS); music industry leadership (MS); sustainable building systems (MS); sustainable urban environments (M Des). Electronic applications accepted. *Expenses:* Contact institution.

Northern Kentucky University, Office of Graduate Programs, College of Informatics, Program in Communication, Highland Heights, KY 41099. Offers communication (MA); communication teaching (Certificate); documentary studies (Certificate); public relations (Certificate); relationships (Certificate). *Program availability:* Part-time, evening/weekend. Terminal master's awarded for partial completion of doctoral program. *Degree requirements:* For master's, comprehensive exams, thesis or applied capstone project. *Entrance requirements:* For master's, GRE, minimum GPA of 3.0, 3 letters of recommendation, letter of intent. Additional exam requirements/recommendations for international students: required—TOEFL (minimum score 79 iBT); recommended—IELTS (minimum score 6.5). Electronic applications accepted.

Northwestern University, The Graduate School, School of Communication, Department of Communication Studies, Evanston, IL 60208. Offers communication studies (PhD), including interaction and social influence, rhetoric and public culture; managerial communication (MSC); media, technology and society (PhD); technology and social behavior (PhD). Terminal master's awarded for partial completion of doctoral program. *Degree requirements:* For doctorate, thesis/dissertation. *Entrance requirements:* For master's and doctorate, GRE General Test. Additional exam requirements/recommendations for international students: required—TOEFL. Electronic applications accepted.

Northwestern University, The Graduate School, School of Communication, Department of Radio, Television and Film, Evanston, IL 60208. Offers documentary media (MFA); screen cultures (MA, PhD); writing for the screen and stage (MFA). *Program availability:* Part-time. Terminal master's awarded for partial completion of doctoral program. *Degree requirements:* For master's, comprehensive exam or thesis; for doctorate, thesis/dissertation, qualifying exam. *Entrance requirements:* For master's and doctorate, GRE General Test. Additional exam requirements/recommendations for international students: required—TOEFL. Electronic applications accepted.

Ohio University, Graduate College, Scripps College of Communication, School of Media Arts and Studies, Athens, OH 45701-2979. Offers communication media arts (MFA); mass communication (PhD); media arts and studies (MA). *Degree requirements:* For master's, comprehensive exam (for some programs), thesis or alternative; for doctorate, comprehensive exam, thesis/dissertation. *Entrance requirements:* For master's, GRE General Test or MAT, minimum GPA of 3.0; for doctorate, GRE General Test or MAT. Additional exam requirements/recommendations for international students: required—TOEFL (minimum score 600 paper-based; 100 iBT) or IELTS (minimum score 7). Electronic applications accepted.

Old Dominion University, College of Arts and Letters, Institute for the Humanities, Norfolk, VA 23529. Offers arts and entrepreneurship (Certificate); cultural and human geography (MA); cultural studies (MA); gender and sexuality studies (MA); health, communication and culture (Certificate); media and popular culture studies (MA); philosophy and religious studies (MA); social justice and entrepreneurship (Certificate); visual studies (MA); world cultures (MA). *Program availability:* Part-time, evening/weekend. *Degree requirements:* For master's, thesis optional, project. *Entrance requirements:* For master's, GRE General Test, minimum GPA of 3.25. Electronic applications accepted.

Pace University, Dyson College of Arts and Sciences, MA Program in Media and Communication Arts, New York, NY 10038. Offers MA. *Program availability:* Part-time, evening/weekend. *Degree requirements:* For master's, comprehensive exam, thesis, internship. *Entrance requirements:* For master's, portfolio containing examples of prior work (press releases, advertisements, presentations, writing samples, etc.) and official transcripts. Additional exam requirements/recommendations for international students: required—TOEFL (minimum score 100 iBT). Electronic applications accepted.

Paris College of Art, Graduate Programs, Paris, France. Offers accessories design (MA); fashion design: new materials and technologies (MA); fashion film and photography (MA); interior design (MA); transdisciplinary new media (MA, MFA). *Entrance requirements:* Additional exam requirements/recommendations for international students: required—TOEFL or IELTS.

Penn State University Park, Graduate School, Donald P. Bellisario College of Communications, Department of Communications, University Park, PA 16802. Offers mass communications (PhD); media studies (MA).

Pepperdine University, Seaver College, Malibu, CA 90263. Offers business (MS), including accounting; communication (MFA), including cinematic media production; humanities (MA, MFA), including American studies (MA), writing for screen and television (MFA); religion (M Div, MA, MS), including ministry (MS), religion (M Div, MA); JD/M Div. *Entrance requirements:* For master's, GRE General Test. Additional exam requirements/recommendations for international students: required—TOEFL. *Expenses:* Contact institution.

Point Park University, School of Communication, Pittsburgh, PA 15222-1984. Offers communication technology (MA); media communication (MA). *Program availability:* Part-time, evening/weekend. *Degree requirements:* For master's, comprehensive exam (for some programs), thesis or alternative. *Entrance requirements:* For master's, GRE (if GPA less than 2.75), minimum GPA of 2.75, 2 letters of recommendation, statement of intent. Additional exam requirements/recommendations for international students: required—TOEFL (minimum score 570 paper-based; 88 iBT), IELTS (minimum score 6.5); recommended—TWE (minimum score 5). Electronic applications accepted.

Pratt Institute, School of Liberal Arts and Sciences, Program in Media Studies, Brooklyn, NY 11205-3899. Offers MA. *Students:* 11 full-time (8 women), 4 part-time (2 women); includes 5 minority (2 Black or African American, non-Hispanic/Latino; 2 Hispanic/Latino; 1 Two or more races, non-Hispanic/Latino), 7 international. Average age 25. 33 applicants, 94% accepted, 5 enrolled. In 2019, 4 master's awarded. *Degree requirements:* For master's, thesis. *Entrance requirements:* For master's, BA, BS, or BFA from accredited institution; statement of purpose; 10-20 pages of relevant writing samples; transcripts of undergraduate coursework; three letters of recommendation. Additional exam requirements/recommendations for international students: required—TOEFL (minimum score 600 paper-based; 100 iBT). *Application deadline:* For fall admission, 1/5 for domestic and international students; for spring admission, 10/1 for domestic and international students. Application fee: $50 ($90 for international students). Electronic applications accepted. *Expenses: Tuition:* Full-time $33,246; part-time $1847 per credit. *Required fees:* $1980. *Financial support:* Career-related internships or fieldwork, Federal Work-Study, institutionally sponsored loans, scholarships/grants, health care benefits, and unspecified assistantships available. Support available to part-time students. Financial award application deadline: 2/1; financial award applicants required to submit FAFSA. *Unit head:* Mendi Obadike, Coordinator, 718-636-5771, E-mail: mobadike@pratt.edu. *Application contact:* Natalie Capannelli, Director of Graduate Admissions, 718-636-3551, Fax: 718-399-4242, E-mail: ncapanne@pratt.edu.
Website: https://www.pratt.edu/academics/liberal-arts-and-sciences/graduate-media-studies/

Queens College of the City University of New York, Arts and Humanities Division, Department of Media Studies, Queens, NY 11367-1597. Offers MA. *Program availability:* Evening/weekend. *Degree requirements:* For master's, thesis. *Entrance requirements:* For master's, minimum GPA of 3.0. Additional exam requirements/recommendations for international students: required—TOEFL; recommended—IELTS.

Rhode Island School of Design, Department of Digital and Media, Providence, RI 02903-2784. Offers MFA. *Students:* 19 full-time (14 women); includes 2 minority (both Hispanic/Latino), 11 international. Average age 27. 161 applicants, 17% accepted, 11 enrolled. In 2019, 11 master's awarded. *Degree requirements:* For master's, thesis, exhibition. *Entrance requirements:* For master's, portfolio, statement of purpose, 3 letters of recommendation. Additional exam requirements/recommendations for international students: required—TOEFL (minimum score 580 paper-based; 93 iBT), IELTS (minimum score 6.5), Duolingo. *Application deadline:* For fall admission, 1/10 for domestic and international students. Application fee: $60. Electronic applications accepted. *Expenses: Tuition:* Full-time $51,800. *Required fees:* $1060. *Financial support:* Fellowships, research assistantships, teaching assistantships, Federal Work-Study, scholarships/grants, and unspecified assistantships available. Financial award application deadline: 2/1; financial award applicants required to submit FAFSA. *Unit head:* Shawn Greenlee, Department Head and Graduate Program Director, 401-454-6139, Fax: 401-277-4966, E-mail: digital@risd.edu. *Application contact:* Molly Pettengill, Associate Director for Graduate Recruitment, 401-454-6312, Fax: 401-454-6309, E-mail: mpetteng@risd.edu.
Website: http://www.risd.edu/academics/digital-media/

Rochester Institute of Technology, Graduate Enrollment Services, College of Imaging Arts and Sciences, School of Media Sciences, MS Program in Media Arts and Technology, Rochester, NY 14623-5603. Offers MS. *Program availability:* Part-time, evening/weekend. *Degree requirements:* For master's, capstone project. *Entrance requirements:* For master's, minimum GPA of 3.0 (recommended), personal statement, resume, two letters of recommendation. Additional exam requirements/recommendations for international students: required—TOEFL (minimum score 80 iBT), IELTS (minimum score 6.5), PTE (minimum score 58). Electronic applications accepted. *Expenses:* Contact institution.

Rochester Institute of Technology, Graduate Enrollment Services, College of Liberal Arts, School of Communication, MS Program in Communication and Media Technologies, Rochester, NY 14623-5603. Offers MS. *Program availability:* Part-time. *Degree requirements:* For master's, thesis or alternative, Thesis or comprehensive exam plus two additional courses. *Entrance requirements:* For master's, minimum GPA of 3.0 (recommended), three writing samples, personal statement, two letters of reference. Additional exam requirements/recommendations for international students: required—TOEFL (minimum score 570 paper-based; 88 iBT), IELTS (minimum score 6.5), PTE (minimum score 61). Electronic applications accepted.

Rowan University, Graduate School, College of Communication and Creative Arts, Integrated Marketing Communication and New Media Certificate of Graduate Study Program, Glassboro, NJ 08028-1701. Offers CGS. Electronic applications accepted. *Expenses: Tuition, area resident:* Part-time $715.50 per semester hour. Tuition, state resident: part-time $715.50 per semester hour. Tuition, nonresident: part-time $715.50 per semester hour. *Required fees:* $161.55 per semester hour.

Saginaw Valley State University, College of Arts and Behavioral Sciences, Program in Communication and Media Administration, University Center, MI 48710. Offers MA. *Program availability:* Part-time, evening/weekend. *Faculty:* 7 full-time (3 women), 1 (woman) part-time/adjunct. *Students:* 7 full-time (0 women), 5 part-time (4 women); includes 1 minority (Black or African American, non-Hispanic/Latino), 7 international. Average age 28. 19 applicants, 68% accepted, 6 enrolled. In 2019, 3 master's awarded.

Degree requirements: For master's, thesis. *Entrance requirements:* For master's, minimum GPA of 3.0. Additional exam requirements/recommendations for international students: required—TOEFL (minimum score 540 paper-based; 76 iBT). *Application deadline:* For fall admission, 7/15 for international students; for winter admission, 11/15 for international students; for spring admission, 4/15 for international students. Applications are processed on a rolling basis. Application fee: $30 ($90 for international students). Electronic applications accepted. *Expenses: Tuition, area resident:* Full-time $11,212; part-time $622.90 per credit hour. Tuition, state resident: full-time $11,212; part-time $622.90 per credit hour. Tuition, nonresident: full-time $11,212; part-time $1253 per credit hour. *Required fees:* $263; $14.60 per credit hour. Tuition and fees vary according to course load, degree level and program. *Financial support:* Federal Work-Study and scholarships/grants available. Support available to part-time students. Financial award application deadline: 4/1; financial award applicants required to submit FAFSA. *Unit head:* Dr. Robert Drew, Professor of Communication, 989-964-7495, E-mail: rdrew@svsu.edu. *Application contact:* Jenna Briggs, Director, Graduate and International Admissions, 989-964-6096, Fax: 989-964-2788, E-mail: gradadm@svsu.edu.

San Diego State University, Graduate and Research Affairs, College of Professional Studies and Fine Arts, School of Communication, San Diego, CA 92182. Offers advertising and public relations (MA); critical-cultural studies (MA); interaction studies (MA); intercultural and international studies (MA); new media studies (MA); news and information studies (MA); telecommunications and media management (MA). *Degree requirements:* For master's, thesis. *Entrance requirements:* For master's, GRE General Test, 3 letters of recommendation. Additional exam requirements/recommendations for international students: required—TOEFL. Electronic applications accepted.

San Francisco State University, Division of Graduate Studies, College of Liberal and Creative Arts, Department of Broadcast and Electronic Communication Arts, San Francisco, CA 94132-1722. Offers MA. *Expenses: Tuition, area resident:* Full-time $7176; part-time $4164 per year. Tuition, state resident: full-time $7176; part-time $4164 per year. Tuition, nonresident: full-time $16,680; part-time $396 per unit. *International tuition:* $16,680 full-time. *Required fees:* $1524; $1524 per unit. $762 per semester. Tuition and fees vary according to degree level and program. *Unit head:* Dr. Nancy Sami Reist, Chair, 415-338-2241, Fax: 415-338-1168, E-mail: sami@sfsu.edu. *Application contact:* Dr. Melissa Camacho, Graduate Coordinator, 415-338-6526, Fax: 415-338-1168, E-mail: mcamacho@sfsu.edu. Website: http://beca.sfsu.edu/

Savannah College of Art and Design, Program in Motion Media Design, Savannah, GA 31402-3146. Offers MA, MFA. *Program availability:* Part-time, 100% online. *Degree requirements:* For master's, final project (for MA); thesis (for MFA). *Entrance requirements:* For master's, GRE (recommended), portfolio (submitted in digital format), audition or writing submission, resume, statement of purpose, two letters of recommendation. Additional exam requirements/recommendations for international students: recommended—TOEFL (minimum score 550 paper-based; 85 iBT), IELTS (minimum score 6.5). Electronic applications accepted.

Savannah College of Art and Design, Program in Performing Arts, Savannah, GA 31402-3146. Offers MFA. *Program availability:* Part-time. *Degree requirements:* For master's, thesis. *Entrance requirements:* For master's, GRE (recommended), portfolio (submitted in digital format), audition or writing submission, resume, statement of purpose, two letters of recommendation. Additional exam requirements/recommendations for international students: recommended—TOEFL (minimum score 550 paper-based; 85 iBT), IELTS (minimum score 6.5). Electronic applications accepted.

Southern Illinois University Carbondale, Graduate School, College of Mass Communication and Media Arts, Department of Mass Communication and Media Arts, Carbondale, IL 62901-4701. Offers MFA, PhD. *Degree requirements:* For doctorate, thesis/dissertation. *Entrance requirements:* For master's, minimum GPA of 2.7; for doctorate, GRE, minimum GPA of 3.25. Additional exam requirements/recommendations for international students: required—TOEFL (minimum score 100 iBT).

Southern Illinois University Carbondale, Graduate School, College of Mass Communication and Media Arts, Department of Professional Media and Media Management Studies, Carbondale, IL 62901-4701. Offers MS. *Entrance requirements:* Additional exam requirements/recommendations for international students: required—TOEFL (minimum score 100 iBT).

Southern Illinois University Carbondale, Graduate School, College of Mass Communication and Media Arts, Program in Media Theory and Research, Carbondale, IL 62901-4701. Offers MA. *Entrance requirements:* For master's, GRE, minimum GPA of 2.7. Additional exam requirements/recommendations for international students: required—TOEFL (minimum score 100 iBT).

Southern Illinois University Edwardsville, Graduate School, College of Arts and Sciences, Department of Mass Communications, Program in Media Literacy, Edwardsville, IL 62026. Offers Postbaccalaureate Certificate. *Program availability:* Part-time, evening/weekend. *Entrance requirements:* Additional exam requirements/recommendations for international students: required—TOEFL (minimum score 550 paper-based; 79 iBT), IELTS (minimum score 6.5). Electronic applications accepted.

Stevens Institute of Technology, Graduate School, Charles V. Schaefer Jr. School of Engineering and Science, Interdisciplinary Program, Hoboken, NJ 07030. Offers MS. *Program availability:* Part-time, evening/weekend. *Faculty:* 276 full-time (74 women), 168 part-time/adjunct (33 women). *Students:* 4 full-time (3 women), 2 part-time (0 women), 3 international. Average age 29. In 2019, 1 master's awarded. *Degree requirements:* For master's, thesis optional, minimum B average in major field and overall. *Entrance requirements:* For master's, International applicants must submit TOEFL/IELTS scores and fulfill the English Language Proficiency Requirement. Applicants to full-time programs who do not qualify for a score waiver are required to submit GRE/GMAT scores. Additional exam requirements/recommendations for international students: required—TOEFL (minimum score 74 iBT), IELTS (minimum score 6). *Application deadline:* For fall admission, 4/15 for domestic and international students; for spring admission, 11/1 for domestic and international students; for summer admission, 5/1 for domestic students. Applications are processed on a rolling basis. Electronic applications accepted. *Expenses: Tuition:* Full-time $52,134. *Required fees:* $1880. Tuition and fees vary according to course load. *Financial support:* Fellowships, research assistantships, teaching assistantships, career-related internships or fieldwork, Federal Work-Study, scholarships/grants, and unspecified assistantships available. Financial award application deadline: 2/15; financial award applicants required to submit FAFSA. *Unit head:* Dr. Jean Zu, Dean of SES, 201-216.8233, Fax: 201-216.8372, E-mail: Jean.Zu@stevens.edu. *Application contact:* Graduate Admissions, 888-783-8367, Fax: 888-555-1306, E-mail: graduate@stevens.edu.

Syracuse University, S. I. Newhouse School of Public Communications, MA Program in Media Studies, Syracuse, NY 13244. Offers MA. *Entrance requirements:* For master's, GRE General Test, resume, official transcripts, personal statement, three letters of recommendation. Additional exam requirements/recommendations for international students: required—TOEFL (minimum score 600 paper-based; 100 iBT). Electronic applications accepted.

Syracuse University, S. I. Newhouse School of Public Communications, MS Program in New Media Management, Syracuse, NY 13244. Offers MS. *Degree requirements:* For master's, thesis optional, capstone course. *Entrance requirements:* For master's, GRE General Test or GMAT, resume, official transcripts, personal statement, three letters of recommendation. Additional exam requirements/recommendations for international students: required—TOEFL (minimum score 600 paper-based; 100 iBT). Electronic applications accepted.

Syracuse University, S. I. Newhouse School of Public Communications, Program in Television, Radio, and Film, Syracuse, NY 13244. Offers MA. *Entrance requirements:* For master's, GRE General Test, resume, official transcripts, personal statement, three letters of recommendation. Additional exam requirements/recommendations for international students: required—TOEFL (minimum score 600 paper-based; 100 iBT). Electronic applications accepted.

Temple University, Klein College of Media and Communication, Department of Media Studies and Production, Philadelphia, PA 19122-6096. Offers MA. *Program availability:* Part-time. *Faculty:* 21 full-time (10 women), 24 part-time/adjunct (12 women). *Students:* 76 full-time (46 women), 13 part-time (7 women); includes 20 minority (11 Black or African American, non-Hispanic/Latino; 2 Asian, non-Hispanic/Latino; 4 Hispanic/Latino; 3 Two or more races, non-Hispanic/Latino), 28 international. 104 applicants, 59% accepted, 28 enrolled. In 2019, 16 master's awarded. *Degree requirements:* For master's, comprehensive exam (for some programs), thesis (for some programs). *Entrance requirements:* For master's, GRE (optional), writing sample/production portfolio, resume. Additional exam requirements/recommendations for international students: required—TOEFL, IELTS, PTE. *Application deadline:* For fall admission, 2/15 for domestic and international students. Application fee: $60. Electronic applications accepted. *Expenses:* Contact institution. *Financial support:* Federal Work-Study available. Financial award applicants required to submit FAFSA. *Unit head:* Matthew Lombard, Co-Chair, 215-204-7182, E-mail: lombard@temple.edu. *Application contact:* Nicole McKenna, Graduate Office Director, 215-204-1497, E-mail: nmckenna@temple.edu.
Website: https://klein.temple.edu/academics/graduate-programs/master-arts-media-studies-and-production

Texas Tech University, Graduate School, College of Media and Communication, Department of Media and Communication, Lubbock, TX 79409-3082. Offers mass communications (MA); media and communication (PhD); strategic communication and innovation (MA). *Program availability:* Part-time, evening/weekend, 100% online, blended/hybrid learning. *Faculty:* 20 full-time (12 women), 7 part-time/adjunct (3 women). *Students:* 97 full-time (56 women), 167 part-time (102 women); includes 66 minority (17 Black or African American, non-Hispanic/Latino; 5 Asian, non-Hispanic/Latino; 36 Hispanic/Latino; 8 Two or more races, non-Hispanic/Latino), 20 international. Average age 31. 161 applicants, 64% accepted, 84 enrolled. In 2019, 98 master's, 6 doctorates awarded. *Degree requirements:* For master's, thesis optional; for doctorate, comprehensive exam, thesis/dissertation. *Entrance requirements:* For doctorate, GRE. Additional exam requirements/recommendations for international students: required—TOEFL (minimum score 550 paper-based; 79 iBT). *Application deadline:* For fall admission, 6/1 priority date for domestic students, 1/15 priority date for international students; for spring admission, 9/1 priority date for domestic students, 6/15 priority date for international students. Applications are processed on a rolling basis. Application fee: $65. Electronic applications accepted. *Expenses:* Contact institution. *Financial support:* In 2019–20, 148 students received support, including 121 fellowships (averaging $4,201 per year), 16 research assistantships (averaging $13,825 per year), 71 teaching assistantships (averaging $12,545 per year); career-related internships or fieldwork, scholarships/grants, and unspecified assistantships also available. Support available to part-time students. Financial award application deadline: 4/15; financial award applicants required to submit FAFSA. *Unit head:* Dr. Coy Callison, Professor and Associate Dean of Graduate Studies, 806-834-5344, E-mail: coy.callison@ttu.edu. *Application contact:* Elaine Taylor, Graduate Program Administrative, 806-834-7064, Fax: 806-742-1085, E-mail: elaine.taylor@ttu.edu.
Website: www.depts.ttu.edu/comc/

Trinity College, Graduate Programs, Program in English, Hartford, CT 06106-3100. Offers literary studies (MA); writing, rhetoric, and media arts (MA). *Program availability:* Part-time, evening/weekend. *Degree requirements:* For master's, thesis (for some programs). *Entrance requirements:* For master's, minimum GPA of 3.0.

University at Buffalo, the State University of New York, Graduate School, College of Arts and Sciences, Department of Media Study, Buffalo, NY 14260. Offers architecture and media (M Arch/MFA); film and media study (MAH); media arts production (MFA); media study (PhD); new media design (Certificate); social media (MAH); M Arch/MFA. *Faculty:* 13 full-time (7 women). *Students:* 36 full-time (18 women); includes 19 minority (1 Black or African American, non-Hispanic/Latino; 14 Asian, non-Hispanic/Latino; 4 Hispanic/Latino). Average age 31. 80 applicants, 30% accepted, 8 enrolled. In 2019, 5 master's, 1 doctorate awarded. Terminal master's awarded for partial completion of doctoral program. *Degree requirements:* For master's, thesis, media project; for doctorate, comprehensive exam, thesis/dissertation, qualifying exam, media project. *Entrance requirements:* For master's, portfolio; for doctorate, GRE, portfolio. Additional exam requirements/recommendations for international students: required—TOEFL (minimum score 550 paper-based; 79 iBT). *Application deadline:* For fall admission, 1/5 priority date for domestic and international students. Applications are processed on a rolling basis. Application fee: $75. Electronic applications accepted. *Expenses:* Approximately $15,000 per year in state tuition + fees, same as normal for institution, with some courses having small (about $100) additional equipment fees; many students are on TAship and pay no tuition, about $1500 per semester in fees; generally 2 years for MAH, 3 for MFA, and 5 for PhD, though not all of PhD years require full courseload. *Financial support:* In 2019–20, 14 students received support, including 10 teaching assistantships with full tuition reimbursements available (averaging $16,000 per year); fellowships, career-related internships or fieldwork, Federal Work-Study, scholarships/grants, and unspecified assistantships also available. Support available to part-time students. Financial award application deadline: 1/5; financial award applicants required to submit FAFSA. *Unit head:* Prof. Tom Feeley, Chair, 716-645-1160, Fax: 716-645-6979, E-mail: thfeeley@buffalo.edu. *Application contact:* Bradley Hendricks, Assistant to the Chair for Student Programs, 716-645-0945, Fax: 716-645-6979, E-mail: bhendric@buffalo.edu.
Website: http://mediastudy.buffalo.edu/

University of Bridgeport, College of Public and International Affairs, Bridgeport, CT 06604. Offers East Asian and Pacific Rim studies (MA); global development and peace (MA); global media and communication studies (MA). *Program availability:* Part-time, evening/weekend. *Degree requirements:* For master's, thesis. *Entrance requirements:* Additional exam requirements/recommendations for international students: recommended—TOEFL (minimum score 550 paper-based; 80 iBT), IELTS (minimum score 6.5).

Media Studies

University of California, Los Angeles, Graduate Division, School of Theater, Film and Television, Department of Film, Television, and Digital Media, Los Angeles, CA 90034. Offers animation (MFA); cinema and media studies (MA, PhD); cinematography (MFA); production (MFA); screenwriting (MFA). *Degree requirements:* For master's, comprehensive exam; for doctorate, one foreign language, thesis/dissertation, oral and written qualifying exams. *Entrance requirements:* For master's, GRE General Test (for MA applicants), bachelor's degree; minimum undergraduate GPA of 3.0 (or its equivalent if letter grade system not used); writing sample (for MA); for doctorate, GRE General Test, master's degree; minimum undergraduate GPA of 3.0 (or its equivalent if letter grade system not used); writing sample. Additional exam requirements/recommendations for international students: required—TOEFL. Electronic applications accepted. *Expenses:* Contact institution.

University of California, Santa Barbara, Graduate Division, College of Letters and Sciences, Division of Humanities and Fine Arts, Department of Film and Media Studies, Santa Barbara, CA 93106-4010. Offers PhD, MA/PhD. Terminal master's awarded for partial completion of doctoral program. *Degree requirements:* For doctorate, one foreign language, comprehensive exam, thesis/dissertation. *Entrance requirements:* For doctorate, GRE, MA in film/media studies or equivalent. Additional exam requirements/recommendations for international students: required—TOEFL (minimum score 600 paper-based; 100 iBT), IELTS (minimum score 7). Electronic applications accepted.

University of California, Santa Barbara, Graduate Division, College of Letters and Sciences, Division of Humanities and Fine Arts, Department of Media Arts and Technology, Santa Barbara, CA 93106-6065. Offers MS, PhD. Terminal master's awarded for partial completion of doctoral program. *Degree requirements:* For master's, thesis; for doctorate, comprehensive exam, thesis/dissertation. *Entrance requirements:* For master's and doctorate, GRE. Additional exam requirements/recommendations for international students: required—TOEFL (minimum score 550 paper-based; 80 iBT), IELTS (minimum score 7). Electronic applications accepted.

University of Chicago, Division of the Humanities, Department of Cinema and Media Studies, Chicago, IL 60637. Offers PhD. *Degree requirements:* For doctorate, 2 foreign languages, comprehensive exam, thesis/dissertation. *Entrance requirements:* For doctorate, GRE General Test, 15-20 page writing sample, statement of purpose, 3 letters of recommendation, transcripts for all previous degrees and institutions attended. Additional exam requirements/recommendations for international students: required—TOEFL (minimum score 104 iBT), IELTS (minimum score 7). Electronic applications accepted.

University of Chicago, Division of the Humanities, Master of Arts Program in the Humanities, Chicago, IL 60637. Offers art history (MA); cinema and media studies (MA); classic languages (MA); comparative literature (MA); creative writing (MA); cultural policy studies (MA); digital humanities (MA); East Asian languages and civilizations (MA); English language and literature (MA); gender and sexuality studies (MA); Germanic studies (MA); linguistics (MA); music (MA); near Eastern languages and civilizations (MA); philosophy (MA); poetics (MA); race, politics and culture (MA); Romance languages and literatures (MA); Slavic languages and literatures (MA); South Asian languages and civilizations (MA); theater and performance studies (MA). *Degree requirements:* For master's, thesis. *Entrance requirements:* For master's, GRE General Test, 10-15 page writing sample, statement of purpose, 3 letters of recommendation, transcripts for all previous degrees and institutions attended. Additional exam requirements/recommendations for international students: required—TOEFL (minimum score 104 iBT), IELTS (minimum score 7). Electronic applications accepted. *Expenses:* Contact institution.

University of Colorado Boulder, Graduate School, College of Engineering and Applied Science, Alliance for Technology, Learning, and Society Program, Boulder, CO 80309. Offers MS, PhD. *Entrance requirements:* For master's, minimum undergraduate GPA of 3.0. Electronic applications accepted. Application fee is waived when completed online.

University of Colorado Boulder, Graduate School, College of Media, Communication and Information, Program in Media Studies, Boulder, CO 80309. Offers PhD. *Entrance requirements:* For doctorate, GRE General Test, minimum undergraduate GPA of 3.25. Additional exam requirements/recommendations for international students: required—TOEFL. Electronic applications accepted. Application fee is waived when completed online.

University of Colorado Denver, College of Arts and Media, Denver, CO 80217-3364. Offers recording arts (MS), including media forensics, recording arts. *Accreditation:* NASM. *Program availability:* Part-time, evening/weekend. *Degree requirements:* For master's, 34 credits, thesis/portfolio. *Entrance requirements:* For master's, GRE General Test (minimum scores higher than 50th percentile for all sections), minimum undergraduate GPA of 3.0, portfolio, resume, interview, 3 letters of recommendation. Additional exam requirements/recommendations for international students: required—TOEFL (minimum score 70 iBT). Electronic applications accepted. Tuition and fees vary according to course load, program and reciprocity agreements.

University of Denver, Division of Arts, Humanities and Social Sciences, Department of Media, Film and Journalism Studies, Denver, CO 80208. Offers international and intercultural communication (MA); media and public communication (MA), including media and globalization, strategic communication. *Program availability:* Part-time. *Faculty:* 18 full-time (8 women), 1 part-time/adjunct (0 women). *Students:* 4 full-time (all women), 23 part-time (19 women); includes 6 minority (1 Black or African American, non-Hispanic/Latino; 1 Asian, non-Hispanic/Latino; 3 Hispanic/Latino; 1 Two or more races, non-Hispanic/Latino), 1 international. Average age 26. 35 applicants, 80% accepted, 13 enrolled. In 2019, 14 master's awarded. *Degree requirements:* For master's, variable foreign language requirement, thesis (for some programs). *Entrance requirements:* For master's, GRE General Test, bachelor's degree, transcripts, personal statement, three letters of recommendation. Additional exam requirements/recommendations for international students: required—TOEFL (minimum score 620 paper-based; 105 iBT). *Application deadline:* For fall admission, 2/1 priority date for domestic and international students; for winter admission, 11/14 for domestic and international students; for spring admission, 1/31 for domestic and international students. Applications are processed on a rolling basis. Application fee: $65. Electronic applications accepted. *Expenses:* Contact institution. *Financial support:* In 2019–20, 24 students received support, including 11 teaching assistantships with tuition reimbursements available (averaging $7,612 per year); career-related internships or fieldwork, Federal Work-Study, institutionally sponsored loans, scholarships/grants, and unspecified assistantships also available. Support available to part-time students. Financial award application deadline: 2/15; financial award applicants required to submit FAFSA. *Unit head:* Dr. Lynn Schofield Clark, Professor and Chair, 303-871-3984, Fax: 303-871-4949, E-mail: lynn.clark@du.edu. *Application contact:* Information Contact, 303-871-2166, E-mail: mfjs@du.edu.
Website: http://www.du.edu/ahss/mfjs

University of Illinois at Urbana-Champaign, Graduate College, College of Fine and Applied Arts, School of Art and Design, Program in Design and Media, Champaign, IL 61820. Offers art and design (MFA), including new media; graphic design (MFA); industrial design (MFA). *Accreditation:* NASAD.

University of Illinois at Urbana-Champaign, Graduate College, College of Media, Institute of Communications Research, Champaign, IL 61820. Offers communications and media (PhD).

The University of Iowa, Graduate College, College of Liberal Arts and Sciences, Department of Communication Studies, Iowa City, IA 52242-1316. Offers interpersonal communication and relationships (MA, PhD); media studies (MA, PhD); rhetoric and public advocacy (MA, PhD). *Degree requirements:* For master's, thesis optional, exam; for doctorate, comprehensive exam, thesis/dissertation. *Entrance requirements:* For master's and doctorate, GRE General Test, minimum GPA of 3.0. Additional exam requirements/recommendations for international students: required—TOEFL (minimum score 550 paper-based; 81 iBT). Electronic applications accepted.

The University of Iowa, Graduate College, College of Liberal Arts and Sciences, School of Journalism and Mass Communication, Iowa City, IA 52242-1316. Offers journalism and media communication (MA); mass communication (PhD); strategic communication (MA); JD/MA; JD/PhD. *Degree requirements:* For master's, thesis optional, exam; for doctorate, comprehensive exam, thesis/dissertation. *Entrance requirements:* For master's and doctorate, GRE General Test, minimum GPA of 3.0. Additional exam requirements/recommendations for international students: required—TOEFL (minimum score 637 paper-based; 110 iBT). Electronic applications accepted.

The University of Kansas, Graduate Studies, College of Liberal Arts and Sciences, Department of Film and Media Studies, Lawrence, KS 66045. Offers MA, PhD. *Students:* 12 full-time (8 women); includes 5 minority (1 Black or African American, non-Hispanic/Latino; 2 American Indian or Alaska Native, non-Hispanic/Latino; 1 Asian, non-Hispanic/Latino; 1 Two or more races, non-Hispanic/Latino), 1 international. Average age 32. 13 applicants, 31% accepted, 2 enrolled. In 2019, 1 master's, 3 doctorates awarded. *Entrance requirements:* For master's, GRE General Test, three recent letters of recommendation, current resume, statement of personal goals, writing sample; for doctorate, GRE General Test, MA in film or related field; three recent letters of recommendation; current resume; statement of personal goals; writing sample; minimum GPA of 3.2 undergraduate, 3.5 graduate. Additional exam requirements/recommendations for international students: required—TOEFL, IELTS, TOEFL or IELTS. *Application deadline:* For fall admission, 1/1 priority date for domestic and international students. Application fee: $65 ($85 for international students). Electronic applications accepted. *Expenses:* Tuition, state resident: full-time $9989. Tuition, nonresident: full-time $23,950. *International tuition:* $23,950 full-time. *Required fees:* $984; $81.99 per credit hour. Tuition and fees vary according to course load, campus/location and program. *Financial support:* Fellowships, research assistantships, teaching assistantships, scholarships/grants, and unspecified assistantships available. Financial award application deadline: 1/1; financial award applicants required to submit FAFSA. *Unit head:* Dr. Michael Baskett, Chair, 785-864-1384, E-mail: eiga@ku.edu. *Application contact:* Julia Reilly, Graduate Admissions Contact, 785-864-9488, E-mail: juliareilly@ku.edu.
Website: http://film.ku.edu/

University of Lethbridge, School of Graduate Studies, Lethbridge, AB T1K 3M4, Canada. Offers addictions counseling (M Sc); agricultural biotechnology (M Sc); agricultural studies (M Sc, MA); anthropology (MA); archaeology (M Sc, MA); art (MA, MFA); biochemistry (M Sc); biological sciences (M Sc); biomolecular science (PhD); biosystems and biodiversity (PhD); Canadian studies (MA); chemistry (M Sc); computer science (M Sc); computer science and geographical information science (M Sc); counseling (MC); counseling psychology (M Ed); dramatic arts (MA); earth, space, and physical science (PhD); economics (MA); education (MA, PhD); educational leadership (M Ed); English (MA); environmental science (M Sc); evolution and behavior (PhD); exercise science (M Sc); French (MA); French/German (MA); French/Spanish (MA); general education (M Ed); geography (M Sc, MA); German (MA); health sciences (M Sc); individualized multidisciplinary (M Sc, MA); kinesiology (M Sc, MA); management (M Sc), including accounting, finance, human resource management and labor relations, information systems, international management, marketing, policy and strategy; mathematics (M Sc); music (M Mus, MA); Native American studies (MA); neuroscience (M Sc, PhD); new media (MA, MFA); nursing (M Sc, MN); philosophy (MA); physics (M Sc); political science (MA); psychology (M Sc, MA); religious studies (MA); sociology (MA); theatre and dramatic arts (MFA); theoretical and computational science (PhD); urban and regional studies (MA); women and gender studies (MA). *Program availability:* Part-time, evening/weekend. *Degree requirements:* For master's, thesis (for some programs); for doctorate, comprehensive exam, thesis/dissertation. *Entrance requirements:* For master's, GMAT (for M Sc in management), bachelor's degree in related field, minimum GPA of 3.0 during previous 20 graded semester courses, 2 years' teaching or related experience (M Ed); for doctorate, master's degree, minimum graduate GPA of 3.5. Additional exam requirements/recommendations for international students: required—TOEFL (minimum score 580 paper-based; 93 iBT). Electronic applications accepted.

University of Maryland, College Park, Academic Affairs, Philip Merrill College of Journalism, College Park, MD 20742. Offers broadcast journalism (MA); journalism (MA); journalism and media studies (PhD); online news (MA); public affairs reporting (MA). *Accreditation:* ACEJMC (one or more programs are accredited). *Program availability:* Part-time, evening/weekend. *Degree requirements:* For doctorate, thesis/dissertation, preliminary written and oral comprehensive exams. *Entrance requirements:* For master's and doctorate, GRE General Test, minimum GPA of 3.0, 3 letters of recommendation. Additional exam requirements/recommendations for international students: required—TOEFL. Electronic applications accepted.

University of Massachusetts Dartmouth, Graduate School, College of Visual and Performing Arts, Department of Art Education, Art History and Media Studies, North Dartmouth, MA 02747-2300. Offers MAE. *Accreditation:* NASAD. *Program availability:* Part-time. *Faculty:* 5 full-time (all women), 3 part-time/adjunct (all women). *Students:* 2 full-time (both women), 14 part-time (10 women); includes 1 minority (Hispanic/Latino). Average age 32. 3 applicants, 100% accepted, 1 enrolled. In 2019, 6 master's awarded. *Degree requirements:* For master's, thesis. *Entrance requirements:* For master's, MTEL (per program description), statement of professional goals and program intent, resume, 2 letters of recommendation, official transcripts, portfolio demonstrating capability for advanced work within a chosen discipline. Additional exam requirements/recommendations for international students: required—TOEFL (minimum score 550 paper-based; 79 iBT). *Application deadline:* For fall admission, 8/15 for domestic students, 7/15 for international students; for spring admission, 10/15 for domestic students, 9/15 for international students. Application fee: $60. Electronic applications accepted. *Expenses: Tuition, area resident:* Full-time $16,390; part-time $682.92 per credit. Tuition, state resident: full-time $16,390; part-time $682.92 per credit. Tuition, nonresident: full-time $29,578; part-time $1232.42 per credit. *Required fees:* $575. *Financial support:* In 2019–20, 1 teaching assistantship (averaging $2,040 per year) was awarded. Financial award application deadline: 3/1; financial award applicants required to submit FAFSA. *Unit head:* Cathy Smilan, Graduate Program Director, Art Education, 508-910-6594, Fax: 508-999-8901, E-mail: csmilan@umassd.edu. *Application contact:* Scott Webster, Director of Graduate Studies and Admissions, 508-999-8604, Fax: 508-999-8183, E-mail: graduate@umassd.edu.
Website: http://www.umassd.edu/cvpa/programs

University of Michigan, Rackham Graduate School, School of Music, Theatre, and Dance, Program in Media Arts, Ann Arbor, MI 48109-2085. Offers MA. *Entrance requirements:* For master's, GRE, portfolio. Additional exam requirements/recommendations for international students: required—TOEFL.

University of Nevada, Las Vegas, Graduate College, Greenspun College of Urban Affairs, Hank Greenspun School of Journalism and Media Studies, Las Vegas, NV 89154-5007. Offers MA. *Program availability:* Part-time. *Faculty:* 4 full-time (0 women). *Students:* 12 full-time (7 women), 7 part-time (3 women); includes 11 minority (2 Black or African American, non-Hispanic/Latino; 7 Hispanic/Latino; 1 Native Hawaiian or other Pacific Islander, non-Hispanic/Latino; 1 Two or more races, non-Hispanic/Latino), 2 international. Average age 29. 14 applicants, 79% accepted, 9 enrolled. In 2019, 5 master's awarded. *Degree requirements:* For master's, comprehensive exam, thesis optional, oral exam. *Entrance requirements:* For master's, GRE General Test, bachelor's degree with minimum GPA 3.0; 3 letters of recommendation; statement of purpose; writing sample. Additional exam requirements/recommendations for international students: required—TOEFL (minimum score 550 paper-based; 80 iBT), IELTS (minimum score 7). *Application deadline:* For fall admission, 3/15 for domestic and international students. Application fee: $60 ($95 for international students). Electronic applications accepted. *Expenses:* Contact institution. *Financial support:* In 2019–20, 7 students received support, including 5 research assistantships with full tuition reimbursements available (averaging $11,500 per year), 6 teaching assistantships with full tuition reimbursements available (averaging $11,250 per year); institutionally sponsored loans, scholarships/grants, health care benefits, and unspecified assistantships also available. Financial award application deadline: 3/15; financial award applicants required to submit FAFSA. *Unit head:* Dr. Kevin Stoker, Chair and Professor, 702-895-2619, Fax: 702-895-0252, E-mail: jms.chair@unlv.edu. *Application contact:* Dr. Ben Burroughs, Graduate Coordinator, 702-895-3647, Fax: 702-895-5189, E-mail: jms.gradcoord@unlv.edu.
Website: http://journalism.unlv.edu/

The University of North Carolina at Chapel Hill, Graduate School, Hussman School of Journalism and Media, Chapel Hill, NC 27599. Offers digital communication (MA, Certificate); media and communication (MA, PhD), including interdisciplinary health communication (MA), journalism (MA), strategic communication (MA), theory and research (MA), visual communication (MA); JD/PhD; MA/JD. *Accreditation:* ACEJMC (one or more programs are accredited). *Program availability:* Part-time, all course instruction online, plus two on-campus experiences totaling seven days. *Faculty:* 30 full-time (15 women), 5 part-time/adjunct (4 women). *Students:* 68 full-time (45 women), 82 part-time (58 women); includes 35 minority (13 Black or African American, non-Hispanic/Latino; 1 American Indian or Alaska Native, non-Hispanic/Latino; 4 Asian, non-Hispanic/Latino; 1 Hispanic/Latino; 16 Two or more races, non-Hispanic/Latino), 9 international. Average age 34. 205 applicants, 49% accepted, 73 enrolled. In 2019, 32 master's, 5 doctorates, 24 other advanced degrees awarded. *Degree requirements:* For master's, comprehensive exam, thesis; for doctorate, comprehensive exam, thesis/dissertation. *Entrance requirements:* For master's, Online master's degree only: GRE General Test (waiver available); Residential master's degree: minimum GPA of 3.0; for doctorate, minimum GPA of 3.0. Additional exam requirements/recommendations for international students: required—TOEFL (minimum iBT score of 105) or IELTS (7.5). Application fee: $95. Electronic applications accepted. *Expenses:* Ph.D.: 7,550 per semester N.C. resident, 15,883 non-res; Residential M.A.: 8,425 per semester N.C., 16,708 non-res; Online M.A./certificate: 2,262 per semester N.C., 4,698 non-res. *Financial support:* In 2019–20, 60 students received support, including 41 fellowships with full tuition reimbursements available (averaging $17,901 per year), 4 research assistantships with full tuition reimbursements available (averaging $17,465 per year); scholarships/grants and health care benefits also available. Financial award application deadline: 12/15; financial award applicants required to submit FAFSA. *Unit head:* Susan King, Dean, 919-962-1204, Fax: 919-962-0620, E-mail: susanking@unc.edu. *Application contact:* Casey Hart, Assistant Director, Graduate Studies, 919-843-9471, Fax: 919-962-0620, E-mail: mjgrad@unc.edu.
Website: http://hussman.unc.edu

The University of North Carolina at Greensboro, Graduate School, College of Arts and Sciences, Department of Media Studies, Greensboro, NC 27412-5001. Offers film and video production (MFA).

University of Oregon, Graduate School, School of Journalism and Communication, Eugene, OR 97403. Offers journalism (MA, MS); media studies (MA, MS, PhD); multimedia journalism (MA, MS); strategic communication (MA, MS). *Accreditation:* ASHA. *Program availability:* Part-time. *Degree requirements:* For master's, thesis or alternative. *Entrance requirements:* For master's, GRE General Test; for doctorate, master's degree.

University of South Carolina, The Graduate School, College of Arts and Sciences, Department of Art, Division of Media Arts, Columbia, SC 29208. Offers MMA. *Degree requirements:* For master's, thesis. *Entrance requirements:* For master's, GRE General Test, interview, portfolio. Additional exam requirements/recommendations for international students: required—TOEFL. Electronic applications accepted.

University of Southern California, Graduate School, Annenberg School for Communication and Journalism, School of Communication, Program in Communication, Los Angeles, CA 90089. Offers culture and community (PhD); global and transnational communication (PhD); groups, organizations and networks (PhD); health communication and social dynamics (PhD); information, political economy and entertainment (PhD); new media and technology (PhD); rhetoric, politics and public media (PhD). *Students:* 88 full-time (63 women); includes 28 minority (2 Black or African American, non-Hispanic/Latino; 6 Asian, non-Hispanic/Latino; 10 Hispanic/Latino; 10 Two or more races, non-Hispanic/Latino), 34 international. Average age 29. 161 applicants, 12% accepted, 14 enrolled. In 2019, 13 doctorates awarded. *Degree requirements:* For doctorate, thesis/dissertation. *Entrance requirements:* For doctorate, GRE General Test, resume or curriculum vitae, scholarly writing, 3 letters of recommendation, statement of purpose. Additional exam requirements/recommendations for international students: required—TOEFL (minimum score 114 iBT), IELTS (minimum score 8); recommended—TWE. *Application deadline:* For fall admission, 12/1 for domestic and international students. Application fee: $90. Electronic applications accepted. *Financial support:* In 2019–20, 15 students received support, including 15 fellowships with full tuition reimbursements available (averaging $52,427 per year); research assistantships, teaching assistantships, Federal Work-Study, health care benefits, and unspecified assistantships also available. Financial award application deadline: 12/1. *Unit head:* Dr. Robeson Taj Frazier, Director of the PhD Program, 213-740-6595, E-mail: rfrazier@usc.edu. *Application contact:* Allyson Hill, Associate Dean for Admissions, 213-821-0770, Fax: 213-740-1933, E-mail: ascadm@usc.edu.
Website: http://www.annenberg.usc.edu

University of Southern California, Graduate School, Annenberg School for Communication and Journalism, School of Communication, Program in Communication Management, Los Angeles, CA 90089. Offers MCM, JD/MCM, MCM/MAJCS. *Program availability:* Part-time, evening/weekend, 100% online. *Students:* 298 full-time, 133 part-time; includes 175 minority (52 Black or African American, non-Hispanic/Latino; 38 Asian, non-Hispanic/Latino; 69 Hispanic/Latino; 3 Native Hawaiian or other Pacific Islander, non-Hispanic/Latino; 13 Two or more races, non-Hispanic/Latino), 132 international. Average age 28. 690 applicants, 45% accepted, 161 enrolled. In 2019, 205 master's awarded. *Degree requirements:* For master's, professional project. *Entrance requirements:* For master's, GRE General Test or GMAT, resume, writing samples, recommendation letters, statement of purpose. Additional exam requirements/recommendations for international students: required—TOEFL (minimum score 114 iBT), IELTS (minimum score 8). *Application deadline:* For fall admission, 3/1 priority date for domestic students, 1/1 priority date for international students. Applications are processed on a rolling basis. Application fee: $90. Electronic applications accepted. *Financial support:* In 2019–20, 10 students received support. Career-related internships or fieldwork, Federal Work-Study, and scholarships/grants available. Support available to part-time students. Financial award application deadline: 1/1; financial award applicants required to submit FAFSA. *Unit head:* Dr. Rebecca Weintraub, Faculty Program Director, 213-821-0764, Fax: 213-740-8036, E-mail: weintrau@usc.edu. *Application contact:* Allyson Hill, Associate Dean for Admissions, 213-821-0770, Fax: 213-740-1933, E-mail: ascadm@usc.edu.
Website: http://www.annenberg.usc.edu

University of Southern California, Graduate School, Annenberg School for Communication and Journalism, School of Communication, Program in Digital Social Media, Los Angeles, CA 90089. Offers MS. *Program availability:* Part-time, evening/weekend. *Students:* 71 full-time, 7 part-time; includes 21 minority (5 Black or African American, non-Hispanic/Latino; 8 Asian, non-Hispanic/Latino; 7 Hispanic/Latino; 1 Two or more races, non-Hispanic/Latino), 43 international. Average age 29. 218 applicants, 39% accepted, 45 enrolled. In 2019, 18 master's awarded. *Degree requirements:* For master's, design, incubate, and execute a rigorous, portfolio-building, capstone project. *Entrance requirements:* For master's, GRE General Test, resume, statement of purpose, writing sample, two letters of recommendation. Additional exam requirements/recommendations for international students: required—TOEFL (minimum score 114 iBT), IELTS (minimum score 8). *Application deadline:* For fall admission, 1/15 for domestic and international students. Applications are processed on a rolling basis. Application fee: $90. Electronic applications accepted. *Financial support:* Career-related internships or fieldwork, Federal Work-Study, and scholarships/grants available. Financial award application deadline: 1/1; financial award applicants required to submit FAFSA. *Unit head:* Dr. Daniela Baroffio, Clinical Professor of Communication/Director, Digital Social Media, 213-821-4431, E-mail: baroffio@usc.edu. *Application contact:* Allyson Hill, Associate Dean of Admissions, 213-821-0770, E-mail: ascadm@usc.edu.
Website: http://www.annenberg.usc.edu

University of Southern California, Graduate School, Dana and David Dornsife College of Letters, Arts and Sciences, Comparative Studies in Literature and Culture Doctoral Program, Los Angeles, CA 90089. Offers comparative literature (PhD); comparative media and culture (PhD); Spanish and Latin American studies (PhD). *Degree requirements:* For doctorate, 2 foreign languages, comprehensive exam, thesis/dissertation. *Entrance requirements:* For doctorate, GRE, competence in language other than English (highly recommended). Additional exam requirements/recommendations for international students: required—TOEFL. Electronic applications accepted.

University of Southern California, Graduate School, School of Cinematic Arts, Interdivisional Program in Media Arts and Practice, Los Angeles, CA 90089. Offers PhD. *Degree requirements:* For doctorate, 2 foreign languages, thesis/dissertation. *Entrance requirements:* For doctorate, GRE, portfolio. Additional exam requirements/recommendations for international students: required—TOEFL. Electronic applications accepted.

University of South Florida, St. Petersburg, College of Arts and Sciences, St. Petersburg, FL 33701. Offers digital journalism and design (MA); environmental science and policy (MA, MS); Florida studies (MLA); journalism and media studies (MA); liberal studies (MLA); psychology (MA). *Program availability:* Part-time, online learning. *Degree requirements:* For master's, comprehensive exam, thesis or project. *Entrance requirements:* For master's, GRE, LSAT, MCAT (varies by program), letter of intent, 3 letters of recommendation, writing samples, bachelor's degree from regionally-accredited institution with minimum GPA of 3.0 overall or in upper two years. Additional exam requirements/recommendations for international students: required—TOEFL (minimum score 550 paper-based; 79 iBT); recommended—IELTS. Electronic applications accepted.

The University of Texas at Austin, Graduate School, College of Communication, Department of Radio-Television-Film, Austin, TX 78712-1111. Offers film and media production (MFA); media studies (MA, PhD); screenwriting (MFA). *Degree requirements:* For master's, thesis (for some programs); for doctorate, thesis/dissertation. *Entrance requirements:* For master's and doctorate, GRE General Test. Electronic applications accepted.

The University of Western Ontario, School of Graduate and Postdoctoral Studies, Faculty of Information and Media Studies, Programs in Media Studies, London, ON N6A 3K7, Canada. Offers MA, PhD. *Program availability:* Part-time. *Degree requirements:* For master's, thesis; for doctorate, comprehensive exam, thesis/dissertation. *Entrance requirements:* For master's, 2 letters of reference; for doctorate, MA in media studies, communications or related field. Additional exam requirements/recommendations for international students: required—TOEFL (minimum score 625 paper-based), TWE (minimum score 5). Electronic applications accepted.

University of Wisconsin–Madison, Graduate School, College of Letters and Science, Department of Communication Arts, Madison, WI 53706-1380. Offers communication science (MA, PhD); film (MA, PhD); media and cultural studies (MA, PhD); rhetoric (MA, PhD). Terminal master's awarded for partial completion of doctoral program. *Degree requirements:* For master's, one foreign language, thesis (for some programs); for doctorate, one foreign language, thesis/dissertation. *Entrance requirements:* For master's and doctorate, GRE General Test, minimum GPA of 3.5. Electronic applications accepted.

University of Wisconsin–Milwaukee, Graduate School, College of Letters and Science, Department of English, Milwaukee, WI 53201-0413. Offers English (MA, PhD), including creative writing, English language and linguistics, English secondary education, literary and critical studies, literature and cultural theory (PhD), literature and language studies, literature, culture, and media, media, cinema and digital studies, professional and technical communication (MA), professional and technical writing, professional writing (PhD), rhetoric and composition (PhD), rhetoric and writing. *Degree requirements:* For master's, thesis or alternative; for doctorate, one foreign language, thesis/dissertation. *Entrance requirements:* For master's, GRE General Test, GRE Subject Test; for doctorate, GRE. Additional exam requirements/recommendations for international students: required—TOEFL (minimum score 550 paper-based; 79 iBT), IELTS (minimum score 6.5). Electronic applications accepted.

University of Wisconsin–Milwaukee, Graduate School, College of Letters and Science, Department of Journalism, Advertising, and Media Studies, Milwaukee, WI 53201-0413. Offers media studies (MA). *Entrance requirements:* Additional exam requirements/recommendations for international students: required—TOEFL (minimum score 550 paper-based; 79 iBT), IELTS (minimum score 6.5). Electronic applications accepted.

Media Studies

University of Wisconsin–Stevens Point, College of Fine Arts and Communication, Division of Communication, Stevens Point, WI 54481-3897. Offers interpersonal communication (MA); media studies (MA); organizational communication (MA); public relations (MA). *Program availability:* Part-time. *Degree requirements:* For master's, thesis or alternative. *Entrance requirements:* For master's, GRE. Additional exam requirements/recommendations for international students: required—TOEFL (minimum score 575 paper-based).

Valparaiso University, Graduate School and Continuing Education, Program in Media and Communication, Valparaiso, IN 46383. Offers digital media (MS, Certificate); sports media (MS, Certificate). *Program availability:* Part-time, evening/weekend. *Entrance requirements:* For master's, minimum GPA of 3.0, undergraduate minor in communication. Additional exam requirements/recommendations for international students: required—TOEFL (minimum score 550 paper-based; 80 iBT), IELTS (minimum score 6). Electronic applications accepted.

Virginia Commonwealth University, Graduate School, College of Humanities and Sciences, Department of English, Richmond, VA 23284-9005. Offers creative writing (MFA), including dual genre, fiction, poetry; English (MA), including literature; media, art, and text (PhD). *Program availability:* Part-time. *Degree requirements:* For master's, thesis optional. *Entrance requirements:* For master's, GRE General Test, portfolio (MFA); for doctorate, GRE General Test. Additional exam requirements/recommendations for international students: required—TOEFL (minimum score 600 paper-based; 100 iBT) or IELTS (minimum score 6.5). Electronic applications accepted.

Virginia Commonwealth University, Graduate School, College of Humanities and Sciences, Richard T. Robertson School of Media and Culture, Program in Media, Art, and Text, Richmond, VA 23284-9005. Offers PhD. *Entrance requirements:* For doctorate, GRE. Additional exam requirements/recommendations for international students: required—TOEFL (minimum score 600 paper-based; 100 iBT); recommended—IELTS (minimum score 6.5). Electronic applications accepted.

Virginia State University, College of Graduate Studies, College of Humanities and Social Sciences, Department of Mass Communications, Petersburg, VA 23806-0001. Offers media management (MA).

Wagner College, Division of Graduate Studies, Nicolais School of Business, Staten Island, NY 10301-4495. Offers accounting (MS); business administration (MBA); finance (MBA); management (Exec MBA); marketing (MBA); media management (MS). *Accreditation:* ACBSP. *Program availability:* Part-time, evening/weekend. *Degree requirements:* For master's, thesis optional. *Entrance requirements:* For master's, minimum GPA of 2.75, proficiency in computers and math. Additional exam requirements/recommendations for international students: required—TOEFL (minimum score 550 paper-based; 79 iBT), IELTS (minimum score 6.5).

Wayne State University, College of Fine, Performing and Communication Arts, Department of Communication, Detroit, MI 48202. Offers communication (PhD), including democratic participation and culture, identity and representation, media, society and culture, risk, crisis and conflict, wellness, work life and relationships; communication and new media (Graduate Certificate); communication studies (MA); dispute resolution (MADR, Graduate Certificate), including community and urban studies (MADR), conflict area studies (MADR), health and family (MADR), international conflict and cooperation (MADR), professional practice (MADR), theory of conflict (MADR), workplace (MADR); health communication (Graduate Certificate); journalism (MA); media arts (MA); media studies (MA); public relations and organizational communication (MA); JD/MADR. *Program availability:* Online learning. *Degree requirements:* For master's, thesis (for some programs), thesis or essay; for doctorate, thesis/dissertation. *Entrance requirements:* For master's, GRE (for MA if undergraduate GPA less than 3.2), personal statement; BA or BS in communication or related field with minimum upper-division GPA of 3.2 and minimum upper-division undergraduate GPA of 3.0, and sample of academic writing (for MA); undergraduate degree with minimum upper-division GPA of 3.0 and three letters of recommendation (for MADR); for doctorate, GRE, undergraduate degree in communication or related field; master's degree in communication or related field with minimum GPA of 3.5; letters of recommendation; personal statement; sample of written scholarship. Additional exam requirements/recommendations for international students: required—TOEFL (minimum score 100 iBT), IELTS, TWE. Electronic applications accepted. *Expenses:* Contact institution.

Wayne State University, College of Liberal Arts and Sciences, Department of English, Detroit, MI 48202. Offers English (MA); film and media studies (PhD); literary and cultural studies (PhD); rhetoric and composition studies (PhD). *Faculty:* 27. *Students:* 59 full-time (36 women), 31 part-time (24 women); includes 17 minority (4 Black or African American, non-Hispanic/Latino; 4 Asian, non-Hispanic/Latino; 3 Hispanic/Latino; 6 Two or more races, non-Hispanic/Latino), 4 international. Average age 33. 87 applicants, 44% accepted, 17 enrolled. In 2019, 12 master's, 9 doctorates awarded. Terminal master's awarded for partial completion of doctoral program. *Degree requirements:* For master's, variable foreign language requirement, essay, thesis, or portfolio of work approved by Director of Graduate Studies; for doctorate, one foreign language, comprehensive exam, thesis/dissertation. *Entrance requirements:* For master's, statement of purpose; two academic letters of reference; sample essay from previous English course; for doctorate, statement of purpose; two academic letters of reference; sample of scholarly or critical writing. Additional exam requirements/recommendations for international students: required—TOEFL (minimum score 550 paper-based; 79 iBT), TWE (minimum score 5.5), Michigan English Language Assessment Battery (minimum score 85); recommended—IELTS (minimum score 6.5). *Application deadline:* For fall admission, 1/15 for domestic students. Applications are processed on a rolling basis. Application fee: $50. Electronic applications accepted. *Expenses:* Tuition: Full-time $34,567. *Financial support:* In 2019–20, 54 students received support, including 5 fellowships with tuition reimbursements available (averaging $21,500 per year), 1 research assistantship with tuition reimbursement available (averaging $19,967 per year), 28 teaching assistantships with tuition reimbursements available (averaging $19,967 per year); scholarships/grants, health care benefits, and unspecified assistantships also available. Financial award applicants required to submit FAFSA. *Unit head:* Dr. Caroline Maun, Chair and Associate Professor, 313-577-7692, E-mail: av4495@wayne.edu. *Application contact:* Dr. Richard Marback, Director of Graduate Studies, 313-577-7694, E-mail: aa4749@wayne.edu. Website: http://clas.wayne.edu/english/

Webster University, George Herbert Walker School of Business and Technology, Department of Business, St. Louis, MO 63119-3194. Offers business and organizational security management (MBA); decision support systems (MBA); environmental management (MBA); finance (MBA, MS); forensic accounting (MS); gerontology (MBA); human resources development (MBA); human resources management (MBA); information technology management (MBA); international business (MA, MBA); international relations (MBA); management and leadership (MBA); marketing (MBA); media communications (MBA); procurement and acquisitions management (MBA); Web services (MBA). *Accreditation:* ACBSP. *Program availability:* Part-time, evening/weekend, online learning. *Degree requirements:* For master's, comprehensive exam (for some programs), thesis (for some programs). *Entrance requirements:* Additional exam requirements/recommendations for international students: required—TOEFL.

Webster University, School of Communications, Program in Media Communications, St. Louis, MO 63119-3194. Offers MA.

Webster University, School of Communications, Program in Media Literacy, St. Louis, MO 63119-3194. Offers MA.

West Virginia State University, Media Studies Graduate Program, Institute, WV 25112-1000. Offers MA. *Degree requirements:* For master's, thesis, comprehensive exam may be taken in lieu of a thesis. *Entrance requirements:* For master's, GRE (950), undergraduate GPA of 3.0, letters of recommendation. Additional exam requirements/recommendations for international students: required—TOEFL (minimum score 550 paper-based). Electronic applications accepted.

West Virginia University, Reed College of Media, Morgantown, WV 26506. Offers data marketing communications (MS); integrated marketing communications (MS, Graduate Certificate); journalism (MSJ); media solutions and innovation (MSJ). *Program availability:* Part-time, online learning. *Degree requirements:* For master's, thesis or alternative. *Entrance requirements:* For master's, GRE General Test, minimum GPA of 3.0, writing samples. Additional exam requirements/recommendations for international students: required—TOEFL (minimum score 550 paper-based). Electronic applications accepted.

Wilfrid Laurier University, Faculty of Graduate and Postdoctoral Studies, Faculty of Arts, Department of Communication Studies, Waterloo, ON N2L 3C5, Canada. Offers media, technology and culture (MA); visual communication and culture (MA). *Degree requirements:* For master's, thesis optional. *Entrance requirements:* For master's, honours BA in communication studies or a cognate discipline from an approved university with a minimum B+ overall in last two years of study and in undergraduate major. Additional exam requirements/recommendations for international students: required—TOEFL (minimum score 89 iBT). Electronic applications accepted.

Publishing

Arizona State University at Tempe, College of Liberal Arts and Sciences, School of Historical, Philosophical and Religious Studies, Tempe, AZ 85287-4301. Offers European history (MA, PhD); medieval studies (Graduate Certificate); North American history (MA, PhD); philosophy (MA, PhD); public history (MA); religious studies (MA, PhD); Renaissance studies (Graduate Certificate); scholarly publishing (Graduate Certificate). *Program availability:* Part-time. Terminal master's awarded for partial completion of doctoral program. *Degree requirements:* For master's, thesis or alternative, interactive Program of Study (iPOS) submitted before completing 50 percent of required credit hours; for doctorate, variable foreign language requirement, comprehensive exam, thesis/dissertation, interactive Program of Study (iPOS) submitted before completing 50 percent of required credit hours. *Entrance requirements:* For master's and doctorate, GRE, minimum GPA of 3.0 or equivalent in last 2 years of work leading to bachelor's degree. Additional exam requirements/recommendations for international students: required—TOEFL, IELTS, or PTE. Electronic applications accepted.

Brown University, Graduate School, School of Engineering, Providence, RI 02912. Offers biomedical engineering (Sc M, PhD); chemical and biochemical engineering (Sc M, PhD); electrical sciences and computer engineering (Sc M, PhD); fluid and thermal sciences (Sc M, PhD); materials science and engineering (Sc M, PhD); mechanics of solids and structures (Sc M, PhD). *Degree requirements:* For doctorate, thesis/dissertation, preliminary exam.

Carnegie Mellon University, Dietrich College of Humanities and Social Sciences, Department of English, Program in Professional Writing, Pittsburgh, PA 15213-3891. Offers editing and publishing (MAPW); policy and non-profit communication (MAPW); public and media relations/corporate communications (MAPW); science or healthcare communication (MAPW); technical writing (MAPW); writing for new media (MAPW); writing for print media (MAPW). *Program availability:* Part-time. *Entrance requirements:* For master's, GRE General Test. Additional exam requirements/recommendations for international students: required—TOEFL, TWE.

DePaul University, College of Liberal Arts and Social Sciences, Chicago, IL 60614. Offers Arabic (MA); Chinese (MA); critical ethnic studies (MA); English (MA); French (MA); German (MA); history (MA); interdisciplinary studies (MA, MS); international public service (MS); international studies (MA); Italian (MA); Japanese (MA); liberal studies (MA); nonprofit management (MNM); public administration (MPA); public health (MPH); public policy (MPP); public service management (MS); refugee and forced migration studies (MS); social work (MSW); sociology (MA); Spanish (MA); sustainable urban development (MA); women's and gender studies (MA); writing and publishing (MA); writing, rhetoric and discourse (MA); MA/PhD. *Accreditation:* CEPH. *Program availability:* Part-time, evening/weekend, online learning. Terminal master's awarded for partial completion of doctoral program. *Degree requirements:* For master's, variable foreign language requirement, comprehensive exam (for some programs), thesis (for some programs). Electronic applications accepted.

The George Washington University, College of Professional Studies, Program in Publishing, Washington, DC 20052. Offers MPS. *Entrance requirements:* For master's, minimum cumulative GPA of 3.0. Electronic applications accepted.

The Graduate Center, City University of New York, Graduate Studies, Program in Digital Humanities, New York, NY 10016-4039. Offers data visualization and mapping (MA); digital pedagogy (MA); textual analysis (MA).

New York University, School of Professional Studies, Center for Publishing, New York, NY 10012-1019. Offers publishing: digital and print media (MS). *Program availability:* Part-time, evening/weekend. *Degree requirements:* For master's, thesis. *Entrance requirements:* For master's, GRE or GMAT (only upon request), bachelor's degree, resume with relevant professional work, internship or volunteer experience, 2 letters of recommendation, personal statement. Additional exam requirements/recommendations for international students: required—TOEFL (minimum score 600 paper-based; 100 iBT), IELTS (minimum score 7). Electronic applications accepted. *Expenses:* Contact institution.

Northwestern University, Medill School of Journalism, Media, and Integrated Marketing Communications, Evanston, IL 60208. Offers integrated marketing communications (MSIMC), including brand strategy, content marketing, direct and interactive marketing, marketing analytics, strategic communications; interactive publishing (MSJ); magazine writing/editing (MSJ); reporting (MSJ); video/broadcast (MSJ). *Entrance requirements:* For master's, GRE General Test, GMAT or LSAT (for MSJ). Additional exam requirements/recommendations for international students: required—TOEFL. Electronic applications accepted. *Expenses:* Contact institution.

Pace University, Dyson College of Arts and Sciences, Program in Publishing, New York, NY 10038. Offers book publishing (Certificate); business side of publishing (Certificate); digital publishing (Certificate); magazine publishing (Certificate); publishing (MS). *Program availability:* Part-time, evening/weekend, 100% online. *Degree requirements:* For master's, internship or thesis. *Entrance requirements:* For master's, GRE General Test, two letters of recommendation, personal statement, resume, all official transcripts. Additional exam requirements/recommendations for international students: required—TOEFL (minimum score 88 iBT), IELTS (minimum score 7) or PTE (minimum score 60). Electronic applications accepted.

Rosemont College, Schools of Graduate and Professional Studies, Publishing Program, Rosemont, PA 19010-1699. Offers MA. *Program availability:* Part-time, online learning. *Degree requirements:* For master's, comprehensive exam (for some programs), thesis. *Entrance requirements:* For master's, 3 letters of recommendation. Additional exam requirements/recommendations for international students: required—TOEFL. Electronic applications accepted. Application fee is waived when completed online.

Rowan University, Graduate School, College of Communication and Creative Arts, Program in Editing and Publishing, Glassboro, NJ 08028-1701. Offers CGS. Electronic applications accepted. *Expenses: Tuition,* area resident: part-time $715.50 per semester hour. Tuition, state resident: part-time $715.50 per semester hour. Tuition, nonresident: part-time $715.50 per semester hour. *Required fees:* $161.55 per semester hour.

Sam Houston State University, College of Humanities and Social Sciences, Department of English, Huntsville, TX 77341. Offers creative writing, editing, and

publishing (MFA); English (MA). *Program availability:* Part-time. *Degree requirements:* For master's, comprehensive exam, thesis optional. *Entrance requirements:* For master's, GRE General Test, creative writing sample, letters of recommendation. Additional exam requirements/recommendations for international students: required—TOEFL (minimum score 550 paper-based; 79 iBT), IELTS (minimum score 6.5). Electronic applications accepted.

Simon Fraser University, Office of Graduate Studies and Postdoctoral Fellows, Faculty of Communication, Art and Technology, Canadian Institute for Studies in Publishing, Vancouver, BC V6B 5K3, Canada. Offers M Pub. *Degree requirements:* For master's, internship, internship project report. *Entrance requirements:* For master's, minimum GPA of 3.0 (on scale of 4.33) or 3.33 based on last 60 credits of undergraduate courses. Additional exam requirements/recommendations for international students: recommended—TOEFL (minimum score 580 paper-based; 93 iBT), IELTS (minimum score 7), TWE (minimum score 5). Electronic applications accepted. *Expenses:* Contact institution.

Stephen F. Austin State University, Graduate School, College of Liberal and Applied Arts, Division of Multidisciplinary Programs, Nacogdoches, TX 75962. Offers cultural heritage (MIS); interdisciplinary studies (MIS); publishing (MA). *Program availability:* Part-time. *Degree requirements:* For master's, comprehensive exam, thesis optional. *Entrance requirements:* For master's, GRE General Test. Additional exam requirements/recommendations for international students: required—TOEFL (minimum score 550 paper-based).

University of Baltimore, Graduate School, Yale Gordon College of Arts and Sciences, Program in Creative Writing and Publishing Arts, Baltimore, MD 21201-5779. Offers MFA. *Program availability:* Part-time, evening/weekend. *Entrance requirements:* Additional exam requirements/recommendations for international students: required—TOEFL.

University of Houston–Victoria, School of Arts and Sciences, Program in Publishing, Victoria, TX 77901-4450. Offers MS. *Entrance requirements:* For master's, GMAT or GRE, 2 letters of recommendation, writing sample. Additional exam requirements/recommendations for international students: required—TOEFL. Electronic applications accepted.

Vermont College of Fine Arts, MFA in Writing and Publishing Program, Montpelier, VT 05602. Offers MFA. *Expenses:* Contact institution.

Rhetoric

Abilene Christian University, Office of Graduate Programs, College of Arts and Sciences, Department of Language and Literature, Abilene, TX 79699. Offers composition/rhetoric (MA); literature (MA); writing (MA). *Program availability:* Part-time. *Faculty:* 9 part-time/adjunct (3 women). *Students:* 6 full-time (4 women), 2 part-time (both women); includes 3 minority (1 Hispanic/Latino; 2 Two or more races, non-Hispanic/Latino), 1 international. 25 applicants, 28% accepted, 4 enrolled. In 2019, 1 master's awarded. *Degree requirements:* For master's, one foreign language, comprehensive exam (for some programs), thesis (for some programs). *Entrance requirements:* For master's, GRE General Test, official transcripts, Recommendations, purpose statement, writing sample. Additional exam requirements/recommendations for international students: required—TOEFL (minimum score 80 iBT), IELTS (minimum score 6), PTE (minimum score 51). *Application deadline:* For fall admission, 8/10 for domestic students; for spring admission, 11/1 for domestic students. Applications are processed on a rolling basis. Application fee: $65. Electronic applications accepted. *Expenses:* $1242 per hour. *Financial support:* In 2019–20, 7 students received support, including 2 teaching assistantships with partial tuition reimbursements available; Federal Work-Study and scholarships/grants also available. Support available to part-time students. Financial award application deadline: 4/1; financial award applicants required to submit FAFSA. *Unit head:* Dr. Todd Womble, Graduate Director, 325-674-2663, Fax: 325-674-2408, E-mail: mtw04b@acu.edu. *Application contact:* Graduate Admissions, 325-674-6911, E-mail: gradinfo@acu.edu.
Website: http://www.acu.edu/on-campus/graduate/college-of-arts-and-sciences/language-and-literature/english.html

Arizona State University at Tempe, College of Liberal Arts and Sciences, Department of English, Tempe, AZ 85287-0302. Offers applied linguistics (PhD); creative writing (MFA); English (MA, PhD), including comparative literature (MA), linguistics (MA), literature, rhetoric and composition (MA), rhetoric, composition, and linguistics (PhD); film and media studies (MAS), including American media and popular culture; linguistics (Graduate Certificate); teaching English to speakers of other languages (MTESOL); translation studies (Graduate Certificate). Terminal master's awarded for partial completion of doctoral program. *Degree requirements:* For master's, variable foreign language requirement, comprehensive exam (for some programs), thesis (for some programs), interactive Program of Study (iPOS) submitted before completing 50 percent of required credit hours; for doctorate, variable foreign language requirement, comprehensive exam, thesis/dissertation, interactive Program of Study (iPOS) submitted before completing 50 percent of required credit hours. *Entrance requirements:* For master's and doctorate, GRE, minimum GPA of 3.0 or equivalent in last 2 years of work leading to bachelor's degree. Additional exam requirements/recommendations for international students: required—TOEFL, IELTS, or PTE. Electronic applications accepted.

Ball State University, Graduate School, College of Sciences and Humanities, Department of English, Muncie, IN 47306. Offers English (MA, PhD), including composition (MA), creative writing (MA), literature, rhetoric and composition; linguistics (MA), including linguistics, teaching English to speakers of other languages (TESOL) and linguistics. *Program availability:* Part-time. *Degree requirements:* For doctorate, variable foreign language requirement, thesis/dissertation. *Entrance requirements:* For master's, GRE General Test, minimum baccalaureate GPA of 2.75 or 3.0 in latter half of baccalaureate, statement of purpose, writing sample, three letters of recommendation; for doctorate, GRE General Test, GRE Subject Test, minimum graduate GPA of 3.2, statement of purpose, writing sample, three letters of recommendation. Additional exam requirements/recommendations for international students: required—TOEFL (minimum score 550 paper-based; 79 iBT), IELTS (minimum score 6.5). Electronic applications accepted. *Expenses: Tuition,* area resident: Full-time $7506; part-time $417 per credit hour. Tuition, nonresident: full-time $20,610; part-time $1145 per credit hour. *Required fees:* $2126. Tuition and fees vary according to course load, campus/location and program.

Bob Jones University, Graduate Programs, Greenville, SC 29614. Offers accountancy (MS); Bible (MA); Bible translation (MA); Biblical studies (Certificate); business administration (MBA); church history (MA, PhD); church ministries (MA); church music (MM); cinema and video production (MA); counseling (MS); curriculum and instruction (Ed D); divinity (M Div); dramatic production (MA); educational leadership (MS, Ed D, Ed S); elementary education (M Ed, MAT); English (M Ed, MA, MAT); fine arts (MA); graphic design (MA); history (M Ed, MA); illustration (MA); interpretative speech (MA); mathematics (M Ed, MAT); medical missions (Certificate); ministry (MM, D Min); multi-categorical special education (M Ed, MAT); music (M Ed); New Testament interpretation (PhD); Old Testament interpretation (PhD); orchestral instrument performance (MM); organ performance (MM); pastoral studies (MA); personnel services (MS, Ed S); piano pedagogy (MM); piano performance (MM); platform arts (MA); rhetoric and public address (MA); secondary education (M Ed); studio art (MA); teaching Bible (MA); theology (MA, PhD); voice performance (MM); youth ministries (MA); M Div/MM.

Boise State University, College of Arts and Sciences, Department of English, Boise, ID 83725-0399. Offers English literature (MA); English, rhetoric and composition (MA); teaching English language (MA); technical communication (MA). *Program availability:* Part-time. *Students:* 21 full-time (13 women), 29 part-time (17 women); includes 7 minority (3 Black or African American, non-Hispanic/Latino; 1 Asian, non-Hispanic/Latino; 1 Hispanic/Latino; 1 Native Hawaiian or other Pacific Islander, non-Hispanic/Latino; 1 Two or more races, non-Hispanic/Latino), 1 international. *Degree requirements:* For master's, thesis (for some programs). *Entrance requirements:* For master's, GRE General Test, minimum GPA of 3.0. Additional exam requirements/recommendations for international students: required—TOEFL, IELTS. Electronic applications accepted. *Expenses: Tuition,* area resident: Full-time $7110; part-time $470 per credit hour. Tuition, state resident: full-time $7110; part-time $470 per credit hour. Tuition, nonresident: full-time $24,030; part-time $827 per credit hour. *International tuition:* $24,030 full-time. *Required fees:* $2536. Tuition and fees vary according to course load and program. *Financial support:* Teaching assistantships, scholarships/grants, and unspecified assistantships available. Financial award application deadline: 2/15; financial award applicants required to submit FAFSA. *Unit head:* Dr. Edward Test, Chair, 208-426-3426, E-mail: edwardtest@boisestate.edu. *Application contact:* Dr. Tom Hillard, Director, 208-426-2991, E-mail: thomashillard@boisestate.edu.
Website: https://www.boisestate.edu/english/graduate-programs/

Bowling Green State University, Graduate College, College of Arts and Sciences, Department of English, Program in English, Bowling Green, OH 43403. Offers English (MA, PhD); literature (MA); rhetoric and writing (PhD); scientific and technical communication (MA). *Program availability:* Part-time. *Degree requirements:* For master's, thesis or alternative; for doctorate, comprehensive exam, thesis/dissertation, foreign language or proficiency in Old English. *Entrance requirements:* For master's and doctorate, GRE General Test. Additional exam requirements/recommendations for international students: required—TOEFL. Electronic applications accepted.

Brigham Young University, Graduate Studies, College of Humanities, Department of English, Provo, UT 84602-1001. Offers creative writing (MFA); literature (MA); rhetoric/composition (MA). *Faculty:* 55 full-time (18 women). *Students:* 66 full-time (52 women), 1 part-time (0 women); includes 5 minority (1 Asian, non-Hispanic/Latino; 4 Hispanic/Latino). Average age 28. 52 applicants, 63% accepted, 26 enrolled. In 2019, 23 master's awarded. *Degree requirements:* For master's, variable foreign language requirement, comprehensive exam, thesis. *Entrance requirements:* For master's, GRE General Test, creative portfolio (for MFA). Additional exam requirements/recommendations for international students: required—E3PT; recommended—TOEFL (minimum score 580 paper-based; 85 iBT), IELTS (minimum score 7), TSE. *Application deadline:* For fall admission, 1/15 for domestic and international students. Application fee: $50. Electronic applications accepted. *Financial support:* In 2019–20, 67 students received support, including 12 research assistantships (averaging $4,000 per year), 62 teaching assistantships (averaging $6,700 per year); career-related internships or fieldwork, institutionally sponsored loans, scholarships/grants, and unspecified assistantships also available. Support available to part-time students. Financial award application deadline: 2/15. *Unit head:* Prof. Lance Larsen, Chair, 801-4228104, Fax: 801-422-0221, E-mail: lance_larsen@byu.edu. *Application contact:* Tessa Hauglid, English Graduate Program Manager, 801-422-4939, Fax: 801-422-0221, E-mail: tessa_hauglid@byu.edu. Website: http://english.byu.edu/

California State University, Dominguez Hills, College of Arts and Humanities, Department of English, Carson, CA 90747-0001. Offers English literature (MA); rhetoric and composition (Certificate); teaching English as a second language (MA, Certificate). *Program availability:* Part-time, evening/weekend. *Degree requirements:* For master's, comprehensive exam (for some programs), thesis or alternative. *Entrance requirements:* For master's, minimum GPA of 3.0 in last 60 units. Additional exam requirements/recommendations for international students: required—TOEFL (minimum score 550 paper-based). Electronic applications accepted.

California State University, Fresno, Division of Research and Graduate Studies, College of Arts and Humanities, Department of English, Fresno, CA 93740-8027. Offers creative writing (MFA); literature (MA); rhetoric and writing studies (MA). *Program availability:* Part-time, evening/weekend. *Degree requirements:* For master's, one foreign language, thesis. *Entrance requirements:* For master's, GRE General Test, minimum GPA of 3.0, writing sample. Additional exam requirements/recommendations for international students: required—TOEFL. Electronic applications accepted. *Expenses:* Tuition, state resident: full-time $4012; part-time $2506 per semester.

California State University, Northridge, Graduate Studies, College of Humanities, Department of English, Northridge, CA 91330. Offers creative writing (MA); literature (MA); rhetoric and composition theory (MA). *Program availability:* Part-time, evening/weekend. *Degree requirements:* For master's, thesis or alternative. *Entrance requirements:* For master's, writing proficiency test, GRE General Test or minimum GPA of 3.0. Additional exam requirements/recommendations for international students: required—TOEFL.

California State University, Stanislaus, College of the Arts, Humanities and Social Sciences, MA Program in English, Turlock, CA 95382. Offers literature (Certificate); rhetoric and teaching writing (MA); teaching English to speakers of other languages (MA). *Program availability:* Part-time. *Degree requirements:* For master's, comprehensive exam, thesis or alternative. *Entrance requirements:* For master's, GRE, minimum GPA of 3.0, 2 letters of reference, personal statement. Additional exam requirements/recommendations for international students: required—TOEFL (minimum score 575 paper-based), TWE (minimum score 4). Electronic applications accepted.

Carnegie Mellon University, Dietrich College of Humanities and Social Sciences, Department of English, Pittsburgh, PA 15213-3891. Offers communication planning and design (M Des); literary and cultural studies (MA, PhD); professional writing (MAPW), including editing and publishing, policy and non-profit communication, public and media relations / corporate communications, science or healthcare communication, technical writing, writing for new media, writing for print media; rhetoric (MA, PhD). *Program availability:* Part-time. Terminal master's awarded for partial completion of doctoral program. *Degree requirements:* For doctorate, 2 foreign languages, comprehensive exam, thesis/dissertation. *Entrance requirements:* For master's and doctorate, GRE General Test. Additional exam requirements/recommendations for international students: required—TOEFL, TWE.

The Catholic University of America, School of Arts and Sciences, Department of English Language and Literature, Washington, DC 20064. Offers English (MA, PhD); rhetoric (Certificate). *Program availability:* Part-time. *Faculty:* 9 full-time (3 women), 3 part-time/adjunct (all women). *Students:* 10 full-time (7 women), 22 part-time (14 women); includes 6 minority (3 Hispanic/Latino; 3 Two or more races, non-Hispanic/Latino). Average age 30. 27 applicants, 59% accepted, 8 enrolled. In 2019, 1 master's, 6 doctorates awarded. *Degree requirements:* For master's, one foreign language, comprehensive exam; for doctorate, 2 foreign languages, comprehensive exam, thesis/dissertation. *Entrance requirements:* For master's and doctorate, GRE General Test, statement of purpose, official copies of academic transcripts, three letters of recommendation, writing sample. Additional exam requirements/recommendations for international students: required—TOEFL (minimum score 550 paper-based; 80 iBT). *Application deadline:* For fall admission, 7/15 priority date for domestic students, 7/1 for international students; for spring admission, 11/15 priority date for domestic students, 11/1 for international students. Applications are processed on a rolling basis. Application fee: $55. Electronic applications accepted. *Expenses:* Contact institution. *Financial support:* Fellowships, research assistantships, teaching assistantships, Federal Work-Study, scholarships/grants, tuition waivers (full and partial), and unspecified assistantships available. Financial award application deadline: 2/1; financial award applicants required to submit FAFSA. *Unit head:* Dr. Ernest Suarez, Chair, 202-319-5488, Fax: 202-319-4188, E-mail: johnsong@cua.edu. *Application contact:* Dr. Steven Brown, Director of Graduate Admissions, 202-319-5057, Fax: 202-319-6533, E-mail: cua-admissions@cua.edu. Website: http://english.cua.edu/

Clemson University, Graduate School, College of Architecture, Arts, and Humanities, Department of English, Clemson, SC 29634. Offers English (MA); rhetoric, communication and information design (PhD); writing, rhetoric and media (MA). *Program availability:* Part-time. *Students:* Average age 32. 52 applicants, 77% accepted, 30 enrolled. In 2019, 21 master's, 7 doctorates awarded. *Degree requirements:* For master's, variable foreign language requirement, thesis (for some programs); for doctorate, comprehensive exam, thesis/dissertation. *Entrance requirements:* For master's, GRE General Test, unofficial transcripts, personal statement, writing sample, letters of recommendation. Additional exam requirements/recommendations for international students: required—TOEFL (minimum score 80 paper-based; 80 iBT); recommended—IELTS (minimum score 6.5), TSE (minimum score 54). *Application deadline:* For fall admission, 4/15 priority date for international students; for spring admission, 10/15 for international students. Applications are processed on a rolling basis. Application fee: $80 ($90 for international students). Electronic applications accepted. *Expenses:* Tuition, area resident: Full-time $10,600; part-time $8688 per semester. Tuition, state resident: full-time $10,600; part-time $8688 per semester. Tuition, nonresident: full-time $22,050; part-time $17,412 per semester. *International tuition:* $22,050 full-time. *Required fees:* $1196; $617 per semester. $617 per semester. Tuition and fees vary according to course load, degree level, campus/location and program. *Financial support:* In 2019–20, 59 students received support, including 6 fellowships with full and partial tuition reimbursements available (averaging $1,667 per year), 43 teaching assistantships with full and partial tuition reimbursements available (averaging $17,154 per year); unspecified assistantships also available. *Unit head:* Dr. Susanna Ashton, Department Chair, 864-656-3151, E-mail: sashton@clemson.edu. *Application contact:* Dr. William Stockton, Graduate Program Coordinator, 864-656-3151, E-mail: wstockt@clemson.edu. Website: https://www.clemson.edu/caah/departments/english/

Colorado State University, College of Liberal Arts, Department of English, Fort Collins, CO 80523-1773. Offers creative writing (MFA); rhetoric and composition (MA). *Faculty:* 24 full-time (12 women), 6 part-time/adjunct (5 women). *Students:* 72 full-time (54 women), 23 part-time (20 women); includes 13 minority (2 Black or African American,

non-Hispanic/Latino; 1 Asian, non-Hispanic/Latino; 5 Hispanic/Latino; 5 Two or more races, non-Hispanic/Latino), 13 international. Average age 30. 170 applicants, 51% accepted, 32 enrolled. In 2019, 32 master's awarded. *Degree requirements:* For master's, thesis (for some programs), portfolio, project or thesis. *Entrance requirements:* For master's, BA/BS or equivalent with minimum cumulative undergraduate GPA of 3.0, transcripts, writing sample, statement of purpose, 3 letters of recommendation. Additional exam requirements/recommendations for international students: recommended—TOEFL (minimum score 550 paper-based; 80 iBT), IELTS (minimum score 6.5). Application fee: $60 ($70 for international students). Electronic applications accepted. *Expenses:* Tuition, state resident: full-time $10,520; part-time $5844 per credit hour. Tuition, nonresident: full-time $25,791; part-time $14,328 per credit hour. *International tuition:* $25,791 full-time. *Required fees:* $2512.80. Part-time tuition and fees vary according to course level, course load, degree level, program and student level. *Financial support:* In 2019–20, 1 fellowship with full and partial tuition reimbursement (averaging $15,210 per year), 1 research assistantship (averaging $7,605 per year), 39 teaching assistantships with full and partial tuition reimbursements (averaging $15,593 per year) were awarded; Federal Work-Study, scholarships/grants, and unspecified assistantships also available. *Unit head:* Dr. Louann Reid, Professor, 970-491-6428, E-mail: louann.reid@colostate.edu. *Application contact:* Marnie Leonard, Administrative Assistant, 970-491-2403, E-mail: marnie.leonard@colostate.edu. Website: http://english.colostate.edu/

DePaul University, College of Liberal Arts and Social Sciences, Chicago, IL 60614. Offers Arabic (MA); Chinese (MA); critical ethnic studies (MA); English (MA); French (MA); German (MA); history (MA); interdisciplinary studies (MA, MS); international public service (MS); international studies (MA); Italian (MA); Japanese (MA); liberal studies (MA); nonprofit management (MNM); public administration (MPA); public health (MPH); public policy (MPP); public service management (MS); refugee and forced migration studies (MS); social work (MSW); sociology (MA); Spanish (MA); sustainable urban development (MA); women's and gender studies (MA); writing and publishing (MA); writing, rhetoric and discourse (MA); MA/PhD. *Accreditation:* CEPH. *Program availability:* Part-time, evening/weekend, online learning. Terminal master's awarded for partial completion of doctoral program. *Degree requirements:* For master's, variable foreign language requirement, comprehensive exam (for some programs), thesis (for some programs). Electronic applications accepted.

Duquesne University, Graduate School of Liberal Arts, Department of Communication and Rhetorical Studies, Pittsburgh, PA 15282-0001. Offers communication (MA); rhetoric (PhD). *Program availability:* Part-time, evening/weekend, 100% online. Terminal master's awarded for partial completion of doctoral program. *Degree requirements:* For master's, thesis optional, practicum; for doctorate, 2 foreign languages, comprehensive exam, thesis/dissertation. *Entrance requirements:* For master's and doctorate, GRE General Test. Additional exam requirements/recommendations for international students: required—TOEFL. Electronic applications accepted.

East Carolina University, Graduate School, Thomas Harriot College of Arts and Sciences, Department of English, Greenville, NC 27858-4353. Offers creative writing (MA); English studies (MA); linguistics (MA); literature (MA); multicultural and transnational literatures (MA, Certificate); professional communication (Certificate); rhetoric and composition (MA); rhetoric, writing, and professional communication (PhD); teaching English in the two-year college (Certificate); teaching English to speakers of other languages (MA, Certificate); technical and professional communication (MA). *Program availability:* Part-time, evening/weekend, online learning. *Application deadline:* For fall admission, 7/31 priority date for domestic students, 2/1 priority date for international students; for spring admission, 11/30 priority date for domestic students, 10/1 priority date for international students. *Expenses:* Tuition, area resident: Full-time $4749; part-time $185 per credit hour. Tuition, state resident: full-time $4749; part-time $185 per credit hour. Tuition, nonresident: full-time $17,898; part-time $864 per credit hour. *International tuition:* $17,898 full-time. *Required fees:* $2787. *Financial support:* Application deadline: 3/1. *Unit head:* Dr. Marianne Montgomery, Chair, 252-328-6041, E-mail: montgomerym@ecu.edu. *Application contact:* Graduate School Admissions, 252-328-6012, Fax: 252-328-6071, E-mail: gradschool@ecu.edu. Website: https://english.ecu.edu/

Eastern Washington University, Graduate Studies, College of Arts, Letters and Education, Department of English, Cheney, WA 99004-2431. Offers literature (MA); rhetoric, composition, and technical communication (MA); teaching English as a second language (MA). *Faculty:* 13 full-time (8 women). *Students:* 59 full-time (40 women), 4 part-time (3 women); includes 1 minority (Asian, non-Hispanic/Latino). Average age 33. 100 applicants, 58% accepted, 33 enrolled. In 2019, 32 master's awarded. *Degree requirements:* For master's, comprehensive exam, thesis or alternative. *Entrance requirements:* For master's, GRE General Test, minimum GPA of 3.0. Additional exam requirements/recommendations for international students: required—TOEFL (minimum score 92 paper-based; 92 iBT), IELTS (minimum score 7), PTE (minimum score 63). *Application deadline:* For fall admission, 4/1 priority date for domestic students; for spring admission, 1/15 for domestic students. Applications are processed on a rolling basis. Application fee: $75. *Financial support:* Teaching assistantships with partial tuition reimbursements, career-related internships or fieldwork, Federal Work-Study, institutionally sponsored loans, scholarships/grants, health care benefits, tuition waivers (partial), and unspecified assistantships available. Support available to part-time students. Financial award application deadline: 2/1; financial award applicants required to submit FAFSA. *Application contact:* Kathy White, Advisor/Recruiter for Graduate Studies, 509-359-2491, E-mail: gradprograms@ewu.edu. Website: http://www.ewu.edu/CALE/Programs/English.xml

Florida State University, The Graduate School, Department of Anthropology, Department of English, Tallahassee, FL 32312. Offers English (MA, MFA, PhD), including creative writing (MFA, PhD), literature (MA, PhD), rhetoric and composition (MA, PhD). *Program availability:* Part-time. *Degree requirements:* For master's, one foreign language, thesis, 33 hours of coursework including capstone essay, thesis or portfolio (MA); 45 hours of coursework including 9-12 thesis hours (MFA); for doctorate, one foreign language, comprehensive exam, thesis/dissertation, 27 hours of coursework, 24 hours of dissertation work. *Entrance requirements:* For master's, GRE General Test, sample of written work, 3 letters of recommendation, resume, statement of purpose; for doctorate, GRE General Test, sample of written work, 3 letters of recommendation, resume. statement of purpose. Additional exam requirements/recommendations for international students: required—TOEFL. Electronic applications accepted.

George Mason University, College of Humanities and Social Sciences, Department of English, Fairfax, VA 22030. Offers college teaching (Certificate), including higher education pedagogy; creative writing (MFA), including fiction, nonfiction writing, poetry; English (MA), including cultural studies, linguistics, literature, professional writing and rhetoric, teaching of writing and literature; English pedagogy (Certificate); folklore studies (Certificate); linguistics (PhD); writing and rhetoric (PhD). *Program availability:* Part-time. *Degree requirements:* For master's, thesis (for some programs), proficiency in a foreign language by course work or translation test; for doctorate, comprehensive exam, thesis/dissertation, 2 papers. *Entrance requirements:* For master's, official transcripts; expanded goals statement; writing sample; portfolio; 2 letters of recommendation; resume; for doctorate, GRE (for linguistics), expanded goals statement; 2 letters of recommendation (writing and rhetoric); 3 letters of recommendation (linguistics); writing sample; introductory course in linguistics; official transcripts; master's degree in relevant field; for Certificate, official transcripts; expanded goals statement; 2 letters of recommendation; writing sample; resume. Additional exam requirements/recommendations for international students: required—TOEFL (minimum score 575 paper-based; 88 iBT), IELTS (minimum score 6.5), PTE (minimum score 59). Electronic applications accepted.

Georgia State University, College of Arts and Sciences, Department of Communication, Atlanta, GA 30302-3083. Offers film, video, and digital imaging (MA), including critical studies, production, screenwriting; human communication and social influence (MA); mass communication (MA); media and society (PhD); moving image studies (PhD); public communication (PhD); rhetoric and politics (PhD). *Program availability:* Part-time. *Faculty:* 22 full-time (16 women), 1 part-time/adjunct (0 women). *Students:* 67 full-time (46 women), 26 part-time (17 women); includes 44 minority (40 Black or African American, non-Hispanic/Latino; 1 Asian, non-Hispanic/Latino; 1 Hispanic/Latino; 1 Native Hawaiian or other Pacific Islander, non-Hispanic/Latino; 1 Two or more races, non-Hispanic/Latino), 12 international. Average age 36. 82 applicants, 49% accepted, 22 enrolled. In 2019, 9 master's, 5 doctorates awarded. *Degree requirements:* For master's, variable foreign language requirement, thesis (for some programs); for doctorate, comprehensive exam, thesis/dissertation. *Entrance requirements:* For master's and doctorate, GRE. Additional exam requirements/ recommendations for international students: required—TOEFL (minimum score 550 paper-based; 80 iBT), IELTS (minimum score 6.5). *Application deadline:* For fall admission, 2/10 for domestic and international students; for spring admission, 10/15 for domestic and international students. Application fee: $50. Electronic applications accepted. *Expenses: Tuition, area resident:* Full-time $7164; part-time $398 per credit hour. Tuition, state resident: full-time $7164; part-time $398 per credit hour. Tuition, nonresident: full-time $22,662; part-time $1259 per credit hour. *International tuition:* $22,662 full-time. *Required fees:* $2128; $312 per credit hour. Tuition and fees vary according to course load and program. *Financial support:* In 2019–20, fellowships with tuition reimbursements (averaging $15,000 per year), teaching assistantships with tuition reimbursements (averaging $15,000 per year) were awarded; career-related internships or fieldwork and unspecified assistantships also available. Financial award applicants required to submit FAFSA. *Unit head:* Dr. Greg Lisby, Chair, 404-413-5639, Fax: 404-413-5634, E-mail: glisby@gsu.edu. *Application contact:* Dr. Greg Lisby, Chair, 404-413-5639, Fax: 404-413-5634, E-mail: glisby@gsu.edu.
Website: http://communication.gsu.edu

Georgia State University, College of Arts and Sciences, Department of English, Atlanta, GA 30302-3083. Offers creative writing (MA, MFA, PhD), including creative writing (PhD), fiction (MA, MFA), poetry (MA, MFA); English (MA, PhD); literary studies (MA, PhD); rhetoric and composition (MA, PhD). *Program availability:* Part-time. *Faculty:* 17 full-time (7 women). *Students:* 102 full-time (65 women), 58 part-time (39 women); includes 33 minority (24 Black or African American, non-Hispanic/Latino; 4 Asian, non-Hispanic/Latino; 3 Hispanic/Latino; 2 Two or more races, non-Hispanic/Latino), 6 international. Average age 37. 137 applicants, 50% accepted, 29 enrolled. In 2019, 10 master's, 21 doctorates awarded. *Entrance requirements:* For master's and doctorate, GRE. Additional exam requirements/recommendations for international students: required—TOEFL (minimum score 550 paper-based; 80 iBT). *Application deadline:* For fall admission, 1/15 for domestic and international students. Application fee: $50. Electronic applications accepted. *Expenses: Tuition, area resident:* Full-time $7164; part-time $398 per credit hour. Tuition, state resident: full-time $7164; part-time $398 per credit hour. Tuition, nonresident: full-time $22,662; part-time $1259 per credit hour. *International tuition:* $22,662 full-time. *Required fees:* $2128; $312 per credit hour. Tuition and fees vary according to course load and program. *Financial support:* In 2019–20, research assistantships with full tuition reimbursements (averaging $6,000 per year), teaching assistantships with full tuition reimbursements (averaging $15,000 per year) were awarded; career-related internships or fieldwork, traineeships, and health care benefits also available. Financial award application deadline: 2/15. *Unit head:* Dr. Lynnee Lewis Gaillet, Chair, 404-413-5842, Fax: 404-413-5830, E-mail: lgaillet@gsu.edu. *Application contact:* Dr. Lynnee Lewis Gaillet, Chair, 404-413-5842, Fax: 404-413-5830, E-mail: lgaillet@gsu.edu.
Website: http://www.english.gsu.edu

Indiana University Bloomington, University Graduate School, College of Arts and Sciences, Department of English, Bloomington, IN 47405. Offers creative writing (MA, MFA), including fiction (MFA), poetry (MFA); literature (PhD); rhetoric (PhD). *Degree requirements:* For master's, 30-36 credit hours plus one language proficiency (for MA); 60 credit hours plus thesis (for MFA); for doctorate, thesis/dissertation, qualifying exam; 90 credit hours; 2nd language proficiency or one language only if acquired at in-depth level. *Entrance requirements:* For master's, GRE General Test, GRE Subject Test (for all but MFA and MA in creative writing), minimum GPA of 3.5; for doctorate, GRE General Test, GRE Subject Test, minimum GPA of 3.7. Additional exam requirements/ recommendations for international students: required—TOEFL (minimum score 550 paper-based; 79 iBT), IELTS (minimum score 6.5). Electronic applications accepted.

Iowa State University of Science and Technology, Department of English, Ames, IA 50011. Offers creative writing (MFA); English (MA); rhetoric and professional communication (PhD). *Degree requirements:* For master's, thesis or alternative; for doctorate, thesis/dissertation. *Entrance requirements:* For master's, GRE General Test, sample of written work, resume, portfolio in creative writing; for doctorate, GRE General Test, sample of written work, resume. Additional exam requirements/recommendations for international students: required—TOEFL (minimum score 600 paper-based; 100 iBT), IELTS (minimum score 7). Electronic applications accepted.

Iowa State University of Science and Technology, Program in Rhetoric and Professional Communication, Ames, IA 50011. Offers PhD. *Entrance requirements:* For doctorate, GRE, official academic transcripts, resume, three letters of recommendation, writing sample. Additional exam requirements/recommendations for international students: required—TOEFL (minimum score 640 paper-based; 111 iBT), IELTS (minimum score 7.5). Electronic applications accepted.

Iowa State University of Science and Technology, Program in Rhetoric, Composition, and Professional Communication, Ames, IA 50011. Offers MA. *Entrance requirements:* For master's, GRE, official academic transcripts, resume, three letters of recommendation, writing sample. Additional exam requirements/recommendations for international students: required—TOEFL (minimum score 600 paper-based; 100 iBT), IELTS (minimum score 7). Electronic applications accepted.

James Madison University, The Graduate School, College of Arts and Letters, Program in Writing, Rhetoric, and Technical Communication, Harrisonburg, VA 22807. Offers MA, MS. *Program availability:* Part-time. *Students:* 10 full-time (6 women), 4 part-time (all women); includes 2 minority (1 Black or African American, non-Hispanic/Latino; 1 Asian, non-Hispanic/Latino). Average age 30. In 2019, 9 master's awarded. Application fee: $60. Electronic applications accepted. *Financial support:* In 2019–20, 10 students received support, including 2 teaching assistantships with full tuition reimbursements available (averaging $9,284 per year); fellowships, career-related internships or fieldwork, Federal Work-Study, and assistantships (averaging $7911) also available. Financial award application deadline: 3/1; financial award applicants required to submit FAFSA. *Unit head:* Dr. Traci A. Zimmerman, Director of the School of Writing, Rhetoric and Technical Communication, 540-568-2334, E-mail: zimmerta@jmu.edu. *Application contact:* Lynette D. Michael, Director of Graduate Admissions, 540-568-6131 Ext. 6395, Fax: 540-568-7860, E-mail: michaeld@jmu.edu.
Website: http://www.jmu.edu/wrtc/

Kent State University, College of Arts and Sciences, Department of English, Kent, OH 44242-0001. Offers creative writing (MFA); English (MA, PhD); English for teachers (MA); literature and writing (MA); rhetoric and composition (PhD); teaching English as a second language (MA). *Program availability:* Part-time. *Faculty:* 19 full-time (9 women), 2 part-time/adjunct (1 woman). *Students:* 101 full-time (64 women), 12 part-time (8 women); includes 5 minority (3 Black or African American, non-Hispanic/Latino; 1 Asian, non-Hispanic/Latino; 1 Hispanic/Latino), 24 international. Average age 34. 69 applicants, 77% accepted, 18 enrolled. In 2019, 19 master's, 3 doctorates awarded. *Degree requirements:* For master's, thesis (for some programs), final portfolio, final exam, practicum or thesis (for MA in teaching English as a second language); for doctorate, one foreign language, comprehensive exam, thesis/dissertation. *Entrance requirements:* For master's, GRE General Test, goal statement, 3 letters of recommendation, 8-15 page writing sample relevant to the field of study (waived for MA in English for teachers concentration), transcripts, for MA - TESL Int'l English proficiency scores: TOEFL (ibT): 79, MELAB 77, IELTS 6.5, PTE 58; for the M.A. - English, TOEFL (ibT): 94, MELAB 82, IELTS 7.0, PTE 65; for doctorate, GRE General Test, statement of purpose, 3 letters of recommendation, 8-15 page writing sample relevant to field of study, transcripts, Master's degree, 3.0 GPA on 4.0 scale; Ph.D Rhetoric & Comp - English proficiency for Int'l: TOEFL (ibT) 102, MELAB 86, IELTS 7.5, PTE 73; Ph.D - English: TOEFL (ibT) 94, MELAB 82, IELTS 7.5, PTE 73. Additional exam requirements/ recommendations for international students: required—See below for scores specific to Masters or Doctorate level. *Application deadline:* Applications are processed on a rolling basis. Application fee: $45 ($70 for international students). Electronic applications accepted. *Financial support:* Fellowships with full tuition reimbursements, teaching assistantships with full tuition reimbursements, and unspecified assistantships available. Financial award application deadline: 1/15. *Unit head:* Dr. Robert Trogdon, Chair, 330-672-2676, E-mail: rtrogdon@kent.edu. *Application contact:* Wesley Raabe, Graduate Studies Coordinator, 330-672-1723, E-mail: wraabe@kent.edu.
Website: http://www.kent.edu/english/

Michigan State University, The Graduate School, College of Arts and Letters, Program in Rhetoric and Writing, East Lansing, MI 48824. Offers critical studies in literacy and pedagogy (MA); digital rhetoric and professional writing (MA); rhetoric and writing (PhD). *Entrance requirements:* Additional exam requirements/recommendations for international students: required—TOEFL. Electronic applications accepted.

Monmouth University, Graduate Studies, Department of English, West Long Branch, NJ 07764-1898. Offers creative writing (MA); literature (MA); rhetoric and writing (MA). *Program availability:* Part-time, evening/weekend. *Faculty:* 7 full-time (5 women). *Students:* 7 full-time (4 women), 34 part-time (22 women); includes 3 minority (2 Hispanic/Latino; 1 Two or more races, non-Hispanic/Latino). Average age 32. In 2019, 14 master's awarded. *Degree requirements:* For master's, comprehensive exam (for some programs), thesis. *Entrance requirements:* For master's, minimum overall GPA of 2.75, fifteen or more credits in literature or related field, essay of 1000 words describing interest and goals, two letters of recommendation, creative writing sample. Additional exam requirements/recommendations for international students: required—TOEFL (minimum score 550 paper-based, 79 iBT), IELTS (minimum score 6), Michigan English Language Assessment Battery (minimum score 77) or Certificate of Advanced English (minimum score of 160). *Application deadline:* For fall admission, 7/15 for domestic students, 6/1 for international students; for spring admission, 12/1 for domestic students, 11/1 for international students; for summer admission, 5/1 for domestic students. Applications are processed on a rolling basis. Application fee: $50. Electronic applications accepted. *Expenses: Tuition:* Full-time $22,194; part-time $14,796 per credit. *Required fees:* $712; $178 per semester. $178 per semester. Tuition and fees vary according to course load. *Financial support:* In 2019–20, 37 students received support. Research assistantships, teaching assistantships, scholarships/grants, and unspecified assistantships available. Support available to part-time students. Financial award applicants required to submit FAFSA. *Unit head:* Dr. Mary Kate Azcuy, Program Director, 732-571-3439, Fax: 732-263-5242, E-mail: mazcuy@monmouth.edu. *Application contact:* Kevin New, Graduate Admission Counselor, 732-571-3452, Fax: 732-263-5123, E-mail: gradadm@monmouth.edu.
Website: https://www.monmouth.edu/graduate/ma-english/

New Mexico Highlands University, Graduate Studies, College of Arts and Sciences, Department of English, Las Vegas, NM 87701. Offers English (MA), including creative writing, language, rhetoric and composition, literature. *Degree requirements:* For master's, comprehensive exam, thesis. *Entrance requirements:* For master's, minimum undergraduate GPA of 3.0. Additional exam requirements/recommendations for international students: required—TOEFL (minimum score 540 paper-based).

New Mexico State University, College of Arts and Sciences, Department of English, Las Cruces, NM 88003-8001. Offers creative writing (MFA); English (MA), including creative writing, English studies for teachers, literature, rhetoric and professional communication; rhetoric and professional communication (PhD). *Program availability:* Part-time. *Faculty:* 17 full-time (7 women), 1 (woman) part-time/adjunct. *Students:* 43 full-time (28 women), 16 part-time (10 women); includes 25 minority (3 Black or African American, non-Hispanic/Latino; 1 Asian, non-Hispanic/Latino; 20 Hispanic/Latino; 1 Two or more races, non-Hispanic/Latino), 6 international. Average age 35. 46 applicants, 57% accepted, 14 enrolled. In 2019, 16 master's, 4 doctorates awarded. *Degree requirements:* For master's, one foreign language, thesis (for some programs); for doctorate, comprehensive exam, thesis/dissertation, internship. *Entrance requirements:* For master's and doctorate, sample of written work. Additional exam requirements/ recommendations for international students: required—TOEFL (minimum score 550 paper-based; 79 iBT), IELTS (minimum score 6.5). *Application deadline:* For fall admission, 2/1 for domestic and international students. Application fee: $40 ($50 for international students). Electronic applications accepted. *Financial support:* In 2019–20, 46 students received support, including 5 fellowships (averaging $4,844 per year), 40 teaching assistantships (averaging $18,521 per year); career-related internships or fieldwork, Federal Work-Study, scholarships/grants, traineeships, health care benefits, and unspecified assistantships also available. Support available to part-time students. Financial award application deadline: 3/1. *Unit head:* Dr. Elizabeth Schirmer, Interim Department Head, 575-646-3931, Fax: 575-646-7725, E-mail: eschirme@nmsu.edu. *Application contact:* Dr. Tracey Eileen Miller-Tomlinson, Director of Graduate Studies, 575-646-2213, Fax: 575-646-7725, E-mail: tomlin@nmsu.edu.
Website: http://english.nmsu.edu

North Carolina State University, Graduate School, College of Humanities and Social Sciences, Program in Communication, Rhetoric, and Digital Media, Raleigh, NC 27695. Offers MS, PhD.

North Dakota State University, College of Graduate and Interdisciplinary Studies, College of Arts, Humanities and Social Sciences, Department of English, Fargo, ND 58102. Offers composition (MA); rhetoric, writing and culture (PhD). *Program* *availability:* Part-time. *Degree requirements:* For master's, one foreign language, thesis. *Entrance requirements:* Additional exam requirements/recommendations for international students: required—TOEFL (minimum score 600 paper-based; 100 iBT), IELTS (minimum score 7). Electronic applications accepted. Tuition and fees vary according to program and reciprocity agreements.

Northern Arizona University, College of Arts and Letters, Department of English, Flagstaff, AZ 86011. Offers applied linguistics (PhD); creative writing (MFA), including creative writing; English (MA), including literature, professional writing, rhetoric, writing, and digital media studies, secondary education; professional writing (Graduate Certificate); rhetoric, writing and digital media studies (Graduate Certificate); teaching English as a second language (MA, Graduate Certificate). *Program availability:* Part-time, 100% online, blended/hybrid learning. *Degree requirements:* For master's, variable foreign language requirement, comprehensive exam (for some programs), thesis (for some programs); for doctorate, variable foreign language requirement, comprehensive exam (for some programs), thesis/dissertation (for some programs); for Graduate Certificate, comprehensive exam (for some programs). *Entrance requirements:* Additional exam requirements/recommendations for international students: required—TOEFL (minimum score 80 iBT), IELTS (minimum score 6.5). Electronic applications accepted.

Northern Kentucky University, Office of Graduate Programs, College of Arts and Sciences, Program in English, Highland Heights, KY 41099. Offers composition and rhetoric (Certificate); creative writing (Certificate); cultural studies and discourses (Certificate); English (MA); professional writing (Certificate). *Program availability:* Part-time, evening/weekend. *Degree requirements:* For master's, comprehensive exam (for some programs), capstone (thesis, portfolio, project, or exams); 30 hours of credit; for Certificate, 18 hours of credit. *Entrance requirements:* For master's, bachelor's degree in English or related field from regionally-accredited institution with minimum GPA of 3.0 in major or cognate area coursework; official transcripts for all undergraduate and graduate work; two letters of reference; for Certificate, official transcripts for all undergraduate and graduate work; bachelor's degree from regionally-accredited institution; minimum undergraduate GPA of 2.5. Additional exam requirements/recommendations for international students: required—TOEFL (minimum score 79 iBT); recommended—IELTS (minimum score 6.5). Electronic applications accepted.

Northwestern University, The Graduate School, School of Communication, Department of Communication Studies, Evanston, IL 60208. Offers communication studies (PhD), including interaction and social influence, rhetoric and public culture; managerial communication (MSC); media, technology and society (PhD); technology and social behavior (PhD). Terminal master's awarded for partial completion of doctoral program. *Degree requirements:* For doctorate, thesis/dissertation. *Entrance requirements:* For master's and doctorate, GRE General Test. Additional exam requirements/recommendations for international students: required—TOEFL. Electronic applications accepted.

Ohio University, Graduate College, Scripps College of Communication, School of Communication Studies, Athens, OH 45701-2979. Offers health communication (PhD); organizational communication (MA); relating and organizing (PhD); rhetoric and public culture (PhD). *Program availability:* Part-time, online learning. Terminal master's awarded for partial completion of doctoral program. *Degree requirements:* For master's, capstone; for doctorate, comprehensive exam, thesis/dissertation. *Entrance requirements:* For master's, GRE; for doctorate, GRE General Test, minimum GPA of 3.0. Additional exam requirements/recommendations for international students: required—TOEFL (minimum score 550 paper-based; 80 iBT) or IELTS (minimum score 6.5). Electronic applications accepted.

Old Dominion University, College of Arts and Letters, Master of Arts in English Program, Norfolk, VA 23529. Offers literature (MA); professional writing (MA); rhetoric and composition (MA). *Program availability:* Part-time, evening/weekend. Terminal master's awarded for partial completion of doctoral program. *Degree requirements:* For master's, comprehensive exam, thesis optional. *Entrance requirements:* For master's, GRE General Test, 24 hours in English, sample of written work, BA. Additional exam requirements/recommendations for international students: required—TOEFL. Electronic applications accepted.

Oregon State University, College of Liberal Arts, Program in English, Corvallis, OR 97331. Offers film and visual studies (MA); literature and culture (MA); rhetoric, writing and composition (MA). *Program availability:* Part-time. *Entrance requirements:* For master's, GRE (recommended). Additional exam requirements/recommendations for international students: required—TOEFL (minimum score 80 iBT), IELTS (minimum score 6.5).

Rensselaer Polytechnic Institute, Graduate School, School of Humanities, Arts, and Social Sciences, Program in Communication and Rhetoric, Troy, NY 12180-3590. Offers MS, PhD. *Faculty:* 9 full-time (6 women). *Students:* 10 full-time (7 women), 1 (woman) part-time. Average age 33. 10 applicants, 30% accepted, 2 enrolled. In 2019, 4 doctorates awarded. Terminal master's awarded for partial completion of doctoral program. *Degree requirements:* For master's, thesis optional; for doctorate, comprehensive exam, thesis/dissertation. *Entrance requirements:* For master's and doctorate, GRE, writing sample. Additional exam requirements/recommendations for international students: required—TOEFL (minimum score 570 paper-based; 88 iBT), IELTS (minimum score 6.5), PTE (minimum score 60). *Application deadline:* For fall admission, 1/1 priority date for domestic and international students; for spring admission, 8/15 priority date for domestic and international students. Applications are processed on a rolling basis. Application fee: $75. Electronic applications accepted. *Financial support:* In 2019–20, research assistantships with full tuition reimbursements (averaging $23,000 per year), teaching assistantships with full tuition reimbursements (averaging $23,000 per year) were awarded; fellowships also available. Financial award application deadline: 1/1. *Unit head:* Dr. Tamar Gordon, Graduate Program Director, 518-276-6933, E-mail: gordot@rpi.edu. *Application contact:* Jarron Decker, Director of Graduate Admissions, 518-276-6216, Fax: 518-276-4072, E-mail: gradadmissions@rpi.edu.
Website: http://www.cm.rpi.edu/pl/graduate

Rowan University, Graduate School, College of Communication and Creative Arts, Writing, Composition, and Rhetoric Certificate of Graduate Study Program, Glassboro, NJ 08028-1701. Offers CGS. *Expenses: Tuition,* area resident: Part-time $715.50 per semester hour. Tuition, state resident: part-time $715.50 per semester hour. Tuition, nonresident: part-time $715.50 per semester hour. *Required fees:* $161.55 per semester hour.

St. Cloud State University, School of Graduate Studies, College of Liberal Arts, Department of English, St. Cloud, MN 56301-4498. Offers English (MS); English studies (MA); rhetoric and writing (MA). *Program availability:* Part-time. *Degree requirements:* For master's, thesis or alternative. *Entrance requirements:* For master's, GRE General Test, minimum GPA of 2.75. Additional exam requirements/recommendations for international students: required—Michigan English Language Assessment Battery; recommended—TOEFL (minimum score 550 paper-based), IELTS (minimum score 6.5). Electronic applications accepted.

San Diego State University, Graduate and Research Affairs, College of Arts and Letters, Department of Rhetoric and Writing Studies, San Diego, CA 92182. Offers MA. *Program availability:* Part-time. *Degree requirements:* For master's, thesis. *Entrance requirements:* For master's, GRE General Test, writing sample, 3 letters of reference. Additional exam requirements/recommendations for international students: required—TOEFL. Electronic applications accepted.

Southern Illinois University Carbondale, Graduate School, College of Liberal Arts, Department of English, Carbondale, IL 62901-4701. Offers composition (MA, PhD), including composition, literature, rhetoric; creative writing (MFA). *Degree requirements:* For master's, one foreign language, thesis; for doctorate, 2 foreign languages, thesis/dissertation. *Entrance requirements:* For master's, GRE General Test, GRE Subject Test, minimum GPA of 2.7; for doctorate, GRE General Test, GRE Subject Test, minimum GPA of 3.25. Additional exam requirements/recommendations for international students: required—TOEFL.

Syracuse University, College of Arts and Sciences, PhD Program in Composition and Cultural Rhetoric, Syracuse, NY 13244. Offers PhD. *Degree requirements:* For doctorate, comprehensive exam, thesis/dissertation. *Entrance requirements:* For doctorate, GRE, three letters of recommendation, essay on intellectual history and academic interests, statement about teaching interests and practical experience, resume, transcripts. Additional exam requirements/recommendations for international students: required—TOEFL (minimum score 100 iBT). Electronic applications accepted.

Syracuse University, College of Visual and Performing Arts, MA Program in Communication and Rhetorical Studies, Syracuse, NY 13244. Offers MA. *Program availability:* Part-time. *Degree requirements:* For master's, comprehensive exam (for some programs), thesis (for some programs). *Entrance requirements:* For master's, GRE General Test, three letters of recommendation, writing sample, transcripts, personal statement, resume. Additional exam requirements/recommendations for international students: required—TOEFL (minimum score 90 iBT). Electronic applications accepted.

Texas Christian University, AddRan College of Liberal Arts, Department of English, Fort Worth, TX 76129-0002. Offers English (MA, PhD); rhetoric and composition (PhD). *Faculty:* 18 full-time (11 women), 1 (woman) part-time/adjunct. *Students:* 54 full-time (38 women); includes 12 minority (3 Black or African American, non-Hispanic/Latino; 7 Hispanic/Latino; 2 Two or more races, non-Hispanic/Latino), 5 international. Average age 29. 33 applicants, 70% accepted, 12 enrolled. In 2019, 5 master's, 6 doctorates awarded. *Degree requirements:* For master's, one foreign language, thesis; for doctorate, one foreign language, comprehensive exam, thesis/dissertation. *Entrance requirements:* For master's and doctorate, GRE General Test. Additional exam requirements/recommendations for international students: required—TOEFL. *Application deadline:* 1/10 for domestic and international students. Application fee: $60. Electronic applications accepted. *Expenses:* Contact institution. *Financial support:* In 2019–20, 47 students received support, including 4 fellowships with full tuition reimbursements available (averaging $21,000 per year), 7 research assistantships with full tuition reimbursements available, 24 teaching assistantships with full tuition reimbursements available (averaging $18,660 per year); career-related internships or fieldwork, health care benefits, tuition waivers (full), and unspecified assistantships also available. Financial award application deadline: 1/10; financial award applicants required to submit FAFSA. *Unit head:* Dr. Brad E. Lucas, Director of Graduate Studies, 817-257-6981, Fax: 817-257-6238, E-mail: b.e.lucas2@tcu.edu. *Application contact:* Merry Roberts, English Department Office Manager, 817-257-6890, Fax: 817-257-6238, E-mail: m.roberts@tcu.edu.
Website: http://www.eng.tcu.edu/

Texas State University, The Graduate College, College of Liberal Arts, Program in Rhetoric and Composition, San Marcos, TX 78666. Offers MA. *Program availability:* Part-time. *Degree requirements:* For master's, comprehensive exam, thesis optional. *Entrance requirements:* For master's, baccalaureate degree from regionally-accredited institution with minimum GPA of 2.75 on last 60 undergraduate semester hours, 3.0 in minimum of 12 hours of undergraduate English courses; 3 letters of recommendation; portfolio; 2 non-fiction documents, one of which demonstrates academic research; statement of purpose. Additional exam requirements/recommendations for international students: required—TOEFL (minimum score 550 paper-based; 78 iBT), IELTS (minimum score 6.5). Electronic applications accepted.

Texas Tech University, Graduate School, College of Arts and Sciences, Department of English, Lubbock, TX 79409-3091. Offers English (MA, PhD); technical communication (MA); technical communication and rhetoric (PhD). *Program availability:* Part-time, evening/weekend, 100% online, blended/hybrid learning. *Faculty:* 67 full-time (34 women), 4 part-time/adjunct (3 women). *Students:* 105 full-time (67 women), 102 part-time (74 women); includes 44 minority (8 Black or African American, non-Hispanic/Latino; 1 American Indian or Alaska Native, non-Hispanic/Latino; 2 Asian, non-Hispanic/Latino; 24 Hispanic/Latino; 9 Two or more races, non-Hispanic/Latino), 11 international. Average age 33. 201 applicants, 54% accepted, 58 enrolled. In 2019, 16 master's, 28 doctorates awarded. Terminal master's awarded for partial completion of doctoral program. *Degree requirements:* For master's, variable foreign language requirement, comprehensive exam, thesis optional; for doctorate, variable foreign language requirement, comprehensive exam, thesis/dissertation. *Entrance requirements:* For master's and doctorate, GRE General Test. Additional exam requirements/recommendations for international students: required—TOEFL (minimum score 550 paper-based; 79 iBT), IELTS (minimum score 6.5). *Application deadline:* For fall admission, 6/1 priority date for domestic students, 1/15 priority date for international students; for spring admission, 9/1 priority date for domestic students, 6/15 priority date for international students. Applications are processed on a rolling basis. Application fee: $65. Electronic applications accepted. *Expenses:* Contact institution. *Financial support:* In 2019–20, 127 students received support, including 103 fellowships (averaging $2,361 per year), 5 research assistantships (averaging $18,968 per year), 101 teaching assistantships (averaging $17,254 per year); career-related internships or fieldwork, Federal Work-Study, scholarships/grants, and unspecified assistantships also available. Financial award application deadline: 1/8; financial award applicants required to submit FAFSA. *Unit head:* Dr. Brian Still, Department Chair, 806-834-6439, Fax: 806-742-0989, E-mail: brian.still@ttu.edu. *Application contact:* Dr. Julie Nelson Couch, Director of Graduate Studies, 806-834-1742, Fax: 806-742-0989, E-mail: english.gradadvisor@ttu.edu.
Website: www.english.ttu.edu/

Texas Woman's University, Graduate School, College of Arts and Sciences, Department of English, Speech, and Foreign Languages, Denton, TX 76204. Offers English (MA, MAT); rhetoric (PhD). *Program availability:* Part-time. *Faculty:* 7 full-time (5 women), 1 (woman) part-time/adjunct. *Students:* 6 full-time (5 women), 47 part-time (43 women); includes 18 minority (5 Black or African American, non-Hispanic/Latino; 2 Asian, non-Hispanic/Latino; 8 Hispanic/Latino; 3 Two or more races, non-Hispanic/Latino), 1 international. Average age 37. 25 applicants, 88% accepted, 14 enrolled. In 2019, 8 master's, 3 doctorates awarded. *Degree requirements:* For master's, comprehensive exam, thesis or alternative, professional paper, thesis or coursework; for doctorate, comprehensive exam, thesis/dissertation, residency for at least 2 consecutive semesters (strongly encouraged), oral defense of dissertation. *Entrance requirements:*

For master's, 3 letters of reference, minimum GPA of 3.0 on previous upper-division undergraduate and graduate work, writing sample, statement of purpose; for doctorate, writing sample, 3 letters of reference, interview (for graduate assistants), minimum GPA of 3.0 on previous upper-division and graduate work, statement of purpose, masters's degree (bachelor's or masters must be in English). Additional exam requirements/recommendations for international students: required—TOEFL (minimum score 600 paper-based; 79 iBT); recommended—IELTS (minimum score 6.5). *Application deadline:* For fall admission, 7/1 priority date for domestic students, 3/1 priority date for international students; for spring admission, 11/1 priority date for domestic students, 7/1 priority date for international students; for summer admission, 4/1 priority date for domestic students, 2/1 priority date for international students. Applications are processed on a rolling basis. Application fee: $50 ($75 for international students). Electronic applications accepted. *Expenses: Tuition, area resident:* Full-time $4973.40; part-time $276.30 per semester hour. Tuition, state resident: full-time $4973.40; part-time $276.30 per semester hour. Tuition, nonresident: full-time $12,569; part-time $698.30 per semester hour. *International tuition:* $12,569.40 full-time. *Required fees:* $2524.30. Tuition and fees vary according to course level, course load, degree level and program. *Financial support:* In 2019–20, 25 students received support, including 16 teaching assistantships (averaging $10,412 per year); career-related internships or fieldwork, scholarships/grants, health care benefits, and unspecified assistantships also available. Support available to part-time students. Financial award application deadline: 3/1; financial award applicants required to submit FAFSA. *Unit head:* Dr. Genevieve West, Chair, 940-898-2324, Fax: 940-898-2297, E-mail: engspfl@twu.edu. *Application contact:* Korie Hawkins, Associate Director of Admissions, Graduate Recruitment, 940-898-3188, Fax: 940-898-3081, E-mail: admissions@twu.edu.
Website: http://www.twu.edu/english-speech-foreign-languages/

The University of Alabama, Graduate School, College of Arts and Sciences, Department of English, Tuscaloosa, AL 35487. Offers composition and rhetoric (PhD); creative writing (MFA), including fiction, poetry; literature (MA, PhD); rhetoric and composition (MA); teaching English as a second language (MATESOL). *Faculty:* 21 full-time (14 women). *Students:* 122 full-time (82 women), 8 part-time (5 women); includes 29 minority (11 Black or African American, non-Hispanic/Latino; 2 American Indian or Alaska Native, non-Hispanic/Latino; 5 Asian, non-Hispanic/Latino; 3 Hispanic/Latino; 8 Two or more races, non-Hispanic/Latino), 8 international. Average age 29. 230 applicants, 25% accepted, 35 enrolled. In 2019, 32 master's awarded. *Degree requirements:* For master's, one foreign language, comprehensive exam, thesis; for doctorate, 2 foreign languages, comprehensive exam, thesis/dissertation. *Entrance requirements:* For master's, GRE (minimum score of 300, except for MFA), minimum GPA of 3.0, critical writing sample; for doctorate, GRE (minimum score of 300), minimum GPA of 3.5 on master's or equivalent graduate work, critical writing sample. Additional exam requirements/recommendations for international students: recommended—TOEFL (minimum score 550 paper-based; 79 iBT). *Application deadline:* For fall admission, 12/31 for domestic and international students. Application fee: $50 ($60 for international students). Electronic applications accepted. *Expenses: Tuition, area resident:* Full-time $10,780; part-time $440 per credit hour. Tuition, nonresident: full-time $30,250; part-time $1550 per credit hour. *Financial support:* In 2019–20, 113 students received support, including fellowships with full tuition reimbursements available (averaging $15,000 per year), research assistantships with full tuition reimbursements available (averaging $13,500 per year), teaching assistantships with full tuition reimbursements available (averaging $13,500 per year); career-related internships or fieldwork, scholarships/grants, health care benefits, and unspecified assistantships also available. Financial award application deadline: 12/31. *Unit head:* Dr. David Ainsworth, Associate Professor and Interim Chair, 205-348-9524, Fax: 205-348-1388, E-mail: dainsworth@ua.edu. *Application contact:* Jennifer Fuqua, Graduate Coordinator, 205-348-0766, Fax: 205-348-1388, E-mail: jfuqua@ua.edu.

The University of Alabama at Birmingham, College of Arts and Sciences, Program in English, Birmingham, AL 35294. Offers creative writing (MA); literature (MA); rhetoric and composition (MA). *Program availability:* Part-time. *Faculty:* 35 full-time (18 women). *Students:* 6 full-time (5 women), 21 part-time (16 women); includes 5 minority (3 Black or African American, non-Hispanic/Latino; 1 American Indian or Alaska Native, non-Hispanic/Latino; 1 Two or more races, non-Hispanic/Latino). Average age 32. 13 applicants, 69% accepted, 5 enrolled. In 2019, 11 master's awarded. *Degree requirements:* For master's, one foreign language, comprehensive exam, thesis or alternative. *Entrance requirements:* For master's, GRE General Test or MAT, minimum GPA of 2.75. *Application deadline:* For fall admission, 7/1 for domestic students; for spring admission, 11/1 for domestic students. Applications are processed on a rolling basis. Application fee: $45 ($60 for international students). Electronic applications accepted. *Financial support:* Teaching assistantships and career-related internships or fieldwork available. *Unit head:* Dr. Gale Temple, Program Director, 205-934-8593, Fax: 205-975-6610, E-mail: gtemple@uab.edu. *Application contact:* Susan Noblitt Banks, Director of Graduate School Operations, 205-934-8227, Fax: 205-934-8413, E-mail: gradschool@uab.edu.
Website: http://www.uab.edu/cas/english/academic-programs

The University of Arizona, College of Humanities, Department of English, Rhetoric, Composition and the Teaching of English Program, Tucson, AZ 85721. Offers MA, PhD. *Accreditation:* NASM. *Degree requirements:* For master's, one foreign language, comprehensive exam; for doctorate, one foreign language, comprehensive exam, thesis/dissertation. *Entrance requirements:* For doctorate, GRE General Test, 3 letters of recommendation, writing sample. Additional exam requirements/recommendations for international students: required—TOEFL (minimum score 550 paper-based; 79 iBT). Electronic applications accepted.

University of Arkansas at Little Rock, Graduate School, College of Social Sciences and Communication, Department of Rhetoric and Writing, Little Rock, AR 72204-1099. Offers professional and technical writing (MA). *Program availability:* Part-time, evening/weekend. *Degree requirements:* For master's, thesis or alternative, oral defense of final project. *Entrance requirements:* For master's, GRE, minimum GPA of 3.0, writing portfolio.

University of California, Berkeley, Graduate Division, College of Letters and Science, Department of Rhetoric, Berkeley, CA 94720. Offers PhD. *Degree requirements:* For doctorate, 2 foreign languages, thesis/dissertation, qualifying exam. *Entrance requirements:* For doctorate, GRE General Test, minimum GPA of 3.0, 3 letters of recommendation. Electronic applications accepted.

University of Central Oklahoma, The Jackson College of Graduate Studies, College of Liberal Arts, Department of English, Edmond, OK 73034-5209. Offers composition and rhetoric (MA); creative writing (MA); literature (MA); teaching English as a second language (MA). *Program availability:* Part-time. *Degree requirements:* For master's, variable foreign language requirement, comprehensive exam (for some programs), thesis (for some programs), portfolio. *Entrance requirements:* For master's, 18-24 hours of course work in English language and literature; writing sample; essay. Additional exam requirements/recommendations for international students: required—TOEFL (minimum score 550 paper-based; 79 iBT), IELTS (minimum score 6.5). Electronic applications accepted.

University of Dayton, Department of English, Dayton, OH 45469. Offers literary and cultural studies (MA); teaching English to speakers of other languages (TESOL) (MA); writing and rhetoric (MA). *Program availability:* Part-time. *Degree requirements:* For master's, thesis optional. *Entrance requirements:* For master's, 24 undergraduate-level semester hours in literature and/or writing; minimum GPA of 3.0; transcripts; personal statement; 8-10 page writing sample; three professional letters of recommendation. Additional exam requirements/recommendations for international students: required—TOEFL (minimum score 550 paper-based, 80 iBT) or IELTS. Electronic applications accepted.

The University of Findlay, Office of Graduate Admissions, Findlay, OH 45840. Offers applied security and analytics (MSAS); athletic training (MAT); business (MBA), including certified management accountant, certified public accountant, health care management, hospitality management; education (MA Ed, Ed D), including children's literature (MA Ed), curriculum and teaching (MA Ed), education (MA Ed), educational administration (MA Ed), human resource development (MA Ed), mathematics (MA Ed), reading (MA Ed), science education (MA Ed), superintendent (Ed D), teaching (Ed D), technology (MA Ed); environmental, safety, and health management (MSEM); health informatics (MS); occupational therapy (MOT); pharmacy (Pharm D); physical therapy (DPT); physician assistant (MPA); rhetoric and writing (MA); teaching English to speakers of other languages (TESOL) and applied linguistics (MA). *Program availability:* Part-time, evening/weekend, 100% online, blended/hybrid learning. *Students:* 688 full-time (430 women), 553 part-time (308 women), 170 international. Average age 28. 865 applicants, 31% accepted, 235 enrolled. In 2019, 363 master's, 141 doctorates awarded. *Degree requirements:* For master's, comprehensive exam (for some programs), thesis (for some programs), cumulative project, capstone project; for doctorate, thesis/dissertation (for some programs). *Entrance requirements:* For master's, GRE/GMAT, bachelor's degree from accredited institution, minimum undergraduate GPA of 2.5 in last 64 hours of course work; for doctorate, GRE, MAT, minimum cumulative GPA of 3.0. Additional exam requirements/recommendations for international students: required—TOEFL (minimum score 79 iBT), IELTS (minimum score 7), PTE (minimum score 61). *Application deadline:* Applications are processed on a rolling basis. Electronic applications accepted. *Financial support:* In 2019–20, 10 research assistantships with partial tuition reimbursements (averaging $7,200 per year), 35 teaching assistantships with partial tuition reimbursements (averaging $7,200 per year) were awarded; Federal Work-Study, institutionally sponsored loans, and unspecified assistantships also available. Financial award applicants required to submit FAFSA. *Unit head:* Dave M. Emsweller, Director of Admissions, Interim, 419-434-4578, E-mail: emsweller@findlay.edu. *Application contact:* Amber Feehan, Graduate Admissions Counselor, 419-434-6933, Fax: 419-434-4898, E-mail: feehan@findlay.edu.
Website: http://www.findlay.edu/admissions/graduate/Pages/default.aspx

University of Houston - Downtown, College of Humanities and Social Sciences, Department of English, Program in Rhetoric and Composition, Houston, TX 77002. Offers MA. *Program availability:* Part-time, evening/weekend. *Faculty:* 4 full-time (1 woman). *Students:* 2 full-time (both women), 10 part-time (6 women); includes 6 minority (3 Black or African American, non-Hispanic/Latino; 1 American Indian or Alaska Native, non-Hispanic/Latino; 1 Asian, non-Hispanic/Latino; 1 Two or more races, non-Hispanic/Latino). Average age 38. 6 applicants, 100% accepted, 4 enrolled. In 2019, 10 master's awarded. *Entrance requirements:* For master's, essay, resume, 2 letters of recommendation, transcripts, 10-15 page sample of academic writing. Additional exam requirements/recommendations for international students: required—TOEFL (minimum score 550 paper-based; 50 iBT). *Application deadline:* For fall admission, 8/9 for domestic students; for spring admission, 12/2 for domestic students; for summer admission, 5/17 for domestic students. Application fee: $35 ($80 for international students). Electronic applications accepted. *Expenses:* $386 in-state resident; $758 non-resident, per credit. *Financial support:* Federal Work-Study and scholarships/grants available. Financial award application deadline: 4/1; financial award applicants required to submit FAFSA. *Unit head:* Dr. Paul Kintzele, Department Chair, English, 713-221-8090, Fax: 713-226-5205, E-mail: kintzelep@uhd.edu. *Application contact:* Ceshia Love, Director of Admissions, 713-221-8093, Fax: 713-223-7408, E-mail: gradadmissions@uhd.edu.
Website: https://www.uhd.edu/academics/humanities/graduate-programs/masters-arts-rhetoric-composition/Pages/marc-index.aspx

The University of Iowa, Graduate College, College of Liberal Arts and Sciences, Department of Communication Studies, Iowa City, IA 52242-1316. Offers interpersonal communication and relationships (MA, PhD); media studies (MA, PhD); rhetoric and public advocacy (MA, PhD). *Degree requirements:* For master's, thesis optional, exam; for doctorate, comprehensive exam, thesis/dissertation. *Entrance requirements:* For master's and doctorate, GRE General Test, minimum GPA of 3.0. Additional exam requirements/recommendations for international students: required—TOEFL (minimum score 550 paper-based; 81 iBT). Electronic applications accepted.

University of Louisiana at Lafayette, College of Liberal Arts, Department of English, Lafayette, LA 70504. Offers American culture (MA, PhD), including history, sociology; American literature and language (PhD); creative writing (MA, PhD), including creative writing (MA), folklore (MA), rhetoric (MA); folklore (MA, PhD); linguistic studies (MA, PhD); professional writing (PhD); rhetoric (MA, PhD); TESOL studies (MA, PhD). *Program availability:* Part-time. Terminal master's awarded for partial completion of doctoral program. *Degree requirements:* For master's, one foreign language, thesis or alternative; for doctorate, 2 foreign languages, comprehensive exam, thesis/dissertation. *Entrance requirements:* For master's, GRE General Test, minimum GPA of 2.75; for doctorate, GRE General Test, minimum GPA of 3.0. Additional exam requirements/recommendations for international students: required—TOEFL (minimum score 550 paper-based). Electronic applications accepted. *Expenses: Tuition, area resident:* Full-time $5511; part-time $1630 per credit hour. Tuition, state resident: full-time $5511; part-time $1630 per credit hour. Tuition, nonresident: full-time $19,239; part-time $2409 per credit hour. *Required fees:* $46,637.

University of Louisville, Graduate School, College of Arts and Sciences, Department of English, Louisville, KY 40292. Offers English (MA), including creative writing, literature, rhetoric and composition (MA, PhD); rhetoric and composition (PhD), including rhetoric and composition (MA, PhD). *Program availability:* Part-time, evening/weekend. *Faculty:* 34 full-time (16 women), 29 part-time/adjunct (15 women). *Students:* 39 full-time (22 women), 19 part-time (12 women); includes 6 minority (3 Black or African American, non-Hispanic/Latino; 1 Hispanic/Latino; 2 Two or more races, non-Hispanic/Latino), 3 international. Average age 31. 42 applicants, 71% accepted, 20 enrolled. In 2019, 12 master's, 5 doctorates awarded. *Degree requirements:* For master's, one foreign language, thesis optional, culminating project of 25-30 pages; for doctorate, comprehensive exam, thesis/dissertation, Year long program; Student teacher program. *Entrance requirements:* For master's, GRE General Test, Two letters of reference, official transcripts; for doctorate, GRE General Test, Three letters of reference, official transcripts. Additional exam requirements/recommendations for international students: required—TOEFL (minimum score 550 paper-based; 79 iBT), IELTS can be used in place of the TOEFL; recommended—IELTS (minimum score 6.5). *Application deadline:* For fall admission, 7/15 priority date for domestic and international students; for spring admission, 12/1 priority date for domestic and international students; for summer admission, 5/15 priority date for domestic and international students. Applications are processed on a rolling basis. Application fee: $65. Electronic applications accepted. *Expenses:* Contact institution. *Financial support:* In 2019–20, 38 students received support, including 3 fellowships with full tuition reimbursements available (averaging $19,992 per year), 13 teaching assistantships with full tuition reimbursements available (averaging $19,992 per year); research assistantships, health care benefits, and unspecified assistantships also available. Financial award application deadline: 1/5. *Unit head:* Dr. Glynis Ridley, Chair, 502-852-6803, E-mail: glynis.ridley@louisville.edu. *Application contact:* Dr. Steven Matthew Biberman, Acting Director of Graduate Studies, 502-852-3052, E-mail: steven.biberman@louisville.edu. Website: http://www.louisville.edu/english

University of Massachusetts Amherst, Graduate School, College of Humanities and Fine Arts, Department of English, Amherst, MA 01003. Offers American studies (PhD); composition and rhetoric (PhD); creative writing (MFA); English and American literature (MA, PhD). *Program availability:* Part-time. Terminal master's awarded for partial completion of doctoral program. *Degree requirements:* For master's, one foreign language, thesis optional; for doctorate, one foreign language, comprehensive exam, thesis/dissertation. *Entrance requirements:* For master's, manuscript; for doctorate, GRE General Test, manuscript. Additional exam requirements/recommendations for international students: required—TOEFL (minimum score 550 paper-based; 80 iBT), IELTS (minimum score 6.5). Electronic applications accepted.

University of Michigan–Flint, College of Arts and Sciences, Program in English Language and Literature, Flint, MI 48502-1950. Offers literature (MA); writing and rhetoric (MA). *Program availability:* Part-time. *Faculty:* 25 full-time (16 women), 5 part-time/adjunct (4 women). *Students:* 11 full-time (6 women), 10 part-time (8 women); includes 2 minority (1 Black or African American, non-Hispanic/Latino; 1 Hispanic/Latino), 2 international. Average age 34. 14 applicants, 93% accepted, 2 enrolled. In 2019, 11 master's awarded. *Entrance requirements:* For master's, bachelor's degree with major or significant coursework in English or related fields from regionally-accredited institution; minimum overall undergraduate GPA of 3.0. Additional exam requirements/recommendations for international students: required—TOEFL (minimum score 84 iBT), IELTS (minimum score 6.5). *Application deadline:* For fall admission, 8/1 for domestic students, 5/1 for international students; for winter admission, 11/15 for domestic students, 10/1 for international students; for spring admission, 3/15 for domestic students, 1/1 for international students; for summer admission, 5/15 for domestic students. Applications are processed on a rolling basis. Application fee: $55. Electronic applications accepted. *Expenses:* Contact institution. *Financial support:* Career-related internships or fieldwork, Federal Work-Study, scholarships/grants, and unspecified assistantships available. Support available to part-time students. Financial award application deadline: 3/1; financial award applicants required to submit FAFSA. *Unit head:* Dr. James Schirmer, Department Chair, 810-762-3285, E-mail: jschirm@umich.edu. *Application contact:* Matt Bohlen, Associate Director of Graduate Programs, 810-762-3171, Fax: 810-766-6789, E-mail: mbohlen@umflint.edu. Website: http://www.umflint.edu/graduateprograms/english-language-and-literature-ma

University of Nebraska–Lincoln, Graduate College, College of Arts and Sciences, Department of Communication Studies, Lincoln, NE 68588. Offers instructional communication (MA, PhD); interpersonal communication (MA, PhD); marketing, communication studies, and advertising (MA, PhD); organizational communication (MA, PhD); rhetoric and culture (MA, PhD). *Degree requirements:* For master's, thesis optional; for doctorate, comprehensive exam, thesis/dissertation. *Entrance requirements:* For master's and doctorate, GRE General Test, writing sample. Additional exam requirements/recommendations for international students: required—TOEFL (minimum score 600 paper-based). Electronic applications accepted.

University of Nebraska–Lincoln, Graduate College, College of Arts and Sciences, Department of English, Lincoln, NE 68588-0333. Offers composition and rhetoric (MA, PhD); creative writing (MA, PhD); literature studies (MA, PhD). *Degree requirements:* For master's, thesis optional; for doctorate, one foreign language, comprehensive exam, thesis/dissertation. *Entrance requirements:* For master's, writing sample; for doctorate, GRE General Test, writing sample. Additional exam requirements/recommendations for international students: required—TOEFL (minimum score 600 paper-based). Electronic applications accepted.

University of North Alabama, College of Arts and Sciences, Department of English, Program in Writing, Florence, AL 35632-0001. Offers creative writing (MA); rhetoric and composition (MA); technical writing (MA). *Program availability:* Part-time, 100% online. *Degree requirements:* For master's, comprehensive exam (for some programs), thesis (for some programs). *Entrance requirements:* For master's, GRE, MAT, three letters of recommendation; writing sample. Additional exam requirements/recommendations for international students: required—TOEFL (minimum score 79 iBT), IELTS (minimum score 6), PTE (minimum score 54). Electronic applications accepted.

The University of North Carolina at Greensboro, Graduate School, College of Arts and Sciences, Department of English, Program in English, Greensboro, NC 27412-5001. Offers American literature (PhD); English (M Ed, MA); English literature (PhD); rhetoric and composition (PhD). *Degree requirements:* For master's, comprehensive exam, thesis or alternative; for doctorate, variable foreign language requirement, thesis/dissertation, preliminary exam. *Entrance requirements:* For master's, GRE General Test, GRE Subject Test, minimum GPA of 3.0; for doctorate, GRE General Test, GRE Subject Test, critical writing sample, minimum GPA of 3.0. Additional exam requirements/recommendations for international students: required—TOEFL. Electronic applications accepted.

University of Oklahoma, College of Arts and Sciences, Department of English, Norman, OK 73019. Offers literary and cultural studies (MA, PhD); writing and rhetoric studies (MA, PhD). *Program availability:* Part-time. *Degree requirements:* For master's, one foreign language, comprehensive exam (for some programs), thesis (for some programs), exam or thesis; for doctorate, one foreign language, comprehensive exam, thesis/dissertation. *Entrance requirements:* For master's, GRE, BA in English or related field; for doctorate, GRE, MA in English or related field. Additional exam requirements/recommendations for international students: required—TOEFL (minimum score 79 iBT) or IELTS (minimum score 6.5). Electronic applications accepted. *Expenses:* Tuition, state resident: full-time $6583.20; part-time $274.30 per credit hour. Tuition, nonresident: full-time $21,242; part-time $885.10 per credit hour. *International tuition:* $21,242.40 full-time. *Required fees:* $1994.20; $72.55 per credit hour. $126.50 per semester. Tuition and fees vary according to course load and degree level.

University of Southern California, Graduate School, Annenberg School for Communication and Journalism, School of Communication, Program in Communication, Los Angeles, CA 90089. Offers culture and community (PhD); global and transnational communication (PhD); groups, organizations and networks (PhD); health communication and social dynamics (PhD); information, political economy and entertainment (PhD); new media and technology (PhD); rhetoric, politics and public media (PhD). *Students:* 88 full-time (63 women); includes 28 minority (2 Black or African American, non-Hispanic/Latino; 6 Asian, non-Hispanic/Latino; 10 Hispanic/Latino; 10 Two or more races, non-Hispanic/Latino), 34 international. Average age 29. 161 applicants, 12% accepted, 14 enrolled. In 2019, 13 doctorates awarded. *Degree*

requirements: For doctorate, thesis/dissertation. *Entrance requirements:* For doctorate, GRE General Test, resume or curriculum vitae, scholarly writing, 3 letters of recommendation, statement of purpose. Additional exam requirements/recommendations for international students: required—TOEFL (minimum score 114 iBT), IELTS (minimum score 8); recommended—TWE. *Application deadline:* For fall admission, 12/1 for domestic and international students. Application fee: $90. Electronic applications accepted. *Financial support:* In 2019–20, 15 students received support, including 15 fellowships with full tuition reimbursements available (averaging $52,427 per year); research assistantships, teaching assistantships, Federal Work-Study, health care benefits, and unspecified assistantships also available. Financial award application deadline: 12/1. *Unit head:* Dr. Robeson Taj Frazier, Director of the PhD Program, 213-740-6595, E-mail: rfrazier@usc.edu. *Application contact:* Allyson Hill, Associate Dean for Admissions, 213-821-0770, Fax: 213-740-1933, E-mail: ascadm@usc.edu. Website: http://www.annenberg.usc.edu

The University of Tennessee at Chattanooga, Program in English, Chattanooga, TN 37403. Offers creative writing (MA); literary study (MA); rhetoric and writing (MA). *Program availability:* Part-time. *Faculty:* 51 full-time (27 women), 22 part-time/adjunct (17 women). *Students:* 15 full-time (9 women), 16 part-time (14 women); includes 4 minority (2 Black or African American, non-Hispanic/Latino; 1 Asian, non-Hispanic/Latino; 1 Native Hawaiian or other Pacific Islander, non-Hispanic/Latino). Average age 33. 15 applicants, 100% accepted, 10 enrolled. In 2019, 8 master's awarded. *Degree requirements:* For master's, comprehensive exam, thesis. *Entrance requirements:* For master's, minimum GPA of 3.0 in English, two letters of recommendation. Additional exam requirements/recommendations for international students: required—TOEFL (minimum score 550 paper-based; 79 iBT), IELTS (minimum score 6). *Application deadline:* For fall admission, 6/15 priority date for domestic students, 7/1 for international students; for spring admission, 11/1 priority date for domestic students, 11/1 for international students. Applications are processed on a rolling basis. Application fee: $35 ($40 for international students). Electronic applications accepted. *Financial support:* Research assistantships, teaching assistantships, career-related internships or fieldwork, scholarships/grants, health care benefits, and unspecified assistantships available. Support available to part-time students. Financial award application deadline: 7/1; financial award applicants required to submit FAFSA. *Unit head:* Dr. Andrew McCarthy, Department Head, 423-425-4615, Fax: 423-425-2282, E-mail: andrew-mccarthy@utc.edu. *Application contact:* Dr. Joanne Romagni, Dean of the Graduate School, 423-425-4478, Fax: 423-425-5223, E-mail: joanne-romagni@utc.edu. Website: http://www.utc.edu/english/

The University of Texas at El Paso, Graduate School, College of Liberal Arts, Department of English, El Paso, TX 79968-0001. Offers bilingual professional writing (Certificate); English and American literature (MA); rhetoric and composition (PhD); rhetoric and writing studies (MA); teaching English (MAT). *Program availability:* Part-time, evening/weekend. *Degree requirements:* For master's, thesis optional. *Entrance requirements:* For master's, GRE General Test, minimum GPA of 3.0. Additional exam requirements/recommendations for international students: required—TOEFL. Electronic applications accepted.

University of Utah, Graduate School, College of Humanities, Department of Communication, Salt Lake City, UT 84112. Offers communicating science, health, environment and risk (MA, MS, PhD); critical cultural studies (MA, MS, PhD); digital media (MA, MS, PhD); rhetoric (MA, MS, PhD). *Program availability:* Part-time, evening/weekend. *Faculty:* 29 full-time (15 women). *Students:* 33 full-time (24 women), 6 part-time (3 women); includes 12 minority (2 Black or African American, non-Hispanic/Latino; 4 Asian, non-Hispanic/Latino; 4 Hispanic/Latino; 1 Native Hawaiian or other Pacific Islander, non-Hispanic/Latino; 1 Two or more races, non-Hispanic/Latino), 3 international. Average age 30. 80 applicants, 19% accepted, 9 enrolled. In 2019, 4 master's, 10 doctorates awarded. Terminal master's awarded for partial completion of doctoral program. *Degree requirements:* For master's, variable foreign language requirement, comprehensive exam (for some programs), thesis (for some programs), Programme of Study; for doctorate, comprehensive exam, thesis/dissertation, Programme of Study; Prospectus. *Entrance requirements:* For master's and doctorate, GRE. Additional exam requirements/recommendations for international students: required—TOEFL (minimum score 80 paper-based), IELTS (minimum score 6.5). *Application deadline:* For fall admission, 12/15 for domestic students, 11/15 for international students. Application fee: $55 ($65 for international students). Electronic applications accepted. *Expenses:* Tuition, state resident: full-time $7085; part-time $272.51 per credit hour. Tuition, nonresident: full-time $24,937; part-time $959.12 per credit hour. *Required fees:* $880.52; $880.52 per semester. Tuition and fees vary according to degree level, program and student level. *Financial support:* In 2019–20, 30 students received support, including 2 fellowships with full tuition reimbursements available (averaging $18,500 per year), 3 research assistantships with tuition reimbursements available (averaging $19,667 per year), 28 teaching assistantships with tuition reimbursements available (averaging $19,929 per year). Financial award application deadline: 12/15. *Unit head:* Kevin Coe, Professor and Chair, 801-581-6888, E-mail: kevin.coe@utah.edu. *Application contact:* Travis Ciaramella, Graduate Advisor, 801-585-6337, E-mail: travis.ciaramella@utah.edu. Website: http://www.communication.utah.edu

University of Utah, Graduate School, College of Humanities, Department of English, Salt Lake City, UT 84112. Offers English (MA, MFA, PhD), including creative writing (MFA, PhD), literary and cultural studies (MA, PhD), rhetoric and composition (MA, PhD). *Faculty:* 17 full-time (9 women). *Students:* 51 full-time (28 women), 19 part-time (9 women); includes 11 minority (1 Black or African American, non-Hispanic/Latino; 4 Asian, non-Hispanic/Latino; 3 Hispanic/Latino; 3 Two or more races, non-Hispanic/Latino), 7 international. Average age 33. 248 applicants, 14% accepted, 18 enrolled. In 2019, 5 master's, 8 doctorates awarded. *Degree requirements:* For master's, one foreign language, thesis (for some programs), for MA - essay written & presented; for MFA - thesis; for doctorate, variable foreign language requirement, comprehensive exam, thesis/dissertation. *Entrance requirements:* For master's, exams required to be admitted, students applying to the MA or MFA degree programs must hold a BA or BS degree from an accredited College or University; a cumulative GPA of 3.3; TOEFL/IELTS scores for International applicants; for doctorate, students applying to the PhD degree programs must hold a BA or BS degree from an accredited College or University; successful completion of a previous Master's degree; a cumulative GPA of 3.3; TOEFL/IELTS scores for International applicants, NA. Additional exam requirements/recommendations for international students: required—TOEFL (minimum score 80 paper-based; 80 iBT), IELTS (minimum score 6.5). *Application deadline:* For fall admission, 12/15 for domestic and international students. Application fee: $55 ($65 for international students). Electronic applications accepted. *Expenses:* Tuition, state resident: full-time $7085; part-time $272.51 per credit hour. Tuition, nonresident: full-time $24,937; part-time $959.12 per credit hour. *Required fees:* $880.52; $880.52 per semester. Tuition and fees vary according to degree level, program and student level. *Financial support:* In 2019–20, 14 students received support, including 14 fellowships with full tuition reimbursements available (averaging $20,000 per year), 34 teaching assistantships with full tuition reimbursements available (averaging $18,000 per year); health care benefits and unspecified assistantships also available. Financial award application deadline: 4/15; financial award applicants required to submit FAFSA. *Unit*

head: Prof. Scott Black, Chair, Department of English, 801-581-3393, Fax: 801-585-5167, E-mail: scott.black@utah.edu. *Application contact:* Prof. Gerri Mackey, Graduate Academic Advisor, Department of English, 801-581-7850, Fax: 801-585-5167, E-mail: gerri.mackey@utah.edu.
Website: http://english.utah.edu/

University of Wisconsin–Madison, Graduate School, College of Letters and Science, Department of Communication Arts, Madison, WI 53706-1380. Offers communication science (MA, PhD); film (MA, PhD); media and cultural studies (MA, PhD); rhetoric (MA, PhD). Terminal master's awarded for partial completion of doctoral program. *Degree requirements:* For master's, one foreign language, thesis (for some programs); for doctorate, one foreign language, thesis/dissertation. *Entrance requirements:* For master's and doctorate, GRE General Test, minimum GPA of 3.5. Electronic applications accepted.

University of Wisconsin–Milwaukee, Graduate School, College of Letters and Science, Department of Communication, Milwaukee, WI 53201-0413. Offers communication (MA, PhD), including rhetorical leadership; rhetorical leadership (Graduate Certificate). *Program availability:* Part-time. *Degree requirements:* For master's, thesis or alternative; for doctorate, comprehensive exam. *Entrance requirements:* For master's, GRE General Test, minimum GPA of 3.0. Additional exam requirements/recommendations for international students: required—TOEFL (minimum score 550 paper-based; 79 iBT), IELTS (minimum score 6). Electronic applications accepted.

University of Wisconsin–Milwaukee, Graduate School, College of Letters and Science, Department of English, Milwaukee, WI 53201-0413. Offers English (MA, PhD), including creative writing, English language and linguistics, English secondary education, literary and critical studies, literature and cultural theory (PhD), literature and language studies, literature, culture, and media, media, cinema and digital studies, professional and technical communication (MA), professional and technical writing, professional writing (PhD), rhetoric and composition (PhD), rhetoric and writing. *Degree requirements:* For master's, thesis or alternative; for doctorate, one foreign language, thesis/dissertation. *Entrance requirements:* For master's, GRE General Test, GRE Subject Test; for doctorate, GRE. Additional exam requirements/recommendations for international students: required—TOEFL (minimum score 550 paper-based; 79 iBT), IELTS (minimum score 6.5). Electronic applications accepted.

Wayne State University, College of Liberal Arts and Sciences, Department of English, Detroit, MI 48202. Offers English (MA); film and media studies (PhD); literary and cultural studies (PhD); rhetoric and composition studies (PhD). *Faculty:* 27. *Students:* 59 full-time (36 women), 31 part-time (24 women); includes 17 minority (4 Black or African American, non-Hispanic/Latino; 4 Asian, non-Hispanic/Latino; 3 Hispanic/Latino; 6 Two or more races, non-Hispanic/Latino), 4 international. Average age 33. 87 applicants, 44% accepted, 17 enrolled. In 2019, 12 master's, 9 doctorates awarded. Terminal master's awarded for partial completion of doctoral program. *Degree requirements:* For master's, variable foreign language requirement, essay, thesis, or portfolio of work approved by Director of Graduate Studies; for doctorate, one foreign language, comprehensive exam, thesis/dissertation. *Entrance requirements:* For master's, statement of purpose; two academic letters of reference; sample essay from previous English course; for doctorate, statement of purpose; two academic letters of reference; sample of scholarly or critical writing. Additional exam requirements/recommendations for international students: required—TOEFL (minimum score 550 paper-based; 79 iBT), TWE (minimum score 5.5), Michigan English Language Assessment Battery (minimum score 85); recommended—IELTS (minimum score 6.5). *Application deadline:* For fall admission, 1/15 for domestic students. Applications are processed on a rolling basis. Application fee: $50. Electronic applications accepted. *Expenses: Tuition:* Full-time $34,567. *Financial support:* In 2019–20, 54 students received support, including 5 fellowships with tuition reimbursements available (averaging $21,500 per year), 1 research assistantship with tuition reimbursement available (averaging $19,967 per year), 28 teaching assistantships with tuition reimbursements available (averaging $19,967 per year); scholarships/grants, health care benefits, and unspecified assistantships also available. Financial award applicants required to submit FAFSA. *Unit head:* Dr. Caroline Maun, Chair and Associate Professor, 313-577-7692, E-mail: av4495@wayne.edu. *Application contact:* Dr. Richard Marback, Director of Graduate Studies, 313-577-7694, E-mail: aa4749@wayne.edu.
Website: http://clas.wayne.edu/english/

Western Carolina University, Graduate School, College of Arts and Sciences, Department of English, Cullowhee, NC 28723. Offers literature (MA); professional writing (MA); rhetoric and composition (MA); teaching English to speakers of other languages (Certificate); technical and professional writing (Certificate). *Program availability:* Part-time, evening/weekend. *Degree requirements:* For master's, one foreign language, comprehensive exam, thesis (for some programs). *Entrance requirements:* For master's, appropriate undergraduate degree, writing sample, 3 letters of recommendation. Additional exam requirements/recommendations for international students: required—TOEFL (minimum score 550 paper-based, 79 iBT) or IELTS (6.5). Electronic applications accepted. *Expenses:* Contact institution.

Speech and Interpersonal Communication

Ball State University, Graduate School, College of Communication, Information, and Media, Department of Communication Studies, Muncie, IN 47306. Offers communication studies (MA), including communication liberal arts and sciences, organization and professional communication and development. *Program availability:* Part-time. *Degree requirements:* For master's, comprehensive exam (for some programs), thesis (for some programs). *Entrance requirements:* For master's, GRE General Test, minimum baccalaureate GPA of 2.75 or 3.0 in latter half of baccalaureate, goal statement, writing sample, three letters of reference. Additional exam requirements/recommendations for international students: required—TOEFL (minimum score 550 paper-based; 79 iBT), IELTS (minimum score 6.5). Electronic applications accepted. *Expenses: Tuition, area resident:* Full-time $7506; part-time $417 per credit hour. Tuition, nonresident: full-time $20,610; part-time $1145 per credit hour. *Required fees:* $2126. Tuition and fees vary according to course load, campus/location and program.

Bob Jones University, Graduate Programs, Greenville, SC 29614. Offers accountancy (MS); Bible (MA); Bible translation (MA); Biblical studies (Certificate); business administration (MBA); church history (MA, PhD); church ministries (MA); church music (MM); cinema and video production (MA); counseling (MS); curriculum and instruction (Ed D); divinity (M Div); dramatic production (MA); educational leadership (MS, Ed D, Ed S); elementary education (M Ed, MAT); English (M Ed, MA, MAT); fine arts (MA); graphic design (MA); history (M Ed, MA); illustration (MA); interpretative speech (MA); mathematics (M Ed, MAT); medical missions (Certificate); ministry (MM, D Min); multi-categorical special education (M Ed, MAT); music (M Ed); New Testament interpretation (PhD); Old Testament interpretation (PhD); orchestral instrument performance (MM); organ performance (MM); pastoral studies (MA); personnel services (MS, Ed S); piano pedagogy (MM); piano performance (MM); platform arts (MA); rhetoric and public address (MA); secondary education (M Ed); studio art (MA); teaching Bible (MA); theology (MA, PhD); voice performance (MM); youth ministries (MA); M Div/MM.

Brooklyn College of the City University of New York, School of Humanities and Social Sciences, Department of Speech Communication Arts and Sciences, Brooklyn, NY 11210-2889. Offers audiology (Au D); speech (MA), including public communication; speech-language pathology (MS). *Accreditation:* ASHA (one or more programs are accredited). *Program availability:* Part-time. Terminal master's awarded for partial completion of doctoral program. *Degree requirements:* For master's, comprehensive exam, NTE. *Entrance requirements:* For master's, GRE, minimum GPA of 3.0, interview, essay. Additional exam requirements/recommendations for international students: required—TOEFL (minimum score 500 paper-based; 61 iBT). Electronic applications accepted.

California State University, Fullerton, Graduate Studies, College of Communications, Department of Human Communication Studies, Fullerton, CA 92831-3599. Offers communication studies (MA). *Program availability:* Part-time. *Degree requirements:* For master's, comprehensive exam, thesis or alternative. *Entrance requirements:* For master's, minimum GPA of 3.0 in major.

California State University, Northridge, Graduate Studies, Mike Curb College of Arts, Media, and Communication, Department of Communication Studies, Northridge, CA 91330. Offers MA. *Entrance requirements:* For master's, GRE General Test. Additional exam requirements/recommendations for international students: required—TOEFL.

Colorado State University, College of Liberal Arts, Department of Communication Studies, Fort Collins, CO 80523-1783. Offers communication (PhD); communication studies (MA), including deliberative practices. *Program availability:* Part-time. *Faculty:* 14 full-time (8 women). *Students:* 29 full-time (21 women), 9 part-time (8 women); includes 8 minority (1 Black or African American, non-Hispanic/Latino; 4 Hispanic/Latino; 3 Two or more races, non-Hispanic/Latino), 2 international. Average age 26. 73 applicants, 34% accepted, 13 enrolled. In 2019, 6 master's awarded. *Degree requirements:* For master's, thesis (for some programs); for doctorate, comprehensive exam, thesis/dissertation. *Entrance requirements:* For master's, GRE, minimum GPA of 3.0, writing sample, 3 letters of reference, statement of purpose, curriculum vitae or resume, transcripts; for doctorate, GRE, minimum GPA of 3.0, writing sample, 3 letters of reference, statement of purpose, transcripts, curriculum vitae or resume. Additional exam requirements/recommendations for international students: required—TOEFL (minimum score 550 paper-based; 80 iBT), IELTS (minimum score 6.5), PTE (minimum score 58). *Application deadline:* For fall admission, 1/5 priority date for domestic and international students; for spring admission, 12/31 for domestic and international students. Electronic applications accepted. *Expenses:* Tuition, state resident: full-time $10,520; part-time $5844 per credit hour. Tuition, nonresident: full-time $25,791; part-time $14,328 per credit hour. *International tuition:* $25,791 full-time. *Required fees:* $2512.80. Part-time tuition and fees vary according to course level, course load, degree level, program and student level. *Financial support:* In 2019–20, 2 students received support, including 30 teaching assistantships with full tuition reimbursements available (averaging $17,012 per year); fellowships with full tuition reimbursements available, research assistantships with full tuition reimbursements available, scholarships/grants, health care benefits, and unspecified assistantships also available. Financial award application deadline: 12/31. *Unit head:* Dr. Greg Dickinson, Department Chair, 970-491-6140, E-mail: greg.dickinson@colostate.edu. *Application contact:* Carly Hennegan, Graduate Studies Support Coordinator, 970-491-4123, E-mail: carly.hennegan@colostate.edu.
Website: http://communicationstudies.colostate.edu/

Georgia State University, College of Arts and Sciences, Department of Communication, Atlanta, GA 30302-3083. Offers film, video, and digital imaging (MA), including critical studies, production, screenwriting; human communication and social influence (MA); mass communication (MA); media and society (PhD); moving image studies (PhD); public communication (PhD); rhetoric and politics (PhD). *Program availability:* Part-time. *Faculty:* 22 full-time (16 women), 1 part-time/adjunct (0 women). *Students:* 67 full-time (46 women), 26 part-time (17 women); includes 44 minority (40 Black or African American, non-Hispanic/Latino; 1 Asian, non-Hispanic/Latino; 1 Hispanic/Latino; 1 Native Hawaiian or other Pacific Islander, non-Hispanic/Latino; 1 Two or more races, non-Hispanic/Latino), 12 international. Average age 36. 82 applicants, 49% accepted, 22 enrolled. In 2019, 9 master's, 5 doctorates awarded. *Degree requirements:* For master's, variable foreign language requirement, thesis (for some programs); for doctorate, comprehensive exam, thesis/dissertation. *Entrance requirements:* For master's and doctorate, GRE. Additional exam requirements/recommendations for international students: required—TOEFL (minimum score 550 paper-based; 80 iBT), IELTS (minimum score 6.5). *Application deadline:* For fall admission, 2/10 for domestic and international students; for spring admission, 10/15 for domestic and international students. Application fee: $50. Electronic applications accepted. *Expenses: Tuition, area resident:* Full-time $7164; part-time $398 per credit hour. Tuition, state resident: full-time $7164; part-time $398 per credit hour. Tuition, nonresident: full-time $22,662; part-time $1259 per credit hour. *International tuition:* $22,662 full-time. *Required fees:* $2128; $312 per credit hour. Tuition and fees vary according to course load and program. *Financial support:* In 2019–20, fellowships with tuition reimbursements (averaging $15,000 per year), teaching assistantships with tuition reimbursements (averaging $15,000 per year) were awarded; career-related internships or fieldwork and unspecified assistantships also available. Financial award applicants required to submit FAFSA. *Unit head:* Dr. Greg Lisby, Chair, 404-413-5639, Fax: 404-413-5634, E-mail: glisby@gsu.edu. *Application contact:* Dr. Greg Lisby, Chair, 404-413-5639, Fax: 404-413-5634, E-mail: glisby@gsu.edu.
Website: http://communication.gsu.edu

Marquette University, Graduate School, College of Communication, Milwaukee, WI 53201-1881. Offers advertising and public relations (MA); communication studies (MA); digital storytelling (Certificate); journalism (MA); mass communication (MA); science, health and environmental communication (MA). *Accreditation:* ACEJMC (one or more programs are accredited). *Program availability:* Part-time, evening/weekend. *Degree* *requirements:* For master's, comprehensive exam, thesis or alternative. *Entrance requirements:* For master's, GRE, official transcripts from all current and previous colleges/universities except Marquette, three letters of recommendation, statement of academic and professional goals. Additional exam requirements/recommendations for international students: required—TOEFL (minimum score 530 paper-based). Electronic applications accepted.

New York University, Steinhardt School of Culture, Education, and Human Development, Department of Media, Culture and Communication, New York, NY 10012. Offers media, culture and communication (MA, PhD); MLIS/MA. *Program availability:* Part-time. Terminal master's awarded for partial completion of doctoral program. *Entrance requirements:* For master's, GRE General Test; for doctorate, GRE General Test, interview. Additional exam requirements/recommendations for international students: required—TOEFL (minimum score 100 iBT). Electronic applications accepted.

North Dakota State University, College of Graduate and Interdisciplinary Studies, College of Arts, Humanities and Social Sciences, Department of Communication, Fargo, ND 58102. Offers communication (PhD); mass communication (MA); speech communication (MS). *Program availability:* Part-time, online learning. Terminal master's awarded for partial completion of doctoral program. *Degree requirements:* For master's, thesis (for some programs); for doctorate, comprehensive exam, thesis/dissertation, 2-3 publications. *Entrance requirements:* For master's, GRE, minimum undergraduate GPA of 3.25; for doctorate, GRE, minimum undergraduate GPA of 3.5. Additional exam requirements/recommendations for international students: required—TOEFL (minimum score 600 paper-based; 100 iBT), IELTS (minimum score 7). Electronic applications accepted. Tuition and fees vary according to program and reciprocity agreements.

Northeastern Illinois University, College of Graduate Studies and Research, College of Arts and Sciences, Program in Communication, Media and Theatre, Chicago, IL 60625. Offers MA. *Program availability:* Part-time, evening/weekend. *Degree requirements:* For master's, comprehensive exam, oral exams, thesis or 3 term papers. *Entrance requirements:* For master's, 15 undergraduate hours in speech and performing arts, minimum GPA of 2.75. Additional exam requirements/recommendations for international students: required—TOEFL (minimum score 550 paper-based; 79 iBT). Electronic applications accepted.

Northwestern University, The Graduate School, School of Communication, Department of Performance Studies, Evanston, IL 60208. Offers MA, PhD. *Program availability:* Part-time. Terminal master's awarded for partial completion of doctoral program. *Degree requirements:* For master's, recital; for doctorate, one foreign language, thesis/dissertation, recital. *Entrance requirements:* For master's and doctorate, GRE General Test. Additional exam requirements/recommendations for international students: required—TOEFL.

Ohio University, Graduate College, Scripps College of Communication, School of Communication Studies, Athens, OH 45701-2979. Offers health communication (PhD); organizational communication (MA); relating and organizing (PhD); rhetoric and public culture (PhD). *Program availability:* Part-time, online learning. Terminal master's awarded for partial completion of doctoral program. *Degree requirements:* For master's, capstone; for doctorate, comprehensive exam, thesis/dissertation. *Entrance requirements:* For master's, GRE; for doctorate, GRE General Test, minimum GPA of 3.0. Additional exam requirements/recommendations for international students: required—TOEFL (minimum score 550 paper-based; 80 iBT) or IELTS (minimum score 6.5). Electronic applications accepted.

Old Dominion University, College of Arts and Letters, Program in Lifespan and Digital Communication, Norfolk, VA 23529. Offers MA. *Accreditation:* NASAD. *Program availability:* Part-time, evening/weekend. *Degree requirements:* For master's, thesis or capstone project. *Entrance requirements:* For master's, GRE. Additional exam requirements/recommendations for international students: required—TOEFL (minimum score 550 paper-based; 79 iBT). Electronic applications accepted. *Expenses:* Contact institution.

Portland State University, Graduate Studies, College of Liberal Arts and Sciences, Department of Communication, Portland, OR 97207-0751. Offers general speech communication (MA, MS, Certificate). *Program availability:* Part-time. *Faculty:* 7 full-time (4 women). *Students:* 12 full-time (7 women), 3 part-time (2 women); includes 3 minority (all Hispanic/Latino). Average age 32. 22 applicants, 59% accepted, 8 enrolled. In 2019, 8 master's awarded. *Degree requirements:* For master's, variable foreign language requirement, comprehensive exam (for some programs), thesis optional. *Entrance requirements:* For master's, GRE (for students who select the thesis option and/or who receive an assistantship), minimum GPA of 3.0 in upper-division course work or 2.75 overall, 3 letters of recommendation, statement of purpose, writing samples. Additional exam requirements/recommendations for international students: required—TOEFL (minimum score 600 paper-based; 100 iBT). *Application deadline:* For fall admission, 5/31 priority date for domestic and international students. Application fee: $65. Electronic applications accepted. *Expenses:* $429 per credit hour resident, $645 per credit hour non-resident. *Financial support:* In 2019–20, 9 teaching assistantships with full and partial tuition reimbursements (averaging $10,200 per year) were awarded; research assistantships, career-related internships or fieldwork, Federal Work-Study, and scholarships/grants also available. Support available to part-time students. Financial award application deadline: 3/1; financial award applicants required to submit FAFSA. *Unit head:* Dr. Jeffrey Robinson, Chair, 503-725-3599, Fax: 503-725-3599, E-mail: jeffreyr@pdx.edu. *Application contact:* Bailey Acord-Becker, Department Coordinator, 503-725-5378, E-mail: commgradinfo@pdx.edu.
Website: http://www.pdx.edu/communication/

Rensselaer Polytechnic Institute, Graduate School, School of Humanities, Arts, and Social Sciences, Program in Communication and Rhetoric, Troy, NY 12180-3590. Offers MS, PhD. *Faculty:* 9 full-time (6 women). *Students:* 10 full-time (7 women), 1 (woman) part-time. Average age 33. 10 applicants, 30% accepted, 2 enrolled. In 2019, 4 doctorates awarded. Terminal master's awarded for partial completion of doctoral program. *Degree requirements:* For master's, thesis optional; for doctorate, comprehensive exam, thesis/dissertation. *Entrance requirements:* For master's and doctorate, GRE, writing sample. Additional exam requirements/recommendations for international students: required—TOEFL (minimum score 570 paper-based; 88 iBT), IELTS (minimum score 6.5), PTE (minimum score 60). *Application deadline:* For fall admission, 1/1 priority date for domestic and international students; for spring admission, 8/15 priority date for domestic and international students. Applications are processed on a rolling basis. Application fee: $75. Electronic applications accepted. *Financial support:* In 2019–20, research assistantships with full tuition reimbursements (averaging $23,000 per year), teaching assistantships with full tuition reimbursements (averaging $23,000 per year) were awarded; fellowships also available. Financial award application deadline: 1/1. *Unit head:* Dr. Tamar Gordon, Graduate Program Director, 518-276-6933, E-mail: gordot@rpi.edu. *Application contact:* Jarron Decker, Director of Graduate Admissions, 518-276-6216, Fax: 518-276-4072, E-mail: gradadmissions@rpi.edu.
Website: http://www.cm.rpi.edu/pl/graduate

San Francisco State University, Division of Graduate Studies, College of Liberal and Creative Arts, Department of Communication Studies, San Francisco, CA 94132-1722. Offers MA. *Program availability:* Part-time. *Application deadline:* Applications are processed on a rolling basis. *Expenses: Tuition, area resident:* Full-time $7176; part-time $4164 per year. Tuition, state resident: full-time $7176; part-time $4164 per year. Tuition, nonresident: full-time $16,680; part-time $396 per unit. *International tuition:* $16,680 full-time. *Required fees:* $1524; $1524 per unit. $762 per semester. Tuition and fees vary according to degree level and program. *Financial support:* Teaching assistantships available. *Unit head:* Prof. Amy Kilgard, Chair, 415-338-1597, Fax: 415-338-6159, E-mail: akilgard@sfsu.edu. *Application contact:* Dr. Fatima Alaoui, Graduate Coordinator, 415-338-1597, Fax: 415-338-6159, E-mail: fzalaoui@sfsu.edu.
Website: http://communicationstudies.sfsu.edu/

San Jose State University, Program in History, San Jose, CA 95192-0117. Offers history (MA); history education (MA). *Program availability:* Part-time, evening/weekend. *Faculty:* 8 full-time (6 women), 2 part-time/adjunct (both women). *Students:* 7 full-time (2 women), 32 part-time (12 women); includes 17 minority (6 Asian, non-Hispanic/Latino; 11 Hispanic/Latino). Average age 36. 15 applicants, 87% accepted, 9 enrolled. In 2019, 12 master's awarded. *Degree requirements:* For master's, variable foreign language requirement, comprehensive exam, thesis optional. *Entrance requirements:* For master's, undergraduate degree and transcripts, statement of purpose, writing sample, 2 letters of recommendation. Additional exam requirements/recommendations for international students: recommended—TOEFL. *Application deadline:* For fall admission, 4/1 for domestic and international students; for spring admission, 11/1 for domestic and international students. Applications are processed on a rolling basis. Application fee: $70. Electronic applications accepted. *Expenses: Tuition, area resident:* Full-time $7176; part-time $4164 per credit hour. Tuition, state resident: full-time $7176; part-time $4164 per credit hour. Tuition, nonresident: full-time $7176; part-time $4165 per credit hour. *International tuition:* $7176 full-time. *Required fees:* $2110; $2110. *Financial support:* In 2019–20, 9 students received support. Scholarships/grants and Instructional Student Assistants available. Financial award application deadline: 5/1; financial award applicants required to submit FAFSA. *Unit head:* Glen Gendzel, Department Chair, 408-924-5514, Fax: 408-924-5531, E-mail: glen.gendzel@sjsu.edu. *Application contact:* Libra Hilde, Graduate Advisor, 408-924-5512, Fax: 408-9244-5531, E-mail: libra.hilde@sjsu.edu.
Website: http://www.sjsu.edu/depts/history/

Seton Hall University, School of Health and Medical Sciences, Program in Speech-Language Pathology, South Orange, NJ 07079-2697. Offers MS. *Accreditation:* ASHA. *Entrance requirements:* For master's, GRE, bachelor's degree, clinical experience; minimum GPA of 3.0, undergraduate preprofessional coursework in communication sciences and disorders. Additional exam requirements/recommendations for international students: recommended—TOEFL. Electronic applications accepted.

Southern Illinois University Carbondale, Graduate School, College of Liberal Arts, Department of Communication Studies, Carbondale, IL 62901-4701. Offers MA, MS, PhD. *Degree requirements:* For master's, one foreign language, thesis or alternative; for doctorate, one foreign language, thesis/dissertation. *Entrance requirements:* For master's, GRE General Test or MAT, minimum GPA of 2.7; for doctorate, GRE General Test or MAT, minimum GPA of 3.25. Additional exam requirements/recommendations for international students: required—TOEFL (minimum score 100 iBT).

Southern Illinois University Edwardsville, Graduate School, College of Arts and Sciences, Department of Applied Communication Studies, Program in Interpersonal Communication, Edwardsville, IL 62026. Offers MA. *Program availability:* Part-time, evening/weekend. *Degree requirements:* For master's, comprehensive exam (for some programs), thesis (for some programs). *Entrance requirements:* Additional exam requirements/recommendations for international students: required—TOEFL (minimum score 550 paper-based, 79 iBT), IELTS (minimum score 6.5), Michigan Test of English Language Proficiency or PTE. Electronic applications accepted.

Texas Christian University, Bob Schieffer College of Communication, Department of Communication Studies, Fort Worth, TX 76129. Offers MS. *Program availability:* Part-time. *Faculty:* 13 full-time (6 women). *Students:* 15 full-time (13 women); includes 2 minority (1 Black or African American, non-Hispanic/Latino; 1 Native Hawaiian or other Pacific Islander, non-Hispanic/Latino). Average age 24. 17 applicants, 76% accepted, 8 enrolled. In 2019, 5 master's awarded. *Degree requirements:* For master's, comprehensive exams or thesis. *Entrance requirements:* For master's, GRE General Test. Additional exam requirements/recommendations for international students: required—TOEFL (minimum score 550 paper-based; 80 iBT). *Application deadline:* For fall and spring admission, 2/15 for domestic and international students. Application fee: $60. Electronic applications accepted. Full-time tuition and fees vary according to program. *Financial support:* In 2019–20, 11 students received support, including 11 teaching assistantships with full tuition reimbursements available (averaging $12,500 per year); tuition waivers (full) also available. Financial award application deadline: 2/15. *Unit head:* Dr. Melissa Schroeder, Associate Professor/Chair, 817-257-7784, Fax: 817-257-6580, E-mail: m.y.schroeder@tcu.edu. *Application contact:* Dr. Paul Schrodt, Professor and Graduate Director, 817-257-5674, Fax: 817-257-6580, E-mail: p.schrodt@tcu.edu.
Website: http://www.commstudies.tcu.edu

The University of Alabama, Graduate School, College of Communication and Information Sciences, Department of Communication Studies, Tuscaloosa, AL 35487. Offers MA. *Program availability:* Part-time, 100% online, blended/hybrid learning. *Faculty:* 17 full-time (9 women). *Students:* 27 full-time (16 women), 52 part-time (37 women); includes 18 minority (14 Black or African American, non-Hispanic/Latino; 3 Hispanic/Latino; 1 Two or more races, non-Hispanic/Latino), 2 international. Average age 31. 52 applicants, 77% accepted, 23 enrolled. In 2019, 24 master's awarded. *Degree requirements:* For master's, comprehensive exam (for some programs), thesis (for some programs), capstone portfolio (for some programs), colloquium presentation. *Entrance requirements:* For master's, GRE, MAT, minimum GPA of 3.0. Additional exam requirements/recommendations for international students: required—TOEFL (minimum score 550 paper-based). *Application deadline:* For fall admission, 5/1 for domestic students, 4/1 for international students; for spring admission, 11/1 for domestic students, 10/1 for international students; for summer admission, 5/1 for domestic students, 3/1 for international students. Applications are processed on a rolling basis. Application fee: $50 ($60 for international students). Electronic applications accepted. *Expenses: Tuition, area resident:* Full-time $10,780; part-time $440 per credit hour. Tuition, nonresident: full-time $30,250; part-time $1550 per credit hour. *Financial support:* In 2019–20, 9 students received support, including teaching assistantships with full tuition reimbursements available (averaging $18,300 per year); fellowships with full tuition reimbursements available, health care benefits, unspecified assistantships, and teaching stipends (averaging $3000 per semester) also available. Financial award application deadline: 3/1. *Unit head:* Dr. Beth S. Bennett, Department Chair, 205-348-8073, E-mail: bbennett@ua.edu. *Application contact:* Dr. Josh R. Pederson, Coordinator of Recruitment, 205-348-0501, E-mail: jrpederson@ua.edu.
Website: http://www.comstudies.ua.edu/

University of Arkansas at Little Rock, Graduate School, College of Social Sciences and Communication, Department of Speech Communication, Little Rock, AR 72204-1099. Offers applied communication studies (MA). *Program availability:* Part-time, evening/weekend. *Degree requirements:* For master's, comprehensive exam, internship, paper, or thesis. *Entrance requirements:* For master's, GRE General Test, MAT, minimum GPA of 2.7.

University of California, Santa Barbara, Graduate Division, College of Letters and Sciences, Division of Social Sciences, Department of Sociology, Santa Barbara, CA 93106-9430. Offers interdisciplinary emphasis: Black studies (PhD); interdisciplinary emphasis: environment and society (PhD); interdisciplinary emphasis: feminist studies (PhD); interdisciplinary emphasis: global studies (PhD); interdisciplinary emphasis: language, interaction and social organization (PhD); interdisciplinary emphasis: quantitative methods in the social sciences (PhD); interdisciplinary emphasis: technology and society (PhD); sociology (PhD); MA/PhD. Terminal master's awarded for partial completion of doctoral program. *Degree requirements:* For doctorate, comprehensive exam, thesis/dissertation. *Entrance requirements:* For doctorate, GRE General Test. Additional exam requirements/recommendations for international students: required—TOEFL (minimum score 550 paper-based; 80 iBT), IELTS (minimum score 7). Electronic applications accepted.

University of Hawaii at Manoa, Office of Graduate Education, College of Arts and Humanities, Department of Communicology, Honolulu, HI 96822. Offers MA. *Program availability:* Part-time. *Degree requirements:* For master's, thesis optional. *Entrance requirements:* For master's, GRE General Test. Additional exam requirements/recommendations for international students: required—TOEFL (minimum score 600 paper-based; 100 iBT), IELTS (minimum score 7).

University of Houston, College of Liberal Arts and Social Sciences, Jack J. Valenti School of Communication, Houston, TX 77204. Offers health communication (MA); mass communication studies (MA); public relations studies (MA); speech communication (MA). *Program availability:* Part-time. *Degree requirements:* For master's, comprehensive exam (for some programs), thesis (for some programs), 30-33 hours. *Entrance requirements:* For master's, GRE. Additional exam requirements/recommendations for international students: required—TOEFL. Electronic applications accepted.

The University of Iowa, Graduate College, College of Liberal Arts and Sciences, Department of Communication Studies, Iowa City, IA 52242-1316. Offers interpersonal communication and relationships (MA, PhD); media studies (MA, PhD); rhetoric and public advocacy (MA, PhD). *Degree requirements:* For master's, thesis optional, exam; for doctorate, comprehensive exam, thesis/dissertation. *Entrance requirements:* For master's and doctorate, GRE General Test, minimum GPA of 3.0. Additional exam requirements/recommendations for international students: required—TOEFL (minimum score 550 paper-based; 81 iBT). Electronic applications accepted.

University of Maryland, College Park, Academic Affairs, College of Behavioral and Social Sciences, Department of Hearing and Speech Sciences, College Park, MD 20742. Offers audiology (MA, PhD); hearing and speech sciences (Au D); language pathology (MA, PhD); neuroscience (PhD); speech (MA, PhD). *Accreditation:* ASHA (one or more programs are accredited). *Degree requirements:* For master's, thesis optional; for doctorate, thesis/dissertation, written and oral exams. *Entrance requirements:* For master's, GRE General Test, minimum GPA of 3.5, 3 letters of recommendation; for doctorate, GRE General Test, minimum GPA of 3.5. Additional exam requirements/recommendations for international students: required—TOEFL. Electronic applications accepted.

University of Nebraska–Lincoln, Graduate College, College of Arts and Sciences, Department of Communication Studies, Lincoln, NE 68588. Offers instructional communication (MA, PhD); interpersonal communication (MA, PhD); marketing, communication studies, and advertising (MA, PhD); organizational communication (MA, PhD); rhetoric and culture (MA, PhD). *Degree requirements:* For master's, thesis optional; for doctorate, comprehensive exam, thesis/dissertation. *Entrance requirements:* For master's and doctorate, GRE General Test, writing sample. Additional exam requirements/recommendations for international students: required—TOEFL (minimum score 600 paper-based). Electronic applications accepted.

University of Nevada, Reno, Graduate School, College of Liberal Arts, Department of Communication Studies, Reno, NV 89557. Offers MA. *Degree requirements:* For master's, thesis optional. *Entrance requirements:* For master's, GRE General Test, minimum GPA of 2.75. Additional exam requirements/recommendations for international

students: required—TOEFL (minimum score 500 paper-based; 61 iBT), IELTS (minimum score 6). Electronic applications accepted.

University of South Carolina, The Graduate School, College of Education, Department of Instruction and Teacher Education, Program in Secondary Education, Columbia, SC 29208. Offers art education (IMA, MAT); business education (IMA, MAT); English (MAT); foreign language (MAT); health education (MAT); mathematics (MAT); science (IMA, MAT); secondary (Ed D); secondary education (MT, PhD); social studies (MAT); theatre and speech (MAT). *Accreditation:* NCATE. *Degree requirements:* For master's, comprehensive exam, thesis (for some programs), foreign language (MA); for doctorate, one foreign language, comprehensive exam, thesis/dissertation. *Entrance requirements:* For master's, GRE General Test or MAT, teaching certificate (IMA, M Ed), interview; for doctorate, GRE General Test or MAT, interview.

University of Wisconsin–Madison, Graduate School, College of Letters and Science, Department of Communication Sciences and Disorders, Madison, WI 53706-1380. Offers audiology (Au D); normal aspects of speech, language and hearing (MS, PhD); speech-language pathology (MS, PhD); MS/PhD. *Accreditation:* ASHA (one or more programs are accredited). *Degree requirements:* For doctorate, thesis/dissertation. *Entrance requirements:* For master's and doctorate, GRE. Electronic applications accepted.

University of Wisconsin–Stevens Point, College of Fine Arts and Communication, Division of Communication, Stevens Point, WI 54481-3897. Offers interpersonal communication (MA); media studies (MA); organizational communication (MA); public relations (MA). *Program availability:* Part-time. *Degree requirements:* For master's, thesis or alternative. *Entrance requirements:* For master's, GRE. Additional exam requirements/recommendations for international students: required—TOEFL (minimum score 575 paper-based).

University of Wisconsin–Superior, Graduate Division, Department of Communicating Arts, Superior, WI 54880-4500. Offers mass communication (MA); speech communication (MA); theater (MA). *Program availability:* Part-time. *Degree requirements:* For master's, comprehensive exam, thesis or alternative, position paper or project. *Entrance requirements:* For master's, minimum GPA of 2.75. Electronic applications accepted.

Wake Forest University, Graduate School of Arts and Sciences, Department of Communication, Winston-Salem, NC 27109. Offers speech communication (MA). *Program availability:* Part-time. *Degree requirements:* For master's, one foreign language, thesis. *Entrance requirements:* For master's, GRE General Test, writing sample. Additional exam requirements/recommendations for international students: required—TOEFL (minimum score 79 iBT). Electronic applications accepted.

Washington University in St. Louis, School of Medicine, Program in Audiology and Communication Sciences, St. Louis, MO 63110. Offers audiology (Au D); deaf education (MS); speech and hearing sciences (PhD). *Accreditation:* ASHA (one or more programs are accredited). *Faculty:* 22 full-time (12 women), 18 part-time/adjunct (12 women). *Students:* 80 full-time (78 women). Average age 23. 117 applicants, 33% accepted, 27 enrolled. In 2019, 7 master's, 15 doctorates awarded. *Degree requirements:* For master's, comprehensive exam, thesis, independent study project, oral exam; for doctorate, comprehensive exam, thesis/dissertation, capstone project. *Entrance requirements:* For master's and doctorate, GRE General Test, minimum B average in previous college/university coursework (recommended). Additional exam requirements/recommendations for international students: required—TOEFL (minimum score 100 iBT). *Application deadline:* For fall admission, 2/15 for domestic and international students. Application fee: $25. Electronic applications accepted. *Expenses:* $40,300 per year. *Financial support:* In 2019–20, 80 students received support, including 80 fellowships with full and partial tuition reimbursements available (averaging $19,000 per year), 6 teaching assistantships with partial tuition reimbursements available (averaging $2,000 per year); Federal Work-Study, scholarships/grants, traineeships, health care benefits, tuition waivers (partial), and unspecified assistantships also available. Financial award application deadline: 2/15; financial award applicants required to submit FAFSA. *Unit head:* Dr. William W. Clark, Program Director, 314-747-0104, Fax: 314-747-0105, E-mail: pacs@wustl.edu. *Application contact:* Beth Elliott, Director, Finance and Student/Academic Affairs, 314-747-0104, Fax: 314-747-0105, E-mail: elliottb@wustl.edu.
Website: http://pacs.wustl.edu/

Technical Communication

Auburn University, Graduate School, College of Liberal Arts, Department of English, Auburn, AL 36849. Offers MA, MTPC, PhD, Graduate Certificate. *Program availability:* Part-time. *Faculty:* 71 full-time (40 women), 7 part-time/adjunct (2 women). *Students:* 22 full-time (13 women), 33 part-time (22 women); includes 9 minority (2 Black or African American, non-Hispanic/Latino; 4 Asian, non-Hispanic/Latino; 1 Hispanic/Latino; 2 Two or more races, non-Hispanic/Latino), 3 international. Average age 32. 53 applicants, 60% accepted, 15 enrolled. In 2019, 16 master's, 2 doctorates, 1 other advanced degree awarded. *Degree requirements:* For master's, one foreign language, thesis optional, written exam; for doctorate, 2 foreign languages, thesis/dissertation, oral and written exams. *Entrance requirements:* For master's, GRE General Test, sample of written work; for doctorate, GRE General Test, GRE Subject Test, sample of written work. Additional exam requirements/recommendations for international students: recommended—TOEFL (minimum score 550 paper-based; 79 iBT), IELTS (minimum score 6.5). *Application deadline:* Applications are processed on a rolling basis. Application fee: $60 ($70 for international students). Electronic applications accepted. *Expenses: Tuition, area resident:* Full-time $9828; part-time $546 per credit hour. Tuition, state resident: full-time $9828; part-time $546 per credit hour. Tuition, nonresident: full-time $29,484; part-time $1638 per credit hour. *International tuition:* $29,744 full-time. Tuition and fees vary according to course load, program and reciprocity agreements. *Financial support:* In 2019–20, 34 fellowships with tuition reimbursements, 1 research assistantship (averaging $21,333 per year), 44 teaching assistantships with tuition reimbursements (averaging $22,830 per year) were awarded; Federal Work-Study also available. Support available to part-time students. Financial award application deadline: 3/15; financial award applicants required to submit FAFSA. *Unit head:* Dr. Jeremy M. Downes, Chair, 334-844-9079. *Application contact:* Dr. George Flowers, Dean of the Graduate School, 334-844-2125.
Website: https://cla.auburn.edu/english/

Boise State University, College of Arts and Sciences, Department of English, Boise, ID 83725-0399. Offers English literature (MA); English, rhetoric and composition (MA); teaching English language (MA); technical communication (MA). *Program availability:*

Part-time. *Students:* 21 full-time (13 women), 29 part-time (17 women); includes 7 minority (3 Black or African American, non-Hispanic/Latino; 1 Asian, non-Hispanic/Latino; 1 Hispanic/Latino; 1 Native Hawaiian or other Pacific Islander, non-Hispanic/Latino; 1 Two or more races, non-Hispanic/Latino), 1 international. *Degree requirements:* For master's, thesis (for some programs). *Entrance requirements:* For master's, GRE General Test, minimum GPA of 3.0. Additional exam requirements/recommendations for international students: required—TOEFL, IELTS. Electronic applications accepted. *Expenses: Tuition, area resident:* Full-time $7110; part-time $470 per credit hour. Tuition, state resident: full-time $7110; part-time $470 per credit hour. Tuition, nonresident: full-time $24,030; part-time $827 per credit hour. *International tuition:* $24,030 full-time. *Required fees:* $2536. Tuition and fees vary according to course load and program. *Financial support:* Teaching assistantships, scholarships/grants, and unspecified assistantships available. Financial award application deadline: 2/15; financial award applicants required to submit FAFSA. *Unit head:* Dr. Edward Test, Chair, 208-426-3426, E-mail: edwardtest@boisestate.edu. *Application contact:* Dr. Tom Hillard, Director, 208-426-2991, E-mail: thomashillard@boisestate.edu.
Website: https://www.boisestate.edu/english/graduate-programs/

Bowling Green State University, Graduate College, College of Arts and Sciences, Department of English, Program in English, Bowling Green, OH 43403. Offers English (MA, PhD); literature (MA); rhetoric and writing (PhD); scientific and technical communication (MA). *Program availability:* Part-time. *Degree requirements:* For master's, thesis or alternative; for doctorate, comprehensive exam, thesis/dissertation, foreign language or proficiency in Old English. *Entrance requirements:* For master's and doctorate, GRE General Test. Additional exam requirements/recommendations for international students: required—TOEFL. Electronic applications accepted.

Drexel University, College of Arts and Sciences, Department of Communication, Culture and Media, Program in Communication, Philadelphia, PA 19104-2875. Offers public communication (MS); science communication (MS); technical communication (MS). *Program availability:* Part-time, evening/weekend. *Degree requirements:* For master's, internship, professional portfolio. *Entrance requirements:* For master's, GRE or minimum GPA of 3.0. Additional exam requirements/recommendations for international students: required—TOEFL. Electronic applications accepted.

East Carolina University, Graduate School, Thomas Harriot College of Arts and Sciences, Department of English, Greenville, NC 27858-4353. Offers creative writing (MA); English studies (MA); linguistics (MA); literature (MA); multicultural and transnational literatures (MA, Certificate); professional communication (Certificate); rhetoric and composition (MA); rhetoric, writing, and professional communication (PhD); teaching English in the two-year college (Certificate); teaching English to speakers of other languages (MA, Certificate); technical and professional communication (MA). *Program availability:* Part-time, evening/weekend, online learning. *Application deadline:* For fall admission, 7/31 priority date for domestic students, 2/1 priority date for international students; for spring admission, 11/30 priority date for domestic students, 10/1 priority date for international students. *Expenses: Tuition, area resident:* Full-time $4749; part-time $185 per credit hour. Tuition, state resident: full-time $4749; part-time $185 per credit hour. Tuition, nonresident: full-time $17,898; part-time $864 per credit hour. *International tuition:* $17,898 full-time. *Required fees:* $2787. *Financial support:* Application deadline: 3/1. *Unit head:* Dr. Marianne Montgomery, Chair, 252-328-6041, E-mail: montgomerym@ecu.edu. *Application contact:* Graduate School Admissions, 252-328-6012, Fax: 252-328-6071, E-mail: gradschool@ecu.edu.
Website: https://english.ecu.edu/

Eastern Michigan University, Graduate School, College of Arts and Sciences, Department of English Language and Literature, Programs in Written Communication, Ypsilanti, MI 48197. Offers technical communication (Graduate Certificate); written communication (MA). *Program availability:* Part-time, evening/weekend, online learning. *Students:* 1 full-time (0 women), 11 part-time (10 women); includes 3 minority (2 Black or African American, non-Hispanic/Latino; 1 Hispanic/Latino). Average age 34. 5 applicants, 100% accepted, 4 enrolled. In 2019, 8 master's awarded. *Entrance requirements:* Additional exam requirements/recommendations for international students: required—TOEFL. *Application deadline:* Applications are processed on a rolling basis. Application fee: $45. *Financial support:* Fellowships, research assistantships with full tuition reimbursements, teaching assistantships with full tuition reimbursements, career-related internships or fieldwork, Federal Work-Study, institutionally sponsored loans, scholarships/grants, tuition waivers (partial), and unspecified assistantships available. Support available to part-time students. Financial award applicants required to submit FAFSA. *Application contact:* Dr. Chalice Randazzo, Program Coordinator, 734-487-4220, Fax: 734-483-9744, E-mail: crandaz1@emich.edu.

Eastern Washington University, Graduate Studies, College of Arts, Letters and Education, Department of English, Cheney, WA 99004-2431. Offers literature (MA); rhetoric, composition, and technical communication (MA); teaching English as a second language (MA). *Faculty:* 13 full-time (8 women). *Students:* 59 full-time (40 women), 4 part-time (3 women); includes 1 minority (Asian, non-Hispanic/Latino). Average age 33. 100 applicants, 58% accepted, 33 enrolled. In 2019, 32 master's awarded. *Degree requirements:* For master's, comprehensive exam, thesis or alternative. *Entrance requirements:* For master's, GRE General Test, minimum GPA of 3.0. Additional exam requirements/recommendations for international students: required—TOEFL (minimum score 92 paper-based; 92 iBT), IELTS (minimum score 7), PTE (minimum score 63). *Application deadline:* For fall admission, 4/1 priority date for domestic students; for spring admission, 1/15 for domestic students. Applications are processed on a rolling basis. Application fee: $75. *Financial support:* Teaching assistantships with partial tuition reimbursements, career-related internships or fieldwork, Federal Work-Study, institutionally sponsored loans, scholarships/grants, health care benefits, tuition waivers (partial), and unspecified assistantships available. Support available to part-time students. Financial award application deadline: 2/1; financial award applicants required to submit FAFSA. *Application contact:* Kathy White, Advisor/Recruiter for Graduate Studies, 509-359-2491, E-mail: gradprograms@ewu.edu.
Website: http://www.ewu.edu/CALE/Programs/English.xml

Harvard University, Harvard Graduate School of Education, Master's Programs in Education, Cambridge, MA 02138. Offers arts in education (Ed M); education policy and management (Ed M); higher education (Ed M); human development and psychology (Ed M); international education policy (Ed M); language and literacy (Ed M); learning and teaching (Ed M); mind, brain, and education (Ed M); prevention science and practice (Ed M); school leadership (Ed M); special studies (Ed M); teacher education (Ed M); technology, innovation, and education (Ed M). *Program availability:* Part-time. *Entrance requirements:* For master's, GRE General Test, statement of purpose, 3 letters of recommendation, resume, official transcripts. Additional exam requirements/recommendations for international students: required—TOEFL (minimum score 613 paper-based; 104 iBT), TWE (minimum score 5). Electronic applications accepted.

Indiana University-Purdue University Indianapolis, School of Engineering and Technology, MS in Technology Program, Indianapolis, IN 46202. Offers applied data management and analytics (MS); facilities management (MS); information security and assurance (MS); motorsports (MS); organizational leadership (MS); technical communication (MS). *Program availability:* Online learning.

Lawrence Technological University, College of Arts and Sciences, Southfield, MI 48075-1058. Offers bioinformatics (Graduate Certificate); computer science (MS), including data science, big data, and data mining, intelligent systems; educational technology (MA), including robotics; instructional design, communication, and presentation (Graduate Certificate); integrated science (MA); science education (MA); technical and professional communication (MS, Graduate Certificate); writing for the digital age (Graduate Certificate). *Program availability:* Part-time, evening/weekend. *Faculty:* 5 full-time (2 women), 2 part-time/adjunct (1 woman). *Students:* 1 (woman) full-time, 25 part-time (15 women); includes 6 minority (3 Black or African American, non-Hispanic/Latino; 2 Asian, non-Hispanic/Latino; 1 Hispanic/Latino), 6 international. Average age 34. 50 applicants, 68% accepted, 3 enrolled. In 2019, 14 master's, 4 other advanced degrees awarded. *Degree requirements:* For master's, thesis (for some programs). *Entrance requirements:* Additional exam requirements/recommendations for international students: required—TOEFL (minimum score 550 paper-based; 79 iBT), IELTS (minimum score 6.5). *Application deadline:* For fall admission, 5/24 for international students; for spring admission, 10/13 for international students; for summer admission, 2/18 for international students. Applications are processed on a rolling basis. Application fee: $50. Electronic applications accepted. *Expenses: Tuition:* Full-time $16,618; part-time $8309 per year. *Required fees:* $600; $600. *Financial support:* In 2019–20, 4 students received support. Scholarships/grants and tuition reduction available. Financial award application deadline: 4/1; financial award applicants required to submit FAFSA. *Unit head:* Glen Bauer, Interim Dean, 248-204-3532, Fax: 248-204-3518, E-mail: scidean@ltu.edu. *Application contact:* Jane Rohrback, Director of Admissions, 248-204-3160, Fax: 248-204-2228, E-mail: admissions@ltu.edu.

Minnesota State University Mankato, College of Graduate Studies and Research, College of Arts and Humanities, Department of English, Mankato, MN 56001. Offers communication and composition (MA); creative writing (MFA); English studies (MA); teaching English as a second language (MA, Certificate); technical communication (MA, Certificate). *Program availability:* Part-time. *Degree requirements:* For master's, one foreign language, comprehensive exam, thesis or alternative. *Entrance requirements:* For master's, minimum GPA of 3.0 during previous 2 years, writing sample (MFA). Additional exam requirements/recommendations for international students: required—TOEFL (minimum score 500 paper-based; 61 iBT). Electronic applications accepted.

Missouri University of Science and Technology, Department of English and Technical Communication, Rolla, MO 65409. Offers technical communication (MS). *Expenses:* Tuition, state resident: full-time $7839; part-time $435.50 per credit hour. Tuition, nonresident: full-time $22,169; part-time $1231.60 per credit hour. *International tuition:* $22,169 full-time. *Required fees:* $649.76. One-time fee: $119. Tuition and fees vary according to course load and program.

New Jersey Institute of Technology, College of Science and Liberal Arts, Newark, NJ 07102. Offers applied mathematics (MS); applied physics (MS, PhD); applied statistics (MS, Certificate); biology (MS, PhD); biostatistics (MS); chemistry (MS, PhD); environmental and sustainability policy (MS); environmental science (MS, PhD); history (MA, MAT); materials science and engineering (MS, PhD); mathematical and computational finance (MS); mathematical sciences (PhD); pharmaceutical chemistry (MS); professional and technical communications (MS); technical communication essentials (Certificate). *Program availability:* Part-time, evening/weekend. *Faculty:* 159 full-time (42 women), 156 part-time/adjunct (61 women). *Students:* 197 full-time (80 women), 58 part-time (14 women); includes 58 minority (18 Black or African American, non-Hispanic/Latino; 22 Asian, non-Hispanic/Latino; 16 Hispanic/Latino; 2 Two or more races, non-Hispanic/Latino), 130 international. Average age 29. 401 applicants, 63% accepted, 73 enrolled. In 2019, 54 master's, 10 doctorates, 1 other advanced degree awarded. Terminal master's awarded for partial completion of doctoral program. *Degree requirements:* For master's, thesis (for some programs); for doctorate, thesis/dissertation. *Entrance requirements:* For master's and doctorate, GRE General Test, Minimum GPA of 3.0, personal statement, 3 letters of recommendation, and transcripts. Additional exam requirements/recommendations for international students: required—TOEFL (minimum score 550 paper-based; 79 iBT), IELTS (minimum score 6.5). *Application deadline:* For fall admission, 6/1 priority date for domestic students, 5/1 priority date for international students; for spring admission, 11/15 priority date for domestic and international students. Applications are processed on a rolling basis. Application fee: $75. Electronic applications accepted. *Expenses:* $23,828 per year (in-state), $33,744 per year (out-of-state). *Financial support:* In 2019–20, 147 students received support, including 13 fellowships with full tuition reimbursements available (averaging $24,000 per year), 41 research assistantships with full tuition reimbursements available (averaging $24,000 per year), 87 teaching assistantships with full tuition reimbursements available (averaging $24,000 per year); scholarships/grants, traineeships, health care benefits, and unspecified assistantships also available. Financial award application deadline: 1/15. *Unit head:* Dr. Kevin Belfield, Dean, 973-596-3676, Fax: 973-565-0586, E-mail: kevin.d.belfield@njit.edu. *Application contact:* Stephen Eck, Director of Admissions, 973-596-3300, Fax: 973-596-3461, E-mail: admissions@njit.edu.
Website: http://csla.njit.edu/

Northeastern University, College of Professional Studies, Boston, MA 02115-5096. Offers applied nutrition (MS); college athletics administration (MSL); commerce and economic development (MS); corporate and organizational communication (MS); criminal justice (MS); digital media (MPS); elearning and instructional design (M Ed); elementary education (MAT); geographic information technology (MPS); global studies and international relations (MS); higher education administration (M Ed); homeland security (MA); human services (MS); informatics (MPS); leadership (MS); learning analytics (M Ed); learning and instruction (M Ed); nonprofit management (MS); professional sports administration (MSL); project management (MS); regulatory affairs for drugs, biologics, and medical devices (MS); respiratory care leadership (MS); special education (M Ed); technical communication (MS). *Program availability:* Part-time, evening/weekend, 100% online, blended/hybrid learning. *Faculty:* 85 full-time (53 women), 892 part-time/adjunct (379 women). *Students:* 5,699 part-time (3,305 women). In 2019, 1,787 master's awarded. *Application deadline:* Applications are processed on a rolling basis. Application fee: $0. Electronic applications accepted. *Expenses:* Contact institution. *Financial support:* Applicants required to submit FAFSA. *Unit head:* Dr. Mary Loeffelholz, Dean of the College of Professional Studies, 617-373-6060. *Application contact:* Dr. Mary Loeffelholz, Dean of the College of Professional Studies, 617-373-6060.
Website: https://cps.northeastern.edu/

Texas State University, The Graduate College, College of Liberal Arts, Program in Technical Communication, San Marcos, TX 78666. Offers MA. *Program availability:* Part-time. *Degree requirements:* For master's, comprehensive exam, thesis optional. *Entrance requirements:* For master's, baccalaureate degree from regionally-accredited institution with minimum GPA of 2.75 on last 60 undergraduate semester hours, 3.0 in minimum of 12 hours of undergraduate English courses; portfolio; 2 non-fiction prose documents with one academic research paper. Additional exam requirements/recommendations for international students: required—TOEFL (minimum score 550 paper-based; 78 iBT), IELTS (minimum score 6.5). Electronic applications accepted.

University of Houston - Downtown, College of Humanities and Social Sciences, Department of English, Program in Technical Communication, Houston, TX 77002. Offers MS. *Program availability:* Part-time, evening/weekend. *Faculty:* 6 full-time (2 women). *Students:* 5 full-time (4 women), 15 part-time (9 women); includes 12 minority (4 Black or African American, non-Hispanic/Latino; 7 Hispanic/Latino; 1 Two or more races, non-Hispanic/Latino), 2 international. Average age 37. 11 applicants, 82% accepted, 6 enrolled. In 2019, 8 master's awarded. *Entrance requirements:* For master's, essay, resume, 2 letters of recommendation, transcripts. Additional exam requirements/recommendations for international students: required—TOEFL (minimum score 600 paper-based; 86 iBT). *Application deadline:* For fall admission, 8/9 for domestic students; for spring admission, 12/2 for domestic students; for summer admission, 5/17 for domestic students. Application fee: $35 ($80 for international students). Electronic applications accepted. *Expenses:* $386 in-state resident; $758 non-resident, per credit. *Financial support:* Federal Work-Study and scholarships/grants available. Financial award application deadline: 4/1; financial award applicants required to submit FAFSA. *Unit head:* Dr. Paul Kintzele, Department Chair, English, 713-221-8090, Fax: 713-226-5205, E-mail: kintzelep@uhd.edu. *Application contact:* Ceshia Love, Director of Admissions, 713-221-8093, Fax: 713-223-7408, E-mail: gradadmissions@uhd.edu.
Website: https://www.uhd.edu/academics/humanities/graduate-programs/master-science-technical-communication/Pages/mstc-index.aspx

University of Nebraska at Omaha, Graduate Studies, College of Arts and Sciences, Department of English, Omaha, NE 68182. Offers advanced writing (Certificate); English (MA); teaching English to speakers of other languages (Certificate); technical communication (Certificate). *Program availability:* Part-time, evening/weekend. *Degree requirements:* For master's, comprehensive exam, thesis (for some programs). *Entrance requirements:* For master's, GRE or MAT, minimum GPA of 3.0, transcripts, 3 letters of recommendation, statement of purpose, writing sample; for Certificate, minimum GPA of 3.0, transcripts, statement of purpose. Additional exam requirements/recommendations for international students: required—TOEFL, IELTS, PTE. Electronic applications accepted.

University of Nebraska at Omaha, Graduate Studies, College of Communication, Fine Arts and Media, School of Communication, Omaha, NE 68182. Offers communication (MA); human resources and training (Certificate); technical communication (Certificate). *Program availability:* Part-time, evening/weekend. *Degree requirements:* For master's, comprehensive exam, thesis (for some programs). *Entrance requirements:* For master's, minimum GPA of 3.0, 15 undergraduate communication courses, resume, statement of purpose, 3 letters of recommendation. Additional exam requirements/recommendations for international students: required—TOEFL, IELTS, PTE. Electronic applications accepted.

University of South Florida, Innovative Education, Tampa, FL 33620-9951. Offers adult, career and higher education (Graduate Certificate), including college teaching, leadership in developing human resources, leadership in higher education; Africana studies (Graduate Certificate), including diasporas and health disparities, genocide and human rights; aging studies (Graduate Certificate), including gerontology; art research (Graduate Certificate), including museum studies; business foundations (Graduate Certificate); chemical and biomedical engineering (Graduate Certificate), including materials science and engineering, water, health and sustainability; child and family studies (Graduate Certificate), including positive behavior support; civil and industrial engineering (Graduate Certificate), including transportation systems analysis; community and family health (Graduate Certificate), including maternal and child health, social marketing and public health, violence and injury: prevention and intervention, women's health; criminology (Graduate Certificate), including criminal justice administration; data science for public administration (Graduate Certificate); digital humanities (Graduate Certificate), including evaluation; English (Graduate Certificate), including comparative literary studies, creative writing, professional and technical communication; entrepreneurship (Graduate Certificate); environmental health (Graduate Certificate), including safety management; epidemiology and biostatistics (Graduate Certificate), including applied biostatistics, biostatistics, concepts and tools of epidemiology, epidemiology, epidemiology of infectious diseases; geography, environment and planning (Graduate Certificate), including community development, environmental policy and management, geographical information systems; geology (Graduate Certificate), including hydrogeology; global health (Graduate Certificate), including disaster management, global health and Latin American and Caribbean studies, global health practice, humanitarian assistance, infection control; government and international affairs (Graduate Certificate), including Cuban studies, globalization studies; health policy and management (Graduate Certificate), including health management and leadership, public health policy and programs; hearing specialist: early intervention (Graduate Certificate); industrial and management systems engineering (Graduate Certificate), including systems engineering, technology management; information studies (Graduate Certificate), including school library media specialist; information systems/decision sciences (Graduate Certificate), including analytics and business intelligence; instructional technology (Graduate Certificate), including distance education, Florida digital/virtual educator, instructional design, multimedia design, Web design; internal medicine, bioethics and medical humanities (Graduate Certificate), including biomedical ethics; Latin American and Caribbean studies (Graduate Certificate); leadership for coastal resiliency planning (Graduate Certificate); mass communications (Graduate Certificate), including multimedia journalism; mathematics and statistics (Graduate Certificate), including mathematics; medicine (Graduate Certificate), including aging and neuroscience, bioinformatics, biotechnology, brain fitness and memory management, clinical investigation, hand and upper limb rehabilitation, health informatics, health sciences, integrative weight management, intellectual property, medicine and gender, metabolic and nutritional medicine, metabolic cardiology, pharmacy sciences; national and competitive intelligence (Graduate Certificate); nursing (Graduate Certificate), including simulation based academic fellowship in advanced pain management; psychological and social foundations (Graduate Certificate), including career counseling, college teaching, diversity in education, mental health counseling, school counseling; public affairs (Graduate Certificate), including nonprofit management, public management, research administration; public health (Graduate Certificate), including assessing chemical toxicity and public health risks, health equity, pharmacoepidemiology, public health generalist, toxicology, translational research in adolescent behavioral health; public health practices (Graduate Certificate), including planning for healthy communities; rehabilitation and mental health counseling (Graduate Certificate), including integrative mental health care, marriage and family therapy, rehabilitation technology; secondary education (Graduate Certificate), including ESOL, foreign language education: culture and content, foreign language education: professional; social work (Graduate Certificate), including geriatric social work/clinical gerontology; special education (Graduate Certificate), including autism spectrum disorder, disabilities education: severe/profound; world languages (Graduate Certificate), including teaching English as a second language (TESL) or foreign language. *Unit head:* Dr. Cynthia DeLuca, Associate Vice President and Assistant Vice Provost, 813-974-3077, Fax: 813-974-7061, E-mail: deluca@usf.edu. *Application contact:* Owen Hooper, Director, Summer and Alternative Calendar Programs, 813-974-6917, E-mail: hooper@usf.edu.
Website: http://www.usf.edu/innovative-education/

University of Wisconsin–Stout, Graduate School, College of Arts, Humanities and Social Sciences, Menomonie, WI 54751. Offers design (MFA); technical and professional communication (MS). *Accreditation:* NASAD.

Section 17
Conflict Resolution and Mediation/Peace Studies

This section contains a directory of institutions offering graduate work in conflict resolution and mediation/peace studies, followed by an in-depth entry submitted by an institution that chose to prepare a detailed program description. Additional information about programs listed in the directory but not augmented by an in-depth entry may be obtained by writing directly to the dean of a graduate school or chair of a department at the address given in the directory.

For programs offering related work, see also in this book *Political Science and International Affairs* and *Public, Regional, and Industrial Affairs.* In another guide in this series:

Graduate Programs in Business, Education, Information Studies, Law & Social Work

See *Business Administration and Management* and *Law*

CONTENTS

Program Directory

Conflict Resolution and Mediation/Peace Studies

American Public University System, AMU/APU Graduate Programs, Charles Town, WV 25414. Offers accounting (MS); applied business analytics (MS); business administration (MBA); criminal justice (MA); cybersecurity studies (MS); educational leadership (M Ed); environmental policy and management (MS); global security (DGS); health information management (MS); history (MA), including American military history, American Revolution, civil war, war since 1945, World War II; information technology (MS); international relations and conflict resolution (MA), including American politics and government, comparative government and development, general, international relations, public policy; national security studies (MA); nursing (MSN); political science (MA); public policy (MPP); reverse logistics management (MA), including comparative and security issues, conflict resolution, international and transnational security issues, peacekeeping; space studies (MS); sports management (MS); strategic intelligence (DSI); teaching (M Ed), including secondary social studies; transportation and logistics management (MA). *Program availability:* Part-time, evening/weekend, online only, 100% online. *Students:* 461 full-time (193 women), 7,322 part-time (3,127 women); includes 3,089 minority (1,404 Black or African American, non-Hispanic/Latino; 30 American Indian or Alaska Native, non-Hispanic/Latino; 210 Asian, non-Hispanic/Latino; 753 Hispanic/Latino; 445 Native Hawaiian or other Pacific Islander, non-Hispanic/Latino; 247 Two or more races, non-Hispanic/Latino), 117 international. Average age 37. In 2019, 2,681 master's awarded. *Degree requirements:* For master's, comprehensive exam or practicum; for doctorate, practicum. *Entrance requirements:* For master's, official transcript showing earned bachelor's degree from institution accredited by recognized accrediting body. Additional exam requirements/recommendations for international students: required—TOEFL (minimum score 550 paper-based), IELTS (minimum score 6.5). *Application deadline:* Applications are processed on a rolling basis. Application fee: $0. Electronic applications accepted. *Financial support:* Scholarships/grants available. Financial award applicants required to submit FAFSA. *Unit head:* Dr. Wallace Boston, President, 877-468-6268, Fax: 304-728-2348, E-mail: president@apus.edu. *Application contact:* Yoci Deal, Associate Vice President, Graduate and International Admissions, 877-468-6268, Fax: 304-724-3764, E-mail: info@apus.edu.
Website: http://www.apus.edu

American University, School of International Service, Washington, DC 20016-8071. Offers comparative and regional studies (Certificate); cross-cultural communication (Certificate); development management (MS); ethics, peace, and global affairs (MA); European studies (Certificate); global environmental policy (MA, Certificate); global information technology (Certificate); global media (MA); international affairs (MA), including comparative and regional studies, global governance, politics, and security, international economic relations, natural resources and sustainable development, U.S. foreign policy and national security; international arts management (Certificate); international communication (MA, Certificate); international development (MA); international economic policy (Certificate); international economic relations (Certificate); international economics (MA); international peace and conflict resolution (MA, Certificate); international politics (Certificate); international relations (MA, PhD); international service (MIS); peacebuilding (Certificate); social enterprise (MA); the Americas (Certificate); United States foreign policy (Certificate); JD/MA. *Program availability:* Part-time, evening/weekend, 100% online, blended/hybrid learning. Terminal master's awarded for partial completion of doctoral program. *Degree requirements:* For master's, one foreign language, comprehensive exam, thesis or alternative; for doctorate, one foreign language, comprehensive exam, thesis/dissertation. *Entrance requirements:* For master's, transcripts, resume, 2 letters of recommendation, statement of purpose; for doctorate, GRE, transcripts, resume, 3 letters of recommendation, statement of purpose. Additional exam requirements/recommendations for international students: required—TOEFL. Electronic applications accepted. *Expenses:* Contact institution.

The American University of Paris, Graduate Programs, Paris, France. Offers cross-cultural and sustainable business management (MA); cultural translation (MA); global communications (MA); global communications and civil society (MA); international affairs (MA); international affairs, conflict resolution and civil society development (MA); Middle East and Islamic studies (MA); Middle East and Islamic studies and international affairs (MA); public policy and international affairs (MA); public policy and international law (MA). *Degree requirements:* For master's, thesis (for some programs). *Entrance requirements:* For master's, minimum undergraduate GPA of 3.0. Additional exam requirements/recommendations for international students: recommended—TOEFL, IELTS. Electronic applications accepted.

The American University of Rome, Graduate School, Rome, Italy. Offers arts management (MA); food studies (MA); peace studies (MA); sustainable cultural heritage (MA). *Degree requirements:* For master's, thesis, internship. *Entrance requirements:* For master's, bachelor's degree in the liberal arts, humanities or social sciences; minimum GPA of 2.75. Additional exam requirements/recommendations for international students: required—TOEFL (minimum score 550 paper-based; 80 iBT), IELTS (minimum score 6.5). Electronic applications accepted.

Anabaptist Mennonite Biblical Seminary, Graduate and Professional Programs, Elkhart, IN 46517-1999. Offers chaplaincy (M Div); Christian faith formation (M Div); Christian formation (MA); Christian spiritual formation (Certificate); divinity (M Div); pastoral ministry (M Div); pastoral theology for financial professionals (Certificate); peace studies (M Div), including environmental sustainability leadership (M Div, MA); theological studies (M Div, Certificate), including peace studies (M Div), theology and ethics (M Div); theology and peace studies (MA), including conflict transformation, environmental sustainability leadership (M Div, MA), international development administration; United Methodist leadership (M Div). *Accreditation:* ACIPE; ATS. *Program availability:* Part-time, 100% online, blended/hybrid learning. *Degree requirements:* For master's, variable foreign language requirement, comprehensive exam (for some programs), thesis optional, senior interview. *Entrance requirements:* For master's, undergraduate degree transcripts, 3 letters of reference, essay. Additional exam requirements/recommendations for international students: required—TOEFL (minimum score 90 iBT); recommended—IELTS (minimum score 7). Electronic applications accepted.

Arcadia University, College of Arts and Sciences, Program in International Peace and Conflict Resolution, Glenside, PA 19038-3295. Offers international peace and conflict resolution (MA). *Program availability:* Part-time, evening/weekend. *Students:* 18 full-time (15 women), 1 part-time (0 women); includes 9 minority (8 Black or African American, non-Hispanic/Latino; 1 Hispanic/Latino), 2 international. In 2019, 13 master's awarded. *Degree requirements:* For master's, Internship, capstone project. *Entrance requirements:* Additional exam requirements/recommendations for international students: required—TOEFL or IELTS. *Application deadline:* Applications are processed on a rolling basis. Application fee: $25. *Expenses:* Contact institution. *Financial support:* Scholarships/grants, unspecified assistantships, and travel purse available. *Unit head:* Amy Widestrom, Chair, 215-572-2917. *Application contact:* 215-572-2910, Fax: 215-572-4049, E-mail: admiss@arcadia.edu.

Bethany Theological Seminary, Graduate and Professional Programs, Richmond, IN 47374-4019. Offers biblical studies (MA Th); ministry studies (M Div); peace studies (M Div, MA Th); theological studies (MA Th, CATS); youth ministry (M Div). *Accreditation:* ACIPE; ATS. *Program availability:* Part-time, online learning. *Degree requirements:* For master's, thesis (for some programs). *Entrance requirements:* For master's, letters of reference. Additional exam requirements/recommendations for international students: required—TOEFL (minimum score 550 paper-based).

Bethel University, Graduate Programs, McKenzie, TN 38201. Offers administration and supervision (MA Ed); business administration (MBA); conflict resolution (MA); physician assistant studies (MS). *Program availability:* Part-time, evening/weekend. *Degree requirements:* For master's, thesis (for some programs). *Entrance requirements:* For master's, GRE General Test or MAT, minimum undergraduate GPA of 2.5.

Brandeis University, Graduate School of Arts and Sciences, Department of Near Eastern and Judaic Studies, Waltham, MA 02454-9110. Offers Near Eastern and Judaic studies (MA); near Eastern and Judaic studies/conflict resolution and coexistence (MA); near Eastern and Judaic studies/Jewish professional leadership (MA); near Eastern and Judaic studies/women's, gender, and sexuality studies (MA); teaching of Hebrew (MAT); the bible and ancient near east (PhD). *Program availability:* Part-time. *Faculty:* 21 full-time (8 women), 5 part-time/adjunct (3 women). *Students:* 34 full-time (15 women), 2 part-time (1 woman); includes 8 minority (1 Black or African American, non-Hispanic/Latino; 2 Asian, non-Hispanic/Latino; 3 Hispanic/Latino; 2 Two or more races, non-Hispanic/Latino), 7 international. Average age 34. 76 applicants, 53% accepted, 5 enrolled. In 2019, 3 master's, 3 doctorates awarded. Terminal master's awarded for partial completion of doctoral program. *Degree requirements:* For master's, one foreign language, thesis or alternative, capstone, thesis, or internship; for doctorate, variable foreign language requirement, comprehensive exam, thesis/dissertation. *Entrance requirements:* For master's and doctorate, GRE General recommended, transcripts, letters of recommendation, resume, writing sample, and statement of purpose. Additional exam requirements/recommendations for international students: required—TOEFL, IELTS, PTE. *Application deadline:* For fall admission, 1/15 priority date for domestic and international students. Applications are processed on a rolling basis. Application fee: $75. Electronic applications accepted. *Financial support:* In 2019–20, 9 fellowships with full tuition reimbursements (averaging $25,000 per year), 8 teaching assistantships (averaging $3,550 per year) were awarded; scholarships/grants, health care benefits, and tuition waivers also available. Support available to part-time students. *Unit head:* Dr. Ilana Szobel, Director of Graduate Studies, 781-736-5230, E-mail: szobel@brandeis.edu. *Application contact:* Jean Mannion, Administrator, 781-736-2950, E-mail: mannion@brandeis.edu.
Website: http://www.brandeis.edu/gsas/programs/nejs.html

Brandeis University, The Heller School for Social Policy and Management, Program in Coexistence and Conflict, Waltham, MA 02454-9110. Offers MA, MA/MA. *Degree requirements:* For master's, thesis, internship. *Entrance requirements:* For master's, 3 letters of recommendation, curriculum vitae or resume, 5 years of field experience. Additional exam requirements/recommendations for international students: required—TOEFL (minimum score 600 paper-based; 100 iBT). Electronic applications accepted.

California State University, Dominguez Hills, College of Arts and Humanities, Program in Negotiation, Conflict Resolution and Peacebuilding, Carson, CA 90747-0001. Offers MA. *Program availability:* Part-time, evening/weekend, online learning. *Degree requirements:* For master's, portfolio. *Entrance requirements:* For master's, minimum GPA of 3.0, 3 letters of recommendation. Additional exam requirements/recommendations for international students: required—TOEFL (minimum score 550 paper-based). Electronic applications accepted.

California University of Pennsylvania, School of Graduate Studies and Research, College of Liberal Arts, Department of Criminal Justice, California, PA 15419-1394. Offers conflict resolution (MA); criminal justice studies (MA). *Program availability:* Part-time, evening/weekend. *Degree requirements:* For master's, comprehensive exam, thesis optional. *Entrance requirements:* For master's, MAT, minimum GPA of 3.0. Additional exam requirements/recommendations for international students: required—TOEFL (minimum score 550 paper-based; 80 iBT). Electronic applications accepted. *Expenses: Tuition, area resident:* Full-time $9288; part-time $516 per credit. Tuition, state resident: full-time $9288; part-time $516 per credit. Tuition, nonresident: full-time $13,932; part-time $774 per credit. *Required fees:* $3631; $291.13 per credit. Part-time tuition and fees vary according to course load.

Cambridge College, School of Management, Boston, MA 02129. Offers business administration (MBA); business negotiation and conflict resolution (M Mgt); general business (M Mgt); health care (MBA); health care management (M Mgt); small business development (M Mgt); technology management (M Mgt). *Program availability:* Part-time, evening/weekend, 100% online, blended/hybrid learning. *Degree requirements:* For master's, thesis, seminars. *Entrance requirements:* For master's, resume, 2 professional references. Additional exam requirements/recommendations for international students: required—TOEFL (minimum score 550 paper-based; 79 iBT), Michigan English Language Assessment Battery (minimum score 85); recommended—IELTS (minimum score 6). Electronic applications accepted. *Expenses:* Contact institution.

Carleton University, Faculty of Graduate Studies, Faculty of Public Affairs and Management, Department of Law, Ottawa, ON K1S 5B6, Canada. Offers conflict resolution (Certificate); legal studies (MA). *Degree requirements:* For master's, thesis. *Entrance requirements:* For master's, honors degree. Additional exam requirements/recommendations for international students: required—TOEFL.

Champlain College, Graduate Studies, Burlington, VT 05402-0670. Offers business (MBA); digital forensic science (MS); early childhood education (M Ed); emergent media (MFA, MS); executive leadership (MS); health care administration (MS); information security operations (MS); law (MS); mediation and applied conflict studies (MS). *Program availability:* Part-time, online learning. *Degree requirements:* For master's, capstone project. *Entrance requirements:* Additional exam requirements/recommendations for international students: required—TOEFL (minimum score 550 paper-based; 80 iBT). Electronic applications accepted.

Colgate Rochester Crozer Divinity School, Graduate and Professional Programs, Rochester, NY 14620-2530. Offers divinity (M Div, MA, Certificate); peace building and interfaith dialogue (D Min); prophetic preaching (D Min); transformative leadership (D Min). *Accreditation:* ACIPE; ATS (one or more programs are accredited). *Program availability:* Part-time, evening/weekend. *Degree requirements:* For master's, thesis (for some programs), supervised ministry year (for M Div); for doctorate, thesis/dissertation. *Entrance requirements:* For master's, BA/BS, personal statement, 4 recommendations;

for doctorate, M Div, 3 years' professional experience, writing sample, personal statement, curriculum vitae, 4 recommendations. Additional exam requirements/recommendations for international students: required—TOEFL (minimum score 600 paper-based; 93 iBT). Electronic applications accepted. *Expenses:* Contact institution.

Colorado Technical University Aurora, Programs in Business Administration and Management, Aurora, CO 80014. Offers accounting (MBA); business administration (MBA); business administration and management (EMBA); finance (MBA); human resource management (MBA); marketing (MBA); mediation and dispute resolution (MBA); operations management (MBA); project management (MBA); technology management (MBA). *Program availability:* Part-time, evening/weekend. *Degree requirements:* For master's, thesis or alternative. *Entrance requirements:* For master's, minimum undergraduate GPA of 3.0, resume.

Colorado Technical University Colorado Springs, Graduate Studies, Program in Management, Colorado Springs, CO 80907. Offers accounting (MBA, MSA); business administration (MBA); finance (MBA); human resources management (MBA); logistics/supply chain management (MBA); management (DM); marketing (MBA); mediation and dispute resolution (MBA); operations management (MBA); project management (MBA); technology management (MBA). *Accreditation:* ACBSP. *Program availability:* Part-time, evening/weekend, online learning. *Degree requirements:* For master's, thesis or alternative; for doctorate, thesis/dissertation. *Entrance requirements:* For doctorate, minimum graduate GPA of 3.0, 5 years of related work experience.

Columbia University, School of Professional Studies, Program in Negotiation and Conflict Resolution, New York, NY 10027. Offers MS. *Program availability:* Part-time. *Entrance requirements:* For master's, 2 letters of recommendation, professional resume. Electronic applications accepted. *Expenses: Tuition:* Full-time $47,600; part-time $1880 per credit. One-time fee: $105.

Cornell University, Graduate School, Graduate Fields of Architecture, Art and Planning, Field of Regional Science, Ithaca, NY 14853. Offers environmental studies (MA, MS, PhD); international spatial problems (MA, MS, PhD); location theory (MA, MS, PhD); multiregional economic analysis (MA, MS, PhD); peace science (MA, MS, PhD); planning methods (MA, MS, PhD); urban and regional economics (MA, MS, PhD). Terminal master's awarded for partial completion of doctoral program. *Degree requirements:* For master's, thesis; for doctorate, comprehensive exam, thesis/dissertation. *Entrance requirements:* For master's and doctorate, GRE General Test, 2 letters of recommendation. Additional exam requirements/recommendations for international students: required—TOEFL (minimum score 600 paper-based; 77 iBT). Electronic applications accepted.

Creighton University, Graduate School, Department of Interdisciplinary Studies, Omaha, NE 68178-0001. Offers health and wellness coaching (MS); health care ethics (MS); healthcare management (MHM); leadership (Ed D); negotiation and conflict resolution (MS); organizational leadership (MS); public health (MPH). *Program availability:* Part-time, online only, blended/hybrid learning. *Degree requirements:* For master's, capstone project or practicum; for doctorate, thesis/dissertation. *Entrance requirements:* Additional exam requirements/recommendations for international students: required—TOEFL (minimum score 90 iBT). Electronic applications accepted. *Expenses:* Contact institution.

Creighton University, School of Law, Program in Negotiation and Conflict Resolution, Omaha, NE 68178-0001. Offers MS, Certificate. *Program availability:* Part-time, evening/weekend, 100% online, blended/hybrid learning. *Degree requirements:* For master's, thesis or alternative, practicum. *Entrance requirements:* For master's, baccalaureate degree, two letters of recommendation, statement of purpose (500-750 words), short writing sample, resume, interview with faculty member, transcripts. Additional exam requirements/recommendations for international students: required—TOEFL (minimum score 90 iBT). Electronic applications accepted. *Expenses:* Contact institution.

Dallas Baptist University, College of Business, Management Program, Dallas, TX 75211-9299. Offers conflict resolution management (MA); general management (MA, MS); health care management (MA); human resource management (MA); professional sales and management optimization (MA). *Program availability:* Part-time, evening/weekend, online learning. *Application deadline:* Applications are processed on a rolling basis. Application fee: $25. Electronic applications accepted. Application fee is waived when completed online. *Expenses: Tuition:* Full-time $18,072; part-time $1004 per credit hour. *Required fees:* $1100; $550 per semester. Tuition and fees vary according to course level and degree level. *Unit head:* Dr. Sandra Reid, Chair, Graduate School of Business, 214-333-6860, E-mail: sandra@dbu.edu. *Application contact:* Dr. Justin Gandy, Program Director, 214-333-6840, E-mail: justing@dbu.edu. Website: https://www.dbu.edu/graduate/degree-programs/ma-management

Drew University, Caspersen School of Graduate Studies, Madison, NJ 07940-1493. Offers conflict resolution and leadership (Certificate), including community leadership, moderation, peace building; education (M Ed); finance (MA); history and culture (MA, PhD), including American history, book history, British history, European history, intellectual history, Irish history, print culture, public history; K-12 education (MAT), including art, biology, chemistry, elementary education, English, French, Italian, math, secondary education, special education, teacher of students with disabilities; liberal studies (M Litt, D Litt), including history, Irish/Irish-American studies, literature (M Litt, MMH, D Litt, DMH, CMH), religion, spirituality, teaching in the two-year college, writing; medical humanities (MMH, DMH, CMH), including arts, health, healthcare, literature (M Litt, MMH, D Litt, DMH, CMH), scientific research; poetry (MFA). *Program availability:* Part-time, evening/weekend. Terminal master's awarded for partial completion of doctoral program. *Degree requirements:* For master's and other advanced degree, thesis (for some programs); for doctorate, one foreign language, comprehensive exam (for some programs), thesis/dissertation. *Entrance requirements:* For master's, PRAXIS Core and Subject Area tests (for MAT), GRE/GMAT (for MFin MS in Data Analytics), resume, transcripts, writing sample, personal statement, letters of recommendation; for doctorate, GRE (PhD in history and culture), resume, transcripts, writing sample, personal statement, letters of recommendation; for other advanced degree, resume, transcripts, personal statement. Additional exam requirements/recommendations for international students: required—TOEFL (minimum score 587 paper-based; 80 iBT), IELTS (minimum score 6), TWE (minimum score 4). Electronic applications accepted.

Eastern Mennonite University, Program in Conflict Transformation, Harrisonburg, VA 22802-2462. Offers MA, Graduate Certificate. *Program availability:* Part-time. *Degree requirements:* For master's, practicum. *Entrance requirements:* For master's, minimum undergraduate GPA of 2.75. Additional exam requirements/recommendations for international students: required—TOEFL (minimum score 550 paper-based). Electronic applications accepted. *Expenses:* Contact institution.

Fresno Pacific University, Graduate Programs, Program in Peacemaking and Conflict Studies, Fresno, CA 93702-4709. Offers church conflict and peacemaking (Certificate); mediation (Certificate); peacemaking and conflict studies (MA); restorative justice (Certificate). *Program availability:* Part-time, evening/weekend. *Degree requirements:* For master's, thesis. *Entrance requirements:* For master's, GMAT, MAT, GRE, interview, writing sample, three references. Additional exam requirements/

recommendations for international students: required—TOEFL (minimum score 550 paper-based). Electronic applications accepted. *Expenses:* Contact institution.

George Mason University, School for Conflict Analysis and Resolution, Arlington, VA 22030. Offers MS, PhD, Certificate. *Program availability:* Part-time, evening/weekend, blended/hybrid learning. *Degree requirements:* For master's, thesis optional; for doctorate, variable foreign language requirement, comprehensive exam, thesis/dissertation, oral defense of dissertation. *Entrance requirements:* For master's and Certificate, goals statement, two letters of recommendation, curriculum vitae or resume, transcripts; for doctorate, goals statement, three letters of recommendation, curriculum vitae or resume, transcripts, writing sample. Additional exam requirements/recommendations for international students: required—TOEFL (minimum score 575 paper-based; 88 iBT), IELTS (minimum score 6.5), PTE (minimum score 59). Electronic applications accepted.

Georgetown University, Graduate School of Arts and Sciences, Department of Government, Program in Conflict Resolution, Washington, DC 20057. Offers MA.

Georgetown University, Graduate School of Arts and Sciences, Walsh School of Foreign Service, Center for Security Studies, Washington, DC 20057. Offers MA, MA/JD, MA/PhD.

Henley-Putnam School of Strategic Security, Master of Science Program in Strategic Security and Protection Management, Rapid City, SD 57701. Offers extremist organizations (MS). *Program availability:* Part-time, online learning. *Degree requirements:* For master's, comprehensive exam, thesis. *Entrance requirements:* For master's, bachelor's degree from institution accredited by an agency recognized by the U.S. Department of Education and/or the Council for Higher Education Accreditation, background check. Additional exam requirements/recommendations for international students: required—TOEFL (minimum score 650 paper-based; 79 iBT); recommended—IELTS. *Expenses:* Contact institution.

Henley-Putnam School of Strategic Security, Master of Science Program in Terrorism and Counterterrorism Studies, Rapid City, SD 57701. Offers intelligence operations (MS); protective intelligence (MS). *Program availability:* Part-time, online learning. *Degree requirements:* For master's, thesis. *Entrance requirements:* For master's, bachelor's degree from institution accredited by an agency recognized by the U.S. Department of Education and/or the Council for Higher Education Accreditation, background check. Additional exam requirements/recommendations for international students: required—TOEFL (minimum score 650 paper-based; 79 iBT); recommended—IELTS (minimum score 7). *Expenses:* Contact institution.

The Institute of World Politics, Graduate Programs in National Security, Intelligence, and International Affairs, Washington, DC 20036. Offers American foreign policy (Certificate); comparative political culture (Certificate); conflict prevention (Certificate); counterintelligence (Certificate); counterterrorism (Certificate); cyber statecraft (Certificate); economic statecraft (Certificate); homeland security (Certificate); intelligence (Certificate); international politics (Certificate); national security affairs (Executive MA, Certificate); nonviolent conflict (Certificate); peace building, stabilization, and humanitarian affairs (Certificate); public diplomacy and strategic influence (Certificate); statecraft and international affairs (MA); statecraft and national security (MA, DSNS); strategic communication (Certificate); strategic intelligence studies (MA, Professional MA); strategic soft power (Certificate). *Program availability:* Part-time, evening/weekend. *Degree requirements:* For master's, 52 credit hours, comprehensive written and oral exam (for MA); proficiency in critical language (for MA in statecraft and international affairs); 28 credit hours (for Executive MA); 36 credit hours (for Professional MA); for doctorate, comprehensive exam, thesis/dissertation; for Certificate, 20 credit hours. *Entrance requirements:* For master's, resume, personal statement, 3 references, essay; 7-10 years of professional experience (for Executive MA); 5-7 years of professional experience (for Professional MA); for doctorate, MA. Additional exam requirements/recommendations for international students: required—TOEFL. Electronic applications accepted.

Kansas State University, Graduate School, College of Human Ecology, School of Family Studies and Human Services, Manhattan, KS 66506-1403. Offers applied family sciences (MS); communication sciences and disorders (MS); conflict resolution (Graduate Certificate); couple and family therapy (MS); early childhood education (MS); family and community service (MS); life-span human development (MS); personal financial planning (MS, PhD, Graduate Certificate); youth development (MS, Graduate Certificate). *Accreditation:* AAMFT/COAMFTE; ASHA. *Program availability:* Part-time, online learning. *Degree requirements:* For master's, comprehensive exam (for some programs), thesis optional. *Entrance requirements:* For master's, GRE, minimum GPA of 3.0 in last 2 years (60 semester hours) of undergraduate study; for doctorate, GRE. Additional exam requirements/recommendations for international students: required—TOEFL (minimum score 600 paper-based). Electronic applications accepted.

Kennesaw State University, College of Humanities and Social Sciences, PhD Program in International Conflict Management, Kennesaw, GA 30144. Offers PhD. *Students:* 24 full-time (8 women), 27 part-time (15 women); includes 15 minority (11 Black or African American, non-Hispanic/Latino; 3 Asian, non-Hispanic/Latino; 1 Hispanic/Latino), 9 international. Average age 40. 32 applicants, 66% accepted, 12 enrolled. In 2019, 9 doctorates awarded. *Degree requirements:* For doctorate, one foreign language, thesis/dissertation. *Entrance requirements:* For doctorate, GRE, portfolio of documents, copy of transcripts from all universities previously attended, resume, statement of goals and objectives, academic writing sample, three letters of recommendation. Additional exam requirements/recommendations for international students: required—TOEFL (minimum score 90 iBT), IELTS (minimum score 7). *Application deadline:* For fall admission, 2/1 for domestic and international students. Application fee: $60. Electronic applications accepted. *Expenses: Tuition, area resident:* Full-time $7104; part-time $296 per credit hour. Tuition, state resident: full-time $7104; part-time $296 per credit hour. Tuition, nonresident: full-time $25,584; part-time $1066 per credit hour. *International tuition:* $25,584 full-time. *Required fees:* $2006; $1706 per unit. $853 per semester. *Financial support:* Applicants required to submit FAFSA. *Unit head:* Director, 470-578-2893, E-mail: conflictphd@kennesaw.edu. *Application contact:* Nicole Densmore, Admissions Counselor, 470-578-6127, Fax: 470-578-9172, E-mail: ksugrad@kennesaw.edu. Website: http://chss.kennesaw.edu/phdincm/

Kennesaw State University, College of Humanities and Social Sciences, Program in Conflict Management, Kennesaw, GA 30144. Offers MSCM. *Program availability:* Evening/weekend. *Students:* 44 full-time (30 women), 1 (woman) part-time; includes 23 minority (19 Black or African American, non-Hispanic/Latino; 2 Asian, non-Hispanic/Latino; 2 Hispanic/Latino), 5 international. Average age 39. 35 applicants, 80% accepted, 22 enrolled. In 2019, 18 master's awarded. *Entrance requirements:* For master's, GMAT, GRE, LSAT. Additional exam requirements/recommendations for international students: required—TOEFL (minimum score 80 iBT), IELTS (minimum score 6.5). *Application deadline:* For fall admission, 6/1 for domestic and international students. Applications are processed on a rolling basis. Application fee: $60. Electronic applications accepted. *Expenses: Tuition, area resident:* Full-time $7104; part-time $296 per credit hour. Tuition, state resident: full-time $7104; part-time $296 per credit hour. Tuition, nonresident: full-time $25,584; part-time $1066 per credit hour. *International tuition:* $25,584 full-time. *Required fees:* $2006; $1706 per unit. $853 per semester.

Conflict Resolution and Mediation/Peace Studies

Financial support: Applicants required to submit FAFSA. *Unit head:* Director, 470-578-6081, E-mail: conflict@kennesaw.edu. *Application contact:* Admissions Counselor, 470-578-4377, Fax: 470-578-9172, E-mail: ksugrad@kennesaw.edu.
Website: http://chss.kennesaw.edu/mscm/

Kent State University, College of Arts and Sciences, Department of Political Science, Kent, OH 44242-0001. Offers political science (MA, PhD), including American politics and policy, conflict analysis and management, transnational and comparative politics and policy; public administration (MPA). *Accreditation:* NASPAA. *Program availability:* Part-time, 100% online. *Faculty:* 15 full-time (5 women), 2 part-time/adjunct (1 woman). *Students:* 39 full-time (19 women), 66 part-time (44 women); includes 14 minority (9 Black or African American, non-Hispanic/Latino; 2 Asian, non-Hispanic/Latino; 3 Two or more races, non-Hispanic/Latino), 12 international. Average age 36. 40 applicants, 90% accepted, 25 enrolled. In 2019, 26 master's, 2 doctorates awarded. *Degree requirements:* For master's, thesis, Capstone for non-thesis option; for doctorate, comprehensive exam, thesis/dissertation. *Entrance requirements:* For master's, GRE - combined verbal and quantitative GRE score above 300, goal statement, transcripts, writing sample, 3 letters of recommendation, minimum GPA of 3.0, resume; for doctorate, GRE -combined verbal and quantitative GRE score above 300, goal statement, transcripts, writing sample, 3 letters of recommendation, minimum GPA of 3.0, resume. Additional exam requirements/recommendations for international students: required—TOEFL (minimum score 79 iBT), IELTS (minimum score 6.5), Michigan English Language Assessment Battery (minimum score 77). *Application deadline:* For fall admission, 1/31 for domestic and international students. Applications are processed on a rolling basis. Application fee: $45 ($70 for international students). Electronic applications accepted. *Financial support:* Research assistantships with full tuition reimbursements, teaching assistantships with full tuition reimbursements, and unspecified assistantships available. Financial award application deadline: 1/31. *Unit head:* Dr. Anthony Molina, Chairperson and Assistant Professor, 330-672-2060, E-mail: amolina4@kent.edu. *Application contact:* Julie Mazzei, Associate Professor and Graduate Coordinator, 330-672-8934, E-mail: jmazzei@kent.edu.
Website: http://www.kent.edu/polisci

Lesley University, Graduate School of Arts and Social Sciences, Cambridge, MA 02138-2790. Offers clinical mental health counseling (MA), including holistic counseling, school and community counseling, trauma studies; counseling psychology (MA, CAGS), including professional counseling (MA), school counseling (MA); creative writing (MFA); expressive therapies (MA, PhD, CAGS), including art (MA), clinical mental health counseling (MA), dance (MA), expressive therapies (MA), music (MA); independent studies (CAGS); independent study (MA); intercultural relations (MA, CAGS); interdisciplinary studies (MA), including individualized studies, integrative holistic health, mindfulness studies, peace and conflict transformation, trauma sensitive assessment, intervention, and consultation, women's studies; urban environmental leadership (MA). *Program availability:* Part-time, online learning. *Degree requirements:* For master's, internship, practicum, thesis (for expressive therapies); for doctorate, thesis/dissertation, arts apprenticeship, field placement; for CAGS, thesis, internship (for counseling psychology, expressive therapies). *Entrance requirements:* For master's, MAT (counseling psychology), interview, writing samples, art portfolio; for doctorate, GRE or MAT, interview, master's degree; for CAGS, interview, master's degree. Additional exam requirements/recommendations for international students: required—TOEFL (minimum score 550 paper-based; 80 iBT). Electronic applications accepted.

Lipscomb University, Institute for Conflict Management, Nashville, TN 37204-3951. Offers MA, Certificate. *Program availability:* Part-time, evening/weekend. *Degree requirements:* For master's, thesis optional, externship. *Entrance requirements:* For master's, GRE, GMAT, LSAT or equivalent, 3 years of work experience. Additional exam requirements/recommendations for international students: required—TOEFL (minimum score 570 paper-based; 80 iBT). Electronic applications accepted. *Expenses:* Contact institution.

London Metropolitan University, Graduate Programs, London, United Kingdom. Offers applied psychology (M Sc); architecture (MA); biomedical science (M Sc); blood science (M Sc); cancer pharmacology (M Sc); computer networking and cyber security (M Sc); computing and information systems (M Sc); conference interpreting (MA); counter-terrorism studies (M Sc); creative, digital and professional writing (MA); crime, violence and prevention (M Sc); criminology (M Sc); curating contemporary art (MA); data analytics (M Sc); digital media (MA); early childhood studies (MA); education (MA, Ed D); financial services law, regulation and compliance (LL M); food science (M Sc); forensic psychology (M Sc); health and social care management and policy (M Sc); human nutrition (M Sc); human resource management (MA); human rights and international conflict (MA); information technology (M Sc); intelligence and security studies (M Sc); international oil, gas and energy law (LL M); international relations (MA); interpreting (MA); learning and teaching in higher education (MA); legal practice (LL M); media and entertainment law (LL M); organizational and consumer psychology (M Sc); psychological therapy (M Sc); psychology of mental health (M Sc); public health (M Sc); public policy and management (MPA); security studies (M Sc); social work (M Sc); spatial planning and urban design (MA); sports therapy (M Sc); supporting older children and young people with dyslexia (MA); teaching languages (MA), including Arabic, English; translation (MA); woman and child abuse (MA).

Middlebury Institute of International Studies at Monterey, Graduate School of International Policy and Management, Program in Nonproliferation and Terrorism Studies, Monterey, CA 93940-2691. Offers MA. *Degree requirements:* For master's, one foreign language. *Entrance requirements:* For master's, minimum GPA of 3.0, proficiency in a foreign language. Additional exam requirements/recommendations for international students: required—TOEFL (minimum score 550 paper-based; 80 iBT). Application fee is waived when completed online.

Montclair State University, The Graduate School, College of Humanities and Social Sciences, Conflict Management in the Workplace Certificate Program, Montclair, NJ 07043-1624. Offers Certificate.

Montclair State University, The Graduate School, College of Humanities and Social Sciences, MA Program in Law and Governance, Montclair, NJ 07043-1624. Offers conflict management and peace studies (MA); governance, compliance and regulation (MA); intellectual property (MA); law and governance (MA); legal management (MA). *Program availability:* Part-time, evening/weekend. *Degree requirements:* For master's, thesis or comprehensive exam. *Entrance requirements:* For master's, GRE General Test, minimum cumulative GPA of 2.75 for undergraduate work, 2 letters of recommendation, essay. Additional exam requirements/recommendations for international students: required—TOEFL (minimum score 83 iBT) or IELTS (minimum score 6.5). Electronic applications accepted.

Naval Postgraduate School, Departments and Academic Groups, Department of National Security Affairs, Monterey, CA 93943. Offers security studies (MA, PhD), including civil-military relations (MA), combating terrorism: policy and strategy (MA), defense decision-making and planning (MA), Europe and Eurasia (MA), Far East, Southeast Asia, and the Pacific (MA), homeland security and defense (MA), Middle East, South Asia, Sub-Saharan Africa (MA), stabilization and reconstruction (MA), western hemisphere (MA). *Program availability:* Part-time. *Degree requirements:* For master's, thesis (for some programs).

Norwich University, College of Graduate and Continuing Studies, Master of Arts in Diplomacy Program, Northfield, VT 05663. Offers diplomacy (MA), including cyber diplomacy - policy, cyber diplomacy - technical, international commerce, international conflict management, international terrorism. *Program availability:* Evening/weekend, online only, mostly all online with a week-long residency requirement. *Degree requirements:* For master's, comprehensive exam, thesis optional. *Entrance requirements:* For master's, minimum undergraduate GPA of 2.75. Additional exam requirements/recommendations for international students: required—TOEFL (minimum score 550 paper-based; 80 iBT), IELTS (minimum score 6.5). Electronic applications accepted. *Expenses:* Contact institution.

Nova Southeastern University, College of Arts, Humanities, and Social Sciences, Fort Lauderdale, FL 33314-7796. Offers advanced conflict resolution practice (Graduate Certificate); child protection (MHS); college student affairs (MS); conflict analysis and resolution (MS, PhD); criminal justice (MS, PhD); cross-disciplinary studies (MA); developmental disabilities (MS); family studies (Graduate Certificate); family systems health care (Graduate Certificate); family therapy (MS, PhD); marriage and family therapy (DMFT); peace studies (Graduate Certificate); qualitative research (Graduate Certificate); solution focused coaching (Graduate Certificate). *Accreditation:* AAMFT/COAMFTE (one or more programs are accredited). *Program availability:* Part-time, evening/weekend, 100% online, blended/hybrid learning. *Faculty:* 60 full-time (37 women), 88 part-time/adjunct (65 women). *Students:* 201 full-time (157 women), 418 part-time (297 women); includes 365 minority (180 Black or African American, non-Hispanic/Latino; 4 American Indian or Alaska Native, non-Hispanic/Latino; 15 Asian, non-Hispanic/Latino; 141 Hispanic/Latino; 25 Two or more races, non-Hispanic/Latino), 49 international. Average age 37. 303 applicants, 84% accepted, 197 enrolled. In 2019, 125 master's, 63 doctorates, 24 other advanced degrees awarded. *Degree requirements:* For master's, comprehensive exam (for some programs), thesis optional, comprehensive exams, portfolios (for some programs), table-top exams (for some programs); for doctorate, comprehensive exam, thesis/dissertation, qualifying exams, portfolios (for some programs). *Entrance requirements:* For master's, interview, minimum GPA of 3.0, writing sample; for doctorate, interview, minimum GPA of 3.5, master's degree in related field, writing sample; for Graduate Certificate, minimum GPA of 3.0. Additional exam requirements/recommendations for international students: required—TOEFL (minimum score 79 paper-based). *Application deadline:* Applications are processed on a rolling basis. Application fee: $50. Electronic applications accepted. *Expenses:* Contact institution. *Financial support:* In 2019–20, 170 students received support. Career-related internships or fieldwork, Federal Work-Study, scholarships/grants, and unspecified assistantships available. Financial award application deadline: 4/1; financial award applicants required to submit FAFSA. *Unit head:* Dr. Honggang Yang, Dean, 954-262-3016, Fax: 954-262-3968, E-mail: yangh@nova.edu. *Application contact:* Marcia Arango, Student Recruitment Coordinator, 954-262-3006, Fax: 954-262-3968, E-mail: marango@nsu.nova.edu.
Website: http://cahss.nova.edu/

Old Dominion University, College of Arts and Letters, Graduate Program in International Studies, Norfolk, VA 23529. Offers conflict and cooperation (MA, PhD); interdependence and transnationalism (MA, PhD); international cultural studies (MA, PhD); international political economy and development (MA, PhD); modeling and simulation (MA, PhD); U.S. foreign policy and international relations (MA, PhD). *Program availability:* Part-time. Terminal master's awarded for partial completion of doctoral program. *Degree requirements:* For master's, one foreign language, comprehensive exam, thesis optional; for doctorate, one foreign language, comprehensive exam, thesis/dissertation. *Entrance requirements:* For master's, GRE General Test, sample of written work, 2 letters of recommendation; for doctorate, GRE General Test, sample of written work, 3 letters of recommendation. Additional exam requirements/recommendations for international students: required—TOEFL (minimum score 570 paper-based). Electronic applications accepted. *Expenses:* Contact institution.

Portland State University, Graduate Studies, College of Liberal Arts and Sciences, Program in Conflict Resolution, Portland, OR 97207-0751. Offers MA, MS. *Program availability:* Part-time. *Faculty:* 7 full-time (3 women), 3 part-time/adjunct (1 woman). *Students:* 7 full-time (1 woman), 13 part-time (10 women); includes 2 minority (1 Hispanic/Latino; 1 Two or more races, non-Hispanic/Latino), 3 international. Average age 40. 9 applicants, 89% accepted, 2 enrolled. In 2019, 13 master's awarded. *Degree requirements:* For master's, variable foreign language requirement, thesis or alternative, practicum, culminating experience. *Entrance requirements:* For master's, personal statement, writing samples, transcripts, 3 letters of recommendation. Additional exam requirements/recommendations for international students: required—TOEFL (minimum score 550 paper-based; 80 iBT), IELTS (minimum score 6.5). *Application deadline:* For fall admission, 5/14 for domestic and international students. Application fee: $65. Electronic applications accepted. *Expenses:* $436 per credit hour resident, $655 per credit hour non-resident. *Financial support:* Teaching assistantships and Federal Work-Study available. Financial award application deadline: 2/1; financial award applicants required to submit FAFSA. *Unit head:* Patricia Schechter, Director/Chair, 503-725-3007, E-mail: schechp@pdx.edu. *Application contact:* Aislyn Matias, Program Coordinator, 503-725-9175, E-mail: ais2@pdx.edu.
Website: http://www.pdx.edu/conflict-resolution/

Regent University, Graduate School, School of Law, Virginia Beach, VA 23464. Offers American legal studies (LL M); human rights (LL M); law (MA, JD), including advanced paralegal studies (MA), alternative dispute resolution (MA), business (MA), criminal justice (MA), general legal studies (MA), human resources management (MA), human rights and rule of law (MA), national security (MA), non-profit organizational law (MA), regulatory compliance (MA), wealth management and financial planning (MA); JD/MA; JD/MBA. *Accreditation:* ABA. *Program availability:* Part-time, 100% online, blended/hybrid learning. *Faculty:* 16 full-time (5 women), 66 part-time/adjunct (22 women). *Students:* 378 full-time (230 women), 349 part-time (246 women); includes 311 minority (207 Black or African American, non-Hispanic/Latino; 5 American Indian or Alaska Native, non-Hispanic/Latino; 17 Asian, non-Hispanic/Latino; 56 Hispanic/Latino; 2 Native Hawaiian or other Pacific Islander, non-Hispanic/Latino; 24 Two or more races, non-Hispanic/Latino), 46 international. Average age 35. 680 applicants, 62% accepted, 223 enrolled. In 2019, 176 master's, 72 doctorates awarded. *Entrance requirements:* For master's, college transcripts, resume, personal statement; for doctorate, LSAT, minimum undergraduate GPA of 3.0, official transcripts, 2 letters of recommendation, resume, personal statement. Additional exam requirements/recommendations for international students: required—TOEFL (minimum score 600 paper-based). *Application deadline:* For fall admission, 3/1 for domestic students. Applications are processed on a rolling basis. Application fee: $50. Electronic applications accepted. *Expenses:* Contact institution. *Financial support:* In 2019–20, 582 students received support. Career-related internships or fieldwork, scholarships/grants, health care benefits, and unspecified assistantships available. Support available to part-time students. Financial award applicants required to submit FAFSA. *Unit head:* Mark Martin, Dean, 757-352-4040, Fax: 757-352-4595, E-mail: mmartin@regent.edu. *Application contact:* Ernie Walton,

Assistant Dean of Admissions, 757-352-4315, E-mail: lawschool@regent.edu. Website: https://www.regent.edu/school-of-law/

Royal Roads University, Graduate Studies, Peace and Conflict Studies Program, Victoria, BC V9B 5Y2, Canada. Offers conflict analysis (G Dip); conflict analysis and management (MA); disaster and emergency management (MA, G Dip); human security and peacebuilding (MA, G Dip); justice studies (G Dip); peace and conflict studies (MAIS). *Program availability:* Blended/hybrid learning. *Degree requirements:* For master's, thesis. *Entrance requirements:* For master's, 5-7 years of related work experience. Additional exam requirements/recommendations for international students: required—TOEFL (minimum score 570 paper-based) or IELTS (7) recommended. Electronic applications accepted.

Saint Mary's College of California, Kalmanovitz School of Education, Leadership Programs, Moraga, CA 94556. Offers coaching and facilitation (MA); organizational leadership and change (MA); peacebuilding and conflict transformation (MA); social justice (MA). *Accreditation:* AACSB. *Program availability:* Part-time, evening/weekend, online learning. *Degree requirements:* For master's, research project. *Entrance requirements:* For master's, letters of recommendation, interview. Electronic applications accepted. *Expenses:* Contact institution.

St. Mary's University, Graduate Studies, Program in International Relations, San Antonio, TX 78228. Offers conflict transformation (Certificate); international conflict resolution (MA); international development (MA); international relations (MA); security policy (MA); JD/MA. *Program availability:* Part-time, evening/weekend, 100% online. *Degree requirements:* For master's, one foreign language, comprehensive exam (for some programs), thesis (for some programs), thesis or comprehensive exam. *Entrance requirements:* For master's, minimum undergraduate cumulative GPA of 3.0. Additional exam requirements/recommendations for international students: required—TOEFL (minimum score 550 paper-based; 80 iBT), IELTS (minimum score 6). Electronic applications accepted.

Saint Paul University, Faculty of Human Sciences, Program in Conflict Studies, Ottawa, ON K1S 1C4, Canada. Offers MA. *Program availability:* Part-time. *Entrance requirements:* For master's, H=honors BA, B average.

Salisbury University, Department of Conflict Analysis and Dispute Resolution, Salisbury, MD 21801-6837. Offers MA. *Program availability:* Part-time, evening/weekend. *Faculty:* 6 full-time (1 woman). *Students:* 25 full-time (10 women), 8 part-time (6 women); includes 10 minority (8 Black or African American, non-Hispanic/Latino; 1 Hispanic/Latino; 1 Two or more races, non-Hispanic/Latino), 3 international. Average age 30. 37 applicants, 89% accepted, 21 enrolled. In 2019, 19 master's awarded. *Entrance requirements:* For master's, transcripts; resume or CV; personal statement; writing sample; minimum GPA of 3.0; three letters of recommendation. Additional exam requirements/recommendations for international students: required—English language proof if degree is not completed in English. *Application deadline:* For fall admission, 5/1 priority date for domestic and international students. Applications are processed on a rolling basis. Application fee: $65. Electronic applications accepted. *Expenses:* Contact institution. *Financial support:* In 2019–20, 13 students received support, including 5 research assistantships with full tuition reimbursements available (averaging $8,400 per year), 9 teaching assistantships with full tuition reimbursements available (averaging $8,027 per year); career-related internships or fieldwork also available. Support available to part-time students. Financial award application deadline: 3/1; financial award applicants required to submit FAFSA. *Unit head:* Dr. Ignaciyas Soosaipillai, Graduate Program Director, 410-543-6435, E-mail: iksoosaipillai@salisbury.edu. *Application contact:* Dr. Ignaciyas Soosaipillai, Graduate Program Director, 410-543-6435, E-mail: iksoosaipillai@salisbury.edu. Website: https://www.salisbury.edu/explore-academics/programs/graduate-degree-programs/cadr-masters/

Salve Regina University, Program in Humanities, Newport, RI 02840-4192. Offers humanitarian assistance (MA); humanities (PhD); public humanities (MA); religion, peace and justice (MA). *Program availability:* Part-time, evening/weekend, online learning. *Degree requirements:* For master's, thesis optional; for doctorate, one foreign language, comprehensive exam, thesis/dissertation. *Entrance requirements:* For master's, GMAT, GRE General Test, or MAT; for doctorate, GRE General Test. Additional exam requirements/recommendations for international students: required—TOEFL (minimum score 600 paper-based; 100 iBT) or IELTS. Electronic applications accepted.

SIT Graduate Institute, Graduate Programs, Master's Programs in Intercultural Service, Leadership, and Management, Master's Program in Peace and Justice Leadership, Brattleboro, VT 05302-0676. Offers MA. *Expenses: Tuition:* Full-time $43,500; part-time $21,750 per credit.

Southern Methodist University, Simmons School of Education and Human Development, Department of Dispute Resolution and Counseling, Dallas, TX 75275. Offers counseling (MS); dispute resolution (MA, Graduate Certificate); healthcare collaboration and conflict engagement (Graduate Certificate). *Program availability:* Part-time. *Entrance requirements:* For master's, minimum undergraduate GPA of 2.75 (for dispute resolution), 3.0 (for counseling); 3 letters of recommendation. Additional exam requirements/recommendations for international students: required—TOEFL. Electronic applications accepted.

Syracuse University, Maxwell School of Citizenship and Public Affairs, CAS Program in Conflict Resolution, Syracuse, NY 13244. Offers CAS. *Program availability:* Part-time. *Entrance requirements:* For degree, resume, three letters of recommendation, personal statement, official transcripts. Additional exam requirements/recommendations for international students: required—TOEFL (minimum score 100 iBT). Electronic applications accepted.

Trident University International, College of Business Administration, Program in Business Administration, Cypress, CA 90630. Offers business administration (PhD); conflict and negotiation management (MBA); criminal justice administration (MBA); entrepreneurship (MBA); finance (MBA); general management (MBA); government accounting (MBA); human resource management (MBA); information security and digital assurance management (MBA); information technology management (MBA); international business (MBA); logistics management (MBA); marketing (MBA); project management (MBA); public management (MBA); quality management (MBA); strategic leadership (MBA). *Program availability:* Part-time, evening/weekend, online learning. *Degree requirements:* For doctorate, comprehensive exam, thesis/dissertation, defense of dissertation. *Entrance requirements:* For master's, minimum GPA of 2.5 (students with GPA 3.0 or greater may transfer up to 30% of graduate level credits); for doctorate, minimum GPA of 3.4, curriculum vitae, course work in research methods or statistics. Additional exam requirements/recommendations for international students: required—TOEFL. Electronic applications accepted.

United States International University–Africa, School of Arts and Sciences, Nairobi, Kenya. Offers counseling psychology (MA), including chemical dependency, health psychology; international relations (MA), including development studies, diplomacy and foreign policy, peace and conflict studies. *Program availability:* Part-time, evening/weekend. *Degree requirements:* For master's, thesis, practicum. *Entrance*

requirements: For master's, GRE General Test, 2 letters of recommendation, resume. Additional exam requirements/recommendations for international students: required—TOEFL.

United Theological Seminary of the Twin Cities, Graduate Programs, New Brighton, MN 55112-2598. Offers advanced theological studies (Diploma); justice and peace studies (M Div, MA); leadership toward racial justice (M Div, MA, Certificate); Methodist studies (M Div, MA, Certificate); ministry (D Min); ministry renewal and professional development (Certificate); pastoral care and counseling (M Div, MA, MARL); religion and theology (MA); theological and religious studies (Certificate); theology and the arts (M Div, MA); urban ministry (M Div, MA, MARL); women's studies: religion, theology and ministry (M Div, MA). *Accreditation:* ACIPE; ATS. *Program availability:* Part-time, evening/weekend. *Degree requirements:* For master's, thesis; for doctorate, comprehensive exam, thesis/dissertation. *Entrance requirements:* For master's, minimum GPA of 2.75; strong analytical, reflective thinking and writing skills; vocational and academic goals compatible with those of Seminary; for doctorate, M Div or equivalent, minimum GPA of 3.0, 3 years experience in professional ministry; for other advanced degree, BA or equivalent life experience; strong analytical, reflective thinking and writing skills (Certificate); proficiency in English language, previous study of theology at a theological school, recommendation of student's denomination (Diploma). Additional exam requirements/recommendations for international students: required—TOEFL (minimum score 550 paper-based).

Universidad del Turabo, Graduate Programs, School of Social Sciences and Humanities, Programs in Public Affairs, Gurabo, PR 00778-3030. Offers arts administration (MPA); conflict and mediation studies (MPA); criminal justice studies (MPA); forensic science (MPA); human services administration (MPA). *Entrance requirements:* For master's, GRE, EXADEP, interview, essay, official transcript, recommendation letters. Electronic applications accepted.

Université de Sherbrooke, Faculty of Law, Sherbrooke, QC J1K 2R1, Canada. Offers alternative dispute resolution (LL M, Diploma); business law (Diploma); common law (JD); criminal and penal law (Diploma); health law (LL M, Diploma); international law (LL M); law (LL D); legal management (Diploma); notarial law (Diploma); transnational law (Diploma). *Program availability:* Part-time, evening/weekend. *Degree requirements:* For master's, thesis; for Diploma, one foreign language. *Entrance requirements:* For master's and Diploma, LL B. Electronic applications accepted.

University of Arkansas at Little Rock, Graduate School, College of Social Sciences and Communication, Program in Conflict Mediation, Little Rock, AR 72204-1099. Offers Graduate Certificate.

University of Baltimore, Graduate School, College of Public Affairs, Program in Negotiations and Conflict Management, Baltimore, MD 21201-5779. Offers MS. *Program availability:* Part-time, evening/weekend. *Degree requirements:* For master's, thesis optional, internship. *Entrance requirements:* For master's, minimum GPA of 3.0. Additional exam requirements/recommendations for international students: required—TOEFL (minimum score 550 paper-based). Electronic applications accepted.

University of Bridgeport, College of Public and International Affairs, Bridgeport, CT 06604. Offers East Asian and Pacific Rim studies (MA); global development and peace (MA); global media and communication studies (MA). *Program availability:* Part-time, evening/weekend. *Degree requirements:* For master's, thesis. *Entrance requirements:* Additional exam requirements/recommendations for international students: recommended—TOEFL (minimum score 550 paper-based; 80 iBT), IELTS (minimum score 6.5).

University of Denver, Josef Korbel School of International Studies, Denver, CO 80208. Offers conflict resolution (MA); global business and corporate social responsibility (Certificate); global finance, trade and economic integration (MA); global health affairs (Certificate); homeland security (Certificate); humanitarian assistance (Certificate); international administration (MA); international development (MA); international human rights (MA); international security (MA); international studies (MA, PhD); public policy studies (MPP); religion and international affairs (Certificate). *Program availability:* Part-time. *Faculty:* 41 full-time (15 women), 14 part-time/adjunct (2 women). *Students:* 208 full-time (112 women), 24 part-time (13 women); includes 50 minority (11 Black or African American, non-Hispanic/Latino; 10 Asian, non-Hispanic/Latino; 15 Hispanic/Latino; 14 Two or more races, non-Hispanic/Latino), 20 international. Average age 27. 718 applicants, 70% accepted, 88 enrolled. In 2019, 134 master's, 2 doctorates, 26 other advanced degrees awarded. *Degree requirements:* For master's, variable foreign language requirement, thesis (for some programs); for doctorate, one foreign language, comprehensive exam, thesis/dissertation, one extended research paper. *Entrance requirements:* For master's, GRE General Test, bachelor's degree, transcripts, two letters of recommendation, personal statement, resume or curriculum vitae; for doctorate, GRE General Test, bachelor's degree (most have a master's degree), transcripts, personal statement, resume or curriculum vitae, writing sample. Additional exam requirements/recommendations for international students: required—TOEFL (minimum score 587 paper-based; 95 iBT). *Application deadline:* For fall admission, 1/23 priority date for domestic and international students; for winter admission, 11/1 for domestic and international students. Applications are processed on a rolling basis. Application fee: $65. Electronic applications accepted. *Expenses:* Contact institution. *Financial support:* In 2019–20, 161 students received support, including 4 teaching assistantships with tuition reimbursements available (averaging $16,875 per year); research assistantships with tuition reimbursements available, career-related internships or fieldwork, Federal Work-Study, institutionally sponsored loans, scholarships/grants, and unspecified assistantships also available. Support available to part-time students. Financial award application deadline: 2/15; financial award applicants required to submit FAFSA. *Unit head:* Dr. Fritz Mayer, Dean, 303-871-6338, E-mail: frederick.mayer@du.edu. *Application contact:* Admissions Contact, 303-871-2324, E-mail: korbeladm@du.edu. Website: http://www.du.edu/korbel

University of Hawaii at Manoa, Office of Graduate Education, College of Social Sciences, Matsunaga Institute for Peace and Conflict Resolution, Honolulu, HI 96822. Offers conflict resolution (Graduate Certificate). *Program availability:* Part-time. *Entrance requirements:* For degree, GRE General Test. Additional exam requirements/recommendations for international students: required—TOEFL (minimum score 540 paper-based; 76 iBT), IELTS (minimum score 5).

The University of Manchester, School of Arts, Languages and Cultures, Manchester, United Kingdom. Offers anthropology, media and performance (PhD); applied theatre (PhD); Arab world studies (PhD); archaeology (PhD); art history and visual studies (PhD); arts and cultural management (PhD); arts management and cultural policy (PhD); Chinese studies (PhD); classics and ancient history (PhD); composition (PhD); creative writing (PhD); drama (PhD); East Asian studies (PhD); electroacoustic composition (PhD); English and American studies (PhD); English language (PhD); French studies (PhD); German studies (PhD); history (PhD); humanitarianism and conflict response (PhD); interpreting studies (PhD); Japanese studies (PhD); Latin American cultural studies (PhD); linguistics (PhD); Middle Eastern studies (PhD); museology (PhD); museum practice (PhD); music (PhD); musicology (PhD); Polish studies (PhD);

Conflict Resolution and Mediation/Peace Studies

Portuguese studies (PhD); religions and theology (PhD); Russian studies (PhD); Spanish studies (PhD); translation and intercultural studies (PhD).

University of Massachusetts Amherst, Graduate School, College of Natural Sciences, Department of Psychological and Brain Sciences, Amherst, MA 01003. Offers clinical psychology (MS, PhD); cognitive psychology (MS, PhD); developmental science (MS, PhD); psychology of peace and violence (MS, PhD); social psychology (MS, PhD). *Accreditation:* APA (one or more programs are accredited). Terminal master's awarded for partial completion of doctoral program. *Degree requirements:* For master's, thesis; for doctorate, comprehensive exam, thesis/dissertation. *Entrance requirements:* For master's and doctorate, GRE General Test, 3 letters of recommendation. Additional exam requirements/recommendations for international students: required—TOEFL (minimum score 550 paper-based; 80 iBT), IELTS (minimum score 6.5). Electronic applications accepted.

University of Massachusetts Boston, McCormack Graduate School of Policy and Global Studies, Program in Conflict Resolution, Boston, MA 02125-3393. Offers MA, Certificate. *Entrance requirements:* For master's, MAT or GRE, minimum GPA of 2.75; for Certificate, minimum GPA of 2.75.

University of Massachusetts Boston, McCormack Graduate School of Policy and Global Studies, Program in Global Governance and Human Security, Boston, MA 02125-3393. Offers MA.

University of Massachusetts Lowell, College of Fine Arts, Humanities and Social Sciences, Program in Peace and Conflict Studies, Lowell, MA 01854. Offers MA. *Degree requirements:* For master's, practicum, project, or thesis. *Entrance requirements:* For master's, GRE, GMAT, or LSAT, bachelor's degree from accredited college or university, minimum undergraduate GPA of 3.0, 18 credits of peace and conflict studies related coursework, three letters of reference, personal statement, resume or curriculum vitae. Additional exam requirements/recommendations for international students: required—TOEFL.

University of Missouri, School of Law, Columbia, MO 65211. Offers dispute resolution (LL M); law (JD). *Accreditation:* ABA. *Entrance requirements:* For doctorate, LSAT. Additional exam requirements/recommendations for international students: required—TOEFL (minimum score 600 paper-based; 100 iBT), IELTS (minimum score 7). *Expenses:* Contact institution.

University of Missouri–St. Louis, College of Arts and Sciences, Department of Sociology, St. Louis, MO 63121. Offers advanced social perspective (MA); community conflict intervention (MA); program design and evaluation research (MA); social policy planning and administration (MA). *Program availability:* Part-time, evening/weekend. *Degree requirements:* For master's, thesis optional. *Entrance requirements:* For master's, 2 letters of recommendation. Additional exam requirements/recommendations for international students: required—TOEFL (minimum score 550 paper-based). Electronic applications accepted. *Expenses: Tuition, area resident:* Full-time $9005.40; part-time $6003.60 per credit hour. Tuition, state resident: full-time $9005.40; part-time $6003.60 per credit hour. Tuition, nonresident: full-time $22,108; part-time $14,738.40 per credit hour. *International tuition:* $22,108 full-time. Tuition and fees vary according to course load.

University of New Haven, Graduate School, College of Arts and Sciences, Program in Industrial and Organizational Psychology, West Haven, CT 06516. Offers conflict management (MA); industrial organizational psychology (MA); industrial-human resources psychology (MA); organizational development and consultation (MA); psychology of conflict management (Graduate Certificate). *Program availability:* Part-time, evening/weekend. *Students:* 63 full-time (37 women), 3 part-time (2 women); includes 15 minority (8 Black or African American, non-Hispanic/Latino; 2 Asian, non-Hispanic/Latino; 5 Hispanic/Latino), 9 international. Average age 27. 80 applicants, 78% accepted, 31 enrolled. In 2019, 41 master's awarded. *Degree requirements:* For master's, thesis or alternative, internship or practicum. *Entrance requirements:* Additional exam requirements/recommendations for international students: required—TOEFL (minimum score 80 iBT), IELTS, PTE. *Application deadline:* Applications are processed on a rolling basis. Application fee: $50. Electronic applications accepted. Application fee is waived when completed online. *Expenses:* Contact institution. *Financial support:* Research assistantships with partial tuition reimbursements, teaching assistantships with partial tuition reimbursements, career-related internships or fieldwork, Federal Work-Study, scholarships/grants, and unspecified assistantships available. Support available to part-time students. Financial award applicants required to submit FAFSA. *Unit head:* Dr. Eric Marcus, Distinguished Lecturer, 203-932-1242, E-mail: emarcus@newhaven.edu. *Application contact:* Selina O'Toole, Senior Associate Director of Graduate Admissions, 203-932-7337, E-mail: SOToole@newhaven.edu.
Website: https://www.newhaven.edu/arts-sciences/graduate-programs/industrial-organizational-psychology/

The University of North Carolina at Greensboro, Graduate School, School of Health and Human Sciences, Department of Peace and Conflict Studies, Greensboro, NC 27412-5001. Offers MA, Certificate. Electronic applications accepted.

The University of North Carolina Wilmington, College of Arts and Sciences, Department of Public and International Affairs, Wilmington, NC 28403-3297. Offers coastal and ocean policy (MS); conflict management and resolution (MA); public administration (MPA), including coastal management. *Accreditation:* NASPAA. *Program availability:* Blended/hybrid learning. *Faculty:* 12 full-time (5 women). *Students:* 51 full-time (32 women), 49 part-time (32 women); includes 21 minority (7 Black or African American, non-Hispanic/Latino; 10 Hispanic/Latino; 4 Two or more races, non-Hispanic/Latino), 1 international. Average age 30. 60 applicants, 93% accepted, 36 enrolled. In 2019, 45 master's awarded. *Degree requirements:* For master's, thesis (for some programs), internship, practicum, capstone project. *Entrance requirements:* For master's, GRE General Test (Coastal and Ocean Policy, or MCOP, degree), 3 letters of recommendation (all degrees); minimum of 3 years of professional work experience, personal statement, resume (for MPA degree); personal statement and resume (MCOP degree); essay and resume (Conflict & Resolution Management degree). Additional exam requirements/recommendations for international students: required—TOEFL (minimum score 79 iBT), IELTS (minimum score 6.5). *Application deadline:* For fall admission, 7/1 for domestic students; for spring admission, 11/15 for domestic students; for summer admission, 4/15 for domestic students. Applications are processed on a rolling basis. Application fee: $75. Electronic applications accepted. *Expenses:* $4,717.97 per year in-state (for Public Administration main campus students), $11,632.47 per year out-of-state (for Public Administration main campus students), $259.01 per credit hour in-state (for online students), $936.91 per credit hour out-of-state (for online students), $3,728.47 per year for the remaining in-state main campus students, $10,642.97 per year for the remaining out-of-state main campus students. *Financial support:* Teaching assistantships and scholarships/grants available. Financial award application deadline: 1/1; financial award applicants required to submit FAFSA. *Unit head:* Dr. Raymonde Kleinberg, Chair, 910-962-4254, Fax: 910-962-3286, E-mail: kleinbergr@uncw.edu. *Application contact:* Dr. Chris Prentice, MPA Program Director, 910-962-2135, E-mail: prenticecr@uncw.edu.
Website: http://www.uncw.edu/pia/graduate/index.html

University of Notre Dame, The Graduate School, Kroc Institute for International Peace Studies, Notre Dame, IN 46556. Offers MA, PhD. *Degree requirements:* For master's, one foreign language, comprehensive exam, thesis optional; for doctorate, one foreign language, comprehensive exam, thesis/dissertation. *Entrance requirements:* For master's, GRE General Test. Additional exam requirements/recommendations for international students: required—TOEFL (minimum score 600 paper-based; 80 iBT). Electronic applications accepted.

University of Phoenix–Online Campus, College of Social Science, Phoenix, AZ 85034-7209. Offers mediation (Certificate); psychology (MS), including behavioral health, industrial-organizational, psychology. *Program availability:* Evening/weekend, online learning. *Entrance requirements:* Additional exam requirements/recommendations for international students: required—TOEFL, TOEIC (Test of English as an International Communication), Berlitz Online English Proficiency Exam, PTE, or IELTS. Electronic applications accepted. *Expenses:* Contact institution.

University of San Diego, Joan B. Kroc School of Peace Studies, San Diego, CA 92110-2492. Offers conflict management and resolution (MS); peace and justice (MA); peace and law (JD/MA); social innovation (MA); JD/MA. *Program availability:* Part-time, evening/weekend. *Faculty:* 10 full-time (3 women), 2 part-time/adjunct (1 woman). *Students:* 73 full-time (58 women), 18 part-time (16 women); includes 49 minority (6 Black or African American, non-Hispanic/Latino; 6 Asian, non-Hispanic/Latino; 19 Hispanic/Latino; 18 Two or more races, non-Hispanic/Latino), 15 international. Average age 31. In 2019, 58 master's awarded. *Degree requirements:* For master's, portfolio project. *Entrance requirements:* For master's, minimum GPA of 3.0, Official transcripts, Current resume, short essays, letters of recommendation. Additional exam requirements/recommendations for international students: required—TOEFL (minimum score 580 paper-based; 83 iBT), TWE. Electronic applications accepted. *Financial support:* In 2019–20, 79 students received support. Career-related internships or fieldwork, Federal Work-Study, institutionally sponsored loans, scholarships/grants, and unspecified assistantships available. Support available to part-time students. Financial award application deadline: 4/1; financial award applicants required to submit FAFSA. *Unit head:* Dr. Patricia Marquez, Dean, Kroc School of Peace Studies, 619-260-7919, E-mail: krocschool@sandiego.edu. *Application contact:* Erika Garwood, Associate Director of Graduate Admissions, 619-260-4524, Fax: 619-260-4158, E-mail: grads@sandiego.edu.
Website: http://www.sandiego.edu/peace/

University of the Sacred Heart, Graduate Programs, Program in Systems of Justice, San Juan, PR 00914-0383. Offers human rights and anti-discriminatory processes (MASJ); mediation and transformation of conflicts (MASJ).

University of Victoria, Faculty of Graduate Studies, Faculty of Human and Social Development, School of Public Administration, Victoria, BC V8W 2Y2, Canada. Offers dispute resolution (MADR); public administration (MPA, PhD); MPA/LL B. *Program availability:* Part-time, evening/weekend, online learning. *Degree requirements:* For master's, thesis (for some programs), report; for doctorate, thesis/dissertation, candidacy exam. *Entrance requirements:* For master's, GMAT or GRE General Test, professional resume; for doctorate, GMAT or GRE General Test. Additional exam requirements/recommendations for international students: required—TOEFL (minimum score 610 paper-based). Electronic applications accepted.

University of Wisconsin–Milwaukee, Graduate School, College of Letters and Science, Interdepartmental Program in Human Resources and Labor Relations, Milwaukee, WI 53201-0413. Offers human resources and labor relations (MHRLR); international human resources and labor relations (Graduate Certificate); mediation and negotiation (Graduate Certificate). *Program availability:* Part-time. *Entrance requirements:* For master's, GMAT or GRE General Test. Additional exam requirements/recommendations for international students: required—TOEFL (minimum score 80 iBT), IELTS (minimum score 6.5). Electronic applications accepted.

University of Wisconsin–Milwaukee, Graduate School, College of Nursing, Milwaukee, WI 53201. Offers clinical nurse specialist (Graduate Certificate); family nurse practitioner (Graduate Certificate); nursing (MN, DNP, PhD); sustainable peacebuilding (MSP). *Accreditation:* AACN. *Program availability:* Part-time. *Entrance requirements:* For master's, GRE General Test or MAT, autobiographical sketch; for doctorate, GRE, minimum GPA of 3.2. Additional exam requirements/recommendations for international students: required—TOEFL (minimum score 550 paper-based; 79 iBT), IELTS (minimum score 6.5). Electronic applications accepted.

Walden University, Graduate Programs, School of Public Policy and Administration, Minneapolis, MN 55401. Offers criminal justice (MPA, MPP, MS, Graduate Certificate), including emergency management (MS, PhD), general program (MS), global leadership (MS, PhD), homeland security and policy coordination (MS, PhD), law and public policy (MS, PhD), policy analysis (MS, PhD), public management and leadership (MS, PhD), self-designed (MS), terrorism, mediation, and peace (MS, PhD); criminal justice and executive management (MS), including global leadership (MS, PhD); criminal justice leadership and executive management (MS), including emergency management (MS, PhD), general program, homeland security and policy coordination (MS, PhD), law and public policy (MS, PhD), policy analysis (MS, PhD), public management and leadership (MS, PhD), self-designed, terrorism, mediation, and peace (MS, PhD); emergency management (MPA, MPP, MS), including criminal justice (MS, PhD), general program (MS), homeland security (MS), public management and leadership (MS, PhD), terrorism and emergency management (MS); general program (MPA, MPP); global leadership (MPA, MPP); government management (Graduate Certificate); health policy (MPA, MPP); homeland security (Graduate Certificate); homeland security and policy coordination (MPA, MPP); international nongovernmental organizations (MPA, MPP); law and public policy (MPA, MPP); local government management for sustainable communities (MPA, MPP); nonprofit management (Graduate Certificate); nonprofit management and leadership (MPA, MPP, MS), including global leadership (MS, PhD), international nongovernmental organization (MS), local government for sustainable communities (MS), self-designed (MS); online teaching in higher education (Post-Master's Certificate); policy analysis (MPA); public management and leadership (MPA, MPP, Graduate Certificate); public policy (Graduate Certificate); public policy and administration (PhD), including criminal justice (MS, PhD), emergency management (MS, PhD), global leadership (MS, PhD), health policy, homeland security and policy coordination (MS, PhD), international nongovernmental organizations, law and public policy (MS, PhD), local government management for sustainable communities, nonprofit management and leadership, policy analysis (MS, PhD), public management and leadership (MS, PhD), terrorism, mediation, and peace (MS, PhD); strategic planning and public policy (Graduate Certificate); terrorism, mediation, and peace (MPA, MPP). *Program availability:* Part-time, evening/weekend, online only, 100% online. *Degree requirements:* For doctorate, thesis/dissertation, residency. *Entrance requirements:* For master's, bachelor's degree or higher; minimum GPA of 2.5; official transcripts; goal statement (for some programs); access to computer and Internet; for doctorate, master's degree or higher; three years of related professional or academic experience (preferred); minimum GPA of 3.0; goal statement and current resume (for select programs); official transcripts; access to computer and Internet; for other advanced degree, relevant work experience; access to computer and Internet. Additional exam requirements/recommendations for international students: required—TOEFL (minimum score 550 paper-based, 79 iBT), IELTS (minimum score 6.5), Michigan English Language Assessment Battery (minimum score 82), or PTE (minimum score 53). Electronic applications accepted.

Walden University, Graduate Programs, School of Social Work and Human Services, Minneapolis, MN 55401. Offers addictions and social work (DSW); advanced clinical practice (MSW); clinical expertise (DSW); criminal justice (DSW); disaster, crisis, and intervention (DSW); family studies and interventions (DSW); human and social services (PhD), including advanced research, community and social services, community intervention and leadership, conflict management, criminal justice, disaster crisis and intervention, family studies and intervention, gerontology, global social services, higher education, human services and nonprofit administration, mental health facilitation; medical social work (DSW); military social work (MSW); policy practice (DSW); social work (PhD), including addictions and social work, clinical expertise, criminal justice, disaster, crisis and intervention, family studies and interventions, medical social work, policy practice, social work administration; social work administration (DSW); social work in healthcare (MSW); social work with children and families (MSW). *Accreditation:* CSWE. *Program availability:* Part-time, evening/weekend, online only, 100% online. *Degree requirements:* For master's, residency (for some programs); for doctorate, thesis/dissertation, residency. *Entrance requirements:* For master's, bachelor's degree or higher; minimum GPA of 2.5; official transcripts; goal statement (for some programs); access to computer and Internet; for doctorate, master's degree or higher; three years of related professional or academic experience (preferred); minimum GPA of 3.0; goal statement and current resume (for select programs); official transcripts; access to computer and Internet. Additional exam requirements/recommendations for international students: required—TOEFL (minimum score 550 paper-based, 79 iBT), IELTS (minimum score 6.5), Michigan English Language Assessment Battery (minimum score 82), or PTE (minimum score 53). Electronic applications accepted.

Wayne State University, College of Fine, Performing and Communication Arts, Department of Communication, Detroit, MI 48202. Offers communication (PhD), including democratic participation and culture, identity and representation, media, society and culture, risk, crisis and conflict, wellness, work life and relationships; communication and new media (Graduate Certificate); communication studies (MA); dispute resolution (MADR, Graduate Certificate), including community and urban studies (MADR), conflict area studies (MADR), health and family (MADR), international conflict and cooperation (MADR), professional practice (MADR), theory of conflict (MADR), workplace (MADR); health communication (Graduate Certificate); journalism (MA); media arts (MA); media studies (MA); public relations and organizational communication (MA); JD/MADR. *Program availability:* Online learning. *Degree requirements:* For master's, thesis (for some programs), thesis or essay; for doctorate, thesis/dissertation. *Entrance requirements:* For master's, GRE (for MA if undergraduate GPA less than 3.2), personal statement; BA or BS in communication or related field with minimum upper-division GPA of 3.2 and minimum upper-division undergraduate GPA of 3.0, and sample of academic writing (for MA); undergraduate degree with minimum upper-division GPA of 3.0 and three letters of recommendation (for MADR); for doctorate, GRE, undergraduate degree in communication or related field; master's degree in communication or related field with minimum GPA of 3.5; letters of recommendation; personal statement; sample of written scholarship. Additional exam requirements/recommendations for international students: required—TOEFL (minimum score 100 iBT), IELTS, TWE. Electronic applications accepted. *Expenses:* Contact institution.

Wilfrid Laurier University, Faculty of Graduate and Postdoctoral Studies, School of International Policy and Governance, Global Governance Program, Waterloo, ON N2L 3C5, Canada. Offers conflict and security (PhD); global environment (PhD); global justice and human rights (PhD); global political economy (PhD); global social governance (PhD); multilateral institutions and diplomacy (PhD). *Degree requirements:* For doctorate, thesis/dissertation. *Entrance requirements:* For master's, MA in political science, history, economics, international development studies, international peace studies, globalization studies, environmental studies or related field with minimum A-. Additional exam requirements/recommendations for international students: required—TOEFL (minimum score 89 iBT). Electronic applications accepted.

Willamette University, College of Law, Salem, OR 97301-3922. Offers dispute resolution (LL M); law (MLS, JD); transnational law (LL M); JD/MBA. *Accreditation:* ABA. *Program availability:* Part-time. *Degree requirements:* For master's, thesis, 25 credit hours (for LL M); 26 credit hours (for MLS); for doctorate, thesis/dissertation, 90 credit hours. *Entrance requirements:* For master's, bachelor's degree (for MLS); domestic or foreign JD (for LL M); for doctorate, LSAT. Additional exam requirements/recommendations for international students: required—TOEFL (minimum score 480 paper-based; 45 iBT); recommended—IELTS (minimum score 5). Electronic applications accepted. Application fee is waived when completed online. *Expenses:* Contact institution.

Yeshiva University, Benjamin N. Cardozo School of Law, New York, NY 10003-4301. Offers comparative legal thought (LL M); dispute resolution and advocacy (LL M); general studies (LL M); intellectual property law (LL M); law (JD). *Accreditation:* ABA. *Program availability:* 100% online. *Entrance requirements:* For master's, LLM program requirements: personal statement, 1 letter of recommendation, English language proficiency score, CV, evaluation of student's transcripts; for doctorate, LSAT, 2 letters of recommendation. Additional exam requirements/recommendations for international students: required—TOEFL (minimum score 100 iBT), Cardozo accepts either a TOEFL or an IELTS score as a part of the English language requirement; recommended—IELTS (minimum score 7). Electronic applications accepted. *Expenses:* Contact institution.

Section 18
Criminology and Forensics

This section contains a directory of institutions offering graduate work in criminology and forensics, followed by an in-depth entry submitted by an institution that chose to prepare a detailed program description. Additional information about programs listed in the directory but not augmented by an in-depth entry may be obtained by writing directly to the dean of a graduate school or chair of a department at the address given in the directory.

For programs offering related work, see also in this book *Political Science and International Affairs, Psychology and Counseling,* and *Sociology, Anthropology, and Archaeology.* In another guide in this series:

Graduate Programs in Business, Education, Information Studies, Law & Social Work

See *Law* and *Social Work*

CONTENTS

Program Directories

Criminal Justice and Criminology

Adler University, Master of Public Administration Program, Chicago, IL 60602. Offers criminal justice (MPA); sustainable communities (MPA). *Program availability:* Part-time, evening/weekend. In 2019, 1 master's awarded. *Degree requirements:* For master's, Social Justice Practicum; Capstone Project. *Unit head:* Phyllis Horton, Director of Admissions, 312-662-4100, E-mail: admissions@adler.edu. *Application contact:* Phyllis Horton, Director of Admissions, 312-662-4100, E-mail: admissions@adler.edu.

Adrian College, Graduate Programs, Adrian, MI 49221-2575. Offers accounting (MS); athletic training (MS); criminal justice (MA). *Degree requirements:* For master's, comprehensive exam (for some programs), thesis (for some programs), thesis, internship or practicum with corresponding in-depth paper and/or presentation. *Entrance requirements:* For master's, appropriate undergraduate degree, minimum cumulative and major GPA of 3.0, personal statement.

Albany State University, College of Arts and Humanities, Albany, GA 31705-2717. Offers criminal justice (MS); English education (M Ed); public administration (MPA), including community and economic development, criminal justice administration, health administration and policy, human resources management, public management, public policy, water resources management and policy; social work (MSW). *Accreditation:* NASPAA. *Program availability:* Part-time. *Degree requirements:* For master's, comprehensive exam, professional portfolio (for MPA), internship, capstone report. *Entrance requirements:* For master's, GRE, MAT, minimum GPA of 3.0, official transcript, pre-medical record/certificate of immunization, letters of reference. Electronic applications accepted.

Albertus Magnus College, Master of Science in Criminal Justice Program, New Haven, CT 06511-1189. Offers corrections administration (MS); juvenile justice (MS). *Program availability:* Part-time, evening/weekend, 100% online, blended/hybrid learning. *Faculty:* 2 full-time (0 women), 1 part-time/adjunct (0 women). *Students:* 18 full-time (13 women), 3 part-time (2 women); includes 10 minority (4 Black or African American, non-Hispanic/Latino; 6 Hispanic/Latino). Average age 33. 10 applicants, 90% accepted, 7 enrolled. In 2019, 11 master's awarded. *Degree requirements:* For master's, comprehensive exam, thesis, min. cumulative GPA of 3.0, completion within 7 years, payment of all tuition and feescapstone. *Entrance requirements:* For master's, A bachelor's degree, min. cumulative GPA of 3.0 in criminal justice and 2.8 in all other coursework, competion of min. 18 undergraduate credits in criminal justice, two letters of recommendation of former professors or professional associates, written essay of 500-600 words. Additional exam requirements/recommendations for international students: required—One of the following: SAT or ACT, TOEFL, IELTS, DUO Lingo English Proficiency Test, 3+ years at a university/college with English as primary language. *Application deadline:* For fall admission, 7/15 for international students; for spring admission, 11/15 for international students. Applications are processed on a rolling basis. Application fee: $50. Electronic applications accepted. *Expenses:* Contact institution. *Financial support:* In 2019–20, 1 student received support. Unspecified assistantships available. Financial award applicants required to submit FAFSA. *Unit head:* John Lawrie, Director of Graduate Leadership Programs, 203-773-4424, E-mail: hfero@albertus.edu. *Application contact:* Dean of the Division of Professional and Graduate Studies, 203-672-6692, E-mail: abosleyboyce@albertus.edu.
Website: https://www.albertus.edu/criminal-justice/ms/

Alliant International University–San Francisco, California School of Forensic Studies, Program in Applied Criminology, San Francisco, CA 94133. Offers victimology (MS). *Entrance requirements:* For master's, 3 essays, resume. Additional exam requirements/recommendations for international students: required—TOEFL (minimum score 550 paper-based; 80 iBT). Electronic applications accepted.

American Public University System, AMU/APU Graduate Programs, Charles Town, WV 25414. Offers accounting (MS); applied business analytics (MS); business administration (MBA); criminal justice (MA); cybersecurity studies (MS); educational leadership (M Ed); environmental policy and management (MS); global security (DGS); health information management (MS); history (MA), including American military history, American Revolution, civil war, war since 1945, World War II; information technology (MS); international relations and conflict resolution (MA), including American politics and government, comparative government and development, general, international relations, public policy; national security studies (MA); nursing (MSN); political science (MA); public policy (MPP); reverse logistics management (MA), including comparative and security issues, conflict resolution, international and transnational security issues, peacekeeping; space studies (MS); sports management (MS); strategic intelligence (DSI); teaching (M Ed), including secondary social studies; transportation and logistics management (MA). *Program availability:* Part-time, evening/weekend, online only, 100% online. *Students:* 461 full-time (193 women), 7,322 part-time (3,127 women); includes 3,089 minority (1,404 Black or African American, non-Hispanic/Latino; 30 American Indian or Alaska Native, non-Hispanic/Latino; 210 Asian, non-Hispanic/Latino; 753 Hispanic/Latino; 445 Native Hawaiian or other Pacific Islander, non-Hispanic/Latino; 247 Two or more races, non-Hispanic/Latino), 117 international. Average age 37. In 2019, 2,681 master's awarded. *Degree requirements:* For master's, comprehensive exam or practicum; for doctorate, practicum. *Entrance requirements:* For master's, official transcript showing earned bachelor's degree from institution accredited by recognized accrediting body. Additional exam requirements/recommendations for international students: required—TOEFL (minimum score 550 paper-based), IELTS (minimum score 6.5). *Application deadline:* Applications are processed on a rolling basis. Application fee: $0. Electronic applications accepted. *Financial support:* Scholarships/grants available. Financial award applicants required to submit FAFSA. *Unit head:* Dr. Wallace Boston, President, 877-468-6268, Fax: 304-728-2348, E-mail: president@apus.edu. *Application contact:* Yoci Deal, Associate Vice President, Graduate and International Admissions, 877-468-6268, Fax: 304-724-3764, E-mail: info@apus.edu.
Website: http://www.apus.edu

American University, School of Public Affairs, Department of Justice, Law and Criminology, Washington, DC 20016-8043. Offers justice, law and criminology (MS, PhD); terrorism, homeland security and policy (MS); JD/MS. *Program availability:* Part-time, evening/weekend, 100% online, blended/hybrid learning. *Degree requirements:* For master's, comprehensive exam; for doctorate, comprehensive exam, thesis/dissertation. *Entrance requirements:* For master's, GRE, 2 recommendations, statement of purpose, resume, transcript; for doctorate, 3 recommendations, statement of purpose, resume, writing sample, transcript. Additional exam requirements/recommendations for international students: required—TOEFL. *Expenses:* Contact institution.

American University of Puerto Rico - Bayamon, Program in Criminal Justice, Bayamon, PR 00960-2037. Offers MA. *Program availability:* Part-time, evening/weekend. *Degree requirements:* For master's, comprehensive exam. *Entrance requirements:* For master's, interviews; recommendations.

Anderson University, Command College of South Carolina, Anderson, SC 29621. Offers criminal justice (MCJ). *Program availability:* Blended/hybrid learning. *Entrance requirements:* For master's, minimum undergraduate GPA of 2.75, 5 years of experience working in criminal justice field, resume. *Application deadline:* Applications are processed on a rolling basis. Electronic applications accepted. *Expenses:* Contact institution. *Financial support:* Scholarships/grants available. Financial award application deadline: 3/1; financial award applicants required to submit FAFSA.
Website: https://www.andersonuniversity.edu/graduate/programs/criminal-justice/command-college

Angelo State University, College of Graduate Studies and Research, College of Arts and Humanities, Department of Security Studies and Criminal Justice, San Angelo, TX 76909. Offers criminal justice (MS); homeland security (MS); intelligence, security studies, and analysis (MSS); security studies (MSS). *Program availability:* Part-time, evening/weekend, online learning. *Entrance requirements:* For master's, essay, letters of recommendation. Additional exam requirements/recommendations for international students: required—TOEFL or IELTS. Electronic applications accepted.

Anna Maria College, Graduate Division, Program in Criminal Justice, Paxton, MA 01612. Offers criminal justice (MS). *Program availability:* Part-time, evening/weekend. *Degree requirements:* For master's, capstone project or thesis. *Entrance requirements:* For master's, bachelor's degree in related field, minimum GPA of 2.7. Additional exam requirements/recommendations for international students: required—TOEFL (minimum score 500 paper-based). Electronic applications accepted.

Arizona State University at Tempe, College of Public Programs, School of Criminology and Criminal Justice, Phoenix, AZ 85004. Offers corrections management (Graduate Certificate); criminal justice (MA); criminology and criminal justice (MS, PhD); law enforcement administration (Graduate Certificate). *Program availability:* Part-time, evening/weekend, online learning. Terminal master's awarded for partial completion of doctoral program. *Degree requirements:* For master's, thesis or alternative, policy analysis project, interactive Program of Study (iPOS) submitted before completing 50 percent of required credit hours; for doctorate, comprehensive exam, thesis/dissertation, interactive Program of Study (iPOS) submitted before completing 50 percent of required credit hours. *Entrance requirements:* For master's, GRE (MS), minimum GPA of 3.0 or equivalent in last 2 years of work leading to bachelor's degree; for doctorate, GRE, minimum GPA of 3.0 or equivalent in last 2 years of work leading to bachelor's degree, 2 letters of recommendation, resume, personal statement. Additional exam requirements/recommendations for international students: required—TOEFL, IELTS, or PTE. Electronic applications accepted.

Arkansas State University, Graduate School, College of Humanities and Social Sciences, Department of Criminology, Sociology, and Geography, State University, AR 72467. Offers criminal justice (MA); sociology (MA); sociology education (SCCT). *Program availability:* Part-time. *Degree requirements:* For master's, one foreign language, comprehensive exam, thesis or alternative; for SCCT, comprehensive exam. *Entrance requirements:* For master's, GRE General Test or MAT, appropriate bachelor's degree, letters of recommendation, official transcripts, immunization records; for SCCT, GRE General Test or MAT, interview, master's degree, official transcript, immunization records. Additional exam requirements/recommendations for international students: required—TOEFL (minimum score 550 paper-based; 79 iBT), IELTS (minimum score 6), PTE (minimum score 56). Electronic applications accepted.

Ashworth College, Graduate Programs, Norcross, GA 30092. Offers business administration (MBA); criminal justice (MS); health care administration (MBA, MS); human resource management (MBA, MS); international business (MBA); management (MS); marketing (MBA, MS).

Ball State University, Graduate School, College of Sciences and Humanities, Department of Political Science, Program in Public Administration, Muncie, IN 47306. Offers public administration (MPA, Certificate), including community and economic development (MPA), criminal justice (MPA), emergency management and homeland security (MPA), information and communication technology (MPA). *Program availability:* Part-time. *Degree requirements:* For master's, comprehensive exam. *Entrance requirements:* For master's, GRE General Test, minimum baccalaureate GPA of 2.8, two letters of recommendation. Additional exam requirements/recommendations for international students: required—TOEFL (minimum score 550 paper-based; 79 iBT), IELTS (minimum score 6.5). Electronic applications accepted. *Expenses: Tuition, area resident:* Full-time $7506; part-time $417 per credit hour. Tuition, nonresident: full-time $20,610; part-time $1145 per credit hour. *Required fees:* $2126. Tuition and fees vary according to course load, campus/location and program.

Bellevue University, Graduate School, College of Information Technology, Bellevue, NE 68005-3098. Offers computer information systems (MS); cybersecurity (MS); management of information systems (MS); project management (MPM).

Bellevue University, Graduate School, College of Professional Studies, Bellevue, NE 68005-3098. Offers instructional design and development (MS); justice administration and criminal management (MS); leadership (MA); organizational performance (MS); public administration (MPA); security management (MS).

Boise State University, School of Public Service, Department of Criminal Justice, Boise, ID 83725-0399. Offers MA. *Students:* 8 full-time (3 women), 3 part-time (2 women); includes 4 minority (1 Asian, non-Hispanic/Latino; 1 Hispanic/Latino; 2 Two or more races, non-Hispanic/Latino), 1 international. *Entrance requirements:* Additional exam requirements/recommendations for international students: required—TOEFL, IELTS. Electronic applications accepted. *Expenses: Tuition, area resident:* Full-time $7110; part-time $470 per credit hour. Tuition, state resident: full-time $7110; part-time $470 per credit hour. Tuition, nonresident: full-time $24,030; part-time $827 per credit hour. *International tuition:* $24,030 full-time. *Required fees:* $2536. Tuition and fees vary according to course load and program. *Financial support:* Scholarships/grants and unspecified assistantships available. Financial award application deadline: 2/15; financial award applicants required to submit FAFSA. *Unit head:* Lisa Growett Bostaph, Program Coordinator, 208-426-3886, E-mail: lisabostaph@boisestate.edu. *Application contact:* Lisa Growett Bostaph, Program Coordinator, 208-426-3886, E-mail: lisabostaph@boisestate.edu.
Website: https://www.boisestate.edu/sps/

Boston University, Metropolitan College, Program in Criminal Justice, Boston, MA 02215. Offers cybercrime investigation and cybersecurity (MCJ); strategic management (MCJ). *Program availability:* Part-time, evening/weekend, online learning. *Faculty:* 6 full-time (2 women), 2 part-time/adjunct (0 women). *Students:* 9 full-time (6 women), 130 part-time (75 women); includes 50 minority (17 Black or African American, non-Hispanic/Latino; 1 American Indian or Alaska Native, non-Hispanic/Latino; 12 Asian, non-Hispanic/Latino; 18 Hispanic/Latino; 2 Two or more races, non-Hispanic/Latino), 8

international. Average age 31. In 2019, 142 master's awarded. *Degree requirements:* For master's, comprehensive examination (for on-campus program only). *Entrance requirements:* Additional exam requirements/recommendations for international students: required—TOEFL (minimum score 84 iBT). *Application deadline:* For fall admission, 8/1 priority date for domestic students, 6/1 priority date for international students; for spring admission, 12/1 priority date for domestic students, 11/15 priority date for international students; for summer admission, 4/1 priority date for domestic students, 3/1 priority date for international students. Applications are processed on a rolling basis. Application fee: $85. Electronic applications accepted. *Expenses:* Contact institution. *Financial support:* In 2019–20, 9 research assistantships (averaging $4,200 per year) were awarded; scholarships/grants and unspecified assistantships also available. Support available to part-time students. Financial award applicants required to submit FAFSA. *Unit head:* Dr. Mary Ellen Mastrorilli, Associate Professor of the Practice and Chair, 617-353-3025, Fax: 617-358-3595, E-mail: memastro@bu.edu. *Application contact:* Enrollment Services, 617-353-9185, E-mail: met@bu.edu.
Website: http://www.bu.edu/met/cj/

Bowling Green State University, Graduate College, College of Health and Human Services, Program in Criminal Justice, Bowling Green, OH 43403. Offers MSCJ. *Program availability:* Part-time, evening/weekend, online learning. *Degree requirements:* For master's, thesis or alternative. *Entrance requirements:* For master's, GRE General Test. Additional exam requirements/recommendations for international students: required—TOEFL. Electronic applications accepted.

Bridgewater State University, College of Graduate Studies, College of Humanities and Social Sciences, Department of Criminal Justice, Bridgewater, MA 02325. Offers MS. *Entrance requirements:* For master's, GRE General Test.

Buffalo State College, State University of New York, The Graduate School, School of the Professions, Department of Criminal Justice, Buffalo, NY 14222-1095. Offers MS. *Program availability:* Part-time, evening/weekend. *Degree requirements:* For master's, comprehensive exam, project. *Entrance requirements:* For master's, minimum GPA of 3.0. Additional exam requirements/recommendations for international students: required—TOEFL (minimum score 550 paper-based).

Cabrini University, Academic Affairs, Radnor, PA 19087. Offers accounting (M Acc); autism spectrum disorder (M Ed); biological sciences (MS), including civic leadership; criminology and criminal justice (MA); curriculum, instruction, and assessment (M Ed); educational leadership (M Ed, Ed D), including curriculum and instructional leadership (Ed D), preK-12 leadership (Ed D); English as a second language (M Ed); organizational leadership (DBA, PhD); preK to 4 (M Ed); reading specialist (M Ed); secondary education (M Ed), including biology, chemistry, English, English/communication, mathematics, social studies; special education grades 7-12 (M Ed); special education preK-8 (M Ed); teaching and learning (M Ed). *Program availability:* Part-time, evening/weekend. *Degree requirements:* For master's, comprehensive exam (for some programs), thesis (for some programs); for doctorate, comprehensive exam (for some programs), thesis/dissertation. *Entrance requirements:* For master's, professional resume, personal statement, two recommendations, official transcripts; for doctorate, official transcripts, minimum master's GPA of 3.0, two recommendations, interview with admissions committee. Additional exam requirements/recommendations for international students: required—TOEFL (minimum score 80 iBT). Electronic applications accepted. Application fee is waived when completed online. *Expenses:* Contact institution.

California Coast University, School of Criminal Justice, Santa Ana, CA 92701. Offers MS.

California State University, Fresno, Division of Research and Graduate Studies, College of Social Sciences, Department of Criminology, Fresno, CA 93740-8027. Offers MS. *Program availability:* Part-time, evening/weekend. *Degree requirements:* For master's, thesis project or comprehensive examination. *Entrance requirements:* For master's, GRE General Test, minimum GPA of 3.0, personal essay. Additional exam requirements/recommendations for international students: required—TOEFL. Electronic applications accepted. *Expenses:* Tuition, state resident: full-time $4012; part-time $2506 per semester.

California State University, Long Beach, Graduate Studies, College of Health and Human Services, Department of Criminology and Criminal Justice, Long Beach, CA 90840. Offers criminal justice (MS); emergency services administration (MS). *Program availability:* Part-time. *Degree requirements:* For master's, comprehensive course or thesis. *Entrance requirements:* For master's, minimum GPA of 3.0. Electronic applications accepted.

California State University, Los Angeles, Graduate Studies, College of Health and Human Services, Department of Criminal Justice and Criminalistics, Los Angeles, CA 90032-8530. Offers criminal justice (MS); criminalistics (MS). *Program availability:* Part-time, evening/weekend. *Degree requirements:* For master's, thesis. *Entrance requirements:* For master's, minimum GPA of 2.75. Additional exam requirements/recommendations for international students: required—TOEFL (minimum score 500 paper-based). *Expenses: Tuition, area resident:* Full-time $7176; part-time $4164 per year. Tuition, state resident: full-time $7176; part-time $4164 per year. Tuition, nonresident: full-time $14,304; part-time $8916 per year. *International tuition:* $14,304 full-time. *Required fees:* $1037.76; $1037.76 per unit. Tuition and fees vary according to degree level and program.

California State University, Sacramento, College of Health and Human Services, Division of Criminal Justice, Sacramento, CA 95819. Offers MS. *Program availability:* Part-time. *Students:* 2 full-time (0 women), 25 part-time (17 women); includes 15 minority (2 Black or African American, non-Hispanic/Latino; 5 Asian, non-Hispanic/Latino; 7 Hispanic/Latino; 1 Native Hawaiian or other Pacific Islander, non-Hispanic/Latino). Average age 27. 36 applicants, 61% accepted, 17 enrolled. In 2019, 6 master's awarded. *Degree requirements:* For master's, thesis, thesis or project. *Entrance requirements:* For master's, GRE, BA in criminal justice or equivalent; minimum GPA of 3.0 during previous 2 years of course work and in major field. Additional exam requirements/recommendations for international students: required—TOEFL (minimum score 550 paper-based; 80 iBT); recommended—IELTS (minimum score 7). *Application deadline:* For fall admission, 3/1 for domestic students, 2/1 for international students. Applications are processed on a rolling basis. Application fee: $70. Electronic applications accepted. *Expenses:* Contact institution. *Financial support:* Teaching assistantships, career-related internships or fieldwork, Federal Work-Study, and scholarships/grants available. Support available to part-time students. Financial award application deadline: 3/1; financial award applicants required to submit FAFSA. *Unit head:* Dr. Ernest Uwazie, Chair, 916-278-6282, E-mail: uwazieee@csus.edu. *Application contact:* Jose Martinez, Graduate Admissions Supervisor, 916-278-6470, E-mail: martinj@skymail.csus.edu.
Website: http://www.csus.edu/hhs/cj

California State University, San Bernardino, Graduate Studies, College of Social and Behavioral Sciences, Program in Criminal Justice, San Bernardino, CA 92407. Offers MA. *Program availability:* Part-time. *Faculty:* 3 full-time (1 woman). *Students:* 3 full-time (2 women), 17 part-time (9 women); includes 14 minority (4 Black or African American, non-Hispanic/Latino; 1 Asian, non-Hispanic/Latino; 9 Hispanic/Latino). Average age 28. 9 applicants, 100% accepted, 7 enrolled. In 2019, 3 master's awarded. *Entrance requirements:* Additional exam requirements/recommendations for international students: required—TOEFL. *Application deadline:* For fall admission, 4/1 for domestic students; for winter admission, 9/1 for domestic students; for spring admission, 12/15 for domestic students. Application fee: $55. *Financial support:* Institutionally sponsored loans available. *Unit head:* Andrea Schoepfer, Graduate Program Coordinator, 909-537-7741, E-mail: cjgradinfo@csusb.edu. *Application contact:* Dr. Dorota Huizinga, Dean of Graduate Studies, 909-537-3064, E-mail: dorota.huizinga@csusb.edu.

California State University, Stanislaus, College of the Arts, Humanities and Social Sciences, Master's in Criminal Justice Program, Turlock, CA 95382. Offers MA. *Program availability:* Part-time. *Degree requirements:* For master's, comprehensive exam, thesis or alternative. *Entrance requirements:* For master's, minimum GPA of 3.0, 3 letters of reference, personal statement. Electronic applications accepted.

California University of Pennsylvania, School of Graduate Studies and Research, College of Liberal Arts, Department of Criminal Justice, California, PA 15419-1394. Offers conflict resolution (MA); criminal justice studies (MA). *Program availability:* Part-time, evening/weekend. *Degree requirements:* For master's, comprehensive exam, thesis optional. *Entrance requirements:* For master's, MAT, minimum GPA of 3.0. Additional exam requirements/recommendations for international students: required—TOEFL (minimum score 550 paper-based; 80 iBT). Electronic applications accepted. *Expenses: Tuition, area resident:* Full-time $9288; part-time $516 per credit. Tuition, state resident: full-time $9288; part-time $516 per credit. Tuition, nonresident: full-time $13,932; part-time $774 per credit. *Required fees:* $3631; $291.13 per credit. Part-time tuition and fees vary according to course load.

California University of Pennsylvania, School of Graduate Studies and Research, College of Liberal Arts, Department of History, Politics, Society and Law, California, PA 15419-1394. Offers legal studies (MS), including criminal justice, homeland security, law and public policy. *Program availability:* Part-time, evening/weekend, online learning. *Degree requirements:* For master's, thesis optional. *Entrance requirements:* For master's, interview, minimum GPA of 3.0. Additional exam requirements/recommendations for international students: required—TOEFL (minimum score 550 paper-based; 80 iBT). Electronic applications accepted. *Expenses: Tuition, area resident:* Full-time $9288; part-time $516 per credit. Tuition, state resident: full-time $9288; part-time $516 per credit. Tuition, nonresident: full-time $13,932; part-time $774 per credit. *Required fees:* $3631; $291.13 per credit. Part-time tuition and fees vary according to course load.

Calumet College of Saint Joseph, Program in Public Safety Administration, Whiting, IN 46394-2195. Offers MS.

Capella University, School of Public Service Leadership, Doctoral Programs in Healthcare, Minneapolis, MN 55402. Offers criminal justice (PhD); emergency management (PhD); epidemiology (Dr PH); general health administration (DHA); general public administration (DPA); health advocacy and leadership (Dr PH); health care administration (PhD); health care leadership (DHA); health policy advocacy (DHA); multidisciplinary human services (PhD); nonprofit management and leadership (PhD); public safety leadership (PhD); social and community services (PhD).

Capella University, School of Public Service Leadership, Master's Programs in Healthcare, Minneapolis, MN 55402. Offers criminal justice (MS); emergency management (MS); general public health (MPH); gerontology (MS); health administration (MHA); health care operations (MHA); health management policy (MPH); health policy (MHA); homeland security (MS); multidisciplinary human services (MS); public administration (MPA); public safety leadership (MS); social and community services (MS); social behavioral sciences (MPH); MS/MPA.

Cardinal Stritch University, College of Business and Management, Milwaukee, WI 53217-3985. Offers cyber security (MBA); healthcare management (MBA); justice administration (MBA); marketing (MBA). *Accreditation:* ACBSP. *Program availability:* Part-time, evening/weekend, 100% online, blended/hybrid learning. *Degree requirements:* For master's, thesis. *Entrance requirements:* For master's, 3 years of management or related experience, minimum GPA of 2.5. Additional exam requirements/recommendations for international students: required—TOEFL (minimum score 79 iBT), IELTS (minimum score 6.5). Electronic applications accepted. *Expenses:* Contact institution.

Caribbean University, Graduate School, Bayamón, PR 00960-0493. Offers administration and supervision (MA Ed); criminal justice (MA); curriculum and instruction (MA Ed, PhD), including elementary education (MA Ed), English education (MA Ed), history education (MA Ed), mathematics education (MA Ed), primary education (MA Ed), science education (MA Ed), Spanish education (MA Ed); educational technology in instructional systems (MA Ed); gerontology (MSN); human resources (MBA); museology, archiving and art history (MA Ed); neonatal pediatrics (MSN); physical education (MA Ed); special education (MA Ed). *Entrance requirements:* For master's, interview, minimum GPA of 2.5.

Carnegie Mellon University, Heinz College, School of Information Systems and Management, Master of Science in Information Security Policy and Management Program, Pittsburgh, PA 15213-3891. Offers MSISPM. *Entrance requirements:* For master's, GRE or GMAT, college-level course in advanced algebra/pre-calculus; college-level courses in economics and statistics (recommended). Additional exam requirements/recommendations for international students: required—TOEFL or IELTS.

The Catholic University of America, School of Arts and Sciences, Department of Sociology, Washington, DC 20064. Offers crime and justice studies (MA); global and comparative sociology (MA); public policy (MA). *Program availability:* Part-time. *Faculty:* 3 full-time (2 women), 2 part-time/adjunct (both women). *Students:* 1 (woman) full-time. Average age 23. 1 applicant, 100% accepted, 1 enrolled. In 2019, 1 master's awarded. *Degree requirements:* For master's, comprehensive exam, thesis or alternative, two seminar papers. *Entrance requirements:* For master's, GRE General Test, statement of purpose, official copies of academic transcripts, three letters of recommendation. Additional exam requirements/recommendations for international students: required—TOEFL (minimum score 550 paper-based; 80 iBT). *Application deadline:* For fall admission, 7/15 priority date for domestic students, 7/1 for international students; for spring admission, 11/15 priority date for domestic students, 11/1 for international students. Applications are processed on a rolling basis. Application fee: $55. Electronic applications accepted. *Financial support:* Fellowships, research assistantships, teaching assistantships, Federal Work-Study, scholarships/grants, tuition waivers (full and partial), and unspecified assistantships available. Financial award application deadline: 2/1; financial award applicants required to submit FAFSA. *Unit head:* Dr. Brandon Vaidyanathan, Chair, 202-319-5941, Fax: 202-319-4980, E-mail: brandonv@cua.edu. *Application contact:* Dr. Steven Brown, Director of Graduate Admissions, 202-319-5057, Fax: 202-319-6533, E-mail: cua-admissions@cua.edu.
Website: http://sociology.cua.edu/

Central Connecticut State University, School of Graduate Studies, College of Liberal Arts and Social Sciences, Department of Criminology and Criminal Justice, New Britain, CT 06050-4010. Offers criminal justice (MS). *Program availability:* Part-time, evening/weekend. *Degree requirements:* For master's, comprehensive exam, thesis or alternative. *Entrance requirements:* For master's, minimum undergraduate GPA of 3.0, essay, resume. Additional exam requirements/recommendations for international students: required—TOEFL (minimum score 550 paper-based; 79 iBT); recommended—IELTS (minimum score 6.5). Electronic applications accepted.

Chaminade University of Honolulu, Graduate, Program in Criminal Justice Administration, Honolulu, HI 96816-1578. Offers correctional (MSCJA); criminal justice (MSCJA); law enforcement (MSCJA). *Program availability:* Part-time, evening/weekend, 100% online, blended/hybrid learning. *Faculty:* 4 full-time (2 women), 1 (woman) part-time/adjunct. *Students:* 15 full-time (10 women), 8 part-time (all women); includes 15 minority (6 Asian, non-Hispanic/Latino; 4 Hispanic/Latino; 3 Native Hawaiian or other Pacific Islander, non-Hispanic/Latino; 2 Two or more races, non-Hispanic/Latino). Average age 30. 10 applicants, 100% accepted, 3 enrolled. In 2019, 15 master's awarded. *Degree requirements:* For master's, comprehensive exam. *Entrance requirements:* For master's, Official transcripts; minimum GPA 3.0, and contact information for three academic/professional references. Additional exam requirements/recommendations for international students: required—TOEFL (minimum score 79 iBT), IELTS (minimum score 6.5), PTE (minimum score 53). *Application deadline:* Applications are processed on a rolling basis. Application fee: $40. Electronic applications accepted. *Expenses:* $1,000 per credit hour; $93 fee per online course. *Financial support:* Applicants required to submit FAFSA. *Unit head:* Ronald Becker, Director, 808-735-4703, Fax: 808-739-4614, E-mail: mscja@chaminade.edu. *Application contact:* Ronald Becker, Director, 808-735-4703, Fax: 808-739-4614, E-mail: mscja@chaminade.edu.
Website: https://chaminade.edu/academic-program/mscja/

Charleston Southern University, Department of Criminal Justice, Charleston, SC 29423-8087. Offers MSCJ. *Program availability:* Part-time, evening/weekend, online learning. *Degree requirements:* For master's, comprehensive exam, thesis optional. *Entrance requirements:* For master's, GRE or MAT, bachelor's degree in criminal justice. Additional exam requirements/recommendations for international students: required—TOEFL (minimum score 550 paper-based; 79 iBT). Electronic applications accepted.

Chicago State University, School of Graduate and Professional Studies, College of Arts and Sciences, Department of Criminal Justice, Philosophy, and Political Science, Chicago, IL 60628. Offers criminal justice (MS). *Program availability:* Part-time, evening/weekend. *Entrance requirements:* For master's, minimum GPA of 2.75.

Clark Atlanta University, School of Arts and Sciences, Department of Sociology and Criminal Justice, Atlanta, GA 30314. Offers MA. *Program availability:* Part-time. *Degree requirements:* For master's, one foreign language, comprehensive exam, thesis. *Entrance requirements:* For master's, GRE General Test, minimum GPA of 2.5. Additional exam requirements/recommendations for international students: required—TOEFL (minimum score 500 paper-based; 61 iBT). Electronic applications accepted.

Clayton State University, School of Graduate Studies, College of Arts and Sciences, Program in Criminal Justice, Morrow, GA 30260-0285. Offers administration of justice (MS); criminology, law, and society (MS).

Clemson University, Graduate School, College of Behavioral, Social and Health Sciences, Department of Sociology, Anthropology and Criminal Justice, Clemson, SC 29634. Offers applied sociology (MS). *Program availability:* Part-time. *Faculty:* 21 full-time (11 women). *Students:* 7 full-time (3 women); includes 1 minority (Black or African American, non-Hispanic/Latino), 1 international. Average age 23. 12 applicants, 75% accepted. In 2019, 4 master's awarded. *Degree requirements:* For master's, thesis optional. *Entrance requirements:* For master's, GRE General Test, unofficial transcripts, letters of recommendation. Additional exam requirements/recommendations for international students: required—TOEFL (minimum score 80 paper-based; 80 iBT); recommended—IELTS (minimum score 6.5), TSE (minimum score 54). *Application deadline:* For fall admission, 4/15 priority date for international students; for spring admission, 10/15 priority date for international students. Applications are processed on a rolling basis. Application fee: $80 ($90 for international students). Electronic applications accepted. *Expenses:* Full-Time Student per Semester: Tuition: $4600 (in-state), $9525 (out-of-state), Fees: $598; Graduate Assistant Per Semester: $1144; Part-Time Student Per Credit Hour: $556 (in-state), $1106 (out-of-state), Fees: $617; other fees apply depending on program, credit hours, campus & residency. *Financial support:* In 2019–20, 7 teaching assistantships with full and partial tuition reimbursements (averaging $11,000 per year) were awarded; career-related internships or fieldwork also available. *Unit head:* Dr. Catherine Weisensee, Department Chair, 864-656-3238, E-mail: kweisen@clemson.edu. *Application contact:* Dr. Bryan Miller, Graduate Program Coordinator, 864-656-3818, E-mail: BLM2@clemson.edu.
Website: http://www.clemson.edu/cbshs/departments/sociology/

Coker College, Graduate Programs, Hartsville, SC 29550. Offers college athletic administration (MS); criminal and social justice policy (MS); curriculum and instructional technology (M Ed); literacy studies (M Ed); management and leadership (MS). *Program availability:* Part-time, 100% online. *Entrance requirements:* For master's, undergraduate overall GPA of 3.0 on 4.0 scale, official transcripts from all undergraduate institutions, 1-page personal statement, resume, 2 professional references, 1 year of teaching in PK-12 and letter of recommendation from principal/assistant principal for MEd in Literacy Studies. Electronic applications accepted.

College of Saint Elizabeth, Program in Justice Administration and Public Service, Morristown, NJ 07960-6989. Offers counter terrorism (Certificate); cyber security investigation (Certificate); justice administration and public service (MA); leadership in community policing (Certificate). *Program availability:* Part-time, 100% online, blended/hybrid learning. *Degree requirements:* For master's, thesis. *Entrance requirements:* Additional exam requirements/recommendations for international students: required—TOEFL (minimum score 550 paper-based; 79 iBT), IELTS (minimum score 6.5). Electronic applications accepted. Application fee is waived when completed online. *Expenses:* Contact institution.

Colorado State University–Global Campus, Graduate Programs, Greenwood Village, CO 80111. Offers criminal justice and law enforcement administration (MS); education leadership (MS); finance (MS); healthcare administration and management (MS); human resource management (MHRM); information technology management (MITM); international management (MS); management (MS); organizational leadership (MS); professional accounting (MPA); project management (MS); teaching and learning (MS). *Accreditation:* ACBSP. *Program availability:* Online learning.

Colorado Technical University Aurora, Program in Computer Science, Aurora, CO 80014. Offers computer systems security (MSCS); database systems (MSCS); software engineering (MSCS). *Program availability:* Part-time, evening/weekend. *Degree requirements:* For master's, thesis or alternative. *Entrance requirements:* For master's, minimum undergraduate GPA of 3.0, resume.

Colorado Technical University Colorado Springs, Graduate Studies, Program in Criminal Justice, Colorado Springs, CO 80907. Offers MSM. *Program availability:* Online learning.

Columbia College, Graduate Programs, Program in Criminal Justice, Columbia, SC 29203-5998. Offers MA. *Expenses: Tuition:* Full-time $10,080; part-time $480 per semester hour.

Columbia College, Master of Science in Criminal Justice Program, Columbia, MO 65216-0002. Offers MSCJ. *Program availability:* Part-time, evening/weekend, 100% online, blended/hybrid learning. *Faculty:* 2 full-time (0 women), 21 part-time/adjunct (12 women). *Students:* 2 full-time (1 woman), 59 part-time (31 women); includes 26 minority (15 Black or African American, non-Hispanic/Latino; 1 American Indian or Alaska Native, non-Hispanic/Latino; 5 Hispanic/Latino; 5 Two or more races, non-Hispanic/Latino). Average age 39. 72 applicants, 79% accepted, 15 enrolled. In 2019, 44 master's awarded. *Entrance requirements:* For master's, bachelor degree, 3.0 GPA, resume, goal statement, application. Additional exam requirements/recommendations for international students: required—TOEFL (minimum score 550 paper-based; 80 iBT), IELTS (minimum score 6.5), PTE (minimum score 58). *Application deadline:* For fall admission, 8/9 priority date for domestic and international students; for spring admission, 12/27 priority date for domestic and international students. Applications are processed on a rolling basis. Application fee: $0. Electronic applications accepted. *Expenses:* 17640 tuition. *Financial support:* In 2019–20, 14 students received support. Scholarships/grants, tuition waivers (full and partial), and unspecified assistantships available. Financial award application deadline: 3/1; financial award applicants required to submit FAFSA. *Unit head:* Dr. Lisa Ford-Brown, Dean of the School of Humanities, Arts and Social Sciences, 573-875-7570, E-mail: labrown@ccis.edu. *Application contact:* Stephanie Johnson, Associate Vice President for Recruiting and Admissions Division, 573-875-7352, Fax: 573-875-7506, E-mail: sgjohnson@ccis.edu.
Website: http://www.ccis.edu/graduate/academics/degrees.asp?MSCJ

Columbia Southern University, College of Safety and Emergency Services, Orange Beach, AL 36561. Offers criminal justice administration (MS); emergency services management (MS); occupational safety and health (MS), including environmental management. *Program availability:* Part-time, evening/weekend, online learning. *Entrance requirements:* For master's, bachelor's degree from accredited/approved institution. Additional exam requirements/recommendations for international students: required—TOEFL. Electronic applications accepted.

Columbus State University, Graduate Studies, College of Letters and Sciences, Department of Political Science and Public Administration, Columbus, GA 31907-5645. Offers public administration (MPA), including criminal justice, environmental policy, government administration, health services administration, political campaigning, urban policy. *Program availability:* Part-time, evening/weekend, 100% online, blended/hybrid learning. *Degree requirements:* For master's, comprehensive exam. *Entrance requirements:* For master's, GRE General Test, minimum GPA of 2.75, three letters of recommendation. Additional exam requirements/recommendations for international students: required—TOEFL (minimum score 550 paper-based; 79 iBT). Electronic applications accepted. *Expenses: Tuition, area resident:* Full-time $210; part-time $210 per credit hour. Tuition, state resident: full-time $210; part-time $210 per credit hour. Tuition, nonresident: full-time $817; part-time $817 per credit hour. *International tuition:* $817 full-time. *Required fees:* $802.50. Tuition and fees vary according to course load, degree level and program.

Concordia University, St. Paul, College of Humanities and Social Sciences, St. Paul, MN 55104-5494. Offers creative writing (MFA); criminal justice leadership (MA); family science (MA); human services (MA), including forensic behavioral health. *Accreditation:* NCATE. *Program availability:* Part-time, evening/weekend, 100% online, blended/hybrid learning. *Degree requirements:* For master's, thesis (for some programs), capstone project. *Entrance requirements:* For master's, official transcripts stating the conferral of a Bachelor's degree with a minimum cumulative GPA of 3.0 based on a 4.0 system; personal statement; writing sample in fiction or non-fiction (MFA students only); resume (MA students only). Additional exam requirements/recommendations for international students: required—TOEFL (minimum score 547 paper-based; 78 iBT), IELTS (minimum score 6), PTE (minimum score 78). Electronic applications accepted. *Expenses:* Contact institution.

Coppin State University, School of Graduate Studies, College of Behavioral and Social Sciences, Department of Criminal Justice, Baltimore, MD 21216-3698. Offers MS. *Program availability:* Part-time, evening/weekend. *Degree requirements:* For master's, thesis optional. *Entrance requirements:* For master's, GRE, minimum GPA of 3.0.

Curry College, Graduate Studies, Program in Criminal Justice, Milton, MA 02186-9984. Offers MA. *Program availability:* Part-time, evening/weekend. *Degree requirements:* For master's, thesis. *Entrance requirements:* For master's, resume, recommendations, interview. Additional exam requirements/recommendations for international students: required—TOEFL (minimum score 550 paper-based; 80 iBT). *Expenses:* Contact institution.

Dallas Baptist University, Professional Development Program, Dallas, TX 75211-9299. Offers accounting (MA); church leadership (MA); communication (MA); counseling (MA); criminal justice (MA); English as a second language (MA); finance (MA); higher education (MA); leadership studies (MA); management (MA). *Program availability:* Part-time, evening/weekend, online learning. *Application deadline:* Applications are processed on a rolling basis. Application fee: $25. Electronic applications accepted. Application fee is waived when completed online. *Expenses: Tuition:* Full-time $18,072; part-time $1004 per credit hour. *Required fees:* $1100; $550 per semester. Tuition and fees vary according to course level and degree level. *Unit head:* Jared Ingram, Program Director, 214-333-5584, E-mail: jaredi@dbu.edu. *Application contact:* Jared Ingram, Program Director, 214-333-5584, E-mail: jaredi@dbu.edu.
Website: https://www.dbu.edu/graduate/degree-programs/ma-professional-development

Delaware Valley University, Program in Criminal Justice, Doylestown, PA 18901-2697. Offers MA.

Delta State University, Graduate Programs, College of Arts and Sciences, Division of Social Sciences and History, Program in Social Justice and Criminology, Cleveland, MS 38733-0001. Offers MSJC. *Program availability:* Part-time, online learning. *Degree requirements:* For master's, thesis or alternative. *Expenses: Tuition, area resident:* Full-time $7501; part-time $417 per credit hour. Tuition, state resident: full-time $7501; part-time $417 per credit hour. Tuition, nonresident: full-time $7501; part-time $417 per credit hour. *International tuition:* $7501 full-time. *Required fees:* $170; $9.45 per credit hour. $9.45 per semester.

DeSales University, Division of Liberal Arts and Social Sciences, Center Valley, PA 18034-9568. Offers criminal justice (MCJ); digital forensics (MCJ, Postbaccalaureate Certificate); education (M Ed), including instructional technology, secondary education, special education, teaching English to speakers of other languages; investigative forensics (MCJ, Postbaccalaureate Certificate). *Program availability:* Part-time, 100% online, blended/hybrid learning. *Faculty:* 5 full-time (3 women), 15 part-time/adjunct (9 women). *Students:* 68 full-time (43 women), 115 part-time (72 women); includes 34 minority (8 Black or African American, non-Hispanic/Latino; 1 Asian, non-Hispanic/Latino; 19 Hispanic/Latino; 1 Native Hawaiian or other Pacific Islander, non-Hispanic/Latino; 5 Two or more races, non-Hispanic/Latino), 1 international. Average age 33. 135 applicants, 48% accepted, 63 enrolled. In 2019, 49 master's awarded. *Entrance* *requirements:* For master's, bachelor's degree from accredited institution, minimum undergraduate GPA of 3.0, personal statement showing potential of graduate work, three letters of recommendation, professional goal statement. Additional exam requirements/recommendations for international students: required—TOEFL. *Application deadline:* Applications are processed on a rolling basis. Application fee: $50. Electronic applications accepted. *Expenses: Tuition:* Full-time $855; part-time $855 per credit hour. Tuition and fees vary according to program. *Financial support:* Applicants required to submit FAFSA. *Unit head:* Ronald Nordone, Dean of Graduate Education, 610-282-1100 Ext. 1289, E-mail: ronald.nordone@desales.edu. *Application contact:* Julia Ferraro, Director of Graduate Admissions, 610-282-1100 Ext. 1768, E-mail: gradadmissions@desales.edu.

East Carolina University, Graduate School, Thomas Harriot College of Arts and Sciences, Department of Criminal Justice, Greenville, NC 27858-4353. Offers criminal justice (MS); criminal justice education (Certificate). *Program availability:* Part-time, evening/weekend, online learning. *Application deadline:* For fall admission, 4/1 priority date for domestic and international students; for spring admission, 10/1 priority date for domestic and international students. *Expenses: Tuition,* area resident: Full-time $4749; part-time $185 per credit hour. Tuition, state resident: full-time $4749; part-time $185 per credit hour. Tuition, nonresident: full-time $17,898; part-time $864 per credit hour. *International tuition:* $17,898 full-time. *Required fees:* $2787. *Financial support:* Application deadline: 3/1. *Unit head:* Dr. Heidi S Bonner, Chair, 252-328-4382, Fax: 252-328-4196, E-mail: bonnerhe@ecu.edu. *Application contact:* Graduate School Admissions, 252-328-6012, Fax: 252-328-6071, E-mail: gradschool@ecu.edu. Website: https://criminal-justice.ecu.edu/

East Carolina University, Graduate School, Thomas Harriot College of Arts and Sciences, Department of Political Science, Greenville, NC 27858-4353. Offers public administration (MPA); security studies (MS, Certificate). *Accreditation:* NASPAA. *Program availability:* Part-time, evening/weekend, online learning. *Application deadline:* For fall admission, 6/1 priority date for domestic students; for spring admission, 10/15 for domestic students. *Expenses: Tuition,* area resident: Full-time $4749; part-time $185 per credit hour. Tuition, state resident: full-time $4749; part-time $185 per credit hour. Tuition, nonresident: full-time $17,898; part-time $864 per credit hour. *International tuition:* $17,898 full-time. *Required fees:* $2787. *Financial support:* Application deadline: 3/1. *Unit head:* Dr. Alethia Cook, Chair, 252-328-5869, E-mail: cooka@ecu.edu. *Application contact:* Graduate School Admissions, 252-328-6012, Fax: 252-328-6071, E-mail: gradschool@ecu.edu. Website: https://politicalscience.ecu.edu/

East Central University, School of Graduate Studies, Department of Professional Programs in Human Services, Ada, OK 74820. Offers clinical rehabilitation and clinical mental health counseling (MSHR); criminal justice (MSHR); human resources (MSHR). *Accreditation:* CORE. *Program availability:* Part-time, evening/weekend. *Degree requirements:* For master's, thesis optional. *Entrance requirements:* For master's, GRE General Test, MAT, minimum GPA of 2.5. Electronic applications accepted.

Eastern Kentucky University, The Graduate School, College of Justice and Safety, Program in Correctional and Juvenile Justice Studies, Richmond, KY 40475-3102. Offers MS. *Degree requirements:* For master's, comprehensive exam (for some programs), thesis (for some programs). *Entrance requirements:* For master's, GRE.

Eastern Kentucky University, The Graduate School, College of Justice and Safety, Program in Criminal Justice and Police Studies, Richmond, KY 40475-3102. Offers criminal justice (MS); criminal justice education (MS); police studies (MS). *Program availability:* Part-time. *Degree requirements:* For master's, thesis optional. *Entrance requirements:* For master's, GRE General Test, minimum GPA of 3.0.

Eastern Kentucky University, The Graduate School, College of Justice and Safety, Program in Loss Prevention and Safety, Richmond, KY 40475-3102. Offers MS. *Entrance requirements:* For master's, GRE.

Eastern Michigan University, Graduate School, College of Arts and Sciences, Department of Sociology, Anthropology and Criminology, Program in Criminology and Criminal Justice, Ypsilanti, MI 48197. Offers MA. *Students:* 7 full-time (4 women), 7 part-time (5 women); includes 2 minority (both Two or more races, non-Hispanic/Latino). Average age 26. 14 applicants, 71% accepted, 5 enrolled. In 2019, 2 master's awarded. Application fee: $45. *Application contact:* Dr. Brian Sellers, Advisor, 734-487-0012, Fax: 734-487-9666, E-mail: bseller3@emich.edu.

East Tennessee State University, College of Graduate and Continuing Studies, College of Arts and Sciences, Department of Criminal Justice and Criminology, Johnson City, TN 37614. Offers criminal justice and criminology (MA); forensic document examination (Postbaccalaureate Certificate). *Program availability:* Part-time, evening/weekend. *Degree requirements:* For master's, comprehensive exam, thesis optional; for Postbaccalaureate Certificate, practicum. *Entrance requirements:* For master's, GRE General Test, minimum GPA of 3.0; for Postbaccalaureate Certificate, minimum GPA of 2.5, three letters of recommendation. Additional exam requirements/recommendations for international students: required—TOEFL (minimum score 550 paper-based; 79 iBT). Electronic applications accepted.

Fairleigh Dickinson University, Metropolitan Campus, University College: Arts, Sciences, and Professional Studies, School of Criminal Justice and Legal Studies, Program in Criminal Justice, Teaneck, NJ 07666-1914. Offers MA.

Fairmont State University, Program in Criminal Justice, Fairmont, WV 26554. Offers MS. *Program availability:* Part-time, evening/weekend, 100% online. *Degree requirements:* For master's, thesis or comprehensive exam. *Entrance requirements:* For master's, GRE, minimum GPA of 3.0. Additional exam requirements/recommendations for international students: required—TOEFL (minimum score 80 iBT), IELTS (minimum score 6.5). Electronic applications accepted.

Faulkner University, Alabama Christian College of Arts and Sciences, Department of Criminal Justice, Montgomery, AL 36109-3398. Offers justice administration (MJA). *Program availability:* Part-time, evening/weekend, online only, 100% online. *Degree requirements:* For master's, research project. *Entrance requirements:* For master's, MAT, bachelor's degree from regionally-accredited college or university; official transcripts from all colleges and universities attended; minimum GPA of 2.5 on undergraduate degree, 3.0 from field of study; letter of intent (300-word minimum); resume; three professional letters of recommendation. Additional exam requirements/recommendations for international students: required—TOEFL (minimum score 500 paper-based). Electronic applications accepted. *Expenses:* Contact institution.

Fayetteville State University, Graduate School, Program in Criminal Justice, Fayetteville, NC 28301. Offers MA. *Program availability:* Part-time, evening/weekend, online learning. *Faculty:* 4 full-time (3 women). *Students:* 9 full-time (4 women), 25 part-time (18 women); includes 26 minority (18 Black or African American, non-Hispanic/Latino; 2 Asian, non-Hispanic/Latino; 4 Hispanic/Latino; 2 Two or more races, non-Hispanic/Latino). Average age 33. 23 applicants, 87% accepted, 17 enrolled. In 2019, 9 master's awarded. *Degree requirements:* For master's, comprehensive exam (for some programs), thesis (for some programs). *Entrance requirements:* For master's, GRE. Additional exam requirements/recommendations for international students: required—TOEFL (minimum score 61 paper-based). *Application deadline:* For fall admission, 6/15

for domestic students; for spring admission, 11/15 for domestic students; for summer admission, 4/15 for domestic students. Applications are processed on a rolling basis. Application fee: $50. Electronic applications accepted. *Financial support:* Application deadline: 3/1; applicants required to submit FAFSA. *Unit head:* Dr. Joe Brown, Interim Chair, 910-672-1478, Fax: 910-672-1908, E-mail: jbrown25@uncfsu.edu. *Application contact:* Dr. Lori Guevara, Graduate Coordinator, 910-672-2190, Fax: 910-672-1908, E-mail: lguevara@uncfsu.edu. Website: https://www.uncfsu.edu/academics/colleges-schools-and-departments/college-of-humanities-and-social-sciences/department-of-criminal-justice

Ferris State University, College of Education and Human Services, School of Criminal Justice, Big Rapids, MI 49307. Offers criminal justice administration (MSCJ). *Program availability:* Part-time, evening/weekend. *Faculty:* 8 full-time (2 women). *Students:* 6 full-time (4 women), 39 part-time (22 women); includes 13 minority (9 Black or African American, non-Hispanic/Latino; 3 Hispanic/Latino; 1 Two or more races, non-Hispanic/Latino). Average age 31. 21 applicants, 100% accepted, 18 enrolled. In 2019, 19 master's awarded. *Degree requirements:* For master's, comprehensive exam or thesis/dissertation. *Entrance requirements:* For master's, bachelor's degree in criminal justice or related field, minimum GPA of 3.0. Additional exam requirements/recommendations for international students: required—TOEFL (minimum score 500 paper-based; 61 iBT). *Application deadline:* For fall admission, 8/15 for domestic students; for winter admission, 12/15 for domestic students; for spring admission, 3/15 for domestic students. Applications are processed on a rolling basis. Application fee: $0 ($30 for international students). Electronic applications accepted. Tuition and fees vary according to degree level, program and student level. *Financial support:* In 2019–20, 5 students received support, including 4 research assistantships (averaging $4,407 per year); Federal Work-Study and unspecified assistantships also available. Support available to part-time students. Financial award applicants required to submit FAFSA. *Unit head:* Dr. Nancy L. Hogan, Professor/Graduate Program Coordinator, 231-591-2664, Fax: 231-591-3792, E-mail: hogann@ferris.edu. *Application contact:* Sara P. Rasmussen, Secretary, 231-591-3652, Fax: 231-591-3792, E-mail: sararasmussen@ferris.edu. Website: http://www.ferris.edu/education/cj/

Florida Agricultural and Mechanical University, Division of Graduate Studies, Research, and Continuing Education, College of Social Sciences, Arts and Humanities, Department of History and Political Science, Program in Applied Social Science, Tallahassee, FL 32307-3200. Offers criminal justice (MASS); history (MASS); political science (MASS); public administration (MASS). *Program availability:* Part-time. *Degree requirements:* For master's, thesis optional. *Entrance requirements:* For master's, GRE General Test, minimum GPA of 3.0.

Florida Atlantic University, College for Design and Social Inquiry, School of Criminology and Criminal Justice, Boca Raton, FL 33431-0991. Offers MS. *Program availability:* Part-time, evening/weekend, online learning. *Faculty:* 8 full-time (2 women). *Students:* 18 full-time (15 women), 21 part-time (20 women); includes 28 minority (13 Black or African American, non-Hispanic/Latino; 1 Asian, non-Hispanic/Latino; 12 Hispanic/Latino; 2 Two or more races, non-Hispanic/Latino), 1 international. Average age 27. 74 applicants, 31% accepted, 19 enrolled. In 2019, 10 master's awarded. *Entrance requirements:* For master's, GRE General Test, minimum GPA of 3.0, undergraduate course work in statistics and criminology. Additional exam requirements/recommendations for international students: required—TOEFL (minimum score 550 paper-based; 61 iBT), IELTS (minimum score 6). *Application deadline:* For fall admission, 5/1 priority date for domestic students, 2/15 for international students; for spring admission, 11/1 priority date for domestic students, 7/15 for international students. Applications are processed on a rolling basis. Application fee: $30. Electronic applications accepted. *Expenses: Tuition:* Full-time $20,536; part-time $371.82 per credit hour. Tuition and fees vary according to program. *Financial support:* Research assistantships, institutionally sponsored loans, scholarships/grants, and unspecified assistantships available. Financial award application deadline: 4/1. *Unit head:* Dawn Lynette Rothe, Director, 561-297-3173, E-mail: rothed@fau.edu. *Application contact:* Dawn Lynette Rothe, Director, 561-297-3173, E-mail: rothed@fau.edu. Website: http://cdsi.fau.edu/sccj/

Florida Gulf Coast University, College of Arts and Sciences, Program in Criminal Justice, Fort Myers, FL 33965-6565. Offers MS. *Entrance requirements:* For master's, GRE General Test, minimum GPA of 3.0. Additional exam requirements/recommendations for international students: required—TOEFL (minimum score 550 paper-based). Electronic applications accepted. *Expenses: Tuition,* area resident: Full-time $6974; part-time $4350 per credit hour. Tuition, state resident: full-time $6974; part-time $4350 per credit hour. Tuition, nonresident: full-time $28,169; part-time $17,595 per credit hour. *International tuition:* $28,169 full-time. *Required fees:* $2027; $1267 per credit hour. $507 per semester. Tuition and fees vary according to course load.

Florida International University, Steven J. Green School of International and Public Affairs, Department of Criminal Justice, Miami, FL 33199. Offers criminal justice (MS); international crime and justice (PhD). *Program availability:* Part-time, evening/weekend. *Faculty:* 20 full-time (10 women), 27 part-time/adjunct (8 women). *Students:* 55 full-time (38 women), 43 part-time (25 women); includes 68 minority (15 Black or African American, non-Hispanic/Latino; 1 Asian, non-Hispanic/Latino; 48 Hispanic/Latino; 4 Two or more races, non-Hispanic/Latino), 8 international. Average age 30. 68 applicants, 44% accepted, 17 enrolled. In 2019, 22 master's awarded. *Entrance requirements:* For master's, minimum undergraduate GPA of 3.0. Additional exam requirements/recommendations for international students: required—TOEFL (minimum score 550 paper-based; 80 iBT). *Application deadline:* For fall admission, 6/1 for domestic students, 4/1 for international students; for spring admission, 10/1 for domestic students, 9/1 for international students. Applications are processed on a rolling basis. Application fee: $30. Electronic applications accepted. *Expenses: Tuition,* area resident: Full-time $8912; part-time $446 per credit hour. Tuition, state resident: full-time $8912; part-time $446 per credit hour. Tuition, nonresident: full-time $21,393; part-time $992 per credit hour. *Required fees:* $2194. *Financial support:* Institutionally sponsored loans and scholarships/grants available. Financial award application deadline: 3/1; financial award applicants required to submit FAFSA. *Unit head:* Dr. Lisa Stolzenberg, Chair, 305-348-5890, E-mail: stolzenb@fiu.edu. *Application contact:* Nanett Rojas, Manager, Admissions Operations, 305-348-7464, Fax: 305-348-7441, E-mail: gradadm@fiu.edu. Website: http://cj.fiu.edu/

Florida State University, The Graduate School, College of Criminology and Criminal Justice, Tallahassee, FL 32306-1127. Offers criminology and criminal justice (MA, MSC, PhD); MPA/MSC; MS/MSW. *Program availability:* Part-time, 100% online. Terminal master's awarded for partial completion of doctoral program. *Degree requirements:* For master's, thesis optional, minimum GPA of 3.0, minimum grade of C in all required courses; for doctorate, comprehensive exam, thesis/dissertation, minimum GPA of 3.0, minimum grade of B in all required courses, minimum of 24 dissertation hours. *Entrance requirements:* For master's, GRE General Test; for doctorate, GRE General Test, area paper or thesis. Additional exam requirements/recommendations for international students: required—TOEFL (minimum score 600 paper-based; 100 iBT). Electronic applications accepted.

Criminal Justice and Criminology

Franklin University, Criminal Justice Administration Program, Columbus, OH 43215-5399. Offers MA.

Gannon University, School of Graduate Studies, College of Humanities, Education, and Social Sciences, School of Humanities, Program in Criminalistics, Erie, PA 16541-0001. Offers MSC. *Program availability:* Online only, 100% online. *Entrance requirements:* For master's, bachelor's degree from accredited college or university; transcripts; minimum overall GPA of 2.75, 3.0 in prerequisite courses; resume; three letters of recommendation; background check. Additional exam requirements/recommendations for international students: required—TOEFL (minimum score 79 iBT). Electronic applications accepted. Application fee is waived when completed online.

George Mason University, College of Humanities and Social Sciences, Department of Criminology, Law and Society, Fairfax, VA 22030. Offers criminal justice (MS); criminology, law, and society (MA, PhD). *Program availability:* Part-time. Terminal master's awarded for partial completion of doctoral program. *Degree requirements:* For master's, thesis (for some programs); for doctorate, comprehensive exam (for some programs), thesis/dissertation, major area paper (depends on catalog year). *Entrance requirements:* For master's, GRE (for MA), college transcripts, goals statement, two letters of recommendation, resume, writing sample; for doctorate, GRE, college transcripts, goals statement, three letters of recommendation, resume, writing sample. Additional exam requirements/recommendations for international students: required—TOEFL (minimum score 575 paper-based; 88 iBT), IELTS (minimum score 6.5), PTE (minimum score 59). Electronic applications accepted.

The George Washington University, Columbian College of Arts and Sciences, Department of Forensic Sciences, Washington, DC 20052. Offers crime scene investigation (MFS); forensic chemistry (MFS); forensic molecular biology (MFS); forensic toxicology (MFS); high-technology crime investigation (MS); security management (MFS). *Program availability:* Part-time, evening/weekend. *Entrance requirements:* For master's, GRE General Test, minimum GPA of 3.0. Additional exam requirements/recommendations for international students: required—TOEFL (minimum score 550 paper-based; 80 iBT). Electronic applications accepted.

The George Washington University, Columbian College of Arts and Sciences, Department of Sociology, Program in Criminology, Washington, DC 20052. Offers MA. *Entrance requirements:* For master's, GRE General Test, minimum GPA of 3.0. Additional exam requirements/recommendations for international students: required—TOEFL (minimum score 550 paper-based). Electronic applications accepted.

Georgia College & State University, The Graduate School, College of Arts and Sciences, Department of Government and Sociology, Program in Criminal Justice, Milledgeville, GA 31061. Offers MSCJ. *Program availability:* Part-time, evening/weekend. *Students:* 7 full-time (5 women), 17 part-time (13 women); includes 11 minority (7 Black or African American, non-Hispanic/Latino; 1 Asian, non-Hispanic/Latino; 3 Hispanic/Latino). Average age 28. 8 applicants, 100% accepted, 4 enrolled. In 2019, 6 master's awarded. *Degree requirements:* For master's, comprehensive exam. *Entrance requirements:* For master's, applicants with an undergraduate GPA 2.75 - 2.99 must submit official scores on either the GRE (290 verb & quant), MAT (score 395) or GMAT (450). Scores must be within the last 5 years, bachelor's degree, resume with relevant work experience; undergraduate GPA of 3.0. Additional exam requirements/recommendations for international students: required—English proficiency must be demonstrated one of the following ways: minimum TOEFL score of 79 on internet test or 550 on paper OR 6.5 on IELTS. *Application deadline:* For fall admission, 7/1 priority date for domestic students, 4/1 priority date for international students; for spring admission, 11/1 priority date for domestic students, 9/1 priority date for international students; for summer admission, 4/1 priority date for domestic students. Applications are processed on a rolling basis. Application fee: $40. Electronic applications accepted. *Expenses:* Full time enrollment per semester: $2592 tuition and $343 fees. *Financial support:* In 2019-20, 4 students received support. Unspecified assistantships available. Financial award application deadline: 7/1; financial award applicants required to submit FAFSA. *Unit head:* Dr. Sara Doude, Program Coordinator, 478-445-4262, E-mail: sara.doude@gcsu.edu. *Application contact:* Kate Marshall, Graduate Admissions Coordinator, 478-445-1184, Fax: 478-445-1336, E-mail: grad-admit@gcsu.edu. Website: http://www.gcsu.edu/artsandsciences/gov/criminal-justice-ms

Georgian Court University, School of Arts and Sciences, Lakewood, NJ 08701. Offers applied behavior analysis (MA); autism spectrum disorders (Certificate); clinical mental health counseling (MA); criminal justice and human rights (MS); holistic health studies (MA); homeland security (Certificate); instructional technology (CPC); integrative health (Certificate); mercy spirituality (Certificate); parish business management (Certificate); professional counselor (Certificate); school psychology (MA, Certificate); theology (MA, Certificate). *Program availability:* Part-time, evening/weekend. *Faculty:* 19 full-time (11 women), 7 part-time/adjunct (3 women). *Students:* 90 full-time (80 women), 71 part-time (59 women); includes 26 minority (8 Black or African American, non-Hispanic/Latino; 2 Asian, non-Hispanic/Latino; 14 Hispanic/Latino; 2 Two or more races, non-Hispanic/Latino), 1 international. Average age 32. 138 applicants, 58% accepted, 57 enrolled. In 2019, 68 master's, 19 other advanced degrees awarded. *Degree requirements:* For master's, comprehensive exam (for some programs), thesis (for some programs); for other advanced degree, comprehensive exam (for some programs). *Entrance requirements:* Additional exam requirements/recommendations for international students: required—TOEFL (minimum score 550 paper-based; 79 iBT). *Application deadline:* For fall admission, 8/15 for domestic students, 5/1 for international students; for spring admission, 1/15 for domestic students, 10/1 for international students. Applications are processed on a rolling basis. Application fee: $40. Electronic applications accepted. *Financial support:* Scholarships/grants, health care benefits, and unspecified assistantships available. Financial award application deadline: 4/15; financial award applicants required to submit FAFSA. *Unit head:* Dr. Mary Chinery, Dean, 732-987-2493, Fax: 732-987-2007, E-mail: mchinery@georgian.edu. *Application contact:* Dr. Mary Chinery, Dean, 732-987-2493, Fax: 732-987-2007, E-mail: mchinery@georgian.edu. Website: https://georgian.edu/academics/school-of-arts-sciences/

Georgia Southern University, Jack N. Averitt College of Graduate Studies, College of Behavioral and Social Sciences, Program in Criminal Justice and Criminology, Statesboro, GA 30458. Offers criminal justice (MS); cyber crime (Certificate). *Program availability:* Part-time, evening/weekend, 100% online. *Faculty:* 13 full-time (9 women). *Students:* 20 full-time (10 women), 10 part-time (6 women); includes 14 minority (12 Black or African American, non-Hispanic/Latino; 2 Hispanic/Latino). Average age 28. 14 applicants, 93% accepted, 10 enrolled. In 2019, 9 master's awarded. *Degree requirements:* For master's, comprehensive exam, field practicum or thesis. *Entrance requirements:* For master's, GRE General Test (minimum score 150 on verbal, 141 on quantitative, or 4 on analytical section) or MAT, minimum GPA of 2.5, 2 letters of recommendation, letter of intent (500-1000 words). Additional exam requirements/recommendations for international students: required—TOEFL (minimum score 523 paper-based; 70 iBT). *Application deadline:* For fall admission, 6/1 priority date for domestic students, 5/1 priority date for international students; for spring admission, 11/15 priority date for domestic students, 9/15 priority date for international students; for summer admission, 4/15 priority date for domestic students, 9/15 for international students. Applications are processed on a rolling basis. Application fee: $30. Electronic applications accepted. *Expenses: Tuition, area resident:* Full-time $4986; part-time $277 per credit hour. Tuition, nonresident: full-time $19,890; part-time $1105 per credit hour. *International tuition:* $19,890 full-time. *Required fees:* $2114; $1057 per semester. $1057 per semester. Tuition and fees vary according to course load, campus/location and program. *Financial support:* In 2019-20, 13 students received support, including 5 research assistantships with full tuition reimbursements available (averaging $8,000 per year); teaching assistantships, career-related internships or fieldwork, Federal Work-Study, scholarships/grants, and unspecified assistantships also available. Support available to part-time students. Financial award application deadline: 3/15; financial award applicants required to submit FAFSA. *Unit head:* Dr. Daniel Skidmore-Hess, Department Head, 912-344-2532, Fax: 912-344-3438, E-mail: daniel.skidmore-hess@armstrong.edu. *Application contact:* McKenzie Peterman, Graduate Admissions Specialist, 912-478-5678, Fax: 912-478-0740, E-mail: mpeterman@georgiasouthern.edu. Website: https://www.armstrong.edu/academic-departments/cjsps-master-of-science-in-criminal-justice

Georgia State University, Andrew Young School of Policy Studies, Department of Criminal Justice and Criminology, Atlanta, GA 30302-3083. Offers criminal justice (MS); criminal justice and criminology (PhD). *Program availability:* Part-time. *Faculty:* 8 full-time (2 women). *Students:* 37 full-time (28 women), 9 part-time (6 women); includes 20 minority (12 Black or African American, non-Hispanic/Latino; 5 Hispanic/Latino; 3 Two or more races, non-Hispanic/Latino), 3 international. Average age 31. 70 applicants, 53% accepted, 22 enrolled. In 2019, 9 master's, 2 doctorates awarded. Terminal master's awarded for partial completion of doctoral program. *Degree requirements:* For master's, thesis optional; for doctorate, comprehensive exam, thesis/dissertation. *Entrance requirements:* For master's and doctorate, GRE. Additional exam requirements/recommendations for international students: required—TOEFL (minimum score 603 paper-based; 100 iBT) or IELTS (minimum score 7). *Application deadline:* For fall admission, 4/1 for domestic and international students; for spring admission, 10/1 for domestic and international students. Application fee: $50. Electronic applications accepted. *Expenses: Tuition, area resident:* Full-time $7164; part-time $398 per credit hour. Tuition, state resident: full-time $7164; part-time $398 per credit hour. Tuition, nonresident: full-time $22,662; part-time $1259 per credit hour. *International tuition:* $22,662 full-time. *Required fees:* $2128; $312 per credit hour. Tuition and fees vary according to course load and program. *Financial support:* In 2019-20, fellowships with full tuition reimbursements (averaging $22,000 per year), research assistantships with full tuition reimbursements (averaging $14,000 per year), teaching assistantships with full tuition reimbursements (averaging $14,000 per year) were awarded; career-related internships or fieldwork, Federal Work-Study, scholarships/grants, traineeships, health care benefits, and unspecified assistantships also available. Financial award application deadline: 2/15. *Unit head:* Dr. Dean Dabney, Professor of Criminal Justice and Criminology/Department Chair, 404-413-1039, Fax: 404-413-1030, E-mail: ddabney@gsu.edu. *Application contact:* Dr. Dean Dabney, Professor of Criminal Justice and Criminology/Department Chair, 404-413-1039, Fax: 404-413-1030, E-mail: ddabney@gsu.edu. Website: http://aysps.gsu.edu/cj/

Georgia State University, Andrew Young School of Policy Studies, Department of Public Management and Policy, Atlanta, GA 30303. Offers criminal justice (MPA); disaster management (Certificate); disaster policy (MPA); environmental policy (PhD); health policy (PhD); management and finance (MPA); nonprofit management (MPA, Certificate); nonprofit policy (MPA); planning and economic development (MPP, Certificate); policy analysis and evaluation (MPA), including planning and economic development; public and nonprofit management (PhD); public finance and budgeting (PhD), including science and technology policy, urban and regional economic development; public finance policy (MPA), including social policy; public health (MPA). *Accreditation:* NASPAA (one or more programs are accredited). *Program availability:* Part-time. *Faculty:* 13 full-time (7 women), 3 part-time/adjunct (1 woman). *Students:* 125 full-time (81 women), 91 part-time (66 women); includes 103 minority (78 Black or African American, non-Hispanic/Latino; 3 Asian, non-Hispanic/Latino; 14 Hispanic/Latino; 8 Two or more races, non-Hispanic/Latino), 31 international. Average age 32. 298 applicants, 60% accepted, 82 enrolled. In 2019, 70 master's, 8 other advanced degrees awarded. Terminal master's awarded for partial completion of doctoral program. *Degree requirements:* For master's, thesis optional; for doctorate, comprehensive exam, thesis/dissertation. *Entrance requirements:* For master's and doctorate, GRE. Additional exam requirements/recommendations for international students: required—TOEFL (minimum score 603 paper-based; 100 iBT) or IELTS (minimum score 7). *Application deadline:* For fall admission, 1/15 for domestic and international students. Application fee: $50. Electronic applications accepted. *Expenses: Tuition, area resident:* Full-time $7164; part-time $398 per credit hour. Tuition, state resident: full-time $7164; part-time $398 per credit hour. Tuition, nonresident: full-time $22,662; part-time $1259 per credit hour. *International tuition:* $22,662 full-time. *Required fees:* $2128; $312 per credit hour. Tuition and fees vary according to course load and program. *Financial support:* In 2019-20, fellowships (averaging $8,194 per year), research assistantships (averaging $8,068 per year), teaching assistantships (averaging $3,600 per year) were awarded; institutionally sponsored loans, scholarships/grants, health care benefits, and unspecified assistantships also available. Financial award application deadline: 2/1. *Unit head:* Dr. Cathy Yang Liu, Chair and Professor, 404-413-0102, Fax: 404-413-0104, E-mail: cyliu@gsu.edu. *Application contact:* Dr. Cathy Yang Liu, Chair and Professor, 404-413-0102, Fax: 404-413-0104, E-mail: cyliu@gsu.edu. Website: https://aysps.gsu.edu/public-management-policy/

Governors State University, College of Arts and Sciences, Program in Criminal Justice, University Park, IL 60484. Offers MA. *Program availability:* Part-time. *Faculty:* 57 full-time (33 women), 72 part-time/adjunct (40 women). *Students:* 10 full-time (8 women), 19 part-time (13 women); includes 23 minority (19 Black or African American, non-Hispanic/Latino; 3 Hispanic/Latino; 1 Two or more races, non-Hispanic/Latino). Average age 37. 19 applicants, 68% accepted, 11 enrolled. In 2019, 9 master's awarded. *Application deadline:* For fall admission, 4/1 for domestic students. Applications are processed on a rolling basis. Application fee: $50. Electronic applications accepted. *Expenses: Tuition, area resident:* Full-time $8472; part-time $353 per credit hour. Tuition, state resident: full-time $8472; part-time $353 per credit hour. Tuition, nonresident: full-time $16,944; part-time $706 per credit hour. *International tuition:* $16,944 full-time. *Required fees:* $2520; $105 per credit hour. $38 per term. Tuition and fees vary according to course load, degree level and program. *Financial support:* Application deadline: 5/1; applicants required to submit FAFSA. *Unit head:* Jason Zingsheim, Chair, Division of Arts and Letters, 708-534-5000 Ext. 7493, E-mail: jzingsheim@govst.edu. *Application contact:* Jason Zingsheim, Chair, Division of Arts and Letters, 708-534-5000 Ext. 7493, E-mail: jzingsheim@govst.edu.

The Graduate Center, City University of New York, Graduate Studies, Program in Criminal Justice, New York, NY 10016-4039. Offers PhD. *Degree requirements:* For doctorate, one foreign language, thesis/dissertation. *Entrance requirements:* For doctorate, GRE General Test, writing sample. Additional exam requirements/recommendations for international students: required—TOEFL. Electronic applications accepted.

Grambling State University, School of Graduate Studies and Research, College of Professional Studies, Department of Criminal Justice, Grambling, LA 71245. Offers MS. *Program availability:* Part-time. *Degree requirements:* For master's, comprehensive exam, thesis optional. *Entrance requirements:* For master's, GRE, minimum GPA of 2.5 on last degree and in four core courses. Additional exam requirements/recommendations for international students: required—TOEFL (minimum score 500 paper-based; 62 iBT). Electronic applications accepted.

Grand Valley State University, College of Community and Public Service, School of Criminal Justice, Allendale, MI 49401-9403. Offers MS. *Program availability:* Part-time, evening/weekend. *Faculty:* 4 full-time (2 women). *Students:* 11 full-time (9 women), 9 part-time (7 women); includes 6 minority (2 Black or African American, non-Hispanic/Latino; 4 Hispanic/Latino), 1 international. Average age 28. 18 applicants, 89% accepted, 8 enrolled. In 2019, 3 master's awarded. *Degree requirements:* For master's, thesis optional, comprehensive exam or thesis. *Entrance requirements:* For master's, minimum GPA of 3.0, three letters of recommendation, personal statement, essay, oral interview. Additional exam requirements/recommendations for international students: required—TOEFL (minimum iBT score of 80), IELTS (6.5), or Michigan English Language Assessment Battery (77). *Application deadline:* For fall admission, 5/1 priority date for domestic students; for winter admission, 11/1 priority date for domestic students; for spring admission, 4/1 priority date for domestic students. Applications are processed on a rolling basis. Application fee: $30. Electronic applications accepted. *Expenses:* Tuition, state resident: full-time $12,654; part-time $3515 per credit hour. Tuition, nonresident: full-time $12,654; part-time $3515 per credit hour. *International tuition:* $12,654 full-time. Tuition and fees vary according to degree level and program. *Financial support:* In 2019–20, 6 students received support, including 2 fellowships, 6 research assistantships with full and partial tuition reimbursements available (averaging $4,000 per year); career-related internships or fieldwork, Federal Work-Study, scholarships/grants, and unspecified assistantships also available. Financial award application deadline: 5/1. *Unit head:* Dr. Patrick Gerkin, Director, 616-331-7130, Fax: 616-331-7155, E-mail: gerkinp@gvsu.edu. *Application contact:* Dr. Tonisha Jones, Graduate Program Director/Recruiting Contact, 616-331-7187, Fax: 616-331-7155, E-mail: jontonis@gvsu.edu.
Website: http://www.gvsu.edu/cj/

Guilford College, Master in Criminal Justice, Greensboro, NC 27410. Offers criminal justice (MS). *Program availability:* Part-time, evening/weekend. *Faculty:* 2 full-time (1 woman), 1 (woman) part-time/adjunct. *Students:* 4 full-time (2 women), 2 part-time (1 woman); includes 2 minority (both Black or African American, non-Hispanic/Latino). Average age 31. 6 applicants, 100% accepted, 6 enrolled. *Degree requirements:* For master's, thesis. *Entrance requirements:* For master's, GRE, statement of purpose, resume, 2 letters of recommendation, transcripts, minimum 3.0 GPA from last two years of undergraduate work. Additional exam requirements/recommendations for international students: recommended—TOEFL (minimum score 550 paper-based; 80 iBT), IELTS (minimum score 6.5). *Application deadline:* Applications are processed on a rolling basis. Application fee: $75. Electronic applications accepted. *Expenses:* Tuition: Part-time $600 per credit. *Financial support:* Applicants required to submit FAFSA. *Unit head:* Will Pizio, Coordinator, 336-316-2418, E-mail: wpizio@guilford.edu. *Application contact:* Will Pizio, Coordinator, 336-316-2418, E-mail: wpizio@guilford.edu.
Website: www.guilford.edu

Hilbert College, Program in Criminal Justice Administration, Hamburg, NY 14075-1597. Offers MS. *Program availability:* Evening/weekend. *Degree requirements:* For master's, final capstone project. *Entrance requirements:* For master's, essay, official transcripts from all prior colleges, two letters of recommendation, current resume, relevant work experience, baccalaureate degree from accredited college or university with minimum cumulative GPA of 3.0, personal interview. Additional exam requirements/recommendations for international students: recommended—TOEFL. Electronic applications accepted. Application fee is waived when completed online. *Expenses:* Contact institution.

Holy Family University, Graduate and Professional Programs, School of Arts and Sciences, Program in Criminal Justice, Philadelphia, PA 19114. Offers MA. *Program availability:* Part-time, evening/weekend. *Degree requirements:* For master's, thesis or alternative. *Entrance requirements:* For master's, 2 letters of recommendation, official transcripts of all college or university work, writing sample. Additional exam requirements/recommendations for international students: required—TOEFL (minimum score 550 paper-based; 79 iBT), IELTS (minimum score 6), PTE (minimum score 54). Electronic applications accepted.

Howard Payne University, Program in Criminal Justice, Brownwood, TX 76801-2715. Offers criminal justice (MS), including corrections, law enforcement. *Program availability:* Part-time, evening/weekend, online only, 100% online. *Entrance requirements:* For master's, baccalaureate degree, minimum cumulative GPA of 3.0, 800-1200 word written essay, official transcripts, three letters of reference. Electronic applications accepted. *Expenses:* Contact institution.

Husson University, Master of Science in Criminal Justice Administration Program, Bangor, ME 04401-2999. Offers MS. *Program availability:* Part-time, evening/weekend. *Degree requirements:* For master's, thesis optional. *Entrance requirements:* For master's, letter of recommendation. Additional exam requirements/recommendations for international students: required—TOEFL (minimum score 550 paper-based; 80 iBT), IELTS (minimum score 6.5). Electronic applications accepted. *Expenses:* Contact institution.

Illinois State University, Graduate School, College of Applied Science and Technology, Department of Criminal Justice Sciences, Normal, IL 61790. Offers MA, MS. *Faculty:* 17 full-time (9 women), 6 part-time/adjunct (2 women). *Students:* 18 full-time (14 women), 6 part-time (2 women). Average age 26. 19 applicants, 84% accepted, 12 enrolled. In 2019, 6 master's awarded. *Degree requirements:* For master's, variable foreign language requirement, thesis or alternative. *Entrance requirements:* For master's, GRE General Test, minimum GPA of 2.6 in last 60 hours of course work. *Application deadline:* Applications are processed on a rolling basis. Application fee: $50. *Expenses:* Tuition, area resident: Full-time $7956; part-time $9767 per year. Tuition, nonresident: full-time $9233; part-time $17,592 per year. *Required fees:* $1797. *Financial support:* In 2019–20, 9 research assistantships were awarded; career-related internships or fieldwork, tuition waivers (full and partial), and unspecified assistantships also available. Financial award application deadline: 4/1. *Unit head:* Dr. Brent Teasdale, Department Chair, 309-438-7617, E-mail: beteasd@ilstu.edu. *Application contact:* Dr. Brent Teasdale, Department Chair, 309-438-7617, E-mail: beteasd@ilstu.edu.
Website: http://criminaljustice.illinoisstate.edu/

Indiana State University, College of Graduate and Professional Studies, College of Arts and Sciences, Department of Criminology and Criminal Justice, Terre Haute, IN 47809. Offers MA, MS. *Program availability:* Part-time, online learning. *Degree requirements:* For master's, comprehensive exam, thesis (for some programs). *Entrance requirements:* For master's, minimum GPA of 2.75 in undergraduate work, 3.0 in previous graduate work. Additional exam requirements/recommendations for international students: required—TOEFL (minimum score 550 paper-based). Electronic applications accepted.

Indiana University Bloomington, University Graduate School, College of Arts and Sciences, Department of Criminal Justice, Bloomington, IN 47405. Offers crime and youth development (MA, PhD); crime, law and psychology (MA, PhD); criminal justice (MA, PhD); criminal justice institutions and practices (MA, PhD); criminology (MA, PhD); developmental criminology (MA, PhD); interdisciplinary studies in crime and punishment (PhD); interdisciplinary studies of crime and punishment (MA); the relationship between crime and gender, race and ethnicity (MA, PhD); theoretical analyses of criminology (MA, PhD). *Program availability:* Part-time. Terminal master's awarded for partial completion of doctoral program. *Degree requirements:* For master's, thesis optional; for doctorate, comprehensive exam, thesis/dissertation, foreign language or research practicum. *Entrance requirements:* For master's and doctorate, GRE General Test. Additional exam requirements/recommendations for international students: required—TOEFL (minimum score 600 paper-based; 100 iBT); recommended—TWE. Electronic applications accepted.

Indiana University Northwest, School of Public and Environmental Affairs, Gary, IN 46408. Offers criminal justice (MPA); environmental affairs (Graduate Certificate); health services (MPA); nonprofit management (Certificate); public management (MPA, Graduate Certificate). *Accreditation:* NASPAA (one or more programs are accredited). *Program availability:* Part-time. *Entrance requirements:* For master's, GRE General Test (minimum combined verbal and quantitative score of 280), GMAT, or LSAT, letters of recommendation. Electronic applications accepted.

Indiana University of Pennsylvania, School of Graduate Studies and Research, College of Health and Human Services, Department of Criminology, Doctoral Program in Criminology, Indiana, PA 15705. Offers PhD. *Program availability:* Part-time. *Faculty:* 12 full-time (7 women). *Students:* 9 full-time (6 women), 12 part-time (7 women), 2 international. Average age 32. 20 applicants, 75% accepted, 4 enrolled. In 2019, 4 doctorates awarded. *Degree requirements:* For doctorate, one foreign language, comprehensive exam, thesis/dissertation. *Entrance requirements:* For doctorate, GRE, 3 letters of recommendation, writing sample, official transcripts, goal statement. Additional exam requirements/recommendations for international students: required—TOEFL (minimum score 540 paper-based; 76 iBT); recommended—IELTS (minimum score 6). *Application deadline:* Applications are processed on a rolling basis. Application fee: $50. Electronic applications accepted. *Expenses:* Contact institution. *Financial support:* In 2019–20, 2 fellowships with tuition reimbursements (averaging $1,000 per year), 7 research assistantships with tuition reimbursements (averaging $13,286 per year), 3 teaching assistantships with partial tuition reimbursements (averaging $25,035 per year) were awarded; Federal Work-Study, scholarships/grants, and unspecified assistantships also available. Support available to part-time students. Financial award application deadline: 4/15; financial award applicants required to submit FAFSA. *Unit head:* Dr. Bitna Kim, Graduate Coordinator, 724-357-5933, E-mail: bitna.kim@iup.edu. *Application contact:* Dr. Bitna Kim, Graduate Coordinator, 724-357-5933, E-mail: bitna.kim@iup.edu.
Website: http://www.iup.edu/grad/criminologyphd/default.aspx

Indiana University of Pennsylvania, School of Graduate Studies and Research, College of Health and Human Services, Department of Criminology, Master's Program in Criminology, Indiana, PA 15705. Offers MA. *Program availability:* Part-time, 100% online, blended/hybrid learning. *Faculty:* 12 full-time (7 women). *Students:* 27 full-time (19 women), 12 part-time (6 women); includes 11 minority (6 Black or African American, non-Hispanic/Latino; 1 Asian, non-Hispanic/Latino; 4 Two or more races, non-Hispanic/Latino), 3 international. Average age 26. 47 applicants, 98% accepted, 24 enrolled. In 2019, 28 master's awarded. *Degree requirements:* For master's, thesis optional. *Entrance requirements:* For master's, 2 letters of recommendation, official transcripts, goal statement. Additional exam requirements/recommendations for international students: required—TOEFL (minimum score 540 paper-based; 76 iBT); recommended—IELTS (minimum score 6). *Application deadline:* Applications are processed on a rolling basis. Application fee: $50. Electronic applications accepted. *Expenses:* Tuition, area resident: Full-time $9288; part-time $516 per credit. Tuition, nonresident: full-time $13,932; part-time $774 per credit. *Required fees:* $4454. One-time fee: $115 full-time. Tuition and fees vary according to course load and program. *Financial support:* In 2019–20, 1 fellowship (averaging $1,300 per year), 15 research assistantships with tuition reimbursements (averaging $1,027 per year) were awarded; career-related internships or fieldwork, Federal Work-Study, scholarships/grants, and unspecified assistantships also available. Support available to part-time students. Financial award application deadline: 4/15; financial award applicants required to submit FAFSA. *Unit head:* Dr. Sadie Miller, Graduate Coordinator, 724-357-1250, E-mail: sadie.mummert@iup.edu. *Application contact:* Dr. Sadie Miller, Graduate Coordinator, 724-357-1250, E-mail: sadie.mummert@iup.edu.
Website: http://www.iup.edu/grad/criminology/default.aspx

Indiana University-Purdue University Indianapolis, School of Public and Environmental Affairs, Indianapolis, IN 46202. Offers criminal justice and public safety (MS); homeland security and emergency management (Graduate Certificate); library management (Graduate Certificate); nonprofit management (Graduate Certificate); public affairs (MPA); public management (Graduate Certificate); social entrepreneurship: nonprofit and public benefit organizations (Graduate Certificate); JD/MPA; MLS/NMC; MLS/PMC; MPA/MA. *Accreditation:* CAHME (one or more programs are accredited); NASPAA. *Program availability:* Part-time, evening/weekend, online learning. *Entrance requirements:* For master's, GRE General Test, GMAT or LSAT, minimum GPA of 3.0 (preferred). Additional exam requirements/recommendations for international students: required—TOEFL (minimum score 93 iBT), IELTS (minimum score 6.5). Electronic applications accepted.

Inter American University of Puerto Rico, Aguadilla Campus, Graduate School, Aguadilla, PR 00605. Offers accounting (MBA); counseling psychology specializing in family (MS); criminal justice (MA); educative management and leadership (MA); elementary education (M Ed); finance (MBA); human resources (MBA); industrial management (MBA); management information systems (MBA); marketing (MBA). *Program availability:* Part-time, evening/weekend. *Faculty:* 6 full-time (all women), 10 part-time/adjunct (5 women). *Students:* 172 full-time (112 women), 23 part-time (16 women); all minorities (all Hispanic/Latino). Average age 30. 102 applicants, 63% accepted, 59 enrolled. *Degree requirements:* For master's, comprehensive exam. *Entrance requirements:* For master's, EXADEP, 2 letters of recommendation, minimum GPA of 2.5. Application fee: $31. Electronic applications accepted. *Expenses:* Tuition: Full-time $3870; part-time $645 per trimester. *Required fees:* $235 per trimester. Tuition and fees vary according to course load. *Unit head:* Dr. Elie Agesilas, Chancellor, 787-891-0925 Ext. 2236, Fax: 787-882-3020, E-mail: eagesila@aguadilla.inter.edu. *Application contact:* Doris Perez, Admission Director, 787-891-0925 Ext. 2740, Fax: 787-882-3020, E-mail: dperez@aguadilla.inter.edu.
Website: http://www.aguadilla.inter.edu/

Inter American University of Puerto Rico, Barranquitas Campus, Program in Criminal Justice, Barranquitas, PR 00794. Offers MA. *Program availability:* Evening/weekend. *Degree requirements:* For master's, 2 foreign languages, comprehensive exam (for some programs), thesis optional, minimum GPA of 3.0; comprehensive examination or integration seminar. *Entrance requirements:* For master's, GRE or EXADEP, bachelor's degree or its equivalent from accredited institution, official academic transcript from institution that conferred bachelor's degree, minimum GPA of 2.5, two recommendation letters, interview (for some programs). Electronic applications accepted. *Expenses:* Contact institution.

Inter American University of Puerto Rico, Metropolitan Campus, Graduate Programs, Program in Criminal Justice, San Juan, PR 00919-1293. Offers MA. *Program availability:* Part-time, evening/weekend. *Degree requirements:* For master's, comprehensive exam. *Entrance requirements:* For master's, GRE or EXADEP, interview. Electronic applications accepted.

Inter American University of Puerto Rico, Ponce Campus, Graduate School, Mercedita, PR 00715-1602. Offers accounting (MBA); biology (M Ed); chemistry (M Ed); criminal justice (MA); elementary education (M Ed); English as a Second Language (M Ed); finance (MBA); history (M Ed); human resources (MBA); marketing (MBA); mathematics (M Ed); Spanish (M Ed). *Entrance requirements:* For master's, minimum GPA of 2.5.

Iona College, School of Arts and Science, Department of Criminal Justice, New Rochelle, NY 10801-1890. Offers criminal justice (MS); cybercrime and security (AC); forensic criminology and criminal justice systems (Certificate). *Program availability:* Part-time, evening/weekend. *Faculty:* 4 full-time (1 woman), 5 part-time/adjunct (1 woman). *Students:* 17 full-time (12 women), 8 part-time (3 women); includes 15 minority (4 Black or African American, non-Hispanic/Latino; 1 Asian, non-Hispanic/Latino; 10 Hispanic/Latino). Average age 26. 20 applicants, 70% accepted, 9 enrolled. In 2019, 13 master's, 5 other advanced degrees awarded. *Degree requirements:* For master's, thesis (for some programs), thesis or literature review. *Entrance requirements:* For master's, minimum GPA of 3.0. Additional exam requirements/recommendations for international students: required—TOEFL (minimum score 550 paper-based; 80 iBT), IELTS (minimum score 6.5). *Application deadline:* For fall admission, 8/1 priority date for domestic students, 5/1 priority date for international students; for spring admission, 1/1 priority date for domestic students, 9/1 priority date for international students. Applications are processed on a rolling basis. Electronic applications accepted. *Financial support:* In 2019–20, 17 students received support. Scholarships/grants and unspecified assistantships available. Financial award application deadline: 4/15; financial award applicants required to submit FAFSA. *Unit head:* Marcus Aldredge, PhD, Chair, 914-633-2594, E-mail: maldredge@iona.edu. *Application contact:* Christopher Kash, Assistant Director of Graduate Admissions, 914-633-2403, Fax: 914-633-2277, E-mail: ckash@iona.edu.
Website: http://www.iona.edu/Academics/School-of-Arts-Science/Departments/Criminal-Justice/Graduate-Programs.aspx

Jackson State University, Graduate School, College of Liberal Arts, Department of Criminal Justice and Sociology, Jackson, MS 39217. Offers criminology and justice services (MA); sociology (MA). *Program availability:* Part-time, evening/weekend. *Degree requirements:* For master's, comprehensive exam, thesis or alternative. *Entrance requirements:* For master's, GRE General Test. Additional exam requirements/recommendations for international students: required—TOEFL (minimum score 520 paper-based; 67 iBT).

Jacksonville State University, Graduate Studies, School of Human Services and Social Sciences, Department of Criminal Justice, Jacksonville, AL 36265-1602. Offers MS. *Program availability:* Part-time, evening/weekend. *Degree requirements:* For master's, comprehensive exam, thesis (for some programs). *Entrance requirements:* For master's, GRE General Test or MAT. Additional exam requirements/recommendations for international students: required—TOEFL (minimum score 500 paper-based; 61 iBT). Electronic applications accepted.

John Jay College of Criminal Justice of the City University of New York, Graduate Studies, MA international Crime and Justice, New York, NY 10019. Offers MA.

John Jay College of Criminal Justice of the City University of New York, Graduate Studies, Program in Protection Management, New York, NY 10019. Offers MS. *Program availability:* Part-time, evening/weekend. *Degree requirements:* For master's, thesis or alternative. *Entrance requirements:* For master's, minimum B average. Additional exam requirements/recommendations for international students: required—TOEFL (minimum score 500 paper-based).

John Jay College of Criminal Justice of the City University of New York, Graduate Studies, Programs in Criminal Justice, New York, NY 10019. Offers criminal justice (MA, PhD); criminology and deviance (PhD); forensic psychology (PhD); forensic science (PhD); international crime and justice (MA); law and philosophy (PhD); organizational behavior (PhD); public policy (PhD). *Program availability:* Part-time, evening/weekend. Terminal master's awarded for partial completion of doctoral program. *Degree requirements:* For master's, thesis or alternative; for doctorate, one foreign language, thesis/dissertation. *Entrance requirements:* For master's, GRE General Test, minimum B average; for doctorate, GRE General Test. Additional exam requirements/recommendations for international students: required—TOEFL (minimum score 500 paper-based).

Johnson & Wales University, Graduate Studies, MS Program in Criminal Justice, Providence, RI 02903-3703. Offers MS. *Program availability:* Online only, 100% online.

Kean University, College of Business and Public Management, Program in Criminal Justice, Union, NJ 07083. Offers MA. *Program availability:* Part-time. *Faculty:* 15 full-time (5 women). *Students:* 11 full-time (6 women), 4 part-time (2 women); includes 3 minority (1 Black or African American, non-Hispanic/Latino; 2 Hispanic/Latino), 2 international. Average age 23. 10 applicants, 100% accepted, 8 enrolled. In 2019, 4 master's awarded. *Degree requirements:* For master's, comprehensive exam, thesis optional. *Entrance requirements:* For master's, GRE (minimum Analytic Writing score of 3.5), 3 reference letters, minimum GPA of 3.0, writing sample, official transcripts from all institutions attended, personal statement, resume, sample of scholarly work from undergraduate studies. Additional exam requirements/recommendations for international students: required—TOEFL (minimum score 550 paper-based; 79 iBT), IELTS (minimum score 6.5). *Application deadline:* For fall admission, 6/30 for domestic and international students; for spring admission, 12/1 for domestic and international students. Applications are processed on a rolling basis. Application fee: $75. Electronic applications accepted. *Expenses:* Tuition, state resident: full-time $15,326; part-time $748 per credit. Tuition, nonresident: full-time $20,288; part-time $902 per credit. *Required fees:* $2149.50; $91.25 per credit. Tuition and fees vary according to course level, course load, degree level and program. *Financial support:* Scholarships/grants and unspecified assistantships available. Financial award applicants required to submit FAFSA. *Unit head:* Dr. Pat McManimon, Program Coordinator, 908-737-4309, E-mail: pmcmanim@kean.edu. *Application contact:* Pedro Lopes, Admissions Counselor, 908-737-7100, E-mail: gradadmissions@kean.edu.
Website: http://grad.kean.edu/masters-programs/criminal-justice

Keiser University, MA in Criminal Justice Program, Fort Lauderdale, FL 33309. Offers MA. *Program availability:* Part-time, online learning.

Keiser University, MA in Homeland Security Program, Fort Lauderdale, FL 33309. Offers MA.

Kennesaw State University, College of Humanities and Social Sciences, Program in Criminal Justice, Kennesaw, GA 30144. Offers MS. *Program availability:* Part-time. *Students:* 23 full-time (20 women), 10 part-time (7 women); includes 12 minority (10 Black or African American, non-Hispanic/Latino; 1 Hispanic/Latino; 1 Two or more races, non-Hispanic/Latino), 1 international. Average age 28. 16 applicants, 100% accepted, 10 enrolled. In 2019, 9 master's awarded. *Degree requirements:* For master's, research project or thesis. *Entrance requirements:* For master's, GRE. Additional exam requirements/recommendations for international students: required—TOEFL (minimum score 80 iBT), IELTS (minimum score 6.5). *Application deadline:* For fall admission, 7/1 for domestic and international students. Applications are processed on a rolling basis. Application fee: $60. Electronic applications accepted. *Expenses: Tuition, area resident:* Full-time $7104; part-time $296 per credit hour. Tuition, state resident: full-time $7104; part-time $296 per credit hour. Tuition, nonresident: full-time $25,584; part-time $1066 per credit hour. *International tuition:* $25,584 full-time. *Required fees:* $2006; $1706 per unit. $853 per semester. *Financial support:* Applicants required to submit FAFSA. *Unit head:* Dr. Chris Totten, Director, 470-578-4413, Fax: 770-499-3423, E-mail: ctotten@kennesaw.edu. *Application contact:* Admissions Counselor, 470-578-4377, Fax: 470-578-9172, E-mail: ksugrad@kennesaw.edu.
Website: http://chss.kennesaw.edu/mscj/

Kent State University, College of Arts and Sciences, Department of Sociology, Kent, OH 44242-0001. Offers criminology and criminal justice (MA), including corrections, global security, policing, victimology; sociology (MA, PhD). *Program availability:* Part-time, 100% online. *Faculty:* 18 full-time (10 women), 2 part-time/adjunct (1 woman). *Students:* 37 full-time (25 women), 37 part-time (30 women); includes 13 minority (5 Black or African American, non-Hispanic/Latino; 1 Asian, non-Hispanic/Latino; 3 Hispanic/Latino; 4 Two or more races, non-Hispanic/Latino), 3 international. Average age 31. 40 applicants, 65% accepted, 17 enrolled. In 2019, 27 master's, 4 doctorates awarded. *Degree requirements:* For master's, thesis, project, or internship; for doctorate, comprehensive exam, thesis/dissertation. *Entrance requirements:* For master's, GRE scores from within the last 5 years (not required for fall 2020 and fall 2021 admissions), three letters of recommendation, official transcript(s), goal statement, resume or vita; for doctorate, GRE scores from within the last 5 years (not required for fall 2020 and fall 2021), minimum undergraduate GPA of 3.0, transcripts, personal statement of 2-4 pages, 3 letters of recommendation, writing samples can be included but are not required. Additional exam requirements/recommendations for international students: required—TOEFL (minimum score 94 iBT), IELTS (minimum score 7), PTE (minimum score 65), Michigan English Language Assessment Battery (minimum score 82). *Application deadline:* For fall admission, 12/1 for domestic and international students. Applications are processed on a rolling basis. Application fee: $45 ($70 for international students). Electronic applications accepted. *Financial support:* Research assistantships with full tuition reimbursements, teaching assistantships with full tuition reimbursements, scholarships/grants, and unspecified assistantships available. Financial award application deadline: 12/1. *Unit head:* Dr. Richard E. Adams, Chair and Full Professor, 330-672-2721, E-mail: radams12@kent.edu. *Application contact:* Dr. William Kalkhoff, Professor and Graduate Coordinator, 330-672-3712, E-mail: wkalkhof@kent.edu.
Website: http://www.kent.edu/sociology/

Lamar University, College of Graduate Studies, College of Arts and Sciences, Department of Sociology, Social Work, and Criminal Justice, Beaumont, TX 77710. Offers MS. *Program availability:* Part-time. *Faculty:* 18 full-time (10 women), 8 part-time/adjunct (3 women). *Students:* 148 part-time (79 women); includes 86 minority (44 Black or African American, non-Hispanic/Latino; 6 Asian, non-Hispanic/Latino; 30 Hispanic/Latino; 6 Two or more races, non-Hispanic/Latino). Average age 34. 154 applicants, 81% accepted, 30 enrolled. In 2019, 70 master's awarded. *Degree requirements:* For master's, thesis or alternative, applied projects. *Entrance requirements:* For master's, GRE General Test. Additional exam requirements/recommendations for international students: required—TOEFL (minimum score 550 paper-based; 79 iBT), IELTS (minimum score 6.5). *Application deadline:* Applications are processed on a rolling basis. Application fee: $25 ($50 for international students). Electronic applications accepted. *Expenses:* $9000 total program cost. *Financial support:* In 2019–20, 2 students received support. Fellowships with partial tuition reimbursements available, career-related internships or fieldwork, Federal Work-Study, and scholarships/grants available. Support available to part-time students. Financial award applicants required to submit FAFSA. *Unit head:* Dr. Stuart Wright, Chair, 409-880-8542, Fax: 409-880-2324. *Application contact:* Celeste Contreas, Director, Admissions and Academic Services, 409-880-8888, Fax: 409-880-7419, E-mail: gradmissions@lamar.edu.
Website: http://artssciences.lamar.edu/sociology-social-work-criminal-justice

Lasell College, Graduate and Professional Studies in Criminal Justice, Newton, MA 02466-2709. Offers emergency and crisis management (MS, Certificate); homeland security and global justice (MS, Certificate); violence prevention and advocacy (MS, Certificate). *Program availability:* Part-time, evening/weekend, online only, 100% online. *Faculty:* 6 full-time (3 women), 1 part-time/adjunct (0 women). *Students:* 28 full-time (5 women), 71 part-time (21 women); includes 27 minority (9 Black or African American, non-Hispanic/Latino; 2 Asian, non-Hispanic/Latino; 13 Hispanic/Latino; 3 Two or more races, non-Hispanic/Latino). Average age 33. 38 applicants, 63% accepted, 17 enrolled. In 2019, 33 master's awarded. *Degree requirements:* For master's, minimum GPA of 3.0; internship or research paper. *Entrance requirements:* For master's, one-page personal statement, 2 letters of recommendation, resume, bachelor's degree transcript; for Certificate, bachelor's transcript, 2 letters of recommendation, 1-page statement, resume. Additional exam requirements/recommendations for international students: required—TOEFL (minimum score 550 paper-based, 79 iBT) or IELTS (minimum score 6). *Application deadline:* For fall admission, 8/31 priority date for domestic students, 6/30 priority date for international students; for spring admission, 12/31 priority date for domestic students, 10/31 priority date for international students. Applications are processed on a rolling basis. Electronic applications accepted. *Expenses: Tuition:* Part-time $600 per credit. *Required fees:* $40 per semester. *Financial support:* Federal Work-Study, scholarships/grants, and tuition discounts available. Support available to part-time students. Financial award application deadline: 8/31; financial award applicants required to submit FAFSA. *Unit head:* Chrystal Porter, Vice President of Graduate and Professional Studies, 617-243-2083, Fax: 617-243-2450, E-mail: gradinfo@lasell.edu. *Application contact:* Adrienne Franciosi, Assistant Vice President of Graduate and Professional Studies, 617-243-2214, Fax: 617-243-2450, E-mail: gradinfo@lasell.edu.
Website: http://www.lasell.edu/academics/graduate-and-professional-studies/programs-of-study/master-of-science-in-criminal-justice-.html

Lewis University, College of Education and Social Sciences, Program in Criminal Justice, Romeoville, IL 60446. Offers MS. *Program availability:* Part-time, evening/weekend, 100% online, blended/hybrid learning. *Students:* 7 full-time (5 women), 33 part-time (17 women); includes 18 minority (4 Black or African American, non-Hispanic/Latino; 1 American Indian or Alaska Native, non-Hispanic/Latino; 11 Hispanic/Latino; 2 Two or more races, non-Hispanic/Latino), 2 international. Average age 33. *Entrance requirements:* For master's, bachelor's degree or a minimum of 12 related hours in criminal/social justice, 2 letters of recommendation, minimum GPA of 3.0, personal statement. Additional exam requirements/recommendations for international students: required—TOEFL (minimum score 79 iBT), IELTS (minimum score 6). *Application deadline:* For fall admission, 5/1 priority date for international students; for spring admission, 11/15 priority date for international students. Applications are processed on a

rolling basis. Application fee: $40. Electronic applications accepted. *Financial support:* Federal Work-Study, scholarships/grants, tuition waivers (full and partial), and unspecified assistantships available. Financial award application deadline: 5/1; financial award applicants required to submit FAFSA. *Unit head:* Dr. Vesna Markovic, Program Chair. *Application contact:* Sheri Vilcek, Graduate Admission Counselor, 815-836-5610, E-mail: grad@lewisu.edu.
Website: http://www.lewisu.edu/academics/masterscrim/index.htm

Liberty University, Helms School of Government, Lynchburg, VA 24515. Offers criminal justice (MS), including forensic psychology, homeland security, public administration (MA, MS); international relations (MS); political science (MS); public administration (MPA), including business and government, healthcare, law and public policy, public and non-profit management; public policy (MA), including campaigns and elections, international affairs, Middle East affairs, public administration (MA, MS). *Program availability:* Part-time, online learning. *Students:* 1,143 full-time (565 women), 572 part-time (408 women); includes 795 minority (499 Black or African American, non-Hispanic/Latino; 16 American Indian or Alaska Native, non-Hispanic/Latino; 23 Asian, non-Hispanic/Latino; 162 Hispanic/Latino; 7 Native Hawaiian or other Pacific Islander, non-Hispanic/Latino; 88 Two or more races, non-Hispanic/Latino), 27 international. Average age 35. 3,017 applicants, 44% accepted, 728 enrolled. In 2019, 415 master's awarded. *Entrance requirements:* For master's, minimum undergraduate GPA of 3.0. Additional exam requirements/recommendations for international students: required—TOEFL (minimum score 600 paper-based; 100 iBT). *Application deadline:* Applications are processed on a rolling basis. Application fee: $50. Electronic applications accepted. *Expenses: Tuition:* Full-time $545; part-time $410 per credit hour. One-time fee: $50. *Financial support:* In 2019–20, 808 students received support. Teaching assistantships and Federal Work-Study available. *Unit head:* Ron Miller, Dean, 434-592-4986, E-mail: govtdean@liberty.edu. *Application contact:* Jay Bridge, Director of Admissions, 800-424-9595, Fax: 800-628-7977, E-mail: gradadmissions@liberty.edu.
Website: https://www.liberty.edu/government/

Liberty University, School of Behavioral Sciences, Lynchburg, VA 24515. Offers applied psychology (MA), including developmental psychology (MA, MS), industrial/organizational psychology (MA, MS); clinical mental health counseling (MA); community care and counseling (Ed D), including marriage and family counseling, pastoral care and counseling, traumatology; counselor education and supervision (PhD); human services counseling (MA), including addictions and recovery, business, child and family law, Christian ministries, criminal justice, crisis response and trauma, executive leadership, health and wellness, life coaching, marriage and family, military resilience; marriage and family counseling (MA); marriage and family therapy (MA); military resilience (Certificate); pastoral counseling (MA), including addictions and recovery, community chaplaincy, crisis response and trauma, discipleship and church ministry, leadership, life coaching, marriage and family, marriage and family studies, military resilience, parenting and child/adolescent, pastoral counseling, theology; professional counseling (MA); psychology (MS), including developmental psychology (MA, MS), industrial/organizational psychology (MA, MS); school counseling (M Ed). *Program availability:* Part-time, online learning. *Students:* 3,786 full-time (3,065 women), 5,193 part-time (4,081 women); includes 2,733 minority (1,967 Black or African American, non-Hispanic/Latino; 48 American Indian or Alaska Native, non-Hispanic/Latino; 103 Asian, non-Hispanic/Latino; 349 Hispanic/Latino; 19 Native Hawaiian or other Pacific Islander, non-Hispanic/Latino; 247 Two or more races, non-Hispanic/Latino), 133 international. Average age 38. 13,324 applicants, 28% accepted, 2,163 enrolled. In 2019, 2,322 master's, 19 doctorates, 112 other advanced degrees awarded. *Entrance requirements:* For master's, Official bachelor's degree transcripts with a 2.0 GPA or higher. *Application deadline:* Applications are processed on a rolling basis. Application fee: $50. Electronic applications accepted. *Expenses: Tuition:* Full-time $545; part-time $410 per credit hour. One-time fee: $50. *Financial support:* In 2019–20, 1,003 students received support. Teaching assistantships and Federal Work-Study available. Financial award applicants required to submit FAFSA. *Unit head:* Dr. Kenyon Knapp, Dean, School of Behavioral Services, E-mail: kcknapp@liberty.edu. *Application contact:* Jay Bridge, Director of Admissions, 800-424-9595, Fax: 800-628-7977, E-mail: gradadmissions@liberty.edu.
Website: https://www.liberty.edu/behavioral-sciences/

Lincoln University, Graduate Studies, Jefferson City, MO 65101. Offers accounting (MBA); counseling (M Ed), including addictions counseling; environmental science (MS); higher education (MA), including hbcu; history (MA); natural sciences (MS); school teaching middle school with certification (M Ed); school teaching-elementary (M Ed); school teaching-secondary (M Ed); sociology (MA); sociology/criminal justice (MA); sustainable agriculture (MS). *Program availability:* Part-time, evening/weekend, 100% online, blended/hybrid learning. *Students:* 47 full-time (33 women), 62 part-time (35 women); includes 42 minority (39 Black or African American, non-Hispanic/Latino; 1 American Indian or Alaska Native, non-Hispanic/Latino; 1 Asian, non-Hispanic/Latino; 1 Native Hawaiian or other Pacific Islander, non-Hispanic/Latino), 13 international. Average age 33. In 2019, 32 master's awarded. *Degree requirements:* For master's, comprehensive exam, thesis optional. *Entrance requirements:* For master's, GRE, MAT, or GMAT, minimum GPA of 2.75 overall, 3.0 in courses related to specialization; 3 letters of recommendation; minimum C average in English composition; personal statement of purpose. Additional exam requirements/recommendations for international students: required—TOEFL (minimum score 500 paper-based; 61 iBT), IELTS (minimum score 5.5), Michigan English Language Assessment Battery (minimum score 80). *Application deadline:* For fall admission, 7/1 priority date for domestic students, 5/1 priority date for international students; for spring admission, 11/1 priority date for domestic students, 10/1 priority date for international students; for summer admission, 6/1 priority date for domestic students. Applications are processed on a rolling basis. Application fee: $30. Electronic applications accepted. *Expenses: Tuition, area resident:* Full-time $511; part-time $511 per credit hour. Tuition, state resident: full-time $511; part-time $511 per credit hour. Tuition, nonresident: full-time $886; part-time $886 per credit hour. *International tuition:* $886 full-time. *Required fees:* $20; $20 per credit hour. $381.10 per semester. *Financial support:* In 2019–20, 8 fellowships (averaging $4,017 per year), 6 research assistantships (averaging $18,500 per year) were awarded; Federal Work-Study, scholarships/grants, and unspecified assistantships also available. Support available to part-time students. Financial award application deadline: 3/1; financial award applicants required to submit FAFSA. *Unit head:* Dr. Benjamin Arnold, Assistant Vice President of Academic Affairs, 573-681-5247, Fax: 573-681-5106, E-mail: gradschool@lincolnu.edu. *Application contact:* James Kendall, Graduate Admission Coordinator/Recruiter, 573-681-5150, Fax: 573-681-5106, E-mail: gradschool@lincolnu.edu.
Website: http://www.lincolnu.edu/web/graduate-studies/graduate-studies

Lindenwood University, Graduate Programs, School of Accelerated Degree Programs, St. Charles, MO 63301-1695. Offers administration (MSA), including management, marketing, project management; business administration (MBA); communications (MA), including digital and multimedia, media management, promotions, training and development; criminal justice and administration (MS); healthcare administration (MS); human resource management (MS); information technology (Certificate); managing information security (MS); managing information technology (MS); managing virtualization and cloud computing (MS); writing (MFA). *Program availability:* Part-time, evening/weekend, 100% online. *Faculty:* 11 full-time (6 women), 66 part-time/adjunct (23 women). *Students:* 408 full-time (262 women), 60 part-time (40 women); includes 149 minority (111 Black or African American, non-Hispanic/Latino; 2 American Indian or Alaska Native, non-Hispanic/Latino; 2 Asian, non-Hispanic/Latino; 18 Hispanic/Latino; 1 Native Hawaiian or other Pacific Islander, non-Hispanic/Latino; 15 Two or more races, non-Hispanic/Latino), 33 international. Average age 39. 268 applicants, 46% accepted, 99 enrolled. In 2019, 347 master's awarded. *Degree requirements:* For master's, thesis (for some programs), minimum cumulative GPA of 3.0; for Certificate, minimum cumulative GPA of 3.0. *Entrance requirements:* For master's, resume, personal statement, official undergraduate transcript, minimum undergraduate cumulative GPA of 3.0. Additional exam requirements/recommendations for international students: required—TOEFL (minimum score 553 paper-based; 81 iBT); recommended—IELTS (minimum score 6.5). *Application deadline:* For fall admission, 9/30 priority date for domestic and international students; for winter admission, 1/6 priority date for domestic and international students; for spring admission, 4/6 priority date for domestic and international students; for summer admission, 7/8 priority date for domestic and international students. Applications are processed on a rolling basis. Application fee: $0 ($100 for international students). Electronic applications accepted. *Expenses:* Contact institution. *Financial support:* In 2019–20, 145 students received support. Career-related internships or fieldwork, institutionally sponsored loans, scholarships/grants, tuition waivers (partial), and unspecified assistantships available. Financial award application deadline: 6/30; financial award applicants required to submit FAFSA. *Unit head:* Dr. Gina Ganahl, Dean, Accelerated Degree Programs, 636-949-4501, Fax: 636-949-4505, E-mail: gganahl@lindenwood.edu. *Application contact:* Kara Schilli, Assistant Vice President, University Admissions, 636-949-4349, Fax: 636-949-4109, E-mail: adultadmissions@lindenwood.edu.
Website: https://www.lindenwood.edu/academics/academic-schools/school-of-accelerated-degree-programs/

Lindenwood University–Belleville, Graduate Programs, Belleville, IL 62226. Offers business administration (MBA); communications (MA), including digital and multimedia, media management, promotions, training and development; counseling (MA); criminal justice administration (MS); education (MA); healthcare administration (MS); human resource management (MS); school administration (MA); teaching (MAT).

Loma Linda University, School of Behavioral Health, Department of Social Work and Social Ecology, Loma Linda, CA 92350. Offers criminal justice (MS); gerontology (MS); social policy and social research (PhD); social work (MSW). *Accreditation:* CSWE. *Degree requirements:* For master's, comprehensive exam, thesis optional; for doctorate, comprehensive exam, thesis/dissertation. *Entrance requirements:* For master's and doctorate, GRE General Test. Additional exam requirements/recommendations for international students: required—TOEFL, Michigan English Language Assessment Battery. Electronic applications accepted.

London Metropolitan University, Graduate Programs, London, United Kingdom. Offers applied psychology (M Sc); architecture (MA); biomedical science (M Sc); blood science (M Sc); cancer pharmacology (M Sc); computer networking and cyber security (M Sc); computing and information systems (M Sc); conference interpreting (MA); counter-terrorism studies (M Sc); creative, digital and professional writing (MA); crime, violence and prevention (M Sc); criminology (M Sc); curating contemporary art (MA); data analytics (M Sc); digital media (MA); early childhood studies (MA); education (MA, Ed D); financial services law, regulation and compliance (LL M); food science (M Sc); forensic psychology (M Sc); health and social care management and policy (M Sc); human nutrition (M Sc); human resource management (MA); human rights and international conflict (MA); information technology (M Sc); intelligence and security studies (M Sc); international oil, gas and energy law (LL M); international relations (MA); interpreting (MA); learning and teaching in higher education (MA); legal practice (LL M); media and entertainment law (LL M); organizational and consumer psychology (M Sc); psychological therapy (M Sc); psychology of mental health (M Sc); public health (M Sc); public policy and management (MPA); security studies (M Sc); social work (M Sc); spatial planning and urban design (MA); sports therapy (M Sc); supporting older children and young people with dyslexia (MA); teaching languages (MA), including Arabic, English; translation (MA); woman and child abuse (MA).

Long Island University - Brentwood Campus, Graduate Programs, Brentwood, NY 11717. Offers childhood education (MS), including grades 1-6; childhood education/literacy B-6 (MS); childhood education/special education (grades 1-6) (MS); clinical mental health counseling (MS, Advanced Certificate); criminal justice (MS); early childhood education (MS); educational leadership (MS Ed); family nurse practitioner (MS, Advanced Certificate); health administration (MPA); library and information science (MS); literacy (B-6) (MS Ed); school counselor (MS, Advanced Certificate); social work (MSW); special education (MS Ed); students with disabilities generalist (grades 7-12) (Advanced Certificate). *Program availability:* Part-time. *Entrance requirements:* For master's and Advanced Certificate, GRE. Additional exam requirements/recommendations for international students: required—TOEFL or IELTS. Electronic applications accepted.

Long Island University - Post, College of Liberal Arts and Sciences, Brookville, NY 11548-1300. Offers applied mathematics (MS); behavior analysis (MA); biology (MS); criminal justice (MS); earth science (MS); English (MA); environmental sustainability (MS); genetic counseling (MS); history (MA); interdisciplinary studies (MA, MS); political science (MA); psychology (MA). *Program availability:* Part-time, evening/weekend, blended/hybrid learning. Terminal master's awarded for partial completion of doctoral program. *Degree requirements:* For master's, comprehensive exam (for some programs), thesis (for some programs). *Entrance requirements:* Additional exam requirements/recommendations for international students: required—TOEFL, IELTS, or PTE. Electronic applications accepted.

Loyola University Chicago, Graduate School, Department of Criminal Justice and Criminology, Chicago, IL 60660. Offers criminal justice (MA). *Program availability:* Part-time, evening/weekend. *Faculty:* 7 full-time (2 women). *Students:* 16 full-time (12 women), 7 part-time (5 women); includes 13 minority (4 Black or African American, non-Hispanic/Latino; 9 Hispanic/Latino). Average age 24. 36 applicants, 64% accepted, 14 enrolled. In 2019, 13 master's awarded. *Degree requirements:* For master's, comprehensive exam, thesis optional. *Entrance requirements:* For master's, minimum GPA of 3.0. Additional exam requirements/recommendations for international students: required—TOEFL (minimum score 550 paper-based). *Application deadline:* For fall admission, 2/1 priority date for domestic students. Applications are processed on a rolling basis. Application fee: $50. Electronic applications accepted. Application fee is waived when completed online. *Expenses:* Contact institution. *Financial support:* In 2019–20, 5 students received support, including 7 research assistantships with partial tuition reimbursements available (averaging $9,000 per year); scholarships/grants also available. Financial award application deadline: 3/1; financial award applicants required to submit FAFSA. *Unit head:* Dr. Don Stemen, Chairperson, 773-508-8594, E-mail: dstemen@luc.edu. *Application contact:* Dr. Christopher Donner, Graduate Program Director, 773-508-8864, E-mail: cdonner@luc.edu.
Website: https://luc.edu/criminaljustice/

Loyola University New Orleans, College of Arts and Sciences, Program in Criminology and Justice, New Orleans, LA 70118. Offers MCJ. *Program availability:* Part-time, evening/weekend. *Faculty:* 2 full-time (1 woman), 4 part-time/adjunct (3 women).

Criminal Justice and Criminology

Students: 9 full-time (6 women), 30 part-time (25 women); includes 17 minority (13 Black or African American, non-Hispanic/Latino; 4 Hispanic/Latino). Average age 30. 37 applicants, 68% accepted, 17 enrolled. In 2019, 4 master's awarded. *Degree requirements:* For master's, comprehensive exam, research and practicum. *Entrance requirements:* For master's, A writing sample (a written response to a specified prompt), a resume, two letters of recommendation, and official undergraduate transcripts from an accredited university. Additional exam requirements/recommendations for international students: required—TOEFL (minimum score 550 paper-based). *Application deadline:* For fall admission, 8/15 priority date for domestic and international students; for winter admission, 10/1 priority date for domestic and international students; for spring admission, 1/1 priority date for domestic and international students; for summer admission, 5/1 priority date for domestic and international students. Applications are processed on a rolling basis. Application fee: $20. Electronic applications accepted. Application fee is waived when completed online. *Expenses:* Contact institution. *Financial support:* In 2019–20, 36 students received support. Research assistantships, scholarships/grants, and unspecified assistantships available. Financial award application deadline: 5/1; financial award applicants required to submit FAFSA. *Unit head:* Dr. Christian Bolden, Chair, 504-865-3124, Fax: 504-865-3883, E-mail: crimjust@loyno.edu. *Application contact:* Kelly Frailing, Assistant Professor, 504-864-7134, Fax: 504-865-3612, E-mail: crimjust@loyno.edu. Website: http://cas.loyno.edu/criminologyjustice/master-criminal-justice

Lynn University, College of Arts and Sciences, Boca Raton, FL 33431-5598. Offers criminal justice (MS); mental health counseling (MS); psychology (MS). *Program availability:* Part-time, evening/weekend, 100% online, blended/hybrid learning. *Faculty:* 15 full-time (7 women), 12 part-time/adjunct (7 women). *Students:* 98 full-time (81 women), 55 part-time (33 women); includes 57 minority (23 Black or African American, non-Hispanic/Latino; 1 American Indian or Alaska Native, non-Hispanic/Latino; 28 Hispanic/Latino; 2 Native Hawaiian or other Pacific Islander, non-Hispanic/Latino; 3 Two or more races, non-Hispanic/Latino), 9 international. Average age 32. 126 applicants, 77% accepted, 69 enrolled. In 2019, 37 master's awarded. *Degree requirements:* For master's, comprehensive exam (for some programs), thesis (for some programs). *Entrance requirements:* For master's, Bachelor's degree from accredited institution, minimum undergraduate GPA of 3.0, official undergraduate transcripts, two letters of recommendation from academic or professional sources, writing sample demonstrating capacity to perform at graduate level. Additional exam requirements/recommendations for international students: required—TOEFL (minimum score 550 paper-based; 80 iBT), IELTS (minimum score 6.5). *Application deadline:* For fall admission, 8/10 for domestic students, 7/31 for international students; for spring admission, 12/18 for domestic students, 12/2 for international students; for summer admission, 4/12 for domestic students, 4/2 for international students. Applications are processed on a rolling basis. Application fee: $45. Electronic applications accepted. *Expenses:* Tuition and fees for degrees offered in the College of Arts and Sciences start at $23,400 and can go to $38,350 depending on the program. Each program has specific credit hour requirements and the cost per credit hour within this college ranges from $650.00 to $740.00 per credit hour. *Financial support:* In 2019–20, 42 students received support. Career-related internships or fieldwork, Federal Work-Study, scholarships/grants, tuition waivers (full and partial), and unspecified assistantships available. Support available to part-time students. Financial award application deadline: 3/1; financial award applicants required to submit FAFSA. *Unit head:* Dr. Gary Villa, Dean, College of Arts and Sciences, 561-237-7025, E-mail: gvilla@lynn.edu. *Application contact:* Steven Pruitt, Director of Graduate and Online Admission, 561-237-7834, Fax: 561-237-7100, E-mail: admissionpm@lynn.edu. Website: https://www.lynn.edu/academics/colleges-schools/arts-and-sciences

Madonna University, School of Business, Livonia, MI 48150-1173. Offers business administration (MBA); international business (MSBA); leadership studies (MSBA); leadership studies in criminal justice (MSBA); quality and operations management (MSBA). *Program availability:* Part-time, evening/weekend, online learning. *Degree requirements:* For master's, thesis (for some programs), foreign language proficiency (international business). *Entrance requirements:* For master's, GMAT, GRE General Test, minimum GPA of 3.0. Electronic applications accepted. *Expenses:* Tuition: Full-time $15,930; part-time $885 per credit hour. Tuition and fees vary according to degree level and program.

Marshall University, Academic Affairs Division, College of Science, Department of Criminal Justice, Huntington, WV 25755. Offers MS. *Program availability:* Evening/weekend. *Degree requirements:* For master's, thesis optional. *Entrance requirements:* For master's, GRE General Test.

Marywood University, Academic Affairs, Munley College of Liberal Arts and Sciences, Department of Social Sciences, Scranton, PA 18509-1598. Offers criminal justice (MS). Electronic applications accepted.

McNeese State University, Doré School of Graduate Studies, College of Liberal Arts, Department of Social Sciences, Lake Charles, LA 70609. Offers criminal justice (MS). *Entrance requirements:* For master's, GRE, minimum undergraduate GPA of 3.0, 3 letters of recommendation, autobiography.

Mercer University, Graduate Studies, Cecil B. Day Campus, College of Professional Advancement, Atlanta, GA 31207. Offers certified rehabilitation counseling (MS); clinical mental health (MS); counselor education and supervision (PhD); criminal justice and public safety leadership (MS); health informatics (MS); human services (MS), including child and adolescent services, gerontology services; organizational leadership (MS), including leadership for the health care professional, leadership for the nonprofit organization, organizational development and change; school counseling (MS). *Program availability:* Part-time, evening/weekend, 100% online, blended/hybrid learning. *Faculty:* 19 full-time (11 women), 34 part-time/adjunct (30 women). *Students:* 193 full-time (156 women), 277 part-time (225 women); includes 260 minority (211 Black or African American, non-Hispanic/Latino; 2 American Indian or Alaska Native, non-Hispanic/Latino; 23 Asian, non-Hispanic/Latino; 19 Hispanic/Latino; 5 Two or more races, non-Hispanic/Latino), 3 international. Average age 32. 300 applicants, 45% accepted, 114 enrolled. In 2019, 183 master's, 7 doctorates awarded. *Degree requirements:* For master's, comprehensive exam (for some programs), thesis (for some programs); for doctorate, thesis/dissertation. *Entrance requirements:* For master's, GRE or MAT, Georgia Professional Standards Commission (GPSC) Certification at the SC-5 level; for doctorate, GRE or MAT. Additional exam requirements/recommendations for international students: recommended—TOEFL (minimum score 550 paper-based; 80 iBT), IELTS (minimum score 6.5). *Application deadline:* For fall admission, 7/1 priority date for domestic and international students; for spring admission, 11/1 priority date for domestic and international students; for summer admission, 4/1 priority date for domestic and international students. Application fee: $35. Electronic applications accepted. Application fee is waived when completed online. *Expenses:* Contact institution. *Financial support:* In 2019–20, 32 students received support. Federal Work-Study, scholarships/grants, and unspecified assistantships available. Financial award applicants required to submit FAFSA. *Unit head:* Dr. Priscilla R. Danheiser, Dean, 678-547-6028, Fax: 678-547-6008, E-mail: danheiser_p@mercer.edu. *Application contact:* Theatis Anderson, Asst VP for Enrollment Management, 678-547-6421, E-mail: anderson_t@mercer.edu. Website: https://professionaladvancement.mercer.edu/.

Mercyhurst University, Graduate Studies, Program in Administration of Justice, Erie, PA 16546. Offers administration of justice (MS). *Program availability:* Part-time, evening/weekend. *Degree requirements:* For master's, thesis optional. *Entrance requirements:* For master's, GRE, resume, essay, three professional references, transcripts. Additional exam requirements/recommendations for international students: required—TOEFL. Electronic applications accepted.

Mercyhurst University, Graduate Studies, Program in Applied Intelligence, Erie, PA 16546. Offers MS, Certificate. *Program availability:* Online learning. *Degree requirements:* For master's, internship. *Entrance requirements:* For master's, GRE or MAT, resume, essay, three professional references, transcripts. Additional exam requirements/recommendations for international students: required—TOEFL. Electronic applications accepted.

Methodist University, School of Graduate Studies, Program in Justice Administration, Fayetteville, NC 28311-1498. Offers MJA. *Program availability:* Part-time, evening/weekend. *Entrance requirements:* For master's, bachelor's degree in criminal justice or related discipline with minimum overall GPA of 3.0 from accredited institution. Additional exam requirements/recommendations for international students: required—TOEFL (minimum score 500 paper-based; 60 iBT).

Metropolitan State University, School of Law Enforcement and Criminal Justice, St. Paul, MN 55106-5000. Offers criminal justice (MS). *Program availability:* Part-time, evening/weekend. *Degree requirements:* For master's, thesis. *Entrance requirements:* For master's, resume, letters of reference, minimum GPA of 3.0. Additional exam requirements/recommendations for international students: required—TOEFL (minimum score 550 paper-based). Electronic applications accepted.

Michigan State University, The Graduate School, College of Social Science, School of Criminal Justice, East Lansing, MI 48824. Offers criminal justice (MS, PhD); forensic science (MS); law enforcement intelligence and analysis (MS). *Program availability:* Online learning. *Entrance requirements:* Additional exam requirements/recommendations for international students: required—TOEFL. Electronic applications accepted.

Middle Tennessee State University, College of Graduate Studies, College of Behavioral and Health Sciences, Department of Criminal Justice Administration, Murfreesboro, TN 37132. Offers MCJ. *Program availability:* Part-time, evening/weekend, online learning. *Degree requirements:* For master's, comprehensive exam, thesis. *Entrance requirements:* For master's, GRE or MAT. Additional exam requirements/recommendations for international students: required—TOEFL (minimum score 525 paper-based; 71 iBT) or IELTS (minimum score 6). Electronic applications accepted.

Midwestern State University, Billie Doris McAda Graduate School, Robert D. and Carol Gunn College of Health Sciences and Human Services, Department of Criminal Justice and Health Services Administration, Wichita Falls, TX 76308. Offers criminal justice (MA); health information management (MHA); health services administration (Graduate Certificate); medical practice management (MHA); public and community sector health care management (MHA); rural and urban hospital management (MHA). *Program availability:* Part-time, evening/weekend. *Degree requirements:* For master's, comprehensive exam, thesis. *Entrance requirements:* For master's, GRE. Additional exam requirements/recommendations for international students: required—TOEFL (minimum score 550 paper-based). Electronic applications accepted.

Minnesota State University Mankato, College of Graduate Studies and Research, College of Social and Behavioral Sciences, Department of Sociology and Corrections, Mankato, MN 56001. Offers sociology (MA); sociology: college teaching (MA); sociology: corrections (MS); sociology: human services planning and administration (MS). *Program availability:* Part-time. *Degree requirements:* For master's, comprehensive exam, thesis or alternative. *Entrance requirements:* For master's, minimum GPA of 3.0 during previous 2 years, 3 letters of reference, resume. Additional exam requirements/recommendations for international students: required—TOEFL. Electronic applications accepted.

Mississippi College, Graduate School, College of Arts and Sciences, School of Humanities and Social Sciences, Department of History and Political Science, Clinton, MS 39058. Offers administration of justice (MSS); history (M Ed, MA, MSS); paralegal studies (Certificate); political science (MSS); social sciences (M Ed, MSS). *Program availability:* Part-time. *Degree requirements:* For master's, one foreign language, comprehensive exam, thesis (for some programs). *Entrance requirements:* For master's, GRE or NTE, minimum GPA of 2.5. Additional exam requirements/recommendations for international students: recommended—TOEFL, IELTS. Electronic applications accepted.

Mississippi Valley State University, Department of Criminal Justice, Itta Bena, MS 38941-1400. Offers MS. *Program availability:* Part-time, evening/weekend, 100% online. *Degree requirements:* For master's, 2 foreign languages, comprehensive exam, thesis optional. *Entrance requirements:* For master's, minimum GPA of 2.5. Additional exam requirements/recommendations for international students: recommended—TOEFL (minimum score 525 paper-based). Electronic applications accepted. *Expenses:* Contact institution.

Missouri Southern State University, Program in Criminal Justice Administration, Joplin, MO 64801-1595. Offers MS. *Program availability:* Online learning. *Degree requirements:* For master's, thesis optional. *Entrance requirements:* For master's, minimum undergraduate GPA of 2.5.

Missouri State University, Graduate College, College of Humanities and Public Affairs, Department of Criminology and Criminal Justice, Springfield, MO 65897. Offers community corrections (Certificate); criminology and criminal justice (MS); homeland security and defense (Certificate). *Program availability:* Part-time, 100% online, blended/hybrid learning. *Degree requirements:* For master's, comprehensive exam, thesis or alternative. *Entrance requirements:* For master's, bachelor's degree in criminology, criminal justice, or sociology; minimum undergraduate GPA of 3.0. Additional exam requirements/recommendations for international students: required—TOEFL (minimum score 550 paper-based; 79 iBT), IELTS (minimum score 6). Electronic applications accepted. *Expenses:* Tuition, area resident: Full-time $2600; part-time $1735 per credit hour. Tuition, nonresident: full-time $5240; part-time $3495 per credit hour. *International tuition:* $5240 full-time. *Required fees:* $530; $438 per credit hour. Tuition and fees vary according to class time, course level, course load, degree level, campus/location and program.

Missouri State University, Graduate College, Interdisciplinary Program in Professional Studies, Springfield, MO 65897. Offers administrative studies (Certificate); applied communication (MS); criminal justice (MS); environmental management (MS); homeland security (MS); individualized (MS); professional studies (MS); screenwriting and producing (MS); sports management (MS). *Program availability:* Part-time, evening/weekend, 100% online, blended/hybrid learning. *Degree requirements:* For master's, comprehensive exam, thesis or alternative. *Entrance requirements:* For master's, GRE, GMAT (if GPA less than 3.0). Additional exam requirements/recommendations for international students: required—TOEFL (minimum score 550 paper-based; 79 iBT),

IELTS (minimum score 6). Electronic applications accepted. *Expenses: Tuition, area resident:* Full-time $2600; part-time $1735 per credit hour. Tuition, nonresident: full-time $5240; part-time $3495 per credit hour. *International tuition:* $5240 full-time. *Required fees:* $530; $438 per credit hour. Tuition and fees vary according to class time, course level, course load, degree level, campus/location and program.

Molloy College, Criminal Justice Program, Rockville Centre, NY 11571. Offers criminal justice (MS). *Program availability:* Part-time, evening/weekend. *Faculty:* 4 full-time (2 women), 2 part-time/adjunct (0 women). *Students:* 9 full-time (5 women), 11 part-time (7 women); includes 10 minority (7 Black or African American, non-Hispanic/Latino; 2 Hispanic/Latino; 1 Native Hawaiian or other Pacific Islander, non-Hispanic/Latino). Average age 31. 11 applicants, 45% accepted, 3 enrolled. In 2019, 12 master's awarded. *Entrance requirements:* Additional exam requirements/recommendations for international students: required—TOEFL (minimum score 550 paper-based; 79 iBT). *Application deadline:* Applications are processed on a rolling basis. Application fee: $60. Electronic applications accepted. *Expenses: Tuition:* Full-time $21,510; part-time $1195 per credit hour. *Required fees:* $1100. Tuition and fees vary according to course load, degree level and program. *Financial support:* Application deadline: 3/1; applicants required to submit FAFSA. *Unit head:* Dr. John Eterno, Associate Dean/Graduate Program Director, 516-323-3804, E-mail: crj@molloy.edu. *Application contact:* Faye Hood, Assistant Director for Admissions, 516-323-4009, E-mail: fhood@molloy.edu. Website: https://www.molloy.edu/academics/graduate-programs/graduate-criminal-justice

Monmouth University, Graduate Studies, Department of Criminal Justice, West Long Branch, NJ 07764-1898. Offers criminal justice (MA), including homeland security; criminal justice administration (Certificate). *Program availability:* Part-time, evening/weekend, 100% online. *Faculty:* 4 full-time (2 women), 1 part-time/adjunct (0 women). *Students:* 20 full-time (7 women), 17 part-time (14 women); includes 7 minority (1 Black or African American, non-Hispanic/Latino; 6 Hispanic/Latino). Average age 26. In 2019, 14 master's, 1 other advanced degree awarded. *Degree requirements:* For master's, comprehensive exam (for some programs), thesis (for some programs). *Entrance requirements:* For master's and Certificate, baccalaureate degree with minimum GPA of 3.0 in major, 2.5 overall; two letters of recommendation; personal essay. Additional exam requirements/recommendations for international students: required—TOEFL (minimum score 550 paper-based; 79 iBT), IELTS (minimum score 6), Michigan English Language Assessment Battery (minimum score 77) or Certificate of Advanced English (minimum score 160). *Application deadline:* For fall admission, 7/15 priority date for domestic students, 6/1 for international students; for spring admission, 12/1 priority date for domestic students, 11/1 for international students; for summer admission, 5/1 for domestic students. Applications are processed on a rolling basis. Application fee: $50. Electronic applications accepted. *Expenses: Tuition:* Full-time $22,194; part-time $14,796 per credit. *Required fees:* $712; $178 per semester. $178 per semester. Tuition and fees vary according to course load. *Financial support:* In 2019–20, 14 students received support. Research assistantships, teaching assistantships, scholarships/grants, and unspecified assistantships available. Support available to part-time students. Financial award applicants required to submit FAFSA. *Unit head:* Dr. Brian Lockwood, Program Director, 732-571-7567, Fax: 732-263-5148, E-mail: blockwoo@monmouth.edu. *Application contact:* Kevin New, Graduate Admission Counselor, 732-571-3452, Fax: 732-263-5123, E-mail: gradadm@monmouth.edu. Website: http://www.monmouth.edu/academics/criminal_justice/default.asp

Monroe College, King Graduate School, Bronx, NY 10468. Offers accounting (MS); business administration (MBA), including entrepreneurship, finance, general business administration, healthcare management, human resources, information technology, marketing; computer science (MS); criminal justice (MS); hospitality management (MS); public health (MPH), including biostatistics and epidemiology, community health, health administration and leadership. *Program availability:* Online learning.

Morehead State University, Graduate School, Caudill College of Arts, Humanities and Social Sciences, School of Humanities and Social Sciences, Morehead, KY 40351. Offers criminology (MA); general sociology (MA); gerontology (MA); sociology regional analysis (MA); sociology/chemical dependency (MA). *Program availability:* Part-time, evening/weekend. *Faculty:* 20 full-time (10 women), 3 part-time/adjunct (2 women). *Students:* 27 full-time (19 women), 15 part-time (9 women); includes 3 minority (2 Black or African American, non-Hispanic/Latino; 1 Hispanic/Latino), 1 international. 53 applicants, 60% accepted, 23 enrolled. In 2019, 8 master's awarded. *Degree requirements:* For master's, comprehensive exam (for some programs), thesis (for some programs), min 3.0 GPA, complete 40 credit hours, option 3 is approved practicum in chemical dependency, written or oral exam, public presentation of thesis or research query or practicum experience (for MPA); demonstration of mastery of skills through individual courses and examinations and taped videos displaying skills (for MA Sociology). *Entrance requirements:* For master's, GRE, 3.0 UG GPA in 18 hours of PA courses; 3.0 UG GPA in all Sociology courses;MA Sociology: UG GPA of 2.75 or higher; submission of 2-page statement of educational and career goals relative to program. Additional exam requirements/recommendations for international students: required—TOEFL (minimum score 525 paper-based). *Application deadline:* Applications are processed on a rolling basis. Application fee: $30. Electronic applications accepted. *Expenses: Tuition, area resident:* Part-time $570 per credit hour. Tuition, state resident: part-time $570 per credit hour. Tuition, nonresident: part-time $570 per credit hour. *Required fees:* $14 per credit hour. *Financial support:* Teaching assistantships, career-related internships or fieldwork, and unspecified assistantships available. Financial award applicants required to submit FAFSA. *Unit head:* Dr. Dianna D. Murphy, Associate Dean/Professor Legal Studies, 606-7832720, E-mail: d.murphy@moreheadstate.edu. *Application contact:* Dr. Dianna D. Murphy, Associate Dean/Professor Legal Studies, 606-7832720, E-mail: d.murphy@moreheadstate.edu.

Mount Mercy University, Program in Criminal Justice, Cedar Rapids, IA 52402-4797. Offers MA. *Program availability:* Evening/weekend, online learning. *Degree requirements:* For master's, capstone.

National American University, Roueche Graduate Center, Austin, TX 78731. Offers accounting (MBA); aviation management (MBA, MM); care coordination (MSN); community college leadership (Ed D); criminal justice (MM); e-marketing (MBA, MM); health care administration (MBA, MM); higher education (MM); human resources management (MBA, MM); information technology management (MBA, MM); international business (MBA); leadership (EMBA); management (MBA); nursing administration (MSN); nursing education (MSN); nursing informatics (MSN); operations and configuration management (MBA, MM); project and process management (MBA, MM). *Program availability:* Part-time, evening/weekend, online learning. *Entrance requirements:* For master's, minimum undergraduate GPA of 2.75. Additional exam requirements/recommendations for international students: required—TOEFL, TWE. Electronic applications accepted.

National University, School of Professional Studies, La Jolla, CA 92037-1011. Offers criminal justice (MCJ); digital cinema production (MFA); digital journalism (MA); homeland security and emergency management (MS); juvenile justice (MS); professional screenwriting (MFA); public administration (MPA), including human resource management, organizational leadership. *Program availability:* Part-time, evening/weekend, 100% online, blended/hybrid learning. *Degree requirements:* For master's, thesis (for some programs). *Entrance requirements:* For master's, interview, minimum GPA of 2.5. Additional exam requirements/recommendations for international students: required—TOEFL (minimum score 550 paper-based; 79 iBT), IELTS (minimum score 6). Electronic applications accepted. *Expenses: Tuition:* Full-time $442; part-time $442 per unit.

New Jersey City University, College of Professional Studies, Department of Criminal Justice, Jersey City, NJ 07305-1597. Offers MS. *Program availability:* Part-time, evening/weekend. *Degree requirements:* For master's, thesis or alternative. *Entrance requirements:* Additional exam requirements/recommendations for international students: required—TOEFL (minimum score 79 iBT).

New Jersey City University, College of Professional Studies, Program in National Security Studies, Jersey City, NJ 07305-1597. Offers civil security leadership (D Sc); national security studies (MS, Certificate). *Program availability:* Part-time. *Entrance requirements:* Additional exam requirements/recommendations for international students: required—TOEFL (minimum score 79 iBT).

New Mexico State University, College of Arts and Sciences, Department of Criminal Justice, Las Cruces, NM 88003-8001. Offers criminal justice (MCJ). *Program availability:* Part-time, evening/weekend, 100% online. *Faculty:* 9 full-time (3 women), 1 part-time/adjunct (0 women). *Students:* 16 full-time (11 women), 21 part-time (14 women); includes 27 minority (3 Black or African American, non-Hispanic/Latino; 1 American Indian or Alaska Native, non-Hispanic/Latino; 23 Hispanic/Latino), 1 international. Average age 31. 25 applicants, 68% accepted, 11 enrolled. In 2019, 12 master's awarded. *Degree requirements:* For master's, comprehensive exam, thesis optional, oral and written exams. *Entrance requirements:* For master's, minimum GPA of 3.0. Additional exam requirements/recommendations for international students: required—TOEFL (minimum score 550 paper-based; 79 iBT), IELTS (minimum score 6.5). *Application deadline:* For spring admission, 4/1 priority date for domestic students. Application fee: $40 ($50 for international students). Electronic applications accepted. *Financial support:* In 2019–20, 12 students received support, including 2 fellowships (averaging $4,844 per year), 1 research assistantship (averaging $18,583 per year), 6 teaching assistantships (averaging $18,495 per year); career-related internships or fieldwork, Federal Work-Study, scholarships/grants, traineeships, health care benefits, and unspecified assistantships also available. Support available to part-time students. Financial award application deadline: 3/1. *Unit head:* Dr. Dennis Giever, Department Head, 575-646-1632, Fax: 575-646-2827, E-mail: dgiever@nmsu.edu. *Application contact:* Dr. Mike Tapia, Graduate Program Director, 575-646-5386, Fax: 575-646-2827, E-mail: mtapia@nmsu.edu. Website: http://crimjust.nmsu.edu

Niagara University, Graduate Division of Arts and Sciences, Department of Criminal Justice, Niagara University, NY 14109. Offers criminal justice administration (MS). *Program availability:* Part-time. *Entrance requirements:* For master's, GRE. Additional exam requirements/recommendations for international students: required—TOEFL (minimum score 550 paper-based; 79 iBT), IELTS (minimum score 6). Electronic applications accepted. *Expenses:* Contact institution.

Norfolk State University, School of Graduate Studies, School of Liberal Arts, Department of Sociology, Program in Criminal Justice, Norfolk, VA 23504. Offers MA.

North Carolina Central University, College of Behavioral and Social Sciences, Department of Criminal Justice, Durham, NC 27707-3129. Offers MS. *Program availability:* Part-time, evening/weekend. *Degree requirements:* For master's, one foreign language, comprehensive exam, thesis or alternative. *Entrance requirements:* For master's, GRE, minimum GPA of 3.0 in major, 2.5 overall. Additional exam requirements/recommendations for international students: required—TOEFL.

North Dakota State University, College of Graduate and Interdisciplinary Studies, College of Arts, Humanities and Social Sciences, Department of Criminal Justice and Political Science, Fargo, ND 58102. Offers criminal justice (PhD); criminal justice administration (MS). *Program availability:* Part-time. Terminal master's awarded for partial completion of doctoral program. *Degree requirements:* For master's, thesis; for doctorate, comprehensive exam, thesis/dissertation. *Entrance requirements:* For master's, minimum GPA of 3.0 in last 60 credit hours, approved bachelor's degree, course work in research methods and statistics; for doctorate, GRE General Test, minimum GPA of 3.0 over last 60 credit hours, 3 letters of recommendation. Additional exam requirements/recommendations for international students: required—TOEFL (minimum score 525 paper-based; 71 iBT). Tuition and fees vary according to program and reciprocity agreements.

Northeastern State University, College of Liberal Arts, Department of Criminal Justice and Legal Studies, Tahlequah, OK 74464-2399. Offers criminal justice (MS). *Program availability:* Part-time, evening/weekend. *Faculty:* 10 full-time (6 women). *Students:* 26 full-time (15 women), 18 part-time (10 women); includes 31 minority (8 Black or African American, non-Hispanic/Latino; 11 American Indian or Alaska Native, non-Hispanic/Latino; 2 Hispanic/Latino; 1 Native Hawaiian or other Pacific Islander, non-Hispanic/Latino; 9 Two or more races, non-Hispanic/Latino). Average age 36. In 2019, 11 master's awarded. *Degree requirements:* For master's, thesis optional, oral exam. *Entrance requirements:* For master's, MAT or GRE, minimum GPA of 2.5. Additional exam requirements/recommendations for international students: required—TOEFL. *Application deadline:* For fall admission, 6/1 priority date for domestic students. Applications are processed on a rolling basis. Application fee: $25. Electronic applications accepted. *Expenses: Tuition, area resident:* Full-time $250; part-time $250 per credit hour. Tuition, state resident: full-time $250; part-time $250 per credit hour. Tuition, nonresident: full-time $556; part-time $555.50 per credit hour. *Required fees:* $33.40 per credit hour. *Financial support:* Teaching assistantships and Federal Work-Study available. Financial award application deadline: 3/1. *Unit head:* Dr. Jennifer Edwards, Graduate Coordinator, 918-444-3529, E-mail: wolynetz@nsuok.edu. *Application contact:* Josh McCollum, Graduate Coordinator, 918-444-2093, E-mail: mccolluj@nsuok.edu. Website: http://academics.nsuok.edu/criminaljustice/GraduateStudies.aspx

Northeastern University, College of Professional Studies, Boston, MA 02115-5096. Offers applied nutrition (MS); college athletics administration (MSL); commerce and economic development (MS); corporate and organizational communication (MS); criminal justice (MS); digital media (MPS); elearning and instructional design (M Ed); elementary education (MAT); geographic information technology (MPS); global studies and international relations (MS); higher education administration (M Ed); homeland security (MA); human services (MS); informatics (MPS); leadership (MS); learning analytics (M Ed); learning and instruction (M Ed); nonprofit management (MS); professional sports administration (MSL); project management (MS); regulatory affairs for drugs, biologics, and medical devices (MS); respiratory care leadership (MS); special education (M Ed); technical communication (MS). *Program availability:* Part-time, evening/weekend, 100% online, blended/hybrid learning. *Faculty:* 85 full-time (53 women), 892 part-time/adjunct (379 women). *Students:* 5,699 part-time (3,305 women). In 2019, 1,787 master's awarded. *Application deadline:* Applications are processed on a rolling basis. Application fee: $0. Electronic applications accepted. *Expenses:* Contact institution. *Financial support:* Applicants required to submit FAFSA. *Unit head:* Dr. Mary Loeffelholz, Dean of the College of Professional Studies, 617-373-6060. *Application*

contact: Dr. Mary Loeffelholz, Dean of the College of Professional Studies, 617-373-6060.
Website: https://cps.northeastern.edu/

Northeastern University, College of Social Sciences and Humanities, Boston, MA 02115. Offers criminology and criminal justice (MSCJ); criminology and justice policy (PhD); economics (MA, PhD); English (MA, PhD); international affairs (MA); law and public policy (PhD); political science (MA, PhD); public administration (MPA); public policy (MPP); security and resilience studies (MS); sociology (MA, PhD); urban and regional policy (MS); urban informatics (MS); world history (MA, PhD). *Program availability:* Online learning. *Degree requirements:* For doctorate, variable foreign language requirement, comprehensive exam, thesis/dissertation. *Entrance requirements:* For master's and doctorate, GRE. Additional exam requirements/recommendations for international students: required—TOEFL, IELTS. Electronic applications accepted. *Expenses:* Contact institution.

Northern Arizona University, College of Social and Behavioral Sciences, Department of Criminology and Criminal Justice, Flagstaff, AZ 86011. Offers applied criminology (MS). *Program availability:* Part-time. *Degree requirements:* For master's, variable foreign language requirement, comprehensive exam (for some programs), thesis (for some programs). *Entrance requirements:* For master's, minimum GPA of 3.0 or the equivalent. Additional exam requirements/recommendations for international students: required—TOEFL (minimum score 80 iBT), IELTS (minimum score 6.5). Electronic applications accepted.

Norwich University, College of Graduate and Continuing Studies, Master of Public Administration Program, Northfield, VT 05663. Offers criminal justice and public safety (MPA); fiscal management (MPA); international development and influence (MPA); municipal governance (MPA); nonprofit management (MPA); policy analysis and analytics (MPA); public administration leadership and crisis management (MPA); public works and sustainability (MPA). *Program availability:* Evening/weekend, online only, mostly all online with a week-long residency requirement. *Degree requirements:* For master's, capstone. *Entrance requirements:* For master's, minimum undergraduate GPA of 2.75. Additional exam requirements/recommendations for international students: required—TOEFL (minimum score 550 paper-based; 80 iBT), IELTS (minimum score 6.5). Electronic applications accepted. *Expenses:* Contact institution.

Norwich University, College of Graduate and Continuing Studies, Master of Science in Criminal Justice Program, Northfield, VT 05663. Offers MS. *Program availability:* Evening/weekend, online only, mostly all online with a week-long residency requirement. *Entrance requirements:* For master's, minimum GPA of 2.75. Additional exam requirements/recommendations for international students: required—TOEFL (minimum score 550 paper-based; 80 iBT), IELTS (minimum score 6.5). Electronic applications accepted. *Expenses:* Contact institution.

Nova Southeastern University, College of Arts, Humanities, and Social Sciences, Fort Lauderdale, FL 33314-7796. Offers advanced conflict resolution practice (Graduate Certificate); child protection (MHS); college student affairs (MS); conflict analysis and resolution (MS, PhD); criminal justice (MS, PhD); cross-disciplinary studies (MA); developmental disabilities (MS); family studies (Graduate Certificate); family systems health care (Graduate Certificate); family therapy (MS, PhD); marriage and family therapy (DMFT); peace studies (Graduate Certificate); qualitative research (Graduate Certificate); solution focused coaching (Graduate Certificate). *Accreditation:* AAMFT/COAMFTE (one or more programs are accredited). *Program availability:* Part-time, evening/weekend, 100% online, blended/hybrid learning. *Faculty:* 60 full-time (37 women), 88 part-time/adjunct (65 women). *Students:* 201 full-time (157 women), 418 part-time (297 women); includes 365 minority (180 Black or African American, non-Hispanic/Latino; 4 American Indian or Alaska Native, non-Hispanic/Latino; 15 Asian, non-Hispanic/Latino; 141 Hispanic/Latino; 25 Two or more races, non-Hispanic/Latino), 49 international. Average age 37. 303 applicants, 84% accepted, 197 enrolled. In 2019, 125 master's, 63 doctorates, 24 other advanced degrees awarded. *Degree requirements:* For master's, comprehensive exam (for some programs), thesis optional, comprehensive exams, portfolios (for some programs), table-top exams (for some programs); for doctorate, comprehensive exam, thesis/dissertation, qualifying exams, portfolios (for some programs). *Entrance requirements:* For master's, interview, minimum GPA of 3.0, writing sample; for doctorate, interview, minimum GPA of 3.5, master's degree in related field, writing sample; for Graduate Certificate, minimum GPA of 3.0. Additional exam requirements/recommendations for international students: required—TOEFL (minimum score 79 paper-based). *Application deadline:* Applications are processed on a rolling basis. Application fee: $50. Electronic applications accepted. *Expenses:* Contact institution. *Financial support:* In 2019–20, 170 students received support. Career-related internships or fieldwork, Federal Work-Study, scholarships/grants, and unspecified assistantships available. Financial award application deadline: 4/1; financial award applicants required to submit FAFSA. *Unit head:* Dr. Honggang Yang, Dean, 954-262-3016, Fax: 954-262-3968, E-mail: yangh@nova.edu. *Application contact:* Marcia Arango, Student Recruitment Coordinator, 954-262-3006, Fax: 954-262-3968, E-mail: marango@nsu.nova.edu.
Website: http://cahss.nova.edu/

Oklahoma City University, Petree College of Arts and Sciences, Oklahoma City, OK 73106-1402. Offers applied behavioral studies (M Ed); applied sociology: nonprofit leadership (MA); creative writing (MFA); criminology (MS); early childhood education (M Ed); elementary education (M Ed); general studies (MLA); leadership/management (MLA); moving image arts (MFA); professional counseling (M Ed); teaching (MA); teaching English to speakers of other languages (MA). *Program availability:* Part-time, evening/weekend. *Degree requirements:* For master's, capstone/practicum. *Entrance requirements:* For master's, bachelor's degree from accredited institution with minimum GPA of 3.0, essay, recommendation letters. Additional exam requirements/recommendations for international students: required—TOEFL (minimum score 550 paper-based; 80 iBT). Electronic applications accepted. *Expenses:* Contact institution.

Old Dominion University, College of Arts and Letters, PhD Program in Criminology and Criminal Justice, Norfolk, VA 23529. Offers criminology and criminal justice (PhD). *Degree requirements:* For doctorate, comprehensive exam, thesis/dissertation. *Entrance requirements:* For doctorate, GRE General Test, MA; minimum graduate GPA of 3.25; theory, methods, and statistics graduate coursework; letters of reference; writing sample. Additional exam requirements/recommendations for international students: required—TOEFL. Electronic applications accepted.

Old Dominion University, College of Arts and Letters, Program in Applied Sociology, Norfolk, VA 23529. Offers criminal justice (MA); general sociology (MA); women's studies (MA). *Program availability:* Part-time, evening/weekend. *Degree requirements:* For master's, thesis. *Entrance requirements:* For master's, GRE General Test, minimum GPA of 3.0; 12 credits in criminal justice, sociology, or women's studies. Additional exam requirements/recommendations for international students: required—TOEFL. Electronic applications accepted. *Expenses:* Contact institution.

Penn State Harrisburg, Graduate School, School of Public Affairs, Middletown, PA 17057. Offers criminal justice (MA); health administration (MHA); health administration: long term care (Certificate); homeland security (MPS, Certificate); public administration (MPA, PhD); public administration: non-profit administration (Certificate); public budgeting and financial management (Certificate); public sector human resource management (Certificate). *Accreditation:* NASPAA.

Penn State University Park, Graduate School, College of the Liberal Arts, Department of Sociology and Criminology, University Park, PA 16802. Offers criminology (MA, PhD); sociology (MA, PhD).

Point Park University, School of Arts and Sciences, Department of Criminal Justice and Intelligence Studies, Pittsburgh, PA 15222-1984. Offers criminal justice administration (MS); intelligence and global security (MA). *Program availability:* Evening/weekend, 100% online. *Degree requirements:* For master's, comprehensive exam (for some programs), thesis or alternative. *Entrance requirements:* For master's, minimum GPA of 2.75, resume, 2 letters of recommendation. Additional exam requirements/recommendations for international students: required—TOEFL (minimum score 550 paper-based; 79 iBT). Electronic applications accepted.

Pontifical Catholic University of Puerto Rico, College of Graduate Studies in Behavioral Science and Community Affairs, Program in Criminology, Ponce, PR 00717-0777. Offers MA. *Program availability:* Part-time, evening/weekend. *Degree requirements:* For master's, thesis. *Entrance requirements:* For master's, EXADEP, 3 letters of recommendation, interview, minimum GPA of 2.75.

Pontificia Universidad Catolica Madre y Maestra, Graduate School, Faculty of Social and Administrative Sciences, Santiago, Dominican Republic. Offers business administration (MBA), including business development, finance, international business, management skills (M Mgmt, MBA), marketing, operations, strategic cost management, strategy, tourist destination planning and management; law (LL M), including civil law, corporate business law, criminal law, international relations, real estate law; management (M Mgmt), including higher financial management, insurance program administration, management skills (M Mgmt, MBA); psychology (MA), including clinical child and adolescent psychology, forensic psychology; strategic human resources (EMBA).

Portland State University, Graduate Studies, College of Urban and Public Affairs, Hatfield School of Government, Department of Criminology and Criminal Justice, Portland, OR 97207-0751. Offers MS. *Program availability:* Part-time. *Faculty:* 10 full-time (4 women), 14 part-time/adjunct (4 women). *Students:* 29 full-time (25 women), 3 part-time (2 women); includes 11 minority (1 American Indian or Alaska Native, non-Hispanic/Latino; 1 Asian, non-Hispanic/Latino; 5 Hispanic/Latino; 1 Native Hawaiian or other Pacific Islander, non-Hispanic/Latino; 3 Two or more races, non-Hispanic/Latino), 1 international. Average age 30. 30 applicants, 77% accepted, 15 enrolled. In 2019, 10 master's awarded. *Degree requirements:* For master's, thesis or alternative, specialization field, culminating experience. *Entrance requirements:* For master's, minimum GPA of 3.2 overall or graduate, statement of purpose, resume/curriculum vitae, 2 letters of recommendation. Additional exam requirements/recommendations for international students: required—TOEFL (minimum score 550 paper-based; 80 iBT). *Application deadline:* For fall admission, 2/1 priority date for domestic and international students. Application fee: $65. *Expenses: Tuition, area resident:* Full-time $13,020; part-time $6510 per year. Tuition, state resident: full-time $13,020; part-time $6510 per year. Tuition, nonresident: full-time $19,830; part-time $9915 per year. *International tuition:* $19,830 full-time. *Required fees:* $1226. One-time fee: $350. Tuition and fees vary according to course load, program and reciprocity agreements. *Financial support:* In 2019–20, 14 students received support, including 8 teaching assistantships with full and partial tuition reimbursements available (averaging $9,232 per year); research assistantships, career-related internships or fieldwork, Federal Work-Study, scholarships/grants, and unspecified assistantships also available. Support available to part-time students. Financial award application deadline: 3/1; financial award applicants required to submit FAFSA. *Unit head:* Dr. Brian Renauer, Chair, 503-725-8090, E-mail: renauer@pdx.edu. *Application contact:* Andrew Nolan, Department Manager, 503-725-9586, E-mail: anolan@pdx.edu.
Website: https://www.pdx.edu/criminology-criminal-justice/

Purdue University Global, School of Criminal Justice, Davenport, IA 52807. Offers corrections (MSCJ); global issues in criminal justice (MSCJ); law (MSCJ); leadership and executive management (MSCJ); policing (MSCJ). *Program availability:* Part-time, evening/weekend, online learning. *Entrance requirements:* Additional exam requirements/recommendations for international students: required—TOEFL (minimum score 550 paper-based; 80 iBT). Electronic applications accepted.

Radford University, College of Graduate Studies and Research, Criminal Justice, MS, Radford, VA 24142. Offers MA, MS, Certificate. *Program availability:* Part-time. *Degree requirements:* For master's, comprehensive exam, thesis optional. *Entrance requirements:* For master's, minimum GPA of 2.9, 2 letters of reference, original writing sample, resume, official transcripts. Additional exam requirements/recommendations for international students: required—TOEFL (minimum score 550 paper-based; 79 iBT), IELTS (minimum score 6.5). Electronic applications accepted.

Regent University, Graduate School, School of Law, Virginia Beach, VA 23464. Offers American legal studies (LL M); human rights (LL M); law (MA, JD), including advanced paralegal studies (MA), alternative dispute resolution (MA), business (MA), criminal justice (MA), general legal studies (MA), human resources management (MA), human rights and rule of law (MA), national security (MA), non-profit organizational law (MA), regulatory compliance (MA), wealth management and financial planning (MA); JD/MA; JD/MBA. *Accreditation:* ABA. *Program availability:* Part-time, 100% online, blended/hybrid learning. *Faculty:* 16 full-time (5 women), 66 part-time/adjunct (22 women). *Students:* 378 full-time (230 women), 349 part-time (246 women); includes 311 minority (207 Black or African American, non-Hispanic/Latino; 5 American Indian or Alaska Native, non-Hispanic/Latino; 17 Asian, non-Hispanic/Latino; 56 Hispanic/Latino; 2 Native Hawaiian or other Pacific Islander, non-Hispanic/Latino; 24 Two or more races, non-Hispanic/Latino), 46 international. Average age 35. 680 applicants, 62% accepted, 223 enrolled. In 2019, 176 master's, 72 doctorates awarded. *Entrance requirements:* For master's, college transcripts, resume, personal statement; for doctorate, LSAT, minimum undergraduate GPA of 3.0, official transcripts, 2 letters of recommendation, resume, personal statement. Additional exam requirements/recommendations for international students: required—TOEFL (minimum score 600 paper-based). *Application deadline:* For fall admission, 3/1 for domestic students. Applications are processed on a rolling basis. Application fee: $50. Electronic applications accepted. *Expenses:* Contact institution. *Financial support:* In 2019–20, 582 students received support. Career-related internships or fieldwork, scholarships/grants, health care benefits, and unspecified assistantships available. Support available to part-time students. Financial award applicants required to submit FAFSA. *Unit head:* Mark Martin, Dean, 757-352-4040, Fax: 757-352-4595, E-mail: mmartin@regent.edu. *Application contact:* Ernie Walton, Assistant Dean of Admissions, 757-352-4315, E-mail: lawschool@regent.edu.
Website: https://www.regent.edu/school-of-law/

Regent University, Graduate School, School of Psychology and Counseling, Virginia Beach, VA 23464-9800. Offers clinical mental health counseling (MA); clinical psychology (Psy D); counseling and psychological studies - clinical (PhD); counseling and psychological studies - research (PhD); counseling studies (CAGS); counselor education and supervision (PhD); general psychology (MS); human services (MA), including addictions counseling, Biblical counseling, Christian counseling, conflict and mediation ministry, criminal justice and ministry, grief counseling, human services counseling, human services for student affairs, life coaching, marriage and family ministry, trauma and crisis counseling; marriage, couple, and family counseling (MA); pastoral counseling (MA); school counseling (MA); M Div/MA; M Ed/MA; MBA/MA. *Accreditation:* ACA; APA (one or more programs are accredited). *Program availability:* Part-time, evening/weekend, 100% online, blended/hybrid learning. *Degree requirements:* For master's, thesis or alternative, internship, practicum, written competency exam; for doctorate, thesis/dissertation or alternative. *Entrance requirements:* For master's, GRE General Test (including writing exam) or MAT, minimum undergraduate GPA of 3.0, resume, transcripts, writing sample, personal goals statement; for doctorate, GRE General Test (including writing exam), minimum undergraduate GPA of 3.0, graduate 3.5; writing sample; 3 recommendations; resume; college transcripts; personal goals statement. Additional exam requirements/recommendations for international students: required—TOEFL (minimum score 577 paper-based). Electronic applications accepted. *Expenses:* Contact institution.

Regis University, College of Contemporary Liberal Studies, Denver, CO 80221-1099. Offers creative writing (MFA); criminology (M Sc); curriculum, instruction and assessment (M Ed); education - teacher leadership (M Ed); educational leadership (M Ed); elementary education (M Ed); literacy (Certificate); reading (M Ed); secondary education (M Ed); special education (M Ed); teacher academic leadership (Certificate); teacher leadership (MA); teacher/educational leadership (M Ed); teaching the linguistically diverse (M Ed). *Program availability:* Part-time, evening/weekend, 100% online, blended/hybrid learning. *Degree requirements:* For master's, thesis (for some programs). *Entrance requirements:* For master's, official transcript reflecting baccalaureate degree awarded from regionally-accredited college or university, work experience, resume, letters of recommendation. Additional exam requirements/recommendations for international students: required—TOEFL (minimum score 550 paper-based; 82 iBT). Electronic applications accepted. *Expenses:* Contact institution.

Robert Morris University Illinois, Morris Graduate School of Management, Chicago, IL 60605. Offers accounting (MBA); accounting/finance (MBA); business analytics (MIS); health care administration (MM); higher education administration (MM); human performance (MS); human resource management (MBA); information security (MIS); information systems management (MIS); law enforcement administration (MM); management (MBA); management/finance (MBA); management/human resource management (MBA); sports administration (MM). *Program availability:* Part-time, evening/weekend. *Entrance requirements:* For master's, official transcripts and letters of recommendation (for some programs); written personal statement. Additional exam requirements/recommendations for international students: required—TOEFL (minimum score 550 paper-based). Electronic applications accepted.

Rochester Institute of Technology, Graduate Enrollment Services, College of Liberal Arts, Criminal Justice Department, MS Program in Criminal Justice, Rochester, NY 14623-5603. Offers MS. *Program availability:* Part-time. *Degree requirements:* For master's, thesis. *Entrance requirements:* For master's, GRE, minimum GPA of 3.0 (recommended); two writing samples, one of which is a personal statement; have completed a statistics course; two letters of recommendation; personal interview. Additional exam requirements/recommendations for international students: required—TOEFL (minimum score 570 paper-based; 88 iBT), IELTS (minimum score 6.5), PTE (minimum score 58). Electronic applications accepted.

Roger Williams University, School of Justice Studies, Bristol, RI 02809. Offers criminal justice (MS); cybersecurity (MS); leadership (MS), including health care administration (MPA, MS); public management (MPA, MS); public administration (MPA), including health care administration (MPA, MS), public management (MPA, MS); MS/JD. *Program availability:* Part-time, evening/weekend, 100% online, blended/hybrid learning. *Faculty:* 1 (woman) full-time, 5 part-time/adjunct (0 women). *Students:* 24 full-time (15 women), 109 part-time (59 women); includes 31 minority (9 Black or African American, non-Hispanic/Latino; 1 Asian, non-Hispanic/Latino; 17 Hispanic/Latino; 4 Two or more races, non-Hispanic/Latino), 2 international. Average age 34. 94 applicants, 83% accepted, 46 enrolled. In 2019, 46 master's awarded. *Degree requirements:* For master's, thesis. *Entrance requirements:* For master's, No, Letter of intent, transcripts, two letters of recommendation, resume, background check (cybersecurity). Additional exam requirements/recommendations for international students: required—TOEFL (minimum score 85 paper-based), IELTS (minimum score 6.5). *Application deadline:* Applications are processed on a rolling basis. Application fee: $50. Electronic applications accepted. Application fee is waived when completed online. *Expenses: Tuition:* Full-time $15,768. *Required fees:* $900; $450. *Financial support:* In 2019–20, 8 students received support. Scholarships/grants and unspecified assistantships available. Financial award application deadline: 3/15; financial award applicants required to submit FAFSA. *Unit head:* Dr. Eric Bronson, Dean and Professor of Criminal Justice, 401-254-3336, E-mail: ebronson@rwu.edu. *Application contact:* Marcus Hanscom, Director of Graduate Admission, 401-254-3345, Fax: 401-254-3557, E-mail: gradadmit@rwu.edu. Website: http://www.rwu.edu/academics/departments/criminaljustice.htm#graduate

Rowan University, Graduate School, College of Humanities and Social Sciences, Department of Law and Justice Studies, Program in Criminal Justice, Glassboro, NJ 08028-1701. Offers MA. *Program availability:* Part-time, evening/weekend. *Degree requirements:* For master's, thesis. *Entrance requirements:* For master's, GRE General Test. Additional exam requirements/recommendations for international students: required—TOEFL. Electronic applications accepted. *Expenses: Tuition, area resident:* Part-time $715.50 per semester hour. Tuition, state resident: part-time $715.50 per semester hour. Tuition, nonresident: part-time $715.50 per semester hour. *Required fees:* $161.55 per semester hour.

Rutgers University - Camden, Graduate School of Arts and Sciences, Program in Criminal Justice, Camden, NJ 08102. Offers MA, MPA/MA. *Program availability:* Part-time, evening/weekend. *Degree requirements:* For master's, comprehensive exam, thesis optional, 30 credits. *Entrance requirements:* For master's, GRE, 3 letters of recommendation; statement of personal, professional, and academic goals. Additional exam requirements/recommendations for international students: required—TOEFL, IELTS. Electronic applications accepted.

Rutgers University - Newark, Graduate School, School of Criminal Justice, Doctoral Program in Criminal Justice, Newark, NJ 07102. Offers PhD. *Degree requirements:* For doctorate, thesis/dissertation. *Entrance requirements:* Additional exam requirements/recommendations for international students: required—TOEFL.

Rutgers University - Newark, Graduate School, School of Criminal Justice, Master's Program in Criminal Justice, Newark, NJ 07102. Offers MA. *Entrance requirements:* For master's, GRE, minimum undergraduate B average. Additional exam requirements/recommendations for international students: required—TOEFL.

Sacred Heart University, Graduate Programs, College of Arts and Sciences, Department of Criminal Justice, Fairfield, CT 06825. Offers MA. *Program availability:* Part-time, evening/weekend. *Degree requirements:* For master's, comprehensive exam, thesis optional. *Entrance requirements:* For master's, BA/BS with minimum GPA of 3.0. Additional exam requirements/recommendations for international students: required—TOEFL (minimum score 570 paper-based, 80 iBT), TWE, or IELTS (6.5). Electronic applications accepted. *Expenses:* Contact institution.

St. Ambrose University, College of Arts and Sciences, Program in Criminal Justice, Davenport, IA 52803-2898. Offers criminal justice (MCJ); juvenile justice education (MCJ). *Program availability:* Part-time, evening/weekend. *Degree requirements:* For master's, thesis (for some programs), practicum or project. *Entrance requirements:* For master's, 2 years of work experience, 2 letters of recommendation, personal interview. Additional exam requirements/recommendations for international students: required—TOEFL. Electronic applications accepted.

St. Cloud State University, School of Graduate Studies, College of Social Sciences, Department of Criminal Justice, Program in Criminal Justice, St. Cloud, MN 56301. Offers criminal justice administration (MS). *Program availability:* Part-time, evening/weekend, online learning. Electronic applications accepted.

St. Cloud State University, School of Graduate Studies, College of Social Sciences, Department of Criminal Justice, Program in Public Safety Executive Leadership, St. Cloud, MN 56301-4498. Offers MS. *Program availability:* Part-time, online learning. *Degree requirements:* For master's, thesis or alternative. *Entrance requirements:* For master's, minimum GPA of 2.75. Additional exam requirements/recommendations for international students: required—TOEFL (minimum score 550 paper-based; 79 iBT), IELTS (minimum score 6.5), Michigan English Language Assessment Battery. Electronic applications accepted.

St. John's University, College of Professional Studies, Department of Criminal Justice, Legal Studies, and Homeland Security, Queens, NY 11439. Offers homeland security and criminal justice leadership (MPS). *Entrance requirements:* For master's, letters of recommendation, transcripts, resume, personal statement, proficiency in a foreign language. Additional exam requirements/recommendations for international students: required—TOEFL (minimum score 90 iBT), IELTS (minimum score 6.5). Electronic applications accepted.

St. John's University, St. John's College of Liberal Arts and Sciences, Department of Sociology and Anthropology, Queens, NY 11439. Offers criminology and justice (MA); sociology (MA). *Program availability:* Part-time, evening/weekend. *Degree requirements:* For master's, comprehensive exam, thesis optional. *Entrance requirements:* For master's, letters of recommendation, transcripts, resume, personal statement. Additional exam requirements/recommendations for international students: required—TOEFL (minimum score 80 iBT), IELTS (minimum score 6.5). Electronic applications accepted.

Saint Joseph's University, College of Arts and Sciences, Department of Criminal Justice, Philadelphia, PA 19131-1395. Offers behavior analysis (MS, Post-Master's Certificate); behavior management (MS); criminal justice (MS); federal law enforcement (MS); intelligence and crime analysis (MS). *Program availability:* Part-time, evening/weekend, 100% online, blended/hybrid learning. *Degree requirements:* For master's, thesis optional. *Entrance requirements:* For master's, 2 letters of recommendation, personal statement, resume, official transcripts, minimum GPA of 3.0. Additional exam requirements/recommendations for international students: required—TOEFL (minimum score 550 paper-based; 80 iBT). Electronic applications accepted. *Expenses:* Contact institution.

Saint Leo University, Graduate Studies in Public Safety Administration, Saint Leo, FL 33574-6665. Offers criminal justice (MS, DCJ), including behavioral studies (MS), corrections (MS), criminal investigation (MS), criminal justice (MS), emergency and disaster management (MS), forensic science (MS), legal studies (MS); emergency and disaster management (MS), including emergency and disaster management, fire science. *Program availability:* Part-time, evening/weekend, 100% online, blended/hybrid learning. *Faculty:* 10 full-time (4 women), 26 part-time/adjunct (6 women). *Students:* 1 (woman) full-time, 761 part-time (490 women); includes 466 minority (252 Black or African American, non-Hispanic/Latino; 4 American Indian or Alaska Native, non-Hispanic/Latino; 5 Asian, non-Hispanic/Latino; 94 Hispanic/Latino; 111 Two or more races, non-Hispanic/Latino). Average age 37. 314 applicants, 82% accepted, 173 enrolled. In 2019, 236 master's, 2 doctorates awarded. *Degree requirements:* For master's, comprehensive project; for doctorate, thesis/dissertation. *Entrance requirements:* For master's, official transcripts, bachelor's degree from regionally-accredited university with minimum GPA of 3.0, statement of professional goals; for doctorate, Official transcript showing completion of Master's degree with a minimum graduate gpa of 3.25, statement of professional goals, two letter of reference (professional or personal). Additional exam requirements/recommendations for international students: required—TOEFL (minimum score 550 paper-based; 78 iBT). *Application deadline:* For fall admission, 7/1 priority date for domestic and international students; for spring admission, 11/1 priority date for domestic and international students. Applications are processed on a rolling basis. Electronic applications accepted. *Expenses:* MS in Criminal Justice $10,770 per FT yr., DCJ $14,101 per FT yr. *Financial support:* In 2019–20, 62 students received support. Scholarships/grants, health care benefits, and tuition remission for Saint Leo employees and their dependents available. Financial award application deadline: 3/1; financial award applicants required to submit FAFSA. *Unit head:* Dr. Robert Diemer, Director of Graduate Studies in Public Safety Administration, 352-588-8974, Fax: 352-588-8660, E-mail: graduatepublicsafety@saintleo.edu. *Application contact:* Saint Leo University Office of Graduate Admissions, 800-707-8846, Fax: 352-588-7873, E-mail: grad.admissions@saintleo.edu.
Website: https://www.saintleo.edu/criminal-justice-master-degree

Saint Louis University, Graduate Programs, College for Public Health and Social Justice, Program in Criminology and Criminal Justice, St. Louis, MO 63103. Offers administration of justice (MA); emergency management (MA); treatment and rehabilitation (MA). *Program availability:* Part-time. *Degree requirements:* For master's, comprehensive exam. *Entrance requirements:* For master's, GRE General Test, two letters of recommendation, resume, transcripts. Additional exam requirements/recommendations for international students: required—TOEFL (minimum score 525 paper-based).

Saint Mary's University, Faculty of Arts, Program in Criminology, Halifax, NS B3H 3C3, Canada. Offers MA. *Program availability:* Part-time. *Degree requirements:* For master's, thesis. *Entrance requirements:* For master's, honors degree, official transcripts, sample of academic written work, 2 letters of recommendation. Electronic applications accepted. *Expenses:* Contact institution.

St. Mary's University, School of Law, Master of Jurisprudence Program, San Antonio, TX 78228. Offers business and entrepreneurship law (MJ); commercial law (MJ); compliance, business law and risk (MJ); criminal justice (MJ); education law (MJ); environmental law (MJ); health law (MJ); healthcare compliance (MJ); international comparative law (MJ); military and national security law (MJ); natural resource law (MJ); tax law (MJ). *Program availability:* Part-time, evening/weekend, 100% online, blended/hybrid learning. *Degree requirements:* For master's, 30 credits, minimum GPA of 2.0. *Entrance requirements:* For master's, official transcripts, personal statement, resume, 2 letters of recommendation, proof of four-year undergraduate degree from accredited U.S. college/university or foreign institution approved by government or accrediting authority. Additional exam requirements/recommendations for international students: required—TOEFL (minimum score 550 paper-based; 80 iBT), IELTS (minimum score 6). Electronic applications accepted. *Expenses:* Contact institution.

Criminal Justice and Criminology

Saint Peter's University, Program in Criminal Justice Administration, Jersey City, NJ 07306-5997. Offers federal law enforcement administration (MA); police administration (MA). *Program availability:* Part-time, evening/weekend. *Entrance requirements:* Additional exam requirements/recommendations for international students: required—TOEFL. Electronic applications accepted.

St. Thomas University - Florida, School of Business, Department of Management, Miami Gardens, FL 33054-6459. Offers accounting (MBA); general management (MSM, Certificate); health management (MBA, MSM, Certificate); human resource management (MBA, MSM, Certificate); international business (MBA, MIB, MSM, Certificate); justice administration (MSM, Certificate); management accounting (MSM, Certificate); public management (MSM, Certificate); sports administration (MS). *Program availability:* Part-time, evening/weekend. *Degree requirements:* For master's, comprehensive exam. *Entrance requirements:* For master's, interview, minimum GPA of 3.0 or GMAT. Additional exam requirements/recommendations for international students: required—TOEFL (minimum score 550 paper-based; 79 iBT). Electronic applications accepted.

Salem State University, School of Graduate Studies, Program in Criminal Justice, Salem, MA 01970-5353. Offers MS. *Program availability:* Part-time, evening/weekend. *Entrance requirements:* For master's, GRE or MAT. Additional exam requirements/recommendations for international students: required—TOEFL (minimum score 550 paper-based; 80 iBT) or IELTS (minimum score 5.5).

Salve Regina University, Program in Administration of Justice and Homeland Security, Newport, RI 02840. Offers administration of justice and homeland security (MS); cybersecurity and intelligence (CGS); digital forensics (CGS); leadership in justice (CGS). *Program availability:* Part-time, evening/weekend, some in-person. *Entrance requirements:* Additional exam requirements/recommendations for international students: required—TOEFL (minimum score 600 paper-based; 100 iBT). *Application deadline:* For fall admission, 7/1 priority date for domestic students, 3/15 priority date for international students; for spring admission, 11/1 priority date for domestic students, 9/5 priority date for international students. Applications are processed on a rolling basis. Application fee: $0. Electronic applications accepted. *Financial support:* Application deadline: 3/1; applicants required to submit FAFSA. *Unit head:* Jeffrey Mace, Director, 401-341-2338, E-mail: jeffrey.mac@salve.edu. *Application contact:* Laurie Reilly, Graduate Admissions Manager, 401-341-2153, Fax: 401-341-2973, E-mail: laurie.reilly@salve.edu.
Website: http://www.salve.edu/graduate-studies/administration-of-justice-and-homeland-security

Sam Houston State University, College of Criminal Justice, Department of Criminal Justice and Criminology, Huntsville, TX 77341. Offers criminal justice (MS, PhD); criminal justice and criminology (MA); criminal justice leadership and management (MS); victim services management (MS). *Program availability:* Part-time, evening/weekend, online learning. *Degree requirements:* For master's, comprehensive exam (for some programs), thesis (for some programs); for doctorate, comprehensive exam, thesis/dissertation. *Entrance requirements:* For master's, GRE, personal essay, official transcripts, three recommendation letters, resume; for doctorate, GRE, personal essay, official transcripts, three recommendation letters, resume, master's degree. Additional exam requirements/recommendations for international students: required—TOEFL (minimum score 550 paper-based; 79 iBT), IELTS (minimum score 6.5). Electronic applications accepted.

San Diego State University, Graduate and Research Affairs, College of Professional Studies and Fine Arts, School of Public Affairs, Program in Criminal Justice Administration, San Diego, CA 92182. Offers MPA. *Program availability:* Part-time. *Entrance requirements:* For master's, GRE General Test, 2 letters of reference. Additional exam requirements/recommendations for international students: required—TOEFL. Electronic applications accepted.

San Diego State University, Graduate and Research Affairs, College of Professional Studies and Fine Arts, School of Public Affairs, Program in Criminal Justice and Criminology, San Diego, CA 92182. Offers MS. *Entrance requirements:* For master's, GRE General Test, 2 letters of reference. Additional exam requirements/recommendations for international students: required—TOEFL. Electronic applications accepted.

San Francisco State University, Division of Graduate Studies, College of Health and Social Sciences, Public Administration Program, San Francisco, CA 94132-1722. Offers criminal justice administration (MPA); environmental administration and policy (MPA); gerontology (MPA); nonprofit administration (MPA); public management (MPA); public policy (MPA); urban administration (MPA). *Accreditation:* NASPAA. *Expenses: Tuition, area resident:* Full-time $7176; part-time $4164 per year. Tuition, state resident: full-time $7176; part-time $4164 per year. Tuition, nonresident: full-time $16,680; part-time $396 per unit. *International tuition:* $16,680 full-time. *Required fees:* $1524; $1524 per unit. $762 per semester. Tuition and fees vary according to degree level and program. *Unit head:* Dr. Janey Wang, Graduate Coordinator, 415-817-4456, Fax: 415-338-0586, E-mail: jqwang@sfsu.edu. *Application contact:* Dr. Janey Wang, Graduate Coordinator, 415-817-4456, Fax: 415-338-0586, E-mail: jqwang@sfsu.edu.
Website: http://mpa.sfsu.edu/

San Jose State University, Program in Justice Studies, San Jose, CA 95192-0001. Offers MS. *Program availability:* Part-time. *Degree requirements:* For master's, thesis or alternative. *Entrance requirements:* For master's, GRE or LSAT, minimum GPA of 3.0. Additional exam requirements/recommendations for international students: required—TOEFL. Electronic applications accepted. *Expenses: Tuition, area resident:* Full-time $7176; part-time $4164 per credit hour. Tuition, state resident: full-time $7176; part-time $4164 per credit hour. Tuition, nonresident: full-time $7176; part-time $4165 per credit hour. *International tuition:* $7176 full-time. *Required fees:* $2110; $2110.

Seattle University, College of Arts and Sciences, Department of Criminal Justice, Seattle, WA 98122-1090. Offers crime analysis (Certificate); criminal justice (MACJ). *Program availability:* Part-time, evening/weekend. *Students:* 18 full-time (14 women), 37 part-time (29 women); includes 24 minority (3 Black or African American, non-Hispanic/Latino; 1 American Indian or Alaska Native, non-Hispanic/Latino; 5 Asian, non-Hispanic/Latino; 7 Hispanic/Latino; 8 Two or more races, non-Hispanic/Latino). Average age 26. 53 applicants, 83% accepted, 28 enrolled. In 2019, 27 master's, 2 Certificates awarded. *Entrance requirements:* For master's, minimum GPA of 3.0; undergraduate degree in criminal justice or related social, behavioral, or physical science, or related coursework and/or volunteer or supervised experience; letters of recommendation; writing sample. Additional exam requirements/recommendations for international students: required—TOEFL, IELTS. *Application deadline:* For fall admission, 3/15 for domestic and international students. Application fee: $55. Electronic applications accepted. *Financial support:* In 2019–20, 27 students received support. Applicants required to submit FAFSA. *Unit head:* Dr. Elaine Gunnison, Graduate Program Director, 206-296-2430, E-mail: gunnisone@seattleu.edu. *Application contact:* Janet Shandley, Associate Dean of Graduate Admissions, 206-296-5900, Fax: 206-298-5656, E-mail: grad_admissions@seattleu.edu.
Website: https://www.seattleu.edu/artsci/criminal-graduate/

Shippensburg University of Pennsylvania, School of Graduate Studies, College of Education and Human Services, Department of Criminal Justice, Shippensburg, PA 17257-2299. Offers criminal justice (MS), including administration of justice, juvenile justice. *Program availability:* Part-time, evening/weekend, 100% online. *Faculty:* 6 full-time (4 women), 4 part-time/adjunct (all women). *Students:* 4 full-time (all women), 20 part-time (9 women); includes 6 minority (3 Black or African American, non-Hispanic/Latino; 3 Hispanic/Latino). Average age 32. 53 applicants, 58% accepted, 14 enrolled. *Degree requirements:* For master's, thesis optional, internship, practicum, or thesis. *Entrance requirements:* For master's, GRE or MAT (if GPA less than 2.75), 500-word statement of interest; optional resume. Additional exam requirements/recommendations for international students: required—TOEFL (minimum score 550 paper-based; 68 iBT), IELTS (minimum score 6), TOEFL (minimum score 550 paper-based, 68 iBT) or IELTS (minimum score 6). *Application deadline:* For fall admission, 4/30 for international students. Applications are processed on a rolling basis. Application fee: $45. Electronic applications accepted. *Expenses:* Tuition, state resident: part-time $516 per credit. Tuition, nonresident: part-time $774 per credit. *Required fees:* $149 per credit. *Financial support:* In 2019–20, 2 students received support. Career-related internships or fieldwork, scholarships/grants, unspecified assistantships, and resident hall director and student payroll positions available. Support available to part-time students. Financial award application deadline: 3/1; financial award applicants required to submit FAFSA. *Unit head:* Dr. Arelys N. Madero, Assistant Professor and Program Coordinator, 717-477-1558, Fax: 717-477-4087, E-mail: anmadero@ship.edu. *Application contact:* Maya T. Mapp, Director of Admissions, 717-477-1231, Fax: 717-477-4016, E-mail: mtmapp@ship.edu.
Website: http://www.ship.edu/criminal_justice/

Simon Fraser University, Office of Graduate Studies and Postdoctoral Fellows, Faculty of Arts and Social Sciences, School of Criminology, Burnaby, BC V5A 1S6, Canada. Offers applied legal studies (MA); criminology (MA, PhD). *Degree requirements:* For master's, thesis or alternative, practicum; for doctorate, thesis/dissertation. *Entrance requirements:* For master's, minimum GPA of 3.0 (on scale of 4.33) or 3.33 based on last 60 credits of undergraduate courses; for doctorate, minimum GPA of 3.5 (on scale of 4.33). Additional exam requirements/recommendations for international students: recommended—TOEFL (minimum score 580 paper-based; 93 iBT), IELTS (minimum score 7), TWE (minimum score 5). Electronic applications accepted.

Simpson College, Department of Social Sciences, Indianola, IA 50125-1297. Offers criminal justice (MACJ). *Program availability:* Evening/weekend.

Slippery Rock University of Pennsylvania, Graduate Studies (Recruitment), College of Liberal Arts, Department of Criminology and Security Studies, Slippery Rock, PA 16057-1383. Offers criminal justice (MA). *Program availability:* Part-time, evening/weekend, online only, 100% online. *Faculty:* 5 full-time (3 women). *Students:* 4 full-time (all women), 15 part-time (8 women); includes 2 minority (both Black or African American, non-Hispanic/Latino). Average age 29. 17 applicants, 53% accepted, 7 enrolled. In 2019, 13 master's awarded. *Degree requirements:* For master's, comprehensive exam (for some programs), thesis (for some programs). *Entrance requirements:* For master's, minimum GPA of 2.75, three letters of recommendation, personal statement. Additional exam requirements/recommendations for international students: required—TOEFL (minimum score 550 paper-based; 80 iBT). *Application deadline:* For fall admission, 3/1 priority date for domestic students, 5/1 priority date for international students; for spring admission, 10/1 priority date for domestic students, 9/1 priority date for international students. Applications are processed on a rolling basis. Application fee: $25 ($30 for international students). Electronic applications accepted. *Expenses:* $516 per credit in-state tuition, $173.61 per credit in-state fees; $774 per credit out-of-state tuition, $224.31 per credit out-of-state fees; $516 per credit in-state tuition, $105.40 per credit in-state fees (for distance education); $526 per credit out-of-state tuition, $118.90 per credit out-of-state fees (for distance education). *Financial support:* In 2019–20, 2 students received support. Career-related internships or fieldwork, Federal Work-Study, institutionally sponsored loans, scholarships/grants, tuition waivers (partial), and unspecified assistantships available. Support available to part-time students. Financial award application deadline: 5/1; financial award applicants required to submit FAFSA. *Unit head:* Dr. David Champion, Graduate Coordinator, 724-738-4462, Fax: 724-738-4822, E-mail: david.champion@sru.edu. *Application contact:* Brandi Weber-Mortimer, Director of Graduate Admissions, 724-738-2051, Fax: 724-738-2146, E-mail: graduate.admissions@sru.edu.
Website: http://www.sru.edu/academics/graduate-programs/criminal-justice-master-of-arts

Southeast Missouri State University, School of Graduate Studies, Department of Criminal Justice and Sociology, Cape Girardeau, MO 63701. Offers criminal justice (MS). *Program availability:* Part-time, 100% online, blended/hybrid learning. *Faculty:* 4 full-time (3 women). *Students:* 9 full-time (8 women), 12 part-time (5 women); includes 3 minority (all Black or African American, non-Hispanic/Latino). Average age 33. 12 applicants, 83% accepted, 9 enrolled. In 2019, 8 master's awarded. *Degree requirements:* For master's, thesis (for some programs), thesis, internship or leadership portfolio. *Entrance requirements:* Additional exam requirements/recommendations for international students: required—TOEFL (minimum score 550 paper-based; 79 iBT), IELTS (minimum score 6), PTE (minimum score 53). *Application deadline:* For fall admission, 8/1 for domestic students, 6/1 priority date for international students; for spring admission, 11/21 for domestic students, 10/1 priority date for international students; for summer admission, 5/15 for domestic students. Applications are processed on a rolling basis. Application fee: $30 ($40 for international students). Electronic applications accepted. *Expenses:* Tuition, state resident: full-time $6989; part-time $291.20 per credit hour. Tuition, nonresident: full-time $13,061; part-time $544.20 per credit hour. *International tuition:* $13,061 full-time. *Required fees:* $955; $39.80 per credit hour. Tuition and fees vary according to degree level. *Financial support:* In 2019–20, 2 students received support, including 2 teaching assistantships with full tuition reimbursements available; career-related internships or fieldwork, Federal Work-Study, scholarships/grants, traineeships, tuition waivers (full), and unspecified assistantships also available. Financial award application deadline: 2/1; financial award applicants required to submit FAFSA. *Unit head:* Dr. Christopher Bradley, Associate Professor & Department Chair, 573-339-3002, E-mail: cbradley@semo.edu. *Application contact:* Dr. Christopher Bradley, Associate Professor & Department Chair, 573-339-3002, E-mail: cbradley@semo.edu.
Website: https://semo.edu/cjsws/index.html

Southern Illinois University Carbondale, Graduate School, College of Liberal Arts, Department of Criminology and Criminal Justice, Carbondale, IL 62901-4701. Offers MA, PhD. *Degree requirements:* For master's, thesis optional; for doctorate, thesis/dissertation. *Entrance requirements:* For master's, GRE General Test, minimum GPA of 2.7; for doctorate, GRE General Test, minimum GPA of 3.25. Additional exam requirements/recommendations for international students: required—TOEFL.

Southern New Hampshire University, School of Arts and Sciences, Manchester, NH 03106-1045. Offers clinical mental health counseling (MS); creative writing (MA); criminal justice (MS); cyber security (MS); English (MA); fiction and nonfiction (MFA); history (MA); political science (MS); psychology (MS). *Program availability:* Part-time, evening/weekend. *Degree requirements:* For master's, one foreign language, thesis.

Entrance requirements: For master's, minimum GPA of 3.0 (for MFA). Additional exam requirements/recommendations for international students: required—TOEFL (minimum score 550 paper-based; 79 iBT), IELTS (minimum score 6.5), TWE (minimum score 5). Electronic applications accepted. *Expenses:* Contact institution.

Southern University and Agricultural and Mechanical College, Graduate School, Nelson Mandela College of Government and Social Sciences, Department of Criminal Justice, Baton Rouge, LA 70813. Offers MS. *Entrance requirements:* Additional exam requirements/recommendations for international students: required—TOEFL (minimum score 525 paper-based).

Southern University at New Orleans, School of Graduate Studies, New Orleans, LA 70126-1009. Offers criminal justice (MA); management information systems (MS); museum studies (MA); social work (MSW). *Accreditation:* CSWE. *Program availability:* Part-time, evening/weekend. *Degree requirements:* For master's, thesis. *Entrance requirements:* For master's, GRE/GMAT. Additional exam requirements/recommendations for international students: required—TOEFL.

South University - Columbia, Program in Criminal Justice, Columbia, SC 29203. Offers MS.

South University - Montgomery, Program in Criminal Justice, Montgomery, AL 36116-1120. Offers MS.

South University - Savannah, Graduate Programs, College of Arts and Sciences, Program in Criminal Justice, Savannah, GA 31406. Offers MS.

South University - Savannah, Graduate Programs, College of Business, Savannah, GA 31406. Offers corrections (MBA); entrepreneurship and small business (MBA); healthcare administration (MBA); hospitality management (MBA); leadership (MS); public administration (MPA); sustainability (MBA).

South University - Tampa, Program in Criminal Justice, Tampa, FL 33614. Offers MS.

South University - West Palm Beach, Program in Criminal Justice, Royal Palm Beach, FL 33411. Offers MS.

Southwestern College, Professional Studies Programs, Wichita, KS 67210. Offers leadership (MS); management (MS); professional business administration (MBA); security administration (MS); specialized ministries (MA). *Program availability:* Part-time, online only, 100% online. *Faculty:* 17 part-time/adjunct (3 women). *Students:* 17 full-time (7 women), 33 part-time (10 women); includes 8 minority (5 Black or African American, non-Hispanic/Latino; 1 Asian, non-Hispanic/Latino; 2 Hispanic/Latino). Average age 36. 30 applicants, 93% accepted, 21 enrolled. In 2019, 37 master's awarded. *Degree requirements:* For master's, practicum/capstone project. *Entrance requirements:* For master's, baccalaureate degree; minimum GPA of 3.0. Additional exam requirements/recommendations for international students: required—TOEFL (minimum score 60 paper-based; 70 iBT), IELTS (minimum score 5.5). *Application deadline:* Applications are processed on a rolling basis. Application fee: $40. Electronic applications accepted. *Expenses:* Professional MBA is $730 per credit hour; MS in Leadership, MS in Security Administration and MS in Management are $660 per credit hour; graduate certificates are $660 per credit hour. *Financial support:* In 2019–20, 7 students received support. Unspecified assistantships and employee tuition waivers available. Financial award applicants required to submit FAFSA. *Unit head:* Jen Caughron, Director of Enrollment Services and Marketing, 888-684-5335 Ext. 3312, Fax: 316-688-5218, E-mail: jennifer.caughron@sckans.edu. *Application contact:* Jen Caughron, Director of Enrollment Services and Marketing, 888-684-5335 Ext. 3312, Fax: 316-688-5218, E-mail: jennifer.caughron@sckans.edu.
Website: https://ps.sckans.edu/

Southwest University, Program in Criminal Justice, Kenner, LA 70062. Offers MS.

Stockton University, Office of Graduate Studies, Program in Criminal Justice, Galloway, NJ 08205-9441. Offers MA. *Program availability:* Part-time, evening/weekend. *Faculty:* 8 full-time (5 women), 1 (woman) part-time/adjunct. *Students:* 3 full-time (1 woman), 28 part-time (20 women); includes 6 minority (1 Black or African American, non-Hispanic/Latino; 1 Asian, non-Hispanic/Latino; 3 Hispanic/Latino; 1 Two or more races, non-Hispanic/Latino). Average age 24. 28 applicants, 71% accepted, 17 enrolled. In 2019, 14 master's awarded. *Degree requirements:* For master's, comprehensive exam (for some programs), thesis, portfolio project. *Entrance requirements:* For master's, GRE General Test, minimum GPA of 3.0. Additional exam requirements/recommendations for international students: required—TOEFL. *Application deadline:* For fall admission, 7/1 for domestic and international students; for spring admission, 12/1 for domestic students, 11/1 for international students. Applications are processed on a rolling basis. Application fee: $50. Electronic applications accepted. *Expenses: Tuition, area resident:* Full-time $750.92; part-time $78.58 per credit hour. Tuition, state resident: full-time $750.92; part-time $78.58 per credit hour. Tuition, nonresident: full-time $846; part-time $78.58 per credit hour. *International tuition:* $1195.96 full-time. *Required fees:* $1464; $78.58 per credit hour. One-time fee: $50 full-time. *Financial support:* Fellowships, research assistantships with partial tuition reimbursements, career-related internships or fieldwork, Federal Work-Study, scholarships/grants, and unspecified assistantships available. Support available to part-time students. Financial award application deadline: 3/1; financial award applicants required to submit FAFSA. *Unit head:* Dr. Christine Tartaro, Director, 609-626-3640, E-mail: christine.tartaro@stockton.edu. *Application contact:* Tara Williams, Assistant Director of Graduate Enrollment Management, 609-626-3640, Fax: 609-626-6050, E-mail: gradschool@stockton.edu.

Suffolk University, College of Arts and Sciences, Department of Sociology, Boston, MA 02108-2770. Offers MSCJS, MSCJS/JD, MSCJS/MPA, MSCJS/MSMHC. *Program availability:* Part-time. *Faculty:* 7 full-time (5 women), 1 (woman) part-time/adjunct. *Students:* 22 full-time (21 women), 14 part-time (all women); includes 8 minority (3 Black or African American, non-Hispanic/Latino; 5 Hispanic/Latino), 2 international. Average age 27. 54 applicants, 59% accepted, 17 enrolled. In 2019, 10 master's awarded. *Entrance requirements:* For master's, 2 letters of recommendation, resume. Additional exam requirements/recommendations for international students: required—TOEFL (minimum score 550 paper-based; 80 iBT). *Application deadline:* For fall admission, 3/15 priority date for domestic students, 3/15 for international students; for spring admission, 10/15 priority date for domestic students, 10/15 for international students. Applications are processed on a rolling basis. Application fee: $50. Electronic applications accepted. *Expenses:* Contact institution. *Financial support:* In 2019–20, 24 students received support, including 7 fellowships (averaging $3,343 per year); career-related internships or fieldwork, Federal Work-Study, institutionally sponsored loans, scholarships/grants, and unspecified assistantships also available. Support available to part-time students. Financial award application deadline: 4/1; financial award applicants required to submit FAFSA. *Unit head:* Dr. Erika Gebo, Professor/Chair, 617-557-1594, E-mail: egebo@suffolk.edu. *Application contact:* Mara Marzocchi, Associate Director of Graduate Admissions, 617-573-8302, Fax: 617-305-1733, E-mail: grad.admission@suffolk.edu.
Website: http://www.suffolk.edu/college/graduate/69297.php

Sul Ross State University, College of Professional Studies, Department of Criminal Justice, Alpine, TX 79832. Offers criminal justice (MS); homeland security (MS); MS/MA. *Entrance requirements:* For master's, GRE General Test, minimum GPA of 2.5 in last 60 hours of undergraduate work.

Tarleton State University, College of Graduate Studies, College of Liberal and Fine Arts, School of Criminology, Criminal Justice and Strategic Studies, Stephenville, TX 76402. Offers criminal justice (MCJ). *Program availability:* Part-time, evening/weekend, 100% online, blended/hybrid learning. *Faculty:* 2 full-time (1 woman), 8 part-time/adjunct (2 women). *Students:* 10 full-time (4 women), 88 part-time (44 women); includes 44 minority (22 Black or African American, non-Hispanic/Latino; 2 Asian, non-Hispanic/Latino; 15 Hispanic/Latino; 5 Two or more races, non-Hispanic/Latino), 2 international. Average age 36. 41 applicants, 83% accepted, 21 enrolled. In 2019, 7 master's awarded. *Degree requirements:* For master's, comprehensive exam (for some programs), thesis optional. *Entrance requirements:* For master's, GRE General Test, minimum GPA of 2.5. Additional exam requirements/recommendations for international students: required—TOEFL (minimum score 520 paper-based; 69 iBT); recommended—IELTS (minimum score 6), TSE (minimum score 50). *Application deadline:* For fall admission, 8/15 priority date for domestic students; for spring admission, 1/7 for domestic students. Applications are processed on a rolling basis. Application fee: $50 ($130 for international students). Electronic applications accepted. *Expenses:* Tuition, state resident: part-time $221.73 per credit hour. Tuition, nonresident: part-time $636.73 per credit hour. *Required fees:* $198 per credit hour. $100 per semester. Tuition and fees vary according to degree level. *Financial support:* Research assistantships, career-related internships or fieldwork, and Federal Work-Study available. Support available to part-time students. Financial award application deadline: 5/1; financial award applicants required to submit FAFSA. *Unit head:* Dr. Alex del Carmen, Associate Dean, 817-717-3669, E-mail: delcarmen@tarleton.edu. *Application contact:* Wendy Weiss, Graduate Admissions Coordinator, 254-968-9104, Fax: 254-968-9670, E-mail: weiss@tarleton.edu.
Website: https://www.tarleton.edu/glsp/index.html

Temple University, College of Liberal Arts, Department of Criminal Justice, Philadelphia, PA 19122-6096. Offers MA, PhD. *Program availability:* Part-time. *Faculty:* 26 full-time (16 women), 14 part-time/adjunct (7 women). *Students:* 38 full-time (29 women), 3 part-time (2 women); includes 11 minority (5 Black or African American, non-Hispanic/Latino; 2 Asian, non-Hispanic/Latino; 3 Hispanic/Latino; 1 Two or more races, non-Hispanic/Latino), 1 international. 63 applicants, 40% accepted, 12 enrolled. In 2019, 6 master's, 2 doctorates awarded. *Degree requirements:* For master's, thesis optional; for doctorate, comprehensive exam, thesis/dissertation. *Entrance requirements:* For master's, GRE, statement of goals, 3 letters of recommendation, writing sample; for doctorate, GRE, 3 letters of recommendation, statement of goals, writing sample. Additional exam requirements/recommendations for international students: required—TOEFL (minimum score 79 iBT), IELTS, PTE, one of three is required. Application fee: $60. Electronic applications accepted. *Financial support:* Fellowships, research assistantships, teaching assistantships, career-related internships or fieldwork, Federal Work-Study, health care benefits, and unspecified assistantships available. Financial award applicants required to submit FAFSA. *Unit head:* Cathy Rosen, Department Chair, 215-204-1089, E-mail: crosen@temple.edu. *Application contact:* Jenisa Ly, Graduate Coordinator, 215-204-9028, E-mail: jenise.ly@temple.edu.
Website: http://www.cla.temple.edu/cj/

Tennessee State University, The School of Graduate Studies and Research, College of Liberal Arts, Department of Criminal Justice, Nashville, TN 37209-1561. Offers MCJ. *Degree requirements:* For master's, thesis. *Entrance requirements:* For master's, GRE General Test or MAT. Electronic applications accepted.

Texas A&M International University, Office of Graduate Studies and Research, College of Arts and Sciences, Department of Social Sciences, Laredo, TX 78041. Offers criminal justice (MS); history and political thought (MA); public administration (MPA); sociology (MA). *Degree requirements:* For master's, comprehensive exam (for some programs), thesis (for some programs). *Entrance requirements:* For master's, GRE General Test. Additional exam requirements/recommendations for international students: required—TOEFL (minimum score 550 paper-based; 79 iBT).

Texas A&M University–Central Texas, Graduate Studies and Research, Killeen, TX 76549. Offers accounting (MS); business administration (MBA); clinical mental health counseling (MS); criminal justice (MCJ); curriculum and instruction (M Ed); educational administration (M Ed); educational psychology - experimental psychology (MS); history (MA); human resource management (MS); information systems (MS); liberal studies (MS); management and leadership (MS); marriage and family therapy (MS); mathematics (MS); political science (MA); school counseling (M Ed); school psychology (Ed S).

Texas A&M University–Commerce, College of Humanities, Social Sciences and Arts, Commerce, TX 75429. Offers applied criminology (MS); applied linguistics (MA, MS); art (MA, MFA); christianity in history (Graduate Certificate); computational linguistics (Graduate Certificate); creative writing (Graduate Certificate); criminal justice management (Graduate Certificate); criminal justice studies (Graduate Certificate); English (MA, MS, PhD); film studies (Graduate Certificate); history (MA, MS); Holocaust studies (Graduate Certificate); homeland security (Graduate Certificate); music (MM); music performance (MM); political science (MA, MS); public history (Graduate Certificate); sociology (MS); Spanish (MA); studies in children's and adolescent literature and culture (Graduate Certificate); teaching English to speakers of other languages (Graduate Certificate); theater (MA, MS); world history (Graduate Certificate). *Program availability:* Part-time. *Faculty:* 49 full-time (28 women), 8 part-time/adjunct (2 women). *Students:* 34 full-time (21 women), 427 part-time (302 women); includes 175 minority (66 Black or African American, non-Hispanic/Latino; 1 American Indian or Alaska Native, non-Hispanic/Latino; 13 Asian, non-Hispanic/Latino; 79 Hispanic/Latino; 16 Two or more races, non-Hispanic/Latino), 15 international. Average age 38. 193 applicants, 49% accepted, 78 enrolled. In 2019, 122 master's, 6 doctorates awarded. *Degree requirements:* For master's, one foreign language, comprehensive exam, thesis (for some programs); for doctorate, one foreign language, comprehensive exam, thesis/dissertation, departmental qualifying exam. *Entrance requirements:* For master's, GRE General Test, official transcripts, letters of recommendation, resume, statement of goals; for doctorate, GRE General Test, official transcripts, letters of recommendation, statement of goals, writing samples, writing sessions, resumes. Additional exam requirements/recommendations for international students: required—TOEFL (minimum score 550 paper-based; 79 iBT), IELTS (minimum score 6), PTE (minimum score 53). *Application deadline:* For fall admission, 6/1 priority date for international students; for spring admission, 10/15 priority date for international students; for summer admission, 3/15 priority date for international students. Applications are processed on a rolling basis. Application fee: $50 ($75 for international students). Electronic applications accepted. *Expenses: Tuition, area resident:* Full-time $3630; part-time $202 per credit hour. Tuition, state resident: full-time $3630; part-time $202 per credit hour. Tuition, nonresident: full-time $11,232; part-time $624 per credit hour. *International tuition:* $11,232 full-time. *Required fees:* $2948. *Financial support:* In 2019–20, 30 students received support, including 18 research assistantships with partial tuition reimbursements available (averaging $3,231 per year), 136 teaching assistantships with partial tuition reimbursements available (averaging $4,053 per year); Federal Work-Study, institutionally sponsored loans, scholarships/grants, health care benefits, and

unspecified assistantships also available. Financial award application deadline: 5/1; financial award applicants required to submit FAFSA. *Unit head:* Dr. William F. Kuracina, Interim Dean, 903-886-5166, Fax: 903-886-5774, E-mail: william.kuracina@tamuc.edu. *Application contact:* Rebecca Stevens, Graduate Student Services Coordinator, 903-468-6049, E-mail: rebecca.stevens@tamuc.edu.
Website: http://www.tamuc.edu/academics/colleges/humanitiesSocialSciencesArts/

Texas A&M University–Kingsville, College of Graduate Studies, College of Arts and Sciences, Department of Psychology and Sociology, Program in Criminology, Kingsville, TX 78363. Offers MS. *Entrance requirements:* Additional exam requirements/recommendations for international students: required—TOEFL (minimum score 550 paper-based; 79 iBT); recommended—IELTS. Electronic applications accepted.

Texas Christian University, AddRan College of Liberal Arts, Department of Criminal Justice, Fort Worth, TX 76129-0002. Offers criminal justice and criminology (MS). *Program availability:* Online only, 100% online. *Faculty:* 7 full-time (4 women), 2 part-time/adjunct (0 women). *Students:* 34 full-time (13 women); includes 15 minority (5 Black or African American, non-Hispanic/Latino; 1 Asian, non-Hispanic/Latino; 9 Hispanic/Latino). Average age 36. 26 applicants, 96% accepted, 19 enrolled. In 2019, 21 master's awarded. *Degree requirements:* For master's, thesis optional. *Application deadline:* For fall admission, 5/1 for domestic and international students. Application fee: $60. Electronic applications accepted. *Expenses:* Contact institution. *Financial support:* In 2019–20, 27 students received support. Scholarships/grants available. Financial award application deadline: 5/1; financial award applicants required to submit FAFSA. *Unit head:* Johnny Nhan, Director/Associate Professor, 626-391-3871, E-mail: j.nhan@tcu.edu. *Application contact:* Pam Carlisle, Program Specialist, 817-257-5846, Fax: 817-257-7737, E-mail: p.carlisle@tcu.edu.
Website: http://cj.tcu.edu

Texas Southern University, Barbara Jordan-Mickey Leland School of Public Affairs, Program in Administration of Justice, Houston, TX 77004-4584. Offers MS, PhD. Electronic applications accepted.

Texas State University, The Graduate College, College of Applied Arts, Program in Criminal Justice, San Marcos, TX 78666. Offers MSCJ, PhD. *Program availability:* Part-time, evening/weekend. *Degree requirements:* For master's, comprehensive exam, thesis (for some programs); for doctorate, comprehensive exam, thesis/dissertation. *Entrance requirements:* For master's, GRE, baccalaureate degree in criminal justice or closely-related field from regionally-accredited university with minimum GPA of 3.0 in last 60 hours of course work; for doctorate, GRE (minimum preferred score of 300 with no less than 150 on the verbal section and 150 on the quantitative section), baccalaureate and master's degrees from regionally-accredited university in criminal justice or related field with minimum GPA of 3.5 in graduate courses; 3 letters of recommendation indicating skills and capacity to be successful in a PhD program; statement of personal history and life goals. Additional exam requirements/recommendations for international students: required—TOEFL (minimum score 550 paper-based; 78 iBT), IELTS (minimum score 6.5). Electronic applications accepted.

Texas State University, The Graduate College, College of Liberal Arts, Program in Public Administration, San Marcos, TX 78666. Offers international relations (MPA); legal and judicial administration (MPA). *Accreditation:* NASPAA. *Program availability:* Part-time, evening/weekend. *Degree requirements:* For master's, comprehensive exam, applied research project. *Entrance requirements:* For master's, baccalaureate degree from regionally-accredited university with minimum GPA of 3.0 on last 60 undergraduate semester hours, statement of purpose, 2 letters of recommendation. Additional exam requirements/recommendations for international students: required—TOEFL (minimum score 550 paper-based; 78 iBT), IELTS (minimum score 6.5). Electronic applications accepted.

Tiffin University, Program in Criminal Justice, Tiffin, OH 44883-2161. Offers criminal justice (MS), including crime analysis, criminal behavior, forensic psychology, homeland security administration, justice administration. *Program availability:* Part-time, evening/weekend, 100% online, blended/hybrid learning. *Degree requirements:* For master's, thesis optional. *Entrance requirements:* For master's, minimum undergraduate GPA of 2.5, work experience. Additional exam requirements/recommendations for international students: required—TOEFL (minimum score 550 paper-based; 79 iBT). Electronic applications accepted. *Expenses:* Contact institution.

Trident University International, College of Business Administration, Program in Business Administration, Cypress, CA 90630. Offers business administration (PhD); conflict and negotiation management (MBA); criminal justice administration (MBA); entrepreneurship (MBA); finance (MBA); general management (MBA); government accounting (MBA); human resource management (MBA); information security and digital assurance management (MBA); information technology management (MBA); international business (MBA); logistics management (MBA); marketing (MBA); project management (MBA); public management (MBA); quality management (MBA); strategic leadership (MBA). *Program availability:* Part-time, evening/weekend, online learning. *Degree requirements:* For doctorate, comprehensive exam, thesis/dissertation, defense of dissertation. *Entrance requirements:* For master's, minimum GPA of 2.5 (students with GPA 3.0 or greater may transfer up to 30% of graduate level credits); for doctorate, minimum GPA of 3.4, curriculum vitae, course work in research methods or statistics. Additional exam requirements/recommendations for international students: required—TOEFL. Electronic applications accepted.

Trine University, Program in Criminal Justice, Angola, IN 46703-1764. Offers emergency management (MS). *Program availability:* Part-time, evening/weekend, online only, 100% online, blended/hybrid learning. *Entrance requirements:* Additional exam requirements/recommendations for international students: required—TOEFL. Electronic applications accepted. *Expenses:* Contact institution.

Troy University, Graduate School, College of Arts and Sciences, Program in Criminal Justice, Troy, AL 36082. Offers MS. *Program availability:* Part-time, evening/weekend, online learning. *Faculty:* 4 full-time (0 women), 3 part-time/adjunct (2 women). *Students:* 36 full-time (21 women), 118 part-time (75 women); includes 87 minority (77 Black or African American, non-Hispanic/Latino; 1 Asian, non-Hispanic/Latino; 4 Hispanic/Latino; 5 Two or more races, non-Hispanic/Latino). Average age 34. 95 applicants, 97% accepted, 57 enrolled. In 2019, 46 master's awarded. *Degree requirements:* For master's, comprehensive exam, research course, minimum GPA of 3.0, admission to candidacy. *Entrance requirements:* For master's, GRE 290 (recommended:150 verbal, 140 quantitative) and GRE writing score. If student has taken the MCAT (recommended: 487), DAT (recommended: 16) or equivalent professional exam, then this may be substituted for the GRE, bachelor's degree; minimum undergraduate GPA of 2.5 or 3.0 on last 30 semester hours, Official transcripts and a letter of recommendation. Additional exam requirements/recommendations for international students: required—TOEFL (minimum score 523 paper-based; 70 iBT), IELTS (minimum score 6). *Application deadline:* Applications are processed on a rolling basis. Application fee: $50. Electronic applications accepted. *Expenses: Tuition, area resident:* Full-time $7650; part-time $2550 per semester hour. Tuition, state resident: full-time $7650; part-time $2550 per semester hour. Tuition, nonresident: full-time $15,300; part-time $5100 per semester hour. *International tuition:* $15,300 full-time. *Required fees:* $856; $352 per semester hour. $176 per semester. *Financial support:* In 2019–20, 50 students received support. Fellowships, research assistantships, teaching assistantships, career-related internships or fieldwork, Federal Work-Study, scholarships/grants, traineeships, tuition waivers, and unspecified assistantships available. Support available to part-time students. Financial award application deadline: 3/1; financial award applicants required to submit FAFSA. *Unit head:* Dr. Jeffrey Rush, Assistant Professor, Division Chair, 334-670-3441, Fax: 334-808-6487, E-mail: rushj@troy.edu. *Application contact:* Haley McKinnon, Director of Graduate Admissions, 334-670-3178, Fax: 334-670-3912, E-mail: hmckinnon@troy.edu.
Website: https://www.troy.edu/academics/academic-programs/criminal-justice.html

Troy University, Graduate School, College of Business, Program in Business Administration, Troy, AL 36082. Offers accounting (EMBA, MBA); criminal justice (EMBA); finance (MBA); general management (EMBA, MBA); healthcare management (EMBA); information systems (EMBA, MBA); international economic development (MBA). *Accreditation:* ACBSP. *Program availability:* Part-time, evening/weekend, online learning. *Faculty:* 15 full-time (5 women), 2 part-time/adjunct (0 women). *Students:* 49 full-time (17 women), 77 part-time (27 women); includes 23 minority (19 Black or African American, non-Hispanic/Latino; 1 Asian, non-Hispanic/Latino; 3 Hispanic/Latino), 21 international. Average age 29. 93 applicants, 60% accepted, 42 enrolled. In 2019, 59 master's awarded. *Degree requirements:* For master's, minimum GPA of 3.0, capstone course, research course. *Entrance requirements:* For master's, GMAT (500 or above) or GRE (1050 or above in verbal and quantitative), or 294 or above on the revised GRE (verbal and quantitative), bachelor's degree; minimum undergraduate GPA of 2.5 or 3.0 on last 30 semester hours, letter of recommendation. Additional exam requirements/recommendations for international students: required—TOEFL (minimum score 523 paper-based; 70 iBT), IELTS (minimum score 6). *Application deadline:* Applications are processed on a rolling basis. Application fee: $50. Electronic applications accepted. *Expenses: Tuition, area resident:* Full-time $7650; part-time $2550 per semester hour. Tuition, state resident: full-time $7650; part-time $2550 per semester hour. Tuition, nonresident: full-time $15,300; part-time $5100 per semester hour. *International tuition:* $15,300 full-time. *Required fees:* $856; $352 per semester hour. $176 per semester. *Financial support:* In 2019–20, 50 students received support. Fellowships, research assistantships, teaching assistantships, career-related internships or fieldwork, Federal Work-Study, scholarships/grants, traineeships, tuition waivers, and unspecified assistantships available. Support available to part-time students. Financial award application deadline: 3/1; financial award applicants required to submit FAFSA. *Unit head:* Dr. Robert Wheatley, Professor, Director of Graduate Business Programs, 334-670-3416, Fax: 334-670-3708, E-mail: rwheat@troy.edu. *Application contact:* Haley McKinnon, Director of Graduate Admissions, 334-670-3178, Fax: 334-670-3733, E-mail: hmckinnon@troy.edu.
Website: https://www.troy.edu/academics/academic-programs/sorrell-college-business-programs.php

Universidad del Este, Graduate School, Carolina, PR 00984. Offers accounting (MBA); adult education (M Ed); agribusiness (MBA); criminal justice and criminology (MA); curriculum and instruction - early education (M Ed); curriculum and instruction - elementary (M Ed); curriculum and instruction - English (M Ed); curriculum and instruction - Spanish (M Ed); human resources (MBA); information security management (MBA); information technology and Web business development (MBA); management (MBA); public policy (MPA); social work (MA), including clinical social work; special education (M Ed); strategic leadership (MBA).

Universidad del Turabo, Graduate Programs, School of Social Sciences and Humanities, Programs in Public Affairs, Program in Criminal Justice Studies, Gurabo, PR 00778-3030. Offers MPA. *Entrance requirements:* For master's, GRE, EXADEP or GMAT, interview, essay, official transcript, recommendation letters. Electronic applications accepted.

Université de Montréal, Faculty of Arts and Sciences, School of Criminology, Montréal, QC H3C 3J7, Canada. Offers M Sc, PhD. Terminal master's awarded for partial completion of doctoral program. *Degree requirements:* For master's, thesis; for doctorate, thesis/dissertation, general exam. *Entrance requirements:* For master's, B Sc in criminology or the equivalent; for doctorate, M Sc in criminology or equivalent. Electronic applications accepted.

University at Albany, State University of New York, School of Criminal Justice, Albany, NY 12222-0001. Offers MA, PhD, MSW/MA. *Program availability:* Part-time, blended/hybrid learning. *Faculty:* 16 full-time (5 women), 10 part-time/adjunct (4 women). *Students:* 63 full-time (38 women), 18 part-time (15 women); includes 24 minority (11 Black or African American, non-Hispanic/Latino; 2 Asian, non-Hispanic/Latino; 10 Hispanic/Latino; 1 Two or more races, non-Hispanic/Latino), 13 international. Average age 27. 106 applicants, 61% accepted, 41 enrolled. In 2019, 39 master's, 4 doctorates awarded. *Degree requirements:* For doctorate, thesis/dissertation. *Entrance requirements:* For master's and doctorate, GRE General Test. Additional exam requirements/recommendations for international students: required—TOEFL (minimum score 550 paper-based). *Application deadline:* For fall admission, 3/15 for domestic and international students; for spring admission, 11/15 for domestic students. Application fee: $75. Electronic applications accepted. *Expenses: Tuition, area resident:* Full-time $11,530; part-time $480 per credit hour. Tuition, nonresident: full-time $23,530; part-time $980 per credit hour. *International tuition:* $23,530 full-time. *Required fees:* $2185; $96 per credit hour. Part-time tuition and fees vary according to course load and program. *Financial support:* Fellowships, research assistantships, teaching assistantships, career-related internships or fieldwork, Federal Work-Study, and institutionally sponsored loans available. Financial award application deadline: 4/1. *Unit head:* William Alex Pridemore, Dean, 518-442-5210, E-mail: pridemore@albany.edu. *Application contact:* Jane Champagne, Director, Graduate Admissions, 518-442-3980, Fax: 518-442-3922, E-mail: graduate@albany.edu.
Website: http://www.albany.edu/scj/

The University of Alabama, Graduate School, College of Arts and Sciences, Department of Criminology and Criminal Justice, Tuscaloosa, AL 35487. Offers MS. *Program availability:* Part-time. *Faculty:* 6 full-time (4 women). *Students:* 18 full-time (12 women), 3 part-time (1 woman); includes 6 minority (2 Black or African American, non-Hispanic/Latino; 1 Asian, non-Hispanic/Latino; 2 Hispanic/Latino; 1 Two or more races, non-Hispanic/Latino), 2 international. Average age 26. 14 applicants, 57% accepted, 6 enrolled. In 2019, 16 master's awarded. *Degree requirements:* For master's, comprehensive exam (for some programs), thesis (for some programs), thesis or comprehensive exam. *Entrance requirements:* For master's, GRE G, except for students with GPA of 3.5 or above. Additional exam requirements/recommendations for international students: recommended—TOEFL. *Application deadline:* For fall admission, 6/15 for domestic and international students; for winter admission, 11/15 for domestic and international students. Applications are processed on a rolling basis. Application fee: $50 ($60 for international students). Electronic applications accepted. *Expenses: Tuition, area resident:* Full-time $10,780; part-time $440 per credit hour. Tuition, nonresident: full-time $30,250; part-time $1550 per credit hour. *Financial support:* In 2019–20, 25 teaching assistantships with partial tuition reimbursements (averaging $6,570 per year) were awarded; fellowships, health care benefits, and unspecified assistantships also available. Financial award application deadline: 6/15. *Unit head:* Dr. Ariane Prohaska, Associate Department Chair and Associate Professor, 205-348-1792,

Fax: 205-348-7795, E-mail: lwreid@ua.edu. *Application contact:* Dr. Adam Lankford, Associate Professor and Director of Graduate Studies, 205-348-9901, Fax: 205-348-9901, E-mail: adam.lankford@ua.edu.
Website: http://cj.ua.edu

The University of Alabama at Birmingham, College of Arts and Sciences, Program in Criminal Justice, Birmingham, AL 35294. Offers MSCJ. *Program availability:* Part-time, evening/weekend. *Faculty:* 13 full-time (5 women). *Students:* 32 full-time (25 women), 10 part-time (7 women); includes 14 minority (12 Black or African American, non-Hispanic/Latino; 1 Asian, non-Hispanic/Latino; 1 Hispanic/Latino). Average age 26. 20 applicants, 30% accepted, 6 enrolled. In 2019, 3 master's awarded. *Degree requirements:* For master's, thesis or demonstration project that shows proficiency in the subject. *Entrance requirements:* Additional exam requirements/recommendations for international students: required—TOEFL, TWE. *Application deadline:* For fall admission, 7/1 for domestic and international students; for spring admission, 11/1 for domestic and international students. Application fee: $45 ($60 for international students). Electronic applications accepted. *Expenses:* Contact institution. *Financial support:* In 2019–20, 1 student received support, including 1 research assistantship (averaging $14,280 per year), 1 teaching assistantship (averaging $14,280 per year); career-related internships or fieldwork and scholarships/grants also available. Financial award application deadline: 7/1; financial award applicants required to submit FAFSA. *Unit head:* Dr. Heith Copes, Director of Graduate Studies in Criminal Justice, 205-934-2069, Fax: 205-934-2067, E-mail: jhcopes@uab.edu. *Application contact:* Susan Noblitt Banks, Director of Graduate School Operations, 205-934-8227, Fax: 205-934-8413, E-mail: gradschool@uab.edu.
Website: http://www.uab.edu/cas/justice-sciences/graduate-programs/master-of-science-in-criminal-justice-mscj

University of Alaska Fairbanks, College of Liberal Arts, Department of Justice, Fairbanks, AK 99775-6120. Offers MA. *Program availability:* Part-time, online only, 100% online. *Degree requirements:* For master's, comprehensive exam, oral defense of project or thesis. *Entrance requirements:* For master's, bachelor's degree from accredited institution with minimum cumulative undergraduate and major GPA of 3.0. Additional exam requirements/recommendations for international students: required—TOEFL (minimum score 550 paper-based; 79 iBT), IELTS (minimum score 6.5). Electronic applications accepted.

University of Alberta, Faculty of Graduate Studies and Research, Department of Sociology, Edmonton, AB T6G 2E1, Canada. Offers criminal justice (MA); demography (MA, PhD); sociology (MA, PhD). *Program availability:* Part-time. *Degree requirements:* For master's, thesis (for some programs); for doctorate, thesis/dissertation.

University of Antelope Valley, Program in Criminal Justice, Lancaster, CA 93534. Offers MS. *Degree requirements:* For master's, capstone project. *Entrance requirements:* For master's, official transcripts documenting earned bachelor's degree from nationally- or regionally-accredited institution with minimum cumulative GPA of 2.0.

University of Arkansas at Little Rock, Graduate School, College of Social Sciences and Communication, Department of Criminal Justice, Little Rock, AR 72204-1099. Offers MA, MS, PhD. *Program availability:* Part-time, evening/weekend. *Degree requirements:* For master's, thesis defense or written comprehensive exam; for doctorate, thesis/dissertation. *Entrance requirements:* For master's, GRE General Test or MAT, interview, minimum GPA of 2.75. Additional exam requirements/recommendations for international students: required—TOEFL (minimum score 550 paper-based; 79 iBT).

University of Baltimore, Graduate School, College of Public Affairs, Program in Criminal Justice, Baltimore, MD 21201-5779. Offers MS, JD/MS. *Program availability:* Part-time, evening/weekend. *Degree requirements:* For master's, thesis or alternative. *Entrance requirements:* For master's, interview, minimum GPA of 2.8. Additional exam requirements/recommendations for international students: required—TOEFL (minimum score 550 paper-based). Electronic applications accepted.

University of California, Irvine, School of Social Ecology, Department of Criminology, Law and Society, Irvine, CA 92697. Offers MAS, PhD. *Students:* 136 full-time (105 women), 75 part-time (65 women); includes 111 minority (18 Black or African American, non-Hispanic/Latino; 22 Asian, non-Hispanic/Latino; 61 Hispanic/Latino; 10 Two or more races, non-Hispanic/Latino), 8 international. Average age 28. 255 applicants, 57% accepted, 98 enrolled. In 2019, 78 master's, 3 doctorates awarded. *Degree requirements:* For doctorate, thesis/dissertation, research project. *Entrance requirements:* For master's and doctorate, GRE General Test, minimum GPA of 3.0. Additional exam requirements/recommendations for international students: required—TOEFL (minimum score 550 paper-based). *Application deadline:* For fall admission, 1/15 priority date for domestic and international students. Application fee: $120 ($140 for international students). Electronic applications accepted. *Financial support:* Fellowships, research assistantships with full tuition reimbursements, teaching assistantships, institutionally sponsored loans, traineeships, health care benefits, and unspecified assistantships available. Financial award application deadline: 3/1; financial award applicants required to submit FAFSA. *Unit head:* Prof. Mona Lynch, Department Chair, 949-824-0047, E-mail: lynchm@uci.edu. *Application contact:* Leslie Noel, Graduate Coordinator, 949-824-1442, Fax: 949-824-3001, E-mail: lknoel@uci.edu.
Website: http://cls.soceco.uci.edu/

University of Central Florida, College of Community Innovation and Education, Department of Criminal Justice, Orlando, FL 32816. Offers corrections leadership (Certificate); criminal justice (MS, PhD); juvenile justice leadership (Certificate); police leadership (Certificate). *Program availability:* Part-time, evening/weekend. *Students:* 94 full-time (64 women), 200 part-time (134 women); includes 144 minority (60 Black or African American, non-Hispanic/Latino; 2 Asian, non-Hispanic/Latino; 72 Hispanic/Latino; 1 Native Hawaiian or other Pacific Islander, non-Hispanic/Latino; 9 Two or more races, non-Hispanic/Latino), 2 international. Average age 30. 200 applicants, 73% accepted, 93 enrolled. In 2019, 79 master's, 27 other advanced degrees awarded. *Degree requirements:* For master's, thesis or alternative; for doctorate, comprehensive exam, thesis/dissertation. *Entrance requirements:* For master's, minimum GPA of 3.0, letters of recommendation, resume, goal statement; for doctorate, GRE, letters of recommendation, curriculum vitae, goal statement, writing sample. Additional exam requirements/recommendations for international students: required—TOEFL. *Application deadline:* For fall admission, 7/15 for domestic students; for spring admission, 12/1 for domestic students. Application fee: $30. Electronic applications accepted. *Financial support:* In 2019–20, 17 students received support, including 11 fellowships with partial tuition reimbursements available (averaging $4,000 per year), 4 research assistantships with partial tuition reimbursements available (averaging $7,822 per year), 12 teaching assistantships with partial tuition reimbursements available (averaging $5,941 per year); career-related internships or fieldwork, Federal Work-Study, institutionally sponsored loans, health care benefits, tuition waivers (partial), and unspecified assistantships also available. Financial award application deadline: 3/1; financial award applicants required to submit FAFSA. *Unit head:* Dr. Eugene Paoline, III, Program Director, 407-823-2603, E-mail: eugene.paoline@ucf.edu. *Application contact:* Associate Director, Graduate Admissions, 407-823-2766, Fax: 407-823-6442, E-mail: gradadmissions@ucf.edu.
Website: https://www.cohpa.ucf.edu/criminaljustice/

University of Central Missouri, The Graduate School, Warrensburg, MO 64093. Offers accountancy (MA); accounting (MBA); applied mathematics (MS); aviation safety (MA); biology (MS); business administration (MBA); career and technology education (MS); college student personnel administration (MS); communication (MA); computer information systems and information technology (MS); computer science (MS); counseling (MS); criminal justice and criminology (MS); educational leadership (Ed S); educational leadership and policy analysis (Ed D); educational technology (MS, Ed S); elementary and early childhood education (MSE); English (MA); english language learners - teaching english as a second language (MA); environmental studies (MA); finance (MBA); history (MA); industrial hygiene (MS); industrial management (MS); information systems (MBA); kinesiology (MS); library science and information services (MS); literacy education (MSE); marketing (MBA); mathematics (MS); music (MA); occupational safety management (MS); professional leadership - adult, career, and technical education (Ed S); professional leadership - counseling (Ed S); psychology (MS); rural family nursing (MS); school administration (MSE); social gerontology (MS); sociology (MA); special education (MSE); speech language pathology (MS); teaching (MAT); technology (MS); technology management (PhD); theatre (MA). *Accreditation:* ASHA. *Program availability:* Part-time, 100% online, blended/hybrid learning. *Faculty:* 236 full-time (113 women), 97 part-time/adjunct (61 women). *Students:* 787 full-time (448 women), 1,459 part-time (997 women); includes 213 minority (72 Black or African American, non-Hispanic/Latino; 5 American Indian or Alaska Native, non-Hispanic/Latino; 27 Asian, non-Hispanic/Latino; 59 Hispanic/Latino; 50 Two or more races, non-Hispanic/Latino), 574 international. Average age 30. 1,477 applicants, 68% accepted, 664 enrolled. In 2019, 831 master's, 93 other advanced degrees awarded. *Degree requirements:* For master's and Ed S, comprehensive exam (for some programs), thesis (for some programs). *Entrance requirements:* For master's, A GRE or GMAT test score may be required by some of the programs, A minimum GPA, letters of recommendation, a statement of purpose may be required by some of the programs; for Ed S, A master's degree is required for the application of an Education Specialist's degree program. Additional exam requirements/recommendations for international students: required—TOEFL (minimum score 550 paper-based; 79 iBT). *Application deadline:* For fall admission, 6/1 priority date for domestic and international students; for spring admission, 10/15 priority date for domestic and international students; for summer admission, 4/1 priority date for domestic and international students. Applications are processed on a rolling basis. Application fee: $30 ($75 for international students). Electronic applications accepted. *Expenses: Tuition, area resident:* Full-time $7524; part-time $313.50 per credit hour. Tuition, state resident: full-time $7524; part-time $313.50 per credit hour. Tuition, nonresident: full-time $15,048; part-time $627 per credit hour. *International tuition:* $15,048 full-time. *Required fees:* $915; $30.50 per credit hour. *Financial support:* In 2019–20, 89 students received support. Research assistantships, teaching assistantships, career-related internships or fieldwork, Federal Work-Study, scholarships/grants, unspecified assistantships, and administrative and laboratory assistantships available. Support available to part-time students. Financial award application deadline: 4/1; financial award applicants required to submit FAFSA. *Unit head:* Shellie Hewitt, Director of Graduate and International Student Services, 660-543-4621, Fax: 660-543-4778, E-mail: hewitt@ucmo.edu. *Application contact:* Shellie Hewitt, Director of Graduate and International Student Services, 660-543-4621, Fax: 660-543-4778, E-mail: hewitt@ucmo.edu.
Website: http://www.ucmo.edu/graduate/

University of Central Oklahoma, The Jackson College of Graduate Studies, College of Liberal Arts, School of Criminal Justice, Edmond, OK 73034-5209. Offers crime and intelligence analysis (MA); criminal justice management and administration (MA). *Program availability:* Part-time. *Degree requirements:* For master's, comprehensive exam (for some programs), thesis (for some programs). *Entrance requirements:* Additional exam requirements/recommendations for international students: required—TOEFL (minimum score 550 paper-based; 79 iBT), IELTS (minimum score 6.5). Electronic applications accepted.

University of Cincinnati, Graduate School, College of Education, Criminal Justice, and Human Services, School of Criminal Justice, Cincinnati, OH 45221. Offers MS, PhD. *Program availability:* Part-time, online learning. *Degree requirements:* For master's, thesis or alternative; for doctorate, thesis/dissertation. *Entrance requirements:* For master's, GRE or MAT, minimum GPA of 3.0; for doctorate, minimum GPA of 3.5. Additional exam requirements/recommendations for international students: required—TOEFL (minimum score 550 paper-based). Electronic applications accepted.

University of Colorado Colorado Springs, School of Public Affairs, Colorado Springs, CO 80918. Offers criminal justice (MCJ); public administration (MPA). *Accreditation:* NASPAA. *Program availability:* Part-time, evening/weekend, 100% online, blended/hybrid learning. *Faculty:* 22 full-time (12 women), 20 part-time/adjunct (10 women). *Students:* 28 full-time (18 women), 194 part-time (127 women); includes 87 minority (19 Black or African American, non-Hispanic/Latino; 4 American Indian or Alaska Native, non-Hispanic/Latino; 6 Asian, non-Hispanic/Latino; 48 Hispanic/Latino; 10 Two or more races, non-Hispanic/Latino), 4 international. Average age 34. 89 applicants, 83% accepted, 58 enrolled. In 2019, 38 master's awarded. *Degree requirements:* For master's, internship, capstone project, or thesis. *Entrance requirements:* For master's, 2 professional and/or academic recommendations by qualified references that establish the applicant's personal qualifications for graduate work; 3.00 (or better) undergraduate GPA for regular admission into the MPA program; current resume; statement of goals (prompts given within the application). Additional exam requirements/recommendations for international students: recommended—TOEFL (minimum score 80 iBT), IELTS (minimum score 6.5). *Application deadline:* Applications are processed on a rolling basis. Application fee: $60 ($100 for international students). Electronic applications accepted. *Expenses:* Contact institution. *Financial support:* In 2019–20, 35 students received support. Career-related internships or fieldwork, Federal Work-Study, scholarships/grants, and tuition waivers available. Support available to part-time students. Financial award application deadline: 3/1; financial award applicants required to submit FAFSA. *Unit head:* Dr. George Reed, Dean, 719-255-4109, E-mail: george.reed@uccs.edu. *Application contact:* Stephani Hosain, Graduate Student Services Specialist, 719-255-4993, E-mail: shosain@uccs.edu.
Website: https://www.uccs.edu/spa/

University of Colorado Denver, School of Public Affairs, Program in Criminology and Criminal Justice, Denver, CO 80217. Offers criminal justice (MCJ), including criminal justice, domestic violence, emergency management and homeland security. *Program availability:* Part-time, evening/weekend. Tuition and fees vary according to course load, program and reciprocity agreements.

University of Colorado Denver, School of Public Affairs, Program in Public Affairs and Administration, Denver, CO 80127. Offers public administration (MPA), including domestic violence, emergency management and homeland security, environmental policy, management and law, homeland security and defense, local government, nonprofit management, public administration; public affairs (PhD). *Accreditation:* NASPAA. *Program availability:* Part-time, evening/weekend, online learning. Tuition and fees vary according to course load, program and reciprocity agreements.

Criminal Justice and Criminology

University of Delaware, College of Arts and Sciences, Department of Sociology and Criminal Justice, Newark, DE 19716. Offers criminology (MA, PhD); sociology (MA, PhD). *Degree requirements:* For master's, thesis; for doctorate, comprehensive exam, thesis/dissertation. *Entrance requirements:* For master's and doctorate, GRE, 3 letters of recommendation. Additional exam requirements/recommendations for international students: required—TOEFL. Electronic applications accepted.

University of Denver, University College, Denver, CO 80208. Offers arts and culture (MA, Certificate); communication management (MS, Certificate), including translation studies (Certificate), world history and culture (Certificate); environmental policy and management (MS); geographic information systems (MS); global affairs (MA, Certificate), including human capital in organizations (Certificate), philanthropic leadership (Certificate); project management (Certificate), strategic innovation and change (Certificate); healthcare leadership (MS); information communications and technology (MS); leadership and organizations (MS); professional creative writing (MA, Certificate), including emergency planning and response (Certificate), organizational security (Certificate); security management (MS, Certificate); strategic human resources (Certificate). *Program availability:* Part-time, evening/weekend, 100% online, blended/hybrid learning. *Faculty:* 104 part-time/adjunct (52 women). *Students:* 59 full-time (33 women), 1,893 part-time (1,210 women); includes 545 minority (133 Black or African American, non-Hispanic/Latino; 16 American Indian or Alaska Native, non-Hispanic/Latino; 64 Asian, non-Hispanic/Latino; 252 Hispanic/Latino; 4 Native Hawaiian or other Pacific Islander, non-Hispanic/Latino; 76 Two or more races, non-Hispanic/Latino), 78 international. Average age 32. 1,290 applicants, 91% accepted, 752 enrolled. In 2019, 457 master's, 181 other advanced degrees awarded. *Degree requirements:* For master's, capstone project. *Entrance requirements:* For master's, baccalaureate degree, transcripts, two letters of recommendation, personal statement, resume, writing sample (Master of Arts in Professional Creative Writing). Additional exam requirements/recommendations for international students: required—TOEFL (minimum score 550 paper-based; 80 iBT). *Application deadline:* For fall admission, 6/19 priority date for domestic students, 6/14 priority date for international students; for winter admission, 10/25 priority date for domestic students, 9/27 priority date for international students; for spring admission, 2/7 priority date for domestic students, 1/10 priority date for international students; for summer admission, 4/24 priority date for domestic students, 3/27 priority date for international students. Applications are processed on a rolling basis. Application fee: $75. Electronic applications accepted. *Expenses:* Contact institution. *Financial support:* In 2019–20, 56 students received support. Teaching assistantships available. Financial award applicants required to submit FAFSA. *Unit head:* Dr. Michael McGuire, Dean, 303-871-3518, E-mail: michael.mcguire@du.edu. *Application contact:* Admission Team, 303-871-2291, E-mail: ucoladm@du.edu.
Website: http://universitycollege.du.edu/

University of Detroit Mercy, College of Liberal Arts and Education, Detroit, MI 48221. Offers addiction counseling (MA); addiction studies (Certificate); clinical mental health counseling (MA); clinical psychology (MA, PhD); computer and information systems (MS); criminal justice (MA); curriculum and instruction (MA); economics (MA); educational administration (MA); financial economics (MA); industrial/organizational psychology (MA); information assurance (MS); intelligence analysis (MA); liberal studies (MALS); religious studies (MA); school counseling (MA, Certificate); school psychology (Spec); security administration (MS); special education: emotionally impaired/behaviorally disordered (MA); special education: learning disabilities (MA). *Program availability:* Part-time, evening/weekend. *Degree requirements:* For doctorate, departmental qualifying exam.

University of Florida, Graduate School, College of Liberal Arts and Sciences, Department of Sociology and Criminology and Law, Gainesville, FL 32611. Offers criminology, law, and society (MA, PhD); sociology (MA, PhD), including sociology, tropical conservation and development, women's and gender studies (PhD); MA/JD. *Program availability:* Part-time. Terminal master's awarded for partial completion of doctoral program. *Degree requirements:* For master's, thesis optional; for doctorate, comprehensive exam, thesis/dissertation. *Entrance requirements:* For master's and doctorate, GRE, minimum GPA of 3.0. Additional exam requirements/recommendations for international students: required—TOEFL (minimum score 550 paper-based; 80 iBT), IELTS (minimum score 6). Electronic applications accepted.

University of Guelph, Office of Graduate and Postdoctoral Studies, College of Social and Applied Human Sciences, Department of Criminology and Criminal Justice Policy, Guelph, ON N1G 2W1, Canada. Offers MA. *Degree requirements:* For master's, thesis or major paper. *Entrance requirements:* For master's, minimum B+ average during previous 2 years of coursework. Electronic applications accepted.

University of Guelph, Office of Graduate and Postdoctoral Studies, College of Social and Applied Human Sciences, Department of Sociology and Anthropology, Guelph, ON N1G 2W1, Canada. Offers anthropology (MA); crime and criminal justice policy (MA); sociology (MA, PhD). *Degree requirements:* For master's, thesis or major paper; for doctorate, comprehensive exam, thesis/dissertation. *Entrance requirements:* For master's, minimum B+ average during previous 2 years of course work, honors BA or equivalent; for doctorate, must have an MA in Sociology, must have 80% or higher in graduate level studies. Additional exam requirements/recommendations for international students: required—TOEFL (minimum score 550 paper-based; 89 iBT) or IELTS (minimum score 6.5). Electronic applications accepted.

University of Houston–Clear Lake, School of Human Sciences and Humanities, Programs in Human Sciences, Houston, TX 77058-1002. Offers behavioral sciences (MA), including criminology, cross cultural studies, general psychology, sociology; clinical psychology (MA); criminology (MA); cross cultural studies (MA); family therapy (MA); fitness and human performance (MA); school psychology (MA). *Accreditation:* AAMFT/COAMFTE. *Program availability:* Part-time, evening/weekend, online learning. *Degree requirements:* For master's, thesis or alternative. *Entrance requirements:* For master's, GRE General Test. Additional exam requirements/recommendations for international students: required—TOEFL (minimum score 550 paper-based). Electronic applications accepted.

University of Houston - Downtown, College of Public Service, Department of Criminal Justice and Social Work, Houston, TX 77002. Offers MS. *Program availability:* Part-time, evening/weekend, online only, 100% online. *Faculty:* 11 full-time (5 women). *Students:* 21 full-time (12 women), 54 part-time (36 women); includes 49 minority (14 Black or African American, non-Hispanic/Latino; 2 Asian, non-Hispanic/Latino; 33 Hispanic/Latino), 3 international. Average age 36. 28 applicants, 89% accepted, 22 enrolled. In 2019, 11 master's awarded. *Degree requirements:* For master's, thesis or project. *Entrance requirements:* For master's, personal statement, 3 letters of recommendation, minimum GPA of 3.0 on last 60 hours. Additional exam requirements/recommendations for international students: required—TOEFL (minimum score 550 paper-based; 50 iBT). *Application deadline:* For fall admission, 7/31 for domestic students; for spring admission, 1/7 for domestic students. Application fee: $35 ($80 for international students). Electronic applications accepted. *Expenses:* $386 in-state resident; $758 non-resident, per credit. *Financial support:* Federal Work-Study and scholarships/grants available. Financial award application deadline: 4/1; financial award applicants required to submit FAFSA. *Unit head:* Dr. Ashley Blackburn, Chair, 713-222-5326, Fax: 713-221-2726, E-mail: blackburna@uhd.edu. *Application contact:* Ceshia Love, Director of Admissions, 713-221-8093, Fax: 713-223-7408, E-mail: gradadmissions@uhd.edu.
Website: http://www.uhd.edu/mscj/

University of Houston - Downtown, Marilyn Davies College of Business, Master of Security Management Program, Houston, TX 77002. Offers MSM. *Program availability:* Part-time, evening/weekend, online only, 100% online. *Faculty:* 1 full-time (0 women), 2 part-time/adjunct (1 woman). *Students:* 62 part-time (20 women); includes 45 minority (32 Black or African American, non-Hispanic/Latino; 5 Asian, non-Hispanic/Latino; 8 Hispanic/Latino), 1 international. Average age 39. 31 applicants, 65% accepted, 18 enrolled. In 2019, 19 master's awarded. *Degree requirements:* For master's, capstone project. *Entrance requirements:* For master's, letter of intent, 3 letters of recommendation from supervisors indicating probability of applicant's success in program, proof of three years of paid work experience with supervisory or managerial responsibilities. Additional exam requirements/recommendations for international students: required—TOEFL (minimum score 81 iBT). *Application deadline:* For fall admission, 7/15 for domestic students. Application fee: $35 ($60 for international students). Electronic applications accepted. *Expenses:* $386 in-state resident; $758 non-resident, per credit. *Financial support:* Federal Work-Study and scholarships/grants available. Financial award application deadline: 4/1; financial award applicants required to submit FAFSA. *Unit head:* Dr. Charles E. Gengler, Dean, 713-221-8179, Fax: 713-221-8675, E-mail: genglerc@uhd.edu. *Application contact:* Ceshia Love, Director of Admissions, 713-221-8093, Fax: 713-223-7408, E-mail: gradadmissions@uhd.edu.
Website: https://www.uhd.edu/academics/business/graduate-programs/Pages/msme-index.aspx

University of Illinois at Chicago, College of Liberal Arts and Sciences, Department of Criminology, Law, and Justice, Chicago, IL 60607-7128. Offers MA, PhD. *Program availability:* Evening/weekend. *Degree requirements:* For master's, thesis. *Entrance requirements:* For master's, GRE General Test, minimum GPA of 3.0. Additional exam requirements/recommendations for international students: required—TOEFL. Electronic applications accepted.

University of Louisiana at Monroe, Graduate School, College of Business and Social Sciences, Department of Criminal Justice, Monroe, LA 71209-0001. Offers MA. *Program availability:* Part-time, evening/weekend, 100% online, blended/hybrid learning. *Faculty:* 3 full-time (2 women). *Students:* 21 full-time (14 women), 14 part-time (11 women); includes 25 minority (23 Black or African American, non-Hispanic/Latino; 1 Hispanic/Latino; 1 Two or more races, non-Hispanic/Latino). Average age 31. 13 applicants, 77% accepted, 9 enrolled. In 2019, 13 master's awarded. *Degree requirements:* For master's, thesis optional. *Entrance requirements:* For master's, GRE General Test, minimum GPA of 2.5. Additional exam requirements/recommendations for international students: required—TOEFL (minimum score 500 paper-based; 61 iBT); recommended—IELTS (minimum score 5.5). *Application deadline:* For fall admission, 8/1 for domestic students, 6/1 for international students; for spring admission, 1/1 for domestic students, 11/1 for international students; for summer admission, 6/1 for domestic students, 3/1 for international students. Applications are processed on a rolling basis. Application fee: $40. Electronic applications accepted. *Expenses: Tuition, area resident:* Full-time $6489. Tuition, state resident: full-time $6489. Tuition, nonresident: full-time $18,989. *Required fees:* $2748. Tuition and fees vary according to course load and program. *Financial support:* In 2019–20, 4 students received support. Career-related internships or fieldwork, Federal Work-Study, scholarships/grants, and unspecified assistantships available. Financial award application deadline: 2/15; financial award applicants required to submit FAFSA. *Unit head:* Dr. Robert D. Hanser, Graduate Coordinator, 318-342-1443, Fax: 318-342-1458, E-mail: hanser@ulm.edu. *Application contact:* Dr. Robert D. Hanser, Graduate Coordinator, 318-342-1443, Fax: 318-342-1458, E-mail: hanser@ulm.edu.
Website: http://www.ulm.edu/criminaljustice

University of Louisville, Graduate School, College of Arts and Sciences, Department of Criminal Justice, Louisville, KY 40292. Offers MS, PhD. *Program availability:* Part-time, evening/weekend, 100% online. *Faculty:* 15 full-time (6 women), 22 part-time/adjunct (8 women). *Students:* 78 full-time (24 women), 50 part-time (13 women); includes 30 minority (14 Black or African American, non-Hispanic/Latino; 1 Asian, non-Hispanic/Latino; 10 Hispanic/Latino; 5 Two or more races, non-Hispanic/Latino), 2 international. Average age 38. 70 applicants, 74% accepted, 35 enrolled. In 2019, 29 master's, 3 doctorates awarded. *Degree requirements:* For master's, thesis or alternative, thesis or professional paper; for doctorate, thesis/dissertation, qualifying project. *Entrance requirements:* For master's, GRE General Test, Two letters of reference, official transcripts. Personal statement; for doctorate, GRE General Test, Three letters of recommendation; personal statement; CV or resume; writing sample; official transcripts. Additional exam requirements/recommendations for international students: required—TOEFL (minimum score 550 paper-based; 79 iBT), IELTS can be used in place of the TOEFL; recommended—IELTS (minimum score 6.5). *Application deadline:* For fall admission, 7/1 priority date for domestic and international students; for spring admission, 11/1 priority date for domestic and international students; for summer admission, 4/1 priority date for domestic and international students. Applications are processed on a rolling basis. Application fee: $65. Electronic applications accepted. *Expenses: Tuition, area resident:* Full-time $13,000; part-time $723 per credit hour. Tuition, state resident: full-time $13,000; part-time $723 per credit hour. Tuition, nonresident: full-time $27,114; part-time $1507 per credit hour. *International tuition:* $27,114 full-time. *Required fees:* $196. Tuition and fees vary according to program and reciprocity agreements. *Financial support:* In 2019–20, 53 students received support, including 9 research assistantships with full tuition reimbursements available (averaging $18,000 per year); fellowships, teaching assistantships, career-related internships or fieldwork, scholarships/grants, health care benefits, and unspecified assistantships also available. Financial award application deadline: 2/15; financial award applicants required to submit FAFSA. *Unit head:* Dr. Cherie Dawson-Edwards, Chair, 502-852-0080, E-mail: bcdaws01@louisville.edu. *Application contact:* Kristin Swartz, Director of Graduate Studies, 502-852-3240, E-mail: kristin.swartz@louisville.edu.
Website: https://louisville.edu/justice/

University of Lynchburg, Graduate Studies, MA Program in Criminal Justice Leadership, Lynchburg, VA 24501-3199. Offers MA. *Program availability:* Part-time. *Degree requirements:* For master's, thesis, professional project/portfolio. *Entrance requirements:* For master's, GRE. Additional exam requirements/recommendations for international students: required—TOEFL (minimum score 550 paper-based; 80 iBT), IELTS (minimum score 6). Electronic applications accepted. Application fee is waived when completed online. *Expenses:* Contact institution.

University of Management and Technology, Program in Criminal Justice, Arlington, VA 22209-1609. Offers homeland security (MS). *Program availability:* Part-time, evening/weekend, online learning. *Entrance requirements:* Additional exam requirements/recommendations for international students: required—TOEFL (minimum score 530 paper-based; 71 iBT). *Expenses: Tuition:* Full-time $7020; part-time $390 per credit hour. *Required fees:* $90; $30 per semester.

University of Management and Technology, Program in Management, Arlington, VA 22209-1609. Offers acquisition management (MS, AC); criminal justice administration (MS); general management (MS); project management (MS, AC). *Program availability:* Part-time, evening/weekend, online learning. *Entrance requirements:* For master's, 3 recommendations, resume. Additional exam requirements/recommendations for international students: required—TOEFL (minimum score 530 paper-based; 71 iBT). Electronic applications accepted. *Expenses: Tuition:* Full-time $7020; part-time $390 per credit hour. *Required fees:* $90; $30 per semester.

The University of Manchester, School of Law, Manchester, United Kingdom. Offers bioethics and medical jurisprudence (PhD); criminology (M Phil, PhD); law (M Phil, PhD).

University of Maryland, College Park, Academic Affairs, College of Behavioral and Social Sciences, Department of Criminology and Criminal Justice, College Park, MD 20742. Offers MA, PhD, JD/MA. *Program availability:* Part-time, evening/weekend. Terminal master's awarded for partial completion of doctoral program. *Degree requirements:* For master's, comprehensive exam, thesis optional; for doctorate, comprehensive exam, thesis/dissertation. *Entrance requirements:* For master's, GRE General Test, minimum GPA of 3.0, 3 letters of recommendation; for doctorate, GRE General Test. Additional exam requirements/recommendations for international students: required—TOEFL. Electronic applications accepted.

University of Maryland Eastern Shore, Graduate Programs, Department of Criminal Justice, Princess Anne, MD 21853. Offers MS. *Program availability:* Part-time, evening/weekend. *Degree requirements:* For master's, comprehensive exam, thesis optional. *Entrance requirements:* For master's, GRE General Test, interview. Additional exam requirements/recommendations for international students: required—TOEFL (minimum score 80 iBT).

University of Massachusetts Lowell, College of Fine Arts, Humanities and Social Sciences, School of Criminology and Justice Studies, Lowell, MA 01854. Offers criminal justice (MA). *Program availability:* Part-time, evening/weekend. *Degree requirements:* For master's, thesis optional. *Entrance requirements:* For master's, GRE General Test or MAT. Electronic applications accepted.

University of Memphis, Graduate School, College of Arts and Sciences, Department of Criminology and Criminal Justice, Memphis, TN 38152. Offers MA. *Program availability:* Part-time, 100% online, blended/hybrid learning. *Students:* 14 full-time (13 women), 5 part-time (3 women); includes 10 minority (8 Black or African American, non-Hispanic/Latino; 2 Two or more races, non-Hispanic/Latino). Average age 28. 9 applicants, 89% accepted, 5 enrolled. In 2019, 7 master's awarded. *Degree requirements:* For master's, comprehensive exam, thesis optional. *Entrance requirements:* For master's, GRE General Test, minimum GPA of 3.0. Additional exam requirements/recommendations for international students: required—TOEFL (minimum score 550 paper-based; 79 iBT). *Application deadline:* For fall admission, 6/1 for domestic students; for spring admission, 11/1 for domestic students. Application fee: $35 ($60 for international students). Electronic applications accepted. *Expenses: Tuition, area resident:* Full-time $9216; part-time $512 per credit hour. Tuition, state resident: full-time $9216; part-time $512 per credit hour. Tuition, nonresident: full-time $12,672; part-time $704 per credit hour. *International tuition:* $16,128 full-time. *Required fees:* $1530; $85 per credit hour. Tuition and fees vary according to program. *Financial support:* Research assistantships with full tuition reimbursements, teaching assistantships with full tuition reimbursements, career-related internships or fieldwork, Federal Work-Study, institutionally sponsored loans, scholarships/grants, tuition waivers (partial), and unspecified assistantships available. Financial award application deadline: 2/1; financial award applicants required to submit FAFSA. *Unit head:* Dr. KB Turner, Chair, 901-678-3397, Fax: 901-678-5279, E-mail: kbturner@memphis.edu. *Application contact:* Dr. James McCutcheon, Graduate Coordinator, 901-678-3399, Fax: 901-678-5279, E-mail: jcmcctch@memphis.edu. Website: http://www.memphis.edu/cjustice/

University of Michigan–Dearborn, College of Arts, Sciences, and Letters, Master of Science in Criminology and Criminal Justice Program, Dearborn, MI 48128. Offers MS. *Program availability:* Part-time, evening/weekend, 100% online, blended/hybrid learning. *Faculty:* 6 full-time (3 women), 11 part-time/adjunct (2 women). *Students:* 9 full-time (6 women), 15 part-time (7 women); includes 10 minority (5 Black or African American, non-Hispanic/Latino; 2 Asian, non-Hispanic/Latino; 3 Hispanic/Latino). Average age 33. 10 applicants, 70% accepted, 4 enrolled. In 2019, 7 master's awarded. *Degree requirements:* For master's, thesis optional. *Entrance requirements:* Additional exam requirements/recommendations for international students: required—TOEFL (minimum score 84 iBT), IELTS (minimum score 6.5). *Application deadline:* For fall admission, 8/1 for domestic students, 5/1 for international students; for winter admission, 12/1 for domestic students, 9/1 for international students; for spring admission, 4/1 for domestic students, 1/1 for international students. Applications are processed on a rolling basis. Application fee: $60. Electronic applications accepted. *Financial support:* Scholarships/grants available. Support available to part-time students. Financial award application deadline: 3/1; financial award applicants required to submit FAFSA. *Unit head:* Dr. Paul Draus, Director, E-mail: draus@umich.edu. *Application contact:* Office of Graduate Studies, 313-583-6321, E-mail: umd-graduatestudies@umich.edu. Website: https://umdearborn.edu/casl/graduate-programs/programs/master-science-criminology-and-criminal-justice

University of Michigan–Flint, Graduate Programs, Program in Public Administration, Flint, MI 48502-1950. Offers administration of non-profit agencies (MPA); criminal justice administration (MPA); educational administration (MPA); general public administration (MPA); healthcare administration (MPA). *Program availability:* Part-time. *Faculty:* 2 part-time/adjunct (1 woman). *Students:* 7 full-time (4 women), 79 part-time (54 women); includes 31 minority (27 Black or African American, non-Hispanic/Latino; 1 American Indian or Alaska Native, non-Hispanic/Latino; 2 Hispanic/Latino; 1 Two or more races, non-Hispanic/Latino), 2 international. Average age 38. 54 applicants, 72% accepted, 19 enrolled. In 2019, 40 master's awarded. *Degree requirements:* For master's, thesis or alternative, internship. *Entrance requirements:* For master's, bachelor's degree from regionally-accredited institution, minimum overall undergraduate GPA of 3.0 on 4.0 scale. Additional exam requirements/recommendations for international students: required—TOEFL (minimum score 84 iBT), IELTS (minimum score 6.5). *Application deadline:* For fall admission, 8/1 for domestic students, 5/1 for international students; for winter admission, 11/15 for domestic students, 10/1 for international students; for spring admission, 3/15 for domestic students, 1/1 for international students; for summer admission, 5/15 for domestic students. Applications are processed on a rolling basis. Application fee: $55. Electronic applications accepted. *Expenses:* Contact institution. *Financial support:* Career-related internships or fieldwork, Federal Work-Study, and scholarships/grants available. Support available to part-time students. Financial award application deadline: 3/1; financial award applicants required to submit FAFSA. *Unit head:* Dr. Kim Sacks McManaway, Director, 810-766-6628, E-mail: kimsaks@umflint.edu. *Application contact:* Matt Bohlen, Associate Director of Graduate Admissions, 810-762-3171, Fax: 810-766-6789, E-mail: mbohlen@umflint.edu. Website: http://www.umflint.edu/graduateprograms/public-administration-mpa

University of Minnesota, Duluth, Graduate School, College of Liberal Arts, Department of Sociology/Anthropology, Program in Criminology, Duluth, MN 55812-2496. Offers MA. *Program availability:* Part-time, evening/weekend. *Degree requirements:* For master's, thesis or alternative. *Entrance requirements:* For master's, minimum GPA of 3.0, letter of recommendation, personal statement. Additional exam requirements/recommendations for international students: required—TOEFL.

University of Mississippi, Graduate School, School of Applied Sciences, University, MS 38677. Offers communicative disorders (MS); criminal justice (MCJ); exercise science (MS); food and nutrition services (MS); health and kinesiology (PhD); health promotion (MS); nutrition and hospitality management (PhD); park and recreation management (MA); social welfare (PhD); social work (MSW). *Students:* 188 full-time (149 women), 37 part-time (18 women); includes 47 minority (35 Black or African American, non-Hispanic/Latino; 2 American Indian or Alaska Native, non-Hispanic/Latino; 1 Asian, non-Hispanic/Latino; 5 Hispanic/Latino; 1 Native Hawaiian or other Pacific Islander, non-Hispanic/Latino; 3 Two or more races, non-Hispanic/Latino), 23 international. Average age 26. *Expenses:* Tuition, state resident: full-time $8718; part-time $484.25 per credit hour. Tuition, nonresident: full-time $24,990; part-time $1388.25 per credit hour. *Required fees:* $100; $4.16 per credit hour. *Unit head:* Dr. Peter Grandjean, Dean of Applied Sciences, 662-915-7900, Fax: 662-915-7901, E-mail: applsci@olemiss.edu. *Application contact:* Temeka Smith, Graduate Activities Specialist for Admissions, 662-915-7474, Fax: 662-915-7577, E-mail: gschool@olemiss.edu. Website: applsci@olemiss.edu

University of Missouri–Kansas City, College of Arts and Sciences, Department of Criminal Justice and Criminology, Kansas City, MO 64110-2499. Offers MS. *Program availability:* Part-time, evening/weekend. *Degree requirements:* For master's, thesis optional. *Entrance requirements:* For master's, GRE, minimum GPA of 3.0 in major, 2.7 overall. Additional exam requirements/recommendations for international students: required—TOEFL (minimum score 550 paper-based; 80 iBT). Electronic applications accepted.

University of Missouri–St. Louis, College of Arts and Sciences, Department of Criminology and Criminal Justice, St. Louis, MO 63121. Offers MA, PhD. *Degree requirements:* For doctorate, thesis/dissertation. *Entrance requirements:* For master's, essay; 2 letters of recommendation; for doctorate, GRE General Test, writing sample, 3 letters of recommendation. Additional exam requirements/recommendations for international students: required—TOEFL (minimum score 550 paper-based; 65 iBT), IELTS (minimum score 6.5). Electronic applications accepted. *Expenses: Tuition, area resident:* Full-time $9005.40; part-time $6003.60 per credit hour. Tuition, state resident: full-time $9005.40; part-time $6003.60 per credit hour. Tuition, nonresident: full-time $22,108; part-time $14,738.40 per credit hour. *International tuition:* $22,108 full-time. Tuition and fees vary according to course load.

University of Montana, Graduate School, College of Humanities and Sciences, Department of Sociology, Missoula, MT 59812. Offers criminology (MA); inequality and social justice (MA); rural and environmental change (MA); sociology (MA). *Entrance requirements:* For master's, GRE General Test. Additional exam requirements/recommendations for international students: required—TOEFL.

University of Nebraska at Omaha, Graduate Studies, College of Public Affairs and Community Service, School of Criminology and Criminal Justice, Omaha, NE 68182. Offers criminology and criminal justice (MA, MS, PhD); managing juvenile and adult populations (Certificate). *Program availability:* Part-time, evening/weekend. Terminal master's awarded for partial completion of doctoral program. *Degree requirements:* For master's, comprehensive exam, thesis (for some programs); for doctorate, comprehensive exam, thesis/dissertation. *Entrance requirements:* For master's, GRE General Test, previous course work in criminal justice, statistics, and research methods; minimum GPA of 3.0; official transcripts; statement of purpose; 2 letters of recommendation; for doctorate, GRE General Test, master's degree, minimum undergraduate GPA of 3.0, 3 letters of recommendation, statement of purpose, writing sample, resume. Additional exam requirements/recommendations for international students: required—TOEFL, IELTS, PTE. Electronic applications accepted.

University of Nevada, Las Vegas, Graduate College, Greenspun College of Urban Affairs, Department of Criminal Justice, Las Vegas, NV 89154-5009. Offers criminal justice (MA); criminology and criminal justice (PhD). *Program availability:* Part-time. *Faculty:* 9 full-time (5 women), 9 part-time/adjunct (2 women). *Students:* 65 full-time (31 women), 5 part-time (4 women); includes 29 minority (6 Black or African American, non-Hispanic/Latino; 15 Hispanic/Latino; 1 Native Hawaiian or other Pacific Islander, non-Hispanic/Latino; 7 Two or more races, non-Hispanic/Latino), 3 international. Average age 31. 69 applicants, 78% accepted, 36 enrolled. In 2019, 13 master's awarded. *Degree requirements:* For master's, comprehensive exam, thesis, oral examination; for doctorate, comprehensive exam, thesis/dissertation. *Entrance requirements:* For master's, GRE General Test, statement of purpose; bachelor's degree; 2 letters of recommendation; for doctorate, GRE General Test (minimum scores: 153 for Quantitative, 155 for Verbal, and 4.5 for Analytical Writing), 3 letters of recommendation; statement of purpose; personal interview. Additional exam requirements/recommendations for international students: required—TOEFL (minimum score 550 paper-based; 80 iBT), IELTS (minimum score 7). *Application deadline:* For fall admission, 4/15 for domestic students. Application fee: $60 ($95 for international students). Electronic applications accepted. *Expenses:* Contact institution. *Financial support:* In 2019–20, 25 students received support, including 6 research assistantships with full tuition reimbursements available (averaging $20,446 per year), 19 teaching assistantships with full tuition reimbursements available (averaging $15,250 per year); institutionally sponsored loans, scholarships/grants, health care benefits, and unspecified assistantships also available. Financial award application deadline: 3/15; financial award applicants required to submit FAFSA. *Unit head:* Dr. Joel Lieberman, Chair/Associate Professor, 702-895-0249, Fax: 702-895-0252, E-mail: crj.chair@unlv.edu. *Application contact:* Dr. Tamara Herold, Graduate Coordinator, 702-895-5903, Fax: 702-895-0252, E-mail: criminaljustice.gradcoord@unlv.edu. Website: http://criminaljustice.unlv.edu/grad/

University of Nevada, Reno, Graduate School, College of Liberal Arts, School of Social Research and Justice Studies, Department of Criminal Justice, Reno, NV 89557. Offers MA. *Degree requirements:* For master's, comprehensive exam, thesis optional. *Entrance requirements:* For master's, GRE or LSAT, undergraduate degree in criminal justice with minimum GPA of 3.0. Additional exam requirements/recommendations for international students: required—TOEFL (minimum score 500 paper-based; 61 iBT), IELTS (minimum score 6). Electronic applications accepted.

University of Nevada, Reno, Graduate School, College of Liberal Arts, School of Social Research and Justice Studies, Program in Justice Management, Reno, NV 89557. Offers MJM. *Program availability:* Part-time, online learning. *Degree requirements:* For master's, thesis optional. *Entrance requirements:* For master's, minimum GPA of 2.75. Additional exam requirements/recommendations for international students: required—TOEFL (minimum score 500 paper-based; 61 iBT), IELTS (minimum score 6). Electronic applications accepted.

University of New Haven, Graduate School, Henry C. Lee College of Criminal Justice and Forensic Sciences, Program in Criminal Justice, West Haven, CT 06516. Offers criminal justice (MS, PhD); criminal justice management (Graduate Certificate). *Program availability:* Part-time, evening/weekend, 100% online, blended/hybrid learning. *Students:* 67 full-time (37 women), 51 part-time (29 women); includes 30 minority (13 Black or African American, non-Hispanic/Latino; 6 Asian, non-Hispanic/Latino; 9 Hispanic/Latino; 2 Two or more races, non-Hispanic/Latino), 14 international. Average age 32. 90 applicants, 72% accepted, 30 enrolled. In 2019, 38 master's, 3 doctorates

awarded. *Entrance requirements:* Additional exam requirements/recommendations for international students: required—TOEFL (minimum score 80 iBT), IELTS, PTE (minimum score 53). *Application deadline:* Applications are processed on a rolling basis. Application fee: $50. Electronic applications accepted. Application fee is waived when completed online. *Financial support:* Research assistantships with partial tuition reimbursements, teaching assistantships with partial tuition reimbursements, Federal Work-Study, scholarships/grants, and unspecified assistantships available. Support available to part-time students. Financial award applicants required to submit FAFSA. *Unit head:* Dr. John DeCarlo, Associate Professor, 203-931-2983, E-mail: JDeCarlo@newhaven.edu. *Application contact:* Selina O'Toole, Senior Associate Director of Graduate Admissions, 203-932-7337, E-mail: SOToole@newhaven.edu.
Website: https://www.newhaven.edu/lee-college/graduate-programs/criminal-justice/

University of New Haven, Graduate School, Henry C. Lee College of Criminal Justice and Forensic Sciences, Program in Investigations, West Haven, CT 06516. Offers criminal investigations (MS); digital forensic investigations (MS); financial crimes investigations (MS). *Program availability:* Part-time, 100% online. *Students:* 55 full-time (36 women), 103 part-time (53 women); includes 54 minority (32 Black or African American, non-Hispanic/Latino; 1 American Indian or Alaska Native, non-Hispanic/Latino; 4 Asian, non-Hispanic/Latino; 16 Hispanic/Latino; 1 Native Hawaiian or other Pacific Islander, non-Hispanic/Latino). Average age 31. 112 applicants, 100% accepted, 67 enrolled. In 2019, 68 master's awarded. *Application deadline:* Applications are processed on a rolling basis. Application fee: $50. Electronic applications accepted. *Unit head:* Dr. Patrick Malloy, Senior Lecturer, 203-932-1046, E-mail: pmalloy@newhaven.edu. *Application contact:* Selina O'Toole, Senior Associate Director of Graduate Admissions, 203-932-7337, E-mail: SOToole@newhaven.edu.
Website: https://online.newhaven.edu/masters-in-investigations/

University of North Alabama, College of Arts and Sciences, Department of Interdisciplinary and Professional Studies, Florence, AL 35632-0001. Offers professional studies (MPS), including community development, higher education administration, information technology, security and safety leadership. *Program availability:* Part-time, 100% online. *Degree requirements:* For master's, thesis optional. *Entrance requirements:* For master's, ETS PPI, personal statement; three letters of recommendation. Additional exam requirements/recommendations for international students: required—TOEFL (minimum score 79 iBT), IELTS (minimum score 6), PTE (minimum score 54). Electronic applications accepted.

University of North Alabama, College of Arts and Sciences, Department of Politics, Justice, and Law, Florence, AL 35632-0001. Offers criminal justice (MSCJ). *Program availability:* Part-time, 100% online. *Degree requirements:* For master's, comprehensive exam (for some programs), thesis optional. *Entrance requirements:* For master's, GRE General Test, MAT, three letters of recommendation; essay. Additional exam requirements/recommendations for international students: required—TOEFL (minimum score 79 iBT), IELTS (minimum score 6), PTE (minimum score 54). Electronic applications accepted.

The University of North Carolina at Charlotte, College of Liberal Arts and Sciences, Department of Criminal Justice and Criminology, Charlotte, NC 28223-0001. Offers crimininal justice (MS). *Program availability:* Part-time, evening/weekend. *Faculty:* 16 full-time (9 women). *Students:* 15 full-time (12 women), 5 part-time (2 women); includes 4 minority (all Black or African American, non-Hispanic/Latino), 1 international. Average age 24. 22 applicants, 64% accepted, 10 enrolled. In 2019, 8 master's awarded. *Degree requirements:* For master's, comprehensive exam (for some programs), thesis optional. *Entrance requirements:* For master's, GRE, official copies of all undergraduate/graduate transcripts; minimum of three letters of recommendation; personal statement; minimum GPA of 3.0 (preferred). Additional exam requirements/recommendations for international students: required—TOEFL (minimum score 557 paper-based; 83 iBT), IELTS (minimum score 6.5), TOEFL (minimum score 557 paper-based, 83 iBT) or IELTS (6.5). *Application deadline:* Applications are processed on a rolling basis. Application fee: $75. Electronic applications accepted. *Expenses:* Tuition, state resident: full-time $4337. Tuition, nonresident: full-time $17,771. *Required fees:* $3093. Tuition and fees vary according to course load, degree level and program. *Financial support:* In 2019–20, 5 students received support, including 5 teaching assistantships (averaging $13,000 per year); fellowships, research assistantships, career-related internships or fieldwork, Federal Work-Study, institutionally sponsored loans, scholarships/grants, and unspecified assistantships also available. Support available to part-time students. Financial award applicants required to submit FAFSA. *Unit head:* Dr. Michael Turner, Professor and Chair, 704-687-0755, E-mail: mgturner@uncc.edu. *Application contact:* Kathy B. Giddings, Director of Graduate Admissions, 704-687-5503, Fax: 704-687-1668, E-mail: gradadm@uncc.edu.
Website: http://criminaljustice.uncc.edu/

The University of North Carolina at Greensboro, Graduate School, College of Arts and Sciences, Department of Sociology, Greensboro, NC 27412-5001. Offers criminology (MA); sociology (MA). *Program availability:* Part-time. *Degree requirements:* For master's, comprehensive exam, thesis. *Entrance requirements:* For master's, GRE General Test. Additional exam requirements/recommendations for international students: required—TOEFL. Electronic applications accepted.

The University of North Carolina at Pembroke, The Graduate School, Department of Political Science and Public Administration, Pembroke, NC 28372-1510. Offers criminal justice (MPA); emergency management (MPA); health administration (MPA); public management (MPA). *Program availability:* Part-time, evening/weekend, online learning. *Degree requirements:* For master's, comprehensive exam, thesis optional. *Entrance requirements:* For master's, GRE General Test or MAT, minimum GPA of 3.0 in major, 2.5 overall; interview. Additional exam requirements/recommendations for international students: required—TOEFL.

The University of North Carolina Wilmington, College of Arts and Sciences, Department of Sociology and Criminology, Wilmington, NC 28403-3297. Offers MA. *Faculty:* 13 full-time (8 women). *Students:* 10 full-time (8 women), 4 part-time (3 women); includes 3 minority (all Black or African American, non-Hispanic/Latino). Average age 24. 20 applicants, 65% accepted, 5 enrolled. In 2019, 8 master's awarded. *Degree requirements:* For master's, thesis or alternative, thesis or internship. *Entrance requirements:* For master's, GRE General Test, 3 letters of recommendation, statement of interest. Additional exam requirements/recommendations for international students: required—TOEFL (minimum score 79 iBT), IELTS (minimum score 6.5). *Application deadline:* For fall admission, 7/1 for domestic students. Applications are processed on a rolling basis. Application fee: $75. Electronic applications accepted. *Expenses: Tuition, area resident:* Full-time $4719; part-time $326 per credit hour. Tuition, state resident: full-time $4719; part-time $326 per credit hour. Tuition, nonresident: full-time $18,548; part-time $1099 per credit hour. *Required fees:* $2738. Tuition and fees vary according to program. *Financial support:* Research assistantships, teaching assistantships, scholarships/grants, and out-of-state tuition awards available. Financial award application deadline: 1/1; financial award applicants required to submit FAFSA. *Unit head:* Dr. Mike Maume, Chair, 910-962-7749, Fax: 910-962-7385, E-mail: maume@uncw.edu. *Application contact:* Dr. Jake Day, Graduate Coordinator, 910-962-7024, Fax: 910-962-7385, E-mail: dayj@uncw.edu.
Website: http://www.uncw.edu/socgrad/index.html

University of North Dakota, Graduate School, College of Arts and Sciences, Program in Criminal Justice, Grand Forks, ND 58202. Offers PhD, JD/PhD. *Program availability:* Part-time. *Entrance requirements:* For doctorate, GRE General Test. Additional exam requirements/recommendations for international students: required—TOEFL (minimum score 550 paper-based; 79 iBT), IELTS (minimum score 6.5). Electronic applications accepted.

University of Northern Colorado, Graduate School, College of Humanities and Social Sciences, Department of Criminology and Criminal Justice, Greeley, CO 80639. Offers criminal justice (MA).

University of North Florida, College of Arts and Sciences, Department of Criminology and Criminal Justice, Jacksonville, FL 32224. Offers criminal justice (MS). *Degree requirements:* For master's, comprehensive exam, thesis optional. *Entrance requirements:* For master's, GRE General Test, minimum GPA of 3.0 in last 60 hours, letters of recommendation. Additional exam requirements/recommendations for international students: required—TOEFL (minimum score 500 paper-based; 61 iBT). Electronic applications accepted.

University of North Georgia, Department of Criminal Justice, Dahlonega, GA 30597. Offers MS. *Students:* 2 full-time (1 woman), 24 part-time (18 women); includes 10 minority (2 Black or African American, non-Hispanic/Latino; 2 Asian, non-Hispanic/Latino; 3 Hispanic/Latino; 3 Two or more races, non-Hispanic/Latino). Average age 32. *Unit head:* Dr. Douglas Orr, Department Head, 706-867-3084, E-mail: douglas.orr@ung.edu. *Application contact:* Cory Thornton, Director of Graduate Admissions, 706-867-2077, E-mail: cory.thornton@ung.edu.
Website: http://ung.edu/criminal-justice/

University of North Texas, Toulouse Graduate School, Denton, TX 76203-5459. Offers accounting (MS); applied anthropology (MA, MS); applied behavior analysis (Certificate); applied geography (MA); applied technology and performance improvement (M Ed, MS); art education (MA); art history (MA); arts leadership (Certificate); audiology (Au D); behavior analysis (MS); behavioral science (PhD); biochemistry and molecular biology (MS); biology (MA, MS); biomedical engineering (MS); business analysis (MS); chemistry (MS); clinical health psychology (PhD); communication studies (MA, MS); computer engineering (MS); computer science (MS); counseling (M Ed, MS), including clinical mental health counseling (MS), college and university counseling, elementary school counseling, secondary school counseling; creative writing (MA); criminal justice (MS); curriculum and instruction (M Ed); decision sciences (MBA); design (MA, MFA), including fashion design (MFA), innovation studies, interior design (MFA); early childhood studies (MS); economics (MS); educational leadership (M Ed, Ed D); educational psychology (MS, PhD), including family studies (MS), gifted and talented (MS), human development (MS), learning and cognition (MS), research, measurement and evaluation (MS); electrical engineering (MS); emergency management (MPA); engineering technology (MS); English (MA); English as a second language (MA); environmental science (MS); finance (MBA, MS); financial management (MPA); French (MA); health services management (MBA); higher education (M Ed, Ed D); history (MA, MS); hospitality management (MS); human resources management (MPA); information science (MS); information systems (PhD); information technologies (MBA); interdisciplinary studies (MA, MS); international studies (MA); international sustainable tourism (MS); jazz studies (MM); journalism (MA, MJ, Graduate Certificate), including interactive and virtual digital communication (Graduate Certificate), narrative journalism (Graduate Certificate), public relations (Graduate Certificate); kinesiology (MS); linguistics (MA); local government management (MPA); logistics (PhD); logistics and supply chain management (MBA); long-term care, senior housing, and aging services (MA); management (PhD); marketing (MBA); mathematics (MA, MS); mechanical and energy engineering (MS, PhD); music (MA), including ethnomusicology, music theory, musicology, performance; music composition (PhD); music education (MM Ed, PhD); nonprofit management (MPA); operations and supply chain management (MBA); performance (MM, DMA); philosophy (MA); political science (MA); professional and technical communication (MA); radio, television and film (MA, MFA); rehabilitation counseling (Certificate); sociology (MA); Spanish (MA); special education (M Ed); speech-language pathology (MA); strategic management (MBA); studio art (MFA); teaching (M Ed); MBA/MS. *Program availability:* Part-time, evening/weekend, online learning. Terminal master's awarded for partial completion of doctoral program. *Degree requirements:* For master's, variable foreign language requirement, comprehensive exam (for some programs), thesis (for some programs); for doctorate, variable foreign language requirement, comprehensive exam (for some programs), thesis/dissertation; for other advanced degree, variable foreign language requirement, comprehensive exam (for some programs). *Entrance requirements:* For master's and doctorate, GRE, GMAT. Additional exam requirements/recommendations for international students: required—TOEFL (minimum score 550 paper-based; 79 iBT). Electronic applications accepted.

University of North Texas at Dallas, Graduate School, Dallas, TX 75241. Offers accounting (MBA); counseling (M Ed, MS); criminal justice (MS); curriculum and instruction (M Ed); educational administration (M Ed); human resources and organizational behavior (MBA); public leadership (MS); strategic management (MBA).

University of Oklahoma, College of Professional and Continuing Studies, Norman, OK 73019. Offers administrative leadership (MA, Graduate Certificate), including government and military leadership (MA), organizational leadership (MA), volunteer and non-profit leadership (MA); corrections management (Graduate Certificate); criminal justice (MS); integrated studies (MA), including human and health services administration, integrated studies; museum studies (MA); prevention science (MPS); restorative justice administration (Graduate Certificate). *Program availability:* Part-time, 100% online, blended/hybrid learning. *Degree requirements:* For master's, comprehensive exam, thesis optional, 33 credit hours; project/internship (for museum studies program only); for Graduate Certificate, 12 graduate credit hours (for Graduate Certificate). *Entrance requirements:* For master's and Graduate Certificate, minimum GPA of 3.0 in last 60 undergraduate hours; statement of goals; resume. Additional exam requirements/recommendations for international students: required—TOEFL (minimum score 79 iBT) or IELTS (minimum score 6.5). Electronic applications accepted. *Expenses:* Tuition, state resident: full-time $6583.20; part-time $274.30 per credit hour. Tuition, nonresident: full-time $21,242; part-time $885.10 per credit hour. *International tuition:* $21,242.40 full-time. *Required fees:* $1994.20; $72.55 per credit hour. $126.50 per semester. Tuition and fees vary according to course load and degree level.

University of Ottawa, Faculty of Graduate and Postdoctoral Studies, Faculty of Social Sciences, Department of Criminology, Ottawa, ON K1N 6N5, Canada. Offers MA, MCA, PhD. *Degree requirements:* For master's, thesis or alternative. *Entrance requirements:* For master's, honors bachelor's degree or equivalent, minimum B average. Electronic applications accepted.

University of Pennsylvania, School of Arts and Sciences, Graduate Group in Criminology, Philadelphia, PA 19104. Offers MA, MS, PhD. *Faculty:* 14 full-time (3 women), 2 part-time/adjunct (0 women). *Students:* 21 full-time (11 women), 1 (woman) part-time; includes 3 minority (1 Black or African American, non-Hispanic/Latino; 2 Asian, non-Hispanic/Latino), 7 international. Average age 27. 60 applicants, 55%

accepted, 19 enrolled. In 2019, 18 master's awarded. Application fee: $90. Website: http://www.sas.upenn.edu/graduate-division

University of Phoenix - Bay Area Campus, College of Criminal Justice and Security, San Jose, CA 95134-1805. Offers administration of justice and security (MS).

University of Phoenix - Dallas Campus, College of Criminal Justice and Security, Dallas, TX 75251. Offers administration of justice and security (MS). *Program availability:* Online learning. *Degree requirements:* For master's, thesis (for some programs). *Entrance requirements:* For master's, minimum undergraduate GPA of 2.5, 3 years of work experience. Additional exam requirements/recommendations for international students: required—TOEFL (minimum score 550 paper-based; 79 iBT). Electronic applications accepted.

University of Phoenix–Online Campus, College of Justice and Security, Phoenix, AZ 85034-7209. Offers administration of justice and security (MS), including administration of justice and security, global and homeland security, law enforcement organizations; public administration (MPA). *Program availability:* Evening/weekend, online learning. *Entrance requirements:* Additional exam requirements/recommendations for international students: required—TOEFL, TOEIC (Test of English as an International Communication), Berlitz Online English Proficiency Exam, PTE, or IELTS. Electronic applications accepted. *Expenses:* Contact institution.

University of Phoenix - Phoenix Campus, College of Criminal Justice and Security, Tempe, AZ 85282-2371. Offers administration of justice and security (MS); global and homeland security (MS); law enforcement organizations (MS); public administration (MPA). *Program availability:* Evening/weekend, online learning. *Entrance requirements:* Additional exam requirements/recommendations for international students: required—TOEFL, TOEIC (Test of English as an International Communication), Berlitz Online English Proficiency Exam, PTE, or IELTS. Electronic applications accepted. *Expenses:* Contact institution.

University of Phoenix - San Antonio Campus, College of Criminal Justice and Security, San Antonio, TX 78230. Offers administration of justice and security (MS).

University of Pittsburgh, School of Law, Master of Studies in Law Program, Pittsburgh, PA 15260. Offers biomedical and health services research (MSL); business law (MSL), including commercial law, corporate law, general business law, international business, tax law; Constitutional law (MSL); criminal law and justice (MSL); disability law (MSL); elder and estate planning law (MSL); employment and labor law (MSL); energy law (MSL); environmental and real estate law (MSL); family law (MSL); health law (MSL); intellectual property and technology law (MSL); international and human rights law (MSL); jurisprudence (MSL); regulatory law (MSL); self-designed (MSL). *Program availability:* Part-time. *Entrance requirements:* Additional exam requirements/recommendations for international students: required—TOEFL (minimum score 600 paper-based; 100 iBT), IELTS (minimum score 7).

University of Providence, Graduate Studies, Program in Criminal Justice, Great Falls, MT 59405. Offers MSM. *Program availability:* Part-time, evening/weekend. *Degree requirements:* For master's, thesis optional. *Entrance requirements:* For master's, GRE General Test or MAT, 3 letters of recommendation. Additional exam requirements/recommendations for international students: required—TOEFL (minimum score 500 paper-based). Electronic applications accepted.

University of Regina, Faculty of Graduate Studies and Research, Faculty of Arts, Department of Justice Studies, Regina, SK S4S 0A2, Canada. Offers justice studies (MA); police studies (MA). *Program availability:* Part-time. *Faculty:* 8 full-time (3 women), 5 part-time/adjunct (2 women). *Students:* 2 full-time (both women). Average age 30. 26 applicants, 8% accepted. In 2019, 1 master's awarded. *Degree requirements:* For master's, thesis. *Entrance requirements:* For master's, transcript, 2 letter of recommendation and writing sample. Additional exam requirements/recommendations for international students: required—TOEFL (minimum score 580 paper-based; 80 iBT), IELTS (minimum score 6.5), PTE (minimum score 59), other options are CANTEST, MELAB, CAEL and U of R ESL; GRE is required for Psychology. *Application deadline:* For fall admission, 1/15 for domestic and international students. Application fee: $100 Canadian dollars. Electronic applications accepted. *Expenses: Tuition:* Full-time $6684 Canadian dollars. *Required fees:* $100 Canadian dollars; $3351.45 Canadian dollars per trimester. $1117.15 Canadian dollars per semester. Tuition and fees vary according to course level, course load, degree level and program. *Financial support:* Fellowships, research assistantships, teaching assistantships, career-related internships or fieldwork, Federal Work-Study, scholarships/grants, unspecified assistantships, and Graduate student base funds and other donor funded schols available. Support available to part-time students. Financial award application deadline: 9/30. *Unit head:* Dr. Gloria DeSantis, Department Head/Graduate coordinator, 306-585-5066, Fax: 306-585-4815, E-mail: Gloria.Desantis@uregina.ca. *Application contact:* Dr. Gloria DeSantis, Graduate Program Coordinator, 306-585-5066, Fax: 306-585-4815, E-mail: Gloria.Desantis@uregina.ca.
Website: http://www.uregina.ca/arts/justice-studies

University of San Diego, Division of Professional and Continuing Education, San Diego, CA 92110-2492. Offers cyber security operations and leadership (MS); law enforcement and public safety leadership (MS). *Program availability:* Part-time-only, evening/weekend, 100% online. *Faculty:* 2 full-time (1 woman), 17 part-time/adjunct (1 woman). *Students:* 329 part-time (82 women); includes 141 minority (28 Black or African American, non-Hispanic/Latino; 2 American Indian or Alaska Native, non-Hispanic/Latino; 20 Asian, non-Hispanic/Latino; 83 Hispanic/Latino; 2 Native Hawaiian or other Pacific Islander, non-Hispanic/Latino; 6 Two or more races, non-Hispanic/Latino). Average age 39. 265 applicants, 86% accepted, 130 enrolled. In 2019, 168 master's awarded. *Entrance requirements:* For master's, GMAT, GRE, or LSAT if GPA is under 2.75. Additional exam requirements/recommendations for international students: required—TOEFL (minimum score 115 iBT). *Application deadline:* For fall admission, 8/3 for domestic and international students; for spring admission, 12/2 for domestic and international students; for summer admission, 4/22 for domestic and international students. Applications are processed on a rolling basis. Application fee: $45. Electronic applications accepted. *Financial support:* Application deadline: 4/1; applicants required to submit FAFSA. *Unit head:* Dr. Chell Roberts, Assoc. Provost for Professional Education and Online Dev., 619-260-4585, Fax: 619-260-2961, E-mail: continuinged@sandiego.edu. *Application contact:* Erika Garwood, Associate Director of Graduate Admissions, 619-260-4524, Fax: 619-260-4158, E-mail: grads@sandiego.edu.
Website: http://pce.sandiego.edu/

University of South Africa, College of Law, Pretoria, South Africa. Offers correctional services management (M Tech); criminology (MA, PhD); law (LL M, LL D); penology (MA, PhD); police science (MA, PhD); policing (M Tech); security risk management (M Tech); social science in criminology (MA).

University of South Carolina, The Graduate School, College of Arts and Sciences, Department of Criminology and Criminal Justice, Columbia, SC 29208. Offers MA, PhD, JD/MA. *Program availability:* Part-time, evening/weekend. *Degree requirements:* For master's, comprehensive exam, thesis; for doctorate, comprehensive exam, thesis/dissertation. *Entrance requirements:* For master's and doctorate, GRE. Additional exam

requirements/recommendations for international students: required—TOEFL. Electronic applications accepted.

University of South Dakota, Graduate School, College of Arts and Sciences, Program in Administrative Studies, Vermillion, SD 57069. Offers addiction studies (MSA); criminal justice studies (MSA); health services administration (MSA); human resources (MSA); interdisciplinary studies (MSA); long term care administration (MSA); organizational leadership (MSA). *Program availability:* Part-time, evening/weekend, 100% online. *Degree requirements:* For master's, thesis or alternative. *Entrance requirements:* For master's, 3 years of work or experience, minimum GPA of 2.7, resume. Additional exam requirements/recommendations for international students: required—TOEFL (minimum score 550 paper-based; 79 iBT). Electronic applications accepted.

University of Southern Mississippi, College of Arts and Sciences, School of Criminal Justice, Forensic Science, and Security, Hattiesburg, MS 39406-0001. Offers criminal justice (MA, MS, PhD); forensic science (MS). *Program availability:* Part-time. *Students:* 2 full-time (both women), 3 part-time (1 woman); includes 1 minority (Black or African American, non-Hispanic/Latino). 18 applicants, 11% accepted. In 2019, 6 master's awarded. *Degree requirements:* For master's, comprehensive exam, thesis; for doctorate, comprehensive exam, thesis/dissertation. *Entrance requirements:* For master's, GRE General Test, minimum GPA of 2.75 in last 60 hours, 3.0 in field of study; for doctorate, GRE General Test, minimum GPA of 3.5. Additional exam requirements/recommendations for international students: required—TOEFL, IELTS. *Application deadline:* For fall admission, 3/15 priority date for domestic students, 3/15 for international students; for spring admission, 1/10 priority date for domestic and international students. Applications are processed on a rolling basis. Application fee: $60. Electronic applications accepted. *Expenses: Tuition, area resident:* Full-time $4393; part-time $488 per credit hour. Tuition, nonresident: full-time $5393; part-time $600 per credit hour. *Required fees:* $6 per semester. *Financial support:* Research assistantships with full tuition reimbursements, teaching assistantships with full tuition reimbursements, career-related internships or fieldwork, Federal Work-Study, institutionally sponsored loans, scholarships/grants, health care benefits, and unspecified assistantships available. Financial award application deadline: 3/15; financial award applicants required to submit FAFSA. *Unit head:* Dr. Lisa Nored, Director, 601-266-4509, Fax: 601-266-4391. *Application contact:* Tera Wright, Manager of Graduate Admissions, 601-266-4509, Fax: 601-266-4391.
Website: https://www.usm.edu/criminal-justice

University of South Florida, College of Behavioral and Community Sciences, Department of Criminology, Tampa, FL 33620-9951. Offers MA, MS, PhD. *Faculty:* 13 full-time (5 women). *Students:* 47 full-time (23 women), 56 part-time (32 women); includes 34 minority (12 Black or African American, non-Hispanic/Latino; 1 Asian, non-Hispanic/Latino; 18 Hispanic/Latino; 3 Two or more races, non-Hispanic/Latino), 3 international. Average age 31. 135 applicants, 62% accepted, 59 enrolled. In 2019, 22 master's, 3 doctorates awarded. *Degree requirements:* For master's, comprehensive exam, thesis (for some programs); for doctorate, comprehensive exam, thesis/dissertation. *Entrance requirements:* For master's, GRE (for Criminology), preferred minimum scores of 153V (61st percentile), 144Q (17th percentile) or higher, 2 letters of recommendation; statement of purpose; writing sample (Criminology and Cybercrime); for doctorate, GRE (preferred minimum score of 153 Verbal (61st percentile), 144 Quantitative (17thh percentile) or higher), masters degree with at least 3.4 GPA; 3 letters of recommendation; statement of purpose; writing sample. Additional exam requirements/recommendations for international students: required—TOEFL, TOEFL (minimum score 550 paper-based; 79 iBT) or IELTS (minimum score 6.5). *Application deadline:* For fall admission, 1/15 for domestic and international students; for spring admission, 9/30 for domestic students, 9/15 for international students. Application fee: $30. Electronic applications accepted. *Financial support:* In 2019–20, 24 students received support, including 2 research assistantships (averaging $14,172 per year), 15 teaching assistantships with tuition reimbursements available (averaging $11,702 per year). *Unit head:* Dr. Michael Leiber, Professor and Chair, 813-974-9704, Fax: 813-974-2803, E-mail: mjleiber@usf.edu. *Application contact:* Dr. Rachel Powers, Associate Professor and Graduate Director, 813-974-9531, E-mail: powersr@usf.edu.
Website: http://criminology.cbcs.usf.edu/

University of South Florida, Innovative Education, Tampa, FL 33620-9951. Offers adult, career and higher education (Graduate Certificate), including college teaching, leadership in developing human resources, leadership in higher education; Africana studies (Graduate Certificate), including diasporas and health disparities, genocide and human rights; aging studies (Graduate Certificate), including gerontology; art research (Graduate Certificate), including museum studies; business foundations (Graduate Certificate); chemical and biomedical engineering (Graduate Certificate), including materials science and engineering, water, health and sustainability; child and family studies (Graduate Certificate), including positive behavior support; civil and industrial engineering (Graduate Certificate), including transportation systems analysis; community and family health (Graduate Certificate), including maternal and child health, social marketing and public health, violence and injury: prevention and intervention, women's health; criminology (Graduate Certificate), including criminal justice administration; data science for public administration (Graduate Certificate); digital humanities (Graduate Certificate); educational measurement and research (Graduate Certificate), including evaluation; English (Graduate Certificate), including comparative literary studies, creative writing, professional and technical communication; entrepreneurship (Graduate Certificate); environmental health (Graduate Certificate), including safety management; epidemiology and biostatistics (Graduate Certificate), including applied biostatistics, biostatistics, concepts and tools of epidemiology, epidemiology, epidemiology of infectious diseases; geography, environment and planning (Graduate Certificate), including community development, environmental policy and management, geographical information systems; geology (Graduate Certificate), including hydrogeology; global health (Graduate Certificate), including disaster management, global health and Latin American and Caribbean studies, global health practice, humanitarian assistance, infection control; government and international affairs (Graduate Certificate), including Cuban studies, globalization studies; health policy and management (Graduate Certificate), including health management and leadership, public health policy and programs; hearing specialist: early intervention (Graduate Certificate); industrial and management systems engineering (Graduate Certificate), including systems engineering, technology management; information studies (Graduate Certificate), including school library media specialist; information systems/decision sciences (Graduate Certificate), including analytics and business intelligence; instructional technology (Graduate Certificate), including distance education, Florida digital/virtual educator, instructional design, multimedia design, Web design; internal medicine, bioethics and medical humanities (Graduate Certificate), including biomedical ethics; Latin American and Caribbean studies (Graduate Certificate); leadership for coastal resiliency planning (Graduate Certificate); mass communications (Graduate Certificate), including multimedia journalism; mathematics and statistics (Graduate Certificate), including mathematics; medicine (Graduate Certificate), including aging and neuroscience, bioinformatics, biotechnology, brain fitness and memory management, clinical investigation, hand and upper limb rehabilitation, health informatics, health sciences, integrative weight management, intellectual property, medicine and gender, metabolic and nutritional medicine, metabolic cardiology, pharmacy sciences; national

and competitive intelligence (Graduate Certificate); nursing (Graduate Certificate), including simulation based academic fellowship in advanced pain management; psychological and social foundations (Graduate Certificate), including career counseling, college teaching, diversity in education, mental health counseling, school counseling; public affairs (Graduate Certificate), including nonprofit management, public management, research administration; public health (Graduate Certificate), including assessing chemical toxicity and public health risks, health equity, pharmacoepidemiology, public health generalist, toxicology, translational research in adolescent behavioral health; public health practices (Graduate Certificate), including planning for healthy communities; rehabilitation and mental health counseling (Graduate Certificate), including integrative mental health care, marriage and family therapy, rehabilitation technology; secondary education (Graduate Certificate), including ESOL, foreign language education: culture and content, foreign language education: professional; social work (Graduate Certificate), including geriatric social work/clinical gerontology; special education (Graduate Certificate), including autism spectrum disorder, disabilities education: severe/profound; world languages (Graduate Certificate), including teaching English as a second language (TESL) or foreign language. *Unit head:* Dr. Cynthia DeLuca, Associate Vice President and Assistant Vice Provost, 813-974-3077, Fax: 813-974-7061, E-mail: deluca@usf.edu. *Application contact:* Owen Hooper, Director, Summer and Alternative Calendar Programs, 813-974-6917, E-mail: hooper@usf.edu.
Website: http://www.usf.edu/innovative-education/

University of South Florida Sarasota-Manatee, College of Liberal Arts and Social Sciences, Sarasota, FL 34243. Offers criminal justice (MA); education (MA); educational leadership (M Ed), including curriculum leadership, K-12 public school leadership, non-public/charter school leadership; elementary education (MAT); English education (MA); social work (MSW). *Program availability:* Part-time, 100% online, blended/hybrid learning. *Degree requirements:* For master's, comprehensive exam (for some programs). *Entrance requirements:* For master's, GRE. Additional exam requirements/recommendations for international students: required—TOEFL (minimum score 550 paper-based; 79 iBT), IELTS (minimum score 6.5). Electronic applications accepted.

The University of Tampa, Program in Criminology and Criminal Justice, Tampa, FL 33606-1490. Offers MS. *Degree requirements:* For master's, thesis optional. *Entrance requirements:* For master's, two letters of recommendation from academic and/or professional sources; writing sample indicating evidence of ability to conduct scholarly research (for thesis option applicants); personal statement; professional resume. Electronic applications accepted.

The University of Tennessee, Graduate School, College of Arts and Sciences, Department of Sociology, Knoxville, TN 37996. Offers criminology (MA, PhD); energy, environment, and resource policy (MA, PhD); political economy (MA, PhD). *Program availability:* Part-time. *Degree requirements:* For master's, thesis or alternative; for doctorate, thesis/dissertation. *Entrance requirements:* For master's, GRE General Test, minimum GPA of 3.0; for doctorate, GRE General Test, minimum GPA of 3.5. Additional exam requirements/recommendations for international students: required—TOEFL. Electronic applications accepted.

The University of Tennessee at Chattanooga, Program in Criminal Justice, Chattanooga, TN 37403. Offers MSCJ. *Program availability:* Part-time. *Students:* 18 full-time (11 women), 9 part-time (4 women); includes 6 minority (3 Black or African American, non-Hispanic/Latino; 1 Hispanic/Latino; 2 Two or more races, non-Hispanic/Latino). Average age 28. 16 applicants, 88% accepted, 13 enrolled. In 2019, 9 master's awarded. *Degree requirements:* For master's, comprehensive exam, thesis optional. *Entrance requirements:* For master's, GRE General Test or MAT, 2 letters of recommendation. Additional exam requirements/recommendations for international students: required—TOEFL (minimum score 550 paper-based; 79 iBT), IELTS (minimum score 6). *Application deadline:* For fall admission, 6/15 priority date for domestic students, 7/1 for international students; for spring admission, 11/1 priority date for domestic students, 11/1 for international students. Applications are processed on a rolling basis. Application fee: $35 ($40 for international students). Electronic applications accepted. *Financial support:* Research assistantships, teaching assistantships, career-related internships or fieldwork, scholarships/grants, and unspecified assistantships available. Support available to part-time students. Financial award application deadline: 7/1; financial award applicants required to submit FAFSA. *Unit head:* Dr. Christina Policastro, Graduate Coordinator, 423-425-5752, Fax: 423-425-2251, E-mail: Christina-Policastro@utc.edu. *Application contact:* Dr. Joanne Romagni, Dean of the Graduate School, 423-425-4478, Fax: 423-425-5223, E-mail: joanne-romagni@utc.edu.
Website: https://www.utc.edu/social-cultural-justice-studies/criminal-justice/index.php

The University of Texas at Arlington, Graduate School, College of Liberal Arts, Department of Criminology and Criminal Justice, Arlington, TX 76019. Offers MA. *Program availability:* Part-time, evening/weekend. *Degree requirements:* For master's, comprehensive exam, thesis or alternative. *Entrance requirements:* For master's, GRE General Test, minimum GPA of 3.0 in last 60 hours of undergraduate course work, 3 letters of recommendation. Additional exam requirements/recommendations for international students: required—TOEFL (minimum score 550 paper-based).

The University of Texas at Dallas, School of Economic, Political and Policy Sciences, Program in Criminology and Criminal Justice, Richardson, TX 75080. Offers criminology (MS, PhD); justice administration and leadership (MS). *Program availability:* Part-time, evening/weekend. *Faculty:* 9 full-time (2 women). *Students:* 29 full-time (23 women), 9 part-time (7 women); includes 13 minority (1 Black or African American, non-Hispanic/Latino; 1 Asian, non-Hispanic/Latino; 8 Hispanic/Latino; 3 Two or more races, non-Hispanic/Latino), 6 international. Average age 31. 38 applicants, 39% accepted, 10 enrolled. In 2019, 14 master's, 3 doctorates awarded. *Degree requirements:* For master's, thesis; for doctorate, thesis/dissertation. *Entrance requirements:* For master's, GRE General Test, minimum GPA of 3.0 in upper-level course work in field; for doctorate, GRE (minimum combined verbal and quantitative score of 1200), minimum GPA of 3.2 in upper-level course work in field. Additional exam requirements/recommendations for international students: required—TOEFL (minimum score 550 paper-based). *Application deadline:* For fall admission, 7/15 for domestic students, 5/1 priority date for international students; for spring admission, 11/15 for domestic students, 9/1 priority date for international students. Applications are processed on a rolling basis. Application fee: $50 ($100 for international students). Electronic applications accepted. *Expenses: Tuition, area resident:* Full-time $16,504. *Tuition, state resident:* full-time $16,504. *Tuition, nonresident:* full-time $34,266. Tuition and fees vary according to course load. *Financial support:* In 2019–20, 15 students received support, including 14 teaching assistantships with partial tuition reimbursements available (averaging $13,500 per year); research assistantships with partial tuition reimbursements available, career-related internships or fieldwork, Federal Work-Study, institutionally sponsored loans, scholarships/grants, and unspecified assistantships also available. Support available to part-time students. Financial award application deadline: 4/30; financial award applicants required to submit FAFSA. *Unit head:* Dr. Richard K Scotch, Interim Program Head, 972-883-2922, Fax: 972-883-2735, E-mail: ph.crim@utdallas.edu. *Application contact:* Rita Medford, Graduate Program Administrator, 972-883-4932, Fax: 972-883-6297, E-mail: gpa.crim@utdallas.edu.
Website: https://epps.utdallas.edu/about/programs/criminology-and-criminal-justice/

The University of Texas at San Antonio, College of Public Policy, Department of Criminal Justice, San Antonio, TX 78207. Offers criminology (MS). *Program availability:* Part-time, evening/weekend. *Degree requirements:* For master's, variable foreign language requirement, minimum of 36 semester credit hours; thesis or written comprehensive exams. *Entrance requirements:* For master's, minimum GPA of 3.0 in last 60 hours of undergraduate course work; 2 letters of recommendation; resume; 18 credit hours in criminal justice, criminology or closely-related discipline. Additional exam requirements/recommendations for international students: required—TOEFL (minimum score 550 paper-based; 79 iBT), IELTS (minimum score 6.5). Electronic applications accepted. *Expenses:* Contact institution.

The University of Texas at Tyler, College of Arts and Sciences, Department of Social Sciences, Tyler, TX 75799-0001. Offers criminal justice (MS); public administration (MPA); sociology (MS). *Program availability:* Part-time, evening/weekend. *Faculty:* 5 full-time (2 women), 5 part-time/adjunct (1 woman). *Students:* 17 full-time (12 women), 36 part-time (25 women); includes 22 minority (7 Black or African American, non-Hispanic/Latino; 1 Asian, non-Hispanic/Latino; 12 Hispanic/Latino; 2 Two or more races, non-Hispanic/Latino), 2 international. Average age 36. 27 applicants, 89% accepted, 16 enrolled. In 2019, 19 master's awarded. *Degree requirements:* For master's, comprehensive exam, thesis optional. *Entrance requirements:* For master's, GRE General Test, minimum GPA of 3.0. Additional exam requirements/recommendations for international students: required—TOEFL. *Application deadline:* For fall admission, 8/17 priority date for domestic students, 7/1 priority date for international students; for spring admission, 12/21 priority date for domestic students, 11/1 priority date for international students. Applications are processed on a rolling basis. Application fee: $25 ($50 for international students). *Financial support:* In 2019–20, 1 fellowship (averaging $1,000 per year) was awarded; research assistantships, teaching assistantships, career-related internships or fieldwork, Federal Work-Study, and scholarships/grants also available. Support available to part-time students. Financial award application deadline: 7/1; financial award applicants required to submit FAFSA. *Unit head:* Dr. Thomas Guderjan, Chair, 903-566-7418, E-mail: tguderjan@uttyler.edu. *Application contact:* Dr. Thomas Guderjan, Chair, 903-566-7418, E-mail: tguderjan@uttyler.edu.
Website: https://www.uttyler.edu/socialsciences/

The University of Texas of the Permian Basin, Office of Graduate Studies, College of Arts and Sciences, Department of Social Sciences, Program in Criminal Justice Administration, Odessa, TX 79762-0001. Offers MS. *Program availability:* Part-time, evening/weekend. *Degree requirements:* For master's, comprehensive exam (for some programs), thesis (for some programs). *Entrance requirements:* For master's, GRE General Test, 3 letters of recommendation. Additional exam requirements/recommendations for international students: required—TOEFL (minimum score 550 paper-based).

The University of Texas Rio Grande Valley, College of Liberal Arts, Department of Criminal Justice, Edinburg, TX 78539. Offers MS. *Faculty:* 6 full-time (3 women). *Students:* 17 full-time (10 women), 21 part-time (10 women); includes 37 minority (1 Asian, non-Hispanic/Latino; 36 Hispanic/Latino). Average age 27. 18 applicants, 89% accepted, 13 enrolled. In 2019, 10 master's awarded. *Entrance requirements:* Additional exam requirements/recommendations for international students: required—TOEFL or IELTS. *Expenses: Tuition, area resident:* Full-time $5959; part-time $440 per credit hour. *Tuition, state resident:* full-time $5959. *Tuition, nonresident:* full-time $5959. *International tuition:* $13,321 full-time. *Required fees:* $1169; $185 per credit hour.
Website: www.utrgv.edu/criminal-justice/index.htm

The University of Texas Rio Grande Valley, College of Liberal Arts, Department of Public Affairs and Security Studies, Edinburg, TX 78539. Offers global security studies and leadership (MPA); public administration (MPA); public policy and management (MPA). *Faculty:* 4 full-time (1 woman), 2 part-time/adjunct (1 woman). *Students:* 14 full-time (8 women), 135 part-time (75 women); includes 126 minority (3 Black or African American, non-Hispanic/Latino; 123 Hispanic/Latino), 2 international. Average age 33. 67 applicants, 93% accepted, 40 enrolled. In 2019, 56 master's awarded. *Expenses: Tuition, area resident:* Full-time $5959; part-time $440 per credit hour. *Tuition, state resident:* full-time $5959. *Tuition, nonresident:* full-time $5959. *International tuition:* $13,321 full-time. *Required fees:* $1169; $185 per credit hour.
Website: utrgv.edu/pass/index.htm

University of the Fraser Valley, Graduate Studies, Abbotsford, BC V2S 7M8, Canada. Offers criminal justice (MA); social work (MSW). *Program availability:* Evening/weekend. *Faculty:* 23 full-time (13 women). *Students:* 46 full-time (32 women), 38 part-time (27 women); includes 26 minority (all American Indian or Alaska Native, non-Hispanic/Latino). Average age 40. 65 applicants, 89% accepted, 58 enrolled. In 2019, 27 master's awarded. *Degree requirements:* For master's, thesis optional, major research paper. *Entrance requirements:* For master's, bachelor's degree, work experience in related field. Additional exam requirements/recommendations for international students: recommended—TOEFL (minimum score 570 paper-based; 88 iBT), IELTS (minimum score 6.5), TWE (minimum score 4.5), TSE (minimum score 61). *Application deadline:* For fall admission, 1/31 priority date for domestic students, 4/1 priority date for international students; for winter admission, 8/31 priority date for domestic students; for spring admission, 12/31 priority date for domestic students. Application fee: $75 Canadian dollars ($250 Canadian dollars for international students). Electronic applications accepted. *Expenses:* Contact institution. *Financial support:* Research assistantships, scholarships/grants, health care benefits, and bursaries available. Financial award application deadline: 5/10. *Unit head:* Dr. Garry Fehr, Associate Vice President for Research, Engagement and Graduate Studies, 604-504-4074, E-mail: Garry.Fehr@ufv.ca. *Application contact:* Educational Advisors, 604-854-4528, Fax: 604-855-7614, E-mail: advising@ufv.ca.
Website: http://www.ufv.ca/Graduate-Studies.htm

The University of Toledo, College of Graduate Studies, College of Health and Human Services, School of Social Justice, Toledo, OH 43606-3390. Offers criminal justice (MA); social work (MSW).

The University of Toledo, College of Graduate Studies, College of Social Justice and Human Service, Department of Criminal Justice and Social Work, Toledo, OH 43606-3390. Offers child advocacy (Certificate); criminal justice (MA); elder law (Certificate); juvenile justice (Certificate); patient advocacy (Certificate); social work (MSW); JD/MA. *Accreditation:* CSWE. *Program availability:* Part-time. *Degree requirements:* For master's, comprehensive exam, thesis. *Entrance requirements:* For master's and Certificate, minimum cumulative GPA of 2.7 for all previous academic work, letters of recommendation. Additional exam requirements/recommendations for international students: required—TOEFL (minimum score 550 paper-based; 80 iBT). Electronic applications accepted.

University of Toronto, School of Graduate Studies, Faculty of Arts and Science, Centre for Criminology and Sociolegal Studies, Toronto, ON M5S 1A1, Canada. Offers MA, PhD, JD/MA. *Program availability:* Part-time. *Degree requirements:* For doctorate, comprehensive exam, thesis/dissertation. *Entrance requirements:* For master's, 2 letters of reference, bachelor's degree in social science or humanities, minimum B+ average in last 2 years of undergraduate study; for doctorate, 2 letters of reference, MA in criminology or equivalent, minimum A- average. Additional exam requirements/

recommendations for international students: required—TOEFL (minimum score 580 paper-based; 93 iBT), TWE (minimum score 5). Electronic applications accepted.

University of West Florida, College of Education and Professional Studies, Department of Criminology and Criminal Justice, Pensacola, FL 32514-5750. Offers criminal justice (MS). *Program availability:* Part-time, evening/weekend. *Degree requirements:* For master's, thesis optional. *Entrance requirements:* For master's, GRE or MAT, official transcripts; minimum undergraduate cumulative GPA of 3.0; 3 letters of recommendation; personal statement. Additional exam requirements/recommendations for international students: required—TOEFL (minimum score 550 paper-based). Electronic applications accepted.

University of Windsor, Faculty of Graduate Studies, Faculty of Arts and Social Sciences, Department of Sociology and Anthropology, Windsor, ON N9B 3P4, Canada. Offers criminology (MA); sociology (MA); sociology-social justice (PhD). *Program availability:* Part-time. *Degree requirements:* For master's, thesis; for doctorate, comprehensive exam, thesis/dissertation. *Entrance requirements:* For master's, minimum B+ average; for doctorate, writing sample, minimum B+ average. Additional exam requirements/recommendations for international students: required—TOEFL (minimum score 560 paper-based). Electronic applications accepted.

University of Wisconsin–Milwaukee, Graduate School, Helen Bader School of Social Welfare, Department of Criminal Justice, Milwaukee, WI 53201-0413. Offers applied data analysis using SAS (Graduate Certificate); crime analytics (MS); criminal justice (MS). *Program availability:* Part-time. *Entrance requirements:* For master's, GRE General Test, MAT. Additional exam requirements/recommendations for international students: required—TOEFL (minimum score 550 paper-based; 79 iBT), IELTS (minimum score 6.5). Electronic applications accepted.

University of Wisconsin–Platteville, School of Graduate Studies, Distance Learning Center, Online Master of Science in Criminal Justice Program, Platteville, WI 53818-3099. Offers MS. *Program availability:* Part-time, online learning. *Degree requirements:* For master's, thesis or alternative. *Entrance requirements:* Additional exam requirements/recommendations for international students: required—TOEFL (minimum score 550 paper-based; 79 iBT), IELTS (minimum score 6.5). Electronic applications accepted. *Expenses:* Contact institution.

Urbana University–A Branch Campus of Franklin University, College of Social and Behavioral Sciences, Urbana, OH 43078-2091. Offers criminal justice administration (MA). *Entrance requirements:* For master's, 3 letters of recommendation.

Utica College, MBA in Economic Crime and Fraud Management, Utica, NY 13502. Offers MBA. *Program availability:* Part-time, evening/weekend, online learning. *Faculty:* 4 full-time (0 women). *Students:* 50 full-time (35 women), 14 part-time (6 women); includes 17 minority (6 Black or African American, non-Hispanic/Latino; 1 American Indian or Alaska Native, non-Hispanic/Latino; 5 Asian, non-Hispanic/Latino; 4 Hispanic/Latino; 1 Two or more races, non-Hispanic/Latino). Average age 33. 31 applicants, 61% accepted, 17 enrolled. In 2019, 49 master's awarded. *Degree requirements:* For master's, thesis. *Entrance requirements:* For master's, BS, minimum GPA of 3.0. Additional exam requirements/recommendations for international students: required—TOEFL (minimum score 525 paper-based). *Application deadline:* Applications are processed on a rolling basis. Application fee: $50. Electronic applications accepted. *Expenses:* Contact institution. *Financial support:* Career-related internships or fieldwork, scholarships/grants, tuition waivers (partial), and unspecified assistantships available. Support available to part-time students. Financial award application deadline: 3/15; financial award applicants required to submit FAFSA. *Unit head:* Dr. R. Bruce McBride, Director of Economic Crime Graduate Programs, 315-792-3808, E-mail: rmcbride@utica.edu. *Application contact:* John D. Rowe, Director of Graduate Admissions, 315-792-3824, Fax: 315-792-3003, E-mail: jrowe@utica.edu.
Website: https://programs.online.utica.edu/programs/mba-fraud-management

Utica College, Program in Economic Crime and Fraud Management, Utica, NY 13502-4892. Offers MS. *Program availability:* Part-time, evening/weekend, 100% online. *Entrance requirements:* For master's, BS, minimum GPA of 3.0. Additional exam requirements/recommendations for international students: required—TOEFL (minimum score 525 paper-based). Electronic applications accepted. *Expenses:* Contact institution.

Virginia Commonwealth University, Graduate School, L. Douglas Wilder School of Government and Public Affairs, Program in Criminal Justice, Richmond, VA 23284-9005. Offers MS, Postbaccalaureate Certificate. *Program availability:* Part-time, evening/weekend. *Degree requirements:* For master's, thesis or comprehensive exam. *Entrance requirements:* For master's, GRE, LSAT or GMAT, minimum cumulative GPA of 3.0. Additional exam requirements/recommendations for international students: required—TOEFL (minimum score 600 paper-based; 100 iBT); recommended—IELTS (minimum score 6.5). Electronic applications accepted.

Virginia State University, College of Graduate Studies, College of Humanities and Social Sciences, Department of Sociology and Criminal Justice, Petersburg, VA 23806-0001. Offers criminal justice (MS).

Walden University, Graduate Programs, School of Public Policy and Administration, Minneapolis, MN 55401. Offers criminal justice (MPA, MPP, MS, Graduate Certificate), including emergency management (MS, PhD), general program (MS), global leadership (MS, PhD), homeland security and policy coordination (MS, PhD), law and public policy (MS, PhD), policy analysis (MS, PhD), public management and leadership (MS, PhD), self-designed (MS), terrorism, mediation, and peace (MS, PhD); criminal justice and executive management (MS), including global leadership (MS, PhD); criminal justice leadership and executive management (MS), including emergency management (MS, PhD), general program, homeland security and policy coordination (MS, PhD), law and public policy (MS, PhD), policy analysis (MS, PhD), public management and leadership (MS, PhD), self-designed, terrorism, mediation, and peace (MS, PhD); emergency management (MPA, MPP, MS), including criminal justice (MS, PhD), general program (MS), homeland security (MS), public management and leadership (MS, PhD), terrorism and emergency management (MS); general program (MPA, MPP); global leadership (MPA, MPP); government management (Graduate Certificate); health policy (MPA, MPP); homeland security (Graduate Certificate); homeland security and policy coordination (MPA, MPP); international nongovernmental organizations (MPA, MPP); law and public policy (MPA, MPP); local government management for sustainable communities (MPA, MPP); nonprofit management (Graduate Certificate); nonprofit management and leadership (MPA, MPP, MS), including global leadership (MS, PhD), international nongovernmental organization (MS), local government for sustainable communities (MS), self-designed (MS); online teaching in higher education (Post-Master's Certificate); policy analysis (MPA); public management and leadership (MPA, MPP, Graduate Certificate); public policy (Graduate Certificate); public policy and administration (PhD), including criminal justice (MS, PhD), emergency management (MS, PhD), global leadership (MS, PhD), health policy, homeland security and policy coordination (MS, PhD), international nongovernmental organizations, law and public policy (MS, PhD), local government management for sustainable communities, nonprofit management and leadership, policy analysis (MS, PhD), public management and leadership (MS, PhD), terrorism, mediation, and peace (MS, PhD); strategic planning and public policy (Graduate Certificate); terrorism, mediation, and peace (MPA, MPP). *Program availability:* Part-time, evening/weekend, online only, 100% online. *Degree requirements:* For doctorate, thesis/dissertation, residency. *Entrance requirements:* For master's, bachelor's degree or higher; minimum GPA of 2.5; official transcripts; goal statement (for some programs); access to computer and Internet; for doctorate, master's degree or higher; three years of related professional or academic experience (preferred); minimum GPA of 3.0; goal statement and current resume (for select programs); official transcripts; access to computer and Internet; for other advanced degree, relevant work experience; access to computer and Internet. Additional exam requirements/recommendations for international students: required—TOEFL (minimum score 550 paper-based, 79 iBT), IELTS (minimum score 6.5), Michigan English Language Assessment Battery (minimum score 82), or PTE (minimum score 53). Electronic applications accepted.

Walden University, Graduate Programs, School of Social Work and Human Services, Minneapolis, MN 55401. Offers addictions and social work (DSW); advanced clinical practice (MSW); clinical expertise (DSW); criminal justice (DSW); disaster, crisis, and intervention (DSW); family studies and interventions (DSW); human and social services (PhD), including advanced research, community and social services, community intervention and leadership, conflict management, criminal justice, disaster crisis and intervention, family studies and intervention, gerontology, global social services, higher education, human services and nonprofit administration, mental health facilitation; medical social work (DSW); military social work (MSW); policy practice (DSW); social work (PhD), including addictions and social work, clinical expertise, criminal justice, disaster, crisis and intervention, family studies and interventions, medical social work, policy practice, social work administration; social work administration (DSW); social work in healthcare (MSW); social work with children and families (MSW). *Accreditation:* CSWE. *Program availability:* Part-time, evening/weekend, online only, 100% online. *Degree requirements:* For master's, residency (for some programs); for doctorate, thesis/dissertation, residency. *Entrance requirements:* For master's, bachelor's degree or higher; minimum GPA of 2.5; official transcripts; goal statement (for some programs); access to computer and Internet; for doctorate, master's degree or higher; three years of related professional or academic experience (preferred); minimum GPA of 3.0; goal statement and current resume (for select programs); official transcripts; access to computer and Internet. Additional exam requirements/recommendations for international students: required—TOEFL (minimum score 550 paper-based, 79 iBT), IELTS (minimum score 6.5), Michigan English Language Assessment Battery (minimum score 82), or PTE (minimum score 53). Electronic applications accepted.

Waldorf University, Program in Organizational Leadership, Forest City, IA 50436. Offers criminal justice leadership (MA); emergency management leadership (MA); fire/rescue executive leadership (MA); human resource development (MA); public administration (MA); sport management (MA); teacher leader (MA).

Washburn University, School of Applied Studies, Department of Criminal Justice and Legal Studies, Topeka, KS 66621. Offers MCJ. *Program availability:* Part-time, evening/weekend, online learning. *Degree requirements:* For master's, thesis or alternative, continuous enrollment each fall and spring semester, completion of all program requirements within seven years of entry (MCJ). *Entrance requirements:* For master's, GRE, 3 letters of reference, minimum GPA of 3.0 for undergraduate degree, short biography, official transcripts. Additional exam requirements/recommendations for international students: required—TOEFL (minimum score 80 iBT). Electronic applications accepted.

Washington State University, College of Arts and Sciences, Department of Criminal Justice and Criminology, Pullman, WA 99164. Offers MA, PhD. *Program availability:* Online learning. *Degree requirements:* For master's, comprehensive exam (for some programs), thesis, oral exam; for doctorate, comprehensive exam, thesis/dissertation, oral or written exam. *Entrance requirements:* For master's, GRE General Test, major in criminal justice, sociology, psychology, liberal arts, or a related field; strong writing and analytical skills; minimum GPA of 3.0; for doctorate, GRE General Test, major in criminal justice, sociology, psychology, liberal arts, or a related field; strong writing and analytical skills. Additional exam requirements/recommendations for international students: required—TOEFL, IELTS. Electronic applications accepted.

Wayland Baptist University, Graduate Programs, Programs in Behavioral and Social Sciences, Plainview, TX 79072-6998. Offers counseling (MA); criminal justice (MACJ); government administration (MPA); history (MA); homeland security (MPA); humanities (MAH); justice administration (MPA). *Program availability:* Part-time, evening/weekend, 100% online, blended/hybrid learning. *Degree requirements:* For master's, comprehensive exam. *Entrance requirements:* For master's, GRE, MAT. Additional exam requirements/recommendations for international students: required—TOEFL (minimum score 500 paper-based; 61 iBT). Electronic applications accepted. *Expenses: Tuition:* Full-time $728; part-time $728 per semester. *Required fees:* $1218. Tuition and fees vary according to degree level, campus/location and program.

Waynesburg University, Graduate and Professional Studies, Canonsburg, PA 15370. Offers business (MBA), including energy management, finance, health systems, human resources, leadership, market development; counseling (MA), including addictions counseling, clinical mental health; counselor education and supervision (PhD); criminal investigation (MA); education (M Ed), including autism, curriculum and instruction, educational leadership, online teaching; nursing (MSN), including administration, education, informatics; nursing practice (DNP); special education (M Ed); technology (M Ed); MSN/MBA. *Accreditation:* AACN. *Program availability:* Part-time, evening/weekend. *Degree requirements:* For doctorate, thesis/dissertation. *Entrance requirements:* Additional exam requirements/recommendations for international students: required—TOEFL. Electronic applications accepted.

Wayne State University, College of Liberal Arts and Sciences, Department of Criminology and Criminal Justice, Detroit, MI 48202. Offers MS, MS/JD. *Program availability:* 100% online. *Faculty:* 8. *Students:* 4 full-time (2 women), 23 part-time (16 women); includes 8 minority (6 Black or African American, non-Hispanic/Latino; 1 Hispanic/Latino; 1 Two or more races, non-Hispanic/Latino). Average age 30. 55 applicants, 31% accepted, 9 enrolled. In 2019, 18 master's awarded. *Degree requirements:* For master's, comprehensive exam, three-credit essay, six-credit thesis, or three-credit capstone seminar. *Entrance requirements:* For master's, GRE (for applicants with a GPA of 2.75-2.99), minimum GPA of 3.0; bachelor's degree from accredited college or university; two letters of recommendation; personal statement. Additional exam requirements/recommendations for international students: required—TOEFL (minimum score 550 paper-based; 79 iBT), TWE (minimum score 5.5), Michigan English Language Assessment Battery (minimum score 85); recommended—IELTS (minimum score 6.5). *Application deadline:* For fall admission, 6/1 for domestic students, 5/1 priority date for international students; for winter admission, 10/1 for domestic students, 9/1 priority date for international students. Application fee: $50. Electronic applications accepted. *Expenses: Tuition:* Full-time $34,567. *Financial support:* In 2019–20, 11 students received support, including 2 research assistantships with tuition reimbursements available (averaging $21,000 per year), 1 teaching assistantship with tuition reimbursement available (averaging $19,967 per year); fellowships with tuition reimbursements available, scholarships/grants, health care benefits, and unspecified assistantships also available. Financial award applicants required to submit FAFSA. *Unit head:* Dr. Bradley Smith, Chair, 313-577-2705, E-mail: bradsmith@wayne.edu.

Criminal Justice and Criminology

Application contact: Dr. Bonnie Wu, Associate Professor/Graduate Director, 313-577-1672, Fax: 313-577-9977, E-mail: yuningwu@wayne.edu.
Website: http://clas.wayne.edu/CRJ/

Webber International University, Graduate School of Business, Babson Park, FL 33827-0096. Offers accounting (MBA); business (MBA); criminal justice management (MBA); international business (MBA); sport business management (MBA). *Program availability:* Part-time, evening/weekend, 100% online, blended/hybrid learning. *Faculty:* 10 full-time (5 women), 2 part-time/adjunct (0 women). *Students:* 65 full-time (33 women), 5 part-time (2 women); includes 19 minority (13 Black or African American, non-Hispanic/Latino; 1 Asian, non-Hispanic/Latino; 5 Hispanic/Latino), 7 international. Average age 28. 86 applicants, 47% accepted, 31 enrolled. In 2019, 41 master's awarded. *Degree requirements:* For master's, International Learning Experience required for the master in International Business, other majors have a practicum project. *Entrance requirements:* For master's, three recommendation letters, resume, essay, official transcripts from all colleges and universities attended. Additional exam requirements/recommendations for international students: required—TOEFL (minimum score 500 paper-based; 61 iBT), IELTS (minimum score 6). *Application deadline:* For fall admission, 8/1 for domestic students, 6/1 for international students; for spring admission, 1/1 for domestic students. Applications are processed on a rolling basis. Application fee: $0. Electronic applications accepted. *Expenses:* Tuition: Full-time $17,496; part-time $8746 per year. *Financial support:* Scholarships/grants and unspecified assistantships available. Financial award application deadline: 8/1; financial award applicants required to submit FAFSA. *Unit head:* Dr. Charles Shieh, Dean, 863-638-2971, E-mail: ShiehCS@webber.edu. *Application contact:* Amanda Amico, Admissions Counselor, 863-638-2910, Fax: 863-638-1591, E-mail: admissions@webber.edu.
Website: www.webber.edu

Webster University, George Herbert Walker School of Business and Technology, Department of Business, St. Louis, MO 63119-3194. Offers business and organizational security management (MBA); decision support systems (MBA); environmental management (MBA); finance (MBA, MS); forensic accounting (MS); gerontology (MBA); human resources development (MBA); human resources management (MBA); information technology management (MBA); international business (MA, MBA); international relations (MBA); management and leadership (MBA); marketing (MBA); media communications (MBA); procurement and acquisitions management (MBA); Web services (MBA). *Accreditation:* ACBSP. *Program availability:* Part-time, evening/weekend, online learning. *Degree requirements:* For master's, comprehensive exam (for some programs), thesis (for some programs). *Entrance requirements:* Additional exam requirements/recommendations for international students: required—TOEFL.

Webster University, George Herbert Walker School of Business and Technology, Department of Management, St. Louis, MO 63119-3194. Offers business and organizational security management (MA); digital marketing management (Graduate Certificate); government contracting (Graduate Certificate); health administration (MHA); health care management (MA); health services management (MA); human resources development (MA); human resources management (MA); information technology management (MA, MS); management (D Mgt); management and leadership (MA); marketing (MA); nonprofit leadership (MA); nonprofit revenue development (Graduate Certificate); organizational development (Graduate Certificate); procurement and acquisitions management (MA); public administration (MPA); space systems operations management (MS). *Program availability:* Part-time, evening/weekend, online learning. *Degree requirements:* For master's, thesis (for some programs); for doctorate, thesis/dissertation, written exam. *Entrance requirements:* For doctorate, GMAT, 3 years of work experience, MBA. Additional exam requirements/recommendations for international students: required—TOEFL.

Western Illinois University, School of Graduate Studies, College of Education and Human Services, School of Law Enforcement and Justice Administration, Macomb, IL 61455-1390. Offers law enforcement and justice administration (MA); police executive administration (Certificate). *Program availability:* Part-time. *Entrance requirements:* For master's, GRE or MAT, minimum GPA of 3.0. Additional exam requirements/recommendations for international students: required—TOEFL (minimum score 520 paper-based; 68 iBT). Electronic applications accepted.

Western Kentucky University, Graduate School, Potter College of Arts and Letters, Department of Sociology, Bowling Green, KY 42101. Offers criminology (MA); sociology (MA). *Program availability:* Online learning. *Degree requirements:* For master's, comprehensive exam, thesis optional, final exam. *Entrance requirements:* For master's, GRE General Test, minimum GPA of 3.0. Additional exam requirements/recommendations for international students: required—TOEFL (minimum score 555 paper-based; 79 iBT).

Western Oregon University, Graduate Programs, College of Liberal Arts and Sciences, Division of Social Science, Monmouth, OR 97361. Offers criminal justice (MA, MS). *Program availability:* Part-time, evening/weekend. *Degree requirements:* For master's, thesis optional, written exams. *Entrance requirements:* For master's, minimum GPA of 3.0. Additional exam requirements/recommendations for international students: required—TOEFL (minimum score 550 paper-based; 79 iBT), IELTS (minimum score 6.5).

Westfield State University, College of Graduate and Continuing Education, Department of Criminal Justice, Westfield, MA 01086. Offers MS. *Program availability:* Part-time, evening/weekend. *Degree requirements:* For master's, comprehensive exam, thesis (for some programs). *Entrance requirements:* For master's, GRE General Test or MAT, minimum undergraduate GPA of 2.8. Additional exam requirements/recommendations for international students: recommended—TOEFL (minimum score 550 paper-based; 79 iBT).

Westfield State University, College of Graduate and Continuing Education, Department of Political Science, Westfield, MA 01086. Offers criminal justice administration (MPA); non-profit management (MPA); public management (MPA). *Program availability:* Part-time, evening/weekend. *Degree requirements:* For master's, comprehensive exam, thesis (for some programs). *Entrance requirements:* For master's, GRE General Test or MAT, minimum undergraduate GPA of 2.8. Additional exam requirements/recommendations for international students: recommended—TOEFL (minimum score 550 paper-based; 79 iBT).

West Texas A&M University, College of Education and Social Sciences, Department of Political Science and Criminal Justice, Canyon, TX 79015. Offers criminal justice (MA). *Program availability:* Part-time, evening/weekend. *Degree requirements:* For master's, comprehensive exam, thesis optional. *Entrance requirements:* For master's, GRE General Test. Additional exam requirements/recommendations for international students: required—TOEFL. Electronic applications accepted.

West Virginia State University, Master of Science Program in Law Enforcement and Administration, Institute, WV 25112-1000. Offers MS. *Degree requirements:* For master's, comprehensive exam, internship, paper. *Entrance requirements:* For master's, GRE (50th Percentile) or MAT (50th Percentile), minimum undergraduate GPA of 2.7, 3 letters of recommendation, completion of course in statistics/research methods, interview. Additional exam requirements/recommendations for international students: required—TOEFL (minimum score 550 paper-based). Electronic applications accepted.

Wichita State University, Graduate School, Fairmount College of Liberal Arts and Sciences, School of Community Affairs, Wichita, KS 67260. Offers criminal justice (MA). *Program availability:* Part-time, 100% online, blended/hybrid learning.

Widener University, College of Arts and Sciences, Program in Criminal Justice, Chester, PA 19013-5792. Offers MA, Psy D/MA. *Program availability:* Part-time, evening/weekend. *Degree requirements:* For master's, project. *Entrance requirements:* For master's, interview, minimum undergraduate GPA of 3.0. *Expenses:* Contact institution.

Wilfrid Laurier University, Laurier Brantford, Brantford, ON N3T 2Y3, Canada. Offers criminology (MA), including culture, crime and policy, international crime and justice, media criminology. *Degree requirements:* For master's, thesis. *Entrance requirements:* For master's, honours bachelor's degree with major in criminology or equivalent degree; minimum B+ average in final year and in all criminology courses. Additional exam requirements/recommendations for international students: required—TOEFL (minimum score 89 iBT). Electronic applications accepted.

Wilmington University, College of Social and Behavioral Sciences, New Castle, DE 19720-6491. Offers administration of human services (MS); administration of justice (MS); clinical mental health counseling (MS); homeland security (MS). *Accreditation:* ACA. *Program availability:* Part-time, evening/weekend. *Entrance requirements:* Additional exam requirements/recommendations for international students: required—TOEFL (minimum score 500 paper-based). Electronic applications accepted.

Wright State University, Graduate School, College of Liberal Arts, Program in Applied Behavioral Science, Criminal Justice and Social Problems, Dayton, OH 45435. Offers criminal justice and social problems (MA). *Degree requirements:* For master's, thesis optional. *Entrance requirements:* Additional exam requirements/recommendations for international students: required—TOEFL.

Xavier University, College of Professional Sciences, Department of Criminal Justice, Cincinnati, OH 45207. Offers MS. *Program availability:* Part-time, evening/weekend. *Degree requirements:* For master's, comprehensive exam, thesis. *Entrance requirements:* For master's, MAT, GRE, or LSAT, minimum GPA of 2.7; official transcript; 2 letters of recommendation. Additional exam requirements/recommendations for international students: required—TOEFL (minimum score 550 paper-based; 79 iBT). Electronic applications accepted. Application fee is waived when completed online. *Expenses:* Contact institution.

Youngstown State University, College of Graduate Studies, Bitonte College of Health and Human Services, Department of Criminal Justice and Forensic Sciences, Youngstown, OH 44555-0001. Offers criminal justice (MS). *Program availability:* Part-time, evening/weekend. *Degree requirements:* For master's, thesis optional. *Entrance requirements:* For master's, minimum GPA of 2.7. Additional exam requirements/recommendations for international students: required—TOEFL.

Forensic Sciences

Alabama State University, College of Science, Mathematics and Technology, Department of Physical Sciences, Montgomery, AL 36101-0271. Offers MS. *Faculty:* 4 full-time (1 woman). *Students:* 7 full-time (all women), 1 (woman) part-time; includes 7 minority (all Black or African American, non-Hispanic/Latino), 1 international. Average age 25. 14 applicants, 7% accepted, 1 enrolled. In 2019, 4 master's awarded. *Degree requirements:* For master's, comprehensive exam, thesis or alternative. *Entrance requirements:* Additional exam requirements/recommendations for international students: required—TOEFL (minimum score 500 paper-based). *Application deadline:* For fall admission, 4/15 for domestic and international students; for spring admission, 11/15 for domestic and international students; for summer admission, 3/15 for domestic and international students. Applications are processed on a rolling basis. Application fee: $25. Electronic applications accepted. *Expenses:* Contact institution. *Financial support:* Research assistantships, teaching assistantships, Federal Work-Study, scholarships/grants, tuition waivers (partial), and unspecified assistantships available. Financial award application deadline: 6/30; financial award applicants required to submit FAFSA. *Unit head:* Dr. Robery L. Green, Chair of Physical Sciences, 334-229-4316, E-mail: rgreen@alasu.edu. *Application contact:* Dr. Ed Brown, Dean of Graduate Studies, 334-229-4274, Fax: 334-229-4928, E-mail: ebrown@alasu.edu.
Website: http://www.alasu.edu/academics/colleges—departments/science-mathematics-technology/physical-sciences/index.aspx

Alliant International University–Irvine, California School of Forensic Studies, Irvine, CA 92606. Offers Psy D. *Degree requirements:* For doctorate, comprehensive exam, thesis/dissertation, internship. *Entrance requirements:* For doctorate, minimum GPA of 3.0, recommendations, essay. Additional exam requirements/recommendations for international students: required—TOEFL (minimum score 80 iBT), TWE (minimum score 5). Electronic applications accepted.

Arcadia University, College of Arts and Sciences, Program in Forensic Science, Glenside, PA 19038-3295. Offers MSFS. *Faculty:* 3 full-time (2 women). *Students:* 21 full-time (19 women), 4 part-time (all women); includes 2 minority (both Black or African American, non-Hispanic/Latino). In 2019, 18 master's awarded. *Degree requirements:* For master's, 12 semester hours of research, 6 to 12 semester hours of practicum/internship, plus mandatory participation in a symposium/seminar series. *Entrance requirements:* For master's, Test scores are not required of applicants with a cumulative science GPA of 3.4 or greater. Test scores from the Graduate Record Examination (GRE) or the Medical College Admission Test (MCAT), taken within the last five years are required for all other applicants. Additional exam requirements/recommendations for international students: required—TOEFL. *Application deadline:* For fall admission, 1/15 for domestic and international students. Applications are processed on a rolling basis. Application fee: $25. *Expenses:* Contact institution. *Unit head:* Dr. Karen Scott, Program

Forensic Sciences

Director, 215-572-2102. *Application contact:* Office of Enrollment Management, 215-572-2910, Fax: 215-572-4049, E-mail: admiss@arcadia.edu.

Bay Path University, Program in Applied Laboratory Science and Operations, Longmeadow, MA 01106-2292. Offers MS. *Program availability:* Part-time, evening/weekend. *Entrance requirements:* For master's, Bachelor of Science in a natural science (such as, Biology, Chemistry, Physics, etc.) is required; completed application; official undergraduate and graduate transcripts (GOA of 3.0 or higher is preferred); original essay of at least 250 words on "Why the MS in Applied Laboratory Science & Operations is important to my goals." Electronic applications accepted. Application fee is waived when completed online. *Expenses:* Contact institution.

Boston University, School of Medicine, Graduate Medical Sciences, Program in Biomedical Forensic Sciences, Boston, MA 02215. Offers MS. *Program availability:* Part-time, evening/weekend, online learning. *Application deadline:* For fall admission, 7/1 for domestic and international students. *Unit head:* Dr. Robin Cotton, Director, E-mail: rwcotton@bu.edu. *Application contact:* GMS Admissions Office, 617-358-9518, Fax: 617-358-2913, E-mail: gmsbusm@bu.edu.
Website: http://www.bumc.bu.edu/gms/bmfs/

Boston University, School of Medicine, Graduate Medical Sciences, Program in Forensic Anthropology, Boston, MA 02215. Offers MS. *Financial support:* Applicants required to submit FAFSA. *Unit head:* Dr. Tara L. Moore, Program Director, E-mail: tlmoore@bu.edu. *Application contact:* GMS Admissions Office, 617-358-9518, Fax: 617-358-2913, E-mail: gmsbusm@bu.edu.
Website: http://www.bumc.bu.edu/gms/forensicanthropology/

Buffalo State College, State University of New York, The Graduate School, School of Natural and Social Sciences, Department of Chemistry, Buffalo, NY 14222-1095. Offers forensic science (MS). *Program availability:* Part-time, evening/weekend. *Degree requirements:* For master's, thesis (for some programs), project. *Entrance requirements:* For master's, minimum GPA of 2.6, New York teaching certificate (MS Ed). Additional exam requirements/recommendations for international students: required—TOEFL (minimum score 550 paper-based).

Carlow University, College of Leadership and Social Change, MBA Program, Pittsburgh, PA 15213-3165. Offers fraud and forensics (MBA); healthcare management (MBA); human resource management (MBA); leadership and management (MBA); project management (MBA). *Program availability:* Part-time, evening/weekend, 100% online, blended/hybrid learning. *Students:* 52 full-time (39 women), 24 part-time (20 women); includes 28 minority (23 Black or African American, non-Hispanic/Latino; 3 Asian, non-Hispanic/Latino; 2 Two or more races, non-Hispanic/Latino). Average age 36. 33 applicants, 100% accepted, 24 enrolled. In 2019, 39 master's awarded. *Entrance requirements:* For master's, minimum undergraduate GPA of 3.0 (preferred); personal essay; resume; official transcripts; two professional recommendations. Additional exam requirements/recommendations for international students: required—TOEFL (minimum score 550 paper-based). *Application deadline:* Applications are processed on a rolling basis. Electronic applications accepted. *Financial support:* Application deadline: 4/1; applicants required to submit FAFSA. *Unit head:* Dr. Howard Stern, Program Director, MBA Program, 412-578-8828, E-mail: hastern@carlow.edu. *Application contact:* Dr. Howard Stern, Program Director, MBA Program, 412-578-8828, E-mail: hastern@carlow.edu.
Website: http://www.carlow.edu/Business_Administration.aspx

Cedar Crest College, Program in Forensic Science, Allentown, PA 18104-6196. Offers MS. *Degree requirements:* For master's, thesis. *Entrance requirements:* For master's, GRE. Electronic applications accepted. *Expenses:* Contact institution.

Champlain College, Graduate Studies, Burlington, VT 05402-0670. Offers business (MBA); digital forensic science (MS); early childhood education (M Ed); emergent media (MFA, MS); executive leadership (MS); health care administration (MS); information security operations (MS); law (MS); mediation and applied conflict studies (MS). *Program availability:* Part-time, online learning. *Degree requirements:* For master's, capstone project. *Entrance requirements:* Additional exam requirements/recommendations for international students: required—TOEFL (minimum score 550 paper-based; 80 iBT). Electronic applications accepted.

DeSales University, Division of Liberal Arts and Social Sciences, Center Valley, PA 18034-9568. Offers criminal justice (MCJ); digital forensics (MCJ, Postbaccalaureate Certificate); education (M Ed), including instructional technology, secondary education, special education, teaching English to speakers of other languages; investigative forensics (MCJ, Postbaccalaureate Certificate). *Program availability:* Part-time, 100% online, blended/hybrid learning. *Faculty:* 5 full-time (3 women), 15 part-time/adjunct (9 women). *Students:* 68 full-time (43 women), 115 part-time (72 women); includes 34 minority (8 Black or African American, non-Hispanic/Latino; 1 Asian, non-Hispanic/Latino; 19 Hispanic/Latino; 1 Native Hawaiian or other Pacific Islander, non-Hispanic/Latino; 5 Two or more races, non-Hispanic/Latino), 1 international. Average age 33. 135 applicants, 48% accepted, 63 enrolled. In 2019, 49 master's awarded. *Entrance requirements:* For master's, bachelor's degree from accredited institution, minimum undergraduate GPA of 3.0, personal statement showing potential of graduate work, three letters of recommendation, professional goal statement. Additional exam requirements/recommendations for international students: required—TOEFL. *Application deadline:* Applications are processed on a rolling basis. Application fee: $50. Electronic applications accepted. *Expenses: Tuition:* Full-time $855; part-time $855 per credit hour. Tuition and fees vary according to program. *Financial support:* Applicants required to submit FAFSA. *Unit head:* Ronald Nordone, Dean of Graduate Education, 610-282-1100 Ext. 1289, E-mail: ronald.nordone@desales.edu. *Application contact:* Julia Ferraro, Director of Graduate Admissions, 610-282-1100 Ext. 1768, E-mail: gradadmissions@desales.edu.

DeSales University, Division of Science and Mathematics, Center Valley, PA 18034-9568. Offers cyber security (Postbaccalaureate Certificate); data analytics (Postbaccalaureate Certificate); information systems (MS), including cyber security, digital forensics, healthcare information management, project management. *Program availability:* Part-time, evening/weekend, 100% online, blended/hybrid learning. *Faculty:* 2 full-time (both women), 5 part-time/adjunct (1 woman). *Students:* 2 full-time (0 women), 17 part-time (4 women); includes 3 minority (2 Asian, non-Hispanic/Latino; 1 Two or more races, non-Hispanic/Latino). Average age 36. 15 applicants, 60% accepted, 9 enrolled. In 2019, 6 master's awarded. *Entrance requirements:* For master's, GRE or GMAT, bachelor's degree in computer-related discipline from accredited college or university, minimum undergraduate GPA of 3.0, personal statement, three letters of recommendation. Additional exam requirements/recommendations for international students: required—TOEFL. *Application deadline:* Applications are processed on a rolling basis. Application fee: $50. Electronic applications accepted. *Expenses:* Contact institution. *Financial support:* Applicants required to submit FAFSA. *Unit head:* Dr. Ronald Nordone, Dean of Graduate Studies, 610-282-1100 Ext. 1289, E-mail: Ronald.Nordone@desale.edu. *Application contact:* Julia Ferraro, Director of Graduate Admissions, 610-282-1100 Ext. 1768, E-mail: gradadmissions@desales.edu.
Website: http://www.desales.edu/home/academics/graduate-studies/programs-of-study/msis—master-of-science-in-information-systems

Duquesne University, Bayer School of Natural and Environmental Sciences, Program in Forensic Science and Law, Pittsburgh, PA 15282-0001. Offers MS. *Degree requirements:* For master's, comprehensive exam. *Entrance requirements:* For master's, SAT or ACT, recommendation form; minimum total QPA of 3.0, 2.5 in math and science. Electronic applications accepted. *Expenses:* Contact institution.

Emporia State University, Department of Biological Sciences, Emporia, KS 66801-5415. Offers botany (MS); environmental biology (MS); forensic science (MS); general biology (MS); microbial and cellular biology (MS); zoology (MS). *Program availability:* Part-time. *Degree requirements:* For master's, comprehensive exam or thesis. *Entrance requirements:* For master's, GRE, appropriate undergraduate degree, interview, letters of reference. Additional exam requirements/recommendations for international students: required—TOEFL (minimum score 520 paper-based; 68 iBT). Electronic applications accepted. *Expenses: Tuition, area resident:* Full-time $6394; part-time $266.41 per credit hour. Tuition, state resident: full-time $6394; part-time $266.41 per credit hour. Tuition, nonresident: full-time $20,128; part-time $828.66 per credit hour. *International tuition:* $20,128 full-time. *Required fees:* $2183; $90.95 per credit hour. Tuition and fees vary according to campus/location and program.

Emporia State University, Department of Physical Sciences, Emporia, KS 66801-5415. Offers forensic science (MS); geospatial analysis (Postbaccalaureate Certificate); physical science (MS). *Program availability:* Part-time, online learning. *Degree requirements:* For master's, comprehensive exam or thesis; qualifying exam. *Entrance requirements:* For master's, appropriate undergraduate degree. Additional exam requirements/recommendations for international students: required—TOEFL (minimum score 520 paper-based; 68 iBT). Electronic applications accepted. *Expenses: Tuition, area resident:* Full-time $6394; part-time $266.41 per credit hour. Tuition, state resident: full-time $6394; part-time $266.41 per credit hour. Tuition, nonresident: full-time $20,128; part-time $828.66 per credit hour. *International tuition:* $20,128 full-time. *Required fees:* $2183; $90.95 per credit hour. Tuition and fees vary according to campus/location and program.

Emporia State University, Program in Forensic Science, Emporia, KS 66801-5415. Offers MS. *Program availability:* Part-time. *Entrance requirements:* For master's, bachelor's degree in a natural science or in forensic science (recommended), three letters of reference, official transcripts, minimum undergraduate GPA of 3.0. Additional exam requirements/recommendations for international students: required—TOEFL. Electronic applications accepted. *Expenses: Tuition, area resident:* Full-time $6394; part-time $266.41 per credit hour. Tuition, state resident: full-time $6394; part-time $266.41 per credit hour. Tuition, nonresident: full-time $20,128; part-time $828.66 per credit hour. *International tuition:* $20,128 full-time. *Required fees:* $2183; $90.95 per credit hour. Tuition and fees vary according to campus/location and program.

Florida Gulf Coast University, College of Arts and Sciences, Program in Forensic Studies, Fort Myers, FL 33965-6565. Offers MS. *Program availability:* Part-time. *Entrance requirements:* For master's, GRE General Test, minimum GPA of 3.0. Additional exam requirements/recommendations for international students: required—TOEFL (minimum score 550 paper-based). Electronic applications accepted. *Expenses: Tuition, area resident:* Full-time $6974; part-time $4350 per credit hour. Tuition, state resident: full-time $6974; part-time $4350 per credit hour. Tuition, nonresident: full-time $28,169; part-time $17,595 per credit hour. *International tuition:* $28,169 full-time. *Required fees:* $2027; $1267 per credit hour. $507 per semester. Tuition and fees vary according to course load.

Florida International University, College of Arts, Sciences, and Education, Department of Chemistry and Biochemistry, Miami, FL 33199. Offers chemistry (MS, PhD); forensic science (MS, PSM, PhD). *Program availability:* Part-time, evening/weekend. *Faculty:* 41 full-time (13 women), 20 part-time/adjunct (9 women). *Students:* 154 full-time (88 women), 9 part-time (5 women); includes 69 minority (13 Black or African American, non-Hispanic/Latino; 5 Asian, non-Hispanic/Latino; 45 Hispanic/Latino; 6 Two or more races, non-Hispanic/Latino), 58 international. Average age 28. 187 applicants, 32% accepted, 43 enrolled. In 2019, 28 master's, 29 doctorates awarded. *Degree requirements:* For master's, thesis (for some programs); for doctorate, comprehensive exam, thesis/dissertation. *Entrance requirements:* For master's and doctorate, GRE General Test, minimum GPA of 3.0, 3 letters of recommendation, resume, letter of intent. Additional exam requirements/recommendations for international students: required—TOEFL (minimum score 550 paper-based; 80 iBT). *Application deadline:* For fall admission, 6/1 for domestic students, 4/1 for international students; for spring admission, 10/1 for domestic students, 9/1 for international students. Applications are processed on a rolling basis. Application fee: $30. Electronic applications accepted. *Expenses: Tuition, area resident:* Full-time $8912; part-time $446 per credit hour. Tuition, state resident: full-time $8912; part-time $446 per credit hour. Tuition, nonresident: full-time $21,393; part-time $992 per credit hour. *Required fees:* $2194. *Financial support:* Institutionally sponsored loans and scholarships/grants available. Financial award application deadline: 3/1; financial award applicants required to submit FAFSA. *Unit head:* Dr. Yong Cai, Chair, 305-348-6210, Fax: 305-348-3772, E-mail: yong.cai@fiu.edu. *Application contact:* Nanett Rojas, Manager, Admissions Operations, 305-348-7464, Fax: 305-348-7441, E-mail: gradadm@fiu.edu.

George Mason University, College of Science, Program in Forensic Science, Fairfax, VA 22030. Offers MS. *Degree requirements:* For master's, comprehensive exam (for some programs), research project or thesis; capstone course; 36 credits, minimum GPA of 3.0. *Entrance requirements:* For master's, undergraduate transcript; 3 letters of recommendation; interest letter; minimum GPA of 3.0. Additional exam requirements/recommendations for international students: required—TOEFL (minimum score 575 paper-based; 88 iBT), IELTS (minimum score 6.5), PTE (minimum score 59). Electronic applications accepted. *Expenses:* Contact institution.

The George Washington University, Columbian College of Arts and Sciences, Department of Forensic Sciences, Washington, DC 20052. Offers crime scene investigation (MFS); forensic chemistry (MFS); forensic molecular biology (MFS); forensic toxicology (MFS); high-technology crime investigation (MS); security management (MFS). *Program availability:* Part-time, evening/weekend. *Entrance requirements:* For master's, GRE General Test, minimum GPA of 3.0. Additional exam requirements/recommendations for international students: required—TOEFL (minimum score 550 paper-based; 80 iBT). Electronic applications accepted.

Georgia State University, Andrew Young School of Policy Studies, School of Social Work, Atlanta, GA 30294. Offers child welfare leadership (Certificate); community partnerships (MSW); forensic social work (Certificate). *Accreditation:* CSWE. *Program availability:* Part-time. *Faculty:* 12 full-time (8 women), 4 part-time/adjunct (2 women). *Students:* 118 full-time (105 women), 19 part-time (18 women); includes 91 minority (76 Black or African American, non-Hispanic/Latino; 3 Asian, non-Hispanic/Latino; 9 Hispanic/Latino; 3 Two or more races, non-Hispanic/Latino). Average age 30. 183 applicants, 56% accepted, 47 enrolled. In 2019, 62 master's awarded. *Entrance requirements:* For master's and Certificate, GRE. Additional exam requirements/recommendations for international students: required—TOEFL (minimum score 550 paper-based; 100 iBT) or IELTS (minimum score 7). *Application deadline:* For fall admission, 2/1 priority date for domestic and international students. Application fee: $50. Electronic applications accepted. *Expenses: Tuition, area resident:* Full-time $7164;

part-time $398 per credit hour. Tuition, state resident: full-time $7164; part-time $398 per credit hour. Tuition, nonresident: full-time $22,662; part-time $1259 per credit hour. *International tuition:* $22,662 full-time. *Required fees:* $2128; $312 per credit hour. Tuition and fees vary according to course load and program. *Financial support:* In 2019–20, research assistantships with tuition reimbursements (averaging $4,000 per year), teaching assistantships with tuition reimbursements (averaging $4,000 per year) were awarded; career-related internships or fieldwork, institutionally sponsored loans, scholarships/grants, tuition waivers, and unspecified assistantships also available. Financial award application deadline: 2/1; financial award applicants required to submit FAFSA. *Unit head:* Brian Bride, Director of School of Social Work, 404-413-1052, Fax: 404-413-1075, E-mail: bbride@gsu.edu. *Application contact:* Brian Bride, Director of School of Social Work, 404-413-1052, Fax: 404-413-1075, E-mail: bbride@gsu.edu.
Website: http://aysps.gsu.edu/socialwork

Golden Gate University, School of Accounting, San Francisco, CA 94105-2968. Offers financial accounting and reporting (M Ac, MSA, Graduate Certificate); forensic accounting (M Ac, MSA, Graduate Certificate); internal auditing (M Ac, MSA, Certificate); management accounting (M Ac, MSA); taxation (M Ac, MSA). *Program availability:* Part-time, evening/weekend. *Entrance requirements:* For master's, minimum GPA of 3.0. Additional exam requirements/recommendations for international students: required—TOEFL (minimum score 550 paper-based), IELTS (minimum score 6.5). Electronic applications accepted. *Expenses:* Contact institution.

Indiana University-Purdue University Indianapolis, School of Science, Forensic and Investigative Sciences Program, Indianapolis, IN 46202. Offers MS. *Degree requirements:* For master's, thesis optional. *Entrance requirements:* For master's, GRE General Test, bachelor's degree in chemistry, biology, forensic science, pharmacology/toxicology, or related science from accredited institution; minimum GPA of 3.0 for all undergraduate work.

Iona College, School of Arts and Science, Department of Criminal Justice, New Rochelle, NY 10801-1890. Offers criminal justice (MS); cybercrime and security (AC); forensic criminology and criminal justice systems (Certificate). *Program availability:* Part-time, evening/weekend. *Faculty:* 4 full-time (1 woman), 5 part-time/adjunct (1 woman). *Students:* 17 full-time (12 women), 8 part-time (3 women); includes 15 minority (4 Black or African American, non-Hispanic/Latino; 1 Asian, non-Hispanic/Latino; 10 Hispanic/Latino). Average age 26. 20 applicants, 70% accepted, 9 enrolled. In 2019, 13 master's, 5 other advanced degrees awarded. *Degree requirements:* For master's, thesis (for some programs), thesis or literature review. *Entrance requirements:* For master's, minimum GPA of 3.0. Additional exam requirements/recommendations for international students: required—TOEFL (minimum score 550 paper-based; 80 iBT), IELTS (minimum score 6.5). *Application deadline:* For fall admission, 8/1 priority date for domestic students, 5/1 priority date for international students; for spring admission, 1/1 priority date for domestic students, 9/1 priority date for international students. Applications are processed on a rolling basis. Electronic applications accepted. *Financial support:* In 2019–20, 17 students received support. Scholarships/grants and unspecified assistantships available. Financial award application deadline: 4/15; financial award applicants required to submit FAFSA. *Unit head:* Marcus Aldredge, PhD, Chair, 914-633-2594, E-mail: maldredge@iona.edu. *Application contact:* Christopher Kash, Assistant Director of Graduate Admissions, 914-633-2403, Fax: 914-633-2277, E-mail: ckash@iona.edu.
Website: http://www.iona.edu/Academics/School-of-Arts-Science/Departments/Criminal-Justice/Graduate-Programs.aspx

James Madison University, The Graduate School, College of Integrated Science and Engineering, Program in Computer Science, Harrisonburg, VA 22807. Offers digital forensics (MS); information security (MS). *Program availability:* Online learning. *Students:* 3 full-time (1 woman), 55 part-time (11 women); includes 14 minority (8 Black or African American, non-Hispanic/Latino; 3 Asian, non-Hispanic/Latino; 3 Hispanic/Latino), 3 international. Average age 30. In 2019, 2 master's awarded. Application fee: $60. Electronic applications accepted. *Financial support:* In 2019–20, 2 students received support. Fellowships, Federal Work-Study, and assistantships (averaging $7911) available. Financial award application deadline: 3/1; financial award applicants required to submit FAFSA. *Unit head:* Dr. Sharon J. Simmons, Department Head, 540-568-4196, E-mail: simmonsj@jmu.edu. *Application contact:* Lynette D. Michael, Director of Graduate Admissions, 540-568-6131 Ext. 6395, Fax: 540-568-7860, E-mail: michaeld@jmu.edu.
Website: http://www.jmu.edu/cs/

John Jay College of Criminal Justice of the City University of New York, Graduate Studies, Programs in Criminal Justice, New York, NY 10019. Offers criminal justice (MA, PhD); criminology and deviance (PhD); forensic psychology (PhD); forensic science (PhD); international crime and justice (MA); law and philosophy (PhD); organizational behavior (PhD); public policy (PhD). *Program availability:* Part-time, evening/weekend. Terminal master's awarded for partial completion of doctoral program. *Degree requirements:* For master's, thesis or alternative; for doctorate, one foreign language, thesis/dissertation. *Entrance requirements:* For master's, GRE General Test, minimum B average; for doctorate, GRE General Test. Additional exam requirements/recommendations for international students: required—TOEFL (minimum score 500 paper-based).

La Salle University, School of Arts and Sciences, Program in Economic Crime Forensics, Philadelphia, PA 19141-1199. Offers corporate fraud (MS); fraud and forensic accounting (Certificate); network security (MS). *Program availability:* Part-time, evening/weekend, online only, 100% online. *Entrance requirements:* For master's, minimum GPA of 3.0; professional resume; letters of recommendation; personal interview; for Certificate, professional resume, 200-word essay. Additional exam requirements/recommendations for international students: required—TOEFL. Electronic applications accepted. Application fee is waived when completed online. *Expenses:* Contact institution.

Long Island University - Brooklyn, School of Health Professions, Brooklyn, NY 11201-8423. Offers athletic training and sport sciences (MS); community health (MS Ed); exercise science (MS); forensic social work (Advanced Certificate); occupational therapy (MS); physical therapy (DPT); physician assistant (MS); public health (MPH); social work (MSW); speech-language pathology (MS). *Accreditation:* AOTA; CEPH. *Degree requirements:* For master's, comprehensive exam (for some programs), thesis (for some programs); for doctorate, comprehensive exam (for some programs). *Entrance requirements:* For master's and doctorate, GRE. Additional exam requirements/recommendations for international students: required—TOEFL (minimum score 550 paper-based; 79 iBT). Electronic applications accepted.

Marshall University, Academic Affairs Division, Forensic Science Center, Huntington, WV 25755. Offers MS, Graduate Certificate. *Degree requirements:* For master's, comprehensive exam, thesis optional. *Entrance requirements:* For master's, GRE General Test, undergraduate degree in a natural science, forensic science, or equivalent course work in a related field; 1 year of undergraduate coursework in general chemistry, organic chemistry, physics and biology, with 1 year of associated laboratory for each course. Additional exam requirements/recommendations for international students: required—TOEFL. *Expenses:* Contact institution.

McGill University, Faculty of Graduate and Postdoctoral Studies, Faculty of Dentistry, Montréal, QC H3A 2T5, Canada. Offers forensic dentistry (Certificate); oral and maxillofacial surgery (M Sc, PhD). *Accreditation:* ADA.

Mercyhurst University, Graduate Studies, Program in Anthropology, Erie, PA 16546. Offers archaeology and geological archaeology (MS); forensic and biological anthropology (MS). *Entrance requirements:* For master's, GRE or MAT, undergraduate degree in related field, interview, resume, essay, three professional references, transcripts. Additional exam requirements/recommendations for international students: required—TOEFL.

Michigan State University, The Graduate School, College of Social Science, School of Criminal Justice, East Lansing, MI 48824. Offers criminal justice (MS, PhD); forensic science (MS); law enforcement intelligence and analysis (MS). *Program availability:* Online learning. *Entrance requirements:* Additional exam requirements/recommendations for international students: required—TOEFL. Electronic applications accepted.

Middle Georgia State University, Office of Graduate Studies, Macon, GA 31206. Offers adult/gerontology acute care nurse practitioner (MSN); information technology (MS), including health informatics, information security and digital forensics, software development. *Entrance requirements:* For master's, GRE. Additional exam requirements/recommendations for international students: required—TOEFL (minimum score 523 paper-based; 69 iBT). *Expenses:* Contact institution.

Missouri Western State University, Program in Forensic Investigations, St. Joseph, MO 64507-2294. Offers MAS, Graduate Certificate. *Program availability:* Part-time. *Students:* 8 full-time (6 women), 10 part-time (5 women); includes 5 minority (1 Black or African American, non-Hispanic/Latino; 2 Asian, non-Hispanic/Latino; 2 Two or more races, non-Hispanic/Latino), 1 international. Average age 25. 18 applicants, 83% accepted, 10 enrolled. In 2019, 7 master's awarded. *Entrance requirements:* For master's, Completion of a B.A. or B.S. degree in any discipline from an accredited college or university; Minimum overall G.P.A. of 2.75. Completion of a 300 or 400 level undergraduate research course with a grade of C or higher. Personal statement describing how the Forensic Investigations degree will further their career goals. 2 letters of reference. Additional exam requirements/recommendations for international students: recommended—TOEFL (minimum score 79 iBT), IELTS (minimum score 6). *Application deadline:* For fall admission, 7/15 for domestic and international students; for spring admission, 11/1 for domestic and international students; for summer admission, 4/29 for domestic and international students. Applications are processed on a rolling basis. Application fee: $45 ($50 for international students). Electronic applications accepted. *Expenses:* Tuition, state resident: full-time $6469.02; part-time $359.39 per credit hour. Tuition, nonresident: full-time $11,581; part-time $643.39 per credit hour. *Required fees:* $345.20; $99.10 per credit hour. Tuition and fees vary according to course load, campus/location and program. *Financial support:* Scholarships/grants and unspecified assistantships available. Support available to part-time students. *Unit head:* Dr. Monty Smith, Forensics Graduate Program Director, 816-271-4434, E-mail: msmith84@missouriwestern.edu. *Application contact:* Dr. Monty Smith, Forensics Graduate Program Director, 816-271-4434, E-mail: msmith84@missouriwestern.edu.
Website: https://www.missouriwestern.edu/criminal-justice-legal-studies/forensic-investigation/

National University, College of Letters and Sciences, La Jolla, CA 92037-1011. Offers biology (MS); counseling psychology (MA), including licensed professional clinical counseling, marriage and family therapy; creative writing (MFA); English (MA); film studies (MA); forensic and crime scene investigations (Certificate); forensic sciences (MFS); human behavior (MA); mathematics for educators (MS); performance psychology (MA); strategic communications (MA). *Program availability:* Part-time, evening/weekend, 100% online, blended/hybrid learning. *Degree requirements:* For master's, thesis (for some programs). *Entrance requirements:* For master's, interview, minimum GPA of 2.5. Additional exam requirements/recommendations for international students: required—TOEFL (minimum score 550 paper-based; 79 iBT), IELTS (minimum score 6). Electronic applications accepted. *Expenses: Tuition:* Full-time $442; part-time $442 per unit.

Niagara University, Graduate Division of Arts and Sciences, Niagara University, NY 14109. Offers criminal justice (MS), including criminal justice administration; information security and digital forensics (MS); interdisciplinary studies (MA). *Program availability:* Part-time. *Entrance requirements:* Additional exam requirements/recommendations for international students: required—TOEFL (minimum score 550 paper-based; 79 iBT), IELTS (minimum score 6). Electronic applications accepted. *Expenses:* Contact institution.

Oklahoma State University Center for Health Sciences, Graduate Program in Forensic Sciences, Tulsa, OK 74107-1898. Offers forensic sciences (MS), including arson and explosives investigation, forensic biology/DNA, forensic document examination, forensic pathology/death scene investigations, forensic psychology, forensic science administration, forensic toxicology/trace evidence. *Program availability:* Part-time, evening/weekend, 100% online, blended/hybrid learning. *Degree requirements:* For master's, comprehensive exam, thesis (for some programs), thesis or creative component. *Entrance requirements:* For master's, GRE (for thesis tracks); GRE or MAT (for options in arson and explosives investigation, forensic science administration, and forensic document examination), professional experience (for options in arson and explosives investigation, forensic science administration and forensic document examination). Additional exam requirements/recommendations for international students: required—TOEFL (minimum score 100 iBT) or IELTS (minimum score 7.0). Electronic applications accepted.

Pace University, Dyson College of Arts and Sciences, Program in Forensic Science, New York, NY 10038. Offers MS. *Program availability:* Part-time, evening/weekend. *Degree requirements:* For master's, thesis. *Entrance requirements:* For master's, two letters of recommendation, personal statement, resume, official transcripts. Additional exam requirements/recommendations for international students: required—TOEFL (minimum score 88 iBT). Electronic applications accepted.

Penn State University Park, Graduate School, Eberly College of Science, Program in Forensic Science, University Park, PA 16802. Offers MPS.

Philadelphia College of Osteopathic Medicine, Graduate and Professional Programs, Programs in Forensic Medicine, Philadelphia, PA 19131. Offers MS. *Program availability:* Evening/weekend. *Faculty:* 2 full-time (0 women), 2 part-time/adjunct (1 woman). *Students:* 70 full-time (56 women); includes 25 minority (12 Black or African American, non-Hispanic/Latino; 3 Asian, non-Hispanic/Latino; 2 Hispanic/Latino; 8 Two or more races, non-Hispanic/Latino), 2 international. Average age 28. 65 applicants, 51% accepted, 19 enrolled. In 2019, 28 master's awarded. *Degree requirements:* For master's, capstone project. *Entrance requirements:* For master's, minimum GPA of 3.0; coursework in biology, chemistry, anatomy and physiology or completion of PCOM pathway program. Additional exam requirements/recommendations for international students: required—TOEFL (minimum score 79 iBT). *Application deadline:* Applications are processed on a rolling basis. Application fee: $75. Electronic applications accepted. *Expenses:* Contact institution. *Financial support:* In 2019–20, 17 students received support. Federal Work-Study, institutionally sponsored loans, and scholarships/grants available. Financial award application deadline: 3/15; financial award applicants required to submit FAFSA. *Unit head:* Dr. Gregory McDonald, Dean, School of Health Sciences, 215-871-6760, Fax: 215-871-6792. *Application contact:* Brianna Rojas, Admissions Recruiter, 215-871-6700, Fax: 215-871-6719, E-mail: briannaro@pcom.edu. Website: http://www.pcom.edu

St. Joseph's College, Long Island Campus, Program in Forensic Computing, Patchogue, NY 11772-2399. Offers MS. *Program availability:* Part-time, evening/weekend. *Faculty:* 1 full-time (0 women), 3 part-time/adjunct (1 woman). *Students:* 7 full-time (4 women), 18 part-time (7 women); includes 9 minority (4 Black or African American, non-Hispanic/Latino; 5 Hispanic/Latino). Average age 28. 18 applicants, 72% accepted, 10 enrolled. In 2019, 2 master's awarded. *Entrance requirements:* For master's, application, official transcripts, 2 letters of recommendation, current resume, 250 word written statement. Additional exam requirements/recommendations for international students: required—TOEFL (minimum score 80 iBT). *Application deadline:* Applications are processed on a rolling basis. Application fee: $25. Electronic applications accepted. *Expenses: Tuition:* Full-time $19,350; part-time $1075 per credit. *Required fees:* $410. *Financial support:* In 2019–20, 7 students received support. *Unit head:* Victoria Hong, Director of M.S. in Forensic Computing, Chairperson, Assistant Professor, 631-687-2646, E-mail: vhong@sjcny.edu. *Application contact:* Victoria Hong, Director of M.S. in Forensic Computing, Chairperson, Assistant Professor, 631-687-2646, E-mail: vhong@sjcny.edu.
Website: https://www.sjcny.edu/long-island/academics/graduate/degree/forensic-computing

St. Joseph's College, New York, Program in Forensic Computing, Brooklyn, NY 11205-3688. Offers MS. *Program availability:* Part-time, evening/weekend. *Faculty:* 1 full-time (0 women), 1 (woman) part-time/adjunct. *Students:* 6 full-time (3 women), 6 part-time (0 women); includes 9 minority (5 Black or African American, non-Hispanic/Latino; 4 Hispanic/Latino). Average age 30. 12 applicants, 83% accepted, 3 enrolled. In 2019, 3 master's awarded. *Entrance requirements:* For master's, application, official transcripts, current resume, 2 letters of recommendation, written statement. Additional exam requirements/recommendations for international students: required—TOEFL (minimum score 80 iBT). *Application deadline:* Applications are processed on a rolling basis. Application fee: $25. Electronic applications accepted. *Expenses: Tuition:* Full-time $19,350; part-time $1075 per credit. *Required fees:* $400. *Financial support:* In 2019–20, 4 students received support. *Unit head:* Dr. Joseph Pascarella, Associate Professor, 718-940-5775, E-mail: jpascarella2@sjcny.edu. *Application contact:* Roberto Figueroa, Director of Transfer, Adult and Graduate Admissions, 718-940-5828, E-mail: rfigueroa@sjcny.edu.
Website: https://www.sjcny.edu/brooklyn/academics/graduate/graduate-degrees/forensic-computing

Saint Leo University, Graduate Studies in Public Safety Administration, Saint Leo, FL 33574-6665. Offers criminal justice (MS, DCJ), including behavioral studies (MS), corrections (MS), criminal investigation (MS), criminal justice (MS), emergency and disaster management (MS), forensic science (MS), legal studies (MS); emergency and disaster management (MS), including emergency and disaster management, fire science. *Program availability:* Part-time, evening/weekend, 100% online, blended/hybrid learning. *Faculty:* 10 full-time (4 women), 26 part-time/adjunct (6 women). *Students:* 1 (woman) full-time, 761 part-time (490 women); includes 466 minority (252 Black or African American, non-Hispanic/Latino; 4 American Indian or Alaska Native, non-Hispanic/Latino; 5 Asian, non-Hispanic/Latino; 94 Hispanic/Latino; 111 Two or more races, non-Hispanic/Latino). Average age 37. 314 applicants, 82% accepted, 173 enrolled. In 2019, 236 master's, 2 doctorates awarded. *Degree requirements:* For master's, comprehensive project; for doctorate, thesis/dissertation. *Entrance requirements:* For master's, official transcripts, bachelor's degree from regionally-accredited university with minimum GPA of 3.0, statement of professional goals; for doctorate, Official transcript showing completion of Master's degree with a minimum graduate gpa of 3.25, statement of professional goals, two letter of reference (professional or personal). Additional exam requirements/recommendations for international students: required—TOEFL (minimum score 550 paper-based; 78 iBT). *Application deadline:* For fall admission, 7/1 priority date for domestic and international students; for spring admission, 11/1 priority date for domestic and international students. Applications are processed on a rolling basis. Electronic applications accepted. *Expenses:* MS in Criminal Justice $10,770 per FT yr., DCJ $14,101 per FT yr. *Financial support:* In 2019–20, 62 students received support. Scholarships/grants, health care benefits, and tuition remission for Saint Leo employees and their dependents available. Financial award application deadline: 3/1; financial award applicants required to submit FAFSA. *Unit head:* Dr. Robert Diemer, Director of Graduate Studies in Public Safety Administration, 352-588-8974, Fax: 352-588-8660, E-mail: graduatepublicsafety@saintleo.edu. *Application contact:* Saint Leo University Office of Graduate Admissions, 800-707-8846, Fax: 352-588-7873, E-mail: grad.admissions@saintleo.edu.
Website: https://www.saintleo.edu/criminal-justice-master-degree

Salve Regina University, Program in Administration of Justice and Homeland Security, Newport, RI 02840. Offers administration of justice and homeland security (MS); cybersecurity and intelligence (CGS); digital forensics (CGS); leadership in justice (CGS). *Program availability:* Part-time, evening/weekend, some in-person. *Entrance requirements:* Additional exam requirements/recommendations for international students: required—TOEFL (minimum score 600 paper-based; 100 iBT). *Application deadline:* For fall admission, 7/1 priority date for domestic students, 3/15 priority date for international students; for spring admission, 11/1 priority date for domestic students, 9/5 priority date for international students. Applications are processed on a rolling basis. Application fee: $0. Electronic applications accepted. *Financial support:* Application deadline: 3/1; applicants required to submit FAFSA. *Unit head:* Jeffrey Mace, Director, 401-341-2338, E-mail: jeffrey.mac@salve.edu. *Application contact:* Laurie Reilly, Graduate Admissions Manager, 401-341-2153, Fax: 401-341-2973, E-mail: laurie.reilly@salve.edu.
Website: http://www.salve.edu/graduate-studies/administration-of-justice-and-homeland-security

Sam Houston State University, College of Criminal Justice, Department of Forensic Science, Huntsville, TX 77341. Offers MS. *Program availability:* Part-time. *Degree requirements:* For master's, comprehensive exam. *Entrance requirements:* For master's, GRE, official transcripts, three letters of recommendation, personal essay. Additional exam requirements/recommendations for international students: required—TOEFL (minimum score 550 paper-based; 79 iBT), IELTS (minimum score 6.5). Electronic applications accepted.

Sam Houston State University, College of Sciences, Department of Computer Science, Huntsville, TX 77341. Offers computing and information science (MS); digital forensics (MS); information assurance and security (MS). *Program availability:* Part-time. *Degree requirements:* For master's, comprehensive exam, thesis optional, internship; for doctorate, comprehensive exam, thesis/dissertation. *Entrance requirements:* For master's, GRE General Test, letters of recommendation. Additional exam requirements/recommendations for international students: required—TOEFL

(minimum score 550 paper-based; 79 iBT), IELTS (minimum score 6.5). Electronic applications accepted.

Seattle University, College of Arts and Sciences, Department of Criminal Justice, Seattle, WA 98122-1090. Offers crime analysis (Certificate); criminal justice (MACJ). *Program availability:* Part-time, evening/weekend. *Students:* 18 full-time (14 women), 37 part-time (29 women); includes 24 minority (3 Black or African American, non-Hispanic/Latino; 1 American Indian or Alaska Native, non-Hispanic/Latino; 5 Asian, non-Hispanic/Latino; 7 Hispanic/Latino; 8 Two or more races, non-Hispanic/Latino). Average age 26. 53 applicants, 83% accepted, 28 enrolled. In 2019, 27 master's, 2 Certificates awarded. *Entrance requirements:* For master's, minimum GPA of 3.0; undergraduate degree in criminal justice or related social, behavioral, or physical science, or related coursework and/or volunteer or supervised experience; letters of recommendation; writing sample. Additional exam requirements/recommendations for international students: required—TOEFL, IELTS. *Application deadline:* For fall admission, 3/15 for domestic and international students. Application fee: $55. Electronic applications accepted. *Financial support:* In 2019–20, 27 students received support. Applicants required to submit FAFSA. *Unit head:* Dr. Elaine Gunnison, Graduate Program Director, 206-296-2430, E-mail: gunnisone@seattleu.edu. *Application contact:* Janet Shandley, Associate Dean of Graduate Admissions, 206-296-5900, Fax: 206-298-5656, E-mail: grad_admissions@seattleu.edu.
Website: https://www.seattleu.edu/artsci/criminal-graduate/

Stevenson University, Master of Forensic Science, Stevenson, MD 21153. Offers biology (MS); chemistry (MS); crime scene investigation (MS). *Program availability:* Part-time. *Faculty:* 1 full-time (0 women), 12 part-time/adjunct (5 women). *Students:* 23 full-time (22 women), 61 part-time (52 women); includes 47 minority (31 Black or African American, non-Hispanic/Latino; 4 Asian, non-Hispanic/Latino; 8 Hispanic/Latino; 4 Two or more races, non-Hispanic/Latino). Average age 28. 53 applicants, 66% accepted, 24 enrolled. In 2019, 15 master's awarded. *Degree requirements:* For master's, thesis or alternative, thesis or a formal scientific paper. *Entrance requirements:* For master's, personal statement (3-5 paragraphs), official college transcript from degree-granting institution, bachelor's degree in a natural science from a regionally accredited institution, minimum cumulative GPA of 3.0 on a 4.0 scale in past academic work. *Application deadline:* For fall admission, 8/9 priority date for domestic students; for spring admission, 1/11 priority date for domestic students; for summer admission, 5/1 priority date for domestic students. Applications are processed on a rolling basis. Application fee: $0. Electronic applications accepted. *Expenses:* $695 per credit. *Financial support:* Unspecified assistantships available. Financial award applicants required to submit FAFSA. *Unit head:* Carolyn Johnson, Department Chair & Professor, 443-352-4074, E-mail: CHJOHNSON@stevenson.edu. *Application contact:* Amanda Millar, Director, Admissions, 443-333-3334, Fax: 443-394-0538, E-mail: amillar@stevenson.edu.
Website: https://www.stevenson.edu/online/academics/online-graduate-programs/forensic-science/

Stevenson University, Program in Forensic Studies, Stevenson, MD 21153. Offers computer forensics (MS); criminalistics (MS); forensic accounting (MS); forensic legal professional (MS); interdisciplinary track (MS); investigations (MS). *Program availability:* Part-time, blended/hybrid learning. *Faculty:* 1 (woman) full-time, 7 part-time/adjunct (3 women). *Students:* 1 (woman) full-time, 19 part-time (14 women); includes 11 minority (6 Black or African American, non-Hispanic/Latino; 1 Asian, non-Hispanic/Latino; 3 Hispanic/Latino; 1 Two or more races, non-Hispanic/Latino). Average age 35. 5 applicants, 40% accepted. In 2019, 25 master's awarded. *Degree requirements:* For master's, capstone course. *Entrance requirements:* For master's, personal statement (3-5 paragraphs); official college transcript from degree-granting institution (additional transcripts may be required to demonstrate satisfaction of program-specific prerequisites); bachelor's degree from a regionally accredited institution; minimum cumulative GPA of 3.0 on a 4.0 scale in past academic work. *Application deadline:* For fall admission, 8/9 priority date for domestic students; for spring admission, 1/11 priority date for domestic students; for summer admission, 5/1 priority date for domestic students. Applications are processed on a rolling basis. Application fee: $0. Electronic applications accepted. *Expenses:* $695 per credit. *Financial support:* Unspecified assistantships available. Financial award applicants required to submit FAFSA. *Unit head:* Carolyn Johnson, Department Chair & Professor, 443-352-4074, E-mail: CHJOHNSON@stevenson.edu. *Application contact:* Amanda Millar, Director, Admissions, 443-334-3334, Fax: 443-394-0538, E-mail: amillar@stevenson.edu.
Website: http://www.stevenson.edu/online/academics/online-graduate-programs/forensic-studies/

Stratford University, School of Graduate Studies, Falls Church, VA 22043. Offers accounting (MS); business administration (MBA, DBA); cyber security (MS); cyber security leadership and policy (MS); digital forensics (MS); healthcare administration (MS); information systems (MS); information technology (DIT); networking and telecommunications (MS); software engineering (MS). *Program availability:* Part-time, evening/weekend, 100% online, blended/hybrid learning. *Degree requirements:* For master's, comprehensive exam, capstone project. *Entrance requirements:* For master's, GRE or GMAT, baccalaureate degree. Additional exam requirements/recommendations for international students: required—TOEFL (minimum score 79 iBT), IELTS (minimum score 6.5), PTE (minimum score 5). Electronic applications accepted.

Syracuse University, College of Arts and Sciences, Programs in Forensic Science, Syracuse, NY 13244. Offers advanced forensic science (MS); biomedical forensic science (MS); firearm and tool mark examination (CAS); general forensic science (MS); medicolegal death investigation (MS, CAS); nuclear forensics (MS); MS/JD. *Entrance requirements:* For master's, GRE General Test, personal statement, three letters of recommendation, transcripts, telephone interview. Additional exam requirements/recommendations for international students: required—TOEFL (minimum score 100 iBT). Electronic applications accepted.

Towson University, Jess and Mildred Fisher College of Science and Mathematics, Program in Forensic Science, Towson, MD 21252-0001. Offers MS. *Students:* 27 full-time (21 women), 6 part-time (5 women); includes 15 minority (10 Black or African American, non-Hispanic/Latino; 3 Asian, non-Hispanic/Latino; 2 Hispanic/Latino). *Entrance requirements:* For master's, minimum GPA of 3.0; bachelor's degree in biological sciences, chemistry, forensic chemistry, or related field. *Application deadline:* For fall admission, 1/17 for domestic students, 5/15 for international students; for spring admission, 10/15 for domestic students, 12/1 for international students. Applications are processed on a rolling basis. Application fee: $45. Electronic applications accepted. *Expenses: Tuition,* area resident: Full-time $7920; part-time $439 per credit. Tuition, nonresident: full-time $16,344; part-time $908 per credit. *International tuition:* $16,344 full-time. *Required fees:* $2628; $146 per credit. $876 per term. *Unit head:* Prof. Mark Profili, Program Director, 410-704-2668, E-mail: mprofili@towson.edu. *Application contact:* Coverley Beidleman, Assistant Director of Graduate Admissions, 410-704-5630, Fax: 410-704-3030, E-mail: grads@towson.edu.
Website: https://www.towson.edu/fcsm/departments/chemistry/grad/forensic/

Universidad del Turabo, Graduate Programs, School of Social Sciences and Humanities, Programs in Public Affairs, Program in Forensic Science, Gurabo, PR 00778-3030. Offers MPA. *Entrance requirements:* For master's, GRE, GMAT or

EXADEP, interview, essay, official transcript, recommendation letters. Electronic applications accepted.

University at Albany, State University of New York, College of Arts and Sciences, Department of Biological Sciences, Albany, NY 12222-0001. Offers forensic biology (MS). *Program availability:* Part-time, blended/hybrid learning. *Faculty:* 28 full-time (11 women), 10 part-time/adjunct (7 women). *Students:* 38 full-time (23 women), 35 part-time (23 women); includes 14 minority (3 Black or African American, non-Hispanic/Latino; 3 Asian, non-Hispanic/Latino; 6 Hispanic/Latino; 2 Two or more races, non-Hispanic/Latino), 14 international. 37 applicants, 59% accepted, 15 enrolled. In 2019, 12 master's awarded. *Degree requirements:* For master's, one foreign language. *Entrance requirements:* For master's, GRE General Test, transcripts of all schools attended, statement of background and goals, departmental questionnaire, resume, names and contact information for 3 recommenders. Additional exam requirements/recommendations for international students: required—TOEFL (minimum score 550 paper-based). *Application deadline:* For fall admission, 1/15 priority date for domestic students, 5/1 for international students; for spring admission, 11/15 for domestic and international students. Applications are processed on a rolling basis. Application fee: $75. Electronic applications accepted. *Expenses: Tuition, area resident:* Full-time $11,530; part-time $480 per credit hour. Tuition, nonresident: full-time $23,530; part-time $980 per credit hour. *International tuition:* $23,530 full-time. *Required fees:* $2185; $96 per credit hour. Part-time tuition and fees vary according to course load and program. *Financial support:* Fellowships, research assistantships, teaching assistantships, and minority assistantships available. Financial award application deadline: 5/1. *Unit head:* Richard cunningham, Chair, 518-442-4300, Fax: 518-442-4354, E-mail: rcunningham@albany.edu. *Application contact:* Michael DeRensis, Director, Graduate Admissions, 518-442-3980, Fax: 518-442-3922, E-mail: graduate@albany.edu.
Website: https://www.albany.edu/biology

University at Albany, State University of New York, School of Business, Department of Accounting and Law, Albany, NY 12222-0001. Offers accounting (MS); forensic accounting (MS); professional accounting (MS); tax practice (MS); taxation (MS). *Accreditation:* AACSB. *Program availability:* Part-time, evening/weekend, 100% online, blended/hybrid learning. *Faculty:* 17 full-time (5 women), 9 part-time/adjunct (1 woman). *Students:* 126 full-time (47 women), 20 part-time (11 women); includes 35 minority (11 Black or African American, non-Hispanic/Latino; 14 Asian, non-Hispanic/Latino; 8 Hispanic/Latino; 2 Two or more races, non-Hispanic/Latino), 11 international. 168 applicants, 63% accepted, 90 enrolled. In 2019, 119 master's awarded. *Degree requirements:* For master's, thesis optional, research project. *Entrance requirements:* For master's, GMAT, transcripts from all schools attended, 3 letters of recommendation, resume, personal statement. Additional exam requirements/recommendations for international students: required—TOEFL (minimum score 550 paper-based). *Application deadline:* For fall admission, 1/15 priority date for domestic students; for spring admission, 11/15 priority date for domestic students. Applications are processed on a rolling basis. Application fee: $75. Electronic applications accepted. *Expenses:* Contact institution. *Financial support:* Teaching assistantships and career-related internships or fieldwork available. *Unit head:* Nillanjan Sen, Dean, 518-956-8311, E-mail: ifisher@albany.edu. *Application contact:* Michael DeRensis, Director, Graduate Admissions, 518-442-3980, Fax: 518-442-3922, E-mail: graduate@albany.edu.
Website: http://www.albany.edu/business/accounting_index.shtml

The University of Alabama at Birmingham, College of Arts and Sciences, Program in Computer Forensics and Security Management, Birmingham, AL 35294. Offers MS. *Students:* 4 full-time (1 woman), 6 part-time (2 women); includes 2 minority (1 Black or African American, non-Hispanic/Latino; 1 Hispanic/Latino), 3 international. Average age 34. In 2019, 3 master's awarded. *Degree requirements:* For master's, field practicum (internship). *Entrance requirements:* For master's, GRE General Test (minimum combined score of 320) or GMAT (minimum total score of 550), minimum GPA of 3.0. *Application deadline:* For fall admission, 3/1 for domestic students. Application fee: $45 ($60 for international students). Electronic applications accepted. *Unit head:* Dr. Anthony Skjellum, Program Co-Director, Computer and Information Sciences, 205-934-2213, Fax: 205-934-5473, E-mail: tony@cis.uab.edu. *Application contact:* Dr. John J. Sloan, III, Program Co-Director, Justice Sciences, 205-934-2069, E-mail: prof@uab.edu.
Website: http://www.uab.edu/cas/justice-sciences/graduate-programs/master-of-science-in-computer-forensics-and-security-management-mscfsm

The University of Alabama at Birmingham, College of Arts and Sciences, Program in Forensic Science, Birmingham, AL 35294. Offers MSFS. *Students:* 11 full-time (8 women), 2 part-time (1 woman); includes 2 minority (1 Black or African American, non-Hispanic/Latino; 1 Two or more races, non-Hispanic/Latino). Average age 23. 36 applicants, 39% accepted, 9 enrolled. In 2019, 10 master's awarded. *Entrance requirements:* For master's, GRE, minimum GPA of 3.0. Additional exam requirements/recommendations for international students: required—TOEFL, TWE. *Application deadline:* For fall admission, 1/31 priority date for domestic students. Application fee: $45 ($60 for international students). Electronic applications accepted. *Financial support:* Research assistantships and scholarships/grants available. *Unit head:* Dr. Elizabeth Gardner, Graduate Program Director, 205-934-0668, E-mail: eagard@uab.edu. *Application contact:* Susan Noblitt Banks, Director of Graduate School Operations, 205-934-8227, Fax: 205-934-8413, E-mail: gradschool@uab.edu.
Website: http://www.uab.edu/cas/justice-sciences/graduate-programs/master-of-science-in-forensic-science-msfs

University of California, Davis, Graduate Studies, Graduate Group in Forensic Science, Davis, CA 95616. Offers MS. *Degree requirements:* For master's, thesis. *Entrance requirements:* Additional exam requirements/recommendations for international students: required—TOEFL (minimum score 550 paper-based), IELTS (minimum score 7). Electronic applications accepted.

University of Central Oklahoma, The Jackson College of Graduate Studies, College of Liberal Arts, School of Criminal Justice, Edmond, OK 73034-5209. Offers crime and intelligence analysis (MA); criminal justice management and administration (MA). *Program availability:* Part-time. *Degree requirements:* For master's, comprehensive exam (for some programs), thesis (for some programs). *Entrance requirements:* Additional exam requirements/recommendations for international students: required—TOEFL (minimum score 550 paper-based; 79 iBT), IELTS (minimum score 6.5). Electronic applications accepted.

University of Central Oklahoma, The Jackson College of Graduate Studies, Forensic Science Institute, Edmond, OK 73034-5209. Offers biology/chemistry (MS); forensic science (MS). *Degree requirements:* For master's, thesis. *Entrance requirements:* For master's, GRE, official transcripts. Additional exam requirements/recommendations for international students: required—TOEFL (minimum score 550 paper-based; 79 iBT), IELTS (minimum score 6.5). Electronic applications accepted.

University of Charleston, Master of Forensic Accounting Program, Charleston, WV 25304-1099. Offers EMFA. *Program availability:* Part-time, blended/hybrid learning. *Entrance requirements:* Additional exam requirements/recommendations for international students: required—TOEFL. Electronic applications accepted.

University of Colorado Denver, College of Arts and Media, Denver, CO 80217-3364. Offers recording arts (MS), including media forensics, recording arts. *Accreditation:* NASM. *Program availability:* Part-time, evening/weekend. *Degree requirements:* For master's, 34 credits, thesis/portfolio. *Entrance requirements:* For master's, GRE General Test (minimum scores higher than 50th percentile for all sections), minimum undergraduate GPA of 3.0, portfolio, resume, interview, 3 letters of recommendation. Additional exam requirements/recommendations for international students: required—TOEFL (minimum score 70 iBT). Electronic applications accepted. Tuition and fees vary according to course load, program and reciprocity agreements.

University of Detroit Mercy, College of Business Administration, Detroit, MI 48221. Offers business administration (MBA); business fundamentals (Certificate); business turnaround management (Certificate); ethical leadership and change management (Certificate); finance (Certificate); forensic accounting (Certificate); JD/MBA; MBA/MHSA. *Program availability:* Part-time, evening/weekend, 100% online, blended/hybrid learning. *Entrance requirements:* For master's, GMAT, resume, letter of recommendation, transcripts; for Certificate, resume, letter of recommendation, transcripts. Electronic applications accepted. Application fee is waived when completed online. *Expenses:* Contact institution.

University of Florida, Graduate School, College of Pharmacy, Programs in Forensic Science, Gainesville, FL 32611. Offers clinical toxicology (Certificate); drug chemistry (Certificate); environmental forensics (Certificate); forensic death investigation (Certificate); forensic DNA and serology (MSP, Certificate); forensic drug chemistry (MSP); forensic science (MSP); forensic toxicology (Certificate). *Program availability:* Part-time, evening/weekend, online learning. *Degree requirements:* For master's, comprehensive exam. *Entrance requirements:* For master's, GRE General Test, minimum GPA of 3.0. Additional exam requirements/recommendations for international students: required—TOEFL (minimum score 550 paper-based; 80 iBT), IELTS (minimum score 6).

University of Houston–Victoria, School of Arts and Sciences, Program in Biomedical Sciences, Victoria, TX 77901-4450. Offers biological sciences (MS); biomedical sciences (MS); forensic science (MS).

University of Illinois at Chicago, College of Pharmacy, Graduate Programs in Pharmacy, Program in Forensic Science, Chicago, IL 60607-7128. Offers MS. *Degree requirements:* For master's, thesis. *Entrance requirements:* For master's, GRE General Test. Additional exam requirements/recommendations for international students: required—TOEFL.

University of Maryland, Baltimore, Graduate School, Program in Forensic Medicine, Baltimore, MD 21201. Offers MS. *Degree requirements:* For master's, comprehensive exam, thesis optional. *Entrance requirements:* For master's, GRE, minimum GPA of 3.0, curriculum vitae, 3 letters of recommendation, essay. Additional exam requirements/recommendations for international students: required—TOEFL (minimum score 80 iBT); recommended—IELTS (minimum score 7). Electronic applications accepted.

University of New Haven, Graduate School, Henry C. Lee College of Criminal Justice and Forensic Sciences, Program in Fire and Explosion Investigation, West Haven, CT 06516. Offers fire science (MS); fire/arson investigation (MS, Graduate Certificate); forensic science (Graduate Certificate); public safety management (MS). *Program availability:* Part-time, evening/weekend. *Students:* Average age 30. 12 applicants, 100% accepted, 5 enrolled. In 2019, 8 master's awarded. *Degree requirements:* For master's, thesis or alternative, research project or internship. *Entrance requirements:* Additional exam requirements/recommendations for international students: required—TOEFL (minimum score 80 iBT), IELTS, PTE (minimum score 53). *Application deadline:* Applications are processed on a rolling basis. Application fee: $50. Electronic applications accepted. Application fee is waived when completed online. *Financial support:* Research assistantships with partial tuition reimbursements, teaching assistantships with partial tuition reimbursements, Federal Work-Study, scholarships/grants, and unspecified assistantships available. Support available to part-time students. Financial award applicants required to submit FAFSA. *Unit head:* Dr. Sorin Iliescu, Assistant Professor, 203-932-7239, E-mail: silliescu@newhaven.edu. *Application contact:* Selina O'Toole, Senior Associate Director of Graduate Admissions, 203-932-7337, E-mail: SOToole@newhaven.edu.
Website: https://www.newhaven.edu/lee-college/graduate-programs/fire-science/

University of New Haven, Graduate School, Henry C. Lee College of Criminal Justice and Forensic Sciences, Program in Forensic Science, West Haven, CT 06516. Offers forensic computer investigation (Graduate Certificate); forensic science (MS); forensic science/fire science (Graduate Certificate). *Program availability:* Part-time, evening/weekend. *Students:* 24 full-time (19 women), 1 (woman) part-time; includes 2 minority (1 Asian, non-Hispanic/Latino; 1 Hispanic/Latino). Average age 23. 59 applicants, 32% accepted, 12 enrolled. In 2019, 15 master's awarded. *Entrance requirements:* For master's, GRE. Additional exam requirements/recommendations for international students: required—TOEFL (minimum score 80 iBT), IELTS, PTE (minimum score 53). *Application deadline:* Applications are processed on a rolling basis. Application fee: $50. Electronic applications accepted. Application fee is waived when completed online. *Financial support:* Research assistantships with partial tuition reimbursements, teaching assistantships with partial tuition reimbursements, Federal Work-Study, scholarships/grants, and unspecified assistantships available. Support available to part-time students. Financial award applicants required to submit FAFSA. *Unit head:* Tim Palmbach, Professor, 203-932-7116, E-mail: TPalmbach@newhaven.edu. *Application contact:* Selina O'Toole, Senior Associate Director of Graduate Admissions, 203-932-7337, E-mail: SOToole@newhaven.edu.
Website: https://www.newhaven.edu/lee-college/graduate-programs/forensic-science/

University of New Haven, Graduate School, Henry C. Lee College of Criminal Justice and Forensic Sciences, Program in Forensic Technology, West Haven, CT 06516. Offers MS. *Program availability:* Part-time. *Students:* 49 full-time (39 women), 9 part-time (8 women); includes 11 minority (1 Black or African American, non-Hispanic/Latino; 10 Hispanic/Latino), 2 international. Average age 25. 54 applicants, 91% accepted, 31 enrolled. In 2019, 19 master's awarded. *Application deadline:* Applications are processed on a rolling basis. Application fee: $50. *Unit head:* Maria Torre, Lecturer, 203-932-1157, E-mail: MTorre@newhaven.edu. *Application contact:* Selina O'Toole, Senior Associate Director of Graduate Admissions, 203-932-7337, E-mail: SOToole@newhaven.edu.
Website: https://www.newhaven.edu/lee-college/graduate-programs/forensic-technology

University of North Texas Health Science Center at Fort Worth, Graduate School of Biomedical Sciences, Fort Worth, TX 76107-2699. Offers biochemistry and cancer biology (MS, PhD); biotechnology (MS); cell biology, immunology and microbiology (MS, PhD); clinical research management (MS); forensic genetics (MS); genetics (MS, PhD); integrative physiology (MS, PhD); medical sciences (MS); pharmaceutical sciences and pharmacotherapy (MS, PhD); pharmacology and neuroscience (MS, PhD); structural anatomy and rehabilitation sciences (MS, PhD); DO/MS; DO/PhD. Terminal master's awarded for partial completion of doctoral program. *Degree requirements:* For master's, thesis; for doctorate, thesis/dissertation. *Entrance requirements:* For master's and doctorate, GRE General Test. Additional exam requirements/recommendations for international students: required—TOEFL. *Expenses:* Contact institution.

University of Rhode Island, Graduate School, College of Arts and Sciences, Department of Computer Science and Statistics, Kingston, RI 02881. Offers computer science (MS, PhD); cyber security (PSM, Graduate Certificate); digital forensics (Graduate Certificate). *Program availability:* Part-time, evening/weekend, 100% online, blended/hybrid learning. *Faculty:* 20 full-time (6 women). *Students:* 29 full-time (13 women), 88 part-time (19 women); includes 16 minority (5 Black or African American, non-Hispanic/Latino; 5 Asian, non-Hispanic/Latino; 5 Hispanic/Latino; 1 Two or more races, non-Hispanic/Latino), 13 international. 77 applicants, 82% accepted, 39 enrolled. In 2019, 47 master's, 3 doctorates, 25 other advanced degrees awarded. Terminal master's awarded for partial completion of doctoral program. *Entrance requirements:* Additional exam requirements/recommendations for international students: required—TOEFL. *Application deadline:* For fall admission, 7/15 for domestic students, 2/1 for international students; for spring admission, 11/15 for domestic students, 7/15 for international students. Application fee: $65. Electronic applications accepted. *Expenses: Tuition, area resident:* Full-time $13,734; part-time $763 per credit. Tuition, state resident: full-time $13,734; part-time $763 per credit. Tuition, nonresident: full-time $26,512; part-time $1473 per credit. *International tuition:* $26,512 full-time. *Required fees:* $1780; $52 per credit. $35 per term. One-time fee: $165. *Financial support:* In 2019–20, 3 research assistantships with tuition reimbursements (averaging $9,645 per year), 15 teaching assistantships with tuition reimbursements (averaging $13,546 per year) were awarded; unspecified assistantships also available. Financial award application deadline: 2/1; financial award applicants required to submit FAFSA. *Unit head:* Dr. Lisa DiPippo, Chair, 401-874-2701, Fax: 401-874-4617, E-mail: dipippo@cs.uri.edu. *Application contact:* Dr. Lutz Hamel, Graduate Program Director, 401-874-2701, E-mail: lutzhamel@uri.edu.
Website: http://www.cs.uri.edu/

University of St. Francis, College of Arts and Sciences, Joliet, IL 60435-6169. Offers forensic social work (Post-Master's Certificate); physician assistant practice (MS); social work (MSW). *Program availability:* Part-time. *Entrance requirements:* For master's, GRE (for MS). Additional exam requirements/recommendations for international students: required—TOEFL (minimum score 550 paper-based; 79 iBT), IELTS (minimum score 6). Electronic applications accepted. Application fee is waived when completed online. *Expenses:* Contact institution.

University of Southern Mississippi, College of Arts and Sciences, School of Criminal Justice, Forensic Science, and Security, Hattiesburg, MS 39406-0001. Offers criminal justice (MA, MS, PhD); forensic science (MS). *Program availability:* Part-time. *Students:* 2 full-time (both women), 3 part-time (1 woman); includes 1 minority (Black or African American, non-Hispanic/Latino). 18 applicants, 11% accepted. In 2019, 6 master's awarded. *Degree requirements:* For master's, comprehensive exam, thesis; for doctorate, comprehensive exam, thesis/dissertation. *Entrance requirements:* For master's, GRE General Test, minimum GPA of 2.75 in last 60 hours, 3.0 in field of study; for doctorate, GRE General Test, minimum GPA of 3.5. Additional exam requirements/recommendations for international students: required—TOEFL, IELTS. *Application deadline:* For fall admission, 3/15 priority date for domestic students, 3/15 for international students; for spring admission, 1/10 priority date for domestic and international students. Applications are processed on a rolling basis. Application fee: $60. Electronic applications accepted. *Expenses: Tuition, area resident:* Full-time $4393; part-time $488 per credit hour. Tuition, nonresident: full-time $5393; part-time $600 per credit hour. *Required fees:* $6 per semester. *Financial support:* Research assistantships with full tuition reimbursements, teaching assistantships with full tuition reimbursements, career-related internships or fieldwork, Federal Work-Study, institutionally sponsored loans, scholarships/grants, health care benefits, and unspecified assistantships available. Financial award application deadline: 3/15; financial award applicants required to submit FAFSA. *Unit head:* Dr. Lisa Nored, Director, 601-266-4509, Fax: 601-266-4391. *Application contact:* Tera Wright, Manager of Graduate Admissions, 601-266-4509, Fax: 601-266-4391.
Website: https://www.usm.edu/criminal-justice

University of South Florida, College of Arts and Sciences, Department of Anthropology, Tampa, FL 33620-9951. Offers applied anthropology (MA), including archaeological and forensic sciences, biocultural medical anthropology, cultural resource management, heritage studies; medical anthropology (Graduate Certificate). *Program availability:* Part-time. *Faculty:* 22 full-time (13 women). *Students:* 67 full-time (51 women), 47 part-time (32 women); includes 30 minority (5 Black or African American, non-Hispanic/Latino; 1 Asian, non-Hispanic/Latino; 23 Hispanic/Latino; 1 Two or more races, non-Hispanic/Latino), 9 international. Average age 32. 152 applicants, 37% accepted, 26 enrolled. In 2019, 11 master's, 11 doctorates awarded. *Degree requirements:* For master's, one foreign language, comprehensive exam, thesis; for doctorate, one foreign language, comprehensive exam, thesis/dissertation. *Entrance requirements:* For master's, GRE (no minimum score requirement), minimum GPA of 3.0, 3 letters of recommendation, statement of purpose, signed research ethics statement, resume or curriculum vitae, writing sample (optional), GA Application (optional); for doctorate, GRE required, minimum GPA of 3.0, 3 letters of recommendation, statement of purpose, signed research ethics statement, resume or curriculum vitae, writing sample (optional), GA Application (optional); for Graduate Certificate, bachelor's degree with minimum GPA of 3.0. Additional exam requirements/recommendations for international students: required—TOEFL, TOEFL (minimum score 550 paper-based; 79 iBT) or IELTS (minimum score 6.5). *Application deadline:* For fall admission, 12/15 priority date for domestic and international students. Application fee:

$30. Electronic applications accepted. *Financial support:* In 2019–20, 17 students received support, including 14 research assistantships with tuition reimbursements available (averaging $14,475 per year), 52 teaching assistantships with partial tuition reimbursements available (averaging $12,540 per year); scholarships/grants and tuition waivers (partial) also available. Financial award application deadline: 1/15; financial award applicants required to submit FAFSA. *Unit head:* Dr. David Himmelgreen, Professor/Chair, 813-974-5455, E-mail: dhimmelg@usf.edu. *Application contact:* Dr. Rebecca Zarger, Associate Professor and Graduate Director, 813-974-0069, E-mail: rzarger@usf.edu.
Website: http://anthropology.usf.edu/graduate/

University of South Florida, College of Graduate Studies, Tampa, FL 33620-9951. Offers cybersecurity (MS), including computer security fundamentals, cyber intelligence, digital forensics, information assurance. *Program availability:* Part-time, evening/weekend, online learning. *Faculty:* 1 (woman) full-time. *Students:* 70 full-time (15 women), 161 part-time (32 women); includes 112 minority (32 Black or African American, non-Hispanic/Latino; 1 American Indian or Alaska Native, non-Hispanic/Latino; 24 Asian, non-Hispanic/Latino; 51 Hispanic/Latino; 4 Two or more races, non-Hispanic/Latino), 4 international. Average age 34. 101 applicants, 76% accepted, 54 enrolled. In 2019, 133 master's awarded. Terminal master's awarded for partial completion of doctoral program. *Degree requirements:* For master's, variable foreign language requirement, comprehensive exam, thesis (for some programs), practicum. *Entrance requirements:* For master's, GRE General Test, 250-500 word essay in which student describes academic and professional background, reasons for pursuing degree, and professional goals pertaining to cybersecurity; 2 letters of recommendation; current resume or CV. Video or phone interview may be required. Additional exam requirements/recommendations for international students: required—TOEFL, TOEFL (minimum score 550 paper-based; 79 iBT) or IELTS (minimum score 6.5). *Application deadline:* For fall admission, 2/15 for domestic and international students; for spring admission, 10/15 for domestic students, 9/15 for international students; for summer admission, 2/15 for domestic and international students. Application fee: $30. Electronic applications accepted. *Financial support:* In 2019–20, 20 students received support. Teaching assistantships available. Financial award application deadline: 2/1; financial award applicants required to submit FAFSA. *Unit head:* Dr. Dwayne Smith, Senior Vice Provost and Dean of the Office of Graduate Studies, 813-974-7359, Fax: 813-974-5762, E-mail: mdsmith8@usf.edu. *Application contact:* Paul Crawford, Associate Director for Graduate Admissions, 813-974-8800, E-mail: pjcrawford@usf.edu.
Website: https://www.usf.edu/graduate-studies/

Virginia Commonwealth University, Graduate School, College of Humanities and Sciences, Department of Forensic Science, Richmond, VA 23284-9005. Offers forensic biology (MS); forensic chemistry/drugs and toxicology (MS); forensic chemistry/trace evidence (MS); forensic physical analysis (MS). *Program availability:* Part-time. *Entrance requirements:* For master's, GRE General Test, bachelor's degree in a natural science discipline, including forensic science, or a degree with equivalent work. Additional exam requirements/recommendations for international students: required—TOEFL (minimum score 600 paper-based; 100 iBT) or IELTS (minimum score 6.5). Electronic applications accepted.

Webster University, George Herbert Walker School of Business and Technology, Department of Business, St. Louis, MO 63119-3194. Offers business and organizational security management (MBA); decision support systems (MBA); environmental management (MBA); finance (MBA, MS); forensic accounting (MS); gerontology (MBA); human resources development (MBA); human resources management (MBA); information technology management (MBA); international business (MA, MBA); international relations (MBA); management and leadership (MBA); marketing (MBA); media communications (MBA); procurement and acquisitions management (MBA); Web services (MBA). *Accreditation:* ACBSP. *Program availability:* Part-time, evening/weekend, online learning. *Degree requirements:* For master's, comprehensive exam (for some programs), thesis (for some programs). *Entrance requirements:* Additional exam requirements/recommendations for international students: required—TOEFL.

West Virginia University, College of Law, Morgantown, WV 26506-6130. Offers energy law and sustainable development (LL M); forensic justice (LL M); law (JD); white collar forensic justice (LL M). *Accreditation:* ABA. *Program availability:* Part-time. *Entrance requirements:* For doctorate, LSAT. Additional exam requirements/recommendations for international students: required—TOEFL (minimum score 600 paper-based; 100 iBT). Electronic applications accepted. *Expenses:* Contact institution.

West Virginia University, Eberly College of Arts and Sciences, Morgantown, WV 26506. Offers biology (MS, PhD); chemistry (MS, PhD); communication studies (MA, PhD); computational statistics (PhD); creative writing (MFA); English (MA, PhD); forensic and investigative science (MS); forensic science (PhD); geography (MA); geology (MA, PhD); history (MA, PhD); legal studies (MLS); mathematics (MS); physics (MS, PhD); political science (MA, PhD); professional writing and editing (MA); psychology (MA); public administration (MPA); social work (MSW); sociology (MA, PhD); statistics (MS). *Program availability:* Part-time, evening/weekend, online learning. Terminal master's awarded for partial completion of doctoral program. *Degree requirements:* For master's, thesis (for some programs); for doctorate, comprehensive exam, thesis/dissertation. *Entrance requirements:* For master's and doctorate, GRE. Additional exam requirements/recommendations for international students: required—TOEFL (minimum score 600 paper-based); recommended—TWE. Electronic applications accepted.

Section 19
Economics

This section contains a directory of institutions offering graduate work in economics. Additional information about programs listed in the directory may be obtained by writing directly to the dean of a graduate school or chair of a department at the address given in the directory.

For programs offering related work, see also in this book *Family and Consumer Sciences, Political Science and International Affairs,* and *Public, Regional, and Industrial Affairs.* In the other guides in this series:

Graduate Programs in the Physical Sciences, Mathematics, Agricultural Sciences, the Environment & Natural Resources
See *Agricultural and Food Sciences* and *Mathematical Sciences*
Graduate Programs in Engineering & Applied Sciences
See *Computer Science and Information Technology; Geological, Mineral/Mining, and Petroleum Engineering;* and *Industrial Engineering*

Graduate Programs in Business, Education, Information Studies, Law & Social Work
See *Business Administration and Management*

CONTENTS

Program Directories

Agricultural Economics and Agribusiness

Alcorn State University, School of Graduate Studies, School of Agriculture and Applied Sciences, Lorman, MS 39096-7500. Offers agricultural economics (MS Ag); agronomy (MS Ag); animal science (MS Ag). *Degree requirements:* For master's, thesis optional.

Arizona State University at Tempe, W. P. Carey School of Business, Morrison School of Agribusiness, Mesa, AZ 85212. Offers PhD. *Program availability:* Part-time, evening/weekend. *Entrance requirements:* Additional exam requirements/recommendations for international students: required—TOEFL (minimum score 550 paper-based; 80 iBT), IELTS (minimum score 6.5); recommended—TWE. Electronic applications accepted.

Auburn University, Graduate School, College of Agriculture, Department of Agricultural Economics and Rural Sociology, Auburn University, AL 36849. Offers agricultural economics (M Ag). *Program availability:* Part-time. *Faculty:* 12 full-time (5 women). *Students:* 3 full-time (1 woman), 3 part-time (0 women); includes 1 minority (Black or African American, non-Hispanic/Latino), 2 international. Average age 31. 7 applicants, 43% accepted, 2 enrolled. In 2019, 2 master's awarded. *Degree requirements:* For master's, thesis (for some programs). *Entrance requirements:* For master's, GRE General Test. Additional exam requirements/recommendations for international students: required—TOEFL (minimum score 550 paper-based; 79 iBT), iTEP; recommended—IELTS (minimum score 6.5). *Application deadline:* Applications are processed on a rolling basis. Application fee: $60 ($70 for international students). Electronic applications accepted. *Expenses: Tuition,* area resident: Full-time $9828; part-time $546 per credit hour. Tuition, state resident: full-time $9828; part-time $546 per credit hour. Tuition, nonresident: full-time $29,484; part-time $1638 per credit hour. *International tuition:* $29,744 full-time. Tuition and fees vary according to course load, program and reciprocity agreements. *Financial support:* In 2019–20, 4 fellowships with tuition reimbursements (averaging $350 per year), 206 research assistantships with tuition reimbursements (averaging $17,715 per year) were awarded; Federal Work-Study also available. Support available to part-time students. Financial award application deadline: 3/15; financial award applicants required to submit FAFSA. *Unit head:* Deacue Fields, Chair, 334-844-4800. *Application contact:* Dr. George Flowers, Dean of the Graduate School, 334-844-2125.
Website: http://www.ag.auburn.edu/agec/

Colorado State University, College of Agricultural Sciences, Department of Agricultural and Resource Economics, Fort Collins, CO 80523-1172. Offers MS, PhD. *Faculty:* 14 full-time (2 women), 3 part-time/adjunct (all women). *Students:* 23 full-time (13 women), 8 part-time (4 women); includes 1 minority (Asian, non-Hispanic/Latino), 18 international. Average age 27. 79 applicants, 56% accepted, 15 enrolled. In 2019, 3 master's, 2 doctorates awarded. *Degree requirements:* For master's, thesis; for doctorate, thesis/dissertation. *Entrance requirements:* For master's and doctorate, GRE, intermediate microeconomics, intermediate econometrics. Additional exam requirements/recommendations for international students: required—TOEFL (minimum score 550 paper-based). *Application deadline:* For fall admission, 2/15 priority date for domestic and international students. Applications are processed on a rolling basis. Application fee: $60 ($70 for international students). Electronic applications accepted. *Expenses:* Tuition, state resident: full-time $10,520; part-time $5844 per credit hour. Tuition, nonresident: full-time $25,791; part-time $14,328 per credit hour. *International tuition:* $25,791 full-time. *Required fees:* $2512.80. Part-time tuition and fees vary according to course level, course load, degree level, program and student level. *Financial support:* In 2019–20, 29 students received support, including 18 research assistantships with full and partial tuition reimbursements available (averaging $16,635 per year), 8 teaching assistantships with full and partial tuition reimbursements available (averaging $16,313 per year); scholarships/grants and health care benefits also available. Financial award application deadline: 2/15. *Unit head:* Dr. Hayley Chouinard, Department Head, 970-491-6955, Fax: 970-491-2067, E-mail: hayley.chouinard@colostate.edu. *Application contact:* Denise Davis, Program Assistant II, 970-491-6955, Fax: 970-491-2067, E-mail: denise.davis@colostate.edu.
Website: http://dare.agsci.colostate.edu/

Cornell University, Graduate School, Graduate Fields of Agriculture and Life Sciences, Field of Applied Economics and Management, Ithaca, NY 14853. Offers agricultural finance (MS, PhD); applied econometrics and qualitative analysis (MS, PhD); economics of development (MS, PhD); environmental economics (MS, PhD); environmental management (MPS); farm management and production economics (MS, PhD); marketing and food distribution (MS, PhD); public policy analysis (MS, PhD); resource economics (PhD). *Entrance requirements:* For master's and doctorate, GRE. Additional exam requirements/recommendations for international students: required—TOEFL.

Cornell University, Graduate School, Graduate Fields of Agriculture and Life Sciences, Field of Global Development, Ithaca, NY 14853. Offers development policy (MPS); international agriculture and development (MPS); international development (MPS); international nutrition (MPS); international planning (MPS); international population (MPS); science and technology policy (MPS). *Degree requirements:* For master's, project paper. *Entrance requirements:* For master's, GRE General Test (recommended), 2 years of development experience, 2 letters of recommendation. Additional exam requirements/recommendations for international students: required—TOEFL (minimum score 550 paper-based; 77 iBT). Electronic applications accepted.

Delaware Valley University, MBA Program, Doylestown, PA 18901-2697. Offers accounting (MBA); entrepreneurship (MBA); finance (MBA); food and agribusiness (MBA); general business (MBA); global executive leadership (MBA); human resource management (MBA); supply chain management (MBA). *Program availability:* Part-time, evening/weekend, online learning. *Entrance requirements:* For master's, minimum undergraduate GPA of 3.0. Electronic applications accepted. *Expenses:* Contact institution.

Illinois State University, Graduate School, College of Applied Science and Technology, Department of Agriculture, Normal, IL 61790. Offers agribusiness (MS). *Faculty:* 17 full-time (6 women), 4 part-time/adjunct (1 woman). *Students:* 7 full-time (1 woman), 4 part-time (all women). Average age 25. 17 applicants, 24% accepted, 4 enrolled. In 2019, 1 master's awarded. *Degree requirements:* For master's, comprehensive exam (for some programs), thesis optional. *Entrance requirements:* For master's, GRE General Test, minimum GPA of 3.0 in last 60 hours. *Application deadline:* Applications are processed on a rolling basis. Application fee: $50. *Expenses: Tuition,* area resident: Full-time $7956; part-time $9767 per year. Tuition, nonresident: full-time $9233; part-time $17,592 per year. *Required fees:* $1797. *Financial support:* Research assistantships, teaching assistantships, tuition waivers (full), and unspecified assistantships available. Financial award application deadline: 4/1. *Unit head:* Dr. Robert Rhykerd, Department Chair, 309-438-8550, E-mail: rrhyker@ilstu.edu. *Application contact:* Dr. Robert Rhykerd, Department Chair, 309-438-8550, E-mail: rrhyker@ilstu.edu.
Website: http://agriculture.illinoisstate.edu/

Instituto Centroamericano de Administracion de Empresas, Graduate Programs, La Garita, Costa Rica. Offers agribusiness management (MIAM); business administration (EMBA); finance (MBA); real estate management (MGREM); sustainable development (MBA); technology (MBA). *Degree requirements:* For master's, comprehensive exam, essay. *Entrance requirements:* For master's, GMAT or GRE General Test, fluency in Spanish, interview, letters of recommendation, minimum 1 year of work experience. Additional exam requirements/recommendations for international students: recommended—TOEFL. Electronic applications accepted.

Iowa State University of Science and Technology, Department of Economics, Ames, IA 50011. Offers agricultural economics (MS, PhD); economics (MS, PhD); JD/MS; JD/PhD. *Degree requirements:* For master's, thesis or alternative; for doctorate, thesis/dissertation. *Entrance requirements:* For master's and doctorate, GRE General Test. Additional exam requirements/recommendations for international students: required—TOEFL (minimum score 570 paper-based; 88 iBT), IELTS (minimum score 6.5). Electronic applications accepted.

Iowa State University of Science and Technology, Program in Agricultural Economics, Ames, IA 50011. Offers MS, PhD. *Degree requirements:* For master's, thesis or alternative; for doctorate, thesis/dissertation. *Entrance requirements:* For master's and doctorate, GRE General Test. Additional exam requirements/recommendations for international students: required—TOEFL (minimum score 570 paper-based; 88 iBT), IELTS (minimum score 6.5). Electronic applications accepted.

Iowa State University of Science and Technology, Program in Seed Technology and Business, Ames, IA 50011. Offers MS. *Degree requirements:* For master's, thesis or alternative. *Entrance requirements:* For master's, resume, 3 letters of recommendation. Additional exam requirements/recommendations for international students: required—TOEFL (minimum score 570 paper-based; 85 iBT), IELTS (minimum score 6.5). Electronic applications accepted.

Kansas State University, Graduate School, College of Agriculture, Department of Agricultural Economics, Manhattan, KS 66506. Offers MAB, MS, PhD. *Program availability:* Part-time, online learning. Terminal master's awarded for partial completion of doctoral program. *Degree requirements:* For master's, thesis or alternative, oral exam; for doctorate, thesis/dissertation, preliminary exams. *Entrance requirements:* For master's and doctorate, GRE General Test. Additional exam requirements/recommendations for international students: required—TOEFL (minimum score 550 paper-based; 79 iBT), IELTS (minimum score 6.5). Electronic applications accepted. *Expenses:* Contact institution.

Louisiana State University and Agricultural & Mechanical College, Graduate School, College of Agriculture, Department of Agricultural Economics and Agribusiness, Baton Rouge, LA 70803. Offers MS, PhD.

McGill University, Faculty of Graduate and Postdoctoral Studies, Faculty of Agricultural and Environmental Sciences, Department of Agricultural Economics, Montréal, QC H3A 2T5, Canada. Offers M Sc.

Michigan State University, The Graduate School, College of Agriculture and Natural Resources, Department of Agricultural, Food, and Resource Economics, East Lansing, MI 48824. Offers agricultural economics (MS, PhD); agricultural, food, and resource economics (MS, PhD). *Entrance requirements:* Additional exam requirements/recommendations for international students: required—TOEFL (minimum score 550 paper-based), Michigan State University ELT (minimum score 85), Michigan English Language Assessment Battery (minimum score 83). Electronic applications accepted.

Mississippi State University, College of Agriculture and Life Sciences, Department of Agricultural Economics, Mississippi State, MS 39762. Offers agricultural economics (MS). *Program availability:* Part-time. *Faculty:* 21 full-time (2 women), 1 part-time/adjunct (0 women). *Students:* 20 full-time (10 women), 9 part-time (1 woman), 5 international. Average age 26. 28 applicants, 57% accepted, 12 enrolled. In 2019, 6 master's awarded. *Degree requirements:* For master's, comprehensive exam, thesis (for some programs), thesis defense. *Entrance requirements:* For master's, GRE, minimum GPA of 3.0. Additional exam requirements/recommendations for international students: required—TOEFL (minimum score 575 paper-based; 84 iBT); recommended—IELTS (minimum score 7). *Application deadline:* For fall admission, 7/1 for domestic students, 5/1 for international students; for spring admission, 11/1 for domestic students, 9/1 for international students. Applications are processed on a rolling basis. Application fee: $60 ($80 for international students). Electronic applications accepted. *Expenses: Tuition,* area resident: Full-time $8880; part-time $456 per credit hour. Tuition, state resident: full-time $8880. Tuition, nonresident: full-time $23,840; part-time $1236 per credit hour. *Required fees:* $110; $11.12 per credit hour. Tuition and fees vary according to course load. *Financial support:* In 2019–20, 14 research assistantships with full tuition reimbursements (averaging $13,681 per year) were awarded; teaching assistantships, career-related internships or fieldwork, Federal Work-Study, institutionally sponsored loans, and unspecified assistantships also available. Financial award application deadline: 4/1; financial award applicants required to submit FAFSA. *Unit head:* Dr. Keith Coble, Professor and Head, 662-325-6670, Fax: 662-325-8777, E-mail: keith.coble@msstate.edu. *Application contact:* Ryan King, Admissions and Enrollment Assistant, 662-325-8951, E-mail: rjk101@grad.msstate.edu.
Website: http://www.agecon.msstate.edu/

New Mexico State University, College of Agricultural, Consumer and Environmental Sciences, Department of Agricultural Economics and Agricultural Business, Las Cruces, NM 88003-8001. Offers agribusiness (MBA); agriculture (M Ag); economic development (DED); water science management (MS). *Program availability:* Part-time. *Faculty:* 8 full-time (2 women), 2 part-time/adjunct (0 women). *Students:* 10 full-time (6 women), 6 part-time (4 women); includes 7 minority (all Hispanic/Latino), 3 international. Average age 25. 14 applicants, 57% accepted, 3 enrolled. In 2019, 4 master's awarded. *Degree requirements:* For master's, thesis (for some programs); for doctorate, comprehensive exam, thesis/dissertation. *Entrance requirements:* For master's, GRE; GMAT (for MBA), previous course work in intermediate microeconomics, intermediate macroeconomics, college-level calculus, statistics; for doctorate, previous course work in intermediate microeconomics, intermediate macroeconomics, college-level calculus, statistics, related MS or equivalent, minimum GPA of 3.0. Additional exam requirements/recommendations for international students: required—TOEFL (minimum score 550 paper-based; 79 iBT), IELTS (minimum score 6.5). *Application deadline:* For fall admission, 7/1 priority date for domestic and international students; for spring admission, 11/1 priority date for domestic and international students. Applications are processed on a rolling basis. Application fee: $40 ($50 for international students). Electronic applications accepted. *Financial support:* In 2019–20, 10 students received support, including 7 research assistantships (averaging $17,353 per year), 6 teaching assistantships (averaging $10,595 per year); career-related internships or fieldwork,

Federal Work-Study, scholarships/grants, traineeships, health care benefits, and unspecified assistantships also available. Support available to part-time students. Financial award application deadline: 3/1. *Unit head:* Dr. Jay Lillywhite, Department Head, 575-646-3215, Fax: 575-646-3808, E-mail: lillywhi@nmsu.edu. *Application contact:* Dr. Ram Acharya, Graduate Committee Chair, 575-646-2524, Fax: 575-646-3808, E-mail: acharyar@nmsu.edu.
Website: http://aces.nmsu.edu/academics/aeab/

New Mexico State University, College of Business, MBA Program, Las Cruces, NM 88003-8001. Offers agribusiness (MBA); finance (MBA); information systems (MBA). *Accreditation:* AACSB. *Program availability:* Part-time-only, evening/weekend, online with required 2-3 day orientation and 2-3 day concluding session in Las Cruces. *Students:* 28 full-time (14 women), 41 part-time (22 women); includes 44 minority (2 Black or African American, non-Hispanic/Latino; 42 Hispanic/Latino), 5 international. Average age 33. 96 applicants, 77% accepted, 17 enrolled. In 2019, 61 master's awarded. *Entrance requirements:* For master's, GMAT or GRE (depending upon undergraduate or graduate degree institution and GPA), minimum GPA of 3.5 from AACSB international or ACBSP-accredited institution or graduate degree from regionally-accredited U.S. university (without GMAT or GRE). Additional exam requirements/recommendations for international students: required—TOEFL (minimum score 550 paper-based; 79 iBT), IELTS (minimum score 6.5). *Application deadline:* For fall admission, 7/15 priority date for domestic students, 4/15 priority date for international students; for spring admission, 4/15 priority date for domestic students, 9/15 priority date for international students; for summer admission, 4/15 for domestic students, 1/15 for international students. Applications are processed on a rolling basis. Application fee: $40 ($50 for international students). Electronic applications accepted. *Financial support:* In 2019–20, 23 students received support, including 1 fellowship (averaging $4,844 per year); Federal Work-Study, institutionally sponsored loans, scholarships/grants, health care benefits, and unspecified assistantships also available. Financial award application deadline: 3/1. *Unit head:* Dr. Kathy Brook, Associate Dean, 575-646-8003, Fax: 575-646-7977, E-mail: kbrook@nmsu.edu. *Application contact:* John Shonk, MBA Advisor, 575-646-8003, Fax: 575-646-7977, E-mail: mbaprog@nmsu.edu.
Website: http://business.nmsu.edu/mba

North Carolina Agricultural and Technical State University, The Graduate College, College of Agriculture and Environmental Sciences, Department of Agribusiness, Applied Economics, and Agriscience Education, Greensboro, NC 27411. Offers agribusiness and food industry management (MS); agricultural education (MS). *Accreditation:* NCATE. *Program availability:* Part-time, evening/weekend. *Degree requirements:* For master's, comprehensive exam, thesis or alternative, qualifying exam. *Entrance requirements:* For master's, GRE General Test, minimum GPA of 3.0.

North Carolina State University, Graduate School, College of Agriculture and Life Sciences, Program in Agricultural and Resource Economics, Raleigh, NC 27695. Offers MS, PhD. *Program availability:* Part-time. *Degree requirements:* For master's, thesis. *Entrance requirements:* Additional exam requirements/recommendations for international students: required—TOEFL. Electronic applications accepted.

North Dakota State University, College of Graduate and Interdisciplinary Studies, College of Agriculture, Food Systems, and Natural Resources, Department of Agribusiness and Applied Economics, Fargo, ND 58102. Offers agribusiness and applied economics (MS); international agribusiness (MS). *Program availability:* Part-time. *Entrance requirements:* For master's, minimum GPA of 3.0. Additional exam requirements/recommendations for international students: required—TOEFL (minimum score 525 paper-based; 79 iBT). Electronic applications accepted. Tuition and fees vary according to program and reciprocity agreements.

Northwest Missouri State University, Graduate School, Melvin and Valorie Booth College of Business and Professional Studies, Maryville, MO 64468-6001. Offers agricultural economics (MBA); business decision and analytics (MBA); general management (MBA); human resource management (MBA); marketing (MBA). *Program availability:* Part-time. *Faculty:* 10 full-time (5 women). *Students:* 52 full-time (29 women), 237 part-time (127 women); includes 41 minority (19 Black or African American, non-Hispanic/Latino; 7 Asian, non-Hispanic/Latino; 11 Hispanic/Latino; 4 Two or more races, non-Hispanic/Latino), 10 international. Average age 32. 110 applicants, 66% accepted, 63 enrolled. In 2019, 48 master's awarded. *Degree requirements:* For master's, comprehensive exam. *Entrance requirements:* For master's, GMAT, GRE, minimum GPA of 2.5. Additional exam requirements/recommendations for international students: required—TOEFL (minimum score 550 paper-based; 79 iBT). *Application deadline:* For fall admission, 7/1 for domestic and international students; for spring admission, 11/15 for domestic and international students; for summer admission, 4/1 for domestic and international students. Applications are processed on a rolling basis. Application fee: $0 ($75 for international students). Electronic applications accepted. *Expenses:* $400 per credit hour (30 credit hours required); $300 total required fees. *Financial support:* Research assistantships with full tuition reimbursements, teaching assistantships with full tuition reimbursements, career-related internships or fieldwork, unspecified assistantships, and administrative assistantships, tutorial assistantships available. Financial award application deadline: 4/1; financial award applicants required to submit FAFSA. *Unit head:* Dr. Steve Ludwig, Director of the Melvin And Valorie Booth School of Business, 660-562-1749, Fax: 660-562-1096, E-mail: sludwig@nwmissouri.edu. *Application contact:* Dr. Steve Ludwig, Director of the Melvin And Valorie Booth School of Business, 660-562-1749, Fax: 660-562-1096, E-mail: sludwig@nwmissouri.edu.
Website: https://www.nwmissouri.edu/business/index.htm

Northwest Missouri State University, Graduate School, School of Agricultural Sciences, Maryville, MO 64468-6001. Offers agricultural economics (MBA); agricultural education (MS Ed); agriculture (MS); teaching: agriculture (MS Ed). *Program availability:* Part-time. *Faculty:* 5 full-time (1 woman). *Students:* 4 full-time (2 women), 2 part-time (1 woman), 5 international. Average age 24. 12 applicants, 50% accepted, 1 enrolled. In 2019, 3 master's awarded. *Degree requirements:* For master's, comprehensive exam, thesis (for some programs). *Entrance requirements:* For master's, GRE General Test, minimum undergraduate GPA of 2.5, writing sample. Additional exam requirements/recommendations for international students: required—TOEFL (minimum score 550 paper-based; 79 iBT). *Application deadline:* For fall admission, 7/1 for domestic and international students; for spring admission, 11/15 for domestic and international students. Applications are processed on a rolling basis. Application fee: $0 ($75 for international students). Electronic applications accepted. *Expenses:* Contact institution. *Financial support:* Research assistantships with full tuition reimbursements, teaching assistantships with full tuition reimbursements, and unspecified assistantships available. Financial award application deadline: 4/1; financial award applicants required to submit FAFSA. *Unit head:* Dr. Rod Barr, Director, 660-562-1620. *Application contact:* Dr. Rod Barr, Director, 660-562-1620.
Website: http://www.nwmissouri.edu/ag/

The Ohio State University, Graduate School, College of Food, Agricultural, and Environmental Sciences, Department of Agricultural, Environmental, and Development Economics, Columbus, OH 43210. Offers MS, PhD. *Entrance requirements:* For master's, GRE General Test (preferred minimum score: 156 quantitative, 153 verbal), minimum undergraduate GPA of 3.1 (recommended); for doctorate, GRE General Test (minimum score: 163 quantitative, 163 verbal), minimum GPA of 3.3 undergraduate, 3.5 graduate (recommended). Additional exam requirements/recommendations for international students: required—TOEFL minimum score 600 paper-based; 100 IBT (for PhD); recommended—TOEFL (minimum score 550 paper-based; 80 iBT). Electronic applications accepted.

Oklahoma State University, College of Agricultural Science and Natural Resources, Department of Agricultural Economics, Stillwater, OK 74078. Offers M Ag, MS, PhD. *Faculty:* 24 full-time (5 women). *Students:* 21 full-time (13 women), 18 part-time (7 women); includes 1 minority (Two or more races, non-Hispanic/Latino), 18 international. Average age 26. 51 applicants, 43% accepted, 10 enrolled. In 2019, 6 master's, 7 doctorates awarded. *Degree requirements:* For master's, thesis or report, oral exam; for doctorate, comprehensive exam, thesis/dissertation. *Entrance requirements:* For master's and doctorate, GRE or GMAT. Additional exam requirements/recommendations for international students: required—TOEFL (minimum score 550 paper-based; 79 iBT). *Application deadline:* For fall admission, 3/1 priority date for international students; for spring admission, 8/1 priority date for international students. Applications are processed on a rolling basis. Application fee: $50 ($75 for international students). Electronic applications accepted. *Expenses: Tuition, area resident:* Full-time $4148.10; part-time $2765.40 per credit hour. Tuition, state resident: full-time $4148.10; part-time $2765.40 per credit hour. Tuition, nonresident: full-time $15,775; part-time $10,516.80 per credit hour. *International tuition:* $15,775.20 full-time. *Required fees:* $2196.90; $122.05 per credit hour. Tuition and fees vary according to course load, campus/location and program. *Financial support:* In 2019–20, 25 research assistantships (averaging $1,500 per year), 5 teaching assistantships (averaging $1,713 per year) were awarded; career-related internships or fieldwork, Federal Work-Study, scholarships/grants, health care benefits, tuition waivers (partial), and unspecified assistantships also available. Support available to part-time students. Financial award application deadline: 3/1; financial award applicants required to submit FAFSA. *Unit head:* Dr. Cheryl DeVuyst, Department Head, 405-744-6161, Fax: 405-744-8210, E-mail: Cheryl.DeVuyst@okstate.edu. *Application contact:* Dr. Sheryl Tucker, Dean, 405-744-6368, Fax: 405-744-0355, E-mail: gradi@okstate.edu.
Website: http://agecon.okstate.edu

Penn State University Park, Graduate School, College of Agricultural Sciences, Department of Agricultural Economics, Sociology, and Education, University Park, PA 16802. Offers agricultural and extension education (M Ed, MS, PhD, Certificate); applied youth, family and community education (M Ed); energy, environmental, and food economics (MS, PhD); rural sociology (MS, PhD).

Purdue University, Graduate School, College of Agriculture, Department of Agricultural Economics, West Lafayette, IN 47907. Offers EMBA, MS, PhD. *Program availability:* Part-time. *Faculty:* 40 full-time (8 women), 1 part-time/adjunct (0 women). *Students:* 59 full-time (28 women), 44 part-time (17 women); includes 5 minority (3 Asian, non-Hispanic/Latino; 2 Hispanic/Latino), 47 international. Average age 30. 178 applicants, 28% accepted, 31 enrolled. In 2019, 40 master's, 8 doctorates awarded. Terminal master's awarded for partial completion of doctoral program. *Degree requirements:* For master's, thesis (for some programs); for doctorate, thesis/dissertation. *Entrance requirements:* For master's and doctorate, GRE General Test, minimum undergraduate GPA of 3.0 or equivalent. Additional exam requirements/recommendations for international students: required—TOEFL (minimum score 550 paper-based; 77 iBT). *Application deadline:* For fall admission, 4/1 priority date for domestic students, 3/1 for international students; for spring admission, 10/1 for domestic students, 8/1 for international students. Applications are processed on a rolling basis. Application fee: $60 ($75 for international students). Electronic applications accepted. *Financial support:* In 2019–20, fellowships with tuition reimbursements (averaging $22,000 per year), research assistantships with tuition reimbursements (averaging $18,000 per year), teaching assistantships with tuition reimbursements (averaging $15,900 per year) were awarded. Financial award application deadline: 3/1; financial award applicants required to submit FAFSA. *Unit head:* Jayson L. Lusk, Head of the Graduate Program, 765-494-4191, E-mail: jlusk@purdue.edu. *Application contact:* Taryn Nance, Graduate Contact, 765-494-2447, E-mail: tnance@purdue.edu.
Website: https://ag.purdue.edu/agecon

Rutgers University - New Brunswick, Graduate School-New Brunswick, Program in Food and Business Economics, Piscataway, NJ 08854-8097. Offers MS. *Degree requirements:* For master's, comprehensive exam, thesis or alternative. *Entrance requirements:* Additional exam requirements/recommendations for international students: required—TOEFL. Electronic applications accepted.

South Carolina State University, College of Graduate and Professional Studies, Department of Business Administration, Orangeburg, SC 29117-0001. Offers agribusiness (MBA); entrepreneurship (MBA); general business administration (MBA); healthcare management (MBA). *Program availability:* Part-time, evening/weekend. *Degree requirements:* For master's, comprehensive exam, business plan. *Entrance requirements:* For master's, GMAT, minimum GPA of 2.8. Additional exam requirements/recommendations for international students: required—TOEFL. Electronic applications accepted.

Southern Illinois University Carbondale, Graduate School, College of Agriculture, Department of Agribusiness Economics, Carbondale, IL 62901-4701. Offers MS, MBA/MS. *Program availability:* Part-time. *Degree requirements:* For master's, thesis. *Entrance requirements:* For master's, minimum GPA of 2.7. Additional exam requirements/recommendations for international students: required—TOEFL (minimum score 550 paper-based; 80 iBT). Electronic applications accepted.

Texas A&M University, College of Agriculture and Life Sciences, Department of Agricultural Economics, College Station, TX 77843. Offers M Agr, MS, PhD. *Program availability:* Part-time. *Faculty:* 32. *Students:* 121 full-time (58 women), 13 part-time (4 women); includes 15 minority (2 Black or African American, non-Hispanic/Latino; 4 Asian, non-Hispanic/Latino; 7 Hispanic/Latino; 2 Two or more races, non-Hispanic/Latino), 69 international. Average age 29. 86 applicants, 77% accepted, 34 enrolled. In 2019, 30 master's, 7 doctorates awarded. Terminal master's awarded for partial completion of doctoral program. *Degree requirements:* For master's, comprehensive exam (for some programs), thesis (for some programs); for doctorate, comprehensive exam, thesis/dissertation. *Entrance requirements:* For master's and doctorate, GRE General Test. Additional exam requirements/recommendations for international students: required—TOEFL (minimum score 550 paper-based; 80 iBT), IELTS (minimum score 6), PTE (minimum score 53). *Application deadline:* For fall admission, 3/1 for domestic students; for spring admission, 8/1 for domestic students. Applications are processed on a rolling basis. Application fee: $50 ($90 for international students). Electronic applications accepted. *Expenses:* Contact institution. *Financial support:* In 2019–20, 108 students received support, including 12 fellowships with tuition reimbursements available (averaging $6,989 per year), 40 research assistantships with tuition reimbursements available (averaging $11,815 per year), 46 teaching assistantships with tuition reimbursements available (averaging $10,789 per year); career-related internships or fieldwork, institutionally sponsored loans, scholarships/grants, traineeships, health care benefits, tuition waivers (full and partial), and unspecified assistantships also available. Support available to part-time students. Financial award application deadline: 3/15; financial award applicants required to submit

FAFSA. *Unit head:* Dr. C. Parr Rosson, III, Professor and Head, 979-845-2116, Fax: 979-847-9378, E-mail: prosson@tamu.edu. *Application contact:* Brandi Blankenship, Program Coordinator, 979-845-5222, Fax: 979-862-1563, E-mail: brandi.blankenship@tamu.edu.
Website: http://agecon.tamu.edu/

Texas A&M University–Kingsville, College of Graduate Studies, Dick and Mary Lewis Kleberg College of Agriculture, Natural Resources and Human Sciences, Department of Agriculture, Agribusiness, and Environmental Sciences, Kingsville, TX 78363. Offers agribusiness (MS); agricultural science (MS); horticulture (PhD); plant and soil science (MS); ranch management (MS). Electronic applications accepted.

Texas Tech University, Graduate School, College of Agricultural Sciences and Natural Resources, Department of Agricultural and Applied Economics, Lubbock, TX 79409-2132. Offers agribusiness (MAB); agricultural and applied economics (MS, PhD); JD/MS. *Program availability:* Part-time, 100% online. *Faculty:* 17 full-time (4 women), 1 part-time/adjunct (0 women). *Students:* 41 full-time (18 women), 11 part-time (3 women); includes 7 minority (2 Black or African American, non-Hispanic/Latino; 1 Asian, non-Hispanic/Latino; 3 Hispanic/Latino; 1 Two or more races, non-Hispanic/Latino), 30 international. Average age 31. 34 applicants, 62% accepted, 7 enrolled. In 2019, 23 master's, 6 doctorates awarded. Terminal master's awarded for partial completion of doctoral program. *Degree requirements:* For master's, thesis or alternative; for doctorate, comprehensive exam, thesis/dissertation. *Entrance requirements:* For master's and doctorate, GRE General Test, formal approval from departmental committee. Additional exam requirements/recommendations for international students: required—TOEFL (minimum score 550 paper-based; 79 iBT). *Application deadline:* For fall admission, 6/1 priority date for domestic students, 1/15 priority date for international students; for spring admission, 9/1 priority date for domestic students, 6/15 priority date for international students. Applications are processed on a rolling basis. Application fee: $65. Electronic applications accepted. *Expenses:* Contact institution. *Financial support:* In 2019–20, 59 students received support, including 55 fellowships (averaging $2,971 per year), 40 research assistantships (averaging $14,878 per year); teaching assistantships, institutionally sponsored loans, scholarships/grants, health care benefits, and unspecified assistantships also available. Financial award application deadline: 5/1; financial award applicants required to submit FAFSA. *Unit head:* Dr. Phillip N. Johnson, Professor, Chair and Charles Thompson Chair, 806-834-0474, Fax: 806-742-1099, E-mail: phil.johnson@ttu.edu. *Application contact:* Dr. Darren Hudson, Graduate Adviser, 806-742-2821, Fax: 806-742-1099, E-mail: darren.hudson@ttu.edu.
Website: www.aaec.ttu.edu

Tropical Agriculture Research and Higher Education Center, Graduate School, Turrialba, Costa Rica. Offers agribusiness management (MS); agroforestry systems (PhD); development practices (MS); ecological agriculture (MS); environmental socioeconomics (MS); forestry in tropical and subtropical zones (PhD); integrated watershed management (MS); international sustainable tourism (MS); management and conservation of tropical rainforests and biodiversity (MS); tropical agriculture (PhD); tropical agroforestry (MS). *Entrance requirements:* For master's, GRE, 2 years of related professional experience, letters of recommendation; for doctorate, GRE, 4 letters of recommendation, letter of support from employing organization, master's degree in agronomy, biological sciences, forestry, natural resources or related field. Additional exam requirements/recommendations for international students: required—TOEFL (minimum score 550 paper-based). Electronic applications accepted.

Tuskegee University, Graduate Programs, College of Agriculture, Environment and Nutrition Sciences, Department of Agricultural and Environmental Sciences, Program in Agricultural and Resource Economics, Tuskegee, AL 36088. Offers MS. *Degree requirements:* For master's, thesis. *Entrance requirements:* For master's, GRE General Test. Additional exam requirements/recommendations for international students: required—TOEFL (minimum score 500 paper-based).

Universidad del Este, Graduate School, Carolina, PR 00984. Offers accounting (MBA); adult education (M Ed); agribusiness (MBA); criminal justice and criminology (MA); curriculum and instruction - early education (M Ed); curriculum and instruction - elementary (M Ed); curriculum and instruction - English (M Ed); curriculum and instruction - Spanish (M Ed); human resources (MBA); information security management (MBA); information technology and Web business development (MBA); management (MBA); public policy (MPA); social work (MA), including clinical social work; special education (M Ed); strategic leadership (MBA).

University of Alberta, Faculty of Graduate Studies and Research, Department of Rural Economy, Edmonton, AB T6G 2E1, Canada. Offers agricultural economics (M Ag, M Sc, PhD); forest economics (M Ag, M Sc, PhD); rural sociology (M Ag, M Sc); MBA/M Ag. *Program availability:* Part-time. *Degree requirements:* For doctorate, thesis/dissertation. *Entrance requirements:* Additional exam requirements/recommendations for international students: required—TOEFL.

The University of Arizona, College of Agriculture and Life Sciences, Department of Agricultural and Resource Economics, Tucson, AZ 85721. Offers applied econometrics and data analytics (MS); applied economics and policy analysis (MS). *Program availability:* Part-time. *Degree requirements:* For master's, thesis or alternative. *Entrance requirements:* For master's, GRE General Test, 3 letters of recommendation, minimum GPA of 3.0. Additional exam requirements/recommendations for international students: required—TOEFL (minimum score 550 paper-based; 79 iBT). Electronic applications accepted.

University of Arkansas, Graduate School, Dale Bumpers College of Agricultural, Food and Life Sciences, Department of Agricultural Economics and Agribusiness, Fayetteville, AR 72701. Offers MS. *Students:* 25 full-time (11 women); includes 4 minority (1 Black or African American, non-Hispanic/Latino; 1 American Indian or Alaska Native, non-Hispanic/Latino; 2 Two or more races, non-Hispanic/Latino), 6 international. 31 applicants, 97% accepted. In 2019, 19 master's awarded. *Application deadline:* For fall admission, 8/1 for domestic students, 4/1 for international students; for spring admission, 12/1 for domestic students, 10/1 for international students; for summer admission, 4/15 for domestic students, 3/1 for international students. Applications are processed on a rolling basis. Application fee: $60. Electronic applications accepted. *Financial support:* In 2019–20, 8 research assistantships, 1 teaching assistantship were awarded; fellowships with tuition reimbursements, career-related internships or fieldwork, and Federal Work-Study also available. Support available to part-time students. Financial award application deadline: 4/1; financial award applicants required to submit FAFSA. *Unit head:* Dr. John D. Anderson, Department Head, 479-575-2281, E-mail: jda042@uark.edu. *Application contact:* Dr. Daniel V. Rainey, Graduate Coordinator, 479-575-5584, E-mail: rainey@uark.edu.
Website: https://agribusiness.uark.edu/index.php

The University of British Columbia, Faculty of Land and Food Systems, Program in Food and Resource Economics, Vancouver, BC V6T 1Z1, Canada. Offers MFRE.

University of California, Berkeley, Graduate Division, College of Natural Resources, Department of Agricultural and Resource Economics, Berkeley, CA 94720. Offers PhD. *Degree requirements:* For doctorate, thesis/dissertation, qualifying exam. *Entrance requirements:* For doctorate, GRE General Test, minimum GPA of 3.0, 3 letters of recommendation. Electronic applications accepted.

University of California, Davis, Graduate Studies, Program in Agricultural and Resource Economics, Davis, CA 95616. Offers MS, PhD, MBA/MS. Terminal master's awarded for partial completion of doctoral program. *Degree requirements:* For master's, thesis optional; for doctorate, thesis/dissertation. *Entrance requirements:* For master's, GRE General Test, minimum GPA of 3.0; for doctorate, GRE General Test, minimum GPA of 3.3. Additional exam requirements/recommendations for international students: required—TOEFL (minimum score 550 paper-based). Electronic applications accepted.

University of California, Santa Barbara, Graduate Division, Donald Bren School of Environmental Science and Management, Santa Barbara, CA 93106-5131. Offers economics and environmental science (PhD); environmental science and management (MESM, PhD); technology and society (PhD). *Degree requirements:* For master's, thesis; for doctorate, thesis/dissertation. *Entrance requirements:* For master's and doctorate, GRE. Additional exam requirements/recommendations for international students: required—TOEFL (minimum score 550 paper-based; 80 iBT), IELTS (minimum score 7). Electronic applications accepted.

University of Connecticut, Graduate School, College of Agriculture, Health and Natural Resources, Department of Agricultural and Resource Economics, Storrs, CT 06269. Offers MS, PhD. Terminal master's awarded for partial completion of doctoral program. *Degree requirements:* For master's, comprehensive exam; for doctorate, thesis/dissertation. *Entrance requirements:* For master's and doctorate, GRE General Test. Additional exam requirements/recommendations for international students: required—TOEFL (minimum score 550 paper-based). Electronic applications accepted.

University of Delaware, College of Agriculture and Natural Resources, Department of Food and Resource Economics, Newark, DE 19716. Offers agricultural and resource economics (MS); agricultural education (MA); operations research (MS); statistics (MS). *Program availability:* Part-time. *Degree requirements:* For master's, thesis. *Entrance requirements:* For master's, GRE General Test, 3 letters of recommendation. Additional exam requirements/recommendations for international students: required—TOEFL (minimum score 550 paper-based). Electronic applications accepted.

University of Florida, Graduate School, College of Agricultural and Life Sciences, Department of Food and Resource Economics, Gainesville, FL 32611. Offers agribusiness (MS); food and resource economics (MAB, MS, PhD); hydrologic sciences (MS, PhD); toxicology (MS, PhD); tropical conservation and development (MAB, MS, PhD). *Program availability:* Part-time. *Degree requirements:* For master's, comprehensive exam, thesis; for doctorate, comprehensive exam, thesis/dissertation. *Entrance requirements:* For master's, GRE (combined minimum score of 300 overall, 145 on quantitative), minimum GPA of 3.0, minimum B grade in prerequisites; for doctorate, GRE (combined minimum score of 305 overall, 150 on quantitative), minimum GPA of 3.0, minimum B grade in prerequisites. Additional exam requirements/recommendations for international students: required—TOEFL (minimum score 550 paper-based; 80 iBT), IELTS (minimum score 6). Electronic applications accepted.

University of Georgia, College of Agricultural and Environmental Sciences, Department of Agricultural and Applied Economics, Athens, GA 30602. Offers agricultural economics (MAE, MS, PhD); environmental economics (MS). *Degree requirements:* For master's, thesis (MS); for doctorate, thesis/dissertation. *Entrance requirements:* For master's and doctorate, GRE General Test. Electronic applications accepted.

University of Guelph, Office of Graduate and Postdoctoral Studies, College of Management and Economics, MBA Program, Guelph, ON N1G 2W1, Canada. Offers food and agribusiness management (MBA); hospitality and tourism management (MBA). *Program availability:* Part-time, evening/weekend, online learning. *Entrance requirements:* For master's, minimum B-average, minimum of 3 years of relevant work experience. Additional exam requirements/recommendations for international students: required—TOEFL (minimum score 550 paper-based). Electronic applications accepted.

University of Guelph, Office of Graduate and Postdoctoral Studies, Ontario Agricultural College, Department of Food, Agricultural and Resource Economics, Guelph, ON N1G 2W1, Canada. Offers agricultural economics (M Sc, PhD); MA/M Sc. *Program availability:* Part-time. *Degree requirements:* For master's, thesis; for doctorate, comprehensive exam, thesis/dissertation. *Entrance requirements:* For master's, minimum B- average during previous 2 years of course work; for doctorate, minimum B standing in recognized master's degree. Additional exam requirements/recommendations for international students: required—TOEFL (minimum score 550 paper-based), IELTS (minimum score 6.5). Electronic applications accepted.

University of Idaho, College of Graduate Studies, College of Agricultural and Life Sciences, Department of Agricultural Economics and Rural Sociology, Moscow, ID 83844-2282. Offers MS. *Faculty:* 9 full-time. *Students:* 12. Average age 26. In 2019, 3 master's awarded. *Entrance requirements:* For master's, minimum GPA of 3.0. Additional exam requirements/recommendations for international students: required—TOEFL (minimum score 79 iBT). *Application deadline:* For fall admission, 7/30 for domestic students; for spring admission, 12/1 for domestic students. Applications are processed on a rolling basis. Application fee: $60. Electronic applications accepted. *Expenses:* Tuition, state resident: full-time $7753.80; part-time $502 per credit hour. Tuition, nonresident: full-time $26,990; part-time $1571 per credit hour. *Required fees:* $2122.20; $47 per credit hour. *Financial support:* Research assistantships and teaching assistantships available. Financial award applicants required to submit FAFSA. *Unit head:* Dr. Christopher McIntosh, Department Head, 208-885-6264, Fax: 208-885-5759, E-mail: ggleason@uidaho.edu. *Application contact:* Dr. Christopher McIntosh, Department Head, 208-885-6264, Fax: 208-885-5759, E-mail: ggleason@uidaho.edu.
Website: https://www.uidaho.edu/cals/agricultural-economics-and-rural-sociology

University of Illinois at Urbana-Champaign, Graduate College, College of Agricultural, Consumer and Environmental Sciences, Department of Agricultural and Consumer Economics, Champaign, IL 61820. Offers agricultural and applied economics (MS, PhD).

University of Kentucky, Graduate School, College of Agriculture, Food and Environment, Program in Agricultural Economics, Lexington, KY 40506-0032. Offers MS, PhD. *Degree requirements:* For master's, comprehensive exam, thesis optional; for doctorate, comprehensive exam, thesis/dissertation. *Entrance requirements:* For master's, GRE General Test, minimum undergraduate GPA of 2.75; for doctorate, GRE General Test, minimum graduate GPA of 3.0. Additional exam requirements/recommendations for international students: required—TOEFL (minimum score 550 paper-based). Electronic applications accepted.

University of Maine, Graduate School, College of Natural Sciences, Forestry, and Agriculture, School of Economics, Orono, ME 04469. Offers economics (MA); financial economics (MA); resource economics and policy (MS). *Program availability:* Part-time. *Faculty:* 12 full-time (4 women), 2 part-time/adjunct (0 women). *Students:* 14 full-time (6 women), 1 part-time (0 women); includes 1 minority (Hispanic/Latino), 3 international. Average age 26. 22 applicants, 55% accepted, 6 enrolled. In 2019, 14 master's awarded. *Degree requirements:* For master's, thesis (for some programs). *Entrance requirements:* For master's, GRE General Test. Additional exam requirements/recommendations for international students: required—TOEFL (minimum score 580 paper-based; 92 iBT), IELTS (minimum score 6.9). *Application deadline:* For spring

admission, 1/30 for domestic and international students. Applications are processed on a rolling basis. Application fee: $65. Electronic applications accepted. *Expenses: Tuition, area resident:* Full-time $8100; part-time $450 per credit hour. Tuition, state resident: full-time $8100; part-time $450 per credit hour. Tuition, nonresident: full-time $26,388; part-time $1466 per credit hour. *International tuition:* $26,388 full-time. *Required fees:* $1257; $278 per semester. Tuition and fees vary according to course load. *Financial support:* In 2019–20, 20 students received support, including 15 research assistantships with full tuition reimbursements available (averaging $15,000 per year), 5 teaching assistantships with full tuition reimbursements available (averaging $15,825 per year); career-related internships or fieldwork, Federal Work-Study, institutionally sponsored loans, scholarships/grants, and tuition waivers (full and partial) also available. Support available to part-time students. Financial award application deadline: 3/1; financial award applicants required to submit FAFSA. *Unit head:* Dr. Mario Teisl, Director, 207-581-3151, Fax: 207-581-4278. *Application contact:* Scott G. Delcourt, Assistant Vice President for Graduate Studies and Senior Associate Dean, 207-581-3291, Fax: 207-581-3232, E-mail: graduate@maine.edu.
Website: http://umaine.edu/soe/

University of Manitoba, Faculty of Graduate Studies, Faculty of Agricultural and Food Sciences, Department of Agribusiness and Agricultural Economics, Winnipeg, MB R3T 2N2, Canada. Offers agribusiness (M Sc, PhD). *Degree requirements:* For master's, thesis or alternative; for doctorate, thesis/dissertation.

University of Maryland, College Park, Academic Affairs, College of Agriculture and Natural Resources, Department of Agricultural and Resource Economics, College Park, MD 20742. Offers agriculture economics (MS, PhD); resource economics (MS, PhD). *Program availability:* Part-time, evening/weekend. *Degree requirements:* For master's, variable foreign language requirement, thesis optional, oral exam; for doctorate, variable foreign language requirement, oral dissertation defense. *Entrance requirements:* For master's, GRE General Test, minimum GPA of 3.0, course work in microeconomics and calculus, 3 letters of recommendation; for doctorate, GRE General Test. Additional exam requirements/recommendations for international students: required—TOEFL. Electronic applications accepted.

University of Massachusetts Amherst, Graduate School, College of Social and Behavioral Sciences, Department of Resource Economics, Amherst, MA 01003. Offers MS, PhD. *Program availability:* Part-time. Terminal master's awarded for partial completion of doctoral program. *Degree requirements:* For master's, thesis or alternative; for doctorate, comprehensive exam, thesis/dissertation. *Entrance requirements:* For master's and doctorate, GRE General Test. Additional exam requirements/recommendations for international students: required—TOEFL (minimum score 550 paper-based; 80 iBT), IELTS (minimum score 6.5). Electronic applications accepted.

University of Missouri, Office of Research and Graduate Studies, College of Agriculture, Food and Natural Resources, Department of Agricultural and Applied Economics, Columbia, MO 65211. Offers agricultural economics (MS, PhD). *Entrance requirements:* For master's and doctorate, GRE General Test, minimum GPA of 3.0.

University of Nebraska–Lincoln, Graduate College, College of Agricultural Sciences and Natural Resources, Department of Agricultural Economics, Lincoln, NE 68588. Offers agribusiness (MBA); agricultural economics (MS, PhD); community development (M Ag). *Degree requirements:* For master's, thesis optional; for doctorate, comprehensive exam, thesis/dissertation. *Entrance requirements:* For master's and doctorate, GRE General Test. Additional exam requirements/recommendations for international students: required—TOEFL (minimum score 550 paper-based). Electronic applications accepted.

University of Puerto Rico at Mayagüez, Graduate Studies, College of Agricultural Sciences, Department of Agricultural Economics and Rural Sociology, Mayagüez, PR 00681-9000. Offers MS. *Program availability:* Part-time. *Degree requirements:* For master's, comprehensive exam, thesis. *Entrance requirements:* For master's, bachelor's degree in agricultural economics or its equivalent. Electronic applications accepted.

University of Saskatchewan, College of Graduate and Postdoctoral Studies, College of Agriculture and Bioresources, Department of Agricultural and Resource Economics, Saskatoon, SK S7N 5A2, Canada. Offers M Sc, PhD, PGD. *Degree requirements:* For master's, thesis; for doctorate, comprehensive exam (for some programs), thesis/dissertation. *Entrance requirements:* Additional exam requirements/recommendations for international students: required—TOEFL (minimum score 80 iBT); recommended—IELTS (minimum score 6.5).

University of Saskatchewan, College of Graduate and Postdoctoral Studies, Edwards School of Business, Program in Business Administration, Saskatoon, SK S7N 5A2, Canada. Offers agribusiness management (MBA).

The University of Tennessee at Martin, Graduate Programs, College of Business and Global Affairs, Program in Business, Martin, TN 38238. Offers agricultural business (MBA); financial services (MBA); general business (MBA). *Accreditation:* AACSB. *Program availability:* Part-time, 100% online, blended/hybrid learning. *Faculty:* 28. *Students:* 12 full-time (10 women), 63 part-time (27 women); includes 15 minority (7 Black or African American, non-Hispanic/Latino; 3 Asian, non-Hispanic/Latino; 2 Hispanic/Latino; 3 Two or more races, non-Hispanic/Latino). Average age 34. 95 applicants, 40% accepted, 36 enrolled. In 2019, 31 master's awarded. *Degree requirements:* For master's, comprehensive exam. *Entrance requirements:* For master's, GMAT, GRE, minimum GPA of 2.5, resume. Additional exam requirements/recommendations for international students: required—TOEFL (minimum score 525 paper-based; 71 iBT). *Application deadline:* For fall admission, 7/28 priority date for domestic students, 7/28 for international students; for spring admission, 12/17 priority date for domestic students, 12/17 for international students; for summer admission, 5/10 priority date for domestic and international students. Applications are processed on a rolling basis. Application fee: $30 ($130 for international students). Electronic applications accepted. *Expenses: Tuition, area resident:* Full-time $9096; part-time $505 per credit hour. Tuition, state resident: full-time $9096; part-time $505 per credit hour. Tuition, nonresident: full-time $15,136; part-time $841 per credit hour. *International tuition:* $23,040 full-time. *Required fees:* $1520; $85 per credit hour. Part-time tuition and fees vary according to course load. *Financial support:* In 2019–20, 39 students

received support, including 5 research assistantships with full tuition reimbursements available (averaging $7,289 per year), 7 teaching assistantships with full tuition reimbursements available (averaging $7,831 per year); scholarships/grants and tuition waivers (full and partial) also available. Financial award application deadline: 2/1; financial award applicants required to submit FAFSA. *Unit head:* Dr. Christie Chen, Coordinator, 731-881-7208, Fax: 731-881-7231, E-mail: mba@utm.edu. *Application contact:* Jolene L. Cunningham, Student Services Specialist, 731-881-7012, Fax: 731-881-7499, E-mail: jcunningham@utm.edu.

University of Vermont, Graduate College, College of Agriculture and Life Sciences, Program in Community Development and Applied Economics, Burlington, VT 05405. Offers community development and applied economics (MS). *Degree requirements:* For master's, thesis. *Entrance requirements:* For master's, GRE General Test. Additional exam requirements/recommendations for international students: required—TOEFL (minimum score 550 paper-based; 90 iBT), IELTS (minimum score 6.5). Electronic applications accepted.

University of Wisconsin–Madison, Graduate School, College of Agricultural and Life Sciences, Department of Agricultural and Applied Economics, Madison, WI 53706. Offers MA, MS, PhD. *Program availability:* Part-time. *Degree requirements:* For doctorate, thesis/dissertation, preliminary exams. *Entrance requirements:* For master's and doctorate, GRE General Test. Additional exam requirements/recommendations for international students: required—TOEFL (minimum score 580 paper-based; 92 iBT). Electronic applications accepted.

University of Wyoming, College of Agriculture and Natural Resources, Department of Agricultural and Applied Economics, Laramie, WY 82071. Offers MS. *Program availability:* Part-time. *Degree requirements:* For master's, thesis (for some programs). *Entrance requirements:* For master's, GRE General Test, minimum GPA of 3.0. Additional exam requirements/recommendations for international students: required—TOEFL. Electronic applications accepted.

Université Laval, Faculty of Agricultural and Food Sciences, Department of Agricultural Economics and Consumer Sciences, Program in Agricultural Economics, Québec, QC G1K 7P4, Canada. Offers M Sc. *Program availability:* Part-time. *Degree requirements:* For master's, thesis (for some programs). *Entrance requirements:* For master's, knowledge of French. Electronic applications accepted.

Utah State University, School of Graduate Studies, College of Agriculture and Applied Sciences, Department of Applied Economics, Logan, UT 84322. Offers applied economics (MAE, MS, PhD); international food and agribusiness (MS). *Program availability:* Part-time. *Degree requirements:* For master's, thesis optional. *Entrance requirements:* For master's, GRE General Test, minimum GPA of 3.0.

Virginia Polytechnic Institute and State University, Graduate School, College of Agriculture and Life Sciences, Blacksburg, VA 24061. Offers agricultural and applied economics (MS, PhD); agricultural and life sciences (MS); agriculture, leadership, and community education (MS, PhD); animal and poultry science (MS, PhD); biochemistry (MS, PhD); crop and soil environmental sciences (MS, PhD); dairy science (MS, PhD); entomology (MS, PhD); food science and technology (MS, PhD); horticulture (PhD); human nutrition, foods and exercise (MS, PhD); plant pathology, physiology, and weed science (MS, PhD). *Faculty:* 246 full-time (83 women). *Students:* 364 full-time (213 women), 106 part-time (68 women); includes 79 minority (29 Black or African American, non-Hispanic/Latino; 1 American Indian or Alaska Native, non-Hispanic/Latino; 13 Asian, non-Hispanic/Latino; 16 Hispanic/Latino; 20 Two or more races, non-Hispanic/Latino), 106 international. Average age 28. 314 applicants, 57% accepted, 130 enrolled. In 2019, 92 master's, 59 doctorates awarded. *Degree requirements:* For master's, comprehensive exam (for some programs), thesis (for some programs); for doctorate, comprehensive exam (for some programs), thesis/dissertation (for some programs). *Entrance requirements:* For master's and doctorate, GRE/GMAT. Additional exam requirements/recommendations for international students: required—TOEFL (minimum score 90 iBT). *Application deadline:* For fall admission, 8/1 for domestic students, 4/1 for international students; for spring admission, 1/1 for domestic students, 9/1 for international students. Applications are processed on a rolling basis. Application fee: $75. Electronic applications accepted. *Expenses:* Tuition, state resident: full-time $13,700; part-time $761.25 per credit hour. Tuition, nonresident: full-time $27,614; part-time $1534 per credit hour. *Required fees:* $886.50 per term. Tuition and fees vary according to campus/location and program. *Financial support:* In 2019–20, 248 research assistantships with full tuition reimbursements (averaging $20,360 per year), 127 teaching assistantships with full tuition reimbursements (averaging $18,183 per year) were awarded; fellowships, scholarships/grants, and unspecified assistantships also available. Financial award application deadline: 3/1; financial award applicants required to submit FAFSA. *Unit head:* Dr. Alan L. Grant, Dean, 540-231-4152, Fax: 540-231-4163, E-mail: algrant@vt.edu. *Application contact:* Crystal Tawney, Administrative Assistant, 540-231-4152, Fax: 540-231-4163, E-mail: cdtawney@vt.edu.
Website: http://www.cals.vt.edu/

Washington State University, College of Agricultural, Human, and Natural Resource Sciences, School of Economic Sciences, Pullman, WA 99164-6210. Offers agricultural economics (PhD); economics (PhD). Terminal master's awarded for partial completion of doctoral program. *Degree requirements:* For master's, comprehensive exam (for some programs), thesis (for some programs), oral exam; for doctorate, comprehensive exam, thesis/dissertation, oral exam, written exam, qualifying exams. *Entrance requirements:* For master's and doctorate, GRE, minimum GPA of 3.0, 3 letters of recommendation. Additional exam requirements/recommendations for international students: required—TOEFL (minimum score 550 paper-based). Electronic applications accepted.

West Texas A&M University, College of Agriculture and Natural Sciences, Department of Agricultural Sciences, Emphasis in Agricultural Business and Economics, Canyon, TX 79015. Offers MS. *Program availability:* Part-time. *Degree requirements:* For master's, comprehensive exam, thesis optional. *Entrance requirements:* For master's, GRE General Test. Additional exam requirements/recommendations for international students: required—TOEFL (minimum score 550 paper-based). Electronic applications accepted.

Applied Economics

Auburn University, Graduate School, College of Liberal Arts, Department of Economics, Auburn, AL 36849. Offers applied economics (PhD); economics (MS). *Program availability:* Part-time. *Faculty:* 17 full-time (6 women), 3 part-time/adjunct (2 women). *Students:* 14 full-time (7 women); includes 1 minority (Black or African

American, non-Hispanic/Latino), 11 international. Average age 31. 42 applicants, 48% accepted, 3 enrolled. In 2019, 2 master's, 2 doctorates awarded. *Degree requirements:* For master's, thesis; for doctorate, thesis/dissertation. *Entrance requirements:* For master's, GMAT, GRE General Test; for doctorate, GRE General Test. Additional exam

requirements/recommendations for international students: recommended—TOEFL (minimum score 550 paper-based; 79 iBT), IELTS (minimum score 6.5). *Application deadline:* Applications are processed on a rolling basis. Application fee: $60 ($70 for international students). Electronic applications accepted. *Expenses: Tuition, area resident:* Full-time $9828; part-time $546 per credit hour. Tuition, state resident: full-time $9828; part-time $546 per credit hour. Tuition, nonresident: full-time $29,484; part-time $1638 per credit hour. *International tuition:* $29,744 full-time. Tuition and fees vary according to course load, program and reciprocity agreements. *Financial support:* In 2019–20, 1 research assistantship with tuition reimbursement (averaging $27,000 per year), 12 teaching assistantships with tuition reimbursements (averaging $21,321 per year) were awarded; fellowships, career-related internships or fieldwork, and Federal Work-Study also available. Support available to part-time students. Financial award application deadline: 3/15; financial award applicants required to submit FAFSA. *Unit head:* Dr. Hyeongwoo Kim, Chair, 334-844-2928, E-mail: hzk0001@auburn.edu. *Application contact:* Dr. George Flowers, Dean of the Graduate School, 334-844-2125.
Website: http://www.cla.auburn.edu/economics/

Auburn University, Graduate School, Interdepartmental Programs, Program in Applied Economics, Auburn University, AL 36849. Offers PhD. *Faculty:* 12 full-time (5 women). *Students:* 3 full-time (1 woman), 3 part-time (0 women); includes 1 minority (Black or African American, non-Hispanic/Latino), 2 international. Average age 28. 14 applicants, 57% accepted, 4 enrolled. In 2019, 4 doctorates awarded. *Degree requirements:* For doctorate, thesis/dissertation. *Entrance requirements:* For doctorate, GRE. Additional exam requirements/recommendations for international students: required—TOEFL (minimum score 550 paper-based; 79 iBT). *Application deadline:* Applications are processed on a rolling basis. Application fee: $60 ($70 for international students). Electronic applications accepted. *Expenses: Tuition, area resident:* Full-time $9828; part-time $546 per credit hour. Tuition, state resident: full-time $9828; part-time $546 per credit hour. Tuition, nonresident: full-time $29,484; part-time $1638 per credit hour. *International tuition:* $29,744 full-time. Tuition and fees vary according to course load, program and reciprocity agreements. *Financial support:* Fellowships available. Financial award application deadline: 3/15; financial award applicants required to submit FAFSA. *Unit head:* Dr. Deacue Fields, Chair, 334-844-5614. *Application contact:* Dr. George Flowers, Dean of the Graduate School, 334-844-2125.
Website: https://agriculture.auburn.edu/academics/graduate-degrees/applied-economics/

Auburn University at Montgomery, College of Liberal Arts & Social Sciences, Department of Economics, Montgomery, AL 36124. Offers applied economics (MS). *Program availability:* Part-time, evening/weekend. *Faculty:* 5 full-time (0 women). *Students:* 15 full-time (6 women), 1 (woman) part-time; includes 3 minority (2 Black or African American, non-Hispanic/Latino; 1 Asian, non-Hispanic/Latino), 5 international. Average age 28. 19 applicants, 100% accepted, 10 enrolled. In 2019, 11 master's awarded. *Entrance requirements:* For master's, GMAT or GRE General Test. Additional exam requirements/recommendations for international students: recommended—TOEFL (minimum score 500 paper-based; 61 iBT), IELTS (minimum score 5.5), TSE (minimum score 44). *Application deadline:* For fall admission, 7/15 for international students; for spring admission, 11/15 for international students; for summer admission, 4/15 for international students. Applications are processed on a rolling basis. Application fee: $25. Electronic applications accepted. *Expenses: Tuition, area resident:* Full-time $7578; part-time $421 per credit hour. Tuition, state resident: full-time $7578; part-time $421 per credit hour. Tuition, nonresident: full-time $17,046; part-time $947 per credit hour. *International tuition:* $17,046 full-time. *Required fees:* $868. *Financial support:* Application deadline: 3/1; applicants required to submit FAFSA. *Unit head:* Dr. Carel Ligeon, Head, 334-244-3486, E-mail: cligeon@aum.edu. *Application contact:* Ashley Warren, Graduate Admissions Coordinator, 334-244-3623, E-mail: awarren3@aum.edu.
Website: http://www.cas.aum.edu/academic-programs/graduate-programs/master-of-science-in-applied-economics

Brandeis University, Brandeis International Business School, Master of Arts in International Economics and Finance Program, Waltham, MA 02454-9110. Offers applied economic analysis (MA). *Students:* Average age 23. 649 applicants, 45% accepted, 92 enrolled. In 2019, 103 master's awarded. *Entrance requirements:* For master's, GMAT or GRE. Additional exam requirements/recommendations for international students: required—TOEFL (minimum score 600 paper-based; 100 iBT), IELTS (minimum score 7), PTE (minimum score 68). *Application deadline:* For fall admission, 11/1 priority date for domestic and international students; for winter admission, 1/15 priority date for domestic and international students; for spring admission, 3/15 priority date for domestic and international students; for summer admission, 4/15 for domestic and international students. Application fee: $100. Electronic applications accepted. *Expenses:* Contact institution. *Financial support:* In 2019–20, 81 students received support. Institutionally sponsored loans and scholarships (averaging $18,384 annually) available. Financial award application deadline: 4/15; financial award applicants required to submit FAFSA. *Unit head:* Peter Petri, Dean, 781-736-2256. *Application contact:* Kelly Sugrue, Assistant Dean of Admissions, 781-736-2252, Fax: 781-736-2263, E-mail: globaladmissions@brandeis.edu.
Website: http://www.brandeis.edu/global/ma

Buffalo State College, State University of New York, The Graduate School, School of Natural and Social Sciences, Department of Economics and Finance, Buffalo, NY 14222-1095. Offers applied economics (MA). *Degree requirements:* For master's, project. *Entrance requirements:* Additional exam requirements/recommendations for international students: required—TOEFL (minimum score 550 paper-based).

Clemson University, Graduate School, College of Agriculture, Forestry and Life Sciences, Department of Agricultural Sciences, Clemson, SC 29634. Offers agricultural education (M Ag Ed); applied economics (PhD); applied economics and statistics (MS). *Faculty:* 21 full-time (3 women). *Students:* 19 full-time (10 women), 8 part-time (6 women); includes 1 minority (Black or African American, non-Hispanic/Latino), 1 international. Average age 27. 23 applicants, 87% accepted, 15 enrolled. In 2019, 15 master's awarded. *Application deadline:* Applications are processed on a rolling basis. Electronic applications accepted. *Expenses: Tuition, area resident:* Full-time $10,600; part-time $8688 per semester. Tuition, state resident: full-time $10,600; part-time $8688 per semester. Tuition, nonresident: full-time $22,050; part-time $17,412 per semester. *International tuition:* $22,050 full-time. *Required fees:* $1196; $617 per semester. $617 per semester. Tuition and fees vary according to course load, degree level, campus/location and program. *Financial support:* In 2019–20, 11 students received support, including 6 research assistantships with full and partial tuition reimbursements available (averaging $13,542 per year), 5 teaching assistantships with full and partial tuition reimbursements available (averaging $7,829 per year); career-related internships or fieldwork also available. *Unit head:* Dr. Charles Privette, Department Chair, 864-656-6247, E-mail: privett@clemson.edu. *Application contact:* Christi Christi, Student Services Manager, 864-656-4082, E-mail: ccampb3@clemson.edu.
Website: http://www.clemson.edu/cafls/departments/agricultural-sciences/index.html

Clemson University, Graduate School, College of Business, John E. Walker Department of Economics, Clemson, SC 29634. Offers applied economics (PhD); applied economics and statistics (MS); economics (MA, PhD). *Faculty:* 28 full-time (3 women), 2 part-time/adjunct (1 woman). *Students:* 65 full-time (23 women), 5 part-time (3 women); includes 5 minority (2 Black or African American, non-Hispanic/Latino; 1 Hispanic/Latino; 2 Two or more races, non-Hispanic/Latino), 40 international. Average age 27. 103 applicants, 73% accepted, 21 enrolled. In 2019, 7 master's, 16 doctorates awarded. Terminal master's awarded for partial completion of doctoral program. *Degree requirements:* For master's, thesis, 24 course hours, 6 thesis hours; for doctorate, comprehensive exam, thesis/dissertation, 42 course hours, 18 dissertation hours. *Entrance requirements:* For master's and doctorate, GRE General Test or GMAT, unofficial transcripts, letters of recommendation, courses in intermediate microeconomic theory and multivariable calculus. Additional exam requirements/recommendations for international students: required—TOEFL (minimum score 80 paper-based; 80 iBT); recommended—IELTS (minimum score 6.5), TSE (minimum score 54). *Application deadline:* For fall admission, 4/15 for international students; for spring admission, 10/15 for international students. Applications are processed on a rolling basis. Application fee: $80 ($90 for international students). Electronic applications accepted. *Expenses:* Full-Time Student per Semester: Tuition: $4600 (in-state), $9525 (out-of-state), Fees: $598; Graduate Assistant Per Semester: $1144; Part-Time Student Per Credit Hour: $556 (in-state), $1106 (out-of-state), Fees: $617; other fees apply depending on credit hours, campus & residency. Doctoral Base Fee per Semester: $4938 (in-state), $10405 (out-of-state). *Financial support:* In 2019–20, 74 students received support, including 25 fellowships with full and partial tuition reimbursements available (averaging $5,310 per year), 18 teaching assistantships with full and partial tuition reimbursements available (averaging $15,889 per year); unspecified assistantships also available. *Unit head:* Dr. Scott Baier, Department Chair, 864-656-4534, E-mail: sbaier@clemson.edu. *Application contact:* Dr. Curtis Simon, PhD Program Coordinator, 864-656-3966, E-mail: cjsmn@clemson.edu.
Website: http://economics.clemson.edu/

Cornell University, Graduate School, Graduate Fields of Agriculture and Life Sciences, Field of Applied Economics and Management, Ithaca, NY 14853. Offers agricultural finance (MS, PhD); applied econometrics and qualitative analysis (MS, PhD); economics of development (MS, PhD); environmental economics (MS, PhD); environmental management (MPS); farm management and production economics (MS, PhD); marketing and food distribution (MS, PhD); public policy analysis (MS, PhD); resource economics (PhD). *Entrance requirements:* For master's and doctorate, GRE. Additional exam requirements/recommendations for international students: required—TOEFL.

Cornell University, Graduate School, Graduate Fields of Arts and Sciences, Field of Economics, Ithaca, NY 14853. Offers applied economics (PhD); basic analytical economics (PhD); econometrics and economic statistics (PhD); economic development and planning (PhD); economic theory (PhD); industrial organization and control (PhD); international economics (PhD); labor economics (PhD); monetary and macro economics (PhD); public finance (PhD). *Degree requirements:* For doctorate, comprehensive exam, thesis/dissertation. *Entrance requirements:* For doctorate, GRE General Test, 3 letters of recommendation. Additional exam requirements/recommendations for international students: required—TOEFL (minimum score 550 paper-based; 77 iBT). Electronic applications accepted.

DePaul University, Kellstadt Graduate School of Business, Chicago, IL 60604. Offers accountancy (MBA, MSA); applied economics (MBA); audit and advisory services (MS); business administration (DBA); business analytics (MS); business strategy and decision-making (MBA); computational finance (MS); economics and policy analysis (MS); enterprise risk management (MS); entrepreneurship (MBA, MS); finance (MBA, MS); general business (MBA); hospitality leadership (MBA); hospitality leadership and operational performance (MS); human resources (MS); international business (MBA); management (MBA, MS); management information systems (MBA); marketing (MBA, MS); marketing analysis (MS); marketing strategy and planning (MBA); real estate (MS); real estate finance and investment (MBA); strategy, execution and valuation (MBA); supply chain management (MS); sustainable management (MS); taxation (MS); JD/MBA. *Accreditation:* AACSB. *Program availability:* Part-time, evening/weekend, online learning. *Entrance requirements:* For master's, GMAT/GRE, 2 letters of recommendation, resume, essay, official transcripts. Additional exam requirements/recommendations for international students: required—TOEFL (minimum score 550 paper-based; 80 iBT). Electronic applications accepted. *Expenses:* Contact institution.

East Carolina University, Graduate School, Thomas Harriot College of Arts and Sciences, Department of Economics, Greenville, NC 27858-4353. Offers quantitative economics and econometrics (MS). *Program availability:* Part-time. *Application deadline:* For fall admission, 8/15 priority date for domestic students, 2/1 priority date for international students; for spring admission, 12/20 priority date for domestic students, 10/1 priority date for international students. *Expenses: Tuition, area resident:* Full-time $4749; part-time $185 per credit hour. Tuition, state resident: full-time $4749; part-time $185 per credit hour. Tuition, nonresident: full-time $17,898; part-time $864 per credit hour. *International tuition:* $17,898 full-time. *Required fees:* $2787. *Financial support:* Application deadline: 3/1. *Unit head:* Dr. Haiyong Liu, Chair, 252-328-1083, E-mail: liuh@ecu.edu. *Application contact:* Graduate School Admissions, 252-328-6012, Fax: 252-328-6071, E-mail: gradschool@ecu.edu.
Website: https://economics.ecu.edu/

Florida State University, The Graduate School, College of Social Sciences and Public Policy, Department of Economics, Tallahassee, FL 32306-2180. Offers applied economics (MS); economics (PhD); JD/MS. *Faculty:* 32 full-time (6 women), 2 part-time/adjunct (1 woman). *Students:* 61 full-time (13 women), 3 part-time (2 women); includes 18 minority (2 Black or African American, non-Hispanic/Latino; 3 Asian, non-Hispanic/Latino; 11 Hispanic/Latino; 2 Two or more races, non-Hispanic/Latino), 3 international. Average age 26. 186 applicants, 48% accepted, 33 enrolled. In 2019, 30 master's, 7 doctorates awarded. Terminal master's awarded for partial completion of doctoral program. *Degree requirements:* For master's, thesis (for some programs), applied project (for some programs); for doctorate, comprehensive exam, thesis/dissertation, dissertation prospectus, workshops. *Entrance requirements:* For master's, GRE General Test, minimum upper-division undergraduate GPA of 3.0, 3.4 on graduate work; minimum 1 course each in statistics and calculus; principles and sufficient upper-level economics courses; for doctorate, GRE General Test, minimum upper-division undergraduate GPA of 3.0, graduate 3.4; minimum 1 course each in statistics and linear algebra, 2 in calculus. Additional exam requirements/recommendations for international students: required—TOEFL (minimum score 90 iBT). *Application deadline:* For fall admission, 2/15 priority date for domestic and international students. Applications are processed on a rolling basis. Application fee: $30. Electronic applications accepted. *Financial support:* In 2019–20, 52 students received support, including 3 fellowships with full tuition reimbursements available (averaging $25,000 per year), 1 research assistantship with full tuition reimbursement available (averaging $19,000 per year), 24 teaching assistantships with full tuition reimbursements available (averaging $19,000 per year); scholarships/grants, tuition waivers (full), and unspecified assistantships also available. Financial award application deadline: 2/15; financial award applicants required to submit FAFSA. *Unit head:* Dr. Manoj Atolia, Chairman, 850-644-5001, Fax: 850-644-4535, E-mail: matolia@fsu.edu. *Application contact:* Dr. Thomas W. Zuehlke, Graduate Director, 850-644-5001, Fax: 850-644-4535, E-mail: tzuehlke@fsu.edu.
Website: http://www.coss.fsu.edu/economics/

Georgia Southern University, Jack N. Averitt College of Graduate Studies, Parker College of Business, Program in Applied Economics, Statesboro, GA 30460. Offers applied economics (MS); information systems (Graduate Certificate). *Program availability:* Part-time-only, online only, 100% online. *Faculty:* 17 full-time (2 women). *Students:* 17 part-time (10 women); includes 4 minority (1 Black or African American, non-Hispanic/Latino; 1 Asian, non-Hispanic/Latino; 2 Two or more races, non-Hispanic/Latino), 1 international. Average age 37. 9 applicants, 78% accepted, 3 enrolled. In 2019, 5 master's awarded. *Entrance requirements:* For master's, GRE, minimum GPA of 3.0, current knowledge of calculus and statistics, introductory micro and macro courses. Additional exam requirements/recommendations for international students: required—TOEFL (minimum score 550 paper-based; 80 iBT), IELTS (minimum score 6). *Application deadline:* For fall admission, 3/1 priority date for domestic students, 3/1 for international students; for spring admission, 10/1 priority date for domestic students, 10/1 for international students. Applications are processed on a rolling basis. Application fee: $50. Electronic applications accepted. *Expenses: Tuition, area resident:* Full-time $4986; part-time $277 per credit hour. Tuition, nonresident: full-time $19,890; part-time $1105 per credit hour. *International tuition:* $19,890 full-time. *Required fees:* $2114; $1057 per semester. $1057 per semester. Tuition and fees vary according to course load, campus/location and program. *Financial support:* Unspecified assistantships available. Financial award application deadline: 4/15; financial award applicants required to submit FAFSA.
Website: http://coba.georgiasouthern.edu/dfe/graduate/master-of-science-in-applied-economics/

HEC Montreal, School of Business Administration, Doctoral Program in Administration, Montréal, QC H3T 2A7, Canada. Offers accounting (PhD); applied economics (PhD); data science (PhD); finance (PhD); financial engineering (PhD); information technology (PhD); international business (PhD); logistics and operations management (PhD); management science (PhD); management, strategy and organizations (PhD); marketing (PhD); organizational behaviour and human resources (PhD). *Accreditation:* AACSB. *Entrance requirements:* For doctorate, TAGE MAGE, GMAT, or GRE, master's degree in administration or related field. Electronic applications accepted.

HEC Montreal, School of Business Administration, Master of Science Programs in Administration, Program in Applied Economics, Montréal, QC H3T 2A7, Canada. Offers M Sc. *Entrance requirements:* For master's, BBA, undergraduate degree in another field, degree deemed equivalent by program director and minimum GPA of 3.0 on 4.3 scale. Additional exam requirements/recommendations for international students: required—TAGE MAGE (minimum recommended score of 300), GMAT (minimum recommended score of 630), or GRE. Electronic applications accepted.

Johns Hopkins University, Advanced Academic Programs, Program in Applied Economics, Washington, DC 21218. Offers MA. *Program availability:* Part-time, evening/weekend. *Entrance requirements:* For master's, minimum GPA of 3.0, coursework in microeconomics and macroeconomics. Additional exam requirements/recommendations for international students: required—TOEFL (minimum score 100 iBT). Electronic applications accepted.

Mills College, Graduate Studies, Lorry I. Lokey Graduate School of Business, Oakland, CA 94613-1000. Offers applied economics (MA); management (MBA, MM). *Program availability:* Part-time. *Entrance requirements:* For master's, GRE, SAT, or ACT, 3 letters of recommendation, 2 transcripts. Additional exam requirements/recommendations for international students: required—TOEFL (minimum score 550 paper-based; 80 iBT) or IELTS (minimum score 6). *Expenses:* Contact institution.

New York University, Graduate School of Arts and Science, Department of Economics, New York, NY 10012-1019. Offers applied economic analysis (Advanced Certificate); economics (MA, PhD); JD/MA; MD/PhD. *Program availability:* Part-time, evening/weekend. Terminal master's awarded for partial completion of doctoral program. *Degree requirements:* For master's, thesis; for doctorate, one foreign language, thesis/dissertation, 4 qualifying exams. *Entrance requirements:* For master's and doctorate, GRE General Test. Additional exam requirements/recommendations for international students: required—TOEFL, IELTS.

Ohio University, Graduate College, College of Arts and Sciences, Department of Economics, Athens, OH 45701-2979. Offers applied economics (MA); financial economics (MFE). *Program availability:* Part-time, evening/weekend. *Degree requirements:* For master's, thesis or alternative. *Entrance requirements:* For master's, GRE or GMAT (recommended), minimum GPA of 3.0. Additional exam requirements/recommendations for international students: required—TOEFL (minimum score 550 paper-based; 80 iBT) or IELTS (minimum score 6.5). Electronic applications accepted.

Oregon State University, College of Agricultural Sciences, Program in Applied Economics, Corvallis, OR 97331. Offers public health economics (MA, MS, PhD). *Program availability:* Part-time. Terminal master's awarded for partial completion of doctoral program. *Entrance requirements:* For master's and doctorate, GRE General Test, minimum GPA of 3.0 in last 90 hours. Additional exam requirements/recommendations for international students: required—TOEFL (minimum score 90 iBT).

St. Cloud State University, School of Graduate Studies, College of Social Sciences, Department of Economics, Program in Applied Economics, St. Cloud, MN 56301-4498. Offers MS.

San Jose State University, Program in Economics, San Jose, CA 95192-0001. Offers applied economics (MA); economics (MA). *Program availability:* Part-time. *Degree requirements:* For master's, comprehensive exam, thesis optional. *Entrance requirements:* For master's, GRE, minimum GPA of 3.0. Electronic applications accepted. *Expenses: Tuition, area resident:* Full-time $7176; part-time $4164 per credit hour. Tuition, state resident: full-time $7176; part-time $4164 per credit hour. Tuition, nonresident: full-time $7176; part-time $4165 per credit hour. *International tuition:* $7176 full-time. *Required fees:* $2110; $2110.

Southern Methodist University, Dedman College of Humanities and Sciences, Department of Economics, Dallas, TX 75205. Offers applied economics (MA); applied economics and predictive analytics (MS); economics (PhD); law and economics (MA). *Program availability:* Part-time, evening/weekend. Terminal master's awarded for partial completion of doctoral program. *Degree requirements:* For master's, thesis, oral qualifying exam; for doctorate, thesis/dissertation, written exams. *Entrance requirements:* For master's, GRE General Test or GMAT, 12 hours of course work in economics, minimum GPA of 3.0, previous course work in calculus and statistics; for doctorate, GRE General Test, minimum GPA of 3.0; 3 semesters of course work in calculus; 1 semester each of course work in statistics and linear algebra. Additional exam requirements/recommendations for international students: required—TOEFL (minimum score 550 paper-based). Electronic applications accepted.

Southern New Hampshire University, School of Business, Manchester, NH 03106-1045. Offers accounting (MBA, Graduate Certificate); accounting finance (MS); accounting/auditing (MS); accounting/forensic accounting (MS); accounting/management accounting (MS); accounting/taxation (MS); applied economics (MS); athletic administration (MBA, Graduate Certificate); business administration (IMBA, Certificate), including business information systems (Certificate), human resource management (Certificate); business analytics (MBA); business intelligence (MBA); communication (MA), including new media and marketing, public relations; community economic development (MBA); criminal justice (MBA); data analytics (MS); economics (MBA); engineering management (MBA); entrepreneurship (MBA); finance (MBA, MS, Graduate Certificate); finance/corporate finance (MS); finance/investments (MS); forensic accounting (MBA); forensic accounting and fraud examination (Graduate Certificate); healthcare informatics (MBA); healthcare management (MBA); human resource management (MS); human resources (MBA); information technology (MS); information technology management (MBA); international business (PhD); Internet marketing (MBA); leadership (MBA); leadership of nonprofit organizations (Graduate Certificate); management (MS); marketing (MBA, MS, Graduate Certificate); music business (MBA); operations and project management (MS); operations and supply chain management (MBA, Graduate Certificate); organizational leadership (MS); project management (MBA, Graduate Certificate); public administration (MBA, Graduate Certificate); quantitative analysis (MBA); Six Sigma (Graduate Certificate); Six Sigma quality (MBA); social media marketing (MBA, Graduate Certificate); sport management (MBA, MS, Graduate Certificate); sustainability and environmental compliance (MBA); MBA/Certificate. *Accreditation:* ACBSP. *Program availability:* Part-time, evening/weekend, online learning. Terminal master's awarded for partial completion of doctoral program. *Degree requirements:* For master's, one foreign language, comprehensive exam (for some programs), thesis or alternative; for doctorate, one foreign language, comprehensive exam, thesis/dissertation. *Entrance requirements:* For master's, minimum GPA of 2.5; for doctorate, GMAT. Additional exam requirements/recommendations for international students: required—TOEFL (minimum score 500 paper-based). Electronic applications accepted.

Texas Tech University, Graduate School, College of Agricultural Sciences and Natural Resources, Department of Agricultural and Applied Economics, Lubbock, TX 79409-2132. Offers agribusiness (MAB); agricultural and applied economics (MS, PhD); JD/MS. *Program availability:* Part-time, 100% online. *Faculty:* 17 full-time (4 women), 1 part-time/adjunct (0 women). *Students:* 41 full-time (18 women), 11 part-time (3 women); includes 7 minority (2 Black or African American, non-Hispanic/Latino; 1 Asian, non-Hispanic/Latino; 3 Hispanic/Latino; 1 Two or more races, non-Hispanic/Latino), 30 international. Average age 31. 34 applicants, 62% accepted, 7 enrolled. In 2019, 23 master's, 6 doctorates awarded. Terminal master's awarded for partial completion of doctoral program. *Degree requirements:* For master's, thesis or alternative; for doctorate, comprehensive exam, thesis/dissertation. *Entrance requirements:* For master's and doctorate, GRE General Test, formal approval from departmental committee. Additional exam requirements/recommendations for international students: required—TOEFL (minimum score 550 paper-based; 79 iBT). *Application deadline:* For fall admission, 6/1 priority date for domestic students, 1/15 priority date for international students; for spring admission, 9/1 priority date for domestic students, 6/15 priority date for international students. Applications are processed on a rolling basis. Application fee: $65. Electronic applications accepted. *Expenses:* Contact institution. *Financial support:* In 2019–20, 59 students received support, including 55 fellowships (averaging $2,971 per year), 40 research assistantships (averaging $14,878 per year); teaching assistantships, institutionally sponsored loans, scholarships/grants, health care benefits, and unspecified assistantships also available. Financial award application deadline: 5/1; financial award applicants required to submit FAFSA. *Unit head:* Dr. Phillip N. Johnson, Professor, Chair and Charles Thompson Chair, 806-834-0474, Fax: 806-742-1099, E-mail: phil.johnson@ttu.edu. *Application contact:* Dr. Darren Hudson, Graduate Adviser, 806-742-2821, Fax: 806-742-1099, E-mail: darren.hudson@ttu.edu.
Website: www.aaec.ttu.edu

Thomas Jefferson University, Jefferson College of Population Health, Philadelphia, PA 19107. Offers applied health economics and outcomes research (MS, PhD, Certificate); behavioral health science (PhD); health policy (MS, Certificate); healthcare quality and safety (MS, PhD); population health (Certificate); public health (MPH, Certificate). *Program availability:* Part-time, evening/weekend, online learning. Terminal master's awarded for partial completion of doctoral program. *Degree requirements:* For master's, thesis; for doctorate, comprehensive exam, thesis/dissertation. *Entrance requirements:* For master's, GRE or other graduate entrance exam (MCAT, LSAT, DAT, etc.), two letters of recommendation, curriculum vitae, transcripts from all undergraduate and graduate institutions; for doctorate, GRE (taken within the last 5 years), three letters of recommendation, curriculum vitae, transcripts from all undergraduate and graduate institutions. Additional exam requirements/recommendations for international students: required—TOEFL. Electronic applications accepted.

UNB Fredericton, School of Graduate Studies, Faculty of Arts - Saint John, Department of Economics, Fredericton, NB E3B 5A3, Canada. Offers applied economics and finance (M Sc); economics (MA). *Faculty:* 12 full-time (2 women). *Students:* 19 full-time (7 women), 16 international. In 2019, 10 master's awarded. *Entrance requirements:* For master's, minimum GPA of 3.0. Additional exam requirements/recommendations for international students: required—TWE (minimum score 4), TOEFL (minimum score 580 paper-based) or IELTS (minimum score 7). *Application deadline:* For fall admission, 1/31 for domestic and international students; for winter admission, 1/15 for domestic students, 1/15 priority date for international students; for spring admission, 1/31 for domestic and international students. Applications are processed on a rolling basis. Application fee: $50 Canadian dollars. Electronic applications accepted. *Expenses: Tuition, area resident:* Full-time $6975 Canadian dollars; part-time $3423 Canadian dollars per year. Tuition, state resident: full-time $6975 Canadian dollars; part-time $3423 Canadian dollars per year. Tuition, Canadian resident: full-time $6975 Canadian dollars; part-time $3423 Canadian dollars per year. *International tuition:* $12,435 Canadian dollars full-time. *Required fees:* $92.25 Canadian dollars per term. Full-time tuition and fees vary according to degree level, campus/location, program, reciprocity agreements and student level. *Financial support:* Fellowships, research assistantships, teaching assistantships, scholarships/grants, health care benefits, and unspecified assistantships available. Financial award application deadline: 1/31. *Unit head:* Dr. Yuri Yevdokimov, Director of Graduate Studies, 506-447-3221, Fax: 506-453-4514, E-mail: yuri@unb.ca. *Application contact:* Dr. Yuri Yevdokimov, Director of Graduate Studies, 506-447-3221, Fax: 506-453-4514, E-mail: yuri@unb.ca.
Website: http://go.unb.ca/gradprograms

The University of Arizona, College of Agriculture and Life Sciences, Department of Agricultural and Resource Economics, Tucson, AZ 85721. Offers applied econometrics and data analytics (MS); applied economics and policy analysis (MS). *Program availability:* Part-time. *Degree requirements:* For master's, thesis or alternative. *Entrance requirements:* For master's, GRE General Test, 3 letters of recommendation, minimum GPA of 3.0. Additional exam requirements/recommendations for international students: required—TOEFL (minimum score 550 paper-based; 79 iBT). Electronic applications accepted.

University of California, Los Angeles, Graduate Division, College of Letters and Science, Department of Economics, Program in Applied Economics, Los Angeles, CA 90095. Offers MAE. *Degree requirements:* For master's, capstone project. *Entrance requirements:* For master's, GRE General Test, bachelor's degree; minimum undergraduate GPA of 3.0 (or equivalent). Additional exam requirements/recommendations for international students: required—TOEFL or IELTS. Electronic applications accepted. *Expenses:* Contact institution.

Applied Economics

University of California, Santa Cruz, Division of Graduate Studies, Division of Social Sciences, Program in Applied Economics and Finance, Santa Cruz, CA 95064. Offers MS. *Degree requirements:* For master's, thesis or alternative, project. *Entrance requirements:* For master's, GRE General Test, GRE Subject Test. Additional exam requirements/recommendations for international students: required—TOEFL (minimum score 550 paper-based; 83 iBT); recommended—IELTS (minimum score 8). Electronic applications accepted.

University of Cincinnati, Carl H. Lindner College of Business, MS Program, Cincinnati, OH 45221. Offers accounting (MS); applied economics (MS); business analytics (MS); finance (MS); information systems (MS); marketing (MS); taxation (MS). *Program availability:* Part-time, evening/weekend. *Faculty:* 88 full-time (25 women), 40 part-time/adjunct (7 women). *Students:* 78 full-time (34 women), 355 part-time (140 women); includes 32 minority (11 Black or African American, non-Hispanic/Latino; 13 Asian, non-Hispanic/Latino; 4 Hispanic/Latino; 4 Two or more races, non-Hispanic/Latino), 296 international. Average age 28. 1,106 applicants, 45% accepted, 433 enrolled. In 2019, 349 master's awarded. *Degree requirements:* For master's, thesis (for some programs), capstone. *Entrance requirements:* For master's, GMAT, GRE, resume, transcripts, essays, letters of recommendation. Additional exam requirements/recommendations for international students: required—TOEFL (minimum score 577 paper-based; 90 iBT), IELTS (minimum score 6.5). *Application deadline:* For fall admission, 6/30 priority date for domestic students, 3/15 for international students; for spring admission, 12/15 for domestic students, 9/15 for international students; for summer admission, 4/15 for domestic and international students. Applications are processed on a rolling basis. Application fee: $65 ($70 for international students). Electronic applications accepted. *Expenses:* Full-time resident $10,961 per term; Full-time non resident $ 15,076 per term; Part-time $920 per credit hour. *Financial support:* In 2019–20, 251 students received support. Teaching assistantships, scholarships/grants, tuition waivers (full and partial), and unspecified assistantships available. Financial award application deadline: 2/1; financial award applicants required to submit FAFSA. *Unit head:* Dr. Marianne Lewis, Dean, 513-556-7001, Fax: 513-556-4891, E-mail: marianne.lewis@uc.edu. *Application contact:* Dona Clary, Executive Director, Graduate Programs, 513-556-3546, Fax: 513-558-7006, E-mail: dona.clary@uc.edu.
Website: http://business.uc.edu/graduate/masters.html

University of Georgia, College of Agricultural and Environmental Sciences, Department of Agricultural and Applied Economics, Athens, GA 30602. Offers agricultural economics (MAE, MS, PhD); environmental economics (MS). *Degree requirements:* For master's, thesis (MS); for doctorate, thesis/dissertation. *Entrance requirements:* For master's and doctorate, GRE General Test. Electronic applications accepted.

University of Houston, College of Liberal Arts and Social Sciences, Department of Economics, Houston, TX 77204. Offers applied economics (MA); economics (MA, PhD). Terminal master's awarded for partial completion of doctoral program. *Degree requirements:* For master's, thesis optional; for doctorate, comprehensive exam, thesis/dissertation. *Entrance requirements:* For master's and doctorate, GRE General Test, minimum GPA of 3.0, statement of purpose, three letters of recommendation. Additional exam requirements/recommendations for international students: required—TOEFL (minimum score 550 paper-based; 79 iBT), IELTS (minimum score 6.5). Electronic applications accepted.

University of Illinois at Urbana-Champaign, Graduate College, College of Agricultural, Consumer and Environmental Sciences, Department of Agricultural and Consumer Economics, Champaign, IL 61820. Offers agricultural and applied economics (MS, PhD).

University of Massachusetts Boston, College of Liberal Arts, Program in Applied Economics, Boston, MA 02125-3393. Offers MA.

University of Michigan, Rackham Graduate School, College of Literature, Science, and the Arts, Department of Economics, Program in Applied Economics, Ann Arbor, MI 48109. Offers AM. *Program availability:* Part-time. *Entrance requirements:* For master's, GRE General Test. Additional exam requirements/recommendations for international students: required—TOEFL (minimum score 600 paper-based).

University of Minnesota, Twin Cities Campus, Graduate School, College of Food, Agricultural and Natural Resource Sciences, Applied Economics Graduate Program, St. Paul, MN 55108. Offers MS, PhD. Terminal master's awarded for partial completion of doctoral program. *Degree requirements:* For master's, thesis; for doctorate, comprehensive exam, thesis/dissertation. *Entrance requirements:* For master's and doctorate, GRE, minimum GPA of 3.0 (preferred). Additional exam requirements/recommendations for international students: required—TOEFL (minimum score 550 paper-based; 79 iBT), IELTS (minimum score 6.5). Electronic applications accepted.

University of Nevada, Las Vegas, Graduate College, Lee Business School, Department of Economics, Las Vegas, NV 89154-6005. Offers applied economics (MA); economics/mathematical science (MA/MS); MA/MS. *Program availability:* Part-time. *Faculty:* 9 full-time (1 woman), 2 part-time/adjunct (0 women). *Students:* 10 full-time (3 women), 6 part-time (1 woman); includes 7 minority (1 Asian, non-Hispanic/Latino; 6 Hispanic/Latino), 3 international. Average age 31. 12 applicants, 67% accepted, 5 enrolled. In 2019, 8 master's awarded. *Degree requirements:* For master's, thesis optional, oral defense of thesis; internship. *Entrance requirements:* For master's, GRE General Test or GMAT, bachelor's degree with minimum GPA 3.0. Additional exam requirements/recommendations for international students: required—TOEFL (minimum score 550 paper-based; 80 iBT), IELTS (minimum score 7). *Application deadline:* For fall admission, 6/15 for domestic students, 5/1 for international students; for spring admission, 11/15 for domestic students, 10/1 for international students. Application fee: $60 ($95 for international students). Electronic applications accepted. *Expenses:* Contact institution. *Financial support:* In 2019–20, 9 students received support, including 1 research assistantship with full tuition reimbursement available (averaging $11,250 per year), 6 teaching assistantships with full tuition reimbursements available (averaging $11,250 per year); institutionally sponsored loans, scholarships/grants, health care benefits, and unspecified assistantships also available. Financial award application deadline: 3/15; financial award applicants required to submit FAFSA. *Unit head:* Dr. Jeff Waddoups, Chair/Professor, 702-895-3497, Fax: 702-895-1354, E-mail: economics.chair@unlv.edu. *Application contact:* Dr. Ian McDonough, Graduate Coordinator, 702-895-3651, Fax: 702-895-3606, E-mail: economics.gradcoord@unlv.edu.
Website: https://www.unlv.edu/economics

University of Nevada, Las Vegas, Graduate College, Lee Business School, Department of Management, Entrepreneurship and Technology, Las Vegas, NV 89154-6034. Offers data analytics (Certificate); data analytics and applied economics (MS); hotel administration/management information systems (MS/MS); management (Certificate); management information systems (MS, Certificate); new venture management (Certificate); MS/MS. *Program availability:* Part-time, evening/weekend. *Faculty:* 9 full-time (1 woman), 2 part-time/adjunct (0 women). *Students:* 70 full-time (27 women), 51 part-time (20 women); includes 46 minority (6 Black or African American, non-Hispanic/Latino; 19 Asian, non-Hispanic/Latino; 15 Hispanic/Latino; 6 Two or more races, non-Hispanic/Latino), 39 international. Average age 31. 80 applicants, 83% accepted, 39 enrolled. In 2019, 28 master's, 8 other advanced degrees awarded. *Entrance requirements:* For master's, GMAT or GRE, bachelor's degree with minimum GPA 3.0; 2 letters of recommendation; for Certificate, GMAT or GRE. Additional exam requirements/recommendations for international students: required—TOEFL (minimum score 550 paper-based; 80 iBT), IELTS (minimum score 7). *Application deadline:* For fall admission, 8/1 for domestic students, 5/1 for international students; for spring admission, 11/15 for domestic students, 10/1 for international students. Application fee: $60 ($95 for international students). Electronic applications accepted. *Expenses:* Contact institution. *Financial support:* In 2019–20, 37 students received support, including 24 research assistantships with full tuition reimbursements available (averaging $11,458 per year), 13 teaching assistantships with full tuition reimbursements available (averaging $11,250 per year); institutionally sponsored loans, scholarships/grants, health care benefits, and unspecified assistantships also available. Financial award application deadline: 3/15; financial award applicants required to submit FAFSA. *Unit head:* Dr. Rajiv Kishore, Chair/ Professor, 702-895-1709, Fax: 702-895-4370, E-mail: met.chair@unlv.edu. *Application contact:* Dr. Han-fen Hu, Graduate Coordinator, 702-895-1365, Fax: 702-895-4370, E-mail: met.gradcoord@unlv.edu.
Website: https://www.unlv.edu/met

The University of North Carolina at Charlotte, Belk College of Business, Department of Economics, Charlotte, NC 28223-0001. Offers applied econometrics (Graduate Certificate); economics (MS). *Program availability:* Part-time, evening/weekend. *Faculty:* 18 full-time (7 women). *Students:* 22 full-time (6 women), 15 part-time (4 women); includes 13 minority (5 Black or African American, non-Hispanic/Latino; 3 Asian, non-Hispanic/Latino; 4 Hispanic/Latino; 1 Two or more races, non-Hispanic/Latino), 10 international. Average age 27. 31 applicants, 97% accepted, 16 enrolled. In 2019, 21 master's, 5 other advanced degrees awarded. *Degree requirements:* For master's, comprehensive exam (for some programs). *Entrance requirements:* For master's, GRE General Test, GMAT, overall GPA of at least 3.0; undergraduate coursework that includes calculus, econometrics (or equivalent), intermediate macroeconomic theory, intermediate microeconomic theory; statement of purpose; three letters of recommendations; resume; transcripts for work attempted beyond high school; for Graduate Certificate, bachelor's degree, or its equivalent, from regionally-accredited college or university; minimum GPA of 2.75 on all previous work completed beyond high school (secondary school); statement of purpose; unofficial transcripts of all college course work; satisfactory scores on TOEFL (if applicable). Additional exam requirements/recommendations for international students: required—TOEFL (minimum score 557 paper-based; 83 iBT), IELTS (minimum score 6.5), TOEFL (minimum score 557 paper-based, 83 iBT) or IELTS (6.5). *Application deadline:* For fall admission, 3/1 for domestic students; for spring admission, 10/1 for domestic students. Applications are processed on a rolling basis. Application fee: $75. Electronic applications accepted. *Expenses:* Contact institution. *Financial support:* Career-related internships or fieldwork, institutionally sponsored loans, scholarships/grants, and unspecified assistantships available. Support available to part-time students. Financial award application deadline: 3/1; financial award applicants required to submit FAFSA. *Unit head:* Dr. Artie Zillante, Department Chair, 704-687-5375, Fax: 704-687-7589, E-mail: azillant@uncc.edu. *Application contact:* Kathy B. Giddings, Director of Graduate Admissions, 704-687-5503, Fax: 704-687-1668, E-mail: gradadm@uncc.edu.
Website: http://msecon.uncc.edu/

The University of North Carolina at Greensboro, Graduate School, Bryan School of Business and Economics, Department of Economics, Program in Applied Economics, Greensboro, NC 27412-5001. Offers MA, MA/PhD. *Degree requirements:* For master's, comprehensive exam, thesis or alternative. *Entrance requirements:* For master's, GRE. Additional exam requirements/recommendations for international students: required—TOEFL. Electronic applications accepted.

University of North Dakota, Graduate School, College of Business and Public Administration, Applied Economics Program, Grand Forks, ND 58202. Offers MSAE. *Program availability:* Part-time, online learning. *Degree requirements:* For master's, comprehensive exam, thesis or alternative. *Entrance requirements:* For master's, GRE General Test. Additional exam requirements/recommendations for international students: required—TOEFL (minimum score 550 paper-based; 79 iBT), IELTS (minimum score 6.5). Electronic applications accepted.

University of Oklahoma, College of Arts and Sciences, Department of Economics, Norman, OK 73019. Offers economics (MA, PhD), including applied economics emphasis (MA), managerial emphasis (MA). Terminal master's awarded for partial completion of doctoral program. *Degree requirements:* For master's, comprehensive exam (for some programs); for doctorate, comprehensive exam, thesis/dissertation. *Entrance requirements:* For master's and doctorate, GRE, undergraduate degree in related field. Additional exam requirements/recommendations for international students: required—TOEFL (minimum score 79 iBT) or IELTS (minimum score 6.5). Electronic applications accepted. *Expenses:* Tuition, state resident: full-time $6583.20; part-time $274.30 per credit hour. Tuition, nonresident: full-time $21,242; part-time $885.10 per credit hour. *International tuition:* $21,242.40 full-time. *Required fees:* $1994.20; $72.55 per credit hour. $126.50 per semester. Tuition and fees vary according to course load and degree level.

University of Pennsylvania, Wharton School, Program in Applied Economics, Philadelphia, PA 19104. Offers PhD.

University of Vermont, Graduate College, College of Agriculture and Life Sciences, Program in Community Development and Applied Economics, Burlington, VT 05405. Offers community development and applied economics (MS). *Degree requirements:* For master's, thesis. *Entrance requirements:* For master's, GRE General Test. Additional exam requirements/recommendations for international students: required—TOEFL (minimum score 550 paper-based; 90 iBT), IELTS (minimum score 6.5). Electronic applications accepted.

University of Wisconsin–Madison, Graduate School, College of Agricultural and Life Sciences, Department of Agricultural and Applied Economics, Madison, WI 53706. Offers MA, MS, PhD. *Program availability:* Part-time. *Degree requirements:* For doctorate, thesis/dissertation, preliminary exams. *Entrance requirements:* For master's and doctorate, GRE General Test. Additional exam requirements/recommendations for international students: required—TOEFL (minimum score 580 paper-based; 92 iBT). Electronic applications accepted.

University of Wyoming, College of Agriculture and Natural Resources, Department of Agricultural and Applied Economics, Laramie, WY 82071. Offers MS. *Program availability:* Part-time. *Degree requirements:* For master's, thesis (for some programs). *Entrance requirements:* For master's, GRE General Test, minimum GPA of 3.0. Additional exam requirements/recommendations for international students: required—TOEFL. Electronic applications accepted.

Utah State University, School of Graduate Studies, College of Agriculture and Applied Sciences, Department of Applied Economics, Logan, UT 84322. Offers applied economics (MAE, MS, PhD); international food and agribusiness (MS). *Program availability:* Part-time. *Degree requirements:* For master's, thesis optional. *Entrance requirements:* For master's, GRE General Test, minimum GPA of 3.0.

Virginia Polytechnic Institute and State University, Graduate School, College of Agriculture and Life Sciences, Blacksburg, VA 24061. Offers agricultural and applied economics (MS, PhD); agricultural and life sciences (MS); agriculture, leadership, and community education (MS, PhD); animal and poultry science (MS, PhD); biochemistry (MS, PhD); crop and soil environmental sciences (MS, PhD); dairy science (MS, PhD); entomology (MS, PhD); food science and technology (MS, PhD); horticulture (PhD); human nutrition, foods and exercise (MS, PhD); plant pathology, physiology, and weed science (MS, PhD). *Faculty:* 246 full-time (83 women). *Students:* 364 full-time (213 women), 106 part-time (68 women); includes 79 minority (29 Black or African American, non-Hispanic/Latino; 1 American Indian or Alaska Native, non-Hispanic/Latino; 13 Asian, non-Hispanic/Latino; 16 Hispanic/Latino; 20 Two or more races, non-Hispanic/Latino), 106 international. Average age 28. 314 applicants, 57% accepted, 130 enrolled. In 2019, 92 master's, 59 doctorates awarded. *Degree requirements:* For master's, comprehensive exam (for some programs), thesis (for some programs); for doctorate, comprehensive exam (for some programs), thesis/dissertation (for some programs). *Entrance requirements:* For master's and doctorate, GRE/GMAT. Additional exam requirements/recommendations for international students: required—TOEFL (minimum score 90 iBT). *Application deadline:* For fall admission, 8/1 for domestic students, 4/1 for international students; for spring admission, 1/1 for domestic students, 9/1 for international students. Applications are processed on a rolling basis. Application fee: $75. Electronic applications accepted. *Expenses:* Tuition, state resident: full-time $13,700; part-time $761.25 per credit hour. Tuition, nonresident: full-time $27,614; part-time $1534 per credit hour. *Required fees:* $886.50 per term. Tuition and fees vary according to campus/location and program. *Financial support:* In 2019–20, 248 research assistantships with full tuition reimbursements (averaging $20,360 per year), 127 teaching assistantships with full tuition reimbursements (averaging $18,183 per year) were awarded; fellowships, scholarships/grants, and unspecified assistantships also available. Financial award application deadline: 3/1; financial award applicants required to submit FAFSA. *Unit head:* Dr. Alan L. Grant, Dean, 540-231-4152, Fax: 540-231-4163, E-mail: algrant@vt.edu. *Application contact:* Crystal Tawney, Administrative Assistant, 540-231-4152, Fax: 540-231-4163, E-mail: cdtawney@vt.edu. Website: http://www.cals.vt.edu/

Washington & Jefferson College, Graduate and Continuing Studies, Washington, PA 15301. Offers applied health care economics and outcomes management (MS); professional accounting (MAC); professional writing (Graduate Certificate); thanatology (Graduate Certificate).

Western Kentucky University, Graduate School, Gordon Ford College of Business, Program in Applied Economics, Bowling Green, KY 42101. Offers MA.

Western Michigan University, Graduate College, College of Arts and Sciences, Department of Economics, Kalamazoo, MI 49008. Offers applied economics (MA, PhD). *Degree requirements:* For master's, thesis; for doctorate, thesis/dissertation.

Wright State University, Graduate School, Raj Soin College of Business, Department of Economics, Program in Social and Applied Economics, Dayton, OH 45435. Offers MS.

Economic Development

Albany State University, College of Arts and Humanities, Albany, GA 31705-2717. Offers criminal justice (MS); English education (M Ed); public administration (MPA), including community and economic development, criminal justice administration, health administration and policy, human resources management, public management, public policy, water resources management and policy; social work (MSW). *Accreditation:* NASPAA. *Program availability:* Part-time. *Degree requirements:* For master's, comprehensive exam, professional portfolio (for MPA), internship, capstone report. *Entrance requirements:* For master's, GRE, MAT, minimum GPA of 3.0, official transcript, pre-medical record/certificate of immunization, letters of reference. Electronic applications accepted.

The American University in Cairo, School of Business, Cairo, Egypt. Offers business administration (MBA); economics (MA); economics in international development (MA, Diploma); finance (MS). *Program availability:* Part-time, evening/weekend. *Degree requirements:* For master's, comprehensive exam (for some programs), thesis (for some programs). *Entrance requirements:* For master's, GMAT, GRE. Additional exam requirements/recommendations for international students: required—TOEFL (minimum score 450 paper-based; 45 iBT), IELTS (minimum score 5). Electronic applications accepted. *Expenses:* Contact institution.

Ball State University, Graduate School, College of Sciences and Humanities, Department of Political Science, Program in Public Administration, Muncie, IN 47306. Offers public administration (MPA, Certificate), including community and economic development (MPA), criminal justice (MPA), emergency management and homeland security (MPA), information and communication technology (MPA). *Program availability:* Part-time. *Degree requirements:* For master's, comprehensive exam. *Entrance requirements:* For master's, GRE General Test, minimum baccalaureate GPA of 2.8, two letters of recommendation. Additional exam requirements/recommendations for international students: required—TOEFL (minimum score 550 paper-based; 79 iBT), IELTS (minimum score 6.5). Electronic applications accepted. *Expenses:* Tuition, area resident: Full-time $7506; part-time $417 per credit hour. Tuition, nonresident: full-time $20,610; part-time $1145 per credit hour. *Required fees:* $2126. Tuition and fees vary according to course load, campus/location and program.

Ball State University, Graduate School, Miller College of Business, Interdepartmental Program in Business Administration, Muncie, IN 47306. Offers business administration (MBA); business essentials (Graduate Certificate); community and economic development (Certificate). *Accreditation:* AACSB. *Program availability:* Part-time, 100% online, blended/hybrid learning. *Entrance requirements:* For master's, GMAT or GRE, minimum baccalaureate GPA of 2.75 or 3.0 in latter half of baccalaureate, resume or curriculum vitae, four professional letters of recommendation. Additional exam requirements/recommendations for international students: required—TOEFL (minimum score 550 paper-based; 79 iBT), IELTS (minimum score 6.5). Electronic applications accepted. *Expenses:* Contact institution.

Boston University, Metropolitan College, Department of Administrative Sciences, Boston, MA 02215. Offers applied business analytics (MS); economic development and tourism management (MSAS); enterprise risk management (MS); financial management (MS); global marketing management (MS); innovation and technology (MSAS); insurance management (MS); project management (MS); supply chain management (MS). *Accreditation:* AACSB. *Program availability:* Part-time, evening/weekend, 100% online, blended/hybrid learning. *Faculty:* 25 full-time (5 women), 40 part-time/adjunct (6 women). *Students:* 596 full-time (316 women), 709 part-time (378 women); includes 175 minority (41 Black or African American, non-Hispanic/Latino; 1 American Indian or Alaska Native, non-Hispanic/Latino; 75 Asian, non-Hispanic/Latino; 52 Hispanic/Latino; 6 Two or more races, non-Hispanic/Latino), 862 international. Average age 27. 3,223 applicants, 61% accepted, 513 enrolled. In 2019, 517 master's awarded. *Degree requirements:* For master's, thesis optional. *Entrance requirements:* For master's, 1 year of work experience, minimum GPA of 3.0. Additional exam requirements/recommendations for international students: required—TOEFL (minimum score 84 iBT). *Application deadline:* For fall admission, 8/1 priority date for domestic students, 6/1 priority date for international students; for spring admission, 12/1 priority date for domestic students, 11/15 priority date for international students; for summer admission, 4/1 priority date for domestic students, 3/1 priority date for international students. Applications are processed on a rolling basis. Application fee: $85. Electronic applications accepted. *Expenses:* Contact institution. *Financial support:* In 2019–20, 15 students received support, including 23 research assistantships (averaging $8,400 per year), 47 teaching assistantships (averaging $4,200 per year); career-related internships or fieldwork, Federal Work-Study, and unspecified assistantships also available. Financial award applicants required to submit FAFSA. *Unit head:* Dr. John Sullivan, Chair, 617-353-3016, E-mail: adminsc@bu.edu. *Application contact:* Enrollment Services, 617-358-8162, E-mail: met@bu.edu. Website: http://www.bu.edu/met/academic-community/departments/administrative-sciences/

The Catholic University of America, Busch School of Business and Economics, Washington, DC 20064. Offers accounting (MS); business analysis (MSBA); integral economic development management (MA); integral economic development policy (MA); management (MS), including Federal contract management, human resource management, leadership and management, project management, sales management. *Program availability:* Part-time. *Faculty:* 25 full-time (3 women), 19 part-time/adjunct (12 women). *Students:* 91 full-time (27 women), 68 part-time (37 women); includes 65 minority (37 Black or African American, non-Hispanic/Latino; 2 American Indian or Alaska Native, non-Hispanic/Latino; 8 Asian, non-Hispanic/Latino; 11 Hispanic/Latino; 7 Two or more races, non-Hispanic/Latino), 26 international. Average age 32. 131 applicants, 88% accepted, 90 enrolled. In 2019, 81 master's awarded. *Degree requirements:* For master's, comprehensive exam (for some programs). *Entrance requirements:* For master's, GRE General Test, statement of purpose, official copies of academic transcripts, three letters of recommendation. Additional exam requirements/recommendations for international students: required—TOEFL (minimum score 550 paper-based; 80 iBT). *Application deadline:* For fall admission, 7/15 priority date for domestic students, 7/1 for international students; for spring admission, 11/15 priority date for domestic students, 11/1 for international students. Applications are processed on a rolling basis. Application fee: $55. Electronic applications accepted. *Expenses:* Contact institution. *Financial support:* Fellowships, research assistantships, teaching assistantships, Federal Work-Study, scholarships/grants, tuition waivers (full and partial), and unspecified assistantships available. Financial award application deadline: 2/1; financial award applicants required to submit FAFSA. *Unit head:* Dr. Andrew Abela, Dean, 202-319-6130, E-mail: DeanAbela@cua.edu. *Application contact:* Dr. Steven Brown, Director of Graduate Admissions, 202-319-5057, Fax: 202-319-6533, E-mail: cua-admissions@cua.edu. Website: https://business.catholic.edu/

Claremont Graduate University, Graduate Programs, School of Social Science, Policy and Evaluation, Department of Economics, Claremont, CA 91711-6160. Offers behavioral economics and neuroeconomics (PhD); business and financial economics (MA, PhD); economic development (Certificate); international economic and development policy (PhD); international economics policy and development (MA); international money and finance (PhD); political economy and public economics (PhD); political economy and public policy (MA); MBA/PhD. *Program availability:* Part-time. *Entrance requirements:* For master's and doctorate, GRE General Test or GMAT. Additional exam requirements/recommendations for international students: required—TOEFL (minimum score 75 iBT). Electronic applications accepted.

Cleveland State University, College of Graduate Studies, Maxine Goodman Levin College of Urban Affairs, Program in Environmental Studies, Cleveland, OH 44115. Offers environmental nonprofit management (MAES); environmental planning (MAES); policy and administration (MAES); sustainable economic development (MAES); urban economic development (Certificate); JD/MAES. *Program availability:* Part-time, evening/weekend. *Degree requirements:* For master's, thesis or alternative, exit project. *Entrance requirements:* For master's, GRE General Test (minimum score: verbal and quantitative combined 40th percentile, analytical writing 4.0), minimum GPA of 3.0. Additional exam requirements/recommendations for international students: required—TOEFL (minimum score 550 paper-based; 78 iBT), IELTS (6.0), or International Test of English Proficiency (iTEP). Electronic applications accepted. *Expenses:* Contact institution.

Cleveland State University, College of Graduate Studies, Maxine Goodman Levin College of Urban Affairs, Program in Public Administration, Cleveland, OH 44115. Offers economic development (MPA); non-profit management (MPA); public management (MPA); JD/MPA. *Accreditation:* NASPAA. *Program availability:* Part-time, evening/weekend. *Students:* Average age 32. 79 applicants, 77% accepted, 12 enrolled. In 2019, 28 master's awarded. *Degree requirements:* For master's, thesis or alternative, exit project. *Entrance requirements:* For master's, GRE General Test (minimum scores in 40th percentile verbal and quantitative, 4.0 writing), minimum GPA of 3.0. Additional exam requirements/recommendations for international students: required—TOEFL (minimum score 550 paper-based; 78 iBT), IELTS (6.0), or International Test of English Proficiency (iTEP). *Application deadline:* For fall admission, 7/1 priority date for domestic students, 5/15 for international students; for spring admission, 11/15 for domestic students, 11/1 for international students; for summer admission, 4/1 for domestic students, 3/15 for international students. Applications are processed on a rolling basis. Application fee: $40. Electronic applications accepted. *Expenses:* Contact institution. *Financial support:* In 2019–20, 16 students received support, including 5 research assistantships with full tuition reimbursements available (averaging $7,200 per year), 1 teaching assistantship with partial tuition reimbursement available (averaging $2,400 per year); scholarships/grants, tuition waivers (full and partial), and unspecified assistantships also available. Support available to part-time students. Financial award application deadline: 3/1; financial award applicants required to submit FAFSA. *Unit head:* Dr. Nicholas Zingale, Director, 216-802-3389, Fax: 216-687-9342, E-mail:

n.zingale@csuohio.edu. *Application contact:* David Arrighi, Graduate Academic Advisor, 216-523-7522, Fax: 216-687-5398, E-mail: d.arrighi@csuohio.edu.
Website: http://urban.csuohio.edu/academics/graduate/mpa/

Cleveland State University, College of Graduate Studies, Maxine Goodman Levin College of Urban Affairs, Program in Urban Planning and Development, Cleveland, OH 44115. Offers economic development (MUPD); environmental sustainability (MUPD); historic preservation (MUPD); housing and neighborhood development (MUPD); real estate development and finance (MUPD); urban economic development (Certificate); urban geographic information systems (MUPD); JD/MUPDD. *Accreditation:* ACSP. *Program availability:* Part-time, evening/weekend. *Degree requirements:* For master's, thesis or alternative, exit project. *Entrance requirements:* For master's, GRE General Test (minimum score: 50th percentile combined verbal and quantitative, 4.0 analytical writing), minimum GPA of 3.0. Additional exam requirements/recommendations for international students: required—TOEFL (minimum score 550 paper-based; 78 iBT), IELTS (6.0), or International Test of English Proficiency (iTEP). Electronic applications accepted. *Expenses:* Contact institution.

Concordia University, School of Graduate Studies, Faculty of Arts and Science, School of Community and Public Affairs, Montréal, QC H3G 1M8, Canada. Offers community economic development (Diploma).

Cornell University, Graduate School, Graduate Fields of Agriculture and Life Sciences, Field of Applied Economics and Management, Ithaca, NY 14853. Offers agricultural finance (MS, PhD); applied econometrics and qualitative analysis (MS, PhD); economics of development (MS, PhD); environmental economics (MS, PhD); environmental management (MPS); farm management and production economics (MS, PhD); marketing and food distribution (MS, PhD); public policy analysis (MS, PhD); resource economics (PhD). *Entrance requirements:* For master's and doctorate, GRE. Additional exam requirements/recommendations for international students: required—TOEFL.

Cornell University, Graduate School, Graduate Fields of Architecture, Art and Planning, Field of City and Regional Planning, Ithaca, NY 14853. Offers city and regional planning (MRP, PhD); environmental planning and design (MRP, PhD); historic preservation planning (MA); international development planning (MRP, PhD); planning theory and systems analysis (MRP, PhD); regional economics and development planning (MRP, PhD); regional science (MRP, PhD); social and health systems planning (MRP, PhD); urban and regional theory (MRP, PhD); urban planning history (MRP, PhD). *Accreditation:* ACSP (one or more programs are accredited). *Degree requirements:* For master's, thesis (MA); for doctorate, comprehensive exam, thesis/dissertation. *Entrance requirements:* For master's and doctorate, GRE General Test, 2 letters of recommendation. Additional exam requirements/recommendations for international students: required—TOEFL (minimum score 600 paper-based; 77 iBT). Electronic applications accepted.

Cornell University, Graduate School, Graduate Fields of Arts and Sciences, Field of Economics, Ithaca, NY 14853. Offers applied economics (PhD); basic analytical economics (PhD); econometrics and economic statistics (PhD); economic development and planning (PhD); economic theory (PhD); industrial organization and control (PhD); international economics (PhD); labor economics (PhD); monetary and macro economics (PhD); public finance (PhD). *Degree requirements:* For doctorate, comprehensive exam, thesis/dissertation. *Entrance requirements:* For doctorate, GRE General Test, 3 letters of recommendation. Additional exam requirements/recommendations for international students: required—TOEFL (minimum score 550 paper-based; 77 iBT). Electronic applications accepted.

East Carolina University, Graduate School, Thomas Harriot College of Arts and Sciences, Department of Geography, Planning, and Environment, Greenville, NC 27858-4353. Offers development and environmental planning (Certificate); economic development (Certificate); geographic information science and technology (Certificate); geography (MA), including geography, planning, rural development. *Program availability:* Part-time, evening/weekend, online learning. *Degree requirements:* For master's, comprehensive exam, thesis optional. *Entrance requirements:* For master's, GRE General Test. *Application deadline:* For fall admission, 4/1 priority date for domestic and international students. Applications are processed on a rolling basis. Electronic applications accepted. *Expenses: Tuition, area resident:* Full-time $4749; part-time $185 per credit hour. Tuition, state resident: full-time $4749; part-time $185 per credit hour. Tuition, nonresident: full-time $17,898; part-time $864 per credit hour. *International tuition:* $17,898 full-time. *Required fees:* $2787. *Financial support:* Research assistantships with partial tuition reimbursements, teaching assistantships with partial tuition reimbursements, and Federal Work-Study available. Support available to part-time students. Financial award application deadline: 3/1. *Unit head:* Dr. Thad Wasklewicz, Chair, 252-328-6230, E-mail: wasklewiczt@ecu.edu. *Application contact:* Graduate Admissions, 252-328-6012, Fax: 252-328-6071, E-mail: gradschool@ecu.edu.
Website: https://geography.ecu.edu/

East Tennessee State University, College of Graduate and Continuing Studies, College of Arts and Sciences, Department of Political Science, International Affairs and Public Administration, Johnson City, TN 37614. Offers economic development (Postbaccalaureate Certificate); economic development and planning (MPA); local government management (MPA); nonprofit and public financial management (MPA); urban planning (Postbaccalaureate Certificate). *Program availability:* Part-time. *Degree requirements:* For master's, internship, capstone. *Entrance requirements:* For master's, GRE General Test, three letters of recommendation. Additional exam requirements/recommendations for international students: required—TOEFL (minimum score 550 paper-based; 79 iBT). Electronic applications accepted.

Fordham University, Graduate School of Arts and Sciences, Program in International Political Economy and Development, New York, NY 10458. Offers MA, Certificate. *Program availability:* Part-time, evening/weekend. *Students:* Average age 27. 81 applicants, 57% accepted, 17 enrolled. In 2019, 21 master's awarded. *Entrance requirements:* For master's, GRE General Test. Additional exam requirements/recommendations for international students: required—TOEFL (minimum score 600 paper-based). *Application deadline:* For fall admission, 1/4 priority date for domestic students; for spring admission, 11/1 for domestic students. Application fee: $70. Electronic applications accepted. *Financial support:* In 2019–20, 35 students received support, including 4 fellowships with tuition reimbursements available (averaging $17,014 per year); research assistantships, career-related internships or fieldwork, institutionally sponsored loans, tuition waivers (full and partial), and unspecified assistantships also available. Financial award application deadline: 1/4; financial award applicants required to submit FAFSA. *Unit head:* Dr. Henry Schwalbenberg, Chair, 718-817-3866, Fax: 718-817-3518. *Application contact:* Garrett Marino, Director of Graduate Admissions, 718-817-4419, Fax: 718-817-3566, E-mail: gmarino10@fordham.edu.

Georgetown University, Graduate School of Arts and Sciences, Department of Economics, Washington, DC 20057. Offers econometrics (PhD); economic development (PhD); economic theory (PhD); industrial organization (PhD); international macro and finance (PhD); international trade (PhD); labor economics (PhD); macroeconomics (PhD); public economics and political economy (PhD); MA/PhD; MS/MA. *Degree requirements:* For doctorate, comprehensive exam, thesis/dissertation. *Entrance requirements:* For doctorate, GRE General Test. Additional exam requirements/recommendations for international students: required—TOEFL.

Georgia Institute of Technology, Graduate Studies, College of Design, School of City and Regional Planning, Atlanta, GA 30332-0001. Offers city and regional planning (PhD); economic development (MCRP); environmental planning and management (MCRP); geographic information systems (MCRP); land and community development (MCRP); land use planning (MCRP); transportation (MCRP); urban design (MCRP); MCP/MSCE. *Accreditation:* ACSP. *Degree requirements:* For master's, thesis, internship. *Entrance requirements:* For master's, GRE General Test, minimum GPA of 2.7. Additional exam requirements/recommendations for international students: required—TOEFL. Electronic applications accepted. *Expenses: Tuition, area resident:* Full-time $14,064; part-time $586 per credit hour. Tuition, state resident: full-time $14,064; part-time $586 per credit hour. Tuition, nonresident: full-time $29,140; part-time $1215 per credit hour. *International tuition:* $29,140 full-time. *Required fees:* $2024; $840 per semester. $2096. Tuition and fees vary according to course load.

Georgia State University, Andrew Young School of Policy Studies, Department of Public Management and Policy, Atlanta, GA 30303. Offers criminal justice (MPA); disaster management (Certificate); disaster policy (MPA); environmental policy (PhD); health policy (PhD); management and finance (MPA); nonprofit management (MPA, Certificate); nonprofit policy (MPA); planning and economic development (MPP, Certificate); policy analysis and evaluation (MPA), including planning and economic development; public and nonprofit management (PhD); public finance and budgeting (PhD), including science and technology policy, urban and regional economic development; public finance policy (MPA), including social policy; public health (MPA). *Accreditation:* NASPAA (one or more programs are accredited). *Program availability:* Part-time. *Faculty:* 13 full-time (7 women), 3 part-time/adjunct (1 woman). *Students:* 125 full-time (81 women), 91 part-time (66 women); includes 103 minority (78 Black or African American, non-Hispanic/Latino; 3 Asian, non-Hispanic/Latino; 14 Hispanic/Latino; 8 Two or more races, non-Hispanic/Latino), 31 international. Average age 32. 298 applicants, 60% accepted, 82 enrolled. In 2019, 70 master's, 8 other advanced degrees awarded. Terminal master's awarded for partial completion of doctoral program. *Degree requirements:* For master's, thesis optional; for doctorate, comprehensive exam, thesis/dissertation. *Entrance requirements:* For master's and doctorate, GRE. Additional exam requirements/recommendations for international students: required—TOEFL (minimum score 603 paper-based; 100 iBT) or IELTS (minimum score 7). *Application deadline:* For fall admission, 1/15 for domestic and international students. Application fee: $50. Electronic applications accepted. *Expenses: Tuition, area resident:* Full-time $7164; part-time $398 per credit hour. Tuition, state resident: full-time $7164; part-time $398 per credit hour. Tuition, nonresident: full-time $22,662; part-time $1259 per credit hour. *International tuition:* $22,662 full-time. *Required fees:* $2128; $312 per credit hour. Tuition and fees vary according to course load and program. *Financial support:* In 2019–20, fellowships (averaging $8,194 per year), research assistantships (averaging $8,068 per year), teaching assistantships (averaging $3,600 per year) were awarded; institutionally sponsored loans, scholarships/grants, health care benefits, and unspecified assistantships also available. Financial award application deadline: 2/1. *Unit head:* Dr. Cathy Yang Liu, Chair and Professor, 404-413-0102, Fax: 404-413-0104, E-mail: cyliu@gsu.edu. *Application contact:* Dr. Cathy Yang Liu, Chair and Professor, 404-413-0102, Fax: 404-413-0104, E-mail: cyliu@gsu.edu.
Website: https://aysps.gsu.edu/public-management-policy/

Indiana University Bloomington, School of Public and Environmental Affairs, Public Affairs Programs, Bloomington, IN 47405. Offers economic development (MPA); energy (MPA); environmental policy (PhD); environmental policy and natural resource management (MPA); information systems (MPA); international development (MPA); local government management (MPA); nonprofit management (MPA, Certificate); policy analysis (MPA); public budgeting and financial management (Certificate); public finance (PhD); public financial administration (MPA); public management (MPA, PhD, Certificate); public policy analysis (PhD); social entrepreneurship (Certificate); specialized public affairs (MPA); sustainability and sustainable development (MPA); JD/MPA; MPA/MA; MPA/MIS; MPA/MLS; MSES/MPA. *Accreditation:* NASPAA (one or more programs are accredited). *Program availability:* Part-time. *Degree requirements:* For master's, capstone, internship; for doctorate, comprehensive exam, thesis/dissertation. *Entrance requirements:* For master's, GRE General Test or GMAT, official transcripts, 3 letters of recommendation, resume, personal statement; for doctorate, GRE General Test, official transcripts, 3 letters of recommendation, statement of purpose. Additional exam requirements/recommendations for international students: required—TOEFL (minimum score 600 paper-based; 96 iBT); recommended—IELTS (minimum score 7). Electronic applications accepted.

Johnson & Wales University, Graduate Studies, MS Program in Global Tourism and Sustainable Economic Development, Providence, RI 02903-3703. Offers MS. *Program availability:* Online learning.

Murray State University, Arthur J. Bauernfeind College of Business, Department of Economics and Finance, Murray, KY 42071. Offers economic development (MS); economics (MS), including finance. *Program availability:* Part-time. *Entrance requirements:* For master's, GRE General Test or GMAT, minimum university GPA of 2.75. Additional exam requirements/recommendations for international students: required—TOEFL (minimum score 527 paper-based; 71 iBT). Electronic applications accepted.

New Mexico State University, College of Business, Department of Economics, Applied Statistics and International Business, Las Cruces, NM 88003. Offers applied statistics (MS); economic development (DED); economics (MA); public utility regulation and economics (Graduate Certificate). *Program availability:* Part-time, online learning. *Faculty:* 16 full-time (3 women). *Students:* 28 full-time (15 women), 25 part-time (11 women); includes 20 minority (2 Black or African American, non-Hispanic/Latino; 1 American Indian or Alaska Native, non-Hispanic/Latino; 5 Asian, non-Hispanic/Latino; 12 Hispanic/Latino), 22 international. Average age 34. 61 applicants, 85% accepted, 21 enrolled. In 2019, 16 master's, 9 doctorates, 14 other advanced degrees awarded. Terminal master's awarded for partial completion of doctoral program. *Degree requirements:* For master's, comprehensive exam, thesis or alternative; for doctorate, comprehensive exam, thesis/dissertation, internship. *Entrance requirements:* For master's, minimum GPA of 3.0; for doctorate, appropriate master's degree, minimum GPA of 3.0 with particular classes required. Additional exam requirements/recommendations for international students: required—TOEFL (minimum score 550 paper-based; 79 iBT), IELTS (minimum score 6.5). *Application deadline:* For fall admission, 3/1 priority date for domestic and international students. Applications are processed on a rolling basis. Application fee: $40 ($50 for international students). Electronic applications accepted. *Financial support:* In 2019–20, 29 students received support, including 2 research assistantships (averaging $18,582 per year), 21 teaching assistantships (averaging $16,789 per year); career-related internships or fieldwork, Federal Work-Study, scholarships/grants, traineeships, health care benefits, and unspecified assistantships also available. Support available to part-time students. Financial award application deadline: 3/1.
Website: http://business.nmsu.edu/departments/economics

Northeastern University, College of Professional Studies, Boston, MA 02115-5096. Offers applied nutrition (MS); college athletics administration (MSL); commerce and economic development (MS); corporate and organizational communication (MS); criminal justice (MS); digital media (MPS); elearning and instructional design (M Ed); elementary education (MAT); geographic information technology (MPS); global studies and international relations (MS); higher education administration (M Ed); homeland security (MA); human services (MS); informatics (MPS); leadership (MS); learning analytics (M Ed); learning and instruction (M Ed); nonprofit management (MS); professional sports administration (MSL); project management (MS); regulatory affairs for drugs, biologics, and medical devices (MS); respiratory care leadership (MS); special education (M Ed); technical communication (MS). *Program availability:* Part-time, evening/weekend, 100% online, blended/hybrid learning. *Faculty:* 85 full-time (53 women), 892 part-time/adjunct (379 women). *Students:* 5,699 part-time (3,305 women). In 2019, 1,787 master's awarded. *Application deadline:* Applications are processed on a rolling basis. Application fee: $0. Electronic applications accepted. *Expenses:* Contact institution. *Financial support:* Applicants required to submit FAFSA. *Unit head:* Dr. Mary Loeffelholz, Dean of the College of Professional Studies, 617-373-6060. *Application contact:* Dr. Mary Loeffelholz, Dean of the College of Professional Studies, 617-373-6060.

Website: https://cps.northeastern.edu/

Southern New Hampshire University, School of Business, Manchester, NH 03106-1045. Offers accounting (MBA, Graduate Certificate); accounting finance (MS); accounting/auditing (MS); accounting/forensic accounting (MS); accounting/management accounting (MS); accounting/taxation (MS); applied economics (MS); athletic administration (MBA, Graduate Certificate); business administration (IMBA, Certificate), including business information systems (Certificate), human resource management (Certificate); business analytics (MBA); business intelligence (MBA); communication (MA), including new media and marketing, public relations; community economic development (MBA); criminal justice (MBA); data analytics (MS); economics (MBA); engineering management (MBA); entrepreneurship (MBA); finance (MBA, MS, Graduate Certificate); finance/corporate finance (MS); finance/investments (MS); forensic accounting (MBA); forensic accounting and fraud examination (Graduate Certificate); healthcare informatics (MBA); healthcare management (MBA); human resource management (MS); human resources (MBA); information technology (MS); information technology management (MBA); international business (PhD); Internet marketing (MBA); leadership (MBA); leadership of nonprofit organizations (Graduate Certificate); management (MS); marketing (MBA, MS, Graduate Certificate); music business (MBA); operations and project management (MS); operations and supply chain management (MBA, Graduate Certificate); organizational leadership (MS); project management (MBA, Graduate Certificate); public administration (MBA, Graduate Certificate); quantitative analysis (MBA); Six Sigma (Graduate Certificate); Six Sigma quality (MBA); social media marketing (MBA, Graduate Certificate); sport management (MBA, MS, Graduate Certificate); sustainability and environmental compliance (MBA); MBA/Certificate. *Accreditation:* ACBSP. *Program availability:* Part-time, evening/weekend, online learning. Terminal master's awarded for partial completion of doctoral program. *Degree requirements:* For master's, one foreign language, comprehensive exam (for some programs), thesis or alternative; for doctorate, one foreign language, comprehensive exam, thesis/dissertation. *Entrance requirements:* For master's, minimum GPA of 2.5; for doctorate, GMAT. Additional exam requirements/recommendations for international students: required—TOEFL (minimum score 500 paper-based). Electronic applications accepted.

State University of New York Empire State College, School for Graduate Studies, Program in Community and Economic Development, Saratoga Springs, NY 12866-4391. Offers MA. *Program availability:* Part-time, evening/weekend, online learning. *Degree requirements:* For master's, thesis, final project. *Entrance requirements:* For master's, undergraduate-level courses in statistics and macroeconomics, bachelor's degree from regionally-accredited college/university. Additional exam requirements/recommendations for international students: required—TOEFL (minimum score 600 paper-based). Electronic applications accepted.

Thomas Edison State University, John S. Watson School of Public Service and Continuing Studies, Trenton, NJ 08608. Offers community and economic development (MSM); environmental policy/environmental justice (MSM); homeland security (MSHS, MSM); information and technology for public service (MSM); nonprofit management (MSM); public and municipal finance (MSM); public health (MSM); public service administration and leadership (MSM); public service leadership (MPSL). *Program availability:* Part-time, online learning. *Entrance requirements:* Additional exam requirements/recommendations for international students: required—TOEFL (minimum score 550 paper-based; 79 iBT). Electronic applications accepted.

Troy University, Graduate School, College of Business, Program in Business Administration, Troy, AL 36082. Offers accounting (EMBA, MBA); criminal justice (EMBA); finance (MBA); general management (EMBA, MBA); healthcare management (EMBA); information systems (EMBA, MBA); international economic development (MBA). *Accreditation:* ACBSP. *Program availability:* Part-time, evening/weekend, online learning. *Faculty:* 15 full-time (5 women), 2 part-time/adjunct (0 women). *Students:* 49 full-time (17 women), 77 part-time (27 women); includes 23 minority (19 Black or African American, non-Hispanic/Latino; 1 Asian, non-Hispanic/Latino; 3 Hispanic/Latino), 21 international. Average age 29. 93 applicants, 60% accepted, 42 enrolled. In 2019, 59 master's awarded. *Degree requirements:* For master's, minimum GPA of 3.0, capstone course, research course. *Entrance requirements:* For master's, GMAT (500 or above) or GRE (1050 or above in verbal and quantitative), or 294 or above on the revised GRE (verbal and quantitative), bachelor's degree; minimum undergraduate GPA of 2.5 or 3.0 on last 30 semester hours, letter of recommendation. Additional exam requirements/recommendations for international students: required—TOEFL (minimum score 523 paper-based; 70 iBT), IELTS (minimum score 6). *Application deadline:* Applications are processed on a rolling basis. Application fee: $50. Electronic applications accepted. *Expenses: Tuition, area resident:* Full-time $7650; part-time $2550 per semester hour. Tuition, state resident: full-time $7650; part-time $2550 per semester hour. Tuition, nonresident: full-time $15,300; part-time $5100 per semester hour. *International tuition:* $15,300 full-time. *Required fees:* $856; $352 per semester hour. $176 per semester. *Financial support:* In 2019–20, 50 students received support. Fellowships, research assistantships, teaching assistantships, career-related internships or fieldwork, Federal Work-Study, scholarships/grants, traineeships, tuition waivers, and unspecified assistantships available. Support available to part-time students. Financial award application deadline: 3/1; financial award applicants required to submit FAFSA. *Unit head:* Dr. Robert Wheatley, Professor, Director of Graduate Business Programs, 334-670-3416, Fax: 334-670-3708, E-mail: rwheat@troy.edu. *Application contact:* Haley McKinnon, Director of Graduate Admissions, 334-670-3178, Fax: 334-670-3733, E-mail: hmckinnon@troy.edu.

Website: https://www.troy.edu/academics/academic-programs/sorrell-college-business-programs.php

Université de Sherbrooke, Faculty of Administration, PhD Program in Economic Development, Sherbrooke, QC J1K 2R1, Canada. Offers PhD. *Degree requirements:* For doctorate, one foreign language, comprehensive exam, thesis/dissertation,

advanced English as a second language. *Entrance requirements:* For doctorate, letters of recommendation, work experience, formal training.

University at Buffalo, the State University of New York, Graduate School, School of Architecture and Planning, Department of Urban and Regional Planning, Buffalo, NY 14214. Offers economic development (MUP); environment/land use (MUP); health and food systems (MUP); historic preservation (MUP, Certificate); neighborhood/community development (MUP); real estate development (MSRED); urban and regional planning (PhD); urban design (MUP); JD/MUP; M Arch/MUP. *Accreditation:* ACSP. *Program availability:* Part-time. *Faculty:* 11 full-time (4 women), 15 part-time/adjunct (6 women). *Students:* 88 full-time (40 women), 25 part-time (10 women); includes 32 minority (16 Black or African American, non-Hispanic/Latino; 2 Asian, non-Hispanic/Latino; 7 Hispanic/Latino; 7 Two or more races, non-Hispanic/Latino), 13 international. Average age 26. 146 applicants, 40% accepted, 40 enrolled. In 2019, 31 master's, 1 doctorate, 4 other advanced degrees awarded. *Degree requirements:* For master's, thesis or alternative, project; for doctorate, comprehensive exam, thesis/dissertation, dissertation. *Entrance requirements:* For master's, resume, two letters of recommendation, personal statement, transcripts; for doctorate, GRE, transcripts, three letters of recommendation, resume, research statement, writing sample. Additional exam requirements/recommendations for international students: required—TOEFL (minimum score 79 iBT), IELTS (minimum score 6.5). *Application deadline:* For fall admission, 3/1 priority date for domestic and international students; for spring admission, 10/31 priority date for domestic students, 10/1 priority date for international students. Applications are processed on a rolling basis. Application fee: $75. Electronic applications accepted. *Expenses: Tuition, area resident:* Full-time $11,310; part-time $471 per credit hour. Tuition, state resident: full-time $11,310; part-time $471 per credit hour. Tuition, nonresident: full-time $23,100; part-time $963 per credit hour. *International tuition:* $23,100 full-time. *Required fees:* $2820. *Financial support:* In 2019–20, 54 students received support, including 5 fellowships with full tuition reimbursements available (averaging $22,560 per year), 1 research assistantship with partial tuition reimbursement available (averaging $16,027 per year), 20 teaching assistantships with partial tuition reimbursements available (averaging $6,912 per year); career-related internships or fieldwork, Federal Work-Study, institutionally sponsored loans, scholarships/grants, health care benefits, tuition waivers (full and partial), and unspecified assistantships also available. Financial award application deadline: 3/1; financial award applicants required to submit FAFSA. *Unit head:* Dr. Daniel B. Hess, Professor and Chair, 716-829-5326, Fax: 716-829-3256, E-mail: dbhess@buffalo.edu. *Application contact:* Norma Everett, Graduate Programs Coordinator, 716-829-3283, Fax: 716-829-3256, E-mail: norma.everett@buffalo.edu.
Website: http://www.ap.buffalo.edu/planning/

University of Central Arkansas, Graduate School, College of Natural Sciences and Math, Department of Geography, Conway, AR 72035-0001. Offers community and economic development (MS); geographic information systems (MGIS, Certificate). *Program availability:* Part-time, online learning. *Entrance requirements:* Additional exam requirements/recommendations for international students: required—TOEFL (minimum score 550 paper-based). Electronic applications accepted.

University of Colorado Denver, College of Architecture and Planning, Program in Urban and Regional Planning, Denver, CO 80217. Offers economic and community development planning (MURP); land use and environmental planning (MURP); urban place making (MURP). *Accreditation:* ACSP. *Program availability:* Part-time. *Degree requirements:* For master's, thesis, minimum of 51 semester hours. *Entrance requirements:* For master's, GRE (for students with an undergraduate GPA below 3.0), sample of writing or work project; statement of interest; resume; three letters of recommendation. Additional exam requirements/recommendations for international students: required—TOEFL (minimum score 75 iBT). Electronic applications accepted. *Expenses:* Contact institution.

University of Houston–Victoria, School of Business Administration, Victoria, TX 77901-4450. Offers accounting (MBA); economic development and entrepreneurship (MS); finance (GMBA, MBA); general business (MBA); international business (MBA); management (GMBA, MBA); marketing (MBA). *Accreditation:* AACSB. *Program availability:* Part-time, evening/weekend, online learning. *Entrance requirements:* For master's, GMAT. Additional exam requirements/recommendations for international students: required—TOEFL (minimum score 550 paper-based). Electronic applications accepted.

University of Massachusetts Lowell, College of Fine Arts, Humanities and Social Sciences, Program in Regional Economic and Social Development, Lowell, MA 01854. Offers MA, Graduate Certificate. *Program availability:* Part-time. *Entrance requirements:* For master's, GRE. Electronic applications accepted.

University of New Hampshire, Graduate School, Carsey School of Public Policy, Program in Community Development Policy and Practice, Durham, NH 03824. Offers MA. *Program availability:* Online learning. *Students:* 1 (woman) full-time, 16 part-time (9 women); includes 4 minority (3 Black or African American, non-Hispanic/Latino; 1 Two or more races, non-Hispanic/Latino), 1 international. Average age 33. 7 applicants, 43% accepted. In 2019, 7 master's awarded. *Entrance requirements:* Additional exam requirements/recommendations for international students: required—TOEFL (minimum score 550 paper-based; 80 iBT), IELTS (minimum score 6.5), PTE. *Application deadline:* For fall admission, 8/15 for domestic students; for spring admission, 12/15 for domestic students; for summer admission, 4/15 for domestic students. Application fee: $65. Electronic applications accepted. *Financial support:* In 2019–20, 5 students received support. Application deadline: 2/15; applicants required to submit FAFSA. *Unit head:* Michael Swack, Chair, 603-862-2821, Fax: 603-862-0275, E-mail: michael.swack@unh.edu. *Application contact:* Robin Husslage, Administrative Assistant, 603-862-2338, E-mail: robin.husslage@unh.edu.
Website: https://carsey.unh.edu/macdpp

University of North Alabama, College of Arts and Sciences, Department of Interdisciplinary and Professional Studies, Florence, AL 35632-0001. Offers professional studies (MPS), including community development, higher education administration, information technology, security and safety leadership. *Program availability:* Part-time, 100% online. *Degree requirements:* For master's, thesis optional. *Entrance requirements:* For master's, ETS PPI, personal statement; three letters of recommendation. Additional exam requirements/recommendations for international students: required—TOEFL (minimum score 79 iBT), IELTS (minimum score 6), PTE (minimum score 54). Electronic applications accepted.

The University of North Carolina at Greensboro, Graduate School, College of Arts and Sciences, Department of Geography, Greensboro, NC 27412-5001. Offers applied geography (MA); geographic information science (Certificate); geography (PhD); urban and economic development (Certificate). *Degree requirements:* For master's, comprehensive exam, thesis or alternative. *Entrance requirements:* For master's, GRE General Test. Additional exam requirements/recommendations for international students: required—TOEFL. Electronic applications accepted.

The University of North Carolina at Greensboro, Graduate School, College of Arts and Sciences, Department of Political Science, Greensboro, NC 27412-5001. Offers nonprofit management (Certificate); public affairs (MPA); urban and economic development (Certificate). *Accreditation:* NASPAA. *Degree requirements:* For master's, comprehensive exam. *Entrance requirements:* For master's, GRE General Test. Additional exam requirements/recommendations for international students: required—TOEFL. Electronic applications accepted.

University of Pennsylvania, School of Arts and Sciences, Fels Institute of Government, Philadelphia, PA 19104. Offers economic development and growth (Certificate); government administration (MGA); nonprofit administration (Certificate); organization dynamics (MS); politics (Certificate); public administration (MPA); public finance (Certificate). *Program availability:* Part-time, evening/weekend. *Students:* 15 full-time (9 women), 49 part-time (24 women); includes 19 minority (8 Black or African American, non-Hispanic/Latino; 6 Asian, non-Hispanic/Latino; 5 Hispanic/Latino), 3 international. Average age 33. 664 applicants, 44% accepted, 130 enrolled. In 2019, 67 master's, 3 other advanced degrees awarded. *Financial support:* Application deadline: 1/1.
Website: http://www.fels.upenn.edu/

University of Puerto Rico at Rio Piedras, Graduate School of Planning, San Juan, PR 00931-3300. Offers economic planning systems (MP); environmental planning (MP); social policy and planning (MP); urban and territorial planning (MP). *Accreditation:* ACSP. *Program availability:* Part-time. *Degree requirements:* For master's, comprehensive exam, thesis, planning project defense. *Entrance requirements:* For master's, PAEG, GRE, minimum GPA of 3.0, 2 letters of recommendation.

University of Southern California, Graduate School, Dana and David Dornsife College of Letters, Arts and Sciences, Department of Economics, Los Angeles, CA 90089. Offers economic development programming (MA, PhD); mathematical finance (MS); M Pl/MA; MA/JD. Terminal master's awarded for partial completion of doctoral program. *Degree requirements:* For master's, comprehensive exam; for doctorate, comprehensive exam, thesis/dissertation. *Entrance requirements:* For master's and doctorate, GRE. Additional exam requirements/recommendations for international students: required—TOEFL (minimum score 93 iBT). Electronic applications accepted.

University of Southern Mississippi, College of Business and Economic Development, School of Finance, Hattiesburg, MS 39406-0001. Offers economic development (MS). *Program availability:* Part-time. *Students:* 14 full-time (6 women), 1 (woman) part-time; includes 7 minority (6 Black or African American, non-Hispanic/Latino; 1 Hispanic/Latino). 18 applicants, 61% accepted, 10 enrolled. In 2019, 10 master's awarded. *Degree requirements:* For master's, comprehensive exam. *Entrance requirements:* Additional exam requirements/recommendations for international students: required—TOEFL, IELTS. *Application deadline:* For fall admission, 8/1 for domestic students, 6/1 for international students; for spring admission, 1/1 for domestic students, 11/1 for international students. Applications are processed on a rolling basis. Application fee: $60. Electronic applications accepted. *Expenses: Tuition, area resident:* Full-time $4393; part-time $488 per credit hour. Tuition, nonresident: full-time $5393; part-time $600 per credit hour. *Required fees:* $6 per semester. *Financial support:* Application deadline: 3/15; applicants required to submit FAFSA. *Unit head:* Dr. Kimberly Goodwin, Director, 601-266-4649. *Application contact:* Dr. Kimberly Goodwin, Director, 601-266-4649.
Website: https://www.usm.edu/finance/index.php

Vanderbilt University, Department of Economics, Nashville, TN 37240-1001. Offers economic development (MA); economics (PhD). *Faculty:* 28 full-time (3 women). *Students:* 113 full-time (55 women), 5 part-time (1 woman); includes 9 minority (2 Asian, non-Hispanic/Latino; 4 Hispanic/Latino; 3 Two or more races, non-Hispanic/Latino), 83 international. Average age 26. 532 applicants, 39% accepted, 48 enrolled. In 2019, 18 master's, 6 doctorates awarded. Terminal master's awarded for partial completion of doctoral program. *Degree requirements:* For master's, thesis or alternative; for doctorate, thesis/dissertation, final and qualifying exams. *Entrance requirements:* For master's and doctorate, GRE General Test, GRE Subject Test (recommended). Additional exam requirements/recommendations for international students: required—TOEFL (minimum score 570 paper-based; 88 iBT). *Application deadline:* For fall admission, 1/15 for domestic and international students; for spring admission, 11/1 for domestic students. Applications are processed on a rolling basis. Electronic applications accepted. *Expenses: Tuition:* Full-time $51,018; part-time $2087 per hour. *Required fees:* $542. Tuition and fees vary according to program. *Financial support:* Fellowships, teaching assistantships, career-related internships or fieldwork, Federal Work-Study, institutionally sponsored loans, scholarships/grants, and health care benefits available. Financial award application deadline: 1/15; financial award applicants required to submit CSS PROFILE or FAFSA. *Unit head:* Dr. Peter Rousseau, Chair, 615-343-2466, Fax: 615-343-8495, E-mail: peter.l.rousseau@vanderbilt.edu. *Application contact:* Mattias Polborn, Director of Graduate Studies, 615-322-8113, Fax: 615-343-8495, E-mail: mattias.polborn@vanderbilt.edu.
Website: http://www.vanderbilt.edu/econ/

Wayne State University, College of Liberal Arts and Sciences, Department of Political Science, Detroit, MI 48202. Offers political science (MA, PhD); public administration (MPA), including economic development policy and management, health and human services policy and management, human and fiscal resource management, nonprofit policy and management, organizational behavior and management, urban and metropolitan policy and management; JD/MA. *Accreditation:* NASPAA. *Program availability:* Part-time, evening/weekend. *Faculty:* 22 full-time (9 women). *Students:* 50 full-time (22 women), 64 part-time (32 women); includes 28 minority (20 Black or African American, non-Hispanic/Latino; 2 Asian, non-Hispanic/Latino; 1 Hispanic/Latino; 5 Two or more races, non-Hispanic/Latino), 10 international. Average age 34. 105 applicants, 40% accepted, 24 enrolled. In 2019, 21 master's, 7 doctorates awarded. Terminal master's awarded for partial completion of doctoral program. *Degree requirements:* For master's, comprehensive exam (for some programs), thesis (for some programs); for doctorate, thesis/dissertation. *Entrance requirements:* For master's, GRE General Test, substantial undergraduate preparation in the social sciences, minimum upper-division undergraduate GPA of 3.0, two letters of recommendation, personal statement; for doctorate, GRE General Test, 3 letters of recommendation; personal statement; interview. Additional exam requirements/recommendations for international students: required—TOEFL (minimum score 550 paper-based; 79 iBT), TWE (minimum score 5.5), Michigan English Language Assessment Battery (minimum score 85); recommended—IELTS (minimum score 6.5). *Application deadline:* For fall admission, 5/15 for domestic students, 5/1 priority date for international students; for winter admission, 10/15 for domestic students, 9/1 priority date for international students. Applications are processed on a rolling basis. Application fee: $50. Electronic applications accepted. *Expenses:* $678.55 per credit in-state tuition, $1,469.75 per credit out-of-state tuition, $54.56 per credit hour student service fee, $315.70 registration fee. *Financial support:* In 2019–20, 48 students received support, including 4 fellowships with partial tuition reimbursements available (averaging $57,000 per year), 1 research assistantship with partial tuition reimbursement available (averaging $45,000 per year), 13 teaching assistantships with partial tuition reimbursements available (averaging $58,000 per year); scholarships/grants, health care benefits, and unspecified assistantships also available. Financial award applicants required to submit FAFSA. *Unit head:* Dr. Daniel Geller, Professor and Chair, 313-577-6328, E-mail: dgeller@wayne.edu. *Application contact:* Dr. Jeffrey Grynaviski, Graduate Director, 313-577-2620, E-mail: gradpolisci@wayne.edu.
Website: http://clas.wayne.edu/politicalscience/

Wayne State University, College of Liberal Arts and Sciences, Department of Urban Studies and Planning, Detroit, MI 48202. Offers economic development (Graduate Certificate); urban studies and planning (MUP). *Accreditation:* ACSP. *Program availability:* Part-time, evening/weekend. *Faculty:* 6 full-time (2 women), 7 part-time/adjunct (2 women). *Students:* 9 full-time (5 women), 53 part-time (32 women); includes 29 minority (24 Black or African American, non-Hispanic/Latino; 1 American Indian or Alaska Native, non-Hispanic/Latino; 1 Hispanic/Latino; 3 Two or more races, non-Hispanic/Latino), 2 international. Average age 30. 84 applicants, 42% accepted, 25 enrolled. In 2019, 8 master's awarded. *Degree requirements:* For master's, 48 credits of coursework; for Graduate Certificate, 12 credits of coursework, at least three of which must be outside of the student's Master's degree. *Entrance requirements:* For master's, transcripts, 2 letters of recommendation, personal statement; for Graduate Certificate, graduate degree or actively pursuing a graduate degree at WSU; personal statement of interest. Additional exam requirements/recommendations for international students: required—TOEFL (minimum score 550 paper-based; 79 iBT), TWE (minimum score 5.5), Michigan English Language Assessment Battery (minimum score 85); recommended—IELTS (minimum score 6.5). *Application deadline:* For fall admission, 6/1 priority date for domestic students, 5/1 priority date for international students; for winter admission, 10/1 priority date for domestic students, 9/1 priority date for international students; for spring admission, 2/1 priority date for domestic students, 1/1 priority date for international students. Applications are processed on a rolling basis. Application fee: $50. Electronic applications accepted. *Expenses: Tuition:* Full-time $34,567. *Financial support:* In 2019–20, 19 students received support. Scholarships/grants available. Financial award application deadline: 6/30; financial award applicants required to submit FAFSA. *Unit head:* Dr. Rayman Mohamed, Chair, 313-577-3356, E-mail: rayman.mohamed@wayne.edu. *Application contact:* Dr. Rayman Mohamed, Chair, 313-577-3356, E-mail: rayman.mohamed@wayne.edu.
Website: http://clas.wayne.edu/dusp/

Western Illinois University, School of Graduate Studies, Illinois Institute for Rural Affairs, Macomb, IL 61455-1390. Offers community and economic development (MA). Electronic applications accepted.

Williams College, Graduate Program in the History of Art, Williamstown, MA 01267. Offers development economics (MA); history of art (MA). *Degree requirements:* For master's, 2 foreign languages, symposium paper and lecture. *Entrance requirements:* For master's, GRE General Test. Additional exam requirements/recommendations for international students: required—TOEFL. Electronic applications accepted. *Expenses: Tuition:* Full-time $55,140.

Yale University, Graduate School of Arts and Sciences, Department of Economics, Program in International and Development Economics, New Haven, CT 06520. Offers MA. *Entrance requirements:* For master's, GRE General Test.

Economics

Albany State University, College of Arts and Humanities, Albany, GA 31705-2717. Offers criminal justice (MS); English education (M Ed); public administration (MPA), including community and economic development, criminal justice administration, health administration and policy, human resources management, public management, public policy, water resources management and policy; social work (MSW). *Accreditation:* NASPAA. *Program availability:* Part-time. *Degree requirements:* For master's, comprehensive exam, professional portfolio (for MPA), internship, capstone report. *Entrance requirements:* For master's, GRE, MAT, minimum GPA of 3.0, official transcript, pre-medical record/certificate of immunization, letters of reference. Electronic applications accepted.

American University, College of Arts and Sciences, Department of Economics, Washington, DC 20016-8029. Offers applied microeconomics (Certificate); economics (MA, PhD); gender analysis in economics (Certificate); international economic relations (Certificate); international economics (MA). *Program availability:* Part-time, evening/weekend, 100% online, blended/hybrid learning. Terminal master's awarded for partial completion of doctoral program. *Degree requirements:* For master's, comprehensive exam, thesis or alternative; for doctorate, comprehensive exam, thesis/dissertation. *Entrance requirements:* For master's, GRE; Please visit website: https://www.american.edu/cas/economics/, statement of purpose, transcripts, 2 letters of recommendation, resume; for doctorate, GRE, statement of purpose, transcripts, 2 letters of recommendation, resume; for Certificate, bachelor's degree, statement of purpose, transcripts, resume. Additional exam requirements/recommendations for international students: required—TOEFL (minimum score 600 paper-based; 100 iBT). Electronic applications accepted. *Expenses:* Contact institution.

American University, School of International Service, Washington, DC 20016-8071. Offers comparative and regional studies (Certificate); cross-cultural communication (Certificate); development management (MS); ethics, peace, and global affairs (MA); European studies (Certificate); global environmental policy (MA, Certificate); global information technology (Certificate); global media (MA); international affairs (MA), including comparative and regional studies, global governance, politics, and security, international economic relations, natural resources and sustainable development, U.S. foreign policy and national security; international arts management (Certificate); international communication (MA, Certificate); international development (MA); international economic policy (Certificate); international economic relations (Certificate); international economics (MA); international peace and conflict resolution (MA, Certificate); international politics (Certificate); international relations (MA, PhD); international service (MIS); peacebuilding (Certificate); social enterprise (MA); the Americas (Certificate); United States foreign policy (Certificate); JD/MA. *Program* *availability:* Part-time, evening/weekend, 100% online, blended/hybrid learning. Terminal master's awarded for partial completion of doctoral program. *Degree requirements:* For master's, one foreign language, comprehensive exam, thesis or alternative; for doctorate, one foreign language, comprehensive exam, thesis/dissertation. *Entrance requirements:* For master's, transcripts, resume, 2 letters of recommendation, statement of purpose; for doctorate, GRE, transcripts, resume, 3 letters of recommendation, statement of purpose. Additional exam requirements/recommendations for international students: required—TOEFL. Electronic applications accepted. *Expenses:* Contact institution.

The American University in Cairo, School of Business, Cairo, Egypt. Offers business administration (MBA); economics (MA); economics in international development (MA, Diploma); finance (MS). *Program availability:* Part-time, evening/weekend. *Degree requirements:* For master's, comprehensive exam (for some programs), thesis (for some programs). *Entrance requirements:* For master's, GMAT, GRE. Additional exam requirements/recommendations for international students: required—TOEFL (minimum score 450 paper-based; 45 iBT), IELTS (minimum score 5). Electronic applications accepted. *Expenses:* Contact institution.

American University of Armenia, Graduate Programs, Yerevan, Armenia. Offers business administration (MBA); computer and information science (MS), including business management, design and manufacturing, energy (ME, MS), industrial engineering and systems management; economics (MS); industrial engineering and systems management (ME), including business, computer aided design/manufacturing, energy (ME, MS), information technology; law (LL M); political science and international affairs (MPSIA); public health (MPH); teaching English as a foreign language (MA). *Program availability:* Part-time, evening/weekend. *Degree requirements:* For master's, thesis (for some programs), capstone/project. *Entrance requirements:* For master's, GRE, GMAT, or LSAT. Additional exam requirements/recommendations for international students: recommended—TOEFL (minimum score 79 iBT), IELTS (minimum score 6.5). *Expenses: Tuition:* Full-time $3100; part-time $165 per credit. Tuition and fees vary according to program.

Andrews University, School of Graduate Studies, College of Professions, College of Professions, Berrien Springs, MI 49104. Offers MBA, MSA. *Faculty:* 8 full-time (3 women). *Students:* 32 full-time (19 women), 38 part-time (17 women); includes 21 minority (7 Black or African American, non-Hispanic/Latino; 6 Asian, non-Hispanic/Latino; 7 Hispanic/Latino; 1 Native Hawaiian or other Pacific Islander, non-Hispanic/Latino), 35 international. Average age 30. In 2019, 22 master's awarded. *Entrance requirements:* For master's, GMAT. Additional exam requirements/recommendations for international students: required—TOEFL (minimum score 550 paper-based). *Application deadline:* Applications are processed on a rolling basis. Application fee: $60. Electronic applications accepted. *Financial support:* Research assistantships, teaching assistantships, Federal Work-Study, and scholarships/grants available. *Application contact:* Jillian Panigot, Director, University Admissions, 800-253-2874, Fax: 269-471-6321, E-mail: graduate@andrews.edu.

Arizona State University at Tempe, W. P. Carey School of Business, Department of Economics, Tempe, AZ 85287-9801. Offers PhD. *Degree requirements:* For doctorate, comprehensive exam, thesis/dissertation, interactive Program of Study (iPOS) submitted before completing 50 percent of required credit hours. *Entrance requirements:* For doctorate, GRE, minimum GPA of 3.0 in last 2 years of work leading to bachelor's degree, 3 letters of recommendation, resume/curriculum vitae, letter of intent, thesis (if applicable), official university transcripts, personal statement. Additional exam requirements/recommendations for international students: required—TOEFL (minimum score 550 paper-based; 80 iBT), IELTS (minimum score 6.5). Electronic applications accepted.

Assumption University, Business Studies Program, Worcester, MA 01609-1296. Offers accounting (MBA); business studies (CAGS); finance/economics (MBA); human resources (MBA); international business (MBA); management (MBA); marketing (MBA); nonprofit leadership (MBA). *Program availability:* Part-time, evening/weekend. *Degree requirements:* For master's, capstone. *Entrance requirements:* For master's, bachelor's degree, three letters of recommendation, official transcripts, personal statement, current resume; for CAGS, MBA or equivalent degree in a closely related field, three letters of recommendation, official transcripts, personal statement, current resume. Additional exam requirements/recommendations for international students: required—TOEFL (minimum score 540 paper-based; 76 iBT), IELTS (minimum score 6). Electronic applications accepted. *Expenses: Tuition:* Full-time $12,690; part-time $705 per credit. *Required fees:* $70 per term.

Auburn University, Graduate School, College of Liberal Arts, Department of Economics, Auburn, AL 36849. Offers applied economics (PhD); economics (MS). *Program availability:* Part-time. *Faculty:* 17 full-time (6 women), 3 part-time/adjunct (2 women). *Students:* 14 full-time (7 women); includes 1 minority (Black or African American, non-Hispanic/Latino), 11 international. Average age 31. 42 applicants, 48% accepted, 3 enrolled. In 2019, 2 master's, 2 doctorates awarded. *Degree requirements:* For master's, thesis; for doctorate, thesis/dissertation. *Entrance requirements:* For master's, GMAT, GRE General Test; for doctorate, GRE General Test. Additional exam requirements/recommendations for international students: recommended—TOEFL (minimum score 550 paper-based; 79 iBT), IELTS (minimum score 6.5). *Application deadline:* Applications are processed on a rolling basis. Application fee: $60 ($70 for international students). Electronic applications accepted. *Expenses: Tuition, area resident:* Full-time $9828; part-time $546 per credit hour. Tuition, state resident: full-time $9828; part-time $546 per credit hour. Tuition, nonresident: full-time $29,484; part-time $1638 per credit hour. *International tuition:* $29,744 full-time. Tuition and fees vary according to course load, program and reciprocity agreements. *Financial support:* In 2019–20, 1 research assistantship with tuition reimbursement (averaging $27,000 per year), 12 teaching assistantships with tuition reimbursements (averaging $21,321 per year) were awarded; fellowships, career-related internships or fieldwork, and Federal Work-Study also available. Support available to part-time students. Financial award application deadline: 3/15; financial award applicants required to submit FAFSA. *Unit head:* Dr. Hyeongwoo Kim, Chair, 334-844-2928, E-mail: hzk0001@auburn.edu. *Application contact:* Dr. George Flowers, Dean of the Graduate School, 334-844-2125. Website: http://www.cla.auburn.edu/economics/

Auburn University at Montgomery, College of Liberal Arts & Social Sciences, Department of Economics, Montgomery, AL 36124. Offers applied economics (MS). *Program availability:* Part-time, evening/weekend. *Faculty:* 5 full-time (0 women). *Students:* 15 full-time (6 women), 1 (woman) part-time; includes 3 minority (2 Black or African American, non-Hispanic/Latino; 1 Asian, non-Hispanic/Latino), 5 international. Average age 28. 19 applicants, 100% accepted, 10 enrolled. In 2019, 11 master's awarded. *Entrance requirements:* For master's, GMAT or GRE General Test. Additional exam requirements/recommendations for international students: recommended—TOEFL (minimum score 500 paper-based; 61 iBT), IELTS (minimum score 5.5), TSE (minimum score 44). *Application deadline:* For fall admission, 7/15 for international students; for spring admission, 11/15 for international students; for summer admission, 4/15 for international students. Applications are processed on a rolling basis. Application fee: $25. Electronic applications accepted. *Expenses: Tuition, area resident:* Full-time $7578; part-time $421 per credit hour. Tuition, state resident: full-time $7578; part-time $421 per credit hour. Tuition, nonresident: full-time $17,046; part-time $947 per credit hour. *International tuition:* $17,046 full-time. *Required fees:* $868. *Financial support:* Application deadline: 3/1; applicants required to submit FAFSA. *Unit head:* Dr. Carel Ligeon, Head, 334-244-3486, E-mail: cligeon@aum.edu. *Application contact:* Ashley Warren, Graduate Admissions Coordinator, 334-244-3623, E-mail: awarren3@aum.edu. Website: http://www.cas.aum.edu/academic-programs/graduate-programs/master-of-science-in-applied-economics

Bard College, Levy Economics Institute, Annandale-on-Hudson, NY 12504. Offers economic theory and policy (MS).

Baruch College of the City University of New York, Zicklin School of Business, Department of Economics and Finance, Program in Economics, New York, NY 10010-5585. Offers MBA. *Program availability:* Part-time, evening/weekend. *Entrance requirements:* For master's, GMAT, 2 letters of recommendation, resume, 2 years of work experience. Additional exam requirements/recommendations for international students: required—TOEFL (minimum score 590 paper-based), TWE (minimum score 5).

Baylor University, Graduate School, Hankamer School of Business, Department of Economics, Waco, TX 76798. Offers MS Eco. *Entrance requirements:* For master's, GMAT or GRE General Test. Additional exam requirements/recommendations for international students: required—TOEFL (minimum score 600 paper-based; 100 iBT), IELTS (minimum score 7). Electronic applications accepted.

Binghamton University, State University of New York, Graduate School, Harpur College of Arts and Sciences, Department of Economics, Binghamton, NY 13902-6000. Offers MA, PhD. *Program availability:* Part-time. Terminal master's awarded for partial completion of doctoral program. *Degree requirements:* For doctorate, comprehensive exam, thesis/dissertation. *Entrance requirements:* For master's and doctorate, GRE General Test. Additional exam requirements/recommendations for international students: required—TOEFL (minimum score 550 paper-based; 80 iBT). Electronic applications accepted.

Boise State University, College of Business and Economics, Department of Economics, Boise, ID 83725-0399. Offers M Ec, MSE. *Students:* 7 full-time (2 women), 2 part-time (0 women); includes 2 minority (1 Black or African American, non-Hispanic/Latino; 1 Asian, non-Hispanic/Latino), 2 international. *Expenses: Tuition, area resident:* Full-time $7110; part-time $470 per credit hour. Tuition, state resident: full-time $7110; part-time $470 per credit hour. Tuition, nonresident: full-time $24,030; part-time $827 per credit hour. *International tuition:* $24,030 full-time. *Required fees:* $2536. Tuition and fees vary according to course load and program. *Unit head:* Dr. Christine A. Loucks, Chair, 208-426-1468, E-mail: cloucks@boisestate.edu. *Application contact:* Dr. Christine A. Loucks, Chair, 208-426-1468, E-mail: cloucks@boisestate.edu. Website: https://www.boisestate.edu/cobe-economics/graduate-programs/

Boston College, Morrissey Graduate School of Arts and Sciences, Department of Economics, Chestnut Hill, MA 02467-3800. Offers PhD. *Degree requirements:* For doctorate, comprehensive exam, thesis/dissertation. *Entrance requirements:* For doctorate, GRE General Test, GRE Subject Test. Additional exam requirements/recommendations for international students: required—TOEFL (minimum score 600 paper-based; 100 iBT), IELTS (minimum score 8). Electronic applications accepted.

Boston University, Graduate School of Arts and Sciences, Department of Economics, Boston, MA 02215. Offers MA, MAEP, MBA/MA. *Students:* 307 full-time (132 women), 38 part-time (18 women); includes 10 minority (5 Asian, non-Hispanic/Latino; 4 Hispanic/Latino; 1 Two or more races, non-Hispanic/Latino), 291 international. Average age 24. 1,595 applicants, 53% accepted, 151 enrolled. In 2019, 143 master's awarded. Terminal master's awarded for partial completion of doctoral program. *Degree requirements:* For master's, comprehensive exam. *Entrance requirements:* For master's, GRE General Test, 2 letters of recommendation, transcripts, personal statement. Additional exam requirements/recommendations for international students: required—TOEFL (minimum score 550 paper-based; 84 iBT). *Application deadline:* For fall admission, 12/1 for domestic and international students; for spring admission, 10/15 for domestic and international students. Application fee: $95. Electronic applications accepted. *Financial support:* In 2019–20, 175 students received support, including 36 fellowships with full tuition reimbursements available (averaging $23,340 per year), 43 research assistantships with full tuition reimbursements available (averaging $23,340 per year), 65 teaching assistantships with full tuition reimbursements available (averaging $23,340 per year); Federal Work-Study, scholarships/grants, and health care benefits also available. Financial award application deadline: 12/1. *Unit head:* Marc Rysman, Chair, 617-353-3086, Fax: 617-353-4449, E-mail: mrysman@bu.edu. *Application contact:* Mirtha Cabello, PhD Program Administrator, 617-353-4454, Fax: 617-353-4449, E-mail: cabello@bu.edu. Website: http://www.bu.edu/econ/

Bowling Green State University, Graduate College, College of Business, Program in Financial Economics, Bowling Green, OH 43403. Offers MA. *Program availability:* Part-time. *Degree requirements:* For master's, thesis or alternative. *Entrance requirements:* For master's, GRE General Test. Additional exam requirements/recommendations for international students: required—TOEFL. Electronic applications accepted.

Brandeis University, Brandeis International Business School, Master of Arts in International Economics and Finance Program, Waltham, MA 02454-9110. Offers applied economic analysis (MA). *Students:* Average age 23. 649 applicants, 45% accepted, 92 enrolled. In 2019, 103 master's awarded. *Entrance requirements:* For master's, GMAT or GRE. Additional exam requirements/recommendations for international students: required—TOEFL (minimum score 600 paper-based; 100 iBT), IELTS (minimum score 7), PTE (minimum score 68). *Application deadline:* For fall admission, 11/1 priority date for domestic and international students; for winter admission, 1/15 priority date for domestic and international students; for spring admission, 3/15 priority date for domestic and international students; for summer admission, 4/15 for domestic and international students. Application fee: $100. Electronic applications accepted. *Expenses:* Contact institution. *Financial support:* In 2019–20, 81 students received support. Institutionally sponsored loans and scholarships (averaging $18,384 annually) available. Financial award application deadline: 4/15; financial award applicants required to submit FAFSA. *Unit head:* Peter Petri, Dean, 781-736-2256. *Application contact:* Kelly Sugrue, Assistant Dean of Admissions, 781-736-2252, Fax: 781-736-2263, E-mail: globaladmissions@brandeis.edu. Website: http://www.brandeis.edu/global/ma

Brandeis University, Brandeis International Business School, PhD in International Economics and Finance Program, Waltham, MA 02454-9110. Offers advanced macroeconomics (PhD); applied microeconomics (PhD). *Faculty:* 43 full-time (17 women), 38 part-time/adjunct (9 women). *Students:* 16 full-time (7 women), 1 part-time (0 women); includes 2 minority (1 American Indian or Alaska Native, non-Hispanic/Latino; 1 Hispanic/Latino), 12 international. Average age 32. In 2019, 3 doctorates awarded. *Degree requirements:* For doctorate, comprehensive exam, thesis/dissertation. *Entrance requirements:* For doctorate, GRE, writing sample. Additional exam requirements/recommendations for international students: required—TOEFL, IELTS, PTE. *Application deadline:* For winter admission, 1/15 priority date for domestic and international students. Application fee: $100. Electronic applications accepted.

Economics

Expenses: Contact institution. *Financial support:* In 2019–20, research assistantships (averaging $6,000 per year), teaching assistantships (averaging $6,000 per year) were awarded; scholarships/grants and health care benefits also available. Financial award application deadline: 1/15; financial award applicants required to submit FAFSA. *Unit head:* Peter Petri, Dean, 781-736-8616. *Application contact:* Kelly Sugrue, Assistant Dean of Admissions, 781-736-2252, Fax: 781-736-2263, E-mail: globaladmissions@brandeis.edu.
Website: https://www.brandeis.edu/global/academics/phd/

Brock University, Faculty of Graduate Studies, Faculty of Social Sciences, Program in Business Economics, St. Catharines, ON L2S 3A1, Canada. Offers MBE. *Degree requirements:* For master's, thesis or alternative. *Entrance requirements:* For master's, honours degree. Additional exam requirements/recommendations for international students: required—TOEFL (minimum score 550 paper-based; 80 iBT), IELTS (minimum score 6.5), TWE (minimum score 4). Electronic applications accepted.

Brooklyn College of the City University of New York, School of Business, Brooklyn, NY 11210-2889. Offers accounting (MS); business administration (MS), including economic analysis, general business, global business and finance. *Program availability:* Part-time, evening/weekend. *Degree requirements:* For master's, comprehensive exam, thesis or alternative. *Entrance requirements:* For master's, GMAT, 2 letters of recommendation. Additional exam requirements/recommendations for international students: required—TOEFL (minimum score 550 paper-based; 79 iBT). Electronic applications accepted.

Brown University, Graduate School, Department of Economics, Providence, RI 02912. Offers PhD. Terminal master's awarded for partial completion of doctoral program. *Degree requirements:* For doctorate, thesis/dissertation. *Entrance requirements:* For doctorate, GRE General Test.

Buffalo State College, State University of New York, The Graduate School, School of Natural and Social Sciences, Department of Economics and Finance, Buffalo, NY 14222-1095. Offers applied economics (MA). *Degree requirements:* For master's, project. *Entrance requirements:* Additional exam requirements/recommendations for international students: required—TOEFL (minimum score 550 paper-based).

California Polytechnic State University, San Luis Obispo, Orfalea College of Business, Program in Economics, San Luis Obispo, CA 93407. Offers MS. *Students:* 10 full-time (1 woman), 1 part-time (0 women); includes 1 minority (Asian, non-Hispanic/Latino), 1 international. Average age 24. In 2019, 13 master's awarded. *Entrance requirements:* For master's, GMAT. Additional exam requirements/recommendations for international students: required—TOEFL (minimum score 80 iBT). *Application deadline:* For fall admission, 4/1 for domestic and international students. Applications are processed on a rolling basis. Application fee: $55. Electronic applications accepted. *Expenses:* Tuition, state resident: full-time $7176; part-time $4164 per year. Tuition, nonresident: full-time $18,690; part-time $8916 per year. *Required fees:* $4206; $3185 per unit. $1061 per term. *Financial support:* Fellowships, career-related internships or fieldwork, Federal Work-Study, institutionally sponsored loans, scholarships/grants, and unspecified assistantships available. Support available to part-time students. Financial award application deadline: 3/2; financial award applicants required to submit FAFSA. *Unit head:* Dr. Scott Dawson, Dean, 805-756-2705, E-mail: scdawson@calpoly.edu. *Application contact:* Dr. Scott Dawson, Dean, 805-756-2705, E-mail: scdawson@calpoly.edu.
Website: http://www.cob.calpoly.edu/gradbusiness/degree-programs/ms-economics/

California State Polytechnic University, Pomona, Program in Economics, Pomona, CA 91768-2557. Offers economics (MS). *Program availability:* Part-time, evening/weekend. *Entrance requirements:* Additional exam requirements/recommendations for international students: required—TOEFL (minimum score 550 paper-based). Electronic applications accepted. *Expenses:* Contact institution.

California State University, East Bay, Office of Graduate Studies, College of Business and Economics, Economics Department, Hayward, CA 94542-3000. Offers MA. *Program availability:* Part-time, evening/weekend. *Degree requirements:* For master's, comprehensive exam, project or thesis. *Entrance requirements:* For master's, GMAT, minimum GPA of 2.75 during previous 2 years of course work. Additional exam requirements/recommendations for international students: required—TOEFL (minimum score 580 paper-based; 92 iBT). Electronic applications accepted.

California State University, Fullerton, Graduate Studies, College of Business and Economics, Department of Economics, Fullerton, CA 92831-3599. Offers MA, MBA. *Program availability:* Part-time. *Entrance requirements:* For master's, GMAT, GRE General Test.

California State University, Long Beach, Graduate Studies, College of Liberal Arts, Department of Economics, Long Beach, CA 90840. Offers economics (MA). *Program availability:* Part-time. *Degree requirements:* For master's, comprehensive exam or thesis. *Entrance requirements:* For master's, GRE General Test, GRE Subject Test, minimum GPA of 3.0. Electronic applications accepted.

California State University, Los Angeles, Graduate Studies, College of Business and Economics, Department of Economics and Statistics, Los Angeles, CA 90032-8530. Offers financial economics (MA); global economics (MA). *Program availability:* Part-time, evening/weekend. *Degree requirements:* For master's, comprehensive exam or thesis. *Entrance requirements:* For master's, GMAT, minimum GPA of 2.5 during previous 2 years of course work. Additional exam requirements/recommendations for international students: required—TOEFL (minimum score 550 paper-based). Electronic applications accepted. *Expenses: Tuition, area resident:* Full-time $7176; part-time $4164 per year. Tuition, state resident: full-time $7176; part-time $4164 per year. Tuition, nonresident: full-time $14,304; part-time $8916 per year. *International tuition:* $14,304 full-time. *Required fees:* $1037.76; $1037.76 per unit. Tuition and fees vary according to degree level and program.

California University of Management and Sciences, Graduate Programs, Anaheim, CA 92801. Offers business administration (MBA, DBA); computer information systems (MS); economics (MS); international business (MS); sports management (MS).

Campbellsville University, School of Business, Economics, and Technology, Campbellsville, KY 42718-2799. Offers business administration (MBA, Professional MBA); information technology management (MS); management (PhD); management and leadership (MML). *Program availability:* Part-time, evening/weekend, 100% online, blended/hybrid learning. *Degree requirements:* For master's, comprehensive exam (for some programs), thesis optional; for doctorate, comprehensive exam, thesis/dissertation. *Entrance requirements:* For master's, GRE or GMAT, letters of recommendation, college transcripts; for doctorate, GMAT, resume, official transcripts, references, personal essay, interview, completion of course in statistics and research methods. Additional exam requirements/recommendations for international students: required—TOEFL (minimum score 550 paper-based; 79 iBT); recommended—IELTS (minimum score 6). Electronic applications accepted. Application fee is waived when completed online. *Expenses:* Contact institution.

Carleton University, Faculty of Graduate Studies, Faculty of Public Affairs and Management, Department of Economics, Ottawa, ON K1S 5B6, Canada. Offers MA, PhD. *Degree requirements:* For master's, thesis optional; for doctorate, comprehensive

exam, thesis/dissertation. *Entrance requirements:* For master's, honors degree; for doctorate, master's degree. Additional exam requirements/recommendations for international students: required—TOEFL.

Carleton University, Faculty of Graduate Studies, Faculty of Public Affairs and Management, Institute of Political Economy, Ottawa, ON K1S 5B6, Canada. Offers MA, PhD. *Degree requirements:* For master's, thesis optional. *Entrance requirements:* For master's, honors degree. Additional exam requirements/recommendations for international students: required—TOEFL.

Carnegie Mellon University, Tepper School of Business, Program in Economics, Pittsburgh, PA 15213-3891. Offers PhD. *Degree requirements:* For doctorate, thesis/dissertation. *Entrance requirements:* For doctorate, GMAT, GRE General Test.

Central European University, Department of Economics, 1051, Hungary. Offers business administration (PhD); business analytics (M Sc); economic policy in global markets (MA); economics (MA, PhD); finance (MS); global economic relations (MA); technology management and innovation (MS). *Program availability:* Part-time. *Degree requirements:* For master's, one foreign language, thesis; for doctorate, one foreign language, comprehensive exam, thesis/dissertation. *Entrance requirements:* For master's and doctorate, interview. Additional exam requirements/recommendations for international students: required—TOEFL (minimum score 570 paper-based); recommended—IELTS (minimum score 6.5). Electronic applications accepted.

Central Michigan University, College of Graduate Studies, College of Business Administration, Department of Economics, Mount Pleasant, MI 48859. Offers MA. *Program availability:* Part-time. *Degree requirements:* For master's, thesis or alternative. Electronic applications accepted. *Expenses: Tuition, area resident:* full-time $12,267; part-time $8178 per year. Tuition, state resident: full-time $12,267; part-time $8178 per year. Tuition, nonresident: full-time $12,267; part-time $8178 per year. *International tuition:* $16,110 full-time. *Required fees:* $225 per semester. Tuition and fees vary according to degree level and program.

City College of the City University of New York, Graduate School, Colin Powell School for Civic and Global Leadership, Department of Economics and Business, New York, NY 10031-9198. Offers economics (MA). *Program availability:* Part-time. *Degree requirements:* For master's, comprehensive exam, proficiency in a foreign language or advanced statistics. *Entrance requirements:* Additional exam requirements/recommendations for international students: required—TOEFL (minimum score 550 paper-based; 79 iBT). Electronic applications accepted.

Claremont Graduate University, Graduate Programs, School of Social Science, Policy and Evaluation, Department of Economics, Claremont, CA 91711-6160. Offers behavioral economics and neuroeconomics (PhD); business and financial economics (MA, PhD); economic development (Certificate); international economic and development policy (PhD); international economics policy and development (MA); international money and finance (PhD); political economy and public economics (PhD); political economy and public policy (MA); MBA/PhD. *Program availability:* Part-time. *Entrance requirements:* For master's and doctorate, GRE General Test or GMAT. Additional exam requirements/recommendations for international students: required—TOEFL (minimum score 75 iBT). Electronic applications accepted.

Claremont Graduate University, Graduate Programs, School of Social Science, Policy and Evaluation, Department of Politics and Policy, Claremont, CA 91711-6160. Offers American politics (MA, PhD); comparative politics (PhD); international political economy (MA); international studies (MA); political philosophy (PhD); political science (PhD); politics, economics and business (MA); public policy (MA, PhD); world politics (PhD); MBA/PhD. *Program availability:* Part-time. Terminal master's awarded for partial completion of doctoral program. *Entrance requirements:* For master's and doctorate, GRE General Test. Additional exam requirements/recommendations for international students: required—TOEFL (minimum score 75 iBT). Electronic applications accepted.

Claremont Graduate University, Graduate Programs, School of Social Science, Policy and Evaluation, Program in Politics, Economics, and Business, Claremont, CA 91711-6160. Offers MA. *Program availability:* Part-time. *Entrance requirements:* For master's, GRE General Test. Additional exam requirements/recommendations for international students: required—TOEFL (minimum score 75 iBT). Electronic applications accepted.

Clark Atlanta University, School of Business Administration, Department of Economics, Atlanta, GA 30314. Offers MA. *Program availability:* Part-time. *Degree requirements:* For master's, thesis optional. *Entrance requirements:* For master's, GRE General Test, minimum GPA of 2.5. Additional exam requirements/recommendations for international students: required—TOEFL (minimum score 500 paper-based; 61 iBT). Electronic applications accepted.

Clark University, Graduate School, Department of Economics, Worcester, MA 01610-1477. Offers PhD. *Faculty:* 11 full-time (3 women), 1 (woman) part-time/adjunct. *Students:* 42 full-time (24 women); includes 3 minority (1 Black or African American, non-Hispanic/Latino; 1 Asian, non-Hispanic/Latino; 1 Hispanic/Latino), 30 international. Average age 30. 49 applicants, 43% accepted, 9 enrolled. In 2019, 5 doctorates awarded. *Degree requirements:* For doctorate, thesis/dissertation. *Entrance requirements:* For doctorate, GRE General Test. Additional exam requirements/recommendations for international students: required—TOEFL (minimum score 575 paper-based; 90 iBT), IELTS (minimum score 6.5). *Application deadline:* For fall admission, 2/1 priority date for domestic students. Application fee: $75. Electronic applications accepted. *Expenses: Tuition:* Full-time $47,650; part-time $4765 per course. *Required fees:* $1850. *Financial support:* Fellowships, research assistantships, teaching assistantships, career-related internships or fieldwork, institutionally sponsored loans, and tuition waivers (full and partial) available. *Unit head:* Dr. Jacqueline Geoghegan, Chair, 508-793-7709, E-mail: jgeoghegan@clarku.edu. *Application contact:* Cindy Rice, Managerial Secretary, 508-793-7226, Fax: 508-793-8849, E-mail: crice@clarku.edu.
Website: http://www.clarku.edu/departments/economics/

Clemson University, Graduate School, College of Business, John E. Walker Department of Economics, Clemson, SC 29634. Offers applied economics (PhD); applied economics and statistics (MS); economics (MA, PhD). *Faculty:* 28 full-time (3 women), 2 part-time/adjunct (1 woman). *Students:* 65 full-time (23 women), 5 part-time (3 women); includes 5 minority (2 Black or African American, non-Hispanic/Latino; 1 Hispanic/Latino; 2 Two or more races, non-Hispanic/Latino), 40 international. Average age 27. 103 applicants, 73% accepted, 21 enrolled. In 2019, 7 master's, 16 doctorates awarded. Terminal master's awarded for partial completion of doctoral program. *Degree requirements:* For master's, thesis, 24 course hours, 6 thesis hours; for doctorate, comprehensive exam, thesis/dissertation, 42 course hours, 18 dissertation hours. *Entrance requirements:* For master's and doctorate, GRE General Test or GMAT, unofficial transcripts, letters of recommendation, courses in intermediate microeconomic theory and multivariable calculus. Additional exam requirements/recommendations for international students: required—TOEFL (minimum score 80 paper-based; 80 iBT); recommended—IELTS (minimum score 6.5), TSE (minimum score 54). *Application deadline:* For fall admission, 4/15 for international students; for spring admission, 10/15 for international students. Applications are processed on a rolling basis. Application fee: $80 ($90 for international students). Electronic applications accepted. *Expenses:* Full-

Time Student per Semester: Tuition: $4600 (in-state), $9525 (out-of-state), Fees: $598; Graduate Assistant Per Semester: $1144; Part-Time Student Per Credit Hour: $556 (in-state), $1106 (out-of-state), Fees: $617; other fees apply depending on credit hours, campus & residency. Doctoral Base Fee per Semester: $4938 (in-state), $10405 (out-of-state). *Financial support:* In 2019–20, 74 students received support, including 25 fellowships with full and partial tuition reimbursements available (averaging $5,310 per year), 18 teaching assistantships with full and partial tuition reimbursements available (averaging $15,889 per year); unspecified assistantships also available. *Unit head:* Dr. Scott Baier, Department Chair, 864-656-4534, E-mail: sbaier@clemson.edu. *Application contact:* Dr. Curtis Simon, PhD Program Coordinator, 864-656-3966, E-mail: cjsmn@clemson.edu.
Website: http://economics.clemson.edu/

Cleveland State University, College of Graduate Studies, College of Liberal Arts and Social Sciences, Department of Economics, Cleveland, OH 44115. Offers MA. *Program availability:* Part-time, evening/weekend. *Faculty:* 6 full-time (1 woman). *Students:* 1 full-time (0 women), 2 part-time (0 women); includes 1 minority (Black or African American, non-Hispanic/Latino). Average age 24. 32 applicants, 72% accepted, 7 enrolled. In 2019, 8 master's awarded. *Entrance requirements:* For master's, minimum GPA of 2.75; coursework in micro theory, macro theory, statistics, and calculus. Additional exam requirements/recommendations for international students: required—TOEFL (minimum score 550 paper-based; 78 iBT), IELTS (minimum score 6). *Application deadline:* For fall admission, 7/1 priority date for domestic students, 5/15 priority date for international students; for spring admission, 11/15 for domestic students, 11/1 for international students; for summer admission, 4/1 for domestic students, 3/15 for international students. Applications are processed on a rolling basis. Application fee: $40. Electronic applications accepted. *Expenses:* Tuition, state resident: full-time $10,215; part-time $6810 per credit hour. Tuition, nonresident: full-time $17,496; part-time $11,664 per credit hour. *International tuition:* $19,316 full-time. Tuition and fees vary according to degree level and program. *Financial support:* In 2019–20, 4 students received support, including 3 teaching assistantships (averaging $6,960 per year). Financial award application deadline: 4/30; financial award applicants required to submit FAFSA. *Unit head:* Dr. Billy Kosteas, Department Chairperson/Associate Professor, 216-687-4526, Fax: 216-687-9206, E-mail: b.kosteas@csuohio.edu. *Application contact:* Dr. Myong Hun Chang, Professor, 216-687-4523, Fax: 216-687-9206, E-mail: m.chang@csuohio.edu.
Website: http://www.csuohio.edu/class/economics/economics

Cleveland State University, College of Graduate Studies, Maxine Goodman Levin College of Urban Affairs, Program in Urban Planning and Development, Cleveland, OH 44115. Offers economic development (MUPD); environmental sustainability (MUPD); historic preservation (MUPD); housing and neighborhood development (MUPD); real estate development and finance (MUPD); urban economic development (Certificate); urban geographic information systems (MUPD); JD/MUPDD. *Accreditation:* ACSP. *Program availability:* Part-time, evening/weekend. *Degree requirements:* For master's, thesis or alternative, exit project. *Entrance requirements:* For master's, GRE General Test (minimum score: 50th percentile combined verbal and quantitative, 4.0 analytical writing), minimum GPA of 3.0. Additional exam requirements/recommendations for international students: required—TOEFL (minimum score 550 paper-based; 78 iBT), IELTS (6.0), or International Test of English Proficiency (iTEP). Electronic applications accepted. *Expenses:* Contact institution.

Colorado State University, College of Liberal Arts, Department of Economics, Fort Collins, CO 80523-1771. Offers MA, PhD. Terminal master's awarded for partial completion of doctoral program. *Degree requirements:* For master's, thesis, minimum GPA of 3.0; for doctorate, comprehensive exam, thesis/dissertation, minimum GPA of 3.0. *Entrance requirements:* For master's and doctorate, GRE, coursework in intermediate micro, intermediate macro, and calculus; minimum GPA of 3.3. Additional exam requirements/recommendations for international students: required—TOEFL (minimum score 550 paper-based; 80 iBT), IELTS (minimum score 6.5). Electronic applications accepted. *Expenses:* Tuition, state resident: full-time $10,520; part-time $5844 per credit hour. Tuition, nonresident: full-time $25,791; part-time $14,328 per credit hour. *International tuition:* $25,791 full-time. *Required fees:* $2512.80. Part-time tuition and fees vary according to course level, course load, degree level, program and student level.

Columbia University, Graduate School of Arts and Sciences, New York, NY 10027. Offers African-American studies (MA); American studies (MA); anthropology (MA, PhD); art history and archaeology (MA, PhD); astronomy (PhD); biological sciences (PhD); biotechnology (MA); chemical physics (PhD); chemistry (PhD); classical studies (MA, PhD); classics (MA, PhD); climate and society (MA); conservation biology (MA); earth and environmental sciences (PhD); East Asia: regional studies (MA); East Asian languages and cultures (MA, PhD); ecology, evolution and environmental biology (MA), including conservation biology; ecology, evolution, and environmental biology (PhD), including ecology and evolutionary biology, evolutionary primatology; economics (MA, PhD); English and comparative literature (MA, PhD); French and Romance philology (MA, PhD); Germanic languages (MA, PhD); global French studies (MA); global thought (MA); Hispanic cultural studies (MA); history (PhD); history and literature (MA); human rights studies (MA); Islamic studies (MA); Italian (MA, PhD); Japanese pedagogy (MA); Jewish studies (MA); Latin America and the Caribbean: regional studies (MA); Latin American and Iberian cultures (PhD); mathematics (MA, PhD), including finance (MA); medieval and Renaissance studies (MA); Middle Eastern, South Asian, and African studies (MA, PhD); modern art: critical and curatorial studies (MA); modern European studies (MA); museum anthropology (MA); music (DMA, PhD); oral history (MA); philosophical foundations of physics (MA); philosophy (MA, PhD); physics (PhD); political science (MA, PhD); psychology (PhD); quantitative methods in the social sciences (MA); religion (MA, PhD); Russia, Eurasia and East Europe: regional studies (MA); Russian translation (MA); Slavic cultures (MA); Slavic languages (MA, PhD); sociology (MA, PhD); South Asian studies (MA); statistics (MA, PhD); theatre (PhD). *Program availability:* Part-time. *Students:* 3,506 full-time (1,844 women), 208 part-time (121 women); includes 864 minority (110 Black or African American, non-Hispanic/Latino; 5 American Indian or Alaska Native, non-Hispanic/Latino; 416 Asian, non-Hispanic/Latino; 147 Hispanic/Latino; 6 Native Hawaiian or other Pacific Islander, non-Hispanic/Latino; 180 Two or more races, non-Hispanic/Latino), 2,065 international. 14,545 applicants, 25% accepted, 1,429 enrolled. In 2019, 1,262 master's, 363 doctorates awarded. Terminal master's awarded for partial completion of doctoral program. *Degree requirements:* For master's, variable foreign language requirement, comprehensive exam (for some programs), thesis (for some programs); for doctorate, variable foreign language requirement, comprehensive exam (for some programs), thesis/dissertation. *Entrance requirements:* For master's and doctorate, GRE General Test, GRE Subject Test (for some programs). Additional exam requirements/recommendations for international students: required—TOEFL (minimum score 600 paper-based; 100 iBT), IELTS (minimum score 7.5). Application fee: $115. Electronic applications accepted. *Expenses:* Tuition: Full-time $47,600; part-time $1880 per credit. One-time fee: $105. *Financial support:* Fellowships, research assistantships, teaching assistantships, career-related internships or fieldwork, Federal Work-Study, institutionally sponsored loans, scholarships/grants, traineeships, health care benefits, tuition waivers, and unspecified assistantships available. Support available to part-time students. Financial award application deadline: 12/15. *Unit head:* Dr. Carlos J. Alonso, Dean of the Graduate School of Arts and Sciences and Vice President for Graduate Education, 212-854-2861, E-mail: gsas-dean@columbia.edu. *Application contact:* GSAS Office of Admissions, 212-854-6729, E-mail: gsas-admissions@columbia.edu. Website: http://gsas.columbia.edu/

Columbia University, Graduate School of Business, Doctoral Program in Business, New York, NY 10027. Offers business (PhD), including accounting, decision, risk, and operations, finance and economics, management, marketing. *Accreditation:* AACSB. *Degree requirements:* For doctorate, comprehensive exam, thesis/dissertation, major field exam, research paper, thesis proposal. *Entrance requirements:* For doctorate, GMAT or GRE (finance), 2 letters of reference, resume. Additional exam requirements/recommendations for international students: required—TOEFL. Electronic applications accepted. *Expenses:* Contact institution.

Columbia University, Graduate School of Business, MBA Program, New York, NY 10027. Offers accounting (MBA); decision, risk, and operations (MBA); entrepreneurship (MBA); finance and economics (MBA); healthcare and pharmaceutical management (MBA); human resource management (MBA); international business (MBA); leadership and ethics (MBA); management (MBA); marketing (MBA); media (MBA); private equity (MBA); real estate (MBA); social enterprise (MBA); value investing (MBA); DDS/MBA; JD/MBA; MBA/MIA; MBA/MPH; MBA/MS; MD/MBA. *Entrance requirements:* For master's, GMAT, 2 letters of recommendation. Additional exam requirements/recommendations for international students: required—TOEFL. Electronic applications accepted. *Expenses:* Contact institution.

Concordia University, School of Graduate Studies, Faculty of Arts and Science, Department of Economics, Montréal, QC H3G 1M8, Canada. Offers MA, PhD, Diploma. *Degree requirements:* For master's, thesis or alternative, research paper; for doctorate, one foreign language, comprehensive exam, thesis/dissertation, research seminar. *Entrance requirements:* For master's and doctorate, honors degree in economics or equivalent.

Copenhagen Business School, Graduate Programs, Copenhagen, Denmark. Offers business administration (Exec MBA, MBA, PhD); business administration and information systems (M Sc); business, language and culture (M Sc); economics and business administration (M Sc); health management (MHM); international business and politics (M Sc); public administration (MPA); shipping and logistics (Exec MBA); technology, market and organization (MBA).

Cornell University, Graduate School, Graduate Fields of Architecture, Art and Planning, Field of Regional Science, Ithaca, NY 14853. Offers environmental studies (MA, MS, PhD); international spatial problems (MA, MS, PhD); location theory (MA, MS, PhD); multiregional economic analysis (MA, MS, PhD); peace science (MA, MS, PhD); planning methods (MA, MS, PhD); urban and regional economics (MA, MS, PhD). Terminal master's awarded for partial completion of doctoral program. *Degree requirements:* For master's, thesis; for doctorate, comprehensive exam, thesis/dissertation. *Entrance requirements:* For master's and doctorate, GRE General Test, 2 letters of recommendation. Additional exam requirements/recommendations for international students: required—TOEFL (minimum score 600 paper-based; 77 iBT). Electronic applications accepted.

Cornell University, Graduate School, Graduate Fields of Arts and Sciences, Field of Economics, Ithaca, NY 14853. Offers applied economics (PhD); basic analytical economics (PhD); econometrics and economic statistics (PhD); economic development and planning (PhD); economic theory (PhD); industrial organization and control (PhD); international economics (PhD); labor economics (PhD); monetary and macro economics (PhD); public finance (PhD). *Degree requirements:* For doctorate, comprehensive exam, thesis/dissertation. *Entrance requirements:* For doctorate, GRE General Test, 3 letters of recommendation. Additional exam requirements/recommendations for international students: required—TOEFL (minimum score 550 paper-based; 77 iBT). Electronic applications accepted.

Dalhousie University, Faculty of Science, Department of Economics, Halifax, NS B3H 4R2, Canada. Offers MA, MDE, PhD. *Degree requirements:* For master's, thesis; for doctorate, thesis/dissertation. *Entrance requirements:* For master's and doctorate, GRE (recommended). Additional exam requirements/recommendations for international students: required—TOEFL, IELTS, CANTEST, CAEL, or Michigan English Language Assessment Battery. Electronic applications accepted.

DePaul University, College of Liberal Arts and Social Sciences, Chicago, IL 60614. Offers Arabic (MA); Chinese (MA); critical ethnic studies (MA); English (MA); French (MA); German (MA); history (MA); interdisciplinary studies (MA, MS); international public service (MS); international studies (MA); Italian (MA); Japanese (MA); liberal studies (MA); nonprofit management (MNM); public administration (MPA); public health (MPH); public policy (MPP); public service management (MS); refugee and forced migration studies (MS); social work (MSW); sociology (MA); Spanish (MA); sustainable urban development (MA); women's and gender studies (MA); writing and publishing (MA); writing, rhetoric and discourse (MA); MA/PhD. *Accreditation:* CEPH. *Program availability:* Part-time, evening/weekend, online learning. Terminal master's awarded for partial completion of doctoral program. *Degree requirements:* For master's, variable foreign language requirement, comprehensive exam (for some programs), thesis (for some programs). Electronic applications accepted.

DePaul University, Kellstadt Graduate School of Business, Chicago, IL 60604. Offers accountancy (MBA, MSA); applied economics (MBA); audit and advisory services (MS); business administration (DBA); business analytics (MS); business strategy and decision-making (MBA); computational finance (MS); economics and policy analysis (MS); enterprise risk management (MS); entrepreneurship (MBA, MS); finance (MBA, MS); general business (MBA); hospitality leadership (MBA); hospitality leadership and operational performance (MS); human resources (MS); international business (MBA); management (MBA, MS); management information systems (MBA); marketing (MBA, MS); marketing analysis (MS); marketing strategy and planning (MBA); real estate (MS); real estate finance and investment (MBA); strategy, execution and valuation (MBA); supply chain management (MS); sustainable management (MS); taxation (MS); JD/MBA. *Accreditation:* AACSB. *Program availability:* Part-time, evening/weekend, online learning. *Entrance requirements:* For master's, GMAT/GRE, 2 letters of recommendation, resume, essay, official transcripts. Additional exam requirements/recommendations for international students: required—TOEFL (minimum score 550 paper-based; 80 iBT). Electronic applications accepted. *Expenses:* Contact institution.

Drexel University, LeBow College of Business, Program in Business Administration, Philadelphia, PA 19104-2875. Offers business administration (MBA, PhD, APC), including accounting (MBA, PhD), decision sciences (PhD), economics (MBA, PhD), finance (MBA, PhD), legal studies (MBA), management (MBA), marketing (MBA, PhD), organizational sciences (PhD), quantitative methods (MBA), strategic management (PhD). *Accreditation:* AACSB. *Program availability:* Part-time, evening/weekend, online learning. Terminal master's awarded for partial completion of doctoral program. *Entrance requirements:* For master's, GMAT, minimum GPA of 2.75; for doctorate, GMAT. Additional exam requirements/recommendations for international students: required—TOEFL. Electronic applications accepted.

Economics

Duke University, Graduate School, Department of Economics, Durham, NC 27708. Offers AM, PhD, JD/AM. *Degree requirements:* For doctorate, thesis/dissertation. *Entrance requirements:* For master's and doctorate, GRE General Test. Additional exam requirements/recommendations for international students: required—TOEFL (minimum score 577 paper-based; 90 iBT) or IELTS (minimum score 7). Electronic applications accepted.

Duke University, Graduate School, Program in Economics and Computation, Durham, NC 27708-0097. Offers MS. *Entrance requirements:* For master's, GRE General Test. Additional exam requirements/recommendations for international students: required—TOEFL (minimum score 577 paper-based; 90 iBT) or IELTS (minimum score 7).

Duke University, Graduate School, Program in Statistical and Economic Modeling, Durham, NC 27708. Offers econometrics (MS); financial economics (MS). *Entrance requirements:* For master's, GRE General Test. Additional exam requirements/recommendations for international students: required—TOEFL (minimum score 577 paper-based; 90 iBT) or IELTS (minimum score 7). Electronic applications accepted.

Eastern Illinois University, Graduate School, College of Liberal Arts and Sciences, Department of Economics, Charleston, IL 61920. Offers MA. *Program availability:* Part-time, evening/weekend. *Degree requirements:* For master's, comprehensive exam (for some programs), thesis (for some programs). *Entrance requirements:* For master's, GMAT or GRE. Additional exam requirements/recommendations for international students: required—TOEFL (minimum score 500 paper-based; 61 iBT), IELTS (minimum score 6). Electronic applications accepted.

Eastern Michigan University, Graduate School, College of Arts and Sciences, Department of Economics, Ypsilanti, MI 48197. Offers MA, Graduate Certificate. *Program availability:* Part-time, evening/weekend, online learning. *Faculty:* 8 full-time (2 women). *Students:* 16 full-time (9 women), 7 part-time (1 woman); includes 2 minority (1 Black or African American, non-Hispanic/Latino; 1 Two or more races, non-Hispanic/Latino), 9 international. Average age 29. 43 applicants, 58% accepted, 11 enrolled. In 2019, 19 master's awarded. *Entrance requirements:* Additional exam requirements/recommendations for international students: required—TOEFL. *Application deadline:* Applications are processed on a rolling basis. Application fee: $45. *Financial support:* Fellowships, research assistantships with full tuition reimbursements, teaching assistantships with full tuition reimbursements, career-related internships or fieldwork, Federal Work-Study, institutionally sponsored loans, scholarships/grants, tuition waivers (partial), and unspecified assistantships available. Support available to part-time students. Financial award applicants required to submit FAFSA. *Unit head:* Dr. Mehmet Yaya, Interim Department Head, 734-487-3395, Fax: 734-487-9666, E-mail: myaya@emich.edu. *Application contact:* Dr. David Crary, Graduate Coordinator, 734-487-0001, Fax: 734-487-9666, E-mail: dcrary@emich.edu. Website: http://www.emich.edu/economics

Emory University, Laney Graduate School, Department of Economics, Atlanta, GA 30322-1100. Offers PhD. *Degree requirements:* For doctorate, comprehensive exam, thesis/dissertation. *Entrance requirements:* For doctorate, GRE General Test. Additional exam requirements/recommendations for international students: recommended—TOEFL. Electronic applications accepted.

Florida Atlantic University, College of Business, Department of Economics, Boca Raton, FL 33431-0991. Offers MS. *Program availability:* Part-time, evening/weekend. *Faculty:* 12 full-time (4 women). *Students:* 14 full-time (2 women), 13 part-time (3 women); includes 13 minority (3 Black or African American, non-Hispanic/Latino; 3 Asian, non-Hispanic/Latino; 5 Hispanic/Latino; 2 Two or more races, non-Hispanic/Latino), 6 international. Average age 28. 27 applicants, 67% accepted, 11 enrolled. In 2019, 12 master's awarded. *Entrance requirements:* For master's, GMAT, GRE General Test, minimum GPA of 3.0. Additional exam requirements/recommendations for international students: required—TOEFL (minimum score 600 paper-based; 61 iBT), IELTS (minimum score 6). *Application deadline:* For fall admission, 7/1 priority date for domestic students, 2/15 priority date for international students; for spring admission, 4/1 priority date for domestic students, 1/15 priority date for international students. Applications are processed on a rolling basis. Application fee: $30. *Expenses: Tuition:* Full-time $20,536; part-time $371.82 per credit hour. Tuition and fees vary according to program. *Financial support:* Teaching assistantships, tuition waivers (partial), and unspecified assistantships available. Financial award application deadline: 3/1. *Unit head:* Dr. Steven B Caudill, Chair, 561-297-2617, E-mail: scaudill@fau.edu. *Application contact:* Dr. Steven B Caudill, Chair, 561-297-2617, E-mail: scaudill@fau.edu. Website: https://business.fau.edu/departments/economics/

Florida International University, Steven J. Green School of International and Public Affairs, Department of Economics, Miami, FL 33199. Offers MA, PhD. *Program availability:* Part-time, evening/weekend. *Faculty:* 18 full-time (3 women), 11 part-time/adjunct (3 women). *Students:* 27 full-time (8 women), 5 part-time (1 woman); includes 13 minority (1 Black or African American, non-Hispanic/Latino; 12 Hispanic/Latino), 16 international. Average age 32. 60 applicants, 20% accepted, 8 enrolled. In 2019, 1 master's, 8 doctorates awarded. *Degree requirements:* For master's, thesis or alternative; for doctorate, comprehensive exam, thesis/dissertation. *Entrance requirements:* For master's, GRE, minimum GPA of 3.0, letters of recommendation; for doctorate, GRE General Test, 3 letters of recommendation, minimum GPA of 3.0. Additional exam requirements/recommendations for international students: required—TOEFL (minimum score 550 paper-based; 80 iBT). *Application deadline:* For fall admission, 4/1 for domestic and international students. Application fee: $30. Electronic applications accepted. *Expenses: Tuition, area resident:* Full-time $8912; part-time $446 per credit hour. Tuition, state resident: full-time $8912; part-time $446 per credit hour. Tuition, nonresident: full-time $21,393; part-time $992 per credit hour. *Required fees:* $2194. *Financial support:* Federal Work-Study, institutionally sponsored loans, and scholarships/grants available. Financial award application deadline: 3/1; financial award applicants required to submit FAFSA. *Unit head:* Dr. Cem Karayalcin, Chair, 305-348-3285, Fax: 305-348-1524, E-mail: ali.karayalcin@fiu.edu. *Application contact:* Nanett Rojas, Manager, Admissions Operations, 305-348-7464, Fax: 305-348-7441, E-mail: gradadm@fiu.edu. Website: http://economics.fiu.edu/

Florida State University, The Graduate School, College of Social Sciences and Public Policy, Department of Economics, Tallahassee, FL 32306-2180. Offers applied economics (MS); economics (PhD); JD/MS. *Faculty:* 32 full-time (6 women), 2 part-time/adjunct (1 woman). *Students:* 61 full-time (13 women), 3 part-time (2 women); includes 18 minority (2 Black or African American, non-Hispanic/Latino; 3 Asian, non-Hispanic/Latino; 11 Hispanic/Latino; 2 Two or more races, non-Hispanic/Latino), 3 international. Average age 26. 186 applicants, 48% accepted, 33 enrolled. In 2019, 30 master's, 7 doctorates awarded. Terminal master's awarded for partial completion of doctoral program. *Degree requirements:* For master's, thesis (for some programs), applied project (for some programs); for doctorate, comprehensive exam, thesis/dissertation, dissertation prospectus, workshops. *Entrance requirements:* For master's, GRE General Test, minimum upper-division undergraduate GPA of 3.0, 3.4 on graduate work; minimum 1 course each in statistics and calculus; principles and sufficient upper-level economics courses; for doctorate, GRE General Test, minimum upper-division undergraduate GPA of 3.0, graduate 3.4; minimum 1 course each in statistics and linear algebra, 2 in calculus. Additional exam requirements/recommendations for international students: required—TOEFL (minimum score 90 iBT). *Application deadline:* For fall admission, 2/15 priority date for domestic and international students. Applications are processed on a rolling basis. Application fee: $30. Electronic applications accepted. *Financial support:* In 2019–20, 52 students received support, including 3 fellowships with full tuition reimbursements available (averaging $25,000 per year), 1 research assistantship with full tuition reimbursement available (averaging $19,000 per year), 24 teaching assistantships with full tuition reimbursements available (averaging $19,000 per year); scholarships/grants, tuition waivers (full), and unspecified assistantships also available. Financial award application deadline: 2/15; financial award applicants required to submit FAFSA. *Unit head:* Dr. Manoj Atolia, Chairman, 850-644-5001, Fax: 850-644-4535, E-mail: matolia@fsu.edu. *Application contact:* Dr. Thomas W. Zuehlke, Graduate Director, 850-644-5001, Fax: 850-644-4535, E-mail: tzuehlke@fsu.edu. Website: http://www.coss.fsu.edu/economics/

Fordham University, Graduate School of Arts and Sciences, Department of Economics, New York, NY 10458. Offers MA, PhD. *Program availability:* Part-time, evening/weekend. *Students:* Average age 32. 154 applicants, 60% accepted, 28 enrolled. In 2019, 19 master's, 6 doctorates awarded. Terminal master's awarded for partial completion of doctoral program. *Degree requirements:* For master's, comprehensive exam; for doctorate, comprehensive exam, thesis/dissertation. *Entrance requirements:* For master's and doctorate, GRE General Test. Additional exam requirements/recommendations for international students: required—TOEFL (minimum score 600 paper-based). *Application deadline:* For fall admission, 1/4 priority date for domestic students; for spring admission, 11/1 for domestic students. Application fee: $70. Electronic applications accepted. *Financial support:* In 2019–20, 29 students received support, including 1 fellowship with tuition reimbursement available (averaging $15,000 per year), 16 teaching assistantships with tuition reimbursements available (averaging $24,350 per year); career-related internships or fieldwork, institutionally sponsored loans, tuition waivers (full and partial), and unspecified assistantships also available. Financial award application deadline: 1/4; financial award applicants required to submit FAFSA. *Unit head:* Dr. Johanna Francis, Associate Chair for Graduate Studies, 718-817-4066, Fax: 718-817-4048, E-mail: ajofrancis@fordham.edu. *Application contact:* Garrett Marino, Director of Graduate Admissions, 718-817-4419, Fax: 718-817-3566, E-mail: tstrattion@fordham.edu.

Fordham University, Graduate School of Arts and Sciences, Program in International Political Economy and Development, New York, NY 10458. Offers MA, Certificate. *Program availability:* Part-time, evening/weekend. *Students:* Average age 27. 81 applicants, 57% accepted, 17 enrolled. In 2019, 21 master's awarded. *Entrance requirements:* For master's, GRE General Test. Additional exam requirements/recommendations for international students: required—TOEFL (minimum score 600 paper-based). *Application deadline:* For fall admission, 1/4 priority date for domestic students; for spring admission, 11/1 for domestic students. Application fee: $70. Electronic applications accepted. *Financial support:* In 2019–20, 35 students received support, including 4 fellowships with tuition reimbursements available (averaging $17,014 per year); research assistantships, career-related internships or fieldwork, institutionally sponsored loans, tuition waivers (full and partial), and unspecified assistantships also available. Financial award application deadline: 1/4; financial award applicants required to submit FAFSA. *Unit head:* Dr. Henry Schwalbenberg, Chair, 718-817-3866, Fax: 718-817-3518. *Application contact:* Garrett Marino, Director of Graduate Admissions, 718-817-4419, Fax: 718-817-3566, E-mail: gmarino10@fordham.edu.

George Mason University, Antonin Scalia Law School, Arlington, VA 22201. Offers global antitrust law and economics (LL M); intellectual property (LL M); law (JD); law and economics (LL M); U.S. law (LL M); JD/MA; JD/MPP; JD/PhD. *Accreditation:* ABA. *Program availability:* Part-time, evening/weekend. *Faculty:* 58 full-time (14 women), 157 part-time/adjunct (41 women). *Students:* 425 full-time (214 women), 116 part-time (49 women); includes 102 minority (8 Black or African American, non-Hispanic/Latino; 1 American Indian or Alaska Native, non-Hispanic/Latino; 32 Asian, non-Hispanic/Latino; 38 Hispanic/Latino; 23 Two or more races, non-Hispanic/Latino), 4 international. Average age 29. 2,964 applicants, 21% accepted, 139 enrolled. In 2019, 165 doctorates awarded. *Entrance requirements:* For master's, JD or international equivalent; for doctorate, LSAT or GRE, baccalaureate degree or international equivalent. Additional exam requirements/recommendations for international students: required—TOEFL or IELTS (for L. M applicants only). *Application deadline:* For fall admission, 6/15 for domestic and international students. Applications are processed on a rolling basis. Application fee: $0. Electronic applications accepted. *Expenses:* Contact institution. *Financial support:* In 2019–20, 451 students received support, including 1 fellowship with full tuition reimbursement available; research assistantships, teaching assistantships, career-related internships or fieldwork, scholarships/grants, and tuition waivers (full and partial) also available. Support available to part-time students. Financial award applicants required to submit FAFSA. *Unit head:* Henry N. Butler, Dean, 703-993-8644, Fax: 703-993-8088. *Application contact:* Sabrina A. Huffman, Director of Admissions, 703-993-8010, Fax: 703-993-8088, E-mail: lawadmit@gmu.edu. Website: http://www.law.gmu.edu/

George Mason University, College of Humanities and Social Sciences, Department of Economics, Fairfax, VA 22030. Offers MA, PhD. *Degree requirements:* For master's, thesis optional, comprehensive exam in applied economic theory; for doctorate, comprehensive exam, thesis/dissertation, 2 preliminary exams, field exams. *Entrance requirements:* For master's, GRE General Test, expanded goals statement; 2 letters of recommendation; undergraduate degree; intermediate microeconomics and macroeconomics; 1 semester of calculus; 1 semester of statistics; for doctorate, GRE General Test, 2 letters of recommendation; resume; official transcripts; expanded goals statement; undergraduate degree; intermediate microeconomics and macroeconomics; 1 year of calculus and statistics; 1 semester of matrix algebra and econometrics. Additional exam requirements/recommendations for international students: required—TOEFL (minimum score 570 paper-based; 80 iBT), IELTS (minimum score 6.5), PTE. Electronic applications accepted.

Georgetown University, Graduate School of Arts and Sciences, Department of Economics, Washington, DC 20057. Offers econometrics (PhD); economic development (PhD); economic theory (PhD); industrial organization (PhD); international macro and finance (PhD); international trade (PhD); labor economics (PhD); macroeconomics (PhD); public economics and political economy (PhD); MA/PhD; MS/MA. *Degree requirements:* For doctorate, comprehensive exam, thesis/dissertation. *Entrance requirements:* For doctorate, GRE General Test. Additional exam requirements/recommendations for international students: required—TOEFL.

The George Washington University, Columbian College of Arts and Sciences, Department of Economics, Washington, DC 20052. Offers MA, PhD. *Program availability:* Part-time, evening/weekend. Terminal master's awarded for partial completion of doctoral program. *Degree requirements:* For master's, comprehensive exam, thesis or alternative; for doctorate, thesis/dissertation, general exam. *Entrance requirements:* For master's and doctorate, GRE General Test, minimum GPA of 3.0. Additional exam requirements/recommendations for international students: required—TOEFL (minimum score 550 paper-based; 80 iBT). Electronic applications accepted.

Georgia Institute of Technology, Graduate Studies, Ivan Allen College of Liberal Arts, School of Economics, Atlanta, GA 30332. Offers MS, PhD. *Program availability:* Part-time. *Faculty:* 13 full-time (4 women), 1 part-time/adjunct. *Students:* 63 full-time (30 women), 8 part-time (2 women); includes 9 minority (1 Black or African American, non-Hispanic/Latino; 3 Asian, non-Hispanic/Latino; 4 Hispanic/Latino; 1 Two or more races, non-Hispanic/Latino), 44 international. Average age 26. 202 applicants, 55% accepted, 41 enrolled. In 2019, 31 master's, 3 doctorates awarded. Terminal master's awarded for partial completion of doctoral program. *Degree requirements:* For master's, thesis; for doctorate, comprehensive exam, thesis/dissertation, teaching of two undergraduate courses. *Entrance requirements:* For master's and doctorate, GRE. Additional exam requirements/recommendations for international students: required—TOEFL (minimum score 577 paper-based; 90 iBT), IELTS (minimum score 7), TOEFL is the preferred method with the requirements shown on the programs. *Application deadline:* For fall admission, 2/15 priority date for domestic and international students. Applications are processed on a rolling basis. Application fee: $75 ($85 for international students). Electronic applications accepted. *Expenses: Tuition, area resident:* Full-time $14,064; part-time $586 per credit hour. Tuition, state resident: full-time $14,064; part-time $586 per credit hour. Tuition, nonresident: full-time $29,140; part-time $1215 per credit hour. *International tuition:* $29,140 full-time. *Required fees:* $2024; $840 per semester. $2096. Tuition and fees vary according to course load. *Financial support:* In 2019–20, 4 research assistantships, 16 teaching assistantships were awarded; fellowships, career-related internships or fieldwork, Federal Work-Study, institutionally sponsored loans, tuition waivers (full and partial), and unspecified assistantships also available. Support available to part-time students. Financial award application deadline: 7/1; financial award applicants required to submit FAFSA. *Unit head:* Laura Taylor, School Chair, 404-385-1363, Fax: 404-894-1809, E-mail: laura.taylor@gatech.edu. *Application contact:* Marla Bruner, Director of Graduate Studies, 404-894-1610, Fax: 404-894-1609, E-mail: gradinfo@mail.gatech.edu.
Website: http://www.econ.gatech.edu

Georgia State University, Andrew Young School of Policy Studies, Department of Economics, Atlanta, GA 30302-3083. Offers economics (MA); environmental economics (PhD); experimental economics (PhD); labor economics (PhD); policy (MA); public finance (PhD); urban and regional economics (PhD). *Program availability:* Part-time. *Faculty:* 22 full-time (4 women). *Students:* 113 full-time (49 women), 14 part-time (6 women); includes 27 minority (11 Black or African American, non-Hispanic/Latino; 10 Asian, non-Hispanic/Latino; 5 Hispanic/Latino; 1 Two or more races, non-Hispanic/Latino), 60 international. Average age 29. 250 applicants, 48% accepted, 31 enrolled. In 2019, 29 master's, 10 doctorates awarded. Terminal master's awarded for partial completion of doctoral program. *Degree requirements:* For master's, thesis optional; for doctorate, comprehensive exam, thesis/dissertation. *Entrance requirements:* For master's and doctorate, GRE. Additional exam requirements/recommendations for international students: required—TOEFL (minimum score 603 paper-based; 100 iBT) or IELTS (minimum score 7). *Application deadline:* For fall admission, 1/15 for domestic and international students. Application fee: $50. Electronic applications accepted. *Expenses: Tuition, area resident:* Full-time $7164; part-time $398 per credit hour. Tuition, state resident: full-time $7164; part-time $398 per credit hour. Tuition, nonresident: full-time $22,662; part-time $1259 per credit hour. *International tuition:* $22,662 full-time. *Required fees:* $2128; $312 per credit hour. Tuition and fees vary according to course load and program. *Financial support:* In 2019–20, fellowships with full tuition reimbursements (averaging $11,333 per year), research assistantships with full tuition reimbursements (averaging $9,788 per year), teaching assistantships with full tuition reimbursements (averaging $3,000 per year) were awarded; career-related internships or fieldwork also available. Financial award application deadline: 2/15; financial award applicants required to submit FAFSA. *Unit head:* Dr. Rusty Tchernis, Director of the Doctoral Program, 404-413-0154, Fax: 404-413-0145, E-mail: rtchernis@gsu.edu. *Application contact:* Dr. Rusty Tchernis, Director of the Doctoral Program, 404-413-0154, Fax: 404-413-0145, E-mail: rtchernis@gsu.edu.
Website: http://economics.gsu.edu/

Georgia State University, College of Education and Human Development, Department of Middle and Secondary Education, Atlanta, GA 30302-3083. Offers curriculum and instruction (Ed D); English education (MAT); mathematics education (M Ed, MAT); middle level education (MAT); reading, language and literacy education (M Ed, MAT), including reading instruction (M Ed); science education (M Ed, MAT), including biology (MAT), broad field science (MAT), chemistry (MAT), earth science (MAT), physics (MAT); social studies education (M Ed, MAT), including economics (MAT), geography (MAT), history (MAT), political science (MAT); teaching and learning (PhD), including language and literacy, mathematics education, music education, science education, social studies education, teaching and teacher education. *Accreditation:* NCATE. *Program availability:* Part-time, evening/weekend, online learning. *Faculty:* 20 full-time (16 women), 8 part-time/adjunct (all women). *Students:* 184 full-time (117 women), 195 part-time (144 women); includes 218 minority (157 Black or African American, non-Hispanic/Latino; 22 Asian, non-Hispanic/Latino; 27 Hispanic/Latino; 12 Two or more races, non-Hispanic/Latino), 3 international. Average age 34. 123 applicants, 61% accepted, 46 enrolled. In 2019, 122 master's, 18 doctorates awarded. *Entrance requirements:* For master's, GRE; GACE I (for initial teacher preparation programs), baccalaureate degree or equivalent, resume, goals statement, two letters of recommendation, minimum undergraduate GPA of 2.5; proof of initial teacher certification in the content area (for M Ed); for doctorate, GRE, resume, goals statement, writing sample, two letters of recommendation, minimum graduate GPA of 3.3, interview. *Application deadline:* For fall admission, 1/15 priority date for domestic and international students; for spring admission, 10/1 for domestic and international students. Application fee: $50. Electronic applications accepted. *Expenses: Tuition, area resident:* Full-time $7164; part-time $398 per credit hour. Tuition, state resident: full-time $7164; part-time $398 per credit hour. Tuition, nonresident: full-time $22,662; part-time $1259 per credit hour. *International tuition:* $22,662 full-time. *Required fees:* $2128; $312 per credit hour. Tuition and fees vary according to course load and program. *Financial support:* In 2019–20, fellowships with full tuition reimbursements (averaging $19,667 per year), research assistantships with full tuition reimbursements (averaging $5,436 per year), teaching assistantships with full tuition reimbursements (averaging $2,779 per year) were awarded; career-related internships or fieldwork, Federal Work-Study, scholarships/grants, health care benefits, tuition waivers (full and partial), and unspecified assistantships also available. Financial award application deadline: 3/15. *Unit head:* Dr. Gertrude Marilyn Tinker Sachs, Chair, 404-413-8384, Fax: 404-413-8063, E-mail: gtinkersachs@gsu.edu. *Application contact:* Shaleen Tibbs, Administrative Specialist, 404-413-8385, Fax: 404-413-8063, E-mail: stibbs@gsu.edu.
Website: http://mse.education.gsu.edu/

The Graduate Center, City University of New York, Graduate Studies, Program in Economics, New York, NY 10016-4039. Offers PhD. *Degree requirements:* For doctorate, thesis/dissertation. *Entrance requirements:* For doctorate, GRE General Test. Additional exam requirements/recommendations for international students: required—TOEFL. Electronic applications accepted.

Harvard University, Graduate School of Arts and Sciences, Committee on Business Economics, Cambridge, MA 02138. Offers PhD. *Degree requirements:* For doctorate, thesis/dissertation. *Entrance requirements:* For doctorate, GMAT or GRE General Test. Additional exam requirements/recommendations for international students: required—TOEFL.

Harvard University, Graduate School of Arts and Sciences, Department of Economics, Cambridge, MA 02138. Offers PhD. *Degree requirements:* For doctorate, thesis/dissertation, oral exam. *Entrance requirements:* For doctorate, GRE General Test, GRE Subject Test. Additional exam requirements/recommendations for international students: required—TOEFL.

Howard University, Graduate School, Department of Economics, Washington, DC 20059-0002. Offers MA, PhD. *Program availability:* Part-time. *Degree requirements:* For master's, comprehensive exam, thesis optional; for doctorate, one foreign language, comprehensive exam, thesis/dissertation. *Entrance requirements:* For master's, GRE General Test, minimum GPA of 3.0; for doctorate, GRE General Test, master's degree in economics or related field, minimum GPA of 3.0. Electronic applications accepted.

Hunter College of the City University of New York, Graduate School, School of Arts and Sciences, Department of Economics, Program in Economics, New York, NY 10065-5085. Offers MA. *Degree requirements:* For master's, thesis.

Illinois State University, Graduate School, College of Arts and Sciences, Department of Economics, Normal, IL 61790. Offers MA, MS. *Faculty:* 16 full-time (2 women), 2 part-time/adjunct (1 woman). *Students:* 26 full-time (14 women). Average age 25. 70 applicants, 79% accepted, 12 enrolled. In 2019, 20 master's awarded. *Degree requirements:* For master's, thesis or alternative. *Entrance requirements:* For master's, GRE General Test, minimum GPA of 2.6 in last 60 hours of course work. *Application deadline:* Applications are processed on a rolling basis. Application fee: $50. *Expenses: Tuition, area resident:* Full-time $7956; part-time $9767 per year. Tuition, nonresident: full-time $9233; part-time $17,592 per year. *Required fees:* $1797. *Financial support:* In 2019–20, 25 research assistantships were awarded; tuition waivers (full) and unspecified assistantships also available. Financial award application deadline: 4/1. *Unit head:* Dr. David Cleeton, Department Chair, 309-438-8588, E-mail: dlcleet@ilstu.edu. *Application contact:* Hassan Mohammadi, Graduate Coordinator, 309-438-7777, E-mail: hmohamma@ilstu.edu.
Website: http://www.econ.ilstu.edu/

Indiana University Bloomington, University Graduate School, College of Arts and Sciences, Department of Economics, Bloomington, IN 47405-7104. Offers MS, PhD. Terminal master's awarded for partial completion of doctoral program. *Degree requirements:* For doctorate, comprehensive exam, thesis/dissertation, main field exam, two supporting fields, 3rd-year paper, tool skill classes, dissertation proposal presentation, oral defense of dissertation. *Entrance requirements:* For doctorate, GRE General Test, three semesters of calculus, semester of linear algebra, semester of statistics or probability. Additional exam requirements/recommendations for international students: required—TOEFL (minimum score 600 paper-based; 100 iBT); recommended—IELTS. Electronic applications accepted.

Indiana University-Purdue University Indianapolis, School of Liberal Arts, Department of Economics, Indianapolis, IN 46202. Offers MA, MA/MA. *Program availability:* Part-time. *Degree requirements:* For master's, thesis (for some programs). *Entrance requirements:* For master's, GRE, minimum GPA of 3.0; courses in economic theory, statistics, and calculus. Additional exam requirements/recommendations for international students: required—TOEFL (minimum score 100 iBT), IELTS (minimum score 6.5). Electronic applications accepted.

Instituto Tecnologico de Santo Domingo, Graduate School, Area of Humanities and Social Sciences, Santo Domingo, Dominican Republic. Offers accounting (Certificate); adult education (Certificate); applied linguistics (MA); economics (MA); education (M Ed); educational psychology (MA, Certificate); gender and development (MA, Certificate); humanistic studies (MA); international marketing management (Certificate); international relations in the Caribbean basin (Certificate); intervention systems in family therapy (MA); linguistic and literary communication (Certificate); pedagogical support (MA); social science education (M Ed); sustainable human development (MA); terminal illness and death psychology (Certificate); youth and adult education (M Ed).

Instituto Tecnológico y de Estudios Superiores de Monterrey, Campus Ciudad de México, School of Business Administration, Ciudad de Mexico, Mexico. Offers business administration (EMBA, MBA, PhD); economy (MBA); finance (MBA). *Program availability:* Part-time, evening/weekend, online learning. *Entrance requirements:* For master's and doctorate, Instituto entrance exam. Additional exam requirements/recommendations for international students: required—TOEFL.

Iowa State University of Science and Technology, Department of Economics, Ames, IA 50011. Offers agricultural economics (MS, PhD); economics (MS, PhD); JD/MS; JD/PhD. *Degree requirements:* For master's, thesis or alternative; for doctorate, thesis/dissertation. *Entrance requirements:* For master's and doctorate, GRE General Test. Additional exam requirements/recommendations for international students: required—TOEFL (minimum score 570 paper-based; 88 iBT), IELTS (minimum score 6.5). Electronic applications accepted.

John Jay College of Criminal Justice of the City University of New York, Graduate Studies, MA in Economics, New York, NY 10019. Offers MA.

Johns Hopkins University, Zanvyl Krieger School of Arts and Sciences, Department of Economics, Baltimore, MD 21218. Offers PhD. Terminal master's awarded for partial completion of doctoral program. *Degree requirements:* For doctorate, comprehensive exam, thesis/dissertation. *Entrance requirements:* For doctorate, GRE General Test. Additional exam requirements/recommendations for international students: required—TOEFL (minimum score 600 paper-based), IELTS. Electronic applications accepted.

Kansas State University, Graduate School, College of Arts and Sciences, Department of Economics, Manhattan, KS 66506. Offers MA, PhD. Terminal master's awarded for partial completion of doctoral program. *Degree requirements:* For master's, comprehensive exam (for some programs), thesis (for some programs), 30 credit hours, including thesis/report or qualifying exams; for doctorate, comprehensive exam, thesis/dissertation, 90 credit hours, including dissertation, qualifying exams, and field exam. *Entrance requirements:* For master's and doctorate, GRE (highly recommended), minimum GPA of 3.0; course work in microeconomics, macroeconomics, calculus and statistics. Additional exam requirements/recommendations for international students: required—TOEFL (minimum score 550 paper-based; 79 iBT), IELTS (minimum score 6.5), TWE (minimum score 5), PTE (minimum score 58). Electronic applications accepted.

Kent State University, College of Business Administration, Master of Arts Program in Economics, Kent, OH 44242-0001. Offers MA. *Program availability:* Part-time. *Faculty:* 12 full-time (3 women). *Students:* 12 full-time (6 women); includes 1 minority (Two or more races, non-Hispanic/Latino), 5 international. Average age 27. 31 applicants, 77% accepted, 5 enrolled. In 2019, 13 master's awarded. *Degree requirements:* For master's, 30 credit hours, minimum GPA of 3.0. *Entrance requirements:* For master's, GMAT or GRE General Test, minimum GPA of 3.0. Additional exam requirements/recommendations for international students: required—TOEFL (minimum score 550 paper-based; 80 iBT), IELTS (minimum score 6.5). *Application deadline:* For fall admission, 2/15 priority date for domestic students, 2/15 for international students; for spring admission, 10/15 for domestic and international students; for summer admission,

5/1 for domestic and international students. Applications are processed on a rolling basis. Application fee: $45 ($70 for international students). Electronic applications accepted. *Financial support:* In 2019–20, 12 students received support, including 12 research assistantships with full tuition reimbursements available (averaging $17,558 per year); Federal Work-Study and scholarships/grants also available. Financial award application deadline: 2/15; financial award applicants required to submit FAFSA. *Unit head:* Dr. Kathryn Wilson, Chair and Professor, 330-672-2366, Fax: 330-672-9808, E-mail: kwilson3@kent.edu. *Application contact:* Roberto Chavez, Administrative Director, 330-672-2282, Fax: 330-672-7303, E-mail: gradbus@kent.edu.
Website: http://www.kent.edu/business/ma-economics

Lakehead University, Graduate Studies, Department of Economics, Thunder Bay, ON P7B 5E1, Canada. Offers MA. *Program availability:* Part-time, evening/weekend. *Degree requirements:* For master's, thesis or comprehensive exams, research papers. *Entrance requirements:* For master's, minimum B average. Additional exam requirements/recommendations for international students: required—TOEFL.

Lee University, Program in Education, Cleveland, TN 37320-3450. Offers art (MAT); curriculum and instruction (M Ed, Ed S); early childhood (MAT); educational leadership (M Ed, Ed S); elementary education (MAT); English and math (MAT); English and science (MAT); English and social studies (MAT); higher education administration (MS); history (MAT); history and economics (MAT); math and science (MAT); math and social studies (MAT); middle grades (MAT); science and social studies (MASW); secondary education (MAT); Spanish (MAT); special education (M Ed, MAT); TESOL (MAT). *Accreditation:* NCATE. *Program availability:* Part-time. *Faculty:* 13 full-time (5 women), 9 part-time/adjunct (6 women). *Students:* 24 full-time (15 women), 72 part-time (46 women); includes 14 minority (8 Black or African American, non-Hispanic/Latino; 1 Hispanic/Latino; 5 Two or more races, non-Hispanic/Latino), 1 international. Average age 29. 44 applicants, 86% accepted, 33 enrolled. In 2019, 60 master's, 3 other advanced degrees awarded. *Degree requirements:* For master's, variable foreign language requirement, thesis optional, internship. *Entrance requirements:* For master's, MAT or GRE General Test, minimum undergraduate GPA of 2.75, 3 letters of recommendation, interview, writing sample, official transcripts, background check; for Ed S, minimum undergraduate and master's GPA of 2.75, official transcripts for undergraduate and master's degrees. Additional exam requirements/recommendations for international students: required—TOEFL (minimum score 61 iBT). *Application deadline:* For fall admission, 6/1 priority date for domestic and international students; for spring admission, 11/1 priority date for domestic and international students; for summer admission, 4/1 priority date for domestic and international students. Applications are processed on a rolling basis. Application fee: $25. Electronic applications accepted. *Expenses: Tuition:* Full-time $13,590; part-time $755 per credit hour. *Required fees:* $25. Tuition and fees vary according to program. *Financial support:* In 2019–20, 40 students received support. Career-related internships or fieldwork, Federal Work-Study, institutionally sponsored loans, scholarships/grants, and unspecified assistantships available. Financial award application deadline: 3/1; financial award applicants required to submit FAFSA. *Unit head:* Dr. William Kamm, Director, 423-614-8544, E-mail: wkamm@leeuniversity.edu. *Application contact:* Jeffery McGirt, Director of Graduate Enrollment, 423-614-8691, Fax: 423-614-8317, E-mail: jmcgirt@leeuniversity.edu.
Website: http://www.leeuniversity.edu/academics/graduate/education

Lehigh University, College of Business, Department of Economics, Bethlehem, PA 18015. Offers MS, PhD. *Faculty:* 12 full-time (1 woman). *Students:* 30 full-time (9 women), 3 part-time (1 woman); includes 2 minority (1 Black or African American, non-Hispanic/Latino; 1 Hispanic/Latino), 23 international. Average age 25. 53 applicants, 75% accepted, 16 enrolled. In 2019, 4 master's, 5 doctorates awarded. Terminal master's awarded for partial completion of doctoral program. *Degree requirements:* For master's, thesis optional; for doctorate, comprehensive exam, thesis/dissertation, proposal defense. *Entrance requirements:* For master's, public finance, investments, applied econometrics, labor economics, health economics; for doctorate, GMAT or GRE General Test. Additional exam requirements/recommendations for international students: required—TOEFL (minimum score 600 paper-based; 94 iBT), IELTS (minimum score 7). *Application deadline:* For fall admission, 7/15 for domestic students, 5/1 for international students; for spring admission, 12/1 for domestic students. Application fee: $75. *Expenses:* Contact institution. *Financial support:* In 2019–20, 18 students received support, including 1 fellowship with full tuition reimbursement available (averaging $33,000 per year), 1 research assistantship with full tuition reimbursement available (averaging $20,600 per year), 13 teaching assistantships with full tuition reimbursements available (averaging $20,600 per year); health care benefits also available. Financial award application deadline: 1/1. *Unit head:* Dr. Shin-yi Chou, Chair, 610-758-3444, Fax: 610-758-4677, E-mail: syc2@lehigh.edu. *Application contact:* Mary Theresa Taglang, Director of Recruitment and Admissions, 610-758-4386, Fax: 610-758-5283, E-mail: mtt4@lehigh.edu.
Website: https://cbe.lehigh.edu/academics/graduate/master-economics

Louisiana State University and Agricultural & Mechanical College, Graduate School, E. J. Ourso College of Business, Department of Economics, Baton Rouge, LA 70803. Offers MS, PhD.

Loyola University Chicago, Quinlan School of Business, MBA Programs, Chicago, IL 60611. Offers accounting (MBA); business ethics (MBA); derivative markets (MBA); economics (MBA); entrepreneurship (MBA); finance (MBA); healthcare management (MBA); human resources management (MBA); information systems management (MBA); international business (MBA); management (MBA); marketing (MBA); risk management (MBA); supply chain management (MBA). *Program availability:* Part-time, evening/weekend. *Entrance requirements:* For master's, GMAT or GRE, official transcripts, two letters of recommendation, statement of purpose, resume. Additional exam requirements/recommendations for international students: required—TOEFL (minimum score 90 iBT) or IELTS (minimum score 6.5). Electronic applications accepted. Application fee is waived when completed online. *Expenses:* Contact institution.

Marquette University, Graduate School of Management, Department of Economics, Milwaukee, WI 53201-1881. Offers business economics (MSAE); financial economics (MSAE); international economics (MSAE); marketing research (MSAE); real estate economics (MSAE). *Program availability:* Part-time, evening/weekend. *Degree requirements:* For master's, comprehensive exam, professional project. *Entrance requirements:* For master's, GMAT or GRE General Test. Additional exam requirements/recommendations for international students: required—TOEFL, IELTS, PTE. Electronic applications accepted.

Marquette University, Graduate School of Management, Executive MBA Program, Milwaukee, WI 53201-1881. Offers economics (MBA); finance (MBA); human resources (MBA); international business (MBA); management information systems (MBA); marketing (MBA); operations and supply chain management (MBA); sports business (MBA). *Accreditation:* AACSB. *Degree requirements:* For master's, international trip. *Entrance requirements:* For master's, GMAT or GRE, two letters of recommendation, official transcripts from current and previous colleges/universities. Additional exam requirements/recommendations for international students: required—TOEFL (minimum score 550 paper-based; 88 iBT), IELTS (minimum score 6.5), PTE. Electronic applications accepted. *Expenses:* Contact institution.

Marquette University, Graduate School of Management, Program in Business Administration, Milwaukee, WI 53201-1881. Offers business administration (MBA); economics (MBA); entrepreneurship (Certificate); finance (MBA); human resources (MBA); international business (MBA); management information systems (MBA); marketing (MBA); operations and supply chain management (MBA); sports business (MBA); JD/MBA; MBA/MA; MBA/MSN. *Accreditation:* AACSB. *Program availability:* Part-time, evening/weekend. *Degree requirements:* For Certificate, business plan. *Entrance requirements:* For master's, GMAT or GRE, letters of recommendation. Additional exam requirements/recommendations for international students: required—TOEFL (minimum score 550 paper-based; 88 iBT), IELTS (minimum score 6.5), PTE. Electronic applications accepted.

Massachusetts Institute of Technology, School of Humanities, Arts, and Social Sciences, Department of Economics, Cambridge, MA 02139. Offers SM, PhD. Terminal master's awarded for partial completion of doctoral program. *Degree requirements:* For master's, thesis; for doctorate, comprehensive exam, thesis/dissertation. *Entrance requirements:* For doctorate, GRE General Test. Additional exam requirements/recommendations for international students: required—TOEFL, IELTS. Electronic applications accepted.

McGill University, Faculty of Graduate and Postdoctoral Studies, Faculty of Arts, Department of Economics, Montréal, QC H3A 2T5, Canada. Offers economics (MA, PhD); social statistics (MA).

McMaster University, School of Graduate Studies, Faculty of Social Sciences, Department of Economics, Hamilton, ON L8S 4M2, Canada. Offers MA, PhD. *Program availability:* Part-time. *Degree requirements:* For doctorate, comprehensive exam, thesis/dissertation. *Entrance requirements:* For master's, GRE (recommended), honors BA in economics; for doctorate, GRE (recommended), B+ average in a master's degree. Additional exam requirements/recommendations for international students: required—TOEFL (minimum score 580 paper-based).

Memorial University of Newfoundland, School of Graduate Studies, Department of Economics, St. John's, NL A1C 5S7, Canada. Offers MA. *Degree requirements:* For master's, thesis optional. *Entrance requirements:* For master's, honors degree (minimum 2nd class standing). Electronic applications accepted.

Miami University, Farmer School of Business, Department of Economics, Oxford, OH 45056. Offers MA.

Michigan State University, The Graduate School, College of Social Science, Department of Economics, East Lansing, MI 48824. Offers MA, PhD. *Entrance requirements:* Additional exam requirements/recommendations for international students: required—TOEFL. Electronic applications accepted.

Middle Tennessee State University, College of Graduate Studies, Jennings A. Jones College of Business, Department of Economics and Finance, Murfreesboro, TN 37132. Offers economics (MA, PhD). *Program availability:* Part-time, evening/weekend, online learning. *Degree requirements:* For master's, comprehensive exam, thesis optional; for doctorate, comprehensive exam, thesis/dissertation. *Entrance requirements:* For master's and doctorate, GRE. Additional exam requirements/recommendations for international students: required—TOEFL (minimum score 525 paper-based; 71 iBT) or IELTS (minimum score 6). Electronic applications accepted.

Mississippi State University, College of Business, Department of Finance and Economics, Mississippi State, MS 39762. Offers applied economics (PhD); economics (MA). *Program availability:* Part-time. *Faculty:* 16 full-time (4 women), 1 part-time/adjunct (0 women). *Students:* 8 full-time (2 women), 1 (woman) part-time, 8 international. Average age 30. 25 applicants, 36% accepted, 2 enrolled. Terminal master's awarded for partial completion of doctoral program. *Degree requirements:* For master's, comprehensive exam, thesis optional; for doctorate, comprehensive exam, thesis/dissertation, written and oral exams. *Entrance requirements:* For master's, GRE, previously-completed intermediate microeconomics and macroeconomics; for doctorate, GRE, BS with minimum GPA of 3.0 cumulative and over last 60 hours of undergraduate work, 3.25 on all graduate work. Additional exam requirements/recommendations for international students: required—TOEFL (minimum score 575 paper-based; 84 iBT); recommended—IELTS (minimum score 6.5). *Application deadline:* For fall admission, 7/1 for domestic students, 5/1 for international students; for spring admission, 11/1 for domestic students, 10/1 for international students. Applications are processed on a rolling basis. Application fee: $60 ($80 for international students). Electronic applications accepted. *Expenses: Tuition, area resident:* Full-time $8880; part-time $456 per credit hour. Tuition, state resident: full-time $8880. Tuition, nonresident: full-time $23,840; part-time $1236 per credit hour. *Required fees:* $110; $11.12 per credit hour. Tuition and fees vary according to course load. *Financial support:* Federal Work-Study, scholarships/grants, health care benefits, and unspecified assistantships available. Financial award application deadline: 4/1; financial award applicants required to submit FAFSA. *Unit head:* Dr. Kathleen Thomas, Professor/Head, 662-325-2561, Fax: 662-325-1977, E-mail: mkt27@msstate.edu. *Application contact:* Robbie Salters, Admissions and Enrollment Management Assistant and Coordinator, 662-325-5188, E-mail: rsalters@grad.msstate.edu.
Website: http://www.business.msstate.edu/programs/fe/index.php

Morgan State University, School of Graduate Studies, James H. Gilliam Jr College of Liberal Arts, Department of Economics, Baltimore, MD 21251. Offers MA. *Program availability:* Part-time, evening/weekend. *Faculty:* 5 full-time (2 women), 2 part-time/adjunct (0 women). *Students:* 1 applicant, 100% accepted. In 2019, 8 master's awarded. *Degree requirements:* For master's, comprehensive exam (for some programs), thesis optional. *Entrance requirements:* For master's, GRE, GMAT. Additional exam requirements/recommendations for international students: required—TOEFL (minimum score 550 paper-based); recommended—IELTS (minimum score 6). *Application deadline:* For fall admission, 2/1 priority date for domestic students; for spring admission, 10/1 priority date for domestic students. Applications are processed on a rolling basis. Application fee: $50 ($70 for international students). Electronic applications accepted. *Expenses:* Tuition, state resident: full-time $455; part-time $455 per credit hour. Tuition, nonresident: full-time $894; part-time $894 per credit hour. *Required fees:* $82; $82 per credit hour. *Financial support:* Fellowships with full and partial tuition reimbursements, research assistantships with full and partial tuition reimbursements, teaching assistantships with full and partial tuition reimbursements, career-related internships or fieldwork, Federal Work-Study, scholarships/grants, tuition waivers (full and partial), and unspecified assistantships available. Support available to part-time students. Financial award application deadline: 2/1. *Unit head:* Dr. Linda Loubert, Interim Chair and Graduate Coordinator, 443-885-1885, E-mail: linda.loubert@morgan.edu. *Application contact:* Dr. Jahmaine Smith, Director of Admission, 443-885-3185, Fax: 443-885-8226, E-mail: Jahmaine.smith@morgan.edu.
Website: https://morgan.edu/cla/economics

Murray State University, Arthur J. Bauernfeind College of Business, Department of Economics and Finance, Murray, KY 42071. Offers economic development (MS); economics (MS), including finance. *Program availability:* Part-time. *Entrance requirements:* For master's, GRE General Test or GMAT, minimum university GPA of 2.75. Additional exam requirements/recommendations for international students:

required—TOEFL (minimum score 527 paper-based; 71 iBT). Electronic applications accepted.

New Mexico State University, College of Business, Department of Economics, Applied Statistics and International Business, Las Cruces, NM 88003. Offers applied statistics (MS); economic development (DED); economics (MA); public utility regulation and economics (Graduate Certificate). *Program availability:* Part-time, online learning. *Faculty:* 16 full-time (3 women). *Students:* 28 full-time (15 women), 25 part-time (11 women); includes 20 minority (2 Black or African American, non-Hispanic/Latino; 1 American Indian or Alaska Native, non-Hispanic/Latino; 5 Asian, non-Hispanic/Latino; 12 Hispanic/Latino), 22 international. Average age 34. 61 applicants, 85% accepted, 21 enrolled. In 2019, 16 master's, 9 doctorates, 14 other advanced degrees awarded. Terminal master's awarded for partial completion of doctoral program. *Degree requirements:* For master's, comprehensive exam, thesis or alternative; for doctorate, comprehensive exam, thesis/dissertation, internship. *Entrance requirements:* For master's, minimum GPA of 3.0; for doctorate, appropriate master's degree, minimum GPA of 3.0 with particular classes required. Additional exam requirements/recommendations for international students: required—TOEFL (minimum score 550 paper-based; 79 iBT), IELTS (minimum score 6.5). *Application deadline:* For fall admission, 3/1 priority date for domestic and international students. Applications are processed on a rolling basis. Application fee: $40 ($50 for international students). Electronic applications accepted. *Financial support:* In 2019–20, 29 students received support, including 2 research assistantships (averaging $18,582 per year), 21 teaching assistantships (averaging $16,789 per year); career-related internships or fieldwork, Federal Work-Study, scholarships/grants, traineeships, health care benefits, and unspecified assistantships also available. Support available to part-time students. Financial award application deadline: 3/1.
Website: http://business.nmsu.edu/departments/economics

The New School, The New School for Social Research, Department of Economics, New York, NY 10003. Offers economics (MA, MS, PhD); global political economy and finance (MA). *Program availability:* Part-time. *Faculty:* 9 full-time (3 women), 2 part-time/adjunct (0 women). *Students:* 80 full-time (30 women), 25 part-time (9 women); includes 22 minority (7 Black or African American, non-Hispanic/Latino; 6 Asian, non-Hispanic/Latino; 8 Hispanic/Latino; 1 Two or more races, non-Hispanic/Latino), 52 international. Average age 32. 147 applicants, 66% accepted, 21 enrolled. In 2019, 39 master's, 8 doctorates awarded. Terminal master's awarded for partial completion of doctoral program. *Degree requirements:* For master's, comprehensive exam (for some programs), mentored research/internship; for doctorate, one foreign language, comprehensive exam, thesis/dissertation. *Entrance requirements:* For master's, GRE, letters of recommendation, writing sample, essays, transcript; for doctorate, letters of recommendation, writing sample, essays, transcript. Additional exam requirements/recommendations for international students: required—TOEFL (minimum score 100 iBT), IELTS (minimum score 7), PTE (minimum score 68). *Application deadline:* For fall admission, 1/5 priority date for domestic and international students; for spring admission, 10/15 priority date for domestic and international students. Applications are processed on a rolling basis. Application fee: $50. Electronic applications accepted. *Expenses:* 2260 per credit. *Financial support:* In 2019–20, 84 students received support, including 14 fellowships (averaging $6,912 per year), 18 research assistantships (averaging $5,253 per year), 19 teaching assistantships with full and partial tuition reimbursements available (averaging $7,989 per year); career-related internships or fieldwork, Federal Work-Study, scholarships/grants, tuition waivers (full and partial), and unspecified assistantships also available. Support available to part-time students. Financial award application deadline: 2/1; financial award applicants required to submit FAFSA. *Unit head:* Mark Setterfield, PhD, Department Chair, 212-229-5717 Ext. 3047, E-mail: setterfm@newschool.edu. *Application contact:* Merida Gasbarro, Director of Graduate Admission, 212-229-5600 Ext. 1108, E-mail: escandom@newschool.edu.
Website: https://www.newschool.edu/nssr/economics/

New York University, Graduate School of Arts and Science, Department of Economics, New York, NY 10012-1019. Offers applied economic analysis (Advanced Certificate); economics (MA, PhD); JD/MA; MD/PhD. *Program availability:* Part-time, evening/weekend. Terminal master's awarded for partial completion of doctoral program. *Degree requirements:* For master's, thesis; for doctorate, one foreign language, thesis/dissertation, 4 qualifying exams. *Entrance requirements:* For master's and doctorate, GRE General Test. Additional exam requirements/recommendations for international students: required—TOEFL, IELTS.

New York University, Leonard N. Stern School of Business, Department of Economics, New York, NY 10012-1019. Offers MBA, PhD.

North Carolina State University, Graduate School, Poole College of Management and College of Agriculture and Life Sciences, Program in Economics, Raleigh, NC 27695. Offers M Econ, MA, PhD. *Program availability:* Part-time. Terminal master's awarded for partial completion of doctoral program. *Degree requirements:* For master's, thesis (for some programs); for doctorate, thesis/dissertation. *Entrance requirements:* For master's and doctorate, GRE General Test. Additional exam requirements/recommendations for international students: required—TOEFL. Electronic applications accepted.

Northeastern University, College of Social Sciences and Humanities, Boston, MA 02115. Offers criminology and criminal justice (MSCJ); criminology and justice policy (PhD); economics (MA, PhD); English (MA, PhD); international affairs (MA); law and public policy (PhD); political science (MA, PhD); public administration (MPA); public policy (MPP); security and resilience studies (MS); sociology (MA, PhD); urban and regional policy (MS); urban informatics (MS); world history (MA, PhD). *Program availability:* Online learning. *Degree requirements:* For doctorate, variable foreign language requirement, comprehensive exam, thesis/dissertation. *Entrance requirements:* For master's and doctorate, GRE. Additional exam requirements/recommendations for international students: required—TOEFL, IELTS. Electronic applications accepted. *Expenses:* Contact institution.

Northern Illinois University, Graduate School, College of Liberal Arts and Sciences, Department of Economics, De Kalb, IL 60115-2854. Offers MA, PhD. *Program availability:* Part-time. *Faculty:* 15 full-time (3 women). *Students:* 23 full-time (9 women), 10 part-time (5 women); includes 2 minority (both Hispanic/Latino), 23 international. Average age 33. 34 applicants, 79% accepted, 7 enrolled. In 2019, 8 master's, 5 doctorates awarded. Terminal master's awarded for partial completion of doctoral program. *Degree requirements:* For master's, comprehensive exam, thesis or alternative; for doctorate, thesis/dissertation, candidacy exam, dissertation defense, research seminar. *Entrance requirements:* For master's, GRE General Test, minimum GPA of 2.75; for doctorate, GRE General Test, minimum GPA of 2.75 (undergraduate), 3.2 (graduate). Additional exam requirements/recommendations for international students: required—TOEFL (minimum score 550 paper-based). *Application deadline:* For fall admission, 6/1 for domestic students, 5/1 for international students; for spring admission, 11/1 for domestic students, 10/1 for international students. Applications are processed on a rolling basis. Application fee: $40. Electronic applications accepted. *Financial support:* In 2019–20, 1 research assistantship with full tuition reimbursement, 25 teaching assistantships with full tuition reimbursements were awarded; fellowships with full tuition reimbursements, career-related internships or fieldwork, Federal Work-Study, scholarships/grants, tuition waivers (full), and unspecified assistantships also

available. Support available to part-time students. Financial award applicants required to submit FAFSA. *Unit head:* Dr. Carl Campbell, Chair, 815-753-6974, Fax: 815-753-1019, E-mail: carlcamp@niu.edu. *Application contact:* Dr. Jeremy Groves, Director, Graduate Studies, 815-753-5747, E-mail: jgroves@niu.edu.
Website: http://www.niu.edu/econ/

Northwestern University, The Graduate School, Judd A. and Marjorie Weinberg College of Arts and Sciences, Department of Economics, Evanston, IL 60208. Offers PhD, JD/PhD. *Degree requirements:* For doctorate, thesis/dissertation, preliminary written exam. *Entrance requirements:* For doctorate, GRE General Test. Additional exam requirements/recommendations for international students: required—TOEFL.

Oakland University, Graduate Study and Lifelong Learning, School of Business Administration, Department of Economics, Rochester, MI 48309-4401. Offers economics (MBA, Certificate). *Program availability:* Part-time. *Entrance requirements:* Additional exam requirements/recommendations for international students: required—TOEFL (minimum score 550 paper-based; 79 iBT), IELTS (minimum score 6.5). Electronic applications accepted. *Expenses: Tuition, area resident:* Full-time $12,328; part-time $770.50 per credit hour. Tuition, state resident: full-time $12,328; part-time $770.50 per credit hour. Tuition, nonresident: full-time $16,432; part-time $1027 per credit hour. *International tuition:* $16,432 full-time. Tuition and fees vary according to degree level and program.

The Ohio State University, Graduate School, College of Arts and Sciences, Division of Social and Behavioral Sciences, Department of Economics, Columbus, OH 43210. Offers MA, PhD. *Entrance requirements:* For doctorate, GRE. Additional exam requirements/recommendations for international students: required—TOEFL (minimum score 550 paper-based; 79 iBT), Michigan English Language Assessment Battery (minimum score 82); recommended—IELTS (minimum score 7). Electronic applications accepted.

Ohio University, Graduate College, College of Arts and Sciences, Department of Economics, Athens, OH 45701-2979. Offers applied economics (MA); financial economics (MFE). *Program availability:* Part-time, evening/weekend. *Degree requirements:* For master's, thesis or alternative. *Entrance requirements:* For master's, GRE or GMAT (recommended), minimum GPA of 3.0. Additional exam requirements/recommendations for international students: required—TOEFL (minimum score 550 paper-based; 80 iBT) or IELTS (minimum score 6.5). Electronic applications accepted.

Oklahoma State University, Spears School of Business, Department of Economics, Stillwater, OK 74078. Offers MS, PhD. *Program availability:* Part-time. *Entrance requirements:* For master's and doctorate, GRE or GMAT. Additional exam requirements/recommendations for international students: required—TOEFL (minimum score 550 paper-based; 79 iBT). Electronic applications accepted. *Expenses: Tuition, area resident:* Full-time $4148.10; part-time $2765.40 per credit hour. Tuition, state resident: full-time $4148.10; part-time $2765.40 per credit hour. Tuition, nonresident: full-time $15,775; part-time $10,516.80 per credit hour. *International tuition:* $15,775.20 full-time. *Required fees:* $2196.90; $122.05 per credit hour. Tuition and fees vary according to course load, campus/location and program.

Old Dominion University, Strome College of Business, Program in Economics, Norfolk, VA 23529. Offers MA. *Program availability:* Part-time, evening/weekend. *Degree requirements:* For master's, comprehensive exam, thesis optional, independent research. *Entrance requirements:* For master's, GMAT or GRE General Test, minimum GPA of 2.5. Additional exam requirements/recommendations for international students: required—TOEFL (minimum score 520 paper-based; 79 iBT). Electronic applications accepted. *Expenses:* Contact institution.

Pace University, Lubin School of Business, Advanced Professional Certificate Program, New York, NY 10038. Offers business economics (APC); e-business (APC); financial management (APC); international business (APC); international economics (APC); investment management (APC); marketing (APC); public accounting (APC). *Program availability:* Part-time, evening/weekend. *Entrance requirements:* For degree, MBA or MS in business discipline, relevant professional experience. Additional exam requirements/recommendations for international students: required—TOEFL (minimum score 90 iBT), IELTS (minimum score 7) or PTE (minimum score 61). Electronic applications accepted.

Penn State University Park, Graduate School, College of the Liberal Arts, Department of Economics, University Park, PA 16802. Offers MA, PhD.

Pepperdine University, School of Public Policy, Malibu, CA 90263. Offers American politics (MPP); economics (MPP); international relations (MPP); state and local policy (MPP); JD/MPP; MBA/MPP; MDR/MPP. *Entrance requirements:* For master's, GRE or GMAT or LSAT, transcripts, 2 letters of recommendation, resume, two essays. Additional exam requirements/recommendations for international students: required—TOEFL (minimum score 95 iBT), IELTS (minimum score 7). Electronic applications accepted. *Expenses:* Contact institution.

Peru State College, Graduate Programs, Program in Organizational Management, Peru, NE 68421. Offers MS. *Program availability:* Part-time, online learning. *Degree requirements:* For master's, thesis (for some programs). *Expenses:* Contact institution.

Portland State University, Graduate Studies, College of Liberal Arts and Sciences, Systems Science Program, Portland, OR 97207-0751. Offers computational intelligence (Certificate); computer modeling and simulation (Certificate); systems science (MS); systems science/anthropology (PhD); systems science/business administration (PhD); systems science/civil engineering (PhD); systems science/economics (PhD); systems science/engineering management (PhD); systems science/general (PhD); systems science/mathematical sciences (PhD); systems science/mechanical engineering (PhD); systems science/psychology (PhD); systems science/sociology (PhD). *Program availability:* Part-time. *Faculty:* 2 full-time (0 women), 6 part-time/adjunct (1 woman). *Students:* 6 full-time (3 women), 25 part-time (8 women); includes 7 minority (2 Asian, non-Hispanic/Latino; 4 Hispanic/Latino; 1 Two or more races, non-Hispanic/Latino), 2 international. Average age 39. 25 applicants, 80% accepted, 15 enrolled. In 2019, 7 master's, 2 doctorates awarded. Terminal master's awarded for partial completion of doctoral program. *Degree requirements:* For master's, comprehensive exam (for some programs), thesis optional; for doctorate, variable foreign language requirement, comprehensive exam (for some programs), thesis/dissertation. *Entrance requirements:* For master's, GRE/GMAT (recommended), minimum GPA of 3.0 on undergraduate or graduate work, 2 letters of recommendation, statement of interest; for doctorate, GRE required, minimum GPA of 3.0 undergraduate, 3.25 graduate; 3 letters of recommendation; statement of interest. Additional exam requirements/recommendations for international students: required—TOEFL (minimum score 550 paper-based; 80 iBT). *Application deadline:* For fall admission, 3/15 priority date for domestic and international students. Application fee: $65. Electronic applications accepted. *Expenses: Tuition, area resident:* Full-time $13,020; part-time $6510 per year. Tuition, state resident: full-time $13,020; part-time $6510 per year. Tuition, nonresident: full-time $19,830; part-time $9915 per year. *International tuition:* $19,830 full-time. *Required fees:* $1226. One-time fee: $350. Tuition and fees vary according to course load, program and reciprocity agreements. *Financial support:* Research assistantships, teaching assistantships, career-related internships or fieldwork, Federal Work-Study,

scholarships/grants, and unspecified assistantships available. Support available to part-time students. Financial award application deadline: 3/1; financial award applicants required to submit FAFSA. *Unit head:* Dr. Wayne Wakeland, Chair, 503-725-4975, E-mail: wakeland@pdx.edu. *Application contact:* Dr. Wayne Wakeland, Chair, 503-725-4975, E-mail: wakeland@pdx.edu.
Website: http://www.pdx.edu/sysc/

Portland State University, Graduate Studies, College of Urban and Public Affairs, Department of Economics, Portland, OR 97207-0751. Offers economics (MA, MS); environmental and resource economics (Certificate). *Program availability:* Part-time. *Faculty:* 15 full-time (4 women), 5 part-time/adjunct (3 women). *Students:* 15 full-time (7 women), 3 part-time (0 women); includes 3 minority (1 American Indian or Alaska Native, non-Hispanic/Latino; 1 Hispanic/Latino; 1 Two or more races, non-Hispanic/Latino), 5 international. Average age 30. 18 applicants, 94% accepted, 8 enrolled. In 2019, 12 master's awarded. *Degree requirements:* For master's, variable foreign language requirement, thesis optional. *Entrance requirements:* For master's, GRE General Test, minimum GPA of 3.0 in economic course work and overall; course work in: calculus, intermediate microeconomics and macroeconomics, statistics, econometrics, linear algebra. Additional exam requirements/recommendations for international students: required—TOEFL (minimum score 550 paper-based; 80 iBT). *Application deadline:* For fall admission, 2/1 for domestic and international students; for winter admission, 9/1 for domestic and international students; for spring admission, 11/1 for domestic and international students. Applications are processed on a rolling basis. Application fee: $65. Electronic applications accepted. *Expenses:* $449 per credit hour resident, $676 per credit hour non-resident. *Financial support:* In 2019–20, 1 research assistantship with full and partial tuition reimbursement (averaging $7,252 per year), 10 teaching assistantships with full and partial tuition reimbursements (averaging $7,416 per year) were awarded; career-related internships or fieldwork, Federal Work-Study, and unspecified assistantships also available. Support available to part-time students. Financial award application deadline: 3/1; financial award applicants required to submit FAFSA. *Unit head:* Dr. Hiro Ito, Chair, 503-725-3930, E-mail: ito@pdx.edu. *Application contact:* Dr. Arnab Mitra, Associate Professor, 503-725-3937, E-mail: amitra@pdx.edu.
Website: https://www.pdx.edu/econ/

Princeton University, Graduate School, Department of Economics, Princeton, NJ 08544-1019. Offers PhD. *Degree requirements:* For doctorate, thesis/dissertation. *Entrance requirements:* For doctorate, GRE General Test, GRE Subject Test (recommended), working knowledge of multivariate calculus and matrix algebra. Additional exam requirements/recommendations for international students: required—TOEFL (minimum score 600 paper-based). Electronic applications accepted.

Princeton University, Graduate School, Program in Population Studies, Princeton, NJ 08544-1019. Offers demography (PhD, Certificate); economics and demography (PhD); public affairs and demography (PhD); sociology and demography (PhD). *Degree requirements:* For doctorate, thesis/dissertation. *Entrance requirements:* For doctorate, GRE General Test. Additional exam requirements/recommendations for international students: required—TOEFL (minimum score 600 paper-based). Electronic applications accepted.

Purdue University, Graduate School, Krannert School of Management, Doctoral Program in Economics, West Lafayette, IN 47907-2076. Offers PhD. *Faculty:* 26 full-time (5 women), 5 part-time/adjunct (2 women). *Students:* 44 full-time (19 women); includes 2 minority (1 Black or African American, non-Hispanic/Latino; 1 Asian, non-Hispanic/Latino), 27 international. Average age 26. 371 applicants, 4% accepted, 9 enrolled. In 2019, 1 doctorate awarded. *Degree requirements:* For doctorate, comprehensive exam, thesis/dissertation, dissertation proposal in 3rd year of study. *Entrance requirements:* For doctorate, GRE, two semesters of calculus, one semester of linear algebra. Additional exam requirements/recommendations for international students: required—TOEFL (minimum score 575 paper-based; 80 iBT). *Application deadline:* For fall admission, 2/15 priority date for domestic and international students. Application fee: $60 ($75 for international students). Electronic applications accepted. *Financial support:* In 2019–20, 30 students received support, including 1 fellowship with full and partial tuition reimbursement available (averaging $25,000 per year), 22 research assistantships with partial tuition reimbursements available (averaging $18,000 per year), 12 teaching assistantships with partial tuition reimbursements available (averaging $18,000 per year); institutionally sponsored loans, scholarships/grants, health care benefits, tuition waivers (partial), unspecified assistantships, and travel funds to present at a major conference also available. Financial award application deadline: 2/15. *Unit head:* Dr. David Hummels, Dean/Professor of Economics, 765-494-4366. *Application contact:* Marcella VanSickle, Krannert Doctoral Programs Coordinator, 765-494-4375, E-mail: krannertphd@purdue.edu.
Website: http://www.krannert.purdue.edu/programs/phd/

Queen's University at Kingston, Smith School of Business, Doctoral Program in Management, Kingston, ON K7L 3N6, Canada. Offers analytics (PhD); business economics (PhD); finance (PhD); management information systems (PhD); marketing (PhD); organizational behavior (PhD); strategy (PhD).

Queen's University at Kingston, Smith School of Business, Master of Science in Management Program, Kingston, ON K7L 3N6, Canada. Offers analytics (M Sc); business economics (M Sc); finance (M Sc); management information systems (M Sc); marketing (M Sc); organizational behavior (M Sc); strategy (M Sc).

Regent University, Graduate School, School of Business and Leadership, Virginia Beach, VA 23464. Offers business administration (MBA), including accounting, economics, entrepreneurship, finance and investing, general management, healthcare management (MA, MBA), human resource management (MA, MBA), innovation management, leadership, marketing, not-for-profit management (MA, MBA); business analytics (MS); business and design management (MA); church leadership (MA); leadership (Certificate); organizational leadership (MA, PhD), including ecclesial leadership (DSL, PhD), entrepreneurial leadership (PhD), healthcare management (MA, MBA), human resource development (PhD), human resource management (MA, MBA), individualized studies (DSL, PhD), interdisciplinary studies (MA), leadership coaching and mentoring (MA), not-for-profit management (MA, MBA), organizational development consulting (MA), servant leadership (MA, DSL); strategic leadership (DSL), including ecclesial leadership (DSL, PhD), global consulting, healthcare leadership, individualized studies (DSL, PhD), leadership coaching, servant leadership (MA, DSL), strategic foresight. *Program availability:* Part-time, evening/weekend, 100% online, blended/hybrid learning. *Faculty:* 9 full-time (2 women), 39 part-time/adjunct (14 women). *Students:* 397 full-time (229 women), 828 part-time (474 women); includes 698 minority (531 Black or African American, non-Hispanic/Latino; 5 American Indian or Alaska Native, non-Hispanic/Latino; 35 Asian, non-Hispanic/Latino; 87 Hispanic/Latino; 5 Native Hawaiian or other Pacific Islander, non-Hispanic/Latino; 35 Two or more races, non-Hispanic/Latino), 45 international. Average age 41. 615 applicants, 76% accepted, 275 enrolled. In 2019, 218 master's, 91 doctorates, 1 other advanced degree awarded. *Degree requirements:* For master's, thesis or alternative, 3-credit hour culminating experience; for doctorate, thesis/dissertation. *Entrance requirements:* For master's, college transcripts, resume, essay; for doctorate, college transcripts, resume, essay, writing sample; for Certificate, writing sample, resume, transcripts. Additional exam requirements/recommendations for international students: required—TOEFL (minimum score 577 paper-based). *Application deadline:* For fall admission, 5/1 priority date for domestic students; for spring admission, 10/1 priority date for domestic students. Applications are processed on a rolling basis. Application fee: $50. Electronic applications accepted. *Expenses:* Contact institution. *Financial support:* In 2019–20, 959 students received support. Career-related internships or fieldwork, scholarships/grants, health care benefits, and unspecified assistantships available. Support available to part-time students. Financial award applicants required to submit FAFSA. *Unit head:* Dr. Doris Gomez, Dean, 757-352-4686, Fax: 757-352-4634, E-mail: dorigom@regent.edu. *Application contact:* Heidi Cece, Assistant Vice President for Enrollment Management, 800-373-5504, Fax: 757-352-4381, E-mail: admissions@regent.edu.
Website: https://www.regent.edu/school-of-business-and-leadership/

Regis University, College of Business and Economics, Denver, CO 80221-1099. Offers accounting (MS); executive leadership (Certificate); finance (MS); finance and accounting (MBA); health industry leadership (MBA); human resource management and leadership (MSOL); management (MBA); marketing (MBA); nonprofit leadership (Post-Graduate Certificate); nonprofit management (MNM); nonprofit organizational capacity building (Certificate); operations management (MBA); organizational leadership and management (MSOL); project leadership and management (MS, MSOL); strategic business management (Certificate); strategic human resource integration (Certificate); strategic management (MBA). *Program availability:* Part-time, evening/weekend, 100% online, blended/hybrid learning. *Degree requirements:* For master's, thesis (for some programs), capstone or final research project. *Entrance requirements:* For master's, official transcript reflecting baccalaureate degree awarded from regionally-accredited college or university, interview, 2 years of full-time related work experience, resume, letters of recommendation. Additional exam requirements/recommendations for international students: required—TOEFL (minimum score 550 paper-based; 82 iBT). Electronic applications accepted. *Expenses:* Contact institution.

Rice University, Graduate Programs, School of Social Sciences, Department of Economics, Houston, TX 77251-1892. Offers economics (PhD); energy economics (MEECON). *Degree requirements:* For doctorate, comprehensive exam, thesis/dissertation. *Entrance requirements:* For doctorate, GRE. Additional exam requirements/recommendations for international students: required—TOEFL (minimum score 600 paper-based; 90 iBT). Electronic applications accepted.

Roosevelt University, Graduate Division, College of Arts and Sciences, Department of Economics, Chicago, IL 60605. Offers economics (MA). *Program availability:* Part-time, evening/weekend. Electronic applications accepted.

Roosevelt University, Graduate Division, College of Arts and Sciences, Department of Math, Actuarial Science, and Economics, Chicago, IL 60605. Offers actuarial science (MS); mathematics (MS), including mathematical sciences. Electronic applications accepted.

Rutgers University - Newark, Graduate School, Program in Economics, Newark, NJ 07102. Offers MA. *Entrance requirements:* For master's, GRE, minimum undergraduate B average.

Rutgers University - Newark, Rutgers Business School–Newark and New Brunswick, Doctoral Programs in Management, Newark, NJ 07102. Offers accounting (PhD); accounting information systems (PhD); economics (PhD); finance (PhD); individualized study (PhD); information technology (PhD); international business (PhD); management science (PhD); marketing science (PhD); organizational management (PhD); science, technology and management (PhD); supply chain management (PhD). *Degree requirements:* For doctorate, comprehensive exam, thesis/dissertation. *Entrance requirements:* For doctorate, GRE or GMAT. Additional exam requirements/recommendations for international students: required—TOEFL (minimum score 550 paper-based; 79 iBT). Electronic applications accepted.

Rutgers University - New Brunswick, Graduate School-New Brunswick, Program in Economics, Piscataway, NJ 08854-8097. Offers MA, PhD. Terminal master's awarded for partial completion of doctoral program. *Degree requirements:* For master's, comprehensive exam (for some programs), thesis or alternative; for doctorate, comprehensive exam, thesis/dissertation. *Entrance requirements:* For master's and doctorate, GRE General Test. Additional exam requirements/recommendations for international students: required—TOEFL. Electronic applications accepted.

St. Cloud State University, School of Graduate Studies, College of Social Sciences, Department of Economics, St. Cloud, MN 56301-4498. Offers applied economics (MS). *Program availability:* Part-time. *Degree requirements:* For master's, thesis or alternative. *Entrance requirements:* For master's, GRE General Test, minimum GPA of 2.75. Additional exam requirements/recommendations for international students: recommended—TOEFL (minimum score 550 paper-based), IELTS (minimum score 6.5). Electronic applications accepted.

San Diego State University, Graduate and Research Affairs, College of Arts and Letters, Department of Economics, San Diego, CA 92182. Offers MA. *Entrance requirements:* For master's, GRE General Test, 2 letters of recommendation. Additional exam requirements/recommendations for international students: required—TOEFL. Electronic applications accepted.

San Francisco State University, Division of Graduate Studies, Lam Family College of Business, Department of Economics, San Francisco, CA 94132-1722. Offers MA. *Expenses: Tuition, area resident:* Full-time $7176; part-time $4164 per year. Tuition, state resident: full-time $7176; part-time $4164 per year. Tuition, nonresident: full-time $16,680; part-time $396 per unit. *International tuition:* $16,680 full-time. *Required fees:* $1524; $1524 per unit. $762 per semester. Tuition and fees vary according to degree level and program. *Unit head:* Dr. Sanjit Sengupta, Faculty Director, 415-817-4366, Fax: 415-817-4340, E-mail: sengupta@sfsu.edu. *Application contact:* Dr. Lisa Takeyama, Graduate Coordinator, 415-338-2499, Fax: 415-817-4340, E-mail: takeyama@sfsu.edu.
Website: http://cob.sfsu.edu/economics

San Jose State University, Program in Economics, San Jose, CA 95192-0001. Offers applied economics (MA); economics (MA). *Program availability:* Part-time. *Degree requirements:* For master's, comprehensive exam, thesis optional. *Entrance requirements:* For master's, GRE, minimum GPA of 3.0. Electronic applications accepted. *Expenses: Tuition, area resident:* Full-time $7176; part-time $4164 per credit hour. Tuition, state resident: full-time $7176; part-time $4164 per credit hour. Tuition, nonresident: full-time $7176; part-time $4165 per credit hour. *International tuition:* $7176 full-time. *Required fees:* $2110; $2110.

Simon Fraser University, Office of Graduate Studies and Postdoctoral Fellows, Faculty of Arts and Social Sciences, Department of Economics, Burnaby, BC V5A 1S6, Canada. Offers MA, PhD. *Degree requirements:* For master's, thesis (for some programs); for doctorate, comprehensive exam, thesis/dissertation. *Entrance requirements:* For master's, GRE, minimum GPA of 3.0 (on scale of 4.33) or 3.33 based on last 60 credits of undergraduate courses; for doctorate, GRE, minimum GPA of 3.5 (on scale of 4.33). Additional exam requirements/recommendations for international students: recommended—TOEFL (minimum score 580 paper-based; 93 iBT), IELTS (minimum score 7), TWE (minimum score 5).

South Dakota State University, Graduate School, College of Agriculture, Food and Environmental Sciences, Department of Economics, Brookings, SD 57007. Offers MS.

Degree requirements: For master's, comprehensive exam, thesis (for some programs), oral exam. *Entrance requirements:* For master's, minimum GPA of 2.75. Additional exam requirements/recommendations for international students: required—TOEFL (minimum score 550 paper-based; 79 iBT).

Southern Illinois University Carbondale, Graduate School, College of Liberal Arts, Department of Economics, Carbondale, IL 62901-4701. Offers MA, MS, PhD. *Degree requirements:* For master's, thesis; for doctorate, thesis/dissertation. *Entrance requirements:* For master's, GRE General Test, minimum GPA of 2.7; for doctorate, GRE General Test, minimum GPA of 3.25. Additional exam requirements/recommendations for international students: required—TOEFL.

Southern Illinois University Edwardsville, Graduate School, School of Business, Department of Economics and Finance, Edwardsville, IL 62026. Offers MA, MS. *Program availability:* Part-time, evening/weekend. *Degree requirements:* For master's, thesis or alternative, final exam, portfolio. *Entrance requirements:* For master's, GMAT or GRE. Additional exam requirements/recommendations for international students: required—TOEFL (minimum score 550 paper-based; 79 iBT), IELTS (minimum score 6.5). Electronic applications accepted.

Southern Methodist University, Dedman College of Humanities and Sciences, Department of Economics, Dallas, TX 75205. Offers applied economics (MA); applied economics and predictive analytics (MS); economics (PhD); law and economics (MA). *Program availability:* Part-time, evening/weekend. Terminal master's awarded for partial completion of doctoral program. *Degree requirements:* For master's, thesis, oral qualifying exam; for doctorate, thesis/dissertation, written exams. *Entrance requirements:* For master's, GRE General Test or GMAT, 12 hours of course work in economics, minimum GPA of 3.0, previous course work in calculus and statistics; for doctorate, GRE General Test, minimum GPA of 3.0; 3 semesters of course work in calculus; 1 semester each of course work in statistics and linear algebra. Additional exam requirements/recommendations for international students: required—TOEFL (minimum score 550 paper-based). Electronic applications accepted.

Southern New Hampshire University, School of Business, Manchester, NH 03106-1045. Offers accounting (MBA, Graduate Certificate); accounting finance (MS); accounting/auditing (MS); accounting/forensic accounting (MS); accounting/management accounting (MS); accounting/taxation (MS); applied economics (MS); athletic administration (MBA, Graduate Certificate); business administration (IMBA, Certificate), including business information systems (Certificate), human resource management (Certificate); business analytics (MBA); business intelligence (MBA); communication (MA), including new media and marketing, public relations; community economic development (MBA); criminal justice (MBA); data analytics (MS); economics (MBA); engineering management (MBA); entrepreneurship (MBA); finance (MBA, MS, Graduate Certificate); finance/corporate finance (MS); finance/investments (MS); forensic accounting (MBA); forensic accounting and fraud examination (Graduate Certificate); healthcare informatics (MBA); healthcare management (MBA); human resource management (MS); human resources (MBA); information technology (MS); information technology management (MBA); international business (PhD); Internet marketing (MBA); leadership (MBA); leadership of nonprofit organizations (Graduate Certificate); management (MS); marketing (MBA, MS, Graduate Certificate); music business (MBA); operations and project management (MS); operations and supply chain management (MBA, Graduate Certificate); organizational leadership (MS); project management (MBA, Graduate Certificate); public administration (MBA, Graduate Certificate); quantitative analysis (MBA); Six Sigma (Graduate Certificate); Six Sigma quality (MBA); social media marketing (MBA, Graduate Certificate); sport management (MBA, MS, Graduate Certificate); sustainability and environmental compliance (MBA); MBA/Certificate. *Accreditation:* ACBSP. *Program availability:* Part-time, evening/weekend, online learning. Terminal master's awarded for partial completion of doctoral program. *Degree requirements:* For master's, one foreign language, comprehensive exam (for some programs), thesis or alternative; for doctorate, one foreign language, comprehensive exam, thesis/dissertation. *Entrance requirements:* For master's, minimum GPA of 2.5; for doctorate, GMAT. Additional exam requirements/recommendations for international students: required—TOEFL (minimum score 500 paper-based). Electronic applications accepted.

Stanford University, School of Humanities and Sciences, Department of Economics, Stanford, CA 94305-2004. Offers PhD. *Expenses: Tuition:* Full-time $52,479; part-time $34,110 per unit. *Required fees:* $672; $224 per quarter. Tuition and fees vary according to program and student level.
Website: http://www-econ.stanford.edu/

State University of New York College of Environmental Science and Forestry, Program in Environmental Science, Syracuse, NY 13210-2779. Offers biophysical and ecological economics (MPS); coupled natural and human systems (MPS); ecosystem restoration (MPS); environmental and community land planning (MPS, MS); environmental and natural resources policy (PhD); environmental communication and participatory processes (PhD); environmental monitoring and modeling (MPS); water and wetland resource studies (MPS, MS). *Program availability:* Part-time. *Faculty:* 1 full-time (0 women), 1 (woman) part-time/adjunct. *Students:* 62 full-time (40 women), 12 part-time (9 women); includes 8 minority (1 Black or African American, non-Hispanic/Latino; 4 American Indian or Alaska Native, non-Hispanic/Latino; 2 Asian, non-Hispanic/Latino; 1 Hispanic/Latino), 28 international. Average age 31. 68 applicants, 84% accepted, 26 enrolled. In 2019, 10 master's, 2 doctorates awarded. Terminal master's awarded for partial completion of doctoral program. *Degree requirements:* For master's, thesis (for some programs); for doctorate, comprehensive exam, thesis/dissertation. *Entrance requirements:* For master's and doctorate, GRE General Test, minimum GPA of 3.0. Additional exam requirements/recommendations for international students: required—TOEFL (minimum score 550 paper-based; 80 iBT), IELTS (minimum score 6). *Application deadline:* For fall admission, 2/1 priority date for domestic and international students; for spring admission, 11/1 priority date for domestic and international students. Applications are processed on a rolling basis. Application fee: $60. Electronic applications accepted. *Expenses:* Tuition, state resident: full-time $11,310; part-time $472 per credit hour. Tuition, nonresident: full-time $23,100; part-time $963 per credit hour. *Required fees:* $1890; $95.21 per credit hour. *Financial support:* In 2019–20, 15 students received support. Unspecified assistantships available. Financial award application deadline: 6/30; financial award applicants required to submit FAFSA. *Unit head:* Dr. Russell Briggs, Director of the Division of Environmental Science, 315-470-6989, Fax: 315-470-6700, E-mail: rdbriggs@esf.edu. *Application contact:* Laura Payne, Office of Instruction and Graduate Studies, 315-470-6599, E-mail: esfgrad@esf.edu.
Website: http://www.esf.edu/environmentalscience/graduate/

Stony Brook University, State University of New York, Graduate School, College of Arts and Sciences, Department of Economics, Stony Brook, NY 11794. Offers MA, PhD. *Faculty:* 15 full-time (7 women), 5 part-time/adjunct (0 women). *Students:* 59 full-time (25 women); includes 4 minority (3 Asian, non-Hispanic/Latino; 1 Hispanic/Latino), 53 international. Average age 27. 152 applicants, 26% accepted, 17 enrolled. In 2019, 9 master's, 7 doctorates awarded. *Degree requirements:* For doctorate, comprehensive exam, thesis/dissertation. *Entrance requirements:* For master's and doctorate, GRE General Test. Additional exam requirements/recommendations for international students: required—TOEFL (minimum score 90 iBT). *Application deadline:* For fall admission, 1/15 for domestic students; for spring admission, 10/1 for domestic students. Application fee: $100. Electronic applications accepted. *Expenses:* Contact institution. *Financial support:* In 2019–20, 34 teaching assistantships were awarded; fellowships and research assistantships also available. *Unit head:* Prof. Marina Azzimonti, Chair, 631-632-7549, Fax: 631-632-7516, E-mail: marina.azzimontirenzo@stonybrook.edu. *Application contact:* Maryann Calvacca, Graduate Program Coordinator, 631-632-7537, Fax: 631-632-7516, E-mail: graduate_economics@stonybrook.edu.
Website: http://www.sunysb.edu/economics/

Syracuse University, Maxwell School of Citizenship and Public Affairs, Dual MA Program in Economics and International Relations, Syracuse, NY 13244. Offers MA/MA. *Entrance requirements:* Additional exam requirements/recommendations for international students: required—TOEFL (minimum score 100 iBT). Electronic applications accepted.

Syracuse University, Maxwell School of Citizenship and Public Affairs, Programs in Economics, Syracuse, NY 13244. Offers MA, PhD. *Degree requirements:* For doctorate, comprehensive exam, thesis/dissertation. *Entrance requirements:* For master's and doctorate, GRE General Test, personal statement, three letters of recommendation, resume, official transcripts. Additional exam requirements/recommendations for international students: required—TOEFL (minimum score 100 iBT). Electronic applications accepted.

Teachers College, Columbia University, Department of Education Policy and Social Analysis, New York, NY 10027-6696. Offers economics and education (Ed M, MA, PhD); education policy (Ed M, MA, Ed D, PhD); politics and education (Ed M, MA, Ed D, PhD); sociology and education (Ed M, MA, Ed D, PhD). *Faculty:* 11 full-time (4 women). *Students:* 89 full-time (71 women), 154 part-time (113 women); includes 91 minority (36 Black or African American, non-Hispanic/Latino; 19 Asian, non-Hispanic/Latino; 29 Hispanic/Latino; 7 Two or more races, non-Hispanic/Latino), 73 international. 433 applicants, 60% accepted, 107 enrolled. *Unit head:* Dr. Aaron Pallas, Chair, 212-678-8119, E-mail: amp155@tc.columbia.edu. *Application contact:* Kelly Sutton-Skinner, Director of Admission and New Student Enrollment, 212-678-3710, E-mail: kms2237@tc.columbia.edu.
Website: http://www.tc.columbia.edu/education-policy-and-social-analysis/

Temple University, College of Liberal Arts, Department of Economics, Philadelphia, PA 19122-6096. Offers MA, PhD. *Program availability:* Part-time, evening/weekend. *Faculty:* 20 full-time (3 women), 6 part-time/adjunct (1 woman). *Students:* 25 full-time (13 women), 5 part-time (2 women); includes 4 minority (3 Black or African American, non-Hispanic/Latino; 1 Asian, non-Hispanic/Latino), 13 international. 63 applicants, 24% accepted, 2 enrolled. In 2019, 6 master's, 6 doctorates awarded. *Entrance requirements:* For master's and doctorate, GRE, statement of goals, 3 letters of recommendation. Additional exam requirements/recommendations for international students: required—TOEFL (minimum score 79 iBT), IELTS, PTE, one of three is required. Application fee: $60. Electronic applications accepted. *Financial support:* Research assistantships, teaching assistantships, Federal Work-Study, and health care benefits available. Financial award applicants required to submit FAFSA. *Unit head:* Michael Leeds, Chairperson, 215-204-8030, E-mail: mleeds@temple.edu. *Application contact:* Linda Wyatt, Graduate Program Coordinator, 215-204-6638, E-mail: ldwyatt@temple.edu.
Website: http://www.cla.temple.edu/economics/

Texas A&M University, College of Liberal Arts, Department of Economics, College Station, TX 77843. Offers economics (MS). *Program availability:* Part-time. *Faculty:* 33. *Students:* 230 full-time (92 women), 5 part-time (3 women); includes 15 minority (2 Black or African American, non-Hispanic/Latino; 2 Asian, non-Hispanic/Latino; 9 Hispanic/Latino; 2 Two or more races, non-Hispanic/Latino), 174 international. Average age 25. 337 applicants, 50% accepted, 74 enrolled. In 2019, 111 master's, 12 doctorates awarded. Terminal master's awarded for partial completion of doctoral program. *Degree requirements:* For master's, comprehensive exam (for some programs), thesis optional; for doctorate, comprehensive exam, thesis/dissertation. *Entrance requirements:* For master's and doctorate, GRE General Test, letters of recommendation. Additional exam requirements/recommendations for international students: required—TOEFL (minimum score 550 paper-based; 80 iBT), IELTS (minimum score 6), PTE (minimum score 53). *Application deadline:* For fall admission, 2/1 for domestic students. Applications are processed on a rolling basis. Application fee: $65 ($90 for international students). Electronic applications accepted. *Expenses:* Contact institution. *Financial support:* In 2019–20, 134 students received support, including 17 fellowships with tuition reimbursements available (averaging $3,235 per year), 10 research assistantships with tuition reimbursements available (averaging $10,811 per year), 57 teaching assistantships with tuition reimbursements available (averaging $20,262 per year); career-related internships or fieldwork, institutionally sponsored loans, scholarships/grants, traineeships, health care benefits, tuition waivers (full and partial), and unspecified assistantships also available. Support available to part-time students. Financial award application deadline: 3/15; financial award applicants required to submit FAFSA. *Unit head:* Dr. Steve Puller, Professor and Department Head, E-mail: spuller@tamu.edu. *Application contact:* Dr. Amy Glass, Director of Doctoral Program, 979-845-8507, Fax: 979-847-8557, E-mail: aglass@tamu.edu.
Website: http://econ.tamu.edu/

Texas Tech University, Graduate School, College of Arts and Sciences, Department of Economics, Lubbock, TX 79409-1014. Offers MA, PhD. *Faculty:* 12 full-time (1 woman). *Students:* 43 full-time (16 women), 2 part-time (both women); includes 3 minority (1 Asian, non-Hispanic/Latino; 2 Hispanic/Latino), 38 international. Average age 31. 46 applicants, 67% accepted, 15 enrolled. In 2019, 1 master's, 6 doctorates awarded. *Degree requirements:* For master's, variable foreign language requirement, comprehensive exam (for some programs), thesis (for some programs); for doctorate, variable foreign language requirement, comprehensive exam, thesis/dissertation. *Entrance requirements:* Additional exam requirements/recommendations for international students: required—TOEFL (minimum score 550 paper-based; 79 iBT). *Application deadline:* For fall admission, 6/1 priority date for domestic students, 1/15 priority date for international students; for spring admission, 9/1 priority date for domestic students, 6/15 priority date for international students. Applications are processed on a rolling basis. Application fee: $65. Electronic applications accepted. *Expenses:* Contact institution. *Financial support:* In 2019–20, 40 students received support, including 38 fellowships (averaging $1,270 per year), 39 teaching assistantships (averaging $14,925 per year); research assistantships, scholarships/grants, unspecified assistantships, and partial tuition and fee waivers also available. Financial award application deadline: 2/1; financial award applicants required to submit FAFSA. *Unit head:* Dr. Klaus G. Becker, Associate Professor/Chair, 806-834-7275, Fax: 806-742-1137, E-mail: klaus.becker@ttu.edu. *Application contact:* Rosie Carrillo, Business Manager, 806-742-2201, Fax: 806-742-1137, E-mail: rosie.carrillo@ttu.edu.
Website: www.depts.ttu.edu/economics/

Troy University, Graduate School, College of Business, Program in Economics, Troy, AL 36082. Offers MA. *Program availability:* Part-time, evening/weekend. *Faculty:* 7 full-time (1 woman). *Students:* 11 full-time (3 women), 1 part-time (0 women), 2 international. Average age 24. 10 applicants, 90% accepted, 8 enrolled. In 2019, 5 master's awarded. *Degree requirements:* For master's, thesis or alternative, minimum

Economics

GPA of 3.0, capstone course, research course, admission to candidacy. *Entrance requirements:* For master's, GMAT (500 or above) or GRE (1050 or above in verbal and quantitative), or 294 or above on the revised GRE (verbal and quantitative), official transcripts; bachelor's degree; minimum GPA of 2.5 in all undergraduate work or 3.0 for last 30 semester hours; letter of recommendation. Additional exam requirements/recommendations for international students: required—TOEFL (minimum score 523 paper-based; 70 iBT), IELTS (minimum score 6). *Application deadline:* Applications are processed on a rolling basis. Application fee: $50. Electronic applications accepted. *Expenses: Tuition, area resident:* Full-time $7650; part-time $2550 per semester hour. Tuition, state resident: full-time $7650; part-time $2550 per semester hour. Tuition, nonresident: full-time $15,300; part-time $5100 per semester hour. *International tuition:* $15,300 full-time. *Required fees:* $856; $352 per semester hour. $176 per semester. *Financial support:* In 2019–20, 11 students received support. Fellowships, research assistantships, teaching assistantships, career-related internships or fieldwork, Federal Work-Study, scholarships/grants, traineeships, tuition waivers, and unspecified assistantships available. Support available to part-time students. Financial award application deadline: 3/1; financial award applicants required to submit FAFSA. *Unit head:* Dr. John Dove, Chair, Economics, 334-808-6604, Fax: 334-670-3708, E-mail: jadove@troy.edu. *Application contact:* Haley McKinnon, Director of Graduate Admissions, 334-670-3178, Fax: 334-670-3733, E-mail: hmckinnon@troy.edu.
Website: https://www.troy.edu/academics/academic-programs/sorrell-college-business-programs.php

Tufts University, The Fletcher School of Law and Diplomacy, Medford, MA 02155. Offers economics and public policy (PhD); international affairs (PhD); international business (MIB); international law (LL M); law and diplomacy (MA, MALD); transatlantic affairs (MA); DVM/MA; JD/MALD; MALD/MA; MALD/MBA; MALD/MS; MD/MA. *Program availability:* Online learning. *Degree requirements:* For master's, one foreign language, thesis; for doctorate, one foreign language, comprehensive exam, thesis/dissertation, dissertation defense. *Entrance requirements:* For master's and doctorate, GMAT or GRE General Test. Additional exam requirements/recommendations for international students: required—TOEFL (minimum score 600 paper-based; 100 iBT), IELTS (minimum score 7). Electronic applications accepted. *Expenses:* Contact institution.

Tufts University, Graduate School of Arts and Sciences, Department of Economics, Medford, MA 02155. Offers economics (MS); economics and public policy (PhD). *Program availability:* Part-time. *Degree requirements:* For master's, thesis optional. *Entrance requirements:* For master's, GRE General Test. Additional exam requirements/recommendations for international students: required—TOEFL (minimum score 550 paper-based; 80 iBT), IELTS (minimum score 6.5). Electronic applications accepted. *Expenses:* Contact institution.

Tulane University, School of Liberal Arts, Department of Economics, New Orleans, LA 70118-5669. Offers MA, PhD. *Degree requirements:* For master's, thesis or alternative; for doctorate, one foreign language, thesis/dissertation. *Entrance requirements:* For master's, GRE General Test, minimum B average in undergraduate course work; for doctorate, GRE General Test. Additional exam requirements/recommendations for international students: required—TOEFL. Electronic applications accepted. *Expenses: Tuition:* Full-time $57,004; part-time $3167 per credit hour. *Required fees:* $2086; $44.50 per credit hour. $80 per term. Tuition and fees vary according to course load, degree level and program.

UNB Fredericton, School of Graduate Studies, Faculty of Arts - Saint John, Department of Economics, Fredericton, NB E3B 5A3, Canada. Offers applied economics and finance (M Sc); economics (MA). *Faculty:* 12 full-time (2 women). *Students:* 19 full-time (7 women), 16 international. In 2019, 10 master's awarded. *Entrance requirements:* For master's, minimum GPA of 3.0. Additional exam requirements/recommendations for international students: required—TWE (minimum score 4), TOEFL (minimum score 580 paper-based) or IELTS (minimum score 7). *Application deadline:* For fall admission, 1/31 for domestic and international students; for winter admission, 1/15 for domestic students, 1/15 priority date for international students; for spring admission, 1/31 for domestic and international students. Applications are processed on a rolling basis. Application fee: $50 Canadian dollars. Electronic applications accepted. *Expenses: Tuition, area resident:* Full-time $6975 Canadian dollars; part-time $3423 Canadian dollars per year. Tuition, state resident: full-time $6975 Canadian dollars; part-time $3423 Canadian dollars per year. Tuition, Canadian resident: full-time $6975 Canadian dollars; part-time $3423 Canadian dollars per year. *International tuition:* $12,435 Canadian dollars full-time. *Required fees:* $92.25 Canadian dollars per term. Full-time tuition and fees vary according to degree level, campus/location, program, reciprocity agreements and student level. *Financial support:* Fellowships, research assistantships, teaching assistantships, scholarships/grants, health care benefits, and unspecified assistantships available. Financial award application deadline: 1/31. *Unit head:* Dr. Yuri Yevdokimov, Director of Graduate Studies, 506-447-3221, Fax: 506-453-4514, E-mail: yuri@unb.ca. *Application contact:* Dr. Yuri Yevdokimov, Director of Graduate Studies, 506-447-3221, Fax: 506-453-4514, E-mail: yuri@unb.ca.
Website: http://go.unb.ca/gradprograms

Universidad de las Américas Puebla, Division of Graduate Studies, School of Social Sciences, Program in Economics, Puebla, Mexico. Offers economics (MA); finance (M Adm). *Program availability:* Part-time, evening/weekend. *Degree requirements:* For master's, one foreign language, thesis.

Université de Moncton, Faculty of Arts and Social Sciences, Department of Economics, Moncton, NB E1A 3E9, Canada. Offers MA. *Degree requirements:* For master's, one foreign language, thesis. *Entrance requirements:* For master's, minimum GPA of 3.0.

Université de Montréal, Faculty of Arts and Sciences, Department of Economic Sciences, Montréal, QC H3C 3J7, Canada. Offers economics (M Sc, PhD); mathematical and computational finance (M Sc). *Degree requirements:* For master's, one foreign language, thesis; for doctorate, one foreign language, thesis/dissertation, general exam. Electronic applications accepted.

Université de Sherbrooke, Faculty of Administration, Program in Economics, Sherbrooke, QC J1K 2R1, Canada. Offers M Sc. Terminal master's awarded for partial completion of doctoral program. *Degree requirements:* For master's, one foreign language, thesis. *Entrance requirements:* For master's, minimum GPA of 3.0 (on 4.3 scale). Electronic applications accepted.

Université de Sherbrooke, Faculty of Letters and Human Sciences, Department of Economics, Sherbrooke, QC J1K 2R1, Canada. Offers MA. *Degree requirements:* For master's, thesis.

Université du Québec à Montréal, Graduate Programs, Program in Economics, Montréal, QC H3C 3P8, Canada. Offers M Sc, PhD. *Program availability:* Part-time. *Degree requirements:* For master's, thesis; for doctorate, thesis/dissertation. *Entrance requirements:* For master's, appropriate bachelor's degree or equivalent, proficiency in French; for doctorate, appropriate master's degree or equivalent, proficiency in French.

University at Albany, State University of New York, College of Arts and Sciences, Department of Economics, Albany, NY 12222-0001. Offers economic forecasting (MA); economics (MA, PhD). *Program availability:* Part-time, blended/hybrid learning. *Faculty:* 21 full-time (4 women), 19 part-time/adjunct (7 women). *Students:* 44 full-time (24 women), 43 part-time (19 women); includes 2 minority (both Hispanic/Latino), 78 international. 156 applicants, 51% accepted, 35 enrolled. In 2019, 28 master's, 4 doctorates awarded. Terminal master's awarded for partial completion of doctoral program. *Degree requirements:* For doctorate, one foreign language, thesis/dissertation. *Entrance requirements:* For master's, transcripts of all schools attended, statement of background and goals, departmental questionnaire, resume, names and contact information for 3 recommenders; for doctorate, GRE General Test, GRE Subject Test, transcripts of all schools attended, statement of background and goals, departmental questionnaire, resume, names and contact information for 3 recommenders. Additional exam requirements/recommendations for international students: required—TOEFL (minimum score 550 paper-based). *Application deadline:* For fall admission, 1/15 for domestic students, 5/1 for international students; for spring admission, 11/15 for domestic students. Applications are processed on a rolling basis. Application fee: $75. Electronic applications accepted. *Expenses: Tuition, area resident:* Full-time $11,530; part-time $480 per credit hour. Tuition, nonresident: full-time $23,530; part-time $980 per credit hour. *International tuition:* $23,530 full-time. *Required fees:* $2185; $96 per credit hour. Part-time tuition and fees vary according to course load and program. *Financial support:* Fellowships, research assistantships, teaching assistantships, career-related internships or fieldwork, institutionally sponsored loans, and lectureships available. Financial award application deadline: 2/15. *Unit head:* Adrian Masters, Chair, 518-442-4735, Fax: 518-442-4736, E-mail: amasters@albany.edu. *Application contact:* Michael DeRensis, Director, Graduate Admissions, 518-442-3980, Fax: 518-442-3922, E-mail: graduate@albany.edu.
Website: https://www.albany.edu/economics

University at Albany, State University of New York, Nelson A. Rockefeller College of Public Affairs and Policy, Department of Public Administration and Policy, Albany, NY 12222-0001. Offers financial management and public economics (MPA); financial market regulation (MPA); health policy (MPA); healthcare management (MPA); homeland security (MPA); human resources management (MPA); information strategy and management (MPA); local government management (MPA); nonprofit management (MPA); nonprofit management and leadership (Certificate); organizational behavior and theory (MPA, PhD); planning and policy analysis (CAS); policy analysis (MPA); politics and administration (PhD); public finance (PhD); public management (PhD); public policy (PhD); public sector management (Certificate); women and public policy (Certificate); JD/MPA. *Accreditation:* NASPAA (one or more programs are accredited). *Program availability:* Blended/hybrid learning. *Faculty:* 19 full-time (8 women), 12 part-time/adjunct (4 women). *Students:* 119 full-time (71 women), 41 part-time (4 women); includes 45 minority (18 Black or African American, non-Hispanic/Latino; 7 Asian, non-Hispanic/Latino; 14 Hispanic/Latino; 6 Two or more races, non-Hispanic/Latino), 28 international. Average age 29. 172 applicants, 81% accepted, 85 enrolled. In 2019, 57 master's, 6 doctorates, 11 other advanced degrees awarded. *Degree requirements:* For doctorate, one foreign language, thesis/dissertation. *Entrance requirements:* For doctorate, GRE General Test. Additional exam requirements/recommendations for international students: required—TOEFL (minimum score 550 paper-based). *Application deadline:* For fall admission, 1/15 priority date for domestic students, 5/1 for international students; for spring admission, 11/15 for domestic students. Applications are processed on a rolling basis. Application fee: $75. Electronic applications accepted. *Expenses: Tuition, area resident:* Full-time $11,530; part-time $480 per credit hour. Tuition, nonresident: full-time $23,530; part-time $980 per credit hour. *International tuition:* $23,530 full-time. *Required fees:* $2185; $96 per credit hour. Part-time tuition and fees vary according to course load and program. *Financial support:* Research assistantships, teaching assistantships, and Federal Work-Study available. Financial award application deadline: 2/1. *Unit head:* Edmund Stazyk, Chair, 518-591-8723, E-mail: estazyk@albany.edu. *Application contact:* Luis Felipe Luna-Reyes, 518-442-5297, E-mail: llunareyes@albany.edu.
Website: http://www.albany.edu/rockefeller/pad.shtml

University at Buffalo, the State University of New York, Graduate School, College of Arts and Sciences, Department of Economics, Buffalo, NY 14260. Offers econometrics and quantitative economics (MS); economics (MA, PhD); financial economics (Certificate); health services (Certificate); information and Internet economics (Certificate); international economics (Certificate); law and regulation (Certificate); urban and regional economics (Certificate). *Program availability:* Part-time. Terminal master's awarded for partial completion of doctoral program. *Degree requirements:* For master's, comprehensive exam; for doctorate, comprehensive exam, thesis/dissertation, field and theory exams. *Entrance requirements:* For master's, GRE General Test or GMAT; for doctorate, GRE General Test. Additional exam requirements/recommendations for international students: required—TOEFL (minimum score 550 paper-based; 79 iBT), TWE. Electronic applications accepted. *Expenses: Tuition, area resident:* Full-time $11,310; part-time $471 per credit hour. Tuition, state resident: full-time $11,310; part-time $471 per credit hour. Tuition, nonresident: full-time $23,100; part-time $963 per credit hour. *International tuition:* $23,100 full-time. *Required fees:* $2820.

University at Buffalo, the State University of New York, Graduate School, Graduate School of Education, Department of Educational Leadership and Policy, Buffalo, NY 14260. Offers economics and education policy analysis (MA); education studies (Ed M); educational administration (Ed M, Ed D, PhD); educational culture, policy and society (PhD); higher education administration (Ed M, PhD); school building leadership (Certificate); school business and human resource administration (Certificate); school district business leadership (Certificate); school district leadership (Certificate). *Program availability:* Part-time, evening/weekend. *Faculty:* 14 full-time (10 women), 8 part-time/adjunct (6 women). *Students:* 101 full-time (69 women), 123 part-time (82 women); includes 55 minority (28 Black or African American, non-Hispanic/Latino; 8 Asian, non-Hispanic/Latino; 13 Hispanic/Latino; 6 Two or more races, non-Hispanic/Latino), 20 international. Average age 35. 238 applicants, 78% accepted, 99 enrolled. In 2019, 48 master's, 5 doctorates, 21 other advanced degrees awarded. *Degree requirements:* For master's, comprehensive exam (for some programs), thesis optional; for doctorate, comprehensive exam, thesis/dissertation. *Entrance requirements:* For master's, interview, letters of reference; for doctorate, GRE General Test or MAT, writing sample, letters of reference. Additional exam requirements/recommendations for international students: required—TOEFL (minimum score 600 paper-based; 79 iBT), IELTS (minimum score 6.5), PTE (minimum score 55), The Graduate School of Education requires international students to submit test scores for at least one of the exams (TOEFL, IELTS, PTE). *Application deadline:* For fall admission, 2/1 priority date for domestic students, 2/1 for international students; for spring admission, 11/15 priority date for domestic students, 10/1 for international students. Applications are processed on a rolling basis. Application fee: $50. Electronic applications accepted. *Expenses: Tuition, area resident:* Full-time $11,310; part-time $471 per credit hour. Tuition, state resident: full-time $11,310; part-time $471 per credit hour. Tuition, nonresident: full-time $23,100; part-time $963 per credit hour. *International tuition:* $23,100 full-time. *Required fees:* $2820. *Financial support:* In 2019–20, 8 fellowships (averaging $20,000 per year), 6 research assistantships with tuition reimbursements (averaging $24,350 per year) were awarded; career-related internships or fieldwork, Federal Work-Study, institutionally sponsored loans, scholarships/grants, health care benefits, tuition waivers (full and partial), and unspecified assistantships also available. Financial award

application deadline: 3/15; financial award applicants required to submit FAFSA. *Unit head:* Dr. Nathan Daun-Barnett, Department Chair, 716-645-2471, Fax: 716-645-2481, E-mail: nbarnett@buffalo.edu. *Application contact:* Renad Aref, Assistant Director of Admission Recruitment, 716-645-2110, Fax: 716-645-7937, E-mail: gseinfo@buffalo.edu.
Website: http://ed.buffalo.edu/leadership

The University of Akron, Graduate School, College of Business Administration, Department of Economics, Akron, OH 44325. Offers MA. *Program availability:* Part-time. *Degree requirements:* For master's, thesis optional. *Entrance requirements:* For master's, GRE or GMAT (recommended), three letters of recommendation (preferably from academics), statement of purpose, resume. Additional exam requirements/ recommendations for international students: required—TOEFL (minimum score 79 iBT), IELTS (minimum score 6.5), GRE or GMAT. Electronic applications accepted.

The University of Alabama, Graduate School, Culverhouse College of Business, Department of Economics, Finance and Legal Studies, Tuscaloosa, AL 35487. Offers economics (MA, PhD); finance (MS, PhD). *Faculty:* 27 full-time (3 women). *Students:* 38 full-time (13 women), 1 part-time (0 women); includes 4 minority (1 Asian, non-Hispanic/ Latino; 1 Hispanic/Latino; 2 Two or more races, non-Hispanic/Latino), 22 international. Average age 29. 164 applicants, 50% accepted, 16 enrolled. In 2019, 49 master's, 6 doctorates awarded. Terminal master's awarded for partial completion of doctoral program. *Degree requirements:* For master's, comprehensive exam (MA), thesis (MS); for doctorate, comprehensive exam, thesis/dissertation. *Entrance requirements:* For master's, GMAT, GRE; for doctorate, GRE or GMAT. Additional exam requirements/ recommendations for international students: required—TOEFL (minimum score 550 paper-based; 79 iBT). *Application deadline:* For fall admission, 7/1 priority date for domestic students, 1/15 for international students. Applications are processed on a rolling basis. Application fee: $50 ($60 for international students). Electronic applications accepted. *Expenses: Tuition, area resident:* Full-time $10,780; part-time $440 per credit hour. Tuition, nonresident: full-time $30,250; part-time $1550 per credit hour. *Financial support:* In 2019–20, 41 students received support. Fellowships, research assistantships with tuition reimbursements available, teaching assistantships with tuition reimbursements available, Federal Work-Study, institutionally sponsored loans, and unspecified assistantships available. Financial award application deadline: 1/15. *Unit head:* Dr. Laura Razzolini, Department Head, 205-348-6683, E-mail: kcwise@cba.ua.edu. *Application contact:* Debra F. Wheatley, Graduate Programs Secretary, 205-348-6683, Fax: 205-348-0590, E-mail: dwheatle@cba.ua.edu.
Website: http://www.cba.ua.edu/

University of Alberta, Faculty of Graduate Studies and Research, Department of Economics, Edmonton, AB T6G 2E1, Canada. Offers economics (MA, PhD); economics and finance (MA); environmental and natural resource economics (PhD). *Program availability:* Part-time. *Degree requirements:* For doctorate, thesis/dissertation. *Entrance requirements:* For master's and doctorate, GRE. Additional exam requirements/ recommendations for international students: required—TOEFL.

The University of Arizona, Eller College of Management, Department of Economics, Tucson, AZ 85721. Offers MA, PhD. Terminal master's awarded for partial completion of doctoral program. *Degree requirements:* For master's, comprehensive exam; for doctorate, thesis/dissertation. *Entrance requirements:* For doctorate, GRE General Test, 3 letters of recommendation. Additional exam requirements/recommendations for international students: required—TOEFL (minimum score 550 paper-based; 79 iBT). Electronic applications accepted.

University of Arkansas, Graduate School, Sam M. Walton College of Business Administration, Department of Economics, Fayetteville, AR 72701. Offers MA, PhD. *Students:* 13 full-time (2 women), 1 part-time (0 women); includes 3 minority (2 Black or African American, non-Hispanic/Latino; 1 Hispanic/Latino), 7 international. In 2019, 6 master's, 3 doctorates awarded. *Degree requirements:* For doctorate, variable foreign language requirement, thesis/dissertation. *Entrance requirements:* For master's and doctorate, GRE General Test. *Application deadline:* For fall admission, 8/1 for domestic students, 4/1 for international students; for spring admission, 12/1 for domestic students, 10/1 for international students; for summer admission, 4/15 for domestic students, 3/1 for international students. Application fee: $60. Electronic applications accepted. *Financial support:* In 2019–20, 5 research assistantships, 8 teaching assistantships were awarded; fellowships with tuition reimbursements, career-related internships or fieldwork, and Federal Work-Study also available. Support available to part-time students. Financial award application deadline: 4/1; financial award applicants required to submit FAFSA. *Unit head:* Dr. Raja Kali, Department Chair, 479-575-6219, Fax: 479-575-3241, E-mail: rkali@uark.edu. *Application contact:* Dr. Gary Ferrier, University Professor, 479-575-6223, Fax: 479-575-3241, E-mail: gferrier@walton.uark.edu.
Website: https://economics.uark.edu/

The University of British Columbia, Faculty of Arts, Vancouver School of Economics, Vancouver, BC V6T 1Z1, Canada. Offers MA, PhD. *Degree requirements:* For master's, thesis (for some programs); for doctorate, comprehensive exam, thesis/dissertation. *Entrance requirements:* For master's and doctorate, GRE General Test. Additional exam requirements/recommendations for international students: required—TOEFL. Electronic applications accepted. *Expenses:* Contact institution.

University of California, Berkeley, Graduate Division, College of Letters and Science, Department of Economics, Berkeley, CA 94720. Offers PhD, JD/MA. *Degree requirements:* For doctorate, thesis/dissertation, field exams, oral qualifying exam. *Entrance requirements:* For doctorate, GRE General Test, minimum GPA of 3.0, 3 letters of recommendation. Additional exam requirements/recommendations for international students: required—TOEFL (minimum score 570 paper-based; 90 iBT). Electronic applications accepted.

University of California, Davis, Graduate Studies, Program in Economics, Davis, CA 95616. Offers MA, PhD. Terminal master's awarded for partial completion of doctoral program. *Degree requirements:* For master's, comprehensive exam (for some programs), thesis (for some programs); for doctorate, thesis/dissertation. *Entrance requirements:* For master's, GRE General Test, minimum GPA of 3.0; for doctorate, GRE General Test, minimum GPA of 3.25. Additional exam requirements/ recommendations for international students: required—TOEFL (minimum score 550 paper-based). Electronic applications accepted.

University of California, Irvine, School of Social Sciences, Department of Economics, Irvine, CA 92697. Offers economics (MA, PhD); public choice (MA, PhD); transportation economics (MA, PhD). *Students:* 110 full-time (35 women), 2 part-time (0 women); includes 22 minority (1 Black or African American, non-Hispanic/Latino; 11 Asian, non-Hispanic/Latino; 9 Hispanic/Latino; 1 Two or more races, non-Hispanic/Latino), 55 international. Average age 29. 228 applicants, 28% accepted, 28 enrolled. In 2019, 8 master's, 13 doctorates awarded. *Entrance requirements:* For master's and doctorate, GRE General Test, minimum GPA of 3.0. Additional exam requirements/ recommendations for international students: required—TOEFL (minimum score 550 paper-based). *Application deadline:* For fall admission, 1/15 priority date for domestic and international students. Applications are processed on a rolling basis. Application fee: $120 ($140 for international students). Electronic applications accepted. *Financial support:* Fellowships, research assistantships with full tuition reimbursements, teaching assistantships, institutionally sponsored loans, traineeships, health care benefits, and unspecified assistantships available. Financial award application deadline: 3/1; financial award applicants required to submit FAFSA. *Unit head:* William Branch, Chair, 949-824-4221, E-mail: wbranch@uci.edu. *Application contact:* Daniel Bogart, Director of Graduate Studies, 949-824-3191, E-mail: dbogart@uci.edu.
Website: http://www.economics.uci.edu/

University of California, Los Angeles, Graduate Division, College of Letters and Science, Department of Economics, Program in Economics, Los Angeles, CA 90095. Offers PhD.

University of California, Riverside, Graduate Division, Department of Economics, Riverside, CA 92521-0102. Offers MA, PhD. Terminal master's awarded for partial completion of doctoral program. *Degree requirements:* For master's, comprehensive exam; for doctorate, thesis/dissertation, qualifying exams. *Entrance requirements:* For master's and doctorate, GRE General Test, minimum GPA of 3.2. Additional exam requirements/recommendations for international students: required—TOEFL (minimum score 550 paper-based; 80 iBT). Electronic applications accepted.

University of California, San Diego, Graduate Division, Department of Economics, La Jolla, CA 92093. Offers PhD. *Students:* 126 full-time (48 women). 735 applicants, 12% accepted, 21 enrolled. In 2019, 17 doctorates awarded. *Degree requirements:* For doctorate, comprehensive exam, thesis/dissertation. *Entrance requirements:* For doctorate, GRE General Test, minimum GPA of 3.5, letters of recommendation, statement of purpose. Additional exam requirements/recommendations for international students: required—TOEFL (minimum score 550 paper-based; 80 iBT), IELTS (minimum score 7), PTE. *Application deadline:* For fall admission, 12/3 for domestic students. Application fee: $105 ($125 for international students). Electronic applications accepted. *Financial support:* Fellowships, research assistantships, teaching assistantships, and scholarships/grants available. Financial award applicants required to submit FAFSA. *Unit head:* Graham Elliot, Chair, 858-534-1055, E-mail: econchair@ucsd.edu. *Application contact:* Jessica Williams, Graduate Coordinator, E-mail: econ-phdadmissions@ucsd.edu.
Website: http://economics.ucsd.edu

University of California, Santa Barbara, Graduate Division, College of Letters and Sciences, Division of Social Sciences, Department of Economics, Santa Barbara, CA 93106-9210. Offers economics (MA); mathematical economics (PhD); public finance (PhD); MA/PhD. Terminal master's awarded for partial completion of doctoral program. *Degree requirements:* For master's, comprehensive exam; for doctorate, comprehensive exam, thesis/dissertation. *Entrance requirements:* For master's and doctorate, GRE General Test, 3 letters of recommendation, statement of purpose, personal achievements/contributions statement, resume/curriculum vitae, transcripts for post-secondary institutions attended. Additional exam requirements/recommendations for international students: required—TOEFL (minimum score 550 paper-based; 80 iBT), IELTS (minimum score 7), TOEFL (minimum score 600 paper-based or 100 iBT) for PhD. Electronic applications accepted.

University of California, Santa Barbara, Graduate Division, College of Letters and Sciences, Division of Social Sciences, Department of Global Studies, Santa Barbara, CA 93106-7065. Offers global culture, ideology, and religion (MA, PhD); global government, human rights, and civil society (MA, PhD); political economy, sustainable development, and the environment (MA, PhD). *Degree requirements:* For master's, one foreign language, thesis, 2 years of a second language; for doctorate, one foreign language, thesis/dissertation, reading proficiency in at least one language other than English. *Entrance requirements:* For master's, GRE, 2 years of a second language with minimum B grade in the final term, statement of purpose, resume or curriculum vitae, 3 letters of recommendation, transcripts (from all post-secondary institutions attended), writing sample (15-20 pages); for doctorate, GRE, statement of purpose, personal achievements/contributions statement, resume or curriculum vitae, 3 letters of recommendation, transcripts from all post-secondary institutions attended, writing sample (15-20 pages). Additional exam requirements/recommendations for international students: required—TOEFL (minimum score 600 paper-based; 94 iBT), IELTS (minimum score 7). Electronic applications accepted.

University of California, Santa Barbara, Graduate Division, Donald Bren School of Environmental Science and Management, Santa Barbara, CA 93106-5131. Offers economics and environmental science (PhD); environmental science and management (MESM, PhD); technology and society (PhD). *Degree requirements:* For master's, thesis; for doctorate, thesis/dissertation. *Entrance requirements:* For master's and doctorate, GRE. Additional exam requirements/recommendations for international students: required—TOEFL (minimum score 550 paper-based; 80 iBT), IELTS (minimum score 7). Electronic applications accepted.

University of California, Santa Cruz, Division of Graduate Studies, Division of Social Sciences, Program in International Economics, Santa Cruz, CA 95064. Offers PhD. *Degree requirements:* For doctorate, thesis/dissertation, 4 field exams, field papers, econometrics project, qualifying exams. *Entrance requirements:* For doctorate, GRE General Test. Additional exam requirements/recommendations for international students: required—TOEFL (minimum score 550 paper-based; 83 iBT); recommended—IELTS (minimum score 8). Electronic applications accepted.

University of Central Florida, College of Business Administration, Department of Economics, Orlando, FL 32816. Offers MS, PhD. *Program availability:* Part-time, evening/weekend. *Students:* 5 full-time (2 women), 1 international. Average age 24. 27 applicants, 44% accepted, 6 enrolled. In 2019, 5 master's awarded. *Degree requirements:* For master's, comprehensive exam, thesis or alternative. *Entrance requirements:* For master's, GMAT, minimum GPA of 3.0 in last 60 hours. Additional exam requirements/recommendations for international students: required—TOEFL. *Application deadline:* For fall admission, 6/15 priority date for domestic students; for spring admission, 11/1 priority date for domestic students. Application fee: $30. Electronic applications accepted. *Financial support:* In 2019–20, 4 students received support, including 4 teaching assistantships with partial tuition reimbursements available (averaging $5,227 per year); institutionally sponsored loans, tuition waivers (partial), and unspecified assistantships also available. Financial award application deadline: 3/1; financial award applicants required to submit FAFSA. *Unit head:* Dr. J. Wally Milon, Chair, 407-823-4429, E-mail: wally.milon@bus.ucf.edu. *Application contact:* Associate Director, Graduate Admissions, 407-823-2766, Fax: 407-823-6442, E-mail: gradadmissions@ucf.edu.
Website: http://web.bus.ucf.edu/economics/

University of Chicago, Booth School of Business, Full-Time MBA Program, Chicago, IL 60637. Offers accounting (MBA); analytic finance (MBA); analytic management (MBA); econometrics and statistics (MBA); economics (MBA); entrepreneurship (MBA); finance (MBA); general management (MBA); health administration and policy (Certificate); international business (MBA); managerial and organizational behavior (MBA); marketing analytics (MBA); marketing management (MBA); operations management (MBA); strategic management (MBA); MBA/AM; MBA/JD; MBA/MA; MBA/MD; MBA/MPP. *Accreditation:* AACSB. *Entrance requirements:* For master's, GMAT or GRE, transcripts, resume, 2 letters of recommendation, essays, interview. Additional exam requirements/

recommendations for international students: required—TOEFL, IELTS, or PTE. Electronic applications accepted. *Expenses:* Contact institution.

University of Chicago, Division of the Social Sciences, The Kenneth C. Griffin Department of Economics, Chicago, IL 60637. Offers PhD. *Degree requirements:* For doctorate, one foreign language, thesis/dissertation, written exams in 2 fields. *Entrance requirements:* For doctorate, GRE General Test, 3 letters of recommendation, statement of purpose, transcripts, resume or curriculum vitae, writing sample (dependent on department). Additional exam requirements/recommendations for international students: required—TOEFL (minimum score 104 iBT), IELTS (minimum score 7). Electronic applications accepted.

University of Cincinnati, Carl H. Lindner College of Business, PhD Programs, Cincinnati, OH 45221. Offers accounting (PhD); business analytics (PhD); economics (PhD); finance (PhD); information systems (PhD); management (PhD); marketing (PhD); operations and business analytics (PhD); operations research (PhD). *Faculty:* 76 full-time (19 women). *Students:* 4 full-time (3 women), 7 part-time (3 women), 8 international. Average age 28. 189 applicants, 10% accepted, 11 enrolled. In 2019, 7 doctorates awarded. *Degree requirements:* For doctorate, comprehensive exam, thesis/dissertation. *Entrance requirements:* For doctorate, GMAT, GRE, transcripts, essays, resume, letters of recommendation. Additional exam requirements/recommendations for international students: required—TOEFL (minimum score 600 paper-based; 100 iBT), IELTS (minimum score 7). *Application deadline:* For fall admission, 1/15 for domestic and international students. Application fee: $65 ($70 for international students). Electronic applications accepted. *Expenses:* Contact institution. *Financial support:* In 2019–20, 38 students received support, including 29 research assistantships with full tuition reimbursements available (averaging $23,250 per year); scholarships/grants, health care benefits, tuition waivers (full), and unspecified assistantships also available. Financial award application deadline: 1/15; financial award applicants required to submit FAFSA. *Unit head:* Dr. Olivier Parent, Director, 513-556-3941, Fax: 513-556-5499, E-mail: olivier.parent@uc.edu. *Application contact:* Patty Kerley, Special Project Coordinator, 513-556-7066, Fax: 513-558-7006, E-mail: patricia.kerley@uc.edu.
Website: http://business.uc.edu/graduate/phd.html

University of Colorado Boulder, Graduate School, College of Arts and Sciences, Department of Economics, Boulder, CO 80309. Offers MA, PhD. Terminal master's awarded for partial completion of doctoral program. *Degree requirements:* For master's, comprehensive exam, thesis or alternative; for doctorate, comprehensive exam, thesis/dissertation, preliminary exam. *Entrance requirements:* For master's, GRE General Test, minimum undergraduate GPA of 2.75; for doctorate, GRE General Test. Additional exam requirements/recommendations for international students: required—TOEFL. Electronic applications accepted. Application fee is waived when completed online.

University of Colorado Denver, Business School, Program in Finance, Denver, CO 80217. Offers economics (MS); finance (MS); financial analysis and management (MS); financial and commodities risk management (MS); risk management and insurance (MS). *Program availability:* Part-time, evening/weekend. *Degree requirements:* For master's, 30 semester hours (18 of required core courses, 9 of finance electives, and 3 of free elective). *Entrance requirements:* For master's, GMAT, essay, resume, two letters of recommendation; financial statements (for international students). Additional exam requirements/recommendations for international students: required—TOEFL (minimum score 537 paper-based; 75 iBT); recommended—IELTS (minimum score 6.5). Electronic applications accepted. *Expenses:* Contact institution.

University of Colorado Denver, College of Liberal Arts and Sciences, Department of Economics, Denver, CO 80217. Offers MA. *Program availability:* Part-time, evening/weekend. *Degree requirements:* For master's, thesis or alternative, 30 credit hours, including 21 of core courses and 9 of electives. *Entrance requirements:* For master's, GRE General Test, 15 hours of course work in economics, minimum GPA of 2.5, three letters of recommendation, calculus and statistics course. Additional exam requirements/recommendations for international students: required—TOEFL (minimum score 537 paper-based; 75 iBT); recommended—IELTS (minimum score 6.5). Electronic applications accepted. Tuition and fees vary according to course load, program and reciprocity agreements.

University of Connecticut, Graduate School, College of Liberal Arts and Sciences, Department of Economics, Storrs, CT 06269-1063. Offers MA, PhD. Terminal master's awarded for partial completion of doctoral program. *Degree requirements:* For master's, comprehensive exam; for doctorate, thesis/dissertation. *Entrance requirements:* For master's and doctorate, GRE General Test, GRE Subject Test. Additional exam requirements/recommendations for international students: required—TOEFL (minimum score 550 paper-based). Electronic applications accepted.

University of Delaware, Alfred Lerner College of Business and Economics, Department of Economics, Newark, DE 19716. Offers economic education (PhD); economics (MA, MS, PhD); economics for entrepreneurship and educators (MA); MA/MBA. *Program availability:* Part-time. *Degree requirements:* For master's, comprehensive exam, thesis (for some programs), mathematics review exam, research project; for doctorate, comprehensive exam, thesis/dissertation, field exam. *Entrance requirements:* For master's, GMAT or GRE General Test, minimum GPA of 2.5; for doctorate, GRE General Test, minimum GPA of 3.5 in graduate economics course work. Additional exam requirements/recommendations for international students: required—TOEFL (minimum score 550 paper-based). Electronic applications accepted.

University of Denver, Division of Arts, Humanities and Social Sciences, Department of Economics, Denver, CO 80208. Offers MA. *Program availability:* Part-time. *Faculty:* 9 full-time (2 women), 1 part-time/adjunct (0 women). *Students:* 1 full-time (0 women), 18 part-time (8 women); includes 2 minority (both Hispanic/Latino), 5 international. Average age 27. 50 applicants, 78% accepted, 10 enrolled. In 2019, 3 master's awarded. *Degree requirements:* For master's, thesis. *Entrance requirements:* For master's, GRE General Test, bachelor's degree with major or minor in economics, 20 quarter hours of economics coursework, or departmental waiver; transcripts; personal statement; three letters of recommendation. Additional exam requirements/recommendations for international students: required—TOEFL (minimum score 550 paper-based; 80 iBT). *Application deadline:* For fall admission, 2/15 priority date for domestic and international students; for winter admission, 12/3 for domestic and international students; for spring admission, 2/26 for domestic and international students. Applications are processed on a rolling basis. Application fee: $65. Electronic applications accepted. *Expenses:* Contact institution. *Financial support:* In 2019–20, 11 students received support, including 4 teaching assistantships with tuition reimbursements available (averaging $7,850 per year); career-related internships or fieldwork, Federal Work-Study, scholarships/grants, and unspecified assistantships also available. Support available to part-time students. Financial award application deadline: 2/15; financial award applicants required to submit FAFSA. *Unit head:* Dr. Yavuz Yasar, Associate Professor and Chair, 303-871-2244, E-mail: yavuz.yasar@du.edu. *Application contact:* Jamie Dinneen, Program Coordinator, 303-871-2243, E-mail: jamie.dinneen@du.edu.
Website: http://www.du.edu/ahss/economics

University of Detroit Mercy, College of Liberal Arts and Education, Detroit, MI 48221. Offers addiction counseling (MA); addiction studies (Certificate); clinical mental health counseling (MA); clinical psychology (MA, PhD); computer and information systems (MS); criminal justice (MA); curriculum and instruction (MA); economics (MA); educational administration (MA); financial economics (MA); industrial/organizational psychology (MA); information assurance (MS); intelligence analysis (MA); liberal studies (MALS); religious studies (MA); school counseling (MA, Certificate); school psychology (Spec); security administration (MS); special education: emotionally impaired/behaviorally disordered (MA); special education: learning disabilities (MA). *Program availability:* Part-time, evening/weekend. *Degree requirements:* For doctorate, departmental qualifying exam.

University of Florida, Graduate School, Warrington College of Business Administration, Hough Graduate School of Business, Department of Economics, Gainesville, FL 32611. Offers MA, PhD. Terminal master's awarded for partial completion of doctoral program. *Degree requirements:* For master's, thesis optional; for doctorate, comprehensive exam, thesis/dissertation. *Entrance requirements:* For master's and doctorate, GMAT (minimum score of 465) or GRE General Test, minimum GPA of 3.0. Additional exam requirements/recommendations for international students: required—TOEFL (minimum score 550 paper-based; 80 iBT), IELTS (minimum score 6). Electronic applications accepted.

University of Georgia, Terry College of Business, Department of Economics, Athens, GA 30602. Offers MA, PhD. *Degree requirements:* For master's, thesis; for doctorate, thesis/dissertation. *Entrance requirements:* For master's and doctorate, GRE General Test. Electronic applications accepted.

University of Guelph, Office of Graduate and Postdoctoral Studies, College of Management and Economics, Department of Economics, Guelph, ON N1G 2W1, Canada. Offers MA, PhD. *Program availability:* Part-time. *Degree requirements:* For master's, thesis or alternative; for doctorate, comprehensive exam, thesis/dissertation. *Entrance requirements:* For master's, minimum B+ average during previous 2 years of course work; for doctorate, minimum A- average, MA in economics. Additional exam requirements/recommendations for international students: required—TOEFL (minimum score 550 paper-based; 89 iBT), IELTS (minimum score 6.5). Electronic applications accepted.

University of Hawaii at Manoa, Office of Graduate Education, College of Social Sciences, Department of Economics, Honolulu, HI 96822. Offers MA, PhD. *Program availability:* Part-time. Terminal master's awarded for partial completion of doctoral program. *Degree requirements:* For master's, thesis optional; for doctorate, comprehensive exam, thesis/dissertation. *Entrance requirements:* For master's and doctorate, GRE General Test. Additional exam requirements/recommendations for international students: required—TOEFL (minimum score 500 paper-based; 61 iBT), IELTS (minimum score 5).

University of Houston, College of Liberal Arts and Social Sciences, Department of Economics, Houston, TX 77204. Offers applied economics (MA); economics (MA, PhD). Terminal master's awarded for partial completion of doctoral program. *Degree requirements:* For master's, thesis optional; for doctorate, comprehensive exam, thesis/dissertation. *Entrance requirements:* For master's and doctorate, GRE General Test, minimum GPA of 3.0, statement of purpose, three letters of recommendation. Additional exam requirements/recommendations for international students: required—TOEFL (minimum score 550 paper-based; 79 iBT), IELTS (minimum score 6.5). Electronic applications accepted.

University of Illinois at Chicago, College of Liberal Arts and Sciences, Department of Economics, Chicago, IL 60607-7128. Offers MA, PhD, MBA/MA. Terminal master's awarded for partial completion of doctoral program. *Degree requirements:* For master's, comprehensive exam; for doctorate, thesis/dissertation. *Entrance requirements:* For master's and doctorate, GRE General Test, minimum GPA of 2.75. Additional exam requirements/recommendations for international students: required—TOEFL. Electronic applications accepted.

University of Illinois at Urbana-Champaign, Graduate College, College of Liberal Arts and Sciences, Department of Economics, Champaign, IL 61820. Offers economics (MS, PhD); policy economics (MS). Terminal master's awarded for partial completion of doctoral program.

The University of Iowa, Tippie College of Business, Department of Economics, Iowa City, IA 52242-1316. Offers PhD. *Degree requirements:* For doctorate, comprehensive exam, thesis/dissertation. *Entrance requirements:* For doctorate, GRE General Test. Additional exam requirements/recommendations for international students: required—TOEFL (minimum score 100 iBT). Electronic applications accepted.

The University of Kansas, Graduate Studies, College of Liberal Arts and Sciences, Department of Economics, Lawrence, KS 66045. Offers MA, PhD, JD/MA. *Program availability:* Part-time. *Students:* 51 full-time (13 women), 2 part-time (0 women), 44 international. Average age 28. 74 applicants, 57% accepted, 15 enrolled. In 2019, 20 master's, 11 doctorates awarded. Terminal master's awarded for partial completion of doctoral program. *Entrance requirements:* For master's and doctorate, statement of personal goals, resume or curriculum vitae, official transcripts, three letters of recommendation. Additional exam requirements/recommendations for international students: required—TOEFL, IELTS. *Application deadline:* For fall admission, 2/1 priority date for domestic and international students; for spring admission, 11/1 priority date for domestic and international students; for summer admission, 5/1 for domestic and international students. Application fee: $65 ($85 for international students). Electronic applications accepted. *Expenses:* Tuition, state resident: full-time $9989. Tuition, nonresident: full-time $23,950. *International tuition:* $23,950 full-time. *Required fees:* $984; $81.99 per credit hour. Tuition and fees vary according to course load, campus/location and program. *Financial support:* Fellowships, research assistantships, teaching assistantships, institutionally sponsored loans, scholarships/grants, health care benefits, and unspecified assistantships available. Financial award application deadline: 2/1. *Unit head:* Milena Stanislavova, Chair, 785-864-5255, E-mail: stanis@ku.edu. *Application contact:* Kate Pleskac, Graduate Admissions Contact, 785-864-6653, E-mail: kate.pleskac@ku.edu.
Website: http://www.economics.ku.edu/

University of Kentucky, Graduate School, Gatton College of Business and Economics, Program in Economics, Lexington, KY 40506-0032. Offers MS, PhD. *Degree requirements:* For master's, comprehensive exam; for doctorate, comprehensive exam, thesis/dissertation. *Entrance requirements:* For master's, GMAT, minimum undergraduate GPA of 2.75; for doctorate, GMAT, minimum undergraduate GPA of 3.0. Additional exam requirements/recommendations for international students: required—TOEFL (minimum score 550 paper-based). Electronic applications accepted.

University of Lethbridge, School of Graduate Studies, Lethbridge, AB T1K 3M4, Canada. Offers addictions counseling (M Sc); agricultural biotechnology (M Sc); agricultural studies (M Sc, MA); anthropology (MA); archaeology (M Sc, MA); art (MA, MFA); biochemistry (M Sc); biological sciences (M Sc); biomolecular science (PhD); biosystems and biodiversity (PhD); Canadian studies (MA); chemistry (M Sc); computer science (M Sc); computer science and geographical information science (M Sc); counseling (MC); counseling psychology (M Ed); dramatic arts (MA); earth, space, and physical science (PhD); economics (MA); education (MA, PhD); educational leadership (M Ed); English (MA); environmental science (M Sc); evolution and behavior (PhD);

exercise science (M Sc); French (MA); French/German (MA); French/Spanish (MA); general education (M Ed); geography (M Sc, MA); German (MA); health sciences (M Sc); individualized multidisciplinary (M Sc, MA); kinesiology (M Sc, MA); management (M Sc), including accounting, finance, human resource management and labor relations, information systems, international management, marketing, policy and strategy; mathematics (M Sc); music (M Mus, MA); Native American studies (MA); neuroscience (M Sc, PhD); new media (MA, MFA); nursing (M Sc, MN); philosophy (MA); physics (M Sc); political science (MA); psychology (M Sc, MA); religious studies (MA); sociology (MA); theatre and dramatic arts (MFA); theoretical and computational science (PhD); urban and regional studies (MA); women and gender studies (MA). *Program availability:* Part-time, evening/weekend. *Degree requirements:* For master's, thesis (for some programs); for doctorate, comprehensive exam, thesis/dissertation. *Entrance requirements:* For master's, GMAT (for M Sc in management), bachelor's degree in related field, minimum GPA of 3.0 during previous 20 graded semester courses, 2 years' teaching or related experience (M Ed); for doctorate, master's degree, minimum graduate GPA of 3.5. Additional exam requirements/recommendations for international students: required—TOEFL (minimum score 580 paper-based; 93 iBT). Electronic applications accepted.

University of Maine, Graduate School, College of Natural Sciences, Forestry, and Agriculture, School of Economics, Orono, ME 04469. Offers economics (MA); financial economics (MA); resource economics and policy (MS). *Program availability:* Part-time. *Faculty:* 12 full-time (4 women), 2 part-time/adjunct (0 women). *Students:* 14 full-time (6 women), 1 part-time (0 women); includes 1 minority (Hispanic/Latino), 3 international. Average age 26. 22 applicants, 55% accepted, 6 enrolled. In 2019, 14 master's awarded. *Degree requirements:* For master's, thesis (for some programs). *Entrance requirements:* For master's, GRE General Test. Additional exam requirements/recommendations for international students: required—TOEFL (minimum score 580 paper-based; 92 iBT), IELTS (minimum score 6.9). *Application deadline:* For spring admission, 1/30 for domestic and international students. Applications are processed on a rolling basis. Application fee: $65. Electronic applications accepted. *Expenses:* Tuition, area resident: Full-time $8100; part-time $450 per credit hour. Tuition, state resident: full-time $8100; part-time $450 per credit hour. Tuition, nonresident: full-time $26,388; part-time $1466 per credit hour. *International tuition:* $26,388 full-time. *Required fees:* $1257; $278 per semester. Tuition and fees vary according to course load. *Financial support:* In 2019–20, 20 students received support, including 15 research assistantships with full tuition reimbursements available (averaging $15,000 per year), 5 teaching assistantships with full tuition reimbursements available (averaging $15,825 per year); career-related internships or fieldwork, Federal Work-Study, institutionally sponsored loans, scholarships/grants, and tuition waivers (full and partial) also available. Support available to part-time students. Financial award application deadline: 3/1; financial award applicants required to submit FAFSA. *Unit head:* Dr. Mario Teisl, Director, 207-581-3151, Fax: 207-581-4278. *Application contact:* Scott G. Delcourt, Assistant Vice President for Graduate Studies and Senior Associate Dean, 207-581-3291, Fax: 207-581-3232, E-mail: graduate@maine.edu.
Website: http://umaine.edu/soe/

University of Manitoba, Faculty of Graduate Studies, Faculty of Arts, Department of Economics, Winnipeg, MB R3T 2N2, Canada. Offers MA, PhD. *Degree requirements:* For master's, thesis or alternative; for doctorate, one foreign language, thesis/dissertation.

University of Maryland, Baltimore County, The Graduate School, College of Arts, Humanities and Social Sciences, Program in Economic Policy Analysis, Baltimore, MD 21250. Offers MA. *Program availability:* Part-time. *Faculty:* 17 full-time (6 women), 4 part-time/adjunct (2 women). *Students:* 5 full-time (1 woman), 7 part-time (3 women); includes 2 minority (1 Black or African American, non-Hispanic/Latino; 1 Hispanic/Latino), 3 international. Average age 29. 14 applicants, 64% accepted, 4 enrolled. In 2019, 4 master's awarded. *Degree requirements:* For master's, comprehensive exam, capstone research project. *Entrance requirements:* For master's, GRE General Test, undergraduate coursework in economic theory, econometrics, and calculus; letters of reference; statement of purpose; transcripts. Additional exam requirements/recommendations for international students: required—TOEFL (minimum score 80 iBT). *Application deadline:* For fall admission, 7/1 priority date for domestic students, 3/1 priority date for international students; for spring admission, 1/1 priority date for domestic students, 9/15 priority date for international students. Applications are processed on a rolling basis. Application fee: $45. Electronic applications accepted. *Expenses:* $14,382 per year. *Financial support:* In 2019–20, 5 students received support, including 5 research assistantships with tuition reimbursements available (averaging $12,560 per year), teaching assistantships with partial tuition reimbursements available (averaging $6,500 per year); Federal Work-Study, health care benefits, tuition waivers (full and partial), and unspecified assistantships also available. Support available to part-time students. Financial award application deadline: 4/15; financial award applicants required to submit FAFSA. *Unit head:* Dr. David F. Mitch, Chair, 410-455-2157, Fax: 410-455-1054, E-mail: mitch@umbc.edu. *Application contact:* Dr. Tim H. Gindling, Graduate Program Director, 410-455-3629, Fax: 410-455-1054, E-mail: econ-masters@umbc.edu.
Website: http://www.umbc.edu/economics/grad_intro.html

University of Maryland, Baltimore County, The Graduate School, College of Arts, Humanities and Social Sciences, School of Public Policy, Baltimore, MD 21250. Offers public policy (MPP, PhD), including economics (PhD), educational policy, emergency services (PhD), environmental policy (MPP), evaluation and analytical methods, health policy, policy history (PhD), public management, urban policy. *Program availability:* Part-time, evening/weekend. *Faculty:* 10 full-time (5 women). *Students:* 49 full-time (29 women), 63 part-time (31 women); includes 39 minority (18 Black or African American, non-Hispanic/Latino; 1 American Indian or Alaska Native, non-Hispanic/Latino; 9 Asian, non-Hispanic/Latino; 9 Hispanic/Latino; 2 Two or more races, non-Hispanic/Latino), 10 international. Average age 36. 73 applicants, 74% accepted, 31 enrolled. In 2019, 17 master's, 8 doctorates awarded. Terminal master's awarded for partial completion of doctoral program. *Degree requirements:* For master's, thesis, policy analysis paper, internship for pre-service; for doctorate, comprehensive exam, thesis/dissertation, comprehensive and field qualifying exams. *Entrance requirements:* For master's, GRE General Test, 3 academic letters of reference, resume, official transcripts; for doctorate, GRE General Test, 3 academic letters of reference, resume, research paper, official transcripts. Additional exam requirements/recommendations for international students: required—TOEFL (minimum score 550 paper-based; 80 iBT), IELTS (minimum score 6.5). *Application deadline:* For fall admission, 1/15 priority date for domestic students, 1/1 priority date for international students; for spring admission, 11/1 priority date for domestic students, 5/1 priority date for international students. Applications are processed on a rolling basis. Application fee: $50. Electronic applications accepted. *Expenses:* $14,382 per year. *Financial support:* In 2019–20, 26 students received support, including 23 research assistantships with full tuition reimbursements available (averaging $20,000 per year), 3 teaching assistantships; Federal Work-Study, scholarships/grants, health care benefits, and unspecified assistantships also available. Financial award application deadline: 1/1; financial award applicants required to submit FAFSA. *Unit head:* Dr. Susan Sterett, Director, 410-455-2140, Fax: 410-455-1172, E-mail: ssterett@umbc.edu. *Application contact:* Shelley Morris, Administrator of Academic Affairs, 410-455-3202, Fax: 410-455-1172, E-mail: shelleym@umbc.edu.
Website: http://publicpolicy.umbc.edu/

University of Maryland, College Park, Academic Affairs, College of Behavioral and Social Sciences, Department of Economics, College Park, MD 20742. Offers MA, PhD. *Program availability:* Part-time, evening/weekend. Terminal master's awarded for partial completion of doctoral program. *Degree requirements:* For master's, comprehensive exam, thesis optional; for doctorate, comprehensive exam, thesis/dissertation, exams. *Entrance requirements:* For master's, GRE General Test, minimum GPA of 3.0, course work in calculus and mathematics, 3 letters of recommendation; for doctorate, GRE General Test, calculus background. Additional exam requirements/recommendations for international students: required—TOEFL. Electronic applications accepted.

University of Maryland, College Park, Academic Affairs, College of Behavioral and Social Sciences, Department of Government and Politics, College Park, MD 20742. Offers American politics (PhD); comparative politics (PhD); international relations (PhD); political economy (PhD); political theory (PhD). *Program availability:* Part-time, evening/weekend. *Degree requirements:* For doctorate, comprehensive exam, thesis/dissertation, written exams in 2 fields. *Entrance requirements:* For doctorate, GRE General Test, minimum GPA of 3.5, writing sample. Additional exam requirements/recommendations for international students: required—TOEFL. Electronic applications accepted.

University of Massachusetts Amherst, Graduate School, College of Social and Behavioral Sciences, Department of Economics, Amherst, MA 01003. Offers MA, PhD. *Program availability:* Part-time. Terminal master's awarded for partial completion of doctoral program. *Degree requirements:* For master's, thesis or alternative; for doctorate, comprehensive exam, thesis/dissertation. *Entrance requirements:* For master's and doctorate, GRE General Test. Additional exam requirements/recommendations for international students: required—TOEFL (minimum score 550 paper-based; 80 iBT), IELTS (minimum score 6.5). Electronic applications accepted.

University of Massachusetts Lowell, College of Fine Arts, Humanities and Social Sciences, Program in Regional Economic and Social Development, Lowell, MA 01854. Offers MA, Graduate Certificate. *Program availability:* Part-time. *Entrance requirements:* For master's, GRE. Electronic applications accepted.

University of Memphis, Graduate School, Fogelman College of Business and Economics, Department of Economics, Memphis, TN 38152. Offers MA, PhD. *Program availability:* Part-time. *Students:* 7 full-time (1 woman), 2 part-time (0 women); includes 3 minority (1 Black or African American, non-Hispanic/Latino; 1 Asian, non-Hispanic/Latino; 1 Hispanic/Latino). Average age 28. 4 applicants, 75% accepted, 2 enrolled. In 2019, 3 master's awarded. Terminal master's awarded for partial completion of doctoral program. *Degree requirements:* For master's, comprehensive exam, thesis or alternative; for doctorate, comprehensive exam, thesis/dissertation, paper presentation. *Entrance requirements:* For master's, GMAT or GRE General Test, previous course work in statistics, intermediate micro and macro theory; one semester of calculus and statistics and matrix or linear algebra; for doctorate, GMAT or GRE, two letters of reference, personal statement, curriculum vitae, interview, minimum GPA of 3.4. Additional exam requirements/recommendations for international students: required—TOEFL (minimum score 550 paper-based; 79 iBT). *Application deadline:* For fall admission, 8/1 for domestic students; for spring admission, 12/1 for domestic students. Application fee: $35 ($60 for international students). Electronic applications accepted. *Expenses:* Tuition, area resident: Full-time $9216; part-time $512 per credit hour. Tuition, state resident: full-time $9216; part-time $512 per credit hour. Tuition, nonresident: full-time $12,672; part-time $704 per credit hour. *International tuition:* $16,128 full-time. *Required fees:* $1530; $85 per credit hour. Tuition and fees vary according to program. *Financial support:* Research assistantships with full tuition reimbursements, teaching assistantships with full tuition reimbursements, Federal Work-Study, scholarships/grants, and unspecified assistantships available. Financial award application deadline: 2/1; financial award applicants required to submit FAFSA. *Unit head:* Dr. William Smith, Chair, 901-678-2785, E-mail: wtsmith@memphis.edu. *Application contact:* Dr. William Smith, Chair, 901-678-2785, E-mail: wtsmith@memphis.edu.
Website: https://www.memphis.edu/economics/

University of Memphis, Graduate School, Fogelman College of Business and Economics, Program in Business Administration, Memphis, TN 38152. Offers accounting (MBA, PhD); business administration (IMBA); economics (PhD); executive business administration (MBA); finance (PhD); management (PhD); marketing (MS); marketing and supply chain management (PhD); real estate development (MS); JD/MBA. *Accreditation:* AACSB. *Students:* 193 full-time (90 women), 402 part-time (160 women); includes 205 minority (97 Black or African American, non-Hispanic/Latino; 2 American Indian or Alaska Native, non-Hispanic/Latino; 83 Asian, non-Hispanic/Latino; 15 Hispanic/Latino; 1 Native Hawaiian or other Pacific Islander, non-Hispanic/Latino; 7 Two or more races, non-Hispanic/Latino), 121 international. Average age 32. 306 applicants, 82% accepted, 136 enrolled. In 2019, 199 master's, 3 doctorates awarded. *Degree requirements:* For master's, comprehensive exam; for doctorate, comprehensive exam, thesis/dissertation. *Entrance requirements:* For master's, GMAT, resume; for doctorate, GMAT, interview, minimum GPA of 3.4, resume, letter of recommendation. Additional exam requirements/recommendations for international students: required—TOEFL (minimum score 550 paper-based). *Application deadline:* For fall admission, 8/1 for domestic students; for spring admission, 12/1 for domestic students. Application fee: $35 ($60 for international students). *Expenses:* Tuition, area resident: Full-time $9216; part-time $512 per credit hour. Tuition, state resident: full-time $9216; part-time $512 per credit hour. Tuition, nonresident: full-time $12,672; part-time $704 per credit hour. *International tuition:* $16,128 full-time. *Required fees:* $1530; $85 per credit hour. Tuition and fees vary according to program. *Financial support:* Research assistantships with full tuition reimbursements, teaching assistantships with full tuition reimbursements, career-related internships or fieldwork, Federal Work-Study, scholarships/grants, and unspecified assistantships available. Financial award application deadline: 2/15; financial award applicants required to submit FAFSA. *Unit head:* Dr. Balaji Krishnan, Director, MBA Programs, 901-678-2786, E-mail: krishnan@memphis.edu. *Application contact:* Dr. Balaji Krishnan, Director, MBA Programs, 901-678-2786, E-mail: krishnan@memphis.edu.
Website: https://www.memphis.edu/mba/index.php

University of Miami, Miami Business School, Coral Gables, FL 33146. Offers accounting (M Acc); business (PhD); business administration (MBA); business analytics (MSBA); economics (PhD); finance (MSF); health administration (MHA); international business (MIBS); real estate (MBA); taxation (MS Tax); JD/MBA; MD/MBA. *Accreditation:* AACSB; CAHME (one or more programs are accredited). *Program availability:* Part-time, evening/weekend, 100% online, blended/hybrid learning. Terminal master's awarded for partial completion of doctoral program. *Degree requirements:* For master's, comprehensive exam; for doctorate, comprehensive exam, thesis/dissertation. *Entrance requirements:* For master's, GMAT or GRE; for doctorate, GRE General Test. Additional exam requirements/recommendations for international students: required—TOEFL (minimum score 94 iBT), IELTS (minimum score 7), TOEFL (minimum score 587 paper-based, 94 iBT) or IELTS (7). Electronic applications accepted. *Expenses:* Contact institution.

Economics

University of Michigan, Rackham Graduate School, College of Literature, Science, and the Arts, Department of Economics, Ann Arbor, MI 48109. Offers applied economics (AM); economics (AM, PhD); public policy and economics (PhD); social work and economics (PhD); JD/PhD; MPP/AM. Terminal master's awarded for partial completion of doctoral program. *Degree requirements:* For doctorate, comprehensive exam, thesis/dissertation, oral defense of dissertation; preliminary exams in microeconomics, macroeconomics, and 2 fields. *Entrance requirements:* For master's and doctorate, GRE General Test. Additional exam requirements/recommendations for international students: required—TOEFL (minimum score 600 paper-based; 100 iBT). Electronic applications accepted.

University of Michigan, School of Social Work, Interdisciplinary PhD Program in Social Work and Social Science, Ann Arbor, MI 48109. Offers social work and anthropology (PhD); social work and economics (PhD); social work and political science (PhD); social work and psychology (PhD); social work and sociology (PhD). *Degree requirements:* For doctorate, thesis/dissertation, oral defense of dissertation, preliminary exam. *Entrance requirements:* For doctorate, GRE General Test. Additional exam requirements/recommendations for international students: required—TOEFL (minimum score 620 paper-based, 88 iBT) or IELTS. Electronic applications accepted. *Expenses:* Contact institution.

University of Minnesota, Twin Cities Campus, Graduate School, College of Liberal Arts, Department of Economics, Minneapolis, MN 55455. Offers MA, PhD. *Faculty:* 19 full-time (3 women), 6 part-time/adjunct (3 women). *Students:* 119 full-time (27 women), 1 part-time; includes 9 minority (5 Asian, non-Hispanic/Latino; 3 Hispanic/Latino; 1 Two or more races, non-Hispanic/Latino), 83 international. Average age 25. 360 applicants, 19% accepted, 26 enrolled. In 2019, 21 master's, 21 doctorates awarded. Terminal master's awarded for partial completion of doctoral program. *Degree requirements:* For master's, comprehensive exam; for doctorate, comprehensive exam, thesis/dissertation, preliminary written and oral exams. *Entrance requirements:* For doctorate, GRE General Test. Additional exam requirements/recommendations for international students: required—TOEFL (minimum score 100 iBT), IELTS (minimum score 7). *Application deadline:* For fall admission, 12/12 priority date for domestic and international students. Application fee: $75 ($95 for international students). Electronic applications accepted. *Financial support:* In 2019–20, 90 students received support, including 13 fellowships with full tuition reimbursements available (averaging $24,000 per year), 4 research assistantships with full tuition reimbursements available (averaging $18,600 per year), 73 teaching assistantships with full tuition reimbursements available (averaging $18,600 per year); scholarships/grants, health care benefits, and unspecified assistantships also available. Financial award application deadline: 12/12. *Unit head:* Prof. Christopher Phelan, Chair, 612-625-6353, Fax: 612-624-0209, E-mail: cphelan@umn.edu. *Application contact:* Prof. Timothy Kehoe, Director of Graduate Studies, 612-625-1589, Fax: 612-624-0209, E-mail: econdgs@umn.edu.
Website: https://cla.umn.edu/economics

University of Mississippi, Graduate School, College of Liberal Arts, University, MS 38677. Offers anthropology (MA); biology (MS, PhD); chemistry (MS, DA, PhD); creative writing (MFA); documentary expression (MFA); economics (MA, PhD); English (MA, PhD); experimental psychology (PhD); history (MA, PhD); mathematics (MS, PhD); modern languages (MA); music (MM); philosophy (MA); physics (MA, MS, PhD); political science (MA, PhD); Southern studies (MA); studio art (MFA). *Program availability:* Part-time. *Faculty:* 481 full-time (215 women), 71 part-time/adjunct (40 women). *Students:* 509 full-time (258 women), 55 part-time (21 women); includes 89 minority (40 Black or African American, non-Hispanic/Latino; 13 Asian, non-Hispanic/Latino; 25 Hispanic/Latino; 11 Two or more races, non-Hispanic/Latino), 157 international. Average age 29. In 2019, 119 master's, 51 doctorates awarded. *Degree requirements:* For doctorate, thesis/dissertation. *Entrance requirements:* For master's, GRE General Test, minimum GPA of 3.0; for doctorate, GRE General Test. Additional exam requirements/recommendations for international students: required—TOEFL. *Application deadline:* Applications are processed on a rolling basis. Application fee: $50. Electronic applications accepted. *Expenses:* Tuition, state resident: full-time $8718; part-time $484.25 per credit hour. Tuition, nonresident: full-time $24,990; part-time $1388.25 per credit hour. *Required fees:* $100; $4.16 per credit hour. *Financial support:* Fellowships, research assistantships, teaching assistantships, career-related internships or fieldwork, Federal Work-Study, institutionally sponsored loans, scholarships/grants, and unspecified assistantships available. Financial award application deadline: 3/1; financial award applicants required to submit FAFSA. *Unit head:* Dr. Lee Michael Cohen, Dean, 662-915-7177, Fax: 662-915-5792, E-mail: libarts@olemiss.edu. *Application contact:* Tameka Smith, Graduate Activities Specialist for Admissions, 662-915-7474, Fax: 662-915-7577, E-mail: gschool@olemiss.edu.
Website: ventress@olemiss.edu

University of Missouri, Office of Research and Graduate Studies, College of Arts and Science, Department of Economics, Columbia, MO 65211. Offers MA, PhD. Terminal master's awarded for partial completion of doctoral program. *Entrance requirements:* For master's, GRE General Test (minimum score 700 quantitative, 400 verbal), minimum GPA of 3.0; bachelor's degree in any field; for doctorate, GRE General Test (minimum score 700 quantitative, 400 verbal), minimum GPA of 3.0.

University of Missouri–Kansas City, College of Arts and Sciences, Department of Economics, Kansas City, MO 64110-2499. Offers MA, PhD. *Program availability:* Part-time, evening/weekend. *Degree requirements:* For doctorate, comprehensive exam, thesis/dissertation. *Entrance requirements:* For master's, GRE or minimum undergraduate GPA of 2.5; for doctorate, GRE, master's degree in economics or equivalent. Additional exam requirements/recommendations for international students: required—TOEFL (minimum score 550 paper-based; 80 iBT). Electronic applications accepted.

University of Missouri–St. Louis, College of Arts and Sciences, Department of Economics, St. Louis, MO 63121. Offers MA. *Program availability:* Part-time, evening/weekend. *Entrance requirements:* For master's, GRE General Test, 2 letters of recommendation. Additional exam requirements/recommendations for international students: required—TOEFL (minimum score 550 paper-based; 79 iBT), IELTS (minimum score 6.5). Electronic applications accepted. *Expenses: Tuition, area resident:* Full-time $9005.40; part-time $6003.60 per credit hour. Tuition, state resident: full-time $9005.40; part-time $6003.60 per credit hour. Tuition, nonresident: full-time $22,108; part-time $14,738.40 per credit hour. *International tuition:* $22,108 full-time. Tuition and fees vary according to course load.

University of Montana, Graduate School, College of Humanities and Sciences, Department of Economics, Missoula, MT 59812. Offers MA. *Degree requirements:* For master's, thesis. *Entrance requirements:* For master's, GRE General Test. Additional exam requirements/recommendations for international students: required—TOEFL (minimum score 525 paper-based).

University of Nebraska at Omaha, Graduate Studies, College of Business Administration, Department of Economics, Omaha, NE 68182. Offers MA, MS. *Program availability:* Part-time, evening/weekend. *Degree requirements:* For master's, comprehensive exam, thesis (for some programs). *Entrance requirements:* For master's, minimum GPA of 2.7, official transcripts. Additional exam requirements/recommendations for international students: required—TOEFL, IELTS, PTE. Electronic applications accepted.

University of Nebraska–Lincoln, Graduate College, College of Business Administration, Department of Economics, Lincoln, NE 68588. Offers MA, PhD, JD/MA. *Degree requirements:* For master's, thesis optional; for doctorate, comprehensive exam, thesis/dissertation. *Entrance requirements:* For master's and doctorate, GRE General Test. Additional exam requirements/recommendations for international students: required—TOEFL (minimum score 550 paper-based). Electronic applications accepted.

University of Nevada, Las Vegas, Graduate College, Lee Business School, Department of Economics, Las Vegas, NV 89154-6005. Offers applied economics (MA); economics/mathematical science (MA/MS); MA/MS. *Program availability:* Part-time. *Faculty:* 9 full-time (1 woman), 2 part-time/adjunct (0 women). *Students:* 10 full-time (3 women), 6 part-time (1 woman); includes 7 minority (1 Asian, non-Hispanic/Latino; 6 Hispanic/Latino), 3 international. Average age 31. 12 applicants, 67% accepted, 5 enrolled. In 2019, 8 master's awarded. *Degree requirements:* For master's, thesis optional, oral defense of thesis; internship. *Entrance requirements:* For master's, GRE General Test or GMAT, bachelor's degree with minimum GPA 3.0. Additional exam requirements/recommendations for international students: required—TOEFL (minimum score 550 paper-based; 80 iBT), IELTS (minimum score 7). *Application deadline:* For fall admission, 6/15 for domestic students, 5/1 for international students; for spring admission, 11/15 for domestic students, 10/1 for international students. Application fee: $60 ($95 for international students). Electronic applications accepted. *Expenses:* Contact institution. *Financial support:* In 2019–20, 9 students received support, including 1 research assistantship with full tuition reimbursement available (averaging $11,250 per year), 6 teaching assistantships with full tuition reimbursements available (averaging $11,250 per year); institutionally sponsored loans, scholarships/grants, health care benefits, and unspecified assistantships also available. Financial award application deadline: 3/15; financial award applicants required to submit FAFSA. *Unit head:* Dr. Jeff Waddoups, Chair/Professor, 702-895-3497, Fax: 702-895-1354, E-mail: economics.chair@unlv.edu. *Application contact:* Dr. Ian McDonough, Graduate Coordinator, 702-895-3651, Fax: 702-895-3606, E-mail: economics.gradcoord@unlv.edu.
Website: https://www.unlv.edu/economics

University of Nevada, Reno, Graduate School, College of Business, Department of Economics, Reno, NV 89557. Offers MA, MS. *Degree requirements:* For master's, thesis. *Entrance requirements:* For master's, GMAT or GRE, minimum GPA of 2.75. Additional exam requirements/recommendations for international students: required—TOEFL (minimum score 500 paper-based; 61 iBT), IELTS (minimum score 6). Electronic applications accepted.

University of New Hampshire, Graduate School, Peter T. Paul College of Business and Economics, Department of Economics, Durham, NH 03824. Offers MA, PhD. *Program availability:* Part-time. *Students:* 19 full-time (9 women), 1 part-time (0 women), 12 international. Average age 28. 9 applicants, 11% accepted. In 2019, 5 master's awarded. Terminal master's awarded for partial completion of doctoral program. *Entrance requirements:* For master's and doctorate, GRE General Test. Additional exam requirements/recommendations for international students: required—TOEFL (minimum score 550 paper-based; 80 iBT), IELTS, PTE. *Application deadline:* For fall admission, 4/15 for domestic students. Application fee: $65. Electronic applications accepted. *Financial support:* In 2019–20, 18 students received support, including 1 fellowship, 2 research assistantships, 12 teaching assistantships; career-related internships or fieldwork, Federal Work-Study, scholarships/grants, and tuition waivers (full and partial) also available. Support available to part-time students. Financial award application deadline: 2/15. *Unit head:* Bruce Elmslie, Chair, 603-862-3347. *Application contact:* Tara Hunter, Administrative Assistant, 603-862-3326, E-mail: tara.hunter@unh.edu.
Website: https://paulcollege.unh.edu/economics

University of New Mexico, Graduate Studies, College of Arts and Sciences, Program in Economics, Albuquerque, NM 87131-2039. Offers econometrics (MA); economic theory (MA); environmental/natural resource economics (MA, PhD); international/development and sustainability economics (MA, PhD); public economics (MA, PhD). *Program availability:* Part-time. Terminal master's awarded for partial completion of doctoral program. *Degree requirements:* For master's, comprehensive exam, thesis (for some programs); for doctorate, comprehensive exam, thesis/dissertation. *Entrance requirements:* For master's and doctorate, GRE General Test, 3 letters of recommendation, letter of intent, curriculum vitae. Additional exam requirements/recommendations for international students: required—TOEFL (minimum score 520 paper-based; 68 iBT). Electronic applications accepted. *Expenses:* Tuition, state resident: full-time $7633; part-time $972 per year. Tuition, nonresident: full-time $22,586; part-time $3840 per year. *International tuition:* $23,292 full-time. *Required fees:* $8608. Tuition and fees vary according to course level, course load, degree level, program and student level.

University of New Orleans, Graduate School, College of Business Administration, Department of Economics and Finance, Program in Financial Economics, New Orleans, LA 70148. Offers PhD. Terminal master's awarded for partial completion of doctoral program. *Degree requirements:* For doctorate, one foreign language, comprehensive exam, thesis/dissertation, general exams. *Entrance requirements:* For doctorate, GRE General Test, minimum GPA of 3.0. Additional exam requirements/recommendations for international students: required—TOEFL (minimum score 550 paper-based; 79 iBT). Electronic applications accepted.

The University of North Carolina at Chapel Hill, Graduate School, College of Arts and Sciences, Department of Economics, Chapel Hill, NC 27599. Offers MS, PhD. Terminal master's awarded for partial completion of doctoral program. *Degree requirements:* For master's, comprehensive exam, thesis or alternative; for doctorate, comprehensive exam, thesis/dissertation. *Entrance requirements:* For master's, GRE General Test, minimum GPA of 3.0; for doctorate, GRE General Test, minimum GPA of 3.5. Additional exam requirements/recommendations for international students: required—TOEFL (minimum score 550 paper-based). Electronic applications accepted.

The University of North Carolina at Charlotte, Belk College of Business, Department of Economics, Charlotte, NC 28223-0001. Offers applied econometrics (Graduate Certificate); economics (MS). *Program availability:* Part-time, evening/weekend. *Faculty:* 18 full-time (7 women). *Students:* 22 full-time (6 women), 15 part-time (4 women); includes 13 minority (5 Black or African American, non-Hispanic/Latino; 3 Asian, non-Hispanic/Latino; 4 Hispanic/Latino; 1 Two or more races, non-Hispanic/Latino), 10 international. Average age 27. 31 applicants, 97% accepted, 16 enrolled. In 2019, 21 master's, 5 other advanced degrees awarded. *Degree requirements:* For master's, comprehensive exam (for some programs). *Entrance requirements:* For master's, GRE General Test, GMAT, overall GPA of at least 3.0; undergraduate coursework that includes calculus, econometrics (or equivalent), intermediate macroeconomic theory, intermediate microeconomic theory; statement of purpose; three letters of recommendations; resume; transcripts for work attempted beyond high school; for Graduate Certificate, bachelor's degree, or its equivalent, from regionally-accredited college or university; minimum GPA of 2.75 on all previous work completed beyond high school (secondary school); statement of purpose; unofficial transcripts of all college course work; satisfactory scores on TOEFL (if applicable). Additional exam requirements/recommendations for international students: required—TOEFL (minimum score 557 paper-based; 83 iBT), IELTS (minimum score 6.5), TOEFL (minimum score 557 paper-based, 83 iBT) or IELTS (6.5). *Application deadline:* For fall admission, 3/1 for domestic students; for spring admission, 10/1 for domestic students. Applications are processed on a rolling basis. Application fee: $75. Electronic applications accepted. *Expenses:* Contact institution. *Financial support:* Career-related internships or fieldwork, institutionally sponsored loans, scholarships/grants, and unspecified assistantships available. Support available to part-time students. Financial award application deadline: 3/1; financial award applicants required to submit FAFSA. *Unit head:* Dr. Artie Zillante, Department Chair, 704-687-5375, Fax: 704-687-7589, E-mail: azillant@uncc.edu. *Application contact:* Kathy B. Giddings, Director of Graduate Admissions, 704-687-5503, Fax: 704-687-1668, E-mail: gradadm@uncc.edu. Website: http://msecon.uncc.edu/

The University of North Carolina at Greensboro, Graduate School, Bryan School of Business and Economics, Department of Economics, Program in Economics, Greensboro, NC 27412-5001. Offers PhD. *Degree requirements:* For doctorate, comprehensive exam, thesis/dissertation. *Entrance requirements:* Additional exam requirements/recommendations for international students: required—TOEFL. Electronic applications accepted.

University of North Florida, Coggin College of Business, MBA Program, Jacksonville, FL 32224. Offers accounting (MBA); construction management (MBA); e-commerce (MBA); economics (MBA); finance (MBA); human resource management (MBA); international business (MBA); logistics (MBA); management applications (MBA). *Accreditation:* AACSB. *Program availability:* Part-time, evening/weekend. *Entrance requirements:* For master's, GMAT or GRE, U.S. bachelor's degree from regionally-accredited university or equivalent foreign degree. Additional exam requirements/recommendations for international students: required—TOEFL (minimum score 550 paper-based; 79 iBT).

University of North Texas, Toulouse Graduate School, Denton, TX 76203-5459. Offers accounting (MS); applied anthropology (MA, MS); applied behavior analysis (Certificate); applied geography (MA); applied technology and performance improvement (M Ed, MS); art education (MA); art history (MA); arts leadership (Certificate); audiology (Au D); behavior analysis (MS); behavioral science (PhD); biochemistry and molecular biology (MS); biology (MA, MS); biomedical engineering (MS); business analysis (MS); chemistry (MS); clinical health psychology (PhD); communication studies (MA, MS); computer engineering (MS); computer science (MS); counseling (M Ed, MS), including clinical mental health counseling (MS), college and university counseling, elementary school counseling, secondary school counseling; creative writing (MA); criminal justice (MS); curriculum and instruction (M Ed); decision sciences (MBA); design (MA, MFA), including fashion design (MFA), innovation studies, interior design (MFA); early childhood studies (MS); economics (MS); educational leadership (M Ed, Ed D); educational psychology (MS, PhD), including family studies (MS), gifted and talented (MS), human development (MS), learning and cognition (MS), research, measurement and evaluation (MS); electrical engineering (MS); emergency management (MPA); engineering technology (MS); English (MA); English as a second language (MA); environmental science (MS); finance (MBA, MS); financial management (MPA); French (MA); health services management (MBA); higher education (M Ed, Ed D); history (MA, MS); hospitality management (MS); human resources management (MPA); information science (MS); information systems (PhD); information technologies (MBA); interdisciplinary studies (MA, MS); international studies (MA); international sustainable tourism (MS); jazz studies (MM); journalism (MA, MJ, Graduate Certificate), including interactive and virtual digital communication (Graduate Certificate), narrative journalism (Graduate Certificate), public relations (Graduate Certificate); kinesiology (MS); linguistics (MA); local government management (MPA); logistics (PhD); logistics and supply chain management (MBA); long-term care, senior housing, and aging services (MA); management (PhD); marketing (MBA); mathematics (MA, MS); mechanical and energy engineering (MS, PhD); music (MA), including ethnomusicology, music theory, musicology, performance; music composition (PhD); music education (MM Ed, PhD); nonprofit management (MPA); operations and supply chain management (MBA); performance (MM, DMA); philosophy (MA); political science (MA); professional and technical communication (MA); radio, television and film (MA, MFA); rehabilitation counseling (Certificate); sociology (MA); Spanish (MA); special education (M Ed); speech-language pathology (MA); strategic management (MBA); studio art (MFA); teaching (M Ed); MBA/MS. *Program availability:* Part-time, evening/weekend, online learning. Terminal master's awarded for partial completion of doctoral program. *Degree requirements:* For master's, variable foreign language requirement, comprehensive exam (for some programs), thesis (for some programs); for doctorate, variable foreign language requirement, comprehensive exam (for some programs), thesis/dissertation; for other advanced degree, variable foreign language requirement, comprehensive exam (for some programs). *Entrance requirements:* For master's and doctorate, GRE, GMAT. Additional exam requirements/recommendations for international students: required—TOEFL (minimum score 550 paper-based; 79 iBT). Electronic applications accepted.

University of Notre Dame, The Graduate School, College of Arts and Letters, Division of Social Sciences, Department of Economics, Notre Dame, IN 46556. Offers PhD. Terminal master's awarded for partial completion of doctoral program. *Degree requirements:* For doctorate, thesis/dissertation, candidacy exam. *Entrance requirements:* For doctorate, GRE General Test. Additional exam requirements/recommendations for international students: required—TOEFL (minimum score 600 paper-based; 80 iBT). Electronic applications accepted.

University of Oklahoma, College of Arts and Sciences, Department of Economics, Norman, OK 73019. Offers economics (MA, PhD), including applied economics emphasis (MA), managerial emphasis (MA). Terminal master's awarded for partial completion of doctoral program. *Degree requirements:* For master's, comprehensive exam (for some programs); for doctorate, comprehensive exam, thesis/dissertation. *Entrance requirements:* For master's and doctorate, GRE, undergraduate degree in related field. Additional exam requirements/recommendations for international students: required—TOEFL (minimum score 79 iBT) or IELTS (minimum score 6.5). Electronic applications accepted. *Expenses:* Tuition, state resident: full-time $6583.20; part-time $274.30 per credit hour. Tuition, nonresident: full-time $21,242; part-time $885.10 per credit hour. International tuition: $21,242.40 full-time. Required fees: $1994.20; $72.55 per credit hour. $126.50 per semester. Tuition and fees vary according to course load and degree level.

University of Oklahoma, David L. Boren College of International Studies, Norman, OK 73019-0390. Offers economics and development (MAIS), including global economics and development, global security studies (MA, MAIS); global affairs (MA), including economics and development, global security studies (MA, MAIS); JD/MAIS; MAIS/MSW. *Program availability:* Part-time, online courses with an 8-10 day study abroad. Terminal master's awarded for partial completion of doctoral program. *Degree requirements:* For master's, variable foreign language requirement, 36 credit hours (33 online); thesis, policy paper or internship project; faculty-led overseas travel program of 8-10 days that will vary in location (online). *Entrance requirements:* For master's, GRE. Additional exam

requirements/recommendations for international students: required—TOEFL (minimum score 79 iBT) or IELTS (minimum score 6.5). Electronic applications accepted. *Expenses:* Tuition, state resident: full-time $6583.20; part-time $274.30 per credit hour. Tuition, nonresident: full-time $21,242; part-time $885.10 per credit hour. *International tuition:* $21,242.40 full-time. *Required fees:* $1994.20; $72.55 per credit hour. $126.50 per semester. Tuition and fees vary according to course load and degree level.

University of Oregon, Graduate School, College of Arts and Sciences, Department of Economics, Eugene, OR 97403. Offers MA, MS, PhD. Terminal master's awarded for partial completion of doctoral program. *Degree requirements:* For master's, thesis or alternative; for doctorate, thesis/dissertation, qualifying exam. *Entrance requirements:* For master's and doctorate, GRE General Test, minimum GPA of 3.0. Additional exam requirements/recommendations for international students: required—TOEFL.

University of Ottawa, Faculty of Graduate and Postdoctoral Studies, Faculty of Social Sciences, Department of Economics, Ottawa, ON K1N 6N5, Canada. Offers MA, PhD. *Program availability:* Part-time. *Degree requirements:* For master's, thesis or alternative; for doctorate, comprehensive exam, thesis/dissertation. *Entrance requirements:* For master's, honors bachelor's degree or equivalent, minimum B average; for doctorate, master's degree, minimum B+ average. Electronic applications accepted.

University of Pennsylvania, School of Arts and Sciences, Graduate Group in Economics, Philadelphia, PA 19104-6297. Offers AM, PhD, JD/AM, JD/PhD. *Faculty:* 39 full-time (5 women), 3 part-time/adjunct (0 women). *Students:* 115 full-time (24 women); includes 11 minority (7 Asian, non-Hispanic/Latino; 3 Hispanic/Latino; 1 Two or more races, non-Hispanic/Latino), 89 international. Average age 28. 624 applicants, 9% accepted, 17 enrolled. In 2019, 14 master's, 15 doctorates awarded. *Entrance requirements:* For doctorate, GRE General Test. Application fee: $90. Website: http://economics.sas.upenn.edu/graduate-program

University of Pittsburgh, Graduate School of Public and International Affairs, Master of Public and International Affairs Program, Pittsburgh, PA 15260. Offers human security (MPIA); international political economy (MPIA); security and intelligence studies (MPIA); JD/MPIA; MBA/MPIA; MPH/MPIA; MPIA/MSW; MSIS/MPIA. *Program availability:* Part-time, evening/weekend. *Faculty:* 33 full-time (11 women), 10 part-time/adjunct (5 women). *Students:* 87 full-time (49 women), 14 part-time (6 women); includes 13 minority (7 Black or African American, non-Hispanic/Latino; 6 Hispanic/Latino), 10 international. Average age 27. 156 applicants, 94% accepted, 49 enrolled. In 2019, 41 master's awarded. *Degree requirements:* For master's, thesis optional, Capstone Seminar. *Entrance requirements:* For master's, Personal essay, resume, two letters of recommendation, transcripts. Additional exam requirements/recommendations for international students: required—TOEFL (minimum score 80 iBT), Duolingo English Test; recommended—IELTS (minimum score 6.5). *Application deadline:* For fall admission, 2/1 priority date for domestic students, 1/15 priority date for international students; for spring admission, 11/1 priority date for domestic students, 8/1 priority date for international students. Application fee: $50. Electronic applications accepted. *Expenses:* $24,480 in-state, $40,848 out-of-state. *Financial support:* In 2019–20, 63 students received support, including 9 fellowships with full tuition reimbursements available (averaging $16,060 per year); scholarships/grants also available. Financial award application deadline: 2/1. *Unit head:* Dr. John Keeler, Dean, 412-648-7605, Fax: 412-648-7601, E-mail: gspia@pitt.edu. *Application contact:* Dr. Michael Rizzi, Director of Student Services, 412-648-7643, Fax: 412-648-7641, E-mail: rizzim@pitt.edu. Website: http://www.gspia.pitt.edu/

University of Pittsburgh, Kenneth P. Dietrich School of Arts and Sciences, Department of Economics, Pittsburgh, PA 15260. Offers MA, PhD. *Faculty:* 22 full-time (8 women). *Students:* 64 full-time (22 women); includes 4 minority (1 Asian, non-Hispanic/Latino; 3 Hispanic/Latino), 33 international. Average age 27. 273 applicants, 11% accepted, 15 enrolled. In 2019, 10 master's, 7 doctorates awarded. *Degree requirements:* For doctorate, comprehensive exam, thesis/dissertation, Comprehensive Research Paper. *Entrance requirements:* For doctorate, GRE, 3 letters of recommendation. Additional exam requirements/recommendations for international students: required—TOEFL (minimum score 90 iBT), IELTS. *Application deadline:* For fall admission, 1/15 for domestic and international students. Application fee: $75. Electronic applications accepted. *Financial support:* In 2019–20, 54 students received support, including 15 fellowships with full tuition reimbursements available (averaging $24,000 per year), 5 research assistantships with full tuition reimbursements available (averaging $20,250 per year), 34 teaching assistantships with full tuition reimbursements available (averaging $20,250 per year). Financial award application deadline: 1/15. *Unit head:* Dr. David Huffman, Department Chair, 412-648-1733, E-mail: huffmand@pitt.edu. *Application contact:* Brian Deutsch, Graduate Administrator, 412-648-7270, E-mail: brd51@pitt.edu. Website: http://www.econ.pitt.edu/

University of Puerto Rico at Rio Piedras, College of Social Sciences, Department of Economics, San Juan, PR 00931-3300. Offers MA. *Program availability:* Part-time. *Degree requirements:* For master's, comprehensive exam, thesis. *Entrance requirements:* For master's, GRE, PAEG, interview, minimum GPA of 3.0, letter of recommendation.

University of Regina, Faculty of Graduate Studies and Research, Johnson-Shoyama Graduate School of Public Policy, Regina, SK S4S 0A2, Canada. Offers economic analysis for public policy (Master's Certificate); health administration (MHA); health systems management (Master's Certificate); public management (MPA, Master's Certificate); public policy (MPA, MPP, PhD); public policy analysis (Master's Certificate). *Program availability:* Part-time. *Faculty:* 9 full-time (4 women), 19 part-time/adjunct (8 women). *Students:* 116 full-time (71 women), 202 part-time (155 women). Average age 30. 328 applicants, 50% accepted. In 2019, 67 master's, 12 other advanced degrees awarded. Terminal master's awarded for partial completion of doctoral program. *Degree requirements:* For master's, thesis (for some programs), course work, in person residencies; for doctorate, comprehensive exam, thesis/dissertation, seminar. *Entrance requirements:* For master's, 4 year undergraduate degree in any area, transcript, 2 letters of recommendation, authorization of release. Students without a background in economics may be required to complete introductory courses in micro and macro economics; for doctorate, master's degree, intended research program in an area of public policy, proposal. Additional exam requirements/recommendations for international students: required—TOEFL (minimum score 585 paper-based; 86 iBT), IELTS (minimum score 6.5), PTE (minimum score 63), Could be one of the listed above. Other options are MELAB, CANTEST, CAEL, and UR ESL. *Application deadline:* For fall admission, 5/1 for domestic and international students; for winter admission, 10/1 for domestic and international students. Application fee: $100. Electronic applications accepted. *Expenses:* Tuition fee is different for each program. See tuition and fees details on each program. *Financial support:* In 2019–20, 78 students received support, including 33 fellowships, 15 teaching assistantships (averaging $2,552 per year); research assistantships, career-related internships or fieldwork, Federal Work-Study, scholarships/grants, unspecified assistantships, and travel award and Graduate Scholarship Base funds also available. Support available to part-time students. Financial award application deadline: 9/30. *Unit head:* Dr. Doug Moen, Executive Director, 306-585-4921, Fax: 306-585-5461, E-mail: doeg.moen@uregina.ca. *Application contact:* John Bird, Academic Advisor, 306-585-5469, Fax: 306-585-5461, E-mail:

john.bird@uregina.ca.
Website: http://www.schoolofpublicpolicy.sk.ca/

University of Rhode Island, Graduate School, College of the Environment and Life Sciences, Department of Environmental and Natural Resource Economics, Kingston, RI 02881. Offers MS, PhD. *Program availability:* Part-time. *Faculty:* 7 full-time (2 women). *Students:* 15 full-time (7 women), 3 part-time (1 woman); includes 2 minority (1 Black or African American, non-Hispanic/Latino; 1 Asian, non-Hispanic/Latino), 8 international. In 2019, 5 master's, 3 doctorates awarded. *Entrance requirements:* Additional exam requirements/recommendations for international students: required—TOEFL. *Application deadline:* For fall admission, 2/1 for domestic and international students. Application fee: $65. Electronic applications accepted. *Expenses: Tuition, area resident:* Full-time $13,734; part-time $763 per credit. Tuition, state resident: full-time $13,734; part-time $763 per credit. Tuition, nonresident: full-time $26,512; part-time $1473 per credit. *International tuition:* $26,512 full-time. *Required fees:* $1780; $52 per credit. $35 per term. One-time fee: $165. *Financial support:* In 2019–20, 21 research assistantships with tuition reimbursements (averaging $9,463 per year) were awarded. Financial award application deadline: 2/1; financial award applicants required to submit FAFSA. *Unit head:* Dr. Hirotsugu Uchida, Chair, 401-874-4586, Fax: 401-874-4766, E-mail: enre_chair@etal.uri.edu. *Application contact:* Corey Lang, Graduate Program Director, 401-874-4569, E-mail: clang@uri.edu.
Website: http://web.uri.edu/enre/

University of Rochester, School of Arts and Sciences, Department of Economics, Rochester, NY 14627. Offers PhD. *Faculty:* 18 full-time (5 women). *Students:* 60 full-time (12 women), 53 international. Average age 28. 270 applicants, 20% accepted, 13 enrolled. In 2019, 3 doctorates awarded. Terminal master's awarded for partial completion of doctoral program. *Degree requirements:* For doctorate, comprehensive exam, thesis/dissertation, qualifying exam. *Entrance requirements:* For doctorate, GRE General Test, transcripts, three letters of recommendation. Additional exam requirements/recommendations for international students: required—TOEFL, IELTS (minimum score 7.5). *Application deadline:* For fall admission, 1/3 for domestic and international students. Application fee: $60. Electronic applications accepted. *Financial support:* In 2019–20, 92 students received support, including 52 fellowships (averaging $22,000 per year), 9 research assistantships (averaging $3,000 per year), 31 teaching assistantships (averaging $3,000 per year); health care benefits, tuition waivers (full), and unspecified assistantships also available. Financial award application deadline: 12/14. *Unit head:* George Alessandria, Chair, 585-275-3096, E-mail: george.alessandria@rochester.edu. *Application contact:* Pamela Young, Administrative Assistant, 585-275-8625, E-mail: pamela.l.young@rochester.edu.
Website: http://www.sas.rochester.edu/eco/graduate/index.html

University of Saskatchewan, College of Graduate and Postdoctoral Studies, College of Arts and Science, Department of Economics, Saskatoon, SK S7N 5A2, Canada. Offers MA, Diploma. *Degree requirements:* For master's, thesis (for some programs). *Entrance requirements:* Additional exam requirements/recommendations for international students: required—TOEFL (minimum score 80 iBT); recommended—IELTS (minimum score 6.5). Electronic applications accepted.

University of South Africa, College of Economic and Management Sciences, Pretoria, South Africa. Offers accounting (D Admin, D Com); accounting science (DA); auditing (D Admin, D Com); business administration (M Tech); business economics (D Admin); business leadership (DBL); business management (D Admin, D Com); economic management analysis (M Tech); economics (D Admin, D Com, PhD); human resource development (M Tech); industrial psychology (D Admin, D Com, PhD); logistics (D Com); marketing (M Tech); public administration (D Admin, D Com, DPA, PhD); public management (M Tech); quantitative management (D Admin, D Com); real estate (M Tech); statistics (D Admin, PhD); tourism management (D Admin, D Com); transport economics (D Admin, D Com).

University of South Carolina, The Graduate School, Darla Moore School of Business, Doctoral Program in Business Administration, Columbia, SC 29208. Offers business administration (PhD); economics (PhD). *Degree requirements:* For doctorate, thesis/dissertation, qualifying and comprehensive exams. *Entrance requirements:* For doctorate, GRE or GMAT. Additional exam requirements/recommendations for international students: required—TOEFL (minimum score 600 paper-based; 100 iBT), IELTS (minimum score 7). Electronic applications accepted. *Expenses:* Contact institution.

University of South Carolina, The Graduate School, Darla Moore School of Business, Master of Arts in Economics Program, Columbia, SC 29208. Offers MA, JD/MA. *Degree requirements:* For master's, thesis optional. *Entrance requirements:* For master's, GMAT or GRE General Test. Additional exam requirements/recommendations for international students: required—TOEFL (minimum score 100 iBT); recommended—IELTS. Electronic applications accepted.

University of Southern California, Graduate School, Dana and David Dornsife College of Letters, Arts and Sciences, Department of Economics, Los Angeles, CA 90089. Offers economic development programming (MA, PhD); mathematical finance (MS); M Pl/MA; MA/JD. Terminal master's awarded for partial completion of doctoral program. *Degree requirements:* For master's, comprehensive exam; for doctorate, comprehensive exam, thesis/dissertation. *Entrance requirements:* For master's and doctorate, GRE. Additional exam requirements/recommendations for international students: required—TOEFL (minimum score 93 iBT). Electronic applications accepted.

University of South Florida, College of Arts and Sciences, Department of Economics, Tampa, FL 33620-9951. Offers MA, PhD. *Program availability:* Part-time, evening/weekend. *Faculty:* 11 full-time (3 women), 1 part-time/adjunct (0 women). *Students:* 32 full-time (8 women), 14 part-time (7 women); includes 5 minority (1 Asian, non-Hispanic/Latino; 3 Hispanic/Latino; 1 Two or more races, non-Hispanic/Latino), 22 international. Average age 29. 82 applicants, 60% accepted, 16 enrolled. In 2019, 16 master's, 4 doctorates awarded. *Degree requirements:* For master's, comprehensive exam, oral exam; for doctorate, comprehensive exam, thesis/dissertation. *Entrance requirements:* For master's, GRE with target scores of 152 (490) on the verbal portion and 152 (670) on the quantitative portion, 3.00 GPA, minimum of 1 course in calculus (grade of B or better), minimum of 1 course in statistics (grade of B or better), undergraduate intermediate-level microeconomics and undergraduate intermediate-level macroeconomics (grade of B or better); for doctorate, Must have taken the GRE within the preceding five years with target scores of 65th percentile on the verbal portion and 65th percentile on the quantitative portion, minimum GPA of 3.00; minimum B grade in calculus (two courses), probability and statistics, undergraduate intermediate-level microeconomics and undergraduate intermediate-level macroeconomics. Additional exam requirements/recommendations for international students: required—TOEFL, TOEFL (minimum score 550 paper-based; 79 iBT) or IELTS (minimum score 6.5). *Application deadline:* For fall admission, 6/1 for domestic and international students; for spring admission, 10/15 for domestic students, 9/15 for international students. Applications are processed on a rolling basis. Application fee: $30. Electronic applications accepted. *Financial support:* In 2019–20, 13 students received support, including 1 research assistantship (averaging $13,082 per year), 15 teaching assistantships with tuition reimbursements available (averaging $11,393 per year); unspecified assistantships also available. Financial award application deadline: 2/1; financial award applicants required to submit FAFSA. *Unit head:* Dr. Bradley Kamp, Associate Professor and Chairperson, 813-974-6549, Fax: 813-974-6510, E-mail: bkamp@usf.edu. *Application contact:* Dr. Michael Loewy, Associate Professor and Graduate Director, 813-974-6532, Fax: 813-974-6510, E-mail: mloewy@usf.edu.
Website: http://www.economics.usf.edu

The University of Tennessee, Graduate School, College of Arts and Sciences, Department of Sociology, Knoxville, TN 37996. Offers criminology (MA, PhD); energy, environment, and resource policy (MA, PhD); political economy (MA, PhD). *Program availability:* Part-time. *Degree requirements:* For master's, thesis or alternative; for doctorate, thesis/dissertation. *Entrance requirements:* For master's, GRE General Test, minimum GPA of 3.0; for doctorate, GRE General Test, minimum GPA of 3.5. Additional exam requirements/recommendations for international students: required—TOEFL. Electronic applications accepted.

The University of Tennessee, Graduate School, College of Business Administration, Department of Economics, Knoxville, TN 37996. Offers MA, PhD. *Degree requirements:* For master's, thesis or alternative; for doctorate, thesis/dissertation. *Entrance requirements:* For master's and doctorate, GRE General Test or GMAT, minimum GPA of 2.7. Additional exam requirements/recommendations for international students: required—TOEFL. Electronic applications accepted.

The University of Texas at Arlington, Graduate School, College of Business, Economics Department, Arlington, TX 76019. Offers MA. *Program availability:* Part-time, evening/weekend. *Degree requirements:* For master's, thesis optional. *Entrance requirements:* For master's, GMAT or GRE. Additional exam requirements/recommendations for international students: required—TOEFL (minimum score 550 paper-based; 79 iBT).

The University of Texas at Austin, Graduate School, College of Liberal Arts, Department of Economics, Austin, TX 78712-1111. Offers MA, MS Econ, PhD. *Program availability:* Part-time. *Degree requirements:* For master's, thesis; for doctorate, comprehensive exam, thesis/dissertation. *Entrance requirements:* For master's and doctorate, GRE General Test, minimum GPA of 3.5 (based on upper-division undergraduate and graduate course work). Additional exam requirements/recommendations for international students: required—TOEFL. Electronic applications accepted.

The University of Texas at Dallas, School of Economic, Political and Policy Sciences, Program in Economics, Richardson, TX 75080. Offers MS, PhD. *Program availability:* Part-time, evening/weekend. *Faculty:* 12 full-time (2 women), 3 part-time/adjunct (0 women). *Students:* 41 full-time (16 women), 15 part-time (5 women); includes 13 minority (5 Black or African American, non-Hispanic/Latino; 7 Asian, non-Hispanic/Latino; 1 Hispanic/Latino), 28 international. Average age 31. 111 applicants, 49% accepted, 19 enrolled. In 2019, 14 master's, 4 doctorates awarded. *Degree requirements:* For master's, internship; for doctorate, thesis/dissertation. *Entrance requirements:* For master's, GRE (minimum combined verbal and quantitative score of 1200), minimum GPA of 3.0 in upper-level course work in field; for doctorate, GRE (minimum combined verbal and quantitative score of 1200, writing 4.5), minimum GPA of 3.25 in upper-level and graduate course work in field. Additional exam requirements/recommendations for international students: required—TOEFL (minimum score 550 paper-based). *Application deadline:* For fall admission, 7/15 for domestic students, 5/1 priority date for international students; for spring admission, 11/15 for domestic students, 9/1 priority date for international students. Applications are processed on a rolling basis. Application fee: $50 ($100 for international students). Electronic applications accepted. *Expenses: Tuition, area resident:* Full-time $16,504. Tuition, state resident: full-time $16,504. Tuition, nonresident: full-time $34,266. Tuition and fees vary according to course load. *Financial support:* In 2019–20, 25 students received support, including 4 research assistantships with partial tuition reimbursements available (averaging $20,891 per year), 20 teaching assistantships with partial tuition reimbursements available (averaging $13,505 per year); career-related internships or fieldwork, Federal Work-Study, institutionally sponsored loans, scholarships/grants, and unspecified assistantships also available. Support available to part-time students. Financial award application deadline: 4/30; financial award applicants required to submit FAFSA. *Unit head:* Dr. Daniel G. Arce, Program Head, 972-883-6857, Fax: 972-883-2735, E-mail: ph.econ@utdallas.edu. *Application contact:* Judy Du, Graduate Program Administrator, 972-883-4964, Fax: 972-883-2735, E-mail: gpa.econ@utdallas.edu.
Website: https://epps.utdallas.edu/about/programs/economics/

The University of Texas at Dallas, School of Economic, Political and Policy Sciences, Program in Public Policy and Political Economy, Richardson, TX 75080. Offers international political economy (MS); public policy (MPP); public policy and political economy (PhD); social data analytics and research (MS). *Program availability:* Part-time, evening/weekend. *Faculty:* 26 full-time (4 women), 3 part-time/adjunct (0 women). *Students:* 51 full-time (25 women), 28 part-time (18 women); includes 29 minority (7 Black or African American, non-Hispanic/Latino; 5 Asian, non-Hispanic/Latino; 14 Hispanic/Latino; 3 Two or more races, non-Hispanic/Latino), 17 international. Average age 34. 48 applicants, 38% accepted, 18 enrolled. In 2019, 22 master's, 7 doctorates awarded. *Degree requirements:* For doctorate, thesis/dissertation. *Entrance requirements:* For master's and doctorate, GRE General Test, minimum GPA of 3.0 in upper-level course work in field. Additional exam requirements/recommendations for international students: required—TOEFL (minimum score 550 paper-based). *Application deadline:* For fall admission, 7/15 for domestic students, 5/1 priority date for international students; for spring admission, 11/15 for domestic students, 9/1 priority date for international students. Applications are processed on a rolling basis. Application fee: $50 ($100 for international students). Electronic applications accepted. *Expenses: Tuition, area resident:* Full-time $16,504. Tuition, state resident: full-time $16,504. Tuition, nonresident: full-time $34,266. Tuition and fees vary according to course load. *Financial support:* In 2019–20, 22 students received support, including 1 fellowship (averaging $2,000 per year), 2 research assistantships with partial tuition reimbursements available (averaging $18,000 per year), 17 teaching assistantships with partial tuition reimbursements available (averaging $13,500 per year); career-related internships or fieldwork, Federal Work-Study, institutionally sponsored loans, scholarships/grants, and unspecified assistantships also available. Support available to part-time students. Financial award application deadline: 4/30; financial award applicants required to submit FAFSA. *Unit head:* Dr. Thomas Brunell, Program Head, 972-883-4963, Fax: 972-883-6297, E-mail: ph.pppe@utdallas.edu. *Application contact:* Marjorie McDonald, Graduate Program Administrator, 972-883-6406, Fax: 972-883-6297, E-mail: pppe@utdallas.edu.
Website: https://epps.utdallas.edu/about/programs/public-policy-and-political-economy/

The University of Texas at El Paso, Graduate School, College of Business Administration, Department of Economics and Finance, El Paso, TX 79968-0001. Offers economics (MS). *Program availability:* Part-time, evening/weekend. *Degree requirements:* For master's, thesis optional, at least 24 credit hours with minimum cumulative GPA of 3.0. *Entrance requirements:* For master's, GRE, undergraduate degree from accredited college or university. Additional exam requirements/recommendations for international students: required—TOEFL. Electronic applications accepted.

The University of Texas at San Antonio, College of Business, Department of Economics, San Antonio, TX 78249-0617. Offers business economics (MBA); economics (MA). *Program availability:* Part-time, evening/weekend. *Degree requirements:* For master's, comprehensive exam, thesis optional. *Entrance requirements:* For master's, GMAT or GRE, transcripts, statement of purpose. Additional exam requirements/recommendations for international students: required—TOEFL (minimum score 550 paper-based; 79 iBT), IELTS (minimum score 6.5). Electronic applications accepted.

The University of Toledo, College of Graduate Studies, College of Languages, Literature and Social Sciences, Department of Economics, Toledo, OH 43606-3390. Offers applied econometric specialization (MA); economics (MA). *Program availability:* Part-time. *Degree requirements:* For master's, comprehensive exam, paper or thesis. *Entrance requirements:* For master's, GRE General Test, minimum cumulative GPA of 2.7 on all previous academic work, three letters of recommendation, statement of purpose, transcripts from all prior institutions attended. Additional exam requirements/recommendations for international students: required—TOEFL (minimum score 550 paper-based; 80 iBT). Electronic applications accepted.

The University of Toledo, College of Graduate Studies, Judith Herb College of Education, Department of Curriculum and Instruction, Toledo, OH 43606-3390. Offers art education (ME); career and technical education (ME, Ed S); curriculum and instruction (ME, PhD, Ed S); early childhood education (Ed S); education and anthropology (MAE); education and biology (MES); education and chemistry (MES); education and classics (MAE); education and economics (MAE); education and English (MAE); education and French (MAE); education and geology (MES); education and German (MAE); education and history (MAE); education and mathematics (MAE, MES); education and physics (MES); education and political science (MAE); education and sociology (MAE); education and Spanish (MAE); educational media (PhD); educational technology (ME); educational technology: virtual educator (Certificate); elementary education (PhD); English as a second language (MAE); gifted and talented education (PhD); middle childhood education (ME); secondary education (ME, PhD); special education (PhD). *Accreditation:* NCATE. *Program availability:* Part-time, evening/weekend. *Degree requirements:* For master's, comprehensive exam, thesis or alternative; for doctorate, comprehensive exam, thesis/dissertation; for other advanced degree, thesis optional. *Entrance requirements:* For master's, doctorate, and other advanced degree, minimum cumulative GPA of 2.7 for all previous academic work, letters of recommendation. Additional exam requirements/recommendations for international students: required—TOEFL (minimum score 550 paper-based; 80 iBT). Electronic applications accepted.

University of Toronto, School of Graduate Studies, Faculty of Arts and Science, Department of Economics, Toronto, ON M5S 1A1, Canada. Offers economics (MA, PhD); financial economics (MFE); JD/MA; JD/PhD. *Program availability:* Part-time. *Degree requirements:* For doctorate, comprehensive exam, thesis/dissertation. *Entrance requirements:* For master's, GRE (for applicants without a degree from a Canadian university), minimum B average in final year, 2 letters of reference; for doctorate, GRE (for applicants without a degree from a Canadian university), master's degree in economics, minimum B+ average, 3 letters of reference. Additional exam requirements/recommendations for international students: required—TOEFL (minimum 580 paper-based; 93 iBT), IELTS (minimum score 7), TWE (minimum score 5), or Michigan English Language Assessment Battery (minimum score 85). Electronic applications accepted.

University of Utah, Graduate School, College of Social and Behavioral Science, Department of Economics, Salt Lake City, UT 84112. Offers econometrics (M Stat); economics (M Phil, MA, MS, PhD). *Faculty:* 18 full-time (4 women), 1 part-time/adjunct (0 women). *Students:* 35 full-time (10 women), 26 part-time (5 women); includes 9 minority (3 Asian, non-Hispanic/Latino; 5 Hispanic/Latino; 1 Two or more races, non-Hispanic/Latino), 29 international. Average age 32. 100 applicants, 23% accepted, 11 enrolled. In 2019, 13 master's, 12 doctorates awarded. Terminal master's awarded for partial completion of doctoral program. *Degree requirements:* For master's, thesis (for some programs); for doctorate, comprehensive exam, thesis/dissertation. *Entrance requirements:* Additional exam requirements/recommendations for international students: required—TOEFL (minimum score 550 paper-based; 80 iBT); recommended—IELTS (minimum score 6.5). *Application deadline:* For fall admission, 2/1 priority date for domestic and international students; for spring admission, 11/1 for domestic and international students; for summer admission, 4/1 for domestic and international students. Application fee: $55 ($65 for international students). Electronic applications accepted. *Expenses:* Tuition, state resident: full-time $7085; part-time $272.51 per credit hour. Tuition, nonresident: full-time $24,937; part-time $959.12 per credit hour. *Required fees:* $880.52; $880.52 per semester. Tuition and fees vary according to degree level, program and student level. *Financial support:* In 2019–20, 5 students received support, including 1 fellowship with full and partial tuition reimbursement available (averaging $6,000 per year), 1 research assistantship with full and partial tuition reimbursement available (averaging $4,000 per year), 27 teaching assistantships with full tuition reimbursements available (averaging $18,259 per year). Financial award application deadline: 4/15. *Unit head:* Dr. Norman Waitzman, Chair, 801-581-7481, E-mail: waitzman@economics.utah.edu. *Application contact:* Alex Francis, Academic Advisor, 801-581-7481, E-mail: grad-advising@economics.utah.edu. Website: http://www.economics.utah.edu

University of Vermont, Graduate College, The Rubenstein School of Environment and Natural Resources, Program in Natural Resources, Burlington, VT 05405. Offers ecological economics (Certificate); natural resources (MS), including aquatic ecology and watershed science, environment thought and culture, environment, science and public affairs, forestry; natural resources (PhD); MELP/MS. *Degree requirements:* For master's, thesis or alternative; for doctorate, thesis/dissertation. *Entrance requirements:* For master's and doctorate, GRE General Test. Additional exam requirements/recommendations for international students: required—TOEFL (minimum score 550 paper-based; 90 iBT), IELTS (minimum score 6.5). Electronic applications accepted.

University of Victoria, Faculty of Graduate Studies, Faculty of Social Sciences, Department of Economics, Victoria, BC V8W 2Y2, Canada. Offers MA, PhD. *Program availability:* Part-time. *Degree requirements:* For master's, comprehensive exam (for some programs), thesis optional; for doctorate, comprehensive exam, thesis/dissertation, candidacy exam. *Entrance requirements:* For master's and doctorate, GRE. Additional exam requirements/recommendations for international students: required—TOEFL (minimum score 575 paper-based), IELTS (minimum score 7). Electronic applications accepted.

University of Virginia, College and Graduate School of Arts and Sciences, Department of Economics, Charlottesville, VA 22903. Offers MA, PhD. *Degree requirements:* For master's, comprehensive exam (for some programs), thesis (for some programs), thesis or comprehensive exam; for doctorate, comprehensive exam, thesis/dissertation. *Entrance requirements:* For master's and doctorate, GRE General Test. Additional exam requirements/recommendations for international students: required—TOEFL (minimum score 600 paper-based; 90 iBT), IELTS (minimum score 7). Electronic applications accepted.

University of Washington, Graduate School, College of Arts and Sciences, Department of Economics, Seattle, WA 98195. Offers PhD. Terminal master's awarded for partial completion of doctoral program. *Degree requirements:* For doctorate, comprehensive exam, thesis/dissertation. *Entrance requirements:* For doctorate, GRE General Test, minimum GPA of 3.0. Additional exam requirements/recommendations for international students: required—TOEFL. Electronic applications accepted.

University of Waterloo, Graduate Studies and Postdoctoral Affairs, Faculty of Arts, Department of Economics, Waterloo, ON N2L 3G1, Canada. Offers MA, PhD. *Program availability:* Part-time. *Entrance requirements:* For master's, honors degree, minimum B average. Additional exam requirements/recommendations for international students: required—TOEFL, IELTS, PTE. Electronic applications accepted.

The University of Western Ontario, School of Graduate and Postdoctoral Studies, Faculty of Social Science, Department of Economics, London, ON N6A 3K7, Canada. Offers MA, PhD. *Degree requirements:* For doctorate, thesis/dissertation. *Entrance requirements:* For master's, GRE, honours BA with B+ average. Additional exam requirements/recommendations for international students: required—TOEFL.

University of Windsor, Faculty of Graduate Studies, Faculty of Science, Department of Economics, Windsor, ON N9B 3P4, Canada. Offers MA. *Program availability:* Part-time. *Degree requirements:* For master's, thesis or alternative. *Entrance requirements:* For master's, minimum B average. Additional exam requirements/recommendations for international students: required—TOEFL (minimum score 560 paper-based). Electronic applications accepted.

University of Wisconsin–Madison, Graduate School, College of Letters and Science, Department of Economics, Madison, WI 53706-1380. Offers PhD. *Degree requirements:* For doctorate, thesis/dissertation. *Entrance requirements:* For doctorate, GRE General Test, 3 semesters of course work in calculus, 1 semester of course work in algebra and mathematics/statistics. Electronic applications accepted.

University of Wisconsin–Milwaukee, Graduate School, College of Letters and Science, Department of Economics, Milwaukee, WI 53201-0413. Offers MA, PhD. *Degree requirements:* For master's, comprehensive exam; for doctorate, comprehensive exam, thesis/dissertation. *Entrance requirements:* For master's, GRE General Test; for doctorate, GRE General Test, GRE Subject Test, minimum GPA of 3.0. Additional exam requirements/recommendations for international students: required—TOEFL (minimum score 550 paper-based; 79 iBT), IELTS (minimum score 6.5). Electronic applications accepted.

University of Wyoming, College of Business, Department of Economics, Laramie, WY 82071. Offers MS, PhD. *Program availability:* Part-time. *Degree requirements:* For master's, thesis; for doctorate, comprehensive exam, thesis/dissertation. *Entrance requirements:* For master's, GRE General Test or GMAT, minimum GPA of 3.0; for doctorate, GRE General Test, minimum GPA of 3.0. Additional exam requirements/recommendations for international students: required—TOEFL (minimum score 525 paper-based).

Université Laval, Faculty of Social Sciences, Department of Economics, Programs in Economics, Québec, QC G1K 7P4, Canada. Offers MA, PhD. Terminal master's awarded for partial completion of doctoral program. *Degree requirements:* For master's, thesis (for some programs); for doctorate, comprehensive exam, thesis/dissertation. *Entrance requirements:* For master's and doctorate, knowledge of French. Electronic applications accepted.

Utah State University, School of Graduate Studies, Jon M. Huntsman School of Business, Department of Economics and Finance, Logan, UT 84322. Offers economics (MS); financial economics (MS). *Degree requirements:* For master's, thesis (for some programs). *Entrance requirements:* For master's, GRE General Test, GMAT, minimum GPA of 3.0. Additional exam requirements/recommendations for international students: required—TOEFL. Electronic applications accepted.

Vanderbilt University, Department of Economics, Nashville, TN 37240-1001. Offers economic development (MA); economics (PhD). *Faculty:* 28 full-time (3 women). *Students:* 113 full-time (55 women), 5 part-time (1 woman); includes 9 minority (2 Asian, non-Hispanic/Latino; 4 Hispanic/Latino; 3 Two or more races, non-Hispanic/Latino), 83 international. Average age 26. 532 applicants, 39% accepted, 48 enrolled. In 2019, 18 master's, 6 doctorates awarded. Terminal master's awarded for partial completion of doctoral program. *Degree requirements:* For master's, thesis or alternative; for doctorate, thesis/dissertation, final and qualifying exams. *Entrance requirements:* For master's and doctorate, GRE General Test, GRE Subject Test (recommended). Additional exam requirements/recommendations for international students: required—TOEFL (minimum score 570 paper-based; 88 iBT). *Application deadline:* For fall admission, 1/15 for domestic and international students; for spring admission, 11/1 for domestic students. Applications are processed on a rolling basis. Electronic applications accepted. *Expenses: Tuition:* Full-time $51,018; part-time $2087 per hour. *Required fees:* $542. Tuition and fees vary according to program. *Financial support:* Fellowships, teaching assistantships, career-related internships or fieldwork, Federal Work-Study, institutionally sponsored loans, scholarships/grants, and health care benefits available. Financial award application deadline: 1/15; financial award applicants required to submit CSS PROFILE or FAFSA. *Unit head:* Dr. Peter Rousseau, Chair, 615-343-2466, Fax: 615-343-8495, E-mail: peter.l.rousseau@vanderbilt.edu. *Application contact:* Mattias Polborn, Director of Graduate Studies, 615-322-8113, Fax: 615-343-8495, E-mail: mattias.polborn@vanderbilt.edu.
Website: http://www.vanderbilt.edu/econ/

Vanderbilt University, Vanderbilt Law School, Nashville, TN 37203. Offers law (LL M, JD); law and economics (PhD); JD/M Div; JD/MA; JD/MBA; JD/MD; JD/MPP; JD/MTS; JD/PhD; LL M/MA. *Accreditation:* ABA. *Degree requirements:* For doctorate, comprehensive exam (for some programs), thesis/dissertation (for some programs), 72 hours of coursework and research (for PhD). *Entrance requirements:* For master's, foreign law degree; for doctorate, GRE (for PhD), LSAT, advanced undergraduate economics (for PhD). Additional exam requirements/recommendations for international students: required—TOEFL. Electronic applications accepted. *Expenses:* Contact institution.

Virginia Commonwealth University, Graduate School, School of Business, Program in Economics, Richmond, VA 23284-9005. Offers MA. *Degree requirements:* For master's, thesis optional. *Entrance requirements:* For master's, GRE General Test (preferred) or GMAT. Additional exam requirements/recommendations for international students: required—TOEFL (minimum score 600 paper-based; 100 iBT). Electronic applications accepted.

Virginia Polytechnic Institute and State University, Graduate School, College of Science, Blacksburg, VA 24061. Offers biological sciences (MS, PhD); biomedical technology development and management (MS); chemistry (MS, PhD); data analysis and applied statistics (MA); economics (PhD); geosciences (MS, PhD); mathematics (MS, PhD); physics (MS, PhD); psychology (MS, PhD); statistics (MS, PhD). *Faculty:* 375 full-time (118 women), 2 part-time/adjunct (1 woman). *Students:* 544 full-time (221 women), 37 part-time (15 women); includes 75 minority (14 Black or African American, non-Hispanic/Latino; 1 American Indian or Alaska Native, non-Hispanic/Latino; 20 Asian, non-Hispanic/Latino; 31 Hispanic/Latino; 9 Two or more races, non-Hispanic/

Latino), 216 international. Average age 27. 962 applicants, 33% accepted, 138 enrolled. In 2019, 75 master's, 69 doctorates awarded. *Degree requirements:* For master's, comprehensive exam (for some programs), thesis (for some programs); for doctorate, comprehensive exam (for some programs), thesis/dissertation (for some programs). *Entrance requirements:* For master's and doctorate, GRE/GMAT. Additional exam requirements/recommendations for international students: required—TOEFL (minimum score 90 iBT). *Application deadline:* For fall admission, 8/1 for domestic students, 4/1 for international students; for spring admission, 1/1 for domestic students, 9/1 for international students. Applications are processed on a rolling basis. Application fee: $75. Electronic applications accepted. *Expenses:* Tuition, state resident: full-time $13,700; part-time $761.25 per credit hour. Tuition, nonresident: full-time $27,614; part-time $1534 per credit hour. *Required fees:* $886.50 per term. Tuition and fees vary according to campus/location and program. *Financial support:* In 2019–20, 5 fellowships with full tuition reimbursements (averaging $25,988 per year), 281 research assistantships with full tuition reimbursements (averaging $15,597 per year), 370 teaching assistantships with full tuition reimbursements (averaging $18,225 per year) were awarded; unspecified assistantships also available. Financial award application deadline: 3/1; financial award applicants required to submit FAFSA. *Unit head:* Dr. Sally C. Morton, Dean, 540-231-5422, Fax: 540-231-3380, E-mail: scmorton@vt.edu. *Application contact:* Allison Craft, Executive Assistant, 540-231-6394, Fax: 540-231-3380, E-mail: crafta@vt.edu.
Website: http://www.science.vt.edu/

Virginia State University, College of Graduate Studies, College of Engineering and Technology, Department of Mathematics and Economics, Petersburg, VA 23806-0001. Offers economics (MA); mathematics (MS). *Degree requirements:* For master's, thesis (for some programs).

Washington State University, College of Agricultural, Human, and Natural Resource Sciences, School of Economic Sciences, Pullman, WA 99164-6210. Offers agricultural economics (PhD); economics (PhD). Terminal master's awarded for partial completion of doctoral program. *Degree requirements:* For master's, comprehensive exam (for some programs), thesis (for some programs), oral exam; for doctorate, comprehensive exam, thesis/dissertation, oral exam, written exam, qualifying exams. *Entrance requirements:* For master's and doctorate, GRE, minimum GPA of 3.0, 3 letters of recommendation. Additional exam requirements/recommendations for international students: required—TOEFL (minimum score 550 paper-based). Electronic applications accepted.

Washington University in St. Louis, The Graduate School, Department of Economics, St. Louis, MO 63130-4899. Offers PhD. Terminal master's awarded for partial completion of doctoral program. *Degree requirements:* For doctorate, one foreign language, thesis/dissertation. *Entrance requirements:* For doctorate, GRE General Test. Additional exam requirements/recommendations for international students: required—TOEFL. Electronic applications accepted.

Wayne State University, College of Liberal Arts and Sciences, Department of Economics, Detroit, MI 48202. Offers applied macroeconomics (MA, PhD); health economics (MA, PhD); industrial organization (MA, PhD); international economics (MA, PhD); labor and human resources (MA, PhD); JD/MA. *Faculty:* 10. *Students:* 47 full-time (13 women), 6 part-time (2 women); includes 8 minority (4 Black or African American, non-Hispanic/Latino; 2 Asian, non-Hispanic/Latino; 2 Hispanic/Latino), 18 international. Average age 31. 67 applicants, 37% accepted, 8 enrolled. In 2019, 4 master's, 2 doctorates awarded. *Degree requirements:* For master's, comprehensive exam; for doctorate, comprehensive exam, thesis/dissertation, oral examination on research, completion of course work in quantitative methods, final lecture. *Entrance requirements:* For master's, minimum upper-division GPA of 3.0; prior coursework in intermediate microeconomic and macroeconomic theory, statistics, and elementary calculus; for doctorate, GRE, minimum upper-division GPA of 3.0, prior coursework in intermediate microeconomic and macroeconomic theory, statistics, two courses in calculus, three letters of recommendation from officials or teaching staff at institution(s) most recently attended, statement of purpose. Additional exam requirements/recommendations for international students: required—TOEFL (minimum score 550 paper-based; 79 iBT), TWE (minimum score 5.5), Michigan English Language Assessment Battery (minimum score 85); recommended—IELTS (minimum score 6.5). *Application deadline:* For fall admission, 5/1 for domestic and international students; for winter admission, 10/1 priority date for domestic students, 9/1 priority date for international students; for spring admission, 1/1 priority date for domestic and international students. Applications are processed on a rolling basis. Application fee: $50. Electronic applications accepted. *Expenses: Tuition:* Full-time $34,567. *Financial support:* In 2019–20, 30 students received support, including 2 fellowships with tuition reimbursements available (averaging $20,000 per year), 17 teaching assistantships with tuition reimbursements available (averaging $19,883 per year); research assistantships, scholarships/grants, health care benefits, and unspecified assistantships also available. Support available to part-time students. Financial award applicants required to submit FAFSA. *Unit head:* Dr. Kevin Cotter, Department Chair, 313-577-3345, E-mail: kevin.cotter@wayne.edu. *Application contact:* Dr. Allen Charles Goodman, Professor and Director of Graduate Studies, 313-577-3235, E-mail: aa1313@wayne.edu.
Website: http://clas.wayne.edu/economics/

Western Illinois University, School of Graduate Studies, College of Business and Technology, Department of Economics and Decision Sciences, Program in Economics, Macomb, IL 61455-1390. Offers MA. Electronic applications accepted.

Western Michigan University, Graduate College, College of Arts and Sciences, Department of Economics, Kalamazoo, MI 49008. Offers applied economics (MA, PhD). *Degree requirements:* For master's, thesis; for doctorate, thesis/dissertation.

West Texas A&M University, College of Business, Department of Accounting, Economics and Finance, Canyon, TX 79015. Offers accounting (MPA); finance and economics (MS). *Program availability:* Part-time, evening/weekend, online learning. *Degree requirements:* For master's, comprehensive exam, thesis optional. *Entrance requirements:* For master's, GMAT. Additional exam requirements/recommendations for international students: required—TOEFL (minimum score 550 paper-based). Electronic applications accepted.

West Virginia University, College of Business and Economics, Morgantown, WV 26506. Offers accountancy (M Acc); accounting (PhD); business administration (MBA); business cyber security management (MS); business data analytics (MS); economics (MA, PhD); finance (MS, PhD); forensic and fraud examination (MS); industrial relations (MS); management (PhD); marketing (PhD). *Program availability:* Part-time, online learning. Terminal master's awarded for partial completion of doctoral program. *Degree requirements:* For master's, thesis optional; for doctorate, comprehensive exam, thesis/dissertation. *Entrance requirements:* For doctorate, GRE General Test, minimum GPA of 3.0. Additional exam requirements/recommendations for international students: required—TOEFL (minimum score 550 paper-based; 92 iBT). Electronic applications accepted. *Expenses:* Contact institution.

Wichita State University, Graduate School, W. Frank Barton School of Business, Department of Economics, Wichita, KS 67260. Offers applied economics (MA), including data analysis, financial economics, international economics. *Program availability:* Part-time, evening/weekend.

Wilfrid Laurier University, Faculty of Graduate and Postdoctoral Studies, Lazaridis School of Business and Economics, Department of Business, Waterloo, ON N2L 3C5, Canada. Offers accounting (PhD); finance (M Fin); financial economics (PhD); marketing (PhD); operations and supply chain management (PhD); organizational behavior and human resource management (M Sc); organizational behaviour and human resource management (PhD); supply chain management (M Sc); technology management (EMTM). *Accreditation:* AACSB. *Program availability:* Part-time, evening/weekend. *Degree requirements:* For master's, thesis optional; for doctorate, comprehensive exam, thesis/dissertation. *Entrance requirements:* For master's, GMAT, 4-year honors degree with minimum B+ average; for doctorate, GMAT, master's degree, minimum B+ average. Additional exam requirements/recommendations for international students: required—TOEFL (minimum score 89 iBT). Electronic applications accepted.

Wilfrid Laurier University, Faculty of Graduate and Postdoctoral Studies, Lazaridis School of Business and Economics, Department of Economics, Waterloo, ON N2L 3C5, Canada. Offers MA. *Entrance requirements:* For master's, honors BA or the equivalent in economics, minimum B average in undergraduate course work. Additional exam requirements/recommendations for international students: required—TOEFL (minimum score 89 iBT). Electronic applications accepted.

Wilfrid Laurier University, Faculty of Graduate and Postdoctoral Studies, School of International Policy and Governance, Global Governance Program, Waterloo, ON N2L 3C5, Canada. Offers conflict and security (PhD); global environment (PhD); global justice and human rights (PhD); global political economy (PhD); global social governance (PhD); multilateral institutions and diplomacy (PhD). *Degree requirements:* For doctorate, thesis/dissertation. *Entrance requirements:* For doctorate, MA in political science, history, economics, international development studies, international peace studies, globalization studies, environmental studies or related field with minimum A-. Additional exam requirements/recommendations for international students: required—TOEFL (minimum score 89 iBT). Electronic applications accepted.

Wright State University, Graduate School, Raj Soin College of Business, Department of Economics, Dayton, OH 45435. Offers social and applied economics (MS). *Entrance requirements:* For master's, GRE General Test. Additional exam requirements/recommendations for international students: required—TOEFL.

Yale University, Graduate School of Arts and Sciences, Department of Economics, New Haven, CT 06520. Offers economics (PhD); international and development economics (MA). *Degree requirements:* For doctorate, thesis/dissertation. *Entrance requirements:* For master's, GRE General Test; for doctorate, GRE General Test, GRE Subject Test.

Yeshiva University, The Katz School, Program in Quantitative Economics, New York, NY 10033-3201. Offers MS.

York University, Faculty of Graduate Studies, Faculty of Liberal Arts and Professional Studies, Program in Economics, Toronto, ON M3J 1P3, Canada. Offers MA, PhD. *Program availability:* Part-time. *Degree requirements:* For doctorate, comprehensive exam, thesis/dissertation. Electronic applications accepted.

Youngstown State University, College of Graduate Studies, College of Liberal Arts and Social Sciences, Department of Economics, Youngstown, OH 44555-0001. Offers economics (MA); financial economics (MA). *Program availability:* Part-time. *Degree requirements:* For master's, comprehensive exam, thesis optional. *Entrance requirements:* For master's, minimum GPA of 2.7, 21 hours in economics. Additional exam requirements/recommendations for international students: required—TOEFL.

International Economics

American University, College of Arts and Sciences, Department of Economics, Washington, DC 20016-8029. Offers applied microeconomics (Certificate); economics (MA, PhD); gender analysis in economics (Certificate); international economic relations (Certificate); international economics (MA). *Program availability:* Part-time, evening/weekend, 100% online, blended/hybrid learning. Terminal master's awarded for partial completion of doctoral program. *Degree requirements:* For master's, comprehensive exam, thesis or alternative; for doctorate, comprehensive exam, thesis/dissertation. *Entrance requirements:* For master's, GRE; Please visit website: https://www.american.edu/cas/economics/, statement of purpose, transcripts, 2 letters of recommendation, resume; for doctorate, GRE, statement of purpose, transcripts, 2 letters of recommendation, resume; for Certificate, bachelor's degree, statement of purpose, transcripts, resume. Additional exam requirements/recommendations for international students: required—TOEFL (minimum score 600 paper-based; 100 iBT). Electronic applications accepted. *Expenses:* Contact institution.

American University, School of International Service, Washington, DC 20016-8071. Offers comparative and regional studies (Certificate); cross-cultural communication (Certificate); development management (MS); ethics, peace, and global affairs (MA); European studies (Certificate); global environmental policy (MA, Certificate); global information technology (Certificate); global media (MA); international affairs (MA), including comparative and regional studies, global governance, politics, and security, international economic relations, natural resources and sustainable development, U.S. foreign policy and national security; international arts management (Certificate); international communication (MA, Certificate); international development (MA); international economic policy (Certificate); international economic relations (Certificate); international economics (MA); international peace and conflict resolution (MA, Certificate); international politics (Certificate); international relations (MA, PhD); international service (MIS); peacebuilding (Certificate); social enterprise (MA); the Americas (Certificate); United States foreign policy (Certificate); JD/MA. *Program availability:* Part-time, evening/weekend, 100% online, blended/hybrid learning. Terminal master's awarded for partial completion of doctoral program. *Degree requirements:* For master's, one foreign language, comprehensive exam, thesis or alternative; for doctorate, one foreign language, comprehensive exam, thesis/dissertation. *Entrance requirements:* For master's, transcripts, resume, 2 letters of recommendation, statement of purpose; for doctorate, GRE, transcripts, resume, 3 letters of recommendation, statement of purpose. Additional exam requirements/recommendations for international students: required—TOEFL. Electronic applications accepted. *Expenses:* Contact institution.

Baruch College of the City University of New York, Austin W. Marxe School of Public and International Affairs, Program in International Affairs, New York, NY 10010-5585. Offers international nongovernmental organizations (MIA); trade policy and global economic governance (MIA); Western Hemisphere affairs (MIA). *Program availability:* Part-time.

Claremont Graduate University, Graduate Programs, School of Social Science, Policy and Evaluation, Department of Economics, Claremont, CA 91711-6160. Offers behavioral economics and neuroeconomics (PhD); business and financial economics (MA, PhD); economic development (Certificate); international economic and development policy (PhD); international economics policy and development (MA); international money and finance (PhD); political economy and public economics (PhD); political economy and public policy (MA); MBA/PhD. *Program availability:* Part-time. *Entrance requirements:* For master's and doctorate, GRE General Test or GMAT. Additional exam requirements/recommendations for international students: required—TOEFL (minimum score 75 iBT). Electronic applications accepted.

Cleveland State University, College of Graduate Studies, College of Liberal Arts and Social Sciences, Department of Political Science, Cleveland, OH 44115. Offers global interactions (MA), including global business interactions, global political interactions. *Entrance requirements:* For master's, minimum undergraduate GPA of 3.0 or GRE (50th percentile or above); two letters of recommendation; undergraduate degree in economics, political science, international relations, or a related discipline; completion of undergraduate macro and micro economics course. Additional exam requirements/recommendations for international students: required—TOEFL (minimum score 550 paper-based; 78 iBT). Electronic applications accepted. *Expenses:* Contact institution.

Fordham University, Gabelli School of Business, New York, NY 10023. Offers accounting (MBA, MS); applied statistics and decision-making (MS); business economics (DPS); capital markets (DPS); communications and media management (MBA); electronic business (MBA); entrepreneurship (MBA); finance (MBA, PhD); global finance (MS); global sustainability (MBA); health administration (MS); healthcare management (MBA); information systems (MBA, MS); investor relations (MS); management (EMBA, MBA, MS, PhD); marketing (MBA); marketing intelligence (MS); media management (MS); nonprofit leadership (MS); quantitative finance (MS); strategy and decision-making (DPS); taxation (MS); JD/MBA; MS/MBA. *Accreditation:* AACSB. *Program availability:* Part-time, evening/weekend, 100% online, blended/hybrid learning. *Faculty:* 130 full-time (49 women), 73 part-time/adjunct (12 women). *Students:* 1,038 full-time, 503 part-time; includes 227 minority (57 Black or African American, non-Hispanic/Latino; 1 American Indian or Alaska Native, non-Hispanic/Latino; 65 Asian, non-Hispanic/Latino; 91 Hispanic/Latino; 1 Native Hawaiian or other Pacific Islander, non-Hispanic/Latino; 12 Two or more races, non-Hispanic/Latino), 985 international. Average age 27. 4,250 applicants, 62% accepted, 764 enrolled. In 2019, 899 master's awarded. Terminal master's awarded for partial completion of doctoral program. *Degree requirements:* For master's, internships (for some degrees); for doctorate, comprehensive exam (for some programs), thesis/dissertation. *Entrance requirements:* For master's, GMAT/GRE, 2 letters of recommendation, resume, 2 essays, transcripts, interview. Additional exam requirements/recommendations for international students: required—TOEFL (minimum score 100 iBT), IELTS (minimum score 7). *Application deadline:* For fall admission, 11/15 for domestic and international students; for winter admission, 1/10 for domestic students, 1/1 for international students; for spring admission, 5/15 for domestic students, 3/1 for international students; for summer admission, 7/10 for domestic students, 6/5 for international students. Application fee: $130. Electronic applications accepted. *Expenses:* Contact institution. *Financial support:* Career-related internships or fieldwork, institutionally sponsored loans, scholarships/grants, and unspecified assistantships available. Support available to part-time students. Financial award application deadline: 6/5; financial award applicants required to submit FAFSA. *Unit head:* Dr. Donna Rapaccioli, Dean, 212-636-6165, Fax: 212-307-1779, E-mail: rapaccioli@fordham.edu. *Application contact:* Lawrence Mur'ray, Senior Assistant Dean of Graduate Admissions and Advising, 212-636-6200, Fax: 212-636-7076, E-mail: admissionsgb@fordham.edu.
Website: http://www.fordham.edu/gabelli

Fordham University, Graduate School of Arts and Sciences, Program in International Political Economy and Development, New York, NY 10458. Offers MA, Certificate. *Program availability:* Part-time, evening/weekend. *Students:* Average age 27. 81 applicants, 57% accepted, 17 enrolled. In 2019, 21 master's awarded. *Entrance requirements:* For master's, GRE General Test. Additional exam requirements/recommendations for international students: required—TOEFL (minimum score 600 paper-based). *Application deadline:* For fall admission, 1/4 priority date for domestic students; for spring admission, 11/1 for domestic students. Application fee: $70. Electronic applications accepted. *Financial support:* In 2019–20, 35 students received support, including 4 fellowships with tuition reimbursements available (averaging $17,014 per year); research assistantships, career-related internships or fieldwork, institutionally sponsored loans, tuition waivers (full and partial), and unspecified assistantships also available. Financial award application deadline: 1/4; financial award applicants required to submit FAFSA. *Unit head:* Dr. Henry Schwalbenberg, Chair, 718-817-3866, Fax: 718-817-3518. *Application contact:* Garrett Marino, Director of Graduate Admissions, 718-817-4419, Fax: 718-817-3566, E-mail: gmarino10@fordham.edu.

The Institute of World Politics, Graduate Programs in National Security, Intelligence, and International Affairs, Washington, DC 20036. Offers American foreign policy (Certificate); comparative political culture (Certificate); conflict prevention (Certificate); counterintelligence (Certificate); counterterrorism (Certificate); cyber statecraft (Certificate); economic statecraft (Certificate); homeland security (Certificate); intelligence (Certificate); international politics (Certificate); national security affairs (Executive MA, Certificate); nonviolent conflict (Certificate); peace building, stabilization, and humanitarian affairs (Certificate); public diplomacy and strategic influence (Certificate); statecraft and international affairs (MA); statecraft and national security (MA, DSNS); strategic communication (Certificate); strategic intelligence studies (MA, Professional MA); strategic soft power (Certificate). *Program availability:* Part-time, evening/weekend. *Degree requirements:* For master's, 52 credit hours, comprehensive written and oral exam (for MA); proficiency in critical language (for MA in statecraft and international affairs); 28 credit hours (for Executive MA); 36 credit hours (for Professional MA); for doctorate, comprehensive exam, thesis/dissertation; for Certificate, 20 credit hours. *Entrance requirements:* For master's, resume, personal statement, 3 references, essay; 7-10 years of professional experience (for Executive MA); 5-7 years of professional experience (for Professional MA); for doctorate, MA. Additional exam requirements/recommendations for international students: required—TOEFL. Electronic applications accepted.

Johns Hopkins University, School of Advanced International Studies, Washington, DC 20036. Offers global risk (MA); international development (MA, Certificate), including international economics (MA); international economics (Certificate); international economics and finance (MA); international public policy (MIPP); international relations (PhD); international studies (Certificate); Japan studies (MA), including international economics; Korea studies (MA), including international economics; South Asia studies (MA), including international economics; Southeast Asia studies (MA), including international economics; JD/MA; MBA/MA; MHS/MA. *Program availability:* Evening/weekend. *Degree requirements:* For master's, 4-6 international economics courses, 5-6 functional or regional concentration courses, 2 core examinations, proficiency in language other than native language, capstone project; for doctorate, 2 foreign languages, thesis/dissertation, 3 comprehensive exams, economics, quantitative and qualitative course, dissertation prospectus and defense. *Entrance requirements:* For master's, GMAT or GRE General Test, previous course work in economics, foreign language, undergraduate degree; for doctorate, GRE General Test, Master's degree. Additional exam requirements/recommendations for international students: required—TOEFL (minimum score 600 paper-based; 100 iBT), IELTS (minimum score 7), TOEFL (minimum score 600 paper-based; 100 iBT) or IELTS (minimum score 7). Electronic applications accepted. *Expenses:* Contact institution.

The New School, The New School for Social Research, Department of Economics, New York, NY 10003. Offers economics (MA, MS, PhD); global political economy and finance (MA). *Program availability:* Part-time. *Faculty:* 9 full-time (3 women), 2 part-time/adjunct (0 women). *Students:* 80 full-time (30 women), 25 part-time (9 women); includes 22 minority (7 Black or African American, non-Hispanic/Latino; 6 Asian, non-Hispanic/Latino; 8 Hispanic/Latino; 1 Two or more races, non-Hispanic/Latino), 52 international. Average age 32. 147 applicants, 66% accepted, 21 enrolled. In 2019, 39 master's, 8 doctorates awarded. Terminal master's awarded for partial completion of doctoral program. *Degree requirements:* For master's, comprehensive exam (for some programs), mentored research/internship; for doctorate, one foreign language, comprehensive exam, thesis/dissertation. *Entrance requirements:* For master's, GRE, letters of recommendation, writing sample, essays, transcript; for doctorate, letters of recommendation, writing sample, essays, transcript. Additional exam requirements/recommendations for international students: required—TOEFL (minimum score 100 iBT), IELTS (minimum score 7), PTE (minimum score 68). *Application deadline:* For fall admission, 1/5 priority date for domestic and international students; for spring admission, 10/15 priority date for domestic and international students. Applications are processed on a rolling basis. Application fee: $50. Electronic applications accepted. *Expenses:* 2260 per credit. *Financial support:* In 2019–20, 84 students received support, including 14 fellowships (averaging $6,912 per year), 18 research assistantships (averaging $5,253 per year), 19 teaching assistantships with full and partial tuition reimbursements available (averaging $7,989 per year); career-related internships or fieldwork, Federal Work-Study, scholarships/grants, tuition waivers (full and partial), and unspecified assistantships also available. Support available to part-time students. Financial award application deadline: 2/1; financial award applicants required to submit FAFSA. *Unit head:* Mark Setterfield, PhD, Department Chair, 212-229-5717 Ext. 3047, E-mail: setterfm@newschool.edu. *Application contact:* Merida Gasbarro, Director of Graduate Admission, 212-229-5600 Ext. 1108, E-mail: escandom@newschool.edu.
Website: https://www.newschool.edu/nssr/economics/

Pace University, Lubin School of Business, Advanced Professional Certificate Program, New York, NY 10038. Offers business economics (APC); e-business (APC); financial management (APC); international business (APC); international economics (APC); investment management (APC); marketing (APC); public accounting (APC). *Program availability:* Part-time, evening/weekend. *Entrance requirements:* For degree, MBA or MS in business discipline, relevant professional experience. Additional exam requirements/recommendations for international students: required—TOEFL (minimum score 90 iBT), IELTS (minimum score 7) or PTE (minimum score 61). Electronic applications accepted.

University of California, San Diego, Graduate Division, School of Global Policy and Strategy, Master of International Affairs Program, La Jolla, CA 92093. Offers international development and nonprofit management (MIA); international economics (MIA); international environmental policy (MIA); international management (MIA); international politics (MIA). *Degree requirements:* For master's, one foreign language. *Entrance requirements:* For master's, GMAT or GRE General Test. Additional exam requirements/recommendations for international students: required—TOEFL (minimum score 90 iBT), IELTS (minimum score 7). Electronic applications accepted.

University of New Mexico, Graduate Studies, College of Arts and Sciences, Program in Economics, Albuquerque, NM 87131-2039. Offers econometrics (MA); economic theory (MA); environmental/natural resource economics (MA, PhD); international/development and sustainability economics (MA, PhD); public economics (MA, PhD). *Program availability:* Part-time. Terminal master's awarded for partial completion of doctoral program. *Degree requirements:* For master's, comprehensive exam, thesis (for some programs); for doctorate, comprehensive exam, thesis/dissertation. *Entrance requirements:* For master's and doctorate, GRE General Test, 3 letters of recommendation, letter of intent, curriculum vitae. Additional exam requirements/recommendations for international students: required—TOEFL (minimum score 520 paper-based; 68 iBT). Electronic applications accepted. *Expenses:* Tuition, state resident: full-time $7633; part-time $972 per year. Tuition, nonresident: full-time $22,586; part-time $3840 per year. *International tuition:* $23,292 full-time. *Required fees:* $8608. Tuition and fees vary according to course level, course load, degree level, program and student level.

Valparaiso University, Graduate School and Continuing Education, Program in International Economics and Finance, Valparaiso, IN 46383. Offers MS. *Program availability:* Part-time, evening/weekend. *Entrance requirements:* For master's, 1 semester of college-level calculus; 1 statistics or quantitative methods class; 2 semesters of introductory economics (course content in introductory economics must include both introductory microeconomics and macroeconomics); 1 introductory accounting course; minimum undergraduate GPA of 3.0; 2 letters of recommendation. Additional exam requirements/recommendations for international students: required—TOEFL (minimum score 550 paper-based; 80 iBT), IELTS (minimum score 6).

Wayne State University, College of Liberal Arts and Sciences, Department of Economics, Detroit, MI 48202. Offers applied macroeconomics (MA, PhD); health economics (MA, PhD); industrial organization (MA, PhD); international economics (MA, PhD); labor and human resources (MA, PhD); JD/MA. *Faculty:* 10. *Students:* 47 full-time (13 women), 6 part-time (2 women); includes 8 minority (4 Black or African American, non-Hispanic/Latino; 2 Asian, non-Hispanic/Latino; 2 Hispanic/Latino), 18 international. Average age 31. 67 applicants, 37% accepted, 8 enrolled. In 2019, 4 master's, 2 doctorates awarded. *Degree requirements:* For master's, comprehensive exam; for doctorate, comprehensive exam, thesis/dissertation, oral examination on research, completion of course work in quantitative methods, final lecture. *Entrance requirements:* For master's, minimum upper-division GPA of 3.0; prior coursework in intermediate microeconomic and macroeconomic theory, statistics, and elementary calculus; for doctorate, GRE, minimum upper-division GPA of 3.0, prior coursework in intermediate microeconomic and macroeconomic theory, statistics, two courses in calculus, three

International Economics

letters of recommendation from officials or teaching staff at institution(s) most recently attended, statement of purpose. Additional exam requirements/recommendations for international students: required—TOEFL (minimum score 550 paper-based; 79 iBT), TWE (minimum score 5.5), Michigan English Language Assessment Battery (minimum score 85); recommended—IELTS (minimum score 6.5). *Application deadline:* For fall admission, 5/1 for domestic and international students; for winter admission, 10/1 priority date for domestic students, 9/1 priority date for international students; for spring admission, 1/1 priority date for domestic and international students. Applications are processed on a rolling basis. Application fee: $50. Electronic applications accepted. *Expenses: Tuition:* Full-time $34,567. *Financial support:* In 2019–20, 30 students received support, including 2 fellowships with tuition reimbursements available (averaging $20,000 per year), 17 teaching assistantships with tuition reimbursements available (averaging $19,883 per year); research assistantships, scholarships/grants, health care benefits, and unspecified assistantships also available. Support available to part-time students. Financial award applicants required to submit FAFSA. *Unit head:* Dr. Kevin Cotter, Department Chair, 313-577-3345, E-mail: kevin.cotter@wayne.edu. *Application contact:* Dr. Allen Charles Goodman, Professor and Director of Graduate Studies, 313-577-3235, E-mail: aa1313@wayne.edu. Website: http://clas.wayne.edu/economics/

Wichita State University, Graduate School, W. Frank Barton School of Business, Department of Economics, Wichita, KS 67260. Offers applied economics (MA), including data analysis, financial economics, international economics. *Program availability:* Part-time, evening/weekend.

Wilfrid Laurier University, Faculty of Graduate and Postdoctoral Studies, School of International Policy and Governance, International Public Policy Program, Waterloo, ON N2L 3C5, Canada. Offers global governance (MIPP); human security (MIPP); international economic relations (MIPP); international environmental policy (MIPP). *Entrance requirements:* For master's, honours BA with minimum B average. Additional exam requirements/recommendations for international students: required—TOEFL (minimum score 89 iBT). Electronic applications accepted.

Yale University, Graduate School of Arts and Sciences, Department of Economics, Program in International and Development Economics, New Haven, CT 06520. Offers MA. *Entrance requirements:* For master's, GRE General Test.

Mineral Economics

Colorado School of Mines, Office of Graduate Studies, Department of Economics and Business, Golden, CO 80401. Offers engineering and technology management (MS); mineral and energy economics (MS, PhD); operations research and engineering (PhD); petroleum economics and management with mineral and energy economics (MS). *Program availability:* Part-time. *Degree requirements:* For master's, thesis (for some programs); for doctorate, comprehensive exam, thesis/dissertation. *Entrance requirements:* For master's and doctorate, GRE General Test. Additional exam requirements/recommendations for international students: required—TOEFL (minimum score 550 paper-based; 79 iBT). Electronic applications accepted. *Expenses:* Tuition, state resident: full-time $16,650; part-time $925 per credit hour. Tuition, nonresident: full-time $37,350; part-time $2075 per credit hour. *International tuition:* $37,350 full-time. *Required fees:* $2412.

Michigan Technological University, Graduate School, College of Business, Houghton, MI 49931. Offers applied natural resource economics (MS); business administration (MBA). *Accreditation:* AACSB. *Program availability:* Part-time, evening/weekend. *Faculty:* 24 full-time (8 women), 1 part-time/adjunct. *Students:* 34 full-time (13 women), 13 part-time (7 women); includes 5 minority (3 Black or African American, non-Hispanic/Latino; 1 Asian, non-Hispanic/Latino; 1 Hispanic/Latino), 8 international. Average age 28. 162 applicants, 27% accepted, 30 enrolled. In 2019, 55 master's awarded. *Degree requirements:* For master's, thesis (for some programs). *Entrance requirements:* For master's, GMAT/GRE (recommended minimum score in the 55th percentile), statement of purpose, personal statement, official transcripts, 2 letters of recommendation, resume/curriculum vitae. Additional exam requirements/recommendations for international students: recommended—TOEFL (minimum score 95 iBT), IELTS (minimum score 7). *Application deadline:* For fall admission, 7/1 for domestic and international students; for spring admission, 12/1 for domestic and international students. Applications are processed on a rolling basis. Application fee: $0. Electronic applications accepted. *Expenses: Tuition, area resident:* Full-time $19,206; part-time $1067 per credit. Tuition, state resident: full-time $19,206; part-time $1067 per credit. Tuition, nonresident: full-time $19,206; part-time $1067 per credit. *International tuition:* $19,206 full-time. *Required fees:* $248; $248 per unit. $124 per semester. Tuition and fees vary according to course load and program. *Financial support:* In 2019–20, 23 students received support, including 4 fellowships with tuition reimbursements available (averaging $16,590 per year), 1 teaching assistantship with tuition reimbursement available (averaging $16,590 per year); health care benefits and unspecified assistantships also available. Financial award application deadline: 4/1; financial award applicants required to submit FAFSA. *Unit head:* Dr. Dean Johnson, Dean, 906-487-2668, Fax: 906-487-1863, E-mail: dean@mtu.edu. *Application contact:* Ashli Wells, Assistant Director of Graduate Enrollment Services, 906-487-3513, Fax: 906-487-2284, E-mail: gradadms@mtu.edu. Website: http://www.mtu.edu/business/

The University of Texas at Austin, Graduate School, Cockrell School of Engineering, Department of Petroleum and Geosystems Engineering, Program in Energy and Earth Resources, Austin, TX 78712-1111. Offers MA. *Degree requirements:* For master's, thesis, seminar. *Entrance requirements:* For master's, GRE General Test. Additional exam requirements/recommendations for international students: required—TOEFL. Electronic applications accepted.

Section 20
Family and Consumer Sciences

This section contains a directory of institutions offering graduate work in family and consumer sciences. Additional information about programs listed in the directory but not augmented by an in-depth entry may be obtained by writing directly to the dean of a graduate school or chair of a department at the address given in the directory.

For programs offering related work, see also in this book *Economics, Psychology and Counseling,* and *Sociology, Anthropology, and Archaeology.* In another guide in this series:

Graduate Programs in Business, Education, Health, Information Studies, Law & Social Work

See *Social Work*

CONTENTS

Program Directories

Family and Consumer Sciences-General

Alabama Agricultural and Mechanical University, School of Graduate Studies, College of Agricultural, Life and Natural Sciences, Department of Family and Consumer Sciences, Huntsville, AL 35811. Offers apparel, merchandising and design (MS); family and consumer sciences (MS); human development and family studies (MS); nutrition and hospitality management (MS). *Program availability:* Part-time, evening/weekend. *Degree requirements:* For master's, comprehensive exam, thesis optional. *Entrance requirements:* For master's, GRE General Test. Additional exam requirements/recommendations for international students: required—TOEFL (minimum score 500 paper-based; 61 iBT). Electronic applications accepted.

Ball State University, Graduate School, Teachers College, Department of Family, Consumer, and Technology Education, Muncie, IN 47306. Offers family and consumer science (MS), including apparel design (MA, MS), fashion merchandising (MA, MS), interior design (MA, MS), residential property management (MA, MS); family and consumer sciences (MA), including apparel design (MA, MS), fashion merchandising (MA, MS), interior design (MA, MS), residential property management (MA, MS); nutrition and dietetics (MA, MS). *Program availability:* Part-time, evening/weekend, 100% online. *Entrance requirements:* For master's, letter of intent, resume, two letters of recommendation, portfolio (for interior design option). Additional exam requirements/recommendations for international students: required—TOEFL (minimum score 550 paper-based; 79 iBT), IELTS (minimum score 6.5). Electronic applications accepted. *Expenses: Tuition, area resident:* Full-time $7506; part-time $417 per credit hour. Tuition, nonresident: full-time $20,610; part-time $1145 per credit hour. *Required fees:* $2126. Tuition and fees vary according to course load, campus/location and program.

California State University, Northridge, Graduate Studies, College of Health and Human Development, Department of Family and Consumer Sciences, Northridge, CA 91330. Offers MS. *Program availability:* Part-time, evening/weekend. *Degree requirements:* For master's, thesis, project, or comprehensive exam. *Entrance requirements:* For master's, GRE General Test or minimum GPA of 3.0. Additional exam requirements/recommendations for international students: required—TOEFL.

Central Michigan University, College of Graduate Studies, College of Education and Human Services, Department of Human Environmental Studies, Mount Pleasant, MI 48859. Offers apparel product development and merchandising technology (MS); gerontology (Graduate Certificate); human development and family studies (MA); nutrition and dietetics (MS). *Program availability:* Part-time, evening/weekend. *Degree requirements:* For master's, thesis or alternative. Electronic applications accepted. *Expenses: Tuition, area resident:* Full-time $12,267; part-time $8178 per year. Tuition, state resident: full-time $12,267; part-time $8178 per year. Tuition, nonresident: full-time $12,267; part-time $8178 per year. *International tuition:* $16,110 full-time. *Required fees:* $225 per semester. Tuition and fees vary according to degree level and program.

Central Washington University, School of Graduate Studies and Research, College of Education and Professional Studies, Department of Family and Consumer Sciences, Ellensburg, WA 98926. Offers career and technical education (MS); family and child life (MS); family and consumer sciences education (MS). *Program availability:* Part-time. *Entrance requirements:* For master's, minimum GPA of 3.0. Additional exam requirements/recommendations for international students: required—TOEFL (minimum score 550 paper-based; 79 iBT). Electronic applications accepted.

Clemson University, Graduate School, College of Behavioral, Social and Health Sciences, PhD Program in International Family and Community Studies, Clemson, SC 29634. Offers international family and community studies (PhD, Certificate). *Faculty:* 2 full-time (both women), 1 part-time/adjunct (0 women). *Students:* 5 full-time (all women), 24 part-time (18 women); includes 1 minority (Hispanic/Latino), 18 international. Average age 39. 23 applicants, 26% accepted. In 2019, 7 doctorates, 1 other advanced degree awarded. *Expenses:* Doctoral Base Fee per Semester: $4938 (in-state), $10405 (out-of-state). Graduate Assistant Per Semester: $1144. *Financial support:* Research assistantships and career-related internships or fieldwork available.
Website: https://www.clemson.edu/cbshs/centers-institutes/ifnl/academics/index.html

Florida State University, The Graduate School, College of Human Sciences, Tallahassee, FL 32306-1490. Offers MS, PhD. *Accreditation:* AAMFT/COAMFTE. *Program availability:* Part-time. *Faculty:* 42 full-time (22 women). *Students:* 107 full-time (71 women), 23 part-time (16 women); includes 28 minority (9 Black or African American, non-Hispanic/Latino; 5 Asian, non-Hispanic/Latino; 1 Hispanic/Latino; 13 Two or more races, non-Hispanic/Latino), 15 international. 157 applicants, 58% accepted, 43 enrolled. In 2019, 20 master's, 15 doctorates awarded. *Degree requirements:* For master's, comprehensive exam (for some programs), thesis optional; for doctorate, thesis/dissertation, pass prelim examination, minimum 24 dissertation credit, pass dissertation defense. *Entrance requirements:* For master's, GRE General Test, minimum upper-division GPA of 3.0; for doctorate, GRE General Test, minimum upper-division GPA of 3.0 or awarded master's degree. Additional exam requirements/recommendations for international students: required—TOEFL (minimum score 550 paper-based; 80 iBT). *Application deadline:* For fall admission, 4/1 for domestic and international students; for spring admission, 10/1 for domestic and international students. Applications are processed on a rolling basis. Application fee: $30. Electronic applications accepted. *Financial support:* In 2019–20, 101 students received support, including 21 research assistantships with full tuition reimbursements available (averaging $23,664 per year), 63 teaching assistantships with full tuition reimbursements available (averaging $23,664 per year); career-related internships or fieldwork, Federal Work-Study, scholarships/grants, and unspecified assistantships also available. Financial award application deadline: 1/15; financial award applicants required to submit FAFSA. *Unit head:* Dr. Michael D. Delp, Dean, 850-644-1281, E-mail: mdelp@fsu.edu. *Application contact:* Tara L. Hartman, Academic Program Specialist, 850-644-7221, E-mail: thartman@fsu.edu.
Website: http://humansciences.fsu.edu

Fontbonne University, Graduate Programs, St. Louis, MO 63105-3098. Offers accounting (MBA, MS); art (MA); art (K-12) (MAT); business (MBA); computer science (MS); deaf education (MA); early intervention in deaf education (MA); education (MA), including autism spectrum disorders, curriculum and instruction, diverse learners, early childhood education, reading, special education; elementary education (MAT); family and consumer sciences (MA), including multidisciplinary health communication studies; fine arts (MFA); instructional design and technology (MS); management and leadership (MM); middle school education (MAT); secondary education (MAT); special education (MAT); speech-language pathology (MS); supply chain management (MS); theatre (MA). *Accreditation:* ASHA. *Program availability:* Part-time, evening/weekend, online learning. *Degree requirements:* For master's, comprehensive exam (for some programs), thesis (for some programs). *Entrance requirements:* Additional exam requirements/recommendations for international students: required—TOEFL (minimum score 500 paper-based; 65 iBT). Electronic applications accepted. *Expenses: Tuition:* Full-time $6975; part-time $775 per credit hour. *Required fees:* $225; $25 per credit hour. Tuition and fees vary according to degree level and program.

Hofstra University, School of Education, Programs in Teacher Education, Hempstead, NY 11549. Offers bilingual education (MA); bilingual extension (Advanced Certificate); business education (MS Ed); curriculum studies (MS Ed); early childhood and childhood education (MS Ed); early childhood education (MA, MS Ed); educational technology (Advanced Certificate); elementary education (MA, MS Ed); English education (MS Ed); family and consumer science (MS Ed); fine arts and music education (Advanced Certificate); fine arts education (MS Ed); foreign language and TESOL (MS Ed); foreign language education (MA, MS Ed); languages other than English and teaching English as a second language (MA); learning and teaching (Ed D); mathematics education (MA, MS Ed); middle childhood extension (Advanced Certificate); music education (MA, MS Ed); science education (MA); secondary education (Advanced Certificate); social studies education (MA, MS Ed); teaching languages other than English and TESOL (MS Ed); technology for learning (MA); TESOL (MS Ed, Advanced Certificate); TESOL with specialization in STEM (MA); work based learning extension (Advanced Certificate). *Program availability:* Part-time, evening/weekend, online only, blended/hybrid learning. *Students:* 131 full-time (96 women), 107 part-time (79 women); includes 60 minority (14 Black or African American, non-Hispanic/Latino; 12 Asian, non-Hispanic/Latino; 33 Hispanic/Latino; 1 Two or more races, non-Hispanic/Latino), 4 international. Average age 29. 228 applicants, 84% accepted, 114 enrolled. In 2019, 96 master's, 5 doctorates, 37 other advanced degrees awarded. *Degree requirements:* For master's, comprehensive exam, thesis (for some programs), exit project, student teaching, fieldwork, electronic portfolio, curriculum project, minimum GPA of 3.0; for doctorate, dissertation; for Advanced Certificate, 3 foreign languages, comprehensive exam (for some programs), thesis project. *Entrance requirements:* For master's, GRE, 2 letters of recommendation, portfolio, teacher certification (MA), interview, essay; for doctorate, GMAT, GRE, LSAT, or MAT; for Advanced Certificate, 2 letters of recommendation, essay, interview and/or portfolio, teaching certificate. Additional exam requirements/recommendations for international students: required—TOEFL (minimum score 550 paper-based; 80 iBT); recommended—IELTS (minimum score 6.5). *Application deadline:* Applications are processed on a rolling basis. Application fee: $75. Electronic applications accepted. *Expenses: Tuition:* Full-time $25,164; part-time $1398 per credit. *Required fees:* $580; $165 per semester. Tuition and fees vary according to course load, degree level and program. *Financial support:* In 2019–20, 112 students received support, including 61 fellowships with full and partial tuition reimbursements available (averaging $5,336 per year), 2 research assistantships with full and partial tuition reimbursements available (averaging $2,075 per year); career-related internships or fieldwork, Federal Work-Study, institutionally sponsored loans, scholarships/grants, traineeships, tuition waivers (full and partial), unspecified assistantships, and scholarships and endowed scholarships also available. Support available to part-time students. Financial award applicants required to submit FAFSA. *Unit head:* Dr. Sandra Stacki, Chairperson, 516-463-5783, Fax: 516-463-6275, E-mail: sandra.l.stacki@hofstra.edu. *Application contact:* Sunil Samuel, Assistant Vice President of Admissions, 516-463-4723, Fax: 516-463-4664, E-mail: graduateadmission@hofstra.edu.
Website: http://www.hofstra.edu/education/

Illinois State University, Graduate School, College of Applied Science and Technology, Department of Family and Consumer Sciences, Normal, IL 61790. Offers MA, MS. *Faculty:* 22 full-time (20 women), 17 part-time/adjunct (15 women). *Students:* 47 full-time (40 women), 15 part-time (all women). Average age 24. 76 applicants, 68% accepted, 36 enrolled. In 2019, 18 master's awarded. *Degree requirements:* For master's, one foreign language, thesis or alternative. *Entrance requirements:* For master's, GRE General Test, minimum GPA of 2.8 in last 60 hours of course work. *Application deadline:* Applications are processed on a rolling basis. Application fee: $50. *Expenses: Tuition, area resident:* Full-time $7956; part-time $9767 per year. Tuition, nonresident: full-time $9233; part-time $17,592 per year. *Required fees:* $1797. *Financial support:* In 2019–20, 2 research assistantships, 22 teaching assistantships were awarded; tuition waivers (full) and unspecified assistantships also available. Financial award application deadline: 4/1. *Unit head:* Dr. Ani Yazedjian, Department Chair, 309-438-2517, Fax: 309-438-5659, E-mail: fcs@ilstu.edu. *Application contact:* Dr. Jennifer Barnes, Graduate Program Coordinator, 309-438-2517, Fax: 309-438-5659, E-mail: jlbarn2@ilstu.edu.
Website: http://fcs.illinoisstate.edu/

Iowa State University of Science and Technology, Program in Family and Consumer Sciences, Ames, IA 50011. Offers MFCS. *Degree requirements:* For master's, thesis or alternative. *Entrance requirements:* For master's, GRE General Test. Additional exam requirements/recommendations for international students: required—TOEFL (minimum score 550 paper-based; 79 iBT), IELTS (minimum score 6.5). Electronic applications accepted.

Kansas State University, Graduate School, College of Human Ecology, Manhattan, KS 66506. Offers MS, PhD, Graduate Certificate. *Program availability:* Part-time, online learning. *Degree requirements:* For master's, residency; for doctorate, thesis/dissertation, residency. Electronic applications accepted.

Lamar University, College of Graduate Studies, College of Education and Human Development, Department of Family and Consumer Sciences, Beaumont, TX 77710. Offers MS. *Program availability:* Part-time, evening/weekend. *Faculty:* 10 full-time (9 women), 3 part-time/adjunct (all women). *Students:* 12 full-time (11 women), 74 part-time (62 women); includes 54 minority (28 Black or African American, non-Hispanic/Latino; 3 Asian, non-Hispanic/Latino; 22 Hispanic/Latino; 1 Two or more races, non-Hispanic/Latino), 1 international. Average age 33. 107 applicants, 90% accepted, 49 enrolled. In 2019, 11 master's awarded. *Degree requirements:* For master's, thesis optional. *Entrance requirements:* For master's, GRE General Test. Additional exam requirements/recommendations for international students: required—TOEFL (minimum score 550 paper-based; 79 iBT), IELTS (minimum score 6.5). *Application deadline:* Applications are processed on a rolling basis. Application fee: $25 ($50 for international students). Electronic applications accepted. *Expenses: Tuition, area resident:* Full-time $6324; part-time $351 per credit. Tuition, state resident: full-time $6324; part-time $351 per credit. Tuition, nonresident: full-time $13,920; part-time $773 per credit. *International tuition:* $13,920 full-time. *Required fees:* $2462; $327 per credit. Tuition and fees vary according to course load, campus/location and reciprocity agreements. *Financial support:* In 2019–20, 7 students received support. Fellowships, research assistantships, teaching assistantships, career-related internships or fieldwork, Federal Work-Study, and institutionally sponsored loans available. Support available to part-time students. Financial award applicants required to submit FAFSA. *Unit head:* Dr. Jill Killough, Department Chair, 409-880-8668, Fax: 409-880-8666. *Application contact:* Celeste Contreas, Director, Admissions and Academic Services, 409-880-8888, Fax:

409-880-7419, E-mail: gradmissions@lamar.edu.
Website: http://education.lamar.edu/family-and-consumer-sciences

Louisiana State University and Agricultural & Mechanical College, Graduate School, College of Agriculture, School of Human Ecology, Baton Rouge, LA 70803. Offers MS, PhD.

New Mexico State University, College of Agricultural, Consumer and Environmental Sciences, Department of Family and Consumer Sciences, Las Cruces, NM 88003-8001. Offers clothing, textiles, and merchandising (MS); family and child science (MS); family and consumer science education (MS); family and consumer sciences (MS); food science and technology (MS); hotel, restaurant, and tourism management (MS); human nutrition and dietetic sciences (MS). *Program availability:* Part-time. *Faculty:* 10 full-time (7 women), 1 (woman) part-time/adjunct. *Students:* 29 full-time (23 women), 11 part-time (10 women); includes 25 minority (1 Black or African American, non-Hispanic/Latino; 3 Asian, non-Hispanic/Latino; 20 Hispanic/Latino; 1 Two or more races, non-Hispanic/Latino), 3 international. Average age 30. 23 applicants, 87% accepted, 16 enrolled. In 2019, 19 master's awarded. *Degree requirements:* For master's, comprehensive exam (for some programs), thesis (for some programs), oral exam. *Entrance requirements:* For master's, GRE, 3 letters of reference from faculty members or employers, resume, letter of interest. Additional exam requirements/recommendations for international students: required—TOEFL (minimum score 550 paper-based; 79 iBT), IELTS (minimum score 6.5). *Application deadline:* For fall admission, 2/1 priority date for domestic and international students; for spring admission, 10/1 for domestic and international students. Applications are processed on a rolling basis. Application fee: $40 ($50 for international students). Electronic applications accepted. *Financial support:* In 2019–20, 24 students received support, including 4 research assistantships (averaging $15,515 per year), 10 teaching assistantships (averaging $14,076 per year); career-related internships or fieldwork, Federal Work-Study, scholarships/grants, traineeships, health care benefits, and unspecified assistantships also available. Support available to part-time students. Financial award application deadline: 3/1. *Application contact:* Dr. Kourtney Vaillancourt, Graduate Program Contact, 575-646-3383, Fax: 575-646-1889, E-mail: kvaillan@nmsu.edu. Website: http://aces.nmsu.edu/academics/fcs

North Carolina Agricultural and Technical State University, The Graduate College, College of Agriculture and Environmental Sciences, Department of Family and Consumer Sciences, Greensboro, NC 27411. Offers child development, early education and family studies (MAT); family and consumer sciences education (MAT); food and nutritional sciences (MS). *Program availability:* Part-time, evening/weekend. *Degree requirements:* For master's, comprehensive exam, thesis or alternative, qualifying exam. *Entrance requirements:* For master's, GRE General Test, minimum GPA of 2.6.

North Dakota State University, College of Graduate and Interdisciplinary Studies, College of Human Development and Education, School of Education, Program in Family and Consumer Sciences Education, Fargo, ND 58102. Offers M Ed, MS. *Accreditation:* NCATE. *Program availability:* Part-time. *Degree requirements:* For master's, comprehensive exam, thesis or alternative. *Entrance requirements:* For master's, MAT. Additional exam requirements/recommendations for international students: required—TOEFL. Tuition and fees vary according to program and reciprocity agreements.

The Ohio State University, Graduate School, College of Education and Human Ecology, Department of Human Sciences, Columbus, OH 43210. Offers consumer sciences (MS, PhD); human development and family science (PhD); human nutrition (MS, PhD); kinesiology (MA, Ed D, PhD). *Program availability:* Part-time. *Degree requirements:* For master's, thesis optional; for doctorate, thesis/dissertation. *Entrance requirements:* For master's and doctorate, GRE. Additional exam requirements/recommendations for international students: required—TOEFL (minimum score 550 paper-based; 79 iBT), Michigan English Language Assessment Battery (minimum score 82); recommended—IELTS (minimum score 7). Electronic applications accepted.

Oklahoma State University, College of Human Sciences, Department of Human Development and Family Science, Stillwater, OK 74078. Offers human development and family science (MS, PhD), including family financial planning (MS), human environmental sciences (PhD). *Accreditation:* AAMFT/COAMFTE (one or more programs are accredited). *Program availability:* Online learning. *Faculty:* 27 full-time (16 women), 4 part-time/adjunct (3 women). *Students:* 36 full-time (30 women), 42 part-time (37 women); includes 17 minority (9 Black or African American, non-Hispanic/Latino; 1 Asian, non-Hispanic/Latino; 3 Hispanic/Latino; 1 Native Hawaiian or other Pacific Islander, non-Hispanic/Latino; 3 Two or more races, non-Hispanic/Latino), 4 international. Average age 30. 54 applicants, 57% accepted, 22 enrolled. In 2019, 28 master's, 6 doctorates awarded. *Entrance requirements:* For master's and doctorate, GRE or GMAT. Additional exam requirements/recommendations for international students: required—TOEFL (minimum score 550 paper-based; 79 iBT). *Application deadline:* For fall admission, 3/1 priority date for international students; for spring admission, 8/1 priority date for international students. Applications are processed on a rolling basis. Application fee: $50 ($75 for international students). Electronic applications accepted. *Expenses:* Tuition, area resident: Full-time $4148.10; part-time $2765.40 per credit hour. Tuition, state resident: full-time $4148.10; part-time $2765.40 per credit hour. Tuition, nonresident: full-time $15,775; part-time $10,516.80 per credit hour. *International tuition:* $15,775.20 full-time. *Required fees:* $2196.90; $122.05 per credit hour. Tuition and fees vary according to course load, campus/location and program. *Financial support:* In 2019–20, 25 research assistantships (averaging $1,431 per year), 20 teaching assistantships (averaging $1,314 per year) were awarded; career-related internships or fieldwork, Federal Work-Study, scholarships/grants, health care benefits, tuition waivers (partial), and unspecified assistantships also available. Support available to part-time students. Financial award application deadline: 3/1; financial award applicants required to submit FAFSA. *Unit head:* Dr. Sissy Osteen, Department Head, 405-744-4741, Fax: 405-744-6344, E-mail: sissy.osteen@okstate.edu. *Application contact:* Dr. Sheryl Tucker, Vice Prov/Dean/Prof, 405-744-6368, E-mail: gradi@okstate.edu. Website: https://education.okstate.edu/departments-programs/human-development-family-science/index.html

Queens College of the City University of New York, Mathematics and Natural Sciences Division, Department of Family, Nutrition and Exercise Sciences, Queens, NY 11367-1597. Offers exercise science specialist (MS); family and consumer science (K-12) (AC); family and consumer science/teaching curriculum (K-12) (MS Ed); nutrition and exercise science (MS); nutrition specialist (MS); physical education (K-12) (AC); physical education/teaching curriculum (pre K-12) (MS Ed). *Program availability:* Part-time, evening/weekend. *Degree requirements:* For master's, research project or comprehensive examination. *Entrance requirements:* For master's, minimum GPA of 3.0. Additional exam requirements/recommendations for international students: required—TOEFL (minimum paper-based score of 600) or IELTS=7 (for program in nutrition). Electronic applications accepted.

Saint Peter's University, Graduate Business Programs, Program in Consumer Science, Jersey City, NJ 07306-5997. Offers mobile intelligence (MS).

Sam Houston State University, College of Health Sciences, Department of Family and Consumer Sciences, Huntsville, TX 77341. Offers dietetics (MS); family and consumer

sciences (MS). *Program availability:* Part-time, evening/weekend. *Degree requirements:* For master's, comprehensive exam, thesis optional, internship. *Entrance requirements:* For master's, GRE General Test, letters of recommendation, personal statement, writing sample. Additional exam requirements/recommendations for international students: required—TOEFL (minimum score 550 paper-based; 79 iBT), IELTS (minimum score 6.5). Electronic applications accepted.

San Francisco State University, Division of Graduate Studies, College of Health and Social Sciences, Department of Family Interiors Nutrition and Apparel, San Francisco, CA 94132-1722. Offers family and consumer sciences (MA). *Program availability:* Part-time. *Application deadline:* Applications are processed on a rolling basis. *Expenses:* Tuition, area resident: Full-time $7176; part-time $4164 per year. Tuition, state resident: full-time $7176; part-time $4164 per year. Tuition, nonresident: full-time $16,680; part-time $396 per unit. *International tuition:* $16,680 full-time. *Required fees:* $1524; $1524 per unit. $762 per semester. Tuition and fees vary according to degree level and program. *Unit head:* Dr. Gus Vouchilas, Chair, 415-338-3420, Fax: 415-338-0947, E-mail: gusv@sfsu.edu. *Application contact:* Dr. Gus Vouchilas, Chair, 415-338-3420, Fax: 415-338-0947, E-mail: gusv@sfsu.edu. Website: http://fina.sfsu.edu/

South Carolina State University, College of Graduate and Professional Studies, Department of Family and Consumer Sciences, Orangeburg, SC 29117-0001. Offers individual and family development (MS); nutritional sciences (MS). *Program availability:* Part-time, evening/weekend. *Degree requirements:* For master's, comprehensive exam, thesis optional, departmental qualifying exam. *Entrance requirements:* For master's, GRE, MAT, or NTE, minimum GPA of 2.7. Electronic applications accepted.

South Dakota State University, Graduate School, College of Education and Human Sciences, Department of Consumer Sciences, Brookings, SD 57007. Offers family financial planning (MS); merchandising (MS). *Entrance requirements:* For master's, resume. Additional exam requirements/recommendations for international students: required—TOEFL (minimum score 525 paper-based).

Stephen F. Austin State University, Graduate School, James I. Perkins College of Education, School of Human Sciences, Nacogdoches, TX 75962. Offers MS. *Degree requirements:* For master's, comprehensive exam, thesis or alternative. *Entrance requirements:* For master's, GRE General Test. Additional exam requirements/recommendations for international students: required—TOEFL.

Tennessee State University, The School of Graduate Studies and Research, College of Agriculture, Human and Natural Sciences, Nashville, TN 37209-1561. Offers agricultural sciences (MS), including agribusiness, agricultural and extension education, animal science, plant and soil science; biological sciences (MS, PhD); biotechnology (PhD); chemistry (MS). *Program availability:* Part-time, evening/weekend. *Degree requirements:* For master's, thesis. *Entrance requirements:* For master's, GRE General Test, GRE Subject Test, MAT.

Texas A&M University–Kingsville, College of Graduate Studies, Dick and Mary Lewis Kleberg College of Agriculture, Natural Resources and Human Sciences, Department of Human Sciences, Kingsville, TX 78363. Offers MS. *Degree requirements:* For master's, variable foreign language requirement, comprehensive exam, thesis (for some programs). *Entrance requirements:* For master's, GRE, MAT, GMAT. Additional exam requirements/recommendations for international students: required—TOEFL (minimum score 550 paper-based; 79 iBT). Electronic applications accepted.

Texas Southern University, College of Liberal Arts and Behavioral Sciences, Department of Human Services and Consumer Sciences, Houston, TX 77004-4584. Offers MS. *Program availability:* Part-time, evening/weekend. *Degree requirements:* For master's, comprehensive exam, thesis (for some programs). *Entrance requirements:* For master's, GRE General Test, minimum GPA of 2.5. Additional exam requirements/recommendations for international students: required—TOEFL. Electronic applications accepted.

Texas State University, The Graduate College, College of Applied Arts, Program in Merchandising and Consumer Studies, San Marcos, TX 78666. Offers MS. *Program availability:* Part-time. *Degree requirements:* For master's, comprehensive exam, thesis optional. *Entrance requirements:* For master's, GRE (General Test Only) required with competitive scores in the verbal reasoning and quantitative reasoning sections or the GMAT, baccalaureate degree from regionally-accredited institution with minimum GPA of 3.0 on last 60 hours of undergraduate coursework; two letters of recommendation; statement of purpose describing professional goals and rationale for pursuing graduate study; resume. Additional exam requirements/recommendations for international students: required—TOEFL (minimum score 550 paper-based; 78 iBT), IELTS (minimum score 6.5). Electronic applications accepted.

Tufts University, Graduate School of Arts and Sciences, Eliot-Pearson Department of Child Study and Human Development, Medford, MA 02155. Offers child study and human development (MA, PhD). *Program availability:* Part-time. *Degree requirements:* For master's, thesis (for some programs); for doctorate, comprehensive exam, thesis/dissertation. *Entrance requirements:* For master's and doctorate, GRE General Test. Additional exam requirements/recommendations for international students: required—TOEFL (minimum score 550 paper-based; 80 iBT), IELTS (minimum score 6.5). Electronic applications accepted. *Expenses:* Contact institution.

The University of Alabama, Graduate School, College of Human Environmental Sciences, Tuscaloosa, AL 35487. Offers MA, MS, MSHES, PhD. *Program availability:* Part-time, evening/weekend, online learning. *Faculty:* 64 full-time (45 women), 2 part-time/adjunct (both women). *Students:* 176 full-time (130 women), 413 part-time (309 women); includes 142 minority (78 Black or African American, non-Hispanic/Latino; 2 American Indian or Alaska Native, non-Hispanic/Latino; 13 Asian, non-Hispanic/Latino; 30 Hispanic/Latino; 1 Native Hawaiian or other Pacific Islander, non-Hispanic/Latino; 18 Two or more races, non-Hispanic/Latino), 11 international. Average age 32. 366 applicants, 74% accepted, 206 enrolled. In 2019, 283 master's, 3 doctorates awarded. *Degree requirements:* For doctorate, thesis/dissertation. *Entrance requirements:* For master's, GRE General Test or MAT (minimum score: 50th percentile), minimum GPA of 3.0; for doctorate, GRE General Test or MAT, minimum GPA of 3.0. *Application deadline:* For fall admission, 7/6 for domestic students. Applications are processed on a rolling basis. Application fee: $50 ($60 for international students). Electronic applications accepted. *Expenses:* Tuition, area resident: Full-time $10,780; part-time $440 per credit hour. Tuition, nonresident: full-time $30,250; part-time $1550 per credit hour. *Financial support:* In 2019–20, 44 students received support. Fellowships with tuition reimbursements available, research assistantships with full tuition reimbursements available, teaching assistantships with full tuition reimbursements available, career-related internships or fieldwork, Federal Work-Study, institutionally sponsored loans, and scholarships/grants available. *Unit head:* Dr. Stuart Usdan, Dean, 205-348-6250, Fax: 205-348-3789, E-mail: susdan@ches.ua.edu. *Application contact:* Patrick D. Fuller, Admissions Officer, 205-348-5923, Fax: 205-348-0400, E-mail: patrick.d.fuller@ua.edu. Website: http://www.ches.ua.edu/

University of Alberta, Faculty of Graduate Studies and Research, Department of Human Ecology, Edmonton, AB T6G 2E1, Canada. Offers family ecology and practice (M Sc, PhD); textiles and clothing (M Sc, MA, PhD). *Program availability:* Online

Family and Consumer Sciences-General

learning. *Degree requirements:* For master's, thesis (for some programs); for doctorate, comprehensive exam, thesis/dissertation. *Entrance requirements:* For master's and doctorate, minimum GPA of 7.0 on a 9.0 scale. Additional exam requirements/recommendations for international students: required—TOEFL (minimum score 580 paper-based).

The University of Arizona, College of Agriculture and Life Sciences, School of Family and Consumer Sciences, Tucson, AZ 85721. Offers PhD. *Program availability:* Part-time. *Entrance requirements:* For doctorate, GRE General Test, minimum GPA of 3.0. Additional exam requirements/recommendations for international students: required—TOEFL (minimum score 550 paper-based; 79 iBT). Electronic applications accepted.

University of Arkansas, Graduate School, Dale Bumpers College of Agricultural, Food and Life Sciences, School of Human Environmental Sciences, Fayetteville, AR 72701. Offers MS. *Program availability:* Part-time, online learning. *Students:* 12 full-time (11 women), 5 part-time (all women); includes 2 minority (1 Black or African American, non-Hispanic/Latino; 1 Hispanic/Latino), 1 international. 7 applicants, 86% accepted. In 2019, 6 master's awarded. *Degree requirements:* For master's, comprehensive exam, thesis (for some programs). *Application deadline:* For fall admission, 8/1 for domestic students, 4/1 for international students; for spring admission, 12/1 for domestic students, 10/1 for international students; for summer admission, 4/15 for domestic students, 3/1 for international students. Application fee: $60. Electronic applications accepted. *Financial support:* In 2019–20, 14 research assistantships were awarded; fellowships, teaching assistantships, and Federal Work-Study also available. Support available to part-time students. Financial award application deadline: 4/1; financial award applicants required to submit FAFSA. *Unit head:* Dr. Betsy Garrison, Director, 479-575-4305, E-mail: megarris@uark.edu. *Application contact:* Dr. Betsy Garrison, Director, 479-575-4305, E-mail: megarris@uark.edu. Website: https://human-environmental-sciences.uark.edu/index.php

University of Central Arkansas, Graduate School, College of Health and Behavioral Sciences, Department of Family and Consumer Sciences, Conway, AR 72035-0001. Offers family and consumer sciences (MS); nutrition (MS). *Program availability:* Part-time, evening/weekend, online learning. *Degree requirements:* For master's, comprehensive exam, thesis optional. *Entrance requirements:* For master's, GRE General Test, minimum GPA of 2.7. Additional exam requirements/recommendations for international students: required—TOEFL (minimum score 550 paper-based). Electronic applications accepted. *Expenses:* Contact institution.

University of Central Oklahoma, The Jackson College of Graduate Studies, College of Education and Professional Studies, Department of Human Environmental Sciences, Edmond, OK 73034-5209. Offers family and child studies (MS), including family life education, infant/child specialist, marriage and family therapy; nutrition-food science (MS). *Program availability:* Part-time. *Degree requirements:* For master's, comprehensive exam (for some programs), thesis (for some programs). *Entrance requirements:* For master's, GRE, essay, physical, CPR and First Aid training. Additional exam requirements/recommendations for international students: required—TOEFL (minimum score 550 paper-based; 79 iBT), IELTS (minimum score 6.5). Electronic applications accepted.

University of Colorado Denver, School of Education and Human Development, Program in Education and Human Development, Denver, CO 80217. Offers administrative leadership and policy (PhD); assessment (MA); early childhood special education/early childhood education (PhD); family science and human development (PhD); human development and family relations (MA); learning (MA); mathematics education (PhD); research and evaluation methods (MA); research, assessment and evaluation (PhD); science education (PhD); urban ecologies (PhD). *Program availability:* Part-time, evening/weekend. *Degree requirements:* For master's, comprehensive exam, 9 hours of core courses embedded within a minimum of 36 to 38 hours of relevant coursework, including an educational psychology practicum, independent study project or thesis (recommended). *Entrance requirements:* For master's, GRE if undergraduate GPA below 2.75, resume, three letters of recommendation, transcripts. Additional exam requirements/recommendations for international students: required—TOEFL (minimum score 537 paper-based; 75 iBT); recommended—IELTS (minimum score 6.5). Electronic applications accepted. *Expenses:* Contact institution.

University of Florida, Graduate School, College of Agricultural and Life Sciences, Department of Family, Youth, and Community Sciences, Gainesville, FL 32611. Offers community studies (MS); family and youth development (MS); family, youth and community sciences (MS); nonprofit organization development (MS). *Program availability:* Part-time, online learning. *Degree requirements:* For master's, comprehensive exam (for some programs), thesis (for some programs). *Entrance requirements:* For master's, GRE General Test, minimum GPA of 3.0. Additional exam requirements/recommendations for international students: required—TOEFL (minimum score 550 paper-based; 80 iBT), IELTS (minimum score 6). Electronic applications accepted.

University of Georgia, College of Family and Consumer Sciences, Athens, GA 30602. Offers MS, PhD. *Degree requirements:* For doctorate, thesis/dissertation. *Entrance requirements:* For master's and doctorate, GRE General Test. Electronic applications accepted.

University of Houston, College of Technology, Department of Human Development and Consumer Sciences, Houston, TX 77204. Offers future studies in commerce (MS); human resources development (MS). *Program availability:* Part-time. *Degree requirements:* For master's, project or thesis. *Entrance requirements:* For master's, GMAT, MAT. Additional exam requirements/recommendations for international students: required—TOEFL (minimum score 550 paper-based; 79 iBT). Electronic applications accepted.

University of Maryland, College Park, Academic Affairs, School of Public Health, Department of Family Science, College Park, MD 20742. Offers family studies (PhD); marriage and family therapy (MS); maternal and child health (PhD). *Accreditation:* AAMFT/COAMFTE. *Program availability:* Part-time, evening/weekend. *Degree requirements:* For master's, thesis or alternative; for doctorate, comprehensive exam, thesis/dissertation, oral defense. *Entrance requirements:* For master's, GRE General Test, minimum GPA of 3.0, 3 letters of recommendation; for doctorate, GRE General Test, minimum GPA of 3.0, 3 letters of recommendation, research sample. Electronic applications accepted.

University of Missouri, Office of Research and Graduate Studies, College of Human Environmental Sciences, Columbia, MO 65211. Offers MA, MS, PhD, Certificate, Graduate Certificate. *Program availability:* Part-time. *Entrance requirements:* For master's and doctorate, GRE General Test, minimum GPA of 3.0. Additional exam requirements/recommendations for international students: required—TOEFL, IELTS.

University of Nebraska–Lincoln, Graduate College, College of Education and Human Sciences, Department of Child, Youth and Family Studies, Lincoln, NE 68588. Offers child development/early childhood education (MS, PhD); child, youth and family studies (MS); family and consumer sciences education (MS, PhD); family financial planning (MS); family science (MS, PhD); gerontology (PhD); human sciences (PhD), including child, youth and family studies, gerontology, medical family therapy; marriage and family therapy (MS); medical family therapy (PhD); youth development (MS). *Accreditation:* AAMFT/COAMFTE (one or more programs are accredited). *Program availability:* Online learning. *Degree requirements:* For master's, thesis optional. *Entrance requirements:* For master's, GRE. Additional exam requirements/recommendations for international students: required—TOEFL (minimum score 550 paper-based). Electronic applications accepted.

University of Puerto Rico at Rio Piedras, College of Education, Program in Family Ecology and Nutrition, San Juan, PR 00931-3300. Offers M Ed. *Program availability:* Part-time. *Degree requirements:* For master's, thesis. *Entrance requirements:* For master's, PAEG or GRE, minimum GPA of 3.0, letter of recommendation.

University of South Africa, College of Agriculture and Environmental Sciences, Pretoria, South Africa. Offers agriculture (MS); consumer science (MCS); environmental management (MA, MS, PhD); environmental science (MA, MS, PhD); geography (MA, MS, PhD); horticulture (M Tech); human ecology (MHE); life sciences (MS); nature conservation (M Tech).

The University of Tennessee, Graduate School, College of Education, Health and Human Sciences, Program in Human Ecology, Knoxville, TN 37996. Offers child and family studies (PhD); community health (PhD); nutrition science (PhD); retailing and consumer sciences (PhD); textile science (PhD). *Degree requirements:* For doctorate, thesis/dissertation. *Entrance requirements:* For doctorate, GRE General Test, minimum GPA of 2.7. Additional exam requirements/recommendations for international students: required—TOEFL. Electronic applications accepted.

The University of Tennessee at Martin, Graduate Programs, College of Agriculture and Applied Sciences, Department of Family and Consumer Sciences, Martin, TN 38238. Offers dietetics (MSFCS); general family and consumer sciences (MSFCS). *Program availability:* Part-time, 100% online. *Faculty:* 7. *Students:* 1 full-time (0 women), 29 part-time (27 women); includes 3 minority (2 Black or African American, non-Hispanic/Latino; 1 Hispanic/Latino). Average age 29. 47 applicants, 70% accepted, 12 enrolled. In 2019, 12 master's awarded. *Degree requirements:* For master's, comprehensive exam, thesis optional. *Entrance requirements:* For master's, GRE General Test, minimum GPA of 2.5. Additional exam requirements/recommendations for international students: required—TOEFL (minimum score 525 paper-based; 71 iBT). *Application deadline:* For fall admission, 7/28 priority date for domestic and international students; for spring admission, 12/17 priority date for domestic and international students; for summer admission, 5/10 priority date for domestic and international students. Applications are processed on a rolling basis. Application fee: $30 ($130 for international students). Electronic applications accepted. *Expenses: Tuition, area resident:* Full-time $9096; part-time $505 per credit hour. Tuition, state resident: full-time $9096; part-time $505 per credit hour. Tuition, nonresident: full-time $15,136; part-time $841 per credit hour. *International tuition:* $23,040 full-time. *Required fees:* $1520; $85 per credit hour. Part-time tuition and fees vary according to course load. *Financial support:* In 2019–20, 10 students received support, including 2 teaching assistantships with full tuition reimbursements available (averaging $6,912 per year); research assistantships with full tuition reimbursements available, scholarships/grants, and tuition waivers (full and partial) also available. Financial award application deadline: 2/1; financial award applicants required to submit FAFSA. *Unit head:* Dr. Lisa LeBleu, Coordinator, 731-881-7116, Fax: 731-881-7106, E-mail: llebleu@utm.edu. *Application contact:* Jolene L. Cunningham, Student Services Specialist, 731-881-7012, Fax: 731-881-7499, E-mail: jcunningham@utm.edu. Website: http://www.utm.edu/departments/caas/fcs/index.php

The University of Texas at Austin, Graduate School, College of Natural Sciences, School of Human Ecology, Austin, TX 78712-1111. Offers human development and family sciences (MA, PhD); nutritional sciences (MA, MS, PhD), including nutrition (MA), nutritional sciences (PhD); textile and apparel technology (MS). *Degree requirements:* For master's, thesis; for doctorate, thesis/dissertation. *Entrance requirements:* For master's and doctorate, GRE General Test. Electronic applications accepted.

University of Wisconsin–Madison, Graduate School, School of Human Ecology, Madison, WI 53706. Offers consumer behavior and family economics (MS, PhD); design studies (MFA, MS, PhD); human development and family studies (MS, PhD). Terminal master's awarded for partial completion of doctoral program. *Degree requirements:* For master's, thesis (for some programs); for doctorate, comprehensive exam, thesis/dissertation. *Entrance requirements:* For master's, GRE General Test, portfolio (design studies), 3 letters of recommendation; for doctorate, GRE General Test. Additional exam requirements/recommendations for international students: required—TOEFL (minimum score 580 paper-based; 92 iBT). Electronic applications accepted.

University of Wisconsin–Stevens Point, College of Professional Studies, School of Health Promotion and Human Development, Program in Family and Consumer Sciences, Stevens Point, WI 54481-3897. Offers Graduate Certificate. *Program availability:* Part-time.

Utah State University, School of Graduate Studies, Emma Eccles Jones College of Education and Human Services, Department of Family, Consumer, and Human Development, Logan, UT 84322. Offers family and human development (MFHD); family, consumer, and human development (MS, PhD), including adolescence/youth (MS), adult development/aging (MS), consumer science (MS), infancy/childhood (MS), marriage and family relations (MS), marriage and family therapy (MS). *Accreditation:* AAMFT/COAMFTE (one or more programs are accredited). *Program availability:* Part-time, evening/weekend, online learning. *Degree requirements:* For master's, thesis; for doctorate, comprehensive exam, thesis/dissertation, competencies. *Entrance requirements:* For master's, GRE General Test or MAT, minimum GPA of 3.0, 3 letters of recommendation; for doctorate, GRE, minimum GPA of 3.0, 3 letters of recommendation. Additional exam requirements/recommendations for international students: required—TOEFL. Electronic applications accepted.

Western Michigan University, Graduate College, College of Education and Human Development, Department of Family and Consumer Sciences, Kalamazoo, MI 49008. Offers career and technical education (MA); family and consumer sciences (MA).

Child and Family Studies

Alabama Agricultural and Mechanical University, School of Graduate Studies, College of Agricultural, Life and Natural Sciences, Department of Family and Consumer Sciences, Huntsville, AL 35811. Offers apparel, merchandising and design (MS); family and consumer sciences (MS); human development and family studies (MS); nutrition and hospitality management (MS). *Program availability:* Part-time, evening/weekend. *Degree requirements:* For master's, comprehensive exam, thesis optional. *Entrance requirements:* For master's, GRE General Test. Additional exam requirements/recommendations for international students: required—TOEFL (minimum score 500 paper-based; 61 iBT). Electronic applications accepted.

Amberton University, Graduate School, Program in Family Studies, Garland, TX 75041-5595. Offers family studies (MS), including Christian counseling.

Arizona State University at Tempe, College of Liberal Arts and Sciences, School of Social and Family Dynamics, Tempe, AZ 85287-3701. Offers family and human development (MS, PhD); infant-family practice (MAS); marriage and family therapy (MAS); sociology (MA, PhD). Terminal master's awarded for partial completion of doctoral program. *Degree requirements:* For master's, thesis or alternative, interactive Program of Study (iPOS) submitted before completing 50 percent of required credit hours; for doctorate, thesis/dissertation, interactive Program of Study (iPOS) submitted before completing 50 percent of required credit hours. *Entrance requirements:* For master's and doctorate, GRE, minimum GPA of 3.0 or equivalent in last 2 years of work leading to bachelor's degree. Additional exam requirements/recommendations for international students: required—TOEFL, IELTS, or PTE. Electronic applications accepted. *Expenses:* Contact institution.

Asbury University, School of Graduate and Professional Studies, Wilmore, KY 40390-1198. Offers biology: alternative certificate (MA Ed); chemistry: alternative certificate (MA Ed); English (MA Ed); English as a second language (MA Ed); ESL (MA Ed); French (MA Ed); Latin: alternative certificate (MA Ed); mathematics: alternative certificate (MA Ed); reading/writing endorsement (MA Ed); social studies (MA Ed); social work (MSW), including child and family services; Spanish (MA Ed); special education (MA Ed); special education: alternative certificate (MA Ed); teacher as leader endorsement (MA Ed). *Accreditation:* NCATE. *Program availability:* Part-time. *Degree requirements:* For master's, action research project, portfolio. *Entrance requirements:* For master's, PRAXIS/NTE, minimum GPA of 2.75, letters of recommendation. Additional exam requirements/recommendations for international students: required—TOEFL (minimum score 550 paper-based). Electronic applications accepted.

Assumption University, Clinical Counseling Psychology Program, Worcester, MA 01609-1296. Offers child and family interventions (MA); clinical counseling psychology (CAGS); cognitive-behavioral therapies (MA). *Program availability:* Part-time, evening/weekend. *Degree requirements:* For master's, comprehensive exam, internship, practicum; for CAGS, comprehensive exam. *Entrance requirements:* For master's, bachelor's degree and at least six psychology courses completed with minimum GPA of 3.0 both overall and in the psychology courses; three letters of recommendation; official transcripts; personal statement; current resume; for CAGS, master's degree in clinical counseling psychology or mental health counseling, or baccalaureate degree and at least six psychology courses with minimum GPA of 3.0 overall and in psychology courses; three letters of recommendation; official transcripts; personal statement; current resume; interview. Additional exam requirements/recommendations for international students: required—TOEFL (minimum score 540 paper-based; 76 iBT), IELTS (minimum score 6). Electronic applications accepted. *Expenses: Tuition:* Full-time $12,690; part-time $705 per credit. *Required fees:* $70 per term.

Auburn University, Graduate School, College of Human Sciences, Department of Human Development and Family Studies, Auburn, AL 36849. Offers MS, PhD. *Accreditation:* AAMFT/COAMFTE (one or more programs are accredited). *Program availability:* Part-time. *Faculty:* 26 full-time (17 women), 1 (woman) part-time/adjunct. *Students:* 26 full-time (15 women), 16 part-time (15 women); includes 9 minority (4 Black or African American, non-Hispanic/Latino; 2 Asian, non-Hispanic/Latino; 2 Hispanic/Latino; 1 Native Hawaiian or other Pacific Islander, non-Hispanic/Latino), 2 international. Average age 28. 50 applicants, 22% accepted, 11 enrolled. In 2019, 8 master's awarded. *Degree requirements:* For master's, thesis, oral exam; for doctorate, thesis/dissertation. *Entrance requirements:* For master's, GRE General Test; for doctorate, GRE General Test, master's degree. Additional exam requirements/recommendations for international students: required—iTEP; recommended—TOEFL (minimum score 550 paper-based; 79 iBT), IELTS (minimum score 6.5). *Application deadline:* Applications are processed on a rolling basis. Application fee: $60 ($70 for international students). Electronic applications accepted. *Expenses: Tuition, area resident:* Full-time $9828; part-time $546 per credit hour. Tuition, state resident: full-time $9828; part-time $546 per credit hour. Tuition, nonresident: full-time $29,484; part-time $1638 per credit hour. *International tuition:* $29,744 full-time. Tuition and fees vary according to course load, program and reciprocity agreements. *Financial support:* In 2019–20, 46 fellowships with tuition reimbursements, 39 research assistantships with tuition reimbursements (averaging $18,077 per year), 9 teaching assistantships with tuition reimbursements (averaging $14,893 per year) were awarded; Federal Work-Study also available. Support available to part-time students. Financial award application deadline: 3/15; financial award applicants required to submit FAFSA. *Unit head:* Dr. Angela Wiley, Head, 334-844-3242, E-mail: arw0044@auburn.edu. *Application contact:* Dr. George Flowers, Dean of the Graduate School, 334-844-2125. Website: http://www.humsci.auburn.edu/hdfs/

Bank Street College of Education, Graduate School, Program in Child Life, New York, NY 10025. Offers MS. *Degree requirements:* For master's, thesis. *Entrance requirements:* For master's, interview, essays, 100 hours of volunteer experience in a child life setting. Additional exam requirements/recommendations for international students: required—TOEFL (minimum score 600 paper-based; 100 iBT), IELTS (minimum score 7).

Bank Street College of Education, Graduate School, Program in Infant and Family Development and Early Intervention, New York, NY 10025. Offers infant and family development (MS Ed); infant and family early childhood special and general education (MS Ed); infant and family/early childhood special education (Ed M). *Degree requirements:* For master's, thesis. *Entrance requirements:* For master's, interview, essays. Additional exam requirements/recommendations for international students: required—TOEFL (minimum score 600 paper-based; 100 iBT), IELTS (minimum score 7). Electronic applications accepted.

Brandeis University, The Heller School for Social Policy and Management, Program in Public Policy, Waltham, MA 02454-9110. Offers aging (MPP); behavioral health (MPP); children, youth and families (MPP); general social policy (MPP); health (MPP); poverty alleviation and development (MPP); MPP/MA. *Degree requirements:* For master's, thesis. *Entrance requirements:* For master's, GRE, 3 letters of recommendation,

statement of purpose, 3 to 5 years of professional experience. Additional exam requirements/recommendations for international students: required—TOEFL (minimum score 600 paper-based; 100 iBT). Electronic applications accepted.

Brandeis University, The Heller School for Social Policy and Management, Program in Social Policy, Waltham, MA 02454-9110. Offers assets and inequalities (PhD); children, youth and families (PhD); global health and development (PhD); health and behavioral health (PhD). *Degree requirements:* For doctorate, comprehensive exam, thesis/dissertation, qualifying paper, 2-year residency. *Entrance requirements:* For doctorate, GRE General Test, 3 letters of recommendation, statement of purpose, writing sample, at least 3-5 years of professional experience. Additional exam requirements/recommendations for international students: required—TOEFL (minimum score 600 paper-based; 100 iBT). Electronic applications accepted.

Brigham Young University, Graduate Studies, College of Family, Home, and Social Sciences, Program in Marriage, Family and Human Development, Provo, UT 84602. Offers MS, PhD. *Accreditation:* AAMFT/COAMFTE. *Faculty:* 24 full-time (5 women). *Students:* 20 full-time (17 women); includes 1 minority (Asian, non-Hispanic/Latino), 1 international. Average age 28. 25 applicants, 56% accepted, 8 enrolled. In 2019, 9 master's awarded. *Degree requirements:* For master's, thesis; for doctorate, comprehensive exam, thesis/dissertation. *Entrance requirements:* For master's and doctorate, GRE General Test, minimum GPA of 3.0 in last 60 semester hours, letters of recommendation. Additional exam requirements/recommendations for international students: required—TOEFL (minimum score 580 paper-based; 85 iBT), IELTS (minimum score 7). *Application deadline:* For fall admission, 1/10 for domestic and international students. Application fee: $50. Electronic applications accepted. *Expenses:* LDS: 2-year masters degree: $14,580 tuition/fees, per credit $430, per course $1,290; 3-year doctorate degree: $21,870 tuition/fees, per credit $430, per course $1,290. NonLDS: 2-year masters degree: $29,160 tuition/fees, per credit $860, per course $2,580; 3-year doctorate degree: $43,740 tuition/fees, per credit $860, per course $2,580. *Financial support:* In 2019–20, 20 students received support, including 20 research assistantships with full and partial tuition reimbursements available (averaging $8,944 per year), 8 teaching assistantships with tuition reimbursements available (averaging $2,800 per year); scholarships/grants and unspecified assistantships also available. Financial award application deadline: 3/20. *Unit head:* Dr. Alan J. Hawkins, Director, School of Life, 801-422-7088, Fax: 801-422-0230, E-mail: alan_hawkins@byu.edu. *Application contact:* Graduate Secretary, 801-422-2060, E-mail: mfhdgrad@byu.edu. Website: http://mfhd.byu.edu

Brock University, Faculty of Graduate Studies, Faculty of Social Sciences, Program in Child and Youth Studies, St. Catharines, ON L2S 3A1, Canada. Offers MA. *Program availability:* Part-time. *Degree requirements:* For master's, thesis. *Entrance requirements:* For master's, honors BA. Additional exam requirements/recommendations for international students: required—TOEFL (minimum score 550 paper-based; 80 iBT), IELTS (minimum score 6.5), TWE (minimum score 4). Electronic applications accepted.

California State University, East Bay, Office of Graduate Studies, College of Letters, Arts, and Social Sciences, Department of Social Work, Hayward, CA 94542-3000. Offers children, youth, and family services (MSW); community mental health services (MSW). *Accreditation:* CSWE. *Degree requirements:* For master's, comprehensive exam. *Entrance requirements:* For master's, minimum GPA of 2.8; courses in statistics and either human biology, physiology, or anatomy; liberal arts or social science baccalaureate degree; 3 letters of recommendation; personal statement; criminal background check; student professional liability insurance. Additional exam requirements/recommendations for international students: required—TOEFL (minimum score 550 paper-based). Electronic applications accepted.

California State University, Los Angeles, Graduate Studies, College of Health and Human Services, Department of Child and Family Studies, Los Angeles, CA 90032-8530. Offers child development (MA). *Program availability:* Part-time, evening/weekend. *Degree requirements:* For master's, comprehensive exam, project or thesis. *Entrance requirements:* Additional exam requirements/recommendations for international students: required—TOEFL (minimum score 500 paper-based). *Expenses: Tuition, area resident:* Full-time $7176; part-time $4164 per year. Tuition, state resident: full-time $7176; part-time $4164 per year. Tuition, nonresident: full-time $14,304; part-time $8916 per year. *International tuition:* $14,304 full-time. *Required fees:* $1037.76; $1037.76 per unit. Tuition and fees vary according to degree level and program.

Capella University, Harold Abel School of Social and Behavioral Science, Master's Programs in Counseling, Minneapolis, MN 55402. Offers child and adolescent development (MS); general addiction counseling (MS); general marriage and family counseling/therapy (MS); general mental health counseling (MS); general school counseling (MS).

Central Michigan University, College of Graduate Studies, College of Education and Human Services, Department of Human Environmental Studies, Mount Pleasant, MI 48859. Offers apparel product development and merchandising technology (MS); gerontology (Graduate Certificate); human development and family studies (MA); nutrition and dietetics (MS). *Program availability:* Part-time, evening/weekend. *Degree requirements:* For master's, thesis or alternative. Electronic applications accepted. *Expenses: Tuition, area resident:* Full-time $12,267; part-time $8178 per year. Tuition, state resident: full-time $12,267; part-time $8178 per year. Tuition, nonresident: full-time $12,267; part-time $8178 per year. *International tuition:* $16,110 full-time. *Required fees:* $225 per semester. Tuition and fees vary according to degree level and program.

Central Washington University, School of Graduate Studies and Research, College of Education and Professional Studies, Department of Family and Consumer Sciences, Ellensburg, WA 98926. Offers career and technical education (MS); family and child life (MS); family and consumer sciences education (MS). *Program availability:* Part-time. *Entrance requirements:* For master's, minimum GPA of 3.0. Additional exam requirements/recommendations for international students: required—TOEFL (minimum score 550 paper-based; 79 iBT). Electronic applications accepted.

Colorado State University, College of Health and Human Sciences, Department of Human Development and Family Studies, Fort Collins, CO 80523-1570. Offers applied developmental science (PhD); family and developmental studies (MS); marriage and family therapy (MS). *Accreditation:* AAMFT/COAMFTE. *Faculty:* 22 full-time (20 women), 2 part-time/adjunct (0 women). *Students:* 32 full-time (28 women), 4 part-time (all women); includes 9 minority (4 Asian, non-Hispanic/Latino; 4 Hispanic/Latino; 1 Two or more races, non-Hispanic/Latino), 2 international. Average age 27. 74 applicants, 42% accepted, 12 enrolled. In 2019, 9 master's, 2 doctorates awarded. Terminal master's awarded for partial completion of doctoral program. *Degree requirements:* For

master's, thesis; for doctorate, comprehensive exam, thesis/dissertation. *Entrance requirements:* For master's, GRE General Test, 3 letters of recommendation; minimum GPA of 3.0; bachelor's degree; curriculum vitae/resume. Additional exam requirements/ recommendations for international students: required—TOEFL (minimum score 550 paper-based; 80 iBT), IELTS (minimum score 6.5), PTE (minimum score 58). *Application deadline:* For fall admission, 1/2 priority date for domestic and international students. Electronic applications accepted. *Expenses:* Tuition, state resident: full-time $10,520; part-time $5844 per credit hour. Tuition, nonresident: full-time $25,791; part-time $14,328 per credit hour. *International tuition:* $25,791 full-time. *Required fees:* $2512.80. Part-time tuition and fees vary according to course level, course load, degree level, program and student level. *Financial support:* In 2019–20, 31 students received support, including 1 fellowship with full and partial tuition reimbursement available (averaging $7,605 per year), 15 research assistantships with full and partial tuition reimbursements available (averaging $13,182 per year), 15 teaching assistantships with full and partial tuition reimbursements available (averaging $9,633 per year); Federal Work-Study and unspecified assistantships also available. Financial award application deadline: 3/1; financial award applicants required to submit FAFSA. *Unit head:* Dr. Julia Braungart-Rieker, Department Head, 970-491-3581, Fax: 970-491-7975, E-mail: JulieBraungart.Rieker@colostate.edu. *Application contact:* Mary Daughtrey, Administrative Assistant III, 970-491-2872, Fax: 970-491-7975, E-mail: mary.daughtrey@colostate.edu.
Website: https://www.chhs.colostate.edu/hdfs

Concordia University, School of Graduate Studies, Faculty of Arts and Science, Department of Education, Program in Child Studies, Montréal, QC H3G 1M8, Canada. Offers MA. *Degree requirements:* For master's, one foreign language, thesis optional. *Entrance requirements:* For master's, minimum B average in undergraduate course work.

Concordia University, St. Paul, College of Humanities and Social Sciences, St. Paul, MN 55104-5494. Offers creative writing (MFA); criminal justice leadership (MA); family science (MA); human services (MA), including forensic behavioral health. *Accreditation:* NCATE. *Program availability:* Part-time, evening/weekend, 100% online, blended/hybrid learning. *Degree requirements:* For master's, thesis (for some programs), capstone project. *Entrance requirements:* For master's, official transcripts stating the conferral of a Bachelor's degree with a minimum cumulative GPA of 3.0 based on a 4.0 system; personal statement; writing sample in fiction or non-fiction (MFA students only); resume (MA students only). Additional exam requirements/recommendations for international students: required—TOEFL (minimum score 547 paper-based; 78 iBT), IELTS (minimum score 6), PTE (minimum score 78). Electronic applications accepted. *Expenses:* Contact institution.

Concordia University Wisconsin, Graduate Programs, School of Education, Program in Family Studies, Mequon, WI 53097-2402. Offers MS Ed. *Degree requirements:* For master's, comprehensive exam, thesis or alternative. *Entrance requirements:* For master's, minimum GPA of 3.0. Additional exam requirements/recommendations for international students: required—TOEFL.

Cornell University, Graduate School, Graduate Fields of Human Ecology, Field of Human Development, Ithaca, NY 14853. Offers developmental psychology (MA, PhD), including cognitive development, developmental psychopathology, ecology of human development, social and personality development; human development and family studies (MA, PhD), including ecology of human development, family studies and the life course. *Degree requirements:* For doctorate, comprehensive exam, thesis/dissertation, pre-doctoral research project, teaching experience. *Entrance requirements:* For doctorate, GRE General Test, 2 letters of recommendation. Additional exam requirements/recommendations for international students: required—TOEFL (minimum score 550 paper-based; 77 iBT). Electronic applications accepted.

Dallas Theological Seminary, Graduate Programs, Dallas, TX 75204-6499. Offers adult education (Th M); apologetics (Th M); Bible backgrounds (Th M); Bible translation (Th M); Biblical and theological studies (Certificate); biblical counseling (MA); biblical exegesis and linguistics (MA); biblical exposition (PhD); biblical studies (MA); Biblical theology (Th M); children's education (Th M); Christian education (MA, D Min); Christian leadership (MA); cross-cultural ministries (MA); educational administration (Th M); educational leadership (Th M); evangelism and discipleship (Th M); exposition of Biblical books (Th M); family life education (Th M); general studies (Th M); Hebrew and cognate studies (Th M); hermeneutics (Th M); historical theology (Th M); homiletics (Th M); intercultural ministries (Th M); Jesus studies (Th M); leadership studies (Th M); media and communication (MA); media arts (Th M); ministry (D Min); ministry with women (Th M); New Testament studies (Th M, PhD); Old Testament studies (Th M, PhD); parachurch ministries (Th M); pastoral care and counseling (Th M); pastoral theology and practice (Th M); philosophy (Th M); sacred theology (STM); spiritual formation (Th M); systematic theology (Th M); teaching in Christian institutions (Th M); theological studies (PhD); urban ministries (Th M); worship studies (Th M); youth education (Th M). *Program availability:* Part-time, online learning. *Degree requirements:* For master's, variable foreign language requirement, thesis (for some programs); for doctorate, 2 foreign languages, thesis/dissertation. *Entrance requirements:* For master's, GRE or MAT (if minimum undergraduate cumulative GPA is below 2.5 or undergraduate degree is unaccredited). Additional exam requirements/recommendations for international students: required—TOEFL (minimum score 575 paper-based; 85 iBT), TWE. Electronic applications accepted.

East Carolina University, Graduate School, College of Health and Human Performance, Department of Human Development and Family Science, Greenville, NC 27858-4353. Offers birth through kindergarten education (MA Ed); human development and family science (MS); marriage and family therapy (MS); medical family therapy (PhD). *Accreditation:* AAMFT/COAMFTE. *Program availability:* Part-time. *Application deadline:* For fall admission, 1/15 for domestic students; for spring admission, 10/15 for domestic students. *Expenses: Tuition, area resident:* Full-time $4749; part-time $185 per credit hour. Tuition, state resident: full-time $4749; part-time $185 per credit hour. Tuition, nonresident: full-time $17,898; part-time $864 per credit hour. *International tuition:* $17,898 full-time. *Required fees:* $2787. *Financial support:* Application deadline: 6/1. *Unit head:* Dr. Sharon Ballard, Chair, 252-328-4220, E-mail: ballards@ecu.edu. *Application contact:* Graduate School Admissions, 252-328-6012, Fax: 252-328-6071, E-mail: gradschool@ecu.edu.
Website: https://hhp.ecu.edu/hdfs/

Fairfield University, Graduate School of Education and Allied Professions, Fairfield, CT 06824. Offers applied behavior analysis (ATC); applied psychology (MA); clinical mental health counseling (MA, CAS); educational technology (MA); elementary education (MA, CAS); family studies (MA); integration of spirituality and religion in counseling (ATC); marriage and family therapy (MA); reading and language development (Sixth Year Certificate); school counseling (MA, CAS); school psychology (MA, CAS); school-based marriage and family therapy (ATC); secondary education (MA); special education (MA, CAS); substance abuse counseling (ATC); teaching (Certificate); teaching and foundations (MA, CAS); TESOL, world languages, and bilingual education (MA, CAS). *Accreditation:* NCATE. *Program availability:* Part-time, evening/weekend. *Faculty:* 24 full-time (18 women), 28 part-time/adjunct (20 women). *Students:* 169 full-time (149 women), 227 part-time (187 women); includes 96 minority (21 Black or African American, non-Hispanic/Latino; 8 Asian, non-Hispanic/Latino; 60 Hispanic/Latino; 7 Two or more races, non-Hispanic/Latino), 1 international. Average age 31. 194 applicants, 60% accepted, 101 enrolled. In 2019, 136 master's, 28 other advanced degrees awarded. *Degree requirements:* For master's, comprehensive exam. *Entrance requirements:* For master's, One of the following for certification programs: Praxis Core, SAT, ACT, or GRE, minimum GPA of 3.0, 2 recommendations, resume. Additional exam requirements/recommendations for international students: required—TOEFL (minimum score 550 paper-based; 84 iBT), IELTS (minimum score 7.5), TOEFL (minimum score 550 paper-based; 84 iBT) or IELTS (minimum score 7.5). *Application deadline:* For fall admission, 2/15 for international students; for spring admission, 10/1 for international students. Application fee: $60. Electronic applications accepted. *Expenses:* Tuition $815/credit hour; Lab Fee (ED598) $300/semester; Lab Fee (CN457,CN467, PY538, PY540) $70/course; Wilson Reading Course Fee $141/credit hour; Registration Fee $50/semester; Graduate Student Activity Fee (Fall and Spring) $65/semester. *Financial support:* In 2019–20, 34 students received support. Career-related internships or fieldwork and unspecified assistantships available. Support available to part-time students. Financial award applicants required to submit FAFSA. *Unit head:* Dr. Laurie Grupp, Dean, 203-254-4250, Fax: 203-254-4241, E-mail: lgrupp@fairfield.edu. *Application contact:* Melanie Rogers, Director of Graduate Admission, 203-254-4184, Fax: 203-254-4073, E-mail: gradadmis@fairfield.edu.
Website: http://www.fairfield.edu/gseap

Florida State University, The Graduate School, College of Human Sciences, Department of Family and Child Sciences, Tallahassee, FL 32306. Offers family and child sciences (MS); human development and family sciences (PhD); marriage and family therapy (PhD). *Accreditation:* AAMFT/COAMFTE. *Program availability:* Part-time. *Faculty:* 17 full-time (11 women). *Students:* 28 full-time (22 women), 4 part-time (2 women); includes 12 minority (7 Black or African American, non-Hispanic/Latino; 1 Asian, non-Hispanic/Latino; 1 Hispanic/Latino; 3 Two or more races, non-Hispanic/ Latino), 2 international. 39 applicants, 46% accepted, 5 enrolled. In 2019, 9 doctorates awarded. Terminal master's awarded for partial completion of doctoral program. *Degree requirements:* For master's, thesis optional, special project for non-thesis students; for doctorate, thesis/dissertation, preliminary examination; clinical examination (for marriage and family therapy). *Entrance requirements:* For master's, GRE General Test, minimum upper division GPA of 3.0; for doctorate, GRE General Test, writing assessment, minimum upper division GPA of 3.0 or master's degree. Additional exam requirements/recommendations for international students: required—TOEFL (minimum score 550 paper-based; 80 iBT). *Application deadline:* For fall admission, 12/1 for domestic and international students. Applications are processed on a rolling basis. Application fee: $30. Electronic applications accepted. *Financial support:* In 2019–20, 34 students received support, including 5 research assistantships with full tuition reimbursements available (averaging $21,020 per year), 29 teaching assistantships with full tuition reimbursements available (averaging $21,020 per year); fellowships with partial tuition reimbursements available, career-related internships or fieldwork, Federal Work-Study, institutionally sponsored loans, scholarships/grants, health care benefits, and unspecified assistantships also available. Financial award application deadline: 1/5; financial award applicants required to submit FAFSA. *Unit head:* Dr. Chester Ray, Interim Department Chair, 850-644-3217, E-mail: caray@fsu.edu. *Application contact:* Mary-Sue McLemore, Academic Support Assistant, 850-644-1117, E-mail: mmclemore@fsu.edu.
Website: https://humansciences.fsu.edu/family-child-sciences/students/graduate-programs/

Iowa State University of Science and Technology, Department of Human Development and Family Studies, Ames, IA 50011. Offers human development and family studies (MFCS, MS, PhD). *Degree requirements:* For master's, thesis; for doctorate, thesis/dissertation. *Entrance requirements:* For master's and doctorate, GRE General Test. Additional exam requirements/recommendations for international students: required—TOEFL (minimum score 550 paper-based; 79 iBT), IELTS (minimum score 6.5). Electronic applications accepted.

Kansas State University, Graduate School, College of Human Ecology, Doctorate in Human Ecology Program, Manhattan, KS 66506-1407. Offers apparel and textiles (PhD); applied family sciences (PhD); couple and family therapy (PhD); hospitality administration (PhD); kinesiology (PhD); life-span human development (PhD). *Program availability:* Part-time. *Degree requirements:* For doctorate, thesis/dissertation. *Entrance requirements:* Additional exam requirements/recommendations for international students: required—TOEFL. Electronic applications accepted.

Kansas State University, Graduate School, College of Human Ecology, School of Family Studies and Human Services, Manhattan, KS 66506-1403. Offers applied family sciences (MS); communication sciences and disorders (MS); conflict resolution (Graduate Certificate); couple and family therapy (MS); early childhood education (MS); family and community service (MS); life-span human development (MS); personal financial planning (MS, PhD, Graduate Certificate); youth development (MS, Graduate Certificate). *Accreditation:* AAMFT/COAMFTE; ASHA. *Program availability:* Part-time, online learning. *Degree requirements:* For master's, comprehensive exam (for some programs), thesis optional. *Entrance requirements:* For master's, GRE, minimum GPA of 3.0 in last 2 years (60 semester hours) of undergraduate study; for doctorate, GRE. Additional exam requirements/recommendations for international students: required—TOEFL (minimum score 600 paper-based). Electronic applications accepted.

Kent State University, College of Education, Health and Human Services, School of Lifespan Development and Educational Sciences, Program in Human Development and Family Studies, Kent, OH 44242-0001. Offers MA. *Degree requirements:* For master's, thesis optional. *Entrance requirements:* For master's, minimum undergraduate GPA of 3.0, 3 letters of reference, goals statement. Additional exam requirements/ recommendations for international students: required—TOEFL (minimum score 550 paper-based; 80 iBT).

Liberty University, School of Behavioral Sciences, Lynchburg, VA 24515. Offers applied psychology (MA), including developmental psychology (MA, MS), industrial/ organizational psychology (MA, MS); clinical mental health counseling (MA); community care and counseling (Ed D), including marriage and family counseling, pastoral care and counseling, traumatology; counselor education and supervision (PhD); human services counseling (MA), including addictions and recovery, business, child and family law, Christian ministries, criminal justice, crisis response and trauma, executive leadership, health and wellness, life coaching, marriage and family, military resilience; marriage and family counseling (MA); marriage and family therapy (MA); military resilience (Certificate); pastoral counseling (MA), including addictions and recovery, community chaplaincy, crisis response and trauma, discipleship and church ministry, leadership, life coaching, marriage and family, marriage and family studies, military resilience, parenting and child/adolescent, pastoral counseling, theology; professional counseling (MA); psychology (MS), including developmental psychology (MA, MS), industrial/ organizational psychology (MA, MS); school counseling (M Ed). *Program availability:* Part-time, online learning. *Students:* 3,786 full-time (3,065 women), 5,193 part-time (4,081 women); includes 2,733 minority (1,967 Black or African American, non-Hispanic/ Latino; 48 American Indian or Alaska Native, non-Hispanic/Latino; 103 Asian, non-Hispanic/Latino; 349 Hispanic/Latino; 19 Native Hawaiian or other Pacific Islander, non-

Hispanic/Latino; 247 Two or more races, non-Hispanic/Latino), 133 international. Average age 38. 13,324 applicants, 28% accepted, 2,163 enrolled. In 2019, 2,322 master's, 19 doctorates, 112 other advanced degrees awarded. *Entrance requirements:* For master's, Official bachelor's degree transcripts with a 2.0 GPA or higher. *Application deadline:* Applications are processed on a rolling basis. Application fee: $50. Electronic applications accepted. *Expenses: Tuition:* Full-time $545; part-time $410 per credit hour. One-time fee: $50. *Financial support:* In 2019–20, 1,003 students received support. Teaching assistantships and Federal Work-Study available. Financial award applicants required to submit FAFSA. *Unit head:* Dr. Kenyon Knapp, Dean, School of Behavioral Services, E-mail: kcknapp@liberty.edu. *Application contact:* Jay Bridge, Director of Admissions, 800-424-9595, Fax: 800-628-7977, E-mail: gradadmissions@liberty.edu.
Website: https://www.liberty.edu/behavioral-sciences/

Loma Linda University, School of Behavioral Health, Department of Counseling and Family Sciences, Loma Linda, CA 92350. Offers child life specialist (MS); clinical mediation (Certificate); counseling (MS); drug and alcohol counseling (Certificate); family life education (Certificate); marital and family therapy (DMFT); school counseling (Certificate). *Degree requirements:* For master's, comprehensive exam, thesis optional; for doctorate, comprehensive exam, thesis/dissertation (for some programs). *Entrance requirements:* For master's, minimum GPA of 3.0; for doctorate, GRE. Additional exam requirements/recommendations for international students: required—TOEFL (minimum score 550 paper-based). Electronic applications accepted.

London Metropolitan University, Graduate Programs, London, United Kingdom. Offers applied psychology (M Sc); architecture (MA); biomedical science (M Sc); blood science (M Sc); cancer pharmacology (M Sc); computer networking and cyber security (M Sc); computing and information systems (M Sc); conference interpreting (MA); counter-terrorism studies (M Sc); creative, digital and professional writing (MA); crime, violence and prevention (M Sc); criminology (M Sc); curating contemporary art (MA); data analytics (M Sc); digital media (MA); early childhood studies (MA); education (MA, Ed D); financial services law, regulation and compliance (LL M); food science (M Sc); forensic psychology (M Sc); health and social care management and policy (M Sc); human nutrition (M Sc); human resource management (MA); human rights and international conflict (MA); information technology (M Sc); intelligence and security studies (M Sc); international oil, gas and energy law (LL M); international relations (MA); interpreting (MA); learning and teaching in higher education (MA); legal practice (LL M); media and entertainment law (LL M); organizational and consumer psychology (M Sc); psychological therapy (M Sc); psychology of mental health (M Sc); public health (M Sc); public policy and management (MPA); security studies (M Sc); social work (M Sc); spatial planning and urban design (MA); sports therapy (M Sc); supporting older children and young people with dyslexia (MA); teaching languages (MA), including Arabic, English; translation (MA); woman and child abuse (MA).

Miami University, College of Education, Health and Society, Department of Family Studies and Social Work, Oxford, OH 45056. Offers MA.

Michigan State University, The Graduate School, College of Social Science, Department of Human Development and Family Studies, East Lansing, MI 48824. Offers child development (MS); family and community services (MA); human development and family studies (MS, PhD); youth development (MA). *Accreditation:* AAMFT/COAMFTE (one or more programs are accredited). *Entrance requirements:* For master's, GRE General Test, minimum GPA of 3.0 in last 2 years of undergraduate course work, 3 letters of recommendation; for doctorate, GRE General Test, minimum GPA of 3.0, 3 letters of recommendation, background in behavioral sciences. Additional exam requirements/recommendations for international students: required—TOEFL. Electronic applications accepted.

Mississippi State University, College of Agriculture and Life Sciences, School of Human Sciences, Mississippi State, MS 39762. Offers agriculture and extension education (MS), including communication, leadership; agriculture science (PhD), including agriculture and extension education; fashion design and merchandising (MS), including design and product development, merchandising; human development and family studies (MS, PhD). *Accreditation:* NCATE (one or more programs are accredited). *Program availability:* Part-time. *Faculty:* 21 full-time (11 women). *Students:* 26 full-time (21 women), 62 part-time (46 women); includes 16 minority (12 Black or African American, non-Hispanic/Latino; 1 American Indian or Alaska Native, non-Hispanic/Latino; 1 Hispanic/Latino; 2 Two or more races, non-Hispanic/Latino), 4 international. Average age 34. 26 applicants, 69% accepted, 16 enrolled. In 2019, 12 master's, 4 doctorates awarded. *Degree requirements:* For master's, thesis optional, comprehensive oral or written exam. *Entrance requirements:* For master's, GRE, minimum GPA of 2.75 in last 4 semesters of course work; for doctorate, minimum GPA of 3.0 on prior graduate work. Additional exam requirements/recommendations for international students: required—TOEFL (minimum score 477 paper-based; 53 iBT); recommended—IELTS (minimum score 4.5). *Application deadline:* For fall admission, 7/1 for domestic students, 5/1 for international students; for spring admission, 11/1 for domestic students, 9/1 for international students. Applications are processed on a rolling basis. Application fee: $60 ($80 for international students). Electronic applications accepted. *Expenses: Tuition, area resident:* Full-time $8880; part-time $456 per credit hour. Tuition, state resident: full-time $8880. Tuition, nonresident: full-time $23,840; part-time $1236 per credit hour. *Required fees:* $110; $11.12 per credit hour. Tuition and fees vary according to course load. *Financial support:* In 2019–20, 15 research assistantships (averaging $12,541 per year) were awarded; Federal Work-Study, institutionally sponsored loans, and unspecified assistantships also available. Financial award application deadline: 4/1; financial award applicants required to submit FAFSA. *Unit head:* Dr. Michael Newman, Professor and Director, 662-325-2950, E-mail: mnewman@humansci.msstate.edu. *Application contact:* Ryan King, Admissions and Enrollment Assistant, 662-325-8951, E-mail: rjk101@grad.msstate.edu.
Website: http://www.humansci.msstate.edu

Missouri State University, Graduate College, College of Education, Department of Childhood Education and Family Studies, Program in Early Childhood and Family Development, Springfield, MO 65897. Offers MS. *Program availability:* Part-time, 100% online, blended/hybrid learning. *Entrance requirements:* For master's, GRE, minimum GPA of 3.0. Additional exam requirements/recommendations for international students: required—TOEFL (minimum score 550 paper-based; 79 iBT), IELTS (minimum score 6). Electronic applications accepted. *Expenses: Tuition, area resident:* Full-time $2600; part-time $1735 per credit hour. Tuition, nonresident: full-time $5240; part-time $3495 per credit hour. *International tuition:* $5240 full-time. *Required fees:* $530; $438 per credit hour. Tuition and fees vary according to class time, course level, course load, degree level, campus/location and program.

Montclair State University, The Graduate School, College of Education and Human Services, Doctoral Program in Family Studies, Montclair, NJ 07043-1624. Offers PhD. *Program availability:* Part-time, evening/weekend. *Degree requirements:* For doctorate, comprehensive exam, thesis/dissertation. *Entrance requirements:* For doctorate, GRE General Test, interview, 3 letters of recommendation, essay. Additional exam requirements/recommendations for international students: required—TOEFL (minimum score 83 iBT), IELTS (minimum score 6.5). Electronic applications accepted.

Montclair State University, The Graduate School, College of Education and Human Services, Program in Family and Child Studies, Montclair, NJ 07043-1624. Offers MA. *Program availability:* Part-time, evening/weekend. *Degree requirements:* For master's, comprehensive exam, thesis or alternative. *Entrance requirements:* For master's, GRE General Test, essay, 2 letters of recommendation. Additional exam requirements/recommendations for international students: required—TOEFL (minimum score 83 iBT), IELTS (minimum score 6.5). Electronic applications accepted.

Montclair State University, The Graduate School, College of Humanities and Social Sciences, Adolescent Advocacy Certificate Program, Montclair, NJ 07043-1624. Offers Certificate.

Montclair State University, The Graduate School, College of Humanities and Social Sciences, Child Advocacy and Policy Certificate Program, Montclair, NJ 07043-1624. Offers Certificate.

Mount Saint Vincent University, Graduate Programs, Department of Child and Youth Study, Halifax, NS B3M 2J6, Canada. Offers MA. *Program availability:* Part-time, evening/weekend. *Degree requirements:* For master's, thesis. *Entrance requirements:* For master's, bachelor's degree in related field, minimum B+ average, professional experience. Electronic applications accepted.

Mount Saint Vincent University, Graduate Programs, Department of Family Studies and Gerontology, Halifax, NS B3M 2J6, Canada. Offers MA. *Program availability:* Part-time, online learning. *Degree requirements:* For master's, thesis. *Entrance requirements:* For master's, minimum GPA of 3.0; course work in statistics, research methods, family and social theories.

North Carolina Agricultural and Technical State University, The Graduate College, College of Agriculture and Environmental Sciences, Department of Family and Consumer Sciences, Greensboro, NC 27411. Offers child development, early education and family studies (MAT); family and consumer sciences education (MAT); food and nutritional sciences (MS). *Program availability:* Part-time, evening/weekend. *Degree requirements:* For master's, comprehensive exam, thesis or alternative, qualifying exam. *Entrance requirements:* For master's, GRE General Test, minimum GPA of 2.6.

North Dakota State University, College of Graduate and Interdisciplinary Studies, College of Human Development and Education, Department of Human Development and Family Science, Fargo, ND 58102. Offers developmental science (PhD); family financial planning (MS, Certificate); gerontology (PhD, Certificate); youth development (MS). *Program availability:* Part-time, evening/weekend, online learning. *Entrance requirements:* Additional exam requirements/recommendations for international students: required—TOEFL (minimum score 525 paper-based; 71 iBT). Tuition and fees vary according to program and reciprocity agreements.

Northern Illinois University, Graduate School, College of Health and Human Sciences, School of Family and Consumer Sciences, De Kalb, IL 60115-2854. Offers applied human development and family sciences (MS). *Accreditation:* AAMFT/COAMFTE. *Program availability:* Part-time. *Faculty:* 16 full-time (14 women), 2 part-time/adjunct (1 woman). *Students:* 25 full-time (23 women), 9 part-time (8 women); includes 10 minority (4 Black or African American, non-Hispanic/Latino; 6 Hispanic/Latino). Average age 27. 32 applicants, 66% accepted, 14 enrolled. In 2019, 15 master's awarded. *Degree requirements:* For master's, comprehensive exam, internship, thesis (for nutrition and dietetics). *Entrance requirements:* For master's, GRE General Test, minimum GPA of 2.75. Additional exam requirements/recommendations for international students: required—TOEFL (minimum score 550 paper-based). *Application deadline:* For fall admission, 6/1 for domestic students, 5/1 for international students; for spring admission, 11/1 for domestic students, 10/1 for international students. Applications are processed on a rolling basis. Application fee: $40. Electronic applications accepted. *Financial support:* In 2019–20, 16 research assistantships with full tuition reimbursements, 7 teaching assistantships with full tuition reimbursements were awarded; fellowships with full tuition reimbursements, career-related internships or fieldwork, Federal Work-Study, scholarships/grants, tuition waivers (full), and staff assistantships also available. Support available to part-time students. Financial award applicants required to submit FAFSA. *Unit head:* Dr. Thomas Pavkov, Chair, 815-753-6342, Fax: 815-753-1321, E-mail: tpavkov@niu.edu. *Application contact:* Graduate School Office, 815-753-0395, E-mail: gradsch@niu.edu.
Website: http://www.chhs.niu.edu/facs/

The Ohio State University, Graduate School, College of Education and Human Ecology, Department of Human Sciences, Columbus, OH 43210. Offers consumer sciences (MS, PhD); human development and family science (PhD); human nutrition (MS, PhD); kinesiology (MA, Ed D, PhD). *Program availability:* Part-time. *Degree requirements:* For master's, thesis optional; for doctorate, thesis/dissertation. *Entrance requirements:* For master's and doctorate, GRE. Additional exam requirements/recommendations for international students: required—TOEFL (minimum score 550 paper-based; 79 iBT), Michigan English Language Assessment Battery (minimum score 82); recommended—IELTS (minimum score 7). Electronic applications accepted.

Ohio University, Graduate College, College of Health Sciences and Professions, Department of Social and Public Health, Athens, OH 45701-2979. Offers early child development and family life (MS); family studies (MS); health administration (MHA); public health (MPH); social work (MSW). *Program availability:* Part-time, evening/weekend, online learning. *Degree requirements:* For master's, capstone (MPH). *Entrance requirements:* For master's, GMAT, GRE General Test, previous course work in accounting, management, and statistics; previous public health background (MHA, MPH). Additional exam requirements/recommendations for international students: required—TOEFL (minimum score 550 paper-based; 80 iBT) or IELTS (minimum score 6.5). Electronic applications accepted. *Expenses:* Contact institution.

Oklahoma State University, College of Human Sciences, Department of Human Development and Family Science, Stillwater, OK 74078. Offers human development and family science (MS, PhD), including family financial planning (MS), human environmental sciences (PhD). *Accreditation:* AAMFT/COAMFTE (one or more programs are accredited). *Program availability:* Online learning. *Faculty:* 27 full-time (16 women), 4 part-time/adjunct (3 women). *Students:* 36 full-time (30 women), 42 part-time (37 women); includes 17 minority (9 Black or African American, non-Hispanic/Latino; 1 Asian, non-Hispanic/Latino; 3 Hispanic/Latino; 1 Native Hawaiian or other Pacific Islander, non-Hispanic/Latino; 3 Two or more races, non-Hispanic/Latino), 4 international. Average age 30. 54 applicants, 57% accepted, 22 enrolled. In 2019, 28 master's, 6 doctorates awarded. *Entrance requirements:* For master's and doctorate, GRE or GMAT. Additional exam requirements/recommendations for international students: required—TOEFL (minimum score 550 paper-based; 79 iBT). *Application deadline:* For fall admission, 3/1 priority date for international students; for spring admission, 8/1 priority date for international students. Applications are processed on a rolling basis. Application fee: $50 ($75 for international students). Electronic applications accepted. *Expenses: Tuition, area resident:* Full-time $4148.10; part-time $2765.40 per credit hour. Tuition, state resident: full-time $4148.10; part-time $2765.40 per credit hour. Tuition, nonresident: full-time $15,775; part-time $10,516.80 per credit hour. *International tuition:* $15,775.20 full-time. *Required fees:* $2196.90; $122.05 per credit hour. Tuition and fees vary according to course load, campus/location and program. *Financial support:* In 2019–20, 25 research assistantships (averaging $1,431 per year),

20 teaching assistantships (averaging $1,314 per year) were awarded; career-related internships or fieldwork, Federal Work-Study, scholarships/grants, health care benefits, tuition waivers (partial), and unspecified assistantships also available. Support available to part-time students. Financial award application deadline: 3/1; financial award applicants required to submit FAFSA. *Unit head:* Dr. Sissy Osteen, Department Head, 405-744-4741, Fax: 405-744-6344, E-mail: sissy.osteen@okstate.edu. *Application contact:* Dr. Sheryl Tucker, Vice Prov/Dean/Prof, 405-744-6368, E-mail: gradi@okstate.edu.
Website: https://education.okstate.edu/departments-programs/human-development-family-science/index.html

Omega Graduate School, Graduate Programs, Dayton, TN 37321-6736. Offers family life education (M Litt); integration of religion and society (D Phil); organizational leadership (M Litt). *Entrance requirements:* For master's, official transcripts, three letters of recommendation, bachelor's degree or its equivalent, minimum undergraduate GPA of 3.0, minimum of 3 years of professional experience; for doctorate, official transcripts, three letters of recommendation, master's degree with minimum GPA of 3.0, minimum of 5 years of professional experience. *Expenses:* Contact institution.

Oregon State University, College of Public Health and Human Sciences, Program in Human Development and Family Studies, Corvallis, OR 97331. Offers MS, PhD. *Entrance requirements:* For master's, GRE; for doctorate, GRE, master's degree (including thesis). Additional exam requirements/recommendations for international students: required—TOEFL (minimum score 80 iBT), IELTS (minimum score 6.5).

Penn State University Park, Graduate School, College of Health and Human Development, Department of Human Development and Family Studies, University Park, PA 16802. Offers MS, PhD.

Purdue University, Graduate School, College of Health and Human Sciences, Department of Child Development and Family Studies, West Lafayette, IN 47907. Offers developmental studies (MS, PhD); family studies (MS, PhD); marriage and family therapy (MS, PhD). *Program availability:* Part-time. *Faculty:* 22 full-time (16 women), 2 part-time/adjunct (1 woman). *Students:* 22 full-time (21 women), 1 (woman) part-time; includes 3 minority (1 Black or African American, non-Hispanic/Latino; 1 Asian, non-Hispanic/Latino; 1 Two or more races, non-Hispanic/Latino), 8 international. Average age 26. 51 applicants, 25% accepted, 4 enrolled. In 2019, 2 master's, 3 doctorates awarded. Terminal master's awarded for partial completion of doctoral program. *Degree requirements:* For master's, thesis; for doctorate, thesis/dissertation. *Entrance requirements:* For master's and doctorate, GRE General Test (minimum score 1000 combined verbal and quantitative), minimum undergraduate GPA of 3.0 or equivalent. Additional exam requirements/recommendations for international students: required—TOEFL (minimum score 600 paper-based; 90 iBT), TWE (minimum score 4). *Application deadline:* For fall admission, 1/4 for domestic and international students. Applications are processed on a rolling basis. Application fee: $60 ($75 for international students). Electronic applications accepted. *Financial support:* Fellowships with full tuition reimbursements, research assistantships with full tuition reimbursements, teaching assistantships with full tuition reimbursements, and career-related internships or fieldwork available. Support available to part-time students. Financial award application deadline: 1/15; financial award applicants required to submit FAFSA. *Unit head:* Dr. Doran C. French, Head, 765-494-9511, E-mail: dcfrench@purdue.edu. *Application contact:* Tina Putz, Graduate Contact, 765-496-3816, E-mail: tputz@purdue.edu.
Website: http://www.purdue.edu/hhs/hdfs/

Purdue University Northwest, Graduate Studies Office, School of Liberal Arts and Social Sciences, Department of Behavioral Sciences, Hammond, IN 46323-2094. Offers child development and family studies (MS); marriage and family therapy (MS). *Accreditation:* AAMFT/COAMFTE. *Program availability:* Part-time. *Degree requirements:* For master's, thesis. *Entrance requirements:* For master's, GRE, interview. Additional exam requirements/recommendations for international students: required—TOEFL.

Queens College of the City University of New York, Mathematics and Natural Sciences Division, Department of Family, Nutrition and Exercise Sciences, Queens, NY 11367-1597. Offers exercise science specialist (MS); family and consumer science (K-12) (AC); family and consumer science/teaching curriculum (K-12) (MS Ed); nutrition and exercise science (MS); nutrition specialist (MS); physical education (K-12) (AC); physical education/teaching curriculum (pre K-12) (MS Ed). *Program availability:* Part-time, evening/weekend. *Degree requirements:* For master's, research project or comprehensive examination. *Entrance requirements:* For master's, minimum GPA of 3.0. Additional exam requirements/recommendations for international students: required—TOEFL (minimum paper-based score of 600) or IELTS=7 (for program in nutrition). Electronic applications accepted.

Roberts Wesleyan College, Department of Social Work, Rochester, NY 14624-1997. Offers child and family practice (MSW); mental health practice (MSW). *Accreditation:* CSWE. *Entrance requirements:* For master's, minimum GPA of 2.75.

St. Cloud State University, School of Graduate Studies, School of Education, Department of Child and Family Studies, St. Cloud, MN 56301-4498. Offers MS. *Degree requirements:* For master's, thesis or alternative. *Entrance requirements:* For master's, GRE General Test, minimum GPA of 2.75. Additional exam requirements/recommendations for international students: required—Michigan English Language Assessment Battery; recommended—TOEFL (minimum score 550 paper-based), IELTS (minimum score 6.5). Electronic applications accepted.

San Diego State University, Graduate and Research Affairs, College of Education, Department of Child and Family Development, San Diego, CA 92182. Offers child development (MS). *Program availability:* Part-time. *Degree requirements:* For master's, thesis. *Entrance requirements:* For master's, GRE General Test, 3 letters of recommendation, interview. Additional exam requirements/recommendations for international students: required—TOEFL. Electronic applications accepted.

San Jose State University, Program in Child & Adolescent Development, San Jose, CA 95192-0075. Offers MA. *Faculty:* 12 full-time (all women), 1 part-time/adjunct (0 women). *Students:* 2 full-time (both women), 9 part-time (all women); includes 5 minority (1 Asian, non-Hispanic/Latino; 4 Hispanic/Latino), 1 international. Average age 28. 17 applicants, 65% accepted, 6 enrolled. In 2019, 9 master's awarded. *Degree requirements:* For master's, thesis or alternative, project. *Entrance requirements:* For master's, application, personal statement, letters of recommendation. Additional exam requirements/recommendations for international students: required—TOEFL. *Application deadline:* For fall admission, 3/1 for domestic and international students. Applications are processed on a rolling basis. Application fee: $70. Electronic applications accepted. *Expenses: Tuition, area resident:* Full-time $7176; part-time $4164 per credit hour. Tuition, state resident: full-time $7176; part-time $4164 per credit hour. Tuition, nonresident: full-time $7176; part-time $4165 per credit hour. *International tuition:* $7176 full-time. *Required fees:* $2110; $2110. *Financial support:* In 2019–20, 5 students received support. Research assistantships, teaching assistantships, Federal Work-Study, and scholarships/grants available. Financial award application deadline: 5/1; financial award applicants required to submit FAFSA. *Unit head:* Dr. Emily Slusser, Department Chair, 408-924-3752, Fax: 408-924-3758, E-mail: emily.slusser@sjsu.edu. *Application contact:* Bryon McIntyre, Administrative Coordinator, 408-924-3614, Fax: 408-924-3758, E-mail: bryon.mcintyre@sjsu.edu.
Website: http://www.sjsu.edu/chad/

South Carolina State University, College of Graduate and Professional Studies, Department of Family and Consumer Sciences, Orangeburg, SC 29117-0001. Offers individual and family development (MS); nutritional sciences (MS). *Program availability:* Part-time, evening/weekend. *Degree requirements:* For master's, comprehensive exam, thesis optional, departmental qualifying exam. *Entrance requirements:* For master's, GRE, MAT, or NTE, minimum GPA of 2.7. Electronic applications accepted.

Spring Arbor University, School of Human Services, Spring Arbor, MI 49283-9799. Offers counseling (MAC); family studies (MAFS); nursing (MSN); social work (MSW). *Program availability:* Part-time, evening/weekend, online learning. *Entrance requirements:* For master's, bachelor's degree from regionally-accredited college or university, minimum GPA of 3.0 for at least the last two years of the bachelor's degree, at least two recommendations from professional/academic individuals. Additional exam requirements/recommendations for international students: required—TOEFL (minimum score 600 paper-based). Electronic applications accepted.

State University of New York at Oswego, Graduate Studies, School of Education, Department of Vocational Teacher Preparation, Oswego, NY 13126. Offers agriculture (MS Ed); business and marketing (MS Ed); family and consumer sciences (MS Ed); health careers (MS Ed); technical education (MS Ed); trade education (MS Ed). *Accreditation:* NCATE. *Program availability:* Part-time, evening/weekend. *Students:* 77. In 2019, 8 master's awarded. *Degree requirements:* For master's, comprehensive exam, thesis or alternative. *Entrance requirements:* Additional exam requirements/recommendations for international students: required—TOEFL (minimum score 560 paper-based). *Application deadline:* For fall admission, 4/1 for domestic students; for spring admission, 10/1 for domestic students. Applications are processed on a rolling basis. Application fee: $65. Electronic applications accepted. *Financial support:* Fellowships with full tuition reimbursements, teaching assistantships with partial tuition reimbursements, career-related internships or fieldwork, Federal Work-Study, institutionally sponsored loans, health care benefits, and unspecified assistantships available. Support available to part-time students. Financial award application deadline: 4/1; financial award applicants required to submit FAFSA. *Unit head:* Dr. Benjamin Ogwo, Chair, 315-312-2480, E-mail: benjamin.ogwo@oswego.edu. *Application contact:* Dr. Benjamin Ogwo, Chair, 315-312-2480, E-mail: benjamin.ogwo@oswego.edu.

Syracuse University, David B. Falk College of Sport and Human Dynamics, Programs in Human Development and Family Science, Syracuse, NY 13244. Offers MA, MS, PhD. *Accreditation:* AAMFT/COAMFTE (one or more programs are accredited). *Program availability:* Part-time. *Degree requirements:* For master's, comprehensive exam (for some programs), thesis; for doctorate, comprehensive exam, thesis/dissertation. *Entrance requirements:* For master's and doctorate, GRE General Test, personal statement, official transcripts, three letters of recommendation, resume. Additional exam requirements/recommendations for international students: required—TOEFL (minimum score 100 iBT). Electronic applications accepted.

Texas State University, The Graduate College, College of Applied Arts, Human Development and Family Studies, San Marcos, TX 78666. Offers MS. *Program availability:* Part-time. *Faculty:* 8 full-time (7 women), 1 (woman) part-time/adjunct. *Students:* 27 full-time (all women), 10 part-time (all women); includes 12 minority (1 Asian, non-Hispanic/Latino; 9 Hispanic/Latino; 2 Two or more races, non-Hispanic/Latino). Average age 24. 39 applicants, 69% accepted, 20 enrolled. In 2019, 7 master's awarded. *Degree requirements:* For master's, comprehensive exam, thesis (for some programs), competitive child life internship (for some programs). *Entrance requirements:* For master's, GRE (general test only) required with competitive scores in the verbal reasoning and quantitative reasoning sections, baccalaureate degree from regionally-accredited university; copy of official transcript from each institution where course credit was granted; minimum GPA of 3.0 in last 60 hours of undergraduate course work (plus any completed graduate courses); resume/curriculum vitae; statement of purpose; three letters of recommendation. Additional exam requirements/recommendations for international students: required—TOEFL (minimum score 550 paper-based; 78 iBT), IELTS (minimum score 6.5). *Application deadline:* For fall admission, 2/15 for domestic and international students. Applications are processed on a rolling basis. Application fee: $55 ($90 for international students). Electronic applications accepted. *Financial support:* In 2019–20, 21 students received support, including 5 fellowships with partial tuition reimbursements available (averaging $488 per year), 7 research assistantships (averaging $12,250 per year), 7 teaching assistantships (averaging $13,870 per year); scholarships/grants and unspecified assistantships also available. Financial award application deadline: 1/15; financial award applicants required to submit FAFSA. *Unit head:* Dr. Christine Gray, Graduate Advisor, 512-245-2904, Fax: 512-245-3829, E-mail: msfamilyandchild@txstate.edu. *Application contact:* Dr. Andrea Golato, Dean of the Graduate College, 512-245-2581, Fax: 512-245-8365, E-mail: er15@txstate.edu.
Website: http://www.fcs.txstate.edu/degrees-programs/fcd/fcdgrad.html

Texas Tech University, Graduate School, College of Human Sciences, Department of Human Development and Family Studies, Lubbock, TX 79409-1230. Offers human development and family studies (MS, PhD), including gerontology (MS). *Accreditation:* AAMFT/COAMFTE (one or more programs are accredited). *Program availability:* 100% online. *Faculty:* 26 full-time (22 women), 2 part-time/adjunct (both women). *Students:* 23 full-time (17 women), 22 part-time (17 women); includes 12 minority (2 Black or African American, non-Hispanic/Latino; 3 Asian, non-Hispanic/Latino; 6 Hispanic/Latino; 1 Two or more races, non-Hispanic/Latino), 3 international. Average age 29. 29 applicants, 59% accepted, 13 enrolled. In 2019, 4 master's, 4 doctorates awarded. *Degree requirements:* For master's, thesis; for doctorate, comprehensive exam, thesis/dissertation. *Entrance requirements:* For master's and doctorate, GRE General Test. Additional exam requirements/recommendations for international students: required—TOEFL (minimum score 550 paper-based; 79 iBT). *Application deadline:* For fall admission, 6/1 priority date for domestic students, 1/15 priority date for international students; for spring admission, 9/1 priority date for domestic students, 6/15 priority date for international students. Applications are processed on a rolling basis. Application fee: $65. Electronic applications accepted. *Expenses:* Contact institution. *Financial support:* In 2019–20, 29 students received support, including 28 fellowships (averaging $6,779 per year), 16 research assistantships (averaging $18,338 per year), 8 teaching assistantships (averaging $14,356 per year); scholarships/grants and unspecified assistantships also available. Financial award application deadline: 12/1; financial award applicants required to submit FAFSA. *Unit head:* Dr. Ann M. Mastergeorge, Chairperson, Rockwell Endowed Child and Family Professor, 806-834-7162, Fax: 806-742-3042, E-mail: ann.mastergeorge@ttu.edu. *Application contact:* Dr. Elizabeth Trejos-Castillo, Graduate Program Director, 806-834-6080, Fax: 806-742-0285, E-mail: elizabeth.trejos@ttu.edu.
Website: www.hdfs.ttu.edu

Texas Woman's University, Graduate School, College of Professional Education, Department of Human Development, Family Studies, and Counseling, Denton, TX 76204. Offers child development (MS); child life (MS); counseling and development (MS); early childhood development and education (PhD); early childhood education (M Ed); family studies (MS, PhD); family therapy (MS, PhD). *Accreditation:* ACA (one or more programs are accredited). *Program availability:* Part-time, evening/weekend,

100% online, blended/hybrid learning. *Faculty:* 27 full-time (22 women), 11 part-time/adjunct (10 women). *Students:* 187 full-time (180 women), 245 part-time (230 women); includes 177 minority (83 Black or African American, non-Hispanic/Latino; 17 Asian, non-Hispanic/Latino; 62 Hispanic/Latino; 15 Two or more races, non-Hispanic/Latino), 8 international. Average age 31. 234 applicants, 49% accepted, 80 enrolled. In 2019, 89 master's, 24 doctorates awarded. *Degree requirements:* For master's, comprehensive exam (for some programs), thesis (for some programs), thesis, professional paper, portfolio, or coursework; practicums (for some programs); for doctorate, comprehensive exam, thesis/dissertation, seminars, qualifying exam, dissertation. *Entrance requirements:* For master's, minimum GPA of 3.0 (3.25 for family therapy), letter of intent, curriculum vitae/resume, interview, writing sample, 2 letters of recommendation, interview (counseling and development); for doctorate, GRE scores (147 verbal, 144 quantitative, 4 analytical), minimum GPA of 3.5 (3.35 for family studies) on all prior graduate work, curriculum vitae/resume, letter of intent, 3 letters of recommendation, master's degree or prerequisite equivalents in core area. Additional exam requirements/recommendations for international students: required—TOEFL (minimum score 79 iBT); recommended—IELTS (minimum score 6.5), TSE (minimum score 53). *Application deadline:* For fall admission, 3/15 for domestic students, 3/1 priority date for international students; for spring admission, 10/1 for domestic students, 7/1 priority date for international students; for summer admission, 2/1 for domestic and international students. Application fee: $50 ($75 for international students). Electronic applications accepted. *Expenses: Tuition, area resident:* Full-time $4973.40; part-time $276.30 per semester hour. Tuition, state resident: full-time $4973.40; part-time $276.30 per semester hour. Tuition, nonresident: full-time $12,569; part-time $698.30 per semester hour. *International tuition:* $12,569.40 full-time. *Required fees:* $2524.30. Tuition and fees vary according to course level, course load, degree level and program. *Financial support:* In 2019–20, 141 students received support, including 2 research assistantships, 17 teaching assistantships (averaging $10,532 per year); career-related internships or fieldwork, scholarships/grants, health care benefits, and unspecified assistantships also available. Support available to part-time students. Financial award application deadline: 3/1; financial award applicants required to submit FAFSA. *Unit head:* Dr. Holly Hansen-Thomas, Interim Chair, 940-898-2685, Fax: 940-898-2676, E-mail: HDFSC@twu.edu. *Application contact:* Korie Hawkins, Associate Director of Admissions, Graduate Recruitment, 940-898-3188, Fax: 940-898-3081, E-mail: admissions@twu.edu.
Website: http://www.twu.edu/family-sciences/

Towson University, College of Liberal Arts, Program in Child Life, Administration and Family Collaboration, Towson, MD 21252-0001. Offers MS. *Entrance requirements:* For master's, bachelor's degree; minimum GPA of 3.0; minimum of 40 hours of volunteer or paid work experience with children with special health care needs in a child life department under the direct supervision of a Certified Child Life Specialist; essay; volunteer/work experience verification form. Electronic applications accepted. *Expenses: Tuition, area resident:* Full-time $7920; part-time $439 per credit. Tuition, nonresident: full-time $16,344; part-time $908 per credit. *International tuition:* $16,344 full-time. *Required fees:* $2628; $146 per credit. $876 per term.

Towson University, College of Liberal Arts, Program in Family-Professional Collaboration, Towson, MD 21252-0001. Offers Postbaccalaureate Certificate. *Entrance requirements:* For degree, minimum GPA of 3.0; bachelor's degree; resume; interview with program director. Electronic applications accepted. *Expenses: Tuition, area resident:* Full-time $7920; part-time $439 per credit. Tuition, nonresident: full-time $16,344; part-time $908 per credit. *International tuition:* $16,344 full-time. *Required fees:* $2628; $146 per credit. $876 per term.

Tufts University, Graduate School of Arts and Sciences, Eliot-Pearson Department of Child Study and Human Development, Medford, MA 02155. Offers child study and human development (MA, PhD). *Program availability:* Part-time. *Degree requirements:* For master's, thesis (for some programs); for doctorate, comprehensive exam, thesis/dissertation. *Entrance requirements:* For master's and doctorate, GRE General Test. Additional exam requirements/recommendations for international students: required—TOEFL (minimum score 550 paper-based; 80 iBT), IELTS (minimum score 6.5). Electronic applications accepted. *Expenses:* Contact institution.

The University of Akron, Graduate School, Buchtel College of Arts and Sciences, Department of Child and Family Development, Akron, OH 44325. Offers child development (MA). *Degree requirements:* For master's, comprehensive exam, project or thesis. *Entrance requirements:* For master's, GRE, minimum GPA of 3.0, three letters of recommendation, statement of purpose, resume. Additional exam requirements/recommendations for international students: required—TOEFL (minimum score 79 iBT), IELTS (minimum score 6.5). Electronic applications accepted.

The University of Alabama, Graduate School, College of Human Environmental Sciences, Department of Human Development and Family Studies, Tuscaloosa, AL 35487. Offers human development and family studies (MSHES); marriage and family therapy (MSHES); parent and family life education (MSHES). *Program availability:* Part-time. *Faculty:* 10 full-time (7 women). *Students:* 17 full-time (12 women), 2 part-time (both women); includes 7 minority (3 Black or African American, non-Hispanic/Latino; 3 Hispanic/Latino; 1 Two or more races, non-Hispanic/Latino). Average age 28. 13 applicants, 69% accepted, 7 enrolled. In 2019, 12 master's awarded. Terminal master's awarded for partial completion of doctoral program. *Degree requirements:* For master's, comprehensive exam (for some programs), thesis optional. *Entrance requirements:* For master's, GRE General Test or MAT, minimum GPA of 3.0. Additional exam requirements/recommendations for international students: required—TOEFL (minimum score 79 iBT), IELTS (minimum score 6.5). *Application deadline:* For fall admission, 12/15 priority date for domestic and international students. Applications are processed on a rolling basis. Application fee: $50 ($60 for international students). Electronic applications accepted. *Expenses: Tuition, area resident:* Full-time $10,780; part-time $440 per credit hour. Tuition, nonresident: full-time $30,250; part-time $1550 per credit hour. *Financial support:* In 2019–20, 15 students received support. Fellowships, research assistantships with full tuition reimbursements available, teaching assistantships, career-related internships or fieldwork, Federal Work-Study, scholarships/grants, health care benefits, and unspecified assistantships available. Financial award application deadline: 3/15. *Unit head:* Dr. Robert Laird, 205-348-9277, E-mail: rdlaird@ches.ua.edu. *Application contact:* Patrick Fuller, Admissions Officer, 205-348-5932, Fax: 205-348-0400, E-mail: patrick.d.fuller@ua.edu.
Website: http://www.hdfs.ches.ua.edu/

The University of Arizona, College of Education, Department of Disability and Psychoeducational Studies, Tucson, AZ 85721. Offers counseling and mental health (MA), including rehabilitation counseling, school counseling; family studies and human development (M Ed); rehabilitation counseling (PhD); school counseling (MA); school psychology (PhD, Ed S); special education (MA, PhD), including cross-categorical special education (MA), deaf and hard of hearing (MA), learning disabilities (MA), severe and multiple disabilities (MA), special education (PhD), visual impairment (MA). *Accreditation:* CORE. *Program availability:* Part-time. Terminal master's awarded for partial completion of doctoral program. *Degree requirements:* For master's, comprehensive exam, thesis optional; for doctorate, comprehensive exam, thesis/dissertation. *Entrance requirements:* For master's, statement of purpose; for doctorate, GRE General Test (minimum score 1100) or MAT, 3 letters of recommendation. Additional exam requirements/recommendations for international students: required—TOEFL (minimum score 550 paper-based; 79 iBT).

University of Central Oklahoma, The Jackson College of Graduate Studies, College of Education and Professional Studies, Department of Human Environmental Sciences, Edmond, OK 73034-5209. Offers family and child studies (MS), including family life education, infant/child specialist, marriage and family therapy; nutrition-food science (MS). *Program availability:* Part-time. *Degree requirements:* For master's, comprehensive exam (for some programs), thesis (for some programs). *Entrance requirements:* For master's, GRE, essay, physical, CPR and First Aid training. Additional exam requirements/recommendations for international students: required—TOEFL (minimum score 550 paper-based; 79 iBT), IELTS (minimum score 6.5). Electronic applications accepted.

University of Colorado Denver, School of Education and Human Development, Program in Education and Human Development, Denver, CO 80217. Offers administrative leadership and policy (PhD); assessment (MA); early childhood special education/early childhood education (PhD); family science and human development (PhD); human development and family relations (MA); learning (MA); mathematics education (PhD); research and evaluation methods (MA); research, assessment and evaluation (PhD); science education (PhD); urban ecologies (PhD). *Program availability:* Part-time, evening/weekend. *Degree requirements:* For master's, comprehensive exam, 9 hours of core courses embedded within a minimum of 36 to 38 hours of relevant coursework, including an educational psychology practicum, independent study project or thesis (recommended). *Entrance requirements:* For master's, GRE if undergraduate GPA below 2.75, resume, three letters of recommendation, transcripts. Additional exam requirements/recommendations for international students: required—TOEFL (minimum score 537 paper-based; 75 iBT); recommended—IELTS (minimum score 6.5). Electronic applications accepted. *Expenses:* Contact institution.

University of Connecticut, Graduate School, College of Liberal Arts and Sciences, Department of Human Development and Family Studies, Storrs, CT 06269. Offers MA, PhD. *Accreditation:* AAMFT/COAMFTE (one or more programs are accredited). Terminal master's awarded for partial completion of doctoral program. *Degree requirements:* For master's, comprehensive exam; for doctorate, thesis/dissertation. *Entrance requirements:* For doctorate, GRE General Test. Additional exam requirements/recommendations for international students: required—TOEFL (minimum score 550 paper-based). Electronic applications accepted.

University of Delaware, College of Education and Human Development, Department of Human Development and Family Studies, Newark, DE 19716. Offers MS, PhD. *Program availability:* Part-time. Terminal master's awarded for partial completion of doctoral program. *Degree requirements:* For master's, thesis or alternative; for doctorate, comprehensive exam, thesis/dissertation. *Entrance requirements:* For master's and doctorate, GRE General Test, 3 letters of recommendation. Additional exam requirements/recommendations for international students: required—TOEFL. Electronic applications accepted.

University of Denver, Morgridge College of Education, Denver, CO 80208. Offers child, family and school psychology (MA, PhD, Ed S); counseling psychology (MA, PhD); curriculum and instruction (MA, Ed D, PhD); curriculum instruction and teaching (Certificate); early childhood special education (MA, Certificate); educational leadership and policy studies (MA, Ed D, PhD, Certificate); higher education (Ed D, PhD); library and information science (MLIS); research methods and statistics (MA, PhD). *Accreditation:* ALA; APA (one or more programs are accredited). *Program availability:* Part-time, evening/weekend, online learning. *Faculty:* 54 full-time (38 women), 28 part-time/adjunct (16 women). *Students:* 477 full-time (385 women), 492 part-time (378 women); includes 266 minority (59 Black or African American, non-Hispanic/Latino; 7 American Indian or Alaska Native, non-Hispanic/Latino; 36 Asian, non-Hispanic/Latino; 128 Hispanic/Latino; 2 Native Hawaiian or other Pacific Islander, non-Hispanic/Latino; 34 Two or more races, non-Hispanic/Latino), 58 international. Average age 31. 1,252 applicants, 68% accepted, 420 enrolled. In 2019, 222 master's, 46 doctorates, 129 other advanced degrees awarded. Terminal master's awarded for partial completion of doctoral program. *Degree requirements:* For master's, comprehensive exam (for some programs); for doctorate, comprehensive exam (for some programs), thesis/dissertation. *Entrance requirements:* For master's, GRE General Test or GMAT, bachelors degree; transcripts; two letters of recommendation; personal statement; resume; for doctorate, GRE General Test or GMAT, Masters degree; transcripts; two letters of recommendation; personal statement(s); resume. Additional exam requirements/recommendations for international students: required—TOEFL (minimum score 550 paper-based; 80 iBT). *Application deadline:* Applications are processed on a rolling basis. Application fee: $65. Electronic applications accepted. *Expenses:* Contact institution. *Financial support:* In 2019–20, 698 students received support, including 19 research assistantships with tuition reimbursements available (averaging $11,372 per year), 3 teaching assistantships with tuition reimbursements available (averaging $4,333 per year); career-related internships or fieldwork, Federal Work-Study, institutionally sponsored loans, scholarships/grants, and unspecified assistantships also available. Support available to part-time students. Financial award application deadline: 2/15; financial award applicants required to submit FAFSA. *Unit head:* Dr. Karen Riley, Dean, 303-871-3665, E-mail: karen.riley@du.edu. *Application contact:* Jodi Dye, Director of Admissions, 303-871-2510, E-mail: jodi.dye@du.edu.
Website: http://morgridge.du.edu

University of Georgia, College of Family and Consumer Sciences, Department of Human Development and Family Science, Athens, GA 30602. Offers child and family development (MS). *Accreditation:* AAMFT/COAMFTE. *Degree requirements:* For master's, thesis (MS). *Entrance requirements:* For master's, GRE General Test. Electronic applications accepted.

University of Guelph, Office of Graduate and Postdoctoral Studies, College of Social and Applied Human Sciences, Department of Family Relations and Applied Nutrition, Guelph, ON N1G 2W1, Canada. Offers applied nutrition (MAN); family relations and human development (M Sc, PhD), including applied human nutrition, couple and family therapy (M Sc), family relations and human development. *Accreditation:* AAMFT/COAMFTE (one or more programs are accredited). *Program availability:* Part-time. *Degree requirements:* For master's, thesis (for some programs); for doctorate, comprehensive exam, thesis/dissertation. *Entrance requirements:* For master's, minimum B+ average; for doctorate, master's degree in family relations and human development or related field with a minimum B+ average or master's degree in applied human nutrition. Additional exam requirements/recommendations for international students: required—TOEFL (minimum score 600 paper-based). Electronic applications accepted.

University of Illinois at Springfield, Graduate Programs, College of Education and Human Services, Program in Human Services, Springfield, IL 62703-5407. Offers alcohol and substance abuse (Graduate Certificate); alcoholism and substance abuse (MA); child and family studies (MA); gerontology (MA); social services administration (MA). *Program availability:* Part-time, 100% online, blended/hybrid learning. *Faculty:* 3 full-time (all women), 3 part-time/adjunct (2 women). *Students:* 12 full-time (all women),

49 part-time (47 women); includes 27 minority (19 Black or African American, non-Hispanic/Latino; 6 Hispanic/Latino; 2 Two or more races, non-Hispanic/Latino), 1 international. Average age 33. 29 applicants, 69% accepted, 12 enrolled. In 2019, 24 master's, 1 other advanced degree awarded. *Degree requirements:* For master's, internship; capstone project. *Entrance requirements:* For master's, minimum undergraduate GPA of 3.0, 2 letters of recommendation from professional or academic sources, statement of intent, interview. Additional exam requirements/recommendations for international students: required—TOEFL (minimum score 500 paper-based; 61 iBT). *Application deadline:* Applications are processed on a rolling basis. Application fee: $60 ($75 for international students). Electronic applications accepted. *Expenses:* $33.25 per credit hour (online fee). *Financial support:* In 2019–20, research assistantships with full tuition reimbursements (averaging $10,562 per year), teaching assistantships with full tuition reimbursements (averaging $10,652 per year) were awarded; fellowships, career-related internships or fieldwork, Federal Work-Study, scholarships/grants, health care benefits, and unspecified assistantships also available. Support available to part-time students. Financial award application deadline: 11/15; financial award applicants required to submit FAFSA. *Unit head:* Dr. Denise Bockmier-Sommers, Program Administrator, 217-206-6908, Fax: 217-206-6775, E-mail: dsomm2@uis.edu. *Application contact:* Dr. Denise Bockmier-Sommers, Program Administrator, 217-206-6908, Fax: 217-206-6775, E-mail: dsomm2@uis.edu.
Website: http://www.uis.edu/humanservices

University of Kentucky, Graduate School, College of Agriculture, Food and Environment, Program in Family Studies, Human Development, and Resource Management, Lexington, KY 40506-0032. Offers MS, PhD. *Accreditation:* AAMFT/COAMFTE. *Degree requirements:* For master's, comprehensive exam, thesis optional. *Entrance requirements:* For master's, GRE General Test, minimum undergraduate GPA of 2.75; for doctorate, GRE General Test, minimum undergraduate GPA of 3.0. Additional exam requirements/recommendations for international students: required—TOEFL (minimum score 550 paper-based). Electronic applications accepted.

University of La Verne, LaFetra College of Education, Programs in Child Development/Child Life, La Verne, CA 91750-4443. Offers child development (MS); child life (MS). *Program availability:* Part-time. *Entrance requirements:* For master's, minimum GPA of 3.0, 3 letters of reference, writing sample. Additional exam requirements/recommendations for international students: required—TOEFL (minimum score 550 paper-based). *Expenses:* Contact institution.

University of Maryland, College Park, Academic Affairs, School of Public Health, Department of Family Science, College Park, MD 20742. Offers family studies (PhD); marriage and family therapy (MS); maternal and child health (PhD). *Accreditation:* AAMFT/COAMFTE. *Program availability:* Part-time, evening/weekend. *Degree requirements:* For master's, thesis or alternative; for doctorate, comprehensive exam, thesis/dissertation, oral defense. *Entrance requirements:* For master's, GRE General Test, minimum GPA of 3.0, 3 letters of recommendation; for doctorate, GRE General Test, minimum GPA of 3.0, 3 letters of recommendation, research sample. Electronic applications accepted.

University of Massachusetts Amherst, Graduate School, College of Education, Program in Education, Amherst, MA 01003. Offers bilingual, English as a second language, and multicultural education (M Ed, Ed S); child study and early education (M Ed); children, families and schools (Ed D, Ed S); early childhood and elementary teacher education (M Ed); educational leadership (M Ed); educational policy and leadership (Ed D); higher education (M Ed); international education (M Ed); language, literacy and culture (Ed D); learning, media and technology (M Ed, Ed S); mathematics, science, and learning technologies (Ed D); reading and writing (M Ed); research, educational measurement and psychometrics (Ed D); school counselor education (M Ed, Ed S); school psychology (Ed S); science education (Ed S); secondary teacher education (M Ed); social justice education (M Ed, Ed D, Ed S); special education (M Ed, Ed D, Ed S); teacher education and school improvement (Ed D, Ed S). *Accreditation:* NCATE. *Program availability:* Part-time, online learning. Terminal master's awarded for partial completion of doctoral program. *Degree requirements:* For doctorate, comprehensive exam, thesis/dissertation. *Entrance requirements:* Additional exam requirements/recommendations for international students: required—TOEFL (minimum score 550 paper-based; 80 iBT), IELTS (minimum score 6.5). Electronic applications accepted.

University of Minnesota, Twin Cities Campus, Graduate School, College of Education and Human Development, Department of Family Social Science, Minneapolis, MN 55455-0213. Offers family education (M Ed); marriage and family therapy (MA, PhD); prevention science (MA). *Accreditation:* AAMFT/COAMFTE (one or more programs are accredited). *Faculty:* 18 full-time (12 women). *Students:* 62 full-time (57 women), 19 part-time (17 women); includes 15 minority (7 Black or African American, non-Hispanic/Latino; 5 Asian, non-Hispanic/Latino; 2 Hispanic/Latino; 1 Two or more races, non-Hispanic/Latino), 14 international. Average age 34. 79 applicants, 67% accepted, 44 enrolled. In 2019, 21 master's, 5 doctorates awarded. *Degree requirements:* For master's, thesis; for doctorate, thesis/dissertation. *Entrance requirements:* For master's and doctorate, GRE General Test, minimum undergraduate GPA of 3.0 (preferred). Additional exam requirements/recommendations for international students: required—TOEFL. *Application deadline:* For fall admission, 12/15 for domestic students. Application fee: $75 ($95 for international students). *Financial support:* In 2019–20, 3 fellowships, 27 research assistantships (averaging $10,086 per year), 19 teaching assistantships (averaging $9,129 per year) were awarded; career-related internships or fieldwork, Federal Work-Study, institutionally sponsored loans, and tuition waivers (partial) also available. Financial award application deadline: 6/30; financial award applicants required to submit FAFSA. *Unit head:* Dr. Jodi Dworkin, Head, 612-625-1900, Fax: 612-625-4227, E-mail: jdworkin@umn.edu. *Application contact:* Dr. Catherine Solheim, Director of Graduate Studies, 612-625-1201, E-mail: csolheim@umn.edu.
Website: http://www.cehd.umn.edu/fsos/

University of Missouri, Office of Research and Graduate Studies, College of Human Environmental Sciences, Department of Human Development and Family Studies, Columbia, MO 65211. Offers MA, MS, PhD. *Entrance requirements:* For master's, GRE General Test, minimum GPA of 3.0. Additional exam requirements/recommendations for international students: required—TOEFL.

University of Montana, Graduate School, Phyllis J. Washington College of Education and Human Sciences, Department of Counselor Education, Missoula, MT 59812. Offers clinical mental health counseling (MA); counseling and supervision (Ed D); counselor education (Ed S); intercultural youth and family development (MA); school counseling (MA). *Accreditation:* ACA. *Degree requirements:* For doctorate, thesis/dissertation. *Entrance requirements:* For master's, doctorate, and Ed S, GRE General Test. Additional exam requirements/recommendations for international students: required—TOEFL.

University of Nebraska–Lincoln, Graduate College, College of Education and Human Sciences, Department of Child, Youth and Family Studies, Lincoln, NE 68588. Offers child development/early childhood education (MS, PhD); child, youth and family studies (MS); family and consumer sciences education (MS, PhD); family financial planning (MS); family science (MS, PhD); gerontology (PhD); human sciences (PhD), including child, youth and family studies, gerontology, medical family therapy; marriage and family therapy (MS); medical family therapy (PhD); youth development (MS). *Accreditation:* AAMFT/COAMFTE (one or more programs are accredited). *Program availability:* Online learning. *Degree requirements:* For master's, thesis optional. *Entrance requirements:* For master's, GRE. Additional exam requirements/recommendations for international students: required—TOEFL (minimum score 550 paper-based). Electronic applications accepted.

University of Nevada, Reno, Graduate School, College of Education, Department of Human Development and Family Studies, Reno, NV 89557. Offers MS. *Degree requirements:* For master's, thesis optional. *Entrance requirements:* For master's, GRE General Test, minimum GPA of 2.75. Additional exam requirements/recommendations for international students: required—TOEFL (minimum score 500 paper-based; 61 iBT), IELTS (minimum score 6). Electronic applications accepted.

University of New Hampshire, Graduate School, College of Health and Human Services, Department of Human Development and Family Studies, Durham, NH 03824. Offers adolescent development (Postbaccalaureate Certificate); human development and family studies (MS), including adolescent development, child development; marriage and family therapy (MS). *Accreditation:* AAMFT/COAMFTE. *Program availability:* Part-time. *Faculty:* 2 full-time (1 woman), 2 part-time/adjunct (1 woman). *Students:* 17 full-time (13 women), 2 part-time (both women); includes 4 minority (2 Black or African American, non-Hispanic/Latino; 1 Hispanic/Latino; 1 Two or more races, non-Hispanic/Latino). Average age 29. 18 applicants, 72% accepted, 7 enrolled. In 2019, 8 master's awarded. *Entrance requirements:* Additional exam requirements/recommendations for international students: required—TOEFL (minimum score 550 paper-based; 80 iBT), IELTS (minimum score 6.5), PTE (minimum score 59), Duolingo. *Application deadline:* For fall admission, 1/15 for domestic and international students. Application fee: $65. Electronic applications accepted. *Financial support:* In 2019–20, 12 students received support, including 4 teaching assistantships; fellowships, research assistantships, Federal Work-Study, scholarships/grants, tuition waivers (full and partial), and unspecified assistantships also available. Support available to part-time students. Financial award application deadline: 1/15. *Unit head:* Kerry Kazura, Chair, 603-862-2135. *Application contact:* Barbara Frankel, Graduate Program Coordinator, 603-862-2153, E-mail: barbara.frankel@unh.edu.
Website: http://www.chhs.unh.edu/hdfs

University of New Mexico, Graduate Studies, College of Education and Human Sciences, Program in Family Studies, Albuquerque, NM 87131-2039. Offers family life education (MA); family relations (MA); family studies (PhD); human development in families (MA). *Program availability:* Part-time, evening/weekend. *Degree requirements:* For master's, comprehensive exam, thesis (for some programs); for doctorate, comprehensive exam, thesis/dissertation. *Entrance requirements:* For master's, written paper, 3 letters of recommendation, personal statement; for doctorate, GRE General Test, written paper, 3 letters of recommendation, personal statement, interview. Additional exam requirements/recommendations for international students: required—TOEFL (minimum score 550 paper-based). Electronic applications accepted. *Expenses:* Tuition, state resident: full-time $7633; part-time $972 per year. Tuition, nonresident: full-time $22,586; part-time $3840 per year. *International tuition:* $23,292 full-time. *Required fees:* $8608. Tuition and fees vary according to course level, course load, degree level, program and student level.

University of North Alabama, College of Arts and Sciences, Department of Sociology and Family Studies, Florence, AL 35632-0001. Offers family studies (MS). *Program availability:* Part-time, online only, 100% online. *Degree requirements:* For master's, comprehensive exam (for some programs), thesis optional. *Entrance requirements:* For master's, GRE or MAT, three professional references; writing sample; essay; resume. Additional exam requirements/recommendations for international students: required—TOEFL (minimum score 79 iBT), IELTS (minimum score 6), PTE (minimum score 54). Electronic applications accepted.

The University of North Carolina at Charlotte, Cato College of Education, Department of Special Education and Child Development, Charlotte, NC 28223-0001. Offers academically or intellectually gifted (Graduate Certificate); autism spectrum disorders (Graduate Certificate); child and family development: birth through kindergarten (Graduate Certificate); child and family studies (M Ed); special education (M Ed, PhD, Graduate Certificate), including academically or intellectually gifted (M Ed). *Program availability:* Part-time, 100% online, blended/hybrid learning. *Faculty:* 26 full-time (20 women), 8 part-time/adjunct (all women). *Students:* 19 full-time (14 women), 95 part-time (88 women); includes 24 minority (17 Black or African American, non-Hispanic/Latino; 4 Hispanic/Latino; 3 Two or more races, non-Hispanic/Latino), 4 international. Average age 35. 96 applicants, 86% accepted, 66 enrolled. In 2019, 14 master's, 6 doctorates, 15 other advanced degrees awarded. *Degree requirements:* For master's, capstone; for doctorate, thesis/dissertation, portfolio. *Entrance requirements:* For master's, GRE or MAT, transcripts, at least three evaluations from professional educators familiar with the applicant's personal and professional qualifications, an essay (one to two pages) describing the applicant's experience and objective in undertaking graduate study; for doctorate, GRE or MAT, 2 official transcripts of all academic work attempted since high school indicating minimum GPA of 3.5 in graduate degree program; at least 3 references of someone who knows applicant's current work and/or academic achievements in previous degree work; two-page essay; current resume or curriculum vitae; writing sample; documentation of teaching; for Graduate Certificate, undergraduate degree from regionally-accredited four-year institution; minimum cumulative undergraduate GPA of 3.0; three recommendations from persons knowledgeable of applicant's interaction with children and families; statement of purpose; clear criminal background check. Additional exam requirements/recommendations for international students: required—TOEFL (minimum score 557 paper-based; 83 iBT), IELTS (minimum score 6.5), TOEFL (minimum score 557 paper-based, 83 iBT) or IELTS (6.5). *Application deadline:* Applications are processed on a rolling basis. Application fee: $75. Electronic applications accepted. *Expenses:* Tuition, state resident: full-time $4337. Tuition, nonresident: full-time $17,771. *Required fees:* $3093. Tuition and fees vary according to course load, degree level and program. *Financial support:* In 2019–20, 15 students received support, including 15 research assistantships (averaging $9,549 per year); teaching assistantships, career-related internships or fieldwork, institutionally sponsored loans, scholarships/grants, and unspecified assistantships also available. Support available to part-time students. Financial award applicants required to submit FAFSA. *Unit head:* Dr. Charles Wood, Department Chair & Professor, 704-687-8395, E-mail: clwood@uncc.edu. *Application contact:* Kathy B. Giddings, Director of Graduate Admissions, 704-687-5503, Fax: 704-687-1668, E-mail: gradadm@uncc.edu.
Website: http://spcd.uncc.edu/

The University of North Carolina at Charlotte, Cato College of Education, Interdisciplinary Education Programs, Charlotte, NC 28223-0001. Offers art education (Graduate Certificate); child and family development: early childhood development (MAT); curriculum and instruction (PhD); elementary education (MAT); foreign language education (MAT); middle grades education (MAT); secondary education (MAT); special education (MAT); teachin (Graduate Certificate); teaching English as a second language

(MAT); theatre education (Graduate Certificate). *Program availability:* Part-time, 100% online, blended/hybrid learning. *Students:* 52 full-time (42 women), 647 part-time (526 women); includes 266 minority (172 Black or African American, non-Hispanic/Latino; 2 American Indian or Alaska Native, non-Hispanic/Latino; 11 Asian, non-Hispanic/Latino; 56 Hispanic/Latino; 25 Two or more races, non-Hispanic/Latino), 8 international. Average age 34. 590 applicants, 84% accepted, 382 enrolled. In 2019, 84 master's, 15 doctorates, 156 other advanced degrees awarded. *Degree requirements:* For master's, capstone/portfolio. *Entrance requirements:* For master's, GRE or MAT, bachelor's degree, or its U.S. equivalent, from regionally-accredited college or university; minimum overall GPA of 3.0 on all previous work beyond high school; statement of purpose (essay); at least three recommendation forms; for doctorate, GRE or MAT, bachelor's degree (or its U.S. equivalent) from regionally-accredited college or university; minimum overall GPA of 3.5 in master's degree program; for Graduate Certificate, bachelor's degree from regionally-accredited university; minimum GPA of 2.75 on all post-secondary work attempted; transcripts; personal statement outlining why the applicant seeks admission to the program. Additional exam requirements/recommendations for international students: required—TOEFL (minimum score 557 paper-based; 83 iBT), IELTS (minimum score 6.5), TOEFL (minimum score 557 paper-based, 83 iBT) or IELTS (6.5). *Application deadline:* Applications are processed on a rolling basis. Application fee: $75. Electronic applications accepted. *Expenses:* Tuition, state resident: full-time $4337. Tuition, nonresident: full-time $17,771. *Required fees:* $3093. Tuition and fees vary according to course load, degree level and program. *Financial support:* Career-related internships or fieldwork, institutionally sponsored loans, scholarships/grants, and unspecified assistantships available. Support available to part-time students. Financial award application deadline: 3/1; financial award applicants required to submit FAFSA. *Unit head:* Dr. Ellen McIntyre, Dean, 704-687-8722, E-mail: ellen.mcintyre@uncc.edu. *Application contact:* Kathy B. Giddings, Director of Graduate Admissions, 704-687-5503, Fax: 704-687-1668, E-mail: gradadm@uncc.edu.
Website: http://education.uncc.edu/academic-programs

The University of North Carolina at Greensboro, Graduate School, School of Health and Human Sciences, Department of Human Development and Family Studies, Greensboro, NC 27412-5001. Offers M Ed, MS, PhD. *Degree requirements:* For master's, one foreign language; for doctorate, one foreign language, thesis/dissertation. *Entrance requirements:* For master's and doctorate, GRE General Test. Additional exam requirements/recommendations for international students: required—TOEFL. Electronic applications accepted. *Expenses:* Contact institution.

University of North Texas, Toulouse Graduate School, Denton, TX 76203-5459. Offers accounting (MS); applied anthropology (MA, MS); applied behavior analysis (Certificate); applied geography (MA); applied technology and performance improvement (M Ed, MS); art education (MA); art history (MA); arts leadership (Certificate); audiology (Au D); behavior analysis (MS); behavioral science (PhD); biochemistry and molecular biology (MS); biology (MA, MS); biomedical engineering (MS); business analysis (MS); chemistry (MS); clinical health psychology (PhD); communication studies (MA, MS); computer engineering (MS); computer science (MS); counseling (M Ed, MS), including clinical mental health counseling (MS), college and university counseling, elementary school counseling, secondary school counseling; creative writing (MA); criminal justice (MS); curriculum and instruction (M Ed); decision sciences (MBA); design (MA, MFA), including fashion design (MFA), innovation studies, interior design (MFA); early childhood studies (MS); economics (MS); educational leadership (M Ed, Ed D); educational psychology (MS, PhD), including family studies (MS), gifted and talented (MS), human development (MS), learning and cognition (MS), research, measurement and evaluation (MS); electrical engineering (MS); emergency management (MPA); engineering technology (MS); English (MA); English as a second language (MA); environmental science (MS); finance (MBA, MS); financial management (MPA); French (MA); health services management (MBA); higher education (M Ed, Ed D); history (MA, MS); hospitality management (MS); human resources management (MPA); information science (MS); information systems (PhD); information technologies (MBA); interdisciplinary studies (MA, MS); international studies (MA); international sustainable tourism (MS); jazz studies (MM); journalism (MA, MJ, Graduate Certificate), including interactive and virtual digital communication (Graduate Certificate), narrative journalism (Graduate Certificate), public relations (Graduate Certificate); kinesiology (MS); linguistics (MA); local government management (MPA); logistics (PhD); logistics and supply chain management (MBA); long-term care, senior housing, and aging services (MA); management (PhD); marketing (MBA); mathematics (MA, MS); mechanical and energy engineering (MS, PhD); music (MA), including ethnomusicology, music theory, musicology, performance; music composition (PhD); music education (MM Ed, PhD); nonprofit management (MPA); operations and supply chain management (MBA); performance (MM, DMA); philosophy (MA); political science (MA); professional and technical communication (MA); radio, television and film (MA, MFA); rehabilitation counseling (Certificate); sociology (MA); Spanish (MA); special education (M Ed); speech-language pathology (MA); strategic management (MBA); studio art (MFA); teaching (M Ed); MBA/MS. *Program availability:* Part-time, evening/weekend, online learning. Terminal master's awarded for partial completion of doctoral program. *Degree requirements:* For master's, variable foreign language requirement, comprehensive exam (for some programs), thesis (for some programs); for doctorate, variable foreign language requirement, comprehensive exam (for some programs), thesis/dissertation; for other advanced degree, variable foreign language requirement, comprehensive exam (for some programs). *Entrance requirements:* For master's and doctorate, GRE, GMAT. Additional exam requirements/recommendations for international students: required—TOEFL (minimum score 550 paper-based; 79 iBT). Electronic applications accepted.

University of Rhode Island, Graduate School, College of Health Sciences, Department of Human Development and Family Studies, Kingston, RI 02881. Offers college student personnel (MS); human development and family studies (MS); marriage and family therapy (MS). *Accreditation:* AAMFT/COAMFTE. *Program availability:* Part-time. *Faculty:* 16 full-time (12 women). *Students:* 50 full-time (40 women), 12 part-time (11 women); includes 14 minority (4 Black or African American, non-Hispanic/Latino; 2 Asian, non-Hispanic/Latino; 5 Hispanic/Latino; 3 Two or more races, non-Hispanic/Latino), 2 international. In 2019, 25 master's awarded. *Entrance requirements:* Additional exam requirements/recommendations for international students: required—TOEFL. *Application deadline:* For fall admission, 1/15 for domestic and international students. Application fee: $65. Electronic applications accepted. *Expenses: Tuition, area resident:* Full-time $13,734; part-time $763 per credit. Tuition, state resident: full-time $13,734; part-time $763 per credit. Tuition, nonresident: full-time $26,512; part-time $1473 per credit. *International tuition:* $26,512 full-time. *Required fees:* $1780; $52 per credit. $35 per term. One-time fee: $165. *Financial support:* In 2019–20, 2 research assistantships with tuition reimbursements (averaging $4,746 per year), 5 teaching assistantships with tuition reimbursements (averaging $11,866 per year) were awarded. Financial award application deadline: 1/15; financial award applicants required to submit FAFSA. *Unit head:* Dr. Sue Adam, Chair, 401-874-5958, E-mail: suekadams@uri.edu. *Application contact:* Dr. Sue Adam, Chair, 401-874-5958, E-mail: suekadams@uri.edu.
Website: http://www.uri.edu/hss/hdf/

University of Southern California, Graduate School, Suzanne Dworak-Peck School of Social Work, Los Angeles, CA 90089. Offers community organization, planning and administration (MSW); families and children (MSW); health (MSW); mental health (MSW); Military Social Work and Veterans Services (MSW); older adults (MSW); public child welfare (MSW); school settings (MSW); social work (MSW, PhD); systems of mental illness recovery (MSW); work and life (MSW); JD/MSW; M Pl/MSW; MPA/MSW; MSW/MBA; MSW/MJCS; MSW/MS. *Accreditation:* CSWE (one or more programs are accredited). *Degree requirements:* For doctorate, comprehensive exam, thesis/dissertation, qualifying exam/publishable paper. *Entrance requirements:* For doctorate, GRE General Test. Additional exam requirements/recommendations for international students: required—TOEFL (minimum score 600 paper-based; 100 iBT), ESL exam. Electronic applications accepted.

University of Southern Mississippi, College of Education and Human Sciences, School of Child and Family Sciences, Hattiesburg, MS 39406-0001. Offers child and family studies (MS); marriage and family therapy (MS); school counseling (M Ed). *Accreditation:* AAMFT/COAMFTE (one or more programs are accredited). *Program availability:* Part-time, online learning. *Students:* 35 full-time (27 women), 57 part-time (all women); includes 33 minority (22 Black or African American, non-Hispanic/Latino; 3 American Indian or Alaska Native, non-Hispanic/Latino; 7 Hispanic/Latino; 1 Two or more races, non-Hispanic/Latino), 1 international. 130 applicants, 21% accepted, 25 enrolled. In 2019, 32 master's awarded. *Degree requirements:* For master's, comprehensive exam, thesis optional. *Entrance requirements:* For master's, GRE General Test, minimum GPA of 2.75 on last 60 hours. Additional exam requirements/recommendations for international students: required—TOEFL. *Application deadline:* For fall admission, 3/1 priority date for domestic students, 3/1 for international students; for spring admission, 1/1 priority date for domestic and international students. Applications are processed on a rolling basis. Application fee: $60. Electronic applications accepted. *Expenses: Tuition, area resident:* Full-time $4393; part-time $488 per credit hour. Tuition, nonresident: full-time $5393; part-time $600 per credit hour. *Required fees:* $6 per semester. *Financial support:* Fellowships, research assistantships with full tuition reimbursements, career-related internships or fieldwork, Federal Work-Study, institutionally sponsored loans, scholarships/grants, health care benefits, and unspecified assistantships available. Financial award application deadline: 3/15; financial award applicants required to submit FAFSA. *Unit head:* Pat Sims, Director, 601-266-6990, Fax: 601-266-4680. *Application contact:* Pat Sims, Director, 601-266-6990, Fax: 601-266-4680.
Website: https://www.usm.edu/family-studies-child-development

University of South Florida, College of Behavioral and Community Sciences, Department of Child and Family Studies, Tampa, FL 33620-9951. Offers applied behavior analysis (MA, MS, PhD); behavioral and community sciences (PhD); child and adolescent behavioral health (MS), including developmental disabilities, leadership in child and adolescent health, translational research and evaluation, youth and behavioral health; rehabilitation and mental health counseling (MA), including addictions and substance abuse counseling, marriage and family therapy. *Accreditation:* ACA. *Faculty:* 21 full-time (13 women), 3 part-time/adjunct (all women). *Students:* 184 full-time (157 women), 104 part-time (88 women); includes 113 minority (42 Black or African American, non-Hispanic/Latino; 4 Asian, non-Hispanic/Latino; 54 Hispanic/Latino; 1 Native Hawaiian or other Pacific Islander, non-Hispanic/Latino; 12 Two or more races, non-Hispanic/Latino), 7 international. Average age 27. 310 applicants, 51% accepted, 92 enrolled. In 2019, 127 master's, 8 doctorates awarded. *Degree requirements:* For master's, comprehensive exam, thesis (for some programs); for doctorate, comprehensive exam, thesis/dissertation, Behavior Analyst Board Certification Exam. *Entrance requirements:* For master's, GRE General Test, 3.00 GPA; 3 letters of reference; resume or CV; statement of purpose; writing sample; undergraduate statistics or research methods course (for Rehab and Mental Health Counseling); for doctorate, GRE General Test, master's degree in behavioral analysis or closely-related field; minimum GPA of 3.5 in graduate course work; three letters of recommendation; campus visit with faculty interview; personal statement; curriculum vitae; evidence of research experiences and expertise; campus visit and interview. Additional exam requirements/recommendations for international students: required—TOEFL, TOEFL (minimum score 550 paper-based; 79 iBT) or IELTS (minimum score 6.5). *Application deadline:* For fall admission, 12/5 for domestic and international students. Application fee: $30. *Financial support:* In 2019–20, 57 students received support. Unspecified assistantships available. *Unit head:* Jason Anthony, Professor and Director, Rightpath Research and Innovation Center, 813-974-6009, E-mail: jasonanthony@usf.edu. *Application contact:* Dr. Raymond G. Miltenberger, Professor/Director of Master's Program, 813-974-5079, Fax: 813-974-6115, E-mail: miltenbe@usf.edu.
Website: http://cfs.cbcs.usf.edu/

University of South Florida, Innovative Education, Tampa, FL 33620-9951. Offers adult, career and higher education (Graduate Certificate), including college teaching, leadership in developing human resources, leadership in higher education; Africana studies (Graduate Certificate), including diasporas and health disparities, genocide and human rights; aging studies (Graduate Certificate), including gerontology; art research (Graduate Certificate), including museum studies; business foundations (Graduate Certificate); chemical and biomedical engineering (Graduate Certificate), including materials science and engineering, water, health and sustainability; child and family studies (Graduate Certificate), including positive behavior support; civil and industrial engineering (Graduate Certificate), including transportation systems analysis; community and family health (Graduate Certificate), including maternal and child health, social marketing and public health, violence and injury: prevention and intervention, women's health; criminology (Graduate Certificate), including criminal justice administration; data science for public administration (Graduate Certificate); digital humanities (Graduate Certificate); educational measurement and research (Graduate Certificate), including evaluation; English (Graduate Certificate), including comparative literary studies, creative writing, professional and technical communication; entrepreneurship (Graduate Certificate); environmental health (Graduate Certificate), including safety management; epidemiology and biostatistics (Graduate Certificate), including applied biostatistics, biostatistics, concepts and tools of epidemiology, epidemiology, epidemiology of infectious diseases; geography, environment and planning (Graduate Certificate), including community development, environmental policy and management, geographical information systems; geology (Graduate Certificate), including hydrogeology; global health (Graduate Certificate), including disaster management, global health and Latin American and Caribbean studies, global health practice, humanitarian assistance, infection control; government and international affairs (Graduate Certificate), including Cuban studies, globalization studies; health policy and management (Graduate Certificate), including health management and leadership, public health policy and programs; hearing specialist: early intervention (Graduate Certificate); industrial and management systems engineering (Graduate Certificate), including systems engineering, technology management; information studies (Graduate Certificate), including school library media specialist; information systems/decision sciences (Graduate Certificate), including analytics and business intelligence; instructional technology (Graduate Certificate), including distance education, Florida digital/virtual educator, instructional design, multimedia design, Web design; internal medicine, bioethics and medical humanities (Graduate Certificate), including biomedical ethics; Latin American and Caribbean studies (Graduate Certificate); leadership for coastal resiliency planning (Graduate Certificate); mass communications (Graduate

Certificate), including multimedia journalism; mathematics and statistics (Graduate Certificate), including mathematics; medicine (Graduate Certificate), including aging and neuroscience, bioinformatics, biotechnology, brain fitness and memory management, clinical investigation, hand and upper limb rehabilitation, health informatics, health sciences, integrative weight management, intellectual property, medicine and gender, metabolic and nutritional medicine, metabolic cardiology, pharmacy sciences; national and competitive intelligence (Graduate Certificate); nursing (Graduate Certificate), including simulation based academic fellowship in advanced pain management; psychological and social foundations (Graduate Certificate), including career counseling, college teaching, diversity in education, mental health counseling, school counseling; public affairs (Graduate Certificate), including nonprofit management, public management, research administration; public health (Graduate Certificate), including assessing chemical toxicity and public health risks, health equity, pharmacoepidemiology, public health generalist, toxicology, translational research in adolescent behavioral health; public health practices (Graduate Certificate), including planning for healthy communities; rehabilitation and mental health counseling (Graduate Certificate), including integrative mental health care, marriage and family therapy, rehabilitation technology; secondary education (Graduate Certificate), including ESOL, foreign language education: culture and content, foreign language education: professional; social work (Graduate Certificate), including geriatric social work/clinical gerontology; special education (Graduate Certificate), including autism spectrum disorder, disabilities education: severe/profound; world languages (Graduate Certificate), including teaching English as a second language (TESL) or foreign language. *Unit head:* Dr. Cynthia DeLuca, Associate Vice President and Assistant Vice Provost, 813-974-3077, Fax: 813-974-7061, E-mail: deluca@usf.edu. *Application contact:* Owen Hooper, Director, Summer and Alternative Calendar Programs, 813-974-6917, E-mail: hooper@usf.edu.
Website: http://www.usf.edu/innovative-education/

The University of Tennessee, Graduate School, College of Education, Health and Human Sciences, Department of Child and Family Studies, Knoxville, TN 37996. Offers child and family studies (MS); early childhood education (MS). *Program availability:* Part-time. *Degree requirements:* For master's, thesis or alternative. *Entrance requirements:* For master's, GRE General Test, minimum GPA of 2.7. Additional exam requirements/recommendations for international students: required—TOEFL. Electronic applications accepted.

The University of Tennessee, Graduate School, College of Education, Health and Human Sciences, Program in Human Ecology, Knoxville, TN 37996. Offers child and family studies (PhD); community health (PhD); nutrition science (PhD); retailing and consumer sciences (PhD); textile science (PhD). *Degree requirements:* For doctorate, thesis/dissertation. *Entrance requirements:* For doctorate, GRE General Test, minimum GPA of 2.7. Additional exam requirements/recommendations for international students: required—TOEFL. Electronic applications accepted.

The University of Tennessee at Martin, Graduate Programs, College of Agriculture and Applied Sciences, Department of Family and Consumer Sciences, Martin, TN 38238. Offers dietetics (MSFCS); general family and consumer sciences (MSFCS). *Program availability:* Part-time, 100% online. *Faculty:* 7. *Students:* 1 full-time (0 women), 29 part-time (27 women); includes 3 minority (2 Black or African American, non-Hispanic/Latino; 1 Hispanic/Latino). Average age 29. 47 applicants, 70% accepted, 12 enrolled. In 2019, 12 master's awarded. *Degree requirements:* For master's, comprehensive exam, thesis optional. *Entrance requirements:* For master's, GRE General Test, minimum GPA of 2.5. Additional exam requirements/recommendations for international students: required—TOEFL (minimum score 525 paper-based; 71 iBT). *Application deadline:* For fall admission, 7/28 priority date for domestic and international students; for spring admission, 12/17 priority date for domestic and international students; for summer admission, 5/10 priority date for domestic and international students. Applications are processed on a rolling basis. Application fee: $30 ($130 for international students). Electronic applications accepted. *Expenses: Tuition, area resident:* Full-time $9096; part-time $505 per credit hour. Tuition, state resident: full-time $9096; part-time $505 per credit hour. Tuition, nonresident: full-time $15,136; part-time $841 per credit hour. *International tuition:* $23,040 full-time. *Required fees:* $1520; $85 per credit hour. Part-time tuition and fees vary according to course load. *Financial support:* In 2019–20, 10 students received support, including 2 teaching assistantships with full tuition reimbursements available (averaging $6,912 per year); research assistantships with full tuition reimbursements available, scholarships/grants, and tuition waivers (full and partial) also available. Financial award application deadline: 2/1; financial award applicants required to submit FAFSA. *Unit head:* Dr. Lisa LeBleu, Coordinator, 731-881-7116, Fax: 731-881-7106, E-mail: llebleu@utm.edu. *Application contact:* Jolene L. Cunningham, Student Services Specialist, 731-881-7012, Fax: 731-881-7499, E-mail: jcunningham@utm.edu.
Website: http://www.utm.edu/departments/caas/fcs/index.php

The University of Texas at Austin, Graduate School, College of Natural Sciences, School of Human Ecology, Program in Human Development and Family Sciences, Austin, TX 78712-1111. Offers MA, PhD. *Degree requirements:* For master's, thesis; for doctorate, thesis/dissertation. *Entrance requirements:* For master's and doctorate, GRE General Test. Additional exam requirements/recommendations for international students: required—TOEFL. Electronic applications accepted.

The University of Texas at Dallas, School of Behavioral and Brain Sciences, Program in Psychological Sciences, Richardson, TX 75080. Offers early childhood disorders (MS); psychological sciences (MS, PhD). *Program availability:* Part-time, evening/weekend. *Faculty:* 21 full-time (17 women), 2 part-time/adjunct (both women). *Students:* 65 full-time (57 women), 11 part-time (9 women); includes 30 minority (7 Black or African American, non-Hispanic/Latino; 7 Asian, non-Hispanic/Latino; 13 Hispanic/Latino; 3 Two or more races, non-Hispanic/Latino), 9 international. Average age 27. 152 applicants, 28% accepted, 24 enrolled. In 2019, 26 master's, 6 doctorates awarded. *Degree requirements:* For master's, directed project or internship; for doctorate, thesis/dissertation. *Entrance requirements:* For master's and doctorate, GRE General Test, minimum GPA of 3.0 in upper-level course work. Additional exam requirements/recommendations for international students: required—TOEFL (minimum score 550 paper-based). *Application deadline:* For fall admission, 7/15 for domestic students, 5/1 priority date for international students; for spring admission, 11/15 for domestic students, 9/1 priority date for international students. Applications are processed on a rolling basis. Application fee: $50 ($100 for international students). Electronic applications accepted. *Expenses: Tuition, area resident:* Full-time $16,504. Tuition, state resident: full-time $16,504. Tuition, nonresident: full-time $34,266. Tuition and fees vary according to course load. *Financial support:* In 2019–20, 25 students received support, including 1 fellowship (averaging $2,000 per year), 6 research assistantships with partial tuition reimbursements available (averaging $29,829 per year), 18 teaching assistantships with partial tuition reimbursements available (averaging $18,900 per year); career-related internships or fieldwork, Federal Work-Study, scholarships/grants, and unspecified assistantships also available. Support available to part-time students. Financial award application deadline: 4/30; financial award applicants required to submit FAFSA. *Unit head:* Dr. Shayla Holub, Area Head, 972-883-4473, Fax: 972-883-3491, E-mail: sholub@utdallas.edu. *Application contact:* Dr. Jackie Nelson, Associate Area Head, 972-883-4478, Fax: 972-883-3491, E-mail: Jackie.Nelson@utdallas.edu.
Website: https://bbs.utdallas.edu/degrees/psy-degrees/

University of Utah, Graduate School, College of Social and Behavioral Science, Department of Family and Consumer Studies, Salt Lake City, UT 84112-0080. Offers human development and social policy (MS). *Program availability:* Part-time. *Faculty:* 8 full-time (6 women), 1 part-time/adjunct (0 women). *Students:* 12 full-time (11 women), 3 part-time (2 women); includes 4 minority (1 Asian, non-Hispanic/Latino; 1 Hispanic/Latino; 2 Two or more races, non-Hispanic/Latino). Average age 31. In 2019, 7 master's awarded. Terminal master's awarded for partial completion of doctoral program. *Application deadline:* For fall admission, 2/1 priority date for domestic and international students. Applications are processed on a rolling basis. Electronic applications accepted. *Expenses:* Tuition, state resident: full-time $7085; part-time $272.51 per credit hour. Tuition, nonresident: full-time $24,937; part-time $959.12 per credit hour. *Required fees:* $880.52; $880.52 per semester. Tuition and fees vary according to degree level, program and student level. *Financial support:* In 2019–20, 10 teaching assistantships (averaging $11,700 per year) were awarded. *Unit head:* Prof. Lori Kowaleski-Jones, PhD, Chair, 801-585-0074, Fax: 801-581-5156, E-mail: lk2700@fcs.utah.edu. *Application contact:* Prof. Jessie Fan, PhD, Graduate Director, 801-581-4170, E-mail: jessie.fan@fcs.utah.edu.
Website: http://fcs.utah.edu/

University of Victoria, Faculty of Graduate Studies, Faculty of Human and Social Development, School of Child and Youth Care, Victoria, BC V8W 2Y2, Canada. Offers MA, PhD. *Program availability:* Part-time. *Degree requirements:* For master's, thesis. *Entrance requirements:* For master's, resume, professional references, sample of academic writing. Additional exam requirements/recommendations for international students: required—TOEFL (minimum score 575 paper-based), IELTS (minimum score 7). Electronic applications accepted.

University of Wisconsin–Madison, Graduate School, School of Human Ecology, Program in Human Development and Family Studies, Madison, WI 53706-1380. Offers MS, PhD. *Program availability:* Part-time. Terminal master's awarded for partial completion of doctoral program. *Degree requirements:* For master's, thesis; for doctorate, comprehensive exam, thesis/dissertation. *Entrance requirements:* For master's, GRE General Test, 3 letters of recommendation; for doctorate, GRE General Test, MS or MA, 3 letters of recommendation. Additional exam requirements/recommendations for international students: required—TOEFL (minimum score 580 paper-based; 92 iBT). Electronic applications accepted.

Utah State University, School of Graduate Studies, Emma Eccles Jones College of Education and Human Services, Department of Family, Consumer, and Human Development, Logan, UT 84322. Offers family and human development (MFHD); family, consumer, and human development (MS, PhD), including adolescence/youth (MS), adult development/aging (MS), consumer science (MS), infancy/childhood (MS), marriage and family relations (MS), marriage and family therapy (MS). *Accreditation:* AAMFT/COAMFTE (one or more programs are accredited). *Program availability:* Part-time, evening/weekend, online learning. *Degree requirements:* For master's, thesis; for doctorate, comprehensive exam, thesis/dissertation, competencies. *Entrance requirements:* For master's, GRE General Test or MAT, minimum GPA of 3.0, 3 letters of recommendation; for doctorate, GRE, minimum GPA of 3.0, 3 letters of recommendation. Additional exam requirements/recommendations for international students: required—TOEFL. Electronic applications accepted.

Vanderbilt University, Peabody College, Department of Psychology and Human Development, Nashville, TN 37240-1001. Offers child studies (M Ed); clinical psychological assessment (M Ed); quantitative methods (M Ed). *Accreditation:* APA. *Program availability:* Part-time. *Degree requirements:* For master's, comprehensive exam (for some programs), thesis optional. *Entrance requirements:* For master's, GRE General Test. Additional exam requirements/recommendations for international students: required—TOEFL (minimum score 550 paper-based; 80 iBT). Electronic applications accepted. *Expenses: Tuition:* Full-time $51,018; part-time $2087 per hour. *Required fees:* $542. Tuition and fees vary according to program.

Walden University, Graduate Programs, School of Counseling, Minneapolis, MN 55401. Offers addiction counseling (MS), including addictions and public health, child and adolescent counseling, family studies and interventions, forensic counseling, general program, military families and culture, trauma and crisis counseling; clinical mental health counseling (MS), including addiction counseling, forensic counseling, military families and culture, trauma and crisis counseling; counselor education and supervision (PhD), including consultation, counseling and social change, forensic mental health counseling, leadership and program evaluation, trauma and crisis; marriage, couple, and family counseling (MS), including addiction counseling, career counseling, forensic counseling, military families and culture, trauma and crisis counseling; school counseling (MS), including addiction counseling, career counseling, crisis and trauma, military families and culture. *Accreditation:* ACA. *Program availability:* Part-time, evening/weekend, online only, 100% online. *Degree requirements:* For master's, residency, field experience, professional development plan, licensure plan; for doctorate, thesis/dissertation, residency, practicum, internship. *Entrance requirements:* For master's, bachelor's degree or higher; minimum GPA of 2.5; official transcripts; goal statement (for some programs); access to computer and Internet; for doctorate, master's degree or higher; three years of related professional or academic experience (preferred); minimum GPA of 3.0; goal statement and current resume (for select programs); official transcripts; access to computer and Internet. Additional exam requirements/recommendations for international students: required—TOEFL (minimum score 550 paper-based, 79 iBT), IELTS (minimum score 6.5), Michigan English Language Assessment Battery (minimum score 82), or PTE (minimum score 53). Electronic applications accepted.

Walden University, Graduate Programs, School of Social Work and Human Services, Minneapolis, MN 55401. Offers addictions and social work (DSW); advanced clinical practice (MSW); clinical expertise (DSW); criminal justice (DSW); disaster, crisis, and intervention (DSW); family studies and interventions (DSW); human and social services (PhD), including advanced research, community and social services, community intervention and leadership, conflict management, criminal justice, disaster crisis and intervention, family studies and intervention, gerontology, global social services, higher education, human services and nonprofit administration, mental health facilitation; medical social work (DSW); military social work (MSW); policy practice (DSW); social work (PhD), including addictions and social work, clinical expertise, criminal justice, disaster, crisis and intervention, family studies and interventions, medical social work, policy practice, social work administration; social work administration (DSW); social work in healthcare (MSW); social work with children and families (MSW). *Accreditation:* CSWE. *Program availability:* Part-time, evening/weekend, online only, 100% online. *Degree requirements:* For master's, residency (for some programs); for doctorate, thesis/dissertation, residency. *Entrance requirements:* For master's, bachelor's degree or higher; minimum GPA of 2.5; official transcripts; goal statement (for some programs); access to computer and Internet; for doctorate, master's degree or higher; three years of related professional or academic experience (preferred); minimum GPA of 3.0; goal statement and current resume (for select programs); official transcripts; access to computer and Internet. Additional exam requirements/recommendations for international students: required—TOEFL (minimum score 550 paper-based, 79 iBT), IELTS (minimum score 6.5), Michigan English Language Assessment Battery (minimum score 82), or PTE (minimum score 53). Electronic applications accepted.

Washington University in St. Louis, Brown School, St. Louis, MO 63130-4899. Offers American Indian/Alaska native (MSW); children, youth and families (MSW); epidemiology/biostatistics (MPH); generalist (MPH); global health (MPH); health (MSW); health policy analysis (MPH); individualized (MSW), including health; mental health (MSW); older adults and aging societies (MSW); public health sciences (PhD); social and economic development (MSW), including domestic, international; social work (PhD); urban design (MPH); violence and injury prevention (MSW); JD/MSW; M Arch/MSW; MPH/MBA; MSW/M Div; MSW/M Ed; MSW/MAPS; MSW/MBA; MSW/MPH; MUD/MSW. *Accreditation:* CEPH; CSWE (one or more programs are accredited). *Faculty:* 54 full-time (31 women), 87 part-time/adjunct (61 women). *Students:* 282 full-time (226 women); includes 90 minority (40 Black or African American, non-Hispanic/Latino; 10 American Indian or Alaska Native, non-Hispanic/Latino; 26 Asian, non-Hispanic/Latino; 13 Hispanic/Latino; 1 Native Hawaiian or other Pacific Islander, non-Hispanic/Latino). Average age 24. *Degree requirements:* For master's, 60 credit hours (for MSW); 52 credit hours (for MPH); practicum; for doctorate, comprehensive exam, thesis/dissertation. *Entrance requirements:* For master's, GRE (preferred), GMAT, LSAT, MCAT, PCAT, or United States Medical Licensing Exam (for MPH); for doctorate, GRE. Additional exam requirements/recommendations for international students: required—TOEFL (minimum score 100 iBT), IELTS (minimum score 7). *Application deadline:* For fall admission, 12/15 priority date for domestic and international students; for winter admission, 3/1 priority date for domestic and international students. Applications are processed on a rolling basis. Electronic applications accepted. *Expenses:* Contact institution. *Financial support:* In 2019–20, 90 research assistantships were awarded; fellowships, teaching assistantships, career-related internships or fieldwork, Federal Work-Study, scholarships/grants, and unspecified assistantships also available. Support available to part-time students. Financial award applicants required to submit FAFSA. *Unit head:* Jamie L. Adkisson-Hennessey, Director of Admissions and Recruitment, 314-935-3524, Fax: 314-935-4859, E-mail: jadkisson@wustl.edu. *Application contact:* Office of Admissions and Recruitment, 314-935-6676, Fax: 314-935-4859, E-mail: brownadmissions@wustl.edu.
Website: http://brownschool.wustl.edu

Child Development

California State University, Los Angeles, Graduate Studies, College of Health and Human Services, Department of Child and Family Studies, Los Angeles, CA 90032-8530. Offers child development (MA). *Program availability:* Part-time, evening/weekend. *Degree requirements:* For master's, comprehensive exam, project or thesis. *Entrance requirements:* Additional exam requirements/recommendations for international students: required—TOEFL (minimum score 500 paper-based). *Expenses: Tuition, area resident:* Full-time $7176; part-time $4164 per year. Tuition, state resident: full-time $7176; part-time $4164 per year. Tuition, nonresident: full-time $14,304; part-time $8916 per year. *International tuition:* $14,304 full-time. *Required fees:* $1037.76; $1037.76 per unit. Tuition and fees vary according to degree level and program.

California State University, Sacramento, College of Education, Graduate and Professional Studies in Education, Sacramento, CA 95819. Offers behavioral science and gender equity (MA); child development (MA); counseling (MS); curriculum and instruction (MA); education (Ed D), including K-12 and community college; education leadership and policy studies (MA), including higher education, PreK-12; education specialist (Ed S), including school psychology; educational technology (MA); language and literacy (MA); multicultural education (MA); school psychology (MA); special education (MA); workforce development advocacy (MA). *Program availability:* Part-time, evening/weekend, blended/hybrid learning. *Students:* 469 full-time (369 women), 155 part-time (124 women); includes 342 minority (58 Black or African American, non-Hispanic/Latino; 12 American Indian or Alaska Native, non-Hispanic/Latino; 92 Asian, non-Hispanic/Latino; 177 Hispanic/Latino; 3 Native Hawaiian or other Pacific Islander, non-Hispanic/Latino), 8 international. Average age 32. 704 applicants, 49% accepted, 265 enrolled. In 2019, 128 master's, 18 other advanced degrees awarded. *Degree requirements:* For master's, comprehensive exam (for some programs), thesis (for some programs), thesis or project; writing proficiency exam. *Entrance requirements:* For master's and doctorate, GRE. Additional exam requirements/recommendations for international students: required—TOEFL (minimum score 550 paper-based; 80 iBT); recommended—IELTS (minimum score 7). *Application deadline:* For fall admission, 3/1 for domestic students, 2/1 for international students. Applications are processed on a rolling basis. Application fee: $70. Electronic applications accepted. *Expenses:* Contact institution. *Financial support:* Career-related internships or fieldwork, Federal Work-Study, and scholarships/grants available. Support available to part-time students. Financial award application deadline: 3/1; financial award applicants required to submit FAFSA. *Unit head:* Dr. Carlos Nevarez, Chair, E-mail: nevarezc@csus.edu. *Application contact:* Jose Martinez, Graduate Admissions Supervisor, 916-278-6470, E-mail: martinj@skymail.csus.edu.
Website: http://www.csus.edu/coe/academics/graduate/index.html

California State University, San Bernardino, Graduate Studies, College of Social and Behavioral Sciences, Department of Psychology, San Bernardino, CA 92407. Offers child development (MA); clinical/counseling psychology (MS); industrial/organizational psychology (MS); psychological science (MA). *Faculty:* 15 full-time (7 women). *Students:* 62 full-time (43 women), 13 part-time (7 women); includes 44 minority (3 Black or African American, non-Hispanic/Latino; 3 Asian, non-Hispanic/Latino; 31 Hispanic/Latino; 7 Two or more races, non-Hispanic/Latino), 5 international. Average age 27. 163 applicants, 24% accepted, 25 enrolled. In 2019, 32 master's awarded. *Degree requirements:* For master's, comprehensive exam, thesis (for some programs). *Entrance requirements:* Additional exam requirements/recommendations for international students: required—TOEFL. Application fee: $55. *Financial support:* Fellowships, research assistantships, and teaching assistantships available. *Unit head:* Dr. Robert Ricco, Chair, 909-537-5485, Fax: 909-537-7003, E-mail: rricco@csusb.edu. *Application contact:* Dr. Dorota Huizinga, Dean of Graduate Studies, 909-537-3064, E-mail: dorota.huizinga@csusb.edu.
Website: https://csbs.csusb.edu/psychology

California State University, San Bernardino, Graduate Studies, College of Social and Behavioral Sciences, Program in Child Development, San Bernardino, CA 92407. Offers psychology-life span (MA). *Students:* 3 full-time (all women), 21 part-time (0 women); includes 17 minority (1 Black or African American, non-Hispanic/Latino; 14 Hispanic/Latino; 2 Two or more races, non-Hispanic/Latino). Average age 28. 22 applicants, 68% accepted, 3 enrolled. In 2019, 1 master's awarded. *Entrance requirements:* Additional exam requirements/recommendations for international students: required—TOEFL. *Application deadline:* For fall admission, 5/1 for domestic students. Application fee: $55. *Unit head:* Dr. Amy Van Schagen, Director, 909-537-3841, E-mail: amy.vanschagen@csusb.edu. *Application contact:* Dr. Dorota Huizinga, Dean of Graduate Studies, 909-537-3064, E-mail: dorota.huizinga@csusb.edu.

Chaminade University of Honolulu, Graduate, Program in Education, Honolulu, HI 96816-1578. Offers child development (M Ed); early childhood education (Montessori) (MAT); early childhood education (PK-3) (MAT); educational leadership (M Ed); elementary education (MAT); instructional leadership (M Ed); Montessori (M Ed); secondary education (MAT); special education (MAT); teacher leader (M Ed). *Program availability:* Part-time, evening/weekend, 100% online, blended/hybrid learning. *Faculty:* 8 full-time (3 women), 15 part-time/adjunct (12 women). *Students:* 72 full-time (56 women), 137 part-time (92 women); includes 126 minority (3 Black or African American, non-Hispanic/Latino; 2 American Indian or Alaska Native, non-Hispanic/Latino; 52 Asian, non-Hispanic/Latino; 8 Hispanic/Latino; 47 Native Hawaiian or other Pacific Islander, non-Hispanic/Latino; 14 Two or more races, non-Hispanic/Latino), 2 international. Average age 35. 85 applicants, 94% accepted, 66 enrolled. In 2019, 61 master's awarded. *Degree requirements:* For master's, thesis or alternative. *Entrance requirements:* For master's, PRAXIS (for MAT), official transcripts, minimum GPA of 3.0 for MAT and 2.75 for MEd, writing sample (for MAT), contact information for academic and or professional references on their application. Additional exam requirements/recommendations for international students: required—TOEFL (minimum score 79 iBT), IELTS (minimum score 6.5), PTE (minimum score 53). *Application deadline:* Applications are processed on a rolling basis. Application fee: $40. Electronic applications accepted. *Expenses:* $825 per credit hour; $93 online fee per online course. *Financial support:* Applicants required to submit FAFSA. *Unit head:* Dr. Dale Fryxell, Dean, 808-739-4652, Fax: 808-739-4607, E-mail: edu-office@chaminade.edu. *Application contact:* 808-739-8340, E-mail: gradserv@chaminade.edu.
Website: https://chaminade.edu/academics/education-behavioral-sciences/

East Carolina University, Graduate School, College of Health and Human Performance, Department of Human Development and Family Science, Greenville, NC 27858-4353. Offers birth through kindergarten education (MA Ed); human development and family science (MS); marriage and family therapy (MS); medical family therapy (PhD). *Accreditation:* AAMFT/COAMFTE. *Program availability:* Part-time. *Application deadline:* For fall admission, 1/15 for domestic students; for spring admission, 10/15 for domestic students. *Expenses: Tuition, area resident:* Full-time $4749; part-time $185 per credit hour. Tuition, state resident: full-time $4749; part-time $185 per credit hour. Tuition, nonresident: full-time $17,898; part-time $864 per credit hour. *International tuition:* $17,898 full-time. *Required fees:* $2787. *Financial support:* Application deadline: 6/1. *Unit head:* Dr. Sharon Ballard, Chair, 252-328-4220, E-mail: ballards@ecu.edu. *Application contact:* Graduate School Admissions, 252-328-6012, Fax: 252-328-6071, E-mail: gradschool@ecu.edu.
Website: https://hhp.ecu.edu/hdfs/

Erikson Institute, Academic Programs, Program in Child Development, Chicago, IL 60654. Offers MS. *Degree requirements:* For master's, comprehensive exam, internship. *Entrance requirements:* For master's, 3 letters of recommendation, minimum GPA of 2.75. Additional exam requirements/recommendations for international students: required—TOEFL.

Fielding Graduate University, Graduate Programs, School of Psychology, Programs in Infant and Early Childhood Development, Santa Barbara, CA 93105-3814. Offers infant and early childhood development (MA, PhD, Graduate Certificate), including early childhood development: education, mental health, and disruptive behaviors (MA), infant mental health and neurodevelopment (MA), reflective practice and supervision (Graduate Certificate). *Program availability:* Part-time, evening/weekend. *Faculty:* 2 full-time (both women), 22 part-time/adjunct (16 women). *Students:* 90 full-time (83 women), 5 part-time (all women); includes 50 minority (20 Black or African American, non-Hispanic/Latino; 3 American Indian or Alaska Native, non-Hispanic/Latino; 5 Asian, non-Hispanic/Latino; 17 Hispanic/Latino; 5 Two or more races, non-Hispanic/Latino). Average age 44. 21 applicants, 81% accepted, 11 enrolled. In 2019, 1 master's, 6 doctorates awarded. *Degree requirements:* For doctorate, comprehensive exam, thesis/dissertation. *Entrance requirements:* For master's and Graduate Certificate, bachelor's degree from regionally-accredited U.S. institution or equivalent; for doctorate, bachelor's or master's degree from regionally-accredited U.S. institution or equivalent, curriculum vitae, statement of purpose, critical thinking writing sample, 2 letters of recommendation, official transcripts. *Application deadline:* For fall admission, 7/16 for domestic and international students; for spring admission, 11/21 for domestic and international students; for summer admission, 2/18 for domestic and international students. Application fee: $75. Electronic applications accepted. *Expenses:* Contact institution. *Financial support:* In 2019–20, 30 students received support. Research assistantships, teaching assistantships, scholarships/grants, and tuition waivers available. Support available to part-time students. Financial award applicants required to submit FAFSA. *Unit head:* Dr. Jenene Craig, Program Director, E-mail: jcraig@fielding.edu. *Application contact:* Enrollment Coordinator, 800-340-1099 Ext. 4098, Fax: 805-687-9793, E-mail: hodadmission@fielding.edu.
Website: http://www.fielding.edu/our-programs/school-of-leadership-studies/phd-infant-early-childhood-development/

Kansas State University, Graduate School, College of Human Ecology, School of Family Studies and Human Services, Manhattan, KS 66506-1403. Offers applied family sciences (MS); communication sciences and disorders (MS); conflict resolution (Graduate Certificate); couple and family therapy (MS); early childhood education (MS); family and community service (MS); life-span human development (MS); personal financial planning (MS, PhD, Graduate Certificate); youth development (MS, Graduate Certificate). *Accreditation:* AAMFT/COAMFTE; ASHA. *Program availability:* Part-time, online learning. *Degree requirements:* For master's, comprehensive exam (for some programs), thesis optional. *Entrance requirements:* For master's, GRE, minimum GPA of 3.0 in last 2 years (60 semester hours) of undergraduate study; for doctorate, GRE. Additional exam requirements/recommendations for international students: required—TOEFL (minimum score 600 paper-based). Electronic applications accepted.

Lee University, Graduate Studies in Counseling, Cleveland, TN 37320-3450. Offers holistic child development (MS). *Program availability:* Part-time, 100% online. *Faculty:* 7 full-time (4 women), 3 part-time/adjunct (1 woman). *Students:* 80 full-time (65 women), 31 part-time (24 women); includes 20 minority (6 Black or African American, non-

Child Development

Hispanic/Latino; 10 Hispanic/Latino; 4 Two or more races, non-Hispanic/Latino), 4 international. Average age 29. 60 applicants, 77% accepted, 36 enrolled. In 2019, 47 master's awarded. *Degree requirements:* For master's, variable foreign language requirement, comprehensive exam (for some programs), thesis (for some programs), internship. *Entrance requirements:* For master's, GRE General Test or MAT (waived if undergraduate GPA is greater than 3.0 or if applicant already has a graduate degree), minimum undergraduate GPA of 3.0, 3 letters of recommendation, interview, official transcripts, essay. Additional exam requirements/recommendations for international students: required—TOEFL (minimum score 61 iBT). *Application deadline:* For fall admission, 4/1 priority date for domestic and international students; for spring admission, 11/1 priority date for domestic and international students. Applications are processed on a rolling basis. Application fee: $25. Electronic applications accepted. *Expenses: Tuition:* Full-time $13,590; part-time $755 per credit hour. *Required fees:* $25. Tuition and fees vary according to program. *Financial support:* In 2019–20, 48 students received support. Career-related internships or fieldwork, Federal Work-Study, institutionally sponsored loans, scholarships/grants, and unspecified assistantships available. Financial award application deadline: 3/1; financial award applicants required to submit FAFSA. *Unit head:* Dr. Heather Quagliana, Director, 423-614-8359, Fax: 423-614-8124, E-mail: heatherlewis@leeuniversity.edu. *Application contact:* Jeffery McGirt, Director of Graduate Enrollment, 423-614-8691, Fax: 423-614-8317, E-mail: jmcgirt@leeuniversity.edu.
Website: http://www.leeuniversity.edu/academics/graduate/counseling/

Michigan State University, The Graduate School, College of Social Science, Department of Human Development and Family Studies, East Lansing, MI 48824. Offers child development (MS); family and community services (MA); human development and family studies (MS, PhD); youth development (MA). *Accreditation:* AAMFT/COAMFTE (one or more programs are accredited). *Entrance requirements:* For master's, GRE General Test, minimum GPA of 3.0 in last 2 years of undergraduate course work, 3 letters of recommendation; for doctorate, GRE General Test, minimum GPA of 3.0, 3 letters of recommendation, background in behavioral sciences. Additional exam requirements/recommendations for international students: required—TOEFL. Electronic applications accepted.

Montclair State University, The Graduate School, College of Education and Human Services, Infant and Early Childhood Mental Health Certificate Program, Montclair, NJ 07043-1624. Offers Certificate.

Montclair State University, The Graduate School, College of Humanities and Social Sciences, MA Program in Child Advocacy and Policy, Montclair, NJ 07043-1624. Offers MA. *Program availability:* Online learning. *Degree requirements:* For master's, seminar. *Entrance requirements:* For master's, minimum GPA of 3.0 in undergraduate major, interview, writing sample.

Mount Saint Mary College, Division of Education, Newburgh, NY 12550. Offers adolescence and special education (MS Ed); childhood education (MS Ed); literacy education (MS Ed). *Accreditation:* NCATE. *Program availability:* Part-time, evening/weekend. *Faculty:* 7 full-time (6 women), 6 part-time/adjunct (4 women). *Students:* 23 full-time (16 women), 83 part-time (64 women); includes 13 minority (1 Black or African American, non-Hispanic/Latino; 1 Asian, non-Hispanic/Latino; 10 Hispanic/Latino; 1 Native Hawaiian or other Pacific Islander, non-Hispanic/Latino). Average age 29. 45 applicants, 58% accepted, 23 enrolled. In 2019, 28 master's awarded. *Entrance requirements:* Additional exam requirements/recommendations for international students: required—TOEFL (minimum score 80 iBT). *Application deadline:* Applications are processed on a rolling basis. Application fee: $45. Electronic applications accepted. Application fee is waived when completed online. *Expenses: Tuition:* Full-time $15,192; part-time $844 per credit. *Required fees:* $180; $90 per semester. *Financial support:* In 2019–20, 18 students received support. Institutionally sponsored loans, scholarships/grants, and unspecified assistantships available. Financial award application deadline: 4/15; financial award applicants required to submit FAFSA. *Unit head:* Dr. Rebecca Norman, Graduate Coordinator, 845-569-3431, Fax: 845-569-3551, E-mail: Rebecca.Norman@msmc.edu. *Application contact:* Eileen Bardney, Director of Admissions, 845-569-3254, Fax: 845-569-3438, E-mail: graduateadmissions@msmc.edu.
Website: http://www.msmc.edu/Academics/Graduate_Programs/Master_of_Science_in_Education

North Carolina Agricultural and Technical State University, The Graduate College, College of Agriculture and Environmental Sciences, Department of Family and Consumer Sciences, Greensboro, NC 27411. Offers child development, early education and family studies (MAT); family and consumer sciences education (MAT); food and nutritional sciences (MS). *Program availability:* Part-time, evening/weekend. *Degree requirements:* For master's, comprehensive exam, thesis or alternative, qualifying exam. *Entrance requirements:* For master's, GRE General Test, minimum GPA of 2.6.

North Dakota State University, College of Graduate and Interdisciplinary Studies, College of Human Development and Education, Department of Human Development and Family Science, Program in Youth Development, Fargo, ND 58102. Offers MS. *Degree requirements:* For master's, comprehensive exam, thesis. *Entrance requirements:* Additional exam requirements/recommendations for international students: required—TOEFL (minimum score 525 paper-based; 71 iBT). Tuition and fees vary according to program and reciprocity agreements.

Ohio University, Graduate College, College of Health Sciences and Professions, Department of Social and Public Health, Athens, OH 45701-2979. Offers early child development and family life (MS); family studies (MS); health administration (MHA); public health (MPH); social work (MSW). *Program availability:* Part-time, evening/weekend, online learning. *Degree requirements:* For master's, capstone (MPH). *Entrance requirements:* For master's, GMAT, GRE General Test, previous course work in accounting, management, and statistics; previous public health background (MHA, MPH). Additional exam requirements/recommendations for international students: required—TOEFL (minimum score 550 paper-based; 80 iBT) or IELTS (minimum score 6.5). Electronic applications accepted. *Expenses:* Contact institution.

Purdue University, Graduate School, College of Health and Human Sciences, Department of Child Development and Family Studies, West Lafayette, IN 47907. Offers developmental studies (MS, PhD); family studies (MS, PhD); marriage and family therapy (MS, PhD). *Program availability:* Part-time. *Faculty:* 22 full-time (16 women), 2 part-time/adjunct (1 woman). *Students:* 22 full-time (21 women), 1 (woman) part-time; includes 3 minority (1 Black or African American, non-Hispanic/Latino; 1 Asian, non-Hispanic/Latino; 1 Two or more races, non-Hispanic/Latino), 8 international. Average age 26. 51 applicants, 25% accepted, 4 enrolled. In 2019, 2 master's, 3 doctorates awarded. Terminal master's awarded for partial completion of doctoral program. *Degree requirements:* For master's, thesis; for doctorate, thesis/dissertation. *Entrance requirements:* For master's and doctorate, GRE General Test (minimum score 1000 combined verbal and quantitative), minimum undergraduate GPA of 3.0 or equivalent. Additional exam requirements/recommendations for international students: required—TOEFL (minimum score 600 paper-based; 90 iBT), TWE (minimum score 4). *Application deadline:* For fall admission, 1/4 for domestic and international students. Applications are processed on a rolling basis. Application fee: $60 ($75 for international students).

Electronic applications accepted. *Financial support:* Fellowships with full tuition reimbursements, research assistantships with full tuition reimbursements, teaching assistantships with full tuition reimbursements, and career-related internships or fieldwork available. Support available to part-time students. Financial award application deadline: 1/15; financial award applicants required to submit FAFSA. *Unit head:* Dr. Doran C. French, Head, 765-494-9511, E-mail: dcfrench@purdue.edu. *Application contact:* Tina Putz, Graduate Contact, 765-496-3816, E-mail: tputz@purdue.edu. Website: http://www.purdue.edu/hhs/hdfs/

Purdue University Northwest, Graduate Studies Office, School of Liberal Arts and Social Sciences, Department of Behavioral Sciences, Hammond, IN 46323-2094. Offers child development and family studies (MS); marriage and family therapy (MS). *Accreditation:* AAMFT/COAMFTE. *Program availability:* Part-time. *Degree requirements:* For master's, thesis. *Entrance requirements:* For master's, GRE, interview. Additional exam requirements/recommendations for international students: required—TOEFL.

Rutgers University - Camden, Graduate School of Arts and Sciences, Program in Childhood Studies, Camden, NJ 08102. Offers MA, PhD. *Program availability:* Part-time, evening/weekend. *Degree requirements:* For master's, comprehensive exam, thesis (for some programs), 30 credits; for doctorate, comprehensive exam, thesis/dissertation, 60 credits. *Entrance requirements:* For master's and doctorate, GRE, 3 letters of recommendation; statement of personal, professional and academic goals. Additional exam requirements/recommendations for international students: required—TOEFL, IELTS. Electronic applications accepted.

San Diego State University, Graduate and Research Affairs, College of Education, Department of Child and Family Development, San Diego, CA 92182. Offers child development (MS). *Program availability:* Part-time. *Degree requirements:* For master's, thesis. *Entrance requirements:* For master's, GRE General Test, 3 letters of recommendation, interview. Additional exam requirements/recommendations for international students: required—TOEFL. Electronic applications accepted.

Sarah Lawrence College, Graduate Studies, Program in Child Development, Bronxville, NY 10708-5999. Offers MA. *Program availability:* Part-time. *Degree requirements:* For master's, thesis, fieldwork. *Entrance requirements:* For master's, minimum B average in undergraduate coursework. Additional exam requirements/recommendations for international students: required—TOEFL. Electronic applications accepted.

Texas Woman's University, Graduate School, College of Professional Education, Department of Human Development, Family Studies, and Counseling, Denton, TX 76204. Offers child development (MS); child life (MS); counseling and development (MS); early childhood development and education (PhD); early childhood education (M Ed); family studies (MS, PhD); family therapy (MS, PhD). *Accreditation:* ACA (one or more programs are accredited). *Program availability:* Part-time, evening/weekend, 100% online, blended/hybrid learning. *Faculty:* 27 full-time (22 women), 11 part-time/adjunct (10 women). *Students:* 187 full-time (180 women), 245 part-time (230 women); includes 177 minority (83 Black or African American, non-Hispanic/Latino; 17 Asian, non-Hispanic/Latino; 62 Hispanic/Latino; 15 Two or more races, non-Hispanic/Latino), 8 international. Average age 31. 234 applicants, 49% accepted, 80 enrolled. In 2019, 89 master's, 24 doctorates awarded. *Degree requirements:* For master's, comprehensive exam (for some programs), thesis (for some programs), thesis, professional paper, portfolio, or coursework; practicums (for some programs); for doctorate, comprehensive exam, thesis/dissertation, seminars, qualifying exam, dissertation. *Entrance requirements:* For master's, minimum GPA of 3.0 (3.25 for family therapy), letter of intent, curriculum vitae/resume, interview, writing sample, 2 letters of recommendation, interview (counseling and development); for doctorate, GRE scores (147 verbal, 144 quantitative, 4 analytical), minimum GPA of 3.5 (3.35 for family studies) on all prior graduate work, curriculum vitae/resume, letter of intent, 3 letters of recommendation, master's degree or prerequisite equivalents in core area. Additional exam requirements/recommendations for international students: required—TOEFL (minimum score 79 iBT); recommended—IELTS (minimum score 6.5), TSE (minimum score 53). *Application deadline:* For fall admission, 3/15 for domestic students, 3/1 priority date for international students; for spring admission, 10/1 for domestic students, 7/1 priority date for international students; for summer admission, 2/1 for domestic and international students. Application fee: $50 ($75 for international students). Electronic applications accepted. *Expenses: Tuition, area resident:* Full-time $4973.40; part-time $276.30 per semester hour. Tuition, state resident: full-time $4973.40; part-time $276.30 per semester hour. Tuition, nonresident: full-time $12,569; part-time $698.30 per semester hour. *International tuition:* $12,569.40 full-time. *Required fees:* $2524.30. Tuition and fees vary according to course level, course load, degree level and program. *Financial support:* In 2019–20, 141 students received support, including 2 research assistantships, 17 teaching assistantships (averaging $10,532 per year); career-related internships or fieldwork, scholarships/grants, health care benefits, and unspecified assistantships also available. Support available to part-time students. Financial award application deadline: 3/1; financial award applicants required to submit FAFSA. *Unit head:* Dr. Holly Hansen-Thomas, Interim Chair, 940-898-2685, Fax: 940-898-2676, E-mail: HDFSC@twu.edu. *Application contact:* Korie Hawkins, Associate Director of Admissions, Graduate Recruitment, 940-898-3188, Fax: 940-898-3081, E-mail: admissions@twu.edu.
Website: http://www.twu.edu/family-sciences/

Tufts University, Graduate School of Arts and Sciences, Eliot-Pearson Department of Child Study and Human Development, Medford, MA 02155. Offers child study and human development (MA, PhD). *Program availability:* Part-time. *Degree requirements:* For master's, thesis (for some programs); for doctorate, comprehensive exam, thesis/dissertation. *Entrance requirements:* For master's and doctorate, GRE General Test. Additional exam requirements/recommendations for international students: required—TOEFL (minimum score 550 paper-based; 80 iBT), IELTS (minimum score 6.5). Electronic applications accepted. *Expenses:* Contact institution.

The University of Akron, Graduate School, Buchtel College of Arts and Sciences, Department of Child and Family Development, Akron, OH 44325. Offers child development (MA). *Degree requirements:* For master's, comprehensive exam, project or thesis. *Entrance requirements:* For master's, GRE, minimum GPA of 3.0, three letters of recommendation, statement of purpose, resume. Additional exam requirements/recommendations for international students: required—TOEFL (minimum score 79 iBT), IELTS (minimum score 6.5). Electronic applications accepted.

University of California, Davis, Graduate Studies, Graduate Group in Child Development, Davis, CA 95616. Offers MS. *Degree requirements:* For master's, comprehensive exam (for some programs), thesis (for some programs). *Entrance requirements:* For master's, GRE General Test, minimum GPA of 3.0. Additional exam requirements/recommendations for international students: required—TOEFL (minimum score 550 paper-based). Electronic applications accepted.

University of Florida, Graduate School, College of Agricultural and Life Sciences, Department of Family, Youth, and Community Sciences, Gainesville, FL 32611. Offers community studies (MS); family and youth development (MS); family, youth and community sciences (MS); nonprofit organization development (MS). *Program* availability: Part-time, online learning. *Degree requirements:* For master's, comprehensive exam (for some programs), thesis (for some programs). *Entrance requirements:* For master's, GRE General Test, minimum GPA of 3.0. Additional exam requirements/recommendations for international students: required—TOEFL (minimum score 550 paper-based; 80 iBT), IELTS (minimum score 6). Electronic applications accepted.

University of La Verne, LaFetra College of Education, Programs in Child Development/Child Life, La Verne, CA 91750-4443. Offers child development (MS); child life (MS). *Program availability:* Part-time. *Entrance requirements:* For master's, minimum GPA of 3.0, 3 letters of reference, writing sample. Additional exam requirements/recommendations for international students: required—TOEFL (minimum score 550 paper-based). *Expenses:* Contact institution.

University of La Verne, Regional and Online Campuses, Graduate Program, ULV Online, La Verne, CA 91750-4443. Offers business administration for experienced professionals (MBA); child development (MS); leadership and management (MS). *Program availability:* Part-time, evening/weekend, online learning. *Entrance requirements:* For master's, GMAT, MAT, or GRE, minimum undergraduate GPA of 3.0, 2 letters of recommendation, resume, statement of purpose.

University of Minnesota, Twin Cities Campus, Graduate School, College of Education and Human Development, Institute of Child Development, Minneapolis, MN 55455-0213. Offers applied child and adolescent development (MA); developmental psychology (PhD); early childhood education (M Ed). *Program availability:* Online learning. *Faculty:* 16 full-time (10 women). *Students:* 109 full-time (100 women), 19 part-time (17 women); includes 25 minority (6 Black or African American, non-Hispanic/Latino; 1 American Indian or Alaska Native, non-Hispanic/Latino; 3 Asian, non-Hispanic/Latino; 10 Hispanic/Latino; 5 Two or more races, non-Hispanic/Latino), 4 international. Average age 29. 226 applicants, 35% accepted, 60 enrolled. In 2019, 17 master's, 5 doctorates awarded. Application fee: $75 ($95 for international students). *Financial support:* In 2019–20, 22 fellowships, 17 research assistantships with full tuition reimbursements (averaging $19,637 per year), 12 teaching assistantships with full tuition reimbursements (averaging $18,974 per year) were awarded. *Unit head:* Dr. Megan Gunnar, Director, 612-624-2713, E-mail: gunnar@umn.edu. *Application contact:* Dr. Kathleen Thomas, Director of Graduate Studies, 612-625-3389, E-mail: thoma114@umn.edu.
Website: http://www.cehd.umn.edu/ICD

University of Nebraska–Lincoln, Graduate College, College of Education and Human Sciences, Department of Child, Youth and Family Studies, Lincoln, NE 68588. Offers child development/early childhood education (MS, PhD); child, youth and family studies (MS); family and consumer sciences education (MS, PhD); family financial planning (MS); family science (MS, PhD); gerontology (PhD); human sciences (PhD), including child, youth and family studies, gerontology, medical family therapy; marriage and family therapy (MS); medical family therapy (PhD); youth development (MS). *Accreditation:* AAMFT/COAMFTE (one or more programs are accredited). *Program availability:* Online learning. *Degree requirements:* For master's, thesis optional. *Entrance requirements:* For master's, GRE. Additional exam requirements/recommendations for international students: required—TOEFL (minimum score 550 paper-based). Electronic applications accepted.

The University of North Carolina at Charlotte, Cato College of Education, Department of Special Education and Child Development, Charlotte, NC 28223-0001. Offers academically or intellectually gifted (Graduate Certificate); autism spectrum disorders (Graduate Certificate); child and family development: birth through kindergarten (Graduate Certificate); child and family studies (M Ed); special education (M Ed, PhD, Graduate Certificate), including academically or intellectually gifted (M Ed). *Program availability:* Part-time, 100% online, blended/hybrid learning. *Faculty:* 26 full-time (20 women), 8 part-time/adjunct (all women). *Students:* 19 full-time (14 women), 95 part-time (88 women); includes 24 minority (17 Black or African American, non-Hispanic/Latino; 4 Hispanic/Latino; 3 Two or more races, non-Hispanic/Latino), 4 international. Average age 35. 96 applicants, 86% accepted, 66 enrolled. In 2019, 14 master's, 6 doctorates, 15 other advanced degrees awarded. *Degree requirements:* For master's, capstone; for doctorate, thesis/dissertation, portfolio. *Entrance requirements:* For master's, GRE or MAT, transcripts, at least three evaluations from professional educators familiar with the applicant's personal and professional qualifications, an essay (one to two pages) describing the applicant's experience and objective in undertaking graduate study; for doctorate, GRE or MAT, 2 official transcripts of all academic work attempted since high school indicating minimum GPA of 3.5 in graduate degree program; at least 3 references of someone who knows applicant's current work and/or academic achievements in previous degree work; two-page essay; current resume or curriculum vitae; writing sample; documentation of teaching; for Graduate Certificate, undergraduate degree from regionally-accredited four-year institution; minimum cumulative undergraduate GPA of 3.0; three recommendations from persons knowledgeable of applicant's interaction with children and families; statement of purpose; clear criminal background check. Additional exam requirements/recommendations for international students: required—TOEFL (minimum score 557 paper-based; 83 iBT), IELTS (minimum score 6.5), TOEFL (minimum score 557 paper-based; 83 iBT) or IELTS (6.5). *Application deadline:* Applications are processed on a rolling basis. Application fee: $75. Electronic applications accepted. *Expenses:* Tuition, state resident: full-time $4337. Tuition, nonresident: full-time $17,771. *Required fees:* $3093. Tuition and fees vary according to course load, degree level and program. *Financial support:* In 2019–20, 15 students received support, including 15 research

assistantships (averaging $9,549 per year); teaching assistantships, career-related internships or fieldwork, institutionally sponsored loans, scholarships/grants, and unspecified assistantships also available. Support available to part-time students. Financial award applicants required to submit FAFSA. *Unit head:* Dr. Charles Wood, Department Chair & Professor, 704-687-8395, E-mail: clwood@uncc.edu. *Application contact:* Kathy B. Giddings, Director of Graduate Admissions, 704-687-5503, Fax: 704-687-1668, E-mail: gradadm@uncc.edu.
Website: http://spcd.uncc.edu/

The University of Tennessee at Martin, Graduate Programs, College of Agriculture and Applied Sciences, Department of Family and Consumer Sciences, Martin, TN 38238. Offers dietetics (MSFCS); general family and consumer sciences (MSFCS). *Program availability:* Part-time, 100% online. *Faculty:* 7. *Students:* 1 full-time (0 women), 29 part-time (27 women); includes 3 minority (2 Black or African American, non-Hispanic/Latino; 1 Hispanic/Latino). Average age 29. 47 applicants, 70% accepted, 12 enrolled. In 2019, 12 master's awarded. *Degree requirements:* For master's, comprehensive exam, thesis optional. *Entrance requirements:* For master's, GRE General Test, minimum GPA of 2.5. Additional exam requirements/recommendations for international students: required—TOEFL (minimum score 525 paper-based; 71 iBT). *Application deadline:* For fall admission, 7/28 priority date for domestic and international students; for spring admission, 12/17 priority date for domestic and international students; for summer admission, 5/10 priority date for domestic and international students. Applications are processed on a rolling basis. Application fee: $30 ($130 for international students). Electronic applications accepted. *Expenses: Tuition, area resident:* Full-time $9096; part-time $505 per credit hour. Tuition, state resident: full-time $9096; part-time $505 per credit hour. Tuition, nonresident: full-time $15,136; part-time $841 per credit hour. *International tuition:* $23,040 full-time. *Required fees:* $1520; $85 per credit hour. Part-time tuition and fees vary according to course load. *Financial support:* In 2019–20, 10 students received support, including 2 teaching assistantships with full tuition reimbursements available (averaging $6,912 per year); research assistantships with full tuition reimbursements available, scholarships/grants, and tuition waivers (full and partial) also available. Financial award application deadline: 2/1; financial award applicants required to submit FAFSA. *Unit head:* Dr. Lisa LeBleu, Coordinator, 731-881-7116, Fax: 731-881-7106, E-mail: llebleu@utm.edu. *Application contact:* Jolene L. Cunningham, Student Services Specialist, 731-881-7012, Fax: 731-881-7499, E-mail: jcunningham@utm.edu.
Website: http://www.utm.edu/departments/caas/fcs/index.php

The University of Texas at Austin, Graduate School, College of Natural Sciences, School of Human Ecology, Austin, TX 78712-1111. Offers human development and family sciences (MA, PhD); nutritional sciences (MA, MS, PhD), including nutrition (MA), nutritional sciences (PhD); textile and apparel technology (MS). *Degree requirements:* For master's, thesis; for doctorate, thesis/dissertation. *Entrance requirements:* For master's and doctorate, GRE General Test. Electronic applications accepted.

The University of West Alabama, School of Graduate Studies, College of Education, Program in Early Childhood Education, Livingston, AL 35470. Offers early childhood development (M Ed); early childhood education P-3 (M Ed, Ed S). *Accreditation:* NCATE. *Program availability:* Part-time, evening/weekend, 100% online. *Faculty:* 5 full-time (all women), 32 part-time/adjunct (22 women). *Students:* 175 full-time (174 women), 11 part-time (9 women); includes 76 minority (70 Black or African American, non-Hispanic/Latino; 1 Asian, non-Hispanic/Latino; 4 Hispanic/Latino; 1 Two or more races, non-Hispanic/Latino), 1 international. Average age 33. 55 applicants, 96% accepted, 46 enrolled. In 2019, 49 master's, 6 Ed Ss awarded. *Degree requirements:* For master's, comprehensive exam, thesis optional; for Ed S, comprehensive exam. *Entrance requirements:* For master's, GRE, minimum GPA of 2.75, verification of background clearance/fingerprints, valid bachelor's-level Professional Educator Certificate in same teaching field. Additional exam requirements/recommendations for international students: required—TOEFL (minimum score 500 paper-based; 61 iBT). *Application deadline:* Applications are processed on a rolling basis. Application fee: $40. Electronic applications accepted. *Expenses: Required fees:* $380; $130. *Financial support:* Teaching assistantships, Federal Work-Study, scholarships/grants, and unspecified assistantships available. Support available to part-time students. Financial award application deadline: 3/1; financial award applicants required to submit FAFSA. *Unit head:* Dr. Jodie Winship, Chair of College of Education, 205-652-5415, Fax: 205-652-3706, E-mail: jwinship@uwa.edu. *Application contact:* Dr. Jodie Winship, Chair of College of Education, 205-652-5415, Fax: 205-652-3706, E-mail: jwinship@uwa.edu.

University of Wyoming, College of Agriculture and Natural Resources, Department of Family and Consumer Sciences, Laramie, WY 82071. Offers early childhood development (MS); family and consumer sciences (MS); food science and human nutrition (MS). *Program availability:* Part-time. *Degree requirements:* For master's, thesis, project. *Entrance requirements:* For master's, GRE General Test or MCAT, minimum GPA of 3.0. Additional exam requirements/recommendations for international students: required—TOEFL (minimum score 540 paper-based; 76 iBT). Electronic applications accepted.

Whittier College, Graduate Programs, Department of Education and Child Development, Whittier, CA 90608-0634. Offers educational administration (MA Ed); elementary education (MA Ed); secondary education (MA Ed). *Program availability:* Part-time, evening/weekend. *Degree requirements:* For master's, thesis. *Entrance requirements:* For master's, GRE General Test, MAT, minimum GPA of 3.5, academic writing sample.

Clothing and Textiles

Alabama Agricultural and Mechanical University, School of Graduate Studies, College of Agricultural, Life and Natural Sciences, Department of Family and Consumer Sciences, Huntsville, AL 35811. Offers apparel, merchandising and design (MS); family and consumer sciences (MS); human development and family studies (MS); nutrition and hospitality management (MS). *Program availability:* Part-time, evening/weekend. *Degree requirements:* For master's, comprehensive exam, thesis optional. *Entrance requirements:* For master's, GRE General Test. Additional exam requirements/recommendations for international students: required—TOEFL (minimum score 500 paper-based; 61 iBT). Electronic applications accepted.

Auburn University, Graduate School, College of Human Sciences, Department of Consumer and Design Sciences, Auburn, AL 36849. Offers MS, PhD. *Program availability:* Part-time. *Faculty:* 20 full-time (18 women). *Students:* 21 full-time (16 women), 6 part-time (5 women); includes 3 minority (all Asian, non-Hispanic/Latino), 15 international. Average age 32. 27 applicants, 37% accepted, 6 enrolled. In 2019, 8

master's, 4 doctorates awarded. *Degree requirements:* For master's, thesis (for some programs); for doctorate, thesis/dissertation. *Entrance requirements:* For master's and doctorate, GRE General Test. Additional exam requirements/recommendations for international students: required—iTEP; recommended—TOEFL (minimum score 550 paper-based; 79 iBT), IELTS (minimum score 6.5). *Application deadline:* Applications are processed on a rolling basis. Application fee: $60 ($70 for international students). Electronic applications accepted. *Expenses:* $546 per credit hour state resident tuition, $1638 per credit hour nonresident tuition, $680 student services fee for GRA/GTA, $2040 differential tuition per semester. *Financial support:* In 2019–20, 9 fellowships with tuition reimbursements, 4 research assistantships with tuition reimbursements (averaging $16,431 per year), 17 teaching assistantships with tuition reimbursements (averaging $16,854 per year) were awarded; career-related internships or fieldwork and Federal Work-Study also available. Support available to part-time students. Financial award application deadline: 3/15; financial award applicants required to submit FAFSA.

Clothing and Textiles

Unit head: Dr. Pamela V. Ulrich, Head, 334-844-1336, E-mail: cwarfiel@humsci.auburn.edu. *Application contact:* Dr. George Flowers, Dean of the Graduate School, 334-844-2125.
Website: http://humsci.auburn.edu/cads/

Central Michigan University, College of Graduate Studies, College of Education and Human Services, Department of Human Environmental Studies, Mount Pleasant, MI 48859. Offers apparel product development and merchandising technology (MS); gerontology (Graduate Certificate); human development and family studies (MA); nutrition and dietetics (MS). *Program availability:* Part-time, evening/weekend. *Degree requirements:* For master's, thesis or alternative. Electronic applications accepted. *Expenses: Tuition, area resident:* Full-time $12,267; part-time $8178 per year. Tuition, state resident: full-time $12,267; part-time $8178 per year. Tuition, nonresident: full-time $12,267; part-time $8178 per year. *International tuition:* $16,110 full-time. *Required fees:* $225 per semester. Tuition and fees vary according to degree level and program.

Cornell University, Graduate School, Graduate Fields of Human Ecology, Field of Fiber Science and Apparel Design, Ithaca, NY 14853. Offers apparel design (MA, MPS); fiber science (MS, PhD); polymer science (MS, PhD); textile science (MS, PhD). *Degree requirements:* For master's, thesis (MA, MS), project paper (MPS); for doctorate, comprehensive exam, thesis/dissertation. *Entrance requirements:* For master's, GRE General Test, 2 letters of recommendation, portfolio (for functional apparel design); for doctorate, GRE General Test, 2 letters of recommendation. Additional exam requirements/recommendations for international students: required—TOEFL (minimum score 600 paper-based; 77 iBT). Electronic applications accepted.

Drexel University, Westphal College of Media Arts and Design, Program in Retail and Merchandising, Philadelphia, PA 19104-2875. Offers MS. *Program availability:* Online learning.

Eastern Michigan University, Graduate School, College of Engineering and Technology, School of Visual and Built Environments, Program in Apparel Textiles and Merchandising, Ypsilanti, MI 48197. Offers MS. *Program availability:* Part-time, evening/weekend, online learning. *Students:* 1 (woman) full-time, 3 part-time (all women); includes 3 minority (2 Black or African American, non-Hispanic/Latino; 1 Asian, non-Hispanic/Latino). Average age 35. 1 applicant. In 2019, 3 master's awarded. *Entrance requirements:* Additional exam requirements/recommendations for international students: required—TOEFL. *Application deadline:* Applications are processed on a rolling basis. Application fee: $45. *Financial support:* Fellowships, research assistantships with full tuition reimbursements, teaching assistantships with full tuition reimbursements, career-related internships or fieldwork, Federal Work-Study, institutionally sponsored loans, scholarships/grants, tuition waivers (partial), and unspecified assistantships available. Support available to part-time students. Financial award applicants required to submit FAFSA. *Application contact:* Dr. Subhas Ghosh, Program Coordinator, 734-487-2476, Fax: 734-487-7690, E-mail: sghosh@emich.edu.

Fashion Institute of Technology, School of Graduate Studies, Program in Fashion and Textile Studies: History, Theory, Museum Practice, New York, NY 10001-5992. Offers MA. *Accreditation:* NASAD. *Degree requirements:* For master's, one foreign language, thesis, internship. *Entrance requirements:* For master's, GRE General Test or GRE Subject Test, previous course work in art history and chemistry, 4 semesters of a foreign language. Additional exam requirements/recommendations for international students: required—TOEFL (minimum score 550 paper-based). Electronic applications accepted.

Fashion Institute of Technology, School of Graduate Studies, Program in Fashion Design, New York, NY 10001-5992. Offers MFA. *Entrance requirements:* For master's, portfolio.

Georgia State University, College of Arts, Ernest G. Welch School of Art and Design, Program in Studio Art, Atlanta, GA 30302-3083. Offers ceramics (MFA); drawing and painting (MFA); graphic design (MFA); interior design (MFA); photography (MFA); printmaking (MFA); sculpture (MFA); textiles (MFA). *Accreditation:* NASAD. Application fee: $50. Electronic applications accepted. *Expenses: Tuition, area resident:* Full-time $7164; part-time $398 per credit hour. Tuition, state resident: full-time $7164; part-time $398 per credit hour. Tuition, nonresident: full-time $22,662; part-time $1259 per credit hour. *International tuition:* $22,662 full-time. *Required fees:* $2128; $312 per credit hour. Tuition and fees vary according to course load and program. *Financial support:* Fellowships, research assistantships, teaching assistantships, scholarships/grants, and unspecified assistantships available. Financial award application deadline: 4/15; financial award applicants required to submit FAFSA. *Unit head:* Joseph Peragine, Director, Welch School of Art and Design, 404-413-5229, E-mail: jperagine@gsu.edu. *Application contact:* Joseph Peragine, Director, Welch School of Art and Design, 404-413-5229, E-mail: jperagine@gsu.edu.
Website: http://artdesign.gsu.edu/graduate/admissions/masters-of-fine-arts-in-studio/

Iowa State University of Science and Technology, Department of Apparel, Events, and Hospitality Management, Ames, IA 50011-1078. Offers apparel, merchandising, and design (MS, PhD); hospitality management (MS, PhD). *Program availability:* Online learning. *Degree requirements:* For doctorate, thesis/dissertation. *Entrance requirements:* For master's and doctorate, GRE General Test. Additional exam requirements/recommendations for international students: required—TOEFL (minimum score 550 paper-based; 79 iBT), IELTS (minimum score 6.5). Electronic applications accepted.

Iowa State University of Science and Technology, Program in Apparel, Merchandising, and Design, Ames, IA 50011. Offers MS, PhD. *Degree requirements:* For master's, thesis; for doctorate, thesis/dissertation. *Entrance requirements:* Additional exam requirements/recommendations for international students: required—TOEFL (minimum score 550 paper-based; 79 iBT), IELTS (minimum score 6.5). Electronic applications accepted.

Kansas State University, Graduate School, College of Human Ecology, Department of Apparel, Textiles, and Interior Design, Manhattan, KS 66506. Offers apparel and textiles (MS), including general apparel and textiles, merchandising. *Program availability:* Online learning. *Degree requirements:* For master's, comprehensive exam (for some programs), thesis (for some programs). *Entrance requirements:* For master's, GRE General Test (except for merchandising applicants), minimum undergraduate GPA of 3.0. Additional exam requirements/recommendations for international students: required—TOEFL (minimum score 550 paper-based; 79 iBT), IELTS (minimum score 6.1). Electronic applications accepted. *Expenses:* Contact institution.

Kansas State University, Graduate School, College of Human Ecology, Doctorate in Human Ecology Program, Manhattan, KS 66506-1407. Offers apparel and textiles (PhD); applied family sciences (PhD); couple and family therapy (PhD); hospitality administration (PhD); kinesiology (PhD); life-span human development (PhD). *Program availability:* Part-time. *Degree requirements:* For doctorate, thesis/dissertation. *Entrance requirements:* Additional exam requirements/recommendations for international students: required—TOEFL. Electronic applications accepted.

LIM College, MPS Program, New York, NY 10022-5268. Offers business of fashion (MPS); fashion marketing (MPS); fashion merchandising and retail management (MPS); global fashion supply chain management (MPS). *Accreditation:* ACBSP. *Program availability:* Part-time, 100% online. *Entrance requirements:* Additional exam

requirements/recommendations for international students: required—TOEFL (minimum score 550 paper-based), IELTS (minimum score 6.5), PTE (minimum score 55). Electronic applications accepted.

Mississippi State University, College of Agriculture and Life Sciences, School of Human Sciences, Mississippi State, MS 39762. Offers agriculture and extension education (MS), including communication, leadership; agriculture science (PhD), including agriculture and extension education; fashion design and merchandising (MS), including design and product development, merchandising; human development and family studies (MS, PhD). *Accreditation:* NCATE (one or more programs are accredited). *Program availability:* Part-time. *Faculty:* 21 full-time (11 women). *Students:* 26 full-time (21 women), 62 part-time (46 women); includes 16 minority (12 Black or African American, non-Hispanic/Latino; 1 American Indian or Alaska Native, non-Hispanic/Latino; 1 Hispanic/Latino; 2 Two or more races, non-Hispanic/Latino), 4 international. Average age 34. 26 applicants, 69% accepted, 16 enrolled. In 2019, 12 master's, 4 doctorates awarded. *Degree requirements:* For master's, thesis optional, comprehensive oral or written exam. *Entrance requirements:* For master's, GRE, minimum GPA of 2.75 in last 4 semesters of course work; for doctorate, minimum GPA of 3.0 on prior graduate work. Additional exam requirements/recommendations for international students: required—TOEFL (minimum score 477 paper-based; 53 iBT); recommended—IELTS (minimum score 4.5). *Application deadline:* For fall admission, 7/1 for domestic students, 5/1 for international students; for spring admission, 11/1 for domestic students, 9/1 for international students. Applications are processed on a rolling basis. Application fee: $60 ($80 for international students). Electronic applications accepted. *Expenses: Tuition, area resident:* Full-time $8880; part-time $456 per credit hour. Tuition, state resident: full-time $8880. Tuition, nonresident: full-time $23,840; part-time $1236 per credit hour. *Required fees:* $110; $11.12 per credit hour. Tuition and fees vary according to course load. *Financial support:* In 2019–20, 15 research assistantships (averaging $12,541 per year) were awarded; Federal Work-Study, institutionally sponsored loans, and unspecified assistantships also available. Financial award application deadline: 4/1; financial award applicants required to submit FAFSA. *Unit head:* Dr. Michael Newman, Professor and Director, 662-325-2950, E-mail: mnewman@humansci.msstate.edu. *Application contact:* Ryan King, Admissions and Enrollment Assistant, 662-325-8951, E-mail: rjk101@grad.msstate.edu.
Website: http://www.humansci.msstate.edu

New Mexico State University, College of Agricultural, Consumer and Environmental Sciences, Department of Family and Consumer Sciences, Las Cruces, NM 88003-8001. Offers clothing, textiles, and merchandising (MS); family and child science (MS); family and consumer science education (MS); family and consumer sciences (MS); food science and technology (MS); hotel, restaurant, and tourism management (MS); human nutrition and dietetic sciences (MS). *Program availability:* Part-time. *Faculty:* 10 full-time (7 women), 1 (woman) part-time/adjunct. *Students:* 29 full-time (23 women), 11 part-time (10 women); includes 25 minority (1 Black or African American, non-Hispanic/Latino; 3 Asian, non-Hispanic/Latino; 20 Hispanic/Latino; 1 Two or more races, non-Hispanic/Latino), 3 international. Average age 30. 23 applicants, 87% accepted, 16 enrolled. In 2019, 19 master's awarded. *Degree requirements:* For master's, comprehensive exam (for some programs), thesis (for some programs), oral exam. *Entrance requirements:* For master's, GRE, 3 letters of reference from faculty members or employers, resume, letter of interest. Additional exam requirements/recommendations for international students: required—TOEFL (minimum score 550 paper-based; 79 iBT), IELTS (minimum score 6.5). *Application deadline:* For fall admission, 2/1 priority date for domestic and international students; for spring admission, 10/1 for domestic and international students. Applications are processed on a rolling basis. Application fee: $40 ($50 for international students). Electronic applications accepted. *Financial support:* In 2019–20, 24 students received support, including 4 research assistantships (averaging $15,515 per year), 10 teaching assistantships (averaging $14,076 per year); career-related internships or fieldwork, Federal Work-Study, scholarships/grants, traineeships, health care benefits, and unspecified assistantships also available. Support available to part-time students. Financial award application deadline: 3/1. *Application contact:* Dr. Kourtney Vaillancourt, Graduate Program Contact, 575-646-3383, Fax: 575-646-1889, E-mail: kvaillan@nmsu.edu.
Website: http://aces.nmsu.edu/academics/fcs

The New School, Parsons Paris, Program in Fashion Studies, New York, NY 10011. Offers MA. *Program availability:* Part-time. *Faculty:* 5 full-time (2 women), 46 part-time/adjunct (31 women). *Students:* 35 full-time (34 women), 1 (woman) part-time; includes 5 minority (4 Black or African American, non-Hispanic/Latino; 1 Hispanic/Latino), 17 international. Average age 25. 35 applicants, 80% accepted, 15 enrolled. In 2019, 8 master's awarded. *Degree requirements:* For master's, thesis. *Entrance requirements:* For master's, transcripts, resume, statement of purpose, recommendation letters, interview. Additional exam requirements/recommendations for international students: required—TOEFL (minimum score 100 iBT), IELTS (minimum score 7), PTE (minimum score 68). *Application deadline:* For fall admission, 1/1 priority date for domestic and international students. Applications are processed on a rolling basis. Application fee: $50. Electronic applications accepted. *Expenses:* $1,390.00 per credit. *Financial support:* In 2019–20, 29 students received support. Career-related internships or fieldwork and scholarships/grants available. Financial award application deadline: 2/1. *Unit head:* Marco Pecorari, Coordinator, 33-176217661, E-mail: pecorarm@newschool.edu. *Application contact:* Mike Fakih, Director of Admissions, Parsons Paris, 33 176 21 76 67, E-mail: thinkparsonsparis@newschool.edu.

North Carolina State University, Graduate School, Wilson College of Textiles, Department of Textile Engineering, Chemistry, and Science, Raleigh, NC 27695. Offers fiber and polymer science (PhD); textile chemistry (MS); textile engineering (MS); textile technology management (PhD). *Degree requirements:* For master's, thesis optional. Electronic applications accepted.

North Carolina State University, Graduate School, Wilson College of Textiles, Program in Textile Technology Management, Raleigh, NC 27695. Offers PhD. *Degree requirements:* For doctorate, one foreign language, thesis/dissertation, cumulative exams. *Entrance requirements:* For doctorate, GRE or GMAT. Electronic applications accepted.

Oklahoma State University, College of Human Sciences, Department of Design, Housing and Merchandising, Stillwater, OK 74078. Offers MS, PhD. *Faculty:* 8 full-time (6 women). *Students:* 11 part-time (4 women); includes 2 minority (both Hispanic/Latino), 5 international. Average age 31. 9 applicants, 56% accepted, 2 enrolled. In 2019, 3 master's, 1 doctorate awarded. *Entrance requirements:* For master's and doctorate, GRE or GMAT. Additional exam requirements/recommendations for international students: required—TOEFL (minimum score 550 paper-based; 79 iBT). *Application deadline:* For fall admission, 3/1 priority date for international students; for spring admission, 8/1 priority date for international students. Applications are processed on a rolling basis. Application fee: $50 ($75 for international students). Electronic applications accepted. *Expenses: Tuition, area resident:* Full-time $4148.10; part-time $2765.40 per credit hour. Tuition, state resident: full-time $4148.10; part-time $2765.40 per credit hour. Tuition, nonresident: full-time $15,775; part-time $10,516.80 per credit hour. *International tuition:* $15,775.20 full-time. *Required fees:* $2196.90; $122.05 per credit hour. Tuition and fees vary according to course load, campus/location and

program. *Financial support:* In 2019–20, 2 research assistantships (averaging $1,660 per year), 4 teaching assistantships (averaging $1,788 per year) were awarded; career-related internships or fieldwork, Federal Work-Study, scholarships/grants, health care benefits, tuition waivers (partial), and unspecified assistantships also available. Support available to part-time students. Financial award application deadline: 3/1; financial award applicants required to submit FAFSA. *Unit head:* Dr. Lynn Boorady, Department Head, 405-744-5035, Fax: 405-744-6910, E-mail: lynn.m.boorady@okstate.edu. *Application contact:* Dr. Sheryl Tucker, Vice Prov/Dean/Prof, 405-744-6368, E-mail: gradi@okstate.edu.
Website: https://education.okstate.edu/

Rutgers University - Newark, Rutgers Business School–Newark and New Brunswick, Program in Business of Fashion, Newark, NJ 07102. Offers MBA.

Savannah College of Art and Design, Program in Accessory Design, Savannah, GA 31402-3146. Offers MA, MFA. *Program availability:* Part-time. *Degree requirements:* For master's, final project (for MA); thesis (for MFA). *Entrance requirements:* For master's, GRE (recommended), portfolio (submitted in digital format), audition or writing submission, resume, statement of purpose, two letters of recommendation. Additional exam requirements/recommendations for international students: recommended—TOEFL (minimum score 550 paper-based; 85 iBT), IELTS (minimum score 6.5). Electronic applications accepted.

Thomas Jefferson University, Kanbar College of Design, Engineering and Commerce, Program in Fashion Design Management, Philadelphia, PA 19107. Offers MS.

Thomas Jefferson University, Kanbar College of Design, Engineering and Commerce, Program in Global Fashion Enterprise, Philadelphia, PA 19107. Offers MS. *Program availability:* Part-time. *Entrance requirements:* For master's, GRE or GMAT, minimum GPA of 2.8, official transcripts, two letters of recommendation, essay. Additional exam requirements/recommendations for international students: required—TOEFL (minimum score 550 paper-based; 79 iBT). Electronic applications accepted.

The University of Akron, Graduate School, Buchtel College of Arts and Sciences, Department of Fashion Merchandising, Akron, OH 44325. Offers clothing, textiles and interiors (MA). *Degree requirements:* For master's, comprehensive exam, thesis or project. *Entrance requirements:* For master's, GRE, minimum GPA of 3.0, three letters of recommendation, statement of purpose, resume. Additional exam requirements/recommendations for international students: required—TOEFL (minimum score 79 iBT), IELTS (minimum score 6.5). Electronic applications accepted.

The University of Alabama, Graduate School, College of Human Environmental Sciences, Department of Clothing, Textiles, and Interior Design, Tuscaloosa, AL 35487. Offers apparel and textiles (MSHES). *Faculty:* 5 full-time (all women). *Students:* 1 (woman) full-time, all international. Average age 32. 1 applicant. *Degree requirements:* For master's, comprehensive exam (for some programs), thesis optional, P-culminating project. *Entrance requirements:* For master's, GRE General Test or MAT, minimum GPA of 3.0. Additional exam requirements/recommendations for international students: required—TOEFL. *Application deadline:* For fall admission, 7/1 for domestic students; for spring admission, 10/30 for domestic students; for summer admission, 4/30 for domestic students. Applications are processed on a rolling basis. Application fee: $50 ($60 for international students). Electronic applications accepted. *Expenses: Tuition,* area resident: Full-time $10,780; part-time $440 per credit hour. Tuition, nonresident: full-time $30,250; part-time $1550 per credit hour. *Financial support:* Fellowships, research assistantships with full tuition reimbursements, teaching assistantships with partial tuition reimbursements, career-related internships or fieldwork, Federal Work-Study, scholarships/grants, and health care benefits available. Financial award application deadline: 4/15. *Unit head:* Dr. Shirley Foster, Chair and Assistant Professor, 205-348-6176, Fax: 205-348-0022, E-mail: sfoster@ches.ua.edu. *Application contact:* Patrick D. Fuller, Admissions Officer, 205-348-5923, Fax: 205-348-0400, E-mail: patrick.d.fuller@ua.edu.
Website: http://www.ctd.ches.ua.edu/

University of Alberta, Faculty of Graduate Studies and Research, Department of Human Ecology, Edmonton, AB T6G 2E1, Canada. Offers family ecology and practice (M Sc, PhD); textiles and clothing (M Sc, MA, PhD). *Program availability:* Online learning. *Degree requirements:* For master's, thesis (for some programs); for doctorate, comprehensive exam, thesis/dissertation. *Entrance requirements:* For master's and doctorate, minimum GPA of 7.0 on a 9.0 scale. Additional exam requirements/recommendations for international students: required—TOEFL (minimum score 580 paper-based).

University of California, Davis, Graduate Studies, Graduate Group in Textiles, Davis, CA 95616. Offers MS. *Degree requirements:* For master's, comprehensive exam (for some programs), thesis (for some programs). *Entrance requirements:* For master's, GRE General Test, minimum GPA of 3.0. Additional exam requirements/recommendations for international students: required—TOEFL (minimum score 550 paper-based). Electronic applications accepted.

University of Delaware, College of Arts and Sciences, Department of Fashion and Apparel Studies, Newark, DE 19716. Offers MS.

University of Georgia, College of Family and Consumer Sciences, Department of Textiles, Merchandising, and Interiors, Athens, GA 30602. Offers historical and cultural aspects of dress and textiles (MS); interior environments (MS); international merchandising (PhD); merchandising and international trade (MS); polymer, fiber and textile science (MS); polymer, fiber, and textile sciences (PhD). *Accreditation:* NASAD. *Degree requirements:* For master's, thesis; for doctorate, thesis/dissertation. *Entrance requirements:* For master's and doctorate, GRE General Test. Electronic applications accepted.

The University of Manchester, School of Materials, Manchester, United Kingdom. Offers advanced aerospace materials engineering (M Sc); advanced metallic systems (PhD); biomedical materials (M Phil, M Sc, PhD); ceramics and glass (M Phil, M Sc, PhD); composite materials (M Sc, PhD); corrosion and protection (M Phil, M Sc, PhD); materials (M Phil, PhD); metallic materials (M Phil, M Sc, PhD); nanostructural materials (M Phil, M Sc, PhD); paper science (M Phil, M Sc, PhD); polymer science and engineering (M Phil, M Sc, PhD); technical textiles (M Sc); textile design, fashion and management (M Phil, M Sc, PhD); textile science and technology (M Phil, M Sc, PhD); textiles (M Phil, PhD); textiles and fashion (M Ent).

University of Minnesota, Twin Cities Campus, Graduate School, College of Design, Department of Design, Housing, and Apparel, Minneapolis, MN 55455-0213. Offers apparel (MA, MS, PhD); design communication (MA, MS, PhD); housing studies (MA, MS, PhD, Postbaccalaureate Certificate); interactive design (MFA); interior design (MA, MS, PhD). *Program availability:* Part-time. *Degree requirements:* For master's and Postbaccalaureate Certificate, comprehensive exam, thesis (for some programs); for doctorate, comprehensive exam, thesis/dissertation. *Entrance requirements:* For

master's, GRE General Test, minimum GPA of 3.0 (preferred), portfolio, 3 letters of recommendation; for doctorate, GRE General Test, minimum GPA of 3.0 (preferred), portfolio, 3 letters of recommendation, writing sample; for Postbaccalaureate Certificate, GRE General Test, minimum GPA of 3.0 (preferred). Additional exam requirements/recommendations for international students: required—TOEFL (minimum score 550 paper-based; 79 iBT). Electronic applications accepted.

University of Missouri, Office of Research and Graduate Studies, College of Human Environmental Sciences, Department of Textile and Apparel Management, Columbia, MO 65211. Offers MS, PhD. *Entrance requirements:* For master's, GRE General Test, minimum GPA of 3.0. Additional exam requirements/recommendations for international students: required—TOEFL. Electronic applications accepted.

University of Nebraska–Lincoln, Graduate College, College of Education and Human Sciences, Department of Textiles, Clothing and Design, Lincoln, NE 68588. Offers human sciences (PhD), including textiles, clothing and design (MS, PhD); merchandising (MS); textile history/quilt studies (MA); textile science (MS); textile-apparel (MA); textiles, clothing and design (MA, MS), including textiles, clothing and design (MS, PhD). *Program availability:* Part-time, online learning. *Degree requirements:* For master's, thesis optional. *Entrance requirements:* For master's, GRE General Test. Additional exam requirements/recommendations for international students: required—TOEFL (minimum score 550 paper-based). Electronic applications accepted.

University of Rhode Island, Graduate School, College of Business, Fashion Merchandising & Design, Kingston, RI 02881. Offers fashion merchandising (Certificate); master seamstress (Certificate); textiles, fashion merchandising and design (MS), including fashion merchandising, historic fashion and textiles, textile conservation, and cultural analysis, textile science. *Program availability:* Part-time. *Faculty:* 8 full-time (6 women). *Students:* 6 full-time (5 women), 4 part-time (3 women); includes 2 minority (1 American Indian or Alaska Native, non-Hispanic/Latino; 1 Asian, non-Hispanic/Latino), 2 international. 10 applicants, 50% accepted, 2 enrolled. In 2019, 5 master's awarded. *Entrance requirements:* Additional exam requirements/recommendations for international students: required—TOEFL. *Application deadline:* For fall admission, 7/1 for domestic students, 2/1 for international students; for spring admission, 11/1 for domestic students, 7/1 for international students. Application fee: $65. Electronic applications accepted. *Expenses: Tuition,* area resident: Full-time $13,734; part-time $763 per credit. Tuition, state resident: full-time $13,734; part-time $763 per credit. Tuition, nonresident: full-time $26,512; part-time $1473 per credit. *International tuition:* $26,512 full-time. *Required fees:* $1780; $52 per credit. $35 per term. One-time fee: $165. *Financial support:* In 2019–20, 2 teaching assistantships with full tuition reimbursements (averaging $9,493 per year) were awarded. Financial award application deadline: 2/1; financial award applicants required to submit FAFSA. *Unit head:* Dr. Susan Hannel, Chair, 401-874-2882, Fax: 401-874-2581, E-mail: susanhannel@uri.edu. *Application contact:* Dr. Linda Welters, Graduate Program Director, 401-874-4525, Fax: 401-874-2581, E-mail: lwelters@uri.edu.
Website: https://web.uri.edu/tmd/ms-textiles-fashion-merchandising-and-design/

The University of Tennessee, Graduate School, College of Education, Health and Human Sciences, Department of Consumer and Industry Services Management, Program in Consumer Services Management, Knoxville, TN 37996. Offers retail and consumer sciences (MS); textile science (MS). *Program availability:* Part-time. *Degree requirements:* For master's, thesis or alternative. *Entrance requirements:* For master's, GRE General Test, minimum GPA of 2.7. Additional exam requirements/recommendations for international students: required—TOEFL. Electronic applications accepted.

The University of Tennessee, Graduate School, College of Education, Health and Human Sciences, Program in Human Ecology, Knoxville, TN 37996. Offers child and family studies (PhD); community health (PhD); nutrition science (PhD); retailing and consumer sciences (PhD); textile science (PhD). *Degree requirements:* For doctorate, thesis/dissertation. *Entrance requirements:* For doctorate, GRE General Test, minimum GPA of 2.7. Additional exam requirements/recommendations for international students: required—TOEFL. Electronic applications accepted.

University of the Incarnate Word, School of Media and Design, San Antonio, TX 78209-6397. Offers communication arts (MA); fashion design (MA). *Program availability:* Part-time, evening/weekend. *Faculty:* 6 full-time (3 women), 2 part-time/adjunct (0 women). *Students:* 21 full-time (11 women), 5 part-time (4 women); includes 16 minority (2 Black or African American, non-Hispanic/Latino; 14 Hispanic/Latino), 3 international. 7 applicants, 100% accepted, 6 enrolled. In 2019, 9 master's awarded. *Degree requirements:* For master's, thesis or alternative, capstone. *Entrance requirements:* For master's, GRE, interview, writing sample. Additional exam requirements/recommendations for international students: required—TOEFL (minimum score 560 paper-based; 83 iBT). *Application deadline:* Applications are processed on a rolling basis. Application fee: $20. Electronic applications accepted. *Expenses: Tuition:* Full-time $11,520; part-time $960 per credit hour. *Required fees:* $1128; $94 per credit hour. Tuition and fees vary according to degree level, campus/location, program and student level. *Financial support:* Federal Work-Study, scholarships/grants, tuition waivers (partial), and unspecified assistantships available. Financial award applicants required to submit FAFSA. *Unit head:* Dr. Sharon Welkey, Dean, 210-829-6091, Fax: 210-829-3196, E-mail: welkey@uiwtx.edu. *Application contact:* Jessica Delarosa, Director of Admissions, 210-8296005, Fax: 210-829-3921, E-mail: admis@uiwtx.edu.
Website: https://www.uiw.edu/smd/index.html

Washington State University, College of Agricultural, Human, and Natural Resource Sciences, Department of Apparel, Merchandising, Design, and Textiles, Pullman, WA 99164-2020. Offers MA. *Program availability:* Part-time. *Degree requirements:* For master's, comprehensive exam (for some programs), thesis, oral exam. *Entrance requirements:* For master's, minimum GPA of 3.0, 2 writing samples, 2 letters of recommendation. Additional exam requirements/recommendations for international students: required—TOEFL, IELTS. Electronic applications accepted.

Wayne State University, College of Fine, Performing and Communication Arts, James Pearson Duffy Department of Art and Art History, Detroit, MI 48202. Offers art (MA, MFA), including ceramics, drawing, fashion design and merchandising (MA), fibers, graphic design, industrial design (MA), interior design (MA), metalsmithing, painting, photography, printmaking, sculpture; art history (MA). *Degree requirements:* For master's, thesis (for some programs), essay or thesis. *Entrance requirements:* For master's, BFA or another degree and equivalent course work, portfolio, personal interview, reference letters, statement of intent (except for art history program). Additional exam requirements/recommendations for international students: required—TOEFL (minimum score 550 paper-based; 79 iBT), TWE (minimum score 5.5), Michigan English Language Assessment Battery (minimum score 85); recommended—IELTS (minimum score 6.5). Electronic applications accepted. *Expenses:* Contact institution.

Consumer Economics

Colorado State University, College of Health and Human Sciences, Department of Design and Merchandising, Fort Collins, CO 80523-1574. Offers apparel and merchandising (MS). *Program availability:* Part-time. *Faculty:* 8 full-time (7 women). *Students:* 8 full-time (6 women), 10 part-time (9 women), 2 international. Average age 30. 23 applicants, 52% accepted, 2 enrolled. In 2019, 8 master's awarded. *Degree requirements:* For master's, thesis or alternative. *Entrance requirements:* For master's, GRE is required for all international applicants and for domestic applicants with a cumulative undergraduate GPA under 3.5 or fewer than five years of relevant post-graduate professional experience, statement of purpose, resume, three letters of reference, portfolio (required for interior design applicants, optional for apparel design applicants). Additional exam requirements/recommendations for international students: required—TOEFL (minimum score 550 paper-based; 80 iBT), IELTS (minimum score 6.5), PTE (minimum score 58), GRE. *Application deadline:* For fall admission, 2/1 priority date for domestic and international students; for spring admission, 10/15 priority date for domestic and international students. Applications are processed on a rolling basis. Application fee: $60 ($70 for international students). Electronic applications accepted. *Expenses:* Tuition, state resident: full-time $10,520; part-time $5844 per credit hour. Tuition, nonresident: full-time $25,791; part-time $14,328 per credit hour. *International tuition:* $25,791 full-time. *Required fees:* $2512.80. Part-time tuition and fees vary according to course level, course load, degree level, program and student level. *Financial support:* In 2019–20, 11 students received support, including 2 fellowships with full tuition reimbursements available (averaging $1,250 per year), 2 research assistantships with full and partial tuition reimbursements available (averaging $11,408 per year), 8 teaching assistantships with full and partial tuition reimbursements available (averaging $11,408 per year); Federal Work-Study, scholarships/grants, health care benefits, and unspecified assistantships also available. Financial award application deadline: 2/1; financial award applicants required to submit FAFSA. *Unit head:* Dr. Karen H. Hyllegard, Professor and Department Head, 970-491-4627, Fax: 970-491-4855, E-mail: karen.hyllegard@colostate.edu. *Application contact:* Dr. Jennifer Paff Ogle, Professor and Graduate Coordinator, 970-491-3794, Fax: 970-491-4855, E-mail: jennifer.ogle@colostate.edu.
Website: http://www.dm.chhs.colostate.edu/

Cornell University, Graduate School, Graduate Fields of Human Ecology, Field of Policy Analysis and Management, Ithaca, NY 14853. Offers consumer policy (PhD); family and social welfare policy (PhD); health administration (MHA); health management and policy (PhD); public policy (PhD). *Degree requirements:* For master's, thesis; for doctorate, thesis/dissertation. *Entrance requirements:* For master's, GRE General Test or GMAT, 2 letters of recommendation; for doctorate, GRE General Test, 2 letters of recommendation. Additional exam requirements/recommendations for international students: required—TOEFL (minimum score 550 paper-based; 77 iBT). Electronic applications accepted.

Kansas State University, Graduate School, College of Human Ecology, Department of Food, Nutrition, Dietetics and Health, Manhattan, KS 66506. Offers dietetics (MS); human nutrition (PhD); nutrition, dietetics and sensory sciences (MS); nutritional sciences (PhD); public health nutrition (PhD); public health physical activity (PhD); sensory analysis and consumer behavior (PhD). *Program availability:* Part-time. *Degree requirements:* For master's, thesis or alternative, residency; for doctorate, thesis/dissertation, residency. *Entrance requirements:* For master's, GRE General Test, minimum undergraduate GPA of 3.0; for doctorate, GRE General Test, minimum graduate GPA of 3.0. Additional exam requirements/recommendations for international students: required—TOEFL (minimum score 550 paper-based; 79 iBT), IELTS (minimum score 6.5). Electronic applications accepted.

Kansas State University, Graduate School, College of Human Ecology, School of Family Studies and Human Services, Manhattan, KS 66506-1403. Offers applied family sciences (MS); communication sciences and disorders (MS); conflict resolution (Graduate Certificate); couple and family therapy (MS); early childhood education (MS); family and community service (MS); life-span human development (MS); personal financial planning (MS, PhD, Graduate Certificate); youth development (MS, Graduate Certificate). *Accreditation:* AAMFT/COAMFTE; ASHA. *Program availability:* Part-time, online learning. *Degree requirements:* For master's, comprehensive exam (for some programs), thesis optional. *Entrance requirements:* For master's, GRE, minimum GPA of 3.0 in last 2 years (60 semester hours) of undergraduate study; for doctorate, GRE. Additional exam requirements/recommendations for international students: required—TOEFL (minimum score 600 paper-based). Electronic applications accepted.

North Dakota State University, College of Graduate and Interdisciplinary Studies, College of Human Development and Education, Department of Human Development and Family Science, Program in Family Financial Planning, Fargo, ND 58102. Offers MS, Certificate. Electronic applications accepted. Tuition and fees vary according to program and reciprocity agreements.

Ohio University, Graduate College, College of Health Sciences and Professions, School of Applied Health Sciences and Wellness, Program in Food and Nutrition, Athens, OH 45701-2979. Offers human and consumer sciences (MS).

Oklahoma State University, College of Human Sciences, Department of Human Development and Family Science, Stillwater, OK 74078. Offers human development and family science (MS, PhD), including family financial planning (MS), human environmental sciences (PhD). *Accreditation:* AAMFT/COAMFTE (one or more programs are accredited). *Program availability:* Online learning. *Faculty:* 27 full-time (16 women), 4 part-time/adjunct (3 women). *Students:* 36 full-time (30 women), 42 part-time (37 women); includes 17 minority (9 Black or African American, non-Hispanic/Latino; 1 Asian, non-Hispanic/Latino; 3 Hispanic/Latino; 1 Native Hawaiian or other Pacific Islander, non-Hispanic/Latino; 3 Two or more races, non-Hispanic/Latino), 4 international. Average age 30. 54 applicants, 57% accepted, 22 enrolled. In 2019, 28 master's, 6 doctorates awarded. *Entrance requirements:* For master's and doctorate, GRE or GMAT. Additional exam requirements/recommendations for international students: required—TOEFL (minimum score 550 paper-based; 79 iBT). *Application deadline:* For fall admission, 3/1 priority date for international students; for spring admission, 8/1 priority date for international students. Applications are processed on a rolling basis. Application fee: $50 ($75 for international students). Electronic applications accepted. *Expenses: Tuition, area resident:* Full-time $4148.10; part-time $2765.40 per credit hour. Tuition, state resident: full-time $4148.10; part-time $2765.40 per credit hour. Tuition, nonresident: full-time $15,775; part-time $10,516.80 per credit hour. *International tuition:* $15,775.20 full-time. *Required fees:* $2196.90; $122.05 per credit hour. Tuition and fees vary according to course load, campus/location and program. *Financial support:* In 2019–20, 25 research assistantships (averaging $1,431 per year), 20 teaching assistantships (averaging $1,314 per year) were awarded; career-related internships or fieldwork, Federal Work-Study, scholarships/grants, health care benefits,

tuition waivers (partial), and unspecified assistantships also available. Support available to part-time students. Financial award application deadline: 3/1; financial award applicants required to submit FAFSA. *Unit head:* Dr. Sissy Osteen, Department Head, 405-744-4741, Fax: 405-744-6344, E-mail: sissy.osteen@okstate.edu. *Application contact:* Dr. Sheryl Tucker, Vice Prov/Dean/Prof, 405-744-6368, E-mail: gradi@okstate.edu.
Website: https://education.okstate.edu/departments-programs/human-development-family-science/index.html

Purdue University, Graduate School, College of Health and Human Sciences, Department of Consumer Sciences and Retailing, West Lafayette, IN 47907. Offers MS, PhD. *Program availability:* Part-time. *Faculty:* 5 full-time (0 women). *Students:* 9 full-time (2 women), 6 part-time (2 women); includes 3 minority (1 Black or African American, non-Hispanic/Latino; 1 Asian, non-Hispanic/Latino; 1 Hispanic/Latino), 8 international. Average age 32. 16 applicants, 13% accepted. In 2019, 2 master's awarded. *Degree requirements:* For master's, thesis, oral presentation, final examination; for doctorate, comprehensive exam, thesis/dissertation, oral presentation, final examination. *Entrance requirements:* For master's, GMAT or GRE General Test (minimum 50th percentile), minimum undergraduate GPA of 3.0 or equivalent; for doctorate, GMAT or GRE General Test (minimum 50th percentile), minimum undergraduate GPA of 3.0 or equivalent; master's degree with minimum GPA of 3.25 or equivalent. Additional exam requirements/recommendations for international students: required—TOEFL (minimum score 550 paper-based; 77 iBT). *Application deadline:* For fall admission, 2/15 priority date for domestic students, 2/15 for international students. Applications are processed on a rolling basis. Application fee: $60 ($75 for international students). Electronic applications accepted. *Financial support:* Fellowships, research assistantships with tuition reimbursements, teaching assistantships with tuition reimbursements, and career-related internships or fieldwork available. Support available to part-time students. Financial award applicants required to submit FAFSA. *Unit head:* Susan Hambrusch, Head of the Graduate Program, 765-494-6003, E-mail: seh@cs.purdue.edu. *Application contact:* Graduate School Admissions, 765-494-2600, Fax: 765-494-0136, E-mail: gradinfo@purdue.edu.
Website: http://www.purdue.edu/hhs/csr/

South Dakota State University, Graduate School, College of Education and Human Sciences, Department of Consumer Sciences, Brookings, SD 57007. Offers family financial planning (MS); merchandising (MS). *Entrance requirements:* For master's, resume. Additional exam requirements/recommendations for international students: required—TOEFL (minimum score 525 paper-based).

State University of New York at Oswego, Graduate Studies, School of Education, Department of Vocational Teacher Preparation, Oswego, NY 13126. Offers agriculture (MS Ed); business and marketing (MS Ed); family and consumer sciences (MS Ed); health careers (MS Ed); technical education (MS Ed); trade education (MS Ed). *Accreditation:* NCATE. *Program availability:* Part-time, evening/weekend. *Students:* 77. In 2019, 8 master's awarded. *Degree requirements:* For master's, comprehensive exam, thesis or alternative. *Entrance requirements:* Additional exam requirements/recommendations for international students: required—TOEFL (minimum score 560 paper-based). *Application deadline:* For fall admission, 4/1 for domestic students; for spring admission, 10/1 for domestic students. Applications are processed on a rolling basis. Application fee: $65. Electronic applications accepted. *Financial support:* Fellowships with full tuition reimbursements, teaching assistantships with partial tuition reimbursements, career-related internships or fieldwork, Federal Work-Study, institutionally sponsored loans, health care benefits, and unspecified assistantships available. Support available to part-time students. Financial award application deadline: 4/1; financial award applicants required to submit FAFSA. *Unit head:* Dr. Benjamin Ogwo, Chair, 315-312-2480, E-mail: benjamin.ogwo@oswego.edu. *Application contact:* Dr. Benjamin Ogwo, Chair, 315-312-2480, E-mail: benjamin.ogwo@oswego.edu.

Texas Tech University, Graduate School, College of Human Sciences, Department of Personal Financial Planning, Lubbock, TX 79409-1210. Offers MS, PhD, JD/MS. *Program availability:* Part-time, blended/hybrid learning. *Faculty:* 12 full-time (6 women), 9 part-time/adjunct (4 women). *Students:* 92 full-time (35 women), 81 part-time (36 women); includes 58 minority (10 Black or African American, non-Hispanic/Latino; 10 Asian, non-Hispanic/Latino; 27 Hispanic/Latino; 11 Two or more races, non-Hispanic/Latino), 24 international. Average age 31. 88 applicants, 70% accepted, 50 enrolled. In 2019, 63 master's, 6 doctorates awarded. Terminal master's awarded for partial completion of doctoral program. *Degree requirements:* For master's, thesis or alternative; for doctorate, comprehensive exam, thesis/dissertation. *Entrance requirements:* For doctorate, GRE, GMAT, or LSAT. Additional exam requirements/recommendations for international students: required—TOEFL (minimum score 550 paper-based; 79 iBT). *Application deadline:* For fall admission, 6/1 priority date for domestic students, 1/15 priority date for international students; for spring admission, 9/1 priority date for domestic students, 6/15 priority date for international students. Applications are processed on a rolling basis. Application fee: $65. Electronic applications accepted. *Expenses:* Contact institution. *Financial support:* In 2019–20, 87 students received support, including 83 fellowships (averaging $3,917 per year), 8 research assistantships (averaging $14,401 per year), 30 teaching assistantships (averaging $17,110 per year); Federal Work-Study, scholarships/grants, health care benefits, and unspecified assistantships also available. Financial award application deadline: 1/15; financial award applicants required to submit FAFSA. *Unit head:* Dr. Vickie Hampton, Department Chairperson, 806-834-1824, E-mail: vickie.hampton@ttu.edu. *Application contact:* Dr. John Gilliam, MS Program Director, 806-834-8864, E-mail: john.gilliam@ttu.edu.
Website: www.pfp.ttu.edu

The University of Alabama, Graduate School, College of Human Environmental Sciences, Department of Consumer Sciences, Tuscaloosa, AL 35487-0158. Offers MS. *Program availability:* Part-time, evening/weekend, online learning. *Faculty:* 10 full-time (6 women), 2 part-time/adjunct (both women). *Students:* 16 full-time (10 women), 50 part-time (19 women); includes 12 minority (8 Black or African American, non-Hispanic/Latino; 1 Hispanic/Latino; 1 Native Hawaiian or other Pacific Islander, non-Hispanic/Latino; 2 Two or more races, non-Hispanic/Latino), 1 international. Average age 34. 29 applicants, 86% accepted, 25 enrolled. In 2019, 32 master's awarded. *Degree requirements:* For master's, thesis (for some programs), alternate accepted requirement - capstone. *Entrance requirements:* For master's, GRE or GMAT, minimum GPA of 3.0. Additional exam requirements/recommendations for international students: required—TOEFL. *Application deadline:* For fall admission, 7/1 priority date for domestic and international students; for winter admission, 1/1 priority date for domestic and international students. Applications are processed on a rolling basis. Application fee: $50 ($60 for international students). Electronic applications accepted. *Expenses: Tuition, area resident:* Full-time $10,780; part-time $440 per credit hour. Tuition, nonresident: full-time $30,250; part-time $1550 per credit hour. *Financial support:* In 2019–20, 4 students received support. Research assistantships with full tuition reimbursements available and teaching assistantships with full tuition reimbursements available available. Financial award application deadline: 1/15. *Unit head:* Dr. Robert Bryan Nielsen, Professor and Department Head, 205-348-6059, Fax: 205-348-3789, E-mail: rbnielsen@ches.ua.edu. *Application contact:* Amber Massey, Program Assistant, 205-348-6178, Fax: 205-348-3789, E-mail: amassey@ches.ua.edu. Website: http://www.csm.ches.ua.edu/

University of Guelph, Office of Graduate and Postdoctoral Studies, College of Management and Economics, Department of Marketing and Consumer Studies, Guelph, ON N1G 2W1, Canada. Offers M Sc. *Degree requirements:* For master's, thesis. *Entrance requirements:* For master's, GMAT or GRE General Test, minimum B average during previous 2 years of course work. Additional exam requirements/recommendations for international students: required—TOEFL (minimum score 575 paper-based). Electronic applications accepted.

University of Idaho, College of Graduate Studies, College of Agricultural and Life Sciences, Margaret Ritchie School of Family and Consumer Sciences, Moscow, ID 83844-3183. Offers MS. *Students:* 9. Average age 33. In 2019, 6 master's awarded. *Entrance requirements:* For master's, minimum GPA of 3.0. Additional exam requirements/recommendations for international students: required—TOEFL (minimum score 79 iBT). *Application deadline:* For fall admission, 7/30 for domestic students; for spring admission, 12/1 for domestic students. Application fee: $60. *Expenses:* Tuition, state resident: full-time $7753.80; part-time $502 per credit hour. Tuition, nonresident: full-time $26,990; part-time $1571 per credit hour. *Required fees:* $2122.20; $47 per credit hour. *Financial support:* Research assistantships and teaching assistantships available. *Unit head:* Dr. Michelle McGuire, Director, 208-885-6546, E-mail: famcon@uidaho.edu. *Application contact:* Dr. Michelle McGuire, Director, 208-885-6546, E-mail: famcon@uidaho.edu. Website: https://www.uidaho.edu/cals/family-and-consumer-sciences

University of Illinois at Urbana-Champaign, Graduate College, College of Agricultural, Consumer and Environmental Sciences, Department of Agricultural and Consumer Economics, Champaign, IL 61820. Offers agricultural and applied economics (MS, PhD).

University of Missouri, Office of Research and Graduate Studies, College of Human Environmental Sciences, Department of Personal Financial Planning, Columbia, MO 65211. Offers PhD. *Entrance requirements:* Additional exam requirements/recommendations for international students: required—TOEFL. Electronic applications accepted.

University of Nebraska–Lincoln, Graduate College, College of Education and Human Sciences, Department of Child, Youth and Family Studies, Lincoln, NE 68588. Offers child development/early childhood education (MS, PhD); child, youth and family studies (MS); family and consumer sciences education (MS, PhD); family financial planning (MS); family science (MS, PhD); gerontology (PhD); human sciences (PhD), including child, youth and family studies, gerontology, medical family therapy; marriage and family therapy (MS); medical family therapy (PhD); youth development (MS). *Accreditation:* AAMFT/COAMFTE (one or more programs are accredited). *Program availability:* Online learning. *Degree requirements:* For master's, thesis optional. *Entrance requirements:* For master's, GRE. Additional exam requirements/recommendations for international students: required—TOEFL (minimum score 550 paper-based). Electronic applications accepted.

University of South Carolina, The Graduate School, College of Hospitality, Retail, and Sport Management, Department of Retailing, Columbia, SC 29208. Offers MR. *Program availability:* Part-time. *Degree requirements:* For master's, comprehensive exam, internship or thesis. *Entrance requirements:* For master's, GMAT or GRE General Test, minimum GPA of 3.0. Additional exam requirements/recommendations for international students: required—TOEFL (minimum score 80 iBT). Electronic applications accepted.

The University of Tennessee, Graduate School, College of Education, Health and Human Sciences, Department of Consumer and Industry Services Management, Program in Consumer Services Management, Knoxville, TN 37996. Offers retail and consumer sciences (MS); textile science (MS). *Program availability:* Part-time. *Degree requirements:* For master's, thesis or alternative. *Entrance requirements:* For master's, GRE General Test, minimum GPA of 2.7. Additional exam requirements/recommendations for international students: required—TOEFL. Electronic applications accepted.

The University of Tennessee, Graduate School, College of Education, Health and Human Sciences, Program in Human Ecology, Knoxville, TN 37996. Offers child and family studies (PhD); community health (PhD); nutrition science (PhD); retailing and consumer sciences (PhD); textile science (PhD). *Degree requirements:* For doctorate, thesis/dissertation. *Entrance requirements:* For doctorate, GRE General Test, minimum GPA of 2.7. Additional exam requirements/recommendations for international students: required—TOEFL. Electronic applications accepted.

University of Wisconsin–Madison, Graduate School, School of Human Ecology, Program in Consumer Behavior and Family Economics, Madison, WI 53706-1380. Offers MS, PhD. Terminal master's awarded for partial completion of doctoral program. *Degree requirements:* For master's, thesis optional; for doctorate, comprehensive exam, thesis/dissertation. *Entrance requirements:* For master's and doctorate, GRE General Test, 3 letters of recommendation. Additional exam requirements/recommendations for international students: required—TOEFL (minimum score 580 paper-based; 92 iBT). Electronic applications accepted.

University of Wyoming, College of Agriculture and Natural Resources, Department of Family and Consumer Sciences, Laramie, WY 82071. Offers early childhood development (MS); family and consumer sciences (MS); food science and human nutrition (MS). *Program availability:* Part-time. *Degree requirements:* For master's, thesis, project. *Entrance requirements:* For master's, GRE General Test or MCAT, minimum GPA of 3.0. Additional exam requirements/recommendations for international students: required—TOEFL (minimum score 540 paper-based; 76 iBT). Electronic applications accepted.

Université Laval, Faculty of Agricultural and Food Sciences, Department of Agricultural Economics and Consumer Sciences, Program in Consumer Sciences, Québec, QC G1K 7P4, Canada. Offers Diploma. *Program availability:* Part-time. *Entrance requirements:* For degree, knowledge of French and English. Electronic applications accepted.

Utah State University, School of Graduate Studies, College of Agriculture and Applied Sciences, School of Applied Sciences, Technology and Education, Logan, UT 84322. Offers agricultural extension and education (MS); family and consumer sciences education and extension (MS); technology and engineering education (MS). *Program availability:* Part-time, online learning. *Degree requirements:* For master's, comprehensive exam (for some programs), thesis (for some programs). *Entrance requirements:* For master's, GRE General Test, MAT, BS in agricultural education, agricultural extension, or related agricultural or science discipline; minimum GPA of 3.0. Additional exam requirements/recommendations for international students: required—TOEFL.

Gerontology

Alliant International University - Los Angeles, California School of Professional Psychology, Program in Couple and Family Therapy, Alhambra, CA 91803. Offers chemical dependency (MA); gerontology (MA); Latin American family therapy (MA). *Accreditation:* AAMFT/COAMFTE. *Program availability:* Part-time, evening/weekend. Terminal master's awarded for partial completion of doctoral program. *Degree requirements:* For master's, comprehensive exam, 50 hours of professional development activities. *Entrance requirements:* Additional exam requirements/recommendations for international students: required—TOEFL (minimum score 550 paper-based). Electronic applications accepted.

Arizona State University at Tempe, College of Public Programs, School of Social Work, Phoenix, AZ 85004-0689. Offers advanced direct practice (MSW); assessment of integrative health modalities (Graduate Certificate); gerontology (Graduate Certificate); Latino cultural competency (Graduate Certificate); planning, administration and community practice (MSW); social work (PhD); trauma and bereavement (Graduate Certificate); MPA/MSW. *Accreditation:* CSWE (one or more programs are accredited). *Program availability:* Part-time. Terminal master's awarded for partial completion of doctoral program. *Degree requirements:* For master's, thesis or alternative, capstone project, interactive Program of Study (iPOS) submitted before completing 50 percent of required credit hours; for doctorate, comprehensive exam, thesis/dissertation, interactive Program of Study (iPOS) submitted before completing 50 percent of required credit hours. *Entrance requirements:* For master's, GRE or MAT, minimum GPA of 3.2 or equivalent in last 2 years of work leading to bachelor's degree; for doctorate, GRE, minimum GPA of 3.0 or equivalent in last 2 years of work leading to bachelor's degree, 3 letters of recommendation, resume, samples of professional writing, personal statement. Additional exam requirements/recommendations for international students: required—TOEFL, IELTS, or PTE. Electronic applications accepted. *Expenses:* Contact institution.

Arkansas State University, Graduate School, College of Nursing and Health Professions, School of Nursing, State University, AR 72467. Offers aging studies (Graduate Certificate); health care management (Graduate Certificate); health sciences (MS); health sciences education (Graduate Certificate); nurse anesthesia (MSN); nursing (MSN); nursing practice (DNP). *Accreditation:* AANA/CANAEP (one or more programs are accredited); ACEN. *Program availability:* Part-time. *Degree requirements:* For master's and Graduate Certificate, comprehensive exam, thesis or alternative; for doctorate, comprehensive exam, thesis/dissertation. *Entrance requirements:* For master's, GRE General Test or MAT, appropriate bachelor's degree, current Arkansas nursing license, CPR certification, physical examination, professional liability insurance, critical care experience, ACLS Certification, PALS Certification, interview, immunization records, personal goal statement, health assessment; for doctorate, GRE or MAT, NCLEX-RN Exam, appropriate master's degree, current Arkansas nursing license, CPR certification, physical examination, professional liability insurance, critical care experience, ACLS Certification, PALS Certification, interview, immunization records, personal goal statement, health assessment, TB skin test, background check; for Graduate Certificate, GRE or MAT, appropriate bachelor's degree, official transcripts, immunization records, proof of employment in healthcare, TB Skin Test, TB Mask Fit Test, CPR Certification. Additional exam requirements/recommendations for international students: required—TOEFL (minimum score 550 paper-based; 79 iBT), IELTS (minimum score 6), PTE (minimum score 56). Electronic applications accepted. *Expenses:* Contact institution.

California State University, Fullerton, Graduate Studies, College of Health and Human Development, Department of Public Health, Fullerton, CA 92831-3599. Offers environmental and occupational health and safety (MPH); gerontological health (MPH); health promotion and disease (MPH). *Accreditation:* CEPH. *Program availability:* Part-time. *Entrance requirements:* For master's, minimum GPA of 3.0 in last 60 units attempted.

California State University, Fullerton, Graduate Studies, College of Humanities and Social Sciences, Program in Gerontology, Fullerton, CA 92831-3599. Offers MS. *Program availability:* Part-time.

California State University, Long Beach, Graduate Studies, College of Health and Human Services, Program in Gerontology, Long Beach, CA 90840. Offers MS. *Program availability:* Part-time. *Degree requirements:* For master's, thesis optional. Electronic applications accepted.

Capella University, School of Public Service Leadership, Master's Programs in Healthcare, Minneapolis, MN 55402. Offers criminal justice (MS); emergency management (MS); general public health (MPH); gerontology (MS); health administration (MHA); health care operations (MHA); health management policy (MPH); health policy (MHA); homeland security (MS); multidisciplinary human services (MS); public administration (MPA); public safety leadership (MS); social and community services (MS); social behavioral sciences (MPH); MS/MPA.

Central Michigan University, College of Graduate Studies, College of Education and Human Services, Department of Human Environmental Studies, Mount Pleasant, MI 48859. Offers apparel product development and merchandising technology (MS); gerontology (Graduate Certificate); human development and family studies (MA); nutrition and dietetics (MS). *Program availability:* Part-time, evening/weekend. *Degree requirements:* For master's, thesis or alternative. Electronic applications accepted. *Expenses: Tuition,* area resident: Full-time $12,267; part-time $8178 per year. Tuition, state resident: full-time $12,267; part-time $8178 per year. Tuition, nonresident: full-time $12,267; part-time $8178 per year. *International tuition:* $16,110 full-time. *Required fees:* $225 per semester. Tuition and fees vary according to degree level and program.

Gerontology

Concordia University Chicago, College of Graduate Studies, Program in Gerontology, River Forest, IL 60305-1499. Offers MA. *Program availability:* Part-time, evening/weekend, 100% online. *Degree requirements:* For master's, comprehensive exam, thesis. *Entrance requirements:* For master's, minimum GPA of 2.9. Additional exam requirements/recommendations for international students: required—TOEFL (minimum score 550 paper-based). Electronic applications accepted.

DeSales University, Division of Healthcare, Center Valley, PA 18034-9568. Offers adult-gerontology acute care (Post Master's Certificate); adult-gerontology acute care nurse practitioner (MSN); adult-gerontology acute certified nurse practitioner (Post Master's Certificate); adult-gerontology clinical nurse specialist (MSN, Post Master's Certificate); clinical leadership (DNP); family nurse practitioner (MSN, Post Master's Certificate); general nursing practice (DNP); nurse anesthetist (MSN); nurse educator (Post Master's Certificate, Postbaccalaureate Certificate); nurse midwife (MSN); nurse practitioner (MSN); psychiatric-mental health nurse practitioner (MSN, Post Master's Certificate); DNP/MBA. *Accreditation:* ACEN. *Program availability:* Part-time. *Faculty:* 31 full-time (23 women), 12 part-time/adjunct (9 women). *Students:* 294 full-time (219 women), 128 part-time (109 women); includes 71 minority (20 Black or African American, non-Hispanic/Latino; 1 American Indian or Alaska Native, non-Hispanic/Latino; 15 Asian, non-Hispanic/Latino; 30 Hispanic/Latino; 5 Two or more races, non-Hispanic/Latino). Average age 28. 2,666 applicants, 6% accepted, 142 enrolled. In 2019, 115 master's, 30 doctorates awarded. *Degree requirements:* For master's, minimum GPA of 3.0, portfolio; for doctorate, minimum GPA of 3.0, scholarly capstone project. *Entrance requirements:* For master's, GRE or MAT (waived if applicant has an undergraduate GPA of 3.0 or higher), BSN from ACEN- or CCNE-accredited program, minimum undergraduate GPA of 3.0, active RN license or eligibility, two letters of recommendation, essay, health care experience, personal interview; for doctorate, BSN or MSN from ACEN- or CCNE-accredited institution, minimum GPA of 3.3 in graduate program, current licensure as an RN. Additional exam requirements/recommendations for international students: required—TOEFL (minimum score 104 iBT). *Application deadline:* Applications are processed on a rolling basis. Application fee: $50. Electronic applications accepted. *Expenses:* Contact institution. *Financial support:* Applicants required to submit FAFSA. *Unit head:* Ronald Nordone, Dean of Graduate Education, 610-282-1100 Ext. 1289, E-mail: ronald.nordone@desales.edu. *Application contact:* Julia Ferraro, Director of Graduate Admissions, 610-282-1100 Ext. 1768, E-mail: gradadmissions@desales.edu.

Duke University, School of Nursing, Durham, NC 27708. Offers acute care pediatric nurse practitioner (MSN, Post-Graduate Certificate); adult-gerontology nurse practitioner (MSN, Post-Graduate Certificate), including acute care, primary care; family nurse practitioner (MSN, Post-Graduate Certificate); neonatal nurse practitioner (MSN, Post-Graduate Certificate); nurse anesthesia (DNP); nurse practitioner (DNP); nursing (PhD); nursing and health care leadership (MSN, Post-Graduate Certificate); nursing education (MSN, Post-Graduate Certificate); nursing informatics (MSN, Post-Graduate Certificate); pediatric nurse practitioner (MSN, Post-Graduate Certificate), including primary care; psychiatric mental health nurse practitioner (MSN, Post-Graduate Certificate); women's health nurse practitioner (MSN, Post-Graduate Certificate). *Accreditation:* AACN; AANA; CANAEP. *Program availability:* Part-time, evening/weekend, online with on-campus intensives. *Faculty:* 48 full-time (40 women), 32 part-time/adjunct (28 women). *Students:* 666 full-time (601 women), 157 part-time (139 women); includes 193 minority (61 Black or African American, non-Hispanic/Latino; 4 American Indian or Alaska Native, non-Hispanic/Latino; 57 Asian, non-Hispanic/Latino; 49 Hispanic/Latino; 1 Native Hawaiian or other Pacific Islander, non-Hispanic/Latino; 21 Two or more races, non-Hispanic/Latino), 8 international. Average age 34. 761 applicants, 33% accepted, 149 enrolled. In 2019, 213 master's, 74 doctorates, 18 other advanced degrees awarded. Terminal master's awarded for partial completion of doctoral program. *Degree requirements:* For master's, thesis optional; for doctorate, capstone project. *Entrance requirements:* For master's, MSN applicants are no longer required to take the GRE, 1 year of nursing experience (recommended), BSN, minimum GPA of 3.0, previous course work in statistics; for doctorate, GRE is required for the DNP in Nurse Anesthesia, BSN or MSN, minimum GPA of 3.0, resume, personal statement, graduate statistics and research methods course, current licensure as a registered nurse, transcripts from all post-secondary institutions; for Post-Graduate Certificate, MSN, licensure or eligibility as a professional nurse, transcripts from all post-secondary institutions, previous course work in statistics. Additional exam requirements/recommendations for international students: required—TOEFL (minimum score 100 iBT), IELTS (minimum score 7). *Application deadline:* For fall admission, 12/1 for domestic and international students; for spring admission, 5/1 for domestic and international students. Application fee: $50. Electronic applications accepted. *Expenses:* Contact institution. *Financial support:* Institutionally sponsored loans, scholarships/grants, and traineeships available. Support available to part-time students. Financial award applicants required to submit FAFSA. *Unit head:* Dr. Marion E. Broome, Dean/Vice Chancellor for Nursing Affairs/Associate Vice President for Academic Affairs for Nursing, 919-684-9446, Fax: 919-684-9414, E-mail: marion.broome@duke.edu. *Application contact:* Dr. Ernie Rushing, Director of Admissions and Recruitment, 919-668-6274, Fax: 919-668-4693, E-mail: ernie.rushing@dm.duke.edu.
Website: http://www.nursing.duke.edu/

East Carolina University, Graduate School, College of Health and Human Performance, School of Social Work, Greenville, NC 27858-4353. Offers gerontology (Certificate); social work (MSW); substance abuse (Certificate). *Accreditation:* CSWE. *Program availability:* Online learning. *Application deadline:* For fall admission, 2/1 priority date for domestic and international students. *Expenses:* Tuition, area resident: Full-time $4749; part-time $185 per credit hour. Tuition, state resident: full-time $4749; part-time $185 per credit hour. Tuition, nonresident: full-time $17,898; part-time $864 per credit hour. International tuition: $17,898 full-time. *Required fees:* $2787. *Financial support:* Application deadline: 6/1. *Unit head:* Dr. Joseph Lee, Director, 252-328-4661, E-mail: leejose14@ecu.edu. *Application contact:* Graduate School Admissions, 252-328-6012, Fax: 252-328-6071, E-mail: gradschool@ecu.edu.
Website: https://hhp.ecu.edu/socw/

Eastern Illinois University, Graduate School, College of Health and Human Services, Program in Aging Studies, Charleston, IL 61920. Offers aging studies (MA). *Program availability:* Part-time, evening/weekend, online learning. *Degree requirements:* For master's, comprehensive exam (for some programs), thesis (for some programs). *Entrance requirements:* For master's, GMAT or GRE. Additional exam requirements/recommendations for international students: required—TOEFL (minimum score 500 paper-based; 61 iBT), IELTS (minimum score 6). Electronic applications accepted.

Eastern Michigan University, Graduate School, College of Health and Human Services, School of Health Sciences, Programs in Gerontology and Dementia, Ypsilanti, MI 48197. Offers dementia (Graduate Certificate); gerontology (Graduate Certificate). *Students:* 1 (woman) part-time. Average age 27. 1 applicant, 100% accepted. In 2019, 4 Graduate Certificates awarded. Application fee: $45. *Application contact:* Dr. Cassandra Barragan, Director, Aging Studies Program, 734-487-5823, Fax: 734-487-4095, E-mail: cbarrag1@emich.edu.

East Tennessee State University, College of Graduate and Continuing Studies, College of Public Health, Program in Public Health, Johnson City, TN 37614. Offers biostatistics (MPH, Postbaccalaureate Certificate); community health (MPH, DPH); environmental health (MPH); epidemiology (MPH, DPH, Postbaccalaureate Certificate); gerontology (Postbaccalaureate Certificate); global health (Postbaccalaureate Certificate); health care management (Postbaccalaureate Certificate); health management and policy (DPH); public health (Postbaccalaureate Certificate); public health services administration (MPH); rural health (Postbaccalaureate Certificate). *Accreditation:* CEPH. *Program availability:* Part-time, online learning. *Degree requirements:* For master's, comprehensive exam, field experience; for doctorate, thesis/dissertation, practicum. *Entrance requirements:* For master's, GRE General Test, minimum GPA of 2.75, SOPHAS application, three letters of recommendation; for doctorate, GRE General Test, SOPHAS application, three letters of recommendation; for Postbaccalaureate Certificate, minimum GPA of 2.5, three letters of recommendation, resume. Additional exam requirements/recommendations for international students: required—TOEFL (minimum score 550 paper-based; 79 iBT), IELTS (minimum score 6.5). Electronic applications accepted.

Georgia State University, College of Arts and Sciences, Gerontology Institute, Atlanta, GA 30302-3083. Offers MA, Certificate. *Program availability:* Part-time. *Faculty:* 4 full-time (all women), 1 (woman) part-time/adjunct. *Students:* 22 full-time (19 women), 14 part-time (10 women); includes 17 minority (14 Black or African American, non-Hispanic/Latino; 2 Asian, non-Hispanic/Latino; 1 Hispanic/Latino), 7 international. Average age 42. 20 applicants, 85% accepted, 14 enrolled. In 2019, 15 master's, 2 other advanced degrees awarded. *Entrance requirements:* For master's, GRE. Additional exam requirements/recommendations for international students: required—TOEFL. *Application deadline:* For fall admission, 4/15 for domestic and international students; for spring admission, 10/15 for domestic and international students. Applications are processed on a rolling basis. Application fee: $50. Electronic applications accepted. *Expenses:* Tuition, area resident: Full-time $7164; part-time $398 per credit hour. Tuition, state resident: full-time $7164; part-time $398 per credit hour. Tuition, nonresident: full-time $22,662; part-time $1259 per credit hour. International tuition: $22,662 full-time. *Required fees:* $2128; $312 per credit hour. Tuition and fees vary according to course load and program. *Financial support:* In 2019–20, research assistantships with full tuition reimbursements (averaging $6,000 per year) were awarded; career-related internships or fieldwork, scholarships/grants, and unspecified assistantships also available. Financial award application deadline: 4/15; financial award applicants required to submit FAFSA. *Unit head:* Dr. Elizabeth O. Burgess, Director, 404-413-5210, Fax: 404-413-5219, E-mail: eburgess@gsu.edu. *Application contact:* Dr. Candace L. Kemp, Director of Graduate Studies, 404-413-5210, Fax: 404-413-5219, E-mail: ckemp@gsu.edu.
Website: http://gerontology.gsu.edu/students/graduate/

Kansas State University, Graduate School, College of Human Ecology, Center on Aging, Manhattan, KS 66506. Offers gerontology (MS, Graduate Certificate). *Program availability:* Part-time, online learning. *Degree requirements:* For master's, comprehensive exam. *Entrance requirements:* For master's, bachelor's degree with minimum GPA of 3.0 from college or university accredited by the cognizant regional accrediting agency. Electronic applications accepted. *Expenses:* Contact institution.

Kent State University, College of Arts and Sciences, Department of Psychological Sciences, Kent, OH 44242-0001. Offers clinical psychology (MA, PhD), including gerontology (MA), psychological sciences (MA); experimental psychology (MA, PhD), including gerontology (MA), psychological sciences (MA). *Accreditation:* APA (one or more programs are accredited). *Faculty:* 28 full-time (15 women), 4 part-time/adjunct (2 women). *Students:* 79 full-time (.63 women); includes 17 minority (6 Black or African American, non-Hispanic/Latino; 5 Asian, non-Hispanic/Latino; 4 Hispanic/Latino; 2 Two or more races, non-Hispanic/Latino), 3 international. Average age 26. 284 applicants, 8% accepted, 16 enrolled. In 2019, 13 master's, 9 doctorates awarded. *Degree requirements:* For master's, thesis, Min grade in Quantitative Statistical Analysis I and II is B-. College of Arts & Sciences requires students to have a 3.0 average from all graduate courses attempted; for doctorate, comprehensive exam, thesis/dissertation. *Entrance requirements:* For master's, GRE General Test, statement of goals and motivations, transcripts, 3 letters of recommendation, minimum junior-senior GPA of 3.0, 18 semester hours of credit in psychology which includes at least one course in statistics and a broad background in psychology; for doctorate, GRE General Test, statement of goals and motivations, transcripts, 3 letters of recommendation, minimum junior-senior GPA of 3.0, 18 semester hours of credit in psychology which includes at least one course in statistics and a broad background in psychology. Additional exam requirements/recommendations for international students: required—TOEFL (minimum score 94 iBT), IELTS (minimum score 7), PTE (minimum score 65), Michigan English Language Assessment Battery (minimum score 82. *Application deadline:* For fall admission, 12/1 for domestic and international students. Applications are processed on a rolling basis. Application fee: $45 ($70 for international students). Electronic applications accepted. *Financial support:* Federal Work-Study, health care benefits, and unspecified assistantships available. Financial award application deadline: 12/1; financial award applicants required to submit FAFSA. *Unit head:* Dr. Maria S. Zaragoza, Professor, Department Chair, 330-672-2166, E-mail: mzaragoz@kent.edu. *Application contact:* Dr. John A. Updegraff, Professor and Graduate Coordinator, 330-672-2166, E-mail: jupdegr1@kent.edu.
Website: https://www.kent.edu/psychology

Lakehead University, Graduate Studies, Faculty of Education, Thunder Bay, ON P7B 5E1, Canada. Offers educational studies (PhD); gerontology (M Ed); women's studies (M Ed). *Program availability:* Part-time, evening/weekend. *Degree requirements:* For master's, project or thesis. *Entrance requirements:* For master's, minimum B average. Additional exam requirements/recommendations for international students: required—TOEFL.

Lakehead University, Graduate Studies, Faculty of Social Sciences and Humanities, Department of History, Thunder Bay, ON P7B 5E1, Canada. Offers gerontology (MA); history (MA); women's studies (MA). *Program availability:* Part-time. *Degree requirements:* For master's, one foreign language, thesis. *Entrance requirements:* For master's, minimum B average. Additional exam requirements/recommendations for international students: required—TOEFL.

Lakehead University, Graduate Studies, Faculty of Social Sciences and Humanities, Department of Sociology, Thunder Bay, ON P7B 5E1, Canada. Offers gerontology (MA); health services and policy research (MA); sociology (MA); women's studies (MA). *Program availability:* Part-time, evening/weekend. *Degree requirements:* For master's, research project or thesis. *Entrance requirements:* For master's, minimum B average. Additional exam requirements/recommendations for international students: required—TOEFL.

Lakehead University, Graduate Studies, Gerontology Collaborative Program-Northern Educational Center for Aging and Health, Thunder Bay, ON P7B 5E1, Canada. Offers gerontology (M Ed, M Sc, MA, MSW). *Program availability:* Part-time. *Degree requirements:* For master's, thesis (for some programs). *Entrance requirements:* Additional exam requirements/recommendations for international students: required—TOEFL.

Lakehead University, Graduate Studies, School of Kinesiology, Thunder Bay, ON P7B 5E1, Canada. Offers kinesiology (M Sc); kinesiology and gerontology (M Sc). *Program availability:* Part-time. *Degree requirements:* For master's, thesis. *Entrance requirements:* For master's, minimum B average. Additional exam requirements/recommendations for international students: required—TOEFL.

Lakehead University, Graduate Studies, School of Social Work, Thunder Bay, ON P7B 5E1, Canada. Offers gerontology (MSW); social work (MSW); women's studies (MSW). *Program availability:* Part-time. *Degree requirements:* For master's, thesis or project. *Entrance requirements:* For master's, minimum B average. Additional exam requirements/recommendations for international students: required—TOEFL.

La Salle University, School of Nursing and Health Sciences, Program in Nursing, Philadelphia, PA 19141-1199. Offers adult gerontology primary care nurse practitioner (MSN, Certificate); adult health and illness clinical nurse specialist (MSN); adult-gerontology clinical nurse specialist (MSN, Certificate); clinical nurse leader (MSN); family primary care nurse practitioner (MSN, Certificate); gerontology (Certificate); nurse anesthetist (MSN, Certificate); nursing (MSN, Certificate); nursing administration (MSN, Certificate); nursing education (Certificate); nursing practice (DNP); nursing service administration (MSN); public health nursing (MSN, Certificate); school nursing (Certificate); MSN/MBA; MSN/MPH. *Accreditation:* AACN. *Program availability:* Part-time, evening/weekend, 100% online. *Degree requirements:* For doctorate, minimum of 1,000 hours of post baccalaureate clinical practice supervised by preceptors. *Entrance requirements:* For master's, GRE, MAT, or GMAT (for students with BSN GPA of less than 3.2), baccalaureate degree in nursing from ACEN- or CCNE-accredited program or an MSN Bridge program; Pennsylvania RN license; 2 letters of reference; resume; statement of philosophy articulating professional values and future educational goal; 1 year of work experience as a registered nurse; for doctorate, GRE (waived for applicants with MSN cumulative GPA of 3.7 or above), MSN, master's degree, MBA or MHA from nationally-accredited program; resume or curriculum vitae; 2 letters of reference; interview; for Certificate, GRE, MAT, or GMAT (for students with BSN GPA of less than 3.2, baccalaureate degree in nursing from ACEN- or CCNE-accredited program or an MSN Bridge program; Pennsylvania RN license; 2 letters of reference; resume; statement of philosophy articulating professional values and future educational goal; 1 year of work experience as a registered nurse. Additional exam requirements/recommendations for international students: required—TOEFL. Electronic applications accepted. Application fee is waived when completed online. *Expenses:* Contact institution.

Loma Linda University, School of Behavioral Health, Department of Social Work and Social Ecology, Loma Linda, CA 92350. Offers criminal justice (MS); gerontology (MS); social policy and social research (PhD); social work (MSW). *Accreditation:* CSWE. *Degree requirements:* For master's, comprehensive exam, thesis optional; for doctorate, comprehensive exam, thesis/dissertation. *Entrance requirements:* For master's and doctorate, GRE General Test. Additional exam requirements/recommendations for international students: required—TOEFL, Michigan English Language Assessment Battery. Electronic applications accepted.

Long Island University - Brooklyn, School of Business, Public Administration and Information Sciences, Brooklyn, NY 11201-8423. Offers accounting (MBA); accounting (MS); business administration (MBA); computer science (MS); gerontology (Advanced Certificate); health administration (MPA); human resources management (MS); not-for-profit management (Advanced Certificate); public administration (MPA); taxation (MS). *Program availability:* Part-time, evening/weekend. *Entrance requirements:* Additional exam requirements/recommendations for international students: required—TOEFL (minimum score 550 paper-based; 75 iBT). Electronic applications accepted.

Long Island University - Post, School of Health Professions and Nursing, Brookville, NY 11548-1300. Offers biomedical science (MS); cardiovascular perfusion (MS); clinical lab sciences (MS); clinical laboratory management (MS); dietetic internship (Advanced Certificate); family nurse practitioner (MS, Advanced Certificate); forensic social work (Advanced Certificate); gerontology (Advanced Certificate); health administration (MPA); non-profit management (Advanced Certificate); nursing education (MS); nutrition (MS); public administration (MPA); social work (MSW). *Program availability:* Part-time, blended/hybrid learning. *Degree requirements:* For master's, comprehensive exam (for some programs), thesis (for some programs). *Entrance requirements:* Additional exam requirements/recommendations for international students: required—TOEFL (minimum score 85 iBT) or IELTS (7.5). Electronic applications accepted.

Marywood University, Academic Affairs, College of Health and Human Services, School of Social Work, Program in Gerontology, Scranton, PA 18509-1598. Offers MS. *Program availability:* Part-time. Electronic applications accepted.

McDaniel College, Graduate and Professional Studies, Program in Gerontology, Westminster, MD 21157-4390. Offers MS, Postbaccalaureate Certificate. *Program availability:* Part-time, evening/weekend, online only, 100% online. *Degree requirements:* For master's, portfolio. *Entrance requirements:* For master's, 3 recommendations. Additional exam requirements/recommendations for international students: required—TOEFL (minimum score 79 iBT), IELTS (minimum score 6). Electronic applications accepted.

Mercer University, Graduate Studies, Cecil B. Day Campus, College of Professional Advancement, Atlanta, GA 31207. Offers certified rehabilitation counseling (MS); clinical mental health (MS); counselor education and supervision (PhD); criminal justice and public safety leadership (MS); health informatics (MS); human services (MS), including child and adolescent services, gerontology services; organizational leadership (MS), including leadership for the health care professional, leadership for the nonprofit organization, organizational development and change; school counseling (MS). *Program availability:* Part-time, evening/weekend, 100% online, blended/hybrid learning. *Faculty:* 19 full-time (11 women), 34 part-time/adjunct (30 women). *Students:* 193 full-time (156 women), 277 part-time (225 women); includes 260 minority (211 Black or African American, non-Hispanic/Latino; 2 American Indian or Alaska Native, non-Hispanic/Latino; 23 Asian, non-Hispanic/Latino; 19 Hispanic/Latino; 5 Two or more races, non-Hispanic/Latino), 3 international. Average age 32. 300 applicants, 45% accepted, 114 enrolled. In 2019, 183 master's, 7 doctorates awarded. *Degree requirements:* For master's, comprehensive exam (for some programs), thesis (for some programs); for doctorate, thesis/dissertation. *Entrance requirements:* For master's, GRE or MAT, Georgia Professional Standards Commission (GPSC) Certification at the SC-5 level; for doctorate, GRE or MAT. Additional exam requirements/recommendations for international students: recommended—TOEFL (minimum score 550 paper-based; 80 iBT), IELTS (minimum score 6.5). *Application deadline:* For fall admission, 7/1 priority date for domestic and international students; for spring admission, 11/1 priority date for domestic and international students; for summer admission, 4/1 priority date for domestic and international students. Application fee: $35. Electronic applications accepted. Application fee is waived when completed online. *Expenses:* Contact institution. *Financial support:* In 2019–20, 32 students received support. Federal Work-Study, scholarships/grants, and unspecified assistantships available. Financial award applicants required to submit FAFSA. *Unit head:* Dr. Priscilla R. Danheiser, Dean, 678-547-6028, Fax: 678-547-6008, E-mail: danheiser_p@mercer.edu. *Application contact:* Theatis Anderson, Asst VP for Enrollment Management, 678-547-6421, E-mail: anderson_t@mercer.edu.
Website: https://professionaladvancement.mercer.edu/

Miami University, College of Arts and Science, Department of Sociology and Gerontology, Oxford, OH 45056. Offers gerontology (MGS); population and social gerontology (MPSG); social gerontology (PhD).

Middle Tennessee State University, College of Graduate Studies, College of Liberal Arts, Program in Gerontology, Murfreesboro, TN 37132. Offers Graduate Certificate. *Program availability:* Part-time, evening/weekend, online learning. *Entrance requirements:* Additional exam requirements/recommendations for international students: required—TOEFL (minimum score 525 paper-based; 71 iBT) or IELTS (minimum score 6). Electronic applications accepted.

Minnesota State University Mankato, College of Graduate Studies and Research, College of Social and Behavioral Sciences, Program in Aging Studies, Mankato, MN 56001. Offers MS. *Degree requirements:* For master's, comprehensive exam, thesis optional. *Entrance requirements:* For master's, GRE, minimum GPA of 3.0 during previous 2 years, letters of recommendation. Additional exam requirements/recommendations for international students: required—TOEFL. Electronic applications accepted.

Morehead State University, Graduate School, Caudill College of Arts, Humanities and Social Sciences, School of Humanities and Social Sciences, Morehead, KY 40351. Offers criminology (MA); general sociology (MA); gerontology (MA); sociology regional analysis (MA); sociology/chemical dependency (MA). *Program availability:* Part-time, evening/weekend. *Faculty:* 20 full-time (10 women), 3 part-time/adjunct (2 women). *Students:* 27 full-time (19 women), 15 part-time (9 women); includes 3 minority (2 Black or African American, non-Hispanic/Latino; 1 Hispanic/Latino), 1 international. 53 applicants, 60% accepted, 23 enrolled. In 2019, 8 master's awarded. *Degree requirements:* For master's, comprehensive exam (for some programs), thesis (for some programs), min 3.0 GPA, complete 40 credit hours, option 3 is approved practicum in chemical dependency, written or oral exam, public presentation of thesis or research query or practicum experience (for MPA); demonstration of mastery of skills through individual courses and examinations and taped videos displaying skills (for MA Sociology). *Entrance requirements:* For master's, GRE, 3.0 UG GPA in 18 hours of PA courses; 3.0 UG GPA in all Sociology courses;MA Sociology: UG GPA of 2.75 or higher; submission of 2-page statement of educational and career goals relative to program. Additional exam requirements/recommendations for international students: required—TOEFL (minimum score 525 paper-based). *Application deadline:* Applications are processed on a rolling basis. Application fee: $30. Electronic applications accepted. *Expenses: Tuition, area resident:* Part-time $570 per credit hour. Tuition, state resident: part-time $570 per credit hour. Tuition, nonresident: part-time $570 per credit hour. *Required fees:* $14 per credit hour. *Financial support:* Teaching assistantships, career-related internships or fieldwork, and unspecified assistantships available. Financial award applicants required to submit FAFSA. *Unit head:* Dr. Dianna D. Murphy, Associate Dean/Professor Legal Studies, 606-7832720, E-mail: d.murphy@moreheadstate.edu. *Application contact:* Dr. Dianna D. Murphy, Associate Dean/Professor Legal Studies, 606-7832720, E-mail: d.murphy@moreheadstate.edu.

Mount Saint Vincent University, Graduate Programs, Department of Family Studies and Gerontology, Halifax, NS B3M 2J6, Canada. Offers MA. *Program availability:* Part-time, online learning. *Degree requirements:* For master's, thesis. *Entrance requirements:* For master's, minimum GPA of 3.0; course work in statistics, research methods, family and social theories.

North Dakota State University, College of Graduate and Interdisciplinary Studies, College of Human Development and Education, Department of Human Development and Family Science, Program in Gerontology, Fargo, ND 58102. Offers PhD, Certificate. Electronic applications accepted. Tuition and fees vary according to program and reciprocity agreements.

Northeastern Illinois University, College of Graduate Studies and Research, College of Arts and Sciences, Program in Gerontology, Chicago, IL 60625. Offers MA. *Program availability:* Part-time, evening/weekend. *Degree requirements:* For master's, comprehensive exam, paper and project or thesis, practicum. *Entrance requirements:* For master's, 15 hours in social sciences (3 hours in gerontology), course in research methods or statistics, minimum GPA of 2.75. Additional exam requirements/recommendations for international students: required—TOEFL (minimum score 550 paper-based; 79 iBT). Electronic applications accepted.

Oregon Health & Science University, School of Nursing, Program in Nursing Education, Portland, OR 97239-3098. Offers MN, Post Master's Certificate. *Program availability:* Part-time, online only, 100% online. *Entrance requirements:* For master's, minimum cumulative GPA of 3.0, 3 letters of recommendation, essay, RN license or eligibility, BS with major in nursing or BSN, statistics taken in last 5 years with minimum B- grade; for Post Master's Certificate, minimum cumulative GPA of 3.0, 3 letters of recommendation, essay, RN license or eligibility, master's degree in nursing, statistics taken in last 5 years with minimum B- grade. Additional exam requirements/recommendations for international students: required—TOEFL (minimum score 83 iBT). Electronic applications accepted. *Expenses:* Contact institution.

Sage Graduate School, School of Management, Program in Health Services Administration, Troy, NY 12180-4115. Offers gerontology (MS). *Program availability:* Part-time, evening/weekend, 100% online, blended/hybrid learning. *Faculty:* 5 full-time (3 women), 4 part-time/adjunct (1 woman). *Students:* 5 full-time (all women), 10 part-time (7 women); includes 4 minority (1 Black or African American, non-Hispanic/Latino; 1 Asian, non-Hispanic/Latino; 1 Hispanic/Latino; 1 Two or more races, non-Hispanic/Latino). Average age 32. 33 applicants, 30% accepted, 7 enrolled. In 2019, 10 master's awarded. *Entrance requirements:* For master's, application, minimum GPA 2.75, current resume, 2 letters of recommendation, career goals essay, official transcripts from each previous college attended. Additional exam requirements/recommendations for international students: required—TOEFL (minimum score 550 paper-based). *Application deadline:* Applications are processed on a rolling basis. Application fee: $30. Electronic applications accepted. *Expenses: Tuition:* Part-time $730 per credit hour. Tuition and fees vary according to course load, degree level and program. *Financial support:* Fellowships, research assistantships, and unspecified assistantships available. Financial award application deadline: 3/1; financial award applicants required to submit FAFSA. *Unit head:* Dr. Kimberly Fredericks, Dean, School of Management, 518-292-1782, Fax: 518-292-1964, E-mail: fredek1@sage.edu. *Application contact:* Michael Jones, SR Associate Director of Graduate Enrollment Management, 518-292-8615, Fax: 518-292-1912, E-mail: jonesm4@sage.edu.

St. Cloud State University, School of Graduate Studies, School of Health and Human Services, Program in Gerontology, St. Cloud, MN 56301-4498. Offers MS, Graduate Certificate. *Program availability:* Part-time. *Degree requirements:* For master's, thesis or alternative. *Entrance requirements:* For master's, GRE General Test, minimum GPA of 2.75. Additional exam requirements/recommendations for international students: required—Michigan English Language Assessment Battery; recommended—TOEFL (minimum score 550 paper-based), IELTS (minimum score 6.5). Electronic applications accepted.

Gerontology

San Diego State University, Graduate and Research Affairs, College of Health and Human Services, Department of Gerontology, San Diego, CA 92182. Offers MS. *Program availability:* Part-time, evening/weekend. *Degree requirements:* For master's, thesis. *Entrance requirements:* For master's, GRE General Test. Additional exam requirements/recommendations for international students: required—TOEFL. Electronic applications accepted.

San Francisco State University, Division of Graduate Studies, College of Health and Social Sciences, Gerontology Program, San Francisco, CA 94132-1722. Offers MA. *Program availability:* Part-time. *Application deadline:* Applications are processed on a rolling basis. *Expenses: Tuition, area resident:* Full-time $7176; part-time $4164 per year. Tuition, state resident: full-time $7176; part-time $4164 per year. Tuition, nonresident: full-time $16,680; part-time $396 per unit. *International tuition:* $16,680 full-time. *Required fees:* $1524; $1524 per unit. $762 per semester. Tuition and fees vary according to degree level and program. *Financial support:* Career-related internships or fieldwork and unspecified assistantships available. *Unit head:* Dr. Darlene Yee-Melichar, Program Coordinator, 415-338-3558, Fax: 415-338-0586, E-mail: dyee@sfsu.edu. *Application contact:* Dr. Darlene Yee-Melichar, Program Coordinator, 415-338-3558, Fax: 415-338-0586, E-mail: dyee@sfsu.edu.
Website: http://gerontology.sfsu.edu/

San Francisco State University, Division of Graduate Studies, College of Health and Social Sciences, Public Administration Program, San Francisco, CA 94132-1722. Offers criminal justice administration (MPA); environmental administration and policy (MPA); gerontology (MPA); nonprofit administration (MPA); public management (MPA); public policy (MPA); urban administration (MPA). *Accreditation:* NASPAA. *Expenses: Tuition, area resident:* Full-time $7176; part-time $4164 per year. Tuition, state resident: full-time $7176; part-time $4164 per year. Tuition, nonresident: full-time $16,680; part-time $396 per unit. *International tuition:* $16,680 full-time. *Required fees:* $1524; $1524 per unit. $762 per semester. Tuition and fees vary according to degree level and program. *Unit head:* Dr. Janey Wang, Graduate Coordinator, 415-817-4456, Fax: 415-338-0586, E-mail: jqwang@sfsu.edu. *Application contact:* Dr. Janey Wang, Graduate Coordinator, 415-817-4456, Fax: 415-338-0586, E-mail: jqwang@sfsu.edu.
Website: http://mpa.sfsu.edu/

Simon Fraser University, Office of Graduate Studies and Postdoctoral Fellows, Faculty of Arts and Social Sciences, Department of Gerontology, Vancouver, BC V6B 5K3, Canada. Offers MA, PhD. *Program availability:* Part-time. *Degree requirements:* For master's, thesis or alternative, internship; for doctorate, comprehensive exam, thesis/dissertation. *Entrance requirements:* For master's, minimum GPA of 3.0 (on scale of 4.33) or 3.33 based on last 60 credits of undergraduate courses; for doctorate, minimum GPA of 3.5 (on scale of 4.33). Additional exam requirements/recommendations for international students: recommended—TOEFL (minimum score 580 paper-based; 93 iBT), IELTS (minimum score 7), TWE (minimum score 5). Electronic applications accepted.

SUNY Brockport, School of Education, Health, and Human Services, Department of Social Work, Brockport, NY 14420-2997. Offers family and community practice (MSW); gerontology (AGC); interdisciplinary health practice (MSW). *Accreditation:* CSWE. *Program availability:* Part-time. *Faculty:* 7 full-time (6 women), 8 part-time/adjunct (6 women). *Students:* 41 full-time (35 women), 59 part-time (51 women); includes 14 minority (10 Black or African American, non-Hispanic/Latino; 4 Hispanic/Latino). 131 applicants, 73% accepted, 71 enrolled. In 2019, 149 master's awarded. *Entrance requirements:* For master's, minimum GPA of 3.0, letters of recommendation, statement of objectives. Additional exam requirements/recommendations for international students: required—TOEFL (minimum score 550 paper-based; 79 iBT), IELTS (minimum score 6.5). *Application deadline:* For fall admission, 1/15 priority date for domestic and international students; for summer admission, 1/15 priority date for domestic and international students. Application fee: $50. Electronic applications accepted. *Expenses: Tuition, area resident:* Part-time $471 per credit hour. Tuition, nonresident: part-time $963 per credit hour. *Financial support:* Federal Work-Study, scholarships/grants, and unspecified assistantships available. Support available to part-time students. Financial award application deadline: 3/15; financial award applicants required to submit FAFSA. *Unit head:* Debra Fromm Faria, Co-Director, 585-395-8455, Fax: 585-395-8603, E-mail: grcmsw@brockport.edu. *Application contact:* Brad Snyder, Coordinator of Admissions, 585-395-3845, Fax: 585-395-8603, E-mail: bsynder@brockport.edu.
Website: https://www.brockport.edu/academics/social_work/graduate/masters.html

Temple University, College of Public Health, Department of Nursing, Philadelphia, PA 19122-6096. Offers adult-gerontology primary care (DNP); family-individual across the lifespan (DNP); nursing (DNP). *Accreditation:* AACN. *Program availability:* Part-time. *Faculty:* 15 full-time (13 women), 6 part-time/adjunct (5 women). *Students:* 3 full-time (1 woman), 55 part-time (50 women); includes 27 minority (13 Black or African American, non-Hispanic/Latino; 11 Asian, non-Hispanic/Latino; 2 Hispanic/Latino; 1 Two or more races, non-Hispanic/Latino). 26 applicants, 54% accepted, 14 enrolled. In 2019, 11 doctorates awarded. *Degree requirements:* For doctorate, evidence-based practice project. *Entrance requirements:* For doctorate, GRE/MAT (waived for those who enter post-master's), 2 letters of reference, statement of goals, RN license, interview, statement of purpose, resume. Additional exam requirements/recommendations for international students: required—TOEFL (minimum score 79 iBT), IELTS (minimum score 6.5), PTE (minimum score 53), one of three is required. *Application deadline:* For fall admission, 3/1 for domestic students. Application fee: $60. Electronic applications accepted. *Expenses:* Contact institution. *Financial support:* Federal Work-Study and scholarships/grants available. Support available to part-time students. Financial award applicants required to submit FAFSA. *Unit head:* Martha Y Kubik, Chairperson, 215-707-4687, E-mail: martha.kubik@temple.edu. *Application contact:* Amy Costik, Assistant Director of Admissions, 215-204-5229, E-mail: amy.costik@temple.edu.
Website: https://cph.temple.edu/nursing/home

Texas Christian University, Harris College of Nursing and Health Sciences, Doctor of Nursing Practice Program, Fort Worth, TX 76129-0002. Offers clinical nurse specialist - adult/gerontology nursing (DNP); clinical nurse specialist - pediatrics (DNP); family nurse practitioner (DNP); general (DNP); nursing administration (DNP). *Accreditation:* AACN. *Program availability:* Part-time, 100% online, blended/hybrid learning. *Faculty:* 29 full-time (26 women), 1 (woman) part-time/adjunct. *Students:* 49 full-time (45 women), 13 part-time (10 women); includes 18 minority (9 Black or African American, non-Hispanic/Latino; 1 American Indian or Alaska Native, non-Hispanic/Latino; 3 Asian, non-Hispanic/Latino; 4 Hispanic/Latino; 1 Two or more races, non-Hispanic/Latino), 2 international. Average age 37. 57 applicants, 70% accepted, 24 enrolled. In 2019, 27 doctorates awarded. *Degree requirements:* For doctorate, thesis/dissertation or alternative, practicum. *Entrance requirements:* For doctorate, three reference letters, essay, resume, two official transcripts from each institution attended, APRN recognition or MSN with experience or certification in nursing administration, as applicable per track, current RN license, successful completion of interview. Additional exam requirements/recommendations for international students: required—TOEFL (minimum score 550 paper-based; 80 iBT). *Application deadline:* For summer admission, 1/15 for domestic and international students. Application fee: $60. Electronic applications accepted. Full-time tuition and fees vary according to program. *Financial support:* In 2019–20, 20 students received support. Scholarships/grants available. Financial award application deadline: 2/15; financial award applicants required to submit FAFSA. *Unit head:* Dr. Kathy Ellis, Division Director, Graduate Nursing, 817-257-6726, Fax: 817-257-7944, E-mail: kathryn.ellis@tcu.edu. *Application contact:* Beth Janke, Academic Program Specialist, 817-257-6726, Fax: 817-257-7944, E-mail: graduatenursing@tcu.edu.
Website: http://dnp.tcu.edu/

Texas State University, The Graduate College, College of Liberal Arts, Program in Dementia and Aging Studies, San Marcos, TX 78666. Offers MS. *Program availability:* Part-time, evening/weekend. *Degree requirements:* For master's, comprehensive exam, thesis (for some programs). *Entrance requirements:* For master's, baccalaureate degree from regionally-accredited university with minimum GPA of 3.0 on last 60 undergraduate semester hours, background course work in social science or gerontology, resume, statement of purpose describing personal goals, 3 letters of recommendation. Additional exam requirements/recommendations for international students: required—TOEFL (minimum score 550 paper-based; 78 iBT), IELTS (minimum score 6.5). Electronic applications accepted.

Texas Tech University, Graduate School, College of Human Sciences, Department of Human Development and Family Studies, Lubbock, TX 79409-1230. Offers human development and family studies (MS, PhD), including gerontology (MS). *Accreditation:* AAMFT/COAMFTE (one or more programs are accredited). *Program availability:* 100% online. *Faculty:* 26 full-time (22 women), 2 part-time/adjunct (both women). *Students:* 23 full-time (17 women), 22 part-time (17 women); includes 12 minority (2 Black or African American, non-Hispanic/Latino; 3 Asian, non-Hispanic/Latino; 6 Hispanic/Latino; 1 Two or more races, non-Hispanic/Latino), 3 international. Average age 29. 29 applicants, 59% accepted, 13 enrolled. In 2019, 4 master's, 4 doctorates awarded. *Degree requirements:* For master's, thesis; for doctorate, comprehensive exam, thesis/dissertation. *Entrance requirements:* For master's and doctorate, GRE General Test. Additional exam requirements/recommendations for international students: required—TOEFL (minimum score 550 paper-based; 79 iBT). *Application deadline:* For fall admission, 6/1 priority date for domestic students, 1/15 priority date for international students; for spring admission, 9/1 priority date for domestic students, 6/15 priority date for international students. Applications are processed on a rolling basis. Application fee: $65. Electronic applications accepted. *Expenses:* Contact institution. *Financial support:* In 2019–20, 29 students received support, including 28 fellowships (averaging $6,779 per year), 16 research assistantships (averaging $18,338 per year), 8 teaching assistantships (averaging $14,356 per year); scholarships/grants and unspecified assistantships also available. Financial award application deadline: 12/1; financial award applicants required to submit FAFSA. *Unit head:* Dr. Ann M. Mastergeorge, Chairperson, Rockwell Endowed Child and Family Professor, 806-834-7162, Fax: 806-742-3042, E-mail: ann.mastergeorge@ttu.edu. *Application contact:* Dr. Elizabeth Trejos-Castillo, Graduate Program Director, 806-834-6080, Fax: 806-742-0285, E-mail: elizabeth.trejos@ttu.edu.
Website: www.hdfs.ttu.edu

Université de Sherbrooke, Faculty of Letters and Human Sciences, Department of Psychology, Sherbrooke, QC J1K 2R1, Canada. Offers gerontology (MA). *Degree requirements:* For master's, thesis.

The University of Akron, Graduate School, Buchtel College of Arts and Sciences, Department of Psychology, Program in Adult Development and Aging, Akron, OH 44325. Offers PhD. *Degree requirements:* For doctorate, one foreign language, comprehensive exam, thesis/dissertation. *Entrance requirements:* For doctorate, GRE, minimum graduate GPA of 3.25, three letters of recommendation, personal statement, resume. Additional exam requirements/recommendations for international students: required—TOEFL (minimum score 79 iBT), IELTS (minimum score 6.5). Electronic applications accepted.

University of Arkansas at Little Rock, Graduate School, College of Education and Health Professions, School of Social Work, Program in Gerontology, Little Rock, AR 72204-1099. Offers Graduate Certificate.

University of Central Missouri, The Graduate School, Warrensburg, MO 64093. Offers accountancy (MA); accounting (MBA); applied mathematics (MS); aviation safety (MA); biology (MS); business administration (MBA); career and technology education (MS); college student personnel administration (MS); communication (MA); computer information systems and information technology (MS); computer science (MS); counseling (MS); criminal justice and criminology (MS); educational leadership (Ed S); educational leadership and policy analysis (Ed D); educational technology (MS, Ed S); elementary and early childhood education (MSE); English (MA); english language learners - teaching english as a second language (MA); environmental studies (MA); finance (MBA); history (MA); industrial hygiene (MS); industrial management (MS); information systems (MBA); kinesiology (MS); library science and information services (MS); literacy education (MSE); marketing (MBA); mathematics (MS); music (MA); occupational safety management (MS); professional leadership - adult, career, and technical education (Ed S); professional leadership - counseling (Ed S); psychology (MS); rural family nursing (MS); school administration (MSE); social gerontology (MS); sociology (MA); special education (MSE); speech language pathology (MS); teaching (MAT); technology (MS); technology management (PhD); theatre (MA). *Accreditation:* ASHA. *Program availability:* Part-time, 100% online, blended/hybrid learning. *Faculty:* 236 full-time (113 women), 97 part-time/adjunct (61 women). *Students:* 787 full-time (448 women), 1,459 part-time (997 women); includes 213 minority (72 Black or African American, non-Hispanic/Latino; 5 American Indian or Alaska Native, non-Hispanic/Latino; 27 Asian, non-Hispanic/Latino; 59 Hispanic/Latino; 50 Two or more races, non-Hispanic/Latino), 574 international. Average age 30. 1,477 applicants, 68% accepted, 664 enrolled. In 2019, 831 master's, 93 other advanced degrees awarded. *Degree requirements:* For master's and Ed S, comprehensive exam (for some programs), thesis (for some programs). *Entrance requirements:* For master's, A GRE or GMAT test score may be required by some of the programs, A minimum GPA, letters of recommendation, a statement of purpose may be required by some of the programs; for Ed S, A master's degree is required for the application of an Education Specialist's degree program. Additional exam requirements/recommendations for international students: required—TOEFL (minimum score 550 paper-based; 79 iBT). *Application deadline:* For fall admission, 6/1 priority date for domestic and international students; for spring admission, 10/15 priority date for domestic and international students; for summer admission, 4/1 priority date for domestic and international students. Applications are processed on a rolling basis. Application fee: $30 ($75 for international students). Electronic applications accepted. *Expenses: Tuition, area resident:* Full-time $7524; part-time $313.50 per credit hour. Tuition, state resident: full-time $7524; part-time $313.50 per credit hour. Tuition, nonresident: full-time $15,048; part-time $627 per credit hour. *International tuition:* $15,048 full-time. *Required fees:* $915; $30.50 per credit hour. *Financial support:* In 2019–20, 89 students received support. Research assistantships, teaching assistantships, career-related internships or fieldwork, Federal Work-Study, scholarships/grants, unspecified assistantships, and administrative and laboratory assistantships available. Support available to part-time students. Financial award application deadline: 4/1; financial award applicants required to submit FAFSA. *Unit head:* Shellie Hewitt, Director of Graduate and International Student Services, 660-543-4621, Fax: 660-543-4778, E-mail: hewitt@ucmo.edu. *Application contact:* Shellie

Hewitt, Director of Graduate and International Student Services, 660-543-4621, Fax: 660-543-4778, E-mail: hewitt@ucmo.edu. Website: http://www.ucmo.edu/graduate/

University of Central Oklahoma, The Jackson College of Graduate Studies, College of Liberal Arts, Department of Sociology, Gerontology, and Substance Abuse Studies, Edmond, OK 73034-5209. Offers gerontology (MA); substance abuse studies (MA), including substance abuse studies. *Program availability:* Part-time. *Degree requirements:* For master's, variable foreign language requirement, comprehensive exam (for some programs), thesis (for some programs). *Entrance requirements:* Additional exam requirements/recommendations for international students: required—TOEFL (minimum score 550 paper-based; 79 iBT), IELTS (minimum score 6.5). Electronic applications accepted.

University of Georgia, College of Public Health, Institute of Gerontology, Athens, GA 30602. Offers Certificate.

University of Illinois at Springfield, Graduate Programs, College of Education and Human Services, Program in Human Services, Springfield, IL 62703-5407. Offers alcohol and substance abuse (Graduate Certificate); alcoholism and substance abuse (MA); child and family studies (MA); gerontology (MA); social services administration (MA). *Program availability:* Part-time, 100% online, blended/hybrid learning. *Faculty:* 3 full-time (all women), 3 part-time/adjunct (2 women). *Students:* 12 full-time (all women), 49 part-time (47 women); includes 27 minority (19 Black or African American, non-Hispanic/Latino; 6 Hispanic/Latino; 2 Two or more races, non-Hispanic/Latino), 1 international. Average age 33. 29 applicants, 69% accepted, 12 enrolled. In 2019, 24 master's, 1 other advanced degree awarded. *Degree requirements:* For master's, internship; capstone project. *Entrance requirements:* For master's, minimum undergraduate GPA of 3.0, 2 letters of recommendation from professional or academic sources, statement of intent, interview. Additional exam requirements/recommendations for international students: required—TOEFL (minimum score 500 paper-based; 61 iBT). *Application deadline:* Applications are processed on a rolling basis. Application fee: $60 ($75 for international students). Electronic applications accepted. *Expenses:* $33.25 per credit hour (online fee). *Financial support:* In 2019–20, research assistantships with full tuition reimbursements (averaging $10,562 per year), teaching assistantships with full tuition reimbursements (averaging $10,652 per year) were awarded; fellowships, career-related internships or fieldwork, Federal Work-Study, scholarships/grants, health care benefits, and unspecified assistantships also available. Support available to part-time students. Financial award application deadline: 11/15; financial award applicants required to submit FAFSA. *Unit head:* Dr. Denise Bockmier-Sommers, Program Administrator, 217-206-6908, Fax: 217-206-6775, E-mail: dsomm2@uis.edu. *Application contact:* Dr. Denise Bockmier-Sommers, Program Administrator, 217-206-6908, Fax: 217-206-6775, E-mail: dsomm2@uis.edu. Website: http://www.uis.edu/humanservices

University of Indianapolis, Graduate Programs, Center for Aging and Community, Indianapolis, IN 46227-3697. Offers gerontology (MS, Certificate). *Program availability:* Part-time, evening/weekend, online learning. *Degree requirements:* For master's, capstone course. *Entrance requirements:* For master's, 3 letters of recommendation. Additional exam requirements/recommendations for international students: required—TOEFL (minimum score 550 paper-based).

University of Indianapolis, Graduate Programs, School of Nursing, Indianapolis, IN 46227-3697. Offers advanced practice nursing (DNP); family nurse practitioner (MSN); gerontological nurse practitioner (MSN); neonatal nurse practitioner (MSN); nurse-midwifery (MSN); nursing (MSN); nursing and health systems leadership (MSN); nursing education (MSN); women's health nurse practitioner (MSN); MBA/MSN. *Accreditation:* AACN. *Entrance requirements:* For master's, minimum GPA of 3.0, interview, letters of recommendation, resume, IN nursing license, 1 year of professional practice; for doctorate, graduate of ACEN- or CCNE-accredited nursing program; MSN or MA with nursing major and minimum cumulative GPA of 3.25; unencumbered RN license with eligibility for licensure in Indiana; completion of graduate-level statistics course within last 5 years with minimum grade of B; resume; essay; official transcripts from all academic institutions. Additional exam requirements/recommendations for international students: required—TOEFL (minimum score 550 paper-based). Electronic applications accepted.

The University of Kansas, Graduate Studies, College of Liberal Arts and Sciences, Program in Gerontology, Lawrence, KS 66045. Offers PhD. *Students:* Average age 32. 3 applicants. *Entrance requirements:* For doctorate, GRE, 3 letters of recommendation; resume; personal statement; transcripts; list of all courses taken in relevant areas such as sociology, psychology, human development, social welfare, biology, and health services. Additional exam requirements/recommendations for international students: required—TOEFL, IELTS. *Application deadline:* For fall admission, 12/1 priority date for domestic and international students. Application fee: $65 ($85 for international students). Electronic applications accepted. *Expenses:* Tuition, state resident: full-time $9989. Tuition, nonresident: full-time $23,950. *International tuition:* $23,950 full-time. *Required fees:* $984; $81.99 per credit hour. Tuition and fees vary according to course load, campus/location and program. *Financial support:* Fellowships, research assistantships, career-related internships or fieldwork, traineeships, and unspecified assistantships available. Financial award application deadline: 12/1. *Unit head:* Tamara Baker, Director, 785-864-6528, E-mail: tbakerthomas@ku.edu. *Application contact:* Corinne Butler, Graduate Admissions Contact, 785-864-9419, Fax: 785-864-2666, E-mail: cleg@ku.edu. Website: http://www.gerontology.ku.edu/

University of Kentucky, Graduate School, College of Public Health, Program in Gerontology, Lexington, KY 40506-0032. Offers PhD, Graduate Certificate. *Degree requirements:* For doctorate, comprehensive exam, thesis/dissertation. *Entrance requirements:* For doctorate, GRE General Test, minimum undergraduate GPA of 2.75, graduate 3.0. Additional exam requirements/recommendations for international students: required—TOEFL (minimum score 550 paper-based). Electronic applications accepted.

University of La Verne, College of Business and Public Management, Master's Program in Public Administration, La Verne, CA 91750-4443. Offers gerontology (MPA); nonprofit (MPA); public health (MPA); urban management and affairs (MPA). *Accreditation:* NASPAA. *Program availability:* Part-time. *Entrance requirements:* For master's, minimum undergraduate GPA of 3.0, statement of purpose, 2 letters of recommendation, resume. Additional exam requirements/recommendations for international students: required—TOEFL (minimum score 550 paper-based). *Expenses:* Contact institution.

University of La Verne, College of Business and Public Management, Program in Gerontology, La Verne, CA 91750-4443. Offers MS, Certificate. *Program availability:* Part-time. *Entrance requirements:* For master's, bachelor's degree, minimum preferred GPA of 2.75, 2 recommendations, personal statement. Additional exam requirements/recommendations for international students: required—TOEFL (minimum score 550 paper-based). *Expenses:* Contact institution.

University of Louisiana at Monroe, Graduate School, College of Business and Social Sciences, Program in Gerontology, Monroe, LA 71209-0001. Offers mental health (MA); small business management (MA). *Program availability:* Part-time, evening/weekend, online learning. *Faculty:* 1 (woman) full-time, 1 part-time/adjunct (0 women). *Students:* 8 full-time (6 women), 15 part-time (14 women); includes 13 minority (all Black or African American, non-Hispanic/Latino). Average age 32. 21 applicants, 57% accepted, 6 enrolled. In 2019, 3 master's awarded. *Degree requirements:* For master's, thesis (for some programs), internship. *Entrance requirements:* For master's, GRE General Test (waived for students with a 2.5 GPA or above). Additional exam requirements/recommendations for international students: required—TOEFL (minimum score 500 paper-based; 61 iBT); recommended—IELTS (minimum score 5.5). *Application deadline:* For fall admission, 8/1 for domestic students, 6/1 for international students; for spring admission, 1/1 for domestic students, 11/1 for international students; for summer admission, 6/1 for domestic students, 3/1 for international students. Applications are processed on a rolling basis. Application fee: $40. Electronic applications accepted. *Expenses: Tuition, area resident:* Full-time $6489. Tuition, state resident: full-time $6489. Tuition, nonresident: full-time $18,989. *Required fees:* $2748. Tuition and fees vary according to course load and program. *Financial support:* In 2019–20, 5 students received support. Career-related internships or fieldwork, Federal Work-Study, scholarships/grants, and unspecified assistantships available. Financial award application deadline: 2/15; financial award applicants required to submit FAFSA. *Unit head:* Dr. Anita Sharma, Director, 318-342-1409, E-mail: asharma@ulm.edu. *Application contact:* Dr. Anita Sharma, Director, 318-342-1409, E-mail: asharma@ulm.edu. Website: http://www.ulm.edu/gerontology/

University of Louisville, Graduate School, Kent School of Social Work, Louisville, KY 40292-0001. Offers marriage and family therapy (PMC), including mental health; social work (MSSW, PhD), including alcohol and drug counseling (MSSW), gerontology (MSSW), marriage and family (PhD), school social work (MSSW). *Accreditation:* AAMFT/COAMFTE; CSWE (one or more programs are accredited). *Program availability:* Part-time, evening/weekend, 100% online, blended/hybrid learning. *Faculty:* 33 full-time (22 women), 90 part-time/adjunct (73 women). *Students:* 385 full-time (333 women), 96 part-time (73 women); includes 143 minority (75 Black or African American, non-Hispanic/Latino; 2 American Indian or Alaska Native, non-Hispanic/Latino; 8 Asian, non-Hispanic/Latino; 26 Hispanic/Latino; 2 Native Hawaiian or other Pacific Islander, non-Hispanic/Latino; 30 Two or more races, non-Hispanic/Latino), 7 international. Average age 32. 313 applicants, 77% accepted, 176 enrolled. In 2019, 243 master's, 4 doctorates awarded. *Degree requirements:* For doctorate, comprehensive exam, thesis/dissertation. *Entrance requirements:* For master's, 3 letters of recommendation, admissions dssay, resume, transcripts; for doctorate, GRE scores, TOFEL scores or equivalent for international students, transcripts (undergraduate and graduate), 3 letters of recommendation, writing sample, personal statement, interview. Additional exam requirements/recommendations for international students: required—TOEFL (minimum score 550 paper-based; 79 iBT), IELTS (minimum score 6.5). *Application deadline:* For fall admission, 5/30 for domestic and international students; for spring admission, 9/30 for domestic and international students; for summer admission, 2/28 for domestic and international students. Applications are processed on a rolling basis. Application fee: $65. Electronic applications accepted. *Expenses: Tuition, area resident:* Full-time $13,000; part-time $723 per credit hour. Tuition, state resident: full-time $13,000; part-time $723 per credit hour. Tuition, nonresident: full-time $27,114; part-time $1507 per credit hour. *International tuition:* $27,114 full-time. *Required fees:* $196. Tuition and fees vary according to program and reciprocity agreements. *Financial support:* In 2019–20, 53 students received support, including 1 fellowship with full tuition reimbursement available (averaging $20,000 per year), 7 research assistantships with full tuition reimbursements available (averaging $20,000 per year), 1 teaching assistantship with full tuition reimbursement available (averaging $20,000 per year); scholarships/grants, health care benefits, and unspecified assistantships also available. Financial award application deadline: 5/15; financial award applicants required to submit FAFSA. *Unit head:* Dr. David Jenkins, Dean, 502-852-3944, Fax: 502-852-0422, E-mail: d.jenkins@louisville.edu. *Application contact:* Sarah Caragianis, Program Manager, MSSW Admissions, 502-852-0414, Fax: 502-852-0422, E-mail: sarah.caragianis@louisville.edu. Website: http://www.louisville.edu/kent

University of Maryland, Baltimore, Graduate School, Graduate Program in Life Sciences, Program in Gerontology, Baltimore, MD 21201. Offers PhD. *Degree requirements:* For doctorate, comprehensive exam, thesis/dissertation. *Entrance requirements:* For doctorate, GRE General Test, minimum GPA of 3.0, curriculum vitae, essay, 3 letters of recommendation. Additional exam requirements/recommendations for international students: required—TOEFL (minimum score 80 iBT); recommended—IELTS (minimum score 7). Electronic applications accepted.

University of Maryland, Baltimore, School of Medicine, Department of Epidemiology and Public Health, Baltimore, MD 21201. Offers biostatistics (MS); clinical research (MS); epidemiology and preventive medicine (MPH, MS, PhD); gerontology (PhD); human genetics and genomic medicine (MS, PhD); molecular epidemiology (MS, PhD); toxicology (MS, PhD); JD/MS; MD/PhD; MS/PhD. *Accreditation:* CEPH. *Program availability:* Part-time. *Students:* 75 full-time (51 women), 32 part-time (28 women); includes 29 minority (11 Black or African American, non-Hispanic/Latino; 11 Asian, non-Hispanic/Latino; 5 Hispanic/Latino; 2 Two or more races, non-Hispanic/Latino), 24 international. Average age 31. In 2019, 27 master's, 9 doctorates awarded. *Degree requirements:* For doctorate, comprehensive exam, thesis/dissertation. *Entrance requirements:* For master's and doctorate, GRE General Test. Additional exam requirements/recommendations for international students: required—TOEFL (minimum score 550 paper-based; 80 iBT); recommended—IELTS (minimum score 7). *Application deadline:* For fall admission, 1/15 for domestic and international students. Application fee: $75. Electronic applications accepted. *Expenses:* Contact institution. *Financial support:* In 2019–20, research assistantships with partial tuition reimbursements (averaging $26,000 per year) were awarded; fellowships, Federal Work-Study, scholarships/grants, and unspecified assistantships also available. Financial award application deadline: 3/1; financial award applicants required to submit FAFSA. *Unit head:* Dr. Laura Hungerford, Program Director, 410-706-8492, Fax: 410-706-4225. *Application contact:* Jessica Kelley, Program Coordinator, 410-706-8492, Fax: 410-706-4225, E-mail: jkelley@som.umaryland.edu. Website: http://lifesciences.umaryland.edu/epidemiology/

University of Maryland, Baltimore County, The Graduate School, College of Arts, Humanities and Social Sciences, PhD Program in Gerontology at UMB/UMBC, Baltimore, MD 21201. Offers aging policy issues (PhD); epidemiology of aging (PhD); social, cultural, and behavioral sciences (PhD); MA/PhD; MS/PhD. *Program availability:* Part-time. *Faculty:* 15 part-time/adjunct (10 women). *Students:* 8 full-time (6 women); includes 4 minority (1 Black or African American, non-Hispanic/Latino; 2 Asian, non-Hispanic/Latino; 1 Hispanic/Latino). Average age 48. 15 applicants, 27% accepted, 1 enrolled. In 2019, 2 doctorates awarded. *Degree requirements:* For doctorate, comprehensive exam, thesis/dissertation. *Entrance requirements:* For doctorate, GRE General Test. Additional exam requirements/recommendations for international students: required—TOEFL, TWE. *Application deadline:* For spring admission, 1/15 for domestic and international students. Application fee: $45. Electronic applications accepted. *Expenses: Tuition, area resident:* Full-time $659. Tuition, state resident: full-

time $659. Tuition, nonresident: full-time $1132. *International tuition:* $1132 full-time. *Required fees:* $140; $140 per credit hour. *Financial support:* In 2019–20, 4 students received support, including fellowships with full tuition reimbursements available (averaging $23,844 per year), 3 research assistantships with full tuition reimbursements available (averaging $20,000 per year), 1 teaching assistantship; health care benefits and dissertation awards also available. Financial award application deadline: 2/1; financial award applicants required to submit FAFSA. *Unit head:* Dr. John Schumacher, Co-Director, UMBC Campus, 410-455-3184, Fax: 410-455-2074, E-mail: jschuma@umbc.edu. *Application contact:* Justine Golden, Academic Coordinator, 410-706-4926, Fax: 410-706-4433, E-mail: jgold002@umaryland.edu.
Website: http://lifesciences.umaryland.edu/gerontologyphd/

University of Maryland, Baltimore County, The Graduate School, Erickson School of Aging Studies, Baltimore, MD 21228. Offers management of aging services (MA). *Program availability:* Part-time. *Faculty:* 4 full-time (1 woman), 7 part-time/adjunct (1 woman). *Students:* 5 full-time (4 women), 7 part-time (all women); includes 5 minority (4 Black or African American, non-Hispanic/Latino; 1 Asian, non-Hispanic/Latino). Average age 32. 7 applicants, 57% accepted, 1 enrolled. In 2019, 13 master's awarded. *Entrance requirements:* For master's, essays. *Application deadline:* For fall admission, 6/1 for domestic students; for spring admission, 12/1 for domestic students. Applications are processed on a rolling basis. Application fee: $50. Electronic applications accepted. *Expenses:* $14,382 per year. *Financial support:* In 2019–20, 1 student received support, including 1 teaching assistantship with full tuition reimbursement available (averaging $21,600 per year). Financial award applicants required to submit FAFSA. *Unit head:* Bill Holman, Graduate Program Director, 443-543-5603, E-mail: holman1@umbc.edu. *Application contact:* Michelle Howell, Administrative Assistant, 443-543-5607, E-mail: mhowell@umbc.edu.
Website: http://www.umbc.edu/erickson/

University of Massachusetts Boston, McCormack Graduate School of Policy and Global Studies, Program in Gerontology, Boston, MA 02125-3393. Offers gerontology (PhD). *Program availability:* Part-time. *Entrance requirements:* For doctorate, GRE General Test, minimum GPA of 3.0.

University of Michigan–Flint, School of Nursing, Flint, MI 48502-1950. Offers adult-gerontology acute care (DNP); adult-gerontology primary care (DNP); family nurse practitioner (DNP); nursing (MSN); psychiatric mental health (DNP); psychiatric mental health nurse practitioner (Certificate). *Accreditation:* AACN. *Program availability:* Part-time, evening/weekend, 100% online. *Faculty:* 32 full-time (31 women), 80 part-time/adjunct (71 women). *Students:* 198 full-time (174 women), 188 part-time (162 women); includes 55 minority (6 Black or African American, non-Hispanic/Latino; 3 American Indian or Alaska Native, non-Hispanic/Latino; 21 Asian, non-Hispanic/Latino; 18 Hispanic/Latino; 1 Native Hawaiian or other Pacific Islander, non-Hispanic/Latino; 6 Two or more races, non-Hispanic/Latino), 1 international. Average age 37. 140 applicants, 84% accepted, 75 enrolled. In 2019, 52 master's, 22 doctorates, 8 other advanced degrees awarded. *Entrance requirements:* For master's, BSN from regionally-accredited college; minimum GPA of 3.2; current unencumbered RN license in the United States; three or more credits in college-level chemistry or statistics with minimum C grade; for doctorate, BSN or MSN (with APRN certification) from regionally-accredited college or university with minimum overall undergraduate GPA of 3.2; college-level statistics with minimum C grade; BSN to DNP Current unencumbered RN license in the United States; MSN to DNP Current unencumbered license as an advanced practice nurse;one year RN experience is preferred; for Certificate, completion of nurse practitioner program with MS from regionally-accredited college or university with minimum overall GPA of 3.2; current unencumbered RN license in the United States; current unencumbered license as nurse practitioner; current certification as nurse practitioner in specialty other than discipline of study. Additional exam requirements/recommendations for international students: required—TOEFL (minimum score 84 iBT), IELTS (minimum score 6.5). *Application deadline:* For fall admission, 7/1 for domestic students, 5/1 for international students; for winter admission, 11/15 for domestic students, 10/1 for international students; for spring admission, 3/15 for domestic students, 1/1 for international students; for summer admission, 5/15 for domestic students. Applications are processed on a rolling basis. Application fee: $55. Electronic applications accepted. *Expenses:* Contact institution. *Financial support:* Federal Work-Study, scholarships/grants, and unspecified assistantships available. Support available to part-time students. Financial award application deadline: 3/1; financial award applicants required to submit FAFSA. *Unit head:* Dr. Constance J. Creech, Director, 810-762-3420, Fax: 810-766-6851, E-mail: ccreech@umflint.edu. *Application contact:* Matt Bohlen, Director of Graduate Admissions, 810-762-3171, Fax: 810-766-6789, E-mail: mbohlen@umflint.edu.
Website: https://www.umflint.edu/nursing/graduate-nursing-programs

University of Nebraska at Omaha, Graduate Studies, College of Public Affairs and Community Service, Department of Gerontology, Omaha, NE 68182. Offers gerontology (PhD, Certificate); social gerontology (MA). *Program availability:* Part-time, evening/weekend. *Degree requirements:* For master's, comprehensive exam, thesis. *Entrance requirements:* For master's, minimum GPA of 3.0, official transcripts, 2 letters of recommendation; for Certificate, minimum GPA of 3.0, official transcripts, 3 letters of recommendation. Additional exam requirements/recommendations for international students: required—TOEFL (minimum score 550 paper-based), IELTS (minimum score 5.5), PTE (minimum score 44). Electronic applications accepted.

University of Nebraska–Lincoln, Graduate College, College of Education and Human Sciences, Department of Child, Youth and Family Studies, Lincoln, NE 68588. Offers child development/early childhood education (MS, PhD); child, youth and family studies (MS); family and consumer sciences education (MS, PhD); family financial planning (MS); family science (MS, PhD); gerontology (PhD); human sciences (PhD), including child, youth and family studies, gerontology, medical family therapy; marriage and family therapy (MS); medical family therapy (PhD); youth development (MS). *Accreditation:* AAMFT/COAMFTE (one or more programs are accredited). *Program availability:* Online learning. *Degree requirements:* For master's, thesis optional. *Entrance requirements:* For master's, GRE. Additional exam requirements/recommendations for international students: required—TOEFL (minimum score 550 paper-based). Electronic applications accepted.

The University of North Carolina at Charlotte, College of Liberal Arts and Sciences, Interdisciplinary Liberal Arts and Sciences Programs, Charlotte, NC 28223-0001. Offers gender, sexuality and women's studies (Graduate Certificate); gerontology (MA, Graduate Certificate); Latin American studies (MA); liberal studies (MA); organizational science (PhD); public policy (PhD). *Program availability:* Part-time, evening/weekend. *Students:* 74 full-time (50 women), 56 part-time (43 women); includes 41 minority (16 Black or African American, non-Hispanic/Latino; 3 Asian, non-Hispanic/Latino; 16 Hispanic/Latino; 6 Two or more races, non-Hispanic/Latino), 16 international. Average age 33. 101 applicants, 51% accepted, 37 enrolled. In 2019, 21 master's, 5 doctorates, 8 other advanced degrees awarded. *Entrance requirements:* For master's, GRE General Test or MAT, bachelor's degree from accredited college or university; official transcripts of all previous academic work attempted beyond high school with minimum overall GPA of 3.0; statement of purpose; recommendation letters; for doctorate, GRE or GMAT, statement of purpose discussing interest in program and objectives for pursuing degree, current resume or curriculum vitae, unofficial transcripts; for Graduate Certificate, bachelor's degree from accredited university and either enrolled and in good standing in a graduate degree program at UNC Charlotte or have a minimum undergraduate GPA of 3.0. Additional exam requirements/recommendations for international students: required—TOEFL (minimum score 557 paper-based; 83 iBT), IELTS (minimum score 6.5), TOEFL (minimum score 557 paper-based, 83 iBT) or IELTS (6.5). *Application deadline:* Applications are processed on a rolling basis. Application fee: $75. Electronic applications accepted. *Expenses:* Tuition, state resident: full-time $4337. Tuition, nonresident: full-time $17,771. *Required fees:* $3093. Tuition and fees vary according to course load, degree level and program. *Financial support:* In 2019–20, 3 students received support, including 2 research assistantships (averaging $6,750 per year), 1 teaching assistantship (averaging $21,000 per year); career-related internships or fieldwork, institutionally sponsored loans, scholarships/grants, unspecified assistantships, and administrative assistantships also available. Support available to part-time students. Financial award applicants required to submit FAFSA. *Unit head:* Dr. Nancy A. Gutierrez, Dean, 704-687-0081, E-mail: ngutierr@uncc.edu. *Application contact:* Kathy B. Giddings, Director of Graduate Admissions, 704-687-5503, Fax: 704-687-3279, E-mail: gradadm@uncc.edu.
Website: http://clas.uncc.edu/academics

The University of North Carolina at Greensboro, Graduate School, School of Health and Human Sciences, Program in Gerontology, Greensboro, NC 27412-5001. Offers MS, Certificate, MS/MBA. Electronic applications accepted.

The University of North Carolina Wilmington, School of Health and Applied Human Sciences, Wilmington, NC 28403-3297. Offers applied gerontology (MS). *Program availability:* Part-time. *Faculty:* 16 full-time (9 women). *Students:* 18 full-time (12 women), 33 part-time (22 women); includes 11 minority (4 Black or African American, non-Hispanic/Latino; 5 Hispanic/Latino; 2 Two or more races, non-Hispanic/Latino). Average age 28. 17 applicants, 88% accepted, 13 enrolled. In 2019, 15 master's awarded. *Degree requirements:* For master's, practicum, final project. *Entrance requirements:* For master's, 3 recommendations, essay. Additional exam requirements/recommendations for international students: required—TOEFL (minimum score 79 iBT), IELTS (minimum score 6.5). *Application deadline:* For fall admission, 7/1 for domestic students; for spring admission, 11/15 for domestic students; for summer admission, 3/15 for domestic students. Applications are processed on a rolling basis. Application fee: $75. Electronic applications accepted. *Expenses: Tuition, area resident:* Full-time $4719; part-time $326 per credit hour. Tuition, state resident: full-time $4719; part-time $326 per credit hour. Tuition, nonresident: full-time $18,548; part-time $1099 per credit hour. *Required fees:* $2738. Tuition and fees vary according to program. *Financial support:* Scholarships/grants and unspecified assistantships available. Financial award application deadline: 1/1; financial award applicants required to submit FAFSA. *Unit head:* Dr. Steve Elliott, Director, 910-962-2115, Fax: 910-962-7073, E-mail: elliotts@uncw.edu. *Application contact:* Dr. Anne Glass, Program Coordinator, 910-962-7509, E-mail: glassa@uncw.edu.
Website: http://www.uncw.edu/shahs/

University of Northern Colorado, Graduate School, College of Natural and Health Sciences, School of Human Sciences, Program in Gerontology, Greeley, CO 80639. Offers MA. *Program availability:* Part-time. *Degree requirements:* For master's, comprehensive exam. *Entrance requirements:* For master's, GRE General Test or MAT, 2 letters of recommendation. Electronic applications accepted.

University of Northern Colorado, Graduate School, College of Natural and Health Sciences, School of Nursing, Greeley, CO 80639. Offers adult-gerontology acute care nurse practitioner (MSN, DNP); family nurse practitioner (MSN, DNP); nursing education (PhD); nursing practice (DNP). *Accreditation:* AACN. *Program availability:* Online learning. *Degree requirements:* For master's, comprehensive exam, thesis or alternative; for doctorate, comprehensive exam, thesis/dissertation. *Entrance requirements:* For master's and doctorate, GRE General Test, minimum GPA of 3.0 in last 60 hours, BS in nursing, 2 letters of recommendation. Electronic applications accepted.

University of North Texas, Toulouse Graduate School, Denton, TX 76203-5459. Offers accounting (MS); applied anthropology (MA, MS); applied behavior analysis (Certificate); applied geography (MA); applied technology and performance improvement (M Ed, MS); art education (MA); art history (MA); arts leadership (Certificate); audiology (Au D); behavior analysis (MS); behavioral science (PhD); biochemistry and molecular biology (MS); biology (MA, MS); biomedical engineering (MS); business analysis (MS); chemistry (MS); clinical health psychology (PhD); communication studies (MA, MS); computer engineering (MS); computer science (MS); counseling (M Ed, MS), including clinical mental health counseling (MS), college and university counseling, elementary school counseling, secondary school counseling; creative writing (MA); criminal justice (MS); curriculum and instruction (M Ed); decision sciences (MBA); design (MA, MFA), including fashion design (MFA), innovation studies, interior design (MFA); early childhood studies (MS); economics (MS); educational leadership (M Ed, Ed D); educational psychology (MS, PhD), including family studies (MS), gifted and talented (MS), human development (MS), learning and cognition (MS), research, measurement and evaluation (MS); electrical engineering (MS); emergency management (MPA); engineering technology (MS); English (MA); English as a second language (MA); environmental science (MS); finance (MBA, MS); financial management (MPA); French (MA); health services management (MBA); higher education (M Ed, Ed D); history (MA, MS); hospitality management (MS); human resources management (MPA); information science (MS); information systems (PhD); information technologies (MBA); interdisciplinary studies (MA, MS); international studies (MA); international sustainable tourism (MS); jazz studies (MM); journalism (MA, MJ, Graduate Certificate), including interactive and virtual digital communication (Graduate Certificate), narrative journalism (Graduate Certificate), public relations (Graduate Certificate); kinesiology (MS); linguistics (MA); local government management (MPA); logistics (PhD); logistics and supply chain management (MBA); long-term care, senior housing, and aging services (MA); management (PhD); marketing (MBA); mathematics (MA, MS); mechanical and energy engineering (MS, PhD); music (MA), including ethnomusicology, music theory, musicology, performance; music composition (PhD); music education (MM Ed, PhD); nonprofit management (MPA); operations and supply chain management (MBA); performance (MM, DMA); philosophy (MA); political science (MA); professional and technical communication (MA); radio, television and film (MA, MFA); rehabilitation counseling (Certificate); sociology (MA); Spanish (MA); special education (M Ed); speech-language pathology (MA); strategic management (MBA); studio art (MFA); teaching (M Ed); MBA/MS. *Program availability:* Part-time, evening/weekend, online learning. Terminal master's awarded for partial completion of doctoral program. *Degree requirements:* For master's, variable foreign language requirement, comprehensive exam (for some programs), thesis (for some programs); for doctorate, variable foreign language requirement, comprehensive exam (for some programs), thesis/dissertation; for other advanced degree, variable foreign language requirement, comprehensive exam (for some programs). *Entrance requirements:* For master's and doctorate, GRE, GMAT. Additional exam requirements/recommendations for international students: required—TOEFL (minimum score 550 paper-based; 79 iBT). Electronic applications accepted.

University of Phoenix - Central Valley Campus, College of Nursing, Fresno, CA 93720-1552. Offers education (MHA); gerontology (MHA); health administration (MHA); nursing (MSN); MSN/MBA.

University of Phoenix - Hawaii Campus, College of Nursing, Honolulu, HI 96813-3800. Offers education (MHA); family nurse practitioner (MSN); gerontology (MHA); health administration (MHA); nursing (MSN); nursing/health care education (MSN); MSN/MBA. *Program availability:* Evening/weekend. *Degree requirements:* For master's, thesis (for some programs). *Entrance requirements:* For master's, minimum undergraduate GPA of 2.5, 3 years of work experience, RN license. Additional exam requirements/recommendations for international students: required—TOEFL (minimum score 550 paper-based; 79 iBT). Electronic applications accepted.

University of Puerto Rico - Medical Sciences Campus, Graduate School of Public Health, Department of Human Development, Program in Gerontology, San Juan, PR 00936-5067. Offers MPH, Certificate. *Program availability:* Part-time, evening/weekend. *Entrance requirements:* For master's, GRE, previous course work in social sciences, biology, psychology, and algebra.

University of Regina, Faculty of Graduate Studies and Research, Faculty of Arts, Program in Gerontology, Regina, SK S4S 0A2, Canada. Offers M Sc, MA. *Program availability:* Part-time. *Faculty:* 10 full-time (4 women). *Students:* 1 (woman) full-time. Average age 30. 14 applicants, 7% accepted. In 2019, 1 master's awarded. *Degree requirements:* For master's, thesis. *Entrance requirements:* For master's, 4-year undergraduate degree in kinesiology, psychology, social work, nursing, biology; or a health professional degree. Some courses (e.g., GERO 890) have undergraduate prerequisites. Students who have not completed these prerequisites or equivalent can still be admitted to the program with the understanding that they will be expected to complete. Additional exam requirements/recommendations for international students: required—TOEFL (minimum score 580 paper-based; 80 iBT), IELTS (minimum score 6.5), PTE (minimum score 59), other options are CAEL, MELAB, Cantest and U of R ESL. *Application deadline:* For fall admission, 3/31 for domestic and international students. Application fee: $100 Canadian dollars. Electronic applications accepted. *Expenses: Tuition:* Full-time $6684 Canadian dollars. *Required fees:* $100 Canadian dollars; $3351.45 Canadian dollars per trimester. $1117.15 Canadian dollars per semester. Tuition and fees vary according to course level, course load, degree level and program. *Financial support:* Fellowships, research assistantships, teaching assistantships, career-related internships or fieldwork, scholarships/grants, and Travel awards, SIES and Graduate Scholarship Base Funds available. Support available to part-time students. Financial award application deadline: 9/30. *Unit head:* Dr. Abigail Wickson-Griffiths, Program Coordinator, 306-337-2132, E-mail: abigail.wickson-griffiths@uregina.ca. *Application contact:* Dr. Abigail Wickson-Griffiths, Program Coordinator, 306-337-2132, E-mail: abigail.wickson-griffiths@uregina.ca.

University of South Carolina, The Graduate School, Program in Gerontology, Columbia, SC 29208. Offers Certificate. *Program availability:* Part-time. *Degree requirements:* For Certificate, practicum. Electronic applications accepted.

University of Southern California, Graduate School, Leonard Davis School of Gerontology, Los Angeles, CA 90089. Offers aging services management (MASM); biology of aging (PhD); gerontology (MA, MS, PhD, Graduate Certificate); long term care administration (MLTCA); JD/MS; M Pl/MS; MBA/MS; MHA/MS; MPA/MS; MS/MSW; Pharm D/MS. *Program availability:* Part-time, online learning. Terminal master's awarded for partial completion of doctoral program. *Degree requirements:* For master's, thesis or alternative; for doctorate, comprehensive exam, thesis/dissertation. *Entrance requirements:* For doctorate, GRE. Electronic applications accepted.

University of Southern California, Graduate School, Suzanne Dworak-Peck School of Social Work, Los Angeles, CA 90089. Offers community organization, planning and administration (MSW); families and children (MSW); health (MSW); mental health (MSW); Military Social Work and Veterans Services (MSW); older adults (MSW); public child welfare (MSW); school settings (MSW); social work (MSW, PhD); systems of mental illness recovery (MSW); work and life (MSW); JD/MSW; M Pl/MSW; MPA/MSW; MSW/MBA; MSW/MJCS; MSW/MS. *Accreditation:* CSWE (one or more programs are accredited). *Degree requirements:* For doctorate, comprehensive exam, thesis/dissertation, qualifying exam/publishable paper. *Entrance requirements:* For doctorate, GRE General Test. Additional exam requirements/recommendations for international students: required—TOEFL (minimum score 600 paper-based; 100 iBT), ESL exam. Electronic applications accepted.

University of Southern Indiana, Graduate Studies, College of Nursing and Health Professions, Program in Nursing, Evansville, IN 47712-3590. Offers adult-gerontology acute care nurse practitioner (MSN, PMC); adult-gerontology clinical nurse specialist (MSN, PMC); adult-gerontology primary care nurse practitioner (MSN, PMC); advanced nursing practice (DNP); family nurse practitioner (MSN, PMC); nursing education (MSN, PMC); nursing management and leadership (MSN, PMC); organizational and systems leadership (DNP); psychiatric mental health nurse practitioner (MSN, PMC). *Accreditation:* AACN. *Program availability:* Part-time, online learning. *Entrance requirements:* For master's, BSN from nationally-accredited school; minimum cumulative GPA of 3.0; satisfactory completion of a course in undergraduate statistics (minimum grade C); one year of full-time experience or 2,000 hours of clinical practice as an RN (recommended); unencumbered U.S. RN license; for doctorate, minimum GPA of 3.0, completion of graduate research course with minimum B grade, unencumbered RN license, resume/curriculum vitae, three professional references, 1-2 page narrative of practice experience and professional goals, Capstone Project Information form. Additional exam requirements/recommendations for international students: required—TOEFL (minimum score 550 paper-based; 79 iBT), IELTS (minimum score 6). Electronic applications accepted. *Expenses:* Contact institution.

University of South Florida, College of Behavioral and Community Sciences, School of Aging Studies, Tampa, FL 33620-9951. Offers MA, PhD. *Program availability:* Part-time, evening/weekend. *Faculty:* 9 full-time (4 women). *Students:* 23 full-time (16 women), 4 part-time (all women); includes 4 minority (1 Black or African American, non-Hispanic/Latino; 1 Asian, non-Hispanic/Latino; 2 Two or more races, non-Hispanic/Latino). Average age 28. 25 applicants, 48% accepted, 6 enrolled. In 2019, 6 master's, 3 doctorates awarded. *Degree requirements:* For master's, comprehensive exam, thesis optional; for doctorate, comprehensive exam, thesis/dissertation. *Entrance requirements:* For master's, GRE is optional for applicants with a 3.25 GPA, a 3.50 GPA in a completed graduate (including professional degrees such as the JD and MD); preferred GRE score of at least 149V (41st percentile), 142Q (16th percentile), 3.5 analytical writing for students submitting GRE scores, minimum GPA of 3.0; statement of purpose; resume; 2 letters of reference; for doctorate, GRE (preferred scores at or above the 50th percentile on Verbal, 30th percentile on quantitative, 50th percentile on analytical writing), minimum GPA of 3.25, three letters of recommendation, summary of career goals, single-authored writing sample. Additional exam requirements/recommendations for international students: required—TOEFL (minimum score 79 iBT). *Application deadline:* For fall admission, 12/11 priority date for domestic and international students; for spring admission, 10/15 for domestic students, 9/15 for international students; for summer admission, 2/15 for domestic students, 1/15 for international students. Application fee: $30. Electronic applications accepted. *Financial support:* In 2019–20, 6 students received support, including 2 research assistantships with tuition reimbursements available (averaging $15,690 per year), 13 teaching assistantships with tuition reimbursements available (averaging $13,503 per year). Financial award application deadline: 2/3. *Unit head:* Dr. Cathy L. McEvoy, Director and Professor, 813-974-1940, Fax: 813-974-9754, E-mail: cmcevoy@usf.edu. *Application contact:* Brent Small, Professor, 813-974-9746, Fax: 813-974-9754, E-mail: bsmall@usf.edu.
Website: http://agingstudies.cbcs.usf.edu/aprog/

University of South Florida, Innovative Education, Tampa, FL 33620-9951. Offers adult, career and higher education (Graduate Certificate), including college teaching, leadership in developing human resources, leadership in higher education; Africana studies (Graduate Certificate), including diasporas and health disparities, genocide and human rights; aging studies (Graduate Certificate), including gerontology; art research (Graduate Certificate), including museum studies; business foundations (Graduate Certificate); chemical and biomedical engineering (Graduate Certificate), including materials science and engineering, water, health and sustainability; child and family studies (Graduate Certificate), including positive behavior support; civil and industrial engineering (Graduate Certificate), including transportation systems analysis; community and family health (Graduate Certificate), including maternal and child health, social marketing and public health, violence and injury: prevention and intervention, women's health; criminology (Graduate Certificate), including criminal justice administration; data science for public administration (Graduate Certificate); digital humanities (Graduate Certificate); educational measurement and research (Graduate Certificate), including evaluation; English (Graduate Certificate), including comparative literary studies, creative writing, professional and technical communication; entrepreneurship (Graduate Certificate); environmental health (Graduate Certificate), including safety management; epidemiology and biostatistics (Graduate Certificate), including applied biostatistics, biostatistics, concepts and tools of epidemiology, epidemiology, epidemiology of infectious diseases; geography, environment and planning (Graduate Certificate), including community development, environmental policy and management, geographical information systems; geology (Graduate Certificate), including hydrogeology; global health (Graduate Certificate), including disaster management, global health and Latin American and Caribbean studies, global health practice, humanitarian assistance, infection control; government and international affairs (Graduate Certificate), including Cuban studies, globalization studies; health policy and management (Graduate Certificate), including health management and leadership, public health policy and programs; hearing specialist: early intervention (Graduate Certificate); industrial and management systems engineering (Graduate Certificate), including systems engineering, technology management; information studies (Graduate Certificate), including school library media specialist; information systems/decision sciences (Graduate Certificate), including analytics and business intelligence; instructional technology (Graduate Certificate), including distance education, Florida digital/virtual educator, instructional design, multimedia design, Web design; internal medicine, bioethics and medical humanities (Graduate Certificate), including biomedical ethics; Latin American and Caribbean studies (Graduate Certificate); leadership for coastal resiliency planning (Graduate Certificate); mass communications (Graduate Certificate), including multimedia journalism; mathematics and statistics (Graduate Certificate), including mathematics; medicine (Graduate Certificate), including aging and neuroscience, bioinformatics, biotechnology, brain fitness and memory management, clinical investigation, hand and upper limb rehabilitation, health informatics, health sciences, integrative weight management, intellectual property, medicine and gender, metabolic and nutritional medicine, metabolic cardiology, pharmacy sciences; national and competitive intelligence (Graduate Certificate); nursing (Graduate Certificate), including simulation based academic fellowship in advanced pain management; psychological and social foundations (Graduate Certificate), including career counseling, college teaching, diversity in education, mental health counseling, school counseling; public affairs (Graduate Certificate), including nonprofit management, public management, research administration; public health (Graduate Certificate), including assessing chemical toxicity and public health risks, health equity, pharmacoepidemiology, public health generalist, toxicology, translational research in adolescent behavioral health; public health practices (Graduate Certificate), including planning for healthy communities; rehabilitation and mental health counseling (Graduate Certificate), including integrative mental health care, marriage and family therapy, rehabilitation technology; secondary education (Graduate Certificate), including ESOL, foreign language education: culture and content, foreign language education: professional; social work (Graduate Certificate), including geriatric social work/clinical gerontology; special education (Graduate Certificate), including autism spectrum disorder, disabilities education: severe/profound; world languages (Graduate Certificate), including teaching English as a second language (TESL) or foreign language. *Unit head:* Dr. Cynthia DeLuca, Associate Vice President and Assistant Vice Provost, 813-974-3077, Fax: 813-974-7061, E-mail: deluca@usf.edu. *Application contact:* Owen Hooper, Director, Summer and Alternative Calendar Programs, 813-974-6917, E-mail: hooper@usf.edu.
Website: http://www.usf.edu/innovative-education/

The University of Tennessee, Graduate School, College of Education, Health and Human Sciences, Program in Public Health, Knoxville, TN 37996. Offers community health education (MPH); gerontology (MPH); health planning/administration (MPH); MS/MPH. *Accreditation:* CEPH. *Degree requirements:* For master's, thesis optional. *Entrance requirements:* For master's, minimum GPA of 2.7. Additional exam requirements/recommendations for international students: required—TOEFL. Electronic applications accepted.

The University of Toledo, College of Graduate Studies, College of Medicine and Life Sciences, Department of Public Health and Preventative Medicine, Toledo, OH 43606-3390. Offers biostatistics and epidemiology (Certificate); contemporary gerontological practice (Certificate); environmental and occupational health and safety (MPH); epidemiology (Certificate); global public health (Certificate); health promotion and education (MPH); industrial hygiene (MSOH); medical and health science teaching and learning (Certificate); occupational health (Certificate); public health administration (MPH); public health and emergency response (Certificate); public health epidemiology (MPH); public health nutrition (MPH); MD/MPH. *Program availability:* Part-time, evening/weekend. *Degree requirements:* For master's, thesis or alternative. *Entrance requirements:* For master's, GRE, minimum undergraduate GPA of 3.0, three letters of recommendation, statement of purpose, transcripts from all prior institutions attended, resume; for Certificate, minimum undergraduate GPA of 3.0, three letters of recommendation, statement of purpose, transcripts from all prior institutions attended, resume. Additional exam requirements/recommendations for international students: required—TOEFL (minimum score 550 paper-based; 80 iBT), IELTS (minimum score 6.5). Electronic applications accepted.

University of Utah, Graduate School, College of Nursing, Gerontology Program, Salt Lake City, UT 84112. Offers MS, Certificate. *Program availability:* Part-time, online only, 100% online. *Faculty:* 9 full-time (8 women), 1 (woman) part-time/adjunct. *Students:* 5 full-time (all women), 9 part-time (all women); includes 1 minority (Two or more races, non-Hispanic/Latino). Average age 41. 7 applicants, 100% accepted, 5 enrolled. In 2019, 2 master's awarded. *Degree requirements:* For master's, thesis optional,

Colloquium Defense, Masters Project. *Entrance requirements:* For master's, Complete application for graduate admission; transcripts for all colleges and universities attended; evidence of bachelors degree from a regionally accredited university or college; minimum 3.0 cumulative GPA on a 4.0 scale; current resume or curriculum vitae; three professional references; goal statement. Additional exam requirements/recommendations for international students: required—TOEFL (minimum score 80 iBT), IELTS (minimum score 6.5). *Application deadline:* For fall admission, 12/1 for domestic and international students. Application fee: $55 ($65 for international students). Electronic applications accepted. *Expenses:* $22,975.43 for completion of three semester program (resident tuition rate); $52,735.55 for completion of three semester program (nonresident tuition rate). *Financial support:* In 2019–20, 8 students received support, including 8 fellowships with partial tuition reimbursements available (averaging $12,563 per year); research assistantships with partial tuition reimbursements available, teaching assistantships with partial tuition reimbursements available, Federal Work-Study, scholarships/grants, and unspecified assistantships also available. Support available to part-time students. Financial award application deadline: 1/20. *Unit head:* Dr. Jacqueline Eaton, Assistant Dean, 801-587-9638, Fax: 801-587-7697, E-mail: jacqueline.eaton@nurs.utah.edu. *Application contact:* Ashley Cadiz, Academic Program Manager, 801-581-8198, Fax: 801-585-2588, E-mail: ashley.cadiz@nurs.utah.edu. Website: http://www.nursing.utah.edu/gerontology/

University of Wisconsin–Milwaukee, Graduate School, Helen Bader School of Social Welfare, Department of Social Work, Milwaukee, WI 53201-0413. Offers applied gerontology (Graduate Certificate); nonprofit management (Graduate Certificate); social welfare (PhD); social work (MSW, PhD). *Program availability:* Part-time. *Entrance requirements:* For doctorate, GRE, bachelor's degree. Additional exam requirements/recommendations for international students: required—TOEFL (minimum score 550 paper-based; 79 iBT), IELTS (minimum score 6.5). Electronic applications accepted.

Université Laval, Faculty of Medicine, Post-Professional Programs in Medical Studies, Québec, QC G1K 7P4, Canada. Offers anatomy–pathology (DESS); anesthesiology (DESS); cardiology (DESS); care of older people (Diploma); clinical research (DESS); community health (DESS); dermatology (DESS); diagnostic radiology (DESS); emergency medicine (Diploma); family medicine (DESS); general surgery (DESS); geriatrics (DESS); hematology (DESS); internal medicine (DESS); maternal and fetal medicine (Diploma); medical biochemistry (DESS); medical microbiology and infectious diseases (DESS); medical oncology (DESS); nephrology (DESS); neurology (DESS); neurosurgery (DESS); obstetrics and gynecology (DESS); ophthalmology (DESS); orthopedic surgery (DESS); oto-rhino-laryngology (DESS); palliative medicine (Diploma); pediatrics (DESS); plastic surgery (DESS); psychiatry (DESS); pulmonary medicine (DESS); radiology–oncology (DESS); thoracic surgery (DESS); urology (DESS). *Degree requirements:* For other advanced degree, comprehensive exam. *Entrance requirements:* For degree, knowledge of French. Electronic applications accepted.

Virginia Commonwealth University, Graduate School, School of Allied Health Professions, Department of Gerontology, Richmond, VA 23284-9005. Offers gerontology (MS). *Program availability:* Part-time. *Entrance requirements:* For master's, GRE General Test or MAT. Additional exam requirements/recommendations for international students: required—TOEFL (minimum score 600 paper-based; 100 iBT); recommended—IELTS (minimum score 6.5). Electronic applications accepted.

Virginia Commonwealth University, Graduate School, School of Allied Health Professions, Doctoral Program in Health Related Sciences, Richmond, VA 23284-9005. Offers clinical laboratory sciences (PhD); gerontology (PhD); health administration (PhD); nurse anesthesia (PhD); occupational therapy (PhD); physical therapy (PhD); radiation sciences (PhD); rehabilitation leadership (PhD). *Entrance requirements:* For doctorate, GRE General Test or MAT, minimum GPA of 3.3 in master's degree. Additional exam requirements/recommendations for international students: required—TOEFL (minimum score 600 paper-based; 100 iBT); recommended—IELTS (minimum score 6.5). Electronic applications accepted.

Walden University, Graduate Programs, School of Social Work and Human Services, Minneapolis, MN 55401. Offers addictions and social work (DSW); advanced clinical practice (MSW); clinical expertise (DSW); criminal justice (DSW); disaster, crisis, and intervention (DSW); family studies and interventions (DSW); human and social services (PhD), including advanced research, community and social services, community intervention and leadership, conflict management, criminal justice, disaster crisis and intervention, family studies and intervention, gerontology, global social services, higher education, human services and nonprofit administration, mental health facilitation; medical social work (DSW); military social work (MSW); policy practice (DSW); social work (PhD), including addictions and social work, clinical expertise, criminal justice, disaster, crisis and intervention, family studies and interventions, medical social work, policy practice, social work administration; social work administration (DSW); social work in healthcare (MSW); social work with children and families (MSW). *Accreditation:* CSWE. *Program availability:* Part-time, evening/weekend, online only, 100% online. *Degree requirements:* For master's, residency (for some programs); for doctorate, thesis/dissertation, residency. *Entrance requirements:* For master's, bachelor's degree or higher; minimum GPA of 2.5; official transcripts; goal statement (for some programs); access to computer and Internet; for doctorate, master's degree or higher; three years of related professional or academic experience (preferred); minimum GPA of 3.0; goal statement and current resume (for select programs); official transcripts; access to computer and Internet. Additional exam requirements/recommendations for international students: required—TOEFL (minimum score 550 paper-based, 79 iBT), IELTS (minimum score 6.5), Michigan English Language Assessment Battery (minimum score 82), or PTE (minimum score 53). Electronic applications accepted.

Washington University in St. Louis, Brown School, St. Louis, MO 63130-4899. Offers American Indian/Alaska native (MSW); children, youth and families (MSW); epidemiology/biostatistics (MPH); generalist (MPH); global health (MPH); health (MSW); health policy analysis (MPH); individualized (MSW), including health; mental health (MSW); older adults and aging societies (MSW); public health sciences (PhD); social and economic development (MSW), including domestic, international; social work (PhD); urban design (MPH); violence and injury prevention (MSW); JD/MSW; M Arch/MSW; MPH/MBA; MSW/M Div; MSW/M Ed; MSW/MAPS; MSW/MBA; MSW/MPH; MUD/MSW. *Accreditation:* CEPH; CSWE (one or more programs are accredited). *Faculty:* 54 full-

time (31 women), 87 part-time/adjunct (61 women). *Students:* 282 full-time (226 women); includes 90 minority (40 Black or African American, non-Hispanic/Latino; 10 American Indian or Alaska Native, non-Hispanic/Latino; 26 Asian, non-Hispanic/Latino; 13 Hispanic/Latino; 1 Native Hawaiian or other Pacific Islander, non-Hispanic/Latino). Average age 24. *Degree requirements:* For master's, 60 credit hours (for MSW); 52 credit hours (for MPH); practicum; for doctorate, comprehensive exam, thesis/dissertation. *Entrance requirements:* For master's, GRE (preferred), GMAT, LSAT, MCAT, PCAT, or United States Medical Licensing Exam (for MPH); for doctorate, GRE. Additional exam requirements/recommendations for international students: required—TOEFL (minimum score 100 iBT), IELTS (minimum score 7). *Application deadline:* For fall admission, 12/15 priority date for domestic and international students; for winter admission, 3/1 priority date for domestic and international students. Applications are processed on a rolling basis. Electronic applications accepted. *Expenses:* Contact institution. *Financial support:* In 2019–20, 90 research assistantships were awarded; fellowships, teaching assistantships, career-related internships or fieldwork, Federal Work-Study, scholarships/grants, and unspecified assistantships also available. Support available to part-time students. Financial award applicants required to submit FAFSA. *Unit head:* Jamie L. Adkisson-Hennessey, Director of Admissions and Recruitment, 314-935-3524, Fax: 314-935-4859, E-mail: jadkisson@wustl.edu. *Application contact:* Office of Admissions and Recruitment, 314-935-6676, Fax: 314-935-4859, E-mail: brownadmissions@wustl.edu. Website: http://brownschool.wustl.edu

Washington University in St. Louis, The Graduate School, Department of Psychological and Brain Sciences, St. Louis, MO 63130-4899. Offers aging and development (PhD). Terminal master's awarded for partial completion of doctoral program. *Degree requirements:* For doctorate, thesis/dissertation. *Entrance requirements:* For doctorate, GRE General Test. Additional exam requirements/recommendations for international students: required—TOEFL. Electronic applications accepted.

Wayne State University, School of Social Work, Detroit, MI 48202. Offers gerontology (Certificate); social work (MSW, PhD). *Accreditation:* CSWE (one or more programs are accredited). *Program availability:* Part-time, evening/weekend, 100% online, blended/hybrid learning. *Faculty:* 27. *Students:* 474 full-time (410 women), 156 part-time (134 women); includes 259 minority (187 Black or African American, non-Hispanic/Latino; 1 American Indian or Alaska Native, non-Hispanic/Latino; 18 Asian, non-Hispanic/Latino; 26 Hispanic/Latino; 27 Two or more races, non-Hispanic/Latino), 16 international. Average age 30. 729 applicants, 20% accepted. In 2019, 315 master's, 2 doctorates, 20 other advanced degrees awarded. Terminal master's awarded for partial completion of doctoral program. *Degree requirements:* For master's, field work; for doctorate, comprehensive exam, thesis/dissertation. *Entrance requirements:* For master's, personal interest statement, resume, 3 reference letters, transcripts; for doctorate, GRE (minimum combined score of 1000 on Verbal and Quantitative components) within last 5 years, minimum undergraduate GPA of 3.5, MSW from CSWE-accredited institution (or working towards one), resume, three letters of reference, personal statement, summary of relevant research and professional experience, writing sample, interview; for Certificate, MSW or actively enrolled in advanced portion of MSW program. Additional exam requirements/recommendations for international students: required—TOEFL (minimum score 550 paper-based; 79 iBT), TWE (minimum score 5.5), Michigan English Language Assessment Battery (minimum score 85); recommended—IELTS (minimum score 6.5). *Application deadline:* For fall admission, 12/18 for domestic students; for spring admission, 4/1 for domestic students. Applications are processed on a rolling basis. Application fee: $50. Electronic applications accepted. *Expenses:* Tuition: Full-time $34,567. *Financial support:* In 2019–20, 139 students received support, including 4 fellowships with tuition reimbursements available (averaging $21,875 per year), 7 research assistantships with tuition reimbursements available (averaging $22,429 per year), 1 teaching assistantship with tuition reimbursement available (averaging $19,967 per year); scholarships/grants and unspecified assistantships also available. Financial award applicants required to submit FAFSA. *Unit head:* Sheryl Kubiak, Dean and Professor, 313-577-4409, E-mail: spk@wayne.edu. *Application contact:* Anwar Najor-Durack, Assistant Dean for Student Affairs, 313-577-4409, E-mail: ac1724@wayne.edu. Website: http://socialwork.wayne.edu/

Webster University, College of Arts and Sciences, Department of Psychology, St. Louis, MO 63119-3194. Offers counseling psychology (MS); gerontology (MS). *Program availability:* Part-time. *Entrance requirements:* Additional exam requirements/recommendations for international students: required—TOEFL.

Webster University, George Herbert Walker School of Business and Technology, Department of Business, St. Louis, MO 63119-3194. Offers business and organizational security management (MBA); decision support systems (MBA); environmental management (MBA); finance (MBA, MS); forensic accounting (MS); gerontology (MBA); human resources development (MBA); human resources management (MBA); information technology management (MBA); international business (MA, MBA); international relations (MBA); management and leadership (MBA); marketing (MBA); media communications (MBA); procurement and acquisitions management (MBA); Web services (MBA). *Accreditation:* ACBSP. *Program availability:* Part-time, evening/weekend, online learning. *Degree requirements:* For master's, comprehensive exam (for some programs), thesis (for some programs). *Entrance requirements:* Additional exam requirements/recommendations for international students: required—TOEFL.

Wichita State University, Graduate School, College of Health Professions, Department of Public Health Sciences, Wichita, KS 67260. Offers aging studies (MA). *Program availability:* Part-time, 100% online, blended/hybrid learning.

Youngstown State University, College of Graduate Studies, College of Liberal Arts and Social Sciences, Program in Gerontology, Youngstown, OH 44555-0001. Offers MA. *Program availability:* Part-time, evening/weekend, online learning. *Degree requirements:* For master's, thesis optional. *Entrance requirements:* For master's, GRE, minimum GPA of 3.0, three letters of recommendation, letter of intent, resume or curriculum vitae, social statistics course at undergraduate or graduate level, minimum of 9 credit hours of aging-related coursework at undergraduate or graduate level.

Section 21
Geography

This section contains a directory of institutions offering graduate work in geography. Additional information about programs listed in the directory may be obtained by writing directly to the dean of a graduate school or chair of a department at the address given in the directory.

For programs offering related work, see also in this book *Area and Cultural Studies* and *Humanities.* In another guide in this series:

Graduate Programs in the Physical Sciences, Mathematics, Agricultural Sciences, the Environment & Natural Resources
See *Geosciences*

CONTENTS

Program Directories

Geographic Information Systems

Acadia University, Faculty of Pure and Applied Science, Program in Applied Geomatics, Wolfville, NS B4P 2R6, Canada. Offers M Sc. *Entrance requirements:* Additional exam requirements/recommendations for international students: required—TOEFL (minimum score 580 paper-based; 93 iBT), IELTS (minimum score 6.5).

Appalachian State University, Cratis D. Williams School of Graduate Studies, Department of Geography and Planning, Boone, NC 28608. Offers geography (MA), including geographic information science. *Program availability:* Part-time, online learning. *Degree requirements:* For master's, comprehensive exam, thesis or alternative. *Entrance requirements:* For master's, GRE General Test, 3 letters of recommendation. Additional exam requirements/recommendations for international students: required—TOEFL (minimum score 570 paper-based; 79 iBT), IELTS (minimum score 6.5). Electronic applications accepted.

Arizona State University at Tempe, College of Liberal Arts and Sciences, School of Geographical Sciences and Urban Planning, Tempe, AZ 85287-5302. Offers geographic information systems (MAS); geographical information science (Graduate Certificate); geography (MA, PhD); transportation systems (Graduate Certificate); urban and environmental planning (MUEP); urban planning (PhD). *Accreditation:* ACSP. Terminal master's awarded for partial completion of doctoral program. *Degree requirements:* For master's, thesis, interactive Program of Study (iPOS) submitted before completing 50 percent of required credit hours; for doctorate, comprehensive exam, thesis/dissertation, interactive Program of Study (iPOS) submitted before completing 50 percent of required credit hours. *Entrance requirements:* For master's and doctorate, GRE, minimum GPA of 3.0 or equivalent in last 2 years of work leading to bachelor's degree. Additional exam requirements/recommendations for international students: required—TOEFL, IELTS, or PTE. Electronic applications accepted. *Expenses:* Contact institution.

Auburn University at Montgomery, College of Liberal Arts & Social Sciences, Department of Sociology, Anthropology and Social Work, Montgomery, AL 36124-4023. Offers geographic information systems (MS). *Students:* Average age 37. 4 applicants, 100% accepted, 3 enrolled. In 2019, 1 master's awarded. *Entrance requirements:* For master's, GRE or MAT. Additional exam requirements/recommendations for international students: recommended—TOEFL (minimum score 500 paper-based; 61 iBT), IELTS (minimum score 5.5), TSE (minimum score 44). *Application deadline:* For fall admission, 7/15 for international students; for spring admission, 11/15 for international students; for summer admission, 4/15 for international students. Applications are processed on a rolling basis. Application fee: $25. Electronic applications accepted. *Expenses: Tuition, area resident:* Full-time $7578; part-time $421 per credit hour. Tuition, state resident: full-time $7578; part-time $421 per credit hour. Tuition, nonresident: full-time $17,046; part-time $947 per credit hour. *International tuition:* $17,046 full-time. *Required fees:* $868. *Financial support:* Applicants required to submit FAFSA. *Unit head:* Dr. Annice Yarber-Allen, Chair, 334-244-3432, Fax: 334-244-3740, E-mail: ayarber@aum.edu. *Application contact:* Dr. Annice Yarber-Allen, Chair, 334-244-3432, Fax: 334-244-3740, E-mail: ayarber@aum.edu.
Website: http://cppj.aum.edu/departments/sociology

Ball State University, Graduate School, College of Sciences and Humanities, Department of Geography, Muncie, IN 47306. Offers geographic information systems (Certificate); geography (MS); professional meteorology and climatology (Certificate). *Program availability:* Part-time. *Entrance requirements:* For master's, minimum baccalaureate GPA of 2.75 or 3.0 in latter half of baccalaureate, letter of interest, three letters of recommendation, resume or curriculum vitae, official transcripts. Additional exam requirements/recommendations for international students: required—TOEFL (minimum score 550 paper-based; 79 iBT), IELTS (minimum score 6.5). Electronic applications accepted. *Expenses: Tuition, area resident:* Full-time $7506; part-time $417 per credit hour. Tuition, nonresident: full-time $20,610; part-time $1145 per credit hour. *Required fees:* $2126. Tuition and fees vary according to course load, campus/location and program.

Boston University, Graduate School of Arts and Sciences, Department of Earth and Environment, Boston, MA 02215. Offers earth and environment (MA, PhD); energy and environment (MA); remote sensing and geospatial sciences (MA). *Students:* 68 full-time (37 women), 11 part-time (7 women); includes 5 minority (1 Asian, non-Hispanic/Latino; 4 Hispanic/Latino), 46 international. Average age 25. 194 applicants, 56% accepted, 31 enrolled. In 2019, 26 master's, 6 doctorates awarded. Terminal master's awarded for partial completion of doctoral program. *Degree requirements:* For master's, comprehensive exam (for some programs), thesis (for some programs); for doctorate, comprehensive exam, thesis/dissertation. *Entrance requirements:* For master's and doctorate, GRE General Test, 3 letters of recommendation, official transcripts, personal statement. Additional exam requirements/recommendations for international students: required—TOEFL (minimum score 550 paper-based; 84 iBT). *Application deadline:* For fall admission, 12/19 for domestic and international students; for winter admission, 11/1 for domestic and international students. Application fee: $95. Electronic applications accepted. *Financial support:* In 2019–20, 52 students received support, including 8 fellowships with full tuition reimbursements available (averaging $23,340 per year), 21 research assistantships with full tuition reimbursements available (averaging $23,340 per year), 17 teaching assistantships with full tuition reimbursements available (averaging $23,340 per year); Federal Work-Study, scholarships/grants, traineeships, and health care benefits also available. Financial award application deadline: 12/19. *Unit head:* Guido Salvucci, Interim Chair, 617-353-8344, E-mail: gdsalvuc@bu.edu. *Application contact:* Matt DiCintio, Graduate Program Coordinator, 617-353-2529, Fax: 617-353-8399, E-mail: dicintio@bu.edu.
Website: http://www.bu.edu/earth/

Central Michigan University, College of Graduate Studies, College of Science and Engineering, Department of Geography and Environmental Studies, Mount Pleasant, MI 48859. Offers geographic information sciences (MS). *Degree requirements:* For master's, thesis optional. *Entrance requirements:* For master's, GRE. *Expenses: Tuition, area resident:* Full-time $12,267; part-time $8178 per year. Tuition, state resident: full-time $12,267; part-time $8178 per year. Tuition, nonresident: full-time $12,267; part-time $8178 per year. *International tuition:* $16,110 full-time. *Required fees:* $225 per semester. Tuition and fees vary according to degree level and program.

Chicago State University, School of Graduate and Professional Studies, College of Arts and Sciences, Department of Geography, Sociology, History, African-American Studies and Anthropology, Chicago, IL 60628. Offers geographic information systems (MA); history (MA). *Entrance requirements:* For master's, minimum GPA of 3.0.

Claremont Graduate University, Graduate Programs, Center for Information Systems and Technology, Claremont, CA 91711-6160. Offers cybersecurity and networking (MS); data science and analytics (MS); electronic commerce (PhD); geographic information systems (MS); health informatics (MS); information systems (Certificate); IT strategy and innovation (MS); knowledge management (PhD); systems development (PhD); telecommunications and networking (PhD); MBA/MS. *Program availability:* Part-time. *Degree requirements:* For doctorate, comprehensive exam, thesis/dissertation, portfolio. *Entrance requirements:* For master's and doctorate, GMAT, GRE General Test. Additional exam requirements/recommendations for international students: required—TOEFL (minimum score 75 iBT). Electronic applications accepted.

Clark University, Graduate School, Department of International Development, Community, and Environment, Program in Geographic Information Science for Development and Environment, Worcester, MA 01610-1477. Offers MS. *Degree requirements:* For master's, thesis. *Entrance requirements:* For master's, 2 references, resume or curriculum vitae, personal statement. Additional exam requirements/recommendations for international students: required—TOEFL (minimum score 575 paper-based; 90 iBT), IELTS (minimum score 6.5). Electronic applications accepted. *Expenses:* Contact institution.

Cleveland State University, College of Graduate Studies, Maxine Goodman Levin College of Urban Affairs, Program in Urban Planning and Development, Cleveland, OH 44115. Offers economic development (MUPD); environmental sustainability (MUPD); historic preservation (MUPD); housing and neighborhood development (MUPD); real estate development and finance (MUPD); urban economic development (Certificate); urban geographic information systems (MUPD); JD/MUPDD. *Accreditation:* ACSP. *Program availability:* Part-time, evening/weekend. *Degree requirements:* For master's, thesis or alternative, exit project. *Entrance requirements:* For master's, GRE General Test (minimum score: 50th percentile combined verbal and quantitative, 4.0 analytical writing), minimum GPA of 3.0. Additional exam requirements/recommendations for international students: required—TOEFL (minimum score 550 paper-based; 78 iBT), IELTS (6.0), or International Test of English Proficiency (iTEP). Electronic applications accepted. *Expenses:* Contact institution.

East Carolina University, Graduate School, Thomas Harriot College of Arts and Sciences, Department of Geography, Planning, and Environment, Greenville, NC 27858-4353. Offers development and environmental planning (Certificate); economic development (Certificate); geographic information science and technology (Certificate); geography (MA), including geography, planning, rural development. *Program availability:* Part-time, evening/weekend, online learning. *Degree requirements:* For master's, comprehensive exam, thesis optional. *Entrance requirements:* For master's, GRE General Test. *Application deadline:* For fall admission, 4/1 priority date for domestic and international students. Applications are processed on a rolling basis. Electronic applications accepted. *Expenses: Tuition, area resident:* Full-time $4749; part-time $185 per credit hour. Tuition, state resident: full-time $4749; part-time $185 per credit hour. Tuition, nonresident: full-time $17,898; part-time $864 per credit hour. *International tuition:* $17,898 full-time. *Required fees:* $2787. *Financial support:* Research assistantships with partial tuition reimbursements, teaching assistantships with partial tuition reimbursements, and Federal Work-Study available. Support available to part-time students. Financial award application deadline: 3/1. *Unit head:* Dr. Thad Wasklewicz, Chair, 252-328-6230, E-mail: wasklewiczt@ecu.edu. *Application contact:* Graduate Admissions, 252-328-6012, Fax: 252-328-6071, E-mail: gradschool@ecu.edu.
Website: https://geography.ecu.edu/

Eastern Illinois University, Graduate School, College of Liberal Arts and Sciences, Department of Geology and Geography, Charleston, IL 61920. Offers geographic information sciences (PSM). *Program availability:* Part-time, evening/weekend. *Entrance requirements:* For master's, GMAT or GRE. Additional exam requirements/recommendations for international students: required—TOEFL (minimum score 500 paper-based; 61 iBT), IELTS (minimum score 6). Electronic applications accepted.

Eastern Illinois University, Graduate School, Lumpkin College of Business and Technology, Program in Business Administration, Charleston, IL 61920. Offers accountancy (MBA); applied management (MBA); geographic information systems (MBA); research (MBA). *Accreditation:* AACSB. *Program availability:* Part-time, evening/weekend. *Entrance requirements:* For master's, GMAT or GRE. Additional exam requirements/recommendations for international students: required—TOEFL (minimum score 500 paper-based; 61 iBT), IELTS (minimum score 6). Electronic applications accepted.

Eastern Michigan University, Graduate School, College of Arts and Sciences, Department of Geography and Geology, Programs in Geographic Information Systems, Ypsilanti, MI 48197. Offers geographic information systems (MS); geographic information systems for educators (Graduate Certificate); geographic information systems for professionals (Graduate Certificate). *Students:* 3 full-time (2 women), 14 part-time (4 women); includes 1 minority (Hispanic/Latino), 5 international. Average age 34. 21 applicants, 62% accepted, 7 enrolled. In 2019, 7 master's awarded. Application fee: $45. *Application contact:* Dr. Hugh Semple, Program Advisor, 734-487-8169, Fax: 734-487-6979, E-mail: hsemple@emich.edu.

East Tennessee State University, College of Graduate and Continuing Studies, College of Arts and Sciences, Department of Geosciences, Johnson City, TN 37614-1709. Offers geographic information systems (Postbaccalaureate Certificate); geospatial analysis (MS); paleontology (MS). *Program availability:* Part-time. *Degree requirements:* For master's, thesis. *Entrance requirements:* For master's, bachelor's degree in geosciences or related discipline, minimum GPA of 3.0, three letters of recommendation, resume, two-page letter that discusses career goals and specific academic and research interests; for Postbaccalaureate Certificate, minimum undergraduate GPA of 2.5, personal essay. Additional exam requirements/recommendations for international students: required—TOEFL (minimum score 550 paper-based; 79 iBT). Electronic applications accepted.

Elizabeth City State University, Department of Mathematics and Computer Science, Master of Science in Mathematics Program, Elizabeth City, NC 27909-7806. Offers applied mathematics (MS); community college teaching (MS); mathematics education (MS); remote sensing (MS). *Program availability:* Part-time, evening/weekend. *Degree requirements:* For master's, thesis. *Entrance requirements:* For master's, MAT and/or GRE, minimum GPA of 3.0, 3 letters of recommendation, two official transcripts from all undergraduate/graduate schools attended, typewritten one-page request for entry into program that includes description of student's educational preparation. Additional exam requirements/recommendations for international students: required—TOEFL (minimum score 550 paper-based, 80 iBT) or IELTS (minimum score 6.5). Electronic applications accepted.

Elmhurst University, Graduate Programs, Program in Geographic Information Systems, Elmhurst, IL 60126-3296. Offers MS. *Program availability:* Part-time, evening/weekend, online only, 100% online. *Faculty:* 7 part-time/adjunct (2 women). *Students:* 19 part-time (8 women); includes 2 minority (1 Black or African American, non-Hispanic/

Latino; 1 Hispanic/Latino). Average age 35. 33 applicants, 39% accepted, 12 enrolled. In 2019, 8 master's awarded. *Entrance requirements:* For master's, 3 recommendations, resume, statement of purpose. Additional exam requirements/recommendations for international students: required—TOEFL (minimum score 550 paper-based; 79 iBT), IELTS (minimum score 6.5). *Application deadline:* Applications are processed on a rolling basis. Application fee: $0. Electronic applications accepted. *Expenses:* $795 per semester hour. *Financial support:* In 2019–20, 5 students received support. Scholarships/grants available. Support available to part-time students. Financial award applicants required to submit FAFSA. *Unit head:* Judy Bock, Director, 630-617-3128, E-mail: judith.bock@elmhurst.edu. *Application contact:* Timothy J. Panfil, Senior Director of Graduate Admission and Enrollment Management, 630-617-3300 Ext. 3256, Fax: 630-617-6471, E-mail: panfilt@elmhurst.edu.
Website: http://www.elmhurst.edu/applied_geospatial_sciences

Florida State University, The Graduate School, College of Social Sciences and Public Policy, Department of Geography, Tallahassee, FL 32306. Offers geographic information science (MS); geography (MA, MS, PhD). *Program availability:* Part-time. *Faculty:* 12 full-time (3 women), 7 part-time/adjunct (5 women). *Students:* 36 full-time (22 women), 16 part-time (6 women); includes 12 minority (4 Black or African American, non-Hispanic/Latino; 3 Hispanic/Latino; 5 Two or more races, non-Hispanic/Latino), 12 international. Average age 32. 82 applicants, 33% accepted, 12 enrolled. In 2019, 26 master's, 6 doctorates awarded. Terminal master's awarded for partial completion of doctoral program. *Degree requirements:* For master's, thesis (for some programs); for doctorate, comprehensive exam, thesis/dissertation. *Entrance requirements:* For master's and doctorate, GRE General Test, minimum GPA of 3.0. Additional exam requirements/recommendations for international students: required—TOEFL (minimum score 80 iBT). *Application deadline:* For fall admission, 3/1 priority date for domestic and international students; for spring admission, 10/1 priority date for domestic and international students. Applications are processed on a rolling basis. Application fee: $30. Electronic applications accepted. *Financial support:* In 2019–20, 44 students received support, including 1 research assistantship with full tuition reimbursement available (averaging $17,687 per year), 16 teaching assistantships with full tuition reimbursements available (averaging $17,687 per year); career-related internships or fieldwork, Federal Work-Study, institutionally sponsored loans, scholarships/grants, health care benefits, tuition waivers (full and partial), and unspecified assistantships also available. Financial award application deadline: 3/1; financial award applicants required to submit FAFSA. *Unit head:* Prof. James Elsner, Chair, 850-644-1706, Fax: 850-644-5913, E-mail: jelsner@fsu.edu. *Application contact:* Dr. Christopher Uejio, Graduate Director, 850-644-1706, Fax: 850-644-5193, E-mail: cuejio@fsu.edu.
Website: http://geography.fsu.edu/

George Mason University, College of Science, Department of Geography and Geoinformation Science, Fairfax, VA 22030. Offers earth system science (MS); earth systems and geoinformation sciences (PhD); environmental geoinformation science and biodiversity conservation (Certificate); geography and geoinformation science (Certificate). *Degree requirements:* For master's, comprehensive exam (for some programs), thesis (for some programs); for doctorate, comprehensive exam, thesis/dissertation. *Entrance requirements:* For master's, GRE, bachelor's degree with minimum GPA of 3.0; 2 copies of official transcripts; current resume; expanded goals statement; 3 letters of recommendation; for doctorate, GRE, bachelor's degree with minimum GPA of 3.0; 2 copies of official transcripts; 3 letters of recommendation; resume; expanded goals statement; for Certificate, GRE, baccalaureate degree with minimum GPA of 3.0; 2 official copies of transcripts; expanded goals statement; 3 letters of recommendation; resume. Additional exam requirements/recommendations for international students: required—TOEFL (minimum score 575 paper-based; 88 iBT), IELTS (minimum score 6.5), PTE (minimum score 59). Electronic applications accepted. *Expenses:* Contact institution.

Georgia Institute of Technology, Graduate Studies, College of Design, School of City and Regional Planning, Atlanta, GA 30332-0001. Offers city and regional planning (PhD); economic development (MCRP); environmental planning and management (MCRP); geographic information systems (MCRP); land and community development (MCRP); land use planning (MCRP); transportation (MCRP); urban design (MCRP); MCP/MSCE. *Accreditation:* ACSP. *Degree requirements:* For master's, thesis, internship. *Entrance requirements:* For master's, GRE General Test, minimum GPA of 2.7. Additional exam requirements/recommendations for international students: required—TOEFL. Electronic applications accepted. *Expenses: Tuition, area resident:* Full-time $14,064; part-time $586 per credit hour. Tuition, state resident: full-time $14,064; part-time $586 per credit hour. Tuition, nonresident: full-time $29,140; part-time $1215 per credit hour. *International tuition:* $29,140 full-time. *Required fees:* $2024; $840 per semester. $2096. Tuition and fees vary according to course load.

Georgia State University, College of Arts and Sciences, Department of Geosciences, Program in Geographic Information Systems, Atlanta, GA 30302-3083. Offers Certificate. *Program availability:* Part-time. *Entrance requirements:* For degree, GRE. Additional exam requirements/recommendations for international students: required—TOEFL (minimum score 550 paper-based; 80 iBT). Electronic applications accepted. *Expenses: Tuition, area resident:* Full-time $7164; part-time $398 per credit hour. Tuition, state resident: full-time $7164; part-time $398 per credit hour. Tuition, nonresident: full-time $22,662; part-time $1259 per credit hour. *International tuition:* $22,662 full-time. *Required fees:* $2128; $312 per credit hour. Tuition and fees vary according to course load and program. *Financial support:* Career-related internships or fieldwork available. *Unit head:* Dr. Katherin Hankins, Chair, 404-413-5775, E-mail: khankings@gsu.edu. *Application contact:* Dr. Katherin Hankins, Chair, 404-413-5775, E-mail: khankings@gsu.edu.
Website: http://geosciences.gsu.edu/grad-programs/

The Graduate Center, City University of New York, Graduate Studies, Program in Digital Humanities, New York, NY 10016-4039. Offers data visualization and mapping (MA); digital pedagogy (MA); textual analysis (MA).

Hood College, Graduate School, Program in Environmental Biology, Frederick, MD 21701-8575. Offers environmental biology (MS); geographic information systems (Certificate). *Program availability:* Part-time, evening/weekend. *Degree requirements:* For master's, thesis or alternative, independent project (A); internship (A); capstone (A). *Entrance requirements:* For master's, minimum GPA of 2.75, 3.0 preferred; official transcripts; essay; completed and earned at least a B in the following five courses: two college-level biology courses (with lab), two college-level chemistry courses (with lab), and one college-level math course (e.g., statistics, algebra, pre-calculus, calculus). Additional exam requirements/recommendations for international students: required—TOEFL (minimum score 575 paper-based; 89 iBT), IELTS (minimum score 6.5). Electronic applications accepted.

Hunter College of the City University of New York, Graduate School, School of Arts and Sciences, Department of Geography, New York, NY 10065-5085. Offers geographic information science (Certificate); geography (MA); geoinformatics (MS). *Program availability:* Part-time, evening/weekend. *Degree requirements:* For master's, comprehensive exam or thesis. *Entrance requirements:* For master's, GRE General Test, minimum B average in major, B- overall; 18 credits of course work in geography; 2 letters of recommendation; for Certificate, minimum B average in major, B- overall. Additional exam requirements/recommendations for international students: required—TOEFL.

Idaho State University, Graduate School, College of Science and Engineering, Department of Geosciences, Pocatello, ID 83209-8072. Offers geographic information science (MS); geology (MNS, MS); geology with emphasis in environmental geoscience (MS); geophysics/hydrology/geology (MS); geotechnology (Postbaccalaureate Certificate). *Program availability:* Part-time. *Degree requirements:* For master's, comprehensive exam, thesis, oral colloquium; for Postbaccalaureate Certificate, thesis optional, minimum 19 credits. *Entrance requirements:* For master's, GRE General Test (minimum 50th percentile in 2 sections), 3 letters of recommendation; for Postbaccalaureate Certificate, GRE General Test, 3 letters of recommendation, bachelor's degree, statement of goals. Additional exam requirements/recommendations for international students: required—TOEFL (minimum score 550 paper-based; 80 iBT). Electronic applications accepted.

Indiana University of Pennsylvania, School of Graduate Studies and Research, College of Humanities and Social Sciences, Department of Geography and Regional Planning, Geographic Information Science/Cartography Track, Indiana, PA 15705. Offers MS. *Program availability:* Part-time. *Faculty:* 8 full-time (2 women). *Students:* 8 full-time (2 women), 1 part-time (0 women), 1 international. Average age 27. 11 applicants, 91% accepted, 4 enrolled. *Degree requirements:* For master's, thesis optional. *Entrance requirements:* For master's, goal statement, letters of recommendation, official transcripts. Additional exam requirements/recommendations for international students: required—TOEFL (minimum score 550 paper-based; 80 iBT), IELTS (minimum score 6.5), TOEFL or IELTS. *Application deadline:* Applications are processed on a rolling basis. Application fee: $50. Electronic applications accepted. *Expenses: Tuition, area resident:* Full-time $9288; part-time $516 per credit. Tuition, nonresident: full-time $13,932; part-time $774 per credit. *Required fees:* $4454. One-time fee: $115 full-time. Tuition and fees vary according to course load and program. *Financial support:* In 2019–20, 6 research assistantships with tuition reimbursements (averaging $2,100 per year) were awarded; career-related internships or fieldwork, Federal Work-Study, scholarships/grants, and unspecified assistantships also available. Financial award application deadline: 4/15; financial award applicants required to submit FAFSA. *Unit head:* Dr. Jennifer Smith, Graduate Coordinator, 724-357-2250, E-mail: jsmith@iup.edu. *Application contact:* Dr. Jennifer Smith, Graduate Coordinator, 724-357-2250, E-mail: jsmith@iup.edu.
Website: http://www.iup.edu/georegionalplan/grad/default.aspx

Indiana University of Pennsylvania, School of Graduate Studies and Research, College of Humanities and Social Sciences, Department of Geography and Regional Planning, Program in Geographic Information Science and Geospatial Techniques, Indiana, PA 15705. Offers Certificate. *Program availability:* Part-time. *Faculty:* 8 full-time (2 women). *Students:* 1 full-time (0 women), 1 part-time (0 women). Average age 29. *Entrance requirements:* Additional exam requirements/recommendations for international students: required—TOEFL (minimum score 550 paper-based; 80 iBT), IELTS (minimum score 6.5), TOEFL or IELTS. *Application deadline:* Applications are processed on a rolling basis. Application fee: $50. Electronic applications accepted. *Expenses: Tuition, area resident:* Full-time $9288; part-time $516 per credit. Tuition, nonresident: full-time $13,932; part-time $774 per credit. *Required fees:* $4454. One-time fee: $115 full-time. Tuition and fees vary according to course load and program. *Financial support:* Research assistantships, career-related internships or fieldwork, Federal Work-Study, scholarships/grants, and unspecified assistantships available. Financial award application deadline: 4/15; financial award applicants required to submit FAFSA. *Unit head:* Dr. Jennifer Smith, Graduate Coordinator, 724-357-2250, E-mail: jsmith@iup.edu. *Application contact:* Dr. Jennifer Smith, Graduate Coordinator, 724-357-2250, E-mail: jsmith@iup.edu.
Website: http://www.iup.edu/georegionalplan/grad/default.aspx

Indiana University-Purdue University Indianapolis, School of Liberal Arts, Department of Geography, Indianapolis, IN 46202. Offers geographic information systems (MS, Certificate). *Program availability:* Part-time. *Degree requirements:* For master's, variable foreign language requirement, thesis; for Certificate, variable foreign language requirement. *Entrance requirements:* For master's, GRE (minimum verbal or quantitative score of 600, with the other score above 500), minimum GPA of 3.0; for Certificate, minimum GPA of 3.0. Additional exam requirements/recommendations for international students: required—TOEFL (minimum score 550 paper-based), IELTS. Electronic applications accepted. *Expenses:* Contact institution.

Johns Hopkins University, Advanced Academic Programs, Program in Environmental Sciences and Policy, Washington, DC 21218. Offers energy policy and climate (MS); environmental sciences (MS); geographic information systems (MS, Certificate). *Program availability:* Part-time, evening/weekend, online learning. *Entrance requirements:* For master's, minimum GPA of 3.0, coursework in chemistry and calculus. Additional exam requirements/recommendations for international students: required—TOEFL (minimum score 100 iBT). Electronic applications accepted.

Kansas State University, Graduate School, College of Arts and Sciences, Department of Geography, Manhattan, KS 66506. Offers geographic information science (Graduate Certificate); geography (MA, PhD). *Degree requirements:* For master's, thesis optional, oral exam; for doctorate, one foreign language, thesis/dissertation. *Entrance requirements:* For master's and doctorate, GRE General Test, minimum GPA of 3.0. Electronic applications accepted.

Kent State University, College of Arts and Sciences, Department of Geography, Kent, OH 44242-0001. Offers geographic information science (MGIS), including cyber geographic information science, environmental geographic information science, geographic information science and health; geography (MA, PhD). *Program availability:* Part-time, 100% online. *Faculty:* 9 full-time (2 women), 2 part-time/adjunct (both women). *Students:* 39 full-time (17 women), 45 part-time (24 women); includes 10 minority (2 Black or African American, non-Hispanic/Latino; 4 Asian, non-Hispanic/Latino; 2 Hispanic/Latino; 2 Two or more races, non-Hispanic/Latino), 19 international. Average age 33. 42 applicants, 83% accepted, 26 enrolled. In 2019, 13 master's, 5 doctorates awarded. *Degree requirements:* For master's, thesis (for some programs), Thesis or two research papers, practicum (MGISc); for doctorate, comprehensive exam, thesis/dissertation. *Entrance requirements:* For master's, GRE, minimum undergraduate GPA of 3.0, undergraduate degree transcripts, three letters of recommendation, goal statement, resume; for doctorate, GRE, Master's degree from accredited college or university, transcripts, three letters of recommendation, goal statement, resume. Additional exam requirements/recommendations for international students: required—TOEFL (minimum score 79 iBT), IELTS (minimum score 6.5), PTE (minimum score 58), Michigan English Language Assessment Battery (minimum score 77). *Application deadline:* For fall admission, 2/1 priority date for domestic and international students; for spring admission, 11/1 for domestic and international students; for summer admission, 4/1 for domestic and international students. Applications are processed on a rolling basis. Application fee: $45 ($70 for international students). Electronic applications accepted. *Financial support:* Fellowships with full tuition reimbursements, research assistantships with full tuition reimbursements, teaching assistantships with full tuition reimbursements, Federal Work-Study, scholarships/grants, and unspecified assistantships available. Financial award application deadline: 2/1. *Unit head:* Dr. Scott

Geographic Information Systems

Sheridan, Professor and Chair, 330-672-3224, Fax: 330-672-4304, E-mail: ssherid1@kent.edu. *Application contact:* Dr. David H. Kaplan, Professor and Graduate Coordinator, 330-672-3221, E-mail: dkaplan@kent.edu.
Website: https://www.kent.edu/geography

Millersville University of Pennsylvania, College of Graduate Studies and Adult Learning, College of Science and Technology, Department of Earth Sciences, Millersville, PA 17551-0302. Offers integrated scientific applications (MS). *Program availability:* Part-time. *Students:* 7 full-time (2 women), 5 part-time (0 women); includes 3 minority (1 Black or African American, non-Hispanic/Latino; 1 Asian, non-Hispanic/Latino; 1 Hispanic/Latino), 1 international. Average age 27. 6 applicants, 100% accepted, 3 enrolled. In 2019, 3 master's awarded. *Entrance requirements:* For master's, GRE or MAT, or GMAT, required only if cumulative GPA is lower than 3.0, resume. Additional exam requirements/recommendations for international students: required—TOEFL, IELTS (minimum score 6), PTE (minimum score 60). *Application deadline:* Applications are processed on a rolling basis. Application fee: $40. Electronic applications accepted. *Expenses: Tuition, area resident:* Part-time $516 per credit. Tuition, state resident: part-time $516 per credit. Tuition, nonresident: part-time $774 per credit. *Required fees:* $118.75 per credit. Tuition and fees vary according to course load, degree level and program. *Financial support:* In 2019–20, 4 students received support. Scholarships/grants and unspecified assistantships available. Financial award application deadline: 3/15; financial award applicants required to submit FAFSA. *Unit head:* Dr. Richard D. Clark, Chairperson and Graduate Program Coordinator, 717-871-7434, Fax: 717-871-7918, E-mail: richard.clark@millersville.edu. *Application contact:* Dr. James A. Delle, Acting Dean of College of Graduate Studies and Adult Learning/ Associate Provost, Academic Administration, 717-871-7462, E-mail: James.Delle@millersville.edu.
Website: https://www.millersville.edu/esci/index.php

Millersville University of Pennsylvania, College of Graduate Studies and Adult Learning, College of Science and Technology, Department of Earth Sciences, Program in Integrated Scientific Applications: GeoInformatics Option, Millersville, PA 17551-0302. Offers integrated scientific applications (MS). *Program availability:* Part-time. *Students:* 1 full-time (0 women), 2 part-time (0 women). Average age 29. *Entrance requirements:* For master's, GRE or MAT or GMAT, required only if cumulative GPA is lower than 3.0, resume. Additional exam requirements/recommendations for international students: required—TOEFL, IELTS (minimum score 6), PTE (minimum score 60). *Application deadline:* Applications are processed on a rolling basis. Application fee: $40. Electronic applications accepted. *Expenses: Tuition, area resident:* Part-time $516 per credit. Tuition, state resident: part-time $516 per credit. Tuition, nonresident: part-time $774 per credit. *Required fees:* $118.75 per credit. Tuition and fees vary according to course load, degree level and program. *Financial support:* In 2019–20, 1 student received support. Scholarships/grants and unspecified assistantships available. Financial award application deadline: 3/15; financial award applicants required to submit FAFSA. *Unit head:* Dr. Richard D. Clark, Chairperson and Graduate Program Coordinator, 717-871-7434, Fax: 717-871-7918, E-mail: richard.clark@millersville.edu. *Application contact:* Dr. James A. Delle, Acting Dean of College of Graduate Studies and Adult Learning/ Associate Provost, Academic Administration, 717-871-7462, E-mail: James.Delle@millersville.edu.
Website: http://www.millersville.edu/esci/msisa/geoinformatics.php

Montclair State University, The Graduate School, College of Science and Mathematics, Geographic Information Science Certificate Program, Montclair, NJ 07043-1624. Offers Certificate.

Naval Postgraduate School, Departments and Academic Groups, Department of Information Sciences, Monterey, CA 93943. Offers electronic warfare systems engineering (MS); information sciences (PhD); information systems and operations (MS); information technology management (MS); information warfare systems engineering (MS); knowledge superiority (Certificate); remote sensing intelligence (MS); system technology (command, control and communications) (MS). *Program availability:* Part-time. *Degree requirements:* For master's, thesis (for some programs); for doctorate, thesis/dissertation.

North Carolina Central University, College of Arts and Sciences, Department of Environmental, Earth and Geospatial Sciences, Durham, NC 27707-3129. Offers earth sciences (MS); environmental and geographic sciences (MS). *Degree requirements:* For master's, one foreign language, comprehensive exam. *Entrance requirements:* For master's, GRE, minimum GPA of 3.0 in major, 2.5 overall. Additional exam requirements/recommendations for international students: required—TOEFL.

North Carolina State University, Graduate School, College of Natural Resources, Department of Parks, Recreation and Tourism Management, Raleigh, NC 27695. Offers natural resource management (MPRTM, MS); park and recreation management (MPRTM, MS); parks, recreation and tourism management (PhD); recreational sport management (MPRTM, MS); spatial information science (MPRTM, MS); tourism policy and development (MPRTM, MS). *Degree requirements:* For master's, thesis (for some programs); for doctorate, thesis/dissertation. *Entrance requirements:* For master's and doctorate, GRE General Test. Additional exam requirements/recommendations for international students: required—TOEFL. Electronic applications accepted.

Northeastern Illinois University, College of Graduate Studies and Research, College of Arts and Sciences, Program in Geography and Environmental Studies, Chicago, IL 60625. Offers geographic information science (Graduate Certificate); geography and environmental studies (MA). *Program availability:* Part-time, evening/weekend. *Degree requirements:* For master's, comprehensive exam, thesis optional. *Entrance requirements:* For master's, undergraduate minor in geography or environmental studies, minimum GPA of 2.75. Additional exam requirements/recommendations for international students: required—TOEFL (minimum score 550 paper-based; 79 iBT). Electronic applications accepted.

Northeastern University, College of Professional Studies, Boston, MA 02115-5096. Offers applied nutrition (MS); college athletics administration (MSL); commerce and economic development (MS); corporate and organizational communication (MS); criminal justice (MS); digital media (MPS); elearning and instructional design (M Ed); elementary education (MAT); geographic information technology (MPS); global studies and international relations (MS); higher education administration (M Ed); homeland security (MA); human services (MS); informatics (MPS); leadership (MS); learning analytics (M Ed); learning and instruction (M Ed); nonprofit management (MS); professional sports administration (MSL); project management (MS); regulatory affairs for drugs, biologics, and medical devices (MS); respiratory care leadership (MS); special education (M Ed); technical communication (MS). *Program availability:* Part-time, evening/weekend, 100% online, blended/hybrid learning. *Faculty:* 85 full-time (53 women), 892 part-time/adjunct (379 women). *Students:* 5,699 part-time (3,305 women). In 2019, 1,787 master's awarded. *Application deadline:* Applications are processed on a rolling basis. Application fee: $0. Electronic applications accepted. *Expenses:* Contact institution. *Financial support:* Applicants required to submit FAFSA. *Unit head:* Dr. Mary Loeffelholz, Dean of the College of Professional Studies, 617-373-6060. *Application contact:* Dr. Mary Loeffelholz, Dean of the College of Professional Studies, 617-373-

6060.
Website: https://cps.northeastern.edu/

Northern Arizona University, College of Social and Behavioral Sciences, Department of Geography, Planning, and Recreation, Flagstaff, AZ 86011. Offers applied geospatial sciences (MS); community planning (Certificate); geographic information systems (Certificate); parks and recreation management (MS). *Program availability:* Part-time, 100% online, blended/hybrid learning. *Degree requirements:* For master's, variable foreign language requirement, comprehensive exam (for some programs), thesis (for some programs); for Certificate, comprehensive exam (for some programs). *Entrance requirements:* Additional exam requirements/recommendations for international students: required—TOEFL (minimum score 80 iBT), IELTS (minimum score 6.5). Electronic applications accepted.

Northern Kentucky University, Office of Graduate Programs, College of Informatics, Department of Computer Science, Highland Heights, KY 41099. Offers computer science (MSCS); geographic information systems (Certificate); secure software engineering (Certificate). *Program availability:* Part-time, evening/weekend. *Degree requirements:* For master's, thesis optional. *Entrance requirements:* For master's, GRE, minimum GPA of 3.0, at least 4 semesters of undergraduate study in computer science including intermediate computer programming and data structures, one year of calculus, one course in discrete mathematics. Additional exam requirements/recommendations for international students: required—TOEFL (minimum score 550 paper-based; 79 iBT); recommended—IELTS (minimum score 6.5). Electronic applications accepted.

Northwest Missouri State University, Graduate School, College of Arts and Sciences, Maryville, MO 64468-6001. Offers biology (MS); elementary mathematics specialist (MS Ed); English (MA); English education (MS Ed); English pedagogy (MA); geographic information science (MS, Certificate); history (MS Ed); mathematics (MS); mathematics education (MS Ed); teaching: science (MS Ed). *Program availability:* Part-time. *Faculty:* 18 full-time (8 women). *Students:* 10 full-time (5 women), 47 part-time (23 women); includes 6 minority (2 American Indian or Alaska Native, non-Hispanic/Latino; 1 Asian, non-Hispanic/Latino; 1 Hispanic/Latino; 1 Native Hawaiian or other Pacific Islander, non-Hispanic/Latino; 1 Two or more races, non-Hispanic/Latino), 1 international. Average age 31. 17 applicants, 65% accepted, 9 enrolled. In 2019, 25 master's, 6 other advanced degrees awarded. *Degree requirements:* For master's, comprehensive exam. *Entrance requirements:* For master's, GRE General Test, writing sample. Additional exam requirements/recommendations for international students: required—TOEFL (minimum score 550 paper-based; 79 iBT). *Application deadline:* For fall admission, 7/1 for domestic and international students; for spring admission, 11/15 for domestic and international students. Applications are processed on a rolling basis. Application fee: $0 ($75 for international students). Electronic applications accepted. *Expenses:* Contact institution. *Financial support:* Research assistantships with full tuition reimbursements, teaching assistantships with full tuition reimbursements, and administrative assistantships, tutorial assistantships available. Financial award application deadline: 4/1; financial award applicants required to submit FAFSA. *Unit head:* Dr. Michael Steiner, Associate Provost-UG Studies & Dean, 660-562-1197. *Application contact:* Dr. Michael Steiner, Associate Provost-UG Studies & Dean, 660-562-1197.
Website: https://www.nwmissouri.edu/academics/departments.htm

Oregon State University, College of Forestry, Program in Natural Resources, Corvallis, OR 97331. Offers fisheries management (MNR); forests and climate change (MNR); geographic information science (MNR); sustainable natural resources (MNR); urban forestry (MNR); water conflict management and transformation (MNR); wildlife management (MNR). *Program availability:* Part-time, online only, 100% online. *Entrance requirements:* For master's, GRE. Additional exam requirements/recommendations for international students: required—TOEFL (minimum score 80 iBT), IELTS (minimum score 6.5). *Expenses:* Contact institution.

Saint Mary's University of Minnesota, Schools of Graduate and Professional Programs, Graduate School of Business and Technology, Data Intelligence and GeoAnalytics, Winona, MN 55987-1399. Offers MS, Certificate. *Unit head:* John Ebert, Director, 507-457-6961, E-mail: jebert@smumn.edu. *Application contact:* Jami Spitzer, Information Contact, 507-457-7500, E-mail: jspitzer@smumn.edu.
Website: http://www.smumn.edu/graduate-home/areas-of-study/graduate-school-of-business-technology/ms-in-geographic-information-science

Salisbury University, Program in Geographic Information Systems Management, Salisbury, MD 21801-6837. Offers MS. *Program availability:* Part-time, evening/weekend, online only, 100% online. *Faculty:* 2 full-time (0 women). *Students:* 3 full-time (1 woman), 10 part-time (2 women); includes 2 minority (both Two or more races, non-Hispanic/Latino). Average age 33. 9 applicants, 89% accepted, 7 enrolled. In 2019, 12 master's awarded. *Degree requirements:* For master's, COOP. *Entrance requirements:* For master's, GRE for recent graduates (less than 3 years), transcripts; resume or CV; personal statement; 2 letters of recommendation; completion of undergraduate coursework in algebra and statistics. Additional exam requirements/recommendations for international students: required—TOEFL (minimum score 550 paper-based; 79 iBT), IELTS (minimum score 6.5). *Application deadline:* For fall admission, 8/1 for domestic and international students; for spring admission, 1/3 for domestic and international students; for summer admission, 5/1 for domestic and international students. Applications are processed on a rolling basis. Application fee: $65. Electronic applications accepted. *Expenses:* Contact institution. *Financial support:* In 2019–20, 2 students received support, including 2 research assistantships with full tuition reimbursements available (averaging $6,500 per year); career-related internships or fieldwork and scholarships/grants also available. Support available to part-time students. Financial award application deadline: 3/1; financial award applicants required to submit FAFSA. *Unit head:* Dr. Stuart Hamilton, Graduate Program Director, 410-543-6459, E-mail: sehamilton@salisbury.edu. *Application contact:* Dr. Stuart Hamilton, Graduate Program Director, 410-543-6459, E-mail: sehamilton@salisbury.edu.
Website: https://www.salisbury.edu/explore-academics/programs/graduate-degree-programs/geo-info-sys-masters/

Sam Houston State University, College of Sciences, Department of Geography and Geology, Huntsville, TX 77341. Offers applied geographic information science (MS); geographic information science (Certificate). *Program availability:* Part-time. *Degree requirements:* For master's, comprehensive exam, thesis (for some programs). *Entrance requirements:* For master's, GRE General Test, letters of recommendation. Additional exam requirements/recommendations for international students: required—TOEFL (minimum score 550 paper-based; 79 iBT), IELTS (minimum score 6.5). Electronic applications accepted.

San Francisco State University, Division of Graduate Studies, College of Science and Engineering, Department of Geography and Environment, San Francisco, CA 94132-1722. Offers geographic information science (MS); geography (MA); resource management and environmental planning (MA). *Expenses: Tuition, area resident:* Full-time $7176; part-time $4164 per year. Tuition, state resident: full-time $7176; part-time $4164 per year. Tuition, nonresident: full-time $16,680; part-time $396 per unit. *International tuition:* $16,680 full-time. *Required fees:* $1524; $1524 per unit. $762 per semester. Tuition and fees vary according to degree level and program. *Unit head:* Dr. Andrew Oliphant, Chair, 415-405-2143, Fax: 415-338-6243, E-mail: andrewo@sfsu.edu.

Application contact: Dr. Nancy Wilkinson, Graduate Coordinator, 415-338-1439, Fax: 415-338-6243, E-mail: nancyw@sfsu.edu.
Website: http://geog.sfsu.edu/

State University of New York College of Environmental Science and Forestry, Department of Environmental Resources Engineering, Syracuse, NY 13210-2779. Offers ecological engineering (MPS, MS, PhD); environmental management (MPS); environmental resources engineering (MPS, MS, PhD); geospatial information science and engineering (MPS, MS, PhD); water resources engineering (MPS, MS, PhD). *Program availability:* Part-time. *Faculty:* 9 full-time (1 woman), 3 part-time/adjunct (0 women). *Students:* 22 full-time (13 women), 4 part-time (1 woman); includes 1 minority (Asian, non-Hispanic/Latino), 15 international. Average age 31. 32 applicants, 31% accepted, 7 enrolled. In 2019, 3 master's, 2 doctorates awarded. Terminal master's awarded for partial completion of doctoral program. *Degree requirements:* For master's, thesis (for some programs); for doctorate, comprehensive exam, thesis/dissertation. *Entrance requirements:* For master's and doctorate, GRE General Test, minimum GPA of 3.0. Additional exam requirements/recommendations for international students: required—TOEFL (minimum score 550 paper-based; 80 iBT), IELTS (minimum score 6). *Application deadline:* For fall admission, 1/15 priority date for domestic and international students; for spring admission, 11/1 priority date for domestic and international students. Applications are processed on a rolling basis. Application fee: $60. Electronic applications accepted. *Expenses:* Tuition, state resident: full-time $11,310; part-time $472 per credit hour. Tuition, nonresident: full-time $23,100; part-time $963 per credit hour. *Required fees:* $1890; $95.21 per credit hour. *Financial support:* In 2019–20, 8 students received support. Unspecified assistantships available. Financial award application deadline: 6/30; financial award applicants required to submit FAFSA. *Unit head:* Dr. Lindi Quackenbush, Chair, 315-470-4727, Fax: 315-470-4710, E-mail: ljquackc@esf.edu. *Application contact:* Laura Payne, Administrative Assistant, Office of Instruction & Graduate Studies, 315-470-6599, Fax: 315-470-6978, E-mail: esfgrad@esf.edu.
Website: http://www.esf.edu/ere

Stony Brook University, State University of New York, Graduate School, School of Marine and Atmospheric Sciences, Sustainability Studies Program, Stony Brook, NY 11794-3352. Offers geospatial sciences (Graduate Certificate). *Students:* 9 part-time (3 women); includes 1 minority (Hispanic/Latino). Average age 25. 2 applicants, 100% accepted, 1 enrolled. In 2019, 6 Graduate Certificates awarded. *Entrance requirements:* For degree, personal statement, letters of recommendation, official transcripts. Additional exam requirements/recommendations for international students: required—TOEFL (minimum score 85 iBT). *Application deadline:* For fall admission, 1/15 for domestic students. Application fee: $100. *Expenses:* Contact institution. *Financial support:* Teaching assistantships available. *Unit head:* Dr. Kate Aubrecht, Director, 631-632-5360, Fax: 631-632-5375, E-mail: katherine.aubrecht@stonybrook.edu. *Application contact:* Dr. Kate Aubrecht, Director, 631-632-5360, Fax: 631-632-5375, E-mail: katherine.aubrecht@stonybrook.edu.
Website: https://www.somas.stonybrook.edu/sustainability-studies/

Temple University, College of Liberal Arts, Department of Geography and Urban Studies, Philadelphia, PA 19122-6096. Offers geographic information systems (PSM, Graduate Certificate); geography and urban studies (MA, PhD). *Program availability:* Part-time, evening/weekend. *Faculty:* 17 full-time (5 women), 3 part-time/adjunct (all women). *Students:* 31 full-time (16 women), 36 part-time (19 women); includes 17 minority (8 Black or African American, non-Hispanic/Latino; 2 Asian, non-Hispanic/Latino; 6 Hispanic/Latino; 1 Two or more races, non-Hispanic/Latino), 8 international. 63 applicants, 33% accepted, 15 enrolled. In 2019, 12 master's, 3 doctorates, 3 other advanced degrees awarded. *Entrance requirements:* For master's, GRE (M.A.), 3 letters of recommendation, statement of goals; for doctorate, GRE, 3 letters of recommendation, statement of goals, writing sample. Additional exam requirements/recommendations for international students: required—TOEFL (minimum score 88 iBT), IELTS, PTE, one of three is required. *Application deadline:* Applications are processed on a rolling basis. Application fee: $60. Electronic applications accepted. *Financial support:* Fellowships, research assistantships, teaching assistantships, Federal Work-Study, health care benefits, tuition waivers, and unspecified assistantships available. Financial award applicants required to submit FAFSA. *Unit head:* Melissa Gilbert, Chairperson, 215-204-7692, E-mail: mgilbert@temple.edu. *Application contact:* Liz Janczewski, Coordinator, 215-204-3386, E-mail: liz.janczewski@temple.edu.
Website: http://www.cla.temple.edu/gus/

Texas A&M University–Corpus Christi, College of Graduate Studies, College of Science and Engineering, Program in Geospatial Computing Sciences, Corpus Christi, TX 78412. Offers PhD. *Degree requirements:* For doctorate, thesis/dissertation. *Entrance requirements:* For doctorate, GRE, essay (500-1000 words in length), three letters of recommendation, curriculum vitae. Additional exam requirements/recommendations for international students: required—TOEFL (minimum score 550 paper-based; 79 iBT), IELTS (minimum score 6.5). Electronic applications accepted.

Texas A&M University–Corpus Christi, College of Graduate Studies, College of Science and Engineering, Program in Geospatial Surveying Engineering, Corpus Christi, TX 78412. Offers MS. *Degree requirements:* For master's, thesis or creative project. *Entrance requirements:* For master's, GRE, essay, two letters of recommendation. Additional exam requirements/recommendations for international students: required—TOEFL (minimum score 550 paper-based; 79 iBT), IELTS (minimum score 6.5). Electronic applications accepted.

Texas State University, The Graduate College, College of Liberal Arts, Doctoral Program in Geographic Information Science, San Marcos, TX 78666. Offers PhD. *Program availability:* Part-time, evening/weekend. *Degree requirements:* For doctorate, comprehensive exam, thesis/dissertation. *Entrance requirements:* For doctorate, official GRE (general test only) required with competitive scores in the verbal reasoning and quantitative reasoning sections, baccalaureate degree from regionally accredited university, master's degree in geography or related field with minimum GPA of 3.5, 3 letters of recommendation, statement of purpose, curriculum vitae, completion of master's thesis or demonstrated evidence of scholarly research. Additional exam requirements/recommendations for international students: required—TOEFL (minimum score 550 paper-based; 78 iBT), IELTS (minimum score 6). Electronic applications accepted.

Texas State University, The Graduate College, College of Liberal Arts, Master's Programs in Geography, San Marcos, TX 78666. Offers environmental geography (MS); geographic education (MAG, MS); geographic information science (MAG); geography (MAG); resources and environmental studies (MAG). *Program availability:* Evening/weekend. *Degree requirements:* For master's, comprehensive exam, thesis (for some programs). *Entrance requirements:* For master's, official GRE (general test only) required with competitive scores in the verbal reasoning and quantitative reasoning sections, baccalaureate degree from regionally-accredited institution with minimum GPA of 3.2 in last 60 hours of course work (for MAG), 3.4 (for MS); 3 letters of recommendation; statement of purpose; current resume. Additional exam requirements/recommendations for international students: required—TOEFL (minimum score 550 paper-based; 78 iBT), IELTS (minimum score 6.5). Electronic applications accepted.

Université du Québec à Montréal, Graduate Programs, Program in Geographical Information Systems, Montréal, QC H3C 3P8, Canada. Offers Diploma. *Program availability:* Part-time. *Entrance requirements:* For degree, appropriate bachelor's degree or equivalent, proficiency in French.

University at Albany, State University of New York, College of Arts and Sciences, Department of Geography and Planning, Albany, NY 12222-0001. Offers geographic information science (Certificate); geography (MA); regional planning (MRP); urban policy (Certificate). *Program availability:* Part-time, blended/hybrid learning. *Faculty:* 12 full-time (3 women), 10 part-time/adjunct (3 women). *Students:* 46 full-time (19 women), 23 part-time (10 women); includes 13 minority (6 Black or African American, non-Hispanic/Latino; 2 Asian, non-Hispanic/Latino; 5 Hispanic/Latino), 9 international. 20 applicants, 100% accepted, 12 enrolled. In 2019, 20 master's, 9 other advanced degrees awarded. *Entrance requirements:* For master's, transcripts of all schools attended, statement of background and goals, departmental questionnaire, resume, names and contact information for 3 recommenders. Additional exam requirements/recommendations for international students: required—TOEFL (minimum score 550 paper-based). *Application deadline:* For fall admission, 7/15 for domestic students, 5/1 for international students; for spring admission, 11/15 for domestic and international students. Applications are processed on a rolling basis. Application fee: $75. Electronic applications accepted. *Expenses: Tuition, area resident:* Full-time $11,530; part-time $480 per credit hour. Tuition, nonresident: full-time $23,530; part-time $980 per credit hour. *International tuition:* $23,530 full-time. *Required fees:* $2185; $96 per credit hour. Part-time tuition and fees vary according to course load and program. *Financial support:* Fellowships, teaching assistantships, career-related internships or fieldwork, Federal Work-Study, and institutionally sponsored loans available. Financial award application deadline: 3/1. *Unit head:* Catherine Lawson, Chair, 518-442-4636, Fax: 518-442-4742, E-mail: lawsonc@albany.edu. *Application contact:* Michael DeRensis, Director, Graduate Admissions, 518-442-3980, Fax: 518-442-3922, E-mail: graduate@albany.edu.
Website: https://www.albany.edu/gp/

University at Buffalo, the State University of New York, Graduate School, College of Arts and Sciences, Department of Geography, N Tonawanda, NY 14261. Offers earth systems science (MA, MS); economic geography and business geographics (MS); environmental modeling and analysis (MA); geographic information science (MA, MS); geography (MA, PhD); health geography (MS); international trade (MA); urban and regional analysis (MA). *Program availability:* Part-time. *Faculty:* 22 full-time (9 women), 3 part-time/adjunct (1 woman). *Students:* 61 full-time (26 women); includes 37 minority (2 Black or African American, non-Hispanic/Latino; 34 Asian, non-Hispanic/Latino; 1 Hispanic/Latino). Average age 28. 120 applicants, 62% accepted, 12 enrolled. In 2019, 23 master's, 3 doctorates awarded. Terminal master's awarded for partial completion of doctoral program. *Degree requirements:* For master's, thesis (for some programs), project or portfolio; for doctorate, thesis/dissertation, dissertation/thesis. *Entrance requirements:* For master's, GRE General Test, minimum GPA of 2.9; for doctorate, GRE General Test, minimum GPA of 3.0. Additional exam requirements/recommendations for international students: required—TOEFL (minimum score 550 paper-based; 79 iBT). *Application deadline:* For fall admission, 5/1 priority date for domestic students, 3/10 priority date for international students; for spring admission, 11/1 priority date for domestic students, 9/1 priority date for international students. Applications are processed on a rolling basis. Application fee: $75. Electronic applications accepted. *Expenses:* Contact institution. *Financial support:* In 2019–20, 15 students received support, including 9 fellowships with full tuition reimbursements available (averaging $4,500 per year), 7 research assistantships with full tuition reimbursements available (averaging $14,000 per year), 13 teaching assistantships with full tuition reimbursements available (averaging $14,080 per year); career-related internships or fieldwork, Federal Work-Study, institutionally sponsored loans, traineeships, health care benefits, and unspecified assistantships also available. Financial award application deadline: 1/10. *Unit head:* Dr. Chris Larsen, Interim Chair, 716-645-0488, Fax: 716-645-2329, E-mail: larsen@buffalo.edu. *Application contact:* Wendy Zitzka, Graduate Secretary, 716-645-0471, Fax: 716-645-2329, E-mail: wzitzka@buffalo.edu.
Website: http://www.geog.buffalo.edu/

The University of Alabama, Graduate School, College of Arts and Sciences, Department of Geography, Tuscaloosa, AL 35487. Offers earth system science (MS, PhD); environment and natural resources (MS, PhD); environment and society (MS, PhD); geographic information science (MS, PhD). *Program availability:* Part-time. *Faculty:* 14 full-time (1 woman), 1 part-time/adjunct (0 women). *Students:* 31 full-time (17 women), 5 part-time (1 woman); includes 17 minority (14 Black or African American, non-Hispanic/Latino; 1 Asian, non-Hispanic/Latino; 2 Two or more races, non-Hispanic/Latino), 7 international. Average age 29. 28 applicants, 54% accepted, 9 enrolled. In 2019, 9 master's awarded. *Degree requirements:* For master's, comprehensive exam, thesis; for doctorate, comprehensive exam, thesis/dissertation. *Entrance requirements:* For master's, GRE, minimum GPA of 3.0. Additional exam requirements/recommendations for international students: required—TOEFL (minimum score 550 paper-based; 79 iBT). *Application deadline:* For fall admission, 2/15 priority date for domestic and international students; for spring admission, 10/1 priority date for domestic and international students. Applications are processed on a rolling basis. Application fee: $50 ($60 for international students). Electronic applications accepted. *Expenses: Tuition, area resident:* Full-time $10,780; part-time $440 per credit hour. Tuition, nonresident: full-time $30,250; part-time $1550 per credit hour. *Financial support:* In 2019–20, 24 students received support, including fellowships with full tuition reimbursements available (averaging $15,000 per year), research assistantships with full tuition reimbursements available (averaging $14,013 per year), teaching assistantships with full tuition reimbursements available (averaging $14,013 per year); career-related internships or fieldwork, health care benefits, and unspecified assistantships also available. Financial award application deadline: 2/15. *Unit head:* Dr. Douglas Sherman, Chair, 205-348-5047, Fax: 205-348-2278, E-mail: douglas.j.sherman@ua.edu. *Application contact:* Dr. Justin Hart, Associate Professor, 205-348-5047, Fax: 205-348-2278, E-mail: hart013@ua.edu.
Website: http://geography.ua.edu

University of Alaska Fairbanks, College of Natural Science and Mathematics, Department of Geosciences, Fairbanks, AK 99775-5780. Offers geophysics (MS), including remote sensing geophysics, snow, ice, and permafrost geophysics, solid-earth geophysics. *Program availability:* Part-time. *Degree requirements:* For master's, comprehensive exam, thesis, oral defense of thesis. *Entrance requirements:* For master's, GRE General Test, bachelor's degree in geology, geophysics, or an appropriate physical science or engineering with minimum cumulative undergraduate and major GPA of 3.0. Additional exam requirements/recommendations for international students: required—TOEFL (minimum score 550 paper-based; 79 iBT), IELTS (minimum score 6.5). Electronic applications accepted.

The University of Arizona, College of Social and Behavioral Sciences, School of Geography and Development, Tucson, AZ 85721. Offers geographic information systems technology (MA); geography (PhD). *Program availability:* Part-time. Terminal master's awarded for partial completion of doctoral program. *Degree requirements:* For master's, thesis or additional course work; for doctorate, variable foreign language requirement, thesis/dissertation. *Entrance requirements:* For master's, GRE General Test, 2 letters of recommendation; for doctorate, GRE General Test, statement of purpose, 2 letters of recommendation, master's degree. Additional exam requirements/recommendations for international students: required—TOEFL (minimum score 550 paper-based; 79 iBT). Electronic applications accepted.

University of Central Arkansas, Graduate School, College of Natural Sciences and Math, Department of Geography, Conway, AR 72035-0001. Offers community and economic development (MS); geographic information systems (MGIS, Certificate). *Program availability:* Part-time, online learning. *Entrance requirements:* Additional exam requirements/recommendations for international students: required—TOEFL (minimum score 550 paper-based). Electronic applications accepted.

University of Colorado Denver, Business School, Program in Information Systems, Denver, CO 80217. Offers accounting and information systems audit and control (MS); business intelligence systems (MS); digital health entrepreneurship (MS); enterprise risk management (MS); enterprise technology management (MS); geographic information systems (MS); health information technology (MS); technology innovation and entrepreneurship (MS); Web and mobile computing (MS). *Program availability:* Part-time, evening/weekend, online learning. *Degree requirements:* For master's, 30 credit hours. *Entrance requirements:* For master's, GMAT, resume, essay, two letters of recommendation, financial statements (for international applicants). Additional exam requirements/recommendations for international students: required—TOEFL (minimum score 525 paper-based; 71 iBT); recommended—IELTS (minimum score 6.5). Electronic applications accepted. *Expenses:* Contact institution.

University of Colorado Denver, College of Engineering, Design and Computing, Department of Civil Engineering, Denver, CO 80217. Offers civil engineering (EASPh D); civil engineering systems (PhD); environmental and sustainability engineering (MS, PhD); geographic information systems (MS); geotechnical engineering (MS, PhD); hydrology and hydraulics (MS, PhD); structural engineering (MS, PhD); transportation engineering (MS, PhD). *Program availability:* Part-time, evening/weekend. *Degree requirements:* For master's, comprehensive exam, 30 credit hours, project or thesis; for doctorate, comprehensive exam, thesis/dissertation, 60 credit hours (30 of which are dissertation research). *Entrance requirements:* For master's, GRE, statement of purpose, transcripts, three references; for doctorate, GRE, statement of purpose, transcripts, references, letter of support from faculty stating willingness to serve as dissertation advisor and outlining plan for financial support. Additional exam requirements/recommendations for international students: required—TOEFL (minimum score 537 paper-based; 75 iBT); recommended—IELTS (minimum score 6.5). Electronic applications accepted. Tuition and fees vary according to course load, program and reciprocity agreements.

University of Colorado Denver, College of Engineering, Design and Computing, Master of Engineering Program, Denver, CO 80217-3364. Offers civil engineering (M Eng), including civil engineering, geographic information systems, transportation systems; electrical engineering (M Eng); mechanical engineering (M Eng). *Program availability:* Part-time. *Entrance requirements:* For master's, GRE (for those with GPA below 2.75), transcripts, references, statement of purpose. Tuition and fees vary according to course load, program and reciprocity agreements.

University of Colorado Denver, College of Liberal Arts and Sciences, Department of Geography and Environmental Sciences, Denver, CO 80217. Offers environmental sciences (MS), including air quality, ecosystems, environmental health, geospatial analysis, hazardous waste, water quality. *Program availability:* Part-time, evening/weekend. *Degree requirements:* For master's, thesis or alternative, 30 credits including 21 of core requirements and 9 of environmental science electives. *Entrance requirements:* For master's, GRE General Test, BA in one of the natural/physical sciences or engineering (or equivalent background); prerequisite coursework in calculus and physics (one semester each); general chemistry with lab and general biology with lab (two semesters each); three letters of recommendation. Additional exam requirements/recommendations for international students: required—TOEFL (minimum score 537 paper-based; 75 iBT); recommended—IELTS (minimum score 6.5). Electronic applications accepted. Tuition and fees vary according to course load, program and reciprocity agreements.

University of Denver, Division of Natural Sciences and Mathematics, Department of Geography and the Environment, Denver, CO 80208. Offers geographic information science (MS); geography (MA, PhD). *Program availability:* Part-time. *Faculty:* 17 full-time (5 women), 9 part-time/adjunct (5 women). *Students:* 1 full-time (0 women), 45 part-time (15 women); includes 3 minority (1 Black or African American, non-Hispanic/Latino; 2 Hispanic/Latino), 5 international. Average age 32. 61 applicants, 41% accepted, 16 enrolled. In 2019, 28 master's, 2 doctorates awarded. Terminal master's awarded for partial completion of doctoral program. *Degree requirements:* For master's, thesis (for some programs), capstone project for some; for doctorate, variable foreign language requirement, comprehensive exam, thesis/dissertation. *Entrance requirements:* For master's, GRE General Test, bachelor's degree, transcripts, personal statement, three letters of recommendation; for doctorate, GRE General Test, master's degree, transcripts, personal statement, three letters of recommendation, resume. Additional exam requirements/recommendations for international students: required—TOEFL (minimum score 570 paper-based; 88 iBT). *Application deadline:* For fall admission, 1/15 priority date for domestic and international students; for winter admission, 3/15 for domestic and international students. Applications are processed on a rolling basis. Application fee: $65. Electronic applications accepted. *Expenses:* Contact institution. *Financial support:* In 2019–20, 46 students received support, including 14 teaching assistantships with tuition reimbursements available (averaging $19,271 per year); research assistantships, career-related internships or fieldwork, Federal Work-Study, institutionally sponsored loans, scholarships/grants, and unspecified assistantships also available. Support available to part-time students. Financial award application deadline: 2/15; financial award applicants required to submit FAFSA. *Unit head:* Dr. Michael Keables, Associate Professor and Chair, 303-871-2653, E-mail: michael.keables@du.edu. *Application contact:* Dr. Eric Boschmann, Associate Professor and Graduate Program Director, 303-871-4387, E-mail: eric.boschmann@du.edu.
Website: http://www.du.edu/nsm/departments/geography

University of Denver, University College, Denver, CO 80208. Offers arts and culture (MA, Certificate); communication management (MS, Certificate), including translation studies (Certificate), world history and culture (Certificate); environmental policy and management (MS); geographic information systems (MS); global affairs (MA, Certificate), including human capital in organizations (Certificate), philanthropic leadership (Certificate), project management (Certificate), strategic innovation and change (Certificate); healthcare leadership (MS); information communications and technology (MS); leadership and organizations (MS); professional creative writing (MA, Certificate), including emergency planning and response (Certificate), organizational security (Certificate); security management (MS, Certificate); strategic human resources (Certificate). *Program availability:* Part-time, evening/weekend, 100% online, blended/hybrid learning. *Faculty:* 104 part-time/adjunct (52 women). *Students:* 59 full-time (33 women), 1,893 part-time (1,210 women); includes 545 minority (133 Black or African American, non-Hispanic/Latino; 16 American Indian or Alaska Native, non-Hispanic/Latino; 64 Asian, non-Hispanic/Latino; 252 Hispanic/Latino; 4 Native Hawaiian or other Pacific Islander, non-Hispanic/Latino; 76 Two or more races, non-Hispanic/Latino), 78 international. Average age 32. 1,290 applicants, 91% accepted, 752 enrolled. In 2019, 457 master's, 181 other advanced degrees awarded. *Degree requirements:* For master's, capstone project. *Entrance requirements:* For master's, baccalaureate degree, transcripts, two letters of recommendation, personal statement, resume, writing sample (Master of Arts in Professional Creative Writing). Additional exam requirements/recommendations for international students: required—TOEFL (minimum score 550 paper-based; 80 iBT). *Application deadline:* For fall admission, 6/19 priority date for domestic students, 6/14 priority date for international students; for winter admission, 10/25 priority date for domestic students, 9/27 priority date for international students; for spring admission, 2/7 priority date for domestic students, 1/10 priority date for international students; for summer admission, 4/24 priority date for domestic students, 3/27 priority date for international students. Applications are processed on a rolling basis. Application fee: $75. Electronic applications accepted. *Expenses:* Contact institution. *Financial support:* In 2019–20, 56 students received support. Teaching assistantships available. Financial award applicants required to submit FAFSA. *Unit head:* Dr. Michael McGuire, Dean, 303-871-3518, E-mail: michael.mcguire@du.edu. *Application contact:* Admission Team, 303-871-2291, E-mail: ucoladm@du.edu.
Website: http://universitycollege.du.edu/

University of Florida, Graduate School, College of Liberal Arts and Sciences, Department of Geography, Gainesville, FL 32611. Offers applications of geographic technologies (MA, MS); geographic information systems (MA, MS, PhD); geography (MA, MS, PhD); hydrologic sciences (MS, PhD); tropical conservation and development (MA, MS, PhD); wetland sciences (MA, MS, PhD). *Degree requirements:* For master's, thesis; for doctorate, comprehensive exam, thesis/dissertation. *Entrance requirements:* For master's and doctorate, GRE General Test, minimum GPA of 3.0. Additional exam requirements/recommendations for international students: required—TOEFL (minimum score 550 paper-based; 80 iBT), IELTS (minimum score 6). Electronic applications accepted.

The University of Iowa, Graduate College, Program in Informatics, Iowa City, IA 52242-1316. Offers bioinformatics (MS, PhD); bioinformatics and computational biology (Certificate); geoinformatics (MS, PhD, Certificate); health informatics (MS, PhD, Certificate); information science (MS, PhD, Certificate). *Degree requirements:* For master's, thesis optional; for doctorate, comprehensive exam, thesis/dissertation. *Entrance requirements:* For master's and doctorate, GRE General Test, minimum GPA of 3.0. Additional exam requirements/recommendations for international students: required—TOEFL (minimum score 550 paper-based; 81 iBT). Electronic applications accepted.

The University of Kansas, Graduate Studies, College of Liberal Arts and Sciences, Department of Geography and Atmospheric Science, Lawrence, KS 66045-7613. Offers atmospheric science (MS); geographic information science (Graduate Certificate); geography (MA, PhD); MUP/MA. *Program availability:* Part-time. *Students:* 50 full-time (24 women), 7 part-time (3 women); includes 13 minority (9 American Indian or Alaska Native, non-Hispanic/Latino; 1 Asian, non-Hispanic/Latino; 1 Hispanic/Latino; 2 Two or more races, non-Hispanic/Latino), 7 international. Average age 28. 33 applicants, 55% accepted, 13 enrolled. In 2019, 3 master's, 8 doctorates, 1 other advanced degree awarded. *Entrance requirements:* For master's and doctorate, GRE General Test, 3 letters of reference, transcripts, statement of interests, resume. Additional exam requirements/recommendations for international students: required—TOEFL, IELTS. *Application deadline:* For fall admission, 1/15 priority date for domestic and international students; for spring admission, 11/1 for domestic and international students; for summer admission, 4/1 for domestic and international students. Application fee: $65 ($85 for international students). Electronic applications accepted. *Expenses:* Tuition, state resident: full-time $9989. Tuition, nonresident: full-time $23,950. *International tuition:* $23,950 full-time. *Required fees:* $984; $81.99 per credit hour. Tuition and fees vary according to course load, campus/location and program. *Financial support:* Fellowships, research assistantships, teaching assistantships, and unspecified assistantships available. Financial award application deadline: 1/15. *Unit head:* Nathaniel Brunsell, Chair, 785-864-2021, E-mail: brunsell@ku.edu. *Application contact:* Cicily Riggs, Graduate Admission Contact, 785-864-0937, E-mail: csriggs@ku.edu.
Website: http://www.geog.ku.edu/

University of Lethbridge, School of Graduate Studies, Lethbridge, AB T1K 3M4, Canada. Offers addictions counseling (M Sc); agricultural biotechnology (M Sc); agricultural studies (M Sc, MA); anthropology (MA); archaeology (M Sc, MA); art (MA, MFA); biochemistry (M Sc); biological sciences (M Sc); biomolecular science (PhD); biosystems and biodiversity (PhD); Canadian studies (MA); chemistry (M Sc); computer science (M Sc); computer science and geographical information science (M Sc); counseling (MC); counseling psychology (M Ed); dramatic arts (MA); earth, space, and physical science (PhD); economics (MA); education (MA, PhD); educational leadership (M Ed); English (MA); environmental science (M Sc); evolution and behavior (PhD); exercise science (M Sc); French (MA); French/German (MA); French/Spanish (MA); general education (M Ed); geography (M Sc, MA); German (MA); health sciences (M Sc); individualized multidisciplinary (M Sc, MA); kinesiology (M Sc, MA); management (M Sc), including accounting, finance, human resource management and labor relations, information systems, international management, marketing, policy and strategy; mathematics (M Sc); music (M Mus, MA); Native American studies (MA); neuroscience (M Sc, PhD); new media (MA, MFA); nursing (M Sc, MN); philosophy (MA); physics (M Sc); political science (MA); psychology (M Sc, MA); religious studies (MA); sociology (MA); theatre and dramatic arts (MFA); theoretical and computational science (PhD); urban and regional studies (MA); women and gender studies (MA). *Program availability:* Part-time, evening/weekend. *Degree requirements:* For master's, thesis (for some programs); for doctorate, comprehensive exam, thesis/dissertation. *Entrance requirements:* For master's, GMAT (for M Sc in management), bachelor's degree in related field, minimum GPA of 3.0 during previous 20 graded semester courses, 2 years' teaching or related experience (M Ed); for doctorate, master's degree, minimum graduate GPA of 3.5. Additional exam requirements/recommendations for international students: required—TOEFL (minimum score 580 paper-based; 93 iBT). Electronic applications accepted.

University of Maryland, Baltimore County, The Graduate School, College of Arts, Humanities and Social Sciences, Department of Geography and Environmental Systems, Program in Geographic Information Systems, Rockville, MD 21250. Offers MPS, Certificate. *Program availability:* Part-time, evening/weekend. *Faculty:* 13 part-time/adjunct (3 women). *Students:* 9 full-time (5 women), 8 part-time (0 women); includes 6 minority (4 Black or African American, non-Hispanic/Latino; 2 Hispanic/Latino), 2 international. Average age 34. 15 applicants, 100% accepted, 8 enrolled. In 2019, 5 master's, 2 Certificates awarded. *Entrance requirements:* Additional exam requirements/recommendations for international students: required—TOEFL (minimum score 99 iBT), IELTS (minimum score 7). *Application deadline:* For fall admission, 8/1 for domestic students, 6/1 for international students; for spring admission, 12/1 for domestic students, 11/1 for international students. Applications are processed on a rolling basis. Application fee: $50. Electronic applications accepted. *Expenses:* $14,382 per year. *Unit head:* Dr. Matthew Baker, Program Director, 301-738-6087, E-mail: mbaker@umbc.edu.

Application contact: Rickeysha Jones, Program Coordinator, 301-738-6285, E-mail: rcjones@umbc.edu.
Website: http://www.umbc.edu/gis

University of Memphis, Graduate School, College of Arts and Sciences, Department of Earth Sciences, Memphis, TN 38152. Offers earth sciences (MA, MS, PhD), including archaeology (MS), geography (MS), geology (MS), geophysics (MS), interdisciplinary studies (MS); geographic information systems (Graduate Certificate), including geographic information systems, GIS educator, GIS planning, GIS professional. *Program availability:* Part-time, evening/weekend. *Students:* 40 full-time (17 women), 22 part-time (7 women); includes 12 minority (2 Black or African American, non-Hispanic/Latino; 8 Asian, non-Hispanic/Latino; 2 Hispanic/Latino), 18 international. Average age 31. 23 applicants, 91% accepted, 18 enrolled. In 2019, 13 master's, 5 doctorates, 8 other advanced degrees awarded. Terminal master's awarded for partial completion of doctoral program. *Degree requirements:* For master's, comprehensive exam, thesis, seminar presentation; for doctorate, comprehensive exam, thesis/dissertation, qualifying exam, submission of two manuscripts for publication in peer-reviewed journal or books. *Entrance requirements:* For master's, GRE General Test, 3 letters of recommendation, statement of research interests; for doctorate, GRE General Test, 2 letters of recommendation, resume, personal statement. Additional exam requirements/recommendations for international students: required—TOEFL (minimum score 550 paper-based; 79 iBT). *Application deadline:* For fall admission, 1/15 for domestic students; for spring admission, 11/1 for domestic students. Applications are processed on a rolling basis. Application fee: $35 ($60 for international students). Electronic applications accepted. *Expenses: Tuition, area resident:* Full-time $9216; part-time $512 per credit hour. Tuition, state resident: full-time $9216; part-time $512 per credit hour. Tuition, nonresident: full-time $12,672; part-time $704 per credit hour. *International tuition:* $16,128 full-time. *Required fees:* $1530; $85 per credit hour. Tuition and fees vary according to program. *Financial support:* Fellowships with full tuition reimbursements, research assistantships with full tuition reimbursements, teaching assistantships with full tuition reimbursements, Federal Work-Study, scholarships/grants, and unspecified assistantships available. Financial award application deadline: 2/1; financial award applicants required to submit FAFSA. *Unit head:* Dr. Daniel Larsen, Chair, 901-678-4358, Fax: 901-678-2178, E-mail: dlarsen@memphis.edu. *Application contact:* Dr. Daniel Larsen, Chair, 901-678-4358, Fax: 901-678-2178, E-mail: dlarsen@memphis.edu.
Website: http://www.memphis.edu/earthsciences/

University of Minnesota, Twin Cities Campus, Graduate School, College of Food, Agricultural and Natural Resource Sciences, Program in Natural Resources Science and Management, St. Paul, MN 55455-0213. Offers assessment, monitoring, and geospatial analysis (MS, PhD); economics, policy, management, and society (MS, PhD); forest hydrology and watershed management (MS, PhD); forest products (MS, PhD); forests: biology, ecology, conservation, and management (MS, PhD); natural resources science and management (MS, PhD); paper science and engineering (MS, PhD); recreation resources, tourism, and environmental education (MS, PhD). *Program availability:* Part-time. *Faculty:* 71 full-time (19 women), 61 part-time/adjunct (12 women). *Students:* 54 full-time (32 women), 34 part-time (17 women); includes 10 minority (1 Black or African American, non-Hispanic/Latino; 2 American Indian or Alaska Native, non-Hispanic/Latino; 5 Asian, non-Hispanic/Latino; 2 Hispanic/Latino), 11 international. Average age 30. 52 applicants, 33% accepted, 11 enrolled. In 2019, 22 master's, 2 doctorates awarded. Terminal master's awarded for partial completion of doctoral program. *Degree requirements:* For master's, comprehensive exam, thesis (for some programs); for doctorate, comprehensive exam, thesis/dissertation. *Entrance requirements:* For master's and doctorate, GRE General Test. Additional exam requirements/recommendations for international students: required—TOEFL (minimum score 550 paper-based; 79 iBT); recommended—IELTS (minimum score 6.5). *Application deadline:* For fall admission, 12/15 priority date for domestic and international students; for spring admission, 10/15 for domestic and international students. Applications are processed on a rolling basis. Application fee: $75 ($95 for international students). Electronic applications accepted. *Financial support:* In 2019–20, 6 students received support, including fellowships with full tuition reimbursements available (averaging $42,000 per year), research assistantships with full tuition reimbursements available (averaging $42,000 per year), teaching assistantships with full tuition reimbursements available (averaging $42,000 per year); scholarships/grants, health care benefits, and unspecified assistantships also available. *Unit head:* Dr. Matt Russell, Director of Graduate Studies, 612-626-4280, E-mail: russellm@umn.edu. *Application contact:* Jennifer Welsh, Graduate Program Coordinator, 612-624-7683, Fax: 612-625-5212, E-mail: nrsm@umn.edu.
Website: http://www.nrsm.umn.edu

University of Minnesota, Twin Cities Campus, Graduate School, College of Liberal Arts, Program in Geographic Information Science, Minneapolis, MN 55455-0213. Offers MGIS. *Program availability:* Part-time. *Degree requirements:* For master's, comprehensive exam, capstone project. *Entrance requirements:* For master's, minimum GPA of 3.0; course work in college-level math, statistics, and computer programming. Additional exam requirements/recommendations for international students: required—TOEFL (minimum score 600 paper-based; 100 iBT). *Expenses:* Contact institution.

University of Missouri, Office of Research and Graduate Studies, College of Agriculture, Food and Natural Resources, School of Natural Resources, Columbia, MO 65211. Offers agroforestry (MS, Certificate); conservation biology (Certificate); fisheries and wildlife sciences (MS, PhD); forestry (MS, PhD); geographical information science (Certificate); human dimensions of natural resources (MS, PhD); parks, recreation and tourism (MS); society and ecosystems (Certificate); soil, environmental and atmospheric sciences (MS, PhD); water resources (MS, PhD). *Program availability:* Part-time. *Degree requirements:* For doctorate, thesis/dissertation. *Entrance requirements:* For master's and doctorate, GRE General Test (minimum score 1200 Verbal and Quantitative), minimum GPA of 3.2. Additional exam requirements/recommendations for international students: required—TOEFL (minimum score 550 paper-based; 80 iBT), IELTS (minimum score 6.5). Electronic applications accepted.

University of Missouri, Office of Research and Graduate Studies, College of Arts and Science, Department of Geography, Columbia, MO 65211. Offers geographic information science (Graduate Certificate); geography (MA). *Entrance requirements:* For master's, GRE General Test (minimum score 1000 verbal and quantitative), minimum GPA of 3.0.

University of Nebraska at Omaha, Graduate Studies, College of Arts and Sciences, Department of Geography and Geology, Omaha, NE 68182. Offers geographic information science (Certificate); geography (MA). *Program availability:* Part-time. *Degree requirements:* For master's, comprehensive exam, thesis (for some programs). *Entrance requirements:* For master's, GRE, minimum GPA of 3.0, 15 undergraduate geography hours, transcripts, resume, statement of purpose, 2 letters of recommendation; for Certificate, minimum GPA of 3.0, transcripts, resume, statement of purpose, 2 letters of recommendation. Additional exam requirements/recommendations for international students: required—TOEFL, IELTS, PTE. Electronic applications accepted.

University of New Hampshire, Graduate School, Interdisciplinary Programs, Program in Geospatial Science, Durham, NH 03824. Offers Postbaccalaureate Certificate. *Students:* 3 part-time (2 women). Average age 31. 5 applicants, 80% accepted, 1 enrolled. In 2019, 3 Postbaccalaureate Certificates awarded. *Entrance requirements:* Additional exam requirements/recommendations for international students: required—TOEFL (minimum score 550 paper-based; 80 iBT), IELTS, PTE. *Application deadline:* For fall admission, 7/1 for domestic students; for spring admission, 12/1 for domestic students; for summer admission, 4/1 for domestic students. Application fee: $25. Electronic applications accepted. *Financial support:* Fellowships, research assistantships, and teaching assistantships available. Financial award application deadline: 2/15. *Unit head:* Michael Palace, Chair, 603-862-4193. *Application contact:* Michael Routhier, 603-862-1792, E-mail: mike.routhier@unh.edu.
Website: http://gss.unh.edu/

University of New Haven, Graduate School, College of Arts and Sciences, Program in Environmental Science, West Haven, CT 06516. Offers environmental ecology (MS); environmental geoscience (MS); environmental health and management (MS); environmental science (MS); geographical information systems (MS). *Program availability:* Part-time, evening/weekend. *Students:* 14 full-time (8 women), 13 part-time (6 women); includes 7 minority (3 Black or African American, non-Hispanic/Latino; 3 Hispanic/Latino; 1 Native Hawaiian or other Pacific Islander, non-Hispanic/Latino), 4 international. Average age 29. 59 applicants, 86% accepted, 10 enrolled. In 2019, 17 master's awarded. *Entrance requirements:* Additional exam requirements/recommendations for international students: required—TOEFL (minimum score 80 iBT), IELTS, PTE. *Application deadline:* Applications are processed on a rolling basis. Application fee: $50. Electronic applications accepted. Application fee is waived when completed online. *Financial support:* Research assistantships with partial tuition reimbursements, teaching assistantships with partial tuition reimbursements, Federal Work-Study, scholarships/grants, and unspecified assistantships available. Support available to part-time students. Financial award applicants required to submit FAFSA. *Unit head:* Dr. Christian Conroy, Assistant Professor, 203-932-7436, E-mail: CWConroy@newhaven.edu. *Application contact:* Selina O'Toole, Senior Associate Director of Graduate Admissions, 203-932-7337, E-mail: SOToole@newhaven.edu.
Website: https://www.newhaven.edu/arts-sciences/graduate-programs/environmental-science/

University of North Alabama, College of Arts and Sciences, Department of Geography, Florence, AL 35632-0001. Offers geospatial science (MS). *Program availability:* Part-time, 100% online. *Degree requirements:* For master's, comprehensive exam (for some programs), thesis optional. *Entrance requirements:* For master's, GRE, three letters of recommendation; personal statement; letter of intent. Additional exam requirements/recommendations for international students: required—TOEFL (minimum score 550 paper-based; 79 iBT), IELTS (minimum score 6), PTE (minimum score 54). Electronic applications accepted.

The University of North Carolina at Charlotte, College of Liberal Arts and Sciences, Department of Geography and Earth Sciences, Charlotte, NC 28223-0001. Offers earth sciences (MS); geography (MA, PhD), including business location and transportation analytics (MA), geographic information science and technology (gis&t) (MA), human environmental systems (MA), urban and regional analysis; earth and environmental systems; geographic information science (PhD), urban regional analysis (MA). *Program availability:* Part-time, evening/weekend. *Faculty:* 30 full-time (13 women), 2 part-time/adjunct (1 woman). *Students:* 49 full-time (27 women), 21 part-time (4 women); includes 13 minority (1 Black or African American, non-Hispanic/Latino; 4 Asian, non-Hispanic/Latino; 7 Hispanic/Latino; 1 Two or more races, non-Hispanic/Latino), 14 international. Average age 28. 53 applicants, 74% accepted, 20 enrolled. In 2019, 17 master's, 2 doctorates awarded. Terminal master's awarded for partial completion of doctoral program. *Degree requirements:* For master's, thesis or alternative, capstone (proposal and defense) for MA; for doctorate, comprehensive exam, thesis/dissertation. *Entrance requirements:* For master's, GRE General Test, minimum GPA of 2.75 (3.0 for junior and senior years), transcripts, three letters of recommendation, and personal essays (for MS); minimum GPA of 3.1 overall or for the last 2 years, 3.2 in major, three letters of reference, and personal essay (for MA); for doctorate, GRE, MA or MS in geography or a field related to the primary emphases of the program; minimum master's-level GPA of 3.5; GIS and quantitative methods proficiency (if missing from coursework), personal statement. Additional exam requirements/recommendations for international students: required—TOEFL (minimum score 557 paper-based; 83 iBT), IELTS (minimum score 6.5), TOEFL (minimum score 557 paper-based, 83 iBT) or IELTS (6.5). *Application deadline:* Applications are processed on a rolling basis. Application fee: $75. Electronic applications accepted. *Expenses:* Tuition, state resident: full-time $4337. Tuition, nonresident: full-time $17,771. *Required fees:* $3093. Tuition and fees vary according to course load, degree level and program. *Financial support:* In 2019–20, 42 students received support, including 3 fellowships (averaging $52,667 per year), 16 research assistantships (averaging $8,489 per year), 23 teaching assistantships (averaging $9,266 per year); career-related internships or fieldwork, institutionally sponsored loans, scholarships/grants, and unspecified assistantships also available. Support available to part-time students. Financial award applicants required to submit FAFSA. *Unit head:* Dr. Deborah S.K. Thomas, Professor and Department Chair, 704-687-5976, E-mail: deborah.thomas@uncc.edu. *Application contact:* Kathy B. Giddings, Director of Graduate Admissions, 704-687-5503, Fax: 704-687-1668, E-mail: gradadm@uncc.edu.
Website: https://geoearth.uncc.edu/

The University of North Carolina at Greensboro, Graduate School, College of Arts and Sciences, Department of Geography, Greensboro, NC 27412-5001. Offers applied geography (MA); geographic information science (Certificate); geography (PhD); urban and economic development (Certificate). *Degree requirements:* For master's, comprehensive exam, thesis or alternative. *Entrance requirements:* For master's, GRE General Test. Additional exam requirements/recommendations for international students: required—TOEFL. Electronic applications accepted.

The University of North Carolina Wilmington, College of Arts and Sciences, Department of Earth and Ocean Sciences, Wilmington, NC 28403-3297. Offers geographic information science (Graduate Certificate); geoscience (MS). *Program availability:* Part-time. *Faculty:* 15 full-time (8 women). *Students:* 10 full-time (4 women), 29 part-time (11 women); includes 6 minority (1 Black or African American, non-Hispanic/Latino; 1 Asian, non-Hispanic/Latino; 2 Hispanic/Latino; 2 Two or more races, non-Hispanic/Latino). Average age 27. 22 applicants, 95% accepted, 13 enrolled. In 2019, 12 master's, 5 other advanced degrees awarded. *Degree requirements:* For master's, comprehensive exam, thesis or alternative. *Entrance requirements:* For master's, GRE General Test, 3 recommendations, research essay. Additional exam requirements/recommendations for international students: required—TOEFL (minimum score 79 iBT), IELTS (minimum score 6.5). *Application deadline:* For fall admission, 5/28 for domestic students; for spring admission, 11/1 for domestic students; for summer admission, 4/15 for domestic students. Applications are processed on a rolling basis. Application fee: $75. Electronic applications accepted. *Expenses: Tuition, area resident:* Full-time $4719; part-time $326 per credit hour. Tuition, state resident: full-time $4719; part-time $326 per credit hour. Tuition, nonresident: full-time $18,548; part-time $1099 per credit hour. *Required fees:* $2738. Tuition and fees vary according to program.

Geographic Information Systems

Financial support: Research assistantships, teaching assistantships, and scholarships/grants available. Financial award application deadline: 1/1; financial award applicants required to submit FAFSA. *Unit head:* Dr. Doug Gamble, Chair, 910-962-3778, Fax: 910-962-7077, E-mail: gambled@uncw.edu. *Application contact:* Dr. Joanne Halls, Graduate Coordinator, 910-962-7614, Fax: 910-962-7077, E-mail: hallsj@uncw.edu. Website: http://uncw.edu/msgeoscience/index.html

University of North Dakota, Graduate School, College of Arts and Sciences, Department of Geography and Geographic Information Science, Grand Forks, ND 58202. Offers MA, MS. *Program availability:* Part-time. *Degree requirements:* For master's, comprehensive exam, thesis or alternative. *Entrance requirements:* For master's, minimum GPA of 3.0. Additional exam requirements/recommendations for international students: required—TOEFL (minimum score 550 paper-based; 79 iBT), IELTS (minimum score 6.5). Electronic applications accepted.

University of North Texas Health Science Center at Fort Worth, School of Public Health, Fort Worth, TX 76107-2699. Offers biostatistics (MS); epidemiology (MPH, MS, PhD); food security and public health (Graduate Certificate); GIS in public health (Graduate Certificate); global health (Graduate Certificate); global health for medical professionals (Graduate Certificate); health administration (MHA); health behavior research (MS, PhD); maternal and child health (MPH); public health (Graduate Certificate); public health practice (MPH); DO/MPH; MS/MPH. *Accreditation:* CAHME; CEPH. *Program availability:* Part-time, evening/weekend, 100% online. *Degree requirements:* For master's, thesis or alternative, supervised internship; for doctorate, thesis/dissertation, supervised internship. *Entrance requirements:* For master's, GRE General Test. Additional exam requirements/recommendations for international students: required—TOEFL. Electronic applications accepted. *Expenses:* Contact institution.

University of Pennsylvania, Stuart Weitzman School of Design, Department of City and Regional Planning, Philadelphia, PA 19104. Offers city and regional planning (PhD); city planning (MCP); GIS and spatial analysis (Certificate); land preservation (Certificate); urban design (Certificate); urban redevelopment (Certificate); urban spatial analytics (MUSA). *Accreditation:* ACSP (one or more programs are accredited). *Program availability:* Part-time. *Faculty:* 24 full-time (10 women), 4 part-time/adjunct (0 women). *Students:* 191 full-time (120 women), 6 part-time (3 women); includes 40 minority (14 Black or African American, non-Hispanic/Latino; 13 Asian, non-Hispanic/Latino; 8 Hispanic/Latino; 5 Two or more races, non-Hispanic/Latino), 94 international. Average age 26. 433 applicants, 59% accepted, 119 enrolled. In 2019, 92 master's, 1 doctorate, 7 other advanced degrees awarded. *Entrance requirements:* Additional exam requirements/recommendations for international students: required—TOEFL (minimum score 100 iBT); recommended—IELTS (minimum score 7), TSE (minimum score 68). *Application deadline:* For spring admission, 1/12 for domestic students. Application fee: $80. Electronic applications accepted. *Financial support:* In 2019–20, 39 teaching assistantships (averaging $2,000 per year) were awarded; fellowships, research assistantships, and Federal Work-Study also available. Financial award application deadline: 2/15; financial award applicants required to submit FAFSA. *Application contact:* Lauren Hoover, Admissions & Recruitment Coordinator, 215-898-6520, E-mail: lhoover@design.upenn.edu. Website: https://www.design.upenn.edu/city-regional-planning

University of Pittsburgh, Kenneth P. Dietrich School of Arts and Sciences, Department of Geology and Environmental Science, Pittsburgh, PA 15260-3332. Offers geographical information systems and remote sensing (Pro-MS); geology and environmental science (MS, PhD). *Program availability:* Part-time. *Faculty:* 11 full-time (3 women). *Students:* 34 full-time (17 women), 1 part-time (0 women); includes 6 minority (1 Black or African American, non-Hispanic/Latino; 1 American Indian or Alaska Native, non-Hispanic/Latino; 4 Asian, non-Hispanic/Latino). Average age 27. 61 applicants, 34% accepted, 9 enrolled. In 2019, 3 master's, 1 doctorate awarded. *Degree requirements:* For master's, thesis; for doctorate, comprehensive exam, thesis/dissertation. *Entrance requirements:* For doctorate, Preliminary Exam. Additional exam requirements/recommendations for international students: required—TOEFL (minimum score 577 paper-based; 90 iBT), IELTS (minimum score 7). *Application deadline:* For fall admission, 1/15 for domestic and international students. Application fee: $75. Electronic applications accepted. *Financial support:* In 2019–20, 30 students received support, including 4 fellowships with full tuition reimbursements available (averaging $11,475 per year), 33 research assistantships with full tuition reimbursements available (averaging $9,482 per year), 21 teaching assistantships with full tuition reimbursements available (averaging $9,455 per year). *Unit head:* Cindy Niznik, Administrative Officer, 412-624-9070, E-mail: niznik@pitt.edu. *Application contact:* Annemarie Lillian Vranesevic, Academic Coordinator, 412-624-8779, E-mail: gpsgrad@pitt.edu. Website: http://geology.pitt.edu/

University of Redlands, College of Arts and Sciences, Program in Geographic Information Science, Redlands, CA 92373-0999. Offers MS. *Entrance requirements:* For master's, 2 years of professional experience using GIS or 2 university-level GIS courses plus internship, minimum undergraduate GPA of 3.0, 2 letters of recommendation. Additional exam requirements/recommendations for international students: required—TOEFL (minimum score 550 paper-based); recommended—IELTS (minimum score 5.5). Electronic applications accepted. *Expenses:* Contact institution.

University of Southern California, Graduate School, Dana and David Dornsife College of Letters, Arts and Sciences, Spatial Sciences Institute, Los Angeles, CA 90089. Offers geographic information science and technology (MS, Graduate Certificate). *Program availability:* Part-time, evening/weekend, online learning. Terminal master's awarded for partial completion of doctoral program. *Degree requirements:* For master's, thesis. *Entrance requirements:* For master's, GRE. Additional exam requirements/recommendations for international students: required—TOEFL. Electronic applications accepted.

University of South Florida, Innovative Education, Tampa, FL 33620-9951. Offers adult, career and higher education (Graduate Certificate), including college teaching, leadership in developing human resources, leadership in higher education; Africana studies (Graduate Certificate), including diasporas and health disparities, genocide and human rights; aging studies (Graduate Certificate), including gerontology; art research (Graduate Certificate), including museum studies; business foundations (Graduate Certificate); chemical and biomedical engineering (Graduate Certificate), including materials science and engineering, water, health and sustainability; child and family studies (Graduate Certificate), including positive behavior support; civil and industrial engineering (Graduate Certificate), including transportation systems analysis; community and family health (Graduate Certificate), including maternal and child health, social marketing and public health, violence and injury: prevention and intervention, women's health; criminology (Graduate Certificate), including criminal justice administration; data science for public administration (Graduate Certificate); digital humanities (Graduate Certificate); educational measurement and research (Graduate Certificate), including evaluation; English (Graduate Certificate), including comparative literary studies, creative writing, professional and technical communication; entrepreneurship (Graduate Certificate); environmental health (Graduate Certificate), including safety management; epidemiology and biostatistics (Graduate Certificate), including applied biostatistics, biostatistics, concepts and tools of epidemiology,

epidemiology, epidemiology of infectious diseases; geography, environment and planning (Graduate Certificate), including community development, environmental policy and management, geographical information systems; geology (Graduate Certificate), including hydrogeology; global health (Graduate Certificate), including disaster management, global health and Latin American and Caribbean studies, global health practice, humanitarian assistance, infection control; government and international affairs (Graduate Certificate), including Cuban studies, globalization studies; health policy and management (Graduate Certificate), including health management and leadership, public health policy and programs; hearing specialist: early intervention (Graduate Certificate); industrial and management systems engineering (Graduate Certificate), including systems engineering, technology management; information studies (Graduate Certificate), including school library media specialist; information systems/decision sciences (Graduate Certificate), including analytics and business intelligence; instructional technology (Graduate Certificate), including distance education, Florida digital/virtual educator, instructional design, multimedia design, Web design; internal medicine, bioethics and medical humanities (Graduate Certificate), including biomedical ethics; Latin American and Caribbean studies (Graduate Certificate); leadership for coastal resiliency planning (Graduate Certificate); mass communications (Graduate Certificate), including multimedia journalism; mathematics and statistics (Graduate Certificate), including mathematics; medicine (Graduate Certificate), including aging and neuroscience, bioinformatics, biotechnology, brain fitness and memory management, clinical investigation, hand and upper limb rehabilitation, health informatics, health sciences, integrative weight management, intellectual property, medicine and gender, metabolic and nutritional medicine, metabolic cardiology, pharmacy sciences; national and competitive intelligence (Graduate Certificate); nursing (Graduate Certificate), including simulation based academic fellowship in advanced pain management; psychological and social foundations (Graduate Certificate), including career counseling, college teaching, diversity in education, mental health counseling, school counseling; public affairs (Graduate Certificate), including nonprofit management, public management, research administration; public health (Graduate Certificate), including assessing chemical toxicity and public health risks, health equity, pharmacoepidemiology, public health generalist, toxicology, translational research in adolescent behavioral health; public health practices (Graduate Certificate), including planning for healthy communities; rehabilitation and mental health counseling (Graduate Certificate), including integrative mental health care, marriage and family therapy, rehabilitation technology; secondary education (Graduate Certificate), including ESOL, foreign language education: culture and content, foreign language education: professional; social work (Graduate Certificate), including geriatric social work/clinical gerontology; special education (Graduate Certificate), including autism spectrum disorder, disabilities education: severe/profound; world languages (Graduate Certificate), including teaching English as a second language (TESL) or foreign language. *Unit head:* Dr. Cynthia DeLuca, Associate Vice President and Assistant Vice Provost, 813-974-3077, Fax: 813-974-7061, E-mail: deluca@usf.edu. *Application contact:* Owen Hooper, Director, Summer and Alternative Calendar Programs, 813-974-6917, E-mail: hooper@usf.edu. Website: http://www.usf.edu/innovative-education/

The University of Texas at Dallas, School of Economic, Political and Policy Sciences, Program in Geospatial Information Sciences, Richardson, TX 75080. Offers MS, PhD. *Program availability:* Part-time, evening/weekend. *Faculty:* 9 full-time (1 woman), 1 part-time/adjunct (0 women). *Students:* 24 full-time (11 women), 23 part-time (7 women); includes 10 minority (1 Black or African American, non-Hispanic/Latino; 5 Asian, non-Hispanic/Latino; 4 Hispanic/Latino), 15 international. Average age 33. 72 applicants, 49% accepted, 22 enrolled. In 2019, 18 master's, 8 doctorates awarded. *Degree requirements:* For master's, thesis (for some programs), project or thesis; internship; for doctorate, comprehensive exam, thesis/dissertation. *Entrance requirements:* For master's and doctorate, GRE General Test, minimum GPA of 3.0 in upper-level coursework in field. Additional exam requirements/recommendations for international students: required—TOEFL (minimum score 550 paper-based). *Application deadline:* For fall admission, 7/15 for domestic students, 5/1 priority date for international students; for spring admission, 11/15 for domestic students, 9/1 priority date for international students. Applications are processed on a rolling basis. Application fee: $50 ($100 for international students). Electronic applications accepted. *Expenses: Tuition, area resident:* Full-time $16,504. Tuition, state resident: full-time $16,504. Tuition, nonresident: full-time $34,266. Tuition and fees vary according to course load. *Financial support:* In 2019–20, 13 students received support, including 2 fellowships (averaging $2,500 per year), 2 research assistantships with partial tuition reimbursements available (averaging $19,002 per year), 10 teaching assistantships with partial tuition reimbursements available (averaging $13,500 per year); career-related internships or fieldwork, Federal Work-Study, institutionally sponsored loans, scholarships/grants, and unspecified assistantships also available. Support available to part-time students. Financial award application deadline: 4/30; financial award applicants required to submit FAFSA. *Unit head:* Dr. Fang Qiu, Program Head, 972-883-4134, Fax: 972-883-2735, E-mail: ph.gis@utdallas.edu. *Application contact:* Judy Du, Graduate Program Administrator, 972-883-4964, Fax: 972-883-6297, E-mail: gpa.gis@utdallas.edu. Website: https://epps.utdallas.edu/about/programs/geospatial-information-sciences/

The University of Toledo, College of Graduate Studies, College of Languages, Literature and Social Sciences, Department of Geography and Planning, Toledo, OH 43606-3390. Offers geographic information science and applied geographics (Certificate); geography and planning (MA); spatially-integrated social science (PhD). *Program availability:* Part-time. *Degree requirements:* For master's, comprehensive exam, thesis; for doctorate, thesis/dissertation. *Entrance requirements:* For master's and doctorate, GRE General Test, minimum cumulative point-hour ratio of 2.7 for all previous academic work, three letters of recommendation; for Certificate, minimum cumulative point-hour ratio of 2.7 for all previous academic work, three letters of recommendation. Additional exam requirements/recommendations for international students: required—TOEFL (minimum score 550 paper-based; 80 iBT). Electronic applications accepted.

University of Utah, Graduate School, College of Social and Behavioral Science, Department of Geography, Salt Lake City, UT 84112. Offers geographic information science (MS); geography (MS, PhD). *Faculty:* 16 full-time (4 women), 1 part-time/adjunct (0 women). *Students:* 38 full-time (19 women), 15 part-time (6 women); includes 8 minority (6 Hispanic/Latino; 1 Native Hawaiian or other Pacific Islander, non-Hispanic/Latino; 1 Two or more races, non-Hispanic/Latino), 10 international. Average age 30. 52 applicants, 69% accepted, 17 enrolled. In 2019, 10 master's, 4 doctorates awarded. *Degree requirements:* For master's, thesis; for doctorate, comprehensive exam, thesis/dissertation. *Entrance requirements:* For master's, GRE (except for MS in geographic information science); for doctorate, GRE. Additional exam requirements/recommendations for international students: required—TOEFL (minimum score 550 paper-based; 7 iBT), IELTS. *Application deadline:* For fall admission, 1/10 priority date for domestic and international students. Application fee: $55 ($65 for international students). *Expenses: Tuition,* state resident: full-time $7085; part-time $272.51 per credit hour. Tuition, nonresident: full-time $24,937; part-time $959.12 per credit hour. *Required fees:* $880.52; $880.52 per semester. Tuition and fees vary according to degree level, program and student level. *Financial support:* In 2019–20, 33 students

received support, including 3 fellowships (averaging $22,667 per year), 16 research assistantships (averaging $13,938 per year), 9 teaching assistantships (averaging $12,333 per year); scholarships/grants and unspecified assistantships also available. Financial award application deadline: 1/20; financial award applicants required to submit CSS PROFILE or FAFSA. *Unit head:* Dr. Philip E. Dennison, epartment Chair, 801-581-8218, Fax: 801-585-5081, E-mail: dennison@geog.utah.edu. *Application contact:* Pamela S. Mitchell, Academic coordinator/graduate secretary, 801-581-8218, Fax: 801-585-5081, E-mail: pam.mitchell@geog.utah.edu.
Website: http://www.geog.utah.edu

University of West Florida, Hal Marcus College of Science and Engineering, Department of Earth and Environmental Sciences, Pensacola, FL 32514-5750. Offers environmental science (MS); geographic information science administration (MS). *Program availability:* Part-time. *Entrance requirements:* For master's, GRE (minimum score: 50th percentile for verbal; 40th percentile for quantitative), official transcripts; formal letter of interest, background, and professional goals; three letters of recommendation by individuals in professionally-relevant fields (waived for graduates of UWF Department of Environmental Sciences); current curriculum vitae/resume. Additional exam requirements/recommendations for international students: required—TOEFL (minimum score 550 paper-based).

University of Wisconsin–Madison, Graduate School, College of Letters and Science, Department of Geography, Madison, WI 53706-1380. Offers cartography and geographic information systems (MS); geographic information systems (Certificate); geography (MS, PhD). *Program availability:* Part-time. *Degree requirements:* For master's, thesis; for doctorate, thesis/dissertation; for Certificate, internship. *Entrance requirements:* For master's and doctorate, GRE General Test, minimum GPA of 3.25. Electronic applications accepted.

University of Wisconsin–Milwaukee, Graduate School, School of Architecture and Urban Planning, Department of Architecture, Milwaukee, WI 53201-0413. Offers architecture (M Arch, MS Arch, PhD); geographic information systems (Graduate Certificate). *Degree requirements:* For master's, comprehensive exam, thesis; for doctorate, comprehensive exam, thesis/dissertation. *Entrance requirements:* For master's, GRE General Test, portfolio. Additional exam requirements/recommendations for international students: required—TOEFL (minimum score 600 paper-based; 100 iBT), IELTS (minimum score 7). Electronic applications accepted.

Université Laval, Faculty of Administrative Sciences, Programs in Business Administration, Québec, QC G1K 7P4, Canada. Offers accounting (MBA); agri-food management (MBA); electronic business (MBA, Diploma); factory management and logistics (MBA); finance (MBA); firm management (MBA); geomatic management (MBA); information technology management (MBA); international management (MBA); management (MBA); management accounting (MBA, Diploma); marketing (MBA); modeling and organizational decision (MBA); occupational health and safety management (MBA); pharmacy management (MBA); social and environmental responsibility (MBA); technological entrepreneurship (Diploma). *Accreditation:* AACSB. *Program availability:* Part-time, evening/weekend, online learning. *Entrance requirements:* For master's and Diploma, knowledge of French and English. Electronic applications accepted.

Virginia Commonwealth University, Graduate School, L. Douglas Wilder School of Government and Public Affairs, Program in Geographic Information Systems, Richmond, VA 23284-9005. Offers Certificate. *Entrance requirements:* Additional exam requirements/recommendations for international students: required—TOEFL (minimum score 600 paper-based; 100 iBT); recommended—IELTS (minimum score 6.5). Electronic applications accepted.

Western Illinois University, School of Graduate Studies, College of Arts and Sciences, Department of Biological Sciences, Macomb, IL 61455-1390. Offers biology (MS); environmental GIS (Certificate); zoo and aquarium studies (Certificate). *Program availability:* Part-time. *Entrance requirements:* Additional exam requirements/recommendations for international students: required—TOEFL (minimum score 550 paper-based; 80 iBT); recommended—IELTS. Electronic applications accepted.

Western Illinois University, School of Graduate Studies, College of Arts and Sciences, Department of Geography, Macomb, IL 61455-1390. Offers geography (MA); GIS analysis: GIS applications (Certificate). *Program availability:* Part-time. *Entrance requirements:* Additional exam requirements/recommendations for international students: required—TOEFL (minimum score 550 paper-based; 80 iBT). Electronic applications accepted.

Western Michigan University, Graduate College, College of Arts and Sciences, Department of Geography, Kalamazoo, MI 49008. Offers geographic information science (Graduate Certificate); geography (MA). *Degree requirements:* For master's, thesis.

Geography

Appalachian State University, Cratis D. Williams School of Graduate Studies, Department of Geography and Planning, Boone, NC 28608. Offers geography (MA), including geographic information science. *Program availability:* Part-time, online learning. *Degree requirements:* For master's, comprehensive exam, thesis or alternative. *Entrance requirements:* For master's, GRE General Test, 3 letters of recommendation. Additional exam requirements/recommendations for international students: required—TOEFL (minimum score 570 paper-based; 79 iBT), IELTS (minimum score 6.5). Electronic applications accepted.

Arizona State University at Tempe, College of Liberal Arts and Sciences, School of Geographical Sciences and Urban Planning, Tempe, AZ 85287-5302. Offers geographic information systems (MAS); geographical information science (Graduate Certificate); geography (MA, PhD); transportation systems (Graduate Certificate); urban and environmental planning (MUEP); urban planning (PhD). *Accreditation:* ACSP. Terminal master's awarded for partial completion of doctoral program. *Degree requirements:* For master's, thesis, interactive Program of Study (iPOS) submitted before completing 50 percent of required credit hours; for doctorate, comprehensive exam, thesis/dissertation, interactive Program of Study (iPOS) submitted before completing 50 percent of required credit hours. *Entrance requirements:* For master's and doctorate, GRE, minimum GPA of 3.0 or equivalent in last 2 years of work leading to bachelor's degree. Additional exam requirements/recommendations for international students: required—TOEFL, IELTS, or PTE. Electronic applications accepted. *Expenses:* Contact institution.

Auburn University, Graduate School, College of Sciences and Mathematics, Department of Geosciences, Auburn, AL 36849. Offers MS. *Program availability:* Part-time. *Faculty:* 24 full-time (9 women), 4 part-time/adjunct (2 women). *Students:* 20 full-time (9 women), 16 part-time (6 women); includes 6 minority (1 Black or African American, non-Hispanic/Latino; 1 American Indian or Alaska Native, non-Hispanic/Latino; 3 Hispanic/Latino; 1 Two or more races, non-Hispanic/Latino), 11 international. Average age 28. 47 applicants, 51% accepted, 11 enrolled. In 2019, 16 master's awarded. *Degree requirements:* For master's, computer language or geographic information systems, field camp. *Entrance requirements:* For master's, GRE General Test. Additional exam requirements/recommendations for international students: required—iTEP; recommended—TOEFL (minimum score 550 paper-based; 79 iBT), IELTS (minimum score 6.5). *Application deadline:* Applications are processed on a rolling basis. Application fee: $60 ($70 for international students). Electronic applications accepted. *Expenses: Tuition, area resident:* Full-time $9828; part-time $546 per credit hour. Tuition, state resident: full-time $9828; part-time $546 per credit hour. Tuition, nonresident: full-time $29,484; part-time $1638 per credit hour. *International tuition:* $29,744 full-time. Tuition and fees vary according to course load, program and reciprocity agreements. *Financial support:* In 2019–20, 25 fellowships with tuition reimbursements, 6 research assistantships with tuition reimbursements (averaging $21,085 per year), 20 teaching assistantships with tuition reimbursements (averaging $24,472 per year) were awarded; Federal Work-Study also available. Support available to part-time students. Financial award application deadline: 3/15; financial award applicants required to submit FAFSA. *Unit head:* Dr. Ming-Kuo Lee, Chair, 334-844-4898, Fax: 334-844-4486, E-mail: leeming@auburn.edu. *Application contact:* Dr. George Flowers, Dean of the Graduate School, 334-844-2125.
Website: http://www.auburn.edu/cosam//departments/geosciences/index.htm

Ball State University, Graduate School, College of Sciences and Humanities, Department of Geography, Muncie, IN 47306. Offers geographic information systems (Certificate); geography (MS); professional meteorology and climatology (Certificate). *Program availability:* Part-time. *Entrance requirements:* For master's, minimum baccalaureate GPA of 2.75 or 3.0 in latter half of baccalaureate, letter of interest, three letters of recommendation, resume or curriculum vitae, official transcripts. Additional exam requirements/recommendations for international students: required—TOEFL (minimum score 550 paper-based; 79 iBT), IELTS (minimum score 6.5). Electronic applications accepted. *Expenses: Tuition, area resident:* Full-time $7506; part-time $417 per credit hour. Tuition, nonresident: full-time $20,610; part-time $1145 per credit hour. *Required fees:* $2126. Tuition and fees vary according to course load, campus/location and program.

Binghamton University, State University of New York, Graduate School, Harpur College of Arts and Sciences, Department of Geography, Binghamton, NY 13902-6000. Offers MA. *Program availability:* Part-time. *Degree requirements:* For master's, one foreign language, thesis (for some programs). *Entrance requirements:* For master's, GRE General Test. Additional exam requirements/recommendations for international students: required—TOEFL (minimum score 550 paper-based; 80 iBT). Electronic applications accepted.

Brock University, Faculty of Graduate Studies, Faculty of Social Sciences, Program in Geography, St. Catharines, ON L2S 3A1, Canada. Offers MA. *Program availability:* Part-time. *Degree requirements:* For master's, thesis optional. *Entrance requirements:* For master's, honors degree. Additional exam requirements/recommendations for international students: required—TOEFL (minimum score 550 paper-based; 80 iBT), IELTS (minimum score 6.5), TWE (minimum score 4).

California State University, East Bay, Office of Graduate Studies, College of Letters, Arts, and Social Sciences, Department of Anthropology, Geography and Environmental Studies, Hayward, CA 94542-3000. Offers anthropology (MA); geography (MA). *Program availability:* Part-time. *Degree requirements:* For master's, variable foreign language requirement, project or thesis. *Entrance requirements:* For master's, minimum GPA of 3.0 in field. Additional exam requirements/recommendations for international students: required—TOEFL (minimum score 550 paper-based). Electronic applications accepted.

California State University, Fullerton, Graduate Studies, College of Humanities and Social Sciences, Department of Geography, Fullerton, CA 92831-3599. Offers MA. *Program availability:* Part-time. *Entrance requirements:* For master's, minimum GPA of 3.0, 18 undergraduate credits in field.

California State University, Long Beach, Graduate Studies, College of Liberal Arts, Department of Geography, Long Beach, CA 90840. Offers MA, MS. *Program availability:* Part-time. *Degree requirements:* For master's, thesis. Electronic applications accepted.

California State University, Los Angeles, Graduate Studies, College of Natural and Social Sciences, Department of Geography and Urban Analysis, Los Angeles, CA 90032-8530. Offers geography (MA). *Program availability:* Part-time, evening/weekend. *Degree requirements:* For master's, one foreign language, comprehensive exam or thesis. *Entrance requirements:* Additional exam requirements/recommendations for international students: required—TOEFL (minimum score 500 paper-based). Electronic applications accepted. *Expenses: Tuition, area resident:* Full-time $7176; part-time $4164 per year. Tuition, state resident: full-time $7176; part-time $4164 per year. Tuition, nonresident: full-time $14,304; part-time $8916 per year. *International tuition:* $14,304 full-time. *Required fees:* $1037.76; $1037.76 per unit. Tuition and fees vary according to degree level and program.

California State University, Northridge, Graduate Studies, College of Social and Behavioral Sciences, Department of Geography, Northridge, CA 91330. Offers MA. *Program availability:* Part-time. *Degree requirements:* For master's, one foreign language, thesis. *Entrance requirements:* For master's, GRE General Test or minimum GPA of 3.0. Additional exam requirements/recommendations for international students: required—TOEFL.

Carleton University, Faculty of Graduate Studies, Faculty of Arts and Social Sciences, Department of Geography and Environmental Studies, Ottawa, ON K1S 5B6, Canada. Offers geography (M Sc, MA, PhD). *Degree requirements:* For master's, thesis, seminar; for doctorate, one foreign language, thesis/dissertation, 2 comprehensive exams. *Entrance requirements:* For master's, honors degree; for doctorate, master's degree in geography. Additional exam requirements/recommendations for international students: required—TOEFL.

Central Connecticut State University, School of Graduate Studies, College of Liberal Arts and Social Sciences, Department of Geography, New Britain, CT 06050-4010.

Geography

Offers MS. *Program availability:* Part-time, evening/weekend. *Degree requirements:* For master's, comprehensive exam, thesis or alternative, special project. *Entrance requirements:* For master's, minimum undergraduate GPA of 3.0, essay. Additional exam requirements/recommendations for international students: required—TOEFL (minimum score 550 paper-based; 79 iBT); recommended—IELTS (minimum score 6.5). Electronic applications accepted.

Central Washington University, School of Graduate Studies and Research, College of the Sciences, Program in Cultural and Environmental Resource Management, Ellensburg, WA 98926. Offers anthropology (MS); geography (MS). *Entrance requirements:* For master's, GRE, minimum GPA of 3.0. Additional exam requirements/recommendations for international students: required—TOEFL (minimum score 550 paper-based; 79 iBT). Electronic applications accepted.

Clark University, Graduate School, School of Geography, Worcester, MA 01610-1477. Offers geography (PhD). *Faculty:* 19 full-time (7 women), 3 part-time/adjunct (2 women). *Students:* 58 full-time (35 women); includes 6 minority (1 Black or African American, non-Hispanic/Latino; 3 Asian, non-Hispanic/Latino; 2 Hispanic/Latino), 26 international. Average age 32. 135 applicants, 13% accepted, 9 enrolled. In 2019, 11 doctorates awarded. *Entrance requirements:* For doctorate, GRE General Test. Additional exam requirements/recommendations for international students: required—TOEFL (minimum score 575 paper-based; 90 iBT), IELTS (minimum score 6.5). *Application deadline:* For fall admission, 12/31 priority date for domestic and international students. Application fee: $75. Electronic applications accepted. *Expenses: Tuition:* Full-time $47,650; part-time $4765 per course. *Required fees:* $1850. *Financial support:* Fellowships, research assistantships, teaching assistantships, career-related internships or fieldwork, and tuition waivers (full) available. *Unit head:* Dr. Deb Martin, Director, 508-793-7104, E-mail: dmartin@clarku.edu. *Application contact:* Dr. Deb Martin, Director, 508-793-7104, E-mail: dmartin@clarku.edu.
Website: http://www.clarku.edu/departments/geography/

Concordia University, School of Graduate Studies, Faculty of Arts and Science, Department of Geography, Planning and Environment, Montréal, QC H3G 1M8, Canada. Offers environmental assessment (M Env, Diploma); geography, urban and environmental studies (M Sc, PhD).

Concordia University, School of Graduate Studies, Faculty of Arts and Science, Department of Political Science, Montréal, QC H3G 1M8, Canada. Offers political science (PhD); public policy and public administration (MA), including geography. *Degree requirements:* For master's, one foreign language, comprehensive exam, thesis optional, internship. *Entrance requirements:* For master's, honors degree or equivalent. Additional exam requirements/recommendations for international students: required—TOEFL.

East Carolina University, Graduate School, Thomas Harriot College of Arts and Sciences, Department of Geography, Planning, and Environment, Greenville, NC 27858-4353. Offers development and environmental planning (Certificate); economic development (Certificate); geographic information science and technology (Certificate); geography (MA), including geography, planning, rural development. *Program availability:* Part-time, evening/weekend, online learning. *Degree requirements:* For master's, comprehensive exam, thesis optional. *Entrance requirements:* For master's, GRE General Test. *Application deadline:* For fall admission, 4/1 priority date for domestic and international students. Applications are processed on a rolling basis. Electronic applications accepted. *Expenses: Tuition, area resident:* Full-time $4749; part-time $185 per credit hour. Tuition, state resident: full-time $4749; part-time $185 per credit hour. Tuition, nonresident: full-time $17,898; part-time $864 per credit hour. *International tuition:* $17,898 full-time. *Required fees:* $2787. *Financial support:* Research assistantships with partial tuition reimbursements, teaching assistantships with partial tuition reimbursements, and Federal Work-Study available. Support available to part-time students. Financial award application deadline: 3/1. *Unit head:* Dr. Thad Wasklewicz, Chair, 252-328-6230, E-mail: wasklewiczt@ecu.edu. *Application contact:* Graduate Admissions, 252-328-6012, Fax: 252-328-6071, E-mail: gradschool@ecu.edu.
Website: https://geography.ecu.edu/

East Stroudsburg University of Pennsylvania, Graduate and Extended Studies, College of Arts and Sciences, Department of History and Geography, East Stroudsburg, PA 18301-2999. Offers M Ed, MA. *Program availability:* Part-time, evening/weekend. *Degree requirements:* For master's, comprehensive exam, thesis, thesis defense. *Entrance requirements:* For master's, Bachelor's degree in History is preferable. Additional exam requirements/recommendations for international students: recommended—TOEFL (minimum score 560 paper-based; 83 iBT), IELTS. Electronic applications accepted.

Florida State University, The Graduate School, College of Social Sciences and Public Policy, Department of Geography, Tallahassee, FL 32306. Offers geographic information science (MS); geography (MA, MS, PhD). *Program availability:* Part-time. *Faculty:* 12 full-time (3 women), 7 part-time/adjunct (5 women). *Students:* 36 full-time (22 women), 16 part-time (6 women); includes 12 minority (4 Black or African American, non-Hispanic/Latino; 3 Hispanic/Latino; 5 Two or more races, non-Hispanic/Latino), 12 international. Average age 32. 82 applicants, 33% accepted, 12 enrolled. In 2019, 26 master's, 6 doctorates awarded. Terminal master's awarded for partial completion of doctoral program. *Degree requirements:* For master's, thesis (for some programs); for doctorate, comprehensive exam, thesis/dissertation. *Entrance requirements:* For master's and doctorate, GRE General Test, minimum GPA of 3.0. Additional exam requirements/recommendations for international students: required—TOEFL (minimum score 80 iBT). *Application deadline:* For fall admission, 3/1 priority date for domestic and international students; for spring admission, 10/1 priority date for domestic and international students. Applications are processed on a rolling basis. Application fee: $30. Electronic applications accepted. *Financial support:* In 2019–20, 44 students received support, including 1 research assistantship with full tuition reimbursement available (averaging $17,687 per year), 16 teaching assistantships with full tuition reimbursements available (averaging $17,687 per year); career-related internships or fieldwork, Federal Work-Study, institutionally sponsored loans, scholarships/grants, health care benefits, tuition waivers (full and partial), and unspecified assistantships also available. Financial award application deadline: 3/1; financial award applicants required to submit FAFSA. *Unit head:* Prof. James Elsner, Chair, 850-644-1706, Fax: 850-644-5913, E-mail: jelsner@fsu.edu. *Application contact:* Dr. Christopher Uejio, Graduate Director, 850-644-1706, Fax: 850-644-5193, E-mail: cuejio@fsu.edu.
Website: http://geography.fsu.edu/

Fort Hays State University, Graduate School, Peter Werth College of Science, Technology and Mathematics, Department of Geosciences, Program in Geosciences, Hays, KS 67601-4099. Offers geography (MS); geology (MS). *Degree requirements:* For master's, comprehensive exam, thesis. *Entrance requirements:* For master's, GRE General Test. Additional exam requirements/recommendations for international students: required—TOEFL (minimum score 550 paper-based). Electronic applications accepted.

George Mason University, College of Science, Department of Geography and Geoinformation Science, Fairfax, VA 22030. Offers earth system science (MS); earth systems and geoinformation sciences (PhD); environmental geoinformation science and biodiversity conservation (Certificate); geography and geoinformation science (Certificate). *Degree requirements:* For master's, comprehensive exam (for some programs), thesis (for some programs); for doctorate, comprehensive exam, thesis/dissertation. *Entrance requirements:* For master's, GRE, bachelor's degree with minimum GPA of 3.0; 2 copies of official transcripts; current resume; expanded goals statement; 3 letters of recommendation; for doctorate, GRE, bachelor's degree with minimum GPA of 3.0; 2 copies of official transcripts; 3 letters of recommendation; resume; expanded goals statement; for Certificate, GRE, baccalaureate degree with minimum GPA of 3.0; 2 official copies of transcripts; expanded goals statement; 3 letters of recommendation; resume. Additional exam requirements/recommendations for international students: required—TOEFL (minimum score 575 paper-based; 88 iBT), IELTS (minimum score 6.5), PTE (minimum score 59). Electronic applications accepted. *Expenses:* Contact institution.

The George Washington University, Columbian College of Arts and Sciences, Department of Geography, Washington, DC 20052. Offers MA, Graduate Certificate. *Degree requirements:* For master's, comprehensive exam, thesis or alternative. *Entrance requirements:* For master's, GRE General Test, BA in geography or related field, minimum GPA of 3.0. Additional exam requirements/recommendations for international students: required—TOEFL (minimum score 550 paper-based; 80 iBT). Electronic applications accepted.

Georgia State University, College of Arts and Sciences, Department of Geosciences, Program in Geography, Atlanta, GA 30302-3083. Offers MS. *Program availability:* Part-time. *Entrance requirements:* For master's, GRE General Test. Additional exam requirements/recommendations for international students: required—TOEFL. *Application deadline:* Applications are processed on a rolling basis. Application fee: $50. Electronic applications accepted. *Expenses: Tuition, area resident:* Full-time $7164; part-time $398 per credit hour. Tuition, state resident: full-time $7164; part-time $398 per credit hour. Tuition, nonresident: full-time $22,662; part-time $1259 per credit hour. *International tuition:* $22,662 full-time. *Required fees:* $2128; $312 per credit hour. Tuition and fees vary according to course load and program. *Financial support:* Research assistantships and teaching assistantships available. *Unit head:* Dr. Katherin Hankings, Chair, 404-413-5775, E-mail: khankins@gsu.edu. *Application contact:* Dr. Katherin Hankings, Chair, 404-413-5775, E-mail: khankins@gsu.edu.
Website: http://geosciences.gsu.edu/grad-programs/

Georgia State University, College of Education and Human Development, Department of Middle and Secondary Education, Atlanta, GA 30302-3083. Offers curriculum and instruction (Ed D); English education (MAT); mathematics education (M Ed, MAT); middle level education (MAT); reading, language and literacy education (M Ed, MAT), including reading instruction (M Ed); science education (M Ed, MAT), including biology (MAT), broad field science (MAT), chemistry (MAT), earth science (MAT), physics (MAT); social studies education (M Ed, MAT), including economics (MAT), geography (MAT), history (MAT), political science (MAT); teaching and learning (PhD), including language and literacy, mathematics education, music education, science education, social studies education, teaching and teacher education. *Accreditation:* NCATE. *Program availability:* Part-time, evening/weekend, online learning. *Faculty:* 20 full-time (16 women), 8 part-time/adjunct (all women). *Students:* 184 full-time (117 women), 195 part-time (144 women); includes 218 minority (157 Black or African American, non-Hispanic/Latino; 22 Asian, non-Hispanic/Latino; 27 Hispanic/Latino; 12 Two or more races, non-Hispanic/Latino), 3 international. Average age 34. 123 applicants, 61% accepted, 46 enrolled. In 2019, 122 master's, 18 doctorates awarded. *Entrance requirements:* For master's, GRE; GACE I (for initial teacher preparation programs), baccalaureate degree or equivalent, resume, goals statement, two letters of recommendation, minimum undergraduate GPA of 2.5; proof of initial teacher certification in the content area (for M Ed); for doctorate, GRE, resume, goals statement, writing sample, two letters of recommendation, minimum graduate GPA of 3.3, interview. *Application deadline:* For fall admission, 1/15 priority date for domestic and international students; for spring admission, 10/1 for domestic and international students. Application fee: $50. Electronic applications accepted. *Expenses: Tuition, area resident:* Full-time $7164; part-time $398 per credit hour. Tuition, state resident: full-time $7164; part-time $398 per credit hour. Tuition, nonresident: full-time $22,662; part-time $1259 per credit hour. *International tuition:* $22,662 full-time. *Required fees:* $2128; $312 per credit hour. Tuition and fees vary according to course load and program. *Financial support:* In 2019–20, fellowships with full tuition reimbursements (averaging $19,667 per year), research assistantships with full tuition reimbursements (averaging $5,436 per year), teaching assistantships with full tuition reimbursements (averaging $2,779 per year) were awarded; career-related internships or fieldwork, Federal Work-Study, scholarships/grants, health care benefits, tuition waivers (full and partial), and unspecified assistantships also available. Financial award application deadline: 3/15. *Unit head:* Dr. Gertrude Marilyn Tinker Sachs, Chair, 404-413-8384, Fax: 404-413-8063, E-mail: gtinkersachs@gsu.edu. *Application contact:* Shaleen Tibbs, Administrative Specialist, 404-413-8385, Fax: 404-413-8063, E-mail: stibbs@gsu.edu.
Website: http://mse.education.gsu.edu/

Hunter College of the City University of New York, Graduate School, School of Arts and Sciences, Department of Geography, New York, NY 10065-5085. Offers geographic information science (Certificate); geography (MA); geoinformatics (MS). *Program availability:* Part-time, evening/weekend. *Degree requirements:* For master's, comprehensive exam or thesis. *Entrance requirements:* For master's, GRE General Test, minimum B average in major, B- overall; 18 credits of course work in geography; 2 letters of recommendation; for Certificate, minimum B average in major, B- overall. Additional exam requirements/recommendations for international students: required—TOEFL.

Indiana University Bloomington, University Graduate School, College of Arts and Sciences, Department of Geography, Bloomington, IN 47405. Offers PhD. *Degree requirements:* For doctorate, comprehensive exam, thesis/dissertation. *Entrance requirements:* For doctorate, GRE General Test, minimum GPA of 3.0. Additional exam requirements/recommendations for international students: required—TOEFL (minimum score 620 paper-based; 105 iBT), IELTS (minimum score 7). Electronic applications accepted.

Indiana University of Pennsylvania, School of Graduate Studies and Research, College of Humanities and Social Sciences, Department of Geography and Regional Planning, Indiana, PA 15705. Offers environmental planning (MS); geographic information science and geospatial techniques (Certificate); geographic information science/cartography (MS); geography (MA); regional planning (MS). *Program availability:* Part-time. *Faculty:* 8 full-time (2 women). *Students:* 16 full-time (4 women), 3 part-time (1 woman); includes 1 minority (Black or African American, non-Hispanic/Latino), 2 international. Average age 28. 23 applicants, 96% accepted, 11 enrolled. In 2019, 3 master's, 1 other advanced degree awarded. *Degree requirements:* For master's, thesis optional. *Entrance requirements:* For master's, GRE, 2 letters of recommendation, official transcripts, goal statement. Additional exam requirements/recommendations for international students: required—TOEFL (minimum score 550 paper-based; 80 iBT), IELTS (minimum score 6.5), TOEFL or IELTS. *Application deadline:* Applications are processed on a rolling basis. Application fee: $50. Electronic applications accepted. *Expenses: Tuition, area resident:* Full-time $9288; part-time $516 per credit. Tuition, nonresident: full-time $13,932; part-time $774 per credit. *Required fees:* $4454. One-time fee: $115 full-time. Tuition and fees vary according to course load and program. *Financial support:* In 2019–20, 1 fellowship with tuition reimbursement (averaging $800 per year), 12 research assistantships with tuition reimbursements (averaging $3,077 per year) were awarded; career-related internships or fieldwork, Federal Work-Study, scholarships/grants, and unspecified assistantships also available. Support available to part-time students. Financial award application deadline: 4/15; financial award applicants required to submit FAFSA. *Unit head:* Dr. John E. Benhart, Jr., Chairperson, 724-357-2250, E-mail: jbenhart@iup.edu. *Application contact:* Dr. Jennifer L. Smith, Graduate Coordinator, 724-357-5990, E-mail: jsmith@iup.edu. Website: http://www.iup.edu/geography

Kansas State University, Graduate School, College of Arts and Sciences, Department of Geography, Manhattan, KS 66506. Offers geographic information science (Graduate Certificate); geography (MA, PhD). *Degree requirements:* For master's, thesis optional, oral exam; for doctorate, one foreign language, thesis/dissertation. *Entrance requirements:* For master's and doctorate, GRE General Test, minimum GPA of 3.0. Electronic applications accepted.

Kent State University, College of Arts and Sciences, Department of Geography, Kent, OH 44242-0001. Offers geographic information science (MGIS), including cyber geographic information science, environmental geographic information science, geographic information science and health; geography (MA, PhD). *Program availability:* Part-time, 100% online. *Faculty:* 9 full-time (2 women), 2 part-time/adjunct (both women). *Students:* 39 full-time (17 women), 45 part-time (24 women); includes 10 minority (2 Black or African American, non-Hispanic/Latino; 4 Asian, non-Hispanic/Latino; 2 Hispanic/Latino; 2 Two or more races, non-Hispanic/Latino), 19 international. Average age 33. 42 applicants, 83% accepted, 26 enrolled. In 2019, 13 master's, 5 doctorates awarded. *Degree requirements:* For master's, thesis (for some programs), Thesis or two research papers, practicum (MGISc); for doctorate, comprehensive exam, thesis/dissertation. *Entrance requirements:* For master's, GRE, minimum undergraduate GPA of 3.0, undergraduate degree transcripts, three letters of recommendation, goal statement, resume; for doctorate, GRE, Master's degree from accredited college or university, transcripts, three letters of recommendation, goal statement, resume. Additional exam requirements/recommendations for international students: required—TOEFL (minimum score 79 iBT), IELTS (minimum score 6.5), PTE (minimum score 58), Michigan English Language Assessment Battery (minimum score 77). *Application deadline:* For fall admission, 2/1 priority date for domestic and international students; for spring admission, 11/1 for domestic and international students; for summer admission, 4/1 for domestic and international students. Applications are processed on a rolling basis. Application fee: $45 ($70 for international students). Electronic applications accepted. *Financial support:* Fellowships with full tuition reimbursements, research assistantships with full tuition reimbursements, teaching assistantships with full tuition reimbursements, Federal Work-Study, scholarships/grants, and unspecified assistantships available. Financial award application deadline: 2/1. *Unit head:* Dr. Scott Sheridan, Professor and Chair, 330-672-3224, Fax: 330-672-4304, E-mail: ssherid1@kent.edu. *Application contact:* Dr. David H. Kaplan, Professor and Graduate Coordinator, 330-672-3221, E-mail: dkaplan@kent.edu. Website: https://www.kent.edu/geography

Louisiana State University and Agricultural & Mechanical College, Graduate School, College of Humanities and Social Sciences, Department of Geography and Anthropology, Baton Rouge, LA 70803. Offers geography (MA, MS); geography and anthropology (PhD).

Marshall University, Academic Affairs Division, College of Liberal Arts, Department of Geography, Huntington, WV 25755. Offers MA, MS, Certificate. *Degree requirements:* For master's, thesis optional. *Entrance requirements:* For master's, GRE General Test (for MS).

McGill University, Faculty of Graduate and Postdoctoral Studies, Faculty of Science, Department of Geography, Montréal, QC H3A 2T5, Canada. Offers geography (M Sc, MA, PhD); neo-tropical environment (MA, PhD); social statistics (MA).

McMaster University, School of Graduate Studies, Faculty of Science, School of Geography and Earth Sciences, Hamilton, ON L8S 4M2, Canada. Offers geochemistry (PhD); geology (M Sc, PhD); human geography (MA, PhD); physical geography (M Sc, PhD). *Program availability:* Part-time. Terminal master's awarded for partial completion of doctoral program. *Degree requirements:* For master's, thesis; for doctorate, comprehensive exam, thesis/dissertation. *Entrance requirements:* For master's, minimum B+ average. Additional exam requirements/recommendations for international students: required—TOEFL (minimum score 550 paper-based).

Memorial University of Newfoundland, School of Graduate Studies, Department of Geography, St. John's, NL A1C 5S7, Canada. Offers M Sc, MA, PhD. *Program availability:* Part-time. *Degree requirements:* For master's, thesis; for doctorate, comprehensive exam, thesis/dissertation, seminar, oral defense of thesis. *Entrance requirements:* For master's, 2nd class degree; for doctorate, master's degree. Electronic applications accepted.

Miami University, College of Arts and Science, Department of Geography, Oxford, OH 45056. Offers MA.

Michigan State University, The Graduate School, College of Social Science, Department of Geography, Environment, and Spatial Sciences, East Lansing, MI 48824. Offers geography (MS, PhD). *Degree requirements:* For master's, comprehensive exam, thesis (for some programs), presentation of poster/paper or oral defense of thesis; for doctorate, comprehensive exam, thesis/dissertation, presentation of poster/paper, presentation and defense of dissertation proposal, oral exam in defense of dissertation. *Entrance requirements:* Additional exam requirements/recommendations for international students: required—TOEFL (minimum score 600 paper-based). Electronic applications accepted.

Minnesota State University Mankato, College of Graduate Studies and Research, College of Social and Behavioral Sciences, Department of Geography, Mankato, MN 56001. Offers MS. *Program availability:* Part-time. *Degree requirements:* For master's, one foreign language, comprehensive exam, thesis optional. *Entrance requirements:* For master's, minimum GPA of 3.0. Electronic applications accepted.

Mississippi State University, College of Arts and Sciences, Department of Geosciences, Mississippi State, MS 39762. Offers applied meteorology (MS); broadcast meteorology (MS); earth and atmospheric science (PhD); environmental geosciences (MS); geography (MS); geology (MS); geospatial sciences (MS); professional meteorology/climatology (MS); teachers in geosciences (MS). *Program availability:* Blended/hybrid learning. *Faculty:* 22 full-time (8 women), 1 part-time/adjunct (0 women). *Students:* 59 full-time (25 women), 201 part-time (92 women); includes 41 minority (13 Black or African American, non-Hispanic/Latino; 1 Asian, non-Hispanic/Latino; 21 Hispanic/Latino; 2 Native Hawaiian or other Pacific Islander, non-Hispanic/Latino; 4 Two or more races, non-Hispanic/Latino), 14 international. Average age 32. 113 applicants, 79% accepted, 70 enrolled. In 2019, 70 master's, 5 doctorates awarded. *Degree requirements:* For master's, thesis (for some programs), comprehensive oral or written

exam; for doctorate, thesis/dissertation, comprehensive oral or written exam. *Entrance requirements:* For master's, GRE (for on-campus applicants), minimum undergraduate GPA of 2.75; for doctorate, thesis-based MS with background in one department emphasis area. Additional exam requirements/recommendations for international students: required—TOEFL (minimum score 477 paper-based; 53 iBT); recommended—IELTS (minimum score 4.5). *Application deadline:* For fall admission, 7/1 for domestic students, 5/1 for international students; for spring admission, 11/1 for domestic students, 9/1 for international students. Applications are processed on a rolling basis. Application fee: $60 ($80 for international students). Electronic applications accepted. *Expenses: Tuition, area resident:* Full-time $8880; part-time $456 per credit hour. Tuition, state resident: full-time $8880. Tuition, nonresident: full-time $23,840; part-time $1236 per credit hour. *Required fees:* $110; $11.12 per credit hour. Tuition and fees vary according to course load. *Financial support:* In 2019–20, 3 research assistantships with full tuition reimbursements (averaging $17,821 per year), 30 teaching assistantships with full tuition reimbursements (averaging $16,617 per year) were awarded; Federal Work-Study, institutionally sponsored loans, scholarships/grants, tuition waivers (partial), and unspecified assistantships also available. Financial award application deadline: 4/1; financial award applicants required to submit FAFSA. *Unit head:* Dr. John C. Rodgers, III, Professor and Department Head, 662-325-1032, Fax: 662-325-9423, E-mail: jcr100@msstate.edu. *Application contact:* Nathan Drake, Manager, Graduate Programs, 662-325-7394, E-mail: ndrake@grad.msstate.edu. Website: http://www.geosciences.msstate.edu

Missouri State University, Graduate College, College of Natural and Applied Sciences, Department of Geography, Geology, and Planning, Springfield, MO 65897. Offers geography, geology, and planning (Certificate); natural and applied science (MNAS), including geography, geology and planning; secondary education (MS Ed), including earth science, physical geography. *Program availability:* Part-time, evening/weekend. *Degree requirements:* For master's, comprehensive exam, thesis (for some programs). *Entrance requirements:* For master's, GRE General Test (MS, MNAS), minimum undergraduate GPA of 3.0 (MS, MNAS), 9-12 teacher certification (MS Ed). Additional exam requirements/recommendations for international students: required—TOEFL (minimum score 550 paper-based; 79 iBT), IELTS (minimum score 6). Electronic applications accepted. *Expenses: Tuition, area resident:* Full-time $2600; part-time $1735 per credit hour. Tuition, nonresident: full-time $5240; part-time $3495 per credit hour. *International tuition:* $5240 full-time. *Required fees:* $530; $438 per credit hour. Tuition and fees vary according to class time, course level, course load, degree level, campus/location and program.

New Mexico State University, College of Arts and Sciences, Department of Geography, Las Cruces, NM 88003-8001. Offers applied geography (MAG). *Program availability:* Part-time. *Faculty:* 6 full-time (2 women). *Students:* 11 full-time (3 women), 11 part-time (3 women); includes 11 minority (10 Hispanic/Latino; 1 Two or more races, non-Hispanic/Latino), 1 international. Average age 32. 10 applicants, 90% accepted, 5 enrolled. In 2019, 1 master's awarded. *Degree requirements:* For master's, comprehensive exam, thesis optional, thesis or residency paper. *Entrance requirements:* For master's, bachelor's degree in geography or related field. Additional exam requirements/recommendations for international students: required—TOEFL (minimum score 550 paper-based; 79 iBT), IELTS (minimum score 6.5). *Application deadline:* For spring admission, 2/1 for domestic students, 2/1 priority date for international students. Applications are processed on a rolling basis. Application fee: $40 ($50 for international students). Electronic applications accepted. *Financial support:* In 2019–20, 12 students received support, including 1 research assistantship (averaging $18,163 per year), 6 teaching assistantships (averaging $17,708 per year); career-related internships or fieldwork, Federal Work-Study, scholarships/grants, traineeships, health care benefits, and unspecified assistantships also available. Support available to part-time students. Financial award application deadline: 3/1. *Unit head:* Dr. Carol Campbell, Department Head, 575-646-3509, Fax: 575-646-7430, E-mail: geobird@nmsu.edu. *Application contact:* Dr. Daniel P. Dugas, Graduate Advisor, 575-646-1045, Fax: 575-646-7430, E-mail: ddugas@nmsu.edu. Website: http://geography.nmsu.edu

Northeastern Illinois University, College of Graduate Studies and Research, College of Arts and Sciences, Program in Geography and Environmental Studies, Chicago, IL 60625. Offers geographic information science (Graduate Certificate); geography and environmental studies (MA). *Program availability:* Part-time, evening/weekend. *Degree requirements:* For master's, comprehensive exam, thesis optional. *Entrance requirements:* For master's, undergraduate minor in geography or environmental studies, minimum GPA of 2.75. Additional exam requirements/recommendations for international students: required—TOEFL (minimum score 550 paper-based; 79 iBT). Electronic applications accepted.

Northern Arizona University, College of Social and Behavioral Sciences, Department of Geography, Planning, and Recreation, Flagstaff, AZ 86011. Offers applied geospatial sciences (MS); community planning (Certificate); geographic information systems (Certificate); parks and recreation management (MS). *Program availability:* Part-time, 100% online, blended/hybrid learning. *Degree requirements:* For master's, variable foreign language requirement, comprehensive exam (for some programs), thesis (for some programs); for Certificate, comprehensive exam (for some programs). *Entrance requirements:* Additional exam requirements/recommendations for international students: required—TOEFL (minimum score 80 iBT), IELTS (minimum score 6.5). Electronic applications accepted.

Northern Illinois University, Graduate School, College of Liberal Arts and Sciences, Department of Geography, De Kalb, IL 60115-2854. Offers MS, PhD. *Program availability:* Part-time. *Faculty:* 8 full-time (2 women). *Students:* 15 full-time (5 women), 5 part-time (2 women), 6 international. Average age 30. 28 applicants, 71% accepted, 2 enrolled. In 2019, 3 master's, 4 doctorates awarded. *Degree requirements:* For master's, comprehensive exam, thesis optional, research seminar. *Entrance requirements:* For master's, GRE General Test, minimum GPA of 2.75; for doctorate, master's degree. Additional exam requirements/recommendations for international students: required—TOEFL (minimum score 550 paper-based). *Application deadline:* For fall admission, 2/1 priority date for domestic students, 5/1 for international students; for spring admission, 10/1 priority date for domestic students, 10/1 for international students. Applications are processed on a rolling basis. Application fee: $40. Electronic applications accepted. *Financial support:* In 2019–20, 1 research assistantship with full tuition reimbursement, 14 teaching assistantships with full tuition reimbursements were awarded; fellowships with full tuition reimbursements, career-related internships or fieldwork, Federal Work-Study, scholarships/grants, tuition waivers (full), and unspecified assistantships also available. Support available to part-time students. Financial award applicants required to submit FAFSA. *Unit head:* Dr. David Changnon, Chair, 815-753-6826, Fax: 815-753-6872, E-mail: dchangnon@niu.edu. *Application contact:* Graduate School Office, 815-753-0395, E-mail: gradsch@niu.edu. Website: http://globe.geog.niu.edu/

The Ohio State University, Graduate School, College of Arts and Sciences, Division of Social and Behavioral Sciences, Department of Geography, Columbus, OH 43210. Offers atmospheric sciences (MS, PhD); geography (MA, PhD). *Degree requirements:* For doctorate, variable foreign language requirement, thesis/dissertation. *Entrance* *requirements:* For master's and doctorate, GRE. Additional exam requirements/ recommendations for international students: required—Michigan English Language Assessment Battery (minimum score 86); recommended—TOEFL (minimum score 600 paper-based; 100 iBT), IELTS (minimum score 8). Electronic applications accepted.

Ohio University, Graduate College, College of Arts and Sciences, Department of Geography, Athens, OH 45701-2979. Offers MA, MS. *Program availability:* Part-time. *Degree requirements:* For master's, thesis or alternative. *Entrance requirements:* For master's, GRE General Test, minimum GPA of 3.0. Additional exam requirements/ recommendations for international students: required—TOEFL (minimum score 600 paper-based; 100 iBT) or IELTS (minimum score 8). Electronic applications accepted.

Oklahoma State University, College of Arts and Sciences, Department of Geography, Stillwater, OK 74078. Offers MS, PhD. *Faculty:* 16 full-time (3 women). *Students:* 3 full-time (0 women), 23 part-time (9 women); includes 3 minority (all Asian, non-Hispanic/ Latino), 3 international. Average age 32. 7 applicants, 29% accepted, 2 enrolled. In 2019, 5 master's, 2 doctorates awarded. *Entrance requirements:* For master's and doctorate, GRE. Additional exam requirements/recommendations for international students: required—TOEFL (minimum score 550 paper-based; 79 iBT). *Application deadline:* For fall admission, 3/1 priority date for international students; for spring admission, 8/1 priority date for international students. Applications are processed on a rolling basis. Application fee: $50 ($75 for international students). Electronic applications accepted. *Expenses: Tuition, area resident:* Full-time $4148.10; part-time $2765.40 per credit hour. Tuition, state resident: full-time $4148.10; part-time $2765.40 per credit hour. Tuition, nonresident: full-time $15,775; part-time $10,516.80 per credit hour. *International tuition:* $15,775.20 full-time. *Required fees:* $2196.90; $122.05 per credit hour. Tuition and fees vary according to course load, campus/location and program. *Financial support:* In 2019–20, 4 research assistantships (averaging $1,517 per year), 14 teaching assistantships (averaging $1,831 per year) were awarded; career-related internships or fieldwork, Federal Work-Study, scholarships/grants, health care benefits, tuition waivers (partial), and unspecified assistantships also available. Support available to part-time students. Financial award application deadline: 3/1; financial award applicants required to submit FAFSA. *Unit head:* Dr. Alyson L. Greiner, Department Head, 405-744-9169, Fax: 405-744-5620, E-mail: alyson.greiner@okstate.edu. *Application contact:* Dr. Sheryl Tucker, Dean, 405-744-6368, Fax: 405-744-0355, E-mail: gradi@okstate.edu.
Website: http://geog.okstate.edu

Oregon State University, College of Earth, Ocean, and Atmospheric Sciences, Program in Geography, Corvallis, OR 97331. Offers geographic information science (MA, MS, PhD); physical geography (MA, MS, PhD); resource geography (MA, MS, PhD). Terminal master's awarded for partial completion of doctoral program. *Entrance requirements:* For master's and doctorate, GRE, minimum GPA of 3.0 in last 90 hours. Additional exam requirements/recommendations for international students: required—TOEFL (minimum score 80 iBT), IELTS (minimum score 6.5).

Penn State University Park, Graduate School, College of Earth and Mineral Sciences, Department of Geography, University Park, PA 16802. Offers geography (MS, PhD).

Portland State University, Graduate Studies, College of Liberal Arts and Sciences, Department of Geography, Portland, OR 97207-0751. Offers geography (MA, MAT, MS, MST, PhD). *Program availability:* Part-time. *Faculty:* 14 full-time (4 women), 9 part-time/ adjunct (4 women). *Students:* 12 full-time (4 women), 14 part-time (9 women); includes 7 minority (1 Asian, non-Hispanic/Latino; 4 Hispanic/Latino; 2 Two or more races, non-Hispanic/Latino). Average age 33. 26 applicants, 77% accepted, 10 enrolled. In 2019, 16 master's awarded. *Degree requirements:* For master's, thesis (for some programs). *Entrance requirements:* For master's, GRE General Test (minimum score of 297), geography degree with minimum GPA of 3.0 overall, 3 letters of recommendation. Additional exam requirements/recommendations for international students: required—TOEFL (minimum score 550 paper-based; 80 iBT), IELTS (minimum score 6.5), PTE (minimum score 60). *Application deadline:* For fall admission, 1/15 priority date for domestic and international students. Application fee: $65. Electronic applications accepted. *Expenses:* $436 per credit hour resident, $655 per credit hour non-resident. *Financial support:* In 2019–20, 7 research assistantships with full and partial tuition reimbursements (averaging $18,433 per year), 9 teaching assistantships with full and partial tuition reimbursements (averaging $11,333 per year) were awarded; career-related internships or fieldwork, Federal Work-Study, scholarships/grants, and unspecified assistantships also available. Support available to part-time students. Financial award application deadline: 3/1; financial award applicants required to submit FAFSA. *Unit head:* Dr. Martin Lafrenz, Chair, 503-725-3163, Fax: 503-725-3162, E-mail: lafrenz@pdx.edu. *Application contact:* Dr. Andres Holz, Graduate Advisor, 503-725-3158, E-mail: lafrenz@pdx.edu.
Website: http://www.pdx.edu/geography/

Queen's University at Kingston, School of Graduate Studies, Faculty of Arts and Science, Department of Geography, Kingston, ON K7L 3N6, Canada. Offers M Sc, MA, PhD. *Degree requirements:* For master's, thesis; for doctorate, comprehensive exam, thesis/dissertation. *Entrance requirements:* Additional exam requirements/ recommendations for international students: required—TOEFL.

Rutgers University - New Brunswick, Graduate School-New Brunswick, Program in Geography, Piscataway, NJ 08854-8097. Offers MA, MS, PhD. Terminal master's awarded for partial completion of doctoral program. *Degree requirements:* For master's, thesis or alternative; for doctorate, comprehensive exam, thesis/dissertation. *Entrance requirements:* For master's and doctorate, GRE General Test. Additional exam requirements/recommendations for international students: required—TOEFL.

St. Cloud State University, School of Graduate Studies, College of Social Sciences, Department of Geography and Planning, St. Cloud, MN 56301-4498. Offers MS, Graduate Certificate. *Degree requirements:* For master's, comprehensive exam (for some programs), thesis or alternative. *Entrance requirements:* For master's, GRE General Test, minimum GPA of 2.75. Additional exam requirements/recommendations for international students: required—Michigan English Language Assessment Battery; recommended—TOEFL (minimum score 550 paper-based), IELTS (minimum score 6.5). Electronic applications accepted.

Salem State University, School of Graduate Studies, Program in Geo-Information Science, Salem, MA 01970-5353. Offers MS. *Program availability:* Part-time, evening/ weekend. *Degree requirements:* For master's, thesis optional. *Entrance requirements:* For master's, GRE or MAT. Additional exam requirements/recommendations for international students: required—TOEFL (minimum score 550 paper-based; 80 iBT) or IELTS (minimum score 5.5).

San Diego State University, Graduate and Research Affairs, College of Arts and Letters, Department of Geography, San Diego, CA 92182. Offers MA, PhD. *Degree requirements:* For master's, thesis; for doctorate, thesis/dissertation. *Entrance requirements:* For master's, GRE General Test, bachelor's degree in related field, 3 letters of recommendation. Additional exam requirements/recommendations for international students: required—TOEFL. Electronic applications accepted.

San Francisco State University, Division of Graduate Studies, College of Science and Engineering, Department of Geography and Environment, San Francisco, CA 94132-1722. Offers geographic information science (MS); geography (MA); resource management and environmental planning (MA). *Expenses: Tuition, area resident:* Full-time $7176; part-time $4164 per year. Tuition, state resident: full-time $7176; part-time $4164 per year. Tuition, nonresident: full-time $16,680; part-time $396 per unit. *International tuition:* $16,680 full-time. *Required fees:* $1524; $1524 per unit. $762 per semester. Tuition and fees vary according to degree level and program. *Unit head:* Dr. Andrew Oliphant, Chair, 415-405-2143, Fax: 415-338-6243, E-mail: andrewo@sfsu.edu. *Application contact:* Dr. Nancy Wilkinson, Graduate Coordinator, 415-338-1439, Fax: 415-338-6243, E-mail: nancyw@sfsu.edu.
Website: http://geog.sfsu.edu/

Shippensburg University of Pennsylvania, School of Graduate Studies, College of Education and Human Services, Department of Teacher Education, Shippensburg, PA 17257-2299. Offers curriculum and instruction (M Ed), including biology, early childhood education, elementary education, geography/earth science, global languages, history, mathematics, middle school education; literacy, technology & reading (M Ed), including reading specialist. *Accreditation:* NCATE. *Program availability:* Part-time, evening/ weekend, 100% online, blended/hybrid learning. *Faculty:* 12 full-time (9 women), 3 part-time/adjunct (all women). *Students:* 14 full-time (11 women), 54 part-time (51 women); includes 4 minority (all Hispanic/Latino). Average age 31. 50 applicants, 74% accepted, 23 enrolled. In 2019, 29 master's awarded. *Degree requirements:* For master's, comprehensive exam (for some programs), thesis optional, practicum or internship; capstone seminar (for some programs). *Entrance requirements:* For master's, MAT or GRE (if GPA less than 2.75), interview, 3 letters of reference, questionnaire of teaching background and future goals, resume. Additional exam requirements/recommendations for international students: required—TOEFL (minimum score 550 paper-based; 68 iBT), IELTS (minimum score 6), TOEFL (minimum score 550 paper-based, 68 iBT) or IELTS (minimum score 6). *Application deadline:* For fall admission, 4/1 priority date for domestic students, 4/30 for international students; for spring admission, 9/1 priority date for domestic students, 9/30 for international students; for summer admission, 2/1 priority date for domestic students. Applications are processed on a rolling basis. Application fee: $45. Electronic applications accepted. *Expenses:* Tuition, state resident: part-time $516 per credit. Tuition, nonresident: part-time $774 per credit. *Required fees:* $149 per credit. *Financial support:* In 2019–20, 6 students received support. Career-related internships or fieldwork, scholarships/grants, unspecified assistantships, and resident hall director and student payroll positions available. Support available to part-time students. Financial award application deadline: 3/1; financial award applicants required to submit FAFSA. *Unit head:* Dr. Janet M. Bufalino, Department Chairperson, 717-477-1688, Fax: 717-477-4046, E-mail: jmbufa@ship.edu. *Application contact:* Maya T. Mapp, Director of Admissions, 717-477-1231, Fax: 717-477-4016, E-mail: mtmapp@ship.edu.
Website: http://www.ship.edu/teacher/

Simon Fraser University, Office of Graduate Studies and Postdoctoral Fellows, Faculty of Environment, Department of Geography, Burnaby, BC V5A 1S6, Canada. Offers M Sc, MA, PhD. *Degree requirements:* For master's, one foreign language, thesis; for doctorate, one foreign language, comprehensive exam, thesis/dissertation. *Entrance requirements:* For master's, minimum GPA of 3.0 (on scale of 4.33) or 3.33 based on last 60 credits of undergraduate courses; for doctorate, minimum GPA of 3.5 (on scale of 4.33). Additional exam requirements/recommendations for international students: recommended—TOEFL (minimum score 580 paper-based; 93 iBT), IELTS (minimum score 7), TWE (minimum score 5). Electronic applications accepted.

South Dakota State University, Graduate School, College of Natural Sciences, Department of Geography, Brookings, SD 57007. Offers MS. *Program availability:* Part-time. *Degree requirements:* For master's, thesis, oral exam. *Entrance requirements:* Additional exam requirements/recommendations for international students: required—TOEFL (minimum score 525 paper-based; 71 iBT).

Southern Illinois University Carbondale, Graduate School, College of Liberal Arts, Department of Geography, Carbondale, IL 62901-4701. Offers MS, PhD. *Degree requirements:* For master's, thesis; for doctorate, thesis/dissertation. *Entrance requirements:* For master's, GRE (recommended), minimum GPA of 2.7; for doctorate, minimum GPA of 3.25. Additional exam requirements/recommendations for international students: required—TOEFL.

Southern Illinois University Edwardsville, Graduate School, College of Arts and Sciences, Department of Geography, Edwardsville, IL 62026. Offers MS. *Program availability:* Part-time, evening/weekend. *Degree requirements:* For master's, thesis optional, final exam. *Entrance requirements:* For master's, GRE (for applicants with a GPA less than 2.8). Additional exam requirements/recommendations for international students: required—TOEFL (minimum score 550 paper-based; 79 iBT), IELTS (minimum score 6.5). Electronic applications accepted.

Syracuse University, Maxwell School of Citizenship and Public Affairs, Programs in Geography, Syracuse, NY 13244. Offers MA, PhD. *Program availability:* Part-time, evening/weekend. *Degree requirements:* For master's, thesis or alternative; for doctorate, comprehensive exam, thesis/dissertation. *Entrance requirements:* For master's and doctorate, GRE General Test, personal statement, three letters of recommendation, official transcripts, resume. Additional exam requirements/ recommendations for international students: required—TOEFL (minimum score 100 iBT). Electronic applications accepted.

Temple University, College of Liberal Arts, Department of Geography and Urban Studies, Philadelphia, PA 19122-6096. Offers geographic information systems (PSM, Graduate Certificate); geography and urban studies (MA, PhD). *Program availability:* Part-time, evening/weekend. *Faculty:* 17 full-time (5 women), 3 part-time/adjunct (all women). *Students:* 31 full-time (16 women), 36 part-time (19 women); includes 17 minority (8 Black or African American, non-Hispanic/Latino; 2 Asian, non-Hispanic/ Latino; 6 Hispanic/Latino; 1 Two or more races, non-Hispanic/Latino), 8 international. 63 applicants, 33% accepted, 15 enrolled. In 2019, 12 master's, 3 doctorates, 3 other advanced degrees awarded. *Entrance requirements:* For master's, GRE (M.A.), 3 letters of recommendation, statement of goals; for doctorate, GRE, 3 letters of recommendation, statement of goals, writing sample. Additional exam requirements/ recommendations for international students: required—TOEFL (minimum score 88 iBT), IELTS, PTE, one of three is required. *Application deadline:* Applications are processed on a rolling basis. Application fee: $60. Electronic applications accepted. *Financial support:* Fellowships, research assistantships, teaching assistantships, Federal Work-Study, health care benefits, tuition waivers, and unspecified assistantships available. Financial award applicants required to submit FAFSA. *Unit head:* Melissa Gilbert, Chairperson, 215-204-7692, E-mail: mgilbert@temple.edu. *Application contact:* Liz Janczewski, Coordinator, 215-204-3386, E-mail: liz.janczewski@temple.edu.
Website: http://www.cla.temple.edu/gus/

Texas A&M University, College of Geosciences, Department of Geography, College Station, TX 77843. Offers geography (MS). *Program availability:* Part-time, 100% online. *Faculty:* 23. *Students:* 76 full-time (33 women), 79 part-time (29 women); includes 49 minority (8 Black or African American, non-Hispanic/Latino; 2 American Indian or Alaska Native, non-Hispanic/Latino; 7 Asian, non-Hispanic/Latino; 29 Hispanic/Latino; 3 Two or more races, non-Hispanic/Latino), 17 international. Average age 32. 97 applicants, 77%

accepted, 40 enrolled. In 2019, 18 master's, 2 doctorates awarded. *Degree requirements:* For master's, comprehensive exam (for some programs), thesis optional; for doctorate, comprehensive exam, thesis/dissertation. *Entrance requirements:* For master's and doctorate, GRE, letters of recommendation. Additional exam requirements/recommendations for international students: required—TOEFL (minimum score 550 paper-based; 80 iBT), IELTS (minimum score 6), PTE (minimum score 53). *Application deadline:* For fall admission, 1/1 priority date for domestic students. Applications are processed on a rolling basis. Application fee: $65 ($90 for international students). Electronic applications accepted. *Expenses:* Contact institution. *Financial support:* In 2019–20, 96 students received support, including 14 fellowships with tuition reimbursements available (averaging $8,490 per year), 36 research assistantships with tuition reimbursements available (averaging $10,713 per year), 28 teaching assistantships with tuition reimbursements available (averaging $12,676 per year); career-related internships or fieldwork, institutionally sponsored loans, scholarships/grants, traineeships, health care benefits, tuition waivers (full and partial), and unspecified assistantships also available. Support available to part-time students. Financial award application deadline: 3/15; financial award applicants required to submit FAFSA. *Unit head:* Dr. David M. Cairns, Department Head, 979-845-2783, E-mail: cairns@tamu.edu. *Application contact:* Dr. Inci Guneralp, Associate Professor and Graduate Director, 979-845-7155, E-mail: iguneralp@geos.tamu.edu.
Website: http://geography.tamu.edu

Texas State University, The Graduate College, College of Liberal Arts, Doctoral Program in Geographic Education, San Marcos, TX 78666. Offers PhD. *Program availability:* Part-time, evening/weekend. *Degree requirements:* For doctorate, comprehensive exam, thesis/dissertation. *Entrance requirements:* For doctorate, official GRE (general test only) required with competitive scores in the verbal reasoning and quantitative reasoning sections, master's degree in geography or related field with minimum GPA of 3.5 on all graduate coursework, 3 letters of recommendation, statement of purpose, curriculum vitae, completion of master's thesis or demonstrated evidence of scholarly research. Additional exam requirements/recommendations for international students: required—TOEFL (minimum score 550 paper-based; 78 iBT), IELTS (minimum score 6). Electronic applications accepted.

Texas State University, The Graduate College, College of Liberal Arts, Doctoral Program in Geography, San Marcos, TX 78666. Offers PhD. *Program availability:* Part-time. *Degree requirements:* For doctorate, comprehensive exam, thesis/dissertation. *Entrance requirements:* For doctorate, official GRE (general test only) required with competitive scores in the verbal reasoning and quantitative reasoning sections, baccalaureate and master's degrees in related field from regionally-accredited institution with minimum GPA of 3.5 in completed graduate course work, 3 letters of recommendation, statement of purpose, curriculum vitae or resume, completion of master's thesis or demonstrated evidence of scholarly research and writing. Additional exam requirements/recommendations for international students: required—TOEFL (minimum score 550 paper-based; 78 iBT), IELTS (minimum score 6). Electronic applications accepted.

Texas State University, The Graduate College, College of Liberal Arts, Master's Programs in Geography, San Marcos, TX 78666. Offers environmental geography (MS); geographic education (MAG, MS); geographic information science (MAG); geography (MAG); resources and environmental studies (MAG). *Program availability:* Evening/weekend. *Degree requirements:* For master's, comprehensive exam, thesis (for some programs). *Entrance requirements:* For master's, official GRE (general test only) required with competitive scores in the verbal reasoning and quantitative reasoning sections, baccalaureate degree from regionally-accredited institution with minimum GPA of 3.2 in last 60 hours of course work (for MAG), 3.4 (for MS); 3 letters of recommendation; statement of purpose; current resume. Additional exam requirements/recommendations for international students: required—TOEFL (minimum score 550 paper-based; 78 iBT), IELTS (minimum score 6.5). Electronic applications accepted.

Texas Tech University, Graduate School, College of Arts and Sciences, Department of Geosciences, Lubbock, TX 79409-1053. Offers atmospheric science (MS); geography (MS); geosciences (MS, PhD). *Program availability:* Part-time. *Faculty:* 28 full-time (4 women), 5 part-time/adjunct (2 women). *Students:* 73 full-time (32 women), 14 part-time (3 women); includes 7 minority (6 Hispanic/Latino; 1 Two or more races, non-Hispanic/Latino), 19 international. Average age 27. 102 applicants, 32% accepted, 24 enrolled. In 2019, 19 master's, 3 doctorates awarded. Terminal master's awarded for partial completion of doctoral program. *Degree requirements:* For master's, thesis; for doctorate, comprehensive exam, thesis/dissertation. *Entrance requirements:* For master's and doctorate, GRE General Test. Additional exam requirements/recommendations for international students: required—TOEFL (minimum score 550 paper-based; 79 iBT). *Application deadline:* For fall admission, 6/1 priority date for domestic students, 1/15 priority date for international students; for spring admission, 9/1 priority date for domestic students, 6/15 priority date for international students. Applications are processed on a rolling basis. Application fee: $65. Electronic applications accepted. *Expenses:* Contact institution. *Financial support:* In 2019–20, 80 students received support, including 66 fellowships (averaging $2,301 per year), 33 research assistantships (averaging $18,558 per year), 41 teaching assistantships (averaging $16,972 per year); Federal Work-Study, scholarships/grants, health care benefits, tuition waivers (partial), and unspecified assistantships also available. Financial award application deadline: 2/1; financial award applicants required to submit FAFSA. *Unit head:* Dr. Kevin Mulligan, Associate Professor and Chair, 806-834-0391, E-mail: kevin.mulligan@ttu.edu. *Application contact:* Dr. Juske Horita, Professor, 806-834-7027, E-mail: juske.horita@ttu.edu.
Website: www.depts.ttu.edu/geosciences/

Thomas Jefferson University, College of Architecture and the Built Environment, Program in Geospatial Technology for Geodesign, Philadelphia, PA 19107. Offers MS. *Program availability:* Part-time.

Towson University, College of Liberal Arts, Program in Geography and Environmental Planning, Towson, MD 21252-0001. Offers MA. *Program availability:* Part-time, evening/weekend. *Students:* 5 full-time (2 women), 9 part-time (2 women); includes 3 minority (2 Hispanic/Latino; 1 Two or more races, non-Hispanic/Latino), 1 international. *Entrance requirements:* For master's, bachelor's degree with minimum of 9 credits of course work in geography, minimum GPA of 3.0 overall and in all geography courses, 2 letters of recommendation, essay. *Application deadline:* For fall admission, 1/17 for domestic students, 5/15 for international students; for spring admission, 10/15 for domestic students, 12/1 for international students. Applications are processed on a rolling basis. Application fee: $45. Electronic applications accepted. *Expenses: Tuition, area resident:* Full-time $7920; part-time $439 per credit. Tuition, nonresident: full-time $16,344; part-time $908 per credit. *International tuition:* $16,344 full-time. *Required fees:* $2628; $146 per credit. $876 per term. *Financial support:* Application deadline: 4/1. *Unit head:* Dr. Todd Moore, Program Director, 410-704-3973, E-mail: tmoore@towson.edu. *Application contact:* Coverley Beidleman, Assistant Director of Graduate Admissions, 410-704-5630, Fax: 410-704-3030, E-mail: grads@towson.edu.
Website: https://www.towson.edu/cla/departments/geography/gradgeography/

Trent University, Graduate Studies, Program in Applications of Modeling in the Natural and Social Sciences, Peterborough, ON K9J 7B8, Canada. Offers applications of modeling in the natural and social sciences (MA); biology (M Sc, PhD); chemistry (M Sc); computer studies (M Sc); geography (M Sc, PhD); physics (M Sc). *Program availability:* Part-time. *Degree requirements:* For master's, thesis. *Entrance requirements:* For master's, honours degree.

Trent University, Graduate Studies, Program in Environmental and Life Sciences, Department of Geography, Peterborough, ON K9J 7B8, Canada. Offers M Sc, PhD. *Program availability:* Part-time. *Degree requirements:* For master's, thesis; for doctorate, thesis/dissertation. *Entrance requirements:* For master's, honors degree; for doctorate, master's degree.

Université de Montréal, Faculty of Arts and Sciences, Department of Geography, Montréal, QC H3C 3J7, Canada. Offers environment and durable development (DESS); geography (M Sc, PhD, DESS). *Degree requirements:* For master's, 2 foreign languages, thesis (for some programs); for doctorate, 3 foreign languages, thesis/dissertation, general exam. *Entrance requirements:* For master's, bachelor's degree in related field; for doctorate, MA in geography or related field. Electronic applications accepted.

Université de Sherbrooke, Faculty of Letters and Human Sciences, Department of Geography and Remote Sensing, Sherbrooke, QC J1K 2R1, Canada. Offers M Sc, PhD. *Degree requirements:* For master's, one foreign language, thesis; for doctorate, thesis/dissertation.

Université du Québec à Montréal, Graduate Programs, Program in Geography, Montréal, QC H3C 3P8, Canada. Offers M Sc. *Program availability:* Part-time. *Degree requirements:* For master's, thesis optional. *Entrance requirements:* For master's, appropriate bachelor's degree or equivalent and proficiency in French.

University at Albany, State University of New York, College of Arts and Sciences, Department of Geography and Planning, Albany, NY 12222-0001. Offers geographic information science (Certificate); geography (MA); regional planning (MRP); urban policy (Certificate). *Program availability:* Part-time, blended/hybrid learning. *Faculty:* 12 full-time (3 women), 10 part-time/adjunct (3 women). *Students:* 46 full-time (19 women), 23 part-time (10 women); includes 13 minority (6 Black or African American, non-Hispanic/Latino; 2 Asian, non-Hispanic/Latino; 5 Hispanic/Latino), 9 international. 20 applicants, 100% accepted, 12 enrolled. In 2019, 20 master's, 9 other advanced degrees awarded. *Entrance requirements:* For master's, transcripts of all schools attended, statement of background and goals, departmental questionnaire, resume, names and contact information for 3 recommenders. Additional exam requirements/recommendations for international students: required—TOEFL (minimum score 550 paper-based). *Application deadline:* For fall admission, 7/15 for domestic students, 5/1 for international students; for spring admission, 11/15 for domestic and international students. Applications are processed on a rolling basis. Application fee: $75. Electronic applications accepted. *Expenses: Tuition, area resident:* Full-time $11,530; part-time $480 per credit hour. Tuition, nonresident: full-time $23,530; part-time $980 per credit hour. *International tuition:* $23,530 full-time. *Required fees:* $2185; $96 per credit hour. Part-time tuition and fees vary according to course load and program. *Financial support:* Fellowships, teaching assistantships, career-related internships or fieldwork, Federal Work-Study, and institutionally sponsored loans available. Financial award application deadline: 3/1. *Unit head:* Catherine Lawson, Chair, 518-442-4636, Fax: 518-442-4742, E-mail: lawsonc@albany.edu. *Application contact:* Michael DeRensis, Director, Graduate Admissions, 518-442-3980, Fax: 518-442-3922, E-mail: graduate@albany.edu.
Website: https://www.albany.edu/gp/

University at Buffalo, the State University of New York, Graduate School, College of Arts and Sciences, Department of Geography, N Tonawanda, NY 14261. Offers earth systems science (MA, MS); economic geography and business geographics (MS); environmental modeling and analysis (MA); geographic information science (MA, MS); geography (MA, PhD); health geography (MS); international trade (MA); urban and regional analysis (MA). *Program availability:* Part-time. *Faculty:* 22 full-time (9 women), 3 part-time/adjunct (1 woman). *Students:* 61 full-time (26 women); includes 37 minority (2 Black or African American, non-Hispanic/Latino; 34 Asian, non-Hispanic/Latino; 1 Hispanic/Latino). Average age 28. 120 applicants, 62% accepted, 12 enrolled. In 2019, 23 master's, 3 doctorates awarded. Terminal master's awarded for partial completion of doctoral program. *Degree requirements:* For master's, thesis (for some programs), project or portfolio; for doctorate, thesis/dissertation, dissertation/thesis. *Entrance requirements:* For master's, GRE General Test, minimum GPA of 2.9; for doctorate, GRE General Test, minimum GPA of 3.0. Additional exam requirements/recommendations for international students: required—TOEFL (minimum score 550 paper-based; 79 iBT). *Application deadline:* For fall admission, 5/1 priority date for domestic students, 3/10 priority date for international students; for spring admission, 11/1 priority date for domestic students, 9/1 priority date for international students. Applications are processed on a rolling basis. Application fee: $75. Electronic applications accepted. *Expenses:* Contact institution. *Financial support:* In 2019–20, 15 students received support, including 9 fellowships with full tuition reimbursements available (averaging $4,500 per year), 7 research assistantships with full tuition reimbursements available (averaging $14,000 per year), 13 teaching assistantships with full tuition reimbursements available (averaging $14,080 per year); career-related internships or fieldwork, Federal Work-Study, institutionally sponsored loans, traineeships, health care benefits, and unspecified assistantships also available. Financial award application deadline: 1/10. *Unit head:* Dr. Chris Larsen, Interim Chair, 716-645-0488, Fax: 716-645-2329, E-mail: larsen@buffalo.edu. *Application contact:* Wendy Zitzka, Graduate Secretary, 716-645-0471, Fax: 716-645-2329, E-mail: wzitzka@buffalo.edu.
Website: http://www.geog.buffalo.edu/

The University of Alabama, Graduate School, College of Arts and Sciences, Department of Geography, Tuscaloosa, AL 35487. Offers earth system science (MS, PhD); environment and natural resources (MS, PhD); environment and society (MS, PhD); geographic information science (MS, PhD). *Program availability:* Part-time. *Faculty:* 14 full-time (1 woman), 1 part-time/adjunct (0 women). *Students:* 31 full-time (17 women), 5 part-time (1 woman); includes 17 minority (14 Black or African American, non-Hispanic/Latino; 1 Asian, non-Hispanic/Latino; 2 Two or more races, non-Hispanic/Latino), 7 international. Average age 29. 28 applicants, 54% accepted, 9 enrolled. In 2019, 9 master's awarded. *Degree requirements:* For master's, comprehensive exam, thesis; for doctorate, comprehensive exam, thesis/dissertation. *Entrance requirements:* For master's, GRE, minimum GPA of 3.0. Additional exam requirements/recommendations for international students: required—TOEFL (minimum score 550 paper-based; 79 iBT). *Application deadline:* For fall admission, 2/15 priority date for domestic and international students; for spring admission, 10/1 priority date for domestic and international students. Applications are processed on a rolling basis. Application fee: $50 ($60 for international students). Electronic applications accepted. *Expenses: Tuition, area resident:* Full-time $10,780; part-time $440 per credit hour. Tuition, nonresident: full-time $30,250; part-time $1550 per credit hour. *Financial support:* In 2019–20, 24 students received support, including fellowships with full tuition reimbursements available (averaging $15,000 per year), research assistantships with full tuition reimbursements available (averaging $14,013 per year), teaching assistantships with full tuition reimbursements available (averaging $14,013 per year); career-related internships or fieldwork, health care benefits, and unspecified

assistantships also available. Financial award application deadline: 2/15. *Unit head:* Dr. Douglas Sherman, Chair, 205-348-5047, Fax: 205-348-2278, E-mail: douglas.j.sherman@ua.edu. *Application contact:* Dr. Justin Hart, Associate Professor, 205-348-5047, Fax: 205-348-2278, E-mail: hart013@ua.edu.
Website: http://geography.ua.edu

The University of Arizona, College of Social and Behavioral Sciences, School of Geography and Development, Tucson, AZ 85721. Offers geographic information systems technology (MA); geography (PhD). *Program availability:* Part-time. Terminal master's awarded for partial completion of doctoral program. *Degree requirements:* For master's, thesis or additional course work; for doctorate, variable foreign language requirement, thesis/dissertation. *Entrance requirements:* For master's, GRE General Test, 2 letters of recommendation; for doctorate, GRE General Test, statement of purpose, 2 letters of recommendation, master's degree. Additional exam requirements/recommendations for international students: required—TOEFL (minimum score 550 paper-based; 79 iBT). Electronic applications accepted.

University of Arkansas, Graduate School, J. William Fulbright College of Arts and Sciences, Department of Geosciences, Program in Geography, Fayetteville, AR 72701. Offers MA. *Program availability:* Part-time. *Students:* 10 full-time (4 women), 6 part-time (2 women); includes 2 minority (1 Hispanic/Latino; 1 Two or more races, non-Hispanic/Latino), 3 international. 19 applicants, 95% accepted. In 2019, 4 master's awarded. *Application deadline:* For fall admission, 8/1 for domestic students, 4/1 for international students; for spring admission, 12/1 for domestic students, 10/1 for international students; for summer admission, 4/15 for domestic students, 3/1 for international students. Applications are processed on a rolling basis. Application fee: $60. Electronic applications accepted. *Financial support:* In 2019–20, 7 research assistantships, 5 teaching assistantships were awarded; fellowships, career-related internships or fieldwork, and Federal Work-Study also available. Support available to part-time students. Financial award application deadline: 4/1; financial award applicants required to submit FAFSA. *Unit head:* Dr. Christopher Liner, Department Chair, 479-575-3355, Fax: 479-575-3469, E-mail: liner@uark.edu. *Application contact:* Dr. Fiona Davidson, Graduate Coordinator, 479-575-3879, Fax: 479-575-3469, E-mail: fdavidso@uark.edu.
Website: https://fulbright.uark.edu/departments/geosciences/

The University of British Columbia, Faculty of Arts, Department of Geography, Vancouver, BC V6T 1Z2, Canada. Offers M Sc, MA, PhD. *Program availability:* Part-time. Terminal master's awarded for partial completion of doctoral program. *Degree requirements:* For master's, thesis; for doctorate, comprehensive exam, thesis/dissertation. *Entrance requirements:* For master's and doctorate, minimum B average, 2nd class honors, upper division (class II, division I). Additional exam requirements/recommendations for international students: required—TOEFL. Electronic applications accepted. *Expenses:* Contact institution.

University of Calgary, Faculty of Graduate Studies, Faculty of Arts, Program in Geography, Calgary, AB T2N 1N4, Canada. Offers M Sc, MA, MGIS, PhD. *Program availability:* Part-time. *Degree requirements:* For master's, thesis, departmental conference; for doctorate, thesis/dissertation, candidacy exam, departmental conference. *Entrance requirements:* For master's, minimum undergraduate GPA of 3.0 during last 2 years; for doctorate, minimum GPA of 3.0 during previous 2 years, master's degree. Additional exam requirements/recommendations for international students: required—TOEFL (minimum score 550 paper-based). Electronic applications accepted.

University of California, Berkeley, Graduate Division, College of Letters and Science, Department of Geography, Berkeley, CA 94720. Offers PhD. *Degree requirements:* For doctorate, thesis/dissertation, qualifying exam. *Entrance requirements:* For doctorate, GRE General Test, minimum GPA of 3.0, 3 letters of recommendation. Additional exam requirements/recommendations for international students: required—TOEFL (minimum score 570 paper-based; 90 iBT). Electronic applications accepted.

University of California, Davis, Graduate Studies, Graduate Group in Geography, Davis, CA 95616. Offers MA, PhD. Terminal master's awarded for partial completion of doctoral program. *Degree requirements:* For master's, comprehensive exam (for some programs), thesis (for some programs); for doctorate, thesis/dissertation. *Entrance requirements:* For master's, GRE General Test, minimum GPA of 3.0; for doctorate, GRE General Test, master's degree, minimum GPA of 3.0. Additional exam requirements/recommendations for international students: required—TOEFL (minimum score 550 paper-based). Electronic applications accepted.

University of California, Los Angeles, Graduate Division, College of Letters and Science, Department of Geography, Los Angeles, CA 90095. Offers MA, PhD. Terminal master's awarded for partial completion of doctoral program. *Degree requirements:* For master's, thesis; for doctorate, thesis/dissertation, oral and written qualifying exams. *Entrance requirements:* For doctorate, GRE General Test, bachelor's degree; minimum undergraduate GPA of 3.3, 3.5 in graduate work (or its equivalent if letter grade system not used); writing sample. Additional exam requirements/recommendations for international students: required—TOEFL. Electronic applications accepted.

University of California, Santa Barbara, Graduate Division, College of Letters and Sciences, Division of Mathematics, Life, and Physical Sciences, Department of Geography, Santa Barbara, CA 93106-4060. Offers cognitive science (PhD); geography (MA, PhD); global studies (PhD); quantitative methods in the social sciences (PhD); technology and society (PhD); transportation (PhD); MA/PhD. Terminal master's awarded for partial completion of doctoral program. *Degree requirements:* For master's, comprehensive exam (for some programs), thesis or alternative; for doctorate, comprehensive exam, thesis/dissertation, 1 quarter of teaching assistantship. *Entrance requirements:* For master's and doctorate, GRE (minimum combined verbal and quantitative scores above 1100 in old scoring system or 301 in new scoring system). Additional exam requirements/recommendations for international students: required—TOEFL (minimum score 550 paper-based; 80 iBT), IELTS (minimum score 7). Electronic applications accepted.

University of Central Arkansas, Graduate School, College of Natural Sciences and Math, Department of Geography, Conway, AR 72035-0001. Offers community and economic development (MS); geographic information systems (MGIS, Certificate). *Program availability:* Part-time, online learning. *Entrance requirements:* Additional exam requirements/recommendations for international students: required—TOEFL (minimum score 550 paper-based). Electronic applications accepted.

University of Cincinnati, Graduate School, McMicken College of Arts and Sciences, Department of Geography, Cincinnati, OH 45221. Offers MA, PhD. Terminal master's awarded for partial completion of doctoral program. *Degree requirements:* For master's, thesis optional; for doctorate, one foreign language, comprehensive exam, thesis/dissertation. *Entrance requirements:* For master's and doctorate, GRE General Test. Additional exam requirements/recommendations for international students: required—TOEFL. Electronic applications accepted.

University of Colorado Boulder, Graduate School, College of Arts and Sciences, Department of Geography, Boulder, CO 80309. Offers MA, PhD. Terminal master's awarded for partial completion of doctoral program. *Degree requirements:* For master's, thesis; for doctorate, one foreign language, comprehensive exam, thesis/dissertation. *Entrance requirements:* For master's, GRE General Test, minimum undergraduate GPA of 3.0; for doctorate, GRE General Test. Electronic applications accepted. Application fee is waived when completed online.

University of Colorado Colorado Springs, College of Letters, Arts and Sciences, Department of Geography and Environmental Studies, Colorado Springs, CO 80918. Offers applied geography (MA). *Program availability:* Part-time. *Faculty:* 13 full-time (5 women), 6 part-time/adjunct (3 women). *Students:* 3 full-time (1 woman), 14 part-time (5 women); includes 5 minority (1 Black or African American, non-Hispanic/Latino; 2 Hispanic/Latino; 2 Two or more races, non-Hispanic/Latino). Average age 33. 16 applicants, 56% accepted, 4 enrolled. In 2019, 2 master's awarded. *Degree requirements:* For master's, comprehensive exam (for some programs), thesis (for some programs). *Entrance requirements:* For master's, beyond the Feb. 1, 2019 GES MA application deadline, the GRE is no longer a required component of the MA application, minimum undergraduate GPA of 3.0, statement of intent (essay). Additional exam requirements/recommendations for international students: required—Applicants who have completed a post-secondary degree at U.S. institution also meet the English proficiency requirements. Applicants with combined sco; recommended—TOEFL (minimum score 89 iBT), IELTS (minimum score 6.5). *Application deadline:* For fall admission, 2/1 priority date for domestic and international students. Applications are processed on a rolling basis. Application fee: $60 ($100 for international students). Electronic applications accepted. *Expenses:* Contact institution. *Financial support:* In 2019–20, 3 students received support, including 4 teaching assistantships (averaging $2,250 per year); Federal Work-Study, scholarships/grants, and unspecified assistantships also available. Support available to part-time students. Financial award application deadline: 3/1; financial award applicants required to submit FAFSA. *Unit head:* Dr. Brandon Vogt, Director of Graduate Studies in GES, 719-255-5146, E-mail: bvogt@uccs.edu. *Application contact:* Monica Killebrew, Department of Geography and Environmental Studies, Administrative Assistant, 719-255-3016, Fax: 719-255-4066, E-mail: mkillebr@uccs.edu.
Website: https://www.uccs.edu/geography/ma-program

University of Connecticut, Graduate School, College of Liberal Arts and Sciences, Department of Geography, Storrs, CT 06269. Offers MA, PhD. *Degree requirements:* For master's, comprehensive exam; for doctorate, thesis/dissertation. *Entrance requirements:* For master's and doctorate, GRE General Test. Additional exam requirements/recommendations for international students: required—TOEFL (minimum score 550 paper-based). Electronic applications accepted.

University of Delaware, College of Earth, Ocean, and Environment, Department of Geography, Newark, DE 19716. Offers MA, MS, PhD. *Degree requirements:* For master's, thesis; for doctorate, thesis/dissertation. *Entrance requirements:* For master's and doctorate, GRE General Test. Additional exam requirements/recommendations for international students: required—TOEFL. Electronic applications accepted.

University of Denver, Division of Natural Sciences and Mathematics, Department of Geography and the Environment, Denver, CO 80208. Offers geographic information science (MS); geography (MA, PhD). *Program availability:* Part-time. *Faculty:* 17 full-time (5 women), 9 part-time/adjunct (5 women). *Students:* 1 full-time (0 women), 45 part-time (15 women); includes 3 minority (1 Black or African American, non-Hispanic/Latino; 2 Hispanic/Latino), 5 international. Average age 32. 61 applicants, 41% accepted, 16 enrolled. In 2019, 28 master's, 2 doctorates awarded. Terminal master's awarded for partial completion of doctoral program. *Degree requirements:* For master's, thesis (for some programs), capstone project for some; for doctorate, variable foreign language requirement, comprehensive exam, thesis/dissertation. *Entrance requirements:* For master's, GRE General Test, bachelor's degree, transcripts, personal statement, three letters of recommendation; for doctorate, GRE General Test, master's degree, transcripts, personal statement, three letters of recommendation, resume. Additional exam requirements/recommendations for international students: required—TOEFL (minimum score 570 paper-based; 88 iBT). *Application deadline:* For fall admission, 1/15 priority date for domestic and international students; for winter admission, 3/15 for domestic and international students. Applications are processed on a rolling basis. Application fee: $65. Electronic applications accepted. *Expenses:* Contact institution. *Financial support:* In 2019–20, 46 students received support, including 14 teaching assistantships with tuition reimbursements available (averaging $19,271 per year); research assistantships, career-related internships or fieldwork, Federal Work-Study, institutionally sponsored loans, scholarships/grants, and unspecified assistantships also available. Support available to part-time students. Financial award application deadline: 2/15; financial award applicants required to submit FAFSA. *Unit head:* Dr. Michael Keables, Associate Professor and Chair, 303-871-2653, E-mail: michael.keables@du.edu. *Application contact:* Dr. Eric Boschmann, Associate Professor and Graduate Program Director, 303-871-4387, E-mail: eric.boschmann@du.edu.
Website: http://www.du.edu/nsm/departments/geography

University of Florida, Graduate School, College of Liberal Arts and Sciences, Department of Geography, Gainesville, FL 32611. Offers applications of geographic technologies (MA, MS); geographic information systems (MA, MS, PhD); geography (MA, MS, PhD); hydrologic sciences (MS, PhD); tropical conservation and development (MA, MS, PhD); wetland sciences (MA, MS, PhD). *Degree requirements:* For master's, thesis; for doctorate, comprehensive exam, thesis/dissertation. *Entrance requirements:* For master's and doctorate, GRE General Test, minimum GPA of 3.0. Additional exam requirements/recommendations for international students: required—TOEFL (minimum score 550 paper-based; 80 iBT), IELTS (minimum score 6). Electronic applications accepted.

University of Georgia, Franklin College of Arts and Sciences, Department of Geography, Athens, GA 30602. Offers MA, MS, PhD. *Degree requirements:* For master's, one foreign language, thesis; for doctorate, one foreign language, thesis/dissertation. *Entrance requirements:* For master's and doctorate, GRE General Test. Electronic applications accepted.

University of Guelph, Office of Graduate and Postdoctoral Studies, College of Social and Applied Human Sciences, Department of Geography, Guelph, ON N1G 2W1, Canada. Offers M Sc, MA, PhD. *Program availability:* Part-time. *Degree requirements:* For master's, thesis (for some programs); for doctorate, comprehensive exam, thesis/dissertation. *Entrance requirements:* For master's, minimum B average during previous 2 years of course work; for doctorate, minimum A- average. Additional exam requirements/recommendations for international students: required—TOEFL (minimum score 550 paper-based). Electronic applications accepted.

University of Hawaii at Manoa, Office of Graduate Education, College of Social Sciences, Department of Geography, Honolulu, HI 96822. Offers geography (MA, PhD); ocean policy (Graduate Certificate). *Program availability:* Part-time. *Degree requirements:* For master's, one foreign language, comprehensive exam, thesis; for doctorate, one foreign language, comprehensive exam, thesis/dissertation. *Entrance requirements:* For master's, GRE General Test; for doctorate, GRE General Test, sample of written work. Additional exam requirements/recommendations for international students: required—TOEFL (minimum score 500 paper-based; 61 iBT), IELTS (minimum score 5).

University of Idaho, College of Graduate Studies, College of Science, Department of Geography, Moscow, ID 83844-2282. Offers MS, PhD. *Faculty:* 8 full-time. *Students:* 10. Average age 29. In 2019, 2 master's, 1 doctorate awarded. *Degree requirements:* For doctorate, thesis/dissertation. *Entrance requirements:* For master's and doctorate, GRE, minimum GPA of 3.0. Additional exam requirements/recommendations for international students: required—TOEFL (minimum score 79 iBT). *Application deadline:* For fall admission, 7/30 for domestic students; for spring admission, 12/1 for domestic students. Applications are processed on a rolling basis. Application fee: $60. Electronic applications accepted. *Expenses:* Tuition, state resident: full-time $7753.80; part-time $502 per credit hour. Tuition, nonresident: full-time $26,990; part-time $1571 per credit hour. *Required fees:* $2122.20; $47 per credit hour. *Financial support:* Research assistantships and teaching assistantships available. Financial award applicants required to submit FAFSA. *Unit head:* Dr. Raymond J. Dezzani, Interim Chair, 208-885-6216, E-mail: geography@uidaho.edu. *Application contact:* Dr. Raymond J. Dezzani, Interim Chair, 208-885-6216, E-mail: geography@uidaho.edu.
Website: https://www.uidaho.edu/sci/geography

University of Illinois at Chicago, College of Liberal Arts and Sciences, Department of Anthropology, Program in Environmental and Urban Geography, Chicago, IL 60607-7128. Offers MA. *Program availability:* Part-time. *Degree requirements:* For master's, thesis. *Entrance requirements:* For master's, GRE General Test, minimum GPA of 2.75. Additional exam requirements/recommendations for international students: required—TOEFL. Electronic applications accepted.

University of Illinois at Urbana-Champaign, Graduate College, College of Liberal Arts and Sciences, School of Earth, Society and Environment, Department of Geography and Geographic Information Science, Champaign, IL 61820. Offers MA, MS, PhD.

The University of Iowa, Graduate College, College of Liberal Arts and Sciences, Department of Geographical and Sustainability Sciences, Iowa City, IA 52242-1316. Offers MA, PhD, Certificate. *Degree requirements:* For master's, thesis optional, exam; for doctorate, comprehensive exam, thesis/dissertation. *Entrance requirements:* For master's and doctorate, GRE General Test, minimum GPA of 3.0. Additional exam requirements/recommendations for international students: required—TOEFL (minimum score 550 paper-based; 81 iBT). Electronic applications accepted.

The University of Kansas, Graduate Studies, College of Liberal Arts and Sciences, Department of Geography and Atmospheric Science, Lawrence, KS 66045-7613. Offers atmospheric science (MS); geographic information science (Graduate Certificate); geography (MA, PhD); MUP/MA. *Program availability:* Part-time. *Students:* 50 full-time (24 women), 7 part-time (3 women); includes 13 minority (9 American Indian or Alaska Native, non-Hispanic/Latino; 1 Asian, non-Hispanic/Latino; 1 Hispanic/Latino; 2 Two or more races, non-Hispanic/Latino), 7 international. Average age 28. 33 applicants, 55% accepted, 13 enrolled. In 2019, 3 master's, 8 doctorates, 1 other advanced degree awarded. *Entrance requirements:* For master's and doctorate, GRE General Test, 3 letters of reference, transcripts, statement of interests, resume. Additional exam requirements/recommendations for international students: required—TOEFL, IELTS. *Application deadline:* For fall admission, 1/15 priority date for domestic and international students; for spring admission, 11/1 for domestic and international students; for summer admission, 4/1 for domestic and international students. Application fee: $65 ($85 for international students). Electronic applications accepted. *Expenses:* Tuition, state resident: full-time $9989. Tuition, nonresident: full-time $23,950. *International tuition:* $23,950 full-time. *Required fees:* $984; $81.99 per credit hour. Tuition and fees vary according to course load, campus/location and program. *Financial support:* Fellowships, research assistantships, teaching assistantships, and unspecified assistantships available. Financial award application deadline: 1/15. *Unit head:* Nathaniel Brunsell, Chair, 785-864-2021, E-mail: brunsell@ku.edu. *Application contact:* Cicily Riggs, Graduate Admission Contact, 785-864-0937, E-mail: csriggs@ku.edu.
Website: http://www.geog.ku.edu/

University of Kentucky, Graduate School, College of Arts and Sciences, Program in Geography, Lexington, KY 40506-0032. Offers MA, PhD. *Degree requirements:* For master's, comprehensive exam, thesis optional; for doctorate, one foreign language, comprehensive exam, thesis/dissertation. *Entrance requirements:* For master's, GRE General Test, minimum undergraduate GPA of 2.75; for doctorate, GRE General Test, minimum graduate GPA of 3.0. Additional exam requirements/recommendations for international students: required—TOEFL (minimum score 550 paper-based). Electronic applications accepted.

University of Lethbridge, School of Graduate Studies, Lethbridge, AB T1K 3M4, Canada. Offers addictions counseling (M Sc); agricultural biotechnology (M Sc); agricultural studies (M Sc, MA); anthropology (MA); archaeology (M Sc, MA); art (MA, MFA); biochemistry (M Sc); biological sciences (M Sc); biomolecular science (PhD); biosystems and biodiversity (PhD); Canadian studies (MA); chemistry (M Sc); computer science (M Sc); computer science and geographical information science (M Sc); counseling (MC); counseling psychology (M Ed); dramatic arts (MA); earth, space, and physical science (PhD); economics (MA); education (MA, PhD); educational leadership (M Ed); English (MA); environmental science (M Sc); evolution and behavior (PhD); exercise science (M Sc); French (MA); French/German (MA); French/Spanish (MA); general education (M Ed); geography (M Sc, MA); German (MA); health sciences (M Sc); individualized multidisciplinary (M Sc, MA); kinesiology (M Sc, MA); management (M Sc), including accounting, finance, human resource management and labor relations, information systems, international management, marketing, policy and strategy; mathematics (M Sc); music (M Mus, MA); Native American studies (MA); neuroscience (M Sc, PhD); new media (MA, MFA); nursing (M Sc, MN); philosophy (MA); physics (M Sc); political science (MA); psychology (M Sc, MA); religious studies (MA); sociology (MA); theatre and dramatic arts (MFA); theoretical and computational science (PhD); urban and regional studies (MA); women and gender studies (MA). *Program availability:* Part-time, evening/weekend. *Degree requirements:* For master's, thesis (for some programs); for doctorate, comprehensive exam, thesis/dissertation. *Entrance requirements:* For master's, GMAT (for M Sc in management), bachelor's degree in related field, minimum GPA of 3.0 during previous 20 graded semester courses, 2 years' teaching or related experience (M Ed); for doctorate, master's degree, minimum graduate GPA of 3.5. Additional exam requirements/recommendations for international students: required—TOEFL (minimum score 580 paper-based; 93 iBT). Electronic applications accepted.

University of Louisville, Graduate School, College of Arts and Sciences, Department of Geography and Geosciences, Louisville, KY 40292-0001. Offers applied geography (MS). *Program availability:* Part-time. *Faculty:* 11 full-time (4 women), 5 part-time/adjunct (3 women). *Students:* 9 full-time (5 women), 2 part-time (0 women); includes 3 minority (all Two or more races, non-Hispanic/Latino), 1 international. Average age 27. 4 applicants, 75% accepted, 2 enrolled. In 2019, 2 master's awarded. *Degree requirements:* For master's, comprehensive exam (for some programs), thesis (for some programs). *Entrance requirements:* For master's, GRE, Two letters of reference, official transcripts. Additional exam requirements/recommendations for international students: required—TOEFL (minimum score 550 paper-based; 79 iBT), IELTS can be used in place of the TOEFL; recommended—IELTS (minimum score 6.5). *Application deadline:* For fall admission, 3/15 priority date for domestic and international students; for spring admission, 11/15 priority date for domestic and international students; for summer admission, 3/15 for domestic and international students. Applications are processed on a rolling basis. Application fee: $65. Electronic applications accepted. *Expenses: Tuition, area resident:* Full-time $13,000; part-time $723 per credit hour. Tuition, state resident: full-time $13,000; part-time $723 per credit hour. Tuition, nonresident: full-time $27,114; part-time $1507 per credit hour. *International tuition:* $27,114 full-time. *Required fees:* $196. Tuition and fees vary according to program and reciprocity agreements. *Financial support:* In 2019–20, 5 students received support, including 2 fellowships (averaging $5,000 per year), 2 research assistantships with full tuition reimbursements available (averaging $14,000 per year); teaching assistantships, scholarships/grants, health care benefits, and unspecified assistantships also available. Financial award application deadline: 3/15. *Unit head:* Dr. David A. Howarth, Professor and Chair, 502-852-2693, Fax: 502-852-4560, E-mail: dahowa01@louisville.edu. *Application contact:* Dr. Christopher Andrew Day, Director of Graduate Studies, 502-852-2703, Fax: 502-852-4560, E-mail: christopher.day@louisville.edu.
Website: http://louisville.edu/geography/

The University of Manchester, School of Environment, Education and Development, Manchester, United Kingdom. Offers architecture (M Phil, PhD); development policy and management (M Phil, PhD); human geography (M Phil, PhD); physical geography (M Phil, PhD); planning and landscape (M Phil, PhD).

The University of Manchester, School of Nursing, Midwifery and Social Work, Manchester, United Kingdom. Offers nursing (M Phil, PhD); social work (M Phil, PhD).

University of Manitoba, Faculty of Graduate Studies, Clayton H. Riddell Faculty of Environment, Earth, and Resources, Department of Environment and Geography, Winnipeg, MB R3T 2N2, Canada. Offers environment (M Env); environment and geography (M Sc); geography (MA, PhD). *Degree requirements:* For master's, thesis; for doctorate, one foreign language, thesis/dissertation.

University of Maryland, Baltimore County, The Graduate School, College of Arts, Humanities and Social Sciences, Department of Geography and Environmental Systems, Program in Geography and Environmental Systems, Baltimore, MD 21250. Offers MS, PhD. *Program availability:* Part-time. *Faculty:* 14 full-time (5 women), 11 part-time/adjunct (2 women). *Students:* 25 full-time (14 women), 7 part-time (4 women); includes 6 minority (1 Black or African American, non-Hispanic/Latino; 1 Asian, non-Hispanic/Latino; 3 Hispanic/Latino; 1 Two or more races, non-Hispanic/Latino), 2 international. Average age 34. 23 applicants, 52% accepted, 3 enrolled. In 2019, 5 master's, 1 doctorate awarded. Terminal master's awarded for partial completion of doctoral program. *Degree requirements:* For master's, thesis optional, annual faculty evaluation, research paper; for doctorate, comprehensive exam, thesis/dissertation, annual faculty evaluation, qualifying exams, proposal and dissertation defense. *Entrance requirements:* For master's and doctorate, GRE, minimum GPA of 3.0 overall, 3.3 in major. Additional exam requirements/recommendations for international students: required—TOEFL (minimum score 550 paper-based; 80 iBT); recommended—IELTS. *Application deadline:* For fall admission, 2/1 for domestic students, 1/1 for international students. Application fee: $50. Electronic applications accepted. *Expenses:* $14,382 per year. *Financial support:* In 2019–20, 15 students received support, including fellowships with full tuition reimbursements available (averaging $19,700 per year), 5 research assistantships with full tuition reimbursements available (averaging $19,700 per year), 12 teaching assistantships with full tuition reimbursements available (averaging $19,700 per year); scholarships/grants, traineeships, health care benefits, and unspecified assistantships also available. Financial award application deadline: 2/1. *Unit head:* Dr. David Lansing, Graduate Program Director, 410-455-2971, E-mail: dlansing@umbc.edu. *Application contact:* Kathryn Nee, Coordinator of Domestic Admissions, 410-455-2944, E-mail: nee@umbc.edu.
Website: http://ges.umbc.edu/graduate/

University of Maryland, College Park, Academic Affairs, College of Behavioral and Social Sciences, Department of Geography, College Park, MD 20742. Offers MA, PhD, MA/MLS. *Program availability:* Part-time, evening/weekend. Terminal master's awarded for partial completion of doctoral program. *Degree requirements:* For master's, thesis, oral exam; for doctorate, comprehensive exam, thesis/dissertation. *Entrance requirements:* For master's, GRE General Test, minimum GPA of 3.0, 3 letters of recommendation; for doctorate, GRE General Test. Additional exam requirements/recommendations for international students: required—TOEFL, TWE. Electronic applications accepted.

University of Massachusetts Amherst, Graduate School, College of Natural Sciences, Department of Geosciences, Program in Geography, Amherst, MA 01003. Offers MS. *Program availability:* Part-time. *Degree requirements:* For master's, thesis or alternative. *Entrance requirements:* For master's, GRE General Test. Additional exam requirements/recommendations for international students: required—TOEFL (minimum score 550 paper-based; 80 iBT), IELTS (minimum score 6.5). Electronic applications accepted.

University of Memphis, Graduate School, College of Arts and Sciences, Department of Earth Sciences, Memphis, TN 38152. Offers earth sciences (MA, MS, PhD), including archaeology (MS), geography (MS), geology (MS), geophysics (MS), interdisciplinary studies (MS); geographic information systems (Graduate Certificate), including geographic information systems, GIS educator, GIS planning, GIS professional. *Program availability:* Part-time, evening/weekend. *Students:* 40 full-time (17 women), 22 part-time (7 women); includes 12 minority (2 Black or African American, non-Hispanic/Latino; 8 Asian, non-Hispanic/Latino; 2 Hispanic/Latino), 18 international. Average age 31. 23 applicants, 91% accepted, 18 enrolled. In 2019, 13 master's, 5 doctorates, 8 other advanced degrees awarded. Terminal master's awarded for partial completion of doctoral program. *Degree requirements:* For master's, comprehensive exam, thesis, seminar presentation; for doctorate, comprehensive exam, thesis/dissertation, qualifying exam, submission of two manuscripts for publication in peer-reviewed journal or books. *Entrance requirements:* For master's, GRE General Test, 3 letters of recommendation, statement of research interests; for doctorate, GRE General Test, 2 letters of recommendation, resume, personal statement. Additional exam requirements/recommendations for international students: required—TOEFL (minimum score 550 paper-based; 79 iBT). *Application deadline:* For fall admission, 1/15 for domestic students; for spring admission, 11/1 for domestic students. Applications are processed on a rolling basis. Application fee: $35 ($60 for international students). Electronic applications accepted. *Expenses: Tuition, area resident:* Full-time $9216; part-time $512 per credit hour. Tuition, state resident: full-time $9216; part-time $512 per credit hour. Tuition, nonresident: full-time $12,672; part-time $704 per credit hour. *International tuition:* $16,128 full-time. *Required fees:* $1530; $85 per credit hour. Tuition and fees vary according to program. *Financial support:* Fellowships with full tuition reimbursements, research assistantships with full tuition reimbursements, teaching assistantships with full tuition reimbursements, Federal Work-Study, scholarships/grants, and unspecified assistantships available. Financial award application deadline: 2/1; financial award applicants required to submit FAFSA. *Unit head:* Dr. Daniel Larsen, Chair, 901-678-4358, Fax: 901-678-2178, E-mail: dlarsen@memphis.edu. *Application contact:* Dr. Daniel Larsen, Chair, 901-678-4358, Fax: 901-678-2178, E-mail: dlarsen@memphis.edu.
Website: http://www.memphis.edu/earthsciences/

Geography

University of Miami, Graduate School, College of Arts and Sciences, Department of Geography and Regional Studies, Coral Gables, FL 33124. Offers geography (MA). *Program availability:* Part-time. *Degree requirements:* For master's, thesis. *Entrance requirements:* For master's, GRE, 3 letters of recommendation, official transcripts. Additional exam requirements/recommendations for international students: required—TOEFL. Electronic applications accepted.

University of Minnesota, Twin Cities Campus, Graduate School, College of Liberal Arts, Department of Geography, Environment and Society, Minneapolis, MN 55455. Offers MA, PhD. *Faculty:* 17 full-time (5 women), 16 part-time/adjunct (8 women). *Students:* 57 full-time (27 women); includes 5 minority (1 Black or African American, non-Hispanic/Latino; 2 Asian, non-Hispanic/Latino; 2 Hispanic/Latino), 16 international. Average age 28. 60 applicants, 27% accepted, 12 enrolled. In 2019, 4 master's, 6 doctorates awarded. Terminal master's awarded for partial completion of doctoral program. *Degree requirements:* For master's, comprehensive exam, thesis or 3 papers; for doctorate, comprehensive exam, thesis/dissertation. *Entrance requirements:* For master's and doctorate, minimum GPA of 3.5. Additional exam requirements/recommendations for international students: required—TOEFL (minimum score 600 paper-based; 100 iBT), IELTS (minimum score 7), MELAB. *Application deadline:* For fall admission, 12/15 for domestic and international students. Application fee: $75 ($95 for international students). Electronic applications accepted. *Financial support:* In 2019–20, 38 students received support, including 5 fellowships with full tuition reimbursements available (averaging $22,500 per year), 1 research assistantship with full tuition reimbursement available (averaging $17,000 per year), 32 teaching assistantships with full and partial tuition reimbursements available (averaging $17,000 per year); career-related internships or fieldwork, scholarships/grants, health care benefits, and unspecified assistantships also available. Financial award application deadline: 12/15. *Unit head:* George Henderson, Chair, 612-625-6080, Fax: 612-624-1044, E-mail: hende057@umn.edu. *Application contact:* Sara C. Braun, Graduate Program Coordinator, 612-625-6080, Fax: 612-624-1044, E-mail: geog-dgs@umn.edu. Website: http://www.geog.umn.edu/

University of Missouri, Office of Research and Graduate Studies, College of Arts and Science, Department of Geography, Columbia, MO 65211. Offers geographic information science (Graduate Certificate); geography (MA). *Entrance requirements:* For master's, GRE General Test (minimum score 1000 verbal and quantitative), minimum GPA of 3.0.

University of Montana, Graduate School, College of Humanities and Sciences, Department of Geography, Missoula, MT 59812. Offers community and environmental planning (MA); geography (MA, MS). *Entrance requirements:* For master's, GRE General Test. Additional exam requirements/recommendations for international students: required—TOEFL.

University of Nebraska at Omaha, Graduate Studies, College of Arts and Sciences, Department of Geography and Geology, Omaha, NE 68182. Offers geographic information science (Certificate); geography (MA). *Program availability:* Part-time. *Degree requirements:* For master's, comprehensive exam, thesis (for some programs). *Entrance requirements:* For master's, GRE, minimum GPA of 3.0, 15 undergraduate geography hours, transcripts, resume, statement of purpose, 2 letters of recommendation; for Certificate, minimum GPA of 3.0, transcripts, resume, statement of purpose, 2 letters of recommendation. Additional exam requirements/recommendations for international students: required—TOEFL, IELTS, PTE. Electronic applications accepted.

University of Nebraska–Lincoln, Graduate College, College of Arts and Sciences, Department of Anthropology and Geography, Program in Geography, Lincoln, NE 68588. Offers MA, PhD. *Degree requirements:* For master's, thesis optional; for doctorate, comprehensive exam, thesis/dissertation. *Entrance requirements:* For master's and doctorate, GRE General Test. Additional exam requirements/recommendations for international students: required—TOEFL (minimum score 550 paper-based). Electronic applications accepted.

University of Nevada, Reno, Graduate School, College of Science, Mackay School of Earth Sciences and Engineering, Department of Geography, Program in Geography, Reno, NV 89557. Offers MS, PhD. Terminal master's awarded for partial completion of doctoral program. *Degree requirements:* For master's, comprehensive exam, thesis; for doctorate, comprehensive exam, thesis/dissertation. *Entrance requirements:* For master's and doctorate, GRE General Test, minimum GPA of 2.75. Additional exam requirements/recommendations for international students: required—TOEFL (minimum score 500 paper-based; 61 iBT), IELTS (minimum score 6). Electronic applications accepted.

University of New Mexico, Graduate Studies, College of Arts and Sciences, Program in Geography and Environmental Studies, Albuquerque, NM 87131-2039. Offers MS. *Program availability:* Part-time. *Degree requirements:* For master's, comprehensive exam (for some programs), thesis (for some programs). *Entrance requirements:* For master's, GRE. Additional exam requirements/recommendations for international students: required—TOEFL. Electronic applications accepted. *Expenses:* Tuition, state resident: full-time $7633; part-time $972 per year. Tuition, nonresident: full-time $22,586; part-time $3840 per year. *International tuition:* $23,292 full-time. *Required fees:* $8608. Tuition and fees vary according to course level, course load, degree level, program and student level.

The University of North Carolina at Chapel Hill, Graduate School, College of Arts and Sciences, Department of Geography, Chapel Hill, NC 27599. Offers MA, PhD. *Degree requirements:* For master's, one foreign language, comprehensive exam, thesis; for doctorate, 2 foreign languages, comprehensive exam, thesis/dissertation. *Entrance requirements:* For master's and doctorate, GRE General Test, minimum GPA of 3.0.

The University of North Carolina at Charlotte, College of Liberal Arts and Sciences, Department of Geography and Earth Sciences, Charlotte, NC 28223-0001. Offers earth sciences (MS); geography (MA, PhD), including business location and transportation analytics (MA), geographic information science and technology (gis&t) (MA), human environmental systems (MA), urban and regional analysis; earth and environmental systems; geographic information science (PhD), urban regional analysis (MA). *Program availability:* Part-time, evening/weekend. *Faculty:* 30 full-time (13 women), 2 part-time/adjunct (1 woman). *Students:* 49 full-time (27 women), 21 part-time (4 women); includes 13 minority (1 Black or African American, non-Hispanic/Latino; 4 Asian, non-Hispanic/Latino; 7 Hispanic/Latino; 1 Two or more races, non-Hispanic/Latino), 14 international. Average age 28. 53 applicants, 74% accepted, 20 enrolled. In 2019, 17 master's, 2 doctorates awarded. Terminal master's awarded for partial completion of doctoral program. *Degree requirements:* For master's, thesis or alternative, capstone (proposal and defense) for MA; for doctorate, comprehensive exam, thesis/dissertation. *Entrance requirements:* For master's, GRE General Test, minimum GPA of 2.75 (3.0 for junior and senior years), transcripts, three letters of recommendation, and personal essays (for MS); minimum GPA of 3.1 overall or for the last 2 years, 3.2 in major, three letters of reference, and personal essay (for MA); for doctorate, GRE, MA or MS in geography or a field related to the primary emphases of the program; minimum master's-level GPA of 3.5; GIS and quantitative methods proficiency (if missing from coursework), personal statement. Additional exam requirements/recommendations for international students: required—TOEFL (minimum score 557 paper-based; 83 iBT), IELTS (minimum score 6.5), TOEFL (minimum score 557 paper-based, 83 iBT) or IELTS (6.5). *Application deadline:* Applications are processed on a rolling basis. Application fee: $75. Electronic applications accepted. *Expenses:* Tuition, state resident: full-time $4337. Tuition, nonresident: full-time $17,771. *Required fees:* $3093. Tuition and fees vary according to course load, degree level and program. *Financial support:* In 2019–20, 42 students received support, including 3 fellowships (averaging $52,667 per year), 16 research assistantships (averaging $8,489 per year), 23 teaching assistantships (averaging $9,266 per year); career-related internships or fieldwork, institutionally sponsored loans, scholarships/grants, and unspecified assistantships also available. Support available to part-time students. Financial award applicants required to submit FAFSA. *Unit head:* Dr. Deborah S.K. Thomas, Professor and Department Chair, 704-687-5976, E-mail: deborah.thomas@uncc.edu. *Application contact:* Kathy B. Giddings, Director of Graduate Admissions, 704-687-5503, Fax: 704-687-1668, E-mail: gradadm@uncc.edu. Website: https://geoearth.uncc.edu/

The University of North Carolina at Greensboro, Graduate School, College of Arts and Sciences, Department of Geography, Greensboro, NC 27412-5001. Offers applied geography (MA); geographic information science (Certificate); geography (PhD); urban and economic development (Certificate). *Degree requirements:* For master's, comprehensive exam, thesis or alternative. *Entrance requirements:* For master's, GRE General Test. Additional exam requirements/recommendations for international students: required—TOEFL. Electronic applications accepted.

University of North Dakota, Graduate School, College of Arts and Sciences, Department of Geography and Geographic Information Science, Grand Forks, ND 58202. Offers MA, MS. *Program availability:* Part-time. *Degree requirements:* For master's, comprehensive exam, thesis or alternative. *Entrance requirements:* For master's, minimum GPA of 3.0. Additional exam requirements/recommendations for international students: required—TOEFL (minimum score 550 paper-based; 79 iBT), IELTS (minimum score 6.5). Electronic applications accepted.

University of Northern Iowa, Graduate College, College of Social and Behavioral Sciences, Department of Geography, Cedar Falls, IA 50614. Offers MA. *Program availability:* Part-time. *Degree requirements:* For master's, thesis or alternative. *Entrance requirements:* For master's, minimum GPA of 3.0; 2 letters of recommendation; brief statement about professional interests and career objectives. Additional exam requirements/recommendations for international students: required—TOEFL (minimum score 500 paper-based; 61 iBT). Electronic applications accepted.

University of North Texas, Toulouse Graduate School, Denton, TX 76203-5459. Offers accounting (MS); applied anthropology (MA, MS); applied behavior analysis (Certificate); applied geography (MA); applied technology and performance improvement (M Ed, MS); art education (MA); art history (MA); arts leadership (Certificate); audiology (Au D); behavior analysis (MS); behavioral science (PhD); biochemistry and molecular biology (MS); biology (MA, MS); biomedical engineering (MS); business analysis (MS); chemistry (MS); clinical health psychology (PhD); communication studies (MA, MS); computer engineering (MS); computer science (MS); counseling (M Ed, MS), including clinical mental health counseling (MS), college and university counseling, elementary school counseling, secondary school counseling; creative writing (MA); criminal justice (MS); curriculum and instruction (M Ed); decision sciences (MBA); design (MA, MFA), including fashion design (MFA), innovation studies, interior design (MFA); early childhood studies (MS); economics (MS); educational leadership (M Ed, Ed D); educational psychology (MS, PhD), including family studies (MS), gifted and talented (MS), human development (MS), learning and cognition (MS), research, measurement and evaluation (MS); electrical engineering (MS); emergency management (MPA); engineering technology (MS); English (MA); English as a second language (MA); environmental science (MS); finance (MBA, MS); financial management (MPA); French (MA); health services management (MBA); higher education (M Ed, Ed D); history (MA, MS); hospitality management (MS); human resources management (MPA); information science (MS); information systems (PhD); information technologies (MBA); interdisciplinary studies (MA, MS); international studies (MA); international sustainable tourism (MS); jazz studies (MM); journalism (MA, MJ, Graduate Certificate), including interactive and virtual digital communication (Graduate Certificate), narrative journalism (Graduate Certificate), public relations (Graduate Certificate); kinesiology (MS); linguistics (MA); local government management (MPA); logistics (PhD); logistics and supply chain management (MBA); long-term care, senior housing, and aging services (MA); management (PhD); marketing (MBA); mathematics (MA, MS); mechanical and energy engineering (MS, PhD); music (MA), including ethnomusicology, music theory, musicology, performance; music composition (PhD); music education (MM Ed, PhD); nonprofit management (MPA); operations and supply chain management (MBA); performance (MM, DMA); philosophy (MA); political science (MA); professional and technical communication (MA); radio, television and film (MA, MFA); rehabilitation counseling (Certificate); sociology (MA); Spanish (MA); special education (M Ed); speech-language pathology (MA); strategic management (MBA); studio art (MFA); teaching (M Ed); MBA/MS. *Program availability:* Part-time, evening/weekend, online learning. Terminal master's awarded for partial completion of doctoral program. *Degree requirements:* For master's, variable foreign language requirement, comprehensive exam (for some programs), thesis (for some programs); for doctorate, variable foreign language requirement, comprehensive exam (for some programs), thesis/dissertation; for other advanced degree, variable foreign language requirement, comprehensive exam (for some programs). *Entrance requirements:* For master's and doctorate, GRE, GMAT. Additional exam requirements/recommendations for international students: required—TOEFL (minimum score 550 paper-based; 79 iBT). Electronic applications accepted.

University of Oklahoma, College of Atmospheric and Geographic Sciences, School of Geosciences, Norman, OK 73019. Offers environmental sustainability (MS); geography (MA, MS, PhD), including geospatial technologies (MS), physical geography (MS). *Program availability:* Part-time. *Degree requirements:* For master's, comprehensive exam (for some programs), thesis (for some programs); for doctorate, comprehensive exam (for some programs), thesis/dissertation (for some programs). *Entrance requirements:* For master's and doctorate, GRE, personal statement, transcripts, two letters of recommendation, writing sample. Additional exam requirements/recommendations for international students: required—TOEFL (minimum score 79 iBT) or IELTS (minimum score 6.5). Electronic applications accepted. *Expenses:* Tuition, state resident: full-time $6583.20; part-time $274.30 per credit hour. Tuition, nonresident: full-time $21,242; part-time $885.10 per credit hour. *International tuition:* $21,242.40 full-time. *Required fees:* $1994.20; $72.55 per credit hour. $126.50 per semester. Tuition and fees vary according to course load and degree level.

University of Oregon, Graduate School, College of Arts and Sciences, Department of Geography, Eugene, OR 97403. Offers MA, MS, PhD. *Degree requirements:* For master's, one foreign language, thesis; for doctorate, one foreign language, thesis/dissertation. *Entrance requirements:* For master's and doctorate, GRE General Test, minimum GPA of 3.0. Additional exam requirements/recommendations for international students: required—TOEFL.

University of Ottawa, Faculty of Graduate and Postdoctoral Studies, Faculty of Arts, Department of Geography, Ottawa, ON K1N 6N5, Canada. Offers M Geog, M Sc, MA,

PhD. *Degree requirements:* For master's, one foreign language, thesis; for doctorate, one foreign language, comprehensive exam, thesis/dissertation. *Entrance requirements:* For master's, honors degree or equivalent, minimum B average; for doctorate, master's degree, minimum B+ average. Electronic applications accepted.

University of Prince Edward Island, Faculty of Arts, Charlottetown, PE C1A 4P3, Canada. Offers island studies (MA). *Program availability:* Part-time. *Degree requirements:* For master's, thesis. *Entrance requirements:* Additional exam requirements/recommendations for international students: required—TOEFL (minimum score 550 paper-based; 80 iBT), Canadian Academic English Language Assessment, Michigan English Language Assessment Battery, Canadian Test of English for Scholars and Trainees.

University of Regina, Faculty of Graduate Studies and Research, Faculty of Arts, Department of Geography, Regina, SK S4S 0A2, Canada. Offers M Sc, MA, PhD. *Program availability:* Part-time. *Faculty:* 10 full-time (5 women). *Students:* 2 full-time (1 woman). Average age 30. In 2019, 1 master's awarded. *Degree requirements:* For master's, thesis; for doctorate, thesis/dissertation. *Entrance requirements:* For master's, thesis proposal, clear and concise statement of the purpose of the research which included the problem to be investigated and the objectives to be met; brief review of the relevant literature and proposed methodology. Additional exam requirements/recommendations for international students: required—TOEFL (minimum score 580 paper-based; 80 iBT), IELTS (minimum score 6.5), PTE (minimum score 59), CANTEST, MAELAB, CAEL and UofR ESL. *Application deadline:* For fall admission, 3/1 for domestic and international students; for winter admission, 10/1 for domestic and international students. Applications are processed on a rolling basis. Application fee: $100. *Expenses: Tuition:* Full-time $6684 Canadian dollars. *Required fees:* $100 Canadian dollars; $3351.45 Canadian dollars per trimester. $1117.15 Canadian dollars per semester. Tuition and fees vary according to course level, course load, degree level and program. *Financial support:* Fellowships, research assistantships, teaching assistantships, career-related internships or fieldwork, scholarships/grants, and travel award and Graduate Scholarship Base Funds available. Support available to part-time students. Financial award application deadline: 9/30. *Unit head:* Dr. Joseph Piwowar, Department Head, 306-585-5273, Fax: 306-585-4815, E-mail: joseph.piwowar@uregina.ca. *Application contact:* Dr. David Sauchyn, Graduate Advisor/Coordinator, 306-337-2299, E-mail: David.Sauchyn@uregina.ca. Website: http://www.uregina.ca/arts/geography

University of Saskatchewan, College of Graduate and Postdoctoral Studies, College of Arts and Science, Department of Geography and Planning, Saskatoon, SK S7N 5A2, Canada. Offers M Sc, MA, PhD. *Degree requirements:* For master's, thesis; for doctorate, comprehensive exam (for some programs), thesis/dissertation. *Entrance requirements:* Additional exam requirements/recommendations for international students: required—TOEFL (minimum score 80 iBT); recommended—IELTS (minimum score 6.5). Electronic applications accepted.

University of South Africa, College of Agriculture and Environmental Sciences, Pretoria, South Africa. Offers agriculture (MS); consumer science (MCS); environmental management (MA, MS, PhD); environmental science (MA, MS, PhD); geography (MA, MS, PhD); horticulture (M Tech); human ecology (MHE); life sciences (MS); nature conservation (M Tech).

University of South Carolina, The Graduate School, College of Arts and Sciences, Department of Geography, Columbia, SC 29208. Offers geography (MA, MS, PhD); geography education (IMA). *Program availability:* Part-time. *Degree requirements:* For master's, comprehensive exam, thesis (for some programs); for doctorate, comprehensive exam, thesis/dissertation. *Entrance requirements:* For master's, GRE General Test; for doctorate, GRE General Test, master's degree. Electronic applications accepted.

University of Southern California, Graduate School, Dana and David Dornsife College of Letters, Arts and Sciences, Spatial Sciences Institute, Los Angeles, CA 90089. Offers geographic information science and technology (MS, Graduate Certificate). *Program availability:* Part-time, evening/weekend, online learning. Terminal master's awarded for partial completion of doctoral program. *Degree requirements:* For master's, thesis. *Entrance requirements:* For master's, GRE. Additional exam requirements/recommendations for international students: required—TOEFL. Electronic applications accepted.

University of South Florida, Innovative Education, Tampa, FL 33620-9951. Offers adult, career and higher education (Graduate Certificate), including college teaching, leadership in developing human resources, leadership in higher education; Africana studies (Graduate Certificate), including diasporas and health disparities, genocide and human rights; aging studies (Graduate Certificate), including gerontology; art research (Graduate Certificate), including museum studies; business foundations (Graduate Certificate); chemical and biomedical engineering (Graduate Certificate), including materials science and engineering, water, health and sustainability; child and family studies (Graduate Certificate), including positive behavior support; civil and industrial engineering (Graduate Certificate), including transportation systems analysis; community and family health (Graduate Certificate), including maternal and child health, social marketing and public health, violence and injury: prevention and intervention, women's health; criminology (Graduate Certificate), including criminal justice administration; data science for public administration (Graduate Certificate); digital humanities (Graduate Certificate); educational measurement and research (Graduate Certificate), including evaluation; English (Graduate Certificate), including comparative literary studies, creative writing, professional and technical communication; entrepreneurship (Graduate Certificate); environmental health (Graduate Certificate), including safety management; epidemiology and biostatistics (Graduate Certificate), including applied biostatistics, biostatistics, concepts and tools of epidemiology, epidemiology, epidemiology of infectious diseases; geography, environment and planning (Graduate Certificate), including community development, environmental policy and management, geographical information systems; geology (Graduate Certificate), including hydrogeology; global health (Graduate Certificate), including disaster management, global health and Latin American and Caribbean studies, global health practice, humanitarian assistance, infection control; government and international affairs (Graduate Certificate), including Cuban studies, globalization studies; health policy and management (Graduate Certificate), including health management and leadership, public health policy and programs; hearing specialist: early intervention (Graduate Certificate); industrial and management systems engineering (Graduate Certificate), including systems engineering, technology management; information studies (Graduate Certificate), including school library media specialist; information systems/decision sciences (Graduate Certificate), including analytics and business intelligence; instructional technology (Graduate Certificate), including distance education, Florida digital/virtual educator, instructional design, multimedia design, Web design; internal medicine, bioethics and medical humanities (Graduate Certificate), including biomedical ethics; Latin American and Caribbean studies (Graduate Certificate); leadership for coastal resiliency planning (Graduate Certificate); mass communications (Graduate Certificate), including multimedia journalism; mathematics and statistics (Graduate Certificate), including mathematics; medicine (Graduate Certificate), including aging and neuroscience, bioinformatics, biotechnology, brain fitness and memory management,

clinical investigation, hand and upper limb rehabilitation, health informatics, health sciences, integrative weight management, intellectual property, medicine and gender, metabolic and nutritional medicine, metabolic cardiology, pharmacy sciences; national and competitive intelligence (Graduate Certificate); nursing (Graduate Certificate), including simulation based academic fellowship in advanced pain management; psychological and social foundations (Graduate Certificate), including career counseling, college teaching, diversity in education, mental health counseling, school counseling; public affairs (Graduate Certificate), including nonprofit management, public management, research administration; public health (Graduate Certificate), including assessing chemical toxicity and public health risks, health equity, pharmacoepidemiology, public health generalist, toxicology, translational research in adolescent behavioral health; public health practices (Graduate Certificate), including planning for healthy communities; rehabilitation and mental health counseling (Graduate Certificate), including integrative mental health care, marriage and family therapy, rehabilitation technology; secondary education (Graduate Certificate), including ESOL, foreign language education: culture and content, foreign language education: professional; social work (Graduate Certificate), including geriatric social work/clinical gerontology; special education (Graduate Certificate), including autism spectrum disorder, disabilities education: severe/profound; world languages (Graduate Certificate), including teaching English as a second language (TESL) or foreign language. *Unit head:* Dr. Cynthia DeLuca, Associate Vice President and Assistant Vice Provost, 813-974-3077, Fax: 813-974-7061, E-mail: deluca@usf.edu. *Application contact:* Owen Hooper, Director, Summer and Alternative Calendar Programs, 813-974-6917, E-mail: hooper@usf.edu.
Website: http://www.usf.edu/innovative-education/

The University of Tennessee, Graduate School, College of Arts and Sciences, Department of Geography, Knoxville, TN 37996. Offers MS, PhD. *Degree requirements:* For master's, thesis or alternative; for doctorate, thesis/dissertation. *Entrance requirements:* For master's and doctorate, GRE General Test, minimum GPA of 2.7. Additional exam requirements/recommendations for international students: required—TOEFL. Electronic applications accepted.

The University of Texas at Austin, Graduate School, College of Liberal Arts, Department of Geography and the Environment, Austin, TX 78712-1111. Offers MA, PhD. *Degree requirements:* For master's, thesis or alternative; for doctorate, thesis/dissertation. *Entrance requirements:* For master's and doctorate, GRE General Test. Additional exam requirements/recommendations for international students: required—TOEFL. Electronic applications accepted.

The University of Texas at Dallas, School of Economic, Political and Policy Sciences, Program in Geospatial Information Sciences, Richardson, TX 75080. Offers MS, PhD. *Program availability:* Part-time, evening/weekend. *Faculty:* 9 full-time (1 woman), 1 part-time/adjunct (0 women). *Students:* 24 full-time (11 women), 23 part-time (7 women); includes 10 minority (1 Black or African American, non-Hispanic/Latino; 5 Asian, non-Hispanic/Latino; 4 Hispanic/Latino), 15 international. Average age 33. 72 applicants, 49% accepted, 22 enrolled. In 2019, 18 master's, 8 doctorates awarded. *Degree requirements:* For master's, thesis (for some programs), project or thesis; internship; for doctorate, comprehensive exam, thesis/dissertation. *Entrance requirements:* For master's and doctorate, GRE General Test, minimum GPA of 3.0 in upper-level coursework in field. Additional exam requirements/recommendations for international students: required—TOEFL (minimum score 550 paper-based). *Application deadline:* For fall admission, 7/15 for domestic students, 5/1 priority date for international students; for spring admission, 11/15 for domestic students, 9/1 priority date for international students. Applications are processed on a rolling basis. Application fee: $50 ($100 for international students). Electronic applications accepted. *Expenses: Tuition, area resident:* Full-time $16,504. Tuition, state resident: full-time $16,504. Tuition, nonresident: full-time $34,266. Tuition and fees vary according to course load. *Financial support:* In 2019–20, 13 students received support, including 2 fellowships (averaging $2,500 per year), 2 research assistantships with partial tuition reimbursements available (averaging $19,002 per year), 10 teaching assistantships with partial tuition reimbursements available (averaging $13,500 per year); career-related internships or fieldwork, Federal Work-Study, institutionally sponsored loans, scholarships/grants, and unspecified assistantships also available. Support available to part-time students. Financial award application deadline: 4/30; financial award applicants required to submit FAFSA. *Unit head:* Dr. Fang Qiu, Program Head, 972-883-4134, Fax: 972-883-2735, E-mail: ph.gis@utdallas.edu. *Application contact:* Judy Du, Graduate Program Administrator, 972-883-4964, Fax: 972-883-6297, E-mail: gpa.gis@utdallas.edu. Website: https://epps.utdallas.edu/about/programs/geospatial-information-sciences/

The University of Toledo, College of Graduate Studies, College of Languages, Literature and Social Sciences, Department of Geography and Planning, Toledo, OH 43606-3390. Offers geographic information science and applied geographics (Certificate); geography and planning (MA); spatially-integrated social science (PhD). *Program availability:* Part-time. *Degree requirements:* For master's, comprehensive exam, thesis; for doctorate, thesis/dissertation. *Entrance requirements:* For master's and doctorate, GRE General Test, minimum cumulative point-hour ratio of 2.7 for all previous academic work, three letters of recommendation; for Certificate, minimum cumulative point-hour ratio of 2.7 for all previous academic work, three letters of recommendation. Additional exam requirements/recommendations for international students: required—TOEFL (minimum score 550 paper-based; 80 iBT). Electronic applications accepted.

University of Toronto, School of Graduate Studies, Faculty of Arts and Science, Department of Geography, Toronto, ON M5S 1A1, Canada. Offers geography (M Sc, MA, PhD); planning (M Sc Pl, MUDS, PhD); urban design (MUD). *Program availability:* Part-time. *Degree requirements:* For master's, thesis optional; for doctorate, thesis/dissertation. *Entrance requirements:* For master's, bachelor's degree or equivalent in geography or a closely related field, minimum B+ average in each of 2 final years of degree, 3 letters of reference; for doctorate, master of geography degree, minimum A-average. Additional exam requirements/recommendations for international students: required—TOEFL (minimum score 580 paper-based; 93 iBT), TWE (minimum score 5). Electronic applications accepted.

University of Utah, Graduate School, College of Social and Behavioral Science, Department of Geography, Salt Lake City, UT 84112. Offers geographic information science (MS); geography (MS, PhD). *Faculty:* 16 full-time (4 women), 1 part-time/adjunct (0 women). *Students:* 38 full-time (19 women), 15 part-time (6 women); includes 8 minority (6 Hispanic/Latino; 1 Native Hawaiian or other Pacific Islander, non-Hispanic/Latino; 1 Two or more races, non-Hispanic/Latino), 10 international. Average age 30. 52 applicants, 69% accepted, 17 enrolled. In 2019, 10 master's, 4 doctorates awarded. *Degree requirements:* For master's, thesis; for doctorate, comprehensive exam, thesis/dissertation. *Entrance requirements:* For master's, GRE (except for MS in geographic information science); for doctorate, GRE. Additional exam requirements/recommendations for international students: required—TOEFL (minimum score 550 paper-based; 7 iBT), IELTS. *Application deadline:* For fall admission, 1/10 priority date for domestic and international students. Application fee: $55 ($65 for international students). *Expenses:* Tuition, state resident: full-time $7085; part-time $272.51 per credit hour. Tuition, nonresident: full-time $24,937; part-time $959.12 per credit hour.

Geography

Required fees: $880.52; $880.52 per semester. Tuition and fees vary according to degree level, program and student level. *Financial support:* In 2019–20, 33 students received support, including 3 fellowships (averaging $22,667 per year), 16 research assistantships (averaging $13,938 per year), 9 teaching assistantships (averaging $12,333 per year); scholarships/grants and unspecified assistantships also available. Financial award application deadline: 1/20; financial award applicants required to submit CSS PROFILE or FAFSA. *Unit head:* Dr. Philip E. Dennison, epartment Chair, 801-581-8218, Fax: 801-585-5081, E-mail: dennison@geog.utah.edu. *Application contact:* Pamela S. Mitchell, Academic coordinator/graduate secretary, 801-581-8218, Fax: 801-585-5081, E-mail: pam.mitchell@geog.utah.edu.
Website: http://www.geog.utah.edu

University of Victoria, Faculty of Graduate Studies, Faculty of Social Sciences, Department of Geography, Victoria, BC V8W 2Y2, Canada. Offers M Sc, MA, PhD. *Program availability:* Part-time. *Degree requirements:* For master's, thesis; for doctorate, comprehensive exam, thesis/dissertation, candidacy exam. *Entrance requirements:* For master's, minimum B+ average in undergraduate course work; for doctorate, master's degree. Additional exam requirements/recommendations for international students: required—TOEFL (minimum score 575 paper-based), IELTS (minimum score 7). Electronic applications accepted.

University of Washington, Graduate School, College of Arts and Sciences, Department of Geography, Seattle, WA 98195. Offers MA, PhD. *Degree requirements:* For master's, thesis; for doctorate, thesis/dissertation. *Entrance requirements:* For master's and doctorate, GRE General Test. Additional exam requirements/recommendations for international students: required—TOEFL. Electronic applications accepted.

University of Waterloo, Graduate Studies and Postdoctoral Affairs, Faculty of Environment, Department of Geography and Environmental Management, Waterloo, ON N2L 3G1, Canada. Offers MA, PhD. *Degree requirements:* For master's, thesis optional; for doctorate, one foreign language, comprehensive exam, thesis/dissertation. *Entrance requirements:* For master's, honors degree, minimum B average; for doctorate, master's degree, minimum A- average. Additional exam requirements/recommendations for international students: required—TOEFL, IELTS, PTE. Electronic applications accepted.

The University of Western Ontario, School of Graduate and Postdoctoral Studies, Faculty of Social Science, Department of Geography, London, ON N6A 3K7, Canada. Offers M Sc, MA, PhD. *Degree requirements:* For master's, thesis; for doctorate, thesis/dissertation. *Entrance requirements:* For master's, GRE, honors degree, minimum B average; for doctorate, honors degree, minimum B average. Additional exam requirements/recommendations for international students: required—TOEFL.

University of Wisconsin–Madison, Graduate School, College of Letters and Science, Department of Geography, Madison, WI 53706-1380. Offers cartography and geographic information systems (MS); geographic information systems (Certificate); geography (MS, PhD). *Program availability:* Part-time. *Degree requirements:* For master's, thesis; for doctorate, thesis/dissertation; for Certificate, internship. *Entrance requirements:* For master's and doctorate, GRE General Test, minimum GPA of 3.25. Electronic applications accepted.

University of Wisconsin–Milwaukee, Graduate School, College of Letters and Science, Department of Geography, Milwaukee, WI 53201-0413. Offers international interests (MA, MS, PhD); physical geography and environmental studies (MA, MS, PhD); urban development (MA, MS, PhD). *Degree requirements:* For master's, comprehensive exam, thesis; for doctorate, thesis/dissertation. *Entrance requirements:* For master's and doctorate, GRE. Additional exam requirements/recommendations for international students: required—TOEFL (minimum score 550 paper-based; 79 iBT), IELTS (minimum score 6.5). Electronic applications accepted.

University of Wyoming, College of Arts and Sciences, Department of Geography, Laramie, WY 82071. Offers geography (MA, MP, MST); geography/water resources (MA); rural planning and natural resources (MP), including community and regional planning and natural resources. *Program availability:* Online learning. *Degree requirements:* For master's, thesis optional. *Entrance requirements:* For master's, GRE General Test, minimum GPA of 3.0. Additional exam requirements/recommendations for international students: required—TOEFL. Electronic applications accepted.

Université Laval, Faculty of Forestry, Geography and Geomatics, Department of Geography, Program in Geographical Sciences, Québec, QC G1K 7P4, Canada. Offers M Sc Geogr, PhD. Terminal master's awarded for partial completion of doctoral program. *Degree requirements:* For master's, thesis; for doctorate, comprehensive exam, thesis/dissertation. *Entrance requirements:* For master's, knowledge of French; for doctorate, knowledge of French, knowledge of a second language. Electronic applications accepted.

Utah State University, School of Graduate Studies, S.J. and Jessie E. Quinney College of Natural Resources, Department of Environment and Society, Logan, UT 84322. Offers bioregional planning (MS); geography (MA, MS); human dimensions of ecosystem science and management (MS, PhD); recreation resource management (MS, PhD). *Degree requirements:* For master's, comprehensive exam, thesis (for some programs). *Entrance requirements:* For master's and doctorate, GRE General Test, minimum GPA of 3.0. Additional exam requirements/recommendations for international students: required—TOEFL. Electronic applications accepted.

Virginia Polytechnic Institute and State University, Graduate School, College of Natural Resources and Environment, Blacksburg, VA 24061. Offers fisheries and wildlife (MS, PhD); forest products (MS/MF); forestry (PhD); geography (MS); geospatial and environmental analysis (PhD); natural resources (MNR); MS/MF. *Faculty:* 84 full-time (20 women). *Students:* 178 full-time (83 women), 69 part-time (43 women); includes 41 minority (6 Black or African American, non-Hispanic/Latino; 9 Asian, non-Hispanic/Latino; 22 Hispanic/Latino; 4 Two or more races, non-Hispanic/Latino), 29 international. Average age 31. 134 applicants, 63% accepted, 65 enrolled. In 2019, 93 master's, 13 doctorates awarded. *Degree requirements:* For master's, comprehensive exam (for some programs), thesis (for some programs); for doctorate, comprehensive exam (for some programs), thesis/dissertation (for some programs). *Entrance requirements:* For master's and doctorate, GRE/GMAT. Additional exam requirements/recommendations for international students: required—TOEFL (minimum score 90 iBT). *Application deadline:* For fall admission, 8/1 for domestic students, 4/1 for international students; for spring admission, 1/1 for domestic students, 9/1 for international students. Applications are processed on a rolling basis. Application fee: $75. Electronic applications accepted. *Expenses:* Tuition, state resident: full-time $13,700; part-time $761.25 per credit hour. Tuition, nonresident: full-time $27,614; part-time $1534 per credit hour. *Required fees:* $886.50 per term. Tuition and fees vary according to campus/location and program. *Financial support:* In 2019–20, 3 fellowships with full tuition reimbursements (averaging $33,250 per year), 90 research assistantships with full tuition reimbursements (averaging $20,262 per year), 45 teaching assistantships with full tuition reimbursements (averaging $17,795 per year) were awarded; scholarships/grants also available. Financial award application deadline: 3/1; financial award applicants required to submit FAFSA. *Unit head:* Dr. Paul M. Winistorfer, Dean, 540-231-5481, Fax: 540-231-7664, E-mail: pstorfer@vt.edu. *Application contact:* Arlice Banks, Executive Assistant, 540-231-7051, Fax: 540-231-7664, E-mail: arbanks@vt.edu.
Website: http://cnre.vt.edu/

Western Illinois University, School of Graduate Studies, College of Arts and Sciences, Department of Geography, Macomb, IL 61455-1390. Offers geography (MA); GIS analysis: GIS applications (Certificate). *Program availability:* Part-time. *Entrance requirements:* Additional exam requirements/recommendations for international students: required—TOEFL (minimum score 550 paper-based; 80 iBT). Electronic applications accepted.

Western Michigan University, Graduate College, College of Arts and Sciences, Department of Geography, Kalamazoo, MI 49008. Offers geographic information science (Graduate Certificate); geography (MA). *Degree requirements:* For master's, thesis.

Western Michigan University, Graduate College, College of Arts and Sciences, Department of Interdisciplinary Arts and Sciences, Kalamazoo, MI 49008. Offers science education (MA, PhD), including biological sciences (PhD), chemistry (PhD), geosciences (PhD), physical geography (PhD), physics (PhD), science education (PhD). *Degree requirements:* For doctorate, thesis/dissertation.

Western Washington University, Graduate School, Huxley College of the Environment, Department of Environmental Studies, Program in Geography, Bellingham, WA 98225-5996. Offers MS. *Entrance requirements:* Additional exam requirements/recommendations for international students: required—TOEFL (minimum score 567 paper-based). Electronic applications accepted.

West Virginia University, Eberly College of Arts and Sciences, Morgantown, WV 26506. Offers biology (MS, PhD); chemistry (MS, PhD); communication studies (MA, PhD); computational statistics (PhD); creative writing (MFA); English (MA, PhD); forensic and investigative science (MS); forensic science (PhD); geography (MA); geology (MA, PhD); history (MA, PhD); legal studies (MLS); mathematics (MS); physics (MS, PhD); political science (MA, PhD); professional writing and editing (MA); psychology (MA); public administration (MPA); social work (MSW); sociology (MA, PhD); statistics (MS). *Program availability:* Part-time, evening/weekend, online learning. Terminal master's awarded for partial completion of doctoral program. *Degree requirements:* For master's, thesis (for some programs); for doctorate, comprehensive exam, thesis/dissertation. *Entrance requirements:* For master's and doctorate, GRE. Additional exam requirements/recommendations for international students: required—TOEFL (minimum score 600 paper-based); recommended—TWE. Electronic applications accepted.

Wilfrid Laurier University, Faculty of Graduate and Postdoctoral Studies, Faculty of Arts, Department of Geography and Environmental Studies, Waterloo, ON N2L 3C5, Canada. Offers environmental and resource management (MA, MES, PhD); environmental science (M Sc, MES, PhD); geomatics (M Sc, MES, PhD); human geography (MES, PhD). *Program availability:* Part-time. *Degree requirements:* For master's, thesis optional; for doctorate, thesis/dissertation. *Entrance requirements:* For master's, honors BA in geography, minimum B average in undergraduate course work; honors BSc with minimum B+ or honors BES or BA in physical geography, environmental or earth sciences or the equivalent; for doctorate, MA in geography, minimum A- average. Additional exam requirements/recommendations for international students: required—TOEFL (minimum score 89 iBT). Electronic applications accepted.

York University, Faculty of Graduate Studies, Faculty of Liberal Arts and Professional Studies, Program in Geography, Toronto, ON M3J 1P3, Canada. Offers M Sc, MA, PhD. *Program availability:* Part-time. *Degree requirements:* For master's, thesis or alternative; for doctorate, comprehensive exam, thesis/dissertation. Electronic applications accepted.

Section 22
Military and Defense Studies

This section contains a directory of institutions offering graduate work in military and defense studies. Additional information about programs listed in the directory may be obtained by writing directly to the dean of a graduate school or chair of a department at the address given in the directory.

For programs offering related work, see also in this book *History* and *Political Science and International Affairs.*

CONTENTS

Military and Defense Studies

American Public University System, AMU/APU Graduate Programs, Charles Town, WV 25414. Offers accounting (MS); applied business analytics (MS); business administration (MBA); criminal justice (MA); cybersecurity studies (MS); educational leadership (M Ed); environmental policy and management (MS); global security (DGS); health information management (MS); history (MA), including American military history, American Revolution, civil war, war since 1945, World War II; information technology (MS); international relations and conflict resolution (MA), including American politics and government, comparative government and development, general, international relations, public policy; national security studies (MA); nursing (MSN); political science (MA); public policy (MPP); reverse logistics management (MA), including comparative and security issues, conflict resolution, international and transnational security issues, peacekeeping; space studies (MS); sports management (MS); strategic intelligence (DSI); teaching (M Ed), including secondary social studies; transportation and logistics management (MA). *Program availability:* Part-time, evening/weekend, online only, 100% online. *Students:* 461 full-time (193 women), 7,322 part-time (3,127 women); includes 3,089 minority (1,404 Black or African American, non-Hispanic/Latino; 30 American Indian or Alaska Native, non-Hispanic/Latino; 210 Asian, non-Hispanic/Latino; 753 Hispanic/Latino; 445 Native Hawaiian or other Pacific Islander, non-Hispanic/Latino; 247 Two or more races, non-Hispanic/Latino), 117 international. Average age 37. In 2019, 2,681 master's awarded. *Degree requirements:* For master's, comprehensive exam or practicum; for doctorate, practicum. *Entrance requirements:* For master's, official transcript showing earned bachelor's degree from institution accredited by recognized accrediting body. Additional exam requirements/recommendations for international students: required—TOEFL (minimum score 550 paper-based), IELTS (minimum score 6.5). *Application deadline:* Applications are processed on a rolling basis. Application fee: $0. Electronic applications accepted. *Financial support:* Scholarships/grants available. Financial award applicants required to submit FAFSA. *Unit head:* Dr. Wallace Boston, President, 877-468-6268, Fax: 304-728-2348, E-mail: president@apus.edu. *Application contact:* Yoci Deal, Associate Vice President, Graduate and International Admissions, 877-468-6268, Fax: 304-724-3764, E-mail: info@apus.edu.
Website: http://www.apus.edu

Austin Peay State University, College of Graduate Studies, College of Arts and Letters, Department of History and Philosophy, Clarksville, TN 37044. Offers military history (MA). *Program availability:* Part-time, online learning. *Faculty:* 12 full-time (2 women). *Students:* 7 full-time (3 women), 22 part-time (7 women); includes 5 minority (2 Black or African American, non-Hispanic/Latino; 3 Two or more races, non-Hispanic/Latino). Average age 37. 11 applicants, 73% accepted, 7 enrolled. In 2019, 14 master's awarded. *Degree requirements:* For master's, comprehensive exam, thesis optional. *Entrance requirements:* For master's, GRE General Test, minimum undergraduate GPA of 2.75, 3 letters of recommendation. Additional exam requirements/recommendations for international students: required—TOEFL (minimum score 500 paper-based). *Application deadline:* For fall admission, 8/5 priority date for domestic students. Applications are processed on a rolling basis. Application fee: $45 ($55 for international students). Electronic applications accepted. *Financial support:* Research assistantships with full tuition reimbursements, career-related internships or fieldwork, Federal Work-Study, institutionally sponsored loans, scholarships/grants, and unspecified assistantships available. Support available to part-time students. Financial award application deadline: 7/1; financial award applicants required to submit FAFSA. *Unit head:* Dr. Cameron Sutt, Chair, 931-221-7919, Fax: 931-221-7917, E-mail: suttc@apsu.edu. *Application contact:* Megan Mitchell, Coordinator of Graduate Admissions, 931-221-6189, Fax: 931-221-7662, E-mail: mitchellm@apsu.edu.
Website: http://www.apsu.edu/history-and-philosophy/

Bellevue University, Graduate School, College of Arts and Sciences, Bellevue, NE 68005-3098. Offers clinical counseling (MS); healthcare administration (MHA); human services (MA); international security and intelligence studies (MS); managerial communication (MA). *Program availability:* Online learning.

The Citadel, The Military College of South Carolina, Citadel Graduate College, Department of Leadership Studies, Charleston, SC 29409. Offers MS, Graduate Certificate. *Program availability:* Part-time, evening/weekend, 100% online, blended/hybrid learning. *Entrance requirements:* For master's, GRE (minimum verbal and quantitative combination of 290) or MAT (minimum of 396), official transcript reflecting highest degree earned from regionally-accredited college or university; for Graduate Certificate, official transcript for baccalaureate degree from regionally-accredited college or university. Additional exam requirements/recommendations for international students: required—TOEFL (minimum score 550 paper-based; 79 iBT). Electronic applications accepted.

The Citadel, The Military College of South Carolina, Citadel Graduate College, School of Humanities and Social Sciences, Department of Criminal Justice, Charleston, SC 29409. Offers homeland security (Graduate Certificate); intelligence analysis (Graduate Certificate); intelligence and security studies (MA). *Program availability:* Part-time, evening/weekend, 100% online, blended/hybrid learning. *Entrance requirements:* For master's, GRE or MAT, writing sample that demonstrates strong critical thinking and communication skills. Additional exam requirements/recommendations for international students: required—TOEFL (minimum score 550 paper-based; 79 iBT). Electronic applications accepted.

East Carolina University, Graduate School, Thomas Harriot College of Arts and Sciences, Department of History, Greenville, NC 27858-4353. Offers American history (MA); Atlantic world (MA); European history (MA); maritime studies (MA); military history (MA); public history (MA). *Program availability:* Part-time. *Application deadline:* For fall admission, 4/1 priority date for domestic and international students; for spring admission, 10/15 priority date for domestic and international students. *Expenses:* Tuition, area resident: Full-time $4749; part-time $185 per credit hour. Tuition, state resident: full-time $4749; part-time $185 per credit hour. Tuition, nonresident: full-time $17,898; part-time $864 per credit hour. *International tuition:* $17,898 full-time. *Required fees:* $2787. *Financial support:* Application deadline: 1/15. *Unit head:* Dr. Christopher Oakley, Chair, 252-328-1025, E-mail: oakleyc@ecu.edu. *Application contact:* Graduate School Admissions, 252-328-6012, E-mail: gradschool@ecu.edu.
Website: https://history.ecu.edu/

Embry-Riddle Aeronautical University–Prescott, Security and Intelligence Program, Prescott, AZ 86301-3720. Offers security and intelligence studies (MSSIS). *Degree requirements:* For master's, variable foreign language requirement, experimental research project, thesis, or comprehensive examination. *Entrance requirements:* For master's, transcripts, statement of goals, letters of recommendation, resume. Additional exam requirements/recommendations for international students: required—TOEFL (minimum score 550 paper-based; 79 iBT), IELTS (minimum score 6). Electronic applications accepted.

George Mason University, Schar School of Policy and Government, Program in International Security, Fairfax, VA 22030. Offers MA. *Program availability:* Part-time, evening/weekend. *Expenses:* Contact institution.

The George Washington University, Elliott School of International Affairs, Program in Security Policy Studies, Washington, DC 20052. Offers MA. *Program availability:* Part-time. *Degree requirements:* For master's, one foreign language, capstone project. *Entrance requirements:* For master's, GRE General Test, 2 semesters of introductory economics, 2 years of a modern foreign language or 1 semester of statistics. Additional exam requirements/recommendations for international students: required—TOEFL (minimum score 100 iBT), IELTS (minimum score 7). Electronic applications accepted.

Hawaii Pacific University, College of Liberal Arts, Program in Diplomacy and Military Studies, Honolulu, HI 96813. Offers MA. *Program availability:* Part-time, evening/weekend. *Entrance requirements:* Additional exam requirements/recommendations for international students: recommended—TOEFL (minimum score 550 paper-based; 80 iBT), IELTS (minimum score 6), TWE (minimum score 5). Electronic applications accepted. *Expenses: Tuition:* Full-time $18,000; part-time $1125 per credit. *Required fees:* $213; $38 per semester.

Henley-Putnam School of Strategic Security, Master of Science Program in Intelligence Management, Rapid City, SD 57701. Offers MS. *Program availability:* Part-time, online learning. *Degree requirements:* For master's, thesis. *Entrance requirements:* For master's, bachelor's degree from an institution accredited by an agency recognized by the U.S. Department of Education and/or the Council for Higher Education Accreditation; background check. Additional exam requirements/recommendations for international students: required—TOEFL (minimum score 650 paper-based; 79 iBT); recommended—IELTS (minimum score 7). *Expenses:* Contact institution.

Henley-Putnam School of Strategic Security, Master of Science Program in Strategic Security and Protection Management, Rapid City, SD 57701. Offers extremist organizations (MS). *Program availability:* Part-time, online learning. *Degree requirements:* For master's, comprehensive exam, thesis. *Entrance requirements:* For master's, bachelor's degree from institution accredited by an agency recognized by the U.S. Department of Education and/or the Council for Higher Education Accreditation, background check. Additional exam requirements/recommendations for international students: required—TOEFL (minimum score 650 paper-based; 79 iBT); recommended—IELTS. *Expenses:* Contact institution.

Henley-Putnam School of Strategic Security, Master of Science Program in Terrorism and Counterterrorism Studies, Rapid City, SD 57701. Offers intelligence operations (MS); protective intelligence (MS). *Program availability:* Part-time, online learning. *Degree requirements:* For master's, thesis. *Entrance requirements:* For master's, bachelor's degree from institution accredited by an agency recognized by the U.S. Department of Education and/or the Council for Higher Education Accreditation, background check. Additional exam requirements/recommendations for international students: required—TOEFL (minimum score 650 paper-based; 79 iBT); recommended—IELTS (minimum score 7). *Expenses:* Contact institution.

The Institute of World Politics, Graduate Programs in National Security, Intelligence, and International Affairs, Washington, DC 20036. Offers American foreign policy (Certificate); comparative political culture (Certificate); conflict prevention (Certificate); counterintelligence (Certificate); counterterrorism (Certificate); cyber statecraft (Certificate); economic statecraft (Certificate); homeland security (Certificate); intelligence (Certificate); international politics (Certificate); national security affairs (Executive MA, Certificate); nonviolent conflict (Certificate); peace building, stabilization, and humanitarian affairs (Certificate); public diplomacy and strategic influence (Certificate); statecraft and international affairs (MA); statecraft and national security (MA, DSNS); strategic communication (Certificate); strategic intelligence studies (MA, Professional MA); strategic soft power (Certificate). *Program availability:* Part-time, evening/weekend. *Degree requirements:* For master's, 52 credit hours, comprehensive written and oral exam (for MA); proficiency in critical language (for MA in statecraft and international affairs); 28 credit hours (for Executive MA); 36 credit hours (for Professional MA); for doctorate, comprehensive exam, thesis/dissertation; for Certificate, 20 credit hours. *Entrance requirements:* For master's, resume, personal statement, 3 references, essay; 7-10 years of professional experience (for Executive MA); 5-7 years of professional experience (for Professional MA); for doctorate, MA. Additional exam requirements/recommendations for international students: required—TOEFL. Electronic applications accepted.

The Judge Advocate General's School, U.S. Army, Graduate Programs, Charlottesville, VA 22903-1781. Offers LL M. *Accreditation:* ABA. *Degree requirements:* For master's, thesis optional. *Entrance requirements:* For master's, active duty military lawyer, international military officer, or DOD civilian attorney; JD or LL B.

Liberty University, School of Divinity, Lynchburg, VA 24515. Offers Biblical exposition (MA); Biblical languages (M Div); Biblical studies (M Div, MA, MAR, Th M, D Min); chaplaincy (M Div, D Min); Christian apologetics (M Div, MA, MAR, Th M); Christian leadership and church ministries (M Div); Christian ministries (M Div); Christian ministry (MA); Christian thought (M Div); church history (M Div, MAR, Th M); community chaplaincy (M Div, MAR); discipleship (D Min); discipleship and church ministry (M Div, MAR, MCM); evangelism and church planting (MAR, MCM, D Min); expository preaching (D Min); global ministry (MA); global studies (M Div, MAR, MCM, MGS, Th M); healthcare chaplaincy (M Div); homiletics (M Div, MAR, Th M); leadership (M Div, MAR); marketplace chaplaincy (M Div, MCM); ministry leadership (Ed D); pastoral counseling (M Div, MA, MAR, D Min), including addictions and recovery (MA), crisis response and trauma (MA), discipleship and church ministries (MA), leadership (MA), life coaching (MA), marketplace chaplaincy (MA), marriage and family (MA), military resilience (MA), pastoral counseling (MA); pastoral leadership (D Min); pastoral ministries (M Div, M Serv Soc, MCM); religious education (MRE); sports chaplaincy (MA); theology (M Div, MAR, MTS, Th M); theology and apologetics (D Min, PhD); worship (M Div, MAR, MCM, D Min); youth and family ministries (M Div). *Program availability:* Part-time, online learning. *Students:* 2,691 full-time (814 women), 2,570 part-time (732 women); includes 1,484 minority (1,046 Black or African American, non-Hispanic/Latino; 33 American Indian or Alaska Native, non-Hispanic/Latino; 120 Asian, non-Hispanic/Latino; 167 Hispanic/Latino; 8 Native Hawaiian or other Pacific Islander, non-Hispanic/Latino; 110 Two or more races, non-Hispanic/Latino), 101 international. Average age 43. 4,508 applicants, 34% accepted, 952 enrolled. In 2019, 1,251 master's, 71 doctorates awarded. *Degree requirements:* For master's, 2 foreign languages, thesis (for some programs); for doctorate, 2 foreign languages, thesis/dissertation. *Entrance requirements:* For master's, minimum undergraduate GPA of 2.0; for doctorate, GRE General Test or MAT, minimum graduate GPA of 3.0. Additional exam requirements/recommendations for international students: required—TOEFL (minimum score 600

paper-based; 100 iBT). *Application deadline:* For fall admission, 6/1 for domestic students; for spring admission, 11/1 for domestic students. Applications are processed on a rolling basis. Application fee: $50. Electronic applications accepted. *Expenses:* Contact institution. *Financial support:* Teaching assistantships with tuition reimbursements, career-related internships or fieldwork, and Federal Work-Study available. Financial award applicants required to submit FAFSA. *Unit head:* Dr. Troy Temple, Interim Dean, School of Divinity, E-mail: divinity@liberty.edu. *Application contact:* Jay Bridge, Director of Graduate Admissions, 800-424-9595, Fax: 800-628-7977, E-mail: gradadmissions@liberty.edu.
Website: https://www.liberty.edu/divinity/

London Metropolitan University, Graduate Programs, London, United Kingdom. Offers applied psychology (M Sc); architecture (MA); biomedical science (M Sc); blood science (M Sc); cancer pharmacology (M Sc); computer networking and cyber security (M Sc); computing and information systems (M Sc); conference interpreting (MA); counter-terrorism studies (M Sc); creative, digital and professional writing (MA); crime, violence and prevention (M Sc); criminology (M Sc); curating contemporary art (MA); data analytics (M Sc); digital media (MA); early childhood studies (MA); education (MA, Ed D); financial services law, regulation and compliance (LL M); food science (M Sc); forensic psychology (M Sc); health and social care management and policy (M Sc); human nutrition (M Sc); human resource management (MA); human rights and international conflict (MA); information technology (M Sc); intelligence and security studies (M Sc); international oil, gas and energy law (LL M); international relations (MA); interpreting (MA); learning and teaching in higher education (MA); legal practice (LL M); media and entertainment law (LL M); organizational and consumer psychology (M Sc); psychological therapy (M Sc); psychology of mental health (M Sc); public health (M Sc); public policy and management (MPA); security studies (M Sc); social work (M Sc); spatial planning and urban design (MA); sports therapy (M Sc); supporting older children and young people with dyslexia (MA); teaching languages (MA), including Arabic, English; translation (MA); woman and child abuse (MA).

Missouri State University, Graduate College, College of Humanities and Public Affairs, Department of Defense and Strategic Studies, Fairfax, VA 22031. Offers defense and strategic studies (Certificate); general weapons of mass destruction (MS). *Program availability:* Part-time. *Degree requirements:* For master's, comprehensive exam, thesis or alternative. *Entrance requirements:* For master's, GRE, minimum GPA of 2.75, 3 letters of recommendation. Additional exam requirements/recommendations for international students: required—TOEFL (minimum score 550 paper-based; 79 iBT), IELTS (minimum score 6). Electronic applications accepted. *Expenses: Tuition, area resident:* Full-time $2600; part-time $1735 per credit hour. Tuition, nonresident: full-time $5240; part-time $3495 per credit hour. *International tuition:* $5240 full-time. *Required fees:* $530; $438 per credit hour. Tuition and fees vary according to class time, course level, course load, degree level, campus/location and program.

National Defense University, The Dwight D. Eisenhower School for National Security and Resource Strategy, Washington, DC 20319-5066. Offers national resource strategy (MS). *Degree requirements:* For master's, comprehensive exam. *Entrance requirements:* Additional exam requirements/recommendations for international students: required—TOEFL.

National Defense University, Joint Advanced Warfighting School, Norfolk, VA 23511. Offers joint campaign planning and strategy (MS). *Degree requirements:* For master's, thesis.

National Defense University, National War College, Washington, DC 20319-5066. Offers national security strategy (MS). *Degree requirements:* For master's, comprehensive exam. *Entrance requirements:* Additional exam requirements/recommendations for international students: required—TOEFL.

National Intelligence University, Graduate Program, Washington, DC 20340-5100. Offers MSSI. *Program availability:* Part-time, evening/weekend. *Degree requirements:* For master's, thesis. *Entrance requirements:* For master's, MAT, authorized nomination.

Naval Postgraduate School, Departments and Academic Groups, Department of Computer Science, Monterey, CA 93943. Offers computer science (MS, PhD); identity management and cyber security (MA); modeling of virtual environments and simulations (MS, PhD); software engineering (MS, PhD). *Program availability:* Part-time, online learning. *Degree requirements:* For master's, thesis; for doctorate, thesis/dissertation.

Naval Postgraduate School, Departments and Academic Groups, Department of Defense Analysis, Monterey, CA 93943. Offers command and control (MS); communications (MS); defense analysis (MS), including astronautics; financial management (MS); information operations (MS); irregular warfare (MS); national security affairs (MS); operations analysis (MS); special operations (MA, MS), including command and control (MS), communications (MS), financial management (MS), information operations (MS), irregular warfare (MS), national security affairs, operations analysis (MS), tactile missiles (MS), terrorist operations and financing (MS); tactile missiles (MS); terrorist operations and financing (MS). *Program availability:* Part-time. *Degree requirements:* For master's, thesis.

Naval Postgraduate School, Departments and Academic Groups, Department of National Security Affairs, Monterey, CA 93943. Offers security studies (MA, PhD), including civil-military relations (MA), combating terrorism: policy and strategy (MA), defense decision-making and planning (MA), Europe and Eurasia (MA), Far East, Southeast Asia, and the Pacific (MA), homeland security and defense (MA), Middle East, South Asia, Sub-Saharan Africa (MA), stabilization and reconstruction (MA), western hemisphere (MA). *Program availability:* Part-time. *Degree requirements:* For master's, thesis (for some programs).

Naval Postgraduate School, Departments and Academic Groups, Graduate School of Business and Public Policy, Monterey, CA 93943. Offers acquisition and contract management (MBA); business administration (EMBA, MBA); contract management (MS); defense business management (MBA); defense systems analysis (MS), including management; defense systems management (international) (MBA); financial management (MBA); information management (MBA); manpower systems analysis (MS); material logistics support management (MBA); program management (MS); resource planning and management for international defense (MBA); supply chain management (MBA); systems acquisition management (MBA); transportation management (MBA). *Accreditation:* AACSB; NASPAA. *Program availability:* Part-time, online learning. *Degree requirements:* For master's, thesis (for some programs), terminal project/capstone (for some programs).

Naval Postgraduate School, Departments and Academic Groups, Undersea Warfare Academic Group, Monterey, CA 93943. Offers applied mathematics (MS); applied physics (MS); applied science (MS), including acoustics, operations research, physical oceanography, signal processing; electrical engineering (MS); engineering acoustics (MS, PhD); engineering science (MS), including electrical engineering, mechanical engineering; mechanical engineer (ME); mechanical engineering (MS, MSME); meteorology (MS); operations research (MS); physical oceanography (MS). *Program availability:* Part-time. *Degree requirements:* For master's, thesis.

Norwich University, College of Graduate and Continuing Studies, Master of Arts in Military History Program, Northfield, VT 05663. Offers MA. *Program availability:* Evening/weekend, online only, mostly all online with a week-long residency requirement. *Degree requirements:* For master's, thesis optional, capstone. *Entrance requirements:* For master's, minimum undergraduate GPA of 2.75. Additional exam requirements/recommendations for international students: required—TOEFL (minimum score 550 paper-based; 80 iBT), IELTS (minimum score 6.5). Electronic applications accepted. *Expenses:* Contact institution.

Royal Military College of Canada, Division of Graduate Studies, Continuing Studies, Department of History, Kingston, ON K7K 7B4, Canada. Offers defense management and policy (MA); history (PhD); war studies (MA). *Degree requirements:* For master's, thesis. *Entrance requirements:* For master's, honours degree with second-class standing; for doctorate, master's degree. Electronic applications accepted.

School of Advanced Air and Space Studies, Program in Airpower Art and Science, Maxwell AFB, AL 36112-6424. Offers MA. *Degree requirements:* For master's, comprehensive exam, thesis. *Entrance requirements:* For master's, less than 16 years total of active commissioned service; master's degree or undergraduate degree with a minimum GPA of 2.75. Additional exam requirements/recommendations for international students: required—TOEFL.

United States Army Command and General Staff College, Graduate Program, Fort Leavenworth, KS 66027-2301. Offers military art and science (MMAS).

University of Calgary, Faculty of Graduate Studies, Faculty of Arts, Program in Military and Strategic Studies, Calgary, AB T2N 1N4, Canada. Offers MSS, PhD. *Program availability:* Part-time. *Degree requirements:* For master's, thesis; for doctorate, comprehensive exam, thesis/dissertation. *Entrance requirements:* For master's, minimum GPA of 3.4. Additional exam requirements/recommendations for international students: recommended—TOEFL (minimum score 550 paper-based).

University of Colorado Denver, School of Public Affairs, Program in Public Affairs and Administration, Denver, CO 80127. Offers public administration (MPA), including domestic violence, emergency management and homeland security, environmental policy, management and law, homeland security and defense, local government, nonprofit management, public administration; public affairs (PhD). *Accreditation:* NASPAA. *Program availability:* Part-time, evening/weekend, online learning. Tuition and fees vary according to course load, program and reciprocity agreements.

University of Pittsburgh, Graduate School of Public and International Affairs, Master of Public and International Affairs Program, Pittsburgh, PA 15260. Offers human security (MPIA); international political economy (MPIA); security and intelligence studies (MPIA); JD/MPIA; MBA/MPIA; MPH/MPIA; MPIA/MSW; MSIS/MPIA. *Program availability:* Part-time, evening/weekend. *Faculty:* 33 full-time (11 women), 10 part-time/adjunct (5 women). *Students:* 87 full-time (49 women), 14 part-time (6 women); includes 13 minority (7 Black or African American, non-Hispanic/Latino; 6 Hispanic/Latino), 10 international. Average age 27. 156 applicants, 94% accepted, 49 enrolled. In 2019, 41 master's awarded. *Degree requirements:* For master's, thesis optional, Capstone Seminar. *Entrance requirements:* For master's, Personal essay, resume, two letters of recommendation, transcripts. Additional exam requirements/recommendations for international students: required—TOEFL (minimum score 80 iBT), Duolingo English Test; recommended—IELTS (minimum score 6.5). *Application deadline:* For fall admission, 2/1 priority date for domestic students, 1/15 priority date for international students; for spring admission, 11/1 priority date for domestic students, 8/1 priority date for international students. Application fee: $50. Electronic applications accepted. *Expenses:* $24,480 in-state, $40,848 out-of-state. *Financial support:* In 2019–20, 63 students received support, including 9 fellowships with full tuition reimbursements available (averaging $16,060 per year); scholarships/grants also available. Financial award application deadline: 2/1. *Unit head:* Dr. John Keeler, Dean, 412-648-7605, Fax: 412-648-7601, E-mail: gspia@pitt.edu. *Application contact:* Dr. Michael Rizzi, Director of Student Services, 412-648-7643, Fax: 412-648-7641, E-mail: rizzim@pitt.edu.
Website: http://www.gspia.pitt.edu/

National Security

American Public University System, AMU/APU Graduate Programs, Charles Town, WV 25414. Offers accounting (MS); applied business analytics (MS); business administration (MBA); criminal justice (MA); cybersecurity studies (MS); educational leadership (M Ed); environmental policy and management (MS); global security (DGS); health information management (MS); history (MA), including American military history, American Revolution, civil war, war since 1945, World War II; information technology (MS); international relations and conflict resolution (MA), including American politics and government, comparative government and development, general, international relations, public policy; national security studies (MA); nursing (MSN); political science (MA); public policy (MPP); reverse logistics management (MA), including comparative and security issues, conflict resolution, international and transnational security issues, peacekeeping; space studies (MS); sports management (MS); strategic intelligence (DSI); teaching (M Ed), including secondary social studies; transportation and logistics management (MA). *Program availability:* Part-time, evening/weekend, online only, 100% online. *Students:* 461 full-time (193 women), 7,322 part-time (3,127 women); includes 3,089 minority (1,404 Black or African American, non-Hispanic/Latino; 30 American Indian or Alaska Native, non-Hispanic/Latino; 210 Asian, non-Hispanic/Latino; 753 Hispanic/Latino; 445 Native Hawaiian or other Pacific Islander, non-Hispanic/Latino; 247 Two or more races, non-Hispanic/Latino), 117 international. Average age 37. In 2019, 2,681 master's awarded. *Degree requirements:* For master's, comprehensive exam or practicum; for doctorate, practicum. *Entrance requirements:* For master's, official transcript showing earned bachelor's degree from institution accredited by recognized accrediting body. Additional exam requirements/recommendations for international students: required—TOEFL (minimum score 550 paper-based), IELTS (minimum score 6.5). *Application deadline:* Applications are processed on a rolling basis. Application fee: $0. Electronic applications accepted. *Financial support:* Scholarships/grants available.

National Security

Financial award applicants required to submit FAFSA. *Unit head:* Dr. Wallace Boston, President, 877-468-6268, Fax: 304-728-2348, E-mail: president@apus.edu. *Application contact:* Yoci Deal, Associate Vice President, Graduate and International Admissions, 877-468-6268, Fax: 304-724-3764, E-mail: info@apus.edu.
Website: http://www.apus.edu

American University, School of International Service, Washington, DC 20016-8071. Offers comparative and regional studies (Certificate); cross-cultural communication (Certificate); development management (MS); ethics, peace, and global affairs (MA); European studies (Certificate); global environmental policy (MA, Certificate); global information technology (Certificate); global media (MA); international affairs (MA), including comparative and regional studies, global governance, politics, and security, international economic relations, natural resources and sustainable development, U.S. foreign policy and national security; international arts management (Certificate); international communication (MA, Certificate); international development (MA); international economic policy (Certificate); international economic relations (Certificate); international economics (MA); international peace and conflict resolution (MA, Certificate); international politics (Certificate); international relations (MA, PhD); international service (MIS); peacebuilding (Certificate); social enterprise (MA); the Americas (Certificate); United States foreign policy (Certificate); JD/MA. *Program availability:* Part-time, evening/weekend, 100% online, blended/hybrid learning. Terminal master's awarded for partial completion of doctoral program. *Degree requirements:* For master's, one foreign language, comprehensive exam, thesis or alternative; for doctorate, one foreign language, comprehensive exam, thesis/dissertation. *Entrance requirements:* For master's, transcripts, resume, 2 letters of recommendation, statement of purpose; for doctorate, GRE, transcripts, resume, 3 letters of recommendation, statement of purpose. Additional exam requirements/recommendations for international students: required—TOEFL. Electronic applications accepted. *Expenses:* Contact institution.

Angelo State University, College of Graduate Studies and Research, College of Arts and Humanities, Department of Security Studies and Criminal Justice, San Angelo, TX 76909. Offers criminal justice (MS); homeland security (MS); intelligence, security studies, and analysis (MSS); security studies (MSS). *Program availability:* Part-time, evening/weekend, online learning. *Entrance requirements:* For master's, essay, letters of recommendation. Additional exam requirements/recommendations for international students: required—TOEFL or IELTS. Electronic applications accepted.

Bellevue University, Graduate School, College of Arts and Sciences, Bellevue, NE 68005-3098. Offers clinical counseling (MS); healthcare administration (MHA); human services (MA); international security and intelligence studies (MS); managerial communication (MA). *Program availability:* Online learning.

California State University, San Bernardino, Graduate Studies, College of Social and Behavioral Sciences, Program in National Security Studies, San Bernardino, CA 92407. Offers MA. *Program availability:* Part-time, evening/weekend. *Students:* 2 full-time (both women), 11 part-time (3 women); includes 6 minority (1 Asian, non-Hispanic/Latino; 3 Hispanic/Latino; 2 Two or more races, non-Hispanic/Latino). Average age 27. 10 applicants, 30% accepted, 2 enrolled. In 2019, 17 master's awarded. *Entrance requirements:* Additional exam requirements/recommendations for international students: required—TOEFL. *Application deadline:* For fall admission, 4/15 for domestic students; for winter admission, 10/16 for domestic students; for spring admission, 1/22 for domestic students. Application fee: $55. *Unit head:* Dr. Mark Clark, Director, 909-537-5491, Fax: 909-537-7018, E-mail: mtclark@csusb.edu. *Application contact:* Dr. Dorota Huizinga, Dean of Graduate Studies, 909-537-3064, E-mail: dorota.huizinga@csusb.edu.

The Citadel, The Military College of South Carolina, Citadel Graduate College, School of Humanities and Social Sciences, Department of Criminal Justice, Charleston, SC 29409. Offers homeland security (Graduate Certificate); intelligence analysis (Graduate Certificate); intelligence and security studies (MA). *Program availability:* Part-time, evening/weekend, 100% online, blended/hybrid learning. *Entrance requirements:* For master's, GRE or MAT, writing sample that demonstrates strong critical thinking and communication skills. Additional exam requirements/recommendations for international students: required—TOEFL (minimum score 550 paper-based; 79 iBT). Electronic applications accepted.

Daniel Morgan Graduate School of National Security, Graduate Programs, Washington, DC 20036. Offers integrated risk value communications (MA); national security (MA).

George Mason University, Schar School of Policy and Government, Program in Biodefense, Arlington, VA 22030. Offers MS, PhD, Certificate. *Program availability:* Evening/weekend, 100% online. *Degree requirements:* For master's, thesis, project; for doctorate, comprehensive exam, thesis/dissertation. *Entrance requirements:* For master's, GRE (taken in the past five years), transcripts from all previous institutions attended in the U.S.; goals statement; 2 letters of recommendation; current resume; writing sample; for doctorate, GRE (taken in the past five years), official transcript from all colleges and universities attended; current resume; two letters of recommendation; statement of goals (not to exceed 500 words); writing sample (approximately 10-25 pages in length). Additional exam requirements/recommendations for international students: required—TOEFL (minimum score 575 paper-based; 88 iBT), IELTS (minimum score 6.5), PTE (minimum score 59). Electronic applications accepted. *Expenses:* Contact institution.

George Mason University, Schar School of Policy and Government, Program in International Security, Fairfax, VA 22030. Offers MA. *Program availability:* Part-time, evening/weekend. *Expenses:* Contact institution.

The George Washington University, Law School, Washington, DC 20052. Offers law (SJD); national security and U.S. foreign relations (LL M). *Accreditation:* ABA. *Program availability:* Part-time, evening/weekend. *Entrance requirements:* For master's, JD or equivalent; for doctorate, LSAT (for JD), LL M or equivalent (for SJD). *Expenses:* Contact institution.

Henley-Putnam School of Strategic Security, Doctorate Program in Strategic Security, Rapid City, SD 57701. Offers DSS. *Program availability:* Part-time, online learning. *Degree requirements:* For doctorate, thesis/dissertation. *Entrance requirements:* For doctorate, 5 years of strategic security experience; background check; interview with dean; copy of master's thesis; master's or bachelor's degree with equivalent of 30 graduate-level semester hours in strategic security or related field from accredited institution. Additional exam requirements/recommendations for international students: required—TOEFL (minimum score 650 paper-based; 79 iBT); recommended—IELTS (minimum score 7). *Expenses:* Contact institution.

The Institute of World Politics, Graduate Programs in National Security, Intelligence, and International Affairs, Washington, DC 20036. Offers American foreign policy (Certificate); comparative political culture (Certificate); conflict prevention (Certificate); counterintelligence (Certificate); counterterrorism (Certificate); cyber statecraft (Certificate); economic statecraft (Certificate); homeland security (Certificate); intelligence (Certificate); international politics (Certificate); national security affairs (Executive MA, Certificate); nonviolent conflict (Certificate); peace building, stabilization, and humanitarian affairs (Certificate); public diplomacy and strategic influence (Certificate); statecraft and international affairs (MA); statecraft and national security (MA, DSNS); strategic communication (Certificate); strategic intelligence studies (MA, Professional MA); strategic soft power (Certificate). *Program availability:* Part-time, evening/weekend. *Degree requirements:* For master's, 52 credit hours, comprehensive written and oral exam (for MA); proficiency in critical language (for MA in statecraft and international affairs); 28 credit hours (for Executive MA); 36 credit hours (for Professional MA); for doctorate, comprehensive exam, thesis/dissertation; for Certificate, 20 credit hours. *Entrance requirements:* For master's, resume, personal statement, 3 references, essay; 7-10 years of professional experience (for Executive MA); 5-7 years of professional experience (for Professional MA); for doctorate, MA. Additional exam requirements/recommendations for international students: required—TOEFL. Electronic applications accepted.

Kansas State University, Graduate School, College of Arts and Sciences, Security Studies Program, Manhattan, KS 66506. Offers MA, PhD. *Program availability:* Part-time. Terminal master's awarded for partial completion of doctoral program. *Degree requirements:* For doctorate, comprehensive exam, thesis/dissertation. *Entrance requirements:* For doctorate, GRE. Additional exam requirements/recommendations for international students: required—TOEFL (minimum score 550 paper-based; 79 iBT), IELTS (minimum score 6.5), PTE (minimum score 58). Electronic applications accepted.

National Defense University, College of International Security Affairs, Washington, DC 20319-5066. Offers strategic security studies (MA), including counterterrorism, homeland defense, international security studies. *Program availability:* Part-time, evening/weekend. *Degree requirements:* For master's, thesis. *Entrance requirements:* Additional exam requirements/recommendations for international students: required—TOEFL.

National Defense University, National War College, Washington, DC 20319-5066. Offers national security strategy (MS). *Degree requirements:* For master's, comprehensive exam. *Entrance requirements:* Additional exam requirements/recommendations for international students: required—TOEFL.

Naval Postgraduate School, Departments and Academic Groups, Department of Defense Analysis, Monterey, CA 93943. Offers command and control (MS); communications (MS); defense analysis (MS), including astronautics; financial management (MS); information operations (MS); irregular warfare (MS); national security affairs (MS); operations analysis (MS); special operations (MA, MS), including command and control (MS), communications (MS), financial management (MS), information operations (MS), irregular warfare (MS), national security affairs, operations analysis (MS), tactile missiles (MS), terrorist operations and financing (MS); tactile missiles (MS); terrorist operations and financing (MS). *Program availability:* Part-time. *Degree requirements:* For master's, thesis.

Naval Postgraduate School, Departments and Academic Groups, Department of National Security Affairs, Monterey, CA 93943. Offers security studies (MA, PhD), including civil-military relations (MA), combating terrorism: policy and strategy (MA), defense decision-making and planning (MA), Europe and Eurasia (MA), Far East, Southeast Asia, and the Pacific (MA), homeland security and defense (MA), Middle East, South Asia, Sub-Saharan Africa (MA), stabilization and reconstruction (MA), western hemisphere (MA). *Program availability:* Part-time. *Degree requirements:* For master's, thesis (for some programs).

Naval War College, Program in National Security and Strategic Studies, Newport, RI 02841-1207. Offers MA.

New Jersey City University, College of Professional Studies, Program in National Security Studies, Jersey City, NJ 07305-1597. Offers civil security leadership (D Sc); national security studies (MS, Certificate). *Program availability:* Part-time. *Entrance requirements:* Additional exam requirements/recommendations for international students: required—TOEFL (minimum score 79 iBT).

Regent University, Graduate School, Robertson School of Government, Virginia Beach, VA 23464. Offers government (MA), including American government, healthcare policy and ethics (MA, MPA), international relations, law and public policy, national security studies, political communication, political theory, religion and politics; national security studies (MA), including cybersecurity, homeland security, international security, Middle East politics; public administration (MPA), including emergency management and homeland security, federal government, general public administration, healthcare policy and ethics (MA, MPA), law, nonprofit administration and faith-based organizations, public leadership and management, servant leadership. *Program availability:* Part-time, evening/weekend, 100% online, blended/hybrid learning. *Faculty:* 5 full-time (1 woman), 19 part-time/adjunct (2 women). *Students:* 36 full-time (22 women), 159 part-time (89 women); includes 82 minority (52 Black or African American, non-Hispanic/Latino; 2 American Indian or Alaska Native, non-Hispanic/Latino; 2 Asian, non-Hispanic/Latino; 23 Hispanic/Latino; 3 Two or more races, non-Hispanic/Latino), 4 international. Average age 36. 181 applicants, 70% accepted, 75 enrolled. In 2019, 58 master's awarded. *Degree requirements:* For master's, thesis optional, internship. *Entrance requirements:* For master's, GRE General Test or LSAT, personal essay, writing sample, resume, college transcripts. Additional exam requirements/recommendations for international students: required—TOEFL (minimum score 577 paper-based). *Application deadline:* For fall admission, 5/1 priority date for domestic students; for spring admission, 11/1 priority date for domestic students. Applications are processed on a rolling basis. Application fee: $50. Electronic applications accepted. *Expenses:* Contact institution. *Financial support:* In 2019–20, 132 students received support. Career-related internships or fieldwork, scholarships/grants, and unspecified assistantships available. Support available to part-time students. Financial award applicants required to submit FAFSA. *Unit head:* Dr. Stephen Perry, Interim Dean, 757-352-4082, E-mail: sperry@regent.edu. *Application contact:* Heidi Cece, Assistant Vice President for Enrollment Management, 800-373-5504, Fax: 757-352-4381, E-mail: admissions@regent.edu.
Website: https://www.regent.edu/robertson-school-of-government/

Regent University, Graduate School, School of Law, Virginia Beach, VA 23464. Offers American legal studies (LL M); human rights (LL M); law (MA, JD), including advanced paralegal studies (MA), alternative dispute resolution (MA), business (MA), criminal justice (MA), general legal studies (MA), human resources management (MA), human rights and rule of law (MA), national security (MA), non-profit organizational law (MA), regulatory compliance (MA), wealth management and financial planning (MA); JD/MA; JD/MBA. *Accreditation:* ABA. *Program availability:* Part-time, 100% online, blended/hybrid learning. *Faculty:* 16 full-time (5 women), 66 part-time/adjunct (22 women). *Students:* 378 full-time (230 women), 349 part-time (246 women); includes 311 minority (207 Black or African American, non-Hispanic/Latino; 5 American Indian or Alaska Native, non-Hispanic/Latino; 17 Asian, non-Hispanic/Latino; 56 Hispanic/Latino; 2 Native Hawaiian or other Pacific Islander, non-Hispanic/Latino; 24 Two or more races, non-Hispanic/Latino), 46 international. Average age 35. 680 applicants, 62% accepted, 223 enrolled. In 2019, 176 master's, 72 doctorates awarded. *Entrance requirements:* For master's, college transcripts, resume, personal statement; for doctorate, LSAT, minimum undergraduate GPA of 3.0, official transcripts, 2 letters of recommendation, resume, personal statement. Additional exam requirements/recommendations for

international students: required—TOEFL (minimum score 600 paper-based). *Application deadline:* For fall admission, 3/1 for domestic students. Applications are processed on a rolling basis. Application fee: $50. Electronic applications accepted. *Expenses:* Contact institution. *Financial support:* In 2019–20, 582 students received support. Career-related internships or fieldwork, scholarships/grants, health care benefits, and unspecified assistantships available. Support available to part-time students. Financial award applicants required to submit FAFSA. *Unit head:* Mark Martin, Dean, 757-352-4040, Fax: 757-352-4595, E-mail: mmartin@regent.edu. *Application contact:* Ernie Walton, Assistant Dean of Admissions, 757-352-4315, E-mail: lawschool@regent.edu.
Website: https://www.regent.edu/school-of-law/

Trinity Washington University, School of Business and Graduate Studies, Washington, DC 20017-1094. Offers business administration (MBA); communication (MA); international security studies (MA); organizational management (MSA), including federal program management, human resource management, nonprofit management, organizational development, public and community health. *Program availability:* Part-time, evening/weekend. *Degree requirements:* For master's, thesis (for some programs), capstone project (MSA). *Entrance requirements:* For master's, minimum GPA of 2.5. Additional exam requirements/recommendations for international students: required—TOEFL (minimum score 550 paper-based).

University of Nebraska at Omaha, Graduate Studies, College of Arts and Sciences, Department of Political Science, Omaha, NE 68182. Offers American government (Certificate); global information operations (Certificate); intelligence and national security (Certificate); political science (MS). *Program availability:* Part-time, evening/weekend, online learning. *Degree requirements:* For master's, comprehensive exam, thesis (for some programs). *Entrance requirements:* For master's, 15 undergraduate political science hours, minimum undergraduate GPA of 3.0, 2 letters of recommendation, official transcripts. Additional exam requirements/recommendations for international students: required—TOEFL, IELTS, PTE. Electronic applications accepted.

University of New Haven, Graduate School, Henry C. Lee College of Criminal Justice and Forensic Sciences, Program in National Security, West Haven, CT 06516. Offers national security (MS, Graduate Certificate); national security administration (Graduate Certificate). *Program availability:* Part-time, evening/weekend. *Students:* 35 full-time (19 women), 18 part-time (7 women); includes 16 minority (5 Black or African American, non-Hispanic/Latino; 1 Asian, non-Hispanic/Latino; 9 Hispanic/Latino; 1 Native Hawaiian or other Pacific Islander, non-Hispanic/Latino), 2 international. Average age 30. 45 applicants, 87% accepted, 22 enrolled. In 2019, 28 master's awarded. *Entrance requirements:* Additional exam requirements/recommendations for international students: required—TOEFL (minimum score 70 iBT), IELTS, or PTE (minimum score of 53). *Application deadline:* Applications are processed on a rolling basis. Application fee: $50. Electronic applications accepted. Application fee is waived when completed online. *Financial support:* Research assistantships with partial tuition reimbursements, teaching assistantships with partial tuition reimbursements, Federal Work-Study, scholarships/grants, and unspecified assistantships available. Support available to part-time students. Financial award applicants required to submit FAFSA. *Unit head:* Dr. Jeffrey Treistman, Assistant Professor, 203-479-4567, E-mail: JTreistman@newhaven.edu. *Application contact:* Selina O'Toole, Senior Associate Director of Graduate Admissions, 203-932-7337, E-mail: SOToole@newhaven.edu.
Website: https://www.newhaven.edu/lee-college/graduate-programs/national-security/

Virginia Polytechnic Institute and State University, VT Online, Blacksburg, VA 24061. Offers advanced transportation systems (Certificate); aerospace engineering (MS); agricultural and life sciences (MSLFS); business information systems (Graduate Certificate); career and technical education (MS); civil engineering (MS); computer engineering (M Eng, MS); decision support systems (Graduate Certificate); eLearning leadership (MA); electrical engineering (M Eng, MS); engineering administration (MEA); environmental engineering (Certificate); environmental politics and policy (Graduate Certificate); environmental sciences and engineering (MS); foundations of political analysis (Graduate Certificate); health product risk management (Graduate Certificate); industrial and systems engineering (MS); information policy and society (Graduate Certificate); information security (Graduate Certificate); information technology (MIT); instructional technology (MA); integrative STEM education (MA Ed); liberal arts (Graduate Certificate); life sciences: health product risk management (MS); natural resources (MNR, Graduate Certificate); networking (Graduate Certificate); nonprofit and nongovernmental organization management (Graduate Certificate); ocean engineering (MS); political science (MA); security studies (Graduate Certificate); software development (Graduate Certificate). *Expenses:* Tuition, state resident: full-time $13,700; part-time $761.25 per credit hour. Tuition, nonresident: full-time $27,614; part-time $1534 per credit hour. *Required fees:* $886.50 per term. Tuition and fees vary according to campus/location and program.

Western Michigan University Cooley Law School, Graduate Programs, Lansing, MI 48901-3038. Offers administrative law (public law) (JD); business transactions (JD); Canadian law practice (JD); corporate law and finance (LL M); environmental law (public law) (JD); general practice (JD), including solo and small firm; general studies (LL M); homeland and national security law (LL M); insurance law (LL M); intellectual property (JD); intellectual property law (LL M); international law (JD); litigation (JD); taxation (LL M); U.S. legal studies for foreign attorneys (LL M); JD/LL M; JD/MBA; JD/MHA; JD/MPA; JD/MSW. *Accreditation:* ABA. *Program availability:* Part-time, evening/weekend, 100% online, blended/hybrid learning. *Degree requirements:* For master's, thesis (for some programs); for doctorate, minimum of 3 credits of clinical experience. *Entrance requirements:* For master's, JD or LL B; for doctorate, LSAT. Additional exam requirements/recommendations for international students: required—TOEFL (for U.S. legal studies for foreign attorneys LL M program); recommended—TOEFL. Electronic applications accepted. *Expenses:* Contact institution.

Section 23
Political Science and International Affairs

This section contains a directory of institutions offering graduate work in political science and international affairs. Additional information about programs listed in the directory but not augmented by an in-depth entry may be obtained by writing directly to the dean of a graduate school or chair of a department at the address given in the directory.

For programs offering related work, see also in this book *Area and Cultural Studies, History, Language and Literature,* and *Public, Regional, and Industrial Affairs.* In another guide in this series:

Graduate Programs in Business, Education, Information Studies, Law & Social Work

See *International Business*

CONTENTS

Program Directories

International Affairs

American Graduate School in Paris, Program in International Relations and Diplomacy, Paris, France. Offers MA, PhD. *Expenses: Tuition:* Full-time 19,117 euros; part-time 2667 euros per unit. *Required fees:* 150 euros. One-time fee: 300 euros full-time; 100 euros part-time.

American Public University System, AMU/APU Graduate Programs, Charles Town, WV 25414. Offers accounting (MS); applied business analytics (MS); business administration (MBA); criminal justice (MA); cybersecurity studies (MS); educational leadership (M Ed); environmental policy and management (MS); global security (DGS); health information management (MS); history (MA), including American military history, American Revolution, civil war, war since 1945, World War II; information technology (MS); international relations and conflict resolution (MA), including American politics and government, comparative government and development, general, international relations, public policy; national security studies (MA); nursing (MSN); political science (MA); public policy (MPP); reverse logistics management (MA), including comparative and security issues, conflict resolution, international and transnational security issues, peacekeeping; space studies (MS); sports management (MS); strategic intelligence (DSI); teaching (M Ed), including secondary social studies; transportation and logistics management (MA). *Program availability:* Part-time, evening/weekend, online only, 100% online. *Students:* 461 full-time (193 women), 7,322 part-time (3,127 women); includes 3,089 minority (1,404 Black or African American, non-Hispanic/Latino; 30 American Indian or Alaska Native, non-Hispanic/Latino; 210 Asian, non-Hispanic/Latino; 753 Hispanic/Latino; 445 Native Hawaiian or other Pacific Islander, non-Hispanic/Latino; 247 Two or more races, non-Hispanic/Latino), 117 international. Average age 37. In 2019, 2,681 master's awarded. *Degree requirements:* For master's, comprehensive exam or practicum; for doctorate, practicum. *Entrance requirements:* For master's, official transcript showing earned bachelor's degree from institution accredited by recognized accrediting body. Additional exam requirements/recommendations for international students: required—TOEFL (minimum score 550 paper-based), IELTS (minimum score 6.5). *Application deadline:* Applications are processed on a rolling basis. Application fee: $0. Electronic applications accepted. *Financial support:* Scholarships/grants available. Financial award applicants required to submit FAFSA. *Unit head:* Dr. Wallace Boston, President, 877-468-6268, Fax: 304-728-2348, E-mail: president@apus.edu. *Application contact:* Yoci Deal, Associate Vice President, Graduate and International Admissions, 877-468-6268, Fax: 304-724-3764, E-mail: info@apus.edu.
Website: http://www.apus.edu

American University, School of International Service, Washington, DC 20016-8071. Offers comparative and regional studies (Certificate); cross-cultural communication (Certificate); development management (MS); ethics, peace, and global affairs (MA); European studies (Certificate); global environmental policy (MA, Certificate); global information technology (Certificate); global media (MA); international affairs (MA), including comparative and regional studies, global governance, politics, and security, international economic relations, natural resources and sustainable development, U.S. foreign policy and national security; international arts management (Certificate); international communication (MA, Certificate); international development (MA); international economic policy (Certificate); international economic relations (Certificate); international economics (MA); international peace and conflict resolution (MA, Certificate); international politics (Certificate); international relations (MA, PhD); international service (MIS); peacebuilding (Certificate); social enterprise (MA); the Americas (Certificate); United States foreign policy (Certificate); JD/MA. *Program availability:* Part-time, evening/weekend, 100% online, blended/hybrid learning. Terminal master's awarded for partial completion of doctoral program. *Degree requirements:* For master's, one foreign language, comprehensive exam, thesis or alternative; for doctorate, one foreign language, comprehensive exam, thesis/dissertation. *Entrance requirements:* For master's, transcripts, resume, 2 letters of recommendation, statement of purpose; for doctorate, GRE, transcripts, resume, 3 letters of recommendation, statement of purpose. Additional exam requirements/recommendations for international students: required—TOEFL. Electronic applications accepted. *Expenses:* Contact institution.

The American University in Cairo, School of Global Affairs and Public Policy, Cairo, Egypt. Offers gender and women's studies (MA); global affairs (MGA); international and comparative law (LL M); international human rights law (MA); journalism and mass communication (MA); Middle East studies (MA); migration and refugee studies (MA, Diploma); public administration (MPA); public policy (MPP); television and digital journalism (MA). *Program availability:* Part-time, evening/weekend. *Degree requirements:* For master's, comprehensive exam (for some programs), thesis (for some programs). *Entrance requirements:* Additional exam requirements/recommendations for international students: required—TOEFL (minimum score 450 paper-based; 45 iBT), IELTS (minimum score 5). Electronic applications accepted. *Expenses:* Contact institution.

American University of Armenia, Graduate Programs, Yerevan, Armenia. Offers business administration (MBA); computer and information science (MS), including business management, design and manufacturing, energy (ME, MS), industrial engineering and systems management; economics (MS); industrial engineering and systems management (ME), including business, computer aided design/manufacturing, energy (ME, MS), information technology; law (LL M); political science and international affairs (MPSIA); public health (MPH); teaching English as a foreign language (MA). *Program availability:* Part-time, evening/weekend. *Degree requirements:* For master's, thesis (for some programs), capstone/project. *Entrance requirements:* For master's, GRE, GMAT, or LSAT. Additional exam requirements/recommendations for international students: recommended—TOEFL (minimum score 79 iBT), IELTS (minimum score 6.5). *Expenses: Tuition:* Full-time $3100; part-time $165 per credit. Tuition and fees vary according to program.

The American University of Paris, Graduate Programs, Paris, France. Offers cross-cultural and sustainable business management (MA); cultural translation (MA); global communications (MA); global communications and civil society (MA); international affairs (MA); international affairs, conflict resolution and civil society development (MA); Middle East and Islamic studies (MA); Middle East and Islamic studies and international affairs (MA); public policy and international affairs (MA); public policy and international law (MA). *Degree requirements:* For master's, thesis (for some programs). *Entrance requirements:* For master's, minimum undergraduate GPA of 3.0. Additional exam requirements/recommendations for international students: recommended—TOEFL, IELTS. Electronic applications accepted.

Anabaptist Mennonite Biblical Seminary, Graduate and Professional Programs, Elkhart, IN 46517-1999. Offers chaplaincy (M Div); Christian faith formation (M Div); Christian formation (MA); Christian spiritual formation (Certificate); divinity (M Div); pastoral ministry (M Div); pastoral theology for financial professionals (Certificate);

peace studies (M Div), including environmental sustainability leadership (M Div, MA); theological studies (M Div, Certificate), including peace studies (M Div), theology and ethics (M Div); theology and peace studies (MA), including conflict transformation, environmental sustainability leadership (M Div, MA), international development administration; United Methodist leadership (M Div). *Accreditation:* ACIPE; ATS. *Program availability:* Part-time, 100% online, blended/hybrid learning. *Degree requirements:* For master's, variable foreign language requirement, comprehensive exam (for some programs), thesis optional, senior interview. *Entrance requirements:* For master's, undergraduate degree transcripts, 3 letters of reference, essay. Additional exam requirements/recommendations for international students: required—TOEFL (minimum score 90 iBT); recommended—IELTS (minimum score 7). Electronic applications accepted.

Baruch College of the City University of New York, Austin W. Marxe School of Public and International Affairs, Program in International Affairs, New York, NY 10010-5585. Offers international nongovernmental organizations (MIA); trade policy and global economic governance (MIA); Western Hemisphere affairs (MIA). *Program availability:* Part-time.

Baylor University, Graduate School, Hankamer School of Business, Department of Economics, Waco, TX 76798. Offers MS Eco. *Entrance requirements:* For master's, GMAT or GRE General Test. Additional exam requirements/recommendations for international students: required—TOEFL (minimum score 600 paper-based; 100 iBT), IELTS (minimum score 7). Electronic applications accepted.

Boston University, Graduate School of Arts and Sciences, Frederick S. Pardee School of Global Studies, Boston, MA 02215. Offers MA, MA/JD, MBA/MA. *Faculty:* 33 full-time (8 women), 10 part-time/adjunct (4 women). *Students:* 70 full-time (43 women), 13 part-time (7 women); includes 14 minority (3 Black or African American, non-Hispanic/Latino; 3 Asian, non-Hispanic/Latino; 7 Hispanic/Latino; 1 Two or more races, non-Hispanic/Latino), 28 international. Average age 25. 296 applicants, 76% accepted, 39 enrolled. In 2019, 54 master's awarded. *Degree requirements:* For master's, one foreign language, thesis (for some programs), master's paper,capstone. *Entrance requirements:* For master's, GRE General Test, 3 letters of recommendation, transcripts of all prior college coursework, personal statement, resume or curriculum vitae. Additional exam requirements/recommendations for international students: required—TOEFL (minimum score 550 paper-based; 84 iBT). *Application deadline:* For fall admission, 1/18 priority date for domestic and international students; for spring admission, 11/1 for domestic and international students. Applications are processed on a rolling basis. Application fee: $95. Electronic applications accepted. *Financial support:* In 2019–20, 60 students received support. Federal Work-Study, scholarships/grants, and unspecified assistantships available. Financial award application deadline: 1/18. *Unit head:* Adil Najam, Dean, 617-358-0988, Fax: 617-358-7238, E-mail: anajam@bu.edu. *Application contact:* Holly Emery, Graduate Admissions Administrator, 617-358-8625, Fax: 617-353-9290, E-mail: psgsgrad@bu.edu.
Website: http://www.bu.edu/PardeeSchool

Brigham Young University, Graduate Studies, BYU Marriott School of Business, MBA Program, Provo, UT 84602. Offers entrepreneurship (MBA); finance (MBA); global supply chain management (MBA); marketing (MBA); strategic human resources (MBA); JD/MBA; MBA/MS. *Accreditation:* AACSB. *Faculty:* 52 full-time (7 women), 18 part-time/adjunct (0 women). *Students:* 103 full-time (22 women); includes 14 minority (8 Asian, non-Hispanic/Latino; 6 Hispanic/Latino). Average age 29. 223 applicants, 59% accepted, 103 enrolled. In 2019, 133 master's awarded. *Entrance requirements:* For master's, GMAT or GRE, commitment to BYU Honor Code, undergraduate degree. Additional exam requirements/recommendations for international students: required—TOEFL (minimum score 590 paper-based; 100 iBT), IELTS (minimum score 7). *Application deadline:* For fall admission, 5/1 for domestic students, 3/1 for international students. Applications are processed on a rolling basis. Application fee: $50. Electronic applications accepted. *Expenses:* $13,450 tuition for 2 semesters (tuition is double for those who are not members of the sponsoring organization, The Church of Jesus Christ of Latter-day Saints); $35,362 living expenses, books and supplies, personal expenses transportation and fees for 2 semesters; program is 4 semesters. *Financial support:* In 2019–20, 15 research assistantships (averaging $3,000 per year), 25 teaching assistantships (averaging $3,000 per year) were awarded; career-related internships or fieldwork, institutionally sponsored loans, and scholarships/grants also available. Financial award application deadline: 3/1; financial award applicants required to submit FAFSA. *Unit head:* Dr. Dan Snow, Director, 801-422-3500, E-mail: mba@byu.edu. *Application contact:* Yvette Anderson, MBA Program Admissions Director, 801-422-3701, Fax: 801-422-0513, E-mail: mba@byu.edu.
Website: http://mba.byu.edu

Brock University, Faculty of Graduate Studies, Faculty of Social Sciences, Program in Political Science, St. Catharines, ON L2S 3A1, Canada. Offers Canadian politics (MA); comparative politics (MA); international relations (MA); political theory or philosophy (MA); public policy (MA). *Program availability:* Part-time. *Degree requirements:* For master's, thesis optional. *Entrance requirements:* For master's, honors degree. Additional exam requirements/recommendations for international students: required—TOEFL (minimum score 550 paper-based; 80 iBT), IELTS (minimum score 6.5), TWE (minimum score 4). Electronic applications accepted.

Brooklyn College of the City University of New York, School of Humanities and Social Sciences, Department of Political Science, Brooklyn, NY 11210-2889. Offers international affairs (MA); political science (MA); urban policy and administration (MA). *Program availability:* Part-time, evening/weekend. *Degree requirements:* For master's, comprehensive exam (for some programs), thesis or alternative, foreign language exam (for international affairs program). *Entrance requirements:* For master's, 2 letters of recommendation, personal statement. Additional exam requirements/recommendations for international students: required—TOEFL (minimum score 500 paper-based; 61 iBT).

Carleton University, Faculty of Graduate Studies, Faculty of Public Affairs and Management, Norman Paterson School of International Affairs, Ottawa, ON K1S 5B6, Canada. Offers MA, PhD. *Program availability:* Part-time. *Degree requirements:* For master's, one foreign language, comprehensive exam, thesis optional. *Entrance requirements:* For master's, honors degree. Additional exam requirements/recommendations for international students: required—TOEFL.

The Catholic University of America, School of Arts and Sciences, Department of Politics, Washington, DC 20064. Offers American government (MA, PhD); Congressional and Presidential studies (MA); international affairs (MA); international political economics (MA); political theory (MA, PhD); world politics (MA, PhD); MA/JD. *Program availability:* Part-time. *Faculty:* 13 full-time (2 women), 6 part-time/adjunct (2 women). *Students:* 11 full-time (6 women), 37 part-time (11 women); includes 7 minority (2 Black or African American, non-Hispanic/Latino; 1 Asian, non-Hispanic/Latino; 2

Hispanic/Latino; 2 Two or more races, non-Hispanic/Latino), 11 international. Average age 34. 43 applicants, 60% accepted, 8 enrolled. In 2019, 14 master's, 5 doctorates awarded. *Degree requirements:* For master's, one foreign language, comprehensive exam, thesis or alternative; for doctorate, variable foreign language requirement, comprehensive exam, thesis/dissertation. *Entrance requirements:* For master's, GRE General Test, statement of purpose, official copies of academic transcripts, three letters of recommendation, minimum GPA of 3.0; for doctorate, GRE General Test, statement of purpose, official copies of academic transcripts, three letters of recommendation. Additional exam requirements/recommendations for international students: required—TOEFL (minimum score 550 paper-based; 80 iBT). *Application deadline:* For fall admission, 7/15 priority date for domestic students, 7/1 for international students; for spring admission, 11/15 priority date for domestic students, 11/1 for international students. Applications are processed on a rolling basis. Application fee: $55. Electronic applications accepted. *Expenses:* Contact institution. *Financial support:* Fellowships, research assistantships, teaching assistantships, Federal Work-Study, scholarships/grants, tuition waivers (full and partial), and unspecified assistantships available. Financial award application deadline: 2/1; financial award applicants required to submit FAFSA. *Unit head:* Dr. Dennis Coyle, Chair, 202-319-5813, Fax: 202-319-6289, E-mail: coyle@cua.edu. *Application contact:* Dr. Steven Brown, Director of Graduate Admissions, 202-319-5057, Fax: 202-319-6533, E-mail: cua-admissions@cua.edu.
Website: http://politics.cua.edu/

Central Connecticut State University, School of Graduate Studies, College of Liberal Arts and Social Sciences, Program in International Studies, New Britain, CT 06050-4010. Offers MS. *Program availability:* Part-time, evening/weekend. *Degree requirements:* For master's, thesis or alternative, special project. *Entrance requirements:* For master's, minimum undergraduate GPA of 3.0, essay, resume. Additional exam requirements/recommendations for international students: required—TOEFL (minimum score 550 paper-based; 79 iBT); recommended—IELTS (minimum score 6.5). Electronic applications accepted.

Central European University, Department of International Relations, 1051, Hungary. Offers global economic relations (MA); international relations (MA, PhD). *Degree requirements:* For master's, one foreign language, thesis; for doctorate, one foreign language, comprehensive exam, thesis/dissertation. *Entrance requirements:* For master's, 500-word essay, statement of purpose; for doctorate, interview. Additional exam requirements/recommendations for international students: required—TOEFL (minimum score 570 paper-based); recommended—IELTS (minimum score 6.5). Electronic applications accepted.

Central Michigan University, Central Michigan University Global Campus, Program in Administration, Mount Pleasant, MI 48859. Offers acquisitions administration (MSA, Certificate); engineering management administration (MSA, Certificate); general administration (MSA, Certificate); health services administration (MSA, Certificate); human resources administration (MSA, Certificate); information resource management (MSA); information resource management administration (Certificate); international administration (MSA, Certificate); leadership (MSA, Certificate); philanthropy and fundraising administration (MSA, Certificate); public administration (MSA, Certificate); recreation and park administration (MSA); research administration (MSA, Certificate). *Program availability:* Part-time, evening/weekend, online learning. *Entrance requirements:* For master's, minimum GPA of 2.7 in major. Electronic applications accepted. *Expenses: Tuition, area resident:* Full-time $12,267; part-time $8178 per year. Tuition, state resident: full-time $12,267; part-time $8178 per year. Tuition, nonresident: full-time $12,267; part-time $8178 per year. *International tuition:* $16,110 full-time. *Required fees:* $225 per semester. Tuition and fees vary according to degree level and program.

Chapman University, Wilkinson College of Arts, Humanities, and Social Sciences, International Studies Program, Orange, CA 92866. Offers MA. *Program availability:* Part-time, evening/weekend. *Students:* 12 full-time (7 women), 7 part-time (4 women); includes 10 minority (1 Asian, non-Hispanic/Latino; 7 Hispanic/Latino; 2 Two or more races, non-Hispanic/Latino), 4 international. Average age 28. 31 applicants, 97% accepted, 8 enrolled. *Degree requirements:* For master's, thesis. *Entrance requirements:* For master's, GRE (if undergraduate GPA less than 3.0), minimum undergraduate GPA of 2.5. Additional exam requirements/recommendations for international students: required—TOEFL (minimum score 80 iBT), IELTS (minimum score 6.5), PTE (minimum score 53). *Application deadline:* For fall admission, 2/1 priority date for domestic students. Applications are processed on a rolling basis. Application fee: $60. Electronic applications accepted. *Expenses:* $1,345 per unit. *Financial support:* Fellowships, Federal Work-Study, scholarships/grants, and unspecified assistantships available. Financial award applicants required to submit FAFSA. *Unit head:* Crystal Murphy, Program Director, 714-628-2763, E-mail: crmurphy@chapman.edu. *Application contact:* David Krausman, Graduate Programs Coordinator, 714-516-7116, E-mail: krausman@chapman.edu.
Website: https://www.chapman.edu/wilkinson/graduate-studies/ma-international-studies/index.aspx

City College of the City University of New York, Graduate School, Colin Powell School for Civic and Global Leadership, Program in International Relations, New York, NY 10031-9198. Offers MA. *Program availability:* Part-time. *Degree requirements:* For master's, one foreign language, thesis. *Entrance requirements:* For master's, GRE, 3 letters of recommendation. Additional exam requirements/recommendations for international students: required—TOEFL (minimum score 600 paper-based; 100 iBT). Electronic applications accepted.

Claremont Graduate University, Graduate Programs, School of Social Science, Policy and Evaluation, Department of Politics and Policy, Claremont, CA 91711-6160. Offers American politics (MA, PhD); comparative politics (PhD); international political economy (MA); international studies (MA); political philosophy (PhD); political science (PhD); politics, economics and business (MA); public policy (MA, PhD); world politics (PhD); MBA/PhD. *Program availability:* Part-time. Terminal master's awarded for partial completion of doctoral program. *Entrance requirements:* For master's and doctorate, GRE General Test. Additional exam requirements/recommendations for international students: required—TOEFL (minimum score 75 iBT). Electronic applications accepted.

Cleveland State University, College of Graduate Studies, College of Liberal Arts and Social Sciences, Department of Political Science, Cleveland, OH 44115. Offers global interactions (MA), including global business interactions, global political interactions. *Entrance requirements:* For master's, minimum undergraduate GPA of 3.0 or GRE (50th percentile or above); two letters of recommendation; undergraduate degree in economics, political science, international relations, or a related discipline; completion of undergraduate macro and micro economics course. Additional exam requirements/recommendations for international students: required—TOEFL (minimum score 550 paper-based; 78 iBT). Electronic applications accepted. *Expenses:* Contact institution.

Columbia University, Graduate School of Arts and Sciences, New York, NY 10027. Offers African-American studies (MA); American studies (MA); anthropology (MA, PhD); art history and archaeology (MA, PhD); astronomy (PhD); biological sciences (PhD); biotechnology (MA); chemical physics (PhD); chemistry (PhD); classical studies (MA, PhD); classics (MA, PhD); climate and society (MA); conservation biology (MA); earth and environmental sciences (PhD); East Asia: regional studies (MA); East Asian languages and cultures (MA, PhD); ecology, evolution and environmental biology (MA), including conservation biology; ecology, evolution, and environmental biology (PhD), including ecology and evolutionary biology, evolutionary primatology; economics (MA, PhD); English and comparative literature (MA, PhD); French and Romance philology (MA, PhD); Germanic languages (MA, PhD); global French studies (MA); global thought (MA); Hispanic cultural studies (MA); history (PhD); history and literature (MA); human rights studies (MA); Islamic studies (MA); Italian (MA, PhD); Japanese pedagogy (MA); Jewish studies (MA); Latin America and the Caribbean: regional studies (MA); Latin American and Iberian cultures (PhD); mathematics (MA, PhD), including finance (MA); medieval and Renaissance studies (MA); Middle Eastern, South Asian, and African studies (MA, PhD); modern art: critical and curatorial studies (MA); modern European studies (MA); museum anthropology (MA); music (DMA, PhD); oral history (MA); philosophical foundations of physics (MA); philosophy (MA, PhD); physics (PhD); political science (MA, PhD); psychology (PhD); quantitative methods in the social sciences (MA); religion (MA, PhD); Russia, Eurasia and East Europe: regional studies (MA); Russian translation (MA); Slavic cultures (MA); Slavic languages (MA, PhD); sociology (MA, PhD); South Asian studies (MA); statistics (MA, PhD); theatre (PhD). *Program availability:* Part-time. *Students:* 3,506 full-time (1,844 women), 208 part-time (121 women); includes 864 minority (110 Black or African American, non-Hispanic/Latino; 5 American Indian or Alaska Native, non-Hispanic/Latino; 416 Asian, non-Hispanic/Latino; 147 Hispanic/Latino; 6 Native Hawaiian or other Pacific Islander, non-Hispanic/Latino; 180 Two or more races, non-Hispanic/Latino), 2,065 international. 14,545 applicants, 25% accepted, 1,429 enrolled. In 2019, 1,262 master's, 363 doctorates awarded. Terminal master's awarded for partial completion of doctoral program. *Degree requirements:* For master's, variable foreign language requirement, comprehensive exam (for some programs), thesis (for some programs); for doctorate, variable foreign language requirement, comprehensive exam (for some programs), thesis/dissertation. *Entrance requirements:* For master's and doctorate, GRE General Test, GRE Subject Test (for some programs). Additional exam requirements/recommendations for international students: required—TOEFL (minimum score 600 paper-based; 100 iBT), IELTS (minimum score 7.5). Application fee: $115. Electronic applications accepted. *Expenses: Tuition:* Full-time $47,600; part-time $1880 per credit. One-time fee: $105. *Financial support:* Fellowships, research assistantships, teaching assistantships, career-related internships or fieldwork, Federal Work-Study, institutionally sponsored loans, scholarships/grants, traineeships, health care benefits, tuition waivers, and unspecified assistantships available. Support available to part-time students. Financial award application deadline: 12/15. *Unit head:* Dr. Carlos J. Alonso, Dean of the Graduate School of Arts and Sciences and Vice President for Graduate Education, 212-854-2861, E-mail: gsas-dean@columbia.edu. *Application contact:* GSAS Office of Admissions, 212-854-6729, E-mail: gsas-admissions@columbia.edu.
Website: http://gsas.columbia.edu/

Columbia University, School of International and Public Affairs, Program in International Affairs, New York, NY 10027. Offers MIA, JD/MIA, MBA/MIA, MIA/MS, MPH/MIA, MSJ/MIA. *Degree requirements:* For master's, one foreign language, comprehensive exam. *Entrance requirements:* For master's, GRE General Test. Additional exam requirements/recommendations for international students: required—TOEFL (minimum score 600 paper-based; 100 iBT), IELTS (minimum score 7), PTE (minimum score 68). Electronic applications accepted. *Expenses: Tuition:* Full-time $47,600; part-time $1880 per credit. One-time fee: $105.

Concordia University Irvine, School of Professional Studies, Irvine, CA 92612-3299. Offers healthcare administration (MHA); international studies (MAIS), including Africa, China; nursing (MSN).

Cornell University, Graduate School, Graduate Fields of Arts and Sciences, Field of Government, Ithaca, NY 14853. Offers American politics (PhD); comparative politics (PhD); international relations (PhD); political methodology (PhD); political thought (PhD); public policy (PhD). *Degree requirements:* For doctorate, comprehensive exam, thesis/dissertation. *Entrance requirements:* For doctorate, GRE General Test, sample of written work, 3 letters of recommendation. Additional exam requirements/recommendations for international students: required—TOEFL (minimum score 550 paper-based; 77 iBT). Electronic applications accepted.

Dallas Baptist University, Gary Cook School of Leadership, Program in International Studies, Dallas, TX 75211-9299. Offers East Asian studies (MA); European studies (MA); general international studies (MA); global business (MA); international immersion (MA); international ministry (MA); international relations (MA). *Program availability:* Part-time, evening/weekend. *Application deadline:* Applications are processed on a rolling basis. Application fee: $25. Electronic applications accepted. Application fee is waived when completed online. *Expenses: Tuition:* Full-time $18,072; part-time $1004 per credit hour. *Required fees:* $1100; $550 per semester. Tuition and fees vary according to course level and degree level. *Unit head:* Dr. Jack Goodyear, Dean, 214-333-5595, Fax: 214-333-6809, E-mail: jackg@dbu.edu. *Application contact:* Lee Bratcher, Program Director, 214-333-5808, E-mail: leeb@dbu.edu.
Website: https://www.dbu.edu/graduate/degree-programs/ma-international-studies

DePaul University, College of Liberal Arts and Social Sciences, Chicago, IL 60614. Offers Arabic (MA); Chinese (MA); critical ethnic studies (MA); English (MA); French (MA); German (MA); history (MA); interdisciplinary studies (MA, MS); international public service (MS); international studies (MA); Italian (MA); Japanese (MA); liberal studies (MA); nonprofit management (MNM); public administration (MPA); public health (MPH); public policy (MPP); public service management (MS); refugee and forced migration studies (MS); social work (MSW); sociology (MA); Spanish (MA); sustainable urban development (MA); women's and gender studies (MA); writing and publishing (MA); writing, rhetoric and discourse (MA); MA/PhD. *Accreditation:* CEPH. *Program availability:* Part-time, evening/weekend, online learning. Terminal master's awarded for partial completion of doctoral program. *Degree requirements:* For master's, variable foreign language requirement, comprehensive exam (for some programs), thesis (for some programs). Electronic applications accepted.

East Carolina University, Graduate School, Thomas Harriot College of Arts and Sciences, Program in International Studies, Greenville, NC 27858-4353. Offers international studies (MA); international teaching (Certificate). *Program availability:* Part-time. *Application deadline:* For fall admission, 7/1 priority date for domestic and international students; for spring admission, 11/15 priority date for domestic and international students; for summer admission, 3/15 priority date for domestic and international students. *Expenses: Tuition, area resident:* Full-time $4749; part-time $185 per credit hour. Tuition, state resident: full-time $4749; part-time $185 per credit hour. Tuition, nonresident: full-time $17,898; part-time $864 per credit hour. *International tuition:* $17,898 full-time. *Required fees:* $2787. *Financial support:* Application deadline: 3/1. *Unit head:* Dr. David L. Smith, Director, 252-328-5524, E-mail: smithdav@ecu.edu. *Application contact:* Graduate School Admissions, 252-328-6012, Fax: 252-328-6071, E-mail: gradschool@ecu.edu.
Website: https://internationalstudies.ecu.edu/#:~:text=ECU's%20International%20Studies%20programs%20help,in%20an%20increasingly%20globalized%20society.&text=Th

International Affairs

Embry-Riddle Aeronautical University–Worldwide, Department of Security and Emergency Services, Daytona Beach, FL 32114-3900. Offers cybersecurity management and policy (MSCMP); human security and resilience (MSHSR). *Program availability:* Part-time, evening/weekend, EagleVision Classroom (between classrooms), EagleVision Home (faculty and students at home), and a blend of Classroom or Home. *Degree requirements:* For master's, capstone project (for MSHSR). *Entrance requirements:* Additional exam requirements/recommendations for international students: required—TOEFL (minimum score 550 paper-based; 79 iBT), IELTS (minimum score 6). Electronic applications accepted.

Fairleigh Dickinson University, Metropolitan Campus, University College: Arts, Sciences, and Professional Studies, School of History, Political and International Studies, Program in International Studies, Teaneck, NJ 07666-1914. Offers MA.

Florida International University, Steven J. Green School of International and Public Affairs, Department of Politics and International Relations, Miami, FL 33199. Offers international relations (MA, PhD), including international relations (PhD), international studies (MA); political science (MA, PhD). *Program availability:* Part-time, evening/weekend. *Faculty:* 28 full-time (10 women), 32 part-time/adjunct (8 women). *Students:* 81 full-time (34 women), 13 part-time (4 women); includes 39 minority (4 Black or African American, non-Hispanic/Latino; 4 Asian, non-Hispanic/Latino; 31 Hispanic/Latino), 35 international. Average age 32. 73 applicants, 45% accepted, 20 enrolled. In 2019, 9 master's, 11 doctorates awarded. *Degree requirements:* For master's, one foreign language, thesis optional; for doctorate, one foreign language, comprehensive exam, thesis/dissertation. *Entrance requirements:* For master's and doctorate, GRE General Test, minimum GPA of 3.0, letters of recommendation. Additional exam requirements/recommendations for international students: required—TOEFL (minimum score 550 paper-based; 80 iBT). *Application deadline:* For fall admission, 3/15 for domestic and international students; for spring admission, 8/15 for domestic and international students. Application fee: $30. Electronic applications accepted. *Expenses: Tuition, area resident:* Full-time $8912; part-time $446 per credit hour. Tuition, state resident: full-time $8912; part-time $446 per credit hour. Tuition, nonresident: full-time $21,393; part-time $992 per credit hour. *Required fees:* $2194. *Financial support:* Institutionally sponsored loans, scholarships/grants, and unspecified assistantships available. Financial award application deadline: 3/1; financial award applicants required to submit FAFSA. *Unit head:* Dr. John Clark, Chair, 305-348-2227, Fax: 305-348-3765, E-mail: john.clark@fiu.edu. *Application contact:* Nanett Rojas, Manager, Admissions Operations, 305-348-7464, Fax: 305-348-7441, E-mail: gradadm@fiu.edu.
Website: http://pir.fiu.edu

Florida State University, The Graduate School, College of Social Sciences and Public Policy, Program in International Affairs, Tallahassee, FL 32306. Offers international affairs (MA); JD/MA; JD/MS. *Program availability:* Part-time. *Faculty:* 4 full-time (all women), 4 part-time/adjunct (0 women). *Students:* 32 full-time (15 women), 33 part-time (17 women); includes 24 minority (6 Black or African American, non-Hispanic/Latino; 1 American Indian or Alaska Native, non-Hispanic/Latino; 3 Asian, non-Hispanic/Latino; 10 Hispanic/Latino; 4 Two or more races, non-Hispanic/Latino), 19 international. Average age 28. 73 applicants, 55% accepted, 20 enrolled. In 2019, 35 master's awarded. *Degree requirements:* For master's, one foreign language, comprehensive exam, thesis optional. *Entrance requirements:* For master's, GRE General Test, minimum GPA of 3.0. Additional exam requirements/recommendations for international students: required—TOEFL (minimum score 550 paper-based; 80 iBT), IELTS (minimum score 6.5). *Application deadline:* For fall admission, 7/1 for domestic and international students; for spring admission, 11/1 for domestic and international students; for summer admission, 3/1 for domestic and international students. Applications are processed on a rolling basis. Application fee: $30. Electronic applications accepted. *Financial support:* In 2019–20, 1 student received support, including research assistantships with full tuition reimbursements available (averaging $6,000 per year), 1 teaching assistantship with full tuition reimbursement available (averaging $6,000 per year); career-related internships or fieldwork, Federal Work-Study, institutionally sponsored loans, scholarships/grants, and unspecified assistantships also available. Financial award application deadline: 2/1; financial award applicants required to submit FAFSA. *Unit head:* Dr. Lee K. Metcalf, Director, 850-644-4418, Fax: 850-645-4981, E-mail: lmetcalf@fsu.edu. *Application contact:* Sabrina Smith, Academic Program Specialist, 850-644-4418, Fax: 850-645-4981, E-mail: ssmith9@fsu.edu.
Website: http://coss.fsu.edu/inaprog/programs/graduate/g-IA

Fordham University, Graduate School of Arts and Sciences, Program in International Political Economy and Development, New York, NY 10458. Offers MA, Certificate. *Program availability:* Part-time, evening/weekend. *Students:* Average age 27. 81 applicants, 57% accepted, 17 enrolled. In 2019, 21 master's awarded. *Entrance requirements:* For master's, GRE General Test. Additional exam requirements/recommendations for international students: required—TOEFL (minimum score 600 paper-based). *Application deadline:* For fall admission, 1/4 priority date for domestic students; for spring admission, 11/1 for domestic students. Application fee: $70. Electronic applications accepted. *Financial support:* In 2019–20, 35 students received support, including 4 fellowships with tuition reimbursements available (averaging $17,014 per year); research assistantships, career-related internships or fieldwork, institutionally sponsored loans, tuition waivers (full and partial), and unspecified assistantships also available. Financial award application deadline: 1/4; financial award applicants required to submit FAFSA. *Unit head:* Dr. Henry Schwalbenberg, Chair, 718-817-3866, Fax: 718-817-3518. *Application contact:* Garrett Marino, Director of Graduate Admissions, 718-817-4419, Fax: 718-817-3566, E-mail: gmarino10@fordham.edu.

George Mason University, College of Humanities and Social Sciences, Program in Global Affairs, Fairfax, VA 22030. Offers MA. *Entrance requirements:* For master's, expanded goals statement, 2 letters of recommendation, writing sample, resume, official transcripts, evidence of professional competency in a second language tested through Language Testing International or other means approved by the department. Additional exam requirements/recommendations for international students: required—TOEFL (minimum score 575 paper-based; 88 iBT), IELTS (minimum score 6.5), PTE (minimum score 59). Electronic applications accepted.

George Mason University, Schar School of Policy and Government, Program in International Commerce and Policy, Arlington, VA 22030. Offers MA. *Entrance requirements:* For master's, GRE/GMAT (for students seeking merit-based scholarships), bachelor's degree with minimum GPA of 3.0; expanded goals statement; current resume; 2 official copies of transcripts; 2 letters of recommendation. Additional exam requirements/recommendations for international students: required—TOEFL (minimum score 575 paper-based; 88 iBT), IELTS (minimum score 6.5), PTE (minimum score 59). Electronic applications accepted. *Expenses:* Contact institution.

Georgetown University, Graduate School of Arts and Sciences, School of Continuing Studies, Washington, DC 20057. Offers American studies (MALS); applied intelligence (MPS); Catholic studies (MALS); classical civilizations (MALS); emergency and disaster management (MPS); ethics and the professions (MALS); global strategic communications (MPS); hospitality management (MPS); human resources management (MPS); humanities (MALS); individualized study (MALS); integrated marketing communications (MPS); international affairs (MALS); Islam and Muslim-Christian relations (MALS); journalism (MPS); liberal studies (DLS); literature and society (MALS); medieval and early modern European studies (MALS); public relations and corporate communications (MPS); real estate (MPS); religious studies (MALS); social and public policy (MALS); sports industry management (MPS); systems engineering management (MPS); technology management (MPS); the theory and practice of American democracy (MALS); urban and regional planning (MPS); visual culture (MALS). *Entrance requirements:* Additional exam requirements/recommendations for international students: required—TOEFL.

Georgetown University, Graduate School of Arts and Sciences, Walsh School of Foreign Service, BMW Center for German and European Studies, Washington, DC 20057. Offers MA, MA/JD, MA/PhD. *Degree requirements:* For master's, 2 foreign languages, comprehensive exam. *Entrance requirements:* For master's, GRE General Test. Additional exam requirements/recommendations for international students: required—TOEFL. Electronic applications accepted.

Georgetown University, Graduate School of Arts and Sciences, Walsh School of Foreign Service, Master of Science in Foreign Service Program, Washington, DC 20057. Offers global business and finance (MS); global politics and security (MS); international development (MS); self-designed studies (MS); JD/MS; MA/MS; MBA/MS; MPP/MS. *Faculty:* 28 full-time (7 women), 41 part-time/adjunct (6 women). *Students:* 203 full-time (105 women); includes 42 minority (9 Black or African American, non-Hispanic/Latino; 1 American Indian or Alaska Native, non-Hispanic/Latino; 14 Asian, non-Hispanic/Latino; 11 Hispanic/Latino; 7 Two or more races, non-Hispanic/Latino), 53 international. Average age 27. 673 applicants, 40% accepted, 100 enrolled. In 2019, 98 master's awarded. *Degree requirements:* For master's, one foreign language, comprehensive exam, internship. *Entrance requirements:* For master's, GRE General Test or GMAT optional, one semester each of micro and macroeconomics with minimum B- grade; two to three years of experience with a second language besides native tongue. Additional exam requirements/recommendations for international students: required—TOEFL (minimum score 100 iBT) or IELTS (minimum score 7) when language of instruction for undergraduate degree was not English. *Application deadline:* For fall admission, 1/15 priority date for domestic and international students. Application fee: $90. Electronic applications accepted. *Expenses:* Contact institution. *Financial support:* In 2019–20, 85 students received support, including 4 research assistantships (averaging $5,000 per year), 4 teaching assistantships (averaging $5,000 per year); career-related internships or fieldwork, scholarships/grants, tuition waivers (partial), and unspecified assistantships also available. Financial award application deadline: 1/15. *Unit head:* Nancy McEldowney, Director, E-mail: Nancy.McEldowney@georgetown.edu. *Application contact:* MSFS Admissions, 202-687-5763, E-mail: msfsinfo@georgetown.edu.
Website: http://msfs.georgetown.edu/

Georgetown University, Law Center, Washington, DC 20001. Offers environmental law (LL M); global health law (LL M); global health law and international institutions (LL M); individualized study (LL M); international business and economic law (LL M); law (JD, SJD); national security law (LL M); securities and financial regulation (LL M); taxation (LL M); JD/LL M; JD/MA; JD/MBA; JD/MPH; JD/PhD. *Accreditation:* ABA. *Program availability:* Part-time, evening/weekend. *Degree requirements:* For master's, thesis; for doctorate, thesis/dissertation (for some programs). *Entrance requirements:* For master's, JD, LL B, or first law degree earned in country of origin; for doctorate, LSAT (for JD). Additional exam requirements/recommendations for international students: required—TOEFL. *Expenses:* Contact institution.

The George Washington University, Elliott School of International Affairs, Program in International Affairs, Washington, DC 20052. Offers MA. *Program availability:* Part-time. *Degree requirements:* For master's, one foreign language, capstone project. *Entrance requirements:* For master's, GRE General Test, 2 years of a modern foreign language, 2 semesters of introductory economics. Additional exam requirements/recommendations for international students: required—TOEFL (minimum score 100 iBT), IELTS (minimum score 7). Electronic applications accepted.

The George Washington University, Elliott School of International Affairs, Program in International Policy and Practice, Washington, DC 20052. Offers MIPP. *Program availability:* Part-time. *Entrance requirements:* For master's, GRE (recommended), advanced degree or 8 years of experience plus BA, introductory microeconomics and macroeconomics. Additional exam requirements/recommendations for international students: required—TOEFL (minimum score 100 iBT), IELTS (minimum score 7). Electronic applications accepted.

The George Washington University, Elliott School of International Affairs, Program in International Studies, Washington, DC 20052. Offers MIS. *Program availability:* Part-time. *Entrance requirements:* For master's, 2 years (or equivalent) of a modern, spoken foreign language; introductory microeconomics/macroeconomics coursework. Additional exam requirements/recommendations for international students: required—TOEFL (minimum score 600 paper-based; 100 iBT), IELTS (minimum score 7). Electronic applications accepted.

The George Washington University, Law School, Washington, DC 20052. Offers law (SJD); national security and U.S. foreign relations (LL M). *Accreditation:* ABA. *Program availability:* Part-time, evening/weekend. *Entrance requirements:* For master's, JD or equivalent; for doctorate, LSAT (for JD), LL M or equivalent (for SJD). *Expenses:* Contact institution.

Georgia Institute of Technology, Graduate Studies, Ivan Allen College of Liberal Arts, Sam Nunn School of International Affairs, Atlanta, GA 30332. Offers MS. *Program availability:* Part-time. *Faculty:* 18 full-time (8 women), 5 part-time/adjunct (1 woman). *Students:* 31 full-time (20 women), 10 part-time (7 women); includes 5 minority (1 Black or African American, non-Hispanic/Latino; 4 Hispanic/Latino), 6 international. Average age 30. 41 applicants, 56% accepted, 12 enrolled. In 2019, 10 master's awarded. Terminal master's awarded for partial completion of doctoral program. *Degree requirements:* For master's, one foreign language, thesis optional, minimum GPA of 3.0, literacy in economics and technology. *Entrance requirements:* For master's, GRE. Additional exam requirements/recommendations for international students: required—TOEFL (minimum score 600 paper-based; 100 iBT), IELTS (minimum score 7.5). *Application deadline:* For fall admission, 1/15 priority date for domestic and international students. Applications are processed on a rolling basis. Application fee: $75 ($85 for international students). Electronic applications accepted. *Expenses: Tuition, area resident:* Full-time $14,064; part-time $586 per credit hour. Tuition, state resident: full-time $14,064; part-time $586 per credit hour. Tuition, nonresident: full-time $29,140; part-time $1215 per credit hour. *International tuition:* $29,140 full-time. *Required fees:* $2024; $840 per semester. $2096. Tuition and fees vary according to course load. *Financial support:* In 2019–20, 2 fellowships, 6 research assistantships, 12 teaching assistantships were awarded; career-related internships or fieldwork, Federal Work-Study, institutionally sponsored loans, tuition waivers (full and partial), and unspecified assistantships also available. Support available to part-time students. Financial award application deadline: 7/1; financial award applicants required to submit FAFSA. *Unit head:* Adam Stulberg, Chair, 404-894-3195, Fax: 404-894-1900, E-mail: adam.stulberg@inta.gatech.edu. *Application contact:* Vince Pedicino, Graduate Coordinator, 404-894-1905, Fax: 404-894-1900, E-mail:

vince.pedicino@inta.gatech.edu.
Website: http://www.inta.gatech.edu

Harvard University, Graduate School of Arts and Sciences, Department of Government, Cambridge, MA 02138. Offers political science (PhD), including American politics, comparative politics, international relations, political thought, quantitative methods. *Degree requirements:* For doctorate, one foreign language, thesis/dissertation, general exams. *Entrance requirements:* For doctorate, GRE General Test. Additional exam requirements/recommendations for international students: required—TOEFL.

Indiana University Bloomington, University Graduate School, College of Arts and Sciences, School of Global and International Studies, Department of International Studies, Bloomington, IN 47405-7000. Offers MA, MS.

Indiana University South Bend, College of Liberal Arts and Sciences, South Bend, IN 46615. Offers advanced computer programming (Graduate Certificate); applied informatics (Graduate Certificate); applied mathematics and computer science (MS); behavior modification (Graduate Certificate); computer applications (Graduate Certificate); computer programming (Graduate Certificate); correctional management and supervision (Graduate Certificate); English (MA); health systems management (Graduate Certificate); international studies (Graduate Certificate); liberal studies (MLS); nonprofit management (Graduate Certificate); paralegal studies (Graduate Certificate); professional writing (Graduate Certificate); public affairs (MPA); public management (Graduate Certificate); social and cultural diversity (Graduate Certificate); strategic sustainability leadership (Graduate Certificate); technology for administration (Graduate Certificate). *Program availability:* Part-time, evening/weekend. *Degree requirements:* For master's, variable foreign language requirement, thesis (for some programs). *Entrance requirements:* For master's, minimum GPA of 3.0. Additional exam requirements/recommendations for international students: required—TOEFL (minimum score 550 paper-based; 80 iBT). *Expenses:* Contact institution.

The Institute of World Politics, Graduate Programs in National Security, Intelligence, and International Affairs, Washington, DC 20036. Offers American foreign policy (Certificate); comparative political culture (Certificate); conflict prevention (Certificate); counterintelligence (Certificate); counterterrorism (Certificate); cyber statecraft (Certificate); economic statecraft (Certificate); homeland security (Certificate); intelligence (Certificate); international politics (Certificate); national security affairs (Executive MA, Certificate); nonviolent conflict (Certificate); peace building, stabilization, and humanitarian affairs (Certificate); public diplomacy and strategic influence (Certificate); statecraft and international affairs (MA); statecraft and national security (MA, DSNS); strategic communication (Certificate); strategic intelligence studies (MA, Professional MA); strategic soft power (Certificate). *Program availability:* Part-time, evening/weekend. *Degree requirements:* For master's, 52 credit hours, comprehensive written and oral exam (for MA); proficiency in critical language (for MA in statecraft and international affairs); 28 credit hours (for Executive MA); 36 credit hours (for Professional MA); for doctorate, comprehensive exam, thesis/dissertation; for Certificate, 20 credit hours. *Entrance requirements:* For master's, resume, personal statement, 3 references, essay; 7-10 years of professional experience (for Executive MA); 5-7 years of professional experience (for Professional MA); for doctorate, MA. Additional exam requirements/recommendations for international students: required—TOEFL. Electronic applications accepted.

Instituto Tecnologico de Santo Domingo, Graduate School, Area of Humanities and Social Sciences, Santo Domingo, Dominican Republic. Offers accounting (Certificate); adult education (Certificate); applied linguistics (MA); economics (MA); education (M Ed); educational psychology (MA, Certificate); gender and development (MA, Certificate); humanistic studies (MA); international marketing management (Certificate); international relations in the Caribbean basin (Certificate); intervention systems in family therapy (MA); linguistic and literary communication (Certificate); pedagogical support (MA); social science education (M Ed); sustainable human development (MA); terminal illness and death psychology (Certificate); youth and adult education (M Ed).

Instituto Tecnológico y de Estudios Superiores de Monterrey, Campus Ciudad Obregón, Program in International Relations, Ciudad Obregón, Mexico. Offers MIR.

International University in Geneva, Leadership Programs, Geneva, Switzerland. Offers international relations and diplomacy (MIRD); media and communication (MA); public administration (DPA). *Degree requirements:* For master's, comprehensive exam. *Entrance requirements:* Additional exam requirements/recommendations for international students: required—TOEFL. Electronic applications accepted.

Johns Hopkins University, School of Advanced International Studies, Washington, DC 20036. Offers global risk (MA); international development (MA, Certificate), including international economics (MA); international economics (Certificate); international economics and finance (MA); international public policy (MIPP); international relations (PhD); international studies (Certificate); Japan studies (MA), including international economics; Korea studies (MA), including international economics; South Asia studies (MA), including international economics; Southeast Asia studies (MA), including international economics; JD/MA; MBA/MA; MHS/MA. *Program availability:* Evening/weekend. *Degree requirements:* For master's, 4-6 international economics courses, 5-6 functional or regional concentration courses, 2 core examinations, proficiency in language other than native language, capstone project; for doctorate, 2 foreign languages, thesis/dissertation, 3 comprehensive exams, economics, quantitative and qualitative course, dissertation prospectus and defense. *Entrance requirements:* For master's, GMAT or GRE General Test, previous course work in economics, foreign language, undergraduate degree; for doctorate, GRE General Test, Master's degree. Additional exam requirements/recommendations for international students: required—TOEFL (minimum score 600 paper-based; 100 iBT), IELTS (minimum score 7), TOEFL (minimum score 600 paper-based; 100 iBT) or IELTS (minimum score 7). Electronic applications accepted. *Expenses:* Contact institution.

Kennesaw State University, College of Humanities and Social Sciences, Program in International Policy Management, Kennesaw, GA 30144. Offers MS. *Program availability:* Online only, 100% online. *Students:* 1 (woman) full-time, 19 part-time (13 women); includes 10 minority (6 Black or African American, non-Hispanic/Latino; 3 Hispanic/Latino; 1 Two or more races, non-Hispanic/Latino). Average age 32. 15 applicants, 93% accepted, 11 enrolled. In 2019, 9 master's awarded. *Degree requirements:* For master's, practicum or thesis. *Entrance requirements:* For master's, GRE, resume, letters of recommendation, writing sample. Additional exam requirements/recommendations for international students: required—TOEFL (minimum score 80 iBT), IELTS (minimum score 6.5). *Application deadline:* For fall admission, 6/1 for domestic and international students. Application fee: $60. Electronic applications accepted. *Expenses: Tuition, area resident:* Full-time $7104; part-time $296 per credit hour. Tuition, state resident: full-time $7104; part-time $296 per credit hour. Tuition, nonresident: full-time $25,584; part-time $1066 per credit hour. *International tuition:* $25,584 full-time. *Required fees:* $2006; $1706 per unit. $853 per semester. *Financial support:* Applicants required to submit FAFSA. *Unit head:* Director, 470-578-6227, E-mail: msipm@kennesaw.edu. *Application contact:* Admissions Counselor, 470-578-4377, Fax: 470-578-9172, E-mail: ksugrad@kennesaw.edu.
Website: http://chss.kennesaw.edu/msipm/

Lebanese American University, School of Arts and Sciences, Beirut, Lebanon. Offers computer science (MS); international affairs (MA).

Lesley University, Graduate School of Arts and Social Sciences, Cambridge, MA 02138-2790. Offers clinical mental health counseling (MA), including holistic counseling, school and community counseling, trauma studies; counseling psychology (MA, CAGS), including professional counseling (MA), school counseling (MA); creative writing (MFA); expressive therapies (MA, PhD, CAGS), including art (MA), clinical mental health counseling (MA), dance (MA), expressive therapies (MA), music (MA); independent studies (CAGS); independent study (MA); intercultural relations (MA, CAGS); interdisciplinary studies (MA), including individualized studies, integrative holistic health, mindfulness studies, peace and conflict transformation, trauma sensitive assessment, intervention, and consultation, women's studies; urban environmental leadership (MA). *Program availability:* Part-time, online learning. *Degree requirements:* For master's, internship, practicum, thesis (for expressive therapies); for doctorate, thesis/dissertation, arts apprenticeship, field placement; for CAGS, thesis, internship (for counseling psychology, expressive therapies). *Entrance requirements:* For master's, MAT (counseling psychology), interview, writing samples, art portfolio; for doctorate, GRE or MAT, interview, master's degree; for CAGS, interview, master's degree. Additional exam requirements/recommendations for international students: required—TOEFL (minimum score 550 paper-based; 80 iBT). Electronic applications accepted.

Liberty University, Helms School of Government, Lynchburg, VA 24515. Offers criminal justice (MS), including forensic psychology, homeland security, public administration (MA, MS); international relations (MS); political science (MS); public administration (MPA), including business and government, healthcare, law and public policy, public and non-profit management; public policy (MA), including campaigns and elections, international affairs, Middle East affairs, public administration (MA, MS). *Program availability:* Part-time, online learning. *Students:* 1,143 full-time (565 women), 572 part-time (408 women); includes 795 minority (499 Black or African American, non-Hispanic/Latino; 16 American Indian or Alaska Native, non-Hispanic/Latino; 23 Asian, non-Hispanic/Latino; 162 Hispanic/Latino; 7 Native Hawaiian or other Pacific Islander, non-Hispanic/Latino; 88 Two or more races, non-Hispanic/Latino), 27 international. Average age 35. 3,017 applicants, 44% accepted, 728 enrolled. In 2019, 415 master's awarded. *Entrance requirements:* For master's, minimum undergraduate GPA of 3.0. Additional exam requirements/recommendations for international students: required—TOEFL (minimum score 600 paper-based; 100 iBT). *Application deadline:* Applications are processed on a rolling basis. Application fee: $50. Electronic applications accepted. *Expenses: Tuition:* Full-time $545; part-time $410 per credit hour. One-time fee: $50. *Financial support:* In 2019–20, 808 students received support. Teaching assistantships and Federal Work-Study available. *Unit head:* Ron Miller, Dean, 434-592-4986, E-mail: govtdean@liberty.edu. *Application contact:* Jay Bridge, Director of Admissions, 800-424-9595, Fax: 800-628-7977, E-mail: gradadmissions@liberty.edu.
Website: https://www.liberty.edu/government/

Liberty University, School of Divinity, Lynchburg, VA 24515. Offers Biblical exposition (MA); Biblical languages (M Div); Biblical studies (M Div, MA, MAR, Th M, D Min); chaplaincy (M Div, D Min); Christian apologetics (M Div, MA, MAR, Th M); Christian leadership and church ministries (M Div); Christian ministries (M Div); Christian ministry (MA); Christian thought (M Div); church history (M Div, MAR, Th M); community chaplaincy (M Div, MAR); discipleship (D Min); discipleship and church ministry (M Div, MAR, MCM); evangelism and church planting (MAR, MCM, D Min); expository preaching (D Min); global ministry (MA); global studies (M Div, MAR, MCM, MGS, Th M); healthcare chaplaincy (M Div); homiletics (M Div, MAR, Th M); leadership (M Div, MAR); marketplace chaplaincy (M Div, MCM); ministry leadership (Ed D); pastoral counseling (M Div, MA, MAR, D Min), including addictions and recovery (MA), crisis response and trauma (MA), discipleship and church ministries (MA), leadership (MA), life coaching (MA), marketplace chaplaincy (MA), marriage and family (MA), military resilience (MA), pastoral counseling (MA); pastoral leadership (D Min); pastoral ministries (M Div, M Serv Soc, MCM); religious education (MRE); sports chaplaincy (MA); theology (M Div, MAR, MTS, Th M); theology and apologetics (D Min, PhD); worship (M Div, MAR, MCM, D Min); youth and family ministries (M Div). *Program availability:* Part-time, online learning. *Students:* 2,691 full-time (814 women), 2,570 part-time (732 women); includes 1,484 minority (1,046 Black or African American, non-Hispanic/Latino; 33 American Indian or Alaska Native, non-Hispanic/Latino; 120 Asian, non-Hispanic/Latino; 167 Hispanic/Latino; 8 Native Hawaiian or other Pacific Islander, non-Hispanic/Latino; 110 Two or more races, non-Hispanic/Latino), 101 international. Average age 43. 4,508 applicants, 34% accepted, 952 enrolled. In 2019, 1,251 master's, 71 doctorates awarded. *Degree requirements:* For master's, 2 foreign languages, thesis (for some programs); for doctorate, 2 foreign languages, thesis/dissertation. *Entrance requirements:* For master's, minimum undergraduate GPA of 2.0; for doctorate, GRE General Test or MAT, minimum graduate GPA of 3.0. Additional exam requirements/recommendations for international students: required—TOEFL (minimum score 600 paper-based; 100 iBT). *Application deadline:* For fall admission, 6/1 for domestic students; for spring admission, 11/1 for domestic students. Applications are processed on a rolling basis. Application fee: $50. Electronic applications accepted. *Expenses:* Contact institution. *Financial support:* Teaching assistantships with tuition reimbursements, career-related internships or fieldwork, and Federal Work-Study available. Financial award applicants required to submit FAFSA. *Unit head:* Dr. Troy Temple, Interim Dean, School of Divinity, E-mail: divinity@liberty.edu. *Application contact:* Jay Bridge, Director of Graduate Admissions, 800-424-9595, Fax: 800-628-7977, E-mail: gradadmissions@liberty.edu.
Website: https://www.liberty.edu/divinity/

Lipscomb University, Program in Organizational Leadership, Nashville, TN 37204-3951. Offers aging services leadership (Certificate); global leadership (Certificate); organizational leadership (MPS); performance coaching (Certificate); strategic leadership (Certificate). *Program availability:* Part-time, online only, blended/hybrid learning. *Entrance requirements:* For master's, GRE or GMAT, two references, resume, interview. Additional exam requirements/recommendations for international students: required—TOEFL (minimum score 550 paper-based). Electronic applications accepted. *Expenses:* Contact institution.

London Metropolitan University, Graduate Programs, London, United Kingdom. Offers applied psychology (M Sc); architecture (MA); biomedical science (M Sc); blood science (M Sc); cancer pharmacology (M Sc); computer networking and cyber security (M Sc); computing and information systems (M Sc); conference interpreting (MA); counter-terrorism studies (M Sc); creative, digital and professional writing (MA); crime, violence and prevention (M Sc); criminology (M Sc); curating contemporary art (MA); data analytics (M Sc); digital media (MA); early childhood studies (MA); education (MA, Ed D); financial services law, regulation and compliance (LL M); food science (M Sc); forensic psychology (M Sc); health and social care management and policy (M Sc); human nutrition (M Sc); human resource management (MA); human rights and international conflict (MA); information technology (M Sc); intelligence and security studies (M Sc); international oil, gas and energy law (LL M); international relations (MA); interpreting (MA); learning and teaching in higher education (MA); legal practice (LL M); media and entertainment law (LL M); organizational and consumer psychology (M Sc); psychological therapy (M Sc); psychology of mental health (M Sc); public health (M Sc);

public policy and management (MPA); security studies (M Sc); social work (M Sc); spatial planning and urban design (MA); sports therapy (M Sc); supporting older children and young people with dyslexia (MA); teaching languages (MA), including Arabic, English; translation (MA); woman and child abuse (MA).

Marquette University, Graduate School, College of Arts and Sciences, Department of History, Milwaukee, WI 53201-1881. Offers European history (MA, PhD); global studies (MA); United States history (MA, PhD). *Program availability:* Part-time. *Degree requirements:* For master's, comprehensive exam, essay, 2 classes of research seminars (6 hours); for doctorate, one foreign language, comprehensive exam, thesis/dissertation, 2 research seminars, dissertation seminar. *Entrance requirements:* For master's, GRE General Test, official transcripts from all current and previous colleges/universities except Marquette, one-page statement of purpose, three letters of recommendation from former teachers; for doctorate, GRE General Test, official transcripts from all current and previous colleges/universities except Marquette, one-page statement of purpose, three letters of recommendation from former teachers, writing sample. Additional exam requirements/recommendations for international students: required—TOEFL. Electronic applications accepted.

Marquette University, Graduate School, College of Arts and Sciences, Department of Political Science, Milwaukee, WI 53201-1881. Offers international affairs (MA); political science (MA); public service (MA); JD/MA; MA/MBA. *Program availability:* Part-time. *Degree requirements:* For master's, comprehensive exam, thesis optional. *Entrance requirements:* For master's, GRE General Test, official transcripts from all current and previous colleges/universities except Marquette, three letters of recommendation, statement of purpose. Additional exam requirements/recommendations for international students: required—TOEFL (minimum score 530 paper-based). Electronic applications accepted.

McMaster University, School of Graduate Studies, Faculty of Social Sciences, Department of Political Science, Hamilton, ON L8S 4M2, Canada. Offers international relations (PhD); political science (MA); public and the global economy (MA); public policy (PhD); public policy and administration (MA). *Program availability:* Part-time. *Degree requirements:* For master's, thesis or alternative. *Entrance requirements:* For master's, minimum B+ average. Additional exam requirements/recommendations for international students: required—TOEFL (minimum score 580 paper-based).

McMaster University, School of Graduate Studies, Faculty of Social Sciences and Faculty of Humanities, Institute on Globalization and the Human Condition, Hamilton, ON L8S 4M2, Canada. Offers globalization studies (MA).

Middlebury Institute of International Studies at Monterey, Graduate School of International Policy and Management, Program in International Policy and Development, Monterey, CA 93940-2691. Offers MA. *Degree requirements:* For master's, one foreign language. *Entrance requirements:* For master's, minimum GPA of 3.0, proficiency in a foreign language. Additional exam requirements/recommendations for international students: required—TOEFL (minimum score 550 paper-based; 80 iBT). Electronic applications accepted.

Middle Tennessee State University, College of Graduate Studies, College of Liberal Arts, Department of Political Science, Murfreesboro, TN 37132. Offers international affairs (MA). *Program availability:* Part-time, evening/weekend, online learning. *Entrance requirements:* Additional exam requirements/recommendations for international students: required—TOEFL (minimum score 525 paper-based; 71 iBT) or IELTS (minimum score 6). Electronic applications accepted.

Missouri State University, Graduate College, College of Humanities and Public Affairs, Department of Political Science, Program in Global Studies, Springfield, MO 65897. Offers MGS. *Program availability:* Part-time. *Degree requirements:* For master's, 2 foreign languages, comprehensive exam, thesis or alternative. *Entrance requirements:* For master's, GRE, minimum GPA of 3.0. Additional exam requirements/recommendations for international students: required—TOEFL (minimum score 550 paper-based; 79 iBT), IELTS (minimum score 6). Electronic applications accepted. *Expenses: Tuition, area resident:* Full-time $2600; part-time $1735 per credit hour. Tuition, nonresident: full-time $5240; part-time $3495 per credit hour. *International tuition:* $5240 full-time. *Required fees:* $530; $438 per credit hour. Tuition and fees vary according to class time, course level, course load, degree level, campus/location and program.

Morgan State University, School of Graduate Studies, James H. Gilliam Jr College of Liberal Arts, Department of World Languages and International Studies, Baltimore, MD 21251. Offers international studies (MA). *Program availability:* Part-time, evening/weekend. *Faculty:* 2 full-time (both women), 9 part-time/adjunct (4 women). *Students:* 4 full-time (1 woman), 2 part-time (1 woman); includes 3 minority (1 Black or African American, non-Hispanic/Latino; 1 Hispanic/Latino; 1 Two or more races, non-Hispanic/Latino), 3 international. Average age 26. 2 applicants, 100% accepted, 2 enrolled. In 2019, 2 master's awarded. *Degree requirements:* For master's, one foreign language, comprehensive exam, thesis. *Entrance requirements:* For master's, GRE, Minimum GPA 3.0. Additional exam requirements/recommendations for international students: required—TOEFL (minimum score 550 paper-based; 70 iBT), IELTS (minimum score 6). *Application deadline:* For fall admission, 2/1 priority date for domestic students, 4/1 for international students; for spring admission, 11/15 for domestic students, 10/1 for international students. Applications are processed on a rolling basis. Application fee: $50 ($70 for international students). Electronic applications accepted. *Expenses:* Tuition, state resident: full-time $455; part-time $455 per credit hour. Tuition, nonresident: full-time $894; part-time $894 per credit hour. *Required fees:* $82; $82 per credit hour. *Financial support:* Fellowships with full and partial tuition reimbursements, research assistantships with full and partial tuition reimbursements, teaching assistantships with full and partial tuition reimbursements, career-related internships or fieldwork, Federal Work-Study, scholarships/grants, tuition waivers (full and partial), and unspecified assistantships available. Support available to part-time students. Financial award application deadline: 2/1. *Unit head:* Dr. Helen Harrison, Interim Department Chair, 443-885-3185, E-mail: helen.harrison@morgan.edu. *Application contact:* Dr. Jahmaine Smith, Director of Admission, 443-885-3185, Fax: 443-885-8226, E-mail: gradapply@morgan.edu.

New England College, Program in Management, Henniker, NH 03242-3293. Offers accounting (MSA); healthcare administration (MS); international relations (MA); marketing management (MS); nonprofit leadership (MS); project management (MS); strategic leadership (MS). *Program availability:* Part-time, evening/weekend. *Degree requirements:* For master's, independent research project. Electronic applications accepted.

The New School, Schools of Public Engagement, Program in International Affairs, New York, NY 10011. Offers cities and social justice (MA); conflict and security (MA); development (MA); governance and rights (MA); international affairs (MS); media and culture (MA). *Program availability:* Part-time. *Faculty:* 13 full-time, 16 part-time/adjunct. *Students:* 82 full-time (66 women), 31 part-time (21 women); includes 33 minority (11 Black or African American, non-Hispanic/Latino; 5 Asian, non-Hispanic/Latino; 13 Hispanic/Latino; 4 Two or more races, non-Hispanic/Latino), 34 international. Average age 28. 156 applicants, 97% accepted, 43 enrolled. In 2019, 68 master's awarded. *Degree requirements:* For master's, thesis or alternative, capstone project. *Entrance requirements:* For master's, academic writing sample, two letters of recommendation, statement of purpose, resume, transcripts. Additional exam requirements/recommendations for international students: required—TOEFL (minimum score 92 iBT), IELTS (minimum score 7), PTE (minimum score 68). *Application deadline:* For fall admission, 1/15 priority date for domestic and international students; for spring admission, 10/15 priority date for domestic and international students. Applications are processed on a rolling basis. Application fee: $50. Electronic applications accepted. *Expenses:* 1710 per credit. *Financial support:* In 2019–20, 97 students received support, including 6 research assistantships (averaging $5,449 per year), 2 teaching assistantships (averaging $5,618 per year); career-related internships or fieldwork, Federal Work-Study, scholarships/grants, and unspecified assistantships also available. Support available to part-time students. Financial award application deadline: 2/1; financial award applicants required to submit FAFSA. *Unit head:* Sakiko Fukuda-Parr, 206-3524 Ext. 2343. *Application contact:* Merida Gasbarro, Director of Graduate Admission, 212-229-5600 Ext. 1108, E-mail: escandom@newschool.edu.
Website: https://www.newschool.edu/public-engagement/ma-ms-international-affairs/

New York University, Graduate School of Arts and Science, Department of Politics, New York, NY 10012-1019. Offers political campaign management (MA); politics (MA, PhD); JD/MA; MBA/MA. *Program availability:* Part-time. Terminal master's awarded for partial completion of doctoral program. *Degree requirements:* For master's, one foreign language, thesis or alternative; for doctorate, 2 foreign languages, comprehensive exam, thesis/dissertation. *Entrance requirements:* For master's and doctorate, GRE General Test. Additional exam requirements/recommendations for international students: required—TOEFL, IELTS.

New York University, School of Professional Studies, Center for Global Affairs, New York, NY 10012-1019. Offers global affairs (MS), including private sector. *Program availability:* Part-time, evening/weekend. *Degree requirements:* For master's, thesis. *Entrance requirements:* For master's, GRE or GMAT (only upon request), bachelor's degree, resume with relevant professional work, internship or volunteer experience, 2 letters of recommendation, personal statement. Additional exam requirements/recommendations for international students: required—TOEFL (minimum score 600 paper-based; 100 iBT), IELTS (minimum score 7). Electronic applications accepted. *Expenses:* Contact institution.

North Carolina State University, Graduate School, College of Humanities and Social Sciences, School of Public and International Affairs, Program in International Studies, Raleigh, NC 27695. Offers MIS. *Degree requirements:* For master's, thesis optional. *Entrance requirements:* For master's, GRE General Test, minimum GPA of 3.0 during previous 2 years. Electronic applications accepted.

Northeastern University, College of Professional Studies, Boston, MA 02115-5096. Offers applied nutrition (MS); college athletics administration (MSL); commerce and economic development (MS); corporate and organizational communication (MS); criminal justice (MS); digital media (MPS); elearning and instructional design (M Ed); elementary education (MAT); geographic information technology (MPS); global studies and international relations (MS); higher education administration (M Ed); homeland security (MA); human services (MS); informatics (MPS); leadership (MS); learning analytics (M Ed); learning and instruction (M Ed); nonprofit management (MS); professional sports administration (MSL); project management (MS); regulatory affairs for drugs, biologics, and medical devices (MS); respiratory care leadership (MS); special education (M Ed); technical communication (MS). *Program availability:* Part-time, evening/weekend, 100% online, blended/hybrid learning. *Faculty:* 85 full-time (53 women), 892 part-time/adjunct (379 women). *Students:* 5,699 part-time (3,305 women). In 2019, 1,787 master's awarded. *Application deadline:* Applications are processed on a rolling basis. Application fee: $0. Electronic applications accepted. *Expenses:* Contact institution. *Financial support:* Applicants required to submit FAFSA. *Unit head:* Dr. Mary Loeffelholz, Dean of the College of Professional Studies, 617-373-6060. *Application contact:* Dr. Mary Loeffelholz, Dean of the College of Professional Studies, 617-373-6060.
Website: https://cps.northeastern.edu/

Northeastern University, College of Social Sciences and Humanities, Boston, MA 02115. Offers criminology and criminal justice (MSCJ); criminology and justice policy (PhD); economics (MA, PhD); English (MA, PhD); international affairs (MA); law and public policy (PhD); political science (MA, PhD); public administration (MPA); public policy (MPP); security and resilience studies (MS); sociology (MA, PhD); urban and regional policy (MS); urban informatics (MS); world history (MA, PhD). *Program availability:* Online learning. *Degree requirements:* For doctorate, variable foreign language requirement, comprehensive exam, thesis/dissertation. *Entrance requirements:* For master's and doctorate, GRE. Additional exam requirements/recommendations for international students: required—TOEFL, IELTS. Electronic applications accepted. *Expenses:* Contact institution.

Northwestern University, The Graduate School, Center for International and Comparative Studies, Evanston, IL 60208. Offers Certificate.

Northwestern University, Pritzker School of Law, Chicago, IL 60611-3069. Offers international human rights (LL M); law (MSL, JD); tax (LL M in Tax); JD/LL M; JD/MBA; JD/PhD; LL M/Certificate. *Accreditation:* ABA. *Program availability:* Part-time, online learning. *Entrance requirements:* For master's, law degree or equivalent, letter of recommendation, resume; for doctorate, LSAT, 1 letter of recommendation, resume. Additional exam requirements/recommendations for international students: required—TOEFL. Electronic applications accepted. *Expenses:* Contact institution.

Norwich University, College of Graduate and Continuing Studies, Master of Arts in Diplomacy Program, Northfield, VT 05663. Offers diplomacy (MA), including cyber diplomacy - policy, cyber diplomacy - technical, international commerce, international conflict management, international terrorism. *Program availability:* Evening/weekend, online only, mostly all online with a week-long residency requirement. *Degree requirements:* For master's, comprehensive exam, thesis optional. *Entrance requirements:* For master's, minimum undergraduate GPA of 2.75. Additional exam requirements/recommendations for international students: required—TOEFL (minimum score 550 paper-based; 80 iBT), IELTS (minimum score 6.5). Electronic applications accepted. *Expenses:* Contact institution.

Norwich University, College of Graduate and Continuing Studies, Master of Arts in International Relations Program, Northfield, VT 05663. Offers international relations (MA), including cyber diplomacy-policy, cyber diplomacy-technical, international development, international security, national security, regions of the world. *Program availability:* Evening/weekend, online only, mostly all online with a week-long residency requirement. *Degree requirements:* For master's, research paper. *Entrance requirements:* For master's, minimum undergraduate GPA of 2.75. Additional exam requirements/recommendations for international students: required—TOEFL (minimum score 550 paper-based; 80 iBT), IELTS (minimum score 6.5). Electronic applications accepted. *Expenses:* Contact institution.

Ohio University, Graduate College, Center for International Studies, Program in Communications and Development Studies, Athens, OH 45701-2979. Offers MA. *Program availability:* Part-time. *Degree requirements:* For master's, one foreign language, thesis optional, internship. *Entrance requirements:* For master's, minimum

GPA of 3.0. Additional exam requirements/recommendations for international students: required—TOEFL (minimum score 550 paper-based; 80 iBT), IELTS (minimum score 6.5). Electronic applications accepted.

Oklahoma State University, Graduate College, Stillwater, OK 74078. Offers aerospace security (Graduate Certificate); bioenergy and sustainable technology (Graduate Certificate); business data mining (Graduate Certificate); business sustainability (Graduate Certificate); environmental science (MS); international studies (MS); non-profit management (Graduate Certificate); teaching English to speakers of other languages (Graduate Certificate); telecommunications management (MS). *Students:* 32 full-time (22 women), 203 part-time (114 women); includes 63 minority (12 Black or African American, non-Hispanic/Latino; 19 American Indian or Alaska Native, non-Hispanic/Latino; 12 Asian, non-Hispanic/Latino; 8 Hispanic/Latino; 12 Two or more races, non-Hispanic/Latino), 38 international. Average age 34. 301 applicants, 83% accepted, 173 enrolled. In 2019, 26 master's, 2 doctorates awarded. *Degree requirements:* For master's, thesis (for some programs); for doctorate, comprehensive exam, thesis/dissertation. *Entrance requirements:* For master's and doctorate, GRE or GMAT. Additional exam requirements/recommendations for international students: required—TOEFL (minimum score 550 paper-based; 79 iBT). *Application deadline:* For fall admission, 3/1 priority date for domestic and international students; for spring admission, 8/1 priority date for domestic and international students. Applications are processed on a rolling basis. Application fee: $50 ($75 for international students). Electronic applications accepted. *Expenses: Tuition, area resident:* Full-time $4148.10; part-time $2765.40 per credit hour. Tuition, state resident: full-time $4148.10; part-time $2765.40 per credit hour. Tuition, nonresident: full-time $15,775; part-time $10,516.80 per credit hour. *International tuition:* $15,775.20 full-time. *Required fees:* $2196.90; $122.05 per credit hour. Tuition and fees vary according to course load, campus/location and program. *Financial support:* Research assistantships, career-related internships or fieldwork, Federal Work-Study, scholarships/grants, health care benefits, tuition waivers (partial), and unspecified assistantships available. Support available to part-time students. Financial award application deadline: 3/1; financial award applicants required to submit FAFSA. *Unit head:* Dr. Sheryl Tucker, Dean, 405-744-6368, Fax: 405-744-0355, E-mail: gradi@okstate.edu. *Application contact:* Dr. Sheryl Tucker, Dean, 405-744-6368, Fax: 405-744-0355, E-mail: gradi@okstate.edu. Website: http://gradcollege.okstate.edu/

Old Dominion University, College of Arts and Letters, Graduate Program in International Studies, Norfolk, VA 23529. Offers conflict and cooperation (MA, PhD); interdependence and transnationalism (MA, PhD); international cultural studies (MA, PhD); international political economy and development (MA, PhD); modeling and simulation (MA, PhD); U.S. foreign policy and international relations (MA, PhD). *Program availability:* Part-time. Terminal master's awarded for partial completion of doctoral program. *Degree requirements:* For master's, one foreign language, comprehensive exam, thesis optional; for doctorate, one foreign language, comprehensive exam, thesis/dissertation. *Entrance requirements:* For master's, GRE General Test, sample of written work, 2 letters of recommendation; for doctorate, GRE General Test, sample of written work, 3 letters of recommendation. Additional exam requirements/recommendations for international students: required—TOEFL (minimum score 570 paper-based). Electronic applications accepted. *Expenses:* Contact institution.

Penn State University Park, Graduate School, School of International Affairs, University Park, PA 16802. Offers MIA. *Program availability:* Part-time, evening/weekend. *Entrance requirements:* Additional exam requirements/recommendations for international students: required—TOEFL (minimum score 550 paper-based; 80 iBT), IELTS. Electronic applications accepted. *Expenses:* Contact institution.

Pepperdine University, School of Public Policy, Malibu, CA 90263. Offers American politics (MPP); economics (MPP); international relations (MPP); state and local policy (MPP); JD/MPP; MBA/MPP; MDR/MPP. *Entrance requirements:* For master's, GRE or GMAT or LSAT, transcripts, 2 letters of recommendation, resume, two essays. Additional exam requirements/recommendations for international students: required—TOEFL (minimum score 95 iBT), IELTS (minimum score 7). Electronic applications accepted. *Expenses:* Contact institution.

Pontificia Universidad Catolica Madre y Maestra, Graduate School, Faculty of Social and Administrative Sciences, Santiago, Dominican Republic. Offers business administration (MBA), including business development, finance, international business, management skills (M Mgmt, MBA), marketing, operations, strategic cost management, strategy, tourist destination planning and management; law (LL M), including civil law, corporate business law, criminal law, international relations, real estate law; management (M Mgmt), including higher financial management, insurance program administration, management skills (M Mgmt, MBA); psychology (MA), including clinical child and adolescent psychology, forensic psychology; strategic human resources (EMBA).

Portland State University, Graduate Studies, College of Urban and Public Affairs, Hatfield School of Government, Department of Political Science, Portland, OR 97207-0751. Offers political science (MA), including American politics, comparative politics, international relations, political theory. *Program availability:* Part-time. *Faculty:* 12 full-time (4 women), 4 part-time/adjunct (1 woman). *Students:* 6 full-time (2 women), 9 part-time (3 women); includes 1 minority (Two or more races, non-Hispanic/Latino), 2 international. Average age 35. 11 applicants, 73% accepted, 4 enrolled. In 2019, 2 master's awarded. *Degree requirements:* For master's, variable foreign language requirement, comprehensive exam, thesis. *Entrance requirements:* For master's, GRE General Test, minimum undergraduate GPA of 3.0 or 3.1 in graduate-level coursework, 2 letters of recommendation, statement of intent. Additional exam requirements/recommendations for international students: required—TOEFL (minimum score 550 paper-based; 90 iBT). *Application deadline:* For fall admission, 2/1 priority date for domestic and international students. Application fee: $65. Electronic applications accepted. *Expenses: Tuition, area resident:* Full-time $13,020; part-time $6510 per year. Tuition, state resident: full-time $13,020; part-time $6510 per year. Tuition, nonresident: full-time $19,830; part-time $9915 per year. *International tuition:* $19,830 full-time. *Required fees:* $1226. One-time fee: $350. Tuition and fees vary according to course load, program and reciprocity agreements. *Financial support:* In 2019–20, 3 teaching assistantships with full and partial tuition reimbursements (averaging $7,209 per year) were awarded; research assistantships, career-related internships or fieldwork, and Federal Work-Study also available. Support available to part-time students. Financial award application deadline: 3/1; financial award applicants required to submit FAFSA. *Unit head:* Melody Valdini, Chair, 503-725-5139, Fax: 503-725-8444, E-mail: mev@pdx.edu. *Application contact:* Dr. David Kinsella, Graduate Committee Chair, 503-725-3035, E-mail: kinsella@pdx.edu. Website: https://www.pdx.edu/hatfieldschool/political-science

Princeton University, Graduate School, Woodrow Wilson School of Public and International Affairs, Princeton, NJ 08544-1019. Offers public affairs (MPA, PhD); public policy (MPP); JD/MPA. Terminal master's awarded for partial completion of doctoral program. *Degree requirements:* For master's, internship; for doctorate, one foreign language, thesis/dissertation. *Entrance requirements:* For master's, GRE General Test, original policy memo; for doctorate, GRE General Test. Additional exam requirements/

recommendations for international students: required—TOEFL (minimum score 600 paper-based). Electronic applications accepted.

Queen's University at Kingston, School of Graduate Studies, Faculty of Arts and Science, Department of Political Studies, Kingston, ON K7L 3N6, Canada. Offers Canadian politics (MA, PhD); comparative politics (MA, PhD); gender and politics (MA, PhD); international relations (MA, PhD); political theory (MA, PhD). *Degree requirements:* For master's, thesis or alternative; for doctorate, one foreign language, thesis/dissertation, qualifying exams. *Entrance requirements:* Additional exam requirements/recommendations for international students: required—TOEFL (minimum score 600 paper-based).

Regent's University London, Webster Graduate School, London, United Kingdom. Offers business (MBA); finance (MS); human resources (MA); information technology management (MA); international business (MA); international non-governmental organizations (MA); international relations (MA); management and leadership (MA); marketing (MA). *Program availability:* Part-time.

Regent University, Graduate School, Robertson School of Government, Virginia Beach, VA 23464. Offers government (MA), including American government, healthcare policy and ethics (MA, MPA), international relations, law and public policy, national security studies, political communication, political theory, religion and politics; national security studies (MA), including cybersecurity, homeland security, international security, Middle East politics; public administration (MPA), including emergency management and homeland security, federal government, general public administration, healthcare policy and ethics (MA, MPA), law, nonprofit administration and faith-based organizations, public leadership and management, servant leadership. *Program availability:* Part-time, evening/weekend, 100% online, blended/hybrid learning. *Faculty:* 5 full-time (1 woman), 19 part-time/adjunct (2 women). *Students:* 36 full-time (22 women), 159 part-time (89 women); includes 82 minority (52 Black or African American, non-Hispanic/Latino; 2 American Indian or Alaska Native, non-Hispanic/Latino; 2 Asian, non-Hispanic/Latino; 23 Hispanic/Latino; 3 Two or more races, non-Hispanic/Latino), 4 international. Average age 36. 181 applicants, 70% accepted, 75 enrolled. In 2019, 58 master's awarded. *Degree requirements:* For master's, thesis optional, internship. *Entrance requirements:* For master's, GRE General Test or LSAT, personal essay, writing sample, resume, college transcripts. Additional exam requirements/recommendations for international students: required—TOEFL (minimum score 577 paper-based). *Application deadline:* For fall admission, 5/1 priority date for domestic students; for spring admission, 11/1 priority date for domestic students. Applications are processed on a rolling basis. Application fee: $50. Electronic applications accepted. *Expenses:* Contact institution. *Financial support:* In 2019–20, 132 students received support. Career-related internships or fieldwork, scholarships/grants, and unspecified assistantships available. Support available to part-time students. Financial award applicants required to submit FAFSA. *Unit head:* Dr. Stephen Perry, Interim Dean, 757-352-4082, E-mail: sperry@regent.edu. *Application contact:* Heidi Cece, Assistant Vice President for Enrollment Management, 800-373-5504, Fax: 757-352-4381, E-mail: admissions@regent.edu. Website: https://www.regent.edu/robertson-school-of-government/

Richmond, The American International University in London, MA in International Relations Program, Richmond, United Kingdom. Offers MA. *Program availability:* Part-time. *Entrance requirements:* Additional exam requirements/recommendations for international students: required—TOEFL, IELTS. Electronic applications accepted.

Rutgers University - Camden, Graduate School of Arts and Sciences, Department of Public Policy and Administration, Camden, NJ 08102. Offers education policy and leadership (MPA); international public service and development (MPA); public management (MPA); JD/MPA; MPA/MA. *Accreditation:* NASPAA. *Program availability:* Part-time, evening/weekend. *Degree requirements:* For master's, directed study, research workshop, 42 credits. *Entrance requirements:* For master's, GRE General Test, GMAT or LSAT, 3 letters of recommendation; resume. Additional exam requirements/recommendations for international students: required—TOEFL (minimum score 550 paper-based), IELTS. Electronic applications accepted.

Rutgers University - Newark, Graduate School, Division of Global Affairs, Newark, NJ 07102. Offers MS, PhD. *Program availability:* Part-time, evening/weekend. *Degree requirements:* For master's, one foreign language, thesis optional. *Entrance requirements:* For master's and doctorate, GRE General Test, minimum B average. Electronic applications accepted.

Rutgers University - Newark, Graduate School, Program in Political Science, Newark, NJ 07102. Offers American political system (MA); international relations (MA); JD/MA. *Program availability:* Part-time, evening/weekend. *Degree requirements:* For master's, comprehensive exam, thesis optional. *Entrance requirements:* For master's, GRE, minimum undergraduate B average. Electronic applications accepted.

Rutgers University - New Brunswick, Graduate School-New Brunswick, Department of Political Science, Piscataway, NJ 08854-8097. Offers American politics (PhD); comparative politics (PhD); international relations (PhD); political theory (PhD); public law (PhD); United Nations and global policy studies (MA); women and politics (PhD). *Degree requirements:* For doctorate, one foreign language, comprehensive exam, thesis/dissertation. *Entrance requirements:* For master's, bachelor's degree from accredited U.S. college or university or a comparable institution in another country; for doctorate, GRE General Test. Additional exam requirements/recommendations for international students: required—TOEFL.

Rutgers University - New Brunswick, Graduate School-New Brunswick, Program in Global and Comparative History, New Brunswick, NJ 08901. Offers MA. *Entrance requirements:* For master's, GRE, minimum GPA of 3.0, official transcripts, two letters of recommendation, 1-2 page personal statement, 10-15 page writing sample. Electronic applications accepted.

St. Mary's University, Graduate Studies, Program in International Relations, San Antonio, TX 78228. Offers conflict transformation (Certificate); international conflict resolution (MA); international development (MA); international relations (MA); security policy (MA); JD/MA. *Program availability:* Part-time, evening/weekend, 100% online. *Degree requirements:* For master's, one foreign language, comprehensive exam (for some programs), thesis (for some programs), thesis or comprehensive exam. *Entrance requirements:* For master's, minimum undergraduate cumulative GPA of 3.0. Additional exam requirements/recommendations for international students: required—TOEFL (minimum score 550 paper-based; 80 iBT), IELTS (minimum score 6). Electronic applications accepted.

Salve Regina University, Program in International Relations, Newport, RI 02840-4192. Offers MA, PhD, CGS. *Program availability:* Part-time, evening/weekend, online learning. *Entrance requirements:* For master's, GMAT, GRE General Test, MAT or LSAT. Additional exam requirements/recommendations for international students: required—TOEFL (minimum score 600 paper-based; 100 iBT) or IELTS. Electronic applications accepted.

San Francisco State University, Division of Graduate Studies, College of Liberal and Creative Arts, Department of International Relations, San Francisco, CA 94132-1722. Offers MA. *Expenses: Tuition, area resident:* Full-time $7176; part-time $4164 per year.

International Affairs

Tuition, state resident: full-time $7176; part-time $4164 per year. Tuition, nonresident: full-time $16,680; part-time $396 per unit. *International tuition:* $16,680 full-time. *Required fees:* $1524; $1524 per unit. $762 per semester. Tuition and fees vary according to degree level and program. *Unit head:* Dr. Mahmood Monshipouri, Chair, 415-338-2239, Fax: 415-338-6159, E-mail: mmonship@sfsu.edu. *Application contact:* Dr. Juanita Darling, Graduate Coordinator, 415-405-3492, Fax: 415-338-6159, E-mail: juanitad@sfsu.edu.
Website: http://internationalrelations.sfsu.edu/

Schiller International University - Paris, Program in International Relations and Diplomacy, Paris, France. Offers MA. *Program availability:* Part-time, evening/weekend. *Degree requirements:* For master's, one foreign language, final comprehensive exam or thesis. *Entrance requirements:* For master's, undergraduate mathematics (strongly advised). Additional exam requirements/recommendations for international students: required—TOEFL (minimum score 550 paper-based).

Seton Hall University, School of Diplomacy and International Relations, South Orange, NJ 07079-2697. Offers diplomacy and international relations (MA); global health management (Graduate Certificate); post-conflict state reconstruction and sustainability (Graduate Certificate); United Nations studies (Graduate Certificate); JD/MA; MA/MA; MBA/MA; MPA/MA. *Program availability:* Part-time, evening/weekend, 100% online, blended/hybrid learning. *Degree requirements:* For master's, thesis (for some programs), 45 credits; for Graduate Certificate, 15 credits. *Entrance requirements:* For master's, GRE, GMAT, or LSAT. Additional exam requirements/recommendations for international students: required—TOEFL. Electronic applications accepted. *Expenses:* Contact institution.

Simon Fraser University, Office of Graduate Studies and Postdoctoral Fellows, Faculty of Arts and Social Sciences, School for International Studies, Burnaby, BC V5A 1S6, Canada. Offers MA. *Entrance requirements:* Additional exam requirements/ recommendations for international students: required—TOEFL (minimum score 580 paper-based; 93 iBT), IELTS (minimum score 7), TWE (minimum score 5). Electronic applications accepted.

SIT Graduate Institute, Graduate Programs, Master's Programs in Intercultural Service, Leadership, and Management, Brattleboro, VT 05302-0676. Offers intercultural service, leadership, and management (self-designed) (MA); international education (MA); peace and justice leadership (MA); sustainable development (MA). *Program availability:* Online learning. *Degree requirements:* For master's, one foreign language, thesis. *Entrance requirements:* For master's, 3 letters of reference. Additional exam requirements/recommendations for international students: required—TOEFL, IELTS. *Expenses:* Tuition: Full-time $43,500; part-time $21,750 per credit.

Syracuse University, Maxwell School of Citizenship and Public Affairs, Dual MA Program in Economics and International Relations, Syracuse, NY 13244. Offers MA/MA. *Entrance requirements:* Additional exam requirements/recommendations for international students: required—TOEFL (minimum score 100 iBT). Electronic applications accepted.

Syracuse University, Maxwell School of Citizenship and Public Affairs, Dual MPA/IR Program in Public Administration and International Relations, Syracuse, NY 13244. Offers MPA/MA. *Entrance requirements:* Additional exam requirements/ recommendations for international students: required—TOEFL (minimum score 100 iBT). Electronic applications accepted.

Syracuse University, Maxwell School of Citizenship and Public Affairs, EMIR Program of International Relations, Syracuse, NY 13244. Offers EMIR. *Program availability:* Part-time. *Entrance requirements:* For master's, resume, personal statement, official transcripts, three letters of recommendation, proof of competence in a second language. Additional exam requirements/recommendations for international students: required—TOEFL (minimum score 100 iBT). Electronic applications accepted.

Syracuse University, Maxwell School of Citizenship and Public Affairs, MA/MS Program in Public Diplomacy, Syracuse, NY 13244. Offers MS/MA. *Entrance requirements:* Additional exam requirements/recommendations for international students: required—TOEFL (minimum score 100 iBT). Electronic applications accepted.

Syracuse University, Maxwell School of Citizenship and Public Affairs, MA Program in International Relations, Syracuse, NY 13244. Offers MA. *Program availability:* Part-time, evening/weekend. *Entrance requirements:* For master's, GRE General Test, resume, personal statement, three letters of recommendation, official transcripts. Additional exam requirements/recommendations for international students: required—TOEFL (minimum score 100 iBT). Electronic applications accepted.

Teachers College, Columbia University, Department of Arts and Humanities, New York, NY 10027. Offers applied linguistics (MA, Ed D); art and art education (Ed M, MA, Ed D, Ed DCT); arts administration (MA); bilingual and bicultural education (MA); global competence (Certificate); history and education (Ed D, PhD); music and music education (Ed DCT); philosophy and education (MA, Ed D, PhD); social studies education (Ed M, PhD); teaching English to speakers of other languages (Ed M); teaching of English and English education (Ed M, MA, Ed D, PhD), including English education (Ed M, Ed D, PhD), teaching of English (MA); teaching of social studies (MA); TESOL (MA, Ed D). *Faculty:* 26 full-time (17 women). *Students:* 426 full-time (358 women), 390 part-time (259 women); includes 222 minority (44 Black or African American, non-Hispanic/Latino; 2 American Indian or Alaska Native, non-Hispanic/Latino; 94 Asian, non-Hispanic/Latino; 65 Hispanic/Latino; 17 Two or more races, non-Hispanic/Latino), 252 international. 957 applicants, 66% accepted, 375 enrolled. *Unit head:* Dr. ZhaoHong Han, Department Chair, E-mail: zhh2@tc.columbia.edu. *Application contact:* Kelly Sutton-Skinner, Director of Admissions and New Student Enrollment, 212-678-3710, E-mail: kms2237@tc.columbia.edu.

Texas A&M University, Bush School of Government and Public Service, College Station, TX 77843. Offers international affairs (MIA). *Accreditation:* NASPAA. *Degree requirements:* For master's, summer internship. *Entrance requirements:* For master's, GRE (preferred) or GMAT. Additional exam requirements/recommendations for international students: required—TOEFL (minimum score 550 paper-based; 80 iBT), IELTS (minimum score 6), PTE (minimum score 53). Electronic applications accepted. *Expenses:* Contact institution.

Texas State University, The Graduate College, College of Liberal Arts, Program in International Studies, San Marcos, TX 78666. Offers MA. *Program availability:* Part-time. *Degree requirements:* For master's, comprehensive exam, thesis (for some programs). *Entrance requirements:* For master's, baccalaureate degree from regionally-accredited university, minimum GPA of 3.0 in last 60 hours leading to bachelor's degree, background courses including 6 hours of economics, proficiency in a language other than English (speaking, reading, and oral comprehension), resume, statement of purpose, 2 letters of recommendation. Additional exam requirements/recommendations for international students: required—TOEFL (minimum score 550 paper-based; 78 iBT), IELTS (minimum score 6.5). Electronic applications accepted.

Texas State University, The Graduate College, College of Liberal Arts, Program in Public Administration, San Marcos, TX 78666. Offers international relations (MPA); legal and judicial administration (MPA). *Accreditation:* NASPAA. *Program availability:* Part-time, evening/weekend. *Degree requirements:* For master's, comprehensive exam,

applied research project. *Entrance requirements:* For master's, baccalaureate degree from regionally-accredited university with minimum GPA of 3.0 on last 60 undergraduate semester hours, statement of purpose, 2 letters of recommendation. Additional exam requirements/recommendations for international students: required—TOEFL (minimum score 550 paper-based; 78 iBT), IELTS (minimum score 6.5). Electronic applications accepted.

Troy University, Graduate School, College of Arts and Sciences, Program in International Relations, Troy, AL 36082. Offers MS. *Program availability:* Part-time, evening/weekend, 100% online, blended/hybrid learning. *Faculty:* 12 full-time (2 women), 10 part-time/adjunct (0 women). *Students:* 43 full-time (10 women), 285 part-time (78 women); includes 67 minority (21 Black or African American, non-Hispanic/Latino; 13 Asian, non-Hispanic/Latino; 30 Hispanic/Latino; 3 Two or more races, non-Hispanic/Latino), 6 international. Average age 32. 187 applicants, 96% accepted, 110 enrolled. In 2019, 66 master's awarded. *Degree requirements:* For master's, comprehensive exam (for some programs), thesis (for some programs), comprehensive exam or thesis, minimum GPA of 3.0, admission to candidacy, minimum B grade on research. *Entrance requirements:* For master's, GRE 290 (recommended:150 verbal, 140 quantitative) and GRE writing score. If student has taken the MCAT (recommended: 487), DAT (recommended: 16) or equivalent professional exam, then this may be substituted for the GRE, bachelor's degree; minimum undergraduate GPA of 2.5 or 3.0 on last 30 semester hours. Additional exam requirements/recommendations for international students: required—TOEFL (minimum score 523 paper-based; 70 iBT), IELTS (minimum score 6). *Application deadline:* Applications are processed on a rolling basis. Application fee: $50. Electronic applications accepted. *Expenses:* Tuition, area resident: Full-time $7650; part-time $2550 per semester hour. Tuition, state resident: full-time $7650; part-time $2550 per semester hour. Tuition, nonresident: full-time $15,300; part-time $5100 per semester hour. *International tuition:* $15,300 full-time. *Required fees:* $856; $352 per semester hour. $176 per semester. *Financial support:* In 2019–20, 257 students received support. Fellowships, research assistantships, teaching assistantships, career-related internships or fieldwork, Federal Work-Study, scholarships/grants, traineeships, tuition waivers, and unspecified assistantships available. Support available to part-time students. Financial award application deadline: 3/1; financial award applicants required to submit FAFSA. *Unit head:* Dr. Doug Davis, Director, International Relations, 334-808-6280, Fax: 334-670-5647, E-mail: gddavis@troy.edu. *Application contact:* Haley McKinnon, Director of Graduate Admissions, 334-670-3178, Fax: 334-670-3912, E-mail: hmckinnon@troy.edu. Website: https://www.troy.edu/academics/academic-programs/graduate/international-relations.html?actualpro-International%20Relations%20-%20Global%20Studies%20%2

Tufts University, The Fletcher School of Law and Diplomacy, Medford, MA 02155. Offers economics and public policy (PhD); international affairs (PhD); international business (MIB); international law (LL M); law and diplomacy (MA, MALD); transatlantic affairs (MA); DVM/MA; JD/MALD; MALD/MA; MALD/MBA; MALD/MS; MD/MA. *Program availability:* Online learning. *Degree requirements:* For master's, one foreign language, thesis; for doctorate, one foreign language, comprehensive exam, thesis/dissertation, dissertation defense. *Entrance requirements:* For master's and doctorate, GMAT or GRE General Test. Additional exam requirements/recommendations for international students: required—TOEFL (minimum score 600 paper-based; 100 iBT), IELTS (minimum score 7). Electronic applications accepted. *Expenses:* Contact institution.

Tufts University, Graduate School of Arts and Sciences, Department of History, Medford, MA 02155. Offers history (MA, PhD), including global history (PhD); history and museum studies (MA). Terminal master's awarded for partial completion of doctoral program. *Degree requirements:* For master's, one foreign language, thesis optional; for doctorate, 2 foreign languages, comprehensive exam, thesis/dissertation. *Entrance requirements:* For master's and doctorate, GRE General Test, writing sample. Additional exam requirements/recommendations for international students: required—TOEFL (minimum score 550 paper-based; 80 iBT), IELTS (minimum score 6.5). Electronic applications accepted. *Expenses:* Contact institution.

United States International University–Africa, School of Arts and Sciences, Nairobi, Kenya. Offers counseling psychology (MA), including chemical dependency, health psychology; international relations (MA), including development studies, diplomacy and foreign policy, peace and conflict studies. *Program availability:* Part-time, evening/weekend. *Degree requirements:* For master's, thesis, practicum. *Entrance requirements:* For master's, GRE General Test, 2 letters of recommendation, resume. Additional exam requirements/recommendations for international students: required—TOEFL.

Universidad de las Americas, A.C., Program in International Organizations and Institutions, Mexico City, Mexico. Offers MA.

Universidad Nacional Pedro Henriquez Urena, Graduate School, Santo Domingo, Dominican Republic. Offers agricultural diversity (MS), including horticultural/fruit production, tropical animal production; conservation of monuments and cultural assets (M Arch); ecology and environment (MS); environmental engineering (MEE); international relations (MA); natural resource management (MS); political science (MA); project feasibility (MPM); project management (MPM); project optimization (MPM); sanitation engineering (ME); science for teachers (MS); tropical Caribbean architecture (M Arch).

Université de Montréal, Faculty of Arts and Sciences, Programs in International Studies, Montréal, QC H3C 3J7, Canada. Offers M Sc, DESS.

University of Bridgeport, College of Public and International Affairs, Bridgeport, CT 06604. Offers East Asian and Pacific Rim studies (MA); global development and peace (MA); global media and communication studies (MA). *Program availability:* Part-time, evening/weekend. *Degree requirements:* For master's, thesis. *Entrance requirements:* Additional exam requirements/recommendations for international students: recommended—TOEFL (minimum score 550 paper-based; 80 iBT), IELTS (minimum score 6.5).

The University of British Columbia, Institute of Asian Research, Vancouver, BC V6T 1Z2, Canada. Offers Asia Pacific policy studies (MAAPPS); public policy and global affairs (MPPGA). *Degree requirements:* For master's, thesis optional. *Entrance requirements:* Additional exam requirements/recommendations for international students: required—TOEFL. Electronic applications accepted. *Expenses:* Contact institution.

University of California, Berkeley, Graduate Division, Program in Global Studies, Berkeley, CA 94720. Offers MA. Electronic applications accepted.

University of California, San Diego, Graduate Division, Department of Political Science, La Jolla, CA 92093. Offers political science (PhD); political science and international affairs (PhD). *Students:* 70 full-time (25 women). 375 applicants, 13% accepted, 16 enrolled. In 2019, 15 doctorates awarded. *Degree requirements:* For doctorate, comprehensive exam, thesis/dissertation. *Entrance requirements:* For doctorate, GRE General Test, letters of recommendation. Additional exam requirements/recommendations for international students: required—TOEFL (minimum score 600 paper-based; 100 iBT), IELTS. *Application deadline:* For fall admission, 12/11 for domestic students. Application fee: $105 ($125 for international students). Electronic

applications accepted. *Financial support:* Fellowships, research assistantships, teaching assistantships, and scholarships/grants available. Financial award applicants required to submit FAFSA. *Unit head:* Thad Kousser, Chair, 858-534-3239, E-mail: tkousser@ucsd.edu. *Application contact:* Julie Choi, Graduate Coordinator, 858-534-2705, E-mail: psgradadmissions@ucsd.edu.
Website: http://polisci.ucsd.edu/

University of California, San Diego, Graduate Division, School of Global Policy and Strategy, Master of International Affairs Program, La Jolla, CA 92093. Offers international development and nonprofit management (MIA); international economics (MIA); international environmental policy (MIA); international management (MIA); international politics (MIA). *Degree requirements:* For master's, one foreign language. *Entrance requirements:* For master's, GMAT or GRE General Test. Additional exam requirements/recommendations for international students: required—TOEFL (minimum score 90 iBT), IELTS (minimum score 7). Electronic applications accepted.

University of California, Santa Barbara, Graduate Division, College of Letters and Sciences, Division of Humanities and Fine Arts, Department of English, Santa Barbara, CA 93106-3170. Offers English (PhD), including environment and society, European medieval studies, feminist studies, global studies, technology and society, translation studies, writing studies; MA/PhD. Terminal master's awarded for partial completion of doctoral program. *Degree requirements:* For doctorate, one foreign language, comprehensive exam, thesis/dissertation. *Entrance requirements:* For doctorate, GRE General Test, GRE Subject Test (English literature). Additional exam requirements/recommendations for international students: required—TOEFL (minimum score 550 paper-based; 80 iBT), IELTS (minimum score 7). Electronic applications accepted.

University of California, Santa Barbara, Graduate Division, College of Letters and Sciences, Division of Humanities and Fine Arts, Department of History, Santa Barbara, CA 93106-9410. Offers European medieval studies (PhD); global studies (PhD); public historical studies (PhD); technology and society (PhD); women's studies (PhD); MA/PhD. *Degree requirements:* For doctorate, variable foreign language requirement, comprehensive exam, thesis/dissertation. *Entrance requirements:* For doctorate, GRE. Additional exam requirements/recommendations for international students: required—TOEFL (minimum score 550 paper-based; 80 iBT), IELTS (minimum score 7). Electronic applications accepted.

University of California, Santa Barbara, Graduate Division, College of Letters and Sciences, Division of Humanities and Fine Arts, Department of Religious Studies, Santa Barbara, CA 93106-3130. Offers ancient Mediterranean studies (PhD); cognitive science (PhD); European medieval studies (PhD); feminist studies (PhD); global studies (PhD); religious studies (MA, PhD); translation studies (PhD); MA/PhD. Terminal master's awarded for partial completion of doctoral program. *Degree requirements:* For master's, one foreign language, comprehensive exam (for some programs), thesis (for some programs); for doctorate, 2 foreign languages, thesis/dissertation, methodology. *Entrance requirements:* For master's and doctorate, GRE General Test. Additional exam requirements/recommendations for international students: required—TOEFL (minimum score 550 paper-based; 80 iBT), IELTS (minimum score 7). Electronic applications accepted.

University of California, Santa Barbara, Graduate Division, College of Letters and Sciences, Division of Humanities and Fine Arts, Program in Comparative Literature, Santa Barbara, CA 93106-4130. Offers comparative literature (PhD); East Asian literatures (PhD); feminist studies (PhD); French (PhD); global studies (PhD); translation studies (PhD); MA/PhD. *Degree requirements:* For doctorate, 2 foreign languages, comprehensive exam, thesis/dissertation. *Entrance requirements:* For doctorate, GRE. Additional exam requirements/recommendations for international students: required—TOEFL (minimum score 550 paper-based; 80 iBT), IELTS (minimum score 7). Electronic applications accepted.

University of California, Santa Barbara, Graduate Division, College of Letters and Sciences, Division of Mathematics, Life, and Physical Sciences, Department of Geography, Santa Barbara, CA 93106-4060. Offers cognitive science (PhD); geography (MA, PhD); global studies (PhD); quantitative methods in the social sciences (PhD); technology and society (PhD); transportation (PhD); MA/PhD. Terminal master's awarded for partial completion of doctoral program. *Degree requirements:* For master's, comprehensive exam (for some programs), thesis or alternative; for doctorate, comprehensive exam, thesis/dissertation, 1 quarter of teaching assistantship. *Entrance requirements:* For master's and doctorate, GRE (minimum combined verbal and quantitative scores above 1100 in old scoring system or 301 in new scoring system). Additional exam requirements/recommendations for international students: required—TOEFL (minimum score 550 paper-based; 80 iBT), IELTS (minimum score 7). Electronic applications accepted.

University of California, Santa Barbara, Graduate Division, College of Letters and Sciences, Division of Social Sciences, Department of Global Studies, Santa Barbara, CA 93106-7065. Offers global culture, ideology, and religion (MA, PhD); global government, human rights, and civil society (MA, PhD); political economy, sustainable development, and the environment (MA, PhD). *Degree requirements:* For master's, one foreign language, thesis, 2 years of a second language; for doctorate, one foreign language, thesis/dissertation, reading proficiency in at least one language other than English. *Entrance requirements:* For master's, GRE, 2 years of a second language with minimum B grade in the final term, statement of purpose, resume or curriculum vitae, 3 letters of recommendation, transcripts (from all post-secondary institutions attended), writing sample (15-20 pages); for doctorate, GRE, statement of purpose, personal achievements/contributions statement, resume or curriculum vitae, 3 letters of recommendation, transcripts from all post-secondary institutions attended, writing sample (15-20 pages). Additional exam requirements/recommendations for international students: required—TOEFL (minimum score 600 paper-based; 94 iBT), IELTS (minimum score 7). Electronic applications accepted.

University of California, Santa Barbara, Graduate Division, College of Letters and Sciences, Division of Social Sciences, Department of Sociology, Santa Barbara, CA 93106-9430. Offers interdisciplinary emphasis: Black studies (PhD); interdisciplinary emphasis: environment and society (PhD); interdisciplinary emphasis: feminist studies (PhD); interdisciplinary emphasis: global studies (PhD); interdisciplinary emphasis: language, interaction and social organization (PhD); interdisciplinary emphasis: quantitative methods in the social sciences (PhD); interdisciplinary emphasis: technology and society (PhD); sociology (PhD); MA/PhD. Terminal master's awarded for partial completion of doctoral program. *Degree requirements:* For doctorate, comprehensive exam, thesis/dissertation. *Entrance requirements:* For doctorate, GRE General Test. Additional exam requirements/recommendations for international students: required—TOEFL (minimum score 550 paper-based; 80 iBT), IELTS (minimum score 7). Electronic applications accepted.

University of California, Santa Cruz, Division of Graduate Studies, Division of Social Sciences, Program in International Economics, Santa Cruz, CA 95064. Offers PhD. *Degree requirements:* For doctorate, thesis/dissertation, 4 field exams, field papers, econometrics project, qualifying exams. *Entrance requirements:* For doctorate, GRE General Test. Additional exam requirements/recommendations for international

students: required—TOEFL (minimum score 550 paper-based; 83 iBT); recommended—IELTS (minimum score 8). Electronic applications accepted.

University of Chicago, Division of the Social Sciences, Committee on International Relations, Chicago, IL 60637. Offers MA. *Degree requirements:* For master's, thesis. *Entrance requirements:* For master's, GRE General Test, 3 letters of recommendation, statement of purpose, transcripts, resume or curriculum vitae, writing sample (dependent on department). Additional exam requirements/recommendations for international students: required—TOEFL (minimum score 104 iBT), IELTS (minimum score 7). Electronic applications accepted. *Expenses:* Contact institution.

University of Colorado Denver, College of Liberal Arts and Sciences, Program in Humanities, Denver, CO 80217. Offers community health (MSS); ethnic studies (MH, MSS); humanities (MH, Graduate Certificate); international studies (MSS); philosophy and theory (MH); social justice (MH, MSS); society and the environment (MSS); visual studies (MH); women's and gender studies (MH, MSS). *Program availability:* Part-time, evening/weekend. *Degree requirements:* For master's, 36 credit hours, project or thesis. *Entrance requirements:* For master's, writing sample, statement of purpose/letter of intent, three letters of recommendation. Additional exam requirements/recommendations for international students: required—TOEFL (minimum score 537 paper-based; 75 iBT); recommended—IELTS (minimum score 6.5). Electronic applications accepted. Tuition and fees vary according to course load, program and reciprocity agreements.

University of Connecticut, Graduate School, College of Liberal Arts and Sciences, Institute of Latina/o, Caribbean, and Latin American Studies, Storrs, CT 06269. Offers Latino and Latin American studies (MA). *Degree requirements:* For master's, comprehensive exam. *Entrance requirements:* For master's, GRE General Test. Additional exam requirements/recommendations for international students: required—TOEFL (minimum score 550 paper-based). Electronic applications accepted.

University of Delaware, College of Arts and Sciences, Department of Political Science and International Relations, Newark, DE 19716. Offers MA, PhD. Terminal master's awarded for partial completion of doctoral program. *Degree requirements:* For master's, research paper; for doctorate, one foreign language, comprehensive exam, thesis/dissertation. *Entrance requirements:* For master's and doctorate, GRE General Test, minimum GPA of 3.2 in major, 3.0 overall. Additional exam requirements/recommendations for international students: required—TOEFL (minimum score 600 paper-based). Electronic applications accepted.

University of Denver, Division of Arts, Humanities and Social Sciences, Department of Media, Film and Journalism Studies, Denver, CO 80208. Offers international and intercultural communication (MA); media and public communication (MA), including media and globalization, strategic communication. *Program availability:* Part-time. *Faculty:* 18 full-time (8 women), 1 part-time/adjunct (0 women). *Students:* 4 full-time (all women), 23 part-time (19 women); includes 6 minority (1 Black or African American, non-Hispanic/Latino; 1 Asian, non-Hispanic/Latino; 3 Hispanic/Latino; 1 Two or more races, non-Hispanic/Latino), 1 international. Average age 26. 35 applicants, 80% accepted, 13 enrolled. In 2019, 14 master's awarded. *Degree requirements:* For master's, variable foreign language requirement, thesis (for some programs). *Entrance requirements:* For master's, GRE General Test, bachelor's degree, transcripts, personal statement, three letters of recommendation. Additional exam requirements/recommendations for international students: required—TOEFL (minimum score 620 paper-based; 105 iBT). *Application deadline:* For fall admission, 2/1 priority date for domestic and international students; for winter admission, 11/14 for domestic and international students; for spring admission, 1/31 for domestic and international students. Applications are processed on a rolling basis. Application fee: $65. Electronic applications accepted. *Expenses:* Contact institution. *Financial support:* In 2019–20, 24 students received support, including 11 teaching assistantships with tuition reimbursements available (averaging $7,612 per year); career-related internships or fieldwork, Federal Work-Study, institutionally sponsored loans, scholarships/grants, and unspecified assistantships also available. Support available to part-time students. Financial award application deadline: 2/15; financial award applicants required to submit FAFSA. *Unit head:* Dr. Lynn Schofield Clark, Professor and Chair, 303-871-3984, Fax: 303-871-4949, E-mail: lynn.clark@du.edu. *Application contact:* Information Contact, 303-871-2166, E-mail: mfjs@du.edu.
Website: http://www.du.edu/ahss/mfjs

University of Denver, Josef Korbel School of International Studies, Denver, CO 80208. Offers conflict resolution (MA); global business and corporate social responsibility (Certificate); global finance, trade and economic integration (MA); global health affairs (Certificate); homeland security (Certificate); humanitarian assistance (Certificate); international administration (MA); international development (MA); international human rights (MA); international security (MA); international studies (MA, PhD); public policy studies (MPP); religion and international affairs (Certificate). *Program availability:* Part-time. *Faculty:* 41 full-time (15 women), 14 part-time/adjunct (2 women). *Students:* 208 full-time (112 women), 24 part-time (13 women); includes 50 minority (11 Black or African American, non-Hispanic/Latino; 10 Asian, non-Hispanic/Latino; 15 Hispanic/Latino; 14 Two or more races, non-Hispanic/Latino), 20 international. Average age 27. 718 applicants, 70% accepted, 88 enrolled. In 2019, 134 master's, 2 doctorates, 26 other advanced degrees awarded. *Degree requirements:* For master's, variable foreign language requirement, thesis (for some programs); for doctorate, one foreign language, comprehensive exam, thesis/dissertation, one extended research paper. *Entrance requirements:* For master's, GRE General Test, bachelor's degree, transcripts, two letters of recommendation, personal statement, resume or curriculum vitae; for doctorate, GRE General Test, bachelor's degree (most have a master's degree), transcripts, personal statement, resume or curriculum vitae, writing sample. Additional exam requirements/recommendations for international students: required—TOEFL (minimum score 587 paper-based; 95 iBT). *Application deadline:* For fall admission, 1/23 priority date for domestic and international students; for winter admission, 11/1 for domestic and international students. Applications are processed on a rolling basis. Application fee: $65. Electronic applications accepted. *Expenses:* Contact institution. *Financial support:* In 2019–20, 161 students received support, including 4 teaching assistantships with tuition reimbursements available (averaging $16,875 per year); research assistantships with tuition reimbursements available, career-related internships or fieldwork, Federal Work-Study, institutionally sponsored loans, scholarships/grants, and unspecified assistantships also available. Support available to part-time students. Financial award application deadline: 2/15; financial award applicants required to submit FAFSA. *Unit head:* Dr. Fritz Mayer, Dean, 303-871-6338, E-mail: frederick.mayer@du.edu. *Application contact:* Admissions Contact, 303-871-2324, E-mail: korbeladm@du.edu.
Website: http://www.du.edu/korbel

University of Denver, University College, Denver, CO 80208. Offers arts and culture (MA, Certificate); communication management (MS, Certificate), including translation studies (Certificate), world history and culture (Certificate); environmental policy and management (MS); geographic information systems (MS); global affairs (MA, Certificate), including human capital in organizations (Certificate), philanthropic leadership (Certificate), project management (Certificate), strategic innovation and change (Certificate); healthcare leadership (MS); information communications and

technology (MS); leadership and organizations (MS); professional creative writing (MA, Certificate), including emergency planning and response (Certificate), organizational security (Certificate); security management (MS, Certificate); strategic human resources (Certificate). *Program availability:* Part-time, evening/weekend, 100% online, blended/hybrid learning. *Faculty:* 104 part-time/adjunct (52 women). *Students:* 59 full-time (33 women), 1,893 part-time (1,210 women); includes 545 minority (133 Black or African American, non-Hispanic/Latino; 16 American Indian or Alaska Native, non-Hispanic/Latino; 64 Asian, non-Hispanic/Latino; 252 Hispanic/Latino; 4 Native Hawaiian or other Pacific Islander, non-Hispanic/Latino; 76 Two or more races, non-Hispanic/Latino), 78 international. Average age 32. 1,290 applicants, 91% accepted, 752 enrolled. In 2019, 457 master's, 181 other advanced degrees awarded. *Degree requirements:* For master's, capstone project. *Entrance requirements:* For master's, baccalaureate degree, transcripts, two letters of recommendation, personal statement, resume, writing sample (Master of Arts in Professional Creative Writing). Additional exam requirements/recommendations for international students: required—TOEFL (minimum score 550 paper-based; 80 iBT). *Application deadline:* For fall admission, 6/19 priority date for domestic students, 6/14 priority date for international students; for winter admission, 10/25 priority date for domestic students, 9/27 priority date for international students; for spring admission, 2/7 priority date for domestic students, 1/10 priority date for international students; for summer admission, 4/24 priority date for domestic students, 3/27 priority date for international students. Applications are processed on a rolling basis. Application fee: $75. Electronic applications accepted. *Expenses:* Contact institution. *Financial support:* In 2019–20, 56 students received support. Teaching assistantships available. Financial award applicants required to submit FAFSA. *Unit head:* Dr. Michael McGuire, Dean, 303-871-3518, E-mail: michael.mcguire@du.edu. *Application contact:* Admission Team, 303-871-2291, E-mail: ucoladm@du.edu.
Website: http://universitycollege.du.edu/

University of Florida, Graduate School, College of Liberal Arts and Sciences, Department of Political Science, Program in International Relations, Gainesville, FL 32611. Offers MA, MAT. *Degree requirements:* For master's, comprehensive exam (for some programs), thesis optional. *Entrance requirements:* For master's, GRE General Test, minimum GPA of 3.0. Additional exam requirements/recommendations for international students: required—TOEFL (minimum score 550 paper-based; 80 iBT), IELTS (minimum score 6). Electronic applications accepted.

University of Georgia, School of Public and International Affairs, Department of International Affairs, Athens, GA 30602. Offers MA, MIP, PhD.

University of Georgia, School of Public and International Affairs, Program in Political Science/International Affairs, Athens, GA 30602. Offers MA, PhD. *Degree requirements:* For master's, one foreign language, thesis; for doctorate, one foreign language, thesis/dissertation. *Entrance requirements:* For master's and doctorate, GRE General Test. Electronic applications accepted.

University of Hawaii at Manoa, Office of Graduate Education, International Cultural Studies Graduate Certificate Program, Honolulu, HI 96822. Offers Graduate Certificate. *Program availability:* Part-time. *Entrance requirements:* For degree, GRE General Test. Additional exam requirements/recommendations for international students: required—TOEFL (minimum score 540 paper-based; 76 iBT), IELTS (minimum score 5).

University of Indianapolis, Graduate Programs, Shaheen College of Arts and Sciences, Department of History and Political Science, Indianapolis, IN 46227-3697. Offers history (MA); international relations (MA). *Program availability:* Part-time, evening/weekend. *Degree requirements:* For master's, thesis optional. *Entrance requirements:* For master's, GRE Subject Test, minimum GPA of 3.0, 3 letters of recommendation. Additional exam requirements/recommendations for international students: required—TOEFL (minimum score 550 paper-based). Electronic applications accepted.

The University of Kansas, Graduate Studies, College of Liberal Arts and Sciences, Center for Global and International Studies, Lawrence, KS 66045. Offers MA. *Program availability:* Part-time, evening/weekend. *Students:* 25 full-time (15 women), 8 part-time (3 women); includes 8 minority (4 Black or African American, non-Hispanic/Latino; 4 Hispanic/Latino). Average age 34. 34 applicants, 97% accepted, 24 enrolled. In 2019, 20 master's awarded. *Entrance requirements:* For master's, GRE, minimum GPA of 3.0, 2 letters of reference, curriculum vitae, reflective essay, 300-500 word statement of interest describing relevant aspects of background and addressing how program will help meet academic and professional goals. Additional exam requirements/recommendations for international students: required—TOEFL (minimum score 80 iBT). *Application deadline:* For fall admission, 1/15 priority date for domestic and international students; for spring admission, 10/1 priority date for domestic and international students. Application fee: $65 ($85 for international students). Electronic applications accepted. *Expenses:* Tuition, state resident: full-time $9989. Tuition, nonresident: full-time $23,950. *International tuition:* $23,950 full-time. *Required fees:* $984; $81.99 per credit hour. Tuition and fees vary according to course load, campus/location and program. *Financial support:* Research assistantships, teaching assistantships, scholarships/grants, health care benefits, and unspecified assistantships available. Support available to part-time students. *Unit head:* Shannon O'Lear, Director, 785-864-2041, E-mail: olear@ku.edu. *Application contact:* Clare Thoman, Graduate Admissions Contact, 785-864-9814, E-mail: clarethoman@ku.edu.
Website: http://global.ku.edu/

University of Kentucky, Graduate School, Patterson School of Diplomacy and International Commerce, Lexington, KY 40506-0027. Offers MA. *Degree requirements:* For master's, one foreign language, comprehensive exam, statistics. *Entrance requirements:* For master's, GRE General Test, minimum undergraduate GPA of 3.0. Additional exam requirements/recommendations for international students: required—TOEFL (minimum score 550 paper-based; 79 iBT). Electronic applications accepted.

University of Maine, Graduate School, College of Liberal Arts and Sciences, School of Policy and International Affairs, Orono, ME 04469. Offers global policy (MA). *Faculty:* 1 (woman) full-time, 2 part-time/adjunct (1 woman). *Students:* 29 full-time (16 women), 1 part-time (0 women); includes 5 minority (3 Black or African American, non-Hispanic/Latino; 1 Asian, non-Hispanic/Latino; 1 Hispanic/Latino), 10 international. Average age 27. 44 applicants, 91% accepted, 15 enrolled. In 2019, 7 master's awarded. *Entrance requirements:* For master's, GRE. Additional exam requirements/recommendations for international students: required—TOEFL (minimum score 80 iBT); recommended—IELTS (minimum score 6.5), TSE (minimum score 60). *Application deadline:* Applications are processed on a rolling basis. Application fee: $65. Electronic applications accepted. *Expenses: Tuition, area resident:* Full-time $8100; part-time $450 per credit hour. Tuition, state resident: full-time $8100; part-time $450 per credit hour. Tuition, nonresident: full-time $26,388; part-time $1466 per credit hour. *International tuition:* $26,388 full-time. *Required fees:* $1257; $278 per semester. Tuition and fees vary according to course load. *Financial support:* In 2019–20, 21 students received support, including 1 research assistantship with full tuition reimbursement available (averaging $8,800 per year), 2 teaching assistantships with full tuition reimbursements available (averaging $15,825 per year); career-related internships or fieldwork, Federal Work-Study, scholarships/grants, and unspecified assistantships also available. Financial award application deadline: 3/1; financial award applicants required to submit FAFSA. *Unit head:* Capt. James Settele, Director, 207-581-3153, E-mail: james.settele@umit.maine.edu. *Application contact:* Scott G. Delcourt, Assistant Vice President for Graduate Studies and Senior Associate Dean, 207-581-3291, Fax: 207-581-3232, E-mail: graduate@maine.edu.
Website: http://spia.umaine.edu/

The University of Manchester, School of Arts, Languages and Cultures, Manchester, United Kingdom. Offers anthropology, media and performance (PhD); applied theatre (PhD); Arab world studies (PhD); archaeology (PhD); art history and visual studies (PhD); arts and cultural management (PhD); arts management and cultural policy (PhD); Chinese studies (PhD); classics and ancient history (PhD); composition (PhD); creative writing (PhD); drama (PhD); East Asian studies (PhD); electroacoustic composition (PhD); English and American studies (PhD); English language (PhD); French studies (PhD); German studies (PhD); history (PhD); humanitarianism and conflict response (PhD); interpreting studies (PhD); Japanese studies (PhD); Latin American cultural studies (PhD); linguistics (PhD); Middle Eastern studies (PhD); museology (PhD); museum practice (PhD); music (PhD); musicology (PhD); Polish studies (PhD); Portuguese studies (PhD); religions and theology (PhD); Russian studies (PhD); Spanish studies (PhD); translation and intercultural studies (PhD).

University of Massachusetts Boston, McCormack Graduate School of Policy and Global Studies, Program in Global Governance and Human Security, Boston, MA 02125-3393. Offers MA.

University of Massachusetts Boston, McCormack Graduate School of Policy and Global Studies, Program in International Relations, Boston, MA 02125-3393. Offers MA.

University of Miami, Graduate School, College of Arts and Sciences, Department of International Studies, Coral Gables, FL 33124. Offers MA, PhD. *Degree requirements:* For master's, one foreign language, comprehensive exam; for doctorate, one foreign language, comprehensive exam, thesis/dissertation. *Entrance requirements:* For master's, GRE General Test, minimum GPA of 3.0; for doctorate, GRE General Test. Additional exam requirements/recommendations for international students: required—TOEFL. Electronic applications accepted.

University of Miami, Graduate School, College of Arts and Sciences, Program in International Administration, Coral Gables, FL 33124. Offers MAIA. *Program availability:* Part-time, evening/weekend. *Degree requirements:* For master's, practicum. *Entrance requirements:* For master's, GRE General Test. Additional exam requirements/recommendations for international students: required—TOEFL (minimum score 550 paper-based), IELTS (minimum score 6.5). Electronic applications accepted.

University of Michigan–Flint, College of Arts and Sciences, Program in Social Sciences, Flint, MI 48502-1950. Offers gender studies (MA); global studies (MA); U.S. history and politics (MA). *Program availability:* Part-time. *Faculty:* 11 full-time (6 women), 4 part-time/adjunct (all women). *Students:* 3 full-time (2 women), 7 part-time (5 women); includes 4 minority (3 Black or African American, non-Hispanic/Latino; 1 Two or more races, non-Hispanic/Latino). Average age 43. 15 applicants, 60% accepted, 2 enrolled. In 2019, 4 master's awarded. *Entrance requirements:* For master's, bachelor's degree from regionally-accredited institution, minimum overall undergraduate GPA of 3.0 on 4.0 scale. Additional exam requirements/recommendations for international students: required—TOEFL (minimum score 84 iBT), IELTS (minimum score 6.5). *Application deadline:* For fall admission, 8/1 for domestic students, 5/1 for international students; for winter admission, 11/15 for domestic students, 10/1 for international students; for spring admission, 3/15 for domestic students, 1/1 for international students; for summer admission, 5/15 for domestic students. Applications are processed on a rolling basis. Application fee: $55. Electronic applications accepted. *Expenses:* Contact institution. *Financial support:* Federal Work-Study, scholarships/grants, and unspecified assistantships available. Financial award application deadline: 3/1; financial award applicants required to submit FAFSA. *Unit head:* Dr. Adam Lutzker, Director, 810-762-3470, Fax: 810-762-3281, E-mail: alutzker@umflint.edu. *Application contact:* Matt Bohlen, Associate Director of Graduate Programs, 810-762-3171, Fax: 810-766-6789, E-mail: mbohlen@umflint.edu.
Website: http://www.umflint.edu/graduateprograms/social-sciences-ma

The University of North Carolina at Chapel Hill, Graduate School, College of Arts and Sciences, Center for Slavic, Eurasian and East European Studies, Chapel Hill, NC 27599. Offers global studies (MA). *Program availability:* Part-time. *Degree requirements:* For master's, one foreign language, thesis. *Entrance requirements:* For master's, GRE General Test. Additional exam requirements/recommendations for international students: required—TOEFL. Electronic applications accepted.

University of Northern British Columbia, Office of Graduate Studies, Prince George, BC V2N 4Z9, Canada. Offers business administration (Diploma); community health science (M Sc); disability management (MA); education (M Ed); first nations studies (MA); gender studies (MA); history (MA); interdisciplinary studies (MA); international studies (MA); mathematical, computer and physical sciences (M Sc); natural resources and environmental studies (M Sc, MA, MNRES, PhD); political science (MA); psychology (M Sc, PhD); social work (MSW). *Program availability:* Part-time, evening/weekend, online learning. *Degree requirements:* For master's, thesis; for doctorate, thesis/dissertation. *Entrance requirements:* For master's, GRE, minimum B average in undergraduate course work; for doctorate, candidacy exam, minimum A average in graduate course work.

University of North Georgia, Program in International Affairs, Dahlonega, GA 30597. Offers MAIA.
Website: http://ung.edu/political-science-international-affairs/

University of North Texas, Toulouse Graduate School, Denton, TX 76203-5459. Offers accounting (MS); applied anthropology (MA, MS); applied behavior analysis (Certificate); applied geography (MA); applied technology and performance improvement (M Ed, MS); art education (MA); art history (MA); arts leadership (Certificate); audiology (Au D); behavior analysis (MS); behavioral science (PhD); biochemistry and molecular biology (MS); biology (MA, MS); biomedical engineering (MS); business analysis (MS); chemistry (MS); clinical health psychology (PhD); communication studies (MA, MS); computer engineering (MS); computer science (MS); counseling (M Ed, MS), including clinical mental health counseling (MS), college and university counseling, elementary school counseling, secondary school counseling; creative writing (MA); criminal justice (MS); curriculum and instruction (M Ed); decision sciences (MBA); design (MA, MFA), including fashion design (MFA), innovation studies, interior design (MFA); early childhood studies (MS); economics (MS); educational leadership (M Ed, Ed D); educational psychology (MS, PhD), including family studies (MS), gifted and talented (MS), human development (MS), learning and cognition (MS), research, measurement and evaluation (MS); electrical engineering (MS); emergency management (MPA); engineering technology (MS); English (MA); English as a second language (MA); environmental science (MS); finance (MBA, MS); financial management (MPA); French (MA); health services management (MBA); higher education (M Ed, Ed D); history (MA, MS); hospitality management (MS); human resources management (MPA); information science (MS); information systems (PhD); information technologies (MBA); interdisciplinary studies (MA, MS); international studies (MA); international sustainable tourism (MS); jazz studies (MM); journalism (MA, MJ, Graduate Certificate), including interactive and virtual digital communication (Graduate Certificate), narrative journalism (Graduate Certificate), public relations (Graduate Certificate); kinesiology (MS); linguistics (MA); local government management (MPA); logistics (PhD); logistics and supply chain management (MBA); long-term care, senior housing, and aging services (MA); management (PhD); marketing (MBA); mathematics (MA, MS); mechanical and energy engineering (MS, PhD); music (MA), including ethnomusicology, music theory, musicology, performance; music composition (PhD); music education (MM Ed, PhD); nonprofit management (MPA); operations and supply chain management (MBA); performance (MM, DMA); philosophy (MA); political science (MA); professional and technical communication (MA); radio, television and film (MA, MFA); rehabilitation counseling (Certificate); sociology (MA); Spanish (MA); special education (M Ed); speech-language pathology (MA); strategic management (MBA); studio art (MFA); teaching (M Ed); MBA/MS. *Program availability:* Part-time, evening/weekend, online learning. Terminal master's awarded for partial completion of doctoral program. *Degree requirements:* For master's, variable foreign language requirement, comprehensive exam (for some programs), thesis (for some programs); for doctorate, variable foreign language requirement, comprehensive exam (for some programs), thesis/dissertation; for other advanced degree, variable foreign language requirement, comprehensive exam (for some programs). *Entrance requirements:* For master's and doctorate, GRE, GMAT. Additional exam requirements/recommendations for international students: required—TOEFL (minimum score 550 paper-based; 79 iBT). Electronic applications accepted.

University of Notre Dame, The Graduate School, Keough School of Global Affairs, Notre Dame, IN 46556. Offers global affairs (MGA); sustainable development (MGA).

University of Oklahoma, David L. Boren College of International Studies, Norman, OK 73019-0390. Offers economics and development (MAIS), including global economics and development, global security studies (MA, MAIS); global affairs (MA), including economics and development, global security studies (MA, MAIS); JD/MAIS; MAIS/MSW. *Program availability:* Part-time, online courses with an 8-10 day study abroad. Terminal master's awarded for partial completion of doctoral program. *Degree requirements:* For master's, variable foreign language requirement, 36 credit hours (33 online); thesis, policy paper or internship project; faculty-led overseas travel program of 8-10 days that will vary in location (online). *Entrance requirements:* For master's, GRE. Additional exam requirements/recommendations for international students: required—TOEFL (minimum score 79 iBT) or IELTS (minimum score 6.5). Electronic applications accepted. *Expenses:* Tuition, state resident: full-time $6583.20; part-time $274.30 per credit hour. Tuition, nonresident: full-time $21,242; part-time $885.10 per credit hour. *International tuition:* $21,242.40 full-time. *Required fees:* $1994.20; $72.55 per credit hour. $126.50 per semester. Tuition and fees vary according to course load and degree level.

University of Oregon, Graduate School, College of Arts and Sciences, Program in International Studies, Eugene, OR 97403. Offers MA. *Program availability:* Part-time. *Degree requirements:* For master's, one foreign language, thesis, internship. *Entrance requirements:* For master's, minimum GPA of 3.0. Additional exam requirements/recommendations for international students: required—TOEFL.

University of Pennsylvania, School of Arts and Sciences, Program in International Studies, Philadelphia, PA 19104. Offers AM. *Faculty:* 7 full-time (1 woman), 3 part-time/adjunct (2 women). *Students:* 6 full-time (5 women); includes 2 minority (1 Hispanic/Latino; 1 Two or more races, non-Hispanic/Latino), 2 international. Average age 30. In 2019, 65 master's awarded. Application fee: $70.
Website: http://www.sas.upenn.edu/graduate-division

University of Pittsburgh, Graduate School of Public and International Affairs, Master of Public Administration Program, Pittsburgh, PA 15260. Offers energy and environment (MPA); governance and international public management (MPA); policy research and analysis (MPA); public and nonprofit management (MPA); urban affairs and planning (MPA); JD/MPA; MPH/MPA; MSIS/MPA; MSW/MPA. *Accreditation:* NASPAA. *Program availability:* Part-time, evening/weekend. *Faculty:* 33 full-time (11 women), 10 part-time/adjunct (5 women). *Students:* 76 full-time (51 women), 17 part-time (10 women); includes 9 minority (5 Black or African American, non-Hispanic/Latino; 1 Asian, non-Hispanic/Latino; 3 Hispanic/Latino), 37 international. Average age 26. 167 applicants, 91% accepted, 44 enrolled. In 2019, 49 master's awarded. *Degree requirements:* For master's, thesis optional, capstone seminar. *Entrance requirements:* For master's, Personal essay, resume, two letters of recommendation, transcripts. Additional exam requirements/recommendations for international students: required—TOEFL (minimum score 80 iBT), Duolingo English Test; recommended—IELTS (minimum score 6.5). *Application deadline:* For fall admission, 2/1 for domestic students, 1/15 priority date for international students; for spring admission, 11/1 for domestic students, 8/1 priority date for international students. Application fee: $50. Electronic applications accepted. *Expenses:* $24,480 in-state, $40,848 out-of-state. *Financial support:* In 2019–20, 30 students received support, including 2 fellowships with full tuition reimbursements available (averaging $16,060 per year); scholarships/grants also available. Financial award application deadline: 2/1; financial award applicants required to submit FAFSA. *Unit head:* Dr. John Keeler, Dean, 412-648-7605, Fax: 412-648-7601, E-mail: gspia@pitt.edu. *Application contact:* Dr. Michael Rizzi, Director of Student Services, 412-648-7643, Fax: 412-648-7641, E-mail: rizzim@pitt.edu.
Website: http://www.gspia.pitt.edu/

University of Pittsburgh, Graduate School of Public and International Affairs, Master of Public and International Affairs Program, Pittsburgh, PA 15260. Offers human security (MPIA); international political economy (MPIA); security and intelligence studies (MPIA); JD/MPIA; MBA/MPIA; MPH/MPIA; MPIA/MSW; MSIS/MPIA. *Program availability:* Part-time, evening/weekend. *Faculty:* 33 full-time (11 women), 10 part-time/adjunct (5 women). *Students:* 87 full-time (49 women), 14 part-time (6 women); includes 13 minority (7 Black or African American, non-Hispanic/Latino; 6 Hispanic/Latino), 10 international. Average age 27. 156 applicants, 94% accepted, 49 enrolled. In 2019, 41 master's awarded. *Degree requirements:* For master's, thesis optional, Capstone Seminar. *Entrance requirements:* For master's, Personal essay, resume, two letters of recommendation, transcripts. Additional exam requirements/recommendations for international students: required—TOEFL (minimum score 80 iBT), Duolingo English Test; recommended—IELTS (minimum score 6.5). *Application deadline:* For fall admission, 2/1 priority date for domestic students, 1/15 priority date for international students; for spring admission, 11/1 priority date for domestic students, 8/1 priority date for international students. Application fee: $50. Electronic applications accepted. *Expenses:* $24,480 in-state, $40,848 out-of-state. *Financial support:* In 2019–20, 63 students received support, including 9 fellowships with full tuition reimbursements available (averaging $16,060 per year); scholarships/grants also available. Financial award application deadline: 2/1. *Unit head:* Dr. John Keeler, Dean, 412-648-7605, Fax: 412-648-7601, E-mail: gspia@pitt.edu. *Application contact:* Dr. Michael Rizzi, Director of Student Services, 412-648-7643, Fax: 412-648-7641, E-mail: rizzim@pitt.edu.
Website: http://www.gspia.pitt.edu/

University of Pittsburgh, Graduate School of Public and International Affairs, PhD Program in Public and International Affairs, Pittsburgh, PA 15260. Offers international affairs (PhD); international development (PhD); public administration (PhD); public policy (PhD). *Faculty:* 33 full-time (11 women), 10 part-time/adjunct (5 women). *Students:* 28 full-time (12 women), 4 part-time (2 women); includes 4 minority (1 Black or African American, non-Hispanic/Latino; 3 Hispanic/Latino), 14 international. Average age 36. 65 applicants, 3% accepted, 2 enrolled. In 2019, 1 doctorate awarded. *Degree requirements:* For doctorate, comprehensive exam, thesis/dissertation. *Entrance requirements:* For doctorate, GRE or GMAT, Personal essay, research proposal essay, two letters of recommendation, transcripts, resume. Additional exam requirements/recommendations for international students: required—TOEFL (minimum score 80 iBT), Duolingo English Test; recommended—IELTS (minimum score 6.5). *Application deadline:* For fall admission, 1/15 for domestic and international students. Application fee: $50. Electronic applications accepted. *Expenses:* $24,480 in-state, $40,848 out-of-state. *Financial support:* In 2019–20, 15 students received support, including 15 research assistantships with full tuition reimbursements available (averaging $16,060 per year). Financial award application deadline: 1/15. *Unit head:* Dr. John Keeler, Dean, 412-648-7605, Fax: 412-648-7601, E-mail: gspia@pitt.edu. *Application contact:* Dr. Michael Rizzi, Director of Student Services, 412-648-7640, Fax: 412-648-7641, E-mail: rizzim@pitt.edu.
Website: http://www.gspia.pitt.edu/

University of Pittsburgh, Katz Graduate School of Business, MBA/Master of Public and International Affairs Dual-Degree Program, Pittsburgh, PA 15260. Offers MBA/MPIA. *Accreditation:* AACSB. *Program availability:* Part-time, evening/weekend. *Faculty:* 95 full-time (30 women), 30 part-time/adjunct (10 women). *Students:* 1 full-time (0 women). 4 applicants, 25% accepted, 1 enrolled. *Entrance requirements:* Additional exam requirements/recommendations for international students: required—TOEFL (minimum score 100 iBT). *Application deadline:* For fall admission, 4/1 priority date for domestic students, 2/1 priority date for international students. Application fee: $50. Electronic applications accepted. *Financial support:* Research assistantships, teaching assistantships, Federal Work-Study, scholarships/grants, health care benefits, and unspecified assistantships available. Financial award application deadline: 6/1; financial award applicants required to submit FAFSA. *Unit head:* Dr. Arjang A. Assad, Dean, 412-648-1556, Fax: 412-648-1552, E-mail: aassad@katz.pitt.edu. *Application contact:* Thomas Keller, Director of Admissions, 412-648-1700, Fax: 412-648-1659, E-mail: admissions@katz.pitt.edu.
Website: https://www.katz.business.pitt.edu/mba/joint-and-dual/international-affairs#section-1

University of Pittsburgh, University Center for International Studies, Pittsburgh, PA 15260. Offers African studies (Certificate); Asian studies (Certificate); European Union studies (Certificate); global studies (Certificate); Latin American studies (Certificate); Russian and East European studies (Certificate); West European studies (Certificate). *Program availability:* Part-time, evening/weekend, online learning. *Degree requirements:* For Certificate, one foreign language, comprehensive exam (for some programs). *Entrance requirements:* Additional exam requirements/recommendations for international students: required—TOEFL. *Expenses:* Contact institution.

University of San Diego, College of Arts and Sciences, Master of Arts Program in International Relations, San Diego, CA 92110-2492. Offers MA, JD/MA. *Program availability:* Part-time, evening/weekend. *Faculty:* 4 full-time (1 woman), 2 part-time/adjunct (1 woman). *Students:* 8 full-time (3 women), 17 part-time (6 women); includes 10 minority (5 Asian, non-Hispanic/Latino; 3 Hispanic/Latino; 2 Two or more races, non-Hispanic/Latino), 1 international. Average age 30. 29 applicants, 52% accepted, 8 enrolled. In 2019, 17 master's awarded. *Degree requirements:* For master's, comprehensive exam. *Entrance requirements:* For master's, GRE General Test (minimum scores: 50-60 percentile verbal/ 40-50 percentile quantitative/4.0 analytical), minimum GPA of 3.2; 24 units in political science, history and/or economics. 3 letters of recommendation. Additional exam requirements/recommendations for international students: required—TOEFL (minimum score 90 iBT), TWE. *Application deadline:* For fall admission, 7/1 for domestic students, 6/1 for international students; for spring admission, 12/1 for domestic students, 11/1 for international students. Applications are processed on a rolling basis. Application fee: $45. Electronic applications accepted. *Financial support:* In 2019–20, 29 students received support. Institutionally sponsored loans, scholarships/grants, and unspecified assistantships available. Support available to part-time students. Financial award application deadline: 4/1; financial award applicants required to submit FAFSA. *Unit head:* Dr. Avi Spiegel, Graduate Program Director, 619-260-2315, Fax: 619-260-6840, E-mail: mair@sandiego.edu. *Application contact:* Erika Garwood, Associate Director of Graduate Admissions, 619-260-4524, Fax: 619-260-4158, E-mail: grads@sandiego.edu.
Website: http://www.sandiego.edu/cas/ma-international-relations/

University of San Francisco, College of Arts and Sciences, International Studies Program, San Francisco, CA 94117. Offers MA. *Program availability:* Part-time. *Faculty:* 8 full-time (5 women), 3 part-time/adjunct (0 women). *Students:* 53 full-time (33 women), 2 part-time (both women); includes 18 minority (4 Black or African American, non-Hispanic/Latino; 2 Asian, non-Hispanic/Latino; 8 Hispanic/Latino; 1 Native Hawaiian or other Pacific Islander, non-Hispanic/Latino; 3 Two or more races, non-Hispanic/Latino), 18 international. Average age 27. 155 applicants, 86% accepted, 28 enrolled. In 2019, 37 master's awarded. *Degree requirements:* For master's, variable foreign language requirement. *Entrance requirements:* Additional exam requirements/recommendations for international students: required—TOEFL (minimum score 90 iBT), IELTS (minimum score 6.5), PTE (minimum score 61). *Application deadline:* For fall admission, 2/15 for domestic and international students. Applications are processed on a rolling basis. Application fee: $55. Electronic applications accepted. Application fee is waived when completed online. *Financial support:* Teaching assistantships with partial tuition reimbursements, career-related internships or fieldwork, and scholarships/grants available. Financial award applicants required to submit FAFSA. *Unit head:* Christie Meno, Graduate Director, 415-422-5122, E-mail: mais@usfca.edu. *Application contact:* Information Contact, 415-422-5101, E-mail: asgraduate@usfca.edu.
Website: https://www.usfca.edu/arts-sciences/graduate-programs/international-studies

University of San Francisco, College of Arts and Sciences, Program in Migration Studies, San Francisco, CA 94117. Offers MMS. *Program availability:* Part-time, evening/weekend. *Faculty:* 3 full-time (1 woman), 3 part-time/adjunct (all women). *Students:* 26 full-time (19 women); includes 16 minority (3 Black or African American, non-Hispanic/Latino; 1 Asian, non-Hispanic/Latino; 11 Hispanic/Latino; 1 Native Hawaiian or other Pacific Islander, non-Hispanic/Latino), 3 international. Average age 27. 78 applicants, 82% accepted, 14 enrolled. In 2019, 6 master's awarded. *Entrance requirements:* For master's, statement of purpose. Additional exam requirements/recommendations for international students: required—TOEFL (minimum score 90 iBT), IELTS (minimum score 6.5), PTE (minimum score 61). *Application deadline:* For fall admission, 2/1 priority date for domestic and international students. Applications are processed on a rolling basis. Application fee: $55. Electronic applications accepted. Application fee is waived when completed online. *Financial support:* Career-related internships or fieldwork and scholarships/grants available. Financial award applicants required to submit FAFSA. *Unit head:* Aide Rodriguez, Graduate Director, 415-422-5101, E-mail: migrationstudies@usfca.edu. *Application contact:* Aide Rodriguez, Graduate Director, 415-422-5101, E-mail: migrationstudies@usfca.edu.
Website: https://www.usfca.edu/arts-sciences/graduate-programs/migration-studies

University of South Carolina, The Graduate School, College of Arts and Sciences, Department of Political Science, Program in International Studies, Columbia, SC 29208. Offers MA, PhD. *Program availability:* Part-time. Terminal master's awarded for partial completion of doctoral program. *Degree requirements:* For master's, one foreign language, thesis or alternative; for doctorate, one foreign language, comprehensive exam, thesis/dissertation. *Entrance requirements:* For master's, GRE General Test, minimum GPA of 3.3; for doctorate, GRE General Test, minimum GPA of 3.5. Additional exam requirements/recommendations for international students: required—TOEFL. Electronic applications accepted.

University of Southern California, Graduate School, Annenberg School for Communication and Journalism, School of Communication, Program in Public Diplomacy, Los Angeles, CA 90089. Offers MPD. *Program availability:* Part-time. *Students:* 25 full-time (22 women); includes 11 minority (1 Black or African American, non-Hispanic/Latino; 2 Asian, non-Hispanic/Latino; 5 Hispanic/Latino; 1 Native Hawaiian or other Pacific Islander, non-Hispanic/Latino; 2 Two or more races, non-Hispanic/Latino), 11 international. Average age 26. 47 applicants, 47% accepted, 13 enrolled. In 2019, 17 master's awarded. *Degree requirements:* For master's, thesis. *Entrance requirements:* For master's, GRE, resume, writing samples, statement of purpose, recommendation letters. Additional exam requirements/recommendations for international students: required—TOEFL (minimum score 114 iBT), IELTS (minimum score 8). *Application deadline:* For fall admission, 1/15 priority date for domestic and international students. Application fee: $90. Electronic applications accepted. *Financial support:* In 2019–20, 6 fellowships (averaging $15,000 per year) were awarded; career-related internships or fieldwork, Federal Work-Study, and scholarships/grants also available. Support available to part-time students. Financial award application deadline: 1/15; financial award applicants required to submit FAFSA. *Unit head:* Dr. Robert David Banks, Faculty Program Co-Director, 213-821-7851, E-mail: robertdb@usc.edu. *Application contact:* Allyson Hill, Associate Dean for Admissions, 213-821-0770, Fax: 213-740-1933, E-mail: ascadm@usc.edu.
Website: http://www.annenberg.usc.edu

University of Southern California, Graduate School, Dana and David Dornsife College of Letters, Arts and Sciences, Political Science and International Relations PhD Program, Los Angeles, CA 90089. Offers PhD. *Degree requirements:* For doctorate, variable foreign language requirement, comprehensive exam, thesis/dissertation. *Entrance requirements:* For doctorate, GRE (minimum score 1000). Additional exam requirements/recommendations for international students: required—TOEFL (minimum score 600 paper-based; 100 iBT). Electronic applications accepted.

University of Southern California, Graduate School, Sol Price School of Public Policy, Master of International Public Policy and Management Program, Los Angeles, CA 90089. Offers MPPM. *Program availability:* Part-time. *Entrance requirements:* Additional exam requirements/recommendations for international students: required—TOEFL (minimum score 71 iBT). Electronic applications accepted. *Expenses:* Contact institution.

University of South Florida, Innovative Education, Tampa, FL 33620-9951. Offers adult, career and higher education (Graduate Certificate), including college teaching, leadership in developing human resources, leadership in higher education; Africana studies (Graduate Certificate), including diasporas and health disparities, genocide and human rights; aging studies (Graduate Certificate), including gerontology; art research (Graduate Certificate), including museum studies; business foundations (Graduate Certificate); chemical and biomedical engineering (Graduate Certificate), including materials science and engineering, water, health and sustainability; child and family studies (Graduate Certificate), including positive behavior support; civil and industrial engineering (Graduate Certificate), including transportation systems analysis; community and family health (Graduate Certificate), including maternal and child health, social marketing and public health, violence and injury: prevention and intervention, women's health; criminology (Graduate Certificate), including criminal justice administration; data science for public administration (Graduate Certificate); digital humanities (Graduate Certificate); educational measurement and research (Graduate Certificate), including evaluation; English (Graduate Certificate), including comparative literary studies, creative writing, professional and technical communication; entrepreneurship (Graduate Certificate); environmental health (Graduate Certificate), including safety management; epidemiology and biostatistics (Graduate Certificate), including applied biostatistics, biostatistics, concepts and tools of epidemiology, epidemiology, epidemiology of infectious diseases; geography, environment and planning (Graduate Certificate), including community development, environmental policy and management, geographical information systems; geology (Graduate Certificate), including hydrogeology; global health (Graduate Certificate), including disaster management, global health and Latin American and Caribbean studies, global health practice, humanitarian assistance, infection control; government and international affairs (Graduate Certificate), including Cuban studies, globalization studies; health policy and management (Graduate Certificate), including health management and leadership, public health policy and programs; hearing specialist: early intervention (Graduate Certificate); industrial and management systems engineering (Graduate Certificate), including systems engineering, technology management; information studies (Graduate Certificate), including school library media specialist; information systems/decision sciences (Graduate Certificate), including analytics and business intelligence; instructional technology (Graduate Certificate), including distance education, Florida digital/virtual educator, instructional design, multimedia design, Web design; internal medicine, bioethics and medical humanities (Graduate Certificate), including biomedical ethics; Latin American and Caribbean studies (Graduate Certificate); leadership for coastal resiliency planning (Graduate Certificate); mass communications (Graduate Certificate), including multimedia journalism; mathematics and statistics (Graduate Certificate), including mathematics; medicine (Graduate Certificate), including aging and neuroscience, bioinformatics, biotechnology, brain fitness and memory management, clinical investigation, hand and upper limb rehabilitation, health informatics, health sciences, integrative weight management, intellectual property, medicine and gender, metabolic and nutritional medicine, metabolic cardiology, pharmacy sciences; national and competitive intelligence (Graduate Certificate); nursing (Graduate Certificate), including simulation based academic fellowship in advanced pain management; psychological and social foundations (Graduate Certificate), including career counseling, college teaching, diversity in education, mental health counseling, school counseling; public affairs (Graduate Certificate), including nonprofit management, public management, research administration; public health (Graduate Certificate), including assessing chemical toxicity and public health risks, health equity, pharmacoepidemiology, public health generalist, toxicology, translational research in adolescent behavioral health; public health practices (Graduate Certificate), including planning for healthy communities; rehabilitation and mental health counseling (Graduate Certificate), including integrative mental health care, marriage and family therapy, rehabilitation technology; secondary education (Graduate Certificate), including ESOL, foreign language education: culture and content, foreign language education: professional; social work (Graduate Certificate), including geriatric social work/clinical gerontology; special education (Graduate Certificate), including autism spectrum disorder, disabilities education: severe/profound; world languages (Graduate Certificate), including teaching English as a second language (TESL) or foreign language. *Unit head:* Dr. Cynthia DeLuca, Associate Vice President and Assistant Vice Provost, 813-974-3077, Fax: 813-974-7061, E-mail: deluca@usf.edu. *Application contact:* Owen Hooper, Director, Summer and Alternative Calendar Programs, 813-974-6917, E-mail: hooper@usf.edu.
Website: http://www.usf.edu/innovative-education/

University of the Pacific, McGeorge School of Law, Sacramento, CA 95817. Offers advocacy (JD); international water resources law (JSD); public policy and law (LL M); JD/MBA; JD/MPPA. *Accreditation:* ABA. *Program availability:* Part-time, evening/weekend. *Degree requirements:* For master's, thesis (for some programs); for doctorate, thesis/dissertation (for some programs). *Entrance requirements:* For master's, JD; for doctorate, LSAT (for JD), LL M (for JSD). Additional exam requirements/recommendations for international students: required—TOEFL (minimum score 600 paper-based; 100 iBT). Electronic applications accepted. *Expenses:* Contact institution.

University of Toronto, School of Graduate Studies, Munk School of Global Affairs, Toronto, ON M5S 1A1, Canada. Offers European, Russian and EurAsian studies (MA); global affairs (MGA); JD/MA. *Entrance requirements:* For master's, GRE General Test, GMAT, or LSAT, Honours (4-year) BA or equivalent, minimum cumulative and final year GPA of 3.5. Additional exam requirements/recommendations for international students: required—TOEFL (minimum score 100 iBT), TWE (minimum score 5). Electronic applications accepted.

University of Utah, Graduate School, College of Social and Behavioral Science, Department of Political Science, Program in Political Science, Salt Lake City, UT 84112-1107. Offers American politics (MA, MS, PhD); comparative politics (MA, MS, PhD); international relations (MA, MS, PhD); political theory (MA, MS, PhD); public administration (MA, MS, PhD). *Program availability:* Part-time. *Faculty:* 21 full-time (6 women), 2 part-time/adjunct (0 women). *Students:* 100 full-time (55 women), 97 part-time (52 women); includes 36 minority (2 Black or African American, non-Hispanic/Latino; 4 Asian, non-Hispanic/Latino; 20 Hispanic/Latino; 1 Native Hawaiian or other Pacific Islander, non-Hispanic/Latino; 9 Two or more races, non-Hispanic/Latino), 6 international. Average age 32. 47 applicants, 66% accepted, 14 enrolled. In 2019, 84 master's, 5 doctorates awarded. Terminal master's awarded for partial completion of doctoral program. *Degree requirements:* For master's, final project, defense; for doctorate, comprehensive exam, thesis/dissertation. *Entrance requirements:* For master's and doctorate, GRE General Test, minimum GPA of 3.2. Additional exam requirements/recommendations for international students: required—TOEFL (minimum score 580 paper-based; 80 iBT), IELTS (minimum score 6.5). *Application deadline:* For fall admission, 1/15 priority date for domestic and international students. Application fee: $55 ($65 for international students). Electronic applications accepted. *Expenses:* General graduate tuition charged by the university. *Financial support:* In 2019–20, 2 students received support, including 1 fellowship (averaging $24,000 per year), 23 teaching assistantships (averaging $11,043 per year); research assistantships and unspecified assistantships also available. Financial award application deadline: 4/1; financial award applicants required to submit CSS PROFILE or FAFSA. *Unit head:* Dr. Brent J. Steele, Department Chair and Professor, 801-581-7031, Fax: 801-585-6492, E-mail: brent.steele@utah.edu. *Application contact:* Sandy Hiskey, Graduate Academic Advisor, 801-581-8608, Fax: 801-585-6492, E-mail: sandy.hiskey@utah.edu.
Website: http://www.poli-sci.utah.edu/

University of Utah, Graduate School, College of Social and Behavioral Science, Master of Science in International Affairs and Global Enterprise Program, Salt Lake City, UT 84112. Offers MS. *Program availability:* Part-time. *Students:* 23 full-time (13 women), 17 part-time (12 women); includes 5 minority (1 Black or African American, non-Hispanic/Latino; 1 Asian, non-Hispanic/Latino; 3 Hispanic/Latino), 3 international. Average age 30. 30 applicants, 90% accepted, 19 enrolled. In 2019, 17 master's awarded. *Degree requirements:* For master's, one foreign language, Project/Nonthesis. *Entrance requirements:* For master's, GRE, LSAT, GMAT, or MAT, undergraduate coursework in statistics, microeconomics theory and macroeconomics theory. Additional exam requirements/recommendations for international students: required—TOEFL (minimum score 100 paper-based; 600 iBT), IELTS (minimum score 7). *Application deadline:* For fall admission, 6/30 priority date for domestic students, 4/1 priority date for international students. Applications are processed on a rolling basis. Application fee: $55 ($65 for international students). Electronic applications accepted. *Expenses:* Base graduate tuition on some core and elective classes and differential tuition on others. *Financial support:* In 2019–20, 11 students received support, including 7 fellowships with full tuition reimbursements available (averaging $16,000 per year); career-related internships or fieldwork, scholarships/grants, health care benefits, and unspecified assistantships also available. Financial award application deadline: 2/15. *Unit head:* Dr. Stephen Bannister, Program Director, 801-581-7481, Fax: 801-585-5081, E-mail: steve.bannister@csbs.utah.edu. *Application contact:* Elizabeth Henke, Program Manager, 801-585-7722, Fax: 801-587-7861, E-mail: elizabeth.henke@cppa.utah.edu.
Website: http://www.miage.utah.edu

University of Virginia, College and Graduate School of Arts and Sciences, Department of Politics, Program in Foreign Affairs, Charlottesville, VA 22903. Offers MA, PhD, JD/MA, MBA/MA. *Degree requirements:* For master's, one foreign language, 2 research/statistics courses or thesis; for doctorate, variable foreign language requirement, thesis/dissertation, 2 research/statistics courses. *Entrance requirements:* For master's and doctorate, GRE General Test, long writing sample; 2 letters of recommendation. Additional exam requirements/recommendations for international students: required—TOEFL (minimum score 600 paper-based; 90 iBT), IELTS (minimum score 7). Electronic applications accepted.

University of Washington, Graduate School, College of Arts and Sciences, Henry M. Jackson School of International Studies, International Studies MA Program, Seattle, WA 98195. Offers MAIS, JD/MAIS, MBA/MAIS, MFR/MAIS, MMA/MAIS, MPA/MAIS, MPH/MAIS. *Degree requirements:* For master's, one foreign language, thesis optional. *Entrance requirements:* For master's, minimum GPA of 3.0 in last two years. Additional exam requirements/recommendations for international students: required—TOEFL (minimum score 500 paper-based; 92 iBT), IELTS (minimum score 7). Electronic applications accepted.

University of Washington, Graduate School, College of Arts and Sciences, Henry M. Jackson School of International Studies, International Studies PhD Program, Seattle, WA 98195. Offers PhD. *Degree requirements:* For doctorate, variable foreign language requirement, comprehensive exam, thesis/dissertation, research tutorial with capstone presentation; dissertation prospectus defense; final examination. *Entrance requirements:* For doctorate, GRE General Test, master's degree. Additional exam requirements/recommendations for international students: required—TOEFL (minimum score 500 paper-based; 92 iBT), IELTS (minimum score 7).

University of Waterloo, Graduate Studies and Postdoctoral Affairs, Faculty of Arts, Department of Political Science, Waterloo, ON N2L 3G1, Canada. Offers global governance (MA, PhD). *Program availability:* Part-time. *Degree requirements:* For master's, thesis (for some programs), research paper. *Entrance requirements:* For master's, honors degree, minimum B average, writing sample. Additional exam requirements/recommendations for international students: required—TOEFL, IELTS, PTE. Electronic applications accepted.

University of Waterloo, Graduate Studies and Postdoctoral Affairs, Faculty of Arts, Global Governance Program, Waterloo, ON N2L 3G1, Canada. Offers MA, PhD. *Entrance requirements:* For doctorate, MA. Additional exam requirements/

recommendations for international students: required—TOEFL, IELTS, PTE. Electronic applications accepted.

University of Wyoming, College of Arts and Sciences, School of Politics, Public Affairs and International Studies, Program in International Studies, Laramie, WY 82071. Offers international peace corps (MA); international studies (MA). *Program availability:* Part-time. *Degree requirements:* For master's, one foreign language, thesis. *Entrance requirements:* For master's, GRE General Test, minimum GPA of 3.0. Additional exam requirements/recommendations for international students: required—TOEFL (minimum score 525 paper-based). Electronic applications accepted.

Université Laval, Québec Institute for Advanced International Studies, Program in International Relations, Québec, QC G1K 7P4, Canada. Offers MA, PhD. *Degree requirements:* For master's, thesis (for some programs). *Entrance requirements:* For master's, English exam, French exam. Electronic applications accepted.

Virginia International University, School of Public and International Affairs, Fairfax, VA 22030. Offers international relations (MS); public administration (MPA).

Virginia Polytechnic Institute and State University, Graduate School, College of Architecture and Urban Studies, Blacksburg, VA 24061. Offers architecture (M Arch, MS); architecture and design research (PhD); building construction science management (MS); creative technologies (MFA); environmental design and planning (PhD); government and international affairs (MPIA); landscape architecture (MLA, PhD); planning, governance, and globalization (PhD); public administration and public affairs (MPA, PhD); urban and regional planning (MURPL). *Accreditation:* ASLA (one or more programs are accredited). *Faculty:* 145 full-time (58 women), 2 part-time/adjunct (1 woman). *Students:* 304 full-time (156 women), 180 part-time (77 women); includes 90 minority (40 Black or African American, non-Hispanic/Latino; 19 Asian, non-Hispanic/Latino; 24 Hispanic/Latino; 7 Two or more races, non-Hispanic/Latino), 130 international. Average age 33. 475 applicants, 72% accepted, 126 enrolled. In 2019, 130 master's, 23 doctorates awarded. *Degree requirements:* For master's, comprehensive exam (for some programs), thesis (for some programs); for doctorate, comprehensive exam (for some programs), thesis/dissertation (for some programs). *Entrance requirements:* For master's and doctorate, GRE/GMAT. Additional exam requirements/recommendations for international students: required—TOEFL (minimum score 90 iBT). *Application deadline:* For fall admission, 8/1 for domestic students, 4/1 for international students; for spring admission, 1/1 for domestic students, 9/1 for international students. Applications are processed on a rolling basis. Application fee: $75. Electronic applications accepted. *Expenses:* Tuition, state resident: full-time $13,700; part-time $761.25 per credit hour. Tuition, nonresident: full-time $27,614; part-time $1534 per credit hour. *Required fees:* $886.50 per term. Tuition and fees vary according to campus/location and program. *Financial support:* In 2019–20, 2 fellowships with full tuition reimbursements (averaging $24,875 per year), 35 research assistantships with full tuition reimbursements (averaging $16,344 per year), 126 teaching assistantships with full tuition reimbursements (averaging $11,525 per year) were awarded; scholarships/grants and unspecified assistantships also available. Financial award application deadline: 3/1; financial award applicants required to submit FAFSA. *Unit head:* Dr. Richard Blythe, Dean, 540-231-6416, Fax: 540-231-6332, E-mail: richbl1@vt.edu. *Application contact:* Christine Mattsson-Coon, Executive Assistant, 540-231-6416, Fax: 540-231-6332, E-mail: cmattsso@vt.edu.
Website: http://www.caus.vt.edu/

Walden University, Graduate Programs, School of Public Policy and Administration, Minneapolis, MN 55401. Offers criminal justice (MPA, MPP, MS, Graduate Certificate), including emergency management (MS, PhD), general program (MS), global leadership (MS, PhD), homeland security and policy coordination (MS, PhD), law and public policy (MS, PhD), policy analysis (MS, PhD), public management and leadership (MS, PhD), self-designed (MS), terrorism, mediation, and peace (MS, PhD); criminal justice and executive management (MS), including global leadership (MS, PhD); criminal justice leadership and executive management (MS), including emergency management (MS, PhD), general program, homeland security and policy coordination (MS, PhD), law and public policy (MS, PhD), policy analysis (MS, PhD), public management and leadership (MS, PhD), self-designed, terrorism, mediation, and peace (MS, PhD); emergency management (MPA, MPP, MS), including criminal justice (MS, PhD), general program (MS), homeland security (MS), public management and leadership (MS, PhD), terrorism and emergency management (MS); general program (MPA, MPP); global leadership (MPA, MPP); government management (Graduate Certificate); health policy (MPA, MPP); homeland security (Graduate Certificate); homeland security and policy coordination (MPA, MPP); international nongovernmental organizations (MPA, MPP); law and public policy (MPA, MPP); local government management for sustainable communities (MPA, MPP); nonprofit management (Graduate Certificate); nonprofit management and leadership (MPA, MPP, MS), including global leadership (MS, PhD), international nongovernmental organization (MS), local government for sustainable communities (MS), self-designed (MS); online teaching in higher education (Post-Master's Certificate); policy analysis (MPA); public management and leadership (MPA, MPP, Graduate Certificate); public policy (Graduate Certificate); public policy and administration (PhD), including criminal justice (MS, PhD), emergency management (MS, PhD), global leadership (MS, PhD), health policy, homeland security and policy coordination (MS, PhD), international nongovernmental organizations, law and public policy (MS, PhD), local government management for sustainable communities, nonprofit management and leadership, policy analysis (MS, PhD), public management and leadership (MS, PhD), terrorism, mediation, and peace (MS, PhD); strategic planning and public policy (Graduate Certificate); terrorism, mediation, and peace (MPA, MPP). *Program availability:* Part-time, evening/weekend, online only, 100% online. *Degree requirements:* For doctorate, thesis/dissertation, residency. *Entrance requirements:* For master's, bachelor's degree or higher; minimum GPA of 2.5; official transcripts; goal statement (for some programs); access to computer and Internet; for doctorate, master's degree or higher; three years of related professional or academic experience (preferred); minimum GPA of 3.0; goal statement and current resume (for select programs); official transcripts; access to computer and Internet; for other advanced degree, relevant work experience; access to computer and Internet. Additional exam requirements/recommendations for international students: required—TOEFL (minimum score 550 paper-based, 79 iBT), IELTS (minimum score 6.5), Michigan English Language Assessment Battery (minimum score 82), or PTE (minimum score 53). Electronic applications accepted.

Webster University, College of Arts and Sciences, Department of History, Politics and International Relations, Program in International Nongovernmental Organizations, St. Louis, MO 63119-3194. Offers MA.

Webster University, College of Arts and Sciences, Department of History, Politics and International Relations, Program in International Relations, St. Louis, MO 63119-3194. Offers MA. *Program availability:* Part-time, evening/weekend. *Degree requirements:* For master's, thesis optional.

Webster University, College of Arts and Sciences, Institute for Human Rights and Humanitarian Studies, St. Louis, MO 63119-3194. Offers international human rights (MA).

Webster University, George Herbert Walker School of Business and Technology, Department of Business, St. Louis, MO 63119-3194. Offers business and organizational security management (MBA); decision support systems (MBA); environmental management (MBA); finance (MBA, MS); forensic accounting (MS); gerontology (MBA); human resources development (MBA); human resources management (MBA); information technology management (MBA); international business (MA, MBA); international relations (MBA); management and leadership (MBA); marketing (MBA); media communications (MBA); procurement and acquisitions management (MBA); Web services (MBA). *Accreditation:* ACBSP. *Program availability:* Part-time, evening/weekend, online learning. *Degree requirements:* For master's, comprehensive exam (for some programs), thesis (for some programs). *Entrance requirements:* Additional exam requirements/recommendations for international students: required—TOEFL.

Western Michigan University, Graduate College, College of Arts and Sciences, Department of Political Science, Kalamazoo, MI 49008. Offers international development administration (MIDA), including Peace Corps; political science (MA, PhD). *Degree requirements:* For master's, thesis optional; for doctorate, thesis/dissertation.

Wilfrid Laurier University, Faculty of Graduate and Postdoctoral Studies, Faculty of Arts, Department of Political Science, Waterloo, ON N2L 3C5, Canada. Offers Canadian political studies (MA); comparative politics/international relations (MA). *Program availability:* Part-time. *Degree requirements:* For master's, thesis optional. *Entrance requirements:* For master's, honors bachelor's degree or the equivalent in political science, minimum B average in undergraduate course work. Additional exam requirements/recommendations for international students: required—TOEFL (minimum score 89 iBT). Electronic applications accepted.

Wilfrid Laurier University, Faculty of Graduate and Postdoctoral Studies, School of International Policy and Governance, Global Governance Program, Waterloo, ON N2L 3C5, Canada. Offers conflict and security (PhD); global environment (PhD); global justice and human rights (PhD); global political economy (PhD); global social governance (PhD); multilateral institutions and diplomacy (PhD). *Degree requirements:* For doctorate, thesis/dissertation. *Entrance requirements:* For doctorate, MA in political science, history, economics, international development studies, international peace studies, globalization studies, environmental studies or related field with minimum A-. Additional exam requirements/recommendations for international students: required—TOEFL (minimum score 89 iBT). Electronic applications accepted.

Wilfrid Laurier University, Faculty of Graduate and Postdoctoral Studies, School of International Policy and Governance, International Public Policy Program, Waterloo, ON N2L 3C5, Canada. Offers global governance (MIPP); human security (MIPP); international economic relations (MIPP); international environmental policy (MIPP). *Entrance requirements:* For master's, honours BA with minimum B average. Additional exam requirements/recommendations for international students: required—TOEFL (minimum score 89 iBT). Electronic applications accepted.

Wilfrid Laurier University, Laurier Brantford, Brantford, ON N3T 2Y3, Canada. Offers criminology (MA), including culture, crime and policy, international crime and justice, media criminology. *Degree requirements:* For master's, thesis. *Entrance requirements:* For master's, honours bachelor's degree with major in criminology or equivalent degree; minimum B+ average in final year and in all criminology courses. Additional exam requirements/recommendations for international students: required—TOEFL (minimum score 89 iBT). Electronic applications accepted.

Yale University, Graduate School of Arts and Sciences, Jackson Institute for Global Affairs, New Haven, CT 06520. Offers MA, JD/MA, MBA/MA, MEM/MA, MF/MA, MFS/MA, MPH/MA. *Faculty:* 38 full-time (12 women). *Students:* 67 full-time (30 women); includes 35 minority (10 Black or African American, non-Hispanic/Latino; 16 Asian, non-Hispanic/Latino; 9 Hispanic/Latino). Average age 28. 404 applicants, 15% accepted, 33 enrolled. In 2019, 28 master's awarded. *Degree requirements:* For master's, one foreign language, summer internship or project. *Entrance requirements:* For master's, GRE General Test for M.A. students (GRE optional for M.A.S. students), professional experience and introductory coursework in microeconomics and macroeconomics (strongly preferred). Additional exam requirements/recommendations for international students: required—TOEFL (minimum score 102 iBT) or IELTS (minimum score 7.5). *Application deadline:* For fall admission, 1/2 for domestic and international students. Application fee: $105. Electronic applications accepted. *Expenses:* $43,300 per year. *Financial support:* In 2019–20, 49 students received support, including 26 fellowships with full and partial tuition reimbursements available (averaging $10,500 per year), 36 teaching assistantships (averaging $6,595 per year); research assistantships, career-related internships or fieldwork, scholarships/grants, tuition waivers (full and partial), unspecified assistantships, and competitive summer fellowships for unpaid internships and projects also available. Financial award application deadline: 1/2. *Unit head:* James Levinsohn, Director, Jackson Institute for Global Affairs, 203-432-6253, Fax: 203-432-9886, E-mail: jackson.institute@yale.edu. *Application contact:* Melissa McGinnis, Assistant Director of Admissions, Jackson Institute for Global Affairs, 203-432-6251, Fax: 203-432-9886, E-mail: melissa.mcginnis@yale.edu.
Website: http://jackson.yale.edu

York University, Faculty of Graduate Studies, Glendon Campus, Program in Public and International Affairs, Toronto, ON M3J 1P3, Canada. Offers MA.

International Development

American University, School of International Service, Washington, DC 20016-8071. Offers comparative and regional studies (Certificate); cross-cultural communication (Certificate); development management (MS); ethics, peace, and global affairs (MA); European studies (Certificate); global environmental policy (MA, Certificate); global information technology (Certificate); global media (MA); international affairs (MA), including comparative and regional studies, global governance, politics, and security, international economic relations, natural resources and sustainable development, U.S. foreign policy and national security; international arts management (Certificate);

international communication (MA, Certificate); international development (MA); international economic policy (Certificate); international economic relations (Certificate); international economics (MA); international peace and conflict resolution (MA, Certificate); international politics (Certificate); international relations (MA, PhD); international service (MIS); peacebuilding (Certificate); social enterprise (MA); the Americas (Certificate); United States foreign policy (Certificate); JD/MA. *Program availability:* Part-time, evening/weekend, 100% online, blended/hybrid learning. Terminal master's awarded for partial completion of doctoral program. *Degree requirements:* For master's, one foreign language, comprehensive exam, thesis or alternative; for doctorate, one foreign language, comprehensive exam, thesis/dissertation. *Entrance requirements:* For master's, transcripts, resume, 2 letters of recommendation, statement of purpose; for doctorate, GRE, transcripts, resume, 3 letters of recommendation, statement of purpose. Additional exam requirements/recommendations for international students: required—TOEFL. Electronic applications accepted. *Expenses:* Contact institution.

Andrews University, School of Graduate Studies, College of Arts and Sciences, Department of Behavioral Science, Program in International Development, Berrien Springs, MI 49104. Offers community and international development (MSCID). *Program availability:* Online learning. *Faculty:* 10 full-time (2 women), 1 part-time/adjunct (0 women). *Students:* 14 full-time (8 women), 13 part-time (6 women); includes 7 minority (5 Black or African American, non-Hispanic/Latino; 1 Asian, non-Hispanic/Latino; 1 Hispanic/Latino), 19 international. Average age 33. In 2019, 8 master's awarded. *Entrance requirements:* For master's, GRE General Test. Additional exam requirements/recommendations for international students: required—TOEFL (minimum score 550 paper-based). *Application deadline:* Applications are processed on a rolling basis. Application fee: $60. Electronic applications accepted. *Unit head:* Dr. Harvey Burnett, Director, 269-471-3152. *Application contact:* Jillian Panigot, Director, University Admissions, 800-253-2874, Fax: 269-471-6321, E-mail: graduate@andrews.edu. Website: http://www.andrews.edu/grad/programs/community-and-international-development-off-campus.html

Athabasca University, Centre for Interdisciplinary Studies, Athabasca, AB T9S 3A3, Canada. Offers adult education (MA); community studies (MA); cultural studies (MA); educational studies (MA); global change (MA); heritage resource management (Postbaccalaureate Certificate); legislative drafting (Postbaccalaureate Certificate); work, organization, and leadership (MA). *Program availability:* Part-time, evening/weekend, online learning. *Degree requirements:* For master's, project. *Entrance requirements:* Additional exam requirements/recommendations for international students: required—TOEFL (minimum score 560 paper-based). Electronic applications accepted.

Clark University, Graduate School, Department of International Development, Community, and Environment, Program in International Development and Social Change, Worcester, MA 01610-1477. Offers MA. *Degree requirements:* For master's, thesis. *Entrance requirements:* For master's, 2 references, resume or curriculum vitae, personal statement. Additional exam requirements/recommendations for international students: required—TOEFL (minimum score 575 paper-based; 90 iBT), IELTS (minimum score 6.5). Electronic applications accepted. *Expenses:* Contact institution.

Dalhousie University, Faculty of Arts and Social Sciences, Department of International Development Studies, Halifax, NS B3H 4R2, Canada. Offers MA. *Entrance requirements:* Additional exam requirements/recommendations for international students: required—TOEFL, IELTS, CANTEST, CAEL, or Michigan English Language Assessment Battery. Electronic applications accepted.

Duke University, Sanford School of Public Policy, Master of International Development Policy Program, Durham, NC 27708-0237. Offers MIDP. *Degree requirements:* For master's, thesis, internship, project. *Entrance requirements:* For master's, minimum five years of professional experience in a development-related field. Additional exam requirements/recommendations for international students: required—TOEFL (minimum score 577 paper-based; 90 iBT), IELTS (minimum score 7), PTE (minimum score 64). Electronic applications accepted. *Expenses:* Contact institution.

Fordham University, Graduate School of Arts and Sciences, Program in International Political Economy and Development, New York, NY 10458. Offers MA, Certificate. *Program availability:* Part-time, evening/weekend. *Students:* Average age 27. 81 applicants, 57% accepted, 17 enrolled. In 2019, 21 master's awarded. *Entrance requirements:* For master's, GRE General Test. Additional exam requirements/recommendations for international students: required—TOEFL (minimum score 600 paper-based). *Application deadline:* For fall admission, 1/4 priority date for domestic students; for spring admission, 11/1 for domestic students. Application fee: $70. Electronic applications accepted. *Financial support:* In 2019–20, 35 students received support, including 4 fellowships with tuition reimbursements available (averaging $17,014 per year); research assistantships, career-related internships or fieldwork, institutionally sponsored loans, tuition waivers (full and partial), and unspecified assistantships also available. Financial award application deadline: 1/4; financial award applicants required to submit FAFSA. *Unit head:* Dr. Henry Schwalbenberg, Chair, 718-817-3866, Fax: 718-817-3518. *Application contact:* Garrett Marino, Director of Graduate Admissions, 718-817-4419, Fax: 718-817-3566, E-mail: gmarino10@fordham.edu.

Georgetown University, McCourt School of Public Policy, Washington, DC, DC 20057. Offers data science for public policy (MDSPP); international development policy (MIDP); policy leadership (EMPL); policy management (MPM); public policy (MPP); MBA/MPP; MPP/JD; MPP/MA; MPP/MSFS; MPP/PhD. *Program availability:* Part-time. *Faculty:* 35 full-time (14 women), 35 part-time/adjunct (16 women). *Students:* 243 full-time (148 women), 25 part-time (16 women); includes 65 minority (24 Black or African American, non-Hispanic/Latino; 16 Asian, non-Hispanic/Latino; 15 Hispanic/Latino; 10 Two or more races, non-Hispanic/Latino), 78 international. 1,353 applicants, 78% accepted, 268 enrolled. *Degree requirements:* For master's, thesis or alternative. *Entrance requirements:* For master's, GRE General Test or GMAT required for MPP, MIDP and MS-DSPP applicants; LSAT accepted for applicants to dual JD/MPP program, minimum B average (3.0 GPA). Additional exam requirements/recommendations for international students: required—TOEFL (minimum score 600 paper-based; 100 iBT), IELTS (minimum score 7), If an applicant did not earn a degree from an institution where English is the primary language of instruction, a TOEFL or IELTS score is required. *Application deadline:* For fall admission, 1/15 priority date for domestic and international students; for summer admission, 1/15 priority date for domestic students, 1/17 priority date for international students. Application fee: $90. Electronic applications accepted. *Financial support:* In 2019–20, 230 students received support, including 5 fellowships with full tuition reimbursements available (averaging $10,000 per year), 40 research assistantships, 60 teaching assistantships; career-related internships or fieldwork, scholarships/grants, and unspecified assistantships also available. Support available to part-time students. Financial award application deadline: 1/15; financial award applicants required to submit FAFSA. *Unit head:* Dr. Maria Cancian, Dean, McCourt School of Public Policy, 202-687-6163, E-mail: mcancian@georgetown.edu. *Application contact:* Julie Ito, Director of Admissions, 202-687-0678, E-mail: mccourtadmissions@georgetown.edu.
Website: https://mccourt.georgetown.edu/

The George Washington University, Columbian College of Arts and Sciences, Department of Anthropology, Washington, DC 20052. Offers anthropology (MA, PhD); international development (MA); medical anthropology (MA); museum training (MA). *Program availability:* Part-time, evening/weekend. *Degree requirements:* For master's, one foreign language, comprehensive exam, thesis or alternative. *Entrance requirements:* For master's, GRE General Test, minimum GPA of 3.0. Additional exam requirements/recommendations for international students: required—TOEFL (minimum score 550 paper-based; 80 iBT). Electronic applications accepted.

The George Washington University, Elliott School of International Affairs, Program in International Development Studies, Washington, DC 20052. Offers MA. *Program availability:* Part-time. *Degree requirements:* For master's, one foreign language, capstone project. *Entrance requirements:* For master's, GRE General Test, 2 years (or the equivalent) of a modern foreign language, introductory courses in microeconomics and macroeconomics. Additional exam requirements/recommendations for international students: required—TOEFL (minimum score 100 iBT), IELTS (minimum score 7). Electronic applications accepted.

Harvard University, John F. Kennedy School of Government, Master in Public Administration in International Development Program, Cambridge, MA 02138. Offers MPAID. *Entrance requirements:* For master's, one course each in microeconomics and macroeconomics; two college-level calculus courses (one must contain multivariable calculus); bachelor's degree; 2-3 years of professional experience in development (strongly encouraged). Additional exam requirements/recommendations for international students: required—TOEFL (minimum score 600 paper-based; 100 iBT). Electronic applications accepted.

Hope International University, School of Graduate and Professional Studies, Program in Business Administration, Fullerton, CA 92831-3138. Offers general management (MBA, MSM); international development (MBA, MSM); marketing management (MBA, MSM); non-profit management (MBA, MSM). *Program availability:* Part-time, online learning. *Degree requirements:* For master's, comprehensive exam (for some programs), thesis (for some programs), project. *Entrance requirements:* For master's, minimum GPA of 3.0; 2 references. Additional exam requirements/recommendations for international students: required—TOEFL (minimum score 550 paper-based; 86 iBT); recommended—IELTS (minimum score 6.5). Electronic applications accepted. *Expenses:* Contact institution.

Indiana University Bloomington, School of Public and Environmental Affairs, Public Affairs Programs, Bloomington, IN 47405. Offers economic development (MPA); energy (MPA); environmental policy (PhD); environmental policy and natural resource management (MPA); information systems (MPA); international development (MPA); local government management (MPA); nonprofit management (MPA, Certificate); policy analysis (MPA); public budgeting and financial management (Certificate); public finance (PhD); public financial administration (MPA); public management (MPA, PhD, Certificate); public policy analysis (PhD); social entrepreneurship (Certificate); specialized public affairs (MPA); sustainability and sustainable development (MPA); JD/MPA; MPA/MA; MPA/MIS; MPA/MLS; MSES/MPA. *Accreditation:* NASPAA (one or more programs are accredited). *Program availability:* Part-time. *Degree requirements:* For master's, capstone, internship; for doctorate, comprehensive exam, thesis/dissertation. *Entrance requirements:* For master's, GRE General Test or GMAT, official transcripts, 3 letters of recommendation, resume, personal statement; for doctorate, GRE General Test, official transcripts, 3 letters of recommendation, statement of purpose. Additional exam requirements/recommendations for international students: required—TOEFL (minimum score 600 paper-based; 96 iBT); recommended—IELTS (minimum score 7). Electronic applications accepted.

Johns Hopkins University, School of Advanced International Studies, Washington, DC 20036. Offers global risk (MA); international development (MA, Certificate), including international economics (MA); international economics (Certificate); international economics and finance (MA); international public policy (MIPP); international relations (PhD); international studies (Certificate); Japan studies (MA), including international economics; Korea studies (MA), including international economics; South Asia studies (MA), including international economics; Southeast Asia studies (MA), including international economics; JD/MA; MBA/MA; MHS/MA. *Program availability:* Evening/weekend. *Degree requirements:* For master's, 4-6 international economics courses, 5-6 functional or regional concentration courses, 2 core examinations, proficiency in language other than native language, capstone project; for doctorate, 2 foreign languages, thesis/dissertation, 3 comprehensive exams, economics, quantitative and qualitative course, dissertation prospectus and defense. *Entrance requirements:* For master's, GMAT or GRE General Test, previous course work in economics, foreign language, undergraduate degree; for doctorate, GRE General Test, Master's degree. Additional exam requirements/recommendations for international students: required—TOEFL (minimum score 600 paper-based; 100 iBT), IELTS (minimum score 7), TOEFL (minimum score 600 paper-based; 100 iBT) or IELTS (minimum score 7). Electronic applications accepted. *Expenses:* Contact institution.

Marymount California University, Program in Leadership and Global Development, Rancho Palos Verdes, CA 90275-6299. Offers MS.

McGill University, Faculty of Graduate and Postdoctoral Studies, Desautels Faculty of Management, Montréal, QC H3A 2T5, Canada. Offers administration (PhD); entrepreneurial studies (MBA); finance (MBA); general management (Post Master's Certificate); global manufacturing and supply chain management (MMM); information systems (MBA); international business (MBA); international practicing management (MM); management (MBA); management for development (MBA); marketing (MBA); operations management (MBA); public accountancy (Diploma); strategic management (MBA); MBA/LL B; MD/MBA.

Middlebury Institute of International Studies at Monterey, Graduate School of International Policy and Management, Program in International Policy and Development, Monterey, CA 93940-2691. Offers MA. *Degree requirements:* For master's, one foreign language. *Entrance requirements:* For master's, minimum GPA of 3.0, proficiency in a foreign language. Additional exam requirements/recommendations for international students: required—TOEFL (minimum score 550 paper-based; 80 iBT). Electronic applications accepted.

Norwich University, College of Graduate and Continuing Studies, Master of Arts in International Relations Program, Northfield, VT 05663. Offers international relations (MA), including cyber diplomacy-policy, cyber diplomacy-technical, international development, international security, national security, regions of the world. *Program availability:* Evening/weekend, online only, mostly all online with a week-long residency requirement. *Degree requirements:* For master's, research paper. *Entrance requirements:* For master's, minimum undergraduate GPA of 2.75. Additional exam requirements/recommendations for international students: required—TOEFL (minimum score 550 paper-based; 80 iBT), IELTS (minimum score 6.5). Electronic applications accepted. *Expenses:* Contact institution.

Norwich University, College of Graduate and Continuing Studies, Master of Public Administration Program, Northfield, VT 05663. Offers criminal justice and public safety (MPA); fiscal management (MPA); international development and influence (MPA); municipal governance (MPA); nonprofit management (MPA); policy analysis and analytics (MPA); public administration leadership and crisis management (MPA); public works and sustainability (MPA). *Program availability:* Evening/weekend, online only, mostly all online with a week-long residency requirement. *Degree requirements:* For master's, capstone. *Entrance requirements:* For master's, minimum undergraduate GPA of 2.75. Additional exam requirements/recommendations for international students: required—TOEFL (minimum score 550 paper-based; 80 iBT), IELTS (minimum score 6.5). Electronic applications accepted. *Expenses:* Contact institution.

Ohio University, Graduate College, Center for International Studies, Program in International Development Studies, Athens, OH 45701-2979. Offers MA. *Program availability:* Part-time. *Degree requirements:* For master's, one foreign language, thesis optional. *Entrance requirements:* For master's, minimum GPA of 3.0. Additional exam requirements/recommendations for international students: required—TOEFL (minimum score 550 paper-based; 80 iBT), IELTS (minimum score 6.5). Electronic applications accepted.

Old Dominion University, College of Arts and Letters, Graduate Program in International Studies, Norfolk, VA 23529. Offers conflict and cooperation (MA, PhD); interdependence and transnationalism (MA, PhD); international cultural studies (MA, PhD); international political economy and development (MA, PhD); modeling and simulation (MA, PhD); U.S. foreign policy and international relations (MA, PhD). *Program availability:* Part-time. Terminal master's awarded for partial completion of doctoral program. *Degree requirements:* For master's, one foreign language, comprehensive exam, thesis optional; for doctorate, one foreign language, comprehensive exam, thesis/dissertation. *Entrance requirements:* For master's, GRE General Test, sample of written work, 2 letters of recommendation; for doctorate, GRE General Test, sample of written work, 3 letters of recommendation. Additional exam requirements/recommendations for international students: required—TOEFL (minimum score 570 paper-based). Electronic applications accepted. *Expenses:* Contact institution.

Rutgers University - Camden, Graduate School of Arts and Sciences, Department of Public Policy and Administration, Camden, NJ 08102. Offers education policy and leadership (MPA); international public service and development (MPA); public management (MPA); JD/MPA; MPA/MA. *Accreditation:* NASPAA. *Program availability:* Part-time, evening/weekend. *Degree requirements:* For master's, directed study, research workshop, 42 credits. *Entrance requirements:* For master's, GRE General Test, GMAT or LSAT, 3 letters of recommendation; resume. Additional exam requirements/recommendations for international students: required—TOEFL (minimum score 550 paper-based), IELTS. Electronic applications accepted.

Saint Mary's University, Faculty of Arts, International Development Studies Program, Halifax, NS B3H 3C3, Canada. Offers MA, Graduate Diploma. *Program availability:* Part-time. *Degree requirements:* For master's, thesis. *Entrance requirements:* For master's, honors degree.

St. Mary's University, Graduate Studies, Program in International Relations, San Antonio, TX 78228. Offers conflict transformation (Certificate); international conflict resolution (MA); international development (MA); international relations (MA); security policy (MA); JD/MA. *Program availability:* Part-time, evening/weekend, 100% online. *Degree requirements:* For master's, one foreign language, comprehensive exam (for some programs), thesis (for some programs), thesis or comprehensive exam. *Entrance requirements:* For master's, minimum undergraduate cumulative GPA of 3.0. Additional exam requirements/recommendations for international students: required—TOEFL (minimum score 550 paper-based; 80 iBT), IELTS (minimum score 6). Electronic applications accepted.

Tufts University, Graduate School of Arts and Sciences, Department of Urban and Environmental Policy and Planning, Medford, MA 02155. Offers community development (MA); environmental policy (MA); health and human welfare (MA); housing policy (MA); international environment/development policy (MA); public policy (MPP); MA/JD; MA/MBA; MA/MPH; MA/MS; MALD/MA. *Accreditation:* ACSP (one or more programs are accredited). *Program availability:* Part-time. *Degree requirements:* For master's, thesis or alternative, internship. *Entrance requirements:* For master's, GRE General Test. Additional exam requirements/recommendations for international students: required—TOEFL (minimum score 550 paper-based; 80 iBT), IELTS (minimum score 6.5). Electronic applications accepted. *Expenses:* Contact institution.

University of California, San Diego, Graduate Division, School of Global Policy and Strategy, Master of International Affairs Program, La Jolla, CA 92093. Offers international development and nonprofit management (MIA); international economics (MIA); international environmental policy (MIA); international management (MIA); international politics (MIA). *Degree requirements:* For master's, one foreign language. *Entrance requirements:* For master's, GMAT or GRE General Test. Additional exam requirements/recommendations for international students: required—TOEFL (minimum score 90 iBT), IELTS (minimum score 7). Electronic applications accepted.

University of Denver, Josef Korbel School of International Studies, Denver, CO 80208. Offers conflict resolution (MA); global business and corporate social responsibility (Certificate); global finance, trade and economic integration (MA); global health affairs (Certificate); homeland security (Certificate); humanitarian assistance (Certificate); international administration (MA); international development (MA); international human rights (MA); international security (MA); international studies (MA, PhD); public policy studies (MPP); religion and international affairs (Certificate). *Program availability:* Part-time. *Faculty:* 41 full-time (15 women), 14 part-time/adjunct (2 women). *Students:* 208 full-time (112 women), 24 part-time (13 women); includes 50 minority (11 Black or African American, non-Hispanic/Latino; 10 Asian, non-Hispanic/Latino; 15 Hispanic/Latino; 14 Two or more races, non-Hispanic/Latino), 20 international. Average age 27. 718 applicants, 70% accepted, 88 enrolled. In 2019, 134 master's, 2 doctorates, 26 other advanced degrees awarded. *Degree requirements:* For master's, variable foreign language requirement, thesis (for some programs); for doctorate, one foreign language, comprehensive exam, thesis/dissertation, one extended research paper. *Entrance requirements:* For master's, GRE General Test, bachelor's degree, transcripts, two letters of recommendation, personal statement, resume or curriculum vitae; for doctorate, GRE General Test, bachelor's degree (most have a master's degree), transcripts, personal statement, resume or curriculum vitae, writing sample. Additional exam requirements/recommendations for international students: required—TOEFL (minimum score 587 paper-based; 95 iBT). *Application deadline:* For fall admission, 1/23 priority date for domestic and international students; for winter admission, 11/1 for domestic and international students. Applications are processed on a rolling basis. Application fee: $65. Electronic applications accepted. *Expenses:* Contact institution. *Financial support:* In 2019–20, 161 students received support, including 4 teaching assistantships with tuition reimbursements available (averaging $16,875 per year); research assistantships with tuition reimbursements available, career-related internships or fieldwork, Federal Work-Study, institutionally sponsored loans, scholarships/grants, and unspecified assistantships also available. Support available to part-time students. Financial award application deadline: 2/15; financial award applicants required to submit FAFSA. *Unit head:* Dr. Fritz Mayer, Dean, 303-871-6338, E-mail: frederick.mayer@du.edu. *Application contact:* Admissions Contact, 303-871-2324, E-mail: korbeladm@du.edu.
Website: http://www.du.edu/korbel

University of Florida, Graduate School, College of Liberal Arts and Sciences, Department of Political Science, Gainesville, FL 32611. Offers educational policy (PhD); international development policy and administration (MA, Certificate); international relations (MA, MAT); political campaigning (MA, Certificate); political science (MA, PhD); public affairs (MA, Certificate); tropical conservation and development (MA, PhD); JD/MA. Terminal master's awarded for partial completion of doctoral program. *Degree requirements:* For master's, variable foreign language requirement, comprehensive exam (for some programs), thesis or alternative, internship (for some programs); for doctorate, variable foreign language requirement, comprehensive exam, thesis/dissertation. *Entrance requirements:* For master's and doctorate, GRE General Test (minimum score: 308 combined verbal/quantitative), minimum GPA of 3.5. Additional exam requirements/recommendations for international students: required—TOEFL (minimum score 550 paper-based; 80 iBT), IELTS (minimum score 6). Electronic applications accepted.

University of Guelph, Office of Graduate and Postdoctoral Studies, Collaborative International Development Studies, Guelph, ON N1G 2W1, Canada. Offers M Eng, M Sc, MA, MBA, PhD. *Program availability:* Part-time. *Degree requirements:* For master's, thesis (for some programs), seminar; for doctorate, comprehensive exam (for some programs), thesis/dissertation. *Entrance requirements:* For master's, honour's degree with courses in economics, social science, and empirical methods.

University of Hawaii at Manoa, Office of Graduate Education, College of Social Sciences, Department of Urban and Regional Planning, Honolulu, HI 96822. Offers community planning (MURP); disaster management and humanitarian assistance (Graduate Certificate); environmental planning and sustainability (MURP); international development planning (MURP); land use, transportation and infrastructure planning (MURP); planning studies (Graduate Certificate); urban and regional planning (PhD, Graduate Certificate). *Accreditation:* ACSP. *Program availability:* Part-time. *Entrance requirements:* For master's, GRE General Test, minimum GPA of 3.0; for doctorate, GRE General Test. Additional exam requirements/recommendations for international students: required—TOEFL (minimum score 500 paper-based; 61 iBT), IELTS (minimum score 5).

The University of Manchester, School of Environment, Education and Development, Manchester, United Kingdom. Offers architecture (M Phil, PhD); development policy and management (M Phil, PhD); human geography (M Phil, PhD); physical geography (M Phil, PhD); planning and landscape (M Phil, PhD).

University of Massachusetts Boston, Graduate School of Global Inclusion and Social Development, Program in Global Inclusion and Social Development, Boston, MA 02125-3393. Offers MA, PhD.

University of Minnesota, Twin Cities Campus, Graduate School, Humphrey School of Public Affairs, Master of Development Practice Program, Minneapolis, MN 55455-0213. Offers MDP. *Students:* 30 full-time (23 women); includes 5 minority (2 Black or African American, non-Hispanic/Latino; 3 Asian, non-Hispanic/Latino), 15 international. Average age 28. 40 applicants, 85% accepted, 12 enrolled. In 2019, 17 master's awarded. *Degree requirements:* For master's, thesis or alternative, international field experience. *Entrance requirements:* For master's, GRE. Additional exam requirements/recommendations for international students: required—TOEFL (minimum score 600 paper-based; 100 iBT), IELTS (minimum score 7). *Application deadline:* For fall admission, 4/1 for domestic and international students. Application fee: $75 ($95 for international students). Electronic applications accepted. *Expenses:* Contact institution. *Financial support:* In 2019–20, 14 students received support, including fellowships with tuition reimbursements available (averaging $11,400 per year), research assistantships with tuition reimbursements available (averaging $26,000 per year); teaching assistantships, scholarships/grants, traineeships, health care benefits, tuition waivers (full and partial), and unspecified assistantships also available. Financial award application deadline: 1/15; financial award applicants required to submit FAFSA. *Unit head:* Laura Bloomberg, Associate Dean, 612-625-0608, Fax: 612-626-0002, E-mail: bloom004@umn.edu. *Application contact:* Jacob Merrifield, Admissions Program Manger, 612-624-3800, Fax: 612-626-0002, E-mail: jmerrifi@umn.edu.
Website: http://www.hhh.umn.edu/degrees/mdp/

University of New Mexico, Graduate Studies, College of Arts and Sciences, Program in Economics, Albuquerque, NM 87131-2039. Offers econometrics (MA); economic theory (MA); environmental/natural resource economics (MA, PhD); international/development and sustainability economics (MA, PhD); public economics (MA, PhD). *Program availability:* Part-time. Terminal master's awarded for partial completion of doctoral program. *Degree requirements:* For master's, comprehensive exam, thesis (for some programs); for doctorate, comprehensive exam, thesis/dissertation. *Entrance requirements:* For master's and doctorate, GRE General Test, 3 letters of recommendation, letter of intent, curriculum vitae. Additional exam requirements/recommendations for international students: required—TOEFL (minimum score 520 paper-based; 68 iBT). Electronic applications accepted. *Expenses:* Tuition, state resident: full-time $7633; part-time $972 per year. Tuition, nonresident: full-time $22,586; part-time $3840 per year. *International tuition:* $23,292 full-time. *Required fees:* $8608. Tuition and fees vary according to course level, course load, degree level, program and student level.

University of Ottawa, Faculty of Graduate and Postdoctoral Studies, Program in Globalization and International Development, Ottawa, ON K1N 6N5, Canada. Offers MA. *Degree requirements:* For master's, thesis or alternative. *Entrance requirements:* For master's, honours bachelor's degree or equivalent, minimum B average.

University of Pittsburgh, Graduate School of Public and International Affairs, Master of International Development Program, Pittsburgh, PA 15260. Offers energy and environment (MID); governance and international public management (MID); human security (MID); nongovernmental organizations and civil society (MID); urban affairs and planning (MID); MID/JD; MID/MBA; MID/MPH; MID/MSIS; MID/MSW. *Program availability:* Part-time, evening/weekend. *Faculty:* 33 full-time (11 women), 10 part-time/adjunct (5 women). *Students:* 61 full-time (42 women), 10 part-time (8 women); includes 11 minority (5 Black or African American, non-Hispanic/Latino; 4 Asian, non-Hispanic/Latino; 1 Hispanic/Latino; 1 Two or more races, non-Hispanic/Latino), 10 international. Average age 27. 89 applicants, 91% accepted, 26 enrolled. In 2019, 20 master's awarded. *Degree requirements:* For master's, thesis optional, capstone seminar. *Entrance requirements:* For master's, Personal essay, resume, two letters of recommendation, transcripts. Additional exam requirements/recommendations for international students: required—TOEFL (minimum score 80 iBT), Duolingo English Test; recommended—IELTS (minimum score 6.5). *Application deadline:* For fall admission, 2/1 for domestic students, 1/15 for international students; for spring admission, 11/1 for domestic students, 8/1 for international students. Application fee: $50. Electronic applications accepted. *Financial support:* In 2019–20, 41 students received support, including 6 fellowships with full tuition reimbursements available (averaging $16,060 per year); scholarships/grants also available. Financial award application deadline: 2/1. *Unit head:* Dr. John Keeler, Dean, 412-648-7605, Fax: 412-648-7601, E-mail: gspia@pitt.edu. *Application contact:* Dr. Michael Rizzi, Director of

Student Services, 412-648-7640, Fax: 412-648-7641, E-mail: rizzim@pitt.edu. Website: http://www.gspia.pitt.edu/

University of Pittsburgh, Graduate School of Public and International Affairs, PhD Program in Public and International Affairs, Pittsburgh, PA 15260. Offers international affairs (PhD); international development (PhD); public administration (PhD); public policy (PhD). *Faculty:* 33 full-time (11 women), 10 part-time/adjunct (5 women). *Students:* 28 full-time (12 women), 4 part-time (2 women); includes 4 minority (1 Black or African American, non-Hispanic/Latino; 3 Hispanic/Latino), 14 international. Average age 36. 65 applicants, 3% accepted, 2 enrolled. In 2019, 1 doctorate awarded. *Degree requirements:* For doctorate, comprehensive exam, thesis/dissertation. *Entrance requirements:* For doctorate, GRE or GMAT, Personal essay, research proposal essay, two letters of recommendation, transcripts, resume. Additional exam requirements/recommendations for international students: required—TOEFL (minimum score 80 iBT), Duolingo English Test; recommended—IELTS (minimum score 6.5). *Application deadline:* For fall admission, 1/15 for domestic and international students. Application fee: $50. Electronic applications accepted. *Expenses:* $24,480 in-state, $40,848 out-of-state. *Financial support:* In 2019–20, 15 students received support, including 15 research assistantships with full tuition reimbursements available (averaging $16,060 per year). Financial award application deadline: 1/15. *Unit head:* Dr. John Keeler, Dean, 412-648-7605, Fax: 412-648-7601, E-mail: gspia@pitt.edu. *Application contact:* Dr. Michael Rizzi, Director of Student Services, 412-648-7640, Fax: 412-648-7641, E-mail: rizzim@pitt.edu.
Website: http://www.gspia.pitt.edu/

University of Pittsburgh, Katz Graduate School of Business, MBA/Master of International Development Joint Degree Program, Pittsburgh, PA 15260. Offers MID/MBA. *Accreditation:* AACSB. *Program availability:* Part-time, evening/weekend. *Faculty:* 95 full-time (30 women), 30 part-time/adjunct (10 women). *Students:* 2 full-time (both women); includes 1 minority (Asian, non-Hispanic/Latino). Average age 32. 6 applicants, 83% accepted, 3 enrolled. *Entrance requirements:* Additional exam requirements/recommendations for international students: required—TOEFL (minimum score 100 iBT). *Application deadline:* For fall admission, 4/1 priority date for domestic students, 2/1 priority date for international students. Application fee: $50. Electronic applications accepted. *Financial support:* Research assistantships, teaching assistantships, Federal Work-Study, scholarships/grants, health care benefits, and unspecified assistantships available. Financial award application deadline: 6/1; financial award applicants required to submit FAFSA. *Unit head:* Dr. Arjang A. Assad, Dean, 412-648-1556, Fax: 412-648-1552, E-mail: aassad@katz.pitt.edu. *Application contact:* Thomas Keller, Director of Admissions, 412-648-1700, Fax: 412-648-1659, E-mail: admissions@katz.pitt.edu.
Website: https://www.katz.business.pitt.edu/mba/joint-and-dual/international-development#section-1

University of San Francisco, College of Arts and Sciences, International and Development Economics Program, San Francisco, CA 94117. Offers MA. *Program availability:* Part-time, evening/weekend. *Students:* 32 full-time (17 women); includes 10 minority (2 Black or African American, non-Hispanic/Latino; 4 Asian, non-Hispanic/Latino; 3 Hispanic/Latino; 1 Two or more races, non-Hispanic/Latino), 15 international. Average age 28. 77 applicants, 77% accepted, 12 enrolled. In 2019, 37 master's awarded. *Entrance requirements:* For master's, Economics courses (macro and micro) and calculus preferred. Additional exam requirements/recommendations for international students: required—TOEFL (minimum score 79 iBT), IELTS (minimum score 6.5), PTE (minimum score 53). *Application deadline:* For fall admission, 3/1 for domestic and international students. Applications are processed on a rolling basis. Application fee: $55. Electronic applications accepted. Application fee is waived when

completed online. *Financial support:* Teaching assistantships with partial tuition reimbursements, career-related internships or fieldwork, and scholarships/grants available. Financial award applicants required to submit FAFSA. *Unit head:* Alessandra Cassar, Graduate Director, 415-422-2711, E-mail: acassar@usfca.edu. *Application contact:* Information Contact, 415-422-5101, Fax: 415-422-6983, E-mail: asgraduate@usfca.edu.
Website: https://www.usfca.edu/arts-sciences/graduate-programs/international-development-economics

Walden University, Graduate Programs, School of Public Policy and Administration, Minneapolis, MN 55401. Offers criminal justice (MPA, MPP, MS, Graduate Certificate), including emergency management (MS, PhD), general program (MS), global leadership (MS, PhD), homeland security and policy coordination (MS, PhD), law and public policy (MS, PhD), policy analysis (MS, PhD), public management and leadership (MS, PhD), self-designed (MS), terrorism, mediation, and peace (MS, PhD); criminal justice and executive management (MS), including global leadership (MS, PhD); criminal justice leadership and executive management (MS), including emergency management (MS, PhD), general program, homeland security and policy coordination (MS, PhD), law and public policy (MS, PhD), policy analysis (MS, PhD), public management and leadership (MS, PhD), self-designed, terrorism, mediation, and peace (MS, PhD); emergency management (MPA, MPP, MS), including criminal justice (MS, PhD), general program (MS), homeland security (MS), public management and leadership (MS, PhD), terrorism and emergency management (MS); general program (MPA, MPP); global leadership (MPA, MPP); government management (Graduate Certificate); health policy (MPA, MPP); homeland security (Graduate Certificate); homeland security and policy coordination (MPA, MPP); international nongovernmental organizations (MPA, MPP); law and public policy (MPA, MPP); local government management for sustainable communities (MPA, MPP); nonprofit management (Graduate Certificate); nonprofit management and leadership (MPA, MPP, MS), including global leadership (MS, PhD), international nongovernmental organization (MS), local government for sustainable communities (MS), self-designed (MS); online teaching in higher education (Post-Master's Certificate); policy analysis (MPA); public management and leadership (MPA, MPP, Graduate Certificate); public policy (Graduate Certificate); public policy and administration (PhD), including criminal justice (MS, PhD), emergency management (MS, PhD), global leadership (MS, PhD), health policy, homeland security and policy coordination (MS, PhD), international nongovernmental organizations, law and public policy (MS, PhD), local government management for sustainable communities, nonprofit management and leadership, policy analysis (MS, PhD), public management and leadership (MS, PhD), terrorism, mediation, and peace (MS, PhD); strategic planning and public policy (Graduate Certificate); terrorism, mediation, and peace (MPA, MPP). *Program availability:* Part-time, evening/weekend, online only, 100% online. *Degree requirements:* For doctorate, thesis/dissertation, residency. *Entrance requirements:* For master's, bachelor's degree or higher; minimum GPA of 2.5; official transcripts; goal statement (for some programs); access to computer and Internet; for doctorate, master's degree or higher; three years of related professional or academic experience (preferred); minimum GPA of 3.0; goal statement and current resume (for select programs); official transcripts; access to computer and Internet; for other advanced degree, relevant work experience; access to computer and Internet. Additional exam requirements/recommendations for international students: required—TOEFL (minimum score 550 paper-based, 79 iBT), IELTS (minimum score 6.5), Michigan English Language Assessment Battery (minimum score 82), or PTE (minimum score 53). Electronic applications accepted.

International Trade Policy

Baruch College of the City University of New York, Austin W. Marxe School of Public and International Affairs, Program in International Affairs, New York, NY 10010-5585. Offers international nongovernmental organizations (MIA); trade policy and global economic governance (MIA); Western Hemisphere affairs (MIA). *Program availability:* Part-time.

The George Washington University, Elliott School of International Affairs, Program in International Trade and Investment Policy, Washington, DC 20052. Offers MA. *Program availability:* Part-time. *Degree requirements:* For master's, one foreign language, capstone project. *Entrance requirements:* For master's, GRE General Test, 2 years of a modern foreign language, 2 semesters of introductory economics. Additional exam requirements/recommendations for international students: required—TOEFL (minimum score 100 iBT), IELTS (minimum score 7). Electronic applications accepted.

Middlebury Institute of International Studies at Monterey, Graduate School of International Policy and Management, Program in International Trade and Economic Diplomacy, Monterey, CA 93940-2691. Offers MA. *Entrance requirements:* For master's, statement of purpose, resume or curriculum vitae, undergraduate transcripts, 2 letters of recommendation, interview. Additional exam requirements/recommendations for international students: required—TOEFL or IELTS.

University at Buffalo, the State University of New York, Graduate School, College of Arts and Sciences, Department of Geography, N Tonawanda, NY 14261. Offers earth systems science (MA, MS); economic geography and business geographics (MS); environmental modeling and analysis (MA); geographic information science (MA, MS); geography (MA, PhD); health geography (MS); international trade (MA); urban and regional analysis (MA). *Program availability:* Part-time. *Faculty:* 22 full-time (9 women), 3 part-time/adjunct (1 woman). *Students:* 61 full-time (26 women); includes 37 minority (2 Black or African American, non-Hispanic/Latino; 34 Asian, non-Hispanic/Latino; 1 Hispanic/Latino). Average age 28. 120 applicants, 62% accepted, 12 enrolled. In 2019, 23 master's, 3 doctorates awarded. Terminal master's awarded for partial completion of

doctoral program. *Degree requirements:* For master's, thesis (for some programs), project or portfolio; for doctorate, thesis/dissertation, dissertation/thesis. *Entrance requirements:* For master's, GRE General Test, minimum GPA of 2.9; for doctorate, GRE General Test, minimum GPA of 3.0. Additional exam requirements/recommendations for international students: required—TOEFL (minimum score 550 paper-based; 79 iBT). *Application deadline:* For fall admission, 5/1 priority date for domestic students, 3/10 priority date for international students; for spring admission, 11/1 priority date for domestic students, 9/1 priority date for international students. Applications are processed on a rolling basis. Application fee: $75. Electronic applications accepted. *Expenses:* Contact institution. *Financial support:* In 2019–20, 15 students received support, including 9 fellowships with full tuition reimbursements available (averaging $4,500 per year), 7 research assistantships with full tuition reimbursements available (averaging $14,000 per year), 13 teaching assistantships with full tuition reimbursements available (averaging $14,080 per year); career-related internships or fieldwork, Federal Work-Study, institutionally sponsored loans, traineeships, health care benefits, and unspecified assistantships also available. Financial award application deadline: 1/10. *Unit head:* Dr. Chris Larsen, Interim Chair, 716-645-0488, Fax: 716-645-2329, E-mail: larsen@buffalo.edu. *Application contact:* Wendy Zitzka, Graduate Secretary, 716-645-0471, Fax: 716-645-2329, E-mail: wzitzka@buffalo.edu.
Website: http://www.geog.buffalo.edu/

Valparaiso University, Graduate School and Continuing Education, Program in International Commerce and Policy, Valparaiso, IN 46383. Offers MS, JD/MS. *Program availability:* Part-time, evening/weekend. *Entrance requirements:* For master's, minimum GPA of 3.0. Additional exam requirements/recommendations for international students: required—TOEFL (minimum score 550 paper-based; 80 iBT), IELTS (minimum score 6). Electronic applications accepted.

Political Science

Acadia University, Faculty of Arts, Department of Political Science, Wolfville, NS B4P 2R6, Canada. Offers MA. *Entrance requirements:* For master's, honors degree or equivalent. Additional exam requirements/recommendations for international students: required—TOEFL (minimum score 580 paper-based; 93 iBT), IELTS (minimum score 6.5).

American Public University System, AMU/APU Graduate Programs, Charles Town, WV 25414. Offers accounting (MS); applied business analytics (MS); business administration (MBA); criminal justice (MA); cybersecurity studies (MS); educational leadership (M Ed); environmental policy and management (MS); global security (DGS); health information management (MS); history (MA), including American military history, American Revolution, civil war, war since 1945, World War II; information technology (MS); international relations and conflict resolution (MA), including American politics and government, comparative government and development, general, international relations, public policy; national security studies (MA); nursing (MSN); political science (MA); public policy (MPP); reverse logistics management (MA), including comparative and security issues, conflict resolution, international and transnational security issues, peacekeeping; space studies (MS); sports management (MS); strategic intelligence (DSI); teaching (M Ed), including secondary social studies; transportation and logistics management (MA). *Program availability:* Part-time, evening/weekend, online only, 100% online. *Students:* 461 full-time (193 women), 7,322 part-time (3,127 women); includes 3,089 minority (1,404 Black or African American, non-Hispanic/Latino; 30 American Indian or Alaska Native, non-Hispanic/Latino; 210 Asian, non-Hispanic/Latino; 753 Hispanic/Latino; 445 Native Hawaiian or other Pacific Islander, non-Hispanic/Latino; 247 Two or more races, non-Hispanic/Latino), 117 international. Average age 37. In 2019, 2,681 master's awarded. *Degree requirements:* For master's, comprehensive exam or practicum; for doctorate, practicum. *Entrance requirements:* For master's, official transcript showing earned bachelor's degree from institution accredited by recognized accrediting body. Additional exam requirements/recommendations for international students: required—TOEFL (minimum score 550 paper-based), IELTS (minimum score 6.5). *Application deadline:* Applications are processed on a rolling basis. Application fee: $0. Electronic applications accepted. *Financial support:* Scholarships/grants available. Financial award applicants required to submit FAFSA. *Unit head:* Dr. Wallace Boston, President, 877-468-6268, Fax: 304-728-2348, E-mail: president@apus.edu. *Application contact:* Yoci Deal, Associate Vice President, Graduate and International Admissions, 877-468-6268, Fax: 304-724-3764, E-mail: info@apus.edu. Website: http://www.apus.edu

American University, School of International Service, Washington, DC 20016-8071. Offers comparative and regional studies (Certificate); cross-cultural communication (Certificate); development management (MS); ethics, peace, and global affairs (MA); European studies (Certificate); global environmental policy (MA, Certificate); global information technology (Certificate); global media (MA); international affairs (MA), including comparative and regional studies, global governance, politics, and security, international economic relations, natural resources and sustainable development, U.S. foreign policy and national security; international arts management (Certificate); international communication (MA, Certificate); international development (MA); international economic policy (Certificate); international economic relations (Certificate); international economics (MA); international peace and conflict resolution (MA, Certificate); international politics (Certificate); international relations (MA, PhD); international service (MIS); peacebuilding (Certificate); social enterprise (MA); the Americas (Certificate); United States foreign policy (Certificate); JD/MA. *Program availability:* Part-time, evening/weekend, 100% online, blended/hybrid learning. Terminal master's awarded for partial completion of doctoral program. *Degree requirements:* For master's, one foreign language, comprehensive exam, thesis or alternative; for doctorate, one foreign language, comprehensive exam, thesis/dissertation. *Entrance requirements:* For master's, transcripts, resume, 2 letters of recommendation, statement of purpose; for doctorate, GRE, transcripts, resume, 3 letters of recommendation, statement of purpose. Additional exam requirements/recommendations for international students: required—TOEFL. Electronic applications accepted. *Expenses:* Contact institution.

American University, School of Public Affairs, Department of Government, Washington, DC 20016-8130. Offers political communication (MA); political science (MA, PhD), including American politics (MA), applied politics (MA); women, policy and political leadership (Certificate). *Program availability:* Part-time, evening/weekend. Terminal master's awarded for partial completion of doctoral program. *Entrance requirements:* Additional exam requirements/recommendations for international students: required—TOEFL. *Expenses:* Contact institution.

American University of Armenia, Graduate Programs, Yerevan, Armenia. Offers business administration (MBA); computer and information science (MS), including business management, design and manufacturing, energy (ME, MS), industrial engineering and systems management; economics (MS); industrial engineering and systems management (ME), including business, computer aided design/manufacturing, energy (ME, MS), information technology; law (LL M); political science and international affairs (MPSIA); public health (MPH); teaching English as a foreign language (MA). *Program availability:* Part-time, evening/weekend. *Degree requirements:* For master's, thesis (for some programs), capstone/project. *Entrance requirements:* For master's, GRE, GMAT, or LSAT. Additional exam requirements/recommendations for international students: recommended—TOEFL (minimum score 79 iBT), IELTS (minimum score 6.5). *Expenses: Tuition:* Full-time $3100; part-time $165 per credit. Tuition and fees vary according to program.

Appalachian State University, Cratis D. Williams School of Graduate Studies, Department of Government and Justice Studies, Boone, NC 28608. Offers political science (MA), including American government; public administration (MPA), including public management. *Accreditation:* NASPAA. *Program availability:* Part-time, online learning. *Degree requirements:* For master's, variable foreign language requirement, comprehensive exam, thesis optional. *Entrance requirements:* For master's, GRE General Test, 3 letters of recommendation. Additional exam requirements/recommendations for international students: required—TOEFL (minimum score 570 paper-based; 79 iBT), IELTS (minimum score 6.5). Electronic applications accepted.

Arizona State University at Tempe, College of Liberal Arts and Sciences, School of Politics and Global Studies, Tempe, AZ 85287-3902. Offers political science (MA, PhD). *Program availability:* Part-time. Terminal master's awarded for partial completion of doctoral program. *Degree requirements:* For master's, thesis or alternative, interactive Program of Study (iPOS) submitted before completing 50 percent of required credit hours; for doctorate, comprehensive exam, thesis/dissertation, interactive Program of Study (iPOS) submitted before completing 50 percent of required credit hours. *Entrance requirements:* For master's and doctorate, GRE, minimum GPA of 3.0 or equivalent in last 2 years of work leading to bachelor's degree. Additional exam requirements/recommendations for international students: required—TOEFL, IELTS, or PTE. Electronic applications accepted.

Arkansas State University, Graduate School, College of Humanities and Social Sciences, Department of Political Science, State University, AR 72467. Offers political science (MA); political science education (SCCT); public administration (MPA). *Accreditation:* NASPAA (one or more programs are accredited). *Program availability:* Part-time. *Degree requirements:* For master's, comprehensive exam, thesis or alternative; for SCCT, comprehensive exam. *Entrance requirements:* For master's, GRE

General Test or MAT, GMAT, appropriate bachelor's degree, letters of recommendation, official transcripts, immunization records, statement of purpose; for SCCT, GRE General Test or MAT, GMAT, interview, master's degree, official transcript, letters of recommendation, immunization records. Additional exam requirements/recommendations for international students: required—TOEFL (minimum score 550 paper-based; 79 iBT), IELTS (minimum score 6), PTE (minimum score 56). Electronic applications accepted.

Ashland University, College of Arts and Sciences, Program in American History and Government, Ashland, OH 44805-3702. Offers American history and government (MAHG). *Program availability:* Part-time, evening/weekend, 100% online, blended/hybrid learning. *Degree requirements:* For master's, capstone project, thesis, or comprehensive exam. *Entrance requirements:* For master's, minimum undergraduate GPA of 2.75, 3.0 graduate. Electronic applications accepted. *Expenses:* Contact institution.

Auburn University, Graduate School, College of Liberal Arts, Department of Political Science, Auburn, AL 36849. Offers public administration (MPA, PhD, Graduate Certificate); MPA/MCP. *Program availability:* Part-time. *Faculty:* 30 full-time (14 women), 5 part-time/adjunct (4 women). *Students:* 93 full-time (51 women), 53 part-time (26 women); includes 33 minority (25 Black or African American, non-Hispanic/Latino; 1 American Indian or Alaska Native, non-Hispanic/Latino; 2 Asian, non-Hispanic/Latino; 5 Hispanic/Latino), 50 international. Average age 32. 74 applicants, 68% accepted, 25 enrolled. In 2019, 64 master's, 2 doctorates, 27 other advanced degrees awarded. *Degree requirements:* For doctorate, thesis/dissertation. *Entrance requirements:* For master's, GRE General Test, minimum GPA of 3.0 in political science, 2.5 overall; for doctorate, GRE General Test. Additional exam requirements/recommendations for international students: required—iTEP; recommended—TOEFL (minimum score 550 paper-based; 79 iBT), IELTS (minimum score 6.5). *Application deadline:* Applications are processed on a rolling basis. Application fee: $60 ($70 for international students). Electronic applications accepted. *Expenses: Tuition, area resident:* Full-time $9828; part-time $546 per credit hour. Tuition, state resident: full-time $9828; part-time $546 per credit hour. Tuition, nonresident: full-time $29,484; part-time $1638 per credit hour. *International tuition:* $29,744 full-time. Tuition and fees vary according to course load, program and reciprocity agreements. *Financial support:* In 2019–20, 17 fellowships with tuition reimbursements, 29 research assistantships with tuition reimbursements (averaging $14,860 per year), 8 teaching assistantships with tuition reimbursements (averaging $20,259 per year) were awarded; career-related internships or fieldwork and Federal Work-Study also available. Support available to part-time students. Financial award application deadline: 3/15; financial award applicants required to submit FAFSA. *Unit head:* Dr. Paul A. Harris, Chair, 334-844-6152, E-mail: paul.harris@auburn.edu. *Application contact:* Dr. George Flowers, Dean of the Graduate School, 334-844-2125. Website: http://cla.auburn.edu/polisci/

Auburn University at Montgomery, College of Liberal Arts & Social Sciences, Department of Political Science and Public Administration, Montgomery, AL 36124. Offers political science (MPS); public administration (MPA); public administration and public policy (PhD). *Accreditation:* NASPAA (one or more programs are accredited). *Program availability:* Part-time, evening/weekend. *Faculty:* 5 full-time (1 woman). *Students:* 8 full-time (3 women), 43 part-time (22 women); includes 18 minority (17 Black or African American, non-Hispanic/Latino; 1 Asian, non-Hispanic/Latino), 6 international. Average age 35. 22 applicants, 95% accepted, 20 enrolled. In 2019, 16 master's awarded. Terminal master's awarded for partial completion of doctoral program. *Degree requirements:* For master's, comprehensive exam; for doctorate, thesis/dissertation. *Entrance requirements:* For master's, GRE General Test or MAT; for doctorate, GRE General Test. Additional exam requirements/recommendations for international students: recommended—TOEFL (minimum score 500 paper-based; 61 iBT), IELTS (minimum score 5.5), TSE (minimum score 44). *Application deadline:* For fall admission, 7/15 for international students; for spring admission, 11/15 for international students; for summer admission, 4/15 for international students. Applications are processed on a rolling basis. Application fee: $25. Electronic applications accepted. *Expenses: Tuition, area resident:* Full-time $7578; part-time $421 per credit hour. Tuition, state resident: full-time $7578; part-time $421 per credit hour. Tuition, nonresident: full-time $17,046; part-time $947 per credit hour. *International tuition:* $17,046 full-time. *Required fees:* $868. *Financial support:* Research assistantships, teaching assistantships, career-related internships or fieldwork, and scholarships/grants available. Support available to part-time students. Financial award application deadline: 3/1; financial award applicants required to submit FAFSA. *Unit head:* Dr. Andrew Cortell, Department Head, 334-244-3622, E-mail: acortell@aum.edu. *Application contact:* Shannon Richardson, Administrative Associate, 244-244-3698, E-mail: sricha17@aum.edu. Website: http://www.cas.aum.edu/academic-programs/graduate-programs/master-of-science-in-political-science

Ball State University, Graduate School, College of Sciences and Humanities, Department of Political Science, Program in Political Science, Muncie, IN 47306. Offers MA. *Program availability:* Part-time. *Degree requirements:* For master's, comprehensive exam. *Entrance requirements:* For master's, GRE General Test, minimum baccalaureate GPA of 2.8. Additional exam requirements/recommendations for international students: required—TOEFL (minimum score 550 paper-based; 79 iBT), IELTS (minimum score 6.5). Electronic applications accepted. *Expenses: Tuition, area resident:* Full-time $7506; part-time $417 per credit hour. Tuition, nonresident: full-time $20,610; part-time $1145 per credit hour. *Required fees:* $2126. Tuition and fees vary according to course load, campus/location and program.

Baylor University, Graduate School, College of Arts and Sciences, Department of Political Science, Waco, TX 76798. Offers MA, MPPA, PhD, JD/MPPA. Terminal master's awarded for partial completion of doctoral program. *Degree requirements:* For master's, variable foreign language requirement, comprehensive exam (for some programs), thesis (for some programs); for doctorate, variable foreign language requirement, comprehensive exam, thesis/dissertation. *Entrance requirements:* For master's and doctorate, GRE General Test. Additional exam requirements/recommendations for international students: required—TOEFL. Electronic applications accepted.

Binghamton University, State University of New York, Graduate School, Harpur College of Arts and Sciences, Department of Political Science, Binghamton, NY 13902-6000. Offers MA, PhD. *Program availability:* Part-time. Terminal master's awarded for partial completion of doctoral program. *Degree requirements:* For master's, comprehensive exam (for some programs), thesis (for some programs); for doctorate, variable foreign language requirement, comprehensive exam, thesis/dissertation. *Entrance requirements:* For master's and doctorate, GRE General Test. Additional exam requirements/recommendations for international students: required—TOEFL (minimum score 550 paper-based; 80 iBT). Electronic applications accepted.

Boise State University, School of Public Service, Department of Political Science, Boise, ID 83725-0399. Offers MA. *Students:* 3 full-time (2 women), 12 part-time (8 women); includes 3 minority (1 American Indian or Alaska Native, non-Hispanic/Latino; 2 Hispanic/Latino). *Degree requirements:* For master's, comprehensive exam, thesis (for some programs), thesis or professional project. *Entrance requirements:* Additional exam requirements/recommendations for international students: required—TOEFL, IELTS.

Electronic applications accepted. *Expenses: Tuition, area resident:* Full-time $7110; part-time $470 per credit hour. Tuition, state resident: full-time $7110; part-time $470 per credit hour. Tuition, nonresident: full-time $24,030; part-time $827 per credit hour. *International tuition:* $24,030 full-time. *Required fees:* $2536. Tuition and fees vary according to course load and program. *Financial support:* Application deadline: 2/15; applicants required to submit FAFSA. *Unit head:* Dr. Lori Hausegger, Chair, 208-426-5804, E-mail: lorihausegger@boisestate.edu. *Application contact:* Dr. Michael Allen, Graduate Program Coordinator, 208-426-2518, E-mail: michaelaallen@boisestate.edu.
Website: https://www.boisestate.edu/sps-politicalscience/graduate/

Boston College, Morrissey Graduate School of Arts and Sciences, Department of Political Science, Chestnut Hill, MA 02467-3800. Offers MA, PhD. Terminal master's awarded for partial completion of doctoral program. *Degree requirements:* For master's, thesis or alternative; for doctorate, one foreign language, thesis/dissertation. *Entrance requirements:* For master's and doctorate, GRE General Test. Additional exam requirements/recommendations for international students: required—TOEFL (minimum score 600 paper-based; 100 iBT), IELTS (minimum score 8). Electronic applications accepted.

Boston University, Graduate School of Arts and Sciences, Department of Political Science, Boston, MA 02215. Offers PhD. *Students:* 35 full-time (19 women), 1 part-time (0 women); includes 5 minority (1 Black or African American, non-Hispanic/Latino; 1 Asian, non-Hispanic/Latino; 3 Hispanic/Latino), 23 international. Average age 28. 93 applicants, 17% accepted, 6 enrolled. In 2019, 9 doctorates awarded. Terminal master's awarded for partial completion of doctoral program. *Degree requirements:* For doctorate, comprehensive exam, thesis/dissertation. *Entrance requirements:* For doctorate, GRE General Test (optional in Fall 2021 admissions), 3 letters of recommendation, transcripts, personal statement, curriculum vitae. Additional exam requirements/recommendations for international students: required—TOEFL (minimum score 600 paper-based; 100 iBT). *Application deadline:* For fall admission, 12/31 for domestic and international students. Application fee: $95. Electronic applications accepted. *Financial support:* In 2019–20, 36 students received support, including 15 fellowships with full tuition reimbursements available (averaging $23,340 per year), 3 research assistantships with full tuition reimbursements available (averaging $23,340 per year), 14 teaching assistantships with full tuition reimbursements available (averaging $23,340 per year); career-related internships or fieldwork, Federal Work-Study, scholarships/grants, and health care benefits also available. Support available to part-time students. Financial award application deadline: 12/31. *Unit head:* Neta Crawford, Chair, 617-353-4040, Fax: 617-353-5508, E-mail: politicschair@bu.edu. *Application contact:* Anastasiya Turcotte, Graduate Program Coordinator, 617-353-2541, Fax: 617-353-5508, E-mail: aturc@bu.edu.
Website: http://www.bu.edu/polisci/

Brandeis University, Graduate School of Arts and Sciences, Department of Politics, Waltham, MA 02454-9110. Offers MA, PhD. *Program availability:* Part-time. *Faculty:* 11 full-time (3 women). *Students:* 13 full-time (6 women), 3 international. Average age 28. 85 applicants, 11% accepted, 3 enrolled. In 2019, 1 master's, 1 doctorate awarded. Terminal master's awarded for partial completion of doctoral program. *Degree requirements:* For master's, thesis or alternative; for doctorate, one foreign language, comprehensive exam, thesis/dissertation. *Entrance requirements:* For master's and doctorate, GRE General, transcripts, letters of recommendation, resume, writing sample. and statement of purpose. Additional exam requirements/recommendations for international students: required—TOEFL, IELTS, PTE. *Application deadline:* For fall admission, 1/15 priority date for domestic and international students. Applications are processed on a rolling basis. Application fee: $75. Electronic applications accepted. *Financial support:* In 2019–20, 7 fellowships with full tuition reimbursements (averaging $25,000 per year), 9 teaching assistantships (averaging $3,550 per year) were awarded; scholarships/grants, health care benefits, and tuition waivers also available. *Unit head:* Dr. Jill Greenlee, Director of Graduate Studies, 781-736-2760, E-mail: greenlee@brandeis.edu. *Application contact:* Rosanne Colocouris, Administrator, 781-736-2755, E-mail: colocour@brandeis.edu.
Website: http://www.brandeis.edu/gsas/programs/politics.html

Brigham Young University, Graduate Studies, BYU Marriott School of Business, Master of Public Administration Program, Provo, UT 84602. Offers healthcare (MPA); local government (MPA); nonprofit management (MPA); state and federal government (MPA); JD/MPA. *Accreditation:* NASPAA. *Faculty:* 10 full-time (2 women), 10 part-time/adjunct (2 women). *Students:* 95 full-time (52 women); includes 10 minority (4 Black or African American, non-Hispanic/Latino; 1 American Indian or Alaska Native, non-Hispanic/Latino; 1 Asian, non-Hispanic/Latino; 2 Hispanic/Latino; 2 Native Hawaiian or other Pacific Islander, non-Hispanic/Latino). Average age 26. 81 applicants, 85% accepted, 57 enrolled. In 2019, 45 master's awarded. *Entrance requirements:* For master's, GMAT or GRE, statement of intent, resume, bachelor's degree, 3 letters or recommendation, ecclesiastical endorsement. Additional exam requirements/recommendations for international students: required—TOEFL (minimum score 580 paper-based; 85 iBT). *Application deadline:* For fall admission, 1/15 for domestic and international students. Application fee: $50. Electronic applications accepted. *Expenses:* Full-time LDS tuition $6,725 a semester in 2019, books, health insurance. *Financial support:* In 2019–20, 93 students received support. Scholarships/grants available. Financial award application deadline: 4/15; financial award applicants required to submit FAFSA. *Unit head:* Dr. Lori Wadsworth, Director, 801-422-5956, E-mail: lori_wadsworth@byu.edu. *Application contact:* Catherine Cooper, Associate Director, 801-422-9173, E-mail: clc@byu.edu.
Website: https://marriottschool.byu.edu/mpa/

Brock University, Faculty of Graduate Studies, Faculty of Social Sciences, Program in Political Science, St. Catharines, ON L2S 3A1, Canada. Offers Canadian politics (MA); comparative politics (MA); international relations (MA); political theory or philosophy (MA); public policy (MA). *Program availability:* Part-time. *Degree requirements:* For master's, thesis optional. *Entrance requirements:* For master's, honors degree. Additional exam requirements/recommendations for international students: required—TOEFL (minimum score 550 paper-based; 80 iBT), IELTS (minimum score 6.5), TWE (minimum score 4). Electronic applications accepted.

Brooklyn College of the City University of New York, School of Humanities and Social Sciences, Department of Political Science, Brooklyn, NY 11210-2889. Offers international affairs (MA); political science (MA); urban policy and administration (MA). *Program availability:* Part-time, evening/weekend. *Degree requirements:* For master's, comprehensive exam (for some programs), thesis or alternative, foreign language exam (for international affairs program). *Entrance requirements:* For master's, 2 letters of recommendation, personal statement. Additional exam requirements/recommendations for international students: required—TOEFL (minimum score 500 paper-based; 61 iBT).

Brown University, Graduate School, Department of Political Science, Providence, RI 02912. Offers PhD. *Degree requirements:* For doctorate, thesis/dissertation. *Entrance requirements:* For doctorate, GRE General Test.

California Polytechnic State University, San Luis Obispo, College of Liberal Arts, Department of Political Science, San Luis Obispo, CA 93407. Offers MPP. *Program availability:* Part-time. *Faculty:* 7 full-time (3 women). *Students:* 5 full-time (2 women), 25 part-time (14 women); includes 11 minority (2 Black or African American, non-Hispanic/Latino; 1 Asian, non-Hispanic/Latino; 4 Hispanic/Latino; 4 Two or more races, non-Hispanic/Latino). Average age 31. 33 applicants, 85% accepted, 15 enrolled. In 2019, 9 master's awarded. *Entrance requirements:* Additional exam requirements/recommendations for international students: required—TOEFL (minimum score 80 iBT). *Application deadline:* For fall admission, 4/1 for domestic and international students. Applications are processed on a rolling basis. Application fee: $55. Electronic applications accepted. *Expenses:* Tuition, state resident: full-time $7176; part-time $4164 per year. Tuition, nonresident: full-time $18,690; part-time $8916 per year. *Required fees:* $4206; $3185 per unit. $1061 per term. *Financial support:* Fellowships, research assistantships, career-related internships or fieldwork, Federal Work-Study, and scholarships/grants available. Support available to part-time students. Financial award application deadline: 3/2; financial award applicants required to submit FAFSA. *Unit head:* Dr. Martin Battle, Graduate Coordinator, 805-756-5717, E-mail: mbattle@calpoly.edu. *Application contact:* Dr. Martin Battle, Graduate Coordinator, 805-756-5717, E-mail: mbattle@calpoly.edu.
Website: http://mpp.calpoly.edu/

California State University, Chico, Office of Graduate Studies, College of Behavioral and Social Sciences, Department of Political Science and Criminal Justice, Program in Political Science, Chico, CA 95929-0722. Offers MA. *Program availability:* Part-time. *Degree requirements:* For master's, thesis or comprehensive examination. *Entrance requirements:* For master's, 2 letters of recommendation, statement of purpose, departmental letter of recommendation access waiver form. Additional exam requirements/recommendations for international students: required—TOEFL (minimum score 550 paper-based; 80 iBT), IELTS (minimum score 6.5), PTE (minimum score 59). Electronic applications accepted.

California State University, Fullerton, Graduate Studies, College of Humanities and Social Sciences, Division of Politics, Administration, and Justice, Fullerton, CA 92831-3599. Offers political science (MA); public administration (MPA). *Accreditation:* NASPAA (one or more programs are accredited). *Program availability:* Part-time. *Degree requirements:* For master's, comprehensive exam, project or thesis. *Entrance requirements:* For master's, minimum GPA of 2.5 in last 60 units of course work, 12 units of course work in social sciences.

California State University, Long Beach, Graduate Studies, College of Liberal Arts, Department of Political Science, Long Beach, CA 90840. Offers MA. *Program availability:* Part-time. *Degree requirements:* For master's, one foreign language, comprehensive exam or thesis. *Entrance requirements:* For master's, GRE General Test, minimum GPA of 3.0 in field. Electronic applications accepted.

California State University, Los Angeles, Graduate Studies, College of Natural and Social Sciences, Department of Political Science, Los Angeles, CA 90032-8530. Offers political science (MA); public administration (MS). *Program availability:* Part-time, evening/weekend. *Degree requirements:* For master's, comprehensive exam or thesis. *Entrance requirements:* Additional exam requirements/recommendations for international students: required—TOEFL (minimum score 500 paper-based). Electronic applications accepted. *Expenses: Tuition, area resident:* Full-time $7176; part-time $4164 per year. Tuition, state resident: full-time $7176; part-time $4164 per year. Tuition, nonresident: full-time $14,304; part-time $8916 per year. *International tuition:* $14,304 full-time. *Required fees:* $1037.76; $1037.76 per unit. Tuition and fees vary according to degree level and program.

California State University, Northridge, Graduate Studies, College of Social and Behavioral Sciences, Department of Political Science, Northridge, CA 91330. Offers MA. *Degree requirements:* For master's, comprehensive exam. *Entrance requirements:* For master's, GRE (if cumulative undergraduate GPA less than 3.0), 2 letters of recommendation. Additional exam requirements/recommendations for international students: required—TOEFL.

California State University, Sacramento, College of Social Sciences and Interdisciplinary Studies, Department of Government, Sacramento, CA 95819. Offers MA. *Program availability:* Part-time. *Students:* 3 full-time (2 women), 22 part-time (11 women); includes 8 minority (3 Black or African American, non-Hispanic/Latino; 2 Asian, non-Hispanic/Latino; 2 Hispanic/Latino; 1 Native Hawaiian or other Pacific Islander, non-Hispanic/Latino). Average age 28. 15 applicants, 73% accepted, 5 enrolled. In 2019, 13 master's awarded. *Degree requirements:* For master's, comprehensive exam, thesis optional, thesis, project or comprehensive exam; writing proficiency exam. *Entrance requirements:* For master's, GRE, minimum GPA of 3.0 during previous 2 years. Additional exam requirements/recommendations for international students: required—TOEFL (minimum score 550 paper-based; 80 iBT); recommended—IELTS (minimum score 7). *Application deadline:* For fall admission, 3/1 for domestic students, 2/1 for international students; for spring admission, 9/15 for domestic students, 8/15 for international students. Applications are processed on a rolling basis. Application fee: $70. Electronic applications accepted. *Expenses:* Contact institution. *Financial support:* Career-related internships or fieldwork, Federal Work-Study, and scholarships/grants available. Support available to part-time students. Financial award application deadline: 3/1; financial award applicants required to submit FAFSA. *Unit head:* Dr. Jim Cox, Professor and Graduate Coordinator, 916-278-6378, E-mail: jhcox@csus.edu. *Application contact:* Jose Martinez, Graduate Admissions Supervisor, 916-278-7871, E-mail: martinj@skymail.csus.edu.
Website: http://www.csus.edu/govt

Carleton University, Faculty of Graduate Studies, Faculty of Public Affairs and Management, Department of Political Science, Ottawa, ON K1S 5B6, Canada. Offers MA, PhD. *Degree requirements:* For master's, one foreign language, comprehensive exam, thesis optional; for doctorate, one foreign language, comprehensive exam, thesis/dissertation. *Entrance requirements:* For master's, honors degree in political science, minimum B average; for doctorate, master's degree in political science. Additional exam requirements/recommendations for international students: required—TOEFL.

Carleton University, Faculty of Graduate Studies, Faculty of Public Affairs and Management, Institute of Political Economy, Ottawa, ON K1S 5B6, Canada. Offers MA, PhD. *Degree requirements:* For master's, thesis optional. *Entrance requirements:* For master's, honors degree. Additional exam requirements/recommendations for international students: required—TOEFL.

Case Western Reserve University, School of Graduate Studies, Department of Political Science, Cleveland, OH 44106. Offers MA, PhD. *Faculty:* 8 full-time (4 women). *Students:* 1 applicant, 100% accepted, 1 enrolled. Terminal master's awarded for partial completion of doctoral program. *Degree requirements:* For master's, comprehensive exam (for some programs), thesis (for some programs); for doctorate, thesis/dissertation. *Entrance requirements:* For master's and doctorate, GRE General Test, undergraduate degree in political science, three letters of recommendation, statement of objectives. Additional exam requirements/recommendations for international students: required—TOEFL (minimum score 577 paper-based; 90 iBT); recommended—IELTS (minimum score 7). *Application deadline:* For fall admission, 6/1 priority date for domestic students; for spring admission, 11/1 for domestic students. Applications are processed on a rolling basis. Application fee: $50. Electronic applications accepted. *Financial support:* Federal Work-Study, institutionally sponsored loans, and health care

benefits available. Financial award application deadline: 2/1; financial award applicants required to submit CSS PROFILE or FAFSA. *Unit head:* Karen Beckwith, Professor and Chair, Department of Political Science, 216-368-4129, Fax: 216-368-4681, E-mail: karen.beckwith@case.edu. *Application contact:* Jessica Jurcak, Department Assistant, 216-368-2424, Fax: 216-368-4681, E-mail: jessica.jurcak@case.edu.
Website: http://politicalscience.case.edu/

The Catholic University of America, School of Arts and Sciences, Department of Politics, Washington, DC 20064. Offers American government (MA, PhD); Congressional and Presidential studies (MA); international affairs (MA); international political economics (MA); political theory (MA, PhD); world politics (MA, PhD); MA/JD. *Program availability:* Part-time. *Faculty:* 13 full-time (2 women), 6 part-time/adjunct (2 women). *Students:* 11 full-time (6 women), 37 part-time (11 women); includes 7 minority (2 Black or African American, non-Hispanic/Latino; 1 Asian, non-Hispanic/Latino; 2 Hispanic/Latino; 2 Two or more races, non-Hispanic/Latino), 11 international. Average age 34. 43 applicants, 60% accepted, 8 enrolled. In 2019, 14 master's, 5 doctorates awarded. *Degree requirements:* For master's, one foreign language, comprehensive exam, thesis or alternative; for doctorate, variable foreign language requirement, comprehensive exam, thesis/dissertation. *Entrance requirements:* For master's, GRE General Test, statement of purpose, official copies of academic transcripts, three letters of recommendation, minimum GPA of 3.0; for doctorate, GRE General Test, statement of purpose, official copies of academic transcripts, three letters of recommendation. Additional exam requirements/recommendations for international students: required—TOEFL (minimum score 550 paper-based; 80 iBT). *Application deadline:* For fall admission, 7/15 priority date for domestic students, 7/1 for international students; for spring admission, 11/15 priority date for domestic students, 11/1 for international students. Applications are processed on a rolling basis. Application fee: $55. Electronic applications accepted. *Expenses:* Contact institution. *Financial support:* Fellowships, research assistantships, teaching assistantships, Federal Work-Study, scholarships/grants, tuition waivers (full and partial), and unspecified assistantships available. Financial award application deadline: 2/1; financial award applicants required to submit FAFSA. *Unit head:* Dr. Dennis Coyle, Chair, 202-319-5813, Fax: 202-319-6289, E-mail: coyle@cua.edu. *Application contact:* Dr. Steven Brown, Director of Graduate Admissions, 202-319-5057, Fax: 202-319-6533, E-mail: cua-admissions@cua.edu.
Website: http://politics.cua.edu/

Central European University, Department of Political Science, Budapest, Hungary. Offers MA, PhD. *Degree requirements:* For master's, one foreign language, thesis; for doctorate, one foreign language, comprehensive exam, thesis/dissertation. *Entrance requirements:* For master's and doctorate, interview. Additional exam requirements/recommendations for international students: required—TOEFL (minimum score 570 paper-based); recommended—IELTS (minimum score 6.5). Electronic applications accepted.

Central European University, Nationalism Studies Program, Budapest, Hungary. Offers MA. *Degree requirements:* For master's, one foreign language, thesis. *Entrance requirements:* For master's, interview. Additional exam requirements/recommendations for international students: required—TOEFL (minimum score 570 paper-based); recommended—IELTS (minimum score 6.5). Electronic applications accepted.

Central Michigan University, Central Michigan University Global Campus, Program in Public Administration, Mount Pleasant, MI 48859. Offers general public administration (MPA); public management (MPA); state and local government (MPA). *Accreditation:* NASPAA. *Program availability:* Part-time, evening/weekend. *Entrance requirements:* For master's, minimum GPA of 2.8. Additional exam requirements/recommendations for international students: required—TOEFL. Electronic applications accepted. *Expenses: Tuition, area resident:* Full-time $12,267; part-time $8178 per year. Tuition, state resident: full-time $12,267; part-time $8178 per year. Tuition, nonresident: full-time $12,267; part-time $8178 per year. *International tuition:* $16,110 full-time. *Required fees:* $225 per semester. Tuition and fees vary according to degree level and program.

Central Michigan University, College of Graduate Studies, College of Liberal Arts and Social Sciences, Department of Political Science and Public Administration, Program in Political Science, Mount Pleasant, MI 48859. Offers American politics (MA), including American politics, comparative/international politics. *Program availability:* Part-time. *Degree requirements:* For master's, thesis or alternative. Electronic applications accepted. *Expenses: Tuition, area resident:* Full-time $12,267; part-time $8178 per year. Tuition, state resident: full-time $12,267; part-time $8178 per year. Tuition, nonresident: full-time $12,267; part-time $8178 per year. *International tuition:* $16,110 full-time. *Required fees:* $225 per semester. Tuition and fees vary according to degree level and program.

Central Michigan University, College of Graduate Studies, College of Liberal Arts and Social Sciences, Department of Political Science and Public Administration, Program in Public Administration, Mount Pleasant, MI 48859. Offers professional development in public administration (Graduate Certificate); public administration (MPA); public management (MPA); state and local government (MPA). *Accreditation:* NASPAA. *Program availability:* Part-time. *Degree requirements:* For master's, thesis or alternative. Electronic applications accepted. *Expenses: Tuition, area resident:* Full-time $12,267; part-time $8178 per year. Tuition, state resident: full-time $12,267; part-time $8178 per year. Tuition, nonresident: full-time $12,267; part-time $8178 per year. *International tuition:* $16,110 full-time. *Required fees:* $225 per semester. Tuition and fees vary according to degree level and program.

The Citadel, The Military College of South Carolina, Citadel Graduate College, School of Humanities and Social Sciences, Department of Political Science, Charleston, SC 29409. Offers international politics and military affairs (MA); social science (MA). *Program availability:* Part-time, evening/weekend, 100% online, blended/hybrid learning. *Entrance requirements:* For master's, GRE (minimum combined score of 290 verbal and quantitative), MAT (minimum raw score of 396), written statement of purpose setting forth intentions, goals, and preparation for graduate study; at least 2 academic letters of recommendation addressing ability to undertake coursework at graduate level. Additional exam requirements/recommendations for international students: required—TOEFL (minimum score 550 paper-based; 79 iBT). Electronic applications accepted.

Claremont Graduate University, Graduate Programs, School of Social Science, Policy and Evaluation, Department of Politics and Policy, Claremont, CA 91711-6160. Offers American politics (MA, PhD); comparative politics (PhD); international political economy (MA); international studies (MA); political philosophy (PhD); political science (PhD); politics, economics and business (MA); public policy (MA, PhD); world politics (PhD); MBA/PhD. *Program availability:* Part-time. Terminal master's awarded for partial completion of doctoral program. *Entrance requirements:* For master's and doctorate, GRE General Test. Additional exam requirements/recommendations for international students: required—TOEFL (minimum score 75 iBT). Electronic applications accepted.

Claremont Graduate University, Graduate Programs, School of Social Science, Policy and Evaluation, Program in Politics, Economics, and Business, Claremont, CA 91711-6160. Offers MA. *Program availability:* Part-time. *Entrance requirements:* For master's, GRE General Test. Additional exam requirements/recommendations for international students: required—TOEFL (minimum score 75 iBT). Electronic applications accepted.

Clark Atlanta University, School of Arts and Sciences, Department of Political Science, Atlanta, GA 30314. Offers MA, PhD. *Program availability:* Part-time. Terminal master's awarded for partial completion of doctoral program. *Degree requirements:* For master's, one foreign language, comprehensive exam, thesis; for doctorate, 2 foreign languages, comprehensive exam, thesis/dissertation. *Entrance requirements:* For master's, GRE General Test, minimum GPA of 2.5; for doctorate, GRE General Test, minimum graduate GPA of 3.0. Additional exam requirements/recommendations for international students: required—TOEFL (minimum score 500 paper-based; 61 iBT).

Colorado State University, College of Liberal Arts, Department of Political Science, Fort Collins, CO 80523-1782. Offers environmental politics and policy (PhD); political science (MA). *Faculty:* 12 full-time (5 women). *Students:* 21 full-time (9 women), 19 part-time (11 women); includes 4 minority (1 Asian, non-Hispanic/Latino; 2 Hispanic/Latino; 1 Two or more races, non-Hispanic/Latino), 4 international. Average age 31. 35 applicants, 49% accepted, 9 enrolled. In 2019, 6 master's, 2 doctorates awarded. Terminal master's awarded for partial completion of doctoral program. *Degree requirements:* For master's, comprehensive exam (for some programs), thesis (for some programs), Thesis or Professional Paper option; for doctorate, thesis/dissertation. *Entrance requirements:* For master's, GRE (waived for 20-21), Completion of B.A; for doctorate, GRE (waived for 20-21), Prospectus,15 page writing sample,Master's degree or 24 credits in CSU's Political Science M.A. program. Additional exam requirements/recommendations for international students: required—TOEFL (minimum score 600 paper-based). *Application deadline:* For fall admission, 2/15 priority date for domestic and international students; for spring admission, 10/15 priority date for domestic students, 8/1 priority date for international students. Applications are processed on a rolling basis. Application fee: $60 ($70 for international students). Electronic applications accepted. *Expenses:* Tuition, state resident: full-time $10,520; part-time $5844 per credit hour. Tuition, nonresident: full-time $25,791; part-time $14,328 per credit hour. *International tuition:* $25,791 full-time. *Required fees:* $2512.80. Part-time tuition and fees vary according to course load, degree level, program and student level. *Financial support:* In 2019–20, 27 students received support, including 25 teaching assistantships with full tuition reimbursements available (averaging $18,083 per year); Federal Work-Study and health care benefits also available. Financial award application deadline: 2/15; financial award applicants required to submit FAFSA. *Unit head:* Dr. Robert Duffy, Professor and Chair, 970-491-5304, E-mail: robert.duffy@colostate.edu. *Application contact:* April Lindgren, Program Assistant, 970-491-5157, E-mail: april.lindgren@colostate.edu.
Website: http://polisci.colostate.edu/

Columbia University, Graduate School of Arts and Sciences, New York, NY 10027. Offers African-American studies (MA); American studies (MA); anthropology (MA, PhD); art history and archaeology (MA, PhD); astronomy (PhD); biological sciences (PhD); biotechnology (MA); chemical physics (PhD); chemistry (PhD); classical studies (MA, PhD); classics (MA, PhD); climate and society (MA); conservation biology (MA); earth and environmental sciences (PhD); East Asia: regional studies (MA); East Asian languages and cultures (MA, PhD); ecology, evolution and environmental biology (MA), including conservation biology; ecology, evolution, and environmental biology (PhD), including ecology and evolutionary biology, evolutionary primatology; economics (MA, PhD); English and comparative literature (MA, PhD); French and Romance philology (MA, PhD); Germanic languages (MA, PhD); global French studies (MA); global thought (MA); Hispanic cultural studies (MA); history (PhD); history and literature (MA); human rights studies (MA); Islamic studies (MA); Italian (MA, PhD); Japanese pedagogy (MA); Jewish studies (MA); Latin America and the Caribbean: regional studies (MA); Latin American and Iberian cultures (PhD); mathematics (MA, PhD), including finance (MA); medieval and Renaissance studies (MA); Middle Eastern, South Asian, and African studies (MA, PhD); modern art: critical and curatorial studies (MA); modern European studies (MA); museum anthropology (MA); music (DMA, PhD); oral history (MA); philosophical foundations of physics (MA); philosophy (MA, PhD); physics (PhD); political science (MA, PhD); psychology (PhD); quantitative methods in the social sciences (MA); religion (MA, PhD); Russia, Eurasia and East Europe: regional studies (MA); Russian translation (MA); Slavic cultures (MA); Slavic languages (MA, PhD); sociology (MA, PhD); South Asian studies (MA); statistics (MA, PhD); theatre (PhD). *Program availability:* Part-time. *Students:* 3,506 full-time (1,844 women), 208 part-time (121 women); includes 864 minority (110 Black or African American, non-Hispanic/Latino; 5 American Indian or Alaska Native, non-Hispanic/Latino; 416 Asian, non-Hispanic/Latino; 147 Hispanic/Latino; 6 Native Hawaiian or other Pacific Islander, non-Hispanic/Latino; 180 Two or more races, non-Hispanic/Latino), 2,065 international. 14,545 applicants, 25% accepted, 1,429 enrolled. In 2019, 1,262 master's, 363 doctorates awarded. Terminal master's awarded for partial completion of doctoral program. *Degree requirements:* For master's, variable foreign language requirement, comprehensive exam (for some programs), thesis (for some programs); for doctorate, variable foreign language requirement, comprehensive exam (for some programs), thesis/dissertation. *Entrance requirements:* For master's and doctorate, GRE General Test, GRE Subject Test (for some programs). Additional exam requirements/recommendations for international students: required—TOEFL (minimum score 600 paper-based; 100 iBT), IELTS (minimum score 7.5). Application fee: $115. Electronic applications accepted. *Expenses: Tuition:* Full-time $47,600; part-time $1880 per credit. One-time fee: $105. *Financial support:* Fellowships, research assistantships, teaching assistantships, career-related internships or fieldwork, Federal Work-Study, institutionally sponsored loans, scholarships/grants, traineeships, health care benefits, tuition waivers, and unspecified assistantships available. Support available to part-time students. Financial award application deadline: 12/15. *Unit head:* Dr. Carlos J. Alonso, Dean of the Graduate School of Arts and Sciences and Vice President for Graduate Education, 212-854-2861, E-mail: gsas-dean@columbia.edu. *Application contact:* GSAS Office of Admissions, 212-854-6729, E-mail: gsas-admissions@columbia.edu.
Website: http://gsas.columbia.edu/

Columbus State University, Graduate Studies, College of Letters and Sciences, Department of Political Science and Public Administration, Columbus, GA 31907-5645. Offers public administration (MPA), including criminal justice, environmental policy, government administration, health services administration, political campaigning, urban policy. *Program availability:* Part-time, evening/weekend, 100% online, blended/hybrid learning. *Degree requirements:* For master's, comprehensive exam. *Entrance requirements:* For master's, GRE General Test, minimum GPA of 2.75, three letters of recommendation. Additional exam requirements/recommendations for international students: required—TOEFL (minimum score 550 paper-based; 79 iBT). Electronic applications accepted. *Expenses: Tuition, area resident:* Full-time $210; part-time $210 per credit hour. Tuition, state resident: full-time $210; part-time $210 per credit hour. Tuition, nonresident: full-time $817; part-time $817 per credit hour. *International tuition:* $817 full-time. *Required fees:* $802.50. Tuition and fees vary according to course load, degree level and program.

Concordia University, School of Graduate Studies, Faculty of Arts and Science, Department of Political Science, Montréal, QC H3G 1M8, Canada. Offers political science (PhD); public policy and public administration (MA), including geography. *Degree requirements:* For master's, one foreign language, comprehensive exam, thesis optional, internship. *Entrance requirements:* For master's, honors degree or equivalent.

Political Science

Additional exam requirements/recommendations for international students: required—TOEFL.

Converse College, Program in Liberal Arts, Spartanburg, SC 29302. Offers English (MLA); history (MLA); political science (MLA). *Degree requirements:* For master's, capstone paper. *Entrance requirements:* For master's, minimum GPA of 3.0, 2 recommendations.

Cornell University, Graduate School, Graduate Fields of Arts and Sciences, Field of Government, Ithaca, NY 14853. Offers American politics (PhD); comparative politics (PhD); international relations (PhD); political methodology (PhD); political thought (PhD); public policy (PhD). *Degree requirements:* For doctorate, comprehensive exam, thesis/dissertation. *Entrance requirements:* For doctorate, GRE General Test, sample of written work, 3 letters of recommendation. Additional exam requirements/recommendations for international students: required—TOEFL (minimum score 550 paper-based; 77 iBT). Electronic applications accepted.

Dalhousie University, Faculty of Arts and Social Sciences, Department of Political Science, Halifax, NS B3H 4R2, Canada. Offers MA, PhD. *Entrance requirements:* Additional exam requirements/recommendations for international students: required—TOEFL, IELTS, CANTEST, CAEL, or Michigan English Language Assessment Battery. Electronic applications accepted.

Duke University, Graduate School, Department of Political Science, Durham, NC 27708. Offers AM, PhD, JD/AM. Terminal master's awarded for partial completion of doctoral program. *Degree requirements:* For doctorate, 2 foreign languages, thesis/dissertation. *Entrance requirements:* For master's and doctorate, GRE General Test. Additional exam requirements/recommendations for international students: required—TOEFL (minimum score 577 paper-based; 90 iBT) or IELTS (minimum score 7). Electronic applications accepted.

East Carolina University, Graduate School, Thomas Harriot College of Arts and Sciences, Department of Political Science, Greenville, NC 27858-4353. Offers public administration (MPA); security studies (MS, Certificate). *Accreditation:* NASPAA. *Program availability:* Part-time, evening/weekend, online learning. *Application deadline:* For fall admission, 6/1 priority date for domestic students; for spring admission, 10/15 for domestic students. *Expenses: Tuition, area resident:* Full-time $4749; part-time $185 per credit hour. Tuition, state resident: full-time $4749; part-time $185 per credit hour. Tuition, nonresident: full-time $17,898; part-time $864 per credit hour. *International tuition:* $17,898 full-time. *Required fees:* $2787. *Financial support:* Application deadline: 3/1. *Unit head:* Dr. Alethia Cook, Chair, 252-328-5869, E-mail: cooka@ecu.edu. *Application contact:* Graduate School Admissions, 252-328-6012, Fax: 252-328-6071, E-mail: gradschool@ecu.edu.
Website: https://politicalscience.ecu.edu/

Eastern Illinois University, Graduate School, College of Liberal Arts and Sciences, Department of Political Science, Charleston, IL 61920. Offers MA. *Program availability:* Part-time, evening/weekend. *Degree requirements:* For master's, comprehensive exam (for some programs), thesis (for some programs). *Entrance requirements:* For master's, GMAT or GRE. Additional exam requirements/recommendations for international students: required—TOEFL (minimum score 500 paper-based; 61 iBT), IELTS (minimum score 6). Electronic applications accepted.

Eastern Kentucky University, The Graduate School, College of Arts and Sciences, Department of Government, Program in Political Science, Richmond, KY 40475-3102. Offers MA. *Entrance requirements:* For master's, GRE General Test, minimum GPA of 2.5.

East Stroudsburg University of Pennsylvania, Graduate and Extended Studies, College of Arts and Sciences, Department of Political Science and Economics, East Stroudsburg, PA 18301-2999. Offers management and leadership in public administration (MS); political science (MA). *Program availability:* Part-time, evening/weekend. *Degree requirements:* For master's, variable foreign language requirement, comprehensive exam, thesis or alternative. *Entrance requirements:* For master's, Goals statement, letters of recommendation. Additional exam requirements/recommendations for international students: recommended—TOEFL (minimum score 560 paper-based; 83 iBT), IELTS. Electronic applications accepted.

Emory University, Laney Graduate School, Department of Political Science, Atlanta, GA 30322-1100. Offers PhD. *Degree requirements:* For doctorate, comprehensive exam, thesis/dissertation. *Entrance requirements:* For doctorate, GRE General Test, minimum GPA of 3.0. Additional exam requirements/recommendations for international students: required—TOEFL. Electronic applications accepted.

Fairleigh Dickinson University, Metropolitan Campus, University College: Arts, Sciences, and Professional Studies, School of History, Political and International Studies, Program in Political Science, Teaneck, NJ 07666-1914. Offers MA.

Florida Agricultural and Mechanical University, Division of Graduate Studies, Research, and Continuing Education, College of Social Sciences, Arts and Humanities, Department of History and Political Science, Program in Applied Social Science, Tallahassee, FL 32307-3200. Offers criminal justice (MASS); history (MASS); political science (MASS); public administration (MASS). *Program availability:* Part-time. *Degree requirements:* For master's, thesis optional. *Entrance requirements:* For master's, GRE General Test, minimum GPA of 3.0.

Florida Atlantic University, Dorothy F. Schmidt College of Arts and Letters, Department of Political Science, Boca Raton, FL 33431-0991. Offers MA. *Program availability:* Part-time. *Faculty:* 15 full-time (3 women). *Students:* 13 full-time (5 women), 8 part-time (7 women); includes 15 minority (4 Black or African American, non-Hispanic/Latino; 2 Asian, non-Hispanic/Latino; 7 Hispanic/Latino; 2 Two or more races, non-Hispanic/Latino). Average age 28. 19 applicants, 58% accepted, 8 enrolled. In 2019, 11 master's awarded. *Degree requirements:* For master's, one foreign language, thesis or alternative. *Entrance requirements:* For master's, GRE General Test, minimum GPA of 3.0 during last 60 hours of course work. Additional exam requirements/recommendations for international students: required—TOEFL (minimum score 500 paper-based; 61 iBT), IELTS (minimum score 6). *Application deadline:* For fall admission, 7/1 for domestic students, 2/15 for international students; for spring admission, 11/1 for domestic students, 7/15 for international students. Applications are processed on a rolling basis. Application fee: $30. Electronic applications accepted. *Expenses: Tuition:* Full-time $20,536; part-time $371.82 per credit hour. Tuition and fees vary according to program. *Financial support:* Research assistantships, teaching assistantships with partial tuition reimbursements, career-related internships or fieldwork, Federal Work-Study, and institutionally sponsored loans available. Support available to part-time students. Financial award application deadline: 4/16. *Unit head:* Dr. Kevin M. Wagner, Chair, 561-297-3211, E-mail: kwagne15@fau.edu. *Application contact:* Dr. Mehmet Gurses, Director of Graduate Studies, 561-297-3213, E-mail: gurses@fau.edu.
Website: http://www.fau.edu/politicalscience/

Florida International University, Steven J. Green School of International and Public Affairs, Department of Politics and International Relations, Miami, FL 33199. Offers international relations (MA, PhD), including international relations (PhD), international studies (MA); political science (MA, PhD). *Program availability:* Part-time, evening/weekend. *Faculty:* 28 full-time (10 women), 32 part-time/adjunct (8 women). *Students:* 81 full-time (34 women), 13 part-time (4 women); includes 39 minority (4 Black or African American, non-Hispanic/Latino; 4 Asian, non-Hispanic/Latino; 31 Hispanic/Latino), 35 international. Average age 32. 73 applicants, 45% accepted, 20 enrolled. In 2019, 9 master's, 11 doctorates awarded. *Degree requirements:* For master's, one foreign language, thesis optional; for doctorate, one foreign language, comprehensive exam, thesis/dissertation. *Entrance requirements:* For master's and doctorate, GRE General Test, minimum GPA of 3.0, letters of recommendation. Additional exam requirements/recommendations for international students: required—TOEFL (minimum score 550 paper-based; 80 iBT). *Application deadline:* For fall admission, 3/15 for domestic and international students; for spring admission, 8/15 for domestic and international students. Application fee: $30. Electronic applications accepted. *Expenses: Tuition, area resident:* Full-time $8912; part-time $446 per credit hour. Tuition, state resident: full-time $8912; part-time $446 per credit hour. Tuition, nonresident: full-time $21,393; part-time $992 per credit hour. *Required fees:* $2194. *Financial support:* Institutionally sponsored loans, scholarships/grants, and unspecified assistantships available. Financial award application deadline: 3/1; financial award applicants required to submit FAFSA. *Unit head:* Dr. John Clark, Chair, 305-348-2227, Fax: 305-348-3765, E-mail: john.clark@fiu.edu. *Application contact:* Nanett Rojas, Manager, Admissions Operations, 305-348-7464, Fax: 305-348-7441, E-mail: gradadm@fiu.edu.
Website: http://pir.fiu.edu

Florida State University, The Graduate School, College of Social Sciences and Public Policy, Department of Political Science, Tallahassee, FL 32306-2230. Offers applied American politics and policy (MS); political science (MS, PhD). *Program availability:* Part-time. *Faculty:* 25 full-time (5 women), 1 part-time/adjunct (0 women). *Students:* 56 full-time (27 women), 18 part-time (9 women); includes 27 minority (8 Black or African American, non-Hispanic/Latino; 2 Asian, non-Hispanic/Latino; 13 Hispanic/Latino; 4 Two or more races, non-Hispanic/Latino), 4 international. Average age 28. 90 applicants, 44% accepted, 28 enrolled. In 2019, 24 master's, 6 doctorates awarded. Terminal master's awarded for partial completion of doctoral program. *Degree requirements:* For master's, thesis optional; for doctorate, comprehensive exam, thesis/dissertation. *Entrance requirements:* For master's, GRE General Test, minimum undergraduate GPA of 3.0; for doctorate, GRE General Test, minimum graduate GPA of 3.5, undergraduate 3.0. Additional exam requirements/recommendations for international students: required—TOEFL (minimum score 600 paper-based; 100 iBT). *Application deadline:* For fall admission, 1/15 priority date for domestic and international students. Applications are processed on a rolling basis. Application fee: $30. Electronic applications accepted. *Financial support:* In 2019–20, 34 students received support, including 16 research assistantships with full tuition reimbursements available (averaging $17,500 per year), 9 teaching assistantships with full tuition reimbursements available (averaging $17,500 per year); Federal Work-Study, institutionally sponsored loans, scholarships/grants, and unspecified assistantships also available. Financial award application deadline: 1/15; financial award applicants required to submit FAFSA. *Unit head:* Dr. Charles Barrilleaux, Department Chair, 850-644-5727, Fax: 850-644-1367, E-mail: cbarrilleaux@fsu.edu. *Application contact:* Elisa Kuchvalek, Academic Coordinator, 850-644-5727, Fax: 850-644-1367, E-mail: ekuchvalek@fsu.edu.
Website: http://coss.fsu.edu/polisci/

Fordham University, Graduate School of Arts and Sciences, Program in Elections and Campaign Management, New York, NY 10458. Offers MA. *Students:* Average age 29. 21 applicants, 38% accepted, 6 enrolled. In 2019, 8 master's awarded. Application fee: $70. *Unit head:* Dr. Monika McDermott, Director, 718-817-3963, E-mail: mmcdermott@fordham.edu. *Application contact:* Garrett Marino, Director of Graduate Admissions, 718-817-4419, Fax: 718-817-3566, E-mail: gmarino10@fordham.edu.
Website: http://www.fordham.edu/academics/programs_at_fordham_/elections__campaign_/

George Mason University, Schar School of Policy and Government, Program in Political Science, Arlington, VA 22030. Offers MA, PhD. *Degree requirements:* For master's, research project or thesis; for doctorate, comprehensive exam, thesis/dissertation. *Entrance requirements:* For master's, GRE (taken in the past five years), transcripts from all previous institutions attended in the U.S.; goals statement; 2 letters of recommendation; current resume; writing sample; for doctorate, GRE (taken in the past five years), official transcript from all colleges and universities attended; current resume; three letters of recommendation; statement of professional goals; writing sample (approximately 10-25 pages in length). Additional exam requirements/recommendations for international students: required—TOEFL (minimum score 575 paper-based; 88 iBT), IELTS (minimum score 6.5), PTE (minimum score 59). Electronic applications accepted.

Georgetown University, Graduate School of Arts and Sciences, Department of Government, Program in Democracy and Governance, Washington, DC 20057. Offers MA.

Georgetown University, Graduate School of Arts and Sciences, School of Continuing Studies, Washington, DC 20057. Offers American studies (MALS); applied intelligence (MPS); Catholic studies (MALS); classical civilizations (MALS); emergency and disaster management (MPS); ethics and the professions (MALS); global strategic communications (MPS); hospitality management (MPS); human resources management (MPS); humanities (MALS); individualized study (MALS); integrated marketing communications (MPS); international affairs (MALS); Islam and Muslim-Christian relations (MALS); journalism (MPS); liberal studies (DLS); literature and society (MALS); medieval and early modern European studies (MALS); public relations and corporate communications (MPS); real estate (MPS); religious studies (MALS); social and public policy (MALS); sports industry management (MPS); systems engineering management (MPS); technology management (MPS); the theory and practice of American democracy (MALS); urban and regional planning (MPS); visual culture (MALS). *Entrance requirements:* Additional exam requirements/recommendations for international students: required—TOEFL.

The George Washington University, College of Professional Studies, Graduate School of Political Management, Program in Legislative Affairs, Washington, DC 20052. Offers MPS. *Program availability:* Part-time, evening/weekend. *Entrance requirements:* For master's, GRE General Test, minimum GPA of 3.0. Additional exam requirements/recommendations for international students: required—TOEFL (minimum score 550 paper-based). Electronic applications accepted.

The George Washington University, Columbian College of Arts and Sciences, Department of Political Science, Washington, DC 20052. Offers legal institutions and theory (MA); political science (MA). *Program availability:* Part-time, evening/weekend. Terminal master's awarded for partial completion of doctoral program. *Degree requirements:* For master's, one foreign language, comprehensive exam, thesis or alternative; for doctorate, 2 foreign languages, thesis/dissertation, general exam. *Entrance requirements:* For master's and doctorate, GRE General Test, minimum GPA of 3.0. Additional exam requirements/recommendations for international students: required—TOEFL (minimum score 550 paper-based; 80 iBT). Electronic applications accepted.

The George Washington University, Elliott School of International Affairs, Program in Security Policy Studies, Washington, DC 20052. Offers MA. *Program availability:* Part-time. *Degree requirements:* For master's, one foreign language, capstone project. *Entrance requirements:* For master's, GRE General Test, 2 semesters of introductory economics, 2 years of a modern foreign language or 1 semester of statistics. Additional exam requirements/recommendations for international students: required—TOEFL (minimum score 100 iBT), IELTS (minimum score 7). Electronic applications accepted.

Georgia State University, College of Arts and Sciences, Department of Communication, Atlanta, GA 30302-3083. Offers film, video, and digital imaging (MA), including critical studies, production, screenwriting; human communication and social influence (MA); mass communication (MA); media and society (PhD); moving image studies (PhD); public communication (PhD); rhetoric and politics (PhD). *Program availability:* Part-time. *Faculty:* 22 full-time (16 women), 1 part-time/adjunct (0 women). *Students:* 67 full-time (46 women), 26 part-time (17 women); includes 44 minority (40 Black or African American, non-Hispanic/Latino; 1 Asian, non-Hispanic/Latino; 1 Hispanic/Latino; 1 Native Hawaiian or other Pacific Islander, non-Hispanic/Latino; 1 Two or more races, non-Hispanic/Latino), 12 international. Average age 36. 82 applicants, 49% accepted, 22 enrolled. In 2019, 9 master's, 5 doctorates awarded. *Degree requirements:* For master's, variable foreign language requirement, thesis (for some programs); for doctorate, comprehensive exam, thesis/dissertation. *Entrance requirements:* For master's and doctorate, GRE. Additional exam requirements/recommendations for international students: required—TOEFL (minimum score 550 paper-based; 80 iBT), IELTS (minimum score 6.5). *Application deadline:* For fall admission, 2/10 for domestic and international students; for spring admission, 10/15 for domestic and international students. Application fee: $50. Electronic applications accepted. *Expenses: Tuition, area resident:* Full-time $7164; part-time $398 per credit hour. Tuition, state resident: full-time $7164; part-time $398 per credit hour. Tuition, nonresident: full-time $22,662; part-time $1259 per credit hour. *International tuition:* $22,662 full-time. *Required fees:* $2128; $312 per credit hour. Tuition and fees vary according to course load and program. *Financial support:* In 2019–20, fellowships with tuition reimbursements (averaging $15,000 per year), teaching assistantships with tuition reimbursements (averaging $15,000 per year) were awarded; career-related internships or fieldwork and unspecified assistantships also available. Financial award applicants required to submit FAFSA. *Unit head:* Dr. Greg Lisby, Chair, 404-413-5639, Fax: 404-413-5634, E-mail: glisby@gsu.edu. *Application contact:* Dr. Greg Lisby, Chair, 404-413-5639, Fax: 404-413-5634, E-mail: glisby@gsu.edu. Website: http://communication.gsu.edu

Georgia State University, College of Arts and Sciences, Department of Political Science, Atlanta, GA 30302-3083. Offers MA, PhD. *Program availability:* Part-time, evening/weekend. *Faculty:* 12 full-time (4 women). *Students:* 68 full-time (42 women), 24 part-time (8 women); includes 31 minority (14 Black or African American, non-Hispanic/Latino; 3 Asian, non-Hispanic/Latino; 6 Hispanic/Latino; 1 Native Hawaiian or other Pacific Islander, non-Hispanic/Latino; 7 Two or more races, non-Hispanic/Latino), 24 international. Average age 31. 68 applicants, 75% accepted, 26 enrolled. In 2019, 16 master's, 5 doctorates awarded. Terminal master's awarded for partial completion of doctoral program. *Entrance requirements:* For master's and doctorate, GRE. *Application deadline:* For fall admission, 2/1 priority date for domestic and international students; for spring admission, 10/15 for domestic and international students. Applications are processed on a rolling basis. Application fee: $50. Electronic applications accepted. *Expenses: Tuition, area resident:* Full-time $7164; part-time $398 per credit hour. Tuition, state resident: full-time $7164; part-time $398 per credit hour. Tuition, nonresident: full-time $22,662; part-time $1259 per credit hour. *International tuition:* $22,662 full-time. *Required fees:* $2128; $312 per credit hour. Tuition and fees vary according to course load and program. *Financial support:* In 2019–20, fellowships with full tuition reimbursements (averaging $19,000 per year), research assistantships with full tuition reimbursements (averaging $14,000 per year), teaching assistantships with full tuition reimbursements (averaging $4,000 per year) were awarded; career-related internships or fieldwork and health care benefits also available. Financial award application deadline: 2/1; financial award applicants required to submit FAFSA. *Unit head:* Dr. Carrie Manning, Chair, 404-413-6162, Fax: 404-413-6156, E-mail: cmanning2@gsu.edu. *Application contact:* Dr. Amy Steigerwalt, Director of Graduate Studies, 404-413-6162, Fax: 404-413-6156, E-mail: asteigerwalt@gsu.edu. Website: http://politicalscience.gsu.edu/home/graduate/degree-requirements/

Georgia State University, College of Education and Human Development, Department of Middle and Secondary Education, Atlanta, GA 30302-3083. Offers curriculum and instruction (Ed D); English education (MAT); mathematics education (M Ed, MAT); middle level education (MAT); reading, language and literacy education (M Ed, MAT), including reading instruction (M Ed); science education (M Ed, MAT), including biology (MAT), broad field science (MAT), chemistry (MAT), earth science (MAT), physics (MAT); social studies education (M Ed, MAT), including economics (MAT), geography (MAT), history (MAT), political science (MAT); teaching and learning (PhD), including language and literacy, mathematics education, music education, science education, social studies education, teaching and teacher education. *Accreditation:* NCATE. *Program availability:* Part-time, evening/weekend, online learning. *Faculty:* 20 full-time (16 women), 8 part-time/adjunct (all women). *Students:* 184 full-time (117 women), 195 part-time (144 women); includes 218 minority (157 Black or African American, non-Hispanic/Latino; 22 Asian, non-Hispanic/Latino; 27 Hispanic/Latino; 12 Two or more races, non-Hispanic/Latino), 3 international. Average age 34. 123 applicants, 61% accepted, 46 enrolled. In 2019, 122 master's, 18 doctorates awarded. *Entrance requirements:* For master's, GRE; GACE I (for initial teacher preparation programs), baccalaureate degree or equivalent, resume, goals statement, two letters of recommendation, minimum undergraduate GPA of 2.5; proof of initial teacher certification in the content area (for M Ed); for doctorate, GRE, resume, goals statement, writing sample, two letters of recommendation, minimum graduate GPA of 3.3, interview. *Application deadline:* For fall admission, 1/15 priority date for domestic and international students; for spring admission, 10/1 for domestic and international students. Application fee: $50. Electronic applications accepted. *Expenses: Tuition, area resident:* Full-time $7164; part-time $398 per credit hour. Tuition, state resident: full-time $7164; part-time $398 per credit hour. Tuition, nonresident: full-time $22,662; part-time $1259 per credit hour. *International tuition:* $22,662 full-time. *Required fees:* $2128; $312 per credit hour. Tuition and fees vary according to course load and program. *Financial support:* In 2019–20, fellowships with full tuition reimbursements (averaging $19,667 per year), research assistantships with full tuition reimbursements (averaging $5,436 per year), teaching assistantships with full tuition reimbursements (averaging $2,779 per year) were awarded; career-related internships or fieldwork, Federal Work-Study, scholarships/grants, health care benefits, tuition waivers (full and partial), and unspecified assistantships also available. Financial award application deadline: 3/15. *Unit head:* Dr. Gertrude Marilyn Tinker Sachs, Chair, 404-413-8384, Fax: 404-413-8063, E-mail: gtinkersachs@gsu.edu. *Application contact:* Shaleen Tibbs, Administrative Specialist, 404-413-8385, Fax: 404-413-8063, E-mail: stibbs@gsu.edu. Website: http://mse.education.gsu.edu/

Governors State University, College of Arts and Sciences, Program in Political and Justice Studies, University Park, IL 60484. Offers MA. *Program availability:* Part-time. *Faculty:* 57 full-time (33 women), 72 part-time/adjunct (32 women). *Students:* 3 part-time (2 women); includes 2 minority (both Black or African American, non-Hispanic/Latino). Average age 38. In 2019, 5 master's awarded. *Application deadline:* For fall admission,

4/1 for domestic students. Applications are processed on a rolling basis. Application fee: $50. Electronic applications accepted. *Expenses: Tuition, area resident:* Full-time $8472; part-time $353 per credit hour. Tuition, state resident: full-time $8472; part-time $353 per credit hour. Tuition, nonresident: full-time $16,944; part-time $706 per credit hour. *International tuition:* $16,944 full-time. *Required fees:* $2520; $105 per credit hour. $38 per term. Tuition and fees vary according to course load, degree level and program. *Financial support:* Application deadline: 5/1; applicants required to submit FAFSA. *Unit head:* Jason Zingsheim, Chair, Division of Arts and Letters, 708-534-5000 Ext. 7493, E-mail: jzingsheim@govst.edu. *Application contact:* Jason Zingsheim, Chair, Division of Arts and Letters, 708-534-5000 Ext. 7493, E-mail: jzingsheim@govst.edu.

The Graduate Center, City University of New York, Graduate Studies, Program in Political Science, New York, NY 10016-4039. Offers MA, PhD. Terminal master's awarded for partial completion of doctoral program. *Degree requirements:* For master's, one foreign language, thesis; for doctorate, one foreign language, thesis/dissertation. *Entrance requirements:* For master's and doctorate, GRE General Test. Additional exam requirements/recommendations for international students: required—TOEFL. Electronic applications accepted.

Grambling State University, School of Graduate Studies and Research, College of Arts and Sciences, Department of Political Science and Public Administration, Grambling, LA 71270. Offers health services administration (MPA); human resource management (MPA); public management (MPA); state and local government (MPA). *Accreditation:* NASPAA. *Program availability:* Part-time. *Degree requirements:* For master's, comprehensive exam (for some programs), thesis optional. *Entrance requirements:* For master's, GRE, minimum GPA of 2.75 on last degree. Additional exam requirements/recommendations for international students: required—TOEFL (minimum score 500 paper-based; 62 iBT). Electronic applications accepted.

Harvard University, Graduate School of Arts and Sciences, Committee on Political Economy and Government, Cambridge, MA 02138. Offers PhD. *Entrance requirements:* For doctorate, GRE General Test or GMAT. Additional exam requirements/ recommendations for international students: required—TOEFL.

Harvard University, Graduate School of Arts and Sciences, Department of Government, Cambridge, MA 02138. Offers political science (PhD), including American politics, comparative politics, international relations, political thought, quantitative methods. *Degree requirements:* For doctorate, one foreign language, thesis/ dissertation, general exams. *Entrance requirements:* For doctorate, GRE General Test. Additional exam requirements/recommendations for international students: required— TOEFL.

Harvard University, John F. Kennedy School of Government, Cambridge, MA 02138. Offers MPA, MPAID, MPP, PhD, JD/MPP, MBA/MPP, MD/MPP. *Degree requirements:* For doctorate, thesis/dissertation. *Entrance requirements:* For master's, GMAT or GRE General Test; for doctorate, GRE General Test. Additional exam requirements/ recommendations for international students: required—TOEFL (minimum score 600 paper-based; 100 iBT), TWE. Electronic applications accepted.

Hillsdale College, Van Andel Graduate School of Statesmanship, Hillsdale, MI 49242-1298. Offers politics (MA, PhD). *Faculty:* 11 full-time. *Students:* 40 full-time (10 women), 11 part-time (3 women). Average age 28. 49 applicants, 37% accepted, 14 enrolled. In 2019, 13 master's, 3 doctorates awarded. Terminal master's awarded for partial completion of doctoral program. *Degree requirements:* For master's, comprehensive exam (for some programs), thesis (for some programs); for doctorate, 2 foreign languages, comprehensive exam, thesis/dissertation. *Entrance requirements:* For master's and doctorate, GRE. Additional exam requirements/recommendations for international students: required—TOEFL. *Application deadline:* For fall admission, 12/15 priority date for domestic and international students; for spring admission, 10/15 for domestic and international students. Application fee: $25. Electronic applications accepted. *Expenses: Tuition:* Full-time $24,370; part-time $1340 per credit hour. *Required fees:* $560; $560 per unit. One-time fee: $25. *Financial support:* In 2019–20, 51 students received support, including 30 fellowships with full tuition reimbursements available (averaging $20,000 per year), 35 research assistantships with full tuition reimbursements available (averaging $4,143 per year); institutionally sponsored loans, scholarships/grants, and unspecified assistantships also available. Financial award application deadline: 12/15. *Unit head:* Dr. Ronald J. Pestritto, Dean, 517-607-2483, E-mail: gradschool@hillsdale.edu. *Application contact:* Mariel Stauff, Graduate Program Coordinator, 517-607-2483, E-mail: gradschool@hillsdale.edu. Website: http://gradschool.hillsdale.edu

Howard University, Graduate School, Department of Political Science, Program in Political Science, Washington, DC 20059-0002. Offers MA, PhD. *Degree requirements:* For master's, comprehensive exam. *Entrance requirements:* For master's, GRE General Test, minimum GPA of 3.0; for doctorate, GRE General Test, minimum GPA of 2.8.

Idaho State University, Graduate School, College of Arts and Letters, Department of Political Science, Pocatello, ID 83209-8073. Offers political science (MA, DA); public administration (MPA). *Program availability:* Part-time. *Degree requirements:* For master's, comprehensive exam, thesis optional; for doctorate, comprehensive exam, thesis/dissertation, teaching internship. *Entrance requirements:* For master's, GRE General Test, minimum GPA of 3.0 in last 2 years of undergraduate study, 3 letters of recommendation; for doctorate, GRE General Test, major field of American politics, minimum GPA of 3.0 in last 2 years of undergraduate study, 3 letters of recommendation. Additional exam requirements/recommendations for international students: required—TOEFL (minimum score 550 paper-based; 80 iBT). Electronic applications accepted.

Illinois State University, Graduate School, College of Arts and Sciences, Department of Politics and Government, Normal, IL 61790. Offers MA, MS. *Faculty:* 21 full-time (9 women), 10 part-time/adjunct (3 women). *Students:* 21 full-time (6 women), 4 part-time (0 women). Average age 26. 27 applicants, 63% accepted, 12 enrolled. In 2019, 10 master's awarded. *Degree requirements:* For master's, thesis or alternative. *Entrance requirements:* For master's, GRE General Test, minimum GPA of 3.0 in last 60 hours of course work, 15 hours of course work in political science. *Application deadline:* Applications are processed on a rolling basis. Application fee: $50. *Expenses: Tuition, area resident:* Full-time $7956; part-time $9767 per year. Tuition, nonresident: full-time $9233; part-time $17,592 per year. *Required fees:* $1797. *Financial support:* In 2019–20, 1 research assistantship, 16 teaching assistantships were awarded; tuition waivers (full) and unspecified assistantships also available. Financial award application deadline: 4/1. *Unit head:* Dr. T.Y. Wang, Department Chair, 309-438-8638, E-mail: tywang@ilstu.edu. *Application contact:* Dr. Jonathan Shapiro, Graduate Coordinator, 309-438-7622, E-mail: jkshapi@ilstu.edu. Website: http://www.politicsandgovernment.ilstu.edu/

Indiana University Bloomington, University Graduate School, College of Arts and Sciences, Department of Political Science, Bloomington, IN 47405-7000. Offers MA, PhD. Terminal master's awarded for partial completion of doctoral program. *Degree requirements:* For master's, thesis, 30 credit hours; for doctorate, comprehensive exam, thesis/dissertation. *Entrance requirements:* For master's, GRE, personal statement, transcripts, 3 letters of recommendation; for doctorate, GRE, sample of written work, 3 letters of recommendation, personal statement. Additional exam requirements/

recommendations for international students: required—TOEFL (minimum score 640 paper-based; 112 iBT). Electronic applications accepted.

Indiana University-Purdue University Indianapolis, School of Liberal Arts, Department of Political Science, Indianapolis, IN 46202. Offers MA.

Institute for Christian Studies, Graduate Programs, Toronto, ON M5S 2E6, Canada. Offers education (M Phil F, PhD); history of philosophy (M Phil F, PhD); philosophical aesthetics (M Phil F, PhD); philosophy of religion (M Phil F, PhD); political theory (M Phil F, PhD); systematic philosophy (M Phil F, PhD); theology (M Phil F, PhD); worldview studies (MWS). *Program availability:* Part-time, online learning. *Degree requirements:* For master's, one foreign language, thesis; for doctorate, 2 foreign languages, thesis/dissertation. *Entrance requirements:* For master's and doctorate, philosophy background. Additional exam requirements/recommendations for international students: required—TOEFL (minimum score 600 paper-based).

The Institute of World Politics, Graduate Programs in National Security, Intelligence, and International Affairs, Washington, DC 20036. Offers American foreign policy (Certificate); comparative political culture (Certificate); conflict prevention (Certificate); counterintelligence (Certificate); counterterrorism (Certificate); cyber statecraft (Certificate); economic statecraft (Certificate); homeland security (Certificate); intelligence (Certificate); international politics (Certificate); national security affairs (Executive MA, Certificate); nonviolent conflict (Certificate); peace building, stabilization, and humanitarian affairs (Certificate); public diplomacy and strategic influence (Certificate); statecraft and international affairs (MA); statecraft and national security (MA, DSNS); strategic communication (Certificate); strategic intelligence studies (MA, Professional MA); strategic soft power (Certificate). *Program availability:* Part-time, evening/weekend. *Degree requirements:* For master's, 52 credit hours, comprehensive written and oral exam (for MA); proficiency in critical language (for MA in statecraft and international affairs); 28 credit hours (for Executive MA); 36 credit hours (for Professional MA); for doctorate, comprehensive exam, thesis/dissertation; for Certificate, 20 credit hours. *Entrance requirements:* For master's, resume, personal statement, 3 references, essay; 7-10 years of professional experience (for Executive MA); 5-7 years of professional experience (for Professional MA); for doctorate, MA. Additional exam requirements/recommendations for international students: required—TOEFL. Electronic applications accepted.

Iowa State University of Science and Technology, Department of Political Science, Ames, IA 50011. Offers political science (MA); public administration (MPA); JD/MA. *Degree requirements:* For master's, thesis (for some programs). *Entrance requirements:* For master's, GRE General Test, GMAT or LSAT. Additional exam requirements/recommendations for international students: required—TOEFL (minimum score 570 paper-based; 80 iBT), IELTS (minimum score 6.5). Electronic applications accepted.

Jackson State University, Graduate School, College of Liberal Arts, Department of Political Science, Jackson, MS 39217. Offers MA. *Program availability:* Part-time, evening/weekend. *Degree requirements:* For master's, comprehensive exam, thesis or alternative. *Entrance requirements:* For master's, GRE General Test. Additional exam requirements/recommendations for international students: required—TOEFL (minimum score 520 paper-based; 67 iBT).

James Madison University, The Graduate School, College of Arts and Letters, Program in Political Science, Harrisonburg, VA 22807. Offers political science (MA), including European Union policy studies. *Students:* 12 full-time (7 women); includes 3 minority (2 Black or African American, non-Hispanic/Latino; 1 Hispanic/Latino). Average age 30. In 2019, 16 master's awarded. Application fee: $60. Electronic applications accepted. *Financial support:* In 2019–20, 2 students received support. Unspecified assistantships available. Financial award application deadline: 3/1; financial award applicants required to submit FAFSA. *Unit head:* Dr. Charles Blake, Academic Unit Head, 540-568-6344, Fax: 540-568-8021, E-mail: blakech@jmu.edu. *Application contact:* Lynette D. Michael, Director of Graduate Admissions, 540-568-6131 Ext. 6395, Fax: 540-568-7860, E-mail: michaeld@jmu.edu.
Website: http://www.jmu.edu/eurounionpolicy.shtml

Johns Hopkins University, Advanced Academic Programs, Program in Government, Washington, DC 21218. Offers global security studies (MA); government (MA); national securities study (Certificate); nonprofit management (Certificate); public management (MA); research administration (MS); MA/MBA. *Program availability:* Part-time, evening/weekend, online learning. *Entrance requirements:* For master's, minimum GPA of 3.0. Additional exam requirements/recommendations for international students: required—TOEFL (minimum score 100 iBT). Electronic applications accepted.

Johns Hopkins University, Zanvyl Krieger School of Arts and Sciences, Department of Political Science, Baltimore, MD 21218. Offers MA, PhD. *Degree requirements:* For doctorate, one foreign language, comprehensive exam, thesis/dissertation. *Entrance requirements:* For doctorate, GRE General Test. Additional exam requirements/recommendations for international students: required—TOEFL (minimum score 600 paper-based; 100 iBT), IELTS. Electronic applications accepted.

Kansas State University, Graduate School, College of Arts and Sciences, Department of Political Science, Manhattan, KS 66506. Offers political science (MA); public administration (MPA). *Accreditation:* NASPAA. *Program availability:* Part-time. *Degree requirements:* For master's, comprehensive exam, thesis or alternative. *Entrance requirements:* For master's, GRE (recommended), minimum GPA of 3.0. Additional exam requirements/recommendations for international students: required—TOEFL (minimum score 550 paper-based; 79 iBT); recommended—IELTS (minimum score 6.5), TSE (minimum score 58). Electronic applications accepted.

Kent State University, College of Arts and Sciences, Department of Political Science, Kent, OH 44242-0001. Offers political science (MA, PhD), including American politics and policy, conflict analysis and management, transnational and comparative politics and policy; public administration (MPA). *Accreditation:* NASPAA. *Program availability:* Part-time, 100% online. *Faculty:* 15 full-time (5 women), 2 part-time/adjunct (1 woman). *Students:* 39 full-time (19 women), 66 part-time (44 women); includes 14 minority (9 Black or African American, non-Hispanic/Latino; 2 Asian, non-Hispanic/Latino; 3 Two or more races, non-Hispanic/Latino), 12 international. Average age 36. 40 applicants, 90% accepted, 25 enrolled. In 2019, 26 master's, 2 doctorates awarded. *Degree requirements:* For master's, thesis, Capstone for non-thesis option; for doctorate, comprehensive exam, thesis/dissertation. *Entrance requirements:* For master's, GRE - combined verbal and quantitative GRE score above 300, goal statement, transcripts, writing sample, 3 letters of recommendation, minimum GPA of 3.0, resume; for doctorate, GRE -combined verbal and quantitative GRE score above 300, goal statement, transcripts, writing sample, 3 letters of recommendation, minimum GPA of 3.0, resume. Additional exam requirements/recommendations for international students: required—TOEFL (minimum score 79 iBT), IELTS (minimum score 6.5), Michigan English Language Assessment Battery (minimum score 77). *Application deadline:* For fall admission, 1/31 for domestic and international students. Applications are processed on a rolling basis. Application fee: $45 ($70 for international students). Electronic applications accepted. *Financial support:* Research assistantships with full tuition reimbursements, teaching assistantships with full tuition reimbursements, and unspecified assistantships available. Financial award application deadline: 1/31. *Unit head:* Dr. Anthony Molina, Chairperson and Assistant Professor, 330-672-2060, E-mail: amolina4@kent.edu. *Application contact:* Julie Mazzei, Associate Professor and Graduate Coordinator, 330-672-8934, E-mail: jmazzei@kent.edu.
Website: http://www.kent.edu/polisci

Lamar University, College of Graduate Studies, College of Arts and Sciences, Department of Political Science, Beaumont, TX 77710. Offers MPA. *Program availability:* Part-time. *Faculty:* 9 full-time (4 women). *Students:* 24 part-time (15 women); includes 15 minority (8 Black or African American, non-Hispanic/Latino; 7 Hispanic/Latino). Average age 38. 56 applicants, 77% accepted, 9 enrolled. In 2019, 4 master's awarded. *Entrance requirements:* For master's, GRE General Test. Additional exam requirements/recommendations for international students: required—TOEFL (minimum score 550 paper-based; 79 iBT), IELTS (minimum score 6.5). *Application deadline:* Applications are processed on a rolling basis. Application fee: $25 ($50 for international students). Electronic applications accepted. *Expenses: Tuition, area resident:* Full-time $6324; part-time $351 per credit. Tuition, state resident: full-time $6324; part-time $351 per credit. Tuition, nonresident: full-time $13,920; part-time $773 per credit. *International tuition:* $13,920 full-time. *Required fees:* $2462; $327 per credit. Tuition and fees vary according to course load, campus/location and reciprocity agreements. *Financial support:* Fellowships, research assistantships, teaching assistantships, career-related internships or fieldwork, Federal Work-Study, and institutionally sponsored loans available. Financial award application deadline: 4/1; financial award applicants required to submit FAFSA. *Unit head:* Dr. Thomas Sowers, Interim Department Chair, 409-880-8285, Fax: 409-880-8710. *Application contact:* Celeste Contreas, Director, Admissions and Academic Services, 409-880-8888, Fax: 409-880-7419, E-mail: gradmissions@lamar.edu.
Website: http://artssciences.lamar.edu/political-science

Lehigh University, College of Arts and Sciences, Department of Political Science, Bethlehem, PA 18015. Offers politics and policy (MA), including political theory. *Program availability:* Part-time, evening/weekend. *Faculty:* 8 full-time (6 women), 1 (woman) part-time/adjunct. *Students:* 10 full-time (4 women), 3 part-time (all women); includes 3 minority (all Hispanic/Latino), 3 international. Average age 26. 15 applicants, 93% accepted, 8 enrolled. In 2019, 9 master's awarded. *Degree requirements:* For master's, thesis or alternative, Either a thesis or research paper is required. But Community Fellows do a paper on their experience. *Entrance requirements:* For master's, transcripts, three letters of recommendation with at least two from academics, resume, statement of objectives, community fellows applicants need additional statement. Additional exam requirements/recommendations for international students: required—TOEFL-iBT only for graduate students who are non-native speakers of English or did not complete undergraduate degree at English speaking university; recommended—TOEFL (minimum score 101 iBT), IELTS (minimum score 7.5). *Application deadline:* For fall admission, 7/15 for domestic students, 4/1 for international students; for spring admission, 12/1 for domestic students; for summer admission, 4/30 for domestic students. Applications are processed on a rolling basis. Application fee: $75. Electronic applications accepted. *Financial support:* In 2019–20, 8 students received support, including 4 fellowships with partial tuition reimbursements available (averaging $14,713 per year), 2 teaching assistantships with full tuition reimbursements available (averaging $22,070 per year); scholarships/grants and tuition waivers (partial) also available. Financial award application deadline: 2/15; financial award applicants required to submit FAFSA. *Unit head:* Dr. Brian L. Fife, Chairperson, 610-758-3338, Fax: 610-758-3348, E-mail: blf218@lehigh.edu. *Application contact:* Dr. Holona Ochs, Director, Graduate Studies, 610-758-6508, Fax: 610-758-3348, E-mail: hlo209@lehigh.edu.
Website: http://polisci.cas2.lehigh.edu/

Liberty University, Helms School of Government, Lynchburg, VA 24515. Offers criminal justice (MS), including forensic psychology, homeland security, public administration (MA, MS); international relations (MS); political science (MS); public administration (MPA), including business and government, healthcare, law and public policy, public and non-profit management; public policy (MA), including campaigns and elections, international affairs, Middle East affairs, public administration (MA, MS). *Program availability:* Part-time, online learning. *Students:* 1,143 full-time (565 women), 572 part-time (408 women); includes 795 minority (499 Black or African American, non-Hispanic/Latino; 16 American Indian or Alaska Native, non-Hispanic/Latino; 23 Asian, non-Hispanic/Latino; 162 Hispanic/Latino; 7 Native Hawaiian or other Pacific Islander, non-Hispanic/Latino; 88 Two or more races, non-Hispanic/Latino), 27 international. Average age 35. 3,017 applicants, 44% accepted, 728 enrolled. In 2019, 415 master's awarded. *Entrance requirements:* For master's, minimum undergraduate GPA of 3.0. Additional exam requirements/recommendations for international students: required—TOEFL (minimum score 600 paper-based; 100 iBT). *Application deadline:* Applications are processed on a rolling basis. Application fee: $50. Electronic applications accepted. *Expenses: Tuition:* Full-time $545; part-time $410 per credit hour. One-time fee: $50. *Financial support:* In 2019–20, 808 students received support. Teaching assistantships and Federal Work-Study available. *Unit head:* Ron Miller, Dean, 434-592-4986, E-mail: govtdean@liberty.edu. *Application contact:* Jay Bridge, Director of Admissions, 800-424-9595, Fax: 800-628-7977, E-mail: gradadmissions@liberty.edu.
Website: https://www.liberty.edu/government/

Long Island University - Brooklyn, Richard L. Conolly College of Liberal Arts and Sciences, Brooklyn, NY 11201-8423. Offers biology (MS); chemistry (MS); clinical psychology (PhD); creative writing (MFA); English (MA); media arts (MA, MFA); political science (MA); psychology (MA); social science (MS); United Nations (Advanced Certificate); urban studies (MA); writing and production for television (MFA). *Program availability:* Part-time. Terminal master's awarded for partial completion of doctoral program. *Degree requirements:* For master's, comprehensive exam (for some programs), thesis (for some programs); for doctorate, thesis/dissertation. *Entrance requirements:* For doctorate, GRE. Additional exam requirements/recommendations for international students: required—TOEFL (minimum score 550 paper-based, 79 iBT) or IELTS. Electronic applications accepted.

Long Island University - Post, College of Liberal Arts and Sciences, Brookville, NY 11548-1300. Offers applied mathematics (MS); behavior analysis (MA); biology (MS); criminal justice (MS); earth science (MS); English (MA); environmental sustainability (MS); genetic counseling (MS); history (MA); interdisciplinary studies (MA, MS); political science (MA); psychology (MA). *Program availability:* Part-time, evening/weekend, blended/hybrid learning. Terminal master's awarded for partial completion of doctoral program. *Degree requirements:* For master's, comprehensive exam (for some programs), thesis (for some programs). *Entrance requirements:* Additional exam requirements/recommendations for international students: required—TOEFL, IELTS, or PTE. Electronic applications accepted.

Louisiana State University and Agricultural & Mechanical College, Graduate School, College of Humanities and Social Sciences, Department of Political Science, Baton Rouge, LA 70803. Offers MA, PhD.

Loyola University Chicago, Graduate School, Department of Political Science, Chicago, IL 60660. Offers global politics (PhD); political science (MA). *Program availability:* Part-time, evening/weekend. *Faculty:* 20 full-time (8 women). *Students:* 18 full-time (9 women), 1 (woman) part-time; includes 1 minority (Hispanic/Latino), 6 international. Average age 30. 46 applicants, 24% accepted, 5 enrolled. In 2019, 6 master's awarded. Terminal master's awarded for partial completion of doctoral program. *Degree requirements:* For master's, comprehensive exam, thesis or alternative; for doctorate, comprehensive exam, thesis/dissertation. *Entrance requirements:* For master's and doctorate, GRE General Test. Additional exam requirements/recommendations for international students: required—TOEFL (minimum score 550 paper-based; 79 iBT). *Application deadline:* For fall admission, 6/1 for domestic and international students; for spring admission, 10/1 for domestic and international students. Applications are processed on a rolling basis. Application fee: $0. Electronic applications accepted. *Expenses:* Contact institution. *Financial support:* In 2019–20, 9 students received support, including 9 fellowships with full tuition reimbursements available (averaging $19,000 per year), 9 research assistantships with full tuition reimbursements available (averaging $19,000 per year); Federal Work-Study, institutionally sponsored loans, scholarships/grants, tuition waivers (full and partial), and unspecified assistantships also available. Financial award application deadline: 2/15. *Unit head:* Prof. Molly Melin, Graduate Program Director, 773-508-8647, Fax: 773-508-3131, E-mail: mmelin@luc.edu. *Application contact:* Jill Schur, Director, Graduate Enrollment Management, 312-915-8902, E-mail: gradinfo@luc.edu. Website: http://www.luc.edu/politicalscience/

Marquette University, Graduate School, College of Arts and Sciences, Department of Political Science, Milwaukee, WI 53201-1881. Offers international affairs (MA); political science (MA); public service (MA); JD/MA; MA/MBA. *Program availability:* Part-time. *Degree requirements:* For master's, comprehensive exam, thesis optional. *Entrance requirements:* For master's, GRE General Test, official transcripts from all current and previous colleges/universities except Marquette, three letters of recommendation, statement of purpose. Additional exam requirements/recommendations for international students: required—TOEFL (minimum score 530 paper-based). Electronic applications accepted.

Marshall University, Academic Affairs Division, College of Liberal Arts, Department of Political Science, Huntington, WV 25755. Offers MA, MPA. *Degree requirements:* For master's, thesis optional. *Entrance requirements:* For master's, GRE General Test.

Massachusetts Institute of Technology, School of Humanities, Arts, and Social Sciences, Department of Political Science, Cambridge, MA 02139. Offers SM, PhD. Terminal master's awarded for partial completion of doctoral program. *Degree requirements:* For master's, thesis, minimum GPA of 3.5 in all subjects; for doctorate, one foreign language, comprehensive exam, thesis/dissertation. *Entrance requirements:* For master's and doctorate, GRE General Test. Additional exam requirements/recommendations for international students: required—TOEFL, IELTS. Electronic applications accepted.

McGill University, Faculty of Graduate and Postdoctoral Studies, Faculty of Arts, Department of Political Science, Montréal, QC H3A 2T5, Canada. Offers MA, PhD.

McMaster University, School of Graduate Studies, Faculty of Social Sciences, Department of Political Science, Hamilton, ON L8S 4M2, Canada. Offers international relations (PhD); political science (MA); public and the global economy (MA); public policy (PhD); public policy and administration (MA). *Program availability:* Part-time. *Degree requirements:* For master's, thesis or alternative. *Entrance requirements:* For master's, minimum B+ average. Additional exam requirements/recommendations for international students: required—TOEFL (minimum score 580 paper-based).

Memorial University of Newfoundland, School of Graduate Studies, Department of Political Science, St. John's, NL A1C 5S7, Canada. Offers MA. *Program availability:* Part-time, evening/weekend. *Degree requirements:* For master's, thesis optional. *Entrance requirements:* For master's, minimum 2nd class bachelor's degree. Electronic applications accepted.

Miami University, College of Arts and Science, Department of Political Science, Oxford, OH 45056. Offers MA.

Michigan State University, The Graduate School, College of Social Science, Department of Political Science, East Lansing, MI 48824. Offers political science (MA, PhD); public policy (MPP). *Degree requirements:* For master's, practicum; for doctorate, comprehensive exam, presentation of dissertation. *Entrance requirements:* Additional exam requirements/recommendations for international students: required—TOEFL. Electronic applications accepted.

Middle Tennessee State University, College of Graduate Studies, College of Liberal Arts, Department of Political Science, Murfreesboro, TN 37132. Offers international affairs (MA). *Program availability:* Part-time, evening/weekend, online learning. *Entrance requirements:* Additional exam requirements/recommendations for international students: required—TOEFL (minimum score 525 paper-based; 71 iBT) or IELTS (minimum score 6). Electronic applications accepted.

Midwestern State University, Billie Doris McAda Graduate School, Prothro-Yeager College of Humanities and Social Sciences, Department of Political Science, Wichita Falls, TX 76308. Offers MA. *Degree requirements:* For master's, one foreign language, comprehensive exam, thesis optional. *Entrance requirements:* For master's, GRE General Test/GMAT/MAT, bachelor's degree from regionally-accredited institution, minimum GPA of 3.0 on last 60 hours of undergraduate work. Additional exam requirements/recommendations for international students: required—TOEFL (minimum score 550 paper-based). Electronic applications accepted.

Mississippi College, Graduate School, College of Arts and Sciences, School of Humanities and Social Sciences, Department of History and Political Science, Clinton, MS 39058. Offers administration of justice (MSS); history (M Ed, MA, MSS); paralegal studies (Certificate); political science (MSS); social sciences (M Ed, MSS). *Program availability:* Part-time. *Degree requirements:* For master's, one foreign language, comprehensive exam, thesis (for some programs). *Entrance requirements:* For master's, GRE or NTE, minimum GPA of 2.5. Additional exam requirements/recommendations for international students: recommended—TOEFL, IELTS. Electronic applications accepted.

Mississippi State University, College of Arts and Sciences, Department of Political Science and Public Administration, Mississippi State, MS 39762. Offers political science (MA); public policy and administration (MPPA, PhD). *Accreditation:* NASPAA (one or more programs are accredited). *Program availability:* Evening/weekend, blended/hybrid learning. *Faculty:* 15 full-time (6 women). *Students:* 24 full-time (13 women), 39 part-time (19 women); includes 18 minority (15 Black or African American, non-Hispanic/Latino; 1 American Indian or Alaska Native, non-Hispanic/Latino; 1 Asian, non-Hispanic/Latino; 1 Hispanic/Latino), 5 international. Average age 32. 29 applicants, 90% accepted, 19 enrolled. In 2019, 11 master's, 1 doctorate awarded. *Degree requirements:* For master's, thesis optional, comprehensive oral or written exam; for doctorate, thesis/dissertation, comprehensive oral and written exam. *Entrance requirements:* For master's, GRE, minimum GPA of 3.0 on the last two years of undergraduate courses or graduate work; for doctorate, GRE General Test, minimum graduate GPA of 3.35. Additional exam requirements/recommendations for international students: required—TOEFL (minimum score 600 paper-based; 100 iBT); recommended—IELTS (minimum score 7.5). *Application deadline:* For fall admission, 8/1 priority date for domestic students, 5/1 for international students; for spring admission, 12/1 priority date for domestic students, 9/1 for international students. Applications are processed on a rolling basis. Application fee: $60 ($80 for international students). Electronic applications

accepted. *Expenses: Tuition, area resident:* Full-time $8880; part-time $456 per credit hour. Tuition, state resident: full-time $8880. Tuition, nonresident: full-time $23,840; part-time $1236 per credit hour. *Required fees:* $110; $11.12 per credit hour. Tuition and fees vary according to course load. *Financial support:* In 2019–20, 9 teaching assistantships with full tuition reimbursements (averaging $11,083 per year) were awarded; Federal Work-Study, institutionally sponsored loans, scholarships/grants, and unspecified assistantships also available. Financial award application deadline: 4/1; financial award applicants required to submit FAFSA. *Unit head:* Dr. P. Edward French, Professor and Head, 662-325-2711, Fax: 662-325-2716, E-mail: efrench@pspa.msstate.edu. *Application contact:* Nathan Drake, Manager, Graduate Programs, 662-325-7394, E-mail: ndrake@grad.msstate.edu. Website: http://www.pspa.msstate.edu

Missouri State University, Graduate College, College of Humanities and Public Affairs, Department of Political Science, Springfield, MO 65897. Offers global studies (MGS); public administration (MPA); public management (Certificate). *Program availability:* Part-time. *Degree requirements:* For master's, variable foreign language requirement, comprehensive exam, thesis or alternative. *Entrance requirements:* For master's, GRE, minimum GPA of 3.0. Additional exam requirements/recommendations for international students: required—TOEFL (minimum score 550 paper-based; 79 iBT), IELTS (minimum score 6). Electronic applications accepted. *Expenses: Tuition, area resident:* Full-time $2600; part-time $1735 per credit hour. Tuition, nonresident: full-time $5240; part-time $3495 per credit hour. *International tuition:* $5240 full-time. *Required fees:* $530; $438 per credit hour. Tuition and fees vary according to class time, course level, course load, degree level, campus/location and program.

Montclair State University, The Graduate School, College of Humanities and Social Sciences, MA Program in Law and Governance, Montclair, NJ 07043-1624. Offers conflict management and peace studies (MA); governance, compliance and regulation (MA); intellectual property (MA); law and governance (MA); legal management (MA). *Program availability:* Part-time, evening/weekend. *Degree requirements:* For master's, thesis or comprehensive exam. *Entrance requirements:* For master's, GRE General Test, minimum cumulative GPA of 2.75 for undergraduate work, 2 letters of recommendation, essay. Additional exam requirements/recommendations for international students: required—TOEFL (minimum score 83 iBT) or IELTS (minimum score 6.5). Electronic applications accepted.

Murray State University, College of Humanities and Fine Arts, Department of Political Science and Sociology, Murray, KY 42071. Offers MPA. *Program availability:* Part-time, evening/weekend. *Entrance requirements:* For master's, GRE or GMAT, minimum university GPA of 2.75. Additional exam requirements/recommendations for international students: required—TOEFL (minimum score 527 paper-based; 71 iBT). Electronic applications accepted.

New Mexico Highlands University, Graduate Studies, College of Arts and Sciences, Department of History, Political Science, and Languages and Culture, Las Vegas, NM 87701. Offers public affairs (MA), including historical and cross-cultural perspectives, history/political science, political and governmental processes. *Degree requirements:* For master's, comprehensive exam, thesis or alternative. *Entrance requirements:* Additional exam requirements/recommendations for international students: required—TOEFL (minimum score 540 paper-based).

New Mexico State University, College of Arts and Sciences, Department of Government, Las Cruces, NM 88003-8001. Offers government (MA); public administration (MPA). *Accreditation:* NASPAA (one or more programs are accredited). *Program availability:* Part-time. *Faculty:* 8 full-time (3 women), 1 (woman) part-time/adjunct. *Students:* 13 full-time (5 women), 18 part-time (6 women); includes 20 minority (3 Black or African American, non-Hispanic/Latino; 17 Hispanic/Latino), 1 international. Average age 33. 12 applicants, 83% accepted, 7 enrolled. In 2019, 14 master's awarded. *Degree requirements:* For master's, comprehensive exam (for some programs), thesis optional. *Entrance requirements:* For master's, GRE (if GPA less than 3.0), writing sample, 3 letters of recommendation, resume. Additional exam requirements/recommendations for international students: required—TOEFL (minimum score 550 paper-based; 79 iBT), IELTS (minimum score 6.5). *Application deadline:* For fall admission, 10/1 for domestic and international students; for spring admission, 3/1 for domestic and international students; for summer admission, 3/1 for domestic and international students. Application fee: $40 ($50 for international students). Electronic applications accepted. *Financial support:* In 2019–20, 13 students received support, including 9 teaching assistantships (averaging $14,126 per year); career-related internships or fieldwork, Federal Work-Study, scholarships/grants, traineeships, health care benefits, and unspecified assistantships also available. Support available to part-time students. Financial award application deadline: 3/1. *Unit head:* Dr. Neil Harvey, Head, 575-646-4935, Fax: 575-646-2052, E-mail: nharvey@nmsu.edu. *Application contact:* Dr. Neil Harvey, Director, Master of Arts in Government Program, 575-646-4935, Fax: 575-646-2052, E-mail: nharvey@nmsu.edu. Website: http://deptofgov.nmsu.edu

The New School, The New School for Social Research, Department of Historical Studies, New York, NY 10003. Offers historical studies (MA); politics (PhD), including historical studies; sociology (PhD), including historical studies. *Program availability:* Part-time, evening/weekend. *Faculty:* 1 (woman) full-time, 2 part-time/adjunct (both women). *Students:* 10 full-time (3 women), 4 part-time (2 women); includes 1 minority (Asian, non-Hispanic/Latino), 4 international. Average age 28. 8 applicants, 100% accepted, 6 enrolled. In 2019, 7 master's awarded. *Degree requirements:* For master's, thesis. *Entrance requirements:* For master's, GRE, two letters of recommendation, writing sample, essays, transcripts. Additional exam requirements/recommendations for international students: required—TOEFL (minimum score 100 iBT), IELTS (minimum score 7), PTE (minimum score 68). *Application deadline:* For fall admission, 1/15 priority date for domestic and international students; for spring admission, 10/15 priority date for domestic and international students. Applications are processed on a rolling basis. Application fee: $50. Electronic applications accepted. *Expenses:* 2260 per credit. *Financial support:* In 2019–20, 11 students received support, including 6 research assistantships (averaging $5,723 per year), 4 teaching assistantships (averaging $7,022 per year); Federal Work-Study, scholarships/grants, traineeships, health care benefits, and tuition waivers (full and partial) also available. Support available to part-time students. Financial award application deadline: 2/1; financial award applicants required to submit FAFSA. *Unit head:* Dr. Oz Frankel, Department Chair, 212-229-5376 Ext. 4924, E-mail: frankelo@newschool.edu. *Application contact:* Merida Gasbarro, Director of Graduate Admission, 212-229-5600 Ext. 1108, E-mail: escandom@newschool.edu. Website: http://www.newschool.edu/nssr/historical-studies/

The New School, The New School for Social Research, Department of Politics, New York, NY 10003. Offers politics (M Phil, MA, PhD). *Program availability:* Part-time. *Faculty:* 12 full-time (5 women), 1 part-time/adjunct (0 women). *Students:* 81 full-time (38 women); includes 4 minority (1 Asian, non-Hispanic/Latino; 1 Hispanic/Latino; 2 Two or more races, non-Hispanic/Latino), 46 international. Average age 33. 96 applicants, 60% accepted, 9 enrolled. In 2019, 20 master's, 11 doctorates awarded. Terminal master's awarded for partial completion of doctoral program. *Degree requirements:* For master's, portfolio of two papers; for doctorate, one foreign language, comprehensive exam, thesis/dissertation. *Entrance requirements:* For master's, GRE, letters of

recommendation, writing sample, essays, transcripts; for doctorate, letters of recommendation, writing sample, essays, transcripts. Additional exam requirements/ recommendations for international students: required—TOEFL (minimum score 100 iBT), IELTS (minimum score 7), PTE (minimum score 68). *Application deadline:* For fall admission, 1/5 priority date for domestic and international students; for spring admission, 10/15 priority date for domestic and international students. Applications are processed on a rolling basis. Application fee: $50. Electronic applications accepted. *Expenses:* 2260 per credit. *Financial support:* In 2019–20, 63 students received support, including 15 fellowships with full and partial tuition reimbursements available (averaging $8,951 per year), 20 research assistantships (averaging $4,777 per year), 22 teaching assistantships (averaging $5,189 per year); Federal Work-Study, scholarships/grants, and tuition waivers (full and partial) also available. Support available to part-time students. Financial award application deadline: 2/1; financial award applicants required to submit FAFSA. *Unit head:* Dr. Anne McNevin, Department Chair, 212-229-5747 Ext. 3382, E-mail: mcnevina@newschool.edu. *Application contact:* Merida Gasbarro, Director of Graduate Admission, 212-229-5600 Ext. 1108, E-mail: escandom@newschool.edu.
Website: http://www.newschool.edu/nssr/politics/

New York University, Graduate School of Arts and Science, Department of Politics, New York, NY 10012-1019. Offers political campaign management (MA); politics (MA, PhD); JD/MA; MBA/MA. *Program availability:* Part-time. Terminal master's awarded for partial completion of doctoral program. *Degree requirements:* For master's, one foreign language, thesis or alternative; for doctorate, 2 foreign languages, comprehensive exam, thesis/dissertation. *Entrance requirements:* For master's and doctorate, GRE General Test. Additional exam requirements/recommendations for international students: required—TOEFL, IELTS.

Northeastern Illinois University, College of Graduate Studies and Research, College of Arts and Sciences, Program in Political Science, Chicago, IL 60625. Offers MA. *Program availability:* Part-time, evening/weekend. *Degree requirements:* For master's, comprehensive exam, thesis optional. *Entrance requirements:* For master's, minimum GPA of 2.75. Additional exam requirements/recommendations for international students: required—TOEFL (minimum score 550 paper-based; 79 iBT). Electronic applications accepted.

Northeastern University, College of Social Sciences and Humanities, Boston, MA 02115. Offers criminology and criminal justice (MSCJ); criminology and justice policy (PhD); economics (MA, PhD); English (MA, PhD); international affairs (MA); law and public policy (PhD); political science (MA, PhD); public administration (MPA); public policy (MPP); security and resilience studies (MS); sociology (MA, PhD); urban and regional policy (MS); urban informatics (MS); world history (MA, PhD). *Program availability:* Online learning. *Degree requirements:* For doctorate, variable foreign language requirement, comprehensive exam, thesis/dissertation. *Entrance requirements:* For master's and doctorate, GRE. Additional exam requirements/ recommendations for international students: required—TOEFL, IELTS. Electronic applications accepted. *Expenses:* Contact institution.

Northern Arizona University, College of Social and Behavioral Sciences, Department of Politics and International Affairs, Flagstaff, AZ 86011. Offers political science (MA, PhD, Graduate Certificate); public administration (MPA); public management (Graduate Certificate). *Program availability:* Part-time, 100% online, blended/hybrid learning. *Degree requirements:* For master's, variable foreign language requirement, comprehensive exam (for some programs), thesis (for some programs); for doctorate, variable foreign language requirement, comprehensive exam (for some programs), thesis/dissertation (for some programs); for Graduate Certificate, comprehensive exam (for some programs). *Entrance requirements:* For master's and doctorate, GRE General Test. Additional exam requirements/recommendations for international students: required—TOEFL (minimum score 93 iBT), IELTS (minimum score 6.5). Electronic applications accepted.

Northern Illinois University, Graduate School, College of Liberal Arts and Sciences, Department of Political Science, De Kalb, IL 60115-2854. Offers MA, PhD. *Program availability:* Part-time, evening/weekend. *Faculty:* 24 full-time (5 women), 8 part-time/ adjunct (2 women). *Students:* 25 full-time (9 women), 9 part-time (5 women); includes 4 minority (2 Asian, non-Hispanic/Latino; 1 Hispanic/Latino; 1 Two or more races, non-Hispanic/Latino), 15 international. Average age 34. 33 applicants, 52% accepted, 6 enrolled. In 2019, 6 master's, 5 doctorates awarded. Terminal master's awarded for partial completion of doctoral program. *Degree requirements:* For master's, comprehensive exam, thesis optional; for doctorate, variable foreign language requirement, thesis/dissertation, candidacy exam, dissertation defense. *Entrance requirements:* For master's, GRE General Test, minimum GPA of 2.75, 9 hours of course work in political science; for doctorate, GRE General Test, minimum GPA of 2.75 (undergraduate), 3.2 (graduate); undergraduate major in related field. Additional exam requirements/recommendations for international students: required—TOEFL (minimum score 550 paper-based). *Application deadline:* For fall admission, 3/1 priority date for domestic students, 5/1 for international students; for spring admission, 11/1 for domestic students, 10/1 for international students. Applications are processed on a rolling basis. Application fee: $40. Electronic applications accepted. *Financial support:* In 2019–20, 22 teaching assistantships with full tuition reimbursements were awarded; fellowships with full tuition reimbursements, research assistantships with full tuition reimbursements, career-related internships or fieldwork, Federal Work-Study, scholarships/grants, tuition waivers (full), and unspecified assistantships also available. Support available to part-time students. Financial award applicants required to submit FAFSA. *Unit head:* Dr. Mitch Pickerill, Chair/Director, Graduate Studies, 815-753-7046, Fax: 815-753-6302. *Application contact:* Dr. Mitch Pickerill, Chair/Director, Graduate Studies, 815-753-7046, Fax: 815-753-6302.
Website: http://polisci.niu.edu/

Northwestern University, The Graduate School, Judd A. and Marjorie Weinberg College of Arts and Sciences, Department of Political Science, Evanston, IL 60208. Offers PhD, JD/PhD. Terminal master's awarded for partial completion of doctoral program. *Degree requirements:* For doctorate, thesis/dissertation, qualifying exams. *Entrance requirements:* For doctorate, GRE General Test, sample of written work. Additional exam requirements/recommendations for international students: required—TOEFL.

The Ohio State University, Graduate School, College of Arts and Sciences, Division of Social and Behavioral Sciences, Department of Political Science, Columbus, OH 43210. Offers PhD. Terminal master's awarded for partial completion of doctoral program. *Entrance requirements:* For doctorate, GRE General Test. Additional exam requirements/recommendations for international students: recommended—TOEFL (minimum score 600 paper-based; 100 iBT), IELTS (minimum score 8). Electronic applications accepted.

Ohio University, Graduate College, College of Arts and Sciences, Department of Political Science, Athens, OH 45701-2979. Offers MA. *Program availability:* Part-time, evening/weekend. *Degree requirements:* For master's, comprehensive exam, thesis or alternative. *Entrance requirements:* For master's, GRE General Test, minimum GPA of 3.0. Additional exam requirements/recommendations for international students: required—TOEFL (minimum score 550 paper-based; 80 iBT) or IELTS (minimum score 6.5). Electronic applications accepted.

Oklahoma State University, College of Arts and Sciences, Department of Political Science, Stillwater, OK 74078. Offers fire and emergency management administration (MS, PhD); political science (MA). *Faculty:* 9 full-time (5 women). *Students:* 9 full-time (1 woman), 4 part-time (3 women); includes 3 minority (2 Black or African American, non-Hispanic/Latino; 1 Asian, non-Hispanic/Latino), 1 international. Average age 25. 12 applicants, 67% accepted, 6 enrolled. In 2019, 11 master's awarded. *Entrance requirements:* For master's and doctorate, GRE. Additional exam requirements/ recommendations for international students: required—TOEFL (minimum score 550 paper-based; 79 iBT). *Application deadline:* For fall admission, 3/1 priority date for international students; for spring admission, 8/1 priority date for international students. Applications are processed on a rolling basis. Application fee: $50 ($75 for international students). Electronic applications accepted. *Expenses: Tuition, area resident:* Full-time $4148.10; part-time $2765.40 per credit hour. Tuition, state resident: full-time $4148.10; part-time $2765.40 per credit hour. Tuition, nonresident: full-time $15,775; part-time $10,516.80 per credit hour. *International tuition:* $15,775.20 full-time. *Required fees:* $2196.90; $122.05 per credit hour. Tuition and fees vary according to course load, campus/location and program. *Financial support:* In 2019–20, 9 teaching assistantships (averaging $1,625 per year) were awarded; research assistantships, career-related internships or fieldwork, Federal Work-Study, scholarships/grants, health care benefits, tuition waivers (partial), and unspecified assistantships also available. Support available to part-time students. Financial award application deadline: 3/1; financial award applicants required to submit FAFSA. *Unit head:* Dr. Rebekah Herrick, Interim Department Head, 405-744-8437, E-mail: rebekah.herrick@okstate.edu. *Application contact:* Dr. Sheryl Tucker, Dean, 405-744-6368, Fax: 405-744-0355, E-mail: gradi@okstate.edu.
Website: http://polsci.okstate.edu

Penn State University Park, Graduate School, College of the Liberal Arts, Department of Political Science, University Park, PA 16802. Offers MA, PhD.

Pepperdine University, School of Public Policy, Malibu, CA 90263. Offers American politics (MPP); economics (MPP); international relations (MPP); state and local policy (MPP); JD/MPP; MBA/MPP; MDR/MPP. *Entrance requirements:* For master's, GRE or GMAT or LSAT, transcripts, 2 letters of recommendation, resume, two essays. Additional exam requirements/recommendations for international students: required—TOEFL (minimum score 95 iBT), IELTS (minimum score 7). Electronic applications accepted. *Expenses:* Contact institution.

Portland State University, Graduate Studies, College of Urban and Public Affairs, Hatfield School of Government, Department of Political Science, Portland, OR 97207-0751. Offers political science (MA), including American politics, comparative politics, international relations, political theory. *Program availability:* Part-time. *Faculty:* 12 full-time (4 women), 4 part-time/adjunct (1 woman). *Students:* 6 full-time (2 women), 9 part-time (3 women); includes 1 minority (Two or more races, non-Hispanic/Latino), 2 international. Average age 35. 11 applicants, 73% accepted, 4 enrolled. In 2019, 2 master's awarded. *Degree requirements:* For master's, variable foreign language requirement, comprehensive exam, thesis. *Entrance requirements:* For master's, GRE General Test, minimum undergraduate GPA of 3.0 or 3.1 in graduate-level coursework, 2 letters of recommendation, statement of intent. Additional exam requirements/ recommendations for international students: required—TOEFL (minimum score 550 paper-based; 90 iBT). *Application deadline:* For fall admission, 2/1 priority date for domestic and international students. Application fee: $65. Electronic applications accepted. *Expenses: Tuition, area resident:* Full-time $13,020; part-time $6510 per year. Tuition, state resident: full-time $13,020; part-time $6510 per year. Tuition, nonresident: full-time $19,830; part-time $9915 per year. *International tuition:* $19,830 full-time. *Required fees:* $1226. One-time fee: $350. Tuition and fees vary according to course load, program and reciprocity agreements. *Financial support:* In 2019–20, 3 teaching assistantships with full and partial tuition reimbursements (averaging $7,209 per year) were awarded; research assistantships, career-related internships or fieldwork, and Federal Work-Study also available. Support available to part-time students. Financial award application deadline: 3/1; financial award applicants required to submit FAFSA. *Unit head:* Melody Valdini, Chair, 503-725-5139, Fax: 503-725-8444, E-mail: mev@pdx.edu. *Application contact:* Dr. David Kinsella, Graduate Committee Chair, 503-725-3035, E-mail: kinsella@pdx.edu.
Website: https://www.pdx.edu/hatfieldschool/political-science

Princeton University, Graduate School, Department of Politics, Princeton, NJ 08544-1019. Offers political philosophy (PhD); politics (PhD). *Degree requirements:* For doctorate, comprehensive exam, thesis/dissertation, teaching experience. *Entrance requirements:* For doctorate, GRE General Test, sample of written work, letters of recommendation. Additional exam requirements/recommendations for international students: required—TOEFL (minimum score 600 paper-based). Electronic applications accepted.

Purdue University, Graduate School, College of Liberal Arts, Department of Political Science, West Lafayette, IN 47907. Offers MA, PhD. *Program availability:* Part-time, evening/weekend. *Faculty:* 19 full-time (10 women), 3 part-time/adjunct (2 women). *Students:* 41 full-time (22 women), 3 part-time (0 women); includes 10 minority (7 Black or African American, non-Hispanic/Latino; 2 Hispanic/Latino; 1 Two or more races, non-Hispanic/Latino), 13 international. Average age 31. 29 applicants, 59% accepted, 8 enrolled. In 2019, 6 master's, 3 doctorates awarded. Terminal master's awarded for partial completion of doctoral program. *Degree requirements:* For master's, comprehensive exam; for doctorate, comprehensive exam, thesis/dissertation. *Entrance requirements:* For master's and doctorate, GRE General Test (minimum score of 160 verbal, 600 on old scoring), minimum undergraduate GPA of 3.0. Additional exam requirements/recommendations for international students: required—TOEFL (minimum score 600 paper-based; 90 iBT). *Application deadline:* For fall admission, 12/15 priority date for domestic and international students; for spring admission, 10/15 for domestic and international students. Applications are processed on a rolling basis. Application fee: $60 ($75 for international students). Electronic applications accepted. *Financial support:* Fellowships, research assistantships, teaching assistantships, and career-related internships or fieldwork available. Support available to part-time students. Financial award application deadline: 2/1; financial award applicants required to submit FAFSA. *Unit head:* Cherie D. Maestas, Dean, 765-494-4162, E-mail: cmaestas@purdue.edu. *Application contact:* Graduate School Admissions, 765-494-2600, Fax: 765-494-0136, E-mail: gradinfo@purdue.edu.
Website: http://www.polsci.purdue.edu/

Purdue University Global, School of Legal Studies, Davenport, IA 52807. Offers health care delivery (MS); pathway to paralegal (Postbaccalaureate Certificate); state and local government (MS). *Program availability:* Part-time, evening/weekend, online learning. *Entrance requirements:* Additional exam requirements/recommendations for international students: required—TOEFL (minimum score 550 paper-based; 80 iBT).

Queen's University at Kingston, School of Graduate Studies, Faculty of Arts and Science, Department of Political Studies, Kingston, ON K7L 3N6, Canada. Offers Canadian politics (MA, PhD); comparative politics (MA, PhD); gender and politics (MA,

PhD); international relations (MA, PhD); political theory (MA, PhD). *Degree requirements:* For master's, thesis or alternative; for doctorate, one foreign language, thesis/dissertation, qualifying exams. *Entrance requirements:* Additional exam requirements/recommendations for international students: required—TOEFL (minimum score 600 paper-based).

Regent University, Graduate School, Robertson School of Government, Virginia Beach, VA 23464. Offers government (MA), including American government, healthcare policy and ethics (MA, MPA), international relations, law and public policy, national security studies, political communication, political theory, religion and politics; national security studies (MA), including cybersecurity, homeland security, international security, Middle East politics; public administration (MPA), including emergency management and homeland security, federal government, general public administration, healthcare policy and ethics (MA, MPA), law, nonprofit administration and faith-based organizations, public leadership and management, servant leadership. *Program availability:* Part-time, evening/weekend, 100% online, blended/hybrid learning. *Faculty:* 5 full-time (1 woman), 19 part-time/adjunct (2 women). *Students:* 36 full-time (22 women), 159 part-time (89 women); includes 82 minority (52 Black or African American, non-Hispanic/Latino; 2 American Indian or Alaska Native, non-Hispanic/Latino; 2 Asian, non-Hispanic/Latino; 23 Hispanic/Latino; 3 Two or more races, non-Hispanic/Latino), 4 international. Average age 36. 181 applicants, 70% accepted, 75 enrolled. In 2019, 58 master's awarded. *Degree requirements:* For master's, thesis optional, internship. *Entrance requirements:* For master's, GRE General Test or LSAT, personal essay, writing sample, resume, college transcripts. Additional exam requirements/recommendations for international students: required—TOEFL (minimum score 577 paper-based). *Application deadline:* For fall admission, 5/1 priority date for domestic students; for spring admission, 11/1 priority date for domestic students. Applications are processed on a rolling basis. Application fee: $50. Electronic applications accepted. *Expenses:* Contact institution. *Financial support:* In 2019–20, 132 students received support. Career-related internships or fieldwork, scholarships/grants, and unspecified assistantships available. Support available to part-time students. Financial award applicants required to submit FAFSA. *Unit head:* Dr. Stephen Perry, Interim Dean, 757-352-4082, E-mail: sperry@regent.edu. *Application contact:* Heidi Cece, Assistant Vice President for Enrollment Management, 800-373-5504, Fax: 757-352-4381, E-mail: admissions@regent.edu.
Website: https://www.regent.edu/robertson-school-of-government/

Rice University, Graduate Programs, School of Social Sciences, Department of Political Science, Houston, TX 77251-1892. Offers PhD. Terminal master's awarded for partial completion of doctoral program. *Degree requirements:* For doctorate, comprehensive exam, thesis/dissertation, 42 hours of coursework. *Entrance requirements:* For doctorate, GRE General Test. Additional exam requirements/recommendations for international students: required—TOEFL (minimum score 600 paper-based; 90 iBT). Electronic applications accepted.

Rutgers University - Newark, Graduate School, Program in Political Science, Newark, NJ 07102. Offers American political system (MA); international relations (MA); JD/MA. *Program availability:* Part-time, evening/weekend. *Degree requirements:* For master's, comprehensive exam, thesis optional. *Entrance requirements:* For master's, GRE, minimum undergraduate B average. Electronic applications accepted.

Rutgers University - New Brunswick, Graduate School-New Brunswick, Department of Political Science, Piscataway, NJ 08854-8097. Offers American politics (PhD); comparative politics (PhD); international relations (PhD); political theory (PhD); public law (PhD); United Nations and global policy studies (MA); women and politics (PhD). *Degree requirements:* For doctorate, one foreign language, comprehensive exam, thesis/dissertation. *Entrance requirements:* For master's, bachelor's degree from accredited U.S. college or university or a comparable institution in another country; for doctorate, GRE General Test. Additional exam requirements/recommendations for international students: required—TOEFL.

St. John's University, St. John's College of Liberal Arts and Sciences, Department of Government and Politics and Division of Library and Information Science, Program in Government and Library and Information Science, Queens, NY 11439. Offers MA/MS. *Program availability:* Part-time, evening/weekend. *Entrance requirements:* Additional exam requirements/recommendations for international students: required—TOEFL (minimum score 80 iBT), IELTS (minimum score 6.5). Electronic applications accepted.

St. John's University, St. John's College of Liberal Arts and Sciences, Department of Government and Politics, Program in Government and Politics, Queens, NY 11439. Offers government and politics (MA); international law and diplomacy (Adv C); public administration (Adv C); JD/MA. *Program availability:* Part-time, evening/weekend. *Degree requirements:* For master's, comprehensive exam, thesis optional. *Entrance requirements:* For master's, letters of recommendation, transcripts, resume, personal statement. Additional exam requirements/recommendations for international students: required—TOEFL (minimum score 80 iBT), IELTS (minimum score 6.5). Electronic applications accepted.

Saint Louis University, Graduate Programs, College of Arts and Sciences, Department of Political Science, St. Louis, MO 63103. Offers MA. *Program availability:* Part-time. *Entrance requirements:* For master's, GRE or LSAT, letters of recommendation, resume, writing sample. Additional exam requirements/recommendations for international students: required—TOEFL (minimum score 525 paper-based). Electronic applications accepted.

Sam Houston State University, College of Humanities and Social Sciences, Department of Political Science, Huntsville, TX 77341. Offers political science (MA); public administration (MPA). *Program availability:* Part-time, online learning. *Degree requirements:* For master's, comprehensive exam, thesis optional, internship. *Entrance requirements:* For master's, GRE General Test, GMAT, writing sample of scholarly work, letters of recommendation, statement of purpose, resume. Additional exam requirements/recommendations for international students: required—TOEFL (minimum score 550 paper-based; 79 iBT), IELTS (minimum score 6.5). Electronic applications accepted.

San Diego State University, Graduate and Research Affairs, College of Arts and Letters, Department of Political Science, San Diego, CA 92182. Offers MA. *Program availability:* Part-time. *Degree requirements:* For master's, thesis. *Entrance requirements:* For master's, GRE General Test, minimum GPA of 3.0, 2 letters of reference. Additional exam requirements/recommendations for international students: required—TOEFL. Electronic applications accepted.

San Francisco State University, Division of Graduate Studies, College of Liberal and Creative Arts, Department of Political Science, San Francisco, CA 94132-1722. Offers MA. *Expenses: Tuition, area resident:* Full-time $7176; part-time $4164 per year. Tuition, state resident: full-time $7176; part-time $4164 per year. Tuition, nonresident: full-time $16,680; part-time $396 per unit. *International tuition:* $16,680 full-time. *Required fees:* $1524; $1524 per unit. $762 per semester. Tuition and fees vary according to degree level and program. *Financial support:* Research assistantships and teaching assistantships available. *Unit head:* Prof. Nicole Watts, Chair, 415-405-2470, Fax: 415-338-2391, E-mail: nfwatts@sfsu.edu. *Application contact:* Dr. Katherine Gordy, Graduate Coordinator, 415-338-7528, Fax: 415-338-2391, E-mail: kgordy@sfsu.edu.
Website: http://politicalscience.sfsu.edu/

Simon Fraser University, Office of Graduate Studies and Postdoctoral Fellows, Faculty of Arts and Social Sciences, Department of Political Science, Burnaby, BC V5A 1S6, Canada. Offers MA, PhD. *Degree requirements:* For master's, thesis or alternative, field exams; for doctorate, one foreign language, comprehensive exam, thesis/dissertation. *Entrance requirements:* For master's, minimum GPA of 3.0 (on scale of 4.33) or 3.33 based on last 60 credits of undergraduate courses; for doctorate, minimum GPA of 3.5 (on scale of 4.33). Additional exam requirements/recommendations for international students: recommended—TOEFL (minimum score 580 paper-based; 93 iBT), IELTS (minimum score 7), TWE (minimum score 5). Electronic applications accepted.

Sonoma State University, School of Social Sciences, Department of Political Science, Rohnert Park, CA 94928. Offers public administration (MPA). *Program availability:* Part-time, evening/weekend. *Entrance requirements:* For master's, GRE General Test, minimum GPA of 3.0. Additional exam requirements/recommendations for international students: required—TOEFL (minimum score 500 paper-based).

Southern Connecticut State University, School of Graduate Studies, School of Arts and Sciences, Department of Political Science, New Haven, CT 06515-1355. Offers MS. *Program availability:* Part-time, evening/weekend. *Degree requirements:* For master's, thesis or alternative. *Entrance requirements:* For master's, interview. Electronic applications accepted.

Southern Illinois University Carbondale, Graduate School, College of Liberal Arts, Department of Political Science, Program in Political Science, Carbondale, IL 62901-4701. Offers MA, PhD, JD/PhD. *Program availability:* Part-time. *Degree requirements:* For doctorate, thesis/dissertation. *Entrance requirements:* For master's, GRE General Test, minimum GPA of 2.7; for doctorate, GRE General Test, minimum GPA of 3.5. Additional exam requirements/recommendations for international students: required—TOEFL.

Southern New Hampshire University, School of Arts and Sciences, Manchester, NH 03106-1045. Offers clinical mental health counseling (MS); creative writing (MA); criminal justice (MS); cyber security (MS); English (MA); fiction and nonfiction (MFA); history (MA); political science (MS); psychology (MS). *Program availability:* Part-time, evening/weekend. *Degree requirements:* For master's, one foreign language, thesis. *Entrance requirements:* For master's, minimum GPA of 3.0 (for MFA). Additional exam requirements/recommendations for international students: required—TOEFL (minimum score 550 paper-based; 79 iBT), IELTS (minimum score 6.5), TWE (minimum score 5). Electronic applications accepted. *Expenses:* Contact institution.

Southern University and Agricultural and Mechanical College, Graduate School, Nelson Mandela College of Government and Social Sciences, Department of Political Science and Geography, Baton Rouge, LA 70813. Offers social sciences (MA). *Degree requirements:* For master's, thesis. *Entrance requirements:* For master's, GMAT or GRE General Test, minimum GPA of 3.0. Additional exam requirements/recommendations for international students: required—TOEFL.

Stanford University, School of Humanities and Sciences, Department of Political Science, Stanford, CA 94305-2004. Offers MA, PhD. *Expenses: Tuition:* Full-time $52,479; part-time $34,110 per unit. *Required fees:* $672; $224 per quarter. Tuition and fees vary according to program and student level.
Website: https://politicalscience.stanford.edu/

Stony Brook University, State University of New York, Graduate School, College of Arts and Sciences, Department of Political Science, Stony Brook, NY 11794. Offers political science (MA, PhD); public policy (MAPP); public policy and urban development (MA). *Program availability:* Evening/weekend. *Faculty:* 18 full-time (5 women), 10 part-time/adjunct (4 women). *Students:* 51 full-time (24 women), 10 part-time (5 women); includes 12 minority (3 Black or African American, non-Hispanic/Latino; 4 Asian, non-Hispanic/Latino; 4 Hispanic/Latino; 1 Two or more races, non-Hispanic/Latino), 12 international. Average age 28. 87 applicants, 59% accepted, 27 enrolled. In 2019, 43 master's, 7 doctorates awarded. *Entrance requirements:* For master's and doctorate, GRE General Test. Additional exam requirements/recommendations for international students: required—TOEFL (minimum score 90 iBT). *Application deadline:* For fall admission, 1/15 for domestic students; for spring admission, 10/1 for domestic students. Application fee: $100. Electronic applications accepted. *Expenses:* Contact institution. *Financial support:* In 2019–20, 1 fellowship, 13 teaching assistantships were awarded; research assistantships also available. *Unit head:* Dr. Leonie Huddy, Chair, 631-632-7639, Fax: 631-632-4116, E-mail: leonie.huddy@stonybrook.edu. *Application contact:* Carri Ann Horner, Coordinator, 631-632-7667, Fax: 631-632-4116, E-mail: carri.horner@stonybrook.edu.
Website: http://www.sunysb.edu/polsci/

Suffolk University, College of Arts and Sciences, Department of Government, Boston, MA 02108-2770. Offers international relations (MSPS); political science (MSPS); professional politics (MSPS, CAGS); MPA/MSPS. *Program availability:* Part-time, evening/weekend. *Faculty:* 11 full-time (4 women), 8 part-time/adjunct (2 women). *Students:* 1 (woman) full-time, 6 part-time (5 women); includes 1 minority (Hispanic/Latino), 2 international. Average age 26. 1 applicant, 100% accepted. In 2019, 12 master's awarded. *Degree requirements:* For master's, thesis optional. *Entrance requirements:* For master's, GRE General Test or MAT, 2 letters of recommendation, resume. Additional exam requirements/recommendations for international students: required—TOEFL (minimum score 550 paper-based; 80 iBT). *Application deadline:* For fall admission, 3/15 priority date for domestic and international students; for spring admission, 10/15 priority date for domestic and international students. Applications are processed on a rolling basis. Application fee: $50. Electronic applications accepted. *Expenses:* Contact institution. *Financial support:* In 2019–20, 4 students received support, including 2 fellowships (averaging $1,800 per year); career-related internships or fieldwork, Federal Work-Study, and institutionally sponsored loans also available. Support available to part-time students. Financial award application deadline: 4/1; financial award applicants required to submit FAFSA. *Unit head:* Rachel Cobb, Department Chair, 617-305-6380, E-mail: rcobb@suffolk.edu. *Application contact:* Mara Marzocchi, Associate Director of Graduate Admissions, 617-573-8302, Fax: 617-305-1733, E-mail: grad.admission@suffolk.edu.
Website: http://www.suffolk.edu/government

Suffolk University, Sawyer Business School, Department of Public Administration, Boston, MA 02108-2770. Offers community health (MPA); information systems, performance management, and big data analytics (MPA); nonprofit management (MPA); state and local government (MPA); JD/MPA; MPA/MS; MPA/MSCJ; MPA/MSMHC; MPA/MSPS. *Accreditation:* NASPAA (one or more programs are accredited). *Program availability:* Part-time, evening/weekend. *Faculty:* 12 full-time (7 women), 4 part-time/adjunct (3 women). *Students:* 13 full-time (5 women), 72 part-time (55 women); includes 35 minority (21 Black or African American, non-Hispanic/Latino; 3 Asian, non-Hispanic/Latino; 9 Hispanic/Latino; 2 Two or more races, non-Hispanic/Latino), 2 international. Average age 35. 89 applicants, 85% accepted, 30 enrolled. In 2019, 40 master's awarded. *Entrance requirements:* Additional exam requirements/recommendations for international students: required—TOEFL (minimum score 550 paper-based; 80 iBT). *Application deadline:* For fall admission, 3/15 priority date for domestic and international

students; for spring admission, 10/15 priority date for domestic and international students. Applications are processed on a rolling basis. Application fee: $50. Electronic applications accepted. *Expenses:* Contact institution. *Financial support:* In 2019–20, 47 students received support, including 2 fellowships (averaging $2,657 per year); career-related internships or fieldwork, Federal Work-Study, institutionally sponsored loans, and scholarships/grants also available. Support available to part-time students. Financial award application deadline: 4/1; financial award applicants required to submit FAFSA. *Unit head:* Brenda Bond, Director/Department Chair, 617-305-1768, E-mail: bbond@suffolk.edu. *Application contact:* Mara Marzocchi, Associate Director of Graduate Admissions, 617-573-8302, Fax: 617-305-1733, E-mail: grad.admission@suffolk.edu.
Website: http://www.suffolk.edu/mpa

Sul Ross State University, College of Arts and Sciences, Department of Behavioral and Social Sciences, Program in Political Science, Alpine, TX 79832. Offers MA. *Program availability:* Part-time, evening/weekend. *Degree requirements:* For master's, thesis optional. *Entrance requirements:* For master's, GRE General Test, minimum undergraduate GPA of 2.5 in last 60 hours.

Syracuse University, Maxwell School of Citizenship and Public Affairs, Programs in Political Science, Syracuse, NY 13244. Offers MA, PhD, JD/MA, JD/PhD, MAIR/PhD. *Degree requirements:* For doctorate, comprehensive exam, thesis/dissertation. *Entrance requirements:* For master's and doctorate, GRE General Test, three letters of recommendation, personal statement, official transcripts, resume. Additional exam requirements/recommendations for international students: required—TOEFL (minimum score 100 iBT). Electronic applications accepted.

Syracuse University, School of Information Studies, CAS Program in E-Government Management and Leadership, Syracuse, NY 13244. Offers CAS. *Program availability:* Part-time. *Entrance requirements:* For degree, resume, personal statement, official transcripts, three letters of recommendation. Additional exam requirements/recommendations for international students: required—TOEFL (minimum score 100 iBT). Electronic applications accepted.

Tarleton State University, College of Graduate Studies, College of Liberal and Fine Arts, History, Sociology and Geography, Stephenville, TX 76402. Offers history (MA). *Program availability:* Part-time. *Faculty:* 20 full-time (8 women), 2 part-time/adjunct (0 women). *Students:* 2 full-time (0 women), 11 part-time (6 women); includes 4 minority (1 Asian, non-Hispanic/Latino; 3 Hispanic/Latino). Average age 29. 60 applicants, 77% accepted, 33 enrolled. *Degree requirements:* For master's, comprehensive exam, thesis optional. *Entrance requirements:* For master's, GRE General Test, minimum GPA of 2.5. Additional exam requirements/recommendations for international students: required—TOEFL (minimum score 520 paper-based; 69 iBT); recommended—IELTS (minimum score 6), TSE (minimum score 50). *Application deadline:* For fall admission, 8/15 priority date for domestic students; for spring admission, 1/7 for domestic students. Applications are processed on a rolling basis. Application fee: $50 ($130 for international students). Electronic applications accepted. *Expenses:* Tuition, state resident: part-time $221.73 per credit hour. Tuition, nonresident: part-time $636.73 per credit hour. *Required fees:* $198 per credit hour. $100 per semester. Tuition and fees vary according to degree level. *Financial support:* Research assistantships, teaching assistantships, career-related internships or fieldwork, and Federal Work-Study available. Support available to part-time students. Financial award application deadline: 5/1; financial award applicants required to submit FAFSA. *Unit head:* Dr. Opeyemi Zubair, Department Head, 254-968-9029, E-mail: zubair@tarleton.edu. *Application contact:* Wendy Weiss, Graduate Admissions Coordinator, 254-968-9104, Fax: 254-968-9670, E-mail: weiss@tarleton.edu.
Website: https://www.tarleton.edu/hsgg/index.html

Teachers College, Columbia University, Department of Education Policy and Social Analysis, New York, NY 10027-6696. Offers economics and education (Ed M, MA, PhD); education policy (Ed M, MA, Ed D, PhD); politics and education (Ed M, MA, Ed D, PhD); sociology and education (Ed M, MA, Ed D, PhD). *Faculty:* 11 full-time (4 women). *Students:* 89 full-time (71 women), 154 part-time (113 women); includes 91 minority (36 Black or African American, non-Hispanic/Latino; 19 Asian, non-Hispanic/Latino; 29 Hispanic/Latino; 7 Two or more races, non-Hispanic/Latino), 73 international. 433 applicants, 60% accepted, 107 enrolled. *Unit head:* Dr. Aaron Pallas, Chair, 212-678-8119, E-mail: amp155@tc.columbia.edu. *Application contact:* Kelly Sutton-Skinner, Director of Admission and New Student Enrollment, 212-678-3710, E-mail: kms2237@tc.columbia.edu.
Website: http://www.tc.columbia.edu/education-policy-and-social-analysis/

Temple University, College of Liberal Arts, Department of Political Science, Philadelphia, PA 19122-6096. Offers MA, PhD. *Program availability:* Part-time, evening/weekend. *Faculty:* 26 full-time (9 women), 7 part-time/adjunct (1 woman). *Students:* 58 full-time (29 women), 20 part-time (12 women); includes 18 minority (7 Black or African American, non-Hispanic/Latino; 2 Asian, non-Hispanic/Latino; 5 Hispanic/Latino; 4 Two or more races, non-Hispanic/Latino), 9 international. 77 applicants, 55% accepted, 26 enrolled. In 2019, 20 master's, 7 doctorates awarded. *Degree requirements:* For master's, seminar paper; for doctorate, thesis/dissertation, preliminary and oral exams. *Entrance requirements:* For master's, GRE (M.A.), writing sample (M.A.), 3 letters of recommendation, statement of goals; for doctorate, GRE, writing sample, statement of goals, 3 letters of recommendation. Additional exam requirements/recommendations for international students: required—TOEFL (minimum score 100 iBT), IELTS, PTE, one of three is required. Application fee: $60. Electronic applications accepted. *Financial support:* Fellowships, research assistantships, teaching assistantships, Federal Work-Study, scholarships/grants, and health care benefits available. Financial award application deadline: 1/15; financial award applicants required to submit FAFSA. *Unit head:* Robin Kolodny, Chair, 215-204-7709, E-mail: rkolodny@temple.edu. *Application contact:* LaTasha R Goodman, Coordinator, 215-204-7796, E-mail: latasha.goodman@temple.edu.
Website: http://www.cla.temple.edu/politicalscience/

Texas A&M International University, Office of Graduate Studies and Research, College of Arts and Sciences, Department of Humanities, Laredo, TX 78041. Offers English (MA); history and political thought (MA); language, literature and translation (MA). *Degree requirements:* For master's, comprehensive exam (for some programs), thesis (for some programs). *Entrance requirements:* For master's, GRE General Test. Additional exam requirements/recommendations for international students: required—TOEFL (minimum score 550 paper-based; 79 iBT).

Texas A&M International University, Office of Graduate Studies and Research, College of Arts and Sciences, Department of Social Sciences, Laredo, TX 78041. Offers criminal justice (MS); history and political thought (MA); public administration (MPA); sociology (MA). *Degree requirements:* For master's, comprehensive exam (for some programs), thesis (for some programs). *Entrance requirements:* For master's, GRE General Test. Additional exam requirements/recommendations for international students: required—TOEFL (minimum score 550 paper-based; 79 iBT).

Texas A&M University, College of Liberal Arts, Department of Political Science, College Station, TX 77843. Offers political science (PhD). *Faculty:* 30. *Students:* 42 full-time (16 women), 3 part-time (2 women); includes 4 minority (1 Asian, non-Hispanic/Latino; 3 Hispanic/Latino), 26 international. Average age 30. 17 applicants, 100% accepted, 6 enrolled. In 2019, 5 master's, 6 doctorates awarded. *Degree requirements:* For master's, comprehensive exam, thesis optional; for doctorate, comprehensive exam, thesis/dissertation. *Entrance requirements:* For master's and doctorate, GRE General Test, letters of recommendation, writing sample. Additional exam requirements/recommendations for international students: required—TOEFL (minimum score 550 paper-based; 80 iBT), IELTS (minimum score 6), PTE (minimum score 53). *Application deadline:* For fall admission, 12/22 for domestic and international students. Application fee: $65 ($90 for international students). Electronic applications accepted. *Expenses:* Contact institution. *Financial support:* In 2019–20, 23 students received support, including 3 fellowships with tuition reimbursements available (averaging $21,333 per year), 26 research assistantships with tuition reimbursements available (averaging $8,268 per year), 22 teaching assistantships with tuition reimbursements available (averaging $15,115 per year); career-related internships or fieldwork, institutionally sponsored loans, scholarships/grants, traineeships, health care benefits, tuition waivers (full and partial), unspecified assistantships, and assistant lecturer positions also available. Support available to part-time students. Financial award application deadline: 3/15; financial award applicants required to submit FAFSA. *Unit head:* Dr. William Clark, Department Head, 979-845-2827, E-mail: wrclark@tamu.edu. *Application contact:* Dr. David Fortunato, Director, Graduate Program, 979-845-2127, E-mail: fortunato@tamu.edu.
Website: http://pols.tamu.edu/

Texas A&M University–Central Texas, Graduate Studies and Research, Killeen, TX 76549. Offers accounting (MS); business administration (MBA); clinical mental health counseling (MS); criminal justice (MCJ); curriculum and instruction (M Ed); educational administration (M Ed); educational psychology - experimental psychology (MS); history (MA); human resource management (MS); information systems (MS); liberal studies (MS); management and leadership (MS); marriage and family therapy (MS); mathematics (MS); political science (MA); school counseling (M Ed); school psychology (Ed S).

Texas A&M University–Commerce, College of Humanities, Social Sciences and Arts, Commerce, TX 75429. Offers applied criminology (MS); applied linguistics (MA, MS); art (MA, MFA); christianity in history (Graduate Certificate); computational linguistics (Graduate Certificate); creative writing (Graduate Certificate); criminal justice management (Graduate Certificate); criminal justice studies (Graduate Certificate); English (MA, MS, PhD); film studies (Graduate Certificate); history (MA, MS); Holocaust studies (Graduate Certificate); homeland security (Graduate Certificate); music (MM); music performance (MM); political science (MA, MS); public history (Graduate Certificate); sociology (MS); Spanish (MA); studies in children's and adolescent literature and culture (Graduate Certificate); teaching English to speakers of other languages (Graduate Certificate); theater (MA, MS); world history (Graduate Certificate). *Program availability:* Part-time. *Faculty:* 49 full-time (28 women), 8 part-time/adjunct (2 women). *Students:* 34 full-time (21 women), 427 part-time (302 women); includes 175 minority (66 Black or African American, non-Hispanic/Latino; 1 American Indian or Alaska Native, non-Hispanic/Latino; 13 Asian, non-Hispanic/Latino; 79 Hispanic/Latino; 16 Two or more races, non-Hispanic/Latino), 15 international. Average age 38. 193 applicants, 49% accepted, 78 enrolled. In 2019, 122 master's, 6 doctorates awarded. *Degree requirements:* For master's, one foreign language, comprehensive exam, thesis (for some programs); for doctorate, one foreign language, comprehensive exam, thesis/dissertation, departmental qualifying exam. *Entrance requirements:* For master's, GRE General Test, official transcripts, letters of recommendation, resume, statement of goals; for doctorate, GRE General Test, official transcripts, letters of recommendation, statement of goals, writing samples, writing sessions, resumes. Additional exam requirements/recommendations for international students: required—TOEFL (minimum score 550 paper-based; 79 iBT), IELTS (minimum score 6), PTE (minimum score 53). *Application deadline:* For fall admission, 6/1 priority date for international students; for spring admission, 10/15 priority date for international students; for summer admission, 3/15 priority date for international students. Applications are processed on a rolling basis. Application fee: $50 ($75 for international students). Electronic applications accepted. *Expenses: Tuition, area resident:* Full-time $3630; part-time $202 per credit hour. Tuition, state resident: full-time $3630; part-time $202 per credit hour. Tuition, nonresident: full-time $11,232; part-time $624 per credit hour. *International tuition:* $11,232 full-time. *Required fees:* $2948. *Financial support:* In 2019–20, 30 students received support, including 18 research assistantships with partial tuition reimbursements available (averaging $3,231 per year), 136 teaching assistantships with partial tuition reimbursements available (averaging $4,053 per year); Federal Work-Study, institutionally sponsored loans, scholarships/grants, health care benefits, and unspecified assistantships also available. Financial award application deadline: 5/1; financial award applicants required to submit FAFSA. *Unit head:* Dr. William F. Kuracina, Interim Dean, 903-886-5166, Fax: 903-886-5774, E-mail: william.kuracina@tamuc.edu. *Application contact:* Rebecca Stevens, Graduate Student Services Coordinator, 903-468-6049, E-mail: rebecca.stevens@tamuc.edu.
Website: http://www.tamuc.edu/academics/colleges/humanitiesSocialSciencesArts/

Texas State University, The Graduate College, College of Liberal Arts, Program in Political Science, San Marcos, TX 78666. Offers MA. *Program availability:* Part-time, evening/weekend. *Degree requirements:* For master's, comprehensive exam, thesis optional. *Entrance requirements:* For master's, baccalaureate degree in political science from regionally-accredited university; minimum GPA of 3.0 on last 60 undergraduate course work; at least 9 hours in upper-level political science or related field; resume; statement of purpose; 3 letters of recommendation; writing sample from political science/humanities courses. Additional exam requirements/recommendations for international students: required—TOEFL (minimum score 550 paper-based; 78 iBT), IELTS (minimum score 6.5). Electronic applications accepted.

Texas Tech University, Graduate School, College of Arts and Sciences, Department of Political Science, Lubbock, TX 79409-1015. Offers political science (MA, PhD); public administration (MPA); JD/MPA. *Accreditation:* NASPAA (one or more programs are accredited). *Program availability:* 100% online, blended/hybrid learning, Regional sites. *Faculty:* 26 full-time (6 women), 5 part-time/adjunct (3 women). *Students:* 43 full-time (21 women), 28 part-time (15 women); includes 18 minority (4 Black or African American, non-Hispanic/Latino; 2 Asian, non-Hispanic/Latino; 10 Hispanic/Latino; 2 Two or more races, non-Hispanic/Latino), 16 international. Average age 32. 46 applicants, 74% accepted, 27 enrolled. In 2019, 22 master's awarded. *Degree requirements:* For master's, thesis or alternative; for doctorate, thesis/dissertation. *Entrance requirements:* For master's and doctorate, GRE General Test, 3 letters of reference. Additional exam requirements/recommendations for international students: required—TOEFL (minimum score 550 paper-based; 79 iBT). *Application deadline:* For fall admission, 6/1 priority date for domestic students, 1/15 priority date for international students; for spring admission, 9/1 priority date for domestic students, 6/15 priority date for international students. Applications are processed on a rolling basis. Application fee: $65. Electronic applications accepted. *Expenses:* Contact institution. *Financial support:* In 2019–20, 47 students received support, including 38 fellowships (averaging $2,581 per year), 44 teaching assistantships (averaging $12,978 per year); research assistantships, scholarships/grants, tuition waivers, and grader positions also available. Financial award application deadline: 4/15; financial award applicants required to submit FAFSA. *Unit*

head: Dr. Timothy Nokken, Associate Professor and Department Chairperson, 806-834-2988, Fax: 806-742-0850, E-mail: timothy.nokken@ttu.edu. *Application contact:* Dr. Toby Rider, Graduate Director, 806-834-8640, Fax: 806-742-0850, E-mail: toby.rider@ttu.edu.
Website: www.depts.ttu.edu/politicalscience/

Texas Woman's University, Graduate School, College of Arts and Sciences, Department of History and Political Science, Denton, TX 76204. Offers government (MA); history (MA). *Program availability:* Part-time, evening/weekend. *Faculty:* 8 full-time (3 women), 1 part-time/adjunct (0 women). *Students:* 8 full-time (5 women), 19 part-time (13 women); includes 11 minority (4 Black or African American, non-Hispanic/Latino; 1 American Indian or Alaska Native, non-Hispanic/Latino; 3 Asian, non-Hispanic/Latino; 2 Hispanic/Latino; 1 Two or more races, non-Hispanic/Latino). Average age 31. 11 applicants, 91% accepted, 8 enrolled. In 2019, 5 master's awarded. *Degree requirements:* For master's, comprehensive exam, thesis or alternative, professional paper or thesis; exam is a defense of the thesis or professional paper. *Entrance requirements:* For master's, minimum GPA of 3.25 on last 60 undergraduate hours, writing sample, curriculum vitae, 3 references. Additional exam requirements/recommendations for international students: required—TOEFL (minimum score 79 iBT); recommended—IELTS (minimum score 6.5), TSE (minimum score 53). *Application deadline:* For fall admission, 3/1 priority date for domestic and international students; for spring admission, 11/1 priority date for domestic students, 7/1 priority date for international students; for summer admission, 5/1 priority date for domestic students, 2/1 priority date for international students. Applications are processed on a rolling basis. Application fee: $50 ($75 for international students). Electronic applications accepted. *Expenses: Tuition, area resident:* Full-time $4973.40; part-time $276.30 per semester hour. Tuition, state resident: full-time $4973.40; part-time $276.30 per semester hour. Tuition, nonresident: full-time $12,569; part-time $698.30 per semester hour. *International tuition:* $12,569.40 full-time. *Required fees:* $2524.30. Tuition and fees vary according to course level, course load, degree level and program. *Financial support:* In 2019–20, 14 students received support, including 12 teaching assistantships (averaging $10,385 per year); career-related internships or fieldwork, scholarships/grants, health care benefits, and unspecified assistantships also available. Support available to part-time students. Financial award application deadline: 3/1; financial award applicants required to submit FAFSA. *Unit head:* Dr. Jonathan Olsen, Chair, 940-898-2133, Fax: 940-898-2130, E-mail: historygov@twu.edu. *Application contact:* Korie Hawkins, Associate Director of Admissions, Graduate Recruitment, 940-898-3188, Fax: 940-898-3081, E-mail: admissions@twu.edu.
Website: http://www.twu.edu/history-government/

Tulane University, School of Liberal Arts, Department of Political Science, New Orleans, LA 70118-5669. Offers PhD. *Degree requirements:* For doctorate, 2 foreign languages, thesis/dissertation. *Entrance requirements:* For doctorate, GRE General Test. Additional exam requirements/recommendations for international students: required—TOEFL. Electronic applications accepted. *Expenses: Tuition:* Full-time $57,004; part-time $3167 per credit hour. *Required fees:* $2086; $44.50 per credit hour. $80 per term. Tuition and fees vary according to course load, degree level and program.

UNB Fredericton, School of Graduate Studies, Faculty of Arts - Saint John, Department of Political Science, Fredericton, NB E3B 5A3, Canada. Offers MA. *Program availability:* Part-time. *Faculty:* 7 full-time (3 women). *Students:* 5 full-time (2 women). Average age 26. In 2019, 3 master's awarded. *Degree requirements:* For master's, thesis (for some programs). *Entrance requirements:* For master's, minimum cumulative GPA of 3.3; 4-year bachelor's degree, or equivalent, in political science. Additional exam requirements/recommendations for international students: required—TOEFL. *Application deadline:* For fall admission, 3/1 for domestic students; for winter admission, 1/15 priority date for domestic and international students. Applications are processed on a rolling basis. Application fee: $50 Canadian dollars. Electronic applications accepted. *Expenses: Tuition, area resident:* Full-time $6975 Canadian dollars; part-time $3423 Canadian dollars per year. Tuition, state resident: full-time $6975 Canadian dollars; part-time $3423 Canadian dollars per year. Tuition, Canadian resident: full-time $6975 Canadian dollars; part-time $3423 Canadian dollars per year. *International tuition:* $12,435 Canadian dollars full-time. *Required fees:* $92.25 Canadian dollars per term. Full-time tuition and fees vary according to degree level, campus/location, program, reciprocity agreements and student level. *Financial support:* Fellowships, research assistantships, and teaching assistantships available. Financial award application deadline: 1/31. *Unit head:* Dr. Suzanne Hindmarch, Director of Graduate Studies, 506-453-3906, Fax: 506-453-4755, E-mail: s.hindmarch@unb.ca. *Application contact:* Zabrina Hamilton, Graduate Secretary, 506-453-4826, Fax: 506-453-4755, E-mail: zhamilto@unb.ca.
Website: http://go.unb.ca/gradprograms

Universidad Nacional Pedro Henriquez Urena, Graduate School, Santo Domingo, Dominican Republic. Offers agricultural diversity (MS), including horticultural/fruit production, tropical animal production; conservation of monuments and cultural assets (M Arch); ecology and environment (MS); environmental engineering (MEE); international relations (MA); natural resource management (MS); political science (MA); project feasibility (MPM); project management (MPM); project optimization (MPM); sanitation engineering (ME); science for teachers (MS); tropical Caribbean architecture (M Arch).

Université de Montréal, Faculty of Arts and Sciences, Department of Political Science, Montréal, QC H3C 3J7, Canada. Offers M Sc, PhD. *Degree requirements:* For master's, thesis; for doctorate, thesis/dissertation, general exam. *Entrance requirements:* For master's, minimum GPA of 2.8; for doctorate, master's degree, minimum GPA of 3.0. Electronic applications accepted.

Université du Québec à Montréal, Graduate Programs, Program in Political Science, Montréal, QC H3C 3P8, Canada. Offers MA, PhD. *Program availability:* Part-time. *Degree requirements:* For master's, thesis; for doctorate, thesis/dissertation. *Entrance requirements:* For master's, appropriate bachelor's degree or equivalent, proficiency in French; for doctorate, appropriate master's degree or equivalent, proficiency in French.

University at Albany, State University of New York, Nelson A. Rockefeller College of Public Affairs and Policy, Department of Political Science, Albany, NY 12222-0001. Offers MA, PhD. *Program availability:* Part-time, 100% online, blended/hybrid learning. *Faculty:* 18 full-time (6 women), 10 part-time/adjunct (2 women). *Students:* 30 full-time (14 women), 34 part-time (18 women); includes 7 minority (2 Black or African American, non-Hispanic/Latino; 1 Asian, non-Hispanic/Latino; 2 Hispanic/Latino; 2 Two or more races, non-Hispanic/Latino), 15 international. Average age 32. 69 applicants, 81% accepted, 18 enrolled. In 2019, 10 master's, 7 doctorates awarded. *Degree requirements:* For doctorate, one foreign language, thesis/dissertation. *Entrance requirements:* For doctorate, GRE General Test. Additional exam requirements/recommendations for international students: required—TOEFL (minimum score 550 paper-based). *Application deadline:* For fall admission, 2/1 priority date for domestic students, 5/1 for international students; for spring admission, 11/15 for domestic students, 11/1 for international students. Applications are processed on a rolling basis. Application fee: $75. Electronic applications accepted. *Expenses: Tuition, area resident:* Full-time $11,530; part-time $480 per credit hour. Tuition, nonresident: full-time $23,530; part-time $980 per credit hour. *International tuition:* $23,530 full-time. *Required fees:* $2185; $96 per credit hour. Part-time tuition and fees vary according to course load and program. *Financial support:* Fellowships, career-related internships or fieldwork, and traineeships available. Financial award application deadline: 2/1. *Unit head:* Meredith Weiss, Chair, 518-442-5256, E-mail: mweiss@albany.edu. *Application contact:* Patricia Strach, 518-442-5256, E-mail: pstrach@albany.edu.
Website: http://www.albany.edu/rockefeller/pos/index.htm

University at Buffalo, the State University of New York, Graduate School, College of Arts and Sciences, Department of Political Science, Buffalo, NY 14260. Offers MA, PhD. *Faculty:* 13 full-time (4 women). *Students:* 22 full-time (2 women), 11 part-time (8 women); includes 8 minority (1 Black or African American, non-Hispanic/Latino; 6 Asian, non-Hispanic/Latino; 1 Native Hawaiian or other Pacific Islander, non-Hispanic/Latino). Average age 28. 29 applicants, 83% accepted, 10 enrolled. In 2019, 4 master's, 4 doctorates awarded. Terminal master's awarded for partial completion of doctoral program. *Degree requirements:* For master's, comprehensive exam, thesis or alternative, paper, project, portfolio; for doctorate, comprehensive exam, thesis/dissertation. *Entrance requirements:* For master's, GRE General Test, minimum GPA of 3.0; for doctorate, GRE General Test, minimum GPA of 3.3. Additional exam requirements/recommendations for international students: required—TOEFL (minimum score 550 paper-based; 79 iBT), IELTS (minimum score 6.5), PTE (minimum score 55). *Application deadline:* For fall admission, 8/1 priority date for domestic students, 3/1 for international students; for spring admission, 11/1 priority date for domestic students, 10/1 for international students. Applications are processed on a rolling basis. Application fee: $75. Electronic applications accepted. *Expenses: Tuition, area resident:* Full-time $11,310; part-time $471 per credit hour. Tuition, state resident: full-time $11,310; part-time $471 per credit hour. Tuition, nonresident: full-time $23,100; part-time $963 per credit hour. *International tuition:* $23,100 full-time. *Required fees:* $2820. *Financial support:* In 2019–20, 12 students received support, including 2 fellowships with full tuition reimbursements available (averaging $6,000 per year), 12 teaching assistantships with full tuition reimbursements available (averaging $13,500 per year); research assistantships, career-related internships or fieldwork, Federal Work-Study, health care benefits, tuition waivers (full), and unspecified assistantships also available. Financial award application deadline: 1/1; financial award applicants required to submit FAFSA. *Unit head:* Dr. Munroe Eagles, Chairman, 716-645-8449, Fax: 716-645-2166, E-mail: eagles@buffalo.edu. *Application contact:* Mary E. O'Brien, Graduate Coordinator, 716-645-3441, Fax: 716-645-2166, E-mail: meobrien@buffalo.edu.
Website: http://arts-sciences.buffalo.edu/political-science.html

The University of Akron, Graduate School, Buchtel College of Arts and Sciences, Department of Political Science, Akron, OH 44325. Offers MA, MAP, JD/MAP. *Program availability:* Part-time. *Entrance requirements:* For master's, minimum GPA of 3.0, three letters of recommendation (two of which must be from faculty members), statement of purpose. Additional exam requirements/recommendations for international students: required—TOEFL (minimum score 79 iBT), IELTS (minimum score 6.5). Electronic applications accepted.

The University of Alabama, Graduate School, College of Arts and Sciences, Department of Political Science, Tuscaloosa, AL 35487. Offers political science (MA, PhD); public administration (MPA). *Program availability:* Part-time. *Faculty:* 20 full-time (5 women). *Students:* 50 full-time (20 women), 4 part-time (3 women); includes 14 minority (10 Black or African American, non-Hispanic/Latino; 2 American Indian or Alaska Native, non-Hispanic/Latino; 1 Asian, non-Hispanic/Latino; 1 Two or more races, non-Hispanic/Latino), 7 international. Average age 29. 37 applicants, 73% accepted, 15 enrolled. In 2019, 21 master's, 5 doctorates awarded. Terminal master's awarded for partial completion of doctoral program. *Degree requirements:* For master's, comprehensive exam, thesis optional; for doctorate, comprehensive exam, thesis/dissertation. *Entrance requirements:* For master's and doctorate, GRE, minimum undergraduate GPA of 3.0. Additional exam requirements/recommendations for international students: required—TOEFL. *Application deadline:* For fall admission, 6/30 for domestic and international students; for spring admission, 10/15 for domestic and international students. Applications are processed on a rolling basis. Application fee: $50 ($60 for international students). Electronic applications accepted. *Expenses: Tuition, area resident:* Full-time $10,780; part-time $440 per credit hour. Tuition, nonresident: full-time $30,250; part-time $1550 per credit hour. *Financial support:* In 2019–20, 19 students received support, including fellowships with full tuition reimbursements available (averaging $15,000 per year), teaching assistantships with full tuition reimbursements available (averaging $12,500 per year); career-related internships or fieldwork and Federal Work-Study also available. Financial award application deadline: 2/15; financial award applicants required to submit FAFSA. *Unit head:* Dr. Joseph Smith, Chair and Professor, 205-348-5981, E-mail: josmith@bama.ua.edu. *Application contact:* Dr. Holger Albrecht, Associate Professor and Director of Graduate Studies, 205-348-5528, Fax: 205-348-5298, E-mail: halbrecht@ua.edu.
Website: http://www.as.ua.edu/psc/

University of Alberta, Faculty of Graduate Studies and Research, Department of Political Science, Edmonton, AB T6G 2E1, Canada. Offers MA, PhD. *Program availability:* Part-time. *Degree requirements:* For master's, thesis (for some programs); for doctorate, one foreign language, thesis/dissertation. *Entrance requirements:* Additional exam requirements/recommendations for international students: required—TOEFL.

The University of Arizona, College of Social and Behavioral Sciences, Department of Political Science, Tucson, AZ 85721. Offers MA, PhD. Terminal master's awarded for partial completion of doctoral program. *Degree requirements:* For master's, thesis or alternative; for doctorate, variable foreign language requirement, comprehensive exam, thesis/dissertation. *Entrance requirements:* For master's, GRE General Test, minimum GPA of 3.2, 3 letters of recommendation, writing sample; for doctorate, GRE General Test, minimum GPA of 3.2, 3 letters of recommendation, statement of purpose, writing sample. Additional exam requirements/recommendations for international students: required—TOEFL (minimum score 550 paper-based; 79 iBT). Electronic applications accepted.

University of Arkansas, Graduate School, J. William Fulbright College of Arts and Sciences, Department of Political Science, Program in Political Science, Fayetteville, AR 72701. Offers MA. *Students:* 11 full-time (6 women), 4 part-time (1 woman); includes 5 minority (2 Black or African American, non-Hispanic/Latino; 2 Hispanic/Latino; 1 Two or more races, non-Hispanic/Latino), 2 international. 11 applicants, 100% accepted. In 2019, 4 master's awarded. *Entrance requirements:* For master's, GRE General Test. *Application deadline:* For fall admission, 8/1 for domestic students, 4/1 for international students; for spring admission, 12/1 for domestic students, 10/1 for international students; for summer admission, 4/15 for domestic students, 3/1 for international students. Applications are processed on a rolling basis. Application fee: $60. Electronic applications accepted. *Financial support:* In 2019–20, 1 research assistantship, 6 teaching assistantships were awarded; fellowships, career-related internships or fieldwork, and Federal Work-Study also available. Support available to part-time students. Financial award application deadline: 4/1; financial award applicants required to submit FAFSA. *Unit head:* Dr. William Schreckhise, 479-575-3356, E-mail: schreckw@uark.edu. *Application contact:* Dr. Pat Conge, 479-575-6434, E-mail:

pconge@uark.edu.
Website: https://fulbright.uark.edu/departments/political-science/

The University of British Columbia, Faculty of Arts, Department of Political Science, Vancouver, BC V6T 1Z1, Canada. Offers MA, PhD. *Program availability:* Part-time. *Degree requirements:* For master's, thesis; for doctorate, comprehensive exam, thesis/ dissertation. *Entrance requirements:* For master's, BA in political science; for doctorate, GRE, BA and MA in political science. Additional exam requirements/recommendations for international students: required—TOEFL, TWE. Electronic applications accepted. *Expenses:* Contact institution.

University of Calgary, Faculty of Graduate Studies, Faculty of Arts, Program in Political Science, Calgary, AB T2N 1N4, Canada. Offers MA, PhD. *Degree requirements:* For master's, thesis; for doctorate, one foreign language, comprehensive exam, thesis/ dissertation, prospectus, oral and written candidacy exams. *Entrance requirements:* For master's, minimum GPA of 3.4; for doctorate, minimum GPA of 3.7. Additional exam requirements/recommendations for international students: required—TOEFL (minimum score 620 paper-based). Electronic applications accepted.

University of California, Berkeley, Graduate Division, College of Letters and Science, Charles and Louise Travers Department of Political Science, Berkeley, CA 94720. Offers PhD. *Degree requirements:* For doctorate, thesis/dissertation, oral qualifying exams. *Entrance requirements:* For doctorate, GRE General Test, minimum GPA of 3.0, 3 letters of recommendation. Additional exam requirements/recommendations for international students: required—TOEFL (minimum score 570 paper-based; 90 iBT). Electronic applications accepted.

University of California, Davis, Graduate Studies, Program in Political Science, Davis, CA 95616. Offers MA, PhD. Terminal master's awarded for partial completion of doctoral program. *Degree requirements:* For master's, thesis; for doctorate, thesis/dissertation. *Entrance requirements:* For master's and doctorate, GRE General Test, minimum GPA of 3.0, writing sample. Additional exam requirements/recommendations for international students: required—TOEFL (minimum score 550 paper-based). Electronic applications accepted.

University of California, Irvine, School of Social Sciences, Department of Political Science, Irvine, CA 92697. Offers political psychology (PhD); political sciences (PhD); public choice (PhD). *Students:* 69 full-time (31 women), 1 part-time (0 women); includes 18 minority (3 Black or African American, non-Hispanic/Latino; 6 Asian, non-Hispanic/ Latino; 4 Hispanic/Latino; 5 Two or more races, non-Hispanic/Latino), 14 international. Average age 30. 98 applicants, 34% accepted, 14 enrolled. In 2019, 6 doctorates awarded. *Entrance requirements:* For doctorate, GRE General Test, minimum GPA of 3.0. Additional exam requirements/recommendations for international students: required—TOEFL (minimum score 550 paper-based). *Application deadline:* For fall admission, 1/15 priority date for domestic students, 1/15 for international students. Applications are processed on a rolling basis. Application fee: $120 ($140 for international students). Electronic applications accepted. *Financial support:* Fellowships, research assistantships with full tuition reimbursements, teaching assistantships, institutionally sponsored loans, traineeships, health care benefits, and unspecified assistantships available. Financial award application deadline: 3/1; financial award applicants required to submit FAFSA. *Unit head:* Jeffrey Kopstein, Chair, 949-824-4012, E-mail: kopstein@uci.edu. *Application contact:* Claudia Cheffs, Department Manager, 949-824-2540, E-mail: ccheffs@uci.edu.
Website: http://www.polisci.uci.edu/

University of California, Los Angeles, Graduate Division, College of Letters and Science, Department of Political Science, Los Angeles, CA 90095. Offers MA, PhD. Terminal master's awarded for partial completion of doctoral program. *Degree requirements:* For master's, comprehensive exam; for doctorate, one foreign language, thesis/dissertation, oral and written qualifying exams. *Entrance requirements:* For doctorate, GRE General Test, bachelor's degree; minimum undergraduate GPA of 3.0 (or its equivalent if letter grade system not used); writing sample. Additional exam requirements/recommendations for international students: required—TOEFL. Electronic applications accepted.

University of California, Riverside, Graduate Division, Department of Political Science, Riverside, CA 92521-0102. Offers MA, PhD. *Program availability:* Part-time. Terminal master's awarded for partial completion of doctoral program. *Degree requirements:* For master's, comprehensive exams or thesis; for doctorate, thesis/ dissertation, qualifying exams. *Entrance requirements:* For master's and doctorate, GRE General Test, minimum GPA of 3.2. Additional exam requirements/recommendations for international students: required—TOEFL (minimum score 550 paper-based; 80 iBT). Electronic applications accepted.

University of California, San Diego, Graduate Division, Department of Political Science, La Jolla, CA 92093. Offers political science (PhD); political science and international affairs (PhD). *Students:* 70 full-time (25 women). 375 applicants, 13% accepted, 16 enrolled. In 2019, 15 doctorates awarded. *Degree requirements:* For doctorate, comprehensive exam, thesis/dissertation. *Entrance requirements:* For doctorate, GRE General Test, letters of recommendation. Additional exam requirements/recommendations for international students: required—TOEFL (minimum score 600 paper-based; 100 iBT), IELTS. *Application deadline:* For fall admission, 12/11 for domestic students. Application fee: $105 ($125 for international students). Electronic applications accepted. *Financial support:* Fellowships, research assistantships, teaching assistantships, and scholarships/grants available. Financial award applicants required to submit FAFSA. *Unit head:* Thad Kousser, Chair, 858-534-3239, E-mail: tkousser@ucsd.edu. *Application contact:* Julie Choi, Graduate Coordinator, 858-534-2705, E-mail: psgradadmissions@ucsd.edu.
Website: http://polisci.ucsd.edu/

University of California, San Diego, Graduate Division, School of Global Policy and Strategy, La Jolla, CA 92093. Offers Chinese economic and political affairs (MCEPA), including Chinese economy, Chinese environment, Chinese foreign relations and security, Chinese politics and public policy; international affairs (MAS, MIA), including international development and nonprofit management (MIA), international economics (MIA), international environmental policy (MIA), international management (MIA), international politics (MIA); political science and international affairs (PhD); public policy (MPP), including American policy in global context, business, government and regulation, energy and environmental policy, health policy, program design and evaluation, security policy. *Program availability:* Part-time. *Degree requirements:* For master's, language requirement (for MIA and MCEPA); for doctorate, thesis/dissertation. *Entrance requirements:* For master's, GMAT or GRE General Test; for doctorate, GRE General Test. Additional exam requirements/recommendations for international students: required—TOEFL (minimum score 90 iBT), IELTS (minimum score 7). Electronic applications accepted. *Expenses:* Contact institution.

University of California, Santa Barbara, Graduate Division, College of Letters and Sciences, Division of Social Sciences, Department of Global Studies, Santa Barbara, CA 93106-7065. Offers global culture, ideology, and religion (MA, PhD); global government, human rights, and civil society (MA, PhD); political economy, sustainable development, and the environment (MA, PhD). *Degree requirements:* For master's, one foreign language, thesis, 2 years of a second language; for doctorate, one foreign language, thesis/dissertation, reading proficiency in at least one language other than English. *Entrance requirements:* For master's, GRE, 2 years of a second language with minimum B grade in the final term, statement of purpose, resume or curriculum vitae, 3 letters of recommendation, transcripts (from all post-secondary institutions attended), writing sample (15-20 pages); for doctorate, GRE, statement of purpose, personal achievements/contributions statement, resume or curriculum vitae, 3 letters of recommendation, transcripts from all post-secondary institutions attended, writing sample (15-20 pages). Additional exam requirements/recommendations for international students: required—TOEFL (minimum score 600 paper-based; 94 iBT), IELTS (minimum score 7). Electronic applications accepted.

University of California, Santa Barbara, Graduate Division, College of Letters and Sciences, Division of Social Sciences, Department of Political Science, Santa Barbara, CA 93106-9420. Offers PhD, MA/PhD. Terminal master's awarded for partial completion of doctoral program. *Degree requirements:* For doctorate, one foreign language, thesis/ dissertation, 2 comprehensive exams or 1 exam and field paper. *Entrance requirements:* For doctorate, GRE General Test. Additional exam requirements/recommendations for international students: required—TOEFL (minimum score 600 paper-based; 100 iBT), IELTS. Electronic applications accepted.

University of California, Santa Cruz, Division of Graduate Studies, Division of Social Sciences, Politics Department, Santa Cruz, CA 95064. Offers PhD. *Degree requirements:* For doctorate, qualifying exam. *Entrance requirements:* For doctorate, GRE. Additional exam requirements/recommendations for international students: required—TOEFL (minimum score 550 paper-based; 83 iBT); recommended—IELTS (minimum score 8). Electronic applications accepted.

University of Central Oklahoma, The Jackson College of Graduate Studies, College of Liberal Arts, Department of Political Science, Edmond, OK 73034-5209. Offers political science (MA), including international affairs; public administration (MPA), including public and nonprofit management, urban management. *Program availability:* Part-time. *Degree requirements:* For master's, comprehensive exam (for some programs), thesis (for some programs). *Entrance requirements:* For master's, 18 undergraduate hours in political science. Additional exam requirements/recommendations for international students: required—TOEFL (minimum score 550 paper-based; 79 iBT), IELTS (minimum score 6.5). Electronic applications accepted.

University of Chicago, Division of the Social Sciences, Department of Political Science, Chicago, IL 60637. Offers PhD. *Degree requirements:* For doctorate, one foreign language, thesis/dissertation, exam, qualifying paper. *Entrance requirements:* For doctorate, GRE General Test, 3 letters of recommendation, statement of purpose, transcripts, resume or curriculum vitae, writing sample (dependent on department). Additional exam requirements/recommendations for international students: required—TOEFL (minimum score 104 iBT), IELTS (minimum score 7). Electronic applications accepted.

University of Cincinnati, Graduate School, McMicken College of Arts and Sciences, Department of Political Science, Cincinnati, OH 45221. Offers MA, PhD. Terminal master's awarded for partial completion of doctoral program. *Degree requirements:* For master's, thesis (for some programs); for doctorate, thesis/dissertation. *Entrance requirements:* For master's and doctorate, GRE General Test, GRE Subject Test. Additional exam requirements/recommendations for international students: required—TOEFL. Electronic applications accepted.

University of Colorado Boulder, Graduate School, College of Arts and Sciences, Department of Political Science, Boulder, CO 80309. Offers MA, PhD. Terminal master's awarded for partial completion of doctoral program. *Degree requirements:* For master's, comprehensive exam, thesis; for doctorate, one foreign language, thesis/dissertation. *Entrance requirements:* For master's, GRE General Test, minimum undergraduate GPA of 3.0; for doctorate, GRE General Test, minimum GPA of 3.5 (undergraduate), 3.0 (graduate). Electronic applications accepted. Application fee is waived when completed online.

University of Colorado Denver, College of Liberal Arts and Sciences, Department of Political Science, Denver, CO 80217. Offers MA. *Program availability:* Part-time, evening/weekend. *Degree requirements:* For master's, project or thesis, minimum of 30 credit hours. *Entrance requirements:* For master's, 18 hours of course work in political science; minimum GPA of 3.0 (3.2 preferred); statement of purpose; academic writing sample. Additional exam requirements/recommendations for international students: required—TOEFL (minimum score 537 paper-based; 75 iBT); recommended—IELTS (minimum score 6.5). Electronic applications accepted. Tuition and fees vary according to course load, program and reciprocity agreements.

University of Colorado Denver, School of Public Affairs, Program in Public Affairs and Administration, Denver, CO 80127. Offers public administration (MPA), including domestic violence, emergency management and homeland security, environmental policy, management and law, homeland security and defense, local government, nonprofit management, public administration; public affairs (PhD). *Accreditation:* NASPAA. *Program availability:* Part-time, evening/weekend, online learning. Tuition and fees vary according to course load, program and reciprocity agreements.

University of Connecticut, Graduate School, College of Liberal Arts and Sciences, Department of Political Science, Storrs, CT 06269. Offers MA, PhD. Terminal master's awarded for partial completion of doctoral program. *Degree requirements:* For master's, comprehensive exam; for doctorate, 2 foreign languages, thesis/dissertation. *Entrance requirements:* For master's and doctorate, GRE General Test. Additional exam requirements/recommendations for international students: required—TOEFL (minimum score 550 paper-based). Electronic applications accepted.

University of Delaware, College of Arts and Sciences, Department of Political Science and International Relations, Newark, DE 19716. Offers MA, PhD. Terminal master's awarded for partial completion of doctoral program. *Degree requirements:* For master's, research paper; for doctorate, one foreign language, comprehensive exam, thesis/ dissertation. *Entrance requirements:* For master's and doctorate, GRE General Test, minimum GPA of 3.2 in major, 3.0 overall. Additional exam requirements/ recommendations for international students: required—TOEFL (minimum score 600 paper-based). Electronic applications accepted.

University of Florida, Graduate School, College of Liberal Arts and Sciences, Department of Political Science, Gainesville, FL 32611. Offers educational policy (PhD); international development policy and administration (MA, Certificate); international relations (MA, MAT); political campaigning (MA, Certificate); political science (MA, PhD); public affairs (MA, Certificate); tropical conservation and development (MA, PhD); JD/ MA. Terminal master's awarded for partial completion of doctoral program. *Degree requirements:* For master's, variable foreign language requirement, comprehensive exam (for some programs), thesis or alternative, internship (for some programs); for doctorate, variable foreign language requirement, comprehensive exam, thesis/ dissertation. *Entrance requirements:* For master's and doctorate, GRE General Test (minimum score: 308 combined verbal/quantitative), minimum GPA of 3.5. Additional exam requirements/recommendations for international students: required—TOEFL (minimum score 550 paper-based; 80 iBT), IELTS (minimum score 6). Electronic applications accepted.

University of Georgia, School of Public and International Affairs, Program in Political Science/International Affairs, Athens, GA 30602. Offers MA, PhD. *Degree requirements:* For master's, one foreign language, thesis; for doctorate, one foreign language, thesis/dissertation. *Entrance requirements:* For master's and doctorate, GRE General Test. Electronic applications accepted.

University of Guelph, Office of Graduate and Postdoctoral Studies, College of Social and Applied Human Sciences, Department of Political Science, Guelph, ON N1G 2W1, Canada. Offers comparative politics (MA); international development (MA); political science (MA); public policy and public administration (MA); the Americas (Canada emphasis) (MA). *Degree requirements:* For master's, thesis or paper. *Entrance requirements:* For master's, minimum B average during previous 2 years of course work, 4 year Honours Degree in Political Science. Additional exam requirements/recommendations for international students: required—TOEFL. Electronic applications accepted.

University of Hawaii at Manoa, Office of Graduate Education, College of Social Sciences, Department of Political Science, Honolulu, HI 96822. Offers MA, PhD. *Program availability:* Part-time. Terminal master's awarded for partial completion of doctoral program. *Degree requirements:* For master's, thesis optional; for doctorate, comprehensive exam, thesis/dissertation. *Entrance requirements:* Additional exam requirements/recommendations for international students: required—TOEFL (minimum score 540 paper-based; 76 iBT), IELTS (minimum score 5).

University of Houston, College of Liberal Arts and Social Sciences, Department of Political Science, Houston, TX 77204. Offers political science (MA, PhD); public administration (MA). *Program availability:* Part-time. Terminal master's awarded for partial completion of doctoral program. *Degree requirements:* For master's, thesis optional; for doctorate, thesis/dissertation. *Entrance requirements:* For master's and doctorate, GRE. Additional exam requirements/recommendations for international students: required—TOEFL (minimum score 550 paper-based; 79 iBT).

University of Idaho, College of Graduate Studies, College of Letters, Arts and Social Sciences, Department of Politics and Philosophy, Moscow, ID 83844-2282. Offers political science (MA, PhD); public administration (MPA). *Faculty:* 5 full-time. *Students:* 25 full-time (13 women), 21 part-time (12 women). Average age 32. In 2019, 10 master's awarded. *Entrance requirements:* For master's, minimum GPA of 3.0. Additional exam requirements/recommendations for international students: required—TOEFL (minimum score 96 iBT). *Expenses:* Tuition, state resident: full-time $7753.80; part-time $502 per credit hour. Tuition, nonresident: full-time $26,990; part-time $1571 per credit hour. *Required fees:* $2122.20; $47 per credit hour. *Unit head:* Dr. Graham Hubbs, Chair, 208-885-6328, E-mail: politics-and-philosophy@uidaho.edu. *Application contact:* Dr. Graham Hubbs, Chair, 208-885-6328, E-mail: politics-and-philosophy@uidaho.edu.
Website: https://www.uidaho.edu/class/politics-and-philosophy

University of Illinois at Chicago, College of Liberal Arts and Sciences, Department of Political Science, Chicago, IL 60607-7128. Offers MA, PhD. *Program availability:* Part-time. Terminal master's awarded for partial completion of doctoral program. *Degree requirements:* For master's, thesis or comprehensive exam. *Entrance requirements:* For master's, GRE General Test, minimum GPA of 3.0. Additional exam requirements/recommendations for international students: required—TOEFL. Electronic applications accepted.

University of Illinois at Springfield, Graduate Programs, College of Public Affairs and Administration, Department of Political Science, Springfield, IL 62703-5407. Offers MA. *Program availability:* Part-time, 100% online, blended/hybrid learning. *Faculty:* 8 full-time (3 women), 2 part-time/adjunct (1 woman). *Students:* 17 full-time (7 women), 62 part-time (30 women); includes 15 minority (8 Black or African American, non-Hispanic/Latino; 4 Hispanic/Latino; 3 Two or more races, non-Hispanic/Latino), 1 international. Average age 33. 87 applicants, 52% accepted, 16 enrolled. In 2019, 21 master's awarded. *Degree requirements:* For master's, comprehensive exam, participant/observer case study, or thesis. *Entrance requirements:* For master's, minimum undergraduate GPA of 3.0; baccalaureate degree, with strong undergraduate background in political science, history, or the social sciences for full admission. Additional exam requirements/recommendations for international students: required—TOEFL (minimum score 500 paper-based; 61 iBT). *Application deadline:* Applications are processed on a rolling basis. Application fee: $60 ($75 for international students). Electronic applications accepted. *Expenses:* $33.25 per credit hour (online fee). *Financial support:* In 2019–20, research assistantships with full tuition reimbursements (averaging $10,562 per year), teaching assistantships with full tuition reimbursements (averaging $10,652 per year) were awarded; fellowships, career-related internships or fieldwork, Federal Work-Study, scholarships/grants, health care benefits, and unspecified assistantships also available. Support available to part-time students. Financial award application deadline: 11/15; financial award applicants required to submit FAFSA. *Unit head:* Dr. Robert Smith, Program Administrator, 217-206-6646, E-mail: rsmit27@uis.edu. *Application contact:* Dr. Robert Smith, Program Administrator, 217-206-6646, E-mail: rsmit27@uis.edu.
Website: http://www.uis.edu/politicalstudies/

University of Illinois at Urbana-Champaign, Graduate College, College of Liberal Arts and Sciences, Department of Political Science, Champaign, IL 61820. Offers MA, PhD, PhD/JD.

The University of Iowa, Graduate College, College of Liberal Arts and Sciences, Department of Political Science, Iowa City, IA 52242-1316. Offers PhD. *Degree requirements:* For doctorate, comprehensive exam, thesis/dissertation. *Entrance requirements:* For doctorate, GRE General Test, minimum GPA of 3.0. Additional exam requirements/recommendations for international students: required—TOEFL (minimum score 600 paper-based; 100 iBT). Electronic applications accepted.

The University of Kansas, Graduate Studies, College of Liberal Arts and Sciences, Department of Political Science, Lawrence, KS 66045. Offers MA, PhD, PhD/MA. *Program availability:* Part-time. *Students:* 33 full-time (16 women), 3 part-time (0 women); includes 5 minority (1 American Indian or Alaska Native, non-Hispanic/Latino; 2 Asian, non-Hispanic/Latino; 1 Hispanic/Latino; 1 Two or more races, non-Hispanic/Latino), 7 international. Average age 34. 39 applicants, 54% accepted, 8 enrolled. In 2019, 3 master's, 6 doctorates awarded. Terminal master's awarded for partial completion of doctoral program. *Entrance requirements:* For master's, GRE General Test, 3 letters of recommendation, curriculum vitae, transcripts, personal statement; for doctorate, GRE General Test, 3 letters of recommendation, transcripts, personal statement, curriculum vitae. Additional exam requirements/recommendations for international students: required—TOEFL, IELTS. *Application deadline:* For fall admission, 4/15 for domestic and international students. Application fee: $65 ($85 for international students). Electronic applications accepted. *Expenses:* Tuition, state resident: full-time $9989. Tuition, nonresident: full-time $23,950. *International tuition:* $23,950 full-time. *Required fees:* $984; $81.99 per credit hour. Tuition and fees vary according to course load, campus/location and program. *Financial support:* Fellowships, research assistantships, teaching assistantships, scholarships/grants, health care benefits, and unspecified assistantships available. Financial award application deadline: 1/7. *Unit head:* Don Haider-Markel, Chair, 785-864-9034, E-mail: dhmarkel@ku.edu. *Application contact:* Megan Wilson, Graduate Admissions Contact, 785-864-3523, E-mail: gradpols@ku.edu.
Website: https://kups.ku.edu/

University of Kentucky, Graduate School, College of Arts and Sciences, Program in Political Science, Lexington, KY 40506-0032. Offers MA, PhD. *Degree requirements:* For master's, comprehensive exam, thesis optional; for doctorate, comprehensive exam, thesis/dissertation. *Entrance requirements:* For master's, GRE General Test, minimum undergraduate GPA of 2.75; for doctorate, GRE General Test, minimum graduate GPA of 3.0. Additional exam requirements/recommendations for international students: required—TOEFL (minimum score 550 paper-based). Electronic applications accepted.

University of Lethbridge, School of Graduate Studies, Lethbridge, AB T1K 3M4, Canada. Offers addictions counseling (M Sc); agricultural biotechnology (M Sc); agricultural studies (M Sc, MA); anthropology (MA); archaeology (M Sc, MA); art (MA, MFA); biochemistry (M Sc); biological sciences (M Sc); biomolecular science (PhD); biosystems and biodiversity (PhD); Canadian studies (MA); chemistry (M Sc); computer science (M Sc); computer science and geographical information science (M Sc); counseling (MC); counseling psychology (M Ed); dramatic arts (MA); earth, space, and physical science (PhD); economics (MA); education (MA, PhD); educational leadership (M Ed); English (MA); environmental science (M Sc); evolution and behavior (PhD); exercise science (M Sc); French (MA); French/German (MA); French/Spanish (MA); general education (M Ed); geography (M Sc, MA); German (MA); health sciences (M Sc); individualized multidisciplinary (M Sc, MA); kinesiology (M Sc, MA); management (M Sc), including accounting, finance, human resource management and labor relations, information systems, international management, marketing, policy and strategy; mathematics (M Sc); music (M Mus, MA); Native American studies (MA); neuroscience (M Sc, PhD); new media (MA, MFA); nursing (M Sc, MN); philosophy (MA); physics (M Sc); political science (MA); psychology (M Sc, MA); religious studies (MA); sociology (MA); theatre and dramatic arts (MFA); theoretical and computational science (PhD); urban and regional studies (MA); women and gender studies (MA). *Program availability:* Part-time, evening/weekend. *Degree requirements:* For master's, thesis (for some programs); for doctorate, comprehensive exam, thesis/dissertation. *Entrance requirements:* For master's, GMAT (for M Sc in management), bachelor's degree in related field, minimum GPA of 3.0 during previous 20 graded semester courses, 2 years' teaching or related experience (M Ed); for doctorate, master's degree, minimum graduate GPA of 3.5. Additional exam requirements/recommendations for international students: required—TOEFL (minimum score 580 paper-based; 93 iBT). Electronic applications accepted.

University of Louisville, Graduate School, College of Arts and Sciences, Department of Political Science, Louisville, KY 40292-0001. Offers digital politics (MA); political science (MA). *Program availability:* Part-time, evening/weekend. *Faculty:* 18 full-time (8 women), 11 part-time/adjunct (5 women). *Students:* 13 full-time (4 women), 6 part-time (2 women); includes 1 minority (Black or African American, non-Hispanic/Latino), 2 international. Average age 27. 19 applicants, 68% accepted, 10 enrolled. In 2019, 11 master's awarded. *Degree requirements:* For master's, thesis optional. *Entrance requirements:* For master's, GRE guidelines (not requirements) reflect average scores of accepted applicants: 153 verbal, 144 quantitative, 4.0 analytic writing, Two letters of reference, official transcripts. Overall undergraduate GPA of 3.0 or 3.2 GPA in the final two years of undergraduate study. Additional exam requirements/recommendations for international students: required—TOEFL (minimum score 550 paper-based; 79 iBT), IELTS can be used in place of the TOEFL; recommended—IELTS (minimum score 6.5). *Application deadline:* For fall admission, 7/15 for domestic and international students; for spring admission, 11/15 for domestic and international students. Applications are processed on a rolling basis. Application fee: $65. Electronic applications accepted. *Expenses: Tuition, area resident:* Full-time $13,000; part-time $723 per credit hour. Tuition, state resident: full-time $13,000; part-time $723 per credit hour. Tuition, nonresident: full-time $27,114; part-time $1507 per credit hour. *International tuition:* $27,114 full-time. *Required fees:* $196. Tuition and fees vary according to program and reciprocity agreements. *Financial support:* In 2019–20, 1 student received support, including 3 research assistantships with full tuition reimbursements available (averaging $12,000 per year); fellowships, teaching assistantships, scholarships/grants, health care benefits, and unspecified assistantships also available. Financial award application deadline: 4/1. *Unit head:* Dr. Jasmine Farrier, Professor/Chair, 502-852-3310, E-mail: j.farrier@louisville.edu. *Application contact:* Amanda LeDuke, Senior Program Coordinator, 502-852-3303, E-mail: amanda.leduke@louisville.edu.
Website: http://louisville.edu/politicalscience

The University of Manchester, School of Social Sciences, Manchester, United Kingdom. Offers ethnographic documentary (M Phil); interdisciplinary study of culture (PhD); philosophy (PhD); politics (PhD); social anthropology (PhD); social anthropology with visual media (PhD); social change (PhD); social statistics (PhD); sociology (PhD); visual anthropology (M Phil).

University of Manitoba, Faculty of Graduate Studies, Faculty of Arts, Department of Political Studies, Winnipeg, MB R3T 2N2, Canada. Offers political studies (MA); public administration (MPA). *Degree requirements:* For master's, one foreign language, thesis or alternative.

University of Maryland, College Park, Academic Affairs, College of Behavioral and Social Sciences, Department of Government and Politics, College Park, MD 20742. Offers American politics (PhD); comparative politics (PhD); international relations (PhD); political economy (PhD); political theory (PhD). *Program availability:* Part-time, evening/weekend. *Degree requirements:* For doctorate, comprehensive exam, thesis/dissertation, written exams in 2 fields. *Entrance requirements:* For doctorate, GRE General Test, minimum GPA of 3.5, writing sample. Additional exam requirements/recommendations for international students: required—TOEFL. Electronic applications accepted.

University of Massachusetts Amherst, Graduate School, College of Social and Behavioral Sciences, Department of Political Science, Amherst, MA 01003. Offers MA, PhD. *Program availability:* Part-time. Terminal master's awarded for partial completion of doctoral program. *Degree requirements:* For master's, one foreign language, thesis or alternative; for doctorate, one foreign language, comprehensive exam, thesis/dissertation. *Entrance requirements:* For master's and doctorate, GRE General Test, writing sample, 3 letters of recommendation. Additional exam requirements/recommendations for international students: required—TOEFL (minimum score 550 paper-based; 80 iBT), IELTS (minimum score 6.5). Electronic applications accepted.

University of Memphis, Graduate School, College of Arts and Sciences, Department of Political Science, Memphis, TN 38152. Offers MA. *Students:* 14 full-time (9 women), 5 part-time (2 women); includes 7 minority (5 Black or African American, non-Hispanic/Latino; 2 Two or more races, non-Hispanic/Latino), 1 international. Average age 27. 9 applicants, 100% accepted, 6 enrolled. In 2019, 8 master's awarded. *Degree requirements:* For master's, comprehensive exam (for some programs), thesis or alternative, internship. *Entrance requirements:* For master's, GRE General Test or LSAT, minimum GPA of 3.0, letters of recommendation, statement of career goals and interests. *Application deadline:* For fall admission, 8/1 for domestic students; for spring admission, 12/1 for domestic students. Applications are processed on a rolling basis. Application fee: $35 ($60 for international students). Electronic applications accepted.

Political Science

Expenses: Tuition, area resident: Full-time $9216; part-time $512 per credit hour. Tuition, state resident: full-time $9216; part-time $512 per credit hour. Tuition, nonresident: full-time $12,672; part-time $704 per credit hour. *International tuition:* $16,128 full-time. *Required fees:* $1530; $85 per credit hour. Tuition and fees vary according to program. *Financial support:* Research assistantships with full tuition reimbursements, Federal Work-Study, scholarships/grants, and unspecified assistantships available. Financial award application deadline: 2/1; financial award applicants required to submit FAFSA. *Unit head:* Dr. Matthias Kaelberer, Chair, 901-678-2395, Fax: 901-678-2983, E-mail: mkaelbrr@memphis.edu. *Application contact:* Dr. Matthias Kaelberer, Chair, 901-678-2395, Fax: 901-678-2983, E-mail: mkaelbrr@memphis.edu.
Website: http://www.memphis.edu/polisci

University of Miami, Graduate School, College of Arts and Sciences, Department of Political Science, Coral Gables, FL 33124. Offers MPA, MPA/JD, MPA/MPH. *Program availability:* Part-time, evening/weekend. *Degree requirements:* For master's, thesis optional. *Entrance requirements:* For master's, GRE General Test. Additional exam requirements/recommendations for international students: required—TOEFL (minimum score 550 paper-based; 80 iBT). Electronic applications accepted.

University of Michigan, Rackham Graduate School, College of Literature, Science, and the Arts, Department of Political Science, Ann Arbor, MI 48109. Offers political science (PhD); political science and public policy (PhD); social work and political science (PhD). Terminal master's awarded for partial completion of doctoral program. *Degree requirements:* For doctorate, comprehensive exam, thesis/dissertation, oral defense of dissertation, preliminary exams. *Entrance requirements:* For doctorate, GRE General Test. Additional exam requirements/recommendations for international students: required—TOEFL. Electronic applications accepted. *Expenses:* Contact institution.

University of Michigan, School of Social Work, Interdisciplinary PhD Program in Social Work and Social Science, Ann Arbor, MI 48109. Offers social work and anthropology (PhD); social work and economics (PhD); social work and political science (PhD); social work and psychology (PhD); social work and sociology (PhD). *Degree requirements:* For doctorate, thesis/dissertation, oral defense of dissertation, preliminary exam. *Entrance requirements:* For doctorate, GRE General Test. Additional exam requirements/recommendations for international students: required—TOEFL (minimum score 620 paper-based, 88 iBT) or IELTS. Electronic applications accepted. *Expenses:* Contact institution.

University of Michigan–Flint, College of Arts and Sciences, Program in Social Sciences, Flint, MI 48502-1950. Offers gender studies (MA); global studies (MA); U.S. history and politics (MA). *Program availability:* Part-time. *Faculty:* 11 full-time (6 women), 4 part-time/adjunct (all women). *Students:* 3 full-time (2 women), 7 part-time (5 women); includes 4 minority (3 Black or African American, non-Hispanic/Latino; 1 Two or more races, non-Hispanic/Latino). Average age 43. 15 applicants, 60% accepted, 2 enrolled. In 2019, 4 master's awarded. *Entrance requirements:* For master's, bachelor's degree from regionally-accredited institution, minimum overall undergraduate GPA of 3.0 on 4.0 scale. Additional exam requirements/recommendations for international students: required—TOEFL (minimum score 84 iBT), IELTS (minimum score 6.5). *Application deadline:* For fall admission, 8/1 for domestic students; 5/1 for international students; for winter admission, 11/15 for domestic students, 10/1 for international students; for spring admission, 3/15 for domestic students, 1/1 for international students; for summer admission, 5/15 for domestic students. Applications are processed on a rolling basis. Application fee: $55. Electronic applications accepted. *Expenses:* Contact institution. *Financial support:* Federal Work-Study, scholarships/grants, and unspecified assistantships available. Financial award application deadline: 3/1; financial award applicants required to submit FAFSA. *Unit head:* Dr. Adam Lutzker, Director, 810-762-3470, Fax: 810-762-3281, E-mail: alutzker@umflint.edu. *Application contact:* Matt Bohlen, Associate Director of Graduate Programs, 810-762-3171, Fax: 810-766-6789, E-mail: mbohlen@umflint.edu.
Website: http://www.umflint.edu/graduateprograms/social-sciences-ma

University of Minnesota, Twin Cities Campus, Graduate School, College of Liberal Arts, Department of Political Science, Minneapolis, MN 55455. Offers PhD. *Degree requirements:* For doctorate, thesis/dissertation, 1 foreign language or statistics. *Entrance requirements:* For doctorate, GRE. Additional exam requirements/recommendations for international students: required—TOEFL; recommended—IELTS. Electronic applications accepted.

University of Mississippi, Graduate School, College of Liberal Arts, University, MS 38677. Offers anthropology (MA); biology (MS, PhD); chemistry (MS, DA, PhD); creative writing (MFA); documentary expression (MFA); economics (MA, PhD); English (MA, PhD); experimental psychology (PhD); history (MA, PhD); mathematics (MS, PhD); modern languages (MA); music (MM); philosophy (MA); physics (MA, MS, PhD); political science (MA, PhD); Southern studies (MA); studio art (MFA). *Program availability:* Part-time. *Faculty:* 481 full-time (215 women), 71 part-time/adjunct (40 women). *Students:* 509 full-time (258 women), 55 part-time (21 women); includes 89 minority (40 Black or African American, non-Hispanic/Latino; 13 Asian, non-Hispanic/Latino; 25 Hispanic/Latino; 11 Two or more races, non-Hispanic/Latino), 157 international. Average age 29. In 2019, 119 master's, 51 doctorates awarded. *Degree requirements:* For doctorate, thesis/dissertation. *Entrance requirements:* For master's, GRE General Test, minimum GPA of 3.0; for doctorate, GRE General Test. Additional exam requirements/recommendations for international students: required—TOEFL. *Application deadline:* Applications are processed on a rolling basis. Application fee: $50. Electronic applications accepted. *Expenses:* Tuition, state resident: full-time $8718; part-time $484.25 per credit hour. Tuition, nonresident: full-time $24,990; part-time $1388.25 per credit hour. *Required fees:* $100; $4.16 per credit hour. *Financial support:* Fellowships, research assistantships, teaching assistantships, career-related internships or fieldwork, Federal Work-Study, institutionally sponsored loans, scholarships/grants, and unspecified assistantships available. Financial award application deadline: 3/1; financial award applicants required to submit FAFSA. *Unit head:* Dr. Lee Michael Cohen, Dean, 662-915-7177, Fax: 662-915-5792, E-mail: libarts@olemiss.edu. *Application contact:* Tameka Smith, Graduate Activities Specialist for Admissions, 662-915-7474, Fax: 662-915-7577, E-mail: gschool@olemiss.edu.
Website: ventress@olemiss.edu

University of Missouri, Office of Research and Graduate Studies, College of Arts and Science, Department of Political Science, Columbia, MO 65211. Offers MA, PhD, Certificate. Terminal master's awarded for partial completion of doctoral program. *Entrance requirements:* For master's, GRE General Test (minimum combined score 1000 Verbal and Quantitative), minimum GPA of 3.0 in last 60 hours and in political science courses; at least 12 hours of upper-level course work in political science; for doctorate, GRE General Test (minimum combined score 1200 Verbal and Quantitative), minimum GPA of 3.0 in last 60 hours and in political science courses; at least 12 hours of upper-level course work in political science.

University of Missouri–Kansas City, College of Arts and Sciences, Department of Political Science, Kansas City, MO 64110-2499. Offers MA. *Program availability:* Part-time, evening/weekend. Terminal master's awarded for partial completion of doctoral program. *Degree requirements:* For master's, thesis optional. *Entrance requirements:*

For master's, GRE, minimum GPA of 3.0, course work in political science, 2 letters of recommendation. Additional exam requirements/recommendations for international students: required—TOEFL (minimum score 550 paper-based; 80 iBT). Electronic applications accepted.

University of Missouri–St. Louis, College of Arts and Sciences, Department of Political Science, St. Louis, MO 63121. Offers American politics (MA); comparative politics (MA); international politics (MA); political process and behavior (MA); political science (PhD); public administration and public policy (MA); urban and regional politics (MA). *Program availability:* Part-time, evening/weekend. Terminal master's awarded for partial completion of doctoral program. *Degree requirements:* For master's, thesis optional; for doctorate, thesis/dissertation. *Entrance requirements:* For master's, GRE General Test, 2 letters of recommendation, statement of purpose; for doctorate, GRE General Test, 3 letters of recommendation, statement of purpose. Additional exam requirements/recommendations for international students: required—TOEFL (minimum score 550 paper-based; 79 iBT), IELTS (minimum score 6.5). Electronic applications accepted. *Expenses: Tuition, area resident:* Full-time $9005.40; part-time $6003.60 per credit hour. Tuition, state resident: full-time $9005.40; part-time $6003.60 per credit hour. Tuition, nonresident: full-time $22,108; part-time $14,738.40 per credit hour. *International tuition:* $22,108 full-time. Tuition and fees vary according to course load.

University of Montana, Graduate School, College of Humanities and Sciences, Department of Political Science, Program in Political Science, Missoula, MT 59812. Offers MA. *Degree requirements:* For master's, thesis. *Entrance requirements:* For master's, GRE General Test.

University of Nebraska at Omaha, Graduate Studies, College of Arts and Sciences, Department of Political Science, Omaha, NE 68182. Offers American government (Certificate); global information operations (Certificate); intelligence and national security (Certificate); political science (MS). *Program availability:* Part-time, evening/weekend, online learning. *Degree requirements:* For master's, comprehensive exam, thesis (for some programs). *Entrance requirements:* For master's, 15 undergraduate political science hours, minimum undergraduate GPA of 3.0, 2 letters of recommendation, official transcripts. Additional exam requirements/recommendations for international students: required—TOEFL, IELTS, PTE. Electronic applications accepted.

University of Nebraska–Lincoln, Graduate College, College of Arts and Sciences, Department of Political Science, Lincoln, NE 68588. Offers political science (MA, PhD); public policy analysis (Graduate Certificate). *Degree requirements:* For master's, thesis optional; for doctorate, variable foreign language requirement, comprehensive exam, thesis/dissertation. *Entrance requirements:* For master's and doctorate, GRE General Test, writing sample. Additional exam requirements/recommendations for international students: required—TOEFL (minimum score 600 paper-based). Electronic applications accepted.

University of Nevada, Las Vegas, Graduate College, College of Liberal Arts, Department of Political Science, Las Vegas, NV 89154-5029. Offers MA, PhD. *Program availability:* Part-time. *Faculty:* 10 full-time (4 women). *Students:* 18 full-time (5 women), 11 part-time (1 woman); includes 7 minority (3 Black or African American, non-Hispanic/Latino; 2 Hispanic/Latino; 2 Two or more races, non-Hispanic/Latino). Average age 34. 16 applicants, 63% accepted, 8 enrolled. In 2019, 2 master's, 2 doctorates awarded. *Degree requirements:* For master's, thesis, professional paper; for doctorate, one foreign language, comprehensive exam, thesis/dissertation, oral examination. *Entrance requirements:* For master's, GRE General Test, 2 letters of recommendation; personal statement; bachelor's degree; minimum GPA of 3.0; for doctorate, GRE General Test, minimum GPA of 3.3 in BA, 3.5 in MA; 3 letters of recommendation; personal statement; writing sample. Additional exam requirements/recommendations for international students: required—TOEFL (minimum score 550 paper-based; 80 iBT), IELTS (minimum score 7). *Application deadline:* For fall admission, 2/1 for domestic and international students. Application fee: $60 ($95 for international students). Electronic applications accepted. *Expenses:* Contact institution. *Financial support:* In 2019–20, 14 students received support, including 6 research assistantships with full tuition reimbursements available (averaging $12,625 per year), 8 teaching assistantships with full tuition reimbursements available (averaging $14,531 per year); institutionally sponsored loans, scholarships/grants, health care benefits, and unspecified assistantships also available. Financial award application deadline: 3/15; financial award applicants required to submit FAFSA. *Unit head:* Dr. David Damore, Chair and Professor, 702-895-5258, Fax: 702-895-1065, E-mail: psc.chair@unlv.edu. *Application contact:* Dr. Christian Jensen, Graduate Coordinator, 702-895-1337, Fax: 702-895-1065, E-mail: psc.gradcoord@unlv.edu.
Website: http://liberalarts.unlv.edu/Political_Science/

University of Nevada, Reno, Graduate School, College of Liberal Arts, Department of Political Science, Program in Political Science, Reno, NV 89557. Offers MA, PhD. Terminal master's awarded for partial completion of doctoral program. *Degree requirements:* For master's, comprehensive exam, oral exam/thesis or professional paper; for doctorate, thesis/dissertation, 2 field exams, oral exam. *Entrance requirements:* For master's, GRE General Test, GMAT, LSAT, minimum GPA of 2.75; for doctorate, GRE General Test, GMAT, LSAT, minimum GPA of 3.0. Additional exam requirements/recommendations for international students: required—TOEFL (minimum score 500 paper-based; 61 iBT), IELTS (minimum score 6). Electronic applications accepted.

University of New Hampshire, Graduate School, College of Liberal Arts, Department of Political Science, Durham, NH 03824. Offers political science (MA, Postbaccalaureate Certificate), including political science (MA), sustainability politics and policy (Postbaccalaureate Certificate). *Program availability:* Part-time. *Students:* 2 full-time (1 woman), 3 part-time (1 woman). Average age 25. 9 applicants, 67% accepted, 2 enrolled. In 2019, 8 master's awarded. *Entrance requirements:* For master's, GRE General Test. Additional exam requirements/recommendations for international students: required—TOEFL (minimum score 550 paper-based; 80 iBT), IELTS, PTE. *Application deadline:* For fall admission, 8/7 for domestic students, 4/1 for international students; for spring admission, 1/1 for domestic students; for summer admission, 5/7 for domestic students. Application fee: $65. Electronic applications accepted. *Financial support:* In 2019–20, 2 students received support, including 2 teaching assistantships; fellowships, research assistantships, career-related internships or fieldwork, Federal Work-Study, scholarships/grants, and tuition waivers (full and partial) also available. Support available to part-time students. Financial award application deadline: 2/15. *Unit head:* Mary Malone, Chair, 603-862-1406. *Application contact:* Heather Austin, Graduate Program Coordinator, 603-862-1750, E-mail: heather.austin@unh.edu.
Website: http://cola.unh.edu/political-science

University of New Mexico, Graduate Studies, College of Arts and Sciences, Program in Political Science, Albuquerque, NM 87131-2039. Offers MA, PhD. *Program availability:* Part-time. Terminal master's awarded for partial completion of doctoral program. *Degree requirements:* For master's, comprehensive exam, thesis optional; for doctorate, comprehensive exam, thesis/dissertation, field research paper, minimum cumulative GPA of 3.5. *Entrance requirements:* For master's and doctorate, GRE General Test, 3 letters of recommendation, writing sample, letter of intent. Additional exam requirements/recommendations for international students: required—TOEFL.

Electronic applications accepted. *Expenses:* Tuition, state resident: full-time $7633; part-time $972 per year. Tuition, nonresident: full-time $22,586; part-time $3840 per year. *International tuition:* $23,292 full-time. *Required fees:* $8608. Tuition and fees vary according to course level, course load, degree level, program and student level.

University of New Orleans, Graduate School, College of Liberal Arts, Education and Human Development, Department of Political Science, New Orleans, LA 70148. Offers political science (MA, PhD); public administration (MPA). *Program availability:* Evening/weekend. *Degree requirements:* For master's, one foreign language, thesis or alternative; for doctorate, one foreign language, thesis/dissertation. *Entrance requirements:* For master's, GRE General Test; for doctorate, GRE General Test, GRE Subject Test. Additional exam requirements/recommendations for international students: required—TOEFL (minimum score 550 paper-based; 79 iBT), IELTS (minimum score 6.5). Electronic applications accepted.

University of North Alabama, College of Arts and Sciences, Department of Politics, Justice, and Law, Florence, AL 35632-0001. Offers criminal justice (MSCJ). *Program availability:* Part-time, 100% online. *Degree requirements:* For master's, comprehensive exam (for some programs), thesis optional. *Entrance requirements:* For master's, GRE General Test, MAT, three letters of recommendation; essay. Additional exam requirements/recommendations for international students: required—TOEFL (minimum score 79 iBT), IELTS (minimum score 6), PTE (minimum score 54). Electronic applications accepted.

The University of North Carolina at Chapel Hill, Graduate School, College of Arts and Sciences, Department of Political Science, Chapel Hill, NC 27599. Offers Latin American studies (Certificate); political science (MA, PhD); trans-Atlantic studies (MA). *Degree requirements:* For master's, comprehensive exam; for doctorate, one foreign language, comprehensive exam, thesis/dissertation. *Entrance requirements:* For master's and doctorate, GRE General Test, minimum GPA of 3.0 recommended. Electronic applications accepted.

The University of North Carolina at Greensboro, Graduate School, College of Arts and Sciences, Department of Political Science, Greensboro, NC 27412-5001. Offers nonprofit management (Certificate); public affairs (MPA); urban and economic development (Certificate). *Accreditation:* NASPAA. *Degree requirements:* For master's, comprehensive exam. *Entrance requirements:* For master's, GRE General Test. Additional exam requirements/recommendations for international students: required—TOEFL. Electronic applications accepted.

University of Northern British Columbia, Office of Graduate Studies, Prince George, BC V2N 4Z9, Canada. Offers business administration (Diploma); community health science (M Sc); disability management (MA); education (M Ed); first nations studies (MA); gender studies (MA); history (MA); interdisciplinary studies (MA); international studies (MA); mathematical, computer and physical sciences (M Sc); natural resources and environmental studies (M Sc, MA, MNRES, PhD); political science (MA); psychology (M Sc, PhD); social work (MSW). *Program availability:* Part-time, evening/weekend, online learning. *Degree requirements:* For master's, thesis; for doctorate, thesis/dissertation. *Entrance requirements:* For master's, GRE, minimum B average in undergraduate course work; for doctorate, candidacy exam, minimum A average in graduate course work.

University of North Texas, Toulouse Graduate School, Denton, TX 76203-5459. Offers accounting (MS); applied anthropology (MA, MS); applied behavior analysis (Certificate); applied geography (MA); applied technology and performance improvement (M Ed, MS); art education (MA); art history (MA); arts leadership (Certificate); audiology (Au D); behavior analysis (MS); behavioral science (PhD); biochemistry and molecular biology (MS); biology (MA, MS); biomedical engineering (MS); business analysis (MS); chemistry (MS); clinical health psychology (PhD); communication studies (MA, MS); computer engineering (MS); computer science (MS); counseling (M Ed, MS), including clinical mental health counseling (MS), college and university counseling, elementary school counseling, secondary school counseling; creative writing (MA); criminal justice (MS); curriculum and instruction (M Ed); decision sciences (MBA); design (MA, MFA), including fashion design (MFA), innovation studies, interior design (MFA); early childhood studies (MS); economics (MS); educational leadership (M Ed, Ed D); educational psychology (MS, PhD), including family studies (MS), gifted and talented (MS), human development (MS), learning and cognition (MS), research, measurement and evaluation (MS); electrical engineering (MS); emergency management (MPA); engineering technology (MS); English (MA); English as a second language (MA); environmental science (MS); finance (MBA, MS); financial management (MPA); French (MA); health services management (MBA); higher education (M Ed, Ed D); history (MA, MS); hospitality management (MS); human resources management (MPA); information science (MS); information systems (PhD); information technologies (MBA); interdisciplinary studies (MA, MS); international studies (MA); international sustainable tourism (MS); jazz studies (MM); journalism (MA, MJ, Graduate Certificate), including interactive and virtual digital communication (Graduate Certificate), narrative journalism (Graduate Certificate), public relations (Graduate Certificate); kinesiology (MS); linguistics (MA); local government management (MPA); logistics (PhD); logistics and supply chain management (MBA); long-term care, senior housing, and aging services (MA); management (PhD); marketing (MBA); mathematics (MA, MS); mechanical and energy engineering (MS, PhD); music (MA), including ethnomusicology, music theory, musicology, performance; music composition (PhD); music education (MM Ed, PhD); nonprofit management (MPA); operations and supply chain management (MBA); performance (MM, DMA); philosophy (MA); political science (MA); professional and technical communication (MA); radio, television and film (MA, MFA); rehabilitation counseling (Certificate); sociology (MA); Spanish (MA); special education (M Ed); speech-language pathology (MA); strategic management (MBA); studio art (MFA); teaching (M Ed); MBA/MS. *Program availability:* Part-time, evening/weekend, online learning. Terminal master's awarded for partial completion of doctoral program. *Degree requirements:* For master's, variable foreign language requirement, comprehensive exam (for some programs), thesis (for some programs); for doctorate, variable foreign language requirement, comprehensive exam (for some programs), thesis/dissertation; for other advanced degree, variable foreign language requirement, comprehensive exam (for some programs). *Entrance requirements:* For master's and doctorate, GRE, GMAT. Additional exam requirements/recommendations for international students: required—TOEFL (minimum score 550 paper-based; 79 iBT). Electronic applications accepted.

University of Notre Dame, The Graduate School, College of Arts and Letters, Division of Social Sciences, Department of Political Science, Notre Dame, IN 46556. Offers PhD. *Degree requirements:* For doctorate, one foreign language, comprehensive exam, thesis/dissertation, candidacy exam. *Entrance requirements:* For doctorate, GRE General Test. Additional exam requirements/recommendations for international students: required—TOEFL (minimum score 600 paper-based; 80 iBT). Electronic applications accepted.

University of Oklahoma, College of Arts and Sciences, Department of Political Science, Norman, OK 73019-0390. Offers political science (MA, PhD); public administration (MPA), including general, nonprofit management, public management, public policy. Terminal master's awarded for partial completion of doctoral program. *Degree requirements:* For master's, comprehensive exam, thesis optional, 36 hours; for doctorate, comprehensive exam, thesis/dissertation, 90 hours. *Entrance requirements:* For master's, GRE, purpose statement, writing sample, and three letters of recommendation (for MA); for doctorate, GRE, purpose statement, writing sample, three letters of recommendation. Additional exam requirements/recommendations for international students: required—TOEFL (minimum score 100 iBT) or IELTS (minimum score 7.0). Electronic applications accepted. *Expenses:* Tuition, state resident: full-time $6583.20; part-time $274.30 per credit hour. Tuition, nonresident: full-time $21,242; part-time $885.10 per credit hour. *International tuition:* $21,242.40 full-time. *Required fees:* $1994.20; $72.55 per credit hour. $126.50 per semester. Tuition and fees vary according to course load and degree level.

University of Oregon, Graduate School, College of Arts and Sciences, Department of Political Science, Eugene, OR 97403. Offers MA, MS, PhD. Terminal master's awarded for partial completion of doctoral program. *Degree requirements:* For master's, thesis or alternative; for doctorate, thesis/dissertation. *Entrance requirements:* For master's and doctorate, GRE General Test, minimum GPA of 3.0. Additional exam requirements/recommendations for international students: required—TOEFL.

University of Ottawa, Faculty of Graduate and Postdoctoral Studies, Faculty of Social Sciences, Department of Political Studies, Ottawa, ON K1N 6N5, Canada. Offers MA, PhD. *Degree requirements:* For master's, thesis or alternative, fluency in English and French; for doctorate, comprehensive exam, thesis/dissertation. *Entrance requirements:* For master's, honors bachelor's degree or equivalent, minimum B average; for doctorate, master's degree, minimum B+ average. Electronic applications accepted.

University of Pennsylvania, School of Arts and Sciences, Fels Institute of Government, Philadelphia, PA 19104. Offers economic development and growth (Certificate); government administration (MGA); nonprofit administration (Certificate); organization dynamics (MS); politics (Certificate); public administration (MPA); public finance (Certificate). *Program availability:* Part-time, evening/weekend. *Students:* 15 full-time (9 women), 49 part-time (24 women); includes 19 minority (8 Black or African American, non-Hispanic/Latino; 6 Asian, non-Hispanic/Latino; 5 Hispanic/Latino), 3 international. Average age 33. 664 applicants, 44% accepted, 130 enrolled. In 2019, 67 master's, 3 other advanced degrees awarded. *Financial support:* Application deadline: 1/1.
Website: http://www.fels.upenn.edu/

University of Pennsylvania, School of Arts and Sciences, Graduate Group in Political Science, Philadelphia, PA 19104-6297. Offers AM, PhD, MGA/AM. *Faculty:* 36 full-time (13 women), 2 part-time/adjunct (1 woman). *Students:* 63 full-time (35 women); includes 13 minority (3 Black or African American, non-Hispanic/Latino; 5 Asian, non-Hispanic/Latino; 4 Hispanic/Latino; 1 Two or more races, non-Hispanic/Latino), 19 international. Average age 29. 323 applicants, 8% accepted, 10 enrolled. In 2019, 5 master's, 12 doctorates awarded. Terminal master's awarded for partial completion of doctoral program. Application fee: $90. *Financial support:* Teaching assistantships available.
Website: http://www.sas.upenn.edu/polisci/content/graduate-program

University of Pittsburgh, Graduate School of Public and International Affairs, Master of Public and International Affairs Program, Pittsburgh, PA 15260. Offers human security (MPIA); international political economy (MPIA); security and intelligence studies (MPIA); JD/MPIA; MBA/MPIA; MPH/MPIA; MPIA/MSW; MSIS/MPIA. *Program availability:* Part-time, evening/weekend. *Faculty:* 33 full-time (11 women), 10 part-time/adjunct (5 women). *Students:* 87 full-time (49 women), 14 part-time (6 women); includes 13 minority (7 Black or African American, non-Hispanic/Latino; 6 Hispanic/Latino), 10 international. Average age 27. 156 applicants, 94% accepted, 49 enrolled. In 2019, 41 master's awarded. *Degree requirements:* For master's, thesis optional, Capstone Seminar. *Entrance requirements:* For master's, Personal essay, resume, two letters of recommendation, transcripts. Additional exam requirements/recommendations for international students: required—TOEFL (minimum score 80 iBT), Duolingo English Test; recommended—IELTS (minimum score 6.5). *Application deadline:* For fall admission, 2/1 priority date for domestic students, 1/15 priority date for international students; for spring admission, 11/1 priority date for domestic students, 8/1 priority date for international students. Application fee: $50. Electronic applications accepted. *Expenses:* $24,480 in-state, $40,848 out-of-state. *Financial support:* In 2019–20, 63 students received support, including 9 fellowships with full tuition reimbursements available (averaging $16,060 per year); scholarships/grants also available. Financial award application deadline: 2/1. *Unit head:* Dr. John Keeler, Dean, 412-648-7605, Fax: 412-648-7601, E-mail: gspia@pitt.edu. *Application contact:* Dr. Michael Rizzi, Director of Student Services, 412-648-7643, Fax: 412-648-7641, E-mail: rizzim@pitt.edu.
Website: http://www.gspia.pitt.edu/

University of Pittsburgh, Kenneth P. Dietrich School of Arts and Sciences, Department of Political Science, Pittsburgh, PA 15260. Offers MA, PhD. *Faculty:* 17 full-time (7 women). *Students:* 55 full-time (22 women), 32 international. Average age 30. 106 applicants, 13% accepted, 7 enrolled. In 2019, 12 master's, 6 doctorates awarded. Terminal master's awarded for partial completion of doctoral program. *Degree requirements:* For doctorate, comprehensive exam, thesis/dissertation, Comprehensive Research Paper. *Entrance requirements:* For doctorate, GRE, 3 letters of recommendation. Additional exam requirements/recommendations for international students: required—TOEFL (minimum score 90 iBT), IELTS. *Application deadline:* For fall admission, 1/15 for domestic and international students. Application fee: $75. Electronic applications accepted. *Financial support:* In 2019–20, 36 students received support, including 16 fellowships with full tuition reimbursements available (averaging $24,000 per year), 10 research assistantships with full tuition reimbursements available (averaging $20,250 per year), 10 teaching assistantships with full tuition reimbursements available (averaging $20,250 per year). Financial award application deadline: 1/15. *Unit head:* Dr. Jonathan Woon, Department Chair, 412-648-7266, E-mail: woon@pitt.edu. *Application contact:* Brian Deutsch, Graduate Administrator, 412-648-7270, E-mail: brd51@pitt.edu.
Website: http://www.polisci.pitt.edu/

University of Rhode Island, Graduate School, College of Arts and Sciences, Department of Political Science, Kingston, RI 02881. Offers international relations (MA), including American politics; public policy and administration (MPA). *Program availability:* Part-time. *Faculty:* 12 full-time (6 women). *Students:* 25 full-time (15 women), 33 part-time (21 women); includes 12 minority (2 Black or African American, non-Hispanic/Latino; 1 American Indian or Alaska Native, non-Hispanic/Latino; 1 Asian, non-Hispanic/Latino; 6 Hispanic/Latino; 2 Two or more races, non-Hispanic/Latino), 2 international. 36 applicants, 94% accepted, 26 enrolled. In 2019, 18 master's awarded. *Entrance requirements:* For master's, GRE, GMAT, or MAT if undergraduate GPA below 3.0, 2 letters of recommendation. Additional exam requirements/recommendations for international students: required—TOEFL. *Application deadline:* For fall admission, 11/15 for domestic students, 2/1 for international students; for spring admission, 7/15 for domestic students, 7/15 priority date for international students. Application fee: $65. Electronic applications accepted. *Expenses: Tuition, area resident:* Full-time $13,734; part-time $763 per credit. Tuition, state resident: full-time $13,734; part-time $763 per credit. Tuition, nonresident: full-time $26,512; part-time $1473 per credit. *International tuition:* $26,512 full-time. *Required fees:* $1780; $52 per credit. $35 per term. One-time fee: $165. *Financial support:* In 2019–20, 1 research assistantship with full tuition

reimbursement (averaging $19,368 per year), 4 teaching assistantships with full tuition reimbursements (averaging $15,189 per year) were awarded; health care benefits also available. Financial award application deadline: 2/1; financial award applicants required to submit FAFSA. *Unit head:* Dr. Marc Hutchison, Department Chair, 401-874-4051, Fax: 401-874-4072, E-mail: mlhutch@uri.edu. *Application contact:* Dr. Kristin Johnson, Director/Associate Professor, 401-874-5495, E-mail: kristin_johnson@uri.edu.
Website: http://www.uri.edu/artsci/psc/

University of Rochester, School of Arts and Sciences, Department of Political Science, Rochester, NY 14627. Offers PhD. *Faculty:* 25 full-time (6 women). *Students:* 39 full-time (19 women), 1 (woman) part-time; includes 6 minority (3 Asian, non-Hispanic/Latino; 2 Hispanic/Latino; 1 Two or more races, non-Hispanic/Latino), 26 international. Average age 29. 91 applicants, 33% accepted, 9 enrolled. In 2019, 9 doctorates awarded. *Degree requirements:* For doctorate, comprehensive exam, thesis/dissertation, prospectus defense. *Entrance requirements:* For doctorate, GRE General Test, three letters of recommendation, personal statement, transcripts, writing sample. Additional exam requirements/recommendations for international students: required—TOEFL. *Application deadline:* For fall admission, 1/15 for domestic and international students. Application fee: $60. Electronic applications accepted. *Financial support:* In 2019–20, 6 students received support, including 6 fellowships with full tuition reimbursements available (averaging $27,000 per year); tuition waivers (full) also available. Financial award application deadline: 1/10. *Unit head:* John Duggan, Chair, 585-275-4999, E-mail: john.duggan@rochester.edu. *Application contact:* AnneMarie Tyll, Secretary, 585-275-8745, E-mail: atyll@ur.rochester.edu.
Website: http://www.sas.rochester.edu/psc/graduate/introduction.php

University of Saskatchewan, College of Graduate and Postdoctoral Studies, College of Arts and Science, Department of Political Studies, Saskatoon, SK S7N 5A2, Canada. Offers MA. *Degree requirements:* For master's, thesis. *Entrance requirements:* Additional exam requirements/recommendations for international students: required—TOEFL (minimum score 80 iBT); recommended—IELTS (minimum score 6.5). Electronic applications accepted.

University of South Africa, College of Human Sciences, Pretoria, South Africa. Offers adult education (M Ed); African languages (MA, PhD); African politics (MA, PhD); Afrikaans (MA, PhD); ancient history (MA, PhD); ancient Near Eastern studies (MA, PhD); anthropology (MA, PhD); applied linguistics (MA); Arabic (MA, PhD); archaeology (MA); art history (MA); Biblical archaeology (MA); Biblical studies (M Th, D Th, PhD); Christian spirituality (M Th, D Th); church history (M Th, D Th); classical studies (MA, PhD); clinical psychology (MA); communication (MA, PhD); comparative education (M Ed, Ed D); consulting psychology (D Admin, D Com, PhD); curriculum studies (M Ed, Ed D); development studies (M Admin, MA, D Admin, PhD); didactics (M Ed, Ed D); education (M Tech); education management (M Ed, Ed D); educational psychology (M Ed); English (MA); environmental education (M Ed); French (MA, PhD); German (MA, PhD); Greek (MA); guidance and counseling (M Ed); health studies (MA, PhD), including health sciences education (MA), health services management (MA), medical and surgical nursing science (critical care general) (MA), midwifery and neonatal nursing science (MA), trauma and emergency care (MA); history (MA, PhD); history of education (Ed D); inclusive education (M Ed, Ed D); information and communications technology policy and regulation (MA); information science (MA, MIS, PhD); international politics (MA, PhD); Islamic studies (MA, PhD); Italian (MA, PhD); Judaica (MA, PhD); linguistics (MA, PhD); mathematical education (M Ed); mathematics education (MA); missiology (M Th, D Th); modern Hebrew (MA, PhD); musicology (MA, MMus, D Mus, PhD); natural science education (M Ed); New Testament (M Th, D Th); Old Testament (D Th); pastoral therapy (M Th, D Th); philosophy (MA); philosophy of education (M Ed, Ed D); politics (MA, PhD); Portuguese (MA, PhD); practical theology (M Th, D Th); psychology (MA, MS, PhD); psychology of education (M Ed, Ed D); public health (MA); religious studies (MA, D Th, PhD); Romance languages (MA); Russian (MA, PhD); Semitic languages (MA, PhD); social behavior studies in HIV/AIDS (MA); social science (mental health) (MA); social science in development studies (MA); social science in psychology (MA); social science in social work (MA); social science in sociology (MA); social work (MSW, DSW, PhD); socio-education (M Ed, Ed D); sociolinguistics (MA); sociology (MA, PhD); Spanish (MA, PhD); systematic theology (M Th, D Th); TESOL (teaching English to speakers of other languages) (MA); theological ethics (M Th, D Th); theory of literature (MA, PhD); urban ministries (D Th); urban ministry (M Th).

University of South Carolina, The Graduate School, College of Arts and Sciences, Department of Political Science, Program in Political Science, Columbia, SC 29208. Offers MA, PhD. *Program availability:* Part-time. Terminal master's awarded for partial completion of doctoral program. *Degree requirements:* For master's, one foreign language, thesis; for doctorate, one foreign language, comprehensive exam, thesis/dissertation. *Entrance requirements:* For master's and doctorate, GRE General Test, minimum GPA of 3.5. Additional exam requirements/recommendations for international students: required—TOEFL. Electronic applications accepted.

University of Southern California, Graduate School, Annenberg School for Communication and Journalism, School of Communication, Program in Public Diplomacy, Los Angeles, CA 90089. Offers MPD. *Program availability:* Part-time. *Students:* 25 full-time (22 women); includes 11 minority (1 Black or African American, non-Hispanic/Latino; 2 Asian, non-Hispanic/Latino; 5 Hispanic/Latino; 1 Native Hawaiian or other Pacific Islander, non-Hispanic/Latino; 2 Two or more races, non-Hispanic/Latino), 11 international. Average age 26. 47 applicants, 47% accepted, 13 enrolled. In 2019, 17 master's awarded. *Degree requirements:* For master's, thesis. *Entrance requirements:* For master's, GRE, resume, writing samples, statement of purpose, recommendation letters. Additional exam requirements/recommendations for international students: required—TOEFL (minimum score 114 iBT), IELTS (minimum score 8). *Application deadline:* For fall admission, 1/15 priority date for domestic and international students. Application fee: $90. Electronic applications accepted. *Financial support:* In 2019–20, 6 fellowships (averaging $15,000 per year) were awarded; career-related internships or fieldwork, Federal Work-Study, and scholarships/grants also available. Support available to part-time students. Financial award application deadline: 1/15; financial award applicants required to submit FAFSA. *Unit head:* Dr. Robert David Banks, Faculty Program Co-Director, 213-821-7851, E-mail: robertdb@usc.edu. *Application contact:* Allyson Hill, Associate Dean for Admissions, 213-821-0770, Fax: 213-740-1933, E-mail: ascadm@usc.edu.
Website: http://www.annenberg.usc.edu

University of Southern California, Graduate School, Dana and David Dornsife College of Letters, Arts and Sciences, Political Science and International Relations PhD Program, Los Angeles, CA 90089. Offers PhD. *Degree requirements:* For doctorate, variable foreign language requirement, comprehensive exam, thesis/dissertation. *Entrance requirements:* For doctorate, GRE (minimum score 1000). Additional exam requirements/recommendations for international students: required—TOEFL (minimum score 600 paper-based; 100 iBT). Electronic applications accepted.

University of South Florida, Innovative Education, Tampa, FL 33620-9951. Offers adult, career and higher education (Graduate Certificate), including college teaching, leadership in developing human resources, leadership in higher education; Africana studies (Graduate Certificate), including diasporas and health disparities, genocide and human rights; aging studies (Graduate Certificate), including gerontology; art research (Graduate Certificate), including museum studies; business foundations (Graduate Certificate); chemical and biomedical engineering (Graduate Certificate), including materials science and engineering, water, health and sustainability; child and family studies (Graduate Certificate), including positive behavior support; civil and industrial engineering (Graduate Certificate), including transportation systems analysis; community and family health (Graduate Certificate), including maternal and child health, social marketing and public health, violence and injury: prevention and intervention, women's health; criminology (Graduate Certificate), including criminal justice administration; data science for public administration (Graduate Certificate); digital humanities (Graduate Certificate); educational measurement and research (Graduate Certificate), including evaluation; English (Graduate Certificate), including comparative literary studies, creative writing, professional and technical communication; entrepreneurship (Graduate Certificate); environmental health (Graduate Certificate), including safety management; epidemiology and biostatistics (Graduate Certificate), including applied biostatistics, biostatistics, concepts and tools of epidemiology, epidemiology, epidemiology of infectious diseases; geography, environment and planning (Graduate Certificate), including community development, environmental policy and management, geographical information systems; geology (Graduate Certificate), including hydrogeology; global health (Graduate Certificate), including disaster management, global health and Latin American and Caribbean studies, global health practice, humanitarian assistance, infection control; government and international affairs (Graduate Certificate), including Cuban studies, globalization studies; health policy and management (Graduate Certificate), including health management and leadership, public health policy and programs; hearing specialist: early intervention (Graduate Certificate); industrial and management systems engineering (Graduate Certificate), including systems engineering, technology management; information studies (Graduate Certificate), including school library media specialist; information systems/decision sciences (Graduate Certificate), including analytics and business intelligence; instructional technology (Graduate Certificate), including distance education, Florida digital/virtual educator, instructional design, multimedia design, Web design; internal medicine, bioethics and medical humanities (Graduate Certificate), including biomedical ethics; Latin American and Caribbean studies (Graduate Certificate); leadership for coastal resiliency planning (Graduate Certificate); mass communications (Graduate Certificate), including multimedia journalism; mathematics and statistics (Graduate Certificate), including mathematics; medicine (Graduate Certificate), including aging and neuroscience, bioinformatics, biotechnology, brain fitness and memory management, clinical investigation, hand and upper limb rehabilitation, health informatics, health sciences, integrative weight management, intellectual property, medicine and gender, metabolic and nutritional medicine, metabolic cardiology, pharmacy sciences; national and competitive intelligence (Graduate Certificate); nursing (Graduate Certificate), including simulation based academic fellowship in advanced pain management; psychological and social foundations (Graduate Certificate), including career counseling, college teaching, diversity in education, mental health counseling, school counseling; public affairs (Graduate Certificate), including nonprofit management, public management, research administration; public health (Graduate Certificate), including assessing chemical toxicity and public health risks, health equity, pharmacoepidemiology, public health generalist, toxicology, translational research in adolescent behavioral health; public health practices (Graduate Certificate), including planning for healthy communities; rehabilitation and mental health counseling (Graduate Certificate), including integrative mental health care, marriage and family therapy, rehabilitation technology; secondary education (Graduate Certificate), including ESOL, foreign language education: culture and content, foreign language education: professional; social work (Graduate Certificate), including geriatric social work/clinical gerontology; special education (Graduate Certificate), including autism spectrum disorder, disabilities education: severe/profound; world languages (Graduate Certificate), including teaching English as a second language (TESL) or foreign language. *Unit head:* Dr. Cynthia DeLuca, Associate Vice President and Assistant Vice Provost, 813-974-3077, Fax: 813-974-7061, E-mail: deluca@usf.edu. *Application contact:* Owen Hooper, Director, Summer and Alternative Calendar Programs, 813-974-6917, E-mail: hooper@usf.edu.
Website: http://www.usf.edu/innovative-education/

The University of Tennessee, Graduate School, College of Arts and Sciences, Department of Political Science, Program in Political Science, Knoxville, TN 37996. Offers MA, PhD. *Program availability:* Part-time. *Degree requirements:* For master's, thesis or alternative; for doctorate, one foreign language, thesis/dissertation. *Entrance requirements:* For master's and doctorate, GRE General Test, minimum GPA of 2.7. Additional exam requirements/recommendations for international students: required—TOEFL. Electronic applications accepted.

The University of Tennessee, Graduate School, College of Arts and Sciences, Department of Sociology, Knoxville, TN 37996. Offers criminology (MA, PhD); energy, environment, and resource policy (MA, PhD); political economy (MA, PhD). *Program availability:* Part-time. *Degree requirements:* For master's, thesis or alternative; for doctorate, thesis/dissertation. *Entrance requirements:* For master's, GRE General Test, minimum GPA of 3.0; for doctorate, GRE General Test, minimum GPA of 3.5. Additional exam requirements/recommendations for international students: required—TOEFL. Electronic applications accepted.

The University of Texas at Arlington, Graduate School, College of Liberal Arts, Department of Political Science, Arlington, TX 76019. Offers MA. *Program availability:* Part-time, evening/weekend. *Degree requirements:* For master's, comprehensive exam, thesis optional. *Entrance requirements:* For master's, GRE, minimum GPA of 3.0 in last 60 hours of course work. Additional exam requirements/recommendations for international students: required—TOEFL (minimum score 550 paper-based). Electronic applications accepted.

The University of Texas at Austin, Graduate School, College of Liberal Arts, Department of Government, Austin, TX 78712-1111. Offers MA, PhD, PhD/JD. *Degree requirements:* For master's, thesis; for doctorate, comprehensive exam, thesis/dissertation. *Entrance requirements:* For master's and doctorate, GRE General Test. Electronic applications accepted.

The University of Texas at Dallas, School of Economic, Political and Policy Sciences, Program in Political Science, Richardson, TX 75080. Offers Constitutional law (MA); legislative studies (MA); political science (MA, PhD). *Program availability:* Part-time, evening/weekend. *Faculty:* 13 full-time (3 women), 1 part-time/adjunct (0 women). *Students:* 23 full-time (8 women), 15 part-time (8 women); includes 10 minority (2 Black or African American, non-Hispanic/Latino; 1 Asian, non-Hispanic/Latino; 5 Hispanic/Latino; 2 Two or more races, non-Hispanic/Latino), 11 international. Average age 33. 24 applicants, 54% accepted, 5 enrolled. In 2019, 7 master's, 5 doctorates awarded. Terminal master's awarded for partial completion of doctoral program. *Degree requirements:* For master's, thesis optional, independent study; for doctorate, thesis/dissertation, practicum research. *Entrance requirements:* For master's, GRE (minimum combined verbal and quantitative score of 1100), minimum undergraduate GPA of 3.0; for doctorate, GRE (minimum combined verbal and quantitative score of 1200, writing 4.5), minimum undergraduate GPA of 3.2. Additional exam requirements/recommendations for international students: required—TOEFL (minimum score 550

paper-based). *Application deadline:* For fall admission, 7/15 for domestic students, 5/1 priority date for international students; for spring admission, 11/15 for domestic students, 9/1 priority date for international students. Applications are processed on a rolling basis. Application fee: $50 ($100 for international students). Electronic applications accepted. *Expenses: Tuition, area resident:* Full-time $16,504. Tuition, state resident: full-time $16,504. Tuition, nonresident: full-time $34,266. Tuition and fees vary according to course load. *Financial support:* In 2019–20, 12 students received support, including 2 research assistantships with partial tuition reimbursements available (averaging $18,000 per year), 10 teaching assistantships with partial tuition reimbursements available (averaging $13,500 per year); career-related internships or fieldwork, Federal Work-Study, institutionally sponsored loans, and scholarships/grants also available. Support available to part-time students. Financial award application deadline: 4/30; financial award applicants required to submit FAFSA. *Unit head:* Dr. Thomas Brunell, Program Head, 972-883-4963, Fax: 972-883-2735, E-mail: ph.psci@utdallas.edu. *Application contact:* Marjorie McDonald, Graduate Program Administrator, 972-883-6406, Fax: 972-883-2735, E-mail: psci@utdallas.edu.
Website: https://epps.utdallas.edu/about/programs/political-science/

The University of Texas at Dallas, School of Economic, Political and Policy Sciences, Program in Public Policy and Political Economy, Richardson, TX 75080. Offers international political economy (MS); public policy (MPP); public policy and political economy (PhD); social data analytics and research (MS). *Program availability:* Part-time, evening/weekend. *Faculty:* 26 full-time (4 women), 3 part-time/adjunct (0 women). *Students:* 51 full-time (25 women), 28 part-time (18 women); includes 29 minority (7 Black or African American, non-Hispanic/Latino; 5 Asian, non-Hispanic/Latino; 14 Hispanic/Latino; 3 Two or more races, non-Hispanic/Latino), 17 international. Average age 34. 48 applicants, 38% accepted, 18 enrolled. In 2019, 22 master's, 7 doctorates awarded. *Degree requirements:* For doctorate, thesis/dissertation. *Entrance requirements:* For master's and doctorate, GRE General Test, minimum GPA of 3.0 in upper-level course work in field. Additional exam requirements/recommendations for international students: required—TOEFL (minimum score 550 paper-based). *Application deadline:* For fall admission, 7/15 for domestic students, 5/1 priority date for international students; for spring admission, 11/15 for domestic students, 9/1 priority date for international students. Applications are processed on a rolling basis. Application fee: $50 ($100 for international students). Electronic applications accepted. *Expenses: Tuition, area resident:* Full-time $16,504. Tuition, state resident: full-time $16,504. Tuition, nonresident: full-time $34,266. Tuition and fees vary according to course load. *Financial support:* In 2019–20, 22 students received support, including 1 fellowship (averaging $2,000 per year), 2 research assistantships with partial tuition reimbursements available (averaging $18,000 per year), 17 teaching assistantships with partial tuition reimbursements available (averaging $13,500 per year); career-related internships or fieldwork, Federal Work-Study, institutionally sponsored loans, scholarships/grants, and unspecified assistantships also available. Support available to part-time students. Financial award application deadline: 4/30; financial award applicants required to submit FAFSA. *Unit head:* Dr. Thomas Brunell, Program Head, 972-883-4963, Fax: 972-883-6297, E-mail: ph.pppe@utdallas.edu. *Application contact:* Marjorie McDonald, Graduate Program Administrator, 972-883-6406, Fax: 972-883-6297, E-mail: pppe@utdallas.edu.
Website: https://epps.utdallas.edu/about/programs/public-policy-and-political-economy/

The University of Texas at El Paso, Graduate School, College of Liberal Arts, Department of Political Science, El Paso, TX 79968-0001. Offers MA. *Program availability:* Part-time, evening/weekend. *Degree requirements:* For master's, thesis optional. *Entrance requirements:* For master's, GRE, letters of recommendation, personal statement, transcripts. Additional exam requirements/recommendations for international students: required—TOEFL; recommended—IELTS. Electronic applications accepted.

The University of Texas at San Antonio, College of Liberal and Fine Arts, Department of Political Science and Geography, San Antonio, TX 78249-0617. Offers geography (MA); political science (MA). *Program availability:* Part-time, evening/weekend. *Degree requirements:* For master's, comprehensive exam (for some programs), thesis optional. *Entrance requirements:* For master's, GRE General Test or LSAT, 18 semester credit hours in upper-division undergraduate or graduate-level courses in political science or directly-related fields in the social or behavioral sciences; 3 letters of recommendation; statement of purpose. Additional exam requirements/recommendations for international students: required—TOEFL (minimum score 550 paper-based; 79 iBT), IELTS (minimum score 6.5). Electronic applications accepted.

The University of Texas of the Permian Basin, Office of Graduate Studies, College of Arts and Sciences, Department of Social Sciences, Odessa, TX 79762-0001. Offers criminal justice administration (MS); political science (MPA). *Program availability:* Part-time, evening/weekend. *Degree requirements:* For master's, comprehensive exam (for some programs), thesis (for some programs). *Entrance requirements:* For master's, GRE General Test. Additional exam requirements/recommendations for international students: required—TOEFL (minimum score 550 paper-based).

The University of Toledo, College of Graduate Studies, College of Languages, Literature and Social Sciences, Department of Political Science and Public Administration, Toledo, OH 43606-3390. Offers health care policy and administration (Certificate); management of non-profit organizations (Certificate); municipal administration (Certificate); political science (MA); public administration (MPA); JD/MPA. *Program availability:* Part-time. *Degree requirements:* For master's, comprehensive exam (for some programs), thesis. *Entrance requirements:* For master's, GRE General Test, minimum cumulative point-hour ratio of 2.7 (3.0 for MPA) for all previous academic work, three letters of recommendation, statement of purpose, transcripts from all prior institutions attended; for Certificate, minimum cumulative point-hour ratio of 2.7 for all previous academic work, three letters of recommendation, statement of purpose, transcripts from all prior institutions attended. Additional exam requirements/recommendations for international students: required—TOEFL (minimum score 550 paper-based; 80 iBT). Electronic applications accepted.

University of Toronto, School of Graduate Studies, Faculty of Arts and Science, Department of Political Science, Toronto, ON M5S 1A1, Canada. Offers MA, PhD, JD/MA, JD/PhD. *Program availability:* Part-time. *Degree requirements:* For master's, thesis optional; for doctorate, one foreign language, thesis/dissertation, reading competency in a language other than English. *Entrance requirements:* For master's, 3 letters of recommendation, writing sample, statement of scholarly intent, minimum cumulative GPA of B+ in a four-year bachelor's program including B+ average over five to eight suitably-distributed full-year political science courses; for doctorate, 4 letters of recommendation, writing sample, minimum A- in most recent political science (or equivalent) degree. Additional exam requirements/recommendations for international students: required—TOEFL (minimum score 580 paper-based; 93 iBT), TWE (minimum score 5). Electronic applications accepted.

University of Utah, Graduate School, College of Humanities, Program in Middle East Studies, Salt Lake City, UT 84112. Offers Arabic (MA, PhD); Hebrew (MA); history (MA, PhD); Persian (MA, PhD); political science (MA, PhD). In 2019, 2 doctorates awarded. *Entrance requirements:* For master's, GRE General Test, minimum GPA of 3.2; for doctorate, GRE General Test, MA in Middle East studies or equivalent, minimum GPA of 3.2. Additional exam requirements/recommendations for international students: required—TOEFL (minimum score 580 paper-based; 92 iBT); recommended—IELTS (minimum score 7). Application fee: $55 ($65 for international students). *Expenses:* Tuition, state resident: full-time $7085; part-time $272.51 per credit hour. Tuition, nonresident: full-time $24,937; part-time $959.12 per credit hour. *Required fees:* $880.52; $880.52 per semester. Tuition and fees vary according to degree level, program and student level. *Unit head:* Johanna Watzinger-Tharp, Director, 801-581-7148, Fax: 801-581-6105, E-mail: j.tharp@utah.edu. *Application contact:* Kellie Hubbard, Academic Advisor, 801-581-5362, Fax: 801-581-6105, E-mail: kellie.hubbard@utah.edu.
Website: http://www.mec.utah.edu

University of Utah, Graduate School, College of Social and Behavioral Science, Department of Political Science, Program in Political Science, Salt Lake City, UT 84112-1107. Offers American politics (MA, MS, PhD); comparative politics (MA, MS, PhD); international relations (MA, MS, PhD); political theory (MA, MS, PhD); public administration (MA, MS, PhD). *Program availability:* Part-time. *Faculty:* 21 full-time (6 women), 2 part-time/adjunct (0 women). *Students:* 100 full-time (55 women), 97 part-time (52 women); includes 36 minority (2 Black or African American, non-Hispanic/Latino; 4 Asian, non-Hispanic/Latino; 20 Hispanic/Latino; 1 Native Hawaiian or other Pacific Islander, non-Hispanic/Latino; 9 Two or more races, non-Hispanic/Latino), 6 international. Average age 32. 47 applicants, 66% accepted, 14 enrolled. In 2019, 84 master's, 5 doctorates awarded. Terminal master's awarded for partial completion of doctoral program. *Degree requirements:* For master's, final project, defense; for doctorate, comprehensive exam, thesis/dissertation. *Entrance requirements:* For master's and doctorate, GRE General Test, minimum GPA of 3.2. Additional exam requirements/recommendations for international students: required—TOEFL (minimum score 580 paper-based; 80 iBT), IELTS (minimum score 6.5). *Application deadline:* For fall admission, 1/15 priority date for domestic and international students. Application fee: $55 ($65 for international students). Electronic applications accepted. *Expenses:* General graduate tuition charged by the university. *Financial support:* In 2019–20, 2 students received support, including 1 fellowship (averaging $24,000 per year), 23 teaching assistantships (averaging $11,043 per year); research assistantships and unspecified assistantships also available. Financial award application deadline: 4/1; financial award applicants required to submit CSS PROFILE or FAFSA. *Unit head:* Dr. Brent J. Steele, Department Chair and Professor, 801-581-7031, Fax: 801-585-6492, E-mail: brent.steele@utah.edu. *Application contact:* Sandy Hiskey, Graduate Academic Advisor, 801-581-8608, Fax: 801-585-6492, E-mail: sandy.hiskey@utah.edu.
Website: http://www.poli-sci.utah.edu/

University of Victoria, Faculty of Graduate Studies, Faculty of Social Sciences, Department of Political Science, Victoria, BC V8W 2Y2, Canada. Offers MA, PhD. *Program availability:* Part-time. *Degree requirements:* For master's, thesis; for doctorate, thesis/dissertation, candidacy exam. *Entrance requirements:* For master's, minimum B+ average in last 2 years of undergraduate course work. Additional exam requirements/recommendations for international students: required—TOEFL (minimum score 600 paper-based). Electronic applications accepted.

University of Virginia, College and Graduate School of Arts and Sciences, Department of Politics, Program in Government, Charlottesville, VA 22903. Offers MA, PhD, JD/MA, MBA/MA. *Degree requirements:* For master's, 2 research/statistics courses or thesis; for doctorate, variable foreign language requirement, thesis/dissertation, 2 research/statistics courses. *Entrance requirements:* For master's and doctorate, GRE General Test, long writing sample; 2 letters of recommendation. Additional exam requirements/recommendations for international students: required—TOEFL (minimum score 600 paper-based; 90 iBT), IELTS (minimum score 7). Electronic applications accepted.

University of Washington, Graduate School, College of Arts and Sciences, Department of Political Science, Seattle, WA 98195. Offers MA, PhD. *Degree requirements:* For doctorate, thesis/dissertation. *Entrance requirements:* For master's and doctorate, GRE General Test, minimum GPA of 3.0. Additional exam requirements/recommendations for international students: required—TOEFL. Electronic applications accepted.

University of Waterloo, Graduate Studies and Postdoctoral Affairs, Faculty of Arts, Department of Political Science, Waterloo, ON N2L 3G1, Canada. Offers global governance (MA, PhD). *Program availability:* Part-time. *Degree requirements:* For master's, thesis (for some programs), research paper. *Entrance requirements:* For master's, honors degree, minimum B average, writing sample. Additional exam requirements/recommendations for international students: required—TOEFL, IELTS, PTE. Electronic applications accepted.

University of Waterloo, Graduate Studies and Postdoctoral Affairs, Faculty of Arts, Global Governance Program, Waterloo, ON N2L 3G1, Canada. Offers MA, PhD. *Entrance requirements:* For doctorate, MA. Additional exam requirements/recommendations for international students: required—TOEFL, IELTS, PTE. Electronic applications accepted.

The University of Western Ontario, School of Graduate and Postdoctoral Studies, Faculty of Social Science, Department of Political Science, London, ON N6A 3K7, Canada. Offers MA, MPA, PhD. *Program availability:* Part-time. *Degree requirements:* For master's, thesis; for doctorate, comprehensive exam, thesis/dissertation. *Entrance requirements:* For master's, minimum B average, honors BA in political science or equivalent, sample of written work; for doctorate, MA in political science or equivalent.

University of West Florida, College of Arts, Social Sciences, and Humanities, Department of Government, Pensacola, FL 32514-5750. Offers political science (MA), including political science, security and diplomacy. *Program availability:* Part-time, evening/weekend. *Degree requirements:* For master's, thesis or alternative. *Entrance requirements:* For master's, GRE, official transcripts; minimum GPA of 3.0; 500-word writing sample in form of letter of intent; resume. Additional exam requirements/recommendations for international students: required—TOEFL (minimum score 550 paper-based).

University of Windsor, Faculty of Graduate Studies, Faculty of Arts and Social Sciences, Department of Political Science, Windsor, ON N9B 3P4, Canada. Offers MA. *Program availability:* Part-time. *Entrance requirements:* For master's, minimum B+ average. Additional exam requirements/recommendations for international students: required—TOEFL (minimum score 600 paper-based). Electronic applications accepted.

University of Wisconsin–Madison, Graduate School, College of Letters and Science, Department of Political Science, Madison, WI 53706-1380. Offers PhD. *Degree requirements:* For doctorate, thesis/dissertation. *Entrance requirements:* For doctorate, GRE General Test. Electronic applications accepted.

University of Wisconsin–Milwaukee, Graduate School, College of Letters and Science, Department of Political Science, Milwaukee, WI 53201-0413. Offers MA, PhD. *Degree requirements:* For master's, thesis or alternative; for doctorate, one foreign language, thesis/dissertation. *Entrance requirements:* For master's and doctorate, GRE General Test, minimum GPA of 3.0. Additional exam requirements/recommendations for international students: required—TOEFL (minimum score 550 paper-based; 79 iBT), IELTS (minimum score 6.5). Electronic applications accepted.

Political Science

University of Wyoming, College of Arts and Sciences, School of Politics, Public Affairs and International Studies, Program in Political Science, Laramie, WY 82071. Offers MA. *Program availability:* Part-time. *Degree requirements:* For master's, thesis or alternative. *Entrance requirements:* For master's, GRE General Test, bachelor's degree in political science, minimum GPA of 3.0. Additional exam requirements/recommendations for international students: required—TOEFL (minimum score 525 paper-based). Electronic applications accepted.

Université Laval, Faculty of Social Sciences, Department of Political Science, Program in Policy Analysis, Québec, QC G1K 7P4, Canada. Offers MA. *Degree requirements:* For master's, thesis (for some programs). *Entrance requirements:* For master's, knowledge of French, comprehension of written English. Electronic applications accepted.

Université Laval, Faculty of Social Sciences, Department of Political Science, Programs in Political Science, Québec, QC G1K 7P4, Canada. Offers MA, PhD. Terminal master's awarded for partial completion of doctoral program. *Degree requirements:* For master's, thesis (for some programs); for doctorate, comprehensive exam, thesis/dissertation. *Entrance requirements:* For master's, knowledge of French; for doctorate, knowledge of French, comprehension of written English. Electronic applications accepted.

Utah State University, School of Graduate Studies, College of Humanities and Social Sciences, Department of Political Science, Logan, UT 84322. Offers MA, MS. *Program availability:* Part-time. *Degree requirements:* For master's, one foreign language, thesis. *Entrance requirements:* For master's, GRE General Test, minimum GPA of 3.0. Additional exam requirements/recommendations for international students: required—TOEFL.

Vanderbilt University, Department of Political Science, Nashville, TN 37240-1001. Offers MA, MAT, PhD. *Faculty:* 20 full-time (7 women). *Students:* 44 full-time (24 women); includes 3 minority (1 Black or African American, non-Hispanic/Latino; 1 Asian, non-Hispanic/Latino; 1 Two or more races, non-Hispanic/Latino), 14 international. Average age 29. 178 applicants, 11% accepted, 8 enrolled. In 2019, 5 master's, 2 doctorates awarded. Terminal master's awarded for partial completion of doctoral program. *Degree requirements:* For master's, thesis; for doctorate, thesis/dissertation, final and qualifying exams. *Entrance requirements:* For master's and doctorate, GRE General Test, writing sample. Additional exam requirements/recommendations for international students: required—TOEFL (minimum score 570 paper-based; 88 iBT). *Application deadline:* For fall admission, 1/15 for domestic and international students. Electronic applications accepted. *Expenses: Tuition:* Full-time $51,018; part-time $2087 per hour. *Required fees:* $542. Tuition and fees vary according to program. *Financial support:* Fellowships with full tuition reimbursements, research assistantships with full tuition reimbursements, teaching assistantships with full tuition reimbursements, Federal Work-Study, institutionally sponsored loans, scholarships/grants, and health care benefits available. Financial award application deadline: 1/15; financial award applicants required to submit CSS PROFILE or FAFSA. *Unit head:* Dr. Alan Wiseman, Chair, 615-322-6222, Fax: 615-343-6003, E-mail: alan.wiseman@vanderbilt.edu. *Application contact:* Emily Ritter, Director of Graduate Studies, 615-936-9795, Fax: 615-343-6003, E-mail: emily.h.ritter@vanderbilt.edu.
Website: http://www.vanderbilt.edu/political-science/

Villanova University, Graduate School of Liberal Arts and Sciences, Department of Political Science, Villanova, PA 19085-1699. Offers MA. *Program availability:* Part-time, evening/weekend, online learning. *Degree requirements:* For master's, comprehensive exam (for some programs). *Entrance requirements:* For master's, GRE, minimum GPA of 3.0. Additional exam requirements/recommendations for international students: required—TOEFL. Electronic applications accepted.

Virginia Commonwealth University, Graduate School, L. Douglas Wilder School of Government and Public Affairs, Richmond, VA 23284-9005. Offers MA, MPA, MS, MURP, PhD, Certificate, Graduate Certificate, Postbaccalaureate Certificate.

Virginia Polytechnic Institute and State University, VT Online, Blacksburg, VA 24061. Offers advanced transportation systems (Certificate); aerospace engineering (MS); agricultural and life sciences (MSLFS); business information systems (Graduate Certificate); career and technical education (MS); civil engineering (MS); computer engineering (M Eng, MS); decision support systems (Graduate Certificate); eLearning leadership (MA); electrical engineering (M Eng, MS); engineering administration (MEA); environmental engineering (Certificate); environmental politics and policy (Graduate Certificate); environmental sciences and engineering (MS); foundations of political analysis (Graduate Certificate); health product risk management (Graduate Certificate); industrial and systems engineering (MS); information policy and society (Graduate Certificate); information security (Graduate Certificate); information technology (MIT); instructional technology (MA); integrative STEM education (MA Ed); liberal arts (Graduate Certificate); life sciences: health product risk management (MS); natural resources (MNR, Graduate Certificate); networking (Graduate Certificate); nonprofit and nongovernmental organization management (Graduate Certificate); ocean engineering (MS); political science (MA); security studies (Graduate Certificate); software development (Graduate Certificate). *Expenses:* Tuition, state resident: full-time $13,700; part-time $761.25 per credit hour. Tuition, nonresident: full-time $27,614; part-time $1534 per credit hour. *Required fees:* $886.50 per term. Tuition and fees vary according to campus/location and program.

Walden University, Graduate Programs, School of Public Policy and Administration, Minneapolis, MN 55401. Offers criminal justice (MPA, MPP, MS, Graduate Certificate), including emergency management (MS, PhD), general program (MS), global leadership (MS, PhD), homeland security and policy coordination (MS, PhD), law and public policy (MS, PhD), policy analysis (MS, PhD), public management and leadership (MS, PhD), self-designed (MS), terrorism, mediation, and peace (MS, PhD); criminal justice and executive management (MS), including global leadership (MS, PhD); criminal justice leadership and executive management (MS), including emergency management (MS, PhD), general program, homeland security and policy coordination (MS, PhD), law and public policy (MS, PhD), policy analysis (MS, PhD), public management and leadership (MS, PhD), self-designed, terrorism, mediation, and peace (MS, PhD); emergency management (MPA, MPP, MS), including criminal justice (MS, PhD), general program (MS), homeland security (MS), public management and leadership (MS, PhD), terrorism and emergency management (MS); general program (MPA, MPP); global leadership (MPA, MPP); government management (Graduate Certificate); health policy (MPA, MPP); homeland security (Graduate Certificate); homeland security and policy coordination (MPA, MPP); international nongovernmental organizations (MPA, MPP); law and public policy (MPA, MPP); local government management for sustainable communities (MPA, MPP); nonprofit management (Graduate Certificate); nonprofit management and leadership (MPA, MPP, MS), including global leadership (MS, PhD), international nongovernmental organization (MS), local government for sustainable communities (MS), self-designed (MS); online teaching in higher education (Post-Master's Certificate); policy analysis (MPA); public management and leadership (MPA, MPP, Graduate Certificate); public policy (Graduate Certificate); public policy and administration (PhD), including criminal justice (MS, PhD), emergency management (MS, PhD), global leadership (MS, PhD), health policy, homeland security and policy

coordination (MS, PhD), international nongovernmental organizations, law and public policy (MS, PhD), local government management for sustainable communities, nonprofit management and leadership, policy analysis (MS, PhD), public management and leadership (MS, PhD), terrorism, mediation, and peace (MS, PhD); strategic planning and public policy (Graduate Certificate); terrorism, mediation, and peace (MPA, MPP). *Program availability:* Part-time, evening/weekend, online only, 100% online. *Degree requirements:* For doctorate, thesis/dissertation, residency. *Entrance requirements:* For master's, bachelor's degree or higher; minimum GPA of 2.5; official transcripts; goal statement (for some programs); access to computer and Internet; for doctorate, master's degree or higher; three years of related professional or academic experience (preferred); minimum GPA of 3.0; goal statement and current resume (for select programs); official transcripts; access to computer and Internet; for other advanced degree, relevant work experience; access to computer and Internet. Additional exam requirements/recommendations for international students: required—TOEFL (minimum score 550 paper-based, 79 iBT), IELTS (minimum score 6.5), Michigan English Language Assessment Battery (minimum score 82), or PTE (minimum score 53). Electronic applications accepted.

Washington State University, College of Arts and Sciences, School of Politics, Philosophy and Public Affairs, Pullman, WA 99164-4880. Offers bioethics (Graduate Certificate); political science (MA, PhD); public affairs (MPA). *Accreditation:* NASPAA. *Program availability:* Online learning. Terminal master's awarded for partial completion of doctoral program. *Degree requirements:* For master's, comprehensive exam (for some programs), thesis, oral exam; for doctorate, comprehensive exam, thesis/dissertation, oral exam, written exam. *Entrance requirements:* For master's, GRE General Test, minimum GPA of 3.0; for doctorate, GRE General Test, minimum GPA of 3.5. Additional exam requirements/recommendations for international students: required—TOEFL. Electronic applications accepted.

Washington University in St. Louis, The Graduate School, Department of Political Science, St. Louis, MO 63130-4899. Offers PhD. *Degree requirements:* For doctorate, thesis/dissertation. *Entrance requirements:* For doctorate, GRE General Test. Additional exam requirements/recommendations for international students: required—TOEFL. Electronic applications accepted.

Wayne State University, College of Liberal Arts and Sciences, Department of Political Science, Detroit, MI 48202. Offers political science (MA, PhD); public administration (MPA), including economic development policy and management, health and human services policy and management, human and fiscal resource management, nonprofit policy and management, organizational behavior and management, urban and metropolitan policy and management; JD/MA. *Accreditation:* NASPAA. *Program availability:* Part-time, evening/weekend. *Faculty:* 22 full-time (9 women). *Students:* 50 full-time (22 women), 64 part-time (32 women); includes 28 minority (20 Black or African American, non-Hispanic/Latino; 2 Asian, non-Hispanic/Latino; 1 Hispanic/Latino; 5 Two or more races, non-Hispanic/Latino), 10 international. Average age 34. 105 applicants, 40% accepted, 24 enrolled. In 2019, 21 master's, 7 doctorates awarded. Terminal master's awarded for partial completion of doctoral program. *Degree requirements:* For master's, comprehensive exam (for some programs), thesis (for some programs); for doctorate, thesis/dissertation. *Entrance requirements:* For master's, GRE General Test, substantial undergraduate preparation in the social sciences, minimum upper-division undergraduate GPA of 3.0, two letters of recommendation, personal statement; for doctorate, GRE General Test, 3 letters of recommendation; personal statement; interview. Additional exam requirements/recommendations for international students: required—TOEFL (minimum score 550 paper-based; 79 iBT), TWE (minimum score 5.5), Michigan English Language Assessment Battery (minimum score 85); recommended—IELTS (minimum score 6.5). *Application deadline:* For fall admission, 5/15 for domestic students, 5/1 priority date for international students; for winter admission, 10/15 for domestic students, 9/1 priority date for international students. Applications are processed on a rolling basis. Application fee: $50. Electronic applications accepted. *Expenses:* $678.55 per credit in-state tuition, $1,469.75 per credit out-of-state tuition, $54.56 per credit hour student service fee, $315.70 registration fee. *Financial support:* In 2019–20, 48 students received support, including 4 fellowships with partial tuition reimbursements available (averaging $57,000 per year), 1 research assistantship with partial tuition reimbursement available (averaging $45,000 per year), 13 teaching assistantships with partial tuition reimbursements available (averaging $58,000 per year); scholarships/grants, health care benefits, and unspecified assistantships also available. Financial award applicants required to submit FAFSA. *Unit head:* Dr. Daniel Geller, Professor and Chair, 313-577-6328, E-mail: dgeller@wayne.edu. *Application contact:* Dr. Jeffrey Grynaviski, Graduate Director, 313-577-2620, E-mail: gradpolisci@wayne.edu.
Website: http://clas.wayne.edu/politicalscience/

Western Illinois University, School of Graduate Studies, College of Arts and Sciences, Department of Political Science, Macomb, IL 61455-1390. Offers MA. *Program availability:* Part-time. *Degree requirements:* For master's, comprehensive exam, thesis or alternative. *Entrance requirements:* Additional exam requirements/recommendations for international students: required—TOEFL (minimum score 550 paper-based; 80 iBT). Electronic applications accepted.

Western Kentucky University, Graduate School, Potter College of Arts and Letters, Department of Political Science, Bowling Green, KY 42101. Offers MPA. *Accreditation:* NASPAA. *Program availability:* Part-time, evening/weekend. *Degree requirements:* For master's, comprehensive exam, final exam. *Entrance requirements:* For master's, GRE General Test, minimum GPA of 2.75. Additional exam requirements/recommendations for international students: required—TOEFL (minimum score 555 paper-based; 79 iBT).

Western Michigan University, Graduate College, College of Arts and Sciences, Department of Political Science, Kalamazoo, MI 49008. Offers international development administration (MIDA), including Peace Corps; political science (MA, PhD). *Degree requirements:* For master's, thesis optional; for doctorate, thesis/dissertation.

Western Washington University, Graduate School, College of Humanities and Social Sciences, Department of Political Science, Bellingham, WA 98225-5996. Offers MA. *Program availability:* Part-time. *Degree requirements:* For master's, comprehensive exam, thesis (for some programs). *Entrance requirements:* For master's, GRE General Test, minimum GPA of 3.0 in last 60 semester hours or last 90 quarter hours. Additional exam requirements/recommendations for international students: required—TOEFL (minimum score 567 paper-based). Electronic applications accepted.

West Virginia University, Eberly College of Arts and Sciences, Morgantown, WV 26506. Offers biology (MS, PhD); chemistry (MS, PhD); communication studies (MA, PhD); computational statistics (PhD); creative writing (MFA); English (MA, PhD); forensic and investigative science (MS); forensic science (PhD); geography (MA); geology (MA, PhD); history (MA, PhD); legal studies (MLS); mathematics (MS); physics (MS, PhD); political science (MA, PhD); professional writing and editing (MA); psychology (MA); public administration (MPA); social work (MSW); sociology (MA, PhD); statistics (MS). *Program availability:* Part-time, evening/weekend, online learning. Terminal master's awarded for partial completion of doctoral program. *Degree requirements:* For master's, thesis (for some programs); for doctorate, comprehensive exam, thesis/dissertation. *Entrance requirements:* For master's and doctorate, GRE.

Additional exam requirements/recommendations for international students: required—TOEFL (minimum score 600 paper-based); recommended—TWE. Electronic applications accepted.

Wilfrid Laurier University, Faculty of Graduate and Postdoctoral Studies, Faculty of Arts, Department of Political Science, Waterloo, ON N2L 3C5, Canada. Offers Canadian political studies (MA); comparative politics/international relations (MA). *Program availability:* Part-time. *Degree requirements:* For master's, thesis optional. *Entrance requirements:* For master's, honors bachelor's degree or the equivalent in political science, minimum B average in undergraduate course work. Additional exam requirements/recommendations for international students: required—TOEFL (minimum score 89 iBT). Electronic applications accepted.

Wilfrid Laurier University, Faculty of Graduate and Postdoctoral Studies, School of International Policy and Governance, Global Governance Program, Waterloo, ON N2L 3C5, Canada. Offers conflict and security (PhD); global environment (PhD); global justice and human rights (PhD); global political economy (PhD); global social governance (PhD); multilateral institutions and diplomacy (PhD). *Degree requirements:* For doctorate, thesis/dissertation. *Entrance requirements:* For doctorate, MA in political science, history, economics, international development studies, international peace studies, globalization studies, environmental studies or related field with minimum A-. Additional exam requirements/recommendations for international students: required—TOEFL (minimum score 89 iBT). Electronic applications accepted.

Wilfrid Laurier University, Faculty of Graduate and Postdoctoral Studies, School of International Policy and Governance, International Public Policy Program, Waterloo, ON N2L 3C5, Canada. Offers global governance (MIPP); human security (MIPP); international economic relations (MIPP); international environmental policy (MIPP). *Entrance requirements:* For master's, honours BA with minimum B average. Additional exam requirements/recommendations for international students: required—TOEFL (minimum score 89 iBT). Electronic applications accepted.

Yale University, Graduate School of Arts and Sciences, Department of Political Science, New Haven, CT 06520. Offers PhD. *Degree requirements:* For doctorate, one foreign language, thesis/dissertation. *Entrance requirements:* For doctorate, GRE General Test.

York University, Faculty of Graduate Studies, Faculty of Liberal Arts and Professional Studies, Program in Political Science, Toronto, ON M3J 1P3, Canada. Offers MA, PhD. *Program availability:* Part-time. *Degree requirements:* For master's, thesis or alternative; for doctorate, one foreign language, comprehensive exam, thesis/dissertation. Electronic applications accepted.

York University, Faculty of Graduate Studies, Program in Social and Political Thought, Toronto, ON M3J 1P3, Canada. Offers MA, PhD. *Program availability:* Part-time. *Degree requirements:* For master's, one foreign language, thesis or alternative, oral exams; for doctorate, one foreign language, comprehensive exam, thesis/dissertation. Electronic applications accepted.

Section 24
Psychology and Counseling

This section contains a directory of institutions offering graduate work in psychology and counseling, followed by in-depth entries submitted by institutions that chose to prepare detailed program descriptions. Additional information about programs listed in the directory but not augmented by an in-depth entry may be obtained by writing directly to the dean of a graduate school or chair of a department at the address given in the directory.

For programs offering related work, see also in this book *Criminology and Forensics, Family and Consumer Sciences,* and *Sociology, Anthropology, and Archaeology.* In the other guides in this series:

Graduate Programs in the Biological/Biomedical Sciences & Health-Related Medical Professions

See *Biological and Biomedical Sciences; Genetics, Developmental Biology, and Reproductive Biology; Neuroscience and Neurobiology; Nursing (Psychiatric Nursing); Pharmacy and Pharmaceutical Sciences; Pharmacology and Toxicology;* and *Public Health*

Graduate Programs in Business, Education, Information Studies, Law & Social Work

See *Education* and *Social Work*

CONTENTS

Program Directories

Psychology—General

Abilene Christian University, Office of Graduate Programs, College of Arts and Sciences, Department of Psychology, Abilene, TX 79699. Offers clinical psychology (MS); counseling psychology (MS); psychology (MS); school psychology (Specialist). *Program availability:* Part-time. *Faculty:* 11 part-time/adjunct (3 women). *Students:* 24 full-time (19 women), 8 part-time (7 women); includes 8 minority (3 Black or African American, non-Hispanic/Latino; 5 Hispanic/Latino), 2 international. 99 applicants, 27% accepted, 10 enrolled. In 2019, 23 master's awarded. *Degree requirements:* For master's, comprehensive exam, thesis (for some programs), practicum; internship. *Entrance requirements:* For master's, official transcripts, purpose statement, Recommendations. Additional exam requirements/recommendations for international students: required—TOEFL (minimum score 80 iBT), IELTS (minimum score 6), PTE (minimum score 51). *Application deadline:* For fall admission, 3/30 priority date for domestic students, 2/15 for international students. Applications are processed on a rolling basis. Application fee: $65. Electronic applications accepted. *Expenses:* *Tuition:* Full-time $22,356; part-time $1242 per credit hour. Tuition and fees vary according to program. *Financial support:* In 2019–20, 25 students received support, including 28 research assistantships with partial tuition reimbursements available; career-related internships or fieldwork, Federal Work-Study, and scholarships/grants also available. Support available to part-time students. Financial award application deadline: 4/1; financial award applicants required to submit FAFSA. *Unit head:* Dr. Cherisse Flanagan, Graduate Program Director, 325-674-2282, Fax: 325-674-6968, E-mail: cyf07a@acu.edu. *Application contact:* Graduate Admissions, 325-674-6911, E-mail: gradinfo@acu.edu.
Website: http://www.acu.edu/on-campus/graduate/college-of-arts-and-sciences/psychology-department.html

Acadia University, Faculty of Pure and Applied Science, Department of Psychology, Wolfville, NS B4P 2R6, Canada. Offers clinical psychology (M Sc). *Entrance requirements:* For master's, GRE General Test, GRE Subject Test, honors degree or equivalent. Additional exam requirements/recommendations for international students: required—TOEFL (minimum score 580 paper-based; 93 iBT), IELTS (minimum score 6.5).

Adelphi University, Gordon F. Derner School of Psychology, Program in General Psychology, Garden City, NY 11530-0701. Offers MA. *Degree requirements:* For master's, comprehensive exam. *Entrance requirements:* For master's, 2 letters of recommendation; minimum GPA of 3.0; course work in psychology including developmental psychology, psychopathology, and research design or experimental psychology; personal essay; transcripts from all previously-attended schools. Additional exam requirements/recommendations for international students: required—TOEFL (minimum score 550 paper-based; 80 iBT). Electronic applications accepted. *Expenses:* Contact institution.

Alabama Agricultural and Mechanical University, School of Graduate Studies, College of Education, Humanities, and Behavioral Sciences, Department of Social Work, Psychology and Counseling, Huntsville, AL 35811. Offers psychology and counseling (MS, Ed S), including clinical psychology (MS), counseling psychology (MS), guidance and counseling, rehabilitation counseling (MS), school counseling (MS), school psychology (MS), school psychometry (MS); social work (MSW). *Accreditation:* CORE; NCATE. *Program availability:* Part-time, evening/weekend. *Degree requirements:* For master's, comprehensive exam. *Entrance requirements:* For master's, GRE General Test. Additional exam requirements/recommendations for international students: required—TOEFL (minimum score 500 paper-based; 61 iBT).

Albizu University - Miami, Graduate Programs, Doral, FL 33172. Offers clinical psychology (PhD, Psy D); entrepreneurship (MBA); exceptional student education (MS); human services (PhD); industrial/organizational psychology (MS); marriage and family therapy (MS); mental health counseling (MS); nonprofit management (MBA); organizational management (MBA); school counseling (MS); speech and language pathology (MS); teaching English for speakers of other languages (MS). *Accreditation:* APA. *Program availability:* Part-time, 100% online, blended/hybrid learning. *Faculty:* 28 full-time (21 women), 27 part-time/adjunct (15 women). *Students:* 410 full-time (351 women), 190 part-time (163 women); includes 519 minority (33 Black or African American, non-Hispanic/Latino; 3 Asian, non-Hispanic/Latino; 477 Hispanic/Latino; 6 Two or more races, non-Hispanic/Latino), 21 international. Average age 33. 286 applicants, 66% accepted, 127 enrolled. In 2019, 96 master's, 54 doctorates awarded. Terminal master's awarded for partial completion of doctoral program. *Degree requirements:* For master's, comprehensive exam (for some programs), integrative project (for MBA); research project (for exceptional student education, teaching English as a second language); comprehensive examination for Speech and Language Pathology; for doctorate, comprehensive exam, thesis/dissertation, comprehensive examinations, internship, project/dissertation. *Entrance requirements:* For master's, GRE/EXADEP, bachelor's degree from accredited institution, minimum GPA of 3.0, 3 letters of recommendation, interview, resume, statement of purpose, official transcripts; for doctorate, GRE (for Psy D), 3 letters of recommendation, resume, interview, statement of purpose, official transcripts; bachelor's degree and minimum GPA of 3.25 (for Psy D); master's degree and minimum GPA of 3.0 (for PhD). Additional exam requirements/recommendations for international students: required—Michigan Test of English Language Proficiency. *Application deadline:* For fall admission, 4/1 priority date for domestic students, 5/1 priority date for international students; for spring admission, 11/1 priority date for domestic students, 9/1 priority date for international students. Applications are processed on a rolling basis. Application fee: $50. Electronic applications accepted. Application fee is waived when completed online. *Expenses:* $600 per credit or $620 per credit or $650 per credit (for master's depending on field); $800 per credit or $1,050 per credit (for doctoral depending on program). *Financial support:* In 2019–20, 158 students received support. Federal Work-Study, scholarships/grants, unspecified assistantships, and tuition discounts available. Financial award application deadline: 6/1; financial award applicants required to submit FAFSA. *Unit head:* Dr. Tilokie Depoo, PhD, Chancellor, 305-593-1223 Ext. 3138, Fax: 305-477-8983, E-mail: tdepoo@albizu.edu. *Application contact:* Nancy Alvarez, Director of Enrollment Management, 305-593-1223 Ext. 3136, Fax: 305-593-1854, E-mail: nalvarez@albizu.edu.
Website: www.albizu.edu

Albizu University - San Juan, Graduate Programs, San Juan, PR 00901. Offers clinical psychology (MS, PhD, Psy D); general psychology (PhD); industrial/organizational psychology (MS, PhD); speech and language pathology (MS). *Accreditation:* APA (one or more programs are accredited). *Program availability:* Part-time, evening/weekend. Terminal master's awarded for partial completion of doctoral program. *Degree requirements:* For master's, one foreign language, comprehensive exam, thesis; for doctorate, one foreign language, comprehensive exam, thesis/dissertation, written qualifying exams. *Entrance requirements:* For master's, GRE General Test or EXADEP, interview; minimum GPA of 2.8 (industrial/organizational psychology); for doctorate, GRE General Test or EXADEP, interview; minimum GPA of 3.0 (PhD in industrial/organizational psychology and clinical psychology), 3.25 (Psy D).

Alliant International University–Fresno, California School of Professional Psychology, Fresno, CA 93727. Offers MA, PhD, Psy D, MA/PhD, Psy D/MA. *Accreditation:* APA. *Degree requirements:* For doctorate, comprehensive exam, thesis/dissertation. *Entrance requirements:* For doctorate, minimum GPA of 3.0, letters of recommendation, essay, interview. Additional exam requirements/recommendations for international students: required—TOEFL (minimum score 550 paper-based), TWE (minimum score 5). Electronic applications accepted.

Alliant International University - Los Angeles, California School of Professional Psychology, Alhambra, CA 91803. Offers MA, PhD, Psy D. *Accreditation:* APA. *Degree requirements:* For doctorate, comprehensive exam, thesis/dissertation. *Entrance requirements:* For doctorate, interview, minimum GPA of 3.0 in psychology and overall, letters of recommendation. Additional exam requirements/recommendations for international students: required—TOEFL (minimum score 600 paper-based), TWE (minimum score 5). Electronic applications accepted.

Alliant International University–Sacramento, California School of Professional Psychology, Sacramento, CA 95833. Offers MA, Psy D. *Program availability:* Part-time. *Degree requirements:* For doctorate, comprehensive exam, thesis/dissertation. *Entrance requirements:* For master's and doctorate, minimum GPA of 3.0, recommendations, essay. Additional exam requirements/recommendations for international students: required—TOEFL (minimum score 550 paper-based), TWE (minimum score 5). Electronic applications accepted.

Alliant International University - San Diego, California School of Professional Psychology, San Diego, CA 92131. Offers MA, MS, PhD, Psy D. *Accreditation:* APA. *Program availability:* Part-time. Terminal master's awarded for partial completion of doctoral program. *Degree requirements:* For master's, practicum; for doctorate, comprehensive exam, thesis/dissertation, internship or practicum. *Entrance requirements:* For master's and doctorate, minimum GPA of 3.0, essay, letters of recommendation, interview. Additional exam requirements/recommendations for international students: required—TOEFL (minimum score 550 paper-based; 80 iBT), TWE (minimum score 5).

Alliant International University–San Francisco, California School of Professional Psychology, San Francisco, CA 94133. Offers MA, Post-Doctoral MS, PhD, Psy D, Certificate. *Accreditation:* APA (one or more programs are accredited). *Degree requirements:* For doctorate, comprehensive exam, thesis/dissertation, internship. *Entrance requirements:* For master's and doctorate, minimum GPA of 3.0, recommendations, essay, interview. Additional exam requirements/recommendations for international students: required—TOEFL (minimum score 550 paper-based; 80 iBT), TWE (minimum score 5). Electronic applications accepted.

American International College, School of Business, Arts and Sciences, Springfield, MA 01109-3189. Offers accounting and taxation (MS); business administration (MBA); clinical psychology (MA); educational psychology (Ed D); forensic psychology (MS); general psychology (MA, CAGS); management (CAGS); resort and casino management (MBA, CAGS). *Program availability:* Part-time, evening/weekend. *Degree requirements:* For master's, practicum; for doctorate, comprehensive exam, thesis/dissertation, practicum. *Entrance requirements:* For master's, BS or BA, minimum undergraduate GPA of 2.75, 2 letters of recommendation, official transcripts, personal goal statement or essay; for doctorate, 3 letters of recommendation; BS or BA; minimum undergraduate GPA of 3.0 (3.25 recommended); official transcripts; personal goal statement or essay. Additional exam requirements/recommendations for international students: required—TOEFL (minimum score 550 paper-based; 80 iBT). *Expenses:* Contact institution.

American University, College of Arts and Sciences, Department of Psychology, Washington, DC 22016-8062. Offers addiction and addictive behavior (Certificate); behavior, cognition, and neuroscience (PhD); clinical psychology (PhD); psychobiology of healing (Certificate); psychology (MA). *Accreditation:* APA. *Program availability:* Part-time. *Degree requirements:* For master's, comprehensive exam, thesis or alternative; for doctorate, comprehensive exam, thesis/dissertation. *Entrance requirements:* For master's, GRE General Test, GRE Subject Test; Please website: https://www.american.edu/cas/psychology/, statement of purpose, transcripts, 2 letters of recommendation; for doctorate, GRE General Test, GRE Subject Test, 3 letters of recommendation, statement of purpose, transcripts, resume. Additional exam requirements/recommendations for international students: required—TOEFL (minimum score 600 paper-based; 100 iBT). *Expenses:* Contact institution.

The American University in Cairo, School of Humanities and Social Sciences, Cairo, Egypt. Offers Arab and Islamic civilizations (Graduate Diploma); Arabic studies (MA); comparative literary studies (Graduate Diploma); Egyptology and Coptology (MA); English and comparative literature (MA); humanities and social sciences (Graduate Diploma); philosophy (MA); psychology (MA); sociology and anthropology (MA); teaching Arabic as a foreign language (MA); teaching English to speakers of other languages (MA). *Program availability:* Part-time, evening/weekend. *Degree requirements:* For master's, comprehensive exam (for some programs), thesis (for some programs). *Entrance requirements:* Additional exam requirements/recommendations for international students: required—TOEFL (minimum score 450 paper-based; 45 iBT), IELTS (minimum score 5). Electronic applications accepted.

Andrews University, School of Graduate Studies, College of Education and International Services, Department of Graduate Psychology and Counseling, Berrien Springs, MI 49104. Offers community counseling (MA), including clinical mental health counseling, community counseling; counseling psychology (MA, PhD); educational and developmental psychology (MA, Ed D, PhD), including educational and developmental psychology (MA), educational psychology (Ed D, PhD); school counseling (MA); school psychology (Ed S); special education (MS). *Accreditation:* ACA (one or more programs are accredited). *Program availability:* Part-time. *Faculty:* 12 full-time (5 women), 4 part-time/adjunct (2 women). *Students:* 86 full-time (65 women), 16 part-time (13 women); includes 38 minority (19 Black or African American, non-Hispanic/Latino; 1 Asian, non-Hispanic/Latino; 17 Hispanic/Latino; 1 Two or more races, non-Hispanic/Latino), 34 international. Average age 34. In 2019, 18 master's, 7 doctorates, 4 other advanced degrees awarded. Terminal master's awarded for partial completion of doctoral program. *Degree requirements:* For master's, thesis optional; for doctorate, thesis/dissertation. *Entrance requirements:* For master's, GRE Subject Test, minimum GPA of 2.6; for doctorate, GRE General Test, MA, minimum GPA of 3.5, sample of research. Additional exam requirements/recommendations for international students: required—TOEFL (minimum score 550 paper-based). *Application deadline:* Applications are processed on a rolling basis. Application fee: $60. Electronic applications accepted.

Financial support: Research assistantships, teaching assistantships, Federal Work-Study, and scholarships/grants available. *Unit head:* Dr. Carole Woolford-Hunt, Chair, 269-471-3473. *Application contact:* Jillian Panigot, Director, University Admissions, 800-253-2874, Fax: 269-471-6321, E-mail: graduate@andrews.edu. Website: https://www.andrews.edu/sed/gpc/

Angelo State University, College of Graduate Studies and Research, Archer College of Health and Human Services, Department of Psychology and Sociology, San Angelo, TX 76909. Offers industrial-organizational psychology (MS). *Program availability:* Part-time, evening/weekend. *Degree requirements:* For master's, comprehensive exam, thesis optional. *Entrance requirements:* For master's, GRE General Test (for industrial and organizational psychology only), essay, letters of recommendation (for industrial and organizational psychology only). Additional exam requirements/recommendations for international students: required—TOEFL or IELTS. Electronic applications accepted.

Antioch University Los Angeles, Program in Psychology, Culver City, CA 90230. Offers clinical psychology (MA); psychology (MA). *Program availability:* Part-time. *Faculty:* 12 full-time (5 women), 52 part-time/adjunct (31 women). *Students:* 456 full-time (322 women), 45 part-time (37 women); includes 136 minority (23 Black or African American, non-Hispanic/Latino; 2 American Indian or Alaska Native, non-Hispanic/Latino; 24 Asian, non-Hispanic/Latino; 62 Hispanic/Latino; 25 Two or more races, non-Hispanic/Latino), 5 international. Average age 36. 169 applicants, 70% accepted, 112 enrolled. In 2019, 182 master's awarded. *Degree requirements:* For master's, thesis (for some programs), internship. *Entrance requirements:* For master's, interview. Additional exam requirements/recommendations for international students: required—TOEFL. *Application deadline:* For fall admission, 8/4 priority date for domestic students; for winter admission, 11/3 priority date for domestic students; for spring admission, 2/4 priority date for domestic students. Applications are processed on a rolling basis. Application fee: $60. *Expenses: Tuition:* Full-time $29,992; part-time $17,996 per credit hour. *Financial support:* Career-related internships or fieldwork, Federal Work-Study, scholarships/grants, and traineeships available. Support available to part-time students. Financial award application deadline: 3/24; financial award applicants required to submit FAFSA. *Unit head:* Joy Turek, Chair, 310-578-1080 Ext. 306, Fax: 310-822-4824, E-mail: joy_turek@antiochla.edu. *Application contact:* Information Contact, 310-578-1090, Fax: 310-822-4824, E-mail: admissions@antiochla.edu. Website: https://www.antioch.edu/los-angeles/degrees-programs/psychology-degree/

Appalachian State University, Cratis D. Williams School of Graduate Studies, Department of Psychology, Boone, NC 28608. Offers clinical health psychology (MA). *Program availability:* Part-time. *Degree requirements:* For master's, comprehensive exam, thesis optional, exit exam. *Entrance requirements:* For master's, GRE General Test, 3 letters of recommendation. Additional exam requirements/recommendations for international students: required—TOEFL (minimum score 550 paper-based; 79 iBT) or IELTS (minimum score 6.5). Electronic applications accepted.

Arcadia University, College of Arts and Sciences, Department of Psychology, Glenside, PA 19038-3295. Offers applied behavior analysis (MAC); autism (MAC); child/family therapy (MAC); community public health (MAC); counseling/international peace and conflict resolution dual degree (MAC); mental health counseling (MAC); trauma (MAC). *Program availability:* Part-time. *Faculty:* 13 full-time (8 women). *Students:* 30 full-time (27 women), 31 part-time (26 women); includes 17 minority (11 Black or African American, non-Hispanic/Latino; 2 Asian, non-Hispanic/Latino; 1 Hispanic/Latino; 3 Two or more races, non-Hispanic/Latino). In 2019, 18 master's awarded. *Degree requirements:* For master's, practicum. *Entrance requirements:* For master's, test scores are not required of applicants with an earned master's degree or who have a GPA greater than a 3.0. Test scores from the Graduate Record Examination (GRE) or the Miller Analogies Test (MAT), taken within the past five years are required for all other applicants. Additional exam requirements/recommendations for international students: required—TOEFL. *Application deadline:* Applications are processed on a rolling basis. Application fee: $25. Electronic applications accepted. *Expenses:* Contact institution. *Financial support:* Research assistantships, career-related internships or fieldwork, and unspecified assistantships available. Support available to part-time students. Financial award application deadline: 8/15. *Unit head:* Dr. Marianne Miserandino, Chair, 215-572-2183. *Application contact:* 215-572-2925, Fax: 215-572-2126, E-mail: grad@arcadia.edu.

Arcadia University, School of Education, Glenside, PA 19038-3295. Offers art education (M Ed); computer education (CAS); curriculum (CAS); curriculum studies (M Ed); early childhood education (M Ed), including individualized, master teacher, research in child development; educational leadership (M Ed, Ed D, CAS); elementary education (M Ed); English education (MA Ed); environmental education (MA Ed); instructional technology (M Ed); language arts (M Ed); library science (M Ed); mathematics education (M Ed, MA Ed); music education (MA Ed); psychology (MA Ed); reading (M Ed, CAS); science education (M Ed, CAS); secondary education (M Ed, CAS); special education (M Ed, Ed D, CAS); theater arts (MA Ed); written communication (MA Ed). *Accreditation:* NASAD. *Program availability:* Part-time, evening/weekend, online learning. *Faculty:* 13 full-time (9 women). *Students:* 32 full-time (28 women), 260 part-time (202 women); includes 66 minority (45 Black or African American, non-Hispanic/Latino; 11 Asian, non-Hispanic/Latino; 5 Hispanic/Latino; 5 Two or more races, non-Hispanic/Latino), 2 international. In 2019, 148 master's, 8 doctorates, 163 CASs awarded. *Entrance requirements:* Additional exam requirements/recommendations for international students: required—Official results from the TOEFL or IELTS are required. *Application deadline:* Applications are processed on a rolling basis. Application fee: $25. Electronic applications accepted. *Expenses:* Contact institution. *Financial support:* Career-related internships or fieldwork, tuition waivers (partial), and unspecified assistantships available. *Unit head:* Kimberly Dean, Chair, 215-572-8629. *Application contact:* 215-572-2925, Fax: 215-572-2126, E-mail: grad@arcadia.edu.

Argosy University, Atlanta, Georgia School of Professional Psychology, Atlanta, GA 30328. Offers clinical psychology (MA, Psy D, Postdoctoral Respecialization Certificate), including child and family psychology (Psy D), general adult clinical (Psy D), health psychology (Psy D), neuropsychology/geropsychology (Psy D); community counseling (MA), including marriage and family therapy; counselor education and supervision (Ed D); forensic psychology (MA); industrial organizational psychology (MA); marriage and family therapy (Certificate); sport-exercise psychology (MA). *Accreditation:* APA.

Argosy University, Chicago, Illinois School of Professional Psychology, Chicago, IL 60601. Offers clinical psychology (MA, Psy D), including child and adolescent psychology (Psy D), client-centered and experiential psychotherapies (Psy D), diversity and multicultural psychology (Psy D), family psychology (Psy D), forensic psychology (Psy D), health psychology (Psy D), neuropsychology (Psy D), organizational consulting (Psy D), psychoanalytic psychology (Psy D), psychology and spirituality (Psy D); community counseling (MA); counseling psychology (Ed D), including counselor education and supervision; counselor education and supervision (Ed D); industrial organizational psychology (MA). *Accreditation:* APA (one or more programs are accredited). *Program availability:* Online learning.

Argosy University, Hawaii, Hawai'i School of Professional Psychology, Honolulu, HI 96813. Offers MA, MS, Ed D, Psy D, Certificate, Postdoctoral Respecialization Certificate. *Accreditation:* APA.

Argosy University, Los Angeles, College of Psychology and Behavioral Sciences, Los Angeles, CA 90045. Offers clinical psychology/marriage and family therapy (MA); counseling psychology (Ed D); counseling psychology/marriage and family therapy (MA); forensic psychology (MA).

Argosy University, Northern Virginia, American School of Professional Psychology, Arlington, VA 22209. Offers clinical psychology (MA, Psy D), including child and family psychology (Psy D), diversity and multicultural psychology (Psy D), forensic psychology (Psy D), health and neuropsychology (Psy D); community counseling (MA); counseling psychology (Ed D), including counselor education and supervision; counselor education and supervision (Ed D); forensic psychology (MA).

Argosy University, Orange County, American School of Professional Psychology, Orange, CA 92868. Offers MA, Ed D, Psy D. *Accreditation:* APA. *Program availability:* Part-time, evening/weekend. *Degree requirements:* For master's, comprehensive exam; for doctorate, comprehensive exam, thesis/dissertation. *Entrance requirements:* For master's and doctorate, 3 letters of recommendation, interview, resume. Additional exam requirements/recommendations for international students: required—TOEFL. Electronic applications accepted.

Argosy University, Phoenix, Arizona School of Professional Psychology, Phoenix, AZ 85021. Offers MA, Psy D.

Argosy University, Seattle, College of Psychology and Behavioral Sciences, Seattle, WA 98121. Offers MA, Ed D, Psy D, Postdoctoral Respecialization Certificate.

Argosy University, Tampa, Florida School of Professional Psychology, Tampa, FL 33607. Offers clinical psychology (MA, Psy D), including clinical psychology; counselor education and supervision (Ed D); industrial organizational psychology (MA); marriage and family therapy (MA); mental health counseling (MA).

Argosy University, Twin Cities, Minnesota School of Professional Psychology, Eagan, MN 55121. Offers clinical psychology (MA, Psy D), including child and family psychology (Psy D), forensic psychology (Psy D), health and neuropsychology (Psy D), trauma (Psy D); forensic counseling (Post-Graduate Certificate); forensic psychology (MA); industrial organizational psychology (MA); marriage and family therapy (MA, DMFT), including forensic counseling (MA). *Accreditation:* AAMFT; AAMFT/COAMFTE; APA.

Arizona State University at Tempe, College of Liberal Arts and Sciences, Department of Psychology, Tempe, AZ 85287-1104. Offers applied behavior analysis (MS); behavioral neuroscience (PhD); clinical psychology (PhD); cognitive science (PhD); developmental psychology (PhD); quantitative psychology (PhD); social psychology (PhD). *Accreditation:* APA. *Degree requirements:* For doctorate, comprehensive exam, thesis/dissertation, interactive Program of Study (iPOS) submitted before completing 50 percent of required credit hours. *Entrance requirements:* For doctorate, GRE General Test, GRE Subject Test, minimum GPA of 3.0 or equivalent in last 2 years of work leading to bachelor's degree. Additional exam requirements/recommendations for international students: required—TOEFL, IELTS, or PTE. Electronic applications accepted.

Arizona State University at Tempe, New College of Interdisciplinary Arts and Sciences, Program in Psychology, Phoenix, AZ 85069-7100. Offers MS. *Program availability:* Part-time, evening/weekend. *Degree requirements:* For master's, thesis or applied project, interactive Program of Study (iPOS) submitted before completing 50 percent of required credit hours. *Entrance requirements:* For master's, GRE, bachelor's degree in psychology or related field; minimum cumulative GPA of 3.0; successful completion of undergraduate statistics and research methods courses; three letters of recommendation from faculty; personal statement of research interests and goals. Additional exam requirements/recommendations for international students: required—TOEFL, IELTS, or PTE. Electronic applications accepted.

Arkansas Tech University, College of Arts and Humanities, Russellville, AR 72801. Offers applied sociology (MS); English (M Ed, MA); history (MA); liberal arts (MLA); multi-media journalism (MA); psychology (MS); teaching English as a second language (MA). *Program availability:* Part-time, 100% online, blended/hybrid learning. *Students:* 32 full-time (19 women), 102 part-time (70 women); includes 22 minority (5 Black or African American, non-Hispanic/Latino; 1 American Indian or Alaska Native, non-Hispanic/Latino; 1 Asian, non-Hispanic/Latino; 12 Hispanic/Latino; 3 Two or more races, non-Hispanic/Latino), 9 international. Average age 32. In 2019, 89 master's awarded. *Degree requirements:* For master's, comprehensive exam (for some programs), thesis (for some programs), project. *Entrance requirements:* Additional exam requirements/recommendations for international students: required—TOEFL (minimum score 550 paper-based; 79 iBT), IELTS (minimum score 6.5), PTE (minimum score 58). *Application deadline:* For fall admission, 3/1 priority date for domestic students, 5/1 priority date for international students; for spring admission, 10/1 priority date for domestic and international students. Applications are processed on a rolling basis. Application fee: $40 ($90 for international students). Electronic applications accepted. *Expenses: Tuition, area resident:* Full-time $7008; part-time $292 per credit hour. Tuition, state resident: full-time $7008; part-time $292 per credit hour. Tuition, nonresident: full-time $14,016; part-time $584 per credit hour. *International tuition:* $14,016 full-time. *Required fees:* $343 per term. *Financial support:* In 2019–20, research assistantships with full and partial tuition reimbursements (averaging $4,800 per year), teaching assistantships with full and partial tuition reimbursements (averaging $4,800 per year) were awarded; career-related internships or fieldwork, Federal Work-Study, scholarships/grants, health care benefits, and unspecified assistantships also available. Support available to part-time students. Financial award application deadline: 4/15; financial award applicants required to submit FAFSA. *Unit head:* Dr. Jeffrey Cass, Dean of College of Arts and Humanities, 479-968-0274, Fax: 479-964-0812, E-mail: jcass@atu.edu. *Application contact:* Dr. Richard Schoephoerster, Dean of Graduate College and Research, 479-968-0398, Fax: 479-964-0542, E-mail: gradcollege@atu.edu. Website: http://www.atu.edu/humanities/

Auburn University, Graduate School, College of Liberal Arts, Department of Psychology, Auburn, AL 36849. Offers MS, PhD. *Accreditation:* APA (one or more programs are accredited). *Program availability:* Part-time. *Faculty:* 31 full-time (15 women), 2 part-time/adjunct (1 woman). *Students:* 43 full-time (32 women), 38 part-time (25 women); includes 15 minority (3 Black or African American, non-Hispanic/Latino; 3 Asian, non-Hispanic/Latino; 7 Hispanic/Latino; 2 Two or more races, non-Hispanic/Latino), 6 international. Average age 27. 320 applicants, 9% accepted, 25 enrolled. In 2019, 15 master's, 11 doctorates awarded. *Degree requirements:* For doctorate, thesis/dissertation. *Entrance requirements:* For master's, GRE General Test, GRE Subject Test, minimum GPA of 3.25 in psychology, 3.0 overall; for doctorate, GRE General Test, GRE Subject Test. Additional exam requirements/recommendations for international students: required—iTEP; recommended—TOEFL (minimum score 550 paper-based; 79 iBT), IELTS (minimum score 6.5). *Application deadline:* Applications are processed on a rolling basis. Application fee: $60 ($70 for international students). Electronic applications accepted. *Expenses: Tuition, area resident:* Full-time $9828; part-time $546

per credit hour. Tuition, state resident: full-time $9828; part-time $546 per credit hour. Tuition, nonresident: full-time $29,484; part-time $1638 per credit hour. *International tuition:* $29,744 full-time. Tuition and fees vary according to course load, program and reciprocity agreements. *Financial support:* In 2019–20, 32 fellowships with tuition reimbursements, 35 research assistantships with tuition reimbursements (averaging $16,135 per year), 25 teaching assistantships with tuition reimbursements (averaging $16,224 per year) were awarded; Federal Work-Study also available. Support available to part-time students. Financial award application deadline: 3/15; financial award applicants required to submit FAFSA. *Unit head:* Dr. Ana Franco-Watkins, Chair, 334-844-6492, E-mail: afrancowatkins@auburn.edu. *Application contact:* Dr. George Flowers, Dean of the Graduate School, 334-844-2125.
Website: https://cla.auburn.edu/psychology/

Auburn University at Montgomery, College of Sciences, Department of Psychology, Montgomery, AL 36124-4023. Offers MS. *Program availability:* Part-time, evening/weekend. *Students:* Average age 27. 12 applicants, 75% accepted, 8 enrolled. In 2019, 8 master's awarded. *Degree requirements:* For master's, comprehensive exam, thesis optional. *Entrance requirements:* For master's, GRE General Test or MAT. Additional exam requirements/recommendations for international students: recommended—TOEFL (minimum score 500 paper-based; 61 iBT), IELTS (minimum score 5.5), TSE (minimum score 44). *Application deadline:* For fall admission, 4/15 for domestic students, 7/15 for international students; for spring admission, 11/15 for international students; for summer admission, 4/15 for international students. Applications are processed on a rolling basis. Application fee: $25. Electronic applications accepted. *Expenses: Tuition, area resident:* Full-time $7578; part-time $421 per credit hour. Tuition, state resident: full-time $7578; part-time $421 per credit hour. Tuition, nonresident: full-time $17,046; part-time $947 per credit hour. *International tuition:* $17,046 full-time. *Required fees:* $868. *Financial support:* In 2019–20, 1 teaching assistantship was awarded; career-related internships or fieldwork and scholarships/grants also available. Support available to part-time students. Financial award application deadline: 3/1; financial award applicants required to submit FAFSA. *Unit head:* Dr. Glen Ray, Acting Head, 334-244-3690, Fax: 334-244-3826, E-mail: gray@aum.edu. *Application contact:* Tonya Sexton, Administrative Associate, 334-244-3306, Fax: 334-244-3826, E-mail: tsexton1@aum.edu.
Website: http://www.cas.aum.edu/departments/psychology

Augusta University, College of Science and Mathematics, Department of Psychological Sciences, Augusta, GA 30912. Offers MS. *Degree requirements:* For master's, thesis optional, written/oral exam. *Entrance requirements:* For master's, GRE General Test, minimum GPA of 3.0, bachelor's degree in psychology or equivalent course work, three letters of recommendation. Additional exam requirements/recommendations for international students: required—TOEFL. Electronic applications accepted.

Austin Peay State University, College of Graduate Studies, College of Behavioral and Health Sciences, Department of Psychological Science and Counseling, Clarksville, TN 37044. Offers industrial-organizational psychology (MS); mental health counseling (MS), including clinical mental health, school counseling; school counseling (MS). *Program availability:* Part-time, online learning. *Faculty:* 9 full-time (6 women), 5 part-time/adjunct (4 women). *Students:* 64 full-time (46 women), 27 part-time (24 women); includes 30 minority (16 Black or African American, non-Hispanic/Latino; 1 Asian, non-Hispanic/Latino; 5 Hispanic/Latino; 8 Two or more races, non-Hispanic/Latino), 1 international. Average age 29. 34 applicants, 68% accepted, 19 enrolled. In 2019, 28 master's awarded. *Degree requirements:* For master's, comprehensive exam, thesis (for some programs). *Entrance requirements:* For master's, GRE General Test, minimum undergraduate GPA of 2.5, 3 letters of recommendation, bachelor's degree. Additional exam requirements/recommendations for international students: required—TOEFL (minimum score 500 paper-based). *Application deadline:* For fall admission, 8/5 priority date for domestic students. Applications are processed on a rolling basis. Application fee: $45 ($55 for international students). Electronic applications accepted. *Financial support:* Research assistantships with full tuition reimbursements, career-related internships or fieldwork, Federal Work-Study, institutionally sponsored loans, scholarships/grants, and unspecified assistantships available. Support available to part-time students. Financial award application deadline: 7/1; financial award applicants required to submit FAFSA. *Unit head:* Dr. Nicole Knickmeyer, Chair, 931-221-7232, Fax: 931-221-6267, E-mail: knickmeyer@apsu.edu. *Application contact:* Megan Mitchell, Coordinator of Graduate Admissions, 800-859-4723, Fax: 931-221-7641, E-mail: gradadmissions@apsu.edu.
Website: http://www.apsu.edu/psychology/index.php

Avila University, Department of Psychology, Kansas City, MO 64145-1698. Offers counseling psychology (MS); psychology (MS). *Program availability:* Part-time. *Faculty:* 6 full-time (all women), 7 part-time/adjunct (4 women). *Students:* 90 full-time (73 women), 20 part-time (17 women); includes 39 minority (23 Black or African American, non-Hispanic/Latino; 1 American Indian or Alaska Native, non-Hispanic/Latino; 3 Asian, non-Hispanic/Latino; 6 Hispanic/Latino; 6 Two or more races, non-Hispanic/Latino), 2 international. Average age 33. 117 applicants, 55% accepted, 52 enrolled. In 2019, 27 master's awarded. *Degree requirements:* For master's, thesis optional, capstone project. *Entrance requirements:* For master's, bachelor's degree, minimum GPA of 3.0 in all previous undergraduate and graduate coursework, 2 letters of recommendation, letter of intent, resume. Additional exam requirements/recommendations for international students: required—TOEFL (minimum score 80 iBT). *Application deadline:* Applications are processed on a rolling basis. Application fee: $0. Electronic applications accepted. *Expenses:* $589 per credit hour. $21,500 - $36,000 total for degree completion depending on major. *Financial support:* In 2019–20, 12 students received support, including 4 research assistantships with partial tuition reimbursements available; career-related internships or fieldwork, scholarships/grants, and unspecified assistantships also available. Support available to part-time students. Financial award applicants required to submit FAFSA. *Unit head:* Phil Gebauer, Director of Graduate Psychology Enrollment Management, 816-501-0419, Fax: 816-501-2455, E-mail: philip.gebauer@avila.edu. *Application contact:* Heather Nobl, Graduate Admissions Advisor, 816-501-2969, E-mail: gradpsych@avila.edu.
Website: https://www.avila.edu/psychology/

Azusa Pacific University, School of Behavioral and Applied Sciences, Department of Psychology, Azusa, CA 91702-7000. Offers child life (MS); research psychology and data analytics (MS).

Ball State University, Graduate School, College of Sciences and Humanities, Department of Psychological Science, Muncie, IN 47306. Offers clinical psychology (MA); cognitive and social processes (MA). *Program availability:* Part-time. *Entrance requirements:* For master's, GRE General Test, minimum baccalaureate GPA of 2.75 or 3.0 in latter half of baccalaureate, goals statements, curriculum vitae, letters of recommendation. Additional exam requirements/recommendations for international students: required—TOEFL (minimum score 550 paper-based; 79 iBT), IELTS (minimum score 6.5). Electronic applications accepted. *Expenses: Tuition, area resident:* Full-time $7506; part-time $417 per credit hour. Tuition, nonresident: full-time $20,610; part-time $1145 per credit hour. *Required fees:* $2126. Tuition and fees vary according to course load, campus/location and program.

Barry University, College of Arts and Sciences, Department of Psychology, Miami Shores, FL 33161-6695. Offers clinical psychology (MS); school psychology (MS, SSP). *Program availability:* Part-time, evening/weekend. *Degree requirements:* For master's, thesis, practicum. *Entrance requirements:* For master's, GRE General Test, minimum GPA of 3.0, course work in psychology. Electronic applications accepted.

Baylor University, Graduate School, College of Arts and Sciences, Department of Psychology and Neuroscience, Program in Psychology, Waco, TX 76798. Offers social, general experimental, behavioral neuroscience (PhD). Terminal master's awarded for partial completion of doctoral program. *Degree requirements:* For master's, thesis; for doctorate, comprehensive exam, thesis/dissertation. *Entrance requirements:* For master's and doctorate, GRE General Test. Additional exam requirements/recommendations for international students: required—TOEFL, IELTS. Electronic applications accepted. *Expenses:* Contact institution.

Binghamton University, State University of New York, Graduate School, Harpur College of Arts and Sciences, Department of Psychology, Binghamton, NY 13902-6000. Offers psychology - behavioral neuroscience (PhD); psychology - clinical psychology (PhD); psychology - cognitive and behavioral science (PhD). *Accreditation:* APA. *Program availability:* Part-time. Terminal master's awarded for partial completion of doctoral program. *Degree requirements:* For doctorate, comprehensive exam (for some programs), thesis/dissertation. *Entrance requirements:* For doctorate, GRE General Test. Additional exam requirements/recommendations for international students: required—TOEFL (minimum score 550 paper-based; 80 iBT). Electronic applications accepted.

Biola University, Rosemead School of Psychology, La Mirada, CA 90639-0001. Offers clinical psychology (PhD, Psy D). *Accreditation:* APA. *Faculty:* 23. *Students:* 115 full-time (94 women), 48 part-time (43 women); includes 48 minority (2 Black or African American, non-Hispanic/Latino; 1 American Indian or Alaska Native, non-Hispanic/Latino; 24 Asian, non-Hispanic/Latino; 16 Hispanic/Latino; 1 Native Hawaiian or other Pacific Islander, non-Hispanic/Latino; 4 Two or more races, non-Hispanic/Latino), 51 international. Average age 30. 126 applicants, 46% accepted, 34 enrolled. In 2019, 29 doctorates awarded. *Degree requirements:* For doctorate, comprehensive exam, thesis/dissertation. *Entrance requirements:* For doctorate, GRE General Test, interview, 30 undergraduate semester hours of credits in psychology, minimum GPA of 3.0. Additional exam requirements/recommendations for international students: required—TOEFL (minimum score 600 paper-based; 100 iBT). *Application deadline:* For fall admission, 12/1 priority date for domestic students, 12/1 for international students. Application fee: $65. Electronic applications accepted. *Expenses:* Contact institution. *Financial support:* Scholarships/grants and unspecified assistantships available. Financial award applicants required to submit FAFSA. *Unit head:* Dr. Tamara Anderson, Dean, 562-903-4867, Fax: 562-903-4864. *Application contact:* Nicholas Perry, Graduate Admissions Counselor, 562-903-4752, E-mail: graduate.admissions@biola.edu.
Website: http://www.rosemead.edu/

Boston College, Morrissey Graduate School of Arts and Sciences, Department of Psychology, Chestnut Hill, MA 02467-3800. Offers PhD. *Degree requirements:* For doctorate, thesis/dissertation, fieldwork. *Entrance requirements:* For doctorate, GRE General Test, GRE Subject Test. Additional exam requirements/recommendations for international students: required—TOEFL (minimum score 600 paper-based; 100 iBT), IELTS (minimum score 8). Electronic applications accepted.

Boston Graduate School of Psychoanalysis, BGSP-New Jersey, Brookline, MA 02446-4602. Offers psychoanalysis (MA); psychoanalytic counseling (MA).

Boston Graduate School of Psychoanalysis, New York Graduate School of Psychoanalysis, New York, NY 10011. Offers MA. *Program availability:* Part-time. *Degree requirements:* For master's, thesis. *Entrance requirements:* For master's, interview, BA, writing sample, letters of recommendation. Additional exam requirements/recommendations for international students: required—TOEFL.

Boston University, Graduate School of Arts and Sciences, Department of Psychological and Brain Sciences, Boston, MA 02215. Offers MA, PhD. *Accreditation:* APA (one or more programs are accredited). *Students:* 104 full-time (76 women), 2 part-time (1 woman); includes 20 minority (3 Black or African American, non-Hispanic/Latino; 7 Asian, non-Hispanic/Latino; 9 Hispanic/Latino; 1 Two or more races, non-Hispanic/Latino), 20 international. Average age 25. 1,006 applicants, 17% accepted, 41 enrolled. In 2019, 32 master's, 12 doctorates awarded. Terminal master's awarded for partial completion of doctoral program. *Degree requirements:* For master's, thesis or alternative, research apprenticeship; for doctorate, comprehensive exam, thesis/dissertation. *Entrance requirements:* For master's and doctorate, GRE General Test, GRE Subject Test (recommended), three letters of recommendation, transcripts, personal statement, curriculum vitae. Additional exam requirements/recommendations for international students: required—TOEFL (minimum score 550 paper-based; 84 iBT). *Application deadline:* For fall admission, 12/1 for domestic and international students. Application fee: $95. Electronic applications accepted. *Financial support:* In 2019–20, 77 students received support, including 5 fellowships with full tuition reimbursements available (averaging $23,340 per year), 30 research assistantships with full tuition reimbursements available (averaging $23,340 per year), 30 teaching assistantships with full tuition reimbursements available (averaging $23,340 per year); career-related internships or fieldwork, Federal Work-Study, scholarships/grants, traineeships, and health care benefits also available. Financial award application deadline: 12/1. *Unit head:* David Somers, Chairman, 617-358-1372, Fax: 617-353-6933, E-mail: somers@bu.edu. *Application contact:* Martin Gastmann, Assistant Director of Admissions and Financial Aid, 617-353-2696, Fax: 617-358-5492, E-mail: grs@bu.edu.
Website: http://www.bu.edu/psych/

Boston University, School of Medicine, Graduate Medical Sciences, Program in Mental Health Counseling and Behavioral Medicine, Boston, MA 02215. Offers MA. *Unit head:* Dr. Stephen Brady, Director, 617-414-2320, Fax: 617-414-2323, E-mail: sbrady@bu.edu. *Application contact:* GMS Admissions Office, 617-358-9518, Fax: 617-358-2913, E-mail: gmsbusm@bu.edu.
Website: http://www.bumc.bu.edu/gms/mhcbm/

Bowling Green State University, Graduate College, College of Arts and Sciences, Department of Psychology, Bowling Green, OH 43403. Offers clinical psychology (MA, PhD); developmental psychology (MA, PhD); experimental psychology (MA, PhD); industrial/organizational psychology (MA, PhD); quantitative psychology (MA, PhD). *Accreditation:* APA (one or more programs are accredited). *Degree requirements:* For doctorate, thesis/dissertation. *Entrance requirements:* For doctorate, GRE General Test, GRE Subject Test. Additional exam requirements/recommendations for international students: required—TOEFL. Electronic applications accepted.

Brandeis University, Graduate School of Arts and Sciences, Department of Psychology, Waltham, MA 02454-9110. Offers brain, body and behavior (PhD); cognitive neuroscience (PhD); general psychology (MA); social/developmental psychology (PhD). *Program availability:* Part-time. *Faculty:* 14 full-time (7 women), 3 part-time/adjunct (all women). *Students:* 31 full-time (21 women), 1 (woman) part-time; includes 6 minority (4 Asian, non-Hispanic/Latino; 2 Hispanic/Latino), 8 international. Average age 26. 157 applicants, 14% accepted, 12 enrolled. In 2019, 18 master's, 2 doctorates awarded. Terminal master's awarded for partial completion of doctoral

program. *Degree requirements:* For master's, thesis (for some programs); for doctorate, thesis/dissertation. *Entrance requirements:* For master's and doctorate, GRE General required; GRE Subject recommended, transcripts, letters of recommendation, resume, and statement of purpose. Additional exam requirements/recommendations for international students: required—TOEFL, IELTS, PTE. *Application deadline:* For fall admission, 12/1 priority date for domestic and international students. Applications are processed on a rolling basis. Application fee: $75. Electronic applications accepted. *Financial support:* In 2019–20, 23 fellowships with full tuition reimbursements (averaging $25,000 per year), 16 teaching assistantships (averaging $3,550 per year) were awarded; research assistantships, scholarships/grants, traineeships, health care benefits, and tuition waivers also available. Support available to part-time students. *Unit head:* Dr. Angela Gutchess, Director of Graduate Studies, 781-736-3247, E-mail: gutchess@brandeis.edu. *Application contact:* Sarah Lupis, Administrator, 781-736-3303, E-mail: slupis@brandeis.edu.
Website: http://www.brandeis.edu/gsas/programs/psychology.html

Brandman University, School of Arts and Sciences, Irvine, CA 92618. Offers psychology (MA), including counseling, marriage and family therapy, professional clinical counseling; social work (MSW).

Brenau University, Sydney O. Smith Graduate School, Ivester College of Health Sciences, Gainesville, GA 30501. Offers family nurse practitioner (MSN); general psychology (MS); nurse educator (MSN); nursing manager (MSN); occupational therapy (MS). *Accreditation:* AOTA. *Program availability:* Part-time, evening/weekend, 100% online, blended/hybrid learning. *Faculty:* 34 full-time (26 women), 11 part-time/adjunct (10 women). *Students:* 321 full-time (242 women), 209 part-time (197 women); includes 177 minority (104 Black or African American, non-Hispanic/Latino; 2 American Indian or Alaska Native, non-Hispanic/Latino; 24 Asian, non-Hispanic/Latino; 36 Hispanic/Latino; 2 Native Hawaiian or other Pacific Islander, non-Hispanic/Latino; 9 Two or more races, non-Hispanic/Latino), 3 international. Average age 29. 517 applicants, 47% accepted, 110 enrolled. In 2019, 174 master's awarded. *Entrance requirements:* For master's, GMAT, GRE, or MAT, minimum GPA 2.5. Additional exam requirements/recommendations for international students: required—TOEFL (minimum score 497 paper-based; 71 iBT); recommended—IELTS (minimum score 5.5). *Application deadline:* Applications are processed on a rolling basis. Application fee: $35. Electronic applications accepted. *Expenses:* $11,763 full-time tuition (average), $4,678 part-time tuition (average). *Financial support:* In 2019–20, 11 students received support. Scholarships/grants available. Financial award applicants required to submit FAFSA. *Unit head:* Dr. Gale Starich, Dean, 777-718-5305, Fax: 770-297-5929, E-mail: gstarich@brenau.edu. *Application contact:* Nathan Goss, Assistant Vice President for Recruitment, 770-534-6162, E-mail: ngoss@brenau.edu.
Website: http://www.brenau.edu/healthsciences/

Bridgewater State University, College of Graduate Studies, College of Humanities and Social Sciences, Department of Psychology, Bridgewater, MA 02325. Offers MA. *Program availability:* Part-time, evening/weekend. *Entrance requirements:* For master's, GRE General Test.

Brigham Young University, Graduate Studies, College of Family, Home, and Social Sciences, Department of Psychology, Provo, UT 84602. Offers clinical psychology (PhD); cognitive and behavioral neuroscience (PhD). *Accreditation:* APA. *Faculty:* 24 full-time (9 women), 3 part-time/adjunct (0 women). *Students:* 62 full-time (39 women); includes 10 minority (3 Black or African American, non-Hispanic/Latino; 1 American Indian or Alaska Native, non-Hispanic/Latino; 5 Asian, non-Hispanic/Latino; 1 Hispanic/Latino), 4 international. Average age 29. 76 applicants, 22% accepted, 11 enrolled. In 2019, 8 doctorates awarded. *Degree requirements:* For doctorate, comprehensive exam, thesis/dissertation, publishable paper. *Entrance requirements:* For doctorate, GRE General Test, minimum GPA of 3.0. Additional exam requirements/recommendations for international students: required—TOEFL (minimum score 580 paper-based; 85 iBT). *Application deadline:* For fall admission, 12/1 for domestic and international students. Application fee: $50. Electronic applications accepted. *Expenses:* $18,226/LDS $25,512/Non-LDS. *Financial support:* In 2019–20, 41 students received support, including 43 research assistantships with partial tuition reimbursements available (averaging $12,000 per year), 7 teaching assistantships with partial tuition reimbursements available (averaging $12,000 per year); scholarships/grants and unspecified assistantships also available. Financial award application deadline: 5/31. *Unit head:* Dr. Gary Burlingame, Chair, 801-422-7557, Fax: 801-422-0602, E-mail: gary_burlingame@byu.edu. *Application contact:* Rachelle Gunderson, Coordinator of Student Programs, 801-422-4560, Fax: 801-422-0602, E-mail: leesa_scott@byu.edu.
Website: http://psychology.byu.edu/

Brock University, Faculty of Graduate Studies, Faculty of Social Sciences, Program in Psychology, St. Catharines, ON L2S 3A1, Canada. Offers behavioral neuroscience (MA, PhD); life span development (MA, PhD); social personality (MA, PhD). *Program availability:* Part-time. *Degree requirements:* For master's, thesis; for doctorate, thesis/dissertation. *Entrance requirements:* For master's, GRE, honors degree; for doctorate, GRE, master's degree. Additional exam requirements/recommendations for international students: required—TOEFL (minimum score 550 paper-based; 80 iBT), IELTS (minimum score 6.5), TWE (minimum score 4). Electronic applications accepted.

Brooklyn College of the City University of New York, School of Natural and Behavioral Sciences, Department of Psychology, Brooklyn, NY 11210-2889. Offers experimental psychology (MA); industrial and organizational psychology (MA), including human relations, organizational behavior; mental health counseling (MA); psychology (PhD). *Program availability:* Part-time. *Degree requirements:* For master's, comprehensive exam, thesis (for some programs). *Entrance requirements:* For master's, minimum GPA of 3.0, 2 letters of recommendation, essay; for doctorate, GRE. Additional exam requirements/recommendations for international students: required—TOEFL (minimum score 520 paper-based; 69 iBT). Electronic applications accepted.

Brown University, Graduate School, Department of Cognitive, Linguistic and Psychological Sciences, Providence, RI 02912. Offers cognitive science (Sc M, PhD); linguistics (AM, PhD); psychology (PhD). *Degree requirements:* For master's, one foreign language, thesis or alternative; for doctorate, 2 foreign languages, thesis/dissertation.

Bucknell University, Graduate Studies, College of Arts and Sciences, Department of Psychology, Lewisburg, PA 17837. Offers MS. *Degree requirements:* For master's, thesis. *Entrance requirements:* For master's, GRE General Test, GRE Subject Test, minimum GPA of 3.0. Additional exam requirements/recommendations for international students: required—TOEFL (minimum score 600 paper-based).

California Coast University, School of Behavioral Science, Santa Ana, CA 92701. Offers psychology (MS). *Program availability:* Online learning.

California Lutheran University, Graduate Studies, Department of Psychology, Thousand Oaks, CA 91360-2787. Offers clinical psychology (MS, Psy D); marital and family therapy (MS). *Accreditation:* APA. *Program availability:* Part-time. *Degree requirements:* For master's, thesis or comprehensive exams; for doctorate, thesis/dissertation, internship. *Entrance requirements:* For master's, GRE General Test, interview, minimum GPA of 3.0; for doctorate, GRE General Test. Electronic applications accepted.

California Polytechnic State University, San Luis Obispo, College of Liberal Arts, Department of Psychology and Child Development, San Luis Obispo, CA 93407. Offers psychology (MS). *Program availability:* Part-time. *Faculty:* 3 full-time (1 woman), 2 part-time/adjunct (1 woman). *Students:* 32 full-time (24 women), 3 part-time (2 women); includes 11 minority (1 Asian, non-Hispanic/Latino; 10 Hispanic/Latino). Average age 27. 69 applicants, 33% accepted, 15 enrolled. In 2019, 13 master's awarded. *Entrance requirements:* For master's, GRE. Additional exam requirements/recommendations for international students: required—TOEFL (minimum score 80 iBT). *Application deadline:* For fall admission, 1/4 for domestic and international students. Application fee: $55. Electronic applications accepted. *Expenses:* Tuition, state resident: full-time $7176; part-time $4164 per year. Tuition, nonresident: full-time $18,690; part-time $8916 per year. *Required fees:* $4206; $3185 per unit. $1061 per term. *Financial support:* Fellowships, research assistantships, career-related internships or fieldwork, Federal Work-Study, and institutionally sponsored loans available. Support available to part-time students. Financial award application deadline: 3/2; financial award applicants required to submit FAFSA. *Unit head:* Dr. Lisa Sweatt, Graduate Coordinator, 805-756-6123, E-mail: lsweatt@calpoly.edu. *Application contact:* Dr. Lisa Sweatt, Graduate Coordinator, 805-756-6123, E-mail: lsweatt@calpoly.edu.
Website: http://psycd.calpoly.edu/graduate/?pid-3

California State Polytechnic University, Pomona, Program in Psychology, Pomona, CA 91768-2557. Offers psychology (MS). *Program availability:* Part-time, evening/weekend. *Entrance requirements:* Additional exam requirements/recommendations for international students: required—TOEFL (minimum score 550 paper-based). Electronic applications accepted. *Expenses:* Contact institution.

California State University, Chico, Office of Graduate Studies, College of Behavioral and Social Sciences, Department of Psychology, Program in Psychological Science, Chico, CA 95929-0722. Offers MA. *Degree requirements:* For master's, thesis, Thesis or Comprehensive Exam. *Entrance requirements:* For master's, GRE General Test or MAT, fall admissions only, deadline February 17th. 3 letters of recommendation, 3 departmental recommendation forms, statement of purpose, departmental application. Additional exam requirements/recommendations for international students: required—TOEFL (minimum score 550 paper-based; 80 iBT), IELTS (minimum score 6.5), PTE (minimum score 59). Electronic applications accepted.

California State University, Dominguez Hills, College of Natural and Behavioral Sciences, Department of Psychology, Carson, CA 90747-0001. Offers clinical psychology (MA); health psychology (MA). *Program availability:* Part-time, evening/weekend. Terminal master's awarded for partial completion of doctoral program. *Degree requirements:* For master's, comprehensive exam, thesis optional. *Entrance requirements:* For master's, GRE General Test or MAT, interview, minimum GPA of 3.0, prerequisite psychology courses. Additional exam requirements/recommendations for international students: required—TOEFL (minimum score 550 paper-based). Electronic applications accepted.

California State University, Fresno, Division of Research and Graduate Studies, College of Science and Mathematics, Department of Psychology, Fresno, CA 93740-8027. Offers applied behavior analysis (MA); general/experimental psychology (MA); school psychology (Ed S). *Degree requirements:* For master's, thesis. *Entrance requirements:* For master's, GRE General Test, GRE Subject Test, minimum GPA of 3.0. Additional exam requirements/recommendations for international students: required—TOEFL. Electronic applications accepted. *Expenses:* Tuition, state resident: full-time $4012; part-time $2506 per semester.

California State University, Fullerton, Graduate Studies, College of Humanities and Social Sciences, Department of Psychology, Fullerton, CA 92831-3599. Offers clinical psychology (MS); psychology (MA). *Program availability:* Part-time. *Entrance requirements:* For master's, GRE General Test, GRE Subject Test, undergraduate major in psychology or related field.

California State University, Long Beach, Graduate Studies, College of Liberal Arts, Department of Psychology, Long Beach, CA 90840. Offers human factors (MS); industrial/organizational psychology (MS); psychology (MA). *Program availability:* Part-time, evening/weekend. *Degree requirements:* For master's, comprehensive exam, thesis. *Entrance requirements:* For master's, GRE General Test, GRE Subject Test. Electronic applications accepted.

California State University, Los Angeles, Graduate Studies, College of Natural and Social Sciences, Department of Psychology, Los Angeles, CA 90032-8530. Offers MA, MS. *Program availability:* Part-time, evening/weekend. *Degree requirements:* For master's, comprehensive exam or thesis. *Entrance requirements:* Additional exam requirements/recommendations for international students: required—TOEFL (minimum score 500 paper-based). Electronic applications accepted. *Expenses:* Tuition, area resident: Full-time $7176; part-time $4164 per year. Tuition, state resident: full-time $7176; part-time $4164 per year. Tuition, nonresident: full-time $14,304; part-time $8916 per year. *International tuition:* $14,304 full-time. *Required fees:* $1037.76; $1037.76 per unit. Tuition and fees vary according to degree level and program.

California State University, Northridge, Graduate Studies, College of Social and Behavioral Sciences, Department of Psychology, Northridge, CA 91330. Offers clinical psychology (MA); general experimental psychology (MA). *Degree requirements:* For master's, thesis. *Entrance requirements:* For master's, GRE General Test, GRE Subject Test, minimum GPA of 3.0, letters of recommendation. Additional exam requirements/recommendations for international students: required—TOEFL.

California State University, Sacramento, College of Social Sciences and Interdisciplinary Studies, Department of Psychology, Sacramento, CA 95819. Offers applied behavior analysis (MA); industrial/organizational psychology (MA). *Program availability:* Part-time. *Students:* 26 full-time (22 women), 30 part-time (21 women); includes 22 minority (1 Black or African American, non-Hispanic/Latino; 2 American Indian or Alaska Native, non-Hispanic/Latino; 4 Asian, non-Hispanic/Latino; 14 Hispanic/Latino; 1 Native Hawaiian or other Pacific Islander, non-Hispanic/Latino), 3 international. Average age 27. 86 applicants, 23% accepted, 16 enrolled. In 2019, 7 master's awarded. *Degree requirements:* For master's, thesis, project; writing proficiency exam. *Entrance requirements:* For master's, GRE, minimum GPA of 3.0 during previous 2 years. Additional exam requirements/recommendations for international students: required—TOEFL (minimum score 550 paper-based; 80 iBT); recommended—IELTS (minimum score 7). *Application deadline:* For fall admission, 3/1 for domestic students, 2/1 for international students. Applications are processed on a rolling basis. Application fee: $70. Electronic applications accepted. *Expenses:* Contact institution. *Financial support:* Teaching assistantships, career-related internships or fieldwork, Federal Work-Study, and scholarships/grants available. Support available to part-time students. Financial award application deadline: 3/1; financial award applicants required to submit FAFSA. *Unit head:* Dr. Rebecca Cameron, Interim Department Chair, 916-278-6254, E-mail: cameron@csus.edu. *Application contact:* Jose Martinez, Graduate Admissions Supervisor, 916-278-7871, E-mail: martinj@skymail.csus.edu.
Website: http://www.csus.edu/psyc

California State University, San Bernardino, Graduate Studies, College of Social and Behavioral Sciences, Department of Psychology, San Bernardino, CA 92407. Offers child development (MA); clinical/counseling psychology (MS); industrial/organizational

psychology (MS); psychological science (MA). *Faculty:* 15 full-time (7 women). *Students:* 62 full-time (43 women), 13 part-time (7 women); includes 44 minority (3 Black or African American, non-Hispanic/Latino; 3 Asian, non-Hispanic/Latino; 31 Hispanic/Latino; 7 Two or more races, non-Hispanic/Latino), 5 international. Average age 27. 163 applicants, 24% accepted, 25 enrolled. In 2019, 32 master's awarded. *Degree requirements:* For master's, comprehensive exam, thesis (for some programs). *Entrance requirements:* Additional exam requirements/recommendations for international students: required—TOEFL. Application fee: $55. *Financial support:* Fellowships, research assistantships, and teaching assistantships available. *Unit head:* Dr. Robert Ricco, Chair, 909-537-5485, Fax: 909-537-7003, E-mail: rricco@csusb.edu. *Application contact:* Dr. Dorota Huizinga, Dean of Graduate Studies, 909-537-3064, E-mail: dorota.huizinga@csusb.edu.
Website: https://csbs.csusb.edu/psychology

California State University, San Marcos, College of Humanities, Arts, Behavioral and Social Sciences, Program in Psychological Science, San Marcos, CA 92606. Offers psychological science (MA). *Entrance requirements:* For master's, GRE General Test, GRE Subject Test in psychology (recommended), 3 letters of recommendation. Additional exam requirements/recommendations for international students: required—TOEFL (minimum score 550 paper-based). *Application deadline:* For fall admission, 2/1 for domestic students. Application fee: $55. Electronic applications accepted. *Expenses: Tuition, area resident:* Full-time $7176. Tuition, state resident: full-time $7176. Tuition, nonresident: full-time $18,640. *International tuition:* $18,640 full-time. *Required fees:* $1960. *Financial support:* Fellowships, research assistantships, teaching assistantships, and tuition waivers available. *Unit head:* Dr. Elisa Grant-Vallone, Chair, 760-750-4145, E-mail: evallone@csusm.edu. *Application contact:* Dr. Charles De Leone, Interim Dean of Office of Graduate Studies and Research, 760-750-8045, Fax: 760-750-8045, E-mail: apply@csusm.edu.
Website: https://www.csusm.edu/psychology/maprogram/index.html

California State University, Stanislaus, College of Science, Programs in Psychology, Turlock, CA 95382. Offers behavior analysis (MA, MS); counseling psychology (MS); general psychology (MA). *Program availability:* Part-time. *Degree requirements:* For master's, thesis. *Entrance requirements:* For master's, GRE, minimum GPA of 3.0, 3 letters of reference, 16 psychology prerequisites, personal statement. Additional exam requirements/recommendations for international students: required—TOEFL (minimum score 550 paper-based). Electronic applications accepted.

Cambridge College, School of Psychology and Counseling, Boston, MA 02129. Offers alcohol and drug counseling (Certificate); behavioral health care management (CAGS); marriage and family therapy (M Ed); mental health and school counseling (M Ed); mental health counseling (M Ed); psychological studies (M Ed); rehabilitation counseling (Certificate); school adjustment and mental health counseling (M Ed); school adjustment counseling for mental health counselors (Certificate); school counseling (M Ed); trauma studies (Certificate). *Program availability:* Part-time, evening/weekend. *Degree requirements:* For master's and other advanced degree, thesis, practicum/internship. *Entrance requirements:* For master's, resume, 2 professional references; for other advanced degree, official transcripts, documents for transfer credit evaluation, resume, written personal statement/essay, 2 professional references, health insurance, immunizations form. Additional exam requirements/recommendations for international students: required—TOEFL (minimum score 550 paper-based; 79 iBT), Michigan English Language Assessment Battery (minimum score 85); recommended—IELTS (minimum score 6). Electronic applications accepted. *Expenses:* Contact institution.

Cameron University, Office of Graduate Studies, Program in Behavioral Sciences, Lawton, OK 73505-6377. Offers MS. *Program availability:* Part-time, evening/weekend. *Degree requirements:* For master's, comprehensive exam, thesis optional. *Entrance requirements:* Additional exam requirements/recommendations for international students: required—TOEFL (minimum score 550 paper-based). Electronic applications accepted.

Capella University, Harold Abel School of Social and Behavioral Science, Doctoral Programs in Psychology, Minneapolis, MN 55402. Offers addiction psychology (PhD); clinical psychology (Psy D); educational psychology (PhD); general advanced studies in human behavior (PhD); general psychology (PhD); industrial/organizational psychology (PhD); school psychology (Psy D).

Capella University, Harold Abel School of Social and Behavioral Science, Master's Programs in Psychology, Minneapolis, MN 55402. Offers applied behavior analysis (MS); clinical psychology (MS); counseling psychology (MS); educational psychology (MS); evaluation, research, and measurement (MS); general advanced studies in human behavior (MS); general psychology (MS); industrial/organizational psychology (MS); leadership coaching psychology (MS); school psychology (MS); sport psychology (MS).

Cardinal Stritch University, College of Arts and Sciences, Department of Psychology, Milwaukee, WI 53217-3985. Offers clinical psychology (MA). *Program availability:* Part-time, evening/weekend. *Degree requirements:* For master's, thesis, portfolio, clinical practicum. *Entrance requirements:* For master's, interview, minimum GPA of 3.0, 3 letters of recommendation. Additional exam requirements/recommendations for international students: required—TOEFL (minimum score 79 iBT), IELTS (minimum score 6.5). Electronic applications accepted. *Expenses:* Contact institution.

Carleton University, Faculty of Graduate Studies, Faculty of Arts and Social Sciences, Department of Psychology, Ottawa, ON K1S 5B6, Canada. Offers neuroscience (M Sc); psychology (MA, PhD). *Program availability:* Part-time. *Degree requirements:* For master's, thesis; for doctorate, comprehensive exam, thesis/dissertation. *Entrance requirements:* For master's, honors degree; for doctorate, GRE, master's degree. Additional exam requirements/recommendations for international students: required—TOEFL.

Carnegie Mellon University, Dietrich College of Humanities and Social Sciences, Department of Psychology, Pittsburgh, PA 15213-3891. Offers cognitive neuroscience (PhD); cognitive psychology (PhD); developmental psychology (PhD); social/personality/health psychology (PhD). *Degree requirements:* For doctorate, comprehensive exam, thesis/dissertation. *Entrance requirements:* For doctorate, GRE General Test. Additional exam requirements/recommendations for international students: required—TOEFL.

Case Western Reserve University, School of Graduate Studies, Psychological Sciences Department, Cleveland, OH 44106. Offers clinical psychology (PhD); communication sciences (MA, PhD), including speech-language pathology; experimental psychology (PhD). *Accreditation:* APA (one or more programs are accredited). *Program availability:* Part-time. *Faculty:* 29 full-time (22 women), 5 part-time/adjunct (4 women). *Students:* 57 full-time (44 women), 2 part-time (both women); includes 11 minority (1 Black or African American, non-Hispanic/Latino; 3 Asian, non-Hispanic/Latino; 6 Hispanic/Latino; 1 Two or more races, non-Hispanic/Latino), 1 international. Average age 27. 293 applicants, 11% accepted, 20 enrolled. In 2019, 17 master's, 7 doctorates awarded. Terminal master's awarded for partial completion of doctoral program. *Degree requirements:* For master's, comprehensive exam, thesis optional; for doctorate, thesis/dissertation, internship. *Entrance requirements:* For doctorate, GRE General Test, GRE Subject Test, personal statement; curriculum vitae. Additional exam requirements/recommendations for international students: required—TOEFL (minimum score 577 paper-based; 90 iBT); recommended—IELTS (minimum score 7). *Application deadline:* For fall admission, 12/1 priority date for domestic students. Application fee: $50. Electronic applications accepted. *Financial support:* Fellowships, research assistantships, teaching assistantships, health care benefits, and tuition waivers (full and partial) available. Financial award application deadline: 12/1; financial award applicants required to submit CSS PROFILE or FAFSA. *Unit head:* Dr. Heath Demaree, Professor and Chair, 216-368-6468, E-mail: psychsciences@case.edu. *Application contact:* Dr. Arin Connell, Associate Professor and Director of Clinical Training, 216-368-1550, E-mail: arin.connell@case.edu.
Website: http://psychsciences.case.edu/

Castleton University, Division of Graduate Studies, Department of Psychology, Castleton, VT 05735. Offers forensic psychology (MA). *Degree requirements:* For master's, thesis. *Entrance requirements:* For master's, GRE General Test, minimum undergraduate GPA of 3.5, previous course work in research methodology and statistics. Additional exam requirements/recommendations for international students: required—TOEFL.

The Catholic University of America, School of Arts and Sciences, Department of Psychology, Washington, DC 20064. Offers applied experimental psychology (PhD); clinical psychology (PhD); general psychology (MA); human development psychology (PhD); human factors (MA); MA/JD. *Accreditation:* APA (one or more programs are accredited). *Program availability:* Part-time. *Faculty:* 9 full-time (5 women), 8 part-time/adjunct (all women). *Students:* 31 full-time (27 women), 40 part-time (33 women); includes 19 minority (3 Black or African American, non-Hispanic/Latino; 3 Asian, non-Hispanic/Latino; 5 Hispanic/Latino; 8 Two or more races, non-Hispanic/Latino), 6 international. Average age 28. 160 applicants, 25% accepted, 17 enrolled. In 2019, 19 master's, 8 doctorates awarded. *Degree requirements:* For master's, comprehensive exam, thesis (for some programs); for doctorate, comprehensive exam, thesis/dissertation. *Entrance requirements:* For master's, GRE General Test, statement of purpose, official copies of academic transcripts, three letters of recommendation; for doctorate, GRE General Test, GRE Subject Test, statement of purpose, official copies of academic transcripts, three letters of recommendation. Additional exam requirements/recommendations for international students: required—TOEFL (minimum score 550 paper-based; 80 iBT). *Application deadline:* For fall admission, 7/15 priority date for domestic students, 7/1 for international students; for spring admission, 11/15 priority date for domestic students, 11/1 for international students. Applications are processed on a rolling basis. Application fee: $55. Electronic applications accepted. *Expenses:* Contact institution. *Financial support:* Fellowships, research assistantships, teaching assistantships, Federal Work-Study, scholarships/grants, tuition waivers (full and partial), and unspecified assistantships available. Financial award application deadline: 2/1; financial award applicants required to submit FAFSA. *Unit head:* Dr. Brendan Rich, Chair, 202-319-5823, Fax: 202-319-6263, E-mail: richb@cua.edu. *Application contact:* Dr. Steven Brown, Director of Graduate Admissions, 202-319-5057, Fax: 202-319-6533, E-mail: cua-admissions@cua.edu.
Website: http://psychology.cua.edu/

Central Connecticut State University, School of Graduate Studies, College of Liberal Arts and Social Sciences, Department of Psychological Science, New Britain, CT 06050-4010. Offers MA. *Program availability:* Part-time, evening/weekend. *Degree requirements:* For master's, thesis or alternative. *Entrance requirements:* For master's, minimum undergraduate GPA of 2.7, letters of recommendation, personal statement. Additional exam requirements/recommendations for international students: required—TOEFL (minimum score 550 paper-based; 79 iBT); recommended—IELTS (minimum score 6.5). Electronic applications accepted.

Central Michigan University, College of Graduate Studies, College of Liberal Arts and Social Sciences, Department of Psychology, Mount Pleasant, MI 48859. Offers clinical psychology (PhD); experimental psychology (MS, PhD), including applied experimental psychology (PhD), experimental psychology (MS); industrial and organizational psychology (MA, PhD), including industrial and organizational psychology, occupational health psychology (PhD); neuroscience (MS, PhD); school psychology (PhD, S Psy S), including psychological services (S Psy S), school psychology (PhD). *Accreditation:* APA (one or more programs are accredited). Terminal master's awarded for partial completion of doctoral program. *Degree requirements:* For master's, thesis or alternative; for doctorate, thesis/dissertation; for S Psy S, thesis. *Entrance requirements:* For doctorate, GRE. Electronic applications accepted. *Expenses: Tuition, area resident:* Full-time $12,267; part-time $8178 per year. Tuition, state resident: full-time $12,267; part-time $8178 per year. Tuition, nonresident: full-time $12,267; part-time $8178 per year. *International tuition:* $16,110 full-time. *Required fees:* $225 per semester. Tuition and fees vary according to degree level and program.

Central Washington University, School of Graduate Studies and Research, College of the Sciences, Department of Psychology, Ellensburg, WA 98926. Offers experimental psychology (MS); mental health counseling (MS); school psychology (Ed S). *Program availability:* Evening/weekend. *Entrance requirements:* For master's, GRE General Test, minimum GPA of 3.0. Additional exam requirements/recommendations for international students: required—TOEFL (minimum score 550 paper-based; 79 iBT). Electronic applications accepted.

Chapman University, Crean College of Health and Behavioral Sciences, Orange, CA 92866. Offers MA, MMS, MS, DPT, TDPT. *Faculty:* 35 full-time (25 women), 9 part-time/adjunct (7 women). *Students:* 283 full-time (189 women), 191 part-time (115 women); includes 228 minority (5 Black or African American, non-Hispanic/Latino; 124 Asian, non-Hispanic/Latino; 69 Hispanic/Latino; 30 Two or more races, non-Hispanic/Latino), 7 international. Average age 27. 2,532 applicants, 10% accepted, 182 enrolled. In 2019, 63 master's, 57 doctorates awarded. *Entrance requirements:* For master's, GRE, Observational Hours, Direct Patient Contact Hours. Application fee: $60. Electronic applications accepted. *Expenses:* Contact institution. *Financial support:* Fellowships and scholarships/grants available. Financial award application deadline: 4/15; financial award applicants required to submit FAFSA. *Unit head:* Dr. Janeen Hill, Dean, 714-628-7223, E-mail: jhill@chapman.edu. *Application contact:* Howard Ying, 714-516-5020, E-mail: hying@chapman.edu.
Website: https://www.chapman.edu/crean/index.aspx

Chestnut Hill College, School of Graduate Studies, Division of Psychology, Philadelphia, PA 19118-2693. Offers clinical and counseling psychology (MS, CAS), including clinical and counseling psychology; clinical psychology (Psy D), including clinical psychology. *Program availability:* Part-time, evening/weekend. *Degree requirements:* For master's, thesis optional, practica; for doctorate, comprehensive exam, thesis/dissertation, internship, practica, clinical competency exam. *Entrance requirements:* For master's, GRE General Test, writing sample, letters of recommendation; for doctorate, GRE General Test, master's degree in counseling/clinical psychology or closely-related field, official transcripts, letters of recommendation, statement of professional goals, writing sample; for CAS, GRE General Test, official transcripts, letters of recommendation, statement of professional goals, writing sample. Additional exam requirements/recommendations for international students: required—TOEFL (minimum score 500 paper-based), IELTS (minimum score 6.0), or TWE (minimum score 22). *Expenses:* Contact institution.

The Chicago School of Professional Psychology, Program in Business Psychology, Chicago, IL 60610. Offers business psychology (PhD); industrial and organizational business psychology (Psy D); industrial and organizational psychology (MA); organizational leadership (MA, PhD). *Degree requirements:* For doctorate, thesis/dissertation optional. *Entrance requirements:* For doctorate, GRE. Additional exam requirements/recommendations for international students: required—TOEFL.

The Chicago School of Professional Psychology at Irvine, Program in Psychology, Irvine, CA 92612. Offers generalist (Psy D); psychodynamic psychotherapy (Psy D).

The Chicago School of Professional Psychology: Online, Program in International Psychology, Chicago, IL 60654. Offers PhD.

The Chicago School of Professional Psychology: Online, Program in Psychology, Chicago, IL 60654. Offers child and adolescent psychology (MA); generalist (MA); gerontology (MA); international psychology (MA); organizational leadership (MA); sport and exercise psychology (MA).

The Citadel, The Military College of South Carolina, Citadel Graduate College, School of Humanities and Social Sciences, Department of Psychology, Charleston, SC 29409. Offers psychology (MA), including clinical counseling; school psychology (Ed S). *Program availability:* Part-time, evening/weekend. *Degree requirements:* For master's, comprehensive exam, practicum; internship (written and oral presentation of a case study as part of internship; for Ed S, comprehensive exam, thesis (for some programs), practicum, internship. *Entrance requirements:* For master's, GRE (minimum combined score of 297, 150 on verbal reasoning and 141 on quantitative reasoning) or MAT (minimum score of 410), minimum undergraduate GPA of 3.0; 12 credit hours in psychology or minimum score on GRE Subject Test in psychology of 600; 2 letters of recommendation; for Ed S, GRE (minimum combined score of 297, 150 on verbal reasoning and 147 on quantitative reasoning) or MAT (minimum score of 410), minimum undergraduate or graduate GPA of 3.0; 2 letters of recommendation. Additional exam requirements/recommendations for international students: required—TOEFL (minimum score 550 paper-based; 79 iBT). Electronic applications accepted.

City College of the City University of New York, Graduate School, Colin Powell School for Civic and Global Leadership, Department of Psychology, New York, NY 10031-9198. Offers clinical psychology (PhD); general psychology (MA); mental health counseling (MA). *Accreditation:* APA (one or more programs are accredited). *Program availability:* Part-time. *Degree requirements:* For master's, one foreign language, comprehensive exam, thesis. *Entrance requirements:* For master's, GRE. Additional exam requirements/recommendations for international students: required—TOEFL (minimum score 550 paper-based; 79 iBT). Electronic applications accepted.

Claremont Graduate University, Graduate Programs, School of Social Science, Policy and Evaluation, Department of Psychology, Claremont, CA 91711-6160. Offers advanced study in evaluation (Certificate); cognitive psychology (MA, PhD); developmental psychology (MA, PhD); evaluation and applied research methods (MA, PhD); health behavior research and evaluation (MA, PhD); human resource development and evaluation (MA); industrial/organizational psychology (MA, PhD); organizational behavior (MA, PhD); organizational psychology (MA, PhD); social psychology (MA, PhD); MBA/PhD. *Program availability:* Part-time. Terminal master's awarded for partial completion of doctoral program. *Entrance requirements:* For master's and doctorate, GRE General Test. Additional exam requirements/recommendations for international students: required—TOEFL (minimum score 75 iBT). Electronic applications accepted.

Clayton State University, School of Graduate Studies, College of Arts and Sciences, Program in Psychology, Morrow, GA 30260-0285. Offers applied developmental psychology (MS); clinical/counseling psychology (MS). *Entrance requirements:* For master's, GRE, 2 official transcripts; 3 letters of recommendation; statement of purpose; on-campus interview; background check. Additional exam requirements/recommendations for international students: required—TOEFL (minimum score 550 paper-based). Electronic applications accepted.

Cleveland State University, College of Graduate Studies, College of Sciences and Health Professions, Department of Psychology, Cleveland, OH 44115. Offers MA, PhD, Psy S. *Accreditation:* APA. *Faculty:* 9 full-time (3 women), 14 part-time/adjunct (5 women). *Students:* 65 full-time (48 women), 27 part-time (19 women); includes 17 minority (10 Black or African American, non-Hispanic/Latino; 1 American Indian or Alaska Native, non-Hispanic/Latino; 1 Asian, non-Hispanic/Latino; 3 Hispanic/Latino; 2 Two or more races, non-Hispanic/Latino), 3 international. Average age 27. 167 applicants, 44% accepted, 36 enrolled. In 2019, 42 master's, 2 doctorates, 10 other advanced degrees awarded. Terminal master's awarded for partial completion of doctoral program. *Entrance requirements:* For master's and doctorate, GRE General Test. Additional exam requirements/recommendations for international students: required—TOEFL (minimum score 550 paper-based; 78 iBT). Application fee: $40. Electronic applications accepted. *Expenses:* Tuition, state resident: full-time $10,215; part-time $6810 per credit hour. Tuition, nonresident: full-time $17,496; part-time $11,664 per credit hour. International tuition: $19,316 full-time. Tuition and fees vary according to degree level and program. *Financial support:* In 2019–20, 40 students received support, including 16 research assistantships with full tuition reimbursements available (averaging $7,200 per year), 16 teaching assistantships with full tuition reimbursements available (averaging $7,200 per year); career-related internships or fieldwork, Federal Work-Study, scholarships/grants, tuition waivers (partial), and unspecified assistantships also available. Financial award application deadline: 3/1; financial award applicants required to submit FAFSA. *Unit head:* Dr. Kathleen M. McNamara, Chairperson, 216-687-2545, Fax: 216-687-9294, E-mail: k.mcnamara@csuohio.edu. *Application contact:* Barbara E. Durfey, Administrative Secretary, 216-687-2544, Fax: 216-687-9294, E-mail: b.durfey@csuohio.edu. Website: http://www.csuohio.edu/sciences/dept/psychology/

College of Saint Elizabeth, Department of Psychology, Morristown, NJ 07960-6989. Offers counseling psychology (MA, Psy D), including mental health counseling (MA), school counseling (MA). *Program availability:* Part-time. *Degree requirements:* For master's, thesis or alternative; for doctorate, thesis/dissertation. *Entrance requirements:* For master's, minimum GPA of 3.0, BA in psychology (preferred), 12 credits of course work in psychology; for doctorate, GRE, 3 letters of recommendation from professionals who can comment on the applicant's qualifications for doctoral study; master's degree in counseling psychology, forensic psychology and counseling, or its equivalent. Additional exam requirements/recommendations for international students: required—TOEFL (minimum score 550 paper-based; 79 iBT), IELTS (minimum score 6.5). Electronic applications accepted. Application fee is waived when completed online. *Expenses:* Contact institution.

College of St. Joseph, Graduate Programs, Division of Psychology and Human Services, Rutland, VT 05701-3899. Offers alcohol and substance abuse counseling (MS); clinical mental health counseling (MS); clinical psychology (MS); community counseling (MS); school guidance counseling (MS). *Program availability:* Part-time, evening/weekend. *Degree requirements:* For master's, comprehensive exam, thesis optional. *Entrance requirements:* For master's, official college transcripts; 2 letters of reference. Additional exam requirements/recommendations for international students: required—TOEFL (minimum score 550 paper-based). Electronic applications accepted.

Colorado State University, College of Natural Sciences, Department of Psychology, Fort Collins, CO 80523-1876. Offers psychology (PhD). *Accreditation:* APA. *Program availability:* 100% online. *Faculty:* 30 full-time (18 women), 8 part-time/adjunct (4 women). *Students:* 75 full-time (54 women), 92 part-time (63 women); includes 32 minority (3 Black or African American, non-Hispanic/Latino; 4 Asian, non-Hispanic/Latino; 17 Hispanic/Latino; 8 Two or more races, non-Hispanic/Latino), 5 international. Average age 29. 415 applicants, 11% accepted, 45 enrolled. In 2019, 36 master's, 12 doctorates awarded. *Degree requirements:* For master's, comprehensive exam, thesis; for doctorate, comprehensive exam, thesis/dissertation. *Entrance requirements:* For master's, GRE General Test, GRE Subject Test in psychology (for some programs; minimum scores within 50th percentile), minimum GPA of 3.0, 3 letters of recommendation, resume/curriculum vitae; for doctorate, GRE, minimum GPA of 3.0, 3 letters of recommendation, resume/curriculum vitae, transcripts. Additional exam requirements/recommendations for international students: required—TOEFL (minimum score 550 paper-based; 80 iBT); recommended—IELTS (minimum score 6.5), TSE (minimum score 58). *Application deadline:* For fall admission, 12/1 for domestic and international students. Application fee: $60 ($70 for international students). Electronic applications accepted. *Expenses:* Contact institution. *Financial support:* In 2019–20, 6 fellowships with full tuition reimbursements (averaging $14,949 per year), 9 research assistantships with full tuition reimbursements (averaging $22,516 per year), 59 teaching assistantships with full tuition reimbursements (averaging $15,962 per year) were awarded; scholarships/grants and traineeships also available. Financial award applicants required to submit FAFSA. *Unit head:* Dr. Don Rojas, Department Chair, 970-491-5213, E-mail: don.rojas@colostate.edu. *Application contact:* Linda Thornton, Administrative Assistant II, 970-491-5212, E-mail: linda.thornton@colostate.edu. Website: https://psychology.colostate.edu/

Columbia University, Graduate School of Arts and Sciences, New York, NY 10027. Offers African-American studies (MA); American studies (MA); anthropology (MA, PhD); art history and archaeology (MA, PhD); astronomy (PhD); biological sciences (PhD); biotechnology (MA); chemical physics (PhD); chemistry (PhD); classical studies (MA, PhD); classics (MA, PhD); climate and society (MA); conservation biology (MA); earth and environmental sciences (PhD); East Asia: regional studies (MA); East Asian languages and cultures (MA, PhD); ecology, evolution and environmental biology (MA), including conservation biology; ecology, evolution, and environmental biology (PhD), including ecology and evolutionary biology, evolutionary primatology; economics (MA, PhD); English and comparative literature (MA, PhD); French and Romance philology (MA, PhD); Germanic languages (MA, PhD); global French studies (MA); global thought (MA); Hispanic cultural studies (MA); history (PhD); history and literature (MA); human rights studies (MA); Islamic studies (MA); Italian (MA, PhD); Japanese pedagogy (MA); Jewish studies (MA); Latin America and the Caribbean: regional studies (MA); Latin American and Iberian cultures (PhD); mathematics (MA, PhD), including finance (MA); medieval and Renaissance studies (MA); Middle Eastern, South Asian, and African studies (MA, PhD); modern art: critical and curatorial studies (MA); modern European studies (MA); museum anthropology (MA); music (DMA, PhD); oral history (MA); philosophical foundations of physics (MA); philosophy (MA, PhD); physics (PhD); political science (MA, PhD); psychology (PhD); quantitative methods in the social sciences (MA); religion (MA, PhD); Russia, Eurasia and East Europe: regional studies (MA); Russian translation (MA); Slavic cultures (MA); Slavic languages (MA, PhD); sociology (MA, PhD); South Asian studies (MA); statistics (MA, PhD); theatre (PhD). *Program availability:* Part-time. *Students:* 3,506 full-time (1,844 women), 208 part-time (121 women); includes 864 minority (110 Black or African American, non-Hispanic/Latino; 5 American Indian or Alaska Native, non-Hispanic/Latino; 416 Asian, non-Hispanic/Latino; 147 Hispanic/Latino; 6 Native Hawaiian or other Pacific Islander, non-Hispanic/Latino; 180 Two or more races, non-Hispanic/Latino), 2,065 international. 14,545 applicants, 25% accepted, 1,429 enrolled. In 2019, 1,262 master's, 363 doctorates awarded. Terminal master's awarded for partial completion of doctoral program. *Degree requirements:* For master's, variable foreign language requirement, comprehensive exam (for some programs), thesis (for some programs); for doctorate, variable foreign language requirement, comprehensive exam (for some programs), thesis/dissertation. *Entrance requirements:* For master's and doctorate, GRE General Test, GRE Subject Test (for some programs). Additional exam requirements/recommendations for international students: required—TOEFL (minimum score 600 paper-based; 100 iBT), IELTS (minimum score 7.5). Application fee: $115. Electronic applications accepted. *Expenses:* Tuition: Full-time $47,600; part-time $1880 per credit. One-time fee: $105. *Financial support:* Fellowships, research assistantships, teaching assistantships, career-related internships or fieldwork, Federal Work-Study, institutionally sponsored loans, scholarships/grants, traineeships, health care benefits, tuition waivers, and unspecified assistantships available. Support available to part-time students. Financial award application deadline: 12/15. *Unit head:* Dr. Carlos J. Alonso, Dean of the Graduate School of Arts and Sciences and Vice President for Graduate Education, 212-854-2861, E-mail: gsas-dean@columbia.edu. *Application contact:* GSAS Office of Admissions, 212-854-6729, E-mail: gsas-admissions@columbia.edu. Website: http://gsas.columbia.edu/

Concordia University, School of Graduate Studies, Faculty of Arts and Science, Department of Psychology, MA Program in Psychology, Montréal, QC H3G 1M8, Canada. Offers MA. *Degree requirements:* For master's, comprehensive exam, thesis. *Entrance requirements:* For master's, GRE General Test, GRE Subject Test, honors degree in psychology or equivalent.

Cornell University, Graduate School, Graduate Fields of Arts and Sciences, Field of Psychology, Ithaca, NY 14853. Offers biopsychology (PhD); human experimental psychology (PhD); personality and social psychology (PhD). *Degree requirements:* For doctorate, comprehensive exam, thesis/dissertation, 2 semesters of teaching experience. *Entrance requirements:* For doctorate, GRE General Test, 3 letters of recommendation. Additional exam requirements/recommendations for international students: required—TOEFL (minimum score 550 paper-based; 77 iBT). Electronic applications accepted.

Dalhousie University, Faculty of Science, Department of Psychology and Neuroscience, Halifax, NS B3H 4R2, Canada. Offers clinical psychology (PhD); psychology (M Sc, PhD); psychology/neuroscience (M Sc, PhD). *Degree requirements:* For master's, thesis; for doctorate, thesis/dissertation. *Entrance requirements:* For doctorate, GRE General Test. Additional exam requirements/recommendations for international students: required—TOEFL, IELTS, CANTEST, CAEL, or Michigan English Language Assessment Battery. Electronic applications accepted.

Dartmouth College, Guarini School of Graduate and Advanced Studies, Department of Psychological and Brain Sciences, Hanover, NH 03755. Offers cognitive neuroscience (PhD); psychology (PhD). *Entrance requirements:* For doctorate, GRE General Test, GRE Subject Test. Additional exam requirements/recommendations for international students: required—TOEFL. Electronic applications accepted.

DePaul University, College of Science and Health, Chicago, IL 60604-2287. Offers applied mathematics (MS); applied statistics (MS); biological sciences (MA, MS); chemistry (MS); environmental science (MS); mathematics education (MA); mathematics for teaching (MS); nursing (MS); nursing practice (DNP); physics (MS);

polymer and coatings science (MS); psychology (MS); pure mathematics (MS); science education (MS); MA/PhD. *Accreditation:* AACN. Electronic applications accepted.

Divine Mercy University, School of Counseling, Arlington, VA 30327. Offers clinical mental health counseling (MS); psychology (MS). *Program availability:* Online learning.

Drexel University, College of Arts and Sciences, Department of Psychology, Philadelphia, PA 19104-2875. Offers clinical psychology (PhD), including clinical psychology, forensic psychology, health psychology, neuropsychology; psychology (MS); JD/PhD. *Accreditation:* APA (one or more programs are accredited). *Degree requirements:* For doctorate, thesis/dissertation, internship. *Entrance requirements:* For doctorate, GRE General Test. Additional exam requirements/recommendations for international students: required—TOEFL. Electronic applications accepted. *Expenses:* Contact institution.

Duke University, Graduate School, Department of Psychology and Neuroscience, Durham, NC 27708. Offers biological psychology (PhD); clinical psychology (PhD); cognitive psychology (PhD); developmental psychology (PhD); experimental psychology (PhD); health psychology (PhD); human social development (PhD); JD/MA. *Accreditation:* APA (one or more programs are accredited). *Degree requirements:* For doctorate, thesis/dissertation. *Entrance requirements:* For doctorate, GRE General Test. Additional exam requirements/recommendations for international students: required—TOEFL (minimum score 577 paper-based; 90 iBT) or IELTS (minimum score 7). Electronic applications accepted.

Duquesne University, Graduate School of Liberal Arts, Department of Psychology, Pittsburgh, PA 15282-0001. Offers clinical psychology (PhD). *Accreditation:* APA. *Degree requirements:* For doctorate, comprehensive exam, thesis/dissertation. *Entrance requirements:* For doctorate, GRE General Test, MA in psychology. Additional exam requirements/recommendations for international students: required—TOEFL. Electronic applications accepted.

East Central University, School of Graduate Studies, Department of Psychology, Ada, OK 74820. Offers MSPS. *Program availability:* Part-time, evening/weekend. *Entrance requirements:* For master's, GRE General Test, MAT. Electronic applications accepted.

Eastern Illinois University, Graduate School, College of Liberal Arts and Sciences, Department of Psychology, Charleston, IL 61920. Offers clinical psychology (MA); school psychology (SSP). *Program availability:* Part-time, evening/weekend. *Degree requirements:* For master's, comprehensive exam, thesis; for SSP, thesis. *Entrance requirements:* For master's and SSP, GMAT or GRE. Additional exam requirements/recommendations for international students: required—TOEFL (minimum score 500 paper-based; 61 iBT), IELTS (minimum score 6). Electronic applications accepted.

Eastern Kentucky University, The Graduate School, College of Arts and Sciences, Department of Psychology, Richmond, KY 40475-3102. Offers clinical psychology (MS); industrial/organizational psychology (MS); school psychology (Psy S). *Program availability:* Part-time. *Entrance requirements:* For master's and Psy S, GRE General Test, minimum GPA of 2.5.

Eastern Michigan University, Graduate School, College of Arts and Sciences, Department of Psychology, Ypsilanti, MI 48197. Offers clinical behavioral psychology (MS); clinical psychology (PhD); general clinical psychology (MS); general experimental psychology (MS). *Accreditation:* APA. *Faculty:* 24 full-time (14 women). *Students:* 41 full-time (36 women), 54 part-time (42 women); includes 31 minority (8 Black or African American, non-Hispanic/Latino; 1 American Indian or Alaska Native, non-Hispanic/Latino; 3 Asian, non-Hispanic/Latino; 11 Hispanic/Latino; 8 Two or more races, non-Hispanic/Latino), 5 international. Average age 26. 165 applicants, 25% accepted, 30 enrolled. In 2019, 25 master's, 7 doctorates awarded. *Entrance requirements:* For master's and doctorate, GRE. *Application deadline:* For fall admission, 2/15 for domestic students. Application fee: $45. *Financial support:* Fellowships available. *Unit head:* Dr. Ellen Koch, Interim Department Head, 734-487-1155, Fax: 734-487-6553, E-mail: ellen.koch@emich.edu. *Application contact:* Dr. Ellen Koch, Interim Department Head, 734-487-1155, Fax: 734-487-6553, E-mail: ellen.koch@emich.edu.

Eastern Washington University, Graduate Studies, College of Social Sciences, Department of Psychology, Cheney, WA 99004-2431. Offers clinical psychology (MS); experimental psychology (MS); mental health counseling (MS), including applied psychology, mental health counseling; school counseling (MS), including applied psychology, school counseling; school psychology respecialization (Ed S). *Faculty:* 22 full-time (15 women). *Students:* 119 full-time (94 women), 13 part-time (10 women); includes 3 minority (all Hispanic/Latino), 6 international. Average age 34. 83 applicants, 42% accepted, 31 enrolled. In 2019, 49 master's awarded. *Degree requirements:* For master's, comprehensive exam, thesis or alternative. *Entrance requirements:* For master's, GRE General Test, minimum GPA of 3.0. Additional exam requirements/recommendations for international students: required—TOEFL (minimum score 580 paper-based; 92 iBT), IELTS (minimum score 7), PTE (minimum score 63). *Application deadline:* For fall admission, 3/1 for domestic students. Applications are processed on a rolling basis. Application fee: $75. Electronic applications accepted. *Financial support:* Teaching assistantships with partial tuition reimbursements, career-related internships or fieldwork, Federal Work-Study, institutionally sponsored loans, scholarships/grants, health care benefits, tuition waivers (partial), and unspecified assistantships available. Support available to part-time students. Financial award application deadline: 2/1; financial award applicants required to submit FAFSA. *Unit head:* Dennis Anderson, 509-359-2087, E-mail: danderson2@ewu.edu. *Application contact:* Kathy White, Advisor/Recruiter for Graduate Studies, 509-359-6297, Fax: 509-359-6044, E-mail: gradprograms@ewu.edu.

East Tennessee State University, College of Graduate and Continuing Studies, College of Arts and Sciences, Department of Psychology, Johnson City, TN 37614. Offers clinical psychology (PhD); experimental psychology (PhD). *Accreditation:* APA. Terminal master's awarded for partial completion of doctoral program. *Degree requirements:* For doctorate, thesis/dissertation, externship. *Entrance requirements:* For doctorate, GRE General Test, minimum GPA of 3.0, three letters of recommendation, interview, minimum of 18 semester hours in undergraduate psychology. Additional exam requirements/recommendations for international students: required—TOEFL (minimum score 550 paper-based; 79 iBT). Electronic applications accepted.

Elizabeth City State University, Department of Education, Psychology and Health, Elizabeth City, NC 27909-7806. Offers M Ed, MSA. *Program availability:* Part-time, evening/weekend. *Degree requirements:* For master's, comprehensive exam (for some programs), thesis. Electronic applications accepted.

Emory University, Laney Graduate School, Department of Psychology, Atlanta, GA 30322-1100. Offers clinical psychology (PhD); cognition and development (PhD); neuroscience and animal behavior (PhD). *Accreditation:* APA. *Degree requirements:* For doctorate, comprehensive exam, thesis/dissertation. *Entrance requirements:* For doctorate, GRE General Test, minimum GPA of 3.25. Additional exam requirements/recommendations for international students: required—TOEFL. Electronic applications accepted.

Emporia State University, Program in Psychology, Emporia, KS 66801-5415. Offers general psychology (MS); industrial/organizational psychology (MS). *Program availability:* Part-time. *Degree requirements:* For master's, comprehensive exam or thesis, internship. *Entrance requirements:* For master's, GRE General Test or MAT, essay exam, appropriate bachelor's degree, letters of recommendation. Additional exam requirements/recommendations for international students: required—TOEFL (minimum score 520 paper-based; 68 iBT). Electronic applications accepted. *Expenses: Tuition, area resident:* Full-time $6394; part-time $266.41 per credit hour. Tuition, state resident: full-time $6394; part-time $266.41 per credit hour. Tuition, nonresident: full-time $20,128; part-time $828.66 per credit hour. *International tuition:* $20,128 full-time. *Required fees:* $2183; $90.95 per credit hour. Tuition and fees vary according to campus/location and program.

Fairleigh Dickinson University, Florham Campus, Maxwell Becton College of Arts and Sciences, Department of Psychology, Madison, NJ 07940-1099. Offers clinical mental health counseling (MA); counseling (MA); industrial/organizational psychology (MA); organizational behavior (MA, Certificate), including organizational behavior (MA), organizational leadership (Certificate); MA/MBA.

Fairleigh Dickinson University, Metropolitan Campus, University College: Arts, Sciences, and Professional Studies, School of Psychology, Teaneck, NJ 07666-1914. Offers clinical psychology (MA, PhD); clinical psychopharmacology (MA); forensic psychology (MA); general-theoretical psychology (MA, Certificate); school psychology (MA, Psy D). *Accreditation:* APA (one or more programs are accredited).

Fayetteville State University, Graduate School, Program in Psychology, Fayetteville, NC 28301. Offers MA. *Program availability:* Part-time, evening/weekend, online only, 100% online. *Faculty:* 5 full-time (3 women). *Students:* 11 full-time (7 women), 3 part-time (2 women); includes 8 minority (6 Black or African American, non-Hispanic/Latino; 1 Hispanic/Latino; 1 Two or more races, non-Hispanic/Latino). Average age 34. 16 applicants, 94% accepted, 9 enrolled. In 2019, 12 master's awarded. *Degree requirements:* For master's, comprehensive exam (for some programs), thesis (for some programs). *Entrance requirements:* For master's, GRE. Additional exam requirements/recommendations for international students: required—TOEFL (minimum score 61 paper-based). *Application deadline:* For fall admission, 4/15 for domestic students. Applications are processed on a rolling basis. Application fee: $50. Electronic applications accepted. *Financial support:* Application deadline: 3/1; applicants required to submit FAFSA. *Unit head:* Dr. Pius Nyutu, Chair, 910-672-1413, E-mail: pnyutu@uncfsu.edu. *Application contact:* Dr. Whitney Wall, Graduate Coordinator, 910-672-1413, E-mail: wwall1@uncfsu.edu.

Fielding Graduate University, Graduate Programs, School of Psychology, Santa Barbara, CA 93105-3814. Offers MA, PhD, Graduate Certificate, Post-Doctoral Certificate, Postbaccalaureate Certificate. *Accreditation:* APA. *Program availability:* Part-time, evening/weekend, 100% online, blended/hybrid learning. Terminal master's awarded for partial completion of doctoral program. *Degree requirements:* For master's, thesis or alternative, capstone; for doctorate, comprehensive exam (for some programs), thesis/dissertation. *Entrance requirements:* For master's, Bachelor's degree from regionally-accredited institution or equivalent, minimum GPA depends on program; for doctorate, Bachelor's or Master's degree from regionally-accredited institution or equivalent, minimum GPA depends on program; for other advanced degree, Bachelor's from regionally-accredited institution or equivalent. Electronic applications accepted. *Expenses:* Contact institution.

Fisk University, Division of Graduate Studies, Department of Psychology, Nashville, TN 37208-3051. Offers clinical psychology (MA); psychology (MA). *Degree requirements:* For master's, thesis. *Entrance requirements:* For master's, GRE General Test, GRE Subject Test, minimum GPA of 3.0. Electronic applications accepted.

Fitchburg State University, Division of Graduate and Continuing Education, Program in Interdisciplinary Studies, Fitchburg, MA 01420-2697. Offers applied communications (CAGS); counseling/psychology (CAGS); individualized track (CAGS); reading specialist (CAGS). *Program availability:* Part-time, evening/weekend. *Entrance requirements:* Additional exam requirements/recommendations for international students: required—TOEFL (minimum score 550 paper-based; 79 iBT). Electronic applications accepted. *Expenses:* Contact institution.

Florida Agricultural and Mechanical University, Division of Graduate Studies, Research, and Continuing Education, College of Social Sciences, Arts and Humanities, Department of Psychology, Tallahassee, FL 32307-3200. Offers community psychology (MS). *Degree requirements:* For master's, thesis. *Entrance requirements:* For master's, GRE General Test, minimum GPA of 3.0. Additional exam requirements/recommendations for international students: required—TOEFL.

Florida Atlantic University, Charles E. Schmidt College of Science, Department of Psychology, Boca Raton, FL 33431-0991. Offers MA. *Faculty:* 26 full-time (10 women). *Students:* 38 full-time (27 women), 18 part-time (12 women); includes 14 minority (1 Black or African American, non-Hispanic/Latino; 3 Asian, non-Hispanic/Latino; 9 Hispanic/Latino; 1 Two or more races, non-Hispanic/Latino), 5 international. Average age 28. 95 applicants, 20% accepted, 18 enrolled. In 2019, 8 master's awarded. Terminal master's awarded for partial completion of doctoral program. *Degree requirements:* For master's, one foreign language, thesis or alternative. *Entrance requirements:* For master's, GRE General Test, minimum GPA of 3.0 during previous 2 years. Additional exam requirements/recommendations for international students: required—TOEFL (minimum score 500 paper-based; 61 iBT), IELTS (minimum score 6). *Application deadline:* For fall admission, 5/1 for domestic students, 5/15 for international students. Application fee: $30. Electronic applications accepted. *Expenses: Tuition:* Full-time $20,536; part-time $371.82 per credit hour. Tuition and fees vary according to program. *Financial support:* Research assistantships with partial tuition reimbursements, teaching assistantships with partial tuition reimbursements, Federal Work-Study, institutionally sponsored loans, scholarships/grants, and unspecified assistantships available. Financial award application deadline: 3/1; financial award applicants required to submit FAFSA.
Website: http://psy.fau.edu/

Florida Institute of Technology, College of Psychology and Liberal Arts, Melbourne, FL 32901-6975. Offers applied behavior analysis (PhD); applied behavior analysis and organizational behavior management (MS); clinical psychology (Psy D); professional behavioral analysis (MA). *Program availability:* Part-time, evening/weekend, 100% online. Terminal master's awarded for partial completion of doctoral program. *Degree requirements:* For master's, comprehensive exam (for some programs), thesis or final exam; for doctorate, comprehensive exam, thesis/dissertation optional, internship. *Entrance requirements:* For master's, GRE General Test, minimum GPA of 3.0, 2 letters of recommendation, resume, statement of objectives; for doctorate, GRE General Test, GRE Subject Test, 3 letters of recommendation, minimum GPA of 3.2, resume, statement of objectives. Additional exam requirements/recommendations for international students: required—TOEFL (minimum score 550 paper-based; 79 iBT). Electronic applications accepted.

Florida International University, College of Arts, Sciences, and Education, Department of Psychology, Miami, FL 33199. Offers behavioral analysis (MS); clinical science (PhD); cognitive neuroscience (PhD); counseling psychology (MS); developmental science (MS, PhD); legal psychology (MS, PhD); organizational psychology (MS, PhD). *Accreditation:* APA. *Program availability:* Part-time, evening/weekend. *Faculty:* 52 full-time (33 women), 50 part-time/adjunct (37 women). *Students:*

203 full-time (159 women), 2 part-time (both women); includes 117 minority (15 Black or African American, non-Hispanic/Latino; 8 Asian, non-Hispanic/Latino; 86 Hispanic/Latino; 8 Two or more races, non-Hispanic/Latino), 15 international. Average age 26. 410 applicants, 19% accepted, 60 enrolled. In 2019, 57 master's, 7 doctorates awarded. Terminal master's awarded for partial completion of doctoral program. *Degree requirements:* For master's, thesis; for doctorate, comprehensive exam, thesis/dissertation. *Entrance requirements:* For master's, GRE General Test, minimum GPA of 3.0, resume, 3 letters of recommendation; for doctorate, GRE General Test, 3 letters of recommendation, resume, letter of intent, two writing samples, minimum GPA of 3.0. Additional exam requirements/recommendations for international students: required—TOEFL (minimum score 550 paper-based; 80 iBT). *Application deadline:* For fall admission, 12/15 for domestic and international students. Application fee: $30. Electronic applications accepted. *Expenses: Tuition, area resident:* Full-time $8912; part-time $446 per credit hour. Tuition, state resident: full-time $8912; part-time $446 per credit hour. Tuition, nonresident: full-time $21,393; part-time $992 per credit hour. *Required fees:* $2194. *Financial support:* Institutionally sponsored loans and scholarships/grants available. Financial award application deadline: 3/1. *Unit head:* Dr. Jeremy Pettit, Interim Chair, 305-348-1671, Fax: 305-348-2880, E-mail: jeremy.pettit@fiu.edu. *Application contact:* Nanett Rojas, Manager, Admissions Operations, 305-348-7464, Fax: 305-348-7441, E-mail: gradadm@fiu.edu.

Florida State University, The Graduate School, Department of Anthropology, Department of Psychology, Tallahassee, FL 32306-4301. Offers applied behavior analysis (MS); clinical psychology (PhD); cognitive psychology (PhD); developmental psychology (PhD); social psychology (PhD). *Accreditation:* APA (one or more programs are accredited). *Faculty:* 44 full-time (16 women). *Students:* 162 full-time (124 women), 7 part-time (5 women); includes 50 minority (6 Black or African American, non-Hispanic/Latino; 16 Asian, non-Hispanic/Latino; 19 Hispanic/Latino; 9 Two or more races, non-Hispanic/Latino), 7 international. Average age 26. 396 applicants, 18% accepted, 45 enrolled. In 2019, 32 master's, 18 doctorates awarded. Terminal master's awarded for partial completion of doctoral program. *Degree requirements:* For master's, comprehensive exam (for some programs), thesis (for some programs); for doctorate, comprehensive exam, thesis/dissertation. *Entrance requirements:* For master's, GRE General Test, minimum GPA of 3.0; for doctorate, GRE General Test. Additional exam requirements/recommendations for international students: required—TOEFL (minimum score 80 iBT). *Application deadline:* For fall admission, 12/1 for domestic and international students. Application fee: $30. Electronic applications accepted. *Financial support:* In 2019–20, 147 students received support, including 13 fellowships with full tuition reimbursements available (averaging $24,324 per year), 32 research assistantships with full tuition reimbursements available (averaging $24,324 per year), 89 teaching assistantships with full tuition reimbursements available (averaging $24,324 per year); career-related internships or fieldwork and health care benefits also available. Financial award applicants required to submit FAFSA. *Unit head:* Dr. Frank Johnson, Chairman, 850-644-2040, Fax: 850-644-7739, E-mail: johnson@psy.fsu.edu. *Application contact:* Lynda L. Gibson, Graduate Program Associate, 850-644-2499, Fax: 850-644-7739, E-mail: grad-info@psy.fsu.edu.
Website: http://www.psy.fsu.edu/

Fordham University, Graduate School of Arts and Sciences, Department of Psychology, New York, NY 10458. Offers applied developmental psychology (PhD); applied psychological methods (MS); clinical psychology (PhD); clinical research methods (MS); psychometrics and quantitative psychology (PhD). *Students:* Average age 31. 929 applicants, 7% accepted, 21 enrolled. In 2019, 14 master's, 14 doctorates awarded. Terminal master's awarded for partial completion of doctoral program. *Degree requirements:* For master's, comprehensive exam; for doctorate, comprehensive exam, thesis/dissertation. *Entrance requirements:* For doctorate, GRE General Test, GRE Subject Test. Additional exam requirements/recommendations for international students: required—TOEFL (minimum score 600 paper-based). *Application deadline:* For fall admission, 12/14 for domestic students. Application fee: $70. Electronic applications accepted. *Financial support:* In 2019–20, 73 students received support, including 16 fellowships with tuition reimbursements available (averaging $24,561 per year), 12 research assistantships with tuition reimbursements available (averaging $15,170 per year), 11 teaching assistantships with tuition reimbursements available (averaging $12,286 per year); career-related internships or fieldwork, institutionally sponsored loans, tuition waivers (full and partial), and unspecified assistantships also available. Financial award application deadline: 12/14; financial award applicants required to submit FAFSA. *Unit head:* Dr. Barry Rosenfeld, Chair, 718-817-3794, Fax: 718-817-3699, E-mail: rosenfeld@fordham.edu. *Application contact:* Garrett Marino, Director of Graduate Admissions, 718-817-4419, Fax: 718-817-3566, E-mail: gmarino10@fordham.edu.

Fort Hays State University, Graduate School, College of Health and Behavioral Sciences, Department of Psychology, Hays, KS 67601-4099. Offers psychology (MS); school psychology (Ed S). *Degree requirements:* For master's and Ed S, comprehensive exam, thesis. *Entrance requirements:* For master's, GRE General Test. Additional exam requirements/recommendations for international students: required—TOEFL (minimum score 550 paper-based). Electronic applications accepted.

Francis Marion University, Graduate Programs, Department of Psychology, Florence, SC 29502-0547. Offers applied psychology (MS), including clinical/counseling psychology, school psychology; school psychology (SSP). *Program availability:* Part-time, evening/weekend. *Degree requirements:* For master's, internship. *Entrance requirements:* For master's, GRE General Test, official transcripts, two letters of recommendation. Additional exam requirements/recommendations for international students: required—TOEFL (minimum score 550 paper-based; 79 iBT). *Expenses: Tuition, area resident:* Full-time $10,612; part-time $530.60 per credit hour. Tuition, state resident: full-time $10,612; part-time $530.60 per credit hour. Tuition, nonresident: full-time $21,224; part-time $1061.20 per credit hour. *International tuition:* $21,224 full-time. *Required fees:* $312; $156 per credit hour. $332 per semester. Tuition and fees vary according to program.

Frostburg State University, College of Liberal Arts and Sciences, Department of Psychology, Frostburg, MD 21532-1099. Offers counseling psychology (MS). *Program availability:* Part-time, evening/weekend. *Degree requirements:* For master's, internship. *Entrance requirements:* For master's, GRE General Test or MAT, interview, minimum GPA of 3.0, resume. Additional exam requirements/recommendations for international students: required—TOEFL. Electronic applications accepted.

Gardner-Webb University, Graduate School, School of Psychology, Boiling Springs, NC 28017. Offers mental health counseling (MA); school counseling (MA). *Program availability:* Part-time, evening/weekend. *Degree requirements:* For master's, comprehensive exam. *Entrance requirements:* For master's, GRE General Test, MAT, minimum GPA of 2.7. Electronic applications accepted. *Expenses:* Contact institution.

Geneva College, Master of Arts in Counseling Program, Beaver Falls, PA 15010. Offers clinical mental health counseling (MA); marriage and family counseling (MA); school counseling (MA). *Accreditation:* ACA. *Program availability:* Part-time, evening/weekend, online only, 100% online, blended/hybrid learning. *Faculty:* 4 full-time (1 woman), 5 part-time/adjunct (2 women). *Students:* 26 full-time (20 women), 22 part-time (17 women); includes 11 minority (9 Black or African American, non-Hispanic/Latino; 1 Asian, non-Hispanic/Latino; 1 Two or more races, non-Hispanic/Latino), 1 international. Average age 33. 24 applicants, 63% accepted, 14 enrolled. In 2019, 34 master's awarded. *Degree requirements:* For master's, comprehensive exam, 60 credits including practicum and internship. *Entrance requirements:* For master's, minimum GPA of 3.0 (preferred), 3 letters of recommendation, essay on career goals, resume of educational and professional experiences. Additional exam requirements/recommendations for international students: required—TOEFL. *Application deadline:* For fall admission, 9/1 for domestic students; for spring admission, 1/10 for domestic students. Applications are processed on a rolling basis. Electronic applications accepted. *Expenses:* $680 per credit. 60 credits required for graduation. *Financial support:* Research assistantships, teaching assistantships, career-related internships or fieldwork, and unspecified assistantships available. Financial award application deadline: 8/1; financial award applicants required to submit FAFSA. *Unit head:* Dr. Shannan Shiderly, Program Director, 724-847-6649, Fax: 724-847-6101, E-mail: slshider@geneva.edu. *Application contact:* Marina Frazier, Graduate Program Manager, 724-847-6697, E-mail: counseling@geneva.edu.
Website: https://www.geneva.edu/graduate/counseling/

George Mason University, College of Humanities and Social Sciences, Department of Psychology, Fairfax, VA 22030. Offers applied developmental psychology (MA, PhD); clinical psychology (PhD); cognitive and behavioral neuroscience (MA, PhD); cognitive neuroscience (Certificate); human factors/applied cognition (MA, PhD, Certificate), including transportation human factors (Certificate), usability (Certificate); industrial/organizational psychology (MA, PhD). *Accreditation:* APA. *Degree requirements:* For master's, comprehensive exam, thesis or practicum research; for doctorate, comprehensive exam, thesis/dissertation, 2nd-year project. *Entrance requirements:* For master's, GRE, 2 official transcripts; goals statement; 15 undergraduate credits in concentration for which the applicant is applying; for doctorate, GRE, 3 letters of recommendation; resume; goals statement; minimum GPA of 3.0 overall for last 60 undergraduate credits, 3.25 in psychology courses; 15 undergraduate credits in concentration for which the applicant is applying; 2 official transcripts; for Certificate, GRE, 2 official transcripts; expanded goals statement; 3 letters of recommendation. Additional exam requirements/recommendations for international students: required—TOEFL (minimum score 575 paper-based; 88 iBT), IELTS (minimum score 6.5), PTE (minimum score 59). Electronic applications accepted.

Georgetown University, Graduate School of Arts and Sciences, Department of Psychology, Washington, DC 20005. Offers human development and public policy (PhD); lifespan cognitive neuroscience (PhD); PhD/MPP. *Faculty:* 14 full-time (9 women). *Students:* 16 full-time (9 women); includes 3 minority (1 Asian, non-Hispanic/Latino; 2 Hispanic/Latino). Average age 25. 101 applicants, 5 enrolled. In 2019, 4 doctorates awarded. *Degree requirements:* For doctorate, thesis/dissertation, area paper. *Entrance requirements:* For doctorate, GRE General Test, GRE Subject Test. Additional exam requirements/recommendations for international students: required—TOEFL. *Application deadline:* For fall admission, 12/1 for domestic and international students. Application fee: $51 ($50 for international students). Electronic applications accepted. *Financial support:* In 2019–20, 16 students received support, including 16 teaching assistantships with full tuition reimbursements available (averaging $28,000 per year); research assistantships also available. Financial award application deadline: 2/1; financial award applicants required to submit FAFSA. *Unit head:* Dr. Jennifer Woolard, Interim Chair, 202-687-9258, Fax: 202-687-6050, E-mail: jlw47@georgetown.edu. *Application contact:* Graduate School Admissions Office, 202-687-5568, E-mail: gradmail@georgetown.edu.
Website: https://psychology.georgetown.edu

The George Washington University, Columbian College of Arts and Sciences, Department of Psychology, Washington, DC 20052. Offers applied social psychology (PhD); clinical psychology (PhD); cognitive neuroscience (PhD). *Accreditation:* APA. *Program availability:* Part-time, evening/weekend. *Degree requirements:* For doctorate, thesis/dissertation or alternative, general exam. *Entrance requirements:* For doctorate, GRE General Test, minimum GPA of 3.0. Additional exam requirements/recommendations for international students: required—TOEFL (minimum score 550 paper-based; 80 iBT).

The George Washington University, Columbian College of Arts and Sciences, Program in Professional Psychology, Washington, DC 20052. Offers MA, Psy D, Graduate Certificate. *Accreditation:* APA. *Entrance requirements:* For doctorate, GRE General Test, interview, minimum GPA of 3.0. Additional exam requirements/recommendations for international students: required—TOEFL (minimum score 550 paper-based; 80 iBT). Electronic applications accepted.

Georgia Institute of Technology, Graduate Studies, College of Sciences, School of Psychology, Atlanta, GA 30332. Offers MS, PhD. *Program availability:* Part-time. *Faculty:* 22 full-time (4 women). *Students:* 75 full-time (55 women), 11 part-time (8 women); includes 20 minority (2 Black or African American, non-Hispanic/Latino; 8 Asian, non-Hispanic/Latino; 5 Hispanic/Latino; 5 Two or more races, non-Hispanic/Latino), 24 international. Average age 28. 228 applicants, 20% accepted, 22 enrolled. In 2019, 11 master's, 10 doctorates awarded. Terminal master's awarded for partial completion of doctoral program. *Degree requirements:* For master's, thesis; for doctorate, thesis/dissertation. *Entrance requirements:* For master's and doctorate, GRE General Test, GRE Subject Test. Additional exam requirements/recommendations for international students: required—TOEFL (minimum score 577 paper-based; 90 iBT), IELTS (minimum score 7), TOEFL is the preferred method with the requirements shown on the programs. *Application deadline:* For fall admission, 12/1 for domestic and international students. Applications are processed on a rolling basis. Application fee: $75 ($85 for international students). Electronic applications accepted. *Expenses: Tuition, area resident:* Full-time $14,064; part-time $586 per credit hour. Tuition, state resident: full-time $14,064; part-time $586 per credit hour. Tuition, nonresident: full-time $29,140; part-time $1215 per credit hour. *International tuition:* $29,140 full-time. *Required fees:* $2024; $840 per semester. $2096. Tuition and fees vary according to course load. *Financial support:* In 2019–20, 5 fellowships, 13 research assistantships, 48 teaching assistantships were awarded; career-related internships or fieldwork, Federal Work-Study, institutionally sponsored loans, tuition waivers (full and partial), and unspecified assistantships also available. Support available to part-time students. Financial award application deadline: 7/1; financial award applicants required to submit FAFSA. *Unit head:* Mark Wheeler, School Chair, 404-894-2680, Fax: 404-894-8905, E-mail: mark.wheeler@psych.gatech.edu. *Application contact:* Marla Bruner, Director of Graduate Studies, 404-894-1610, Fax: 404-894-1609, E-mail: gradinfo@mail.gatech.edu.
Website: http://www.psychology.gatech.edu

Georgia Southern University, Jack N. Averitt College of Graduate Studies, College of Behavioral and Social Sciences, Program in Psychology, Statesboro, GA 30460. Offers clinical psychology (Psy D); psychology (MS). *Faculty:* 27 full-time (14 women), 1 (woman) part-time/adjunct. *Students:* 55 full-time (40 women), 8 part-time (5 women); includes 16 minority (4 Black or African American, non-Hispanic/Latino; 2 Asian, non-Hispanic/Latino; 9 Hispanic/Latino; 1 Two or more races, non-Hispanic/Latino), 1 international. Average age 25. 33 applicants, 58% accepted, 14 enrolled. In 2019, 17 master's, 6 doctorates awarded. Terminal master's awarded for partial completion of

doctoral program. *Degree requirements:* For master's, comprehensive exam, thesis (for some programs), terminal exam; for doctorate, comprehensive exam, thesis/dissertation, clinical qualifying exam, practicum, internship. *Entrance requirements:* For master's, GRE General Test, minimum GPA of 3.0, introductory courses in psychology and statistics, letters of recommendation; for doctorate, GRE General Test; GRE Subject Test (if no undergraduate degree in psychology), minimum undergraduate GPA of 3.25; 3 letters of reference; statement of purpose. Additional exam requirements/recommendations for international students: required—TOEFL (minimum score 550 paper-based; 80 iBT), IELTS (minimum score 6). *Application deadline:* For fall admission, 1/15 priority date for domestic students, 1/15 for international students. Application fee: $50. Electronic applications accepted. *Expenses: Tuition, area resident:* Full-time $4986; part-time $277 per credit hour. Tuition, nonresident: full-time $19,890; part-time $1105 per credit hour. *International tuition:* $19,890 full-time. *Required fees:* $2114; $1057 per semester. $1057 per semester. Tuition and fees vary according to course load, campus/location and program. *Financial support:* In 2019–20, 46 students received support, including 4 fellowships with full tuition reimbursements available (averaging $7,750 per year), 6 research assistantships with full tuition reimbursements available (averaging $7,750 per year), 17 teaching assistantships with full tuition reimbursements available (averaging $7,750 per year); career-related internships or fieldwork, Federal Work-Study, scholarships/grants, tuition waivers (full), and unspecified assistantships also available. Support available to part-time students. Financial award application deadline: 4/15; financial award applicants required to submit FAFSA. *Unit head:* Dr. Ty W. Boyer, Graduate Director, 912-478-5539, Fax: 912-478-0751, E-mail: tboyer@georgiasouthern.edu.
Website: http://class.georgiasouthern.edu/psychology/

Georgia State University, College of Arts and Sciences, Department of Psychology, Atlanta, GA 30302-3083. Offers clinical psychology (PhD); cognitive sciences (PhD); community psychology (PhD); developmental psychology (PhD); neuropsychology and behavioral neuroscience (PhD). *Accreditation:* APA. *Faculty:* 29 full-time (17 women). *Students:* 107 full-time (85 women), 2 part-time (both women); includes 23 minority (9 Black or African American, non-Hispanic/Latino; 6 Asian, non-Hispanic/Latino; 7 Hispanic/Latino; 1 Two or more races, non-Hispanic/Latino), 13 international. Average age 28. 498 applicants, 5% accepted, 17 enrolled. In 2019, 18 doctorates awarded. *Entrance requirements:* For doctorate, GRE. Additional exam requirements/recommendations for international students: required—TOEFL (minimum score 550 paper-based; 80 iBT). *Application deadline:* For fall admission, 12/1 for domestic and international students. Application fee: $50. Electronic applications accepted. *Expenses: Tuition, area resident:* Full-time $7164; part-time $398 per credit hour. Tuition, state resident: full-time $7164; part-time $398 per credit hour. Tuition, nonresident: full-time $22,662; part-time $1259 per credit hour. *International tuition:* $22,662 full-time. *Required fees:* $2128; $312 per credit hour. Tuition and fees vary according to course load and program. *Financial support:* In 2019–20, fellowships with full tuition reimbursements (averaging $19,282 per year), research assistantships with full tuition reimbursements (averaging $5,173 per year), teaching assistantships with full tuition reimbursements (averaging $6,389 per year) were awarded; scholarships/grants, traineeships, health care benefits, and unspecified assistantships also available. Financial award applicants required to submit FAFSA. *Unit head:* Dr. Lisa Armistead, Professor, Associate Provost for Graduate Programs, 404-413-2091, Fax: 404-413-6207, E-mail: lparmistead@gsu.edu. *Application contact:* Dr. Lindsey Cohen, Director of Graduate Studies, 404-413-6263, Fax: 404-413-6207, E-mail: llcohen@gsu.edu.
Website: https://psychology.gsu.edu/

Goddard College, Graduate Division, Master of Arts in Psychology Program, Plainfield, VT 05667-9432. Offers expressive arts therapy (MA); psychology (MA); sexual orientation (MA). *Program availability:* Part-time, online learning. *Degree requirements:* For master's, thesis or alternative, clinical internship. *Entrance requirements:* For master's, eight specific undergraduate prerequisite courses taken within previous five years (or preparatory semester at Goddard), statement of purpose, 3 letters of recommendation, interview. Electronic applications accepted.

Golden Gate University, Ageno School of Business, San Francisco, CA 94105-2968. Offers accounting (MBA); adaptive leadership (MBA); advanced financial planning (MS); business administration (EMBA, MBA, DBA); business analytics (MBA, MS); entrepreneurship (MBA); finance (MBA, MS, Certificate); financial life planning (Certificate); financial planning (MS, Certificate); global supply chain management (MBA, Certificate); human resource management (MBA, MS, Certificate); information technology management (MBA, MS, Certificate); international business (MBA); marketing (MBA, MS, Certificate); project management (MBA, MS, Certificate); psychology (MA, Certificate); public administration (EMPA, MBA); public administration leadership (Certificate); JD/MBA. *Program availability:* Part-time, evening/weekend. *Degree requirements:* For doctorate, thesis/dissertation, qualifying examination. *Entrance requirements:* For master's, GMAT (for MBA), minimum GPA of 2.5 (MS). Additional exam requirements/recommendations for international students: required—TOEFL (minimum score 550 paper-based; 79 iBT). Electronic applications accepted. *Expenses:* Contact institution.

Governors State University, College of Education, Program in Psychology, University Park, IL 60484. Offers MA. *Program availability:* Part-time. *Faculty:* 23 full-time (15 women), 51 part-time/adjunct (38 women). *Students:* 30 full-time (21 women), 51 part-time (45 women); includes 50 minority (32 Black or African American, non-Hispanic/Latino; 15 Hispanic/Latino; 3 Two or more races, non-Hispanic/Latino), 1 international. Average age 34. 55 applicants, 56% accepted, 28 enrolled. In 2019, 23 master's awarded. *Application deadline:* For fall admission, 4/1 for domestic students. Applications are processed on a rolling basis. Application fee: $50. Electronic applications accepted. *Expenses:* $353/credit hour; $4,236 in tuition/term; $5,534 in tuition and fees/term; $11,068/year. *Financial support:* Application deadline: 5/1; applicants required to submit FAFSA. *Unit head:* Patricia Robey, Chair, Division of Psychology and Counseling, 708-534-5000 Ext. 4975, E-mail: sdermer@govst.edu. *Application contact:* Patricia Robey, Chair, Division of Psychology and Counseling, 708-534-5000 Ext. 4975, E-mail: sdermer@govst.edu.

The Graduate Center, City University of New York, Graduate Studies, Program in Psychology, New York, NY 10016-4039. Offers basic applied neurocognition (PhD); biopsychology (PhD); clinical psychology (PhD); developmental psychology (PhD); environmental psychology (PhD); experimental psychology (PhD); industrial psychology (PhD); learning processes (PhD); neuropsychology (PhD); psychology (PhD); social personality (PhD). *Degree requirements:* For doctorate, one foreign language, thesis/dissertation. *Entrance requirements:* For doctorate, GRE General Test. Additional exam requirements/recommendations for international students: required—TOEFL. Electronic applications accepted.

Grand Canyon University, College of Doctoral Studies, Phoenix, AZ 85017-1097. Offers data analytics (DBA); general psychology (PhD), including cognition and instruction, industrial and organizational psychology, integrating technology, learning, and psychology, performance psychology; management (DBA); marketing (DBA); organizational leadership (Ed D), including behavioral health, Christian ministry, health care administration, organizational development. *Degree requirements:* For doctorate, comprehensive exam, thesis/dissertation. *Entrance requirements:* For doctorate, minimum GPA of 3.4 on earned advanced degree from regionally-accredited institution; transcripts; goals statement.

Hampton University, School of Liberal Arts and Education, Program in Psychology, Hampton, VA 23668. Offers marriage and family studies (MS); psychology (MS). *Program availability:* Part-time. *Students:* 4 part-time (all women); all minorities (all Black or African American, non-Hispanic/Latino). Average age 26. 9 applicants. In 2019, 1 master's awarded. *Degree requirements:* For master's, thesis. *Entrance requirements:* For master's, GRE. Additional exam requirements/recommendations for international students: required—TOEFL (minimum score 525 paper-based) or IELTS (6.5). *Application deadline:* For fall admission, 6/1 priority date for domestic students, 4/1 priority date for international students; for spring admission, 11/1 priority date for domestic students, 9/1 priority date for international students; for summer admission, 4/1 priority date for domestic and international students. Application fee: $35. Electronic applications accepted. *Expenses:* Contact institution. *Financial support:* Unspecified assistantships available. Financial award application deadline: 6/30; financial award applicants required to submit FAFSA. *Unit head:* Dr. Tamara Williams, Interim Chairperson, 757-727-5301. *Application contact:* Dr. Tamara Williams, Interim Chairperson, 757-727-5301.

Hardin-Simmons University, Graduate School, Cynthia Ann Parker College of Liberal Arts, Department of Psychology, Abilene, TX 79698-0001. Offers clinical counseling and marriage and family therapy (MA). *Program availability:* Part-time. *Degree requirements:* For master's, comprehensive exam, clinical experience, project. *Entrance requirements:* For master's, 21 semester hours of course work in psychology (18 in upper-division classes); minimum undergraduate GPA of 3.0 in major, 2.7 overall; writing sample; letters of recommendation. Additional exam requirements/recommendations for international students: required—TOEFL (minimum score 550 paper-based; 79 iBT). Electronic applications accepted.

Harvard University, Graduate School of Arts and Sciences, Department of Psychology, Cambridge, MA 02138. Offers psychology (PhD), including behavior and decision analysis, cognition, developmental psychology, experimental psychology, personality, psychobiology, psychopathology; social psychology (PhD). *Accreditation:* APA. *Degree requirements:* For doctorate, thesis/dissertation, general exams. *Entrance requirements:* For doctorate, GRE General Test. Additional exam requirements/recommendations for international students: required—TOEFL.

Hofstra University, College of Liberal Arts and Sciences, Programs in Psychology, Hempstead, NY 11549. Offers applied organizational psychology (PhD); clinical psychology (PhD); industrial/organizational psychology (MA); school-community psychology (Psy D). *Accreditation:* APA. *Program availability:* Part-time, evening/weekend. *Students:* 193 full-time (138 women), 22 part-time (10 women); includes 42 minority (6 Black or African American, non-Hispanic/Latino; 1 American Indian or Alaska Native, non-Hispanic/Latino; 9 Asian, non-Hispanic/Latino; 23 Hispanic/Latino; 3 Two or more races, non-Hispanic/Latino), 21 international. Average age 26. 338 applicants, 36% accepted, 61 enrolled. In 2019, 60 master's, 33 doctorates awarded. Terminal master's awarded for partial completion of doctoral program. *Degree requirements:* For master's, comprehensive exam, thesis optional, internship, minimum GPA of 3.0; for doctorate, comprehensive exam, thesis/dissertation, 1st year qualifying examination, 2nd year research project, successful practicum/externship placements, written presentation and successful oral defense of dissertation, completion of full-time internship. *Entrance requirements:* For master's, GRE General Test, minimum GPA of 3.0, essay, interview; for doctorate, GRE General Test, GRE Subject Test (psychology), 3 letters of recommendation, interview, essay, curriculum vitae. Additional exam requirements/recommendations for international students: required—TOEFL (minimum score 550 paper-based; 80 iBT); recommended—IELTS (minimum score 6.5). *Application deadline:* For fall admission, 12/31 for domestic and international students. Application fee: $75. Electronic applications accepted. *Expenses: Tuition:* Full-time $25,164; part-time $1398 per credit. *Required fees:* $580; $165 per semester. Tuition and fees vary according to course load, degree level and program. *Financial support:* In 2019–20, 152 students received support, including 125 fellowships with full and partial tuition reimbursements available (averaging $8,256 per year), 4 research assistantships with full and partial tuition reimbursements available (averaging $5,531 per year); career-related internships or fieldwork, Federal Work-Study, institutionally sponsored loans, scholarships/grants, traineeships, tuition waivers (full and partial), unspecified assistantships, and scholarships and endowed scholarships also available. Support available to part-time students. Financial award applicants required to submit FAFSA. *Unit head:* Dr. Craig Johnson, Chairperson, 516-463-5636, E-mail: craig.a.johnson@hofstra.edu. *Application contact:* Sunil Samuel, Assistant Vice President of Admissions, 516-463-4723, Fax: 516-463-4664, E-mail: graduateadmission@hofstra.edu.
Website: http://www.hofstra.edu/hclas

Howard University, Graduate School, Department of Psychology, Washington, DC 20059-0002. Offers clinical psychology (PhD); developmental psychology (PhD); experimental psychology (PhD); neuropsychology (PhD); personality psychology (PhD); psychology (MS); social psychology (PhD). *Accreditation:* APA (one or more programs are accredited). *Program availability:* Part-time. *Degree requirements:* For master's, thesis; for doctorate, comprehensive exam, thesis/dissertation, qualifying exam. *Entrance requirements:* For master's, GRE General Test, minimum GPA of 2.5, bachelor's degree in psychology or related field; for doctorate, GRE General Test, minimum GPA of 3.0.

Humboldt State University, Academic Programs, College of Professional Studies, Department of Psychology, Arcata, CA 95521-8299. Offers psychology (MA), including biological psychology, counseling, developmental psychopathology, school psychology, social and environmental psychology. *Program availability:* Part-time. *Faculty:* 14 full-time (9 women), 13 part-time/adjunct (8 women). *Students:* 76 full-time (54 women), 11 part-time (4 women); includes 37 minority (1 Black or African American, non-Hispanic/Latino; 3 American Indian or Alaska Native, non-Hispanic/Latino; 4 Asian, non-Hispanic/Latino; 22 Hispanic/Latino; 7 Two or more races, non-Hispanic/Latino), 1 international. Average age 28. 89 applicants, 42% accepted, 31 enrolled. In 2019, 38 master's awarded. *Degree requirements:* For master's, thesis. *Entrance requirements:* For master's, appropriate bachelor's degree, minimum GPA of 2.5. Additional exam requirements/recommendations for international students: required—TOEFL (minimum score 500 paper-based). *Application deadline:* For fall admission, 2/1 for domestic students, 2/15 for international students. Applications are processed on a rolling basis. Application fee: $55. *Expenses:* Tuition, state resident: full-time $7176; part-time $4164 per term. *Required fees:* $2120; $1672 per term. *Financial support:* Career-related internships or fieldwork available. Financial award application deadline: 3/1; financial award applicants required to submit FAFSA. *Unit head:* Dr. Carrie Aigner, Graduate Program Coordinator, 707-826-3757, E-mail: carrie.aigner@humboldt.edu. *Application contact:* Dr. Carrie Aigner, Graduate Program Coordinator, 707-826-3757, E-mail: carrie.aigner@humboldt.edu.
Website: http://www2.humboldt.edu/psychology/programs-child/graduate-programs-psychology

Hunter College of the City University of New York, Graduate School, School of Arts and Sciences, Department of Psychology, New York, NY 10065-5085. Offers animal behavior and conservation (MA, Certificate); general psychology (MA). *Program availability:* Part-time, evening/weekend. *Degree requirements:* For master's, comprehensive exam, thesis. *Entrance requirements:* For master's, GRE General Test, minimum 12 credits of course work in psychology, including statistics and experimental psychology; 2 letters of recommendation. Additional exam requirements/recommendations for international students: required—TOEFL.

Idaho State University, Graduate School, College of Arts and Letters, Department of Psychology, Pocatello, ID 83209-8112. Offers clinical psychology (PhD); experimental psychology (PhD). *Accreditation:* APA. *Program availability:* Part-time. *Degree requirements:* For doctorate, comprehensive exam, thesis/dissertation, 1 year full-time clinical internship. *Entrance requirements:* For doctorate, GRE General Test, GRE Subject Test, MS in psychology, recommendation from Clinical Admissions Committee. Additional exam requirements/recommendations for international students: required—TOEFL (minimum score 550 paper-based; 80 iBT). Electronic applications accepted.

Illinois Institute of Technology, Graduate College, Lewis College of Human Sciences, Department of Psychology, Chicago, IL 60616. Offers clinical psychology (PhD); industrial and organizational psychology (PhD); personnel and human resource development (MS); rehabilitation and mental health counseling (MS); rehabilitation counseling education (PhD). *Accreditation:* APA (one or more programs are accredited); CORE. *Program availability:* Part-time, evening/weekend. Terminal master's awarded for partial completion of doctoral program. *Degree requirements:* For master's, thesis (for some programs); for doctorate, comprehensive exam, thesis/dissertation, minimum of 107 credit hours, 1-year full-time internship. *Entrance requirements:* For master's, GRE General Test (minimum score 298 Quantitative and Verbal, 3.0 Analytical Writing), minimum GPA of 3.0; 3 letters of recommendation; bachelor's degree from accredited institution (for personnel and human resource development); for doctorate, GRE General Test (minimum score 298 Quantitative and Verbal, 3.0 Analytical Writing), bachelor's or master's degree from accredited institution, recommendations. Additional exam requirements/recommendations for international students: required—TOEFL (minimum score 550 paper-based; 80 iBT). Electronic applications accepted.

Illinois State University, Graduate School, College of Arts and Sciences, Department of Psychology, Normal, IL 61790. Offers psychology (MA, MS), including clinical-counseling psychology, cognitive and behavioral sciences, developmental psychology, industrial/organizational-social psychology; school psychology (PhD, SSP). *Accreditation:* APA. *Faculty:* 32 full-time (14 women), 6 part-time/adjunct (5 women). *Students:* 92 full-time (77 women), 18 part-time (14 women). Average age 25. 154 applicants, 32% accepted, 37 enrolled. In 2019, 27 master's, 3 doctorates, 5 other advanced degrees awarded. *Degree requirements:* For master's, thesis or alternative; for doctorate, variable foreign language requirement, thesis/dissertation, 2 terms of residency, internship, practicum. *Entrance requirements:* For master's, GRE General Test, GRE Subject Test, minimum GPA of 3.0 in last 60 hours of course work; for doctorate, GRE General Test. *Application deadline:* Applications are processed on a rolling basis. Application fee: $50. *Expenses: Tuition, area resident:* Full-time $7956; part-time $9767 per year. Tuition, nonresident: full-time $9233; part-time $17,592 per year. *Required fees:* $1797. *Financial support:* In 2019–20, 26 research assistantships, 34 teaching assistantships were awarded; tuition waivers (full) and unspecified assistantships also available. Financial award application deadline: 4/1. *Unit head:* Dr. J Scott Jordan, Department Chair, 309-438-2484, E-mail: jsjorda@illinoisState.edu. *Application contact:* Dr. Karen Mark, Graduate Coordinator, 309-438-8130, E-mail: kimark@ilstu.edu.
Website: http://psychology.illinoisstate.edu/

Immaculata University, College of Graduate Studies, Department of Psychology, Immaculata, PA 19345. Offers clinical mental health counseling (MA); clinical psychology (Psy D); forensic psychology (Graduate Certificate); integrative psychotherapy (Graduate Certificate); neuropsychology (Graduate Certificate); psychodynamic psychotherapy (Graduate Certificate); psychological testing (Graduate Certificate); school counseling (MA, Graduate Certificate); school psychology (MA). *Accreditation:* APA. *Program availability:* Part-time, evening/weekend. Terminal master's awarded for partial completion of doctoral program. *Degree requirements:* For master's, comprehensive exam, thesis optional; for doctorate, comprehensive exam, thesis/dissertation. *Entrance requirements:* For master's, GRE General Test or MAT, minimum GPA of 3.0; for doctorate, GRE General Test or MAT, minimum GPA of 3.5. Additional exam requirements/recommendations for international students: required—TOEFL, IELTS. Electronic applications accepted.

Indiana State University, College of Graduate and Professional Studies, College of Arts and Sciences, Department of Psychology, Terre Haute, IN 47809. Offers clinical psychology (Psy D); general psychology (MA, MS). *Accreditation:* APA (one or more programs are accredited). Terminal master's awarded for partial completion of doctoral program. *Degree requirements:* For master's, thesis (for some programs); for doctorate, comprehensive exam, thesis/dissertation, internship, professional research project. *Entrance requirements:* For master's, GRE General Test, 12 semester hours of course work in psychology, minimum GPA of 2.75; for doctorate, GRE General Test, minimum GPA of 3.0. Additional exam requirements/recommendations for international students: required—TOEFL (minimum score 550 paper-based). Electronic applications accepted.

Indiana Tech, Program in Psychology, Fort Wayne, IN 46803-1297. Offers MS.

Indiana University Bloomington, University Graduate School, College of Arts and Sciences, Department of Psychological and Brain Sciences, Bloomington, IN 47405. Offers clinical science (PhD); cognitive neuroscience (PhD); cognitive psychology (PhD); developmental psychology (PhD); methods of behavior (PhD); molecular systems neuroscience (PhD); social psychology (PhD). *Accreditation:* APA. *Degree requirements:* For doctorate, comprehensive exam, 90 credit hours, 2 advanced statistics/methods courses, 2 written research projects, the teaching of psychology course, teaching 1 semester of undergraduate methods course, qualifying examination, minor or a second major, first-year research seminar course, dissertation defense, written dissertation. *Entrance requirements:* For doctorate, GRE. Additional exam requirements/recommendations for international students: required—TOEFL (minimum score 550 paper-based; 79 iBT). Electronic applications accepted.

Indiana University of Pennsylvania, School of Graduate Studies and Research, College of Natural Sciences and Mathematics, Department of Psychology, Indiana, PA 15705. Offers clinical psychology (Psy D); psychology (MA). *Accreditation:* APA (one or more programs are accredited). *Program availability:* Part-time. *Faculty:* 10 full-time (6 women). *Students:* 48 full-time (34 women), 15 part-time (9 women); includes 16 minority (4 Black or African American, non-Hispanic/Latino; 6 Asian, non-Hispanic/Latino; 5 Hispanic/Latino; 1 Two or more races, non-Hispanic/Latino), 2 international. Average age 27. 146 applicants, 20% accepted, 15 enrolled. In 2019, 14 master's, 13 doctorates awarded. Terminal master's awarded for partial completion of doctoral program. *Degree requirements:* For doctorate, comprehensive exam, thesis/dissertation, doctoral project/dissertation. *Entrance requirements:* For doctorate, GRE General Test, minimum GPA of 3.0, interview, 3 letters of recommendation, official transcripts, goal statement. Additional exam requirements/recommendations for international students: required—TOEFL (minimum score 540 paper-based; 76 iBT), IELTS (minimum score 6), TOEFL or IELTS. *Application deadline:* Applications are

processed on a rolling basis. Application fee: $50. Electronic applications accepted. *Expenses: Tuition, area resident:* Full-time $9288; part-time $516 per credit. Tuition, nonresident: full-time $13,932; part-time $774 per credit. *Required fees:* $4454. One-time fee: $115 full-time. Tuition and fees vary according to course load and program. *Financial support:* In 2019–20, 15 fellowships with tuition reimbursements (averaging $533 per year), 49 research assistantships with tuition reimbursements (averaging $8,189 per year), 3 teaching assistantships with partial tuition reimbursements (averaging $25,035 per year) were awarded; career-related internships or fieldwork, Federal Work-Study, scholarships/grants, and unspecified assistantships also available. Support available to part-time students. Financial award application deadline: 4/15; financial award applicants required to submit FAFSA. *Unit head:* Dr. Lisa Newell, Chairperson, 724-357-2426, E-mail: newell@iup.edu. *Application contact:* Dr. Derek Hatfield, Director of Doctoral Studies, 724-357- Ext. 4527, E-mail: derek.hatfield@iup.edu.
Website: http://www.iup.edu/psychology

Indiana University-Purdue University Indianapolis, School of Science, Department of Psychology, Indianapolis, IN 46202-3275. Offers addiction neuroscience (PhD); applied social and organizational psychology (PhD); clinical psychology (PhD); industrial/organizational psychology (MS). *Accreditation:* APA (one or more programs are accredited). Terminal master's awarded for partial completion of doctoral program. *Degree requirements:* For master's, thesis; for doctorate, thesis/dissertation. *Entrance requirements:* For master's, GRE General Test, minimum undergraduate GPA of 3.0; for doctorate, GRE General Test, GRE Subject Test (clinical psychology), minimum undergraduate GPA of 3.2. Additional exam requirements/recommendations for international students: required—TOEFL (minimum score 567 paper-based; 86 iBT), IELTS (minimum score 6.5). Electronic applications accepted.

Inter American University of Puerto Rico, Metropolitan Campus, Graduate Programs, Program in Psychology, San Juan, PR 00919-1293. Offers counseling psychology (MA, PhD); industrial/organizational psychology (MA, PhD); labor relations (MA); school psychology (MA, PhD). *Degree requirements:* For master's, comprehensive exam. *Entrance requirements:* For master's, GRE or EXADEP, interview. Electronic applications accepted.

Inter American University of Puerto Rico, San Germán Campus, Graduate Studies Center, Program in Psychology, San Germán, PR 00683-5008. Offers counseling psychology (MA, PhD); school psychology (MA, PhD). *Program availability:* Part-time, evening/weekend. *Degree requirements:* For master's, comprehensive exam, thesis; for doctorate, comprehensive exam, thesis/dissertation. *Entrance requirements:* For master's, GRE General Test or EXADEP, minimum GPA of 3.0; for doctorate, GRE, EXADEP or MAT, minimum GPA of 3.0.

Iona College, School of Arts and Science, Department of Psychology, New Rochelle, NY 10801-1890. Offers general-experimental psychology (MA); human resources (Certificate); industrial-organizational psychology (MA); mental health counseling (MA); organizational behavior (Certificate); psychology (MA); school psychology (MA). *Program availability:* Part-time. *Faculty:* 8 full-time (4 women), 12 part-time/adjunct (8 women). *Students:* 71 full-time (64 women), 41 part-time (34 women); includes 51 minority (12 Black or African American, non-Hispanic/Latino; 5 Asian, non-Hispanic/Latino; 28 Hispanic/Latino; 1 Native Hawaiian or other Pacific Islander, non-Hispanic/Latino; 5 Two or more races, non-Hispanic/Latino), 3 international. Average age 25. 104 applicants, 85% accepted, 34 enrolled. In 2019, 29 master's, 15 other advanced degrees awarded. *Degree requirements:* For master's, thesis (for some programs), literature review (for some programs). *Entrance requirements:* For master's, BA in psychology including 3 credits each in psychology statistics and experimental research methods, or 9 credits in psychology including 3 credits each in psychology statistics, psychology research methods and upper-level coursework. Additional exam requirements/recommendations for international students: required—TOEFL (minimum score 550 paper-based), IELTS (minimum score 6.5). *Application deadline:* For fall admission, 8/15 for domestic students, 5/1 for international students; for spring admission, 1/15 for domestic students, 9/1 for international students. Applications are processed on a rolling basis. Electronic applications accepted. *Financial support:* In 2019–20, 51 students received support, including 4 research assistantships with partial tuition reimbursements available (averaging $10,143 per year); scholarships/grants, tuition waivers (partial), and unspecified assistantships also available. Support available to part-time students. Financial award application deadline: 4/15; financial award applicants required to submit FAFSA. *Unit head:* Colleen Jacobsen, PhD, Chair, 914-637-2770, E-mail: cjacobsen@iona.edu. *Application contact:* Shantell Smith, Associate Director of Graduate Admissions, Arts and Science, 914-633-2440, Fax: 914-633-2277, E-mail: ssmith@iona.edu.
Website: http://www.iona.edu/Academics/School-of-Arts-Science/Departments/Psychology/Graduate-Programs.aspx

Iowa State University of Science and Technology, Department of Psychology, Ames, IA 50011. Offers cognitive psychology (PhD); counseling psychology (PhD); psychology (MS, PhD); social psychology (PhD). *Accreditation:* APA (one or more programs are accredited). *Entrance requirements:* For doctorate, GRE General Test, GRE Subject Test (psychology), 3 letters of recommendation. Additional exam requirements/recommendations for international students: required—TOEFL (minimum score 560 paper-based; 79 iBT), IELTS (minimum score 6.5). Electronic applications accepted.

Jackson State University, Graduate School, College of Liberal Arts, Department of Psychology, Jackson, MS 39217. Offers clinical psychology (PhD). *Accreditation:* APA. *Degree requirements:* For doctorate, comprehensive exam, thesis/dissertation. *Entrance requirements:* For doctorate, MAT, GRE. Additional exam requirements/recommendations for international students: required—TOEFL (minimum score 520 paper-based; 67 iBT).

Jacksonville State University, Graduate Studies, School of Human Services and Social Sciences, Department of Psychology, Jacksonville, AL 36265-1602. Offers MS. *Program availability:* Part-time, evening/weekend. *Degree requirements:* For master's, comprehensive exam, thesis (for some programs). *Entrance requirements:* For master's, GRE General Test or MAT. Additional exam requirements/recommendations for international students: required—TOEFL (minimum score 500 paper-based; 61 iBT). Electronic applications accepted.

James Madison University, The Graduate School, College of Health and Behavioral Studies, Program in Psychological Sciences, Harrisonburg, VA 22807. Offers applied research (MA); behavior analysis (MA); experimental psychology (MA); quantitative psychology (MA). *Program availability:* Part-time, evening/weekend. *Students:* 24 full-time (20 women); includes 7 minority (1 Black or African American, non-Hispanic/Latino; 3 Asian, non-Hispanic/Latino; 3 Hispanic/Latino), 1 international. Average age 30. In 2019, 12 master's awarded. Application fee: $60. Electronic applications accepted. *Financial support:* In 2019–20, 22 students received support, including 1 teaching assistantship with full tuition reimbursement available (averaging $9,284 per year); career-related internships or fieldwork, Federal Work-Study, and assistantships (averaging $7911) also available. Financial award application deadline: 3/1; financial award applicants required to submit FAFSA. *Unit head:* Dr. Jeff S. Dyche, Graduate Program Director, 540-568-4965, E-mail: dychejs@jmu.edu. *Application contact:*

Lynette D. Michael, Director of Graduate Admissions, 540-568-6131 Ext. 6395, Fax: 540-568-7860, E-mail: michaeld@jmu.edu.
Website: http://www.psyc.jmu.edu/psycsciences/

John F. Kennedy University, College of Psychology, Pleasant Hill, CA 94523-4817. Offers MA, Psy D, Certificate, Graduate Certificate. *Accreditation:* APA. *Program availability:* Part-time, evening/weekend. *Entrance requirements:* Additional exam requirements/recommendations for international students: required—TOEFL.

Johns Hopkins University, Zanvyl Krieger School of Arts and Sciences, Department of Psychological and Brain Sciences, Baltimore, MD 21218. Offers PhD. *Degree requirements:* For doctorate, thesis/dissertation, research project, teaching experience. *Entrance requirements:* For doctorate, GRE General Test. Additional exam requirements/recommendations for international students: required—TOEFL (minimum score 600 paper-based; 100 iBT), IELTS (minimum score 7). Electronic applications accepted. *Expenses:* Contact institution.

Kansas State University, Graduate School, College of Arts and Sciences, Department of Psychological Sciences, Manhattan, KS 66506. Offers MS, PhD. *Program availability:* Part-time. *Degree requirements:* For master's, thesis or alternative; for doctorate, thesis/dissertation, preliminary exam. *Entrance requirements:* For master's, GRE General Test, minimum undergraduate GPA of 3.0; for doctorate, GRE General Test, minimum GPA of 3.0. Additional exam requirements/recommendations for international students: required—TOEFL (minimum score 600 paper-based). Electronic applications accepted.

Kean University, College of Liberal Arts, Program in Psychology, Union, NJ 07083. Offers human behavior and organizational psychology (MA); psychological services (MA). *Program availability:* Part-time. *Faculty:* 18 full-time (14 women). *Students:* 68 full-time (56 women), 52 part-time (40 women); includes 70 minority (32 Black or African American, non-Hispanic/Latino; 5 Asian, non-Hispanic/Latino; 32 Hispanic/Latino; 1 Two or more races, non-Hispanic/Latino), 4 international. Average age 28. 68 applicants, 84% accepted, 42 enrolled. In 2019, 52 master's awarded. *Degree requirements:* For master's, comprehensive exam, research component, two semesters of advanced seminar. *Entrance requirements:* For master's, GRE General Test, minimum GPA of 3.0; official transcripts from all institutions attended; two letters of recommendation; professional resume/curriculum vitae; 12 credits in behavioral sciences on the undergraduate level. Additional exam requirements/recommendations for international students: required—TOEFL (minimum score 550 paper-based; 79 iBT), IELTS (minimum score 6.5). *Application deadline:* For fall admission, 6/30 for domestic and international students; for spring admission, 12/1 for domestic and international students. Applications are processed on a rolling basis. Application fee: $75. Electronic applications accepted. *Expenses:* Tuition, state resident: full-time $15,326; part-time $748 per credit. Tuition, nonresident: full-time $20,288; part-time $902 per credit. *Required fees:* $2149.50; $91.25 per credit. Tuition and fees vary according to course level, course load, degree level and program. *Financial support:* Scholarships/grants and unspecified assistantships available. Financial award applicants required to submit FAFSA. *Unit head:* Dr. Zandra Gratz, Program Coordinator, 908-737-5881, E-mail: zgratz@kean.edu. *Application contact:* Amy Clark, Program Assistant, 908-737-7100, E-mail: gradadmissions@kean.edu.
Website: http://grad.kean.edu/masters-programs/psychological-services

Keiser University, MS in Psychology Program, Fort Lauderdale, FL 33309. Offers MS.

Keiser University, PhD in Psychology Program, Fort Lauderdale, FL 33309. Offers PhD.

Kent State University, College of Arts and Sciences, Department of Psychological Sciences, Kent, OH 44242-0001. Offers clinical psychology (MA, PhD), including gerontology (MA), psychological sciences (MA); experimental psychology (MA, PhD), including gerontology (MA), psychological sciences (MA). *Accreditation:* APA (one or more programs are accredited). *Faculty:* 28 full-time (15 women), 4 part-time/adjunct (2 women). *Students:* 79 full-time (63 women); includes 17 minority (6 Black or African American, non-Hispanic/Latino; 5 Asian, non-Hispanic/Latino; 4 Hispanic/Latino; 2 Two or more races, non-Hispanic/Latino), 3 international. Average age 26. 284 applicants, 8% accepted, 16 enrolled. In 2019, 13 master's, 9 doctorates awarded. *Degree requirements:* For master's, thesis, Min grade in Quantitative Statistical Analysis I and II is B-. College of Arts & Sciences requires students to have a 3.0 average from all graduate courses attempted; for doctorate, comprehensive exam, thesis/dissertation. *Entrance requirements:* For master's, GRE General Test, statement of goals and motivations, transcripts, 3 letters of recommendation, minimum junior-senior GPA of 3.0, 18 semester hours of credit in psychology which includes at least one course in statistics and a broad background in psychology; for doctorate, GRE General Test, statement of goals and motivations, transcripts, 3 letters of recommendation, minimum junior-senior GPA of 3.0, 18 semester hours of credit in psychology which includes at least one course in statistics and a broad background in psychology. Additional exam requirements/recommendations for international students: required—TOEFL (minimum score 94 iBT), IELTS (minimum score 7), PTE (minimum score 65), Michigan English Language Assessment Battery (minimum score 82. *Application deadline:* For fall admission, 12/1 for domestic and international students. Applications are processed on a rolling basis. Application fee: $45 ($70 for international students). Electronic applications accepted. *Financial support:* Federal Work-Study, health care benefits, and unspecified assistantships available. Financial award application deadline: 12/1; financial award applicants required to submit FAFSA. *Unit head:* Dr. Maria S. Zaragoza, Professor, Department Chair, 330-672-2166, E-mail: mzaragoz@kent.edu. *Application contact:* Dr. John A. Updegraff, Professor and Graduate Coordinator, 330-672-2166, E-mail: jupdegr1@kent.edu.
Website: https://www.kent.edu/psychology

Kent State University, College of Public Health, Kent, OH 44242-0001. Offers public health (MPH, PhD), including biostatistics (MPH), environmental health sciences (MPH), epidemiology, health policy and management, prevention science (PhD), social and behavioral sciences (MPH). *Accreditation:* CEPH. *Program availability:* Part-time, 100% online. *Faculty:* 23 full-time (12 women), 4 part-time/adjunct (1 woman). *Students:* 136 full-time (98 women), 158 part-time (129 women); includes 71 minority (45 Black or African American, non-Hispanic/Latino; 12 Asian, non-Hispanic/Latino; 8 Hispanic/Latino; 6 Two or more races, non-Hispanic/Latino), 40 international. Average age 31. 187 applicants, 79% accepted, 85 enrolled. In 2019, 93 master's, 7 doctorates awarded. *Degree requirements:* For master's, comprehensive exam, between 150 - 300 hours' placement at public health agency, final portfolio and presentation; for doctorate, comprehensive exam, thesis/dissertation. *Entrance requirements:* For master's, GRE or other standardized graduate admission exam (GMAT, MCAT, LSAT or PCAT), minimum GPA of 3.0, transcripts, goal statement, 3 letters of recommendation; for doctorate, GRE or other standardized graduate admission exam with a quantitative component, Master's degree in related discipline, minimum GPA of 3.0, personal statement, resume, interview with faculty, 3 letters of recommendation, transcript(s). Additional exam requirements/recommendations for international students: required—TOEFL (minimum score 94 iBT), IELTS (minimum score 7), PTE (minimum score 65), For MPH: TOEFL iBT 79, Michigan English Language Assessment Battery (minimum score of 77), IELTS 6.5, PTE 58; For Ph.D.: see below and min MELAB 82. *Application deadline:* For fall admission, 6/15 for domestic and international students; for spring admission, 10/15 for domestic and international students; for summer admission, 3/15 for domestic and international students. Applications are processed on a rolling basis. Application fee: $45 ($70 for international students). Electronic applications accepted. *Financial support:* Career-related internships or fieldwork, Federal Work-Study, scholarships/grants, and unspecified assistantships available. *Unit head:* Dr. Sonia Alemagno, Dean and Professor of Health Policy and Management, 330-672-6500, E-mail: salemagn@kent.edu. *Application contact:* Dr. Jeffrey S. Hallam, Professor/Associate Dean for Research and Graduate Studies, 330-672-0679, E-mail: jhallam1@kent.edu.
Website: http://www.kent.edu/publichealth/

Lakehead University, Graduate Studies, Department of Psychology, Thunder Bay, ON P7B 5E1, Canada. Offers clinical psychology (PhD); experimental psychology (MA). *Program availability:* Part-time, evening/weekend. *Degree requirements:* For master's, thesis optional; for doctorate, thesis/dissertation, 2 comprehensive exams, internship. *Entrance requirements:* For master's, GRE, honors degree in psychology, advanced course work in statistics, minimum B average; for doctorate, GRE, minimum B average. Additional exam requirements/recommendations for international students: required—TOEFL.

Lamar University, College of Graduate Studies, College of Arts and Sciences, Department of Psychology, Beaumont, TX 77710. Offers MS. *Program availability:* Part-time. *Faculty:* 9 full-time (4 women), 3 part-time/adjunct (1 woman). *Students:* 19 full-time (14 women), 9 part-time (5 women); includes 11 minority (4 Black or African American, non-Hispanic/Latino; 1 Asian, non-Hispanic/Latino; 4 Hispanic/Latino; 2 Two or more races, non-Hispanic/Latino). Average age 27. 19 applicants, 63% accepted, 10 enrolled. In 2019, 3 master's awarded. *Degree requirements:* For master's, thesis, practicum. *Entrance requirements:* For master's, GRE General Test, minimum GPA of 2.75 in last 60 hours of undergraduate course work. Additional exam requirements/recommendations for international students: required—TOEFL (minimum score 550 paper-based; 79 iBT), IELTS (minimum score 6.5). Application fee: $25 ($50 for international students). *Expenses: Tuition, area resident:* Full-time $6324; part-time $351 per credit. Tuition, state resident: full-time $6324; part-time $351 per credit. Tuition, nonresident: full-time $13,920; part-time $773 per credit. *International tuition:* $13,920 full-time. *Required fees:* $2462; $327 per credit. Tuition and fees vary according to course load, campus/location and reciprocity agreements. *Financial support:* In 2019–20, 23 students received support, including 3 teaching assistantships (averaging $4,500 per year); fellowships, research assistantships, career-related internships or fieldwork, Federal Work-Study, scholarships/grants, and tuition waivers (partial) also available. Support available to part-time students. Financial award application deadline: 4/1. *Unit head:* Dr. Edythe E. Kirk, Chair, 409-880-8285, Fax: 409-880-1710. *Application contact:* Celeste Contreas, Director, Admissions and Academic Services, 409-880-8888, Fax: 409-880-7419, E-mail: gradmissions@lamar.edu.
Website: http://artssciences.lamar.edu/psychology

La Salle University, School of Arts and Sciences, Program in Clinical Psychology, Philadelphia, PA 19141-1199. Offers child clinical psychology (Psy D); clinical health psychology (Psy D); clinical psychology (MA); general practice psychology (Psy D). *Accreditation:* AAMFT/COAMFTE. *Program availability:* Part-time, evening/weekend. Terminal master's awarded for partial completion of doctoral program. *Degree requirements:* For doctorate, comprehensive exam, thesis/dissertation. *Entrance requirements:* For doctorate, GRE (minimum scores of 148 on both the Verbal Reasoning and Quantitative Reasoning sections strongly recommended); GRE Subject Test in psychology (for those entering with bachelor's degree), baccalaureate degree from accredited institution with major in psychology or related discipline; minimum undergraduate GPA of 3.0, 3.2 graduate; three letters of recommendation; statement of interest and intent; curriculum vitae or resume; personal interview. Additional exam requirements/recommendations for international students: required—TOEFL. Electronic applications accepted. Application fee is waived when completed online. *Expenses:* Contact institution.

Laurentian University, School of Graduate Studies and Research, Programme in Psychology, Sudbury, ON P3E 2C6, Canada. Offers applied psychology (MA); experimental psychology (MA).

Lehigh University, College of Arts and Sciences, Department of Psychology, Bethlehem, PA 18015. Offers MS, PhD. *Faculty:* 16 full-time (11 women). *Students:* 19 full-time (14 women), 2 part-time (both women); includes 4 minority (1 Black or African American, non-Hispanic/Latino; 3 Hispanic/Latino), 7 international. Average age 26. 63 applicants, 17% accepted, 5 enrolled. In 2019, 3 master's, 4 doctorates awarded. Terminal master's awarded for partial completion of doctoral program. *Degree requirements:* For master's, thesis; for doctorate, comprehensive exam, thesis/dissertation. *Entrance requirements:* For master's and doctorate, GRE General Test. Additional exam requirements/recommendations for international students: required—TOEFL. *Application deadline:* For fall admission, 1/1 for domestic and international students. Application fee: $75. *Financial support:* In 2019–20, 14 students received support, including 2 research assistantships with full tuition reimbursements available (averaging $21,630 per year), 12 teaching assistantships with full tuition reimbursements available (averaging $21,630 per year); tuition waivers (full) also available. Financial award application deadline: 1/1. *Unit head:* Dr. Michael Gill, Chairperson, 610-758-6577, Fax: 610-758-6277, E-mail: mjg6@lehigh.edu. *Application contact:* Dr. Almut Hupbach, Program Director, 610-758-6762, Fax: 610-758-6277, E-mail: alh309@lehigh.edu.
Website: http://psychology.cas.lehigh.edu/

Lesley University, Graduate School of Arts and Social Sciences, Cambridge, MA 02138-2790. Offers clinical mental health counseling (MA), including holistic counseling, school and community counseling, trauma studies; counseling psychology (MA, CAGS), including professional counseling (MA), school counseling (MA); creative writing (MFA); expressive therapies (MA, PhD, CAGS), including art (MA), clinical mental health counseling (MA), dance (MA), expressive therapies (MA), music (MA); independent studies (CAGS); independent study (MA); intercultural relations (MA, CAGS); interdisciplinary studies (MA), including individualized studies, integrative holistic health, mindfulness studies, peace and conflict transformation, trauma sensitive assessment, intervention, and consultation, women's studies; urban environmental leadership (MA). *Program availability:* Part-time, online learning. *Degree requirements:* For master's, internship, practicum, thesis (for expressive therapies); for doctorate, thesis/dissertation, arts apprenticeship, field placement; for CAGS, thesis, internship (for counseling psychology, expressive therapies). *Entrance requirements:* For master's, MAT (counseling psychology), interview, writing samples, art portfolio; for doctorate, GRE or MAT, interview, master's degree; for CAGS, interview, master's degree. Additional exam requirements/recommendations for international students: required—TOEFL (minimum score 550 paper-based; 80 iBT). Electronic applications accepted.

LeTourneau University, Graduate Programs, Longview, TX 75607-7001. Offers business administration (MBA); counseling (MA); curriculum and instruction (M Ed); educational administration (M Ed); engineering (ME, MS); engineering management (MEM); health care administration (MS); marriage and family therapy (MA); psychology (MA); strategic leadership (MSL); teacher leadership (M Ed); teaching and learning (M Ed). *Program availability:* Part-time, 100% online, blended/hybrid learning. *Students:* 45 full-time (34 women), 243 part-time (186 women); includes 142 minority (89 Black or

African American, non-Hispanic/Latino; 1 Asian, non-Hispanic/Latino; 26 Hispanic/Latino; 26 Two or more races, non-Hispanic/Latino), 2 international. Average age 37. In 2019, 143 master's awarded. *Entrance requirements:* Additional exam requirements/recommendations for international students: required—TOEFL (minimum score 525 paper-based; 80 iBT), IELTS (minimum score 6), Either a TOEFL or IELTS is required for graduate students. One or the other. *Application deadline:* Applications are processed on a rolling basis. Application fee: $0. Electronic applications accepted. *Financial support:* Unspecified assistantships and employee tuition waivers and institutionally sponsored loans available. Financial award applicants required to submit FAFSA.
Website: http://www.letu.edu

Liberty University, School of Behavioral Sciences, Lynchburg, VA 24515. Offers applied psychology (MA), including developmental psychology (MA, MS), industrial/organizational psychology (MA, MS); clinical mental health counseling (MA); community care and counseling (Ed D), including marriage and family counseling, pastoral care and counseling, traumatology; counselor education and supervision (PhD); human services counseling (MA), including addictions and recovery, business, child and family law, Christian ministries, criminal justice, crisis response and trauma, executive leadership, health and wellness, life coaching, marriage and family, military resilience; marriage and family counseling (MA); marriage and family therapy (MA); military resilience (Certificate); pastoral counseling (MA), including addictions and recovery, community chaplaincy, crisis response and trauma, discipleship and church ministry, leadership, life coaching, marriage and family, marriage and family studies, military resilience, parenting and child/adolescent, pastoral counseling, theology; professional counseling (MA); psychology (MS), including developmental psychology (MA, MS), industrial/organizational psychology (MA, MS); school counseling (M Ed). *Program availability:* Part-time, online learning. *Students:* 3,786 full-time (3,065 women), 5,193 part-time (4,081 women); includes 2,733 minority (1,967 Black or African American, non-Hispanic/Latino; 48 American Indian or Alaska Native, non-Hispanic/Latino; 103 Asian, non-Hispanic/Latino; 349 Hispanic/Latino; 19 Native Hawaiian or other Pacific Islander, non-Hispanic/Latino; 247 Two or more races, non-Hispanic/Latino), 133 international. Average age 38. 13,324 applicants, 28% accepted, 2,163 enrolled. In 2019, 2,322 master's, 19 doctorates, 112 other advanced degrees awarded. *Entrance requirements:* For master's, Official bachelor's degree transcripts with a 2.0 GPA or higher. *Application deadline:* Applications are processed on a rolling basis. Application fee: $50. Electronic applications accepted. *Expenses: Tuition:* Full-time $545; part-time $410 per credit hour. One-time fee: $50. *Financial support:* In 2019–20, 1,003 students received support. Teaching assistantships and Federal Work-Study available. Financial award applicants required to submit FAFSA. *Unit head:* Dr. Kenyon Knapp, Dean, School of Behavioral Services, E-mail: kcknapp@liberty.edu. *Application contact:* Jay Bridge, Director of Admissions, 800-424-9595, Fax: 800-628-7977, E-mail: gradadmissions@liberty.edu.
Website: https://www.liberty.edu/behavioral-sciences/

Lipscomb University, Department of Psychology, Counseling, and Family Science, Nashville, TN 37204-3951. Offers clinical mental health counseling (MS); counseling psychology (Certificate); marriage and family therapy (MMFT); psychology (MS). *Program availability:* Part-time, evening/weekend. *Degree requirements:* For master's, thesis (for some programs), practicum, internship, capstone. *Entrance requirements:* For master's, GRE, resume, 3 reference letters, transcripts, goals statement. Additional exam requirements/recommendations for international students: required—TOEFL (minimum score 570 paper-based; 80 iBT). Electronic applications accepted. *Expenses:* Contact institution.

Loma Linda University, School of Behavioral Health, Department of Psychology, Loma Linda, CA 92350. Offers clinical psychology (PhD, Psy D). *Accreditation:* APA. *Degree requirements:* For doctorate, comprehensive exam, thesis/dissertation. *Entrance requirements:* For doctorate, GRE General Test, three letters of recommendation. Additional exam requirements/recommendations for international students: required—TOEFL (minimum score 550 paper-based; 80 iBT). Electronic applications accepted.

Long Island University - Brooklyn, Richard L. Conolly College of Liberal Arts and Sciences, Brooklyn, NY 11201-8423. Offers biology (MS); chemistry (MS); clinical psychology (PhD); creative writing (MFA); English (MA); media arts (MA, MFA); political science (MA); psychology (MA); social science (MS); United Nations (Advanced Certificate); urban studies (MA); writing and production for television (MFA). *Program availability:* Part-time. Terminal master's awarded for partial completion of doctoral program. *Degree requirements:* For master's, comprehensive exam (for some programs), thesis (for some programs); for doctorate, thesis/dissertation. *Entrance requirements:* For doctorate, GRE. Additional exam requirements/recommendations for international students: required—TOEFL (minimum score 550 paper-based, 79 iBT) or IELTS. Electronic applications accepted.

Long Island University - Post, College of Liberal Arts and Sciences, Brookville, NY 11548-1300. Offers applied mathematics (MS); behavior analysis (MA); biology (MS); criminal justice (MS); earth science (MS); English (MA); environmental sustainability (MS); genetic counseling (MS); history (MA); interdisciplinary studies (MA, MS); political science (MA); psychology (MA). *Program availability:* Part-time, evening/weekend, blended/hybrid learning. Terminal master's awarded for partial completion of doctoral program. *Degree requirements:* For master's, comprehensive exam (for some programs), thesis (for some programs). *Entrance requirements:* Additional exam requirements/recommendations for international students: required—TOEFL, IELTS, or PTE. Electronic applications accepted.

Louisiana State University and Agricultural & Mechanical College, Graduate School, College of Humanities and Social Sciences, Department of Psychology, Baton Rouge, LA 70803. Offers biological psychology (MA, PhD); clinical psychology (MA, PhD); cognitive psychology (MA, PhD); developmental psychology (MA, PhD); school psychology (MA, PhD). *Accreditation:* APA (one or more programs are accredited).

Loyola University Maryland, Graduate Programs, Loyola College of Arts and Sciences, Department of Psychology, Baltimore, MD 21210-2699. Offers clinical psychology (MS, Psy D, CAS); counseling psychology (MS, CAS). *Accreditation:* APA. *Students:* 132 full-time (109 women), 39 part-time (32 women); includes 55 minority (21 Black or African American, non-Hispanic/Latino; 19 Asian, non-Hispanic/Latino; 11 Hispanic/Latino; 4 Two or more races, non-Hispanic/Latino), 5 international. Average age 27. 427 applicants, 25% accepted, 44 enrolled. In 2019, 59 master's, 11 doctorates awarded. *Degree requirements:* For doctorate, comprehensive exam, thesis/dissertation. *Entrance requirements:* For master's, GRE (optional), essay, application, transcripts, letters of recommendation, CV/resume, interview; for doctorate, GRE, essay, application, transcripts, letters of recommendation, CV/resume, interview. Additional exam requirements/recommendations for international students: required—TOEFL (minimum score 550 paper-based; 80 iBT), IELTS (minimum score 7), TOEFL (minimum score 550 paper-based, 80iBT) or ILETS (minimum score 7). *Application deadline:* For fall admission, 12/1 for domestic and international students. Application fee: $60. Electronic applications accepted. *Expenses:* Contact institution. *Financial support:* Scholarships/grants and unspecified assistantships available. Financial award application deadline: 4/15; financial award applicants required to submit FAFSA. *Unit head:* Carolyn M. Barry, Chair, 410-617-5325, E-mail: cbarry@loyola.edu. *Application*

contact: Office of Graduate Admission, 410-617-5020, E-mail: graduate@loyola.edu. Website: https://www.loyola.edu/academics/psychology

Lynn University, College of Arts and Sciences, Boca Raton, FL 33431-5598. Offers criminal justice (MS); mental health counseling (MS); psychology (MS). *Program availability:* Part-time, evening/weekend, 100% online, blended/hybrid learning. *Faculty:* 15 full-time (7 women), 12 part-time/adjunct (7 women). *Students:* 98 full-time (81 women), 55 part-time (33 women); includes 57 minority (23 Black or African American, non-Hispanic/Latino; 1 American Indian or Alaska Native, non-Hispanic/Latino; 28 Hispanic/Latino; 2 Native Hawaiian or other Pacific Islander, non-Hispanic/Latino; 3 Two or more races, non-Hispanic/Latino), 9 international. Average age 32. 126 applicants, 77% accepted, 69 enrolled. In 2019, 37 master's awarded. *Degree requirements:* For master's, comprehensive exam (for some programs), thesis (for some programs). *Entrance requirements:* For master's, Bachelor's degree from accredited institution, minimum undergraduate GPA of 3.0, official undergraduate transcripts, two letters of recommendation from academic or professional sources, writing sample demonstrating capacity to perform at graduate level. Additional exam requirements/recommendations for international students: required—TOEFL (minimum score 550 paper-based; 80 iBT), IELTS (minimum score 6.5). *Application deadline:* For fall admission, 8/10 for domestic students, 7/31 for international students; for spring admission, 12/18 for domestic students, 12/2 for international students; for summer admission, 4/12 for domestic students, 4/2 for international students. Applications are processed on a rolling basis. Application fee: $45. Electronic applications accepted. *Expenses:* Tuition and fees for degrees offered in the College of Arts and Sciences start at $23,400 and can go to $38,350 depending on the program. Each program has specific credit hour requirements and the cost per credit hour within this college ranges from $650.00 to $740.00 per credit hour. *Financial support:* In 2019–20, 42 students received support. Career-related internships or fieldwork, Federal Work-Study, scholarships/grants, tuition waivers (full and partial), and unspecified assistantships available. Support available to part-time students. Financial award application deadline: 3/1; financial award applicants required to submit FAFSA. *Unit head:* Dr. Gary Villa, Dean, College of Arts and Sciences, 561-237-7025, E-mail: gvilla@lynn.edu. *Application contact:* Steven Pruitt, Director of Graduate and Online Admission, 561-237-7834, Fax: 561-237-7100, E-mail: admissionpm@lynn.edu.
Website: https://www.lynn.edu/academics/colleges-schools/arts-and-sciences

Madonna University, Department of Psychology, Livonia, MI 48150-1173. Offers clinical psychology (MSCP). *Program availability:* Part-time, evening/weekend. *Degree requirements:* For master's, thesis or alternative. *Entrance requirements:* Additional exam requirements/recommendations for international students: required—TOEFL. Electronic applications accepted. *Expenses: Tuition:* Full-time $15,930; part-time $885 per credit hour. Tuition and fees vary according to degree level and program.

Mansfield University of Pennsylvania, Graduate Studies, Program in Organizational Leadership, Mansfield, PA 16933. Offers MA. *Program availability:* Online learning.

Marietta College, Master of Arts in Psychology, Marietta, OH 45750-4000. Offers MAP. *Program availability:* Part-time. *Faculty:* 3 full-time (2 women). *Students:* 1 part-time. Average age 24. In 2019, 3 master's awarded. *Degree requirements:* For master's, thesis. *Entrance requirements:* For master's, GRE, transcripts, essay, two letters of recommendation. Additional exam requirements/recommendations for international students: required—TOEFL. *Application deadline:* Applications are processed on a rolling basis. Application fee: $25. *Expenses:* $790 per credit hour. *Financial support:* Unspecified assistantships available. *Unit head:* Dr. Mary Barnas, Director, 740-376-4766, E-mail: barnasm@marietta.edu. *Application contact:* Dr. Mary Barnas, Director, 740-376-4766, E-mail: barnasm@marietta.edu.

Marist College, Graduate Programs, School of Social and Behavioral Sciences, Poughkeepsie, NY 12601-1387. Offers education (M Ed, MA); mental health counseling (MA); school psychology (MA, Adv C). *Program availability:* Part-time, evening/weekend. *Degree requirements:* For master's, thesis optional. *Entrance requirements:* For master's, GRE General Test, letters of recommendation, minimum undergraduate GPA of 3.0, interview. Additional exam requirements/recommendations for international students: required—TOEFL (minimum score 550 paper-based; 80 iBT); recommended—IELTS (minimum score 6.5). Electronic applications accepted.

Marquette University, Graduate School, College of Arts and Sciences, Department of Psychology, Milwaukee, WI 53201-1881. Offers PhD. *Accreditation:* APA. Terminal master's awarded for partial completion of doctoral program. *Degree requirements:* For doctorate, thesis/dissertation, internship, qualifying exam. *Entrance requirements:* For doctorate, GRE General Test, sample of scholarly writing, official transcripts from all current and previous colleges/universities except Marquette, personal statement, three letters of reference. Additional exam requirements/recommendations for international students: required—TOEFL (minimum score 530 paper-based). Electronic applications accepted.

Marshall University, Academic Affairs Division, College of Liberal Arts, Department of Psychology, Huntington, WV 25755. Offers clinical psychology (Certificate); psychology (MA, Psy D). *Accreditation:* APA. *Degree requirements:* For master's, thesis optional. *Entrance requirements:* For master's, GRE General Test or MAT.

Martin University, Division of Psychology, Indianapolis, IN 46218-3867. Offers community psychology (MS). *Program availability:* Part-time, evening/weekend. *Degree requirements:* For master's, thesis. *Entrance requirements:* For master's, GRE General Test, GRE Subject Test.

Marywood University, Academic Affairs, Reap College of Education and Human Development, Department of Psychology and Counseling, Program in Psychology, Scranton, PA 18509-1598. Offers clinical services (MA); general theoretical psychology (MA). *Program availability:* Part-time. Electronic applications accepted.

McGill University, Faculty of Graduate and Postdoctoral Studies, Faculty of Medicine, Department of Psychiatry, Montréal, QC H3A 2T5, Canada. Offers M Sc.

McGill University, Faculty of Graduate and Postdoctoral Studies, Faculty of Science, Department of Psychology, Montréal, QC H3A 2T5, Canada. Offers clinical psychology (PhD); experimental psychology (M Sc, MA, PhD).

McMaster University, School of Graduate Studies, Faculty of Science, Department of Psychology, Hamilton, ON L8S 4M2, Canada. Offers M Sc, PhD. *Degree requirements:* For doctorate, comprehensive exam, thesis/dissertation. *Entrance requirements:* For doctorate, GRE General Test, honors degree, minimum B+ average. Additional exam requirements/recommendations for international students: required—TOEFL (minimum score 550 paper-based).

McNeese State University, Doré School of Graduate Studies, Burton College of Education, Department of Psychology, Lake Charles, LA 70609. Offers applied behavior analysis (MA, Graduate Certificate); counseling psychology (MA); general/experimental psychology (MA). *Program availability:* Evening/weekend. *Entrance requirements:* For master's, GRE.

Medaille College, Programs in Psychology, Buffalo, NY 14214-2695. Offers clinical psychology (Psy D); marriage and family therapy (MA); mental health counseling (MA); psychology (MA). *Accreditation:* ACA. *Program availability:* Part-time, evening/weekend.

Degree requirements: For master's, comprehensive exam (for some programs), thesis (for some programs). *Entrance requirements:* For master's, GRE General Test (psychology), minimum GPA of 2.75 (psychology). Additional exam requirements/recommendations for international students: required—TOEFL (minimum score 550 paper-based). Electronic applications accepted.

Memorial University of Newfoundland, School of Graduate Studies, Department of Psychology, St. John's, NL A1C 5S7, Canada. Offers applied psychological sciences (MAPS); clinical psychology (Psy D); experimental psychology (M Sc, PhD). *Program availability:* Part-time. *Degree requirements:* For master's, workterms (MASP), thesis (M Sc); for doctorate, comprehensive exam, thesis/dissertation, oral thesis defense. *Entrance requirements:* For master's, GRE, honors bachelor's degree of high second class standing or equivalent; for doctorate, GRE, master's or honors degree. Electronic applications accepted.

Mercy College, School of Social and Behavioral Sciences, Program in Psychology, Dobbs Ferry, NY 10522-1189. Offers MS. *Program availability:* Part-time, evening/weekend, 100% online, blended/hybrid learning. *Students:* 22 full-time (19 women), 25 part-time (19 women); includes 32 minority (13 Black or African American, non-Hispanic/Latino; 19 Hispanic/Latino), 1 international. Average age 30. 38 applicants, 47% accepted, 13 enrolled. In 2019, 13 master's awarded. *Degree requirements:* For master's, comprehensive exam (for some programs), thesis (for some programs), must complete thesis or comprehensive exam. *Entrance requirements:* For master's, transcript(s); two letters of recommendation; resume; essay; interview. Additional exam requirements/recommendations for international students: required—TOEFL (minimum score 80 iBT), IELTS (minimum score 6.5). *Application deadline:* Applications are processed on a rolling basis. Application fee: $40. Electronic applications accepted. *Expenses: Tuition:* Full-time $16,146; part-time $897 per credit. *Required fees:* $332; $166 per semester. Tuition and fees vary according to course load and program. *Financial support:* Career-related internships or fieldwork, Federal Work-Study, scholarships/grants, and unspecified assistantships available. Support available to part-time students. Financial award applicants required to submit FAFSA. *Unit head:* Dr. Diana Juettner, Interim Dean, School of Social and Behavioral Sciences, 914-674-7546, E-mail: djuettner@mercy.edu. *Application contact:* Allison Gurdineer, Executive Director of Admissions, 877-637-2946, Fax: 914-674-7382, E-mail: admissions@mercy.edu.
Website: https://www.mercy.edu/degrees-programs/ms-psychology

Meredith College, School of Education, Health and Human Sciences, Master of Arts in Psychology Program, Raleigh, NC 27607-5298. Offers industrial/organizational psychology (MA). *Students:* 20 full-time (17 women), 7 part-time (6 women); includes 8 minority (4 Black or African American, non-Hispanic/Latino; 1 Asian, non-Hispanic/Latino; 3 Hispanic/Latino). Average age 30. *Degree requirements:* For master's, internship. *Entrance requirements:* For master's, GRE, official transcripts, two recommendation forms, resume or curriculum vitae, essay. *Application deadline:* Applications are processed on a rolling basis. Application fee: $60. *Unit head:* Lori Kelley, Program Manager/Admissions Counselor, 919-760-8723, E-mail: lrkelley@meredith.edu. *Application contact:* Lori Kelley, Program Manager/Admissions Counselor, 919-760-8723, E-mail: lrkelley@meredith.edu.
Website: https://www.meredith.edu/master-of-psychology

Miami University, College of Arts and Science, Department of Psychology, Oxford, OH 45056. Offers MA, PhD. *Accreditation:* APA (one or more programs are accredited).

Michigan School of Psychology, MA and Psy D Programs in Clinical Psychology, Farmington Hills, MI 48334. Offers MA, Psy D. *Accreditation:* APA. *Program availability:* Part-time, evening/weekend. *Faculty:* 14 full-time (7 women), 16 part-time/adjunct (11 women). *Students:* 125 full-time (97 women), 60 part-time (43 women); includes 47 minority (29 Black or African American, non-Hispanic/Latino; 3 Asian, non-Hispanic/Latino; 6 Hispanic/Latino; 9 Two or more races, non-Hispanic/Latino). Average age 30. 205 applicants, 54% accepted, 86 enrolled. In 2019, 61 master's, 13 doctorates awarded. *Degree requirements:* For master's, practicum; for doctorate, comprehensive exam, thesis/dissertation, internship, practicum. *Entrance requirements:* For master's, undergraduate degree from accredited institution with minimum GPA of 2.5; major in psychology, social work, or counseling (prerequisites apply without one of these degrees); for doctorate, GRE General Test, undergraduate degree from accredited institution with minimum GPA of 2.5; graduate degree in psychology, social work, or counseling from accredited institution with minimum GPA of 3.25; graduate-level practicum. Additional exam requirements/recommendations for international students: required—TOEFL (minimum score 550 paper-based; 79 iBT). *Application deadline:* For fall admission, 2/15 for domestic students. Application fee: $75. Electronic applications accepted. *Expenses: Tuition:* Full-time $40,000; part-time $15,000 per year. *Required fees:* $2265; $780 per semester. $260 per semester. One-time fee: $75. Tuition and fees vary according to course load, degree level and program. *Financial support:* In 2019–20, 12 students received support, including 1 research assistantship (averaging $8,566 per year), 5 teaching assistantships (averaging $14,436 per year); institutionally sponsored loans, scholarships/grants, and unspecified assistantships also available. Financial award application deadline: 8/30; financial award applicants required to submit FAFSA. *Unit head:* Dr. Shannon Chavez-Korell, Program Director, 248-476-1122, Fax: 248-476-1125. *Application contact:* Carrie Pyeatt, Coordinator of Admissions and Student Engagement, 248-476-1122 Ext. 117, Fax: 248-476-1125, E-mail: cpyeatt@msp.edu.
Website: msp.edu

Michigan State University, The Graduate School, College of Social Science, Department of Psychology, East Lansing, MI 48824. Offers MA, PhD. *Accreditation:* APA (one or more programs are accredited). *Entrance requirements:* Additional exam requirements/recommendations for international students: required—TOEFL (minimum score 550 paper-based), Michigan State University ELT (minimum score 85), Michigan English Language Assessment Battery (minimum score 83). Electronic applications accepted.

Middle Tennessee State University, College of Graduate Studies, College of Behavioral and Health Sciences, Department of Psychology, Murfreesboro, TN 37132. Offers clinical psychology (MA); experimental psychology (MA); industrial/organizational psychology (MA); psychology (MA, Ed S); quantitative psychology (MA); school psychology (MA). *Program availability:* Part-time, evening/weekend, online learning. *Degree requirements:* For master's, comprehensive exam, thesis. *Entrance requirements:* For master's, GRE. Additional exam requirements/recommendations for international students: required—TOEFL (minimum score 525 paper-based; 71 iBT) or IELTS (minimum score 6). Electronic applications accepted.

Millersville University of Pennsylvania, College of Graduate Studies and Adult Learning, College of Education and Human Services, Department of Psychology, Millersville, PA 17551-0302. Offers psychology (MS), including clinical psychology, school psychology; school counseling (M Ed). *Program availability:* Part-time. *Faculty:* 11 full-time (6 women), 3 part-time/adjunct (0 women). *Students:* 63 full-time (52 women), 84 part-time (65 women); includes 19 minority (3 Black or African American, non-Hispanic/Latino; 3 Asian, non-Hispanic/Latino; 11 Hispanic/Latino; 2 Two or more races, non-Hispanic/Latino), 2 international. Average age 27. 77 applicants, 75% accepted, 43 enrolled. In 2019, 42 master's awarded. *Degree requirements:* For master's, comprehensive exam (for some programs), thesis optional, internship, practicum, portfolio. *Entrance requirements:* For master's, GRE required only if cumulative GPA is lower than 3.0, At least 1 academic reference, interview, 18 undergraduate credits in Psychology (Clinical and School), 6 undergraduate credits in Psychology (school counseling). Additional exam requirements/recommendations for international students: required—TOEFL, IELTS (minimum score 6), PTE (minimum score 60). *Application deadline:* For fall admission, 1/15 for domestic students; for winter admission, 4/15 for domestic students; for spring admission, 10/1 for domestic students. Application fee: $40. Electronic applications accepted. *Expenses: Tuition, area resident:* Part-time $516 per credit. Tuition, state resident: part-time $516 per credit. Tuition, nonresident: part-time $774 per credit. *Required fees:* $118.75 per credit. Tuition and fees vary according to course load, degree level and program. *Financial support:* In 2019–20, 55 students received support. Scholarships/grants and unspecified assistantships available. Financial award application deadline: 3/15; financial award applicants required to submit FAFSA. *Unit head:* Dr. Debra S. Vredenburg-Rudy, Chair, 717-871-7279, Fax: 717-871-7946, E-mail: debra.vredenburg@millersville.edu. *Application contact:* Dr. James A. Delle, Acting Dean of College of Graduate Studies and Adult Learning/Associate Provost, Academic Administration, 717-871-7462, E-mail: James.Delle@millersville.edu.
Website: https://www.millersville.edu/psychology/index.php

Minnesota State University Mankato, College of Graduate Studies and Research, College of Social and Behavioral Sciences, Department of Psychology, Mankato, MN 56001. Offers clinical psychology (MA); industrial/organizational psychology (MA); school psychology (Psy D). *Program availability:* Part-time. *Degree requirements:* For master's, one foreign language, comprehensive exam, thesis (for some programs). *Entrance requirements:* For master's, GRE General Test, GRE Subject Test (clinical psychology), minimum GPA of 3.0 during previous 2 years, 3 letters of reference. Additional exam requirements/recommendations for international students: required—TOEFL. Electronic applications accepted.

Mississippi State University, College of Arts and Sciences, Department of Psychology, Mississippi State, MS 39762. Offers applied psychology (PhD), including clinical, cognitive science; psychology (MS). *Accreditation:* APA. *Faculty:* 18 full-time (7 women). *Students:* 37 full-time (24 women), 9 part-time (4 women); includes 8 minority (4 Black or African American, non-Hispanic/Latino; 3 Asian, non-Hispanic/Latino; 1 Hispanic/Latino). Average age 28. 79 applicants, 20% accepted, 8 enrolled. In 2019, 6 master's, 1 doctorate awarded. Terminal master's awarded for partial completion of doctoral program. *Degree requirements:* For master's, comprehensive exam, thesis; for doctorate, thesis/dissertation, qualifying exam, comprehensive written and oral exam. *Entrance requirements:* For master's, GRE General Test, minimum GPA of 2.75 on last two years of undergraduate courses; for doctorate, GRE General Test, proficiency in at least 1 computer language, minimum GPA of 3.0. Additional exam requirements/recommendations for international students: required—TOEFL (minimum score 477 paper-based; 53 iBT); recommended—IELTS (minimum score 4.5). *Application deadline:* For fall admission, 4/1 priority date for domestic students, 5/1 for international students; for spring admission, 11/1 priority date for domestic students, 9/1 for international students. Applications are processed on a rolling basis. Application fee: $60 ($80 for international students). Electronic applications accepted. *Expenses: Tuition, area resident:* Full-time $8880; part-time $456 per credit hour. Tuition, state resident: full-time $8880. Tuition, nonresident: full-time $23,840; part-time $1236 per credit hour. *Required fees:* $110; $11.12 per credit hour. Tuition and fees vary according to course load. *Financial support:* In 2019–20, 6 research assistantships with full tuition reimbursements (averaging $13,607 per year), 28 teaching assistantships with full tuition reimbursements (averaging $11,864 per year) were awarded; career-related internships or fieldwork, Federal Work-Study, institutionally sponsored loans, scholarships/grants, and unspecified assistantships also available. Financial award application deadline: 4/1; financial award applicants required to submit FAFSA. *Unit head:* Dr. Mitchell E. Berman, Professor and Head, 662-325-3202, Fax: 662-325-7212, E-mail: mberman@psychology.msstate.edu. *Application contact:* Angie Campbell, Admissions and Enrollment Assistant, 662-325-9514, E-mail: acampbell@grad.msstate.edu.
Website: http://www.psychology.msstate.edu/

Missouri State University, Graduate College, College of Health and Human Services, Department of Psychology, Springfield, MO 65897. Offers applied behavior analysis (MS); clinical psychology (MS); experimental psychology (MS); forensic child psychology (Certificate); industrial/organizational psychology (MS). *Degree requirements:* For master's, comprehensive exam, thesis. *Entrance requirements:* For master's, GRE General Test, GRE Subject Test, minimum GPA of 3.25 in major, 3.0 overall; 20 hours of course work in psychology. Additional exam requirements/recommendations for international students: required—TOEFL (minimum score 550 paper-based; 79 iBT), IELTS (minimum score 6). Electronic applications accepted. *Expenses: Tuition, area resident:* Full-time $2600; part-time $1735 per credit hour. Tuition, nonresident: full-time $5240; part-time $3495 per credit hour. *International tuition:* $5240 full-time. *Required fees:* $530; $438 per credit hour. Tuition and fees vary according to class time, course level, course load, degree level, campus/location and program.

Monmouth University, Graduate Studies, Department of Professional Counseling, West Long Branch, NJ 07764-1898. Offers addiction studies (MA); clinical mental health counseling (MS); professional counseling (PMC). *Accreditation:* ACA. *Program availability:* Part-time, evening/weekend. *Faculty:* 9 full-time (5 women), 4 part-time/adjunct (3 women). *Students:* 91 full-time (78 women), 53 part-time (38 women); includes 28 minority (11 Black or African American, non-Hispanic/Latino; 1 Asian, non-Hispanic/Latino; 12 Hispanic/Latino; 4 Two or more races, non-Hispanic/Latino). Average age 30. In 2019, 57 master's awarded. *Degree requirements:* For master's, comprehensive exam (for some programs), thesis optional, fieldwork. *Entrance requirements:* For master's, GRE, minimum GPA of 3.0 overall, 12 credits in psychology or closely-related field, two Monmouth University psychological counseling recommendation forms, narrative essay; for PMC, degree or current enrollment in CACREP-accredited master's program in counseling with minimum cumulative GPA of 3.0. Additional exam requirements/recommendations for international students: required—TOEFL (minimum score 550 paper-based; 79 iBT), IELTS (minimum score 6), Michigan English Language Assessment Battery (minimum score 77) or Certificate of Advanced English (minimum score 160). *Application deadline:* For fall admission, 7/15 priority date for domestic students, 6/1 for international students; for spring admission, 12/1 priority date for domestic students, 11/1 for international students; for summer admission, 5/1 for domestic students. Applications are processed on a rolling basis. Application fee: $50. Electronic applications accepted. *Expenses: Tuition:* Full-time $22,194; part-time $14,796 per credit. *Required fees:* $712; $178 per semester. $178 per semester. Tuition and fees vary according to course load. *Financial support:* In 2019–20, 149 students received support. Research assistantships, teaching assistantships, scholarships/grants, and unspecified assistantships available. Support available to part-time students. Financial award applicants required to submit FAFSA. *Unit head:* Dr. Joanne Jodry, Program Director, 732-263-5115, Fax: 732-923-4661, E-mail: jjodry@monmouth.edu. *Application contact:* Kevin New, Graduate Admission Counselor, 732-571-3452, Fax: 732-263-5123, E-mail: gradadm@monmouth.edu.

Website: https://www.monmouth.edu/school-of-humanities-social-sciences/professional-counseling.aspx

Montana State University, The Graduate School, College of Letters and Science, Department of Psychology, Bozeman, MT 59717. Offers MS. *Program availability:* Part-time. *Degree requirements:* For master's, comprehensive exam, thesis (for some programs). *Entrance requirements:* For master's, GRE General Test. Additional exam requirements/recommendations for international students: required—TOEFL (minimum score 550 paper-based). Electronic applications accepted.

Montana State University Billings, College of Arts and Sciences, Department of Psychology, Billings, MT 59101. Offers MS. *Program availability:* Part-time. *Degree requirements:* For master's, thesis optional. *Entrance requirements:* For master's, GRE General Test, 3 letters of recommendation, resume. Additional exam requirements/recommendations for international students: required—TOEFL (minimum score 79 iBT), IELTS (minimum score 6.5). Electronic applications accepted.

Montclair State University, The Graduate School, College of Humanities and Social Sciences, Program in Psychology, Montclair, NJ 07043-1624. Offers MA. *Program availability:* Part-time, evening/weekend. *Degree requirements:* For master's, thesis. *Entrance requirements:* For master's, GRE General Test, 2 letters of recommendation, essay. Additional exam requirements/recommendations for international students: required—TOEFL (minimum score 83 iBT), IELTS (minimum score 6.5). Electronic applications accepted.

Morehead State University, Graduate School, College of Science, Department of Psychology, Morehead, KY 40351. Offers clinical/counseling psychology (MS); general/experimental psychology (MS). *Program availability:* Part-time, evening/weekend. *Faculty:* 8 full-time (5 women), 1 part-time/adjunct (0 women). *Students:* 10 full-time (9 women), 1 (woman) part-time; includes 2 minority (both Two or more races, non-Hispanic/Latino). 20 applicants, 60% accepted, 6 enrolled. In 2019, 11 master's awarded. *Degree requirements:* For master's, comprehensive exam, Minimum 3.0 GPA, internship, pass a comprehensive oral examination administered by a committee of three faculty. *Entrance requirements:* For master's, GRE, 3.5 UG GPA preferred, 3.0 is minimum required, 18 hrs in psychology, interview, 3 letters of recommendation, statement of purpose for seeking graduate-level training in clinical/counseling psychology. *Application deadline:* For fall admission, 3/1 priority date for domestic and international students. Applications are processed on a rolling basis. Application fee: $30. Electronic applications accepted. *Expenses: Tuition, area resident:* Part-time $570 per credit hour. Tuition, state resident: part-time $570 per credit hour. Tuition, nonresident: part-time $570 per credit hour. *Required fees:* $14 per credit hour. *Financial support:* Research assistantships, career-related internships or fieldwork, and unspecified assistantships available. Financial award applicants required to submit FAFSA. *Unit head:* Dr. Gregory Corso, Department Chair Psychology, 606-783-2981, E-mail: g.corso@moreheadstate.edu. *Application contact:* Dr. Gregory Corso, Department Chair Psychology, 606-783-2981, E-mail: g.corso@moreheadstate.edu. Website: https://www.moreheadstate.edu/College-of-Science/Psychology

Morgan State University, School of Graduate Studies, James H. Gilliam Jr College of Liberal Arts, Department of Psychology, Baltimore, MD 21251. Offers psychometrics (MS, PhD). *Program availability:* Part-time, evening/weekend. *Faculty:* 12 full-time (10 women), 3 part-time/adjunct (2 women). *Students:* 11 full-time (8 women); includes 8 minority (all Black or African American, non-Hispanic/Latino). Average age 36. 7 applicants, 43% accepted, 2 enrolled. In 2019, 1 doctorate awarded. *Degree requirements:* For master's, comprehensive exam, thesis; for doctorate, comprehensive exam, thesis/dissertation. *Entrance requirements:* For master's and doctorate, GRE, Minimum GPA 3.0. Additional exam requirements/recommendations for international students: required—TOEFL (minimum score 70 iBT); recommended—IELTS (minimum score 6). *Application deadline:* For fall admission, 4/15 for domestic and international students. Applications are processed on a rolling basis. Application fee: $50 ($70 for international students). Electronic applications accepted. *Expenses:* Tuition, state resident: full-time $455; part-time $455 per credit hour. Tuition, nonresident: full-time $894; part-time $894 per credit hour. *Required fees:* $82; $82 per credit hour. *Financial support:* In 2019–20, 2 students received support. Fellowships with full and partial tuition reimbursements available, research assistantships with full and partial tuition reimbursements available, teaching assistantships with full and partial tuition reimbursements available, career-related internships or fieldwork, Federal Work-Study, scholarships/grants, tuition waivers (full and partial), and unspecified assistantships available. Support available to part-time students. Financial award application deadline: 2/1. *Unit head:* Dr. Jocelyn Turner-Musa, Chair Department of Psychology, 443-885-3290, E-mail: ocelyn.turnermusa@morgan.edu. *Application contact:* Dr. Jahmaine Smith, Director of Admissions, 443-885-3185, Fax: 443-885-8226, E-mail: gradapply@morgan.edu.

Murray State University, College of Humanities and Fine Arts, Department of Psychology, Murray, KY 42071. Offers clinical psychology (MA, MS); general experimental psychology (MA, MS); research design and analysis (Certificate). *Program availability:* Part-time. *Entrance requirements:* For master's and Certificate, GRE or GMAT, minimum university GPA of 2.75. Additional exam requirements/recommendations for international students: required—TOEFL (minimum score 527 paper-based; 71 iBT). Electronic applications accepted.

Naropa University, Graduate Programs, Program in Ecopsychology, Boulder, CO 80302-6697. Offers MA. *Program availability:* Part-time, blended/hybrid learning. *Degree requirements:* For master's, thesis, service learning. *Entrance requirements:* For master's, curriculum vitae/resume with pertinent academic, employment and volunteer activities; 2 letters of recommendation; transcripts; letter of interest. Additional exam requirements/recommendations for international students: required—TOEFL (minimum score 550 paper-based; 80 iBT). Electronic applications accepted. *Expenses:* Contact institution.

National Louis University, College of Arts and Sciences, Chicago, IL 60603. Offers adult education (Ed D); counseling and human services (MS); language and academic development (M Ed, Certificate); psychology (MA, PhD, Certificate); public policy (MA); written communication (MS, Certificate). *Program availability:* Part-time, evening/weekend, online learning. *Degree requirements:* For master's and Certificate, comprehensive exam (for some programs), thesis (for some programs); for doctorate, thesis/dissertation. *Entrance requirements:* For master's, MAT or GRE, 3 professional or academic references, interview, minimum GPA of 3.0; for doctorate, GRE General Test, MAT, or Watson-Glaser Critical Thinking Appraisal, three professional or academic references, statement of academic and professional goals, 3 years of experience in field, interview, master's degree, resume, writing sample; for Certificate, GRE, MAT, or Watson-Glaser Critical Thinking Appraisal, three professional or academic references, statement of academic and professional goals, interview, minimum GPA of 3.0. Additional exam requirements/recommendations for international students: required—Department of Language Studies Assessment or TOEFL (minimum score 550 paper-based; 79 iBT). Electronic applications accepted.

New Mexico Highlands University, Graduate Studies, College of Arts and Sciences, Department of Social and Behavioral Sciences, Las Vegas, NM 87701. Offers psychology (MS), including clinical psychology/counseling, general psychology; public

affairs (MA), including applied sociology; Southwest studies (MA), including anthropology. *Program availability:* Part-time. *Degree requirements:* For master's, comprehensive exam, thesis or alternative. *Entrance requirements:* For master's, minimum undergraduate GPA of 3.0. Additional exam requirements/recommendations for international students: required—TOEFL (minimum score 540 paper-based).

New Mexico State University, College of Arts and Sciences, Department of Psychology, Las Cruces, NM 88003-8001. Offers experimental psychology (MA, PhD). *Faculty:* 10 full-time (3 women). *Students:* 20 full-time (13 women), 5 part-time (4 women); includes 11 minority (1 Black or African American, non-Hispanic/Latino; 1 American Indian or Alaska Native, non-Hispanic/Latino; 1 Asian, non-Hispanic/Latino; 6 Hispanic/Latino; 2 Two or more races, non-Hispanic/Latino), 1 international. Average age 28. 32 applicants, 59% accepted, 12 enrolled. In 2019, 3 master's, 6 doctorates awarded. *Degree requirements:* For master's, thesis; for doctorate, comprehensive exam, thesis/dissertation, work-related experience (teaching or internship). *Entrance requirements:* For master's, GRE General Test, letters of recommendation, curriculum vitae, personal statement, writing sample; for doctorate, GRE General Test, letters of recommendation, master's thesis, curriculum vitae, personal statement, writing sample. Additional exam requirements/recommendations for international students: required—TOEFL (minimum score 550 paper-based; 79 iBT), IELTS (minimum score 6.5). *Application deadline:* For fall admission, 1/15 priority date for domestic students, 1/15 for international students. Applications are processed on a rolling basis. Application fee: $40 ($50 for international students). Electronic applications accepted. *Financial support:* In 2019–20, 22 students received support, including 3 fellowships (averaging $4,844 per year), 6 research assistantships (averaging $14,740 per year), 15 teaching assistantships (averaging $17,121 per year); career-related internships or fieldwork, Federal Work-Study, scholarships/grants, traineeships, health care benefits, and unspecified assistantships also available. Support available to part-time students. Financial award application deadline: 3/1. *Unit head:* Dr. Dominic A. Simon, Department Head, 575-646-2502, Fax: 575-646-6212, E-mail: domsimon@nmsu.edu. *Application contact:* Dr. Laura J. Madson, Chair of Graduate Committee, 575-646-6207, Fax: 575-646-6212, E-mail: lmadson@nmsu.edu. Website: http://psych.nmsu.edu

The New School, The New School for Social Research, Department of Psychology, New York, NY 10011. Offers clinical psychology (PhD); cognitive, social, and developmental psychology (PhD); psychology (MA). *Accreditation:* APA (one or more programs are accredited). *Program availability:* Part-time. *Faculty:* 17 full-time (9 women), 8 part-time/adjunct (2 women). *Students:* 173 full-time (135 women), 32 part-time (28 women); includes 36 minority (8 Black or African American, non-Hispanic/Latino; 8 Asian, non-Hispanic/Latino; 17 Hispanic/Latino; 1 Native Hawaiian or other Pacific Islander, non-Hispanic/Latino; 2 Two or more races, non-Hispanic/Latino), 42 international. Average age 29. 217 applicants, 85% accepted, 58 enrolled. In 2019, 75 master's, 14 doctorates awarded. Terminal master's awarded for partial completion of doctoral program. *Degree requirements:* For master's, comprehensive exam, thesis (for some programs); for doctorate, comprehensive exam, thesis/dissertation. *Entrance requirements:* For master's, GRE, letters of recommendation, writing sample, essays, transcripts; for doctorate, letters of recommendation, writing sample, essays, transcripts. Additional exam requirements/recommendations for international students: required—TOEFL (minimum score 100 iBT), IELTS (minimum score 7), PTE (minimum score 68). *Application deadline:* For fall admission, 1/5 priority date for domestic and international students; for spring admission, 10/15 priority date for domestic and international students. Applications are processed on a rolling basis. Application fee: $50. Electronic applications accepted. *Expenses:* 2260 per credit. *Financial support:* In 2019–20, 191 students received support, including 21 fellowships with full and partial tuition reimbursements available (averaging $6,560 per year), 43 research assistantships (averaging $5,556 per year), 52 teaching assistantships with full and partial tuition reimbursements available (averaging $7,423 per year); career-related internships or fieldwork, Federal Work-Study, scholarships/grants, and tuition waivers (full and partial) also available. Support available to part-time students. Financial award application deadline: 2/1; financial award applicants required to submit FAFSA. *Unit head:* Dr. Howard Steele, Department Chair, 212-2295727 Ext. 3118, E-mail: steeleh@newschool.edu. *Application contact:* Merida Gasbarro, Director of Graduate Admission, 212-229-5600 Ext. 1108, E-mail: escandom@newschool.edu. Website: https://www.newschool.edu/nssr/psychology/

New York Medical College, School of Health Sciences and Practice, Valhalla, NY 10595. Offers behavioral sciences and health promotion (MPH); biostatistics (MS); children with special health care (Graduate Certificate); emergency preparedness (Graduate Certificate); environmental health science (MPH); epidemiology (MPH, MS); global health (Graduate Certificate); health education (Graduate Certificate); health policy and management (MPH, Dr PH); industrial hygiene (Graduate Certificate); pediatric dysphagia (Post-Graduate Certificate); physical therapy (DPT); public health (Graduate Certificate); speech-language pathology (MS). *Accreditation:* ASHA; CEPH. *Program availability:* Part-time, evening/weekend, 100% online, blended/hybrid learning. *Faculty:* 47 full-time (34 women), 203 part-time/adjunct (125 women). *Students:* 230 full-time (171 women), 292 part-time (207 women); includes 204 minority (73 Black or African American, non-Hispanic/Latino; 4 American Indian or Alaska Native, non-Hispanic/Latino; 59 Asian, non-Hispanic/Latino; 54 Hispanic/Latino; 1 Native Hawaiian or other Pacific Islander, non-Hispanic/Latino; 13 Two or more races, non-Hispanic/Latino), 35 international. Average age 29. 790 applicants, 61% accepted, 162 enrolled. In 2019, 113 master's, 47 doctorates awarded. *Degree requirements:* For master's, comprehensive exam (for some programs), thesis (for some programs); for doctorate, thesis/dissertation. *Entrance requirements:* For master's, GRE (for MS in speech-language pathology); for doctorate, GRE (for Doctor of Physical Therapy and Doctor of Public Health). Additional exam requirements/recommendations for international students: required—TOEFL (minimum score 96 paper-based; 24 iBT), IELTS (minimum score 7). *Application deadline:* For fall admission, 8/1 for domestic students, 4/15 for international students; for spring admission, 12/1 for domestic students; for summer admission, 5/1 for domestic students, 4/15 for international students. Applications are processed on a rolling basis. Application fee: $128 ($120 for international students). Electronic applications accepted. *Expenses:* $1195 credit fee, academic support fee $200, Student activities fee $140 per year, technology fee $150. *Financial support:* In 2019–20, 18 students received support. Federal Work-Study, scholarships/grants, unspecified assistantships, and Federal student loans available. Financial award application deadline: 4/30; financial award applicants required to submit FAFSA. *Unit head:* Ben Johnson, PhD, Vice Dean, 914-594-4531, E-mail: bjohnson23@nymc.edu. *Application contact:* Irene Bundziak, Assistant to Director of Admissions, 914-594-4905, E-mail: irene_bundziak@nymc.edu. Website: http://www.nymc.edu/school-of-health-sciences-and-practice-shsp/

New York University, Graduate School of Arts and Science, Department of Psychology, New York, NY 10012-1019. Offers cognition and perception (PhD); general psychology (MA); industrial/organizational psychology (MA); psychotherapy and psychoanalysis (Advanced Certificate); social psychology (PhD). *Program availability:* Part-time. Terminal master's awarded for partial completion of doctoral program. *Degree requirements:* For master's, comprehensive exam, thesis or alternative; for doctorate, thesis/dissertation. *Entrance requirements:* For master's and doctorate, GRE General

Test. Additional exam requirements/recommendations for international students: required—TOEFL, IELTS.

New York University, Steinhardt School of Culture, Education, and Human Development, Department of Applied Psychology, Programs in Educational and Developmental Psychology, New York, NY 10012. Offers developmental psychology (PhD); human development and social intervention (MA); psychology and social intervention (PhD). *Accreditation:* APA (one or more programs are accredited). *Program availability:* Part-time. *Entrance requirements:* For doctorate, GRE General Test, interview. Additional exam requirements/recommendations for international students: required—TOEFL. Electronic applications accepted.

Norfolk State University, School of Graduate Studies, School of Liberal Arts, Department of Psychology, Norfolk, VA 23504. Offers community/clinical psychology (MA); psychology (Psy D). *Program availability:* Part-time. *Degree requirements:* For master's, comprehensive exam, thesis or alternative; for doctorate, comprehensive exam, thesis/dissertation. *Entrance requirements:* For master's, minimum GPA of 2.7.

North Carolina Central University, College of Behavioral and Social Sciences, Department of Psychology, Durham, NC 27707-3129. Offers clinical psychology (MA); general psychology (MA). *Program availability:* Part-time, evening/weekend. *Degree requirements:* For master's, one foreign language, comprehensive exam, thesis. *Entrance requirements:* For master's, GRE, minimum GPA of 3.0 in major, 2.5 overall. Additional exam requirements/recommendations for international students: required—TOEFL.

North Carolina State University, Graduate School, College of Humanities and Social Sciences, Department of Psychology, Raleigh, NC 27695. Offers applied social and community psychology (PhD); human factors and applied cognition (PhD); industrial/organizational psychology (PhD); lifespan developmental psychology (PhD); school psychology (PhD). *Accreditation:* APA. *Degree requirements:* For doctorate, comprehensive exam, thesis/dissertation. *Entrance requirements:* For doctorate, GRE General Test, GRE Subject Test (industrial/organizational psychology), MAT (recommended), minimum GPA of 3.0 in major. Electronic applications accepted.

Northcentral University, Graduate Studies, San Diego, CA 92106. Offers business (MBA, DBA, PhD, Postbaccalaureate Certificate); education (M Ed, Ed D, PhD, Ed S, Post-Master's Certificate, Postbaccalaureate Certificate); marriage and family therapy (MA, DMFT, PhD, Post-Master's Certificate, Postbaccalaureate Certificate); psychology (MA, PhD, Post-Master's Certificate, Postbaccalaureate Certificate); technology (MS, PhD), including computer science, cybersecurity (MS), data science, technology and innovation management (PhD). *Program availability:* Part-time, evening/weekend, online only, 100% online. *Degree requirements:* For doctorate, comprehensive exam, thesis/dissertation. *Entrance requirements:* For master's, bachelor's degree from regionally- or nationally-accredited institution, current resume or curriculum vitae, statement of intent, interview, and background check (for marriage and family therapy); for doctorate, post-baccalaureate master's degree and/or doctoral degree from nationally- or regionally-accredited academic institution; for other advanced degree, bachelor's-level or higher degree from accredited institution or university (for Post-Baccalaureate Certificate); master's and/or doctoral degree from regionally- or nationally-accredited academic institution (for Post-Master's Certificate). Additional exam requirements/recommendations for international students: required—TOEFL (minimum score 550 paper-based; 79 iBT), IELTS (minimum score 6.5), PTE (minimum score 53). Electronic applications accepted. *Expenses: Tuition:* Part-time $1053 per credit. *Required fees:* $95 per course. Full-time tuition and fees vary according to degree level and program.

North Dakota State University, College of Graduate and Interdisciplinary Studies, College of Science and Mathematics, Department of Psychology, Fargo, ND 58102. Offers clinical psychology (MS); health and social psychology (PhD); psychological clinical science (PhD); psychology (MS); visual and cognitive neuroscience (PhD). *Entrance requirements:* Additional exam requirements/recommendations for international students: required—TOEFL. Electronic applications accepted. Tuition and fees vary according to program and reciprocity agreements.

Northeastern State University, College of Education, Department of Psychology and Counseling, Tahlequah, OK 74464-2399. Offers counseling (MS). *Program availability:* Part-time, evening/weekend. *Faculty:* 10 full-time (5 women), 5 part-time/adjunct (4 women). *Students:* 78 full-time (57 women), 47 part-time (39 women); includes 54 minority (10 Black or African American, non-Hispanic/Latino; 20 American Indian or Alaska Native, non-Hispanic/Latino; 2 Asian, non-Hispanic/Latino; 2 Hispanic/Latino; 20 Two or more races, non-Hispanic/Latino). Average age 32. In 2019, 48 master's awarded. *Degree requirements:* For master's, thesis (for some programs), written and oral examinations. *Entrance requirements:* For master's, GRE, minimum GPA of 2.5. *Application deadline:* Applications are processed on a rolling basis. Application fee: $25. Electronic applications accepted. *Expenses: Tuition, area resident:* Full-time $250; part-time $250 per credit hour. Tuition, state resident: full-time $250; part-time $250 per credit hour. Tuition, nonresident: full-time $556; part-time $555.50 per credit hour. *Required fees:* $33.40 per credit hour. *Financial support:* Teaching assistantships, career-related internships or fieldwork, and Federal Work-Study available. Financial award application deadline: 3/1. *Unit head:* Dr. Elizabeth Keller-Dupree, Program Chair, 918-449-6534, E-mail: kellere@nsuok.edu. *Application contact:* Josh McCollum, Graduate Coordinator, 918-444-2093, E-mail: mccolluj@nsuok.edu.
Website: https://academics.nsuok.edu/education/EducationHome/COEDepartments/PsychologyCounseling.aspx

Northeastern University, College of Science, Boston, MA 02115-5096. Offers applied mathematics (MS); bioinformatics (MS); biology (PhD); biotechnology (MS); chemistry and chemical biology (MS, PhD); environmental science and policy (MS); marine and environmental sciences (PhD); marine biology (MS); mathematics (MS, PhD); operations research (MSOR); physics (MS, PhD); psychology (PhD). *Program availability:* Part-time. Terminal master's awarded for partial completion of doctoral program. *Degree requirements:* For master's, comprehensive exam (for some programs), thesis; for doctorate, comprehensive exam (for some programs), thesis/dissertation. *Entrance requirements:* For master's, GRE General Test. Electronic applications accepted. *Expenses:* Contact institution.

Northern Arizona University, College of Social and Behavioral Sciences, Department of Psychological Sciences, Flagstaff, AZ 86011. Offers psychological sciences (MA). *Program availability:* Part-time. *Degree requirements:* For master's, variable foreign language requirement, comprehensive exam (for some programs), thesis (for some programs). *Entrance requirements:* For master's, GRE General Test. Additional exam requirements/recommendations for international students: required—TOEFL (minimum score 80 iBT), IELTS (minimum score 6.5). Electronic applications accepted.

Northern Illinois University, Graduate School, College of Liberal Arts and Sciences, Department of Psychology, De Kalb, IL 60115-2854. Offers MA, PhD. *Accreditation:* APA (one or more programs are accredited). *Faculty:* 26 full-time (11 women), 5 part-time/adjunct (1 woman). *Students:* 70 full-time (53 women), 31 part-time (26 women); includes 22 minority (4 Black or African American, non-Hispanic/Latino; 6 Asian, non-Hispanic/Latino; 11 Hispanic/Latino; 1 Two or more races, non-Hispanic/Latino), 4 international. Average age 27. 287 applicants, 10% accepted, 21 enrolled. In 2019, 17 master's, 18 doctorates awarded. *Degree requirements:* For master's, comprehensive exam, thesis optional; for doctorate, thesis/dissertation, candidacy exam, dissertation defense. *Entrance requirements:* For master's, GRE General Test, minimum GPA of 3.0 for last 2 years of undergraduate work; for doctorate, GRE General Test, minimum undergraduate GPA of 2.75, graduate 3.2; master's degree with research thesis. Additional exam requirements/recommendations for international students: required—TOEFL (minimum score 550 paper-based). *Application deadline:* For fall admission, 3/1 for domestic students, 5/1 for international students; for spring admission, 11/1 for domestic students, 10/1 for international students. Applications are processed on a rolling basis. Application fee: $40. Electronic applications accepted. *Financial support:* In 2019–20, 33 research assistantships with full tuition reimbursements, 58 teaching assistantships with full tuition reimbursements were awarded; fellowships with full tuition reimbursements, career-related internships or fieldwork, Federal Work-Study, scholarships/grants, tuition waivers (full), and staff assistantships also available. Support available to part-time students. Financial award applicants required to submit FAFSA. *Unit head:* Dr. Amanda M Durik, Chair, 815-753-7065. *Application contact:* Graduate School Office, 815-753-0395, E-mail: gradsch@niu.edu.
Website: http://www.niu.edu/psyc/

Northern Michigan University, Office of Graduate Education and Research, College of Arts and Sciences, Department of Psychological Science, Marquette, MI 49855-5301. Offers applied behavior analysis (MS); psychological science (MS). *Program availability:* Part-time. *Degree requirements:* For master's, thesis or alternative. *Entrance requirements:* For master's, minimum GPA of 3.0; bachelor's degree (preferably in psychology); undergraduate courses in introduction to psychology and statistics; personal statement; 3 letters of recommendation. Additional exam requirements/recommendations for international students: required—TOEFL (minimum score 500 paper-based; 61 iBT), IELTS (minimum score 6). *Application deadline:* For fall admission, 2/1 for domestic students. Applications are processed on a rolling basis. Application fee: $50. Electronic applications accepted. *Financial support:* Teaching assistantships with full tuition reimbursements available. Financial award application deadline: 3/1; financial award applicants required to submit FAFSA. *Unit head:* Dr. Adam Prus, Department Head and Professor, 906-227-2935, E-mail: psych@nmu.edu. *Application contact:* Dr. Adam Prus, Department Head and Professor, 906-227-2935, E-mail: psych@nmu.edu.
Website: http://www.nmu.edu/psychology/

Northwestern State University of Louisiana, Graduate Studies and Research, Department of Psychology, Natchitoches, LA 71497. Offers clinical psychology (MS). *Degree requirements:* For master's, comprehensive exam, thesis or alternative. *Entrance requirements:* For master's, GRE General Test, GRE Subject Test, minimum undergraduate GPA of 2.5. Additional exam requirements/recommendations for international students: required—TOEFL. Electronic applications accepted.

Northwestern University, The Graduate School, Judd A. and Marjorie Weinberg College of Arts and Sciences, Department of Psychology, Evanston, IL 60208. Offers brain, behavior and cognition (PhD); clinical psychology (PhD); cognitive psychology (PhD); personality psychology (PhD); social psychology (PhD); JD/PhD. *Accreditation:* APA (one or more programs are accredited). *Program availability:* Part-time. *Degree requirements:* For doctorate, thesis/dissertation. *Entrance requirements:* For doctorate, GRE General Test, GRE Subject Test. Additional exam requirements/recommendations for international students: required—TOEFL. Electronic applications accepted.

Northwest University, College of Social and Behavioral Sciences, Kirkland, WA 98033. Offers counseling psychology (MA, Psy D); international community development (MA). *Program availability:* Evening/weekend. *Entrance requirements:* For master's, 3 character references. Additional exam requirements/recommendations for international students: required—TOEFL (minimum score 580 paper-based). *Expenses:* Contact institution.

Nova Southeastern University, College of Psychology, Fort Lauderdale, FL 33314-7796. Offers clinical mental health counseling (MS); clinical psychology (PhD, Psy D); counseling (MS); experimental psychology (MS); forensic psychology (MS); general psychology (MS); school counseling (MS); school psychology (Psy D, Psy S); substance abuse counseling (MS); substance abuse counseling and education (MS). *Accreditation:* APA (one or more programs are accredited). *Program availability:* Part-time, 100% online, blended/hybrid learning. *Faculty:* 72 full-time (34 women), 111 part-time/adjunct (76 women). *Students:* 1,263 full-time (1,068 women), 868 part-time (761 women); includes 1,221 minority (368 Black or African American, non-Hispanic/Latino; 3 American Indian or Alaska Native, non-Hispanic/Latino; 111 Asian, non-Hispanic/Latino; 668 Hispanic/Latino; 1 Native Hawaiian or other Pacific Islander, non-Hispanic/Latino; 70 Two or more races, non-Hispanic/Latino), 59 international. Average age 31. 935 applicants, 56% accepted, 375 enrolled. In 2019, 400 master's, 72 doctorates, 13 other advanced degrees awarded. Terminal master's awarded for partial completion of doctoral program. *Degree requirements:* For master's, comprehensive exam, 3 practica; for doctorate, thesis/dissertation, clinical internship, competency exam; for Psy S, comprehensive exam, internship. *Entrance requirements:* For master's and Psy S, GRE General Test, letters of recommendation, research/personal statement, interview; for doctorate, GRE General Test, GRE Subject Test (recommended), minimum undergraduate GPA of 3.0, letters of recommendation, research/personal statement, interview, curriculum vitae/resume. Additional exam requirements/recommendations for international students: required—TOEFL (minimum score 550 paper-based). *Application deadline:* Applications are processed on a rolling basis. Application fee: $50. Electronic applications accepted. *Expenses:* Contact institution. *Financial support:* In 2019–20, 197 students received support, including 15 research assistantships (averaging $5,600 per year), 68 teaching assistantships (averaging $2,000 per year); career-related internships or fieldwork, Federal Work-Study, institutionally sponsored loans, scholarships/grants, and unspecified assistantships also available. Support available to part-time students. Financial award application deadline: 4/15; financial award applicants required to submit FAFSA. *Unit head:* Dr. Karen Grosby, Dean, 954-262-5712, Fax: 954-262-3859, E-mail: grosby@nova.edu. *Application contact:* Gregory Gayle, Director, Recruitment and Admissions, 954-262-5903, Fax: 954-262-3893, E-mail: ggayle1@nova.edu.
Website: http://psychology.nova.edu/

The Ohio State University, Graduate School, College of Arts and Sciences, Division of Social and Behavioral Sciences, Department of Psychology, Columbus, OH 43210. Offers behavioral neuroscience (PhD); clinical psychology (PhD); cognitive psychology (PhD); developmental psychology (PhD); intellectual and developmental disabilities psychology (PhD); quantitative psychology (PhD); social psychology (PhD). *Accreditation:* APA. *Entrance requirements:* For doctorate, GRE General Test. Additional exam requirements/recommendations for international students: required—TOEFL (minimum score 600 paper-based; 100 iBT); recommended—IELTS (minimum score 8). Electronic applications accepted.

Ohio University, Graduate College, College of Arts and Sciences, Department of Psychology, Athens, OH 45701-2979. Offers clinical psychology (PhD); experimental psychology (PhD); organizational psychology (PhD). *Accreditation:* APA. *Degree requirements:* For doctorate, one foreign language, comprehensive exam, thesis/dissertation. *Entrance requirements:* For doctorate, GRE General Test, GRE Subject Test. Additional exam requirements/recommendations for international students:

required—TOEFL (minimum score 550 paper-based; 80 iBT) or IELTS (minimum score 6.5). Electronic applications accepted.

Oklahoma State University, College of Arts and Sciences, Department of Psychology, Stillwater, OK 74078. Offers clinical psychology (PhD); general psychology (MS). *Accreditation:* APA (one or more programs are accredited). *Faculty:* 23 full-time (13 women), 2 part-time/adjunct (1 woman). *Students:* 39 full-time (32 women), 23 part-time (18 women); includes 14 minority (2 Black or African American, non-Hispanic/Latino; 2 American Indian or Alaska Native, non-Hispanic/Latino; 2 Asian, non-Hispanic/Latino; 4 Hispanic/Latino; 1 Native Hawaiian or other Pacific Islander, non-Hispanic/Latino; 3 Two or more races, non-Hispanic/Latino), 1 international. Average age 27. 154 applicants, 9% accepted, 14 enrolled. In 2019, 10 master's, 5 doctorates awarded. *Entrance requirements:* For master's and doctorate, GRE General Test. Additional exam requirements/recommendations for international students: required—TOEFL (minimum score 550 paper-based; 79 iBT). *Application deadline:* For fall admission, 3/1 priority date for international students; for spring admission, 8/1 priority date for international students. Applications are processed on a rolling basis. Application fee: $50 ($75 for international students). Electronic applications accepted. *Expenses: Tuition, area resident:* Full-time $4148.10; part-time $2765.40 per credit hour. *Tuition, state resident:* full-time $4148.10; part-time $2765.40 per credit hour. *Tuition, nonresident:* full-time $15,775; part-time $10,516.80 per credit hour. *International tuition:* $15,775.20 full-time. *Required fees:* $2196.90; $122.05 per credit hour. Tuition and fees vary according to course load, campus/location and program. *Financial support:* In 2019–20, 16 research assistantships (averaging $1,711 per year), 38 teaching assistantships (averaging $1,798 per year) were awarded; career-related internships or fieldwork, Federal Work-Study, scholarships/grants, health care benefits, tuition waivers (partial), and unspecified assistantships also available. Support available to part-time students. Financial award application deadline: 3/1; financial award applicants required to submit FAFSA. *Unit head:* Dr. Thad Leffingwell, Department Head, 405-744-7494, Fax: 405-744-8067, E-mail: thad.leffingwell@okstate.edu. *Application contact:* Dr. Sheryl Tucker, Vice Prov/Dean/Prof, 405-744-6368, E-mail: gradi@okstate.edu.
Website: http://psychology.okstate.edu

Old Dominion University, College of Sciences, Doctoral Program in Psychology, Norfolk, VA 23529. Offers applied psychological sciences (PhD); human factors psychology (PhD); industrial/organizational psychology (PhD). *Degree requirements:* For doctorate, comprehensive exam, thesis/dissertation, candidacy exam. *Entrance requirements:* For doctorate, GRE General Test, GRE Subject Test, 3 recommendation letters. Additional exam requirements/recommendations for international students: required—TOEFL. Electronic applications accepted. *Expenses:* Contact institution.

Old Dominion University, College of Sciences, Master of Science in Psychology Program, Norfolk, VA 23529. Offers MS. *Program availability:* Part-time. Terminal master's awarded for partial completion of doctoral program. *Degree requirements:* For master's, thesis. *Entrance requirements:* For master's, GRE General Test, minimum GPA of 3.0 in major, previous course work in psychology. Additional exam requirements/recommendations for international students: required—TOEFL (minimum score 550 paper-based; 79 iBT), GRE. Electronic applications accepted. *Expenses:* Contact institution.

Oregon State University, College of Liberal Arts, Program in Psychology, Corvallis, OR 97331. Offers applied cognition (MS, PhD); engineering psychology (MS, PhD); health psychology (MS, PhD).

Our Lady of the Lake University, College of Professional Studies, Program in Psychology, San Antonio, TX 78207-4689. Offers marriage and family therapy (MS); school psychology (MS). *Accreditation:* APA. *Program availability:* Part-time. *Degree requirements:* For master's, comprehensive exam, practicum. *Entrance requirements:* For master's, GRE General Test or MAT, bachelor's degree with at least 12 undergraduate semester hours in psychology including one course in statistics and minimum cumulative GPA of 3.0; criminal background check; personal statement addressing background in psychology, expectations of the MS program, and professional goals; statement of purpose; 2 letters of recommendation. Additional exam requirements/recommendations for international students: required—TOEFL. Electronic applications accepted. Application fee is waived when completed online.

Pace University, Dyson College of Arts and Sciences, Department of Psychology, Program in Psychology, New York, NY 10038. Offers psychology (MA). *Program availability:* Part-time, evening/weekend. *Entrance requirements:* For master's, GRE, two letters of recommendation, resume, statement of purpose, all official transcripts, bachelor's degree from accredited institution, at least 9 hours of undergraduate psychology course prerequisites. Additional exam requirements/recommendations for international students: required—TOEFL (minimum score 88 iBT), IELTS (minimum score 7) or PTE (minimum score 60). Electronic applications accepted.

Pacifica Graduate Institute, Graduate Programs, Carpinteria, CA 93013. Offers clinical psychology (PhD); counseling psychology (MA); depth psychology (MA, PhD); mythological studies (MA, PhD). Terminal master's awarded for partial completion of doctoral program. *Degree requirements:* For master's, thesis (for some programs), practicum; for doctorate, comprehensive exam, thesis/dissertation, internship. *Entrance requirements:* For master's, resume, 3 letters of recommendation, writing sample, interview; for doctorate, resumé, 4 letters of recommendation, writing sample, interview. Additional exam requirements/recommendations for international students: required—TOEFL.

Pacific University, School of Professional Psychology, Forest Grove, OR 97116-1797. Offers applied psychological science (MA, MS); clinical psychology (PhD, Psy D). *Accreditation:* APA (one or more programs are accredited). *Program availability:* Part-time. *Degree requirements:* For master's, comprehensive exam (for some programs), thesis (for some programs); for doctorate, comprehensive exam, thesis/dissertation. *Entrance requirements:* For master's, course work in introductory psychology, statistics, and abnormal psychology; minimum GPA of 3.0; for doctorate, GRE General Test, minimum GPA of 3.0, undergraduate course work in psychology, minimum GPA of 3.1 in last 2 years. Additional exam requirements/recommendations for international students: required—TOEFL (minimum score 600 paper-based). Electronic applications accepted. *Expenses:* Contact institution.

Palo Alto University, MS in Psychology (PhD Prep) Program, Palo Alto, CA 94304. Offers MS. *Program availability:* Part-time, online only, online program with 1-week on-campus intensive. *Degree requirements:* For master's, online program with a 1-week on-campus intensive. *Entrance requirements:* For master's, undergraduate degree in psychology with minimum GPA of 3.3. Additional exam requirements/recommendations for international students: required—TOEFL. Electronic applications accepted. *Expenses:* Contact institution.

Palo Alto University, PhD in Clinical Psychology Program, Palo Alto, CA 94304. Offers PhD. *Accreditation:* APA. *Degree requirements:* For doctorate, comprehensive exam, thesis/dissertation, 2000-hour clinical internship. *Entrance requirements:* For doctorate, GRE General Test, undergraduate or graduate degree in psychology or related area; 4 course prerequisites: biopsychology, abnormal psychology, developmental psychology, and statistics. Additional exam requirements/recommendations for international

students: required—TOEFL, IELTS. Electronic applications accepted. *Expenses:* Contact institution.

Penn State Harrisburg, Graduate School, School of Behavioral Sciences and Education, Middletown, PA 17057. Offers adult education in the health and medical professions (Certificate); applied behavior analysis (MA); applied clinical psychology (MA); applied psychological research (MA); community psychology and social change (MA); English as a second language (ESL) program specialist and leadership (Certificate); health education (M Ed); lifelong learning and adult education (M Ed, D Ed); literacy education (M Ed); literacy leadership (Certificate); psychology: applications in clinical psychology (Certificate); psychology: health psychology (Certificate); teaching and curriculum (M Ed); training and development (M Ed, Certificate). *Program availability:* Part-time, evening/weekend.

Penn State University Park, Graduate School, College of the Liberal Arts, Department of Psychology, University Park, PA 16802. Offers psychology (MS, PhD). *Accreditation:* APA (one or more programs are accredited)

Philadelphia College of Osteopathic Medicine, Graduate and Professional Programs, School of Professional and Applied Psychology, Philadelphia, PA 19131. Offers applied behavior analysis (Certificate); clinical health psychology (Post-Doctoral Certificate); clinical neuropsychology (Post-Doctoral Certificate); clinical psychology (Psy D); educational psychology (PhD); mental health counseling (MS); organizational development and leadership (MS); psychology (Certificate); public health management and administration (MS); school psychology (MS, Psy D, Ed S). *Accreditation:* APA. *Faculty:* 19 full-time (11 women), 122 part-time/adjunct (58 women). *Students:* 342 (285 women); includes 108 minority (65 Black or African American, non-Hispanic/Latino; 1 American Indian or Alaska Native, non-Hispanic/Latino; 10 Asian, non-Hispanic/Latino; 14 Hispanic/Latino; 18 Two or more races, non-Hispanic/Latino). Average age 25. 357 applicants, 51% accepted, 113 enrolled. In 2019, 79 master's, 38 doctorates, 16 other advanced degrees awarded. Terminal master's awarded for partial completion of doctoral program. *Degree requirements:* For master's, comprehensive exam (for some programs), thesis (for some programs); for doctorate, comprehensive exam, thesis/dissertation. *Entrance requirements:* For master's, GRE or MAT, minimum GPA of 3.0; bachelor's degree from regionally-accredited college or university; for doctorate, PRAXIS II (for Psy D in school psychology), minimum undergraduate GPA of 3.0; for other advanced degree, GRE (for Ed S). Additional exam requirements/recommendations for international students: required—TOEFL (minimum score 79 iBT). *Application deadline:* Applications are processed on a rolling basis. Application fee: $50. Electronic applications accepted. *Financial support:* In 2019–20, 28 teaching assistantships were awarded; Federal Work-Study, institutionally sponsored loans, and scholarships/grants also available. Financial award application deadline: 3/15; financial award applicants required to submit FAFSA. *Unit head:* Dr. Robert DiTomasso, Chairman, 215-871-6442, Fax: 215-871-6458, E-mail: robertd@pcom.edu. *Application contact:* Johnathan Cox, Associate Director of Admissions, 215-871-6700, Fax: 215-871-6719, E-mail: johnathancox@pcom.edu.
Website: pcom.edu

Phillips Graduate University, Master's Program in Psychology, Chatsworth, CA 91311. Offers art therapy (MA); marriage and family therapy (MA); school counseling (MA); school psychology (MA). *Program availability:* Evening/weekend. *Degree requirements:* For master's, comprehensive exam, thesis. *Entrance requirements:* For master's, minimum GPA of 2.5. Electronic applications accepted.

Pittsburg State University, Graduate School, College of Education, Department of Psychology and Counseling, Program in Psychology, Pittsburg, KS 66762. Offers psychology (MS), including clinical psychology, general psychology. *Degree requirements:* For master's, thesis or alternative. *Entrance requirements:* For master's, GRE General Test, minimum GPA of 2.8. Additional exam requirements/recommendations for international students: required—TOEFL (minimum score 550 paper-based; 79 iBT), IELTS (minimum score 6.5), PTE (minimum score 53). Electronic applications accepted. *Expenses:* Contact institution.

Pontifical Catholic University of Puerto Rico, College of Graduate Studies in Behavioral Science and Community Affairs, Ponce, PR 00717-0777. Offers clinical psychology (PhD, Psy D); clinical social work (MSW); criminology (MA); industrial psychology (PhD); psychology (PhD); public administration (MSS); rehabilitation counseling (MA). *Program availability:* Part-time, evening/weekend. *Degree requirements:* For master's, thesis; for doctorate, comprehensive exam, thesis/dissertation. *Entrance requirements:* For master's, EXADEP, GRE General Test, 3 letters of recommendation, interview, minimum GPA of 2.75.

Pontificia Universidad Catolica Madre y Maestra, Graduate School, Faculty of Social and Administrative Sciences, Santiago, Dominican Republic. Offers business administration (MBA), including business development, finance, international business, management skills (M Mgmt, MBA), marketing, operations, strategic cost management, strategy, tourist destination planning and management; law (LL M), including civil law, corporate business law, criminal law, international relations, real estate law; management (M Mgmt), including higher financial management, insurance program administration, management skills (M Mgmt, MBA); psychology (MA), including clinical child and adolescent psychology, forensic psychology; strategic human resources (EMBA).

Portland State University, Graduate Studies, College of Liberal Arts and Sciences, Department of Psychology, Portland, OR 97207-0751. Offers MA, MS, PhD. *Faculty:* 22 full-time (11 women), 21 part-time/adjunct (16 women). *Students:* 42 full-time (32 women), 10 part-time (9 women); includes 8 minority (4 Asian, non-Hispanic/Latino; 2 Hispanic/Latino; 2 Two or more races, non-Hispanic/Latino). Average age 30. 168 applicants, 7% accepted, 10 enrolled. In 2019, 9 master's, 4 doctorates awarded. Terminal master's awarded for partial completion of doctoral program. *Degree requirements:* For master's, variable foreign language requirement, thesis; for doctorate, variable foreign language requirement, comprehensive exam, thesis/dissertation. *Entrance requirements:* For master's, GRE General Test, personal statement, 3 letters of reference; for doctorate, Completed the GRE and scored in the 70-80th percentile (or above) in Verbal, 60-70th percentile (or above) in Quantitative, and 4.5 or above on the Analytical Writing section. Additional exam requirements/recommendations for international students: required—TOEFL (minimum score 550 paper-based). *Application deadline:* For fall admission, 12/15 for domestic and international students. Application fee: $65. Electronic applications accepted. *Expenses:* $429 per credit hour resident, $645 per credit hour non-resident. *Financial support:* In 2019–20, 6 research assistantships with full and partial tuition reimbursements (averaging $14,554 per year), 26 teaching assistantships with full and partial tuition reimbursements (averaging $12,404 per year) were awarded; career-related internships or fieldwork, Federal Work-Study, scholarships/grants, and unspecified assistantships also available. Support available to part-time students. Financial award application deadline: 3/1; financial award applicants required to submit FAFSA. *Unit head:* Dr. Ellen Skinner, Chair, 503-725-3966, Fax: 503-725-3904, E-mail: skinnere@pdx.edu. *Application contact:* Dr. Thomas Kindermann, 503-725-3970, E-mail: kindermannt@pdx.edu.
Website: http://www.pdx.edu/psy/

Psychology—General

Portland State University, Graduate Studies, College of Liberal Arts and Sciences, Systems Science Program, Portland, OR 97207-0751. Offers computational intelligence (Certificate); computer modeling and simulation (Certificate); systems science (MS); systems science/anthropology (PhD); systems science/business administration (PhD); systems science/civil engineering (PhD); systems science/economics (PhD); systems science/engineering management (PhD); systems science/general (PhD); systems science/mathematical sciences (PhD); systems science/mechanical engineering (PhD); systems science/psychology (PhD); systems science/sociology (PhD). *Program availability:* Part-time. *Faculty:* 2 full-time (0 women), 6 part-time/adjunct (1 woman). *Students:* 6 full-time (3 women), 25 part-time (8 women); includes 7 minority (2 Asian, non-Hispanic/Latino; 4 Hispanic/Latino; 1 Two or more races, non-Hispanic/Latino), 2 international. Average age 39. 25 applicants, 80% accepted, 15 enrolled. In 2019, 7 master's, 2 doctorates awarded. Terminal master's awarded for partial completion of doctoral program. *Degree requirements:* For master's, comprehensive exam (for some programs), thesis optional; for doctorate, variable foreign language requirement, comprehensive exam (for some programs), thesis/dissertation. *Entrance requirements:* For master's, GRE/GMAT (recommended), minimum GPA of 3.0 on undergraduate or graduate work, 2 letters of recommendation, statement of interest; for doctorate, GRE required, minimum GPA of 3.0 undergraduate, 3.25 graduate; 3 letters of recommendation; statement of interest. Additional exam requirements/recommendations for international students: required—TOEFL (minimum score 550 paper-based; 80 iBT). *Application deadline:* For fall admission, 3/15 priority date for domestic and international students. Application fee: $65. Electronic applications accepted. *Expenses: Tuition, area resident:* Full-time $13,020; part-time $6510 per year. Tuition, state resident: full-time $13,020; part-time $6510 per year. Tuition, nonresident: full-time $19,830; part-time $9915 per year. *International tuition:* $19,830 full-time. *Required fees:* $1226. One-time fee: $350. Tuition and fees vary according to course load, program and reciprocity agreements. *Financial support:* Research assistantships, teaching assistantships, career-related internships or fieldwork, Federal Work-Study, scholarships/grants, and unspecified assistantships available. Support available to part-time students. Financial award application deadline: 3/1; financial award applicants required to submit FAFSA. *Unit head:* Dr. Wayne Wakeland, Chair, 503-725-4975, E-mail: wakeland@pdx.edu. *Application contact:* Dr. Wayne Wakeland, Chair, 503-725-4975, E-mail: wakeland@pdx.edu.
Website: http://www.pdx.edu/sysc/

Princeton University, Graduate School, Department of Psychology, Princeton, NJ 08544-1019. Offers neuroscience (PhD); psychology (PhD). *Degree requirements:* For doctorate, thesis/dissertation. *Entrance requirements:* For doctorate, GRE General Test, GRE Subject Test. Additional exam requirements/recommendations for international students: required—TOEFL (minimum score 550 paper-based). Electronic applications accepted.

Purdue University, Graduate School, College of Health and Human Sciences, Department of Psychological Sciences, West Lafayette, IN 47907. Offers behavioral neuroscience (PhD); clinical psychology (PhD); cognitive psychology (PhD); industrial/organizational psychology (PhD); mathematical and computational cognitive science (PhD). *Accreditation:* APA. *Faculty:* 43 full-time (17 women), 2 part-time/adjunct (both women). *Students:* 69 full-time (55 women), 4 part-time (2 women); includes 18 minority (2 Black or African American, non-Hispanic/Latino; 2 Asian, non-Hispanic/Latino; 11 Hispanic/Latino; 3 Two or more races, non-Hispanic/Latino), 19 international. Average age 28. 314 applicants, 15% accepted, 28 enrolled. In 2019, 12 doctorates awarded. Terminal master's awarded for partial completion of doctoral program. *Degree requirements:* For doctorate, thesis/dissertation. *Entrance requirements:* For doctorate, GRE General Test, minimum undergraduate GPA of 3.0 or equivalent. Additional exam requirements/recommendations for international students: required—TOEFL (minimum score 550 paper-based; 77 iBT); recommended—TWE. *Application deadline:* For fall admission, 12/3 for domestic and international students. Applications are processed on a rolling basis. Application fee: $60 ($75 for international students). Electronic applications accepted. *Financial support:* Fellowships with partial tuition reimbursements, research assistantships with partial tuition reimbursements, teaching assistantships with partial tuition reimbursements, and career-related internships or fieldwork available. Support available to part-time students. Financial award applicants required to submit FAFSA. *Unit head:* Dr. Jefferey D. Karpicke, Head, 765-494-6061, E-mail: karpicke@purdue.edu. *Application contact:* Nancy A. O'Brien, Graduate Contact, 765-494-6067, E-mail: nobrien@psych.pardue.edu.
Website: http://www.psych.purdue.edu/

Queens College of the City University of New York, Mathematics and Natural Sciences Division, Department of Psychology, Queens, NY 11367-1597. Offers applied behavior analysis (MA); behavioral neuroscience (MA); general psychology (MA). *Program availability:* Part-time. Terminal master's awarded for partial completion of doctoral program. *Degree requirements:* For master's, comprehensive exam (for some programs), thesis (for some programs). *Entrance requirements:* For master's, GRE for Behavioral Neuroscience MA, minimum GPA of 3.0. Additional exam requirements/recommendations for international students: required—TOEFL (minimum score 100 iBT), IELTS (minimum score 7). Electronic applications accepted.

Queen's University at Kingston, School of Graduate Studies, Faculty of Arts and Science, Department of Psychology, Kingston, ON K7L 3N6, Canada. Offers brain behavior and cognitive science (MA, PhD); clinical psychology (MA, PhD); developmental psychology (MA, PhD); social personality psychology (MA, PhD). *Degree requirements:* For master's, thesis; for doctorate, comprehensive exam, thesis/dissertation. *Entrance requirements:* For master's and doctorate, GRE General Test. Additional exam requirements/recommendations for international students: required—TOEFL.

Radford University, College of Graduate Studies and Research, Psychology, MA/MS, Radford, VA 24142. Offers clinical-counseling psychology (MA, MS); experimental psychology (MA); industrial-organizational psychology (MA, MS). *Program availability:* Part-time. *Degree requirements:* For master's, comprehensive exam, thesis (for some programs). *Entrance requirements:* For master's, GRE, minimum GPA of 3.0, 3 letters of reference, essay, resume, official transcripts. Additional exam requirements/recommendations for international students: required—TOEFL (minimum score 550 paper-based; 79 iBT), IELTS (minimum score 6.5). Electronic applications accepted.

Rhode Island College, School of Graduate Studies, Faculty of Arts and Sciences, Department of Psychology, Providence, RI 02908-1991. Offers health psychology (CGS); psychology (MA). *Program availability:* Part-time, evening/weekend. *Faculty:* 5 full-time (all women). *Students:* 6 full-time (4 women), 2 part-time (1 woman); includes 1 minority (Hispanic/Latino). Average age 26. In 2019, 6 master's awarded. *Degree requirements:* For master's, comprehensive exam. *Entrance requirements:* For master's, GRE, 3 letters of recommendation. Additional exam requirements/recommendations for international students: required—TOEFL (minimum score 550 paper-based; 80 iBT). *Application deadline:* For fall admission, 3/1 for domestic students; for spring admission, 11/1 for domestic students. Applications are processed on a rolling basis. Application fee: $50. Electronic applications accepted. *Expenses: Tuition, area resident:* Part-time $462 per credit hour. Tuition, state resident: part-time $462 per credit hour. *Required fees:* $720. One-time fee: $140. *Financial support:* Teaching assistantships, Federal Work-Study, scholarships/grants, health care benefits, and unspecified assistantships available. Support available to part-time students. Financial award application deadline: 5/15; financial award applicants required to submit FAFSA. *Unit head:* Bethany Lewis, Chair, 401-456-8015. *Application contact:* Bethany Lewis, Chair, 401-456-8015.
Website: http://www.ric.edu/psychology/Pages/Graduate-Studies-in-Psychology.aspx

Rice University, Graduate Programs, School of Humanities, Department of Religious Studies, Houston, TX 77251-1892. Offers African religions (PhD); African-American religions (PhD); contemplative studies (PhD); ghosticism, esotericism, mysticism (PhD); Islam (PhD); Jewish thought and philosophy (PhD); modern Christianity in thought and popular culture (PhD); psychology of religion (PhD); the Bible and beyond (PhD). *Degree requirements:* For doctorate, 2 foreign languages, comprehensive exam, thesis/dissertation. *Entrance requirements:* For doctorate, GRE, letters of recommendation, writing sample. Additional exam requirements/recommendations for international students: required—TOEFL (minimum score 600 paper-based; 90 iBT). Electronic applications accepted.

Rice University, Graduate Programs, School of Social Sciences, Department of Psychology, Houston, TX 77251-1892. Offers cognitive sciences (MA, PhD); industrial-organizational/social psychology (MA, PhD); psychology (MA, PhD). Terminal master's awarded for partial completion of doctoral program. *Degree requirements:* For master's, thesis; for doctorate, thesis/dissertation. *Entrance requirements:* For doctorate, GRE General Test, minimum GPA of 3.0. Additional exam requirements/recommendations for international students: required—TOEFL. Electronic applications accepted.

Rivier University, School of Graduate Studies, Department of Psychology, Nashua, NH 03060. Offers clinical psychology (MS); experimental psychology (MS).

Roberts Wesleyan College, Graduate Psychology Programs, Rochester, NY 14624-1997. Offers clinical/school psychology (Psy D); school counseling (MS); school psychology (MS). *Program availability:* Part-time, evening/weekend. *Degree requirements:* For master's, comprehensive exam, PRAXIS II (for school psychology). *Entrance requirements:* For master's, GRE. Electronic applications accepted. Application fee is waived when completed online.

Rochester Institute of Technology, Graduate Enrollment Services, College of Liberal Arts, Psychology Department, Rochester, NY 14623-5603. Offers engineering psychology (Advanced Certificate); experimental psychology (MS); school psychology (MS, Advanced Certificate). *Program availability:* Part-time. *Entrance requirements:* For master's, GRE, minimum GPA of 3.0 (recommended). Electronic applications accepted. *Expenses:* Contact institution.

Roosevelt University, Graduate Division, College of Arts and Sciences, Department of Psychology, Program in Clinical Psychology, Chicago, IL 60605. Offers MA, Psy D. Electronic applications accepted.

Rosalind Franklin University of Medicine and Science, College of Health Professions, Department of Psychology, North Chicago, IL 60064-3095. Offers clinical psychology (MS, PhD). *Accreditation:* APA. Terminal master's awarded for partial completion of doctoral program. *Degree requirements:* For master's, capstone experience. *Entrance requirements:* For master's, minimum GPA of 3.0, bachelor's degree (preferably in related subject); for doctorate, GRE, minimum GPA of 3.0, bachelor's or master's degree. Additional exam requirements/recommendations for international students: required—TOEFL.

Rowan University, Graduate School, College of Science and Mathematics, Department of Psychology, Glassboro, NJ 08028-1701. Offers MA, CAGS. Electronic applications accepted. *Expenses: Tuition, area resident:* Part-time $715.50 per semester hour. Tuition, state resident: part-time $715.50 per semester hour. Tuition, nonresident: part-time $715.50 per semester hour. *Required fees:* $161.55 per semester hour.

Rutgers University - Camden, Graduate School of Arts and Sciences, Program in Psychology, Camden, NJ 08102. Offers MA. *Program availability:* Part-time, evening/weekend. *Degree requirements:* For master's, thesis, 30 credits. *Entrance requirements:* For master's, GRE, 3 letters of recommendation; statement of personal, professional, and academic goals; prerequisite course work in introductory psychology, statistics and experimental psychology. Additional exam requirements/recommendations for international students: required—TOEFL, IELTS. Electronic applications accepted.

Rutgers University - Newark, Graduate School, Program in Psychology, Newark, NJ 07102. Offers cognitive neuroscience (PhD); cognitive science (PhD); perception (PhD); psychobiology (PhD); social cognition (PhD). *Degree requirements:* For doctorate, comprehensive exam, thesis/dissertation. *Entrance requirements:* For doctorate, GRE General Test, GRE Subject Test, minimum undergraduate B average. Electronic applications accepted.

Rutgers University - New Brunswick, Graduate School-New Brunswick, Program in Psychology, Piscataway, NJ 08854-8097. Offers behavioral neuroscience (PhD); clinical psychology (PhD); cognitive psychology (PhD); interdisciplinary health psychology (PhD); social psychology (PhD). *Accreditation:* APA. *Degree requirements:* For doctorate, comprehensive exam, thesis/dissertation. *Entrance requirements:* For doctorate, GRE General Test, 3 letters of recommendation. Additional exam requirements/recommendations for international students: required—TOEFL (minimum score 577 paper-based). Electronic applications accepted.

Sage Graduate School, School of Health Sciences, Department of Psychology, Troy, NY 12180-4115. Offers MA, Certificate. *Program availability:* Part-time, evening/weekend. *Faculty:* 4 full-time (all women), 2 part-time/adjunct (both women). *Students:* 51 full-time (46 women), 44 part-time (34 women); includes 22 minority (6 Black or African American, non-Hispanic/Latino; 3 Asian, non-Hispanic/Latino; 10 Hispanic/Latino; 3 Two or more races, non-Hispanic/Latino). Average age 28. 100 applicants, 37% accepted, 35 enrolled. In 2019, 26 master's awarded. *Degree requirements:* For master's, thesis or alternative. *Entrance requirements:* Additional exam requirements/recommendations for international students: required—TOEFL (minimum score 550 paper-based). *Application deadline:* Applications are processed on a rolling basis. Application fee: $30. Electronic applications accepted. *Expenses: Tuition:* Part-time $730 per credit hour. Tuition and fees vary according to course load, degree level and program. *Financial support:* Fellowships, research assistantships, scholarships/grants, and unspecified assistantships available. Financial award application deadline: 3/1; financial award applicants required to submit FAFSA. *Unit head:* Dr. Kathleen Kelly, Dean, School of Health Sciences, 518-244-2030, Fax: 518-244-4571, E-mail: kellyk5@sage.edu. *Application contact:* Dr. Gayle Morse, Graduate Program Director, 518-292-1819, E-mail: morseg@sage.edu.

St. John's University, St. John's College of Liberal Arts and Sciences, Department of Psychology, Psychology Program, Queens, NY 11439. Offers MA. *Program availability:* Part-time, evening/weekend. Terminal master's awarded for partial completion of doctoral program. *Degree requirements:* For master's, comprehensive exam (for some programs), thesis (for some programs), core courses in history and systems of psychology, inferential statistics, research methods, and psychological measurement. *Entrance requirements:* For master's, GRE General Test, letters of recommendation, transcripts, resume, personal statement, 24 credits of psychology prerequisites, lab paper, term paper. Additional exam requirements/recommendations for international students: required—TOEFL (minimum score 80 iBT), IELTS (minimum score 6.5). Electronic applications accepted.

Saint Joseph's University, College of Arts and Sciences, Department of Criminal Justice, Philadelphia, PA 19131-1395. Offers behavior analysis (MS, Post-Master's Certificate); behavior management (MS); criminal justice (MS); federal law enforcement (MS); intelligence and crime analysis (MS). *Program availability:* Part-time, evening/ weekend, 100% online, blended/hybrid learning. *Degree requirements:* For master's, thesis optional. *Entrance requirements:* For master's, 2 letters of recommendation, personal statement, resume, official transcripts, minimum GPA of 3.0. Additional exam requirements/recommendations for international students: required—TOEFL (minimum score 550 paper-based; 80 iBT). Electronic applications accepted. *Expenses:* Contact institution.

Saint Joseph's University, College of Arts and Sciences, Department of Psychology, Philadelphia, PA 19131-1395. Offers MS. *Program availability:* Evening/weekend. *Entrance requirements:* For master's, GRE General Test, 2 letters of recommendation, official transcripts, personal statement. Additional exam requirements/recommendations for international students: required—TOEFL (minimum score 550 paper-based; 80 iBT). Electronic applications accepted. *Expenses:* Contact institution.

Saint Leo University, Graduate Studies in Psychology, Saint Leo, FL 33574-6665. Offers psychology (MS). *Program availability:* Part-time-only, evening/weekend, online only, 100% online. *Faculty:* 6 full-time (3 women), 4 part-time/adjunct (1 woman). *Students:* 83 part-time (59 women); includes 43 minority (22 Black or African American, non-Hispanic/Latino; 1 Asian, non-Hispanic/Latino; 8 Hispanic/Latino; 12 Two or more races, non-Hispanic/Latino), 1 international. Average age 32. 53 applicants, 62% accepted, 23 enrolled. In 2019, 5 master's awarded. *Degree requirements:* For master's, thesis. *Entrance requirements:* For master's, A score of 1000 or higher on the GRE when UG gpa is between 2.8 and 2.9, Official transcripts from all postsecondary institutions, personal statement of professional goals, two letters of recommendation, undergraduate coursework in Psychology (Intro), Research Methods (including Statistics) in Psychology, Social Work or Sociology disciplines with minimum 3.0 average. Additional exam requirements/recommendations for international students: required—TOEFL (minimum score 550 paper-based; 78 iBT). *Application deadline:* For fall admission, 7/1 priority date for domestic students, 7/1 for international students; for spring admission, 11/1 priority date for domestic students, 11/1 for international students. Applications are processed on a rolling basis. Electronic applications accepted. *Expenses:* MS in Psychology $11,805 per FT yr. *Financial support:* In 2019–20, 16 students received support. Scholarships/grants, health care benefits, and tuition remission for Saint Leo employees and their dependents available. Financial award application deadline: 3/1; financial award applicants required to submit FAFSA. *Unit head:* Dr. Cathleen Dunn, Director, Graduate Studies in Psychology, 352-588-8294, Fax: 352-588-8300. *Application contact:* Saint Leo University Office of Graduate Admissions, 800-707-8846, Fax: 352-588-7873, E-mail: grad.admissions@saintleo.edu. Website: https://www.saintleo.edu/online-masters-in-psychology

Saint Louis University, Graduate Programs, College of Arts and Sciences, Department of Psychology, St. Louis, MO 63103. Offers clinical psychology (MS-R, PhD); experimental psychology (MS-R, PhD); industrial-organizational psychology (PhD); psychology (PhD). *Accreditation:* APA (one or more programs are accredited). *Program availability:* Part-time. *Degree requirements:* For master's, comprehensive exam, thesis; for doctorate, thesis/dissertation, clinical internship (for clinical psychology PhD). *Entrance requirements:* For master's, GRE General Test, interview, letters of recommendation, resume; for doctorate, GRE General Test, interview, letters of recommendation, resumé, transcripts, goal statement. Additional exam requirements/recommendations for international students: required—TOEFL (minimum score 550 paper-based). Electronic applications accepted.

Saint Mary's University, Faculty of Science, Department of Psychology, Halifax, NS B3H 3C3, Canada. Offers applied psychology (M Sc, PhD), including industrial/ organizational psychology (M Sc). *Program availability:* Part-time. *Degree requirements:* For master's, thesis, 500-hour internship; for doctorate, comprehensive exam, thesis/ dissertation, research project. *Entrance requirements:* For master's and doctorate, GRE General Test.

Salem State University, School of Graduate Studies, Program in Counseling and Psychological Services, Salem, MA 01970-5353. Offers MS, Graduate Certificate. *Program availability:* Part-time, evening/weekend. *Entrance requirements:* For master's, GRE or MAT. Additional exam requirements/recommendations for international students: required—TOEFL (minimum score 550 paper-based; 80 iBT) or IELTS (minimum score 5.5).

Sam Houston State University, College of Humanities and Social Sciences, Department of Psychology and Philosophy, Huntsville, TX 77341. Offers psychology (MA, PhD, SSP), including clinical psychology (MA, PhD), psychology (MA), school psychology (SSP). *Accreditation:* APA. *Program availability:* Part-time. Terminal master's awarded for partial completion of doctoral program. *Degree requirements:* For master's, comprehensive exam, thesis optional; for doctorate, comprehensive exam, thesis/dissertation. *Entrance requirements:* For master's, GRE General Test, personal statement, letters of recommendation; for doctorate, GRE General Test, GRE Subject Test (advanced psychology), personal essay, letters of recommendation, resume. Additional exam requirements/recommendations for international students: required—TOEFL (minimum score 550 paper-based; 79 iBT), IELTS (minimum score 6.5). Electronic applications accepted.

San Diego State University, Graduate and Research Affairs, College of Sciences, Department of Psychology, San Diego, CA 92182. Offers clinical psychology (MS, PhD); industrial and organizational psychology (MS); program evaluation (MS); psychology (MA). *Accreditation:* APA (one or more programs are accredited). Terminal master's awarded for partial completion of doctoral program. *Degree requirements:* For master's, thesis, oral exam; for doctorate, thesis/dissertation. *Entrance requirements:* For master's, GRE General Test, GRE Subject Test, 3 letters of recommendation; for doctorate, GRE General Test, GRE Subject Test, minimum GPA of 3.0, 3 letters of recommendation. Additional exam requirements/recommendations for international students: required—TOEFL. Electronic applications accepted.

San Francisco State University, Division of Graduate Studies, College of Science and Engineering, Department of Psychology, San Francisco, CA 94132-1722. Offers clinical psychology (MS); developmental psychology (MA); industrial/organizational psychology (MS); mind, brain, and behavior (MA); school psychology (MS, Credential); social, personality, and affective science psychology (MA). *Expenses: Tuition, area resident:* Full-time $7176; part-time $4164 per year. Tuition, state resident: full-time $7176; part-time $4164 per year. Tuition, nonresident: full-time $16,680; part-time $396 per unit. *International tuition:* $16,680 full-time. *Required fees:* $1524; $1524 per unit. $762 per semester. Tuition and fees vary according to degree level and program. *Financial support:* Teaching assistantships available. Financial award application deadline: 3/1. *Unit head:* Dr. Chris Wright, Chair, 415-338-7555, Fax: 415-338-2398, E-mail: cwright@sfsu.edu. *Application contact:* Dr. Ryan Howell, Department Graduate Program Coordinator, 415-405-2140, Fax: 415-338-2398, E-mail: rhowell@sfsu.edu. Website: http://psychology.sfsu.edu/graduate/application.html

San Jose State University, Program in Psychology, San Jose, CA 95192-0120. Offers clinical psychology (MS); experimental psychology (MA); industrial/organizational psychology (MS); psychology (MA). *Faculty:* 19 full-time (12 women), 2 part-time/adjunct (1 woman). *Students:* 51 full-time (44 women), 30 part-time (21 women); includes 37 minority (2 Black or African American, non-Hispanic/Latino; 14 Asian, non-Hispanic/ Latino; 21 Hispanic/Latino), 4 international. Average age 27. 184 applicants, 23% accepted, 31 enrolled. In 2019, 35 master's awarded. *Application deadline:* For fall admission, 2/1 for domestic and international students. Application fee: $70. Electronic applications accepted. *Expenses: Tuition, area resident:* Full-time $7176; part-time $4164 per credit hour. Tuition, state resident: full-time $7176; part-time $4164 per credit hour. Tuition, nonresident: full-time $7176; part-time $4165 per credit hour. *International tuition:* $7176 full-time. *Required fees:* $2110; $2110. *Financial support:* In 2019–20, 22 students received support, including 1 research assistantship (averaging $500 per year); scholarships/grants also available. Financial award application deadline: 5/1; financial award applicants required to submit FAFSA. *Unit head:* Clifton Oyamot, Professor and Chair, 408-924-5650, E-mail: clifton.oyamot@sjsu.edu. *Application contact:* Psychology Department, 408-408-924-5600, E-mail: psychology@sjsu.edu. Website: http://www.sjsu.edu/psych/

Saybrook University, LIOS MA Residential Programs, Kirkland, WA 98033. Offers leadership and organization development (MA); psychology counseling (MA). *Degree requirements:* For master's, thesis (for some programs), oral exams. *Entrance requirements:* For master's, bachelor's degree from an accredited university or college. Additional exam requirements/recommendations for international students: recommended—TOEFL, IELTS, TWE.

Saybrook University, School of Psychology and Interdisciplinary Inquiry, San Francisco, CA 94612. Offers human science (MA, PhD), including consciousness and spirituality, humanistic and transpersonal psychology, integrative health studies, organizational systems, social transformation; organizational systems (MA, PhD), including consciousness and spirituality, humanistic and transpersonal psychology, integrative health studies, leadership of sustainable systems (MA), organizational systems, social transformation; psychology (MA, PhD), including consciousness and spirituality, creativity studies (MA), humanistic and transpersonal psychology, integrative health studies, Jungian studies, marriage and family therapy (MA), organizational systems, social transformation. *Program availability:* Online learning. Terminal master's awarded for partial completion of doctoral program. *Degree requirements:* For master's, thesis or alternative; for doctorate, thesis/dissertation. *Entrance requirements:* Additional exam requirements/recommendations for international students: required—TOEFL (minimum score 580 paper-based; 93 iBT). Electronic applications accepted.

The Seattle School of Theology and Psychology, Graduate Programs, Seattle, WA 98121. Offers Christian studies (MA); counseling psychology (MA); divinity (M Div). *Program availability:* Part-time. *Entrance requirements:* For master's, MAT.

Seattle University, College of Arts and Sciences, Department of Psychology, Seattle, WA 98122-1090. Offers existential and phenomenological therapeutic psychology (MA Psych). *Faculty:* 13 full-time (10 women), 12 part-time/adjunct (10 women). *Students:* 39 full-time (22 women), 2 part-time (both women); includes 11 minority (3 Black or African American, non-Hispanic/Latino; 1 American Indian or Alaska Native, non-Hispanic/Latino; 2 Asian, non-Hispanic/Latino; 3 Hispanic/Latino; 2 Two or more races, non-Hispanic/Latino), 2 international. Average age 30. 56 applicants, 45% accepted, 24 enrolled. In 2019, 10 master's awarded. *Entrance requirements:* For master's, interview, minimum GPA of 3.0, previous undergraduate course work in psychology, experience (paid or volunteer) in counseling or human services. *Application deadline:* For fall admission, 1/15 for domestic and international students. Application fee: $55. Electronic applications accepted. *Financial support:* In 2019–20, 30 students received support. Career-related internships or fieldwork and Federal Work-Study available. Support available to part-time students. Financial award applicants required to submit FAFSA. *Unit head:* Dr. Kevin Krycka, Director of Graduate Programs, 206-296-5398, Fax: 206-296-2141, E-mail: krycka@seattleu.edu. *Application contact:* Janet Shandley, Associate Dean of Graduate Admissions, 206-296-5900, Fax: 206-298-5656, E-mail: grad_admissions@seattleu.edu. Website: http://www.seattleu.edu/artsci/departments/psychology/

Seton Hall University, College of Arts and Sciences, Department of Psychology, South Orange, NJ 07079-2697. Offers experimental psychology (MS). *Program availability:* Part-time, evening/weekend. *Degree requirements:* For master's, thesis optional. *Entrance requirements:* For master's, GRE, minimum of 18 credits in psychology with minimum GPA of 3.0. Additional exam requirements/recommendations for international students: required—TOEFL. Electronic applications accepted.

Shippensburg University of Pennsylvania, School of Graduate Studies, College of Arts and Sciences, Department of Psychology, Shippensburg, PA 17257-2299. Offers psychological science (MS). *Program availability:* Part-time, evening/weekend. *Faculty:* 6 full-time (3 women). *Students:* 2 full-time (1 woman), 4 part-time (3 women), 1 international. Average age 24. 17 applicants. In 2019, 5 master's awarded. *Degree requirements:* For master's, comprehensive exam (for some programs), thesis (for some programs), thesis, field experience, or competency exam. *Entrance requirements:* For master's, minimum GPA of 2.75, course in statistics, 9 undergraduate credit hours in psychology, supplemental form with personal goals statement. Additional exam requirements/recommendations for international students: required—TOEFL (minimum score 550 paper-based; 68 iBT), IELTS (minimum score 6), TOEFL (minimum score 550 paper-based, 68 iBT) or IELTS (minimum score 6). *Application deadline:* For fall admission, 3/1 priority date for domestic students, 3/1 for international students; for summer admission, 3/1 for domestic students. Applications are processed on a rolling basis. Application fee: $45. Electronic applications accepted. *Expenses:* Tuition, state resident: part-time $516 per credit. Tuition, nonresident: part-time $774 per credit. *Required fees:* $149 per credit. *Financial support:* In 2019–20, 4 students received support. Career-related internships or fieldwork, scholarships/grants, unspecified assistantships, and resident hall director and student payroll positions available. Support available to part-time students. Financial award application deadline: 3/1; financial award applicants required to submit FAFSA. *Unit head:* Dr. Thomas C. Hatvany, Assistant Professor and Program Coordinator, 717-477-1657, Fax: 717-477-4057, E-mail: tchatvany@ship.edu. *Application contact:* Maya T. Mapp, Director of Admissions, 717-477-1231, Fax: 717-477-4016, E-mail: mtmapp@ship.edu. Website: http://www.ship.edu/psychology

Simon Fraser University, Office of Graduate Studies and Postdoctoral Fellows, Faculty of Arts and Social Sciences, Department of Psychology, Burnaby, BC V5A 1S6, Canada. Offers MA, PhD. *Degree requirements:* For master's, thesis; for doctorate, comprehensive exam, thesis/dissertation, clinical training (for some programs). *Entrance requirements:* For master's, GRE General Test, GRE Subject Test (psychology), minimum GPA of 3.0 (on scale of 4.33) or 3.33 based on last 60 credits of undergraduate courses; for doctorate, GRE General Test, GRE Subject Test (psychology), minimum GPA of 3.5 (on scale of 4.33). Additional exam requirements/ recommendations for international students: recommended—TOEFL (minimum score 580 paper-based; 93 iBT), IELTS (minimum score 7), TWE (minimum score 5). Electronic applications accepted. *Expenses:* Contact institution.

Psychology—General

Sofia University, Hybrid: Face-to-Face/Online Programs, Palo Alto, CA 94303. Offers transpersonal psychology (MA, PhD), including transpersonal psychology (PhD). *Program availability:* Online learning. *Entrance requirements:* For master's, bachelor's degree; for doctorate, bachelor's degree; master's degree. Electronic applications accepted.

Sofia University, Residential Programs, Palo Alto, CA 94303. Offers clinical psychology (Psy D); computer science (MS); counseling psychology (MA); transpersonal psychology (MA, PhD). *Program availability:* Part-time, evening/weekend. Terminal master's awarded for partial completion of doctoral program. *Degree requirements:* For doctorate, thesis/dissertation. *Entrance requirements:* For master's, bachelor's degree; for doctorate, bachelor's degree; master's degree (for some programs). Electronic applications accepted.

Southeastern Baptist Theological Seminary, Graduate and Professional Programs, Wake Forest, NC 27587. Offers advanced biblical studies (M Div); Christian education (M Div, MACE); Christian ethics (PhD); Christian ministry (M Div); Christian planting (M Div); church music (MACM); counseling (MACO); evangelism (PhD); language (M Div); ministry (D Min); New Testament (PhD); Old Testament (PhD); philosophy (PhD); theology (Th M, PhD); women's studies (M Div). *Accreditation:* ACIPE; ATS (one or more programs are accredited). *Degree requirements:* For master's, thesis (for some programs), oral exam; for doctorate, thesis/dissertation, fieldwork. *Entrance requirements:* For master's, Cooperative English Test, minimum GPA of 2.0, M Div or equivalent (Th M); for doctorate, GRE General Test or MAT, Cooperative English Test, M Div or equivalent, 3 years of professional experience.

Southeastern Louisiana University, College of Arts, Humanities and Social Sciences, Department of Psychology, Hammond, LA 70402. Offers psychology (MA), including industrial/organizational psychology. *Program availability:* Part-time. *Faculty:* 7 full-time (5 women). *Students:* 18 full-time (11 women), 7 part-time (4 women); includes 6 minority (1 Black or African American, non-Hispanic/Latino; 2 Asian, non-Hispanic/Latino; 1 Native Hawaiian or other Pacific Islander, non-Hispanic/Latino; 2 Two or more races, non-Hispanic/Latino). Average age 26. 11 applicants, 100% accepted, 5 enrolled. In 2019, 9 master's awarded. *Degree requirements:* For master's, comprehensive exam, thesis optional, 38 hours of psychology course work; either a thesis or non-thesis project. *Entrance requirements:* For master's, GRE; for regular admission status a combined score of 294, for provisional admission status a combined score of 289, 3 letters of reference; 3.0 undergraduate GPA; 18 semester hours of undergraduate credit in psychology and/or educational psychology, including at least 3 semester hours each in a statistics course and in a general experimental (laboratory) course. Additional exam requirements/recommendations for international students: required—TOEFL (minimum score 500 paper-based; 61 iBT). *Application deadline:* For fall admission, 3/15 priority date for domestic and international students; for spring admission, 10/15 priority date for domestic students, 10/1 priority date for international students. Applications are processed on a rolling basis. Application fee: $20 ($30 for international students). Electronic applications accepted. *Expenses: Tuition, area resident:* Full-time $6684; part-time $489 per credit hour. Tuition, state resident: full-time $6684; part-time $489 per credit hour. Tuition, nonresident: full-time $19,162; part-time $1183 per credit hour. *International tuition:* $19,162 full-time. *Required fees:* $2124. *Financial support:* In 2019–20, 15 students received support, including 11 research assistantships with tuition reimbursements available (averaging $9,300 per year); career-related internships or fieldwork, institutionally sponsored loans, traineeships, and unspecified assistantships also available. Financial award application deadline: 5/1; financial award applicants required to submit FAFSA. *Unit head:* Dr. Susan Coats, Department Head, 985-549-2154, Fax: 985-549-6892, E-mail: scoats@southeastern.edu. *Application contact:* Dr. Susan Coats, Department Head, 985-549-2154, Fax: 985-549-6892, E-mail: scoats@southeastern.edu.
Website: http://www.southeastern.edu/acad_research/depts/psyc/index.html

Southern Adventist University, School of Education and Psychology, Collegedale, TN 37315-0370. Offers clinical mental health counseling (MS); instructional leadership (MS Ed); literacy education (MS Ed); outdoor education (MS Ed); professional school counseling (MS). *Accreditation:* NCATE. *Program availability:* Part-time, evening/weekend, 100% online, blended/hybrid learning. *Degree requirements:* For master's, comprehensive exam (for some programs), thesis optional, portfolio (MS) portfolio (MS Ed in outdoor education). *Entrance requirements:* For master's, interview (MS); 9 semester hours of upper-division course work in psychology or related field, including 1 course in psychology research or statistics; 9 semester hours of education (MS Ed). Additional exam requirements/recommendations for international students: required—TOEFL (minimum score 100 iBT). Electronic applications accepted.

Southern California Seminary, Graduate and Professional Programs, El Cajon, CA 92019. Offers Biblical studies (MABS); counseling psychology (MACP); marriage and family therapy (MAMFT); psychology (Psy D); religious studies (MRS); theology (M Div). *Program availability:* Part-time, evening/weekend, online learning. *Degree requirements:* For master's, thesis (for some programs); for doctorate, thesis/dissertation. *Entrance requirements:* For doctorate, master's degree in psychology. Additional exam requirements/recommendations for international students: required—TOEFL (minimum score 550 paper-based). Electronic applications accepted.

Southern Connecticut State University, School of Graduate Studies, School of Arts and Sciences, Department of Psychology, New Haven, CT 06515-1355. Offers MA. *Program availability:* Part-time, evening/weekend. *Degree requirements:* For master's, thesis or alternative. *Entrance requirements:* For master's, interview, previous course work in psychology. Electronic applications accepted.

Southern Illinois University Carbondale, Graduate School, College of Education and Human Services, Program in Behavior Analysis and Therapy, Carbondale, IL 62901-4701. Offers MS. *Entrance requirements:* Additional exam requirements/recommendations for international students: required—TOEFL.

Southern Illinois University Carbondale, Graduate School, College of Liberal Arts, Department of Psychology, Carbondale, IL 62901-4701. Offers clinical psychology (PhD); counseling psychology (PhD); experimental psychology (MA, MS). *Accreditation:* APA (one or more programs are accredited). *Degree requirements:* For master's, thesis; for doctorate, thesis/dissertation. *Entrance requirements:* For master's, GRE General Test, GRE Subject Test, minimum GPA of 2.7; for doctorate, GRE General Test, GRE Subject Test, minimum GPA of 3.25. Additional exam requirements/recommendations for international students: required—TOEFL.

Southern Illinois University Edwardsville, Graduate School, School of Education, Health, and Human Behavior, Department of Psychology, Edwardsville, IL 62026. Offers clinical child and school psychology (MS); clinical psychology (MA); industrial-organizational psychology (MA); school psychology (SD). *Program availability:* Part-time, evening/weekend. *Degree requirements:* For master's, thesis (for some programs), research paper; for SD, thesis. *Entrance requirements:* For master's, GRE. Additional exam requirements/recommendations for international students: required—TOEFL (minimum score 550 paper-based; 79 iBT), IELTS (minimum score 6.5). Electronic applications accepted.

Southern Methodist University, Dedman College of Humanities and Sciences, Department of Psychology, Dallas, TX 75275. Offers clinical psychology (PhD). *Accreditation:* APA. Terminal master's awarded for partial completion of doctoral program. *Degree requirements:* For doctorate, comprehensive exam, thesis/dissertation, oral exam, practicum, research presentation and publication. *Entrance requirements:* For doctorate, GRE General Test, minimum GPA of 3.4. Additional exam requirements/recommendations for international students: required—TOEFL (minimum score 550 paper-based). Electronic applications accepted.

Southern Nazarene University, College of Professional and Graduate Studies, Department of Psychology and Counseling, Bethany, OK 73008. Offers counseling psychology (MA, MSCP); marital and family therapy (MA). *Degree requirements:* For master's, thesis optional. *Entrance requirements:* For master's, English proficiency exam, minimum GPA of 3.0 in last 60 hours/major, 2.7 overall.

Southern New Hampshire University, School of Arts and Sciences, Manchester, NH 03106-1045. Offers clinical mental health counseling (MS); creative writing (MA); criminal justice (MS); cyber security (MS); English (MA); fiction and nonfiction (MFA); history (MA); political science (MS); psychology (MS). *Program availability:* Part-time, evening/weekend. *Degree requirements:* For master's, one foreign language, thesis. *Entrance requirements:* For master's, minimum GPA of 3.0 (for MFA). Additional exam requirements/recommendations for international students: required—TOEFL (minimum score 550 paper-based; 79 iBT), IELTS (minimum score 6.5), TWE (minimum score 5). Electronic applications accepted. *Expenses:* Contact institution.

Southern Oregon University, Graduate Studies, Department of Psychology, Ashland, OR 97520. Offers MHC. *Accreditation:* ACA. *Program availability:* Part-time, online learning. *Degree requirements:* For master's, thesis, portfolio, oral defense. *Entrance requirements:* For master's, GRE General Test, minimum cumulative GPA of 3.0 in the last 90 quarter credits (60 semester credits) of undergraduate coursework. Additional exam requirements/recommendations for international students: required—TOEFL (minimum score 540 paper-based; 76 iBT), IELTS (minimum score 6), ELPT (minimum score 964) or ELS (minimum score 112). Electronic applications accepted.

Southern University and Agricultural and Mechanical College, Graduate School, Nelson Mandela College of Government and Social Sciences, Department of Psychology, Baton Rouge, LA 70813. Offers rehabilitation counseling (MS). *Degree requirements:* For master's, comprehensive exam, thesis optional. *Entrance requirements:* For master's, GMAT or GRE General Test. Additional exam requirements/recommendations for international students: required—TOEFL (minimum score 525 paper-based).

Southwestern College, Program in Psychodrama and Action Methods, Santa Fe, NM 87502-4788. Offers Certificate. *Entrance requirements:* For degree, 3 letters of reference.

Spalding University, Graduate Studies, Kosair College of Health and Natural Sciences, School of Professional Psychology, Louisville, KY 40203-2188. Offers clinical psychology (MA, Psy D). *Accreditation:* APA (one or more programs are accredited). *Program availability:* Part-time. Terminal master's awarded for partial completion of doctoral program. *Degree requirements:* For master's, comprehensive exam; for doctorate, thesis/dissertation. *Entrance requirements:* For master's and doctorate, GRE General Test, 18 hours of undergraduate course work in psychology, interview, letters of recommendation, writing sample, autobiographical statement. Additional exam requirements/recommendations for international students: required—TOEFL (minimum score 535 paper-based).

Stanford University, School of Humanities and Sciences, Department of Psychology, Stanford, CA 94305-2004. Offers PhD. *Expenses: Tuition:* Full-time $52,479; part-time $34,110 per unit. *Required fees:* $672; $224 per quarter. Tuition and fees vary according to program and student level.
Website: http://www-psych.stanford.edu/

State University of New York at New Paltz, Graduate and Extended Learning School, School of Liberal Arts and Sciences, Department of Psychology, New Paltz, NY 12561. Offers clinical mental health counseling (MS); mental health counseling (AC); psychological science (MS); school counseling (MS); trauma and disaster mental health (AC). *Program availability:* Part-time, evening/weekend. *Faculty:* 14 full-time (5 women), 1 part-time/adjunct (0 women). *Students:* 57 full-time (43 women), 34 part-time (27 women); includes 25 minority (3 Black or African American, non-Hispanic/Latino; 3 Asian, non-Hispanic/Latino; 16 Hispanic/Latino; 1 Native Hawaiian or other Pacific Islander, non-Hispanic/Latino; 2 Two or more races, non-Hispanic/Latino). 147 applicants, 39% accepted, 45 enrolled. In 2019, 32 master's, 5 other advanced degrees awarded. *Degree requirements:* For master's, comprehensive exam, thesis. *Entrance requirements:* For master's, GRE General Test, minimum GPA of 3.0. Additional exam requirements/recommendations for international students: required—TOEFL (minimum score 550 paper-based; 80 iBT), IELTS (minimum score 6.5). *Application deadline:* For fall admission, 2/1 priority date for domestic and international students; for spring admission, 11/15 priority date for domestic and international students. Application fee: $50. Electronic applications accepted. *Expenses: Tuition, area resident:* Full-time $11,310; part-time $471 per credit. Tuition, state resident: full-time $11,310; part-time $471 per credit. Tuition, nonresident: full-time $23,100; part-time $963 per credit. *International tuition:* $23,100 full-time. *Required fees:* $1432; $41.83 per credit. *Financial support:* In 2019–20, 6 teaching assistantships with partial tuition reimbursements (averaging $5,000 per year) were awarded. Financial award application deadline: 8/1. *Unit head:* Dr. Jonathan Raskin, Chair, 845-257-3471, E-mail: raskinj@newpaltz.edu. *Application contact:* Vika Shock, Director of Graduate Admissions, 845-257-3286, E-mail: gradstudies@newpaltz.edu.
Website: http://www.newpaltz.edu/psychology/

State University of New York at Plattsburgh, School of Arts and Sciences, Department of Psychology, Plattsburgh, NY 12901-2681. Offers school psychology (MA, CAS). *Program availability:* Part-time. *Entrance requirements:* For master's, GRE General Test, minimum GPA of 3.0. Additional exam requirements/recommendations for international students: required—TOEFL.

Stephen F. Austin State University, Graduate School, College of Liberal and Applied Arts, Department of Psychology, Nacogdoches, TX 75962. Offers MA. *Degree requirements:* For master's, comprehensive exam, thesis. *Entrance requirements:* For master's, GRE General Test. Additional exam requirements/recommendations for international students: required—TOEFL.

Stony Brook University, State University of New York, Graduate School, College of Arts and Sciences, Department of Psychology, Stony Brook, NY 11794. Offers psychology (MA). *Accreditation:* APA (one or more programs are accredited). *Faculty:* 29 full-time (17 women), 5 part-time/adjunct (2 women). *Students:* 90 full-time (76 women); includes 21 minority (6 Black or African American, non-Hispanic/Latino; 7 Asian, non-Hispanic/Latino; 6 Hispanic/Latino; 2 Two or more races, non-Hispanic/Latino), 12 international. Average age 27. 491 applicants, 7% accepted, 15 enrolled. In 2019, 42 master's, 16 doctorates awarded. *Entrance requirements:* For doctorate, GRE General Test, GRE Subject Test. Additional exam requirements/recommendations for international students: required—TOEFL (minimum score 90 iBT). *Application deadline:* For fall admission, 1/15 for domestic students; for spring admission, 10/1 for domestic students. Application fee: $100. *Expenses:* Contact institution. *Financial support:* In

2019–20, 14 fellowships, 24 research assistantships, 52 teaching assistantships were awarded; career-related internships or fieldwork also available. *Unit head:* Dr. Sheri Levy, Chair, 631-632-4355, E-mail: sheri.levy@stonybrook.edu. *Application contact:* Marilynn Wollmuth, Coordinator, 631-632-7855, Fax: 631-632-7876, E-mail: marilyn.wollmuth@stonybrook.edu.
Website: http://www.psychology.sunysb.edu/psychology/

Suffolk University, College of Arts and Sciences, Department of Psychology, Boston, MA 02108-2770. Offers clinical psychology (PhD); college admission counseling (Certificate); mental health counseling (MS); school counseling (MS). *Accreditation:* APA. *Faculty:* 17 full-time (12 women), 1 (woman) part-time/adjunct. *Students:* 46 full-time (45 women), 22 part-time (19 women); includes 8 minority (2 Black or African American, non-Hispanic/Latino; 3 Asian, non-Hispanic/Latino; 1 Hispanic/Latino; 2 Two or more races, non-Hispanic/Latino). Average age 26. 299 applicants, 15% accepted, 22 enrolled. In 2019, 11 master's, 6 doctorates, 1 other advanced degree awarded. Terminal master's awarded for partial completion of doctoral program. *Degree requirements:* For master's, practicum, internship; for doctorate, thesis/dissertation, practicum. *Entrance requirements:* For doctorate, GRE General Test or MAT, 2 letters of recommendation, resume. Additional exam requirements/recommendations for international students: required—TOEFL (minimum score 550 paper-based; 80 iBT). *Application deadline:* For fall admission, 12/1 for domestic and international students. Applications are processed on a rolling basis. Application fee: $50. Electronic applications accepted. *Expenses:* Contact institution. *Financial support:* In 2019–20, 66 students received support, including 7 fellowships (averaging $3,375 per year); career-related internships or fieldwork, Federal Work-Study, institutionally sponsored loans, scholarships/grants, and unspecified assistantships also available. Support available to part-time students. Financial award application deadline: 4/1; financial award applicants required to submit FAFSA. *Unit head:* Dr. Amy Marks, Chairperson, 617-573-8017, E-mail: akmarks@suffolk.edu. *Application contact:* Mara Marzocchi, Associate Director of Graduate Admissions, 617-573-8302, Fax: 617-305-1733, E-mail: grad.admission@suffolk.edu.
Website: http://www.suffolk.edu/college/graduate/69299.php

Sul Ross State University, College of Arts and Sciences, Department of Behavioral and Social Sciences, Program in Psychology, Alpine, TX 79832. Offers MA. *Entrance requirements:* For master's, GRE General Test, minimum GPA of 2.5 in last 60 hours of undergraduate work.

SUNY Brockport, School of Arts and Sciences, Department of Psychology, Brockport, NY 14420-2997. Offers clinical psychology (with applied emphasis) (MA); clinical psychology (with research emphasis) (MA); general psychology (MA). *Program availability:* Part-time. *Faculty:* 12 full-time (10 women), 1 (woman) part-time/adjunct. *Students:* 11 full-time (7 women), 8 part-time (6 women). 28 applicants, 25% accepted, 6 enrolled. In 2019, 7 master's awarded. *Entrance requirements:* For master's, GRE General Test, letters of recommendation, interview, minimum GPA of 3.0. Additional exam requirements/recommendations for international students: required—TOEFL (minimum score 550 paper-based; 79 iBT), IELTS (minimum score 6.5). *Application deadline:* For fall admission, 4/1 priority date for domestic and international students. Application fee: $50. Electronic applications accepted. *Expenses: Tuition, area resident:* Part-time $471 per credit hour. Tuition, nonresident: part-time $963 per credit hour. *Financial support:* In 2019–20, 3 teaching assistantships with full tuition reimbursements (averaging $6,000 per year) were awarded; Federal Work-Study, scholarships/grants, and unspecified assistantships also available. Support available to part-time students. Financial award application deadline: 3/15; financial award applicants required to submit FAFSA. *Unit head:* Dr. Sara Margolin, Graduate Director, 585-395-2908, Fax: 585-395-2116, E-mail: smargoli@brockport.edu. *Application contact:* Danielle A. Welch, Graduate Counselor, 585-295-5430, Fax: 585-395-2115, E-mail: dwelch@brockport.edu.
Website: https://www.brockport.edu/academics/psychology/graduate/masters.html

Syracuse University, College of Arts and Sciences, Department of Psychology, Syracuse, NY 13244. Offers clinical psychology (PhD); cognition, brain, and behavior (PhD); school psychology (PhD); social psychology (PhD). *Accreditation:* APA. Terminal master's awarded for partial completion of doctoral program. *Degree requirements:* For doctorate, comprehensive exam, thesis/dissertation. *Entrance requirements:* For doctorate, GRE General Test, GRE Subject Test, resume, personal statement, three letters of recommendation. Additional exam requirements/recommendations for international students: required—TOEFL (minimum score 100 iBT). Electronic applications accepted.

Teachers College, Columbia University, Department of Counseling and Clinical Psychology, New York, NY 10027-6696. Offers clinical psychology (PhD); counseling psychology (Ed M, Ed D, PhD); mental health counseling (ME); psychological counseling (ME, ND); psychology in education (MA, ND); school counselor (ME). *Accreditation:* APA (one or more programs are accredited). *Program availability:* Part-time.

Temple University, College of Liberal Arts, Department of Psychology, Philadelphia, PA 19122-6096. Offers MA, MS, PhD. *Accreditation:* APA. *Faculty:* 42 full-time (22 women), 22 part-time/adjunct (13 women). *Students:* 103 full-time (86 women), 11 part-time (10 women); includes 18 minority (5 Black or African American, non-Hispanic/Latino; 3 Asian, non-Hispanic/Latino; 5 Hispanic/Latino; 5 Two or more races, non-Hispanic/Latino), 11 international. 583 applicants, 6% accepted, 24 enrolled. In 2019, 16 master's, 18 doctorates awarded. *Entrance requirements:* For master's, GRE (mininum 150 verbal, 150 quantitative, 4 in analytical writing), writing sample, statement of goals, 3 letters of recommendation; for doctorate, GRE General Test, GRE Subject Exam in Psychology strongly recommended, 3 letters of recommendation, statement of goals. Additional exam requirements/recommendations for international students: required—TOEFL (minimum score 105 iBT), IELTS (minimum score 7), PTE (minimum score 72), one of three required. Application fee: $60. Electronic applications accepted. *Financial support:* Research assistantships, teaching assistantships, Federal Work-Study, health care benefits, and unspecified assistantships available. Financial award applicants required to submit FAFSA. *Unit head:* Peter Marshall, Chairperson, 215-204-7630, E-mail: peter.marshall@temple.edu. *Application contact:* Deborah Drabick, Director of Graduate Studies, 215-204-0957, E-mail: deborah.drabick@temple.edu.
Website: http://www.cla.temple.edu/psychology/

Tennessee State University, The School of Graduate Studies and Research, College of Education, Department of Psychology, Nashville, TN 37209-1561. Offers counseling psychology (MS). *Entrance requirements:* For master's, GRE General Test or MAT. Electronic applications accepted.

Texas A&M International University, Office of Graduate Studies and Research, College of Arts and Sciences, Department of Psychology and Communication, Laredo, TX 78041. Offers counseling psychology (MACP); psychology (MS). *Degree requirements:* For master's, thesis (for some programs). *Entrance requirements:* For master's, GRE General Test. Additional exam requirements/recommendations for international students: required—TOEFL (minimum score 550 paper-based; 79 iBT).

Texas A&M University, College of Liberal Arts, Department of Psychological and Brain Sciences, College Station, TX 77843. Offers clinical psychology (PhD); psychology (MS). *Accreditation:* APA (one or more programs are accredited). *Degree requirements:* For doctorate, comprehensive exam (for some programs), thesis/dissertation. *Entrance requirements:* For doctorate, GRE General Test. Additional exam requirements/recommendations for international students: required—TOEFL (minimum score 550 paper-based; 80 iBT), IELTS (minimum score 6), PTE (minimum score 53). Electronic applications accepted. *Expenses:* Contact institution.

Texas A&M University–Commerce, College of Education and Human Services, Commerce, TX 75429. Offers counseling (M Ed, MS, PhD); early childhood education (M Ed, MS); educational administration (M Ed, MS, Ed D); educational psychology (PhD); educational technology leadership (M Ed, MS); educational technology library science (M Ed, MS); elementary education (M Ed); health, kinesiology and sports studies (MS); higher education (MS, Ed D); psychology (MS); reading (M Ed, MS); school psychology (SSP); secondary education (M Ed, MS); social work (MSW); special education (M Ed, MS); supervision, curriculum and instruction-elementary education (Ed D); training and development (MS). *Program availability:* Part-time, evening/weekend, 100% online, blended/hybrid learning. *Faculty:* 88 full-time (52 women), 23 part-time/adjunct (19 women). *Students:* 261 full-time (202 women), 1,180 part-time (943 women); includes 597 minority (300 Black or African American, non-Hispanic/Latino; 8 American Indian or Alaska Native, non-Hispanic/Latino; 30 Asian, non-Hispanic/Latino; 211 Hispanic/Latino; 48 Two or more races, non-Hispanic/Latino), 11 international. Average age 37. 689 applicants, 52% accepted, 291 enrolled. In 2019, 527 master's, 64 doctorates awarded. *Degree requirements:* For master's, comprehensive exam, thesis optional, departmental qualifying exams (for some programs); for doctorate, comprehensive exam, thesis/dissertation, departmental qualifying exam; for SSP, comprehensive exam (for some programs). *Entrance requirements:* For master's, GRE General Test, official transcripts, letters of recommendation, resume, statement of goals; for doctorate, GRE General Test, letters of recommendation, statement of goals, writing samples, writing sessions, resumes. Additional exam requirements/recommendations for international students: required—TOEFL (minimum score 550 paper-based; 79 iBT), IELTS (minimum score 6), PTE (minimum score 53). *Application deadline:* For fall admission, 6/1 priority date for international students; for spring admission, 10/15 priority date for international students; for summer admission, 3/15 priority date for international students. Applications are processed on a rolling basis. Application fee: $50 ($75 for international students). Electronic applications accepted. *Expenses: Tuition, area resident:* Full-time $3630; part-time $202 per credit hour. Tuition, state resident: full-time $3630; part-time $202 per credit hour. Tuition, nonresident: full-time $11,232; part-time $624 per credit hour. *International tuition:* $11,232 full-time. *Required fees:* $2948. *Financial support:* In 2019–20, 82 students received support, including 109 research assistantships with partial tuition reimbursements available (averaging $3,657 per year), 42 teaching assistantships with partial tuition reimbursements available (averaging $4,705 per year); career-related internships or fieldwork, Federal Work-Study, institutionally sponsored loans, scholarships/grants, health care benefits, and unspecified assistantships also available. Financial award application deadline: 5/1; financial award applicants required to submit FAFSA. *Unit head:* Dr. Kimberly McLeod, Dean, 903-886-5181, Fax: 903-886-5905, E-mail: kimberly.mcleod@tamuc.edu. *Application contact:* Dayla Burgin, Graduate Student Services Coordinator, 903-886-5134, E-mail: dayla.burgin@tamuc.edu.
Website: http://www.tamuc.edu/academics/graduateSchool/programs/education/default.aspx

Texas A&M University–Corpus Christi, College of Graduate Studies, College of Liberal Arts, Program in Psychology, Corpus Christi, TX 78412. Offers clinical psychology (MA); general psychology (MA). *Program availability:* Part-time, evening/weekend. *Degree requirements:* For master's, comprehensive exam. *Entrance requirements:* For master's, GRE (taken within 5 years; waived if candidate already has master's degree), minimum GPA of 3.0 in last 60 hours, essay (500-1000 words), 2 letters of recommendation. Additional exam requirements/recommendations for international students: required—TOEFL (minimum score 550 paper-based; 79 iBT), IELTS (minimum score 6.5). Electronic applications accepted.

Texas A&M University–Kingsville, College of Graduate Studies, College of Arts and Sciences, Department of Psychology and Sociology, Program in Psychology, Kingsville, TX 78363. Offers MA, MS. *Entrance requirements:* Additional exam requirements/recommendations for international students: required—TOEFL (minimum score 550 paper-based; 79 iBT); recommended—IELTS. Electronic applications accepted.

Texas A&M University–Texarkana, Graduate Studies and Research, College of Health and Behavioral Sciences, Texarkana, TX 75503. Offers counseling psychology (MS). *Program availability:* Part-time, evening/weekend. *Degree requirements:* For master's, comprehensive exam (for some programs), thesis or alternative. *Entrance requirements:* For master's, minimum GPA of 3.0 in last 60 hours of bachelor's degree. Additional exam requirements/recommendations for international students: required—TOEFL. Electronic applications accepted.

Texas Christian University, College of Science and Engineering, Department of Psychology, Fort Worth, TX 76129-0002. Offers developmental trauma (MS); experimental psychology (PhD), including cognition/developmental, learning, neuroscience, social. *Faculty:* 14 full-time (7 women), 1 part-time/adjunct (0 women). *Students:* 31 full-time (26 women); includes 2 minority (both Asian, non-Hispanic/Latino), 2 international. Average age 25. 52 applicants, 35% accepted, 13 enrolled. In 2019, 10 master's, 4 doctorates awarded. Terminal master's awarded for partial completion of doctoral program. *Entrance requirements:* For doctorate, GRE General Test. Additional exam requirements/recommendations for international students: required—TOEFL (minimum score 550 paper-based; 80 iBT). *Application deadline:* For fall admission, 1/1 for domestic and international students. Application fee: $60 ($0 for international students). Electronic applications accepted. Full-time tuition and fees vary according to program. *Financial support:* In 2019–20, 23 students received support, including 23 teaching assistantships with full tuition reimbursements available (averaging $19,750 per year); scholarships/grants also available. Financial award application deadline: 1/1; financial award applicants required to submit FAFSA. *Unit head:* Dr. Anna I. Petursdottir, Chair, 817-257-7410, Fax: 817-257-7681, E-mail: a.petursdottir@tcu.edu. *Application contact:* Cindy Hayes, Administrative Assistant, 817-257-7410, Fax: 817-257-7681, E-mail: c.hayes@tcu.edu.
Website: https://psychology.tcu.edu/

Texas Southern University, College of Liberal Arts and Behavioral Sciences, Department of Psychology, Houston, TX 77004-4584. Offers MA. Electronic applications accepted.

Texas State University, The Graduate College, College of Liberal Arts, Program in Psychological Research, San Marcos, TX 78666. Offers MA. *Program availability:* Part-time. *Degree requirements:* For master's, comprehensive exam, thesis optional. *Entrance requirements:* For master's, official GRE (general test only) required with competitive scores, baccalaureate degree from regionally-accredited university with minimum GPA of 3.0 on last 60 undergraduate semester hours and in psychology, statistics, and experimental and research methods courses; statement of research interest; resume; statement of purpose; 3 letters of recommendation. Additional exam requirements/recommendations for international students: required—TOEFL (minimum score 550 paper-based; 78 iBT), IELTS (minimum score 6.5). Electronic applications accepted.

Texas Tech University, Graduate School, College of Arts and Sciences, Department of Psychological Sciences, Lubbock, TX 79409-2051. Offers clinical psychology (PhD); counseling psychology (MA, PhD); general experimental psychology (MA, PhD); psychology (MA). *Accreditation:* APA (one or more programs are accredited). *Faculty:* 33 full-time (14 women), 2 part-time/adjunct (both women). *Students:* 105 full-time (63 women), 24 part-time (22 women); includes 39 minority (6 Black or African American, non-Hispanic/Latino; 1 American Indian or Alaska Native, non-Hispanic/Latino; 11 Asian, non-Hispanic/Latino; 21 Hispanic/Latino), 7 international. Average age 28. 162 applicants, 14% accepted, 16 enrolled. In 2019, 21 master's, 10 doctorates awarded. *Degree requirements:* For doctorate, comprehensive exam, thesis/dissertation, 100 credit hours of organized courses, research credits, and practica. *Entrance requirements:* For master's, GRE General Test, GRE Subject Test, essays, letters of recommendation; for doctorate, GRE General Test, essays, letters of recommendation. Additional exam requirements/recommendations for international students: required—TOEFL (minimum score 550 paper-based; 79 iBT). *Application deadline:* For fall admission, 6/1 priority date for domestic students, 1/15 priority date for international students; for spring admission, 9/1 priority date for domestic students, 6/15 priority date for international students. Applications are processed on a rolling basis. Application fee: $65. Electronic applications accepted. *Expenses:* Contact institution. *Financial support:* In 2019–20, 121 students received support, including 115 fellowships (averaging $2,803 per year), 39 research assistantships (averaging $12,832 per year), 77 teaching assistantships (averaging $13,684 per year); Federal Work-Study, institutionally sponsored loans, health care benefits, and unspecified assistantships also available. Financial award application deadline: 4/15; financial award applicants required to submit FAFSA. *Unit head:* Dr. Robert Morgan, Professor and Chair, 806-834-7117, Fax: 806-742-0818, E-mail: robert.morgan@ttu.edu. *Application contact:* Kay Hill, Admissions Coordinator, 806-834-1350, Fax: 806-742-0818, E-mail: kay.hill@ttu.edu.
Website: www.depts.ttu.edu/psy/

Texas Woman's University, Graduate School, College of Arts and Sciences, Department of Psychology and Philosophy, Denton, TX 76204. Offers counseling psychology (MA, PhD); psychological science (MS); school psychology (PhD, SSP). *Accreditation:* APA (one or more programs are accredited). *Faculty:* 16 full-time (12 women), 5 part-time/adjunct (3 women). *Students:* 88 full-time (81 women), 50 part-time (42 women); includes 65 minority (16 Black or African American, non-Hispanic/Latino; 14 Asian, non-Hispanic/Latino; 33 Hispanic/Latino; 2 Two or more races, non-Hispanic/Latino). Average age 28. 132 applicants, 33% accepted, 33 enrolled. In 2019, 20 master's, 6 doctorates awarded. Terminal master's awarded for partial completion of doctoral program. *Degree requirements:* For master's, comprehensive exam (for some programs), thesis or alternative, practica (for MA); thesis or coursework; written exam required for those who do not complete a thesis; for doctorate, comprehensive exam, thesis/dissertation, internship, residency; for SSP, comprehensive exam, SSP-internship, capstone evaluation. *Entrance requirements:* For master's, GRE (preferred minimum score 153 Verbal, 144 Quantitative), BA/BS or 18 hours in psychology; minimum GPA of 3.0, 3.5 in psychology classes; 3 letters of reference; curriculum vitae/resume; essay, interview; for doctorate, GRE (preferred minimum score 153 [500 old version] Verbal, 144 [500 old version] Quantitative, 4 Analytical), 3 letters of reference, minimum GPA of 3.0 overall and 3.5 in psychology classes, MA in psychology or related discipline with thesis, curriculum vitae, essays; for SSP, GRE (preferred minimum score 153 [500 old version] Verbal, 144 [500 old version] Quantitative, 4 Analytical), BA/BS or 18 hours in psychology; minimum GPA of 3.0, 3.5 in psychology classes; 3 letters of reference; curriculum vitae; personal essay. Additional exam requirements/recommendations for international students: required—TOEFL (minimum score 550 paper-based; 79 iBT); recommended—IELTS (minimum score 6.5), TSE (minimum score 53). *Application deadline:* For fall admission, 2/1 for domestic and international students. Application fee: $50 ($75 for international students). Electronic applications accepted. *Expenses: Tuition, area resident:* Full-time $4973.40; part-time $276.30 per semester hour. Tuition, state resident: full-time $4973.40; part-time $276.30 per semester hour. Tuition, nonresident: full-time $12,569; part-time $698.30 per semester hour. *International tuition:* $12,569.40 full-time. *Required fees:* $2524.30. Tuition and fees vary according to course level, course load, degree level and program. *Financial support:* In 2019–20, 93 students received support, including 53 teaching assistantships (averaging $6,217 per year); career-related internships or fieldwork, scholarships/grants, health care benefits, and unspecified assistantships also available. Support available to part-time students. Financial award application deadline: 3/1; financial award applicants required to submit FAFSA. *Unit head:* Dr. Brian Harding, Acting Chair, 940-898-2303, Fax: 940-898-2301, E-mail: psychology@twu.edu. *Application contact:* Korie Hawkins, Associate Director of Admissions, Graduate Recruitment, 940-898-3188, Fax: 940-898-3081, E-mail: admissions@twu.edu.
Website: http://www.twu.edu/psychology-philosophy/

Tiffin University, Program in Psychology, Tiffin, OH 44883-2161. Offers MS. *Program availability:* Part-time, evening/weekend, online only, 100% online. *Entrance requirements:* Additional exam requirements/recommendations for international students: recommended—TOEFL. Electronic applications accepted. *Expenses:* Contact institution.

Towson University, College of Liberal Arts, Program in Psychology, Towson, MD 21252-0001. Offers clinical psychology (MA); counseling psychology (MA); experimental psychology (MA); school psychology (MA). *Program availability:* Part-time, evening/weekend. *Students:* 97 full-time (79 women), 25 part-time (20 women); includes 27 minority (15 Black or African American, non-Hispanic/Latino; 3 Asian, non-Hispanic/Latino; 2 Hispanic/Latino; 7 Two or more races, non-Hispanic/Latino), 3 international. *Entrance requirements:* For master's, GRE, minimum GPA of 3.0, letters of recommendation. *Application deadline:* For fall admission, 1/17 for domestic students, 5/15 for international students; for spring admission, 10/15 for domestic students, 12/1 for international students. Applications are processed on a rolling basis. Application fee: $45. Electronic applications accepted. *Expenses: Tuition, area resident:* Full-time $7920; part-time $439 per credit. Tuition, nonresident: full-time $16,344; part-time $908 per credit. *International tuition:* $16,344 full-time. *Required fees:* $2628; $146 per credit. $876 per term. *Financial support:* Application deadline: 4/1. *Unit head:* Dr. Geoffrey Munro, Department Chair, 410-704-2634, E-mail: psycdept@towson.edu. *Application contact:* Coverley Beidleman, Assistant Director of Graduate Admissions, 410-704-5630, Fax: 410-704-3030, E-mail: grads@towson.edu.
Website: https://www.towson.edu/cla/departments/psychology/grad/

Tufts University, Graduate School of Arts and Sciences, Department of Psychology, Medford, MA 02155. Offers cognitive science (PhD); psychology (MS, PhD). Terminal master's awarded for partial completion of doctoral program. *Degree requirements:* For master's, thesis; for doctorate, thesis/dissertation. *Entrance requirements:* For master's and doctorate, GRE General Test, GRE Subject Test. Additional exam requirements/recommendations for international students: required—TOEFL (minimum score 550 paper-based; 80 iBT), IELTS (minimum score 6.5). Electronic applications accepted. *Expenses:* Contact institution.

Tulane University, School of Science and Engineering, Department of Psychology, New Orleans, LA 70118-5669. Offers MS, PhD. *Accreditation:* APA (one or more programs are accredited). Terminal master's awarded for partial completion of doctoral program. *Degree requirements:* For master's, variable foreign language requirement, thesis; for doctorate, thesis/dissertation. *Entrance requirements:* For master's, GRE General Test, minimum B average in undergraduate course work; for doctorate, GRE General Test. Additional exam requirements/recommendations for international students: required—TOEFL. Electronic applications accepted. *Expenses: Tuition:* Full-time $57,004; part-time $3167 per credit hour. *Required fees:* $2086; $44.50 per credit hour. $80 per term. Tuition and fees vary according to course load, degree level and program.

UNB Fredericton, School of Graduate Studies, Faculty of Science, Applied Science, and Engineering, Psychology, Fredericton, NB E3B 5A3, Canada. Offers MA, PhD. *Program availability:* Part-time. *Faculty:* 16 full-time (11 women), 3 part-time/adjunct (all women). *Students:* 37 full-time (32 women), 3 part-time (1 woman), 2 international. Average age 30. In 2019, 6 doctorates awarded. *Degree requirements:* For doctorate, comprehensive exam, thesis/dissertation. *Entrance requirements:* For master's, BA (honors) in psychology or equivalent research experience; for doctorate, minimum GPA of 3.7. Additional exam requirements/recommendations for international students: required—TOEFL (minimum score 600 paper-based). *Application deadline:* For fall admission, 1/15 for domestic and international students; for winter admission, 1/15 priority date for domestic and international students. Applications are processed on a rolling basis. Application fee: $50 Canadian dollars. Electronic applications accepted. *Expenses: Tuition, area resident:* Full-time $6975 Canadian dollars; part-time $3423 Canadian dollars per year. Tuition, state resident: full-time $6975 Canadian dollars; part-time $3423 Canadian dollars per year. Tuition, Canadian resident: full-time $6975 Canadian dollars; part-time $3423 Canadian dollars per year. *International tuition:* $12,435 Canadian dollars full-time. *Required fees:* $92.25 Canadian dollars per term. Full-time tuition and fees vary according to degree level, campus/location, program, reciprocity agreements and student level. *Financial support:* Fellowships, research assistantships, and teaching assistantships available. Financial award application deadline: 1/15. *Unit head:* Dr. Suzanne Hindmarch, Director of Graduate Studies, 506-443 3906, Fax: 506-447-3063, E-mail: s.hindmarch@unb.ca. *Application contact:* Jessica Carter, Graduate Secretary, 506-453-4707, Fax: 506-447-3063, E-mail: j.carter4@unb.ca.
Website: http://go.unb.ca/gradprograms

Uniformed Services University of the Health Sciences, F. Edward Hebert School of Medicine, Graduate Programs in the Biomedical Sciences and Public Health, Department of Medical and Clinical Psychology, Bethesda, MD 20814. Offers clinical psychology (PhD); medical psychology (PhD). *Accreditation:* APA. Terminal master's awarded for partial completion of doctoral program. *Degree requirements:* For doctorate, comprehensive exam, thesis/dissertation, qualifying exam. *Entrance requirements:* For doctorate, GRE General Test, minimum GPA of 3.0, U.S. citizenship. Additional exam requirements/recommendations for international students: required—TOEFL. Electronic applications accepted.

Union College, Graduate Programs, Department of Psychology, Barbourville, KY 40906-1499. Offers clinical psychology (MA); counseling psychology (MA); school psychology (MA).

Universidad de las Americas, A.C., Program in Psychology, Mexico City, Mexico. Offers family therapy (MA).

Universidad de las Américas Puebla, Division of Graduate Studies, School of Social Sciences, Program in Psychology, Puebla, Mexico. Offers MA. *Program availability:* Part-time, evening/weekend. *Degree requirements:* For master's, one foreign language, thesis. *Entrance requirements:* For master's, minimum B+ average.

Université de Montréal, Faculty of Arts and Sciences, Department of Psychology, Montréal, QC H3C 3J7, Canada. Offers M Sc, PhD. Terminal master's awarded for partial completion of doctoral program. *Degree requirements:* For master's, one foreign language, thesis; for doctorate, one foreign language, thesis/dissertation, general exam. Electronic applications accepted.

Université de Sherbrooke, Faculty of Letters and Human Sciences, Department of Psychology, Sherbrooke, QC J1K 2R1, Canada. Offers gerontology (MA). *Degree requirements:* For master's, thesis.

Université du Québec à Montréal, Graduate Programs, Program in Psychology, Montréal, QC H3C 3P8, Canada. Offers D Ps, PhD. *Program availability:* Part-time. *Degree requirements:* For doctorate, thesis/dissertation. *Entrance requirements:* For doctorate, appropriate master's degree or equivalent, proficiency in French.

Université du Québec à Trois-Rivières, Graduate Programs, Program in Psychology, Trois-Rivières, QC G9A 5H7, Canada. Offers PhD, Certificate. *Program availability:* Part-time. *Degree requirements:* For doctorate, thesis/dissertation. *Entrance requirements:* For doctorate, appropriate master's degree, proficiency in French.

University at Albany, State University of New York, College of Arts and Sciences, Department of Psychology, Albany, NY 12222-0001. Offers behavioral neuroscience (PhD); clinical psychology (PhD); cognitive psychology (PhD); industrial/organizational psychology (MA, PhD); social-personality psychology (PhD). *Accreditation:* APA (one or more programs are accredited). *Program availability:* Blended/hybrid learning. *Faculty:* 31 full-time (14 women), 6 part-time/adjunct (4 women). *Students:* 68 full-time (44 women), 53 part-time (35 women); includes 30 minority (3 Black or African American, non-Hispanic/Latino; 10 Asian, non-Hispanic/Latino; 11 Hispanic/Latino; 6 Two or more races, non-Hispanic/Latino), 9 international. 253 applicants, 21% accepted, 28 enrolled. In 2019, 22 master's, 11 doctorates awarded. *Degree requirements:* For doctorate, thesis/dissertation. *Entrance requirements:* For master's, transcripts of all schools attended, statement of background and goals, departmental questionnaire, resume, names and contact information for 3 recommenders; for doctorate, GRE General Test, GRE Subject Test, transcripts of all schools attended, statement of background and goals, departmental questionnaire, resume, names and contact information for 3 recommenders. Additional exam requirements/recommendations for international students: required—TOEFL (minimum score 550 paper-based). *Application deadline:* For fall admission, 1/15 for domestic and international students; for spring admission, 11/15 for domestic students. Application fee: $75. Electronic applications accepted. *Expenses: Tuition, area resident:* Full-time $11,530; part-time $480 per credit hour. Tuition, nonresident: full-time $23,530; part-time $980 per credit hour. *International tuition:* $23,530 full-time. *Required fees:* $2185; $96 per credit hour. Part-time tuition and fees vary according to course load and program. *Financial support:* Fellowships, research assistantships, teaching assistantships, and career-related internships or fieldwork available. Financial award application deadline: 2/1. *Unit head:* Christine K. Wagner, Chair, 518-442-4820, Fax: 518-442-4867, E-mail: cwagner@albany.edu. *Application contact:* Michael DeRensis, Director, Graduate Admissions, 518-442-3980, Fax: 518-442-3922, E-mail: graduate@albany.edu.
Website: https://www.albany.edu/psychology/

University at Buffalo, the State University of New York, Graduate School, College of Arts and Sciences, Department of Psychology, Buffalo, NY 14260. Offers MA, PhD.

Accreditation: APA (one or more programs are accredited). *Faculty:* 27 full-time (11 women), 7 part-time/adjunct (3 women). *Students:* 81 full-time (66 women), 8 part-time (4 women); includes 17 minority (1 Black or African American, non-Hispanic/Latino; 11 Asian, non-Hispanic/Latino; 3 Hispanic/Latino; 2 Two or more races, non-Hispanic/Latino), 11 international. Average age 27. 220 applicants, 18% accepted, 15 enrolled. In 2019, 22 master's, 9 doctorates awarded. Terminal master's awarded for partial completion of doctoral program. *Degree requirements:* For master's, thesis optional, Project or Thesis required; for doctorate, thesis/dissertation. *Entrance requirements:* For master's and doctorate, GRE General Test. Additional exam requirements/recommendations for international students: required—TOEFL (minimum score 550 paper-based; 79 iBT). *Application deadline:* For fall admission, 12/1 for domestic and international students. Application fee: $75. Electronic applications accepted. *Expenses: Tuition, area resident:* Full-time $11,310; part-time $471 per credit hour. Tuition, state resident: Full-time $11,310; part-time $471 per credit hour. Tuition, nonresident: full-time $23,100; part-time $963 per credit hour. *International tuition:* $23,100 full-time. *Required fees:* $2820. *Financial support:* In 2019–20, 58 students received support, including fellowships with full tuition reimbursements available (averaging $20,000 per year), 19 research assistantships with full tuition reimbursements available (averaging $20,000 per year), 39 teaching assistantships with full tuition reimbursements available (averaging $20,000 per year); career-related internships or fieldwork, scholarships/grants, health care benefits, and unspecified assistantships also available. Financial award application deadline: 12/1; financial award applicants required to submit FAFSA. *Unit head:* Dr. Peter Q. Pfordresher, Chair, 716-645-0234, Fax: 716-645-3801, E-mail: pqp@buffalo.edu. *Application contact:* Mary Wlodarczyk, Admissions Officer, 716-645-8617, Fax: 716-645-3801, E-mail: psych@buffalo.edu.
Website: https://arts-sciences.buffalo.edu/psychology.html

The University of Akron, Graduate School, Buchtel College of Arts and Sciences, Department of Psychology, Akron, OH 44325. Offers adult development and aging (PhD); counseling psychology (MA, PhD); industrial/organizational psychology (MA, PhD); psychology (MA). *Accreditation:* APA (one or more programs are accredited). Terminal master's awarded for partial completion of doctoral program. *Degree requirements:* For master's, thesis or specialty exam; for doctorate, one foreign language, comprehensive exam, thesis/dissertation. *Entrance requirements:* For master's, GRE, baccalaureate degree in psychology or extensive background in psychology; minimum cumulative undergraduate GPA of 3.0; three letters of recommendation; for doctorate, GRE, baccalaureate degree in psychology or 30 credits of psychology coursework; minimum cumulative undergraduate GPA of 3.0, 3.25 on all psychology coursework; current vita; declaration of intent; three letters of recommendation. Additional exam requirements/recommendations for international students: required—TOEFL (minimum score 79 iBT), IELTS (minimum score 6.5). Electronic applications accepted.

The University of Alabama, Graduate School, College of Arts and Sciences, Department of Psychology, Tuscaloosa, AL 35487. Offers clinical psychology (PhD); experimental psychology (PhD). *Faculty:* 31 full-time (18 women), 1 (woman) part-time/adjunct. *Students:* 84 full-time (68 women), 15 part-time (11 women); includes 17 minority (7 Black or African American, non-Hispanic/Latino; 1 Asian, non-Hispanic/Latino; 7 Hispanic/Latino; 2 Two or more races, non-Hispanic/Latino), 7 international. Average age 28. 269 applicants, 9% accepted, 17 enrolled. In 2019, 21 doctorates awarded. *Degree requirements:* For doctorate, thesis/dissertation, internship (for clinical psychology). *Entrance requirements:* For doctorate, GRE. Additional exam requirements/recommendations for international students: required—TOEFL (minimum score 550 paper-based). *Application deadline:* For fall admission, 11/16 for domestic and international students. Application fee: $50 ($60 for international students). Electronic applications accepted. *Expenses: Tuition, area resident:* Full-time $10,780; part-time $440 per credit hour. Tuition, nonresident: full-time $30,250; part-time $1550 per credit hour. *Financial support:* In 2019–20, 65 students received support, including fellowships with full tuition reimbursements available (averaging $17,000 per year), research assistantships with tuition reimbursements available (averaging $12,744 per year), teaching assistantships with tuition reimbursements available (averaging $13,824 per year); career-related internships or fieldwork, institutionally sponsored loans, scholarships/grants, health care benefits, and unspecified assistantships also available. Financial award application deadline: 11/16. *Unit head:* Dr. Frances A. Conners, Chair, 205-348-1913, Fax: 205-348-8648, E-mail: fconners@ua.edu. *Application contact:* Mary Beth Hubbard, Information Contact, 205-348-1919, Fax: 205-348-8648, E-mail: mary.b.hubbard@ua.edu.
Website: http://www.psychology.ua.edu

The University of Alabama at Birmingham, College of Arts and Sciences, Program in Psychology, Birmingham, AL 35294. Offers behavioral neuroscience (PhD); lifespan developmental psychology (PhD); medical/clinical psychology (PhD); psychology (MA). *Accreditation:* APA (one or more programs are accredited). *Faculty:* 27 full-time (12 women), 1 (woman) part-time/adjunct. *Students:* 81 full-time (55 women), 3 part-time (all women); includes 22 minority (10 Black or African American, non-Hispanic/Latino; 4 Asian, non-Hispanic/Latino; 6 Hispanic/Latino; 2 Two or more races, non-Hispanic/Latino), 3 international. Average age 27. 199 applicants, 7% accepted, 12 enrolled. In 2019, 8 master's, 15 doctorates awarded. *Entrance requirements:* For master's and doctorate, GRE General Test, letters of recommendation. *Application deadline:* Applications are processed on a rolling basis. Electronic applications accepted. *Financial support:* Fellowships, research assistantships, and teaching assistantships available. *Unit head:* Dr. Karlene K. Ball, Chair, 205-934-2610, Fax: 205-975-2295, E-mail: psych-dept@uab.edu. *Application contact:* Susan Noblitt Banks, Director of Graduate School Operations, 205-934-8227, Fax: 205-934-8413, E-mail: gradschool@uab.edu.
Website: http://www.uab.edu/cas/psychology/graduate

The University of Alabama in Huntsville, School of Graduate Studies, College of Arts, Humanities, and Social Sciences, Department of Psychology, Huntsville, AL 35899. Offers industrial/organizational psychology (MA); psychology (MA). *Program availability:* Part-time. *Degree requirements:* For master's, comprehensive exam, thesis or alternative, oral and written exams. *Entrance requirements:* For master's, GRE General Test, 15 hours of course work in psychology, minimum GPA of 3.25, sample of written work. Additional exam requirements/recommendations for international students: required—TOEFL (minimum score 500 paper-based; 80 iBT), IELTS (minimum score 6.5). Electronic applications accepted.

University of Alaska Anchorage, College of Arts and Sciences, Department of Psychology, Anchorage, AK 99508. Offers clinical psychology (MS); clinical-community psychology with rural and indigenous emphasis (PhD). *Accreditation:* APA. *Program availability:* Part-time. *Degree requirements:* For master's, thesis. *Entrance requirements:* For master's, GRE General Test, GRE Subject Test, interview, references; for doctorate, interview, bachelor's or master's degree in psychology. Additional exam requirements/recommendations for international students: required—TOEFL (minimum score 550 paper-based).

University of Alberta, Faculty of Graduate Studies and Research, Department of Psychology, Edmonton, AB T6G 2E1, Canada. Offers M Sc, MA, PhD. Terminal master's awarded for partial completion of doctoral program. *Degree requirements:* For

master's, thesis (for some programs); for doctorate, thesis/dissertation. *Entrance requirements:* For master's and doctorate, GRE. Additional exam requirements/recommendations for international students: required—TOEFL (minimum score 550 paper-based). Electronic applications accepted.

The University of Arizona, College of Science, Department of Psychology, Tucson, AZ 85721. Offers MA, PhD. *Accreditation:* APA (one or more programs are accredited). *Degree requirements:* For doctorate, comprehensive exam, thesis/dissertation. *Entrance requirements:* For master's, GRE General Test, 3 letters of recommendation, statement of purpose; for doctorate, GRE General Test, 3 letters of recommendation. Additional exam requirements/recommendations for international students: required—TOEFL (minimum score 550 paper-based; 79 iBT). Electronic applications accepted.

University of Arkansas, Graduate School, J. William Fulbright College of Arts and Sciences, Department of Psychology, Fayetteville, AR 72701. Offers MA, PhD. *Accreditation:* APA (one or more programs are accredited). *Students:* 44 full-time (34 women), 4 part-time (2 women); includes 12 minority (2 Black or African American, non-Hispanic/Latino; 1 American Indian or Alaska Native, non-Hispanic/Latino; 2 Asian, non-Hispanic/Latino; 5 Hispanic/Latino; 2 Two or more races, non-Hispanic/Latino). 146 applicants, 5% accepted. In 2019, 9 master's, 5 doctorates awarded. *Degree requirements:* For master's, thesis; for doctorate, variable foreign language requirement, thesis/dissertation. *Entrance requirements:* For doctorate, GRE General Test, GRE Subject Test. *Application deadline:* For fall admission, 8/1 for domestic students, 4/1 for international students; for spring admission, 12/1 for domestic students, 10/1 for international students; for summer admission, 4/15 for domestic students, 3/1 for international students. Applications are processed on a rolling basis. Application fee: $60. Electronic applications accepted. *Financial support:* In 2019–20, 24 research assistantships, 8 teaching assistantships were awarded; fellowships with tuition reimbursements, career-related internships or fieldwork, Federal Work-Study, and traineeships also available. Support available to part-time students. Financial award application deadline: 4/1; financial award applicants required to submit FAFSA. *Unit head:* Dr. Douglas A. Behrend, Department Chair, 479-575-4256, E-mail: dbehrend@uark.edu. *Application contact:* Dr. James Lampinen, 479-575-4256, E-mail: lampinen@uark.edu.
Website: https://fulbright.uark.edu/departments/psychological-science/

University of Arkansas at Little Rock, Graduate School, College of Social Sciences and Communication, Department of Psychology, Little Rock, AR 72204-1099. Offers applied psychology (MAP). *Program availability:* Part-time, evening/weekend. *Entrance requirements:* For master's, GRE General Test, minimum GPA of 2.7.

The University of British Columbia, Faculty of Arts, Department of Psychology, Vancouver, BC V6T 1Z4, Canada. Offers behavioral neuroscience (MA, PhD); clinical psychology (MA, PhD); cognitive science (MA, PhD); developmental psychology (MA, PhD); health psychology (MA, PhD); quantitative methods (MA, PhD); social/personality psychology (MA, PhD). *Accreditation:* APA (one or more programs are accredited). Terminal master's awarded for partial completion of doctoral program. *Degree requirements:* For master's, thesis; for doctorate, comprehensive exam, thesis/dissertation. *Entrance requirements:* For master's and doctorate, GRE General Test. Additional exam requirements/recommendations for international students: required—TOEFL. Electronic applications accepted. *Expenses:* Contact institution.

University of Calgary, Faculty of Graduate Studies, Faculty of Arts, Program in Psychology, Calgary, AB T2N 1N4, Canada. Offers clinical psychology (M Sc, PhD); psychology (M Sc, PhD). *Degree requirements:* For master's, thesis; for doctorate, thesis/dissertation. *Entrance requirements:* For master's, GRE General Test, bachelor's degree in psychology, minimum GPA of 3.4. Additional exam requirements/recommendations for international students: required—TOEFL (minimum score 550 paper-based). Electronic applications accepted.

University of California, Berkeley, Graduate Division, College of Letters and Science, Department of Psychology, Berkeley, CA 94720. Offers PhD. *Accreditation:* APA. *Degree requirements:* For doctorate, thesis/dissertation, qualifying exam. *Entrance requirements:* For doctorate, GRE General Test, GRE Subject Test, minimum GPA of 3.0, 3 letters of recommendation. Electronic applications accepted.

University of California, Davis, Graduate Studies, Program in Psychology, Davis, CA 95616. Offers PhD. *Degree requirements:* For doctorate, thesis/dissertation. *Entrance requirements:* For doctorate, GRE General Test, GRE Subject Test, minimum GPA of 3.0. Additional exam requirements/recommendations for international students: required—TOEFL (minimum score 550 paper-based). Electronic applications accepted.

University of California, Irvine, School of Social Ecology, Psycological Science, Irvine, CA 92697. Offers PhD. *Students:* 76 full-time (53 women); includes 31 minority (6 Black or African American, non-Hispanic/Latino; 1 American Indian or Alaska Native, non-Hispanic/Latino; 10 Asian, non-Hispanic/Latino; 12 Hispanic/Latino; 2 Two or more races, non-Hispanic/Latino), 12 international. Average age 28. 288 applicants, 10% accepted, 16 enrolled. In 2019, 9 doctorates awarded. *Degree requirements:* For doctorate, thesis/dissertation, research project. *Entrance requirements:* For doctorate, GRE General Test, minimum GPA of 3.0. Additional exam requirements/recommendations for international students: required—TOEFL (minimum score 550 paper-based). *Application deadline:* For fall admission, 12/15 priority date for domestic and international students. Applications are processed on a rolling basis. Application fee: $120 ($140 for international students). Electronic applications accepted. *Financial support:* Fellowships, research assistantships with full tuition reimbursements, teaching assistantships, institutionally sponsored loans, traineeships, health care benefits, and unspecified assistantships available. Financial award application deadline: 3/1; financial award applicants required to submit FAFSA. *Unit head:* Susan Charles, Chair, 949-824-5574, E-mail: scharles@uci.edu. *Application contact:* Roxane C. Silver, Professor, 949-824-2192, Fax: 949-824-3002, E-mail: rsilver@uci.edu.
Website: http://psb.soceco.uci.edu/

University of California, Irvine, School of Social Sciences, Department of Cognitive Sciences, Irvine, CA 92697. Offers psychology (PhD). *Students:* 58 full-time (30 women), 1 part-time (0 women); includes 16 minority (11 Asian, non-Hispanic/Latino; 5 Hispanic/Latino), 16 international. Average age 28. 135 applicants, 25% accepted, 21 enrolled. In 2019, 10 doctorates awarded. *Entrance requirements:* For doctorate, GRE General Test, minimum GPA of 3.0. Additional exam requirements/recommendations for international students: required—TOEFL (minimum score 550 paper-based). *Application deadline:* For fall admission, 1/15 priority date for domestic and international students. Applications are processed on a rolling basis. Application fee: $120 ($140 for international students). Electronic applications accepted. *Financial support:* Fellowships, research assistantships with full tuition reimbursements, teaching assistantships, institutionally sponsored loans, traineeships, health care benefits, and unspecified assistantships available. Financial award application deadline: 3/1; financial award applicants required to submit FAFSA. *Unit head:* Prof. Ramesh Srinivasan, Department Chair, 949-824-2969, E-mail: r.srinivasan@uci.edu. *Application contact:* Joachim Vandekerckhove, Graduate Director, 949-824-5958, E-mail: joachim@uci.edu.
Website: http://www.cogsci.uci.edu/cs_graduates

University of California, Los Angeles, Graduate Division, College of Letters and Science, Department of Psychology, Los Angeles, CA 90034. Offers MA, PhD.

Psychology—General

Accreditation: APA (one or more programs are accredited). Terminal master's awarded for partial completion of doctoral program. *Degree requirements:* For master's, comprehensive exam; for doctorate, thesis/dissertation, oral and written qualifying exams, teaching experience. *Entrance requirements:* For doctorate, GRE General Test, GRE Subject Test (psychology), bachelor's degree; minimum undergraduate GPA of 3.0 (or its equivalent if letter grade system not used); interview. Additional exam requirements/recommendations for international students: required—TOEFL. Electronic applications accepted.

University of California, Merced, Graduate Division, School of Social Sciences, Humanities and Arts, Merced, CA 95343. Offers cognitive and information sciences (PhD); interdisciplinary humanities (MA, PhD); psychological sciences (MA, PhD); social sciences (MA, PhD); sociology (MA, PhD). *Faculty:* 113 full-time (57 women), 2 part-time/adjunct (0 women). *Students:* 194 full-time (128 women), 1 (woman) part-time; includes 81 minority (5 Black or African American, non-Hispanic/Latino; 18 Asian, non-Hispanic/Latino; 54 Hispanic/Latino; 4 Two or more races, non-Hispanic/Latino), 39 international. Average age 31. 218 applicants, 48% accepted, 36 enrolled. In 2019, 12 master's, 23 doctorates awarded. Terminal master's awarded for partial completion of doctoral program. *Degree requirements:* For master's, variable foreign language requirement, comprehensive exam, thesis or alternative, oral defense; for doctorate, variable foreign language requirement, comprehensive exam, thesis/dissertation, oral defense. *Entrance requirements:* For master's and doctorate, GRE. Additional exam requirements/recommendations for international students: required—TOEFL (minimum score 550 paper-based; 80 iBT); recommended—IELTS (minimum score 6.5). *Application deadline:* For fall admission, 1/15 for domestic and international students. Application fee: $105 ($125 for international students). Electronic applications accepted. *Expenses: Tuition, area resident:* Full-time $11,442; part-time $5721 per semester. Tuition, state resident: full-time $11,442; part-time $5721 per semester. Tuition, nonresident: full-time $26,544; part-time $13,272 per semester. *International tuition:* $26,544 full-time. *Required fees:* $564 per semester. *Financial support:* In 2019–20, 183 students received support, including 7 fellowships with full tuition reimbursements available (averaging $22,005 per year), 5 research assistantships with full tuition reimbursements available (averaging $21,420 per year), 171 teaching assistantships with full tuition reimbursements available (averaging $21,911 per year); scholarships/grants, traineeships, and health care benefits also available. *Unit head:* Dr. Jeffrey Gilger, Dean, 209-228-4343, E-mail: jgilger@ucmerced.edu. *Application contact:* Tsu Ya, Director of Admissions and Academic Services, 209-228-4521, Fax: 209-228-6906, E-mail: tya@ucmerced.edu.

University of California, Riverside, Graduate Division, Department of Psychology, Riverside, CA 92521-0102. Offers PhD. *Accreditation:* APA. *Degree requirements:* For doctorate, comprehensive exam, thesis/dissertation, 3 quarters of teaching experience, qualifying exams. *Entrance requirements:* For doctorate, GRE General Test, minimum GPA of 3.2. Additional exam requirements/recommendations for international students: required—TOEFL (minimum score 550 paper-based; 80 iBT). Electronic applications accepted.

University of California, San Diego, Graduate Division, Department of Psychology, La Jolla, CA 92093. Offers PhD. *Students:* 57 full-time (34 women). 315 applicants, 8% accepted, 15 enrolled. In 2019, 5 doctorates awarded. *Degree requirements:* For doctorate, comprehensive exam, thesis/dissertation, 4 quarters of teaching assistantship. *Entrance requirements:* For doctorate, GRE General Test, minimum GPA of 3.0. Additional exam requirements/recommendations for international students: required—TOEFL (minimum score 550 paper-based; 80 iBT), IELTS (minimum score 7). *Application deadline:* For fall admission, 12/3 for domestic students. Application fee: $105 ($125 for international students). Electronic applications accepted. *Financial support:* Fellowships, research assistantships, teaching assistantships, scholarships/grants, and unspecified assistantships available. Financial award applicants required to submit FAFSA. *Unit head:* Michael Gorman, Chair, 858-822-2466. *Application contact:* Samantha Llanos, Graduate Coordinator, 858-534-4416, E-mail: psycphdinfo@ucsd.edu.
Website: http://psychology.ucsd.edu/

University of California, Santa Barbara, Graduate Division, College of Letters and Sciences, Division of Mathematics, Life, and Physical Sciences, Department of Psychological and Brain Sciences, Santa Barbara, CA 93106-9660. Offers cognitive science (PhD); psychology (PhD); quantitative methods in the social sciences (PhD); technology and society (PhD). Terminal master's awarded for partial completion of doctoral program. *Degree requirements:* For doctorate, comprehensive exam, thesis/dissertation, teaching assistant training, progress report, papers, mini-convention presentation, 1 quarter of student teaching or teaching assistant class with section lab, continued participation in research and weekly area meetings. *Entrance requirements:* For doctorate, GRE General Test. Additional exam requirements/recommendations for international students: required—TOEFL (minimum score 550 paper-based; 80 iBT) or IELTS (minimum score 7). Electronic applications accepted.

University of California, Santa Cruz, Division of Graduate Studies, Division of Social Sciences, Department of Psychology, Santa Cruz, CA 95064. Offers PhD. *Degree requirements:* For doctorate, thesis/dissertation, qualifying exam, seminars. *Entrance requirements:* For doctorate, GRE General Test. Additional exam requirements/recommendations for international students: required—TOEFL (minimum score 550 paper-based; 83 iBT); recommended—IELTS (minimum score 8). Electronic applications accepted.

University of Central Arkansas, Graduate School, College of Health and Behavioral Sciences, Department of Counseling and Psychology, Conway, AR 72035-0001. Offers community counseling (MS); counseling psychology (MS); school psychology (MS, PhD, PMC). *Accreditation:* APA. Terminal master's awarded for partial completion of doctoral program. *Degree requirements:* For master's, comprehensive exam, thesis optional, internship; for doctorate, comprehensive exam, thesis/dissertation, internship. *Entrance requirements:* For master's, GRE General Test, minimum GPA of 2.75; for doctorate, GRE General Test, minimum GPA of 3.25. Additional exam requirements/recommendations for international students: required—TOEFL (minimum score 550 paper-based). Electronic applications accepted.

University of Central Florida, College of Sciences, Department of Psychology, Orlando, FL 32816. Offers clinical psychology (PhD). *Accreditation:* APA. *Program availability:* Part-time. *Students:* 153 full-time (103 women), 17 part-time (14 women); includes 56 minority (6 Black or African American, non-Hispanic/Latino; 1 American Indian or Alaska Native, non-Hispanic/Latino; 12 Asian, non-Hispanic/Latino; 31 Hispanic/Latino; 6 Two or more races, non-Hispanic/Latino), 13 international. Average age 27. 545 applicants, 13% accepted, 47 enrolled. In 2019, 39 master's, 12 doctorates awarded. *Degree requirements:* For master's, thesis; for doctorate, thesis/dissertation, candidacy exam. *Entrance requirements:* For master's, GRE General Test, minimum GPA of 3.0 in last 60 hours, resume or curriculum vitae, personal statement, letters of recommendation; for doctorate, GRE General Test, curriculum vitae, personal statement, letters of recommendation. Additional exam requirements/recommendations for international students: required—TOEFL. *Application deadline:* For fall admission, 1/1 for domestic students. Application fee: $30. Electronic applications accepted. *Financial support:* In 2019–20, 103 students received support, including 34 fellowships with partial tuition reimbursements available (averaging $7,110 per year), 27 research assistantships with partial tuition reimbursements available (averaging $6,976 per year), 72 teaching assistantships with partial tuition reimbursements available (averaging $8,411 per year); career-related internships or fieldwork, Federal Work-Study, institutionally sponsored loans, health care benefits, tuition waivers (partial), and unspecified assistantships also available. Financial award application deadline: 3/1; financial award applicants required to submit FAFSA. *Unit head:* Dr. Clint Bowers, Interim Chair, 407-823-3576, E-mail: clint.bowers@ucf.edu. *Application contact:* Associate Director, Graduate Admissions, 407-823-2766, Fax: 407-823-6442, E-mail: gradadmissions@ucf.edu.
Website: http://sciences.ucf.edu/psychology/

University of Central Missouri, The Graduate School, Warrensburg, MO 64093. Offers accountancy (MA); accounting (MBA); applied mathematics (MS); aviation safety (MA); biology (MS); business administration (MBA); career and technology education (MS); college student personnel administration (MS); communication (MA); computer information systems and information technology (MS); computer science (MS); counseling (MS); criminal justice and criminology (MS); educational leadership (Ed S); educational leadership and policy analysis (Ed D); educational technology (MS, Ed S); elementary and early childhood education (MSE); English (MA); english language learners - teaching english as a second language (MA); environmental studies (MA); finance (MBA); history (MA); industrial hygiene (MS); industrial management (MS); information systems (MBA); kinesiology (MS); library science and information services (MS); literacy education (MSE); marketing (MBA); mathematics (MS); music (MA); occupational safety management (MS); professional leadership - adult, career, and technical education (Ed S); professional leadership - counseling (Ed S); psychology (MS); rural family nursing (MS); school administration (MSE); social gerontology (MS); sociology (MA); special education (MSE); speech language pathology (MS); teaching (MAT); technology (MS); technology management (PhD); theatre (MA). *Accreditation:* ASHA. *Program availability:* Part-time, 100% online, blended/hybrid learning. *Faculty:* 236 full-time (113 women), 97 part-time/adjunct (61 women). *Students:* 787 full-time (448 women), 1,459 part-time (997 women); includes 213 minority (72 Black or African American, non-Hispanic/Latino; 5 American Indian or Alaska Native, non-Hispanic/Latino; 27 Asian, non-Hispanic/Latino; 59 Hispanic/Latino; 50 Two or more races, non-Hispanic/Latino), 574 international. Average age 30. 1,477 applicants, 68% accepted, 664 enrolled. In 2019, 831 master's, 93 other advanced degrees awarded. *Degree requirements:* For master's and Ed S, comprehensive exam (for some programs), thesis (for some programs). *Entrance requirements:* For master's, A GRE or GMAT test score may be required by some of the programs, A minimum GPA, letters of recommendation, a statement of purpose may be required by some of the programs; for Ed S, A master's degree is required for the application of an Education Specialist's degree program. Additional exam requirements/recommendations for international students: required—TOEFL (minimum score 550 paper-based; 79 iBT). *Application deadline:* For fall admission, 6/1 priority date for domestic and international students; for spring admission, 10/15 priority date for domestic and international students; for summer admission, 4/1 priority date for domestic and international students. Applications are processed on a rolling basis. Application fee: $30 ($75 for international students). Electronic applications accepted. *Expenses: Tuition, area resident:* Full-time $7524; part-time $313.50 per credit hour. Tuition, state resident: full-time $7524; part-time $313.50 per credit hour. Tuition, nonresident: full-time $15,048; part-time $627 per credit hour. *International tuition:* $15,048 full-time. *Required fees:* $915; $30.50 per credit hour. *Financial support:* In 2019–20, 89 students received support. Research assistantships, teaching assistantships, career-related internships or fieldwork, Federal Work-Study, scholarships/grants, unspecified assistantships, and administrative and laboratory assistantships available. Support available to part-time students. Financial award application deadline: 4/1; financial award applicants required to submit FAFSA. *Unit head:* Shellie Hewitt, Director of Graduate and International Student Services, 660-543-4621, Fax: 660-543-4778, E-mail: hewitt@ucmo.edu. *Application contact:* Shellie Hewitt, Director of Graduate and International Student Services, 660-543-4621, Fax: 660-543-4778, E-mail: hewitt@ucmo.edu.
Website: http://www.ucmo.edu/graduate/

University of Central Oklahoma, The Jackson College of Graduate Studies, College of Education and Professional Studies, Department of Psychology, Edmond, OK 73034-5209. Offers psychology (MA), including counseling psychology, experimental psychology, forensic psychology, general psychology, school psychology. *Degree requirements:* For master's, thesis (for some programs). *Entrance requirements:* For master's, GRE. Additional exam requirements/recommendations for international students: required—TOEFL (minimum score 550 paper-based; 79 iBT), IELTS (minimum score 6.5). Electronic applications accepted.

University of Chicago, Division of the Social Sciences, Department of Psychology, Chicago, IL 60637. Offers PhD. *Degree requirements:* For doctorate, one foreign language, thesis/dissertation. *Entrance requirements:* For doctorate, GRE General Test, 3 letters of recommendation, statement of purpose, transcripts, resume or curriculum vitae, writing sample (dependent on department). Additional exam requirements/recommendations for international students: required—TOEFL (minimum score 104 iBT), IELTS (minimum score 7). Electronic applications accepted.

University of Cincinnati, Graduate School, McMicken College of Arts and Sciences, Department of Psychology, Cincinnati, OH 45221. Offers clinical psychology (PhD); experimental psychology (PhD). *Accreditation:* APA. *Degree requirements:* For doctorate, comprehensive exam, thesis/dissertation. *Entrance requirements:* For doctorate, GRE General Test. Additional exam requirements/recommendations for international students: required—TOEFL.

University of Colorado Boulder, Graduate School, College of Arts and Sciences, Department of Psychology and Neuroscience, Boulder, CO 80309. Offers MA, PhD. *Accreditation:* APA (one or more programs are accredited). Terminal master's awarded for partial completion of doctoral program. *Degree requirements:* For master's, comprehensive exam; for doctorate, thesis/dissertation. *Entrance requirements:* For master's, GRE General Test, minimum undergraduate GPA of 2.75; for doctorate, GRE General Test. Electronic applications accepted. Application fee is waived when completed online.

University of Colorado Colorado Springs, College of Letters, Arts and Sciences, Department of Psychology, Colorado Springs, CO 80918. Offers psychology (PhD). *Accreditation:* APA. *Program availability:* Part-time. *Faculty:* 19 full-time (11 women), 8 part-time/adjunct (5 women). *Students:* 38 full-time (36 women), 24 part-time (17 women); includes 10 minority (1 Black or African American, non-Hispanic/Latino; 2 Asian, non-Hispanic/Latino; 4 Hispanic/Latino; 3 Two or more races, non-Hispanic/Latino). Average age 27. 265 applicants, 17% accepted, 21 enrolled. In 2019, 27 master's awarded. *Degree requirements:* For master's, thesis; for doctorate, comprehensive exam, thesis/dissertation. *Entrance requirements:* For master's, GRE, BA or BS degree or an equivalent from an accredited college or university; minimum GPA of 3.0 or above. Competitive applicants have Graduate Record Exam scores of the 50th percentile or higher on both the verbal and quantitative sections. The advanced psychology subject test is strongly recommended. Four letters of recommendation; for doctorate, Graduate Record Exam scores (Verbal, Quantitative, Written Analysis) are

required for application and are taken into account in the admissions process; the GRE Psychology test is NOT required, but it is recommended, An average of 3.0 on a 4.00 point scale or above in all undergraduate courses, and 3.5 or better on graduate coursework. An adequate undergraduate program in psychology including college-level mathematics, statistics, experimental psychology, and some background in the biological, physical, and social sciences. Four letters of recommendation. Additional exam requirements/recommendations for international students: required—TOEFL (minimum score 80 iBT), IELTS (minimum score 6.5). *Application deadline:* For fall admission, 12/1 for domestic and international students. Applications are processed on a rolling basis. Application fee: $60 ($100 for international students). Electronic applications accepted. *Expenses:* Contact institution. *Financial support:* In 2019–20, 47 students received support, including 7 fellowships (averaging $10,000 per year), 2 research assistantships (averaging $10,400 per year), 5 teaching assistantships (averaging $4,000 per year); career-related internships or fieldwork, Federal Work-Study, scholarships/grants, and unspecified assistantships also available. Support available to part-time students. Financial award application deadline: 3/1; financial award applicants required to submit FAFSA. *Unit head:* Dr. Mary Coussons-Read, Department Chair, 719-255-3107, Fax: 719-255-4166, E-mail: mcousson@uccs.edu. *Application contact:* David Dubois, Graduate Student Advisor, 719-255-4500, Fax: 719-255-4166, E-mail: ddubois@uccs.edu.
Website: https://www.uccs.edu/psych/#graduate

University of Connecticut, Graduate School, College of Liberal Arts and Sciences, Department of Psychological Sciences, Storrs, CT 06269. Offers behavioral neuroscience (PhD); biopsychology (PhD); clinical psychology (MA, PhD); cognition and instruction (PhD); developmental psychology (MA, PhD); ecological psychology (PhD); experimental psychology (PhD); general psychology (MA, PhD); industrial/organizational psychology (PhD); language and cognition (PhD); neuroscience (PhD); social psychology (MA, PhD). *Accreditation:* APA. Terminal master's awarded for partial completion of doctoral program. *Degree requirements:* For master's, comprehensive exam; for doctorate, thesis/dissertation. *Entrance requirements:* For master's and doctorate, GRE General Test, GRE Subject Test. Additional exam requirements/recommendations for international students: required—TOEFL (minimum score 550 paper-based). Electronic applications accepted.

University of Dayton, Program in General Psychology, Dayton, OH 45469. Offers MA. *Degree requirements:* For master's, thesis. *Entrance requirements:* For master's, GRE General Test, GRE Subject Test (recommended), minimum undergraduate GPA of 2.7, 15 undergraduate course credits in psychology, psychology statistics, research methods. Additional exam requirements/recommendations for international students: required—TOEFL (minimum score 550 paper-based; 80 iBT); recommended—IELTS. Electronic applications accepted.

University of Delaware, College of Arts and Sciences, Department of Psychology, Newark, DE 19716. Offers behavioral neuroscience (PhD); clinical psychology (PhD); cognitive psychology (PhD); social psychology (PhD). *Accreditation:* APA. *Degree requirements:* For doctorate, thesis/dissertation. *Entrance requirements:* For doctorate, GRE General Test. Additional exam requirements/recommendations for international students: required—TOEFL (minimum score 600 paper-based). Electronic applications accepted.

University of Denver, Division of Arts, Humanities and Social Sciences, Department of Psychology, Denver, CO 80208. Offers affective/cognitive/social psychology (PhD); clinical child psychology (PhD); developmental psychology (PhD). *Accreditation:* APA. *Faculty:* 29 full-time (20 women). *Students:* 30 full-time (24 women); includes 8 minority (2 Asian, non-Hispanic/Latino; 5 Hispanic/Latino; 1 Two or more races, non-Hispanic/Latino), 2 international. Average age 27. 457 applicants, 4% accepted, 10 enrolled. In 2019, 5 doctorates awarded. Terminal master's awarded for partial completion of doctoral program. *Degree requirements:* For doctorate, comprehensive exam (for some programs), thesis/dissertation. *Entrance requirements:* For doctorate, GRE General Test, master's degree, transcripts, biographical statement, three letters of recommendation, resume, essay on diversity (for clinical child program only). Additional exam requirements/recommendations for international students: required—TOEFL (minimum score 550 paper-based; 80 iBT). *Application deadline:* For fall admission, 12/21 for domestic and international students. Application fee: $65. Electronic applications accepted. *Expenses:* Contact institution. *Financial support:* In 2019–20, 30 students received support, including 13 research assistantships with tuition reimbursements available (averaging $15,392 per year), 15 teaching assistantships with tuition reimbursements available (averaging $13,800 per year); Federal Work-Study, institutionally sponsored loans, scholarships/grants, and unspecified assistantships also available. Support available to part-time students. Financial award application deadline: 2/15; financial award applicants required to submit FAFSA. *Unit head:* Dr. Sarah Watamura, Associate Professor and Chair, 303-871-4130, E-mail: sarah.watamura@du.edu. *Application contact:* Paula Plank-Houghtaling, Graduate Program Administrator, 303-871-3803, E-mail: phoughta@du.edu.
Website: http://www.du.edu/ahss/psychology

University of Denver, Graduate School of Professional Psychology, Denver, CO 80208. Offers clinical psychology (Psy D); forensic psychology (MA); international disaster psychology (MA); sport and performance psychology (MA); sport coaching (MA); strength and conditioning and fitness coaching (Certificate). *Accreditation:* APA. *Faculty:* 23 full-time (15 women), 16 part-time/adjunct (9 women). *Students:* 243 full-time (192 women), 84 part-time (44 women); includes 95 minority (18 Black or African American, non-Hispanic/Latino; 1 American Indian or Alaska Native, non-Hispanic/Latino; 18 Asian, non-Hispanic/Latino; 46 Hispanic/Latino; 1 Native Hawaiian or other Pacific Islander, non-Hispanic/Latino; 11 Two or more races, non-Hispanic/Latino), 9 international. Average age 27. 953 applicants, 27% accepted, 137 enrolled. In 2019, 117 master's, 35 doctorates, 152 other advanced degrees awarded. *Degree requirements:* For master's, comprehensive exam (for some programs); for doctorate, comprehensive exam, community field placement, paper, clinical internship, complete 4 assessments, professional psychology clinic. *Entrance requirements:* For master's and doctorate, GRE General Test, psychology major/minor or 660 or higher on psychology subject GRE exam, transcripts, resume, two letters of recommendation, essay. Additional exam requirements/recommendations for international students: required—TOEFL (minimum score 550 paper-based; 80 iBT). *Application deadline:* For fall admission, 1/11 for domestic and international students. Application fee: $65. Electronic applications accepted. *Expenses:* Contact institution. *Financial support:* In 2019–20, 249 students received support, including 20 teaching assistantships with tuition reimbursements available (averaging $2,835 per year); career-related internships or fieldwork, Federal Work-Study, institutionally sponsored loans, scholarships/grants, unspecified assistantships, and clinical assistantships also available. Support available to part-time students. Financial award application deadline: 2/15; financial award applicants required to submit FAFSA. *Unit head:* Dr. Shelly Smith-Acuna, Dean, 303-871-3880, Fax: 303-871-4220, E-mail: shelly.smith-acuna@du.edu. *Application contact:* Julie Schellman, Director of Enrollment, 303-871-2908, E-mail: Julie.Schellman@du.edu.
Website: http://www.du.edu/gspp

University of Florida, Graduate School, College of Liberal Arts and Sciences, Department of Psychology, Gainesville, FL 32611. Offers counseling psychology (PhD);

psychology (MA, MS, PhD), including psychology (PhD), women's and gender studies (PhD); JD/PhD. *Degree requirements:* For master's, comprehensive exam, thesis or alternative; for doctorate, comprehensive exam, thesis/dissertation. *Entrance requirements:* For master's and doctorate, GRE General Test, minimum GPA of 3.0. Additional exam requirements/recommendations for international students: required—TOEFL (minimum score 550 paper-based; 80 iBT), IELTS (minimum score 6). Electronic applications accepted.

University of Florida, Graduate School, College of Public Health and Health Professions, Department of Clinical and Health Psychology, Gainesville, FL 32611. Offers clinical and translational science (PhD); psychology (MS). *Accreditation:* APA (one or more programs are accredited). *Degree requirements:* For doctorate, comprehensive exam, thesis/dissertation, pre-doctoral internship. *Entrance requirements:* For master's and doctorate, GRE General Test, minimum GPA of 3.0. Additional exam requirements/recommendations for international students: required—TOEFL (minimum score 550 paper-based; 80 iBT), IELTS (minimum score 6). Electronic applications accepted.

University of Georgia, Franklin College of Arts and Sciences, Department of Psychology, Athens, GA 30602. Offers PhD. *Accreditation:* APA. *Degree requirements:* For doctorate, one foreign language, thesis/dissertation. *Entrance requirements:* For doctorate, GRE General Test. Additional exam requirements/recommendations for international students: required—TOEFL. Electronic applications accepted.

University of Guelph, Office of Graduate and Postdoctoral Studies, College of Social and Applied Human Sciences, Department of Psychology, Guelph, ON N1G 2W1, Canada. Offers applied social psychology (MA, PhD); clinical psychology: applied development emphasis (PhD); clinical psychology: applied developmental emphasis (MA); industrial/organizational psychology (MA, PhD); neuroscience and applied cognitive science (MA, PhD). *Degree requirements:* For master's, thesis; for doctorate, comprehensive exam, thesis/dissertation. *Entrance requirements:* For master's, GRE General Test, GRE Subject Test, minimum B+ average during previous 2 years of course work; for doctorate, GRE General Test, GRE Subject Test, minimum A- average. Additional exam requirements/recommendations for international students: required—TOEFL (minimum score 89 iBT). Electronic applications accepted.

University of Hawaii at Manoa, Office of Graduate Education, College of Social Sciences, Department of Psychology, Honolulu, HI 96822. Offers clinical psychology (PhD); community and cultural psychology (PhD); community and culture (MA); psychology (MA, PhD, Graduate Certificate). *Accreditation:* APA (one or more programs are accredited). *Program availability:* Part-time. Terminal master's awarded for partial completion of doctoral program. *Degree requirements:* For master's, comprehensive exam, thesis; for doctorate, comprehensive exam, thesis/dissertation. *Entrance requirements:* For master's and doctorate, GRE General Test, GRE Subject Test. Additional exam requirements/recommendations for international students: required—TOEFL (minimum score 600 paper-based; 100 iBT), IELTS (minimum score 7).

University of Houston, College of Liberal Arts and Social Sciences, Department of Psychology, Houston, TX 77204. Offers clinical psychology (PhD); developmental psychology (PhD); industrial/organizational psychology (PhD); psychology (MA); social psychology (PhD). *Accreditation:* APA (one or more programs are accredited). *Degree requirements:* For master's, comprehensive exam, thesis; for doctorate, comprehensive exam, thesis/dissertation. *Entrance requirements:* For master's, GRE General Test, career statement, 3 letters of recommendation; for doctorate, GRE General Test, 3 letters of recommendation. Additional exam requirements/recommendations for international students: required—TOEFL (minimum score 550 paper-based; 79 iBT). Electronic applications accepted.

University of Houston–Clear Lake, School of Human Sciences and Humanities, Programs in Human Sciences, Houston, TX 77058-1002. Offers behavioral sciences (MA), including criminology, cross cultural studies, general psychology, sociology; clinical psychology (MA); criminology (MA); cross cultural studies (MA); family therapy (MA); fitness and human performance (MA); school psychology (MA). *Accreditation:* AAMFT/COAMFTE. *Program availability:* Part-time, evening/weekend, online learning. *Degree requirements:* For master's, thesis or alternative. *Entrance requirements:* For master's, GRE General Test. Additional exam requirements/recommendations for international students: required—TOEFL (minimum score 550 paper-based). Electronic applications accepted.

University of Houston–Victoria, School of Arts and Sciences, Program in Psychology, Victoria, TX 77901-4450. Offers counseling psychology (MA); forensic psychology (MA); school psychology (MA). *Program availability:* Part-time, evening/weekend, online learning. *Degree requirements:* For master's, project or thesis. *Entrance requirements:* For master's, GRE General Test. Additional exam requirements/recommendations for international students: required—TOEFL (minimum score 550 paper-based). Electronic applications accepted.

University of Idaho, College of Graduate Studies, College of Letters, Arts and Social Sciences, Department of Psychology and Communication Studies, Moscow, ID 83844-2282. Offers experimental psychology (PhD); psychology and communication studies (MS). *Faculty:* 9. *Students:* 19 full-time (7 women), 13 part-time (6 women). Average age 32. In 2019, 6 master's awarded. *Entrance requirements:* For master's, GRE, minimum GPA of 3.0. Additional exam requirements/recommendations for international students: required—TOEFL (minimum score 79 iBT). *Application deadline:* For fall admission, 7/30 for domestic students; for spring admission, 12/1 for domestic students. Applications are processed on a rolling basis. Application fee: $60. Electronic applications accepted. *Expenses:* Tuition, state resident: full-time $7753.80; part-time $502 per credit hour. Tuition, nonresident: full-time $26,990; part-time $1571 per credit hour. *Required fees:* $2122.20; $47 per credit hour. *Financial support:* Fellowships, research assistantships, and teaching assistantships available. Financial award applicants required to submit FAFSA. *Unit head:* Dr. Benjamin Barton, Chair, 208-885-6324, E-mail: psyc-comm@uidaho.edu. *Application contact:* Dr. Benjamin Barton, Chair, 208-885-6324, E-mail: psyc-comm@uidaho.edu.
Website: https://www.uidaho.edu/class/psychcomm

University of Illinois at Chicago, College of Liberal Arts and Sciences, Department of Psychology, Chicago, IL 60607-7128. Offers MA, PhD. *Accreditation:* APA. *Degree requirements:* For doctorate, thesis/dissertation, departmental qualifying exam. *Entrance requirements:* For doctorate, GRE General Test, minimum GPA of 2.75. Additional exam requirements/recommendations for international students: required—TOEFL. Electronic applications accepted. *Expenses:* Contact institution.

University of Illinois at Urbana-Champaign, Graduate College, College of Liberal Arts and Sciences, Department of Psychology, Champaign, IL 61820. Offers MA, MS, PhD. *Accreditation:* APA (one or more programs are accredited).

University of Indianapolis, Graduate Programs, College of Applied Behavioral Sciences, Indianapolis, IN 46227-3697. Offers addictions counseling (MA); clinical psychology (Psy D); mental health counseling (MA); psychology (MA); social work (MSW). *Accreditation:* APA. *Degree requirements:* For master's, practicum; for doctorate, comprehensive exam, thesis/dissertation, 1200 hours of clinical practicum, 2000-hour internship. *Entrance requirements:* For master's, GRE, 3 letters of recommendation; for doctorate, GRE, minimum GPA of 3.0, 18 hours of course work in psychology, 3 letters of recommendation. Additional exam requirements/recommendations for international students: required—TOEFL (minimum score 550 paper-based).

The University of Iowa, Graduate College, College of Education, Department of Psychological and Quantitative Foundations, Iowa City, IA 52242-1316. Offers counseling psychology (PhD); educational measurement and statistics (MA, PhD); educational psychology (MA, PhD); school psychology (PhD, Ed S). *Accreditation:* APA. *Degree requirements:* For master's, thesis optional, exam; for doctorate, comprehensive exam, thesis/dissertation; for Ed S, exam. *Entrance requirements:* For master's, doctorate, and Ed S, GRE General Test, minimum GPA of 3.0. Additional exam requirements/recommendations for international students: required—TOEFL (minimum score 550 paper-based; 81 iBT). Electronic applications accepted.

The University of Iowa, Graduate College, College of Liberal Arts and Sciences, Department of Psychology, Iowa City, IA 52242-1316. Offers MA, PhD. *Degree requirements:* For master's, thesis optional, exam; for doctorate, comprehensive exam, thesis/dissertation. *Entrance requirements:* For master's and doctorate, GRE General Test, minimum GPA of 3.0. Additional exam requirements/recommendations for international students: required—TOEFL (minimum score 550 paper-based; 81 iBT). Electronic applications accepted.

The University of Kansas, Graduate Studies, College of Liberal Arts and Sciences, Department of Applied Behavioral Science, Lawrence, KS 66045. Offers applied behavioral science (MA); behavioral psychology (PhD); community health and development (Graduate Certificate); PhD/MPH. *Program availability:* Part-time. *Students:* 42 full-time (29 women), 45 part-time (40 women); includes 10 minority (2 Black or African American, non-Hispanic/Latino; 3 Asian, non-Hispanic/Latino; 2 Hispanic/Latino; 1 Native Hawaiian or other Pacific Islander, non-Hispanic/Latino; 2 Two or more races, non-Hispanic/Latino). Average age 35. 110 applicants, 42% accepted, 32 enrolled. In 2019, 7 master's, 4 doctorates, 12 other advanced degrees awarded. Terminal master's awarded for partial completion of doctoral program. *Entrance requirements:* For master's, GRE, curriculum vitae; 3 letters of recommendation; personal statement; all academic transcripts; copies of pertinent written work, published or not, as well as presented papers; for doctorate, GRE, curriculum vitae; 3 letters of recommendation; personal statement; copies of pertinent written work, published or not, as well as presented papers. Additional exam requirements/recommendations for international students: required—TOEFL, IELTS. *Application deadline:* For fall admission, 12/15 priority date for domestic students, 12/15 for international students. Application fee: $65 ($85 for international students). Electronic applications accepted. *Expenses:* Tuition, state resident: full-time $9989. Tuition, nonresident: full-time $23,950. *International tuition:* $23,950 full-time. *Required fees:* $984; $81.99 per credit hour. Tuition and fees vary according to course load, campus/location and program. *Financial support:* Fellowships, research assistantships, teaching assistantships, career-related internships or fieldwork, traineeships, tuition waivers (full), and unspecified assistantships available. Financial award application deadline: 12/15; financial award applicants required to submit CSS PROFILE or FAFSA. *Unit head:* Dr. Florence DiGennaro Reed, Chairperson, 785-864-0521, E-mail: fdreed@ku.edu. *Application contact:* Brittney Tyler-Milholland, Graduate Representative, 785-864-3625, E-mail: tylermil@ku.edu.
Website: http://absc.ku.edu

The University of Kansas, Graduate Studies, College of Liberal Arts and Sciences, Department of Psychology, Lawrence, KS 66045. Offers clinical psychology (MA, PhD); cognitive and brain sciences (MA, PhD); developmental psychology (MA, PhD); quantitative psychology (PhD); social psychology (MA, PhD). *Accreditation:* APA (one or more programs are accredited). *Program availability:* Part-time. *Students:* 72 full-time (51 women), 1 (woman) part-time; includes 16 minority (6 Black or African American, non-Hispanic/Latino; 3 Asian, non-Hispanic/Latino; 1 Hispanic/Latino; 6 Two or more races, non-Hispanic/Latino), 9 international. Average age 27. 343 applicants, 9% accepted, 17 enrolled. In 2019, 15 master's, 14 doctorates awarded. Terminal master's awarded for partial completion of doctoral program. *Entrance requirements:* For doctorate, GRE General Test, three letters of recommendation, resume/curriculum vitae, statement of purpose/personal statement, writing sample. Additional exam requirements/recommendations for international students: required—TOEFL, IELTS. *Application deadline:* For fall admission, 12/1 for domestic and international students. Application fee: $65 ($85 for international students). Electronic applications accepted. *Expenses:* Tuition, state resident: full-time $9989. Tuition, nonresident: full-time $23,950. *International tuition:* $23,950 full-time. *Required fees:* $984; $81.99 per credit hour. Tuition and fees vary according to course load, campus/location and program. *Financial support:* Fellowships, research assistantships, teaching assistantships, career-related internships or fieldwork, Federal Work-Study, scholarships/grants, health care benefits, and unspecified assistantships available. Financial award application deadline: 12/1; financial award applicants required to submit FAFSA. *Unit head:* Michael Vitevitch, Chair, 785-864-9312, E-mail: mvitevit@ku.edu. *Application contact:* Kirsten Hermreck, Graduate Admissions Contact, 785-864-4195, E-mail: psycgrad@ku.edu.
Website: http://www.psych.ku.edu/

University of Kentucky, Graduate School, College of Arts and Sciences, Program in Psychology, Lexington, KY 40506-0032. Offers MA, PhD. *Accreditation:* APA (one or more programs are accredited). *Degree requirements:* For master's, comprehensive exam, thesis; for doctorate, comprehensive exam, thesis/dissertation. *Entrance requirements:* For master's, GRE General Test, minimum undergraduate GPA of 2.75; for doctorate, GRE General Test, minimum graduate GPA of 3.0. Additional exam requirements/recommendations for international students: required—TOEFL (minimum score 550 paper-based). Electronic applications accepted.

University of La Verne, College of Arts and Sciences, Department of Psychology, La Verne, CA 91750-4443. Offers clinical psychology (Psy D); marriage and family therapy (MFT, MS). *Accreditation:* APA (one or more programs are accredited). *Program availability:* Part-time. *Degree requirements:* For master's, thesis, competency exam, fieldwork, culminating project; for doctorate, thesis/dissertation, clinical practica, clinical internship, competency exams, personal psychotherapy. *Entrance requirements:* For master's, minimum undergraduate GPA of 3.0, 5- to 7-page statement of purpose and autobiography, 3 letters of recommendation, interview, curriculum vitae; for doctorate, GRE, minimum GPA of 3.1, statement of professional goals and aspirations, 3 recommendations, interview, curriculum vitae. Additional exam requirements/recommendations for international students: required—TOEFL (minimum score 600 paper-based; 100 iBT); recommended—IELTS (minimum score 6.5). *Expenses:* Contact institution.

University of Lethbridge, School of Graduate Studies, Lethbridge, AB T1K 3M4, Canada. Offers addictions counseling (M Sc); agricultural biotechnology (M Sc); agricultural studies (M Sc, MA); anthropology (MA); archaeology (M Sc, MA); art (MA, MFA); biochemistry (M Sc); biological sciences (M Sc); biomolecular science (PhD); biosystems and biodiversity (PhD); Canadian studies (MA); chemistry (M Sc); computer science (M Sc); computer science and geographical information science (M Sc); counseling (MC); counseling psychology (M Ed); dramatic arts (MA); earth, space, and physical science (PhD); economics (MA); education (MA, PhD); educational leadership (M Ed); English (MA); environmental science (M Sc); evolution and behavior (PhD); exercise science (M Sc); French (MA); French/German (MA); French/Spanish (MA); general education (M Ed); geography (M Sc, MA); German (MA); health sciences (M Sc); individualized multidisciplinary (M Sc, MA); kinesiology (M Sc, MA); management (M Sc), including accounting, finance, human resource management and labor relations, information systems, international management, marketing, policy and strategy; mathematics (M Sc); music (M Mus, MA); Native American studies (MA); neuroscience (M Sc, PhD); new media (MA, MFA); nursing (M Sc, MN); philosophy (MA); physics (M Sc); political science (MA); psychology (M Sc, MA); religious studies (MA); sociology (MA); theatre and dramatic arts (MFA); theoretical and computational science (PhD); urban and regional studies (MA); women and gender studies (MA). *Program availability:* Part-time, evening/weekend. *Degree requirements:* For master's, thesis (for some programs); for doctorate, comprehensive exam, thesis/dissertation. *Entrance requirements:* For master's, GMAT (for M Sc in management), bachelor's degree in related field, minimum GPA of 3.0 during previous 20 graded semester courses, 2 years' teaching or related experience (M Ed); for doctorate, master's degree, minimum graduate GPA of 3.5. Additional exam requirements/recommendations for international students: required—TOEFL (minimum score 580 paper-based; 93 iBT). Electronic applications accepted.

University of Louisiana at Lafayette, College of Liberal Arts, Department of Psychology, Lafayette, LA 70504. Offers psychology (MS). *Program availability:* Part-time. *Degree requirements:* For master's, comprehensive exam, thesis or alternative. *Entrance requirements:* For master's, GRE General Test, minimum GPA of 3.0. Electronic applications accepted. *Expenses: Tuition, area resident:* Full-time $5511; part-time $1630 per credit hour. Tuition, state resident: full-time $5511; part-time $1630 per credit hour. Tuition, nonresident: full-time $19,239; part-time $2409 per credit hour. *Required fees:* $46,637.

University of Louisiana at Monroe, Graduate School, College of Business and Social Sciences, Department of Psychology, Monroe, LA 71209-0001. Offers forensic psychology (MS); general psychology (MS); psychometrics (MS). *Program availability:* Part-time, evening/weekend, online learning. *Faculty:* 5 full-time (1 woman). *Students:* 71 full-time (67 women), 19 part-time (18 women); includes 38 minority (26 Black or African American, non-Hispanic/Latino; 2 American Indian or Alaska Native, non-Hispanic/Latino; 1 Asian, non-Hispanic/Latino; 3 Hispanic/Latino; 6 Two or more races, non-Hispanic/Latino), 3 international. Average age 28. 98 applicants, 55% accepted, 41 enrolled. In 2019, 20 master's awarded. *Degree requirements:* For master's, thesis optional. *Entrance requirements:* For master's, GRE General Test, minimum GPA of 2.75. Additional exam requirements/recommendations for international students: required—TOEFL (minimum score 500 paper-based; 61 iBT); recommended—IELTS (minimum score 5.5). *Application deadline:* For fall admission, 8/1 for domestic students, 6/1 for international students; for spring admission, 1/1 for domestic students, 11/1 for international students; for summer admission, 6/1 for domestic students, 3/1 for international students. Applications are processed on a rolling basis. Application fee: $40. Electronic applications accepted. *Expenses: Tuition, area resident:* Full-time $6489. Tuition, state resident: full-time $6489. Tuition, nonresident: full-time $18,989. *Required fees:* $2748. Tuition and fees vary according to course load and program. *Financial support:* In 2019–20, 30 students received support. Research assistantships with full tuition reimbursements available, career-related internships or fieldwork, Federal Work-Study, scholarships/grants, and unspecified assistantships available. Financial award application deadline: 2/15; financial award applicants required to submit FAFSA. *Unit head:* Dr. Pamela Saulsberry, Director, 318-342-1445, E-mail: saulsberry@ulm.edu. *Application contact:* Dr. Jack Palmer, Graduate Coordinator, 318-342-1345, E-mail: palmer@ulm.edu.
Website: http://www.ulm.edu/psychology

University of Louisville, Graduate School, College of Arts and Sciences, Department of Psychological and Brain Sciences, Louisville, KY 40292-0001. Offers clinical psychology (PhD); experimental psychology (PhD), including cognition and development, vision and hearing. *Accreditation:* APA. *Program availability:* Part-time. *Faculty:* 24 full-time (14 women), 9 part-time/adjunct (5 women). *Students:* 50 full-time (42 women), 1 (woman) part-time; includes 5 minority (1 Black or African American, non-Hispanic/Latino; 2 Hispanic/Latino; 2 Two or more races, non-Hispanic/Latino), 6 international. Average age 29. 144 applicants, 1% accepted, 2 enrolled. In 2019, 14 doctorates awarded. *Degree requirements:* For doctorate, comprehensive exam, thesis/dissertation, coursework; internship for clinical. *Entrance requirements:* For doctorate, GRE General Test, Three letters of reference, official transcripts. Additional exam requirements/recommendations for international students: required—TOEFL (minimum score 550 paper-based; 79 iBT), IELTS can be used in place of TOEFL; recommended—IELTS (minimum score 6.5). *Application deadline:* For fall admission, 12/1 for domestic and international students. Applications are processed on a rolling basis. Application fee: $65. Electronic applications accepted. *Expenses: Tuition, area resident:* Full-time $13,000; part-time $723 per credit hour. Tuition, state resident: full-time $13,000; part-time $723 per credit hour. Tuition, nonresident: full-time $27,114; part-time $1507 per credit hour. *International tuition:* $27,114 full-time. *Required fees:* $196. Tuition and fees vary according to program and reciprocity agreements. *Financial support:* In 2019–20, 49 students received support, including 8 fellowships with full tuition reimbursements available (averaging $22,000 per year), 3 research assistantships with full tuition reimbursements available (averaging $22,000 per year), 30 teaching assistantships with full tuition reimbursements available (averaging $22,000 per year); scholarships/grants, health care benefits, and unspecified assistantships also available. Financial award application deadline: 12/1. *Unit head:* Dr. Benjamin Mast, Professor and Chair, 502-852-3280, Fax: 502-852-8904, E-mail: b.mast@louisville.edu. *Application contact:* Maggie Leahy, Administrative Assistant, 502-852-4364, Fax: 502-852-8904, E-mail: maggie.leahy@louisville.edu.
Website: http://louisville.edu/psychology

University of Maine, Graduate School, College of Liberal Arts and Sciences, Department of Psychology, Orono, ME 04469. Offers psychological sciences (PhD). *Accreditation:* APA (one or more programs are accredited). *Faculty:* 6 full-time (5 women), 6 part-time/adjunct (4 women). *Students:* 26 full-time (24 women); includes 5 minority (1 Asian, non-Hispanic/Latino; 4 Hispanic/Latino). Average age 28. 140 applicants, 6% accepted, 7 enrolled. In 2019, 4 master's, 4 doctorates awarded. Terminal master's awarded for partial completion of doctoral program. *Degree requirements:* For master's, thesis; for doctorate, comprehensive exam, thesis/dissertation. *Entrance requirements:* For master's and doctorate, GRE General Test, GRE Subject Test. Additional exam requirements/recommendations for international students: required—TOEFL (minimum score 80 iBT), IELTS (minimum score 6.5), PTE (minimum score 60). *Application deadline:* For fall admission, 12/1 for domestic and international students. Applications are processed on a rolling basis. Application fee: $65. Electronic applications accepted. *Expenses: Tuition, area resident:* Full-time $8100; part-time $450 per credit hour. Tuition, state resident: full-time $8100; part-time $450 per credit hour. Tuition, nonresident: full-time $26,388; part-time $1466 per credit hour. *International tuition:* $26,388 full-time. *Required fees:* $1257; $278 per semester. Tuition and fees vary according to course load. *Financial support:* In 2019–20, 24 students received support, including 1 fellowship with full tuition reimbursement available (averaging $34,000 per year), 1 research assistantship with full tuition

reimbursement available (averaging $17,000 per year), 17 teaching assistantships with full tuition reimbursements available (averaging $17,000 per year); Federal Work-Study, institutionally sponsored loans, tuition waivers (full and partial), and unspecified assistantships also available. Financial award application deadline: 3/1; financial award applicants required to submit FAFSA. *Unit head:* Dr. Michael Robbins, Chair, 207-581-2051, Fax: 207-581-6128. *Application contact:* Scott G. Delcourt, Assistant Vice President for Graduate Studies and Senior Associate Dean, 207-581-3291, Fax: 207-581-3232, E-mail: graduate@maine.edu.
Website: https://umaine.edu/psychology/clinicalpsychology/

The University of Manchester, School of Psychological Sciences, Manchester, United Kingdom. Offers audiology (M Phil, PhD); clinical psychology (M Phil, PhD, Psy D); psychology (M Phil, PhD).

University of Manitoba, Faculty of Graduate Studies, Faculty of Arts, Department of Psychology, Winnipeg, MB R3T 2N2, Canada. Offers clinical psychology (PhD); psychology (MA, PhD); school psychology (MA). *Degree requirements:* For master's, thesis; for doctorate, one foreign language, thesis/dissertation. *Entrance requirements:* For master's and doctorate, GRE General Test.

University of Maryland, Baltimore County, The Graduate School, College of Arts, Humanities and Social Sciences, Department of Psychology, Baltimore, MD 21250. Offers applied developmental psychology (PhD); human services psychology (MA, PhD), including applied behavioral analysis (MA), human services psychology (PhD); industrial/organizational psychology (MPS). *Accreditation:* APA (one or more programs are accredited). *Faculty:* 25 full-time (14 women), 22 part-time/adjunct (8 women). *Students:* 94 full-time (77 women), 175 part-time (126 women); includes 110 minority (58 Black or African American, non-Hispanic/Latino; 22 Asian, non-Hispanic/Latino; 20 Hispanic/Latino; 1 Native Hawaiian or other Pacific Islander, non-Hispanic/Latino; 9 Two or more races, non-Hispanic/Latino), 13 international. Average age 28. 361 applicants, 37% accepted, 85 enrolled. In 2019, 72 master's, 11 doctorates awarded. Terminal master's awarded for partial completion of doctoral program. *Degree requirements:* For master's, thesis or alternative; for doctorate, comprehensive exam, thesis/dissertation. *Entrance requirements:* For master's, GRE General Test; for doctorate, GRE General Test, GRE Subject Test, minimum GPA of 3.0. Additional exam requirements/recommendations for international students: required—TOEFL. *Application deadline:* For fall admission, 12/1 for domestic and international students. Application fee: $50. Electronic applications accepted. *Expenses:* $14,382 per year. *Financial support:* In 2019–20, 54 students received support, including 6 fellowships with full tuition reimbursements available (averaging $22,000 per year), 23 research assistantships with full tuition reimbursements available (averaging $20,400 per year), 25 teaching assistantships with full tuition reimbursements available; career-related internships or fieldwork, Federal Work-Study, health care benefits, and unspecified assistantships also available. Financial award application deadline: 3/1; financial award applicants required to submit FAFSA. *Unit head:* Dr. Christopher Murphy, Chair, 410-455-2415, Fax: 410-455-1055, E-mail: chmurphy@umbc.edu. *Application contact:* Beverly McDougall, Program Management Specialist, 410-455-2567, Fax: 410-455-1055, E-mail: psycdept@umbc.edu.
Website: http://psychology.umbc.edu/

University of Maryland, College Park, Academic Affairs, College of Behavioral and Social Sciences, Department of Psychology, College Park, MD 20742. Offers clinical psychology (PhD); developmental psychology (PhD); experimental psychology (PhD); industrial psychology (MA, MS, PhD); social psychology (PhD). *Accreditation:* APA (one or more programs are accredited). *Degree requirements:* For master's, thesis; for doctorate, variable foreign language requirement, comprehensive exam, thesis/dissertation. *Entrance requirements:* For master's and doctorate, GRE General Test, GRE Subject Test, minimum GPA of 3.5, research and/or work experience, 3 letters of recommendation. Electronic applications accepted.

University of Massachusetts Amherst, Graduate School, College of Natural Sciences, Department of Psychological and Brain Sciences, Amherst, MA 01003. Offers clinical psychology (MS, PhD); cognitive psychology (MS, PhD); developmental science (MS, PhD); psychology of peace and violence (MS, PhD); social psychology (MS, PhD). *Accreditation:* APA (one or more programs are accredited). Terminal master's awarded for partial completion of doctoral program. *Degree requirements:* For master's, thesis; for doctorate, comprehensive exam, thesis/dissertation. *Entrance requirements:* For master's and doctorate, GRE General Test, 3 letters of recommendation. Additional exam requirements/recommendations for international students: required—TOEFL (minimum score 550 paper-based; 80 iBT), IELTS (minimum score 6.5). Electronic applications accepted.

University of Massachusetts Dartmouth, Graduate School, College of Arts and Sciences, Department of Psychology, North Dartmouth, MA 02747-2300. Offers autism studies (Graduate Certificate); psychology - applied behavioral analysis (MA, Post-Master's Certificate); psychology - clinical (MA); psychology - research (MA). *Program availability:* Part-time. *Faculty:* 18 full-time (11 women), 7 part-time/adjunct (4 women). *Students:* 40 full-time (32 women), 54 part-time (47 women); includes 16 minority (5 Black or African American, non-Hispanic/Latino; 2 Asian, non-Hispanic/Latino; 5 Hispanic/Latino; 4 Two or more races, non-Hispanic/Latino), 3 international. Average age 29. 97 applicants, 58% accepted, 34 enrolled. In 2019, 26 master's, 1 other advanced degree awarded. *Degree requirements:* For master's, thesis (for some programs), thesis. *Entrance requirements:* For master's, GRE (recommended), statement of purpose (minimum of 300 words), resume, 3 letters of recommendation, official transcripts; for other advanced degree, statement of purpose (minimum of 300 words), resume, 3 letters of recommendation, official transcripts. Additional exam requirements/recommendations for international students: required—TOEFL (minimum score 80 iBT). *Application deadline:* For fall admission, 4/15 for domestic students, 3/15 for international students. Application fee: $60. Electronic applications accepted. *Expenses: Tuition, area resident:* Full-time $16,390; part-time $682.92 per credit. Tuition, state resident: full-time $16,390; part-time $682.92 per credit. Tuition, nonresident: full-time $29,578; part-time $1232.42 per credit. *Required fees:* $575. *Financial support:* In 2019–20, 1 research assistantship (averaging $9,000 per year), 2 teaching assistantships (averaging $14,000 per year) were awarded; tuition waivers (full and partial) and unspecified assistantships also available. Financial award application deadline: 3/1; financial award applicants required to submit FAFSA. *Unit head:* R. Thomas Boone, Graduate Program Director, Psychology, 508-999-8440, E-mail: tboone@umassd.edu. *Application contact:* Scott Webster, Director of Graduate Studies and Admissions, 508-999-8604, Fax: 508-999-8183, E-mail: graduate@umassd.edu.
Website: http://www.umassd.edu/cas/psychology/graduate-programs

University of Massachusetts Lowell, College of Fine Arts, Humanities and Social Sciences, Department of Psychology, Lowell, MA 01854. Offers community social psychology (MA). *Program availability:* Part-time. *Degree requirements:* For master's, thesis optional. *Entrance requirements:* For master's, GRE General Test or MAT. Electronic applications accepted.

University of Memphis, Graduate School, College of Arts and Sciences, Department of Psychology, Memphis, TN 38152-3230. Offers clinical psychology (PhD); experimental psychology (PhD); general psychology (MS); school psychology (MA, PhD, Ed S). *Accreditation:* APA. *Students:* 102 full-time (74 women), 24 part-time (18 women); includes 31 minority (13 Black or African American, non-Hispanic/Latino; 6 Asian, non-Hispanic/Latino; 6 Hispanic/Latino; 6 Two or more races, non-Hispanic/Latino), 6 international. Average age 28. 57 applicants, 84% accepted, 32 enrolled. In 2019, 21 master's, 12 doctorates, 6 other advanced degrees awarded. *Degree requirements:* For master's, comprehensive exam (for some programs), thesis (for some programs), 37 credit hours (for MA); 33 credit hours with thesis or 36 with exam (for MS); for doctorate, comprehensive exam, thesis/dissertation, 80 semester hours, major area paper; 1-year placement and 1-year internship (for clinical psychology); internship (for school psychology); for Ed S, 30 credit hours. *Entrance requirements:* For master's, GRE, 3 letters of recommendation, 18 undergraduate hours in psychology; for doctorate, GRE, minimum GPA of 2.75, 18 hours of undergraduate psychology courses, transcripts, personal statement, 3 letters of recommendation, interview; for Ed S, GRE, minimum GPA of 2.75, 18 hours of undergraduate psychology courses, 3 letters of recommendation. Additional exam requirements/recommendations for international students: required—TOEFL (minimum score 550 paper-based; 79 iBT). *Application deadline:* For fall admission, 12/5 for domestic students. Applications are processed on a rolling basis. Application fee: $35 ($60 for international students). Electronic applications accepted. *Expenses: Tuition, area resident:* Full-time $9216; part-time $512 per credit hour. Tuition, state resident: full-time $9216; part-time $512 per credit hour. Tuition, nonresident: full-time $12,672; part-time $704 per credit hour. *International tuition:* $16,128 full-time. *Required fees:* $1530; $85 per credit hour. Tuition and fees vary according to program. *Financial support:* Fellowships with full tuition reimbursements, research assistantships with full tuition reimbursements, teaching assistantships with full tuition reimbursements, Federal Work-Study, scholarships/grants, tuition waivers (partial), and unspecified assistantships available. Financial award application deadline: 2/1; financial award applicants required to submit FAFSA. *Unit head:* Dr. Randy Floyd, Chair, 901-678-2146, Fax: 901-678-2579, E-mail: rgfloyd@memphis.edu. *Application contact:* Dr. Robert Cohen, Graduate Programs Coordinator, 901-678-4679, Fax: 901-678-2579, E-mail: rcohen@memphis.edu.
Website: http://www.memphis.edu/psychology

University of Miami, Graduate School, College of Arts and Sciences, Department of Psychology, Coral Gables, FL 33124. Offers adult clinical (PhD); behavioral neuroscience (PhD); child clinical (PhD); developmental psychology (PhD); health clinical (PhD); psychology (MS). *Accreditation:* APA (one or more programs are accredited). *Degree requirements:* For doctorate, comprehensive exam, thesis/dissertation. *Entrance requirements:* For doctorate, GRE General Test, minimum GPA of 3.5. Additional exam requirements/recommendations for international students: required—TOEFL. Electronic applications accepted.

University of Michigan, Rackham Graduate School, College of Literature, Science, and the Arts, Department of Psychology, Ann Arbor, MI 48109. Offers biopsychology (PhD); clinical science (PhD); cognition and cognitive neuroscience (PhD); developmental psychology (PhD); personality and social contexts (PhD); social psychology (PhD). *Accreditation:* APA. Terminal master's awarded for partial completion of doctoral program. *Degree requirements:* For doctorate, comprehensive exam, thesis/dissertation, oral defense of dissertation, preliminary exam. *Entrance requirements:* For doctorate, GRE (Biopsychology, Cognition and Cognitive Neuroscience, Developmental, Social, and Clinical); GRE Subject Test also strongly recommended (Clinical); GRE not required (Personality and Social Contexts). Additional exam requirements/recommendations for international students: required—TOEFL. Electronic applications accepted.

University of Michigan, Rackham Graduate School, College of Literature, Science, and the Arts, Department of Women's Studies, Ann Arbor, MI 48109. Offers English and women's studies (PhD); history and women's studies (PhD); LGBTQ studies (Certificate); psychology and women's studies (PhD); women's studies (Certificate). *Degree requirements:* For doctorate, variable foreign language requirement, comprehensive exam (for some programs), thesis/dissertation. *Entrance requirements:* For doctorate, previous undergraduate coursework in women's studies. Electronic applications accepted.

University of Michigan, Rackham Graduate School, Combined Program in Education and Psychology, Ann Arbor, MI 48109. Offers PhD. *Accreditation:* TEAC. *Degree requirements:* For doctorate, thesis/dissertation, independent research project, preliminary exam, oral defense of dissertation. *Entrance requirements:* For doctorate, GRE General Test with Analytical Writing Test. Additional exam requirements/recommendations for international students: required—TOEFL (minimum score 600 paper-based; 100 iBT). Electronic applications accepted. *Expenses:* Contact institution.

University of Michigan, School of Social Work, Interdisciplinary PhD Program in Social Work and Social Science, Ann Arbor, MI 48109. Offers social work and anthropology (PhD); social work and economics (PhD); social work and political science (PhD); social work and psychology (PhD); social work and sociology (PhD). *Degree requirements:* For doctorate, thesis/dissertation, oral defense of dissertation, preliminary exam. *Entrance requirements:* For doctorate, GRE General Test. Additional exam requirements/recommendations for international students: required—TOEFL (minimum score 620 paper-based, 88 iBT) or IELTS. Electronic applications accepted. *Expenses:* Contact institution.

University of Minnesota, Twin Cities Campus, Graduate School, College of Liberal Arts, Department of Psychology, Minneapolis, MN 55455-0213. Offers biological psychopathology (PhD); clinical psychology (PhD); cognitive and biological psychology (PhD); counseling psychology (PhD); industrial/organizational psychology (PhD); personality, individual differences, and behavior genetics (PhD); quantitative/psychometric methods (PhD); school psychology (PhD); social psychology (PhD). *Accreditation:* APA. *Degree requirements:* For doctorate, comprehensive exam, thesis/dissertation. *Entrance requirements:* For doctorate, GRE General Test, GRE Subject Test (recommended), 12 credits of upper-level psychology courses, including a course in statistics or psychological measurement. Additional exam requirements/recommendations for international students: required—TOEFL (minimum score 79 iBT).

University of Missouri, Office of Research and Graduate Studies, College of Arts and Science, Department of Psychological Sciences, Columbia, MO 65211. Offers MA, PhD, Certificate. *Accreditation:* APA (one or more programs are accredited). Terminal master's awarded for partial completion of doctoral program. *Entrance requirements:* For master's, GRE General Test, minimum GPA of 3.0; for doctorate, GRE General Test; GRE Subject Test (strongly recommended), minimum GPA of 3.0.

University of Missouri–Kansas City, College of Arts and Sciences, Department of Psychology, Kansas City, MO 64110-2499. Offers community psychology (PhD). *Accreditation:* APA. Terminal master's awarded for partial completion of doctoral program. *Degree requirements:* For master's, thesis; for doctorate, comprehensive exam, thesis/dissertation, residency. *Entrance requirements:* For master's, GRE, minimum GPA of 3.5, letter of recommendation; for doctorate, GRE, minimum GPA of 3.25. Additional exam requirements/recommendations for international students: required—TOEFL (minimum score 550 paper-based; 80 iBT). Electronic applications accepted.

Psychology—General

University of Missouri–St. Louis, College of Arts and Sciences, Department of Psychological Sciences, St. Louis, MO 63121. Offers behavioral neuroscience (MA, PhD); clinical psychology (PhD); trauma studies (Certificate). *Accreditation:* APA (one or more programs are accredited). *Program availability:* Evening/weekend. Terminal master's awarded for partial completion of doctoral program. *Degree requirements:* For master's, thesis; for doctorate, thesis/dissertation. *Entrance requirements:* For master's, GRE General Test, 3 letters of recommendation; for doctorate, GRE General Test, GRE Subject Test, 3 letters of recommendation. Additional exam requirements/recommendations for international students: required—TOEFL (minimum score 550 paper-based; 79 iBT), IELTS (minimum score 6.5). Electronic applications accepted. *Expenses: Tuition, area resident:* Full-time $9005.40; part-time $6003.60 per credit hour. Tuition, state resident: full-time $9005.40; part-time $6003.60 per credit hour. Tuition, nonresident: full-time $22,108; part-time $14,738.40 per credit hour. *International tuition:* $22,108 full-time. Tuition and fees vary according to course load.

University of Montana, Graduate School, College of Humanities and Sciences, Department of Psychology, Missoula, MT 59812. Offers clinical psychology (PhD); experimental psychology (PhD), including animal behavior psychology, developmental psychology; school psychology (MA, PhD, Ed S). *Accreditation:* APA (one or more programs are accredited). Terminal master's awarded for partial completion of doctoral program. *Degree requirements:* For master's, thesis; for doctorate, thesis/dissertation. *Entrance requirements:* For master's, doctorate, and Ed S, GRE General Test. Additional exam requirements/recommendations for international students: required—TOEFL.

University of Nebraska at Omaha, Graduate Studies, College of Arts and Sciences, Department of Psychology, Omaha, NE 68182. Offers applied behavior analysis (Certificate); human resources and training (Certificate); industrial/organizational psychology (MS); psychology (MA, PhD); school psychology (MS, Ed S). *Program availability:* Part-time. *Degree requirements:* For master's, comprehensive exam, thesis (for some programs); for doctorate, comprehensive exam, thesis/dissertation. *Entrance requirements:* For master's and doctorate, GRE, minimum GPA of 3.0, official transcripts, 3 letters of recommendation, statement of purpose, writing sample, resume. Additional exam requirements/recommendations for international students: required—TOEFL, IELTS, PTE. Electronic applications accepted.

University of Nebraska–Lincoln, Graduate College, College of Arts and Sciences, Department of Psychology, Lincoln, NE 68588. Offers biopsychology (PhD); clinical psychology (PhD); cognitive psychology (PhD); developmental psychology (PhD); psychology (MA); social/personality psychology (PhD); JD/MA; JD/PhD. *Accreditation:* APA (one or more programs are accredited). *Degree requirements:* For master's, thesis optional; for doctorate, comprehensive exam, thesis/dissertation. *Entrance requirements:* For master's and doctorate, GRE General Test. Additional exam requirements/recommendations for international students: required—TOEFL (minimum score 550 paper-based). Electronic applications accepted.

University of Nevada, Las Vegas, Graduate College, College of Liberal Arts, Department of Psychology, Las Vegas, NV 89154-5030. Offers quantitative psychology (Certificate). *Program availability:* Part-time. *Faculty:* 18 full-time (7 women), 3 part-time/adjunct (2 women). *Students:* 68 full-time (50 women), 16 part-time (11 women); includes 26 minority (2 Black or African American, non-Hispanic/Latino; 1 American Indian or Alaska Native, non-Hispanic/Latino; 4 Asian, non-Hispanic/Latino; 13 Hispanic/Latino; 6 Two or more races, non-Hispanic/Latino), 5 international. Average age 28. 149 applicants, 17% accepted, 18 enrolled. In 2019, 14 master's, 9 doctorates awarded. *Degree requirements:* For doctorate, comprehensive exam, thesis/dissertation, oral defense of dissertation. *Entrance requirements:* For doctorate, GRE General and Subject Tests, bachelor's degree with minimum GPA of 3.2 or master's degree with minimum GPA of 3.5; 3 recommendation letters; statement of purpose; interview. Additional exam requirements/recommendations for international students: required—TOEFL (minimum score 550 paper-based; 80 iBT), IELTS (minimum score 7). *Application deadline:* For fall admission, 12/1 for domestic students, 10/1 for international students. Application fee: $60 ($95 for international students). Electronic applications accepted. *Expenses:* Contact institution. *Financial support:* In 2019–20, 66 students received support, including 4 fellowships with full tuition reimbursements available (averaging $22,500 per year), 45 research assistantships with full tuition reimbursements available (averaging $15,800 per year), 17 teaching assistantships with full tuition reimbursements available (averaging $15,500 per year); institutionally sponsored loans, scholarships/grants, health care benefits, and unspecified assistantships also available. Financial award application deadline: 3/15; financial award applicants required to submit FAFSA. *Unit head:* Dr. Christopher Kearney, Chair/Professor, 702-895-0183, Fax: 702-895-0195, E-mail: psychology.chair@unlv.edu. *Application contact:* Dr. Jennifer Rennels, Graduate Coordinator, 702-895-0648, Fax: 702-895-0195, E-mail: psychology.gradcoord@unlv.edu.
Website: http://psychology.unlv.edu/

University of Nevada, Reno, Graduate School, College of Liberal Arts, Department of Psychology, Reno, NV 89557. Offers behavior analysis (MA, PhD); clinical psychology (MA, PhD); cognitive brain science (MA, PhD). *Accreditation:* APA (one or more programs are accredited). Terminal master's awarded for partial completion of doctoral program. *Degree requirements:* For master's, thesis optional; for doctorate, thesis/dissertation. *Entrance requirements:* For master's, GRE General Test, GRE Subject Test, minimum GPA of 2.75; for doctorate, GRE General Test, GRE Subject Test, minimum GPA of 3.0. Additional exam requirements/recommendations for international students: required—TOEFL (minimum score 500 paper-based; 61 iBT), IELTS (minimum score 6). Electronic applications accepted.

University of New Brunswick Saint John, Department of Psychology, Saint John, NE E2L 4L5, Canada. Offers clinical psychology (PhD); experimental psychology (MA, PhD). *Program availability:* Part-time. *Faculty:* 10 full-time (6 women). *Students:* 12 full-time (8 women), 1 part-time (0 women), 1 international. In 2019, 4 master's awarded. *Degree requirements:* For master's, thesis. *Entrance requirements:* For master's, GRE General and Subject Tests, honors thesis; minimum GPA of 3.7. Additional exam requirements/recommendations for international students: required—TOEFL (minimum score 550 paper-based), TWE. *Application deadline:* For fall admission, 1/15 priority date for domestic students. Application fee: $50. Electronic applications accepted. *Expenses: Tuition, area resident:* Full-time $6975 Canadian dollars; part-time $3423 Canadian dollars per year. Tuition, state resident: full-time $6975 Canadian dollars; part-time $3423 Canadian dollars per year. Tuition, Canadian resident: full-time $6975 Canadian dollars; part-time $3423 Canadian dollars per year. *International tuition:* $12,435 Canadian dollars full-time. *Required fees:* $132.75 Canadian dollars; $92.25 Canadian dollars per term. Tuition and fees vary according to campus/location, program and student level. *Financial support:* Fellowships, research assistantships, teaching assistantships, and unspecified assistantships available. Support available to part-time students. Financial award application deadline: 2/1. *Unit head:* Dr. Mary Ann Campbell, Director of Graduate Studies, 506-648 5969, Fax: 506-648-5780, E-mail: mcampbel@unb.ca. *Application contact:* Mary Miernicki, Administrative Assistant, 506-648-5640, Fax: 506-648-5780, E-mail: Mary.Miernicki@unb.ca.
Website: http://go.unb.ca/gradprograms

University of New Hampshire, Graduate School, College of Liberal Arts, Department of Psychology, Durham, NH 03824. Offers PhD. *Students:* 10 full-time (7 women), 11 part-time (5 women), 2 international. Average age 28. 40 applicants, 20% accepted, 6 enrolled. In 2019, 6 doctorates awarded. *Entrance requirements:* For doctorate, GRE General Test, GRE Subject Test. Additional exam requirements/recommendations for international students: required—TOEFL (minimum score 550 paper-based; 80 iBT), IELTS, PTE. *Application deadline:* For fall admission, 1/15 for domestic and international students. Application fee: $65. Electronic applications accepted. *Financial support:* In 2019–20, 20 students received support, including 1 fellowship, 19 teaching assistantships; research assistantships, career-related internships or fieldwork, Federal Work-Study, scholarships/grants, and tuition waivers (full and partial) also available. Support available to part-time students. Financial award application deadline: 2/15. *Unit head:* Dr. William Stine, Chair, 603-862-2823. *Application contact:* Robin Scholefield, Administrative Assistant, 603-862-2369, E-mail: psychology.ph.d@unh.edu.
Website: http://cola.unh.edu/psychology

University of New Mexico, Graduate Studies, College of Arts and Sciences, Program in Psychology, Albuquerque, NM 87131-2039. Offers behavioral neuroscience (PhD); clinical psychology (PhD); cognitive neuroimaging (PhD); developmental psychology (PhD); evolution (PhD); health psychology (PhD); quantitative methodology (PhD). *Accreditation:* APA. *Degree requirements:* For doctorate, comprehensive exam, thesis/dissertation. *Entrance requirements:* For doctorate, GRE General Test, GRE Subject Test (psychology), minimum GPA of 3.0. Additional exam requirements/recommendations for international students: required—TOEFL (minimum score 550 paper-based; 79 iBT), IELTS (minimum score 6.5). Electronic applications accepted. *Expenses:* Tuition, state resident: full-time $7633; part-time $972 per year. Tuition, nonresident: full-time $22,586; part-time $3840 per year. *International tuition:* $23,292 full-time. *Required fees:* $8608. Tuition and fees vary according to course level, course load, degree level, program and student level.

University of New Orleans, Graduate School, College of Sciences, Department of Psychology, New Orleans, LA 70148. Offers MS, PhD. *Degree requirements:* For doctorate, thesis/dissertation. *Entrance requirements:* For doctorate, GRE General Test, minimum GPA of 3.0, 21 hours of course work in psychology. Additional exam requirements/recommendations for international students: required—TOEFL (minimum score 550 paper-based; 79 iBT), IELTS. Electronic applications accepted.

The University of North Carolina at Chapel Hill, Graduate School, College of Arts and Sciences, Department of Psychology, Chapel Hill, NC 27599-3270. Offers behavioral neuroscience psychology (PhD); clinical psychology (PhD); cognitive psychology (PhD); developmental psychology (PhD); quantitative psychology (PhD); social psychology (PhD). *Accreditation:* APA. *Degree requirements:* For doctorate, comprehensive exam, thesis/dissertation. *Entrance requirements:* For doctorate, GRE General Test, minimum GPA of 3.0. Additional exam requirements/recommendations for international students: required—TOEFL (minimum score 550 paper-based; 79 iBT), IELTS (minimum score 7). Electronic applications accepted.

The University of North Carolina at Charlotte, College of Liberal Arts and Sciences, Department of Psychology, Charlotte, NC 28223-0001. Offers cognitive science (Graduate Certificate); health psychology (PhD), including general; community; clinical; interdisciplinary; industrial/organizational psychology (MA); psychology (MA). *Accreditation:* APA. *Program availability:* Part-time. *Faculty:* 29 full-time (19 women), 2 part-time/adjunct (both women). *Students:* 42 full-time (35 women), 32 part-time (24 women); includes 18 minority (6 Black or African American, non-Hispanic/Latino; 4 Asian, non-Hispanic/Latino; 3 Hispanic/Latino; 5 Two or more races, non-Hispanic/Latino), 2 international. Average age 27. 164 applicants, 15% accepted, 14 enrolled. In 2019, 31 master's, 5 doctorates, 3 other advanced degrees awarded. *Degree requirements:* For master's, thesis (for some programs); for doctorate, comprehensive exam, thesis/dissertation. *Entrance requirements:* For master's, GRE, GMAT, MAT, bachelor's degree; statement of purpose addressing motivation for degree, preparation for graduate studies and impact of the degree; 2 letters of recommendation; (MA, Psychology) minimum 3.0 GPA in psychology courses; 18 credit hours of undergraduate psychology courses, undergraduate course in statistics; for doctorate, GRE and/or GMAT (Org. Science), at least 18 hours of coursework in psychology including introductory psychology and research methods, undergraduate course in statistics, transcripts of all academic work attempted since high school including evidence of the completion of a bachelor's degree, at least three references, personal statement, resume or curriculum vitae; for Graduate Certificate, enrolled and in good standing in a graduate degree program at UNC Charlotte, or have minimum GPA of 3.0 for undergraduate courses. Additional exam requirements/recommendations for international students: required—TOEFL (minimum score 557 paper-based; 83 iBT), IELTS (minimum score 6.5), TOEFL (minimum score 557 paper-based, 83 iBT) or IELTS (6.5). *Application deadline:* Applications are processed on a rolling basis. Application fee: $75. Electronic applications accepted. *Expenses:* Contact institution. *Financial support:* In 2019–20, 15 students received support, including 9 research assistantships (averaging $10,659 per year), 6 teaching assistantships (averaging $9,454 per year); fellowships, career-related internships or fieldwork, Federal Work-Study, institutionally sponsored loans, scholarships/grants, and unspecified assistantships also available. Support available to part-time students. Financial award applicants required to submit FAFSA. *Unit head:* Dr. Eric Heggestad, Chair & Associate Professor, 704-687-1338, E-mail: edhegges@uncc.edu. *Application contact:* Kathy B. Giddings, Director of Graduate Admissions, 704-687-5503, Fax: 704-687-1668, E-mail: gradadm@uncc.edu.
Website: http://psych.uncc.edu

The University of North Carolina at Greensboro, Graduate School, College of Arts and Sciences, Department of Psychology, Greensboro, NC 27412-5001. Offers clinical psychology (MA, PhD); cognitive psychology (MA, PhD); developmental psychology (MA, PhD); social psychology (MA, PhD). *Accreditation:* APA (one or more programs are accredited). Terminal master's awarded for partial completion of doctoral program. *Degree requirements:* For master's, comprehensive exam, thesis; for doctorate, one foreign language, thesis/dissertation, preliminary exam. *Entrance requirements:* For master's and doctorate, GRE General Test. Additional exam requirements/recommendations for international students: required—TOEFL. Electronic applications accepted.

The University of North Carolina Wilmington, College of Arts and Sciences, Department of Psychology, Wilmington, NC 28403-3297. Offers clinical psychology (PhD); psychology (MA), including applied behavior analysis, psychological science. *Faculty:* 27 full-time (15 women). *Students:* 44 full-time (36 women), 34 part-time (29 women); includes 12 minority (3 Black or African American, non-Hispanic/Latino; 5 Hispanic/Latino; 4 Two or more races, non-Hispanic/Latino), 1 international. Average age 25. 112 applicants, 38% accepted, 38 enrolled. In 2019, 19 master's awarded. *Degree requirements:* For master's, comprehensive exam, thesis; for doctorate, thesis/dissertation, 1-year external APA-accredited or APPIC-member internship. *Entrance requirements:* For master's, GRE General Test, GRE Subject Test (psychology) only if bachelor's degree was not in the area of psychology, 3 letters of recommendation, psychology research interest form, resume, essay; for doctorate, GRE General Test, GRE Subject Test (psychology) only if bachelor's degree was not in the area of

psychology, 3 letters of recommendation, resume, statement of interest. Additional exam requirements/recommendations for international students: required—TOEFL (minimum score 79 iBT), IELTS (minimum score 6.5). *Application deadline:* For fall admission, 4/15 for domestic students. Applications are processed on a rolling basis. Application fee: $75. Electronic applications accepted. *Expenses: Tuition, area resident:* Full-time $4719; part-time $326 per credit hour. Tuition, state resident: full-time $4719; part-time $326 per credit hour. Tuition, nonresident: full-time $18,548; part-time $1099 per credit hour. *Required fees:* $2738. Tuition and fees vary according to program. *Financial support:* Research assistantships, teaching assistantships, Federal Work-Study, scholarships/grants, unspecified assistantships, and out-of-state tuition remission available. Financial award application deadline: 1/1; financial award applicants required to submit FAFSA. *Unit head:* Dr. Julian Keith, Chair, 910-962-3378, Fax: 910-962-7010, E-mail: keithj@uncw.edu. *Application contact:* Dr. Kate Nooner, Graduate Coordinator, 910-962-2140, Fax: 910-962-7010, E-mail: psygradprogram@uncw.edu.
Website: http://www.uncw.edu/psy/grad/

University of North Dakota, Graduate School, College of Arts and Sciences, Department of Psychology, Grand Forks, ND 58202. Offers clinical psychology (PhD); forensic psychology (MA, MS). *Accreditation:* APA (one or more programs are accredited). *Degree requirements:* For master's, thesis, final exam; for doctorate, comprehensive exam, thesis/dissertation, internship, final exam. *Entrance requirements:* For master's, GRE General Test, GRE Subject Test, minimum GPA of 3.0; for doctorate, GRE General Test, GRE Subject Test, minimum GPA of 3.5. Additional exam requirements/recommendations for international students: required—TOEFL (minimum score 550 paper-based; 79 iBT), IELTS (minimum score 6.5). Electronic applications accepted.

University of Northern British Columbia, Office of Graduate Studies, Prince George, BC V2N 4Z9, Canada. Offers business administration (Diploma); community health science (M Sc); disability management (MA); education (M Ed); first nations studies (MA); gender studies (MA); history (MA); interdisciplinary studies (MA); international studies (MA); mathematical, computer and physical sciences (M Sc); natural resources and environmental studies (M Sc, MA, MNRES, PhD); political science (MA); psychology (M Sc, PhD); social work (MSW). *Program availability:* Part-time, evening/weekend, online learning. *Degree requirements:* For master's, thesis; for doctorate, thesis/dissertation. *Entrance requirements:* For master's, GRE, minimum B average in undergraduate course work; for doctorate, candidacy exam, minimum A average in graduate course work.

University of Northern Iowa, Graduate College, College of Social and Behavioral Sciences, Department of Psychology, Cedar Falls, IA 50614. Offers MA. *Program availability:* Part-time. *Degree requirements:* For master's, comprehensive exam, thesis. *Entrance requirements:* For master's, GRE, minimum GPA of 3.0, 3 letters of recommendation. Additional exam requirements/recommendations for international students: required—TOEFL (minimum score 500 paper-based; 61 iBT). Electronic applications accepted.

University of North Florida, College of Arts and Sciences, Department of Psychology, Jacksonville, FL 32224. Offers counseling psychology (MAC); general psychology (MA). *Program availability:* Part-time, evening/weekend. *Degree requirements:* For master's, comprehensive exam, thesis optional, practicum. *Entrance requirements:* For master's, GRE General Test, 2 letters of recommendation, minimum GPA of 3.0 in last 60 hours of course work. Additional exam requirements/recommendations for international students: required—TOEFL (minimum score 500 paper-based; 61 iBT). Electronic applications accepted.

University of North Texas, Toulouse Graduate School, Denton, TX 76203-5459. Offers accounting (MS); applied anthropology (MA, MS); applied behavior analysis (Certificate); applied geography (MA); applied technology and performance improvement (M Ed, MS); art education (MA); art history (MA); arts leadership (Certificate); audiology (Au D); behavior analysis (MS); behavioral science (PhD); biochemistry and molecular biology (MS); biology (MA, MS); biomedical engineering (MS); business analysis (MS); chemistry (MS); clinical health psychology (PhD); communication studies (MA, MS); computer engineering (MS); computer science (MS); counseling (M Ed, MS), including clinical mental health counseling (MS), college and university counseling, elementary school counseling, secondary school counseling; creative writing (MA); criminal justice (MS); curriculum and instruction (M Ed); decision sciences (MBA); design (MA, MFA), including fashion design (MFA), innovation studies, interior design (MFA); early childhood studies (MS); economics (MS); educational leadership (M Ed, Ed D); educational psychology (MS, PhD), including family studies (MS), gifted and talented (MS), human development (MS), learning and cognition (MS), research, measurement and evaluation (MS); electrical engineering (MS); emergency management (MPA); engineering technology (MS); English (MA); English as a second language (MA); environmental science (MS); finance (MBA, MS); financial management (MPA); French (MA); health services management (MBA); higher education (M Ed, Ed D); history (MA, MS); hospitality management (MS); human resources management (MPA); information science (MS); information systems (PhD); information technologies (MBA); interdisciplinary studies (MA, MS); international studies (MA); international sustainable tourism (MS); jazz studies (MM); journalism (MA, MJ, Graduate Certificate), including interactive and virtual digital communication (Graduate Certificate), narrative journalism (Graduate Certificate), public relations (Graduate Certificate); kinesiology (MS); linguistics (MA); local government management (MPA); logistics (PhD); logistics and supply chain management (MBA); long-term care, senior housing, and aging services (MA); management (PhD); marketing (MBA); mathematics (MA, MS); mechanical and energy engineering (MS, PhD); music (MA), including ethnomusicology, music theory, musicology, performance; music composition (PhD); music education (MM Ed, PhD); nonprofit management (MPA); operations and supply chain management (MBA); performance (MM, DMA); philosophy (MA); political science (MA); professional and technical communication (MA); radio, television and film (MA, MFA); rehabilitation counseling (Certificate); sociology (MA); Spanish (MA); special education (M Ed); speech-language pathology (MA); strategic management (MBA); studio art (MFA); teaching (M Ed); MBA/MS. *Program availability:* Part-time, evening/weekend, online learning. Terminal master's awarded for partial completion of doctoral program. *Degree requirements:* For master's, variable foreign language requirement, comprehensive exam (for some programs), thesis (for some programs); for doctorate, variable foreign language requirement, comprehensive exam (for some programs), thesis/dissertation; for other advanced degree, variable foreign language requirement, comprehensive exam (for some programs). *Entrance requirements:* For master's and doctorate, GRE, GMAT. Additional exam requirements/recommendations for international students: required—TOEFL (minimum score 550 paper-based; 79 iBT). Electronic applications accepted.

University of Notre Dame, The Graduate School, College of Arts and Letters, Division of Social Sciences, Department of Psychology, Notre Dame, IN 46556. Offers cognitive psychology (PhD); counseling psychology (PhD); developmental psychology (PhD); quantitative psychology (PhD). *Accreditation:* APA. *Degree requirements:* For doctorate, comprehensive exam, thesis/dissertation, candidacy exam. *Entrance requirements:* For doctorate, GRE General Test, GRE Subject Test (strongly recommended). Additional exam requirements/recommendations for international students: required—TOEFL (minimum score 600 paper-based; 80 iBT). Electronic applications accepted.

University of Oklahoma, College of Arts and Sciences, Department of Psychology, Norman, OK 73019. Offers organizational dynamics (MA, Graduate Certificate), including human resource management (Graduate Certificate), organizational dynamics (MA), project management (Graduate Certificate); psychology (MS, PhD), including psychology. Terminal master's awarded for partial completion of doctoral program. *Degree requirements:* For master's, comprehensive exam, thesis; for doctorate, comprehensive exam, thesis/dissertation. *Entrance requirements:* For master's and doctorate, GRE. Additional exam requirements/recommendations for international students: required—TOEFL (minimum score 79 iBT) or IELTS (minimum score 6.5). Electronic applications accepted. *Expenses:* Tuition, state resident: full-time $6583.20; part-time $274.30 per credit hour. Tuition, nonresident: full-time $21,242; part-time $885.10 per credit hour. *International tuition:* $21,242.40 full-time. *Required fees:* $1994.20; $72.55 per credit hour. $126.50 per semester. Tuition and fees vary according to course load and degree level.

University of Oregon, Graduate School, College of Arts and Sciences, Department of Psychology, Eugene, OR 97403. Offers clinical psychology (PhD); cognitive psychology (MA, MS, PhD); developmental psychology (MA, MS, PhD); physiological psychology (MA, MS, PhD); psychology (MA, MS, PhD); social/personality psychology (MA, MS, PhD). *Accreditation:* APA (one or more programs are accredited). Terminal master's awarded for partial completion of doctoral program. *Degree requirements:* For doctorate, thesis/dissertation. *Entrance requirements:* For master's, GRE General Test, minimum GPA of 3.0; for doctorate, GRE General Test. Additional exam requirements/recommendations for international students: required—TOEFL.

University of Ottawa, Faculty of Graduate and Postdoctoral Studies, Faculty of Social Sciences, School of Psychology, Ottawa, ON K1N 6N5, Canada. Offers PhD. *Degree requirements:* For doctorate, thesis/dissertation. *Entrance requirements:* For doctorate, minimum B+ average. Electronic applications accepted.

University of Pennsylvania, School of Arts and Sciences, Graduate Group in Psychology, Philadelphia, PA 19104-6241. Offers PhD. *Accreditation:* APA. *Faculty:* 67 full-time (24 women), 19 part-time/adjunct (5 women). *Students:* 53 full-time (34 women); includes 13 minority (1 Black or African American, non-Hispanic/Latino; 7 Asian, non-Hispanic/Latino; 2 Hispanic/Latino; 3 Two or more races, non-Hispanic/Latino), 16 international. Average age 28. 575 applicants, 3% accepted, 12 enrolled. In 2019, 8 doctorates awarded. Application fee: $90.
Website: http://psychology.sas.upenn.edu/graduate-program

University of Philosophical Research, Master's in Transformational Psychology Program, Los Angeles, CA 90027. Offers MA. *Degree requirements:* For master's, thesis. Electronic applications accepted.

University of Phoenix–Online Campus, College of Social Science, Phoenix, AZ 85034-7209. Offers mediation (Certificate); psychology (MS), including behavioral health, industrial-organizational, psychology. *Program availability:* Evening/weekend, online learning. *Entrance requirements:* Additional exam requirements/recommendations for international students: required—TOEFL, TOEIC (Test of English as an International Communication), Berlitz Online English Proficiency Exam, PTE, or IELTS. Electronic applications accepted. *Expenses:* Contact institution.

University of Phoenix - Phoenix Campus, College of Social Sciences, Tempe, AZ 85282-2371. Offers counseling (MS), including clinical mental health counseling, community counseling, counseling, marriage, family and child therapy; psychology (MS). *Program availability:* Evening/weekend, online learning. *Entrance requirements:* Additional exam requirements/recommendations for international students: required—TOEFL, TOEIC (Test of English as an International Communication), Berlitz Online English Proficiency Exam, PTE, or IELTS. Electronic applications accepted. *Expenses:* Contact institution.

University of Pittsburgh, Kenneth P. Dietrich School of Arts and Sciences, Department of Psychology, Pittsburgh, PA 15260. Offers biological and health psychology (PhD); clinical psychology (PhD); cognitive psychology (PhD); developmental psychology (PhD); social psychology (PhD). *Accreditation:* APA. *Faculty:* 33 full-time (18 women), 10 part-time/adjunct (3 women). *Students:* 90 full-time (73 women); includes 25 minority (4 Black or African American, non-Hispanic/Latino; 2 American Indian or Alaska Native, non-Hispanic/Latino; 10 Asian, non-Hispanic/Latino; 2 Hispanic/Latino; 7 Two or more races, non-Hispanic/Latino). Average age 25. 580 applicants, 6% accepted, 18 enrolled. In 2019, 16 doctorates awarded. Terminal master's awarded for partial completion of doctoral program. *Degree requirements:* For doctorate, comprehensive exam, thesis/dissertation. *Entrance requirements:* For doctorate, GRE General Test, minimum GPA of 3.0. Additional exam requirements/recommendations for international students: required—TOEFL (minimum score 550 paper-based; 90 iBT). *Application deadline:* For fall admission, 12/1 for domestic and international students. Application fee: $75. Electronic applications accepted. *Financial support:* In 2019–20, 90 students received support, including 38 fellowships with full tuition reimbursements available (averaging $30,378 per year), 19 research assistantships with full tuition reimbursements available (averaging $29,220 per year), 33 teaching assistantships with full tuition reimbursements available (averaging $29,220 per year); career-related internships or fieldwork, scholarships/grants, health care benefits, and unspecified assistantships also available. Financial award application deadline: 12/1. *Unit head:* Dr. Julie Fiez, Chair, 412-624-7078, Fax: 412-422-9149, E-mail: fiez@pitt.edu. *Application contact:* Francesca Sirianni, Graduate Administrator, 412-624-4502, Fax: 412-624-4428, E-mail: psygrad@pitt.edu.
Website: http://www.psychology.pitt.edu/

University of Puerto Rico at Rio Piedras, College of Social Sciences, Department of Psychology, San Juan, PR 00931-3300. Offers clinical psychology (MA); industrial organizational psychology (MA); investigative academic psychology (MA); psychology (PhD); social-community psychology (MA). *Program availability:* Part-time. *Degree requirements:* For master's, comprehensive exam, thesis; for doctorate, comprehensive exam, thesis/dissertation, internship. *Entrance requirements:* For master's, GRE or PAEG, interview, minimum GPA of 3.0; for doctorate, GRE or PAEG, interview, master's degree, minimum GPA of 3.0.

University of Regina, Faculty of Graduate Studies and Research, Faculty of Arts, Department of Psychology, Regina, SK S4S 0A2, Canada. Offers clinical psychology (MA, PhD); experimental and applied psychology (MA, PhD). *Faculty:* 20 full-time (9 women), 11 part-time/adjunct (7 women). *Students:* 55 full-time (47 women). Average age 30. 116 applicants, 18% accepted. In 2019, 4 master's, 1 doctorate awarded. *Degree requirements:* For master's, thesis; for doctorate, comprehensive exam, thesis/dissertation. *Entrance requirements:* For master's, GRE General Test, post secondary transcripts, 2 letter of recommendations; for doctorate, GRE General Test and GRE Subject Test (optional for those with a master's degree from a Canadian university). Additional exam requirements/recommendations for international students: required—TOEFL (minimum score 580 paper-based; 80 iBT), IELTS (minimum score 6.5), PTE (minimum score 59), other option is CAEL, MELAB and U of R ESL. *Application deadline:* For fall admission, 1/15 for domestic and international students. Application fee: $100. Electronic applications accepted. *Expenses: Tuition:* Full-time $6684

Canadian dollars. *Required fees:* $100 Canadian dollars; $3351.45 Canadian dollars per trimester. $1117.15 Canadian dollars per semester. Tuition and fees vary according to course level, course load, degree level and program. *Financial support:* Fellowships, research assistantships, teaching assistantships, career-related internships or fieldwork, Federal Work-Study, scholarships/grants, unspecified assistantships, and travel award and Graduate Scholarship Base Funds available. Support available to part-time students. Financial award application deadline: 9/30. *Unit head:* Dr. Richard MacLennan, Department Head, 306-585-4458, Fax: 306-585-5429, E-mail: richard.maclennan@uregina.ca. *Application contact:* Dr. Richard MacLennan, Department Head, 306-585-4458, Fax: 306-585-5429, E-mail: richard.maclennan@uregina.ca.
Website: http://www.uregina.ca/arts/psychology

University of Rhode Island, Graduate School, College of Health Sciences, Department of Psychology, Kingston, RI 02881. Offers behavioral science (PhD); clinical psychology (PhD); school psychology (MS, PhD). *Accreditation:* APA (one or more programs are accredited). *Program availability:* Part-time. *Faculty:* 23 full-time (13 women), 1 part-time/adjunct (0 women). *Students:* 59 full-time (50 women), 5 part-time (2 women); includes 10 minority (5 Black or African American, non-Hispanic/Latino; 2 Asian, non-Hispanic/Latino; 3 Hispanic/Latino), 4 international. 353 applicants, 11% accepted, 11 enrolled. In 2019, 11 master's, 15 doctorates awarded. *Entrance requirements:* Additional exam requirements/recommendations for international students: required—TOEFL. *Application deadline:* For fall admission, 12/1 for domestic and international students. Application fee: $65. Electronic applications accepted. *Expenses: Tuition, area resident:* Full-time $13,734; part-time $763 per credit. Tuition, state resident: full-time $13,734; part-time $763 per credit. Tuition, nonresident: full-time $26,512; part-time $1473 per credit. *International tuition:* $26,512 full-time. *Required fees:* $1780; $52 per credit. $35 per term. One-time fee: $165. *Financial support:* In 2019–20, 9 research assistantships with tuition reimbursements (averaging $10,024 per year), 20 teaching assistantships with tuition reimbursements (averaging $17,045 per year) were awarded. Financial award application deadline: 12/1; financial award applicants required to submit FAFSA. *Unit head:* Dr. Mark Robbins, Chair, 401-874-5082, E-mail: markrobb@uri.edu. *Application contact:* Dr. Mark Robbins, Chair, 401-874-5082, E-mail: markrobb@uri.edu.
Website: http://www.uri.edu/artsci/psy/

University of Rochester, School of Arts and Sciences, Psychology, Rochester, NY 14627. Offers clinical psychology (PhD); developmental psychology (PhD); social-personality psychology (PhD). *Accreditation:* APA. *Faculty:* 16 full-time (9 women). *Students:* 42 full-time (35 women); includes 10 minority (1 Black or African American, non-Hispanic/Latino; 5 Asian, non-Hispanic/Latino; 3 Hispanic/Latino; 1 Two or more races, non-Hispanic/Latino), 5 international. Average age 28. 240 applicants, 6% accepted, 9 enrolled. In 2019, 10 doctorates awarded. Terminal master's awarded for partial completion of doctoral program. *Degree requirements:* For doctorate, thesis/dissertation. *Entrance requirements:* For doctorate, GRE General Test (optional for Fall 2021 admission cycle), personal statement, official transcripts, three letters of recommendation, curriculum vitae or resume. Additional exam requirements/recommendations for international students: required—TOEFL. *Application deadline:* For fall admission, 12/1 for domestic and international students. Application fee: $20. Electronic applications accepted. *Financial support:* In 2019–20, 35 students received support, including 5 fellowships with full tuition reimbursements available, 8 research assistantships with full tuition reimbursements available (averaging $24,000 per year), 22 teaching assistantships with full tuition reimbursements available (averaging $24,000 per year); career-related internships or fieldwork, scholarships/grants, and tuition waivers (full) also available. Financial award application deadline: 4/15. *Unit head:* Loisa Bennetto, Chair, 585-275-8712, E-mail: loisa.bennetto@rochester.edu. *Application contact:* Loisa Bennetto, Chair, 585-275-8712, E-mail: loisa.bennetto@rochester.edu.
Website: http://www.sas.rochester.edu/psy/graduate/index.html

University of Saint Mary, Graduate Programs, Program in Psychology, Leavenworth, KS 66048-5082. Offers MA. *Program availability:* Part-time, evening/weekend. *Students:* 9 full-time (8 women); includes 1 minority (Two or more races, non-Hispanic/Latino). Average age 29. *Entrance requirements:* For master's, Bachelor's degree in psychology from accredited college, official transcripts, minimum GPA of 2.75, three professional recommendations, essay. *Application deadline:* Applications are processed on a rolling basis. Application fee: $25. Electronic applications accepted. *Expenses:* $640 per credit hour. *Financial support:* Unspecified assistantships available. Financial award applicants required to submit FAFSA. *Unit head:* Dr. David Strohm, Director of Undergraduate and Graduate Psychology Programs, 913-319-3012, E-mail: strohm57@stmary.edu. *Application contact:* Dr. David Strohm, Director of Undergraduate and Graduate Psychology Programs, 913-319-3012, E-mail: strohm57@stmary.edu.
Website: http://www.stmary.edu/success/Grad-Program/Master-of-Arts-Psychology.aspx

University of Saskatchewan, College of Graduate and Postdoctoral Studies, College of Arts and Science, Department of Psychology, Saskatoon, SK S7N 5A2, Canada. Offers MA, PhD. *Degree requirements:* For master's, thesis; for doctorate, comprehensive exam (for some programs), thesis/dissertation. *Entrance requirements:* Additional exam requirements/recommendations for international students: required—TOEFL (minimum score 80 iBT); recommended—IELTS (minimum score 6.5). Electronic applications accepted.

University of South Africa, College of Human Sciences, Pretoria, South Africa. Offers adult education (M Ed); African languages (MA, PhD); African politics (MA, PhD); Afrikaans (MA, PhD); ancient history (MA, PhD); ancient Near Eastern studies (MA, PhD); anthropology (MA, PhD); applied linguistics (MA); Arabic (MA, PhD); archaeology (MA); art history (MA); Biblical archaeology (MA); Biblical studies (M Th, D Th, PhD); Christian spirituality (M Th, D Th); church history (M Th, D Th); classical studies (MA, PhD); clinical psychology (MA); communication (MA, PhD); comparative education (M Ed, Ed D); consulting psychology (D Admin, D Com, PhD); curriculum studies (M Ed, Ed D); development studies (M Admin, MA, D Admin, PhD); didactics (M Ed, Ed D); education (M Tech); education management (M Ed, Ed D); educational psychology (M Ed); English (MA); environmental education (M Ed); French (MA, PhD); German (MA, PhD); Greek (MA); guidance and counseling (M Ed); health studies (MA, PhD), including health sciences education (MA), health services management (MA), medical and surgical nursing science (critical care general) (MA), midwifery and neonatal nursing science (MA), trauma and emergency care (MA); history (MA, PhD); history of education (Ed D); inclusive education (M Ed, Ed D); information and communications technology policy and regulation (MA); information science (MA, MIS, PhD); international politics (MA, PhD); Islamic studies (MA, PhD); Italian (MA, PhD); Judaica (MA, PhD); linguistics (MA, PhD); mathematical education (M Ed); mathematics education (MA); missiology (M Th, D Th); modern Hebrew (MA, PhD); musicology (MA, MMus, D Mus, PhD); natural science education (M Ed); New Testament (M Th, D Th); Old Testament (D Th); pastoral therapy (M Th, D Th); philosophy (MA); philosophy of education (M Ed, Ed D); politics (MA, PhD); Portuguese (MA, PhD); practical theology (M Th, D Th); psychology (MA, MS, PhD); psychology of education (M Ed, Ed D); public health (MA); religious studies (MA, D Th, PhD); Romance languages (MA); Russian (MA, PhD); Semitic languages (MA, PhD); social behavior studies in HIV/AIDS (MA); social science (mental health) (MA); social science in development studies (MA); social science in psychology (MA); social science in social work (MA); social science in sociology (MA); social work (MSW, DSW, PhD); socio-education (M Ed, Ed D); sociolinguistics (MA); sociology (MA, PhD); Spanish (MA, PhD); systematic theology (M Th, D Th); TESOL (teaching English to speakers of other languages) (MA); theological ethics (M Th, D Th); theory of literature (MA, PhD); urban ministries (D Th); urban ministry (M Th).

University of South Alabama, College of Arts and Sciences, Department of Psychology, Mobile, AL 36688. Offers MS. *Accreditation:* APA. *Program availability:* Part-time, evening/weekend. *Faculty:* 4 full-time (2 women). *Students:* 11 full-time (7 women), 1 (woman) part-time; includes 3 minority (1 Hispanic/Latino; 2 Two or more races, non-Hispanic/Latino). Average age 29. 4 applicants, 100% accepted, 3 enrolled. In 2019, 6 master's awarded. *Degree requirements:* For master's, comprehensive exam, thesis optional. *Entrance requirements:* For master's, GRE. Additional exam requirements/recommendations for international students: required—TOEFL (minimum score 71 iBT). *Application deadline:* For fall admission, 2/15 for domestic students, 1/15 for international students. Application fee: $35. Electronic applications accepted. *Expenses: Tuition, area resident:* Part-time $442 per credit hour. Tuition, state resident: full-time $10,608; part-time $442 per credit hour. Tuition, nonresident: full-time $21,216; part-time $884 per credit hour. *Financial support:* Fellowships, research assistantships, teaching assistantships, career-related internships or fieldwork, Federal Work-Study, institutionally sponsored loans, scholarships/grants, and unspecified assistantships available. Support available to part-time students. Financial award application deadline: 3/31; financial award applicants required to submit FAFSA. *Unit head:* Dr. John Shelley-Tremblay, Chair, Psychology, 251-460-6371, E-mail: jstrembplay@southalabama.edu. *Application contact:* Lisa Nash, Department Secretary, 251-460-6371, E-mail: lnash@southalabama.edu.
Website: http://www.southalabama.edu/colleges/artsandsci/psychology/index.html

University of South Carolina, The Graduate School, College of Arts and Sciences, Department of Psychology, Columbia, SC 29208. Offers clinical/community psychology (MA, PhD), including clinical/community psychology (PhD), general psychology (MA); experimental psychology (MA, PhD); school psychology (PhD). *Accreditation:* APA (one or more programs are accredited). Terminal master's awarded for partial completion of doctoral program. *Degree requirements:* For master's, thesis; for doctorate, comprehensive exam, thesis/dissertation. *Entrance requirements:* For master's and doctorate, GRE General Test. Additional exam requirements/recommendations for international students: required—TOEFL. Electronic applications accepted.

University of South Dakota, Graduate School, College of Arts and Sciences, Department of Psychology, Vermillion, SD 57069. Offers clinical psychology (MA, PhD); human factors (MA, PhD). *Accreditation:* APA (one or more programs are accredited). *Degree requirements:* For master's, comprehensive exam, thesis; for doctorate, comprehensive exam, thesis/dissertation. *Entrance requirements:* For master's, GRE, minimum GPA of 3.0; for doctorate, GRE General Test, GRE Subject Test, minimum GPA of 3.0. Additional exam requirements/recommendations for international students: required—TOEFL (minimum score 550 paper-based; 79 iBT). Electronic applications accepted.

University of Southern California, Graduate School, Dana and David Dornsife College of Letters, Arts and Sciences, Department of Psychology, Los Angeles, CA 90089. Offers brain and cognitive science (PhD); clinical science (PhD); developmental psychology (PhD); human behavior (MHB); quantitative methods (PhD); social psychology (PhD). *Accreditation:* APA. *Degree requirements:* For doctorate, comprehensive exam, thesis/dissertation, one-year internship (for clinical science students). *Entrance requirements:* For doctorate, GRE. Additional exam requirements/recommendations for international students: recommended—TOEFL (minimum score 600 paper-based; 100 iBT). Electronic applications accepted.

University of Southern Mississippi, College of Education and Human Sciences, School of Psychology, Hattiesburg, MS 39406-0001. Offers MS, PhD. *Accreditation:* APA (one or more programs are accredited). *Students:* 103 full-time (75 women), 14 part-time (all women); includes 20 minority (8 Black or African American, non-Hispanic/Latino; 1 American Indian or Alaska Native, non-Hispanic/Latino; 2 Asian, non-Hispanic/Latino; 3 Hispanic/Latino; 6 Two or more races, non-Hispanic/Latino), 2 international. 282 applicants, 15% accepted, 37 enrolled. In 2019, 34 master's, 23 doctorates awarded. Terminal master's awarded for partial completion of doctoral program. *Degree requirements:* For master's, comprehensive exam, thesis; for doctorate, comprehensive exam, thesis/dissertation. *Entrance requirements:* For master's, GRE General Test, minimum GPA of 3.0; for doctorate, GRE General Test, interview, minimum GPA of 3.5. Additional exam requirements/recommendations for international students: required—TOEFL, IELTS. *Application deadline:* Applications are processed on a rolling basis. Application fee: $60. *Expenses: Tuition, area resident:* Full-time $4393; part-time $488 per credit hour. Tuition, nonresident: full-time $5393; part-time $600 per credit hour. *Required fees:* $6 per semester. *Financial support:* Research assistantships with full tuition reimbursements, teaching assistantships with full tuition reimbursements, career-related internships or fieldwork, Federal Work-Study, institutionally sponsored loans, scholarships/grants, health care benefits, and unspecified assistantships available. Financial award application deadline: 3/15; financial award applicants required to submit FAFSA. *Unit head:* Dr. Sara Jordan, Director, 601-266-4177, E-mail: d.olmi@usm.edu. *Application contact:* Dr. Sara Jordan, Director, 601-266-4177, E-mail: d.olmi@usm.edu.
Website: https://www.usm.edu/psychology

University of South Florida, College of Arts and Sciences, Department of Psychology, Tampa, FL 33620-9951. Offers psychology (PhD), including clinical psychology, cognition, neuroscience and social psychology, industrial-organizational psychology. *Accreditation:* APA. *Faculty:* 30 full-time (11 women). *Students:* 79 full-time (55 women), 12 part-time (8 women); includes 16 minority (2 Black or African American, non-Hispanic/Latino; 6 Asian, non-Hispanic/Latino; 6 Hispanic/Latino; 2 Two or more races, non-Hispanic/Latino), 8 international. Average age 28. 355 applicants, 5% accepted, 19 enrolled. In 2019, 17 doctorates awarded. *Degree requirements:* For doctorate, comprehensive exam, thesis/dissertation, internship. *Entrance requirements:* For doctorate, a GRE Score Report with a strong preference for GRE V and Q scores each at the 50th percentile or better, statement of purpose; Research Interests and Faculty Matches Form (http://psychology.usf.edu/forms/ResearchInterest.aspx); 3 letters of recommendation; GPA worksheet (http://www.grad.usf.edu/inc/linked-files/gpa.pdf). Additional exam requirements/recommendations for international students: required—TOEFL, TOEFL (minimum score 550 paper-based; 79 iBT) or IELTS (minimum score 6.5). *Application deadline:* For fall admission, 12/1 priority date for domestic and international students. Application fee: $30. Electronic applications accepted. *Expenses:* Contact institution. *Financial support:* In 2019–20, 44 students received support, including 18 research assistantships with tuition reimbursements available (averaging $14,727 per year), 57 teaching assistantships with tuition reimbursements available (averaging $14,543 per year); tuition waivers (partial) and unspecified assistantships also available. Financial award applicants required to submit FAFSA. *Unit head:* Dr. Toru Shimizu, Chairperson, 813-974-0352, Fax: 813-974-4617, E-mail: shimizu@usf.edu. *Application contact:* Dr. Sandra Schneider, Professor and Graduate Program Director, 813-974-0928, E-mail: sandra@usf.edu.
Website: http://psychology.usf.edu/

University of South Florida, St. Petersburg, College of Arts and Sciences, St. Petersburg, FL 33701. Offers digital journalism and design (MA); environmental science and policy (MA, MS); Florida studies (MLA); journalism and media studies (MA); liberal studies (MLA); psychology (MA). *Program availability:* Part-time, online learning. *Degree requirements:* For master's, comprehensive exam, thesis or project. *Entrance requirements:* For master's, GRE, LSAT, MCAT (varies by program), letter of intent, 3 letters of recommendation, writing samples, bachelor's degree from regionally-accredited institution with minimum GPA of 3.0 overall or in upper two years. Additional exam requirements/recommendations for international students: required—TOEFL (minimum score 550 paper-based; 79 iBT); recommended—IELTS. Electronic applications accepted.

The University of Tennessee, Graduate School, College of Arts and Sciences, Department of Psychology, Knoxville, TN 37996. Offers clinical psychology (PhD); experimental psychology (MA, PhD); psychology (MA). *Accreditation:* APA (one or more programs are accredited). Terminal master's awarded for partial completion of doctoral program. *Degree requirements:* For master's, thesis; for doctorate, thesis/dissertation. *Entrance requirements:* For master's and doctorate, GRE General Test, GRE Subject Test, minimum GPA of 2.7. Additional exam requirements/recommendations for international students: required—TOEFL. Electronic applications accepted.

The University of Tennessee at Chattanooga, Program in Psychology, Chattanooga, TN 37403. Offers industrial/organizational psychology (MS); research psychology (MS). *Program availability:* Part-time. *Faculty:* 17 full-time (10 women), 4 part-time/adjunct (2 women). *Students:* 44 full-time (35 women), 4 part-time (3 women); includes 6 minority (1 Black or African American, non-Hispanic/Latino; 3 Hispanic/Latino; 2 Two or more races, non-Hispanic/Latino), 1 international. Average age 25. 98 applicants, 24% accepted, 20 enrolled. In 2019, 26 master's awarded. *Degree requirements:* For master's, comprehensive exam (for some programs), thesis (for some programs). *Entrance requirements:* For master's, GRE General Test. Additional exam requirements/recommendations for international students: required—TOEFL (minimum score 550 paper-based; 79 iBT), IELTS (minimum score 6). *Application deadline:* For fall admission, 6/15 priority date for domestic students, 7/1 for international students; for spring admission, 11/1 priority date for domestic students, 11/1 for international students. Applications are processed on a rolling basis. Application fee: $35 ($40 for international students). Electronic applications accepted. *Financial support:* Research assistantships, teaching assistantships, career-related internships or fieldwork, scholarships/grants, and unspecified assistantships available. Support available to part-time students. Financial award application deadline: 7/1; financial award applicants required to submit FAFSA. *Unit head:* Dr. Brian O'Leary, Department Head, 423-425-4283, Fax: 423-425-4284, E-mail: Boleary@utc.edu. *Application contact:* Dr. Joanne Romagni, Dean of the Graduate School, 423-425-4478, Fax: 423-425-5223, E-mail: joanne-romagni@utc.edu.
Website: http://www.utc.edu/psychology/

The University of Texas at Arlington, Graduate School, College of Science, Department of Psychology, Arlington, TX 76019. Offers experimental health psychology (PhD); experimental psychology (MS, PhD); health/neuroscience psychology (MS, PhD); industrial and organizational psychology (MS). *Program availability:* Part-time. Terminal master's awarded for partial completion of doctoral program. *Degree requirements:* For master's, comprehensive exam or thesis; for doctorate, thesis/dissertation (for some programs). *Entrance requirements:* For master's and doctorate, GRE General Test, minimum GPA of 3.0 in last 60 hours of course work. Additional exam requirements/recommendations for international students: required—TOEFL (minimum score 550 paper-based).

The University of Texas at Austin, Graduate School, College of Liberal Arts, Department of Psychology, Austin, TX 78712-1111. Offers behavioral neuroscience (PhD); clinical psychology (PhD); cognitive systems (PhD); developmental psychology (PhD); individual differences and evolutionary psychology (PhD); perceptual systems (PhD); social psychology (PhD). *Accreditation:* APA. *Degree requirements:* For doctorate, thesis/dissertation. *Entrance requirements:* For doctorate, GRE General Test. Electronic applications accepted.

The University of Texas at Dallas, School of Behavioral and Brain Sciences, Program in Psychological Sciences, Richardson, TX 75080. Offers early childhood disorders (MS); psychological sciences (MS, PhD). *Program availability:* Part-time, evening/weekend. *Faculty:* 21 full-time (17 women), 2 part-time/adjunct (both women). *Students:* 65 full-time (57 women), 11 part-time (9 women); includes 30 minority (7 Black or African American, non-Hispanic/Latino; 7 Asian, non-Hispanic/Latino; 13 Hispanic/Latino; 3 Two or more races, non-Hispanic/Latino), 9 international. Average age 27. 152 applicants, 28% accepted, 24 enrolled. In 2019, 26 master's, 6 doctorates awarded. *Degree requirements:* For master's, directed project or internship; for doctorate, thesis/dissertation. *Entrance requirements:* For master's and doctorate, GRE General Test, minimum GPA of 3.0 in upper-level course work. Additional exam requirements/recommendations for international students: required—TOEFL (minimum score 550 paper-based). *Application deadline:* For fall admission, 7/15 for domestic students, 5/1 priority date for international students; for spring admission, 11/15 for domestic students, 9/1 priority date for international students. Applications are processed on a rolling basis. Application fee: $50 ($100 for international students). Electronic applications accepted. *Expenses: Tuition, area resident:* Full-time $16,504. Tuition, state resident: full-time $16,504. Tuition, nonresident: full-time $34,266. Tuition and fees vary according to course load. *Financial support:* In 2019–20, 25 students received support, including 1 fellowship (averaging $2,000 per year), 6 research assistantships with partial tuition reimbursements available (averaging $29,829 per year), 18 teaching assistantships with partial tuition reimbursements available (averaging $18,900 per year); career-related internships or fieldwork, Federal Work-Study, scholarships/grants, and unspecified assistantships also available. Support available to part-time students. Financial award application deadline: 4/30; financial award applicants required to submit FAFSA. *Unit head:* Dr. Shayla Holub, Area Head, 972-883-4473, Fax: 972-883-3491, E-mail: sholub@utdallas.edu. *Application contact:* Dr. Jackie Nelson, Associate Area Head, 972-883-4478, Fax: 972-883-3491, E-mail: Jackie.Nelson@utdallas.edu.
Website: https://bbs.utdallas.edu/degrees/psy-degrees/

The University of Texas at El Paso, Graduate School, College of Liberal Arts, Department of Psychology, El Paso, TX 79968-0001. Offers clinical psychology (MA); experimental psychology (MA); psychology (PhD). *Program availability:* Part-time, evening/weekend. *Degree requirements:* For master's, thesis; for doctorate, thesis/dissertation. *Entrance requirements:* For master's, GRE, letters of recommendation; for doctorate, GRE, statement of purpose, letters of recommendation. Additional exam requirements/recommendations for international students: required—TOEFL; recommended—IELTS. Electronic applications accepted.

The University of Texas at San Antonio, College of Liberal and Fine Arts, Department of Psychology, San Antonio, TX 78249-0617. Offers MS, PhD. *Program availability:* Part-time. *Degree requirements:* For master's, comprehensive exam, thesis or alternative; for doctorate, comprehensive exam, thesis/dissertation. *Entrance requirements:* For master's, GRE, minimum GPA of 3.2 in last 60 hours and in all psychology courses; 18 hours of psychology courses including inferential statistics and research methods; two letters of recommendation; statement of purpose; for doctorate, GRE, master's degree with minimum GPA of 3.5, three letters of recommendation, statement of purpose. Additional exam requirements/recommendations for international students: required—TOEFL (minimum score 550 paper-based; 79 iBT), IELTS (minimum score 6.5). Electronic applications accepted. *Expenses:* Contact institution.

The University of Texas at Tyler, College of Education and Psychology, Department of Psychology and Counseling, Tyler, TX 75799-0001. Offers clinical psychology (MS), including neuropsychology, school psychology; counseling psychology (MA), including general, marriage and family; interdisciplinary studies (MSIS); school counseling (MA). *Program availability:* Part-time, evening/weekend. *Faculty:* 12 full-time (5 women), 6 part-time/adjunct (3 women). *Students:* 131 full-time (103 women), 83 part-time (67 women); includes 67 minority (10 Black or African American, non-Hispanic/Latino; 1 American Indian or Alaska Native, non-Hispanic/Latino; 7 Asian, non-Hispanic/Latino; 41 Hispanic/Latino; 8 Two or more races, non-Hispanic/Latino), 8 international. Average age 30. 130 applicants, 65% accepted, 47 enrolled. In 2019, 94 master's awarded. *Degree requirements:* For master's, comprehensive exam, thesis optional. *Entrance requirements:* For master's, GRE General Test, minimum GPA of 3.0. Additional exam requirements/recommendations for international students: required—TOEFL. *Application deadline:* For fall admission, 8/17 priority date for domestic students, 7/1 priority date for international students; for spring admission, 12/21 priority date for domestic students, 11/1 priority date for international students. Application fee: $25 ($50 for international students). Electronic applications accepted. *Financial support:* In 2019–20, fellowships with partial tuition reimbursements (averaging $3,000 per year) were awarded; research assistantships, teaching assistantships, career-related internships or fieldwork, Federal Work-Study, and institutionally sponsored loans also available. Support available to part-time students. Financial award application deadline: 7/1. *Unit head:* Dr. Charles B. Barke, Chair, 903-565-5875, E-mail: cbarke@uttyler.edu. *Application contact:* Dr. Charles B. Barke, Chair, 903-565-5875, E-mail: cbarke@uttyler.edu.
Website: http://www.uttyler.edu/psychology/

The University of Texas of the Permian Basin, Office of Graduate Studies, College of Arts and Sciences, Department of Psychology, Odessa, TX 79762-0001. Offers clinical psychology (MA); experimental psychology (MA). *Program availability:* Part-time, evening/weekend. *Degree requirements:* For master's, comprehensive exam, thesis, practicum. *Entrance requirements:* For master's, GRE General Test, 3 letters of recommendation. Additional exam requirements/recommendations for international students: required—TOEFL (minimum score 550 paper-based).

The University of Texas Rio Grande Valley, College of Liberal Arts, Department of Psychological Science, Edinburg, TX 78539. Offers psychology (MA), including clinical psychology, experimental psychology. *Faculty:* 15 full-time (3 women), 4 part-time/adjunct (2 women). *Students:* 42 full-time (32 women), 22 part-time (12 women); includes 57 minority (1 Asian, non-Hispanic/Latino; 56 Hispanic/Latino), 6 international. Average age 27. 50 applicants, 56% accepted, 23 enrolled. In 2019, 12 master's awarded. *Expenses: Tuition, area resident:* Full-time $5959; part-time $440 per credit hour. Tuition, state resident: full-time $5959. Tuition, nonresident: full-time $5959. *International tuition:* $13,321 full-time. *Required fees:* $1169; $185 per credit hour.
Website: utrgv.edu/psychology/index.htm

University of the Pacific, College of the Pacific, Department of Psychology, Stockton, CA 95211-0197. Offers MA. *Degree requirements:* For master's, thesis. *Entrance requirements:* For master's, GRE General Test. Additional exam requirements/recommendations for international students: required—TOEFL.

University of the West, Department of Psychology, Rosemead, CA 91770. Offers Buddhist psychology (MA); multicultural counseling (MA). *Program availability:* Part-time, evening/weekend. *Degree requirements:* For master's, fieldwork; comprehensive exam or thesis.

The University of Toledo, College of Graduate Studies, College of Languages, Literature and Social Sciences, Department of Psychology, Toledo, OH 43606-3390. Offers clinical psychology (MA, PhD); experimental psychology (MA, PhD). *Accreditation:* APA. *Degree requirements:* For master's, comprehensive exam, thesis; for doctorate, comprehensive exam, thesis/dissertation. *Entrance requirements:* For master's and doctorate, GRE General Test, GRE Subject Test, minimum cumulative point-hour ratio of 2.7 for all previous academic work, three letters of recommendation, statement of purpose, transcripts from all prior institutions attended. Additional exam requirements/recommendations for international students: required—TOEFL (minimum score 550 paper-based; 80 iBT). Electronic applications accepted.

University of Toronto, School of Graduate Studies, Faculty of Arts and Science, Department of Psychology, Toronto, ON M5S 1A1, Canada. Offers MA, PhD. *Degree requirements:* For master's, thesis; for doctorate, thesis/dissertation, oral exam. *Entrance requirements:* For master's, minimum A- average in last two years, 6 full courses in psychology, laboratory experience; for doctorate, minimum A- average, research experience. Additional exam requirements/recommendations for international students: required—TOEFL (minimum score 580 paper-based; 93 iBT), TWE (minimum score 5). Electronic applications accepted.

The University of Tulsa, Graduate School, Kendall College of Arts and Sciences, Department of Psychology, Tulsa, OK 74104-3189. Offers clinical psychology (MA, PhD); industrial/organizational psychology (MA, PhD); JD/MA. *Accreditation:* APA (one or more programs are accredited). *Program availability:* Part-time. Terminal master's awarded for partial completion of doctoral program. *Degree requirements:* For doctorate, comprehensive exam, thesis/dissertation. *Entrance requirements:* For master's and doctorate, GRE General Test. Additional exam requirements/recommendations for international students: required—TOEFL (minimum score 577 paper-based; 91 iBT), IELTS (minimum score 6.5). Electronic applications accepted. *Expenses: Tuition:* Full-time $22,896; part-time $1272 per credit hour. *Required fees:* $6 per credit hour. Tuition and fees vary according to course load and program.

University of Utah, Graduate School, College of Social and Behavioral Science, Department of Psychology, Salt Lake City, UT 84112. Offers clinical psychology (PhD); psychology (PhD), including cognitive neuroscience, developmental psychology, social psychology. *Accreditation:* APA. *Faculty:* 27 full-time (14 women), 1 (woman) part-time/adjunct. *Students:* 53 full-time (40 women); includes 8 minority (1 Black or African American, non-Hispanic/Latino; 4 Hispanic/Latino; 3 Two or more races, non-Hispanic/Latino), 6 international. Average age 28. 295 applicants, 8% accepted, 13 enrolled. In 2019, 11 doctorates awarded. *Degree requirements:* For doctorate, thesis/dissertation. *Entrance requirements:* For doctorate, GRE General Test. Additional exam requirements/recommendations for international students: required—TOEFL (minimum score 500 paper-based). *Application deadline:* For fall admission, 12/1 for domestic and international students. Application fee: $55 ($65 for international students). Electronic applications accepted. *Expenses:* Tuition, state resident: full-time $7085; part-time $272.51 per credit hour. Tuition, nonresident: full-time $24,937; part-time $959.12 per credit hour. *Required fees:* $880.52; $880.52 per semester. Tuition and fees vary according to degree level, program and student level. *Financial support:* In 2019–20, 5 fellowships (averaging $13,400 per year), 22 research assistantships (averaging $15,000 per year), 33 teaching assistantships (averaging $14,909 per year) were awarded; unspecified assistantships also available. Financial award applicants required

to submit FAFSA. *Unit head:* Dr. Bert N. Uchino, Chair, 801-581-8925, Fax: 801-581-5841, E-mail: bert.uchino@psych.utah.edu. *Application contact:* Nancy Seegmiller, Program Manager, 801-581-8925, Fax: 801-581-5841, E-mail: nancy.seegmiller@psych.utah.edu.
Website: http://www.psych.utah.edu/

University of Vermont, Graduate College, College of Arts and Sciences, Program in General/Experimental Psychology, Burlington, VT 05405-0134. Offers psychology (PhD), including biobehavioral psychology, developmental psychology, human behavioral pharmacology, social psychology. *Accreditation:* APA. *Degree requirements:* For doctorate, thesis/dissertation. *Entrance requirements:* For doctorate, GRE General Test. Additional exam requirements/recommendations for international students: required—TOEFL (minimum score 550 paper-based, 100 iBT) or IELTS (7). Electronic applications accepted.

University of Victoria, Faculty of Graduate Studies, Faculty of Social Sciences, Department of Psychology, Victoria, BC V8W 2Y2, Canada. Offers clinical psychology (PhD); clinical psychology (neuropsychology) (M Sc); cognition and brain science (M Sc, PhD); experimental neuropsychology (M Sc, PhD); individualized study (M Sc, PhD); life span development psychology (PhD); life span developmental psychology (M Sc); social psychology (M Sc, PhD). *Degree requirements:* For master's, thesis; for doctorate, thesis/dissertation, candidacy exam. *Entrance requirements:* For master's and doctorate, GRE General Test. Additional exam requirements/recommendations for international students: required—TOEFL (minimum score 600 paper-based). Electronic applications accepted.

University of Virginia, College and Graduate School of Arts and Sciences, Department of Psychology, Charlottesville, VA 22903. Offers MA, PhD. *Accreditation:* APA (one or more programs are accredited). *Degree requirements:* For master's, pre-dissertation research project; for doctorate, comprehensive exam, thesis/dissertation. *Entrance requirements:* For master's and doctorate, GRE General Test, 3 or more letters of recommendation. Additional exam requirements/recommendations for international students: required—TOEFL (minimum score 600 paper-based; 90 iBT), IELTS (minimum score 7). Electronic applications accepted.

University of Washington, Graduate School, College of Arts and Sciences, Department of Psychology, Seattle, WA 98195. Offers animal behavior (PhD); applied child and adolescent psychology: prevention and treatment (MA); behavioral neuroscience (PhD); clinical psychology (PhD); cognition and perception (PhD); developmental psychology (PhD); quantitative psychology (PhD); social psychology and personality (PhD). *Accreditation:* APA (one or more programs are accredited). *Degree requirements:* For doctorate, thesis/dissertation. *Entrance requirements:* For doctorate, GRE General Test, minimum GPA of 3.0. Electronic applications accepted.

University of Waterloo, Graduate Studies and Postdoctoral Affairs, Faculty of Arts, Department of Psychology, Waterloo, ON N2L 3G1, Canada. Offers MA, MA Sc, PhD. Terminal master's awarded for partial completion of doctoral program. *Degree requirements:* For master's, thesis (for some programs); for doctorate, thesis/dissertation. *Entrance requirements:* For master's, GRE, honors degree in psychology, minimum B average; for doctorate, GRE, master's degree in psychology, minimum B average. Additional exam requirements/recommendations for international students: required—TOEFL, IELTS, PTE. Electronic applications accepted.

The University of Western Ontario, School of Graduate and Postdoctoral Studies, Faculty of Science, Department of Psychology, London, ON N6A 3K7, Canada. Offers MA, PhD. *Degree requirements:* For master's, thesis; for doctorate, thesis/dissertation. *Entrance requirements:* For master's, minimum B average during last 2 years; for doctorate, MA in psychology. Additional exam requirements/recommendations for international students: required—TOEFL.

University of West Florida, Usha Kundu, MD College of Health, Department of Psychology, Pensacola, FL 32514-5750. Offers applied experimental (MA); counseling (MA); industrial-organizational (MA). *Program availability:* Part-time. *Degree requirements:* For master's, thesis (for some programs). *Entrance requirements:* For master's, GRE, official transcripts; minimum GPA of 3.0; writing sample; three letters of reference; field experience or skill sets; oral interview (for counseling specialization). Additional exam requirements/recommendations for international students: required—TOEFL (minimum score 550 paper-based).

University of Windsor, Faculty of Graduate Studies, Faculty of Arts and Social Sciences, Department of Psychology, Windsor, ON N9B 3P4, Canada. Offers adult clinical (MA, PhD); applied social psychology (MA, PhD); child clinical (MA, PhD); clinical neuropsychology (MA, PhD). *Degree requirements:* For master's, thesis; for doctorate, comprehensive exam, thesis/dissertation. *Entrance requirements:* For master's, GRE General Test, GRE Subject Test in psychology, minimum B average; for doctorate, GRE General Test, GRE Subject Test in psychology, master's degree. Additional exam requirements/recommendations for international students: required—TOEFL (minimum score 600 paper-based). Electronic applications accepted.

University of Wisconsin–Eau Claire, College of Arts and Sciences, Department of Psychology, Eau Claire, WI 54702-4004. Offers school psychology (MSE, Ed S). *Program availability:* Part-time. *Degree requirements:* For master's, comprehensive exam, thesis, National Certified School Psychologist Professional Exam, written exam, externship. *Entrance requirements:* For master's, GRE, minimum undergraduate GPA of 3.0; courses in exceptional children and youth, statistics, psychopathology, and theories of counseling. Additional exam requirements/recommendations for international students: required—TOEFL (minimum score 79 iBT).

University of Wisconsin–La Crosse, College of Arts, Social Sciences, and Humanities, Department of Psychology, La Crosse, WI 54601-3742. Offers school psychology (MS Ed, Ed S). *Faculty:* 4 full-time (2 women), 1 (woman) part-time/adjunct. *Students:* 24 full-time (20 women), 12 part-time (11 women). Average age 24. 57 applicants, 32% accepted, 13 enrolled. In 2019, 28 master's, 28 Ed Ss awarded. *Degree requirements:* For master's, thesis, seminar, or comprehensive exams. *Entrance requirements:* For master's and Ed S, GRE. Additional exam requirements/recommendations for international students: required—TOEFL (minimum score 550 paper-based; 79 iBT). *Application deadline:* For fall admission, 1/31 for domestic and international students. Electronic applications accepted. *Financial support:* Research assistantships, Federal Work-Study, scholarships/grants, and health care benefits available. Support available to part-time students. *Unit head:* Dr. Robert Dixon, Director of School Psychology, 608-785-6893, E-mail: rdixon@uwlax.edu. *Application contact:* Jennifer Weber, Senior Student Services Coordinator Graduate Admissions, 608-785-8939, E-mail: admissions@uwlax.edu.
Website: https://www.uwlax.edu/Psychology/Graduate-program/

University of Wisconsin–Madison, Graduate School, College of Letters and Science, Department of Psychology, Madison, WI 53706-1380. Offers biology of brain and behavior (PhD); clinical psychology (PhD); cognitive neurosciences (PhD); developmental psychology (PhD); perception (PhD); psychology (PhD); social and personality psychology (PhD). *Accreditation:* APA. *Degree requirements:* For doctorate, comprehensive exam, thesis/dissertation. *Entrance requirements:* For doctorate, GRE General Test, minimum undergraduate GPA of 3.0. Additional exam requirements/recommendations for international students: required—TOEFL. Electronic applications accepted.

University of Wisconsin–Milwaukee, Graduate School, College of Letters and Science, Department of Psychology, Milwaukee, WI 53201-0413. Offers psychology (MS, PhD). *Accreditation:* APA (one or more programs are accredited). *Degree requirements:* For master's, thesis; for doctorate, variable foreign language requirement, thesis/dissertation. *Entrance requirements:* For master's and doctorate, GRE General Test, GRE Subject Test. Additional exam requirements/recommendations for international students: required—TOEFL (minimum score 550 paper-based; 79 iBT), IELTS (minimum score 6.5). Electronic applications accepted.

University of Wisconsin–Oshkosh, Graduate Studies, College of Letters and Science, Department of Psychology, Oshkosh, WI 54901. Offers experimental psychology (MS); industrial/organizational psychology (MS). *Degree requirements:* For master's, thesis. *Entrance requirements:* For master's, GRE, 10 semester hours of undergraduate course work in psychology. Additional exam requirements/recommendations for international students: required—TOEFL (minimum score 550 paper-based; 79 iBT). Electronic applications accepted.

University of Wisconsin–Whitewater, School of Graduate Studies, College of Letters and Sciences, Department of Psychology, Whitewater, WI 53190-1790. Offers school psychology (MSE, Ed S). *Program availability:* Part-time, evening/weekend, online learning. *Degree requirements:* For master's, comprehensive exam or thesis. *Entrance requirements:* For master's, MAT or GRE, interview, minimum GPA of 3.0, 3 letters of recommendation. Additional exam requirements/recommendations for international students: required—TOEFL (minimum score 550 paper-based; 80 iBT), IELTS (minimum score 6). Electronic applications accepted.

University of Wyoming, College of Arts and Sciences, Department of Psychology, Laramie, WY 82071. Offers MA, MS, PhD. *Accreditation:* APA (one or more programs are accredited). Terminal master's awarded for partial completion of doctoral program. *Degree requirements:* For master's, thesis; for doctorate, comprehensive exam, thesis/dissertation. *Entrance requirements:* For master's and doctorate, GRE General Test, GRE Subject Test, minimum GPA of 3.0. Additional exam requirements/recommendations for international students: required—TOEFL.

Université Laval, Faculty of Social Sciences, School of Psychology, Programs in Psychology, Québec, QC G1K 7P4, Canada. Offers clinical psychology (PhD); community psychology (PhD); psychology (PhD, Psy D). *Degree requirements:* For doctorate, comprehensive exam, thesis/dissertation. *Entrance requirements:* For doctorate, comprehension of written English, knowledge of French, interview. Electronic applications accepted.

Utah State University, School of Graduate Studies, Emma Eccles Jones College of Education and Human Services, Department of Psychology, Logan, UT 84322. Offers clinical/counseling/school psychology (PhD); research and evaluation methodology (PhD); school counseling (MS); school psychology (MS). *Accreditation:* APA (one or more programs are accredited). *Program availability:* Part-time, evening/weekend, online learning. Terminal master's awarded for partial completion of doctoral program. *Degree requirements:* For master's, thesis (for some programs); for doctorate, thesis/dissertation. *Entrance requirements:* For master's, GRE General Test (school psychology), MAT (school counseling), minimum GPA of 3.5; for doctorate, GRE General Test, minimum GPA of 3.5. Additional exam requirements/recommendations for international students: required—TOEFL.

Valdosta State University, Department of Psychology, Counseling, and Family Therapy, Valdosta, GA 31698. Offers industrial/organizational psychology (MS); marriage and family therapy (MS); school counseling (M Ed, Ed S). *Accreditation:* AAMFT/COAMFTE. *Program availability:* Part-time, evening/weekend, 100% online, blended/hybrid learning. *Degree requirements:* For master's, thesis or alternative, comprehensive written and/or oral exams; for Ed S, thesis. *Entrance requirements:* For master's, GRE General Test or MAT, GACE; for Ed S, GRE General Test or MAT. Additional exam requirements/recommendations for international students: required—TOEFL (minimum score 523 paper-based); recommended—IELTS. Electronic applications accepted. *Expenses:* Contact institution.

Vanderbilt University, Program in Psychological Sciences, Nashville, TN 37240-1001. Offers PhD. *Accreditation:* APA. *Faculty:* 51 full-time (22 women). *Students:* 82 full-time (48 women); includes 9 minority (1 Black or African American, non-Hispanic/Latino; 2 Asian, non-Hispanic/Latino; 3 Hispanic/Latino; 3 Two or more races, non-Hispanic/Latino), 29 international. Average age 26. 520 applicants, 3% accepted, 10 enrolled. In 2019, 6 doctorates awarded. *Degree requirements:* For doctorate, comprehensive exam, thesis/dissertation, final and qualifying exams. *Entrance requirements:* For doctorate, GRE General Test, GRE Subject Test. Additional exam requirements/recommendations for international students: required—TOEFL (minimum score 570 paper-based; 88 iBT). *Application deadline:* For fall admission, 12/1 for domestic and international students. Application fee: $0. Electronic applications accepted. *Expenses:* Contact institution. *Financial support:* Fellowships with full tuition reimbursements, research assistantships with full tuition reimbursements, teaching assistantships with full tuition reimbursements, career-related internships or fieldwork, Federal Work-Study, institutionally sponsored loans, scholarships/grants, traineeships, and health care benefits available. Financial award application deadline: 1/15; financial award applicants required to submit CSS PROFILE or FAFSA. *Unit head:* Bethany Rittle-Johnson, Chair, 615-322-8301, Fax: 615-343-9494, E-mail: Bethany.rittle-johnson@vanderbilt.edu. *Application contact:* Dr. Rene Marois, Chair, 615-322-2874, Fax: 615-343-5027, E-mail: r.marois@vanderbilt.edu.
Website: http://peabody.vanderbilt.edu/departments/psych/

Villanova University, Graduate School of Liberal Arts and Sciences, Department of Psychology, Villanova, PA 19085-1699. Offers MA, MS. *Program availability:* Part-time, evening/weekend. *Degree requirements:* For master's, thesis. *Entrance requirements:* For master's, GRE General Test, minimum GPA of 3.0, statement of goals. Additional exam requirements/recommendations for international students: required—TOEFL. Electronic applications accepted.

Virginia Polytechnic Institute and State University, Graduate School, College of Science, Blacksburg, VA 24061. Offers biological sciences (MS, PhD); biomedical technology development and management (MS); chemistry (MS, PhD); data analysis and applied statistics (MA); economics (PhD); geosciences (MS, PhD); mathematics (MS, PhD); physics (MS, PhD); psychology (MS, PhD); statistics (MS, PhD). *Faculty:* 375 full-time (118 women), 2 part-time/adjunct (1 woman). *Students:* 544 full-time (221 women), 37 part-time (15 women); includes 75 minority (14 Black or African American, non-Hispanic/Latino; 1 American Indian or Alaska Native, non-Hispanic/Latino; 20 Asian, non-Hispanic/Latino; 31 Hispanic/Latino; 9 Two or more races, non-Hispanic/Latino), 216 international. Average age 27. 962 applicants, 33% accepted, 138 enrolled. In 2019, 75 master's, 69 doctorates awarded. *Degree requirements:* For master's, comprehensive exam (for some programs), thesis (for some programs); for doctorate, comprehensive exam (for some programs), thesis/dissertation (for some programs). *Entrance requirements:* For master's and doctorate, GRE/GMAT. Additional exam requirements/recommendations for international students: required—TOEFL (minimum score 90 iBT). *Application deadline:* For fall admission, 8/1 for domestic students, 4/1 for

international students; for spring admission, 1/1 for domestic students, 9/1 for international students. Applications are processed on a rolling basis. Application fee: $75. Electronic applications accepted. *Expenses:* Tuition, state resident: full-time $13,700; part-time $761.25 per credit hour. Tuition, nonresident: full-time $27,614; part-time $1534 per credit hour. *Required fees:* $886.50 per term. Tuition and fees vary according to campus/location and program. *Financial support:* In 2019–20, 5 fellowships with full tuition reimbursements (averaging $25,988 per year), 281 research assistantships with full tuition reimbursements (averaging $15,597 per year), 370 teaching assistantships with full tuition reimbursements (averaging $18,225 per year) were awarded; unspecified assistantships also available. Financial award application deadline: 3/1; financial award applicants required to submit FAFSA. *Unit head:* Dr. Sally C. Morton, Dean, 540-231-5422, Fax: 540-231-3380, E-mail: scmorton@vt.edu. *Application contact:* Allison Craft, Executive Assistant, 540-231-6394, Fax: 540-231-3380, E-mail: crafta@vt.edu.
Website: http://www.science.vt.edu/

Virginia State University, College of Graduate Studies, College of Natural and Health Sciences, Department of Psychology, Petersburg, VA 23806-0001. Offers behavioral and community health sciences (PhD); clinical health psychology (PhD); clinical psychology (MS); general psychology (MS). *Degree requirements:* For master's, one foreign language, thesis. *Entrance requirements:* For master's, GRE General Test.

Wake Forest University, Graduate School of Arts and Sciences, Department of Psychology, Winston-Salem, NC 27109. Offers MA. *Degree requirements:* For master's, one foreign language, comprehensive exam, thesis. *Entrance requirements:* For master's, GRE General Test. Additional exam requirements/recommendations for international students: required—TOEFL (minimum score 79 iBT). Electronic applications accepted.

Walden University, Graduate Programs, School of Psychology, Minneapolis, MN 55401. Offers clinical psychology (MS), including counseling, general program; forensic psychology (MS), including forensic psychology in the community, general program, mental health applications, program planning and evaluation in forensic settings, psychology and legal systems; industrial organizational (MS, PhD), including consulting psychology, forensic (MS), forensic psychology (PhD), general practice, leadership development and coaching (MS), organizational diversity and social change, research evaluation (PhD); online teaching in psychology (Post-Master's Certificate); organizational psychology and development (Postbaccalaureate Certificate); psychology (MS, PhD), including applied psychology (MS), clinical psychology (PhD), crisis management and response (MS), educational psychology, forensic psychology (PhD), general psychology (MS), general psychology research (PhD), general psychology teaching (PhD), health psychology, leadership development and coaching (MS), psychology of culture (MS), psychology, public administration, and social change (MS), social psychology, terrorism and security (MS); psychology respecialization (Post-Doctoral Certificate). *Program availability:* Part-time, evening/weekend, online only, 100% online. Terminal master's awarded for partial completion of doctoral program. *Degree requirements:* For master's, thesis optional; for doctorate, thesis/dissertation, residency. *Entrance requirements:* For master's, bachelor's degree or higher; minimum GPA of 2.5; official transcripts; goal statement (for some programs); access to computer and Internet; for doctorate, master's degree or higher; three years of related professional or academic experience (preferred); minimum GPA of 3.0; goal statement and current resume (for select programs); official transcripts; access to computer and Internet; for other advanced degree, relevant work experience; access to computer and Internet. Additional exam requirements/recommendations for international students: required—TOEFL (minimum score 550 paper-based, 79 iBT), IELTS (minimum score 6.5), Michigan English Language Assessment Battery (minimum score 82), or PTE (minimum score 53). Electronic applications accepted.

Washburn University, College of Arts and Sciences, Department of Psychology, Topeka, KS 66621. Offers clinical psychology (MA). *Program availability:* Part-time. *Degree requirements:* For master's, comprehensive exam (for some programs), thesis or alternative. *Entrance requirements:* For master's, GRE General Test, 15 hours of undergraduate course work in psychology. Additional exam requirements/recommendations for international students: required—TOEFL (minimum score 80 iBT). Electronic applications accepted.

Washington State University, College of Arts and Sciences, Department of Psychology, Pullman, WA 99164. Offers clinical psychology (PhD); experimental psychology (PhD). *Accreditation:* APA (one or more programs are accredited). *Degree requirements:* For doctorate, comprehensive exam, thesis/dissertation, oral exam, written exam. *Entrance requirements:* For doctorate, GRE General Test, three letters of reference; summary data form; at least 18 credits of study in psychology; at least one course in statistics and research methodology; official transcripts; minimum cumulative undergraduate GPA of 3.0 or master's degree in psychology. Additional exam requirements/recommendations for international students: required—TOEFL, IELTS. Electronic applications accepted.

Washington University in St. Louis, The Graduate School, Department of Philosophy, Program in Philosophy-Neuroscience-Psychology, St. Louis, MO 63130-4899. Offers PhD. *Degree requirements:* For doctorate, thesis/dissertation. *Entrance requirements:* For doctorate, GRE General Test, sample of written work. Additional exam requirements/recommendations for international students: required—TOEFL. Electronic applications accepted.

Washington University in St. Louis, The Graduate School, Department of Psychological and Brain Sciences, St. Louis, MO 63130-4899. Offers aging and development (PhD). Terminal master's awarded for partial completion of doctoral program. *Degree requirements:* For doctorate, thesis/dissertation. *Entrance requirements:* For doctorate, GRE General Test. Additional exam requirements/recommendations for international students: required—TOEFL. Electronic applications accepted.

Wayne State University, College of Liberal Arts and Sciences, Department of Psychology, Detroit, MI 48202. Offers behavioral and cognitive neuroscience (PhD); clinical psychology (PhD); developmental science (PhD); industrial/organizational psychology (MA, PhD); social personality (PhD). *Accreditation:* APA (one or more programs are accredited). *Faculty:* 40. *Students:* 92 full-time (66 women), 42 part-time (27 women); includes 23 minority (4 Black or African American, non-Hispanic/Latino; 2 Asian, non-Hispanic/Latino; 9 Hispanic/Latino; 8 Two or more races, non-Hispanic/Latino), 10 international. Average age 27. 433 applicants, 15% accepted, 36 enrolled. In 2019, 28 master's, 13 doctorates awarded. Terminal master's awarded for partial completion of doctoral program. *Degree requirements:* For master's, thesis (for some programs); for doctorate, comprehensive exam, thesis/dissertation, training assignments. *Entrance requirements:* For master's, GRE General Test, minimum undergraduate upper-division cumulative GPA of 3.0, courses in psychology and statistics; for doctorate, GRE General Test, bachelor's, master's, or other advanced degree; at least twelve credits in psychology with minimum GPA of 3.0; courses in laboratory psychology and statistical methods in psychology; at least three letters of recommendation; statement of purpose. Additional exam requirements/recommendations for international students: required—TOEFL (minimum score 550

paper-based; 79 iBT), TWE (minimum score 5.5), Michigan English Language Assessment Battery (minimum score 85); recommended—IELTS (minimum score 6.5). Application fee: $50. Electronic applications accepted. *Expenses: Tuition:* Full-time $34,567. *Financial support:* In 2019–20, 93 students received support, including 11 fellowships with tuition reimbursements available (averaging $21,181 per year), 8 research assistantships with tuition reimbursements available (averaging $20,965 per year), 48 teaching assistantships with tuition reimbursements available (averaging $19,952 per year); scholarships/grants, health care benefits, and unspecified assistantships also available. Financial award applicants required to submit FAFSA. *Unit head:* Scott Bowen, PhD, Chair/Professor, 313-577-2803, E-mail: ad4771@wayne.edu. *Application contact:* Alia Allen, Academic Services Officer III, 313-577-2823, E-mail: aallen@wayne.edu.
Website: http://clas.wayne.edu/psychology/

Webster University, College of Arts and Sciences, Department of Psychology, St. Louis, MO 63119-3194. Offers counseling psychology (MS); gerontology (MS). *Program availability:* Part-time. *Entrance requirements:* Additional exam requirements/recommendations for international students: required—TOEFL.

Western Carolina University, Graduate School, College of Education and Allied Professions, Department of Psychology, Cullowhee, NC 28723. Offers general psychology (MA). *Program availability:* Part-time. *Degree requirements:* For master's, comprehensive exam, thesis. *Entrance requirements:* For master's, GRE General Test, appropriate undergraduate degree, interview, 3 letters of recommendation. Additional exam requirements/recommendations for international students: required—TOEFL (minimum score 550 paper-based; 79 iBT). *Expenses: Tuition,* area resident: Full-time $2217.50; part-time $1664 per semester. Tuition, state resident: full-time $2217.50; part-time $1664 per semester. Tuition, nonresident: full-time $7421; part-time $5566 per semester. *International tuition:* $7421 full-time. *Required fees:* $5598; $1954 per semester. Tuition and fees vary according to course load, campus/location and program.

Western Illinois University, School of Graduate Studies, College of Arts and Sciences, Department of Psychology, Macomb, IL 61455-1390. Offers clinical/community mental health (MS); general experimental psychology (MS); school psychology (SSP). *Program availability:* Part-time. *Degree requirements:* For master's, comprehensive exam (for some programs), thesis or alternative. *Entrance requirements:* For master's and SSP, GRE General Test. Additional exam requirements/recommendations for international students: required—TOEFL (minimum score 550 paper-based; 80 iBT). Electronic applications accepted.

Western Kentucky University, Graduate School, College of Education and Behavioral Sciences, Department of Psychology, Bowling Green, KY 42101. Offers clinical psychology (MA); experimental psychology (MA); general psychology (MA); industrial/organizational psychology (MA); school psychology (Ed S). *Degree requirements:* For master's, comprehensive exam, thesis (for some programs); for Ed S, thesis, oral exam. *Entrance requirements:* For master's, GRE General Test; for Ed S, GRE General Test, minimum GPA of 3.5. Additional exam requirements/recommendations for international students: required—TOEFL (minimum score 555 paper-based; 79 iBT).

Western Michigan University, Graduate College, College of Arts and Sciences, Department of Psychology, Kalamazoo, MI 49008. Offers behavior analysis (MA, PhD); clinical psychology (PhD); industrial/organizational behavior management (MA). *Accreditation:* APA (one or more programs are accredited). *Degree requirements:* For master's, variable foreign language requirement, thesis; for doctorate, 2 foreign languages, comprehensive exam, thesis/dissertation.

Western Washington University, Graduate School, College of Humanities and Social Sciences, Department of Psychology, Bellingham, WA 98225-5996. Offers experimental psychology (MS); mental health counseling (MS); school counseling (M Ed). *Accreditation:* ACA (one or more programs are accredited). *Degree requirements:* For master's, comprehensive exam, thesis (for some programs). *Entrance requirements:* For master's, GRE General Test, minimum GPA of 3.0 in last 60 semester hours or last 90 quarter hours. Additional exam requirements/recommendations for international students: required—TOEFL (minimum score 567 paper-based).

Westfield State University, College of Graduate and Continuing Education, Department of Psychology, Westfield, MA 01086. Offers applied behavior analysis (MA); counseling (MA), including forensic mental health counseling, mental health counseling, school adjustment counseling, school guidance counseling. *Program availability:* Part-time, evening/weekend. *Degree requirements:* For master's, comprehensive exam, practicum. *Entrance requirements:* For master's, GRE General Test, MAT, minimum undergraduate GPA of 3.0. Additional exam requirements/recommendations for international students: recommended—TOEFL (minimum score 550 paper-based; 79 iBT).

West Texas A&M University, College of Education and Social Sciences, Department of Psychology, Sociology and Social Work, Canyon, TX 79015. Offers psychology (MA); social work (MS). *Accreditation:* CSWE. *Program availability:* Part-time, evening/weekend. *Degree requirements:* For master's, comprehensive exam, thesis optional. *Entrance requirements:* For master's, GRE General Test, 3 letters of recommendation; interview; minimum GPA of 3.25 in psychology, 3.0 overall. Additional exam requirements/recommendations for international students: required—TOEFL. Electronic applications accepted.

West Virginia University, Eberly College of Arts and Sciences, Morgantown, WV 26506. Offers biology (MS, PhD); chemistry (MS, PhD); communication studies (MA, PhD); computational statistics (PhD); creative writing (MFA); English (MA, PhD); forensic and investigative science (MS); forensic science (PhD); geography (MA); geology (MA, PhD); history (MA, PhD); legal studies (MLS); mathematics (MS); physics (MS, PhD); political science (MA, PhD); professional writing and editing (MA); psychology (MA); public administration (MPA); social work (MSW); sociology (MA, PhD); statistics (MS). *Program availability:* Part-time, evening/weekend, online learning. Terminal master's awarded for partial completion of doctoral program. *Degree requirements:* For master's, thesis (for some programs); for doctorate, comprehensive exam, thesis/dissertation. *Entrance requirements:* For master's and doctorate, GRE. Additional exam requirements/recommendations for international students: required—TOEFL (minimum score 600 paper-based); recommended—TWE. Electronic applications accepted.

Wheaton College, Graduate School, School of Psychology Counseling and Family Therapy, Wheaton, IL 60187-5593. Offers clinical mental health counseling (MA); clinical psychology (Psy D); marriage and family therapy (MA). *Accreditation:* APA (one or more programs are accredited). Terminal master's awarded for partial completion of doctoral program. *Degree requirements:* For master's, thesis or alternative; for doctorate, thesis/dissertation, internship. *Entrance requirements:* For master's, GRE General Test, 18 hours of course work in psychology; for doctorate, GRE General Test. Additional exam requirements/recommendations for international students: required—TOEFL (minimum score 550 paper-based; 80 iBT), IELTS (minimum score 6.5). *Expenses: Tuition:* Full-time $16,800; part-time $700 per credit hour. Tuition and fees vary according to degree level and program.

Psychology—General

Wichita State University, Graduate School, Fairmount College of Liberal Arts and Sciences, Department of Psychology, Wichita, KS 67260. Offers clinical (PhD); community (PhD); human factors (PhD). *Accreditation:* APA. *Program availability:* Part-time.

Widener University, School of Human Service Professions, Institute for Graduate Clinical Psychology, Law-Psychology Program, Chester, PA 19013-5792. Offers JD/Psy D. Electronic applications accepted. *Expenses: Tuition:* Full-time $48,750; part-time $917 per credit hour. Tuition and fees vary according to class time, degree level, campus/location and program.

Wilfrid Laurier University, Faculty of Graduate and Postdoctoral Studies, Faculty of Science, Department of Psychology, Waterloo, ON N2L 3C5, Canada. Offers behavioral neuroscience (M Sc, PhD); cognitive neuroscience (M Sc, PhD); community psychology (MA, PhD); social and developmental psychology (MA, PhD). *Program availability:* Part-time. *Degree requirements:* For master's, thesis; for doctorate, thesis/dissertation. *Entrance requirements:* For master's, GRE General Test, honors BA or the equivalent in psychology, minimum B average in undergraduate course work; for doctorate, GRE General Test, master's degree, minimum A- average. Additional exam requirements/recommendations for international students: required—TOEFL (minimum score 89 iBT). Electronic applications accepted.

William Carey University, Department of Psychology and Graduate Counseling, Hattiesburg, MS 39401. Offers counseling psychology (MS). *Program availability:* Part-time. *Entrance requirements:* For master's, GRE, PRAXIS, MAT, minimum GPA of 2.5. Additional exam requirements/recommendations for international students: required—TOEFL (minimum score 550 paper-based). *Expenses:* Contact institution.

William James College, Graduate Programs, Newton, MA 02459. Offers applied psychology in higher education student personnel administration (MA); clinical psychology (Psy D); counseling psychology (MA); counseling psychology and community mental health (MA); counseling psychology and global mental health (MA); executive coaching (Graduate Certificate); forensic and counseling psychology (MA); leadership psychology (Psy D); organizational psychology (MA); primary care psychology (MA); respecialization in clinical psychology (Certificate); school psychology (Psy D); MA/CAGS. *Accreditation:* APA. *Degree requirements:* For master's, comprehensive exam (for some programs); for doctorate, thesis/dissertation (for some programs). Electronic applications accepted.

Winthrop University, College of Arts and Sciences, Department of Psychology, Rock Hill, SC 29733. Offers MS, SSP. *Degree requirements:* For master's, comprehensive exam; for SSP, thesis or alternative, portfolio. *Entrance requirements:* For master's, GRE General Test, interview, minimum GPA of 3.0, 3 letters of recommendation, 15 hours of psychology courses in specified subject areas. Additional exam requirements/recommendations for international students: required—TOEFL (minimum score 550 paper-based; 79 iBT), IELTS (minimum score 6). Electronic applications accepted. *Expenses: Tuition,* area resident: Full-time $7659; part-time $641 per credit hour. Tuition, state resident: full-time $7659; part-time $641 per credit hour. Tuition, nonresident: full-time $14,753; part-time $1234 per credit hour.

Wisconsin School of Professional Psychology, Program in Clinical Psychology, Milwaukee, WI 53225-4960. Offers MA, Psy D. *Accreditation:* APA. *Program availability:* Part-time, evening/weekend. Terminal master's awarded for partial completion of doctoral program. *Degree requirements:* For master's, candidacy exam, 500 hours of supervised clinical practica; for doctorate, thesis/dissertation, 1 year clinical intern and practicum experience (2000 hrs), candidacy and clinical exams. *Entrance requirements:*

For master's, GRE General Test, GRE Subject Test, bachelor's degree in psychology, writing sample; for doctorate, GRE General Test, GRE Subject Test, master's degree in clinical psychology or equivalent, writing sample.

The Wright Institute, Doctoral Program in Clinical Psychology, Berkeley, CA 94704-1796. Offers Psy D. *Degree requirements:* For doctorate, comprehensive exam, thesis/dissertation. *Entrance requirements:* For doctorate, GRE General Test, statistics, human development, theories of personality and/or abnormal psychology. Additional exam requirements/recommendations for international students: required—TOEFL (minimum score 600 paper-based). Electronic applications accepted.

Wright State University, Graduate School, College of Science and Mathematics, Department of Psychology, Dayton, OH 45435. Offers human factors and industrial/organizational psychology (MS, PhD). *Degree requirements:* For master's, thesis; for doctorate, thesis/dissertation. *Entrance requirements:* For master's, GRE General Test. Additional exam requirements/recommendations for international students: required—TOEFL.

Wright State University, School of Professional Psychology, Dayton, OH 45435. Offers clinical psychology (Psy D). *Accreditation:* APA. *Degree requirements:* For doctorate, thesis/dissertation. *Entrance requirements:* For doctorate, GRE General Test, GRE Subject Test. Additional exam requirements/recommendations for international students: required—TOEFL. *Expenses:* Contact institution.

Xavier University, College of Professional Sciences, Department of Psychology, Cincinnati, OH 45207. Offers clinical psychology (Psy D); industrial-organizational psychology (MA). *Accreditation:* APA (one or more programs are accredited). *Degree requirements:* For master's, one foreign language, comprehensive exam, thesis, internship; for doctorate, one foreign language, comprehensive exam, thesis/dissertation, internship. *Entrance requirements:* For master's, GRE, official transcript; 3 letters of recommendation; for doctorate, GRE General Test; GRE Subject Test in psychology (if no undergraduate degree in psychology), bachelor's or master's degree; 18 semester hours of psychology coursework; minimum GPA of 3.0; work and research experience; official transcript; 3 letters of recommendation; statement of purpose. Additional exam requirements/recommendations for international students: required—TOEFL (minimum score 550 paper-based; 79 iBT), IELTS (minimum score 6.5). Electronic applications accepted. *Expenses:* Contact institution.

Yale University, Graduate School of Arts and Sciences, Department of Psychology, New Haven, CT 06520. Offers behavioral neuroscience (PhD); clinical psychology (PhD); cognitive psychology (PhD); developmental psychology (PhD); social/personality psychology (PhD). *Accreditation:* APA. *Degree requirements:* For doctorate, thesis/dissertation. *Entrance requirements:* For doctorate, GRE General Test.

Yeshiva University, Ferkauf Graduate School of Psychology, New York, NY 10033-3201. Offers MA, PhD, Psy D. *Accreditation:* APA (one or more programs are accredited). *Program availability:* Part-time. *Degree requirements:* For doctorate, comprehensive exam, thesis/dissertation. *Entrance requirements:* For master's and doctorate, GRE General Test.

York University, Faculty of Graduate Studies, Faculty of Health, Program in Psychology, Toronto, ON M3J 1P3, Canada. Offers MA, PhD. *Program availability:* Part-time. *Degree requirements:* For master's, thesis, practicum; for doctorate, thesis/dissertation, practicum. *Entrance requirements:* For master's, GRE. Electronic applications accepted.

Addictions/Substance Abuse Counseling

Alliant International University - Los Angeles, California School of Professional Psychology, Program in Couple and Family Therapy, Alhambra, CA 91803. Offers chemical dependency (MA); gerontology (MA); Latin American family therapy (MA). *Accreditation:* AAMFT/COAMFTE. *Program availability:* Part-time, evening/weekend. Terminal master's awarded for partial completion of doctoral program. *Degree requirements:* For master's, comprehensive exam, 50 hours of professional development activities. *Entrance requirements:* Additional exam requirements/recommendations for international students: required—TOEFL (minimum score 550 paper-based). Electronic applications accepted.

Antioch University New England, Graduate School, Department of Applied Psychology, Keene, NH 03431-3552. Offers autism spectrum disorders (Certificate), including applied behavioral analysis internship, autism spectrum disorders; clinical mental health counseling (MA), including clinical mental health counseling, substance abuse counseling; dance/movement therapy and counseling (M Ed, MA, PMC); marriage and family therapy (MA, PhD, Certificate). *Faculty:* 15 full-time (12 women), 30 part-time/adjunct (25 women). *Students:* 264 full-time (217 women), 79 part-time (64 women); includes 67 minority (25 Black or African American, non-Hispanic/Latino; 2 American Indian or Alaska Native, non-Hispanic/Latino; 8 Asian, non-Hispanic/Latino; 27 Hispanic/Latino; 5 Two or more races, non-Hispanic/Latino), 5 international. Average age 35. 149 applicants, 52% accepted, 77 enrolled. In 2019, 49 master's awarded. *Degree requirements:* For master's, internship, practicum. *Entrance requirements:* For master's, previous course work and work experience in psychology. Additional exam requirements/recommendations for international students: required—TOEFL (minimum score 550 paper-based). *Application deadline:* For fall admission, 7/15 for domestic and international students; for spring admission, 12/1 for domestic and international students. Applications are processed on a rolling basis. Application fee: $50. Electronic applications accepted. *Expenses:* Contact institution. *Financial support:* In 2019–20, 56 students received support. Fellowships, research assistantships, career-related internships or fieldwork, Federal Work-Study, and scholarships/grants available. Financial award application deadline: 6/1; financial award applicants required to submit FAFSA. *Unit head:* Dr. Kevin Lyness, Department Chair, 603-283-2149, E-mail: klyness@antioch.edu. *Application contact:* Admissions, 800-552-8380, Fax: 603-357-0718, E-mail: admissions.ane@antioch.edu.
Website: https://www.antioch.edu/new-england/degrees-programs/counseling-wellness/

Argosy University, Hawaii, Hawai'i School of Professional Psychology, Program in Substance Abuse Counseling, Honolulu, HI 96813. Offers Certificate.

Arkansas State University, Graduate School, College of Nursing and Health Professions, Department of Social Work, State University, AR 72467. Offers addiction studies (Graduate Certificate); social work (MSW). *Accreditation:* CSWE. *Program availability:* Part-time. *Degree requirements:* For master's and Graduate Certificate, comprehensive exam, thesis (for some programs). *Entrance requirements:* For master's and Graduate Certificate, GRE or MAT, appropriate bachelor's degree, letters of

reference, personal statement, resume, official transcript, immunization records. Additional exam requirements/recommendations for international students: required—TOEFL (minimum score 550 paper-based; 79 iBT), IELTS (minimum score 6), PTE (minimum score 56). Electronic applications accepted. *Expenses:* Contact institution.

Assumption University, Addiction Counseling Program, Worcester, MA 01609-1296. Offers CGS. *Program availability:* Part-time, evening/weekend. *Entrance requirements:* For degree, bachelor's degree, three letters of recommendation, official transcripts, personal statement, current resume. Additional exam requirements/recommendations for international students: required—TOEFL (minimum score 540 paper-based; 76 iBT), IELTS (minimum score 6). Electronic applications accepted. *Expenses: Tuition:* Full-time $12,690; part-time $705 per credit. *Required fees:* $70 per term.

Bay Path University, Program in Clinical Mental Health Counseling, Longmeadow, MA 01106-2292. Offers clinical mental health counseling (MS), including alcohol and drug abuse counseling, early intervention. *Program availability:* Part-time, blended/hybrid learning. *Entrance requirements:* For master's, completed application; official undergraduate and graduate transcripts (a GPA of 3.0 or higher is preferred); original essay of 300-500 words on the topic "Why the MS in Clinical Mental Health Counseling is important to my personal and professional goals"; current resume; 2 recommendations. Electronic applications accepted. Application fee is waived when completed online. *Expenses:* Contact institution.

Cambridge College, School of Psychology and Counseling, Boston, MA 02129. Offers alcohol and drug counseling (Certificate); behavioral health care management (CAGS); marriage and family therapy (M Ed); mental health and school counseling (M Ed); mental health counseling (M Ed); psychological studies (M Ed); rehabilitation counseling (Certificate); school adjustment and mental health counseling (M Ed); school adjustment counseling for mental health counselors (Certificate); school counseling (M Ed); trauma studies (Certificate). *Program availability:* Part-time, evening/weekend. *Degree requirements:* For master's and other advanced degree, thesis, practicum/internship. *Entrance requirements:* For master's, resume, 2 professional references; for other advanced degree, official transcripts, documents for transfer credit evaluation, resume, written personal statement/essay, 2 professional references, health insurance, immunizations form. Additional exam requirements/recommendations for international students: required—TOEFL (minimum score 550 paper-based; 79 iBT), Michigan English Language Assessment Battery (minimum score 85); recommended—IELTS (minimum score 6). Electronic applications accepted. *Expenses:* Contact institution.

Capella University, Harold Abel School of Social and Behavioral Science, Doctoral Programs in Psychology, Minneapolis, MN 55402. Offers addiction psychology (PhD); clinical psychology (Psy D); educational psychology (PhD); general advanced studies in human behavior (PhD); general psychology (PhD); industrial/organizational psychology (PhD); school psychology (Psy D).

Capella University, Harold Abel School of Social and Behavioral Science, Master's Programs in Counseling, Minneapolis, MN 55402. Offers child and adolescent development (MS); general addiction counseling (MS); general marriage and family counseling/therapy (MS); general mental health counseling (MS); general school counseling (MS).

The College of New Jersey, Office of Graduate and Advancing Education, School of Education, Department of Counselor Education, Program in Community Counseling: Substance Abuse and Addiction Specialization, Ewing, NJ 08628. Offers MA, Certificate. *Program availability:* Part-time. *Degree requirements:* For master's, comprehensive exam. *Entrance requirements:* For master's, GRE, minimum GPA of 3.0 in field or 2.75 overall; for Certificate, previous master's degree or higher. Additional exam requirements/recommendations for international students: required—TOEFL. Electronic applications accepted.

College of St. Joseph, Graduate Programs, Division of Psychology and Human Services, Program in Alcohol and Substance Abuse Counseling, Rutland, VT 05701-3899. Offers MS. *Program availability:* Part-time. *Degree requirements:* For master's, comprehensive exam. *Entrance requirements:* For master's, official college transcripts; 2 letters of reference. Additional exam requirements/recommendations for international students: required—TOEFL (minimum score 550 paper-based). Electronic applications accepted.

Coppin State University, School of Graduate Studies, College of Behavioral and Social Sciences, Department of Applied Psychology and Rehabilitation Counseling, Program in Alcohol and Substance Abuse Counseling, Baltimore, MD 21216-3698. Offers MS. *Program availability:* Part-time. *Degree requirements:* For master's, comprehensive exam (for some programs), thesis optional, internship, clinical requirement. *Entrance requirements:* For master's, GRE General Test, interview, minimum GPA of 3.0.

East Carolina University, Graduate School, College of Allied Health Sciences, Department of Addictions and Rehabilitation Studies, Greenville, NC 27858-4353. Offers clinical counseling (MS); military and trauma counseling (Certificate); rehabilitation and career counseling (MS); rehabilitation counseling (Certificate); rehabilitation counseling and administration (PhD); substance abuse counseling (Certificate); vocational evaluation (Certificate). *Accreditation:* CORE. *Program availability:* Part-time, evening/weekend. *Students:* Average age 33. 51 applicants, 73% accepted, 31 enrolled. In 2019, 19 master's, 5 doctorates, 34 other advanced degrees awarded. *Degree requirements:* For master's, comprehensive exam, thesis or alternative, internship; for doctorate, thesis/dissertation, internship. *Entrance requirements:* For master's and doctorate, GRE General Test or MAT. Additional exam requirements/recommendations for international students: recommended—TOEFL (minimum score 78 iBT), IELTS (minimum score 6.5). *Application deadline:* For fall admission, 3/1 priority date for domestic students; for spring admission, 10/1 priority date for domestic students. Applications are processed on a rolling basis. Application fee: $75. Electronic applications accepted. *Expenses: Tuition, area resident:* Full-time $4749; part-time $185 per credit hour. Tuition, state resident: full-time $4749; part-time $185 per credit hour. Tuition, nonresident: full-time $17,898; part-time $864 per credit hour. *International tuition:* $17,898 full-time. *Required fees:* $2787. *Financial support:* Research assistantships with partial tuition reimbursements, teaching assistantships with partial tuition reimbursements, Federal Work-Study, scholarships/grants, and unspecified assistantships available. Support available to part-time students. Financial award application deadline: 3/1; financial award applicants required to submit FAFSA. *Unit head:* Dr. Paul Toriello, Chair, 252-744-6292, E-mail: toriellop@ecu.edu. *Application contact:* Graduate School Admissions, 252-328-6013, Fax: 252-328-6071, E-mail: gradschool@ecu.edu. Website: http://www.ecu.edu/rehb/

East Carolina University, Graduate School, College of Health and Human Performance, School of Social Work, Greenville, NC 27858-4353. Offers gerontology (Certificate); social work (MSW); substance abuse (Certificate). *Accreditation:* CSWE. *Program availability:* Online learning. *Application deadline:* For fall admission, 2/1 priority date for domestic and international students. *Expenses: Tuition, area resident:* Full-time $4749; part-time $185 per credit hour. Tuition, state resident: full-time $4749; part-time $185 per credit hour. Tuition, nonresident: full-time $17,898; part-time $864 per credit hour. *International tuition:* $17,898 full-time. *Required fees:* $2787. *Financial support:* Application deadline: 6/1. *Unit head:* Dr. Joseph Lee, Director, 252-328-4661, E-mail: leejose14@ecu.edu. *Application contact:* Graduate School Admissions, 252-328-6012, Fax: 252-328-6071, E-mail: gradschool@ecu.edu. Website: https://hhp.ecu.edu/socw/

Fairfield University, Graduate School of Education and Allied Professions, Fairfield, CT 06824. Offers applied behavior analysis (ATC); applied psychology (MA); clinical mental health counseling (MA, CAS); educational technology (MA); elementary education (MA, CAS); family studies (MA); integration of spirituality and religion in counseling (ATC); marriage and family therapy (MA); reading and language development (Sixth Year Certificate); school counseling (MA, CAS); school psychology (MA, CAS); school-based marriage and family therapy (ATC); secondary education (MA); special education (MA, CAS); substance abuse counseling (ATC); teaching (Certificate); teaching and foundations (MA, CAS); TESOL, world languages, and bilingual education (MA, CAS). *Accreditation:* NCATE. *Program availability:* Part-time, evening/weekend. *Faculty:* 24 full-time (18 women), 28 part-time/adjunct (20 women). *Students:* 169 full-time (149 women), 227 part-time (187 women); includes 96 minority (21 Black or African American, non-Hispanic/Latino; 8 Asian, non-Hispanic/Latino; 60 Hispanic/Latino; 7 Two or more races, non-Hispanic/Latino), 1 international. Average age 31. 194 applicants, 60% accepted, 101 enrolled. In 2019, 136 master's, 28 other advanced degrees awarded. *Degree requirements:* For master's, comprehensive exam. *Entrance requirements:* For master's, One of the following for certification programs: Praxis Core, SAT, ACT, or GRE, minimum GPA of 3.0, 2 recommendations, resume. Additional exam requirements/recommendations for international students: required—TOEFL (minimum score 550 paper-based; 84 iBT), IELTS (minimum score 7.5), TOEFL (minimum score 550 paper-based; 84 iBT) or IELTS (minimum score 7.5). *Application deadline:* For fall admission, 2/15 for international students; for spring admission, 10/1 for international students. Application fee: $60. Electronic applications accepted. *Expenses:* Tuition $815/credit hour; Lab Fee (ED598) $300/semester; Lab Fee (CN457,CN467, PY538, PY540) $70/course; Wilson Reading Course Fee $141/credit hour; Registration Fee $50/semester; Graduate Student Activity Fee (Fall and Spring) $65/semester. *Financial support:* In 2019–20, 34 students received support. Career-related internships or fieldwork and unspecified assistantships available. Support available to part-time students. Financial award applicants required to submit FAFSA. *Unit head:* Dr. Laurie Grupp, Dean, 203-254-4250, Fax: 203-254-4241, E-mail: lgrupp@fairfield.edu. *Application contact:* Melanie Rogers, Director of Graduate Admission, 203-254-4184, Fax: 203-254-4073, E-mail: gradadmis@fairfield.edu. Website: http://www.fairfield.edu/gseap

The George Washington University, Graduate School of Education and Human Development, Department of Counseling and Human Development, Program in Rehabilitation Counseling, Washington, DC 20052. Offers autism spectrum disorder (MA Ed/HD); substance abuse and psychiatric disabilities (MA Ed/HD); traumatic brain injury (MA Ed/HD). *Accreditation:* CORE. *Program availability:* Online learning. *Entrance requirements:* For master's, GRE or MAT, two letters of recommendation, 1- to 2-page statement of purpose, official transcripts from all institutions attended, resume. Additional exam requirements/recommendations for international students: required—TOEFL or IELTS. Electronic applications accepted.

Governors State University, College of Health and Human Services, Program in Addiction Studies and Behavioral Health, University Park, IL 60484. Offers MHS. *Program availability:* Part-time. *Faculty:* 8 full-time (5 women), 9 part-time/adjunct (7 women). *Students:* 12 full-time (10 women), 89 part-time (69 women); includes 72 minority (70 Black or African American, non-Hispanic/Latino; 1 Hispanic/Latino; 1 Two or more races, non-Hispanic/Latino), 1 international. Average age 43. 44 applicants, 48% accepted, 16 enrolled. In 2019, 25 master's awarded. *Application deadline:* For fall admission, 4/1 for domestic students. Applications are processed on a rolling basis. Application fee: $50. Electronic applications accepted. *Expenses: Tuition, area resident:* Full-time $8472; part-time $353 per credit hour. Tuition, state resident: full-time $8472; part-time $353 per credit hour. Tuition, nonresident: full-time $16,944; part-time $706 per credit hour. *International tuition:* $16,944 full-time. *Required fees:* $2520; $105 per credit hour. $38 per term. Tuition and fees vary according to course load, degree level and program. *Financial support:* Application deadline: 5/1; applicants required to submit FAFSA. *Unit head:* Cheryl Mejta, Chair, Department of Addictions Studies and Behavioral Health, 708-534-5000 Ext. 4911, E-mail: cmejta@govst.edu. *Application contact:* Cheryl Mejta, Chair, Department of Addictions Studies and Behavioral Health, 708-534-5000 Ext. 4911, E-mail: cmejta@govst.edu.

Hazelden Betty Ford Graduate School of Addiction Studies, Graduate Programs, Center City, MN 55012. Offers addiction counseling (MA, Certificate). *Program availability:* Part-time. *Entrance requirements:* Additional exam requirements/recommendations for international students: required—TOEFL.

Indiana University Northwest, College of Arts and Sciences, Gary, IN 46408. Offers clinical counseling (MS), including drug and alcohol counseling; community development/urban studies (Graduate Certificate); computer information systems (Graduate Certificate); liberal studies (MLS); race-ethnic studies (Graduate Certificate); women's and gender studies (Graduate Certificate). *Program availability:* Part-time, evening/weekend. *Entrance requirements:* For master's, GRE (recommended for MS), minimum undergraduate GPA of 3.0, bachelor's degree from accredited university (for MS). Electronic applications accepted. *Expenses:* Contact institution.

Indiana University Northwest, School of Social Work, Gary, IN 46408-1197. Offers health (MSW); mental health and addictions (MSW). *Program availability:* Part-time, evening/weekend. *Degree requirements:* For master's, practicum. *Entrance requirements:* For master's, minimum GPA of 3.0; bachelor's degree from accredited university including the successful completion of 6 courses in social or behavioral sciences and 1 course in statistics; 3 professional references. Electronic applications accepted. *Expenses:* Contact institution.

Indiana University South Bend, School of Education, South Bend, IN 46615. Offers addiction counseling (MS Ed); alcohol and drug counseling (Graduate Certificate); clinical mental health counseling (MS Ed); educational leadership (MS Ed); elementary education (MS Ed); marriage, couple, and family counseling (MS Ed); school counseling (MS Ed); secondary education (MS Ed); special education (MAT, MS Ed), including intense intervention (MS Ed), mild intervention (MS Ed). *Accreditation:* NCATE. *Program availability:* Part-time, evening/weekend. *Degree requirements:* For master's, thesis or alternative, exit project. *Entrance requirements:* For master's, letters of recommendation, GRE or minimum GPA of 3.0. Additional exam requirements/recommendations for international students: required—TOEFL. Electronic applications accepted. *Expenses:* Contact institution.

Indiana Wesleyan University, Graduate School, College of Arts and Sciences, Marion, IN 46953. Offers addictions counseling (MS); clinical mental health counseling (MS); community counseling (MS); marriage and family therapy (MS); school counseling (MS); student development counseling and administration (MS). *Accreditation:* ACA. *Program availability:* Part-time. *Degree requirements:* For master's, thesis or alternative. *Entrance requirements:* For master's, GRE General Test. Additional exam requirements/recommendations for international students: required—TOEFL. Electronic applications accepted. *Expenses:* Contact institution.

Johnson & Wales University, Graduate Studies, MS Program in Counseling, Providence, RI 02903-3703. Offers addiction counseling (MS); clinical mental health counseling (MS). *Program availability:* Part-time.

Kean University, Nathan Weiss Graduate College, Program in Counselor Education, Union, NJ 07083. Offers alcohol and drug abuse counseling (MA); clinical mental health counseling (MA); school counseling (MA). *Accreditation:* ACA; NCATE. *Program availability:* Part-time. *Faculty:* 10 full-time (7 women). *Students:* 128 full-time (100 women), 164 part-time (126 women); includes 137 minority (63 Black or African American, non-Hispanic/Latino; 2 American Indian or Alaska Native, non-Hispanic/Latino; 9 Asian, non-Hispanic/Latino; 58 Hispanic/Latino; 2 Native Hawaiian or other Pacific Islander, non-Hispanic/Latino; 3 Two or more races, non-Hispanic/Latino). Average age 33. 217 applicants, 37% accepted, 52 enrolled. In 2019, 90 master's awarded. *Degree requirements:* For master's, practicum, internship, portfolio. *Entrance requirements:* For master's, minimum GPA of 3.0, 2 letters of recommendation, personal statement, resume. Additional exam requirements/recommendations for international students: required—TOEFL (minimum score 550 paper-based; 79 iBT), IELTS (minimum score 6.5). *Application deadline:* For fall admission, 3/1 for domestic and international students; for spring admission, 11/1 for domestic and international students. Applications are processed on a rolling basis. Application fee: $75. Electronic applications accepted. *Expenses:* Tuition, state resident: full-time $15,326; part-time $748 per credit. Tuition, nonresident: full-time $20,288; part-time $902 per credit. *Required fees:* $2149.50; $91.25 per credit. Tuition and fees vary according to course level, course load, degree level and program. *Financial support:* Scholarships/grants and unspecified assistantships available. Financial award applicants required to submit FAFSA. *Unit head:* Dr. J. Barry Mascari, Program Coordinator, 908-737-5954, E-mail: jmascari@kean.edu. *Application contact:* Pedro Lopes, Admissions Counselor, 908-737-7100, E-mail: gradadmissions@kean.edu. Website: http://grad.kean.edu/counseling

Lenoir-Rhyne University, Graduate Programs, School of Education, Program in Human Services, Hickory, NC 28601. Offers management (MA); substance abuse (MA); vocational strategies (MA). *Program availability:* Part-time, online only, 100% online. *Degree requirements:* For master's, comprehensive exam. *Entrance requirements:* For master's, GRE General Test or MAT, essay; minimum GPA of 2.7 undergraduate, 3.0 graduate. Additional exam requirements/recommendations for international students: required—TOEFL (minimum score 600 paper-based). Electronic applications accepted. *Expenses:* Contact institution.

Lewis & Clark College, Graduate School of Education and Counseling, Department of Counseling Psychology, Program in Professional Mental Health Counseling - Addictions, Portland, OR 97219-7899. Offers MA, MS. *Program availability:* Part-time, evening/weekend. *Degree requirements:* For master's, thesis (MS). *Entrance requirements:* For master's, GRE General Test, minimum undergraduate GPA of 2.75. Additional exam requirements/recommendations for international students: required—TOEFL (minimum score 575 paper-based). Electronic applications accepted.

Addictions/Substance Abuse Counseling

Liberty University, School of Behavioral Sciences, Lynchburg, VA 24515. Offers applied psychology (MA), including developmental psychology (MA, MS), industrial/organizational psychology (MA, MS); clinical mental health counseling (MA); community care and counseling (Ed D), including marriage and family counseling, pastoral care and counseling, traumatology; counselor education and supervision (PhD); human services counseling (MA), including addictions and recovery, business, child and family law, Christian ministries, criminal justice, crisis response and trauma, executive leadership, health and wellness, life coaching, marriage and family, military resilience; marriage and family counseling (MA); marriage and family therapy (MA); military resilience (Certificate); pastoral counseling (MA), including addictions and recovery, community chaplaincy, crisis response and trauma, discipleship and church ministry, leadership, life coaching, marriage and family, marriage and family studies, military resilience, parenting and child/adolescent, pastoral counseling, theology; professional counseling (MA); psychology (MS), including developmental psychology (MA, MS), industrial/organizational psychology (MA, MS); school counseling (M Ed). *Program availability:* Part-time, online learning. *Students:* 3,786 full-time (3,065 women), 5,193 part-time (4,081 women); includes 2,733 minority (1,967 Black or African American, non-Hispanic/Latino; 48 American Indian or Alaska Native, non-Hispanic/Latino; 103 Asian, non-Hispanic/Latino; 349 Hispanic/Latino; 19 Native Hawaiian or other Pacific Islander, non-Hispanic/Latino; 247 Two or more races, non-Hispanic/Latino), 133 international. Average age 38. 13,324 applicants, 28% accepted, 2,163 enrolled. In 2019, 2,322 master's, 19 doctorates, 112 other advanced degrees awarded. *Entrance requirements:* For master's, Official bachelor's degree transcripts with a 2.0 GPA or higher. *Application deadline:* Applications are processed on a rolling basis. Application fee: $50. Electronic applications accepted. *Expenses: Tuition:* Full-time $545; part-time $410 per credit hour. One-time fee: $50. *Financial support:* In 2019–20, 1,003 students received support. Teaching assistantships and Federal Work-Study available. Financial award applicants required to submit FAFSA. *Unit head:* Dr. Kenyon Knapp, Dean, School of Behavioral Services, E-mail: kcknapp@liberty.edu. *Application contact:* Jay Bridge, Director of Admissions, 800-424-9595, Fax: 800-628-7977, E-mail: gradadmissions@liberty.edu.
Website: https://www.liberty.edu/behavioral-sciences/

Liberty University, School of Divinity, Lynchburg, VA 24515. Offers Biblical exposition (MA); Biblical languages (M Div); Biblical studies (M Div, MA, MAR, Th M, D Min); chaplaincy (M Div, D Min); Christian apologetics (M Div, MA, MAR, Th M); Christian leadership and church ministries (M Div); Christian ministries (M Div); Christian ministry (MA); Christian thought (M Div); church history (M Div, MAR, Th M); community chaplaincy (M Div, MAR); discipleship (D Min); discipleship and church ministry (M Div, MAR, MCM); evangelism and church planting (MAR, MCM, D Min); expository preaching (D Min); global ministry (MA); global studies (M Div, MAR, MCM, MGS, Th M); healthcare chaplaincy (M Div); homiletics (M Div, MAR, Th M); leadership (M Div, MAR); marketplace chaplaincy (M Div, MCM); ministry leadership (Ed D); pastoral counseling (M Div, MA, MAR, D Min), including addictions and recovery (MA), crisis response and trauma (MA), discipleship and church ministries (MA), leadership (MA), life coaching (MA), marketplace chaplaincy (MA), marriage and family (MA), military resilience (MA), pastoral counseling (MA); pastoral leadership (D Min); pastoral ministries (M Div, M Serv Soc, MCM); religious education (MRE); sports chaplaincy (MA); theology (M Div, MAR, MTS, Th M); theology and apologetics (D Min, PhD); worship (M Div, MAR, MCM, D Min); youth and family ministries (M Div). *Program availability:* Part-time, online learning. *Students:* 2,691 full-time (814 women), 2,570 part-time (732 women); includes 1,484 minority (1,046 Black or African American, non-Hispanic/Latino; 33 American Indian or Alaska Native, non-Hispanic/Latino; 120 Asian, non-Hispanic/Latino; 167 Hispanic/Latino; 8 Native Hawaiian or other Pacific Islander, non-Hispanic/Latino; 110 Two or more races, non-Hispanic/Latino), 101 international. Average age 43. 4,508 applicants, 34% accepted, 952 enrolled. In 2019, 1,251 master's, 71 doctorates awarded. *Degree requirements:* For master's, 2 foreign languages, thesis (for some programs); for doctorate, 2 foreign languages, thesis/dissertation. *Entrance requirements:* For master's, minimum undergraduate GPA of 2.0; for doctorate, GRE General Test or MAT, minimum graduate GPA of 3.0. Additional exam requirements/recommendations for international students: required—TOEFL (minimum score 600 paper-based; 100 iBT). *Application deadline:* For fall admission, 6/1 for domestic students; for spring admission, 11/1 for domestic students. Applications are processed on a rolling basis. Application fee: $50. Electronic applications accepted. *Expenses:* Contact institution. *Financial support:* Teaching assistantships with tuition reimbursements, career-related internships or fieldwork, and Federal Work-Study available. Financial award applicants required to submit FAFSA. *Unit head:* Dr. Troy Temple, Interim Dean, School of Divinity, E-mail: divinity@liberty.edu. *Application contact:* Jay Bridge, Director of Graduate Admissions, 800-424-9595, Fax: 800-628-7977, E-mail: gradadmissions@liberty.edu.
Website: https://www.liberty.edu/divinity/

Loma Linda University, School of Behavioral Health, Department of Counseling and Family Sciences, Loma Linda, CA 92350. Offers child life specialist (MS); clinical mediation (Certificate); counseling (MS); drug and alcohol counseling (Certificate); family life education (Certificate); marital and family therapy (DMFT); school counseling (Certificate). *Degree requirements:* For master's, comprehensive exam, thesis optional; for doctorate, comprehensive exam, thesis/dissertation (for some programs). *Entrance requirements:* For master's, minimum GPA of 3.0; for doctorate, GRE. Additional exam requirements/recommendations for international students: required—TOEFL (minimum score 550 paper-based). Electronic applications accepted.

Long Island University - Hudson, Graduate School, Purchase, NY 10577. Offers autism (Advanced Certificate); bilingual education (Advanced Certificate); childhood education (MS Ed); crisis management (Advanced Certificate); early childhood education (MS Ed); educational leadership (MS Ed); health administration (MPA); literacy (MS Ed); marriage and family therapy (MS); mental health counseling (MS, Advanced Certificate), including credentialed alcoholism and substance abuse counselor (MS); middle childhood and adolescence education (MS Ed); pharmaceutics (MS), including cosmetic science, industrial pharmacy; public administration (MPA); school counseling (MS Ed, Advanced Certificate); school psychology (MS Ed); special education (MS Ed); TESOL (MS Ed); TESOL (all grades) (Advanced Certificate). *Program availability:* Part-time, evening/weekend. *Entrance requirements:* Additional exam requirements/recommendations for international students: required—TOEFL. Electronic applications accepted. *Expenses:* Contact institution.

Maryville University of Saint Louis, Myrtle E. and Earl E. Walker College of Health Professions, Program in Rehabilitation Counseling, St. Louis, MO 63141-7299. Offers marriage and family therapy (MARC); music therapy (MARC); substance abuse (MARC). *Accreditation:* CORE. *Program availability:* Part-time. *Faculty:* 3 full-time (1 woman). *Students:* 18 full-time (16 women), 16 part-time (12 women); includes 9 minority (7 Black or African American, non-Hispanic/Latino; 2 Two or more races, non-Hispanic/Latino). Average age 31. In 2019, 7 master's awarded. *Degree requirements:* For master's, internship, seminar. *Entrance requirements:* For master's, Bachelors degree from regionally accredited institution. minimum cumulative GPA of 3.0, 2 letters of recommendation, interview, essay, transcripts, resume. Additional exam requirements/recommendations for international students: required—TOEFL (minimum score 563 paper-based; 92 iBT). *Application deadline:* For fall admission, 1/15 for domestic students; for spring admission, 10/1 for domestic students. Applications are processed on a rolling basis. Electronic applications accepted. *Expenses:* Contact institution. *Financial support:* Career-related internships or fieldwork, Federal Work-Study, and campus employment available. Financial award application deadline: 4/1; financial award applicants required to submit FAFSA. *Unit head:* Dr. Michael Kiener, Director, 314-529-9443, Fax: 314-529-9495, E-mail: mkiener@maryville.edu. *Application contact:* Jeannie DeLuca, Director, Admissions and Advising, 314-529-9355, Fax: 314-529-9927, E-mail: jdeluca@maryville.edu.
Website: http://www.maryville.edu/hp/rehabilitation-counseling/

Metropolitan State University, College of Community Studies and Public Affairs, St. Paul, MN 55106-5000. Offers alcohol and drug counseling (MS); co-occurring disorders recovery counseling (MS); public administration (MPA); public and nonprofit administration (MPNA).

Monmouth University, Graduate Studies, Department of Professional Counseling, West Long Branch, NJ 07764-1898. Offers addiction studies (MA); clinical mental health counseling (MS); professional counseling (PMC). *Accreditation:* ACA. *Program availability:* Part-time, evening/weekend. *Faculty:* 9 full-time (5 women), 4 part-time/adjunct (3 women). *Students:* 91 full-time (78 women), 53 part-time (38 women); includes 28 minority (11 Black or African American, non-Hispanic/Latino; 1 Asian, non-Hispanic/Latino; 12 Hispanic/Latino; 4 Two or more races, non-Hispanic/Latino). Average age 30. In 2019, 57 master's awarded. *Degree requirements:* For master's, comprehensive exam (for some programs), thesis optional, fieldwork. *Entrance requirements:* For master's, GRE, minimum GPA of 3.0 overall, 12 credits in psychology or closely-related field, two Monmouth University psychological counseling recommendation forms, narrative essay; for PMC, degree or current enrollment in CACREP-accredited master's program in counseling with minimum cumulative GPA of 3.0. Additional exam requirements/recommendations for international students: required—TOEFL (minimum score 550 paper-based; 79 iBT), IELTS (minimum score 6), Michigan English Language Assessment Battery (minimum score 77) or Certificate of Advanced English (minimum score 160). *Application deadline:* For fall admission, 7/15 priority date for domestic students, 6/1 for international students; for spring admission, 12/1 priority date for domestic students, 11/1 for international students; for summer admission, 5/1 for domestic students. Applications are processed on a rolling basis. Application fee: $50. Electronic applications accepted. *Expenses: Tuition:* Full-time $22,194; part-time $14,796 per credit. *Required fees:* $712; $178 per semester. $178 per semester. Tuition and fees vary according to course load. *Financial support:* In 2019–20, 149 students received support. Research assistantships, teaching assistantships, scholarships/grants, and unspecified assistantships available. Support available to part-time students. Financial award applicants required to submit FAFSA. *Unit head:* Dr. Joanne Jodry, Program Director, 732-263-5115, Fax: 732-923-4661, E-mail: jjodry@monmouth.edu. *Application contact:* Kevin New, Graduate Admission Counselor, 732-571-3452, Fax: 732-263-5123, E-mail: gradadm@monmouth.edu.
Website: https://www.monmouth.edu/school-of-humanities-social-sciences/professional-counseling.aspx

Montclair State University, The Graduate School, College of Education and Human Services, Certified Alcohol and Drug Counselor Certificate Program, Montclair, NJ 07043-1624. Offers Certificate.

Northern Vermont University–Johnson, Program in Counseling, Johnson, VT 05656. Offers addictions counseling (MA); clinical mental health counseling (MA); general counseling (MA); school counseling (MA). *Program availability:* Part-time. *Degree requirements:* For master's, comprehensive exam. *Entrance requirements:* For master's, interview. Additional exam requirements/recommendations for international students: required—TOEFL. Electronic applications accepted.

Northwest Nazarene University, Program in Social Work, Nampa, ID 83686-5897. Offers clinical mental health and addictions practice (MSW). *Accreditation:* CSWE. *Program availability:* Part-time-only, evening/weekend. *Degree requirements:* For master's, comprehensive exam, thesis or alternative. *Entrance requirements:* For master's, interview, letters of reference, degree from regionally-accredited college/university, written personal statement. Electronic applications accepted.

Nova Southeastern University, College of Psychology, Fort Lauderdale, FL 33314-7796. Offers clinical mental health counseling (MS); clinical psychology (PhD, Psy D); counseling (MS); experimental psychology (MS); forensic psychology (MS); general psychology (MS); school counseling (MS); school psychology (Psy D, Psy S); substance abuse counseling (MS); substance abuse counseling and education (MS). *Accreditation:* APA (one or more programs are accredited). *Program availability:* Part-time, 100% online, blended/hybrid learning. *Faculty:* 72 full-time (34 women), 111 part-time/adjunct (76 women). *Students:* 1,263 full-time (1,068 women), 868 part-time (761 women); includes 1,221 minority (368 Black or African American, non-Hispanic/Latino; 3 American Indian or Alaska Native, non-Hispanic/Latino; 111 Asian, non-Hispanic/Latino; 668 Hispanic/Latino; 1 Native Hawaiian or other Pacific Islander, non-Hispanic/Latino; 70 Two or more races, non-Hispanic/Latino), 59 international. Average age 31. 935 applicants, 56% accepted, 375 enrolled. In 2019, 400 master's, 72 doctorates, 13 other advanced degrees awarded. Terminal master's awarded for partial completion of doctoral program. *Degree requirements:* For master's, comprehensive exam, 3 practica; for doctorate, thesis/dissertation, clinical internship, competency exam; for Psy S, comprehensive exam, internship. *Entrance requirements:* For master's and Psy S, GRE General Test, letters of recommendation, research/personal statement, interview; for doctorate, GRE General Test, GRE Subject Test (recommended), minimum undergraduate GPA of 3.0, letters of recommendation, research/personal statement, interview, curriculum vitae/resume. Additional exam requirements/recommendations for international students: required—TOEFL (minimum score 550 paper-based). *Application deadline:* Applications are processed on a rolling basis. Application fee: $50. Electronic applications accepted. *Expenses:* Contact institution. *Financial support:* In 2019–20, 197 students received support, including 15 research assistantships (averaging $5,600 per year), 68 teaching assistantships (averaging $2,000 per year); career-related internships or fieldwork, Federal Work-Study, institutionally sponsored loans, scholarships/grants, and unspecified assistantships also available. Support available to part-time students. Financial award application deadline: 4/15; financial award applicants required to submit FAFSA. *Unit head:* Dr. Karen Grosby, Dean, 954-262-5712, Fax: 954-262-3859, E-mail: grosby@nova.edu. *Application contact:* Gregory Gayle, Director, Recruitment and Admissions, 954-262-5903, Fax: 954-262-3893, E-mail: ggayle1@nova.edu.
Website: http://psychology.nova.edu/

Oral Roberts University, School of Theology and Missions, Tulsa, OK 74171. Offers biblical literature (MA), including advanced languages, Judaic-Christian studies; church ministries and leadership (D Min); clinical pastoral education (M Div); missions (MA); pastoral care and chaplaincy (M Div, D Min); practical theology (MA), including teaching ministries, urban ministries; professional counseling (MA), including addiction studies, marriage and family therapy; theological/historical studies (MA). *Accreditation:* ATS. *Program availability:* Part-time, online learning. *Faculty:* 17 full-time (2 women). *Students:* 268 full-time (146 women), 96 part-time (52 women); includes 66 minority (48 Black or African American, non-Hispanic/Latino; 9 American Indian or Alaska Native, non-Hispanic/Latino; 8 Asian, non-Hispanic/Latino; 1 Native Hawaiian or other Pacific Islander, non-Hispanic/Latino), 65 international. Average age 40. 661 applicants, 24% accepted, 136 enrolled. In 2019, 113 master's, 19 doctorates awarded. *Degree*

requirements: For master's, thesis (for some programs), practicum/internship; for doctorate, thesis/dissertation, applied research project. *Entrance requirements:* For master's, GRE General Test or MAT (waived for those with undergraduate degree from regionally accredited institution and 3.0 or higher GPA), minimum GPA of 2.5 (professional) or 3.0 (academic); for doctorate, M Div, minimum GPA of 3.0, 3 years of full-time ministry experience. Additional exam requirements/recommendations for international students: recommended—TOEFL (minimum score 550 paper-based; 79 iBT), IELTS (minimum score 7). *Application deadline:* Applications are processed on a rolling basis. Application fee: $35. Electronic applications accepted. Application fee is waived when completed online. *Expenses: Tuition:* Full-time $11,052; part-time $5526 per year. *Required fees:* $1230; $615 per unit. Tuition and fees vary according to program. *Financial support:* Fellowships and scholarships/grants available. Financial award application deadline: 6/1. *Unit head:* Dr. Bill Buker, Chair, 918-495-6493, E-mail: bbuker@oru.edu. *Application contact:* Joe Sims, Enrollment Counselor, 918-495-6618, E-mail: jsims@oru.edu.
Website: http://www.gradtheology.oru.edu/

Pace University, Dyson College of Arts and Sciences, Department of Psychology, Program in Mental Health Counseling, New York, NY 10038. Offers grief and loss (MS); mental health counseling (MS, PhD); substance abuse (MS). *Program availability:* Part-time, evening/weekend. Terminal master's awarded for partial completion of doctoral program. *Degree requirements:* For master's, comprehensive exam, qualifying exams, internship; for doctorate, comprehensive exam, thesis/dissertation, internships. *Entrance requirements:* For master's, GRE, resume, personal statement, two letters of reference, official transcripts, interview; for doctorate, three letters of recommendation (two of which are academic in nature); personal statement; official transcripts; internship(s); interview; master's degree in mental health counseling or program with curriculum equivalent to that of Pace's graduate program in mental health counseling. Additional exam requirements/recommendations for international students: required—TOEFL (minimum score 88 iBT), IELTS (minimum score 7) or PTE (minimum score 60). Electronic applications accepted.

Palm Beach Atlantic University, School of Education and Behavioral Studies, West Palm Beach, FL 33416-4708. Offers counseling psychology (MS), including addictions/mental health, general counseling, marriage and family therapy, mental health counseling, school guidance counseling. *Program availability:* Part-time, evening/weekend. *Entrance requirements:* For master's, GRE or MAT, minimum GPA of 3.0; essay. Additional exam requirements/recommendations for international students: required—TOEFL (minimum score 550 paper-based; 79 iBT). Electronic applications accepted. *Expenses: Tuition:* Part-time $570 per credit hour. *Required fees:* $580 per unit. Tuition and fees vary according to degree level, campus/location and program.

Plymouth State University, College of Graduate Studies, Graduate Studies in Education, Programs in Counseling, Plymouth, NH 03264-1595. Offers addictions treatment (MS); couples and family therapy (MS); play therapy (MS). *Accreditation:* ACA; NCATE. *Program availability:* Part-time, evening/weekend. *Entrance requirements:* For master's, MAT, minimum GPA of 3.0.

Post University, Program in Counseling and Human Services, Waterbury, CT 06723-2540. Offers counseling and human services (MS); counseling and human services/alcohol and drug counseling (MS); counseling and human services/clinical mental health counseling (MS); counseling and human services/forensic mental health counseling (MS); counseling and human services/non-profit management (MS). *Program availability:* Part-time, evening/weekend, online learning. *Entrance requirements:* For master's, resume.

Regent University, Graduate School, School of Psychology and Counseling, Virginia Beach, VA 23464-9800. Offers clinical mental health counseling (MA); clinical psychology (Psy D); counseling and psychological studies - clinical (PhD); counseling and psychological studies - research (PhD); counseling studies (CAGS); counselor education and supervision (PhD); general psychology (MS); human services (MA), including addictions counseling, Biblical counseling, Christian counseling, conflict and mediation ministry, criminal justice and ministry, grief counseling, human services counseling, human services for student affairs, life coaching, marriage and family ministry, trauma and crisis counseling; marriage, couple, and family counseling (MA); pastoral counseling (MA); school counseling (MA); M Div/MA; M Ed/MA; MBA/MA. *Accreditation:* ACA; APA (one or more programs are accredited). *Program availability:* Part-time, evening/weekend, 100% online, blended/hybrid learning. *Degree requirements:* For master's, thesis or alternative, internship, practicum, written competency exam; for doctorate, thesis/dissertation or alternative. *Entrance requirements:* For master's, GRE General Test (including writing exam) or MAT, minimum undergraduate GPA of 3.0, resume, transcripts, writing sample, personal goals statement; for doctorate, GRE General Test (including writing exam), minimum undergraduate GPA of 3.0, graduate 3.5; writing sample; 3 recommendations; resume; college transcripts; personal goals statement. Additional exam requirements/recommendations for international students: required—TOEFL (minimum score 577 paper-based). Electronic applications accepted. *Expenses:* Contact institution.

Salve Regina University, Program in Rehabilitation Counseling, Newport, RI 02840-4192. Offers clinical rehabilitation and mental health counseling (MA); mental health (CAGS), including rehabilitation counseling; rehabilitation (CAGS), including substance abuse counseling; rehabilitation counseling (MA); substance abuse and treatment (CAGS). *Accreditation:* CORE. *Program availability:* Part-time, evening/weekend. *Entrance requirements:* For master's, GMAT, GRE General Test or MAT. Additional exam requirements/recommendations for international students: required—TOEFL (minimum score 600 paper-based; 100 iBT) or IELTS. Electronic applications accepted.

Stephens College, Division of Graduate and Continuing Studies, Columbia, MO 65215-0002. Offers counseling (M Ed), including addictions counseling, clinical mental health counseling, school counseling; health information administration (Postbaccalaureate Certificate); physician assistant studies (MPAS); TV and screenwriting (MFA). *Program availability:* Part-time, evening/weekend, online learning. *Entrance requirements:* For master's, minimum GPA of 3.0 in last 60 hours. Additional exam requirements/recommendations for international students: required—TOEFL (minimum score 79 iBT). Electronic applications accepted.

Stony Brook University, State University of New York, Stony Brook Medicine, Renaissance School of Medicine, Program in Public Health, Stony Brook, NY 11794. Offers community health (MPH); evaluation sciences (MPH); family violence (MPH); health communication (Certificate); health economics (MPH); health education and promotion (Certificate); population health (MPH); substance abuse (MPH). *Accreditation:* CEPH. *Program availability:* Part-time, evening/weekend. *Students:* 39 full-time (30 women), 17 part-time (12 women); includes 24 minority (3 Black or African American, non-Hispanic/Latino; 13 Asian, non-Hispanic/Latino; 7 Hispanic/Latino; 1 Two or more races, non-Hispanic/Latino), 2 international. Average age 28. 174 applicants, 67% accepted, 70 enrolled. In 2019, 22 master's awarded. *Entrance requirements:* For master's, GRE, 3 references, bachelor's degree from accredited college or university with minimum GPA of 3.0, essays, interview. Additional exam requirements/recommendations for international students: required—TOEFL (minimum score 90 iBT). *Application deadline:* For fall admission, 7/15 for domestic students. Application fee: $100. Electronic applications accepted. *Expenses:* Contact institution. *Financial support:* In 2019–20, 4 research assistantships were awarded; fellowships also available. *Unit head:* Dr. Lisa A. Benz Scott, Director, 631-444-9396, E-mail: publichealth@stonybrookmedicine.edu. *Application contact:* Joanie Maniaci, Assistant Director for Student Affairs, 631-444-2074, Fax: 631-444-6035, E-mail: joanmarie.maniaci@stonybrook.edu.
Website: https://publichealth.stonybrookmedicine.edu/

Syracuse University, David B. Falk College of Sport and Human Dynamics, Programs in Addiction Studies, Syracuse, NY 13244. Offers MA, CAS. *Program availability:* Part-time. *Entrance requirements:* For master's, GRE, personal statement, official transcripts, three letters of recommendation, resume; for CAS, personal statement, official transcripts, three letters of recommendation, resume. Additional exam requirements/recommendations for international students: required—TOEFL (minimum score 100 iBT). Electronic applications accepted.

Texas Tech University Health Sciences Center, School of Health Professions, Program in Addiction Counseling, Lubbock, TX 79430. Offers MS. *Program availability:* Part-time, 100% online, blended/hybrid learning. *Faculty:* 7 full-time (4 women). *Students:* 8 full-time (7 women), 13 part-time (10 women); includes 9 minority (2 Black or African American, non-Hispanic/Latino; 2 Asian, non-Hispanic/Latino; 5 Hispanic/Latino). Average age 39. 3 applicants, 100% accepted, 3 enrolled. In 2019, 1 master's awarded. *Degree requirements:* For master's, internship. *Entrance requirements:* Additional exam requirements/recommendations for international students: required—TOEFL (minimum score 550 paper-based; 79 iBT). *Application deadline:* For fall admission, 6/1 for domestic students; for spring admission, 11/1 for domestic students. Applications are processed on a rolling basis. Application fee: $75. Electronic applications accepted. *Expenses:* Contact institution. *Financial support:* In 2019–20, 9 students received support. Available to part-time students. Application deadline: 9/1; applicants required to submit FAFSA. *Unit head:* Dr. Zach Sneed, Program Director, 806-743-2590, Fax: 806-743-3244, E-mail: health.professions@ttuhsc.edu. *Application contact:* Lindsay Johnson, Associate Dean for Admissions and Student Affairs, 806-743-3220, Fax: 806-743-2994, E-mail: health.professions@ttuhsc.edu.
Website: http://www.ttuhsc.edu/health-professions/master-of-science-addiction-counseling/

United States International University–Africa, School of Arts and Sciences, Nairobi, Kenya. Offers counseling psychology (MA), including chemical dependency, health psychology; international relations (MA), including development studies, diplomacy and foreign policy, peace and conflict studies. *Program availability:* Part-time, evening/weekend. *Degree requirements:* For master's, thesis, practicum. *Entrance requirements:* For master's, GRE General Test, 2 letters of recommendation, resume. Additional exam requirements/recommendations for international students: required—TOEFL.

Universidad Central del Caribe, Program in Substance Abuse Counseling, Bayamón, PR 00960-6032. Offers MHS.

University of California, Berkeley, UC Berkeley Extension, Certificate Programs in Behavioral and Health Sciences, Berkeley, CA 94720. Offers alcohol and drug abuse studies (Certificate). *Accreditation:* APA.

University of Central Oklahoma, The Jackson College of Graduate Studies, College of Liberal Arts, Department of Sociology, Gerontology, and Substance Abuse Studies, Edmond, OK 73034-5209. Offers gerontology (MA); substance abuse studies (MA), including substance abuse studies. *Program availability:* Part-time. *Degree requirements:* For master's, variable foreign language requirement, comprehensive exam (for some programs), thesis (for some programs). *Entrance requirements:* Additional exam requirements/recommendations for international students: required—TOEFL (minimum score 550 paper-based; 79 iBT), IELTS (minimum score 6.5). Electronic applications accepted.

University of Cincinnati, Graduate School, College of Education, Criminal Justice, and Human Services, School of Human Services, Counseling Program, Cincinnati, OH 45221-0068. Offers counselor education (Ed D); mental health (MA); school counseling (M Ed); substance abuse prevention (Graduate Certificate). *Accreditation:* ACA (one or more programs are accredited); NCATE. *Program availability:* Part-time. *Faculty:* 8 full-time (5 women), 4 part-time/adjunct (3 women). *Students:* 73 full-time (62 women), 16 part-time (14 women); includes 17 minority (10 Black or African American, non-Hispanic/Latino; 1 Asian, non-Hispanic/Latino; 2 Hispanic/Latino; 4 Two or more races, non-Hispanic/Latino), 7 international. Average age 24. 112 applicants, 64% accepted, 40 enrolled. In 2019, 19 master's, 2 doctorates awarded. Terminal master's awarded for partial completion of doctoral program. *Degree requirements:* For master's, comprehensive exam, thesis or alternative; for doctorate, comprehensive exam, thesis/dissertation. *Entrance requirements:* For master's and doctorate, GRE General Test, interview. Additional exam requirements/recommendations for international students: required—TOEFL (minimum score 620 paper-based). *Application deadline:* For fall admission, 12/1 priority date for domestic and international students. Application fee: $65 ($70 for international students). Electronic applications accepted. *Financial support:* In 2019–20, 24 students received support, including 4 teaching assistantships with full tuition reimbursements available (averaging $12,540 per year); career-related internships or fieldwork, scholarships/grants, tuition waivers (full), and unspecified assistantships also available. Support available to part-time students. Financial award application deadline: 12/1. *Unit head:* Dr. Michael Brubaker, Program Director, 513-556-9196, Fax: 513-556-3898, E-mail: michael.brubaker@uc.edu. *Application contact:* Amanda Carlisle, Program Coordinator, 513-556-3335, Fax: 513-556-3898, E-mail: amanda.carlisle@uc.edu.
Website: https://cech.uc.edu/schools/human-services/graduate-programs/counseling-graduate-programs.html

University of Detroit Mercy, College of Liberal Arts and Education, Detroit, MI 48221. Offers addiction counseling (MA); addiction studies (Certificate); clinical mental health counseling (MA); clinical psychology (MA, PhD); computer and information systems (MS); criminal justice (MA); curriculum and instruction (MA); economics (MA); educational administration (MA); financial economics (MA); industrial/organizational psychology (MA); information assurance (MS); intelligence analysis (MA); liberal studies (MALS); religious studies (MA); school counseling (MA, Certificate); school psychology (Spec); security administration (MS); special education: emotionally impaired/behaviorally disordered (MA); special education: learning disabilities (MA). *Program availability:* Part-time, evening/weekend. *Degree requirements:* For doctorate, departmental qualifying exam.

University of Illinois at Springfield, Graduate Programs, College of Education and Human Services, Program in Human Services, Springfield, IL 62703-5407. Offers alcohol and substance abuse (Graduate Certificate); alcoholism and substance abuse (MA); child and family studies (MA); gerontology (MA); social services administration (MA). *Program availability:* Part-time, 100% online, blended/hybrid learning. *Faculty:* 3 full-time (all women), 3 part-time/adjunct (2 women). *Students:* 12 full-time (all women), 49 part-time (47 women); includes 27 minority (19 Black or African American, non-Hispanic/Latino; 6 Hispanic/Latino; 2 Two or more races, non-Hispanic/Latino), 1 international. Average age 33. 29 applicants, 69% accepted, 12 enrolled. In 2019, 24

master's, 1 other advanced degree awarded. *Degree requirements:* For master's, internship; capstone project. *Entrance requirements:* For master's, minimum undergraduate GPA of 3.0, 2 letters of recommendation from professional or academic sources, statement of intent, interview. Additional exam requirements/recommendations for international students: required—TOEFL (minimum score 500 paper-based; 61 iBT). *Application deadline:* Applications are processed on a rolling basis. Application fee: $60 ($75 for international students). Electronic applications accepted. *Expenses:* $33.25 per credit hour (online fee). *Financial support:* In 2019–20, research assistantships with full tuition reimbursements (averaging $10,562 per year), teaching assistantships with full tuition reimbursements (averaging $10,652 per year) were awarded; fellowships, career-related internships or fieldwork, Federal Work-Study, scholarships/grants, health care benefits, and unspecified assistantships also available. Support available to part-time students. Financial award application deadline: 11/15; financial award applicants required to submit FAFSA. *Unit head:* Dr. Denise Bockmier-Sommers, Program Administrator, 217-206-6908, Fax: 217-206-6775, E-mail: dsomm2@uis.edu. *Application contact:* Dr. Denise Bockmier-Sommers, Program Administrator, 217-206-6908, Fax: 217-206-6775, E-mail: dsomm2@uis.edu.
Website: http://www.uis.edu/humanservices

University of Indianapolis, Graduate Programs, College of Applied Behavioral Sciences, Indianapolis, IN 46227-3697. Offers addictions counseling (MA); clinical psychology (Psy D); mental health counseling (MA); psychology (MA); social work (MSW). *Accreditation:* APA. *Degree requirements:* For master's, practicum; for doctorate, comprehensive exam, thesis/dissertation, 1200 hours of clinical practicum, 2000-hour internship. *Entrance requirements:* For master's, GRE, 3 letters of recommendation; for doctorate, GRE, minimum GPA of 3.0, 18 hours of course work in psychology, 3 letters of recommendation. Additional exam requirements/recommendations for international students: required—TOEFL (minimum score 550 paper-based).

University of Lethbridge, School of Graduate Studies, Lethbridge, AB T1K 3M4, Canada. Offers addictions counseling (M Sc); agricultural biotechnology (M Sc); agricultural studies (M Sc, MA); anthropology (MA); archaeology (M Sc, MA); art (MA, MFA); biochemistry (M Sc); biological sciences (M Sc); biomolecular science (PhD); biosystems and biodiversity (PhD); Canadian studies (MA); chemistry (M Sc); computer science (M Sc); computer science and geographical information science (M Sc); counseling (MC); counseling psychology (M Ed); dramatic arts (MA); earth, space, and physical science (PhD); economics (MA); education (MA, PhD); educational leadership (M Ed); English (MA); environmental science (M Sc); evolution and behavior (PhD); exercise science (M Sc); French (MA); French/German (MA); French/Spanish (MA); general education (M Ed); geography (M Sc, MA); German (MA); health sciences (M Sc); individualized multidisciplinary (M Sc, MA); kinesiology (M Sc, MA); management (M Sc), including accounting, finance, human resource management and labor relations, information systems, international management, marketing, policy and strategy; mathematics (M Sc); music (M Mus, MA); Native American studies (MA); neuroscience (M Sc, PhD); new media (MA, MFA); nursing (M Sc, MN); philosophy (MA); physics (M Sc); political science (MA); psychology (M Sc, MA); religious studies (MA); sociology (MA); theatre and dramatic arts (MFA); theoretical and computational science (PhD); urban and regional studies (MA); women and gender studies (MA). *Program availability:* Part-time, evening/weekend. *Degree requirements:* For master's, thesis (for some programs); for doctorate, comprehensive exam, thesis/dissertation. *Entrance requirements:* For master's, GMAT (for M Sc in management), bachelor's degree in related field, minimum GPA of 3.0 during previous 20 graded semester courses, 2 years' teaching or related experience (M Ed); for doctorate, master's degree, minimum graduate GPA of 3.5. Additional exam requirements/recommendations for international students: required—TOEFL (minimum score 580 paper-based; 93 iBT). Electronic applications accepted.

University of Louisville, Graduate School, Kent School of Social Work, Louisville, KY 40292-0001. Offers marriage and family therapy (PMC), including mental health; social work (MSSW, PhD), including alcohol and drug counseling (MSSW), gerontology (MSSW), marriage and family (PhD), school social work (MSSW). *Accreditation:* AAMFT/COAMFTE; CSWE (one or more programs are accredited). *Program availability:* Part-time, evening/weekend, 100% online, blended/hybrid learning. *Faculty:* 33 full-time (22 women), 90 part-time/adjunct (73 women). *Students:* 385 full-time (333 women), 96 part-time (73 women); includes 143 minority (75 Black or African American, non-Hispanic/Latino; 2 American Indian or Alaska Native, non-Hispanic/Latino; 8 Asian, non-Hispanic/Latino; 26 Hispanic/Latino; 2 Native Hawaiian or other Pacific Islander, non-Hispanic/Latino; 30 Two or more races, non-Hispanic/Latino), 7 international. Average age 32. 313 applicants, 77% accepted, 176 enrolled. In 2019, 243 master's, 4 doctorates awarded. *Degree requirements:* For doctorate, comprehensive exam, thesis/dissertation. *Entrance requirements:* For master's, 3 letters of recommendation, admissions essay, resume, transcripts; for doctorate, GRE scores, TOFEL scores or equivalent for international students, transcripts (undergraduate and graduate), 3 letters of recommendation, writing sample, personal statement, interview. Additional exam requirements/recommendations for international students: required—TOEFL (minimum score 550 paper-based; 79 iBT), IELTS (minimum score 6.5). *Application deadline:* For fall admission, 5/30 for domestic and international students; for spring admission, 9/30 for domestic and international students; for summer admission, 2/28 for domestic and international students. Applications are processed on a rolling basis. Application fee: $65. Electronic applications accepted. *Expenses: Tuition, area resident:* Full-time $13,000; part-time $723 per credit hour. Tuition, state resident: full-time $13,000; part-time $723 per credit hour. Tuition, nonresident: full-time $27,114; part-time $1507 per credit hour. *International tuition:* $27,114 full-time. *Required fees:* $196. Tuition and fees vary according to program and reciprocity agreements. *Financial support:* In 2019–20, 53 students received support, including 1 fellowship with full tuition reimbursement available (averaging $20,000 per year), 7 research assistantships with full tuition reimbursements available (averaging $20,000 per year), 1 teaching assistantship with full tuition reimbursement available (averaging $20,000 per year); scholarships/grants, health care benefits, and unspecified assistantships also available. Financial award application deadline: 5/15; financial award applicants required to submit FAFSA. *Unit head:* Dr. David Jenkins, Dean, 502-852-3944, Fax: 502-852-0422, E-mail: d.jenkins@louisville.edu. *Application contact:* Sarah Caragianis, Program Manager, MSSW Admissions, 502-852-0414, Fax: 502-852-0422, E-mail: sarah.caragianis@louisville.edu.
Website: http://www.louisville.edu/kent

University of Nevada, Las Vegas, Graduate College, College of Education, Department of Early Childhood, Multilingual, and Special Education, Las Vegas, NV 89154-3066. Offers addiction studies (Advanced Certificate); counselor education (M Ed, MS), including clinical mental health (MS), school counseling (M Ed); early childhood education (M Ed); early childhood special education (Certificate), including infancy, preschool; English language learning (M Ed); mental health counseling (Advanced Certificate); special education (M Ed, PhD); PhD/JD. *Program availability:* Part-time. *Faculty:* 14 full-time (9 women), 18 part-time/adjunct (16 women). *Students:* 235 full-time (192 women), 225 part-time (180 women); includes 225 minority (57 Black or African American, non-Hispanic/Latino; 3 American Indian or Alaska Native, non-Hispanic/Latino; 16 Asian, non-Hispanic/Latino; 108 Hispanic/Latino; 5 Native Hawaiian or other Pacific Islander, non-Hispanic/Latino; 36 Two or more races, non-Hispanic/Latino), 15 international. Average age 35. 238 applicants, 70% accepted, 134 enrolled. In 2019, 168 master's, 3 doctorates, 1 other advanced degree awarded. *Degree requirements:* For master's, comprehensive exam (for some programs); for doctorate, comprehensive exam, thesis/dissertation; for other advanced degree, final project. *Entrance requirements:* For master's, bachelor's degree; letter of recommendation; statement of purpose; for doctorate, GRE General Test, statement of purpose; writing sample; 3 letters of recommendation. Additional exam requirements/recommendations for international students: required—TOEFL (minimum score 550 paper-based; 80 iBT), IELTS (minimum score 7). Application fee: $60 ($95 for international students). Electronic applications accepted. *Expenses:* Contact institution. *Financial support:* In 2019–20, 40 students received support, including 13 research assistantships with full tuition reimbursements available (averaging $14,231 per year), 27 teaching assistantships with full tuition reimbursements available (averaging $15,933 per year); institutionally sponsored loans, scholarships/grants, health care benefits, and unspecified assistantships also available. Financial award application deadline: 3/15; financial award applicants required to submit FAFSA. *Unit head:* Dr. Joseph Morgan, Department Chair/Professor, 702-895-3167, Fax: 702-895-3205, E-mail: ems.chair@unlv.edu. *Application contact:* Dr. Sharolyn D. Pollard-Durodola, Graduate Coordinator, 702-895-3329, Fax: 702-895-3205, E-mail: ems.gradcoord@unlv.edu.
Website: http://education.unlv.edu/ecs/

University of New Hampshire, Graduate School, College of Health and Human Services, Department of Social Work, Durham, NH 03824. Offers child welfare (Postbaccalaureate Certificate); intellectual and development disabilities (Postbaccalaureate Certificate); social work (MSW); substance use disorders (Postbaccalaureate Certificate); MSW/JD; MSW/MS. *Accreditation:* CSWE. *Program availability:* Part-time, online learning. *Students:* 190 full-time (168 women), 33 part-time (25 women); includes 15 minority (4 Black or African American, non-Hispanic/Latino; 1 Asian, non-Hispanic/Latino; 7 Hispanic/Latino; 3 Two or more races, non-Hispanic/Latino), 2 international. Average age 31. 177 applicants, 72% accepted, 71 enrolled. In 2019, 79 master's, 4 other advanced degrees awarded. *Entrance requirements:* Additional exam requirements/recommendations for international students: required—TOEFL (minimum score 550 paper-based; 80 iBT), IELTS, PTE. *Application deadline:* For fall admission, 4/1 for domestic students. Application fee: $65. Electronic applications accepted. *Financial support:* In 2019–20, 18 students received support, including 8 teaching assistantships; fellowships, research assistantships, career-related internships or fieldwork, Federal Work-Study, and scholarships/grants also available. Support available to part-time students. Financial award application deadline: 2/15. *Unit head:* Melissa Wells, Chair, 603-862-0076. *Application contact:* Kerrin Edelman, Administrative Assistant, 603-862-0215, E-mail: kerrin.edelman@unh.edu.
Website: https://chhs.unh.edu/sw/master-social-work-msw

University of New Hampshire, Graduate School Manchester Campus, Manchester, NH 03101. Offers business administration (MBA); cybersecurity policy and risk management (MS); educational administration and supervision (Ed S); educational studies (M Ed); elementary education (M Ed); information technology (MS); public administration (MPA); public health (MPH, Certificate); secondary education (M Ed, MAT); social work (MSW); substance use disorders (Certificate). *Program availability:* Part-time, evening/weekend. *Students:* 118 full-time (56 women), 110 part-time (47 women); includes 23 minority (4 Black or African American, non-Hispanic/Latino; 5 Asian, non-Hispanic/Latino; 13 Hispanic/Latino; 1 Two or more races, non-Hispanic/Latino), 39 international. Average age 32. 231 applicants, 78% accepted, 64 enrolled. In 2019, 47 master's, 3 other advanced degrees awarded. *Entrance requirements:* Additional exam requirements/recommendations for international students: required—TOEFL (minimum score 550 paper-based; 80 iBT), IELTS, PTE. *Application deadline:* For fall admission, 6/1 for domestic students, 4/1 for international students; for spring admission, 12/1 for domestic students. Application fee: $65. Electronic applications accepted. *Financial support:* In 2019–20, 11 students received support, including 1 teaching assistantship; fellowships, research assistantships, Federal Work-Study, scholarships/grants, health care benefits, and unspecified assistantships also available. Support available to part-time students. Financial award application deadline: 2/15; financial award applicants required to submit FAFSA. *Unit head:* Candice Morey, Educational Programs Coordinator, 603-641-4313, E-mail: unhm.gradcenter@unh.edu. *Application contact:* Candice Morey, Educational Programs Coordinator, 603-641-4313, E-mail: unhm.gradcenter@unh.edu.
Website: http://www.gradschool.unh.edu/manchester/

The University of North Carolina at Charlotte, Cato College of Education, Department of Counseling, Charlotte, NC 28223-0001. Offers counseling (MA); counselor education and supervision (PhD); play therapy (Postbaccalaureate Certificate); school counseling (Post-Master's Certificate); substance abuse counseling (Postbaccalaureate Certificate). *Accreditation:* ACA. *Program availability:* Part-time, evening/weekend. *Faculty:* 8 full-time (2 women), 11 part-time/adjunct (9 women). *Students:* 132 full-time (108 women), 85 part-time (75 women); includes 73 minority (51 Black or African American, non-Hispanic/Latino; 2 Asian, non-Hispanic/Latino; 17 Hispanic/Latino; 3 Two or more races, non-Hispanic/Latino), 1 international. Average age 31. 261 applicants, 54% accepted, 86 enrolled. In 2019, 74 master's, 5 doctorates, 15 other advanced degrees awarded. Terminal master's awarded for partial completion of doctoral program. *Degree requirements:* For master's, comprehensive exam; for doctorate, comprehensive exam, thesis/dissertation. *Entrance requirements:* For master's, GRE or MAT, bachelor's degree from regionally-accredited university, minimum overall GPA of 3.0, brief statement of purpose, professional references, official transcripts; for doctorate, GRE or MAT, master's degree in counseling from a CACREP-accredited program with minimum cumulative GPA of 3.5; one year of experience as a professional counselor (preferred); letters of reference; essay; interview; for other advanced degree, statement of purpose, three reference letters. Additional exam requirements/recommendations for international students: required—TOEFL (minimum score 557 paper-based; 83 iBT), IELTS (minimum score 6.5), TOEFL (minimum score 557 paper-based, 83 iBT) or IELTS (6.5). *Application deadline:* For fall admission, 12/1 for domestic students. Applications are processed on a rolling basis. Application fee: $75. Electronic applications accepted. *Expenses:* Tuition, state resident: full-time $4337. Tuition, nonresident: full-time $17,771. *Required fees:* $3093. Tuition and fees vary according to course load, degree level and program. *Financial support:* In 2019–20, 8 students received support, including 2 research assistantships (averaging $13,500 per year), 5 teaching assistantships (averaging $4,200 per year); career-related internships or fieldwork, institutionally sponsored loans, scholarships/grants, and unspecified assistantships also available. Support available to part-time students. Financial award application deadline: 3/1; financial award applicants required to submit FAFSA. *Unit head:* Dr. Henry L. Harris, Chair, 704-687-8971, E-mail: hharris2@uncc.edu. *Application contact:* Kathy B. Giddings, Director of Graduate Admissions, 704-687-5503, Fax: 704-687-1668, E-mail: gradadm@uncc.edu.
Website: http://counseling.uncc.edu/

University of South Dakota, Graduate School, College of Arts and Sciences, Program in Administrative Studies, Vermillion, SD 57069. Offers addiction studies (MSA); criminal justice studies (MSA); health services administration (MSA); human resources (MSA); interdisciplinary studies (MSA); long term care administration (MSA); organizational leadership (MSA). *Program availability:* Part-time, evening/weekend, 100% online. *Degree requirements:* For master's, thesis or alternative. *Entrance requirements:* For master's, 3 years of work or experience, minimum GPA of 2.7, resume. Additional exam requirements/recommendations for international students: required—TOEFL (minimum score 550 paper-based; 79 iBT). Electronic applications accepted.

University of Southern Maine, College of Management and Human Service, School of Education and Human Development, Program in Counselor Education, Portland, ME 04103. Offers clinical mental health counseling (MS); counseling (CAS); culturally responsive practices in education and human development (CGS); mental health rehabilitation technician/community (CGS); rehabilitation counseling (MS); school counseling (MS); substance abuse counseling (CGS). *Accreditation:* ACA (one or more programs are accredited); CORE; TEAC. *Program availability:* Part-time, evening/weekend. *Degree requirements:* For master's, comprehensive exam, thesis or alternative; for other advanced degree, thesis or alternative. *Entrance requirements:* For master's, GRE General Test or MAT, interview; for other advanced degree, master's degree. Additional exam requirements/recommendations for international students: required—TOEFL (minimum score 550 paper-based; 79 iBT). Electronic applications accepted. *Expenses: Tuition, area resident:* Full-time $864; part-time $432 per credit hour. Tuition, state resident: full-time $864; part-time $432 per credit hour. Tuition, nonresident: full-time $2372; part-time $1186 per credit hour. *Required fees:* $141; $108 per credit hour. Tuition and fees vary according to course load.

University of South Florida, College of Behavioral and Community Sciences, Department of Child and Family Studies, Tampa, FL 33620-9951. Offers applied behavior analysis (MA, MS, PhD); behavioral and community sciences (PhD); child and adolescent behavioral health (MS), including developmental disabilities, leadership in child and adolescent health, translational research and evaluation, youth and behavioral health; rehabilitation and mental health counseling (MA), including addictions and substance abuse counseling, marriage and family therapy. *Accreditation:* ACA. *Faculty:* 21 full-time (13 women), 3 part-time/adjunct (all women). *Students:* 184 full-time (157 women), 104 part-time (88 women); includes 113 minority (42 Black or African American, non-Hispanic/Latino; 4 Asian, non-Hispanic/Latino; 54 Hispanic/Latino; 1 Native Hawaiian or other Pacific Islander, non-Hispanic/Latino; 12 Two or more races, non-Hispanic/Latino), 7 international. Average age 27. 310 applicants, 51% accepted, 92 enrolled. In 2019, 127 master's, 8 doctorates awarded. *Degree requirements:* For master's, comprehensive exam, thesis (for some programs); for doctorate, comprehensive exam, thesis/dissertation, Behavior Analyst Board Certification Exam. *Entrance requirements:* For master's, GRE General Test, 3.00 GPA; 3 letters of reference; resume or CV; statement of purpose; writing sample; undergraduate statistics or research methods course (for Rehab and Mental Health Counseling); for doctorate, GRE General Test, master's degree in behavioral analysis or closely-related field; minimum GPA of 3.5 in graduate course work; three letters of recommendation; campus visit with faculty interview; personal statement; curriculum vitae; evidence of research experiences and expertise; campus visit and interview. Additional exam requirements/recommendations for international students: required—TOEFL, TOEFL (minimum score 550 paper-based; 79 iBT) or IELTS (minimum score 6.5). *Application deadline:* For fall admission, 12/5 for domestic and international students. Application fee: $30. *Financial support:* In 2019–20, 57 students received support. Unspecified assistantships available. *Unit head:* Jason Anthony, Professor and Director, Rightpath Research and Innovation Center, 813-974-6009, E-mail: jasonanthony@usf.edu. *Application contact:* Dr. Raymond G. Miltenberger, Professor/Director of Master's Program, 813-974-5079, Fax: 813-974-6115, E-mail: miltenbe@usf.edu.
Website: http://cfs.cbcs.usf.edu/

The University of Tennessee at Martin, Graduate Programs, College of Education, Health and Behavioral Sciences, Program in Counseling, Martin, TN 38238. Offers addictions counseling (MS Ed); clinical mental health counseling (MS Ed); school counseling (MS Ed); student affairs and college counseling (MS Ed). *Accreditation:* NCATE. *Program availability:* Part-time, online only, 100% online. *Students:* 26 full-time (24 women), 53 part-time (47 women); includes 9 minority (all Black or African American, non-Hispanic/Latino). Average age 32. 101 applicants, 38% accepted, 28 enrolled. In 2019, 16 master's awarded. *Degree requirements:* For master's, comprehensive exam. *Entrance requirements:* For master's, minimum GPA of 2.5, resume, letters of reference. Additional exam requirements/recommendations for international students: required—TOEFL (minimum score 525 paper-based; 71 iBT). *Application deadline:* For fall admission, 7/28 priority date for domestic and international students; for spring admission, 12/17 priority date for domestic and international students; for summer admission, 5/10 priority date for domestic and international students. Applications are processed on a rolling basis. Application fee: $30 ($130 for international students). Electronic applications accepted. *Expenses: Tuition, area resident:* Full-time $9096; part-time $505 per credit hour. Tuition, state resident: full-time $9096; part-time $505 per credit hour. Tuition, nonresident: full-time $15,136; part-time $841 per credit hour. *International tuition:* $23,040 full-time. *Required fees:* $1520; $85 per credit hour. Part-time tuition and fees vary according to course load. *Financial support:* In 2019–20, 12 students received support, including 1 teaching assistantship with full tuition reimbursement available (averaging $6,283 per year); research assistantships with full tuition reimbursements available, scholarships/grants, and tuition waivers (full and partial) also available. Financial award application deadline: 2/1; financial award applicants required to submit FAFSA. *Unit head:* Cynthia West, Dean, 731-881-7125, Fax: 731-881-7975, E-mail: cwest@utm.edu. *Application contact:* Jolene L. Cunningham, Student Services Specialist, 731-881-7012, Fax: 731-881-7499, E-mail: jcunningham@utm.edu.

Viterbo University, Master of Science in Mental Health Counseling Program, La Crosse, WI 54601-4797. Offers addiction counseling (MS); child and adolescent counseling (MS); complementary health and wellness counseling (MS). *Accreditation:*

ACA. *Program availability:* Part-time, evening/weekend. *Degree requirements:* For master's, comprehensive exam, thesis, 54 credits of core program courses; 6 elective credits; minimum GPA of 3.0; action research project; practicum/internship experience. *Entrance requirements:* For master's, MAT, BS in a human service or social science discipline; prerequisite coursework in general psychology, behavior disorders/abnormal psychology, and research methods/statistics; minimum undergraduate cumulative GPA of 3.0; background check; personal statement; undergraduate transcripts; interview. Additional exam requirements/recommendations for international students: required—TOEFL (minimum score 525 paper-based). Electronic applications accepted. Application fee is waived when completed online. *Expenses:* Contact institution.

Walden University, Graduate Programs, School of Counseling, Minneapolis, MN 55401. Offers addiction counseling (MS), including addictions and public health, child and adolescent counseling, family studies and interventions, forensic counseling, general program, military families and culture, trauma and crisis counseling; clinical mental health counseling (MS), including addiction counseling, forensic counseling, military families and culture, trauma and crisis counseling; counselor education and supervision (PhD), including consultation, counseling and social change, forensic mental health counseling, leadership and program evaluation, trauma and crisis; marriage, couple, and family counseling (MS), including addiction counseling, career counseling, forensic counseling, military families and culture, trauma and crisis counseling; school counseling (MS), including addiction counseling, career counseling, crisis and trauma, military families and culture. *Accreditation:* ACA. *Program availability:* Part-time, evening/weekend, online only, 100% online. *Degree requirements:* For master's, residency, field experience, professional development plan, licensure plan; for doctorate, thesis/dissertation, residency, practicum, internship. *Entrance requirements:* For master's, bachelor's degree or higher; minimum GPA of 2.5; official transcripts; goal statement (for some programs); access to computer and Internet; for doctorate, master's degree or higher; three years of related professional or academic experience (preferred); minimum GPA of 3.0; goal statement and current resume (for select programs); official transcripts; access to computer and Internet. Additional exam requirements/recommendations for international students: required—TOEFL (minimum score 550 paper-based, 79 iBT), IELTS (minimum score 6.5), Michigan English Language Assessment Battery (minimum score 82), or PTE (minimum score 53). Electronic applications accepted.

Walden University, Graduate Programs, School of Social Work and Human Services, Minneapolis, MN 55401. Offers addictions and social work (DSW); advanced clinical practice (MSW); clinical expertise (DSW); criminal justice (DSW); disaster, crisis, and intervention (DSW); family studies and interventions (DSW); human and social services (PhD), including advanced research, community and social services, community intervention and leadership, conflict management, criminal justice, disaster crisis and intervention, family studies and intervention, gerontology, global social services, higher education, human services and nonprofit administration, mental health facilitation; medical social work (DSW); military social work (MSW); policy practice (DSW); social work (PhD), including addictions and social work, clinical expertise, criminal justice, disaster, crisis and intervention, family studies and interventions, medical social work, policy practice, social work administration; social work administration (DSW); social work in healthcare (MSW); social work with children and families (MSW). *Accreditation:* CSWE. *Program availability:* Part-time, evening/weekend, online only, 100% online. *Degree requirements:* For master's, residency (for some programs); for doctorate, thesis/dissertation, residency. *Entrance requirements:* For master's, bachelor's degree or higher; minimum GPA of 2.5; official transcripts; goal statement (for some programs); access to computer and Internet; for doctorate, master's degree or higher; three years of related professional or academic experience (preferred); minimum GPA of 3.0; goal statement and current resume (for select programs); official transcripts; access to computer and Internet. Additional exam requirements/recommendations for international students: required—TOEFL (minimum score 550 paper-based, 79 iBT), IELTS (minimum score 6.5), Michigan English Language Assessment Battery (minimum score 82), or PTE (minimum score 53). Electronic applications accepted.

Washburn University, School of Applied Studies, Department of Human Services, Topeka, KS 66621. Offers addiction counseling (MA). *Program availability:* Evening/weekend. *Entrance requirements:* For master's, minimum GPA of 3.0 in last 60 hours of coursework. Additional exam requirements/recommendations for international students: required—TOEFL (minimum score 80 iBT).

Waynesburg University, Graduate and Professional Studies, Canonsburg, PA 15370. Offers business (MBA), including energy management, finance, health systems, human resources, leadership, market development; counseling (MA), including addictions counseling, clinical mental health; counselor education and supervision (PhD); criminal investigation (MA); education (M Ed), including autism, curriculum and instruction, educational leadership, online teaching; nursing (MSN), including administration, education, informatics; nursing practice (DNP); special education (M Ed); technology (M Ed); MSN/MBA. *Accreditation:* AACN. *Program availability:* Part-time, evening/weekend. *Degree requirements:* For doctorate, thesis/dissertation. *Entrance requirements:* Additional exam requirements/recommendations for international students: required—TOEFL. Electronic applications accepted.

Winona State University, College of Education, Department of Counselor Education, Winona, MN 55987. Offers addiction counseling (Certificate); clinical mental health counseling (MS); human services (MS); school counseling (MS). *Accreditation:* ACA (one or more programs are accredited); NCATE. *Program availability:* Part-time, evening/weekend. *Degree requirements:* For master's, thesis or alternative. *Entrance requirements:* For master's, letters of reference, interview, group activity, on-site writing. Electronic applications accepted.

Applied Behavior Analysis

Antioch University New England, Graduate School, Department of Applied Psychology, Keene, NH 03431-3552. Offers autism spectrum disorders (Certificate), including applied behavioral analysis internship, autism spectrum disorders; clinical mental health counseling (MA), including clinical mental health counseling, substance abuse counseling; dance/movement therapy and counseling (M Ed, MA, PMC); marriage and family therapy (MA, PhD, Certificate). *Faculty:* 15 full-time (12 women), 30 part-time/adjunct (25 women). *Students:* 264 full-time (217 women), 79 part-time (64 women); includes 67 minority (25 Black or African American, non-Hispanic/Latino; 2 American Indian or Alaska Native, non-Hispanic/Latino; 8 Asian, non-Hispanic/Latino; 27 Hispanic/Latino; 5 Two or more races, non-Hispanic/Latino), 5 international. Average

age 35. 149 applicants, 52% accepted, 77 enrolled. In 2019, 49 master's awarded. *Degree requirements:* For master's, internship, practicum. *Entrance requirements:* For master's, previous course work and work experience in psychology. Additional exam requirements/recommendations for international students: required—TOEFL (minimum score 550 paper-based). *Application deadline:* For fall admission, 7/15 for domestic and international students; for spring admission, 12/1 for domestic and international students. Applications are processed on a rolling basis. Application fee: $50. Electronic applications accepted. *Expenses:* Contact institution. *Financial support:* In 2019–20, 56 students received support. Fellowships, research assistantships, career-related internships or fieldwork, Federal Work-Study, and scholarships/grants available.

Financial award application deadline: 6/1; financial award applicants required to submit FAFSA. *Unit head:* Dr. Kevin Lyness, Department Chair, 603-283-2149, E-mail: klyness@antioch.edu. *Application contact:* Admissions, 800-552-8380, Fax: 603-357-0718, E-mail: admissions.ane@antioch.edu.
Website: https://www.antioch.edu/new-england/degrees-programs/counseling-wellness/

Arcadia University, College of Arts and Sciences, Department of Psychology, Glenside, PA 19038-3295. Offers applied behavior analysis (MAC); autism (MAC); child/family therapy (MAC); community public health (MAC); counseling/international peace and conflict resolution dual degree (MAC); mental health counseling (MAC); trauma (MAC). *Program availability:* Part-time. *Faculty:* 13 full-time (8 women). *Students:* 30 full-time (27 women), 31 part-time (26 women); includes 17 minority (11 Black or African American, non-Hispanic/Latino; 2 Asian, non-Hispanic/Latino; 1 Hispanic/Latino; 3 Two or more races, non-Hispanic/Latino). In 2019, 18 master's awarded. *Degree requirements:* For master's, practicum. *Entrance requirements:* For master's, test scores are not required of applicants with an earned master's degree or who have a GPA greater than a 3.0. Test scores from the Graduate Record Examination (GRE) or the Miller Analogies Test (MAT), taken within the past five years are required for all other applicants. Additional exam requirements/recommendations for international students: required—TOEFL. *Application deadline:* Applications are processed on a rolling basis. Application fee: $25. Electronic applications accepted. *Expenses:* Contact institution. *Financial support:* Research assistantships, career-related internships or fieldwork, and unspecified assistantships available. Support available to part-time students. Financial award application deadline: 8/15. *Unit head:* Dr. Marianne Miserandino, Chair, 215-572-2183. *Application contact:* 215-572-2925, Fax: 215-572-2126, E-mail: grad@arcadia.edu.

Arizona State University at Tempe, College of Liberal Arts and Sciences, Department of Psychology, Tempe, AZ 85287-1104. Offers applied behavior analysis (MS); behavioral neuroscience (PhD); clinical psychology (PhD); cognitive science (PhD); developmental psychology (PhD); quantitative psychology (PhD); social psychology (PhD). *Accreditation:* APA. *Degree requirements:* For doctorate, comprehensive exam, thesis/dissertation, interactive Program of Study (iPOS) submitted before completing 50 percent of required credit hours. *Entrance requirements:* For doctorate, GRE General Test, GRE Subject Test, minimum GPA of 3.0 or equivalent in last 2 years of work leading to bachelor's degree. Additional exam requirements/recommendations for international students: required—TOEFL, IELTS, or PTE. Electronic applications accepted.

Assumption University, Applied Behavior Analysis Program, Worcester, MA 01609-1296. Offers MA, CAGS. *Program availability:* Part-time, evening/weekend. *Degree requirements:* For master's, thesis optional, practicum; for CAGS, practicum. *Entrance requirements:* For master's, BA with minimum GPA of 3.0, three letters of recommendation, official transcripts, personal statement, current resume; for CAGS, MA/MS in related field, three letters of recommendation, official transcripts, personal statement, current resume. Additional exam requirements/recommendations for international students: required—TOEFL (minimum score 540 paper-based; 76 iBT), IELTS (minimum score 6). Electronic applications accepted. *Expenses: Tuition:* Full-time $12,690; part-time $705 per credit. *Required fees:* $70 per term.

Aurora University, School of Education and Human Performance, Aurora, IL 60506-4892. Offers applied behavioral analysis (MS); bilingual-ESL education (MA); educational leadership with principal endorsement (MA); educational technology (MA); leadership in adult learning higher education (Ed D); leadership in curriculum and instruction (Ed D); leadership in educational administration (Ed D); reading instruction (MA); special education (MA). *Accreditation:* NCATE. *Program availability:* Part-time, evening/weekend, 100% online. *Faculty:* 13 full-time (5 women), 36 part-time/adjunct (20 women). *Students:* 43 full-time (34 women), 564 part-time (407 women); includes 123 minority (31 Black or African American, non-Hispanic/Latino; 10 Asian, non-Hispanic/Latino; 68 Hispanic/Latino; 1 Native Hawaiian or other Pacific Islander, non-Hispanic/Latino; 13 Two or more races, non-Hispanic/Latino), 2 international. Average age 37. 291 applicants, 98% accepted, 136 enrolled. In 2019, 133 master's, 27 doctorates awarded. *Degree requirements:* For master's, student teaching, research seminar, and practicum; for doctorate, comprehensive exam, thesis/dissertation. *Entrance requirements:* For master's, 2 years of teaching experience, valid teaching certificate, resume; for doctorate, appropriate master's degree, two references, curriculum vitae, personal statement, professional project, reflective essay. Additional exam requirements/recommendations for international students: required—TOEFL (minimum score 550 paper-based; 79 iBT). *Application deadline:* For fall admission, 6/1 for international students; for spring admission, 10/1 for international students. Applications are processed on a rolling basis. Application fee: $0. Electronic applications accepted. *Expenses:* The reported tuition amount is for the program with the greatest enrollment, MA in Educational Leadership with Principal Endorsement. Other programs may require more semester hours and thus have greater cost. The Education doctoral programs are roughly double the amount of the master's programs. *Financial support:* In 2019–20, 28 students received support. Federal Work-Study, scholarships/grants, and unspecified assistantships available. Financial award applicants required to submit FAFSA. *Unit head:* Dr. Jen Buckley, Dean, School of Education and Human Performance, 630-844-1542, Fax: 630-844-6155, E-mail: jbuckley@aurora.edu. *Application contact:* Jason Harmon, Dean of Adult and Graduate Studies, 630-947-8955, E-mail: AUadmission@aurora.edu.
Website: https://aurora.edu/academics/colleges-schools/education

Ball State University, Graduate School, Teachers College, Department of Special Education, Program in Applied Behavior Analysis, Muncie, IN 47306. Offers applied behavior analysis (MA), including autism. *Program availability:* Part-time, online only, 100% online. *Entrance requirements:* For master's, minimum baccalaureate GPA of 2.75 or 3.0 in latter half of baccalaureate. Additional exam requirements/recommendations for international students: required—TOEFL (minimum score 550 paper-based; 79 iBT), IELTS (minimum score 6.5). Electronic applications accepted. *Expenses: Tuition, area resident:* Full-time $7506; part-time $417 per credit hour. Tuition, nonresident: full-time $20,610; part-time $1145 per credit hour. *Required fees:* $2126. Tuition and fees vary according to course load, campus/location and program.

Bay Path University, Program in Applied Behavior Analysis, Longmeadow, MA 01106-2292. Offers applied behavior analysis (MS); autism spectrum disorders (MS). *Program availability:* Part-time, blended/hybrid learning. *Entrance requirements:* For master's, completed application; official undergraduate and graduate transcripts (GPA of 3.0 or higher is preferred); original essay of 300-500 words on the topic "Why the MS/EdS in Applied Behavior Analysis is important to my personal and professional goals"; current resume; 2 recommendations; signed program requirement form. Electronic applications accepted. Application fee is waived when completed online. *Expenses:* Contact institution.

Cairn University, School of Education, Langhorne, PA 19047-2990. Offers applied behavior analysis (MS Sp Ed, Certificate); educational leadership and administration (MS El); instruction (MS Sp Ed); teacher education (MS Ed). *Program availability:* Part-time, evening/weekend, 100% online, blended/hybrid learning. *Entrance requirements:* Additional exam requirements/recommendations for international students: required—TOEFL (minimum score 550 paper-based). Electronic applications accepted. Application fee is waived when completed online. *Expenses:* Contact institution.

Caldwell University, Department of Applied Behavior Analysis, Caldwell, NJ 07006-6195. Offers MA, PhD, Post-Master's Certificate. *Program availability:* Part-time. Terminal master's awarded for partial completion of doctoral program. *Degree requirements:* For master's, comprehensive exam, thesis; for doctorate, comprehensive exam, thesis/dissertation. *Entrance requirements:* For master's, GRE, MAT, Minimum undergraduate GPA of 3.3; 2 letters of recommendation; writing sample; personal statement; interview; bachelor's degree or higher; for doctorate, GRE, MAT, ABA Certification, M.A. in Applied Behavior Analysis, Psychology, Special Education, or a related field, minimum GPA of 3.6 in master's coursework, 3 letters of recommendation, writing sample, personal statement, and interview; for Post-Master's Certificate, M.A. in ABA, Psychology, Special Education, or a related field; minimum GPA of 3.3 in master's coursework, writing sample, 2 letters of recommendation, personal statement, and interview. Additional exam requirements/recommendations for international students: required—The TOEFL or IELTS is required of international students who were not educated at the Bachelors level in English; recommended—TOEFL (minimum score 580 paper-based; 92 iBT), IELTS (minimum score 7.5). Electronic applications accepted. *Expenses:* Contact institution.

California State University, Fresno, Division of Research and Graduate Studies, College of Science and Mathematics, Department of Psychology, Fresno, CA 93740-8027. Offers applied behavior analysis (MA); general/experimental psychology (MA); school psychology (Ed S). *Degree requirements:* For master's, thesis. *Entrance requirements:* For master's, GRE General Test, GRE Subject Test, minimum GPA of 3.0. Additional exam requirements/recommendations for international students: required—TOEFL. Electronic applications accepted. *Expenses:* Tuition, state resident: full-time $4012; part-time $2506 per semester.

California State University, Sacramento, College of Social Sciences and Interdisciplinary Studies, Department of Psychology, Sacramento, CA 95819. Offers applied behavior analysis (MA); industrial/organizational psychology (MA). *Program availability:* Part-time. *Students:* 26 full-time (22 women), 30 part-time (21 women); includes 22 minority (1 Black or African American, non-Hispanic/Latino; 2 American Indian or Alaska Native, non-Hispanic/Latino; 4 Asian, non-Hispanic/Latino; 14 Hispanic/Latino; 1 Native Hawaiian or other Pacific Islander, non-Hispanic/Latino), 3 international. Average age 27. 86 applicants, 23% accepted, 16 enrolled. In 2019, 7 master's awarded. *Degree requirements:* For master's, thesis, project; writing proficiency exam. *Entrance requirements:* For master's, GRE, minimum GPA of 3.0 during previous 2 years. Additional exam requirements/recommendations for international students: required—TOEFL (minimum score 550 paper-based; 80 iBT); recommended—IELTS (minimum score 7). *Application deadline:* For fall admission, 3/1 for domestic students, 2/1 for international students. Applications are processed on a rolling basis. Application fee: $70. Electronic applications accepted. *Expenses:* Contact institution. *Financial support:* Teaching assistantships, career-related internships or fieldwork, Federal Work-Study, and scholarships/grants available. Support available to part-time students. Financial award application deadline: 3/1; financial award applicants required to submit FAFSA. *Unit head:* Dr. Rebecca Cameron, Interim Department Chair, 916-278-6254, E-mail: cameron@csus.edu. *Application contact:* Jose Martinez, Graduate Admissions Supervisor, 916-278-7871, E-mail: martinj@skymail.csus.edu.
Website: http://www.csus.edu/psyc

California State University, Stanislaus, College of Science, Programs in Psychology, Turlock, CA 95382. Offers behavior analysis (MA, MS); counseling psychology (MS); general psychology (MA). *Program availability:* Part-time. *Degree requirements:* For master's, thesis. *Entrance requirements:* For master's, GRE, minimum GPA of 3.0, 3 letters of reference, 16 psychology prerequisites, personal statement. Additional exam requirements/recommendations for international students: required—TOEFL (minimum score 550 paper-based). Electronic applications accepted.

Capella University, Harold Abel School of Social and Behavioral Science, Master's Programs in Psychology, Minneapolis, MN 55402. Offers applied behavior analysis (MS); clinical psychology (MS); counseling psychology (MS); educational psychology (MS); evaluation, research, and measurement (MS); general advanced studies in human behavior (MS); general psychology (MS); industrial/organizational psychology (MS); leadership coaching psychology (MS); school psychology (MS); sport psychology (MS).

The Chicago School of Professional Psychology, Program in Applied Behavior Analysis, Chicago, IL 60610. Offers MS, PhD. *Degree requirements:* For master's, thesis, practicum; for doctorate, thesis/dissertation, practicum. *Entrance requirements:* For doctorate, GRE. Additional exam requirements/recommendations for international students: required—TOEFL.

The Chicago School of Professional Psychology at Downtown Los Angeles, Program in Applied Behavior Analysis, Los Angeles, CA 90017. Offers Psy D.

The Chicago School of Professional Psychology at Downtown Los Angeles, Program in Clinical Psychology, Los Angeles, CA 90017. Offers applied behavior analysis (MA); clinical psychology (Psy D); marital and family therapy (MA).

The Chicago School of Professional Psychology at San Diego, Graduate Programs, San Diego, CA 92101. Offers applied behavior analysis (MS, PhD); applied clinical psychology (Psy D); clinical psychology (MA); industrial and organizational psychology (MA).

College of Saint Elizabeth, Program in Applied Behavior Analysis, Morristown, NJ 07960-6989. Offers MA, Certificate. *Program availability:* Part-time. *Degree requirements:* For master's, thesis. *Entrance requirements:* Additional exam requirements/recommendations for international students: required—TOEFL (minimum score 550 paper-based; 79 iBT), IELTS (minimum score 6.5). Electronic applications accepted. Application fee is waived when completed online.

Drake University, School of Education, Des Moines, IA 50311-4516. Offers applied behavior analysis (MS); counseling (MS); education (PhD); education administration (Ed D); educational leadership (MSE); leadership development (MS); literacy (Ed S); literacy education (MSE); rehabilitation administration (MS); rehabilitation placement (MS); teacher education (5-12) (MAT); teacher education (K-8) (MST). *Program availability:* Part-time, evening/weekend, 100% online, blended/hybrid learning. *Students:* 99 full-time (78 women), 666 part-time (500 women); includes 76 minority (33 Black or African American, non-Hispanic/Latino; 11 Asian, non-Hispanic/Latino; 21 Hispanic/Latino; 11 Two or more races, non-Hispanic/Latino), 2 international. Average age 35. In 2019, 212 master's, 30 doctorates awarded. *Degree requirements:* For master's and Ed S, comprehensive exam, internships (for some programs); for doctorate, comprehensive exam, thesis/dissertation, internships (for some programs). *Entrance requirements:* For master's, GRE General Test, MAT, or Drake Writing Assessment, resume, 2 letters of recommendation; for doctorate, GRE General Test or MAT, master's degree, 3 letters of recommendation; for Ed S, GRE General Test or MAT. Additional exam requirements/recommendations for international students: required—TOEFL (minimum score 550 paper-based). *Application deadline:* For fall admission, 7/1 priority date for domestic students, 6/1 priority date for international

students; for spring admission, 11/1 priority date for domestic students, 10/1 priority date for international students. Applications are processed on a rolling basis. Application fee: $25. Electronic applications accepted. *Expenses:* Contact institution. *Financial support:* Research assistantships, career-related internships or fieldwork, and unspecified assistantships available. Support available to part-time students. *Unit head:* Dr. Ryan Wise, Dean, 515-271-3829, E-mail: ryan.wise@drake.edu. *Application contact:* Dr. Ryan Wise, Dean, 515-271-3829, E-mail: ryan.wise@drake.edu.
Website: http://www.drake.edu/soe/

Drexel University, Goodwin College of Professional Studies, School of Education, Philadelphia, PA 19104-2875. Offers applied behavior analysis (MS); creativity and innovation (MS); education improvement and transformation (MS); educational administration (MS); educational leadership and management (Ed D); educational leadership development and learning technologies (PhD); global and international education (MS); higher education (MS); human resources development (MS); learning technologies (MS); mathematics, learning and teaching (MS); special education (MS); teaching, learning and curriculum (MS). *Program availability:* Part-time, evening/weekend, online learning. *Degree requirements:* For doctorate, thesis/dissertation. *Entrance requirements:* For doctorate, GRE or GMAT. Additional exam requirements/recommendations for international students: required—TOEFL, IELTS. Electronic applications accepted. Application fee is waived when completed online. *Expenses:* Contact institution.

Elms College, Division of Social Sciences, Chicopee, MA 01013-2839. Offers applied behavior analysis (MS); autism spectrum disorders (MS, CAGS); communication sciences and disorders (CAGS). *Program availability:* Part-time. *Faculty:* 2 full-time (1 woman), 3 part-time/adjunct (2 women). *Students:* 12 part-time (11 women); includes 1 minority (Hispanic/Latino). Average age 30. 13 applicants, 85% accepted, 11 enrolled. In 2019, 8 master's, 1 other advanced degree awarded. *Entrance requirements:* For degree, minimum GPA of 3.0. Additional exam requirements/recommendations for international students: required—TOEFL (minimum score 80 iBT). *Application deadline:* Applications are processed on a rolling basis. Application fee: $0. Electronic applications accepted. *Financial support:* Applicants required to submit FAFSA. *Unit head:* Dr. Jennifer Rivers, Chair, Division of Social Sciences, 413-265-2422, E-mail: riversj@elms.edu. *Application contact:* Nancy Davis, Director, Office of Graduate and Continuing Education Admissions, 413-265-2456, E-mail: grad@elms.edu.

Endicott College, Van Loan School of Graduate and Professional Studies, Program in Applied Behavior Analysis, Beverly, MA 01915. Offers applied behavior analysis (M Ed, PhD); autism (Certificate); autism and applied behavior analysis (M Ed). *Program availability:* Part-time, evening/weekend, online only, 100% online. *Faculty:* 5 full-time (4 women), 57 part-time/adjunct (47 women). *Students:* 41 full-time (40 women), 376 part-time (324 women); includes 92 minority (22 Black or African American, non-Hispanic/Latino; 27 Asian, non-Hispanic/Latino; 33 Hispanic/Latino; 10 Two or more races, non-Hispanic/Latino), 3 international. Average age 31. 235 applicants, 64% accepted, 114 enrolled. In 2019, 59 master's, 5 doctorates, 7 other advanced degrees awarded. *Degree requirements:* For master's, thesis; for doctorate, comprehensive exam, thesis/dissertation, Research Projects; Practicum. *Entrance requirements:* For master's, official transcript of all post-secondary academic work; 3 or more-page essay on specific topic in APA format with required citations; 2 letters of recommendation; interview with program director; for doctorate, GRE or MAT, official transcript of all post-secondary academic work; 3 letters of recommendations; Current resume and/or curriculum vitae; 6-10 page (double-spaced, 12 pt. font) personal essay on specified topic; A short paper (limit 10 pages), double-spaced, in APA format, responding to specified question; Admission interview; for Certificate, Same as Master's. Additional exam requirements/recommendations for international students: required—TOEFL. *Application deadline:* Applications are processed on a rolling basis. Application fee: $50. Electronic applications accepted. *Expenses:* Tuition varies by program. *Financial support:* Applicants required to submit FAFSA. *Unit head:* Aubry Threlkeld, Associate Dean of Graduate Education, 978-232-2408, E-mail: athrelke@endicott.edu. *Application contact:* Ian Menchini, Director, Graduate Enrollment and Advising, 978-232-5292, Fax: 978-232-3000, E-mail: imenchin@endicott.edu.
Website: https://www.endicott.edu/academics/schools/school-of-education/graduate-programs

Fairfield University, Graduate School of Education and Allied Professions, Fairfield, CT 06824. Offers applied behavior analysis (ATC); applied psychology (MA); clinical mental health counseling (MA, CAS); educational technology (MA); elementary education (MA, CAS); family studies (MA); integration of spirituality and religion in counseling (ATC); marriage and family therapy (MA); reading and language development (Sixth Year Certificate); school counseling (MA, CAS); school psychology (MA, CAS); school-based marriage and family therapy (ATC); secondary education (MA); special education (MA, CAS); substance abuse counseling (ATC); teaching (Certificate); teaching and foundations (MA, CAS); TESOL, world languages, and bilingual education (MA, CAS). *Accreditation:* NCATE. *Program availability:* Part-time, evening/weekend. *Faculty:* 24 full-time (18 women), 28 part-time/adjunct (20 women). *Students:* 169 full-time (149 women), 227 part-time (187 women); includes 96 minority (21 Black or African American, non-Hispanic/Latino; 8 Asian, non-Hispanic/Latino; 60 Hispanic/Latino; 7 Two or more races, non-Hispanic/Latino), 1 international. Average age 31. 194 applicants, 60% accepted, 101 enrolled. In 2019, 136 master's, 28 other advanced degrees awarded. *Degree requirements:* For master's, comprehensive exam. *Entrance requirements:* For master's, One of the following for certification programs: Praxis Core, SAT, ACT, or GRE, minimum GPA of 3.0, 2 recommendations, resume. Additional exam requirements/recommendations for international students: required—TOEFL (minimum score 550 paper-based; 84 iBT), IELTS (minimum score 7.5), TOEFL (minimum score 550 paper-based; 84 iBT) or IELTS (minimum score 7.5). *Application deadline:* For fall admission, 2/15 for international students; for spring admission, 10/1 for international students. Application fee: $60. Electronic applications accepted. *Expenses:* Tuition $815/credit hour; Lab Fee (ED598) $300/semester; Lab Fee (CN457,CN467, PY538, PY540) $70/course; Wilson Reading Course Fee $141/credit hour; Registration Fee $50/semester; Graduate Student Activity Fee (Fall and Spring) $65/semester. *Financial support:* In 2019–20, 34 students received support. Career-related internships or fieldwork and unspecified assistantships available. Support available to part-time students. Financial award applicants required to submit FAFSA. *Unit head:* Dr. Laurie Grupp, Dean, 203-254-4250, Fax: 203-254-4241, E-mail: lgrupp@fairfield.edu. *Application contact:* Melanie Rogers, Director of Graduate Admission, 203-254-4184, Fax: 203-254-4073, E-mail: gradadmis@fairfield.edu.
Website: http://www.fairfield.edu/gseap

Florida Institute of Technology, College of Psychology and Liberal Arts, Program in Applied Behavior Analysis, Melbourne, FL 32901-6975. Offers applied behavior analysis (MS). *Program availability:* Part-time. *Degree requirements:* For master's, comprehensive exam, thesis optional, minimum of 44 credit hours, all courses at least grade of B or better. *Entrance requirements:* For master's, GRE General Test, minimum GPA of 3.0, 3 letters of recommendation, resume, statement of objectives. Additional exam requirements/recommendations for international students: required—TOEFL (minimum score 550 paper-based; 79 iBT). Electronic applications accepted.

Florida Institute of Technology, College of Psychology and Liberal Arts, Program in Applied Behavior Analysis and Organizational Behavior Management, Melbourne, FL 32901-6975. Offers applied behavior analysis and organizational behavior management (MS). *Program availability:* Part-time. *Degree requirements:* For master's, comprehensive exam, thesis, minimum of 50 credits, all course grades of B or higher. *Entrance requirements:* For master's, GRE General Test, 3 letters of recommendation, resume, statement of objectives. Additional exam requirements/recommendations for international students: required—TOEFL (minimum score 550 paper-based; 79 iBT). Electronic applications accepted.

Florida Institute of Technology, College of Psychology and Liberal Arts, Program in Professional Behavior Analysis, Melbourne, FL 32901-6975. Offers professional behavior analysis (MA). *Accreditation:* APA. *Program availability:* Part-time, 100% online. *Degree requirements:* For master's, comprehensive exam, minimum of 45 credit hours. *Entrance requirements:* Additional exam requirements/recommendations for international students: required—TOEFL (minimum score 550 paper-based; 79 iBT). Electronic applications accepted.

Florida International University, College of Arts, Sciences, and Education, Department of Psychology, Miami, FL 33199. Offers behavioral analysis (MS); clinical science (PhD); cognitive neuroscience (PhD); counseling psychology (MS); developmental science (MS, PhD); legal psychology (MS, PhD); organizational psychology (MS, PhD). *Accreditation:* APA. *Program availability:* Part-time, evening/weekend. *Faculty:* 52 full-time (33 women), 50 part-time/adjunct (37 women). *Students:* 203 full-time (159 women), 2 part-time (both women); includes 117 minority (15 Black or African American, non-Hispanic/Latino; 8 Asian, non-Hispanic/Latino; 86 Hispanic/Latino; 8 Two or more races, non-Hispanic/Latino), 15 international. Average age 26. 410 applicants, 19% accepted, 60 enrolled. In 2019, 57 master's, 7 doctorates awarded. Terminal master's awarded for partial completion of doctoral program. *Degree requirements:* For master's, thesis; for doctorate, comprehensive exam, thesis/dissertation. *Entrance requirements:* For master's, GRE General Test, minimum GPA of 3.0, resume, 3 letters of recommendation; for doctorate, GRE General Test, 3 letters of recommendation, resume, letter of intent, two writing samples, minimum GPA of 3.0. Additional exam requirements/recommendations for international students: required—TOEFL (minimum score 550 paper-based; 80 iBT). *Application deadline:* For fall admission, 12/15 for domestic and international students. Application fee: $30. Electronic applications accepted. *Expenses: Tuition, area resident:* Full-time $8912; part-time $446 per credit hour. *Tuition, state resident:* full-time $8912; part-time $446 per credit hour. *Tuition, nonresident:* full-time $21,393; part-time $992 per credit hour. *Required fees:* $2194. *Financial support:* Institutionally sponsored loans and scholarships/grants available. Financial award application deadline: 3/1. *Unit head:* Dr. Jeremy Pettit, Interim Chair, 305-348-1671, Fax: 305-348-2880, E-mail: jeremy.pettit@fiu.edu. *Application contact:* Nanett Rojas, Manager, Admissions Operations, 305-348-7464, Fax: 305-348-7441, E-mail: gradadm@fiu.edu.

Florida State University, The Graduate School, Department of Anthropology, Department of Psychology, Program in Applied Behavior Analysis, Panama City, FL 32405. Offers MS. *Faculty:* 4 full-time (2 women). *Students:* 33 full-time (28 women); includes 10 minority (1 Black or African American, non-Hispanic/Latino; 8 Hispanic/Latino; 1 Two or more races, non-Hispanic/Latino). Average age 25. 64 applicants, 42% accepted, 17 enrolled. In 2019, 16 master's awarded. *Degree requirements:* For master's, comprehensive exam. *Entrance requirements:* For master's, GRE General Test, minimum GPA of 3.0. *Application deadline:* For fall admission, 1/15 for domestic and international students. Application fee: $30. Electronic applications accepted. *Financial support:* In 2019–20, 33 students received support, including 33 teaching assistantships with full tuition reimbursements available (averaging $17,000 per year); career-related internships or fieldwork and health care benefits also available. Financial award application deadline: 1/15; financial award applicants required to submit FAFSA. *Unit head:* Dr. Jon Bailey, Head, 850-644-6443, Fax: 850-645-7518, E-mail: bailey@psy.fsu.edu. *Application contact:* Lynda L. Gibson, Graduate Program Associate, 850-644-2499, Fax: 850-644-7739, E-mail: grad-info@psy.fsu.edu.
Website: http://www.psy.fsu.edu/

Georgian Court University, School of Arts and Sciences, Lakewood, NJ 08701. Offers applied behavior analysis (MA); autism spectrum disorders (Certificate); clinical mental health counseling (MA); criminal justice and human rights (MS); holistic health studies (MA); homeland security (Certificate); instructional technology (CPC); integrative health (Certificate); mercy spirituality (Certificate); parish business management (Certificate); professional counselor (Certificate); school psychology (MA, Certificate); theology (MA, Certificate). *Program availability:* Part-time, evening/weekend. *Faculty:* 19 full-time (11 women), 7 part-time/adjunct (3 women). *Students:* 90 full-time (80 women), 71 part-time (59 women); includes 26 minority (8 Black or African American, non-Hispanic/Latino; 2 Asian, non-Hispanic/Latino; 14 Hispanic/Latino; 2 Two or more races, non-Hispanic/Latino), 1 international. Average age 32. 138 applicants, 58% accepted, 57 enrolled. In 2019, 68 master's, 19 other advanced degrees awarded. *Degree requirements:* For master's, comprehensive exam (for some programs), thesis (for some programs); for other advanced degree, comprehensive exam (for some programs). *Entrance requirements:* Additional exam requirements/recommendations for international students: required—TOEFL (minimum score 550 paper-based; 79 iBT). *Application deadline:* For fall admission, 8/15 for domestic students, 5/1 for international students; for spring admission, 1/15 for domestic students, 10/1 for international students. Applications are processed on a rolling basis. Application fee: $40. Electronic applications accepted. *Financial support:* Scholarships/grants, health care benefits, and unspecified assistantships available. Financial award application deadline: 4/15; financial award applicants required to submit FAFSA. *Unit head:* Dr. Mary Chinery, Dean, 732-987-2493, Fax: 732-987-2007, E-mail: mchinery@georgian.edu. *Application contact:* Dr. Mary Chinery, Dean, 732-987-2493, Fax: 732-987-2007, E-mail: mchinery@georgian.edu.
Website: https://georgian.edu/academics/school-of-arts-sciences/

Hofstra University, School of Education, Specialized Programs in Education, Hempstead, NY 11549. Offers applied behavior analysis (Advanced Certificate); childhood special education (MS Ed); early childhood special education (MS Ed, Advanced Certificate); educational and policy leadership (Ed D); educational leadership (Advanced Certificate); educational leadership and policy studies (MS Ed), including K-12; elementary special education (MS Ed); gifted education (Advanced Certificate); health education (MS); health professions pedagogy and leadership (MS); higher education leadership and policy studies (MS Ed); inclusive early childhood special education (MS Ed); inclusive elementary special education (MS Ed); inclusive secondary special education (MS Ed); literacy studies (MA, MS Ed, Ed D, Advanced Certificate); pedagogy for health professions (Advanced Certificate); physical education (MS); school district business leader (Advanced Certificate); secondary education generalist - students with disabilities 7-12 (MS Ed); secondary special education generalist - secondary education (MS Ed); special education (MS Ed, Advanced Certificate); special education assessment and diagnosis (Advanced Certificate); special education early childhood intervention (MS Ed); special education: international perspectives (MS Ed); teaching students with severe or multiple disabilities (Advanced Certificate). *Program availability:* Part-time, evening/weekend, online only, blended/

hybrid learning. *Students:* 109 full-time (83 women), 209 part-time (155 women); includes 89 minority (41 Black or African American, non-Hispanic/Latino; 3 American Indian or Alaska Native, non-Hispanic/Latino; 8 Asian, non-Hispanic/Latino; 31 Hispanic/Latino; 6 Two or more races, non-Hispanic/Latino), 2 international. Average age 31. 194 applicants, 87% accepted, 108 enrolled. In 2019, 120 master's, 25 doctorates, 27 other advanced degrees awarded. *Degree requirements:* For master's, one foreign language, comprehensive exam (for some programs), thesis (for some programs), electronic portfolio, capstone course, internship, practicum, student teaching, seminars, minimum GPA of 3.0; for doctorate, one foreign language, comprehensive exam, thesis/dissertation, qualifying hearing. *Entrance requirements:* For master's, GRE, interview, letters of recommendation, portfolio, essay, certification; for doctorate, GRE or MAT, interview, resume, essay, master's degree, 3 letters of recommendation, writing sample; for Advanced Certificate, GRE, interview, letters of recommendation, essay, professional experience, resume, master's degree. Additional exam requirements/recommendations for international students: required—TOEFL (minimum score 550 paper-based; 80 iBT); recommended—IELTS (minimum score 6.5). *Application deadline:* Applications are processed on a rolling basis. Application fee: $75. Electronic applications accepted. *Expenses: Tuition:* Full-time $25,164; part-time $1398 per credit. *Required fees:* $580; $165 per semester. Tuition and fees vary according to course load, degree level and program. *Financial support:* In 2019–20, 177 students received support, including 99 fellowships with full and partial tuition reimbursements available (averaging $4,221 per year), 12 research assistantships with full and partial tuition reimbursements available (averaging $5,577 per year); career-related internships or fieldwork, Federal Work-Study, institutionally sponsored loans, scholarships/grants, traineeships, tuition waivers (full and partial), unspecified assistantships, and scholarships and endowed scholarships also available. Support available to part-time students. Financial award applicants required to submit FAFSA. *Unit head:* Dr. Alan Flurkey, Chairperson, 516-463-5237, E-mail: alan.d.flurkey@hofstra.edu. *Application contact:* Sunil Samuel, Assistant Vice President of Admissions, 516-463-4723, Fax: 516-463-4664, E-mail: graduateadmission@hofstra.edu.
Website: http://www.hofstra.edu/education/

James Madison University, The Graduate School, College of Health and Behavioral Studies, Program in Psychological Sciences, Harrisonburg, VA 22807. Offers applied research (MA); behavior analysis (MA); experimental psychology (MA); quantitative psychology (MA). *Program availability:* Part-time, evening/weekend. *Students:* 24 full-time (20 women); includes 7 minority (1 Black or African American, non-Hispanic/Latino; 3 Asian, non-Hispanic/Latino; 3 Hispanic/Latino), 1 international. Average age 30. In 2019, 12 master's awarded. Application fee: $60. Electronic applications accepted. *Financial support:* In 2019–20, 22 students received support, including 1 teaching assistantship with full tuition reimbursement available (averaging $9,284 per year); career-related internships or fieldwork, Federal Work-Study, and assistantships (averaging $7911) also available. Financial award application deadline: 3/1; financial award applicants required to submit FAFSA. *Unit head:* Dr. Jeff S. Dyche, Graduate Program Director, 540-568-4965, E-mail: dychejs@jmu.edu. *Application contact:* Lynette D. Michael, Director of Graduate Admissions, 540-568-6131 Ext. 6395, Fax: 540-568-7860, E-mail: michaeld@jmu.edu.
Website: http://www.psyc.jmu.edu/psycsciences/

Lindenwood University, Graduate Programs, School of Education, St. Charles, MO 63301-1695. Offers behavioral analysis (MA); education (MA), including autism spectrum disorders, character education, early intervention in autism and sensory impairment, gifted, technology; educational administration (MA, Ed D, Ed S); English to speakers of other languages (MA); instructional leadership (Ed D, Ed S); library media (MA); professional counseling (MA); school administration (MA, Ed S); school counseling (MA); teaching (MA). *Program availability:* Part-time, evening/weekend, 100% online, blended/hybrid learning. *Faculty:* 39 full-time (28 women), 133 part-time/adjunct (83 women). *Students:* 391 full-time (287 women), 1,149 part-time (889 women); includes 358 minority (284 Black or African American, non-Hispanic/Latino; 8 American Indian or Alaska Native, non-Hispanic/Latino; 6 Asian, non-Hispanic/Latino; 32 Hispanic/Latino; 28 Two or more races, non-Hispanic/Latino), 11 international. Average age 35. 465 applicants, 71% accepted, 229 enrolled. In 2019, 432 master's, 60 doctorates, 77 other advanced degrees awarded. *Degree requirements:* For master's, thesis (for some programs), minimum GPA of 3.0; for doctorate, thesis/dissertation, minimum GPA of 3.0; for Ed S, comprehensive exam, project, minimum GPA of 3.0. *Entrance requirements:* For master's, interview, minimum undergraduate cumulative GPA of 3.0, writing sample, letter of recommendation; for doctorate, minimum graduate GPA of 3.4, resume, interview, writing sample, 4 letters of recommendation; for Ed S, master's degree in education, relevant work experience. Additional exam requirements/recommendations for international students: required—TOEFL (minimum score 553 paper-based; 81 iBT); recommended—IELTS (minimum score 6.5). *Application deadline:* For fall admission, 8/9 priority date for domestic students, 6/1 priority date for international students; for spring admission, 12/20 priority date for domestic students, 11/1 priority date for international students; for summer admission, 5/15 priority date for domestic students, 3/27 priority date for international students. Applications are processed on a rolling basis. Application fee: $0 ($100 for international students). Electronic applications accepted. *Expenses: Tuition:* Full-time $8910; part-time $495 per credit. Tuition and fees vary according to course load, degree level and program. *Financial support:* In 2019–20, 198 students received support. Career-related internships or fieldwork, Federal Work-Study, institutionally sponsored loans, scholarships/grants, tuition waivers (partial), and unspecified assistantships available. Financial award application deadline: 6/30; financial award applicants required to submit FAFSA. *Unit head:* Dr. Anthony Scheffler, Dean, School of Education, 636-949-4618, Fax: 636-949-4197, E-mail: ascheffler@lindenwood.edu. *Application contact:* Kara Schilli, Assistant Vice President, University Admissions, 636-949-4349, Fax: 636-949-4109, E-mail: adultadmissions@lindenwood.edu.
Website: https://www.lindenwood.edu/academics/academic-schools/school-of-education/

Lipscomb University, College of Education, Nashville, TN 37204-3951. Offers applied behavior analysis (MS, Certificate); coaching for learning (M Ed, Certificate, Ed S); educational leadership (M Ed, Ed S); English language learning (M Ed, Ed S); instructional coaching (M Ed, Certificate, Ed S); instructional practice (M Ed); learning organizations and strategic change (Ed D); literacy coaching (Certificate, Ed S); reading specialty (M Ed, Ed S); school counseling (M Ed, Ed S); special education (M Ed); teaching, learning, and leading (M Ed); technology integration (M Ed, Ed S); technology integration specialist (Certificate). *Accreditation:* NCATE. *Program availability:* Part-time, evening/weekend, 100% online. *Degree requirements:* For master's, comprehensive exam, portfolio, research project and presentation; for doctorate, practical capstone project in experiential setting. *Entrance requirements:* For master's, MAT (minimum score 31) or GRE General Test (minimum score 294), 2 reference letters, goals statement, writing sample, interview; for doctorate, MAT or GRE General Test, 3 reference letters, artifact of demonstrated academic excellence, written personal statements, interview. Additional exam requirements/recommendations for international students: required—TOEFL (minimum score 570 paper-based; 80 iBT). Electronic applications accepted. *Expenses:* Contact institution.

Long Island University - Brooklyn, School of Education, Brooklyn, NY 11201-8423. Offers adolescence urban education (MS Ed); applied behavior analysis (Advanced Certificate); bilingual education (Advanced Certificate); bilingual education in urban setting (MS Ed); bilingual school counselor (MS Ed, Advanced Certificate); childhood urban education (MS Ed); childhood/early childhood education (MS Ed); childhood/early childhood urban education (MS Ed); early childhood urban education (MS Ed, Advanced Certificate); educational leadership (Advanced Certificate); marriage and family therapy (MS, Advanced Certificate); mental health counseling (MS, Advanced Certificate); school building district leader (Advanced Certificate); school counselor (MS Ed, Advanced Certificate); school psychologist (MS Ed); teaching students with disabilities (MS Ed); teaching urban children with disabilities (MS Ed); TESOL (MS Ed, Advanced Certificate). *Accreditation:* TEAC. *Program availability:* Part-time, evening/weekend, 100% online. *Entrance requirements:* For master's, GRE. Additional exam requirements/recommendations for international students: required—TOEFL (minimum score 527 paper-based, 75 iBT), IELTS, or PTE. Electronic applications accepted.

Long Island University - Post, College of Liberal Arts and Sciences, Brookville, NY 11548-1300. Offers applied mathematics (MS); behavior analysis (MA); biology (MS); criminal justice (MS); earth science (MS); English (MA); environmental sustainability (MS); genetic counseling (MS); history (MA); interdisciplinary studies (MA, MS); political science (MA); psychology (MA). *Program availability:* Part-time, evening/weekend, blended/hybrid learning. Terminal master's awarded for partial completion of doctoral program. *Degree requirements:* For master's, comprehensive exam (for some programs), thesis (for some programs). *Entrance requirements:* Additional exam requirements/recommendations for international students: required—TOEFL, IELTS, or PTE. Electronic applications accepted.

Long Island University - Riverhead, Graduate Programs, Riverhead, NY 11901. Offers applied behavior analysis (Advanced Certificate); childhood education (MS), including grades 1-6; cybersecurity policy (Advanced Certificate); homeland security management (MS, Advanced Certificate); literacy education (MS); literacy education B-6 (MS); teaching students with disabilities (MS), including grades 1-6; TESOL (Advanced Certificate). *Accreditation:* TEAC. *Program availability:* Part-time. *Entrance requirements:* Additional exam requirements/recommendations for international students: required—TOEFL or IELTS. Electronic applications accepted. *Expenses:* Contact institution.

Mary Baldwin University, Graduate Studies, Programs in Education, Staunton, VA 24401-3610. Offers applied behavior analysis (MS); autism spectrum disorders (M Ed); elementary education (M Ed, MAT); English as a second language (M Ed); environment-based learning (M Ed); gifted education (M Ed); higher education (MS); leadership (M Ed); middle grades education (MAT); reading education (M Ed); special education (M Ed). *Accreditation:* TEAC.

McNeese State University, Doré School of Graduate Studies, Burton College of Education, Department of Psychology, Lake Charles, LA 70609. Offers applied behavior analysis (MA, Graduate Certificate); counseling psychology (MA); general/experimental psychology (MA). *Program availability:* Evening/weekend. *Entrance requirements:* For master's, GRE.

Mercyhurst University, Graduate Studies, Program in Applied Behavior Analysis, Erie, PA 16546. Offers MABA. *Degree requirements:* For master's, thesis, project.

Mercyhurst University, Graduate Studies, Program in Special Education, Erie, PA 16546. Offers applied behavior analysis (MS); autism (MS); generalist (MS); higher education leadership and disabilities (MS). *Program availability:* Part-time, evening/weekend. *Degree requirements:* For master's, thesis optional. *Entrance requirements:* For master's, GRE or PRAXIS I, interview, resume, essay, three professional references, transcripts. Additional exam requirements/recommendations for international students: required—TOEFL. Electronic applications accepted.

Missouri State University, Graduate College, College of Health and Human Services, Department of Psychology, Springfield, MO 65897. Offers applied behavior analysis (MS); clinical psychology (MS); experimental psychology (MS); forensic child psychology (Certificate); industrial/organizational psychology (MS). *Degree requirements:* For master's, comprehensive exam, thesis. *Entrance requirements:* For master's, GRE General Test, GRE Subject Test, minimum GPA of 3.25 in major, 3.0 overall; 20 hours of course work in psychology. Additional exam requirements/recommendations for international students: required—TOEFL (minimum score 550 paper-based; 79 iBT), IELTS (minimum score 6). Electronic applications accepted. *Expenses: Tuition, area resident:* Full-time $2600; part-time $1735 per credit hour. Tuition, nonresident: full-time $5240; part-time $3495 per credit hour. *International tuition:* $5240 full-time. *Required fees:* $530; $438 per credit hour. Tuition and fees vary according to class time, course level, course load, degree level, campus/location and program.

Monmouth University, Graduate Studies, School of Education, West Long Branch, NJ 07764-1898. Offers applied behavior analysis (Certificate); autism (Certificate); director of school counseling services (Post-Master's Certificate); early childhood (M Ed); educational leadership (Ed D); elementary education (MAT), including elementary level, secondary level; English as a second language (M Ed); learning disabilities teacher-consultant (Post-Master's Certificate); literacy (MS Ed); school counseling (MS Ed); special education (MS Ed), including autism, learning disabilities teacher-consultant, teacher of students with disabilities, teaching in inclusive settings; speech-language pathology (MS Ed); student affairs and college counseling (MS Ed); supervisor (Post-Master's Certificate); teaching English to speakers of other languages (Certificate). *Accreditation:* NCATE. *Program availability:* Part-time, evening/weekend, 100% online, blended/hybrid learning. *Faculty:* 28 full-time (19 women), 34 part-time/adjunct (25 women). *Students:* 168 full-time (144 women), 225 part-time (197 women); includes 66 minority (20 Black or African American, non-Hispanic/Latino; 6 Asian, non-Hispanic/Latino; 37 Hispanic/Latino; 3 Two or more races, non-Hispanic/Latino), 2 international. Average age 30. In 2019, 108 master's, 9 other advanced degrees awarded. *Degree requirements:* For master's, thesis (for some programs); for doctorate, thesis/dissertation, Project. *Entrance requirements:* For master's, GRE taken within last 5 years (for MS Ed in speech-language pathology); SAT (minimum combined score of 1660 in 3 sections), ACT (23), GRE (minimum score of 4.0 on analytical writing section and minimum combined score of 310 on quantitative and verbal sections), or passing scores on 3 parts of Core Academic Skills Educators, minimum GPA of 3.0 in major; 2 letters of recommendation (for some programs); resume, personal statement or essay (depending on program). Additional exam requirements/recommendations for international students: required—TOEFL (minimum score 550 paper-based; 79 iBT), IELTS (minimum score 6), Michigan English Language Assessment Battery (minimum score 77) or Certificate of Advanced English (minimum score 160). *Application deadline:* For fall admission, 7/15 priority date for domestic students, 7/1 for international students; for spring admission, 12/1 priority date for domestic students, 11/1 for international students; for summer admission, 5/1 for domestic students. Applications are processed on a rolling basis. Application fee: $50. Electronic applications accepted. *Expenses: Tuition:* Full-time $22,194; part-time $14,796 per credit. *Required fees:* $712; $178 per semester. $178 per semester. Tuition and fees vary according to course load. *Financial support:* In 2019–20, 337 students received support. Research assistantships, teaching

assistantships, scholarships/grants, and unspecified assistantships available. Support available to part-time students. Financial award applicants required to submit FAFSA. *Unit head:* Dr. John E. Henning, Dean, 732-263-5513, Fax: 732-263-5277, E-mail: kodonnel@monmouth.edu. *Application contact:* Kirsten Sneeringer, Graduate Admission Counselor, 732-571-3452, Fax: 732-263-5123, E-mail: gradadm@monmouth.edu.
Website: http://www.monmouth.edu/academics/schools/education/default.asp

Montana State University Billings, College of Education, Department of Educational Theory and Practice, Program in Special Education, Billings, MT 59101. Offers advanced studies (MS Sp Ed); applied behavior analysis (MS Sp Ed); generalist (MS Sp Ed). *Accreditation:* NCATE. *Program availability:* Part-time. *Degree requirements:* For master's, thesis or professional paper and/or field experience. *Entrance requirements:* For master's, GRE General Test or MAT, minimum GPA of 3.0. Additional exam requirements/recommendations for international students: required—TOEFL (minimum score 79 iBT), IELTS (minimum score 6.5). Electronic applications accepted.

National University, Sanford College of Education, La Jolla, CA 92037-1011. Offers advanced teaching practices (MS); applied behavior analysis (MS); applied school leadership (MS); e-teaching and learning (Certificate); education (MA); educational administration (MS); educational and instructional technology (MS); educational counseling (MS); higher education administration (MS); inspired teaching and learning (M Ed); school psychology (MS); special education (MA, MS). *Program availability:* Part-time, evening/weekend, 100% online, blended/hybrid learning. *Degree requirements:* For master's, thesis (for some programs). *Entrance requirements:* For master's, interview, minimum GPA of 2.5. Additional exam requirements/recommendations for international students: required—TOEFL (minimum score 550 paper-based; 79 iBT), IELTS (minimum score 6). Electronic applications accepted. *Expenses: Tuition:* Full-time $442; part-time $442 per unit.

Niagara University, Graduate Division of Education, Niagara University, NY 14109. Offers applied behavior analysis (Certificate); educational leadership (MS Ed, PhD, Certificate), including leadership and policy (PhD); school building leader (MS Ed); school district business leader (Certificate), school district leader (MS Ed, Certificate); literacy instruction (MS Ed); mental health counseling (MS, Certificate); school counseling (MS Ed, Certificate); school psychology (MS); teacher education (MS, MS Ed, Certificate), including early childhood and childhood education (MS Ed, Certificate), early childhood special education (MS), middle and adolescence education (Certificate), special education (MS Ed), special education (grades 1-6) (Certificate), special education (grades 7-12) (Certificate), teaching English to speakers of other languages (TESOL) (Certificate). *Accreditation:* NCATE (one or more programs are accredited). *Program availability:* Part-time, evening/weekend, 100% online, blended/hybrid learning. *Entrance requirements:* For master's, GRE General Test or MAT. Additional exam requirements/recommendations for international students: required—TOEFL (minimum score 550 paper-based; 79 iBT), IELTS (minimum score 6). Electronic applications accepted. *Expenses:* Contact institution.

Northeastern University, Bouvé College of Health Sciences, Boston, MA 02115-5096. Offers applied behavior analysis (MS); audiology (Au D); counseling psychology (MS, PhD, CAGS); exercise science (MS); nursing (MS, PhD, CAGS), including administration (MS), adult-gerontology acute care nurse practitioner (MS, CAGS), adult-gerontology primary care nurse practitioner (MS, CAGS), anesthesia (MS), family nurse practitioner (MS, CAGS), neonatal nurse practitioner (MS, CAGS), pediatric nurse practitioner (MS, CAGS), psychiatric mental health nurse practitioner (MS, CAGS); nursing practice (DNP); pharmaceutical sciences (MS, PhD), including interdisciplinary concentration, pharmaceutics and drug delivery systems; pharmacology (MS); pharmacy (Pharm D); school psychology (PhD); speech-language pathology (MS); urban health (MPH); MS/MBA. *Accreditation:* AANA/CANAEP; ACPE (one or more programs are accredited); ASHA; CEPH. *Program availability:* Part-time, evening/weekend, online learning. *Degree requirements:* For doctorate, thesis/dissertation (for some programs); for CAGS, comprehensive exam. Electronic applications accepted. *Expenses:* Contact institution.

Northern Michigan University, Office of Graduate Education and Research, College of Arts and Sciences, Department of Psychological Science, Marquette, MI 49855-5301. Offers applied behavior analysis (MS); psychological science (MS). *Program availability:* Part-time. *Degree requirements:* For master's, thesis or alternative. *Entrance requirements:* For master's, minimum GPA of 3.0; bachelor's degree (preferably in psychology); undergraduate courses in introduction to psychology and statistics; personal statement; 3 letters of recommendation. Additional exam requirements/recommendations for international students: required—TOEFL (minimum score 500 paper-based; 61 iBT), IELTS (minimum score 6). *Application deadline:* For fall admission, 2/1 for domestic students. Applications are processed on a rolling basis. Application fee: $50. Electronic applications accepted. *Financial support:* Teaching assistantships with full tuition reimbursements available. Financial award application deadline: 3/1; financial award applicants required to submit FAFSA. *Unit head:* Dr. Adam Prus, Department Head and Professor, 906-227-2935, E-mail: psych@nmu.edu. *Application contact:* Dr. Adam Prus, Department Head and Professor, 906-227-2935, E-mail: psych@nmu.edu.
Website: http://www.nmu.edu/psychology/

Northern Vermont University–Johnson, Program in Education, Johnson, VT 05656. Offers applied behavior analysis (MA Ed); curriculum and instruction (MA Ed); foundations of education (MA Ed); special education (MA Ed). *Program availability:* Part-time. *Degree requirements:* For master's, thesis or alternative, exit interview. *Entrance requirements:* For master's, interview. Additional exam requirements/recommendations for international students: required—TOEFL. Electronic applications accepted.

Oakland University, Graduate Study and Lifelong Learning, School of Education and Human Services, Department of Human Development and Child Studies, Program in Special Education, Rochester, MI 48309-4401. Offers applied behavior analysis (Graduate Certificate); autism spectrum disorder (Graduate Certificate); emotional impairment (Graduate Certificate); special education (M Ed), including applied behavior analysis, autism spectrum disorder, emotional impairment, specific learning disabilities; specific learning disabilities (Graduate Certificate). *Accreditation:* TEAC. *Entrance requirements:* For master's, supplemental application form, 2 recommendation forms, Copy of current (or most recent) teaching certificate, interview may be required for candidates under consideration, Goal statement, which includes the reason for application, cumulative grade point average (GPA) of 3.0 or above. Additional exam requirements/recommendations for international students: required—TOEFL (minimum score 550 paper-based; 79 iBT), IELTS (minimum score 6.5). Electronic applications accepted. *Expenses: Tuition, area resident:* Full-time $12,328; part-time $770.50 per credit hour. Tuition, state resident: full-time $12,328; part-time $770.50 per credit hour. Tuition, nonresident: full-time $16,432; part-time $1027 per credit hour. *International tuition:* $16,432 full-time. Tuition and fees vary according to degree level and program.

Oklahoma City University, Petree College of Arts and Sciences, Oklahoma City, OK 73106-1402. Offers applied behavioral studies (M Ed); applied sociology: nonprofit leadership (MA); creative writing (MFA); criminology (MS); early childhood education

(M Ed); elementary education (M Ed); general studies (MLA); leadership/management (MLA); moving image arts (MFA); professional counseling (M Ed); teaching (MA); teaching English to speakers of other languages (MA). *Program availability:* Part-time, evening/weekend. *Degree requirements:* For master's, capstone/practicum. *Entrance requirements:* For master's, bachelor's degree from accredited institution with minimum GPA of 3.0, essay, recommendation letters. Additional exam requirements/recommendations for international students: required—TOEFL (minimum score 550 paper-based; 80 iBT). Electronic applications accepted. *Expenses:* Contact institution.

Penn State Harrisburg, Graduate School, School of Behavioral Sciences and Education, Middletown, PA 17057. Offers adult education in the health and medical professions (Certificate); applied behavior analysis (MA); applied clinical psychology (MA); applied psychological research (MA); community psychology and social change (MA); English as a second language (ESL) program specialist and leadership (Certificate); health education (M Ed); lifelong learning and adult education (M Ed, D Ed); literacy education (M Ed); literacy leadership (Certificate); psychology: applications in clinical psychology (Certificate); psychology: health psychology (Certificate); teaching and curriculum (M Ed); training and development (M Ed, Certificate). *Program availability:* Part-time, evening/weekend.

Philadelphia College of Osteopathic Medicine, Graduate and Professional Programs, School of Professional and Applied Psychology, Philadelphia, PA 19131. Offers applied behavior analysis (Certificate); clinical health psychology (Post-Doctoral Certificate); clinical neuropsychology (Post-Doctoral Certificate); clinical psychology (Psy D); educational psychology (PhD); mental health counseling (MS); organizational development and leadership (MS); psychology (Certificate); public health management and administration (MS); school psychology (MS, Psy D, Ed S). *Accreditation:* APA. *Faculty:* 19 full-time (11 women), 122 part-time/adjunct (58 women). *Students:* 342 (285 women); includes 108 minority (65 Black or African American, non-Hispanic/Latino; 1 American Indian or Alaska Native, non-Hispanic/Latino; 10 Asian, non-Hispanic/Latino; 14 Hispanic/Latino; 18 Two or more races, non-Hispanic/Latino). Average age 25. 357 applicants, 51% accepted, 113 enrolled. In 2019, 79 master's, 38 doctorates, 16 other advanced degrees awarded. Terminal master's awarded for partial completion of doctoral program. *Degree requirements:* For master's, comprehensive exam (for some programs), thesis (for some programs); for doctorate, comprehensive exam, thesis/dissertation. *Entrance requirements:* For master's, GRE or MAT, minimum GPA of 3.0; bachelor's degree from regionally-accredited college or university; for doctorate, PRAXIS II (for Psy D in school psychology), minimum undergraduate GPA of 3.0; for other advanced degree, GRE (for Ed S). Additional exam requirements/recommendations for international students: required—TOEFL (minimum score 79 iBT). *Application deadline:* Applications are processed on a rolling basis. Application fee: $50. Electronic applications accepted. *Financial support:* In 2019–20, 28 teaching assistantships were awarded; Federal Work-Study, institutionally sponsored loans, and scholarships/grants also available. Financial award application deadline: 3/15; financial award applicants required to submit FAFSA. *Unit head:* Dr. Robert DiTomasso, Chairman, 215-871-6442, Fax: 215-871-6458, E-mail: robertd@pcom.edu. *Application contact:* Johnathan Cox, Associate Director of Admissions, 215-871-6700, Fax: 215-871-6719, E-mail: johnathancox@pcom.edu.
Website: pcom.edu

Queens College of the City University of New York, Mathematics and Natural Sciences Division, Department of Psychology, Queens, NY 11367-1597. Offers applied behavior analysis (MA); behavioral neuroscience (MA); general psychology (MA). *Program availability:* Part-time. Terminal master's awarded for partial completion of doctoral program. *Degree requirements:* For master's, comprehensive exam (for some programs), thesis (for some programs). *Entrance requirements:* For master's, GRE for Behavioral Neuroscience MA, minimum GPA of 3.0. Additional exam requirements/recommendations for international students: required—TOEFL (minimum score 100 iBT), IELTS (minimum score 7). Electronic applications accepted.

Regis College, Nursing and Health Sciences School, Weston, MA 02493. Offers applied behavior analysis (MS); counseling psychology (MA); health administration (MS); nurse practitioner (Certificate); nursing (MS, DNP); nursing education (Certificate); occupational therapy (MS). *Accreditation:* ACEN. *Program availability:* Part-time, evening/weekend, 100% online, blended/hybrid learning. *Degree requirements:* For doctorate, thesis/dissertation. *Entrance requirements:* For master's, minimum GPA of 3.0, official transcripts, recommendations, personal statement, resume/curriculum vitae, interview; for doctorate, GRE if GPA from master's lower than 3.5. Additional exam requirements/recommendations for international students: required—TOEFL (minimum score 560 paper-based; 79 iBT); recommended—IELTS (minimum score 6.5). *Application deadline:* Applications are processed on a rolling basis. Application fee: $75. Electronic applications accepted. *Financial support:* Federal Work-Study, scholarships/grants, and unspecified assistantships available. Support available to part-time students. Financial award applicants required to submit FAFSA. *Application contact:* Thomas May, Graduate Admission Counselor, 781-768-7162, E-mail: thomas.may@regiscollege.edu.

Rollins College, Hamilton Holt School, Master of Arts in Applied Behavior Analysis and Clinical Science Program, Winter Park, FL 32789-4499. Offers MA. *Program availability:* Part-time, evening/weekend. *Faculty:* 3 full-time (all women), 2 part-time/adjunct (both women). *Students:* 25 full-time (22 women), 13 part-time (10 women); includes 15 minority (4 Black or African American, non-Hispanic/Latino; 2 Asian, non-Hispanic/Latino; 8 Hispanic/Latino; 1 Two or more races, non-Hispanic/Latino), 1 international. Average age 28. In 2019, 9 master's awarded. *Degree requirements:* For master's, thesis, Board Certified Behavior Analyst Examination; intensive practicum. *Entrance requirements:* For master's, GRE, official transcripts, three letters of recommendation, essay, resume. Additional exam requirements/recommendations for international students: required—TOEFL (minimum score 550 paper-based). *Application deadline:* For fall admission, 3/1 priority date for domestic students. Applications are processed on a rolling basis. Application fee: $50. Electronic applications accepted. *Expenses:* $2,534 per credit hour; typcal course is 4 credit hours. *Financial support:* In 2019–20, 1 student received support. Scholarships/grants and unspecified assistantships available. Support available to part-time students. Financial award applicants required to submit FAFSA. *Unit head:* Dr. Michele Williams, Director, Health Professions, 407-646-2036, E-mail: amwilliams2@rollins.edu. *Application contact:* Graduate Program Admission, 407-646-2232, Fax: 407-646-1551.

Rowan University, Graduate School, College of Science and Mathematics, Program in Applied Behavioral Analysis, Glassboro, NJ 08028-1701. Offers MA, CAGS. *Entrance requirements:* For master's, GRE General Test. Additional exam requirements/recommendations for international students: required—TOEFL. *Expenses: Tuition, area resident:* Part-time $715.50 per semester hour. Tuition, state resident: part-time $715.50 per semester hour. Tuition, nonresident: part-time $715.50 per semester hour. *Required fees:* $161.55 per semester hour.

Sage Graduate School, Esteves School of Education, Program in Applied Behavior Analysis and Autism, Troy, NY 12180-4115. Offers MS, Post Master's Certificate. *Program availability:* Part-time, evening/weekend, online only, 100% online. *Faculty:* 6 full-time (5 women), 8 part-time/adjunct (2 women). *Students:* 24 full-time (18 women), 148 part-time (130 women); includes 57 minority (11 Black or African American, non-

Hispanic/Latino; 1 American Indian or Alaska Native, non-Hispanic/Latino; 13 Asian, non-Hispanic/Latino; 27 Hispanic/Latino; 5 Two or more races, non-Hispanic/Latino). Average age 29. 267 applicants, 52% accepted, 60 enrolled. In 2019, 79 master's, 9 other advanced degrees awarded. *Entrance requirements:* For master's, undergraduate degree with minimum GPA of 2.75. Additional exam requirements/recommendations for international students: required—TOEFL (minimum score 550 paper-based). *Application deadline:* Applications are processed on a rolling basis. Application fee: $30. Electronic applications accepted. *Expenses: Tuition:* Part-time $730 per credit hour. Tuition and fees vary according to course load, degree level and program. *Financial support:* Scholarships/grants and unspecified assistantships available. Financial award applicants required to submit FAFSA. *Unit head:* Dr. John Pelizza, Dean, Esteves School of Education, 518-244-2051, Fax: 518-244-2334, E-mail: pelizj@sage.edu. *Application contact:* Dr. Lori Finn, Department Chair, Center for Applied Behavior Analysis, 518-244-6873, Fax: 518-244-6880, E-mail: caba@sage.edu.
Website: http://www.sage.edu

St. Cloud State University, School of Graduate Studies, School of Health and Human Services, Department of Counseling and Community Psychology, Program in Applied Behavior Analysis, St. Cloud, MN 56301-4498. Offers MS. *Program availability:* Part-time, online learning. *Degree requirements:* For master's, comprehensive exam (for some programs), thesis or alternative. *Entrance requirements:* For master's, GRE General Test, minimum GPA of 2.75. Additional exam requirements/recommendations for international students: required—Michigan English Language Assessment Battery; recommended—TOEFL (minimum score 550 paper-based), IELTS (minimum score 6.5).

Saint Louis University, Graduate Programs, College for Public Health and Social Justice, School of Social Work, St. Louis, MO 63103. Offers applied behavior analysis (MS); social work (MSW, PhD). *Accreditation:* CSWE. *Program availability:* Part-time. *Entrance requirements:* For master's, minimum GPA of 3.0, letters of recommendation. Additional exam requirements/recommendations for international students: required—TOEFL (minimum score 550 paper-based). *Expenses:* Contact institution.

Saint Peter's University, Graduate Programs in Education, Jersey City, NJ 07306-5997. Offers director of school counseling services (Certificate); educational leadership (MA Ed, Ed D); higher education (MHE, Ed D), including educational leadership (Ed D), general administration (MHE); middle school mathematics (Certificate); professional/associate counselor (Certificate); reading (MA Ed); school business administrator (Certificate); school counseling (MA, Certificate); special education (MA Ed, Certificate), including applied behavioral analysis (MA Ed), literacy (MA Ed), teacher of students with disabilities (Certificate); teaching (MA Ed, Certificate), including 6-8 middle school education, K-12 secondary education, K-5 elementary education. *Accreditation:* TEAC. *Program availability:* Part-time, evening/weekend. *Degree requirements:* For master's, comprehensive exam; for doctorate, comprehensive exam, thesis/dissertation. *Entrance requirements:* For master's and doctorate, GRE or MAT. Additional exam requirements/recommendations for international students: required—TOEFL. Electronic applications accepted.

Salve Regina University, Program in Applied Behavior Analysis, Newport, RI 02840-4192. Offers MA, CAGS. *Program availability:* Part-time, some fully in person classes offered. *Entrance requirements:* Additional exam requirements/recommendations for international students: required—TOEFL. *Application deadline:* For fall admission, 8/1 for domestic students; for winter admission, 12/1 for domestic students; for spring admission, 2/1 for domestic students; for summer admission, 4/1 for domestic students. Applications are processed on a rolling basis. Application fee: $0. Electronic applications accepted. *Financial support:* Application deadline: 3/1; applicants required to submit FAFSA. *Unit head:* Dr. Cody Morris, Graduate Program Director, E-mail: cody.morris@salve.edu. *Application contact:* Laurie Reilly, Graduate Admissions Manager, 401-341-2153, Fax: 401-341-2973, E-mail: laurie.reilly@salve.edu.

Shenandoah University, College of Arts and Sciences, Winchester, VA 22601. Offers applied behavior analysis (MS). *Program availability:* Part-time, evening/weekend. *Degree requirements:* For master's, thesis or alternative, minimum of 37 credit hours of 3.0 or better, including 21 in coursework, 12 of supervised practical experience, and 4 for capstone project. *Entrance requirements:* For master's, bachelor's degree (minimum 3.0 GPA); essay; 3 letters of recommendation written by professors, supervisors, or other persons engaged in the practice of Applied Behavior Analysis or other human services professions. Additional exam requirements/recommendations for international students: required—TOEFL (minimum score 550 paper-based; 79 iBT), IELTS (minimum score 6.5), TOEFL (minimum score 550 paper-based, 79 iBT) OR IELTS (6.5). Electronic applications accepted. *Expenses:* Contact institution.

Simmons University, Gwen Ifill College of Media, Arts, and Humanities, Boston, MA 02115. Offers behavior analysis (MS, PhD, Ed S); children's literature (MA); dietetics (Certificate); elementary education (MAT); English (MA); gender/cultural studies (MA); history (MA); nutrition and health promotion (MS); physical therapy (DPT); public health (MPH); public policy (MPP); special education: moderate and severe disabilities (MS Ed); sports nutrition (Certificate); writing for children (MFA). *Program availability:* Part-time. *Faculty:* 10 full-time (9 women), 7 part-time/adjunct (6 women). *Students:* 2 full-time (both women), 67 part-time (57 women); includes 13 minority (3 Black or African American, non-Hispanic/Latino; 4 Asian, non-Hispanic/Latino; 3 Hispanic/Latino; 3 Two or more races, non-Hispanic/Latino), 1 international. Average age 31. 42 applicants, 62% accepted, 23 enrolled. In 2019, 24 master's awarded. *Degree requirements:* For master's, thesis optional. *Entrance requirements:* For master's, GRE, bachelor's degree from accredited college or university; minimum B average (preferred). Additional exam requirements/recommendations for international students: required—TOEFL (minimum score 600 paper-based; 100 iBT). *Application deadline:* For fall admission, 8/1 for domestic and international students; for spring admission, 12/15 for domestic and international students; for summer admission, 5/1 for domestic and international students. Applications are processed on a rolling basis. Application fee: $35. Electronic applications accepted. *Expenses:* Contact institution. *Financial support:* In 2019–20, 14 students received support, including 1 fellowship (averaging $15,360 per year), 13 teaching assistantships (averaging $2,000 per year); scholarships/grants also available. Financial award applicants required to submit FAFSA. *Unit head:* Dr. Brian Norman, Dean, 617-521-2472, E-mail: brian.norman@simmons.edu. *Application contact:* Patricia Flaherty, Director, Graduate Studies Admission, 617-521-3902, Fax: 617-521-3058, E-mail: gsa@simmons.edu.
Website: https://www.simmons.edu/academics/colleges-schools-departments/ifill

Teachers College, Columbia University, Department of Health and Behavior Studies, New York, NY 10027-6696. Offers applied behavior analysis (MA, PhD); applied educational psychology: school psychology (Ed M, PhD); behavioral nutrition (PhD), including nutrition (Ed D, PhD); community health education (MS); community nutrition education (Ed M), including community nutrition education; education of deaf and hard of hearing (MA, PhD); health education (MA, Ed D); hearing impairment (Ed D); intellectual disability/autism (MA, Ed D, PhD); nursing education (Ed D, Advanced Certificate); nutrition and education (MS); nutrition and exercise physiology (MS); nutrition and public health (MS); nutrition education (Ed D), including nutrition (Ed D, PhD); physical disabilities (Ed D); reading specialist (MA); severe or multiple disabilities (MA); special education (Ed M, MA, Ed D); teaching of sign language (MA). *Faculty:* 17 full-time (11 women). *Students:* 243 full-time (225 women), 246 part-time (211 women); includes 172 minority (33 Black or African American, non-Hispanic/Latino; 2 American Indian or Alaska Native, non-Hispanic/Latino; 63 Asian, non-Hispanic/Latino; 63 Hispanic/Latino; 11 Two or more races, non-Hispanic/Latino), 67 international. 515 applicants, 68% accepted, 170 enrolled. *Unit head:* Dr. Dolores Perin, Chair, 212-678-3091, E-mail: dp111@tc.columbia.edu. *Application contact:* Kelly Sutton-Skinner, Director of Admission and New Student Enrollment, E-mail: kms2237@tc.columbia.edu.
Website: http://www.tc.columbia.edu/health-and-behavior-studies/

Temple University, College of Education and Human Development, Department of Psychological Studies in Education, Philadelphia, PA 19122-6096. Offers applied behavior analysis (MS Ed); counseling psychology (Ed M), including agency counseling, school counseling; educational psychology (Ed M); school psychology (PhD, Ed S). *Accreditation:* APA (one or more programs are accredited). *Program availability:* Part-time, evening/weekend. *Faculty:* 19 full-time (10 women), 19 part-time/adjunct (9 women). *Students:* 165 full-time (122 women), 49 part-time (37 women); includes 74 minority (39 Black or African American, non-Hispanic/Latino; 13 Asian, non-Hispanic/Latino; 17 Hispanic/Latino; 5 Two or more races, non-Hispanic/Latino), 11 international. 374 applicants, 49% accepted, 100 enrolled. In 2019, 73 master's, 5 doctorates, 16 other advanced degrees awarded. *Degree requirements:* For master's, comprehensive exam (for some programs); for doctorate, thesis/dissertation. *Entrance requirements:* For master's, statement of goals, 2 recommendation letters; for doctorate, GRE, statement of goals, academic writing sample, 2 recommendation letters. Additional exam requirements/recommendations for international students: required—TOEFL (minimum score 79 iBT), IELTS, PTE, one of three is required. Application fee: $60. Electronic applications accepted. *Financial support:* Fellowships, research assistantships, teaching assistantships, career-related internships or fieldwork, Federal Work-Study, health care benefits, and unspecified assistantships available. Financial award applicants required to submit FAFSA. *Unit head:* Renee Tobin, Prof. of Counseling Psychology and Dept. Chairperson, 215-204-7884, E-mail: renee.tobin@temple.edu. *Application contact:* Remy Van Wyk, Academic Coordinator, 215-204-1474, E-mail: remy.van.wyk@temple.edu.
Website: http://education.temple.edu/pse

Tennessee Technological University, College of Graduate Studies, College of Education, Department of Curriculum and Instruction, Program in Exceptional Learning, Cookeville, TN 38505. Offers applied behavior analysis (PhD); literacy (PhD); program planning and evaluation (PhD); STEM education (PhD). *Program availability:* Part-time, evening/weekend. *Students:* 12 full-time (7 women), 22 part-time (12 women); includes 1 minority (Black or African American, non-Hispanic/Latino), 3 international. 16 applicants, 50% accepted, 7 enrolled. In 2019, 5 doctorates awarded. *Degree requirements:* For doctorate, comprehensive exam, thesis/dissertation. *Entrance requirements:* For doctorate, GRE, minimum GPA of 3.0. Additional exam requirements/recommendations for international students: required—TOEFL (minimum score 550 paper-based; 79 iBT), IELTS (minimum score 5.5), PTE (minimum score 53), or TOEIC (Test of English as an International Communication). *Application deadline:* For fall admission, 8/1 for domestic students, 5/1 for international students; for spring admission, 12/1 for domestic students, 10/1 for international students; for summer admission, 5/1 for domestic students, 2/1 for international students. Applications are processed on a rolling basis. Application fee: $35 ($40 for international students). Electronic applications accepted. *Expenses: Tuition, area resident:* Part-time $597 per credit hour. Tuition, state resident: part-time $597 per credit hour. Tuition, nonresident: part-time $1323 per credit hour. *Financial support:* Fellowships, research assistantships, and teaching assistantships available. Financial award application deadline: 4/1. *Unit head:* Dr. Lisa Zagumny, Dean, College of Education, 931-372-3078, Fax: 931-372-3517, E-mail: lzagumny@tntech.edu. *Application contact:* Shelia K. Kendrick, Coordinator of Graduate Studies, 931-372-3808, Fax: 931-372-3497, E-mail: skendrick@tntech.edu.
Website: https://www.tntech.edu/education/elphd/

University of California, Riverside, Graduate Division, Graduate School of Education, Riverside, CA 92521. Offers applied behavior analysis (M Ed); diversity and equity (M Ed); education policy analysis and leadership (PhD); education specialist (Credential); education, society, and culture (MA, PhD); educational psychology (MA, PhD); general education (M Ed); higher education administration and policy (M Ed, PhD); multiple subject (Credential); research, evaluation, measurement and statistics (MA); school psychology (PhD); single subject (Credential); special education (M Ed, PhD); special education and autism (MA); TESOL (M Ed). Terminal master's awarded for partial completion of doctoral program. *Degree requirements:* For master's, comprehensive exams or thesis (MA), case study or analytical report (M Ed); for doctorate, comprehensive exam, thesis/dissertation, written and oral qualifying exams, college teaching practicum. *Entrance requirements:* For master's, GRE General Test (for MA); CBEST and CSET (for M Ed in general education only), UCR Extension TESOL certificate (for M Ed with TESOL emphasis only); for doctorate, GRE General Test, writing sample; for Credential, CBEST, CSET. Additional exam requirements/recommendations for international students: required—TOEFL (minimum score 550 paper-based; 80 iBT), IELTS (minimum score 7). Electronic applications accepted.

The University of Kansas, Graduate Studies, College of Liberal Arts and Sciences, Department of Applied Behavioral Science, Lawrence, KS 66045. Offers applied behavioral science (MA); behavioral psychology (PhD); community health and development (Graduate Certificate); PhD/MPH. *Program availability:* Part-time. *Students:* 42 full-time (29 women), 45 part-time (40 women); includes 10 minority (2 Black or African American, non-Hispanic/Latino; 3 Asian, non-Hispanic/Latino; 2 Hispanic/Latino; 1 Native Hawaiian or other Pacific Islander, non-Hispanic/Latino; 2 Two or more races, non-Hispanic/Latino). Average age 35. 110 applicants, 42% accepted, 32 enrolled. In 2019, 7 master's, 4 doctorates, 12 other advanced degrees awarded. Terminal master's awarded for partial completion of doctoral program. *Entrance requirements:* For master's, GRE, curriculum vitae; 3 letters of recommendation; personal statement; all academic transcripts; copies of pertinent written work, published or not, as well as presented papers; for doctorate, GRE, curriculum vitae; 3 letters of recommendation; personal statement; copies of pertinent written work, published or not, as well as presented papers. Additional exam requirements/recommendations for international students: required—TOEFL, IELTS. *Application deadline:* For fall admission, 12/15 priority date for domestic students, 12/15 for international students. Application fee: $65 ($85 for international students). Electronic applications accepted. *Expenses:* Tuition, state resident: full-time $9989. Tuition, nonresident: full-time $23,950. *International tuition:* $23,950 full-time. *Required fees:* $984; $81.99 per credit hour. Tuition and fees vary according to course load, campus/location and program. *Financial support:* Fellowships, research assistantships, teaching assistantships, career-related internships or fieldwork, traineeships, tuition waivers (full), and unspecified assistantships available. Financial award application deadline: 12/15; financial award applicants required to submit CSS PROFILE or FAFSA. *Unit head:* Dr. Florence DiGennaro Reed, Chairperson, 785-864-0521, E-mail: fdreed@ku.edu. *Application contact:* Brittney Tyler-Milholland, Graduate Representative, 785-864-3625, E-mail: tylermil@ku.edu.
Website: http://absc.ku.edu

University of Louisville, Graduate School, College of Education and Human Development, Department of Elementary, Middle & Secondary Education, Louisville, KY 40292-0001. Offers art education (MAT); autism and applied behavior analysis (Certificate); curriculum and instruction (PhD); early elementary education (MAT); exercise physiology (MS); health and physical education (MAT); health professions education (Certificate); higher education (MA); human resources and organization development (MS); instructional technology (M Ed); interdisciplinary early childhood education (MAT); middle school education (MAT); music education (MAT); secondary education (MAT); special education (MAT); sport administration (MS); teacher leadership (M Ed). *Program availability:* Part-time, evening/weekend. *Faculty:* 15 full-time (11 women), 14 part-time/adjunct (8 women). *Students:* 19 full-time (15 women), 110 part-time (58 women); includes 33 minority (12 Black or African American, non-Hispanic/Latino; 7 Asian, non-Hispanic/Latino; 6 Hispanic/Latino; 1 Native Hawaiian or other Pacific Islander, non-Hispanic/Latino; 7 Two or more races, non-Hispanic/Latino). Average age 29. 23 applicants, 83% accepted, 17 enrolled. In 2019, 62 master's awarded. *Degree requirements:* For doctorate, comprehensive exam, thesis/dissertation. *Entrance requirements:* For master's, GRE (for most programs), PRAXIS (for educator preparation programs), professional statement, recommendation letters, resume, transcripts, minimum of one year of teaching experience is required for admission to this program, formal interview; for doctorate, GRE, professional statement, recommendation letters, resume, transcripts. Additional exam requirements/recommendations for international students: required—TOEFL (minimum score 550 paper-based; 79 iBT); recommended—IELTS (minimum score 6.5). *Application deadline:* For fall admission, 4/15 priority date for domestic and international students; for spring admission, 12/1 for domestic students, 10/1 for international students; for summer admission, 4/1 for domestic and international students. Application fee: $65. Electronic applications accepted. *Expenses: Tuition, area resident:* Full-time $13,000; part-time $723 per credit hour. Tuition, state resident: full-time $13,000; part-time $723 per credit hour. Tuition, nonresident: full-time $27,114; part-time $1507 per credit hour. *International tuition:* $27,114 full-time. *Required fees:* $196. Tuition and fees vary according to program and reciprocity agreements. *Financial support:* In 2019–20, 34 students received support, including 4 research assistantships with full tuition reimbursements available (averaging $21,024 per year), 1 teaching assistantship with full tuition reimbursement available (averaging $21,024 per year); fellowships, scholarships/grants, health care benefits, tuition waivers (full), and unspecified assistantships also available. Financial award application deadline: 2/1; financial award applicants required to submit FAFSA. *Unit head:* Dr. Caroline C. Sheffield, Chair, 502-852-6493, E-mail: midsecnd@louisville.edu. *Application contact:* Dr. Margaret Pentecost, Assistant Dean for Graduate Student Success, 502-852-6437, Fax: 502-852-1417, E-mail: gedadm@louisville.edu.
Website: http://louisville.edu/delphi

University of Massachusetts Dartmouth, Graduate School, College of Arts and Sciences, Department of Psychology, North Dartmouth, MA 02747-2300. Offers autism studies (Graduate Certificate); psychology - applied behavioral analysis (MA, Post-Master's Certificate); psychology - clinical (MA); psychology - research (MA). *Program availability:* Part-time. *Faculty:* 18 full-time (11 women), 7 part-time/adjunct (4 women). *Students:* 40 full-time (32 women), 54 part-time (47 women); includes 16 minority (5 Black or African American, non-Hispanic/Latino; 2 Asian, non-Hispanic/Latino; 5 Hispanic/Latino; 4 Two or more races, non-Hispanic/Latino), 3 international. Average age 29. 97 applicants, 58% accepted, 34 enrolled. In 2019, 26 master's, 1 other advanced degree awarded. *Degree requirements:* For master's, thesis (for some programs), thesis. *Entrance requirements:* For master's, GRE (recommended), statement of purpose (minimum of 300 words), resume, 3 letters of recommendation, official transcripts; for other advanced degree, statement of purpose (minimum of 300 words), resume, 3 letters of recommendation, official transcripts. Additional exam requirements/recommendations for international students: required—TOEFL (minimum score 80 iBT). *Application deadline:* For fall admission, 4/15 for domestic students, 3/15 for international students. Application fee: $60. Electronic applications accepted. *Expenses: Tuition, area resident:* Full-time $16,390; part-time $682.92 per credit. Tuition, state resident: full-time $16,390; part-time $682.92 per credit. Tuition, nonresident: full-time $29,578; part-time $1232.42 per credit. *Required fees:* $575. *Financial support:* In 2019–20, 1 research assistantship (averaging $9,000 per year), 2 teaching assistantships (averaging $14,000 per year) were awarded; tuition waivers (full and partial) and unspecified assistantships also available. Financial award application deadline: 3/1; financial award applicants required to submit FAFSA. *Unit head:* R. Thomas Boone, Graduate Program Director, Psychology, 508-999-8440, E-mail: tboone@umassd.edu. *Application contact:* Scott Webster, Director of Graduate Studies and Admissions, 508-999-8604, Fax: 508-999-8183, E-mail: graduate@umassd.edu.
Website: http://www.umassd.edu/cas/psychology/graduate-programs

University of Memphis, Graduate School, College of Education, Department of Instruction and Curriculum Leadership, Memphis, TN 38152. Offers advanced studies in teaching and learning (M Ed); applied behavior analysis (Graduate Certificate); autism studies (Graduate Certificate); early childhood education (MAT, MS, Ed D); elementary education (MAT); instruction and curriculum (MS, Ed D); instruction design and technology (MS, Ed D); instructional design and technology (Graduate Certificate); literacy, leadership, and coaching (Graduate Certificate); reading (MS, Ed D); school library information specialist (Graduate Certificate); secondary education (MAT); special education (MAT, MS, Ed D); STEM teacher leadership (Graduate Certificate); urban education (Graduate Certificate). *Accreditation:* NCATE (one or more programs are accredited). *Program availability:* Part-time, 100% online, blended/hybrid learning. *Students:* 61 full-time (48 women), 444 part-time (340 women); includes 250 minority (203 Black or African American, non-Hispanic/Latino; 2 American Indian or Alaska Native, non-Hispanic/Latino; 12 Asian, non-Hispanic/Latino; 25 Hispanic/Latino; 8 Two or more races, non-Hispanic/Latino), 5 international. Average age 35. 290 applicants, 99% accepted, 181 enrolled. In 2019, 121 master's, 13 doctorates, 29 other advanced degrees awarded. Terminal master's awarded for partial completion of doctoral program. *Degree requirements:* For master's, comprehensive exam, thesis or alternative; for doctorate, comprehensive exam, thesis/dissertation. *Entrance requirements:* For master's, GRE General Test, PRAXIS, minimum GPA of 2.5, letters of reference; for doctorate, GRE General Test, GRE Subject Test, 2 years of teaching experience, letters of reference, statement of purpose, interview. Additional exam requirements/recommendations for international students: required—TOEFL (minimum score 550 paper-based; 79 iBT). *Application deadline:* For fall admission, 4/1 priority date for domestic students; for spring admission, 10/1 priority date for domestic students; for summer admission, 2/1 priority date for domestic students. Applications are processed on a rolling basis. Application fee: $35 ($60 for international students). Electronic applications accepted. *Expenses: Tuition, area resident:* Full-time $9216; part-time $512 per credit hour. Tuition, state resident: full-time $9216; part-time $512 per credit hour. Tuition, nonresident: full-time $12,672; part-time $704 per credit hour. *International tuition:* $16,128 full-time. *Required fees:* $1530; $85 per credit hour. Tuition and fees vary according to program. *Financial support:* Research assistantships with full tuition reimbursements, teaching assistantships with full tuition reimbursements, career-related internships or fieldwork, Federal Work-Study, institutionally sponsored loans, scholarships/grants, traineeships, and unspecified assistantships available. Support available to part-time students. Financial award application deadline: 2/1; financial award applicants required to submit FAFSA. *Unit head:* Dr. Sandra Cooley Nichols, Chair, 901-678-2365, E-mail: smcooley@memphis.edu. *Application contact:* Dr. Lee Allen, Director of Graduate Programs, 901-678-4073, E-mail: allenlee@memphis.edu.
Website: http://www.memphis.edu/icl/

University of Michigan–Dearborn, College of Education, Health, and Human Services, Master of Science Program in Applied Behavior Analysis, Dearborn, MI 48128. Offers MS. *Program availability:* Part-time, evening/weekend. *Faculty:* 2 full-time (1 woman), 1 (woman) part-time/adjunct. *Students:* 3 full-time (all women), 23 part-time (21 women); includes 5 minority (3 Black or African American, non-Hispanic/Latino; 1 Asian, non-Hispanic/Latino; 1 Native Hawaiian or other Pacific Islander, non-Hispanic/Latino). Average age 29. 33 applicants, 73% accepted, 10 enrolled. *Entrance requirements:* For master's, bachelor's degree from accredited institution, official transcripts from all post-secondary institutions attended, minimum GPA of 3.0, three professional letters of recommendation, personal statement. Additional exam requirements/recommendations for international students: required—TOEFL (minimum score 560 paper-based; 84 iBT), IELTS (minimum score 6.5). *Application deadline:* For fall admission, 8/1 for domestic students, 5/1 for international students; for winter admission, 12/1 for domestic students, 9/1 for international students; for spring admission, 4/1 for domestic students, 1/1 for international students. Applications are processed on a rolling basis. Application fee: $60. Electronic applications accepted. *Financial support:* Scholarships/grants available. Financial award application deadline: 3/1; financial award applicants required to submit FAFSA. *Unit head:* Dr. Paul Fossum, Director, Master's Programs, 313-593-0982, E-mail: pfossum@umich.edu. *Application contact:* Office of Graduate Studies, 313-583-6321, E-mail: umd-graduatestudies@umich.edu.
Website: https://umdearborn.edu/cehhs/graduate-programs/areas-study/ms-applied-behavior-analysis

University of Nebraska at Omaha, Graduate Studies, College of Arts and Sciences, Department of Psychology, Omaha, NE 68182. Offers applied behavior analysis (Certificate); human resources and training (Certificate); industrial/organizational psychology (MS); psychology (MA, PhD); school psychology (MS, Ed S). *Program availability:* Part-time. *Degree requirements:* For master's, comprehensive exam, thesis (for some programs); for doctorate, comprehensive exam, thesis/dissertation. *Entrance requirements:* For master's and doctorate, GRE, minimum GPA of 3.0, official transcripts, 3 letters of recommendation, statement of purpose, writing sample, resume. Additional exam requirements/recommendations for international students: required—TOEFL, IELTS, PTE. Electronic applications accepted.

University of Nebraska Medical Center, Medical Sciences Interdepartmental Area, Omaha, NE 68198. Offers applied behavior analysis (PhD); clinical translational research (MS, PhD); health practice and medical education research (MS); oral biology (MS, PhD). *Program availability:* Part-time. Terminal master's awarded for partial completion of doctoral program. *Degree requirements:* For master's, comprehensive exam, thesis; for doctorate, comprehensive exam, thesis/dissertation. *Entrance requirements:* For master's, GRE General Test; for doctorate, GRE General Test, MCAT, DAT, LSAT. Additional exam requirements/recommendations for international students: required—TOEFL (minimum score 550 paper-based; 80 iBT), IELTS. Electronic applications accepted. *Expenses:* Contact institution.

University of Nevada, Reno, Graduate School, College of Liberal Arts, Department of Psychology, Program in Behavior Analysis, Reno, NV 89557. Offers MA, PhD. *Degree requirements:* For master's, thesis optional; for doctorate, thesis/dissertation. *Entrance requirements:* For master's, GRE General Test, minimum GPA of 2.75; for doctorate, GRE General Test, minimum GPA of 3.0. Additional exam requirements/recommendations for international students: required—TOEFL (minimum score 500 paper-based; 61 iBT), IELTS (minimum score 6). Electronic applications accepted.

The University of North Carolina Wilmington, College of Arts and Sciences, Department of Psychology, Wilmington, NC 28403-3297. Offers clinical psychology (PhD); psychology (MA), including applied behavior analysis, psychological science. *Faculty:* 27 full-time (15 women). *Students:* 44 full-time (36 women), 34 part-time (29 women); includes 12 minority (3 Black or African American, non-Hispanic/Latino; 5 Hispanic/Latino; 4 Two or more races, non-Hispanic/Latino), 1 international. Average age 25. 112 applicants, 38% accepted, 38 enrolled. In 2019, 19 master's awarded. *Degree requirements:* For master's, comprehensive exam, thesis; for doctorate, thesis/dissertation, 1-year external APA-accredited or APPIC-member internship. *Entrance requirements:* For master's, GRE General Test, GRE Subject Test (psychology) only if bachelor's degree was not in the area of psychology, 3 letters of recommendation, psychology research interest form, resume, essay; for doctorate, GRE General Test, GRE Subject Test (psychology) only if bachelor's degree was not in the area of psychology, 3 letters of recommendation, resume, statement of interest. Additional exam requirements/recommendations for international students: required—TOEFL (minimum score 79 iBT), IELTS (minimum score 6.5). *Application deadline:* For fall admission, 4/15 for domestic students. Applications are processed on a rolling basis. Application fee: $75. Electronic applications accepted. *Expenses: Tuition, area resident:* Full-time $4719; part-time $326 per credit hour. Tuition, state resident: full-time $4719; part-time $326 per credit hour. Tuition, nonresident: full-time $18,548; part-time $1099 per credit hour. *Required fees:* $2738. Tuition and fees vary according to program. *Financial support:* Research assistantships, teaching assistantships, Federal Work-Study, scholarships/grants, unspecified assistantships, and out-of-state tuition remission available. Financial award application deadline: 1/1; financial award applicants required to submit FAFSA. *Unit head:* Dr. Julian Keith, Chair, 910-962-3378, Fax: 910-962-7010, E-mail: keithj@uncw.edu. *Application contact:* Dr. Kate Nooner, Graduate Coordinator, 910-962-2140, Fax: 910-962-7010, E-mail: psygradprogram@uncw.edu.
Website: http://www.uncw.edu/psy/grad/

University of North Florida, College of Education and Human Services, Department of Exceptional, Deaf, and Interpreter Education, Jacksonville, FL 32224. Offers American Sign Language (MS); American Sign Language/English interpreting (M Ed); applied behavior analysis (M Ed); autism (M Ed); deaf education (M Ed); disability services (M Ed); exceptional student education (M Ed). *Accreditation:* NCATE. *Program availability:* Part-time, evening/weekend. *Entrance requirements:* For master's, GRE General Test, minimum GPA of 3.0 in last 60 hours, interview, 3 letters of recommendation. Additional exam requirements/recommendations for international students: required—TOEFL (minimum score 500 paper-based). Electronic applications accepted.

University of North Texas, Toulouse Graduate School, Denton, TX 76203-5459. Offers accounting (MS); applied anthropology (MA, MS); applied behavior analysis (Certificate); applied geography (MA); applied technology and performance improvement (M Ed, MS); art education (MA); art history (MA); arts leadership (Certificate); audiology (Au D); behavior analysis (MS); behavioral science (PhD); biochemistry and molecular biology (MS); biology (MA, MS); biomedical engineering (MS); business analysis (MS); chemistry (MS); clinical health psychology (PhD); communication studies (MA, MS); computer engineering (MS); computer science (MS); counseling (M Ed, MS), including clinical mental health counseling (MS), college and university counseling, elementary school counseling, secondary school counseling; creative writing (MA); criminal justice (MS); curriculum and instruction (M Ed); decision sciences (MBA); design (MA, MFA), including fashion design (MFA), innovation studies, interior design (MFA); early childhood studies (MS); economics (MS); educational leadership (M Ed, Ed D); educational psychology (MS, PhD), including family studies (MS), gifted and talented (MS), human development (MS), learning and cognition (MS), research, measurement and evaluation (MS); electrical engineering (MS); emergency management (MPA); engineering technology (MS); English (MA); English as a second language (MA); environmental science (MS); finance (MBA, MS); financial management (MPA); French (MA); health services management (MBA); higher education (M Ed, Ed D); history (MA, MS); hospitality management (MS); human resources management (MPA); information science (MS); information systems (PhD); information technologies (MBA); interdisciplinary studies (MA, MS); international studies (MA); international sustainable tourism (MS); jazz studies (MM); journalism (MA, MJ, Graduate Certificate), including interactive and virtual digital communication (Graduate Certificate), narrative journalism (Graduate Certificate), public relations (Graduate Certificate); kinesiology (MS); linguistics (MA); local government management (MPA); logistics (PhD); logistics and supply chain management (MBA); long-term care, senior housing, and aging services (MA); management (PhD); marketing (MBA); mathematics (MA, MS); mechanical and energy engineering (MS, PhD); music (MA), including ethnomusicology, music theory, musicology, performance; music composition (PhD); music education (MM Ed, PhD); nonprofit management (MPA); operations and supply chain management (MBA); performance (MM, DMA); philosophy (MA); political science (MA); professional and technical communication (MA); radio, television and film (MA, MFA); rehabilitation counseling (Certificate); sociology (MA); Spanish (MA); special education (M Ed); speech-language pathology (MA); strategic management (MBA); studio art (MFA); teaching (M Ed); MBA/MS. *Program availability:* Part-time, evening/weekend, online learning. Terminal master's awarded for partial completion of doctoral program. *Degree requirements:* For master's, variable foreign language requirement, comprehensive exam (for some programs), thesis (for some programs); for doctorate, variable foreign language requirement, comprehensive exam (for some programs), thesis/dissertation; for other advanced degree, variable foreign language requirement, comprehensive exam (for some programs). *Entrance requirements:* For master's and doctorate, GRE, GMAT. Additional exam requirements/recommendations for international students: required—TOEFL (minimum score 550 paper-based; 79 iBT). Electronic applications accepted.

University of Oklahoma, Jeannine Rainbolt College of Education, Department of Educational Psychology, Norman, OK 73019. Offers instructional psychology and technology (M Ed, PhD), including educational psychology (M Ed), instructional design and technology (M Ed), instructional psychology and technology (PhD), integrating technology in teaching (M Ed); professional counseling (M Ed), including professional counseling; special education (M Ed, PhD), including applied behavior analysis (M Ed), higher education and community support (PhD), higher education professor (PhD), school instruction and leadership (PhD), secondary transition education (M Ed). *Accreditation:* NCATE. *Program availability:* Part-time, 100% online, blended/hybrid learning. Terminal master's awarded for partial completion of doctoral program. *Degree requirements:* For master's, comprehensive exam (for some programs), thesis (for some programs); for doctorate, comprehensive exam (for some programs), thesis/dissertation. *Entrance requirements:* For doctorate, GRE. Additional exam requirements/recommendations for international students: required—TOEFL (minimum score 79 iBT) or IELTS (minimum score 6.5). Electronic applications accepted. *Expenses:* Tuition, state resident: full-time $6583.20; part-time $274.30 per credit hour. Tuition, nonresident: full-time $21,242; part-time $885.10 per credit hour. *International tuition:* $21,242.40 full-time. *Required fees:* $1994.20; $72.55 per credit hour. $126.50 per semester. Tuition and fees vary according to course load and degree level.

University of Southern Maine, College of Management and Human Service, School of Education and Human Development, Program in Educational Psychology, Portland, ME 04103. Offers applied behavior analysis (MS, CGS). *Program availability:* Part-time, evening/weekend. *Entrance requirements:* For master's, GRE or MAT. Additional exam requirements/recommendations for international students: required—TOEFL (minimum score 550 paper-based; 79 iBT). Electronic applications accepted. *Expenses: Tuition, area resident:* Full-time $864; part-time $432 per credit hour. Tuition, state resident: full-time $864; part-time $432 per credit hour. Tuition, nonresident: full-time $2372; part-time $1186 per credit hour. *Required fees:* $141; $108 per credit hour. Tuition and fees vary according to course load.

University of South Florida, College of Behavioral and Community Sciences, Department of Child and Family Studies, Tampa, FL 33620-9951. Offers applied behavior analysis (MA, MS, PhD); behavioral and community sciences (PhD); child and adolescent behavioral health (MS), including developmental disabilities, leadership in child and adolescent health, translational research and evaluation, youth and behavioral health; rehabilitation and mental health counseling (MA), including addictions and substance abuse counseling, marriage and family therapy. *Accreditation:* ACA. *Faculty:* 21 full-time (13 women), 3 part-time/adjunct (all women). *Students:* 184 full-time (157 women), 104 part-time (88 women); includes 113 minority (42 Black or African American, non-Hispanic/Latino; 4 Asian, non-Hispanic/Latino; 54 Hispanic/Latino; 1 Native Hawaiian or other Pacific Islander, non-Hispanic/Latino; 12 Two or more races, non-Hispanic/Latino), 7 international. Average age 27. 310 applicants, 51% accepted, 92 enrolled. In 2019, 127 master's, 8 doctorates awarded. *Degree requirements:* For master's, comprehensive exam, thesis (for some programs); for doctorate, comprehensive exam, thesis/dissertation, Behavior Analyst Board Certification Exam. *Entrance requirements:* For master's, GRE General Test, 3.00 GPA; 3 letters of reference; resume or CV; statement of purpose; writing sample; undergraduate statistics or research methods course (for Rehab and Mental Health Counseling); for doctorate, GRE General Test, master's degree in behavioral analysis or closely-related field; minimum GPA of 3.5 in graduate course work; three letters of recommendation; campus visit with faculty interview; personal statement; curriculum vitae; evidence of research experiences and expertise; campus visit and interview. Additional exam requirements/recommendations for international students: required—TOEFL, TOEFL (minimum score 550 paper-based; 79 iBT) or IELTS (minimum score 6.5). *Application deadline:* For fall admission, 12/5 for domestic and international students. Application fee: $30. *Financial support:* In 2019–20, 57 students received support. Unspecified assistantships available. *Unit head:* Jason Anthony, Professor and Director, Rightpath Research and Innovation Center, 813-974-6009, E-mail: jasonanthony@usf.edu. *Application contact:* Dr. Raymond G. Miltenberger, Professor/Director of Master's Program, 813-974-5079, Fax: 813-974-6115, E-mail: miltenbe@usf.edu.
Website: http://cfs.cbcs.usf.edu/

The University of Texas at San Antonio, College of Education and Human Development, Department of Educational Psychology, San Antonio, TX 78207. Offers applied behavior analysis (Certificate); educational psychology (MA), including applied educational psychology, behavior assessment and intervention, general educational psychology, program evaluation; language acquisition and bilingual psychoeducational assessment (Certificate); school psychology (MA). *Program availability:* Part-time. *Degree requirements:* For master's, comprehensive exam, thesis (for some programs). *Entrance requirements:* For master's, GRE, bachelor's degree with 18 credit hours in field of study or in another appropriate field of study, two letters of recommendation, statement of purpose; for Certificate, 18 hours in psychology, sociology, education, or anything related (for applied behavioral analysis); minimum GPA of 2.7 in last 30 hours (for language acquisition and bilingual psychoeducational assessment). Additional exam requirements/recommendations for international students: required—TOEFL (minimum score 550 paper-based; 79 iBT), IELTS (minimum score 6.5). Electronic applications accepted.

University of Utah, Graduate School, College of Education, Department of Special Education, Salt Lake City, UT 84112. Offers board certified behavior analyst (M Ed, MS, PhD); deaf and hard of hearing (M Ed); deafblind (M Ed, MS); early childhood deaf and hard of hearing (MS); early childhood special education (M Ed, MS, PhD); early childhood visual impairments (M Ed); mild/moderate disabilities (M Ed, MS, PhD); severe disabilities (M Ed, MS, PhD); visual impairments (M Ed, MS). *Program availability:* Part-time, blended/hybrid learning, Interactive Video Conferencing. *Faculty:* 16 full-time (13 women), 4 part-time/adjunct (3 women). *Students:* 70 full-time (64 women), 22 part-time (21 women); includes 14 minority (1 Black or African American, non-Hispanic/Latino; 2 Asian, non-Hispanic/Latino; 9 Hispanic/Latino; 1 Native Hawaiian or other Pacific Islander, non-Hispanic/Latino; 1 Two or more races, non-Hispanic/Latino). Average age 33. 30 applicants, 87% accepted, 22 enrolled. In 2019, 20 master's, 2 doctorates awarded. Terminal master's awarded for partial completion of doctoral program. *Degree requirements:* For master's, comprehensive exam, thesis optional; for doctorate, comprehensive exam, thesis/dissertation. *Entrance requirements:* For master's, minimum GPA of 3.0; for doctorate, GRE General Test, minimum GPA of 3.5, Master's Degree. Additional exam requirements/recommendations for international students: required—TOEFL (minimum score 600 paper-based; 250 iBT). *Application deadline:* For fall admission, 10/1 for domestic and international students; for spring admission, 3/1 for domestic and international students; for summer admission, 5/16 for domestic and international students. Application fee: $55 ($65 for international students). Electronic applications accepted. *Expenses:* Contact institution. *Financial support:* In 2019–20, 51 students received support, including 41 fellowships with full and partial tuition reimbursements available (averaging $4,634 per year), 2 research assistantships with full and partial tuition reimbursements available (averaging $12,500 per year), 1 teaching assistantship with full tuition reimbursement available (averaging $9,000 per year); career-related internships or fieldwork, scholarships/grants, health care benefits, and unspecified assistantships also available. Financial award application deadline: 3/15. *Unit head:* Matt Jameson, PhD, Department Chair, 801-581-8121, E-mail: matt.jameson@utah.edu. *Application contact:* Matt Jameson, PhD, Department Chair, 801-581-8121, E-mail: matt.jameson@utah.edu.
Website: http://special-ed.utah.edu/

University of West Florida, College of Education and Professional Studies, Department of Teacher Education and Educational Leadership, Program in Exceptional Student Education, Pensacola, FL 32514-5750. Offers applied behavior analysis (MA); special and alternative education (MA). *Accreditation:* NCATE. *Program availability:* Part-time, evening/weekend, online learning. *Entrance requirements:* For master's, GRE (minimum score 450 verbal) or MAT (minimum score 396) if bachelor's GPA less than 3.0, state teaching certification; letter of intent; two professional references. Additional exam requirements/recommendations for international students: required—TOEFL (minimum score 550 paper-based).

Wayne State University, College of Education, Division of Theoretical and Behavioral Foundations, Detroit, MI 48202. Offers applied behavior analysis (Certificate); counseling (M Ed, MA, Ed D, Ed S); counseling psychology (MA, PhD); education evaluation and research (M Ed, Ed D); educational psychology (M Ed, PhD), including learning and instruction sciences (PhD); rehabilitation counseling and community inclusion (MA); school and community psychology (MA, Certificate). *Accreditation:* ACA (one or more programs are accredited); CORE (one or more programs are accredited). *Program availability:* Part-time, evening/weekend. *Faculty:* 10. *Students:* 199 full-time (171 women), 142 part-time (107 women); includes 135 minority (90 Black or African American, non-Hispanic/Latino; 2 American Indian or Alaska Native, non-Hispanic/Latino; 6 Asian, non-Hispanic/Latino; 16 Hispanic/Latino; 21 Two or more races, non-Hispanic/Latino), 10 international. Average age 32. 364 applicants, 25% accepted, 72 enrolled. In 2019, 101 master's, 11 doctorates, 19 other advanced degrees awarded. *Degree requirements:* For master's, thesis (for some programs); for doctorate, comprehensive exam, thesis/dissertation. *Entrance requirements:* For master's, GRE, interview, personal statement, portfolio (only art therapy); references; program application; for doctorate, GRE, departmental writing exam, interview, curriculum vitae, references, master's degree in closely-related field with minimum GPA of 3.5, demonstration of counseling skills (for Ed D in counseling); autobiographical statement; letter of application; personal statement; for other advanced degree, education specialist certificate: master's degree in counseling or closely related field and licensure; personal statement; recommendations; autobiographical statement; interview. Additional exam requirements/recommendations for international students: required—TOEFL (minimum score 550 paper-based; 79 iBT); recommended—IELTS (minimum score 6.5), TWE (minimum score 5.5), TSE (minimum score 58). *Application deadline:* Applications are processed on a rolling basis. Application fee: $50. Electronic applications accepted. *Expenses: Tuition:* Full-time $34,567. *Financial support:* In 2019–20, 92 students received support, including 1 fellowship (averaging $20,000 per year), 1 research assistantship with tuition reimbursement available (averaging $19,967 per year); teaching assistantships, Federal Work-Study, scholarships/grants, health care benefits, and unspecified assistantships also available. Support available to part-time students. Financial award applicants required to submit FAFSA. *Unit head:* Dr. William Hill, Assistant Dean, 313-577-9316, E-mail: ad2107@wayne.edu. *Application contact:* Dr. Mary L Waker, Graduate Admissions Officer, 313-577-1601, Fax: 313-577-7904, E-mail: m.waker@wayne.edu.
Website: https://education.wayne.edu/counseling-educational-psychology

Western New England University, College of Arts and Sciences, Program in Behavior Analysis, Springfield, MA 01119. Offers applied behavior analysis (MS); behavior analysis (PhD). *Program availability:* Part-time, evening/weekend. *Degree requirements:* For doctorate, thesis/dissertation. *Entrance requirements:* For master's, GRE, official transcript, personal statement, resume, three letters of recommendation; for doctorate, GRE, master's degree in behavior analysis with minimum GPA of 3.6, official transcript, personal statement, resume, three letters of recommendation. Additional exam requirements/recommendations for international students: required—TOEFL (minimum score 79 iBT). Electronic applications accepted. *Expenses:* Contact institution.

Westfield State University, College of Graduate and Continuing Education, Department of Psychology, Program in Applied Behavior Analysis, Westfield, MA 01086. Offers MA. *Program availability:* Part-time, evening/weekend. *Degree requirements:* For master's, comprehensive exam, thesis (for some programs). *Entrance requirements:* For master's, GRE General Test or MAT, minimum undergraduate GPA of 2.8. Additional exam requirements/recommendations for international students: recommended—TOEFL (minimum score 550 paper-based; 79 iBT).

Wright State University, Graduate School, College of Liberal Arts, Program in Applied Behavioral Science, Criminal Justice and Social Problems, Dayton, OH 45435. Offers criminal justice and social problems (MA). *Degree requirements:* For master's, thesis optional. *Entrance requirements:* Additional exam requirements/recommendations for international students: required—TOEFL.

Applied Psychology

Antioch University New England, Graduate School, Department of Applied Psychology, Keene, NH 03431-3552. Offers autism spectrum disorders (Certificate), including applied behavioral analysis internship, autism spectrum disorders; clinical mental health counseling (MA), including clinical mental health counseling, substance abuse counseling; dance/movement therapy and counseling (M Ed, MA, PMC); marriage and family therapy (MA, PhD, Certificate). *Faculty:* 15 full-time (12 women), 30 part-time/adjunct (25 women). *Students:* 264 full-time (217 women), 79 part-time (64 women); includes 67 minority (25 Black or African American, non-Hispanic/Latino; 2 American Indian or Alaska Native, non-Hispanic/Latino; 8 Asian, non-Hispanic/Latino; 27 Hispanic/Latino; 5 Two or more races, non-Hispanic/Latino), 5 international. Average age 35. 149 applicants, 52% accepted, 77 enrolled. In 2019, 49 master's awarded. *Degree requirements:* For master's, internship, practicum. *Entrance requirements:* For master's, previous course work and work experience in psychology. Additional exam requirements/recommendations for international students: required—TOEFL (minimum score 550 paper-based). *Application deadline:* For fall admission, 7/15 for domestic and international students; for spring admission, 12/1 for domestic and international students. Applications are processed on a rolling basis. Application fee: $50. Electronic applications accepted. *Expenses:* Contact institution. *Financial support:* In 2019–20, 56 students received support. Fellowships, research assistantships, career-related internships or fieldwork, Federal Work-Study, and scholarships/grants available. Financial award application deadline: 6/1; financial award applicants required to submit FAFSA. *Unit head:* Dr. Kevin Lyness, Department Chair, 603-283-2149, E-mail: klyness@antioch.edu. *Application contact:* Admissions, 800-552-8380, Fax: 603-357-0718, E-mail: admissions.ane@antioch.edu.
Website: https://www.antioch.edu/new-england/degrees-programs/counseling-wellness/

Arizona State University at Tempe, Ira A. Fulton Schools of Engineering, The Polytechnic School, Applied Psychology Program, Mesa, AZ 85212. Offers MS. *Program availability:* Part-time. Terminal master's awarded for partial completion of doctoral program. *Degree requirements:* For master's, thesis or applied project with oral defense and exam; interactive Program of Study (iPOS) submitted before completing 50 percent of required credit hours. *Entrance requirements:* For master's, GRE, minimum GPA of 3.0 or equivalent in last 2 years of work leading to bachelor's degree. Additional exam requirements/recommendations for international students: required—TOEFL, IELTS, or PTE. Electronic applications accepted.

Athabasca University, Program in Counseling, Athabasca, AB T9S 3A3, Canada. Offers applied psychology (Post Master's Certificate); art therapy (MC); career counseling (MC); counseling (Advanced Certificate); counseling psychology (MC); school counseling (MC).

California State University, Chico, Office of Graduate Studies, College of Behavioral and Social Sciences, Department of Psychology, Program in Applied/School Psychology, Chico, CA 95929-0722. Offers MA. *Degree requirements:* For master's, thesis or comprehensive exam. *Entrance requirements:* For master's, GRE General Test or MAT, fall admissions only, deadline February 17th. 3 letters of recommendation, 3 departmental recommendation forms, statement of purpose, departmental application. Additional exam requirements/recommendations for international students: required—TOEFL (minimum score 550 paper-based; 80 iBT), IELTS (minimum score 6.5), PTE. Electronic applications accepted.

The Catholic University of America, School of Arts and Sciences, Department of Psychology, Washington, DC 20064. Offers applied experimental psychology (PhD); clinical psychology (PhD); general psychology (MA); human development psychology (PhD); human factors (MA); MA/JD. *Accreditation:* APA (one or more programs are accredited). *Program availability:* Part-time. *Faculty:* 9 full-time (5 women), 8 part-time/adjunct (all women). *Students:* 31 full-time (27 women), 40 part-time (33 women); includes 19 minority (3 Black or African American, non-Hispanic/Latino; 3 Asian, non-Hispanic/Latino; 5 Hispanic/Latino; 8 Two or more races, non-Hispanic/Latino), 6 international. Average age 28. 160 applicants, 25% accepted, 17 enrolled. In 2019, 19 master's, 8 doctorates awarded. *Degree requirements:* For master's, comprehensive exam, thesis (for some programs); for doctorate, comprehensive exam, thesis/dissertation. *Entrance requirements:* For master's, GRE General Test, statement of purpose, official copies of academic transcripts, three letters of recommendation; for doctorate, GRE General Test, GRE Subject Test, statement of purpose, official copies of academic transcripts, three letters of recommendation. Additional exam requirements/recommendations for international students: required—TOEFL (minimum score 550 paper-based; 80 iBT). *Application deadline:* For fall admission, 7/15 priority date for domestic students, 7/1 for international students; for spring admission, 11/15 priority date for domestic students, 11/1 for international students. Applications are processed on a rolling basis. Application fee: $55. Electronic applications accepted. *Expenses:* Contact institution. *Financial support:* Fellowships, research assistantships, teaching assistantships, Federal Work-Study, scholarships/grants, tuition waivers (full and partial), and unspecified assistantships available. Financial award application deadline: 2/1; financial award applicants required to submit FAFSA. *Unit head:* Dr. Brendan Rich, Chair, 202-319-5823, Fax: 202-319-6263, E-mail: richb@cua.edu. *Application contact:* Dr. Steven Brown, Director of Graduate Admissions, 202-319-5057, Fax: 202-319-6533, E-mail: cua-admissions@cua.edu.
Website: http://psychology.cua.edu/

Central Michigan University, College of Graduate Studies, College of Liberal Arts and Social Sciences, Department of Psychology, Program in Experimental Psychology, Mount Pleasant, MI 48859. Offers applied experimental psychology (PhD); experimental psychology (MS). *Program availability:* Part-time. *Degree requirements:* For master's, thesis or alternative; for doctorate, thesis/dissertation. Electronic applications accepted. *Expenses: Tuition, area resident:* Full-time $12,267; part-time $8178 per year. Tuition, state resident: full-time $12,267; part-time $8178 per year. Tuition, nonresident: full-time $12,267; part-time $8178 per year. *International tuition:* $16,110 full-time. *Required fees:* $225 per semester. Tuition and fees vary according to degree level and program.

The Chicago School of Professional Psychology at San Diego, Graduate Programs, San Diego, CA 92101. Offers applied behavior analysis (MS, PhD); applied clinical psychology (Psy D); clinical psychology (MA); industrial and organizational psychology (MA).

The Chicago School of Professional Psychology: Online, Program in Applied Industrial and Organizational Psychology, Chicago, IL 60654. Offers MA, Certificate.

Clayton State University, School of Graduate Studies, College of Arts and Sciences, Program in Psychology, Morrow, GA 30260-0285. Offers applied developmental psychology (MS); clinical/counseling psychology (MS). *Entrance requirements:* For master's, GRE, 2 official transcripts; 3 letters of recommendation; statement of purpose; on-campus interview; background check. Additional exam requirements/

recommendations for international students: required—TOEFL (minimum score 550 paper-based). Electronic applications accepted.

Clemson University, Graduate School, College of Behavioral, Social and Health Sciences, Department of Psychology, Clemson, SC 29634. Offers applied psychology (MS); human factors psychology (PhD); industrial-organizational psychology (PhD). *Faculty:* 32 full-time (15 women). *Students:* 40 full-time (28 women), 4 part-time (2 women); includes 8 minority (2 Black or African American, non-Hispanic/Latino; 1 Asian, non-Hispanic/Latino; 5 Hispanic/Latino), 1 international. Average age 26. 168 applicants, 11% accepted, 14 enrolled. In 2019, 13 master's, 6 doctorates awarded. *Expenses:* Full-Time Student per Semester: Tuition: $6225 (in-state), $13425 (out-of-state), Fees: $598; Graduate Assistant Per Semester: $1144; Part-Time Student Per Credit Hour: $833 (in-state), $1731 (out-of-state), Fees: $617. Doctoral Base Fee per Semester: $4938 (in-state), $10405 (out-of-state). *Financial support:* In 2019–20, 43 students received support, including 5 fellowships with full and partial tuition reimbursements available (averaging $12,800 per year), 9 research assistantships with full and partial tuition reimbursements available (averaging $14,408 per year), 28 teaching assistantships with full and partial tuition reimbursements available (averaging $15,268 per year); career-related internships or fieldwork and unspecified assistantships also available. *Application contact:* Dr. Robert Sinclair, Graduate Program Coordinator, 864-656-3931, E-mail: RSINCLA@clemson.edu.
Website: http://www.clemson.edu/cbshs/departments/psychology/index.html

DEREE - The American College of Greece, Graduate Programs, Athens, Greece. Offers applied psychology (MS); communication (MA); leadership (MS); marketing (MS).

Eastern Washington University, Graduate Studies, College of Social Sciences, Department of Psychology, Cheney, WA 99004-2431. Offers clinical psychology (MS); experimental psychology (MS); mental health counseling (MS), including applied psychology, mental health counseling; school counseling (MS), including applied psychology, school counseling; school psychology respecialization (Ed S). *Faculty:* 22 full-time (15 women). *Students:* 119 full-time (94 women), 13 part-time (10 women); includes 3 minority (all Hispanic/Latino), 6 international. Average age 34. 83 applicants, 42% accepted, 31 enrolled. In 2019, 49 master's awarded. *Degree requirements:* For master's, comprehensive exam, thesis or alternative. *Entrance requirements:* For master's, GRE General Test, minimum GPA of 3.0. Additional exam requirements/recommendations for international students: required—TOEFL (minimum score 580 paper-based; 92 iBT), IELTS (minimum score 7), PTE (minimum score 63). *Application deadline:* For fall admission, 3/1 for domestic students. Applications are processed on a rolling basis. Application fee: $75. Electronic applications accepted. *Financial support:* Teaching assistantships with partial tuition reimbursements, career-related internships or fieldwork, Federal Work-Study, institutionally sponsored loans, scholarships/grants, health care benefits, tuition waivers (partial), and unspecified assistantships available. Support available to part-time students. Financial award application deadline: 2/1; financial award applicants required to submit FAFSA. *Unit head:* Dennis Anderson, 509-359-2087, E-mail: danderson2@ewu.edu. *Application contact:* Kathy White, Advisor/Recruiter for Graduate Studies, 509-359-6297, Fax: 509-359-6044, E-mail: gradprograms@ewu.edu.

Fairfield University, Graduate School of Education and Allied Professions, Fairfield, CT 06824. Offers applied behavior analysis (ATC); applied psychology (MA); clinical mental health counseling (MA, CAS); educational technology (MA); elementary education (MA, CAS); family studies (MA); integration of spirituality and religion in counseling (ATC); marriage and family therapy (MA); reading and language development (Sixth Year Certificate); school counseling (MA, CAS); school psychology (MA, CAS); school-based marriage and family therapy (ATC); secondary education (MA); special education (MA, CAS); substance abuse counseling (ATC); teaching (Certificate); teaching and foundations (MA, CAS); TESOL, world languages, and bilingual education (MA, CAS). *Accreditation:* NCATE. *Program availability:* Part-time, evening/weekend. *Faculty:* 24 full-time (18 women), 28 part-time/adjunct (20 women). *Students:* 169 full-time (149 women), 227 part-time (187 women); includes 96 minority (21 Black or African American, non-Hispanic/Latino; 8 Asian, non-Hispanic/Latino; 60 Hispanic/Latino; 7 Two or more races, non-Hispanic/Latino), 1 international. Average age 31. 194 applicants, 60% accepted, 101 enrolled. In 2019, 136 master's, 28 other advanced degrees awarded. *Degree requirements:* For master's, comprehensive exam. *Entrance requirements:* For master's, One of the following for certification programs: Praxis Core, SAT, ACT, or GRE, minimum GPA of 3.0, 2 recommendations, resume. Additional exam requirements/recommendations for international students: required—TOEFL (minimum score 550 paper-based; 84 iBT), IELTS (minimum score 7.5), TOEFL (minimum score 550 paper-based; 84 iBT) or IELTS (minimum score 7.5). *Application deadline:* For fall admission, 2/15 for international students; for spring admission, 10/1 for international students. Application fee: $60. Electronic applications accepted. *Expenses:* Tuition $815/credit hour; Lab Fee (ED598) $300/semester; Lab Fee (CN457,CN467, PY538, PY540) $70/course; Wilson Reading Course Fee $141/credit hour; Registration Fee $50/semester; Graduate Student Activity Fee (Fall and Spring) $65/semester. *Financial support:* In 2019–20, 34 students received support. Career-related internships or fieldwork and unspecified assistantships available. Support available to part-time students. Financial award applicants required to submit FAFSA. *Unit head:* Dr. Laurie Grupp, Dean, 203-254-4250, Fax: 203-254-4241, E-mail: lgrupp@fairfield.edu. *Application contact:* Melanie Rogers, Director of Graduate Admission, 203-254-4184, Fax: 203-254-4073, E-mail: gradadmis@fairfield.edu.
Website: http://www.fairfield.edu/gseap

Fordham University, Graduate School of Arts and Sciences, Department of Psychology, Program in Applied Developmental Psychology, New York, NY 10458. Offers PhD. *Accreditation:* APA. *Students:* Average age 31. 35 applicants, 29% accepted, 3 enrolled. In 2019, 3 doctorates awarded. *Degree requirements:* For doctorate, comprehensive exam, thesis/dissertation. *Entrance requirements:* For doctorate, GRE General Test, GRE Subject Test. Additional exam requirements/recommendations for international students: required—TOEFL (minimum score 600 paper-based). *Application deadline:* For fall admission, 12/14 for domestic students. Application fee: $70. Electronic applications accepted. *Financial support:* In 2019–20, 15 students received support, including 4 fellowships with tuition reimbursements available (averaging $26,065 per year), 2 research assistantships with tuition reimbursements available (averaging $17,529 per year), 2 teaching assistantships with tuition reimbursements available (averaging $10,600 per year); career-related internships or fieldwork, institutionally sponsored loans, tuition waivers (full and partial), and unspecified assistantships also available. Financial award application deadline: 12/14. *Unit head:* Dr. Tiffany Yip, Program Director, 718-817-3797, Fax: 718-817-3785, E-mail: tyip@fordham.edu. *Application contact:* Garrett Marino, Director of Graduate Admissions, 718-817-4419, Fax: 718-817-3566, E-mail: gmarino10@fordham.edu.

Applied Psychology

Fordham University, Graduate School of Arts and Sciences, Department of Psychology, Program in Applied Psychological Methods, New York, NY 10458. Offers MS. *Students:* Average age 27. 21 applicants, 38% accepted, 1 enrolled. In 2019, 3 master's awarded. *Entrance requirements:* For master's, GRE General Test. Additional exam requirements/recommendations for international students: required—TOEFL. *Application deadline:* For fall admission, 1/4 priority date for domestic students, 1/4 for international students; for spring admission, 10/31 for domestic and international students. Application fee: $70. *Unit head:* Dr. Andrew Rasmussen, Program Director, 718-817-3775, E-mail: arasmussen@fordham.edu. *Application contact:* Garrett Marino, Director of Graduate Admissions, 718-817-4419, Fax: 718-817-3566, E-mail: gmarino10@fordham.edu.

Francis Marion University, Graduate Programs, Department of Psychology, Florence, SC 29502-0547. Offers applied psychology (MS), including clinical/counseling psychology, school psychology; school psychology (SSP). *Program availability:* Part-time, evening/weekend. *Degree requirements:* For master's, internship. *Entrance requirements:* For master's, GRE General Test, official transcripts, two letters of recommendation. Additional exam requirements/recommendations for international students: required—TOEFL (minimum score 550 paper-based; 79 iBT). *Expenses: Tuition, area resident:* Full-time $10,612; part-time $530.60 per credit hour. Tuition, state resident: full-time $10,612; part-time $530.60 per credit hour. Tuition, nonresident: full-time $21,224; part-time $1061.20 per credit hour. *International tuition:* $21,224 full-time. *Required fees:* $312; $156 per credit hour. $332 per semester. Tuition and fees vary according to program.

The George Washington University, Columbian College of Arts and Sciences, Department of Psychology, Washington, DC 20052. Offers applied social psychology (PhD); clinical psychology (PhD); cognitive neuroscience (PhD). *Accreditation:* APA. *Program availability:* Part-time, evening/weekend. *Degree requirements:* For doctorate, thesis/dissertation or alternative, general exam. *Entrance requirements:* For doctorate, GRE General Test, minimum GPA of 3.0. Additional exam requirements/recommendations for international students: required—TOEFL (minimum score 550 paper-based; 80 iBT).

Laurentian University, School of Graduate Studies and Research, Programme in Psychology, Sudbury, ON P3E 2C6, Canada. Offers applied psychology (MA); experimental psychology (MA).

Liberty University, School of Behavioral Sciences, Lynchburg, VA 24515. Offers applied psychology (MA), including developmental psychology (MA, MS), industrial/organizational psychology (MA, MS); clinical mental health counseling (MA); community care and counseling (Ed D), including marriage and family counseling, pastoral care and counseling, traumatology; counselor education and supervision (PhD); human services counseling (MA), including addictions and recovery, business, child and family law, Christian ministries, criminal justice, crisis response and trauma, executive leadership, health and wellness, life coaching, marriage and family, military resilience; marriage and family counseling (MA); marriage and family therapy (MA); military resilience (Certificate); pastoral counseling (MA), including addictions and recovery, community chaplaincy, crisis response and trauma, discipleship and church ministry, leadership, life coaching, marriage and family, marriage and family studies, military resilience, parenting and child/adolescent, pastoral counseling, theology; professional counseling (MA); psychology (MS), including developmental psychology (MA, MS), industrial/organizational psychology (MA, MS); school counseling (M Ed). *Program availability:* Part-time, online learning. *Students:* 3,786 full-time (3,065 women), 5,193 part-time (4,081 women); includes 2,733 minority (1,967 Black or African American, non-Hispanic/Latino; 48 American Indian or Alaska Native, non-Hispanic/Latino; 103 Asian, non-Hispanic/Latino; 349 Hispanic/Latino; 19 Native Hawaiian or other Pacific Islander, non-Hispanic/Latino; 247 Two or more races, non-Hispanic/Latino), 133 international. Average age 38. 13,324 applicants, 28% accepted, 2,163 enrolled. In 2019, 2,322 master's, 19 doctorates, 112 other advanced degrees awarded. *Entrance requirements:* For master's, Official bachelor's degree transcripts with a 2.0 GPA or higher. *Application deadline:* Applications are processed on a rolling basis. Application fee: $50. Electronic applications accepted. *Expenses: Tuition:* Full-time $545; part-time $410 per credit hour. One-time fee: $50. *Financial support:* In 2019–20, 1,003 students received support. Teaching assistantships and Federal Work-Study available. Financial award applicants required to submit FAFSA. *Unit head:* Dr. Kenyon Knapp, Dean, School of Behavioral Services, E-mail: kcknapp@liberty.edu. *Application contact:* Jay Bridge, Director of Admissions, 800-424-9595, Fax: 800-628-7977, E-mail: gradadmissions@liberty.edu. Website: https://www.liberty.edu/behavioral-sciences/

London Metropolitan University, Graduate Programs, London, United Kingdom. Offers applied psychology (M Sc); architecture (MA); biomedical science (M Sc); blood science (M Sc); cancer pharmacology (M Sc); computer networking and cyber security (M Sc); computing and information systems (M Sc); conference interpreting (MA); counter-terrorism studies (M Sc); creative, digital and professional writing (MA); crime, violence and prevention (M Sc); criminology (M Sc); curating contemporary art (MA); data analytics (M Sc); digital media (MA); early childhood studies (MA); education (MA, Ed D); financial services law, regulation and compliance (LL M); food science (M Sc); forensic psychology (M Sc); health and social care management and policy (M Sc); human nutrition (M Sc); human resource management (MA); human rights and international conflict (MA); information technology (M Sc); intelligence and security studies (M Sc); international oil, gas and energy law (LL M); international relations (MA); interpreting (MA); learning and teaching in higher education (MA); legal practice (LL M); media and entertainment law (LL M); organizational and consumer psychology (M Sc); psychological therapy (M Sc); psychology of mental health (M Sc); public health (M Sc); public policy and management (MPA); security studies (M Sc); social work (M Sc); spatial planning and urban design (MA); sports therapy (M Sc); supporting older children and young people with dyslexia (MA); teaching languages (MA), including Arabic, English; translation (MA); woman and child abuse (MA).

Loras College, Graduate Division, Program in Applied Psychology, Dubuque, IA 52004-0178. Offers MA. *Program availability:* Part-time, evening/weekend. *Degree requirements:* For master's, comprehensive exam, thesis (for some programs). *Entrance requirements:* For master's, Ohio State University Psychological Test or GRE General Test, minimum undergraduate GPA of 2.75.

Lynn University, College of Arts and Sciences, Boca Raton, FL 33431-5598. Offers criminal justice (MS); mental health counseling (MS); psychology (MS). *Program availability:* Part-time, evening/weekend, 100% online, blended/hybrid learning. *Faculty:* 15 full-time (7 women), 12 part-time/adjunct (7 women). *Students:* 98 full-time (81 women), 55 part-time (33 women); includes 57 minority (23 Black or African American, non-Hispanic/Latino; 1 American Indian or Alaska Native, non-Hispanic/Latino; 28 Hispanic/Latino; 2 Native Hawaiian or other Pacific Islander, non-Hispanic/Latino; 3 Two or more races, non-Hispanic/Latino), 9 international. Average age 32. 126 applicants, 77% accepted, 69 enrolled. In 2019, 37 master's awarded. *Degree requirements:* For master's, comprehensive exam (for some programs), thesis (for some programs). *Entrance requirements:* For master's, Bachelor's degree from accredited institution, minimum undergraduate GPA of 3.0, official undergraduate transcripts, two letters of recommendation from academic or professional sources, writing sample demonstrating capacity to perform at graduate level. Additional exam requirements/recommendations for international students: required—TOEFL (minimum score 550 paper-based; 80 iBT), IELTS (minimum score 6.5). *Application deadline:* For fall admission, 8/10 for domestic students, 7/31 for international students; for spring admission, 12/18 for domestic students, 12/2 for international students; for summer admission, 4/12 for domestic students, 4/2 for international students. Applications are processed on a rolling basis. Application fee: $45. Electronic applications accepted. *Expenses:* Tuition and fees for degrees offered in the College of Arts and Sciences start at $23,400 and can go to $38,350 depending on the program. Each program has specific credit hour requirements and the cost per credit hour within this college ranges from $650.00 to $740.00 per credit hour. *Financial support:* In 2019–20, 42 students received support. Career-related internships or fieldwork, Federal Work-Study, scholarships/grants, tuition waivers (full and partial), and unspecified assistantships available. Support available to part-time students. Financial award application deadline: 3/1; financial award applicants required to submit FAFSA. *Unit head:* Dr. Gary Villa, Dean, College of Arts and Sciences, 561-237-7025, E-mail: gvilla@lynn.edu. *Application contact:* Steven Pruitt, Director of Graduate and Online Admission, 561-237-7834, Fax: 561-237-7100, E-mail: admissionpm@lynn.edu.
Website: https://www.lynn.edu/academics/colleges-schools/arts-and-sciences

Mississippi State University, College of Arts and Sciences, Department of Psychology, Mississippi State, MS 39762. Offers applied psychology (PhD), including clinical, cognitive science; psychology (MS). *Accreditation:* APA. *Faculty:* 18 full-time (7 women). *Students:* 37 full-time (24 women), 9 part-time (4 women); includes 8 minority (4 Black or African American, non-Hispanic/Latino; 3 Asian, non-Hispanic/Latino; 1 Hispanic/Latino). Average age 28. 79 applicants, 20% accepted, 8 enrolled. In 2019, 6 master's, 1 doctorate awarded. Terminal master's awarded for partial completion of doctoral program. *Degree requirements:* For master's, comprehensive exam, thesis; for doctorate, thesis/dissertation, qualifying exam, comprehensive written and oral exam. *Entrance requirements:* For master's, GRE General Test, minimum GPA of 2.75 on last two years of undergraduate courses; for doctorate, GRE General Test, proficiency in at least 1 computer language, minimum GPA of 3.0. Additional exam requirements/recommendations for international students: required—TOEFL (minimum score 477 paper-based; 53 iBT); recommended—IELTS (minimum score 4.5). *Application deadline:* For fall admission, 4/1 priority date for domestic students, 5/1 for international students; for spring admission, 11/1 priority date for domestic students, 9/1 for international students. Applications are processed on a rolling basis. Application fee: $60 ($80 for international students). Electronic applications accepted. *Expenses: Tuition, area resident:* Full-time $8880; part-time $456 per credit hour. Tuition, state resident: full-time $8880. Tuition, nonresident: full-time $23,840; part-time $1236 per credit hour. *Required fees:* $110; $11.12 per credit hour. Tuition and fees vary according to course load. *Financial support:* In 2019–20, 6 research assistantships with full tuition reimbursements (averaging $13,607 per year), 28 teaching assistantships with full tuition reimbursements (averaging $11,864 per year) were awarded; career-related internships or fieldwork, Federal Work-Study, institutionally sponsored loans, scholarships/grants, and unspecified assistantships also available. Financial award application deadline: 4/1; financial award applicants required to submit FAFSA. *Unit head:* Dr. Mitchell E. Berman, Professor and Head, 662-325-3202, Fax: 662-325-7212, E-mail: mberman@psychology.msstate.edu. *Application contact:* Angie Campbell, Admissions and Enrollment Assistant, 662-325-9514, E-mail: acampbell@grad.msstate.edu.
Website: http://www.psychology.msstate.edu/

New York University, Steinhardt School of Culture, Education, and Human Development, Department of Applied Psychology, New York, NY 10012. Offers counseling (MA, PhD, Advanced Certificate), including counseling and guidance (MA, Advanced Certificate), counseling for mental health and wellness (MA), counseling psychology (PhD), LGBT health, education, and social services (Advanced Certificate); educational and developmental psychology (MA, PhD), including developmental psychology (PhD), human development and social intervention (MA), psychology and social intervention (PhD); Advanced Certificate/MPH; MA/Advanced Certificate. *Accreditation:* APA (one or more programs are accredited). *Program availability:* Part-time. Terminal master's awarded for partial completion of doctoral program. *Entrance requirements:* For doctorate, GRE General Test, interview. Additional exam requirements/recommendations for international students: required—TOEFL (minimum score 100 iBT). Electronic applications accepted.

North Carolina State University, Graduate School, College of Humanities and Social Sciences, Department of Psychology, Raleigh, NC 27695. Offers applied social and community psychology (PhD); human factors and applied cognition (PhD); industrial/organizational psychology (PhD); lifespan developmental psychology (PhD); school psychology (PhD). *Accreditation:* APA. *Degree requirements:* For doctorate, comprehensive exam, thesis/dissertation. *Entrance requirements:* For doctorate, GRE General Test, GRE Subject Test (industrial/organizational psychology), MAT (recommended), minimum GPA of 3.0 in major. Electronic applications accepted.

Old Dominion University, College of Sciences, Doctoral Program in Psychology, Norfolk, VA 23529. Offers applied psychological sciences (PhD); human factors psychology (PhD); industrial/organizational psychology (PhD). *Degree requirements:* For doctorate, comprehensive exam, thesis/dissertation, candidacy exam. *Entrance requirements:* For doctorate, GRE General Test, GRE Subject Test, 3 recommendation letters. Additional exam requirements/recommendations for international students: required—TOEFL. Electronic applications accepted. *Expenses:* Contact institution.

Penn State Erie, The Behrend College, Graduate School, Erie, PA 16563. Offers accounting (MPAC); applied clinical psychology (MA); business administration (MBA); quality and manufacturing management (MMM). *Accreditation:* AACSB. *Program availability:* Part-time. *Entrance requirements:* Additional exam requirements/recommendations for international students: required—TOEFL (minimum score 550 paper-based; 80 iBT), IELTS. Electronic applications accepted.

Penn State Harrisburg, Graduate School, School of Behavioral Sciences and Education, Middletown, PA 17057. Offers adult education in the health and medical professions (Certificate); applied behavior analysis (MA); applied clinical psychology (MA); applied psychological research (MA); community psychology and social change (MA); English as a second language (ESL) program specialist and leadership (Certificate); health education (M Ed); lifelong learning and adult education (M Ed, D Ed); literacy education (M Ed); literacy leadership (Certificate); psychology: applications in clinical psychology (Certificate); psychology: health psychology (Certificate); teaching and curriculum (M Ed); training and development (M Ed, Certificate). *Program availability:* Part-time, evening/weekend.

Rutgers University - New Brunswick, Graduate School of Applied and Professional Psychology, Piscataway, NJ 08854. Offers Psy M, Psy D. *Accreditation:* APA (one or more programs are accredited). *Degree requirements:* For doctorate, comprehensive exam, thesis/dissertation, 1 year internship. *Entrance requirements:* For doctorate, GRE General Test, GRE Subject Test, bachelor's degree in psychology or equivalent. Additional exam requirements/recommendations for international students: required—TOEFL. Electronic applications accepted. *Expenses:* Contact institution.

Sacred Heart University, Graduate Programs, College of Arts and Sciences, Department of Psychology, Fairfield, CT 06825. Offers applied psychology (MS), including community psychology, general applied psychology, industrial-organizational psychology. *Program availability:* Part-time, evening/weekend, online learning. *Degree requirements:* For master's, comprehensive exam, thesis optional. *Entrance requirements:* For master's, minimum overall GPA of 3.0, bachelor's degree from accredited college or university. Additional exam requirements/recommendations for international students: required—TOEFL (minimum score 570 paper-based, 80 iBT), TWE, or IELTS (6.5). Electronic applications accepted. *Expenses:* Contact institution.

Saint Mary's University, Faculty of Science, Department of Psychology, Halifax, NS B3H 3C3, Canada. Offers applied psychology (M Sc, PhD), including industrial/organizational psychology (M Sc). *Program availability:* Part-time. *Degree requirements:* For master's, thesis, 500-hour internship; for doctorate, comprehensive exam, thesis/dissertation, research project. *Entrance requirements:* For master's and doctorate, GRE General Test.

Tarleton State University, College of Graduate Studies, College of Education, Department of Psychological Sciences, Stephenville, TX 76402. Offers applied psychology (MS). *Program availability:* Part-time. *Faculty:* 7 full-time (3 women). *Students:* 16 full-time (11 women), 33 part-time (26 women); includes 15 minority (4 Black or African American, non-Hispanic/Latino; 9 Hispanic/Latino; 2 Two or more races, non-Hispanic/Latino). Average age 31. 30 applicants, 83% accepted, 18 enrolled. In 2019, 4 master's awarded. *Degree requirements:* For master's, comprehensive exam, thesis optional. *Entrance requirements:* For master's, GRE General Test, minimum GPA of 2.5. Additional exam requirements/recommendations for international students: required—TOEFL (minimum score 520 paper-based; 69 iBT); recommended—IELTS (minimum score 6). *Application deadline:* For fall admission, 8/15 priority date for domestic students; for spring admission, 1/7 for domestic students. Applications are processed on a rolling basis. Application fee: $50 ($130 for international students). Electronic applications accepted. *Expenses:* Tuition, state resident: part-time $221.73 per credit hour. Tuition, nonresident: part-time $636.73 per credit hour. *Required fees:* $198 per credit hour. $100 per semester. Tuition and fees vary according to degree level. *Financial support:* Research assistantships, teaching assistantships, career-related internships or fieldwork, Federal Work-Study, institutionally sponsored loans, and tuition waivers available. Support available to part-time students. Financial award application deadline: 5/1; financial award applicants required to submit FAFSA. *Unit head:* Dr. Jamie Borchardt, Department Head, 254-968-1970, E-mail: borchardt@tarleton.edu. *Application contact:* Wendy Weiss, Graduate Admissions Coordinator, 254-968-9104, Fax: 254-968-9670, E-mail: weiss@tarleton.edu.

Teachers College, Columbia University, Department of Human Development, New York, NY 10027-6696. Offers applied statistics (MS); cognitive studies in education (MA, Ed D, PhD); developmental psychology (MA, Ed D, PhD); educational psychology-human cognition and learning (Ed M, MA, Ed D, PhD); learning analytics (MS); measurement and evaluation (ME, Ed D, PhD); measurement, evaluation, and statistics (MA, MS, Ed D, PhD). *Faculty:* 10 full-time (4 women). *Students:* 123 full-time (94 women), 129 part-time (91 women); includes 58 minority (12 Black or African American, non-Hispanic/Latino; 32 Asian, non-Hispanic/Latino; 13 Hispanic/Latino; 1 Two or more races, non-Hispanic/Latino), 131 international. 429 applicants, 60% accepted, 108 enrolled. *Unit head:* Dr. James Corter, Chair, 212-678-3843, E-mail: jec34@tc.columbia.edu. *Application contact:* Kelly Sutton-Skinner, Director of Admission and New Student Enrollment, E-mail: kms2237@tc.columbia.edu.
Website: http://www.tc.columbia.edu/human-development/

University of Arkansas at Little Rock, Graduate School, College of Social Sciences and Communication, Department of Psychology, Little Rock, AR 72204-1099. Offers applied psychology (MAP). *Program availability:* Part-time, evening/weekend. *Entrance requirements:* For master's, GRE General Test, minimum GPA of 2.7.

University of Baltimore, Graduate School, Yale Gordon College of Arts and Sciences, Program in Applied Psychology, Baltimore, MD 21201-5779. Offers counseling psychology (MS). *Program availability:* Part-time, evening/weekend. *Degree requirements:* For master's, thesis optional. *Entrance requirements:* For master's, GRE, minimum GPA of 3.0. Additional exam requirements/recommendations for international students: required—TOEFL (minimum score 550 paper-based). Electronic applications accepted. *Expenses:* Contact institution.

University of Calgary, Faculty of Graduate Studies, Werklund School of Education, Program in School of Applied Child Psychology, Calgary, AB T2N 1N4, Canada. Offers counseling psychology (M Sc, MC, PhD); school and applied child psychology (M Ed, M Sc, PhD). *Program availability:* Part-time. *Degree requirements:* For master's, thesis (for some programs), final oral exam; for doctorate, thesis/dissertation, candidacy exam, final oral exam. *Entrance requirements:* For master's, minimum GPA of 3.0, 3 letters of reference; for doctorate, minimum GPA of 3.5, 3 letters of reference.

University of Guelph, Office of Graduate and Postdoctoral Studies, College of Social and Applied Human Sciences, Department of Psychology, Guelph, ON N1G 2W1, Canada. Offers applied social psychology (MA, PhD); clinical psychology: applied development emphasis (PhD); clinical psychology: applied developmental emphasis (MA); industrial/organizational psychology (MA, PhD); neuroscience and applied cognitive science (MA, PhD). *Degree requirements:* For master's, thesis; for doctorate, comprehensive exam, thesis/dissertation. *Entrance requirements:* For master's, GRE General Test, GRE Subject Test, minimum B+ average during previous 2 years of course work; for doctorate, GRE General Test, GRE Subject Test, minimum A- average. Additional exam requirements/recommendations for international students: required—TOEFL (minimum score 89 iBT). Electronic applications accepted.

University of Maryland, Baltimore County, The Graduate School, College of Arts, Humanities and Social Sciences, Department of Psychology, Program in Applied Developmental Psychology, Baltimore, MD 21250. Offers PhD. *Faculty:* 8 full-time (6 women), 11 part-time/adjunct (4 women). *Students:* 21 full-time (19 women), 1 (woman) part-time; includes 6 minority (2 Black or African American, non-Hispanic/Latino; 3 Asian, non-Hispanic/Latino; 1 Hispanic/Latino), 7 international. Average age 28. 31 applicants, 16% accepted, 3 enrolled. In 2019, 2 doctorates awarded. *Degree requirements:* For doctorate, comprehensive exam, thesis/dissertation. *Entrance requirements:* For doctorate, GRE General Test, minimum GPA of 3.0. Additional exam requirements/recommendations for international students: required—TOEFL. *Application deadline:* For fall admission, 12/1 for domestic and international students. Application fee: $50. Electronic applications accepted. *Expenses:* $14,382 per year. *Financial support:* In 2019–20, 16 students received support, including 2 fellowships with partial tuition reimbursements available (averaging $17,250 per year), 3 research assistantships with full tuition reimbursements available (averaging $20,400 per year), 11 teaching assistantships with full tuition reimbursements available (averaging $17,250 per year); career-related internships or fieldwork, Federal Work-Study, health care benefits, and unspecified assistantships also available. Financial award application deadline: 3/1; financial award applicants required to submit FAFSA. *Unit head:* Dr. Susan Sonnenschein, Director, 410-455-2361, Fax: 410-455-1055, E-mail: sonnenschein@umbc.edu. *Application contact:* Beverly McDougall, Program Management Specialist, 410-455-2567, Fax: 410-455-1055, E-mail: psycdept@umbc.edu.
Website: http://psychology.umbc.edu/

University of Pennsylvania, School of Arts and Sciences, College of Liberal and Professional Studies, Philadelphia, PA 19104. Offers applied geosciences (MSAG); applied positive psychology (MAP); chemical sciences (MCS); environmental studies (MES); individualized study (MLA); liberal arts (M Phil); medical physics (MMP); organization dynamics (M Phil). *Students:* 240 full-time (161 women), 290 part-time (180 women); includes 91 minority (31 Black or African American, non-Hispanic/Latino; 31 Asian, non-Hispanic/Latino; 14 Hispanic/Latino; 15 Two or more races, non-Hispanic/Latino), 136 international. Average age 33. 955 applicants, 44% accepted, 272 enrolled. In 2019, 203 master's awarded. *Unit head:* Nora Lewis, Vice Dean, Professional and Liberal Education, 215-898-7326, E-mail: nlewis@sas.upenn.edu. *Application contact:* Nora Lewis, Vice Dean, Professional and Liberal Education, 215-898-7326, E-mail: nlewis@sas.upenn.edu.
Website: http://www.sas.upenn.edu/lps/graduate

University of Regina, Faculty of Graduate Studies and Research, Faculty of Arts, Department of Psychology, Regina, SK S4S 0A2, Canada. Offers clinical psychology (MA, PhD); experimental and applied psychology (MA, PhD). *Faculty:* 20 full-time (9 women), 11 part-time/adjunct (7 women). *Students:* 55 full-time (47 women). Average age 30. 116 applicants, 18% accepted. In 2019, 4 master's, 1 doctorate awarded. *Degree requirements:* For master's, thesis; for doctorate, comprehensive exam, thesis/dissertation. *Entrance requirements:* For master's, GRE General Test, post secondary transcripts, 2 letter of recommendations; for doctorate, GRE General Test and GRE Subject Test (optional for those with a master's degree from a Canadian university). Additional exam requirements/recommendations for international students: required—TOEFL (minimum score 580 paper-based; 80 iBT), IELTS (minimum score 6.5), PTE (minimum score 59), other option is CAEL, MELAB and U of R ESL. *Application deadline:* For fall admission, 1/15 for domestic and international students. Application fee: $100. Electronic applications accepted. *Expenses:* *Tuition:* Full-time $6684 Canadian dollars. *Required fees:* $100 Canadian dollars; $3351.45 Canadian dollars per trimester. $1117.15 Canadian dollars per semester. Tuition and fees vary according to course level, course load, degree level and program. *Financial support:* Fellowships, research assistantships, teaching assistantships, career-related internships or fieldwork, Federal Work-Study, scholarships/grants, unspecified assistantships, and travel award and Graduate Scholarship Base Funds available. Support available to part-time students. Financial award application deadline: 9/30. *Unit head:* Dr. Richard MacLennan, Department Head, 306-585-4458, Fax: 306-585-5429, E-mail: richard.maclennan@uregina.ca. *Application contact:* Dr. Richard MacLennan, Department Head, 306-585-4458, Fax: 306-585-5429, E-mail: richard.maclennan@uregina.ca.
Website: http://www.uregina.ca/arts/psychology

University of South Carolina Aiken, Program in Applied Clinical Psychology, Aiken, SC 29801. Offers MS. *Program availability:* Part-time. *Faculty:* 8 full-time (6 women), 1 part-time/adjunct (0 women). *Students:* 17 full-time (16 women), 8 part-time (5 women); includes 3 minority (1 Black or African American, non-Hispanic/Latino; 1 Hispanic/Latino; 1 Two or more races, non-Hispanic/Latino), 1 international. Average age 26. 38 applicants, 29% accepted, 7 enrolled. In 2019, 16 master's awarded. *Degree requirements:* For master's, thesis. *Entrance requirements:* For master's, GRE. Additional exam requirements/recommendations for international students: required—TOEFL (minimum score 551 paper-based; 80 iBT), IELTS (minimum score 6), PTE (minimum score 53), USC Aiken accepts the TOEFL, IELTS, or PTE exams to demonstrate English proficiency. *Application deadline:* For fall admission, 6/1 priority date for domestic and international students. Applications are processed on a rolling basis. Application fee: $45 ($100 for international students). Electronic applications accepted. *Expenses:* *Tuition, area resident:* Full-time $13,734; part-time $572.25 per credit hour. Tuition, state resident: full-time $13,734; part-time $572.25 per credit hour. Tuition, nonresident: full-time $29,760; part-time $1240 per credit hour. *International tuition:* $29,760 full-time. *Required fees:* $13 per credit hour. $25 per semester. Tuition and fees vary according to course load and program. *Financial support:* In 2019–20, 20 students received support, including 18 research assistantships with partial tuition reimbursements available (averaging $3,788 per year), 5 teaching assistantships with partial tuition reimbursements available (averaging $2,857 per year); career-related internships or fieldwork, Federal Work-Study, scholarships/grants, tuition waivers (partial), and unspecified assistantships also available. Financial award application deadline: 3/1; financial award applicants required to submit FAFSA. *Unit head:* Dr. Jane Stafford, Director, 803-641-3358, Fax: 803-641-3720, E-mail: jstafford@usca.edu. *Application contact:* Dan Robb, Associate Vice Chancellor for Enrollment Management, 803-641-3487, Fax: 803-641-3727, E-mail: danr@usca.edu.
Website: https://www.usca.edu/majors-programs/graduate/applied-clinical-psychology

The University of Tennessee, Graduate School, College of Education, Health and Human Sciences, Department of Educational Psychology and Counseling, Knoxville, TN 37996. Offers adult education (MS); applied educational psychology (MS); collaborative learning (Ed D); college student personnel (MS); mental health counseling (MS); rehabilitation counseling (MS); school counseling (MS). *Accreditation:* ACA (one or more programs are accredited); CORE (one or more programs are accredited); NCATE. *Program availability:* Part-time, evening/weekend. *Degree requirements:* For master's, thesis optional. *Entrance requirements:* For master's, GRE General Test, minimum GPA of 2.7. Additional exam requirements/recommendations for international students: required—TOEFL. Electronic applications accepted.

The University of Texas at El Paso, Graduate School, College of Liberal Arts, Department of Sociology and Anthropology, El Paso, TX 79968-0001. Offers applied anthropology (Certificate); applied social sciences (Certificate); sociology (MA). *Program availability:* Part-time, evening/weekend. *Degree requirements:* For master's, thesis. *Entrance requirements:* For master's, GRE General Test, minimum GPA of 3.0. Additional exam requirements/recommendations for international students: required—TOEFL. Electronic applications accepted.

University of West Florida, Usha Kundu, MD College of Health, Department of Psychology, Pensacola, FL 32514-5750. Offers applied experimental (MA); counseling (MA); industrial-organizational (MA). *Program availability:* Part-time. *Degree requirements:* For master's, thesis (for some programs). *Entrance requirements:* For master's, GRE, official transcripts; minimum GPA of 3.0; writing sample; three letters of reference; field experience or skill sets; oral interview (for counseling specialization). Additional exam requirements/recommendations for international students: required—TOEFL (minimum score 550 paper-based).

University of Windsor, Faculty of Graduate Studies, Faculty of Arts and Social Sciences, Department of Psychology, Windsor, ON N9B 3P4, Canada. Offers adult clinical (MA, PhD); applied social psychology (MA, PhD); child clinical (MA, PhD); clinical neuropsychology (MA, PhD). *Degree requirements:* For master's, thesis; for doctorate, comprehensive exam, thesis/dissertation. *Entrance requirements:* For master's, GRE General Test, GRE Subject Test in psychology, minimum B average; for doctorate, GRE General Test, GRE Subject Test in psychology, master's degree. Additional exam requirements/recommendations for international students: required—TOEFL (minimum score 600 paper-based). Electronic applications accepted.

University of Wisconsin–Stout, Graduate School, College of Education, Health and Human Sciences, Program in Applied Psychology, Menomonie, WI 54751. Offers MS. *Program availability:* Part-time. *Degree requirements:* For master's, thesis. *Entrance requirements:* For master's, GRE General Test, GRE Subject Test, minimum GPA of 3.0, 15 semester credits of undergraduate course work in psychology, 8 semester credits in research methods and statistics. Additional exam requirements/recommendations for international students: required—TOEFL (minimum score 500 paper-based; 61 iBT). Electronic applications accepted.

Walden University, Graduate Programs, School of Psychology, Minneapolis, MN 55401. Offers clinical psychology (MS), including counseling, general program; forensic psychology (MS), including forensic psychology in the community, general program, mental health applications, program planning and evaluation in forensic settings, psychology and legal systems; industrial organizational (MS, PhD), including consulting psychology, forensic (MS), forensic psychology (PhD), general practice, leadership development and coaching (MS), organizational diversity and social change, research evaluation (PhD); online teaching in psychology (Post-Master's Certificate); organizational psychology and development (Postbaccalaureate Certificate); psychology (MS, PhD), including applied psychology (MS), clinical psychology (PhD), crisis management and response (MS), educational psychology, forensic psychology (PhD), general psychology (MS), general psychology research (PhD), general psychology teaching (PhD), health psychology, leadership development and coaching (MS), psychology of culture (MS), psychology, public administration, and social change (MS), social psychology, terrorism and security (MS); psychology respecialization (Post-Doctoral Certificate). *Program availability:* Part-time, evening/weekend, online only, 100% online. Terminal master's awarded for partial completion of doctoral program. *Degree requirements:* For master's, thesis optional; for doctorate, thesis/dissertation, residency. *Entrance requirements:* For master's, bachelor's degree or higher; minimum GPA of 2.5; official transcripts; goal statement (for some programs); access to computer and Internet; for doctorate, master's degree or higher; three years of related professional or academic experience (preferred); minimum GPA of 3.0; goal statement and current resume (for select programs); official transcripts; access to computer and Internet; for other advanced degree, relevant work experience; access to computer and Internet. Additional exam requirements/recommendations for international students: required—TOEFL (minimum score 550 paper-based, 79 iBT), IELTS (minimum score 6.5), Michigan English Language Assessment Battery (minimum score 82), or PTE (minimum score 53). Electronic applications accepted.

William James College, Graduate Programs, Newton, MA 02459. Offers applied psychology in higher education student personnel administration (MA); clinical psychology (Psy D); counseling psychology (MA); counseling psychology and community mental health (MA); counseling psychology and global mental health (MA); executive coaching (Graduate Certificate); forensic and counseling psychology (MA); leadership psychology (Psy D); organizational psychology (MA); primary care psychology (MA); respecialization in clinical psychology (Certificate); school psychology (Psy D); MA/CAGS. *Accreditation:* APA. *Degree requirements:* For master's, comprehensive exam (for some programs); for doctorate, thesis/dissertation (for some programs). Electronic applications accepted.

Clinical Psychology

Abilene Christian University, Office of Graduate Programs, College of Arts and Sciences, Department of Psychology, Abilene, TX 79699. Offers clinical psychology (MS); counseling psychology (MS); psychology (MS); school psychology (Specialist). *Program availability:* Part-time. *Faculty:* 11 part-time/adjunct (3 women). *Students:* 24 full-time (19 women), 8 part-time (7 women); includes 8 minority (3 Black or African American, non-Hispanic/Latino; 5 Hispanic/Latino), 2 international. 99 applicants, 27% accepted, 10 enrolled. In 2019, 23 master's awarded. *Degree requirements:* For master's, comprehensive exam, thesis (for some programs), practicum; internship. *Entrance requirements:* For master's, official transcripts, purpose statement, Recommendations. Additional exam requirements/recommendations for international students: required—TOEFL (minimum score 80 iBT), IELTS (minimum score 6), PTE (minimum score 51). *Application deadline:* For fall admission, 3/30 priority date for domestic students, 2/15 for international students. Applications are processed on a rolling basis. Application fee: $65. Electronic applications accepted. *Expenses: Tuition:* Full-time $22,356; part-time $1242 per credit hour. Tuition and fees vary according to program. *Financial support:* In 2019–20, 25 students received support, including 28 research assistantships with partial tuition reimbursements available; career-related internships or fieldwork, Federal Work-Study, and scholarships/grants also available. Support available to part-time students. Financial award application deadline: 4/1; financial award applicants required to submit FAFSA. *Unit head:* Dr. Cherisse Flanagan, Graduate Program Director, 325-674-2282, Fax: 325-674-6968, E-mail: cyf07a@acu.edu. *Application contact:* Graduate Admissions, 325-674-6911, E-mail: gradinfo@acu.edu.
Website: http://www.acu.edu/on-campus/graduate/college-of-arts-and-sciences/psychology-department.html

Acadia University, Faculty of Pure and Applied Science, Department of Psychology, Wolfville, NS B4P 2R6, Canada. Offers clinical psychology (M Sc). *Entrance requirements:* For master's, GRE General Test, GRE Subject Test, honors degree or equivalent. Additional exam requirements/recommendations for international students: required—TOEFL (minimum score 580 paper-based; 93 iBT), IELTS (minimum score 6.5).

Adams State University, Office of Graduate Studies, Department of Counselor Education, Alamosa, CO 81101. Offers counselor education (MA), including clinical mental health counseling, school counseling; counselor education and supervision (PhD). *Accreditation:* ACA (one or more programs are accredited). *Program availability:* Part-time. *Degree requirements:* For master's, internship, qualifying exam. *Entrance requirements:* For master's, GRE General Test or MAT, minimum undergraduate GPA of 2.75. *Application deadline:* For fall admission, 5/15 priority date for domestic students; for spring admission, 10/15 for domestic students. Applications are processed on a rolling basis. Application fee: $30. *Financial support:* In 2019–20, fellowships with partial tuition reimbursements (averaging $4,000 per year) were awarded; career-related internships or fieldwork, Federal Work-Study, institutionally sponsored loans, and unspecified assistantships also available. Support available to part-time students. Financial award application deadline: 4/15; financial award applicants required to submit FAFSA. *Unit head:* Dr. Mark Manzanares, Chair, 719-587-7626, Fax: 719-587-7522, E-mail: ceonline@adams.edu. *Application contact:* Leslie Boutillette, Assistant Coordinator, 719-587-8138, Fax: 719-587-7522, E-mail: ceonline@adams.edu.
Website: http://counselored.adams.edu/

Adelphi University, Gordon F. Derner School of Psychology, Program in Clinical Psychology, Garden City, NY 11530-0701. Offers PhD. *Degree requirements:* For doctorate, thesis/dissertation, research component (second-year), 1-year internship. *Entrance requirements:* For doctorate, GRE General Test, GRE Subject Test, interview; resume; undergraduate course work in psychology, experimental psychology, statistics, developmental psychology, and abnormal psychology. Additional exam requirements/recommendations for international students: required—TOEFL (minimum score 550 paper-based; 80 iBT), IELTS (minimum score 6.5). Electronic applications accepted. *Expenses:* Contact institution.

Adler University, Doctor of Psychology (Psy.D.) in Clinical Psychology, Vancouver, BC V6B 3J5, Canada. Offers advanced Adlerian psychotherapy (Psy D); child and adolescent clinical psychology (Psy D); military clinical psychology (Psy D); primary care psychology and behavioral medicine (Psy D); substance abuse treatment (Psy D); traumatic stress psychology (Psy D). In 2019, 1 doctorate awarded. *Degree requirements:* For doctorate, Dissertation Required, Social Justice Practicum; Clinical Practicum; Internships. *Unit head:* Phyllis Horton, Director of Admissions, 312-662-4100, E-mail: admissions@adler.edu. *Application contact:* Michelle Brice, Director of Admissions, 312-662-4113, Fax: 312-662-4199, E-mail: admissions@adler.edu.

Adler University, Master of Arts (M.A.) in Counseling: Specialization in Clinical Mental Health Counseling, Chicago, IL 60602. Offers MAC. *Program availability:* Part-time, evening/weekend, 100% online, blended/hybrid learning. In 2019, 2 master's awarded. *Degree requirements:* For master's, thesis optional, Social Justice Practicum; Internship. *Unit head:* Phyllis Horton, Director of Admissions, 312-662-4100, E-mail: admissions@adler.edu. *Application contact:* Phyllis Horton, Director of Admissions, 312-662-4100, E-mail: admissions@adler.edu.

Alabama Agricultural and Mechanical University, School of Graduate Studies, College of Education, Humanities, and Behavioral Sciences, Department of Social Work, Psychology and Counseling, Huntsville, AL 35811. Offers psychology and counseling (MS, Ed S), including clinical psychology (MS), counseling psychology (MS), guidance and counseling, rehabilitation counseling (MS), school counseling (MS), school psychology (MS), school psychometry (MS); social work (MSW). *Accreditation:* CORE; NCATE. *Program availability:* Part-time, evening/weekend. *Degree requirements:* For master's, comprehensive exam. *Entrance requirements:* For master's, GRE General Test. Additional exam requirements/recommendations for international students: required—TOEFL (minimum score 500 paper-based; 61 iBT).

Albizu University - Miami, Graduate Programs, Doral, FL 33172. Offers clinical psychology (PhD, Psy D); entrepreneurship (MBA); exceptional student education (MS); human services (PhD); industrial/organizational psychology (MS); marriage and family therapy (MS); mental health counseling (MS); nonprofit management (MBA); organizational management (MBA); school counseling (MS); speech and language pathology (MS); teaching English for speakers of other languages (MS). *Accreditation:* APA. *Program availability:* Part-time, 100% online, blended/hybrid learning. *Faculty:* 28 full-time (21 women), 27 part-time/adjunct (15 women). *Students:* 410 full-time (351 women), 190 part-time (163 women); includes 519 minority (33 Black or African American, non-Hispanic/Latino; 3 Asian, non-Hispanic/Latino; 477 Hispanic/Latino; 6 Two or more races, non-Hispanic/Latino), 21 international. Average age 33. 286 applicants, 66% accepted, 127 enrolled. In 2019, 96 master's, 54 doctorates awarded. Terminal master's awarded for partial completion of doctoral program. *Degree requirements:* For master's, comprehensive exam (for some programs), integrative project (for MBA); research project (for exceptional student education, teaching English as a second language); comprehensive examination for Speech and Language Pathology; for doctorate, comprehensive exam, thesis/dissertation, comprehensive examinations, internship, project/dissertation. *Entrance requirements:* For master's, GRE/EXADEP, bachelor's degree from accredited institution, minimum GPA of 3.0, 3 letters of recommendation, interview, resume, statement of purpose, official transcripts; for doctorate, GRE (for Psy D), 3 letters of recommendation, resume, interview, statement of purpose, official transcripts; bachelor's degree and minimum GPA of 3.25 (for Psy D); master's degree and minimum GPA of 3.0 (for PhD). Additional exam requirements/recommendations for international students: required—Michigan Test of English Language Proficiency. *Application deadline:* For fall admission, 4/1 priority date for domestic students, 5/1 priority date for international students; for spring admission, 11/1 priority date for domestic students, 9/1 priority date for international students. Applications are processed on a rolling basis. Application fee: $50. Electronic applications accepted. Application fee is waived when completed online. *Expenses:* $600 per credit or $620 per credit or $650 per credit (for master's depending on field); $800 per credit or $1,050 per credit (for doctoral depending on program). *Financial support:* In 2019–20, 158 students received support. Federal Work-Study, scholarships/grants, unspecified assistantships, and tuition discounts available. Financial award application deadline: 6/1; financial award applicants required to submit FAFSA. *Unit head:* Dr. Tilokie Depoo, PhD, Chancellor, 305-593-1223 Ext. 3138, Fax: 305-477-8983, E-mail: tdepoo@albizu.edu. *Application contact:* Nancy Alvarez, Director of Enrollment Management, 305-593-1223 Ext. 3136, Fax: 305-593-1854, E-mail: nalvarez@albizu.edu.
Website: www.albizu.edu

Albizu University - San Juan, Graduate Programs, San Juan, PR 00901. Offers clinical psychology (MS, PhD, Psy D); general psychology (PhD); industrial/organizational psychology (MS, PhD); speech and language pathology (MS). *Accreditation:* APA (one or more programs are accredited). *Program availability:* Part-time, evening/weekend. Terminal master's awarded for partial completion of doctoral program. *Degree requirements:* For master's, one foreign language, comprehensive exam, thesis; for doctorate, one foreign language, comprehensive exam, thesis/dissertation, written qualifying exams. *Entrance requirements:* For master's, GRE General Test or EXADEP, interview; minimum GPA of 2.8 (industrial/organizational psychology); for doctorate, GRE General Test or EXADEP, interview; minimum GPA of 3.0 (PhD in industrial/organizational psychology and clinical psychology), 3.25 (Psy D).

Alliant International University–Fresno, California School of Professional Psychology, PhD Program in Clinical Psychology, Fresno, CA 93727. Offers PhD. *Degree requirements:* For doctorate, comprehensive exam, thesis/dissertation. *Entrance requirements:* For doctorate, minimum GPA of 3.0 in both psychology and overall, letters of recommendation, interview. Additional exam requirements/recommendations for international students: required—TOEFL (minimum score 550 paper-based; 80 iBT), TWE (minimum score 5). Electronic applications accepted.

Alliant International University–Fresno, California School of Professional Psychology, Psy D Program in Clinical Psychology, Fresno, CA 93727. Offers Psy D. *Accreditation:* APA. *Degree requirements:* For doctorate, comprehensive exam, thesis/dissertation. *Entrance requirements:* For doctorate, minimum GPA of 3.0 in both psychology and overall, letters of recommendation, interview. Additional exam requirements/recommendations for international students: required—TOEFL (minimum score 550 paper-based; 80 iBT), TWE (minimum score 5). Electronic applications accepted.

Alliant International University - Los Angeles, California School of Professional Psychology, PhD Program in Clinical Psychology, Alhambra, CA 91803. Offers PhD. *Accreditation:* APA. *Degree requirements:* For doctorate, comprehensive exam, thesis/dissertation. *Entrance requirements:* For doctorate, interview, minimum GPA of 3.0 in both psychology and overall. Additional exam requirements/recommendations for international students: required—TOEFL (minimum score 600 paper-based), TWE (minimum score 5). Electronic applications accepted.

Alliant International University - Los Angeles, California School of Professional Psychology, Psy D Program in Clinical Psychology, Alhambra, CA 91803. Offers clinical health psychology (Psy D); family/child and couple clinical psychology (Psy D); multi-interest option (Psy D); multicultural community-clinical psychology (Psy D). *Accreditation:* APA. *Degree requirements:* For doctorate, comprehensive exam, thesis/dissertation. *Entrance requirements:* For doctorate, interview, minimum GPA of 3.0 in both psychology and overall. Additional exam requirements/recommendations for international students: required—TOEFL (minimum score 600 paper-based), TWE. Electronic applications accepted.

Alliant International University–Sacramento, California School of Professional Psychology, Program in Clinical Psychology, Sacramento, CA 95833. Offers Psy D. *Degree requirements:* For doctorate, comprehensive exam, thesis/dissertation, internship. *Entrance requirements:* For doctorate, minimum GPA of 3.0, letters of recommendation, interview. Additional exam requirements/recommendations for international students: required—TOEFL (minimum score 600 paper-based; 80 iBT), TWE (minimum score 5). Electronic applications accepted.

Alliant International University - San Diego, California School of Professional Psychology, Organizational Psychology Division, San Diego, CA 92131. Offers clinical/industrial organizational psychology (PhD); consulting psychology (PhD); industrial/organizational psychology (MA, MS, PhD); leadership (PhD). *Program availability:* Part-time, evening/weekend. Terminal master's awarded for partial completion of doctoral program. *Degree requirements:* For doctorate, comprehensive exam, thesis/dissertation, internship/practicum. *Entrance requirements:* For master's and doctorate, minimum GPA of 3.0, recommendations, essay, interview. Additional exam requirements/recommendations for international students: required—TOEFL (minimum score 550 paper-based; 80 iBT), TWE (minimum score 5). Electronic applications accepted.

Alliant International University - San Diego, California School of Professional Psychology, PhD Program in Clinical Psychology, San Diego, CA 92131. Offers PhD. *Accreditation:* APA. *Degree requirements:* For doctorate, comprehensive exam, thesis/dissertation, internship. *Entrance requirements:* For doctorate, interview, minimum GPA of 3.0, recommendations, essay, interview. Additional exam requirements/recommendations for international students: required—TOEFL (minimum score 600 paper-based; 80 iBT), TWE (minimum score 5). Electronic applications accepted.

Alliant International University - San Diego, California School of Professional Psychology, Psy D Program in Clinical Psychology, San Diego, CA 92131. Offers Psy D. *Accreditation:* APA. *Degree requirements:* For doctorate, comprehensive exam, thesis/dissertation, internship. *Entrance requirements:* For doctorate, minimum GPA of 3.0, recommendations, essay, interview. Additional exam requirements/recommendations for international students: required—TOEFL (minimum score 550 paper-based; 80 iBT), TWE (minimum score 5). Electronic applications accepted.

Alliant International University–San Francisco, California School of Forensic Studies, San Francisco, CA 94133. Offers applied criminology (MS), including victimology; clinical forensic psychology (PhD, Psy D). *Degree requirements:* For doctorate, comprehensive exam, thesis/dissertation, internship. *Entrance requirements:* For master's, minimum GPA of 3.0, recommendations, essay; for doctorate, minimum GPA of 3.0, recommendations, essay, interview. Additional exam requirements/recommendations for international students: required—TOEFL (minimum score 550 paper-based; 80 iBT), TWE (minimum score 5).

Alliant International University–San Francisco, California School of Professional Psychology, PhD Program in Clinical Psychology, San Francisco, CA 94133. Offers PhD. *Degree requirements:* For doctorate, comprehensive exam, thesis/dissertation, internship. *Entrance requirements:* For doctorate, minimum GPA of 3.0, recommendations, essay, interview. Additional exam requirements/recommendations for international students: required—TOEFL (minimum score 550 paper-based; 80 iBT), TWE (minimum score 5). Electronic applications accepted.

Alliant International University–San Francisco, California School of Professional Psychology, Psy D Program in Clinical Psychology, San Francisco, CA 94133. Offers Psy D, Certificate. *Accreditation:* APA (one or more programs are accredited). *Degree requirements:* For doctorate, comprehensive exam, thesis/dissertation, internship. *Entrance requirements:* For doctorate, minimum GPA of 3.0, recommendations, essay, interview. Additional exam requirements/recommendations for international students: required—TOEFL (minimum score 550 paper-based; 80 iBT), TWE (minimum score 5). Electronic applications accepted.

American International College, School of Business, Arts and Sciences, Springfield, MA 01109-3189. Offers accounting and taxation (MS); business administration (MBA); clinical psychology (MA); educational psychology (Ed D); forensic psychology (MS); general psychology (MA, CAGS); management (CAGS); resort and casino management (MBA, CAGS). *Program availability:* Part-time, evening/weekend. *Degree requirements:* For master's, practicum; for doctorate, comprehensive exam, thesis/dissertation, practicum. *Entrance requirements:* For master's, BS or BA, minimum undergraduate GPA of 2.75, 2 letters of recommendation, official transcripts, personal goal statement or essay; for doctorate, 3 letters of recommendation; BS or BA, minimum undergraduate GPA of 3.0 (3.25 recommended); official transcripts; personal goal statement or essay. Additional exam requirements/recommendations for international students: required—TOEFL (minimum score 550 paper-based; 80 iBT). *Expenses:* Contact institution.

American International College, School of Education, Low Residency Programs, Springfield, MA 01109-3189. Offers counseling psychology (MA); educational leadership and supervision (Ed D); professional counseling and supervision (Ed D); teaching and learning (Ed D). *Program availability:* Evening/weekend. *Degree requirements:* For doctorate, thesis/dissertation. *Entrance requirements:* For master's, minimum undergraduate GPA of 3.0, 2 letters of recommendation, personal goal statement, official transcript of all academic work (graduate and undergraduate); for doctorate, minimum master's GPA of 3.0, 3 letters of recommendation, personal goal statement/essay (6-8 pages), official transcript of all academic work (graduate and undergraduate). Additional exam requirements/recommendations for international students: required—TOEFL. *Expenses:* Contact institution.

American University, College of Arts and Sciences, Department of Psychology, Washington, DC 22016-8062. Offers addiction and addictive behavior (Certificate); behavior, cognition, and neuroscience (PhD); clinical psychology (PhD); psychobiology of healing (Certificate); psychology (MA). *Accreditation:* APA. *Program availability:* Part-time. *Degree requirements:* For master's, comprehensive exam, thesis or alternative; for doctorate, comprehensive exam, thesis/dissertation. *Entrance requirements:* For master's, GRE General Test, GRE Subject Test; Please website: https://www.american.edu/cas/psychology/, statement of purpose, transcripts, 2 letters of recommendation; for doctorate, GRE General Test, GRE Subject Test, 3 letters of recommendation, statement of purpose, transcripts, resume. Additional exam requirements/recommendations for international students: required—TOEFL (minimum score 600 paper-based; 100 iBT). *Expenses:* Contact institution.

Andrews University, School of Graduate Studies, College of Education and International Services, Department of Graduate Psychology and Counseling, Program in Community Counseling, Berrien Springs, MI 49104. Offers clinical mental health counseling (MA); community counseling (MA). *Students:* 25 full-time (19 women), 4 part-time (3 women); includes 14 minority (4 Black or African American, non-Hispanic/Latino; 1 Asian, non-Hispanic/Latino; 9 Hispanic/Latino), 9 international. Average age 32. In 2019, 10 master's awarded. *Degree requirements:* For master's, thesis optional. *Entrance requirements:* For master's, GRE. Additional exam requirements/recommendations for international students: required—TOEFL (minimum score 550 paper-based). *Application deadline:* Applications are processed on a rolling basis. Application fee: $60. Electronic applications accepted. *Unit head:* Dr. Nancy Carbonell, Coordinator, 269-471-3472. *Application contact:* Jillian Panigot, Director, University Admissions, 800-253-2874, Fax: 269-471-6321, E-mail: graduate@andrews.edu.

Antioch University Los Angeles, Program in Psychology, Culver City, CA 90230. Offers clinical psychology (MA); psychology (MA). *Program availability:* Part-time. *Faculty:* 12 full-time (5 women), 52 part-time/adjunct (31 women). *Students:* 456 full-time (322 women), 45 part-time (37 women); includes 136 minority (23 Black or African American, non-Hispanic/Latino; 2 American Indian or Alaska Native, non-Hispanic/Latino; 24 Asian, non-Hispanic/Latino; 62 Hispanic/Latino; 25 Two or more races, non-Hispanic/Latino), 5 international. Average age 36. 169 applicants, 70% accepted, 112 enrolled. In 2019, 182 master's awarded. *Degree requirements:* For master's, thesis (for some programs), internship. *Entrance requirements:* For master's, interview. Additional exam requirements/recommendations for international students: required—TOEFL. *Application deadline:* For fall admission, 8/4 priority date for domestic students; for winter admission, 11/3 priority date for domestic students; for spring admission, 2/4 priority date for domestic students. Applications are processed on a rolling basis. Application fee: $60. *Expenses: Tuition:* Full-time $29,992; part-time $17,996 per credit hour. *Financial support:* Career-related internships or fieldwork, Federal Work-Study, scholarships/grants, and traineeships available. Support available to part-time students. Financial award application deadline: 3/24; financial award applicants required to submit FAFSA. *Unit head:* Joy Turek, Chair, 310-578-1080 Ext. 306, Fax: 310-822-4824, E-mail: joy_turek@antiochla.edu. *Application contact:* Information Contact, 310-578-1090, Fax: 310-822-4824, E-mail: admissions@antiochla.edu.
Website: https://www.antioch.edu/los-angeles/degrees-programs/psychology-degree/

Antioch University New England, Graduate School, Department of Applied Psychology, Keene, NH 03431-3552. Offers autism spectrum disorders (Certificate), including applied behavioral analysis internship, autism spectrum disorders; clinical mental health counseling (MA), including clinical mental health counseling, substance abuse counseling; dance/movement therapy and counseling (M Ed, MA, PMC); marriage and family therapy (MA, PhD, Certificate). *Faculty:* 15 full-time (12 women), 30 part-time/adjunct (25 women). *Students:* 264 full-time (217 women), 79 part-time (64 women); includes 67 minority (25 Black or African American, non-Hispanic/Latino; 2 American Indian or Alaska Native, non-Hispanic/Latino; 8 Asian, non-Hispanic/Latino; 27 Hispanic/Latino; 5 Two or more races, non-Hispanic/Latino), 5 international. Average age 35. 149 applicants, 52% accepted, 77 enrolled. In 2019, 49 master's awarded. *Degree requirements:* For master's, internship, practicum. *Entrance requirements:* For master's, previous course work and work experience in psychology. Additional exam requirements/recommendations for international students: required—TOEFL (minimum score 550 paper-based). *Application deadline:* For fall admission, 7/15 for domestic and international students; for spring admission, 12/1 for domestic and international students. Applications are processed on a rolling basis. Application fee: $50. Electronic applications accepted. *Expenses:* Contact institution. *Financial support:* In 2019–20, 56 students received support. Fellowships, research assistantships, career-related internships or fieldwork, Federal Work-Study, and scholarships/grants available. Financial award application deadline: 6/1; financial award applicants required to submit FAFSA. *Unit head:* Dr. Kevin Lyness, Department Chair, 603-283-2149, E-mail: klyness@antioch.edu. *Application contact:* Admissions, 800-552-8380, Fax: 603-357-0718, E-mail: admissions.ane@antioch.edu.
Website: https://www.antioch.edu/new-england/degrees-programs/counseling-wellness/

Antioch University New England, Graduate School, Department of Clinical Psychology, Keene, NH 03431-3552. Offers Psy D. *Accreditation:* APA. *Faculty:* 12 full-time (8 women), 13 part-time/adjunct (9 women). *Students:* 124 full-time (106 women), 4 part-time (2 women); includes 18 minority (3 Black or African American, non-Hispanic/Latino; 1 American Indian or Alaska Native, non-Hispanic/Latino; 4 Asian, non-Hispanic/Latino; 2 Hispanic/Latino; 8 Two or more races, non-Hispanic/Latino), 3 international. Average age 38. 77 applicants, 60% accepted, 21 enrolled. In 2019, 26 doctorates awarded. *Degree requirements:* For doctorate, thesis/dissertation, internship, practicum. *Entrance requirements:* For doctorate, GRE General Test, GRE Subject Test, previous course work in psychology, work sample. Additional exam requirements/recommendations for international students: required—TOEFL (minimum score 550 paper-based). *Application deadline:* For fall admission, 1/7 for domestic and international students. Application fee: $75. *Expenses:* Contact institution. *Financial support:* Applicants required to submit FAFSA. *Unit head:* Dr. Kathi Borden, Chairperson, 603-283-2191, Fax: 603-357-0718, E-mail: kborden@antioch.edu. *Application contact:* Jennifer Fritz, Director of Admissions, 800-552-8380, Fax: 603-357-0718, E-mail: admissions.ane@antiochne.edu.
Website: https://www.antioch.edu/new-england/degrees-programs/psychology-degree/

Antioch University Santa Barbara, Psychology, Santa Barbara, CA 93101-1581. Offers MA, Psy D. *Faculty:* 3 full-time (2 women), 30 part-time/adjunct (19 women). *Students:* 162 full-time (126 women), 25 part-time (11 women); includes 49 minority (3 Black or African American, non-Hispanic/Latino; 2 Asian, non-Hispanic/Latino; 37 Hispanic/Latino; 7 Two or more races, non-Hispanic/Latino), 12 international. Average age 36. 113 applicants, 61% accepted, 54 enrolled. In 2019, 57 master's, 16 doctorates awarded. *Entrance requirements:* Additional exam requirements/recommendations for international students: required—TOEFL (minimum score 550 paper-based). *Application deadline:* Applications are processed on a rolling basis. Application fee: $60. Electronic applications accepted. *Expenses: Tuition:* Full-time $15,936. *Required fees:* $100. *Unit head:* Dr. Sandra Kenny, Chair, 805-962-8179 Ext. 5116, Fax: 805-962-4786, E-mail: skenny@antioch.edu. *Application contact:* Dr. Sandra Kenny, Chair, 805-962-8179 Ext. 5116, Fax: 805-962-4786, E-mail: skenny@antioch.edu.

Clinical Psychology

Antioch University Seattle, Program in Clinical Psychology, Seattle, WA 98121. Offers psychology (Psy D). *Program availability:* Part-time, evening/weekend. *Faculty:* 34 full-time (23 women), 26 part-time/adjunct (21 women). *Students:* 347 full-time (295 women), 147 part-time (121 women); includes 92 minority (13 Black or African American, non-Hispanic/Latino; 1 American Indian or Alaska Native, non-Hispanic/Latino; 26 Asian, non-Hispanic/Latino; 35 Hispanic/Latino; 17 Two or more races, non-Hispanic/Latino), 10 international. Average age 40. 83 applicants, 54% accepted, 16 enrolled. In 2019, 14 doctorates awarded. *Degree requirements:* For doctorate, thesis/dissertation. *Application deadline:* For fall admission, 9/1 for domestic students; for winter admission, 12/1 for domestic students; for spring admission, 3/1 for domestic students; for summer admission, 6/1 for domestic students. Applications are processed on a rolling basis. Application fee: $50. Electronic applications accepted. *Expenses: Tuition:* Full-time $18,604. *Required fees:* $75. *Financial support:* Fellowships, research assistantships with tuition reimbursements, Federal Work-Study, scholarships/grants, and unspecified assistantships available. Financial award applicants required to submit FAFSA. *Unit head:* Dana Waters, Associate Chair, 206-268-4865, E-mail: dwaters@antioch.edu. *Application contact:* Dana Waters, Associate Chair, 206-268-4865, E-mail: dwaters@antioch.edu.
Website: http://www.antiochseattle.edu/academics/psychology/

Antioch University Seattle, Program in Counseling, Therapy and Wellness, Seattle, WA 98121. Offers clinical mental health counseling (MA); counselor education and supervision (PhD); couple and family therapy (MA). *Program availability:* Part-time, evening/weekend. *Faculty:* 34 full-time (23 women), 26 part-time/adjunct (21 women). *Students:* 150 full-time (129 women), 56 part-time (47 women); includes 37 minority (6 Black or African American, non-Hispanic/Latino; 10 Asian, non-Hispanic/Latino; 13 Hispanic/Latino; 8 Two or more races, non-Hispanic/Latino). Average age 35. 223 applicants, 32% accepted, 69 enrolled. In 2019, 88 master's awarded. *Application deadline:* For fall admission, 9/1 for domestic students; for winter admission, 12/1 for domestic students; for spring admission, 3/1 for domestic students; for summer admission, 6/1 for domestic students. Applications are processed on a rolling basis. Application fee: $50. Electronic applications accepted. *Expenses: Tuition:* Full-time $18,604. *Required fees:* $75. *Unit head:* Kathrine Fort, Chair & Core Faculty, Clinical Mental Health CounselingChair & Core F, 206-268-4875, E-mail: kfort@antioch.edu. *Application contact:* Kathrine Fort, Chair & Core Faculty, Clinical Mental Health CounselingChair & Core F, 206-268-4875, E-mail: kfort@antioch.edu.

Appalachian State University, Cratis D. Williams School of Graduate Studies, Department of Human Development and Psychological Counseling, Boone, NC 28608. Offers clinical mental health counseling (MA); college student development (MA); marriage and family therapy (MA); school counseling (MA). *Accreditation:* AAMFT/COAMFTE; ACA; NCATE. *Program availability:* Part-time. *Degree requirements:* For master's, comprehensive exam (for some programs), thesis optional, internships. *Entrance requirements:* For master's, GRE General Test, 3 letters of recommendation. Additional exam requirements/recommendations for international students: required—TOEFL (minimum score 570 paper-based; 79 iBT), IELTS (minimum score 6.5). Electronic applications accepted.

Appalachian State University, Cratis D. Williams School of Graduate Studies, Department of Psychology, Boone, NC 28608. Offers clinical health psychology (MA). *Program availability:* Part-time. *Degree requirements:* For master's, comprehensive exam, thesis optional, exit exam. *Entrance requirements:* For master's, GRE General Test, 3 letters of recommendation. Additional exam requirements/recommendations for international students: required—TOEFL (minimum score 550 paper-based; 79 iBT) or IELTS (minimum score 6.5). Electronic applications accepted.

Argosy University, Atlanta, Georgia School of Professional Psychology, Atlanta, GA 30328. Offers clinical psychology (MA, Psy D, Postdoctoral Respecialization Certificate), including child and family psychology (Psy D), general adult clinical (Psy D), health psychology (Psy D), neuropsychology/geropsychology (Psy D); community counseling (MA), including marriage and family therapy; counselor education and supervision (Ed D); forensic psychology (MA); industrial organizational psychology (MA); marriage and family therapy (Certificate); sport-exercise psychology (MA). *Accreditation:* APA.

Argosy University, Chicago, Illinois School of Professional Psychology, Doctoral Program in Clinical Psychology, Chicago, IL 60601. Offers child and adolescent psychology (Psy D); client-centered and experiential psychotherapies (Psy D); diversity and multicultural psychology (Psy D); family psychology (Psy D); forensic psychology (Psy D); health psychology (Psy D); neuropsychology (Psy D); organizational consulting (Psy D); psychoanalytic psychology (Psy D); psychology and spirituality (Psy D). *Accreditation:* APA.

Argosy University, Chicago, Illinois School of Professional Psychology, Master's Program in Clinical Psychology, Chicago, IL 60601. Offers MA.

Argosy University, Hawaii, Hawai'i School of Professional Psychology, Program in Clinical Psychology, Honolulu, HI 96813. Offers clinical psychology (MA, Psy D, Postdoctoral Respecialization Certificate), including child and family clinical practice (Psy D), diversity in clinical practice (Psy D). *Accreditation:* APA.

Argosy University, Los Angeles, College of Psychology and Behavioral Sciences, Los Angeles, CA 90045. Offers clinical psychology/marriage and family therapy (MA); counseling psychology (Ed D); counseling psychology/marriage and family therapy (MA); forensic psychology (MA).

Argosy University, Northern Virginia, American School of Professional Psychology, Arlington, VA 22209. Offers clinical psychology (MA, Psy D), including child and family psychology (Psy D), diversity and multicultural psychology (Psy D), forensic psychology (Psy D), health and neuropsychology (Psy D); community counseling (MA); counseling psychology (Ed D), including counselor education and supervision; counselor education and supervision (Ed D); forensic psychology (MA).

Argosy University, Orange County, American School of Professional Psychology, Program in Clinical Psychology, Orange, CA 92868. Offers child and adolescent psychology (Psy D); forensic psychology (Psy D); marriage and family therapy (MA).

Argosy University, Phoenix, Arizona School of Professional Psychology, Program in Clinical Psychology, Phoenix, AZ 85021. Offers clinical psychology (MA); neuropsychology (Psy D); sports-exercise psychology (Psy D).

Argosy University, Seattle, College of Psychology and Behavioral Sciences, Program in Clinical Psychology, Seattle, WA 98121. Offers MA, Psy D, Postdoctoral Respecialization Certificate.

Argosy University, Tampa, Florida School of Professional Psychology, Program in Clinical Psychology, Tampa, FL 33607. Offers clinical psychology (MA, Psy D), including child and adolescent psychology (Psy D), geropsychology (Psy D), marriage/couples and family therapy (Psy D), neuropsychology (Psy D). *Accreditation:* APA.

Argosy University, Twin Cities, Minnesota School of Professional Psychology, Eagan, MN 55121. Offers clinical psychology (MA, Psy D), including child and family psychology (Psy D), forensic psychology (Psy D), health and neuropsychology (Psy D), trauma (Psy D); forensic counseling (Post-Graduate Certificate); forensic psychology (MA); industrial organizational psychology (MA); marriage and family therapy (MA, DMFT), including forensic counseling (MA). *Accreditation:* AAMFT; AAMFT/COAMFTE; APA.

Arizona State University at Tempe, College of Liberal Arts and Sciences, Department of Psychology, Tempe, AZ 85287-1104. Offers applied behavior analysis (MS); behavioral neuroscience (PhD); clinical psychology (PhD); cognitive science (PhD); developmental psychology (PhD); quantitative psychology (PhD); social psychology (PhD). *Accreditation:* APA. *Degree requirements:* For doctorate, comprehensive exam, thesis/dissertation, interactive Program of Study (iPOS) submitted before completing 50 percent of required credit hours. *Entrance requirements:* For doctorate, GRE General Test, GRE Subject Test, minimum GPA of 3.0 or equivalent in last 2 years of work leading to bachelor's degree. Additional exam requirements/recommendations for international students: required—TOEFL, IELTS, or PTE. Electronic applications accepted.

Arkansas State University, Graduate School, College of Education and Behavioral Science, Department of Psychology and Counseling, State University, AR 72467. Offers clinical mental health counseling (Graduate Certificate); college student personnel services (MS); dyslexia therapy (Graduate Certificate); psychological science (MS); psychology and counseling (Ed S); rehabilitation counseling (MRC); school counseling (MSE); student affairs (Graduate Certificate). *Accreditation:* ACA (one or more programs are accredited); CORE (one or more programs are accredited); NCATE. *Program availability:* Part-time. *Degree requirements:* For master's and other advanced degree, comprehensive exam, thesis or alternative. *Entrance requirements:* For master's, GRE General Test or MAT (for MSE), appropriate bachelor's degree, interview, letters of reference, official transcripts, immunization records, written statement, 2-3 page autobiography; for other advanced degree, GRE General Test, interview, master's degree, letters of reference, official transcript, personal statement, immunization records. Additional exam requirements/recommendations for international students: required—TOEFL (minimum score 550 paper-based; 79 iBT), IELTS (minimum score 6), PTE (minimum score 56). Electronic applications accepted.

Ashland Theological Seminary, Graduate Programs, Ashland, OH 44805. Offers Biblical studies (MA); Christian ministries (MACM), including Black church studies (MACM, D Min), general Christian ministries, leadership, spiritual formation (MACM, D Min); clinical mental health counseling (MA); counseling (MAC); historical and theological studies (MA), including Anabaptism and Pietism, Christian theology, church history, New Testament, Old Testament; ministry (D Min), including Black church studies (MACM, D Min), chaplaincy (M Div, D Min), independent design, spiritual formation (MACM, D Min), transformational leadership; pastoral ministry (M Div), including chaplaincy (M Div, D Min), general ministry. *Accreditation:* ATS. *Program availability:* Part-time. *Degree requirements:* For master's, 2 foreign languages, comprehensive exam (for some programs), thesis (for some programs); for doctorate, thesis/dissertation. *Entrance requirements:* For master's, bachelor's degree from accredited institution with minimum undergraduate GPA of 2.75; for doctorate, M Div, minimum undergraduate GPA of 3.0. Additional exam requirements/recommendations for international students: required—TOEFL (minimum score 500 paper-based; 65 iBT). Electronic applications accepted.

Auburn University at Montgomery, College of Education, Department of Counselor, Leadership, and Special Education, Montgomery, AL 36124. Offers counselor education (M Ed, Ed S), including clinical mental health counseling, school counseling; early childhood special education (M Ed); instructional leadership (M Ed, Ed S); special education/collaborative teacher (M Ed, Ed S). *Accreditation:* ACA; NCATE. *Program availability:* Part-time, evening/weekend. *Faculty:* 6 full-time (3 women), 4 part-time/adjunct (2 women). *Students:* 64 full-time (45 women), 53 part-time (42 women); includes 59 minority (56 Black or African American, non-Hispanic/Latino; 1 Asian, non-Hispanic/Latino; 2 Hispanic/Latino), 1 international. Average age 36. 90 applicants, 79% accepted, 71 enrolled. In 2019, 34 master's awarded. *Degree requirements:* For master's, 3 letters of recommendation from company/school. *Entrance requirements:* For master's, GRE General Test or MAT, certification, BS in teaching; for Ed S, GRE General Test or MAT, certification. Additional exam requirements/recommendations for international students: recommended—TOEFL (minimum score 500 paper-based; 61 iBT), IELTS (minimum score 5.5), TSE (minimum score 44). *Application deadline:* For fall admission, 7/15 for international students; for spring admission, 11/15 for international students; for summer admission, 4/15 for international students. Applications are processed on a rolling basis. Application fee: $25. Electronic applications accepted. *Expenses: Tuition, area resident:* Full-time $7578; part-time $421 per credit hour. Tuition, state resident: full-time $7578; part-time $421 per credit hour. Tuition, nonresident: full-time $17,046; part-time $947 per credit hour. *International tuition:* $17,046 full-time. *Required fees:* $868. *Financial support:* Career-related internships or fieldwork and scholarships/grants available. Support available to part-time students. Financial award application deadline: 3/1; financial award applicants required to submit FAFSA. *Unit head:* Dr. Alan Miller, Department Head, 334-244-3036, E-mail: sflynt@aum.edu. *Application contact:* Lessie Garcia-Latimore, Administrative Associate, 334-244-3879, E-mail: lgarcia@aum.edu.
Website: http://education.aum.edu/academic-departments/counselor-leadership-and-special-education

Augusta University, College of Education, Department of Counselor Education, Leadership, and Research, Augusta, GA 30912. Offers counselor education (M Ed, Ed S), including clinical mental health counseling (M Ed), school counselor (M Ed). *Accreditation:* ACA; NCATE. *Program availability:* Part-time, evening/weekend. *Degree requirements:* For master's, comprehensive exam; for Ed S, comprehensive exam, thesis. *Entrance requirements:* For master's, GRE, MAT, minimum GPA of 2.5; for Ed S, GRE, MAT.

Austin Peay State University, College of Graduate Studies, College of Behavioral and Health Sciences, Department of Psychological Science and Counseling, Clarksville, TN 37044. Offers industrial-organizational psychology (MS); mental health counseling (MS), including clinical mental health, school counseling; school counseling (MS). *Program availability:* Part-time, online learning. *Faculty:* 9 full-time (6 women), 5 part-time/adjunct (4 women). *Students:* 64 full-time (46 women), 27 part-time (24 women); includes 30 minority (16 Black or African American, non-Hispanic/Latino; 1 Asian, non-Hispanic/Latino; 5 Hispanic/Latino; 8 Two or more races, non-Hispanic/Latino), 1 international. Average age 29. 34 applicants, 68% accepted, 19 enrolled. In 2019, 28 master's awarded. *Degree requirements:* For master's, comprehensive exam, thesis (for some programs). *Entrance requirements:* For master's, GRE General Test, minimum undergraduate GPA of 2.5, 3 letters of recommendation, bachelor's degree. Additional exam requirements/recommendations for international students: required—TOEFL (minimum score 500 paper-based). *Application deadline:* For fall admission, 8/5 priority date for domestic students. Applications are processed on a rolling basis. Application fee: $45 ($55 for international students). Electronic applications accepted. *Financial support:* Research assistantships with full tuition reimbursements, career-related internships or fieldwork, Federal Work-Study, institutionally sponsored loans, scholarships/grants, and unspecified assistantships available. Support available to part-time students. Financial award application deadline: 7/1; financial award applicants required to submit FAFSA. *Unit head:* Dr. Nicole Knickmeyer, Chair, 931-221-7232, Fax: 931-221-6267, E-mail: knickmeyer@apsu.edu. *Application contact:* Megan Mitchell,

Coordinator of Graduate Admissions, 800-859-4723, Fax: 931-221-7641, E-mail: gradadmissions@apsu.edu.
Website: http://www.apsu.edu/psychology/index.php

Azusa Pacific University, School of Behavioral and Applied Sciences, Department of Clinical Psychology, Azusa, CA 91702-7000. Offers family psychology (Psy D). *Accreditation:* APA. *Program availability:* Part-time, evening/weekend. *Degree requirements:* For doctorate, comprehensive exam. *Entrance requirements:* Additional exam requirements/recommendations for international students: required—TOEFL (minimum score 600 paper-based). *Expenses:* Contact institution.

Ball State University, Graduate School, College of Health, Department of Counseling Psychology, Social Psychology, and Counseling, Program in Counseling Psychology, Muncie, IN 47306. Offers counseling (MA), including clinical mental health counseling, mental health counseling, rehabilitation counseling, school counseling; counseling psychology (PhD). *Accreditation:* ACA; APA. *Program availability:* Part-time. *Degree requirements:* For doctorate, thesis/dissertation. *Entrance requirements:* For master's, GRE General Test (minimum scores 144 quantitative, 153 verbal), minimum baccalaureate GPA of 2.75 or 3.0 in latter half of baccalaureate, minimum GPA of 3.0 in psychology coursework, three letters of recommendation; for doctorate, GRE General Test, interview, minimum graduate GPA of 3.2, resume. Additional exam requirements/recommendations for international students: required—TOEFL (minimum score 550 paper-based; 79 iBT), IELTS (minimum score 6.5). Electronic applications accepted. *Expenses: Tuition, area resident:* Full-time $7506; part-time $417 per credit hour. Tuition, nonresident: full-time $20,610; part-time $1145 per credit hour. *Required fees:* $2126. Tuition and fees vary according to course load, campus/location and program.

Ball State University, Graduate School, College of Health, Department of Counseling Psychology, Social Psychology, and Counseling, Program in Social Psychology, Muncie, IN 47306. Offers social psychology (MA); social psychology and clinical mental health counseling (MA). *Entrance requirements:* For master's, GRE General Test (minimum scores 144 quantitative, 153 verbal), minimum baccalaureate GPA of 2.75 or 3.0 in latter half of baccalaureate, minimum GPA of 3.0 in psychology coursework, three letters of recommendation. Additional exam requirements/recommendations for international students: required—TOEFL (minimum score 550 paper-based; 79 iBT), IELTS (minimum score 6.5). Electronic applications accepted. *Expenses: Tuition, area resident:* Full-time $7506; part-time $417 per credit hour. Tuition, nonresident: full-time $20,610; part-time $1145 per credit hour. *Required fees:* $2126. Tuition and fees vary according to course load, campus/location and program.

Ball State University, Graduate School, College of Sciences and Humanities, Department of Psychological Science, Program in Clinical Psychology, Muncie, IN 47306. Offers MA. *Entrance requirements:* For master's, GRE General Test, minimum baccalaureate GPA of 2.75 or 3.0 in latter half of baccalaureate, goals statements, curriculum vitae, letters of recommendation. Additional exam requirements/recommendations for international students: required—TOEFL (minimum score 550 paper-based; 79 iBT), IELTS (minimum score 6.5). Electronic applications accepted. *Expenses: Tuition, area resident:* Full-time $7506; part-time $417 per credit hour. Tuition, nonresident: full-time $20,610; part-time $1145 per credit hour. *Required fees:* $2126. Tuition and fees vary according to course load, campus/location and program.

Barry University, College of Arts and Sciences, Department of Psychology, Miami Shores, FL 33161-6695. Offers clinical psychology (MS); school psychology (MS, SSP). *Program availability:* Part-time, evening/weekend. *Degree requirements:* For master's, thesis, practicum. *Entrance requirements:* For master's, GRE General Test, minimum GPA of 3.0, course work in psychology. Electronic applications accepted.

Baylor University, Graduate School, College of Arts and Sciences, Department of Psychology and Neuroscience, Program in Clinical Psychology, Waco, TX 76798. Offers Psy D. *Accreditation:* APA. *Degree requirements:* For doctorate, comprehensive exam, thesis/dissertation, Year-long internship at APA-accredited internship site. *Entrance requirements:* For doctorate, GRE General Test, In-person interview. Additional exam requirements/recommendations for international students: required—TOEFL, IELTS. Electronic applications accepted. *Expenses:* Contact institution.

Bay Path University, Program in Clinical Mental Health Counseling, Longmeadow, MA 01106-2292. Offers clinical mental health counseling (MS), including alcohol and drug abuse counseling, early intervention. *Program availability:* Part-time, blended/hybrid learning. *Entrance requirements:* For master's, completed application; official undergraduate and graduate transcripts (a GPA of 3.0 or higher is preferred); original essay of 300-500 words on the topic "Why the MS in Clinical Mental Health Counseling is important to my personal and professional goals"; current resume; 2 recommendations. Electronic applications accepted. Application fee is waived when completed online. *Expenses:* Contact institution.

Benedictine University, Graduate Programs, Program in Clinical Psychology, Lisle, IL 60532. Offers MS. *Program availability:* Part-time. *Entrance requirements:* For master's, autobiographical statement. Additional exam requirements/recommendations for international students: required—TOEFL (minimum score 550 paper-based; 79 iBT), IELTS (minimum score 6.5). Electronic applications accepted.

Bethel Seminary, Graduate and Professional Programs, St. Paul, MN 55112-6998. Offers Anglican studies (Certificate); children's and family ministry (MA); Christian studies (Certificate); Christian thought (MA); church planting (Certificate); Greek and Hebrew language (M Div); Greek language (M Div); Hebrew language (M Div); marriage and family therapy (MA, Certificate); mental health counseling (MA); ministry (MA, D Min); ministry practice (Certificate); theological studies (MA, Certificate); transformational leadership (MA); young life youth ministry (Certificate). *Accreditation:* ACIPE. *Program availability:* Part-time, evening/weekend, 100% online, blended/hybrid learning. *Degree requirements:* For master's, variable foreign language requirement, thesis (for some programs); for doctorate, thesis/dissertation. *Entrance requirements:* For master's, letters of reference, transcripts, personal statement; for doctorate, M Div, letters of reference, organizational support; for Certificate, letters of reference, family essay, personal statement, and family of origin paper (for marriage and family therapy). Additional exam requirements/recommendations for international students: required—TOEFL (minimum score 550 paper-based; 87 iBT). Electronic applications accepted. *Expenses:* Contact institution.

Binghamton University, State University of New York, Graduate School, Harpur College of Arts and Sciences, Department of Psychology, Program in Psychology - Clinical Psychology, Binghamton, NY 13902-6000. Offers PhD. *Accreditation:* APA. *Program availability:* Part-time. Terminal master's awarded for partial completion of doctoral program. *Degree requirements:* For doctorate, comprehensive exam, thesis/dissertation. *Entrance requirements:* For doctorate, GRE General Test. Additional exam requirements/recommendations for international students: required—TOEFL (minimum score 550 paper-based; 80 iBT). Electronic applications accepted.

Biola University, Rosemead School of Psychology, La Mirada, CA 90639-0001. Offers clinical psychology (PhD, Psy D). *Accreditation:* APA. *Faculty:* 23. *Students:* 115 full-time (94 women), 48 part-time (43 women); includes 48 minority (2 Black or African American, non-Hispanic/Latino; 1 American Indian or Alaska Native, non-Hispanic/Latino; 24 Asian, non-Hispanic/Latino; 16 Hispanic/Latino; 1 Native Hawaiian or other Pacific Islander, non-Hispanic/Latino; 4 Two or more races, non-Hispanic/Latino), 51 international. Average age 30. 126 applicants, 46% accepted, 34 enrolled. In 2019, 29 doctorates awarded. *Degree requirements:* For doctorate, comprehensive exam, thesis/dissertation. *Entrance requirements:* For doctorate, GRE General Test, interview, 30 undergraduate semester hours of credits in psychology, minimum GPA of 3.0. Additional exam requirements/recommendations for international students: required—TOEFL (minimum score 600 paper-based; 100 iBT). *Application deadline:* For fall admission, 12/1 priority date for domestic students, 12/1 for international students. Application fee: $65. Electronic applications accepted. *Expenses:* Contact institution. *Financial support:* Scholarships/grants and unspecified assistantships available. Financial award applicants required to submit FAFSA. *Unit head:* Dr. Tamara Anderson, Dean, 562-903-4867, Fax: 562-903-4864. *Application contact:* Nicholas Perry, Graduate Admissions Counselor, 562-903-4752, E-mail: graduate.admissions@biola.edu.
Website: http://www.rosemead.edu/

Bowling Green State University, Graduate College, College of Arts and Sciences, Department of Psychology, Bowling Green, OH 43403. Offers clinical psychology (MA, PhD); developmental psychology (MA, PhD); experimental psychology (MA, PhD); industrial/organizational psychology (MA, PhD); quantitative psychology (MA, PhD). *Accreditation:* APA (one or more programs are accredited). *Degree requirements:* For doctorate, thesis/dissertation. *Entrance requirements:* For doctorate, GRE General Test, GRE Subject Test. Additional exam requirements/recommendations for international students: required—TOEFL. Electronic applications accepted.

Bowling Green State University, Graduate College, College of Education and Human Development, School of Intervention Services, Program in Clinical Mental Health Counseling, Bowling Green, OH 43403. Offers clinical mental health counseling (MA); school counseling (M Ed). *Accreditation:* ACA; NCATE. *Program availability:* Part-time. *Degree requirements:* For master's, thesis or alternative. *Entrance requirements:* For master's, GRE General Test. Additional exam requirements/recommendations for international students: required—TOEFL. Electronic applications accepted.

Bradley University, The Graduate School, College of Education and Health Sciences, Education, Counseling and Leadership Department, Peoria, IL 61625-0002. Offers counseling (MA), including clinical mental health counseling, professional school counseling; leadership in educational administration (MA); nonprofit leadership (MA). *Accreditation:* ACA; NCATE. *Program availability:* Part-time, evening/weekend, blended/hybrid learning. *Faculty:* 24 full-time (15 women), 10 part-time/adjunct (6 women). *Students:* 48 full-time (43 women), 246 part-time (197 women); includes 62 minority (35 Black or African American, non-Hispanic/Latino; 3 American Indian or Alaska Native, non-Hispanic/Latino; 4 Asian, non-Hispanic/Latino; 17 Hispanic/Latino; 3 Two or more races, non-Hispanic/Latino), 3 international. Average age 33. 125 applicants, 74% accepted, 68 enrolled. In 2019, 67 master's awarded. *Degree requirements:* For master's, comprehensive exam, thesis optional. *Entrance requirements:* For master's, GRE General Test or MAT, interview, 3 letters of recommendation. Additional exam requirements/recommendations for international students: required—TOEFL (minimum score 550 paper-based; 79 iBT), IELTS (minimum score 6.5), PTE (minimum score 58). *Application deadline:* For fall admission, 5/15 priority date for domestic and international students; for spring admission, 10/15 priority date for domestic and international students. Applications are processed on a rolling basis. Application fee: $40 ($50 for international students). Electronic applications accepted. *Expenses: Tuition:* Part-time $930 per credit hour. *Financial support:* In 2019–20, 40 students received support, including 13 research assistantships with full tuition reimbursements available (averaging $11,040 per year); fellowships, career-related internships or fieldwork, scholarships/grants, tuition waivers (full), and unspecified assistantships also available. Support available to part-time students. Financial award application deadline: 4/1. *Unit head:* Dean Cantu, Associate Dean and Director, Professor, 309-677-3190, E-mail: dcantu@bradley.edu. *Application contact:* Rachel Webb, Director of On-Campus Graduate Admissions and International Student and Scholar Services, 309-677-2375, E-mail: rkwebb@bradley.edu.
Website: https://www.bradley.edu/academic/departments/ecl/

Brigham Young University, Graduate Studies, College of Family, Home, and Social Sciences, Department of Psychology, Provo, UT 84602. Offers clinical psychology (PhD); cognitive and behavioral neuroscience (PhD). *Accreditation:* APA. *Faculty:* 24 full-time (9 women), 3 part-time/adjunct (0 women). *Students:* 62 full-time (39 women); includes 10 minority (3 Black or African American, non-Hispanic/Latino; 1 American Indian or Alaska Native, non-Hispanic/Latino; 5 Asian, non-Hispanic/Latino; 1 Hispanic/Latino), 4 international. Average age 29. 76 applicants, 22% accepted, 11 enrolled. In 2019, 8 doctorates awarded. *Degree requirements:* For doctorate, comprehensive exam, thesis/dissertation, publishable paper. *Entrance requirements:* For doctorate, GRE General Test, minimum GPA of 3.0. Additional exam requirements/recommendations for international students: required—TOEFL (minimum score 580 paper-based; 85 iBT). *Application deadline:* For fall admission, 12/1 for domestic and international students. Application fee: $50. Electronic applications accepted. *Expenses:* $18,226/LDS $25,512/Non-LDS. *Financial support:* In 2019–20, 41 students received support, including 43 research assistantships with partial tuition reimbursements available (averaging $12,000 per year), 7 teaching assistantships with partial tuition reimbursements available (averaging $12,000 per year); scholarships/grants and unspecified assistantships also available. Financial award application deadline: 5/31. *Unit head:* Dr. Gary Burlingame, Chair, 801-422-7557, Fax: 801-422-0602, E-mail: gary_burlingame@byu.edu. *Application contact:* Rachelle Gunderson, Coordinator of Student Programs, 801-422-4560, Fax: 801-422-0602, E-mail: leesa_scott@byu.edu.
Website: http://psychology.byu.edu/

California Lutheran University, Graduate Studies, Department of Psychology, Thousand Oaks, CA 91360-2787. Offers clinical psychology (MS, Psy D); marital and family therapy (MS). *Accreditation:* APA. *Program availability:* Part-time. *Degree requirements:* For master's, thesis or comprehensive exams; for doctorate, thesis/dissertation, internship. *Entrance requirements:* For master's, GRE General Test, interview, minimum GPA of 3.0; for doctorate, GRE General Test. Electronic applications accepted.

California State University, Dominguez Hills, College of Natural and Behavioral Sciences, Department of Psychology, Carson, CA 90747-0001. Offers clinical psychology (MA); health psychology (MA). *Program availability:* Part-time, evening/weekend. Terminal master's awarded for partial completion of doctoral program. *Degree requirements:* For master's, comprehensive exam, thesis optional. *Entrance requirements:* For master's, GRE General Test or MAT, interview, minimum GPA of 3.0, prerequisite psychology courses. Additional exam requirements/recommendations for international students: required—TOEFL (minimum score 550 paper-based). Electronic applications accepted.

California State University, Fullerton, Graduate Studies, College of Humanities and Social Sciences, Department of Psychology, Fullerton, CA 92831-3599. Offers clinical psychology (MS); psychology (MA). *Program availability:* Part-time. *Entrance requirements:* For master's, GRE General Test, GRE Subject Test, undergraduate major in psychology or related field.

Clinical Psychology

California State University, Northridge, Graduate Studies, College of Social and Behavioral Sciences, Department of Psychology, Northridge, CA 91330. Offers clinical psychology (MA); general experimental psychology (MA). *Degree requirements:* For master's, thesis. *Entrance requirements:* For master's, GRE General Test, GRE Subject Test, minimum GPA of 3.0, letters of recommendation. Additional exam requirements/recommendations for international students: required—TOEFL.

California State University, San Bernardino, Graduate Studies, College of Social and Behavioral Sciences, Department of Psychology, San Bernardino, CA 92407. Offers child development (MA); clinical/counseling psychology (MS); industrial/organizational psychology (MS); psychological science (MA). *Faculty:* 15 full-time (7 women). *Students:* 62 full-time (43 women), 13 part-time (7 women); includes 44 minority (3 Black or African American, non-Hispanic/Latino; 3 Asian, non-Hispanic/Latino; 31 Hispanic/Latino; 7 Two or more races, non-Hispanic/Latino, 5 international. Average age 27. 163 applicants, 24% accepted, 25 enrolled. In 2019, 32 master's awarded. *Degree requirements:* For master's, comprehensive exam, thesis (for some programs). *Entrance requirements:* Additional exam requirements/recommendations for international students: required—TOEFL. Application fee: $55. *Financial support:* Fellowships, research assistantships, and teaching assistantships available. *Unit head:* Dr. Robert Ricco, Chair, 909-537-5485, Fax: 909-537-7003, E-mail: rricco@csusb.edu. *Application contact:* Dr. Dorota Huizinga, Dean of Graduate Studies, 909-537-3064, E-mail: dorota.huizinga@csusb.edu. Website: https://csbs.csusb.edu/psychology

California University of Pennsylvania, School of Graduate Studies and Research, College of Education and Human Services, Department of Counselor Education, California, PA 15419-1394. Offers clinical mental health counseling (MS); school counseling (M Ed). *Accreditation:* ACA; NCATE. *Program availability:* Part-time, evening/weekend. *Degree requirements:* For master's, comprehensive exam, thesis optional. *Entrance requirements:* For master's, MAT, minimum GPA of 3.0, resume, letters of reference. Additional exam requirements/recommendations for international students: required—TOEFL (minimum score 550 paper-based; 80 iBT). Electronic applications accepted. *Expenses: Tuition, area resident:* Full-time $9288; part-time $516 per credit. Tuition, state resident: full-time $9288; part-time $516 per credit. Tuition, nonresident: full-time $13,932; part-time $774 per credit. *Required fees:* $3631; $291.13 per credit. Part-time tuition and fees vary according to course load.

Capella University, Harold Abel School of Social and Behavioral Science, Doctoral Programs in Psychology, Minneapolis, MN 55402. Offers addiction psychology (PhD); clinical psychology (Psy D); educational psychology (PhD); general advanced studies in human behavior (PhD); general psychology (PhD); industrial/organizational psychology (PhD); school psychology (Psy D).

Capella University, Harold Abel School of Social and Behavioral Science, Master's Programs in Psychology, Minneapolis, MN 55402. Offers applied behavior analysis (MS); clinical psychology (MS); counseling psychology (MS); educational psychology (MS); evaluation, research, and measurement (MS); general advanced studies in human behavior (MS); general psychology (MS); industrial/organizational psychology (MS); leadership coaching psychology (MS); school psychology (MS); sport psychology (MS).

Cardinal Stritch University, College of Arts and Sciences, Department of Psychology, Milwaukee, WI 53217-3985. Offers clinical psychology (MA). *Program availability:* Part-time, evening/weekend. *Degree requirements:* For master's, thesis, portfolio, clinical practicum. *Entrance requirements:* For master's, interview, minimum GPA of 3.0, 3 letters of recommendation. Additional exam requirements/recommendations for international students: required—TOEFL (minimum score 79 iBT), IELTS (minimum score 6.5). Electronic applications accepted. *Expenses:* Contact institution.

Case Western Reserve University, School of Graduate Studies, Psychological Sciences Department, Program in Clinical Psychology, Cleveland, OH 44106. Offers PhD. *Accreditation:* APA. *Program availability:* Part-time. *Faculty:* 7 full-time (4 women). *Students:* 20 full-time (14 women), 1 (woman) part-time; includes 4 minority (1 Asian, non-Hispanic/Latino; 3 Hispanic/Latino). Average age 28. 187 applicants, 3% accepted, 4 enrolled. In 2019, 4 doctorates awarded. *Degree requirements:* For doctorate, thesis/dissertation, internship. *Entrance requirements:* For doctorate, GRE General Test, GRE Subject Test, personal statement; curriculum vitae; three letters of recommendation. Additional exam requirements/recommendations for international students: required—TOEFL (minimum score 577 paper-based; 90 iBT); recommended—IELTS (minimum score 7). *Application deadline:* For fall admission, 12/1 priority date for domestic students. Application fee: $50. Electronic applications accepted. *Financial support:* Fellowships, research assistantships, teaching assistantships, and health care benefits available. Financial award application deadline: 12/1; financial award applicants required to submit FAFSA. *Unit head:* Dr. Heath Demaree, Professor and Chair, 216-368-6468, E-mail: psychsciences@case.edu. *Application contact:* Arin Connell, Associate Professor and Director of Clinical Training, 216-368-1550, E-mail: arin.connell@case.edu. Website: http://psychsciences.case.edu/graduate/

The Catholic University of America, School of Arts and Sciences, Department of Psychology, Washington, DC 20064. Offers applied experimental psychology (PhD); clinical psychology (PhD); general psychology (MA); human development psychology (PhD); human factors (MA); MA/JD. *Accreditation:* APA (one or more programs are accredited). *Program availability:* Part-time. *Faculty:* 9 full-time (5 women), 8 part-time/adjunct (all women). *Students:* 31 full-time (27 women), 40 part-time (33 women); includes 19 minority (3 Black or African American, non-Hispanic/Latino; 3 Asian, non-Hispanic/Latino; 5 Hispanic/Latino; 8 Two or more races, non-Hispanic/Latino), 6 international. Average age 28. 160 applicants, 25% accepted, 17 enrolled. In 2019, 19 master's, 8 doctorates awarded. *Degree requirements:* For master's, comprehensive exam, thesis (for some programs); for doctorate, comprehensive exam, thesis/dissertation. *Entrance requirements:* For master's, GRE General Test, statement of purpose, official copies of academic transcripts, three letters of recommendation; for doctorate, GRE General Test, GRE Subject Test, statement of purpose, official copies of academic transcripts, three letters of recommendation. Additional exam requirements/recommendations for international students: required—TOEFL (minimum score 550 paper-based; 80 iBT). *Application deadline:* For fall admission, 7/15 priority date for domestic students, 7/1 for international students; for spring admission, 11/15 priority date for domestic students, 11/1 for international students. Applications are processed on a rolling basis. Application fee: $55. Electronic applications accepted. *Expenses:* Contact institution. *Financial support:* Fellowships, research assistantships, teaching assistantships, Federal Work-Study, scholarships/grants, tuition waivers (full and partial), and unspecified assistantships available. Financial award application deadline: 2/1; financial award applicants required to submit FAFSA. *Unit head:* Dr. Brendan Rich, Chair, 202-319-5823, Fax: 202-319-6263, E-mail: richb@cua.edu. *Application contact:* Dr. Steven Brown, Director of Graduate Admissions, 202-319-5057, Fax: 202-319-6533, E-mail: cua-admissions@cua.edu. Website: http://psychology.cua.edu/

Central Michigan University, College of Graduate Studies, College of Liberal Arts and Social Sciences, Department of Psychology, Program in Clinical Psychology, Mount Pleasant, MI 48859. Offers PhD. *Accreditation:* APA. *Degree requirements:* For doctorate, thesis/dissertation. *Entrance requirements:* For doctorate, GRE. Electronic applications accepted. *Expenses: Tuition, area resident:* Full-time $12,267; part-time $8178 per year. Tuition, state resident: full-time $12,267; part-time $8178 per year. Tuition, nonresident: full-time $12,267; part-time $8178 per year. *International tuition:* $16,110 full-time. *Required fees:* $225 per semester. Tuition and fees vary according to degree level and program.

Chestnut Hill College, School of Graduate Studies, Division of Psychology, Program in Clinical and Counseling Psychology, Philadelphia, PA 19118-2693. Offers clinical and counseling psychology (MS, CAS), including child and adolescent therapy, child and adolescent therapy with autism spectrum disorders, co-occurring disorders, couple and family therapy, diverse and underserved communities, generalist (MS), trauma studies. *Program availability:* Part-time, evening/weekend. *Degree requirements:* For master's, thesis optional, practica. *Entrance requirements:* For master's, GRE General Test, writing sample, letters of recommendation. Additional exam requirements/recommendations for international students: required—TOEFL (minimum score 500 paper-based), IELTS (minimum score 6.0), or TWE (minimum score 22). Electronic applications accepted. *Expenses:* Contact institution.

Chestnut Hill College, School of Graduate Studies, Division of Psychology, Program in Clinical Psychology, Philadelphia, PA 19118-2693. Offers clinical psychology (Psy D), including clinical psychology, couple and family therapy, psychological assessment. *Accreditation:* APA. *Program availability:* Part-time, evening/weekend. *Degree requirements:* For doctorate, comprehensive exam, thesis/dissertation, internship, practica, clinical competency exam. *Entrance requirements:* For doctorate, GRE General Test, letters of recommendation, writing sample, master's degree in clinical/counseling psychology or closely-related field. Additional exam requirements/recommendations for international students: required—TOEFL (minimum score 500 paper-based), IELTS (minimum score 6.0), or TWE (minimum score 22). Electronic applications accepted. *Expenses:* Contact institution.

The Chicago School of Professional Psychology, Program in Clinical Forensic Psychology, Chicago, IL 60610. Offers Psy D. *Degree requirements:* For doctorate, thesis/dissertation. *Entrance requirements:* For doctorate, GRE. Additional exam requirements/recommendations for international students: required—TOEFL, IELTS.

The Chicago School of Professional Psychology, Program in Clinical Mental Health Counseling, Chicago, IL 60610. Offers MA. *Program availability:* Part-time.

The Chicago School of Professional Psychology, Program in Clinical Psychology, Chicago, IL 60610. Offers Psy D. *Accreditation:* APA. *Degree requirements:* For doctorate, comprehensive exam, thesis/dissertation. *Entrance requirements:* For doctorate, GRE, 18 hours of psychology credit (including courses in statistics, normal psychology and human development); minimum GPA of 3.2. Additional exam requirements/recommendations for international students: required—TOEFL. Electronic applications accepted.

The Chicago School of Professional Psychology at Downtown Los Angeles, Program in Clinical Forensic Psychology, Los Angeles, CA 90017. Offers Psy D.

The Chicago School of Professional Psychology at Downtown Los Angeles, Program in Clinical Psychology, Los Angeles, CA 90017. Offers applied behavior analysis (MA); clinical psychology (Psy D); marital and family therapy (MA).

The Chicago School of Professional Psychology at Irvine, Program in Clinical Forensic Psychology, Irvine, CA 92612. Offers Psy D.

The Chicago School of Professional Psychology at San Diego, Graduate Programs, San Diego, CA 92101. Offers applied behavior analysis (MS, PhD); applied clinical psychology (Psy D); clinical psychology (MA); industrial and organizational psychology (MA).

The Chicago School of Professional Psychology at Xavier University of Louisiana, Graduate Program, New Orleans, LA 70125. Offers Psy D.

The Chicago School of Professional Psychology: Online, Program in Clinical Psychopharmacology, Chicago, IL 60654. Offers MS. *Program availability:* Online learning.

Chicago State University, School of Graduate and Professional Studies, College of Arts and Sciences, Department of Psychology, Chicago, IL 60628. Offers counseling (MA), including bilingual specialization, clinical mental health counseling, school counseling. *Accreditation:* ACA; NCATE. *Degree requirements:* For master's, comprehensive exam, thesis optional. *Entrance requirements:* For master's, minimum GPA of 3.0 for last 60 semester hours of course work or essay; interview.

City College of the City University of New York, Graduate School, Colin Powell School for Civic and Global Leadership, Department of Psychology, New York, NY 10031-9198. Offers clinical psychology (PhD); general psychology (MA); mental health counseling (MA). *Accreditation:* APA (one or more programs are accredited). *Program availability:* Part-time. *Degree requirements:* For master's, one foreign language, comprehensive exam, thesis. *Entrance requirements:* For master's, GRE. Additional exam requirements/recommendations for international students: required—TOEFL (minimum score 550 paper-based; 79 iBT). Electronic applications accepted.

Clark University, Graduate School, Hiatt School of Psychology, Program in Clinical Psychology, Worcester, MA 01610-1477. Offers PhD. *Accreditation:* APA. *Students:* Average age 28. *Entrance requirements:* For doctorate, GRE General Test. Additional exam requirements/recommendations for international students: required—TOEFL. *Application deadline:* For fall admission, 12/15 priority date for domestic and international students. Applications are processed on a rolling basis. Application fee: $75. *Expenses: Tuition:* Full-time $47,650; part-time $4765 per course. *Required fees:* $1850. *Financial support:* Fellowships, research assistantships, teaching assistantships, and tuition waivers (full) available. *Unit head:* Dr. Wendy Grolnick, Professor, 508-793-7276, E-mail: wgrolnick@clarku.edu. *Application contact:* Dr. Wendy Grolnick, Professor, 508-793-7276, E-mail: wgrolnick@clarku.edu. Website: http://www.clarku.edu/departments/psychology/grad/clinical/index.cfm

Clayton State University, School of Graduate Studies, College of Arts and Sciences, Program in Psychology, Morrow, GA 30260-0285. Offers applied developmental psychology (MS); clinical/counseling psychology (MS). *Entrance requirements:* For master's, GRE, 2 official transcripts; 3 letters of recommendation; statement of purpose; on-campus interview; background check. Additional exam requirements/recommendations for international students: required—TOEFL (minimum score 550 paper-based). Electronic applications accepted.

Clemson University, Graduate School, College of Education, Department of Education and Human Development, Clemson, SC 29634. Offers counselor education (M Ed, Ed S), including mental health counseling, school counseling, student affairs (M Ed); learning sciences (PhD); literacy (M Ed); literacy, language and culture (PhD); special education (M Ed, MAT, PhD). *Faculty:* 35 full-time (25 women). *Students:* 96 full-time (76 women), 175 part-time (169 women); includes 36 minority (20 Black or African American, non-Hispanic/Latino; 1 Asian, non-Hispanic/Latino; 11 Hispanic/Latino; 4 Two or more races, non-Hispanic/Latino), 10 international. Average age 32. 367 applicants, 74% accepted, 150 enrolled. In 2019, 53 master's, 7 doctorates, 32 other advanced

degrees awarded. *Expenses: Tuition, area resident:* Full-time $10,600; part-time $8688 per semester. Tuition, state resident: full-time $10,600; part-time $8688 per semester. Tuition, nonresident: full-time $22,050; part-time $17,412 per semester. *International tuition:* $22,050 full-time. *Required fees:* $1196; $617 per semester. $617 per semester. Tuition and fees vary according to course load, degree level, campus/location and program. *Financial support:* In 2019–20, 120 students received support, including 7 fellowships with full and partial tuition reimbursements available (averaging $11,238 per year), 6 research assistantships with full and partial tuition reimbursements available (averaging $14,250 per year), 25 teaching assistantships with full and partial tuition reimbursements available (averaging $15,355 per year); career-related internships or fieldwork and unspecified assistantships also available. *Unit head:* Dr. Debi Switzer, Department Chair, 864-656-5098, E-mail: debi@clemson.edu. *Application contact:* Julie Search, Student Services Program Coordinator, 864-250-250, E-mail: alisonp@clemson.edu.
Website: http://www.clemson.edu/education/departments/education-human-development/index.html

College of St. Joseph, Graduate Programs, Division of Psychology and Human Services, Program in Clinical Mental Health Counseling, Rutland, VT 05701-3899. Offers MS. *Program availability:* Part-time. *Degree requirements:* For master's, comprehensive exam. *Entrance requirements:* For master's, official college transcripts; 2 letters of reference. Additional exam requirements/recommendations for international students: required—TOEFL (minimum score 550 paper-based). Electronic applications accepted.

College of St. Joseph, Graduate Programs, Division of Psychology and Human Services, Program in Clinical Psychology, Rutland, VT 05701-3899. Offers MS. *Program availability:* Part-time, evening/weekend. *Degree requirements:* For master's, comprehensive exam, thesis optional. *Entrance requirements:* For master's, official college transcripts; 2 letters of reference. Additional exam requirements/recommendations for international students: required—TOEFL (minimum score 550 paper-based). Electronic applications accepted.

College of Staten Island of the City University of New York, Graduate Programs, Division of Humanities and Social Sciences, Program in Clinical Mental Health Counseling, Staten Island, NY 10314-6600. Offers clinical mental health counseling (MA). *Faculty:* 6. *Students:* 62. 67 applicants, 39% accepted, 2 enrolled. In 2019, 19 master's awarded. *Degree requirements:* For master's, 16 required courses, one practicum, three internship courses. *Entrance requirements:* For master's, BA/BS with a 3.0 GPA and 15-19 credits in certain areas of psychology. 2 letters of recommendation, a 1-2 page statement of experience and interest in the field. An on-site interview and writing sample will be completed if invited. Additional exam requirements/recommendations for international students: required—TOEFL (minimum score 600 paper-based; 100 iBT), IELTS (minimum score 7). *Application deadline:* For fall admission, 3/10 for domestic and international students. Applications are processed on a rolling basis. Application fee: $75. Electronic applications accepted. *Expenses: Tuition, area resident:* Full-time $11,090; part-time $470 per credit. Tuition, state resident: full-time $11,090; part-time $470 per credit. Tuition, nonresident: full-time $20,520; part-time $855 per credit. *International tuition:* $20,520 full-time. *Required fees:* $559; $181 per semester. Tuition and fees vary according to program. *Unit head:* Dr. Frances Melendez, Graduate Program Coordinator, 718-982-3960, E-mail: frances.melendez@csi.cuny.edu. *Application contact:* Sasha Spence, Associate Director for Graduate Admissions, 718-982-2019, Fax: 718-982-2500, E-mail: sasha.spence@csi.cuny.edu.
Website: https://www.csi.cuny.edu/admissions/graduate-admissions/graduate-programs-and-requirements/clinical-mental-health-counseling-ma

Columbus State University, Graduate Studies, College of Education and Health Professions, Department of Counseling, Foundations, and Leadership, Columbus, GA 31907-5645. Offers clinical mental health counseling (MS); curriculum and leadership (Ed D), including curriculum, educational leadership, higher education (M Ed, Ed D); educational leadership (M Ed, Ed S), including higher education (M Ed, Ed D); school counseling (M Ed, Ed S). *Accreditation:* ACA; NCATE. *Program availability:* Part-time, evening/weekend, 100% online, blended/hybrid learning. *Degree requirements:* For master's, thesis, exit exam; for doctorate, comprehensive exam, thesis/dissertation; for Ed S, thesis or alternative. *Entrance requirements:* For master's, GRE General Test, minimum undergraduate GPA of 2.75; for doctorate, GRE General Test, minimum graduate GPA of 3.5, four years of professional service; for Ed S, GRE General Test, minimum undergraduate GPA of 2.75, graduate 3.0. Additional exam requirements/recommendations for international students: required—TOEFL (minimum score 550 paper-based; 79 iBT). Electronic applications accepted. *Expenses: Tuition, area resident:* Full-time $210; part-time $210 per credit hour. Tuition, state resident: full-time $210; part-time $210 per credit hour. Tuition, nonresident: full-time $817; part-time $817 per credit hour. *International tuition:* $817 full-time. *Required fees:* $802.50. Tuition and fees vary according to course load, degree level and program.

Concordia University, School of Graduate Studies, Faculty of Arts and Science, Department of Psychology, PhD Program in Psychology, Montréal, QC H3G 1M8, Canada. Offers PhD, Certificate. *Degree requirements:* For doctorate, comprehensive exam, thesis/dissertation. *Entrance requirements:* For doctorate, master's degree in psychology.

Dalhousie University, Faculty of Science, Department of Psychology and Neuroscience, Halifax, NS B3H 4R2, Canada. Offers clinical psychology (PhD); psychology (M Sc, PhD); psychology/neuroscience (M Sc, PhD). *Degree requirements:* For master's, thesis; for doctorate, thesis/dissertation. *Entrance requirements:* For doctorate, GRE General Test. Additional exam requirements/recommendations for international students: required—TOEFL, IELTS, CANTEST, CAEL, or Michigan English Language Assessment Battery. Electronic applications accepted.

DePaul University, College of Education, Chicago, IL 60614. Offers bilingual-bicultural education (M Ed, MA); counseling (M Ed, MA), including clinical mental health counseling, college student development, school counseling; curriculum studies (M Ed, MA, Ed D); early childhood education (M Ed, MA, Ed D); educational leadership (M Ed, MA, Ed D), including Catholic leadership (M Ed, MA), general (M Ed, MA), higher education (M Ed, MA), physical education (M Ed, MA), principal preparation (M Ed), teacher preparation (M Ed); elementary education (M Ed, MA); middle grades education (M Ed); middle school mathematics education (MS); reading specialist (M Ed, MA); secondary education (M Ed, MA); social and cultural foundations in education (M Ed, MA); special education (M Ed); sport, fitness and recreation leadership (MS); value-creating education for global citizenship (M Ed); world languages education (M Ed, MA). *Program availability:* Part-time, evening/weekend, online learning. *Degree requirements:* For doctorate, thesis/dissertation. Electronic applications accepted.

Divine Mercy University, Institute for the Psychological Sciences, Arlington, VA 30327. Offers clinical psychology (Psy D). *Program availability:* Part-time. *Degree requirements:* For doctorate, comprehensive exam, thesis/dissertation. *Entrance requirements:* For doctorate, GRE. Additional exam requirements/recommendations for international students: required—TOEFL.

Divine Mercy University, School of Counseling, Arlington, VA 30327. Offers clinical mental health counseling (MS); psychology (MS). *Program availability:* Online learning.

Drexel University, College of Arts and Sciences, Department of Psychology, Clinical Psychology Program, Philadelphia, PA 19104-2875. Offers clinical psychology (PhD); forensic psychology (PhD); health psychology (PhD); neuropsychology (PhD). *Accreditation:* APA. Terminal master's awarded for partial completion of doctoral program. *Degree requirements:* For doctorate, thesis/dissertation, qualifying exam. *Entrance requirements:* For doctorate, GRE General Test, GRE Subject Test, minimum GPA of 3.0. Electronic applications accepted. *Expenses:* Contact institution.

Drexel University, College of Arts and Sciences, Department of Psychology, Program in Law-Psychology, Philadelphia, PA 19104-2875. Offers JD/PhD. Electronic applications accepted. *Expenses:* Contact institution.

Duke University, Graduate School, Department of Psychology and Neuroscience, Durham, NC 27708. Offers biological psychology (PhD); clinical psychology (PhD); cognitive psychology (PhD); developmental psychology (PhD); experimental psychology (PhD); health psychology (PhD); human social development (PhD); JD/MA. *Accreditation:* APA (one or more programs are accredited). *Degree requirements:* For doctorate, thesis/dissertation. *Entrance requirements:* For doctorate, GRE General Test. Additional exam requirements/recommendations for international students: required—TOEFL (minimum score 577 paper-based; 90 iBT) or IELTS (minimum score 7). Electronic applications accepted.

Duquesne University, Graduate School of Liberal Arts, Department of Psychology, Pittsburgh, PA 15282-0001. Offers clinical psychology (PhD). *Accreditation:* APA. *Degree requirements:* For doctorate, comprehensive exam, thesis/dissertation. *Entrance requirements:* For doctorate, GRE General Test, MA in psychology. Additional exam requirements/recommendations for international students: required—TOEFL. Electronic applications accepted.

Duquesne University, School of Education, Department of Counseling, Psychology, and Special Education, Program in Counselor Education, Pittsburgh, PA 15282-0001. Offers clinical mental health counseling (MS Ed, Post-Master's Certificate); counselor education and supervision (Ed D); counselor licensure (Post-Master's Certificate); marriage and family counseling (MS Ed); school counseling (MS Ed). *Accreditation:* ACA (one or more programs are accredited). *Program availability:* Part-time, evening/weekend. *Degree requirements:* For master's, thesis optional; for doctorate, thesis/dissertation. *Entrance requirements:* For master's, letters of recommendation, essay, interview, bachelor's degree; for doctorate, GRE, letters of recommendation, essay, interview, master's degree; for Post-Master's Certificate, GRE, letters of recommendation, essay, interview, bachelor's/master's degree. Additional exam requirements/recommendations for international students: required—TOEFL (minimum score 550 paper-based), IELTS (minimum score 6.5). Electronic applications accepted.

East Carolina University, Graduate School, College of Allied Health Sciences, Department of Addictions and Rehabilitation Studies, Greenville, NC 27858-4353. Offers clinical counseling (MS); military and trauma counseling (Certificate); rehabilitation and career counseling (MS); rehabilitation counseling (Certificate); rehabilitation counseling and administration (PhD); substance abuse counseling (Certificate); vocational evaluation (Certificate). *Accreditation:* CORE. *Program availability:* Part-time, evening/weekend. *Students:* Average age 33. 51 applicants, 73% accepted, 31 enrolled. In 2019, 19 master's, 5 doctorates, 34 other advanced degrees awarded. *Degree requirements:* For master's, comprehensive exam, thesis or alternative, internship; for doctorate, thesis/dissertation, internship. *Entrance requirements:* For master's and doctorate, GRE General Test or MAT. Additional exam requirements/recommendations for international students: recommended—TOEFL (minimum score 78 iBT), IELTS (minimum score 6.5). *Application deadline:* For fall admission, 3/1 priority date for domestic students; for spring admission, 10/1 priority date for domestic students. Applications are processed on a rolling basis. Application fee: $75. Electronic applications accepted. *Expenses: Tuition, area resident:* Full-time $4749; part-time $185 per credit hour. Tuition, state resident: full-time $4749; part-time $185 per credit hour. Tuition, nonresident: full-time $17,898; part-time $864 per credit hour. *International tuition:* $17,898 full-time. *Required fees:* $2787. *Financial support:* Research assistantships with partial tuition reimbursements, teaching assistantships with partial tuition reimbursements, Federal Work-Study, scholarships/grants, and unspecified assistantships available. Support available to part-time students. Financial award application deadline: 3/1; financial award applicants required to submit FAFSA. *Unit head:* Dr. Paul Toriello, Chair, 252-744-6292, E-mail: toriellop@ecu.edu. *Application contact:* Graduate School Admissions, 252-328-6013, Fax: 252-328-6071, E-mail: gradschool@ecu.edu.
Website: http://www.ecu.edu/rehb/

East Carolina University, Graduate School, Thomas Harriot College of Arts and Sciences, Department of Psychology, Greenville, NC 27858-4353. Offers health psychology (PhD), including clinical health psychology, occupational health psychology, pediatric school psychology; industrial and organizational psychology (MA); quantitative methods for the social and behavioral sciences (Certificate); MA/CAS. *Program availability:* Part-time, evening/weekend. *Application deadline:* For fall admission, 12/1 priority date for domestic and international students. *Expenses: Tuition, area resident:* Full-time $4749; part-time $185 per credit hour. Tuition, state resident: full-time $4749; part-time $185 per credit hour. Tuition, nonresident: full-time $17,898; part-time $864 per credit hour. *International tuition:* $17,898 full-time. *Required fees:* $2787. *Financial support:* Application deadline: 6/1. *Unit head:* Dr. Alan Christensen, Chair, E-mail: christensenal19@ecu.edu. *Application contact:* Graduate School Admissions, 252-328-6012, Fax: 252-328-6071, E-mail: gradschool@ecu.edu.
Website: https://psychology.ecu.edu/

East Central University, School of Graduate Studies, Department of Professional Programs in Human Services, Ada, OK 74820. Offers clinical rehabilitation and clinical mental health counseling (MSHR); criminal justice (MSHR); human resources (MSHR). *Accreditation:* CORE. *Program availability:* Part-time, evening/weekend. *Degree requirements:* For master's, thesis optional. *Entrance requirements:* For master's, GRE General Test, MAT, minimum GPA of 2.5. Electronic applications accepted.

Eastern Illinois University, Graduate School, College of Liberal Arts and Sciences, Department of Psychology, Charleston, IL 61920. Offers clinical psychology (MA); school psychology (SSP). *Program availability:* Part-time, evening/weekend. *Degree requirements:* For master's, comprehensive exam, thesis; for SSP, thesis. *Entrance requirements:* For master's and SSP, GMAT or GRE. Additional exam requirements/recommendations for international students: required—TOEFL (minimum score 500 paper-based; 61 iBT), IELTS (minimum score 6). Electronic applications accepted.

Eastern Kentucky University, The Graduate School, College of Arts and Sciences, Department of Psychology, Richmond, KY 40475-3102. Offers clinical psychology (MS); industrial/organizational psychology (MS); school psychology (Psy S). *Program availability:* Part-time. *Entrance requirements:* For master's and Psy S, GRE General Test, minimum GPA of 2.5.

Eastern Michigan University, Graduate School, College of Arts and Sciences, Department of Psychology, Ypsilanti, MI 48197. Offers clinical behavioral psychology (MS); clinical psychology (PhD); general clinical psychology (MS); general experimental psychology (MS). *Accreditation:* APA. *Faculty:* 24 full-time (14 women). *Students:* 41 full-time (36 women), 54 part-time (42 women); includes 31 minority (8 Black or African American, non-Hispanic/Latino; 1 American Indian or Alaska Native, non-Hispanic/Latino; 3 Asian, non-Hispanic/Latino; 11 Hispanic/Latino; 8 Two or more races, non-Hispanic/Latino), 5 international. Average age 26. 165 applicants, 25% accepted, 30 enrolled. In 2019, 25 master's, 7 doctorates awarded. *Entrance requirements:* For master's and doctorate, GRE. *Application deadline:* For fall admission, 2/15 for domestic students. Application fee: $45. *Financial support:* Fellowships available. *Unit head:* Dr. Ellen Koch, Interim Department Head, 734-487-1155, Fax: 734-487-6553, E-mail: ellen.koch@emich.edu. *Application contact:* Dr. Ellen Koch, Interim Department Head, 734-487-1155, Fax: 734-487-6553, E-mail: ellen.koch@emich.edu.

Eastern Virginia Medical School, The Virginia Consortium Program in Clinical Psychology, Norfolk, VA 23501-1980. Offers Psy D. *Entrance requirements:* For doctorate, GRE, BS in behavioral sciences or equivalent. Additional exam requirements/recommendations for international students: required—TOEFL. *Expenses:* Contact institution.

Eastern Washington University, Graduate Studies, College of Social Sciences, Department of Psychology, Cheney, WA 99004-2431. Offers clinical psychology (MS); experimental psychology (MS); mental health counseling (MS), including applied psychology, mental health counseling; school counseling (MS), including applied psychology, school counseling; school psychology respecialization (Ed S). *Faculty:* 22 full-time (15 women). *Students:* 119 full-time (94 women), 13 part-time (10 women); includes 3 minority (all Hispanic/Latino), 6 international. Average age 34. 83 applicants, 42% accepted, 31 enrolled. In 2019, 49 master's awarded. *Degree requirements:* For master's, comprehensive exam, thesis or alternative. *Entrance requirements:* For master's, GRE General Test, minimum GPA of 3.0. Additional exam requirements/recommendations for international students: required—TOEFL (minimum score 580 paper-based; 92 iBT), IELTS (minimum score 7), PTE (minimum score 63). *Application deadline:* For fall admission, 3/1 for domestic students. Applications are processed on a rolling basis. Application fee: $75. Electronic applications accepted. *Financial support:* Teaching assistantships with partial tuition reimbursements, career-related internships or fieldwork, Federal Work-Study, institutionally sponsored loans, scholarships/grants, health care benefits, tuition waivers (partial), and unspecified assistantships available. Support available to part-time students. Financial award application deadline: 2/1; financial award applicants required to submit FAFSA. *Unit head:* Dennis Anderson, 509-359-2087, E-mail: danderson2@ewu.edu. *Application contact:* Kathy White, Advisor/Recruiter for Graduate Studies, 509-359-6297, Fax: 509-359-6044, E-mail: gradprograms@ewu.edu.

East Tennessee State University, College of Graduate and Continuing Studies, Clemmer College, Department of Counseling and Human Services, Johnson City, TN 37614. Offers clinical mental health counseling (MA); college counseling/student affairs higher education (MA); couples and family therapy (MA); human services (MS); school counseling (MA). *Accreditation:* ACA; NCATE. *Program availability:* Part-time. *Degree requirements:* For master's, comprehensive exam, thesis optional, internship, student teaching, culminating experience. *Entrance requirements:* For master's, GRE General Test, minimum GPA of 3.0, three letters of recommendation, interview, 2-3 page essay detailing experiences that have shaped pursuit of degree, resume. Additional exam requirements/recommendations for international students: required—TOEFL (minimum score 550 paper-based; 79 iBT). Electronic applications accepted.

East Tennessee State University, College of Graduate and Continuing Studies, College of Arts and Sciences, Department of Psychology, Johnson City, TN 37614. Offers clinical psychology (PhD); experimental psychology (PhD). *Accreditation:* APA. Terminal master's awarded for partial completion of doctoral program. *Degree requirements:* For doctorate, thesis/dissertation, externship. *Entrance requirements:* For doctorate, GRE General Test, minimum GPA of 3.0, three letters of recommendation, interview, minimum of 18 semester hours in undergraduate psychology. Additional exam requirements/recommendations for international students: required—TOEFL (minimum score 550 paper-based; 79 iBT). Electronic applications accepted.

Edinboro University of Pennsylvania, Department of Counseling, School Psychology and Special Education, Edinboro, PA 16444. Offers counseling (MA), including art therapy, clinical mental health counseling, college counseling, rehabilitation counseling, school counseling; educational psychology (M Ed); school psychology (Ed S); special education (M Ed), including autism, behavior management. *Accreditation:* ACA. *Program availability:* Part-time, evening/weekend. *Faculty:* 19 full-time (13 women), 2 part-time/adjunct (1 woman). *Students:* 180 full-time (146 women), 215 part-time (186 women); includes 42 minority (18 Black or African American, non-Hispanic/Latino; 2 American Indian or Alaska Native, non-Hispanic/Latino; 4 Asian, non-Hispanic/Latino; 12 Hispanic/Latino; 1 Native Hawaiian or other Pacific Islander, non-Hispanic/Latino; 5 Two or more races, non-Hispanic/Latino), 3 international. Average age 31. 197 applicants, 63% accepted, 71 enrolled. In 2019, 87 master's, 8 other advanced degrees awarded. *Degree requirements:* For master's, thesis or alternative, competency exam; for Ed S, thesis or alternative. *Entrance requirements:* For master's and Ed S, GRE or MAT, minimum QPA of 2.5. Additional exam requirements/recommendations for international students: required—TOEFL (minimum score 550 paper-based; 213 iBT), IELTS (minimum score 6.5). *Application deadline:* Applications are processed on a rolling basis. Application fee: $30. Electronic applications accepted. *Expenses: Tuition, area resident:* Full-time $11,261; part-time $625.60 per credit. Tuition, state resident: full-time $11,261; part-time $625.60 per credit. Tuition, nonresident: full-time $16,850; part-time $936.10 per credit. *International tuition:* $16,850 full-time. *Required fees:* $57.75 per credit. *Financial support:* In 2019–20, 35 students received support. Research assistantships with tuition reimbursements available, career-related internships or fieldwork, Federal Work-Study, scholarships/grants, and unspecified assistantships available. Support available to part-time students. Financial award application deadline: 2/15; financial award applicants required to submit FAFSA. *Unit head:* Dr. Penelope Orr, Chairperson, 814-732-1684, E-mail: porr@edinboro.edu. *Application contact:* Dr. Penelope Orr, Chairperson, 814-732-1684, E-mail: porr@edinboro.edu.
Website: https://www.edinboro.edu/academics/schools-and-departments/soe/departments/cspe/

Emory University, Laney Graduate School, Department of Psychology, Atlanta, GA 30322-1100. Offers clinical psychology (PhD); cognition and development (PhD); neuroscience and animal behavior (PhD). *Accreditation:* APA. *Degree requirements:* For doctorate, comprehensive exam, thesis/dissertation. *Entrance requirements:* For doctorate, GRE General Test, minimum GPA of 3.25. Additional exam requirements/recommendations for international students: required—TOEFL. Electronic applications accepted.

Emporia State University, Program in Clinical Psychology, Emporia, KS 66801-5415. Offers MS. *Program availability:* Part-time. *Degree requirements:* For master's, comprehensive exam, clinical internship. *Entrance requirements:* For master's, GRE or MAT, 24 hours of course work in undergraduate psychology, 3 letters of recommendation. Additional exam requirements/recommendations for international students: required—TOEFL (minimum score 520 paper-based; 68 iBT). Electronic applications accepted. *Expenses: Tuition, area resident:* Full-time $6394; part-time $266.41 per credit hour. Tuition, state resident: full-time $6394; part-time $266.41 per credit hour. Tuition, nonresident: full-time $20,128; part-time $828.66 per credit hour. *International tuition:* $20,128 full-time. *Required fees:* $2183; $90.95 per credit hour. Tuition and fees vary according to campus/location and program.

Evangel University, Department of Behavioral and Social Sciences, Springfield, MO 65802. Offers clinical mental health counseling (MS). *Program availability:* Part-time. *Degree requirements:* For master's, comprehensive exam. *Entrance requirements:* For master's, GRE General Test, minimum undergraduate GPA of 3.0. Additional exam requirements/recommendations for international students: required—TOEFL (minimum score 550 paper-based). Electronic applications accepted. Application fee is waived when completed online.

Fairfield University, Graduate School of Education and Allied Professions, Fairfield, CT 06824. Offers applied behavior analysis (ATC); applied psychology (MA); clinical mental health counseling (MA, CAS); educational technology (MA); elementary education (MA, CAS); family studies (MA); integration of spirituality and religion in counseling (ATC); marriage and family therapy (MA); reading and language development (Sixth Year Certificate); school counseling (MA, CAS); school psychology (MA, CAS); school-based marriage and family therapy (ATC); secondary education (MA); special education (MA, CAS); substance abuse counseling (ATC); teaching (Certificate); teaching and foundations (MA, CAS); TESOL, world languages, and bilingual education (MA, CAS). *Accreditation:* NCATE. *Program availability:* Part-time, evening/weekend. *Faculty:* 24 full-time (18 women), 28 part-time/adjunct (20 women). *Students:* 169 full-time (149 women), 227 part-time (187 women); includes 96 minority (21 Black or African American, non-Hispanic/Latino; 8 Asian, non-Hispanic/Latino; 60 Hispanic/Latino; 7 Two or more races, non-Hispanic/Latino), 1 international. Average age 31. 194 applicants, 60% accepted, 101 enrolled. In 2019, 136 master's, 28 other advanced degrees awarded. *Degree requirements:* For master's, comprehensive exam. *Entrance requirements:* For master's, One of the following for certification programs: Praxis Core, SAT, ACT, or GRE, minimum GPA of 3.0, 2 recommendations, resume. Additional exam requirements/recommendations for international students: required—TOEFL (minimum score 550 paper-based; 84 iBT), IELTS (minimum score 7.5), TOEFL (minimum score 550 paper-based; 84 iBT) or IELTS (minimum score 7.5). *Application deadline:* For fall admission, 2/15 for international students; for spring admission, 10/1 for international students. Application fee: $60. Electronic applications accepted. *Expenses:* Tuition $815/credit hour; Lab Fee (ED598) $300/semester; Lab Fee (CN457,CN467, PY538, PY540) $70/course; Wilson Reading Course Fee $141/credit hour; Registration Fee $50/semester; Graduate Student Activity Fee (Fall and Spring) $65/semester. *Financial support:* In 2019–20, 34 students received support. Career-related internships or fieldwork and unspecified assistantships available. Support available to part-time students. Financial award applicants required to submit FAFSA. *Unit head:* Dr. Laurie Grupp, Dean, 203-254-4250, Fax: 203-254-4241, E-mail: lgrupp@fairfield.edu. *Application contact:* Melanie Rogers, Director of Graduate Admission, 203-254-4184, Fax: 203-254-4073, E-mail: gradadmis@fairfield.edu.
Website: http://www.fairfield.edu/gseap

Fairleigh Dickinson University, Florham Campus, Maxwell Becton College of Arts and Sciences, Department of Psychology, Program in Clinical Mental Health Counseling, Madison, NJ 07940-1099. Offers MA. *Accreditation:* ACA.

Fairleigh Dickinson University, Metropolitan Campus, University College: Arts, Sciences, and Professional Studies, School of Psychology, Program in Clinical Psychology, Teaneck, NJ 07666-1914. Offers MA, PhD. *Accreditation:* APA.

Fairleigh Dickinson University, Metropolitan Campus, University College: Arts, Sciences, and Professional Studies, School of Psychology, Program in Clinical Psychopharmacology, Teaneck, NJ 07666-1914. Offers MA.

Fielding Graduate University, Graduate Programs, School of Psychology, Programs in Clinical Psychology, Santa Barbara, CA 93105-3814. Offers clinical psychology (PhD, Postbaccalaureate Certificate); respecialization in clinical psychology (Post-Doctoral Certificate). *Program availability:* Part-time, evening/weekend, 100% online, blended/hybrid learning. *Degree requirements:* For doctorate, thesis/dissertation. *Entrance requirements:* For doctorate, bachelor's degree, minimum GPA of 3.0, curriculum vitae, statement of purpose, critical thinking writing sample, 3 letters of recommendation, official transcript; for other advanced degree, bachelor's degree (for Postbaccalaureate Certificate); doctoral degree in psychology (for Post-Doctoral Certificate); minimum GPA of 3.0, curriculum vitae, statement of purpose, 3 letters of recommendation, official transcript. Electronic applications accepted. *Expenses:* Contact institution.

Fisk University, Division of Graduate Studies, Department of Psychology, Nashville, TN 37208-3051. Offers clinical psychology (MA); psychology (MA). *Degree requirements:* For master's, thesis. *Entrance requirements:* For master's, GRE General Test, GRE Subject Test, minimum GPA of 3.0. Electronic applications accepted.

Florida Gulf Coast University, Elaine Nicpon Marieb College of Health and Human Services, Program in School Counseling, Fort Myers, FL 33965-6565. Offers clinical mental health counseling (MA); school counseling (MA). *Accreditation:* ACA. *Program availability:* Part-time, evening/weekend. *Degree requirements:* For master's, thesis or alternative. *Entrance requirements:* For master's, GRE General Test, MAT, minimum GPA of 3.0. Additional exam requirements/recommendations for international students: required—TOEFL (minimum score 550 paper-based). Electronic applications accepted. *Expenses: Tuition, area resident:* Full-time $6974; part-time $4350 per credit hour. Tuition, state resident: full-time $6974; part-time $4350 per credit hour. Tuition, nonresident: full-time $28,169; part-time $17,595 per credit hour. *International tuition:* $28,169 full-time. *Required fees:* $2027; $1267 per credit hour. $507 per semester. Tuition and fees vary according to course load.

Florida Institute of Technology, College of Psychology and Liberal Arts, Program in Clinical Psychology, Melbourne, FL 32901-6975. Offers clinical psychology (Psy D). *Accreditation:* APA. *Degree requirements:* For doctorate, comprehensive exam, thesis/dissertation or alternative, minimum of 4 years residency on campus (full-time status), minimum 123 credit hours beyond bachelor's degree, CPE exam, 2nd-year student review, minimum GPA of 3.2, research project, accredited internship of at least 2,000 hours. *Entrance requirements:* For doctorate, GRE General Test, GRE Subject Test (psychology), résumé of professional experience; statement of professional career objectives; 3 letters of recommendation from psychologists familiar with the applicant's academic and/or clinical work, to be mailed directly by the recommenders (forms are available online from the graduate admissions website at www.fit.edu/grad/forms/php); transcripts. Additional exam requirements/recommendations for international students: required—TOEFL (minimum score 550 paper-based; 79 iBT). Electronic applications accepted.

Florida International University, College of Arts, Sciences, and Education, Department of Psychology, Miami, FL 33199. Offers behavioral analysis (MS); clinical science (PhD); cognitive neuroscience (PhD); counseling psychology (MS); developmental science (MS, PhD); legal psychology (MS, PhD); organizational psychology (MS, PhD). *Accreditation:* APA. *Program availability:* Part-time, evening/weekend. *Faculty:* 52 full-time (33 women), 50 part-time/adjunct (37 women). *Students:* 203 full-time (159 women), 2 part-time (both women); includes 117 minority (15 Black or African American, non-Hispanic/Latino; 8 Asian, non-Hispanic/Latino; 86 Hispanic/

Latino; 8 Two or more races, non-Hispanic/Latino), 15 international. Average age 26. 410 applicants, 19% accepted, 60 enrolled. In 2019, 57 master's, 7 doctorates awarded. Terminal master's awarded for partial completion of doctoral program. *Degree requirements:* For master's, thesis; for doctorate, comprehensive exam, thesis/dissertation. *Entrance requirements:* For master's, GRE General Test, minimum GPA of 3.0, resume, 3 letters of recommendation; for doctorate, GRE General Test, 3 letters of recommendation, resume, letter of intent, two writing samples, minimum GPA of 3.0. Additional exam requirements/recommendations for international students: required—TOEFL (minimum score 550 paper-based; 80 iBT). *Application deadline:* For fall admission, 12/15 for domestic and international students. Application fee: $30. Electronic applications accepted. *Expenses: Tuition, area resident:* Full-time $8912; part-time $446 per credit hour. Tuition, state resident: full-time $8912; part-time $446 per credit hour. Tuition, nonresident: full-time $21,393; part-time $992 per credit hour. *Required fees:* $2194. *Financial support:* Institutionally sponsored loans and scholarships/grants available. Financial award application deadline: 3/1. *Unit head:* Dr. Jeremy Pettit, Interim Chair, 305-348-1671, Fax: 305-348-2880, E-mail: jeremy.pettit@fiu.edu. *Application contact:* Nanett Rojas, Manager, Admissions Operations, 305-348-7464, Fax: 305-348-7441, E-mail: gradadm@fiu.edu.

Florida State University, The Graduate School, Department of Anthropology, Department of Psychology, Program in Clinical Psychology, Tallahassee, FL 32306-4301. Offers PhD. *Accreditation:* APA. *Faculty:* 13 full-time (5 women). *Students:* 60 full-time (43 women), 5 part-time (4 women); includes 18 minority (9 Asian, non-Hispanic/Latino; 5 Hispanic/Latino; 4 Two or more races, non-Hispanic/Latino), 3 international. Average age 27. 213 applicants, 8% accepted, 11 enrolled. In 2019, 12 doctorates awarded. Terminal master's awarded for partial completion of doctoral program. *Degree requirements:* For doctorate, comprehensive exam, thesis/dissertation. *Entrance requirements:* For doctorate, GRE General Test, minimum GPA of 3.3, research experience, letters of recommendation. Additional exam requirements/recommendations for international students: required—TOEFL (minimum score 80 iBT). *Application deadline:* For fall admission, 12/1 for domestic and international students. Application fee: $30. Electronic applications accepted. *Financial support:* In 2019–20, 58 students received support, including 9 fellowships with full tuition reimbursements available (averaging $24,324 per year), 23 research assistantships with full tuition reimbursements available (averaging $24,324 per year), 21 teaching assistantships with full tuition reimbursements available (averaging $24,324 per year); career-related internships or fieldwork, traineeships, and health care benefits also available. Financial award application deadline: 12/1; financial award applicants required to submit FAFSA. *Unit head:* Dr. Jesse Cougle, Director, 850-645-8729, Fax: 850-644-7739, E-mail: cougle@psy.fsu.edu. *Application contact:* Lynda L. Gibson, Graduate Program Associate, 850-644-2499, Fax: 850-644-7739, E-mail: grad-info@psy.fsu.edu. Website: http://www.psy.fsu.edu/

Fordham University, Graduate School of Arts and Sciences, Department of Psychology, Program in Clinical Psychology, New York, NY 10458. Offers PhD. *Students:* Average age 30. 607 applicants, 2% accepted, 9 enrolled. In 2019, 13 doctorates awarded. Terminal master's awarded for partial completion of doctoral program. *Degree requirements:* For doctorate, comprehensive exam, thesis/dissertation, clinical internship. *Entrance requirements:* For doctorate, GRE General Test, GRE Subject Test. Additional exam requirements/recommendations for international students: required—TOEFL (minimum score 600 paper-based). *Application deadline:* For fall admission, 12/14 for domestic students. Application fee: $70. Electronic applications accepted. *Financial support:* In 2019–20, 55 students received support, including 8 fellowships with tuition reimbursements available (averaging $26,390 per year), 10 research assistantships with tuition reimbursements available (averaging $12,285 per year), 7 teaching assistantships with tuition reimbursements available (averaging $12,871 per year); career-related internships or fieldwork, institutionally sponsored loans, tuition waivers (full and partial), and unspecified assistantships also available. Financial award application deadline: 12/14. *Unit head:* Dr. Monica Rivera-Mindt, Program Director, 212-636-7453, E-mail: riveramindt@fordham.edu. *Application contact:* Garrett Marino, Director of Graduate Admissions, 718-817-4419, Fax: 718-817-3566, E-mail: gmarino10@fordham.edu.

Franciscan University of Steubenville, Graduate Programs, Department of Clinical Mental Health Counseling, Steubenville, OH 43952-1763. Offers MA. *Accreditation:* ACA. *Program availability:* Part-time. *Degree requirements:* For master's, case presentation, integrative paper. *Entrance requirements:* For master's, GRE General Test or MAT for those with a GPA below 3.0, minimum undergraduate GPA of 2.5. Additional exam requirements/recommendations for international students: required—TOEFL. Electronic applications accepted. *Expenses:* Contact institution.

Francis Marion University, Graduate Programs, Department of Psychology, Florence, SC 29502-0547. Offers applied psychology (MS), including clinical/counseling psychology, school psychology; school psychology (SSP). *Program availability:* Part-time, evening/weekend. *Degree requirements:* For master's, internship. *Entrance requirements:* For master's, GRE General Test, official transcripts, two letters of recommendation. Additional exam requirements/recommendations for international students: required—TOEFL (minimum score 550 paper-based; 79 iBT). *Expenses: Tuition, area resident:* Full-time $10,612; part-time $530.60 per credit hour. Tuition, state resident: full-time $10,612; part-time $530.60 per credit hour. Tuition, nonresident: full-time $21,224; part-time $1061.20 per credit hour. *International tuition:* $21,224 full-time. *Required fees:* $312; $156 per credit hour. $332 per semester. Tuition and fees vary according to program.

Fuller Theological Seminary, Graduate Programs, Pasadena, CA 91182. Offers Christian leadership (MACL); clinical psychology (PhD, Psy D); family studies (MA); global leadership (MA); global ministries (D Min); global ministries (Korean language) (D Min); intercultural studies (MA, Th M, PhD); intercultural studies (Korean language) (MA); marital and family therapy (MS); marriage and family enrichment (Certificate); ministry (M Div, D Min); missiology (D Miss); missiology (Korean language) (Th M); theology (MA, Th M, PhD), including evangelism (MA), family life education (MA), pastoral ministry (MA), recovery ministry (MA), worship music ministry (MA), worship, theology, and the arts (MA), youth, family, and culture (MA); theology and ministry (MA).

Gallaudet University, The Graduate School, Washington, DC 20002. Offers American Sign Language/English bilingual early childhood deaf education: birth to 5 (Certificate); audiology (Au D); clinical psychology (PhD); deaf and hard of hearing infants, toddlers, and their families (Certificate); deaf education (MA, Ed S); deaf history (Certificate); deaf studies (Certificate); educating deaf students with disabilities (Certificate); education: teacher preparation (MA), including deaf education, early childhood education and deaf education, elementary education and deaf education, secondary education and deaf education; educational neuroscience (PhD); hearing, speech and language sciences (MS, PhD); international development (MA); interpretation (MA, PhD), including combined interpreting practice and research (MA), interpreting research (MA); linguistics (MA, PhD); mental health counseling (MA); peer mentoring (Certificate); public administration (MPA); school counseling (MA); school psychology (Psy S); sign language teaching (MA); social work (MSW); speech-language pathology (MS). *Program availability:* Part-time. *Faculty:* 101 full-time (70 women). *Students:* 267 full-time (208 women), 139 part-time (95 women); includes 120 minority (38 Black or African

American, non-Hispanic/Latino; 20 Asian, non-Hispanic/Latino; 44 Hispanic/Latino; 18 Two or more races, non-Hispanic/Latino), 19 international. Average age 30. 484 applicants, 50% accepted, 162 enrolled. In 2019, 138 master's, 25 doctorates, 14 other advanced degrees awarded. Terminal master's awarded for partial completion of doctoral program. *Degree requirements:* For master's, comprehensive exam (for some programs), thesis optional; for doctorate, comprehensive exam, thesis/dissertation. *Entrance requirements:* For master's and doctorate, GRE General Test or MAT, letters of recommendation, interviews, goals statement, American Sign Language proficiency interview, written English competency. Additional exam requirements/recommendations for international students: required—TOEFL. *Application deadline:* For fall admission, 2/15 for domestic students. Applications are processed on a rolling basis. Application fee: $75. Electronic applications accepted. *Expenses: Tuition:* Full-time $18,180; part-time $688 per credit. *Required fees:* $526; $526. Tuition and fees vary according to course load. *Financial support:* In 2019–20, 50 students received support. Fellowships, research assistantships, teaching assistantships, career-related internships or fieldwork, Federal Work-Study, scholarships/grants, tuition waivers (partial), and unspecified assistantships available. Support available to part-time students. Financial award application deadline: 7/1; financial award applicants required to submit FAFSA. *Unit head:* Dr. Gaurav Mathur, Dean, Graduate School and Continuing Studies, 202-250-2380, Fax: 202-651-5027, E-mail: gaurav.mathur@gallaudet.edu. *Application contact:* Heidi Zornes-Foster, Senior Graduate Admissions Counselor, 202-650-5436, Fax: 202-651-5295, E-mail: graduate.school@gallaudet.edu. Website: www.gallaudet.edu

Gannon University, School of Graduate Studies, College of Humanities, Education, and Social Sciences, School of Humanities, Program in Clinical Mental Health Counseling, Erie, PA 16541-0001. Offers MS. *Accreditation:* ACA. *Program availability:* Part-time, evening/weekend. *Degree requirements:* For master's, thesis, internship. *Entrance requirements:* For master's, bachelor's degree from approved institution, resume, 3 letters of recommendation, essay, interview, minimum GPA of 2.8, PA child abuse clearances and PA State Police criminal record check dated within a year of application. Additional exam requirements/recommendations for international students: required—TOEFL (minimum score 79 iBT). Electronic applications accepted. Application fee is waived when completed online.

Geneva College, Master of Arts in Counseling Program, Beaver Falls, PA 15010. Offers clinical mental health counseling (MA); marriage and family counseling (MA); school counseling (MA). *Accreditation:* ACA. *Program availability:* Part-time, evening/weekend, online only, 100% online, blended/hybrid learning. *Faculty:* 4 full-time (1 woman), 5 part-time/adjunct (2 women). *Students:* 26 full-time (20 women), 22 part-time (17 women); includes 11 minority (9 Black or African American, non-Hispanic/Latino; 1 Asian, non-Hispanic/Latino; 1 Two or more races, non-Hispanic/Latino), 1 international. Average age 33. 24 applicants, 63% accepted, 14 enrolled. In 2019, 34 master's awarded. *Degree requirements:* For master's, comprehensive exam, 60 credits including practicum and internship. *Entrance requirements:* For master's, minimum GPA of 3.0 (preferred), 3 letters of recommendation, essay on career goals, resume of educational and professional experiences. Additional exam requirements/recommendations for international students: required—TOEFL. *Application deadline:* For fall admission, 9/1 for domestic students; for spring admission, 1/10 for domestic students. Applications are processed on a rolling basis. Electronic applications accepted. *Expenses:* $680 per credit. 60 credits required for graduation. *Financial support:* Research assistantships, teaching assistantships, career-related internships or fieldwork, and unspecified assistantships available. Financial award application deadline: 8/1; financial award applicants required to submit FAFSA. *Unit head:* Dr. Shannan Shiderly, Program Director, 724-847-6649, Fax: 724-847-6101, E-mail: slshider@geneva.edu. *Application contact:* Marina Frazier, Graduate Program Manager, 724-847-6697, E-mail: counseling@geneva.edu. Website: https://www.geneva.edu/graduate/counseling/

George Fox University, College of Education, Graduate Department of Counseling, Newberg, OR 97132-2697. Offers clinical mental health counseling (MA); marriage, couple and family counseling (MA, Certificate); school counseling (MA, Certificate); school psychology (Ed S). *Program availability:* Part-time. *Degree requirements:* For master's, clinical project. *Entrance requirements:* For master's, MAT or GRE, bachelor's degree from regionally-accredited college or university, minimum cumulative GPA of 3.0, 1 professional and 1 academic reference, resume, on-campus interview, official transcripts. Additional exam requirements/recommendations for international students: required—TOEFL (minimum score 577 paper-based; 90 iBT), IELTS (minimum score 7). Electronic applications accepted. *Expenses:* Contact institution.

George Fox University, Program in Clinical Psychology, Newberg, OR 97132-2697. Offers Psy D. *Accreditation:* APA. *Degree requirements:* For doctorate, thesis/dissertation, internship. *Entrance requirements:* For doctorate, GRE General Test, bachelor's degree from regionally-accredited university or college, minimum undergraduate GPA of 3.0 during previous 2 years, interview, official transcripts. Additional exam requirements/recommendations for international students: required—TOEFL (minimum score 80 iBT), IELTS (minimum score 6.5). Electronic applications accepted. *Expenses:* Contact institution.

George Mason University, College of Humanities and Social Sciences, Department of Psychology, Fairfax, VA 22030. Offers applied developmental psychology (MA, PhD); clinical psychology (PhD); cognitive and behavioral neuroscience (MA, PhD); cognitive neuroscience (Certificate); human factors/applied cognition (MA, PhD, Certificate), including transportation human factors (Certificate), usability (Certificate); industrial/organizational psychology (MA, PhD). *Accreditation:* APA. *Degree requirements:* For master's, comprehensive exam, thesis or practicum research; for doctorate, comprehensive exam, thesis/dissertation, 2nd-year project. *Entrance requirements:* For master's, GRE, 2 official transcripts; goals statement; 15 undergraduate credits in concentration for which the applicant is applying; for doctorate, GRE, 3 letters of recommendation; resume; goals statement; minimum GPA of 3.0 overall for last 60 undergraduate credits, 3.25 in psychology courses; 15 undergraduate credits in concentration for which the applicant is applying; 2 official transcripts; for Certificate, GRE, 2 official transcripts; expanded goals statement; 3 letters of recommendation. Additional exam requirements/recommendations for international students: required—TOEFL (minimum score 575 paper-based; 88 iBT), IELTS (minimum score 6.5), PTE (minimum score 59). Electronic applications accepted.

The George Washington University, Columbian College of Arts and Sciences, Department of Psychology, Washington, DC 20052. Offers applied social psychology (PhD); clinical psychology (PhD); cognitive neuroscience (PhD). *Accreditation:* APA. *Program availability:* Part-time, evening/weekend. *Degree requirements:* For doctorate, thesis/dissertation or alternative, general exam. *Entrance requirements:* For doctorate, GRE General Test, minimum GPA of 3.0. Additional exam requirements/recommendations for international students: required—TOEFL (minimum score 550 paper-based; 80 iBT).

The George Washington University, Graduate School of Education and Human Development, Department of Counseling and Human Development, Program in Clinical Mental Health Counseling, Washington, DC 20052. Offers MA. *Entrance requirements:* For master's, GRE or MAT, two letters of recommendation, 1- to 2-page statement of purpose, official transcripts from all institutions attended, resume. Additional exam requirements/recommendations for international students: required—TOEFL or IELTS.

Georgian Court University, School of Arts and Sciences, Lakewood, NJ 08701. Offers applied behavior analysis (MA); autism spectrum disorders (Certificate); clinical mental health counseling (MA); criminal justice and human rights (MS); holistic health studies (MA); homeland security (Certificate); instructional technology (CPC); integrative health (Certificate); mercy spirituality (Certificate); parish business management (Certificate); professional counselor (Certificate); school psychology (MA, Certificate); theology (MA, Certificate). *Program availability:* Part-time, evening/weekend. *Faculty:* 19 full-time (11 women), 7 part-time/adjunct (3 women). *Students:* 90 full-time (80 women), 71 part-time (59 women); includes 26 minority (8 Black or African American, non-Hispanic/Latino; 2 Asian, non-Hispanic/Latino; 14 Hispanic/Latino; 2 Two or more races, non-Hispanic/Latino), 1 international. Average age 32. 138 applicants, 58% accepted, 57 enrolled. In 2019, 68 master's, 19 other advanced degrees awarded. *Degree requirements:* For master's, comprehensive exam (for some programs), thesis (for some programs); for other advanced degree, comprehensive exam (for some programs). *Entrance requirements:* Additional exam requirements/recommendations for international students: required—TOEFL (minimum score 550 paper-based; 79 iBT). *Application deadline:* For fall admission, 8/15 for domestic students, 5/1 for international students; for spring admission, 1/15 for domestic students, 10/1 for international students. Applications are processed on a rolling basis. Application fee: $40. Electronic applications accepted. *Financial support:* Scholarships/grants, health care benefits, and unspecified assistantships available. Financial award application deadline: 4/15; financial award applicants required to submit FAFSA. *Unit head:* Dr. Mary Chinery, Dean, 732-987-2493, Fax: 732-987-2007, E-mail: mchinery@georgian.edu. *Application contact:* Dr. Mary Chinery, Dean, 732-987-2493, Fax: 732-987-2007, E-mail: mchinery@georgian.edu.
Website: https://georgian.edu/academics/school-of-arts-sciences/

Georgia Southern University, Jack N. Averitt College of Graduate Studies, College of Behavioral and Social Sciences, Program in Psychology, Statesboro, GA 30460. Offers clinical psychology (Psy D); psychology (MS). *Faculty:* 27 full-time (14 women), 1 (woman) part-time/adjunct. *Students:* 55 full-time (40 women), 8 part-time (5 women); includes 16 minority (4 Black or African American, non-Hispanic/Latino; 2 Asian, non-Hispanic/Latino; 9 Hispanic/Latino; 1 Two or more races, non-Hispanic/Latino), 1 international. Average age 25. 33 applicants, 58% accepted, 14 enrolled. In 2019, 17 master's, 6 doctorates awarded. Terminal master's awarded for partial completion of doctoral program. *Degree requirements:* For master's, comprehensive exam, thesis (for some programs), terminal exam; for doctorate, comprehensive exam, thesis/dissertation, clinical qualifying exam, practicum, internship. *Entrance requirements:* For master's, GRE General Test, minimum GPA of 3.0, introductory courses in psychology and statistics, letters of recommendation; for doctorate, GRE General Test; GRE Subject Test (if no undergraduate degree in psychology), minimum undergraduate GPA of 3.25; 3 letters of reference; statement of purpose. Additional exam requirements/recommendations for international students: required—TOEFL (minimum score 550 paper-based; 80 iBT), IELTS (minimum score 6). *Application deadline:* For fall admission, 1/15 priority date for domestic students, 1/15 for international students. Application fee: $50. Electronic applications accepted. *Expenses: Tuition, area resident:* Full-time $4986; part-time $277 per credit hour. Tuition, nonresident: full-time $19,890; part-time $1105 per credit hour. *International tuition:* $19,890 full-time. *Required fees:* $2114; $1057 per semester. $1057 per semester. Tuition and fees vary according to course load, campus/location and program. *Financial support:* In 2019–20, 46 students received support, including 4 fellowships with full tuition reimbursements available (averaging $7,750 per year), 6 research assistantships with full tuition reimbursements available (averaging $7,750 per year), 17 teaching assistantships with full tuition reimbursements available (averaging $7,750 per year); career-related internships or fieldwork, Federal Work-Study, scholarships/grants, tuition waivers (full), and unspecified assistantships also available. Support available to part-time students. Financial award application deadline: 4/15; financial award applicants required to submit FAFSA. *Unit head:* Dr. Ty W. Boyer, Graduate Director, 912-478-5539, Fax: 912-478-0751, E-mail: tboyer@georgiasouthern.edu.
Website: http://class.georgiasouthern.edu/psychology/

Georgia State University, College of Arts and Sciences, Department of Psychology, Atlanta, GA 30302-3083. Offers clinical psychology (PhD); cognitive sciences (PhD); community psychology (PhD); developmental psychology (PhD); neuropsychology and behavioral neuroscience (PhD). *Accreditation:* APA. *Faculty:* 29 full-time (17 women). *Students:* 107 full-time (85 women), 2 part-time (both women); includes 23 minority (9 Black or African American, non-Hispanic/Latino; 6 Asian, non-Hispanic/Latino; 7 Hispanic/Latino; 1 Two or more races, non-Hispanic/Latino), 13 international. Average age 28. 498 applicants, 5% accepted, 17 enrolled. In 2019, 18 doctorates awarded. *Entrance requirements:* For doctorate, GRE. Additional exam requirements/recommendations for international students: required—TOEFL (minimum score 550 paper-based; 80 iBT). *Application deadline:* For fall admission, 12/1 for domestic and international students. Application fee: $50. Electronic applications accepted. *Expenses: Tuition, area resident:* Full-time $7164; part-time $398 per credit hour. Tuition, state resident: full-time $7164; part-time $398 per credit hour. Tuition, nonresident: full-time $22,662; part-time $1259 per credit hour. *International tuition:* $22,662 full-time. *Required fees:* $2128; $312 per credit hour. Tuition and fees vary according to course load and program. *Financial support:* In 2019–20, fellowships with full tuition reimbursements (averaging $19,282 per year), research assistantships with full tuition reimbursements (averaging $5,173 per year), teaching assistantships with full tuition reimbursements (averaging $6,389 per year) were awarded; scholarships/grants, traineeships, health care benefits, and unspecified assistantships also available. Financial award applicants required to submit FAFSA. *Unit head:* Dr. Lisa Armistead, Professor, Associate Provost for Graduate Programs, 404-413-2091, Fax: 404-413-6207, E-mail: lparmistead@gsu.edu. *Application contact:* Dr. Lindsey Cohen, Director of Graduate Studies, 404-413-6263, Fax: 404-413-6207, E-mail: llcohen@gsu.edu.
Website: https://psychology.gsu.edu/

Goddard College, Graduate Division, Master of Arts in Clinical Mental Health Counseling Program, Plainfield, VT 05667-9432. Offers MA.

Grace College, Department of Graduate Counseling, Winona Lake, IN 46590-1294. Offers clinical mental health counseling (MA). *Accreditation:* ACA. *Program availability:* Part-time. *Degree requirements:* For master's, comprehensive exam, portfolio, internships. *Entrance requirements:* For master's, GRE, references, background check, interview, minimum GPA of 3.0. Additional exam requirements/recommendations for international students: required—TOEFL. Electronic applications accepted. Application fee is waived when completed online.

The Graduate Center, City University of New York, Graduate Studies, Program in Psychology, New York, NY 10016-4039. Offers basic applied neurocognition (PhD); biopsychology (PhD); clinical psychology (PhD); developmental psychology (PhD); environmental psychology (PhD); experimental psychology (PhD); industrial psychology (PhD); learning processes (PhD); neuropsychology (PhD); psychology (PhD); social personality (PhD). *Degree requirements:* For doctorate, one foreign language, thesis/dissertation. *Entrance requirements:* For doctorate, GRE General Test. Additional exam requirements/recommendations for international students: required—TOEFL. Electronic applications accepted.

Hawaii Pacific University, College of Liberal Arts, Program in Clinical Mental Health Counseling, Honolulu, HI 96813. Offers MA. *Program availability:* Part-time, evening/weekend. *Entrance requirements:* For master's, GRE, transcripts, two letters of recommendation, statement of purpose, resume. Additional exam requirements/recommendations for international students: recommended—TOEFL (minimum score 550 paper-based; 80 iBT), IELTS (minimum score 6), TWE (minimum score 5). Electronic applications accepted. *Expenses: Tuition:* Full-time $18,000; part-time $1125 per credit. *Required fees:* $213; $38 per semester.

Hodges University, Graduate Programs, Naples, FL 34119. Offers accounting (M Acc); business administration (MBA); clinical mental health counseling (MS); health services administration (MS); information systems management (MIS); legal studies (MS); management (MSM). *Program availability:* Part-time, evening/weekend, 100% online, blended/hybrid learning. *Degree requirements:* For master's, comprehensive exam (for some programs), thesis (for some programs). *Entrance requirements:* For master's, essay. Additional exam requirements/recommendations for international students: recommended—TOEFL. Electronic applications accepted.

Hofstra University, College of Liberal Arts and Sciences, Programs in Psychology, Hempstead, NY 11549. Offers applied organizational psychology (PhD); clinical psychology (PhD); industrial/organizational psychology (MA); school-community psychology (Psy D). *Accreditation:* APA. *Program availability:* Part-time, evening/weekend. *Students:* 193 full-time (138 women), 22 part-time (10 women); includes 42 minority (6 Black or African American, non-Hispanic/Latino; 1 American Indian or Alaska Native, non-Hispanic/Latino; 9 Asian, non-Hispanic/Latino; 23 Hispanic/Latino; 3 Two or more races, non-Hispanic/Latino), 21 international. Average age 26. 338 applicants, 36% accepted, 61 enrolled. In 2019, 60 master's, 33 doctorates awarded. Terminal master's awarded for partial completion of doctoral program. *Degree requirements:* For master's, comprehensive exam, thesis optional, internship, minimum GPA of 3.0; for doctorate, comprehensive exam, thesis/dissertation, 1st year qualifying examination, 2nd year research project, successful practicum/externship placements, written presentation and successful oral defense of dissertation, completion of full-time internship. *Entrance requirements:* For master's, GRE General Test, minimum GPA of 3.0, essay, interview; for doctorate, GRE General Test, GRE Subject Test (psychology), 3 letters of recommendation, interview, essay, curriculum vitae. Additional exam requirements/recommendations for international students: required—TOEFL (minimum score 550 paper-based; 80 iBT); recommended—IELTS (minimum score 6.5). *Application deadline:* For fall admission, 12/31 for domestic and international students. Application fee: $75. Electronic applications accepted. *Expenses: Tuition:* Full-time $25,164; part-time $1398 per credit. *Required fees:* $580; $165 per semester. Tuition and fees vary according to course load, degree level and program. *Financial support:* In 2019–20, 152 students received support, including 125 fellowships with full and partial tuition reimbursements available (averaging $8,256 per year), 4 research assistantships with full and partial tuition reimbursements available (averaging $5,531 per year); career-related internships or fieldwork, Federal Work-Study, institutionally sponsored loans, scholarships/grants, traineeships, tuition waivers (full and partial), unspecified assistantships, and scholarships and endowed scholarships also available. Support available to part-time students. Financial award applicants required to submit FAFSA. *Unit head:* Dr. Craig Johnson, Chairperson, 516-463-5636, E-mail: craig.a.johnson@hofstra.edu. *Application contact:* Sunil Samuel, Assistant Vice President of Admissions, 516-463-4723, Fax: 516-463-4664, E-mail: graduateadmission@hofstra.edu.
Website: http://www.hofstra.edu/hclas

Hood College, Graduate School, Program in Counseling, Frederick, MD 21701-8575. Offers clinical mental health counseling (MS); school counseling (MS). *Program availability:* Part-time, evening/weekend. *Degree requirements:* For master's, 700 hour practicum and internship (R). *Entrance requirements:* For master's, minimum GPA of 3.0 (or if below 3.0 applicant may submit GRE scores for possible consideration), official transcripts, personal statement, essay, resume, two letters of recommendation. Additional exam requirements/recommendations for international students: required—TOEFL (minimum score 575 paper-based; 89 iBT), IELTS (minimum score 6.5). Electronic applications accepted. *Expenses:* Contact institution.

Howard University, Graduate School, Department of Psychology, Washington, DC 20059-0002. Offers clinical psychology (PhD); developmental psychology (PhD); experimental psychology (PhD); neuropsychology (PhD); personality psychology (PhD); psychology (MS); social psychology (PhD). *Accreditation:* APA (one or more programs are accredited). *Program availability:* Part-time. *Degree requirements:* For master's, thesis; for doctorate, comprehensive exam, thesis/dissertation, qualifying exam. *Entrance requirements:* For master's, GRE General Test, minimum GPA of 2.5, bachelor's degree in psychology or related field; for doctorate, GRE General Test, minimum GPA of 3.0.

Husson University, Graduate Programs in Counseling and Human Relations, Bangor, ME 04401-2999. Offers clinical mental health counseling (MS); human relations (MS); school counseling (MS). *Accreditation:* ACA. *Program availability:* Part-time, evening/weekend. *Degree requirements:* For master's, comprehensive exam (for some programs), thesis optional. *Entrance requirements:* For master's, BS with minimum GPA of 3.0, letters of recommendation, interview. Additional exam requirements/recommendations for international students: required—TOEFL (minimum score 550 paper-based; 80 iBT), IELTS (minimum score 6.5). Electronic applications accepted. *Expenses:* Contact institution.

Idaho State University, Graduate School, College of Arts and Letters, Department of Psychology, Program in Clinical Psychology, Pocatello, ID 83209-8112. Offers PhD. *Degree requirements:* For doctorate, comprehensive exam, thesis/dissertation, 1 year full-time clinical internship. *Entrance requirements:* For doctorate, GRE General Test, GRE Subject Test, MS in psychology. Additional exam requirements/recommendations for international students: required—TOEFL (minimum score 550 paper-based; 80 iBT). Electronic applications accepted.

Illinois Institute of Technology, Graduate College, Lewis College of Human Sciences, Department of Psychology, Chicago, IL 60616. Offers clinical psychology (PhD); industrial and organizational psychology (PhD); personnel and human resource development (MS); rehabilitation and mental health counseling (MS); rehabilitation counseling education (PhD). *Accreditation:* APA (one or more programs are accredited); CORE. *Program availability:* Part-time, evening/weekend. Terminal master's awarded for partial completion of doctoral program. *Degree requirements:* For master's, thesis (for some programs); for doctorate, comprehensive exam, thesis/dissertation, minimum of 107 credit hours, 1-year full-time internship. *Entrance requirements:* For master's, GRE General Test (minimum score 298 Quantitative and Verbal, 3.0 Analytical Writing), minimum GPA of 3.0; 3 letters of recommendation; bachelor's degree from accredited institution (for personnel and human resource development); for doctorate, GRE General Test (minimum score 298 Quantitative and Verbal, 3.0 Analytical Writing), bachelor's or master's degree from accredited institution, recommendations. Additional exam requirements/recommendations for international students: required—TOEFL (minimum score 550 paper-based; 80 iBT). Electronic applications accepted.

Illinois State University, Graduate School, College of Arts and Sciences, Department of Psychology, Normal, IL 61790. Offers psychology (MA, MS), including clinical-counseling psychology, cognitive and behavioral sciences, developmental psychology, industrial/organizational-social psychology; school psychology (PhD, SSP). *Accreditation:* APA. *Faculty:* 32 full-time (14 women), 6 part-time/adjunct (5 women). *Students:* 92 full-time (77 women), 18 part-time (14 women). Average age 25. 154 applicants, 32% accepted, 37 enrolled. In 2019, 27 master's, 3 doctorates, 5 other advanced degrees awarded. *Degree requirements:* For master's, thesis or alternative; for doctorate, variable foreign language requirement, thesis/dissertation, 2 terms of residency, internship, practicum. *Entrance requirements:* For master's, GRE General Test, GRE Subject Test, minimum GPA of 3.0 in last 60 hours of course work; for doctorate, GRE General Test. *Application deadline:* Applications are processed on a rolling basis. Application fee: $50. *Expenses: Tuition, area resident:* Full-time $7956; part-time $9767 per year. Tuition, nonresident: full-time $9233; part-time $17,592 per year. *Required fees:* $1797. *Financial support:* In 2019–20, 26 research assistantships, 34 teaching assistantships were awarded; tuition waivers (full) and unspecified assistantships also available. Financial award application deadline: 4/1. *Unit head:* Dr. J Scott Jordan, Department Chair, 309-438-2484, E-mail: jsjorda@illinoisState.edu. *Application contact:* Dr. Karen Mark, Graduate Coordinator, 309-438-8130, E-mail: kimark@ilstu.edu.
Website: http://psychology.illinoisstate.edu/

Immaculata University, College of Graduate Studies, Department of Psychology, Immaculata, PA 19345. Offers clinical mental health counseling (MA); clinical psychology (Psy D); forensic psychology (Graduate Certificate); integrative psychotherapy (Graduate Certificate); neuropsychology (Graduate Certificate); psychodynamic psychotherapy (Graduate Certificate); psychological testing (Graduate Certificate); school counseling (MA, Graduate Certificate); school psychology (MA). *Accreditation:* APA. *Program availability:* Part-time, evening/weekend. Terminal master's awarded for partial completion of doctoral program. *Degree requirements:* For master's, comprehensive exam, thesis optional; for doctorate, comprehensive exam, thesis/dissertation. *Entrance requirements:* For master's, GRE General Test or MAT, minimum GPA of 3.0; for doctorate, GRE General Test or MAT, minimum GPA of 3.5. Additional exam requirements/recommendations for international students: required—TOEFL, IELTS. Electronic applications accepted.

Indiana State University, College of Graduate and Professional Studies, Bayh College of Education, Department of Communication Disorders and Counseling, School, and Educational Psychology, Terre Haute, IN 47809. Offers clinical mental health counseling (MS); communication disorders (MS); school counseling (M Ed); school psychology (PhD, Ed S); MA/MS. *Accreditation:* ACA; ASHA; NCATE. *Program availability:* Part-time, evening/weekend. *Degree requirements:* For master's, thesis optional; for doctorate, thesis/dissertation, research tools proficiency tests. *Entrance requirements:* For master's, GRE General Test or MAT, minimum undergraduate GPA of 2.75; for doctorate, GRE General Test, master's degree, minimum undergraduate GPA of 3.5. Electronic applications accepted.

Indiana State University, College of Graduate and Professional Studies, College of Arts and Sciences, Department of Psychology, Terre Haute, IN 47809. Offers clinical psychology (Psy D); general psychology (MA, MS). *Accreditation:* APA (one or more programs are accredited). Terminal master's awarded for partial completion of doctoral program. *Degree requirements:* For master's, thesis (for some programs); for doctorate, comprehensive exam, thesis/dissertation, internship, professional research project. *Entrance requirements:* For master's, GRE General Test, 12 semester hours of course work in psychology, minimum GPA of 2.75; for doctorate, GRE General Test, minimum GPA of 3.0. Additional exam requirements/recommendations for international students: required—TOEFL (minimum score 550 paper-based). Electronic applications accepted.

Indiana University of Pennsylvania, School of Graduate Studies and Research, College of Education and Communications, Department of Counseling, Program in Clinical Mental Health Counseling, Indiana, PA 15705. Offers MA. *Program availability:* Part-time, evening/weekend. *Faculty:* 10 full-time (9 women), 6 part-time/adjunct (3 women). *Students:* 67 full-time (52 women), 35 part-time (30 women); includes 12 minority (4 Black or African American, non-Hispanic/Latino; 1 Hispanic/Latino; 7 Two or more races, non-Hispanic/Latino), 2 international. Average age 29. 82 applicants, 68% accepted, 46 enrolled. In 2019, 30 master's awarded. *Entrance requirements:* For master's, minimum undergraduate GPA of 2.8, official transcripts, goal statement, letters of recommendation. Additional exam requirements/recommendations for international students: required—TOEFL (minimum score 540 paper-based; 76 iBT); recommended—IELTS (minimum score 6). *Application deadline:* For fall admission, 3/6 priority date for domestic students. Application fee: $50. Electronic applications accepted. *Expenses: Tuition, area resident:* Full-time $9288; part-time $516 per credit. Tuition, nonresident: full-time $13,932; part-time $774 per credit. *Required fees:* $4454. One-time fee: $115 full-time. Tuition and fees vary according to course load and program. *Financial support:* In 2019–20, 6 fellowships with tuition reimbursements (averaging $667 per year), 14 research assistantships with full and partial tuition reimbursements (averaging $5,681 per year) were awarded; career-related internships or fieldwork, Federal Work-Study, scholarships/grants, and unspecified assistantships also available. Financial award application deadline: 4/15; financial award applicants required to submit FAFSA. *Unit head:* Dr. Claire Dandeneau, Program Coordinator, 724-357-2306, E-mail: cdanden@iup.edu. *Application contact:* Amber Dworek, Director of Graduate Admissions, 724-357-2222, E-mail: amber.dworek@iup.edu.

Indiana University of Pennsylvania, School of Graduate Studies and Research, College of Natural Sciences and Mathematics, Department of Psychology, Program in Clinical Psychology, Indiana, PA 15705. Offers Psy D. *Accreditation:* APA. *Program availability:* Part-time. *Faculty:* 10 full-time (6 women). *Students:* 48 full-time (34 women), 15 part-time (9 women); includes 16 minority (4 Black or African American, non-Hispanic/Latino; 6 Asian, non-Hispanic/Latino; 5 Hispanic/Latino; 1 Two or more races, non-Hispanic/Latino), 2 international. Average age 27. 146 applicants, 20% accepted, 15 enrolled. In 2019, 13 doctorates awarded. *Degree requirements:* For doctorate, comprehensive exam, thesis/dissertation. *Entrance requirements:* For doctorate, GRE General Test, minimum GPA of 3.0, 3 letters of recommendation, interview, goal statement, official transcripts. Additional exam requirements/recommendations for international students: required—TOEFL (minimum score 540 paper-based; 76 iBT), IELTS (minimum score 6), TOEFL or IELTS. *Application deadline:* For fall admission, 12/15 priority date for domestic students. Application fee: $50. Electronic applications accepted. *Expenses:* Contact institution. *Financial support:* In 2019–20, 15 fellowships (averaging $533 per year), 49 research assistantships with tuition reimbursements (averaging $8,189 per year), 3 teaching assistantships with tuition reimbursements (averaging $25,035 per year) were awarded; career-related internships or fieldwork, Federal Work-Study, scholarships/grants, and unspecified assistantships also available. Financial award application deadline: 4/15; financial award applicants required to submit FAFSA. *Unit head:* Dr. Derek Hatfield, Coordinator, 724-357-4527, E-mail: Derek.Hatfield@iup.edu. *Application contact:* Dr. Derek Hatfield,

Coordinator, 724-357-4527, E-mail: Derek.Hatfield@iup.edu.
Website: http://www.iup.edu/psychology/grad/clinical-psychology-psyd/default.aspx

Indiana University-Purdue University Indianapolis, School of Science, Department of Psychology, Indianapolis, IN 46202-3275. Offers addiction neuroscience (PhD); applied social and organizational psychology (PhD); clinical psychology (PhD); industrial/organizational psychology (MS). *Accreditation:* APA (one or more programs are accredited). Terminal master's awarded for partial completion of doctoral program. *Degree requirements:* For master's, thesis; for doctorate, thesis/dissertation. *Entrance requirements:* For master's, GRE General Test, minimum undergraduate GPA of 3.0; for doctorate, GRE General Test, GRE Subject Test (clinical psychology), minimum undergraduate GPA of 3.2. Additional exam requirements/recommendations for international students: required—TOEFL (minimum score 567 paper-based; 86 iBT), IELTS (minimum score 6.5). Electronic applications accepted.

Indiana University South Bend, School of Education, South Bend, IN 46615. Offers addiction counseling (MS Ed); alcohol and drug counseling (Graduate Certificate); clinical mental health counseling (MS Ed); educational leadership (MS Ed); elementary education (MS Ed); marriage, couple, and family counseling (MS Ed); school counseling (MS Ed); secondary education (MS Ed); special education (MAT, MS Ed), including intense intervention (MS Ed), mild intervention (MS Ed). *Accreditation:* NCATE. *Program availability:* Part-time, evening/weekend. *Degree requirements:* For master's, thesis or alternative, exit project. *Entrance requirements:* For master's, letters of recommendation, GRE or minimum GPA of 3.0. Additional exam requirements/recommendations for international students: required—TOEFL. Electronic applications accepted. *Expenses:* Contact institution.

Jackson State University, Graduate School, College of Education and Human Development, Department of Counseling, Rehabilitation and Psychometric Services, Jackson, MS 39217. Offers clinical mental health (MS); rehabilitation counseling (MS); school counseling (MS Ed). *Accreditation:* ACA; CORE (one or more programs are accredited); NCATE. *Program availability:* Part-time, evening/weekend, 100% online, blended/hybrid learning. *Degree requirements:* For master's, comprehensive exam, thesis. *Entrance requirements:* For master's, GRE General Test. Additional exam requirements/recommendations for international students: required—TOEFL (minimum score 520 paper-based; 67 iBT). Electronic applications accepted. *Expenses:* Contact institution.

Jackson State University, Graduate School, College of Liberal Arts, Department of Psychology, Jackson, MS 39217. Offers clinical psychology (PhD). *Accreditation:* APA. *Degree requirements:* For doctorate, comprehensive exam, thesis/dissertation. *Entrance requirements:* For doctorate, MAT, GRE. Additional exam requirements/recommendations for international students: required—TOEFL (minimum score 520 paper-based; 67 iBT).

James Madison University, The Graduate School, College of Health and Behavioral Studies, Clinical Mental Health Counseling Program, Harrisonburg, VA 22807. Offers MA/Ed S. *Accreditation:* ACA. *Program availability:* Part-time, evening/weekend. *Students:* 73 full-time (59 women), 22 part-time (20 women); includes 21 minority (13 Black or African American, non-Hispanic/Latino; 3 Asian, non-Hispanic/Latino; 5 Two or more races, non-Hispanic/Latino). Average age 30. Application fee: $60. *Financial support:* In 2019–20, 60 students received support, including 1 teaching assistantship; career-related internships or fieldwork, Federal Work-Study, and assistantships (averaging $7911) also available. Financial award application deadline: 3/1; financial award applicants required to submit FAFSA.

James Madison University, The Graduate School, College of Health and Behavioral Studies, Program in Combined-Integrated Clinical and School Psychology, Harrisonburg, VA 22807. Offers Psy D. *Program availability:* Part-time, evening/weekend. *Students:* 23 full-time (20 women), 3 part-time (all women); includes 6 minority (2 Black or African American, non-Hispanic/Latino; 1 Asian, non-Hispanic/Latino; 2 Hispanic/Latino; 1 Two or more races, non-Hispanic/Latino), 3 international. Average age 30. In 2019, 4 doctorates awarded. Application fee: $60. Electronic applications accepted. *Financial support:* In 2019–20, 18 students received support. Fellowships, teaching assistantships, Federal Work-Study, unspecified assistantships, and 17 doctoral assistantships (stipend varies) available. Financial award application deadline: 3/1; financial award applicants required to submit FAFSA. *Unit head:* Dr. Gregg R. Henriques, Graduate Program Director, 540-568-7857, E-mail: henrigg@jmu.edu. *Application contact:* Lynette D. Michael, Director of Graduate Admissions, 540-568-6131 Ext. 6395, Fax: 540-568-7860, E-mail: michaeld@jmu.edu.
Website: http://www.psyc.jmu.edu/cipsyd/

John Brown University, Graduate Counseling Programs, Siloam Springs, AR 72761-2121. Offers clinical mental health counseling (MS); marriage and family therapy (MS); play therapy (Graduate Certificate); school counseling (MS). *Accreditation:* NCATE. *Program availability:* Part-time, evening/weekend. *Degree requirements:* For master's, practica or internships. *Entrance requirements:* For master's, GRE (minimum score of 300), recommendation forms from three people, 200-word essay describing professional plans and reason for seeking acceptance. Additional exam requirements/recommendations for international students: required—TOEFL (minimum score 550 paper-based; 79 iBT). Electronic applications accepted. *Expenses:* Contact institution.

Johns Hopkins University, Bloomberg School of Public Health, Department of Mental Health, Baltimore, MD 21218. Offers children's mental health services (PhD); mental health (MHS). *Degree requirements:* For master's, thesis (for some programs); for doctorate, thesis/dissertation, 1-year full-time residency, oral and written exams. *Entrance requirements:* For master's, GRE General Test, MCAT, 3 letters of recommendation, curriculum vitae; for doctorate, GRE General Test, MCAT or GMAT, 3 letters of recommendation, curriculum vitae. Additional exam requirements/recommendations for international students: required—TOEFL (minimum score 600 paper-based; 100 iBT), IELTS. Electronic applications accepted.

Johnson & Wales University, Graduate Studies, MS Program in Counseling, Providence, RI 02903-3703. Offers addiction counseling (MS); clinical mental health counseling (MS). *Program availability:* Part-time.

Johnson University, Graduate and Professional Programs, Knoxville, TN 37998. Offers biblical interpretation (Graduate Certificate); business administration (MBA); Christian ministries (Graduate Certificate); clinical mental health counseling (MA); educational technology (MA); intercultural studies (MA); leadership (MBA); leadership studies (PhD); New Testament (MA); nonprofit management (MBA); school counseling (MA); spiritual formation and leadership (Graduate Certificate); strategic ministry (MA); teacher education (MA). *Program availability:* Part-time, 100% online, blended/hybrid learning. *Faculty:* 26 full-time (10 women), 32 part-time/adjunct (9 women). *Students:* 116 full-time (56 women), 196 part-time (91 women); includes 40 minority (23 Black or African American, non-Hispanic/Latino; 1 American Indian or Alaska Native, non-Hispanic/Latino; 4 Asian, non-Hispanic/Latino; 6 Hispanic/Latino; 6 Two or more races, non-Hispanic/Latino), 31 international. Average age 36. In 2019, 87 master's, 6 doctorates, 14 other advanced degrees awarded. *Degree requirements:* For master's, variable foreign language requirement, comprehensive exam, thesis (for some programs), internships; for doctorate, variable foreign language requirement, comprehensive exam, thesis/dissertation, internships. *Entrance requirements:* For

master's, PRAXIS (for MA in teacher education); MAT (for counseling); GRE or GMAT (for MBA), interview, 3 references, transcripts, essay, minimum GPA of 2.5 or 3.0 (depending on program); for doctorate, GRE or MAT (taken not less than 5 years prior), interview, 3 references, transcripts, essay, minimum GPA of 3.0; for Graduate Certificate, interview, 3 references, transcripts, essay, minimum GPA of 3.0. Additional exam requirements/recommendations for international students: required—TOEFL (minimum score 527 paper-based; 71 iBT). *Application deadline:* For fall admission, 7/1 for domestic students; for spring admission, 11/1 for domestic students; for summer admission, 4/1 for domestic students. Application fee: $50. Electronic applications accepted. *Expenses:* Contact institution. *Financial support:* Scholarships/grants available. Financial award application deadline: 4/15; financial award applicants required to submit FAFSA. *Unit head:* Lisa Tarwater, Chief Admissions Officer, 865-251-3400, E-mail: ltarwater@johnsonu.edu. *Application contact:* Lisa Tarwater, Chief Admissions Officer, 865-251-3400, E-mail: ltarwater@johnsonu.edu.
Website: www.johnsonu.edu

Judson University, Master of Arts in Clinical Mental Health Counseling Program, Elgin, IL 60123. Offers MA. *Program availability:* Evening/weekend. *Faculty:* 6 full-time (4 women), 8 part-time/adjunct (5 women). *Students:* 44 full-time (38 women), 2 part-time (both women); includes 12 minority (10 Black or African American, non-Hispanic/Latino; 1 Asian, non-Hispanic/Latino; 1 Hispanic/Latino). Average age 39. 58 applicants, 53% accepted, 9 enrolled. In 2019, 19 master's awarded. *Application deadline:* Applications are processed on a rolling basis. Application fee: $35. Electronic applications accepted. *Expenses: Required fees:* $250. One-time fee: $125 full-time. *Financial support:* Unspecified assistantships available. *Unit head:* Dr. Amber Randolph, Program Director, 847-628-1544, E-mail: amber.randolph@judsonu.edu. *Application contact:* Kim Surin, Enrollment Manager, 847-628-5033, E-mail: kim.surin@info.judsonu.edu.
Website: https://www.judsonu.edu/Graduate/CMHC/Overview/

Kean University, Nathan Weiss Graduate College, Doctorate Program in Combined School and Clinical Psychology, Union, NJ 07083. Offers Psy D. *Program availability:* Part-time. *Faculty:* 7 full-time (4 women). *Students:* 43 full-time (30 women), 12 part-time (8 women); includes 13 minority (4 Black or African American, non-Hispanic/Latino; 4 Asian, non-Hispanic/Latino; 5 Hispanic/Latino), 1 international. Average age 28. 117 applicants, 23% accepted, 12 enrolled. In 2019, 7 doctorates awarded. *Degree requirements:* For doctorate, comprehensive exam, thesis/dissertation, externship. *Entrance requirements:* For doctorate, GRE General Test, GRE Subject Test in psychology (taken within last 5 years), minimum undergraduate GPA of 3.3, graduate 3.5; 3 letters of recommendation; personal interview; prerequisite coursework in theories of personality, abnormal psychology, tests and measurements, statistics, and experimental psychology; personal statement. Additional exam requirements/recommendations for international students: required—TOEFL (minimum score 550 paper-based; 79 iBT), IELTS (minimum score 6.5). *Application deadline:* For fall admission, 1/1 for domestic and international students. Applications are processed on a rolling basis. Application fee: $75. Electronic applications accepted. *Expenses:* Contact institution. *Financial support:* Scholarships/grants and unspecified assistantships available. Financial award applicants required to submit FAFSA. *Unit head:* Dr. Jennifer Block-Lerner, Program Coordinator, 908-737-5864, E-mail: jlerner@kean.edu. *Application contact:* Pedro Lopes, Admissions Counselor, 908-737-7100, E-mail: gradadmissions@kean.edu.
Website: http://grad.kean.edu/doctoral-programs/combined-school-and-clinical-psychology

Kean University, Nathan Weiss Graduate College, Program in Counselor Education, Union, NJ 07083. Offers alcohol and drug abuse counseling (MA); clinical mental health counseling (MA); school counseling (MA). *Accreditation:* ACA; NCATE. *Program availability:* Part-time. *Faculty:* 10 full-time (7 women). *Students:* 128 full-time (100 women), 164 part-time (126 women); includes 137 minority (63 Black or African American, non-Hispanic/Latino; 2 American Indian or Alaska Native, non-Hispanic/Latino; 9 Asian, non-Hispanic/Latino; 58 Hispanic/Latino; 2 Native Hawaiian or other Pacific Islander, non-Hispanic/Latino; 3 Two or more races, non-Hispanic/Latino). Average age 33. 217 applicants, 37% accepted, 52 enrolled. In 2019, 90 master's awarded. *Degree requirements:* For master's, practicum, internship, portfolio. *Entrance requirements:* For master's, minimum GPA of 3.0, 2 letters of recommendation, personal statement, resume. Additional exam requirements/recommendations for international students: required—TOEFL (minimum score 550 paper-based; 79 iBT), IELTS (minimum score 6.5). *Application deadline:* For fall admission, 3/1 for domestic and international students; for spring admission, 11/1 for domestic and international students. Applications are processed on a rolling basis. Application fee: $75. Electronic applications accepted. *Expenses:* Tuition, state resident: full-time $15,326; part-time $748 per credit. Tuition, nonresident: full-time $20,288; part-time $902 per credit. *Required fees:* $2149.50; $91.25 per credit. Tuition and fees vary according to course level, course load, degree level and program. *Financial support:* Scholarships/grants and unspecified assistantships available. Financial award applicants required to submit FAFSA. *Unit head:* Dr. J. Barry Mascari, Program Coordinator, 908-737-5954, E-mail: jmascari@kean.edu. *Application contact:* Pedro Lopes, Admissions Counselor, 908-737-7100, E-mail: gradadmissions@kean.edu.
Website: http://grad.kean.edu/counseling

Kent State University, College of Arts and Sciences, Department of Psychological Sciences, Kent, OH 44242-0001. Offers clinical psychology (MA, PhD), including gerontology (MA), psychological sciences (MA); experimental psychology (MA, PhD), including gerontology (MA), psychological sciences (MA). *Accreditation:* APA (one or more programs are accredited). *Faculty:* 28 full-time (15 women), 4 part-time/adjunct (2 women). *Students:* 79 full-time (63 women); includes 17 minority (6 Black or African American, non-Hispanic/Latino; 5 Asian, non-Hispanic/Latino; 4 Hispanic/Latino; 2 Two or more races, non-Hispanic/Latino), 3 international. Average age 26. 284 applicants, 8% accepted, 16 enrolled. In 2019, 13 master's, 9 doctorates awarded. *Degree requirements:* For master's, thesis, Min grade in Quantitative Statistical Analysis I and II is B-. College of Arts & Sciences requires students to have a 3.0 average from all graduate courses attempted; for doctorate, comprehensive exam, thesis/dissertation. *Entrance requirements:* For master's, GRE General Test, statement of goals and motivations, transcripts, 3 letters of recommendation, minimum junior-senior GPA of 3.0, 18 semester hours of credit in psychology which includes at least one course in statistics and a broad background in psychology; for doctorate, GRE General Test, statement of goals and motivations, transcripts, 3 letters of recommendation, minimum junior-senior GPA of 3.0, 18 semester hours of credit in psychology which includes at least one course in statistics and a broad background in psychology. Additional exam requirements/recommendations for international students: required—TOEFL (minimum score 94 iBT), IELTS (minimum score 7), PTE (minimum score 65), Michigan English Language Assessment Battery (minimum score 82. *Application deadline:* For fall admission, 12/1 for domestic and international students. Applications are processed on a rolling basis. Application fee: $45 ($70 for international students). Electronic applications accepted. *Financial support:* Federal Work-Study, health care benefits, and unspecified assistantships available. Financial award application deadline: 12/1; financial award applicants required to submit FAFSA. *Unit head:* Dr. Maria S. Zaragoza, Professor, Department Chair, 330-672-2166, E-mail: mzaragoz@kent.edu. *Application contact:* Dr. John A. Updegraff, Professor and Graduate Coordinator, 330-672-2166, E-mail: jupdegr1@kent.edu.
Website: https://www.kent.edu/psychology

LaGrange College, Graduate Programs, Program in Clinical Mental Health Counseling, LaGrange, GA 30240-2999. Offers MS. *Entrance requirements:* For master's, GRE or MAT, bachelor's degree, 3 letters of reference, essay, background check.

Lakehead University, Graduate Studies, Department of Psychology, Thunder Bay, ON P7B 5E1, Canada. Offers clinical psychology (PhD); experimental psychology (MA). *Program availability:* Part-time, evening/weekend. *Degree requirements:* For master's, thesis optional; for doctorate, thesis/dissertation, 2 comprehensive exams, internship. *Entrance requirements:* For master's, GRE, honors degree in psychology, advanced course work in statistics, minimum B average; for doctorate, GRE, minimum B average. Additional exam requirements/recommendations for international students: required—TOEFL.

Lamar University, College of Graduate Studies, College of Education and Human Development, Department of Counseling, Beaumont, TX 77710. Offers clinical mental health counseling (M Ed); school counseling (M Ed); special education (M Ed). *Accreditation:* ACA. *Faculty:* 19 full-time (16 women), 20 part-time/adjunct (17 women). *Students:* 196 full-time (176 women), 1,263 part-time (1,124 women); includes 757 minority (382 Black or African American, non-Hispanic/Latino; 6 American Indian or Alaska Native, non-Hispanic/Latino; 19 Asian, non-Hispanic/Latino; 314 Hispanic/Latino; 2 Native Hawaiian or other Pacific Islander, non-Hispanic/Latino; 34 Two or more races, non-Hispanic/Latino). Average age 36. 1,097 applicants, 66% accepted, 360 enrolled. In 2019, 434 master's awarded. *Entrance requirements:* Additional exam requirements/recommendations for international students: required—TOEFL (minimum score 550 paper-based; 79 iBT), IELTS (minimum score 6.5). *Application deadline:* Applications are processed on a rolling basis. Application fee: $25 ($50 for international students). Electronic applications accepted. *Expenses:* $18000 total program cost. *Financial support:* In 2019–20, 19 students received support. Fellowships, research assistantships, teaching assistantships, career-related internships or fieldwork, scholarships/grants, and unspecified assistantships available. Financial award applicants required to submit FAFSA. *Application contact:* Celeste Contreas, Director, Admissions and Academic Services, 409-880-8888, Fax: 409-880-7419, E-mail: gradmissions@lamar.edu.
Website: https://www.lamar.edu/education/counseling/index.html

La Salle University, School of Arts and Sciences, Program in Clinical Psychology, Philadelphia, PA 19141-1199. Offers child clinical psychology (Psy D); clinical health psychology (Psy D); clinical psychology (MA); general practice psychology (Psy D). *Accreditation:* AAMFT/COAMFTE. *Program availability:* Part-time, evening/weekend. Terminal master's awarded for partial completion of doctoral program. *Degree requirements:* For doctorate, comprehensive exam, thesis/dissertation. *Entrance requirements:* For doctorate, GRE (minimum scores of 148 on both the Verbal Reasoning and Quantitative Reasoning sections strongly recommended); GRE Subject Test in psychology (for those entering with bachelor's degree), baccalaureate degree from accredited institution with major in psychology or related discipline; minimum undergraduate GPA of 3.0, 3.2 graduate; three letters of recommendation; statement of interest and intent; curriculum vitae or resume; personal interview. Additional exam requirements/recommendations for international students: required—TOEFL. Electronic applications accepted. Application fee is waived when completed online. *Expenses:* Contact institution.

La Salle University, School of Arts and Sciences, Program in Counseling and Family Therapy, Philadelphia, PA 19141-1199. Offers industrial/organizational psychology (MA); marriage and family therapy (MA); professional clinical counseling (MA). *Accreditation:* ACA; APA. *Program availability:* Part-time, evening/weekend. *Degree requirements:* For master's, comprehensive exam. *Entrance requirements:* For master's, GRE or MAT (waived for applicants that already possess a master's degree in any field or for applicants that have a cumulative GPA of 3.5 or higher), minimum of 15 hours in psychology, counseling, or marriage and family studies; minimum GPA of 3.0; three letters of recommendation; personal statement; work experience (paid or volunteer). Additional exam requirements/recommendations for international students: required—TOEFL. Electronic applications accepted. Application fee is waived when completed online. *Expenses:* Contact institution.

Lenoir-Rhyne University, Graduate Programs, School of Counseling and Human Services, Program in Clinical Mental Health Counseling, Hickory, NC 28601. Offers MA. *Accreditation:* ACA. *Program availability:* Part-time, evening/weekend. *Degree requirements:* For master's, comprehensive exam, thesis optional. *Entrance requirements:* For master's, GRE General Test or MAT, writing sample; minimum undergraduate GPA of 2.7, graduate 3.0. Additional exam requirements/recommendations for international students: required—TOEFL (minimum score 600 paper-based). Electronic applications accepted. *Expenses:* Contact institution.

Lesley University, Graduate School of Arts and Social Sciences, Cambridge, MA 02138-2790. Offers clinical mental health counseling (MA), including holistic counseling, school and community counseling, trauma studies; counseling psychology (MA, CAGS), including professional counseling (MA), school counseling (MA); creative writing (MFA); expressive therapies (MA, PhD, CAGS), including art (MA), clinical mental health counseling (MA), dance (MA), expressive therapies (MA), music (MA); independent studies (CAGS); independent study (MA); intercultural relations (MA, CAGS); interdisciplinary studies (MA), including individualized studies, integrative holistic health, mindfulness studies, peace and conflict transformation, trauma sensitive assessment, intervention, and consultation, women's studies; urban environmental leadership (MA). *Program availability:* Part-time, online learning. *Degree requirements:* For master's, internship, practicum, thesis (for expressive therapies); for doctorate, thesis/dissertation, arts apprenticeship, field placement; for CAGS, thesis, internship (for counseling psychology, expressive therapies). *Entrance requirements:* For master's, MAT (counseling psychology), interview, writing samples, art portfolio; for doctorate, GRE or MAT, interview, master's degree; for CAGS, interview, master's degree. Additional exam requirements/recommendations for international students: required—TOEFL (minimum score 550 paper-based; 80 iBT). Electronic applications accepted.

Lewis University, College of Education and Social Sciences, Program in Clinical Mental Health Counseling, Romeoville, IL 60446. Offers adult mental health counseling (MA). *Program availability:* Part-time, evening/weekend. *Students:* 54 full-time (48 women), 56 part-time (49 women); includes 40 minority (9 Black or African American, non-Hispanic/Latino; 1 Asian, non-Hispanic/Latino; 27 Hispanic/Latino; 1 Native Hawaiian or other Pacific Islander, non-Hispanic/Latino; 2 Two or more races, non-Hispanic/Latino), 1 international. Average age 28. In 2019, 27 master's awarded. *Degree requirements:* For master's, comprehensive exam, thesis optional, practicum, internship. *Entrance requirements:* For master's, bachelor's degree, 15 hours of undergraduate psychology, including statistics or research; 2 letters of recommendation; minimum GPA of 3.0 in last 60 hours; interview, personal statement. Additional exam requirements/recommendations for international students: required—TOEFL (minimum score 550 paper-based; 79 iBT), IELTS (minimum score 6). *Application deadline:* For fall admission, 5/1 priority date for international students; for spring admission, 11/15 priority date for international students. Applications are processed on a rolling basis. Application

fee: $40. Electronic applications accepted. *Financial support:* Federal Work-Study and unspecified assistantships available. Financial award application deadline: 5/1; financial award applicants required to submit FAFSA. *Unit head:* Dr. Katherine Helm-Lewis, Program Director. *Application contact:* Sheri Vilcek, Graduate Admissions Counselor, 815-836-5610, E-mail: grad@lewisu.edu.
Website: http://www.lewisu.edu/academics/grad.htm/

Liberty University, School of Behavioral Sciences, Lynchburg, VA 24515. Offers applied psychology (MA), including developmental psychology (MA, MS), industrial/organizational psychology (MA, MS); clinical mental health counseling (MA); community care and counseling (Ed D), including marriage and family counseling, pastoral care and counseling, traumatology; counselor education and supervision (PhD); human services counseling (MA), including addictions and recovery, business, child and family law, Christian ministries, criminal justice, crisis response and trauma, executive leadership, health and wellness, life coaching, marriage and family, military resilience; marriage and family counseling (MA); marriage and family therapy (MA); military resilience (Certificate); pastoral counseling (MA), including addictions and recovery, community chaplaincy, crisis response and trauma, discipleship and church ministry, leadership, life coaching, marriage and family, marriage and family studies, military resilience, parenting and child/adolescent, pastoral counseling, theology; professional counseling (MA); psychology (MS), including developmental psychology (MA, MS), industrial/organizational psychology (MA, MS); school counseling (M Ed). *Program availability:* Part-time, online learning. *Students:* 3,786 full-time (3,065 women), 5,193 part-time (4,081 women); includes 2,733 minority (1,967 Black or African American, non-Hispanic/Latino; 48 American Indian or Alaska Native, non-Hispanic/Latino; 103 Asian, non-Hispanic/Latino; 349 Hispanic/Latino; 19 Native Hawaiian or other Pacific Islander, non-Hispanic/Latino; 247 Two or more races, non-Hispanic/Latino), 133 international. Average age 38. 13,324 applicants, 28% accepted, 2,163 enrolled. In 2019, 2,322 master's, 19 doctorates, 112 other advanced degrees awarded. *Entrance requirements:* For master's, Official bachelor's degree transcripts with a 2.0 GPA or higher. *Application deadline:* Applications are processed on a rolling basis. Application fee: $50. Electronic applications accepted. *Expenses: Tuition:* Full-time $545; part-time $410 per credit hour. One-time fee: $50. *Financial support:* In 2019–20, 1,003 students received support. Teaching assistantships and Federal Work-Study available. Financial award applicants required to submit FAFSA. *Unit head:* Dr. Kenyon Knapp, Dean, School of Behavioral Services, E-mail: kcknapp@liberty.edu. *Application contact:* Jay Bridge, Director of Admissions, 800-424-9595, Fax: 800-628-7977, E-mail: gradadmissions@liberty.edu.
Website: https://www.liberty.edu/behavioral-sciences/

Lipscomb University, Department of Psychology, Counseling, and Family Science, Nashville, TN 37204-3951. Offers clinical mental health counseling (MS); counseling psychology (Certificate); marriage and family therapy (MMFT); psychology (MS). *Program availability:* Part-time, evening/weekend. *Degree requirements:* For master's, thesis (for some programs), practicum, internship, capstone. *Entrance requirements:* For master's, GRE, resume, 3 reference letters, transcripts, goals statement. Additional exam requirements/recommendations for international students: required—TOEFL (minimum score 570 paper-based; 80 iBT). Electronic applications accepted. *Expenses:* Contact institution.

Lock Haven University of Pennsylvania, The Stephen Poorman College of Business, Information Systems, and Human Services, Lock Haven, PA 17745-2390. Offers clinical mental health counseling (MS); sport science (MS). *Program availability:* Online learning. *Degree requirements:* For master's, thesis. *Entrance requirements:* For master's, minimum undergraduate GPA of 3.0. Additional exam requirements/recommendations for international students: required—TOEFL. Electronic applications accepted.

Loma Linda University, School of Behavioral Health, Department of Psychology, Loma Linda, CA 92350. Offers clinical psychology (PhD, Psy D). *Accreditation:* APA. *Degree requirements:* For doctorate, comprehensive exam, thesis/dissertation. *Entrance requirements:* For doctorate, GRE General Test, three letters of recommendation. Additional exam requirements/recommendations for international students: required—TOEFL (minimum score 550 paper-based; 80 iBT). Electronic applications accepted.

London Metropolitan University, Graduate Programs, London, United Kingdom. Offers applied psychology (M Sc); architecture (MA); biomedical science (M Sc); blood science (M Sc); cancer pharmacology (M Sc); computer networking and cyber security (M Sc); computing and information systems (M Sc); conference interpreting (MA); counter-terrorism studies (M Sc); creative, digital and professional writing (MA); crime, violence and prevention (M Sc); criminology (M Sc); curating contemporary art (MA); data analytics (M Sc); digital media (MA); early childhood studies (MA); education (MA, Ed D); financial services law, regulation and compliance (LL M); food science (M Sc); forensic psychology (M Sc); health and social care management and policy (M Sc); human nutrition (M Sc); human resource management (MA); human rights and international conflict (MA); information technology (M Sc); intelligence and security studies (M Sc); international oil, gas and energy law (LL M); international relations (MA); interpreting (MA); learning and teaching in higher education (MA); legal practice (LL M); media and entertainment law (LL M); organizational and consumer psychology (M Sc); psychological therapy (M Sc); psychology of mental health (M Sc); public health (M Sc); public policy and management (MPA); security studies (M Sc); social work (M Sc); spatial planning and urban design (MA); sports therapy (M Sc); supporting older children and young people with dyslexia (MA); teaching languages (MA), including Arabic, English; translation (MA); woman and child abuse (MA).

Long Island University - Brentwood Campus, Graduate Programs, Brentwood, NY 11717. Offers childhood education (MS), including grades 1-6; childhood education/literacy B-6 (MS); childhood education/special education (grades 1-6) (MS); clinical mental health counseling (MS, Advanced Certificate); criminal justice (MS); early childhood education (MS); educational leadership (MS Ed); family nurse practitioner (MS, Advanced Certificate); health administration (MPA); library and information science (MS); literacy (B-6) (MS Ed); school counselor (MS, Advanced Certificate); social work (MSW); special education (MS Ed); students with disabilities generalist (grades 7-12) (Advanced Certificate). *Program availability:* Part-time. *Entrance requirements:* For master's and Advanced Certificate, GRE. Additional exam requirements/recommendations for international students: required—TOEFL or IELTS. Electronic applications accepted.

Long Island University - Brooklyn, Richard L. Conolly College of Liberal Arts and Sciences, Brooklyn, NY 11201-8423. Offers biology (MS); chemistry (MS); clinical psychology (PhD); creative writing (MFA); English (MA); media arts (MA, MFA); political science (MA); psychology (MA); social science (MS); United Nations (Advanced Certificate); urban studies (MA); writing and production for television (MFA). *Program availability:* Part-time. Terminal master's awarded for partial completion of doctoral program. *Degree requirements:* For master's, comprehensive exam (for some programs), thesis (for some programs); for doctorate, thesis/dissertation. *Entrance requirements:* For doctorate, GRE. Additional exam requirements/recommendations for international students: required—TOEFL (minimum score 550 paper-based, 79 iBT) or IELTS. Electronic applications accepted.

Long Island University - Post, College of Education, Information and Technology, Brookville, NY 11548-1300. Offers adolescence education (MS); adolescence education 7-12 (MS); archives and records management (AC); art education (MS); childhood education (MS); childhood education/literacy B-6 (MS); childhood education/special education (MS); clinical mental health counseling (MS, AC); early childhood education (MS); early childhood education/childhood education (MS); educational leadership (AC); educational technology (MS); information studies (PhD); interdisciplinary educational studies (Ed D); middle childhood education (MS); music education (MS); public library administration (AC); school counselor (MS); special education (MS Ed); speech-language pathology (MA); students with disabilities, 7-12 generalist (AC); TESOL (MA). *Accreditation:* ASHA; TEAC. *Program availability:* Part-time, 100% online, blended/hybrid learning. Terminal master's awarded for partial completion of doctoral program. *Degree requirements:* For master's, variable foreign language requirement, comprehensive exam (for some programs), thesis optional; for doctorate, comprehensive exam, thesis/dissertation. *Entrance requirements:* For master's and AC, GRE (for some programs). Additional exam requirements/recommendations for international students: required—TOEFL (minimum score 550 paper-based, 75 iBT), IELTS, or PTE. Electronic applications accepted.

Louisiana State University and Agricultural & Mechanical College, Graduate School, College of Humanities and Social Sciences, Department of Psychology, Baton Rouge, LA 70803. Offers biological psychology (MA, PhD); clinical psychology (MA, PhD); cognitive psychology (MA, PhD); developmental psychology (MA, PhD); school psychology (MA, PhD). *Accreditation:* APA (one or more programs are accredited).

Louisiana Tech University, Graduate School, College of Education, Ruston, LA 71272. Offers counseling and guidance (MA), including clinical mental health counseling, human services, orientation and mobility; counseling psychology (PhD); curriculum and instruction (M Ed); cyber education (Graduate Certificate); dynamics of domestic and family violence (Graduate Certificate); early childhood education - PreK-3 (MAT); educational leadership (M Ed, Ed D); elementary education and special education mild/moderate grades 1-5 (MAT); higher education administration (Graduate Certificate); industrial/organizational psychology (MA, PhD); kinesiology (MS); middle school education (MAT), including mathematics; orientation and mobility (Graduate Certificate); rehabilitation teaching for the blind (Graduate Certificate); secondary education (MAT), including agriculture, biology, business, chemistry, English; special education: visually impaired (MAT); teacher leader education (Graduate Certificate); visual impairments - blind education (Graduate Certificate). *Accreditation:* NCATE. *Program availability:* Part-time. *Degree requirements:* For master's, thesis; for doctorate, thesis/dissertation. *Entrance requirements:* For master's and doctorate, GRE General Test. Additional exam requirements/recommendations for international students: required—TOEFL (minimum score 550 paper-based; 80 iBT), IELTS (minimum score 6.5). Electronic applications accepted. *Expenses: Tuition, area resident:* Full-time $6592; part-time $400 per credit. Tuition, state resident: full-time $6592; part-time $400 per credit. Tuition, nonresident: full-time $13,333; part-time $681 per credit. *International tuition:* $13,333 full-time. *Required fees:* $3011; $3011 per unit.

Loyola University Chicago, Graduate School, Program in Clinical Psychology, Chicago, IL 60660. Offers MA, PhD. *Accreditation:* APA. *Faculty:* 9 full-time (7 women). *Students:* 33 full-time (30 women); includes 7 minority (3 Black or African American, non-Hispanic/Latino; 1 Asian, non-Hispanic/Latino; 3 Hispanic/Latino). Average age 27. 192 applicants, 3% accepted, 5 enrolled. In 2019, 5 master's, 8 doctorates awarded. Terminal master's awarded for partial completion of doctoral program. *Degree requirements:* For master's, thesis; for doctorate, comprehensive exam, thesis/dissertation, clinical internship. *Entrance requirements:* For doctorate, GRE General Test, letters of recommendation, personal statement, curriculum vitae, transcript. Additional exam requirements/recommendations for international students: recommended—TOEFL. *Application deadline:* For fall admission, 12/1 for domestic students. Application fee: $0. Electronic applications accepted. *Expenses: Tuition:* Full-time $18,540; part-time $1033 per credit hour. *Required fees:* $904; $230 per credit hour. *Financial support:* In 2019–20, 22 students received support, including 2 fellowships with full tuition reimbursements available (averaging $22,000 per year), 20 research assistantships with full tuition reimbursements available (averaging $19,000 per year), 5 teaching assistantships with full tuition reimbursements available (averaging $19,000 per year); career-related internships or fieldwork and scholarships/grants also available. Financial award application deadline: 12/1. *Unit head:* Dr. Grayson Holmbeck, Director of Clinical Training, 773-508-2967, Fax: 773-508-8713, E-mail: gholmbe@luc.edu. *Application contact:* Adrienne Riessle, Senior Secretary, 773-508-3011, Fax: 773-508-8713, E-mail: ariessle@luc.edu.
Website: https://luc.edu/psychology/graduate/clinicalpsychologyprogram/

Loyola University Chicago, School of Education, Program in Community Counseling, Chicago, IL 60660. Offers clinical mental health counseling (Ed S); community counseling (M Ed, MA). *Program availability:* Part-time. *Faculty:* 5 full-time (2 women), 5 part-time/adjunct (4 women). *Students:* 24 full-time (21 women), 4 part-time (0 women); includes 7 minority (3 Black or African American, non-Hispanic/Latino; 3 Hispanic/Latino; 1 Two or more races, non-Hispanic/Latino), 1 international. Average age 28. 60 applicants, 72% accepted, 13 enrolled. In 2019, 9 master's awarded. *Degree requirements:* For master's, comprehensive exam (for some programs), thesis (for some programs). *Entrance requirements:* For master's, GRE General Test, minimum GPA of 3.0, letters of recommendation, resume. Additional exam requirements/recommendations for international students: required—TOEFL (minimum score 550 paper-based; 79 iBT). *Application deadline:* For fall admission, 1/1 for domestic and international students. Application fee: $50. Electronic applications accepted. Application fee is waived when completed online. *Expenses:* 17082. *Financial support:* Career-related internships or fieldwork, institutionally sponsored loans, scholarships/grants, and unspecified assistantships available. Support available to part-time students. Financial award application deadline: 2/1; financial award applicants required to submit FAFSA. *Unit head:* Dr. Matt Miller, Director, 312-915-6800, E-mail: mmill11@luc.edu. *Application contact:* Dr. Matt Miller, Director, 312-915-6800, E-mail: mmill11@luc.edu.

Loyola University Maryland, Graduate Programs, Loyola College of Arts and Sciences, Department of Psychology, Baltimore, MD 21210-2699. Offers clinical psychology (MS, Psy D, CAS); counseling psychology (MS, CAS). *Accreditation:* APA. *Students:* 132 full-time (109 women), 39 part-time (32 women); includes 55 minority (21 Black or African American, non-Hispanic/Latino; 19 Asian, non-Hispanic/Latino; 11 Hispanic/Latino; 4 Two or more races, non-Hispanic/Latino), 5 international. Average age 27. 427 applicants, 25% accepted, 44 enrolled. In 2019, 59 master's, 11 doctorates awarded. *Degree requirements:* For doctorate, comprehensive exam, thesis/dissertation. *Entrance requirements:* For master's, GRE (optional), essay, application, transcripts, letters of recommendation, CV/resume, interview; for doctorate, GRE, essay, application, transcripts, letters of recommendation, CV/resume, interview. Additional exam requirements/recommendations for international students: required—TOEFL (minimum score 550 paper-based; 80 iBT), IELTS (minimum score 7), TOEFL (minimum score 550 paper-based, 80iBT) or ILETS (minimum score 7). *Application deadline:* For fall admission, 12/1 for domestic and international students. Application fee: $60. Electronic applications accepted. *Expenses:* Contact institution. *Financial support:* Scholarships/grants and unspecified assistantships available. Financial award application deadline: 4/15; financial award applicants required to submit FAFSA. *Unit head:* Carolyn M. Barry, Chair, 410-617-5325, E-mail: cbarry@loyola.edu. *Application contact:* Office of Graduate Admission, 410-617-5020, E-mail: graduate@loyola.edu. Website: https://www.loyola.edu/academics/psychology

Loyola University New Orleans, College of Nursing and Health, Department of Counseling, New Orleans, LA 70118. Offers counseling (MS), including marriage and family. *Program availability:* Part-time, evening/weekend. *Faculty:* 5 full-time (3 women), 3 part-time/adjunct (2 women). *Students:* 42 full-time (33 women), 40 part-time (36 women); includes 18 minority (9 Black or African American, non-Hispanic/Latino; 8 Hispanic/Latino; 1 Two or more races, non-Hispanic/Latino), 3 international. Average age 29. 50 applicants, 68% accepted, 27 enrolled. In 2019, 19 master's awarded. *Degree requirements:* For master's, comprehensive exam, minimum GPA of 3.0 in counseling coursework. *Entrance requirements:* For master's, GRE if undergraduate GPA is below 3.0, resume, transcripts, 3 letters of recommendation, statement of objectives (1-3 pgs), bachelors degree from regionally-accredited institution, interview, writing sample. Additional exam requirements/recommendations for international students: required—TOEFL (minimum score 550 paper-based; 79 iBT). *Application deadline:* For fall admission, 12/1 priority date for domestic and international students. Applications are processed on a rolling basis. Electronic applications accepted. *Expenses:* Contact institution. *Financial support:* In 2019–20, 58 students received support. Research assistantships, career-related internships or fieldwork, and tuition waivers (partial) available. Support available to part-time students. Financial award application deadline: 5/1; financial award applicants required to submit FAFSA. *Unit head:* Dr. John Dewell, Chair, 504-864-7858, Fax: 504-864-7844, E-mail: counselingdept@loyno.edu. *Application contact:* Dianna Whitfield, Department Assistant, 504-864-7848, Fax: 504-864-7844, E-mail: counselingdept@loyno.edu. Website: http://css.loyno.edu/counseling

Madonna University, Department of Psychology, Livonia, MI 48150-1173. Offers clinical psychology (MSCP). *Program availability:* Part-time, evening/weekend. *Degree requirements:* For master's, thesis or alternative. *Entrance requirements:* Additional exam requirements/recommendations for international students: required—TOEFL. Electronic applications accepted. *Expenses: Tuition:* Full-time $15,930; part-time $885 per credit hour. Tuition and fees vary according to degree level and program.

Marquette University, Graduate School, College of Education, Department of Counselor Education and Counseling Psychology, Milwaukee, WI 53201-1881. Offers clinical mental health counseling (MS); community counseling (MA); counseling psychology (PhD); school counseling (MA). *Accreditation:* ACA. *Program availability:* Part-time. Terminal master's awarded for partial completion of doctoral program. *Degree requirements:* For master's, comprehensive exam, thesis (for some programs); for doctorate, thesis/dissertation, qualifying exam. *Entrance requirements:* For master's, GRE General Test or MAT, official transcripts from all current and previous colleges/universities except Marquette, three letters of recommendation, statement of purpose; for doctorate, GRE General Test, MAT, sample of written work, official transcripts from all current and previous colleges/universities except Marquette, three letters of recommendation, statement of purpose, resume/curriculum vitae. Additional exam requirements/recommendations for international students: required—TOEFL (minimum score 530 paper-based).

Marshall University, Academic Affairs Division, College of Liberal Arts, Department of Psychology, Huntington, WV 25755. Offers clinical psychology (Certificate); psychology (MA, Psy D). *Accreditation:* APA. *Degree requirements:* For master's, thesis optional. *Entrance requirements:* For master's, GRE General Test or MAT.

Marymount University, School of Sciences, Mathematics, and Education, Program in Counseling, Arlington, VA 22207-4299. Offers clinical mental health counseling (MA); counseling with forensic and legal studies (MA/MA); pastoral counseling (MA); school counseling (MA); MA/MA. *Accreditation:* ACA (one or more programs are accredited). *Program availability:* Part-time, evening/weekend. *Faculty:* 11 full-time (9 women), 3 part-time/adjunct (all women). *Students:* 119 full-time (100 women), 39 part-time (33 women); includes 54 minority (20 Black or African American, non-Hispanic/Latino; 8 Asian, non-Hispanic/Latino; 20 Hispanic/Latino; 6 Two or more races, non-Hispanic/Latino), 2 international. Average age 28. 122 applicants, 89% accepted, 58 enrolled. In 2019, 41 master's awarded. *Degree requirements:* For master's, thesis or alternative, capstone/internship. *Entrance requirements:* For master's, GRE, 2 letters of recommendation, interview, resume, personal statement. Additional exam requirements/recommendations for international students: required—TOEFL (minimum score 600 paper-based; 96 iBT), IELTS (minimum score 6.5), PTE (minimum score 58). *Application deadline:* For fall admission, 1/15 priority date for domestic and international students. Applications are processed on a rolling basis. Application fee: $40. Electronic applications accepted. *Expenses: Tuition:* Part-time $1050 per credit. *Required fees:* $22 per credit. One-time fee: $270 part-time. Tuition and fees vary according to program. *Financial support:* In 2019–20, 19 students received support. Research assistantships, teaching assistantships, career-related internships or fieldwork, scholarships/grants, and unspecified assistantships available. Support available to part-time students. Financial award application deadline: 3/1; financial award applicants required to submit FAFSA. *Unit head:* Dr. Lisa Jackson-Cherry, Chair, Counseling, 703-284-1633, E-mail: lisa.jackson-cherry@marymount.edu. *Application contact:* Fiona McDonnell, Administrative Assistant, 703-284-5901, E-mail: gadmissi@marymount.edu. Website: https://www.marymount.edu/Academics/School-of-Sciences-Mathematics-and-Education/Graduate-Programs/Counseling-(M-A-)

Marywood University, Academic Affairs, Reap College of Education and Human Development, Department of Psychology and Counseling, Program in Clinical Psychology, Scranton, PA 18509-1598. Offers Psy D. *Accreditation:* APA. *Program availability:* Part-time. Electronic applications accepted. *Expenses:* Contact institution.

Marywood University, Academic Affairs, Reap College of Education and Human Development, Department of Psychology and Counseling, Program in Psychology, Scranton, PA 18509-1598. Offers clinical services (MA); general theoretical psychology (MA). *Program availability:* Part-time. Electronic applications accepted.

McGill University, Faculty of Graduate and Postdoctoral Studies, Faculty of Science, Department of Psychology, Montréal, QC H3A 2T5, Canada. Offers clinical psychology (PhD); experimental psychology (M Sc, MA, PhD).

McKendree University, Graduate Programs, Master of Arts Program in Clinical Mental Health Counseling, Lebanon, IL 62254-1299. Offers MA. *Program availability:* Part-time, evening/weekend. *Degree requirements:* For master's, comprehensive exam, internship. *Entrance requirements:* For master's, official transcripts from each college or university attended, minimum undergraduate GPA of 3.0, three letters of recommendation, personal statement, completion of six undergraduate credit hours in a behavior science, curriculum vitae or resume. Electronic applications accepted.

Medaille College, Programs in Psychology, Buffalo, NY 14214-2695. Offers clinical psychology (Psy D); marriage and family therapy (MA); mental health counseling (MA); psychology (MA). *Accreditation:* ACA. *Program availability:* Part-time, evening/weekend. *Degree requirements:* For master's, comprehensive exam (for some programs), thesis (for some programs). *Entrance requirements:* For master's, GRE General Test (psychology), minimum GPA of 2.75 (psychology). Additional exam requirements/recommendations for international students: required—TOEFL (minimum score 550 paper-based). Electronic applications accepted.

Memorial University of Newfoundland, School of Graduate Studies, Department of Psychology, St. John's, NL A1C 5S7, Canada. Offers applied psychological sciences (MAPS); clinical psychology (Psy D); experimental psychology (M Sc, PhD). *Program availability:* Part-time. *Degree requirements:* For master's, workterms (MASP), thesis (M Sc); for doctorate, comprehensive exam, thesis/dissertation, oral thesis defense. *Entrance requirements:* For master's, GRE, honors bachelor's degree of high second class standing or equivalent; for doctorate, GRE, master's or honors degree. Electronic applications accepted.

Mercer University, Graduate Studies, Cecil B. Day Campus, College of Professional Advancement, Atlanta, GA 31207. Offers certified rehabilitation counseling (MS); clinical mental health (MS); counselor education and supervision (PhD); criminal justice and public safety leadership (MS); health informatics (MS); human services (MS), including child and adolescent services, gerontology services; organizational leadership (MS), including leadership for the health care professional, leadership for the nonprofit organization, organizational development and change; school counseling (MS). *Program availability:* Part-time, evening/weekend, 100% online, blended/hybrid learning. *Faculty:* 19 full-time (11 women), 34 part-time/adjunct (30 women). *Students:* 193 full-time (156 women), 277 part-time (225 women); includes 260 minority (211 Black or African American, non-Hispanic/Latino; 2 American Indian or Alaska Native, non-Hispanic/Latino; 23 Asian, non-Hispanic/Latino; 19 Hispanic/Latino; 5 Two or more races, non-Hispanic/Latino), 3 international. Average age 32. 300 applicants, 45% accepted, 114 enrolled. In 2019, 183 master's, 7 doctorates awarded. *Degree requirements:* For master's, comprehensive exam (for some programs), thesis (for some programs); for doctorate, thesis/dissertation. *Entrance requirements:* For master's, GRE or MAT, Georgia Professional Standards Commission (GPSC) Certification at the SC-5 level; for doctorate, GRE or MAT. Additional exam requirements/recommendations for international students: recommended—TOEFL (minimum score 550 paper-based; 80 iBT), IELTS (minimum score 6.5). *Application deadline:* For fall admission, 7/1 priority date for domestic and international students; for spring admission, 11/1 priority date for domestic and international students; for summer admission, 4/1 priority date for domestic and international students. Application fee: $35. Electronic applications accepted. Application fee is waived when completed online. *Expenses:* Contact institution. *Financial support:* In 2019–20, 32 students received support. Federal Work-Study, scholarships/grants, and unspecified assistantships available. Financial award applicants required to submit FAFSA. *Unit head:* Dr. Priscilla R. Danheiser, Dean, 678-547-6028, Fax: 678-547-6008, E-mail: danheiser_p@mercer.edu. *Application contact:* Theatis Anderson, Asst VP for Enrollment Management, 678-547-6421, E-mail: anderson_t@mercer.edu.
Website: https://professionaladvancement.mercer.edu/

Merrimack College, School of Liberal Arts, North Andover, MA 01845-5800. Offers clinical mental health counseling (MS); interfaith spirituality (Certificate); public affairs (MPA); spiritual direction (MA, Certificate); spirituality (MA). *Program availability:* Part-time, evening/weekend. *Degree requirements:* For master's, internship/strategic capstone (for MPA); 700-hour fieldwork placement (for MS); practicum (for MA in spiritual direction); for Certificate, practicum (for spiritual direction). *Entrance requirements:* For master's, official college transcripts, resume, personal statement, 2 recommendations (3 for MS in clinical mental health counseling); interview (for MA in spirituality). Additional exam requirements/recommendations for international students: required—TOEFL (minimum score 84 iBT), IELTS (minimum score 6.5), PTE (minimum score 56). Electronic applications accepted. Application fee is waived when completed online. *Expenses:* Contact institution.

Messiah University, Program in Counseling, Mechanicsburg, PA 17055. Offers clinical mental health counseling (MAC); counseling (CAGS); marriage, couple, and family counseling (MAC); school counseling (MAC). *Accreditation:* ACA. *Program availability:* Part-time, online learning. *Entrance requirements:* For master's, minimum undergraduate cumulative GPA of 3.0, 2 recommendations, resume or curriculum vitae, interview; for CAGS, bachelor's degree, minimum undergraduate cumulative GPA of 3.0, essay, two recommendations, resume or curriculum vitae, interview. Electronic applications accepted.

Michigan School of Psychology, MA and Psy D Programs in Clinical Psychology, Farmington Hills, MI 48334. Offers MA, Psy D. *Accreditation:* APA. *Program availability:* Part-time, evening/weekend. *Faculty:* 14 full-time (7 women), 16 part-time/adjunct (11 women). *Students:* 125 full-time (97 women), 60 part-time (43 women); includes 47 minority (29 Black or African American, non-Hispanic/Latino; 3 Asian, non-Hispanic/Latino; 6 Hispanic/Latino; 9 Two or more races, non-Hispanic/Latino). Average age 30. 205 applicants, 54% accepted, 86 enrolled. In 2019, 61 master's, 13 doctorates awarded. *Degree requirements:* For master's, practicum; for doctorate, comprehensive exam, thesis/dissertation, internship, practicum. *Entrance requirements:* For master's, undergraduate degree from accredited institution with minimum GPA of 2.5; major in psychology, social work, or counseling (prerequisites apply without one of these degrees); for doctorate, GRE General Test, undergraduate degree from accredited institution with minimum GPA of 2.5; graduate degree in psychology, social work, or counseling from accredited institution with minimum GPA of 3.25; graduate-level practicum. Additional exam requirements/recommendations for international students: required—TOEFL (minimum score 550 paper-based; 79 iBT). *Application deadline:* For fall admission, 2/15 for domestic students. Application fee: $75. Electronic applications accepted. *Expenses: Tuition:* Full-time $40,000; part-time $15,000 per year. *Required fees:* $2265; $780 per semester. $260 per semester. One-time fee: $75. Tuition and fees vary according to course load, degree level and program. *Financial support:* In 2019–20, 12 students received support, including 1 research assistantship (averaging $8,566 per year), 5 teaching assistantships (averaging $14,436 per year); institutionally sponsored loans, scholarships/grants, and unspecified assistantships also available. Financial award application deadline: 8/30; financial award applicants required to submit FAFSA. *Unit head:* Dr. Shannon Chavez-Korell, Program Director, 248-476-1122, Fax: 248-476-1125. *Application contact:* Carrie Pyeatt, Coordinator of Admissions and Student Engagement, 248-476-1122 Ext. 117, Fax: 248-476-1125, E-mail: cpyeatt@msp.edu.
Website: msp.edu

MidAmerica Nazarene University, School of Behavioral Sciences and Counseling, Olathe, KS 66062-1899. Offers counseling (MA), including clinical mental health, marriage, couple and family, school counseling, spiritual formation in counseling. *Accreditation:* ACA. *Program availability:* 100% online. *Faculty:* 7 full-time (2 women), 14 part-time/adjunct (9 women). *Students:* 64 full-time (52 women), 143 part-time (113 women); includes 33 minority (20 Black or African American, non-Hispanic/Latino; 2 American Indian or Alaska Native, non-Hispanic/Latino; 2 Asian, non-Hispanic/Latino; 8 Hispanic/Latino; 1 Two or more races, non-Hispanic/Latino), 1 international. Average age 34. 131 applicants, 73% accepted, 84 enrolled. In 2019, 50 master's awarded. *Degree requirements:* For master's, comprehensive exam. *Entrance requirements:* For master's, on-site writing assessment, official transcript, three recommendations, personal interview, background check. Additional exam requirements/recommendations for international students: required—TOEFL (minimum score 81 iBT). *Application* *deadline:* For winter admission, 2/15 for domestic and international students; for spring admission, 4/1 for domestic and international students. Electronic applications accepted. *Expenses:* Technology fee ($2,040), Graduation fee ($100), carrying fee ($286), professional fee($811), lab fee ($325), other fee ($1,068). *Financial support:* Applicants required to submit FAFSA. *Unit head:* Dr. Todd Frye, Dean, School of Behavioral Sciences and Counseling, 913-971-3449, Fax: 913-971-3402, E-mail: tmfrye@mnu.edu. *Application contact:* Jeanne Blades, Administrative Assistant, 913-971-3730, E-mail: jmblades@mnu.edu.

Middle Tennessee State University, College of Graduate Studies, College of Behavioral and Health Sciences, Department of Psychology, Murfreesboro, TN 37132. Offers clinical psychology (MA); experimental psychology (MA); industrial/organizational psychology (MA); psychology (MA, Ed S); quantitative psychology (MA); school psychology (MA). *Program availability:* Part-time, evening/weekend, online learning. *Degree requirements:* For master's, comprehensive exam, thesis. *Entrance requirements:* For master's, GRE. Additional exam requirements/recommendations for international students: required—TOEFL (minimum score 525 paper-based; 71 iBT) or IELTS (minimum score 6). Electronic applications accepted.

Midwestern State University, Billie Doris McAda Graduate School, Prothro-Yeager College of Humanities and Social Sciences, Department of Psychology, Wichita Falls, TX 76308. Offers clinical/counseling psychology (MA). *Program availability:* Part-time, evening/weekend. *Degree requirements:* For master's, one foreign language, comprehensive exam, thesis optional. *Entrance requirements:* For master's, GRE General Test, 3 recommendation forms. Additional exam requirements/recommendations for international students: required—TOEFL (minimum score 550 paper-based). Electronic applications accepted.

Midwestern University, Downers Grove Campus, College of Health Sciences, Illinois Campus, Program in Clinical Psychology, Downers Grove, IL 60515-1235. Offers Psy D. *Accreditation:* APA. *Degree requirements:* For doctorate, thesis/dissertation, qualifying examination. *Entrance requirements:* For doctorate, GRE, minimum overall GPA of 2.75, 3 letters of recommendation. Additional exam requirements/recommendations for international students: required—TOEFL.

Midwestern University, Glendale Campus, College of Health Sciences, Arizona Campus, Program in Clinical Psychology, Glendale, AZ 85308. Offers Psy D. *Accreditation:* APA.

Millersville University of Pennsylvania, College of Graduate Studies and Adult Learning, College of Education and Human Services, Department of Psychology, Millersville, PA 17551-0302. Offers psychology (MS), including clinical psychology, school psychology; school counseling (M Ed). *Program availability:* Part-time. *Faculty:* 11 full-time (6 women), 3 part-time/adjunct (0 women). *Students:* 63 full-time (52 women), 84 part-time (65 women); includes 19 minority (3 Black or African American, non-Hispanic/Latino; 3 Asian, non-Hispanic/Latino; 11 Hispanic/Latino; 2 Two or more races, non-Hispanic/Latino), 2 international. Average age 27. 77 applicants, 75% accepted, 43 enrolled. In 2019, 42 master's awarded. *Degree requirements:* For master's, comprehensive exam (for some programs), thesis optional, internship, practicum, portfolio. *Entrance requirements:* For master's, GRE required only if cumulative GPA is lower than 3.0, At least 1 academic reference, interview, 18 undergraduate credits in Psychology (Clinical and School), 6 undergraduate credits in Psychology (school counseling). Additional exam requirements/recommendations for international students: required—TOEFL, IELTS (minimum score 6), PTE (minimum score 60). *Application deadline:* For fall admission, 1/15 for domestic students; for winter admission, 4/15 for domestic students; for spring admission, 10/1 for domestic students. Application fee: $40. Electronic applications accepted. *Expenses: Tuition, area resident:* Part-time $516 per credit. Tuition, state resident: part-time $516 per credit. Tuition, nonresident: part-time $774 per credit. *Required fees:* $118.75 per credit. Tuition and fees vary according to course load, degree level and program. *Financial support:* In 2019–20, 55 students received support. Scholarships/grants and unspecified assistantships available. Financial award application deadline: 3/15; financial award applicants required to submit FAFSA. *Unit head:* Dr. Debra S. Vredenburg-Rudy, Chair, 717-871-7279, Fax: 717-871-7946, E-mail: debra.vredenburg@millersville.edu. *Application contact:* Dr. James A. Delle, Acting Dean of College of Graduate Studies and Adult Learning/Associate Provost, Academic Administration, 717-871-7462, E-mail: James.Delle@millersville.edu.
Website: https://www.millersville.edu/psychology/index.php

Millersville University of Pennsylvania, College of Graduate Studies and Adult Learning, College of Education and Human Services, Department of Psychology, Program in Clinical Psychology, Millersville, PA 17551-0302. Offers psychology (MS). *Program availability:* Part-time. *Students:* 25 full-time (20 women), 30 part-time (19 women); includes 8 minority (1 Black or African American, non-Hispanic/Latino; 1 Asian, non-Hispanic/Latino; 5 Hispanic/Latino; 1 Two or more races, non-Hispanic/Latino), 2 international. Average age 25. 37 applicants, 65% accepted, 19 enrolled. In 2019, 16 master's awarded. *Degree requirements:* For master's, comprehensive exam, thesis optional, internship. *Entrance requirements:* For master's, GRE required only if cumulative GPA is lower than 3.0, at least 1 academic reference; interview; 18 undergraduate credits in psychology. Additional exam requirements/recommendations for international students: required—TOEFL, IELTS (minimum score 6), PTE (minimum score 60). *Application deadline:* For fall admission, 1/15 for domestic students; for winter admission, 4/15 for domestic students; for spring admission, 10/1 for domestic students. Application fee: $40. Electronic applications accepted. *Expenses: Tuition, area resident:* Part-time $516 per credit. Tuition, state resident: part-time $516 per credit. Tuition, nonresident: part-time $774 per credit. *Required fees:* $118.75 per credit. Tuition and fees vary according to course load, degree level and program. *Financial support:* In 2019–20, 19 students received support. Scholarships/grants and unspecified assistantships available. Financial award application deadline: 3/15; financial award applicants required to submit FAFSA. *Unit head:* Dr. Karena Rush, Coordinator, 717-871-7276, Fax: 717-871-7946, E-mail: karena.rush@millersville.edu. *Application contact:* Dr. James A. Delle, Acting Dean of College of Graduate Studies and Adult Learning/Associate Provost, Academic Administration, 717-871-7462, E-mail: James.Delle@millersville.edu.
Website: https://www.millersville.edu/psychology/graduate-programs-webpages/clinical-psychology/index.php

Milligan University, Area of Counselor Education Programs, Milligan College, TN 37682. Offers clinical mental health counseling (MSC); counseling ministry (Graduate Certificate); school counseling (MSC). *Program availability:* Part-time. *Faculty:* 3 full-time (all women), 2 part-time/adjunct (1 woman). *Students:* 24 full-time (20 women), 4 part-time (3 women); includes 2 minority (1 Black or African American, non-Hispanic/Latino; 1 Two or more races, non-Hispanic/Latino). Average age 30. 33 applicants, 67% accepted, 16 enrolled. In 2019, 15 master's awarded. *Degree requirements:* For master's, thesis or alternative. *Entrance requirements:* For master's, GRE General Test if undergraduate GPA is less than 3.0, undergraduate degree and supporting transcripts, essay/personal statement, professional recommendations, interview. Additional exam requirements/recommendations for international students: required—TOEFL (minimum score 550 paper-based, 79 iBT) or IELTS (6.5). *Application deadline:* For fall admission, 8/1 for domestic students, 6/1 for international students. Applications are processed on a

rolling basis. Application fee: $30. Electronic applications accepted. *Expenses:* Up to 60 hr program; $460/hr; $75 one-time records fee; $325/semester (technology and activity fees). *Financial support:* Scholarships/grants available. Financial award application deadline: 12/1; financial award applicants required to submit FAFSA. *Unit head:* Dr. Rebecca Sapp, Director of Master of Science in Counseling Program, 423-461-3071, E-mail: rlsapp@milligan.edu. *Application contact:* Stacy Shankle, Graduate Admissions Recruiter, Healthcare Programs, 423-461-8424, Fax: 423-461-8789, E-mail: srshankle@milligan.edu.

Minnesota State University Mankato, College of Graduate Studies and Research, College of Social and Behavioral Sciences, Department of Psychology, Mankato, MN 56001. Offers clinical psychology (MA); industrial/organizational psychology (MA); school psychology (Psy D). *Program availability:* Part-time. *Degree requirements:* For master's, one foreign language, comprehensive exam, thesis (for some programs). *Entrance requirements:* For master's, GRE General Test, GRE Subject Test (clinical psychology), minimum GPA of 3.0 during previous 2 years, 3 letters of reference. Additional exam requirements/recommendations for international students: required—TOEFL. Electronic applications accepted.

Mississippi State University, College of Arts and Sciences, Department of Psychology, Mississippi State, MS 39762. Offers applied psychology (PhD), including clinical, cognitive science; psychology (MS). *Accreditation:* APA. *Faculty:* 18 full-time (7 women). *Students:* 37 full-time (24 women), 9 part-time (4 women); includes 8 minority (4 Black or African American, non-Hispanic/Latino; 3 Asian, non-Hispanic/Latino; 1 Hispanic/Latino). Average age 28. 79 applicants, 20% accepted, 8 enrolled. In 2019, 6 master's, 1 doctorate awarded. Terminal master's awarded for partial completion of doctoral program. *Degree requirements:* For master's, comprehensive exam, thesis; for doctorate, thesis/dissertation, qualifying exam, comprehensive written and oral exam. *Entrance requirements:* For master's, GRE General Test, minimum GPA of 2.75 on last two years of undergraduate courses; for doctorate, GRE General Test, proficiency in at least 1 computer language, minimum GPA of 3.0. Additional exam requirements/recommendations for international students: required—TOEFL (minimum score 477 paper-based; 53 iBT); recommended—IELTS (minimum score 4.5). *Application deadline:* For fall admission, 4/1 priority date for domestic students, 5/1 for international students; for spring admission, 11/1 priority date for domestic students, 9/1 for international students. Applications are processed on a rolling basis. Application fee: $60 ($80 for international students). Electronic applications accepted. *Expenses: Tuition, area resident:* Full-time $8880; part-time $456 per credit hour. Tuition, state resident: full-time $8880. Tuition, nonresident: full-time $23,840; part-time $1236 per credit hour. *Required fees:* $110; $11.12 per credit hour. Tuition and fees vary according to course load. *Financial support:* In 2019–20, 6 research assistantships with full tuition reimbursements (averaging $13,607 per year), 28 teaching assistantships with full tuition reimbursements (averaging $11,864 per year) were awarded; career-related internships or fieldwork, Federal Work-Study, institutionally sponsored loans, scholarships/grants, and unspecified assistantships also available. Financial award application deadline: 4/1; financial award applicants required to submit FAFSA. *Unit head:* Dr. Mitchell E. Berman, Professor and Head, 662-325-3202, Fax: 662-325-7212, E-mail: mberman@psychology.msstate.edu. *Application contact:* Angie Campbell, Admissions and Enrollment Assistant, 662-325-9514, E-mail: acampbell@grad.msstate.edu.
Website: http://www.psychology.msstate.edu/

Mississippi State University, College of Education, Department of Counseling, Educational Psychology, and Foundations, Mississippi State, MS 39762. Offers clinical mental health (MS); college counseling (MS); counseling/mental health (PhD); counseling/school psychology (PhD); counselor education (Ed S); educational psychology/general educational psychology (PhD); educational psychology/school psychology (PhD); general educational psychology (MS); psychometry (MS); rehabilitation counseling (MS); school counseling (MS); school psychology (Ed S); student affairs (MS). *Accreditation:* ACA (one or more programs are accredited); APA; CORE (one or more programs are accredited); NCATE. *Program availability:* Part-time, blended/hybrid learning. *Faculty:* 15 full-time (10 women), 3 part-time/adjunct (all women). *Students:* 105 full-time (87 women), 47 part-time (37 women); includes 58 minority (49 Black or African American, non-Hispanic/Latino; 1 Asian, non-Hispanic/Latino; 6 Hispanic/Latino; 2 Two or more races, non-Hispanic/Latino), 7 international. Average age 30. 83 applicants, 69% accepted, 40 enrolled. In 2019, 39 master's, 3 doctorates, 7 other advanced degrees awarded. Terminal master's awarded for partial completion of doctoral program. *Degree requirements:* For master's, comprehensive exam, thesis optional; for doctorate, thesis/dissertation, comprehensive oral and written exam. *Entrance requirements:* For master's, GRE (taken within the last five years), BS with minimum GPA of 2.75 on last 60 hours; for doctorate, GRE, MS from CACREP- or CORE-accredited program in counseling; for Ed S, GRE, MS in counseling or related field, minimum GPA of 3.3 on all graduate work. Additional exam requirements/recommendations for international students: required—TOEFL (minimum score 550 paper-based; 79 iBT); recommended—IELTS (minimum score 6.5). *Application deadline:* For fall admission, 2/1 priority date for domestic and international students. Applications are processed on a rolling basis. Application fee: $60 ($80 for international students). Electronic applications accepted. *Expenses: Tuition, area resident:* Full-time $8880; part-time $456 per credit hour. Tuition, state resident: full-time $8880. Tuition, nonresident: full-time $23,840; part-time $1236 per credit hour. *Required fees:* $110; $11.12 per credit hour. Tuition and fees vary according to course load. *Financial support:* In 2019–20, 3 research assistantships (averaging $9,000 per year), 7 teaching assistantships with full tuition reimbursements (averaging $8,401 per year) were awarded; career-related internships or fieldwork, Federal Work-Study, institutionally sponsored loans, and unspecified assistantships also available. Financial award application deadline: 2/1; financial award applicants required to submit FAFSA. *Unit head:* Dr. Daniel Gadke, Professor and Interim Head, 662-325-3426, Fax: 662-325-3263, E-mail: dgadke@colled.msstate.edu. *Application contact:* Ryan King, Admissions and Enrollment Assistant, 662-325-8951, E-mail: rjk101@grad.msstate.edu.
Website: http://www.cep.msstate.edu/

Missouri State University, Graduate College, College of Health and Human Services, Department of Psychology, Springfield, MO 65897. Offers applied behavior analysis (MS); clinical psychology (MS); experimental psychology (MS); forensic child psychology (Certificate); industrial/organizational psychology (MS). *Degree requirements:* For master's, comprehensive exam, thesis. *Entrance requirements:* For master's, GRE General Test, GRE Subject Test, minimum GPA of 3.25 in major, 3.0 overall; 20 hours of course work in psychology. Additional exam requirements/recommendations for international students: required—TOEFL (minimum score 550 paper-based; 79 iBT), IELTS (minimum score 6). Electronic applications accepted. *Expenses: Tuition, area resident:* Full-time $2600; part-time $1735 per credit hour. Tuition, nonresident: full-time $5240; part-time $3495 per credit hour. *International tuition:* $5240 full-time. *Required fees:* $530; $438 per credit hour. Tuition and fees vary according to class time, course level, course load, degree level, campus/location and program.

Molloy College, Program in Clinical Mental Health Counseling, Rockville Centre, NY 11571. Offers clinical mental health counseling (MS). *Program availability:* Part-time-

only, evening/weekend. *Faculty:* 3 full-time (2 women), 1 (woman) part-time/adjunct. *Students:* 14 full-time (12 women), 30 part-time (24 women); includes 14 minority (7 Black or African American, non-Hispanic/Latino; 1 Asian, non-Hispanic/Latino; 5 Hispanic/Latino; 1 Two or more races, non-Hispanic/Latino). Average age 33. 33 applicants, 45% accepted, 14 enrolled. In 2019, 13 master's awarded. *Degree requirements:* For master's, A practicum (100 clock hours) course and a one year (600 clock hours) supervised internship in mental health counseling in a Molloy College approved mental health setting. *Entrance requirements:* For master's, Graduate Record Examination - verbal, quantitative, and writing, Baccalaureate degree with a minimum G.P.A. of 3.0 or higher from an accredited college or university, or successful completion of another master's degree demonstrating prerequisite coursework; Official copies of undergraduate and/or graduate transcripts; Current resume; Personal statement; Three academic or professional letters of recommendation; P. Additional exam requirements/recommendations for international students: required—TOEFL (minimum score 550 paper-based; 79 iBT). *Application deadline:* Applications are processed on a rolling basis. Application fee: $60. Electronic applications accepted. *Expenses: Tuition:* Full-time $21,510; part-time $1195 per credit hour. *Required fees:* $1100. Tuition and fees vary according to course load, degree level and program. *Financial support:* Application deadline: 3/1; applicants required to submit FAFSA. *Unit head:* Dr. Laura B. Kestemberg, Associate Dean and Director, Master of Science Program Department of Clinical Mental Health Counseling, 516-323-3842, E-mail: lkestemberg@molloy.edu. *Application contact:* Faye Hood, Assistant Director for Admissions, 516-323-4009, E-mail: fhood@molloy.edu.
Website: https://www.molloy.edu/academics/graduate-programs/master-of-science-in-clinical-mental-health-counseling

Montclair State University, The Graduate School, College of Humanities and Social Sciences, Program in Clinical Psychology, Montclair, NJ 07043-1624. Offers MA. *Program availability:* Part-time, evening/weekend. *Entrance requirements:* For master's, GRE General Test, 2 letters of recommendation, essay. Additional exam requirements/recommendations for international students: required—TOEFL (minimum score 83 iBT), IELTS (minimum score 6.5). Electronic applications accepted.

Morehead State University, Graduate School, College of Science, Department of Psychology, Morehead, KY 40351. Offers clinical/counseling psychology (MS); general/experimental psychology (MS). *Program availability:* Part-time, evening/weekend. *Faculty:* 8 full-time (5 women), 1 part-time/adjunct (0 women). *Students:* 10 full-time (9 women), 1 (woman) part-time; includes 2 minority (both Two or more races, non-Hispanic/Latino). 20 applicants, 60% accepted, 6 enrolled. In 2019, 11 master's awarded. *Degree requirements:* For master's, comprehensive exam, Minimum 3.0 GPA, internship, pass a comprehensive oral examination administered by a committee of three faculty. *Entrance requirements:* For master's, GRE, 3.5 UG GPA preferred, 3.0 is minimum required, 18 hrs in psychology, interview, 3 letters of recommendation, statement of purpose for seeking graduate-level training in clinical/counseling psychology. *Application deadline:* For fall admission, 3/1 priority date for domestic and international students. Applications are processed on a rolling basis. Application fee: $30. Electronic applications accepted. *Expenses: Tuition, area resident:* Part-time $570 per credit hour. Tuition, state resident: part-time $570 per credit hour. Tuition, nonresident: part-time $570 per credit hour. *Required fees:* $14 per credit hour. *Financial support:* Research assistantships, career-related internships or fieldwork, and unspecified assistantships available. Financial award applicants required to submit FAFSA. *Unit head:* Dr. Gregory Corso, Department Chair Psychology, 606-783-2981, E-mail: g.corso@moreheadstate.edu. *Application contact:* Dr. Gregory Corso, Department Chair Psychology, 606-783-2981, E-mail: g.corso@moreheadstate.edu.
Website: https://www.moreheadstate.edu/College-of-Science/Psychology

Mount Mary University, Graduate Programs, Program in Counseling, Milwaukee, WI 53222-4597. Offers clinical mental health counseling (MS, Certificate); clinical rehabilitation counseling (MS, Certificate); school counseling (MS, Certificate); vocational rehabilitation counseling (MS, Certificate). *Accreditation:* ACA. *Program availability:* Part-time, evening/weekend. *Degree requirements:* For master's, comprehensive exam, thesis or alternative. *Entrance requirements:* For master's, minimum GPA of 3.0. Additional exam requirements/recommendations for international students: required—TOEFL (minimum score 550 paper-based; 80 iBT); recommended—IELTS (minimum score 6.5). Electronic applications accepted. *Expenses:* Contact institution.

Murray State University, College of Humanities and Fine Arts, Department of Psychology, Murray, KY 42071. Offers clinical psychology (MA, MS); general experimental psychology (MA, MS); research design and analysis (Certificate). *Program availability:* Part-time. *Entrance requirements:* For master's and Certificate, GRE or GMAT, minimum university GPA of 2.75. Additional exam requirements/recommendations for international students: required—TOEFL (minimum score 527 paper-based; 71 iBT). Electronic applications accepted.

National University, College of Letters and Sciences, La Jolla, CA 92037-1011. Offers biology (MS); counseling psychology (MA), including licensed professional clinical counseling, marriage and family therapy; creative writing (MFA); English (MA); film studies (MA); forensic and crime scene investigations (Certificate); forensic sciences (MFS); human behavior (MA); mathematics for educators (MS); performance psychology (MA); strategic communications (MA). *Program availability:* Part-time, evening/weekend, 100% online, blended/hybrid learning. *Degree requirements:* For master's, thesis (for some programs). *Entrance requirements:* For master's, interview, minimum GPA of 2.5. Additional exam requirements/recommendations for international students: required—TOEFL (minimum score 550 paper-based; 79 iBT), IELTS (minimum score 6). Electronic applications accepted. *Expenses: Tuition:* Full-time $442; part-time $442 per unit.

Neumann University, Program in Pastoral Clinical Mental Health Counseling, Aston, PA 19014-1298. Offers pastoral care specialist (Certificate); pastoral clinical mental health counseling (MS); pastoral clinical mental health counseling certificate of advanced study (Certificate); pastoral counseling (PhD); spiritual formation and direction (CSD); spiritual formation and direction supervision certificate of advanced study (Certificate). *Program availability:* Part-time, evening/weekend. *Degree requirements:* For doctorate, comprehensive exam, thesis/dissertation. *Entrance requirements:* For master's and other advanced degree, official transcripts from all institutions attended, letter of intent, three letters of recommendation; for doctorate, MAT, master's degree, official transcripts from all institutions attended, resume or curriculum vitae, letter of intent, two official letters of recommendation. Additional exam requirements/recommendations for international students: required—TOEFL (minimum score 70 iBT). Electronic applications accepted. *Expenses:* Contact institution.

New Mexico Highlands University, Graduate Studies, College of Arts and Sciences, Department of Social and Behavioral Sciences, Las Vegas, NM 87701. Offers psychology (MS), including clinical psychology/counseling, general psychology; public affairs (MA), including applied sociology; Southwest studies (MA), including anthropology. *Program availability:* Part-time. *Degree requirements:* For master's, comprehensive exam, thesis or alternative. *Entrance requirements:* For master's, minimum undergraduate GPA of 3.0. Additional exam requirements/recommendations for international students: required—TOEFL (minimum score 540 paper-based).

The New School, The New School for Social Research, Department of Psychology, New York, NY 10011. Offers clinical psychology (PhD); cognitive, social, and developmental psychology (PhD); psychology (MA). *Accreditation:* APA (one or more programs are accredited). *Program availability:* Part-time. *Faculty:* 17 full-time (9 women), 8 part-time/adjunct (2 women). *Students:* 173 full-time (135 women), 32 part-time (28 women); includes 36 minority (8 Black or African American, non-Hispanic/Latino; 8 Asian, non-Hispanic/Latino; 17 Hispanic/Latino; 1 Native Hawaiian or other Pacific Islander, non-Hispanic/Latino; 2 Two or more races, non-Hispanic/Latino), 42 international. Average age 29. 217 applicants, 85% accepted, 58 enrolled. In 2019, 75 master's, 14 doctorates awarded. Terminal master's awarded for partial completion of doctoral program. *Degree requirements:* For master's, comprehensive exam, thesis (for some programs); for doctorate, comprehensive exam, thesis/dissertation. *Entrance requirements:* For master's, GRE, letters of recommendation, writing sample, essays, transcripts; for doctorate, letters of recommendation, writing sample, essays, transcripts. Additional exam requirements/recommendations for international students: required—TOEFL (minimum score 100 iBT), IELTS (minimum score 7), PTE (minimum score 68). *Application deadline:* For fall admission, 1/5 priority date for domestic and international students; for spring admission, 10/15 priority date for domestic and international students. Applications are processed on a rolling basis. Application fee: $50. Electronic applications accepted. *Expenses:* 2260 per credit. *Financial support:* In 2019–20, 191 students received support, including 21 fellowships with full and partial tuition reimbursements available (averaging $6,560 per year), 43 research assistantships (averaging $5,556 per year), 52 teaching assistantships with full and partial tuition reimbursements available (averaging $7,423 per year); career-related internships or fieldwork, Federal Work-Study, scholarships/grants, and tuition waivers (full and partial) also available. Support available to part-time students. Financial award application deadline: 2/1; financial award applicants required to submit FAFSA. *Unit head:* Dr. Howard Steele, Department Chair, 212-2295727 Ext. 3118, E-mail: steeleh@newschool.edu. *Application contact:* Merida Gasbarro, Director of Graduate Admission, 212-229-5600 Ext. 1108, E-mail: escandom@newschool.edu.
Website: https://www.newschool.edu/nssr/psychology/

Nicholls State University, Graduate Studies, College of Education, Department of Psychology, Counseling and Family Studies, Thibodaux, LA 70310. Offers clinical mental health counseling (MA); school counseling (M Ed); school psychology (SSP). *Accreditation:* NCATE. *Program availability:* Part-time, evening/weekend. *Degree requirements:* For master's, comprehensive exam; for SSP, comprehensive exam, internship. *Entrance requirements:* For master's, GRE General Test. Electronic applications accepted.

Norfolk State University, School of Graduate Studies, School of Liberal Arts, Department of Psychology, Program in Community/Clinical Psychology, Norfolk, VA 23504. Offers MA. *Degree requirements:* For master's, comprehensive exam, thesis or alternative. *Entrance requirements:* For master's, minimum GPA of 2.7.

North Carolina Agricultural and Technical State University, The Graduate College, College of Education, Department of Counseling, Greensboro, NC 27411. Offers mental health counseling (MS); rehabilitation counseling and rehabilitation counselor education (PhD); school counseling (MS). *Accreditation:* ACA. *Program availability:* Part-time, evening/weekend. *Degree requirements:* For master's, comprehensive exam, thesis, qualifying exam. *Entrance requirements:* For master's, GRE General Test, minimum GPA of 3.0.

North Carolina Central University, College of Behavioral and Social Sciences, Department of Psychology, Durham, NC 27707-3129. Offers clinical psychology (MA); general psychology (MA). *Program availability:* Part-time, evening/weekend. *Degree requirements:* For master's, one foreign language, comprehensive exam, thesis. *Entrance requirements:* For master's, GRE, minimum GPA of 3.0 in major, 2.5 overall. Additional exam requirements/recommendations for international students: required—TOEFL.

North Carolina Central University, School of Education, Program in Counselor Education, Durham, NC 27707-3129. Offers career counseling (MA); clinical mental health counseling (MA); school counseling (MA). *Accreditation:* ACA; NCATE. *Program availability:* Part-time, evening/weekend. *Degree requirements:* For master's, comprehensive exam, thesis or alternative. *Entrance requirements:* For master's, GRE, minimum GPA of 3.0 in major, 2.5 overall. Additional exam requirements/recommendations for international students: required—TOEFL.

North Dakota State University, College of Graduate and Interdisciplinary Studies, College of Science and Mathematics, Department of Psychology, Fargo, ND 58102. Offers clinical psychology (MS); health and social psychology (PhD); psychological clinical science (PhD); psychology (MS); visual and cognitive neuroscience (PhD). *Entrance requirements:* Additional exam requirements/recommendations for international students: required—TOEFL. Electronic applications accepted. Tuition and fees vary according to program and reciprocity agreements.

Northeastern Illinois University, College of Graduate Studies and Research, Daniel L. Goodwin College of Education, Program in Clinical Mental Health Counseling, Chicago, IL 60625-4699. Offers MA.

Northern Kentucky University, Office of Graduate Programs, College of Education and Human Services, Clinical Mental Health Counseling Program, Highland Heights, KY 41099. Offers MS. *Accreditation:* ACA. *Program availability:* Part-time, evening/weekend. *Degree requirements:* For master's, comprehensive exam. *Entrance requirements:* For master's, GRE or MAT. Additional exam requirements/recommendations for international students: required—TOEFL (minimum score 550 paper-based; 79 iBT); recommended—IELTS (minimum score 6.5). Electronic applications accepted.

Northern State University, MS Ed Program in Counseling, Aberdeen, SD 57401-7198. Offers clinical mental health counseling (MS Ed); school counseling (MS Ed). *Accreditation:* ACA; NCATE. *Program availability:* Part-time, online learning. *Faculty:* 5 full-time (all women). *Students:* 21 full-time (16 women), 2 part-time (1 woman); includes 4 minority (1 American Indian or Alaska Native, non-Hispanic/Latino; 1 Hispanic/Latino; 2 Two or more races, non-Hispanic/Latino), 1 international. Average age 29. 17 applicants, 47% accepted, 8 enrolled. In 2019, 12 master's awarded. *Degree requirements:* For master's, comprehensive exam, thesis optional. *Entrance requirements:* For master's, minimum GPA of 2.75. Additional exam requirements/recommendations for international students: required—TOEFL (minimum score 550 paper-based; 78 iBT), IELTS (minimum score 6). *Application deadline:* For fall admission, 8/15 for domestic and international students; for spring admission, 12/15 for domestic and international students. Applications are processed on a rolling basis. Application fee: $35. Electronic applications accepted. *Expenses: Tuition, area resident:* Full-time $5939; part-time $5939 per year. Tuition, state resident: full-time $8816; part-time $8816 per year. Tuition, nonresident: full-time $11,088; part-time $11,088 per year. *International tuition:* $7392 full-time. *Required fees:* $484; $242. *Financial support:* In 2019–20, 11 students received support, including 5 teaching assistantships with partial tuition reimbursements available (averaging $7,764 per year); career-related internships or fieldwork, Federal Work-Study, institutionally sponsored loans, scholarships/grants, and unspecified assistantships also available. Support available to part-time students.

Financial award application deadline: 3/1; financial award applicants required to submit FAFSA. *Unit head:* Dr. Doug Ohmer, Dean of Professional Studies, 605-626-2400, Fax: 605-626-2980, E-mail: doug.ohmer@northern.edu. *Application contact:* Tammy K. Griffith, Program Assistant, 605-626-2558, Fax: 605-626-7190, E-mail: tammy.griffith@northern.edu.
Website: https://www.northern.edu/programs/graduate/counseling-masters

Northwestern State University of Louisiana, Graduate Studies and Research, Department of Psychology, Natchitoches, LA 71497. Offers clinical psychology (MS). *Degree requirements:* For master's, comprehensive exam, thesis or alternative. *Entrance requirements:* For master's, GRE General Test, GRE Subject Test, minimum undergraduate GPA of 2.5. Additional exam requirements/recommendations for international students: required—TOEFL. Electronic applications accepted.

Northwestern University, Feinberg School of Medicine and The Graduate School, Program in Clinical Psychology, Evanston, IL 60208. Offers clinical psychology (PhD), including clinical neuropsychology. *Accreditation:* APA. *Degree requirements:* For doctorate, thesis/dissertation, clinical internship. *Entrance requirements:* For doctorate, GRE General Test, GRE Subject Test, minimum GPA of 3.2, course work in psychology. Additional exam requirements/recommendations for international students: required—TOEFL.

Northwestern University, The Graduate School, Judd A. and Marjorie Weinberg College of Arts and Sciences, Department of Psychology, Evanston, IL 60208. Offers brain, behavior and cognition (PhD); clinical psychology (PhD); cognitive psychology (PhD); personality psychology (PhD); social psychology (PhD); JD/PhD. *Accreditation:* APA (one or more programs are accredited). *Program availability:* Part-time. *Degree requirements:* For doctorate, thesis/dissertation. *Entrance requirements:* For doctorate, GRE General Test, GRE Subject Test. Additional exam requirements/recommendations for international students: required—TOEFL. Electronic applications accepted.

Northwest Nazarene University, Program in Social Work, Nampa, ID 83686-5897. Offers clinical mental health and addictions practice (MSW). *Accreditation:* CSWE. *Program availability:* Part-time-only, evening/weekend. *Degree requirements:* For master's, comprehensive exam, thesis or alternative. *Entrance requirements:* For master's, interview, letters of reference, degree from regionally-accredited college/university, written personal statement. Electronic applications accepted.

Notre Dame de Namur University, Division of Academic Affairs, School of Education and Psychology, Program in Clinical Psychology, Belmont, CA 94002-1908. Offers MS. *Program availability:* Part-time. *Degree requirements:* For master's, thesis. *Entrance requirements:* Additional exam requirements/recommendations for international students: required—TOEFL (minimum score 550 paper-based; 79 iBT). Electronic applications accepted.

Nova Southeastern University, College of Psychology, Fort Lauderdale, FL 33314-7796. Offers clinical mental health counseling (MS); clinical psychology (PhD, Psy D); counseling (MS); experimental psychology (MS); forensic psychology (MS); general psychology (MS); school counseling (MS); school psychology (Psy D, Psy S); substance abuse counseling (MS); substance abuse counseling and education (MS). *Accreditation:* APA (one or more programs are accredited). *Program availability:* Part-time, 100% online, blended/hybrid learning. *Faculty:* 72 full-time (34 women), 111 part-time/adjunct (76 women). *Students:* 1,263 full-time (1,068 women), 868 part-time (761 women); includes 1,221 minority (368 Black or African American, non-Hispanic/Latino; 3 American Indian or Alaska Native, non-Hispanic/Latino; 111 Asian, non-Hispanic/Latino; 668 Hispanic/Latino; 1 Native Hawaiian or other Pacific Islander, non-Hispanic/Latino; 70 Two or more races, non-Hispanic/Latino), 59 international. Average age 31. 935 applicants, 56% accepted, 375 enrolled. In 2019, 400 master's, 72 doctorates, 13 other advanced degrees awarded. Terminal master's awarded for partial completion of doctoral program. *Degree requirements:* For master's, comprehensive exam, 3 practica; for doctorate, thesis/dissertation, clinical internship, competency exam; for Psy S, comprehensive exam, internship. *Entrance requirements:* For master's and Psy S, GRE General Test, letters of recommendation, research/personal statement, interview; for doctorate, GRE General Test, GRE Subject Test (recommended), minimum undergraduate GPA of 3.0, letters of recommendation, research/personal statement, interview, curriculum vitae/resume. Additional exam requirements/recommendations for international students: required—TOEFL (minimum score 550 paper-based). *Application deadline:* Applications are processed on a rolling basis. Application fee: $50. Electronic applications accepted. *Expenses:* Contact institution. *Financial support:* In 2019–20, 197 students received support, including 15 research assistantships (averaging $5,600 per year), 68 teaching assistantships (averaging $2,000 per year); career-related internships or fieldwork, Federal Work-Study, institutionally sponsored loans, scholarships/grants, and unspecified assistantships also available. Support available to part-time students. Financial award application deadline: 4/15; financial award applicants required to submit FAFSA. *Unit head:* Dr. Karen Grosby, Dean, 954-262-5712, Fax: 954-262-3859, E-mail: grosby@nova.edu. *Application contact:* Gregory Gayle, Director, Recruitment and Admissions, 954-262-5903, Fax: 954-262-3893, E-mail: ggayle1@nova.edu.
Website: http://psychology.nova.edu/

The Ohio State University, Graduate School, College of Arts and Sciences, Division of Social and Behavioral Sciences, Department of Psychology, Columbus, OH 43210. Offers behavioral neuroscience (PhD); clinical psychology (PhD); cognitive psychology (PhD); developmental psychology (PhD); intellectual and developmental disabilities psychology (PhD); quantitative psychology (PhD); social psychology (PhD). *Accreditation:* APA. *Entrance requirements:* For doctorate, GRE General Test. Additional exam requirements/recommendations for international students: required—TOEFL (minimum score 600 paper-based; 100 iBT); recommended—IELTS (minimum score 8). Electronic applications accepted.

Ohio University, Graduate College, College of Arts and Sciences, Department of Psychology, Program in Clinical Psychology, Athens, OH 45701-2979. Offers PhD. *Accreditation:* APA. *Degree requirements:* For doctorate, one foreign language, comprehensive exam, thesis/dissertation. *Entrance requirements:* For doctorate, GRE General Test, GRE Subject Test, minimum graduate GPA of 3.4. Additional exam requirements/recommendations for international students: required—TOEFL.

Oklahoma State University, College of Arts and Sciences, Department of Psychology, Stillwater, OK 74078. Offers clinical psychology (PhD); general psychology (MS). *Accreditation:* APA (one or more programs are accredited). *Faculty:* 23 full-time (13 women), 2 part-time/adjunct (1 woman). *Students:* 39 full-time (32 women), 23 part-time (18 women); includes 14 minority (2 Black or African American, non-Hispanic/Latino; 2 American Indian or Alaska Native, non-Hispanic/Latino; 2 Asian, non-Hispanic/Latino; 4 Hispanic/Latino; 1 Native Hawaiian or other Pacific Islander, non-Hispanic/Latino; 3 Two or more races, non-Hispanic/Latino), 1 international. Average age 27. 154 applicants, 9% accepted, 14 enrolled. In 2019, 10 master's, 5 doctorates awarded. *Entrance requirements:* For master's and doctorate, GRE General Test. Additional exam requirements/recommendations for international students: required—TOEFL (minimum score 550 paper-based; 79 iBT). *Application deadline:* For fall admission, 3/1 priority date for international students; for spring admission, 8/1 priority date for international students. Applications are processed on a rolling basis. Application fee: $50 ($75 for international students). Electronic applications accepted. *Expenses: Tuition, area*

resident: Full-time $4148.10; part-time $2765.40 per credit hour. Tuition, state resident: full-time $4148.10; part-time $2765.40 per credit hour. Tuition, nonresident: full-time $15,775; part-time $10,516.80 per credit hour. *International tuition:* $15,775.20 full-time. *Required fees:* $2196.90; $122.05 per credit hour. Tuition and fees vary according to course load, campus/location and program. *Financial support:* In 2019–20, 16 research assistantships (averaging $1,711 per year), 38 teaching assistantships (averaging $1,798 per year) were awarded; career-related internships or fieldwork, Federal Work-Study, scholarships/grants, health care benefits, tuition waivers (partial), and unspecified assistantships also available. Support available to part-time students. Financial award application deadline: 3/1; financial award applicants required to submit FAFSA. *Unit head:* Dr. Thad Leffingwell, Department Head, 405-744-7494, Fax: 405-744-8067, E-mail: thad.leffingwell@okstate.edu. *Application contact:* Dr. Sheryl Tucker, Vice Prov/Dean/Prof, 405-744-6368, E-mail: gradi@okstate.edu.
Website: http://psychology.okstate.edu

Old Dominion University, College of Sciences, Virginia Consortium Program in Clinical Psychology, Norfolk, VA 23529. Offers PhD. *Degree requirements:* For doctorate, comprehensive exam, thesis/dissertation, internship. *Entrance requirements:* For doctorate, GRE General Test. Additional exam requirements/recommendations for international students: required—TOEFL. Electronic applications accepted. *Expenses:* Contact institution.

Oregon State University, College of Education, Program in Counseling, Corvallis, OR 97331. Offers clinical mental health counseling (M Coun); counseling (PhD); school counseling (M Coun). *Accreditation:* ACA (one or more programs are accredited); NCATE. *Program availability:* Part-time, blended/hybrid learning. *Degree requirements:* For master's, thesis or alternative; for doctorate, one foreign language, thesis/dissertation. *Entrance requirements:* For master's, minimum GPA of 3.0 in last 90 hours; for doctorate, GRE or MAT, master's degree, minimum GPA of 3.0 in last 90 hours of course work, 2 years of teaching experience. Additional exam requirements/recommendations for international students: required—TOEFL (minimum score 575 paper-based).

Pace University, Dyson College of Arts and Sciences, Department of Psychology, Program in School-Clinical Child Psychology, New York, NY 10038. Offers school psychology (MS Ed); school-clinical child psychology (Psy D). *Accreditation:* APA (one or more programs are accredited). Terminal master's awarded for partial completion of doctoral program. *Degree requirements:* For master's, qualifying exams, internship; for doctorate, comprehensive exam, thesis/dissertation, qualifying exams, externship, internship. *Entrance requirements:* For master's, GRE General Test, GRE Subject Test in psychology (recommended), interview, 3 letters of recommendation, resume, personal statement; for doctorate, GRE General Test, GRE Subject Test in psychology (recommended), interview, transcripts, 3 letters of recommendation. Additional exam requirements/recommendations for international students: required—TOEFL (minimum score 88 iBT), IELTS (minimum score 7) or PTE (minimum score 60). Electronic applications accepted.

Pacifica Graduate Institute, Graduate Programs, Carpinteria, CA 93013. Offers clinical psychology (PhD); counseling psychology (MA); depth psychology (MA, PhD); mythological studies (MA, PhD). Terminal master's awarded for partial completion of doctoral program. *Degree requirements:* For master's, thesis (for some programs), practicum; for doctorate, comprehensive exam, thesis/dissertation, internship. *Entrance requirements:* For master's, resume, 3 letters of recommendation, writing sample, interview; for doctorate, resumé, 4 letters of recommendation, writing sample, interview. Additional exam requirements/recommendations for international students: required—TOEFL.

Pacific University, School of Professional Psychology, Forest Grove, OR 97116-1797. Offers applied psychological science (MA, MS); clinical psychology (PhD, Psy D). *Accreditation:* APA (one or more programs are accredited). *Program availability:* Part-time. *Degree requirements:* For master's, comprehensive exam (for some programs), thesis (for some programs); for doctorate, comprehensive exam, thesis/dissertation. *Entrance requirements:* For master's, course work in introductory psychology, statistics, and abnormal psychology; minimum GPA of 3.0; for doctorate, GRE General Test, minimum GPA of 3.0, undergraduate course work in psychology, minimum GPA of 3.1 in last 2 years. Additional exam requirements/recommendations for international students: required—TOEFL (minimum score 600 paper-based). Electronic applications accepted. *Expenses:* Contact institution.

Palo Alto University, MA in Counseling Program, Palo Alto, CA 94304. Offers clinical mental health (MA); marriage, family and child (MA). *Program availability:* Part-time, 100% online, blended/hybrid learning. *Degree requirements:* For master's, capstone project. *Entrance requirements:* For master's, undergraduate degree in psychology with minimum GPA of 3.3. Additional exam requirements/recommendations for international students: required—TOEFL. Electronic applications accepted. *Expenses:* Contact institution.

Palo Alto University, PGSP-Stanford Psy D Consortium Program, Palo Alto, CA 94304. Offers Psy D. *Accreditation:* APA. *Degree requirements:* For doctorate, comprehensive exam, thesis/dissertation, 2000-hour clinical internship. *Entrance requirements:* For doctorate, GRE General Test (minimum overall score 1200); GRE Subject Test in psychology (highly recommended), undergraduate degree in psychology or related area with minimum GPA of 3.3. Additional exam requirements/recommendations for international students: required—TOEFL, IELTS. Electronic applications accepted. *Expenses:* Contact institution.

Palo Alto University, PhD in Clinical Psychology Program, Palo Alto, CA 94304. Offers PhD. *Accreditation:* APA. *Degree requirements:* For doctorate, comprehensive exam, thesis/dissertation, 2000-hour clinical internship. *Entrance requirements:* For doctorate, GRE General Test, undergraduate or graduate degree in psychology or related area; 4 course prerequisites: biopsychology, abnormal psychology, developmental psychology, and statistics. Additional exam requirements/recommendations for international students: required—TOEFL, IELTS. Electronic applications accepted. *Expenses:* Contact institution.

Penn State Erie, The Behrend College, Graduate School, Erie, PA 16563. Offers accounting (MPAC); applied clinical psychology (MA); business administration (MBA); quality and manufacturing management (MMM). *Accreditation:* AACSB. *Program availability:* Part-time. *Entrance requirements:* Additional exam requirements/recommendations for international students: required—TOEFL (minimum score 550 paper-based; 80 iBT), IELTS. Electronic applications accepted.

Penn State Harrisburg, Graduate School, School of Behavioral Sciences and Education, Middletown, PA 17057. Offers adult education in the health and medical professions (Certificate); applied behavior analysis (MA); applied clinical psychology (MA); applied psychological research (MA); community psychology and social change (MA); English as a second language (ESL) program specialist and leadership (Certificate); health education (M Ed); lifelong learning and adult education (M Ed, D Ed); literacy education (M Ed); literacy leadership (Certificate); psychology: applications in clinical psychology (Certificate); psychology: health psychology (Certificate); teaching and curriculum (M Ed); training and development (M Ed, Certificate). *Program availability:* Part-time, evening/weekend.

Clinical Psychology

Philadelphia College of Osteopathic Medicine, Graduate and Professional Programs, School of Professional and Applied Psychology, Philadelphia, PA 19131. Offers applied behavior analysis (Certificate); clinical health psychology (Post-Doctoral Certificate); clinical neuropsychology (Post-Doctoral Certificate); clinical psychology (Psy D); educational psychology (PhD); mental health counseling (MS); organizational development and leadership (MS); psychology (Certificate); public health management and administration (MS); school psychology (MS, Psy D, Ed S). *Accreditation:* APA. *Faculty:* 19 full-time (11 women), 122 part-time/adjunct (58 women). *Students:* 342 (285 women); includes 108 minority (65 Black or African American, non-Hispanic/Latino; 1 American Indian or Alaska Native, non-Hispanic/Latino; 10 Asian, non-Hispanic/Latino; 14 Hispanic/Latino; 18 Two or more races, non-Hispanic/Latino). Average age 25. 357 applicants, 51% accepted, 113 enrolled. In 2019, 79 master's, 38 doctorates, 16 other advanced degrees awarded. Terminal master's awarded for partial completion of doctoral program. *Degree requirements:* For master's, comprehensive exam (for some programs), thesis (for some programs); for doctorate, comprehensive exam, thesis/dissertation. *Entrance requirements:* For master's, GRE or MAT, minimum GPA of 3.0; bachelor's degree from regionally-accredited college or university; for doctorate, PRAXIS II (for Psy D in school psychology), minimum undergraduate GPA of 3.0; for other advanced degree, GRE (for Ed S). Additional exam requirements/recommendations for international students: required—TOEFL (minimum score 79 iBT). *Application deadline:* Applications are processed on a rolling basis. Application fee: $50. Electronic applications accepted. *Financial support:* In 2019–20, 28 teaching assistantships were awarded; Federal Work-Study, institutionally sponsored loans, and scholarships/grants also available. Financial award application deadline: 3/15; financial award applicants required to submit FAFSA. *Unit head:* Dr. Robert DiTomasso, Chairman, 215-871-6442, Fax: 215-871-6458, E-mail: robertd@pcom.edu. *Application contact:* Johnathan Cox, Associate Director of Admissions, 215-871-6700, Fax: 215-871-6719, E-mail: johnathancox@pcom.edu.
Website: pcom.edu

Pillar College, Program in Counseling, Newark, NJ 07102. Offers MA.

Pittsburg State University, Graduate School, College of Education, Department of Psychology and Counseling, Program in Psychology, Pittsburg, KS 66762. Offers psychology (MS), including clinical psychology, general psychology. *Degree requirements:* For master's, thesis or alternative. *Entrance requirements:* For master's, GRE General Test, minimum GPA of 2.8. Additional exam requirements/recommendations for international students: required—TOEFL (minimum score 550 paper-based; 79 iBT), IELTS (minimum score 6.5), PTE (minimum score 53). Electronic applications accepted. *Expenses:* Contact institution.

Plymouth State University, College of Graduate Studies, Graduate Studies in Education, Certificate of Advanced Graduate Studies Programs, Plymouth, NH 03264-1595. Offers clinical mental health counseling (CAGS); educational leadership (CAGS); higher education (CAGS); school psychology (CAGS). *Program availability:* Part-time, evening/weekend.

Point Loma Nazarene University, College of Extended Learning, Program in Clinical Counseling, San Diego, CA 92108. Offers marriage and family therapy (MA); professional clinical counselor (MA). *Faculty:* 1 (woman) full-time, 12 part-time/adjunct (6 women). *Students:* 81 full-time (70 women), 10 part-time (all women); includes 45 minority (4 Black or African American, non-Hispanic/Latino; 4 Asian, non-Hispanic/Latino; 31 Hispanic/Latino; 6 Two or more races, non-Hispanic/Latino). Average age 29. 32 applicants, 91% accepted, 28 enrolled. In 2019, 19 master's awarded. *Degree requirements:* For master's, comprehensive exam. Application fee: $50. *Expenses:* $790 per unit. *Financial support:* In 2019–20, 18 students received support. Scholarships/grants available. Financial award applicants required to submit FAFSA. *Unit head:* Dr. Daniel Lee Jenkins, Ph.D, Program Director, 619-849-7850, E-mail: DanJenkins@pointloma.edu. *Application contact:* Dana Barger, Director of Recruitment and Admissions, Graduate and Professional Students, 619-329-6799, E-mail: gradinfo@pointloma.edu.
Website: https://www.pointloma.edu/graduate-studies/programs/clinical-counseling-ma

Point Park University, School of Arts and Sciences, Department of Humanities and Human Sciences, Pittsburgh, PA 15222-1984. Offers clinical-community psychology (MA, Psy D).

Ponce Health Sciences University, PhD Program in Clinical Psychology, Ponce, PR 00732-7004. Offers PhD, Psy D. *Accreditation:* APA. *Degree requirements:* For doctorate, one foreign language, comprehensive exam, thesis/dissertation, internship. *Entrance requirements:* For doctorate, GRE General Test or EXADEP, proficiency in Spanish and English; 2 letters of recommendation; minimum undergraduate GPA of 2.7, graduate 3.0; criminal background check.

Pontifical Catholic University of Puerto Rico, College of Graduate Studies in Behavioral Science and Community Affairs, Program in Clinical Psychology, Ponce, PR 00717-0777. Offers PhD, Psy D. *Program availability:* Part-time, evening/weekend. *Degree requirements:* For doctorate, comprehensive exam, thesis/dissertation. *Entrance requirements:* For doctorate, EXADEP, minimum GPA of 2.75.

Pontificia Universidad Catolica Madre y Maestra, Graduate School, Faculty of Social and Administrative Sciences, Santiago, Dominican Republic. Offers business administration (MBA), including business development, finance, international business, management skills (M Mgmt, MBA), marketing, operations, strategic cost management, strategy, tourist destination planning and management; law (LL M), including civil law, corporate business law, criminal law, international relations, real estate law; management (M Mgmt), including higher financial management, insurance program administration, management skills (M Mgmt, MBA); psychology (MA), including clinical child and adolescent psychology, forensic psychology; strategic human resources (EMBA).

Post University, Program in Counseling and Human Services, Waterbury, CT 06723-2540. Offers counseling and human services (MS); counseling and human services/alcohol and drug counseling (MS); counseling and human services/clinical mental health counseling (MS); counseling and human services/forensic mental health counseling (MS); counseling and human services/non-profit management (MS). *Program availability:* Part-time, evening/weekend, online learning. *Entrance requirements:* For master's, resume.

Prairie View A&M University, College of Juvenile Justice and Psychology, Prairie View, TX 77446. Offers clinical adolescent psychology (PhD); juvenile forensic psychology (MSJFP); juvenile justice (MSJJ, PhD). *Program availability:* Part-time, evening/weekend, online only, 100% online, Master's in Juvenile Justice. *Faculty:* 11 full-time (5 women), 3 part-time/adjunct (all women). *Students:* 19 full-time (13 women), 35 part-time (26 women); includes 45 minority (44 Black or African American, non-Hispanic/Latino; 1 Hispanic/Latino), 7 international. Average age 31. 24 applicants, 79% accepted, 19 enrolled. In 2019, 6 master's, 4 doctorates awarded. *Degree requirements:* For master's, comprehensive exam; for doctorate, thesis/dissertation. *Entrance requirements:* For master's, GRE, minimum GPA of 2.75; for doctorate, GRE, previous course work in clinical adolescent psychology, minimum GPA of 3.5. Additional exam requirements/recommendations for international students: required—TOEFL (minimum score 550 paper-based; 79 iBT). *Application deadline:* For fall admission, 5/1 priority date for domestic and international students; for spring admission, 10/1 priority date for domestic students, 9/1 priority date for international students; for summer admission, 3/1 priority date for domestic students, 2/1 priority date for international students. Applications are processed on a rolling basis. Application fee: $50. Electronic applications accepted. *Expenses: Tuition, area resident:* Full-time $5479.68. Tuition, state resident: full-time $5479.68. Tuition, nonresident: full-time $15,439. *International tuition:* $15,439 full-time. *Required fees:* $2149.32. *Financial support:* In 2019–20, 26 students received support, including 24 research assistantships with full tuition reimbursements available (averaging $24,000 per year), 8 teaching assistantships with full tuition reimbursements available (averaging $18,000 per year); career-related internships or fieldwork, institutionally sponsored loans, scholarships/grants, health care benefits, tuition waivers (full), and unspecified assistantships also available. Support available to part-time students. Financial award application deadline: 4/1; financial award applicants required to submit FAFSA. *Unit head:* Dr. Camille Gibson, Interim Dean, 936-261-5265 Ext. 5265, Fax: 936-261-5253, E-mail: cbgibson@pvamu.edu. *Application contact:* Pauline Walker, Executive Secretary, Graduate Program, 936-261-3521, Fax: 936-261-3529, E-mail: gradadmissions@pvamu.edu.

Purdue University, Graduate School, College of Health and Human Sciences, Department of Psychological Sciences, West Lafayette, IN 47907. Offers behavioral neuroscience (PhD); clinical psychology (PhD); cognitive psychology (PhD); industrial/organizational psychology (PhD); mathematical and computational cognitive science (PhD). *Accreditation:* APA. *Faculty:* 43 full-time (17 women), 2 part-time/adjunct (both women). *Students:* 69 full-time (55 women), 4 part-time (2 women); includes 18 minority (2 Black or African American, non-Hispanic/Latino; 2 Asian, non-Hispanic/Latino; 11 Hispanic/Latino; 3 Two or more races, non-Hispanic/Latino), 19 international. Average age 28. 314 applicants, 15% accepted, 28 enrolled. In 2019, 12 doctorates awarded. Terminal master's awarded for partial completion of doctoral program. *Degree requirements:* For doctorate, thesis/dissertation. *Entrance requirements:* For doctorate, GRE General Test, minimum undergraduate GPA of 3.0 or equivalent. Additional exam requirements/recommendations for international students: required—TOEFL (minimum score 550 paper-based; 77 iBT); recommended—TWE. *Application deadline:* For fall admission, 12/3 for domestic and international students. Applications are processed on a rolling basis. Application fee: $60 ($75 for international students). Electronic applications accepted. *Financial support:* Fellowships with partial tuition reimbursements, research assistantships with partial tuition reimbursements, teaching assistantships with partial tuition reimbursements, and career-related internships or fieldwork available. Support available to part-time students. Financial award applicants required to submit FAFSA. *Unit head:* Dr. Jefferey D. Karpicke, Head, 765-494-6061, E-mail: karpicke@purdue.edu. *Application contact:* Nancy A. O'Brien, Graduate Contact, 765-494-6067, E-mail: nobrien@psych.pardue.edu.
Website: http://www.psych.purdue.edu/

Queen's University at Kingston, School of Graduate Studies, Faculty of Arts and Science, Department of Psychology, Kingston, ON K7L 3N6, Canada. Offers brain behavior and cognitive science (MA, PhD); clinical psychology (MA, PhD); developmental psychology (MA, PhD); social personality psychology (MA, PhD). *Degree requirements:* For master's, thesis; for doctorate, comprehensive exam, thesis/dissertation. *Entrance requirements:* For master's and doctorate, GRE General Test. Additional exam requirements/recommendations for international students: required—TOEFL.

Quincy University, Master of Science in Education Counseling Program, Quincy, IL 62301-2699. Offers clinical mental health counseling (MS Ed); college student personnel (MS Ed); school counseling (MS Ed). *Program availability:* Part-time, evening/weekend. *Degree requirements:* For master's, comprehensive exam, practicum, internship. *Entrance requirements:* For master's, MAT or GRE. Additional exam requirements/recommendations for international students: required—TOEFL (minimum score 550 paper-based; 79 iBT). Electronic applications accepted.

Radford University, College of Graduate Studies and Research, Psychology, MA/MS, Radford, VA 24142. Offers clinical-counseling psychology (MA, MS); experimental psychology (MA); industrial-organizational psychology (MA, MS). *Program availability:* Part-time. *Degree requirements:* For master's, comprehensive exam, thesis (for some programs). *Entrance requirements:* For master's, GRE, minimum GPA of 3.0, 3 letters of reference, essay, resume, official transcripts. Additional exam requirements/recommendations for international students: required—TOEFL (minimum score 550 paper-based; 79 iBT), IELTS (minimum score 6.5). Electronic applications accepted.

Regent University, Graduate School, School of Psychology and Counseling, Virginia Beach, VA 23464-9800. Offers clinical mental health counseling (MA); clinical psychology (Psy D); counseling and psychological studies - clinical (PhD); counseling and psychological studies - research (PhD); counseling studies (CAGS); counselor education and supervision (PhD); general psychology (MS); human services (MA), including addictions counseling, Biblical counseling, Christian counseling, conflict and mediation ministry, criminal justice and ministry, grief counseling, human services counseling, human services for student affairs, life coaching, marriage and family ministry, trauma and crisis counseling; marriage, couple, and family counseling (MA); pastoral counseling (MA); school counseling (MA); M Div/MA; M Ed/MA; MBA/MA. *Accreditation:* ACA; APA (one or more programs are accredited). *Program availability:* Part-time, evening/weekend, 100% online, blended/hybrid learning. *Degree requirements:* For master's, thesis or alternative, internship, practicum, written competency exam; for doctorate, thesis/dissertation or alternative. *Entrance requirements:* For master's, GRE General Test (including writing exam) or MAT, minimum undergraduate GPA of 3.0, resume, transcripts, writing sample, personal goals statement; for doctorate, GRE General Test (including writing exam), minimum undergraduate GPA of 3.0, graduate 3.5; writing sample; 3 recommendations; resume; college transcripts; personal goals statement. Additional exam requirements/recommendations for international students: required—TOEFL (minimum score 577 paper-based). Electronic applications accepted. *Expenses:* Contact institution.

Richmont Graduate University, School of Counseling, Atlanta, GA 30339. Offers clinical mental health counseling (MA); marriage and family therapy (MA). *Accreditation:* ACA. *Program availability:* Part-time, evening/weekend. *Degree requirements:* For master's, comprehensive exam, thesis optional. *Entrance requirements:* For master's, GRE or MAT. Electronic applications accepted.

Rider University, College of Education and Human Services, Program in Counseling Services, Lawrenceville, NJ 08648-3001. Offers clinical mental health counseling (MA); director of counseling services (Ed S); school counseling (MA, Certificate, Ed S). *Accreditation:* ACA; NCATE. *Program availability:* Part-time, evening/weekend. *Degree requirements:* For master's, comprehensive exam, research project; for other advanced degree, specialty seminar. *Entrance requirements:* For master's, GRE or MAT, interview, resume, 2 letters of recommendation; for other advanced degree, GRE or MAT. Additional exam requirements/recommendations for international students: required—TOEFL (minimum score 540 paper-based; 79 iBT). Electronic applications accepted.

Rivier University, School of Graduate Studies, Department of Psychology, Nashua, NH 03060. Offers clinical psychology (MS); experimental psychology (MS).

Roberts Wesleyan College, Graduate Psychology Programs, Rochester, NY 14624-1997. Offers clinical/school psychology (Psy D); school counseling (MS); school psychology (MS). *Program availability:* Part-time, evening/weekend. *Degree requirements:* For master's, comprehensive exam, PRAXIS II (for school psychology). *Entrance requirements:* For master's, GRE. Electronic applications accepted. Application fee is waived when completed online.

Roger Williams University, Feinstein School of Social and Natural Sciences, Bristol, RI 02809. Offers clinical psychology (MA); forensic psychology (MA). *Faculty:* 1 (woman) full-time, 1 part-time/adjunct (0 women). *Students:* 34 full-time (31 women), 1 part-time (0 women); includes 5 minority (1 Black or African American, non-Hispanic/Latino; 1 Asian, non-Hispanic/Latino; 3 Hispanic/Latino). Average age 23. 84 applicants, 57% accepted, 19 enrolled. In 2019, 22 master's awarded. *Degree requirements:* For master's, thesis. *Entrance requirements:* For master's, GRE, Letter of intent, transcripts, three letters of recommendation. Additional exam requirements/recommendations for international students: required—TOEFL (minimum score 85 paper-based), IELTS (minimum score 6.5). *Application deadline:* For fall admission, 2/15 for domestic students, 2/1 for international students. Application fee: $50. *Expenses:* Tuition: Full-time $15,768. *Required fees:* $900; $450. *Financial support:* In 2019–20, 29 students received support. Scholarships/grants and unspecified assistantships available. Financial award application deadline: 3/15; financial award applicants required to submit FAFSA. *Unit head:* Alejandro Leguizamo, Graduate Program Director, 401-254-3934, E-mail: aleguizamo@rwu.edu. *Application contact:* Marcus Hanscom, Director of Graduate Admissions, 401-254-3345, Fax: 401-254-3557, E-mail: gradadmit@rwu.edu. Website: http://www.rwu.edu/academics/schools-and-colleges/fssns

Roosevelt University, Graduate Division, College of Arts and Sciences, Department of Psychology, Program in Clinical Psychology - Counseling Practice, Chicago, IL 60605. Offers MA. *Accreditation:* APA. Electronic applications accepted.

Roosevelt University, Graduate Division, College of Education, Program in Clinical Mental Health Counseling and School Counseling, Chicago, IL 60605. Offers clinical mental health counseling (MA); school counseling (MA). *Accreditation:* ACA.

Rosalind Franklin University of Medicine and Science, College of Health Professions, Department of Psychology, North Chicago, IL 60064-3095. Offers clinical psychology (MS, PhD). *Accreditation:* APA. Terminal master's awarded for partial completion of doctoral program. *Degree requirements:* For master's, capstone experience. *Entrance requirements:* For master's, minimum GPA of 3.0, bachelor's degree (preferably in related subject); for doctorate, GRE, minimum GPA of 3.0, bachelor's or master's degree. Additional exam requirements/recommendations for international students: required—TOEFL.

Rowan University, Graduate School, College of Science and Mathematics, Program in Clinical Mental Health Counseling, Glassboro, NJ 08028-1701. Offers MA, CAGS. *Program availability:* Part-time, evening/weekend. *Entrance requirements:* For master's, GRE General Test. Additional exam requirements/recommendations for international students: required—TOEFL. *Expenses: Tuition, area resident:* Part-time $715.50 per semester hour. Tuition, state resident: part-time $715.50 per semester hour. Tuition, nonresident: part-time $715.50 per semester hour. *Required fees:* $161.55 per semester hour.

Rutgers University - New Brunswick, Graduate School-New Brunswick, Program in Psychology, Piscataway, NJ 08854-8097. Offers behavioral neuroscience (PhD); clinical psychology (PhD); cognitive psychology (PhD); interdisciplinary health psychology (PhD); social psychology (PhD). *Accreditation:* APA. *Degree requirements:* For doctorate, comprehensive exam, thesis/dissertation. *Entrance requirements:* For doctorate, GRE General Test, 3 letters of recommendation. Additional exam requirements/recommendations for international students: required—TOEFL (minimum score 577 paper-based). Electronic applications accepted.

Rutgers University - New Brunswick, Graduate School of Applied and Professional Psychology, Department of Clinical Psychology, Piscataway, NJ 08854-8097. Offers Psy M, Psy D. *Accreditation:* APA (one or more programs are accredited). *Degree requirements:* For doctorate, comprehensive exam, thesis/dissertation, 1 year internship. *Entrance requirements:* For doctorate, GRE General Test, GRE Subject Test, bachelor's degree in psychology or equivalent. Additional exam requirements/recommendations for international students: required—TOEFL. Electronic applications accepted. *Expenses:* Contact institution.

St. John's University, St. John's College of Liberal Arts and Sciences, Department of Psychology, Program in Clinical Psychology, Queens, NY 11439. Offers clinical psychology-child (PhD); clinical psychology-general (PhD). *Accreditation:* APA. *Degree requirements:* For doctorate, comprehensive exam, thesis/dissertation. *Entrance requirements:* For doctorate, GRE General Test, GRE Subject Test, letters of recommendation, transcripts, resume, personal statement, 24 credits of psychology prerequisites, lab paper, term paper. Additional exam requirements/recommendations for international students: required—TOEFL (minimum score 80 iBT), IELTS (minimum score 6.5). Electronic applications accepted. *Expenses:* Contact institution.

St. John's University, The School of Education, Department of Counselor Education, Program in Clinical Mental Health Counseling, Queens, NY 11439. Offers MS Ed, Adv C. *Entrance requirements:* For master's, 2 letters of recommendation, interview; for Adv C, official master's transcripts, statement of purpose. Electronic applications accepted.

Saint Louis University, Graduate Programs, College of Arts and Sciences, Department of Psychology, St. Louis, MO 63103. Offers clinical psychology (MS-R, PhD); experimental psychology (MS-R, PhD); industrial-organizational psychology (PhD); psychology (PhD). *Accreditation:* APA (one or more programs are accredited). *Program availability:* Part-time. *Degree requirements:* For master's, comprehensive exam, thesis; for doctorate, thesis/dissertation, clinical internship (for clinical psychology PhD). *Entrance requirements:* For master's, GRE General Test, interview, letters of recommendation, resume; for doctorate, GRE General Test, interview, letters of recommendation, resumé, transcripts, goal statement. Additional exam requirements/recommendations for international students: required—TOEFL (minimum score 550 paper-based). Electronic applications accepted.

Saint Michael's College, Graduate Programs, Program in Clinical Psychology, Colchester, VT 05439. Offers MA. *Program availability:* Part-time, evening/weekend. *Degree requirements:* For master's, thesis or alternative, internship, practicum, research seminar. *Entrance requirements:* For master's, GRE General Test, GRE Subject Test, undergraduate major in psychology or related area, minimum 12 credits in psychology, minimum GPA of 3.0, official transcripts, 2 references, resume. Additional exam requirements/recommendations for international students: required—TOEFL (minimum score 79 iBT). Electronic applications accepted.

Sam Houston State University, College of Humanities and Social Sciences, Department of Psychology and Philosophy, Huntsville, TX 77341. Offers psychology (MA, PhD, SSP), including clinical psychology (MA, PhD), psychology (MA), school psychology (SSP). *Accreditation:* APA. *Program availability:* Part-time. Terminal master's awarded for partial completion of doctoral program. *Degree requirements:* For master's, comprehensive exam, thesis optional; for doctorate, comprehensive exam,

thesis/dissertation. *Entrance requirements:* For master's, GRE General Test, personal statement, letters of recommendation; for doctorate, GRE General Test, GRE Subject Test (advanced psychology), personal essay, letters of recommendation, resume. Additional exam requirements/recommendations for international students: required—TOEFL (minimum score 550 paper-based; 79 iBT), IELTS (minimum score 6.5). Electronic applications accepted.

San Diego State University, Graduate and Research Affairs, College of Sciences, Department of Psychology, San Diego, CA 92182. Offers clinical psychology (MS, PhD); industrial and organizational psychology (MS); program evaluation (MS); psychology (MA). *Accreditation:* APA (one or more programs are accredited). Terminal master's awarded for partial completion of doctoral program. *Degree requirements:* For master's, thesis, oral exam; for doctorate, thesis/dissertation. *Entrance requirements:* For master's, GRE General Test, GRE Subject Test, 3 letters of recommendation; for doctorate, GRE General Test, GRE Subject Test, minimum GPA of 3.0, 3 letters of recommendation. Additional exam requirements/recommendations for international students: required—TOEFL. Electronic applications accepted.

San Francisco State University, Division of Graduate Studies, College of Health and Social Sciences, Department of Counseling, San Francisco, CA 94132-1722. Offers clinical mental health counseling (MS); marriage, family and child counseling (MS). *Accreditation:* ACA. *Program availability:* Part-time. *Application deadline:* Applications are processed on a rolling basis. *Expenses: Tuition, area resident:* Full-time $7176; part-time $4164 per year. Tuition, state resident: full-time $7176; part-time $4164 per year. Tuition, nonresident: full-time $16,680; part-time $396 per unit. *International tuition:* $16,680 full-time. *Required fees:* $1524; $1524 per unit. $762 per semester. Tuition and fees vary according to degree level and program. *Unit head:* Dr. Rebecca Toporek, Chair, 415-338-2005, Fax: 415-338-0594, E-mail: counsel@sfsu.edu. *Application contact:* Dr. Graciela Orozco, College Counseling Coordinator, 415-338-1064, Fax: 415-338-0594, E-mail: orozco@sfsu.edu. Website: http://counseling.sfsu.edu

San Francisco State University, Division of Graduate Studies, College of Science and Engineering, Department of Psychology, San Francisco, CA 94132-1722. Offers clinical psychology (MS); developmental psychology (MA); industrial/organizational psychology (MS); mind, brain, and behavior (MA); school psychology (MS, Credential); social, personality, and affective science psychology (MA). *Expenses: Tuition, area resident:* Full-time $7176; part-time $4164 per year. Tuition, state resident: full-time $7176; part-time $4164 per year. Tuition, nonresident: full-time $16,680; part-time $396 per unit. *International tuition:* $16,680 full-time. *Required fees:* $1524; $1524 per unit. $762 per semester. Tuition and fees vary according to degree level and program. *Financial support:* Teaching assistantships available. Financial award application deadline: 3/1. *Unit head:* Dr. Chris Wright, Chair, 415-338-7555, Fax: 415-338-2398, E-mail: cwright@sfsu.edu. *Application contact:* Dr. Ryan Howell, Department Graduate Program Coordinator, 415-405-2140, Fax: 415-338-2398, E-mail: rhowell@sfsu.edu. Website: http://psychology.sfsu.edu/graduate/application.html

San Jose State University, Program in Psychology, San Jose, CA 95192-0120. Offers clinical psychology (MS); experimental psychology (MA); industrial/organizational psychology (MS); psychology (MA). *Faculty:* 19 full-time (12 women), 2 part-time/adjunct (1 woman). *Students:* 51 full-time (44 women), 30 part-time (21 women); includes 37 minority (2 Black or African American, non-Hispanic/Latino; 14 Asian, non-Hispanic/Latino; 21 Hispanic/Latino), 4 international. Average age 27. 184 applicants, 23% accepted, 31 enrolled. In 2019, 35 master's awarded. *Application deadline:* For fall admission, 2/1 for domestic and international students. Application fee: $70. Electronic applications accepted. *Expenses: Tuition, area resident:* Full-time $7176; part-time $4164 per credit hour. Tuition, state resident: full-time $7176; part-time $4164 per credit hour. Tuition, nonresident: full-time $7176; part-time $4165 per credit hour. *International tuition:* $7176 full-time. *Required fees:* $2110; $2110. *Financial support:* In 2019–20, 22 students received support, including 1 research assistantship (averaging $500 per year); scholarships/grants also available. Financial award application deadline: 5/1; financial award applicants required to submit FAFSA. *Unit head:* Clifton Oyamot, Professor and Chair, 408-924-5650, E-mail: clifton.oyamot@sjsu.edu. *Application contact:* Psychology Department, 408-408-924-5600, E-mail: psychology@sjsu.edu. Website: http://www.sjsu.edu/psych/

Saybrook University, School of Clinical Psychology, San Francisco, CA 94612. Offers MA. *Degree requirements:* For master's, thesis (for some programs), oral exams. *Entrance requirements:* For master's, bachelor's degree from an accredited university or college.

Seattle Pacific University, PhD in Clinical Psychology Program, Seattle, WA 98119-1997. Offers PhD. *Accreditation:* APA. *Students:* 48 full-time (36 women), 21 part-time (18 women); includes 21 minority (3 Black or African American, non-Hispanic/Latino; 8 Asian, non-Hispanic/Latino; 7 Hispanic/Latino; 3 Two or more races, non-Hispanic/Latino), 4 international. Average age 28. 91 applicants, 13% accepted, 12 enrolled. In 2019, 5 doctorates awarded. *Degree requirements:* For doctorate, thesis/dissertation, clinical internship, practicum. *Entrance requirements:* For doctorate, GRE (preferred minimum score 1100 verbal and quantitative, taken within the last five years), BA, personal statement. Additional exam requirements/recommendations for international students: required—TOEFL (minimum score 600 paper-based). *Application deadline:* For fall admission, 12/15 for domestic and international students. Electronic applications accepted. *Expenses:* Contact institution. *Financial support:* Fellowships and scholarships/grants available. Financial award applicants required to submit FAFSA. *Unit head:* Dr. Amy Mezuli, Chair of Clinical Psychology, 206-281-2820, E-mail: mezulis@spu.edu. *Application contact:* Dr. Amy Mezuli, Chair of Clinical Psychology, 206-281-2820, E-mail: mezulis@spu.edu. Website: https://spu.edu/academics/school-of-psychology-family-community/graduate-programs/clinical-psychology-phd

Shippensburg University of Pennsylvania, School of Graduate Studies, College of Education and Human Services, Department of Counseling, Shippensburg, PA 17257-2299. Offers college counseling (MS); college student personnel (MS); counselor education and supervision (Ed D); mental health counseling (MS); school counseling (M Ed). *Accreditation:* ACA (one or more programs are accredited); NCATE. *Program availability:* Part-time, evening/weekend, online only, blended/hybrid learning. *Faculty:* 7 full-time (2 women), 4 part-time/adjunct (all women). *Students:* 78 full-time (67 women), 32 part-time (27 women); includes 23 minority (13 Black or African American, non-Hispanic/Latino; 4 Asian, non-Hispanic/Latino; 5 Hispanic/Latino; 1 Two or more races, non-Hispanic/Latino), 3 international. Average age 31. 104 applicants, 48% accepted, 22 enrolled. In 2019, 36 master's awarded. *Degree requirements:* For master's, fieldwork, research project, internship, candidacy; for doctorate, thesis/dissertation, practicum, internship. *Entrance requirements:* For master's, GRE or MAT (for MS if GPA is less than 2.75), minimum GPA of 2.75 (3.0 for M Ed), resume, 3 letter of recommendation forms, one year of relevant work experience, on-campus interview, autobiographical statement; for doctorate, master's degree in counseling or related discipline; resume; three recommendation letters (1 each from employer, clinical supervisor, and prior graduate school faculty member); personal essay; interview with department chair. Additional exam requirements/recommendations for international students: required—TOEFL (minimum score 550 paper-based; 68 iBT), IELTS

(minimum score 6), TOEFL (minimum score 550 paper-based, 68 iBT) or IELTS (minimum score 6). *Application deadline:* Applications are processed on a rolling basis. Application fee: $45. Electronic applications accepted. *Expenses:* Tuition, state resident: part-time $516 per credit. Tuition, nonresident: part-time $774 per credit. *Required fees:* $149 per credit. *Financial support:* In 2019–20, 55 students received support. Career-related internships or fieldwork, scholarships/grants, unspecified assistantships, and resident hall director and student payroll positions available. Support available to part-time students. Financial award application deadline: 3/1; financial award applicants required to submit FAFSA. *Unit head:* Dr. Kurt L. Kraus, Departmental Chair and Program Coordinator, 717-477-1603, Fax: 717-477-4056, E-mail: klkrau@ship.edu. *Application contact:* Maya T. Mapp, Director of Admissions, 717-477-1231, Fax: 717-477-4016, E-mail: mtmapp@ship.edu.
Website: http://www.ship.edu/counsel/

Siena Heights University, Graduate College, Adrian, MI 49221-1796. Offers clinical mental health counseling (MA); educational leadership (Specialist); leadership (MA), including health care leadership, organizational leadership; teacher education (MA), including early childhood education, early childhood education: Montessori, education leadership: principal, elementary education: reading K-12, leadership: higher education, secondary education: reading K-12, special education: cognitive impairment, special education: learning disabilities. *Program availability:* Part-time, evening/weekend. *Degree requirements:* For master's, thesis, Presentation. *Entrance requirements:* For master's, Minimum GPA of 3.0, current resume, essay, all post-secondary transcripts, 3 letters of reference, conviction disclosure form; copy of teaching certificate (for some education programs); for Specialist, Master's degree, minimum GPA of 3.0, current resume, essay, all post-secondary transcripts, 3 letters of reference, conviction disclosure form; copy of teaching certificate (for some education programs). Additional exam requirements/recommendations for international students: recommended—TOEFL, IELTS, TWE, TSE. Electronic applications accepted.

Slippery Rock University of Pennsylvania, Graduate Studies (Recruitment), College of Education, Department of Counseling and Development, Slippery Rock, PA 16057-1383. Offers M Ed, MA. *Accreditation:* ACA (one or more programs are accredited); NCATE. *Program availability:* Part-time, evening/weekend. *Faculty:* 10 full-time (4 women), 2 part-time/adjunct (both women). *Students:* 73 full-time (59 women), 26 part-time (25 women); includes 13 minority (7 Black or African American, non-Hispanic/Latino; 6 Hispanic/Latino), 1 international. Average age 25. 100 applicants, 42% accepted, 28 enrolled. In 2019, 36 master's awarded. *Degree requirements:* For master's, comprehensive exam, thesis (for some programs). *Entrance requirements:* For master's, GRE General Test or MAT, official transcripts, personal statement, three letters of recommendation, interview. Additional exam requirements/recommendations for international students: required—TOEFL (minimum score 550 paper-based; 80 iBT). *Application deadline:* For fall admission, 1/15 priority date for domestic and international students. Applications are processed on a rolling basis. Application fee: $25 ($30 for international students). Electronic applications accepted. *Expenses:* $516 per credit in-state tuition, $173.61 per credit in-state fees; $774 per credit out-of-state tuition, $224.31 per credit out-of-state fees; $516 per credit in-state tuition, $105.40 per credit in-state fees (for distance education); $526 per credit out-of-state tuition, $118.90 per credit out-of-state fees (for distance education). *Financial support:* In 2019–20, 50 students received support. Career-related internships or fieldwork, Federal Work-Study, institutionally sponsored loans, scholarships/grants, tuition waivers (partial), and unspecified assistantships available. Support available to part-time students. Financial award application deadline: 5/1; financial award applicants required to submit FAFSA. *Unit head:* Dr. Jane Hale, Graduate Coordinator, 724-738-2035, Fax: 724-738-4859, E-mail: stacy.jacob@sru.edu. *Application contact:* Brandi Weber-Mortimer, Director of Graduate Admissions, 724-738-2051, Fax: 724-738-2146, E-mail: graduate.admissions@sru.edu.
Website: http://www.sru.edu/academics/colleges-and-departments/coe/departments/counseling-and-development

Sofia University, Residential Programs, Palo Alto, CA 94303. Offers clinical psychology (Psy D); computer science (MS); counseling psychology (MA); transpersonal psychology (MA, PhD). *Program availability:* Part-time, evening/weekend. Terminal master's awarded for partial completion of doctoral program. *Degree requirements:* For doctorate, thesis/dissertation. *Entrance requirements:* For master's, bachelor's degree; for doctorate, bachelor's degree; master's degree (for some programs). Electronic applications accepted.

Sonoma State University, School of Social Sciences, Department of Counseling, Rohnert Park, CA 94928-3609. Offers clinical mental health counseling (MA); school counseling (MA). *Accreditation:* ACA. *Program availability:* Part-time. *Entrance requirements:* For master's, minimum GPA of 3.0. Additional exam requirements/recommendations for international students: required—TOEFL (minimum score 500 paper-based).

Southeastern Oklahoma State University, School of Behavioral Sciences, Durant, OK 74701-0609. Offers clinical mental health counseling (MS). *Accreditation:* ACA. *Program availability:* Part-time, evening/weekend. *Degree requirements:* For master's, comprehensive exam, thesis optional. *Entrance requirements:* For master's, GRE General Test, minimum GPA of 3.0 in last 60 hours or 2.75 overall. Additional exam requirements/recommendations for international students: required—TOEFL (minimum score 550 paper-based; 79 iBT). Electronic applications accepted.

Southern Illinois University Carbondale, Graduate School, College of Liberal Arts, Department of Psychology, Carbondale, IL 62901-4701. Offers clinical psychology (PhD); counseling psychology (PhD); experimental psychology (MA, MS). *Accreditation:* APA (one or more programs are accredited). *Degree requirements:* For master's, thesis; for doctorate, thesis/dissertation. *Entrance requirements:* For master's, GRE General Test, GRE Subject Test, minimum GPA of 2.7; for doctorate, GRE General Test, GRE Subject Test, minimum GPA of 3.25. Additional exam requirements/recommendations for international students: required—TOEFL.

Southern Illinois University Edwardsville, Graduate School, School of Education, Health, and Human Behavior, Department of Psychology, Program in Clinical Child and School Psychology, Edwardsville, IL 62026. Offers MS. *Program availability:* Part-time. *Degree requirements:* For master's, thesis (for some programs), research project. *Entrance requirements:* For master's, GRE. Additional exam requirements/recommendations for international students: required—TOEFL (minimum score 550 paper-based, 79 iBT), IELTS (minimum score 6.5), Michigan Test of English Language Proficiency or PTE. Electronic applications accepted.

Southern Illinois University Edwardsville, Graduate School, School of Education, Health, and Human Behavior, Department of Psychology, Program in Clinical Psychology, Edwardsville, IL 62026. Offers MA. *Program availability:* Part-time, evening/weekend. *Degree requirements:* For master's, comprehensive exam (for some programs), thesis (for some programs). *Entrance requirements:* For master's, GRE. Additional exam requirements/recommendations for international students: required—TOEFL (minimum score 550 paper-based; 79 iBT), IELTS (minimum score 6.5). Electronic applications accepted.

Southern Methodist University, Dedman College of Humanities and Sciences, Department of Psychology, Dallas, TX 75275. Offers clinical psychology (PhD). *Accreditation:* APA. Terminal master's awarded for partial completion of doctoral program. *Degree requirements:* For doctorate, comprehensive exam, thesis/dissertation, oral exam, practicum, research presentation and publication. *Entrance requirements:* For doctorate, GRE General Test, minimum GPA of 3.4. Additional exam requirements/recommendations for international students: required—TOEFL (minimum score 550 paper-based). Electronic applications accepted.

Southern New Hampshire University, School of Arts and Sciences, Manchester, NH 03106-1045. Offers clinical mental health counseling (MS); creative writing (MA); criminal justice (MS); cyber security (MS); English (MA); fiction and nonfiction (MFA); history (MA); political science (MS); psychology (MS). *Program availability:* Part-time, evening/weekend. *Degree requirements:* For master's, one foreign language, thesis. *Entrance requirements:* For master's, minimum GPA of 3.0 (for MFA). Additional exam requirements/recommendations for international students: required—TOEFL (minimum score 550 paper-based; 79 iBT), IELTS (minimum score 6.5), TWE (minimum score 5). Electronic applications accepted. *Expenses:* Contact institution.

Spalding University, Graduate Studies, Kosair College of Health and Natural Sciences, School of Professional Psychology, Louisville, KY 40203-2188. Offers clinical psychology (MA, Psy D). *Accreditation:* APA (one or more programs are accredited). *Program availability:* Part-time. Terminal master's awarded for partial completion of doctoral program. *Degree requirements:* For master's, comprehensive exam; for doctorate, thesis/dissertation. *Entrance requirements:* For master's and doctorate, GRE General Test, 18 hours of undergraduate course work in psychology, interview, letters of recommendation, writing sample, autobiographical statement. Additional exam requirements/recommendations for international students: required—TOEFL (minimum score 535 paper-based).

Springfield College, Graduate Programs, Program in Human Services, Springfield, MA 01109-3797. Offers mental health counseling (MS); organizational management and leadership (MS). *Program availability:* Part-time, evening/weekend, blended/hybrid learning. *Degree requirements:* For master's, comprehensive exam, thesis (for some programs), Community Action Research Project. *Entrance requirements:* Additional exam requirements/recommendations for international students: required—TOEFL (minimum score 550 paper-based). Electronic applications accepted. *Expenses:* Contact institution.

Springfield College, Graduate Programs, Programs in Psychology, Springfield, MA 01109-3797. Offers athletic counseling (MS, CAGS); clinical mental health counseling (M Ed, CAGS); counseling psychology (Psy D); general counseling (M Ed); industrial/organizational psychology (M Ed, CAGS); school counseling (M Ed, CAGS); student personnel administration in higher education (M Ed, CAGS). *Accreditation:* APA. *Program availability:* Part-time. *Degree requirements:* For master's, research project, portfolio; for doctorate, dissertation project, 1500 hours of counseling psychology practicum, full-year internship. *Entrance requirements:* For doctorate, GRE. Additional exam requirements/recommendations for international students: required—TOEFL (minimum score 550 paper-based); recommended—IELTS (minimum score 7). Electronic applications accepted.

State University of New York at New Paltz, Graduate and Extended Learning School, School of Liberal Arts and Sciences, Department of Psychology, New Paltz, NY 12561. Offers clinical mental health counseling (MS); mental health counseling (AC); psychological science (MS); school counseling (MS); trauma and disaster mental health (AC). *Program availability:* Part-time, evening/weekend. *Faculty:* 14 full-time (5 women), 1 part-time/adjunct (0 women). *Students:* 57 full-time (43 women), 34 part-time (27 women); includes 25 minority (3 Black or African American, non-Hispanic/Latino; 3 Asian, non-Hispanic/Latino; 16 Hispanic/Latino; 1 Native Hawaiian or other Pacific Islander, non-Hispanic/Latino; 2 Two or more races, non-Hispanic/Latino). 147 applicants, 39% accepted, 45 enrolled. In 2019, 32 master's, 5 other advanced degrees awarded. *Degree requirements:* For master's, comprehensive exam, thesis. *Entrance requirements:* For master's, GRE General Test, minimum GPA of 3.0. Additional exam requirements/recommendations for international students: required—TOEFL (minimum score 550 paper-based; 80 iBT), IELTS (minimum score 6.5). *Application deadline:* For fall admission, 2/1 priority date for domestic and international students; for spring admission, 11/15 priority date for domestic and international students. Application fee: $50. Electronic applications accepted. *Expenses: Tuition, area resident:* Full-time $11,310; part-time $471 per credit. Tuition, state resident: full-time $11,310; part-time $471 per credit. Tuition, nonresident: full-time $23,100; part-time $963 per credit. *International tuition:* $23,100 full-time. *Required fees:* $1432; $41.83 per credit. *Financial support:* In 2019–20, 6 teaching assistantships with partial tuition reimbursements (averaging $5,000 per year) were awarded. Financial award application deadline: 8/1. *Unit head:* Dr. Jonathan Raskin, Chair, 845-257-3471, E-mail: raskinj@newpaltz.edu. *Application contact:* Vika Shock, Director of Graduate Admissions, 845-257-3286, E-mail: gradstudies@newpaltz.edu.
Website: http://www.newpaltz.edu/psychology/

State University of New York at Plattsburgh, School of Education, Health, and Human Services, Department of Counselor Education, Plattsburgh, NY 12901-2681. Offers clinical mental health counseling (MS, Advanced Certificate); school counselor (MS Ed, CAS); student affairs counseling (MS). *Accreditation:* ACA (one or more programs are accredited); TEAC. *Program availability:* Part-time. *Entrance requirements:* For master's, GRE General Test or MAT, minimum GPA of 2.8. Additional exam requirements/recommendations for international students: required—TOEFL.

Stephens College, Division of Graduate and Continuing Studies, Columbia, MO 65215-0002. Offers counseling (M Ed), including addictions counseling, clinical mental health counseling, school counseling; health information administration (Postbaccalaureate Certificate); physician assistant studies (MPAS); TV and screenwriting (MFA). *Program availability:* Part-time, evening/weekend, online learning. *Entrance requirements:* For master's, minimum GPA of 3.0 in last 60 hours. Additional exam requirements/recommendations for international students: required—TOEFL (minimum score 79 iBT). Electronic applications accepted.

Stony Brook University, State University of New York, Graduate School, College of Arts and Sciences, Department of Psychology, Program in Clinical Psychology, Stony Brook, NY 11794. Offers PhD. *Accreditation:* APA. *Students:* 39 full-time (32 women); includes 7 minority (2 Black or African American, non-Hispanic/Latino; 3 Asian, non-Hispanic/Latino; 2 Hispanic/Latino), 6 international. Average age 27. 377 applicants, 4% accepted, 8 enrolled. In 2019, 5 doctorates awarded. *Entrance requirements:* For doctorate, GRE General Test, GRE Subject Test. Additional exam requirements/recommendations for international students: required—TOEFL (minimum score 90 iBT). *Application deadline:* For fall admission, 1/15 for domestic students; for spring admission, 10/1 for domestic students. Application fee: $100. *Expenses:* Contact institution. *Financial support:* In 2019–20, 5 fellowships, 5 research assistantships, 19 teaching assistantships were awarded. *Unit head:* Dr. Sheri Levy, Chair, 631-632-4355, E-mail: sheri.levy@stonybrook.edu. *Application contact:* Marilynn Wollmuth, Coordinator, 631-632-7855, Fax: 631-632-7876, E-mail:

marilyn.wollmuth@stonybrook.edu.
Website: https://www.stonybrook.edu/commcms/psychology/clinical/overview.html

Suffolk University, College of Arts and Sciences, Department of Psychology, Boston, MA 02108-2770. Offers clinical psychology (PhD); college admission counseling (Certificate); mental health counseling (MS); school counseling (MS). *Accreditation:* APA. *Faculty:* 17 full-time (12 women), 1 (woman) part-time/adjunct. *Students:* 46 full-time (45 women), 22 part-time (19 women); includes 8 minority (2 Black or African American, non-Hispanic/Latino; 3 Asian, non-Hispanic/Latino; 1 Hispanic/Latino; 2 Two or more races, non-Hispanic/Latino). Average age 26. 299 applicants, 15% accepted, 22 enrolled. In 2019, 11 master's, 6 doctorates, 1 other advanced degree awarded. Terminal master's awarded for partial completion of doctoral program. *Degree requirements:* For master's, practicum, internship; for doctorate, thesis/dissertation, practicum. *Entrance requirements:* For doctorate, GRE General Test or MAT, 2 letters of recommendation, resume. Additional exam requirements/recommendations for international students: required—TOEFL (minimum score 550 paper-based; 80 iBT). *Application deadline:* For fall admission, 12/1 for domestic and international students. Applications are processed on a rolling basis. Application fee: $50. Electronic applications accepted. *Expenses:* Contact institution. *Financial support:* In 2019–20, 66 students received support, including 7 fellowships (averaging $3,375 per year); career-related internships or fieldwork, Federal Work-Study, institutionally sponsored loans, scholarships/grants, and unspecified assistantships also available. Support available to part-time students. Financial award application deadline: 4/1; financial award applicants required to submit FAFSA. *Unit head:* Dr. Amy Marks, Chairperson, 617-573-8017, E-mail: akmarks@suffolk.edu. *Application contact:* Mara Marzocchi, Associate Director of Graduate Admissions, 617-573-8302, Fax: 617-305-1733, E-mail: grad.admission@suffolk.edu.
Website: http://www.suffolk.edu/college/graduate/69299.php

Syracuse University, College of Arts and Sciences, Department of Psychology, Syracuse, NY 13244. Offers clinical psychology (PhD); cognition, brain, and behavior (PhD); school psychology (PhD); social psychology (PhD). *Accreditation:* APA. Terminal master's awarded for partial completion of doctoral program. *Degree requirements:* For doctorate, comprehensive exam, thesis/dissertation. *Entrance requirements:* For doctorate, GRE General Test, GRE Subject Test, resume, personal statement, three letters of recommendation. Additional exam requirements/recommendations for international students: required—TOEFL (minimum score 100 iBT). Electronic applications accepted.

Syracuse University, School of Education, MS Program in Clinical Mental Health Counseling, Syracuse, NY 13244. Offers MS. *Program availability:* Part-time. *Entrance requirements:* For master's, GRE or MAT, baccalaureate degree from regionally-accredited college/university, relevant work experience, three letters of recommendation, personal statement, interview, transcripts. Additional exam requirements/recommendations for international students: required—TOEFL (minimum score 100 iBT). Electronic applications accepted.

Teachers College, Columbia University, Department of Counseling and Clinical Psychology, New York, NY 10027-6696. Offers clinical psychology (PhD); counseling psychology (Ed M, Ed D, PhD); mental health counseling (ME); psychological counseling (ME, ND); psychology in education (MA, ND); school counselor (ME). *Accreditation:* APA (one or more programs are accredited). *Program availability:* Part-time.

Texas A&M University–Central Texas, Graduate Studies and Research, Killeen, TX 76549. Offers accounting (MS); business administration (MBA); clinical mental health counseling (MS); criminal justice (MCJ); curriculum and instruction (M Ed); educational administration (M Ed); educational psychology - experimental psychology (MS); history (MA); human resource management (MS); information systems (MS); liberal studies (MS); management and leadership (MS); marriage and family therapy (MS); mathematics (MS); political science (MA); school counseling (M Ed); school psychology (Ed S).

Texas A&M University–Corpus Christi, College of Graduate Studies, College of Liberal Arts, Program in Psychology, Corpus Christi, TX 78412. Offers clinical psychology (MA); general psychology (MA). *Program availability:* Part-time, evening/weekend. *Degree requirements:* For master's, comprehensive exam. *Entrance requirements:* For master's, GRE (taken within 5 years; waived if candidate already has master's degree), minimum GPA of 3.0 in last 60 hours, essay (500-1000 words), 2 letters of recommendation. Additional exam requirements/recommendations for international students: required—TOEFL (minimum score 550 paper-based; 79 iBT), IELTS (minimum score 6.5). Electronic applications accepted.

Texas A&M University–San Antonio, Department of Counseling, Health and Kinesiology, San Antonio, TX 78224. Offers clinical mental health counseling (MA); counseling and guidance (MA); kinesiology (MS); marriage and family counseling (MA). *Program availability:* Part-time, evening/weekend, online learning. *Degree requirements:* For master's, comprehensive exam, thesis or alternative. *Entrance requirements:* For master's, MAT or GRE (composite quantitative and verbal). Additional exam requirements/recommendations for international students: required—TOEFL (minimum score 550 paper-based; 79 iBT), IELTS (minimum score 6). Electronic applications accepted. *Expenses: Tuition, area resident:* Full-time $3822; part-time $1068 per semester. *Required fees:* $2146; $1412 per unit. $706 per semester.

Texas State University, The Graduate College, College of Education, Program in Professional Counseling, San Marcos, TX 78666. Offers clinical mental health counseling (MA); marriage and family counseling (MA); school counseling (MA). *Accreditation:* ACA. *Program availability:* Part-time. *Degree requirements:* For master's, comprehensive exam, thesis optional, internship. *Entrance requirements:* For master's, Official GRE (general test only) required with competitive scores in the verbal and quantitative reasoning sections, baccalaureate degree from regionally-accredited institution with minimum GPA of 3.0 in last 60 hours of undergraduate work; resume; statement of purpose addressing professional goals, reasoning for specified emphasis (i.e., community, school, marital), strengths and weaknesses, and perspective on diversity; 3 references. Additional exam requirements/recommendations for international students: required—TOEFL (minimum iBT scores: 22 listening, 22 reading, 24 speaking, 21 writing). Electronic applications accepted.

Texas Tech University, Graduate School, College of Arts and Sciences, Department of Psychological Sciences, Lubbock, TX 79409-2051. Offers clinical psychology (PhD); counseling psychology (MA, PhD); general experimental psychology (MA, PhD); psychology (MA). *Accreditation:* APA (one or more programs are accredited). *Faculty:* 33 full-time (14 women), 2 part-time/adjunct (both women). *Students:* 105 full-time (63 women), 24 part-time (22 women); includes 39 minority (6 Black or African American, non-Hispanic/Latino; 1 American Indian or Alaska Native, non-Hispanic/Latino; 11 Asian, non-Hispanic/Latino; 21 Hispanic/Latino), 7 international. Average age 28. 162 applicants, 14% accepted, 16 enrolled. In 2019, 21 master's, 10 doctorates awarded. *Degree requirements:* For doctorate, comprehensive exam, thesis/dissertation, 100 credit hours of organized courses, research credits, and practica. *Entrance requirements:* For master's, GRE General Test, GRE Subject Test, essays, letters of recommendation; for doctorate, GRE General Test, essays, letters of recommendation. Additional exam requirements/recommendations for international students: required—TOEFL (minimum score 550 paper-based; 79 iBT). *Application deadline:* For fall admission, 6/1 priority date for domestic students, 1/15 priority date for international students; for spring admission, 9/1 priority date for domestic students, 6/15 priority date for international students. Applications are processed on a rolling basis. Application fee: $65. Electronic applications accepted. *Expenses:* Contact institution. *Financial support:* In 2019–20, 121 students received support, including 115 fellowships (averaging $2,803 per year), 39 research assistantships (averaging $12,832 per year), 77 teaching assistantships (averaging $13,684 per year); Federal Work-Study, institutionally sponsored loans, health care benefits, and unspecified assistantships also available. Financial award application deadline: 4/15; financial award applicants required to submit FAFSA. *Unit head:* Dr. Robert Morgan, Professor and Chair, 806-834-7117, Fax: 806-742-0818, E-mail: robert.morgan@ttu.edu. *Application contact:* Kay Hill, Admissions Coordinator, 806-834-1350, Fax: 806-742-0818, E-mail: kay.hill@ttu.edu.
Website: www.depts.ttu.edu/psy/

Texas Tech University Health Sciences Center, School of Health Professions, Program in Clinical Mental Health Counseling, Lubbock, TX 79430. Offers MS. *Program availability:* Part-time, online only. *Faculty:* 7 full-time (4 women). *Students:* 75 full-time (62 women), 57 part-time (51 women); includes 56 minority (14 Black or African American, non-Hispanic/Latino; 1 American Indian or Alaska Native, non-Hispanic/Latino; 2 Asian, non-Hispanic/Latino; 34 Hispanic/Latino; 5 Two or more races, non-Hispanic/Latino), 1 international. Average age 34. 81 applicants, 81% accepted, 62 enrolled. *Entrance requirements:* Additional exam requirements/recommendations for international students: required—TOEFL (minimum score 550 paper-based; 79 iBT). *Application deadline:* For fall admission, 6/1 for domestic students; for spring admission, 11/1 for domestic students. Applications are processed on a rolling basis. Application fee: $75. Electronic applications accepted. *Financial support:* In 2019–20, 28 students received support. Available to part-time students. Application deadline: 9/1; applicants required to submit FAFSA. *Unit head:* Dr. Logan Winkelman, Director, 806-743-3220, Fax: 806-743-3244, E-mail: health.professions@ttuhsc.edu. *Application contact:* Lindsay Johnson, Associate Dean for Admissions and Student Affairs, 806-743-3220, Fax: 806-743-2994, E-mail: health.professions@ttuhsc.edu.
Website: http://www.ttuhsc.edu/health-professions/master-of-science-clinical-mental-health-counseling/

Trinity Washington University, School of Education, Washington, DC 20017-1094. Offers clinical mental health counseling (MA); early childhood education (MAT); educating for change (M Ed); educational administration (MSA); elementary education (MAT); reading (M Ed); school counseling (MA); secondary education (MAT), including English, social studies; special education (MAT). *Accreditation:* NCATE. *Program availability:* Part-time, evening/weekend. *Degree requirements:* For master's, thesis (for some programs), capstone project(s). *Entrance requirements:* For master's, PRAXIS I, minimum GPA of 2.8. Additional exam requirements/recommendations for international students: required—TOEFL (minimum score 550 paper-based).

Uniformed Services University of the Health Sciences, F. Edward Hebert School of Medicine, Graduate Programs in the Biomedical Sciences and Public Health, Department of Medical and Clinical Psychology, Bethesda, MD 20814. Offers clinical psychology (PhD); medical psychology (PhD). *Accreditation:* APA. Terminal master's awarded for partial completion of doctoral program. *Degree requirements:* For doctorate, comprehensive exam, thesis/dissertation, qualifying exam. *Entrance requirements:* For doctorate, GRE General Test, minimum GPA of 3.0, U.S. citizenship. Additional exam requirements/recommendations for international students: required—TOEFL. Electronic applications accepted.

Union College, Graduate Programs, Department of Psychology, Barbourville, KY 40906-1499. Offers clinical psychology (MA); counseling psychology (MA); school psychology (MA).

Union Institute & University, Master of Arts Program in Clinical Mental Health Counseling, Cincinnati, OH 45206-1925. Offers MA. *Program availability:* Part-time, online only, blended/hybrid learning. Terminal master's awarded for partial completion of doctoral program. *Degree requirements:* For master's, thesis, internship. *Entrance requirements:* For master's, transcripts, letters of recommendation, essay. Additional exam requirements/recommendations for international students: recommended—TOEFL. Electronic applications accepted. *Expenses:* Contact institution.

Universidad de Iberoamerica, Graduate School, San Jose, Costa Rica. Offers clinical neuropsychology (PhD); clinical psychology (M Psych); educational psychology (M Psych); forensic psychology (M Psych); hospital management (MHA); intensive care nursing (MN); medicine (MD).

University at Albany, State University of New York, College of Arts and Sciences, Department of Psychology, Albany, NY 12222-0001. Offers behavioral neuroscience (PhD); clinical psychology (PhD); cognitive psychology (PhD); industrial/organizational psychology (MA, PhD); social-personality psychology (PhD). *Accreditation:* APA (one or more programs are accredited). *Program availability:* Blended/hybrid learning. *Faculty:* 31 full-time (14 women), 6 part-time/adjunct (4 women). *Students:* 68 full-time (44 women), 53 part-time (35 women); includes 30 minority (3 Black or African American, non-Hispanic/Latino; 10 Asian, non-Hispanic/Latino; 11 Hispanic/Latino; 6 Two or more races, non-Hispanic/Latino), 9 international. 253 applicants, 21% accepted, 28 enrolled. In 2019, 22 master's, 11 doctorates awarded. *Degree requirements:* For doctorate, thesis/dissertation. *Entrance requirements:* For master's, transcripts of all schools attended, statement of background and goals, departmental questionnaire, resume, names and contact information for 3 recommenders; for doctorate, GRE General Test, GRE Subject Test, transcripts of all schools attended, statement of background and goals, departmental questionnaire, resume, names and contact information for 3 recommenders. Additional exam requirements/recommendations for international students: required—TOEFL (minimum score 550 paper-based). *Application deadline:* For fall admission, 1/15 for domestic and international students; for spring admission, 11/15 for domestic students. Application fee: $75. Electronic applications accepted. *Expenses: Tuition, area resident:* Full-time $11,530; part-time $480 per credit hour. Tuition, nonresident: full-time $23,530; part-time $980 per credit hour. *International tuition:* $23,530 full-time. *Required fees:* $2185; $96 per credit hour. Part-time tuition and fees vary according to course load and program. *Financial support:* Fellowships, research assistantships, teaching assistantships, and career-related internships or fieldwork available. Financial award application deadline: 2/1. *Unit head:* Christine K. Wagner, Chair, 518-442-4820, Fax: 518-442-4867, E-mail: cwagner@albany.edu. *Application contact:* Michael DeRensis, Director, Graduate Admissions, 518-442-3980, Fax: 518-442-3922, E-mail: graduate@albany.edu.
Website: https://www.albany.edu/psychology/

The University of Akron, Graduate School, College of Health Professions, School of Counseling, Program in Clinical Mental Health Counseling, Akron, OH 44325. Offers MA. *Accreditation:* ACA; NCATE. *Degree requirements:* For master's, comprehensive exam. *Entrance requirements:* For master's, minimum GPA of 2.75, letters of recommendation, interview. Additional exam requirements/recommendations for international students: required—TOEFL (minimum score 79 iBT), IELTS (minimum score 6.5). Electronic applications accepted.

Clinical Psychology

The University of Alabama, Graduate School, College of Arts and Sciences, Department of Psychology, Tuscaloosa, AL 35487. Offers clinical psychology (PhD); experimental psychology (PhD). *Faculty:* 31 full-time (18 women), 1 (woman) part-time/adjunct. *Students:* 84 full-time (68 women), 15 part-time (11 women); includes 17 minority (7 Black or African American, non-Hispanic/Latino; 1 Asian, non-Hispanic/Latino; 7 Hispanic/Latino; 2 Two or more races, non-Hispanic/Latino), 7 international. Average age 28. 269 applicants, 9% accepted, 17 enrolled. In 2019, 21 doctorates awarded. *Degree requirements:* For doctorate, thesis/dissertation, internship (for clinical psychology). *Entrance requirements:* For doctorate, GRE. Additional exam requirements/recommendations for international students: required—TOEFL (minimum score 550 paper-based). *Application deadline:* For fall admission, 11/16 for domestic and international students. Application fee: $50 ($60 for international students). Electronic applications accepted. *Expenses: Tuition, area resident:* Full-time $10,780; part-time $440 per credit hour. Tuition, nonresident: full-time $30,250; part-time $1550 per credit hour. *Financial support:* In 2019–20, 65 students received support, including fellowships with full tuition reimbursements available (averaging $17,000 per year), research assistantships with tuition reimbursements available (averaging $12,744 per year), teaching assistantships with tuition reimbursements available (averaging $13,824 per year); career-related internships or fieldwork, institutionally sponsored loans, scholarships/grants, health care benefits, and unspecified assistantships also available. Financial award application deadline: 11/16. *Unit head:* Dr. Frances A. Conners, Chair, 205-348-1913, Fax: 205-348-8648, E-mail: fconners@ua.edu. *Application contact:* Mary Beth Hubbard, Information Contact, 205-348-1919, Fax: 205-348-8648, E-mail: mary.b.hubbard@ua.edu.
Website: http://www.psychology.ua.edu

The University of Alabama at Birmingham, College of Arts and Sciences, Program in Psychology, Birmingham, AL 35294. Offers behavioral neuroscience (PhD); lifespan developmental psychology (PhD); medical/clinical psychology (PhD); psychology (MA). *Accreditation:* APA (one or more programs are accredited). *Faculty:* 27 full-time (12 women), 1 (woman) part-time/adjunct. *Students:* 81 full-time (55 women), 3 part-time (all women); includes 22 minority (10 Black or African American, non-Hispanic/Latino; 4 Asian, non-Hispanic/Latino; 6 Hispanic/Latino; 2 Two or more races, non-Hispanic/Latino), 3 international. Average age 27. 199 applicants, 7% accepted, 12 enrolled. In 2019, 8 master's, 15 doctorates awarded. *Entrance requirements:* For master's and doctorate, GRE General Test, letters of recommendation. *Application deadline:* Applications are processed on a rolling basis. Electronic applications accepted. *Financial support:* Fellowships, research assistantships, and teaching assistantships available. *Unit head:* Dr. Karlene K. Ball, Chair, 205-934-2610, Fax: 205-975-2295, E-mail: psych-dept@uab.edu. *Application contact:* Susan Noblitt Banks, Director of Graduate School Operations, 205-934-8227, Fax: 205-934-8413, E-mail: gradschool@uab.edu.
Website: http://www.uab.edu/cas/psychology/graduate

University of Alaska Anchorage, College of Arts and Sciences, Department of Psychology, Anchorage, AK 99508. Offers clinical psychology (MS); clinical-community psychology with rural and indigenous emphasis (PhD). *Accreditation:* APA. *Program availability:* Part-time. *Degree requirements:* For master's, thesis. *Entrance requirements:* For master's, GRE General Test, GRE Subject Test, interview, references; for doctorate, interview, bachelor's or master's degree in psychology. Additional exam requirements/recommendations for international students: required—TOEFL (minimum score 550 paper-based).

University of Bridgeport, School of Arts and Sciences, Department of Counseling, Bridgeport, CT 06604. Offers clinical mental health counseling (MS); college student personnel (MS); community counseling (MS); human resource development (MS); human service (MS). *Program availability:* Part-time, evening/weekend. *Degree requirements:* For master's, thesis, project. *Entrance requirements:* Additional exam requirements/recommendations for international students: recommended—TOEFL (minimum score 550 paper-based; 80 iBT), IELTS (minimum score 6.5). Electronic applications accepted. *Expenses:* Contact institution.

The University of British Columbia, Faculty of Arts, Department of Psychology, Vancouver, BC V6T 1Z4, Canada. Offers behavioral neuroscience (MA, PhD); clinical psychology (MA, PhD); cognitive science (MA, PhD); developmental psychology (MA, PhD); health psychology (MA, PhD); quantitative methods (MA, PhD); social/personality psychology (MA, PhD). *Accreditation:* APA (one or more programs are accredited). Terminal master's awarded for partial completion of doctoral program. *Degree requirements:* For master's, thesis; for doctorate, comprehensive exam, thesis/dissertation. *Entrance requirements:* For master's and doctorate, GRE General Test. Additional exam requirements/recommendations for international students: required—TOEFL. Electronic applications accepted. *Expenses:* Contact institution.

University of Calgary, Faculty of Graduate Studies, Faculty of Arts, Program in Psychology, Calgary, AB T2N 1N4, Canada. Offers clinical psychology (M Sc, PhD); psychology (M Sc, PhD). *Degree requirements:* For master's, thesis; for doctorate, thesis/dissertation. *Entrance requirements:* For master's, GRE General Test, bachelor's degree in psychology, minimum GPA of 3.4. Additional exam requirements/recommendations for international students: required—TOEFL (minimum score 550 paper-based). Electronic applications accepted.

University of California, San Diego, Graduate Division, Program in Clinical Psychology, San Diego, CA 92093. Offers PhD. *Students:* 59 part-time (48 women). In 2019, 10 doctorates awarded. *Degree requirements:* For doctorate, comprehensive exam, thesis/dissertation, 1-year full-time internship. *Entrance requirements:* For doctorate, GRE General Test, GRE Subject Test, minimum GPA of 3.25. Additional exam requirements/recommendations for international students: required—TOEFL (minimum score 550 paper-based; 80 iBT), IELTS (minimum score 7). Electronic applications accepted. *Financial support:* Fellowships, research assistantships, teaching assistantships, scholarships/grants, and unspecified assistantships available. Financial award applicants required to submit FAFSA. *Unit head:* Lauren Brookman-Frazee, Co-Director, 858-534-5370, E-mail: lbrookman@ucsd.edu. *Application contact:* Kristin Deveraux, Program Coordinator, 858-534-7653, E-mail: kdeveraux@ucsd.edu.
Website: http://clinpsyc.sdsu.edu/

University of California, Santa Barbara, Graduate Division, Gevirtz Graduate School of Education, Santa Barbara, CA 93106-9490. Offers counseling, clinical and school psychology (MA, PhD, Credential), including clinical psychology (PhD), counseling psychology (MA, PhD), pupil personnel services (Credential), school psychology (PhD); education (MA, PhD); teacher education (M Ed, Credential), including multiple subject teaching (Credential), single subject teaching (Credential), special education (Credential), teaching (M Ed); MA/PhD. *Accreditation:* APA (one or more programs are accredited). Terminal master's awarded for partial completion of doctoral program. *Degree requirements:* For master's, comprehensive exam (for some programs), thesis (for some programs); for doctorate, comprehensive exam (for some programs), thesis/dissertation. *Entrance requirements:* For master's and doctorate, GRE; for Credential, GRE or MAT, CSET, CBEST. Additional exam requirements/recommendations for international students: required—TOEFL (minimum score 550 paper-based; 80 iBT), IELTS (minimum score 7). Electronic applications accepted.

University of Central Florida, College of Sciences, Department of Psychology, Program in Clinical Psychology, Orlando, FL 32816. Offers MA, PhD. *Accreditation:* APA. *Students:* 61 full-time (47 women), 8 part-time (6 women); includes 24 minority (3 Black or African American, non-Hispanic/Latino; 5 Asian, non-Hispanic/Latino; 12 Hispanic/Latino; 4 Two or more races, non-Hispanic/Latino), 3 international. Average age 27. 302 applicants, 10% accepted, 20 enrolled. In 2019, 18 master's, 6 doctorates awarded. *Degree requirements:* For master's, thesis or alternative, clinical internship; for doctorate, thesis/dissertation, candidacy exam, internship. *Entrance requirements:* For master's, GRE General Test, minimum GPA of 3.0 in last 60 hours, resume, personal statement, letters of recommendation; for doctorate, GRE General Test, minimum GPA of 3.0 in last 60 hours, curriculum vitae, personal statement, letters of recommendation. Additional exam requirements/recommendations for international students: required—TOEFL. *Application deadline:* For fall admission, 1/1 for domestic students. Application fee: $30. Electronic applications accepted. *Financial support:* In 2019–20, 35 students received support, including 12 fellowships with partial tuition reimbursements available (averaging $7,874 per year), 8 research assistantships with partial tuition reimbursements available (averaging $7,085 per year), 26 teaching assistantships with partial tuition reimbursements available (averaging $8,242 per year); career-related internships or fieldwork, Federal Work-Study, institutionally sponsored loans, health care benefits, tuition waivers (partial), and unspecified assistantships also available. Financial award application deadline: 3/1; financial award applicants required to submit FAFSA. *Unit head:* Dr. Brian Fisak, Program Director, 407-823-2822, E-mail: brian.fisak@ucf.edu. *Application contact:* Associate Director, Graduate Admissions, 407-823-2766, Fax: 407-823-6442, E-mail: gradadmissions@ucf.edu.
Website: http://psychology.cos.ucf.edu/graduate/

University of Cincinnati, Graduate School, McMicken College of Arts and Sciences, Department of Psychology, Cincinnati, OH 45221. Offers clinical psychology (PhD); experimental psychology (PhD). *Accreditation:* APA. *Degree requirements:* For doctorate, comprehensive exam, thesis/dissertation. *Entrance requirements:* For doctorate, GRE General Test. Additional exam requirements/recommendations for international students: required—TOEFL.

University of Colorado Denver, College of Liberal Arts and Sciences, Department of Psychology, Denver, CO 80217. Offers clinical health psychology (PhD). *Program availability:* Part-time, evening/weekend. *Degree requirements:* For doctorate, comprehensive exam, thesis/dissertation, 69 credits of coursework, minimum of 12 clinical practicum hours, 30 dissertation hours, three credits of pre-doctoral internship. *Entrance requirements:* For doctorate, GRE General Test; GRE Subject Test (recommended), minimum GPA of 3.5; undergraduate courses in introductory psychology, psychological statistics, research methods and abnormal psychology; letters of recommendation; personal statement; resume. Additional exam requirements/recommendations for international students: required—TOEFL (minimum score 537 paper-based; 75 iBT); recommended—IELTS (minimum score 6.5). Electronic applications accepted. Tuition and fees vary according to course load, program and reciprocity agreements.

University of Colorado Denver, School of Education and Human Development, Program in Counseling Psychology and Counselor Education, Denver, CO 80217. Offers counseling (MA), including clinical mental health counseling, couple and family counseling, multicultural counseling, school counseling; school counseling (MA). *Accreditation:* ACA; NCATE. *Program availability:* Part-time, evening/weekend. *Entrance requirements:* For master's, GRE or MAT (unless applicant already holds a graduate degree), letters of recommendation, interview, resume, transcripts from all colleges/universities attended. Tuition and fees vary according to course load, program and reciprocity agreements.

University of Connecticut, Graduate School, College of Liberal Arts and Sciences, Department of Psychological Sciences, Storrs, CT 06269. Offers behavioral neuroscience (PhD); biopsychology (PhD); clinical psychology (MA, PhD); cognition and instruction (PhD); developmental psychology (MA, PhD); ecological psychology (PhD); experimental psychology (PhD); general psychology (MA, PhD); industrial/organizational psychology (PhD); language and cognition (PhD); neuroscience (PhD); social psychology (MA, PhD). *Accreditation:* APA. Terminal master's awarded for partial completion of doctoral program. *Degree requirements:* For master's, comprehensive exam; for doctorate, thesis/dissertation. *Entrance requirements:* For master's and doctorate, GRE General Test, GRE Subject Test. Additional exam requirements/recommendations for international students: required—TOEFL (minimum score 550 paper-based). Electronic applications accepted.

University of Dayton, Department of Counselor Education and Human Services, Dayton, OH 45469. Offers clinical mental health counseling (MS Ed); college student personnel (MS Ed); higher education administration (MS Ed); human services (MS Ed); school counseling (MS Ed); school psychology (MS Ed, Ed S). *Accreditation:* ACA; NCATE. *Program availability:* Part-time. *Degree requirements:* For master's, thesis (for some programs); for Ed S, thesis (for some programs), professional portfolio. *Entrance requirements:* For master's, MAT or GRE (if GPA less than 2.75), essays (for some programs). Additional exam requirements/recommendations for international students: required—TOEFL (minimum score 550 paper-based; 80 iBT). Electronic applications accepted. *Expenses:* Contact institution.

University of Dayton, Program in Clinical Psychology, Dayton, OH 45469. Offers MA. *Degree requirements:* For master's, thesis, clinical practicum. *Entrance requirements:* For master's, GRE (minimum combined Verbal and Quantitative score 300; neither subtest below 148), minimum undergraduate GPA of 3.2. Additional exam requirements/recommendations for international students: required—TOEFL (minimum score 550 paper-based; 80 iBT). Electronic applications accepted.

University of Delaware, College of Arts and Sciences, Department of Psychology, Newark, DE 19716. Offers behavioral neuroscience (PhD); clinical psychology (PhD); cognitive psychology (PhD); social psychology (PhD). *Accreditation:* APA. *Degree requirements:* For doctorate, thesis/dissertation. *Entrance requirements:* For doctorate, GRE General Test. Additional exam requirements/recommendations for international students: required—TOEFL (minimum score 600 paper-based). Electronic applications accepted.

University of Denver, Division of Arts, Humanities and Social Sciences, Department of Psychology, Denver, CO 80208. Offers affective/cognitive/social psychology (PhD); clinical child psychology (PhD); developmental psychology (PhD). *Accreditation:* APA. *Faculty:* 29 full-time (20 women). *Students:* 30 full-time (24 women); includes 8 minority (2 Asian, non-Hispanic/Latino; 5 Hispanic/Latino; 1 Two or more races, non-Hispanic/Latino), 2 international. Average age 27. 457 applicants, 4% accepted, 10 enrolled. In 2019, 5 doctorates awarded. Terminal master's awarded for partial completion of doctoral program. *Degree requirements:* For doctorate, comprehensive exam (for some programs), thesis/dissertation. *Entrance requirements:* For doctorate, GRE General Test, master's degree, transcripts, biographical statement, three letters of recommendation, resume, essay on diversity (for clinical child program only). Additional exam requirements/recommendations for international students: required—TOEFL (minimum score 550 paper-based; 80 iBT). *Application deadline:* For fall admission, 12/21 for domestic and international students. Application fee: $65. Electronic applications

accepted. *Expenses:* Contact institution. *Financial support:* In 2019–20, 30 students received support, including 13 research assistantships with tuition reimbursements available (averaging $15,392 per year), 15 teaching assistantships with tuition reimbursements available (averaging $13,800 per year); Federal Work-Study, institutionally sponsored loans, scholarships/grants, and unspecified assistantships also available. Support available to part-time students. Financial award application deadline: 2/15; financial award applicants required to submit FAFSA. *Unit head:* Dr. Sarah Watamura, Associate Professor and Chair, 303-871-4130, E-mail: sarah.watamura@du.edu. *Application contact:* Paula Plank-Houghtaling, Graduate Program Administrator, 303-871-3803, E-mail: phoughta@du.edu.
Website: http://www.du.edu/ahss/psychology

University of Denver, Graduate School of Professional Psychology, Denver, CO 80208. Offers clinical psychology (Psy D); forensic psychology (MA); international disaster psychology (MA); sport and performance psychology (MA); sport coaching (MA); strength and conditioning and fitness coaching (Certificate). *Accreditation:* APA. *Faculty:* 23 full-time (15 women), 16 part-time/adjunct (9 women). *Students:* 243 full-time (192 women), 84 part-time (44 women); includes 95 minority (18 Black or African American, non-Hispanic/Latino; 1 American Indian or Alaska Native, non-Hispanic/Latino; 18 Asian, non-Hispanic/Latino; 46 Hispanic/Latino; 1 Native Hawaiian or other Pacific Islander, non-Hispanic/Latino; 11 Two or more races, non-Hispanic/Latino), 9 international. Average age 27. 953 applicants, 27% accepted, 137 enrolled. In 2019, 117 master's, 35 doctorates, 152 other advanced degrees awarded. *Degree requirements:* For master's, comprehensive exam (for some programs); for doctorate, comprehensive exam, community field placement, paper, clinical internship, complete 4 assessments, professional psychology clinic. *Entrance requirements:* For master's and doctorate, GRE General Test, psychology major/minor or 660 or higher on psychology subject GRE exam, transcripts, resume, two letters of recommendation, essay. Additional exam requirements/recommendations for international students: required—TOEFL (minimum score 550 paper-based; 80 iBT). *Application deadline:* For fall admission, 1/11 for domestic and international students. Application fee: $65. Electronic applications accepted. *Expenses:* Contact institution. *Financial support:* In 2019–20, 249 students received support, including 20 teaching assistantships with tuition reimbursements available (averaging $2,835 per year); career-related internships or fieldwork, Federal Work-Study, institutionally sponsored loans, scholarships/grants, unspecified assistantships, and clinical assistantships also available. Support available to part-time students. Financial award application deadline: 2/15; financial award applicants required to submit FAFSA. *Unit head:* Dr. Shelly Smith-Acuna, Dean, 303-871-3880, Fax: 303-871-4220, E-mail: shelly.smith-acuna@du.edu. *Application contact:* Julie Schellman, Director of Enrollment, 303-871-2908, E-mail: Julie.Schellman@du.edu.
Website: http://www.du.edu/gspp

University of Detroit Mercy, College of Liberal Arts and Education, Detroit, MI 48221. Offers addiction counseling (MA); addiction studies (Certificate); clinical mental health counseling (MA); clinical psychology (MA, PhD); computer and information systems (MS); criminal justice (MA); curriculum and instruction (MA); economics (MA); educational administration (MA); financial economics (MA); industrial/organizational psychology (MA); information assurance (MS); intelligence analysis (MA); liberal studies (MALS); religious studies (MA); school counseling (MA, Certificate); school psychology (Spec); security administration (MS); special education: emotionally impaired/behaviorally disordered (MA); special education: learning disabilities (MA). *Program availability:* Part-time, evening/weekend. *Degree requirements:* For doctorate, departmental qualifying exam.

University of Florida, Graduate School, College of Public Health and Health Professions, Department of Clinical and Health Psychology, Gainesville, FL 32611. Offers clinical and translational science (PhD); psychology (MS). *Accreditation:* APA (one or more programs are accredited). *Degree requirements:* For doctorate, comprehensive exam, thesis/dissertation, pre-doctoral internship. *Entrance requirements:* For master's and doctorate, GRE General Test, minimum GPA of 3.0. Additional exam requirements/recommendations for international students: required—TOEFL (minimum score 550 paper-based; 80 iBT), IELTS (minimum score 6). Electronic applications accepted.

University of Guelph, Office of Graduate and Postdoctoral Studies, College of Social and Applied Human Sciences, Department of Psychology, Guelph, ON N1G 2W1, Canada. Offers applied social psychology (MA, PhD); clinical psychology: applied development emphasis (PhD); clinical psychology: applied developmental emphasis (MA); industrial/organizational psychology (MA, PhD); neuroscience and applied cognitive science (MA, PhD). *Degree requirements:* For master's, thesis; for doctorate, comprehensive exam, thesis/dissertation. *Entrance requirements:* For master's, GRE General Test, GRE Subject Test, minimum B+ average during previous 2 years of course work; for doctorate, GRE General Test, GRE Subject Test, minimum A- average. Additional exam requirements/recommendations for international students: required—TOEFL (minimum score 89 iBT). Electronic applications accepted.

University of Hartford, College of Arts and Sciences, Department of Psychology, Program in Clinical Practices, West Hartford, CT 06117-1599. Offers clinical practices (Psy D); psychology (MA). *Accreditation:* APA. *Faculty:* 5 full-time (4 women), 6 part-time/adjunct (4 women). *Students:* 68 full-time (58 women), 65 part-time (56 women); includes 32 minority (5 Black or African American, non-Hispanic/Latino; 1 American Indian or Alaska Native, non-Hispanic/Latino; 14 Asian, non-Hispanic/Latino; 9 Hispanic/Latino; 3 Two or more races, non-Hispanic/Latino), 3 international. Average age 28. 195 applicants, 41% accepted, 37 enrolled. In 2019, 34 master's, 38 doctorates awarded. *Degree requirements:* For master's, comprehensive exam, thesis optional. *Entrance requirements:* For master's, GRE General Test, GRE Subject Test, minimum GPA of 3.0, 3 letters of recommendation. Additional exam requirements/recommendations for international students: required—TOEFL (minimum score 550 paper-based). *Application deadline:* For fall admission, 2/15 priority date for domestic students. Applications are processed on a rolling basis. Application fee: $45. Electronic applications accepted. *Expenses: Tuition:* Full-time $23,700; part-time $645 per credit. *Required fees:* $510; $510 per unit. Tuition and fees vary according to course load, degree level and program. *Financial support:* In 2019–20, 5 research assistantships (averaging $2,000 per year), 4 teaching assistantships (averaging $2,600 per year) were awarded. Financial award application deadline: 6/1; financial award applicants required to submit FAFSA. *Unit head:* Dr. Tony Crespi, Director, 860-768-5081, Fax: 860-768-5292, E-mail: crespi@hartford.edu. *Application contact:* Renee Murphy, Assistant Director of Graduate Admissions, 860-768-4371, Fax: 860-768-5160, E-mail: rmurphy@hartford.edu.
Website: http://uhaweb.hartford.edu/psych/

University of Hawaii at Manoa, Office of Graduate Education, College of Social Sciences, Department of Psychology, Honolulu, HI 96822. Offers clinical psychology (PhD); community and cultural psychology (PhD); community and culture (MA); psychology (MA, PhD, Graduate Certificate). *Accreditation:* APA (one or more programs are accredited). *Program availability:* Part-time. Terminal master's awarded for partial completion of doctoral program. *Degree requirements:* For master's, comprehensive exam, thesis; for doctorate, comprehensive exam, thesis/dissertation. *Entrance requirements:* For master's and doctorate, GRE General Test, GRE Subject Test. Additional exam requirements/recommendations for international students: required—TOEFL (minimum score 600 paper-based; 100 iBT), IELTS (minimum score 7).

University of Houston, College of Liberal Arts and Social Sciences, Department of Psychology, Houston, TX 77204. Offers clinical psychology (PhD); developmental psychology (PhD); industrial/organizational psychology (PhD); psychology (MA); social psychology (PhD). *Accreditation:* APA (one or more programs are accredited). *Degree requirements:* For master's, comprehensive exam, thesis; for doctorate, comprehensive exam, thesis/dissertation. *Entrance requirements:* For master's, GRE General Test, career statement, 3 letters of recommendation; for doctorate, GRE General Test, 3 letters of recommendation. Additional exam requirements/recommendations for international students: required—TOEFL (minimum score 550 paper-based; 79 iBT). Electronic applications accepted.

University of Houston–Clear Lake, School of Human Sciences and Humanities, Programs in Human Sciences, Houston, TX 77058-1002. Offers behavioral sciences (MA), including criminology, cross cultural studies, general psychology, sociology; clinical psychology (MA); criminology (MA); cross cultural studies (MA); family therapy (MA); fitness and human performance (MA); school psychology (MA). *Accreditation:* AAMFT/COAMFTE. *Program availability:* Part-time, evening/weekend, online learning. *Degree requirements:* For master's, thesis or alternative. *Entrance requirements:* For master's, GRE General Test. Additional exam requirements/recommendations for international students: required—TOEFL (minimum score 550 paper-based). Electronic applications accepted.

University of Indianapolis, Graduate Programs, College of Applied Behavioral Sciences, Indianapolis, IN 46227-3697. Offers addictions counseling (MA); clinical psychology (Psy D); mental health counseling (MA); psychology (MA); social work (MSW). *Accreditation:* APA. *Degree requirements:* For master's, practicum; for doctorate, comprehensive exam, thesis/dissertation, 1200 hours of clinical practicum, 2000-hour internship. *Entrance requirements:* For master's, GRE, 3 letters of recommendation; for doctorate, GRE, minimum GPA of 3.0, 18 hours of course work in psychology, 3 letters of recommendation. Additional exam requirements/recommendations for international students: required—TOEFL (minimum score 550 paper-based).

The University of Kansas, Graduate Studies, College of Liberal Arts and Sciences, Department of Psychology, Lawrence, KS 66045. Offers clinical psychology (MA, PhD); cognitive and brain sciences (MA, PhD); developmental psychology (MA, PhD); quantitative psychology (PhD); social psychology (MA, PhD). *Accreditation:* APA (one or more programs are accredited). *Program availability:* Part-time. *Students:* 72 full-time (51 women), 1 (woman) part-time; includes 16 minority (6 Black or African American, non-Hispanic/Latino; 3 Asian, non-Hispanic/Latino; 1 Hispanic/Latino; 6 Two or more races, non-Hispanic/Latino), 9 international. Average age 27. 343 applicants, 9% accepted, 17 enrolled. In 2019, 15 master's, 14 doctorates awarded. Terminal master's awarded for partial completion of doctoral program. *Entrance requirements:* For doctorate, GRE General Test, three letters of recommendation, resume/curriculum vitae, statement of purpose/personal statement, writing sample. Additional exam requirements/recommendations for international students: required—TOEFL, IELTS. *Application deadline:* For fall admission, 12/1 for domestic and international students. Application fee: $65 ($85 for international students). Electronic applications accepted. *Expenses:* Tuition, state resident: full-time $9989. Tuition, nonresident: full-time $23,950. *International tuition:* $23,950 full-time. *Required fees:* $984; $81.99 per credit hour. Tuition and fees vary according to course load, campus/location and program. *Financial support:* Fellowships, research assistantships, teaching assistantships, career-related internships or fieldwork, Federal Work-Study, scholarships/grants, health care benefits, and unspecified assistantships available. Financial award application deadline: 12/1; financial award applicants required to submit FAFSA. *Unit head:* Michael Vitevitch, Chair, 785-864-9312, E-mail: mvitevit@ku.edu. *Application contact:* Kirsten Hermreck, Graduate Admissions Contact, 785-864-4195, E-mail: psycgrad@ku.edu.
Website: http://www.psych.ku.edu/

University of La Verne, College of Arts and Sciences, Department of Psychology, Program in Clinical Psychology, La Verne, CA 91750-4443. Offers Psy D. *Degree requirements:* For doctorate, thesis/dissertation, clinical practica, clinical internship, competency exams, personal psychotherapy. *Entrance requirements:* For doctorate, GRE, minimum undergraduate GPA of 3.1, statement of professional goals and aspirations, 3 recommendations, interview, curriculum vitae. Additional exam requirements/recommendations for international students: required—TOEFL (minimum score 600 paper-based; 100 iBT), IELTS (minimum score 6.5). Electronic applications accepted. *Expenses:* Contact institution.

University of Louisiana at Monroe, Graduate School, College of Health Sciences, Programs in Counseling Studies, Monroe, LA 71209-0001. Offers clinical mental health counseling (MS); school counseling (MS). *Accreditation:* ACA; NCATE. *Program availability:* Part-time, evening/weekend, online learning. *Faculty:* 1 (woman) full-time, 4 part-time/adjunct (2 women). *Students:* 25 full-time (22 women), 18 part-time (15 women); includes 10 minority (7 Black or African American, non-Hispanic/Latino; 1 Hispanic/Latino; 2 Two or more races, non-Hispanic/Latino). Average age 35. 89 applicants, 16% accepted, 8 enrolled. In 2019, 18 master's awarded. *Degree requirements:* For master's, thesis optional, internship. *Entrance requirements:* For master's, GRE General Test, minimum undergraduate GPA of 2.5. Additional exam requirements/recommendations for international students: required—TOEFL (minimum score 500 paper-based; 61 iBT); recommended—IELTS (minimum score 5.5). *Application deadline:* For fall admission, 3/15 for domestic and international students. Applications are processed on a rolling basis. Application fee: $55. Electronic applications accepted. *Expenses: Tuition, area resident:* Full-time $6489. Tuition, state resident: full-time $6489. Tuition, nonresident: full-time $18,989. *Required fees:* $2748. Tuition and fees vary according to course load and program. *Financial support:* In 2019–20, 7 students received support. Career-related internships or fieldwork, Federal Work-Study, scholarships/grants, and unspecified assistantships available. Financial award application deadline: 2/15; financial award applicants required to submit FAFSA. *Unit head:* Dr. Thomas Foster, Program Director of Counseling, 318-342-1298, E-mail: tfoster@ulm.edu. *Application contact:* Dr. Thomas Foster, Program Director of Counseling, 318-342-1298, E-mail: tfoster@ulm.edu.
Website: http://www.ulm.edu/counseling/

University of Louisville, Graduate School, College of Arts and Sciences, Department of Psychological and Brain Sciences, Louisville, KY 40292-0001. Offers clinical psychology (PhD); experimental psychology (PhD), including cognition and development, vision and hearing. *Accreditation:* APA. *Program availability:* Part-time. *Faculty:* 24 full-time (14 women), 9 part-time/adjunct (5 women). *Students:* 50 full-time (42 women), 1 (woman) part-time; includes 5 minority (1 Black or African American, non-Hispanic/Latino; 2 Hispanic/Latino; 2 Two or more races, non-Hispanic/Latino), 6 international. Average age 29. 144 applicants, 1% accepted, 2 enrolled. In 2019, 14 doctorates awarded. *Degree requirements:* For doctorate, comprehensive exam, thesis/dissertation, coursework; internship for clinical. *Entrance requirements:* For doctorate, GRE General Test, Three letters of reference, official transcripts. Additional exam requirements/recommendations for international students: required—TOEFL (minimum score 550 paper-based; 79 iBT), IELTS can be used in place of TOEFL;

recommended—IELTS (minimum score 6.5). *Application deadline:* For fall admission, 12/1 for domestic and international students. Applications are processed on a rolling basis. Application fee: $65. Electronic applications accepted. *Expenses: Tuition, area resident:* Full-time $13,000; part-time $723 per credit hour. Tuition, state resident: full-time $13,000; part-time $723 per credit hour. Tuition, nonresident: full-time $27,114; part-time $1507 per credit hour. *International tuition:* $27,114 full-time. *Required fees:* $196. Tuition and fees vary according to program and reciprocity agreements. *Financial support:* In 2019–20, 49 students received support, including 8 fellowships with full tuition reimbursements available (averaging $22,000 per year), 3 research assistantships with full tuition reimbursements available (averaging $22,000 per year), 30 teaching assistantships with full tuition reimbursements available (averaging $22,000 per year); scholarships/grants, health care benefits, and unspecified assistantships also available. Financial award application deadline: 12/1. *Unit head:* Dr. Benjamin Mast, Professor and Chair, 502-852-3280, Fax: 502-852-8904, E-mail: b.mast@louisville.edu. *Application contact:* Maggie Leahy, Administrative Assistant, 502-852-4364, Fax: 502-852-8904, E-mail: maggie.leahy@louisville.edu.
Website: http://louisville.edu/psychology

University of Lynchburg, Graduate Studies, M Ed Program in Clinical Mental Health Counseling, Lynchburg, VA 24501-3199. Offers M Ed. *Accreditation:* ACA. *Program availability:* Part-time, evening/weekend. *Degree requirements:* For master's, counseling internship. *Entrance requirements:* For master's, GRE, minimum GPA of 3.0 (preferred), official transcripts (bachelor's, others as relevant), three letters of recommendation, career goals statement, personal interview. Additional exam requirements/recommendations for international students: required—TOEFL (minimum score 550 paper-based; 80 iBT), IELTS (minimum score 6). Electronic applications accepted. Application fee is waived when completed online. *Expenses:* Contact institution.

The University of Manchester, School of Psychological Sciences, Manchester, United Kingdom. Offers audiology (M Phil, PhD); clinical psychology (M Phil, PhD, Psy D); psychology (M Phil, PhD).

University of Manitoba, Faculty of Graduate Studies, Faculty of Arts, Department of Psychology, Winnipeg, MB R3T 2N2, Canada. Offers clinical psychology (PhD); psychology (MA, PhD); school psychology (MA). *Degree requirements:* For master's, thesis; for doctorate, one foreign language, thesis/dissertation. *Entrance requirements:* For master's and doctorate, GRE General Test.

University of Mary Hardin-Baylor, Graduate Studies in Counseling, Belton, TX 76513. Offers clinical and mental health counseling (MA); marriage, family and child counseling (MA); non-clinical professional studies (MA). *Accreditation:* ACA. *Program availability:* Part-time, evening/weekend. *Faculty:* 6 full-time (3 women), 4 part-time/adjunct (2 women). *Students:* 54 full-time (41 women), 23 part-time (19 women); includes 36 minority (13 Black or African American, non-Hispanic/Latino; 1 American Indian or Alaska Native, non-Hispanic/Latino; 1 Asian, non-Hispanic/Latino; 18 Hispanic/Latino; 3 Two or more races, non-Hispanic/Latino). Average age 31. 57 applicants, 75% accepted, 25 enrolled. In 2019, 32 master's awarded. *Degree requirements:* For master's, comprehensive exam. *Entrance requirements:* For master's, GRE General Test with minimum cumulative score of 300 on verbal and quantitative portions and 3.0 on analytical section (if overall undergraduate GPA is below a 3.0), minimum cumulative undergraduate GPA of 2.75 or 3.0 on last 60 hours of course work; three letters of recommendation; interview with departmental graduate admissions committee. Additional exam requirements/recommendations for international students: required—TOEFL (minimum score 60 iBT), IELTS (minimum score 4.5). *Application deadline:* For fall admission, 6/1 for domestic students, 4/30 priority date for international students; for spring admission, 11/1 for domestic students, 9/30 priority date for international students. Applications are processed on a rolling basis. Application fee: $35 ($135 for international students). Electronic applications accepted. *Expenses: Tuition:* Full-time $16,200; part-time $10,800 per credit hour. *Required fees:* $1350; $75 per credit hour. $50 per term. Tuition and fees vary according to course load and degree level. *Financial support:* In 2019–20, 58 students received support. Federal Work-Study, unspecified assistantships, and scholarships for some active duty military personnel available. Support available to part-time students. Financial award applicants required to submit FAFSA. *Unit head:* Dr. Ty Leonard, Interim Director, Graduate Counseling, 254-295-5532, E-mail: hleonard@umhb.edu. *Application contact:* Katherine Moore, Assistant Director, Graduate Admissions, 254-295-4924, E-mail: kmoore@umhb.edu.
Website: https://go.umhb.edu/graduate/counseling/home

University of Maryland, Baltimore County, The Graduate School, College of Arts, Humanities and Social Sciences, Department of Psychology, Program in Human Services Psychology, Baltimore, MD 21250. Offers applied behavioral analysis (MA); human services psychology (PhD), including behavioral medicine, clinical psychology, community psychology. *Faculty:* 17 full-time (9 women), 11 part-time/adjunct (4 women). *Students:* 58 full-time (47 women), 17 part-time (12 women); includes 19 minority (8 Black or African American, non-Hispanic/Latino; 5 Asian, non-Hispanic/Latino; 5 Hispanic/Latino; 1 Two or more races, non-Hispanic/Latino), 3 international. Average age 27. 212 applicants, 18% accepted, 17 enrolled. In 2019, 15 master's, 9 doctorates awarded. *Degree requirements:* For master's, thesis; for doctorate, comprehensive exam, thesis/dissertation. *Entrance requirements:* For master's, GRE General Test, minimum GPA of 3.0; for doctorate, GRE General Test, GRE Subject Test, minimum GPA of 3.0. Additional exam requirements/recommendations for international students: required—TOEFL. *Application deadline:* For fall admission, 12/1 for domestic and international students. Application fee: $50. Electronic applications accepted. *Expenses:* $14,382 per year. *Financial support:* In 2019–20, 34 students received support, including 4 fellowships with full tuition reimbursements available (averaging $26,000 per year), 20 research assistantships with full tuition reimbursements available (averaging $20,400 per year), 10 teaching assistantships with full tuition reimbursements available (averaging $17,250 per year); career-related internships or fieldwork, Federal Work-Study, scholarships/grants, health care benefits, tuition waivers, and unspecified assistantships also available. Financial award application deadline: 3/1; financial award applicants required to submit FAFSA. *Unit head:* Dr. Steve Pitts, Program Director, 410-455-2362, Fax: 410-455-1055, E-mail: spitts@umbc.edu. *Application contact:* Beverly McDougall, Program Management Specialist, 410-455-2613, Fax: 410-455-1055, E-mail: psycdept@umbc.edu.
Website: http://psychology.umbc.edu/

University of Maryland, College Park, Academic Affairs, College of Behavioral and Social Sciences, Department of Psychology, College Park, MD 20742. Offers clinical psychology (PhD); developmental psychology (PhD); experimental psychology (PhD); industrial psychology (MA, MS, PhD); social psychology (PhD). *Accreditation:* APA (one or more programs are accredited). *Degree requirements:* For master's, thesis; for doctorate, variable foreign language requirement, comprehensive exam, thesis/dissertation. *Entrance requirements:* For master's and doctorate, GRE General Test, GRE Subject Test, minimum GPA of 3.5, research and/or work experience, 3 letters of recommendation. Electronic applications accepted.

University of Massachusetts Amherst, Graduate School, College of Natural Sciences, Department of Psychological and Brain Sciences, Amherst, MA 01003. Offers clinical psychology (MS, PhD); cognitive psychology (MS, PhD); developmental science (MS, PhD); psychology of peace and violence (MS, PhD); social psychology (MS, PhD). *Accreditation:* APA (one or more programs are accredited). Terminal master's awarded for partial completion of doctoral program. *Degree requirements:* For master's, thesis; for doctorate, comprehensive exam, thesis/dissertation. *Entrance requirements:* For master's and doctorate, GRE General Test, 3 letters of recommendation. Additional exam requirements/recommendations for international students: required—TOEFL (minimum score 550 paper-based; 80 iBT), IELTS (minimum score 6.5). Electronic applications accepted.

University of Massachusetts Boston, College of Liberal Arts, Program in Clinical Psychology, Boston, MA 02125-3393. Offers PhD. *Accreditation:* APA. *Entrance requirements:* For doctorate, GRE General Test, GRE Subject Test, minimum GPA of 2.75. Electronic applications accepted.

University of Massachusetts Dartmouth, Graduate School, College of Arts and Sciences, Department of Psychology, North Dartmouth, MA 02747-2300. Offers autism studies (Graduate Certificate); psychology - applied behavioral analysis (MA, Post-Master's Certificate); psychology - clinical (MA); psychology - research (MA). *Program availability:* Part-time. *Faculty:* 18 full-time (11 women), 7 part-time/adjunct (4 women). *Students:* 40 full-time (32 women), 54 part-time (47 women); includes 16 minority (5 Black or African American, non-Hispanic/Latino; 2 Asian, non-Hispanic/Latino; 5 Hispanic/Latino; 4 Two or more races, non-Hispanic/Latino), 3 international. Average age 29. 97 applicants, 58% accepted, 34 enrolled. In 2019, 26 master's, 1 other advanced degree awarded. *Degree requirements:* For master's, thesis (for some programs), thesis. *Entrance requirements:* For master's, GRE (recommended), statement of purpose (minimum of 300 words), resume, 3 letters of recommendation, official transcripts; for other advanced degree, statement of purpose (minimum of 300 words), resume, 3 letters of recommendation, official transcripts. Additional exam requirements/recommendations for international students: required—TOEFL (minimum score 80 iBT). *Application deadline:* For fall admission, 4/15 for domestic students, 3/15 for international students. Application fee: $60. Electronic applications accepted. *Expenses: Tuition, area resident:* Full-time $16,390; part-time $682.92 per credit. Tuition, state resident: full-time $16,390; part-time $682.92 per credit. Tuition, nonresident: full-time $29,578; part-time $1232.42 per credit. *Required fees:* $575. *Financial support:* In 2019–20, 1 research assistantship (averaging $9,000 per year), 2 teaching assistantships (averaging $14,000 per year) were awarded; tuition waivers (full and partial) and unspecified assistantships also available. Financial award application deadline: 3/1; financial award applicants required to submit FAFSA. *Unit head:* R. Thomas Boone, Graduate Program Director, Psychology, 508-999-8440, E-mail: tboone@umassd.edu. *Application contact:* Scott Webster, Director of Graduate Studies and Admissions, 508-999-8604, Fax: 508-999-8183, E-mail: graduate@umassd.edu.
Website: http://www.umassd.edu/cas/psychology/graduate-programs

University of Memphis, Graduate School, College of Arts and Sciences, Department of Psychology, Memphis, TN 38152-3230. Offers clinical psychology (PhD); experimental psychology (PhD); general psychology (MS); school psychology (MA, PhD, Ed S). *Accreditation:* APA. *Students:* 102 full-time (74 women), 24 part-time (18 women); includes 31 minority (13 Black or African American, non-Hispanic/Latino; 6 Asian, non-Hispanic/Latino; 6 Hispanic/Latino; 6 Two or more races, non-Hispanic/Latino), 6 international. Average age 28. 57 applicants, 84% accepted, 32 enrolled. In 2019, 21 master's, 12 doctorates, 6 other advanced degrees awarded. *Degree requirements:* For master's, comprehensive exam (for some programs), thesis (for some programs), 37 credit hours (for MA); 33 credit hours with thesis or 36 with exam (for MS); for doctorate, comprehensive exam, thesis/dissertation, 80 semester hours, major area paper; 1-year placement and 1-year internship (for clinical psychology); internship (for school psychology); for Ed S, 30 credit hours. *Entrance requirements:* For master's, GRE, 3 letters of recommendation, 18 undergraduate hours in psychology; for doctorate, GRE, minimum GPA of 2.75, 18 hours of undergraduate psychology courses, transcripts, personal statement, 3 letters of recommendation, interview; for Ed S, GRE, minimum GPA of 2.75, 18 hours of undergraduate psychology courses, 3 letters of recommendation. Additional exam requirements/recommendations for international students: required—TOEFL (minimum score 550 paper-based; 79 iBT). *Application deadline:* For fall admission, 12/5 for domestic students. Applications are processed on a rolling basis. Application fee: $35 ($60 for international students). Electronic applications accepted. *Expenses: Tuition, area resident:* Full-time $9216; part-time $512 per credit hour. Tuition, state resident: full-time $9216; part-time $512 per credit hour. Tuition, nonresident: full-time $12,672; part-time $704 per credit hour. *International tuition:* $16,128 full-time. *Required fees:* $1530; $85 per credit hour. Tuition and fees vary according to program. *Financial support:* Fellowships with full tuition reimbursements, research assistantships with full tuition reimbursements, teaching assistantships with full tuition reimbursements, Federal Work-Study, scholarships/grants, tuition waivers (partial), and unspecified assistantships available. Financial award application deadline: 2/1; financial award applicants required to submit FAFSA. *Unit head:* Dr. Randy Floyd, Chair, 901-678-2146, Fax: 901-678-2579, E-mail: rgfloyd@memphis.edu. *Application contact:* Dr. Robert Cohen, Graduate Programs Coordinator, 901-678-4679, Fax: 901-678-2579, E-mail: rcohen@memphis.edu.
Website: http://www.memphis.edu/psychology

University of Memphis, Graduate School, College of Education, Department of Counseling, Educational Psychology and Research, Memphis, TN 38152. Offers counseling (MS, Ed D), including clinical mental health counseling (MS), clinical rehabilitation counseling (MS), rehabilitation counseling (MS), school counseling (MS); counseling psychology (PhD); educational psychology and research (MS, PhD), including educational psychology, educational research. *Accreditation:* ACA (one or more programs are accredited); APA (one or more programs are accredited); CORE (one or more programs are accredited); NCATE. *Program availability:* 100% online, blended/hybrid learning. *Students:* 136 full-time (110 women), 145 part-time (117 women); includes 107 minority (81 Black or African American, non-Hispanic/Latino; 10 Asian, non-Hispanic/Latino; 11 Hispanic/Latino; 5 Two or more races, non-Hispanic/Latino), 4 international. Average age 32. 149 applicants, 53% accepted, 61 enrolled. In 2019, 30 master's, 19 doctorates awarded. *Degree requirements:* For master's, comprehensive exam, thesis or alternative, internship; for doctorate, comprehensive exam, thesis/dissertation, practicum, internship, residency, scholarly work. *Entrance requirements:* For master's, GRE General Test or MAT, minimum GPA of 2.5, letters of reference, interview; for doctorate, GRE General Test, master's degree or equivalent, letters of reference, interview, curriculum vitae, personal statement. Additional exam requirements/recommendations for international students: required—TOEFL (minimum score 550 paper-based; 79 iBT). *Application deadline:* For fall admission, 10/1 priority date for domestic students; for spring admission, 4/1 priority date for domestic students. Applications are processed on a rolling basis. Application fee: $35 ($60 for international students). Electronic applications accepted. *Expenses: Tuition, area resident:* Full-time $9216; part-time $512 per credit hour. Tuition, state resident: full-time $9216; part-time $512 per credit hour. Tuition, nonresident: full-time $12,672; part-time $704 per credit hour. *International tuition:* $16,128 full-time. *Required fees:* $1530; $85 per credit hour. Tuition and fees vary according to program. *Financial support:* Fellowships with full tuition reimbursements, research assistantships with full tuition reimbursements, teaching assistantships with full tuition reimbursements, career-related internships or fieldwork, Federal Work-Study, scholarships/grants, and unspecified assistantships available. Financial award application deadline: 2/1; financial award applicants required

to submit FAFSA. *Unit head:* Dr. Steve West, Chair, 901-678-2841, Fax: 901-678-5114, E-mail: slwest@memphis.edu. *Application contact:* Stormey Warren, Graduate Programs, 901-678-2363, Fax: 901-678-4778, E-mail: shutsell@memphis.edu.
Website: http://www.memphis.edu/cepr/

University of Miami, Graduate School, College of Arts and Sciences, Department of Psychology, Coral Gables, FL 33124. Offers adult clinical (PhD); behavioral neuroscience (PhD); child clinical (PhD); developmental psychology (PhD); health clinical (PhD); psychology (MS). *Accreditation:* APA (one or more programs are accredited). *Degree requirements:* For doctorate, comprehensive exam, thesis/dissertation. *Entrance requirements:* For doctorate, GRE General Test, minimum GPA of 3.5. Additional exam requirements/recommendations for international students: required—TOEFL. Electronic applications accepted.

University of Michigan, Rackham Graduate School, College of Literature, Science, and the Arts, Department of Psychology, Ann Arbor, MI 48109. Offers biopsychology (PhD); clinical science (PhD); cognition and cognitive neuroscience (PhD); developmental psychology (PhD); personality and social contexts (PhD); social psychology (PhD). *Accreditation:* APA. Terminal master's awarded for partial completion of doctoral program. *Degree requirements:* For doctorate, comprehensive exam, thesis/dissertation, oral defense of dissertation, preliminary exam. *Entrance requirements:* For doctorate, GRE (Biopsychology, Cognition and Cognitive Neuroscience, Developmental, Social, and Clinical); GRE Subject Test also strongly recommended (Clinical); GRE not required (Personality and Social Contexts). Additional exam requirements/recommendations for international students: required—TOEFL. Electronic applications accepted.

University of Michigan–Dearborn, College of Arts, Sciences, and Letters, Master of Science in Psychology Program, Dearborn, MI 48128. Offers clinical health psychology (MS); health psychology (MS). *Program availability:* Part-time. *Faculty:* 17 full-time (9 women). *Students:* 19 full-time (16 women), 8 part-time (4 women); includes 6 minority (1 Black or African American, non-Hispanic/Latino; 3 Asian, non-Hispanic/Latino; 2 Hispanic/Latino). Average age 27. 54 applicants, 50% accepted, 10 enrolled. In 2019, 11 master's awarded. *Degree requirements:* For master's, thesis optional. *Entrance requirements:* For master's, GRE, 3 letters of recommendation. Additional exam requirements/recommendations for international students: required—TOEFL (minimum score 560 paper-based; 84 iBT), IELTS (minimum score 6.5). *Application deadline:* For fall admission, 3/15 for domestic and international students. Application fee: $60. Electronic applications accepted. *Financial support:* Career-related internships or fieldwork, scholarships/grants, and non-resident tuition scholarships available. Financial award application deadline: 3/1; financial award applicants required to submit FAFSA. *Unit head:* Dr. Michelle Leonard, Program Director, 313-593-5608, E-mail: mtleon@umich.edu. *Application contact:* Office of Graduate Studies, 313-583-6321, E-mail: umd-graduatestudies@umich.edu.
Website: http://umdearborn.edu/casl/psychology/

University of Minnesota, Twin Cities Campus, Graduate School, College of Liberal Arts, Department of Psychology, Program in Clinical Psychology, Minneapolis, MN 55455-0213. Offers PhD. *Accreditation:* APA. *Degree requirements:* For doctorate, comprehensive exam, thesis/dissertation, internship. *Entrance requirements:* For doctorate, GRE General Test, minimum GPA of 3.5; 12 credits of upper-level psychology courses, including statistics or psychological measurement; previous course work in abnormal psychology. Additional exam requirements/recommendations for international students: required—TOEFL (minimum score 550 paper-based; 79 iBT).

University of Missouri–St. Louis, College of Arts and Sciences, Department of Psychological Sciences, St. Louis, MO 63121. Offers behavioral neuroscience (MA, PhD); clinical psychology (PhD); trauma studies (Certificate). *Accreditation:* APA (one or more programs are accredited). *Program availability:* Evening/weekend. Terminal master's awarded for partial completion of doctoral program. *Degree requirements:* For master's, thesis; for doctorate, thesis/dissertation. *Entrance requirements:* For master's, GRE General Test, 3 letters of recommendation; for doctorate, GRE General Test, GRE Subject Test, 3 letters of recommendation. Additional exam requirements/recommendations for international students: required—TOEFL (minimum score 550 paper-based; 79 iBT), IELTS (minimum score 6.5). Electronic applications accepted. *Expenses: Tuition, area resident:* Full-time $9005.40; part-time $6003.60 per credit hour. Tuition, state resident: full-time $9005.40; part-time $6003.60 per credit hour. Tuition, nonresident: full-time $22,108; part-time $14,738.40 per credit hour. *International tuition:* $22,108 full-time. Tuition and fees vary according to course load.

University of Montana, Graduate School, College of Humanities and Sciences, Department of Psychology, Missoula, MT 59812. Offers clinical psychology (PhD); experimental psychology (PhD), including animal behavior psychology, developmental psychology; school psychology (MA, PhD, Ed S). *Accreditation:* APA (one or more programs are accredited). Terminal master's awarded for partial completion of doctoral program. *Degree requirements:* For master's, thesis; for doctorate, thesis/dissertation. *Entrance requirements:* For master's, doctorate, and Ed S, GRE General Test. Additional exam requirements/recommendations for international students: required—TOEFL.

University of Montana, Graduate School, Phyllis J. Washington College of Education and Human Sciences, Department of Counselor Education, Missoula, MT 59812. Offers clinical mental health counseling (MA); counseling and supervision (Ed D); counselor education (Ed S); intercultural youth and family development (MA); school counseling (MA). *Accreditation:* ACA. *Degree requirements:* For doctorate, thesis/dissertation. *Entrance requirements:* For master's, doctorate, and Ed S, GRE General Test. Additional exam requirements/recommendations for international students: required—TOEFL.

University of Nebraska–Lincoln, Graduate College, College of Arts and Sciences, Department of Psychology, Lincoln, NE 68588. Offers biopsychology (PhD); clinical psychology (PhD); cognitive psychology (PhD); developmental psychology (PhD); psychology (MA); social/personality psychology (PhD); JD/MA; JD/PhD. *Accreditation:* APA (one or more programs are accredited). *Degree requirements:* For master's, thesis optional; for doctorate, comprehensive exam, thesis/dissertation. *Entrance requirements:* For master's and doctorate, GRE General Test. Additional exam requirements/recommendations for international students: required—TOEFL (minimum score 550 paper-based). Electronic applications accepted.

University of Nevada, Las Vegas, Graduate College, College of Education, Department of Early Childhood, Multilingual, and Special Education, Las Vegas, NV 89154-3066. Offers addiction studies (Advanced Certificate); counselor education (M Ed, MS), including clinical mental health (MS), school counseling (M Ed); early childhood education (M Ed); early childhood special education (Certificate), including infancy, preschool; English language learning (M Ed); mental health counseling (Advanced Certificate); special education (M Ed, PhD); PhD/JD. *Program availability:* Part-time. *Faculty:* 14 full-time (9 women), 18 part-time/adjunct (16 women). *Students:* 235 full-time (192 women), 225 part-time (180 women); includes 225 minority (57 Black or African American, non-Hispanic/Latino; 3 American Indian or Alaska Native, non-Hispanic/Latino; 16 Asian, non-Hispanic/Latino; 108 Hispanic/Latino; 5 Native Hawaiian or other Pacific Islander, non-Hispanic/Latino; 36 Two or more races, non-Hispanic/Latino), 15 international. Average age 35. 238 applicants, 70% accepted, 134 enrolled. In 2019, 168 master's, 3 doctorates, 1 other advanced degree awarded. *Degree requirements:* For master's, comprehensive exam (for some programs); for doctorate, comprehensive exam, thesis/dissertation; for other advanced degree, final project. *Entrance requirements:* For master's, bachelor's degree; letter of recommendation; statement of purpose; for doctorate, GRE General Test, statement of purpose; writing sample; 3 letters of recommendation. Additional exam requirements/recommendations for international students: required—TOEFL (minimum score 550 paper-based; 80 iBT), IELTS (minimum score 7). Application fee: $60 ($95 for international students). Electronic applications accepted. *Expenses:* Contact institution. *Financial support:* In 2019–20, 40 students received support, including 13 research assistantships with full tuition reimbursements available (averaging $14,231 per year), 27 teaching assistantships with full tuition reimbursements available (averaging $15,933 per year); institutionally sponsored loans, scholarships/grants, health care benefits, and unspecified assistantships also available. Financial award application deadline: 3/15; financial award applicants required to submit FAFSA. *Unit head:* Dr. Joseph Morgan, Department Chair/Professor, 702-895-3167, Fax: 702-895-3205, E-mail: ems.chair@unlv.edu. *Application contact:* Dr. Sharolyn D. Pollard-Durodola, Graduate Coordinator, 702-895-3329, Fax: 702-895-3205, E-mail: ems.gradcoord@unlv.edu.
Website: http://education.unlv.edu/ecs/

University of Nevada, Reno, Graduate School, College of Liberal Arts, Department of Psychology, Program in Clinical Psychology, Reno, NV 89557. Offers PhD. Terminal master's awarded for partial completion of doctoral program. *Degree requirements:* For doctorate, comprehensive exam, thesis/dissertation. *Entrance requirements:* For doctorate, GRE Subject Test (psychology), minimum GPA of 3.0. Additional exam requirements/recommendations for international students: required—TOEFL (minimum score 500 paper-based; 61 iBT), IELTS (minimum score 6). Electronic applications accepted.

University of New Brunswick Saint John, Department of Psychology, Saint John, NE E2L 4L5, Canada. Offers clinical psychology (PhD); experimental psychology (MA, PhD). *Program availability:* Part-time. *Faculty:* 10 full-time (6 women). *Students:* 12 full-time (8 women), 1 part-time (0 women), 1 international. In 2019, 4 master's awarded. *Degree requirements:* For master's, thesis. *Entrance requirements:* For master's, GRE General and Subject Tests, honors thesis; minimum GPA of 3.7. Additional exam requirements/recommendations for international students: required—TOEFL (minimum score 550 paper-based), TWE. *Application deadline:* For fall admission, 1/15 priority date for domestic students. Application fee: $50. Electronic applications accepted. *Expenses: Tuition, area resident:* Full-time $6975 Canadian dollars; part-time $3423 Canadian dollars per year. Tuition, state resident: full-time $6975 Canadian dollars; part-time $3423 Canadian dollars per year. Tuition, Canadian resident: full-time $6975 Canadian dollars; part-time $3423 Canadian dollars per year. *International tuition:* $12,435 Canadian dollars full-time. *Required fees:* $132.75 Canadian dollars; $92.25 Canadian dollars per term. Tuition and fees vary according to campus/location, program and student level. *Financial support:* Fellowships, research assistantships, teaching assistantships, and unspecified assistantships available. Support available to part-time students. Financial award application deadline: 2/1. *Unit head:* Dr. Mary Ann Campbell, Director of Graduate Studies, 506-648 5969, Fax: 506-648-5780, E-mail: mcampbel@unb.ca. *Application contact:* Mary Miernicki, Administrative Assistant, 506-648-5640, Fax: 506-648-5780, E-mail: Mary.Miernicki@unb.ca.
Website: http://go.unb.ca/gradprograms

University of New Mexico, Graduate Studies, College of Arts and Sciences, Program in Psychology, Albuquerque, NM 87131-2039. Offers behavioral neuroscience (PhD); clinical psychology (PhD); cognitive neuroimaging (PhD); developmental psychology (PhD); evolution (PhD); health psychology (PhD); quantitative methodology (PhD). *Accreditation:* APA. *Degree requirements:* For doctorate, comprehensive exam, thesis/dissertation. *Entrance requirements:* For doctorate, GRE General Test, GRE Subject Test (psychology), minimum GPA of 3.0. Additional exam requirements/recommendations for international students: required—TOEFL (minimum score 550 paper-based; 79 iBT), IELTS (minimum score 6.5). Electronic applications accepted. *Expenses:* Tuition, state resident: full-time $7633; part-time $972 per year. Tuition, nonresident: full-time $22,586; part-time $3840 per year. *International tuition:* $23,292 full-time. *Required fees:* $8608. Tuition and fees vary according to course level, course load, degree level, program and student level.

University of North Alabama, College of Education, Department of Counselor Education, Florence, AL 35632-0001. Offers clinical mental health counseling (MA); counseling (MA Ed). *Accreditation:* ACA; NCATE. *Program availability:* Part-time. *Degree requirements:* For master's, comprehensive exam. *Entrance requirements:* For master's, GRE, MAT, or NTE, minimum GPA of 2.5, Alabama Class B Certificate or equivalent, teaching experience. Additional exam requirements/recommendations for international students: required—TOEFL (minimum score 79 iBT), IELTS (minimum score 6), PTE (minimum score 54). Electronic applications accepted.

The University of North Carolina at Chapel Hill, Graduate School, College of Arts and Sciences, Department of Psychology, Chapel Hill, NC 27599-3270. Offers behavioral neuroscience psychology (PhD); clinical psychology (PhD); cognitive psychology (PhD); developmental psychology (PhD); quantitative psychology (PhD); social psychology (PhD). *Accreditation:* APA. *Degree requirements:* For doctorate, comprehensive exam, thesis/dissertation. *Entrance requirements:* For doctorate, GRE General Test, minimum GPA of 3.0. Additional exam requirements/recommendations for international students: required—TOEFL (minimum score 550 paper-based; 79 iBT), IELTS (minimum score 7). Electronic applications accepted.

The University of North Carolina at Greensboro, Graduate School, College of Arts and Sciences, Department of Psychology, Greensboro, NC 27412-5001. Offers clinical psychology (MA, PhD); cognitive psychology (MA, PhD); developmental psychology (MA, PhD); social psychology (MA, PhD). *Accreditation:* APA (one or more programs are accredited). Terminal master's awarded for partial completion of doctoral program. *Degree requirements:* For master's, comprehensive exam, thesis; for doctorate, one foreign language, thesis/dissertation, preliminary exam. *Entrance requirements:* For master's and doctorate, GRE General Test. Additional exam requirements/recommendations for international students: required—TOEFL. Electronic applications accepted.

The University of North Carolina Wilmington, College of Arts and Sciences, Department of Psychology, Wilmington, NC 28403-3297. Offers clinical psychology (PhD); psychology (MA), including applied behavior analysis, psychological science. *Faculty:* 27 full-time (15 women). *Students:* 44 full-time (36 women), 34 part-time (29 women); includes 12 minority (3 Black or African American, non-Hispanic/Latino; 5 Hispanic/Latino; 4 Two or more races, non-Hispanic/Latino), 1 international. Average age 25. 112 applicants, 38% accepted, 38 enrolled. In 2019, 19 master's awarded. *Degree requirements:* For master's, comprehensive exam, thesis; for doctorate, thesis/dissertation, 1-year external APA-accredited or APPIC-member internship. *Entrance requirements:* For master's, GRE General Test, GRE Subject Test (psychology) only if bachelor's degree was not in the area of psychology, 3 letters of recommendation, psychology research interest form, resume, essay; for doctorate, GRE General Test, GRE Subject Test (psychology) only if bachelor's degree was not in the area of

psychology, 3 letters of recommendation, resume, statement of interest. Additional exam requirements/recommendations for international students: required—TOEFL (minimum score 79 iBT), IELTS (minimum score 6.5). *Application deadline:* For fall admission, 4/15 for domestic students. Applications are processed on a rolling basis. Application fee: $75. Electronic applications accepted. *Expenses: Tuition, area resident:* Full-time $4719; part-time $326 per credit hour. Tuition, state resident: full-time $4719; part-time $326 per credit hour. Tuition, nonresident: full-time $18,548; part-time $1099 per credit hour. *Required fees:* $2738. Tuition and fees vary according to program. *Financial support:* Research assistantships, teaching assistantships, Federal Work-Study, scholarships/grants, unspecified assistantships, and out-of-state tuition remission available. Financial award application deadline: 1/1; financial award applicants required to submit FAFSA. *Unit head:* Dr. Julian Keith, Chair, 910-962-3378, Fax: 910-962-7010, E-mail: keithj@uncw.edu. *Application contact:* Dr. Kate Nooner, Graduate Coordinator, 910-962-2140, Fax: 910-962-7010, E-mail: psygradprogram@uncw.edu.
Website: http://www.uncw.edu/psy/grad/

University of North Dakota, Graduate School, College of Arts and Sciences, Department of Psychology, Grand Forks, ND 58202. Offers clinical psychology (PhD); forensic psychology (MA, MS). *Accreditation:* APA (one or more programs are accredited). *Degree requirements:* For master's, thesis, final exam; for doctorate, comprehensive exam, thesis/dissertation, internship, final exam. *Entrance requirements:* For master's, GRE General Test, GRE Subject Test, minimum GPA of 3.0; for doctorate, GRE General Test, GRE Subject Test, minimum GPA of 3.5. Additional exam requirements/recommendations for international students: required—TOEFL (minimum score 550 paper-based; 79 iBT), IELTS (minimum score 6.5). Electronic applications accepted.

University of Northern Colorado, Graduate School, College of Education and Behavioral Sciences, Department of Applied Psychology and Counselor Education, Program in Clinical Counseling, Greeley, CO 80639. Offers MA. *Program availability:* Part-time. Electronic applications accepted.

University of North Texas, Toulouse Graduate School, Denton, TX 76203-5459. Offers accounting (MS); applied anthropology (MA, MS); applied behavior analysis (Certificate); applied geography (MA); applied technology and performance improvement (M Ed, MS); art education (MA); art history (MA); arts leadership (Certificate); audiology (Au D); behavior analysis (MS); behavioral science (PhD); biochemistry and molecular biology (MS); biology (MA, MS); biomedical engineering (MS); business analysis (MS); chemistry (MS); clinical health psychology (PhD); communication studies (MA, MS); computer engineering (MS); computer science (MS); counseling (M Ed, MS), including clinical mental health counseling (MS), college and university counseling, elementary school counseling, secondary school counseling; creative writing (MA); criminal justice (MS); curriculum and instruction (M Ed); decision sciences (MBA); design (MA, MFA), including fashion design (MFA), innovation studies, interior design (MFA); early childhood studies (MS); economics (MS); educational leadership (M Ed, Ed D); educational psychology (MS, PhD), including family studies (MS), gifted and talented (MS), human development (MS), learning and cognition (MS), research, measurement and evaluation (MS); electrical engineering (MS); emergency management (MPA); engineering technology (MS); English (MA); English as a second language (MA); environmental science (MS); finance (MBA, MS); financial management (MPA); French (MA); health services management (MBA); higher education (M Ed, Ed D); history (MA, MS); hospitality management (MS); human resources management (MPA); information science (MS); information systems (PhD); information technologies (MBA); interdisciplinary studies (MA, MS); international studies (MA); international sustainable tourism (MS); jazz studies (MM); journalism (MA, MJ, Graduate Certificate), including interactive and virtual digital communication (Graduate Certificate), narrative journalism (Graduate Certificate), public relations (Graduate Certificate); kinesiology (MS); linguistics (MA); local government management (MPA); logistics (PhD); logistics and supply chain management (MBA); long-term care, senior housing, and aging services (MA); management (PhD); marketing (MBA); mathematics (MA, MS); mechanical and energy engineering (MS, PhD); music (MA), including ethnomusicology, music theory, musicology, performance; music composition (PhD); music education (MM Ed, PhD); nonprofit management (MPA); operations and supply chain management (MBA); performance (MM, DMA); philosophy (MA); political science (MA); professional and technical communication (MA); radio, television and film (MA, MFA); rehabilitation counseling (Certificate); sociology (MA); Spanish (MA); special education (M Ed); speech-language pathology (MA); strategic management (MBA); studio art (MFA); teaching (M Ed); MBA/MS. *Program availability:* Part-time, evening/weekend, online learning. Terminal master's awarded for partial completion of doctoral program. *Degree requirements:* For master's, variable foreign language requirement, comprehensive exam (for some programs), thesis (for some programs); for doctorate, variable foreign language requirement, comprehensive exam (for some programs), thesis/dissertation; for other advanced degree, variable foreign language requirement, comprehensive exam (for some programs). *Entrance requirements:* For master's and doctorate, GRE, GMAT. Additional exam requirements/recommendations for international students: required—TOEFL (minimum score 550 paper-based; 79 iBT). Electronic applications accepted.

University of North Texas at Dallas, Graduate School, Dallas, TX 75241. Offers accounting (MBA); counseling (M Ed, MS); criminal justice (MS); curriculum and instruction (M Ed); educational administration (M Ed); human resources and organizational behavior (MBA); public leadership (MS); strategic management (MBA).

University of Oklahoma, College of Arts and Sciences, Department of Human Relations, Norman, OK 73019-0390. Offers clinical mental health (MHR); helping skills in human relations (Graduate Certificate); human relations (MHR); human resource diversity and development (Graduate Certificate); human resources (MHR); licensed professional counselor (MHR). *Program availability:* Part-time, evening/weekend. *Entrance requirements:* For degree, minimum GPA of 3.0. Additional exam requirements/recommendations for international students: required—TOEFL (minimum score 79 iBT) or IELTS (minimum score 6.5). Electronic applications accepted. *Expenses:* Tuition, state resident: full-time $6583.20; part-time $274.30 per credit hour. Tuition, nonresident: full-time $21,242; part-time $885.10 per credit hour. *International tuition:* $21,242.40 full-time. *Required fees:* $1994.20; $72.55 per credit hour. $126.50 per semester. Tuition and fees vary according to course load and degree level.

University of Oregon, Graduate School, College of Arts and Sciences, Department of Psychology, Program in Clinical Psychology, Eugene, OR 97403. Offers PhD. *Accreditation:* APA. *Degree requirements:* For doctorate, thesis/dissertation. *Entrance requirements:* For doctorate, GRE General Test. Additional exam requirements/recommendations for international students: required—TOEFL.

University of Phoenix - Phoenix Campus, College of Social Sciences, Tempe, AZ 85282-2371. Offers counseling (MS), including clinical mental health counseling, community counseling, counseling, marriage, family and child therapy; psychology (MS). *Program availability:* Evening/weekend, online learning. *Entrance requirements:* Additional exam requirements/recommendations for international students: required—TOEFL, TOEIC (Test of English as an International Communication), Berlitz Online English Proficiency Exam, PTE, or IELTS. Electronic applications accepted. *Expenses:* Contact institution.

University of Pittsburgh, Kenneth P. Dietrich School of Arts and Sciences, Department of Psychology, Pittsburgh, PA 15260. Offers biological and health psychology (PhD); clinical psychology (PhD); cognitive psychology (PhD); developmental psychology (PhD); social psychology (PhD). *Accreditation:* APA. *Faculty:* 33 full-time (18 women), 10 part-time/adjunct (3 women). *Students:* 90 full-time (73 women); includes 25 minority (4 Black or African American, non-Hispanic/Latino; 2 American Indian or Alaska Native, non-Hispanic/Latino; 10 Asian, non-Hispanic/Latino; 2 Hispanic/Latino; 7 Two or more races, non-Hispanic/Latino). Average age 25. 580 applicants, 6% accepted, 18 enrolled. In 2019, 16 doctorates awarded. Terminal master's awarded for partial completion of doctoral program. *Degree requirements:* For doctorate, comprehensive exam, thesis/dissertation. *Entrance requirements:* For doctorate, GRE General Test, minimum GPA of 3.0. Additional exam requirements/recommendations for international students: required—TOEFL (minimum score 550 paper-based; 90 iBT). *Application deadline:* For fall admission, 12/1 for domestic and international students. Application fee: $75. Electronic applications accepted. *Financial support:* In 2019–20, 90 students received support, including 38 fellowships with full tuition reimbursements available (averaging $30,378 per year), 19 research assistantships with full tuition reimbursements available (averaging $29,220 per year), 33 teaching assistantships with full tuition reimbursements available (averaging $29,220 per year); career-related internships or fieldwork, scholarships/grants, health care benefits, and unspecified assistantships also available. Financial award application deadline: 12/1. *Unit head:* Dr. Julie Fiez, Chair, 412-624-7078, Fax: 412-422-9149, E-mail: fiez@pitt.edu. *Application contact:* Francesca Sirianni, Graduate Administrator, 412-624-4502, Fax: 412-624-4428, E-mail: psygrad@pitt.edu.
Website: http://www.psychology.pitt.edu/

University of Pittsburgh, School of Health and Rehabilitation Sciences, Department of Rehabilitation Science and Technology, Pittsburgh, PA 15260. Offers clinical rehabilitation and mental health counseling (MS); physician assistant studies (MS); prosthetics and orthotics (DPT); rehabilitation technology (MS). *Program availability:* Part-time, blended/hybrid learning. *Faculty:* 26 full-time (15 women), 6 part-time/adjunct (3 women). *Students:* 97 full-time (57 women), 16 part-time (13 women); includes 19 minority (3 Black or African American, non-Hispanic/Latino; 5 Asian, non-Hispanic/Latino; 3 Hispanic/Latino; 8 Two or more races, non-Hispanic/Latino), 9 international. Average age 26. 187 applicants, 58% accepted, 49 enrolled. In 2019, 50 master's awarded. *Degree requirements:* For master's, comprehensive exam (for some programs), thesis (for some programs). *Entrance requirements:* For master's, Varies by program, Varies by program. Additional exam requirements/recommendations for international students: required—International applicants may provide Duolingo English Test, IELTS or TOEFL scores to verify English language proficiency. Electronic applications accepted. *Financial support:* In 2019–20, 14 students received support, including 1 fellowship with full tuition reimbursement available (averaging $30,000 per year), 9 research assistantships with full tuition reimbursements available (averaging $30,000 per year); scholarships/grants also available. *Unit head:* Dr. Jonathan Pearlman, Chair and Associate Professor, Department of Rehabilitation Science and Technology, 412-383-3955, E-mail: jpearlman@pitt.edu. *Application contact:* Jessica Maguire, Director of Admissions, 412-383-6557, Fax: 412-383-6535, E-mail: maguire@pitt.edu.
Website: http://www.shrs.pitt.edu/rst

University of Puerto Rico at Rio Piedras, College of Social Sciences, Department of Psychology, San Juan, PR 00931-3300. Offers clinical psychology (MA); industrial organizational psychology (MA); investigative academic psychology (MA); psychology (PhD); social-community psychology (MA). *Program availability:* Part-time. *Degree requirements:* For master's, comprehensive exam, thesis; for doctorate, comprehensive exam, thesis/dissertation, internship. *Entrance requirements:* For master's, GRE or PAEG, interview, minimum GPA of 3.0; for doctorate, GRE or PAEG, interview, master's degree, minimum GPA of 3.0.

University of Regina, Faculty of Graduate Studies and Research, Faculty of Arts, Department of Psychology, Regina, SK S4S 0A2, Canada. Offers clinical psychology (MA, PhD); experimental and applied psychology (MA, PhD). *Faculty:* 20 full-time (9 women), 11 part-time/adjunct (7 women). *Students:* 55 full-time (47 women). Average age 30. 116 applicants, 18% accepted. In 2019, 4 master's, 1 doctorate awarded. *Degree requirements:* For master's, thesis; for doctorate, comprehensive exam, thesis/dissertation. *Entrance requirements:* For master's, GRE General Test, post secondary transcripts, 2 letter of recommendations; for doctorate, GRE General Test and GRE Subject Test (optional for those with a master's degree from a Canadian university). Additional exam requirements/recommendations for international students: required—TOEFL (minimum score 580 paper-based; 80 iBT), IELTS (minimum score 6.5), PTE (minimum score 59), other option is CAEL, MELAB and U of R ESL. *Application deadline:* For fall admission, 1/15 for domestic and international students. Application fee: $100. Electronic applications accepted. *Expenses: Tuition:* Full-time $6684 Canadian dollars. *Required fees:* $100 Canadian dollars; $3351.45 Canadian dollars per trimester. $1117.15 Canadian dollars per semester. Tuition and fees vary according to course level, course load, degree level and program. *Financial support:* Fellowships, research assistantships, teaching assistantships, career-related internships or fieldwork, Federal Work-Study, scholarships/grants, unspecified assistantships, and travel award and Graduate Scholarship Base Funds available. Support available to part-time students. Financial award application deadline: 9/30. *Unit head:* Dr. Richard MacLennan, Department Head, 306-585-4458, Fax: 306-585-5429, E-mail: richard.maclennan@uregina.ca. *Application contact:* Dr. Richard MacLennan, Department Head, 306-585-4458, Fax: 306-585-5429, E-mail: richard.maclennan@uregina.ca.
Website: http://www.uregina.ca/arts/psychology

University of Rhode Island, Graduate School, College of Health Sciences, Department of Psychology, Kingston, RI 02881. Offers behavioral science (PhD); clinical psychology (PhD); school psychology (MS, PhD). *Accreditation:* APA (one or more programs are accredited). *Program availability:* Part-time. *Faculty:* 23 full-time (13 women), 1 part-time/adjunct (0 women). *Students:* 59 full-time (50 women), 5 part-time (2 women); includes 10 minority (5 Black or African American, non-Hispanic/Latino; 2 Asian, non-Hispanic/Latino; 3 Hispanic/Latino), 4 international. 353 applicants, 11% accepted, 11 enrolled. In 2019, 11 master's, 15 doctorates awarded. *Entrance requirements:* Additional exam requirements/recommendations for international students: required—TOEFL. *Application deadline:* For fall admission, 12/1 for domestic and international students. Application fee: $65. Electronic applications accepted. *Expenses: Tuition, area resident:* Full-time $13,734; part-time $763 per credit. Tuition, state resident: full-time $13,734; part-time $763 per credit. Tuition, nonresident: full-time $26,512; part-time $1473 per credit. *International tuition:* $26,512 full-time. *Required fees:* $1780; $52 per credit. $35 per term. One-time fee: $165. *Financial support:* In 2019–20, 9 research assistantships with tuition reimbursements (averaging $10,024 per year), 20 teaching assistantships with tuition reimbursements (averaging $17,045 per year) were awarded. Financial award application deadline: 12/1; financial award applicants required to submit FAFSA. *Unit head:* Dr. Mark Robbins, Chair, 401-874-5082, E-mail: markrobb@uri.edu. *Application contact:* Dr. Mark Robbins, Chair, 401-874-5082, E-mail: markrobb@uri.edu.
Website: http://www.uri.edu/artsci/psy/

University of Rochester, School of Arts and Sciences, Psychology, Rochester, NY 14627. Offers clinical psychology (PhD); developmental psychology (PhD); social-personality psychology (PhD). *Accreditation:* APA. *Faculty:* 16 full-time (9 women). *Students:* 42 full-time (35 women); includes 10 minority (1 Black or African American, non-Hispanic/Latino; 5 Asian, non-Hispanic/Latino; 3 Hispanic/Latino; 1 Two or more races, non-Hispanic/Latino), 5 international. Average age 28. 240 applicants, 6% accepted, 9 enrolled. In 2019, 10 doctorates awarded. Terminal master's awarded for partial completion of doctoral program. *Degree requirements:* For doctorate, thesis/dissertation. *Entrance requirements:* For doctorate, GRE General Test (optional for Fall 2021 admission cycle), personal statement, official transcripts, three letters of recommendation, curriculum vitae or resume. Additional exam requirements/recommendations for international students: required—TOEFL. *Application deadline:* For fall admission, 12/1 for domestic and international students. Application fee: $20. Electronic applications accepted. *Financial support:* In 2019–20, 35 students received support, including 5 fellowships with full tuition reimbursements available, 8 research assistantships with full tuition reimbursements available (averaging $24,000 per year), 22 teaching assistantships with full tuition reimbursements available (averaging $24,000 per year); career-related internships or fieldwork, scholarships/grants, and tuition waivers (full) also available. Financial award application deadline: 4/15. *Unit head:* Loisa Bennetto, Chair, 585-275-8712, E-mail: loisa.bennetto@rochester.edu. *Application contact:* Loisa Bennetto, Chair, 585-275-8712, E-mail: loisa.bennetto@rochester.edu. Website: http://www.sas.rochester.edu/psy/graduate/index.html

University of Saint Francis, Graduate School, Department of Behavioral and Social Sciences, Fort Wayne, IN 46808-3994. Offers clinical mental health counseling (MS, Post Master's Certificate); psychology (MS); school counseling (MS Ed). *Program availability:* Part-time, evening/weekend. *Faculty:* 6 full-time (2 women), 1 part-time/adjunct (0 women). *Students:* 21 full-time (17 women), 9 part-time (8 women); includes 4 minority (2 Black or African American, non-Hispanic/Latino; 1 Asian, non-Hispanic/Latino; 1 Hispanic/Latino), 1 international. Average age 29. 25 applicants, 92% accepted, 17 enrolled. In 2019, 13 master's awarded. *Entrance requirements:* Additional exam requirements/recommendations for international students: required—TOEFL (minimum score 550 paper-based), IELTS (minimum score 6.5). *Application deadline:* Applications are processed on a rolling basis. Electronic applications accepted. *Expenses: Tuition:* Full-time $9450; part-time $525 per semester hour. *Required fees:* $330 per semester. Tuition and fees vary according to course load, degree level, campus/location and program. *Financial support:* Applicants required to submit FAFSA. *Unit head:* Dr. John Brinkman, Director for the Department of Psychology and Counseling, 260-399-7700 Ext. 8425, E-mail: jbrinkman@sf.edu. *Application contact:* Kyle Richardson, Associate Director of Enrollment Management, 260-399-7700 Ext. 6310, Fax: 260-399-8152, E-mail: krichardson@sf.edu. Website: https://admissions.sf.edu/graduate/

University of Saint Joseph, Department of Counseling and Applied Behavioral Studies, West Hartford, CT 06117-2700. Offers clinical mental health counseling (MA); school counseling (MA). *Accreditation:* ACA. *Program availability:* Part-time, evening/weekend. *Degree requirements:* For master's, comprehensive exam, thesis optional. *Entrance requirements:* For master's, 2 letters of recommendation. Electronic applications accepted. Application fee is waived when completed online.

University of San Francisco, School of Nursing and Health Professions, Program in Clinical Psychology, San Francisco, CA 94117. Offers Psy D. *Faculty:* 10 full-time (6 women), 4 part-time/adjunct (3 women). *Students:* 43 full-time (36 women), 26 part-time (20 women); includes 38 minority (7 Black or African American, non-Hispanic/Latino; 10 Asian, non-Hispanic/Latino; 15 Hispanic/Latino; 6 Two or more races, non-Hispanic/Latino), 2 international. Average age 31. 81 applicants, 44% accepted, 14 enrolled. In 2019, 8 doctorates awarded. *Entrance requirements:* For doctorate, GRE General Test and GRE Subject Test in psychology (taken within five years of application), bachelor's degree from accredited institution; official transcripts; personal statement of interest; professional resume or curriculum vitae; three letters of recommendation; minimum undergraduate GPA of 3.0 in major and overall. Additional exam requirements/recommendations for international students: required—TOEFL (minimum score 600 paper-based; 100 iBT), IELTS, TOEFL or IELTS. *Application deadline:* For fall admission, 12/1 for domestic students. Applications are processed on a rolling basis. Application fee: $55. Electronic applications accepted. *Financial support:* Scholarships/grants available. *Unit head:* Dr. June Madsen Clausen, Program Director, 415-422-6681, E-mail: nursing@usfca.edu. *Application contact:* Carolyn Aorroyo, Graduate Enrollment Manager, 415-422-2806, E-mail: carroyo2@usfca.edu. Website: http://www.usfca.edu/nursing/psyd/

The University of Scranton, Panuska College of Professional Studies, Department of Counseling and Human Services, Program in Clinical Mental Health Counseling, Scranton, PA 18510. Offers MS. *Accreditation:* ACA. *Program availability:* Part-time, evening/weekend. *Degree requirements:* For master's, comprehensive exam (for some programs), thesis (for some programs), capstone experience. *Entrance requirements:* For master's, minimum GPA of 3.0, three letters of reference. Additional exam requirements/recommendations for international students: required—TOEFL (minimum score 500 paper-based; 80 iBT), IELTS (minimum score 6.5). Electronic applications accepted.

University of South Africa, College of Human Sciences, Pretoria, South Africa. Offers adult education (M Ed); African languages (MA, PhD); African politics (MA, PhD); Afrikaans (MA, PhD); ancient history (MA, PhD); ancient Near Eastern studies (MA, PhD); anthropology (MA, PhD); applied linguistics (MA); Arabic (MA, PhD); archaeology (MA); art history (MA); Biblical archaeology (MA); Biblical studies (M Th, D Th, PhD); Christian spirituality (M Th, D Th); church history (M Th, D Th); classical studies (MA, PhD); clinical psychology (MA); communication (MA, PhD); comparative education (M Ed, Ed D); consulting psychology (D Admin, D Com, PhD); curriculum studies (M Ed, Ed D); development studies (M Admin, MA, D Admin, PhD); didactics (M Ed, Ed D); education (M Tech); education management (M Ed, Ed D); educational psychology (M Ed); English (MA); environmental education (M Ed); French (MA, PhD); German (MA, PhD); Greek (MA); guidance and counseling (M Ed); health studies (MA, PhD), including health sciences education (MA), health services management (MA), medical and surgical nursing science (critical care general) (MA), midwifery and neonatal nursing science (MA), trauma and emergency care (MA); history (MA, PhD); history of education (Ed D); inclusive education (M Ed, Ed D); information and communications technology policy and regulation (MA); information science (MA, MIS, PhD); international politics (MA, PhD); Islamic studies (MA, PhD); Italian (MA, PhD); Judaica (MA, PhD); linguistics (MA, PhD); mathematical education (M Ed); mathematics education (MA); missiology (M Th, D Th); modern Hebrew (MA, PhD); musicology (MA, MMus, D Mus, PhD); natural science education (M Ed); New Testament (M Th, D Th); Old Testament (D Th); pastoral therapy (M Th, D Th); philosophy (MA); philosophy of education (M Ed, Ed D); politics (MA, PhD); Portuguese (MA, PhD); practical theology (M Th, D Th); psychology (MA, MS, PhD); psychology of education (M Ed, Ed D); public health (MA); religious studies (MA, D Th, PhD); Romance languages (MA); Russian (MA, PhD); Semitic languages (MA, PhD); social behavior studies in HIV/AIDS (MA); social science (mental health) (MA); social science in development studies (MA); social science in psychology (MA); social science in social work (MA); social science in sociology (MA); social work

(MSW, DSW, PhD); socio-education (M Ed, Ed D); sociolinguistics (MA); sociology (MA, PhD); Spanish (MA, PhD); systematic theology (M Th, D Th); TESOL (teaching English to speakers of other languages) (MA); theological ethics (M Th, D Th); theory of literature (MA, PhD); urban ministries (D Th); urban ministry (M Th).

University of South Alabama, College of Education and Professional Studies, Department of Counseling and Instructional Sciences, Mobile, AL 36688-0002. Offers clinical mental health counseling (MS); educational media (M Ed); educational media and technology (MS); instructional design and development (MS, PhD); instructional leadership (Ed S); school counseling (M Ed). *Accreditation:* NCATE. *Program availability:* Part-time. *Faculty:* 9 full-time (6 women), 5 part-time/adjunct (all women). *Students:* 105 full-time (85 women), 22 part-time (19 women); includes 42 minority (34 Black or African American, non-Hispanic/Latino; 1 American Indian or Alaska Native, non-Hispanic/Latino; 2 Asian, non-Hispanic/Latino; 2 Hispanic/Latino; 3 Two or more races, non-Hispanic/Latino), 4 international. Average age 35. 51 applicants, 96% accepted, 38 enrolled. In 2019, 27 master's, 2 doctorates, 1 other advanced degree awarded. *Degree requirements:* For master's, comprehensive exam, thesis optional; for doctorate, comprehensive exam, thesis/dissertation. *Entrance requirements:* For master's, GRE General Test or MAT; for doctorate, GRE. Additional exam requirements/recommendations for international students: required—TOEFL (minimum score 525 paper-based; 71 iBT). *Application deadline:* For fall admission, 8/18 for domestic students, 7/18 for international students; for spring admission, 1/10 for domestic students, 12/10 for international students; for summer admission, 5/31 for domestic and international students. Applications are processed on a rolling basis. Application fee: $35. Electronic applications accepted. *Expenses: Tuition, area resident:* Part-time $442 per credit hour. Tuition, state resident: full-time $10,608; part-time $442 per credit hour. Tuition, nonresident: full-time $21,216; part-time $884 per credit hour. *Financial support:* Fellowships, research assistantships, teaching assistantships, career-related internships or fieldwork, Federal Work-Study, institutionally sponsored loans, scholarships/grants, and unspecified assistantships available. Support available to part-time students. Financial award application deadline: 3/31; financial award applicants required to submit FAFSA. *Unit head:* Dr. Tres Stefurak, Department Chair, 251-380-2734, Fax: 251-380-2713, E-mail: jstefurak@southalabama.edu. *Application contact:* Dr. James Van Haneghan, Graduate Coordinator, 251-380-2760, Fax: 251-380-2713, E-mail: jvanhane@southalabama.edu. Website: http://www.southalabama.edu/colleges/ceps/cins/

University of South Alabama, Graduate School, Program in Clinical and Counseling Psychology, Mobile, AL 36688-0002. Offers PhD. *Accreditation:* ACA. *Faculty:* 7 full-time (2 women). *Students:* 22 full-time (16 women), 8 part-time (5 women); includes 6 minority (4 Black or African American, non-Hispanic/Latino; 1 Asian, non-Hispanic/Latino; 1 Two or more races, non-Hispanic/Latino), 1 international. Average age 29. 7 applicants, 100% accepted, 7 enrolled. In 2019, 7 doctorates awarded. *Degree requirements:* For doctorate, thesis/dissertation, capstone internship. *Entrance requirements:* For doctorate, GRE. Additional exam requirements/recommendations for international students: required—TOEFL (minimum score 525 paper-based; 71 iBT). *Application deadline:* For fall admission, 12/15 for domestic and international students. Application fee: $50. Electronic applications accepted. *Expenses: Tuition, area resident:* Part-time $442 per credit hour. Tuition, state resident: full-time $10,608; part-time $442 per credit hour. Tuition, nonresident: full-time $21,216; part-time $884 per credit hour. *Financial support:* Fellowships, research assistantships, teaching assistantships, career-related internships or fieldwork, institutionally sponsored loans, scholarships/grants, and unspecified assistantships available. Support available to part-time students. Financial award application deadline: 3/31; financial award applicants required to submit FAFSA. *Unit head:* Dr. Tres Stefurak, Chair, Department of Counseling & Instructional Sciences, College of Education & Professional Studies, 251-460-6622, E-mail: jstefurak@southalabama.edu. *Application contact:* Dr. Joe Currier, Director of Clinical Training, 251-460-6622, E-mail: jcurrier@southalabama.edu. Website: http://www.southalabama.edu/graduateschool/ccp

University of South Carolina, The Graduate School, College of Arts and Sciences, Department of Psychology, Program in Clinical/Community Psychology, Columbia, SC 29208. Offers clinical/community psychology (PhD); general psychology (MA). *Accreditation:* APA. *Degree requirements:* For master's, comprehensive exam, thesis; for doctorate, comprehensive exam, thesis/dissertation. *Entrance requirements:* For doctorate, GRE General Test, minimum GPA of 3.2. Additional exam requirements/recommendations for international students: required—TOEFL. Electronic applications accepted.

University of South Carolina Aiken, Program in Applied Clinical Psychology, Aiken, SC 29801. Offers MS. *Program availability:* Part-time. *Faculty:* 8 full-time (6 women), 1 part-time/adjunct (0 women). *Students:* 17 full-time (16 women), 8 part-time (5 women); includes 3 minority (1 Black or African American, non-Hispanic/Latino; 1 Hispanic/Latino; 1 Two or more races, non-Hispanic/Latino), 1 international. Average age 26. 38 applicants, 29% accepted, 7 enrolled. In 2019, 16 master's awarded. *Degree requirements:* For master's, thesis. *Entrance requirements:* For master's, GRE. Additional exam requirements/recommendations for international students: required—TOEFL (minimum score 551 paper-based; 80 iBT), IELTS (minimum score 6), PTE (minimum score 53), USC Aiken accepts the TOEFL, IELTS, or PTE exams to demonstrate English proficiency. *Application deadline:* For fall admission, 6/1 priority date for domestic and international students. Applications are processed on a rolling basis. Application fee: $45 ($100 for international students). Electronic applications accepted. *Expenses: Tuition, area resident:* Full-time $13,734; part-time $572.25 per credit hour. Tuition, state resident: full-time $13,734; part-time $572.25 per credit hour. Tuition, nonresident: full-time $29,760; part-time $1240 per credit hour. *International tuition:* $29,760 full-time. *Required fees:* $13 per credit hour. $25 per semester. Tuition and fees vary according to course load and program. *Financial support:* In 2019–20, 20 students received support, including 18 research assistantships with partial tuition reimbursements available (averaging $3,788 per year), 5 teaching assistantships with partial tuition reimbursements available (averaging $2,857 per year); career-related internships or fieldwork, Federal Work-Study, scholarships/grants, tuition waivers (partial), and unspecified assistantships also available. Financial award application deadline: 3/1; financial award applicants required to submit FAFSA. *Unit head:* Dr. Jane Stafford, Director, 803-641-3358, Fax: 803-641-3720, E-mail: jstafford@usca.edu. *Application contact:* Dan Robb, Associate Vice Chancellor for Enrollment Management, 803-641-3487, Fax: 803-641-3727, E-mail: danr@usca.edu. Website: https://www.usca.edu/majors-programs/graduate/applied-clinical-psychology

University of South Dakota, Graduate School, College of Arts and Sciences, Department of Psychology, Vermillion, SD 57069. Offers clinical psychology (MA, PhD); human factors (MA, PhD). *Accreditation:* APA (one or more programs are accredited). *Degree requirements:* For master's, comprehensive exam, thesis; for doctorate, comprehensive exam, thesis/dissertation. *Entrance requirements:* For master's, GRE, minimum GPA of 3.0; for doctorate, GRE General Test, GRE Subject Test, minimum GPA of 3.0. Additional exam requirements/recommendations for international students: required—TOEFL (minimum score 550 paper-based; 79 iBT). Electronic applications accepted.

Clinical Psychology

University of Southern California, Graduate School, Dana and David Dornsife College of Letters, Arts and Sciences, Department of Psychology, Los Angeles, CA 90089. Offers brain and cognitive science (PhD); clinical science (PhD); developmental psychology (PhD); human behavior (MHB); quantitative methods (PhD); social psychology (PhD). *Accreditation:* APA. *Degree requirements:* For doctorate, comprehensive exam, thesis/dissertation, one-year internship (for clinical science students). *Entrance requirements:* For doctorate, GRE. Additional exam requirements/recommendations for international students: recommended—TOEFL (minimum score 600 paper-based; 100 iBT). Electronic applications accepted.

University of South Florida, College of Arts and Sciences, Department of Psychology, Tampa, FL 33620-9951. Offers psychology (PhD), including clinical psychology, cognition, neuroscience and social psychology, industrial-organizational psychology. *Accreditation:* APA. *Faculty:* 30 full-time (11 women). *Students:* 79 full-time (55 women), 12 part-time (8 women); includes 16 minority (2 Black or African American, non-Hispanic/Latino; 6 Asian, non-Hispanic/Latino; 6 Hispanic/Latino; 2 Two or more races, non-Hispanic/Latino), 8 international. Average age 28. 355 applicants, 5% accepted, 19 enrolled. In 2019, 17 doctorates awarded. *Degree requirements:* For doctorate, comprehensive exam, thesis/dissertation, internship. *Entrance requirements:* For doctorate, a GRE Score Report with a strong preference for GRE V and Q scores each at the 50th percentile or better, statement of purpose; Research Interests and Faculty Matches Form (http://psychology.usf.edu/forms/ResearchInterest.aspx); 3 letters of recommendation; GPA worksheet (http://www.grad.usf.edu/inc/linked-files/gpa.pdf). Additional exam requirements/recommendations for international students: required—TOEFL, TOEFL (minimum score 550 paper-based; 79 iBT) or IELTS (minimum score 6.5). *Application deadline:* For fall admission, 12/1 priority date for domestic and international students. Application fee: $30. Electronic applications accepted. *Expenses:* Contact institution. *Financial support:* In 2019–20, 44 students received support, including 18 research assistantships with tuition reimbursements available (averaging $14,727 per year), 57 teaching assistantships with tuition reimbursements available (averaging $14,543 per year); tuition waivers (partial) and unspecified assistantships also available. Financial award applicants required to submit FAFSA. *Unit head:* Dr. Toru Shimizu, Chairperson, 813-974-0352, Fax: 813-974-4617, E-mail: shimizu@usf.edu. *Application contact:* Dr. Sandra Schneider, Professor and Graduate Program Director, 813-974-0928, E-mail: sandra@usf.edu.
Website: http://psychology.usf.edu/

The University of Tennessee, Graduate School, College of Arts and Sciences, Department of Psychology, Knoxville, TN 37996. Offers clinical psychology (PhD); experimental psychology (MA, PhD); psychology (MA). *Accreditation:* APA (one or more programs are accredited). Terminal master's awarded for partial completion of doctoral program. *Degree requirements:* For master's, thesis; for doctorate, thesis/dissertation. *Entrance requirements:* For master's and doctorate, GRE General Test, GRE Subject Test, minimum GPA of 2.7. Additional exam requirements/recommendations for international students: required—TOEFL. Electronic applications accepted.

The University of Texas at Austin, Graduate School, College of Liberal Arts, Department of Psychology, Austin, TX 78712-1111. Offers behavioral neuroscience (PhD); clinical psychology (PhD); cognitive systems (PhD); developmental psychology (PhD); individual differences and evolutionary psychology (PhD); perceptual systems (PhD); social psychology (PhD). *Accreditation:* APA. *Degree requirements:* For doctorate, thesis/dissertation. *Entrance requirements:* For doctorate, GRE General Test. Electronic applications accepted.

The University of Texas at El Paso, Graduate School, College of Liberal Arts, Department of Psychology, El Paso, TX 79968-0001. Offers clinical psychology (MA); experimental psychology (MA); psychology (PhD). *Program availability:* Part-time, evening/weekend. *Degree requirements:* For master's, thesis; for doctorate, thesis/dissertation. *Entrance requirements:* For master's, GRE, letters of recommendation; for doctorate, GRE, statement of purpose, letters of recommendation. Additional exam requirements/recommendations for international students: required—TOEFL; recommended—IELTS. Electronic applications accepted.

The University of Texas at Tyler, College of Education and Psychology, Department of Psychology and Counseling, Tyler, TX 75799-0001. Offers clinical psychology (MS), including neuropsychology, school psychology; counseling psychology (MA), including general, marriage and family; interdisciplinary studies (MSIS); school counseling (MA). *Program availability:* Part-time, evening/weekend. *Faculty:* 12 full-time (5 women), 6 part-time/adjunct (3 women). *Students:* 131 full-time (103 women), 83 part-time (67 women); includes 67 minority (10 Black or African American, non-Hispanic/Latino; 1 American Indian or Alaska Native, non-Hispanic/Latino; 7 Asian, non-Hispanic/Latino; 41 Hispanic/Latino; 8 Two or more races, non-Hispanic/Latino), 8 international. Average age 30. 130 applicants, 65% accepted, 47 enrolled. In 2019, 94 master's awarded. *Degree requirements:* For master's, comprehensive exam, thesis optional. *Entrance requirements:* For master's, GRE General Test, minimum GPA of 3.0. Additional exam requirements/recommendations for international students: required—TOEFL. *Application deadline:* For fall admission, 8/17 priority date for domestic students, 7/1 priority date for international students; for spring admission, 12/21 priority date for domestic students, 11/1 priority date for international students. Application fee: $25 ($50 for international students). Electronic applications accepted. *Financial support:* In 2019–20, fellowships with partial tuition reimbursements (averaging $3,000 per year) were awarded; research assistantships, teaching assistantships, career-related internships or fieldwork, Federal Work-Study, and institutionally sponsored loans also available. Support available to part-time students. Financial award application deadline: 7/1. *Unit head:* Dr. Charles B. Barke, Chair, 903-565-5875, E-mail: cbarke@uttyler.edu. *Application contact:* Dr. Charles B. Barke, Chair, 903-565-5875, E-mail: cbarke@uttyler.edu.
Website: http://www.uttyler.edu/psychology/

The University of Texas of the Permian Basin, Office of Graduate Studies, College of Arts and Sciences, Department of Psychology, Odessa, TX 79762-0001. Offers clinical psychology (MA); experimental psychology (MA). *Program availability:* Part-time, evening/weekend. *Degree requirements:* For master's, comprehensive exam, thesis, practicum. *Entrance requirements:* For master's, GRE General Test, 3 letters of recommendation. Additional exam requirements/recommendations for international students: required—TOEFL (minimum score 550 paper-based).

The University of Texas Rio Grande Valley, College of Education and P-16 Integration, Department of Counseling, Edinburg, TX 78539. Offers clinical mental health counseling (M Ed); school counseling (M Ed). *Faculty:* 13 full-time (8 women), 6 part-time/adjunct (3 women). *Students:* 14 full-time (11 women), 160 part-time (130 women); includes 163 minority (1 Black or African American, non-Hispanic/Latino; 162 Hispanic/Latino), 2 international. Average age 30. 39 applicants, 67% accepted, 23 enrolled. In 2019, 36 master's awarded. *Expenses: Tuition, area resident:* Full-time $5959; part-time $440 per credit hour. Tuition, state resident: full-time $5959. Tuition, nonresident: full-time $5959. *International tuition:* $13,321 full-time. *Required fees:* $1169; $185 per credit hour. *Financial support:* Application deadline: 1/15.
Website: utrgv.edu/cg/

The University of Texas Rio Grande Valley, College of Liberal Arts, Department of Psychological Science, Edinburg, TX 78539. Offers psychology (MA), including clinical psychology, experimental psychology. *Faculty:* 15 full-time (3 women), 4 part-time/adjunct (2 women). *Students:* 42 full-time (32 women), 22 part-time (12 women); includes 57 minority (1 Asian, non-Hispanic/Latino; 56 Hispanic/Latino), 6 international. Average age 27. 50 applicants, 56% accepted, 23 enrolled. In 2019, 12 master's awarded. *Expenses: Tuition, area resident:* Full-time $5959; part-time $440 per credit hour. Tuition, state resident: full-time $5959. Tuition, nonresident: full-time $5959. *International tuition:* $13,321 full-time. *Required fees:* $1169; $185 per credit hour.
Website: utrgv.edu/psychology/index.htm

The University of Texas Southwestern Medical Center, Southwestern Graduate School of Biomedical Sciences, Clinical Psychology Program, Dallas, TX 75390. Offers PhD. *Accreditation:* APA. *Degree requirements:* For doctorate, thesis/dissertation, clinical and qualifying exams. *Entrance requirements:* For doctorate, GRE General Test, minimum undergraduate GPA of 3.0. Electronic applications accepted.

University of the Cumberlands, Program in Clinical Psychology, Williamsburg, KY 40769-1372. Offers PhD. *Program availability:* Part-time, evening/weekend, online learning.

The University of Toledo, College of Graduate Studies, College of Languages, Literature and Social Sciences, Department of Psychology, Toledo, OH 43606-3390. Offers clinical psychology (MA, PhD); experimental psychology (MA, PhD). *Accreditation:* APA. *Degree requirements:* For master's, comprehensive exam, thesis; for doctorate, comprehensive exam, thesis/dissertation. *Entrance requirements:* For master's and doctorate, GRE General Test, GRE Subject Test, minimum cumulative point-hour ratio of 2.7 for all previous academic work, three letters of recommendation, statement of purpose, transcripts from all prior institutions attended. Additional exam requirements/recommendations for international students: required—TOEFL (minimum score 550 paper-based; 80 iBT). Electronic applications accepted.

The University of Tulsa, Graduate School, Kendall College of Arts and Sciences, Department of Psychology, Program in Clinical Psychology, Tulsa, OK 74104-3189. Offers MA, PhD, JD/MA. *Accreditation:* APA (one or more programs are accredited). *Program availability:* Part-time. Terminal master's awarded for partial completion of doctoral program. *Degree requirements:* For master's, thesis (for some programs), 6 credit hours of practicum training; for doctorate, comprehensive exam, thesis/dissertation, 1-year pre-doctoral internship. *Entrance requirements:* For master's and doctorate, GRE General Test, interview, resume. Additional exam requirements/recommendations for international students: required—TOEFL (minimum score 577 paper-based; 91 iBT), IELTS (minimum score 6.5). Electronic applications accepted. *Expenses: Tuition:* Full-time $22,896; part-time $1272 per credit hour. *Required fees:* $6 per credit hour. Tuition and fees vary according to course load and program.

University of Utah, Graduate School, College of Education, Department of Educational Psychology, Salt Lake City, UT 84112. Offers clinical mental health counseling (M Ed); counseling psychology (PhD); elementary education (M Ed); instructional design and educational technology (M Ed); instructional design and technology (MS); learning and cognition (MS, PhD); reading and literacy (M Ed, PhD); school counseling (M Ed); school psychology (M Ed, PhD, Ed S); statistics (M Stat). *Accreditation:* APA (one or more programs are accredited). *Faculty:* 25 full-time (15 women), 7 part-time/adjunct (4 women). *Students:* 237 full-time (159 women); includes 37 minority (19 Asian, non-Hispanic/Latino; 9 Hispanic/Latino; 9 Two or more races, non-Hispanic/Latino). Average age 27. 262 applicants, 24% accepted, 54 enrolled. In 2019, 62 master's, 8 doctorates awarded. Terminal master's awarded for partial completion of doctoral program. *Degree requirements:* For master's, comprehensive exam, thesis (for some programs); for doctorate, comprehensive exam, thesis/dissertation. *Entrance requirements:* For master's and doctorate, graduation application, transcripts, GRE scores, CV/resume, personal statement, letters of recommendataion. Additional exam requirements/recommendations for international students: required—TOEFL (minimum score 80 paper-based; 80 iBT), IELTS (minimum score 6.5). *Application deadline:* For fall admission, 12/15 for domestic and international students; for spring admission, 7/15 for domestic and international students; for summer admission, 3/15 for domestic and international students. Application fee: $55 ($75 for international students). Electronic applications accepted. *Expenses:* Tuition, state resident: full-time $7085; part-time $272.51 per credit hour. Tuition, nonresident: full-time $24,937; part-time $959.12 per credit hour. *Required fees:* $880.52; $880.52 per semester. Tuition and fees vary according to degree level, program and student level. *Financial support:* In 2019–20, 86 students received support, including 5 fellowships with full and partial tuition reimbursements available (averaging $11,500 per year), 14 research assistantships with full and partial tuition reimbursements available (averaging $15,900 per year), 2 teaching assistantships with full and partial tuition reimbursements available (averaging $12,560 per year); scholarships/grants, health care benefits, and unspecified assistantships also available. Financial award application deadline: 3/30. *Unit head:* Dr. Jason Burrow-Sanchez, Chair, Educational Psychology, 801-581-7148, Fax: 801-581-5566, E-mail: jason.burrow-sanchez@utah.edu. *Application contact:* JoLynn N. Yates, Academic Coordinator, 801-581-6811, Fax: 801-581-5566, E-mail: jo.yates@utah.edu.
Website: http://www.ed.utah.edu/edps/

University of Utah, Graduate School, College of Social and Behavioral Science, Department of Psychology, Salt Lake City, UT 84112. Offers clinical psychology (PhD); psychology (PhD), including cognitive neuroscience, developmental psychology, social psychology. *Accreditation:* APA. *Faculty:* 27 full-time (14 women), 1 (woman) part-time/adjunct. *Students:* 53 full-time (40 women); includes 8 minority (1 Black or African American, non-Hispanic/Latino; 4 Hispanic/Latino; 3 Two or more races, non-Hispanic/Latino), 6 international. Average age 28. 295 applicants, 8% accepted, 13 enrolled. In 2019, 11 doctorates awarded. *Degree requirements:* For doctorate, thesis/dissertation. *Entrance requirements:* For doctorate, GRE General Test. Additional exam requirements/recommendations for international students: required—TOEFL (minimum score 500 paper-based). *Application deadline:* For fall admission, 12/1 for domestic and international students. Application fee: $55 ($65 for international students). Electronic applications accepted. *Expenses:* Tuition, state resident: full-time $7085; part-time $272.51 per credit hour. Tuition, nonresident: full-time $24,937; part-time $959.12 per credit hour. *Required fees:* $880.52; $880.52 per semester. Tuition and fees vary according to degree level, program and student level. *Financial support:* In 2019–20, 5 fellowships (averaging $13,400 per year), 22 research assistantships (averaging $15,000 per year), 33 teaching assistantships (averaging $14,909 per year) were awarded; unspecified assistantships also available. Financial award applicants required to submit FAFSA. *Unit head:* Dr. Bert N. Uchino, Chair, 801-581-8925, Fax: 801-581-5841, E-mail: bert.uchino@psych.utah.edu. *Application contact:* Nancy Seegmiller, Program Manager, 801-581-8925, Fax: 801-581-5841, E-mail: nancy.seegmiller@psych.utah.edu.
Website: http://www.psych.utah.edu/

University of Vermont, Graduate College, College of Arts and Sciences, Program in Clinical Psychology, Burlington, VT 05405. Offers clinical developmental psychology (PhD); clinical psychology (PhD). *Degree requirements:* For doctorate, thesis/dissertation. *Entrance requirements:* For doctorate, GRE General Test, writing sample, resume. Additional exam requirements/recommendations for international students:

required—TOEFL (minimum iBT score of 100) or IELTS (7). Electronic applications accepted.

University of Vermont, Graduate College, College of Education and Social Services, Counseling Program, Burlington, VT 05405. Offers counseling (MS), including clinical mental health, school counseling. *Accreditation:* ACA; NCATE. *Entrance requirements:* For master's, resume. Additional exam requirements/recommendations for international students: required—TOEFL (minimum score 550 paper-based, 90 iBT) or IELTS (6.5). Electronic applications accepted.

University of Victoria, Faculty of Graduate Studies, Faculty of Social Sciences, Department of Psychology, Victoria, BC V8W 2Y2, Canada. Offers clinical psychology (PhD); clinical psychology (neuropsychology) (M Sc); cognition and brain science (M Sc, PhD); experimental neuropsychology (M Sc, PhD); individualized study (M Sc, PhD); life span development psychology (PhD); life span developmental psychology (M Sc); social psychology (M Sc, PhD). *Degree requirements:* For master's, thesis; for doctorate, thesis/dissertation, candidacy exam. *Entrance requirements:* For master's and doctorate, GRE General Test. Additional exam requirements/recommendations for international students: required—TOEFL (minimum score 600 paper-based). Electronic applications accepted.

University of Virginia, Curry School of Education, Department of Human Services, Program in Clinical and School Psychology, Charlottesville, VA 22903. Offers PhD.

University of Washington, Graduate School, College of Arts and Sciences, Department of Psychology, Seattle, WA 98195. Offers animal behavior (PhD); applied child and adolescent psychology: prevention and treatment (MA); behavioral neuroscience (PhD); clinical psychology (PhD); cognition and perception (PhD); developmental psychology (PhD); quantitative psychology (PhD); social psychology and personality (PhD). *Accreditation:* APA (one or more programs are accredited). *Degree requirements:* For doctorate, thesis/dissertation. *Entrance requirements:* For doctorate, GRE General Test, minimum GPA of 3.0. Electronic applications accepted.

The University of West Alabama, School of Graduate Studies, College of Education, Program in Clinical Mental Health Counseling, Livingston, AL 35470. Offers MS. *Program availability:* Part-time, evening/weekend, 100% online. *Faculty:* 9 full-time (7 women), 21 part-time/adjunct (12 women). *Students:* 168 full-time (149 women); includes 90 minority (84 Black or African American, non-Hispanic/Latino; 1 Asian, non-Hispanic/Latino; 2 Hispanic/Latino; 2 Native Hawaiian or other Pacific Islander, non-Hispanic/Latino; 1 Two or more races, non-Hispanic/Latino), 1 international. Average age 32. 52 applicants, 98% accepted, 41 enrolled. In 2019, 3 master's awarded. *Degree requirements:* For master's, comprehensive exam. *Entrance requirements:* For master's, GRE, minimum GPA of 2.75, verification of background clearance/fingerprints, essay, 3 academic references, resume. Additional exam requirements/recommendations for international students: required—TOEFL (minimum score 500 paper-based; 61 iBT). *Application deadline:* Applications are processed on a rolling basis. Application fee: $40. Electronic applications accepted. *Expenses: Required fees:* $380; $130. *Financial support:* Teaching assistantships, Federal Work-Study, scholarships/grants, and unspecified assistantships available. Support available to part-time students. Financial award application deadline: 3/1. *Unit head:* Dr. Jodie Winship, Chair of College of Education, 205-652-5415, E-mail: jwinship@uwa.edu. *Application contact:* Dr. Jodie Winship, Chair of College of Education, 205-652-5415, E-mail: jwinship@uwa.edu.

University of Windsor, Faculty of Graduate Studies, Faculty of Arts and Social Sciences, Department of Psychology, Windsor, ON N9B 3P4, Canada. Offers adult clinical (MA, PhD); applied social psychology (MA, PhD); child clinical (MA, PhD); clinical neuropsychology (MA, PhD). *Degree requirements:* For master's, thesis; for doctorate, comprehensive exam, thesis/dissertation. *Entrance requirements:* For master's, GRE General Test, GRE Subject Test in psychology, minimum B average; for doctorate, GRE General Test, GRE Subject Test in psychology, master's degree. Additional exam requirements/recommendations for international students: required—TOEFL (minimum score 600 paper-based). Electronic applications accepted.

University of Wisconsin–Madison, Graduate School, College of Letters and Science, Department of Psychology, Program in Clinical Psychology, Madison, WI 53706-1380. Offers PhD. *Accreditation:* APA. *Degree requirements:* For doctorate, comprehensive exam, thesis/dissertation. *Entrance requirements:* For doctorate, GRE General Test, minimum undergraduate GPA of 3.0. Additional exam requirements/recommendations for international students: required—TOEFL. Electronic applications accepted.

University of Wisconsin–Parkside, College of Natural and Health Sciences, Program in Clinical Mental Health Counseling, Kenosha, WI 53141-2000. Offers MS. *Expenses: Tuition, area resident:* Full-time $9173; part-time $509.64 per credit. *Tuition, state resident:* full-time $9173; part-time $509.64 per credit. *Tuition, nonresident:* full-time $18,767; part-time $1042.64 per credit. *International tuition:* $18,767 full-time. *Required fees:* $1123.20; $63.64 per credit. Tuition and fees vary according to campus/location, program and reciprocity agreements.

University of Wisconsin–Stout, Graduate School, College of Education, Health and Human Sciences, Program in Clinical Mental Health Counseling, Menomonie, WI 54751. Offers MS. *Accreditation:* ACA. *Program availability:* Part-time. *Degree requirements:* For master's, comprehensive exam or thesis. *Entrance requirements:* For master's, minimum GPA of 2.75. Additional exam requirements/recommendations for international students: required—TOEFL (minimum score 500 paper-based; 61 iBT). Electronic applications accepted.

Université Laval, Faculty of Social Sciences, School of Psychology, Programs in Psychology, Québec, QC G1K 7P4, Canada. Offers clinical psychology (PhD); community psychology (PhD); psychology (PhD, Psy D). *Degree requirements:* For doctorate, comprehensive exam, thesis/dissertation. *Entrance requirements:* For doctorate, comprehension of written English, knowledge of French, interview. Electronic applications accepted.

Utah State University, School of Graduate Studies, Emma Eccles Jones College of Education and Human Services, Department of Psychology, Logan, UT 84322. Offers clinical/counseling/school psychology (PhD); research and evaluation methodology (PhD); school counseling (MS); school psychology (MS). *Accreditation:* APA (one or more programs are accredited). *Program availability:* Part-time, evening/weekend, online learning. Terminal master's awarded for partial completion of doctoral program. *Degree requirements:* For master's, thesis (for some programs); for doctorate, thesis/dissertation. *Entrance requirements:* For master's, GRE General Test (school psychology), MAT (school counseling), minimum GPA of 3.5; for doctorate, GRE General Test, minimum GPA of 3.5. Additional exam requirements/recommendations for international students: required—TOEFL.

Valparaiso University, Graduate School and Continuing Education, Program in Clinical Mental Health Counseling, Valparaiso, IN 46383. Offers clinical mental health counseling (MA); JD/MA. *Program availability:* Part-time, evening/weekend. *Degree requirements:* For master's, thesis or alternative, internship. *Entrance requirements:* For master's, minimum GPA of 3.0; 15 credits in the social/behavioral sciences (psychology, sociology, human development, etc.) with minimum GPA of 3.0; course in introductory psychology; recent statistics course with minimum B average. Additional exam

requirements/recommendations for international students: required—TOEFL (minimum score 550 paper-based; 80 iBT), IELTS (minimum score 6). Electronic applications accepted.

Vanguard University of Southern California, Graduate Program in Clinical Psychology, Costa Mesa, CA 92626. Offers MS. *Program availability:* Part-time, evening/weekend. *Degree requirements:* For master's, thesis or alternative, completion of personal therapy. *Entrance requirements:* For master's, minimum GPA of 3.0. Additional exam requirements/recommendations for international students: required—TOEFL (minimum score 550 paper-based; 79 iBT). Electronic applications accepted. *Expenses:* Contact institution.

Virginia Commonwealth University, Graduate School, College of Humanities and Sciences, Department of Psychology, Program in Clinical Psychology, Richmond, VA 23284-9005. Offers behavioral medicine (PhD); clinical child psychology (PhD). *Accreditation:* APA. *Degree requirements:* For doctorate, thesis/dissertation. *Entrance requirements:* For doctorate, GRE General Test. Additional exam requirements/recommendations for international students: required—TOEFL (minimum score 600 paper-based; 100 iBT); recommended—IELTS (minimum score 6.5). Electronic applications accepted.

Virginia State University, College of Graduate Studies, College of Natural and Health Sciences, Department of Psychology, Petersburg, VA 23806-0001. Offers behavioral and community health sciences (PhD); clinical health psychology (PhD); clinical psychology (MS); general psychology (MS). *Degree requirements:* For master's, one foreign language, thesis. *Entrance requirements:* For master's, GRE General Test.

Walden University, Graduate Programs, School of Psychology, Minneapolis, MN 55401. Offers clinical psychology (MS), including counseling, general program; forensic psychology (MS), including forensic psychology in the community, general program, mental health applications, program planning and evaluation in forensic settings, psychology and legal systems; industrial organizational (MS, PhD), including consulting psychology, forensic (MS), forensic psychology (PhD), general practice, leadership development and coaching (MS), organizational diversity and social change, research evaluation (PhD); online teaching in psychology (Post-Master's Certificate); organizational psychology and development (Postbaccalaureate Certificate); psychology (MS, PhD), including applied psychology (MS), clinical psychology (PhD), crisis management and response (MS), educational psychology, forensic psychology (PhD), general psychology (MS), general psychology research (PhD), general psychology teaching (PhD), health psychology, leadership development and coaching (MS), psychology of culture (MS), psychology, public administration, and social change (MS), social psychology, terrorism and security (MS); psychology respecialization (Post-Doctoral Certificate). *Program availability:* Part-time, evening/weekend, online only, 100% online. Terminal master's awarded for partial completion of doctoral program. *Degree requirements:* For master's, thesis optional; for doctorate, thesis/dissertation, residency. *Entrance requirements:* For master's, bachelor's degree or higher; minimum GPA of 2.5; official transcripts; goal statement (for some programs); access to computer and Internet; for doctorate, master's degree or higher; three years of related professional or academic experience (preferred); minimum GPA of 3.0; goal statement and current resume (for select programs); official transcripts; access to computer and Internet; for other advanced degree, relevant work experience; access to computer and Internet. Additional exam requirements/recommendations for international students: required—TOEFL (minimum score 550 paper-based, 79 iBT), IELTS (minimum score 6.5), Michigan English Language Assessment Battery (minimum score 82), or PTE (minimum score 53). Electronic applications accepted.

Washburn University, College of Arts and Sciences, Department of Psychology, Topeka, KS 66621. Offers clinical psychology (MA). *Program availability:* Part-time. *Degree requirements:* For master's, comprehensive exam (for some programs), thesis or alternative. *Entrance requirements:* For master's, GRE General Test, 15 hours of undergraduate course work in psychology. Additional exam requirements/recommendations for international students: required—TOEFL (minimum score 80 iBT). Electronic applications accepted.

Washington State University, College of Arts and Sciences, Department of Psychology, Pullman, WA 99164. Offers clinical psychology (PhD); experimental psychology (PhD). *Accreditation:* APA (one or more programs are accredited). *Degree requirements:* For doctorate, comprehensive exam, thesis/dissertation, oral exam, written exam. *Entrance requirements:* For doctorate, GRE General Test, three letters of reference; summary data form; at least 18 credits of study in psychology; at least one course in statistics and research methodology; official transcripts; minimum cumulative undergraduate GPA of 3.0 or master's degree in psychology. Additional exam requirements/recommendations for international students: required—TOEFL, IELTS. Electronic applications accepted.

Waynesburg University, Graduate and Professional Studies, Canonsburg, PA 15370. Offers business (MBA), including energy management, finance, health systems, human resources, leadership, market development; counseling (MA), including addictions counseling, clinical mental health; counselor education and supervision (PhD); criminal investigation (MA); education (M Ed), including autism, curriculum and instruction, educational leadership, online teaching; nursing (MSN), including administration, education, informatics; nursing practice (DNP); special education (M Ed); technology (M Ed); MSN/MBA. *Accreditation:* AACN. *Program availability:* Part-time, evening/weekend. *Degree requirements:* For doctorate, thesis/dissertation. *Entrance requirements:* Additional exam requirements/recommendations for international students: required—TOEFL. Electronic applications accepted.

Wayne State University, College of Liberal Arts and Sciences, Department of Psychology, Detroit, MI 48202. Offers behavioral and cognitive neuroscience (PhD); clinical psychology (PhD); developmental science (PhD); industrial/organizational psychology (MA, PhD); social personality (PhD). *Accreditation:* APA (one or more programs are accredited). *Faculty:* 40. *Students:* 92 full-time (66 women), 42 part-time (27 women); includes 23 minority (4 Black or African American, non-Hispanic/Latino; 2 Asian, non-Hispanic/Latino; 9 Hispanic/Latino; 8 Two or more races, non-Hispanic/Latino), 10 international. Average age 27. 433 applicants, 15% accepted, 36 enrolled. In 2019, 28 master's, 13 doctorates awarded. Terminal master's awarded for partial completion of doctoral program. *Degree requirements:* For master's, thesis (for some programs); for doctorate, comprehensive exam, thesis/dissertation, training assignments. *Entrance requirements:* For master's, GRE General Test, minimum undergraduate upper-division cumulative GPA of 3.0, courses in psychology and statistics; for doctorate, GRE General Test, bachelor's, master's, or other advanced degree; at least twelve credits in psychology with minimum GPA of 3.0; courses in laboratory psychology and statistical methods in psychology; at least three letters of recommendation; statement of purpose. Additional exam requirements/recommendations for international students: required—TOEFL (minimum score 550 paper-based; 79 iBT), TWE (minimum score 5.5), Michigan English Language Assessment Battery (minimum score 85); recommended—IELTS (minimum score 6.5). Application fee: $50. Electronic applications accepted. *Expenses: Tuition:* Full-time $34,567. *Financial support:* In 2019–20, 93 students received support, including 11 fellowships with tuition reimbursements available (averaging $21,181 per year), 8

research assistantships with tuition reimbursements available (averaging $20,965 per year), 48 teaching assistantships with tuition reimbursements available (averaging $19,952 per year); scholarships/grants, health care benefits, and unspecified assistantships also available. Financial award applicants required to submit FAFSA. *Unit head:* Scott Bowen, PhD, Chair/Professor, 313-577-2803, E-mail: ad4771@wayne.edu. *Application contact:* Alia Allen, Academic Services Officer III, 313-577-2823, E-mail: aallen@wayne.edu.
Website: http://clas.wayne.edu/psychology/

Western Connecticut State University, Division of Graduate Studies, School of Professional Studies, Department of Education and Educational Psychology, Program in Clinical Mental Health Counseling, Danbury, CT 06810-6885. Offers MS. *Accreditation:* ACA. *Program availability:* Part-time. *Entrance requirements:* For master's, minimum GPA of 2.8, 3 letters of reference, interview, 9 hours of psychology. Additional exam requirements/recommendations for international students: recommended—TOEFL (minimum score 550 paper-based; 79 iBT), IELTS (minimum score 6).

Western Illinois University, School of Graduate Studies, College of Arts and Sciences, Department of Psychology, Macomb, IL 61455-1390. Offers clinical/community mental health (MS); general experimental psychology (MS); school psychology (SSP). *Program availability:* Part-time. *Degree requirements:* For master's, comprehensive exam (for some programs), thesis or alternative. *Entrance requirements:* For master's and SSP, GRE General Test. Additional exam requirements/recommendations for international students: required—TOEFL (minimum score 550 paper-based; 80 iBT). Electronic applications accepted.

Western Kentucky University, Graduate School, College of Education and Behavioral Sciences, Department of Psychology, Bowling Green, KY 42101. Offers clinical psychology (MA); experimental psychology (MA); general psychology (MA); industrial/organizational psychology (MA); school psychology (Ed S). *Degree requirements:* For master's, comprehensive exam, thesis (for some programs); for Ed S, thesis, oral exam. *Entrance requirements:* For master's, GRE General Test; for Ed S, GRE General Test, minimum GPA of 3.5. Additional exam requirements/recommendations for international students: required—TOEFL (minimum score 555 paper-based; 79 iBT).

Western Michigan University, Graduate College, College of Arts and Sciences, Department of Psychology, Kalamazoo, MI 49008. Offers behavior analysis (MA, PhD); clinical psychology (PhD); industrial/organizational behavior management (MA). *Accreditation:* APA (one or more programs are accredited). *Degree requirements:* For master's, variable foreign language requirement, thesis; for doctorate, 2 foreign languages, comprehensive exam, thesis/dissertation.

West Virginia University, College of Education and Human Services, Morgantown, WV 26506. Offers audiology (Au D); autism spectrum disorder (MA); clinical rehabilitation and mental health counseling (MS); communication science and disorders (PhD); counseling (MA); counseling psychology (PhD); curriculum and instruction (Ed D); early childhood education (MA); early intervention/ early childhood special education (MA); education (PhD); educational leadership (MA); educational leadership/ public school administration (Ed D); educational leadership/public school administration (MA); educational psychology (MA, Ed D); elementary education (MA); gifted education (MA); higher education administration (MA, Ed D); higher education curriculum and teaching (MA); institutional design and technology (MA); instructional design and technology (Ed D); literacy education (MA); secondary education (MA); secondary education/ English (MA); special education (Ed D); speech pathology (MS). *Accreditation:* ASHA; NCATE. *Program availability:* Part-time, evening/weekend, online learning. *Degree requirements:* For master's, content exams; for doctorate, comprehensive exam, thesis/dissertation. *Entrance requirements:* Additional exam requirements/recommendations for international students: required—TOEFL (minimum score 500 paper-based; 61 iBT). Electronic applications accepted.

Wheaton College, Graduate School, School of Psychology Counseling and Family Therapy, Wheaton, IL 60187-5593. Offers clinical mental health counseling (MA); clinical psychology (Psy D); marriage and family therapy (MA). *Accreditation:* APA (one or more programs are accredited). Terminal master's awarded for partial completion of doctoral program. *Degree requirements:* For master's, thesis or alternative; for doctorate, thesis/dissertation, internship. *Entrance requirements:* For master's, GRE General Test, 18 hours of course work in psychology; for doctorate, GRE General Test. Additional exam requirements/recommendations for international students: required—TOEFL (minimum score 550 paper-based; 80 iBT), IELTS (minimum score 6.5). *Expenses: Tuition:* Full-time $16,800; part-time $700 per credit hour. Tuition and fees vary according to degree level and program.

Wichita State University, Graduate School, Fairmount College of Liberal Arts and Sciences, Department of Psychology, Wichita, KS 67260. Offers clinical (PhD); community (PhD); human factors (PhD). *Accreditation:* APA. *Program availability:* Part-time.

Widener University, School of Human Service Professions, Institute for Graduate Clinical Psychology, Program in Clinical Psychology, Chester, PA 19013-5792. Offers Psy D, Psy D/M Ed, Psy D/MA, Psy D/MBA, Psy D/MHA, Psy D/MPA. *Accreditation:* APA. *Degree requirements:* For doctorate, thesis/dissertation, final oral and written qualifying exams. *Entrance requirements:* For doctorate, GRE General Test or MAT. Electronic applications accepted. *Expenses:* Contact institution.

Widener University, School of Human Service Professions, Institute for Graduate Clinical Psychology, Program in Clinical Psychology and Health and Medical Services Administration, Chester, PA 19013-5792. Offers Psy D/MBA, Psy D/MHA. *Accreditation:* APA (one or more programs are accredited). Electronic applications accepted.

Expenses: Tuition: Full-time $48,750; part-time $917 per credit hour. Tuition and fees vary according to class time, degree level, campus/location and program.

William James College, Graduate Programs, Newton, MA 02459. Offers applied psychology in higher education student personnel administration (MA); clinical psychology (Psy D); counseling psychology (MA); counseling psychology and community mental health (MA); counseling psychology and global mental health (MA); executive coaching (Graduate Certificate); forensic and counseling psychology (MA); leadership psychology (Psy D); organizational psychology (MA); primary care psychology (MA); respecialization in clinical psychology (Certificate); school psychology (Psy D); MA/CAGS. *Accreditation:* APA. *Degree requirements:* For master's, comprehensive exam (for some programs); for doctorate, thesis/dissertation (for some programs). Electronic applications accepted.

Wilmington University, College of Social and Behavioral Sciences, New Castle, DE 19720-6491. Offers administration of human services (MS); administration of justice (MS); clinical mental health counseling (MS); homeland security (MS). *Accreditation:* ACA. *Program availability:* Part-time, evening/weekend. *Entrance requirements:* Additional exam requirements/recommendations for international students: required—TOEFL (minimum score 500 paper-based). Electronic applications accepted.

Winona State University, College of Education, Department of Counselor Education, Winona, MN 55987. Offers addiction counseling (Certificate); clinical mental health counseling (MS); human services (MS); school counseling (MS). *Accreditation:* ACA (one or more programs are accredited); NCATE. *Program availability:* Part-time, evening/weekend. *Degree requirements:* For master's, thesis or alternative. *Entrance requirements:* For master's, letters of reference, interview, group activity, on-site writing. Electronic applications accepted.

Wisconsin School of Professional Psychology, Program in Clinical Psychology, Milwaukee, WI 53225-4960. Offers MA, Psy D. *Accreditation:* APA. *Program availability:* Part-time, evening/weekend. Terminal master's awarded for partial completion of doctoral program. *Degree requirements:* For master's, candidacy exam, 500 hours of supervised clinical practica; for doctorate, thesis/dissertation, 1 year clinical intern and practicum experience (2000 hrs), candidacy and clinical exams. *Entrance requirements:* For master's, GRE General Test, GRE Subject Test, bachelor's degree in psychology, writing sample; for doctorate, GRE General Test, GRE Subject Test, master's degree in clinical psychology or equivalent, writing sample.

The Wright Institute, Doctoral Program in Clinical Psychology, Berkeley, CA 94704-1796. Offers Psy D. *Degree requirements:* For doctorate, comprehensive exam, thesis/dissertation. *Entrance requirements:* For doctorate, GRE General Test, statistics, human development, theories of personality and/or abnormal psychology. Additional exam requirements/recommendations for international students: required—TOEFL (minimum score 600 paper-based). Electronic applications accepted.

Wright State University, School of Professional Psychology, Dayton, OH 45435. Offers clinical psychology (Psy D). *Accreditation:* APA. *Degree requirements:* For doctorate, thesis/dissertation. *Entrance requirements:* For doctorate, GRE General Test, GRE Subject Test. Additional exam requirements/recommendations for international students: required—TOEFL. *Expenses:* Contact institution.

Xavier University, College of Professional Sciences, Department of Psychology, Cincinnati, OH 45207. Offers clinical psychology (Psy D); industrial-organizational psychology (MA). *Accreditation:* APA (one or more programs are accredited). *Degree requirements:* For master's, one foreign language, comprehensive exam, thesis, internship; for doctorate, one foreign language, comprehensive exam, thesis/dissertation, internship. *Entrance requirements:* For master's, GRE, official transcript; 3 letters of recommendation; for doctorate, GRE General Test; GRE Subject Test in psychology (if no undergraduate degree in psychology), bachelor's or master's degree; 18 semester hours of psychology coursework; minimum GPA of 3.0; work and research experience; official transcript; 3 letters of recommendation; statement of purpose. Additional exam requirements/recommendations for international students: required—TOEFL (minimum score 550 paper-based; 79 iBT), IELTS (minimum score 6.5). Electronic applications accepted. *Expenses:* Contact institution.

Xavier University, College of Professional Sciences, School of Education, Department of Counseling, Cincinnati, OH 45207. Offers clinical mental health counseling (MA); school counseling (MA). *Program availability:* Part-time, evening/weekend. *Degree requirements:* For master's, internship. *Entrance requirements:* For master's, GRE or MAT, minimum GPA of 3.0; 2 letters of recommendation; resume; official transcript; statement of purpose. Additional exam requirements/recommendations for international students: required—TOEFL (minimum score 550 paper-based; 79 iBT). Electronic applications accepted. Application fee is waived when completed online. *Expenses:* Contact institution.

Yale University, Graduate School of Arts and Sciences, Department of Psychology, New Haven, CT 06520. Offers behavioral neuroscience (PhD); clinical psychology (PhD); cognitive psychology (PhD); developmental psychology (PhD); social/personality psychology (PhD). *Accreditation:* APA. *Degree requirements:* For doctorate, thesis/dissertation. *Entrance requirements:* For doctorate, GRE General Test.

Yeshiva University, Ferkauf Graduate School of Psychology, Program in Clinical Psychology, New York, NY 10033-3201. Offers Psy D. *Accreditation:* APA. *Program availability:* Part-time. *Degree requirements:* For doctorate, comprehensive exam, thesis/dissertation. *Entrance requirements:* For doctorate, GRE General Test.

Yeshiva University, Ferkauf Graduate School of Psychology, Program in School/Clinical-Child Psychology, New York, NY 10033-3201. Offers Psy D. *Accreditation:* APA. *Program availability:* Part-time. *Degree requirements:* For doctorate, comprehensive exam, thesis/dissertation. *Entrance requirements:* For doctorate, GRE General Test.

Cognitive Sciences

American University, College of Arts and Sciences, Department of Psychology, Washington, DC 22016-8062. Offers addiction and addictive behavior (Certificate); behavior, cognition, and neuroscience (PhD); clinical psychology (PhD); psychobiology of healing (Certificate); psychology (MA). *Accreditation:* APA. *Program availability:* Part-time. *Degree requirements:* For master's, comprehensive exam, thesis or alternative; for doctorate, comprehensive exam, thesis/dissertation. *Entrance requirements:* For master's, GRE General Test, GRE Subject Test; Please website: https://www.american.edu/cas/psychology/, statement of purpose, transcripts, 2 letters of recommendation; for doctorate, GRE General Test, GRE Subject Test, 3 letters of recommendation, statement of purpose, transcripts, resume. Additional exam

requirements/recommendations for international students: required—TOEFL (minimum score 600 paper-based; 100 iBT). *Expenses:* Contact institution.

Arizona State University at Tempe, College of Liberal Arts and Sciences, Department of Psychology, Tempe, AZ 85287-1104. Offers applied behavior analysis (MS); behavioral neuroscience (PhD); clinical psychology (PhD); cognitive science (PhD); developmental psychology (PhD); quantitative psychology (PhD); social psychology (PhD). *Accreditation:* APA. *Degree requirements:* For doctorate, comprehensive exam, thesis/dissertation, interactive Program of Study (iPOS) submitted before completing 50 percent of required credit hours. *Entrance requirements:* For doctorate, GRE General Test, GRE Subject Test, minimum GPA of 3.0 or equivalent in last 2 years of work leading to bachelor's degree. Additional exam requirements/recommendations for international students: required—TOEFL, IELTS, or PTE. Electronic applications accepted.

Arizona State University at Tempe, Ira A. Fulton Schools of Engineering, The Polytechnic School, Department of Engineering, Mesa, AZ 85212. Offers simulation, modeling, and applied cognitive science (PhD). *Program availability:* Part-time. *Degree requirements:* For doctorate, comprehensive exam, thesis/dissertation, interactive Program of Study (iPOS) submitted before completing 50 percent of required credit hours. *Entrance requirements:* For doctorate, GRE, master's degree in psychology, engineering, cognitive science, or computer science; 3 letters of recommendation; statement of research interests. Additional exam requirements/recommendations for international students: required—TOEFL, IELTS, or PTE. Electronic applications accepted.

Ball State University, Graduate School, College of Sciences and Humanities, Department of Psychological Science, Program in Cognitive and Social Processes, Muncie, IN 47306. Offers MA. *Entrance requirements:* For master's, GRE General Test, minimum baccalaureate GPA of 2.75 or 3.0 in latter half of baccalaureate, goals statements, curriculum vitae, letters of recommendation. Additional exam requirements/recommendations for international students: required—TOEFL (minimum score 550 paper-based; 79 iBT), IELTS (minimum score 6.5). Electronic applications accepted. *Expenses: Tuition, area resident:* Full-time $7506; part-time $417 per credit hour. Tuition, nonresident: full-time $20,610; part-time $1145 per credit hour. *Required fees:* $2126. Tuition and fees vary according to course load, campus/location and program.

Binghamton University, State University of New York, Graduate School, Harpur College of Arts and Sciences, Department of Psychology, Program in Psychology - Cognitive and Behavioral Science, Binghamton, NY 13902-6000. Offers PhD. *Program availability:* Part-time. Terminal master's awarded for partial completion of doctoral program. *Degree requirements:* For doctorate, thesis/dissertation. *Entrance requirements:* For doctorate, GRE General Test. Additional exam requirements/recommendations for international students: required—TOEFL (minimum score 550 paper-based; 80 iBT). Electronic applications accepted.

Brandeis University, Graduate School of Arts and Sciences, Department of Psychology, Waltham, MA 02454-9110. Offers brain, body and behavior (PhD); cognitive neuroscience (PhD); general psychology (MA); social/developmental psychology (PhD). *Program availability:* Part-time. *Faculty:* 14 full-time (7 women), 3 part-time/adjunct (all women). *Students:* 31 full-time (21 women), 1 (woman) part-time; includes 6 minority (4 Asian, non-Hispanic/Latino; 2 Hispanic/Latino), 8 international. Average age 26. 157 applicants, 14% accepted, 12 enrolled. In 2019, 18 master's, 2 doctorates awarded. Terminal master's awarded for partial completion of doctoral program. *Degree requirements:* For master's, thesis (for some programs); for doctorate, thesis/dissertation. *Entrance requirements:* For master's and doctorate, GRE General required; GRE Subject recommended, transcripts, letters of recommendation, resume, and statement of purpose. Additional exam requirements/recommendations for international students: required—TOEFL, IELTS, PTE. *Application deadline:* For fall admission, 12/1 priority date for domestic and international students. Applications are processed on a rolling basis. Application fee: $75. Electronic applications accepted. *Financial support:* In 2019–20, 23 fellowships with full tuition reimbursements (averaging $25,000 per year), 16 teaching assistantships (averaging $3,550 per year) were awarded; research assistantships, scholarships/grants, traineeships, health care benefits, and tuition waivers also available. Support available to part-time students. *Unit head:* Dr. Angela Gutchess, Director of Graduate Studies, 781-736-3247, E-mail: gutchess@brandeis.edu. *Application contact:* Sarah Lupis, Administrator, 781-736-3303, E-mail: slupis@brandeis.edu.
Website: http://www.brandeis.edu/gsas/programs/psychology.html

Brigham Young University, Graduate Studies, College of Family, Home, and Social Sciences, Department of Psychology, Provo, UT 84602. Offers clinical psychology (PhD); cognitive and behavioral neuroscience (PhD). *Accreditation:* APA. *Faculty:* 24 full-time (9 women), 3 part-time/adjunct (0 women). *Students:* 62 full-time (39 women); includes 10 minority (3 Black or African American, non-Hispanic/Latino; 1 American Indian or Alaska Native, non-Hispanic/Latino; 5 Asian, non-Hispanic/Latino; 1 Hispanic/Latino), 4 international. Average age 29. 76 applicants, 22% accepted, 11 enrolled. In 2019, 8 doctorates awarded. *Degree requirements:* For doctorate, comprehensive exam, thesis/dissertation, publishable paper. *Entrance requirements:* For doctorate, GRE General Test, minimum GPA of 3.0. Additional exam requirements/recommendations for international students: required—TOEFL (minimum score 580 paper-based; 85 iBT). *Application deadline:* For fall admission, 12/1 for domestic and international students. Application fee: $50. Electronic applications accepted. *Expenses:* $18,226/LDS $25,512/Non-LDS. *Financial support:* In 2019–20, 41 students received support, including 43 research assistantships with partial tuition reimbursements available (averaging $12,000 per year), 7 teaching assistantships with partial tuition reimbursements available (averaging $12,000 per year); scholarships/grants and unspecified assistantships also available. Financial award application deadline: 5/31. *Unit head:* Dr. Gary Burlingame, Chair, 801-422-7557, Fax: 801-422-0602, E-mail: gary_burlingame@byu.edu. *Application contact:* Rachelle Gunderson, Coordinator of Student Programs, 801-422-4560, Fax: 801-422-0602, E-mail: leesa_scott@byu.edu.
Website: http://psychology.byu.edu/

Brown University, Graduate School, Department of Cognitive, Linguistic and Psychological Sciences, Providence, RI 02912. Offers cognitive science (Sc M, PhD); linguistics (AM, PhD); psychology (PhD). *Degree requirements:* For master's, one foreign language, thesis or alternative; for doctorate, 2 foreign languages, thesis/dissertation.

Carleton University, Faculty of Graduate Studies, Faculty of Arts and Social Sciences, Program in Cognitive Science, Ottawa, ON K1S 5B6, Canada. Offers PhD. *Degree requirements:* For doctorate, thesis/dissertation. *Entrance requirements:* For doctorate, master's degree.

Carnegie Mellon University, Dietrich College of Humanities and Social Sciences, Department of Psychology, Area of Cognitive Neuroscience, Pittsburgh, PA 15213-3891. Offers PhD. *Degree requirements:* For doctorate, comprehensive exam, thesis/dissertation. *Entrance requirements:* For doctorate, GRE General Test. Additional exam requirements/recommendations for international students: required—TOEFL.

Carnegie Mellon University, Dietrich College of Humanities and Social Sciences, Department of Psychology, Area of Cognitive Psychology, Pittsburgh, PA 15213-3891. Offers PhD. *Degree requirements:* For doctorate, comprehensive exam, thesis/dissertation. *Entrance requirements:* For doctorate, GRE General Test. Additional exam requirements/recommendations for international students: required—TOEFL.

Case Western Reserve University, School of Graduate Studies, Department of Cognitive Science, Cleveland, OH 44106. Offers cognitive linguistics (MA). *Program availability:* Part-time. *Degree requirements:* For master's, thesis. *Entrance requirements:* For master's, GRE, statement of purpose, three letters of recommendation, writing sample. Additional exam requirements/recommendations for international students: required—TOEFL (minimum score 577 paper-based; 90 iBT); recommended—IELTS (minimum score 7). Electronic applications accepted.

Central European University, Department of Cognitive Science, 1051, Hungary. Offers PhD. *Degree requirements:* For doctorate, one foreign language, comprehensive exam, thesis/dissertation. *Entrance requirements:* For doctorate, essay, interview. Additional exam requirements/recommendations for international students: required—TOEFL (minimum score 570 paper-based); recommended—IELTS (minimum score 6.5). Electronic applications accepted.

Claremont Graduate University, Graduate Programs, School of Social Science, Policy and Evaluation, Department of Psychology, Claremont, CA 91711-6160. Offers advanced study in evaluation (Certificate); cognitive psychology (MA, PhD); developmental psychology (MA, PhD); evaluation and applied research methods (MA, PhD); health behavior research and evaluation (MA, PhD); human resource development and evaluation (MA); industrial/organizational psychology (MA, PhD); organizational behavior (MA, PhD); organizational psychology (MA, PhD); social psychology (MA, PhD); MBA/PhD. *Program availability:* Part-time. Terminal master's awarded for partial completion of doctoral program. *Entrance requirements:* For master's and doctorate, GRE General Test. Additional exam requirements/recommendations for international students: required—TOEFL (minimum score 75 iBT). Electronic applications accepted.

Cornell University, Graduate School, Graduate Fields of Arts and Sciences, Field of Information Science, Ithaca, NY 14853. Offers cognition (PhD); human computer interaction (PhD); information science (PhD); information systems (PhD); social aspects of information (PhD). *Degree requirements:* For doctorate, comprehensive exam, thesis/dissertation. *Entrance requirements:* For doctorate, GRE General Test, 3 letters of recommendation. Additional exam requirements/recommendations for international students: required—TOEFL (minimum score 550 paper-based; 77 iBT). Electronic applications accepted.

Dartmouth College, Guarini School of Graduate and Advanced Studies, Department of Psychological and Brain Sciences, Program in Cognitive Neuroscience, Hanover, NH 03755. Offers PhD. *Entrance requirements:* Additional exam requirements/recommendations for international students: required—TOEFL. Electronic applications accepted.

Duke University, Graduate School, Department of Psychology and Neuroscience, Durham, NC 27708. Offers biological psychology (PhD); clinical psychology (PhD); cognitive psychology (PhD); developmental psychology (PhD); experimental psychology (PhD); health psychology (PhD); human social development (PhD); JD/MA. *Accreditation:* APA (one or more programs are accredited). *Degree requirements:* For doctorate, thesis/dissertation. *Entrance requirements:* For doctorate, GRE General Test. Additional exam requirements/recommendations for international students: required—TOEFL (minimum score 577 paper-based; 90 iBT) or IELTS (minimum score 7). Electronic applications accepted.

Emory University, Laney Graduate School, Department of Psychology, Atlanta, GA 30322-1100. Offers clinical psychology (PhD); cognition and development (PhD); neuroscience and animal behavior (PhD). *Accreditation:* APA. *Degree requirements:* For doctorate, comprehensive exam, thesis/dissertation. *Entrance requirements:* For doctorate, GRE General Test, minimum GPA of 3.25. Additional exam requirements/recommendations for international students: required—TOEFL. Electronic applications accepted.

Florida International University, College of Arts, Sciences, and Education, Department of Psychology, Miami, FL 33199. Offers behavioral analysis (MS); clinical science (PhD); cognitive neuroscience (PhD); counseling psychology (MS); developmental science (MS, PhD); legal psychology (MS, PhD); organizational psychology (MS, PhD). *Accreditation:* APA. *Program availability:* Part-time, evening/weekend. *Faculty:* 52 full-time (33 women), 50 part-time/adjunct (37 women). *Students:* 203 full-time (159 women), 2 part-time (both women); includes 117 minority (15 Black or African American, non-Hispanic/Latino; 8 Asian, non-Hispanic/Latino; 86 Hispanic/Latino; 8 Two or more races, non-Hispanic/Latino), 15 international. Average age 26. 410 applicants, 19% accepted, 60 enrolled. In 2019, 57 master's, 7 doctorates awarded. Terminal master's awarded for partial completion of doctoral program. *Degree requirements:* For master's, thesis; for doctorate, comprehensive exam, thesis/dissertation. *Entrance requirements:* For master's, GRE General Test, minimum GPA of 3.0, resume, 3 letters of recommendation; for doctorate, GRE General Test, 3 letters of recommendation, resume, letter of intent, two writing samples, minimum GPA of 3.0. Additional exam requirements/recommendations for international students: required—TOEFL (minimum score 550 paper-based; 80 iBT). *Application deadline:* For fall admission, 12/15 for domestic and international students. Application fee: $30. Electronic applications accepted. *Expenses: Tuition, area resident:* Full-time $8912; part-time $446 per credit hour. Tuition, state resident: full-time $8912; part-time $446 per credit hour. Tuition, nonresident: full-time $21,393; part-time $992 per credit hour. *Required fees:* $2194. *Financial support:* Institutionally sponsored loans and scholarships/grants available. Financial award application deadline: 3/1. *Unit head:* Dr. Jeremy Pettit, Interim Chair, 305-348-1671, Fax: 305-348-2880, E-mail: jeremy.pettit@fiu.edu. *Application contact:* Nanett Rojas, Manager, Admissions Operations, 305-348-7464, Fax: 305-348-7441, E-mail: gradadm@fiu.edu.

Florida State University, The Graduate School, Department of Anthropology, Department of Psychology, Program in Cognitive Psychology, Tallahassee, FL 32306-4301. Offers PhD. *Faculty:* 7 full-time (1 woman). *Students:* 15 full-time (8 women), 2 part-time (1 woman); includes 7 minority (2 Black or African American, non-Hispanic/Latino; 3 Asian, non-Hispanic/Latino; 1 Hispanic/Latino; 1 Two or more races, non-Hispanic/Latino), 1 international. Average age 27. 24 applicants, 29% accepted, 5 enrolled. In 2019, 2 doctorates awarded. Terminal master's awarded for partial completion of doctoral program. *Degree requirements:* For doctorate, comprehensive exam, thesis/dissertation. *Entrance requirements:* For doctorate, GRE General Test, minimum GPA of 3.0, research experience, letters of recommendation. Additional exam requirements/recommendations for international students: required—TOEFL (minimum score 80 iBT). *Application deadline:* For fall admission, 12/1 for domestic and international students. Application fee: $30. Electronic applications accepted. *Financial support:* In 2019–20, 16 students received support, including 2 fellowships with full tuition reimbursements available, 5 research assistantships with full tuition reimbursements available (averaging $24,324 per year), 10 teaching assistantships with full tuition reimbursements available (averaging $24,324 per year); health care benefits also available. Financial award application deadline: 12/1; financial award applicants required to submit FAFSA. *Unit head:* Dr. Walter Boot, Director, 850-645-8734, Fax: 850-644-7739, E-mail: boot@psy.fsu.edu. *Application contact:* Lynda L. Gibson, Graduate Program Associate, 850-644-2499, Fax: 850-644-7739, E-mail: grad-info@psy.fsu.edu.
Website: http://www.psy.fsu.edu/

George Mason University, College of Humanities and Social Sciences, Department of Psychology, Fairfax, VA 22030. Offers applied developmental psychology (MA, PhD); clinical psychology (PhD); cognitive and behavioral neuroscience (MA, PhD); cognitive neuroscience (Certificate); human factors/applied cognition (MA, PhD, Certificate), including transportation human factors (Certificate), usability (Certificate); industrial/organizational psychology (MA, PhD). *Accreditation:* APA. *Degree requirements:* For master's, comprehensive exam, thesis or practicum research; for doctorate, comprehensive exam, thesis/dissertation, 2nd-year project. *Entrance requirements:* For master's, GRE, 2 official transcripts; goals statement; 15 undergraduate credits in concentration for which the applicant is applying; for doctorate, GRE, 3 letters of recommendation; resume; goals statement; minimum GPA of 3.0 overall for last 60 undergraduate credits, 3.25 in psychology courses; 15 undergraduate credits in concentration for which the applicant is applying; 2 official transcripts; for Certificate, GRE, 2 official transcripts; expanded goals statement; 3 letters of recommendation. Additional exam requirements/recommendations for international students: required—TOEFL (minimum score 575 paper-based; 88 iBT), IELTS (minimum score 6.5), PTE (minimum score 59). Electronic applications accepted.

The George Washington University, Columbian College of Arts and Sciences, Department of Psychology, Washington, DC 20052. Offers applied social psychology (PhD); clinical psychology (PhD); cognitive neuroscience (PhD). *Accreditation:* APA. *Program availability:* Part-time, evening/weekend. *Degree requirements:* For doctorate, thesis/dissertation or alternative, general exam. *Entrance requirements:* For doctorate, GRE General Test, minimum GPA of 3.0. Additional exam requirements/recommendations for international students: required—TOEFL (minimum score 550 paper-based; 80 iBT).

Georgia State University, College of Arts and Sciences, Department of Psychology, Atlanta, GA 30302-3083. Offers clinical psychology (PhD); cognitive sciences (PhD); community psychology (PhD); developmental psychology (PhD); neuropsychology and behavioral neuroscience (PhD). *Accreditation:* APA. *Faculty:* 29 full-time (17 women). *Students:* 107 full-time (85 women), 2 part-time (both women); includes 23 minority (9 Black or African American, non-Hispanic/Latino; 6 Asian, non-Hispanic/Latino; 7 Hispanic/Latino; 1 Two or more races, non-Hispanic/Latino), 13 international. Average age 28. 498 applicants, 5% accepted, 17 enrolled. In 2019, 18 doctorates awarded. *Entrance requirements:* For doctorate, GRE. Additional exam requirements/recommendations for international students: required—TOEFL (minimum score 550 paper-based; 80 iBT). *Application deadline:* For fall admission, 12/1 for domestic and international students. Application fee: $50. Electronic applications accepted. *Expenses: Tuition, area resident:* Full-time $7164; part-time $398 per credit hour. Tuition, state resident: full-time $7164; part-time $398 per credit hour. Tuition, nonresident: full-time $22,662; part-time $1259 per credit hour. *International tuition:* $22,662 full-time. *Required fees:* $2128; $312 per credit hour. Tuition and fees vary according to course load and program. *Financial support:* In 2019–20, fellowships with full tuition reimbursements (averaging $19,282 per year), research assistantships with full tuition reimbursements (averaging $5,173 per year), teaching assistantships with full tuition reimbursements (averaging $6,389 per year) were awarded; scholarships/grants, traineeships, health care benefits, and unspecified assistantships also available. Financial award applicants required to submit FAFSA. *Unit head:* Dr. Lisa Armistead, Professor, Associate Provost for Graduate Programs, 404-413-2091, Fax: 404-413-6207, E-mail: lparmistead@gsu.edu. *Application contact:* Dr. Lindsey Cohen, Director of Graduate Studies, 404-413-6263, Fax: 404-413-6207, E-mail: llcohen@gsu.edu.
Website: https://psychology.gsu.edu/

The Graduate Center, City University of New York, Graduate Studies, Program in Psychology, New York, NY 10016-4039. Offers basic applied neurocognition (PhD); biopsychology (PhD); clinical psychology (PhD); developmental psychology (PhD); environmental psychology (PhD); experimental psychology (PhD); industrial psychology (PhD); learning processes (PhD); neuropsychology (PhD); psychology (PhD); social personality (PhD). *Degree requirements:* For doctorate, one foreign language, thesis/dissertation. *Entrance requirements:* For doctorate, GRE General Test. Additional exam requirements/recommendations for international students: required—TOEFL. Electronic applications accepted.

Grand Canyon University, College of Doctoral Studies, Phoenix, AZ 85017-1097. Offers data analytics (DBA); general psychology (PhD), including cognition and instruction, industrial and organizational psychology, integrating technology, learning, and psychology, performance psychology; management (DBA); marketing (DBA); organizational leadership (Ed D), including behavioral health, Christian ministry, health care administration, organizational development. *Degree requirements:* For doctorate, comprehensive exam, thesis/dissertation. *Entrance requirements:* For doctorate, minimum GPA of 3.4 on earned advanced degree from regionally-accredited institution; transcripts; goals statement.

Harvard University, Graduate School of Arts and Sciences, Department of Psychology, Cambridge, MA 02138. Offers psychology (PhD), including behavior and decision analysis, cognition, developmental psychology, experimental psychology, personality, psychobiology, psychopathology; social psychology (PhD). *Accreditation:* APA. *Degree requirements:* For doctorate, thesis/dissertation, general exams. *Entrance requirements:* For doctorate, GRE General Test. Additional exam requirements/recommendations for international students: required—TOEFL.

Harvard University, Harvard Graduate School of Education, Master's Programs in Education, Cambridge, MA 02138. Offers arts in education (Ed M); education policy and management (Ed M); higher education (Ed M); human development and psychology (Ed M); international education policy (Ed M); language and literacy (Ed M); learning and teaching (Ed M); mind, brain, and education (Ed M); prevention science and practice (Ed M); school leadership (Ed M); special studies (Ed M); teacher education (Ed M); technology, innovation, and education (Ed M). *Program availability:* Part-time. *Entrance requirements:* For master's, GRE General Test, statement of purpose, 3 letters of recommendation, resume, official transcripts. Additional exam requirements/recommendations for international students: required—TOEFL (minimum score 613 paper-based; 104 iBT), TWE (minimum score 5). Electronic applications accepted.

Illinois State University, Graduate School, College of Arts and Sciences, Department of Psychology, Normal, IL 61790. Offers psychology (MA, MS), including clinical-counseling psychology, cognitive and behavioral sciences, developmental psychology, industrial/organizational-social psychology; school psychology (PhD, SSP). *Accreditation:* APA. *Faculty:* 32 full-time (14 women), 6 part-time/adjunct (5 women). *Students:* 92 full-time (77 women), 18 part-time (14 women). Average age 25. 154 applicants, 32% accepted, 37 enrolled. In 2019, 27 master's, 3 doctorates, 5 other advanced degrees awarded. *Degree requirements:* For master's, thesis or alternative; for doctorate, variable foreign language requirement, thesis/dissertation, 2 terms of residency, internship, practicum. *Entrance requirements:* For master's, GRE General Test, GRE Subject Test, minimum GPA of 3.0 in last 60 hours of course work; for doctorate, GRE General Test. *Application deadline:* Applications are processed on a rolling basis. Application fee: $50. *Expenses: Tuition, area resident:* Full-time $7956; part-time $9767 per year. Tuition, nonresident: full-time $9233; part-time $17,592 per year. *Required fees:* $1797. *Financial support:* In 2019–20, 26 research assistantships, 34 teaching assistantships were awarded; tuition waivers (full) and unspecified assistantships also available. Financial award application deadline: 4/1. *Unit head:* Dr. J Scott Jordan, Department Chair, 309-438-2484, E-mail: jsjorda@illinoisState.edu. *Application contact:* Dr. Karen Mark, Graduate Coordinator, 309-438-8130, E-mail: kimark@ilstu.edu.
Website: http://psychology.illinoisstate.edu/

Indiana University Bloomington, University Graduate School, College of Arts and Sciences, Cognitive Science Program, Bloomington, IN 47406-7512. Offers PhD. *Degree requirements:* For doctorate, comprehensive exam, thesis/dissertation, research project; colloquia course. *Entrance requirements:* For doctorate, GRE, 3 letters of reference. Additional exam requirements/recommendations for international students: required—TOEFL (minimum score 600 paper-based; 94 iBT), IELTS (minimum score 6.5). Electronic applications accepted. *Expenses:* Contact institution.

Indiana University Bloomington, University Graduate School, College of Arts and Sciences, Department of Psychological and Brain Sciences, Bloomington, IN 47405. Offers clinical science (PhD); cognitive neuroscience (PhD); cognitive psychology (PhD); developmental psychology (PhD); methods of behavior (PhD); molecular systems neuroscience (PhD); social psychology (PhD). *Accreditation:* APA. *Degree requirements:* For doctorate, comprehensive exam, 90 credit hours, 2 advanced statistics/methods courses, 2 written research projects, the teaching of psychology course, teaching 1 semester of undergraduate methods course, qualifying examination, minor or a second major, first-year research seminar course, dissertation defense, written dissertation. *Entrance requirements:* For doctorate, GRE. Additional exam requirements/recommendations for international students: required—TOEFL (minimum score 550 paper-based; 79 iBT). Electronic applications accepted.

Iowa State University of Science and Technology, Department of Psychology, Ames, IA 50011. Offers cognitive psychology (PhD); counseling psychology (PhD); psychology (MS, PhD); social psychology (PhD). *Accreditation:* APA (one or more programs are accredited). *Entrance requirements:* For doctorate, GRE General Test, GRE Subject Test (psychology), 3 letters of recommendation. Additional exam requirements/recommendations for international students: required—TOEFL (minimum score 560 paper-based; 79 iBT), IELTS (minimum score 6.5). Electronic applications accepted.

Johns Hopkins University, Zanvyl Krieger School of Arts and Sciences, Department of Cognitive Science, Baltimore, MD 21218. Offers MA, PhD. Terminal master's awarded for partial completion of doctoral program. *Degree requirements:* For master's, thesis, portfolio, or 1st research paper (depending on track); for doctorate, thesis/dissertation, 2 research papers. *Entrance requirements:* For master's, GRE, minimum GPA of 3.0, undergraduate degree relevant to cognitive science, resume or curriculum vitae, statement of purpose, transcripts from previous post-secondary institutions, 2 recommendation letters, research or course proposal; for doctorate, GRE General Test, 3 letters of recommendation, sample of work, statement of purpose, original transcripts from all previous post-secondary institutions. Additional exam requirements/recommendations for international students: required—TOEFL (minimum score 600 paper-based; 100 iBT), IELTS (minimum score 7). Electronic applications accepted. *Expenses:* Contact institution.

Louisiana State University and Agricultural & Mechanical College, Graduate School, College of Humanities and Social Sciences, Department of Psychology, Baton Rouge, LA 70803. Offers biological psychology (MA, PhD); clinical psychology (MA, PhD); cognitive psychology (MA, PhD); developmental psychology (MA, PhD); school psychology (MA, PhD). *Accreditation:* APA (one or more programs are accredited).

Massachusetts Institute of Technology, School of Science, Department of Brain and Cognitive Sciences, Cambridge, MA 02139. Offers cognitive science (PhD); neuroscience (PhD). *Degree requirements:* For doctorate, comprehensive exam, thesis/dissertation. *Entrance requirements:* For doctorate, GRE General Test. Additional exam requirements/recommendations for international students: required—TOEFL, IELTS. Electronic applications accepted.

Michigan Technological University, Graduate School, College of Sciences and Arts, Department of Cognitive and Learning Sciences, Houghton, MI 49931. Offers applied cognitive science and human factors (MS, PhD); applied science education (MS); post-secondary STEM education (Graduate Certificate). *Program availability:* Part-time, blended/hybrid learning. *Faculty:* 25 full-time (12 women), 6 part-time/adjunct. *Students:* 12 full-time (8 women), 16 part-time (14 women); includes 3 minority (2 Black or African American, non-Hispanic/Latino; 1 Hispanic/Latino), 5 international. Average age 37. 47 applicants, 32% accepted, 4 enrolled. In 2019, 10 master's, 1 doctorate, 3 other advanced degrees awarded. Terminal master's awarded for partial completion of doctoral program. *Degree requirements:* For master's, comprehensive exam (for some programs), thesis (for some programs); for doctorate, comprehensive exam, thesis/dissertation, applied internship experience. *Entrance requirements:* For master's, GRE (for applied cognitive science and human factors program only), statement of purpose, personal statement, official transcripts, 3 letters of recommendation, resume/curriculum vitae; for doctorate, GRE, statement of purpose, personal statement, official transcripts, 3 letters of recommendation, resume/curriculum vitae. Additional exam requirements/recommendations for international students: required—TOEFL (minimum score 90 iBT), TOEFL (recommended minimum score 90 iBT) or IELTS. *Application deadline:* For fall admission, 2/1 priority date for domestic and international students. Applications are processed on a rolling basis. Application fee: $0. Electronic applications accepted. *Expenses: Tuition, area resident:* Full-time $19,206; part-time $1067 per credit. Tuition, state resident: full-time $19,206; part-time $1067 per credit. Tuition, nonresident: full-time $19,206; part-time $1067 per credit. *International tuition:* $19,206 full-time. *Required fees:* $248; $248 per unit. $124 per semester. Tuition and fees vary according to course load and program. *Financial support:* In 2019–20, 13 students received support, including 2 fellowships (averaging $16,590 per year), 5 research assistantships with tuition reimbursements available (averaging $16,590 per year), 4 teaching assistantships (averaging $16,590 per year); career-related internships or fieldwork, scholarships/grants, health care benefits, unspecified assistantships, and adjunct instructor positions also available. Financial award application deadline: 12/15; financial award applicants required to submit FAFSA. *Unit head:* Dr. Kelly S. Steelman, Interim Department Chair, 906-487-2792, Fax: 906-487-2468, E-mail: steelman@mtu.edu. *Application contact:* Dr. Kelly S. Steelman, Graduate Program Director, 906-487-2792, Fax: 906-487-2468, E-mail: steelman@mtu.edu.
Website: http://www.mtu.edu/cls/

Mississippi State University, College of Arts and Sciences, Department of Psychology, Mississippi State, MS 39762. Offers applied psychology (PhD), including clinical, cognitive science; psychology (MS). *Accreditation:* APA. *Faculty:* 18 full-time (7 women). *Students:* 37 full-time (24 women), 9 part-time (4 women); includes 8 minority (4 Black or African American, non-Hispanic/Latino; 3 Asian, non-Hispanic/Latino; 1 Hispanic/Latino). Average age 28. 79 applicants, 20% accepted, 8 enrolled. In 2019, 6 master's, 1 doctorate awarded. Terminal master's awarded for partial completion of doctoral program. *Degree requirements:* For master's, comprehensive exam, thesis; for doctorate, thesis/dissertation, qualifying exam, comprehensive written and oral exam. *Entrance requirements:* For master's, GRE General Test, minimum GPA of 2.75 on last two years of undergraduate courses; for doctorate, GRE General Test, proficiency in at least 1 computer language, minimum GPA of 3.0. Additional exam requirements/recommendations for international students: required—TOEFL (minimum score 477 paper-based; 53 iBT); recommended—IELTS (minimum score 4.5). *Application deadline:* For fall admission, 4/1 priority date for domestic students, 5/1 for international students; for spring admission, 11/1 priority date for domestic students, 9/1 for international students. Applications are processed on a rolling basis. Application fee: $60 ($80 for international students). Electronic applications accepted. *Expenses:*

Tuition, area resident: Full-time $8880; part-time $456 per credit hour. Tuition, state resident: full-time $8880. Tuition, nonresident: full-time $23,840; part-time $1236 per credit hour. *Required fees:* $110; $11.12 per credit hour. Tuition and fees vary according to course load. *Financial support:* In 2019–20, 6 research assistantships with full tuition reimbursements (averaging $13,607 per year), 28 teaching assistantships with full tuition reimbursements (averaging $11,864 per year) were awarded; career-related internships or fieldwork, Federal Work-Study, institutionally sponsored loans, scholarships/grants, and unspecified assistantships also available. Financial award application deadline: 4/1; financial award applicants required to submit FAFSA. *Unit head:* Dr. Mitchell E. Berman, Professor and Head, 662-325-3202, Fax: 662-325-7212, E-mail: mberman@psychology.msstate.edu. *Application contact:* Angie Campbell, Admissions and Enrollment Assistant, 662-325-9514, E-mail: acampbell@grad.msstate.edu.
Website: http://www.psychology.msstate.edu/

The New School, The New School for Social Research, Department of Psychology, New York, NY 10011. Offers clinical psychology (PhD); cognitive, social, and developmental psychology (PhD); psychology (MA). *Accreditation:* APA (one or more programs are accredited). *Program availability:* Part-time. *Faculty:* 17 full-time (9 women), 8 part-time/adjunct (2 women). *Students:* 173 full-time (135 women), 32 part-time (28 women); includes 36 minority (8 Black or African American, non-Hispanic/Latino; 8 Asian, non-Hispanic/Latino; 17 Hispanic/Latino; 1 Native Hawaiian or other Pacific Islander, non-Hispanic/Latino; 2 Two or more races, non-Hispanic/Latino), 42 international. Average age 29. 217 applicants, 85% accepted, 58 enrolled. In 2019, 75 master's, 14 doctorates awarded. Terminal master's awarded for partial completion of doctoral program. *Degree requirements:* For master's, comprehensive exam, thesis (for some programs); for doctorate, comprehensive exam, thesis/dissertation. *Entrance requirements:* For master's, GRE, letters of recommendation, writing sample, essays, transcripts; for doctorate, letters of recommendation, writing sample, essays, transcripts. Additional exam requirements/recommendations for international students: required—TOEFL (minimum score 100 iBT), IELTS (minimum score 7), PTE (minimum score 68). *Application deadline:* For fall admission, 1/5 priority date for domestic and international students; for spring admission, 10/15 priority date for domestic and international students. Applications are processed on a rolling basis. Application fee: $50. Electronic applications accepted. *Expenses:* 2260 per credit. *Financial support:* In 2019–20, 191 students received support, including 21 fellowships with full and partial tuition reimbursements available (averaging $6,560 per year), 43 research assistantships (averaging $5,556 per year), 52 teaching assistantships with full and partial tuition reimbursements available (averaging $7,423 per year); career-related internships or fieldwork, Federal Work-Study, scholarships/grants, and tuition waivers (full and partial) also available. Support available to part-time students. Financial award application deadline: 2/1; financial award applicants required to submit FAFSA. *Unit head:* Dr. Howard Steele, Department Chair, 212-2295727 Ext. 3118, E-mail: steeleh@newschool.edu. *Application contact:* Merida Gasbarro, Director of Graduate Admission, 212-229-5600 Ext. 1108, E-mail: escandom@newschool.edu.
Website: https://www.newschool.edu/nssr/psychology/

New York University, Graduate School of Arts and Science, Department of Psychology, New York, NY 10012-1019. Offers cognition and perception (PhD); general psychology (MA); industrial/organizational psychology (MA); psychotherapy and psychoanalysis (Advanced Certificate); social psychology (PhD). *Program availability:* Part-time. Terminal master's awarded for partial completion of doctoral program. *Degree requirements:* For master's, comprehensive exam, thesis or alternative; for doctorate, thesis/dissertation. *Entrance requirements:* For master's and doctorate, GRE General Test. Additional exam requirements/recommendations for international students: required—TOEFL, IELTS.

North Carolina State University, Graduate School, College of Humanities and Social Sciences, Department of Psychology, Raleigh, NC 27695. Offers applied social and community psychology (PhD); human factors and applied cognition (PhD); industrial/organizational psychology (PhD); lifespan developmental psychology (PhD); school psychology (PhD). *Accreditation:* APA. *Degree requirements:* For doctorate, comprehensive exam, thesis/dissertation. *Entrance requirements:* For doctorate, GRE General Test, GRE Subject Test (industrial/organizational psychology), MAT (recommended), minimum GPA of 3.0 in major. Electronic applications accepted.

North Dakota State University, College of Graduate and Interdisciplinary Studies, College of Science and Mathematics, Department of Psychology, Fargo, ND 58102. Offers clinical psychology (MS); health and social psychology (PhD); psychological clinical science (PhD); psychology (MS); visual and cognitive neuroscience (PhD). *Entrance requirements:* Additional exam requirements/recommendations for international students: required—TOEFL. Electronic applications accepted. Tuition and fees vary according to program and reciprocity agreements.

Northwestern University, The Graduate School, Judd A. and Marjorie Weinberg College of Arts and Sciences, Department of Psychology, Evanston, IL 60208. Offers brain, behavior and cognition (PhD); clinical psychology (PhD); cognitive psychology (PhD); personality psychology (PhD); social psychology (PhD); JD/PhD. *Accreditation:* APA (one or more programs are accredited). *Program availability:* Part-time. *Degree requirements:* For doctorate, thesis/dissertation. *Entrance requirements:* For doctorate, GRE General Test, GRE Subject Test. Additional exam requirements/recommendations for international students: required—TOEFL. Electronic applications accepted.

The Ohio State University, Graduate School, College of Arts and Sciences, Division of Social and Behavioral Sciences, Department of Psychology, Columbus, OH 43210. Offers behavioral neuroscience (PhD); clinical psychology (PhD); cognitive psychology (PhD); developmental psychology (PhD); intellectual and developmental disabilities psychology (PhD); quantitative psychology (PhD); social psychology (PhD). *Accreditation:* APA. *Entrance requirements:* For doctorate, GRE General Test. Additional exam requirements/recommendations for international students: required—TOEFL (minimum score 600 paper-based; 100 iBT); recommended—IELTS (minimum score 8). Electronic applications accepted.

Oregon State University, College of Liberal Arts, Program in Psychology, Corvallis, OR 97331. Offers applied cognition (MS, PhD); engineering psychology (MS, PhD); health psychology (MS, PhD).

Purdue University, Graduate School, College of Health and Human Sciences, Department of Psychological Sciences, West Lafayette, IN 47907. Offers behavioral neuroscience (PhD); clinical psychology (PhD); cognitive psychology (PhD); industrial/organizational psychology (PhD); mathematical and computational cognitive science (PhD). *Accreditation:* APA. *Faculty:* 43 full-time (17 women), 2 part-time/adjunct (both women). *Students:* 69 full-time (55 women), 4 part-time (2 women); includes 18 minority (2 Black or African American, non-Hispanic/Latino; 2 Asian, non-Hispanic/Latino; 11 Hispanic/Latino; 3 Two or more races, non-Hispanic/Latino), 19 international. Average age 28. 314 applicants, 15% accepted, 28 enrolled. In 2019, 12 doctorates awarded. Terminal master's awarded for partial completion of doctoral program. *Degree requirements:* For doctorate, thesis/dissertation. *Entrance requirements:* For doctorate, GRE General Test, minimum undergraduate GPA of 3.0 or equivalent. Additional exam requirements/recommendations for international students: required—TOEFL (minimum score 550 paper-based; 77 iBT); recommended—TWE. *Application deadline:* For fall admission, 12/3 for domestic and international students. Applications are processed on a rolling basis. Application fee: $60 ($75 for international students). Electronic applications accepted. *Financial support:* Fellowships with partial tuition reimbursements, research assistantships with partial tuition reimbursements, teaching assistantships with partial tuition reimbursements, and career-related internships or fieldwork available. Support available to part-time students. Financial award applicants required to submit FAFSA. *Unit head:* Dr. Jefferey D. Karpicke, Head, 765-494-6061, E-mail: karpicke@purdue.edu. *Application contact:* Nancy A. O'Brien, Graduate Contact, 765-494-6067, E-mail: nobrien@psych.pardue.edu.
Website: http://www.psych.purdue.edu/

Queen's University at Kingston, School of Graduate Studies, Faculty of Arts and Science, Department of Psychology, Kingston, ON K7L 3N6, Canada. Offers brain behavior and cognitive science (MA, PhD); clinical psychology (MA, PhD); developmental psychology (MA, PhD); social personality psychology (MA, PhD). *Degree requirements:* For master's, thesis; for doctorate, comprehensive exam, thesis/dissertation. *Entrance requirements:* For master's and doctorate, GRE General Test. Additional exam requirements/recommendations for international students: required—TOEFL.

Rensselaer Polytechnic Institute, Graduate School, School of Humanities, Arts, and Social Sciences, Program in Cognitive Science, Troy, NY 12180-3590. Offers PhD. *Faculty:* 21 full-time (5 women), 2 part-time/adjunct (0 women). *Students:* 22 full-time (9 women); includes 6 minority (2 Asian, non-Hispanic/Latino; 1 Hispanic/Latino; 3 Two or more races, non-Hispanic/Latino), 8 international. Average age 27. 15 applicants, 33% accepted, 2 enrolled. In 2019, 5 doctorates awarded. *Degree requirements:* For doctorate, thesis/dissertation. *Entrance requirements:* For doctorate, GRE. Additional exam requirements/recommendations for international students: required—TOEFL (minimum score 600 paper-based; 100 iBT), IELTS (minimum score 7), PTE (minimum score 68). *Application deadline:* For fall admission, 1/1 priority date for domestic and international students. Applications are processed on a rolling basis. Application fee: $75. Electronic applications accepted. *Financial support:* In 2019–20, research assistantships (averaging $23,000 per year), teaching assistantships (averaging $23,000 per year) were awarded; fellowships also available. Financial award application deadline: 1/1. *Unit head:* Dr. Wayne Gray, Graduate Program Director, 518-276-3315, E-mail: grayw@rpi.edu. *Application contact:* Jarron Decker, Director of Graduate Admissions, 518-276-6216, Fax: 518-276-4072, E-mail: gradadmissions@rpi.edu.
Website: http://www.cogsci.rpi.edu/pl/phd-cognitive-science

Rice University, Graduate Programs, School of Social Sciences, Department of Psychology, Houston, TX 77251-1892. Offers cognitive sciences (MA, PhD); industrial-organizational/social psychology (MA, PhD); psychology (MA, PhD). Terminal master's awarded for partial completion of doctoral program. *Degree requirements:* For master's, thesis; for doctorate, thesis/dissertation. *Entrance requirements:* For doctorate, GRE General Test, minimum GPA of 3.0. Additional exam requirements/recommendations for international students: required—TOEFL. Electronic applications accepted.

Rochester Institute of Technology, Graduate Enrollment Services, College of Liberal Arts, Psychology Department, Advanced Certificate Program in Engineering Psychology, Rochester, NY 14623-5603. Offers Advanced Certificate. *Program availability:* Part-time. *Entrance requirements:* For degree, minimum GPA of 3.0 (recommended). Additional exam requirements/recommendations for international students: required—TOEFL (minimum score 550 paper-based; 79 iBT), IELTS (minimum score 6.5), PTE (minimum score 58). Electronic applications accepted.

Rutgers University - Newark, Graduate School, Program in Psychology, Newark, NJ 07102. Offers cognitive neuroscience (PhD); cognitive science (PhD); perception (PhD); psychobiology (PhD); social cognition (PhD). *Degree requirements:* For doctorate, comprehensive exam, thesis/dissertation. *Entrance requirements:* For doctorate, GRE General Test, GRE Subject Test, minimum undergraduate B average. Electronic applications accepted.

Rutgers University - New Brunswick, Graduate School-New Brunswick, Program in Psychology, Piscataway, NJ 08854-8097. Offers behavioral neuroscience (PhD); clinical psychology (PhD); cognitive psychology (PhD); interdisciplinary health psychology (PhD); social psychology (PhD). *Accreditation:* APA. *Degree requirements:* For doctorate, comprehensive exam, thesis/dissertation. *Entrance requirements:* For doctorate, GRE General Test, 3 letters of recommendation. Additional exam requirements/recommendations for international students: required—TOEFL (minimum score 577 paper-based). Electronic applications accepted.

Stony Brook University, State University of New York, Graduate School, College of Arts and Sciences, Department of Psychology, Program in Cognitive Psychology, Stony Brook, NY 11794. Offers PhD. *Students:* 12 full-time (9 women); includes 3 minority (1 Asian, non-Hispanic/Latino; 1 Hispanic/Latino; 1 Two or more races, non-Hispanic/Latino), 4 international. Average age 28. 39 applicants, 21% accepted, 3 enrolled. In 2019, 5 doctorates awarded. *Entrance requirements:* For doctorate, GRE General Test, GRE Subject Test. Additional exam requirements/recommendations for international students: required—TOEFL (minimum score 90 iBT). *Application deadline:* For fall admission, 1/15 for domestic students; for spring admission, 10/1 for domestic students. Application fee: $100. Electronic applications accepted. *Expenses:* Contact institution. *Financial support:* In 2019–20, 3 research assistantships, 9 teaching assistantships were awarded; fellowships also available. *Unit head:* Dr. Sheri Levy, Chair, 631-632-4355, E-mail: sheri.levy@stonybrook.edu. *Application contact:* Marilynn Wollmuth, Graduate Director, 631-632-7855, Fax: 631-632-7876, E-mail: marilyn.wollmuth@stonybrook.edu.
Website: http://www.stonybrook.edu/commcms/psychology/cognitive/overview.html

Syracuse University, College of Arts and Sciences, Department of Psychology, Syracuse, NY 13244. Offers clinical psychology (PhD); cognition, brain, and behavior (PhD); school psychology (PhD); social psychology (PhD). *Accreditation:* APA. Terminal master's awarded for partial completion of doctoral program. *Degree requirements:* For doctorate, comprehensive exam, thesis/dissertation. *Entrance requirements:* For doctorate, GRE General Test, GRE Subject Test, resume, personal statement, three letters of recommendation. Additional exam requirements/recommendations for international students: required—TOEFL (minimum score 100 iBT). Electronic applications accepted.

Texas Christian University, College of Science and Engineering, Department of Psychology, Fort Worth, TX 76129-0002. Offers developmental trauma (MS); experimental psychology (PhD), including cognition/developmental, learning, neuroscience, social. *Faculty:* 14 full-time (7 women), 1 part-time/adjunct (0 women). *Students:* 31 full-time (26 women); includes 2 minority (both Asian, non-Hispanic/Latino), 2 international. Average age 25. 52 applicants, 35% accepted, 13 enrolled. In 2019, 10 master's, 4 doctorates awarded. Terminal master's awarded for partial completion of doctoral program. *Entrance requirements:* For doctorate, GRE General Test. Additional exam requirements/recommendations for international students: required—TOEFL (minimum score 550 paper-based; 80 iBT). *Application deadline:* For fall admission, 1/1 for domestic and international students. Application fee: $60 ($0 for international students). Electronic applications accepted. Full-time tuition and fees vary

according to program. *Financial support:* In 2019–20, 23 students received support, including 23 teaching assistantships with full tuition reimbursements available (averaging $19,750 per year); scholarships/grants also available. Financial award application deadline: 1/1; financial award applicants required to submit FAFSA. *Unit head:* Dr. Anna I. Petursdottir, Chair, 817-257-7410, Fax: 817-257-7681, E-mail: a.petursdottir@tcu.edu. *Application contact:* Cindy Hayes, Administrative Assistant, 817-257-7410, Fax: 817-257-7681, E-mail: c.hayes@tcu.edu.
Website: https://psychology.tcu.edu/

Tufts University, Graduate School of Arts and Sciences, Department of Psychology, Medford, MA 02155. Offers cognitive science (PhD); psychology (MS, PhD). Terminal master's awarded for partial completion of doctoral program. *Degree requirements:* For master's, thesis; for doctorate, thesis/dissertation. *Entrance requirements:* For master's and doctorate, GRE General Test, GRE Subject Test. Additional exam requirements/recommendations for international students: required—TOEFL (minimum score 550 paper-based; 80 iBT), IELTS (minimum score 6.5). Electronic applications accepted. *Expenses:* Contact institution.

Tufts University, School of Engineering, Department of Computer Science, Medford, MA 02155. Offers bioengineering (MS), including bioinformatics; cognitive science/computer science (PhD); computer science (MS, PhD); soft material robotics (PhD). *Program availability:* Part-time. Terminal master's awarded for partial completion of doctoral program. *Entrance requirements:* For master's and doctorate, GRE General Test. Additional exam requirements/recommendations for international students: required—TOEFL (minimum score 550 paper-based; 80 iBT), IELTS (minimum score 6.5). Electronic applications accepted. *Expenses: Tuition:* Part-time $1799 per credit hour. Full-time tuition and fees vary according to degree level, program and student level. Part-time tuition and fees vary according to course load.

University at Albany, State University of New York, College of Arts and Sciences, Department of Psychology, Albany, NY 12222-0001. Offers behavioral neuroscience (PhD); clinical psychology (PhD); cognitive psychology (PhD); industrial/organizational psychology (MA, PhD); social-personality psychology (PhD). *Accreditation:* APA (one or more programs are accredited). *Program availability:* Blended/hybrid learning. *Faculty:* 31 full-time (14 women), 6 part-time/adjunct (4 women). *Students:* 68 full-time (44 women), 53 part-time (35 women); includes 30 minority (3 Black or African American, non-Hispanic/Latino; 10 Asian, non-Hispanic/Latino; 11 Hispanic/Latino; 6 Two or more races, non-Hispanic/Latino), 9 international. 253 applicants, 21% accepted, 28 enrolled. In 2019, 22 master's, 11 doctorates awarded. *Degree requirements:* For doctorate, thesis/dissertation. *Entrance requirements:* For master's, transcripts of all schools attended, statement of background and goals, departmental questionnaire, resume, names and contact information for 3 recommenders; for doctorate, GRE General Test, GRE Subject Test, transcripts of all schools attended, statement of background and goals, departmental questionnaire, resume, names and contact information for 3 recommenders. Additional exam requirements/recommendations for international students: required—TOEFL (minimum score 550 paper-based). *Application deadline:* For fall admission, 1/15 for domestic and international students; for spring admission, 11/15 for domestic students. Application fee: $75. Electronic applications accepted. *Expenses: Tuition, area resident:* Full-time $11,530; part-time $480 per credit hour. Tuition, nonresident: full-time $23,530; part-time $980 per credit hour. *International tuition:* $23,530 full-time. *Required fees:* $2185; $96 per credit hour. Part-time tuition and fees vary according to course load and program. *Financial support:* Fellowships, research assistantships, teaching assistantships, and career-related internships or fieldwork available. Financial award application deadline: 2/1. *Unit head:* Christine K. Wagner, Chair, 518-442-4820, Fax: 518-442-4867, E-mail: cwagner@albany.edu. *Application contact:* Michael DeRensis, Director, Graduate Admissions, 518-442-3980, Fax: 518-442-3922, E-mail: graduate@albany.edu.
Website: https://www.albany.edu/psychology/

The University of British Columbia, Faculty of Arts, Department of Psychology, Vancouver, BC V6T 1Z4, Canada. Offers behavioral neuroscience (MA, PhD); clinical psychology (MA, PhD); cognitive science (MA, PhD); developmental psychology (MA, PhD); health psychology (MA, PhD); quantitative methods (MA, PhD); social/personality psychology (MA, PhD). *Accreditation:* APA (one or more programs are accredited). Terminal master's awarded for partial completion of doctoral program. *Degree requirements:* For master's, thesis; for doctorate, comprehensive exam, thesis/dissertation. *Entrance requirements:* For master's and doctorate, GRE General Test. Additional exam requirements/recommendations for international students: required—TOEFL. Electronic applications accepted. *Expenses:* Contact institution.

University of California, Merced, Graduate Division, School of Social Sciences, Humanities and Arts, Merced, CA 95343. Offers cognitive and information sciences (PhD); interdisciplinary humanities (MA, PhD); psychological sciences (MA, PhD); social sciences (MA, PhD); sociology (MA, PhD). *Faculty:* 113 full-time (57 women), 2 part-time/adjunct (0 women). *Students:* 194 full-time (128 women), 1 (woman) part-time; includes 81 minority (5 Black or African American, non-Hispanic/Latino; 18 Asian, non-Hispanic/Latino; 54 Hispanic/Latino; 4 Two or more races, non-Hispanic/Latino), 39 international. Average age 31. 218 applicants, 48% accepted, 36 enrolled. In 2019, 12 master's, 23 doctorates awarded. Terminal master's awarded for partial completion of doctoral program. *Degree requirements:* For master's, variable foreign language requirement, comprehensive exam, thesis or alternative, oral defense; for doctorate, variable foreign language requirement, comprehensive exam, thesis/dissertation, oral defense. *Entrance requirements:* For master's and doctorate, GRE. Additional exam requirements/recommendations for international students: required—TOEFL (minimum score 550 paper-based; 80 iBT); recommended—IELTS (minimum score 6.5). *Application deadline:* For fall admission, 1/15 for domestic and international students. Application fee: $105 ($125 for international students). Electronic applications accepted. *Expenses: Tuition, area resident:* Full-time $11,442; part-time $5721 per semester. Tuition, state resident: full-time $11,442; part-time $5721 per semester. Tuition, nonresident: full-time $26,544; part-time $13,272 per semester. *International tuition:* $26,544 full-time. *Required fees:* $564 per semester. *Financial support:* In 2019–20, 183 students received support, including 7 fellowships with full tuition reimbursements available (averaging $22,005 per year), 5 research assistantships with full tuition reimbursements available (averaging $21,420 per year), 171 teaching assistantships with full tuition reimbursements available (averaging $21,911 per year); scholarships/grants, traineeships, and health care benefits also available. *Unit head:* Dr. Jeffrey Gilger, Dean, 209-228-4343, E-mail: jgilger@ucmerced.edu. *Application contact:* Tsu Ya, Director of Admissions and Academic Services, 209-228-4521, Fax: 209-228-6906, E-mail: tya@ucmerced.edu.

University of California, San Diego, Graduate Division, Department of Cognitive Science, La Jolla, CA 92093. Offers cognitive science (PhD). *Students:* 57 full-time (28 women), 1 part-time (0 women). 198 applicants, 12% accepted, 13 enrolled. In 2019, 4 doctorates awarded. *Degree requirements:* For doctorate, one foreign language, thesis/dissertation, 1-quarter teaching assistantship for each academic year in residence. *Entrance requirements:* For doctorate, GRE General Test, minimum GPA of 3.0, letters of recommendation, statement of purpose. Additional exam requirements/recommendations for international students: required—TOEFL (minimum score 550 paper-based; 80 iBT), IELTS (minimum score 7), PTE. *Application deadline:* For fall admission, 12/6 for domestic students. Application fee: $105 ($125 for international students). Electronic applications accepted. *Financial support:* Fellowships, research assistantships, teaching assistantships, scholarships/grants, and unspecified assistantships available. Financial award applicants required to submit FAFSA. *Unit head:* Douglas Nitz, Chair, 858-653-1132, E-mail: dnitz@ucsd.edu. *Application contact:* Ethel Lu, Graduate Coordinator, 858-534-7141, E-mail: cogsphd@ucsd.edu.
Website: http://www.cogsci.ucsd.edu

University of California, Santa Barbara, Graduate Division, College of Engineering, Department of Computer Science, Santa Barbara, CA 93106-5110. Offers computer science (MS, PhD), including cognitive science (PhD), computational science and engineering (PhD), technology and society (PhD). Terminal master's awarded for partial completion of doctoral program. *Degree requirements:* For master's, comprehensive exam (for some programs), thesis (for some programs), project (for some programs); for doctorate, thesis/dissertation. *Entrance requirements:* For master's and doctorate, GRE. Additional exam requirements/recommendations for international students: required—TOEFL (minimum score 600 paper-based; 100 iBT), IELTS (minimum score 7). Electronic applications accepted.

University of California, Santa Barbara, Graduate Division, College of Letters and Sciences, Division of Humanities and Fine Arts, Department of Religious Studies, Santa Barbara, CA 93106-3130. Offers ancient Mediterranean studies (PhD); cognitive science (PhD); European medieval studies (PhD); feminist studies (PhD); global studies (PhD); religious studies (MA, PhD); translation studies (PhD); MA/PhD. Terminal master's awarded for partial completion of doctoral program. *Degree requirements:* For master's, one foreign language, comprehensive exam (for some programs), thesis (for some programs); for doctorate, 2 foreign languages, thesis/dissertation, methodology. *Entrance requirements:* For master's and doctorate, GRE General Test. Additional exam requirements/recommendations for international students: required—TOEFL (minimum score 550 paper-based; 80 iBT), IELTS (minimum score 7). Electronic applications accepted.

University of California, Santa Barbara, Graduate Division, College of Letters and Sciences, Division of Mathematics, Life, and Physical Sciences, Department of Geography, Santa Barbara, CA 93106-4060. Offers cognitive science (PhD); geography (MA, PhD); global studies (PhD); quantitative methods in the social sciences (PhD); technology and society (PhD); transportation (PhD); MA/PhD. Terminal master's awarded for partial completion of doctoral program. *Degree requirements:* For master's, comprehensive exam (for some programs), thesis or alternative; for doctorate, comprehensive exam, thesis/dissertation, 1 quarter of teaching assistantship. *Entrance requirements:* For master's and doctorate, GRE (minimum combined verbal and quantitative scores above 1100 in old scoring system or 301 in new scoring system). Additional exam requirements/recommendations for international students: required—TOEFL (minimum score 550 paper-based; 80 iBT), IELTS (minimum score 7). Electronic applications accepted.

University of California, Santa Barbara, Graduate Division, College of Letters and Sciences, Division of Mathematics, Life, and Physical Sciences, Department of Psychological and Brain Sciences, Santa Barbara, CA 93106-9660. Offers cognitive science (PhD); psychology (PhD); quantitative methods in the social sciences (PhD); technology and society (PhD). Terminal master's awarded for partial completion of doctoral program. *Degree requirements:* For doctorate, comprehensive exam, thesis/dissertation, teaching assistant training, progress report, papers, mini-convention presentation, 1 quarter of student teaching or teaching assistant class with section lab, continued participation in research and weekly area meetings. *Entrance requirements:* For doctorate, GRE General Test. Additional exam requirements/recommendations for international students: required—TOEFL (minimum score 550 paper-based; 80 iBT) or IELTS (minimum score 7). Electronic applications accepted.

University of California, Santa Barbara, Graduate Division, College of Letters and Sciences, Division of Social Sciences, Department of Communication, Santa Barbara, CA 93106-4020. Offers cognitive science (PhD); communication (PhD); feminist studies (PhD); language, interaction and social organization (PhD); quantitative methods in the social sciences (PhD); society and technology (PhD); MA/PhD. Terminal master's awarded for partial completion of doctoral program. *Degree requirements:* For doctorate, comprehensive exam, thesis/dissertation. *Entrance requirements:* For doctorate, GRE. Additional exam requirements/recommendations for international students: required—TOEFL (minimum score 80 iBT), IELTS (minimum score 7). Electronic applications accepted.

University of Central Florida, College of Sciences, Department of Psychology, Program in Human Factors and Cognitive Psychology, Orlando, FL 32816. Offers human factors and cognitive psychology (PhD). *Students:* 31 full-time (18 women), 3 part-time (all women); includes 12 minority (1 American Indian or Alaska Native, non-Hispanic/Latino; 3 Asian, non-Hispanic/Latino; 8 Hispanic/Latino), 1 international. Average age 29. 35 applicants, 14% accepted, 4 enrolled. In 2019, 3 doctorates awarded. *Degree requirements:* For doctorate, thesis/dissertation, departmental candidacy exam. *Entrance requirements:* For doctorate, GRE General Test, degree in psychology or allied area, resume or curriculum vitae, personal statement, letters of recommendation, evidence of successful completion of undergraduate courses in statistics and general areas of experimental psychology. Additional exam requirements/recommendations for international students: required—TOEFL. *Application deadline:* For fall admission, 1/1 for domestic students. Application fee: $30. Electronic applications accepted. *Financial support:* In 2019–20, 29 students received support, including 15 fellowships with partial tuition reimbursements available (averaging $6,803 per year), 7 research assistantships with partial tuition reimbursements available (averaging $6,863 per year), 22 teaching assistantships with partial tuition reimbursements available (averaging $8,850 per year); career-related internships or fieldwork, Federal Work-Study, institutionally sponsored loans, health care benefits, tuition waivers (partial), and unspecified assistantships also available. Financial award application deadline: 3/1; financial award applicants required to submit FAFSA. *Unit head:* Dr. James Szalma, Program Director, 407-823-0920, E-mail: james.szalma@ucf.edu. *Application contact:* Associate Director, Graduate Admissions, 407-823-2766, Fax: 407-823-6442, E-mail: gradadmissions@ucf.edu.
Website: http://psychology.cos.ucf.edu/graduate/

University of Connecticut, Graduate School, College of Liberal Arts and Sciences, Department of Psychological Sciences, Storrs, CT 06269. Offers behavioral neuroscience (PhD); biopsychology (PhD); clinical psychology (MA, PhD); cognition and instruction (PhD); developmental psychology (MA, PhD); ecological psychology (PhD); experimental psychology (PhD); general psychology (MA, PhD); industrial/organizational psychology (PhD); language and cognition (PhD); neuroscience (PhD); social psychology (MA, PhD). *Accreditation:* APA. Terminal master's awarded for partial completion of doctoral program. *Degree requirements:* For master's, comprehensive exam; for doctorate, thesis/dissertation. *Entrance requirements:* For master's and doctorate, GRE General Test, GRE Subject Test. Additional exam requirements/recommendations for international students: required—TOEFL (minimum score 550 paper-based). Electronic applications accepted.

University of Connecticut, Graduate School, Neag School of Education, Department of Educational Psychology, Cognition, Instruction, and Learning Technology Program, Storrs, CT 06269. Offers MA, PhD. *Degree requirements:* For master's, comprehensive exam; for doctorate, thesis/dissertation. *Entrance requirements:* For doctorate, GRE General Test. Additional exam requirements/recommendations for international students: required—TOEFL (minimum score 550 paper-based). Electronic applications accepted.

University of Delaware, College of Arts and Sciences, Department of Linguistics and Cognitive Science, Newark, DE 19716. Offers linguistics (PhD); linguistics and cognitive science (MA). *Degree requirements:* For doctorate, one foreign language, comprehensive exam, thesis/dissertation, publishable research papers. *Entrance requirements:* For master's, GRE General Test; for doctorate, GRE General Test, writing sample. Additional exam requirements/recommendations for international students: required—TOEFL (minimum score 600 paper-based). Electronic applications accepted.

University of Delaware, College of Arts and Sciences, Department of Psychology, Newark, DE 19716. Offers behavioral neuroscience (PhD); clinical psychology (PhD); cognitive psychology (PhD); social psychology (PhD). *Accreditation:* APA. *Degree requirements:* For doctorate, thesis/dissertation. *Entrance requirements:* For doctorate, GRE General Test. Additional exam requirements/recommendations for international students: required—TOEFL (minimum score 600 paper-based). Electronic applications accepted.

University of Guelph, Office of Graduate and Postdoctoral Studies, College of Social and Applied Human Sciences, Department of Psychology, Guelph, ON N1G 2W1, Canada. Offers applied social psychology (MA, PhD); clinical psychology: applied development emphasis (PhD); clinical psychology: applied developmental emphasis (MA); industrial/organizational psychology (MA, PhD); neuroscience and applied cognitive science (MA, PhD). *Degree requirements:* For master's, thesis; for doctorate, comprehensive exam, thesis/dissertation. *Entrance requirements:* For master's, GRE General Test, GRE Subject Test, minimum B+ average during previous 2 years of course work; for doctorate, GRE General Test, GRE Subject Test, minimum A- average. Additional exam requirements/recommendations for international students: required—TOEFL (minimum score 89 iBT). Electronic applications accepted.

The University of Kansas, Graduate Studies, College of Liberal Arts and Sciences, Department of Psychology, Lawrence, KS 66045. Offers clinical psychology (MA, PhD); cognitive and brain sciences (MA, PhD); developmental psychology (MA, PhD); quantitative psychology (PhD); social psychology (MA, PhD). *Accreditation:* APA (one or more programs are accredited). *Program availability:* Part-time. *Students:* 72 full-time (51 women), 1 (woman) part-time; includes 16 minority (6 Black or African American, non-Hispanic/Latino; 3 Asian, non-Hispanic/Latino; 1 Hispanic/Latino; 6 Two or more races, non-Hispanic/Latino), 9 international. Average age 27. 343 applicants, 9% accepted, 17 enrolled. In 2019, 15 master's, 14 doctorates awarded. Terminal master's awarded for partial completion of doctoral program. *Entrance requirements:* For doctorate, GRE General Test, three letters of recommendation, resume/curriculum vitae, statement of purpose/personal statement, writing sample. Additional exam requirements/recommendations for international students: required—TOEFL, IELTS. *Application deadline:* For fall admission, 12/1 for domestic and international students. Application fee: $65 ($85 for international students). Electronic applications accepted. *Expenses:* Tuition, state resident: full-time $9989. Tuition, nonresident: full-time $23,950. *International tuition:* $23,950 full-time. *Required fees:* $984; $81.99 per credit hour. Tuition and fees vary according to course load, campus/location and program. *Financial support:* Fellowships, research assistantships, teaching assistantships, career-related internships or fieldwork, Federal Work-Study, scholarships/grants, health care benefits, and unspecified assistantships available. Financial award application deadline: 12/1; financial award applicants required to submit FAFSA. *Unit head:* Michael Vitevitch, Chair, 785-864-9312, E-mail: mvitevit@ku.edu. *Application contact:* Kirsten Hermreck, Graduate Admissions Contact, 785-864-4195, E-mail: psycgrad@ku.edu. Website: http://www.psych.ku.edu/

University of Louisville, Graduate School, College of Arts and Sciences, Department of Psychological and Brain Sciences, Louisville, KY 40292-0001. Offers clinical psychology (PhD); experimental psychology (PhD), including cognition and development, vision and hearing. *Accreditation:* APA. *Program availability:* Part-time. *Faculty:* 24 full-time (14 women), 9 part-time/adjunct (5 women). *Students:* 50 full-time (42 women), 1 (woman) part-time; includes 5 minority (1 Black or African American, non-Hispanic/Latino; 2 Hispanic/Latino; 2 Two or more races, non-Hispanic/Latino), 6 international. Average age 29. 144 applicants, 1% accepted, 2 enrolled.. In 2019, 14 doctorates awarded. *Degree requirements:* For doctorate, comprehensive exam, thesis/ dissertation, coursework; internship for clinical. *Entrance requirements:* For doctorate, GRE General Test, Three letters of reference, official transcripts. Additional exam requirements/recommendations for international students: required—TOEFL (minimum score 550 paper-based; 79 iBT), IELTS can be used in place of TOEFL; recommended—IELTS (minimum score 6.5). *Application deadline:* For fall admission, 12/1 for domestic and international students. Applications are processed on a rolling basis. Application fee: $65. Electronic applications accepted. *Expenses: Tuition, area resident:* Full-time $13,000; part-time $723 per credit hour. Tuition, state resident: full-time $13,000; part-time $723 per credit hour. Tuition, nonresident: full-time $27,114; part-time $1507 per credit hour. *International tuition:* $27,114 full-time. *Required fees:* $196. Tuition and fees vary according to program and reciprocity agreements. *Financial support:* In 2019–20, 49 students received support, including 8 fellowships with full tuition reimbursements available (averaging $22,000 per year), 3 research assistantships with full tuition reimbursements available (averaging $22,000 per year), 30 teaching assistantships with full tuition reimbursements available (averaging $22,000 per year); scholarships/grants, health care benefits, and unspecified assistantships also available. Financial award application deadline: 12/1. *Unit head:* Dr. Benjamin Mast, Professor and Chair, 502-852-3280, Fax: 502-852-8904, E-mail: b.mast@louisville.edu. *Application contact:* Maggie Leahy, Administrative Assistant, 502-852-4364, Fax: 502-852-8904, E-mail: maggie.leahy@louisville.edu. Website: http://louisville.edu/psychology

University of Maryland, Baltimore County, The Graduate School, College of Natural and Mathematical Sciences, Department of Biological Sciences, Program in Neuroscience and Cognitive Sciences, Baltimore, MD 21250. Offers PhD. *Faculty:* 6 full-time (3 women). *Students:* 6 full-time (4 women); includes 3 minority (1 Black or African American, non-Hispanic/Latino; 2 Asian, non-Hispanic/Latino). Average age 25. 7 applicants. *Degree requirements:* For doctorate, thesis/dissertation. *Entrance requirements:* For doctorate, GRE General Test, minimum GPA of 3.0. Additional exam requirements/recommendations for international students: required—TOEFL (minimum score 80 iBT), IELTS (minimum score 6.5). *Application deadline:* For fall admission, 4/15 priority date for domestic and international students. Application fee: $50. Electronic applications accepted. *Expenses: Tuition, area resident:* Full-time $659. Tuition, state resident: full-time $659. Tuition, nonresident: full-time $1132. *International tuition:* $1132 full-time. *Required fees:* $140; $140 per credit hour. *Financial support:* In 2019–20, 5 students received support, including 1 research assistantship with full tuition reimbursement available (averaging $24,600 per year), 4 teaching assistantships with full tuition reimbursements available (averaging $23,518 per year); health care benefits and unspecified assistantships also available. *Unit head:* Dr. Michelle Starz-Gaiano, Director, 410-455-2217, Fax: 410-455-3875, E-mail: biograd@umbc.edu. *Application contact:* Brandy Darcey, Graduate Program Coordinator, 410-455-3669, E-mail: bdarcey@umbc.edu. Website: http://biology.umbc.edu

University of Maryland, College Park, Academic Affairs, College of Behavioral and Social Sciences, Program in Neurosciences and Cognitive Sciences, College Park, MD 20742. Offers PhD. *Degree requirements:* For doctorate, comprehensive exam, thesis/ dissertation. *Entrance requirements:* For doctorate, GRE General Test, 3 letters of recommendation. Additional exam requirements/recommendations for international students: required—TOEFL. Electronic applications accepted.

University of Massachusetts Amherst, Graduate School, College of Natural Sciences, Department of Psychological and Brain Sciences, Amherst, MA 01003. Offers clinical psychology (MS, PhD); cognitive psychology (MS, PhD); developmental science (MS, PhD); psychology of peace and violence (MS, PhD); social psychology (MS, PhD). *Accreditation:* APA (one or more programs are accredited). Terminal master's awarded for partial completion of doctoral program. *Degree requirements:* For master's, thesis; for doctorate, comprehensive exam, thesis/dissertation. *Entrance requirements:* For master's and doctorate, GRE General Test, 3 letters of recommendation. Additional exam requirements/recommendations for international students: required—TOEFL (minimum score 550 paper-based; 80 iBT), IELTS (minimum score 6.5). Electronic applications accepted.

University of Massachusetts Amherst, Graduate School, Interdisciplinary Programs, Program in Neuroscience and Behavior, Amherst, MA 01003. Offers animal behavior and learning (PhD); molecular and cellular neuroscience (PhD); neural and behavioral development (PhD); neuroendocrinology (PhD); neuroscience and behavior (MS); sensorimotor, cognitive, and computational neuroscience (PhD). Terminal master's awarded for partial completion of doctoral program. *Degree requirements:* For master's, thesis or alternative; for doctorate, comprehensive exam, thesis/dissertation. *Entrance requirements:* For master's, GRE General Test; for doctorate, GRE General Test; GRE Subject Test in psychology, biology, or mathematics (recommended). Additional exam requirements/recommendations for international students: required—TOEFL (minimum score 550 paper-based; 80 iBT), IELTS (minimum score 6.5). Electronic applications accepted.

University of Massachusetts Boston, College of Liberal Arts, Program in Developmental and Brain Sciences, Boston, MA 02125-3393. Offers MA. *Entrance requirements:* Additional exam requirements/recommendations for international students: required—TOEFL; recommended—IELTS. Electronic applications accepted.

University of Michigan, Rackham Graduate School, College of Literature, Science, and the Arts, Department of Psychology, Ann Arbor, MI 48109. Offers biopsychology (PhD); clinical science (PhD); cognition and cognitive neuroscience (PhD); developmental psychology (PhD); personality and social contexts (PhD); social psychology (PhD). *Accreditation:* APA. Terminal master's awarded for partial completion of doctoral program. *Degree requirements:* For doctorate, comprehensive exam, thesis/ dissertation, oral defense of dissertation, preliminary exam. *Entrance requirements:* For doctorate, GRE (Biopsychology, Cognition and Cognitive Neuroscience, Developmental, Social, and Clinical); GRE Subject Test also strongly recommended (Clinical); GRE not required (Personality and Social Contexts). Additional exam requirements/ recommendations for international students: required—TOEFL. Electronic applications accepted.

University of Minnesota, Twin Cities Campus, Graduate School, College of Liberal Arts, Department of Psychology, Program in Cognitive and Biological Psychology, Minneapolis, MN 55455-0213. Offers PhD. *Degree requirements:* For doctorate, comprehensive exam, thesis/dissertation. *Entrance requirements:* For doctorate, GRE General Test, GRE Subject Test (recommended), 12 credits of upper-level psychology courses, including a course in statistics or psychological measurement. Additional exam requirements/recommendations for international students: required—TOEFL (minimum score 550 paper-based; 79 iBT).

University of Nebraska–Lincoln, Graduate College, College of Arts and Sciences, Department of Psychology, Lincoln, NE 68588. Offers biopsychology (PhD); clinical psychology (PhD); cognitive psychology (PhD); developmental psychology (PhD); psychology (MA); social/personality psychology (PhD); JD/MA; JD/PhD. *Accreditation:* APA (one or more programs are accredited). *Degree requirements:* For master's, thesis optional; for doctorate, comprehensive exam, thesis/dissertation. *Entrance requirements:* For master's and doctorate, GRE General Test. Additional exam requirements/recommendations for international students: required—TOEFL (minimum score 550 paper-based). Electronic applications accepted.

University of Nebraska–Lincoln, Graduate College, College of Education and Human Sciences, Department of Educational Psychology, Lincoln, NE 68588. Offers cognition, learning and development (MA); counseling psychology (MA); educational psychology (MA, Ed S); psychological studies in education (PhD), including cognition, learning and development, counseling psychology, quantitative, qualitative, and psychometric methods, school psychology; quantitative, qualitative, and psychometric methods (MA); school psychology (MA, Ed S). *Accreditation:* APA (one or more programs are accredited); NCATE. *Degree requirements:* For master's, thesis optional. *Entrance requirements:* For master's, GRE General Test. Additional exam requirements/ recommendations for international students: required—TOEFL (minimum score 500 paper-based). Electronic applications accepted.

University of Nevada, Reno, Graduate School, College of Liberal Arts, Department of Psychology, Program in Cognitive Brain Science, Reno, NV 89557. Offers MA, PhD. Terminal master's awarded for partial completion of doctoral program. *Degree requirements:* For master's, thesis optional; for doctorate, comprehensive exam, thesis/ dissertation. *Entrance requirements:* For master's, GRE General Test, minimum GPA of 2.75; for doctorate, GRE General Test, minimum GPA of 3.0. Additional exam requirements/recommendations for international students: required—TOEFL (minimum score 500 paper-based; 61 iBT), IELTS (minimum score 6). Electronic applications accepted.

University of New Mexico, Graduate Studies, College of Arts and Sciences, Program in Psychology, Albuquerque, NM 87131-2039. Offers behavioral neuroscience (PhD); clinical psychology (PhD); cognitive neuroimaging (PhD); developmental psychology (PhD); evolution (PhD); health psychology (PhD); quantitative methodology (PhD). *Accreditation:* APA. *Degree requirements:* For doctorate, comprehensive exam, thesis/ dissertation. *Entrance requirements:* For doctorate, GRE General Test, GRE Subject Test (psychology), minimum GPA of 3.0. Additional exam requirements/ recommendations for international students: required—TOEFL (minimum score 550 paper-based; 79 iBT), IELTS (minimum score 6.5). Electronic applications accepted. *Expenses:* Tuition, state resident: full-time $7633; part-time $972 per year. Tuition, nonresident: full-time $22,586; part-time $3840 per year. *International tuition:* $23,292 full-time. *Required fees:* $8608. Tuition and fees vary according to course level, course load, degree level, program and student level.

Cognitive Sciences

The University of North Carolina at Chapel Hill, Graduate School, College of Arts and Sciences, Department of Psychology, Chapel Hill, NC 27599-3270. Offers behavioral neuroscience psychology (PhD); clinical psychology (PhD); cognitive psychology (PhD); developmental psychology (PhD); quantitative psychology (PhD); social psychology (PhD). *Accreditation:* APA. *Degree requirements:* For doctorate, comprehensive exam, thesis/dissertation. *Entrance requirements:* For doctorate, GRE General Test, minimum GPA of 3.0. Additional exam requirements/recommendations for international students: required—TOEFL (minimum score 550 paper-based; 79 iBT), IELTS (minimum score 7). Electronic applications accepted.

The University of North Carolina at Charlotte, College of Liberal Arts and Sciences, Department of Psychology, Charlotte, NC 28223-0001. Offers cognitive science (Graduate Certificate); health psychology (PhD), including general; community; clinical; interdisciplinary; industrial/organizational psychology (MA); psychology (MA). *Accreditation:* APA. *Program availability:* Part-time. *Faculty:* 29 full-time (19 women), 2 part-time/adjunct (both women). *Students:* 42 full-time (35 women), 32 part-time (24 women); includes 18 minority (6 Black or African American, non-Hispanic/Latino; 4 Asian, non-Hispanic/Latino; 3 Hispanic/Latino; 5 Two or more races, non-Hispanic/Latino; 2 international. Average age 27. 164 applicants, 15% accepted, 14 enrolled. In 2019, 31 master's, 5 doctorates, 3 other advanced degrees awarded. *Degree requirements:* For master's, thesis (for some programs); for doctorate, comprehensive exam, thesis/dissertation. *Entrance requirements:* For master's, GRE, GMAT, MAT, bachelor's degree; statement of purpose addressing motivation for degree, preparation for graduate studies and impact of the degree; 2 letters of recommendation; (MA, Psychology) minimum 3.0 GPA in psychology courses; 18 credit hours of undergraduate psychology courses, undergraduate course in statistics; for doctorate, GRE and/or GMAT (Org. Science), at least 18 hours of coursework in psychology including introductory psychology and research methods, undergraduate course in statistics, transcripts of all academic work attempted since high school including evidence of the completion of a bachelor's degree, at least three references, personal statement, resume or curriculum vitae; for Graduate Certificate, enrolled and in good standing in a graduate degree program at UNC Charlotte, or have minimum GPA of 3.0 for undergraduate courses. Additional exam requirements/recommendations for international students: required—TOEFL (minimum score 557 paper-based; 83 iBT), IELTS (minimum score 6.5), TOEFL (minimum score 557 paper-based, 83 iBT) or IELTS (6.5). *Application deadline:* Applications are processed on a rolling basis. Application fee: $75. Electronic applications accepted. *Expenses:* Contact institution. *Financial support:* In 2019–20, 15 students received support, including 9 research assistantships (averaging $10,659 per year), 6 teaching assistantships (averaging $9,454 per year); fellowships, career-related internships or fieldwork, Federal Work-Study, institutionally sponsored loans, scholarships/grants, and unspecified assistantships also available. Support available to part-time students. Financial award applicants required to submit FAFSA. *Unit head:* Dr. Eric Heggestad, Chair & Associate Professor, 704-687-1338, E-mail: edhegges@uncc.edu. *Application contact:* Kathy B. Giddings, Director of Graduate Admissions, 704-687-5503, Fax: 704-687-1668, E-mail: gradadm@uncc.edu.
Website: http://psych.uncc.edu

The University of North Carolina at Greensboro, Graduate School, College of Arts and Sciences, Department of Psychology, Greensboro, NC 27412-5001. Offers clinical psychology (MA, PhD); cognitive psychology (MA, PhD); developmental psychology (MA, PhD); social psychology (MA, PhD). *Accreditation:* APA (one or more programs are accredited). Terminal master's awarded for partial completion of doctoral program. *Degree requirements:* For master's, comprehensive exam, thesis; for doctorate, one foreign language, thesis/dissertation, preliminary exam. *Entrance requirements:* For master's and doctorate, GRE General Test. Additional exam requirements/recommendations for international students: required—TOEFL. Electronic applications accepted.

University of Notre Dame, The Graduate School, College of Arts and Letters, Division of Social Sciences, Department of Psychology, Notre Dame, IN 46556. Offers cognitive psychology (PhD); counseling psychology (PhD); developmental psychology (PhD); quantitative psychology (PhD). *Accreditation:* APA. *Degree requirements:* For doctorate, comprehensive exam, thesis/dissertation, candidacy exam. *Entrance requirements:* For doctorate, GRE General Test, GRE Subject Test (strongly recommended). Additional exam requirements/recommendations for international students: required—TOEFL (minimum score 600 paper-based; 80 iBT). Electronic applications accepted.

University of Oregon, Graduate School, College of Arts and Sciences, Department of Psychology, Eugene, OR 97403. Offers clinical psychology (PhD); cognitive psychology (MA, MS, PhD); developmental psychology (MA, MS, PhD); physiological psychology (MA, MS, PhD); psychology (MA, MS, PhD); social/personality psychology (MA, MS, PhD). *Accreditation:* APA (one or more programs are accredited). Terminal master's awarded for partial completion of doctoral program. *Degree requirements:* For doctorate, thesis/dissertation. *Entrance requirements:* For master's, GRE General Test, minimum GPA of 3.0; for doctorate, GRE General Test. Additional exam requirements/recommendations for international students: required—TOEFL.

University of Rochester, School of Arts and Sciences, Department of Brain and Cognitive Sciences, Rochester, NY 14627. Offers PhD. *Faculty:* 15 full-time (2 women). *Students:* 34 full-time (14 women); includes 6 minority (3 Asian, non-Hispanic/Latino; 1 Hispanic/Latino; 2 Two or more races, non-Hispanic/Latino; 16 international. Average age 28. 63 applicants, 21% accepted, 7 enrolled. In 2019, 8 doctorates awarded. *Degree requirements:* For doctorate, thesis/dissertation, qualifying exam. *Entrance requirements:* For doctorate, GRE, two letters of recommendation, personal statement, official transcripts. Additional exam requirements/recommendations for international students: required—TOEFL (minimum score 100 iBT). *Application deadline:* For fall admission, 12/1 for domestic and international students. Application fee: $20. Electronic applications accepted. *Financial support:* In 2019–20, 31 students received support, including 1 fellowship (averaging $29,870 per year), 30 research assistantships (averaging $28,870 per year); scholarships/grants, traineeships, health care benefits, and tuition waivers (full) also available. Financial award application deadline: 12/1. *Unit head:* Duje Tadin, Professor and Chair, 585-275-8682, E-mail: dtadin@ur.rochester.edu. *Application contact:* Kathleen Corser, Graduate Program Coordinator, 585-275-1844, E-mail: kcorser@ur.rochester.edu.
Website: http://www.sas.rochester.edu/bcs/graduate/index.html

University of Southern California, Graduate School, Dana and David Dornsife College of Letters, Arts and Sciences, Department of Psychology, Los Angeles, CA 90089. Offers brain and cognitive science (PhD); clinical science (PhD); developmental psychology (PhD); human behavior (MHB); quantitative methods (PhD); social psychology (PhD). *Accreditation:* APA. *Degree requirements:* For doctorate, comprehensive exam, thesis/dissertation, one-year internship (for clinical science students). *Entrance requirements:* For doctorate, GRE. Additional exam requirements/recommendations for international students: recommended—TOEFL (minimum score 600 paper-based; 100 iBT). Electronic applications accepted.

University of South Florida, College of Arts and Sciences, Department of Psychology, Tampa, FL 33620-9951. Offers psychology (PhD), including clinical psychology, cognition, neuroscience and social psychology, industrial-organizational psychology.

Accreditation: APA. *Faculty:* 30 full-time (11 women). *Students:* 79 full-time (55 women), 12 part-time (8 women); includes 16 minority (2 Black or African American, non-Hispanic/Latino; 6 Asian, non-Hispanic/Latino; 6 Hispanic/Latino; 2 Two or more races, non-Hispanic/Latino; 8 international. Average age 28. 355 applicants, 5% accepted, 19 enrolled. In 2019, 17 doctorates awarded. *Degree requirements:* For doctorate, comprehensive exam, thesis/dissertation, internship. *Entrance requirements:* For doctorate, a GRE Score Report with a strong preference for GRE V and Q scores each at the 50th percentile or better, statement of purpose; Research Interests and Faculty Matches Form (http://psychology.usf.edu/forms/ResearchInterest.aspx); 3 letters of recommendation; GPA worksheet (http://www.grad.usf.edu/inc/linked-files/gpa.pdf). Additional exam requirements/recommendations for international students: required—TOEFL, TOEFL (minimum score 550 paper-based; 79 iBT) or IELTS (minimum score 6.5). *Application deadline:* For fall admission, 12/1 priority date for domestic and international students. Application fee: $30. Electronic applications accepted. *Expenses:* Contact institution. *Financial support:* In 2019–20, 44 students received support, including 18 research assistantships with tuition reimbursements available (averaging $14,727 per year), 57 teaching assistantships with tuition reimbursements available (averaging $14,543 per year); tuition waivers (partial) and unspecified assistantships also available. Financial award applicants required to submit FAFSA. *Unit head:* Dr. Toru Shimizu, Chairperson, 813-974-0352, Fax: 813-974-4617, E-mail: shimizu@usf.edu. *Application contact:* Dr. Sandra Schneider, Professor and Graduate Program Director, 813-974-0928, E-mail: sandra@usf.edu.
Website: http://psychology.usf.edu/

The University of Texas at Dallas, School of Behavioral and Brain Sciences, Program in Cognition and Neuroscience, Richardson, TX 75080. Offers applied cognition and neuroscience (MS); cognition and neuroscience (PhD). *Program availability:* Part-time, evening/weekend. *Faculty:* 24 full-time (4 women), 7 part-time/adjunct (4 women). *Students:* 189 full-time (113 women), 43 part-time (25 women); includes 65 minority (6 Black or African American, non-Hispanic/Latino; 1 American Indian or Alaska Native, non-Hispanic/Latino; 31 Asian, non-Hispanic/Latino; 18 Hispanic/Latino; 9 Two or more races, non-Hispanic/Latino), 54 international. Average age 28. 182 applicants, 47% accepted, 69 enrolled. In 2019, 63 master's, 5 doctorates awarded. *Degree requirements:* For master's, internship; for doctorate, thesis/dissertation. *Entrance requirements:* For master's and doctorate, GRE General Test, minimum GPA of 3.0 in upper-level coursework in field. Additional exam requirements/recommendations for international students: required—TOEFL (minimum score 550 paper-based). *Application deadline:* For fall admission, 7/15 for domestic students, 5/1 priority date for international students; for spring admission, 11/15 for domestic students, 9/1 priority date for international students. Applications are processed on a rolling basis. Application fee: $50 ($100 for international students). Electronic applications accepted. *Expenses: Tuition, area resident:* Full-time $16,504. *Tuition, state resident:* full-time $16,504. Tuition, nonresident: full-time $34,266. Tuition and fees vary according to course load. *Financial support:* In 2019–20, 75 students received support, including 2 fellowships (averaging $3,000 per year), 32 research assistantships with partial tuition reimbursements available (averaging $28,597 per year), 43 teaching assistantships with partial tuition reimbursements available (averaging $19,530 per year); career-related internships or fieldwork, Federal Work-Study, institutionally sponsored loans, scholarships/grants, and unspecified assistantships also available. Support available to part-time students. Financial award application deadline: 4/30; financial award applicants required to submit FAFSA. *Unit head:* Dr. Kristen Kennedy, Area Head, 972-883-3739, Fax: 972-883-3491, E-mail: kmk082000@utdallas.edu. *Application contact:* Dr. Theodore Price, Area Head, 972-883-4311, Fax: 972-883-3491, E-mail: theodore.price@utdallas.edu.
Website: https://bbs.utdallas.edu/degrees/cn-degrees/

University of Washington, Graduate School, College of Arts and Sciences, Department of Psychology, Seattle, WA 98195. Offers animal behavior (PhD); applied child and adolescent psychology: prevention and treatment (MA); behavioral neuroscience (PhD); clinical psychology (PhD); cognition and perception (PhD); developmental psychology (PhD); quantitative psychology (PhD); social psychology and personality (PhD). *Accreditation:* APA (one or more programs are accredited). *Degree requirements:* For doctorate, thesis/dissertation. *Entrance requirements:* For doctorate, GRE General Test, minimum GPA of 3.0. Electronic applications accepted.

University of Wisconsin–Madison, Graduate School, College of Letters and Science, Department of Psychology, Program in Cognitive Neurosciences, Madison, WI 53706-1380. Offers PhD. *Degree requirements:* For doctorate, comprehensive exam, thesis/dissertation. *Entrance requirements:* For doctorate, GRE General Test, minimum undergraduate GPA of 3.0. Additional exam requirements/recommendations for international students: required—TOEFL. Electronic applications accepted.

University of Wisconsin–Madison, Graduate School, College of Letters and Science, Department of Psychology, Program in Perception, Madison, WI 53706-1380. Offers PhD. *Degree requirements:* For doctorate, comprehensive exam, thesis/dissertation. *Entrance requirements:* For doctorate, GRE General Test, minimum GPA of 3.0. Electronic applications accepted.

Wayne State University, College of Liberal Arts and Sciences, Department of Psychology, Detroit, MI 48202. Offers behavioral and cognitive neuroscience (PhD); clinical psychology (PhD); developmental science (PhD); industrial/organizational psychology (MA, PhD); social personality (PhD). *Accreditation:* APA (one or more programs are accredited). *Faculty:* 40. *Students:* 92 full-time (66 women), 42 part-time (27 women); includes 23 minority (4 Black or African American, non-Hispanic/Latino; 2 Asian, non-Hispanic/Latino; 9 Hispanic/Latino; 8 Two or more races, non-Hispanic/Latino), 10 international. Average age 27. 433 applicants, 15% accepted, 36 enrolled. In 2019, 28 master's, 13 doctorates awarded. Terminal master's awarded for partial completion of doctoral program. *Degree requirements:* For master's, thesis (for some programs); for doctorate, comprehensive exam, thesis/dissertation, training assignments. *Entrance requirements:* For master's, GRE General Test, minimum undergraduate upper-division cumulative GPA of 3.0, courses in psychology and statistics; for doctorate, GRE General Test, bachelor's, master's, or other advanced degree; at least twelve credits in psychology with minimum GPA of 3.0; courses in laboratory psychology and statistical methods in psychology; at least three letters of recommendation; statement of purpose. Additional exam requirements/recommendations for international students: required—TOEFL (minimum score 550 paper-based; 79 iBT), TWE (minimum score 5.5), Michigan English Language Assessment Battery (minimum score 85); recommended—IELTS (minimum score 6.5). Application fee: $50. Electronic applications accepted. *Expenses: Tuition:* Full-time $34,567. *Financial support:* In 2019–20, 93 students received support, including 11 fellowships with tuition reimbursements available (averaging $21,181 per year), 8 research assistantships with tuition reimbursements available (averaging $20,965 per year), 48 teaching assistantships with tuition reimbursements available (averaging $19,952 per year); scholarships/grants, health care benefits, and unspecified assistantships also available. Financial award applicants required to submit FAFSA. *Unit head:* Scott Bowen, PhD, Chair/Professor, 313-577-2803, E-mail: ad4771@wayne.edu. *Application contact:* Alia Allen, Academic Services Officer III, 313-577-2823, E-mail:

aallen@wayne.edu.
Website: http://clas.wayne.edu/psychology/

Wilfrid Laurier University, Faculty of Graduate and Postdoctoral Studies, Faculty of Science, Department of Psychology, Waterloo, ON N2L 3C5, Canada. Offers behavioral neuroscience (M Sc, PhD); cognitive neuroscience (M Sc, PhD); community psychology (MA, PhD); social and developmental psychology (MA, PhD). *Program availability:* Part-time. *Degree requirements:* For master's, thesis; for doctorate, thesis/dissertation. *Entrance requirements:* For master's, GRE General Test, honors BA or the equivalent in psychology, minimum B average in undergraduate course work; for doctorate, GRE

General Test, master's degree, minimum A- average. Additional exam requirements/recommendations for international students: required—TOEFL (minimum score 89 iBT). Electronic applications accepted.

Yale University, Graduate School of Arts and Sciences, Department of Psychology, New Haven, CT 06520. Offers behavioral neuroscience (PhD); clinical psychology (PhD); cognitive psychology (PhD); developmental psychology (PhD); social/personality psychology (PhD). *Accreditation:* APA. *Degree requirements:* For doctorate, thesis/dissertation. *Entrance requirements:* For doctorate, GRE General Test.

Counseling Psychology

Abilene Christian University, Office of Graduate Programs, College of Arts and Sciences, Department of Psychology, Abilene, TX 79699. Offers clinical psychology (MS); counseling psychology (MS); psychology (MS); school psychology (Specialist). *Program availability:* Part-time. *Faculty:* 11 part-time/adjunct (3 women). *Students:* 24 full-time (19 women), 8 part-time (7 women); includes 8 minority (3 Black or African American, non-Hispanic/Latino; 5 Hispanic/Latino), 2 international. 99 applicants, 27% accepted, 10 enrolled. In 2019, 23 master's awarded. *Degree requirements:* For master's, comprehensive exam, thesis (for some programs), practicum; internship. *Entrance requirements:* For master's, official transcripts, purpose statement, Recommendations. Additional exam requirements/recommendations for international students: required—TOEFL (minimum score 80 iBT), IELTS (minimum score 6), PTE (minimum score 51). *Application deadline:* For fall admission, 3/30 priority date for domestic students, 2/15 for international students. Applications are processed on a rolling basis. Application fee: $65. Electronic applications accepted. *Expenses: Tuition:* Full-time $22,356; part-time $1242 per credit hour. Tuition and fees vary according to program. *Financial support:* In 2019–20, 25 students received support, including 28 research assistantships with partial tuition reimbursements available; career-related internships or fieldwork, Federal Work-Study, and scholarships/grants also available. Support available to part-time students. Financial award application deadline: 4/1; financial award applicants required to submit FAFSA. *Unit head:* Dr. Cherisse Flanagan, Graduate Program Director, 325-674-2282, Fax: 325-674-6968, E-mail: cyf07a@acu.edu. *Application contact:* Graduate Admissions, 325-674-6911, E-mail: gradinfo@acu.edu.
Website: http://www.acu.edu/on-campus/graduate/college-of-arts-and-sciences/psychology-department.html

Adelphi University, Gordon F. Derner School of Psychology, Program in Mental Health Counseling, Garden City, NY 11530-0701. Offers MA. *Degree requirements:* For master's, comprehensive exam. *Entrance requirements:* For master's, GRE General Test, minimum cumulative GPA of 3.1; interview; course work in developmental psychology, research methods, and psycho-pathology; 2 letters of recommendation. Additional exam requirements/recommendations for international students: required—TOEFL (minimum score 550 paper-based; 80 iBT), IELTS (minimum score 6.5). Electronic applications accepted. *Expenses:* Contact institution.

Alabama Agricultural and Mechanical University, School of Graduate Studies, College of Education, Humanities, and Behavioral Sciences, Department of Social Work, Psychology and Counseling, Huntsville, AL 35811. Offers psychology and counseling (MS, Ed S), including clinical psychology (MS), counseling psychology (MS), guidance and counseling, rehabilitation counseling (MS), school counseling (MS), school psychology (MS), school psychometry (MS); social work (MSW). *Accreditation:* CORE; NCATE. *Program availability:* Part-time, evening/weekend. *Degree requirements:* For master's, comprehensive exam. *Entrance requirements:* For master's, GRE General Test. Additional exam requirements/recommendations for international students: required—TOEFL (minimum score 500 paper-based; 61 iBT).

Alaska Pacific University, Graduate Programs, Department of Counseling, Psychological Studies, and Human Services, Program in Counseling Psychology, Anchorage, AK 99508-4672. Offers MSCP.

Albizu University - Miami, Graduate Programs, Doral, FL 33172. Offers clinical psychology (PhD, Psy D); entrepreneurship (MBA); exceptional student education (MS); human services (PhD); industrial/organizational psychology (MS); marriage and family therapy (MS); mental health counseling (MS); nonprofit management (MBA); organizational management (MBA); school counseling (MS); speech and language pathology (MS); teaching English for speakers of other languages (MS). *Accreditation:* APA. *Program availability:* Part-time, 100% online, blended/hybrid learning. *Faculty:* 28 full-time (21 women), 27 part-time/adjunct (15 women). *Students:* 410 full-time (351 women), 190 part-time (163 women); includes 519 minority (33 Black or African American, non-Hispanic/Latino; 3 Asian, non-Hispanic/Latino; 477 Hispanic/Latino; 6 Two or more races, non-Hispanic/Latino), 21 international. Average age 33. 286 applicants, 66% accepted, 127 enrolled. In 2019, 96 master's, 54 doctorates awarded. Terminal master's awarded for partial completion of doctoral program. *Degree requirements:* For master's, comprehensive exam (for some programs), integrative project (for MBA); research project (for exceptional student education, teaching English as a second language); comprehensive examination for Speech and Language Pathology; for doctorate, comprehensive exam, thesis/dissertation, comprehensive examinations, internship, project/dissertation. *Entrance requirements:* For master's, GRE/EXADEP, bachelor's degree from accredited institution, minimum GPA of 3.0, 3 letters of recommendation, interview, resume, statement of purpose, official transcripts; for doctorate, GRE (for Psy D), 3 letters of recommendation, resume, interview, statement of purpose, official transcripts; bachelor's degree and minimum GPA of 3.25 (for Psy D); master's degree and minimum GPA of 3.0 (for PhD). Additional exam requirements/recommendations for international students: required—Michigan Test of English Language Proficiency. *Application deadline:* For fall admission, 4/1 priority date for domestic students, 5/1 priority date for international students; for spring admission, 11/1 priority date for domestic students, 9/1 priority date for international students. Applications are processed on a rolling basis. Application fee: $50. Electronic applications accepted. Application fee is waived when completed online. *Expenses:* $600 per credit or $620 per credit or $650 per credit (for master's depending on field); $800 per credit or $1,050 per credit (for doctoral depending on program). *Financial support:* In 2019–20, 158 students received support. Federal Work-Study, scholarships/grants, unspecified assistantships, and tuition discounts available. Financial award application deadline: 6/1; financial award applicants required to submit FAFSA. *Unit head:* Dr. Tilokie Depoo, PhD, Chancellor, 305-593-1223 Ext. 3138, Fax: 305-477-8983, E-mail: tdepoo@albizu.edu. *Application contact:* Nancy Alvarez, Director of Enrollment Management, 305-593-1223 Ext. 3136, Fax: 305-593-1854, E-mail:

nalvarez@albizu.edu.
Website: www.albizu.edu

Alfred University, Graduate School, Counseling and School Psychology Program, Alfred, NY 14802-1205. Offers mental health counseling (MS Ed); school counseling (MS Ed, CAS); school psychology (MA, Psy D, CAS). *Accreditation:* APA. *Program availability:* Part-time, evening/weekend. *Faculty:* 14 full-time (7 women), 24 part-time/adjunct (12 women). *Students:* 56 full-time (41 women), 394 part-time (317 women); includes 256 minority (120 Black or African American, non-Hispanic/Latino; 2 American Indian or Alaska Native, non-Hispanic/Latino; 7 Asian, non-Hispanic/Latino; 127 Hispanic/Latino), 2 international. Average age 33. 249 applicants, 98% accepted, 224 enrolled. In 2019, 172 master's, 5 doctorates, 111 other advanced degrees awarded. *Degree requirements:* For master's, thesis (for some programs), internship; for doctorate, thesis/dissertation, internship. *Entrance requirements:* For master's and doctorate, GRE General Test. Additional exam requirements/recommendations for international students: required—TOEFL (minimum score 590 paper-based; 90 iBT), IELTS (minimum score 6.5). *Application deadline:* For fall admission, 1/15 priority date for domestic and international students. Applications are processed on a rolling basis. Application fee: $60. Electronic applications accepted. Application fee is waived when completed online. *Expenses:* $7,580 per year. *Financial support:* Research assistantships with partial tuition reimbursements, career-related internships or fieldwork, and unspecified assistantships available. Financial award application deadline: 3/15; financial award applicants required to submit FAFSA. *Unit head:* Dr. Jay Cerio, Dean, 607-871-2757, E-mail: fcerio@alfred.edu. *Application contact:* Lindsey Gertin, Assistant Director of Graduate Admissions, 607-871-2017, Fax: 607-871-2198, E-mail: gradinquiry@alfred.edu.

Amberton University, Graduate School, Programs in Counseling, Garland, TX 75041-5595. Offers marriage and family therapy (MA); professional counseling (MA); school counseling (MA). *Entrance requirements:* For master's, minimum GPA of 3.0.

American International College, School of Education, Low Residency Programs, Springfield, MA 01109-3189. Offers counseling psychology (MA); educational leadership and supervision (Ed D); professional counseling and supervision (Ed D); teaching and learning (Ed D). *Program availability:* Evening/weekend. *Degree requirements:* For doctorate, thesis/dissertation. *Entrance requirements:* For master's, minimum undergraduate GPA of 3.0, 2 letters of recommendation, personal goal statement, official transcript of all academic work (graduate and undergraduate); for doctorate, minimum master's GPA of 3.0, 3 letters of recommendation, personal goal statement/essay (6-8 pages), official transcript of all academic work (graduate and undergraduate). Additional exam requirements/recommendations for international students: required—TOEFL. *Expenses:* Contact institution.

Amridge University, Graduate and Professional Programs, Montgomery, AL 36117. Offers Biblical studies (MA, PhD); Christian ministry (MS); family therapy (D Min); human services (MS); leadership and management (MS); marriage and family therapy (M Div, MA, PhD); ministerial leadership (M Div, MS); New Testament studies (MA); Old Testament studies (MA); professional counseling (M Div, MA, PhD); theology (M Div, D Min). *Program availability:* Part-time, evening/weekend, online learning. *Degree requirements:* For master's, one foreign language, comprehensive exam (for some programs), thesis (for some programs); for doctorate, one foreign language, comprehensive exam (for some programs), thesis/dissertation (for some programs). *Entrance requirements:* For master's, official transcript showing an earned 4-year BA or BS from regionally- or nationally-accredited institution; for doctorate, official transcript showing earned graduate degree from regionally- or nationally-accredited institution; writing sample (e.g. career monograph, published journal article, term paper from master's degree or doctoral dissertation); interview. Additional exam requirements/recommendations for international students: required—TOEFL (minimum score 79 iBT). Electronic applications accepted.

Andrews University, School of Graduate Studies, College of Education and International Services, Department of Graduate Psychology and Counseling, Program in Community Counseling, Berrien Springs, MI 49104. Offers clinical mental health counseling (MA); community counseling (MA). *Students:* 25 full-time (19 women), 4 part-time (3 women); includes 14 minority (4 Black or African American, non-Hispanic/Latino; 1 Asian, non-Hispanic/Latino; 9 Hispanic/Latino), 9 international. Average age 32. In 2019, 10 master's awarded. *Degree requirements:* For master's, thesis optional. *Entrance requirements:* For master's, GRE. Additional exam requirements/recommendations for international students: required—TOEFL (minimum score 550 paper-based). *Application deadline:* Applications are processed on a rolling basis. Application fee: $60. Electronic applications accepted. *Unit head:* Dr. Nancy Carbonell, Coordinator, 269-471-3472. *Application contact:* Jillian Panigot, Director, University Admissions, 800-253-2874, Fax: 269-471-6321, E-mail: graduate@andrews.edu.

Andrews University, School of Graduate Studies, College of Education and International Services, Department of Graduate Psychology and Counseling, Program in Counseling Psychology, Berrien Springs, MI 49104. Offers MA, PhD. *Students:* 26 full-time (18 women), 2 part-time (both women); includes 12 minority (8 Black or African American, non-Hispanic/Latino; 3 Hispanic/Latino; 1 Two or more races, non-Hispanic/Latino), 2 international. Average age 36. In 2019, 1 master's, 6 doctorates awarded. *Degree requirements:* For doctorate, thesis/dissertation. *Entrance requirements:* For master's, GRE. Additional exam requirements/recommendations for international students: required—TOEFL (minimum score 550 paper-based). *Application deadline:* Applications are processed on a rolling basis. Application fee: $60. Electronic applications accepted. *Unit head:* Dr. Carole Woolford, Coordinator, 269-471-6074. *Application contact:* Jillian Panigot, Direrctor, University Admissions, 800-253-2874, Fax: 269-471-6321, E-mail: graduate@andrews.edu.

Anna Maria College, Graduate Division, Program in Counseling Psychology, Paxton, MA 01612. Offers counseling psychology (MA). *Program availability:* Part-time, evening/

weekend. *Degree requirements:* For master's, comprehensive exam, practicum. *Entrance requirements:* Additional exam requirements/recommendations for international students: required—TOEFL (minimum score 500 paper-based). Electronic applications accepted.

Antioch University New England, Graduate School, Department of Applied Psychology, Keene, NH 03431-3552. Offers autism spectrum disorders (Certificate), including applied behavioral analysis internship, autism spectrum disorders; clinical mental health counseling (MA), including clinical mental health counseling, substance abuse counseling; dance/movement therapy and counseling (M Ed, MA, PMC); marriage and family therapy (MA, PhD, Certificate). *Faculty:* 15 full-time (12 women), 30 part-time/adjunct (25 women). *Students:* 264 full-time (217 women), 79 part-time (64 women); includes 67 minority (25 Black or African American, non-Hispanic/Latino; 2 American Indian or Alaska Native, non-Hispanic/Latino; 8 Asian, non-Hispanic/Latino; 27 Hispanic/Latino; 5 Two or more races, non-Hispanic/Latino), 5 international. Average age 35. 149 applicants, 52% accepted, 77 enrolled. In 2019, 49 master's awarded. *Degree requirements:* For master's, internship, practicum. *Entrance requirements:* For master's, previous course work and work experience in psychology. Additional exam requirements/recommendations for international students: required—TOEFL (minimum score 550 paper-based). *Application deadline:* For fall admission, 7/15 for domestic and international students; for spring admission, 12/1 for domestic and international students. Applications are processed on a rolling basis. Application fee: $50. Electronic applications accepted. *Expenses:* Contact institution. *Financial support:* In 2019–20, 56 students received support. Fellowships, research assistantships, career-related internships or fieldwork, Federal Work-Study, and scholarships/grants available. Financial award application deadline: 6/1; financial award applicants required to submit FAFSA. *Unit head:* Dr. Kevin Lyness, Department Chair, 603-283-2149, E-mail: klyness@antioch.edu. *Application contact:* Admissions, 800-552-8380, Fax: 603-357-0718, E-mail: admissions.ane@antioch.edu.
Website: https://www.antioch.edu/new-england/degrees-programs/counseling-wellness/

Appalachian State University, Cratis D. Williams School of Graduate Studies, Department of Human Development and Psychological Counseling, Boone, NC 28608. Offers clinical mental health counseling (MA); college student development (MA); marriage and family therapy (MA); school counseling (MA). *Accreditation:* AAMFT/COAMFTE; ACA; NCATE. *Program availability:* Part-time. *Degree requirements:* For master's, comprehensive exam (for some programs), thesis optional, internships. *Entrance requirements:* For master's, GRE General Test, 3 letters of recommendation. Additional exam requirements/recommendations for international students: required—TOEFL (minimum score 570 paper-based; 79 iBT), IELTS (minimum score 6.5). Electronic applications accepted.

Arcadia University, College of Arts and Sciences, Department of Psychology, Glenside, PA 19038-3295. Offers applied behavior analysis (MAC); autism (MAC); child/family therapy (MAC); community public health (MAC); counseling/international peace and conflict resolution dual degree (MAC); mental health counseling (MAC); trauma (MAC). *Program availability:* Part-time. *Faculty:* 13 full-time (8 women). *Students:* 30 full-time (27 women), 31 part-time (26 women); includes 17 minority (11 Black or African American, non-Hispanic/Latino; 2 Asian, non-Hispanic/Latino; 1 Hispanic/Latino; 3 Two or more races, non-Hispanic/Latino). In 2019, 18 master's awarded. *Degree requirements:* For master's, practicum. *Entrance requirements:* For master's, test scores are not required of applicants with an earned master's degree or who have a GPA greater than a 3.0. Test scores from the Graduate Record Examination (GRE) or the Miller Analogies Test (MAT), taken within the past five years are required for all other applicants. Additional exam requirements/recommendations for international students: required—TOEFL. *Application deadline:* Applications are processed on a rolling basis. Application fee: $25. Electronic applications accepted. *Expenses:* Contact institution. *Financial support:* Research assistantships, career-related internships or fieldwork, and unspecified assistantships available. Support available to part-time students. Financial award application deadline: 8/15. *Unit head:* Dr. Marianne Miserandino, Chair, 215-572-2183. *Application contact:* 215-572-2925, Fax: 215-572-2126, E-mail: grad@arcadia.edu.

Argosy University, Chicago, Illinois School of Professional Psychology, Doctoral Program in Clinical Psychology, Chicago, IL 60601. Offers child and adolescent psychology (Psy D); client-centered and experiential psychotherapies (Psy D); diversity and multicultural psychology (Psy D); family psychology (Psy D); forensic psychology (Psy D); health psychology (Psy D); neuropsychology (Psy D); organizational consulting (Psy D); psychoanalytic psychology (Psy D); psychology and spirituality (Psy D). *Accreditation:* APA.

Argosy University, Chicago, Illinois School of Professional Psychology, Program in Counseling Psychology, Chicago, IL 60601. Offers counselor education and supervision (Ed D). *Accreditation:* ACA. *Program availability:* Online learning.

Argosy University, Hawaii, Hawai'i School of Professional Psychology, Program in Counseling Psychology, Honolulu, HI 96813. Offers Ed D.

Argosy University, Los Angeles, College of Psychology and Behavioral Sciences, Los Angeles, CA 90045. Offers clinical psychology/marriage and family therapy (MA); counseling psychology (Ed D); counseling psychology/marriage and family therapy (MA); forensic psychology (MA).

Argosy University, Northern Virginia, American School of Professional Psychology, Arlington, VA 22209. Offers clinical psychology (MA, Psy D), including child and family psychology (Psy D), diversity and multicultural psychology (Psy D), forensic psychology (Psy D), health and neuropsychology (Psy D); community counseling (MA); counseling psychology (Ed D), including counselor education and supervision; counselor education and supervision (Ed D); forensic psychology (MA).

Argosy University, Orange County, American School of Professional Psychology, Program in Counseling Psychology, Orange, CA 92868. Offers counseling psychology (Ed D); marriage and family therapy (MA).

Argosy University, Phoenix, Arizona School of Professional Psychology, Program in Mental Health Counseling, Phoenix, AZ 85021. Offers MA.

Argosy University, Seattle, College of Psychology and Behavioral Sciences, Program in Counseling Psychology, Seattle, WA 98121. Offers MA, Ed D.

Argosy University, Tampa, Florida School of Professional Psychology, Tampa, FL 33607. Offers clinical psychology (MA, Psy D), including clinical psychology; counselor education and supervision (Ed D); industrial organizational psychology (MA); marriage and family therapy (MA); mental health counseling (MA).

Arizona State University at Tempe, School of Letters and Sciences, Program in Counseling Psychology, Tempe, AZ 85287-0811. Offers PhD. *Accreditation:* APA. *Degree requirements:* For doctorate, comprehensive exam, thesis/dissertation, internship/practica, interactive Program of Study (iPOS) submitted before completing 50 percent of required credit hours. *Entrance requirements:* For doctorate, GRE, minimum GPA of 3.0 or equivalent in last 2 years of work leading to bachelor's degree, 3 letters of recommendation, personal statement describing history and academic/professional goals, completed Biographical Information form, 7-page sample of expository writing. Additional exam requirements/recommendations for international students: required—TOEFL, IELTS, or PTE. Electronic applications accepted.

Assumption University, Clinical Counseling Psychology Program, Worcester, MA 01609-1296. Offers child and family interventions (MA); clinical counseling psychology (CAGS); cognitive-behavioral therapies (MA). *Program availability:* Part-time, evening/weekend. *Degree requirements:* For master's, comprehensive exam, internship, practicum; for CAGS, comprehensive exam. *Entrance requirements:* For master's, bachelor's degree and at least six psychology courses completed with minimum GPA of 3.0 both overall and in the psychology courses; three letters of recommendation; official transcripts; personal statement; current resume; for CAGS, master's degree in clinical counseling psychology or mental health counseling, or baccalaureate degree and at least six psychology courses with minimum GPA of 3.0 overall and in psychology courses; three letters of recommendation; official transcripts; personal statement; current resume; interview. Additional exam requirements/recommendations for international students: required—TOEFL (minimum score 540 paper-based; 76 iBT), IELTS (minimum score 6). Electronic applications accepted. *Expenses: Tuition:* Full-time $12,690; part-time $705 per credit. *Required fees:* $70 per term.

Athabasca University, Program in Counseling, Athabasca, AB T9S 3A3, Canada. Offers applied psychology (Post Master's Certificate); art therapy (MC); career counseling (MC); counseling (Advanced Certificate); counseling psychology (MC); school counseling (MC).

Austin Peay State University, College of Graduate Studies, College of Behavioral and Health Sciences, Department of Psychological Science and Counseling, Clarksville, TN 37044. Offers industrial-organizational psychology (MS); mental health counseling (MS), including clinical mental health, school counseling; school counseling (MS). *Program availability:* Part-time, online learning. *Faculty:* 9 full-time (6 women), 5 part-time/adjunct (4 women). *Students:* 64 full-time (46 women), 27 part-time (24 women); includes 30 minority (16 Black or African American, non-Hispanic/Latino; 1 Asian, non-Hispanic/Latino; 5 Hispanic/Latino; 8 Two or more races, non-Hispanic/Latino), 1 international. Average age 29. 34 applicants, 68% accepted, 19 enrolled. In 2019, 28 master's awarded. *Degree requirements:* For master's, comprehensive exam, thesis (for some programs). *Entrance requirements:* For master's, GRE General Test, minimum undergraduate GPA of 2.5, 3 letters of recommendation, bachelor's degree. Additional exam requirements/recommendations for international students: required—TOEFL (minimum score 500 paper-based). *Application deadline:* For fall admission, 8/5 priority date for domestic students. Applications are processed on a rolling basis. Application fee: $45 ($55 for international students). Electronic applications accepted. *Financial support:* Research assistantships with full tuition reimbursements, career-related internships or fieldwork, Federal Work-Study, institutionally sponsored loans, scholarships/grants, and unspecified assistantships available. Support available to part-time students. Financial award application deadline: 7/1; financial award applicants required to submit FAFSA. *Unit head:* Dr. Nicole Knickmeyer, Chair, 931-221-7232, Fax: 931-221-6267, E-mail: knickmeyer@apsu.edu. *Application contact:* Megan Mitchell, Coordinator of Graduate Admissions, 800-859-4723, Fax: 931-221-7641, E-mail: gradadmissions@apsu.edu.
Website: http://www.apsu.edu/psychology/index.php

Avila University, Department of Psychology, Kansas City, MO 64145-1698. Offers counseling psychology (MS); psychology (MS). *Program availability:* Part-time. *Faculty:* 6 full-time (all women), 7 part-time/adjunct (4 women). *Students:* 90 full-time (73 women), 20 part-time (17 women); includes 39 minority (23 Black or African American, non-Hispanic/Latino; 1 American Indian or Alaska Native, non-Hispanic/Latino; 3 Asian, non-Hispanic/Latino; 6 Hispanic/Latino; 6 Two or more races, non-Hispanic/Latino), 2 international. Average age 33. 117 applicants, 55% accepted, 52 enrolled. In 2019, 27 master's awarded. *Degree requirements:* For master's, thesis optional, capstone project. *Entrance requirements:* For master's, bachelor's degree, minimum GPA of 3.0 in all previous undergraduate and graduate coursework, 2 letters of recommendation, letter of intent, resume. Additional exam requirements/recommendations for international students: required—TOEFL (minimum score 80 iBT). *Application deadline:* Applications are processed on a rolling basis. Application fee: $0. Electronic applications accepted. *Expenses:* $589 per credit hour. $21,500 - $36,000 total for degree completion depending on major. *Financial support:* In 2019–20, 12 students received support, including 4 research assistantships with partial tuition reimbursements available; career-related internships or fieldwork, scholarships/grants, and unspecified assistantships also available. Support available to part-time students. Financial award applicants required to submit FAFSA. *Unit head:* Phil Gebauer, Director of Graduate Psychology Enrollment Management, 816-501-0419, Fax: 816-501-2455, E-mail: philip.gebauer@avila.edu. *Application contact:* Heather Nobl, Graduate Admissions Advisor, 816-501-2969, E-mail: gradpsych@avila.edu.
Website: https://www.avila.edu/psychology/

Ball State University, Graduate School, College of Health, Department of Counseling Psychology, Social Psychology, and Counseling, Program in Counseling Psychology, Muncie, IN 47306. Offers counseling (MA), including clinical mental health counseling, mental health counseling, rehabilitation counseling, school counseling; counseling psychology (PhD). *Accreditation:* ACA; APA. *Program availability:* Part-time. *Degree requirements:* For doctorate, thesis/dissertation. *Entrance requirements:* For master's, GRE General Test (minimum scores 144 quantitative, 153 verbal), minimum baccalaureate GPA of 2.75 or 3.0 in latter half of baccalaureate, minimum GPA of 3.0 in psychology coursework, three letters of recommendation; for doctorate, GRE General Test, interview, minimum graduate GPA of 3.2, resume. Additional exam requirements/recommendations for international students: required—TOEFL (minimum score 550 paper-based; 79 iBT), IELTS (minimum score 6.5). Electronic applications accepted. *Expenses: Tuition, area resident:* Full-time $7506; part-time $417 per credit hour. Tuition, nonresident: full-time $20,610; part-time $1145 per credit hour. *Required fees:* $2126. Tuition and fees vary according to course load, campus/location and program.

Baruch College of the City University of New York, Weissman School of Arts and Sciences, Program in Mental Health Counseling, New York, NY 10010-5585. Offers MA. *Entrance requirements:* For master's, bachelor's degree from accredited institution, minimum undergraduate GPA of 3.2, relevant professional or volunteer experience, minimum of 15 credits in psychology, personal statement, three letters of recommendation, official transcript. Additional exam requirements/recommendations for international students: required—TOEFL. Electronic applications accepted.

Bastyr University, School of Natural Health Arts and Sciences, Kenmore, WA 98028-4966. Offers counseling psychology (MA); maternal-child health systems (MA); midwifery (MS); nutrition (Certificate); nutrition and clinical health psychology (MS); nutrition and wellness (MS). *Accreditation:* AND; MEAC. *Program availability:* Part-time. *Degree requirements:* For master's, thesis optional. *Entrance requirements:* For master's, 1-2 years' basic sciences course work (depending on program). Additional exam requirements/recommendations for international students: required—TOEFL (minimum score 550 paper-based; 79 iBT).

Becker College, Program in Mental Health Counseling, Worcester, MA 01609. Offers community mental health (MA); school consultation (MA). *Entrance requirements:* For master's, GRE, interview, official transcript, three letters of recommendation, essay. Electronic applications accepted.

Bethel University, Graduate School, St. Paul, MN 55112-6999. Offers business administration (MBA); classroom management (Certificate); counseling (MA); K-12 education (MA); leadership (Ed D); leadership foundations (Certificate); nurse educator (MS, Certificate); nurse-midwifery (MS); physician assistant (MS); special education (MA); strategic leadership (MA); teaching (MA); teaching and learning (Certificate). *Program availability:* Part-time, evening/weekend, 100% online, blended/hybrid learning. *Faculty:* 36 full-time (24 women), 112 part-time/adjunct (73 women). *Students:* 428 full-time (318 women), 825 part-time (482 women); includes 245 minority (95 Black or African American, non-Hispanic/Latino; 13 American Indian or Alaska Native, non-Hispanic/Latino; 52 Asian, non-Hispanic/Latino; 50 Hispanic/Latino; 2 Native Hawaiian or other Pacific Islander, non-Hispanic/Latino; 33 Two or more races, non-Hispanic/Latino), 28 international. Average age 38. 810 applicants, 45% accepted, 256 enrolled. In 2019, 320 master's, 34 doctorates, 112 other advanced degrees awarded. *Degree requirements:* For master's, comprehensive exam (for some programs), thesis (for some programs); for doctorate, comprehensive exam, thesis/dissertation. *Entrance requirements:* Additional exam requirements/recommendations for international students: required—TOEFL (minimum score 550 paper-based; 80 iBT), TOEFL (minimum score 550 paper-based, 80 iBT) or IELTS. *Application deadline:* Applications are processed on a rolling basis. Application fee: $0. Electronic applications accepted. *Expenses:* $420-$850/credit dependent on the program. *Financial support:* Teaching assistantships, career-related internships or fieldwork, and scholarships/grants available. Support available to part-time students. Financial award applicants required to submit FAFSA. *Unit head:* Dr. Randy Bergen, Associate Provost, 651-635-8000, Fax: 651-635-8004, E-mail: r-bergen@bethel.edu. *Application contact:* Director of Admissions, 651-635-8000, Fax: 651-635-8004, E-mail: gs@bethel.edu.
Website: https://www.bethel.edu/graduate/

Boston College, Lynch School of Education and Human Development, Department of Counseling, Developmental, and Educational Psychology, Chestnut Hill, MA 02467-3800. Offers applied developmental and education psychology (MA, PhD); counseling psychology (PhD); mental health counseling (MA); school counseling (MA); theology and ministry and counseling (MA/MA); MA/MA. *Accreditation:* APA (one or more programs are accredited). *Program availability:* Part-time, evening/weekend. Terminal master's awarded for partial completion of doctoral program. *Degree requirements:* For master's, comprehensive exam; for doctorate, comprehensive exam, thesis/dissertation. Electronic applications accepted.

Boston Graduate School of Psychoanalysis, Master's Programs, Brookline, MA 02446-4602. Offers mental health counseling (MA); psychoanalysis (MA); psychoanalysis, society and culture (MA). *Program availability:* Part-time. Terminal master's awarded for partial completion of doctoral program. *Degree requirements:* For master's, thesis. *Entrance requirements:* For master's, interview, BA, personal statement, writing sample, 3 letters of recommendation. Additional exam requirements/recommendations for international students: required—TOEFL (minimum score 550 paper-based; 79 iBT).

Boston University, School of Medicine, Graduate Medical Sciences, Program in Mental Health Counseling and Behavioral Medicine, Boston, MA 02215. Offers MA. *Unit head:* Dr. Stephen Brady, Director, 617-414-2320, Fax: 617-414-2323, E-mail: sbrady@bu.edu. *Application contact:* GMS Admissions Office, 617-358-9518, Fax: 617-358-2913, E-mail: gmsbusm@bu.edu.
Website: http://www.bumc.bu.edu/gms/mhcbm/

Bowie State University, Graduate Programs, Program in Counseling Psychology, Bowie, MD 20715-9465. Offers MA. *Program availability:* Part-time, evening/weekend. *Degree requirements:* For master's, comprehensive exam, thesis optional, research paper, practicum. *Entrance requirements:* For master's, minimum GPA of 2.5, 3 recommendations. Electronic applications accepted. *Expenses: Tuition, area resident:* Full-time $11,942; part-time $423 per credit hour. Tuition, state resident: full-time $11,942; part-time $423 per credit hour. Tuition, nonresident: full-time $18,806; part-time $709 per credit hour. *International tuition:* $18,806 full-time. *Required fees:* $1106; $1106 per semester. $553 per semester.

Bowie State University, Graduate Programs, Program in Mental Health Counseling, Bowie, MD 20715-9465. Offers MA. *Accreditation:* ACA. *Program availability:* Part-time, evening/weekend. *Degree requirements:* For master's, comprehensive exam. *Entrance requirements:* For master's, 3 letters of recommendation, minimum GPA of 3.0, 12 undergraduate credit hours in counseling or psychology. Electronic applications accepted. *Expenses: Tuition, area resident:* Full-time $11,942; part-time $423 per credit hour. Tuition, state resident: full-time $11,942; part-time $423 per credit hour. Tuition, nonresident: full-time $18,806; part-time $709 per credit hour. *International tuition:* $18,806 full-time. *Required fees:* $1106; $1106 per semester. $553 per semester.

Bradley University, The Graduate School, College of Education and Health Sciences, Education, Counseling and Leadership Department, Peoria, IL 61625-0002. Offers counseling (MA), including clinical mental health counseling, professional school counseling; leadership in educational administration (MA); nonprofit leadership (MA). *Accreditation:* ACA; NCATE. *Program availability:* Part-time, evening/weekend, blended/hybrid learning. *Faculty:* 24 full-time (15 women), 10 part-time/adjunct (6 women). *Students:* 48 full-time (43 women), 246 part-time (197 women); includes 62 minority (35 Black or African American, non-Hispanic/Latino; 3 American Indian or Alaska Native, non-Hispanic/Latino; 4 Asian, non-Hispanic/Latino; 17 Hispanic/Latino; 3 Two or more races, non-Hispanic/Latino), 3 international. Average age 33. 125 applicants, 74% accepted, 68 enrolled. In 2019, 67 master's awarded. *Degree requirements:* For master's, comprehensive exam, thesis optional. *Entrance requirements:* For master's, GRE General Test or MAT, interview, 3 letters of recommendation. Additional exam requirements/recommendations for international students: required—TOEFL (minimum score 550 paper-based; 79 iBT), IELTS (minimum score 6.5), PTE (minimum score 58). *Application deadline:* For fall admission, 5/15 priority date for domestic and international students; for spring admission, 10/15 priority date for domestic and international students. Applications are processed on a rolling basis. Application fee: $40 ($50 for international students). Electronic applications accepted. *Expenses: Tuition:* Part-time $930 per credit hour. *Financial support:* In 2019–20, 40 students received support, including 13 research assistantships with full tuition reimbursements available (averaging $11,040 per year); fellowships, career-related internships or fieldwork, scholarships/grants, tuition waivers (full), and unspecified assistantships also available. Support available to part-time students. Financial award application deadline: 4/1. *Unit head:* Dean Cantu, Associate Dean and Director, Professor, 309-677-3190, E-mail: dcantu@bradley.edu. *Application contact:* Rachel Webb, Director of On-Campus Graduate Admissions and International Student and Scholar Services, 309-677-2375, E-mail: rkwebb@bradley.edu.
Website: https://www.bradley.edu/academic/departments/ecl/

Brandman University, School of Arts and Sciences, Irvine, CA 92618. Offers psychology (MA), including counseling, marriage and family therapy, professional clinical counseling; social work (MSW).

Brigham Young University, Graduate Studies, David O. McKay School of Education, Department of Counseling Psychology and Special Education, Provo, UT 84602-1001. Offers counseling psychology (PhD); school psychology (Ed S); special education (MS). *Program availability:* Part-time, evening/weekend. *Faculty:* 14 full-time (4 women), 6 part-time/adjunct (2 women). *Students:* 71 full-time (46 women), 18 part-time (17 women); includes 16 minority (1 Black or African American, non-Hispanic/Latino; 4 American Indian or Alaska Native, non-Hispanic/Latino; 6 Asian, non-Hispanic/Latino; 4 Hispanic/Latino; 1 Native Hawaiian or other Pacific Islander, non-Hispanic/Latino), 7 international. Average age 31. 86 applicants, 29% accepted, 25 enrolled. In 2019, 7 master's, 6 doctorates, 14 other advanced degrees awarded. *Degree requirements:* For master's and Ed S, comprehensive exam, thesis; for doctorate, comprehensive exam, thesis/dissertation. *Entrance requirements:* For master's, doctorate, and Ed S, GRE General Test, application & application fee; unofficial transcripts; honor code commitment; 3 letters of recommendation. Additional exam requirements/recommendations for international students: required—TOEFL (minimum score 580 paper-based; 85 iBT), IELTS (minimum score 7), E3PT. *Application deadline:* For fall admission, 12/15 for domestic and international students. Application fee: $50. Electronic applications accepted. *Financial support:* In 2019–20, 91 students received support, including 87 fellowships (averaging $7,100 per year), 57 research assistantships (averaging $6,400 per year), 10 teaching assistantships (averaging $5,250 per year); institutionally sponsored loans also available. Financial award application deadline: 5/1. *Unit head:* Dr. Lane Fischer, Department Chair, 801-422-8293, E-mail: lane_fischer@byu.edu. *Application contact:* Diane Hancock, Executive Secretary, 801-422-3859, E-mail: diane_hancock@byu.edu.
Website: https://education.byu.edu/cpse

Brooklyn College of the City University of New York, School of Natural and Behavioral Sciences, Department of Health and Nutrition Sciences, Brooklyn, NY 11210-2889. Offers community health (MA), including community health education, thanatology; grief counseling (CAS); nutrition (MS); public health (MPH), including general public health, health care policy and administration. *Program availability:* Part-time, evening/weekend. *Degree requirements:* For master's, thesis or alternative. *Entrance requirements:* For master's, GRE, essay, 2 letters of recommendation. Additional exam requirements/recommendations for international students: required—TOEFL. Electronic applications accepted.

Brooklyn College of the City University of New York, School of Natural and Behavioral Sciences, Department of Psychology, Brooklyn, NY 11210-2889. Offers experimental psychology (MA); industrial and organizational psychology (MA), including human relations, organizational behavior; mental health counseling (MA); psychology (PhD). *Program availability:* Part-time. *Degree requirements:* For master's, comprehensive exam, thesis (for some programs). *Entrance requirements:* For master's, minimum GPA of 3.0, 2 letters of recommendation, essay; for doctorate, GRE. Additional exam requirements/recommendations for international students: required—TOEFL (minimum score 520 paper-based; 69 iBT). Electronic applications accepted.

Bushnell University, School of Education and Counseling, Eugene, OR 97401-3745. Offers clinical mental health counseling (MA); elementary teaching (MAT); English for speakers of other languages (MAT); physical education (MAT); school counseling (MA); secondary teaching (MAT); special education (MAT). *Program availability:* Part-time, evening/weekend, online learning. *Degree requirements:* For master's, thesis (for some programs). *Entrance requirements:* For master's, GRE or MAT, minimum undergraduate GPA of 3.0, interview, 2-3 page statement of purpose, two letters of recommendation, resume, background check. Additional exam requirements/recommendations for international students: required—TOEFL (minimum score 550 paper-based; 80 iBT). Electronic applications accepted. *Expenses:* Contact institution.

Caldwell University, School of Psychology and Counseling, Caldwell, NJ 07006-6195. Offers MA, Post-Master's Certificate. *Accreditation:* ACA. *Program availability:* Part-time. *Degree requirements:* For master's, comprehensive exam, practicum, internship; for Post-Master's Certificate, comprehensive exam. *Entrance requirements:* For master's, minimum GPA of 3.2; two letters of recommendation; interview; writing sample. Additional exam requirements/recommendations for international students: required—The TOEFL or IELTS is required of international students who were not educated at the Bachelors level in English; recommended—TOEFL (minimum score 580 paper-based; 92 iBT), IELTS (minimum score 7.5). Electronic applications accepted. *Expenses:* Contact institution.

California Baptist University, Program in Counseling Ministry and Counseling Psychology (Dual Master's), Riverside, CA 92504-3206. Offers MA/MS. *Program availability:* Part-time. *Entrance requirements:* Additional exam requirements/recommendations for international students: required—TOEFL (minimum score 80 iBT). Electronic applications accepted. *Expenses:* Contact institution.

California Baptist University, Program in Counseling Psychology, Riverside, CA 92504-3206. Offers counseling psychology (MS); forensic psychology (MS); professional clinical counseling (MS). *Program availability:* Part-time, evening/weekend, 100% online, blended/hybrid learning. *Degree requirements:* For master's, comprehensive exam, 24 (individual) or 50 hours (group) of psychotherapy, practicum. *Entrance requirements:* For master's, minimum undergraduate GPA of 2.75; official transcripts; three recommendations; 500-word essay; interview; 3 prerequisite courses completed with minimum C grade. Additional exam requirements/recommendations for international students: required—TOEFL (minimum score 80 iBT). Electronic applications accepted. *Expenses:* Contact institution.

California State University, Fresno, Division of Research and Graduate Studies, Kremen School of Education and Human Development, Department of Counselor Education and Rehabilitation, Program in Clinical Rehabilitation and Mental Health Counseling, Fresno, CA 93740-8027. Offers MS. *Accreditation:* ACA; CORE. *Program availability:* Part-time, evening/weekend. *Degree requirements:* For master's, internship; project, thesis, or comprehensive exam. *Entrance requirements:* For master's, GRE General Test, MAT, minimum GPA of 3.0, official transcripts. Additional exam requirements/recommendations for international students: required—TOEFL. Electronic applications accepted. *Expenses:* Tuition, state resident: full-time $4012; part-time $2506 per semester.

California State University, San Bernardino, Graduate Studies, College of Social and Behavioral Sciences, Department of Psychology, San Bernardino, CA 92407. Offers child development (MA); clinical/counseling psychology (MS); industrial/organizational psychology (MS); psychological science (MA). *Faculty:* 15 full-time (7 women). *Students:* 62 full-time (43 women), 13 part-time (7 women); includes 44 minority (3 Black or African American, non-Hispanic/Latino; 3 Asian, non-Hispanic/Latino; 31 Hispanic/Latino; 7 Two or more races, non-Hispanic/Latino), 5 international. Average age 27. 163 applicants, 24% accepted, 25 enrolled. In 2019, 32 master's awarded. *Degree requirements:* For master's, comprehensive exam, thesis (for some programs). *Entrance requirements:* Additional exam requirements/recommendations for international students: required—TOEFL. Application fee: $55. *Financial support:* Fellowships, research assistantships, and teaching assistantships available. *Unit head:* Dr. Robert Ricco, Chair, 909-537-5485, Fax: 909-537-7003, E-mail: rricco@csusb.edu. *Application contact:* Dr. Dorota Huizinga, Dean of Graduate Studies, 909-537-3064, E-mail:

dorota.huizinga@csusb.edu.
Website: https://csbs.csusb.edu/psychology

California State University, Stanislaus, College of Science, Programs in Psychology, Turlock, CA 95382. Offers behavior analysis (MA, MS); counseling psychology (MS); general psychology (MA). *Program availability:* Part-time. *Degree requirements:* For master's, thesis. *Entrance requirements:* For master's, GRE, minimum GPA of 3.0, 3 letters of reference, 16 psychology prerequisites, personal statement. Additional exam requirements/recommendations for international students: required—TOEFL (minimum score 550 paper-based). Electronic applications accepted.

California University of Pennsylvania, School of Graduate Studies and Research, College of Education and Human Services, Department of Counselor Education, California, PA 15419-1394. Offers clinical mental health counseling (MS); school counseling (M Ed). *Accreditation:* ACA; NCATE. *Program availability:* Part-time, evening/weekend. *Degree requirements:* For master's, comprehensive exam, thesis optional. *Entrance requirements:* For master's, MAT, minimum GPA of 3.0, resume, letters of reference. Additional exam requirements/recommendations for international students: required—TOEFL (minimum score 550 paper-based; 80 iBT). Electronic applications accepted. *Expenses: Tuition, area resident:* Full-time $9288; part-time $516 per credit. Tuition, state resident: full-time $9288; part-time $516 per credit. Tuition, nonresident: full-time $13,932; part-time $774 per credit. *Required fees:* $3631; $291.13 per credit. Part-time tuition and fees vary according to course load.

Cambridge College, School of Psychology and Counseling, Boston, MA 02129. Offers alcohol and drug counseling (Certificate); behavioral health care management (CAGS); marriage and family therapy (M Ed); mental health and school counseling (M Ed); mental health counseling (M Ed); psychological studies (M Ed); rehabilitation counseling (Certificate); school adjustment and mental health counseling (M Ed); school adjustment counseling for mental health counselors (Certificate); school counseling (M Ed); trauma studies (Certificate). *Program availability:* Part-time, evening/weekend. *Degree requirements:* For master's and other advanced degree, thesis, practicum/internship. *Entrance requirements:* For master's, resume, 2 professional references; for other advanced degree, official transcripts, documents for transfer credit evaluation, resume, written personal statement/essay, 2 professional references, health insurance, immunizations form. Additional exam requirements/recommendations for international students: required—TOEFL (minimum score 550 paper-based; 79 iBT), Michigan English Language Assessment Battery (minimum score 85); recommended—IELTS (minimum score 6). Electronic applications accepted. *Expenses:* Contact institution.

Capella University, Harold Abel School of Social and Behavioral Science, Master's Programs in Counseling, Minneapolis, MN 55402. Offers child and adolescent development (MS); general addiction counseling (MS); general marriage and family counseling/therapy (MS); general mental health counseling (MS); general school counseling (MS).

Capella University, Harold Abel School of Social and Behavioral Science, Master's Programs in Psychology, Minneapolis, MN 55402. Offers applied behavior analysis (MS); clinical psychology (MS); counseling psychology (MS); educational psychology (MS); evaluation, research, and measurement (MS); general advanced studies in human behavior (MS); general psychology (MS); industrial/organizational psychology (MS); leadership coaching psychology (MS); school psychology (MS); sport psychology (MS).

Carlow University, College of Leadership and Social Change, Doctor of Counseling Psychology, Pittsburgh, PA 15213-3165. Offers Psy D. *Accreditation:* APA. *Program availability:* Part-time, evening/weekend. *Students:* 34 full-time (28 women), 9 part-time (7 women); includes 7 minority (3 Black or African American, non-Hispanic/Latino; 1 Asian, non-Hispanic/Latino; 1 Hispanic/Latino; 2 Two or more races, non-Hispanic/Latino), 1 international. Average age 32. 27 applicants, 44% accepted, 11 enrolled. In 2019, 11 doctorates awarded. *Degree requirements:* For doctorate, thesis/dissertation, internship. *Entrance requirements:* For doctorate, GRE, resume or curriculum vitae; personal essay; reflective essay; official transcripts from all previous undergraduate and graduate institutions; three letters of recommendation; master's degree in closely-related field; interview. Additional exam requirements/recommendations for international students: required—TOEFL (minimum score 550 paper-based). *Application deadline:* Applications are processed on a rolling basis. Electronic applications accepted. *Expenses:* Contact institution. *Financial support:* Unspecified assistantships available. Financial award application deadline: 4/1; financial award applicants required to submit FAFSA. *Unit head:* Dr. Joseph M. Roberts, Chair, Psy D Program, 412-575-6331, Fax: 412-578-6357, E-mail: jmroberts@carlow.edu. *Application contact:* Dr. Joseph M. Roberts, Chair, Psy D Program, 412-575-6331, Fax: 412-578-6357, E-mail: jmroberts@carlow.edu.
Website: http://www.carlow.edu/PsyD_Counseling_Psychology.aspx

Carlow University, College of Leadership and Social Change, Program in Professional Counseling, Pittsburgh, PA 15213-3165. Offers child and family (MS). *Program availability:* Part-time, evening/weekend. *Students:* 114 full-time (99 women), 23 part-time (20 women); includes 26 minority (18 Black or African American, non-Hispanic/Latino; 1 Asian, non-Hispanic/Latino; 5 Hispanic/Latino; 2 Two or more races, non-Hispanic/Latino). Average age 30. 63 applicants, 100% accepted, 39 enrolled. In 2019, 42 master's, 3 other advanced degrees awarded. *Entrance requirements:* For master's, personal essay; resume or curriculum vitae; three recommendations; official transcripts; interview; minimum undergraduate GPA of 3.0. Additional exam requirements/recommendations for international students: required—TOEFL (minimum score 550 paper-based). *Application deadline:* Applications are processed on a rolling basis. Electronic applications accepted. *Financial support:* Application deadline: 4/1; applicants required to submit FAFSA. *Unit head:* Dr. Travis W. Schermer, Director, 412-575-6650, Fax: 412-575-6357, E-mail: twschermer@carlow.edu. *Application contact:* Dr. Travis W. Schermer, Director, 412-575-6650, Fax: 412-575-6357, E-mail: twschermer@carlow.edu.
Website: http://www.carlow.edu/Master_of_Science_in_Professional_Counseling.aspx

Carlow University, College of Leadership and Social Change, Student Affairs/Professional Counseling Dual Degree Program, Pittsburgh, PA 15213-3165. Offers MA/MS. *Program availability:* Part-time, evening/weekend. *Students:* 10 full-time (7 women), 1 (woman) part-time; includes 5 minority (4 Black or African American, non-Hispanic/Latino; 1 Two or more races, non-Hispanic/Latino). Average age 28. 10 applicants, 100% accepted, 5 enrolled. *Entrance requirements:* Additional exam requirements/recommendations for international students: required—TOEFL (minimum score 550 paper-based). *Application deadline:* Applications are processed on a rolling basis. Electronic applications accepted. *Financial support:* Application deadline: 4/1; applicants required to submit FAFSA. *Unit head:* Dr. Harriet Schwartz, Chair, 412-578-8720, E-mail: hlschwartz@carlow.edu. *Application contact:* Dr. Harriet Schwartz, Chair, 412-578-8720, E-mail: hlschwartz@carlow.edu.
Website: https://www.carlow.edu/MA_studentaffairs.aspx

Centenary University, Program in Counseling Psychology, Hackettstown, NJ 07840-2100. Offers counseling (MA); counseling psychology (MA). *Program availability:* Part-time, evening/weekend, online learning. *Degree requirements:* For master's, thesis, fieldwork.

Central Michigan University, Central Michigan University Global Campus, Program in Counseling, Mount Pleasant, MI 48859. Offers professional counseling (MA); school counseling (MA). *Accreditation:* TEAC. *Program availability:* Part-time, evening/weekend. *Entrance requirements:* For master's, MAT, minimum GPA of 2.7. Additional exam requirements/recommendations for international students: required—TOEFL. Electronic applications accepted. *Expenses: Tuition, area resident:* Full-time $12,267; part-time $8178 per year. Tuition, state resident: full-time $12,267; part-time $8178 per year. Tuition, nonresident: full-time $12,267; part-time $8178 per year. *International tuition:* $16,110 full-time. *Required fees:* $225 per semester. Tuition and fees vary according to degree level and program.

Central Michigan University, College of Graduate Studies, College of Liberal Arts and Social Sciences, Department of Psychology, Mount Pleasant, MI 48859. Offers clinical psychology (PhD); experimental psychology (MS, PhD), including applied experimental psychology (PhD), experimental psychology (MS); industrial and organizational psychology (MA, PhD), including industrial and organizational psychology, occupational health psychology (PhD); neuroscience (MS, PhD); school psychology (PhD, S Psy S), including psychological services (S Psy S), school psychology (PhD). *Accreditation:* APA (one or more programs are accredited). Terminal master's awarded for partial completion of doctoral program. *Degree requirements:* For master's, thesis or alternative; for doctorate, thesis/dissertation; for S Psy S, thesis. *Entrance requirements:* For doctorate, GRE. Electronic applications accepted. *Expenses: Tuition, area resident:* Full-time $12,267; part-time $8178 per year. Tuition, state resident: full-time $12,267; part-time $8178 per year. Tuition, nonresident: full-time $12,267; part-time $8178 per year. *International tuition:* $16,110 full-time. *Required fees:* $225 per semester. Tuition and fees vary according to degree level and program.

Central Washington University, School of Graduate Studies and Research, College of the Sciences, Department of Psychology, Program in Mental Health Counseling, Ellensburg, WA 98926. Offers MS. *Accreditation:* ACA. *Degree requirements:* For master's, thesis or alternative, internship. *Entrance requirements:* For master's, GRE General Test, minimum GPA of 3.0. Additional exam requirements/recommendations for international students: required—TOEFL (minimum score 550 paper-based; 79 iBT). Electronic applications accepted.

Chatham University, Program in Counseling Psychology, Pittsburgh, PA 15232-2826. Offers child, adolescent and family (MSCP); counseling psychology (Psy D); health and holistic (MSCP); organization and supervision (MSCP); sport and exercise (MSCP). *Accreditation:* APA. *Program availability:* Part-time, evening/weekend. *Faculty:* 13 full-time (8 women), 21 part-time/adjunct (17 women). *Students:* 93 full-time (79 women), 56 part-time (44 women); includes 29 minority (16 Black or African American, non-Hispanic/Latino; 4 Asian, non-Hispanic/Latino; 6 Hispanic/Latino; 3 Two or more races, non-Hispanic/Latino), 2 international. Average age 29. 172 applicants, 46% accepted, 54 enrolled. In 2019, 30 master's, 7 doctorates awarded. *Degree requirements:* For master's, thesis optional, supervised internship; for doctorate, thesis/dissertation, internship. *Entrance requirements:* For master's, minimum GPA of 3.0; 2 letters of recommendation; resume; prerequisite coursework in statistics, biology, and psychology; for doctorate, GRE. Additional exam requirements/recommendations for international students: required—TOEFL (minimum score 600 paper-based; 100 iBT), IELTS (minimum score 7), TWE. *Application deadline:* For fall admission, 4/1 priority date for domestic and international students; for spring admission, 11/1 for domestic students, 10/1 for international students. Applications are processed on a rolling basis. Application fee: $45. Electronic applications accepted. Application fee is waived when completed online. *Expenses:* $1,017 per credit hour. *Financial support:* Career-related internships or fieldwork available. Financial award applicants required to submit FAFSA. *Unit head:* Dr. Mary Jo Loughran, Director, 412-365-2783, Fax: 412-365-1505, E-mail: mloughran@chatham.edu. *Application contact:* Melanie Elmer, Assistant Director of Graduate Admission, 412-365-1394, Fax: 412-365-1609, E-mail: gradadmissions@chatham.edu.
Website: http://www.chatham.edu/mscp

Chestnut Hill College, School of Graduate Studies, Division of Psychology, Program in Clinical and Counseling Psychology, Philadelphia, PA 19118-2693. Offers clinical and counseling psychology (MS, CAS), including child and adolescent therapy, child and adolescent therapy with autism spectrum disorders, co-occurring disorders, couple and family therapy, diverse and underserved communities, generalist (MS), trauma studies. *Program availability:* Part-time, evening/weekend. *Degree requirements:* For master's, thesis optional, practica. *Entrance requirements:* For master's, GRE General Test, writing sample, letters of recommendation. Additional exam requirements/recommendations for international students: required—TOEFL (minimum score 500 paper-based), IELTS (minimum score 6.0), or TWE (minimum score 22). Electronic applications accepted. *Expenses:* Contact institution.

City University of Seattle, Graduate Division, Division of Arts and Sciences, Seattle, WA 98121. Offers counseling psychology (MA). *Accreditation:* ACA. *Program availability:* Part-time, evening/weekend, online learning. *Degree requirements:* For master's, comprehensive exam (for some programs), thesis (for some programs). *Entrance requirements:* For master's, baccalaureate degree or equivalent from an accredited or otherwise recognized institution. Additional exam requirements/recommendations for international students: recommended—TOEFL (minimum score 567 paper-based; 87 iBT), IELTS, TWE. Electronic applications accepted. *Expenses:* Contact institution.

Cleveland State University, College of Graduate Studies, College of Education and Human Services, Department of Counseling, Administration, Supervision and Adult Learning (CASAL), Cleveland, OH 44115. Offers adult learning and development (M Ed); counselor education (PhD); early childhood mental health counseling (Certificate); educational administration and supervision (M Ed). *Accreditation:* ACA (one or more programs are accredited). *Program availability:* Part-time, evening/weekend. *Degree requirements:* For master's, comprehensive exam (for some programs), thesis optional, internship. *Entrance requirements:* For master's, GRE General Test or MAT, letter of recommendation and minimum GPA of 2.75 (for counseling); 2 letters of recommendation and interviews (for organizational leadership). Additional exam requirements/recommendations for international students: required—TOEFL (minimum score 550 paper-based; 78 iBT), IELTS (minimum score 6). Electronic applications accepted. *Expenses:* Tuition, state resident: full-time $10,215; part-time $6810 per credit hour. Tuition, nonresident: full-time $17,496; part-time $11,664 per credit hour. *International tuition:* $19,316 full-time. Tuition and fees vary according to degree level and program.

Cleveland State University, College of Graduate Studies, College of Education and Human Services, Doctoral Studies in Education, Specialization in Counseling Psychology, Cleveland, OH 44115. Offers PhD. *Entrance requirements:* For doctorate, GRE (Verbal, Quantitative, and Writing), minimum undergraduate GPA of 2.75, graduate 3.0; 3 letters of recommendation; personal statement; curriculum vitae; interview. Additional exam requirements/recommendations for international students: required—TOEFL (minimum score 550 paper-based; 78 iBT), IELTS (minimum score 6). Electronic applications accepted. *Expenses:* Tuition, state resident: full-time $10,215; part-time $6810 per credit hour. Tuition, nonresident: full-time $17,496; part-time

$11,664 per credit hour. *International tuition:* $19,316 full-time. Tuition and fees vary according to degree level and program.

The College of New Rochelle, Graduate School, Division of Human Services, Program in Guidance and Counseling, New Rochelle, NY 10805-2308. Offers MS, Advanced Certificate. *Program availability:* Part-time. *Degree requirements:* For master's, internship. *Entrance requirements:* For master's, interview.

The College of New Rochelle, Graduate School, Division of Human Services, Program in Mental Health Counseling, New Rochelle, NY 10805-2308. Offers mental health counseling (MS); thanatology (Certificate). *Degree requirements:* For Certificate, internship.

College of Saint Elizabeth, Department of Psychology, Morristown, NJ 07960-6989. Offers counseling psychology (MA, Psy D), including mental health counseling (MA); school counseling (MA). *Program availability:* Part-time. *Degree requirements:* For master's, thesis or alternative; for doctorate, thesis/dissertation. *Entrance requirements:* For master's, minimum GPA of 3.0, BA in psychology (preferred), 12 credits of course work in psychology; for doctorate, GRE, 3 letters of recommendation from professionals who can comment on the applicant's qualifications for doctoral study; master's degree in counseling psychology, forensic psychology and counseling, or its equivalent. Additional exam requirements/recommendations for international students: required—TOEFL (minimum score 550 paper-based; 79 iBT), IELTS (minimum score 6.5). Electronic applications accepted. Application fee is waived when completed online. *Expenses:* Contact institution.

College of St. Joseph, Graduate Programs, Division of Psychology and Human Services, Program in Clinical Mental Health Counseling, Rutland, VT 05701-3899. Offers MS. *Program availability:* Part-time. *Degree requirements:* For master's, comprehensive exam. *Entrance requirements:* For master's, official college transcripts; 2 letters of reference. Additional exam requirements/recommendations for international students: required—TOEFL (minimum score 550 paper-based). Electronic applications accepted.

The College of Saint Rose, Graduate Studies, Thelma P. Lally School of Education, Programs in Clinical Mental Health Counseling, Albany, NY 12203-1419. Offers clinical mental health counseling (Certificate); school counseling (MS Ed, Certificate), including mental health counseling (MS Ed). *Students:* 28 full-time (26 women), 22 part-time (18 women); includes 9 minority (5 Black or African American, non-Hispanic/Latino; 1 Asian, non-Hispanic/Latino; 1 Hispanic/Latino; 2 Two or more races, non-Hispanic/Latino). Average age 29. 40 applicants, 55% accepted, 12 enrolled. In 2019, 18 master's awarded. *Entrance requirements:* For master's, minimum undergraduate GPA of 3.0. Additional exam requirements/recommendations for international students: required—TOEFL (minimum score 550 paper-based; 80 iBT), IELTS (minimum score 6), PTE (minimum score 56). *Application deadline:* For fall admission, 4/1 for domestic and international students; for spring admission, 10/15 priority date for domestic and international students; for summer admission, 3/15 for domestic and international students. Applications are processed on a rolling basis. Application fee: $40. Electronic applications accepted. *Expenses: Tuition:* Full-time $14,382; part-time $799 per credit hour. *Required fees:* $954; $698. Tuition and fees vary according to course load. *Financial support:* Career-related internships or fieldwork, scholarships/grants, tuition waivers (partial), and unspecified assistantships available. Support available to part-time students. Financial award application deadline: 4/15. *Unit head:* Claudia Lingertat-Putnam, Chair, 518-337-4311, E-mail: lingertc@strose.edu. *Application contact:* Daniel Gallagher, Assistant Vice President for Graduate Recruitment and Enrollment, 518-485-3390, Fax: 518-458-5479, E-mail: grad@strose.edu.
Website: https://www.strose.edu/counseling/

College of Staten Island of the City University of New York, Graduate Programs, Division of Humanities and Social Sciences, Staten Island, NY 10314-6600. Offers autism spectrum disorders (Advanced Certificate); cinema and media studies (MA); clinical mental health counseling (MA), including clinical mental health counseling; English (MA), including English; history (MA), including history; liberal studies (MA); public history (Advanced Certificate). *Expenses: Tuition,* area resident: Full-time $11,090; part-time $470 per credit. Tuition, state resident: full-time $11,090; part-time $470 per credit. Tuition, nonresident: full-time $20,520; part-time $855 per credit. *International tuition:* $20,520 full-time. *Required fees:* $559; $181 per semester. Tuition and fees vary according to program. *Unit head:* Dr. Sarolta Takacs, Dean of Humanities and Social Sciences, 718-982-2315, Fax: 718-982-2316, E-mail: sarolta.takacs@csi.cuny.edu. *Application contact:* Sasha Spence, Associate Director for Graduate Admissions, 718-982-2019, Fax: 718-982-2500, E-mail: sasha.spence@csi.cuny.edu.
Website: http://www.csi.cuny.edu/academicsresearch/deanhumanities/

Colorado Christian University, Program in Counseling, Lakewood, CO 80226. Offers MAC. *Accreditation:* ACA. *Program availability:* Part-time, evening/weekend. *Degree requirements:* For master's, thesis optional. *Entrance requirements:* For master's, GRE General Test, 3 letters of recommendation. Additional exam requirements/recommendations for international students: required—TOEFL. Electronic applications accepted. *Expenses:* Contact institution.

Concordia University Chicago, College of Graduate Studies, Program in Clinical Mental Health Counseling, River Forest, IL 60305-1499. Offers MA. *Accreditation:* ACA. *Program availability:* Blended/hybrid learning. *Degree requirements:* For master's, final project. *Entrance requirements:* For master's, minimum GPA of 2.9. Additional exam requirements/recommendations for international students: required—TOEFL (minimum score 550 paper-based). Electronic applications accepted.

Dallas Baptist University, College of Humanities and Social Sciences, Dallas, TX 75211-9299. Offers professional counseling (MA). *Expenses: Tuition:* Full-time $18,072; part-time $1004 per credit hour. *Required fees:* $1100; $550 per semester. Tuition and fees vary according to course level and degree level. *Unit head:* Dr. Rob Sullivan, Dean, 214-333-5238. *Application contact:* Dr. Mary Becerril, Program Director, 214-333-5265, Fax: 214-333-6819, E-mail: maryb@dbu.edu.
Website: https://www.dbu.edu/graduate/degree-programs/ma-professional-counseling

Delaware Valley University, Program in Counseling Psychology, Doylestown, PA 18901-2697. Offers child and adolescent therapy (MA); social justice community counseling (MA).

DePaul University, College of Education, Chicago, IL 60614. Offers bilingual-bicultural education (M Ed, MA); counseling (M Ed, MA), including clinical mental health counseling, college student development, school counseling; curriculum studies (M Ed, MA, Ed D); early childhood education (M Ed, MA, Ed D); educational leadership (M Ed, MA, Ed D), including Catholic leadership (M Ed, MA), general (M Ed, MA), higher education (M Ed, MA), physical education (M Ed, MA), principal preparation (M Ed), teacher preparation (M Ed); elementary education (M Ed, MA); middle grades education (M Ed); middle school mathematics education (MS); reading specialist (M Ed, MA); secondary education (M Ed, MA); social and cultural foundations in education (M Ed, MA); special education (M Ed); sport, fitness and recreation leadership (MS); value-creating education for global citizenship (M Ed); world languages education (M Ed, MA).

Program availability: Part-time, evening/weekend, online learning. *Degree requirements:* For doctorate, thesis/dissertation. Electronic applications accepted.

Duquesne University, School of Education, Department of Counseling, Psychology, and Special Education, Program in Counselor Education, Pittsburgh, PA 15282-0001. Offers clinical mental health counseling (MS Ed, Post-Master's Certificate); counselor education and supervision (Ed D); counselor licensure (Post-Master's Certificate); marriage and family counseling (MS Ed); school counseling (MS Ed). *Accreditation:* ACA (one or more programs are accredited). *Program availability:* Part-time, evening/weekend. *Degree requirements:* For master's, thesis optional; for doctorate, thesis/dissertation. *Entrance requirements:* For master's, letters of recommendation, essay, interview, bachelor's degree; for doctorate, GRE, letters of recommendation, essay, interview, master's degree; for Post-Master's Certificate, GRE, letters of recommendation, essay, interview, bachelor's/master's degree. Additional exam requirements/recommendations for international students: required—TOEFL (minimum score 550 paper-based), IELTS (minimum score 6.5). Electronic applications accepted.

Eastern Nazarene College, Adult and Graduate Studies, Program in Marriage and Family Therapy, Quincy, MA 02170. Offers MS. *Program availability:* Part-time, evening/weekend. *Entrance requirements:* For master's, 3 letters of recommendation, resume. Additional exam requirements/recommendations for international students: required—TOEFL (minimum score 550 paper-based).

Eastern Washington University, Graduate Studies, College of Social Sciences, Department of Psychology, Cheney, WA 99004-2431. Offers clinical psychology (MS); experimental psychology (MS); mental health counseling (MS), including applied psychology, mental health counseling; school counseling (MS), including applied psychology, school counseling; school psychology respecialization (Ed S). *Faculty:* 22 full-time (15 women). *Students:* 119 full-time (94 women), 13 part-time (10 women); includes 3 minority (all Hispanic/Latino), 6 international. Average age 34. 83 applicants, 42% accepted, 31 enrolled. In 2019, 49 master's awarded. *Degree requirements:* For master's, comprehensive exam, thesis or alternative. *Entrance requirements:* For master's, GRE General Test, minimum GPA of 3.0. Additional exam requirements/recommendations for international students: required—TOEFL (minimum score 580 paper-based; 92 iBT), IELTS (minimum score 7), PTE (minimum score 63). *Application deadline:* For fall admission, 3/1 for domestic students. Applications are processed on a rolling basis. Application fee: $75. Electronic applications accepted. *Financial support:* Teaching assistantships with partial tuition reimbursements, career-related internships or fieldwork, Federal Work-Study, institutionally sponsored loans, scholarships/grants, health care benefits, tuition waivers (partial), and unspecified assistantships available. Support available to part-time students. Financial award application deadline: 2/1; financial award applicants required to submit FAFSA. *Unit head:* Dennis Anderson, 509-359-2087, E-mail: danderson2@ewu.edu. *Application contact:* Kathy White, Advisor/Recruiter for Graduate Studies, 509-359-6297, Fax: 509-359-6044, E-mail: gradprograms@ewu.edu.

East Texas Baptist University, Master of Arts in Clinical Mental Health Counseling, Marshall, TX 75670-1498. Offers MA. *Program availability:* Part-time, evening/weekend. *Faculty:* 3 full-time (2 women). *Students:* 5 full-time (3 women), 15 part-time (all women); includes 11 minority (8 Black or African American, non-Hispanic/Latino; 1 American Indian or Alaska Native, non-Hispanic/Latino; 2 Hispanic/Latino). Average age 32. 11 applicants, 73% accepted, 6 enrolled. In 2019, 11 master's awarded. *Entrance requirements:* Additional exam requirements/recommendations for international students: recommended—TOEFL (minimum score 550 paper-based; 79 iBT). *Application deadline:* For fall admission, 8/13 for domestic students; for spring admission, 1/7 for domestic students; for summer admission, 5/5 for domestic students. Applications are processed on a rolling basis. Application fee: $50. Electronic applications accepted. *Expenses:* $725 per credit hour tuition; $155 per semester fees (6 or more hours enrolled); $77 per semester fees (1-5 hours enrolled). *Financial support:* In 2019–20, 4 students received support. Scholarships/grants, unspecified assistantships, and staff grants available. Financial award applicants required to submit FAFSA. *Unit head:* Dr. Allen Appiah-Boateng, Director, 903-923-2318, E-mail: gradadmissions@etbu.edu. *Application contact:* Den Murley, Director of Graduate Admissions, 903-923-2079, Fax: 903-934-8115, E-mail: gradadmissions@etbu.edu.
Website: https://www.etbu.edu/academics/academic-schools/school-natural-and-social-sciences/department-behavioral-sciences/programs

Edinboro University of Pennsylvania, Department of Counseling, School Psychology and Special Education, Edinboro, PA 16444. Offers counseling (MA), including art therapy, clinical mental health counseling, college counseling, rehabilitation counseling, school counseling; educational psychology (M Ed); school psychology (Ed S); special education (M Ed), including autism, behavior management. *Accreditation:* ACA. *Program availability:* Part-time, evening/weekend. *Faculty:* 19 full-time (13 women), 2 part-time/adjunct (1 woman). *Students:* 180 full-time (146 women), 215 part-time (186 women); includes 42 minority (18 Black or African American, non-Hispanic/Latino; 2 American Indian or Alaska Native, non-Hispanic/Latino; 4 Asian, non-Hispanic/Latino; 12 Hispanic/Latino; 1 Native Hawaiian or other Pacific Islander, non-Hispanic/Latino; 5 Two or more races, non-Hispanic/Latino), 3 international. Average age 31. 197 applicants, 63% accepted, 71 enrolled. In 2019, 87 master's, 8 other advanced degrees awarded. *Degree requirements:* For master's, thesis or alternative, competency exam; for Ed S, thesis or alternative. *Entrance requirements:* For master's and Ed S, GRE or MAT, minimum QPA of 2.5. Additional exam requirements/recommendations for international students: required—TOEFL (minimum score 550 paper-based; 213 iBT), IELTS (minimum score 6.5). *Application deadline:* Applications are processed on a rolling basis. Application fee: $30. Electronic applications accepted. *Expenses: Tuition,* area resident: Full-time $11,261; part-time $625.60 per credit. Tuition, state resident: full-time $11,261; part-time $625.60 per credit. Tuition, nonresident: full-time $16,850; part-time $936.10 per credit. *International tuition:* $16,850 full-time. *Required fees:* $57.75 per credit. *Financial support:* In 2019–20, 35 students received support. Research assistantships with tuition reimbursements available, career-related internships or fieldwork, Federal Work-Study, scholarships/grants, and unspecified assistantships available. Support available to part-time students. Financial award application deadline: 2/15; financial award applicants required to submit FAFSA. *Unit head:* Dr. Penelope Orr, Chairperson, 814-732-1684, E-mail: porr@edinboro.edu. *Application contact:* Dr. Penelope Orr, Chairperson, 814-732-1684, E-mail: porr@edinboro.edu.
Website: https://www.edinboro.edu/academics/schools-and-departments/soe/departments/cspe/

Emporia State University, Program in Clinical Counseling, Emporia, KS 66801-5415. Offers MS. *Accreditation:* ACA. *Program availability:* Part-time. *Degree requirements:* For master's, comprehensive exam, internship. *Entrance requirements:* For master's, GRE or MAT. Additional exam requirements/recommendations for international students: required—TOEFL (minimum score 520 paper-based; 68 iBT). Electronic applications accepted. *Expenses: Tuition,* area resident: Full-time $6394; part-time $266.41 per credit hour. Tuition, state resident: full-time $6394; part-time $266.41 per credit hour. Tuition, nonresident: full-time $20,128; part-time $828.66 per credit hour. *International tuition:* $20,128 full-time. *Required fees:* $2183; $90.95 per credit hour. Tuition and fees vary according to campus/location and program.

Counseling Psychology

Evangel University, Department of Behavioral and Social Sciences, Springfield, MO 65802. Offers clinical mental health counseling (MS). *Program availability:* Part-time. *Degree requirements:* For master's, comprehensive exam. *Entrance requirements:* For master's, GRE General Test, minimum undergraduate GPA of 3.0. Additional exam requirements/recommendations for international students: required—TOEFL (minimum score 550 paper-based). Electronic applications accepted. Application fee is waived when completed online.

Fairfield University, Graduate School of Education and Allied Professions, Fairfield, CT 06824. Offers applied behavior analysis (ATC); applied psychology (MA); clinical mental health counseling (MA, CAS); educational technology (MA); elementary education (MA, CAS); family studies (MA); integration of spirituality and religion in counseling (ATC); marriage and family therapy (MA); reading and language development (Sixth Year Certificate); school counseling (MA, CAS); school psychology (MA, CAS); school-based marriage and family therapy (ATC); secondary education (MA); special education (MA, CAS); substance abuse counseling (ATC); teaching (Certificate); teaching and foundations (MA, CAS); TESOL, world languages, and bilingual education (MA, CAS). *Accreditation:* NCATE. *Program availability:* Part-time, evening/weekend. *Faculty:* 24 full-time (18 women), 28 part-time/adjunct (20 women). *Students:* 169 full-time (149 women), 227 part-time (187 women); includes 96 minority (21 Black or African American, non-Hispanic/Latino; 8 Asian, non-Hispanic/Latino; 60 Hispanic/Latino; 7 Two or more races, non-Hispanic/Latino), 1 international. Average age 31. 194 applicants, 60% accepted, 101 enrolled. In 2019, 136 master's, 28 other advanced degrees awarded. *Degree requirements:* For master's, comprehensive exam. *Entrance requirements:* For master's, One of the following for certification programs: Praxis Core, SAT, ACT, or GRE, minimum GPA of 3.0, 2 recommendations, resume. Additional exam requirements/recommendations for international students: required—TOEFL (minimum score 550 paper-based; 84 iBT), IELTS (minimum score 7.5), TOEFL (minimum score 550 paper-based; 84 iBT) or IELTS (minimum score 7.5). *Application deadline:* For fall admission, 2/15 for international students; for spring admission, 10/1 for international students. Application fee: $60. Electronic applications accepted. *Expenses:* Tuition $815/credit hour; Lab Fee (ED598) $300/semester; Lab Fee (CN457,CN467, PY538, PY540) $70/course; Wilson Reading Course Fee $141/credit hour; Registration Fee $50/semester; Graduate Student Activity Fee (Fall and Spring) $65/semester. *Financial support:* In 2019–20, 34 students received support. Career-related internships or fieldwork and unspecified assistantships available. Support available to part-time students. Financial award applicants required to submit FAFSA. *Unit head:* Dr. Laurie Grupp, Dean, 203-254-4250, Fax: 203-254-4241, E-mail: lgrupp@fairfield.edu. *Application contact:* Melanie Rogers, Director of Graduate Admission, 203-254-4184, Fax: 203-254-4073, E-mail: gradadmis@fairfield.edu. Website: http://www.fairfield.edu/gseap

Fairleigh Dickinson University, Florham Campus, Maxwell Becton College of Arts and Sciences, Department of Psychology, Program in Clinical Mental Health Counseling, Madison, NJ 07940-1099. Offers MA. *Accreditation:* ACA.

Fairleigh Dickinson University, Florham Campus, Maxwell Becton College of Arts and Sciences, Department of Psychology, Program in Counseling, Madison, NJ 07940-1099. Offers MA. *Accreditation:* ACA.

Felician University, Program in Counseling Psychology, Lodi, NJ 07644-2117. Offers MA, Psy D. *Program availability:* Part-time, evening/weekend. Terminal master's awarded for partial completion of doctoral program. *Degree requirements:* For master's, comprehensive exam, thesis, presentation; for doctorate, thesis/dissertation, scholarly project. *Entrance requirements:* For master's, two letters of recommendation, interview, resume, personal statement, graduation from accredited baccalaureate program. Additional exam requirements/recommendations for international students: required—TOEFL (minimum score 550 paper-based; 79 iBT), IELTS (minimum score 6.5), PTE (minimum score 56). Electronic applications accepted. Application fee is waived when completed online. *Expenses:* Contact institution.

Fitchburg State University, Division of Graduate and Continuing Education, Programs in Counseling, Fitchburg, MA 01420-2697. Offers clinical mental health counseling (MS); school guidance counseling (MS). *Accreditation:* NCATE. *Program availability:* Part-time, evening/weekend. *Entrance requirements:* Additional exam requirements/recommendations for international students: required—TOEFL (minimum score 550 paper-based; 79 iBT). Electronic applications accepted. *Expenses:* Contact institution.

Florida International University, College of Arts, Sciences, and Education, Department of Psychology, Miami, FL 33199. Offers behavioral analysis (MS); clinical science (PhD); cognitive neuroscience (PhD); counseling psychology (MS); developmental science (MS, PhD); legal psychology (MS, PhD); organizational psychology (MS, PhD). *Accreditation:* APA. *Program availability:* Part-time, evening/weekend. *Faculty:* 52 full-time (33 women), 50 part-time/adjunct (37 women). *Students:* 203 full-time (159 women), 2 part-time (both women); includes 117 minority (15 Black or African American, non-Hispanic/Latino; 8 Asian, non-Hispanic/Latino; 86 Hispanic/Latino; 8 Two or more races, non-Hispanic/Latino), 15 international. Average age 26. 410 applicants, 19% accepted, 60 enrolled. In 2019, 57 master's, 7 doctorates awarded. Terminal master's awarded for partial completion of doctoral program. *Degree requirements:* For master's, thesis; for doctorate, comprehensive exam, thesis/dissertation. *Entrance requirements:* For master's, GRE General Test, minimum GPA of 3.0, resume, 3 letters of recommendation; for doctorate, GRE General Test, 3 letters of recommendation, resume, letter of intent, two writing samples, minimum GPA of 3.0. Additional exam requirements/recommendations for international students: required—TOEFL (minimum score 550 paper-based; 80 iBT). *Application deadline:* For fall admission, 12/15 for domestic and international students. Application fee: $30. Electronic applications accepted. *Expenses: Tuition, area resident:* Full-time $8912; part-time $446 per credit hour. *Tuition, state resident:* full-time $8912; part-time $446 per credit hour. *Tuition, nonresident:* full-time $21,393; part-time $992 per credit hour. *Required fees:* $2194. *Financial support:* Institutionally sponsored loans and scholarships/grants available. Financial award application deadline: 3/1. *Unit head:* Dr. Jeremy Pettit, Interim Chair, 305-348-1671, Fax: 305-348-2880, E-mail: jeremy.pettit@fiu.edu. *Application contact:* Nanett Rojas, Manager, Admissions Operations, 305-348-7464, Fax: 305-348-7441, E-mail: gradadm@fiu.edu.

Fordham University, Graduate School of Education, Division of Psychological and Educational Services, New York, NY 10023. Offers counseling and personnel services (MSE); counseling psychology (PhD); school psychology (PhD). *Accreditation:* APA (one or more programs are accredited); NCATE. *Program availability:* Part-time, evening/weekend. Terminal master's awarded for partial completion of doctoral program. *Degree requirements:* For master's, comprehensive exam (for some programs); for doctorate, comprehensive exam (for some programs), thesis/dissertation. *Entrance requirements:* For doctorate, GRE General Test. Additional exam requirements/recommendations for international students: required—TOEFL (minimum score 577 paper-based; 90 iBT), IELTS (minimum score 7). Electronic applications accepted.

Fort Valley State University, College of Graduate Studies and Extended Education, Department of Counseling Psychology, Program in Mental Health Counseling, Fort Valley, GA 31030. Offers MS. *Accreditation:* ACA. *Program availability:* Part-time.

Degree requirements: For master's, comprehensive exam (for some programs), thesis optional. *Entrance requirements:* For master's, GRE General Test or MAT. Additional exam requirements/recommendations for international students: recommended—TOEFL.

Framingham State University, Graduate Studies, Program in Counseling Psychology, Framingham, MA 01701-9101. Offers MA. *Program availability:* Part-time, evening/weekend.

Franciscan University of Steubenville, Graduate Programs, Department of Clinical Mental Health Counseling, Steubenville, OH 43952-1763. Offers MA. *Accreditation:* ACA. *Program availability:* Part-time. *Degree requirements:* For master's, case presentation, integrative paper. *Entrance requirements:* For master's, GRE General Test or MAT for those with a GPA below 3.0, minimum undergraduate GPA of 2.5. Additional exam requirements/recommendations for international students: required—TOEFL. Electronic applications accepted. *Expenses:* Contact institution.

Francis Marion University, Graduate Programs, Department of Psychology, Florence, SC 29502-0547. Offers applied psychology (MS), including clinical/counseling psychology, school psychology; school psychology (SSP). *Program availability:* Part-time, evening/weekend. *Degree requirements:* For master's, internship. *Entrance requirements:* For master's, GRE General Test, official transcripts, two letters of recommendation. Additional exam requirements/recommendations for international students: required—TOEFL (minimum score 550 paper-based; 79 iBT). *Expenses: Tuition, area resident:* Full-time $10,612; part-time $530.60 per credit hour. *Tuition, state resident:* full-time $10,612; part-time $530.60 per credit hour. *Tuition, nonresident:* full-time $21,224; part-time $1061.20 per credit hour. *International tuition:* $21,224 full-time. *Required fees:* $312; $156 per credit hour. $332 per semester. Tuition and fees vary according to program.

Frostburg State University, College of Liberal Arts and Sciences, Department of Psychology, Program in Counseling Psychology, Frostburg, MD 21532-1099. Offers MS. *Program availability:* Part-time, evening/weekend. *Degree requirements:* For master's, internship. *Entrance requirements:* For master's, GRE General Test or MAT, interview, minimum GPA of 3.0, resume. Additional exam requirements/recommendations for international students: required—TOEFL. Electronic applications accepted.

Gallaudet University, The Graduate School, Washington, DC 20002. Offers American Sign Language/English bilingual early childhood deaf education: birth to 5 (Certificate); audiology (Au D); clinical psychology (PhD); deaf and hard of hearing infants, toddlers, and their families (Certificate); deaf education (MA, Ed S); deaf history (Certificate); deaf studies (Certificate); educating deaf students with disabilities (Certificate); education: teacher preparation (MA), including deaf education, early childhood education and deaf education, elementary education and deaf education, secondary education and deaf education; educational neuroscience (PhD); hearing, speech and language sciences (MS, PhD); international development (MA); interpretation (MA, PhD), including combined interpreting practice and research (MA), interpreting research (MA); linguistics (MA, PhD); mental health counseling (MA); peer mentoring (Certificate); public administration (MPA); school counseling (MA); school psychology (Psy S); sign language teaching (MA); social work (MSW); speech-language pathology (MS). *Program availability:* Part-time. *Faculty:* 101 full-time (70 women). *Students:* 267 full-time (208 women), 139 part-time (95 women); includes 120 minority (38 Black or African American, non-Hispanic/Latino; 20 Asian, non-Hispanic/Latino; 44 Hispanic/Latino; 18 Two or more races, non-Hispanic/Latino), 19 international. Average age 30. 484 applicants, 50% accepted, 162 enrolled. In 2019, 138 master's, 25 doctorates, 14 other advanced degrees awarded. Terminal master's awarded for partial completion of doctoral program. *Degree requirements:* For master's, comprehensive exam (for some programs), thesis optional; for doctorate, comprehensive exam, thesis/dissertation. *Entrance requirements:* For master's and doctorate, GRE General Test or MAT, letters of recommendation, interviews, goals statement, American Sign Language proficiency interview, written English competency. Additional exam requirements/recommendations for international students: required—TOEFL. *Application deadline:* For fall admission, 2/15 for domestic students. Applications are processed on a rolling basis. Application fee: $75. Electronic applications accepted. *Expenses: Tuition:* Full-time $18,180; part-time $688 per credit. *Required fees:* $526; $526. Tuition and fees vary according to course load. *Financial support:* In 2019–20, 50 students received support. Fellowships, research assistantships, teaching assistantships, career-related internships or fieldwork, Federal Work-Study, scholarships/grants, tuition waivers (partial), and unspecified assistantships available. Support available to part-time students. Financial award application deadline: 7/1; financial award applicants required to submit FAFSA. *Unit head:* Dr. Gaurav Mathur, Dean, Graduate School and Continuing Studies, 202-250-2380, Fax: 202-651-5027, E-mail: gaurav.mathur@gallaudet.edu. *Application contact:* Heidi Zornes-Foster, Senior Graduate Admissions Counselor, 202-650-5436, Fax: 202-651-5295, E-mail: graduate.school@gallaudet.edu. Website: www.gallaudet.edu

Gannon University, School of Graduate Studies, College of Humanities, Education, and Social Sciences, School of Humanities, Program in Clinical Mental Health Counseling, Erie, PA 16541-0001. Offers MS. *Accreditation:* ACA. *Program availability:* Part-time, evening/weekend. *Degree requirements:* For master's, thesis, internship. *Entrance requirements:* For master's, bachelor's degree from approved institution, resume, 3 letters of recommendation, essay, interview, minimum GPA of 2.8, PA child abuse clearances and PA State Police criminal record check dated within a year of application. Additional exam requirements/recommendations for international students: required—TOEFL (minimum score 79 iBT). Electronic applications accepted. Application fee is waived when completed online.

Gardner-Webb University, Graduate School, School of Psychology, Boiling Springs, NC 28017. Offers mental health counseling (MA); school counseling (MA). *Program availability:* Part-time, evening/weekend. *Degree requirements:* For master's, comprehensive exam. *Entrance requirements:* For master's, GRE General Test, MAT, minimum GPA of 2.7. Electronic applications accepted. *Expenses:* Contact institution.

Geneva College, Master of Arts in Counseling Program, Beaver Falls, PA 15010. Offers clinical mental health counseling (MA); marriage and family counseling (MA); school counseling (MA). *Accreditation:* ACA. *Program availability:* Part-time, evening/weekend, online only, 100% online, blended/hybrid learning. *Faculty:* 4 full-time (1 woman), 5 part-time/adjunct (2 women). *Students:* 26 full-time (20 women), 22 part-time (17 women); includes 11 minority (9 Black or African American, non-Hispanic/Latino; 1 Asian, non-Hispanic/Latino; 1 Two or more races, non-Hispanic/Latino), 1 international. Average age 33. 24 applicants, 63% accepted, 14 enrolled. In 2019, 34 master's awarded. *Degree requirements:* For master's, comprehensive exam, 60 credits including practicum and internship. *Entrance requirements:* For master's, minimum GPA of 3.0 (preferred), 3 letters of recommendation, essay on career goals, resume of educational and professional experiences. Additional exam requirements/recommendations for international students: required—TOEFL. *Application deadline:* For fall admission, 9/1 for domestic students; for spring admission, 1/10 for domestic students. Applications are processed on a rolling basis. Electronic applications accepted. *Expenses:* $680 per credit. 60 credits required for graduation. *Financial support:* Research assistantships,

teaching assistantships, career-related internships or fieldwork, and unspecified assistantships available. Financial award application deadline: 8/1; financial award applicants required to submit FAFSA. *Unit head:* Dr. Shannan Shiderly, Program Director, 724-847-6649, Fax: 724-847-6101, E-mail: slshider@geneva.edu. *Application contact:* Marina Frazier, Graduate Program Manager, 724-847-6697, E-mail: counseling@geneva.edu.
Website: https://www.geneva.edu/graduate/counseling/

George Fox University, College of Education, Graduate Department of Counseling, Newberg, OR 97132-2697. Offers clinical mental health counseling (MA); marriage, couple and family counseling (MA, Certificate); school counseling (MA, Certificate); school psychology (Ed S). *Program availability:* Part-time. *Degree requirements:* For master's, clinical project. *Entrance requirements:* For master's, MAT or GRE, bachelor's degree from regionally-accredited college or university, minimum cumulative GPA of 3.0, 1 professional and 1 academic reference, resume, on-campus interview, official transcripts. Additional exam requirements/recommendations for international students: required—TOEFL (minimum score 577 paper-based; 90 iBT), IELTS (minimum score 7). Electronic applications accepted. *Expenses:* Contact institution.

Georgian Court University, School of Arts and Sciences, Lakewood, NJ 08701. Offers applied behavior analysis (MA); autism spectrum disorders (Certificate); clinical mental health counseling (MA); criminal justice and human rights (MS); holistic health studies (MA); homeland security (Certificate); instructional technology (CPC); integrative health (Certificate); mercy spirituality (Certificate); parish business management (Certificate); professional counselor (Certificate); school psychology (MA, Certificate); theology (MA, Certificate). *Program availability:* Part-time, evening/weekend. *Faculty:* 19 full-time (11 women), 7 part-time/adjunct (3 women). *Students:* 90 full-time (80 women), 71 part-time (59 women); includes 26 minority (8 Black or African American, non-Hispanic/Latino; 2 Asian, non-Hispanic/Latino; 14 Hispanic/Latino; 2 Two or more races, non-Hispanic/Latino), 1 international. Average age 32. 138 applicants, 58% accepted, 57 enrolled. In 2019, 68 master's, 19 other advanced degrees awarded. *Degree requirements:* For master's, comprehensive exam (for some programs), thesis (for some programs); for other advanced degree, comprehensive exam (for some programs). *Entrance requirements:* Additional exam requirements/recommendations for international students: required—TOEFL (minimum score 550 paper-based; 79 iBT). *Application deadline:* For fall admission, 8/15 for domestic students, 5/1 for international students; for spring admission, 1/15 for domestic students, 10/1 for international students. Applications are processed on a rolling basis. Application fee: $40. Electronic applications accepted. *Financial support:* Scholarships/grants, health care benefits, and unspecified assistantships available. Financial award application deadline: 4/15; financial award applicants required to submit FAFSA. *Unit head:* Dr. Mary Chinery, Dean, 732-987-2493, Fax: 732-987-2007, E-mail: mchinery@georgian.edu. *Application contact:* Dr. Mary Chinery, Dean, 732-987-2493, Fax: 732-987-2007, E-mail: mchinery@georgian.edu.
Website: https://georgian.edu/academics/school-of-arts-sciences/

Georgia Southern University, Jack N. Averitt College of Graduate Studies, College of Education, Department of Leadership, Technology, and Human Development, Program in Counselor Education, Statesboro, GA 30460. Offers mental health counseling (M Ed); school counseling (M Ed). *Accreditation:* ACA; NCATE. *Program availability:* Part-time, evening/weekend. *Students:* 46 full-time (39 women), 2 part-time (1 woman); includes 18 minority (13 Black or African American, non-Hispanic/Latino; 4 Hispanic/Latino; 1 Two or more races, non-Hispanic/Latino). Average age 27. 52 applicants, 48% accepted, 13 enrolled. In 2019, 16 master's awarded. *Degree requirements:* For master's, comprehensive exam, transition point assessments. *Entrance requirements:* For master's, minimum GPA of 2.5, letters of recommendation, interview. Additional exam requirements/recommendations for international students: required—TOEFL (minimum score 550 paper-based; 80 iBT), IELTS (minimum score 6). *Application deadline:* For fall admission, 3/2 for domestic students, 3/15 for international students; for spring admission, 3/2 for domestic students, 10/1 for international students. Application fee: $50. Electronic applications accepted. *Expenses: Tuition, area resident:* Full-time $4986; part-time $277 per credit hour. Tuition, nonresident: full-time $19,890; part-time $1105 per credit hour. *International tuition:* $19,890 full-time. *Required fees:* $2114; $1057 per semester. $1057 per semester. Tuition and fees vary according to course load, campus/location and program. *Financial support:* In 2019–20, 27 students received support, including 3 research assistantships with full tuition reimbursements available (averaging $7,750 per year); career-related internships or fieldwork, scholarships/grants, and unspecified assistantships also available. Financial award application deadline: 4/15; financial award applicants required to submit FAFSA. *Unit head:* Dr. Brandon Hunt, Program Director, 912-478-0502, Fax: 912-478-7104, E-mail: bhunt@georgiasouthern.edu. *Application contact:* Dr. Lydia Cross, Graduate Academic Services Center, 912-478-8664, E-mail: lcross@georgiasouthern.edu.
Website: http://coe.georgiasouthern.edu/coun/

Georgia State University, College of Education and Human Development, Department of Counseling and Psychological Services, Program in Mental Health Counseling, Atlanta, GA 30302-3083. Offers MS, Ed S. *Accreditation:* ACA (one or more programs are accredited); APA (one or more programs are accredited). *Entrance requirements:* For master's, GRE, goal statement, resume, 3 letters of recommendation, transcripts. Additional exam requirements/recommendations for international students: required—TOEFL. Application fee: $50. Electronic applications accepted. *Expenses: Tuition, area resident:* Full-time $7164; part-time $398 per credit hour. Tuition, state resident: full-time $7164; part-time $398 per credit hour. Tuition, nonresident: full-time $22,662; part-time $1259 per credit hour. *International tuition:* $22,662 full-time. *Required fees:* $2128; $312 per credit hour. Tuition and fees vary according to course load and program. *Financial support:* Research assistantships, teaching assistantships, career-related internships or fieldwork, scholarships/grants, health care benefits, and unspecified assistantships available. Financial award application deadline: 4/1. *Unit head:* Dr. Brian Dew, Chairperson, 404-413-8168, Fax: 404-413-8013, E-mail: bdew@gsu.edu. *Application contact:* Dr. Brian Dew, Chairperson, 404-413-8168, Fax: 404-413-8013, E-mail: bdew@gsu.edu.
Website: https://education.gsu.edu/cps/

Governors State University, College of Education, Program in Counseling, University Park, IL 60484. Offers MA. *Accreditation:* ACA. *Program availability:* Part-time. *Faculty:* 23 full-time (15 women), 50 part-time/adjunct (37 women). *Students:* 79 full-time (70 women), 106 part-time (96 women); includes 103 minority (72 Black or African American, non-Hispanic/Latino; 3 Asian, non-Hispanic/Latino; 23 Hispanic/Latino; 5 Two or more races, non-Hispanic/Latino), 3 international. Average age 37. 81 applicants, 32% accepted, 23 enrolled. In 2019, 46 master's awarded. *Application deadline:* For fall admission, 4/1 for domestic students. Applications are processed on a rolling basis. Application fee: $50. Electronic applications accepted. *Expenses:* $477/credit hour; $5,724 in tuition/term; $7,022 in tuition and fees/term; $14,044/year. *Financial support:* Application deadline: 5/1; applicants required to submit FAFSA. *Unit head:* Patricia Robey, Chair, Division of Psychology and Counseling, 708-534-5000 Ext. 4975, E-mail: probey@govst.edu. *Application contact:* Patricia Robey, Chair, Division of Psychology and Counseling, 708-534-5000 Ext. 4975, E-mail: probey@govst.edu.

Hardin-Simmons University, Graduate School, Cynthia Ann Parker College of Liberal Arts, Department of Psychology, Abilene, TX 79698-0001. Offers clinical counseling and marriage and family therapy (MA). *Program availability:* Part-time. *Degree requirements:* For master's, comprehensive exam, clinical experience, project. *Entrance requirements:* For master's, 21 semester hours of course work in psychology (18 in upper-division classes); minimum undergraduate GPA of 3.0 in major, 2.7 overall; writing sample; letters of recommendation. Additional exam requirements/recommendations for international students: required—TOEFL (minimum score 550 paper-based; 79 iBT). Electronic applications accepted.

Heidelberg University, Master of Arts in Counseling Program, Tiffin, OH 44883-2462. Offers school counseling (MA). *Accreditation:* ACA. *Program availability:* Part-time, evening/weekend. *Students:* 47 full-time (36 women), 23 part-time (18 women). 43 applicants, 88% accepted, 21 enrolled. In 2019, 7 master's awarded. *Degree requirements:* For master's, counseling practicum, internship. *Entrance requirements:* For master's, bachelor's degree with minimum GPA of 2.9; 12 hours of coursework in behavioral sciences; 3 letters of recommendation; 2-3 page goal statement. Additional exam requirements/recommendations for international students: required—TOEFL (minimum score 79 paper-based), IELTS (minimum score 6.5), TOEFL (minimum score 550 paper-based, 79 iBT) or IELTS (minimum score 6.5). *Application deadline:* For fall admission, 8/15 for domestic students, 6/1 for international students; for spring admission, 12/3 for domestic students, 11/1 for international students; for summer admission, 5/1 for domestic students, 4/1 for international students. Applications are processed on a rolling basis. Application fee: $0. Electronic applications accepted. Application fee is waived when completed online. *Expenses: Tuition:* Full-time $15,580; part-time $744 per credit hour. One-time fee: $240. *Financial support:* Unspecified assistantships available. Financial award applicants required to submit FAFSA. *Unit head:* Dr. Marjorie Shavers, Director of Graduate Studies in Counseling, 419-448-2308, E-mail: mshavers@heidelberg.edu. *Application contact:* Katie Zeyen, Graduate Admissions Coordinator, 419-448-2602, Fax: 419-448-2565, E-mail: kzeyen@heidelberg.edu.
Website: https://www.heidelberg.edu/academics/programs/master-of-counseling

Henderson State University, Graduate Studies, Teachers College, Department of Counselor Education, Arkadelphia, AR 71999-0001. Offers clinical mental health counseling (MS); developmental therapy (MS, Graduate Certificate); secondary school counseling (MSE). *Accreditation:* NCATE. *Program availability:* Part-time. *Entrance requirements:* For master's, GRE General Test or MAT, letters of recommendation, minimum GPA of 2.7, teacher certification. Additional exam requirements/recommendations for international students: required—TOEFL (minimum score 600 paper-based); recommended—IELTS (minimum score 6.5).

Hodges University, Graduate Programs, Naples, FL 34119. Offers accounting (M Acc); business administration (MBA); clinical mental health counseling (MS); health services administration (MS); information systems management (MIS); legal studies (MS); management (MSM). *Program availability:* Part-time, evening/weekend, 100% online, blended/hybrid learning. *Degree requirements:* For master's, comprehensive exam (for some programs), thesis (for some programs). *Entrance requirements:* For master's, essay. Additional exam requirements/recommendations for international students: recommended—TOEFL. Electronic applications accepted.

Hofstra University, School of Health Professions and Human Services, Programs in Counseling, Hempstead, NY 11549. Offers counseling (MS Ed, PD); creative arts therapy (MA); interdisciplinary transition specialist (Advanced Certificate); marriage and family therapy (MA); mental health counseling (MA, Advanced Certificate); rehabilitation administration (PD); rehabilitation counseling (MS Ed, Advanced Certificate); rehabilitation counseling in mental health (MS Ed, Advanced Certificate). *Accreditation:* ACA. *Program availability:* Part-time, evening/weekend. *Students:* 124 full-time (105 women), 69 part-time (64 women); includes 68 minority (23 Black or African American, non-Hispanic/Latino; 10 Asian, non-Hispanic/Latino; 32 Hispanic/Latino; 3 Native Hawaiian or other Pacific Islander, non-Hispanic/Latino), 4 international. Average age 28. 188 applicants, 77% accepted, 75 enrolled. In 2019, 58 master's, 3 other advanced degrees awarded. *Degree requirements:* For master's, comprehensive exam (for some programs), thesis (for some programs), internship, practicum, student teaching, seminars, minimum GPA of 3.0. *Entrance requirements:* For master's, GRE, interview, letters of recommendation, portfolio, essay, professional experience, certification; for other advanced degree, GRE, interview, letters of recommendation, essay, professional experience, resume, master's degree. Additional exam requirements/recommendations for international students: required—TOEFL (minimum score 550 paper-based; 80 iBT); recommended—IELTS (minimum score 6.5). *Application deadline:* Applications are processed on a rolling basis. Application fee: $75. Electronic applications accepted. *Expenses: Tuition:* Full-time $25,164; part-time $1398 per credit. *Required fees:* $580; $165 per semester. Tuition and fees vary according to course load, degree level and program. *Financial support:* In 2019–20, 77 students received support, including 44 fellowships with full and partial tuition reimbursements available (averaging $3,811 per year), 9 research assistantships with full and partial tuition reimbursements available (averaging $6,586 per year); career-related internships or fieldwork, Federal Work-Study, institutionally sponsored loans, scholarships/grants, traineeships, tuition waivers (full and partial), unspecified assistantships, and scholarships and endowed scholarships also available. Support available to part-time students. Financial award applicants required to submit FAFSA. *Unit head:* Dr. Jamie Mitus, Chairperson, 516-463-5759, E-mail: jamie.s.mitus@hofstra.edu. *Application contact:* Sunil Samuel, Assistant Vice President of Admissions, 516-463-4723, Fax: 516-463-4664, E-mail: graduateadmission@hofstra.edu.
Website: http://www.hofstra.edu/academics/colleges/healthscienceshumanservices/

Holy Family University, Graduate and Professional Programs, School of Arts and Sciences, Program in Counseling Psychology, Philadelphia, PA 19114. Offers MS. *Program availability:* Part-time, evening/weekend. *Degree requirements:* For master's, comprehensive exam, thesis optional. *Entrance requirements:* For master's, GRE or MAT (if GPA is below 3.0), baccalaureate degree from accredited college or university; minimum undergraduate cumulative GPA of 3.0; 2 letters of recommendation; personal statement; official transcripts; interview. Additional exam requirements/recommendations for international students: required—TOEFL (minimum score 550 paper-based; 79 iBT), IELTS (minimum score 6), PTE (minimum score 54). Electronic applications accepted.

Holy Names University, Graduate Division, Department of Counseling Psychology, Oakland, CA 94619-1699. Offers counseling and forensic counseling (MA); counseling psychology (MA); forensic psychology (MA). *Program availability:* Part-time, evening/weekend. *Degree requirements:* For master's, comprehensive paper, seminars. *Entrance requirements:* For master's, minimum undergraduate GPA of 2.6 overall, 3.0 in major. Additional exam requirements/recommendations for international students: required—TOEFL (minimum score 550 paper-based; 79 iBT). Electronic applications accepted. Application fee is waived when completed online. *Expenses:* Contact institution.

Howard University, School of Education, Department of Human Development and Psychoeducational Studies, Program in Counseling Psychology, Washington, DC 20059-0002. Offers PhD. *Accreditation:* APA. *Program availability:* Part-time. *Degree* *requirements:* For doctorate, one foreign language, comprehensive exam, thesis/dissertation, expository writing exam, internship. *Entrance requirements:* For doctorate, GRE General Test, minimum GPA of 3.4. Additional exam requirements/recommendations for international students: required—TOEFL (minimum score 550 paper-based; 79 iBT). Electronic applications accepted.

Humboldt State University, Academic Programs, College of Professional Studies, Department of Psychology, Arcata, CA 95521-8299. Offers psychology (MA), including biological psychology, counseling, developmental psychopathology, school psychology, social and environmental psychology. *Program availability:* Part-time. *Faculty:* 14 full-time (9 women), 13 part-time/adjunct (8 women). *Students:* 76 full-time (54 women), 11 part-time (4 women); includes 37 minority (1 Black or African American, non-Hispanic/Latino; 3 American Indian or Alaska Native, non-Hispanic/Latino; 4 Asian, non-Hispanic/Latino; 22 Hispanic/Latino; 7 Two or more races, non-Hispanic/Latino), 1 international. Average age 28. 89 applicants, 42% accepted, 31 enrolled. In 2019, 38 master's awarded. *Degree requirements:* For master's, thesis. *Entrance requirements:* For master's, appropriate bachelor's degree, minimum GPA of 2.5. Additional exam requirements/recommendations for international students: required—TOEFL (minimum score 500 paper-based). *Application deadline:* For fall admission, 2/1 for domestic students, 2/15 for international students. Applications are processed on a rolling basis. Application fee: $55. *Expenses:* Tuition, state resident: full-time $7176; part-time $4164 per term. *Required fees:* $2120; $1672 per term. *Financial support:* Career-related internships or fieldwork available. Financial award application deadline: 3/1; financial award applicants required to submit FAFSA. *Unit head:* Dr. Carrie Aigner, Graduate Program Coordinator, 707-826-3757, E-mail: carrie.aigner@humboldt.edu. *Application contact:* Dr. Carrie Aigner, Graduate Program Coordinator, 707-826-3757, E-mail: carrie.aigner@humboldt.edu.
Website: http://www2.humboldt.edu/psychology/programs-child/graduate-programs-psychology

Husson University, Graduate Programs in Counseling and Human Relations, Bangor, ME 04401-2999. Offers clinical mental health counseling (MS); human relations (MS); school counseling (MS). *Accreditation:* ACA. *Program availability:* Part-time, evening/weekend. *Degree requirements:* For master's, comprehensive exam (for some programs), thesis optional. *Entrance requirements:* For master's, BS with minimum GPA of 3.0, letters of recommendation, interview. Additional exam requirements/recommendations for international students: required—TOEFL (minimum score 550 paper-based; 80 iBT), IELTS (minimum score 6.5). Electronic applications accepted. *Expenses:* Contact institution.

Idaho State University, Graduate School, College of Health Professions, Department of Counseling, Pocatello, ID 83209-8120. Offers counseling (M Coun, Ed S), including marriage and family counseling (M Coun), mental health counseling (M Coun), school counseling (M Coun), student affairs and college counseling (M Coun); counselor education and counseling (PhD). *Accreditation:* ACA (one or more programs are accredited). *Program availability:* Part-time. *Degree requirements:* For master's, comprehensive exam, thesis, 4 semesters resident graduate study, practicum/internship; for doctorate, comprehensive exam, thesis/dissertation, 3 semesters internship, 4 consecutive semesters doctoral-level study on campus; for Ed S, comprehensive exam, thesis, case studies, oral exam. *Entrance requirements:* For master's, GRE General Test, MAT, minimum GPA of 3.0, bachelors degree, interview, 3 letters of recommendation; for doctorate, GRE General Test, MAT, minimum graduate GPA of 3.0, resume, interview, counseling license, master's degree; for Ed S, GRE General Test, minimum graduate GPA of 3.0, master's degree in counseling, 3 letters of recommendation, 2 years work experience. Additional exam requirements/recommendations for international students: required—TOEFL (minimum score 600 paper-based; 80 iBT). Electronic applications accepted.

Illinois State University, Graduate School, College of Arts and Sciences, Department of Psychology, Normal, IL 61790. Offers psychology (MA, MS), including clinical-counseling psychology, cognitive and behavioral sciences, developmental psychology, industrial/organizational-social psychology; school psychology (PhD, SSP). *Accreditation:* APA. *Faculty:* 32 full-time (14 women), 6 part-time/adjunct (5 women). *Students:* 92 full-time (77 women), 18 part-time (14 women). Average age 25. 154 applicants, 32% accepted, 37 enrolled. In 2019, 27 master's, 3 doctorates, 5 other advanced degrees awarded. *Degree requirements:* For master's, thesis or alternative; for doctorate, variable foreign language requirement, thesis/dissertation, 2 terms of residency, internship, practicum. *Entrance requirements:* For master's, GRE General Test, GRE Subject Test, minimum GPA of 3.0 in last 60 hours of course work; for doctorate, GRE General Test. *Application deadline:* Applications are processed on a rolling basis. Application fee: $50. *Expenses:* Tuition, area resident: full-time $7956; part-time $9767 per year. Tuition, nonresident: full-time $9233; part-time $17,592 per year. *Required fees:* $1797. *Financial support:* In 2019–20, 26 research assistantships, 34 teaching assistantships were awarded; tuition waivers (full) and unspecified assistantships also available. Financial award application deadline: 4/1. *Unit head:* Dr. J Scott Jordan, Department Chair, 309-438-2484, E-mail: jsjorda@illinoisState.edu. *Application contact:* Dr. Karen Mark, Graduate Coordinator, 309-438-8130, E-mail: kimark@ilstu.edu.
Website: http://psychology.illinoisstate.edu/

Immaculata University, College of Graduate Studies, Department of Psychology, Immaculata, PA 19345. Offers clinical mental health counseling (MA); clinical psychology (Psy D); forensic psychology (Graduate Certificate); integrative psychotherapy (Graduate Certificate); neuropsychology (Graduate Certificate); psychodynamic psychotherapy (Graduate Certificate); psychological testing (Graduate Certificate); school counseling (MA, Graduate Certificate); school psychology (MA). *Accreditation:* APA. *Program availability:* Part-time, evening/weekend. Terminal master's awarded for partial completion of doctoral program. *Degree requirements:* For master's, comprehensive exam, thesis optional; for doctorate, comprehensive exam, thesis/dissertation. *Entrance requirements:* For master's, GRE General Test or MAT, minimum GPA of 3.0; for doctorate, GRE General Test or MAT, minimum GPA of 3.5. Additional exam requirements/recommendations for international students: required—TOEFL, IELTS. Electronic applications accepted.

Indiana University Northwest, College of Arts and Sciences, Gary, IN 46408. Offers clinical counseling (MS), including drug and alcohol counseling; community development/urban studies (Graduate Certificate); computer information systems (Graduate Certificate); liberal studies (MLS); race-ethnic studies (Graduate Certificate); women's and gender studies (Graduate Certificate). *Program availability:* Part-time, evening/weekend. *Entrance requirements:* For master's, GRE (recommended for MS), minimum undergraduate GPA of 3.0, bachelor's degree from accredited university (for MS). Electronic applications accepted. *Expenses:* Contact institution.

Indiana University South Bend, School of Education, South Bend, IN 46615. Offers addiction counseling (MS Ed); alcohol and drug counseling (Graduate Certificate); clinical mental health counseling (MS Ed); educational leadership (MS Ed); elementary education (MS Ed); marriage, couple, and family counseling (MS Ed); school counseling (MS Ed); secondary education (MS Ed); special education (MAT, MS Ed), including intense intervention (MS Ed), mild intervention (MS Ed). *Accreditation:* NCATE. *Program availability:* Part-time, evening/weekend. *Degree requirements:* For master's,

thesis or alternative, exit project. *Entrance requirements:* For master's, letters of recommendation, GRE or minimum GPA of 3.0. Additional exam requirements/recommendations for international students: required—TOEFL. Electronic applications accepted. *Expenses:* Contact institution.

Indiana Wesleyan University, Graduate School, College of Arts and Sciences, Marion, IN 46953. Offers addictions counseling (MS); clinical mental health counseling (MS); community counseling (MS); marriage and family therapy (MS); school counseling (MS); student development counseling and administration (MS). *Accreditation:* ACA. *Program availability:* Part-time. *Degree requirements:* For master's, thesis or alternative. *Entrance requirements:* For master's, GRE General Test. Additional exam requirements/recommendations for international students: required—TOEFL. Electronic applications accepted. *Expenses:* Contact institution.

Instituto Tecnologico de Santo Domingo, Graduate School, Area of Humanities and Social Sciences, Santo Domingo, Dominican Republic. Offers accounting (Certificate); adult education (Certificate); applied linguistics (MA); economics (MA); education (M Ed); educational psychology (MA, Certificate); gender and development (MA, Certificate); humanistic studies (MA); international marketing management (Certificate); international relations in the Caribbean basin (Certificate); intervention systems in family therapy (MA); linguistic and literary communication (Certificate); pedagogical support (MA); social science education (M Ed); sustainable human development (MA); terminal illness and death psychology (Certificate); youth and adult education (M Ed).

Inter American University of Puerto Rico, Aguadilla Campus, Graduate School, Aguadilla, PR 00605. Offers accounting (MBA); counseling psychology specializing in family (MS); criminal justice (MA); educative management and leadership (MA); elementary education (M Ed); finance (MBA); human resources (MBA); industrial management (MBA); management information systems (MBA); marketing (MBA). *Program availability:* Part-time, evening/weekend. *Faculty:* 6 full-time (all women), 10 part-time/adjunct (5 women). *Students:* 172 full-time (112 women), 23 part-time (16 women); all minorities (all Hispanic/Latino). Average age 30. 102 applicants, 63% accepted, 59 enrolled. *Degree requirements:* For master's, comprehensive exam. *Entrance requirements:* For master's, EXADEP, 2 letters of recommendation, minimum GPA of 2.5. Application fee: $31. Electronic applications accepted. *Expenses: Tuition:* Full-time $3870; part-time $645 per trimester. *Required fees:* $235 per trimester. Tuition and fees vary according to course load. *Unit head:* Dr. Elie Agesilas, Chancellor, 787-891-0925 Ext. 2236, Fax: 787-882-3020, E-mail: eagesila@aguadilla.inter.edu. *Application contact:* Doris Perez, Admission Director, 787-891-0925 Ext. 2740, Fax: 787-882-3020, E-mail: dperez@aguadilla.inter.edu.
Website: http://www.aguadilla.inter.edu/

Inter American University of Puerto Rico, Metropolitan Campus, Graduate Programs, Program in Psychology, San Juan, PR 00919-1293. Offers counseling psychology (MA, PhD); industrial/organizational psychology (MA, PhD); labor relations (MA); school psychology (MA, PhD). *Degree requirements:* For master's, comprehensive exam. *Entrance requirements:* For master's, GRE or EXADEP, interview. Electronic applications accepted.

Inter American University of Puerto Rico, San Germán Campus, Graduate Studies Center, Program in Psychology, San Germán, PR 00683-5008. Offers counseling psychology (MA, PhD); school psychology (MA, PhD). *Program availability:* Part-time, evening/weekend. *Degree requirements:* For master's, comprehensive exam, thesis; for doctorate, comprehensive exam, thesis/dissertation. *Entrance requirements:* For master's, GRE General Test or EXADEP, minimum GPA of 3.0; for doctorate, GRE, EXADEP or MAT, minimum GPA of 3.0.

Iona College, School of Arts and Science, Department of Psychology, New Rochelle, NY 10801-1890. Offers general-experimental psychology (MA); human resources (Certificate); industrial-organizational psychology (MA); mental health counseling (MA); organizational behavior (Certificate); psychology (MA); school psychology (MA). *Program availability:* Part-time. *Faculty:* 8 full-time (4 women), 12 part-time/adjunct (8 women). *Students:* 71 full-time (64 women), 41 part-time (34 women); includes 51 minority (12 Black or African American, non-Hispanic/Latino; 5 Asian, non-Hispanic/Latino; 28 Hispanic/Latino; 1 Native Hawaiian or other Pacific Islander, non-Hispanic/Latino; 5 Two or more races, non-Hispanic/Latino), 3 international. Average age 25. 104 applicants, 85% accepted, 34 enrolled. In 2019, 29 master's, 15 other advanced degrees awarded. *Degree requirements:* For master's, thesis (for some programs), literature review (for some programs). *Entrance requirements:* For master's, BA in psychology including 3 credits each in psychology statistics and experimental research methods, or 9 credits in psychology including 3 credits each in psychology statistics, psychology research methods and upper-level coursework. Additional exam requirements/recommendations for international students: required—TOEFL (minimum score 550 paper-based), IELTS (minimum score 6.5). *Application deadline:* For fall admission, 8/15 for domestic students, 5/1 for international students; for spring admission, 1/15 for domestic students, 9/1 for international students. Applications are processed on a rolling basis. Electronic applications accepted. *Financial support:* In 2019–20, 51 students received support, including 4 research assistantships with partial tuition reimbursements available (averaging $10,143 per year); scholarships/grants, tuition waivers (partial), and unspecified assistantships also available. Support available to part-time students. Financial award application deadline: 4/15; financial award applicants required to submit FAFSA. *Unit head:* Colleen Jacobsen, PhD, Chair, 914-637-2770, E-mail: cjacobsen@iona.edu. *Application contact:* Shantell Smith, Associate Director of Graduate Admissions, Arts and Science, 914-633-2440, Fax: 914-633-2277, E-mail: ssmith@iona.edu.
Website: http://www.iona.edu/Academics/School-of-Arts-Science/Departments/Psychology/Graduate-Programs.aspx

Iowa State University of Science and Technology, Department of Psychology, Ames, IA 50011. Offers cognitive psychology (PhD); counseling psychology (PhD); psychology (MS, PhD); social psychology (PhD). *Accreditation:* APA (one or more programs are accredited). *Entrance requirements:* For doctorate, GRE General Test, GRE Subject Test (psychology), 3 letters of recommendation. Additional exam requirements/recommendations for international students: required—TOEFL (minimum score 560 paper-based; 79 iBT), IELTS (minimum score 6.5). Electronic applications accepted.

Jacksonville University, Brooks Rehabilitation College of Healthcare Sciences, School of Applied Health Sciences, Program in Clinical Mental Health Counseling, Jacksonville, FL 32211. Offers clinical mental health counseling (MS), including marriage and family therapy. *Program availability:* Part-time, blended/hybrid learning. *Students:* 39 full-time (35 women); includes 9 minority (6 Black or African American, non-Hispanic/Latino; 1 Asian, non-Hispanic/Latino; 2 Hispanic/Latino), 3 international. Average age 40. 63 applicants, 59% accepted, 22 enrolled. *Entrance requirements:* For master's, baccalaureate degree from accredited college or university with minimum GPA of 3.0; background check; 1-2 page essay stating intent; resume (education, work experience); 3 letters of recommendation; interview. Additional exam requirements/recommendations for international students: required—TOEFL (minimum score 650 paper-based; 114 iBT), IELTS (minimum score 8). *Application deadline:* Applications are processed on a rolling basis. Application fee: $50. Electronic applications accepted. *Expenses:* Contact institution. *Financial support:* Federal Work-Study, institutionally sponsored loans,

scholarships/grants, and health care benefits available. Support available to part-time students. Financial award application deadline: 3/15; financial award applicants required to submit FAFSA. *Unit head:* Dr. Whitney George, Department Chair, Clinical Mental Health Counseling, 904-256-7620, E-mail: wgeorge@ju.edu. *Application contact:* Pamela Adrian, Assistant Director, Graduate Admissions, 904-256-7245, E-mail: padrian@ju.edu.
Website: https://www.ju.edu/mentalhealth/

James Madison University, The Graduate School, College of Health and Behavioral Studies, Clinical Mental Health Counseling Program, Harrisonburg, VA 22807. Offers MA/Ed S. *Accreditation:* ACA. *Program availability:* Part-time, evening/weekend. *Students:* 73 full-time (59 women), 22 part-time (20 women); includes 21 minority (13 Black or African American, non-Hispanic/Latino; 3 Asian, non-Hispanic/Latino; 5 Two or more races, non-Hispanic/Latino). Average age 30. Application fee: $60. *Financial support:* In 2019–20, 60 students received support, including 1 teaching assistantship; career-related internships or fieldwork, Federal Work-Study, and assistantships (averaging $7911) also available. Financial award application deadline: 3/1; financial award applicants required to submit FAFSA.

James Madison University, The Graduate School, College of Health and Behavioral Studies, Program in Counseling and Supervision, Harrisonburg, VA 22807. Offers PhD. *Program availability:* Part-time, evening/weekend. *Students:* 6 full-time (5 women), 7 part-time (2 women); includes 4 minority (3 Black or African American, non-Hispanic/Latino; 1 Hispanic/Latino), 1 international. Average age 30. In 2019, 5 doctorates awarded. Application fee: $60. Electronic applications accepted. *Financial support:* In 2019–20, 3 students received support. Fellowships, Federal Work-Study, and assistantships (averaging $7911) available. Financial award application deadline: 3/1; financial award applicants required to submit FAFSA. *Unit head:* Dr. Robin Anderson, Department Head, 540-568-3293, E-mail: ander2rd@jmu.edu. *Application contact:* Lynette D. Michael, Director of Graduate Admissions, 540-568-6131 Ext. 6395, Fax: 540-568-7860, E-mail: michaeld@jmu.edu.
Website: http://psyc.jmu.edu/counseling/supervision/

John Brown University, Graduate Counseling Programs, Siloam Springs, AR 72761-2121. Offers clinical mental health counseling (MS); marriage and family therapy (MS); play therapy (Graduate Certificate); school counseling (MS). *Accreditation:* NCATE. *Program availability:* Part-time, evening/weekend. *Degree requirements:* For master's, practica or internships. *Entrance requirements:* For master's, GRE (minimum score of 300), recommendation forms from three people, 200-word essay describing professional plans and reason for seeking acceptance. Additional exam requirements/recommendations for international students: required—TOEFL (minimum score 550 paper-based; 79 iBT). Electronic applications accepted. *Expenses:* Contact institution.

John Carroll University, Graduate School, Department of Counseling, University Heights, OH 44118. Offers clinical counseling (Certificate); community counseling (MA). *Accreditation:* ACA. *Program availability:* Part-time, evening/weekend. *Degree requirements:* For master's, internship, practicum. *Entrance requirements:* Additional exam requirements/recommendations for international students: required—TOEFL. *Application deadline:* Applications are processed on a rolling basis. Electronic applications accepted. *Financial support:* Scholarships/grants and unspecified assistantships available. Financial award applicants required to submit FAFSA. *Unit head:* Dr. Nathan Gehlert, Chair, 216-397-4697, Fax: 216-397-3045, E-mail: ngehlert@jcu.edu. *Application contact:* Colleen K. Sommerfeld, Assistant Dean for Graduate Admission & Retention, 216-397-4902, Fax: 216-397-1835, E-mail: csommerfeld@jcu.edu.
Website: https://jcu.edu/academics/counseling

John F. Kennedy University, College of Psychology, Program in Counseling Psychology, Pleasant Hill, CA 94523-4817. Offers MA. *Program availability:* Part-time, evening/weekend, blended/hybrid learning. *Degree requirements:* For master's, thesis or alternative. *Entrance requirements:* For master's, interview. Additional exam requirements/recommendations for international students: required—TOEFL.

John F. Kennedy University, College of Psychology, Program in Holistic Psychology, Pleasant Hill, CA 94523-4817. Offers depth and transpersonal psychotherapy (MA); expressive arts (MA); holistic studies (MA); somatic psychology (MA). *Program availability:* Part-time, evening/weekend. *Degree requirements:* For master's, thesis or alternative. *Entrance requirements:* For master's, interview. Additional exam requirements/recommendations for international students: required—TOEFL.

Kean University, College of Liberal Arts, Program in Psychology, Union, NJ 07083. Offers human behavior and organizational psychology (MA); psychological services (MA). *Program availability:* Part-time. *Faculty:* 18 full-time (14 women). *Students:* 68 full-time (56 women), 52 part-time (40 women); includes 70 minority (32 Black or African American, non-Hispanic/Latino; 5 Asian, non-Hispanic/Latino; 32 Hispanic/Latino; 1 Two or more races, non-Hispanic/Latino), 4 international. Average age 28. 68 applicants, 84% accepted, 42 enrolled. In 2019, 52 master's awarded. *Degree requirements:* For master's, comprehensive exam, research component, two semesters of advanced seminar. *Entrance requirements:* For master's, GRE General Test, minimum GPA of 3.0; official transcripts from all institutions attended; two letters of recommendation; professional resume/curriculum vitae; 12 credits in behavioral sciences on the undergraduate level. Additional exam requirements/recommendations for international students: required—TOEFL (minimum score 550 paper-based; 79 iBT), IELTS (minimum score 6.5). *Application deadline:* For fall admission, 6/30 for domestic and international students; for spring admission, 12/1 for domestic and international students. Applications are processed on a rolling basis. Application fee: $75. Electronic applications accepted. *Expenses:* Tuition, state resident: full-time $15,326; part-time $748 per credit. Tuition, nonresident: full-time $20,288; part-time $902 per credit. *Required fees:* $2149.50; $91.25 per credit. Tuition and fees vary according to course level, course load, degree level and program. *Financial support:* Scholarships/grants and unspecified assistantships available. Financial award applicants required to submit FAFSA. *Unit head:* Dr. Zandra Gratz, Program Coordinator, 908-737-5881, E-mail: zgratz@kean.edu. *Application contact:* Amy Clark, Program Assistant, 908-737-7100, E-mail: gradadmissions@kean.edu.
Website: http://grad.kean.edu/masters-programs/psychological-services

Kean University, Nathan Weiss Graduate College, Program in Counselor Education, Union, NJ 07083. Offers alcohol and drug abuse counseling (MA); clinical mental health counseling (MA); school counseling (MA). *Accreditation:* ACA; NCATE. *Program availability:* Part-time. *Faculty:* 10 full-time (7 women). *Students:* 128 full-time (100 women), 164 part-time (126 women); includes 137 minority (63 Black or African American, non-Hispanic/Latino; 2 American Indian or Alaska Native, non-Hispanic/Latino; 9 Asian, non-Hispanic/Latino; 58 Hispanic/Latino; 2 Native Hawaiian or other Pacific Islander, non-Hispanic/Latino; 3 Two or more races, non-Hispanic/Latino). Average age 33. 217 applicants, 37% accepted, 52 enrolled. In 2019, 90 master's awarded. *Degree requirements:* For master's, practicum, internship, portfolio. *Entrance requirements:* For master's, minimum GPA of 3.0, 2 letters of recommendation, personal statement, resume. Additional exam requirements/recommendations for international students: required—TOEFL (minimum score 550 paper-based; 79 iBT), IELTS (minimum score 6.5). *Application deadline:* For fall admission, 3/1 for domestic and international students; for spring admission, 11/1 for domestic and international students. Applications are processed on a rolling basis. Application fee: $75. Electronic applications accepted. *Expenses:* Tuition, state resident: full-time $15,326; part-time $748 per credit. Tuition, nonresident: full-time $20,288; part-time $902 per credit. *Required fees:* $2149.50; $91.25 per credit. Tuition and fees vary according to course level, course load, degree level and program. *Financial support:* Scholarships/grants and unspecified assistantships available. Financial award applicants required to submit FAFSA. *Unit head:* Dr. J. Barry Mascari, Program Coordinator, 908-737-5954, E-mail: jmascari@kean.edu. *Application contact:* Pedro Lopes, Admissions Counselor, 908-737-7100, E-mail: gradadmissions@kean.edu.
Website: http://grad.kean.edu/counseling

Kent State University, College of Education, Health and Human Services, School of Lifespan Development and Educational Sciences, Program in Clinical Mental Health Counseling, Kent, OH 44242-0001. Offers M Ed. *Accreditation:* ACA; NCATE. *Entrance requirements:* For master's, minimum GPA of 2.75, 2 letters of reference, goals statement, moral character form, interview. Additional exam requirements/recommendations for international students: required—TOEFL (minimum score 550 paper-based; 80 iBT). Electronic applications accepted.

Kutztown University of Pennsylvania, College of Education, Program in Counseling Psychology, Kutztown, PA 19530-0730. Offers MA. *Program availability:* Part-time, evening/weekend. *Faculty:* 10 full-time (7 women), 1 part-time/adjunct (0 women). *Students:* 72 full-time (58 women), 57 part-time (49 women); includes 30 minority (16 Black or African American, non-Hispanic/Latino; 6 Hispanic/Latino; 8 Two or more races, non-Hispanic/Latino), 2 international. Average age 28. 59 applicants, 76% accepted, 32 enrolled. In 2019, 29 master's awarded. *Degree requirements:* For master's, comprehensive exam, thesis optional. *Entrance requirements:* For master's, GRE General Test, 3 letters of recommendation, minimum undergraduate GPA of 3.0, psychobiographical statement, resume. Additional exam requirements/recommendations for international students: required—TOEFL (minimum score 550 paper-based, 79 iBT), IELTS (minimum score 6.5), or PTE (minimum score 53). *Application deadline:* For fall admission, 3/1 for domestic and international students; for spring admission, 10/1 for domestic and international students. Application fee: $35. Electronic applications accepted. *Expenses: Tuition, area resident:* Full-time $9288; part-time $515 per credit. Tuition, state resident: full-time $9288. Tuition, nonresident: full-time $13,932; part-time $774 per credit. *Required fees:* $1688; $94 per credit. *Financial support:* Career-related internships or fieldwork, Federal Work-Study, and unspecified assistantships available. Financial award application deadline: 3/1; financial award applicants required to submit FAFSA. *Unit head:* Dr. Helen S Hamlet, Department Chair, 610-683-4204, Fax: 610-683-1585, E-mail: hamlet@kutztown.edu. *Application contact:* Dr. Helen S Hamlet, Department Chair, 610-683-4204, Fax: 610-683-1585, E-mail: hamlet@kutztown.edu.
Website: https://www.kutztown.edu/academics/graduate-programs/counseling.htm

Lamar University, College of Graduate Studies, College of Education and Human Development, Department of Counseling, Beaumont, TX 77710. Offers clinical mental health counseling (M Ed); school counseling (M Ed); special education (M Ed). *Accreditation:* ACA. *Faculty:* 19 full-time (16 women), 20 part-time/adjunct (17 women). *Students:* 196 full-time (176 women), 1,263 part-time (1,124 women); includes 757 minority (382 Black or African American, non-Hispanic/Latino; 6 American Indian or Alaska Native, non-Hispanic/Latino; 19 Asian, non-Hispanic/Latino; 314 Hispanic/Latino; 2 Native Hawaiian or other Pacific Islander, non-Hispanic/Latino; 34 Two or more races, non-Hispanic/Latino). Average age 36. 1,097 applicants, 66% accepted, 360 enrolled. In 2019, 434 master's awarded. *Entrance requirements:* Additional exam requirements/recommendations for international students: required—TOEFL (minimum score 550 paper-based; 79 iBT), IELTS (minimum score 6.5). *Application deadline:* Applications are processed on a rolling basis. Application fee: $25 ($50 for international students). Electronic applications accepted. *Expenses:* $18000 total program cost. *Financial support:* In 2019–20, 19 students received support. Fellowships, research assistantships, teaching assistantships, career-related internships or fieldwork, scholarships/grants, and unspecified assistantships available. Financial award applicants required to submit FAFSA. *Application contact:* Celeste Contreas, Director, Admissions and Academic Services, 409-880-8888, Fax: 409-880-7419, E-mail: gradmissions@lamar.edu.
Website: https://www.lamar.edu/education/counseling/index.html

Lancaster Bible College, Graduate School, Lancaster, PA 17601-5036. Offers adult ministries (MA); Bible (MA); children and family ministry (MA); church planting (MA); consulting resource teacher (M Ed); elementary school counseling (M Ed); leadership (PhD); leadership studies (MA); marriage and family counseling (MA); mental health counseling (MA); pastoral studies (MA); secondary school counseling (M Ed); sports ministry (MA); student ministry (MA); town and country ministry (MA). *Program availability:* Part-time, evening/weekend. *Degree requirements:* For master's, comprehensive exam (for some programs), thesis (for some programs). *Entrance requirements:* For master's, bachelor's degree with a minimum of 30 credits of course work in Bible, minimum undergraduate GPA of 3.0, interview. Additional exam requirements/recommendations for international students: required—TOEFL.

La Salle University, School of Arts and Sciences, Program in Counseling and Family Therapy, Philadelphia, PA 19141-1199. Offers industrial/organizational psychology (MA); marriage and family therapy (MA); professional clinical counseling (MA). *Accreditation:* ACA; APA. *Program availability:* Part-time, evening/weekend. *Degree requirements:* For master's, comprehensive exam. *Entrance requirements:* For master's, GRE or MAT (waived for applicants that already possess a master's degree in any field or for applicants that have a cumulative GPA of 3.5 or higher), minimum of 15 hours in psychology, counseling, or marriage and family studies; minimum GPA of 3.0; three letters of recommendation; personal statement; work experience (paid or volunteer). Additional exam requirements/recommendations for international students: required—TOEFL. Electronic applications accepted. Application fee is waived when completed online. *Expenses:* Contact institution.

Lee University, Graduate Studies in Counseling, Cleveland, TN 37320-3450. Offers holistic child development (MS). *Program availability:* Part-time, 100% online. *Faculty:* 7 full-time (4 women), 3 part-time/adjunct (1 woman). *Students:* 80 full-time (65 women), 31 part-time (24 women); includes 20 minority (6 Black or African American, non-Hispanic/Latino; 10 Hispanic/Latino; 4 Two or more races, non-Hispanic/Latino), 4 international. Average age 29. 60 applicants, 77% accepted, 36 enrolled. In 2019, 47 master's awarded. *Degree requirements:* For master's, variable foreign language requirement, comprehensive exam (for some programs), thesis (for some programs), internship. *Entrance requirements:* For master's, GRE General Test or MAT (waived if undergraduate GPA is greater than 3.0 or if applicant already has a graduate degree), minimum undergraduate GPA of 3.0, 3 letters of recommendation, interview, official transcripts, essay. Additional exam requirements/recommendations for international students: required—TOEFL (minimum score 61 iBT). *Application deadline:* For fall admission, 4/1 priority date for domestic and international students; for spring admission, 11/1 priority date for domestic and international students. Applications are processed on a rolling basis. Application fee: $25. Electronic applications accepted. *Expenses: Tuition:* Full-time $13,590; part-time $755 per credit hour. *Required fees:*

$25. Tuition and fees vary according to program. *Financial support:* In 2019–20, 48 students received support. Career-related internships or fieldwork, Federal Work-Study, institutionally sponsored loans, scholarships/grants, and unspecified assistantships available. Financial award application deadline: 3/1; financial award applicants required to submit FAFSA. *Unit head:* Dr. Heather Quagliana, Director, 423-614-8359, Fax: 423-614-8124, E-mail: heatherlewis@leeuniversity.edu. *Application contact:* Jeffery McGirt, Director of Graduate Enrollment, 423-614-8691, Fax: 423-614-8317, E-mail: jmcgirt@leeuniversity.edu.
Website: http://www.leeuniversity.edu/academics/graduate/counseling/

Lehigh University, College of Education, Program in Counseling Psychology, Bethlehem, PA 18015. Offers counseling and human services (M Ed); counseling psychology (PhD); international counseling (M Ed, Certificate); school counseling (M Ed). *Accreditation:* APA (one or more programs are accredited). *Program availability:* Part-time. *Faculty:* 7 full-time (4 women), 13 part-time/adjunct (11 women). *Students:* 50 full-time (45 women), 38 part-time (32 women); includes 23 minority (3 Black or African American, non-Hispanic/Latino; 5 Asian, non-Hispanic/Latino; 14 Hispanic/Latino; 1 Two or more races, non-Hispanic/Latino), 12 international. Average age 30. 174 applicants, 36% accepted, 16 enrolled. In 2019, 30 master's, 2 doctorates awarded. *Degree requirements:* For master's, thesis (for some programs); for doctorate, comprehensive exam, thesis/dissertation. *Entrance requirements:* For master's, minimum GPA of 3.0, 2 letters of recommendation, essay, transcript; for doctorate, GRE General Test, 2 letters of recommendation, transcript, essay, GRE; for Certificate, minimum GPA of 3.0 (undergraduate), 3.5 (graduate). Additional exam requirements/recommendations for international students: required—TOEFL (minimum score 600 paper-based; 93 iBT), Either TOEFL or IELTS is required of international students for whom English is not their main language; recommended—IELTS. *Application deadline:* For fall admission, 1/15 for domestic and international students. Application fee: $65. Electronic applications accepted. Application fee is waived when completed online. *Expenses:* $565/credit; $125/semester internships fee. *Financial support:* In 2019–20, 23 students received support, including 1 fellowship with full and partial tuition reimbursement available (averaging $32,000 per year), 6 research assistantships with full and partial tuition reimbursements available (averaging $14,000 per year); scholarships/grants and unspecified assistantships also available. Financial award application deadline: 1/15; financial award applicants required to submit FAFSA. *Unit head:* Dr. Grace Caskie, Director, 610-758-6094, Fax: 610-758-3227, E-mail: caskie@lehigh.edu. *Application contact:* Lori Anderson, Coordinator, Counseling Psychology, 610-758-3250, Fax: 610-758-6223, E-mail: lja320@lehigh.edu.
Website: https://ed.lehigh.edu/academics/programs/counseling-psychology

Lenoir-Rhyne University, Graduate Programs, School of Counseling and Human Services, Program in Clinical Mental Health Counseling, Hickory, NC 28601. Offers MA. *Accreditation:* ACA. *Program availability:* Part-time, evening/weekend. *Degree requirements:* For master's, comprehensive exam, thesis optional. *Entrance requirements:* For master's, GRE General Test or MAT, writing sample; minimum undergraduate GPA of 2.7, graduate 3.0. Additional exam requirements/recommendations for international students: required—TOEFL (minimum score 600 paper-based). Electronic applications accepted. *Expenses:* Contact institution.

Lesley University, Graduate School of Arts and Social Sciences, Cambridge, MA 02138-2790. Offers clinical mental health counseling (MA), including holistic counseling, school and community counseling, trauma studies; counseling psychology (MA, CAGS), including professional counseling (MA), school counseling (MA); creative writing (MFA); expressive therapies (MA, PhD, CAGS), including art (MA), clinical mental health counseling (MA), dance (MA), expressive therapies (MA), music (MA); independent studies (CAGS); independent study (MA); intercultural relations (MA, CAGS); interdisciplinary studies (MA), including individualized studies, integrative holistic health, mindfulness studies, peace and conflict transformation, trauma sensitive assessment, intervention, and consultation, women's studies; urban environmental leadership (MA). *Program availability:* Part-time, online learning. *Degree requirements:* For master's, internship, practicum, thesis (for expressive therapies); for doctorate, thesis/dissertation, arts apprenticeship, field placement; for CAGS, thesis, internship (for counseling psychology, expressive therapies). *Entrance requirements:* For master's, MAT (counseling psychology), interview, writing samples, art portfolio; for doctorate, GRE or MAT, interview, master's degree; for CAGS, interview, master's degree. Additional exam requirements/recommendations for international students: required—TOEFL (minimum score 550 paper-based; 80 iBT). Electronic applications accepted.

LeTourneau University, Graduate Programs, Longview, TX 75607-7001. Offers business administration (MBA); counseling (MA); curriculum and instruction (M Ed); educational administration (M Ed); engineering (ME, MS); engineering management (MEM); health care administration (MS); marriage and family therapy (MA); psychology (MA); strategic leadership (MSL); teacher leadership (M Ed); teaching and learning (M Ed). *Program availability:* Part-time, 100% online, blended/hybrid learning. *Students:* 45 full-time (34 women), 243 part-time (186 women); includes 142 minority (89 Black or African American, non-Hispanic/Latino; 1 Asian, non-Hispanic/Latino; 26 Hispanic/Latino; 26 Two or more races, non-Hispanic/Latino), 2 international. Average age 37. In 2019, 143 master's awarded. *Entrance requirements:* Additional exam requirements/recommendations for international students: required—TOEFL (minimum score 525 paper-based; 80 iBT), IELTS (minimum score 6), Either a TOEFL or IELTS is required for graduate students. One or the other. *Application deadline:* Applications are processed on a rolling basis. Application fee: $0. Electronic applications accepted. *Financial support:* Unspecified assistantships and employee tuition waivers and institutionally sponsored loans available. Financial award applicants required to submit FAFSA.
Website: http://www.letu.edu

Lewis & Clark College, Graduate School of Education and Counseling, Department of Counseling Psychology, Program in Professional Mental Health Counseling, Portland, OR 97219-7899. Offers MA, MS. *Accreditation:* ACA. *Program availability:* Part-time, evening/weekend. *Degree requirements:* For master's, thesis (MS). *Entrance requirements:* For master's, GRE General Test, minimum undergraduate GPA of 2.75. Additional exam requirements/recommendations for international students: required—TOEFL (minimum score 575 paper-based). Electronic applications accepted.

Lewis University, College of Education and Social Sciences, Program in Clinical Mental Health Counseling, Romeoville, IL 60446. Offers adult mental health counseling (MA). *Program availability:* Part-time, evening/weekend. *Students:* 54 full-time (48 women), 56 part-time (49 women); includes 40 minority (9 Black or African American, non-Hispanic/Latino; 1 Asian, non-Hispanic/Latino; 27 Hispanic/Latino; 1 Native Hawaiian or other Pacific Islander, non-Hispanic/Latino; 2 Two or more races, non-Hispanic/Latino), 1 international. Average age 28. In 2019, 27 master's awarded. *Degree requirements:* For master's, comprehensive exam, thesis optional, practicum, internship. *Entrance requirements:* For master's, bachelor's degree, 15 hours of undergraduate psychology, including statistics or research; 2 letters of recommendation; minimum GPA of 3.0 in last 60 hours; interview, personal statement. Additional exam requirements/recommendations for international students: required—TOEFL (minimum score 550 paper-based; 79 iBT), IELTS (minimum score 6). *Application deadline:* For fall admission, 5/1 priority date for international students; for spring admission, 11/15 priority date for international students. Applications are processed on a rolling basis. Application fee: $40. Electronic applications accepted. *Financial support:* Federal Work-Study and unspecified assistantships available. Financial award application deadline: 5/1; financial award applicants required to submit FAFSA. *Unit head:* Dr. Katherine Helm-Lewis, Program Director. *Application contact:* Sheri Vilcek, Graduate Admissions Counselor, 815-836-5610, E-mail: grad@lewisu.edu.
Website: http://www.lewisu.edu/academics/grad.htm/

Liberty University, School of Behavioral Sciences, Lynchburg, VA 24515. Offers applied psychology (MA), including developmental psychology (MA, MS), industrial/organizational psychology (MA, MS); clinical mental health counseling (MA); community care and counseling (Ed D), including marriage and family counseling, pastoral care and counseling, traumatology; counselor education and supervision (PhD); human services counseling (MA), including addictions and recovery, business, child and family law, Christian ministries, criminal justice, crisis response and trauma, executive leadership, health and wellness, life coaching, marriage and family, military resilience; marriage and family counseling (MA); marriage and family therapy (MA); military resilience (Certificate); pastoral counseling (MA), including addictions and recovery, community chaplaincy, crisis response and trauma, discipleship and church ministry, leadership, life coaching, marriage and family, marriage and family studies, military resilience, parenting and child/adolescent, pastoral counseling, theology; professional counseling (MA); psychology (MS), including developmental psychology (MA, MS), industrial/organizational psychology (MA, MS); school counseling (M Ed). *Program availability:* Part-time, online learning. *Students:* 3,786 full-time (3,065 women), 5,193 part-time (4,081 women); includes 2,733 minority (1,967 Black or African American, non-Hispanic/Latino; 48 American Indian or Alaska Native, non-Hispanic/Latino; 103 Asian, non-Hispanic/Latino; 349 Hispanic/Latino; 19 Native Hawaiian or other Pacific Islander, non-Hispanic/Latino; 247 Two or more races, non-Hispanic/Latino), 133 international. Average age 38. 13,324 applicants, 28% accepted, 2,163 enrolled. In 2019, 2,322 master's, 19 doctorates, 112 other advanced degrees awarded. *Entrance requirements:* For master's, Official bachelor's degree transcripts with a 2.0 GPA or higher. *Application deadline:* Applications are processed on a rolling basis. Application fee: $50. Electronic applications accepted. *Expenses: Tuition:* Full-time $545; part-time $410 per credit hour. One-time fee: $50. *Financial support:* In 2019–20, 1,003 students received support. Teaching assistantships and Federal Work-Study available. Financial award applicants required to submit FAFSA. *Unit head:* Dr. Kenyon Knapp, Dean, School of Behavioral Services, E-mail: kcknapp@liberty.edu. *Application contact:* Jay Bridge, Director of Admissions, 800-424-9595, Fax: 800-628-7977, E-mail: gradadmissions@liberty.edu.
Website: https://www.liberty.edu/behavioral-sciences/

Lindenwood University, Graduate Programs, School of Education, St. Charles, MO 63301-1695. Offers behavioral analysis (MA); education (MA), including autism spectrum disorders, character education, early intervention in autism and sensory impairment, gifted, technology; educational administration (MA, Ed D, Ed S); English to speakers of other languages (MA); instructional leadership (Ed D, Ed S); library media (MA); professional counseling (MA); school administration (MA, Ed S); school counseling (MA); teaching (MA). *Program availability:* Part-time, evening/weekend, 100% online, blended/hybrid learning. *Faculty:* 39 full-time (28 women), 133 part-time/adjunct (83 women). *Students:* 391 full-time (287 women), 1,149 part-time (889 women); includes 358 minority (284 Black or African American, non-Hispanic/Latino; 8 American Indian or Alaska Native, non-Hispanic/Latino; 6 Asian, non-Hispanic/Latino; 32 Hispanic/Latino; 28 Two or more races, non-Hispanic/Latino), 11 international. Average age 35. 465 applicants, 71% accepted, 229 enrolled. In 2019, 432 master's, 60 doctorates, 77 other advanced degrees awarded. *Degree requirements:* For master's, thesis (for some programs), minimum GPA of 3.0; for doctorate, thesis/dissertation, minimum GPA of 3.0; for Ed S, comprehensive exam, project, minimum GPA of 3.0. *Entrance requirements:* For master's, interview, minimum undergraduate cumulative GPA of 3.0, writing sample, letter of recommendation; for doctorate, minimum graduate GPA of 3.4, resume, interview, writing sample, 4 letters of recommendation; for Ed S, master's degree in education, relevant work experience. Additional exam requirements/recommendations for international students: required—TOEFL (minimum score 553 paper-based; 81 iBT); recommended—IELTS (minimum score 6.5). *Application deadline:* For fall admission, 8/9 priority date for domestic students, 6/1 priority date for international students; for spring admission, 12/20 priority date for domestic students, 11/1 priority date for international students; for summer admission, 5/15 priority date for domestic students, 3/27 priority date for international students. Applications are processed on a rolling basis. Application fee: $0 ($100 for international students). Electronic applications accepted. *Expenses: Tuition:* Full-time $8910; part-time $495 per credit. Tuition and fees vary according to course load, degree level and program. *Financial support:* In 2019–20, 198 students received support. Career-related internships or fieldwork, Federal Work-Study, institutionally sponsored loans, scholarships/grants, tuition waivers (partial), and unspecified assistantships available. Financial award application deadline: 6/30; financial award applicants required to submit FAFSA. *Unit head:* Dr. Anthony Scheffler, Dean, School of Education, 636-949-4618, Fax: 636-949-4197, E-mail: ascheffler@lindenwood.edu. *Application contact:* Kara Schilli, Assistant Vice President, University Admissions, 636-949-4349, Fax: 636-949-4109, E-mail: adultadmissions@lindenwood.edu.
Website: https://www.lindenwood.edu/academics/academic-schools/school-of-education/

Lindsey Wilson College, School of Professional Counseling, Columbia, KY 42728. Offers counseling and human development (M Ed); counselor education and supervision (PhD). *Accreditation:* ACA (one or more programs are accredited). *Program availability:* Part-time, evening/weekend, online learning.

Lipscomb University, Department of Psychology, Counseling, and Family Science, Nashville, TN 37204-3951. Offers clinical mental health counseling (MS); counseling psychology (Certificate); marriage and family therapy (MMFT); psychology (MS). *Program availability:* Part-time, evening/weekend. *Degree requirements:* For master's, thesis (for some programs), practicum, internship, capstone. *Entrance requirements:* For master's, GRE, resume, 3 reference letters, transcripts, goals statement. Additional exam requirements/recommendations for international students: required—TOEFL (minimum score 570 paper-based; 80 iBT). Electronic applications accepted. *Expenses:* Contact institution.

Lock Haven University of Pennsylvania, The Stephen Poorman College of Business, Information Systems, and Human Services, Lock Haven, PA 17745-2390. Offers clinical mental health counseling (MS); sport science (MS). *Program availability:* Online learning. *Degree requirements:* For master's, thesis. *Entrance requirements:* For master's, minimum undergraduate GPA of 3.0. Additional exam requirements/recommendations for international students: required—TOEFL. Electronic applications accepted.

London Metropolitan University, Graduate Programs, London, United Kingdom. Offers applied psychology (M Sc); architecture (MA); biomedical science (M Sc); blood science (M Sc); cancer pharmacology (M Sc); computer networking and cyber security (M Sc); computing and information systems (M Sc); conference interpreting (MA); counter-terrorism studies (M Sc); creative, digital and professional writing (MA); crime, violence and prevention (M Sc); criminology (M Sc); curating contemporary art (MA);

data analytics (M Sc); digital media (MA); early childhood studies (MA); education (MA, Ed D); financial services law, regulation and compliance (LL M); food science (M Sc); forensic psychology (M Sc); health and social care management and policy (M Sc); human nutrition (M Sc); human resource management (MA); human rights and international conflict (MA); information technology (M Sc); intelligence and security studies (M Sc); international oil, gas and energy law (LL M); international relations (MA); interpreting (MA); learning and teaching in higher education (MA); legal practice (LL M); media and entertainment law (LL M); organizational and consumer psychology (M Sc); psychological therapy (M Sc); psychology of mental health (M Sc); public health (M Sc); public policy and management (MPA); security studies (M Sc); social work (M Sc); spatial planning and urban design (MA); sports therapy (M Sc); supporting older children and young people with dyslexia (MA); teaching languages (MA), including Arabic, English; translation (MA); woman and child abuse (MA).

Long Island University - Brentwood Campus, Graduate Programs, Brentwood, NY 11717. Offers childhood education (MS), including grades 1-6; childhood education/literacy B-6 (MS); childhood education/special education (grades 1-6) (MS); clinical mental health counseling (MS, Advanced Certificate); criminal justice (MS); early childhood education (MS); educational leadership (MS Ed); family nurse practitioner (MS, Advanced Certificate); health administration (MPA); library and information science (MS); literacy (B-6) (MS Ed); school counselor (MS, Advanced Certificate); social work (MSW); special education (MS Ed); students with disabilities generalist (grades 7-12) (Advanced Certificate). *Program availability:* Part-time. *Entrance requirements:* For master's and Advanced Certificate, GRE. Additional exam requirements/recommendations for international students: required—TOEFL or IELTS. Electronic applications accepted.

Long Island University - Brooklyn, School of Education, Brooklyn, NY 11201-8423. Offers adolescence urban education (MS Ed); applied behavior analysis (Advanced Certificate); bilingual education (Advanced Certificate); bilingual education in urban setting (MS Ed); bilingual school counselor (MS Ed, Advanced Certificate); childhood urban education (MS Ed); childhood/early childhood education (MS Ed); childhood/early childhood urban education (MS Ed); early childhood urban education (MS Ed, Advanced Certificate); educational leadership (Advanced Certificate); marriage and family therapy (MS, Advanced Certificate); mental health counseling (MS, Advanced Certificate); school building district leader (Advanced Certificate); school counselor (MS Ed, Advanced Certificate); school psychologist (MS Ed); teaching students with disabilities (MS Ed); teaching urban children with disabilities (MS Ed); TESOL (MS Ed, Advanced Certificate). *Accreditation:* TEAC. *Program availability:* Part-time, evening/weekend, 100% online. *Entrance requirements:* For master's, GRE. Additional exam requirements/recommendations for international students: required—TOEFL (minimum score 527 paper-based, 75 iBT), IELTS, or PTE. Electronic applications accepted.

Long Island University - Hudson, Graduate School, Purchase, NY 10577. Offers autism (Advanced Certificate); bilingual education (Advanced Certificate); childhood education (MS Ed); crisis management (Advanced Certificate); early childhood education (MS Ed); educational leadership (MS Ed); health administration (MPA); literacy (MS Ed); marriage and family therapy (MS); mental health counseling (MS, Advanced Certificate), including credentialed alcoholism and substance abuse counselor (MS); middle childhood and adolescence education (MS Ed); pharmaceutics (MS), including cosmetic science, industrial pharmacy; public administration (MPA); school counseling (MS Ed, Advanced Certificate); school psychology (MS Ed); special education (MS Ed); TESOL (MS Ed); TESOL (all grades) (Advanced Certificate). *Program availability:* Part-time, evening/weekend. *Entrance requirements:* Additional exam requirements/recommendations for international students: required—TOEFL. Electronic applications accepted. *Expenses:* Contact institution.

Long Island University - Post, College of Education, Information and Technology, Brookville, NY 11548-1300. Offers adolescence education (MS); adolescence education 7-12 (MS); archives and records management (AC); art education (MS); childhood education (MS); childhood education/literacy B-6 (MS); childhood education/special education (MS); clinical mental health counseling (MS, AC); early childhood education (MS); early childhood education/childhood education (MS); educational leadership (AC); educational technology (MS); information studies (PhD); interdisciplinary educational studies (Ed D); middle childhood education (MS); music education (MS); public library administration (AC); school counselor (MS); special education (MS Ed); speech-language pathology (MA); students with disabilities, 7-12 generalist (AC); TESOL (MA). *Accreditation:* ASHA; TEAC. *Program availability:* Part-time, 100% online, blended/hybrid learning. Terminal master's awarded for partial completion of doctoral program. *Degree requirements:* For master's, variable foreign language requirement, comprehensive exam (for some programs), thesis optional; for doctorate, comprehensive exam, thesis/dissertation. *Entrance requirements:* For master's and AC, GRE (for some programs). Additional exam requirements/recommendations for international students: required—TOEFL (minimum score 550 paper-based, 75 iBT), IELTS, or PTE. Electronic applications accepted.

Louisiana Tech University, Graduate School, College of Education, Ruston, LA 71272. Offers counseling and guidance (MA), including clinical mental health counseling, human services, orientation and mobility; counseling psychology (PhD); curriculum and instruction (M Ed); cyber education (Graduate Certificate); dynamics of domestic and family violence (Graduate Certificate); early childhood education - PreK-3 (MAT); educational leadership (M Ed, Ed D); elementary education and special education mild/moderate grades 1-5 (MAT); higher education administration (Graduate Certificate); industrial/organizational psychology (MA, PhD); kinesiology (MS); middle school education (MAT), including mathematics; orientation and mobility (Graduate Certificate); rehabilitation teaching for the blind (Graduate Certificate); secondary education (MAT), including agriculture, biology, business, chemistry, English; special education: visually impaired (MAT); teacher leader education (Graduate Certificate); visual impairments - blind education (Graduate Certificate). *Accreditation:* NCATE. *Program availability:* Part-time. *Degree requirements:* For master's, thesis; for doctorate, thesis/dissertation. *Entrance requirements:* For master's and doctorate, GRE General Test. Additional exam requirements/recommendations for international students: required—TOEFL (minimum score 550 paper-based; 80 iBT), IELTS (minimum score 6.5). Electronic applications accepted. *Expenses: Tuition, area resident:* Full-time $6592; part-time $400 per credit. Tuition, state resident: full-time $6592; part-time $400 per credit. Tuition, nonresident: full-time $13,333; part-time $681 per credit. *International tuition:* $13,333 full-time. *Required fees:* $3011; $3011 per unit.

Loyola Marymount University, School of Education, Program in Counseling, Los Angels, CA 90045. Offers MA. *Students:* 48 full-time (40 women); includes 34 minority (8 Black or African American, non-Hispanic/Latino; 2 Asian, non-Hispanic/Latino; 21 Hispanic/Latino; 3 Two or more races, non-Hispanic/Latino), 2 international. Average age 28. 44 applicants, 32% accepted, 14 enrolled. In 2019, 21 master's awarded. *Entrance requirements:* For master's, graduate admissions application; undergrad GPA of at least 3.0; 2 letters of recommendation; official transcripts; personal statement; CBEST (School and guidance counseling only). Additional exam requirements/recommendations for international students: required—TOEFL, IELTS. *Application deadline:* For fall admission, 6/15 for domestic students; for spring admission, 11/15 for domestic students; for summer admission, 3/15 for domestic students. Application fee: $50. Electronic applications accepted. *Financial support:* Federal Work-Study and scholarships/grants available. Financial award applicants required to submit FAFSA. *Unit head:* Dr. Sheri Atwater, Director, Counseling Program, E-mail: sheri.atwater@lmu.edu. *Application contact:* Ammar Dalal, Assistant Vice Provost for Graduate Enrollment, 310-338-2721, Fax: 310-338-6086, E-mail: graduateadmission@lmu.edu.
Website: http://soe.lmu.edu/academics/counseling

Loyola University Chicago, School of Education, Program in Community Counseling, Chicago, IL 60660. Offers clinical mental health counseling (Ed S); community counseling (M Ed, MA). *Program availability:* Part-time. *Faculty:* 5 full-time (2 women), 5 part-time/adjunct (4 women). *Students:* 24 full-time (21 women), 4 part-time (0 women); includes 7 minority (3 Black or African American, non-Hispanic/Latino; 3 Hispanic/Latino; 1 Two or more races, non-Hispanic/Latino), 1 international. Average age 28. 60 applicants, 72% accepted, 13 enrolled. In 2019, 9 master's awarded. *Degree requirements:* For master's, comprehensive exam (for some programs), thesis (for some programs). *Entrance requirements:* For master's, GRE General Test, minimum GPA of 3.0, letters of recommendation, resume. Additional exam requirements/recommendations for international students: required—TOEFL (minimum score 550 paper-based; 79 iBT). *Application deadline:* For fall admission, 1/1 for domestic and international students. Application fee: $50. Electronic applications accepted. Application fee is waived when completed online. *Expenses:* 17082. *Financial support:* Career-related internships or fieldwork, institutionally sponsored loans, scholarships/grants, and unspecified assistantships available. Support available to part-time students. Financial award application deadline: 2/1; financial award applicants required to submit FAFSA. *Unit head:* Dr. Matt Miller, Director, 312-915-6800, E-mail: mmill11@luc.edu. *Application contact:* Dr. Matt Miller, Director, 312-915-6800, E-mail: mmill11@luc.edu.

Loyola University Chicago, School of Education, Program in Counseling Psychology, Chicago, IL 60660. Offers PhD. *Accreditation:* APA. *Faculty:* 5 full-time (2 women), 5 part-time/adjunct (4 women). *Students:* 15 full-time (11 women); includes 8 minority (4 Black or African American, non-Hispanic/Latino; 2 Asian, non-Hispanic/Latino; 2 Hispanic/Latino), 4 international. Average age 29. 29 applicants, 21% accepted, 3 enrolled. In 2019, 3 doctorates awarded. *Degree requirements:* For doctorate, comprehensive exam, thesis/dissertation. *Entrance requirements:* For doctorate, GRE General Test, GRE Subject Test, interview; minimum graduate GPA of 3.5, undergraduate 3.0; letters of recommendation. Additional exam requirements/recommendations for international students: required—TOEFL (minimum score 550 paper-based; 79 iBT). *Application deadline:* For fall admission, 12/1 for domestic and international students. Application fee: $50. Electronic applications accepted. Application fee is waived when completed online. *Expenses:* 17082. *Financial support:* In 2019–20, 7 research assistantships with full tuition reimbursements (averaging $14,000 per year), 18 teaching assistantships with full tuition reimbursements (averaging $4,000 per year) were awarded; career-related internships or fieldwork, institutionally sponsored loans, scholarships/grants, traineeships, health care benefits, and unspecified assistantships also available. Financial award application deadline: 2/1; financial award applicants required to submit FAFSA. *Unit head:* Dr. Matt Miller, Director, 312-915-6800, E-mail: mmill11@luc.edu. *Application contact:* Dr. Matt Miller, Director, 312-915-6800, E-mail: mmill11@luc.edu.

Loyola University Maryland, Graduate Programs, Loyola College of Arts and Sciences, Department of Psychology, Baltimore, MD 21210-2699. Offers clinical psychology (MS, Psy D, CAS); counseling psychology (MS, CAS). *Accreditation:* APA. *Students:* 132 full-time (109 women), 39 part-time (32 women); includes 55 minority (21 Black or African American, non-Hispanic/Latino; 19 Asian, non-Hispanic/Latino; 11 Hispanic/Latino; 4 Two or more races, non-Hispanic/Latino), 5 international. Average age 27. 427 applicants, 25% accepted, 44 enrolled. In 2019, 59 master's, 11 doctorates awarded. *Degree requirements:* For doctorate, comprehensive exam, thesis/dissertation. *Entrance requirements:* For master's, GRE (optional), essay, application, transcripts, letters of recommendation, CV/resume, interview; for doctorate, GRE, essay, application, transcripts, letters of recommendation, CV/resume, interview. Additional exam requirements/recommendations for international students: required—TOEFL (minimum score 550 paper-based; 80 iBT), IELTS (minimum score 7), TOEFL (minimum score 550 paper-based, 80iBT) or ILETS (minimum score 7). *Application deadline:* For fall admission, 12/1 for domestic and international students. Application fee: $60. Electronic applications accepted. *Expenses:* Contact institution. *Financial support:* Scholarships/grants and unspecified assistantships available. Financial award application deadline: 4/15; financial award applicants required to submit FAFSA. *Unit head:* Carolyn M. Barry, Chair, 410-617-5325, E-mail: cbarry@loyola.edu. *Application contact:* Office of Graduate Admission, 410-617-5020, E-mail: graduate@loyola.edu.
Website: https://www.loyola.edu/academics/psychology

Lynn University, College of Arts and Sciences, Boca Raton, FL 33431-5598. Offers criminal justice (MS); mental health counseling (MS); psychology (MS). *Program availability:* Part-time, evening/weekend, 100% online, blended/hybrid learning. *Faculty:* 15 full-time (7 women), 12 part-time/adjunct (7 women). *Students:* 98 full-time (81 women), 55 part-time (33 women); includes 57 minority (23 Black or African American, non-Hispanic/Latino; 1 American Indian or Alaska Native, non-Hispanic/Latino; 28 Hispanic/Latino; 2 Native Hawaiian or other Pacific Islander, non-Hispanic/Latino; 3 Two or more races, non-Hispanic/Latino), 9 international. Average age 32. 126 applicants, 77% accepted, 69 enrolled. In 2019, 37 master's awarded. *Degree requirements:* For master's, comprehensive exam (for some programs), thesis (for some programs). *Entrance requirements:* For master's, Bachelor's degree from accredited institution, minimum undergraduate GPA of 3.0, official undergraduate transcripts, two letters of recommendation from academic or professional sources, writing sample demonstrating capacity to perform at graduate level. Additional exam requirements/recommendations for international students: required—TOEFL (minimum score 550 paper-based; 80 iBT), IELTS (minimum score 6.5). *Application deadline:* For fall admission, 8/10 for domestic students, 7/31 for international students; for spring admission, 12/18 for domestic students, 12/2 for international students; for summer admission, 4/12 for domestic students, 4/2 for international students. Applications are processed on a rolling basis. Application fee: $45. Electronic applications accepted. *Expenses:* Tuition and fees for degrees offered in the College of Arts and Sciences start at $23,400 and can go to $38,350 depending on the program. Each program has specific credit hour requirements and the cost per credit hour within this college ranges from $650.00 to $740.00 per credit hour. *Financial support:* In 2019–20, 42 students received support. Career-related internships or fieldwork, Federal Work-Study, scholarships/grants, tuition waivers (full and partial), and unspecified assistantships available. Support available to part-time students. Financial award application deadline: 3/1; financial award applicants required to submit FAFSA. *Unit head:* Dr. Gary Villa, Dean, College of Arts and Sciences, 561-237-7025, E-mail: gvilla@lynn.edu. *Application contact:* Steven Pruitt, Director of Graduate and Online Admission, 561-237-7834, Fax: 561-237-7100, E-mail: admissionpm@lynn.edu.
Website: https://www.lynn.edu/academics/colleges-schools/arts-and-sciences

Manhattan College, Graduate Programs, School of Education and Health, Program in Mental Health Counseling, Riverdale, NY 10471. Offers MS, Advanced Certificate. *Program availability:* Part-time. *Degree requirements:* For master's, thesis. *Entrance* *requirements:* Additional exam requirements/recommendations for international students: required—TOEFL. Electronic applications accepted. *Expenses:* Contact institution.

Marian University, Master of Science in Counseling Program, Indianapolis, IN 46222-1997. Offers clinical mental health counseling (MS); school counseling (MS). *Program availability:* Part-time. *Degree requirements:* For master's, 60 credit hours plus 1000 hours of supervised practicum (for clinical mental health counseling track); 48 credit hours plus 700 hours of supervised practicum (for school counseling track). *Entrance requirements:* For master's, GRE (preferred scores: combined 295, verbal 150, quantitative 145, writing 4), bachelor's degree (in related field preferred); minimum undergraduate and major GPA of 3.0; completion of undergraduate psychology courses in development, abnormal psychology, statistics or research methods; official transcripts from all postsecondary institutions attended; personal statement; 3 letters of recommendation; resume; interview. Additional exam requirements/recommendations for international students: required—TOEFL (minimum score 550 paper-based; 79 iBT). Electronic applications accepted. Application fee is waived when completed online. *Expenses:* Contact institution.

Marist College, Graduate Programs, School of Social and Behavioral Sciences, Poughkeepsie, NY 12601-1387. Offers education (M Ed, MA); mental health counseling (MA); school psychology (MA, Adv C). *Program availability:* Part-time, evening/weekend. *Degree requirements:* For master's, thesis optional. *Entrance requirements:* For master's, GRE General Test, letters of recommendation, minimum undergraduate GPA of 3.0, interview. Additional exam requirements/recommendations for international students: required—TOEFL (minimum score 550 paper-based; 80 iBT); recommended—IELTS (minimum score 6.5). Electronic applications accepted.

Marquette University, Graduate School, College of Education, Department of Counselor Education and Counseling Psychology, Milwaukee, WI 53201-1881. Offers clinical mental health counseling (MS); community counseling (MA); counseling psychology (PhD); school counseling (MA). *Accreditation:* ACA. *Program availability:* Part-time. Terminal master's awarded for partial completion of doctoral program. *Degree requirements:* For master's, comprehensive exam, thesis (for some programs); for doctorate, thesis/dissertation, qualifying exam. *Entrance requirements:* For master's, GRE General Test or MAT, official transcripts from all current and previous colleges/universities except Marquette, three letters of recommendation, statement of purpose; for doctorate, GRE General Test, MAT, sample of written work, official transcripts from all current and previous colleges/universities except Marquette, three letters of recommendation, statement of purpose, resume/curriculum vitae. Additional exam requirements/recommendations for international students: required—TOEFL (minimum score 530 paper-based).

Marymount University, School of Sciences, Mathematics, and Education, Program in Counseling, Arlington, VA 22207-4299. Offers clinical mental health counseling (MA); counseling with forensic and legal studies (MA/MA); pastoral counseling (MA); school counseling (MA); MA/MA. *Accreditation:* ACA (one or more programs are accredited). *Program availability:* Part-time, evening/weekend. *Faculty:* 11 full-time (9 women), 3 part-time/adjunct (all women). *Students:* 119 full-time (100 women), 39 part-time (33 women); includes 54 minority (20 Black or African American, non-Hispanic/Latino; 8 Asian, non-Hispanic/Latino; 20 Hispanic/Latino; 6 Two or more races, non-Hispanic/Latino), 2 international. Average age 28. 122 applicants, 89% accepted, 58 enrolled. In 2019, 41 master's awarded. *Degree requirements:* For master's, thesis or alternative, capstone/internship. *Entrance requirements:* For master's, GRE, 2 letters of recommendation, interview, resume, personal statement. Additional exam requirements/recommendations for international students: required—TOEFL (minimum score 600 paper-based; 96 iBT), IELTS (minimum score 6.5), PTE (minimum score 58). *Application deadline:* For fall admission, 1/15 priority date for domestic and international students. Applications are processed on a rolling basis. Application fee: $40. Electronic applications accepted. *Expenses: Tuition:* Part-time $1050 per credit. *Required fees:* $22 per credit. One-time fee: $270 part-time. Tuition and fees vary according to program. *Financial support:* In 2019–20, 19 students received support. Research assistantships, teaching assistantships, career-related internships or fieldwork, scholarships/grants, and unspecified assistantships available. Support available to part-time students. Financial award application deadline: 3/1; financial award applicants required to submit FAFSA. *Unit head:* Dr. Lisa Jackson-Cherry, Chair, Counseling, 703-284-1633, E-mail: lisa.jackson-cherry@marymount.edu. *Application contact:* Fiona McDonnell, Administrative Assistant, 703-284-5901, E-mail: gadmissi@marymount.edu. Website: https://www.marymount.edu/Academics/School-of-Sciences-Mathematics-and-Education/Graduate-Programs/Counseling-(M-A-)

Marywood University, Academic Affairs, Reap College of Education and Human Development, Department of Psychology and Counseling, Program in Mental Health Counseling, Scranton, PA 18509-1598. Offers MA. *Accreditation:* ACA. Electronic applications accepted.

McGill University, Faculty of Graduate and Postdoctoral Studies, Faculty of Education, Department of Educational and Counseling Psychology, Montréal, QC H3A 2T5, Canada. Offers counseling psychology (MA, PhD); educational psychology (M Ed, MA, PhD); school/applied child psychology and applied developmental psychology (M Ed, MA, PhD, Diploma), including school psychology. *Accreditation:* APA.

McKendree University, Graduate Programs, Master of Arts Program in Clinical Mental Health Counseling, Lebanon, IL 62254-1299. Offers MA. *Program availability:* Part-time, evening/weekend. *Degree requirements:* For master's, comprehensive exam, internship. *Entrance requirements:* For master's, official transcripts from each college or university attended, minimum undergraduate GPA of 3.0, three letters of recommendation, personal statement, completion of six undergraduate credit hours in a behavior science, curriculum vitae or resume. Electronic applications accepted.

McNeese State University, Doré School of Graduate Studies, Burton College of Education, Department of Psychology, Lake Charles, LA 70609. Offers applied behavior analysis (MA, Graduate Certificate); counseling psychology (MA); general/experimental psychology (MA). *Program availability:* Evening/weekend. *Entrance requirements:* For master's, GRE.

Medaille College, Programs in Psychology, Buffalo, NY 14214-2695. Offers clinical psychology (Psy D); marriage and family therapy (MA); mental health counseling (MA); psychology (MA). *Accreditation:* ACA. *Program availability:* Part-time, evening/weekend. *Degree requirements:* For master's, comprehensive exam (for some programs), thesis (for some programs). *Entrance requirements:* For master's, GRE General Test (psychology), minimum GPA of 2.75 (psychology). Additional exam requirements/recommendations for international students: required—TOEFL (minimum score 550 paper-based). Electronic applications accepted.

Mercy College, School of Social and Behavioral Sciences, Program in Counseling, Dobbs Ferry, NY 10522-1189. Offers counseling (MS); family counseling (Certificate). *Program availability:* Part-time, evening/weekend, blended/hybrid learning. *Students:* 53 full-time (48 women), 112 part-time (95 women); includes 125 minority (59 Black or African American, non-Hispanic/Latino; 1 Asian, non-Hispanic/Latino; 62 Hispanic/Latino; 1 Native Hawaiian or other Pacific Islander, non-Hispanic/Latino; 2 Two or more races, non-Hispanic/Latino). Average age 33. 216 applicants, 71% accepted, 63 enrolled. In 2019, 65 master's awarded. *Degree requirements:* For master's, comprehensive exam, Internship. *Entrance requirements:* For master's, transcript(s); two letters of recommendation; resume; essay; interview. Additional exam requirements/recommendations for international students: required—TOEFL (minimum score 80 iBT), IELTS (minimum score 6.5). *Application deadline:* Applications are processed on a rolling basis. Application fee: $40. Electronic applications accepted. *Expenses: Tuition:* Full-time $16,146; part-time $897 per credit. *Required fees:* $332; $166 per semester. Tuition and fees vary according to course load and program. *Financial support:* Career-related internships or fieldwork, Federal Work-Study, scholarships/grants, and unspecified assistantships available. Support available to part-time students. Financial award applicants required to submit FAFSA. *Unit head:* Dr. Diana Juettner, Interim Dean, School of Social and Behavioral Sciences, 914-674-7546, E-mail: djuettner@mercy.edu. *Application contact:* Allison Gurdineer, Executive Director of Admissions, 877-637-2946, Fax: 914-674-7382, E-mail: admissions@mercy.edu. Website: https://www.mercy.edu/degrees-programs/ms-counseling

Mercy College, School of Social and Behavioral Sciences, Program in Mental Health Counseling, Dobbs Ferry, NY 10522-1189. Offers MS. *Program availability:* Part-time, evening/weekend, blended/hybrid learning. *Students:* 65 full-time (56 women), 106 part-time (87 women); includes 129 minority (71 Black or African American, non-Hispanic/Latino; 2 Asian, non-Hispanic/Latino; 53 Hispanic/Latino; 1 Native Hawaiian or other Pacific Islander, non-Hispanic/Latino; 2 Two or more races, non-Hispanic/Latino), 1 international. Average age 36. 128 applicants, 55% accepted, 49 enrolled. In 2019, 53 master's awarded. *Degree requirements:* For master's, comprehensive exam, Internship. *Entrance requirements:* For master's, transcript(s); two letters of recommendation; resume; essay; interview. Additional exam requirements/recommendations for international students: required—TOEFL (minimum score 80 iBT), IELTS (minimum score 6.5). *Application deadline:* Applications are processed on a rolling basis. Application fee: $40. Electronic applications accepted. *Expenses: Tuition:* Full-time $16,146; part-time $897 per credit. *Required fees:* $332; $166 per semester. Tuition and fees vary according to course load and program. *Financial support:* Career-related internships or fieldwork, Federal Work-Study, scholarships/grants, and unspecified assistantships available. Support available to part-time students. Financial award applicants required to submit FAFSA. *Unit head:* Dr. Diana Juettner, Interim Dean, School of Social and Behavioral Sciences, 914-674-7546, E-mail: djuettner@mercy.edu. *Application contact:* Allison Gurdineer, Executive Director of Admissions, 877-637-2946, Fax: 914-674-7382, E-mail: admissions@mercy.edu. Website: https://www.mercy.edu/degrees-programs/ms-mental-health-counseling

Messiah University, Program in Counseling, Mechanicsburg, PA 17055. Offers clinical mental health counseling (MAC); counseling (CAGS); marriage, couple, and family counseling (MAC); school counseling (MAC). *Accreditation:* ACA. *Program availability:* Part-time, online learning. *Entrance requirements:* For master's, minimum undergraduate cumulative GPA of 3.0, 2 recommendations, resume or curriculum vitae, interview; for CAGS, bachelor's degree, minimum undergraduate cumulative GPA of 3.0, essay, two recommendations, resume or curriculum vitae, interview. Electronic applications accepted.

Mid-America Christian University, Program in Counseling, Oklahoma City, OK 73170-4504. Offers marital and family therapy (MS); pastoral/spiritual direction (MS); professional counselor (MS). *Entrance requirements:* For master's, MAT, bachelor's degree from a regionally accredited college or university, minimum overall cumulative GPA of 2.75 of bachelor course work. Additional exam requirements/recommendations for international students: required—TOEFL (minimum score 550 paper-based).

Middle Tennessee State University, College of Graduate Studies, College of Education, Department of Educational Leadership, Program in Professional Counseling, Murfreesboro, TN 37132. Offers mental health counseling (M Ed); school counseling (M Ed). *Accreditation:* ACA; NCATE. *Program availability:* Part-time, evening/weekend, online learning. *Degree requirements:* For master's, comprehensive exam, thesis. *Entrance requirements:* For master's, GRE or MAT. Additional exam requirements/recommendations for international students: required—TOEFL (minimum score 525 paper-based; 71 iBT) or IELTS (minimum score 6). Electronic applications accepted.

Midwestern State University, Billie Doris McAda Graduate School, Prothro-Yeager College of Humanities and Social Sciences, Department of Psychology, Wichita Falls, TX 76308. Offers clinical/counseling psychology (MA). *Program availability:* Part-time, evening/weekend. *Degree requirements:* For master's, one foreign language, comprehensive exam, thesis optional. *Entrance requirements:* For master's, GRE General Test, 3 recommendation forms. Additional exam requirements/recommendations for international students: required—TOEFL (minimum score 550 paper-based). Electronic applications accepted.

Minnesota State University Mankato, College of Graduate Studies and Research, College of Education, Department of Counseling and Student Personnel, Mankato, MN 56001. Offers college student affairs (MS); counselor education and supervision (Ed D); mental health counseling (MS); professional school counseling (K-12) (MS). *Accreditation:* ACA (one or more programs are accredited); NCATE. *Degree requirements:* For master's, comprehensive exam, thesis or alternative. *Entrance requirements:* For master's, GRE General Test or MAT (if GPA less than 3.0 for last 2 years), minimum GPA of 3.0 during previous 2 years, 3 letters of reference. Additional exam requirements/recommendations for international students: required—TOEFL. Electronic applications accepted.

Mississippi College, Graduate School, School of Education, Department of Psychology and Counseling, Clinton, MS 39058. Offers counseling (Ed S); marriage and family counseling (MS); mental health counseling (MS); school counseling (M Ed). *Program availability:* Part-time. *Degree requirements:* For master's and Ed S, comprehensive exam, thesis optional. *Entrance requirements:* For master's, GRE or NTE. Additional exam requirements/recommendations for international students: recommended—TOEFL, IELTS. Electronic applications accepted.

Missouri State University, Graduate College, College of Education, Department of Counseling, Leadership, and Special Education, Program in Counseling, Springfield, MO 65897. Offers mental health counseling (MS). *Accreditation:* ACA. *Program availability:* Part-time, evening/weekend. *Degree requirements:* For master's, comprehensive exam, thesis or alternative. *Entrance requirements:* For master's, GRE or MAT, minimum GPA of 2.75. Additional exam requirements/recommendations for international students: required—TOEFL (minimum score 550 paper-based; 79 iBT), IELTS (minimum score 6). Electronic applications accepted. *Expenses: Tuition, area resident:* Full-time $2600; part-time $1735 per credit hour. Tuition, nonresident: full-time $5240; part-time $3495 per credit hour. *International tuition:* $5240 full-time. *Required fees:* $530; $438 per credit hour. Tuition and fees vary according to class time, course level, course load, degree level, campus/location and program.

Monmouth University, Graduate Studies, Department of Professional Counseling, West Long Branch, NJ 07764-1898. Offers addiction studies (MA); clinical mental health counseling (MS); professional counseling (PMC). *Accreditation:* ACA. *Program availability:* Part-time, evening/weekend. *Faculty:* 9 full-time (5 women), 4 part-time/adjunct (3 women). *Students:* 91 full-time (78 women), 53 part-time (38 women); includes 28 minority (11 Black or African American, non-Hispanic/Latino; 1 Asian, non-

Hispanic/Latino; 12 Hispanic/Latino; 4 Two or more races, non-Hispanic/Latino). Average age 30. In 2019, 57 master's awarded. *Degree requirements:* For master's, comprehensive exam (for some programs), thesis optional, fieldwork. *Entrance requirements:* For master's, GRE, minimum GPA of 3.0 overall, 12 credits in psychology or closely-related field, two Monmouth University psychological counseling recommendation forms, narrative essay; for PMC, degree or current enrollment in CACREP-accredited master's program in counseling with minimum cumulative GPA of 3.0. Additional exam requirements/recommendations for international students: required—TOEFL (minimum score 550 paper-based; 79 iBT), IELTS (minimum score 6), Michigan English Language Assessment Battery (minimum score 77) or Certificate of Advanced English (minimum score 160). *Application deadline:* For fall admission, 7/15 priority date for domestic students, 6/1 for international students; for spring admission, 12/1 priority date for domestic students, 11/1 for international students; for summer admission, 5/1 for domestic students. Applications are processed on a rolling basis. Application fee: $50. Electronic applications accepted. *Expenses: Tuition:* Full-time $22,194; part-time $14,796 per credit. *Required fees:* $712; $178 per semester. $178 per semester. Tuition and fees vary according to course load. *Financial support:* In 2019–20, 149 students received support. Research assistantships, teaching assistantships, scholarships/grants, and unspecified assistantships available. Support available to part-time students. Financial award applicants required to submit FAFSA. *Unit head:* Dr. Joanne Jodry, Program Director, 732-263-5115, Fax: 732-923-4661, E-mail: jjodry@monmouth.edu. *Application contact:* Kevin New, Graduate Admission Counselor, 732-571-3452, Fax: 732-263-5123, E-mail: gradadm@monmouth.edu. Website: https://www.monmouth.edu/school-of-humanities-social-sciences/professional-counseling.aspx

Montana State University Billings, College of Allied Health Professions, Program in Clinical Rehabilitation and Mental Health Counseling, Billings, MT 59101. Offers MS. *Accreditation:* ACA; CORE. *Program availability:* Part-time. *Degree requirements:* For master's, thesis or professional paper and/or field experience. *Entrance requirements:* For master's, GRE General Test or MAT, minimum GPA of 3.0, letters of recommendation, letter of intent. Additional exam requirements/recommendations for international students: required—TOEFL (minimum score 79 iBT), IELTS (minimum score 6.5). Electronic applications accepted.

Moody Theological Seminary–Michigan, Graduate Programs, Plymouth, MI 48170. Offers Bible (Graduate Certificate); Christian education (MA); counseling psychology (MA); divinity (M Div); theological studies (MA). *Accreditation:* ATS. *Program availability:* Part-time, evening/weekend. *Degree requirements:* For master's, one foreign language, thesis.

Morehead State University, Graduate School, College of Science, Department of Psychology, Morehead, KY 40351. Offers clinical/counseling psychology (MS); general/experimental psychology (MS). *Program availability:* Part-time, evening/weekend. *Faculty:* 8 full-time (5 women), 1 part-time/adjunct (0 women). *Students:* 10 full-time (9 women), 1 (woman) part-time; includes 2 minority (both Two or more races, non-Hispanic/Latino). 20 applicants, 60% accepted, 6 enrolled. In 2019, 11 master's awarded. *Degree requirements:* For master's, comprehensive exam, Minimum 3.0 GPA, internship, pass a comprehensive oral examination administered by a committee of three faculty. *Entrance requirements:* For master's, GRE, 3.5 UG GPA preferred, 3.0 is minimum required, 18 hrs in psychology, interview, 3 letters of recommendation, statement of purpose for seeking graduate-level training in clinical/counseling psychology. *Application deadline:* For fall admission, 3/1 priority date for domestic and international students. Applications are processed on a rolling basis. Application fee: $30. Electronic applications accepted. *Expenses: Tuition, area resident:* Part-time $570 per credit hour. Tuition, state resident: part-time $570 per credit hour. Tuition, nonresident: part-time $570 per credit hour. *Required fees:* $14 per credit hour. *Financial support:* Research assistantships, career-related internships or fieldwork, and unspecified assistantships available. Financial award applicants required to submit FAFSA. *Unit head:* Dr. Gregory Corso, Department Chair Psychology, 606-783-2981, E-mail: g.corso@moreheadstate.edu. *Application contact:* Dr. Gregory Corso, Department Chair Psychology, 606-783-2981, E-mail: g.corso@moreheadstate.edu. Website: https://www.moreheadstate.edu/College-of-Science/Psychology

Mount Mary University, Graduate Programs, Program in Counseling, Milwaukee, WI 53222-4597. Offers clinical mental health counseling (MS, Certificate); clinical rehabilitation counseling (MS, Certificate); school counseling (MS, Certificate); vocational rehabilitation counseling (MS, Certificate). *Accreditation:* ACA. *Program availability:* Part-time, evening/weekend. *Degree requirements:* For master's, comprehensive exam, thesis or alternative. *Entrance requirements:* For master's, minimum GPA of 3.0. Additional exam requirements/recommendations for international students: required—TOEFL (minimum score 550 paper-based; 80 iBT); recommended—IELTS (minimum score 6.5). Electronic applications accepted. *Expenses:* Contact institution.

Mount Saint Mary's University, Graduate Division, Los Angeles, CA 90049. Offers business administration (MBA); counseling psychology (MS); creative writing (MFA); education (MS, Certificate); film and television (MFA); health policy and management (MS); humanities (MA); nursing (MSN, Certificate); physical therapy (DPT); religious studies (MA). *Program availability:* Part-time, evening/weekend. *Entrance requirements:* Additional exam requirements/recommendations for international students: required—TOEFL. Electronic applications accepted. *Expenses: Tuition:* Full-time $18,648; part-time $9324 per year. *Required fees:* $540; $540 per unit.

Naropa University, Graduate Programs, Program in Clinical Mental Health Counseling, Boulder, CO 80302-6697. Offers contemplative psychotherapy and Buddhist psychology (MA); mindfulness-based transpersonal counseling (MA); somatic counseling: body psychotherapy (MA); somatic counseling: dance/movement therapy (MA); transpersonal art therapy (MA); transpersonal wilderness therapy (MA). *Degree requirements:* For master's, internships, counseling practicum, paper. *Entrance requirements:* For master's, interview, 2 letters of recommendation, professional resume, statement of interest essay, supplementary essay; minimum 100 hours of paid or volunteer work in a helping profession (for some concentrations); wilderness experience (for some concentrations). Additional exam requirements/recommendations for international students: required—TOEFL (minimum score 550 paper-based; 80 iBT). Electronic applications accepted. *Expenses:* Contact institution.

National University, College of Letters and Sciences, La Jolla, CA 92037-1011. Offers biology (MS); counseling psychology (MA), including licensed professional clinical counseling, marriage and family therapy; creative writing (MFA); English (MA); film studies (MA); forensic and crime scene investigations (Certificate); forensic sciences (MFS); human behavior (MA); mathematics for educators (MS); performance psychology (MA); strategic communications (MA). *Program availability:* Part-time, evening/weekend, 100% online, blended/hybrid learning. *Degree requirements:* For master's, thesis (for some programs). *Entrance requirements:* For master's, interview, minimum GPA of 2.5. Additional exam requirements/recommendations for international students: required—TOEFL (minimum score 550 paper-based; 79 iBT), IELTS (minimum score 6). Electronic applications accepted. *Expenses: Tuition:* Full-time $442; part-time $442 per unit.

Nebraska Christian College of Hope International University, Graduate Programs, Papillion, NE 68046. Offers biblical studies (M Div); business as mission/social entrepreneurship (MBA); children, youth, and family (M Div); church planting (M Div); counseling psychology (MS); educational administration (MA); elementary education (M Ed); general management (MBA); gifted and talented education (M Ed); intercultural studies (M Div); international development (MBA); marketing management (MBA); ministry (MA); ministry and leadership (M Div); music education (M Ed); non-profit management (MBA); pastoral care (M Div); secondary education (M Ed); spiritual formation (M Div); worship ministry (M Div).

New England College, Program in Community Mental Health Counseling, Henniker, NH 03242-3293. Offers human services (MS); mental health counseling (MS). *Program availability:* Part-time, evening/weekend. *Degree requirements:* For master's, internship.

New Mexico Highlands University, Graduate Studies, College of Arts and Sciences, Department of Social and Behavioral Sciences, Las Vegas, NM 87701. Offers psychology (MS), including clinical psychology/counseling, general psychology; public affairs (MA), including applied sociology; Southwest studies (MA), including anthropology. *Program availability:* Part-time. *Degree requirements:* For master's, comprehensive exam, thesis or alternative. *Entrance requirements:* For master's, minimum undergraduate GPA of 3.0. Additional exam requirements/recommendations for international students: required—TOEFL (minimum score 540 paper-based).

New Mexico State University, College of Education, Department of Counseling and Educational Psychology, Las Cruces, NM 88003-8001. Offers counseling psychology (PhD); educational diagnostics (MA), including clinical mental health counseling, educational diagnostics; school psychology (Ed S). *Accreditation:* ACA; APA (one or more programs are accredited); NCATE. *Program availability:* Part-time, evening/weekend. *Faculty:* 12 full-time (9 women), 4 part-time/adjunct (all women). *Students:* 90 full-time (71 women), 59 part-time (43 women); includes 82 minority (6 Black or African American, non-Hispanic/Latino; 4 American Indian or Alaska Native, non-Hispanic/Latino; 3 Asian, non-Hispanic/Latino; 63 Hispanic/Latino; 6 Two or more races, non-Hispanic/Latino), 5 international. Average age 33. 140 applicants, 51% accepted, 54 enrolled. In 2019, 21 master's, 8 doctorates, 6 other advanced degrees awarded. *Degree requirements:* For master's, comprehensive exam, thesis optional, internship; for doctorate, comprehensive exam, thesis/dissertation, internship; for Ed S, comprehensive exam, thesis or alternative, internship as alternate. *Entrance requirements:* For master's, doctorate, and Ed S, GRE General Test, minimum GPA of 3.0. Additional exam requirements/recommendations for international students: required—TOEFL (minimum score 550 paper-based; 79 iBT), IELTS (minimum score 6.5). *Application deadline:* For fall admission, 12/15 for domestic and international students; for spring admission, 2/1 priority date for domestic students, 2/1 for international students. Application fee: $40 ($50 for international students). Electronic applications accepted. *Financial support:* In 2019–20, 87 students received support, including 10 fellowships (averaging $4,844 per year), 3 research assistantships (averaging $9,959 per year), 25 teaching assistantships (averaging $15,189 per year); career-related internships or fieldwork, Federal Work-Study, scholarships/grants, traineeships, health care benefits, and unspecified assistantships also available. Support available to part-time students. Financial award application deadline: 3/1. *Unit head:* Dr. Barbara Gormley, Department Head, 575-646-2121, Fax: 575-646-8035, E-mail: bgormley@nmsu.edu. *Application contact:* Norma Arrieta, Student Program Coordinator, 575-646-2121, Fax: 575-646-8035, E-mail: cep@nmsu.edu. Website: http://cep.education.nmsu.edu

New York University, Steinhardt School of Culture, Education, and Human Development, Department of Applied Psychology, Programs in Counseling, New York, NY 10012. Offers counseling and guidance (MA, Advanced Certificate), including bilingual school counseling K-12 (MA), school counseling K-12 (MA); counseling for mental health and wellness (MA); counseling psychology (PhD); LGBT health, education, and social services (Advanced Certificate); Advanced Certificate/MPH; MA/Advanced Certificate. *Accreditation:* APA (one or more programs are accredited). *Program availability:* Part-time. *Entrance requirements:* For doctorate, GRE General Test, interview. Additional exam requirements/recommendations for international students: required—TOEFL (minimum score 100 iBT). Electronic applications accepted.

Niagara University, Graduate Division of Education, Niagara University, NY 14109. Offers applied behavior analysis (Certificate); educational leadership (MS Ed, PhD, Certificate), including leadership and policy (PhD), school building leader (MS Ed), school district business leader (Certificate), school district leader (MS Ed, Certificate); literacy instruction (MS Ed); mental health counseling (MS, Certificate); school counseling (MS Ed, Certificate); school psychology (MS); teacher education (MS, MS Ed, Certificate), including early childhood and childhood education (MS Ed, Certificate), early childhood special education (MS), middle and adolescence education (Certificate), special education (MS Ed), special education (grades 1-6) (Certificate), special education (grades 7-12) (Certificate), teaching English to speakers of other languages (TESOL) (Certificate). *Accreditation:* NCATE (one or more programs are accredited). *Program availability:* Part-time, evening/weekend, 100% online, blended/hybrid learning. *Entrance requirements:* For master's, GRE General Test or MAT. Additional exam requirements/recommendations for international students: required—TOEFL (minimum score 550 paper-based; 79 iBT), IELTS (minimum score 6). Electronic applications accepted. *Expenses:* Contact institution.

North Dakota State University, College of Graduate and Interdisciplinary Studies, College of Human Development and Education, School of Education, Program in Counselor Education, Fargo, ND 58102. Offers clinical mental health counseling (M Ed, MS); counselor education and supervision (PhD); school counseling (M Ed, MS). *Accreditation:* ACA; NCATE. *Program availability:* Part-time, online learning. *Degree requirements:* For master's, comprehensive exam, thesis or alternative; for doctorate, comprehensive exam, thesis/dissertation. *Entrance requirements:* For master's, GRE, MAT, interview. Additional exam requirements/recommendations for international students: required—TOEFL. Tuition and fees vary according to program and reciprocity agreements.

Northeastern University, Bouvé College of Health Sciences, Boston, MA 02115-5096. Offers applied behavior analysis (MS); audiology (Au D); counseling psychology (MS, PhD, CAGS); exercise science (MS); nursing (MS, PhD, CAGS), including administration (MS), adult-gerontology acute care nurse practitioner (MS, CAGS), adult-gerontology primary care nurse practitioner (MS, CAGS), anesthesia (MS), family nurse practitioner (MS, CAGS), neonatal nurse practitioner (MS, CAGS), pediatric nurse practitioner (MS, CAGS), psychiatric mental health nurse practitioner (MS, CAGS); nursing practice (DNP); pharmaceutical sciences (MS, PhD), including interdisciplinary concentration, pharmaceutics and drug delivery systems; pharmacology (MS); pharmacy (Pharm D); school psychology (PhD); speech-language pathology (MS); urban health (MPH); MS/MBA. *Accreditation:* AANA/CANAEP; ACPE (one or more programs are accredited); ASHA; CEPH. *Program availability:* Part-time, evening/weekend, online learning. *Degree requirements:* For doctorate, thesis/dissertation (for some programs); for CAGS, comprehensive exam. Electronic applications accepted. *Expenses:* Contact institution.

Counseling Psychology

Northern Arizona University, College of Education, Department of Educational Psychology, Flagstaff, AZ 86011. Offers clinical mental health counseling (MA); combined counseling/school psychology (PhD), including counseling psychology; counseling (M Ed), including school counseling, student affairs; human relations (M Ed); psychology of human development and learning (Graduate Certificate); school psychology (Ed S). *Program availability:* Part-time, 100% online, blended/hybrid learning. Terminal master's awarded for partial completion of doctoral program. *Degree requirements:* For master's, variable foreign language requirement, comprehensive exam (for some programs), thesis (for some programs); for doctorate, variable foreign language requirement, comprehensive exam (for some programs), thesis/dissertation (for some programs); for other advanced degree, comprehensive exam (for some programs). *Entrance requirements:* Additional exam requirements/recommendations for international students: required—TOEFL (minimum score 80 iBT), IELTS (minimum score 6.5). Electronic applications accepted.

Northern Kentucky University, Office of Graduate Programs, College of Education and Human Services, Clinical Mental Health Counseling Program, Highland Heights, KY 41099. Offers MS. *Accreditation:* ACA. *Program availability:* Part-time, evening/weekend. *Degree requirements:* For master's, comprehensive exam. *Entrance requirements:* For master's, GRE or MAT. Additional exam requirements/recommendations for international students: required—TOEFL (minimum score 550 paper-based; 79 iBT); recommended—IELTS (minimum score 6.5). Electronic applications accepted.

Northern State University, MS Ed Program in Counseling, Aberdeen, SD 57401-7198. Offers clinical mental health counseling (MS Ed); school counseling (MS Ed). *Accreditation:* ACA; NCATE. *Program availability:* Part-time, online learning. *Faculty:* 5 full-time (all women). *Students:* 21 full-time (16 women), 2 part-time (1 woman); includes 4 minority (1 American Indian or Alaska Native, non-Hispanic/Latino; 1 Hispanic/Latino; 2 Two or more races, non-Hispanic/Latino), 1 international. Average age 29. 17 applicants, 47% accepted, 8 enrolled. In 2019, 12 master's awarded. *Degree requirements:* For master's, comprehensive exam, thesis optional. *Entrance requirements:* For master's, minimum GPA of 2.75. Additional exam requirements/recommendations for international students: required—TOEFL (minimum score 550 paper-based; 78 iBT), IELTS (minimum score 6). *Application deadline:* For fall admission, 8/15 for domestic and international students; for spring admission, 12/15 for domestic and international students. Applications are processed on a rolling basis. Application fee: $35. Electronic applications accepted. *Expenses: Tuition, area resident:* Full-time $5939; part-time $5939 per year. Tuition, state resident: full-time $8816; part-time $8816 per year. Tuition, nonresident: full-time $11,088; part-time $11,088 per year. *International tuition:* $7392 full-time. *Required fees:* $484; $242. *Financial support:* In 2019–20, 11 students received support, including 5 teaching assistantships with partial tuition reimbursements available (averaging $7,764 per year); career-related internships or fieldwork, Federal Work-Study, institutionally sponsored loans, scholarships/grants, and unspecified assistantships also available. Support available to part-time students. Financial award application deadline: 3/1; financial award applicants required to submit FAFSA. *Unit head:* Dr. Doug Ohmer, Dean of Professional Studies, 605-626-2400, Fax: 605-626-2980, E-mail: doug.ohmer@northern.edu. *Application contact:* Tammy K. Griffith, Program Assistant, 605-626-2558, Fax: 605-626-7190, E-mail: tammy.griffith@northern.edu.
Website: https://www.northern.edu/programs/graduate/counseling-masters

Northwestern Oklahoma State University, School of Professional Studies, Program in Counseling Psychology, Alva, OK 73717-2799. Offers MCP. *Program availability:* Part-time. *Degree requirements:* For master's, comprehensive exam. *Entrance requirements:* For master's, GRE General Test or MAT, minimum GPA of 2.75.

Northwest University, College of Social and Behavioral Sciences, Kirkland, WA 98033. Offers counseling psychology (MA, Psy D); international community development (MA). *Program availability:* Evening/weekend. *Entrance requirements:* For master's, 3 character references. Additional exam requirements/recommendations for international students: required—TOEFL (minimum score 580 paper-based). *Expenses:* Contact institution.

Nova Southeastern University, College of Psychology, Fort Lauderdale, FL 33314-7796. Offers clinical mental health counseling (MS); clinical psychology (PhD, Psy D); counseling (MS); experimental psychology (MS); forensic psychology (MS); general psychology (MS); school counseling (MS); school psychology (Psy D, Psy S); substance abuse counseling (MS); substance abuse counseling and education (MS). *Accreditation:* APA (one or more programs are accredited). *Program availability:* Part-time, 100% online, blended/hybrid learning. *Faculty:* 72 full-time (34 women), 111 part-time/adjunct (76 women). *Students:* 1,263 full-time (1,068 women), 868 part-time (761 women); includes 1,221 minority (368 Black or African American, non-Hispanic/Latino; 3 American Indian or Alaska Native, non-Hispanic/Latino; 111 Asian, non-Hispanic/Latino; 668 Hispanic/Latino; 1 Native Hawaiian or other Pacific Islander, non-Hispanic/Latino; 70 Two or more races, non-Hispanic/Latino), 59 international. Average age 31. 935 applicants, 56% accepted, 375 enrolled. In 2019, 400 master's, 72 doctorates, 13 other advanced degrees awarded. Terminal master's awarded for partial completion of doctoral program. *Degree requirements:* For master's, comprehensive exam, 3 practica; for doctorate, thesis/dissertation, clinical internship, competency exam; for Psy S, comprehensive exam, internship. *Entrance requirements:* For master's and Psy S, GRE General Test, letters of recommendation, research/personal statement, interview; for doctorate, GRE General Test, GRE Subject Test (recommended), minimum undergraduate GPA of 3.0, letters of recommendation, research/personal statement, interview, curriculum vitae/resume. Additional exam requirements/recommendations for international students: required—TOEFL (minimum score 550 paper-based). *Application deadline:* Applications are processed on a rolling basis. Application fee: $50. Electronic applications accepted. *Expenses:* Contact institution. *Financial support:* In 2019–20, 197 students received support, including 15 research assistantships (averaging $5,600 per year), 68 teaching assistantships (averaging $2,000 per year); career-related internships or fieldwork, Federal Work-Study, institutionally sponsored loans, scholarships/grants, and unspecified assistantships also available. Support available to part-time students. Financial award application deadline: 4/15; financial award applicants required to submit FAFSA. *Unit head:* Dr. Karen Grosby, Dean, 954-262-5712, Fax: 954-262-3859, E-mail: grosby@nova.edu. *Application contact:* Gregory Gayle, Director, Recruitment and Admissions, 954-262-5903, Fax: 954-262-3893, E-mail: ggayle1@nova.edu.
Website: http://psychology.nova.edu/

Nyack College, Alliance Graduate School of Counseling, New York, NY 10004. Offers marriage and family therapy (MA); mental health counseling (MA). *Program availability:* Part-time, evening/weekend, 100% online, blended/hybrid learning. *Students:* 62 full-time (56 women), 128 part-time (102 women); includes 157 minority (62 Black or African American, non-Hispanic/Latino; 1 American Indian or Alaska Native, non-Hispanic/Latino; 40 Asian, non-Hispanic/Latino; 48 Hispanic/Latino; 6 Two or more races, non-Hispanic/Latino), 4 international. Average age 37. In 2019, 60 master's awarded. *Degree requirements:* For master's, comprehensive exam, counselor-in-training therapy, internship, CPCE exam. *Entrance requirements:* For master's, Millon Clinical Multiaxial Inventory-3, Minnesota Multiphasic Personality Inventory-2, transcripts, statement of Christian life and experience, statement of support systems. Additional exam requirements/recommendations for international students: required—TOEFL (minimum score 550 paper-based; 80 iBT). *Application deadline:* For fall admission, 8/1 for domestic students, 2/15 for international students; for spring admission, 12/15 for domestic students, 7/15 for international students. Applications are processed on a rolling basis. Application fee: $30. Electronic applications accepted. *Expenses:* $800 per credit. *Financial support:* Career-related internships or fieldwork and scholarships/grants available. Financial award applicants required to submit FAFSA. *Unit head:* Dr. Antoinette Gines-Rivera, Director, 646-378-6160. *Application contact:* Dr. Antoinette Gines-Rivera, Director, 646-378-6160.
Website: http://www.nyack.edu/agsc

Oakland University, Graduate Study and Lifelong Learning, School of Education and Human Services, Department of Counseling, Rochester, MI 48309-4401. Offers MA, PhD, Certificate. *Accreditation:* ACA (one or more programs are accredited). *Program availability:* Part-time. *Degree requirements:* For doctorate, thesis/dissertation. *Entrance requirements:* Additional exam requirements/recommendations for international students: required—TOEFL (minimum score 550 paper-based; 79 iBT), IELTS (minimum score 6.5). Electronic applications accepted. *Expenses: Tuition, area resident:* Full-time $12,328; part-time $770.50 per credit hour. Tuition, state resident: full-time $12,328; part-time $770.50 per credit hour. Tuition, nonresident: full-time $16,432; part-time $1027 per credit hour. *International tuition:* $16,432 full-time. Tuition and fees vary according to degree level and program.

Old Dominion University, Darden College of Education, Counseling Program, Norfolk, VA 23529. Offers clinical mental health counseling (MS Ed); college counseling (MS Ed); counseling (Ed S); counselor education (PhD); school counseling (MS Ed). *Accreditation:* ACA. *Program availability:* Part-time, evening/weekend. *Degree requirements:* For master's and Ed S, comprehensive exam; for doctorate, comprehensive exam, thesis/dissertation. *Entrance requirements:* For master's and Ed S, GRE General Test, resume, essay, transcripts, recommendations; for doctorate, GRE General Test, resume, interview, essay, transcripts, recommendations. Additional exam requirements/recommendations for international students: required—TOEFL. Electronic applications accepted. *Expenses:* Contact institution.

Ottawa University, Graduate Studies-Arizona, Program in Professional Counseling, Ottawa, KS 66067-3399. Offers Christian counseling (MA); expressive arts therapy (MA); marriage and family therapy (MA); treatment of trauma, abuse and deprivation (MA). *Program availability:* Part-time, evening/weekend, online learning. *Degree requirements:* For master's, comprehensive exam, thesis or alternative, field experience, practicum. *Entrance requirements:* For master's, minimum undergraduate GPA of 3.0; course work in theories of personality, abnormal psychology, and human growth and development. Additional exam requirements/recommendations for international students: required—TOEFL (minimum score 550 paper-based).

Our Lady of the Lake University, College of Professional Studies, Program in Counseling Psychology, San Antonio, TX 78207-4689. Offers Psy D. *Degree requirements:* For doctorate, comprehensive exam, thesis/dissertation, internship, 3-years of residency in San Antonio. *Entrance requirements:* For doctorate, GRE General Test, GRE Subject Test (psychology), master's degree in psychology or closely-related discipline of at least 45 hours from regionally-accredited institution; minimum cumulative GPA of 3.5 in the master's program; criminal background check; 3 letters of recommendation; pertinent professional experience; personal statement. Additional exam requirements/recommendations for international students: required—TOEFL. Electronic applications accepted. Application fee is waived when completed online. *Expenses:* Contact institution.

Pace University, Dyson College of Arts and Sciences, Department of Psychology, Program in Mental Health Counseling, New York, NY 10038. Offers grief and loss (MS); mental health counseling (MS, PhD); substance abuse (MS). *Program availability:* Part-time, evening/weekend. Terminal master's awarded for partial completion of doctoral program. *Degree requirements:* For master's, comprehensive exam, qualifying exams, internship; for doctorate, comprehensive exam, thesis/dissertation, internships. *Entrance requirements:* For master's, GRE, resume, personal statement, two letters of reference, official transcripts, interview; for doctorate, three letters of recommendation (two of which are academic in nature); personal statement; official transcripts; internship(s); interview; master's degree in mental health counseling or program with curriculum equivalent to that of Pace's graduate program in mental health counseling. Additional exam requirements/recommendations for international students: required—TOEFL (minimum score 88 iBT), IELTS (minimum score 7) or PTE (minimum score 60). Electronic applications accepted.

Pacifica Graduate Institute, Graduate Programs, Carpinteria, CA 93013. Offers clinical psychology (PhD); counseling psychology (MA); depth psychology (MA, PhD); mythological studies (MA, PhD). Terminal master's awarded for partial completion of doctoral program. *Degree requirements:* For master's, thesis (for some programs), practicum; for doctorate, comprehensive exam, thesis/dissertation, internship. *Entrance requirements:* For master's, resume, 3 letters of recommendation, writing sample, interview; for doctorate, resumé, 4 letters of recommendation, writing sample, interview. Additional exam requirements/recommendations for international students: required—TOEFL.

Palm Beach Atlantic University, School of Education and Behavioral Studies, West Palm Beach, FL 33416-4708. Offers counseling psychology (MS), including addictions/mental health, general counseling, marriage and family therapy, mental health counseling, school guidance counseling. *Program availability:* Part-time, evening/weekend. *Entrance requirements:* For master's, GRE or MAT, minimum GPA of 3.0; essay. Additional exam requirements/recommendations for international students: required—TOEFL (minimum score 550 paper-based; 79 iBT). Electronic applications accepted. *Expenses: Tuition:* Part-time $570 per credit hour. *Required fees:* $580 per unit. Tuition and fees vary according to degree level, campus/location and program.

Palo Alto University, MA in Counseling Program, Palo Alto, CA 94304. Offers clinical mental health (MA); marriage, family and child (MA). *Program availability:* Part-time, 100% online, blended/hybrid learning. *Degree requirements:* For master's, capstone project. *Entrance requirements:* For master's, undergraduate degree in psychology with minimum GPA of 3.3. Additional exam requirements/recommendations for international students: required—TOEFL. Electronic applications accepted. *Expenses:* Contact institution.

Philadelphia College of Osteopathic Medicine, Graduate and Professional Programs, School of Professional and Applied Psychology, Philadelphia, PA 19131. Offers applied behavior analysis (Certificate); clinical health psychology (Post-Doctoral Certificate); clinical neuropsychology (Post-Doctoral Certificate); clinical psychology (Psy D); educational psychology (PhD); mental health counseling (MS); organizational development and leadership (MS); psychology (Certificate); public health management and administration (MS); school psychology (MS, Psy D, Ed S). *Accreditation:* APA. *Faculty:* 19 full-time (11 women), 122 part-time/adjunct (58 women). *Students:* 342 (285 women); includes 108 minority (65 Black or African American, non-Hispanic/Latino; 1 American Indian or Alaska Native, non-Hispanic/Latino; 10 Asian, non-Hispanic/Latino; 14 Hispanic/Latino; 18 Two or more races, non-Hispanic/Latino). Average age 25. 357 applicants, 51% accepted, 113 enrolled. In 2019, 79 master's, 38 doctorates, 16 other

advanced degrees awarded. Terminal master's awarded for partial completion of doctoral program. *Degree requirements:* For master's, comprehensive exam (for some programs), thesis (for some programs); for doctorate, comprehensive exam, thesis/dissertation. *Entrance requirements:* For master's, GRE or MAT, minimum GPA of 3.0; bachelor's degree from regionally-accredited college or university; for doctorate, PRAXIS II (for Psy D in school psychology), minimum undergraduate GPA of 3.0; for other advanced degree, GRE (for Ed S). Additional exam requirements/recommendations for international students: required—TOEFL (minimum score 79 iBT). *Application deadline:* Applications are processed on a rolling basis. Application fee: $50. Electronic applications accepted. *Financial support:* In 2019–20, 28 teaching assistantships were awarded; Federal Work-Study, institutionally sponsored loans, and scholarships/grants also available. Financial award application deadline: 3/15; financial award applicants required to submit FAFSA. *Unit head:* Dr. Robert DiTomasso, Chairman, 215-871-6442, Fax: 215-871-6458, E-mail: robertd@pcom.edu. *Application contact:* Johnathan Cox, Associate Director of Admissions, 215-871-6700, Fax: 215-871-6719, E-mail: johnathancox@pcom.edu.
Website: pcom.edu

Phoenix Seminary, Graduate Programs, Phoenix, AZ 85018. Offers Biblical and theological studies (Graduate Diploma); Biblical communication (M Div); Biblical leadership (MA); Christian counseling (Graduate Diploma); counseling and family (M Div); leadership development (M Div); ministry (D Min); professional counseling (MA). *Accreditation:* ATS (one or more programs are accredited). *Program availability:* Part-time, evening/weekend. *Degree requirements:* For master's, 2 foreign languages, comprehensive exam; for doctorate, 2 foreign languages, thesis/dissertation. *Entrance requirements:* For master's, undergraduate degree with minimum GPA of 2.5; for doctorate, M Div (94 hours) with minimum GPA of 3.0. Additional exam requirements/recommendations for international students: required—TOEFL (minimum score 587 paper-based; 92 iBT), TWE (minimum score 4.5).

Prescott College, Graduate Programs, Program in Counseling and Psychology, Prescott, AZ 86301. Offers adventure-based psychotherapy (MA); counseling psychology (MA); ecopsychology (MA); ecotherapy (MA); equine-assisted mental health (MA); expressive arts therapy (MA); somatic psychology (MA); student-directed independent study (MA). *Program availability:* Part-time, online learning. Terminal master's awarded for partial completion of doctoral program. *Degree requirements:* For master's, thesis, fieldwork or internship, practicum. *Entrance requirements:* For master's, 2 letters of recommendation, resume. Additional exam requirements/recommendations for international students: required—TOEFL (minimum score 500 paper-based). Electronic applications accepted.

Providence University College & Theological Seminary, Theological Seminary, Otterburne, MB R0A 1G0, Canada. Offers children's ministry (Certificate); Christian studies (MA, Certificate); counseling (MA); cross-cultural discipleship (Certificate); divinity (M Div); educational studies (MA), including counseling psychology, educational ministries, student development, teaching English to speakers of other languages, training teachers of English to speakers of other languages; global studies (MA); lay counseling (Diploma); ministry (D Min); teaching English to speakers of other languages (Certificate); theological studies (MA); training teacher of English to speakers of other languages (Certificate); youth ministry (Certificate). *Accreditation:* ATS. *Program availability:* Part-time. *Degree requirements:* For master's, variable foreign language requirement, thesis (for some programs); for doctorate, thesis/dissertation. *Entrance requirements:* Additional exam requirements/recommendations for international students: recommended—TOEFL (minimum score 550 paper-based).

Purdue University Northwest, Graduate Studies Office, School of Education, Program in Counseling, Hammond, IN 46323-2094. Offers human services (MS Ed); mental health counseling (MS Ed); school counseling (MS Ed). *Accreditation:* ACA. *Entrance requirements:* Additional exam requirements/recommendations for international students: required—TOEFL.

Queens College of the City University of New York, Division of Education, Department of Educational and Community Programs, Queens, NY 11367-1597. Offers bilingual pupil personnel (AC); counselor education (MS Ed); mental health counseling (MS); school building leader (AC); school district leader (AC); school psychologist (MS Ed); special education-childhood education (AC); special education-early childhood (MS Ed); teacher of special education 1-6 (MS Ed); teacher of special education birth-2 (MS Ed); teaching students with disabilities, grades 7-12 (MS Ed, AC). *Program availability:* Part-time. *Degree requirements:* For master's, research project; for AC, internship, research project. *Entrance requirements:* For master's, minimum GPA of 3.0. Additional exam requirements/recommendations for international students: required—TOEFL, IELTS. Electronic applications accepted.

Radford University, College of Graduate Studies and Research, Counseling Psychology, Psy.D., Radford, VA 24142. Offers Psy D. *Degree requirements:* For doctorate, comprehensive exam, thesis/dissertation. *Entrance requirements:* For doctorate, GRE General Test, master's degree; minimum graduate GPA of 3.5; letter of interest describing professional and/or research experience; curriculum vitae/resume; essay on cultural background and experiences; 3 letters of recommendation; official transcripts. Additional exam requirements/recommendations for international students: required—TOEFL (minimum score 550 paper-based; 79 iBT), IELTS (minimum score 6.5). Electronic applications accepted.

Regent University, Graduate School, School of Psychology and Counseling, Virginia Beach, VA 23464-9800. Offers clinical mental health counseling (MA); clinical psychology (Psy D); counseling and psychological studies - clinical (PhD); counseling and psychological studies - research (PhD); counseling studies (CAGS); counselor education and supervision (PhD); general psychology (MS); human services (MA), including addictions counseling, Biblical counseling, Christian counseling, conflict and mediation ministry, criminal justice and ministry, grief counseling, human services counseling, human services for student affairs, life coaching, marriage and family ministry, trauma and crisis counseling; marriage, couple, and family counseling (MA); pastoral counseling (MA); school counseling (MA); M Div/MA; M Ed/MA; MBA/MA. *Accreditation:* ACA; APA (one or more programs are accredited). *Program availability:* Part-time, evening/weekend, 100% online, blended/hybrid learning. *Degree requirements:* For master's, thesis or alternative, internship, practicum, written competency exam; for doctorate, thesis/dissertation or alternative. *Entrance requirements:* For master's, GRE General Test (including writing exam) or MAT, minimum undergraduate GPA of 3.0, resume, transcripts, writing sample, personal goals statement; for doctorate, GRE General Test (including writing exam), minimum undergraduate GPA of 3.0, graduate 3.5; writing sample; 3 recommendations; resume; college transcripts; personal goals statement. Additional exam requirements/recommendations for international students: required—TOEFL (minimum score 577 paper-based). Electronic applications accepted. *Expenses:* Contact institution.

Regis College, Nursing and Health Sciences School, Weston, MA 02493. Offers applied behavior analysis (MS); counseling psychology (MA); health administration (MS); nurse practitioner (Certificate); nursing (MS, DNP); nursing education (Certificate); occupational therapy (MS). *Accreditation:* ACEN. *Program availability:* Part-time, evening/weekend, 100% online, blended/hybrid learning. *Degree requirements:* For

doctorate, thesis/dissertation. *Entrance requirements:* For master's, minimum GPA of 3.0, official transcripts, recommendations, personal statement, resume/curriculum vitae, interview; for doctorate, GRE if GPA from master's lower than 3.5. Additional exam requirements/recommendations for international students: required—TOEFL (minimum score 560 paper-based; 79 iBT); recommended—IELTS (minimum score 6.5). *Application deadline:* Applications are processed on a rolling basis. Application fee: $75. Electronic applications accepted. *Financial support:* Federal Work-Study, scholarships/grants, and unspecified assistantships available. Support available to part-time students. Financial award applicants required to submit FAFSA. *Application contact:* Thomas May, Graduate Admission Counselor, 781-768-7162, E-mail: thomas.may@regiscollege.edu.

Rhode Island College, School of Graduate Studies, Feinstein School of Education and Human Development, Department of Counseling, Educational Leadership, and School Psychology, Providence, RI 02908-1991. Offers advanced counseling (CGS); agency counseling (MA); clinical mental health counseling (MS); co-occurring disorders (MA, CGS); educational leadership (M Ed); mental health counseling (CAGS); school counseling (MA); school psychology (CAGS); teacher leadership (CGS). *Accreditation:* ACA; NCATE. *Program availability:* Part-time, evening/weekend. *Faculty:* 10 full-time (7 women), 5 part-time/adjunct (4 women). *Students:* 51 full-time (37 women), 73 part-time (57 women); includes 21 minority (8 Black or African American, non-Hispanic/Latino; 11 Hispanic/Latino; 2 Two or more races, non-Hispanic/Latino). Average age 33. In 2019, 13 master's, 27 other advanced degrees awarded. *Degree requirements:* For master's and other advanced degree, comprehensive exam (for some programs), thesis (for some programs). *Entrance requirements:* For master's, GRE General Test or MAT, undergraduate transcripts; minimum undergraduate GPA of 3.0; for other advanced degree, GRE or MAT (for most programs), undergraduate transcripts; minimum undergraduate GPA of 3.0; 3 letters of recommendation; current resume. Additional exam requirements/recommendations for international students: required—TOEFL (minimum score 550 paper-based; 80 iBT). *Application deadline:* For fall admission, 3/1 for domestic students; for spring admission, 11/1 for domestic students. Applications are processed on a rolling basis. Application fee: $50. Electronic applications accepted. *Expenses:* Tuition, area resident: Part-time $462 per credit hour. Tuition, state resident: part-time $462 per credit hour. Required fees: $720. One-time fee: $140. *Financial support:* Teaching assistantships, career-related internships or fieldwork, Federal Work-Study, scholarships/grants, health care benefits, and unspecified assistantships available. Support available to part-time students. Financial award application deadline: 5/15; financial award applicants required to submit FAFSA. *Unit head:* Charles Boisvert, Chair, 401-456-8023. *Application contact:* Charles Boisvert, Chair, 401-456-8023. Website: http://www.ric.edu/counselingEducationalLeadershipSchoolPsychology/index.php

Rivier University, School of Graduate Studies, Department of Education, Nashua, NH 03060. Offers curriculum and instruction (M Ed); early childhood education (M Ed); educational administration (M Ed); educational studies (M Ed); elementary education (M Ed); elementary education and general special education (M Ed); emotional and behavioral disorders (M Ed); general social education (M Ed); leadership and learning (Ed D, CAGS); learning disabilities (M Ed); learning disabilities and reading (M Ed); mental health counseling (MA); reading (M Ed); school counseling (M Ed). *Program availability:* Part-time, evening/weekend. *Degree requirements:* For master's, comprehensive exam (for some programs), internships. *Entrance requirements:* For master's, GRE General Test or MAT.

Rosemont College, Schools of Graduate and Professional Studies, Counseling Psychology Program, Rosemont, PA 19010-1699. Offers human services (MA); school counseling (MA). *Program availability:* Part-time, evening/weekend. *Degree requirements:* For master's, thesis or alternative, practicum. *Entrance requirements:* For master's, minimum undergraduate GPA of 3.0, 3 letters of recommendation. Additional exam requirements/recommendations for international students: required—TOEFL. Electronic applications accepted. Application fee is waived when completed online. *Expenses:* Contact institution.

Rutgers University - New Brunswick, Graduate School of Education, Department of Educational Psychology, Programs in School Counseling and Counseling Psychology, Piscataway, NJ 08854-8097. Offers Ed M. *Accreditation:* ACA. *Program availability:* Part-time, evening/weekend. *Entrance requirements:* For master's, GRE General Test, 3 letters of recommendation. Additional exam requirements/recommendations for international students: required—TOEFL (minimum score 550 paper-based; 83 iBT). Electronic applications accepted.

Sage Graduate School, School of Health Sciences, Department of Psychology, Program in Counseling and Community Psychology, Troy, NY 12180-4115. Offers MA. *Program availability:* Part-time, evening/weekend. *Faculty:* 4 full-time (all women), 2 part-time/adjunct (both women). *Students:* 39 full-time (36 women), 35 part-time (27 women); includes 16 minority (3 Black or African American, non-Hispanic/Latino; 2 Asian, non-Hispanic/Latino; 9 Hispanic/Latino; 2 Two or more races, non-Hispanic/Latino). Average age 27. 77 applicants, 65% accepted, 30 enrolled. In 2019, 11 master's awarded. *Degree requirements:* For master's, externship, internship, thesis or research seminar. *Entrance requirements:* For master's, Completed application; minimum GPA of 3.0 or higher; official transcripts of all previous undergraduate study; 2 letters of reference (academic or professional); undergraduate courses in statistics, history and systems of psychology; 3 other courses in behavioral science; personal prospectus statement; current resume. Additional exam requirements/recommendations for international students: required—TOEFL (minimum score 550 paper-based). *Application deadline:* Applications are processed on a rolling basis. Application fee: $30. Electronic applications accepted. *Expenses:* Tuition: Part-time $730 per credit hour. Tuition and fees vary according to course load, degree level and program. *Financial support:* Fellowships, research assistantships, scholarships/grants, and unspecified assistantships available. Financial award applicants required to submit FAFSA. *Unit head:* Dr. Kathleen Kelly, Dean, School of Health Sciences, 518-244-2030, Fax: 518-244-4571, E-mail: kellyk5@sage.edu. *Application contact:* Dr. Gayle Morse, Graduate Program Director, 518-292-1819, E-mail: morseg@sage.edu.
Website: http://www.sage.edu/academics/psychology/programs/counseling/

St. Bonaventure University, School of Graduate Studies, School of Education, Program in Counselor Education, St. Bonaventure, NY 14778-2284. Offers community mental health counseling (MS Ed); rehabilitation counseling (MS Ed); school counseling (MS Ed); school counselor (Adv C). *Accreditation:* ACA. *Program availability:* Part-time, 100% online. *Faculty:* 7 full-time (4 women), 10 part-time/adjunct (7 women). *Students:* 43 full-time (37 women), 213 part-time (175 women); includes 39 minority (2 Black or African American, non-Hispanic/Latino; 2 American Indian or Alaska Native, non-Hispanic/Latino; 7 Asian, non-Hispanic/Latino; 18 Hispanic/Latino; 1 Native Hawaiian or other Pacific Islander, non-Hispanic/Latino; 9 Two or more races, non-Hispanic/Latino). Average age 32. 167 applicants, 85% accepted, 64 enrolled. In 2019, 17 master's, 7 Adv Cs awarded. *Degree requirements:* For master's, comprehensive exam, thesis optional, internship, portfolio, two consecutive summer residencies; for Adv C, internship. *Entrance requirements:* For master's, statement of intent/writing sample; transcripts from all colleges previously attended; two references; interview; minimum undergraduate GPA of 3.0; for Adv C, interview, writing sample, minimum

undergraduate GPA of 3.0, two letters of recommendation, master's degree, transcripts from all colleges previously attended. Additional exam requirements/recommendations for international students: required—TOEFL (minimum score 550 paper-based; 79 iBT). *Application deadline:* For fall admission, 3/15 priority date for domestic students, 2/1 priority date for international students; for spring admission, 10/15 priority date for domestic students, 7/1 priority date for international students. Applications are processed on a rolling basis. Electronic applications accepted. *Expenses: Tuition:* Full-time $770; part-time $770 per credit hour. *Required fees:* $35; $35 per credit hour. Tuition and fees vary according to course load. *Financial support:* Scholarships/grants, health care benefits, and unspecified assistantships available. Financial award application deadline: 4/15; financial award applicants required to submit FAFSA. *Unit head:* Dr. LaToya Pierce, Director, 716-375-2038, Fax: 716-375-2360, E-mail: lpierce@sbu.edu. *Application contact:* Matthew Retchless, Director of Graduate Admissions, 716-375-2021, Fax: 716-375-4015, E-mail: gradsch@sbu.edu.
Website: http://www.sbu.edu/academics/msed-in-school-counseling

St. Edward's University, School of Education, Master of Arts in Counseling Program, Austin, TX 78704. Offers MA. *Program availability:* Part-time, evening/weekend. *Entrance requirements:* Additional exam requirements/recommendations for international students: required—TOEFL, IELTS. Electronic applications accepted.

St. John Fisher College, Wegmans School of Nursing, Program in Mental Health Counseling, Rochester, NY 14618-3597. Offers MS. *Accreditation:* ACA. *Program availability:* Part-time. *Faculty:* 5 full-time (4 women), 1 part-time/adjunct (0 women). *Students:* 50 full-time (46 women), 23 part-time (18 women); includes 18 minority (10 Black or African American, non-Hispanic/Latino; 2 Asian, non-Hispanic/Latino; 6 Hispanic/Latino). Average age 28. 76 applicants, 72% accepted, 36 enrolled. In 2019, 32 master's awarded. *Degree requirements:* For master's, practicum experience, internship. *Entrance requirements:* For master's, GRE (if GPA below 3.0), 2 letters of recommendation, personal statement, current resume, interview. Additional exam requirements/recommendations for international students: required—TOEFL (minimum score 575 paper-based; 80 iBT). *Application deadline:* Applications are processed on a rolling basis. Application fee: $30. Electronic applications accepted. *Expenses:* Contact institution. *Financial support:* Scholarships/grants available. Financial award applicants required to submit FAFSA. *Unit head:* Dr. Rachel Jordan, Director, 585-899-3858, E-mail: rjordan@sjfc.edu. *Application contact:* Michelle Gosier, Director of Transfer and Graduate Admissions, 585-385-8064, E-mail: mgosier@sjfc.edu.
Website: https://www.sjfc.edu/graduate-programs/ms-in-mental-health-counseling/

St. John's University, The School of Education, Department of Counselor Education, Program in Clinical Mental Health Counseling, Queens, NY 11439. Offers MS Ed, Adv C. *Entrance requirements:* For master's, 2 letters of recommendation, interview; for Adv C, official master's transcripts, statement of purpose. Electronic applications accepted.

Saint Martin's University, Office of Graduate Studies, Program in Counseling, Lacey, WA 98503. Offers MAC. *Program availability:* Part-time. *Students:* 73 full-time (54 women), 21 part-time (17 women); includes 26 minority (10 Black or African American, non-Hispanic/Latino; 3 American Indian or Alaska Native, non-Hispanic/Latino; 2 Asian, non-Hispanic/Latino; 7 Hispanic/Latino; 4 Two or more races, non-Hispanic/Latino), 3 international. Average age 36. In 2019, 33 master's awarded. *Degree requirements:* For master's, clinical experience, interview. *Entrance requirements:* For master's, clinical experience. Additional exam requirements/recommendations for international students: required—TOEFL (minimum score 550 paper-based; 79 iBT); recommended—IELTS (minimum score 6.5). *Application deadline:* For fall admission, 4/1 priority date for domestic and international students; for spring admission, 11/1 priority date for domestic and international students. Applications are processed on a rolling basis. Application fee: $50. Electronic applications accepted. *Expenses: Tuition:* Full-time $22,950; part-time $15,300 per year. Tuition and fees vary according to course level, course load, degree level, campus/location and program. *Financial support:* Career-related internships or fieldwork, Federal Work-Study, and institutionally sponsored loans available. Support available to part-time students. Financial award application deadline: 3/1; financial award applicants required to submit FAFSA. *Unit head:* Dr. Alexandra Onno, Chair, 360-438-4560, E-mail: aonno@stmartin.edu. *Application contact:* Timothy Greer, Graduate Admissions Counselor, 360-412-6128, E-mail: tgreer@stmartin.edu.
Website: https://www.stmartin.edu

St. Mary's University, Graduate Studies, Program in Clinical Mental Health Counseling, San Antonio, TX 78228. Offers MA. *Program availability:* Part-time, evening/weekend. *Degree requirements:* For master's, comprehensive exam, 700-hour clinical experience (practicum/internship). *Entrance requirements:* For master's, GRE General Test or MAT, bachelor's degree from accredited college or university; recommendations from past employers and/or from faculty members of previous undergraduate studies; personal statement indicating interest in becoming professional counselor or doing work that requires counseling skills. Additional exam requirements/recommendations for international students: required—TOEFL (minimum score 550 paper-based; 80 iBT), IELTS (minimum score 6). Electronic applications accepted.

Saint Mary's University of Minnesota, Schools of Graduate and Professional Programs, Graduate School of Health and Human Services, Counseling and Psychological Services Program, Winona, MN 55987-1399. Offers MA, Certificate. *Unit head:* Dr. Mary Louise Wise, Associate Program Director, 612-728-5104, Fax: 612-728-5121, E-mail: mlwise@smumn.edu. *Application contact:* Laurie Roy, Director of Admission of Schools of Graduate and Professional Programs, 507-457-8606, Fax: 612-728-5121, E-mail: lroy@smumn.edu.
Website: http://www.smumn.edu/graduate-home/areas-of-study/graduate-school-of-health-human-services/ma-in-counseling-psychological-services

Saint Mary's University of Minnesota, Schools of Graduate and Professional Programs, Graduate School of Health and Human Services, Counseling Psychology Program, Winona, MN 55987-1399. Offers Psy D. *Unit head:* Dr. Ashley Sovereign, Director, 612-238-4557, E-mail: asoverei@smumn.edu. *Application contact:* Laurie Roy, Director of Admission of Schools of Graduate and Professional Programs, 507-457-8606, Fax: 612-728-5121, E-mail: lroy@smumn.edu.
Website: http://www.smumn.edu/graduate-home/areas-of-study/graduate-school-of-health-human-services/doctor-of-psychology-in-counseling-psychology

Saint Paul University, Faculty of Human Sciences, Program in Counseling and Spirituality, Ottawa, ON K1S 1C4, Canada. Offers individual or marital/couple counseling (MA); spiritual care (MA). *Program availability:* Part-time. *Degree requirements:* For master's, research project or thesis. *Entrance requirements:* For master's, honors BA in human sciences, minimum B average, 12 theology credits.

St. Thomas University - Florida, Biscayne College, Department of Social Sciences and Counseling, Program in Mental Health Counseling, Miami Gardens, FL 33054-6459. Offers MS. *Program availability:* Part-time, evening/weekend. *Degree requirements:* For master's, comprehensive exam. *Entrance requirements:* For master's, interview, minimum GPA of 3.0 or GRE. Additional exam requirements/recommendations for international students: required—TOEFL (minimum score 550 paper-based; 79 iBT). Electronic applications accepted.

Salem State University, School of Graduate Studies, Program in Counseling and Psychological Services, Salem, MA 01970-5353. Offers MS, Graduate Certificate. *Program availability:* Part-time, evening/weekend. *Entrance requirements:* For master's, GRE or MAT. Additional exam requirements/recommendations for international students: required—TOEFL (minimum score 550 paper-based; 80 iBT) or IELTS (minimum score 5.5).

Salem State University, School of Graduate Studies, Program of Advanced Professional Studies in Counseling, Salem, MA 01970-5353. Offers Graduate Certificate. *Program availability:* Part-time, evening/weekend. *Entrance requirements:* Additional exam requirements/recommendations for international students: required—TOEFL (minimum score 550 paper-based; 80 iBT) or IELTS (minimum score 5.5).

Salve Regina University, Program in Rehabilitation Counseling, Newport, RI 02840-4192. Offers clinical rehabilitation and mental health counseling (MA); mental health (CAGS), including rehabilitation counseling; rehabilitation (CAGS), including substance abuse counseling; rehabilitation counseling (MA); substance abuse and treatment (CAGS). *Accreditation:* CORE. *Program availability:* Part-time, evening/weekend. *Entrance requirements:* For master's, GMAT, GRE General Test or MAT. Additional exam requirements/recommendations for international students: required—TOEFL (minimum score 600 paper-based; 100 iBT) or IELTS. Electronic applications accepted.

Santa Clara University, School of Education and Counseling Psychology, Santa Clara, CA 95053. Offers alternative and correctional education (Certificate); counseling (MA); counseling psychology (MA); educational leadership (MA); interdisciplinary education (MA); teaching + clear teaching certificate for catholic school teachers (MAT); teaching + teaching credential (mattc) - multiple subjects (MAT); teaching + teaching credential (mattc) - single subjects (MAT). *Program availability:* Part-time, online learning. *Entrance requirements:* For master's, statement of purpose, resume or cv, official transcript; other requirements vary by degree. Additional exam requirements/recommendations for international students: required—TOEFL (minimum score 90 iBT), IELTS (minimum score 6.5), A TOEFL score of 90 or above or IELTS score of 6.5 or above is required for international students. Electronic applications accepted.

Saybrook University, LIOS MA Residential Programs, Kirkland, WA 98033. Offers leadership and organization development (MA); psychology counseling (MA). *Degree requirements:* For master's, thesis (for some programs), oral exams. *Entrance requirements:* For master's, bachelor's degree from an accredited university or college. Additional exam requirements/recommendations for international students: recommended—TOEFL, IELTS, TWE.

The Seattle School of Theology and Psychology, Graduate Programs, Seattle, WA 98121. Offers Christian studies (MA); counseling psychology (MA); divinity (M Div). *Program availability:* Part-time. *Entrance requirements:* For master's, MAT.

Seton Hall University, College of Education and Human Services, Department of Professional Psychology and Family Therapy, Program in Counseling Psychology, South Orange, NJ 07079-2697. Offers counseling psychology (PhD); school counseling (MA). *Accreditation:* APA. *Faculty:* 10 full-time (7 women). *Students:* 15 full-time (12 women), 107 part-time (73 women); includes 51 minority (23 Black or African American, non-Hispanic/Latino; 6 Asian, non-Hispanic/Latino; 19 Hispanic/Latino; 3 Two or more races, non-Hispanic/Latino). Average age 32. 133 applicants, 39% accepted, 28 enrolled. In 2019, 30 master's, 5 doctorates awarded. *Degree requirements:* For master's, comprehensive exam (for some programs); for doctorate, comprehensive exam, thesis/dissertation, internship. *Entrance requirements:* For master's and doctorate, GRE, interview. Additional exam requirements/recommendations for international students: required—TOEFL. *Application deadline:* For fall admission, 1/15 for domestic students. Application fee: $50. *Financial support:* In 2019–20, 1 research assistantship with full tuition reimbursement (averaging $4,500 per year) was awarded; career-related internships or fieldwork also available. Financial award application deadline: 2/1. *Unit head:* Dr. Thomas Massarelli, Chair, 973-761-9668, E-mail: beitinbe@shu.edu. *Application contact:* Diana Minakakis, Director of Graduate Admissions, 973-275-2824, Fax: 973-275-2181, E-mail: diana.minakakis@shu.edu.
Website: http://www.shu.edu/academics/education/professional-psychology/

Siena Heights University, Graduate College, Adrian, MI 49221-1796. Offers clinical mental health counseling (MA); educational leadership (Specialist); leadership (MA), including health care leadership, organizational leadership; teacher education (MA), including early childhood education, early childhood education: Montessori, education leadership: principal, elementary education: reading K-12, leadership: higher education, secondary education: reading K-12, special education: cognitive impairment, special education: learning disabilities. *Program availability:* Part-time, evening/weekend. *Degree requirements:* For master's, thesis, Presentation. *Entrance requirements:* For master's, Minimum GPA of 3.0, current resume, essay, all post-secondary transcripts, 3 letters of reference, conviction disclosure form; copy of teaching certificate (for some education programs); for Specialist, Master's degree, minimum GPA of 3.0, current resume, essay, all post-secondary transcripts, 3 letters of reference, conviction disclosure form; copy of teaching certificate (for some education programs). Additional exam requirements/recommendations for international students: recommended—TOEFL, IELTS, TWE, TSE. Electronic applications accepted.

Simpson University, School of Graduate Studies, Redding, CA 96003-8606. Offers counseling psychology (MA); organizational leadership (MA). *Program availability:* Evening/weekend, 100% online, blended/hybrid learning. *Degree requirements:* For master's, thesis optional, portfolio capstone, integrative essay. *Entrance requirements:* For master's, three letters of recommendation, personal statement, resume, transcripts, personal interview, bachelor's degree in psychology or related field with minimum GPA of 3.0 in final 60 credits (for counseling psychology); two references (for organizational leadership). Additional exam requirements/recommendations for international students: required—TOEFL (minimum score 550 paper-based; 79 iBT). Electronic applications accepted. *Expenses:* Contact institution.

Slippery Rock University of Pennsylvania, Graduate Studies (Recruitment), College of Education, Department of Counseling and Development, Slippery Rock, PA 16057-1383. Offers M Ed, MA. *Accreditation:* ACA (one or more programs are accredited); NCATE. *Program availability:* Part-time, evening/weekend. *Faculty:* 10 full-time (4 women), 2 part-time/adjunct (both women). *Students:* 73 full-time (59 women), 26 part-time (25 women); includes 13 minority (7 Black or African American, non-Hispanic/Latino; 6 Hispanic/Latino), 1 international. Average age 25. 100 applicants, 42% accepted, 28 enrolled. In 2019, 36 master's awarded. *Degree requirements:* For master's, comprehensive exam, thesis (for some programs). *Entrance requirements:* For master's, GRE General Test or MAT, official transcripts, personal statement, three letters of recommendation, interview. Additional exam requirements/recommendations for international students: required—TOEFL (minimum score 550 paper-based; 80 iBT). *Application deadline:* For fall admission, 1/15 priority date for domestic and international students. Applications are processed on a rolling basis. Application fee: $25 ($30 for international students). Electronic applications accepted. *Expenses:* $516 per credit in-state tuition, $173.61 per credit in-state fees; $774 per credit out-of-state tuition, $224.31 per credit out-of-state fees; $516 per credit in-state tuition, $105.40 per credit in-state fees (for distance education); $526 per credit out-of-state tuition, $118.90 per credit out-of-state fees (for distance education). *Financial support:* In 2019–20, 50 students

received support. Career-related internships or fieldwork, Federal Work-Study, institutionally sponsored loans, scholarships/grants, tuition waivers (partial), and unspecified assistantships available. Support available to part-time students. Financial award application deadline: 5/1; financial award applicants required to submit FAFSA. *Unit head:* Dr. Jane Hale, Graduate Coordinator, 724-738-2035, Fax: 724-738-4859, E-mail: stacy.jacob@sru.edu. *Application contact:* Brandi Weber-Mortimer, Director of Graduate Admissions, 724-738-2051, Fax: 724-738-2146, E-mail: graduate.admissions@sru.edu.
Website: http://www.sru.edu/academics/colleges-and-departments/coe/departments/counseling-and-development

Sofia University, Residential Programs, Palo Alto, CA 94303. Offers clinical psychology (Psy D); computer science (MS); counseling psychology (MA); transpersonal psychology (MA, PhD). *Program availability:* Part-time, evening/weekend. Terminal master's awarded for partial completion of doctoral program. *Degree requirements:* For doctorate, thesis/dissertation. *Entrance requirements:* For master's, bachelor's degree; for doctorate, bachelor's degree; master's degree (for some programs). Electronic applications accepted.

Sonoma State University, School of Social Sciences, Department of Counseling, Rohnert Park, CA 94928-3609. Offers clinical mental health counseling (MA); school counseling (MA). *Accreditation:* ACA. *Program availability:* Part-time. *Entrance requirements:* For master's, minimum GPA of 3.0. Additional exam requirements/recommendations for international students: required—TOEFL (minimum score 500 paper-based).

Southeastern Oklahoma State University, School of Behavioral Sciences, Durant, OK 74701-0609. Offers clinical mental health counseling (MS). *Accreditation:* ACA. *Program availability:* Part-time, evening/weekend. *Degree requirements:* For master's, comprehensive exam, thesis optional. *Entrance requirements:* For master's, GRE General Test, minimum GPA of 3.0 in last 60 hours or 2.75 overall. Additional exam requirements/recommendations for international students: required—TOEFL (minimum score 550 paper-based; 79 iBT). Electronic applications accepted.

Southeastern University, College of Behavioral & Social Sciences, Lakeland, FL 33801. Offers human services (MA); international community development (MA); pastoral care and counseling (MS); professional counseling (MS); school counseling (MS); social work (MSW). *Program availability:* Evening/weekend. *Faculty:* 17 full-time (12 women). *Students:* 95 full-time (80 women), 9 part-time (6 women); includes 49 minority (18 Black or African American, non-Hispanic/Latino; 3 Asian, non-Hispanic/Latino; 25 Hispanic/Latino; 1 Native Hawaiian or other Pacific Islander, non-Hispanic/Latino; 2 Two or more races, non-Hispanic/Latino), 1 international. Average age 28. In 2019, 50 master's awarded. *Entrance requirements:* Additional exam requirements/recommendations for international students: required—TOEFL (minimum score 76 iBT), IELTS (minimum score 6). Application fee: $50. Electronic applications accepted. *Unit head:* Dr. Erica H. Sirrine, Dean, 863-667-5341, E-mail: ehsirrine@seu.edu. *Application contact:* Dr. Erica H. Sirrine, Dean, 863-667-5341, E-mail: ehsirrine@seu.edu. Website: http://www.seu.edu/behavior/

Southeast Missouri State University, School of Graduate Studies, Leadership, Middle and Secondary Education, Cape Girardeau, MO 63701-4799. Offers counseling (MA, Ed S), including career counseling (MA), counseling education (Ed S), mental health counseling (MA), school counseling (MA); educational administration (MA, Ed D, Ed S), including educational administration (Ed S), educational leadership (Ed D); elementary administration (MA), higher education administration (MA), secondary administration (MA), teacher leadership (MA, Ed S). *Accreditation:* NCATE. *Program availability:* Part-time, evening/weekend, online only, 100% online, blended/hybrid learning. *Degree requirements:* For master's and Ed S, comprehensive exam, thesis or alternative, paper; for doctorate, comprehensive exam, thesis/dissertation. *Entrance requirements:* For master's, minimum GPA of 3.5; for doctorate, minimum GPA of 3.7. Additional exam requirements/recommendations for international students: required—TOEFL (minimum score 550 paper-based; 79 iBT), IELTS (minimum score 6), PTE (minimum score 53). Electronic applications accepted. *Expenses:* Contact institution.

Southern Adventist University, School of Education and Psychology, Collegedale, TN 37315-0370. Offers clinical mental health counseling (MS); instructional leadership (MS Ed); literacy education (MS Ed); outdoor education (MS Ed); professional school counseling (MS). *Accreditation:* NCATE. *Program availability:* Part-time, evening/weekend, 100% online, blended/hybrid learning. *Degree requirements:* For master's, comprehensive exam (for some programs), thesis optional, portfolio (MS) portfolio (MS Ed in outdoor education). *Entrance requirements:* For master's, interview (MS); 9 semester hours of upper-division course work in psychology or related field, including 1 course in psychology research or statistics; 9 semester hours of education (MS Ed). Additional exam requirements/recommendations for international students: required—TOEFL (minimum score 100 iBT). Electronic applications accepted.

Southern California Seminary, Graduate and Professional Programs, El Cajon, CA 92019. Offers Biblical studies (MABS); counseling psychology (MACP); marriage and family therapy (MAMFT); psychology (Psy D); religious studies (MRS); theology (M Div). *Program availability:* Part-time, evening/weekend, online learning. *Degree requirements:* For master's, thesis (for some programs); for doctorate, thesis/dissertation. *Entrance requirements:* For doctorate, master's degree in psychology. Additional exam requirements/recommendations for international students: required—TOEFL (minimum score 550 paper-based). Electronic applications accepted.

Southern Illinois University Carbondale, Graduate School, College of Liberal Arts, Department of Psychology, Carbondale, IL 62901-4701. Offers clinical psychology (PhD); counseling psychology (PhD); experimental psychology (MA, MS). *Accreditation:* APA (one or more programs are accredited). *Degree requirements:* For master's, thesis; for doctorate, thesis/dissertation. *Entrance requirements:* For master's, GRE General Test, GRE Subject Test, minimum GPA of 2.7; for doctorate, GRE General Test, GRE Subject Test, minimum GPA of 3.25. Additional exam requirements/recommendations for international students: required—TOEFL.

Southern Nazarene University, College of Professional and Graduate Studies, Department of Psychology and Counseling, Bethany, OK 73008. Offers counseling psychology (MA, MSCP); marital and family therapy (MA). *Degree requirements:* For master's, thesis optional. *Entrance requirements:* For master's, English proficiency exam, minimum GPA of 3.0 in last 60 hours/major, 2.7 overall.

Southern Oregon University, Graduate Studies, Department of Psychology, Ashland, OR 97520. Offers MHC. *Accreditation:* ACA. *Program availability:* Part-time, online learning. *Degree requirements:* For master's, thesis, portfolio, oral defense. *Entrance requirements:* For master's, GRE General Test, minimum cumulative GPA of 3.0 in the last 90 quarter credits (60 semester credits) of undergraduate coursework. Additional exam requirements/recommendations for international students: required—TOEFL (minimum score 540 paper-based; 76 iBT), IELTS (minimum score 6), ELPT (minimum score 964) or ELS (minimum score 112). Electronic applications accepted.

South University - Austin, Program in Clinical Mental Health Counseling, Round Rock, TX 78681. Offers MA.

South University - Columbia, Program in Clinical Mental Health Counseling, Columbia, SC 29203. Offers MA.

South University - Montgomery, Program in Clinical Mental Health Counseling, Montgomery, AL 36116-1120. Offers MA.

South University - Richmond, Program in Clinical Mental Health Counseling, Glen Allen, VA 23060. Offers MA. *Accreditation:* ACA.

South University - Savannah, Graduate Programs, College of Arts and Sciences, Program in Clinical Mental Health Counseling, Savannah, GA 31406. Offers MA. *Accreditation:* ACA.

South University - Virginia Beach, Program in Clinical Mental Health Counseling, Virginia Beach, VA 23452. Offers MA. *Accreditation:* ACA.

South University - West Palm Beach, Program in Clinical Mental Health Counseling, Royal Palm Beach, FL 33411. Offers MA.

Southwestern Assemblies of God University, Thomas F. Harrison School of Graduate Studies, Program in Counseling Psychology, Waxahachie, TX 75165-5735. Offers counseling psychology (clinical) (MCP); human services counseling (MS). *Program availability:* Part-time. *Degree requirements:* For master's, comprehensive written and oral exams. *Entrance requirements:* For master's, GRE General Test, minimum GPA of 2.5. Electronic applications accepted.

Southwestern College, Program in Art Therapy/Counseling, Santa Fe, NM 87502-4788. Offers MA. *Program availability:* Part-time, evening/weekend. *Degree requirements:* For master's, internship. *Entrance requirements:* For master's, resume, slide portfolio, interview, 3 letters of reference. Additional exam requirements/recommendations for international students: required—TOEFL.

Southwestern College, Program in Counseling, Santa Fe, NM 87502-4788. Offers MA. *Program availability:* Part-time, evening/weekend. *Degree requirements:* For master's, internship. *Entrance requirements:* For master's, resume, 3 letters of reference, interview. Additional exam requirements/recommendations for international students: required—TOEFL.

Southwestern College, Program in Grief, Loss and Trauma Counseling, Santa Fe, NM 87502-4788. Offers MA, Certificate. *Program availability:* Part-time, evening/weekend, online learning. *Entrance requirements:* For master's, interview, references, resume; for Certificate, 3 letters of reference, interview.

Spring Arbor University, School of Human Services, Spring Arbor, MI 49283-9799. Offers counseling (MAC); family studies (MAFS); nursing (MSN); social work (MSW). *Program availability:* Part-time, evening/weekend, online learning. *Entrance requirements:* For master's, bachelor's degree from regionally-accredited college or university, minimum GPA of 3.0 for at least the last two years of the bachelor's degree, at least two recommendations from professional/academic individuals. Additional exam requirements/recommendations for international students: required—TOEFL (minimum score 600 paper-based). Electronic applications accepted.

Springfield College, Graduate Programs, Programs in Psychology, Springfield, MA 01109-3797. Offers athletic counseling (MS, CAGS); clinical mental health counseling (M Ed, CAGS); counseling psychology (Psy D); general counseling (M Ed); industrial/organizational psychology (M Ed, CAGS); school counseling (M Ed, CAGS); student personnel administration in higher education (M Ed, CAGS). *Accreditation:* APA. *Program availability:* Part-time. *Degree requirements:* For master's, research project, portfolio; for doctorate, dissertation project, 1500 hours of counseling psychology practicum, full-year internship. *Entrance requirements:* For doctorate, GRE. Additional exam requirements/recommendations for international students: required—TOEFL (minimum score 550 paper-based); recommended—IELTS (minimum score 7). Electronic applications accepted.

State University of New York at New Paltz, Graduate and Extended Learning School, School of Liberal Arts and Sciences, Department of Psychology, New Paltz, NY 12561. Offers clinical mental health counseling (MS); mental health counseling (AC); psychological science (MS); school counseling (MS); trauma and disaster mental health (AC). *Program availability:* Part-time, evening/weekend. *Faculty:* 14 full-time (5 women), 1 part-time/adjunct (0 women). *Students:* 57 full-time (43 women), 34 part-time (27 women); includes 25 minority (3 Black or African American, non-Hispanic/Latino; 3 Asian, non-Hispanic/Latino; 16 Hispanic/Latino; 1 Native Hawaiian or other Pacific Islander, non-Hispanic/Latino; 2 Two or more races, non-Hispanic/Latino). 147 applicants, 39% accepted, 45 enrolled. In 2019, 32 master's, 5 other advanced degrees awarded. *Degree requirements:* For master's, comprehensive exam, thesis. *Entrance requirements:* For master's, GRE General Test, minimum GPA of 3.0. Additional exam requirements/recommendations for international students: required—TOEFL (minimum score 550 paper-based; 80 iBT), IELTS (minimum score 6.5). *Application deadline:* For fall admission, 2/1 priority date for domestic and international students; for spring admission, 11/15 priority date for domestic and international students. Application fee: $50. Electronic applications accepted. *Expenses: Tuition, area resident:* Full-time $11,310; part-time $471 per credit. Tuition, state resident: full-time $11,310; part-time $471 per credit. Tuition, nonresident: full-time $23,100; part-time $963 per credit. *International tuition:* $23,100 full-time. *Required fees:* $1432; $41.83 per credit. *Financial support:* In 2019–20, 6 teaching assistantships with partial tuition reimbursements (averaging $5,000 per year) were awarded. Financial award application deadline: 8/1. *Unit head:* Dr. Jonathan Raskin, Chair, 845-257-3471, E-mail: raskinj@newpaltz.edu. *Application contact:* Vika Shock, Director of Graduate Admissions, 845-257-3286, E-mail: gradstudies@newpaltz.edu. Website: http://www.newpaltz.edu/psychology/

State University of New York at Oswego, Graduate Studies, School of Education, Department of Counseling and Psychological Services, Oswego, NY 13126. Offers mental health counseling (MS); MS/CAS. *Students:* 230. In 2019, 77 master's awarded. *Degree requirements:* For master's, comprehensive exam, thesis optional. *Entrance requirements:* For master's, GRE General Test, interview, minimum GPA of 3.0. Additional exam requirements/recommendations for international students: required—TOEFL (minimum score 560 paper-based). *Application deadline:* For fall admission, 2/1 for domestic and international students. Applications are processed on a rolling basis. Application fee: $65. Electronic applications accepted. *Financial support:* Fellowships with full tuition reimbursements, teaching assistantships with partial tuition reimbursements, career-related internships or fieldwork, Federal Work-Study, institutionally sponsored loans, scholarships/grants, health care benefits, and unspecified assistantships available. Support available to part-time students. Financial award application deadline: 4/1; financial award applicants required to submit FAFSA. *Unit head:* Dr. Michael LeBlanc, Chair, 315-312-3282, E-mail: michael.leblanc@oswego.edu. *Application contact:* Dr. Michael LeBlanc, Chair, 315-312-3282, E-mail: michael.leblanc@oswego.edu.

State University of New York at Plattsburgh, School of Education, Health, and Human Services, Department of Counselor Education, Plattsburgh, NY 12901-2681. Offers clinical mental health counseling (MS, Advanced Certificate); school counselor (MS Ed, CAS); student affairs counseling (MS). *Accreditation:* ACA (one or more programs are accredited); TEAC. *Program availability:* Part-time. *Entrance* *requirements:* For master's, GRE General Test or MAT, minimum GPA of 2.8. Additional exam requirements/recommendations for international students: required—TOEFL.

State University of New York College at Old Westbury, Program in Mental Health Counseling, Old Westbury, NY 11568-0210. Offers MS. *Entrance requirements:* For master's, essay, letters of recommendation.

Suffolk University, College of Arts and Sciences, Department of Psychology, Boston, MA 02108-2770. Offers clinical psychology (PhD); college admission counseling (Certificate); mental health counseling (MS); school counseling (MS). *Accreditation:* APA. *Faculty:* 17 full-time (12 women), 1 (woman) part-time/adjunct. *Students:* 46 full-time (45 women), 22 part-time (19 women); includes 8 minority (2 Black or African American, non-Hispanic/Latino; 3 Asian, non-Hispanic/Latino; 1 Hispanic/Latino; 2 Two or more races, non-Hispanic/Latino). Average age 26. 299 applicants, 15% accepted, 22 enrolled. In 2019, 11 master's, 6 doctorates, 1 other advanced degree awarded. Terminal master's awarded for partial completion of doctoral program. *Degree requirements:* For master's, practicum, internship; for doctorate, thesis/dissertation, practicum. *Entrance requirements:* For doctorate, GRE General Test or MAT, 2 letters of recommendation, resume. Additional exam requirements/recommendations for international students: required—TOEFL (minimum score 550 paper-based; 80 iBT). *Application deadline:* For fall admission, 12/1 for domestic and international students. Applications are processed on a rolling basis. Application fee: $50. Electronic applications accepted. *Expenses:* Contact institution. *Financial support:* In 2019–20, 66 students received support, including 7 fellowships (averaging $3,375 per year); career-related internships or fieldwork, Federal Work-Study, institutionally sponsored loans, scholarships/grants, and unspecified assistantships also available. Support available to part-time students. Financial award application deadline: 4/1; financial award applicants required to submit FAFSA. *Unit head:* Dr. Amy Marks, Chairperson, 617-573-8017, E-mail: akmarks@suffolk.edu. *Application contact:* Mara Marzocchi, Associate Director of Graduate Admissions, 617-573-8302, Fax: 617-305-1733, E-mail: grad.admission@suffolk.edu.
Website: http://www.suffolk.edu/college/graduate/69299.php

SUNY Brockport, School of Education, Health, and Human Services, Department of Counselor Education, Brockport, NY 14420-2997. Offers college counseling (MS Ed, CAS); mental health counseling (MS, CAS); school counseling (MS Ed, CAS); school counselor supervision (CAS). *Accreditation:* ACA (one or more programs are accredited). *Program availability:* Part-time. *Faculty:* 7 full-time (3 women), 5 part-time/adjunct (4 women). *Students:* 47 full-time (32 women), 127 part-time (97 women); includes 7 minority (all Black or African American, non-Hispanic/Latino). 130 applicants, 52% accepted, 46 enrolled. In 2019, 39 master's, 6 other advanced degrees awarded. *Degree requirements:* For master's, thesis, internship. *Entrance requirements:* For master's, group interview, letters of recommendation, written objectives, audio response; for CAS, master's degree, New York state school counselor certificate. Additional exam requirements/recommendations for international students: required—TOEFL (minimum score 550 paper-based; 79 iBT), IELTS (minimum score 6.5). *Application deadline:* For fall admission, 2/1 priority date for domestic and international students; for spring admission, 9/1 priority date for domestic and international students; for summer admission, 2/1 priority date for domestic and international students. Application fee: $80. Electronic applications accepted. *Expenses: Tuition, area resident:* Part-time $471 per credit hour. Tuition, nonresident: part-time $963 per credit hour. *Financial support:* In 2019–20, 1 fellowship with full tuition reimbursement (averaging $7,500 per year), 1 teaching assistantship with full tuition reimbursement (averaging $6,000 per year) were awarded; Federal Work-Study, scholarships/grants, and unspecified assistantships also available. Support available to part-time students. Financial award application deadline: 3/15; financial award applicants required to submit FAFSA. *Unit head:* Dr. Robert Dobmeier, Chair, 585-395-5090, Fax: 585-395-2366, E-mail: rdobmeie@brockport.edu. *Application contact:* Danielle A. Welch, Graduate Admissions Counselor, 585-395-5465, Fax: 585-395-2515.
Website: https://www.brockport.edu/academics/counselor_education/

Tarleton State University, College of Graduate Studies, College of Education, Department of Psychological Sciences, Stephenville, TX 76402. Offers applied psychology (MS). *Program availability:* Part-time. *Faculty:* 7 full-time (3 women). *Students:* 16 full-time (11 women), 33 part-time (26 women); includes 15 minority (4 Black or African American, non-Hispanic/Latino; 9 Hispanic/Latino; 2 Two or more races, non-Hispanic/Latino). Average age 31. 30 applicants, 83% accepted, 18 enrolled. In 2019, 4 master's awarded. *Degree requirements:* For master's, comprehensive exam, thesis optional. *Entrance requirements:* For master's, GRE General Test, minimum GPA of 2.5. Additional exam requirements/recommendations for international students: required—TOEFL (minimum score 520 paper-based; 69 iBT); recommended—IELTS (minimum score 6). *Application deadline:* For fall admission, 8/15 priority date for domestic students; for spring admission, 1/7 for domestic students. Applications are processed on a rolling basis. Application fee: $50 ($130 for international students). Electronic applications accepted. *Expenses:* Tuition, state resident: part-time $221.73 per credit hour. Tuition, nonresident: part-time $636.73 per credit hour. *Required fees:* $198 per credit hour. $100 per semester. Tuition and fees vary according to degree level. *Financial support:* Research assistantships, teaching assistantships, career-related internships or fieldwork, Federal Work-Study, institutionally sponsored loans, and tuition waivers available. Support available to part-time students. Financial award application deadline: 5/1; financial award applicants required to submit FAFSA. *Unit head:* Dr. Jamie Borchardt, Department Head, 254-968-1970, E-mail: borchardt@tarleton.edu. *Application contact:* Wendy Weiss, Graduate Admissions Coordinator, 254-968-9104, Fax: 254-968-9670, E-mail: weiss@tarleton.edu.

Teachers College, Columbia University, Department of Counseling and Clinical Psychology, New York, NY 10027-6696. Offers clinical psychology (PhD); counseling psychology (Ed M, Ed D, PhD); mental health counseling (ME); psychological counseling (ME, ND); psychology in education (MA, ND); school counselor (ME). *Accreditation:* APA (one or more programs are accredited). *Program availability:* Part-time.

Temple University, College of Education and Human Development, Department of Psychological Studies in Education, Philadelphia, PA 19122-6096. Offers applied behavior analysis (MS Ed); counseling psychology (Ed M), including agency counseling, school counseling; educational psychology (Ed M); school psychology (PhD, Ed S). *Accreditation:* APA (one or more programs are accredited). *Program availability:* Part-time, evening/weekend. *Faculty:* 19 full-time (10 women), 19 part-time/adjunct (9 women). *Students:* 165 full-time (122 women), 49 part-time (37 women); includes 74 minority (39 Black or African American, non-Hispanic/Latino; 13 Asian, non-Hispanic/Latino; 17 Hispanic/Latino; 5 Two or more races, non-Hispanic/Latino), 11 international. 374 applicants, 49% accepted, 100 enrolled. In 2019, 73 master's, 5 doctorates, 16 other advanced degrees awarded. *Degree requirements:* For master's, comprehensive exam (for some programs); for doctorate, thesis/dissertation. *Entrance requirements:* For master's, statement of goals, 2 recommendation letters; for doctorate, GRE, statement of goals, academic writing sample, 2 recommendation letters. Additional exam requirements/recommendations for international students: required—TOEFL (minimum score 79 iBT), IELTS, PTE, one of three is required. Application fee: $60. Electronic applications accepted. *Financial support:* Fellowships, research assistantships, teaching assistantships, career-related internships or fieldwork, Federal Work-Study, health care benefits, and unspecified assistantships available. Financial award applicants required to submit FAFSA. *Unit head:* Renee Tobin, Prof. of Counseling Psychology and Dept. Chairperson, 215-204-7884, E-mail: renee.tobin@temple.edu. *Application contact:* Remy Van Wyk, Academic Coordinator, 215-204-1474, E-mail: remy.van.wyk@temple.edu.
Website: http://education.temple.edu/pse

Tennessee State University, The School of Graduate Studies and Research, College of Education, Department of Psychology, Nashville, TN 37209-1561. Offers counseling psychology (MS). *Entrance requirements:* For master's, GRE General Test or MAT. Electronic applications accepted.

Texas A&M International University, Office of Graduate Studies and Research, College of Arts and Sciences, Department of Psychology and Communication, Laredo, TX 78041. Offers counseling psychology (MACP); psychology (MS). *Degree requirements:* For master's, thesis (for some programs). *Entrance requirements:* For master's, GRE General Test. Additional exam requirements/recommendations for international students: required—TOEFL (minimum score 550 paper-based; 79 iBT).

Texas A&M University, College of Education and Human Development, Department of Educational Psychology, College Station, TX 77843. Offers bilingual education (M Ed, MS); counseling psychology (PhD); educational psychology (M Ed, MS, PhD); educational technology (M Ed); school psychology (PhD); special education (M Ed, MS). *Accreditation:* APA (one or more programs are accredited). *Program availability:* Part-time, evening/weekend, blended/hybrid learning. *Faculty:* 47. *Students:* 162 full-time (135 women), 248 part-time (205 women); includes 154 minority (26 Black or African American, non-Hispanic/Latino; 1 American Indian or Alaska Native, non-Hispanic/Latino; 20 Asian, non-Hispanic/Latino; 97 Hispanic/Latino; 1 Native Hawaiian or other Pacific Islander, non-Hispanic/Latino; 9 Two or more races, non-Hispanic/Latino), 49 international. Average age 33. 174 applicants, 51% accepted, 61 enrolled. In 2019, 107 master's, 21 doctorates awarded. *Degree requirements:* For master's, thesis optional; for doctorate, thesis/dissertation. *Entrance requirements:* For master's and doctorate, GRE General Test. Additional exam requirements/recommendations for international students: required—TOEFL (minimum score 550 paper-based; 80 iBT), IELTS (minimum score 6), PTE (minimum score 53). Application fee: $65 ($90 for international students). Electronic applications accepted. *Expenses:* Contact institution. *Financial support:* In 2019–20, 272 students received support, including 16 fellowships with tuition reimbursements available (averaging $13,000 per year), 122 research assistantships with tuition reimbursements available (averaging $14,333 per year), 23 teaching assistantships with tuition reimbursements available (averaging $9,052 per year); career-related internships or fieldwork, institutionally sponsored loans, scholarships/grants, traineeships, health care benefits, tuition waivers (full and partial), and unspecified assistantships also available. Support available to part-time students. Financial award application deadline: 3/15; financial award applicants required to submit FAFSA. *Unit head:* Dr. Fuhui Tong, Interim Department Head, E-mail: fuhuitong@tamu.edu. *Application contact:* Sally Kallina, Academic Advisor IV, E-mail: skallina@tamu.edu.
Website: http://epsy.tamu.edu

Texas A&M University–Texarkana, Graduate Studies and Research, College of Health and Behavioral Sciences, Texarkana, TX 75503. Offers counseling psychology (MS). *Program availability:* Part-time, evening/weekend. *Degree requirements:* For master's, comprehensive exam (for some programs), thesis or alternative. *Entrance requirements:* For master's, minimum GPA of 3.0 in last 60 hours of bachelor's degree. Additional exam requirements/recommendations for international students: required—TOEFL. Electronic applications accepted.

Texas Tech University, Graduate School, College of Arts and Sciences, Department of Psychological Sciences, Lubbock, TX 79409-2051. Offers clinical psychology (PhD); counseling psychology (MA, PhD); general experimental psychology (MA, PhD); psychology (MA). *Accreditation:* APA (one or more programs are accredited). *Faculty:* 33 full-time (14 women), 2 part-time/adjunct (both women). *Students:* 105 full-time (63 women), 24 part-time (22 women); includes 39 minority (6 Black or African American, non-Hispanic/Latino; 1 American Indian or Alaska Native, non-Hispanic/Latino; 11 Asian, non-Hispanic/Latino; 21 Hispanic/Latino), 7 international. Average age 28. 162 applicants, 14% accepted, 16 enrolled. In 2019, 21 master's, 10 doctorates awarded. *Degree requirements:* For doctorate, comprehensive exam, thesis/dissertation, 100 credit hours of organized courses, research credits, and practica. *Entrance requirements:* For master's, GRE General Test, GRE Subject Test, essays, letters of recommendation; for doctorate, GRE General Test, essays, letters of recommendation. Additional exam requirements/recommendations for international students: required—TOEFL (minimum score 550 paper-based; 79 iBT). *Application deadline:* For fall admission, 6/1 priority date for domestic students, 1/15 priority date for international students; for spring admission, 9/1 priority date for domestic students, 6/15 priority date for international students. Applications are processed on a rolling basis. Application fee: $65. Electronic applications accepted. *Expenses:* Contact institution. *Financial support:* In 2019–20, 121 students received support, including 115 fellowships (averaging $2,803 per year), 39 research assistantships (averaging $12,832 per year), 77 teaching assistantships (averaging $13,684 per year); Federal Work-Study, institutionally sponsored loans, health care benefits, and unspecified assistantships also available. Financial award application deadline: 4/15; financial award applicants required to submit FAFSA. *Unit head:* Dr. Robert Morgan, Professor and Chair, 806-834-7117, Fax: 806-742-0818, E-mail: robert.morgan@ttu.edu. *Application contact:* Kay Hill, Admissions Coordinator, 806-834-1350, Fax: 806-742-0818, E-mail: kay.hill@ttu.edu.
Website: www.depts.ttu.edu/psy/

Texas Woman's University, Graduate School, College of Arts and Sciences, Department of Psychology and Philosophy, Denton, TX 76204. Offers counseling psychology (MA, PhD); psychological science (MS); school psychology (PhD, SSP). *Accreditation:* APA (one or more programs are accredited). *Faculty:* 16 full-time (12 women), 5 part-time/adjunct (3 women). *Students:* 88 full-time (81 women), 50 part-time (42 women); includes 65 minority (16 Black or African American, non-Hispanic/Latino; 14 Asian, non-Hispanic/Latino; 33 Hispanic/Latino; 2 Two or more races, non-Hispanic/Latino). Average age 28. 132 applicants, 33% accepted, 33 enrolled. In 2019, 20 master's, 6 doctorates awarded. Terminal master's awarded for partial completion of doctoral program. *Degree requirements:* For master's, comprehensive exam (for some programs), thesis or alternative, practica (for MA); thesis or coursework; written exam required for those who do not complete a thesis; for doctorate, comprehensive exam, thesis/dissertation, internship, residency; for SSP, comprehensive exam, SSP-internship, capstone evaluation. *Entrance requirements:* For master's, GRE (preferred minimum score 153 Verbal, 144 Quantitative), BA/BS or 18 hours in psychology; minimum GPA of 3.0, 3.5 in psychology classes; 3 letters of reference; curriculum vitae/resume; essay, interview; for doctorate, GRE (preferred minimum score 153 [500 old version] Verbal, 144 [500 old version] Quantitative, 4 Analytical), 3 letters of reference, minimum GPA of 3.0 overall and 3.5 in psychology classes, MA in psychology or related discipline with thesis, curriculum vitae, essays; for SSP, GRE (preferred minimum score 153 [500 old version] Verbal, 144 [500 old version] Quantitative, 4 Analytical), BA/BS or 18 hours in psychology; minimum GPA of 3.0, 3.5 in psychology classes; 3 letters of

reference; curriculum vitae; personal essay. Additional exam requirements/recommendations for international students: required—TOEFL (minimum score 550 paper-based; 79 iBT); recommended—IELTS (minimum score 6.5), TSE (minimum score 53). *Application deadline:* For fall admission, 2/1 for domestic and international students. Application fee: $50 ($75 for international students). Electronic applications accepted. *Expenses: Tuition, area resident:* Full-time $4973.40; part-time $276.30 per semester hour. Tuition, state resident: full-time $4973.40; part-time $276.30 per semester hour. Tuition, nonresident: full-time $12,569; part-time $698.30 per semester hour. *International tuition:* $12,569.40 full-time. *Required fees:* $2524.30. Tuition and fees vary according to course level, course load, degree level and program. *Financial support:* In 2019–20, 93 students received support, including 53 teaching assistantships (averaging $6,217 per year); career-related internships or fieldwork, scholarships/grants, health care benefits, and unspecified assistantships also available. Support available to part-time students. Financial award application deadline: 3/1; financial award applicants required to submit FAFSA. *Unit head:* Dr. Brian Harding, Acting Chair, 940-898-2303, Fax: 940-898-2301, E-mail: psychology@twu.edu. *Application contact:* Korie Hawkins, Associate Director of Admissions, Graduate Recruitment, 940-898-3188, Fax: 940-898-3081, E-mail: admissions@twu.edu.
Website: http://www.twu.edu/psychology-philosophy/

Towson University, College of Liberal Arts, Program in Psychology, Towson, MD 21252-0001. Offers clinical psychology (MA); counseling psychology (MA); experimental psychology (MA); school psychology (MA). *Program availability:* Part-time, evening/weekend. *Students:* 97 full-time (79 women), 25 part-time (20 women); includes 27 minority (15 Black or African American, non-Hispanic/Latino; 3 Asian, non-Hispanic/Latino; 2 Hispanic/Latino; 7 Two or more races, non-Hispanic/Latino), 3 international. *Entrance requirements:* For master's, GRE, minimum GPA of 3.0, letters of recommendation. *Application deadline:* For fall admission, 1/17 for domestic students, 5/15 for international students; for spring admission, 10/15 for domestic students, 12/1 for international students. Applications are processed on a rolling basis. Application fee: $45. Electronic applications accepted. *Expenses: Tuition, area resident:* Full-time $7920; part-time $439 per credit. Tuition, nonresident: full-time $16,344; part-time $908 per credit. *International tuition:* $16,344 full-time. *Required fees:* $2628; $146 per credit. $876 per term. *Financial support:* Application deadline: 4/1. *Unit head:* Dr. Geoffrey Munro, Department Chair, 410-704-2634, E-mail: psycdept@towson.edu. *Application contact:* Coverley Beidleman, Assistant Director of Graduate Admissions, 410-704-5630, Fax: 410-704-3030, E-mail: grads@towson.edu.
Website: https://www.towson.edu/cla/departments/psychology/grad/

Trinity Christian College, Program in Counseling Psychology, Palos Heights, IL 60463-0929. Offers MA. *Program availability:* Evening/weekend, online learning.

Trinity International University, Trinity Evangelical Divinity School, Deerfield, IL 60015-1284. Offers academic ministry (M Div); Biblical and Near Eastern archaeology and languages (MA); chaplaincy and ministry care (MA); Christian studies (Certificate); church and parachurch ministry (M Div); church history (MA, Th M); counseling (Th M); educational ministries (MA); educational ministry (Th M); educational studies (PhD); intercultural studies (MA, PhD); leadership and management (D Min); mental health counseling (MA); military chaplaincy (D Min); ministry (MA); missions (Th M); missions and evangelism (D Min); New Testament (MA, Th M); Old Testament (Th M); Old Testament and Semitic languages (MA); pastoral ministry and care (D Min); pastoral theology (Th M); preaching and teaching (D Min); spiritual formation and education (D Min); systematic theology (MA, Th M); theological studies (MA, PhD); urban ministry (MA). *Program availability:* Part-time, online learning. *Degree requirements:* For master's, comprehensive exam, thesis, fieldwork; for doctorate, comprehensive exam (for some programs), thesis/dissertation; for Certificate, comprehensive exam, integrative papers. *Entrance requirements:* For master's, GRE, MAT, minimum cumulative undergraduate GPA of 3.0; for doctorate, GRE, minimum cumulative graduate GPA of 3.2; for Certificate, GRE, MAT, minimum undergraduate GPA of 2.5. Additional exam requirements/recommendations for international students: required—TOEFL (minimum score 580 paper-based), TWE (minimum score 4). Electronic applications accepted.

Trinity International University, Trinity Graduate School, Deerfield, IL 60015-1284. Offers athletic training (MA); bioethics (MA); counseling psychology (MA); diverse learning (M Ed); leadership (MA); teaching (MA). *Program availability:* Part-time, evening/weekend, online learning. *Degree requirements:* For master's, comprehensive exam. *Entrance requirements:* For master's, GRE General Test or MAT, minimum undergraduate GPA of 3.0. Additional exam requirements/recommendations for international students: required—TOEFL (minimum score 580 paper-based), TWE (minimum score 4). Electronic applications accepted.

Trinity International University Florida, Graduate School, Davie, FL 33324. Offers MA. *Expenses: Tuition:* Full-time $5040; part-time $720 per credit hour. *Required fees:* $900; $300 per semester.

Trinity Washington University, School of Education, Washington, DC 20017-1094. Offers clinical mental health counseling (MA); early childhood education (MAT); educating for change (M Ed); educational administration (MSA); elementary education (MAT); reading (M Ed); school counseling (MA); secondary education (MAT), including English, social studies; special education (MAT). *Accreditation:* NCATE. *Program availability:* Part-time, evening/weekend. *Degree requirements:* For master's, thesis (for some programs), capstone project(s). *Entrance requirements:* For master's, PRAXIS I, minimum GPA of 2.8. Additional exam requirements/recommendations for international students: required—TOEFL (minimum score 550 paper-based).

Trinity Western University, School of Graduate Studies, Master of Arts in Counselling Psychology, Langley, BC V2Y 1Y1, Canada. Offers MA. *Accreditation:* ACA. *Program availability:* Part-time. *Degree requirements:* For master's, comprehensive exam, thesis. *Entrance requirements:* For master's, GRE (if out of school for 5 years prior to applying), BA in honors psychology, minimum GPA of 3.0 for 3rd and 4th year of BA. Additional exam requirements/recommendations for international students: required—TOEFL (minimum score 600 paper-based; 100 iBT), IELTS (minimum score 7). *Application deadline:* For fall admission, 1/31 priority date for domestic and international students; for spring admission, 10/15 priority date for domestic and international students. Application fee: $0 Canadian dollars. *Expenses: Tuition:* Full-time $13,000 Canadian dollars; part-time $8700 Canadian dollars per semester hour. *Required fees:* $504 Canadian dollars; $336 Canadian dollars per semester hour. $168 Canadian dollars per semester. Tuition and fees vary according to course load, campus/location, program, reciprocity agreements and student level. *Financial support:* Research assistantships, teaching assistantships, and scholarships/grants available. *Unit head:* Janelle Kwee, Program Director, MA Counselling Psychology, E-mail: janelle.kwee@twu.ca. *Application contact:* Phil Kay, Director of Graduate and International Admissions, 604-513-2121 Ext. 3444, E-mail: phil.kay@twu.ca.
Website: http://www.twu.ca/cpsy/

Truett McConnell University, The Leonhard Schiemer School of Psychology and Biblical Counseling, Cleveland, GA 30528. Offers professional counseling (MA). *Program availability:* Part-time. *Students:* 14 full-time (12 women), 9 part-time (6 women); includes 4 minority (1 Black or African American, non-Hispanic/Latino; 3 Hispanic/Latino). Average age 32. 17 applicants, 47% accepted, 6 enrolled. In 2019, 1 master's awarded. *Entrance requirements:* For master's, bachelor's degree from accredited institution, minimum GPA of 2.5, interview with faculty, personal statement. *Application deadline:* For fall admission, 8/1 for domestic students; for spring admission, 12/1 for domestic students; for summer admission, 5/1 for domestic students. Applications are processed on a rolling basis. Electronic applications accepted. *Expenses: Tuition:* Full-time $6300; part-time $350 per credit hour. *Required fees:* $1010; $1010. Tuition and fees vary according to course load. *Financial support:* Applicants required to submit FAFSA. *Unit head:* Dr. Holly Haynes, Dean, 706-865-2134 Ext. 6205, E-mail: hhaynes@truett.edu. *Application contact:* Timothy Agee, Graduate Admissions Coordinator, 706-865-2134 Ext. 4305, E-mail: tagee@truett.edu.
Website: https://truett.edu/degrees/master-arts-professional-counseling/

Union College, Graduate Programs, Department of Psychology, Barbourville, KY 40906-1499. Offers clinical psychology (MA); counseling psychology (MA); school psychology (MA).

United States International University–Africa, School of Arts and Sciences, Nairobi, Kenya. Offers counseling psychology (MA), including chemical dependency, health psychology; international relations (MA), including development studies, diplomacy and foreign policy, peace and conflict studies. *Program availability:* Part-time, evening/weekend. *Degree requirements:* For master's, thesis, practicum. *Entrance requirements:* For master's, GRE General Test, 2 letters of recommendation, resume. Additional exam requirements/recommendations for international students: required—TOEFL.

Universidad del Turabo, Graduate Programs, School of Social Sciences and Humanities, Programs in Psychology, Program in Counseling Psychology, Gurabo, PR 00778-3030. Offers M Psych, Psy D, Certificate. *Entrance requirements:* For master's, GRE, GMAT or EXADEP, interview, essay, official transcript, recommendation letters. Electronic applications accepted.

Universidad Metropolitana, School of Social Sciences, Humanities and Communications, Program in Counseling Psychology, San Juan, PR 00928-1150. Offers MA.

University at Albany, State University of New York, School of Education, Department of Educational and Counseling Psychology, Albany, NY 12222-0001. Offers counseling psychology (PhD, CAS); mental health counseling (MS). *Program availability:* Part-time, evening/weekend, 100% online, blended/hybrid learning. *Faculty:* 31 full-time (14 women), 6 part-time/adjunct (4 women). *Students:* 266 full-time (204 women), 122 part-time (90 women); includes 91 minority (20 Black or African American, non-Hispanic/Latino; 23 Asian, non-Hispanic/Latino; 31 Hispanic/Latino; 17 Two or more races, non-Hispanic/Latino), 34 international. Average age 27. 128 applicants, 55% accepted, 51 enrolled. In 2019, 80 master's, 14 doctorates, 14 other advanced degrees awarded. *Degree requirements:* For doctorate, thesis/dissertation. *Entrance requirements:* For master's, GRE General Test. Additional exam requirements/recommendations for international students: required—TOEFL (minimum score 550 paper-based). *Application deadline:* For fall admission, 2/15 for domestic and international students; for spring admission, 11/15 for domestic students. Application fee: $75. Electronic applications accepted. *Expenses: Tuition, area resident:* Full-time $11,530; part-time $480 per credit hour. Tuition, nonresident: full-time $23,530; part-time $980 per credit hour. *International tuition:* $23,530 full-time. *Required fees:* $2185; $96 per credit hour. Part-time tuition and fees vary according to course load and program. *Financial support:* Teaching assistantships and career-related internships or fieldwork available. *Unit head:* Kevin Quinn, Chair, 518-442-5049, E-mail: kquinn@albany.edu. *Application contact:* Kevin Quinn, Chair, 518-442-5049, E-mail: kquinn@albany.edu.
Website: https://www.albany.edu/graduatebulletin/department_educational_counseling_psychology.htm

University at Buffalo, the State University of New York, Graduate School, Graduate School of Education, Department of Counseling, School, and Educational Psychology, Buffalo, NY 14260. Offers applied statistical analysis (Advanced Certificate); counseling/school psychology (PhD); counselor education (PhD); education studies (Ed M); educational psychology (MA, PhD); mental health counseling (MS, Certificate); mindful counseling for wellness and engagement (Advanced Certificate); rehabilitation counseling (MS, Advanced Certificate); school counseling (Ed M, Certificate). *Accreditation:* CORE (one or more programs are accredited). *Program availability:* Part-time, 100% online. *Faculty:* 23 full-time (12 women), 23 part-time/adjunct (16 women). *Students:* 147 full-time (117 women), 125 part-time (109 women); includes 52 minority (24 Black or African American, non-Hispanic/Latino; 8 Asian, non-Hispanic/Latino; 14 Hispanic/Latino; 6 Two or more races, non-Hispanic/Latino), 18 international. Average age 32. 349 applicants, 52% accepted, 125 enrolled. In 2019, 77 master's, 9 doctorates, 59 other advanced degrees awarded. Terminal master's awarded for partial completion of doctoral program. *Degree requirements:* For master's, comprehensive exam (for some programs), thesis (for some programs); for doctorate, comprehensive exam, thesis/dissertation. *Entrance requirements:* For master's, GRE General Test, interview, letters of reference, personal statement; for doctorate, GRE General Test, interview, letters of reference, writing sample, personal statement; for other advanced degree, proof of previous degrees for specific counseling certificates. Additional exam requirements/recommendations for international students: required—TOEFL (minimum score 600 paper-based; 79 iBT), IELTS (minimum score 6.5), PTE (minimum score 55), The Graduate School of Education requires international students to submit test scores for at least one of the exams (TOEFL, IELTS, PTE). *Application deadline:* For fall admission, 2/1 priority date for domestic and international students. Applications are processed on a rolling basis. Application fee: $50. Electronic applications accepted. *Expenses: Tuition, area resident:* Full-time $11,310; part-time $471 per credit hour. Tuition, state resident: full-time $11,310; part-time $471 per credit hour. Tuition, nonresident: full-time $23,100; part-time $963 per credit hour. *International tuition:* $23,100 full-time. *Required fees:* $2820. *Financial support:* In 2019–20, 10 fellowships (averaging $20,000 per year), 14 research assistantships with tuition reimbursements (averaging $26,000 per year) were awarded; teaching assistantships, career-related internships or fieldwork, Federal Work-Study, institutionally sponsored loans, scholarships/grants, tuition waivers (full and partial), and unspecified assistantships also available. Financial award application deadline: 2/1; financial award applicants required to submit FAFSA. *Unit head:* Dr. Myles Faith, Department Chair, 716-645-2484, Fax: 716-645-6616, E-mail: mfaith@buffalo.edu. *Application contact:* Renad Aref, Assistant Director of Admission Recruitment, 716-645-2110, Fax: 716-645-7937, E-mail: gseinfo@buffalo.edu.
Website: http://ed.buffalo.edu/counseling

The University of Akron, Graduate School, Buchtel College of Arts and Sciences, Department of Psychology, Program in Counseling Psychology, Akron, OH 44325. Offers MA, PhD. *Accreditation:* APA (one or more programs are accredited). *Degree requirements:* For doctorate, one foreign language, comprehensive exam, thesis/dissertation. *Entrance requirements:* For doctorate, GRE, bachelor's degree in psychology or 30 credits of psychology coursework; current curriculum vitae; declaration of intent outlining goals and interests; three letters of recommendation. Additional exam requirements/recommendations for international students: required—TOEFL (minimum score 79 iBT), IELTS (minimum score 6.5). Electronic applications accepted.

Counseling Psychology

The University of Akron, Graduate School, College of Health Professions, School of Counseling, Program in Clinical Mental Health Counseling, Akron, OH 44325. Offers MA. *Accreditation:* ACA; NCATE. *Degree requirements:* For master's, comprehensive exam. *Entrance requirements:* For master's, minimum GPA of 2.75, letters of recommendation, interview. Additional exam requirements/recommendations for international students: required—TOEFL (minimum score 79 iBT), IELTS (minimum score 6.5). Electronic applications accepted.

University of Alberta, Faculty of Graduate Studies and Research, Department of Educational Psychology, Edmonton, AB T6G 2E1, Canada. Offers counseling psychology (M Ed, PhD); educational psychology (M Ed, PhD); instructional technology (M Ed); school counseling (M Ed); school psychology (M Ed, PhD); special education (M Ed, PhD); special education-deafness studies (M Ed); teaching English as a second language (M Ed). *Program availability:* Part-time. *Degree requirements:* For master's, thesis optional; for doctorate, comprehensive exam, thesis/dissertation. *Entrance requirements:* For master's and doctorate, minimum GPA of 3.0. Additional exam requirements/recommendations for international students: required—TOEFL.

The University of Arizona, College of Education, Department of Disability and Psychoeducational Studies, Program in Counseling and Mental Health, Tucson, AZ 85721. Offers rehabilitation counseling (MA); school counseling (MA). *Accreditation:* ACA. *Entrance requirements:* Additional exam requirements/recommendations for international students: required—TOEFL (minimum score 550 paper-based; 80 iBT).

University of Baltimore, Graduate School, Yale Gordon College of Arts and Sciences, Program in Applied Psychology, Baltimore, MD 21201-5779. Offers counseling psychology (MS). *Program availability:* Part-time, evening/weekend. *Degree requirements:* For master's, thesis optional. *Entrance requirements:* For master's, GRE, minimum GPA of 3.0. Additional exam requirements/recommendations for international students: required—TOEFL (minimum score 550 paper-based). Electronic applications accepted. *Expenses:* Contact institution.

University of Bridgeport, School of Arts and Sciences, Department of Counseling, Bridgeport, CT 06604. Offers clinical mental health counseling (MS); college student personnel (MS); community counseling (MS); human resource development (MS); human service (MS). *Program availability:* Part-time, evening/weekend. *Degree requirements:* For master's, thesis, project. *Entrance requirements:* Additional exam requirements/recommendations for international students: recommended—TOEFL (minimum score 550 paper-based; 80 iBT), IELTS (minimum score 6.5). Electronic applications accepted. *Expenses:* Contact institution.

The University of British Columbia, Faculty of Education, Department of Educational and Counseling Psychology, and Special Education, Vancouver, BC V6T 1Z4, Canada. Offers counseling psychology (M Ed, MA, PhD); guidance studies (Diploma); human development, learning and culture (M Ed, MA, PhD); measurement, evaluation, and research methodology (M Ed, MA, PhD); school psychology (M Ed, MA, PhD); special education (M Ed, MA, PhD, Diploma). *Program availability:* Part-time. *Degree requirements:* For master's, thesis (for some programs); for doctorate, comprehensive exam, thesis/dissertation. *Entrance requirements:* For master's, GRE General Test (for MA in counseling psychology); for doctorate, GRE General Test. Additional exam requirements/recommendations for international students: required—TOEFL. Electronic applications accepted. *Expenses:* Contact institution.

University of Calgary, Faculty of Graduate Studies, Werklund School of Education, Program in School of Applied Child Psychology, Calgary, AB T2N 1N4, Canada. Offers counseling psychology (M Sc, MC, PhD); school and applied child psychology (M Ed, M Sc, PhD). *Program availability:* Part-time. *Degree requirements:* For master's, thesis (for some programs), final oral exam; for doctorate, thesis/dissertation, candidacy exam, final oral exam. *Entrance requirements:* For master's, minimum GPA of 3.0, 3 letters of reference; for doctorate, minimum GPA of 3.5, 3 letters of reference.

University of California, Berkeley, UC Berkeley Extension, Certificate Programs in Behavioral and Health Sciences, Berkeley, CA 94720. Offers alcohol and drug abuse studies (Certificate). *Accreditation:* APA.

University of California, Santa Barbara, Graduate Division, Gevirtz Graduate School of Education, Santa Barbara, CA 93106-9490. Offers counseling, clinical and school psychology (MA, PhD, Credential), including clinical psychology (PhD); counseling psychology (MA, PhD); pupil personnel services (Credential), school psychology (PhD); education (MA, PhD); teacher education (M Ed, Credential), including multiple subject teaching (Credential), single subject teaching (Credential), special education (Credential), teaching (M Ed); MA/PhD. *Accreditation:* APA (one or more programs are accredited). Terminal master's awarded for partial completion of doctoral program. *Degree requirements:* For master's, comprehensive exam (for some programs), thesis (for some programs); for doctorate, comprehensive exam (for some programs), thesis/dissertation. *Entrance requirements:* For master's and doctorate, GRE; for Credential, GRE or MAT, CSET, CBEST. Additional exam requirements/recommendations for international students: required—TOEFL (minimum score 550 paper-based; 80 iBT), IELTS (minimum score 7). Electronic applications accepted.

University of Central Arkansas, Graduate School, College of Health and Behavioral Sciences, Department of Counseling and Psychology, Program in Counseling Psychology, Conway, AR 72035-0001. Offers MS. *Degree requirements:* For master's, comprehensive exam, thesis optional. *Entrance requirements:* For master's, GRE General Test, minimum GPA of 2.7. Additional exam requirements/recommendations for international students: required—TOEFL (minimum score 550 paper-based). Electronic applications accepted.

University of Central Missouri, The Graduate School, Warrensburg, MO 64093. Offers accountancy (MA); accounting (MBA); applied mathematics (MS); aviation safety (MA); biology (MS); business administration (MBA); career and technology education (MS); college student personnel administration (MS); communication (MA); computer information systems and information technology (MS); computer science (MS); counseling (MS); criminal justice and criminology (MS); educational leadership (Ed S); educational leadership and policy analysis (Ed D); educational technology (MS, Ed S); elementary and early childhood education (MSE); English (MA); english language learners - teaching english as a second language (MA); environmental studies (MA); finance (MBA); history (MA); industrial hygiene (MS); industrial management (MS); information systems (MBA); kinesiology (MS); library science and information services (MS); literacy education (MSE); marketing (MBA); mathematics (MS); music (MA); occupational safety management (MS); professional leadership - adult, career, and technical education (Ed S); professional leadership - counseling (Ed S); psychology (MS); rural family nursing (MS); school administration (MSE); social gerontology (MS); sociology (MA); special education (MSE); speech language pathology (MS); teaching (MAT); technology (MS); technology management (PhD); theatre (MA). *Accreditation:* ASHA. *Program availability:* Part-time, 100% online, blended/hybrid learning. *Faculty:* 236 full-time (113 women), 97 part-time/adjunct (61 women). *Students:* 787 full-time (448 women), 1,459 part-time (997 women); includes 213 minority (72 Black or African American, non-Hispanic/Latino; 5 American Indian or Alaska Native, non-Hispanic/Latino; 27 Asian, non-Hispanic/Latino; 59 Hispanic/Latino; 50 Two or more races, non-Hispanic/Latino), 574 international. Average age 30. 1,477 applicants, 68% accepted, 664 enrolled. In 2019, 831 master's, 93 other advanced degrees awarded. *Degree*

requirements: For master's and Ed S, comprehensive exam (for some programs), thesis (for some programs). *Entrance requirements:* For master's, A GRE or GMAT test score may be required by some of the programs, A minimum GPA, letters of recommendation, a statement of purpose may be required by some of the programs; for Ed S, A master's degree is required for the application of an Education Specialist's degree program. Additional exam requirements/recommendations for international students: required—TOEFL (minimum score 550 paper-based; 79 iBT). *Application deadline:* For fall admission, 6/1 priority date for domestic and international students; for spring admission, 10/15 priority date for domestic and international students; for summer admission, 4/1 priority date for domestic and international students. Applications are processed on a rolling basis. Application fee: $30 ($75 for international students). Electronic applications accepted. *Expenses: Tuition, area resident:* Full-time $7524; part-time $313.50 per credit hour. Tuition, state resident: full-time $7524; part-time $313.50 per credit hour. Tuition, nonresident: full-time $15,048; part-time $627 per credit hour. *International tuition:* $15,048 full-time. *Required fees:* $915; $30.50 per credit hour. *Financial support:* In 2019–20, 89 students received support. Research assistantships, teaching assistantships, career-related internships or fieldwork, Federal Work-Study, scholarships/grants, unspecified assistantships, and administrative and laboratory assistantships available. Support available to part-time students. Financial award application deadline: 4/1; financial award applicants required to submit FAFSA. *Unit head:* Shellie Hewitt, Director of Graduate and International Student Services, 660-543-4621, Fax: 660-543-4778, E-mail: hewitt@ucmo.edu. *Application contact:* Shellie Hewitt, Director of Graduate and International Student Services, 660-543-4621, Fax: 660-543-4778, E-mail: hewitt@ucmo.edu.
Website: http://www.ucmo.edu/graduate/

University of Central Oklahoma, The Jackson College of Graduate Studies, College of Education and Professional Studies, Department of Psychology, Edmond, OK 73034-5209. Offers psychology (MA), including counseling psychology, experimental psychology, forensic psychology, general psychology, school psychology. *Degree requirements:* For master's, thesis (for some programs). *Entrance requirements:* For master's, GRE. Additional exam requirements/recommendations for international students: required—TOEFL (minimum score 550 paper-based; 79 iBT), IELTS (minimum score 6.5). Electronic applications accepted.

University of Colorado Denver, School of Education and Human Development, Program in Counseling Psychology and Counselor Education, Denver, CO 80217. Offers counseling (MA), including clinical mental health counseling, couple and family counseling, multicultural counseling, school counseling; school counseling (MA). *Accreditation:* ACA; NCATE. *Program availability:* Part-time, evening/weekend. *Entrance requirements:* For master's, GRE or MAT (unless applicant already holds a graduate degree), letters of recommendation, interview, resume, transcripts from all colleges/universities attended. Tuition and fees vary according to course load, program and reciprocity agreements.

University of Connecticut, Graduate School, Neag School of Education, Department of Educational Psychology, Program in Counseling Psychology, Storrs, CT 06269. Offers counseling psychology (PhD); school counseling (MA). *Accreditation:* ACA. Terminal master's awarded for partial completion of doctoral program. *Degree requirements:* For master's, comprehensive exam, thesis or alternative; for doctorate, thesis/dissertation. *Entrance requirements:* For doctorate, GRE General Test. Additional exam requirements/recommendations for international students: required—TOEFL (minimum score 550 paper-based). Electronic applications accepted.

University of Dayton, Department of Counselor Education and Human Services, Dayton, OH 45469. Offers clinical mental health counseling (MS Ed); college student personnel (MS Ed); higher education administration (MS Ed); human services (MS Ed); school counseling (MS Ed); school psychology (MS Ed, Ed S). *Accreditation:* ACA; NCATE. *Program availability:* Part-time. *Degree requirements:* For master's, thesis (for some programs); for Ed S, thesis (for some programs), professional portfolio. *Entrance requirements:* For master's, MAT or GRE (if GPA less than 2.75), essays (for some programs). Additional exam requirements/recommendations for international students: required—TOEFL (minimum score 550 paper-based; 80 iBT). Electronic applications accepted. *Expenses:* Contact institution.

University of Denver, Morgridge College of Education, Denver, CO 80208. Offers child, family and school psychology (MA, PhD, Ed S); counseling psychology (MA, PhD); curriculum and instruction (MA, Ed D, PhD); curriculum instruction and teaching (Certificate); early childhood special education (MA, Certificate); educational leadership and policy studies (MA, Ed D, PhD, Certificate); higher education (Ed D, PhD); library and information science (MLIS); research methods and statistics (MA, PhD). *Accreditation:* ALA; APA (one or more programs are accredited). *Program availability:* Part-time, evening/weekend, online learning. *Faculty:* 54 full-time (38 women), 28 part-time/adjunct (16 women). *Students:* 477 full-time (385 women), 492 part-time (378 women); includes 266 minority (59 Black or African American, non-Hispanic/Latino; 7 American Indian or Alaska Native, non-Hispanic/Latino; 36 Asian, non-Hispanic/Latino; 128 Hispanic/Latino; 2 Native Hawaiian or other Pacific Islander, non-Hispanic/Latino; 34 Two or more races, non-Hispanic/Latino), 58 international. Average age 31. 1,252 applicants, 68% accepted, 420 enrolled. In 2019, 222 master's, 46 doctorates, 129 other advanced degrees awarded. Terminal master's awarded for partial completion of doctoral program. *Degree requirements:* For master's, comprehensive exam (for some programs); for doctorate, comprehensive exam (for some programs), thesis/dissertation. *Entrance requirements:* For master's, GRE General Test or GMAT, bachelors degree; transcripts; two letters of recommendation; personal statement; resume; for doctorate, GRE General Test or GMAT, Masters degree; transcripts; two letters of recommendation; personal statement(s); resume. Additional exam requirements/recommendations for international students: required—TOEFL (minimum score 550 paper-based; 80 iBT). *Application deadline:* Applications are processed on a rolling basis. Application fee: $65. Electronic applications accepted. *Expenses:* Contact institution. *Financial support:* In 2019–20, 698 students received support, including 19 research assistantships with tuition reimbursements available (averaging $11,372 per year), 3 teaching assistantships with tuition reimbursements available (averaging $4,333 per year); career-related internships or fieldwork, Federal Work-Study, institutionally sponsored loans, scholarships/grants, and unspecified assistantships also available. Support available to part-time students. Financial award application deadline: 2/15; financial award applicants required to submit FAFSA. *Unit head:* Dr. Karen Riley, Dean, 303-871-3665, E-mail: karen.riley@du.edu. *Application contact:* Jodi Dye, Director of Admissions, 303-871-2510, E-mail: jodi.dye@du.edu.
Website: http://morgridge.du.edu

University of Florida, Graduate School, College of Liberal Arts and Sciences, Department of Psychology, Gainesville, FL 32611. Offers counseling psychology (PhD); psychology (MA, MS, PhD), including psychology (PhD); women's and gender studies (PhD); JD/PhD. *Degree requirements:* For master's, comprehensive exam, thesis or alternative; for doctorate, comprehensive exam, thesis/dissertation. *Entrance requirements:* For master's and doctorate, GRE General Test, minimum GPA of 3.0. Additional exam requirements/recommendations for international students: required—TOEFL (minimum score 550 paper-based; 80 iBT), IELTS (minimum score 6). Electronic applications accepted.

University of Hawaii at Hilo, Program in Counseling Psychology, Hilo, HI 96720-4091. Offers MA. *Entrance requirements:* Additional exam requirements/recommendations for international students: required—TOEFL, IELTS.

University of Houston, College of Education, Department of Psychological, Health and Learning Sciences, Houston, TX 77204-5023. Offers administration and supervision - higher education (M Ed); counseling (M Ed); counseling psychology (PhD); educational psychology (M Ed); school psychology (PhD); school psychology and individual differences (PhD); special education (M Ed). *Accreditation:* NCATE. *Program availability:* Part-time, evening/weekend, 100% online, blended/hybrid learning. *Faculty:* 29 full-time (21 women), 1 (woman) part-time/adjunct. *Students:* 163 full-time (138 women), 57 part-time (50 women); includes 124 minority (45 Black or African American, non-Hispanic/Latino; 2 American Indian or Alaska Native, non-Hispanic/Latino; 22 Asian, non-Hispanic/Latino; 48 Hispanic/Latino; 7 Two or more races, non-Hispanic/Latino), 16 international. Average age 30. 179 applicants, 55% accepted, 60 enrolled. In 2019, 33 master's, 8 doctorates awarded. Terminal master's awarded for partial completion of doctoral program. *Degree requirements:* For master's, comprehensive exam; for doctorate, comprehensive exam, thesis/dissertation. *Entrance requirements:* For master's, GRE, transcripts, 3 letters of recommendation, curriculum vita, goal statement; for doctorate, GRE, transcripts, 3 letters of recommendation, curriculum vita, goal statement, writing sample, interview. Additional exam requirements/recommendations for international students: required—TOEFL (minimum score 550 paper-based; 79 iBT), Duolingo English Test. *Application deadline:* For fall admission, 1/15 for domestic and international students; for spring admission, 9/15 for domestic and international students. Applications are processed on a rolling basis. Application fee: $80 ($75 for international students). Electronic applications accepted. *Financial support:* In 2019–20, 10 students received support, including 5 fellowships with full tuition reimbursements available (averaging $2,000 per year), 38 research assistantships with full tuition reimbursements available (averaging $8,203 per year), 43 teaching assistantships with full tuition reimbursements available (averaging $8,152 per year); career-related internships or fieldwork, Federal Work-Study, institutionally sponsored loans, scholarships/grants, health care benefits, and unspecified assistantships also available. Support available to part-time students. Financial award application deadline: 2/1. *Unit head:* Dr. Nathan Grant Smith, Department Chair, 713-743-7648, Fax: 713-743-4996, E-mail: ngsmith@uh.edu. *Application contact:* Bridgette Jones, Director of Student Affairs, 713-743-2978, E-mail: bajones5@uh.edu. Website: https://uh.edu/education/departments/phls/

University of Houston–Victoria, School of Arts and Sciences, Program in Psychology, Victoria, TX 77901-4450. Offers counseling psychology (MA); forensic psychology (MA); school psychology (MA). *Program availability:* Part-time, evening/weekend, online learning. *Degree requirements:* For master's, project or thesis. *Entrance requirements:* For master's, GRE General Test. Additional exam requirements/recommendations for international students: required—TOEFL (minimum score 550 paper-based). Electronic applications accepted.

University of Indianapolis, Graduate Programs, College of Applied Behavioral Sciences, Indianapolis, IN 46227-3697. Offers addictions counseling (MA); clinical psychology (Psy D); mental health counseling (MA); psychology (MA); social work (MSW). *Accreditation:* APA. *Degree requirements:* For master's, practicum; for doctorate, comprehensive exam, thesis/dissertation, 1200 hours of clinical practicum, 2000-hour internship. *Entrance requirements:* For master's, GRE, 3 letters of recommendation; for doctorate, GRE, minimum GPA of 3.0, 18 hours of course work in psychology, 3 letters of recommendation. Additional exam requirements/recommendations for international students: required—TOEFL (minimum score 550 paper-based).

The University of Iowa, Graduate College, College of Education, Department of Psychological and Quantitative Foundations, Iowa City, IA 52242-1316. Offers counseling psychology (PhD); educational measurement and statistics (MA, PhD); educational psychology (MA, PhD); school psychology (PhD, Ed S). *Accreditation:* APA. *Degree requirements:* For master's, thesis optional, exam; for doctorate, comprehensive exam, thesis/dissertation; for Ed S, exam. *Entrance requirements:* For master's, doctorate, and Ed S, GRE General Test, minimum GPA of 3.0. Additional exam requirements/recommendations for international students: required—TOEFL (minimum score 550 paper-based; 81 iBT). Electronic applications accepted.

The University of Iowa, Graduate College, College of Education, Department of Rehabilitation and Counselor Education, Iowa City, IA 52242-1316. Offers counselor education and supervision (PhD); couple and family therapy (PhD); rehabilitation and mental health counseling (MA); rehabilitation counselor education (PhD); school counseling (MA). *Accreditation:* ACA (one or more programs are accredited); CORE (one or more programs are accredited). *Degree requirements:* For master's, thesis optional, exam; for doctorate, comprehensive exam, thesis/dissertation. *Entrance requirements:* For master's and doctorate, GRE General Test, minimum GPA of 3.0. Additional exam requirements/recommendations for international students: required—TOEFL (minimum score 550 paper-based; 81 iBT). Electronic applications accepted.

The University of Kansas, Graduate Studies, School of Education, Department of Educational Psychology, Program in Counseling Psychology, Lawrence, KS 66045. Offers MS, PhD. *Accreditation:* APA (one or more programs are accredited). *Program availability:* Part-time. *Students:* 56 full-time (39 women), 1 (woman) part-time; includes 14 minority (6 Black or African American, non-Hispanic/Latino; 1 Asian, non-Hispanic/Latino; 4 Hispanic/Latino; 3 Two or more races, non-Hispanic/Latino), 3 international. Average age 27. 91 applicants, 27% accepted, 18 enrolled. In 2019, 12 master's, 4 doctorates awarded. *Entrance requirements:* For master's and doctorate, GRE General Test, minimum GPA of 3.0, resume, statement of purpose, official transcript, three letters of recommendation. Additional exam requirements/recommendations for international students: required—TOEFL, IELTS. *Application deadline:* For fall admission, 12/1 priority date for domestic and international students. Application fee: $65 ($85 for international students). Electronic applications accepted. *Expenses:* Tuition, state resident: full-time $9989. Tuition, nonresident: full-time $23,950. *International tuition:* $23,950 full-time. *Required fees:* $984; $81.99 per credit hour. Tuition and fees vary according to course load, campus/location and program. *Financial support:* Fellowships, research assistantships, teaching assistantships, career-related internships or fieldwork, scholarships/grants, and unspecified assistantships available. Financial award application deadline: 12/1. *Unit head:* Dr. David Hansen, Chair, 785-864-1874, E-mail: dhansen@ku.edu. *Application contact:* Penny Fritts, Graduate Admissions Contact, 785-864-9645, E-mail: fritts@ku.edu. Website: http://pre.soe.ku.edu/academics/cpsy/masters

University of Kentucky, Graduate School, College of Education, Program in Educational and Counseling Psychology, Lexington, KY 40506-0032. Offers counseling psychology (MS, PhD, Ed S); educational psychology (MS, PhD); school psychology (PhD, Ed S). *Accreditation:* APA (one or more programs are accredited); NCATE. *Degree requirements:* For doctorate, comprehensive exam, thesis/dissertation; for Ed S, comprehensive exam. *Entrance requirements:* For doctorate, GRE General Test, minimum graduate GPA of 3.0; for Ed S, GRE General Test. Additional exam requirements/recommendations for international students: required—TOEFL (minimum score 550 paper-based). Electronic applications accepted.

University of Lethbridge, School of Graduate Studies, Lethbridge, AB T1K 3M4, Canada. Offers addictions counseling (M Sc); agricultural biotechnology (M Sc); agricultural studies (M Sc, MA); anthropology (MA); archaeology (M Sc, MA); art (MA, MFA); biochemistry (M Sc); biological sciences (M Sc); biomolecular science (PhD); biosystems and biodiversity (PhD); Canadian studies (MA); chemistry (M Sc); computer science (M Sc); computer science and geographical information science (M Sc); counseling (MC); counseling psychology (M Ed); dramatic arts (MA); earth, space, and physical science (PhD); economics (MA); education (MA, PhD); educational leadership (M Ed); English (MA); environmental science (M Sc); evolution and behavior (PhD); exercise science (M Sc); French (MA); French/German (MA); French/Spanish (MA); general education (M Ed); geography (M Sc, MA); German (MA); health sciences (M Sc); individualized multidisciplinary (M Sc, MA); kinesiology (M Sc, MA); management (M Sc), including accounting, finance, human resource management and labor relations, information systems, international management, marketing, policy and strategy; mathematics (M Sc); music (M Mus, MA); Native American studies (MA); neuroscience (M Sc, PhD); new media (MA, MFA); nursing (M Sc, MN); philosophy (MA); physics (M Sc); political science (MA); psychology (M Sc, MA); religious studies (MA); sociology (MA); theatre and dramatic arts (MFA); theoretical and computational science (PhD); urban and regional studies (MA); women and gender studies (MA). *Program availability:* Part-time, evening/weekend. *Degree requirements:* For master's, thesis (for some programs); for doctorate, comprehensive exam, thesis/dissertation. *Entrance requirements:* For master's, GMAT (for M Sc in management), bachelor's degree in related field, minimum GPA of 3.0 during previous 20 graded semester courses, 2 years' teaching or related experience (M Ed); for doctorate, master's degree, minimum graduate GPA of 3.5. Additional exam requirements/recommendations for international students: required—TOEFL (minimum score 580 paper-based; 93 iBT). Electronic applications accepted.

University of Louisiana at Monroe, Graduate School, College of Health Sciences, Programs in Counseling Studies, Monroe, LA 71209-0001. Offers clinical mental health counseling (MS); school counseling (MS). *Accreditation:* ACA; NCATE. *Program availability:* Part-time, evening/weekend, online learning. *Faculty:* 1 (woman) full-time, 4 part-time/adjunct (2 women). *Students:* 25 full-time (22 women), 18 part-time (15 women); includes 10 minority (7 Black or African American, non-Hispanic/Latino; 1 Hispanic/Latino; 2 Two or more races, non-Hispanic/Latino). Average age 35. 89 applicants, 16% accepted, 8 enrolled. In 2019, 18 master's awarded. *Degree requirements:* For master's, thesis optional, internship. *Entrance requirements:* For master's, GRE General Test, minimum undergraduate GPA of 2.5. Additional exam requirements/recommendations for international students: required—TOEFL (minimum score 500 paper-based; 61 iBT); recommended—IELTS (minimum score 5.5). *Application deadline:* For fall admission, 3/15 for domestic and international students. Applications are processed on a rolling basis. Application fee: $55. Electronic applications accepted. *Expenses: Tuition, area resident:* Full-time $6489. Tuition, state resident: full-time $6489. Tuition, nonresident: full-time $18,989. *Required fees:* $2748. Tuition and fees vary according to course load and program. *Financial support:* In 2019–20, 7 students received support. Career-related internships or fieldwork, Federal Work-Study, scholarships/grants, and unspecified assistantships available. Financial award application deadline: 2/15; financial award applicants required to submit FAFSA. *Unit head:* Dr. Thomas Foster, Program Director of Counseling, 318-342-1298, E-mail: tfoster@ulm.edu. *Application contact:* Dr. Thomas Foster, Program Director of Counseling, 318-342-1298, E-mail: tfoster@ulm.edu. Website: http://www.ulm.edu/counseling/

University of Louisville, Graduate School, College of Education and Human Development, Department of Counseling and Human Development, Louisville, KY 40292-0001. Offers counseling and personnel services (M Ed, PhD), including art therapy (M Ed), college student personnel, counseling psychology, counselor education and supervision (PhD), educational psychology, measurement, and evaluation (PhD), mental health counseling (M Ed), school counseling (M Ed). *Accreditation:* APA; NCATE. *Program availability:* Part-time. *Faculty:* 11 full-time (7 women), 10 part-time/adjunct (6 women). *Students:* 118 full-time (95 women), 60 part-time (45 women); includes 54 minority (32 Black or African American, non-Hispanic/Latino; 1 American Indian or Alaska Native, non-Hispanic/Latino; 2 Asian, non-Hispanic/Latino; 12 Hispanic/Latino; 1 Native Hawaiian or other Pacific Islander, non-Hispanic/Latino; 6 Two or more races, non-Hispanic/Latino), 3 international. Average age 29. 118 applicants, 52% accepted, 43 enrolled. In 2019, 61 master's, 11 doctorates awarded. Terminal master's awarded for partial completion of doctoral program. *Degree requirements:* For master's, thesis optional; for doctorate, comprehensive exam, thesis/dissertation. *Entrance requirements:* For master's, professional statement, recommendation letters, resume, transcripts; for doctorate, GRE, professional statement, recommendation letters, resume, transcripts. Additional exam requirements/recommendations for international students: required—TOEFL (minimum score 550 paper-based; 79 iBT); recommended—IELTS (minimum score 6.5). *Application deadline:* For fall admission, 3/1 priority date for domestic and international students; for spring admission, 10/1 priority date for domestic and international students; for summer admission, 3/1 priority date for domestic and international students. Application fee: $65. Electronic applications accepted. *Expenses: Tuition, area resident:* Full-time $13,000; part-time $723 per credit hour. Tuition, state resident: full-time $13,000; part-time $723 per credit hour. Tuition, nonresident: full-time $27,114; part-time $1507 per credit hour. *International tuition:* $27,114 full-time. *Required fees:* $196. Tuition and fees vary according to program and reciprocity agreements. *Financial support:* In 2019–20, 73 students received support, including 3 fellowships with full tuition reimbursements available (averaging $21,024 per year), 5 research assistantships with full tuition reimbursements available (averaging $21,024 per year), 3 teaching assistantships with full tuition reimbursements available (averaging $21,024 per year); scholarships/grants, health care benefits, and unspecified assistantships also available. Financial award application deadline: 3/1; financial award applicants required to submit FAFSA. *Unit head:* Dr. Mark M. Leach, Department Chair, 502-852-0588, Fax: 502-852-0629, E-mail: m.leach@louisville.edu. *Application contact:* Dr. Margaret Pentecost, Assistant Dean for Graduate Student Success, 502-852-2628, Fax: 502-852-1417, E-mail: gedadm@louisville.edu. Website: http://www.louisville.edu/education/departments/ecpy

University of Lynchburg, Graduate Studies, M Ed Program in Clinical Mental Health Counseling, Lynchburg, VA 24501-3199. Offers M Ed. *Accreditation:* ACA. *Program availability:* Part-time, evening/weekend. *Degree requirements:* For master's, counseling internship. *Entrance requirements:* For master's, GRE, minimum GPA of 3.0 (preferred), official transcripts (bachelor's, others as relevant), three letters of recommendation, career goals statement, personal interview. Additional exam requirements/recommendations for international students: required—TOEFL (minimum score 550 paper-based; 80 iBT), IELTS (minimum score 6). Electronic applications accepted. Application fee is waived when completed online. *Expenses:* Contact institution.

The University of Manchester, Manchester Institute of Education, Manchester, United Kingdom. Offers counseling (D Couns); counseling psychology (D Couns); education (M Phil, Ed D, PhD); educational and child psychology (Ed D); educational psychology (Ed D).

Counseling Psychology

University of Mary Hardin-Baylor, Graduate Studies in Counseling, Belton, TX 76513. Offers clinical and mental health counseling (MA); marriage, family and child counseling (MA); non-clinical professional studies (MA). *Accreditation:* ACA. *Program availability:* Part-time, evening/weekend. *Faculty:* 6 full-time (3 women), 4 part-time/adjunct (2 women). *Students:* 54 full-time (41 women), 23 part-time (19 women); includes 36 minority (13 Black or African American, non-Hispanic/Latino; 1 American Indian or Alaska Native, non-Hispanic/Latino; 1 Asian, non-Hispanic/Latino; 18 Hispanic/Latino; 3 Two or more races, non-Hispanic/Latino). Average age 31. 57 applicants, 75% accepted, 25 enrolled. In 2019, 32 master's awarded. *Degree requirements:* For master's, comprehensive exam. *Entrance requirements:* For master's, GRE General Test with minimum cumulative score of 300 on verbal and quantitative portions and 3.0 on analytical section (if overall undergraduate GPA is below a 3.0), minimum cumulative undergraduate GPA of 2.75 or 3.0 on last 60 hours of course work; three letters of recommendation; interview with departmental graduate admissions committee. Additional exam requirements/recommendations for international students: required—TOEFL (minimum score 60 iBT), IELTS (minimum score 4.5). *Application deadline:* For fall admission, 6/1 for domestic students, 4/30 priority date for international students; for spring admission, 11/1 for domestic students, 9/30 priority date for international students. Applications are processed on a rolling basis. Application fee: $35 ($135 for international students). Electronic applications accepted. *Expenses: Tuition:* Full-time $16,200; part-time $10,800 per credit hour. *Required fees:* $1350; $75 per credit hour. $50 per term. Tuition and fees vary according to course load and degree level. *Financial support:* In 2019–20, 58 students received support. Federal Work-Study, unspecified assistantships, and scholarships for some active duty military personnel available. Support available to part-time students. Financial award applicants required to submit FAFSA. *Unit head:* Dr. Ty Leonard, Interim Director, Graduate Counseling, 254-295-5532, E-mail: hleonard@umhb.edu. *Application contact:* Katherine Moore, Assistant Director, Graduate Admissions, 254-295-4924, E-mail: kmoore@umhb.edu.
Website: https://go.umhb.edu/graduate/counseling/home

University of Maryland, College Park, Academic Affairs, College of Education, Department of Counseling, Higher Education and Special Education, College Park, MD 20742. Offers college student personnel (M Ed, MA); college student personnel administration (PhD); community counseling (CAGS); community/career counseling (M Ed, MA); counseling and personnel services (M Ed, MA, PhD), including art therapy (M Ed), college student personnel (M Ed), counseling and personnel services (PhD), counseling psychology (M Ed), mental health counseling (M Ed), school counseling (M Ed); counseling psychology (PhD); counselor education (PhD); rehabilitation counseling (M Ed, MA, AGSC); school counseling (M Ed, MA); school psychology (M Ed, MA, PhD). *Accreditation:* APA (one or more programs are accredited); NCATE. *Program availability:* Part-time, evening/weekend, online learning. *Degree requirements:* For master's, thesis (for some programs); for doctorate, thesis/dissertation. *Entrance requirements:* For master's, GRE General Test or MAT, minimum GPA of 3.0, 3 letters of recommendation; for doctorate, GRE General Test or MAT, minimum GPA of 3.5, 3 letters of recommendation. Additional exam requirements/recommendations for international students: required—TOEFL. Electronic applications accepted.

University of Massachusetts Boston, College of Education and Human Development, Program in Counseling and School Psychology, Boston, MA 02125-3393. Offers PhD. *Accreditation:* ACA; CORE. *Program availability:* Part-time, evening/weekend. Electronic applications accepted.

University of Massachusetts Boston, College of Education and Human Development, Program in Mental Health Counseling, Boston, MA 02125-3393. Offers MS. Electronic applications accepted.

University of Memphis, Graduate School, College of Education, Department of Counseling, Educational Psychology and Research, Memphis, TN 38152. Offers counseling (MS, Ed D), including clinical mental health counseling (MS), clinical rehabilitation counseling (MS), rehabilitation counseling (MS), school counseling (MS); counseling psychology (PhD); educational psychology and research (MS, PhD), including educational psychology, educational research. *Accreditation:* ACA (one or more programs are accredited); APA (one or more programs are accredited); CORE (one or more programs are accredited); NCATE. *Program availability:* 100% online, blended/hybrid learning. *Students:* 136 full-time (110 women), 145 part-time (117 women); includes 107 minority (81 Black or African American, non-Hispanic/Latino; 10 Asian, non-Hispanic/Latino; 11 Hispanic/Latino; 5 Two or more races, non-Hispanic/Latino), 4 international. Average age 32. 149 applicants, 53% accepted, 61 enrolled. In 2019, 30 master's, 19 doctorates awarded. *Degree requirements:* For master's, comprehensive exam, thesis or alternative, internship; for doctorate, comprehensive exam, thesis/dissertation, practicum, internship, residency, scholarly work. *Entrance requirements:* For master's, GRE General Test or MAT, minimum GPA of 2.5, letters of reference, interview; for doctorate, GRE General Test, master's degree or equivalent, letters of reference, interview, curriculum vitae, personal statement. Additional exam requirements/recommendations for international students: required—TOEFL (minimum score 550 paper-based; 79 iBT). *Application deadline:* For fall admission, 10/1 priority date for domestic students; for spring admission, 4/1 priority date for domestic students. Applications are processed on a rolling basis. Application fee: $35 ($60 for international students). Electronic applications accepted. *Expenses: Tuition, area resident:* Full-time $9216; part-time $512 per credit hour. Tuition, state resident: full-time $9216; part-time $512 per credit hour. Tuition, nonresident: full-time $12,672; part-time $704 per credit hour. *International tuition:* $16,128 full-time. *Required fees:* $1530; $85 per credit hour. Tuition and fees vary according to program. *Financial support:* Fellowships with full tuition reimbursements, research assistantships with full tuition reimbursements, teaching assistantships with full tuition reimbursements, career-related internships or fieldwork, Federal Work-Study, scholarships/grants, and unspecified assistantships available. Financial award application deadline: 2/1; financial award applicants required to submit FAFSA. *Unit head:* Dr. Steve West, Chair, 901-678-2841, Fax: 901-678-5114, E-mail: slwest@memphis.edu. *Application contact:* Stormey Warren, Graduate Programs, 901-678-2363, Fax: 901-678-4778, E-mail: shutsell@memphis.edu.
Website: http://www.memphis.edu/cepr/

University of Miami, Graduate School, School of Education and Human Development, Department of Educational and Psychological Studies, Program in Counseling Psychology, Coral Gables, FL 33124. Offers PhD. *Accreditation:* APA. *Students:* 25 full-time (18 women), 2 part-time (both women); includes 11 minority (5 Black or African American, non-Hispanic/Latino; 1 Asian, non-Hispanic/Latino; 5 Hispanic/Latino), 2 international. Average age 29. 130 applicants, 6% accepted, 5 enrolled. In 2019, 3 doctorates awarded. *Degree requirements:* For doctorate, thesis/dissertation, qualifying exam. *Entrance requirements:* For doctorate, GRE General Test. Additional exam requirements/recommendations for international students: required—TOEFL (minimum score 550 paper-based; 80 iBT); recommended—IELTS (minimum score 6.5). *Application deadline:* For fall admission, 12/1 priority date for domestic students, 10/1 priority date for international students. Application fee: $85. Electronic applications accepted. *Financial support:* Research assistantships, teaching assistantships, scholarships/grants, health care benefits, tuition waivers (full), and unspecified assistantships available. Financial award application deadline: 3/1; financial award applicants required to submit FAFSA. *Unit head:* Dr. Lydia Buki, Associate Professor and Director of Training, 305-284-2230, Fax: 305-284-3003, E-mail: l.buki@miami.edu. *Application contact:* Dr. Lydia Buki, Associate Professor and Director of Training, 305-284-2230, Fax: 305-284-3003, E-mail: l.buki@miami.edu.
Website: https://sites.education.miami.edu/counseling-psychology/

University of Minnesota, Twin Cities Campus, Graduate School, College of Liberal Arts, Department of Psychology, Program in Counseling Psychology, Minneapolis, MN 55455-0213. Offers PhD. *Accreditation:* APA. *Degree requirements:* For doctorate, comprehensive exam, thesis/dissertation, internship. *Entrance requirements:* For doctorate, GRE General Test, GRE Subject Test (recommended), 12 credits of upper-level psychology courses, including a course in statistics or psychological measurement. Additional exam requirements/recommendations for international students: required—TOEFL (minimum score 550 paper-based; 79 iBT).

University of Missouri, Office of Research and Graduate Studies, College of Education, Department of Educational, School, and Counseling Psychology, Columbia, MO 65211. Offers counseling psychology (M Ed, MA, PhD, Ed S); educational psychology (M Ed, MA, PhD, Ed S); learning and instruction (M Ed); school psychology (M Ed, MA, PhD, Ed S). *Accreditation:* APA (one or more programs are accredited). *Program availability:* Part-time. *Entrance requirements:* For master's, doctorate, and Ed S, GRE General Test, minimum GPA of 3.0. Additional exam requirements/recommendations for international students: required—TOEFL.

University of Missouri–Kansas City, School of Education, Kansas City, MO 64110-2499. Offers administration (Ed D); counseling and guidance (MA, Ed S), including mental health counseling (Ed S), school counseling (Ed S); counseling psychology (PhD); curriculum and instruction (MA, Ed S), including language and literacy (Ed S); education (PhD), including higher education administration, PK-12 education administration; educational administration (MA, Ed S), including advanced principal (Ed S), beginning principal (Ed S), district-level administration (Ed S); reading education (MA); special education (MA). *Accreditation:* NCATE. *Program availability:* Part-time, evening/weekend. *Degree requirements:* For doctorate, thesis/dissertation, internship, practicum. *Entrance requirements:* For master's, GRE, minimum GPA of 2.75, 2 letters of reference, written statement of purpose; for doctorate, GRE, minimum GPA of 3.0; for Ed S, minimum GPA of 3.0. Additional exam requirements/recommendations for international students: required—TOEFL (minimum score 550 paper-based; 80 iBT).

University of Montana, Graduate School, Phyllis J. Washington College of Education and Human Sciences, Department of Counselor Education, Missoula, MT 59812. Offers clinical mental health counseling (MA); counseling and supervision (Ed D); counselor education (Ed S); intercultural youth and family development (MA); school counseling (MA). *Accreditation:* ACA. *Degree requirements:* For doctorate, thesis/dissertation. *Entrance requirements:* For master's, doctorate, and Ed S, GRE General Test. Additional exam requirements/recommendations for international students: required—TOEFL.

University of Nebraska at Kearney, College of Education, Department of Counseling and School Psychology, Kearney, NE 68849. Offers clinical mental health counseling (MS Ed); school counseling (MS Ed), including elementary, secondary; school psychology (Ed S); student affairs (MS Ed). *Accreditation:* ACA; NCATE. *Program availability:* Part-time, evening/weekend, 100% online, blended/hybrid learning. *Faculty:* 7 full-time (4 women). *Students:* 76 full-time (63 women), 124 part-time (91 women); includes 25 minority (1 Black or African American, non-Hispanic/Latino; 3 Asian, non-Hispanic/Latino; 17 Hispanic/Latino; 4 Two or more races, non-Hispanic/Latino), 6 international. Average age 30. 61 applicants, 85% accepted, 44 enrolled. In 2019, 38 master's, 15 Ed Ss awarded. *Degree requirements:* For master's, comprehensive exam, thesis optional; for Ed S, comprehensive exam. *Entrance requirements:* For master's and Ed S, personal statement, recommendations, resume, interview. Additional exam requirements/recommendations for international students: required—TOEFL (minimum score 550 paper-based; 79 iBT), IELTS (minimum score 6.5). *Application deadline:* For fall admission, 6/15 for domestic students, 5/15 for international students; for spring admission, 10/15 for domestic students, 9/15 for international students; for summer admission, 4/15 for domestic students, 1/15 for international students. Application fee: $45. Electronic applications accepted. *Expenses: Tuition, area resident:* Full-time $4662; part-time $259 per credit hour. Tuition, nonresident: full-time $10,242; part-time $569 per credit hour. *International tuition:* $10,242 full-time. *Required fees:* $1222; $381.50 per term. Full-time tuition and fees vary according to course load, campus/location and program. *Financial support:* In 2019–20, 8 students received support, including 7 research assistantships with full tuition reimbursements available (averaging $10,980 per year), 1 teaching assistantship with full tuition reimbursement available (averaging $10,980 per year); career-related internships or fieldwork, scholarships/grants, health care benefits, and unspecified assistantships also available. Support available to part-time students. Financial award application deadline: 2/28; financial award applicants required to submit FAFSA. *Unit head:* Dr. David Hof, Chair, Counseling & School Psychology, 308-865-8320, E-mail: hofdd@unk.edu. *Application contact:* Linda Johnson, Director, Graduate Admissions and Programs, 800-717-7881, Fax: 308-865-8837, E-mail: gradstudies@unk.edu.
Website: http://www.unk.edu/academics/csp/

University of Nebraska–Lincoln, Graduate College, College of Education and Human Sciences, Department of Educational Psychology, Lincoln, NE 68588. Offers cognition, learning and development (MA); counseling psychology (MA); educational psychology (MA, Ed S); psychological studies in education (PhD), including cognition, learning and development, counseling psychology, quantitative, qualitative, and psychometric methods, school psychology; quantitative, qualitative, and psychometric methods (MA); school psychology (MA, Ed S). *Accreditation:* APA (one or more programs are accredited); NCATE. *Degree requirements:* For master's, thesis optional. *Entrance requirements:* For master's, GRE General Test. Additional exam requirements/recommendations for international students: required—TOEFL (minimum score 500 paper-based). Electronic applications accepted.

University of Nevada, Las Vegas, Graduate College, College of Education, Department of Early Childhood, Multilingual, and Special Education, Las Vegas, NV 89154-3066. Offers addiction studies (Advanced Certificate); counselor education (M Ed, MS), including clinical mental health (MS), school counseling (M Ed); early childhood education (M Ed); early childhood special education (Certificate), including infancy, preschool; English language learning (M Ed); mental health counseling (Advanced Certificate); special education (M Ed, PhD); PhD/JD. *Program availability:* Part-time. *Faculty:* 14 full-time (9 women), 18 part-time/adjunct (16 women). *Students:* 235 full-time (192 women), 225 part-time (180 women); includes 225 minority (57 Black or African American, non-Hispanic/Latino; 3 American Indian or Alaska Native, non-Hispanic/Latino; 16 Asian, non-Hispanic/Latino; 108 Hispanic/Latino; 5 Native Hawaiian or other Pacific Islander, non-Hispanic/Latino; 36 Two or more races, non-Hispanic/Latino), 15 international. Average age 35. 238 applicants, 70% accepted, 134 enrolled. In 2019, 168 master's, 3 doctorates, 1 other advanced degree awarded. *Degree requirements:* For master's, comprehensive exam (for some programs); for doctorate, comprehensive exam, thesis/dissertation; for other advanced degree, final project. *Entrance requirements:* For master's, bachelor's degree; letter of recommendation; statement of purpose; for doctorate, GRE General Test, statement of purpose; writing sample; 3 letters of recommendation. Additional exam requirements/recommendations for international students: required—TOEFL (minimum score 550 paper-based; 80 iBT), IELTS (minimum score 7). Application fee: $60 ($95 for international students). Electronic applications accepted. *Expenses:* Contact institution. *Financial support:* In 2019–20, 40 students received support, including 13 research assistantships with full tuition reimbursements available (averaging $14,231 per year), 27 teaching assistantships with full tuition reimbursements available (averaging $15,933 per year); institutionally sponsored loans, scholarships/grants, health care benefits, and unspecified assistantships also available. Financial award application deadline: 3/15; financial award applicants required to submit FAFSA. *Unit head:* Dr. Joseph Morgan, Department Chair/Professor, 702-895-3167, Fax: 702-895-3205, E-mail: ems.chair@unlv.edu. *Application contact:* Dr. Sharolyn D. Pollard-Durodola, Graduate Coordinator, 702-895-3329, Fax: 702-895-3205, E-mail: ems.gradcoord@unlv.edu. Website: http://education.unlv.edu/ecs/

The University of North Carolina at Greensboro, Graduate School, School of Education, Department of Counseling and Educational Development, Greensboro, NC 27412-5001. Offers advanced school counseling (PMC); counseling and counselor education (PhD); counseling and educational development (MS); couple and family counseling (PMC); school counseling (PMC); MS/Ed S. *Accreditation:* ACA (one or more programs are accredited); NCATE. *Degree requirements:* For master's, comprehensive exam, practicum, internship; for doctorate, comprehensive exam, thesis/dissertation. *Entrance requirements:* For master's, doctorate, and PMC, GRE General Test. Additional exam requirements/recommendations for international students: required—TOEFL. Electronic applications accepted.

The University of North Carolina at Pembroke, The Graduate School, School of Education, Programs in Counseling, Pembroke, NC 28372-1510. Offers clinical mental health counseling (MA Ed); professional school counseling (MA Ed). *Accreditation:* NCATE. *Program availability:* Part-time, evening/weekend. *Degree requirements:* For master's, comprehensive exam, thesis optional. *Entrance requirements:* For master's, GRE General Test or MAT, minimum GPA of 3.0 in major, 2.5 overall. Additional exam requirements/recommendations for international students: required—TOEFL.

University of North Dakota, Graduate School, College of Education and Human Development, Department of Counseling Psychology and Community Services, Grand Forks, ND 58202. Offers counseling (MA); counseling psychology (PhD). *Degree requirements:* For master's, comprehensive exam, thesis or alternative; for doctorate, comprehensive exam, thesis/dissertation, final examination. *Entrance requirements:* For master's, GRE General Test or MAT, minimum GPA of 3.0; for doctorate, GRE General Test, minimum GPA of 3.0. Additional exam requirements/recommendations for international students: required—TOEFL (minimum score 550 paper-based; 79 iBT), IELTS (minimum score 6.5). Electronic applications accepted.

University of Northern Colorado, Graduate School, College of Education and Behavioral Sciences, Department of Applied Psychology and Counselor Education, Program in Counseling Psychology, Greeley, CO 80639. Offers PhD. *Accreditation:* ACA; APA; NCATE. *Program availability:* Part-time, evening/weekend. *Degree requirements:* For doctorate, comprehensive exam, thesis/dissertation. *Entrance requirements:* For doctorate, GRE General Test, 3 letters of reference.

University of Northern Iowa, Graduate College, College of Social and Behavioral Sciences, School of Applied Human Sciences, MA Program in Counseling, Cedar Falls, IA 50614. Offers mental health counseling (MA); school counseling (MA). *Accreditation:* ACA. *Program availability:* Part-time, evening/weekend. *Degree requirements:* For master's, comprehensive exam, thesis or alternative. *Entrance requirements:* For master's, minimum GPA of 3.0. Additional exam requirements/recommendations for international students: required—TOEFL (minimum score 500 paper-based; 61 iBT). Electronic applications accepted.

University of North Florida, College of Arts and Sciences, Department of Psychology, Jacksonville, FL 32224. Offers counseling psychology (MAC); general psychology (MA). *Program availability:* Part-time, evening/weekend. *Degree requirements:* For master's, comprehensive exam, thesis optional, practicum. *Entrance requirements:* For master's, GRE General Test, 2 letters of recommendation, minimum GPA of 3.0 in last 60 hours of course work. Additional exam requirements/recommendations for international students: required—TOEFL (minimum score 500 paper-based; 61 iBT). Electronic applications accepted.

University of North Georgia, Department of Counseling, Cumming, GA 30040. Offers counseling (MS). Website: http://ung.edu/counseling/

University of North Texas, Toulouse Graduate School, Denton, TX 76203-5459. Offers accounting (MS); applied anthropology (MA, MS); applied behavior analysis (Certificate); applied geography (MA); applied technology and performance improvement (M Ed, MS); art education (MA); art history (MA); arts leadership (Certificate); audiology (Au D); behavior analysis (MS); behavioral science (PhD); biochemistry and molecular biology (MS); biology (MA, MS); biomedical engineering (MS); business analysis (MS); chemistry (MS); clinical health psychology (PhD); communication studies (MA, MS); computer engineering (MS); computer science (MS); counseling (M Ed, MS), including clinical mental health counseling (MS), college and university counseling, elementary school counseling, secondary school counseling; creative writing (MA); criminal justice (MS); curriculum and instruction (M Ed); decision sciences (MBA); design (MA, MFA), including fashion design (MFA), innovation studies, interior design (MFA); early childhood studies (MS); economics (MS); educational leadership (M Ed, Ed D); educational psychology (MS, PhD), including family studies (MS), gifted and talented (MS), human development (MS), learning and cognition (MS), research, measurement and evaluation (MS); electrical engineering (MS); emergency management (MPA); engineering technology (MS); English (MA); English as a second language (MA); environmental science (MS); finance (MBA, MS); financial management (MPA); French (MA); health services management (MBA); higher education (M Ed, Ed D); history (MA, MS); hospitality management (MS); human resources management (MPA); information science (MS); information systems (PhD); information technologies (MBA); interdisciplinary studies (MA, MS); international studies (MA); international sustainable tourism (MS); jazz studies (MM); journalism (MA, MJ, Graduate Certificate), including interactive and virtual digital communication (Graduate Certificate), narrative journalism (Graduate Certificate), public relations (Graduate Certificate); kinesiology (MS); linguistics (MA); local government management (MPA); logistics (PhD); logistics and supply chain management (MBA); long-term care, senior housing, and aging services (MA); management (PhD); marketing (MBA); mathematics (MA, MS); mechanical and energy engineering (MS, PhD); music (MA), including ethnomusicology, music theory, musicology, performance; music composition (PhD); music education (MM Ed, PhD); nonprofit management (MPA); operations and supply chain management (MBA); performance (MM, DMA); philosophy (MA); political science (MA); professional and technical communication (MA); radio, television and film (MA, MFA); rehabilitation counseling (Certificate); sociology (MA); Spanish (MA); special education (M Ed); speech-language pathology (MA); strategic management (MBA); studio art (MFA); teaching (M Ed); MBA/MS. *Program availability:* Part-time, evening/weekend, online learning. Terminal master's awarded for partial completion of doctoral program. *Degree requirements:* For master's, variable foreign language requirement,

comprehensive exam (for some programs), thesis (for some programs); for doctorate, variable foreign language requirement, comprehensive exam (for some programs), thesis/dissertation; for other advanced degree, variable foreign language requirement, comprehensive exam (for some programs). *Entrance requirements:* For master's and doctorate, GRE, GMAT. Additional exam requirements/recommendations for international students: required—TOEFL (minimum score 550 paper-based; 79 iBT). Electronic applications accepted.

University of Notre Dame, The Graduate School, College of Arts and Letters, Division of Social Sciences, Department of Psychology, Notre Dame, IN 46556. Offers cognitive psychology (PhD); counseling psychology (PhD); developmental psychology (PhD); quantitative psychology (PhD). *Accreditation:* APA. *Degree requirements:* For doctorate, comprehensive exam, thesis/dissertation, candidacy exam. *Entrance requirements:* For doctorate, GRE General Test, GRE Subject Test (strongly recommended). Additional exam requirements/recommendations for international students: required—TOEFL (minimum score 600 paper-based; 80 iBT). Electronic applications accepted.

University of Oregon, Graduate School, College of Education, Eugene, OR 97403. Offers communication disorders and sciences (MA, MS, PhD); counseling psychology (PhD); couples and family therapy (MS); critical and sociocultural studies in education (PhD); curriculum and teacher education (MA, MS); educational leadership (MS, D Ed, PhD); prevention science (M Ed, MS, PhD); school psychology (MS, PhD); special education (M Ed, MA, MS, PhD). *Accreditation:* ASHA. *Program availability:* Part-time. Terminal master's awarded for partial completion of doctoral program. *Degree requirements:* For master's, exam, paper, or project; for doctorate, comprehensive exam, thesis/dissertation. *Entrance requirements:* Additional exam requirements/recommendations for international students: required—TOEFL.

University of Pennsylvania, Graduate School of Education, Division of Human Development and Quantitative Methods, Program in Counseling and Mental Health Services, Philadelphia, PA 19104. Offers M Phil, MS Ed. *Students:* 82 full-time (72 women), 3 part-time (all women); includes 26 minority (6 Black or African American, non-Hispanic/Latino; 13 Asian, non-Hispanic/Latino; 6 Hispanic/Latino; 1 Two or more races, non-Hispanic/Latino), 37 international. Average age 25. 257 applicants, 54% accepted, 82 enrolled. In 2019, 73 master's awarded. Application fee: $75. Website: http://www.gse.upenn.edu/aphd/cmhs/msed

University of Phoenix - Las Vegas Campus, College of Human Services, Las Vegas, NV 89135. Offers marriage, family, and child therapy (MSC); mental health counseling (MSC); school counseling (MSC). *Program availability:* Online learning. *Entrance requirements:* For master's, minimum undergraduate GPA of 2.5, 3 years of work experience. Additional exam requirements/recommendations for international students: required—TOEFL (minimum score 550 paper-based; 79 iBT). Electronic applications accepted.

University of Phoenix - Phoenix Campus, College of Social Sciences, Tempe, AZ 85282-2371. Offers counseling (MS), including clinical mental health counseling, community counseling, counseling, marriage, family and child therapy; psychology (MS). *Program availability:* Evening/weekend, online learning. *Entrance requirements:* Additional exam requirements/recommendations for international students: required—TOEFL, TOEIC (Test of English as an International Communication), Berlitz Online English Proficiency Exam, PTE, or IELTS. Electronic applications accepted. *Expenses:* Contact institution.

University of Providence, Graduate Studies, Program in Counseling, Great Falls, MT 59405. Offers MSC. *Program availability:* Part-time, evening/weekend. *Degree requirements:* For master's, thesis optional, internship. *Entrance requirements:* For master's, GRE General Test, 3 letters of recommendation. Additional exam requirements/recommendations for international students: required—TOEFL (minimum score 500 paper-based). Electronic applications accepted.

University of Puget Sound, School of Education, Program in Counseling, Tacoma, WA 98416. Offers mental health counseling (M Ed); school counseling (M Ed). *Program availability:* Part-time. *Degree requirements:* For master's, capstone course. *Entrance requirements:* For master's, GRE General Test, interview. Additional exam requirements/recommendations for international students: required—TOEFL (minimum score 550 paper-based; 90 iBT). Electronic applications accepted. *Expenses:* Contact institution.

University of Rhode Island, Graduate School, College of Health Sciences, Department of Human Development and Family Studies, Kingston, RI 02881. Offers college student personnel (MS); human development and family studies (MS); marriage and family therapy (MS). *Accreditation:* AAMFT/COAMFTE. *Program availability:* Part-time. *Faculty:* 16 full-time (12 women). *Students:* 50 full-time (40 women), 12 part-time (11 women); includes 14 minority (4 Black or African American, non-Hispanic/Latino; 2 Asian, non-Hispanic/Latino; 5 Hispanic/Latino; 3 Two or more races, non-Hispanic/Latino), 2 international. In 2019, 25 master's awarded. *Entrance requirements:* Additional exam requirements/recommendations for international students: required—TOEFL. *Application deadline:* For fall admission, 1/15 for domestic and international students. Application fee: $65. Electronic applications accepted. *Expenses: Tuition, area resident:* Full-time $13,734; part-time $763 per credit. Tuition, state resident: full-time $13,734; part-time $763 per credit. Tuition, nonresident: full-time $26,512; part-time $1473 per credit. *International tuition:* $26,512 full-time. *Required fees:* $1780; $52 per credit. $35 per term. One-time fee: $165. *Financial support:* In 2019–20, 2 research assistantships with tuition reimbursements (averaging $4,746 per year), 5 teaching assistantships with tuition reimbursements (averaging $11,866 per year) were awarded. Financial award application deadline: 1/15; financial award applicants required to submit FAFSA. *Unit head:* Dr. Sue Adam, Chair, 401-874-5958, E-mail: suekadams@uri.edu. *Application contact:* Dr. Sue Adam, Chair, 401-874-5958, E-mail: suekadams@uri.edu. Website: http://www.uri.edu/hss/hdf/

University of Saint Francis, Graduate School, Department of Behavioral and Social Sciences, Fort Wayne, IN 46808-3994. Offers clinical mental health counseling (MS, Post Master's Certificate); psychology (MS); school counseling (MS Ed). *Program availability:* Part-time, evening/weekend. *Faculty:* 6 full-time (2 women), 1 part-time/adjunct (0 women). *Students:* 21 full-time (17 women), 9 part-time (8 women); includes 4 minority (2 Black or African American, non-Hispanic/Latino; 1 Asian, non-Hispanic/Latino; 1 Hispanic/Latino), 1 international. Average age 29. 25 applicants, 92% accepted, 17 enrolled. In 2019, 13 master's awarded. *Entrance requirements:* Additional exam requirements/recommendations for international students: required—TOEFL (minimum score 550 paper-based), IELTS (minimum score 6.5). *Application deadline:* Applications are processed on a rolling basis. Electronic applications accepted. *Expenses: Tuition:* Full-time $9450; part-time $525 per semester hour. *Required fees:* $330 per semester. Tuition and fees vary according to course load, degree level, campus/location and program. *Financial support:* Applicants required to submit FAFSA. *Unit head:* Dr. John Brinkman, Director for the Department of Psychology and Counseling, 260-399-7700 Ext. 8425, E-mail: jbrinkman@sf.edu. *Application contact:* Kyle Richardson, Associate Director of Enrollment Management, 260-399-7700 Ext. 6310, Fax: 260-399-8152, E-mail: krichardson@sf.edu. Website: https://admissions.sf.edu/graduate/

Counseling Psychology

University of Saint Joseph, Department of Counseling and Applied Behavioral Studies, West Hartford, CT 06117-2700. Offers clinical mental health counseling (MA); school counseling (MA). *Accreditation:* ACA. *Program availability:* Part-time, evening/weekend. *Degree requirements:* For master's, comprehensive exam, thesis optional. *Entrance requirements:* For master's, 2 letters of recommendation. Electronic applications accepted. Application fee is waived when completed online.

University of Saint Mary, Graduate Programs, Program in Counseling Psychology, Leavenworth, KS 66048-5082. Offers MA. *Program availability:* Part-time, evening/weekend. *Students:* 34 full-time (29 women), 5 part-time (4 women); includes 9 minority (1 Asian, non-Hispanic/Latino; 7 Hispanic/Latino; 1 Two or more races, non-Hispanic/Latino). Average age 35. In 2019, 11 master's awarded. *Entrance requirements:* For master's, Bachelor's degree in psychology from accredited college, official transcripts, minimum GPA of 2.75, three professional recommendations, essay. *Application deadline:* Applications are processed on a rolling basis. Application fee: $25. Electronic applications accepted. *Expenses:* $640 per credit hour. *Financial support:* Unspecified assistantships available. Financial award applicants required to submit FAFSA. *Unit head:* Dr. David Strohm, Director of Undergraduate and Graduate Psychology Programs, 913-319-3012, E-mail: strohm57@stmary.edu. *Application contact:* Dr. David Strohm, Director of Undergraduate and Graduate Psychology Programs, 913-319-3012, E-mail: strohm57@stmary.edu.
Website: https://www.stmary.edu/success/masters-counseling-psych

University of St. Thomas, College of Education, Leadership and Counseling, Graduate School of Professional Psychology, St. Paul, MN 55105-1096. Offers counseling psychology (MA, Psy D). *Accreditation:* APA. *Program availability:* Part-time, evening/weekend. *Degree requirements:* For master's, comprehensive exam, practicum; for doctorate, comprehensive exam, thesis/dissertation, qualifying exam, practicum, internship. *Entrance requirements:* For master's, GRE, minimum GPA of 2.75, letters of recommendation, personal statement; for doctorate, GRE, minimum GPA of 3.2, letters of recommendation, personal statement. Additional exam requirements/recommendations for international students: required—TOEFL (minimum score 550 paper-based; 80 iBT). Electronic applications accepted. *Expenses:* Contact institution.

University of San Diego, School of Leadership and Education Sciences, Department of Counseling and Marital and Family Therapy, San Diego, CA 92110-2492. Offers clinical mental health counseling (MA); marital and family therapy (MA); school counseling (MA). *Accreditation:* ACA. *Program availability:* Part-time, evening/weekend. *Faculty:* 14 full-time (8 women), 24 part-time/adjunct (14 women). *Students:* 178 full-time (160 women), 47 part-time (41 women); includes 106 minority (9 Black or African American, non-Hispanic/Latino; 21 Asian, non-Hispanic/Latino; 59 Hispanic/Latino; 17 Two or more races, non-Hispanic/Latino), 5 international. Average age 27. 391 applicants, 42% accepted, 88 enrolled. In 2019, 96 master's awarded. *Degree requirements:* For master's, comprehensive exam, international experience. *Entrance requirements:* For master's, GRE or GMAT (minimum overall score in 50th percentile), group interview with faculty. Additional exam requirements/recommendations for international students: required—TOEFL (minimum score 580 paper-based; 83 iBT), TWE. *Application deadline:* For fall admission, 2/10 for domestic and international students. Applications are processed on a rolling basis. Application fee: $45. Electronic applications accepted. *Financial support:* In 2019–20, 199 students received support. Career-related internships or fieldwork, Federal Work-Study, institutionally sponsored loans, scholarships/grants, unspecified assistantships, and stipends available. Support available to part-time students. Financial award application deadline: 4/1; financial award applicants required to submit FAFSA. *Unit head:* Dr. Wendell Callahan, Director, 619-260-7988, E-mail: wcallahan@sandiego.edu. *Application contact:* Erika Garwood, Director of Admissions and Enrollment, 619-260-4524, Fax: 619-260-4158, E-mail: grads@sandiego.edu.
Website: http://www.sandiego.edu/soles/counseling-and-marital-and-family-therapy//

University of San Francisco, School of Education, Department of Counseling Psychology, San Francisco, CA 94117. Offers counseling (MA), including educational counseling, life transitions counseling, marital and family therapy. *Program availability:* Part-time. *Faculty:* 8 full-time (all women), 30 part-time/adjunct (18 women). *Students:* 364 full-time (302 women), 6 part-time (3 women); includes 215 minority (22 Black or African American, non-Hispanic/Latino; 2 American Indian or Alaska Native, non-Hispanic/Latino; 48 Asian, non-Hispanic/Latino; 123 Hispanic/Latino; 1 Native Hawaiian or other Pacific Islander, non-Hispanic/Latino; 19 Two or more races, non-Hispanic/Latino), 3 international. Average age 29. 351 applicants, 66% accepted, 137 enrolled. In 2019, 119 master's awarded. *Entrance requirements:* Additional exam requirements/recommendations for international students: required—TOEFL, IELTS, PTE. *Application deadline:* For fall admission, 3/1 priority date for domestic students, 3/1 for international students; for spring admission, 10/15 priority date for domestic students, 10/15 for international students. Applications are processed on a rolling basis. Application fee: $55 ($65 for international students). Electronic applications accepted. *Financial support:* Fellowships, research assistantships, and teaching assistantships available. Financial award application deadline: 3/2; financial award applicants required to submit FAFSA. *Unit head:* Dr. Christine Yeh, Chair, 415-422-6868. *Application contact:* Peter Cole, Admission Coordinator, 415-422-5467, E-mail: schoolofeducation@usfca.edu.

University of Saskatchewan, College of Graduate and Postdoctoral Studies, College of Education, Department of Educational Psychology and Special Education, Saskatoon, SK S7N 5A2, Canada. Offers measurement and evaluation (M Ed, PhD); school and counseling psychology (M Ed, PhD); special education (M Ed, PhD). *Degree requirements:* For master's, thesis (for some programs); for doctorate, comprehensive exam (for some programs), thesis/dissertation. *Entrance requirements:* Additional exam requirements/recommendations for international students: required—TOEFL (minimum score 80 iBT); recommended—IELTS (minimum score 6.5). Electronic applications accepted.

The University of Scranton, Panuska College of Professional Studies, Department of Counseling and Human Services, Program in Clinical Mental Health Counseling, Scranton, PA 18510. Offers MS. *Accreditation:* ACA. *Program availability:* Part-time, evening/weekend. *Degree requirements:* For master's, comprehensive exam (for some programs), thesis (for some programs), capstone experience. *Entrance requirements:* For master's, minimum GPA of 3.0, three letters of reference. Additional exam requirements/recommendations for international students: required—TOEFL (minimum score 500 paper-based; 80 iBT), IELTS (minimum score 6.5). Electronic applications accepted.

University of South Africa, College of Human Sciences, Pretoria, South Africa. Offers adult education (M Ed); African languages (MA, PhD); African politics (MA, PhD); Afrikaans (MA, PhD); ancient history (MA, PhD); ancient Near Eastern studies (MA, PhD); anthropology (MA, PhD); applied linguistics (MA); Arabic (MA, PhD); archaeology (MA); art history (MA); Biblical archaeology (MA); Biblical studies (M Th, D Th, PhD); Christian spirituality (M Th, D Th); church history (M Th, D Th); classical studies (MA, PhD); clinical psychology (MA); communication (MA, PhD); comparative education (M Ed, Ed D); consulting psychology (D Admin, D Com, PhD); curriculum studies (M Ed, Ed D); development studies (M Admin, MA, D Admin, PhD); didactics (M Ed, Ed D); education (M Tech); education management (M Ed, Ed D); educational psychology (M Ed); English (MA); environmental education (M Ed); French (MA, PhD); German (MA, PhD); Greek (MA); guidance and counseling (M Ed); health studies (MA, PhD), including health sciences education (MA), health services management (MA), medical and surgical nursing science (critical care general) (MA), midwifery and neonatal nursing science (MA), trauma and emergency care (MA); history (MA, PhD); history of education (Ed D); inclusive education (M Ed, Ed D); information and communications technology policy and regulation (MA); information science (MA, MIS, PhD); international politics (MA, PhD); Islamic studies (MA, PhD); Italian (MA, PhD); Judaica (MA, PhD); linguistics (MA, PhD); mathematical education (M Ed); mathematics education (MA); missiology (M Th, D Th); modern Hebrew (MA, PhD); musicology (MA, MMus, D Mus, PhD); natural science education (M Ed); New Testament (M Th, D Th); Old Testament (D Th); pastoral therapy (M Th, D Th); philosophy (MA); philosophy of education (M Ed, Ed D); politics (MA, PhD); Portuguese (MA, PhD); practical theology (M Th, D Th); psychology (MA, MS, PhD); psychology of education (M Ed, Ed D); public health (MA); religious studies (MA, D Th, PhD); Romance languages (MA); Russian (MA, PhD); Semitic languages (MA, PhD); social behavior studies in HIV/AIDS (MA); social science (mental health) (MA); social science in development studies (MA); social science in psychology (MA); social science in social work (MA); social science in sociology (MA); social work (MSW, DSW, PhD); socio-education (M Ed, Ed D); sociolinguistics (MA); sociology (MA, PhD); Spanish (MA, PhD); systematic theology (M Th, D Th); TESOL (teaching English to speakers of other languages) (MA); theological ethics (M Th, D Th); theory of literature (MA, PhD); urban ministries (D Th); urban ministry (M Th).

University of South Alabama, College of Education and Professional Studies, Department of Counseling and Instructional Sciences, Mobile, AL 36688-0002. Offers clinical mental health counseling (MS); educational media (M Ed); educational media and technology (MS); instructional design and development (MS, PhD); instructional leadership (Ed S); school counseling (M Ed). *Accreditation:* NCATE. *Program availability:* Part-time. *Faculty:* 9 full-time (6 women), 5 part-time/adjunct (all women). *Students:* 105 full-time (85 women), 22 part-time (19 women); includes 42 minority (34 Black or African American, non-Hispanic/Latino; 1 American Indian or Alaska Native, non-Hispanic/Latino; 2 Asian, non-Hispanic/Latino; 2 Hispanic/Latino; 3 Two or more races, non-Hispanic/Latino), 4 international. Average age 35. 51 applicants, 96% accepted, 38 enrolled. In 2019, 27 master's, 2 doctorates, 1 other advanced degree awarded. *Degree requirements:* For master's, comprehensive exam, thesis optional; for doctorate, comprehensive exam, thesis/dissertation. *Entrance requirements:* For master's, GRE General Test or MAT; for doctorate, GRE. Additional exam requirements/recommendations for international students: required—TOEFL (minimum score 525 paper-based; 71 iBT). *Application deadline:* For fall admission, 8/18 for domestic students, 7/18 for international students; for spring admission, 1/10 for domestic students, 12/10 for international students; for summer admission, 5/31 for domestic and international students. Applications are processed on a rolling basis. Application fee: $35. Electronic applications accepted. *Expenses: Tuition, area resident:* Part-time $442 per credit hour. Tuition, state resident: full-time $10,608; part-time $442 per credit hour. Tuition, nonresident: full-time $21,216; part-time $884 per credit hour. *Financial support:* Fellowships, research assistantships, teaching assistantships, career-related internships or fieldwork, Federal Work-Study, institutionally sponsored loans, scholarships/grants, and unspecified assistantships available. Support available to part-time students. Financial award application deadline: 3/31; financial award applicants required to submit FAFSA. *Unit head:* Dr. Tres Stefurak, Department Chair, 251-380-2734, Fax: 251-380-2713, E-mail: jstefurak@southalabama.edu. *Application contact:* Dr. James Van Haneghan, Graduate Coordinator, 251-380-2760, Fax: 251-380-2713, E-mail: jvanhane@southalabama.edu.
Website: http://www.southalabama.edu/colleges/ceps/cins/

University of South Alabama, Graduate School, Program in Clinical and Counseling Psychology, Mobile, AL 36688-0002. Offers PhD. *Accreditation:* ACA. *Faculty:* 7 full-time (2 women). *Students:* 22 full-time (16 women), 8 part-time (5 women); includes 6 minority (4 Black or African American, non-Hispanic/Latino; 1 Asian, non-Hispanic/Latino; 1 Two or more races, non-Hispanic/Latino), 1 international. Average age 29. 7 applicants, 100% accepted, 7 enrolled. In 2019, 7 doctorates awarded. *Degree requirements:* For doctorate, thesis/dissertation, capstone internship. *Entrance requirements:* For doctorate, GRE. Additional exam requirements/recommendations for international students: required—TOEFL (minimum score 525 paper-based; 71 iBT). *Application deadline:* For fall admission, 12/15 for domestic and international students. Application fee: $50. Electronic applications accepted. *Expenses: Tuition, area resident:* Part-time $442 per credit hour. Tuition, state resident: full-time $10,608; part-time $442 per credit hour. Tuition, nonresident: full-time $21,216; part-time $884 per credit hour. *Financial support:* Fellowships, research assistantships, teaching assistantships, career-related internships or fieldwork, institutionally sponsored loans, scholarships/grants, and unspecified assistantships available. Support available to part-time students. Financial award application deadline: 3/31; financial award applicants required to submit FAFSA. *Unit head:* Dr. Tres Stefurak, Chair, Department of Counseling & Instructional Sciences, College of Education & Professional Studies, 251-460-6622, E-mail: jstefurak@southalabama.edu. *Application contact:* Dr. Joe Currier, Director of Clinical Training, 251-460-6622, E-mail: jcurrier@southalabama.edu.
Website: http://www.southalabama.edu/graduateschool/ccp

University of South Dakota, Graduate School, School of Education, Division of Counseling and Psychology in Education, Vermillion, SD 57069. Offers counseling (MA, PhD, Ed S); human development and educational psychology (MA, PhD, Ed S); mental health counseling (Certificate); school psychology (PhD, Ed S). *Accreditation:* ACA (one or more programs are accredited); NCATE. *Program availability:* Part-time. *Degree requirements:* For master's and other advanced degree, comprehensive exam, thesis or alternative; for doctorate, comprehensive exam, thesis/dissertation. *Entrance requirements:* For master's and doctorate, GRE General Test, minimum GPA of 3.0. Additional exam requirements/recommendations for international students: required—TOEFL (minimum score 550 paper-based; 79 iBT). Electronic applications accepted.

University of Southern Maine, College of Management and Human Service, School of Education and Human Development, Program in Counselor Education, Portland, ME 04103. Offers clinical mental health counseling (MS); counseling (CAS); culturally responsive practices in education and human development (CGS); mental health rehabilitation technician/community (CGS); rehabilitation counseling (MS); school counseling (MS); substance abuse counseling (CGS). *Accreditation:* ACA (one or more programs are accredited); CORE; TEAC. *Program availability:* Part-time, evening/weekend. *Degree requirements:* For master's, comprehensive exam, thesis or alternative; for other advanced degree, thesis or alternative. *Entrance requirements:* For master's, GRE General Test or MAT, interview; for other advanced degree, master's degree. Additional exam requirements/recommendations for international students: required—TOEFL (minimum score 550 paper-based; 79 iBT). Electronic applications accepted. *Expenses: Tuition, area resident:* Full-time $864; part-time $432 per credit hour. Tuition, state resident: full-time $864; part-time $432 per credit hour. Tuition, nonresident: full-time $2372; part-time $1186 per credit hour. *Required fees:* $141; $108 per credit hour. Tuition and fees vary according to course load.

University of South Florida, College of Behavioral and Community Sciences, Department of Child and Family Studies, Tampa, FL 33620-9951. Offers applied behavior analysis (MA, MS, PhD); behavioral and community sciences (PhD); child and

adolescent behavioral health (MS), including developmental disabilities, leadership in child and adolescent health, translational research and evaluation, youth and behavioral health; rehabilitation and mental health counseling (MA), including addictions and substance abuse counseling, marriage and family therapy. *Accreditation:* ACA. *Faculty:* 21 full-time (13 women), 3 part-time/adjunct (all women). *Students:* 184 full-time (157 women), 104 part-time (88 women); includes 113 minority (42 Black or African American, non-Hispanic/Latino; 4 Asian, non-Hispanic/Latino; 54 Hispanic/Latino; 1 Native Hawaiian or other Pacific Islander, non-Hispanic/Latino; 12 Two or more races, non-Hispanic/Latino), 7 international. Average age 27. 310 applicants, 51% accepted, 92 enrolled. In 2019, 127 master's, 8 doctorates awarded. *Degree requirements:* For master's, comprehensive exam, thesis (for some programs); for doctorate, comprehensive exam, thesis/dissertation, Behavior Analyst Board Certification Exam. *Entrance requirements:* For master's, GRE General Test, 3.00 GPA; 3 letters of reference; resume or CV; statement of purpose; writing sample; undergraduate statistics or research methods course (for Rehab and Mental Health Counseling); for doctorate, GRE General Test, master's degree in behavioral analysis or closely-related field; minimum GPA of 3.5 in graduate course work; three letters of recommendation; campus visit with faculty interview; personal statement; curriculum vitae; evidence of research experiences and expertise; campus visit and interview. Additional exam requirements/recommendations for international students: required—TOEFL, TOEFL (minimum score 550 paper-based; 79 iBT) or IELTS (minimum score 6.5). *Application deadline:* For fall admission, 12/5 for domestic and international students. Application fee: $30. *Financial support:* In 2019–20, 57 students received support. Unspecified assistantships available. *Unit head:* Jason Anthony, Professor and Director, Rightpath Research and Innovation Center, 813-974-6009, E-mail: jasonanthony@usf.edu. *Application contact:* Dr. Raymond G. Miltenberger, Professor/Director of Master's Program, 813-974-5079, Fax: 813-974-6115, E-mail: miltenbe@usf.edu.
Website: http://cfs.cbcs.usf.edu/

University of South Florida, Innovative Education, Tampa, FL 33620-9951. Offers adult, career and higher education (Graduate Certificate), including college teaching, leadership in developing human resources, leadership in higher education; Africana studies (Graduate Certificate), including diasporas and health disparities, genocide and human rights; aging studies (Graduate Certificate), including gerontology; art research (Graduate Certificate), including museum studies; business foundations (Graduate Certificate); chemical and biomedical engineering (Graduate Certificate), including materials science and engineering, water, health and sustainability; child and family studies (Graduate Certificate), including positive behavior support; civil and industrial engineering (Graduate Certificate), including transportation systems analysis; community and family health (Graduate Certificate), including maternal and child health, social marketing and public health, violence and injury: prevention and intervention, women's health; criminology (Graduate Certificate), including criminal justice administration; data science for public administration (Graduate Certificate); digital humanities (Graduate Certificate); educational measurement and research (Graduate Certificate), including evaluation; English (Graduate Certificate), including comparative literary studies, creative writing, professional and technical communication; entrepreneurship (Graduate Certificate); environmental health (Graduate Certificate), including safety management; epidemiology and biostatistics (Graduate Certificate), including applied biostatistics, biostatistics, concepts and tools of epidemiology, epidemiology, epidemiology of infectious diseases; geography, environment and planning (Graduate Certificate), including community development, environmental policy and management, geographical information systems; geology (Graduate Certificate), including hydrogeology; global health (Graduate Certificate), including disaster management, global health and Latin American and Caribbean studies, global health practice, humanitarian assistance, infection control; government and international affairs (Graduate Certificate), including Cuban studies, globalization studies; health policy and management (Graduate Certificate), including health management and leadership, public health policy and programs; hearing specialist: early intervention (Graduate Certificate); industrial and management systems engineering (Graduate Certificate), including systems engineering, technology management; information studies (Graduate Certificate), including school library media specialist; information systems/decision sciences (Graduate Certificate), including analytics and business intelligence; instructional technology (Graduate Certificate), including distance education, Florida digital/virtual educator, instructional design, multimedia design, Web design; internal medicine, bioethics and medical humanities (Graduate Certificate), including biomedical ethics; Latin American and Caribbean studies (Graduate Certificate); leadership for coastal resiliency planning (Graduate Certificate); mass communications (Graduate Certificate), including multimedia journalism; mathematics and statistics (Graduate Certificate), including mathematics; medicine (Graduate Certificate), including aging and neuroscience, bioinformatics, biotechnology, brain fitness and memory management, clinical investigation, hand and upper limb rehabilitation, health informatics, health sciences, integrative weight management, intellectual property, medicine and gender, metabolic and nutritional medicine, metabolic cardiology, pharmacy sciences; national and competitive intelligence (Graduate Certificate); nursing (Graduate Certificate), including simulation based academic fellowship in advanced pain management; psychological and social foundations (Graduate Certificate), including career counseling, college teaching, diversity in education, mental health counseling, school counseling; public affairs (Graduate Certificate), including nonprofit management, public management, research administration; public health (Graduate Certificate), including assessing chemical toxicity and public health risks, health equity, pharmacoepidemiology, public health generalist, toxicology, translational research in adolescent behavioral health; public health practices (Graduate Certificate), including planning for healthy communities; rehabilitation and mental health counseling (Graduate Certificate), including integrative mental health care, marriage and family therapy, rehabilitation technology; secondary education (Graduate Certificate), including ESOL, foreign language education: culture and content, foreign language education: professional; social work (Graduate Certificate), including geriatric social work/clinical gerontology; special education (Graduate Certificate), including autism spectrum disorder, disabilities education: severe/profound; world languages (Graduate Certificate), including teaching English as a second language (TESL) or foreign language. *Unit head:* Dr. Cynthia DeLuca, Associate Vice President and Assistant Vice Provost, 813-974-3077, Fax: 813-974-7061, E-mail: deluca@usf.edu. *Application contact:* Owen Hooper, Director, Summer and Alternative Calendar Programs, 813-974-6917, E-mail: hooper@usf.edu.
Website: http://www.usf.edu/innovative-education/

The University of Tennessee, Graduate School, College of Education, Health and Human Sciences, Department of Educational Psychology and Counseling, Knoxville, TN 37996. Offers adult education (MS); applied educational psychology (MS); collaborative learning (Ed D); college student personnel (MS); mental health counseling (MS); rehabilitation counseling (MS); school counseling (MS). *Accreditation:* ACA (one or more programs are accredited); CORE (one or more programs are accredited); NCATE. *Program availability:* Part-time, evening/weekend. *Degree requirements:* For master's, thesis optional. *Entrance requirements:* For master's, GRE General Test, minimum GPA of 2.7. Additional exam requirements/recommendations for international students: required—TOEFL. Electronic applications accepted.

The University of Texas at Austin, Graduate School, College of Education, Department of Educational Psychology, Austin, TX 78712-1111. Offers academic educational psychology (M Ed, MA); counseling psychology (PhD); counselor education (M Ed); human development, culture and learning sciences (PhD); program evaluation (MA); quantitative methods (M Ed, MA, PhD); school psychology (MA, PhD). *Accreditation:* APA (one or more programs are accredited). *Degree requirements:* For master's, thesis optional; for doctorate, thesis/dissertation. *Entrance requirements:* For master's and doctorate, GRE General Test, 3 letters of recommendation. Additional exam requirements/recommendations for international students: required—TOEFL.

The University of Texas at Tyler, College of Education and Psychology, Department of Psychology and Counseling, Tyler, TX 75799-0001. Offers clinical psychology (MS), including neuropsychology, school psychology; counseling psychology (MA), including general, marriage and family; interdisciplinary studies (MSIS); school counseling (MA). *Program availability:* Part-time, evening/weekend. *Faculty:* 12 full-time (5 women), 6 part-time/adjunct (3 women). *Students:* 131 full-time (103 women), 83 part-time (67 women); includes 67 minority (10 Black or African American, non-Hispanic/Latino; 1 American Indian or Alaska Native, non-Hispanic/Latino; 7 Asian, non-Hispanic/Latino; 41 Hispanic/Latino; 8 Two or more races, non-Hispanic/Latino), 8 international. Average age 30. 130 applicants, 65% accepted, 47 enrolled. In 2019, 94 master's awarded. *Degree requirements:* For master's, comprehensive exam, thesis optional. *Entrance requirements:* For master's, GRE General Test, minimum GPA of 3.0. Additional exam requirements/recommendations for international students: required—TOEFL. *Application deadline:* For fall admission, 8/17 priority date for domestic students, 7/1 priority date for international students; for spring admission, 12/21 priority date for domestic students, 11/1 priority date for international students. Application fee: $25 ($50 for international students). Electronic applications accepted. *Financial support:* In 2019–20, fellowships with partial tuition reimbursements (averaging $3,000 per year) were awarded; research assistantships, teaching assistantships, career-related internships or fieldwork, Federal Work-Study, and institutionally sponsored loans also available. Support available to part-time students. Financial award application deadline: 7/1. *Unit head:* Dr. Charles B. Barke, Chair, 903-565-5875, E-mail: cbarke@uttyler.edu. *Application contact:* Dr. Charles B. Barke, Chair, 903-565-5875, E-mail: cbarke@uttyler.edu.
Website: http://www.uttyler.edu/psychology/

University of the Cumberlands, Program in Professional Counseling, Williamsburg, KY 40769-1372. Offers MA. *Accreditation:* ACA. *Program availability:* Part-time, evening/weekend, online learning. Electronic applications accepted.

University of the District of Columbia, College of Arts and Sciences, Program in Counseling, Washington, DC 20008-1175. Offers MS. *Accreditation:* ACA.

University of the Southwest, Graduate Programs, Hobbs, NM 88240-9129. Offers business administration (MBA); curriculum and instruction (MSE); curriculum and instruction: bilingual (MSE); curriculum and instruction: TESOL (MSE); early childhood education (MSE); educational administration (MSE); mental health counseling (MSE); school counseling (MSE); special education (MSE); sports management (MBA). *Program availability:* Part-time, evening/weekend, online learning. *Degree requirements:* For master's, comprehensive exam, thesis (for some programs). *Entrance requirements:* Additional exam requirements/recommendations for international students: recommended—TOEFL. Electronic applications accepted.

University of Utah, Graduate School, College of Education, Department of Educational Psychology, Salt Lake City, UT 84112. Offers clinical mental health counseling (M Ed); counseling psychology (PhD); elementary education (M Ed); instructional design and educational technology (M Ed); instructional design and technology (MS); learning and cognition (MS, PhD); reading and literacy (M Ed, PhD); school counseling (M Ed); school psychology (M Ed, PhD, Ed S); statistics (M Stat). *Accreditation:* APA (one or more programs are accredited). *Faculty:* 25 full-time (15 women), 7 part-time/adjunct (4 women). *Students:* 237 full-time (159 women); includes 37 minority (19 Asian, non-Hispanic/Latino; 9 Hispanic/Latino; 9 Two or more races, non-Hispanic/Latino). Average age 27. 262 applicants, 24% accepted, 54 enrolled. In 2019, 62 master's, 8 doctorates awarded. Terminal master's awarded for partial completion of doctoral program. *Degree requirements:* For master's, comprehensive exam, thesis (for some programs); for doctorate, comprehensive exam, thesis/dissertation. *Entrance requirements:* For master's and doctorate, graduation application, transcripts, GRE scores, CV/resume, personal statement, letters of recommendation. Additional exam requirements/recommendations for international students: required—TOEFL (minimum score 80 paper-based; 80 iBT), IELTS (minimum score 6.5). *Application deadline:* For fall admission, 12/15 for domestic and international students; for spring admission, 7/15 for domestic and international students; for summer admission, 3/15 for domestic and international students. Application fee: $55 ($75 for international students). Electronic applications accepted. *Expenses:* Tuition, state resident: full-time $7085; part-time $272.51 per credit hour. Tuition, nonresident: full-time $24,937; part-time $959.12 per credit hour. *Required fees:* $880.52; $880.52 per semester. Tuition and fees vary according to degree level, program and student level. *Financial support:* In 2019–20, 86 students received support, including 5 fellowships with full and partial tuition reimbursements available (averaging $11,500 per year), 14 research assistantships with full and partial tuition reimbursements available (averaging $15,900 per year), 2 teaching assistantships with full and partial tuition reimbursements available (averaging $12,560 per year); scholarships/grants, health care benefits, and unspecified assistantships also available. Financial award application deadline: 3/30. *Unit head:* Dr. Jason Burrow-Sanchez, Chair, Educational Psychology, 801-581-7148, Fax: 801-581-5566, E-mail: jason.burrow-sanchez@utah.edu. *Application contact:* JoLynn N. Yates, Academic Coordinator, 801-581-6811, Fax: 801-581-5566, E-mail: jo.yates@utah.edu.
Website: http://www.ed.utah.edu/edps/

University of Vermont, Graduate College, College of Education and Social Services, Counseling Program, Burlington, VT 05405. Offers counseling (MS), including clinical mental health, school counseling. *Accreditation:* ACA; NCATE. *Entrance requirements:* For master's, resume. Additional exam requirements/recommendations for international students: required—TOEFL (minimum score 550 paper-based, 90 iBT) or IELTS (6.5). Electronic applications accepted.

University of Victoria, Faculty of Graduate Studies, Faculty of Education, Department of Educational Psychology and Leadership Studies, Victoria, BC V8W 2Y2, Canada. Offers aboriginal communities counseling (M Ed); counseling (M Ed, MA); educational psychology (M Ed, MA, PhD), including counseling psychology (M Ed, MA), leadership studies (PhD), learning and development (MA, PhD), measurement and evaluation, special education (M Ed, MA); leadership studies (M Ed, MA). *Program availability:* Part-time. *Degree requirements:* For master's, thesis (for some programs), comprehensive exam (M Ed); for doctorate, comprehensive exam, thesis/dissertation, candidacy exam. *Entrance requirements:* For master's, 2 years of work experience in a relevant field; for doctorate, GRE, 2 years of work experience in a relevant field, minimum B average. Additional exam requirements/recommendations for international students: required—TOEFL (minimum score 575 paper-based), IELTS (minimum score 7).

The University of Western Ontario, School of Graduate and Postdoctoral Studies, Faculty of Social Science, Faculty of Education, Program in Counseling Psychology,

London, ON N6A 3K7, Canada. Offers M Ed. *Program availability:* Part-time. *Entrance requirements:* For master's, minimum B average, 3 years' experience in helping profession.

University of West Florida, Usha Kundu, MD College of Health, Department of Psychology, Pensacola, FL 32514-5750. Offers applied experimental (MA); counseling (MA); industrial-organizational (MA). *Program availability:* Part-time. *Degree requirements:* For master's, thesis (for some programs). *Entrance requirements:* For master's, GRE, official transcripts; minimum GPA of 3.0; writing sample; three letters of reference; field experience or skill sets; oral interview (for counseling specialization). Additional exam requirements/recommendations for international students: required—TOEFL (minimum score 550 paper-based).

University of Wisconsin–Madison, Graduate School, School of Education, Department of Counseling Psychology, Program in Counseling Psychology, Madison, WI 53706-1380. Offers PhD. *Accreditation:* APA. *Degree requirements:* For doctorate, thesis/dissertation.

University of Wisconsin–Milwaukee, Graduate School, School of Education, Department of Educational Psychology, Milwaukee, WI 53201-0413. Offers children's mental health for school professionals (Graduate Certificate); counseling psychology (PhD); educational statistics and measurement (MS, PhD); learning and development (MS, PhD); multicultural knowledge of mental health practices (Graduate Certificate); school counseling (MS, Graduate Certificate); school psychology (MS, PhD, Ed S). *Accreditation:* APA. *Program availability:* Part-time. *Degree requirements:* For master's, comprehensive exam, thesis; for doctorate, thesis/dissertation. *Entrance requirements:* For master's, minimum GPA of 3.0; for doctorate, GRE General Test, minimum GPA of 3.0. Additional exam requirements/recommendations for international students: required—TOEFL (minimum score 550 paper-based; 79 iBT), IELTS (minimum score 6.5). Electronic applications accepted.

University of Wisconsin–Stout, Graduate School, College of Education, Health and Human Sciences, School of Education, Program in School Counseling, Menomonie, WI 54751. Offers MS. *Accreditation:* ACA. *Program availability:* Part-time. *Degree requirements:* For master's, thesis. *Entrance requirements:* For master's, minimum GPA of 2.75. Additional exam requirements/recommendations for international students: required—TOEFL (minimum score 500 paper-based; 61 iBT). Electronic applications accepted.

Utah State University, School of Graduate Studies, Emma Eccles Jones College of Education and Human Services, Department of Psychology, Logan, UT 84322. Offers clinical/counseling/school psychology (PhD); research and evaluation methodology (PhD); school counseling (MS); school psychology (MS). *Accreditation:* APA (one or more programs are accredited). *Program availability:* Part-time, evening/weekend, online learning. Terminal master's awarded for partial completion of doctoral program. *Degree requirements:* For master's, thesis (for some programs); for doctorate, thesis/dissertation. *Entrance requirements:* For master's, GRE General Test (school psychology), MAT (school counseling), minimum GPA of 3.5; for doctorate, GRE General Test, minimum GPA of 3.5. Additional exam requirements/recommendations for international students: required—TOEFL.

Virginia Commonwealth University, Graduate School, College of Humanities and Sciences, Department of Psychology, Program in Counseling Psychology, Richmond, VA 23284-9005. Offers PhD. *Accreditation:* ACA; APA. *Degree requirements:* For doctorate, thesis/dissertation. *Entrance requirements:* For doctorate, GRE General Test, GRE Subject Test. Additional exam requirements/recommendations for international students: required—TOEFL (minimum score 600 paper-based; 100 iBT); recommended—IELTS (minimum score 6.5). Electronic applications accepted.

Virginia Commonwealth University, Graduate School, School of Allied Health Professions, Program in Patient Counseling, Richmond, VA 23284-9005. Offers MS. *Accreditation:* ACA. *Entrance requirements:* For master's, GRE General Test. Additional exam requirements/recommendations for international students: required—TOEFL (minimum score 600 paper-based; 100 iBT). Electronic applications accepted.

Viterbo University, Master of Science in Mental Health Counseling Program, La Crosse, WI 54601-4797. Offers addiction counseling (MS); child and adolescent counseling (MS); complementary health and wellness counseling (MS). *Accreditation:* ACA. *Program availability:* Part-time, evening/weekend. *Degree requirements:* For master's, comprehensive exam, thesis, 54 credits of core program courses; 6 elective credits; minimum GPA of 3.0; action research project; practicum/internship experience. *Entrance requirements:* For master's, MAT, BS in a human service or social science discipline; prerequisite coursework in general psychology, behavior disorders/abnormal psychology, and research methods/statistics; minimum undergraduate cumulative GPA of 3.0; background check; personal statement; undergraduate transcripts; interview. Additional exam requirements/recommendations for international students: required—TOEFL (minimum score 525 paper-based). Electronic applications accepted. Application fee is waived when completed online. *Expenses:* Contact institution.

Walden University, Graduate Programs, School of Counseling, Minneapolis, MN 55401. Offers addiction counseling (MS), including addictions and public health, child and adolescent counseling, family studies and interventions, forensic counseling, general program, military families and culture, trauma and crisis counseling; clinical mental health counseling (MS), including addiction counseling, forensic counseling, military families and culture, trauma and crisis counseling; counselor education and supervision (PhD), including consultation, counseling and social change, forensic mental health counseling, leadership and program evaluation, trauma and crisis; marriage, couple, and family counseling (MS), including addiction counseling, career counseling, forensic counseling, military families and culture, trauma and crisis counseling; school counseling (MS), including addiction counseling, career counseling, crisis and trauma, military families and culture. *Accreditation:* ACA. *Program availability:* Part-time, evening/weekend, online only, 100% online. *Degree requirements:* For master's, residency, field experience, professional development plan, licensure plan; for doctorate, thesis/dissertation, residency, practicum, internship. *Entrance requirements:* For master's, bachelor's degree or higher; minimum GPA of 2.5; official transcripts; goal statement (for some programs); access to computer and Internet; for doctorate, master's degree or higher; three years of related professional or academic experience (preferred); minimum GPA of 3.0; goal statement and current resume (for select programs); official transcripts; access to computer and Internet. Additional exam requirements/recommendations for international students: required—TOEFL (minimum score 550 paper-based, 79 iBT), IELTS (minimum score 6.5), Michigan English Language Assessment Battery (minimum score 82), or PTE (minimum score 53). Electronic applications accepted.

Walden University, Graduate Programs, School of Psychology, Minneapolis, MN 55401. Offers clinical psychology (MS), including counseling, general program; forensic psychology (MS), including forensic psychology in the community, general program, mental health applications, program planning and evaluation in forensic settings, psychology and legal systems; industrial organizational (MS, PhD), including consulting psychology, forensic (MS), forensic psychology (PhD), general practice, leadership development and coaching (MS), organizational diversity and social change, research evaluation (PhD); online teaching in psychology (Post-Master's Certificate); organizational psychology and development (Postbaccalaureate Certificate); psychology (MS, PhD), including applied psychology (MS), clinical psychology (PhD), crisis management and response (MS), educational psychology, forensic psychology (PhD), general psychology (MS), general psychology research (PhD), general psychology teaching (PhD), health psychology, leadership development and coaching (MS), psychology of culture (MS), psychology, public administration, and social change (MS), social psychology, terrorism and security (MS); psychology respecialization (Post-Doctoral Certificate). *Program availability:* Part-time, evening/weekend, online only, 100% online. Terminal master's awarded for partial completion of doctoral program. *Degree requirements:* For master's, thesis optional; for doctorate, thesis/dissertation, residency. *Entrance requirements:* For master's, bachelor's degree or higher; minimum GPA of 2.5; official transcripts; goal statement (for some programs); access to computer and Internet; for doctorate, master's degree or higher; three years of related professional or academic experience (preferred); minimum GPA of 3.0; goal statement and current resume (for select programs); official transcripts; access to computer and Internet; for other advanced degree, relevant work experience; access to computer and Internet. Additional exam requirements/recommendations for international students: required—TOEFL (minimum score 550 paper-based, 79 iBT), IELTS (minimum score 6.5), Michigan English Language Assessment Battery (minimum score 82), or PTE (minimum score 53). Electronic applications accepted.

Walden University, Graduate Programs, School of Social Work and Human Services, Minneapolis, MN 55401. Offers addictions and social work (DSW); advanced clinical practice (MSW); clinical expertise (DSW); criminal justice (DSW); disaster, crisis, and intervention (DSW); family studies and interventions (DSW); human and social services (PhD), including advanced research, community and social services, community intervention and leadership, conflict management, criminal justice, disaster crisis and intervention, family studies and intervention, gerontology, global social services, higher education, human services and nonprofit administration, mental health facilitation; medical social work (DSW); military social work (MSW); policy practice (DSW); social work (PhD), including addictions and social work, clinical expertise, criminal justice, disaster, crisis and intervention, family studies and interventions, medical social work, policy practice, social work administration; social work administration (DSW); social work in healthcare (MSW); social work with children and families (MSW). *Accreditation:* CSWE. *Program availability:* Part-time, evening/weekend, online only, 100% online. *Degree requirements:* For master's, residency (for some programs); for doctorate, thesis/dissertation, residency. *Entrance requirements:* For master's, bachelor's degree or higher; minimum GPA of 2.5; official transcripts; goal statement (for some programs); access to computer and Internet; for doctorate, master's degree or higher; three years of related professional or academic experience (preferred); minimum GPA of 3.0; goal statement and current resume (for select programs); official transcripts; access to computer and Internet. Additional exam requirements/recommendations for international students: required—TOEFL (minimum score 550 paper-based, 79 iBT), IELTS (minimum score 6.5), Michigan English Language Assessment Battery (minimum score 82), or PTE (minimum score 53). Electronic applications accepted.

Walsh University, Master of Arts in Counseling and Human Development (CHD), North Canton, OH 44720-3396. Offers clinical mental health counseling (MA); school counseling (MA); student affairs in higher education (MA). *Accreditation:* ACA. *Program availability:* Part-time, evening/weekend, blended/hybrid learning. *Faculty:* 6 full-time (5 women), 8 part-time/adjunct (7 women). *Students:* 38 full-time (30 women), 36 part-time (28 women); includes 7 minority (5 Black or African American, non-Hispanic/Latino; 1 Asian, non-Hispanic/Latino; 1 Two or more races, non-Hispanic/Latino), 3 international. Average age 28. 43 applicants, 84% accepted, 19 enrolled. In 2019, 27 master's awarded. *Entrance requirements:* For master's, applicants with a minimum cumulative GPA of 2.99 or less must submit results from the graduate record examination (GRE) or the miller analogies test (MAT), application, resume, official college transcripts, 3 letters of recommendation, notarized affidavit of good moral character, writing sample, interview with department. Additional exam requirements/recommendations for international students: recommended—TOEFL (minimum score 500 paper-based; 61 iBT), IELTS (minimum score 5.5). *Application deadline:* For fall admission, 7/15 priority date for domestic students. Applications are processed on a rolling basis. Application fee: $0. Electronic applications accepted. *Expenses:* $745/credit hour, $50 technology fee. *Financial support:* In 2019–20, 5 students received support. Research assistantships and unspecified assistantships available. Financial award application deadline: 12/31. *Unit head:* Dr. Lisa Zimmerman, Program Director, 330-490-7266, E-mail: lzimmerman@walsh.edu. *Application contact:* Dr. Lisa Zimmerman, Program Director, 330-490-7266, E-mail: lzimmerman@walsh.edu.
Website: http://www.walsh.edu/

Washington Adventist University, Program in Counseling Psychology, Takoma Park, MD 20912. Offers MA. *Program availability:* Part-time. *Entrance requirements:* Additional exam requirements/recommendations for international students: required—TOEFL (minimum score 550 paper-based), IELTS (minimum score 5).

Washington Adventist University, Program in Professional Counseling Psychology, Takoma Park, MD 20912. Offers MA. *Program availability:* Part-time. *Entrance requirements:* Additional exam requirements/recommendations for international students: required—TOEFL (minimum score 550 paper-based), IELTS (minimum score 5).

Washington State University, College of Education, Department of Educational Leadership, Sports Studies, and Educational/Counseling Psychology, Pullman, WA 99164-2136. Offers counseling psychology (PhD); educational leadership (Ed M, MA, Ed D, PhD); educational psychology (MA, PhD); sport management (MA). *Program availability:* Part-time, online learning. *Degree requirements:* For master's, comprehensive exam (for some programs), thesis (for some programs), oral or written exam; for doctorate, comprehensive exam, thesis/dissertation, oral and written exam, internship. *Entrance requirements:* For master's and doctorate, GRE General Test, minimum GPA of 3.0, 3 letters of recommendation, transcripts showing all college or university course work, statement of professional objectives, current curriculum vitae/resume. Additional exam requirements/recommendations for international students: required—TOEFL (minimum score 550 paper-based; 80 iBT). Electronic applications accepted.

Wayland Baptist University, Graduate Programs, Programs in Behavioral and Social Sciences, Plainview, TX 79072-6998. Offers counseling (MA); criminal justice (MACJ); government administration (MPA); history (MA); homeland security (MPA); humanities (MAH); justice administration (MPA). *Program availability:* Part-time, evening/weekend, 100% online, blended/hybrid learning. *Degree requirements:* For master's, comprehensive exam. *Entrance requirements:* For master's, GRE, MAT. Additional exam requirements/recommendations for international students: required—TOEFL (minimum score 500 paper-based; 61 iBT). Electronic applications accepted. *Expenses: Tuition:* Full-time $728; part-time $728 per semester. *Required fees:* $1218. Tuition and fees vary according to degree level, campus/location and program.

Waynesburg University, Graduate and Professional Studies, Canonsburg, PA 15370. Offers business (MBA), including energy management, finance, health systems, human resources, leadership, market development; counseling (MA), including addictions counseling, clinical mental health; counselor education and supervision (PhD); criminal investigation (MA); education (M Ed), including autism, curriculum and instruction, educational leadership, online teaching; nursing (MSN), including administration, education, informatics; nursing practice (DNP); special education (M Ed); technology (M Ed); MSN/MBA. *Accreditation:* AACN. *Program availability:* Part-time, evening/weekend. *Degree requirements:* For doctorate, thesis/dissertation. *Entrance requirements:* Additional exam requirements/recommendations for international students: required—TOEFL. Electronic applications accepted.

Wayne State University, College of Education, Division of Theoretical and Behavioral Foundations, Detroit, MI 48202. Offers applied behavior analysis (Certificate); counseling (M Ed, MA, Ed D, Ed S); counseling psychology (MA, PhD); education evaluation and research (M Ed, Ed D); educational psychology (M Ed, PhD), including learning and instruction sciences (PhD); rehabilitation counseling and community inclusion (MA); school and community psychology (MA, Certificate). *Accreditation:* ACA (one or more programs are accredited); CORE (one or more programs are accredited). *Program availability:* Part-time, evening/weekend. *Faculty:* 10. *Students:* 199 full-time (171 women), 142 part-time (107 women); includes 135 minority (90 Black or African American, non-Hispanic/Latino; 2 American Indian or Alaska Native, non-Hispanic/Latino; 6 Asian, non-Hispanic/Latino; 16 Hispanic/Latino; 21 Two or more races, non-Hispanic/Latino), 10 international. Average age 32. 364 applicants, 25% accepted, 72 enrolled. In 2019, 101 master's, 11 doctorates, 19 other advanced degrees awarded. *Degree requirements:* For master's, thesis (for some programs); for doctorate, comprehensive exam, thesis/dissertation. *Entrance requirements:* For master's, GRE, interview, personal statement, portfolio (only art therapy); references; program application; for doctorate, GRE, departmental writing exam, interview, curriculum vitae, references, master's degree in closely-related field with minimum GPA of 3.5, demonstration of counseling skills (for Ed D in counseling); autobiographical statement; letter of application; personal statement; for other advanced degree, education specialist certificate: master's degree in counseling or closely related field and licensure; personal statement; recommendations; autobiographical statement; interview. Additional exam requirements/recommendations for international students: required—TOEFL (minimum score 550 paper-based; 79 iBT); recommended—IELTS (minimum score 6.5), TWE (minimum score 5.5), TSE (minimum score 58). *Application deadline:* Applications are processed on a rolling basis. Application fee: $50. Electronic applications accepted. *Expenses: Tuition:* Full-time $34,567. *Financial support:* In 2019–20, 92 students received support, including 1 fellowship (averaging $20,000 per year), 1 research assistantship with tuition reimbursement available (averaging $19,967 per year); teaching assistantships, Federal Work-Study, scholarships/grants, health care benefits, and unspecified assistantships also available. Support available to part-time students. Financial award applicants required to submit FAFSA. *Unit head:* Dr. William Hill, Assistant Dean, 313-577-9316, E-mail: ad2107@wayne.edu. *Application contact:* Dr. Mary L Waker, Graduate Admissions Officer, 313-577-1601, Fax: 313-577-7904, E-mail: m.waker@wayne.edu.
Website: https://education.wayne.edu/counseling-educational-psychology

Webster University, College of Arts and Sciences, Department of Professional Counseling, St. Louis, MO 63119-3194. Offers counseling (MA). *Accreditation:* ACA. *Program availability:* Part-time. *Entrance requirements:* Additional exam requirements/recommendations for international students: required—TOEFL.

Webster University, College of Arts and Sciences, Department of Psychology, St. Louis, MO 63119-3194. Offers counseling psychology (MS); gerontology (MS). *Program availability:* Part-time. *Entrance requirements:* Additional exam requirements/recommendations for international students: required—TOEFL.

Western Kentucky University, Graduate School, College of Education and Behavioral Sciences, Department of Counseling and Student Affairs, Bowling Green, KY 42101. Offers counseling (MA Ed), including marriage and family therapy, mental health counseling; school counseling (P-12) (MA Ed); student affairs in higher education (MA Ed). *Accreditation:* ACA; NCATE. *Program availability:* Part-time, evening/weekend. *Degree requirements:* For master's, comprehensive exam, thesis optional. *Entrance requirements:* For master's, GRE General Test. Additional exam requirements/recommendations for international students: required—TOEFL (minimum score 555 paper-based; 79 iBT).

Western Michigan University, Graduate College, College of Education and Human Development, Department of Counselor Education and Counseling Psychology, Kalamazoo, MI 49008. Offers counseling psychology (MA, PhD); counselor education (MA, PhD), including counselor education (MA). *Accreditation:* ACA (one or more programs are accredited); APA (one or more programs are accredited); CORE; NCATE. *Degree requirements:* For doctorate, thesis/dissertation.

Western Washington University, Graduate School, College of Humanities and Social Sciences, Department of Psychology, Program in Mental Health Counseling, Bellingham, WA 98225-5996. Offers MS. *Accreditation:* ACA. *Degree requirements:* For master's, thesis optional. *Entrance requirements:* For master's, GRE General Test, minimum GPA of 3.0 in last 60 semester hours or last 90 quarter hours. Additional exam requirements/recommendations for international students: required—TOEFL (minimum score 567 paper-based). Electronic applications accepted.

Westfield State University, College of Graduate and Continuing Education, Department of Psychology, Program in Counseling, Westfield, MA 01086. Offers forensic mental health counseling (MA); mental health counseling (MA); school adjustment counseling (MA); school guidance counseling (MA). *Program availability:* Part-time, evening/weekend. *Degree requirements:* For master's, comprehensive exam, practicum. *Entrance requirements:* For master's, GRE General Test, MAT, minimum undergraduate GPA of 3.0. Additional exam requirements/recommendations for international students: recommended—TOEFL (minimum score 550 paper-based; 79 iBT).

Westminster College, School of Arts and Sciences, Master of Science in Mental Health Counseling Program, SALT LAKE CITY, UT 84105. Offers MSMHC. *Faculty:* 2 full-time (both women), 5 part-time/adjunct (2 women). *Students:* 25 full-time (20 women), 9 part-time (4 women); includes 5 minority (all Hispanic/Latino). Average age 33. 39 applicants, 56% accepted, 12 enrolled. In 2019, 9 master's awarded. *Degree requirements:* For master's, comprehensive exam, internship, meet all credit hour and other course requirements, maintain an overall grade point average of 3.0 or above, be enrolled at Westminster College during the semester in which they wish to graduate, maintain good academic standing, earn a grade of B- or higher in all graduate courses. *Entrance requirements:* For master's, GRE (waived if undergraduate GPA is 3.4 or higher), baccalaureate degree from regionally-accredited college or university or a recognized

international college or university; personal statement, personal resume, official copies of transcripts sent by the registrar of each college or university attended; 3 letters of recommendation; proof of clear state and federal background checks. Additional exam requirements/recommendations for international students: required—TOEFL (minimum score 84 iBT), IELTS (minimum score 7). *Application deadline:* For fall admission, 12/15 priority date for domestic and international students. Application fee: $50. Electronic applications accepted. *Expenses:* $811 per credit hour tuition, $13 per credit hour fees. *Financial support:* In 2019–20, 3 students received support. Career-related internships or fieldwork, scholarships/grants, and tuition remission available. *Unit head:* Lance Newman, Dean of the School of Arts and Sciences, 801-832-2300, E-mail: lnewman@westminstercollege.edu. *Application contact:* Elhom Gosink, Graduate Enrollment Coordinator, 801-832-2292, Fax: 801-832-3101, E-mail: egosink@westminstercollege.edu.
Website: https://westminstercollege.edu/graduate/programs/master-of-science-in-mental-health-counseling

West Virginia University, College of Education and Human Services, Morgantown, WV 26506. Offers audiology (Au D); autism spectrum disorder (MA); clinical rehabilitation and mental health counseling (MS); communication science and disorders (PhD); counseling (MA); counseling psychology (PhD); curriculum and instruction (Ed D); early childhood education (MA); early intervention/ early childhood special education (MA); education (PhD); educational leadership (MA); educational leadership/ public school administration (Ed D); educational leadership/public school administration (MA); educational psychology (MA, Ed D); elementary education (MA); gifted education (MA); higher education administration (MA, Ed D); higher education curriculum and teaching (MA); institutional design and technology (MA); instructional design and technology (Ed D); literacy education (MA); secondary education (MA); secondary education/English (MA); special education (Ed D); speech pathology (MS). *Accreditation:* ASHA; NCATE. *Program availability:* Part-time, evening/weekend, online learning. *Degree requirements:* For master's, content exams; for doctorate, comprehensive exam, thesis/dissertation. *Entrance requirements:* Additional exam requirements/recommendations for international students: required—TOEFL (minimum score 500 paper-based; 61 iBT). Electronic applications accepted.

Wheaton College, Graduate School, School of Psychology Counseling and Family Therapy, Wheaton, IL 60187-5593. Offers clinical mental health counseling (MA); clinical psychology (Psy D); marriage and family therapy (MA). *Accreditation:* APA (one or more programs are accredited). Terminal master's awarded for partial completion of doctoral program. *Degree requirements:* For master's, thesis or alternative; for doctorate, thesis/dissertation, internship. *Entrance requirements:* For master's, GRE General Test, 18 hours of course work in psychology; for doctorate, GRE General Test. Additional exam requirements/recommendations for international students: required—TOEFL (minimum score 550 paper-based; 80 iBT), IELTS (minimum score 6.5). *Expenses: Tuition:* Full-time $16,800; part-time $700 per credit hour. Tuition and fees vary according to degree level and program.

William Carey University, Department of Psychology and Graduate Counseling, Hattiesburg, MS 39401. Offers counseling psychology (MS). *Program availability:* Part-time. *Entrance requirements:* For master's, GRE, PRAXIS, MAT, minimum GPA of 2.5. Additional exam requirements/recommendations for international students: required—TOEFL (minimum score 550 paper-based). *Expenses:* Contact institution.

William James College, Graduate Programs, Newton, MA 02459. Offers applied psychology in higher education student personnel administration (MA); clinical psychology (Psy D); counseling psychology (MA); counseling psychology and community mental health (MA); counseling psychology and global mental health (MA); executive coaching (Graduate Certificate); forensic and counseling psychology (MA); leadership psychology (Psy D); organizational psychology (MA); primary care psychology (MA); respecialization in clinical psychology (Certificate); school psychology (Psy D); MA/CAGS. *Accreditation:* APA. *Degree requirements:* For master's, comprehensive exam (for some programs); for doctorate, thesis/dissertation (for some programs). Electronic applications accepted.

Wilmington University, College of Social and Behavioral Sciences, New Castle, DE 19720-6491. Offers administration of human services (MS); administration of justice (MS); clinical mental health counseling (MS); homeland security (MS). *Accreditation:* ACA. *Program availability:* Part-time, evening/weekend. *Entrance requirements:* Additional exam requirements/recommendations for international students: required—TOEFL (minimum score 500 paper-based). Electronic applications accepted.

Winebrenner Theological Seminary, Graduate Programs, Findlay, OH 45840. Offers clinical counseling (MA); family ministry (MA); practical theology (MA); theological and ministerial studies (M Div, D Min); theological studies (MA). *Accreditation:* ATS (one or more programs are accredited). *Program availability:* Part-time, 100% online, blended/hybrid learning. *Degree requirements:* For master's, variable foreign language requirement, thesis (for some programs); for doctorate, thesis/dissertation. *Entrance requirements:* For doctorate, 3 years of post-M Div full-time ministry. Additional exam requirements/recommendations for international students: required—TOEFL (minimum score 550 paper-based; 80 iBT). Electronic applications accepted. *Expenses: Tuition:* Full-time $9450; part-time $525 per credit. Tuition and fees vary according to course load, degree level and program.

The Wright Institute, Master of Arts in Counseling Psychology Program, Berkeley, CA 94704-1796. Offers MA. *Program availability:* Part-time, evening/weekend. *Degree requirements:* For master's, comprehensive exam. *Entrance requirements:* Additional exam requirements/recommendations for international students: required—TOEFL. Electronic applications accepted.

Xavier University, College of Professional Sciences, School of Education, Department of Counseling, Cincinnati, OH 45207. Offers clinical mental health counseling (MA); school counseling (MA). *Program availability:* Part-time, evening/weekend. *Degree requirements:* For master's, internship. *Entrance requirements:* For master's, GRE or MAT, minimum GPA of 3.0; 2 letters of recommendation; resume; official transcript; statement of purpose. Additional exam requirements/recommendations for international students: required—TOEFL (minimum score 550 paper-based; 79 iBT). Electronic applications accepted. Application fee is waived when completed online. *Expenses:* Contact institution.

Yeshiva University, Ferkauf Graduate School of Psychology, Program in Mental Health Counseling Psychology, New York, NY 10033-3201. Offers MA. *Program availability:* Part-time. *Entrance requirements:* For master's, GRE General Test.

Developmental Psychology

Andrews University, School of Graduate Studies, College of Education and International Services, Department of Graduate Psychology and Counseling, Program in Educational and Developmental Psychology, Berrien Springs, MI 49104. Offers educational and developmental psychology (MA); educational psychology (Ed D, PhD). *Students:* 17 full-time (14 women), 8 part-time (7 women); includes 4 minority (2 Black or African American, non-Hispanic/Latino; 2 Hispanic/Latino), 15 international. Average age 36. In 2019, 5 master's, 1 doctorate awarded. *Degree requirements:* For master's, thesis optional. *Entrance requirements:* For master's, GRE. Additional exam requirements/recommendations for international students: required—TOEFL (minimum score 550 paper-based). *Application deadline:* Applications are processed on a rolling basis. Application fee: $60. Electronic applications accepted. *Unit head:* Dr. Jimmy Kijai, Coordinator, 269-471-6240. *Application contact:* Jillian Panigot, Director, University Admissions, 800-253-2874, Fax: 269-471-6321, E-mail: graduate@andrews.edu.

Arizona State University at Tempe, College of Liberal Arts and Sciences, Department of Psychology, Tempe, AZ 85287-1104. Offers applied behavior analysis (MS); behavioral neuroscience (PhD); clinical psychology (PhD); cognitive science (PhD); developmental psychology (PhD); quantitative psychology (PhD); social psychology (PhD). *Accreditation:* APA. *Degree requirements:* For doctorate, comprehensive exam, thesis/dissertation, interactive Program of Study (iPOS) submitted before completing 50 percent of required credit hours. *Entrance requirements:* For doctorate, GRE General Test, GRE Subject Test, minimum GPA of 3.0 or equivalent in last 2 years of work leading to bachelor's degree. Additional exam requirements/recommendations for international students: required—TOEFL, IELTS, or PTE. Electronic applications accepted.

Azusa Pacific University, School of Behavioral and Applied Sciences, Department of Psychology, Azusa, CA 91702-7000. Offers child life (MS); research psychology and data analytics (MS).

Bay Path University, Program in Developmental Psychology, Longmeadow, MA 01106-2292. Offers developmental psychology (MS). *Program availability:* Part-time, 100% online. *Entrance requirements:* For master's, completed application; official undergraduate and graduate transcripts (a GPA of 3.0 or higher is preferred); original essay of 300-500 words on the topic: "Why the MS in Developmental Psychology is important to my personal and professional goals"; current resume; 2 recommendations; signed program requirement form. Electronic applications accepted. Application fee is waived when completed online. *Expenses:* Contact institution.

Boston College, Lynch School of Education and Human Development, Department of Counseling, Developmental, and Educational Psychology, Chestnut Hill, MA 02467-3800. Offers applied developmental and education psychology (MA, PhD); counseling psychology (PhD); mental health counseling (MA); school counseling (MA); theology and ministry and counseling (MA/MA); MA/MA. *Accreditation:* APA (one or more programs are accredited). *Program availability:* Part-time, evening/weekend. Terminal master's awarded for partial completion of doctoral program. *Degree requirements:* For master's, comprehensive exam; for doctorate, comprehensive exam, thesis/dissertation. Electronic applications accepted.

Boston Graduate School of Psychoanalysis, CAGS and Certificate Programs, Brookline, MA 02446-4602. Offers child and adolescent intervention (CAGS); psychoanalysis (Certificate); psychoanalytic psychotherapy (CAGS). *Program availability:* Part-time. *Degree requirements:* For other advanced degree, thesis. *Entrance requirements:* For degree, interview, BA, writing sample, 3 letters of reference, transcripts. Additional exam requirements/recommendations for international students: required—TOEFL (minimum score 550 paper-based; 79 iBT).

Bowling Green State University, Graduate College, College of Arts and Sciences, Department of Psychology, Bowling Green, OH 43403. Offers clinical psychology (MA, PhD); developmental psychology (MA, PhD); experimental psychology (MA, PhD); industrial/organizational psychology (MA, PhD); quantitative psychology (MA, PhD). *Accreditation:* APA (one or more programs are accredited). *Degree requirements:* For doctorate, thesis/dissertation. *Entrance requirements:* For doctorate, GRE General Test, GRE Subject Test. Additional exam requirements/recommendations for international students: required—TOEFL. Electronic applications accepted.

Brandeis University, Graduate School of Arts and Sciences, Department of Psychology, Waltham, MA 02454-9110. Offers brain, body and behavior (PhD); cognitive neuroscience (PhD); general psychology (MA); social/developmental psychology (PhD). *Program availability:* Part-time. *Faculty:* 14 full-time (7 women), 3 part-time/adjunct (all women). *Students:* 31 full-time (21 women), 1 (woman) part-time; includes 6 minority (4 Asian, non-Hispanic/Latino; 2 Hispanic/Latino), 8 international. Average age 26. 157 applicants, 14% accepted, 12 enrolled. In 2019, 18 master's, 2 doctorates awarded. Terminal master's awarded for partial completion of doctoral program. *Degree requirements:* For master's, thesis (for some programs); for doctorate, thesis/dissertation. *Entrance requirements:* For master's and doctorate, GRE General required; GRE Subject recommended, transcripts, letters of recommendation, resume, and statement of purpose. Additional exam requirements/recommendations for international students: required—TOEFL, IELTS, PTE. *Application deadline:* For fall admission, 12/1 priority date for domestic and international students. Applications are processed on a rolling basis. Application fee: $75. Electronic applications accepted. *Financial support:* In 2019–20, 23 fellowships with full tuition reimbursements (averaging $25,000 per year), 16 teaching assistantships (averaging $3,550 per year) were awarded; research assistantships, scholarships/grants, traineeships, health care benefits, and tuition waivers also available. Support available to part-time students. *Unit head:* Dr. Angela Gutchess, Director of Graduate Studies, 781-736-3247, E-mail: gutchess@brandeis.edu. *Application contact:* Sarah Lupis, Administrator, 781-736-3303, E-mail: slupis@brandeis.edu.
Website: http://www.brandeis.edu/gsas/programs/psychology.html

Capella University, Harold Abel School of Social and Behavioral Science, Master's Programs in Counseling, Minneapolis, MN 55402. Offers child and adolescent development (MS); general addiction counseling (MS); general marriage and family counseling/therapy (MS); general mental health counseling (MS); general school counseling (MS).

Carnegie Mellon University, Dietrich College of Humanities and Social Sciences, Department of Psychology, Area of Developmental Psychology, Pittsburgh, PA 15213-3891. Offers PhD. *Degree requirements:* For doctorate, comprehensive exam, thesis/dissertation. *Entrance requirements:* For doctorate, GRE General Test. Additional exam requirements/recommendations for international students: required—TOEFL.

Chatham University, Program in Counseling Psychology, Pittsburgh, PA 15232-2826. Offers child, adolescent and family (MSCP); counseling psychology (Psy D); health and holistic (MSCP); organization and supervision (MSCP); sport and exercise (MSCP).

Accreditation: APA. *Program availability:* Part-time, evening/weekend. *Faculty:* 13 full-time (8 women), 21 part-time/adjunct (17 women). *Students:* 93 full-time (79 women), 56 part-time (44 women); includes 29 minority (16 Black or African American, non-Hispanic/Latino; 4 Asian, non-Hispanic/Latino; 6 Hispanic/Latino; 3 Two or more races, non-Hispanic/Latino), 2 international. Average age 29. 172 applicants, 46% accepted, 54 enrolled. In 2019, 30 master's, 7 doctorates awarded. *Degree requirements:* For master's, thesis optional, supervised internship; for doctorate, thesis/dissertation, internship. *Entrance requirements:* For master's, minimum GPA of 3.0; 2 letters of recommendation; resume; prerequisite coursework in statistics, biology, and psychology; for doctorate, GRE. Additional exam requirements/recommendations for international students: required—TOEFL (minimum score 600 paper-based; 100 iBT), IELTS (minimum score 7), TWE. *Application deadline:* For fall admission, 4/1 priority date for domestic and international students; for spring admission, 11/1 for domestic students, 10/1 for international students. Applications are processed on a rolling basis. Application fee: $45. Electronic applications accepted. Application fee is waived when completed online. *Expenses:* $1,017 per credit hour. *Financial support:* Career-related internships or fieldwork available. Financial award applicants required to submit FAFSA. *Unit head:* Dr. Mary Jo Loughran, Director, 412-365-2783, Fax: 412-365-1505, E-mail: mloughran@chatham.edu. *Application contact:* Melanie Elmer, Assistant Director of Graduate Admission, 412-365-1394, Fax: 412-365-1609, E-mail: gradadmissions@chatham.edu.
Website: http://www.chatham.edu/mscp

Claremont Graduate University, Graduate Programs, School of Social Science, Policy and Evaluation, Department of Psychology, Claremont, CA 91711-6160. Offers advanced study in evaluation (Certificate); cognitive psychology (MA, PhD); developmental psychology (MA, PhD); evaluation and applied research methods (MA, PhD); health behavior research and evaluation (MA, PhD); human resource development and evaluation (MA); industrial/organizational psychology (MA, PhD); organizational behavior (MA, PhD); organizational psychology (MA, PhD); social psychology (MA, PhD); MBA/PhD. *Program availability:* Part-time. Terminal master's awarded for partial completion of doctoral program. *Entrance requirements:* For master's and doctorate, GRE General Test. Additional exam requirements/recommendations for international students: required—TOEFL (minimum score 75 iBT). Electronic applications accepted.

Clark University, Graduate School, Hiatt School of Psychology, Program in Developmental Psychology, Worcester, MA 01610-1477. Offers PhD. *Students:* Average age 28. *Entrance requirements:* For doctorate, GRE General Test. Additional exam requirements/recommendations for international students: required—TOEFL. *Application deadline:* For fall admission, 12/15 priority date for domestic students, 12/15 for international students. Applications are processed on a rolling basis. Application fee: $75. *Expenses:* Tuition: Full-time $47,650; part-time $4765 per course. *Required fees:* $1850. *Financial support:* Fellowships, research assistantships, teaching assistantships, and tuition waivers (full) available. *Unit head:* Dr. Michael Bamberg, Chair, 508-793-7135, E-mail: mbamberg@clarku.edu. *Application contact:* Kelly Boulay, Departmental Administrator, 508-793-7274, Fax: 508-793-7265, E-mail: psychology@clarku.edu.
Website: http://www.clarku.edu/departments/psychology/grad/developmental/index.cfm

Clayton State University, School of Graduate Studies, College of Arts and Sciences, Program in Psychology, Morrow, GA 30260-0285. Offers applied developmental psychology (MS); clinical/counseling psychology (MS). *Entrance requirements:* For master's, GRE, 2 official transcripts; 3 letters of recommendation; statement of purpose; on-campus interview; background check. Additional exam requirements/recommendations for international students: required—TOEFL (minimum score 550 paper-based). Electronic applications accepted.

Cornell University, Graduate School, Graduate Fields of Human Ecology, Field of Human Development, Ithaca, NY 14853. Offers developmental psychology (MA, PhD), including cognitive development, developmental psychopathology, ecology of human development, social and personality development; human development and family studies (MA, PhD), including ecology of human development, family studies and the life course. *Degree requirements:* For doctorate, comprehensive exam, thesis/dissertation, pre-doctoral research project, teaching experience. *Entrance requirements:* For doctorate, GRE General Test, 2 letters of recommendation. Additional exam requirements/recommendations for international students: required—TOEFL (minimum score 550 paper-based; 77 iBT). Electronic applications accepted.

Delaware Valley University, Program in Counseling Psychology, Doylestown, PA 18901-2697. Offers child and adolescent therapy (MA); social justice community counseling (MA).

Duke University, Graduate School, Department of Psychology and Neuroscience, Durham, NC 27708. Offers biological psychology (PhD); clinical psychology (PhD); cognitive psychology (PhD); developmental psychology (PhD); experimental psychology (PhD); health psychology (PhD); human social development (PhD); JD/MA. *Accreditation:* APA (one or more programs are accredited). *Degree requirements:* For doctorate, thesis/dissertation. *Entrance requirements:* For doctorate, GRE General Test. Additional exam requirements/recommendations for international students: required—TOEFL (minimum score 577 paper-based; 90 iBT) or IELTS (minimum score 7). Electronic applications accepted.

Emory University, Laney Graduate School, Department of Psychology, Atlanta, GA 30322-1100. Offers clinical psychology (PhD); cognition and development (PhD); neuroscience and animal behavior (PhD). *Accreditation:* APA. *Degree requirements:* For doctorate, comprehensive exam, thesis/dissertation. *Entrance requirements:* For doctorate, GRE General Test, minimum GPA of 3.25. Additional exam requirements/recommendations for international students: required—TOEFL. Electronic applications accepted.

Erikson Institute, Academic Programs, Chicago, IL 60654. Offers administration (Certificate); bilingual/ESL (Certificate); child development (MS); early childhood education (MS); infant mental health (Certificate); infant studies (Certificate); social work (MSW); MS/MSW. *Program availability:* Part-time, evening/weekend. *Degree requirements:* For master's, comprehensive exam, internship; for Certificate, internship. *Entrance requirements:* For master's and Certificate, minimum GPA of 2.75. Additional exam requirements/recommendations for international students: required—TOEFL.

Fielding Graduate University, Graduate Programs, School of Psychology, Programs in Infant and Early Childhood Development, Santa Barbara, CA 93105-3814. Offers infant and early childhood development (MA, PhD, Graduate Certificate), including early childhood development: education, mental health, and disruptive behaviors (MA), infant mental health and neurodevelopment (MA), reflective practice and supervision (Graduate Certificate). *Program availability:* Part-time, evening/weekend. *Faculty:* 2 full-

time (both women), 22 part-time/adjunct (16 women). *Students:* 90 full-time (83 women), 5 part-time (all women); includes 50 minority (20 Black or African American, non-Hispanic/Latino; 3 American Indian or Alaska Native, non-Hispanic/Latino; 5 Asian, non-Hispanic/Latino; 17 Hispanic/Latino; 5 Two or more races, non-Hispanic/Latino). Average age 44. 21 applicants, 81% accepted, 11 enrolled. In 2019, 1 master's, 6 doctorates awarded. *Degree requirements:* For doctorate, comprehensive exam, thesis/dissertation. *Entrance requirements:* For master's and Graduate Certificate, bachelor's degree from regionally-accredited U.S. institution or equivalent; for doctorate, bachelor's or master's degree from regionally-accredited U.S. institution or equivalent, curriculum vitae, statement of purpose, critical thinking writing sample, 2 letters of recommendation, official transcripts. *Application deadline:* For fall admission, 7/16 for domestic and international students; for spring admission, 11/21 for domestic and international students; for summer admission, 2/18 for domestic and international students. Application fee: $75. Electronic applications accepted. *Expenses:* Contact institution. *Financial support:* In 2019–20, 30 students received support. Research assistantships, teaching assistantships, scholarships/grants, and tuition waivers available. Support available to part-time students. Financial award applicants required to submit FAFSA. *Unit head:* Dr. Jenene Craig, Program Director, E-mail: jcraig@fielding.edu. *Application contact:* Enrollment Coordinator, 800-340-1099 Ext. 4098, Fax: 805-687-9793, E-mail: hodadmission@fielding.edu.
Website: http://www.fielding.edu/our-programs/school-of-leadership-studies/phd-infant-early-childhood-development/

Florida International University, College of Arts, Sciences, and Education, Department of Psychology, Miami, FL 33199. Offers behavioral analysis (MS); clinical science (PhD); cognitive neuroscience (PhD); counseling psychology (MS); developmental science (MS, PhD); legal psychology (MS, PhD); organizational psychology (MS, PhD). *Accreditation:* APA. *Program availability:* Part-time, evening/weekend. *Faculty:* 52 full-time (33 women), 50 part-time/adjunct (37 women). *Students:* 203 full-time (159 women), 2 part-time (both women); includes 117 minority (15 Black or African American, non-Hispanic/Latino; 8 Asian, non-Hispanic/Latino; 86 Hispanic/Latino; 8 Two or more races, non-Hispanic/Latino), 15 international. Average age 26. 410 applicants, 19% accepted, 60 enrolled. In 2019, 57 master's, 7 doctorates awarded. Terminal master's awarded for partial completion of doctoral program. *Degree requirements:* For master's, thesis; for doctorate, comprehensive exam, thesis/dissertation. *Entrance requirements:* For master's, GRE General Test, minimum GPA of 3.0, resume, 3 letters of recommendation; for doctorate, GRE General Test, 3 letters of recommendation, resume, letter of intent, two writing samples, minimum GPA of 3.0. Additional exam requirements/recommendations for international students: required—TOEFL (minimum score 550 paper-based; 80 iBT). *Application deadline:* For fall admission, 12/15 for domestic and international students. Application fee: $30. Electronic applications accepted. *Expenses: Tuition, area resident:* Full-time $8912; part-time $446 per credit hour. Tuition, state resident: full-time $8912; part-time $446 per credit hour. Tuition, nonresident: full-time $21,393; part-time $992 per credit hour. *Required fees:* $2194. *Financial support:* Institutionally sponsored loans and scholarships/grants available. Financial award application deadline: 3/1. *Unit head:* Dr. Jeremy Pettit, Interim Chair, 305-348-1671, Fax: 305-348-2880, E-mail: jeremy.pettit@fiu.edu. *Application contact:* Nanett Rojas, Manager, Admissions Operations, 305-348-7464, Fax: 305-348-7441, E-mail: gradadm@fiu.edu.

Florida State University, The Graduate School, Department of Anthropology, Department of Psychology, Program in Developmental Psychology, Tallahassee, FL 32306-4301. Offers PhD. *Faculty:* 6 full-time (2 women). *Students:* 15 full-time (all women); includes 6 minority (2 Black or African American, non-Hispanic/Latino; 1 Asian, non-Hispanic/Latino; 3 Hispanic/Latino), 2 international. Average age 27. 14 applicants, 36% accepted, 4 enrolled. Terminal master's awarded for partial completion of doctoral program. *Degree requirements:* For doctorate, comprehensive exam, thesis/dissertation. *Entrance requirements:* For doctorate, GRE General Test, minimum GPA of 3.2, research experience, letters of recommendation. Additional exam requirements/recommendations for international students: required—TOEFL (minimum score 80 iBT). *Application deadline:* For fall admission, 12/1 for domestic and international students. Application fee: $30. Electronic applications accepted. *Financial support:* In 2019–20, 15 students received support, including 3 fellowships with full tuition reimbursements available (averaging $24,324 per year), 9 research assistantships with full tuition reimbursements available (averaging $24,324 per year), 6 teaching assistantships with full tuition reimbursements available (averaging $24,324 per year); health care benefits also available. Financial award application deadline: 12/1; financial award applicants required to submit FAFSA. *Unit head:* Dr. Sara Hart, Director, 850-645-9693, Fax: 850-644-7739, E-mail: shart@fcrr.org. *Application contact:* Lynda L. Gibson, Graduate Program Associate, 850-644-2499, Fax: 850-644-7739, E-mail: grad-info@psy.fsu.edu.
Website: http://www.psy.fsu.edu

Fordham University, Graduate School of Arts and Sciences, Department of Psychology, Program in Applied Developmental Psychology, New York, NY 10458. Offers PhD. *Accreditation:* APA. *Students:* Average age 31. 35 applicants, 29% accepted, 3 enrolled. In 2019, 3 doctorates awarded. *Degree requirements:* For doctorate, comprehensive exam, thesis/dissertation. *Entrance requirements:* For doctorate, GRE General Test, GRE Subject Test. Additional exam requirements/recommendations for international students: required—TOEFL (minimum score 600 paper-based). *Application deadline:* For fall admission, 12/14 for domestic students. Application fee: $70. Electronic applications accepted. *Financial support:* In 2019–20, 15 students received support, including 4 fellowships with tuition reimbursements available (averaging $26,065 per year), 2 research assistantships with tuition reimbursements available (averaging $17,529 per year), 2 teaching assistantships with tuition reimbursements available (averaging $10,600 per year); career-related internships or fieldwork, institutionally sponsored loans, tuition waivers (full and partial), and unspecified assistantships also available. Financial award application deadline: 12/14. *Unit head:* Dr. Tiffany Yip, Program Director, 718-817-3797, Fax: 718-817-3785, E-mail: tyip@fordham.edu. *Application contact:* Garrett Marino, Director of Graduate Admissions, 718-817-4419, Fax: 718-817-3566, E-mail: gmarino10@fordham.edu.

George Mason University, College of Humanities and Social Sciences, Department of Psychology, Fairfax, VA 22030. Offers applied developmental psychology (MA, PhD); clinical psychology (PhD); cognitive and behavioral neuroscience (MA, PhD); cognitive neuroscience (Certificate); human factors/applied cognition (MA, PhD, Certificate, including transportation human factors (Certificate), usability (Certificate); industrial/organizational psychology (MA, PhD). *Accreditation:* APA. *Degree requirements:* For master's, comprehensive exam, thesis or practicum research; for doctorate, comprehensive exam, thesis/dissertation, 2nd-year project. *Entrance requirements:* For master's, GRE, 2 official transcripts; goals statement; 15 undergraduate credits in concentration for which the applicant is applying; for doctorate, GRE, 3 letters of recommendation; resume; goals statement; minimum GPA of 3.0 overall for last 60 undergraduate credits, 3.25 in psychology courses; 15 undergraduate credits in concentration for which the applicant is applying; 2 official transcripts; for Certificate, GRE, 2 official transcripts; expanded goals statement; 3 letters of recommendation. Additional exam requirements/recommendations for international students: required—TOEFL (minimum score 575 paper-based; 88 iBT), IELTS (minimum score 6.5), PTE (minimum score 59). Electronic applications accepted.

Georgia State University, College of Arts and Sciences, Department of Psychology, Atlanta, GA 30302-3083. Offers clinical psychology (PhD); cognitive sciences (PhD); community psychology (PhD); developmental psychology (PhD); neuropsychology and behavioral neuroscience (PhD). *Accreditation:* APA. *Faculty:* 29 full-time (17 women). *Students:* 107 full-time (85 women), 2 part-time (both women); includes 23 minority (9 Black or African American, non-Hispanic/Latino; 6 Asian, non-Hispanic/Latino; 7 Hispanic/Latino; 1 Two or more races, non-Hispanic/Latino), 13 international. Average age 28. 498 applicants, 5% accepted, 17 enrolled. In 2019, 18 doctorates awarded. *Entrance requirements:* For doctorate, GRE. Additional exam requirements/recommendations for international students: required—TOEFL (minimum score 550 paper-based; 80 iBT). *Application deadline:* For fall admission, 12/1 for domestic and international students. Application fee: $50. Electronic applications accepted. *Expenses: Tuition, area resident:* Full-time $7164; part-time $398 per credit hour. Tuition, state resident: full-time $7164; part-time $398 per credit hour. Tuition, nonresident: full-time $22,662; part-time $1259 per credit hour. *International tuition:* $22,662 full-time. *Required fees:* $2128; $312 per credit hour. Tuition and fees vary according to course load and program. *Financial support:* In 2019–20, fellowships with full tuition reimbursements (averaging $19,282 per year), research assistantships with full tuition reimbursements (averaging $5,173 per year), teaching assistantships with full tuition reimbursements (averaging $6,389 per year) were awarded; scholarships/grants, traineeships, health care benefits, and unspecified assistantships also available. Financial award applicants required to submit FAFSA. *Unit head:* Dr. Lisa Armistead, Professor, Associate Provost for Graduate Programs, 404-413-2091, Fax: 404-413-6207, E-mail: lparmistead@gsu.edu. *Application contact:* Dr. Lindsey Cohen, Director of Graduate Studies, 404-413-6263, Fax: 404-413-6207, E-mail: llcohen@gsu.edu.
Website: https://psychology.gsu.edu/

The Graduate Center, City University of New York, Graduate Studies, Program in Psychology, New York, NY 10016-4039. Offers basic applied neurocognition (PhD); biopsychology (PhD); clinical psychology (PhD); developmental psychology (PhD); environmental psychology (PhD); experimental psychology (PhD); industrial psychology (PhD); learning processes (PhD); neuropsychology (PhD); psychology (PhD); social personality (PhD). *Degree requirements:* For doctorate, one foreign language, thesis/dissertation. *Entrance requirements:* For doctorate, GRE General Test. Additional exam requirements/recommendations for international students: required—TOEFL. Electronic applications accepted.

Harvard University, Graduate School of Arts and Sciences, Department of Psychology, Cambridge, MA 02138. Offers psychology (PhD), including behavior and decision analysis, cognition, developmental psychology, experimental psychology, personality, psychobiology, psychopathology; social psychology (PhD). *Accreditation:* APA. *Degree requirements:* For doctorate, thesis/dissertation, general exams. *Entrance requirements:* For doctorate, GRE General Test. Additional exam requirements/recommendations for international students: required—TOEFL.

Howard University, Graduate School, Department of Psychology, Washington, DC 20059-0002. Offers clinical psychology (PhD); developmental psychology (PhD); experimental psychology (PhD); neuropsychology (PhD); personality psychology (PhD); psychology (MS); social psychology (PhD). *Accreditation:* APA (one or more programs are accredited). *Program availability:* Part-time. *Degree requirements:* For master's, thesis; for doctorate, comprehensive exam, thesis/dissertation, qualifying exam. *Entrance requirements:* For master's, GRE General Test, minimum GPA of 2.5, bachelor's degree in psychology or related field; for doctorate, GRE General Test, minimum GPA of 3.0.

Humboldt State University, Academic Programs, College of Professional Studies, Department of Psychology, Arcata, CA 95521-8299. Offers psychology (MA), including biological psychology, counseling, developmental psychopathology, school psychology, social and environmental psychology. *Program availability:* Part-time. *Faculty:* 14 full-time (9 women), 13 part-time/adjunct (8 women). *Students:* 76 full-time (54 women), 11 part-time (4 women); includes 37 minority (1 Black or African American, non-Hispanic/Latino; 3 American Indian or Alaska Native, non-Hispanic/Latino; 4 Asian, non-Hispanic/Latino; 22 Hispanic/Latino; 7 Two or more races, non-Hispanic/Latino), 1 international. Average age 28. 89 applicants, 42% accepted, 31 enrolled. In 2019, 38 master's awarded. *Degree requirements:* For master's, thesis. *Entrance requirements:* For master's, appropriate bachelor's degree, minimum GPA of 2.5. Additional exam requirements/recommendations for international students: required—TOEFL (minimum score 500 paper-based). *Application deadline:* For fall admission, 2/1 for domestic students, 2/15 for international students. Applications are processed on a rolling basis. Application fee: $55. *Expenses:* Tuition, state resident: full-time $7176; part-time $4164 per term. *Required fees:* $2120; $1672 per term. *Financial support:* Career-related internships or fieldwork available. Financial award application deadline: 3/1; financial award applicants required to submit FAFSA. *Unit head:* Dr. Carrie Aigner, Graduate Program Coordinator, 707-826-3757, E-mail: carrie.aigner@humboldt.edu. *Application contact:* Dr. Carrie Aigner, Graduate Program Coordinator, 707-826-3757, E-mail: carrie.aigner@humboldt.edu.
Website: http://www2.humboldt.edu/psychology/programs-child/graduate-programs-psychology

Illinois State University, Graduate School, College of Arts and Sciences, Department of Psychology, Normal, IL 61790. Offers psychology (MA, MS), including clinical-counseling psychology, cognitive and behavioral sciences, developmental psychology, industrial/organizational-social psychology; school psychology (PhD, SSP). *Accreditation:* APA. *Faculty:* 32 full-time (14 women), 6 part-time/adjunct (5 women). *Students:* 92 full-time (77 women), 18 part-time (14 women). Average age 25. 154 applicants, 32% accepted, 37 enrolled. In 2019, 27 master's, 3 doctorates, 5 other advanced degrees awarded. *Degree requirements:* For master's, thesis or alternative; for doctorate, variable foreign language requirement, thesis/dissertation, 2 terms of residency, internship, practicum. *Entrance requirements:* For master's, GRE General Test, GRE Subject Test, minimum GPA of 3.0 in last 60 hours of course work; for doctorate, GRE General Test. *Application deadline:* Applications are processed on a rolling basis. Application fee: $50. *Expenses:* Tuition, area resident: Full-time $7956; part-time $9767 per year. Tuition, nonresident: full-time $9233; part-time $17,592 per year. *Required fees:* $1797. *Financial support:* In 2019–20, 26 research assistantships, 34 teaching assistantships were awarded; tuition waivers (full) and unspecified assistantships also available. Financial award application deadline: 4/1. *Unit head:* Dr. J Scott Jordan, Department Chair, 309-438-2484, E-mail: jsjorda@illinoisState.edu. *Application contact:* Dr. Karen Mark, Graduate Coordinator, 309-438-8130, E-mail: kimark@ilstu.edu.
Website: http://psychology.illinoisstate.edu/

Indiana University Bloomington, University Graduate School, College of Arts and Sciences, Department of Psychological and Brain Sciences, Bloomington, IN 47405. Offers clinical science (PhD); cognitive neuroscience (PhD); cognitive psychology (PhD); developmental psychology (PhD); methods of behavior (PhD); molecular systems neuroscience (PhD); social psychology (PhD). *Accreditation:* APA. *Degree requirements:* For doctorate, comprehensive exam, 90 credit hours, 2 advanced statistics/methods courses, 2 written research projects, the teaching of psychology course, teaching 1 semester of undergraduate methods course, qualifying examination, minor or a second major, first-year research seminar course, dissertation defense, written dissertation. *Entrance requirements:* For doctorate, GRE. Additional exam requirements/recommendations for international students: required—TOEFL (minimum score 550 paper-based; 79 iBT). Electronic applications accepted.

La Salle University, School of Arts and Sciences, Program in Clinical Psychology, Philadelphia, PA 19141-1199. Offers child clinical psychology (Psy D); clinical health psychology (Psy D); clinical psychology (MA); general practice psychology (Psy D). *Accreditation:* AAMFT/COAMFTE. *Program availability:* Part-time, evening/weekend. Terminal master's awarded for partial completion of doctoral program. *Degree requirements:* For doctorate, comprehensive exam, thesis/dissertation. *Entrance requirements:* For doctorate, GRE (minimum scores of 148 on both the Verbal Reasoning and Quantitative Reasoning sections strongly recommended); GRE Subject Test in psychology (for those entering with bachelor's degree), baccalaureate degree from accredited institution with major in psychology or related discipline; minimum undergraduate GPA of 3.0, 3.2 graduate; three letters of recommendation; statement of interest and intent; curriculum vitae or resume; personal interview. Additional exam requirements/recommendations for international students: required—TOEFL. Electronic applications accepted. Application fee is waived when completed online. *Expenses:* Contact institution.

Liberty University, School of Behavioral Sciences, Lynchburg, VA 24515. Offers applied psychology (MA), including developmental psychology (MA, MS), industrial/organizational psychology (MA, MS); clinical mental health counseling (MA); community care and counseling (Ed D), including marriage and family counseling, pastoral care and counseling, traumatology; counselor education and supervision (PhD); human services counseling (MA), including addictions and recovery, business, child and family law, Christian ministries, criminal justice, crisis response and trauma, executive leadership, health and wellness, life coaching, marriage and family, military resilience; marriage and family counseling (MA); marriage and family therapy (MA); military resilience (Certificate); pastoral counseling (MA), including addictions and recovery, community chaplaincy, crisis response and trauma, discipleship and church ministry, leadership, life coaching, marriage and family, marriage and family studies, military resilience, parenting and child/adolescent, pastoral counseling, theology; professional counseling (MA); psychology (MS), including developmental psychology (MA, MS), industrial/organizational psychology (MA, MS); school counseling (M Ed). *Program availability:* Part-time, online learning. *Students:* 3,786 full-time (3,065 women), 5,193 part-time (4,081 women); includes 2,733 minority (1,967 Black or African American, non-Hispanic/Latino; 48 American Indian or Alaska Native, non-Hispanic/Latino; 103 Asian, non-Hispanic/Latino; 349 Hispanic/Latino; 19 Native Hawaiian or other Pacific Islander, non-Hispanic/Latino; 247 Two or more races, non-Hispanic/Latino), 133 international. Average age 38. 13,324 applicants, 28% accepted, 2,163 enrolled. In 2019, 2,322 master's, 19 doctorates, 112 other advanced degrees awarded. *Entrance requirements:* For master's, Official bachelor's degree transcripts with a 2.0 GPA or higher. *Application deadline:* Applications are processed on a rolling basis. Application fee: $50. Electronic applications accepted. *Expenses: Tuition:* Full-time $545; part-time $410 per credit hour. One-time fee: $50. *Financial support:* In 2019–20, 1,003 students received support. Teaching assistantships and Federal Work-Study available. Financial award applicants required to submit FAFSA. *Unit head:* Dr. Kenyon Knapp, Dean, School of Behavioral Services, E-mail: kcknapp@liberty.edu. *Application contact:* Jay Bridge, Director of Admissions, 800-424-9595, Fax: 800-628-7977, E-mail: gradadmissions@liberty.edu. Website: https://www.liberty.edu/behavioral-sciences/

Louisiana State University and Agricultural & Mechanical College, Graduate School, College of Humanities and Social Sciences, Department of Psychology, Baton Rouge, LA 70803. Offers biological psychology (MA, PhD); clinical psychology (MA, PhD); cognitive psychology (MA, PhD); developmental psychology (MA, PhD); school psychology (MA, PhD). *Accreditation:* APA (one or more programs are accredited).

Loyola University Chicago, Graduate School, Program in Developmental Psychology, Chicago, IL 60660. Offers MA, PhD. *Faculty:* 7 full-time (6 women). *Students:* 20 full-time (all women), 3 part-time (all women); includes 6 minority (1 Black or African American, non-Hispanic/Latino; 1 Asian, non-Hispanic/Latino; 4 Hispanic/Latino), 1 international. Average age 31. 23 applicants, 4% accepted, 1 enrolled. In 2019, 2 master's, 5 doctorates awarded. Terminal master's awarded for partial completion of doctoral program. *Degree requirements:* For doctorate, comprehensive exam, thesis/dissertation. *Entrance requirements:* For doctorate, GRE General Test, Sample of written work. Additional exam requirements/recommendations for international students: required—TOEFL. *Application deadline:* For fall admission, 1/15 for domestic and international students. Application fee: $50. Electronic applications accepted. Application fee is waived when completed online. *Expenses:* Contact institution. *Financial support:* In 2019–20, 1 fellowship with tuition reimbursement (averaging $9,000 per year), 5 research assistantships with tuition reimbursements (averaging $18,000 per year), 1 teaching assistantship with tuition reimbursement (averaging $9,000 per year) were awarded; career-related internships or fieldwork, Federal Work-Study, and scholarships/grants also available. Financial award application deadline: 12/15; financial award applicants required to submit FAFSA. *Unit head:* Dr. Christine Pajunar Li-Grining, Training Track Coordinator, 773-508-8225, Fax: 773-508-8713, E-mail: cligrining@luc.edu. *Application contact:* Jill Schur, Director, Graduate Enrollment Management, 312-915-8902, E-mail: gradinfo@luc.edu.
Website: https://www.luc.edu/psychology/graduate/developmentalpsychologyprogram/

McGill University, Faculty of Graduate and Postdoctoral Studies, Faculty of Education, Department of Educational and Counseling Psychology, Montréal, QC H3A 2T5, Canada. Offers counseling psychology (MA, PhD); educational psychology (M Ed, MA, PhD); school/applied child psychology and applied developmental psychology (M Ed, MA, PhD, Diploma), including school psychology. *Accreditation:* APA.

New York University, Steinhardt School of Culture, Education, and Human Development, Department of Applied Psychology, Programs in Educational and Developmental Psychology, New York, NY 10012. Offers developmental psychology (PhD); human development and social intervention (MA); psychology and social intervention (PhD). *Accreditation:* APA (one or more programs are accredited). *Program availability:* Part-time. *Entrance requirements:* For doctorate, GRE General Test, interview. Additional exam requirements/recommendations for international students: required—TOEFL. Electronic applications accepted.

North Carolina State University, Graduate School, College of Humanities and Social Sciences, Department of Psychology, Raleigh, NC 27695. Offers applied social and community psychology (PhD); human factors and applied cognition (PhD); industrial/organizational psychology (PhD); lifespan developmental psychology (PhD); school psychology (PhD). *Accreditation:* APA. *Degree requirements:* For doctorate, comprehensive exam, thesis/dissertation. *Entrance requirements:* For doctorate, GRE General Test, GRE Subject Test (industrial/organizational psychology), MAT (recommended), minimum GPA of 3.0 in major. Electronic applications accepted.

North Dakota State University, College of Graduate and Interdisciplinary Studies, College of Human Development and Education, Department of Human Development and Family Science, Program in Developmental Science, Fargo, ND 58102. Offers PhD. Electronic applications accepted. Tuition and fees vary according to program and reciprocity agreements.

The Ohio State University, Graduate School, College of Arts and Sciences, Division of Social and Behavioral Sciences, Department of Psychology, Columbus, OH 43210. Offers behavioral neuroscience (PhD); clinical psychology (PhD); cognitive psychology (PhD); developmental psychology (PhD); intellectual and developmental disabilities psychology (PhD); quantitative psychology (PhD); social psychology (PhD). *Accreditation:* APA. *Entrance requirements:* For doctorate, GRE General Test. Additional exam requirements/recommendations for international students: required—TOEFL (minimum score 600 paper-based; 100 iBT); recommended—IELTS (minimum score 8). Electronic applications accepted.

Pace University, Dyson College of Arts and Sciences, Department of Psychology, Program in School-Clinical Child Psychology, New York, NY 10038. Offers school psychology (MS Ed); school-clinical child psychology (Psy D). *Accreditation:* APA (one or more programs are accredited). Terminal master's awarded for partial completion of doctoral program. *Degree requirements:* For master's, qualifying exams, internship; for doctorate, comprehensive exam, thesis/dissertation, qualifying exams, externship, internship. *Entrance requirements:* For master's, GRE General Test, GRE Subject Test in psychology (recommended), interview, 3 letters of recommendation, resume, personal statement; for doctorate, GRE General Test, GRE Subject Test in psychology (recommended), interview, transcripts, 3 letters of recommendation. Additional exam requirements/recommendations for international students: required—TOEFL (minimum score 88 iBT), IELTS (minimum score 7) or PTE (minimum score 60). Electronic applications accepted.

Pontificia Universidad Catolica Madre y Maestra, Graduate School, Faculty of Social and Administrative Sciences, Santiago, Dominican Republic. Offers business administration (MBA), including business development, finance, international business, management skills (M Mgmt, MBA), marketing, operations, strategic cost management, strategy, tourist destination planning and management; law (LL M), including civil law, corporate business law, criminal law, international relations, real estate law; management (M Mgmt), including higher financial management, insurance program administration, management skills (M Mgmt, MBA); psychology (MA), including clinical child and adolescent psychology, forensic psychology; strategic human resources (EMBA).

Queen's University at Kingston, School of Graduate Studies, Faculty of Arts and Science, Department of Psychology, Kingston, ON K7L 3N6, Canada. Offers brain behavior and cognitive science (MA, PhD); clinical psychology (MA, PhD); developmental psychology (MA, PhD); social personality psychology (MA, PhD). *Degree requirements:* For master's, thesis; for doctorate, comprehensive exam, thesis/dissertation. *Entrance requirements:* For master's and doctorate, GRE General Test. Additional exam requirements/recommendations for international students: required—TOEFL.

Regis University, Rueckert-Hartman College for Health Professions, Denver, CO 80221-1099. Offers advanced practice nurse (DNP); counseling (MA); counseling children and adolescents (Post-Graduate Certificate); counseling military families (Post-Graduate Certificate); depth psychotherapy (Post-Graduate Certificate); fellowship in orthopedic manual physical therapy (Certificate); health care business management (Certificate); health care quality and patient safety (Certificate); health industry leadership (MBA); health services administration (MS); marriage and family therapy (MA, Post-Graduate Certificate); neonatal nurse practitioner (MSN); nursing education (MSN); nursing leadership (MSN); occupational therapy (OTD); pharmacy (Pharm D); physical therapy (DPT). *Accreditation:* ACPE. *Program availability:* Part-time, evening/weekend, 100% online, blended/hybrid learning. *Degree requirements:* For master's, thesis (for some programs), internship. *Entrance requirements:* For master's, official transcript reflecting baccalaureate degree awarded from regionally-accredited college or university. Additional exam requirements/recommendations for international students: required—TOEFL (minimum score 550 paper-based; 82 iBT). Electronic applications accepted. *Expenses:* Contact institution.

San Francisco State University, Division of Graduate Studies, College of Science and Engineering, Department of Psychology, San Francisco, CA 94132-1722. Offers clinical psychology (MS); developmental psychology (MA); industrial/organizational psychology (MS); mind, brain, and behavior (MA); school psychology (MS, Credential); social, personality, and affective science psychology (MA). *Expenses: Tuition, area resident:* Full-time $7176; part-time $4164 per year. Tuition, state resident: full-time $7176; part-time $4164 per year. Tuition, nonresident: full-time $16,680; part-time $396 per unit. *International tuition:* $16,680 full-time. *Required fees:* $1524; $1524 per unit. $762 per semester. Tuition and fees vary according to degree level and program. *Financial support:* Teaching assistantships available. Financial award application deadline: 3/1. *Unit head:* Dr. Chris Wright, Chair, 415-338-7555, Fax: 415-338-2398, E-mail: cwright@sfsu.edu. *Application contact:* Dr. Ryan Howell, Department Graduate Program Coordinator, 415-405-2140, Fax: 415-338-2398, E-mail: rhowell@sfsu.edu.
Website: http://psychology.sfsu.edu/graduate/application.html

Teachers College, Columbia University, Department of Human Development, New York, NY 10027-6696. Offers applied statistics (MS); cognitive studies in education (MA, Ed D, PhD); developmental psychology (MA, Ed D, PhD); educational psychology-human cognition and learning (Ed M, MA, Ed D, PhD); learning analytics (MS); measurement and evaluation (ME, Ed D, PhD); measurement, evaluation, and statistics (MA, MS, Ed D, PhD). *Faculty:* 10 full-time (4 women). *Students:* 123 full-time (94 women), 129 part-time (91 women); includes 58 minority (12 Black or African American, non-Hispanic/Latino; 32 Asian, non-Hispanic/Latino; 13 Hispanic/Latino; 1 Two or more races, non-Hispanic/Latino), 131 international. 429 applicants, 60% accepted, 108 enrolled. *Unit head:* Dr. James Corter, Chair, 212-678-3843, E-mail: jec34@tc.columbia.edu. *Application contact:* Kelly Sutton-Skinner, Director of Admission and New Student Enrollment, E-mail: kms2237@tc.columbia.edu.
Website: http://www.tc.columbia.edu/human-development/

Texas Christian University, College of Science and Engineering, Department of Psychology, Fort Worth, TX 76129-0002. Offers developmental trauma (MS); experimental psychology (PhD), including cognition/developmental, learning, neuroscience, social. *Faculty:* 14 full-time (7 women), 1 part-time/adjunct (0 women). *Students:* 31 full-time (26 women); includes 2 minority (both Asian, non-Hispanic/Latino), 2 international. Average age 25. 52 applicants, 35% accepted, 13 enrolled. In 2019, 10 master's, 4 doctorates awarded. Terminal master's awarded for partial completion of doctoral program. *Entrance requirements:* For doctorate, GRE General Test. Additional exam requirements/recommendations for international students: required—TOEFL (minimum score 550 paper-based; 80 iBT). *Application deadline:* For fall admission, 1/1 for domestic and international students. Application fee: $60 ($0 for international students). Electronic applications accepted. Full-time tuition and fees vary according to program. *Financial support:* In 2019–20, 23 students received support, including 23 teaching assistantships with full tuition reimbursements available (averaging $19,750 per year); scholarships/grants also available. Financial award application deadline: 1/1; financial award applicants required to submit FAFSA. *Unit head:* Dr. Anna I. Petursdottir, Chair, 817-257-7410, Fax: 817-257-7681, E-mail:

a.petursdottir@tcu.edu. *Application contact:* Cindy Hayes, Administrative Assistant, 817-257-7410, Fax: 817-257-7681, E-mail: c.hayes@tcu.edu.
Website: https://psychology.tcu.edu/

Université de Montréal, Faculty of Arts and Sciences, School of Psychoeducation, Montréal, QC H3C 3J7, Canada. Offers M Sc, PhD. *Program availability:* Part-time. *Degree requirements:* For master's, one foreign language, thesis. Electronic applications accepted.

The University of Alabama at Birmingham, College of Arts and Sciences, Program in Psychology, Birmingham, AL 35294. Offers behavioral neuroscience (PhD); lifespan developmental psychology (PhD); medical/clinical psychology (PhD); psychology (MA). *Accreditation:* APA (one or more programs are accredited). *Faculty:* 27 full-time (12 women), 1 (woman) part-time/adjunct. *Students:* 81 full-time (55 women), 3 part-time (all women); includes 22 minority (10 Black or African American, non-Hispanic/Latino; 4 Asian, non-Hispanic/Latino; 6 Hispanic/Latino; 2 Two or more races, non-Hispanic/Latino), 3 international. Average age 27. 199 applicants, 7% accepted, 12 enrolled. In 2019, 8 master's, 15 doctorates awarded. *Entrance requirements:* For master's and doctorate, GRE General Test, letters of recommendation. *Application deadline:* Applications are processed on a rolling basis. Electronic applications accepted. *Financial support:* Fellowships, research assistantships, and teaching assistantships available. *Unit head:* Dr. Karlene K. Ball, Chair, 205-934-2610, Fax: 205-975-2295, E-mail: psych-dept@uab.edu. *Application contact:* Susan Noblitt Banks, Director of Graduate School Operations, 205-934-8227, Fax: 205-934-8413, E-mail: gradschool@uab.edu.
Website: http://www.uab.edu/cas/psychology/graduate

The University of British Columbia, Faculty of Arts, Department of Psychology, Vancouver, BC V6T 1Z4, Canada. Offers behavioral neuroscience (MA, PhD); clinical psychology (MA, PhD); cognitive science (MA, PhD); developmental psychology (MA, PhD); health psychology (MA, PhD); quantitative methods (MA, PhD); social/personality psychology (MA, PhD). *Accreditation:* APA (one or more programs are accredited). Terminal master's awarded for partial completion of doctoral program. *Degree requirements:* For master's, thesis; for doctorate, comprehensive exam, thesis/dissertation. *Entrance requirements:* For master's and doctorate, GRE General Test. Additional exam requirements/recommendations for international students: required—TOEFL. Electronic applications accepted. *Expenses:* Contact institution.

University of Connecticut, Graduate School, College of Liberal Arts and Sciences, Department of Psychological Sciences, Storrs, CT 06269. Offers behavioral neuroscience (PhD); biopsychology (PhD); clinical psychology (MA, PhD); cognition and instruction (PhD); developmental psychology (MA, PhD); ecological psychology (PhD); experimental psychology (PhD); general psychology (MA, PhD); industrial/organizational psychology (PhD); language and cognition (PhD); neuroscience (PhD); social psychology (MA, PhD). *Accreditation:* APA. Terminal master's awarded for partial completion of doctoral program. *Degree requirements:* For master's, comprehensive exam; for doctorate, thesis/dissertation. *Entrance requirements:* For master's and doctorate, GRE General Test, GRE Subject Test. Additional exam requirements/recommendations for international students: required—TOEFL (minimum score 550 paper-based). Electronic applications accepted.

University of Denver, Division of Arts, Humanities and Social Sciences, Department of Psychology, Denver, CO 80208. Offers affective/cognitive/social psychology (PhD); clinical child psychology (PhD); developmental psychology (PhD). *Accreditation:* APA. *Faculty:* 29 full-time (20 women). *Students:* 30 full-time (24 women); includes 8 minority (2 Asian, non-Hispanic/Latino; 5 Hispanic/Latino; 1 Two or more races, non-Hispanic/Latino), 2 international. Average age 27. 457 applicants, 4% accepted, 10 enrolled. In 2019, 5 doctorates awarded. Terminal master's awarded for partial completion of doctoral program. *Degree requirements:* For doctorate, comprehensive exam (for some programs), thesis/dissertation. *Entrance requirements:* For doctorate, GRE General Test, master's degree, transcripts, biographical statement, three letters of recommendation, resume, essay on diversity (for clinical child program only). Additional exam requirements/recommendations for international students: required—TOEFL (minimum score 550 paper-based; 80 iBT). *Application deadline:* For fall admission, 12/21 for domestic and international students. Application fee: $65. Electronic applications accepted. *Expenses:* Contact institution. *Financial support:* In 2019–20, 30 students received support, including 13 research assistantships with tuition reimbursements available (averaging $15,392 per year), 15 teaching assistantships with tuition reimbursements available (averaging $13,800 per year); Federal Work-Study, institutionally sponsored loans, scholarships/grants, and unspecified assistantships also available. Support available to part-time students. Financial award application deadline: 2/15; financial award applicants required to submit FAFSA. *Unit head:* Dr. Sarah Watamura, Associate Professor and Chair, 303-871-4130, E-mail: sarah.watamura@du.edu. *Application contact:* Paula Plank-Houghtaling, Graduate Program Administrator, 303-871-3803, E-mail: phoughta@du.edu.
Website: http://www.du.edu/ahss/psychology

University of Houston, College of Liberal Arts and Social Sciences, Department of Psychology, Houston, TX 77204. Offers clinical psychology (PhD); developmental psychology (PhD); industrial/organizational psychology (PhD); psychology (MA); social psychology (PhD). *Accreditation:* APA (one or more programs are accredited). *Degree requirements:* For master's, comprehensive exam, thesis; for doctorate, comprehensive exam, thesis/dissertation. *Entrance requirements:* For master's, GRE General Test, career statement, 3 letters of recommendation; for doctorate, GRE General Test, 3 letters of recommendation. Additional exam requirements/recommendations for international students: required—TOEFL (minimum score 550 paper-based; 79 iBT). Electronic applications accepted.

University of Illinois at Chicago, College of Education, Department of Educational Psychology, Chicago, IL 60607-7128. Offers early childhood education (M Ed); educational psychology (PhD); measurement, evaluation, statistics, and assessment (M Ed); youth development (M Ed). *Program availability:* Part-time, online learning.

The University of Kansas, Graduate Studies, College of Liberal Arts and Sciences, Department of Psychology, Lawrence, KS 66045. Offers clinical psychology (MA, PhD); cognitive and brain sciences (MA, PhD); developmental psychology (MA, PhD); quantitative psychology (PhD); social psychology (MA, PhD). *Accreditation:* APA (one or more programs are accredited). *Program availability:* Part-time. *Students:* 72 full-time (51 women), 1 (woman) part-time; includes 16 minority (6 Black or African American, non-Hispanic/Latino; 3 Asian, non-Hispanic/Latino; 1 Hispanic/Latino; 6 Two or more races, non-Hispanic/Latino), 9 international. Average age 27. 343 applicants, 9% accepted, 17 enrolled. In 2019, 15 master's, 14 doctorates awarded. Terminal master's awarded for partial completion of doctoral program. *Entrance requirements:* For doctorate, GRE General Test, three letters of recommendation, resume/curriculum vitae, statement of purpose/personal statement, writing sample. Additional exam requirements/recommendations for international students: required—TOEFL, IELTS. *Application deadline:* For fall admission, 12/1 for domestic and international students. Application fee: $65 ($85 for international students). Electronic applications accepted. *Expenses:* Tuition, state resident: full-time $9989. Tuition, nonresident: full-time $23,950. *International tuition:* $23,950 full-time. *Required fees:* $984; $81.99 per credit hour. Tuition and fees vary according to course load, campus/location and program. *Financial support:* Fellowships, research assistantships, teaching assistantships, career-related internships or fieldwork, Federal Work-Study, scholarships/grants, health care benefits, and unspecified assistantships available. Financial award application deadline: 12/1; financial award applicants required to submit FAFSA. *Unit head:* Michael Vitevitch, Chair, 785-864-9312, E-mail: mvitevit@ku.edu. *Application contact:* Kirsten Hermreck, Graduate Admissions Contact, 785-864-4195, E-mail: psycgrad@ku.edu.
Website: http://www.psych.ku.edu/

The University of Kansas, Graduate Studies, College of Liberal Arts and Sciences, Program in Child Language, Lawrence, KS 66045. Offers MA, PhD. *Students:* Average age 32. 2 applicants, 100% accepted, 2 enrolled. In 2019, 1 master's awarded. *Entrance requirements:* For master's and doctorate, GRE, official transcripts, three letters of recommendation, personal statement, curriculum vitae. Additional exam requirements/recommendations for international students: required—TOEFL, IELTS. *Application deadline:* For fall admission, 1/15 priority date for domestic and international students. Applications are processed on a rolling basis. Application fee: $65 ($85 for international students). Electronic applications accepted. *Expenses:* Tuition, state resident: full-time $9989. Tuition, nonresident: full-time $23,950. *International tuition:* $23,950 full-time. *Required fees:* $984; $81.99 per credit hour. Tuition and fees vary according to course load, campus/location and program. *Financial support:* Fellowships, research assistantships, teaching assistantships, career-related internships or fieldwork, traineeships, and unspecified assistantships available. Financial award application deadline: 1/15. *Unit head:* Mabel L. Rice, Director, 785-864-4570, E-mail: mabel@ku.edu. *Application contact:* Suzanne Scales, Graduate Admissions Contact, 785-864-4804, E-mail: sscales@ku.edu.
Website: http://cldp.ku.edu/

University of Louisville, Graduate School, College of Arts and Sciences, Department of Psychological and Brain Sciences, Louisville, KY 40292-0001. Offers clinical psychology (PhD); experimental psychology (PhD), including cognition and development, vision and hearing. *Accreditation:* APA. *Program availability:* Part-time. *Faculty:* 24 full-time (14 women), 9 part-time/adjunct (5 women). *Students:* 50 full-time (42 women), 1 (woman) part-time; includes 5 minority (1 Black or African American, non-Hispanic/Latino; 2 Hispanic/Latino; 2 Two or more races, non-Hispanic/Latino), 6 international. Average age 29. 144 applicants, 1% accepted, 2 enrolled. In 2019, 14 doctorates awarded. *Degree requirements:* For doctorate, comprehensive exam, thesis/dissertation, coursework; internship for clinical. *Entrance requirements:* For doctorate, GRE General Test, Three letters of reference, official transcripts. Additional exam requirements/recommendations for international students: required—TOEFL (minimum score 550 paper-based; 79 iBT), IELTS can be used in place of TOEFL; recommended—IELTS (minimum score 6.5). *Application deadline:* For fall admission, 12/1 for domestic and international students. Applications are processed on a rolling basis. Application fee: $65. Electronic applications accepted. *Expenses: Tuition, area resident:* Full-time $13,000; part-time $723 per credit hour. Tuition, state resident: full-time $13,000; part-time $723 per credit hour. Tuition, nonresident: full-time $27,114; part-time $1507 per credit hour. *International tuition:* $27,114 full-time. *Required fees:* $196. Tuition and fees vary according to program and reciprocity agreements. *Financial support:* In 2019–20, 49 students received support, including 8 fellowships with full tuition reimbursements available (averaging $22,000 per year), 3 research assistantships with full tuition reimbursements available (averaging $22,000 per year), 30 teaching assistantships with full tuition reimbursements available (averaging $22,000 per year); scholarships/grants, health care benefits, and unspecified assistantships also available. Financial award application deadline: 12/1. *Unit head:* Dr. Benjamin Mast, Professor and Chair, 502-852-3280, Fax: 502-852-8904, E-mail: b.mast@louisville.edu. *Application contact:* Maggie Leahy, Administrative Assistant, 502-852-4364, Fax: 502-852-8904, E-mail: maggie.leahy@louisville.edu.
Website: http://louisville.edu/psychology

The University of Manchester, Manchester Institute of Education, Manchester, United Kingdom. Offers counseling (D Couns); counseling psychology (D Couns); education (M Phil, Ed D, PhD); educational and child psychology (Ed D); educational psychology (Ed D).

University of Maryland, Baltimore County, The Graduate School, College of Arts, Humanities and Social Sciences, Department of Psychology, Program in Applied Developmental Psychology, Baltimore, MD 21250. Offers PhD. *Faculty:* 8 full-time (6 women), 11 part-time/adjunct (4 women). *Students:* 21 full-time (19 women), 1 (woman) part-time; includes 6 minority (2 Black or African American, non-Hispanic/Latino; 3 Asian, non-Hispanic/Latino; 1 Hispanic/Latino), 7 international. Average age 28. 31 applicants, 16% accepted, 3 enrolled. In 2019, 2 doctorates awarded. *Degree requirements:* For doctorate, comprehensive exam, thesis/dissertation. *Entrance requirements:* For doctorate, GRE General Test, minimum GPA of 3.0. Additional exam requirements/recommendations for international students: required—TOEFL. *Application deadline:* For fall admission, 12/1 for domestic and international students. Application fee: $50. Electronic applications accepted. *Expenses:* $14,382 per year. *Financial support:* In 2019–20, 16 students received support, including 2 fellowships with partial tuition reimbursements available (averaging $17,250 per year), 3 research assistantships with full tuition reimbursements available (averaging $20,400 per year), 11 teaching assistantships with full tuition reimbursements available (averaging $17,250 per year); career-related internships or fieldwork, Federal Work-Study, health care benefits, and unspecified assistantships also available. Financial award application deadline: 3/1; financial award applicants required to submit FAFSA. *Unit head:* Dr. Susan Sonnenschein, Director, 410-455-2361, Fax: 410-455-1055, E-mail: sonnenschein@umbc.edu. *Application contact:* Beverly McDougall, Program Management Specialist, 410-455-2567, Fax: 410-455-1055, E-mail: psycdept@umbc.edu.
Website: http://psychology.umbc.edu/

University of Maryland, College Park, Academic Affairs, College of Behavioral and Social Sciences, Department of Psychology, College Park, MD 20742. Offers clinical psychology (PhD); developmental psychology (PhD); experimental psychology (PhD); industrial psychology (MA, MS, PhD); social psychology (PhD). *Accreditation:* APA (one or more programs are accredited). *Degree requirements:* For master's, thesis; for doctorate, variable foreign language requirement, comprehensive exam, thesis/dissertation. *Entrance requirements:* For master's and doctorate, GRE General Test, GRE Subject Test, minimum GPA of 3.5, research and/or work experience, 3 letters of recommendation. Electronic applications accepted.

University of Massachusetts Amherst, Graduate School, College of Natural Sciences, Department of Psychological and Brain Sciences, Amherst, MA 01003. Offers clinical psychology (MS, PhD); cognitive psychology (MS, PhD); developmental science (MS, PhD); psychology of peace and violence (MS, PhD); social psychology (MS, PhD). *Accreditation:* APA (one or more programs are accredited). Terminal master's awarded for partial completion of doctoral program. *Degree requirements:* For master's, thesis; for doctorate, comprehensive exam, thesis/dissertation. *Entrance requirements:* For master's and doctorate, GRE General Test, 3 letters of recommendation. Additional exam requirements/recommendations for international students: required—TOEFL (minimum score 550 paper-based; 80 iBT), IELTS (minimum score 6.5). Electronic applications accepted.

University of Miami, Graduate School, College of Arts and Sciences, Department of Psychology, Coral Gables, FL 33124. Offers adult clinical (PhD); behavioral neuroscience (PhD); child clinical (PhD); developmental psychology (PhD); health clinical (PhD); psychology (MS). *Accreditation:* APA (one or more programs are accredited). *Degree requirements:* For doctorate, comprehensive exam, thesis/dissertation. *Entrance requirements:* For doctorate, GRE General Test, minimum GPA of 3.5. Additional exam requirements/recommendations for international students: required—TOEFL. Electronic applications accepted.

University of Michigan, Rackham Graduate School, College of Literature, Science, and the Arts, Department of Psychology, Ann Arbor, MI 48109. Offers biopsychology (PhD); clinical science (PhD); cognition and cognitive neuroscience (PhD); developmental psychology (PhD); personality and social contexts (PhD); social psychology (PhD). *Accreditation:* APA. Terminal master's awarded for partial completion of doctoral program. *Degree requirements:* For doctorate, comprehensive exam, thesis/dissertation, oral defense of dissertation, preliminary exam. *Entrance requirements:* For doctorate, GRE (Biopsychology, Cognition and Cognitive Neuroscience, Developmental, Social, and Clinical); GRE Subject Test also strongly recommended (Clinical); GRE not required (Personality and Social Contexts). Additional exam requirements/recommendations for international students: required—TOEFL. Electronic applications accepted.

University of Montana, Graduate School, College of Humanities and Sciences, Department of Psychology, Missoula, MT 59812. Offers clinical psychology (PhD); experimental psychology (PhD), including animal behavior psychology, developmental psychology; school psychology (MA, PhD, Ed S). *Accreditation:* APA (one or more programs are accredited). Terminal master's awarded for partial completion of doctoral program. *Degree requirements:* For master's, thesis; for doctorate, thesis/dissertation. *Entrance requirements:* For master's, doctorate, and Ed S, GRE General Test. Additional exam requirements/recommendations for international students: required—TOEFL.

University of Nebraska–Lincoln, Graduate College, College of Arts and Sciences, Department of Psychology, Lincoln, NE 68588. Offers biopsychology (PhD); clinical psychology (PhD); cognitive psychology (PhD); developmental psychology (PhD); psychology (MA); social/personality psychology (PhD); JD/MA; JD/PhD. *Accreditation:* APA (one or more programs are accredited). *Degree requirements:* For master's, thesis optional; for doctorate, comprehensive exam, thesis/dissertation. *Entrance requirements:* For master's and doctorate, GRE General Test. Additional exam requirements/recommendations for international students: required—TOEFL (minimum score 550 paper-based). Electronic applications accepted.

University of Nebraska–Lincoln, Graduate College, College of Education and Human Sciences, Department of Educational Psychology, Lincoln, NE 68588. Offers cognition, learning and development (MA); counseling psychology (MA); educational psychology (MA, Ed S); psychological studies in education (PhD), including cognition, learning and development, counseling psychology, quantitative, qualitative, and psychometric methods, school psychology; quantitative, qualitative, and psychometric methods (MA); school psychology (MA, Ed S). *Accreditation:* APA (one or more programs are accredited); NCATE. *Degree requirements:* For master's, thesis optional. *Entrance requirements:* For master's, GRE General Test. Additional exam requirements/recommendations for international students: required—TOEFL (minimum score 500 paper-based). Electronic applications accepted.

University of New Mexico, Graduate Studies, College of Arts and Sciences, Program in Psychology, Albuquerque, NM 87131-2039. Offers behavioral neuroscience (PhD); clinical psychology (PhD); cognitive neuroimaging (PhD); developmental psychology (PhD); evolution (PhD); health psychology (PhD); quantitative methodology (PhD). *Accreditation:* APA. *Degree requirements:* For doctorate, comprehensive exam, thesis/dissertation. *Entrance requirements:* For doctorate, GRE General Test, GRE Subject Test (psychology), minimum GPA of 3.0. Additional exam requirements/recommendations for international students: required—TOEFL (minimum score 550 paper-based; 79 iBT), IELTS (minimum score 6.5). Electronic applications accepted. *Expenses:* Tuition, state resident: full-time $7633; part-time $972 per year. Tuition, nonresident: full-time $22,586; part-time $3840 per year. *International tuition:* $23,292 full-time. *Required fees:* $8608. Tuition and fees vary according to course level, course load, degree level, program and student level.

The University of North Carolina at Chapel Hill, Graduate School, College of Arts and Sciences, Department of Psychology, Chapel Hill, NC 27599-3270. Offers behavioral neuroscience psychology (PhD); clinical psychology (PhD); cognitive psychology (PhD); developmental psychology (PhD); quantitative psychology (PhD); social psychology (PhD). *Accreditation:* APA. *Degree requirements:* For doctorate, comprehensive exam, thesis/dissertation. *Entrance requirements:* For doctorate, GRE General Test, minimum GPA of 3.0. Additional exam requirements/recommendations for international students: required—TOEFL (minimum score 550 paper-based; 79 iBT), IELTS (minimum score 7). Electronic applications accepted.

The University of North Carolina at Greensboro, Graduate School, College of Arts and Sciences, Department of Psychology, Greensboro, NC 27412-5001. Offers clinical psychology (MA, PhD); cognitive psychology (MA, PhD); developmental psychology (MA, PhD); social psychology (MA, PhD). *Accreditation:* APA (one or more programs are accredited). Terminal master's awarded for partial completion of doctoral program. *Degree requirements:* For master's, comprehensive exam, thesis; for doctorate, one foreign language, thesis/dissertation, preliminary exam. *Entrance requirements:* For master's and doctorate, GRE General Test. Additional exam requirements/recommendations for international students: required—TOEFL. Electronic applications accepted.

University of Notre Dame, The Graduate School, College of Arts and Letters, Division of Social Sciences, Department of Psychology, Notre Dame, IN 46556. Offers cognitive psychology (PhD); counseling psychology (PhD); developmental psychology (PhD); quantitative psychology (PhD). *Accreditation:* APA. *Degree requirements:* For doctorate, comprehensive exam, thesis/dissertation, candidacy exam. *Entrance requirements:* For doctorate, GRE General Test, GRE Subject Test (strongly recommended). Additional exam requirements/recommendations for international students: required—TOEFL (minimum score 600 paper-based; 80 iBT). Electronic applications accepted.

University of Oregon, Graduate School, College of Arts and Sciences, Department of Psychology, Eugene, OR 97403. Offers clinical psychology (PhD); cognitive psychology (MA, MS, PhD); developmental psychology (MA, MS, PhD); physiological psychology (MA, MS, PhD); psychology (MA, MS, PhD); social/personality psychology (MA, MS, PhD). *Accreditation:* APA (one or more programs are accredited). Terminal master's awarded for partial completion of doctoral program. *Degree requirements:* For doctorate, thesis/dissertation. *Entrance requirements:* For master's, GRE General Test, minimum GPA of 3.0; for doctorate, GRE General Test. Additional exam requirements/recommendations for international students: required—TOEFL.

University of Pittsburgh, Kenneth P. Dietrich School of Arts and Sciences, Department of Psychology, Pittsburgh, PA 15260. Offers biological and health psychology (PhD); clinical psychology (PhD); cognitive psychology (PhD); developmental psychology (PhD); social psychology (PhD). *Accreditation:* APA. *Faculty:* 33 full-time (18 women), 10 part-time/adjunct (3 women). *Students:* 90 full-time (73 women); includes 25 minority (4 Black or African American, non-Hispanic/Latino; 2 American Indian or Alaska Native, non-Hispanic/Latino; 10 Asian, non-Hispanic/Latino; 2 Hispanic/Latino; 7 Two or more races, non-Hispanic/Latino). Average age 25. 580 applicants, 6% accepted, 18 enrolled. In 2019, 16 doctorates awarded. Terminal master's awarded for partial completion of doctoral program. *Degree requirements:* For doctorate, comprehensive exam, thesis/dissertation. *Entrance requirements:* For doctorate, GRE General Test, minimum GPA of 3.0. Additional exam requirements/recommendations for international students: required—TOEFL (minimum score 550 paper-based; 90 iBT). *Application deadline:* For fall admission, 12/1 for domestic and international students. Application fee: $75. Electronic applications accepted. *Financial support:* In 2019–20, 90 students received support, including 38 fellowships with full tuition reimbursements available (averaging $30,378 per year), 19 research assistantships with full tuition reimbursements available (averaging $29,220 per year), 33 teaching assistantships with full tuition reimbursements available (averaging $29,220 per year); career-related internships or fieldwork, scholarships/grants, health care benefits, and unspecified assistantships also available. Financial award application deadline: 12/1. *Unit head:* Dr. Julie Fiez, Chair, 412-624-7078, Fax: 412-422-9149, E-mail: fiez@pitt.edu. *Application contact:* Francesca Sirianni, Graduate Administrator, 412-624-4502, Fax: 412-624-4428, E-mail: psygrad@pitt.edu.
Website: http://www.psychology.pitt.edu/

University of Rochester, School of Arts and Sciences, Psychology, Rochester, NY 14627. Offers clinical psychology (PhD); developmental psychology (PhD); social-personality psychology (PhD). *Accreditation:* APA. *Faculty:* 16 full-time (9 women). *Students:* 42 full-time (35 women); includes 10 minority (1 Black or African American, non-Hispanic/Latino; 5 Asian, non-Hispanic/Latino; 3 Hispanic/Latino; 1 Two or more races, non-Hispanic/Latino), 5 international. Average age 28. 240 applicants, 6% accepted, 9 enrolled. In 2019, 10 doctorates awarded. Terminal master's awarded for partial completion of doctoral program. *Degree requirements:* For doctorate, thesis/dissertation. *Entrance requirements:* For doctorate, GRE General Test (optional for Fall 2021 admission cycle), personal statement, official transcripts, three letters of recommendation, curriculum vitae or resume. Additional exam requirements/recommendations for international students: required—TOEFL. *Application deadline:* For fall admission, 12/1 for domestic and international students. Application fee: $20. Electronic applications accepted. *Financial support:* In 2019–20, 35 students received support, including 5 fellowships with full tuition reimbursements available, 8 research assistantships with full tuition reimbursements available (averaging $24,000 per year), 22 teaching assistantships with full tuition reimbursements available (averaging $24,000 per year); career-related internships or fieldwork, scholarships/grants, and tuition waivers (full) also available. Financial award application deadline: 4/15. *Unit head:* Loisa Bennetto, Chair, 585-275-8712, E-mail: loisa.bennetto@rochester.edu. *Application contact:* Loisa Bennetto, Chair, 585-275-8712, E-mail: loisa.bennetto@rochester.edu.
Website: http://www.sas.rochester.edu/psy/graduate/index.html

University of Southern California, Graduate School, Dana and David Dornsife College of Letters, Arts and Sciences, Department of Psychology, Los Angeles, CA 90089. Offers brain and cognitive science (PhD); clinical science (PhD); developmental psychology (PhD); human behavior (MHB); quantitative methods (PhD); social psychology (PhD). *Accreditation:* APA. *Degree requirements:* For doctorate, comprehensive exam, thesis/dissertation, one-year internship (for clinical science students). *Entrance requirements:* For doctorate, GRE. Additional exam requirements/recommendations for international students: recommended—TOEFL (minimum score 600 paper-based; 100 iBT). Electronic applications accepted.

The University of Texas at Austin, Graduate School, College of Liberal Arts, Department of Psychology, Austin, TX 78712-1111. Offers behavioral neuroscience (PhD); clinical psychology (PhD); cognitive systems (PhD); developmental psychology (PhD); individual differences and evolutionary psychology (PhD); perceptual systems (PhD); social psychology (PhD). *Accreditation:* APA. *Degree requirements:* For doctorate, thesis/dissertation. *Entrance requirements:* For doctorate, GRE General Test. Electronic applications accepted.

University of Utah, Graduate School, College of Social and Behavioral Science, Department of Psychology, Salt Lake City, UT 84112. Offers clinical psychology (PhD); psychology (PhD), including cognitive neuroscience, developmental psychology, social psychology. *Accreditation:* APA. *Faculty:* 27 full-time (14 women), 1 (woman) part-time/adjunct. *Students:* 53 full-time (40 women); includes 8 minority (1 Black or African American, non-Hispanic/Latino; 4 Hispanic/Latino; 3 Two or more races, non-Hispanic/Latino), 6 international. Average age 28. 295 applicants, 8% accepted, 13 enrolled. In 2019, 11 doctorates awarded. *Degree requirements:* For doctorate, thesis/dissertation. *Entrance requirements:* For doctorate, GRE General Test. Additional exam requirements/recommendations for international students: required—TOEFL (minimum score 500 paper-based). *Application deadline:* For fall admission, 12/1 for domestic and international students. Application fee: $55 ($65 for international students). Electronic applications accepted. *Expenses:* Tuition, state resident: full-time $7085; part-time $272.51 per credit hour. Tuition, nonresident: full-time $24,937; part-time $959.12 per credit hour. *Required fees:* $880.52; $880.52 per semester. Tuition and fees vary according to degree level, program and student level. *Financial support:* In 2019–20, 5 fellowships (averaging $13,400 per year), 22 research assistantships (averaging $15,000 per year), 33 teaching assistantships (averaging $14,909 per year) were awarded; unspecified assistantships also available. Financial award applicants required to submit FAFSA. *Unit head:* Dr. Bert N. Uchino, Chair, 801-581-8925, Fax: 801-581-5841, E-mail: bert.uchino@psych.utah.edu. *Application contact:* Nancy Seegmiller, Program Manager, 801-581-8925, Fax: 801-581-5841, E-mail: nancy.seegmiller@psych.utah.edu.
Website: http://www.psych.utah.edu/

University of Vermont, Graduate College, College of Arts and Sciences, Program in General/Experimental Psychology, Burlington, VT 05405-0134. Offers psychology (PhD), including biobehavioral psychology, developmental psychology, human behavioral pharmacology, social psychology. *Accreditation:* APA. *Degree requirements:* For doctorate, thesis/dissertation. *Entrance requirements:* For doctorate, GRE General Test. Additional exam requirements/recommendations for international students: required—TOEFL (minimum score 550 paper-based, 100 iBT) or IELTS (7). Electronic applications accepted.

University of Victoria, Faculty of Graduate Studies, Faculty of Social Sciences, Department of Psychology, Victoria, BC V8W 2Y2, Canada. Offers clinical psychology (PhD); clinical psychology (neuropsychology) (M Sc); cognition and brain science (M Sc, PhD); experimental neuropsychology (M Sc, PhD); individualized study (M Sc, PhD); life span development psychology (PhD); life span developmental psychology (M Sc); social psychology (M Sc, PhD). *Degree requirements:* For master's, thesis; for doctorate, thesis/dissertation, candidacy exam. *Entrance requirements:* For master's and doctorate, GRE General Test. Additional exam requirements/recommendations for international students: required—TOEFL (minimum score 600 paper-based). Electronic applications accepted.

University of Washington, Graduate School, College of Arts and Sciences, Department of Psychology, Seattle, WA 98195. Offers animal behavior (PhD); applied child and adolescent psychology: prevention and treatment (MA); behavioral neuroscience (PhD); clinical psychology (PhD); cognition and perception (PhD); developmental psychology (PhD); quantitative psychology (PhD); social psychology and personality (PhD). *Accreditation:* APA (one or more programs are accredited). *Degree requirements:* For doctorate, thesis/dissertation. *Entrance requirements:* For doctorate, GRE General Test, minimum GPA of 3.0. Electronic applications accepted.

University of Wisconsin–Madison, Graduate School, College of Letters and Science, Department of Psychology, Program in Developmental Psychology, Madison, WI 53706-1380. Offers PhD. *Degree requirements:* For doctorate, comprehensive exam, thesis/dissertation. *Entrance requirements:* For doctorate, GRE General Test, minimum undergraduate GPA of 3.0. Additional exam requirements/recommendations for international students: required—TOEFL. Electronic applications accepted.

University of Wisconsin–Milwaukee, Graduate School, School of Education, Department of Educational Psychology, Milwaukee, WI 53201-0413. Offers children's mental health for school professionals (Graduate Certificate); counseling psychology (PhD); educational statistics and measurement (MS, PhD); learning and development (MS, PhD); multicultural knowledge of mental health practices (Graduate Certificate); school counseling (MS, Graduate Certificate); school psychology (MS, PhD, Ed S). *Accreditation:* APA. *Program availability:* Part-time. *Degree requirements:* For master's, comprehensive exam, thesis; for doctorate, thesis/dissertation. *Entrance requirements:* For master's, minimum GPA of 3.0; for doctorate, GRE General Test, minimum GPA of 3.0. Additional exam requirements/recommendations for international students: required—TOEFL (minimum score 550 paper-based; 79 iBT), IELTS (minimum score 6.5). Electronic applications accepted.

Viterbo University, Master of Science in Mental Health Counseling Program, La Crosse, WI 54601-4797. Offers addiction counseling (MS); child and adolescent counseling (MS); complementary health and wellness counseling (MS). *Accreditation:* ACA. *Program availability:* Part-time, evening/weekend. *Degree requirements:* For master's, comprehensive exam, thesis, 54 credits of core program courses; 6 elective credits; minimum GPA of 3.0; action research project; practicum/internship experience. *Entrance requirements:* For master's, MAT, BS in a human service or social science discipline; prerequisite coursework in general psychology, behavior disorders/abnormal psychology, and research methods/statistics; minimum undergraduate cumulative GPA of 3.0; background check; personal statement; undergraduate transcripts; interview. Additional exam requirements/recommendations for international students: required—TOEFL (minimum score 525 paper-based). Electronic applications accepted. Application fee is waived when completed online. *Expenses:* Contact institution.

Washington University in St. Louis, The Graduate School, Department of Psychological and Brain Sciences, St. Louis, MO 63130-4899. Offers aging and development (PhD). Terminal master's awarded for partial completion of doctoral program. *Degree requirements:* For doctorate, thesis/dissertation. *Entrance requirements:* For doctorate, GRE General Test. Additional exam requirements/recommendations for international students: required—TOEFL. Electronic applications accepted.

Wilfrid Laurier University, Faculty of Graduate and Postdoctoral Studies, Faculty of Science, Department of Psychology, Waterloo, ON N2L 3C5, Canada. Offers behavioral neuroscience (M Sc, PhD); cognitive neuroscience (M Sc, PhD); community psychology (MA, PhD); social and developmental psychology (MA, PhD). *Program availability:* Part-time. *Degree requirements:* For master's, thesis; for doctorate, thesis/dissertation. *Entrance requirements:* For master's, GRE General Test, honors BA or the equivalent in psychology, minimum B average in undergraduate course work; for doctorate, GRE General Test, master's degree, minimum A- average. Additional exam requirements/recommendations for international students: required—TOEFL (minimum score 89 iBT). Electronic applications accepted.

Yale University, Graduate School of Arts and Sciences, Department of Psychology, New Haven, CT 06520. Offers behavioral neuroscience (PhD); clinical psychology (PhD); cognitive psychology (PhD); developmental psychology (PhD); social/personality psychology (PhD). *Accreditation:* APA. *Degree requirements:* For doctorate, thesis/dissertation. *Entrance requirements:* For doctorate, GRE General Test.

Experimental Psychology

Azusa Pacific University, School of Behavioral and Applied Sciences, Department of Psychology, Azusa, CA 91702-7000. Offers child life (MS); research psychology and data analytics (MS).

Bowling Green State University, Graduate College, College of Arts and Sciences, Department of Psychology, Bowling Green, OH 43403. Offers clinical psychology (MA, PhD); developmental psychology (MA, PhD); experimental psychology (MA, PhD); industrial/organizational psychology (MA, PhD); quantitative psychology (MA, PhD). *Accreditation:* APA (one or more programs are accredited). *Degree requirements:* For doctorate, thesis/dissertation. *Entrance requirements:* For doctorate, GRE General Test, GRE Subject Test. Additional exam requirements/recommendations for international students: required—TOEFL. Electronic applications accepted.

Brooklyn College of the City University of New York, School of Natural and Behavioral Sciences, Department of Psychology, Brooklyn, NY 11210-2889. Offers experimental psychology (MA); industrial and organizational psychology (MA), including human relations, organizational behavior; mental health counseling (MA); psychology (PhD). *Program availability:* Part-time. *Degree requirements:* For master's, comprehensive exam, thesis (for some programs). *Entrance requirements:* For master's, minimum GPA of 3.0, 2 letters of recommendation, essay; for doctorate, GRE. Additional exam requirements/recommendations for international students: required—TOEFL (minimum score 520 paper-based; 69 iBT). Electronic applications accepted.

California State University, Fresno, Division of Research and Graduate Studies, College of Science and Mathematics, Department of Psychology, Fresno, CA 93740-8027. Offers applied behavior analysis (MA); general/experimental psychology (MA); school psychology (Ed S). *Degree requirements:* For master's, thesis. *Entrance requirements:* For master's, GRE General Test, GRE Subject Test, minimum GPA of 3.0. Additional exam requirements/recommendations for international students: required—TOEFL. Electronic applications accepted. *Expenses:* Tuition, state resident: full-time $4012; part-time $2506 per semester.

California State University, Northridge, Graduate Studies, College of Social and Behavioral Sciences, Department of Psychology, Northridge, CA 91330. Offers clinical psychology (MA); general experimental psychology (MA). *Degree requirements:* For master's, thesis. *Entrance requirements:* For master's, GRE General Test, GRE Subject Test, minimum GPA of 3.0, letters of recommendation. Additional exam requirements/recommendations for international students: required—TOEFL.

Case Western Reserve University, School of Graduate Studies, Psychological Sciences Department, Program in Experimental Psychology, Cleveland, OH 44106. Offers PhD. *Faculty:* 10 full-time (5 women). *Students:* 4 full-time (3 women); includes 1 minority (Asian, non-Hispanic/Latino), 1 international. Average age 28. 187 applicants, 3% accepted, 4 enrolled. In 2019, 3 doctorates awarded. *Degree requirements:* For doctorate, thesis/dissertation, internship. *Entrance requirements:* For doctorate, GRE General Test, GRE Subject Test, personal statement, three letters of recommendation, curriculum vitae. Additional exam requirements/recommendations for international students: required—TOEFL (minimum score 577 paper-based; 90 iBT); recommended—IELTS (minimum score 7). *Application deadline:* For fall admission, 1/15 priority date for domestic students. Application fee: $50. Electronic applications accepted. *Financial support:* Research assistantships, teaching assistantships, and health care benefits available. Financial award application deadline: 1/15; financial award applicants required to submit FAFSA. *Unit head:* Dr. Heath Demaree, Professor and Chair, 216-368-6468, E-mail: psychsciences@case.edu. *Application contact:* Arin Connell, Associate Professor and Director of Clinical Training, 216-368-1550, E-mail: arin.connell@case.edu.
Website: http://psychsciences.case.edu/graduate/

The Catholic University of America, School of Arts and Sciences, Department of Psychology, Washington, DC 20064. Offers applied experimental psychology (PhD); clinical psychology (PhD); general psychology (MA); human development psychology (PhD); human factors (MA); MA/JD. *Accreditation:* APA (one or more programs are accredited). *Program availability:* Part-time. *Faculty:* 9 full-time (5 women), 8 part-time/adjunct (all women). *Students:* 31 full-time (27 women), 40 part-time (33 women); includes 19 minority (3 Black or African American, non-Hispanic/Latino; 3 Asian, non-Hispanic/Latino; 5 Hispanic/Latino; 8 Two or more races, non-Hispanic/Latino), 6 international. Average age 28. 160 applicants, 25% accepted, 17 enrolled. In 2019, 19 master's, 8 doctorates awarded. *Degree requirements:* For master's, comprehensive exam, thesis (for some programs); for doctorate, comprehensive exam, thesis/dissertation. *Entrance requirements:* For master's, GRE General Test, statement of purpose, official copies of academic transcripts, three letters of recommendation; for doctorate, GRE General Test, GRE Subject Test, statement of purpose, official copies of academic transcripts, three letters of recommendation. Additional exam requirements/recommendations for international students: required—TOEFL (minimum score 550 paper-based; 80 iBT). *Application deadline:* For fall admission, 7/15 priority date for domestic students, 7/1 for international students; for spring admission, 11/15 priority date for domestic students, 11/1 for international students. Applications are processed on a rolling basis. Application fee: $55. Electronic applications accepted. *Expenses:* Contact institution. *Financial support:* Fellowships, research assistantships, teaching assistantships, Federal Work-Study, scholarships/grants, tuition waivers (full and partial), and unspecified assistantships available. Financial award application deadline: 2/1; financial award applicants required to submit FAFSA. *Unit head:* Dr. Brendan Rich, Chair, 202-319-5823, Fax: 202-319-6263, E-mail: richb@cua.edu. *Application contact:* Dr. Steven Brown, Director of Graduate Admissions, 202-319-5057, Fax: 202-319-6533, E-mail: cua-admissions@cua.edu.
Website: http://psychology.cua.edu

Central Michigan University, College of Graduate Studies, College of Liberal Arts and Social Sciences, Department of Psychology, Program in Experimental Psychology, Mount Pleasant, MI 48859. Offers applied experimental psychology (PhD); experimental psychology (MS). *Program availability:* Part-time. *Degree requirements:* For master's, thesis or alternative; for doctorate, thesis/dissertation. Electronic applications accepted. *Expenses: Tuition, area resident:* Full-time $12,267; part-time $8178 per year. *Tuition, state resident:* full-time $12,267; part-time $8178 per year. *Tuition, nonresident:* full-time $12,267; part-time $8178 per year. *International tuition:* $16,110 full-time. *Required fees:* $225 per semester. Tuition and fees vary according to degree level and program.

Central Washington University, School of Graduate Studies and Research, College of the Sciences, Department of Psychology, Program in Experimental Psychology, Ellensburg, WA 98926. Offers MS. *Entrance requirements:* For master's, GRE General Test, minimum GPA of 3.0. Additional exam requirements/recommendations for international students: required—TOEFL (minimum score 550 paper-based; 79 iBT). Electronic applications accepted.

Cornell University, Graduate School, Graduate Fields of Arts and Sciences, Field of Psychology, Ithaca, NY 14853. Offers biopsychology (PhD); human experimental psychology (PhD); personality and social psychology (PhD). *Degree requirements:* For doctorate, comprehensive exam, thesis/dissertation, 2 semesters of teaching experience. *Entrance requirements:* For doctorate, GRE General Test, 3 letters of recommendation. Additional exam requirements/recommendations for international students: required—TOEFL (minimum score 550 paper-based; 77 iBT). Electronic applications accepted.

Duke University, Graduate School, Department of Psychology and Neuroscience, Durham, NC 27708. Offers biological psychology (PhD); clinical psychology (PhD); cognitive psychology (PhD); developmental psychology (PhD); experimental psychology (PhD); health psychology (PhD); human social development (PhD); JD/MA. *Accreditation:* APA (one or more programs are accredited). *Degree requirements:* For doctorate, thesis/dissertation. *Entrance requirements:* For doctorate, GRE General Test. Additional exam requirements/recommendations for international students: required—TOEFL (minimum score 577 paper-based; 90 iBT) or IELTS (minimum score 7). Electronic applications accepted.

Eastern Washington University, Graduate Studies, College of Social Sciences, Department of Psychology, Cheney, WA 99004-2431. Offers clinical psychology (MS); experimental psychology (MS); mental health counseling (MS), including applied psychology, mental health counseling; school counseling (MS), including applied psychology, school counseling; school psychology respecialization (Ed S). *Faculty:* 22 full-time (15 women). *Students:* 119 full-time (94 women), 13 part-time (10 women); includes 3 minority (all Hispanic/Latino), 6 international. Average age 34. 83 applicants,

42% accepted, 31 enrolled. In 2019, 49 master's awarded. *Degree requirements:* For master's, comprehensive exam, thesis or alternative. *Entrance requirements:* For master's, GRE General Test, minimum GPA of 3.0. Additional exam requirements/recommendations for international students: required—TOEFL (minimum score 580 paper-based; 92 iBT), IELTS (minimum score 7), PTE (minimum score 63). *Application deadline:* For fall admission, 3/1 for domestic students. Applications are processed on a rolling basis. Application fee: $75. Electronic applications accepted. *Financial support:* Teaching assistantships with partial tuition reimbursements, career-related internships or fieldwork, Federal Work-Study, institutionally sponsored loans, scholarships/grants, health care benefits, tuition waivers (partial), and unspecified assistantships available. Support available to part-time students. Financial award application deadline: 2/1; financial award applicants required to submit FAFSA. *Unit head:* Dennis Anderson, 509-359-2087, E-mail: danderson2@ewu.edu. *Application contact:* Kathy White, Advisor/Recruiter for Graduate Studies, 509-359-6297, Fax: 509-359-6044, E-mail: gradprograms@ewu.edu.

East Tennessee State University, College of Graduate and Continuing Studies, College of Arts and Sciences, Department of Psychology, Johnson City, TN 37614. Offers clinical psychology (PhD); experimental psychology (PhD). *Accreditation:* APA. Terminal master's awarded for partial completion of doctoral program. *Degree requirements:* For doctorate, thesis/dissertation, externship. *Entrance requirements:* For doctorate, GRE General Test, minimum GPA of 3.0, three letters of recommendation, interview, minimum of 18 semester hours in undergraduate psychology. Additional exam requirements/recommendations for international students: required—TOEFL (minimum score 550 paper-based; 79 iBT). Electronic applications accepted.

Fairleigh Dickinson University, Metropolitan Campus, University College: Arts, Sciences, and Professional Studies, School of Psychology, Program in General-Theoretical Psychology, Teaneck, NJ 07666-1914. Offers MA, Certificate.

The Graduate Center, City University of New York, Graduate Studies, Program in Psychology, New York, NY 10016-4039. Offers basic applied neurocognition (PhD); biopsychology (PhD); clinical psychology (PhD); developmental psychology (PhD); environmental psychology (PhD); experimental psychology (PhD); industrial psychology (PhD); learning processes (PhD); neuropsychology (PhD); psychology (PhD); social personality (PhD). *Degree requirements:* For doctorate, one foreign language, thesis/dissertation. *Entrance requirements:* For doctorate, GRE General Test. Additional exam requirements/recommendations for international students: required—TOEFL. Electronic applications accepted.

Harvard University, Graduate School of Arts and Sciences, Department of Psychology, Cambridge, MA 02138. Offers psychology (PhD), including behavior and decision analysis, cognition, developmental psychology, experimental psychology, personality, psychobiology, psychopathology; social psychology (PhD). *Accreditation:* APA. *Degree requirements:* For doctorate, thesis/dissertation, general exams. *Entrance requirements:* For doctorate, GRE General Test. Additional exam requirements/recommendations for international students: required—TOEFL.

Howard University, Graduate School, Department of Psychology, Washington, DC 20059-0002. Offers clinical psychology (PhD); developmental psychology (PhD); experimental psychology (PhD); neuropsychology (PhD); personality psychology (PhD); psychology (MS); social psychology (PhD). *Accreditation:* APA (one or more programs are accredited). *Program availability:* Part-time. *Degree requirements:* For master's, thesis; for doctorate, comprehensive exam, thesis/dissertation, qualifying exam. *Entrance requirements:* For master's, GRE General Test, minimum GPA of 2.5, bachelor's degree in psychology or related field; for doctorate, GRE General Test, minimum GPA of 3.0.

Idaho State University, Graduate School, College of Arts and Letters, Department of Psychology, Program in Experimental Psychology, Pocatello, ID 83209. Offers PhD. *Entrance requirements:* For doctorate, GRE, BA/BS in psychology or the equivalent, minimum undergraduate GPA of 3.0 for the last two years.

Iona College, School of Arts and Science, Department of Psychology, New Rochelle, NY 10801-1890. Offers general-experimental psychology (MA); human resources (Certificate); industrial-organizational psychology (MA); mental health counseling (MA); organizational behavior (Certificate); psychology (MA); school psychology (MA). *Program availability:* Part-time. *Faculty:* 8 full-time (4 women), 12 part-time/adjunct (8 women). *Students:* 71 full-time (64 women), 41 part-time (34 women); includes 51 minority (12 Black or African American, non-Hispanic/Latino; 5 Asian, non-Hispanic/Latino; 28 Hispanic/Latino; 1 Native Hawaiian or other Pacific Islander, non-Hispanic/Latino; 5 Two or more races, non-Hispanic/Latino), 3 international. Average age 25. 104 applicants, 85% accepted, 34 enrolled. In 2019, 29 master's, 15 other advanced degrees awarded. *Degree requirements:* For master's, thesis (for some programs), literature review (for some programs). *Entrance requirements:* For master's, BA in psychology including 3 credits each in psychology statistics and experimental research methods, or 9 credits in psychology including 3 credits each in psychology statistics, psychology research methods and upper-level coursework. Additional exam requirements/recommendations for international students: required—TOEFL (minimum score 550 paper-based), IELTS (minimum score 6.5). *Application deadline:* For fall admission, 8/15 for domestic students, 5/1 for international students; for spring admission, 1/15 for domestic students, 9/1 for international students. Applications are processed on a rolling basis. Electronic applications accepted. *Financial support:* In 2019–20, 51 students received support, including 4 research assistantships with partial tuition reimbursements available (averaging $10,143 per year); scholarships/grants, tuition waivers (partial), and unspecified assistantships also available. Support available to part-time students. Financial award application deadline: 4/15; financial award applicants required to submit FAFSA. *Unit head:* Colleen Jacobsen, PhD, Chair, 914-637-2770, E-mail: cjacobsen@iona.edu. *Application contact:* Shantell Smith, Associate Director of Graduate Admissions, Arts and Science, 914-633-2440, Fax: 914-633-2277, E-mail: ssmith@iona.edu.
Website: http://www.iona.edu/Academics/School-of-Arts-Science/Departments/Psychology/Graduate-Programs.aspx

James Madison University, The Graduate School, College of Health and Behavioral Studies, Program in Psychological Sciences, Harrisonburg, VA 22807. Offers applied research (MA); behavior analysis (MA); experimental psychology (MA); quantitative psychology (MA). *Program availability:* Part-time, evening/weekend. *Students:* 24 full-time (20 women); includes 7 minority (1 Black or African American, non-Hispanic/Latino; 3 Asian, non-Hispanic/Latino; 3 Hispanic/Latino), 1 international. Average age 30. In 2019, 12 master's awarded. Application fee: $60. Electronic applications accepted. *Financial support:* In 2019–20, 22 students received support, including 1 teaching assistantship with full tuition reimbursement available (averaging $9,284 per year); career-related internships or fieldwork, Federal Work-Study, and assistantships (averaging $7911) also available. Financial award application deadline: 3/1; financial award applicants required to submit FAFSA. *Unit head:* Dr. Jeff S. Dyche, Graduate Program Director, 540-568-4965, E-mail: dychejs@jmu.edu. *Application contact:* Lynette D. Michael, Director of Graduate Admissions, 540-568-6131 Ext. 6395, Fax: 540-568-7860, E-mail: michaeld@jmu.edu.
Website: http://www.psyc.jmu.edu/psycsciences/

Kent State University, College of Arts and Sciences, Department of Psychological Sciences, Kent, OH 44242-0001. Offers clinical psychology (MA, PhD), including gerontology (MA), psychological sciences (MA); experimental psychology (MA, PhD), including gerontology (MA), psychological sciences (MA). *Accreditation:* APA (one or more programs are accredited). *Faculty:* 28 full-time (15 women), 4 part-time/adjunct (2 women). *Students:* 79 full-time (63 women); includes 17 minority (6 Black or African American, non-Hispanic/Latino; 5 Asian, non-Hispanic/Latino; 4 Hispanic/Latino; 2 Two or more races, non-Hispanic/Latino), 3 international. Average age 26. 284 applicants, 8% accepted, 16 enrolled. In 2019, 13 master's, 9 doctorates awarded. *Degree requirements:* For master's, thesis, Min grade in Quantitative Statistical Analysis I and II is B-. College of Arts & Sciences requires students to have a 3.0 average from all graduate courses attempted; for doctorate, comprehensive exam, thesis/dissertation. *Entrance requirements:* For master's, GRE General Test, statement of goals and motivations, transcripts, 3 letters of recommendation, minimum junior-senior GPA of 3.0, 18 semester hours of credit in psychology which includes at least one course in statistics and a broad background in psychology; for doctorate, GRE General Test, statement of goals and motivations, transcripts, 3 letters of recommendation, minimum junior-senior GPA of 3.0, 18 semester hours of credit in psychology which includes at least one course in statistics and a broad background in psychology. Additional exam requirements/recommendations for international students: required—TOEFL (minimum score 94 iBT), IELTS (minimum score 7), PTE (minimum score 65), Michigan English Language Assessment Battery (minimum score 82. *Application deadline:* For fall admission, 12/1 for domestic and international students. Applications are processed on a rolling basis. Application fee: $45 ($70 for international students). Electronic applications accepted. *Financial support:* Federal Work-Study, health care benefits, and unspecified assistantships available. Financial award application deadline: 12/1; financial award applicants required to submit FAFSA. *Unit head:* Dr. Maria S. Zaragoza, Professor, Department Chair, 330-672-2166, E-mail: mzaragoz@kent.edu. *Application contact:* Dr. John A. Updegraff, Professor and Graduate Coordinator, 330-672-2166, E-mail: jupdegr1@kent.edu.
Website: https://www.kent.edu/psychology

Lakehead University, Graduate Studies, Department of Psychology, Thunder Bay, ON P7B 5E1, Canada. Offers clinical psychology (PhD); experimental psychology (MA). *Program availability:* Part-time, evening/weekend. *Degree requirements:* For master's, thesis optional; for doctorate, thesis/dissertation, 2 comprehensive exams, internship. *Entrance requirements:* For master's, GRE, honors degree in psychology, advanced course work in statistics, minimum B average; for doctorate, GRE, minimum B average. Additional exam requirements/recommendations for international students: required—TOEFL.

Laurentian University, School of Graduate Studies and Research, Programme in Psychology, Sudbury, ON P3E 2C6, Canada. Offers applied psychology (MA); experimental psychology (MA).

McGill University, Faculty of Graduate and Postdoctoral Studies, Faculty of Science, Department of Psychology, Montréal, QC H3A 2T5, Canada. Offers clinical psychology (PhD); experimental psychology (M Sc, MA, PhD).

McNeese State University, Doré School of Graduate Studies, Burton College of Education, Department of Psychology, Lake Charles, LA 70609. Offers applied behavior analysis (MA, Graduate Certificate); counseling psychology (MA); general/experimental psychology (MA). *Program availability:* Evening/weekend. *Entrance requirements:* For master's, GRE.

Memorial University of Newfoundland, School of Graduate Studies, Department of Psychology, St. John's, NL A1C 5S7, Canada. Offers applied psychological sciences (MAPS); clinical psychology (Psy D); experimental psychology (M Sc, PhD). *Program availability:* Part-time. *Degree requirements:* For master's, workterms (MASP), thesis (M Sc); for doctorate, comprehensive exam, thesis/dissertation, oral thesis defense. *Entrance requirements:* For master's, GRE, honors bachelor's degree of high second class standing or equivalent; for doctorate, GRE, master's or honors degree. Electronic applications accepted.

Middle Tennessee State University, College of Graduate Studies, College of Behavioral and Health Sciences, Department of Psychology, Murfreesboro, TN 37132. Offers clinical psychology (MA); experimental psychology (MA); industrial/organizational psychology (MA); psychology (MA, Ed S); quantitative psychology (MA); school psychology (MA). *Program availability:* Part-time, evening/weekend, online learning. *Degree requirements:* For master's, comprehensive exam, thesis. *Entrance requirements:* For master's, GRE. Additional exam requirements/recommendations for international students: required—TOEFL (minimum score 525 paper-based; 71 iBT) or IELTS (minimum score 6). Electronic applications accepted.

Missouri State University, Graduate College, College of Health and Human Services, Department of Psychology, Springfield, MO 65897. Offers applied behavior analysis (MS); clinical psychology (MS); experimental psychology (MS); forensic child psychology (Certificate); industrial/organizational psychology (MS). *Degree requirements:* For master's, comprehensive exam, thesis. *Entrance requirements:* For master's, GRE General Test, GRE Subject Test, minimum GPA of 3.25 in major, 3.0 overall; 20 hours of course work in psychology. Additional exam requirements/recommendations for international students: required—TOEFL (minimum score 550 paper-based; 79 iBT), IELTS (minimum score 6). Electronic applications accepted. *Expenses: Tuition, area resident:* Full-time $2600; part-time $1735 per credit hour. Tuition, nonresident: full-time $5240; part-time $3495 per credit hour. *International tuition:* $5240 full-time. *Required fees:* $530; $438 per credit hour. Tuition and fees vary according to class time, course level, course load, degree level, campus/location and program.

Morehead State University, Graduate School, College of Science, Department of Psychology, Morehead, KY 40351. Offers clinical/counseling psychology (MS); general/experimental psychology (MS). *Program availability:* Part-time, evening/weekend. *Faculty:* 8 full-time (5 women), 1 part-time/adjunct (0 women). *Students:* 10 full-time (9 women), 1 (woman) part-time; includes 2 minority (both Two or more races, non-Hispanic/Latino). 20 applicants, 60% accepted, 6 enrolled. In 2019, 11 master's awarded. *Degree requirements:* For master's, comprehensive exam, Minimum 3.0 GPA, internship, pass a comprehensive oral examination administered by a committee of three faculty. *Entrance requirements:* For master's, GRE, 3.5 UG GPA preferred, 3.0 is minimum required, 18 hrs in psychology, interview, 3 letters of recommendation, statement of purpose for seeking graduate-level training in clinical/counseling psychology. *Application deadline:* For fall admission, 3/1 priority date for domestic and international students. Applications are processed on a rolling basis. Application fee: $30. Electronic applications accepted. *Expenses: Tuition, area resident:* Part-time $570 per credit hour. Tuition, state resident: part-time $570 per credit hour. Tuition, nonresident: part-time $570 per credit hour. *Required fees:* $14 per credit hour. *Financial support:* Research assistantships, career-related internships or fieldwork, and unspecified assistantships available. Financial award applicants required to submit FAFSA. *Unit head:* Dr. Gregory Corso, Department Chair Psychology, 606-783-2981, E-mail: g.corso@moreheadstate.edu. *Application contact:* Dr. Gregory Corso,

Department Chair Psychology, 606-783-2981, E-mail: g.corso@moreheadstate.edu.
Website: https://www.moreheadstate.edu/College-of-Science/Psychology

Murray State University, College of Humanities and Fine Arts, Department of Psychology, Murray, KY 42071. Offers clinical psychology (MA, MS); general experimental psychology (MA, MS); research design and analysis (Certificate). *Program availability:* Part-time. *Entrance requirements:* For master's and Certificate, GRE or GMAT, minimum university GPA of 2.75. Additional exam requirements/recommendations for international students: required—TOEFL (minimum score 527 paper-based; 71 iBT). Electronic applications accepted.

Nova Southeastern University, College of Psychology, Fort Lauderdale, FL 33314-7796. Offers clinical mental health counseling (MS); clinical psychology (PhD, Psy D); counseling (MS); experimental psychology (MS); forensic psychology (MS); general psychology (MS); school counseling (MS); school psychology (Psy D, Psy S); substance abuse counseling (MS); substance abuse counseling and education (MS). *Accreditation:* APA (one or more programs are accredited). *Program availability:* Part-time, 100% online, blended/hybrid learning. *Faculty:* 72 full-time (34 women), 111 part-time/adjunct (76 women). *Students:* 1,263 full-time (1,068 women), 868 part-time (761 women); includes 1,221 minority (368 Black or African American, non-Hispanic/Latino; 3 American Indian or Alaska Native, non-Hispanic/Latino; 111 Asian, non-Hispanic/Latino; 668 Hispanic/Latino; 1 Native Hawaiian or other Pacific Islander, non-Hispanic/Latino; 70 Two or more races, non-Hispanic/Latino), 59 international. Average age 31. 935 applicants, 56% accepted, 375 enrolled. In 2019, 400 master's, 72 doctorates, 13 other advanced degrees awarded. Terminal master's awarded for partial completion of doctoral program. *Degree requirements:* For master's, comprehensive exam, 3 practica; for doctorate, thesis/dissertation, clinical internship, competency exam; for Psy S, comprehensive exam, internship. *Entrance requirements:* For master's and Psy S, GRE General Test, letters of recommendation, research/personal statement, interview; for doctorate, GRE General Test, GRE Subject Test (recommended), minimum undergraduate GPA of 3.0, letters of recommendation, research/personal statement, interview, curriculum vitae/resume. Additional exam requirements/recommendations for international students: required—TOEFL (minimum score 550 paper-based). *Application deadline:* Applications are processed on a rolling basis. Application fee: $50. Electronic applications accepted. *Expenses:* Contact institution. *Financial support:* In 2019–20, 197 students received support, including 15 research assistantships (averaging $5,600 per year), 68 teaching assistantships (averaging $2,000 per year); career-related internships or fieldwork, Federal Work-Study, institutionally sponsored loans, scholarships/grants, and unspecified assistantships also available. Support available to part-time students. Financial award application deadline: 4/15; financial award applicants required to submit FAFSA. *Unit head:* Dr. Karen Grosby, Dean, 954-262-5712, Fax: 954-262-3859, E-mail: grosby@nova.edu. *Application contact:* Gregory Gayle, Director, Recruitment and Admissions, 954-262-5903, Fax: 954-262-3893, E-mail: ggayle1@nova.edu.
Website: http://psychology.nova.edu/

Ohio University, Graduate College, College of Arts and Sciences, Department of Psychology, Program in Experimental Psychology, Athens, OH 45701-2979. Offers PhD. *Degree requirements:* For doctorate, one foreign language, comprehensive exam, thesis/dissertation. *Entrance requirements:* For doctorate, GRE General Test, GRE Subject Test, minimum graduate GPA of 3.4. Additional exam requirements/recommendations for international students: required—TOEFL.

Radford University, College of Graduate Studies and Research, Psychology, MA/MS, Radford, VA 24142. Offers clinical-counseling psychology (MA, MS); experimental psychology (MA); industrial-organizational psychology (MA, MS). *Program availability:* Part-time. *Degree requirements:* For master's, comprehensive exam, thesis (for some programs). *Entrance requirements:* For master's, GRE, minimum GPA of 3.0, 3 letters of reference, essay, resume, official transcripts. Additional exam requirements/recommendations for international students: required—TOEFL (minimum score 550 paper-based; 79 iBT), IELTS (minimum score 6.5). Electronic applications accepted.

Rivier University, School of Graduate Studies, Department of Psychology, Nashua, NH 03060. Offers clinical psychology (MS); experimental psychology (MS).

Rochester Institute of Technology, Graduate Enrollment Services, College of Liberal Arts, Psychology Department, MS Program in Experimental Psychology, Rochester, NY 14623-5603. Offers MS. *Program availability:* Part-time. *Degree requirements:* For master's, thesis. *Entrance requirements:* For master's, GRE, minimum GPA of 3.0 (recommended). Additional exam requirements/recommendations for international students: required—TOEFL (minimum score 550 paper-based; 79 iBT), IELTS (minimum score 6.5), PTE (minimum score 58). Electronic applications accepted.

Saint Louis University, Graduate Programs, College of Arts and Sciences, Department of Psychology, St. Louis, MO 63103. Offers clinical psychology (MS-R, PhD); experimental psychology (MS-R, PhD); industrial-organizational psychology (PhD); psychology (PhD). *Accreditation:* APA (one or more programs are accredited). *Program availability:* Part-time. *Degree requirements:* For master's, comprehensive exam, thesis; for doctorate, thesis/dissertation, clinical internship (for clinical psychology PhD). *Entrance requirements:* For master's, GRE General Test, interview, letters of recommendation, resume; for doctorate, GRE General Test, interview, letters of recommendation, resumé, transcripts, goal statement. Additional exam requirements/recommendations for international students: required—TOEFL (minimum score 550 paper-based). Electronic applications accepted.

San Jose State University, Program in Psychology, San Jose, CA 95192-0120. Offers clinical psychology (MS); experimental psychology (MA); industrial/organizational psychology (MS); psychology (MA). *Faculty:* 19 full-time (12 women), 2 part-time/adjunct (1 woman). *Students:* 51 full-time (44 women), 30 part-time (21 women); includes 37 minority (2 Black or African American, non-Hispanic/Latino; 14 Asian, non-Hispanic/Latino; 21 Hispanic/Latino), 4 international. Average age 27. 184 applicants, 23% accepted, 31 enrolled. In 2019, 35 master's awarded. *Application deadline:* For fall admission, 2/1 for domestic and international students. Application fee: $70. Electronic applications accepted. *Expenses: Tuition, area resident:* Full-time $7176; part-time $4164 per credit hour. Tuition, state resident: full-time $7176; part-time $4164 per credit hour. Tuition, nonresident: full-time $7176; part-time $4165 per credit hour. *International tuition:* $7176 full-time. *Required fees:* $2110; $2110. *Financial support:* In 2019–20, 22 students received support, including 1 research assistantship (averaging $500 per year); scholarships/grants also available. Financial award application deadline: 5/1; financial award applicants required to submit FAFSA. *Unit head:* Clifton Oyamot, Professor and Chair, 408-924-5650, E-mail: clifton.oyamot@sjsu.edu. *Application contact:* Psychology Department, 408-408-924-5600, E-mail: psychology@sjsu.edu.
Website: http://www.sjsu.edu/psych/

Seton Hall University, College of Arts and Sciences, Department of Psychology, South Orange, NJ 07079-2697. Offers experimental psychology (MS). *Program availability:* Part-time, evening/weekend. *Degree requirements:* For master's, thesis optional. *Entrance requirements:* For master's, GRE, minimum of 18 credits in psychology with minimum GPA of 3.0. Additional exam requirements/recommendations for international students: required—TOEFL. Electronic applications accepted.

Southern Illinois University Carbondale, Graduate School, College of Liberal Arts, Department of Psychology, Carbondale, IL 62901-4701. Offers clinical psychology (PhD); counseling psychology (PhD); experimental psychology (MA, MS). *Accreditation:* APA (one or more programs are accredited). *Degree requirements:* For master's, thesis; for doctorate, thesis/dissertation. *Entrance requirements:* For master's, GRE General Test, GRE Subject Test, minimum GPA of 2.7; for doctorate, GRE General Test, GRE Subject Test, minimum GPA of 3.25. Additional exam requirements/recommendations for international students: required—TOEFL.

Texas A&M University–Central Texas, Graduate Studies and Research, Killeen, TX 76549. Offers accounting (MS); business administration (MBA); clinical mental health counseling (MS); criminal justice (MCJ); curriculum and instruction (M Ed); educational administration (M Ed); educational psychology - experimental psychology (MS); history (MA); human resource management (MS); information systems (MS); liberal studies (MS); management and leadership (MS); marriage and family therapy (MS); mathematics (MS); political science (MA); school counseling (M Ed); school psychology (Ed S).

Texas Christian University, College of Science and Engineering, Department of Psychology, Fort Worth, TX 76129-0002. Offers developmental trauma (MS); experimental psychology (PhD), including cognition/developmental, learning, neuroscience, social. *Faculty:* 14 full-time (7 women), 1 part-time/adjunct (0 women). *Students:* 31 full-time (26 women); includes 2 minority (both Asian, non-Hispanic/Latino), 2 international. Average age 25. 52 applicants, 35% accepted, 13 enrolled. In 2019, 10 master's, 4 doctorates awarded. Terminal master's awarded for partial completion of doctoral program. *Entrance requirements:* For doctorate, GRE General Test. Additional exam requirements/recommendations for international students: required—TOEFL (minimum score 550 paper-based; 80 iBT). *Application deadline:* For fall admission, 1/1 for domestic and international students. Application fee: $60 ($0 for international students). Electronic applications accepted. Full-time tuition and fees vary according to program. *Financial support:* In 2019–20, 23 students received support, including 23 teaching assistantships with full tuition reimbursements available (averaging $19,750 per year); scholarships/grants also available. Financial award application deadline: 1/1; financial award applicants required to submit FAFSA. *Unit head:* Dr. Anna I. Petursdottir, Chair, 817-257-7410, Fax: 817-257-7681, E-mail: a.petursdottir@tcu.edu. *Application contact:* Cindy Hayes, Administrative Assistant, 817-257-7410, Fax: 817-257-7681, E-mail: c.hayes@tcu.edu.
Website: https://psychology.tcu.edu/

Texas Tech University, Graduate School, College of Arts and Sciences, Department of Psychological Sciences, Lubbock, TX 79409-2051. Offers clinical psychology (PhD); counseling psychology (MA, PhD); general experimental psychology (MA, PhD); psychology (MA). *Accreditation:* APA (one or more programs are accredited). *Faculty:* 33 full-time (14 women), 2 part-time/adjunct (both women). *Students:* 105 full-time (63 women), 24 part-time (22 women); includes 39 minority (6 Black or African American, non-Hispanic/Latino; 1 American Indian or Alaska Native, non-Hispanic/Latino; 11 Asian, non-Hispanic/Latino; 21 Hispanic/Latino), 7 international. Average age 28. 162 applicants, 14% accepted, 16 enrolled. In 2019, 21 master's, 10 doctorates awarded. *Degree requirements:* For doctorate, comprehensive exam, thesis/dissertation, 100 credit hours of organized courses, research credits, and practica. *Entrance requirements:* For master's, GRE General Test, GRE Subject Test, essays, letters of recommendation; for doctorate, GRE General Test, essays, letters of recommendation. Additional exam requirements/recommendations for international students: required—TOEFL (minimum score 550 paper-based; 79 iBT). *Application deadline:* For fall admission, 6/1 priority date for domestic students, 1/15 priority date for international students; for spring admission, 9/1 priority date for domestic students, 6/15 priority date for international students. Applications are processed on a rolling basis. Application fee: $65. Electronic applications accepted. *Expenses:* Contact institution. *Financial support:* In 2019–20, 121 students received support, including 115 fellowships (averaging $2,803 per year), 39 research assistantships (averaging $12,832 per year), 77 teaching assistantships (averaging $13,684 per year); Federal Work-Study, institutionally sponsored loans, health care benefits, and unspecified assistantships also available. Financial award application deadline: 4/15; financial award applicants required to submit FAFSA. *Unit head:* Dr. Robert Morgan, Professor and Chair, 806-834-7117, Fax: 806-742-0818, E-mail: robert.morgan@ttu.edu. *Application contact:* Kay Hill, Admissions Coordinator, 806-834-1350, Fax: 806-742-0818, E-mail: kay.hill@ttu.edu.
Website: www.depts.ttu.edu/psy/

Towson University, College of Liberal Arts, Program in Psychology, Towson, MD 21252-0001. Offers clinical psychology (MA); counseling psychology (MA); experimental psychology (MA); school psychology (MA). *Program availability:* Part-time, evening/weekend. *Students:* 97 full-time (79 women), 25 part-time (20 women); includes 27 minority (15 Black or African American, non-Hispanic/Latino; 3 Asian, non-Hispanic/Latino; 2 Hispanic/Latino; 7 Two or more races, non-Hispanic/Latino), 3 international. *Entrance requirements:* For master's, GRE, minimum GPA of 3.0, letters of recommendation. *Application deadline:* For fall admission, 1/17 for domestic students, 5/15 for international students; for spring admission, 10/15 for domestic students, 12/1 for international students. Applications are processed on a rolling basis. Application fee: $45. Electronic applications accepted. *Expenses: Tuition, area resident:* Full-time $7920; part-time $439 per credit. Tuition, nonresident: full-time $16,344; part-time $908 per credit. *International tuition:* $16,344 full-time. *Required fees:* $2628; $146 per credit. $876 per term. *Financial support:* Application deadline: 4/1. *Unit head:* Dr. Geoffrey Munro, Department Chair, 410-704-2634, E-mail: psycdept@towson.edu. *Application contact:* Coverley Beidleman, Assistant Director of Graduate Admissions, 410-704-5630, Fax: 410-704-3030, E-mail: grads@towson.edu.
Website: https://www.towson.edu/cla/departments/psychology/grad/

The University of Alabama, Graduate School, College of Arts and Sciences, Department of Psychology, Tuscaloosa, AL 35487. Offers clinical psychology (PhD); experimental psychology (PhD). *Faculty:* 31 full-time (18 women), 1 (woman) part-time/adjunct. *Students:* 84 full-time (68 women), 15 part-time (11 women); includes 17 minority (7 Black or African American, non-Hispanic/Latino; 1 Asian, non-Hispanic/Latino; 7 Hispanic/Latino; 2 Two or more races, non-Hispanic/Latino), 7 international. Average age 28. 269 applicants, 9% accepted, 17 enrolled. In 2019, 21 doctorates awarded. *Degree requirements:* For doctorate, thesis/dissertation, internship (for clinical psychology). *Entrance requirements:* For doctorate, GRE. Additional exam requirements/recommendations for international students: required—TOEFL (minimum score 550 paper-based). *Application deadline:* For fall admission, 11/16 for domestic and international students. Application fee: $50 ($60 for international students). Electronic applications accepted. *Expenses: Tuition, area resident:* Full-time $10,780; part-time $440 per credit hour. Tuition, nonresident: full-time $30,250; part-time $1550 per credit hour. *Financial support:* In 2019–20, 65 students received support, including fellowships with full tuition reimbursements available (averaging $17,000 per year), research assistantships with tuition reimbursements available (averaging $12,744 per year), teaching assistantships with tuition reimbursements available (averaging $13,824 per year); career-related internships or fieldwork, institutionally sponsored loans, scholarships/grants, health care benefits, and unspecified assistantships also available. Financial award application deadline: 11/16. *Unit head:* Dr. Frances A. Conners, Chair, 205-348-1913, Fax: 205-348-8648, E-mail: fconners@ua.edu. *Application contact:* Mary Beth Hubbard, Information Contact, 205-348-1919, Fax: 205-348-8648, E-mail:

mary.b.hubbard@ua.edu.
Website: http://www.psychology.ua.edu

University of Central Oklahoma, The Jackson College of Graduate Studies, College of Education and Professional Studies, Department of Psychology, Edmond, OK 73034-5209. Offers psychology (MA), including counseling psychology, experimental psychology, forensic psychology, general psychology, school psychology. *Degree requirements:* For master's, thesis (for some programs). *Entrance requirements:* For master's, GRE. Additional exam requirements/recommendations for international students: required—TOEFL (minimum score 550 paper-based; 79 iBT), IELTS (minimum score 6.5). Electronic applications accepted.

University of Cincinnati, Graduate School, McMicken College of Arts and Sciences, Department of Psychology, Cincinnati, OH 45221. Offers clinical psychology (PhD); experimental psychology (PhD). *Accreditation:* APA. *Degree requirements:* For doctorate, comprehensive exam, thesis/dissertation. *Entrance requirements:* For doctorate, GRE General Test. Additional exam requirements/recommendations for international students: required—TOEFL.

University of Connecticut, Graduate School, College of Liberal Arts and Sciences, Department of Psychological Sciences, Storrs, CT 06269. Offers behavioral neuroscience (PhD); biopsychology (PhD); clinical psychology (MA, PhD); cognition and instruction (PhD); developmental psychology (MA, PhD); ecological psychology (PhD); experimental psychology (PhD); general psychology (MA, PhD); industrial/organizational psychology (PhD); language and cognition (PhD); neuroscience (PhD); social psychology (MA, PhD). *Accreditation:* APA. Terminal master's awarded for partial completion of doctoral program. *Degree requirements:* For master's, comprehensive exam; for doctorate, thesis/dissertation. *Entrance requirements:* For master's and doctorate, GRE General Test, GRE Subject Test. Additional exam requirements/recommendations for international students: required—TOEFL (minimum score 550 paper-based). Electronic applications accepted.

University of Idaho, College of Graduate Studies, College of Letters, Arts and Social Sciences, Department of Psychology and Communication Studies, Moscow, ID 83844-2282. Offers experimental psychology (PhD); psychology and communication studies (MS). *Faculty:* 9. *Students:* 19 full-time (7 women), 13 part-time (6 women). Average age 32. In 2019, 6 master's awarded. *Entrance requirements:* For master's, GRE, minimum GPA of 3.0. Additional exam requirements/recommendations for international students: required—TOEFL (minimum score 79 iBT). *Application deadline:* For fall admission, 7/30 for domestic students; for spring admission, 12/1 for domestic students. Applications are processed on a rolling basis. Application fee: $60. Electronic applications accepted. *Expenses:* Tuition, state resident: full-time $7753.80; part-time $502 per credit hour. Tuition, nonresident: full-time $26,990; part-time $1571 per credit hour. *Required fees:* $2122.20; $47 per credit hour. *Financial support:* Fellowships, research assistantships, and teaching assistantships available. Financial award applicants required to submit FAFSA. *Unit head:* Dr. Benjamin Barton, Chair, 208-885-6324, E-mail: psyc-comm@uidaho.edu. *Application contact:* Dr. Benjamin Barton, Chair, 208-885-6324, E-mail: psyc-comm@uidaho.edu.
Website: https://www.uidaho.edu/class/psychcomm

University of Louisville, Graduate School, College of Arts and Sciences, Department of Psychological and Brain Sciences, Louisville, KY 40292-0001. Offers clinical psychology (PhD); experimental psychology (PhD), including cognition and development, vision and hearing. *Accreditation:* APA. *Program availability:* Part-time. *Faculty:* 24 full-time (14 women), 9 part-time/adjunct (5 women). *Students:* 50 full-time (42 women), 1 (woman) part-time; includes 5 minority (1 Black or African American, non-Hispanic/Latino; 2 Hispanic/Latino; 2 Two or more races, non-Hispanic/Latino), 6 international. Average age 29. 144 applicants, 1% accepted, 2 enrolled. In 2019, 14 doctorates awarded. *Degree requirements:* For doctorate, comprehensive exam, thesis/dissertation, coursework; internship for clinical. *Entrance requirements:* For doctorate, GRE General Test, Three letters of reference, official transcripts. Additional exam requirements/recommendations for international students: required—TOEFL (minimum score 550 paper-based; 79 iBT), IELTS can be used in place of TOEFL; recommended—IELTS (minimum score 6.5). *Application deadline:* For fall admission, 12/1 for domestic and international students. Applications are processed on a rolling basis. Application fee: $65. Electronic applications accepted. *Expenses: Tuition, area resident:* Full-time $13,000; part-time $723 per credit hour. Tuition, state resident: full-time $13,000; part-time $723 per credit hour. Tuition, nonresident: full-time $27,114; part-time $1507 per credit hour. *International tuition:* $27,114 full-time. *Required fees:* $196. Tuition and fees vary according to program and reciprocity agreements. *Financial support:* In 2019–20, 49 students received support, including 8 fellowships with full tuition reimbursements available (averaging $22,000 per year), 3 research assistantships with full tuition reimbursements available (averaging $22,000 per year), 30 teaching assistantships with full tuition reimbursements available (averaging $22,000 per year); scholarships/grants, health care benefits, and unspecified assistantships also available. Financial award application deadline: 12/1. *Unit head:* Dr. Benjamin Mast, Professor and Chair, 502-852-3280, Fax: 502-852-8904, E-mail: b.mast@louisville.edu. *Application contact:* Maggie Leahy, Administrative Assistant, 502-852-4364, Fax: 502-852-8904, E-mail: maggie.leahy@louisville.edu.
Website: http://louisville.edu/psychology

University of Maryland, College Park, Academic Affairs, College of Behavioral and Social Sciences, Department of Psychology, College Park, MD 20742. Offers clinical psychology (PhD); developmental psychology (PhD); experimental psychology (PhD); industrial psychology (MA, MS, PhD); social psychology (PhD). *Accreditation:* APA (one or more programs are accredited). *Degree requirements:* For master's, thesis; for doctorate, variable foreign language requirement, comprehensive exam, thesis/dissertation. *Entrance requirements:* For master's and doctorate, GRE General Test, GRE Subject Test, minimum GPA of 3.5, research and/or work experience, 3 letters of recommendation. Electronic applications accepted.

University of Massachusetts Dartmouth, Graduate School, College of Arts and Sciences, Department of Psychology, North Dartmouth, MA 02747-2300. Offers autism studies (Graduate Certificate); psychology - applied behavioral analysis (MA, Post-Master's Certificate); psychology - clinical (MA); psychology - research (MA). *Program availability:* Part-time. *Faculty:* 18 full-time (11 women), 7 part-time/adjunct (4 women). *Students:* 40 full-time (32 women), 54 part-time (47 women); includes 16 minority (5 Black or African American, non-Hispanic/Latino; 2 Asian, non-Hispanic/Latino; 5 Hispanic/Latino; 4 Two or more races, non-Hispanic/Latino), 3 international. Average age 29. 97 applicants, 58% accepted, 34 enrolled. In 2019, 26 master's, 1 other advanced degree awarded. *Degree requirements:* For master's, thesis (for some programs), thesis. *Entrance requirements:* For master's, GRE (recommended), statement of purpose (minimum of 300 words), resume, 3 letters of recommendation, official transcripts; for other advanced degree, statement of purpose (minimum of 300 words), resume, 3 letters of recommendation, official transcripts. Additional exam requirements/recommendations for international students: required—TOEFL (minimum score 80 iBT). *Application deadline:* For fall admission, 4/15 for domestic students, 3/15 for international students. Application fee: $60. Electronic applications accepted. *Expenses: Tuition, area resident:* Full-time $16,390; part-time $682.92 per credit. Tuition, state resident: full-time $16,390; part-time $682.92 per credit. Tuition, nonresident: full-time $29,578; part-time $1232.42 per credit. *Required fees:* $575. *Financial support:* In 2019–20, 1 research assistantship (averaging $9,000 per year), 2 teaching assistantships (averaging $14,000 per year) were awarded; tuition waivers (full and partial) and unspecified assistantships also available. Financial award application deadline: 3/1; financial award applicants required to submit FAFSA. *Unit head:* R. Thomas Boone, Graduate Program Director, Psychology, 508-999-8440, E-mail: tboone@umassd.edu. *Application contact:* Scott Webster, Director of Graduate Studies and Admissions, 508-999-8604, Fax: 508-999-8183, E-mail: graduate@umassd.edu.
Website: http://www.umassd.edu/cas/psychology/graduate-programs

University of Memphis, Graduate School, College of Arts and Sciences, Department of Psychology, Memphis, TN 38152-3230. Offers clinical psychology (PhD); experimental psychology (PhD); general psychology (MS); school psychology (MA, PhD, Ed S). *Accreditation:* APA. *Students:* 102 full-time (74 women), 24 part-time (18 women); includes 31 minority (13 Black or African American, non-Hispanic/Latino; 6 Asian, non-Hispanic/Latino; 6 Hispanic/Latino; 6 Two or more races, non-Hispanic/Latino), 6 international. Average age 28. 57 applicants, 84% accepted, 32 enrolled. In 2019, 21 master's, 12 doctorates, 6 other advanced degrees awarded. *Degree requirements:* For master's, comprehensive exam (for some programs), thesis (for some programs), 37 credit hours (for MA); 33 credit hours with thesis or 36 with exam (for MS); for doctorate, comprehensive exam, thesis/dissertation, 80 semester hours, major area paper; 1-year placement and 1-year internship (for clinical psychology); internship (for school psychology); for Ed S, 30 credit hours. *Entrance requirements:* For master's, GRE, 3 letters of recommendation, 18 undergraduate hours in psychology; for doctorate, GRE, minimum GPA of 2.75, 18 hours of undergraduate psychology courses, transcripts, personal statement, 3 letters of recommendation, interview; for Ed S, GRE, minimum GPA of 2.75, 18 hours of undergraduate psychology courses, 3 letters of recommendation. Additional exam requirements/recommendations for international students: required—TOEFL (minimum score 550 paper-based; 79 iBT). *Application deadline:* For fall admission, 12/5 for domestic students. Applications are processed on a rolling basis. Application fee: $35 ($60 for international students). Electronic applications accepted. *Expenses: Tuition, area resident:* Full-time $9216; part-time $512 per credit hour. Tuition, state resident: full-time $9216; part-time $512 per credit hour. Tuition, nonresident: full-time $12,672; part-time $704 per credit hour. *International tuition:* $16,128 full-time. *Required fees:* $1530; $85 per credit hour. Tuition and fees vary according to program. *Financial support:* Fellowships with full tuition reimbursements, research assistantships with full tuition reimbursements, teaching assistantships with full tuition reimbursements, Federal Work-Study, scholarships/grants, tuition waivers (partial), and unspecified assistantships available. Financial award application deadline: 2/1; financial award applicants required to submit FAFSA. *Unit head:* Dr. Randy Floyd, Chair, 901-678-2146, Fax: 901-678-2579, E-mail: rgfloyd@memphis.edu. *Application contact:* Dr. Robert Cohen, Graduate Programs Coordinator, 901-678-4679, Fax: 901-678-2579, E-mail: rcohen@memphis.edu.
Website: http://www.memphis.edu/psychology

University of Mississippi, Graduate School, College of Liberal Arts, University, MS 38677. Offers anthropology (MA); biology (MS, PhD); chemistry (MS, DA, PhD); creative writing (MFA); documentary expression (MFA); economics (MA, PhD); English (MA, PhD); experimental psychology (PhD); history (MA, PhD); mathematics (MS, PhD); modern languages (MA); music (MM); philosophy (MA); physics (MA, MS, PhD); political science (MA, PhD); Southern studies (MA); studio art (MFA). *Program availability:* Part-time. *Faculty:* 481 full-time (215 women), 71 part-time/adjunct (40 women). *Students:* 509 full-time (258 women), 55 part-time (21 women); includes 89 minority (40 Black or African American, non-Hispanic/Latino; 13 Asian, non-Hispanic/Latino; 25 Hispanic/Latino; 11 Two or more races, non-Hispanic/Latino), 157 international. Average age 29. In 2019, 119 master's, 51 doctorates awarded. *Degree requirements:* For doctorate, thesis/dissertation. *Entrance requirements:* For master's, GRE General Test, minimum GPA of 3.0; for doctorate, GRE General Test. Additional exam requirements/recommendations for international students: required—TOEFL. *Application deadline:* Applications are processed on a rolling basis. Application fee: $50. Electronic applications accepted. *Expenses:* Tuition, state resident: full-time $8718; part-time $484.25 per credit hour. Tuition, nonresident: full-time $24,990; part-time $1388.25 per credit hour. *Required fees:* $100; $4.16 per credit hour. *Financial support:* Fellowships, research assistantships, teaching assistantships, career-related internships or fieldwork, Federal Work-Study, institutionally sponsored loans, scholarships/grants, and unspecified assistantships available. Financial award application deadline: 3/1; financial award applicants required to submit FAFSA. *Unit head:* Dr. Lee Michael Cohen, Dean, 662-915-7177, Fax: 662-915-5792, E-mail: libarts@olemiss.edu. *Application contact:* Tameka Smith, Graduate Activities Specialist for Admissions, 662-915-7474, Fax: 662-915-7577, E-mail: gschool@olemiss.edu.
Website: ventress@olemiss.edu

University of Montana, Graduate School, College of Humanities and Sciences, Department of Psychology, Missoula, MT 59812. Offers clinical psychology (PhD); experimental psychology (PhD), including animal behavior psychology, developmental psychology; school psychology (MA, PhD, Ed S). *Accreditation:* APA (one or more programs are accredited). Terminal master's awarded for partial completion of doctoral program. *Degree requirements:* For master's, thesis; for doctorate, thesis/dissertation. *Entrance requirements:* For master's, doctorate, and Ed S, GRE General Test. Additional exam requirements/recommendations for international students: required—TOEFL.

University of New Brunswick Saint John, Department of Psychology, Saint John, NE E2L 4L5, Canada. Offers clinical psychology (PhD); experimental psychology (MA, PhD). *Program availability:* Part-time. *Faculty:* 10 full-time (6 women). *Students:* 12 full-time (8 women), 1 part-time (0 women), 1 international. In 2019, 4 master's awarded. *Degree requirements:* For master's, thesis. *Entrance requirements:* For master's, GRE General and Subject Tests, honors thesis; minimum GPA of 3.7. Additional exam requirements/recommendations for international students: required—TOEFL (minimum score 550 paper-based), TWE. *Application deadline:* For fall admission, 1/15 priority date for domestic students. Application fee: $50. Electronic applications accepted. *Expenses: Tuition, area resident:* Full-time $6975 Canadian dollars; part-time $3423 Canadian dollars per year. Tuition, state resident: full-time $6975 Canadian dollars; part-time $3423 Canadian dollars per year. Tuition, Canadian resident: full-time $6975 Canadian dollars; part-time $3423 Canadian dollars per year. *International tuition:* $12,435 Canadian dollars full-time. *Required fees:* $132.75 Canadian dollars; $92.25 Canadian dollars per term. Tuition and fees vary according to campus/location, program and student level. *Financial support:* Fellowships, research assistantships, teaching assistantships, and unspecified assistantships available. Support available to part-time students. Financial award application deadline: 2/1. *Unit head:* Dr. Mary Ann Campbell, Director of Graduate Studies, 506-648 5969, Fax: 506-648-5780, E-mail: mcampbel@unb.ca. *Application contact:* Mary Miernicki, Administrative Assistant, 506-648-5640, Fax: 506-648-5780, E-mail: Mary.Miernicki@unb.ca.
Website: http://go.unb.ca/gradprograms

University of Regina, Faculty of Graduate Studies and Research, Faculty of Arts, Department of Psychology, Regina, SK S4S 0A2, Canada. Offers clinical psychology (MA, PhD); experimental and applied psychology (MA, PhD). *Faculty:* 20 full-time (9

women), 11 part-time/adjunct (7 women). *Students:* 55 full-time (47 women). Average age 30. 116 applicants, 18% accepted. In 2019, 4 master's, 1 doctorate awarded. *Degree requirements:* For master's, thesis; for doctorate, comprehensive exam, thesis/dissertation. *Entrance requirements:* For master's, GRE General Test, post secondary transcripts, 2 letter of recommendations; for doctorate, GRE General Test and GRE Subject Test (optional for those with a master's degree from a Canadian university). Additional exam requirements/recommendations for international students: required—TOEFL (minimum score 580 paper-based; 80 iBT), IELTS (minimum score 6.5), PTE (minimum score 59), other option is CAEL, MELAB and U of R ESL. *Application deadline:* For fall admission, 1/15 for domestic and international students. Application fee: $100. Electronic applications accepted. *Expenses: Tuition:* Full-time $6684 Canadian dollars. *Required fees:* $100 Canadian dollars; $3351.45 Canadian dollars per trimester. $1117.15 Canadian dollars per semester. Tuition and fees vary according to course level, course load, degree level and program. *Financial support:* Fellowships, research assistantships, teaching assistantships, career-related internships or fieldwork, Federal Work-Study, scholarships/grants, unspecified assistantships, and travel award and Graduate Scholarship Base Funds available. Support available to part-time students. Financial award application deadline: 9/30. *Unit head:* Dr. Richard MacLennan, Department Head, 306-585-4458, Fax: 306-585-5429, E-mail: richard.maclennan@uregina.ca. *Application contact:* Dr. Richard MacLennan, Department Head, 306-585-4458, Fax: 306-585-5429, E-mail: richard.maclennan@uregina.ca.
Website: http://www.uregina.ca/arts/psychology

University of South Carolina, The Graduate School, College of Arts and Sciences, Department of Psychology, Program in Experimental Psychology, Columbia, SC 29208. Offers MA, PhD. Terminal master's awarded for partial completion of doctoral program. *Degree requirements:* For master's, comprehensive exam, thesis; for doctorate, comprehensive exam, thesis/dissertation. *Entrance requirements:* For master's and doctorate, GRE General Test. Additional exam requirements/recommendations for international students: required—TOEFL. Electronic applications accepted.

The University of Tennessee, Graduate School, College of Arts and Sciences, Department of Psychology, Knoxville, TN 37996. Offers clinical psychology (PhD); experimental psychology (MA, PhD); psychology (MA). *Accreditation:* APA (one or more programs are accredited). Terminal master's awarded for partial completion of doctoral program. *Degree requirements:* For master's, thesis; for doctorate, thesis/dissertation. *Entrance requirements:* For master's and doctorate, GRE General Test, GRE Subject Test, minimum GPA of 2.7. Additional exam requirements/recommendations for international students: required—TOEFL. Electronic applications accepted.

The University of Tennessee at Chattanooga, Program in Psychology, Chattanooga, TN 37403. Offers industrial/organizational psychology (MS); research psychology (MS). *Program availability:* Part-time. *Faculty:* 17 full-time (10 women), 4 part-time/adjunct (2 women). *Students:* 44 full-time (35 women), 4 part-time (3 women); includes 6 minority (1 Black or African American, non-Hispanic/Latino; 3 Hispanic/Latino; 2 Two or more races, non-Hispanic/Latino), 1 international. Average age 25. 98 applicants, 24% accepted, 20 enrolled. In 2019, 26 master's awarded. *Degree requirements:* For master's, comprehensive exam (for some programs), thesis (for some programs). *Entrance requirements:* For master's, GRE General Test. Additional exam requirements/recommendations for international students: required—TOEFL (minimum score 550 paper-based; 79 iBT), IELTS (minimum score 6). *Application deadline:* For fall admission, 6/15 priority date for domestic students, 7/1 for international students; for spring admission, 11/1 priority date for domestic students, 11/1 for international students. Applications are processed on a rolling basis. Application fee: $35 ($40 for international students). Electronic applications accepted. *Financial support:* Research assistantships, teaching assistantships, career-related internships or fieldwork, scholarships/grants, and unspecified assistantships available. Support available to part-time students. Financial award application deadline: 7/1; financial award applicants required to submit FAFSA. *Unit head:* Dr. Brian O'Leary, Department Head, 423-425-4283, Fax: 423-425-4284, E-mail: Boleary@utc.edu. *Application contact:* Dr. Joanne Romagni, Dean of the Graduate School, 423-425-4478, Fax: 423-425-5223, E-mail: joanne-romagni@utc.edu.
Website: http://www.utc.edu/psychology/

The University of Texas at Arlington, Graduate School, College of Science, Department of Psychology, Arlington, TX 76019. Offers experimental health psychology (PhD); experimental psychology (MS, PhD); health/neuroscience psychology (MS, PhD); industrial and organizational psychology (MS). *Program availability:* Part-time. Terminal master's awarded for partial completion of doctoral program. *Degree requirements:* For master's, comprehensive exam or thesis; for doctorate, thesis/dissertation (for some programs). *Entrance requirements:* For master's and doctorate, GRE General Test, minimum GPA of 3.0 in last 60 hours of course work. Additional exam requirements/recommendations for international students: required—TOEFL (minimum score 550 paper-based).

The University of Texas at El Paso, Graduate School, College of Liberal Arts, Department of Psychology, El Paso, TX 79968-0001. Offers clinical psychology (MA); experimental psychology (MA); psychology (PhD). *Program availability:* Part-time, evening/weekend. *Degree requirements:* For master's, thesis; for doctorate, thesis/dissertation. *Entrance requirements:* For master's, GRE, letters of recommendation; for doctorate, GRE, statement of purpose, letters of recommendation. Additional exam requirements/recommendations for international students: required—TOEFL; recommended—IELTS. Electronic applications accepted.

The University of Texas of the Permian Basin, Office of Graduate Studies, College of Arts and Sciences, Department of Psychology, Odessa, TX 79762-0001. Offers clinical psychology (MA); experimental psychology (MA). *Program availability:* Part-time, evening/weekend. *Degree requirements:* For master's, comprehensive exam, thesis, practicum. *Entrance requirements:* For master's, GRE General Test, 3 letters of recommendation. Additional exam requirements/recommendations for international students: required—TOEFL (minimum score 550 paper-based).

The University of Texas Rio Grande Valley, College of Liberal Arts, Department of Psychological Science, Edinburg, TX 78539. Offers psychology (MA), including clinical psychology, experimental psychology. *Faculty:* 15 full-time (3 women), 4 part-time/adjunct (2 women). *Students:* 42 full-time (32 women), 22 part-time (12 women); includes 57 minority (1 Asian, non-Hispanic/Latino; 56 Hispanic/Latino), 6 international. Average age 27. 50 applicants, 56% accepted, 23 enrolled. In 2019, 12 master's awarded. *Expenses: Tuition, area resident:* Full-time $5959; part-time $440 per credit hour. Tuition, state resident: full-time $5959. Tuition, nonresident: full-time $5959. *International tuition:* $13,321 full-time. *Required fees:* $1169; $185 per credit hour.
Website: utrgv.edu/psychology/index.htm

The University of Toledo, College of Graduate Studies, College of Languages, Literature and Social Sciences, Department of Psychology, Toledo, OH 43606-3390. Offers clinical psychology (MA, PhD); experimental psychology (MA, PhD). *Accreditation:* APA. *Degree requirements:* For master's, comprehensive exam, thesis; for doctorate, comprehensive exam, thesis/dissertation. *Entrance requirements:* For master's and doctorate, GRE General Test, GRE Subject Test, minimum cumulative point-hour ratio of 2.7 for all previous academic work, three letters of recommendation, statement of purpose, transcripts from all prior institutions attended. Additional exam requirements/recommendations for international students: required—TOEFL (minimum score 550 paper-based; 80 iBT). Electronic applications accepted.

University of Vermont, Graduate College, College of Arts and Sciences, Program in General/Experimental Psychology, Burlington, VT 05405-0134. Offers psychology (PhD), including biobehavioral psychology, developmental psychology, human behavioral pharmacology, social psychology. *Accreditation:* APA. *Degree requirements:* For doctorate, thesis/dissertation. *Entrance requirements:* For doctorate, GRE General Test. Additional exam requirements/recommendations for international students: required—TOEFL (minimum score 550 paper-based, 100 iBT) or IELTS (7). Electronic applications accepted.

University of Victoria, Faculty of Graduate Studies, Faculty of Social Sciences, Department of Psychology, Victoria, BC V8W 2Y2, Canada. Offers clinical psychology (PhD); clinical psychology (neuropsychology) (M Sc); cognition and brain science (M Sc, PhD); experimental neuropsychology (M Sc, PhD); individualized study (M Sc, PhD); life span development psychology (PhD); life span developmental psychology (M Sc); social psychology (M Sc, PhD). *Degree requirements:* For master's, thesis; for doctorate, thesis/dissertation, candidacy exam. *Entrance requirements:* For master's and doctorate, GRE General Test. Additional exam requirements/recommendations for international students: required—TOEFL (minimum score 600 paper-based). Electronic applications accepted.

The University of West Alabama, School of Graduate Studies, College of Liberal Arts, Livingston, AL 35470. Offers experimental psychology (MS). *Program availability:* Part-time, evening/weekend, 100% online. *Faculty:* 7 full-time (2 women), 7 part-time/adjunct (5 women). *Students:* 39 full-time (36 women), 6 part-time (5 women); includes 21 minority (18 Black or African American, non-Hispanic/Latino; 1 Hispanic/Latino; 2 Two or more races, non-Hispanic/Latino), 1 international. Average age 26. 24 applicants, 92% accepted, 20 enrolled. In 2019, 2 master's awarded. *Degree requirements:* For master's, thesis. *Entrance requirements:* For master's, Depends on degree program, Depends on degree program. Additional exam requirements/recommendations for international students: required—TOEFL (minimum score 500 paper-based; 61 iBT). *Application deadline:* Applications are processed on a rolling basis. Application fee: $40. Electronic applications accepted. *Expenses: Required fees:* $380; $130. *Financial support:* In 2019–20, 3 teaching assistantships (averaging $7,344 per year) were awarded; Federal Work-Study, scholarships/grants, and unspecified assistantships also available. Support available to part-time students. Financial award application deadline: 3/1; financial award applicants required to submit FAFSA. *Unit head:* Dr. Mark Davis, Dean of College of Liberal Arts, 205-652-3570, Fax: 205-652-3717, E-mail: mdavis@uwa.edu. *Application contact:* Dr. Mark Davis, Dean of College of Liberal Arts, 205-652-3570, Fax: 205-652-3717, E-mail: mdavis@uwa.edu.
Website: http://www.uwa.edu/academics/collegeofliberalarts

University of West Florida, Usha Kundu, MD College of Health, Department of Psychology, Pensacola, FL 32514-5750. Offers applied experimental (MA); counseling (MA); industrial-organizational (MA). *Program availability:* Part-time. *Degree requirements:* For master's, thesis (for some programs). *Entrance requirements:* For master's, GRE, official transcripts; minimum GPA of 3.0; writing sample; three letters of reference; field experience or skill sets; oral interview (for counseling specialization). Additional exam requirements/recommendations for international students: required—TOEFL (minimum score 550 paper-based).

University of Wisconsin–Oshkosh, Graduate Studies, College of Letters and Science, Department of Psychology, Oshkosh, WI 54901. Offers experimental psychology (MS); industrial/organizational psychology (MS). *Degree requirements:* For master's, thesis. *Entrance requirements:* For master's, GRE, 10 semester hours of undergraduate course work in psychology. Additional exam requirements/recommendations for international students: required—TOEFL (minimum score 550 paper-based; 79 iBT). Electronic applications accepted.

Washington State University, College of Arts and Sciences, Department of Psychology, Pullman, WA 99164. Offers clinical psychology (PhD); experimental psychology (PhD). *Accreditation:* APA (one or more programs are accredited). *Degree requirements:* For doctorate, comprehensive exam, thesis/dissertation, oral exam, written exam. *Entrance requirements:* For doctorate, GRE General Test, three letters of reference; summary data form; at least 18 credits of study in psychology; at least one course in statistics and research methodology; official transcripts; minimum cumulative undergraduate GPA of 3.0 or master's degree in psychology. Additional exam requirements/recommendations for international students: required—TOEFL, IELTS. Electronic applications accepted.

Western Illinois University, School of Graduate Studies, College of Arts and Sciences, Department of Psychology, Macomb, IL 61455-1390. Offers clinical/community mental health (MS); general experimental psychology (MS); school psychology (SSP). *Program availability:* Part-time. *Degree requirements:* For master's, comprehensive exam (for some programs), thesis or alternative. *Entrance requirements:* For master's and SSP, GRE General Test. Additional exam requirements/recommendations for international students: required—TOEFL (minimum score 550 paper-based; 80 iBT). Electronic applications accepted.

Western Kentucky University, Graduate School, College of Education and Behavioral Sciences, Department of Psychology, Bowling Green, KY 42101. Offers clinical psychology (MA); experimental psychology (MA); general psychology (MA); industrial/organizational psychology (MA); school psychology (Ed S). *Degree requirements:* For master's, comprehensive exam, thesis (for some programs); for Ed S, thesis, oral exam. *Entrance requirements:* For master's, GRE General Test; for Ed S, GRE General Test, minimum GPA of 3.5. Additional exam requirements/recommendations for international students: required—TOEFL (minimum score 555 paper-based; 79 iBT).

Western Washington University, Graduate School, College of Humanities and Social Sciences, Department of Psychology, Program in Experimental Psychology, Bellingham, WA 98225-5996. Offers MS. *Degree requirements:* For master's, thesis. *Entrance requirements:* For master's, GRE General Test, minimum GPA of 3.0 in last 60 semester hours or last 90 quarter hours. Additional exam requirements/recommendations for international students: required—TOEFL (minimum score 567 paper-based). Electronic applications accepted.

Forensic Psychology

Adler University, Master of Arts (M.A.) in Forensic Mental Health Leadership, Chicago, IL 60602. Offers MAC. In 2019, 1 master's awarded. *Degree requirements:* For master's, Social Justice Practicum. *Unit head:* Phyllis Horton, Director of Admissions, 312-662-4100, E-mail: admissions@adler.edu. *Application contact:* Phyllis Horton, Director of Admissions, 312-662-4100, E-mail: admissions@adler.edu.

Alliant International University–Fresno, California School of Forensic Studies, PhD Program in Clinical Forensic Psychology, Fresno, CA 93727. Offers PhD. *Degree requirements:* For doctorate, comprehensive exam, thesis/dissertation, research internship. *Entrance requirements:* For doctorate, minimum GPA of 3.0, letters of recommendation, essay, interview. Additional exam requirements/recommendations for international students: required—TOEFL (minimum score 550 paper-based), TWE (minimum score 5).

Alliant International University–Fresno, California School of Forensic Studies, PsyD Program in Clinical Forensic Psychology, Fresno, CA 93727. Offers victimology (Psy D). *Degree requirements:* For doctorate, comprehensive exam, thesis/dissertation, internship. *Entrance requirements:* For doctorate, minimum GPA of 3.0, recommendations, essay, interview. Additional exam requirements/recommendations for international students: required—TOEFL (minimum score 550 paper-based), TWE (minimum score 5). Electronic applications accepted.

Alliant International University–Irvine, California School of Forensic Studies, Irvine, CA 92606. Offers Psy D. *Degree requirements:* For doctorate, comprehensive exam, thesis/dissertation, internship. *Entrance requirements:* For doctorate, minimum GPA of 3.0, recommendations, essay. Additional exam requirements/recommendations for international students: required—TOEFL (minimum score 80 iBT), TWE (minimum score 5). Electronic applications accepted.

Alliant International University - Los Angeles, California School of Forensic Studies, Alhambra, CA 91803. Offers forensic psychology (Psy D). *Degree requirements:* For doctorate, comprehensive exam, thesis/dissertation. *Entrance requirements:* For doctorate, interview; master's degree in psychology, forensic psychology, criminology, criminal justice, social work or law; minimum GPA of 3.0 in psychology and overall. Additional exam requirements/recommendations for international students: required—TOEFL (minimum score 600 paper-based), TWE (minimum score 5).

Alliant International University–Sacramento, California School of Forensic Studies, Program in Clinical Forensic Psychology, Sacramento, CA 95833. Offers Psy D. *Degree requirements:* For doctorate, comprehensive exam, thesis/dissertation. *Entrance requirements:* For doctorate, minimum GPA of 3.0, recommendations, essay. Additional exam requirements/recommendations for international students: required—TOEFL (minimum score 550 paper-based; 80 iBT), TWE (minimum score 5). Electronic applications accepted.

Alliant International University–San Francisco, California School of Forensic Studies, San Francisco, CA 94133. Offers applied criminology (MS), including victimology; clinical forensic psychology (PhD, Psy D). *Degree requirements:* For doctorate, comprehensive exam, thesis/dissertation, internship. *Entrance requirements:* For master's, minimum GPA of 3.0, recommendations, essay; for doctorate, minimum GPA of 3.0, recommendations, essay, interview. Additional exam requirements/recommendations for international students: required—TOEFL (minimum score 550 paper-based; 80 iBT), TWE (minimum score 5).

American International College, School of Business, Arts and Sciences, Springfield, MA 01109-3189. Offers accounting and taxation (MS); business administration (MBA); clinical psychology (MA); educational psychology (Ed D); forensic psychology (MS); general psychology (MA, CAGS); management (CAGS); resort and casino management (MBA, CAGS). *Program availability:* Part-time, evening/weekend. *Degree requirements:* For master's, practicum; for doctorate, comprehensive exam, thesis/dissertation, practicum. *Entrance requirements:* For master's, BS or BA, minimum undergraduate GPA of 2.75, 2 letters of recommendation, official transcripts, personal goal statement or essay; for doctorate, 3 letters of recommendation; BS or BA; minimum undergraduate GPA of 3.0 (3.25 recommended); official transcripts; personal goal statement or essay. Additional exam requirements/recommendations for international students: required—TOEFL (minimum score 550 paper-based; 80 iBT). *Expenses:* Contact institution.

Argosy University, Atlanta, Georgia School of Professional Psychology, Atlanta, GA 30328. Offers clinical psychology (MA, Psy D, Postdoctoral Respecialization Certificate), including child and family psychology (Psy D), general adult clinical (Psy D), health psychology (Psy D), neuropsychology/geropsychology (Psy D); community counseling (MA), including marriage and family therapy; counselor education and supervision (Ed D); forensic psychology (MA); industrial organizational psychology (MA); marriage and family therapy (Certificate); sport-exercise psychology (MA). *Accreditation:* APA.

Argosy University, Chicago, Illinois School of Professional Psychology, Doctoral Program in Clinical Psychology, Chicago, IL 60601. Offers child and adolescent psychology (Psy D); client-centered and experiential psychotherapies (Psy D); diversity and multicultural psychology (Psy D); family psychology (Psy D); forensic psychology (Psy D); health psychology (Psy D); neuropsychology (Psy D); organizational consulting (Psy D); psychoanalytic psychology (Psy D); psychology and spirituality (Psy D). *Accreditation:* APA.

Argosy University, Hawaii, Hawai'i School of Professional Psychology, Program in Forensic Psychology, Honolulu, HI 96813. Offers MA.

Argosy University, Los Angeles, College of Psychology and Behavioral Sciences, Los Angeles, CA 90045. Offers clinical psychology/marriage and family therapy (MA); counseling psychology (Ed D); counseling psychology/marriage and family therapy (MA); forensic psychology (MA).

Argosy University, Northern Virginia, American School of Professional Psychology, Arlington, VA 22209. Offers clinical psychology (MA, Psy D), including child and family psychology (Psy D), diversity and multicultural psychology (Psy D), forensic psychology (Psy D), health and neuropsychology (Psy D); community counseling (MA); counseling psychology (Ed D), including counselor education and supervision; counselor education and supervision (Ed D); forensic psychology (MA).

Argosy University, Orange County, American School of Professional Psychology, Program in Forensic Psychology, Orange, CA 92868. Offers MA.

Argosy University, Phoenix, Arizona School of Professional Psychology, Program in Forensic Psychology, Phoenix, AZ 85021. Offers MA.

Argosy University, Twin Cities, Minnesota School of Professional Psychology, Eagan, MN 55121. Offers clinical psychology (MA, Psy D), including child and family psychology (Psy D), forensic psychology (Psy D), health and neuropsychology (Psy D), trauma (Psy D); forensic counseling (Post-Graduate Certificate); forensic psychology (MA); industrial organizational psychology (MA); marriage and family therapy (MA, DMFT), including forensic counseling (MA). *Accreditation:* AAMFT; AAMFT/COAMFTE; APA.

California Baptist University, Program in Counseling Psychology, Riverside, CA 92504-3206. Offers counseling psychology (MS); forensic psychology (MS); professional clinical counseling (MS). *Program availability:* Part-time, evening/weekend, 100% online, blended/hybrid learning. *Degree requirements:* For master's, comprehensive exam, 24 (individual) or 50 hours (group) of psychotherapy, practicum. *Entrance requirements:* For master's, minimum undergraduate GPA of 2.75; official transcripts; three recommendations; 500-word essay; interview; 3 prerequisite courses completed with minimum C grade. Additional exam requirements/recommendations for international students: required—TOEFL (minimum score 80 iBT). Electronic applications accepted. *Expenses:* Contact institution.

California Baptist University, Program in Forensic Psychology, Riverside, CA 92504-3206. Offers MA. *Program availability:* Part-time. *Degree requirements:* For master's, comprehensive exam, thesis or alternative, 9-month practicum. *Entrance requirements:* For master's, minimum undergraduate GPA of 2.75; three recommendations; 500-word essay; interview; four prerequisite courses completed with minimum C grade. Additional exam requirements/recommendations for international students: required—TOEFL (minimum score 80 iBT). Electronic applications accepted. *Expenses:* Contact institution.

Castleton University, Division of Graduate Studies, Department of Psychology, Castleton, VT 05735. Offers forensic psychology (MA). *Degree requirements:* For master's, thesis. *Entrance requirements:* For master's, GRE General Test, minimum undergraduate GPA of 3.5, previous course work in research methodology and statistics. Additional exam requirements/recommendations for international students: required—TOEFL.

The Chicago School of Professional Psychology, Program in Clinical Forensic Psychology, Chicago, IL 60610. Offers Psy D. *Degree requirements:* For doctorate, thesis/dissertation. *Entrance requirements:* For doctorate, GRE. Additional exam requirements/recommendations for international students: required—TOEFL, IELTS.

The Chicago School of Professional Psychology, Program in Forensic Psychology, Chicago, IL 60610. Offers MA. *Degree requirements:* For master's, thesis optional. *Entrance requirements:* For master's, GRE (highly recommended), 1 course each in research methods, statistics, and psychology. Additional exam requirements/recommendations for international students: required—TOEFL (minimum score 550 paper-based; 79 iBT).

The Chicago School of Professional Psychology at Downtown Los Angeles, Program in Clinical Forensic Psychology, Los Angeles, CA 90017. Offers Psy D.

The Chicago School of Professional Psychology at Irvine, Program in Clinical Forensic Psychology, Irvine, CA 92612. Offers Psy D.

The Chicago School of Professional Psychology: Online, Program in Forensic Psychology, Chicago, IL 60654. Offers MA, Certificate.

Drexel University, College of Arts and Sciences, Department of Psychology, Clinical Psychology Program, Philadelphia, PA 19104-2875. Offers clinical psychology (PhD); forensic psychology (PhD); health psychology (PhD); neuropsychology (PhD). *Accreditation:* APA. Terminal master's awarded for partial completion of doctoral program. *Degree requirements:* For doctorate, thesis/dissertation, qualifying exam. *Entrance requirements:* For doctorate, GRE General Test, GRE Subject Test, minimum GPA of 3.0. Electronic applications accepted. *Expenses:* Contact institution.

Fairleigh Dickinson University, Metropolitan Campus, University College: Arts, Sciences, and Professional Studies, School of Psychology, Program in Forensic Psychology, Teaneck, NJ 07666-1914. Offers MA.

The George Washington University, Graduate School of Education and Human Development, Department of Counseling and Human Development, Washington, DC 20052. Offers clinical mental health counseling (MA); counseling (PhD, Ed S); counseling culturally and linguistically diverse persons (MA Ed/HD, Certificate); forensic rehabilitation counseling (Graduate Certificate); job development and placement (Graduate Certificate); rehabilitation counseling (MA Ed/HD), including autism spectrum disorder, substance abuse and psychiatric disabilities, traumatic brain injury; school counseling (MA Ed, Graduate Certificate). *Accreditation:* ACA (one or more programs are accredited). *Program availability:* Part-time, evening/weekend. *Degree requirements:* For master's and other advanced degree, comprehensive exam; for doctorate, comprehensive exam, thesis/dissertation. *Entrance requirements:* For master's, GRE General Test or MAT, minimum GPA of 2.75; for doctorate, GRE General Test or MAT, interview, minimum GPA of 3.3; for other advanced degree, GRE General Test or MAT, minimum GPA of 3.3.

Holy Names University, Graduate Division, Department of Counseling Psychology, Oakland, CA 94619-1699. Offers counseling and forensic counseling (MA); counseling psychology (MA); forensic psychology (MA). *Program availability:* Part-time, evening/weekend. *Degree requirements:* For master's, comprehensive paper, seminars. *Entrance requirements:* For master's, minimum undergraduate GPA of 2.6 overall, 3.0 in major. Additional exam requirements/recommendations for international students: required—TOEFL (minimum score 550 paper-based; 79 iBT). Electronic applications accepted. Application fee is waived when completed online. *Expenses:* Contact institution.

Immaculata University, College of Graduate Studies, Department of Psychology, Immaculata, PA 19345. Offers clinical mental health counseling (MA); clinical psychology (Psy D); forensic psychology (Graduate Certificate); integrative psychotherapy (Graduate Certificate); neuropsychology (Graduate Certificate); psychodynamic psychotherapy (Graduate Certificate); psychological testing (Graduate Certificate); school counseling (MA, Graduate Certificate); school psychology (MA). *Accreditation:* APA. *Program availability:* Part-time, evening/weekend. Terminal master's awarded for partial completion of doctoral program. *Degree requirements:* For master's, comprehensive exam, thesis optional; for doctorate, comprehensive exam, thesis/dissertation. *Entrance requirements:* For master's, GRE General Test or MAT, minimum GPA of 3.0; for doctorate, GRE General Test or MAT, minimum GPA of 3.5. Additional exam requirements/recommendations for international students: required—TOEFL, IELTS. Electronic applications accepted.

John Jay College of Criminal Justice of the City University of New York, Graduate Studies, MA in Forensics Mental Health Counseling, New York, NY 10019. Offers MA.

John Jay College of Criminal Justice of the City University of New York, Graduate Studies, Program in Forensic Psychology, New York, NY 10019. Offers MA, PhD, MA/JD. *Accreditation:* APA. *Program availability:* Part-time, evening/weekend. *Degree requirements:* For master's, thesis or alternative, externship. *Entrance requirements:* For master's, GRE General Test, minimum B average in major. Additional exam requirements/recommendations for international students: required—TOEFL (minimum score 500 paper-based).

John Jay College of Criminal Justice of the City University of New York, Graduate Studies, Programs in Criminal Justice, New York, NY 10019. Offers criminal justice (MA, PhD); criminology and deviance (PhD); forensic psychology (PhD); forensic science (PhD); international crime and justice (MA); law and philosophy (PhD); organizational behavior (PhD); public policy (PhD). *Program availability:* Part-time, evening/weekend. Terminal master's awarded for partial completion of doctoral program. *Degree requirements:* For master's, thesis or alternative; for doctorate, one foreign language, thesis/dissertation. *Entrance requirements:* For master's, GRE General Test, minimum B average; for doctorate, GRE General Test. Additional exam requirements/recommendations for international students: required—TOEFL (minimum score 500 paper-based).

Kean University, College of Liberal Arts, Program in Forensic Psychology, Union, NJ 07083. Offers MA. *Faculty:* 18 full-time (14 women). *Students:* 41 full-time (37 women), 22 part-time (18 women); includes 33 minority (5 Black or African American, non-Hispanic/Latino; 2 Asian, non-Hispanic/Latino; 26 Hispanic/Latino), 1 international. Average age 26. 62 applicants, 65% accepted, 26 enrolled. In 2019, 27 master's awarded. *Degree requirements:* For master's, project. *Entrance requirements:* For master's, baccalaureate degree from accredited college or university in psychology or related field; minimum cumulative GPA of 3.0; official transcripts; two letters of recommendation; professional resume/curriculum vitae; personal statement. Additional exam requirements/recommendations for international students: required—TOEFL (minimum score 550 paper-based, 79 iBT) or IELTS (6.5). *Application deadline:* For fall admission, 6/30 for domestic and international students; for spring admission, 12/1 for domestic and international students. Application fee: $75. Electronic applications accepted. *Expenses:* Tuition, state resident: full-time $15,326; part-time $748 per credit. Tuition, nonresident: full-time $20,288; part-time $902 per credit. *Required fees:* $2149.50; $91.25 per credit. Tuition and fees vary according to course level, course load, degree level and program. *Financial support:* Scholarships/grants and unspecified assistantships available. Financial award applicants required to submit FAFSA. *Unit head:* Dr. Richard Conti, Director, 908-737-5883, E-mail: rconti@kean.edu. *Application contact:* Amy Clark, Program Assistant, 908-737-7100, E-mail: grad-adm@kean.edu. Website: http://grad.kean.edu/masters-programs/forensic-psychology

Liberty University, Helms School of Government, Lynchburg, VA 24515. Offers criminal justice (MS), including forensic psychology, homeland security, public administration (MA, MS); international relations (MS); political science (MS); public administration (MPA), including business and government, healthcare, law and public policy, public and non-profit management; public policy (MA), including campaigns and elections, international affairs, Middle East affairs, public administration (MA, MS). *Program availability:* Part-time, online learning. *Students:* 1,143 full-time (565 women), 572 part-time (408 women); includes 795 minority (499 Black or African American, non-Hispanic/Latino; 16 American Indian or Alaska Native, non-Hispanic/Latino; 23 Asian, non-Hispanic/Latino; 162 Hispanic/Latino; 7 Native Hawaiian or other Pacific Islander, non-Hispanic/Latino; 88 Two or more races, non-Hispanic/Latino), 27 international. Average age 35. 3,017 applicants, 44% accepted, 728 enrolled. In 2019, 415 master's awarded. *Entrance requirements:* For master's, minimum undergraduate GPA of 3.0. Additional exam requirements/recommendations for international students: required—TOEFL (minimum score 600 paper-based; 100 iBT). *Application deadline:* Applications are processed on a rolling basis. Application fee: $50. Electronic applications accepted. *Expenses:* Tuition: Full-time $545; part-time $410 per credit hour. One-time fee: $50. *Financial support:* In 2019–20, 808 students received support. Teaching assistantships and Federal Work-Study available. *Unit head:* Ron Miller, Dean, 434-592-4986, E-mail: govtdean@liberty.edu. *Application contact:* Jay Bridge, Director of Admissions, 800-424-9595, Fax: 800-628-7977, E-mail: gradadmissions@liberty.edu. Website: https://www.liberty.edu/government/

London Metropolitan University, Graduate Programs, London, United Kingdom. Offers applied psychology (M Sc); architecture (MA); biomedical science (M Sc); blood science (M Sc); cancer pharmacology (M Sc); computer networking and cyber security (M Sc); computing and information systems (M Sc); conference interpreting (MA); counter-terrorism studies (M Sc); creative, digital and professional writing (MA); crime, violence and prevention (M Sc); criminology (M Sc); curating contemporary art (MA); data analytics (M Sc); digital media (MA); early childhood studies (MA); education (MA, Ed D); financial services law, regulation and compliance (LL M); food science (M Sc); forensic psychology (M Sc); health and social care management and policy (M Sc); human nutrition (M Sc); human resource management (MA); human rights and international conflict (MA); information technology (M Sc); intelligence and security studies (M Sc); international oil, gas and energy law (LL M); international relations (MA); interpreting (MA); learning and teaching in higher education (MA); legal practice (LL M); media and entertainment law (LL M); organizational and consumer psychology (M Sc); psychological therapy (M Sc); psychology of mental health (M Sc); public health (M Sc); public policy and management (MPA); security studies (M Sc); social work (M Sc); spatial planning and urban design (MA); sports therapy (M Sc); supporting older children and young people with dyslexia (MA); teaching languages (MA), including Arabic, English; translation (MA); woman and child abuse (MA).

Marymount University, School of Sciences, Mathematics, and Education, Program in Forensic and Legal Psychology, Arlington, VA 22207-4299. Offers forensic and legal psychology (MA); forensic and legal psychology with counseling (MA/MA); MA/MA. *Program availability:* Part-time, evening/weekend. *Faculty:* 6 full-time (4 women), 9 part-time/adjunct (7 women). *Students:* 156 full-time (142 women), 29 part-time (27 women); includes 55 minority (20 Black or African American, non-Hispanic/Latino; 4 Asian, non-Hispanic/Latino; 25 Hispanic/Latino; 6 Two or more races, non-Hispanic/Latino), 2 international. Average age 24. 212 applicants, 95% accepted, 99 enrolled. In 2019, 77 master's awarded. *Degree requirements:* For master's, thesis or alternative, internship. *Entrance requirements:* For master's, GRE, 2 letters of recommendation, resume, personal statement. Additional exam requirements/recommendations for international students: required—TOEFL (minimum score 600 paper-based; 96 iBT), IELTS (minimum score 6.5), PTE (minimum score 58). *Application deadline:* For fall admission, 2/15 for domestic and international students. Application fee: $40. Electronic applications accepted. *Expenses: Tuition:* Part-time $1050 per credit. *Required fees:* $22 per credit. One-time fee: $270 part-time. Tuition and fees vary according to program. *Financial support:* In 2019–20, 18 students received support. Research assistantships, teaching assistantships, career-related internships or fieldwork, scholarships/grants, and unspecified assistantships available. Support available to part-time students. Financial award application deadline: 3/1; financial award applicants required to submit FAFSA. *Unit head:* Dr. Jason Doll, Chair, Forensic and Legal Psychology, 703-526-6821, E-mail: jason.doll@marymount.edu. *Application contact:* Fiona McDonnell, Administrative Assistant, 703-284-5901, E-mail: gadmissi@marymount.edu. Website: https://www.marymount.edu/Academics/School-of-Sciences-Mathematics-and-Education/Graduate-Programs/Forensic-Legal-Psychology-(M-A-)

Montclair State University, The Graduate School, College of Humanities and Social Sciences, Family/Civil Forensic Psychology Certificate Program, Montclair, NJ 07043-1624. Offers Certificate.

Montclair State University, The Graduate School, College of Humanities and Social Sciences, Forensic Psychology Certificate Program, Montclair, NJ 07043-1624. Offers Certificate. *Program availability:* Part-time, evening/weekend. *Entrance requirements:* For degree, 2 letters of recommendation, essay. Additional exam requirements/recommendations for international students: required—TOEFL (minimum score 83 iBT), IELTS (minimum score 6.5). Electronic applications accepted.

Nova Southeastern University, College of Psychology, Fort Lauderdale, FL 33314-7796. Offers clinical mental health counseling (MS); clinical psychology (PhD, Psy D); counseling (MS); experimental psychology (MS); forensic psychology (MS); general psychology (MS); school counseling (MS); school psychology (Psy D, Psy S); substance abuse counseling (MS); substance abuse counseling and education (MS). *Accreditation:* APA (one or more programs are accredited). *Program availability:* Part-time, 100% online, blended/hybrid learning. *Faculty:* 72 full-time (34 women), 111 part-time/adjunct (76 women). *Students:* 1,263 full-time (1,068 women), 868 part-time (761 women); includes 1,221 minority (368 Black or African American, non-Hispanic/Latino; 3 American Indian or Alaska Native, non-Hispanic/Latino; 111 Asian, non-Hispanic/Latino; 668 Hispanic/Latino; 1 Native Hawaiian or other Pacific Islander, non-Hispanic/Latino; 70 Two or more races, non-Hispanic/Latino), 59 international. Average age 31. 935 applicants, 56% accepted, 375 enrolled. In 2019, 400 master's, 72 doctorates, 13 other advanced degrees awarded. Terminal master's awarded for partial completion of doctoral program. *Degree requirements:* For master's, comprehensive exam, 3 practica; for doctorate, thesis/dissertation, clinical internship, competency exam; for Psy S, comprehensive exam, internship. *Entrance requirements:* For master's and Psy S, GRE General Test, letters of recommendation, research/personal statement, interview; for doctorate, GRE General Test, GRE Subject Test (recommended), minimum undergraduate GPA of 3.0, letters of recommendation, research/personal statement, interview, curriculum vitae/resume. Additional exam requirements/recommendations for international students: required—TOEFL (minimum score 550 paper-based). *Application deadline:* Applications are processed on a rolling basis. Application fee: $50. Electronic applications accepted. *Expenses:* Contact institution. *Financial support:* In 2019–20, 197 students received support, including 15 research assistantships (averaging $5,600 per year), 68 teaching assistantships (averaging $2,000 per year); career-related internships or fieldwork, Federal Work-Study, institutionally sponsored loans, scholarships/grants, and unspecified assistantships also available. Support available to part-time students. Financial award application deadline: 4/15; financial award applicants required to submit FAFSA. *Unit head:* Dr. Karen Grosby, Dean, 954-262-5712, Fax: 954-262-3859, E-mail: grosby@nova.edu. *Application contact:* Gregory Gayle, Director, Recruitment and Admissions, 954-262-5903, Fax: 954-262-3893, E-mail: ggayle1@nova.edu. Website: http://psychology.nova.edu/

Pontificia Universidad Catolica Madre y Maestra, Graduate School, Faculty of Social and Administrative Sciences, Santiago, Dominican Republic. Offers business administration (MBA), including business development, finance, international business, management skills (M Mgmt, MBA), marketing, operations, strategic cost management, strategy, tourist destination planning and management; law (LL M), including civil law, corporate business law, criminal law, international relations, real estate law; management (M Mgmt), including higher financial management, insurance program administration, management skills (M Mgmt, MBA); psychology (MA), including clinical child and adolescent psychology, forensic psychology; strategic human resources (EMBA).

Post University, Program in Counseling and Human Services, Waterbury, CT 06723-2540. Offers counseling and human services (MS); counseling and human services/alcohol and drug counseling (MS); counseling and human services/clinical mental health counseling (MS); counseling and human services/forensic mental health counseling (MS); counseling and human services/non-profit management (MS). *Program availability:* Part-time, evening/weekend, online learning. *Entrance requirements:* For master's, resume.

Prairie View A&M University, College of Juvenile Justice and Psychology, Prairie View, TX 77446. Offers clinical adolescent psychology (PhD); juvenile forensic psychology (MSJFP); juvenile justice (MSJJ, PhD). *Program availability:* Part-time, evening/weekend, online only, 100% online, Master's in Juvenile Justice. *Faculty:* 11 full-time (5 women), 3 part-time/adjunct (all women). *Students:* 19 full-time (13 women), 35 part-time (26 women); includes 45 minority (44 Black or African American, non-Hispanic/Latino; 1 Hispanic/Latino), 7 international. Average age 31. 24 applicants, 79% accepted, 19 enrolled. In 2019, 6 master's, 4 doctorates awarded. *Degree requirements:* For master's, comprehensive exam; for doctorate, thesis/dissertation. *Entrance requirements:* For master's, GRE, minimum GPA of 2.75; for doctorate, GRE, previous course work in clinical adolescent psychology, minimum GPA of 3.5. Additional exam requirements/recommendations for international students: required—TOEFL (minimum score 550 paper-based; 79 iBT). *Application deadline:* For fall admission, 5/1 priority date for domestic and international students; for spring admission, 10/1 priority date for domestic students, 9/1 priority date for international students; for summer admission, 3/1 priority date for domestic students, 2/1 priority date for international students. Applications are processed on a rolling basis. Application fee: $50. Electronic applications accepted. *Expenses: Tuition,* area resident: Full-time $5479.68. Tuition, state resident: full-time $5479.68. Tuition, nonresident: full-time $15,439. *International tuition:* $15,439 full-time. *Required fees:* $2149.32. *Financial support:* In 2019–20, 26 students received support, including 24 research assistantships with full tuition reimbursements available (averaging $24,000 per year), 8 teaching assistantships with full tuition reimbursements available (averaging $18,000 per year); career-related internships or fieldwork, institutionally sponsored loans, scholarships/grants, health care benefits, tuition waivers (full), and unspecified assistantships also available. Support available to part-time students. Financial award application deadline: 4/1; financial award applicants required to submit FAFSA. *Unit head:* Dr. Camille Gibson, Interim Dean, 936-261-5265 Ext. 5265, Fax: 936-261-5253, E-mail: cbgibson@pvamu.edu. *Application contact:* Pauline Walker, Executive Secretary, Graduate Program, 936-261-3521, Fax: 936-261-3529, E-mail: gradadmissions@pvamu.edu.

Roger Williams University, Feinstein School of Social and Natural Sciences, Bristol, RI 02809. Offers clinical psychology (MA); forensic psychology (MA). *Faculty:* 1 (woman) full-time, 1 part-time/adjunct (0 women). *Students:* 34 full-time (31 women), 1 part-time (0 women); includes 5 minority (1 Black or African American, non-Hispanic/Latino; 1 Asian, non-Hispanic/Latino; 3 Hispanic/Latino). Average age 23. 84 applicants, 57% accepted, 19 enrolled. In 2019, 22 master's awarded. *Degree requirements:* For master's, thesis. *Entrance requirements:* For master's, GRE, Letter of intent, transcripts, three letters of recommendation. Additional exam requirements/recommendations for international students: required—TOEFL (minimum score 85 paper-based), IELTS (minimum score 6.5). *Application deadline:* For fall admission, 2/15 for domestic students, 2/1 for international students. Application fee: $50. *Expenses: Tuition:* Full-time $15,768. *Required fees:* $900; $450. *Financial support:* In 2019–20, 29 students received support. Scholarships/grants and unspecified assistantships available. Financial award application deadline: 3/15; financial award applicants required to submit

FAFSA. *Unit head:* Alejandro Leguizamo, Graduate Program Director, 401-254-3934, E-mail: aleguizamo@rwu.edu. *Application contact:* Marcus Hanscom, Director of Graduate Admissions, 401-254-3345, Fax: 401-254-3557, E-mail: gradadmit@rwu.edu. Website: http://www.rwu.edu/academics/schools-and-colleges/fssns

Sage Graduate School, School of Health Sciences, Program in Forensic Mental Health, Troy, NY 12180-4115. Offers MS, Certificate. *Program availability:* Part-time, evening/weekend. *Faculty:* 1 (woman) full-time, 3 part-time/adjunct (all women). *Students:* 12 full-time (10 women), 9 part-time (7 women); includes 6 minority (3 Black or African American, non-Hispanic/Latino; 1 Asian, non-Hispanic/Latino; 1 Hispanic/Latino; 1 Two or more races, non-Hispanic/Latino). Average age 31. 22 applicants, 77% accepted, 5 enrolled. In 2019, 14 master's awarded. *Entrance requirements:* For master's, a minimum UG GPA of 3.0 or higher; satisfactory completion of UG or GR course work in statistics; satisfactory completion of 2 courses in social and behavioral sciences; completion of the FMH application form; 2 letters of recommendation, including at least one academic reference. Additional exam requirements/recommendations for international students: required—TOEFL (minimum score 550 paper-based). *Application deadline:* Applications are processed on a rolling basis. Application fee: $30. Electronic applications accepted. *Expenses: Tuition:* Part-time $730 per credit hour. Tuition and fees vary according to course load, degree level and program. *Financial support:* Fellowships, research assistantships, scholarships/grants, and unspecified assistantships available. Financial award applicants required to submit FAFSA. *Unit head:* Kimberly Brayton, Program Director, Forensic Mental Health, 518-244-4425, E-mail: braytk@sage.edu. *Application contact:* Michael Jones, SR Associate Director of Graduate Enrollment Management, 518-292-8615, Fax: 518-292-1912, E-mail: jonesm4@sage.edu.

Tiffin University, Program in Criminal Justice, Tiffin, OH 44883-2161. Offers criminal justice (MS), including crime analysis, criminal behavior, forensic psychology, homeland security administration, justice administration. *Program availability:* Part-time, evening/weekend, 100% online, blended/hybrid learning. *Degree requirements:* For master's, thesis optional. *Entrance requirements:* For master's, minimum undergraduate GPA of 2.5, work experience. Additional exam requirements/recommendations for international students: required—TOEFL (minimum score 550 paper-based; 79 iBT). Electronic applications accepted. *Expenses:* Contact institution.

Universidad de Iberoamerica, Graduate School, San Jose, Costa Rica. Offers clinical neuropsychology (PhD); clinical psychology (M Psych); educational psychology (M Psych); forensic psychology (M Psych); hospital management (MHA); intensive care nursing (MN); medicine (MD).

Universidad del Turabo, Graduate Programs, School of Social Sciences and Humanities, Programs in Psychology, Gurabo, PR 00778-3030. Offers counseling psychology (M Psych, Psy D, Certificate); forensic psychology (Certificate); psychology (M Psych). *Entrance requirements:* For master's, GRE, GMAT or EXADEP, interview, essay, official transcript, recommendation letters; for doctorate, GRE, GMAT or EXADEP, interview, essay, official transcript, recommendation letters, curriculum vitae. Electronic applications accepted.

University of Central Oklahoma, The Jackson College of Graduate Studies, College of Education and Professional Studies, Department of Psychology, Edmond, OK 73034-5209. Offers psychology (MA), including counseling psychology, experimental psychology, forensic psychology, general psychology, school psychology. *Degree requirements:* For master's, thesis (for some programs). *Entrance requirements:* For master's, GRE. Additional exam requirements/recommendations for international students: required—TOEFL (minimum score 550 paper-based; 79 iBT), IELTS (minimum score 6.5). Electronic applications accepted.

University of Denver, Graduate School of Professional Psychology, Denver, CO 80208. Offers clinical psychology (Psy D); forensic psychology (MA); international disaster psychology (MA); sport and performance psychology (MA); sport coaching (MA); strength and conditioning and fitness coaching (Certificate). *Accreditation:* APA. *Faculty:* 23 full-time (15 women), 16 part-time/adjunct (9 women). *Students:* 243 full-time (192 women), 84 part-time (44 women); includes 95 minority (18 Black or African American, non-Hispanic/Latino; 1 American Indian or Alaska Native, non-Hispanic/Latino; 18 Asian, non-Hispanic/Latino; 46 Hispanic/Latino; 1 Native Hawaiian or other Pacific Islander, non-Hispanic/Latino; 11 Two or more races, non-Hispanic/Latino), 9 international. Average age 27. 953 applicants, 27% accepted, 137 enrolled. In 2019, 117 master's, 35 doctorates, 152 other advanced degrees awarded. *Degree requirements:* For master's, comprehensive exam (for some programs); for doctorate, comprehensive exam, community field placement, paper, clinical internship, complete 4 assessments, professional psychology clinic. *Entrance requirements:* For master's and doctorate, GRE General Test, psychology major/minor or 660 or higher on psychology subject GRE exam, transcripts, resume, two letters of recommendation, essay. Additional exam requirements/recommendations for international students: required—TOEFL (minimum score 550 paper-based; 80 iBT). *Application deadline:* For fall admission, 1/11 for domestic and international students. Application fee: $65. Electronic applications accepted. *Expenses:* Contact institution. *Financial support:* In 2019–20, 249 students received support, including 20 teaching assistantships with tuition reimbursements available (averaging $2,835 per year); career-related internships or fieldwork, Federal Work-Study, institutionally sponsored loans, scholarships/grants, unspecified assistantships, and clinical assistantships also available. Support available to part-time students. Financial award application deadline: 2/15; financial award applicants required to submit FAFSA. *Unit head:* Dr. Shelly Smith-Acuna, Dean, 303-871-3880, Fax: 303-871-4220, E-mail: shelly.smith-acuna@du.edu. *Application contact:* Julie Schellman, Director of Enrollment, 303-871-2908, E-mail: Julie.Schellman@du.edu. Website: http://www.du.edu/gspp

University of Houston–Victoria, School of Arts and Sciences, Program in Psychology, Victoria, TX 77901-4450. Offers counseling psychology (MA); forensic psychology (MA); school psychology (MA). *Program availability:* Part-time, evening/weekend, online learning. *Degree requirements:* For master's, project or thesis. *Entrance requirements:* For master's, GRE General Test. Additional exam requirements/recommendations for international students: required—TOEFL (minimum score 550 paper-based). Electronic applications accepted.

University of Louisiana at Monroe, Graduate School, College of Business and Social Sciences, Department of Psychology, Monroe, LA 71209-0001. Offers forensic psychology (MS); general psychology (MS); psychometrics (MS). *Program availability:* Part-time, evening/weekend, online learning. *Faculty:* 5 full-time (1 woman). *Students:* 71 full-time (67 women), 19 part-time (18 women); includes 38 minority (26 Black or African American, non-Hispanic/Latino; 2 American Indian or Alaska Native, non-Hispanic/Latino; 1 Asian, non-Hispanic/Latino; 3 Hispanic/Latino; 6 Two or more races, non-Hispanic/Latino), 3 international. Average age 28. 98 applicants, 55% accepted, 41 enrolled. In 2019, 20 master's awarded. *Degree requirements:* For master's, thesis optional. *Entrance requirements:* For master's, GRE General Test, minimum GPA of 2.75. Additional exam requirements/recommendations for international students: required—TOEFL (minimum score 500 paper-based; 61 iBT); recommended—IELTS (minimum score 5.5). *Application deadline:* For fall admission, 8/1 for domestic students, 6/1 for international students; for spring admission, 1/1 for domestic students, 11/1 for international students; for summer admission, 6/1 for domestic students, 3/1 for international students. Applications are processed on a rolling basis. Application fee: $40. Electronic applications accepted. *Expenses: Tuition, area resident:* Full-time $6489. Tuition, state resident: full-time $6489. Tuition, nonresident: full-time $18,989. *Required fees:* $2748. Tuition and fees vary according to course load and program. *Financial support:* In 2019–20, 30 students received support. Research assistantships with full tuition reimbursements available, career-related internships or fieldwork, Federal Work-Study, scholarships/grants, and unspecified assistantships available. Financial award application deadline: 2/15; financial award applicants required to submit FAFSA. *Unit head:* Dr. Pamela Saulsberry, Director, 318-342-1445, E-mail: saulsberry@ulm.edu. *Application contact:* Dr. Jack Palmer, Graduate Coordinator, 318-342-1345, E-mail: palmer@ulm.edu.
Website: http://www.ulm.edu/psychology

University of New Haven, Graduate School, College of Arts and Sciences, Program in Community Psychology, West Haven, CT 06516. Offers applications of psychology (Graduate Certificate); community clinical services (MA); community psychology (MA); forensic psychology (MA); program development (MA). *Program availability:* Part-time, evening/weekend. *Students:* 24 full-time (20 women), 9 part-time (8 women); includes 11 minority (7 Black or African American, non-Hispanic/Latino; 2 Asian, non-Hispanic/Latino; 2 Hispanic/Latino), 6 international. Average age 28. 28 applicants, 79% accepted, 10 enrolled. In 2019, 10 master's awarded. *Degree requirements:* For master's, thesis or alternative, fieldwork. *Entrance requirements:* Additional exam requirements/recommendations for international students: required—TOEFL (minimum score 80 iBT), IELTS, PTE. *Application deadline:* Applications are processed on a rolling basis. Application fee: $50. Electronic applications accepted. Application fee is waived when completed online. *Financial support:* Research assistantships with partial tuition reimbursements, teaching assistantships with partial tuition reimbursements, Federal Work-Study, scholarships/grants, and unspecified assistantships available. Support available to part-time students. Financial award application deadline: 5/1; financial award applicants required to submit FAFSA. *Unit head:* Dr. Melissa Whitson, Associate Professor, 203-479-4589, E-mail: mwhitson@newhaven.edu. *Application contact:* Selina O'Toole, Senior Associate Director of Graduate Admissions, 203-932-7337, E-mail: SOToole@newhaven.edu.
Website: http://www.newhaven.edu/4725/

University of North Dakota, Graduate School, College of Arts and Sciences, Department of Psychology, Grand Forks, ND 58202. Offers clinical psychology (PhD); forensic psychology (MA, MS). *Accreditation:* APA (one or more programs are accredited). *Degree requirements:* For master's, thesis, final exam; for doctorate, comprehensive exam, thesis/dissertation, internship, final exam. *Entrance requirements:* For master's, GRE General Test, GRE Subject Test, minimum GPA of 3.0; for doctorate, GRE General Test, GRE Subject Test, minimum GPA of 3.5. Additional exam requirements/recommendations for international students: required—TOEFL (minimum score 550 paper-based; 79 iBT), IELTS (minimum score 6.5). Electronic applications accepted.

Walden University, Graduate Programs, School of Counseling, Minneapolis, MN 55401. Offers addiction counseling (MS), including addictions and public health, child and adolescent counseling, family studies and interventions, forensic counseling, general program, military families and culture, trauma and crisis counseling; clinical mental health counseling (MS), including addiction counseling, forensic counseling, military families and culture, trauma and crisis counseling; counselor education and supervision (PhD), including consultation, counseling and social change, forensic mental health counseling, leadership and program evaluation, trauma and crisis; marriage, couple, and family counseling (MS), including addiction counseling, career counseling, forensic counseling, military families and culture, trauma and crisis counseling; school counseling (MS), including addiction counseling, career counseling, crisis and trauma, military families and culture. *Accreditation:* ACA. *Program availability:* Part-time, evening/weekend, online only, 100% online. *Degree requirements:* For master's, residency, field experience, professional development plan, licensure plan; for doctorate, thesis/dissertation, residency, practicum, internship. *Entrance requirements:* For master's, bachelor's degree or higher; minimum GPA of 2.5; official transcripts; goal statement (for some programs); access to computer and Internet; for doctorate, master's degree or higher; three years of related professional or academic experience (preferred); minimum GPA of 3.0; goal statement and current resume (for select programs); official transcripts; access to computer and Internet. Additional exam requirements/recommendations for international students: required—TOEFL (minimum score 550 paper-based, 79 iBT), IELTS (minimum score 6.5), Michigan English Language Assessment Battery (minimum score 82), or PTE (minimum score 53). Electronic applications accepted.

Walden University, Graduate Programs, School of Psychology, Minneapolis, MN 55401. Offers clinical psychology (MS), including counseling, general program; forensic psychology (MS), including forensic psychology in the community, general program, mental health applications, program planning and evaluation in forensic settings, psychology and legal systems; industrial organizational (MS, PhD), including consulting psychology, forensic (MS), forensic psychology (PhD), general practice, leadership development and coaching (MS), organizational diversity and social change, research evaluation (PhD); online teaching in psychology (Post-Master's Certificate); organizational psychology and development (Postbaccalaureate Certificate); psychology (MS, PhD), including applied psychology (MS), clinical psychology (PhD), crisis management and response (MS), educational psychology, forensic psychology (PhD), general psychology (MS), general psychology research (PhD), general psychology teaching (PhD), health psychology, leadership development and coaching (MS), psychology of culture (MS), psychology, public administration, and social change (MS), social psychology, terrorism and security (MS); psychology respecialization (Post-Doctoral Certificate). *Program availability:* Part-time, evening/weekend, online only, 100% online. Terminal master's awarded for partial completion of doctoral program. *Degree requirements:* For master's, thesis optional; for doctorate, thesis/dissertation, residency. *Entrance requirements:* For master's, bachelor's degree or higher; minimum GPA of 2.5; official transcripts; goal statement (for some programs); access to computer and Internet; for doctorate, master's degree or higher; three years of related professional or academic experience (preferred); minimum GPA of 3.0; goal statement and current resume (for select programs); official transcripts; access to computer and Internet; for other advanced degree, relevant work experience; access to computer and Internet. Additional exam requirements/recommendations for international students: required—TOEFL (minimum score 550 paper-based, 79 iBT), IELTS (minimum score 6.5), Michigan English Language Assessment Battery (minimum score 82), or PTE (minimum score 53). Electronic applications accepted.

Westfield State University, College of Graduate and Continuing Education, Department of Psychology, Program in Counseling, Westfield, MA 01086. Offers forensic mental health counseling (MA); mental health counseling (MA); school adjustment counseling (MA); school guidance counseling (MA). *Program availability:* Part-time, evening/weekend. *Degree requirements:* For master's, comprehensive exam, practicum. *Entrance requirements:* For master's, GRE General Test, MAT, minimum undergraduate GPA of 3.0. Additional exam requirements/recommendations for international students: recommended—TOEFL (minimum score 550 paper-based; 79 iBT).

William James College, Graduate Programs, Newton, MA 02459. Offers applied psychology in higher education student personnel administration (MA); clinical psychology (Psy D); counseling psychology (MA); counseling psychology and community mental health (MA); counseling psychology and global mental health (MA); executive coaching (Graduate Certificate); forensic and counseling psychology (MA); leadership psychology (Psy D); organizational psychology (MA); primary care psychology (MA); respecialization in clinical psychology (Certificate); school psychology (Psy D); MA/CAGS. *Accreditation:* APA. *Degree requirements:* For master's, comprehensive exam (for some programs); for doctorate, thesis/dissertation (for some programs). Electronic applications accepted.

Genetic Counseling

Augustana University, Augustana-Sanford Genetic Counseling Program, Sioux Falls, SD 57197. Offers MS. *Degree requirements:* For master's, thesis, clinical rotation with satisfactory evaluations; ACGC logbook with minimum 50 core-qualifying cases. *Entrance requirements:* For master's, GRE or GMAT. Additional exam requirements/ recommendations for international students: required—TOEFL. Electronic applications accepted. *Expenses:* Contact institution.

Baylor College of Medicine, School of Health Professions, Genetic Counseling Program, Houston, TX 77030-3498. Offers MS.

Bay Path University, Program in Genetic Counseling, Longmeadow, MA 01106-2292. Offers MS. *Program availability:* Evening/weekend, blended/hybrid learning. *Entrance requirements:* For master's, GRE, completed application; official undergraduate and graduate transcripts; original essay on the topic: "Why is achieving an MS in Genetic Counseling from Bay Path University important to my life and professional goals?"; current resume; 3 recommendations. Applicants selected for an interview will be contacted by phone or email. Electronic applications accepted. Application fee is waived when completed online. *Expenses:* Contact institution.

Boston University, School of Medicine, Graduate Medical Sciences, Program in Genetic Counseling, Boston, MA 02215. Offers MS. *Application deadline:* For fall admission, 2/1 for domestic students. *Financial support:* In 2019–20, 15 students received support. Institutionally sponsored loans and unspecified assistantships available. Financial award application deadline: 1/1; financial award applicants required to submit FAFSA. *Unit head:* Kathleen Berentsen Swenson, Program Director, E-mail: kbb2010@bu.edu. *Application contact:* GMS Admissions Office, 617-358-9518, Fax: 617-358-2913, E-mail: gmsbusm@bu.edu.
Website: http://www.bumc.bu.edu/gms/genetic-counseling/

Brandeis University, Graduate School of Arts and Sciences, Program in Genetic Counseling, Waltham, MA 02454-9110. Offers MS. *Program availability:* Part-time. *Faculty:* 1 (woman) full-time, 5 part-time/adjunct (all women). *Students:* 20 full-time (all women); includes 5 minority (3 Asian, non-Hispanic/Latino; 2 Hispanic/Latino), 1 international. Average age 27. 163 applicants, 6% accepted, 10 enrolled. In 2019, 10 master's awarded. *Degree requirements:* For master's, thesis, internship/fieldwork. *Entrance requirements:* For master's, General GRE, transcripts, letters of recommendation, resume, statement of purpose, and prerequisite courses. Additional exam requirements/recommendations for international students: required—TOEFL, IELTS, PTE. *Application deadline:* For fall admission, 1/1 for domestic and international students. Application fee: $75. Electronic applications accepted. *Financial support:* Scholarships/grants available. *Unit head:* Dr. Gretchen Schneider, Director of Graduate Studies, 781-736-3108, E-mail: gretchen@brandeis.edu. *Application contact:* Amanda Ogilby, Administrator, 781-736-3179, E-mail: amandaogilby@brandeis.edu.
Website: http://www.brandeis.edu/gsas/programs/genetic_counseling.html

California State University, Stanislaus, College of Natural Sciences, MS Program in Genetic Counseling, Turlock, CA 95382. Offers MS. *Degree requirements:* For master's, thesis. *Entrance requirements:* For master's, GRE, minimum GPA of 3.0, 3 letters of reference, personal statement. Additional exam requirements/recommendations for international students: required—TOEFL (minimum score 550 paper-based). Electronic applications accepted. *Expenses:* Contact institution.

Case Western Reserve University, School of Medicine and School of Graduate Studies, Graduate Programs in Medicine, Department of Genetics and Genome Sciences, Cleveland, OH 44106. Offers genetic counseling (MS); genetics and genome sciences (PhD); MD/PhD. Terminal master's awarded for partial completion of doctoral program. *Degree requirements:* For master's, thesis; for doctorate, comprehensive exam, thesis/dissertation. *Entrance requirements:* For master's, GRE General Test; for doctorate, GRE General Test, GRE Subject Test. Additional exam requirements/ recommendations for international students: required—TOEFL.

Emory University, School of Medicine, Programs in Allied Health Professions, Genetic Counseling Training Program, Atlanta, GA 30322. Offers MM Sc. *Degree requirements:* For master's, thesis, capstone project. *Entrance requirements:* For master's, GRE General Test, minimum GPA of 3.0; prerequisites: genetics, statistics, psychology, and biochemistry. Additional exam requirements/recommendations for international students: required—TOEFL.

Icahn School of Medicine at Mount Sinai, Graduate School of Biomedical Sciences, New York, NY 10029-6504. Offers biomedical sciences (MS, PhD); clinical research education (MS, PhD); community medicine (MPH); genetic counseling (MS); neurosciences (PhD); MD/PhD. Terminal master's awarded for partial completion of doctoral program. *Degree requirements:* For master's, thesis; for doctorate, comprehensive exam, thesis/dissertation. *Entrance requirements:* For master's, GRE General Test; for doctorate, GRE General Test, GRE Subject Test, 3 years of college pre-med course work. Additional exam requirements/recommendations for international students: required—TOEFL. Electronic applications accepted.

Johns Hopkins University, Bloomberg School of Public Health, Department of Health, Behavior and Society, Baltimore, MD 21218. Offers genetic counseling (Sc M); health education and health communication (MSPH); social and behavioral sciences (PhD); social factors in health (MHS). *Degree requirements:* For master's, comprehensive exam (for some programs), thesis (for some programs); for doctorate, comprehensive exam, thesis/dissertation. *Entrance requirements:* For master's, GRE, curriculum vitae, 3 letters of recommendation; for doctorate, GRE, transcripts, curriculum vitae, 3 recommendation letters. Additional exam requirements/recommendations for international students: required—TOEFL (minimum score 100 iBT), IELTS (minimum score 7). Electronic applications accepted.

Long Island University - Post, College of Liberal Arts and Sciences, Brookville, NY 11548-1300. Offers applied mathematics (MS); behavior analysis (MA); biology (MS); criminal justice (MS); earth science (MS); English (MA); environmental sustainability (MS); genetic counseling (MS); history (MA); interdisciplinary studies (MA, MS); political science (MA); psychology (MA). *Program availability:* Part-time, evening/weekend, blended/hybrid learning. Terminal master's awarded for partial completion of doctoral program. *Degree requirements:* For master's, comprehensive exam (for some programs), thesis (for some programs). *Entrance requirements:* Additional exam requirements/recommendations for international students: required—TOEFL, IELTS, or PTE. Electronic applications accepted.

McGill University, Faculty of Graduate and Postdoctoral Studies, Faculty of Medicine, Department of Human Genetics, Montréal, QC H3A 2T5, Canada. Offers genetic counseling (M Sc); human genetics (M Sc, PhD).

Northwestern University, The Graduate School, Program in Genetic Counseling, Evanston, IL 60208. Offers MS. *Degree requirements:* For master's, thesis. *Entrance requirements:* For master's, GRE General Test, interview. Additional exam requirements/recommendations for international students: required—TOEFL.

Sarah Lawrence College, Graduate Studies, Joan H. Marks Graduate Program in Human Genetics, Bronxville, NY 10708-5999. Offers MS. *Program availability:* Part-time. *Degree requirements:* For master's, thesis, fieldwork. *Entrance requirements:* For master's, previous course work in biology, chemistry, developmental biology, genetics, probability and statistics. Additional exam requirements/recommendations for international students: required—TOEFL (minimum score 600 paper-based). Electronic applications accepted. *Expenses:* Contact institution.

Thomas Jefferson University, Jefferson College of Life Sciences, MS Program in Human Genetics and Genetic Counseling, Philadelphia, PA 19107. Offers MS. *Entrance requirements:* For master's, BA, personal statement, official transcripts, recommendation letters. Additional exam requirements/recommendations for international students: required—TOEFL, IELTS (minimum score 7). Electronic applications accepted.

Université de Montréal, Faculty of Medicine, Program in Genetic Counseling, Montréal, QC H3C 3J7, Canada. Offers DESS.

The University of Alabama at Birmingham, School of Health Professions, Program in Genetic Counseling, Birmingham, AL 35294. Offers MS. *Students:* Average age 30. 129 applicants, 4% accepted, 5 enrolled. In 2019, 5 master's awarded. *Entrance requirements:* For master's, GRE, minimum undergraduate GPA of 3.0, letters of recommendation, paid or volunteer experience, personal statement. Additional exam requirements/recommendations for international students: required—TOEFL, TWE. *Application deadline:* For fall admission, 1/15 for domestic students. Application fee: $0 ($60 for international students). Electronic applications accepted. *Unit head:* Dr. Christina B. Hurst, Graduate Program Director, 205-934-7299, E-mail: cbhurst@uab.edu. *Application contact:* Susan Noblitt Banks, Director of Graduate School Operations, 205-934-8227, Fax: 205-934-8413, E-mail: gradschool@uab.edu. Website: http://www.uab.edu/shp/cds/genetic-counseling

University of Arkansas for Medical Sciences, College of Health Professions, Little Rock, AR 72205-7199. Offers audiology (Au D); communication sciences and disorders (MS, PhD); genetic counseling (MS); nuclear medicine advanced associate (MIS); physician assistant studies (MPAS); radiologist assistant (MIS). *Accreditation:* ASHA. *Program availability:* Part-time, online learning. *Degree requirements:* For master's, thesis (for some programs); for doctorate, comprehensive exam (for some programs), thesis/dissertation (for some programs). *Entrance requirements:* For master's, GRE. Additional exam requirements/recommendations for international students: required—TOEFL (minimum score 550 paper-based; 79 iBT). Electronic applications accepted. *Expenses:* Contact institution.

The University of British Columbia, Faculty of Medicine, Department of Medical Genetics, M Sc Program in Genetic Counselling, Vancouver, BC V6H 3N1, Canada. Offers M Sc. Electronic applications accepted. *Expenses:* Contact institution.

University of California, Irvine, School of Medicine, Program in Genetic Counseling, Irvine, CA 92697. Offers MS. *Students:* 15 full-time (13 women); includes 5 minority (4 Asian, non-Hispanic/Latino; 1 Hispanic/Latino). Average age 26. 215 applicants, 4% accepted, 8 enrolled. In 2019, 7 master's awarded. *Entrance requirements:* For master's, GRE General Test, minimum GPA of 3.0. Additional exam requirements/ recommendations for international students: required—TOEFL (minimum score 550 paper-based). *Application deadline:* For fall admission, 1/15 priority date for domestic students, 1/15 for international students. Applications are processed on a rolling basis. Application fee: $120 ($140 for international students). Electronic applications accepted. *Financial support:* In 2019–20, 3 students received support. Research assistantships with full tuition reimbursements available, teaching assistantships, career-related internships or fieldwork, institutionally sponsored loans, traineeships, health care benefits, and unspecified assistantships available. Financial award application deadline: 3/1; financial award applicants required to submit FAFSA. *Unit head:* Pamela Flodman, Director, 714-456-8470, E-mail: pflodman@uci.edu. *Application contact:* Pamela Flodman, Director, 714-456-8470, E-mail: pflodman@uci.edu.
Website: http://www.pediatrics.uci.edu/masters-genetic-counseling.asp

University of Cincinnati, Graduate School, College of Allied Health Sciences, Program in Genetic Counseling, Cincinnati, OH 45221. Offers medical genetics (MS). *Program availability:* Part-time. *Degree requirements:* For master's, thesis. *Entrance requirements:* For master's, GRE General Test. Additional exam requirements/ recommendations for international students: required—TOEFL. Electronic applications accepted.

University of Colorado Denver, School of Medicine, Graduate Program in Genetic Counseling, Aurora, CO 80045. Offers biophysics and genetics (MS). *Degree requirements:* For master's, 44 core semester hours, project or thesis. *Entrance requirements:* For master's, GRE, minimum undergraduate GPA of 3.0; 4 letters of recommendation; prerequisite coursework in biology, general chemistry, general biochemistry, general genetics, and general psychology; experience in counseling and laboratory settings and strong understanding of genetic counseling field (highly recommended). Additional exam requirements/recommendations for international students: required—TOEFL (minimum score 570 paper-based; 89 iBT). Electronic applications accepted. Tuition and fees vary according to course load, program and reciprocity agreements.

Genetic Counseling

University of Manitoba, Max Rady College of Medicine and Faculty of Graduate Studies, Graduate Programs in Medicine, Department of Biochemistry and Medical Genetics, Winnipeg, MB R3T 2N2, Canada. Offers biochemistry and medical genetics (M Sc, PhD); genetic counseling (M Sc). Terminal master's awarded for partial completion of doctoral program. *Degree requirements:* For master's, thesis; for doctorate, thesis/dissertation.

University of Maryland, Baltimore, School of Medicine, Genetic Counseling Training Program, Baltimore, MD 21201. Offers MGC. *Students:* 15 full-time (13 women), 1 international. Average age 24. 134 applicants, 6% accepted, 8 enrolled. In 2019, 8 master's awarded. *Expenses:* Contact institution. *Unit head:* Shannan DeLany Dixon, Director, 410-706-4713, Fax: 410-706-1644, E-mail: sdelany@som.umaryland.edu. *Application contact:* Shannan DeLany Dixon, Director, 410-706-4713, Fax: 410-706-1644, E-mail: sdelany@som.umaryland.edu.

University of Michigan, Rackham Graduate School, Program in Biomedical Sciences (PIBS), Department of Human Genetics, Ann Arbor, MI 48109. Offers genetic counseling (MS); human genetics (MS, PhD). Terminal master's awarded for partial completion of doctoral program. *Degree requirements:* For master's, thesis optional, research project (for MS in genetic counseling); for doctorate, thesis/dissertation, oral preliminary exam, oral defense of dissertation. *Entrance requirements:* For master's, GRE General Test, bachelor's degree; 3 letters of recommendation; advocacy experience (for the MS in genetic counseling); for doctorate, bachelor's degree; 3 letters of recommendation. Additional exam requirements/recommendations for international students: required—TOEFL (minimum score 84 iBT). Electronic applications accepted.

University of Minnesota, Twin Cities Campus, Graduate School, Program in Molecular, Cellular, Developmental Biology and Genetics, Minneapolis, MN 55455-0213. Offers genetic counseling (MS); molecular, cellular, developmental biology and genetics (PhD). Terminal master's awarded for partial completion of doctoral program. *Degree requirements:* For master's, thesis optional; for doctorate, thesis/dissertation. *Entrance requirements:* For master's and doctorate, GRE General Test. Additional exam requirements/recommendations for international students: required—TOEFL (minimum score 625 paper-based; 80 iBT). Electronic applications accepted.

The University of North Carolina at Greensboro, Graduate School, School of Health and Human Sciences, Program in Genetic Counseling, Greensboro, NC 27412-5001. Offers MS. Electronic applications accepted.

University of Oklahoma Health Sciences Center, College of Medicine and Graduate College, Department of Genetic Counseling, Oklahoma City, OK 73190. Offers MS. *Entrance requirements:* For master's, GRE General Test, 3 letters of recommendation.

University of Pittsburgh, Graduate School of Public Health, Department of Human Genetics, Pittsburgh, PA 15261. Offers genetic counseling (MS); human genetics (MS, PhD); public health genetics (MPH, Certificate); MD/PhD; MS/MPH. *Program availability:* Part-time. *Faculty:* 17 full-time (7 women), 91 part-time/adjunct (64 women). *Students:* 63 full-time (52 women), 15 part-time (13 women); includes 13 minority (2 Black or African American, non-Hispanic/Latino; 5 Asian, non-Hispanic/Latino; 3 Hispanic/Latino; 1 Native Hawaiian or other Pacific Islander, non-Hispanic/Latino; 2 Two or more races, non-Hispanic/Latino), 19 international. Average age 26. 251 applicants, 31% accepted, 32 enrolled. In 2019, 26 master's, 7 doctorates awarded. *Degree requirements:* For master's, comprehensive exam, thesis; for doctorate, comprehensive exam, thesis/dissertation, Qualifying Exam (Required). *Entrance requirements:* For master's and doctorate, GRE (Domestic and International)*, TOEFL or IELTS (International ONLY), *Will accept MCAT in Lieu of GRE, previous course work in biochemistry and behavioral or social sciences (recommended); bachelor's degree in a discipline related to the biological or behavioral sciences from accredited college or university with minimum GPA of 3.0, introductory courses in genetics and calculus. Additional exam requirements/recommendations for international students: required—TOEFL (minimum score 550 paper-based; 80 iBT), IELTS (minimum score 6.5), GRE, WES Evaluation for foreign education. *Application deadline:* For fall admission, 7/15 priority date for domestic students, 4/1 priority date for international students; for spring admission, 10/15 priority date for domestic students, 8/1 priority date for international students. Applications are processed on a rolling basis. Application fee: $135. Electronic applications accepted. *Expenses:* $13,379 per term full-time in-state, $23,407 per term full-time out-of-state; $1122 per credit part-time in-state, $1916 per credit part-time out-of-state; $500 per term for full-time dissertation research; $475 per term full-time fees; $295 per term part-time fees. *Financial support:* In 2019–20, 8 students received support. Career-related internships or fieldwork, scholarships/grants, and unspecified assistantships available. Financial award application deadline: 4/15; financial award applicants required to submit CSS PROFILE or FAFSA. *Unit head:* Jennifer Heinemann Palaski, MBA, Department Administrator, Human Genetics and Biostatistics, 412-648-1560, Fax: 412-624-3020, E-mail: JDH150@pitt.edu. *Application contact:* Noel C. Harrie, Recruitment and Academic Affairs Administrator, 412-624-3066, Fax: 412-624-3020, E-mail: nce1@pitt.edu. Website: http://www.publichealth.pitt.edu/hugen

University of South Carolina, School of Medicine and The Graduate School, Graduate Programs in Medicine, Program in Genetic Counseling, Columbia, SC 29203. Offers MS. *Degree requirements:* For master's, comprehensive exam, internship, practicum. *Entrance requirements:* For master's, GRE General Test. Electronic applications accepted. *Expenses:* Contact institution.

The University of Texas Health Science Center at Houston, MD Anderson UTHealth Graduate School, Houston, TX 77225-0036. Offers biochemistry and cell biology (PhD); biomedical sciences (MS); cancer biology (PhD); genetic counseling (MS); genetics and epigenetics (PhD); immunology (PhD); medical physics (MS, PhD); microbiology and infectious diseases (PhD); neuroscience (PhD); quantitative sciences (PhD); therapeutics and pharmacology (PhD); MD/PhD. Terminal master's awarded for partial completion of doctoral program. *Degree requirements:* For master's, thesis; for doctorate, thesis/dissertation. *Entrance requirements:* For master's and doctorate, GRE General Test. Additional exam requirements/recommendations for international students: required—TOEFL. Electronic applications accepted.

University of Toronto, Faculty of Medicine, Department of Molecular Genetics, Toronto, ON M5S 1A1, Canada. Offers genetic counseling (M Sc); molecular genetics (M Sc, PhD). *Degree requirements:* For master's, thesis; for doctorate, thesis/dissertation. *Entrance requirements:* For master's, B Sc or equivalent; for doctorate, M Sc or equivalent, minimum B+ average. Additional exam requirements/recommendations for international students: required—TOEFL, IELTS (minimum score 7), Michigan English Language Assessment Battery (minimum score 85), or COPE (minimum score 4). Electronic applications accepted.

University of Wisconsin–Madison, Graduate School, College of Agricultural and Life Sciences and School of Medicine and Public Health, Department of Genetics, Madison, WI 53706-1380. Offers genetic counseling (MS); genetics (PhD). *Degree requirements:* For doctorate, thesis/dissertation.

University of Wisconsin–Madison, School of Medicine and Public Health, Master of Genetic Counselor Studies Program, Madison, WI 53706-1380. Offers MGCS.

Health Psychology

Adler University, Master of Science (M.S.) in Sport and Human Performance, Chicago, IL 60602. Offers MAC. In 2019, 1 master's awarded. *Degree requirements:* For master's, Social Justice Practicum; Sports Externship. *Unit head:* Phyllis Horton, Director of Admissions, 312-662-4100, E-mail: admissions@adler.edu. *Application contact:* Phyllis Horton, Director of Admissions, 312-662-4100, E-mail: admissions@adler.edu.

Alliant International University - Los Angeles, California School of Professional Psychology, Psy D Program in Clinical Psychology, Alhambra, CA 91803. Offers clinical health psychology (Psy D); family/child and couple clinical psychology (Psy D); multi-interest option (Psy D); multicultural community-clinical psychology (Psy D). *Accreditation:* APA. *Degree requirements:* For doctorate, comprehensive exam, thesis/dissertation. *Entrance requirements:* For doctorate, interview, minimum GPA of 3.0 in both psychology and overall. Additional exam requirements/recommendations for international students: required—TOEFL (minimum score 600 paper-based), TWE. Electronic applications accepted.

Appalachian State University, Cratis D. Williams School of Graduate Studies, Department of Psychology, Boone, NC 28608. Offers clinical health psychology (MA). *Program availability:* Part-time. *Degree requirements:* For master's, comprehensive exam, thesis optional, exit exam. *Entrance requirements:* For master's, GRE General Test, 3 letters of recommendation. Additional exam requirements/recommendations for international students: required—TOEFL (minimum score 550 paper-based; 79 iBT) or IELTS (minimum score 6.5). Electronic applications accepted.

Argosy University, Atlanta, Georgia School of Professional Psychology, Atlanta, GA 30328. Offers clinical psychology (MA, Psy D, Postdoctoral Respecialization Certificate), including child and family psychology (Psy D), general adult clinical (Psy D), health psychology (Psy D), neuropsychology/geropsychology (Psy D); community counseling (MA), including marriage and family therapy; counselor education and supervision (Ed D); forensic psychology (MA); industrial organizational psychology (MA); marriage and family therapy (Certificate); sport-exercise psychology (MA). *Accreditation:* APA.

Argosy University, Chicago, Illinois School of Professional Psychology, Doctoral Program in Clinical Psychology, Chicago, IL 60601. Offers child and adolescent psychology (Psy D); client-centered and experiential psychotherapies (Psy D); diversity and multicultural psychology (Psy D); family psychology (Psy D); forensic psychology (Psy D); health psychology (Psy D); neuropsychology (Psy D); organizational consulting (Psy D); psychoanalytic psychology (Psy D); psychology and spirituality (Psy D). *Accreditation:* APA.

Argosy University, Northern Virginia, American School of Professional Psychology, Arlington, VA 22209. Offers clinical psychology (MA, Psy D), including child and family psychology (Psy D), diversity and multicultural psychology (Psy D), forensic psychology (Psy D), health and neuropsychology (Psy D); community counseling (MA); counseling psychology (Ed D), including counselor education and supervision; counselor education and supervision (Ed D); forensic psychology (MA).

Argosy University, Twin Cities, Minnesota School of Professional Psychology, Eagan, MN 55121. Offers clinical psychology (MA, Psy D), including child and family psychology (Psy D), forensic psychology (Psy D), health and neuropsychology (Psy D), trauma (Psy D); forensic counseling (Post-Graduate Certificate); forensic psychology (MA); industrial organizational psychology (MA); marriage and family therapy (MA, DMFT), including forensic counseling (MA). *Accreditation:* AAMFT; AAMFT/COAMFTE; APA.

Bastyr University, School of Natural Health Arts and Sciences, Kenmore, WA 98028-4966. Offers counseling psychology (MA); maternal-child health systems (MA); midwifery (MS); nutrition (Certificate); nutrition and clinical health psychology (MS); nutrition and wellness (MS). *Accreditation:* AND; MEAC. *Program availability:* Part-time. *Degree requirements:* For master's, thesis optional. *Entrance requirements:* For master's, 1-2 years' basic sciences course work (depending on program). Additional exam requirements/recommendations for international students: required—TOEFL (minimum score 550 paper-based; 79 iBT).

California State University, Dominguez Hills, College of Natural and Behavioral Sciences, Department of Psychology, Carson, CA 90747-0001. Offers clinical psychology (MA); health psychology (MA). *Program availability:* Part-time, evening/weekend. Terminal master's awarded for partial completion of doctoral program. *Degree requirements:* For master's, comprehensive exam, thesis optional. *Entrance requirements:* For master's, GRE General Test or MAT, interview, minimum GPA of 3.0, prerequisite psychology courses. Additional exam requirements/recommendations for international students: required—TOEFL (minimum score 550 paper-based). Electronic applications accepted.

Central Michigan University, College of Graduate Studies, College of Liberal Arts and Social Sciences, Department of Psychology, Program in Industrial and Organizational Psychology, Mount Pleasant, MI 48859. Offers industrial and organizational psychology (MA, PhD); occupational health psychology (PhD). *Degree requirements:* For master's, thesis; for doctorate, comprehensive exam, thesis/dissertation. *Entrance requirements:* For master's and doctorate, GRE. Electronic applications accepted. *Expenses: Tuition, area resident:* Full-time $12,267; part-time $8178 per year. Tuition, state resident: full-time $12,267; part-time $8178 per year. Tuition, nonresident: full-time $12,267; part-time $8178 per year. *International tuition:* $16,110 full-time. *Required fees:* $225 per semester. Tuition and fees vary according to degree level and program.

Chatham University, Program in Counseling Psychology, Pittsburgh, PA 15232-2826. Offers child, adolescent and family (MSCP); counseling psychology (Psy D); health and holistic (MSCP); organization and supervision (MSCP); sport and exercise (MSCP). *Accreditation:* APA. *Program availability:* Part-time, evening/weekend. *Faculty:* 13 full-time (8 women), 21 part-time/adjunct (17 women). *Students:* 93 full-time (79 women), 56 part-time (44 women); includes 29 minority (16 Black or African American, non-Hispanic/

Latino; 4 Asian, non-Hispanic/Latino; 6 Hispanic/Latino; 3 Two or more races, non-Hispanic/Latino), 2 international. Average age 29. 172 applicants, 46% accepted, 54 enrolled. In 2019, 30 master's, 7 doctorates awarded. *Degree requirements:* For master's, thesis optional, supervised internship; for doctorate, thesis/dissertation, internship. *Entrance requirements:* For master's, minimum GPA of 3.0; 2 letters of recommendation; resume; prerequisite coursework in statistics, biology, and psychology; for doctorate, GRE. Additional exam requirements/recommendations for international students: required—TOEFL (minimum score 600 paper-based; 100 iBT), IELTS (minimum score 7), TWE. *Application deadline:* For fall admission, 4/1 priority date for domestic and international students; for spring admission, 11/1 for domestic students, 10/1 for international students. Applications are processed on a rolling basis. Application fee: $45. Electronic applications accepted. Application fee is waived when completed online. *Expenses:* $1,017 per credit hour. *Financial support:* Career-related internships or fieldwork available. Financial award applicants required to submit FAFSA. *Unit head:* Dr. Mary Jo Loughran, Director, 412-365-2783, Fax: 412-365-1505, E-mail: mloughran@chatham.edu. *Application contact:* Melanie Elmer, Assistant Director of Graduate Admission, 412-365-1394, Fax: 412-365-1609, E-mail: gradadmissions@chatham.edu.
Website: http://www.chatham.edu/mscp

Claremont Graduate University, Graduate Programs, School of Social Science, Policy and Evaluation, Department of Psychology, Claremont, CA 91711-6160. Offers advanced study in evaluation (Certificate); cognitive psychology (MA, PhD); developmental psychology (MA, PhD); evaluation and applied research methods (MA, PhD); health behavior research and evaluation (MA, PhD); human resource development and evaluation (MA); industrial/organizational psychology (MA, PhD); organizational behavior (MA, PhD); organizational psychology (MA, PhD); social psychology (MA, PhD); MBA/PhD. *Program availability:* Part-time. Terminal master's awarded for partial completion of doctoral program. *Entrance requirements:* For master's and doctorate, GRE General Test. Additional exam requirements/recommendations for international students: required—TOEFL (minimum score 75 iBT). Electronic applications accepted.

Drexel University, College of Arts and Sciences, Department of Psychology, Clinical Psychology Program, Philadelphia, PA 19104-2875. Offers clinical psychology (PhD); forensic psychology (PhD); health psychology (PhD); neuropsychology (PhD). *Accreditation:* APA. Terminal master's awarded for partial completion of doctoral program. *Degree requirements:* For doctorate, thesis/dissertation, qualifying exam. *Entrance requirements:* For doctorate, GRE General Test, GRE Subject Test, minimum GPA of 3.0. Electronic applications accepted. *Expenses:* Contact institution.

Drexel University, College of Arts and Sciences, Department of Psychology, Program in Law-Psychology, Philadelphia, PA 19104-2875. Offers JD/PhD. Electronic applications accepted. *Expenses:* Contact institution.

Duke University, Graduate School, Department of Psychology and Neuroscience, Durham, NC 27708. Offers biological psychology (PhD); clinical psychology (PhD); cognitive psychology (PhD); developmental psychology (PhD); experimental psychology (PhD); health psychology (PhD); human social development (PhD); JD/MA. *Accreditation:* APA (one or more programs are accredited). *Degree requirements:* For doctorate, thesis/dissertation. *Entrance requirements:* For doctorate, GRE General Test. Additional exam requirements/recommendations for international students: required—TOEFL (minimum score 577 paper-based; 90 iBT) or IELTS (minimum score 7). Electronic applications accepted.

East Carolina University, Graduate School, Thomas Harriot College of Arts and Sciences, Department of Psychology, Greenville, NC 27858-4353. Offers health psychology (PhD), including clinical health psychology, occupational health psychology, pediatric school psychology; industrial and organizational psychology (MA); quantitative methods for the social and behavioral sciences (Certificate); MA/CAS. *Program availability:* Part-time, evening/weekend. *Application deadline:* For fall admission, 12/1 priority date for domestic and international students. *Expenses: Tuition, area resident:* Full-time $4749; part-time $185 per credit hour. *Tuition, state resident:* full-time $4749; part-time $185 per credit hour. *Tuition, nonresident:* full-time $17,898; part-time $864 per credit hour. *International tuition:* $17,898 full-time. *Required fees:* $2787. *Financial support:* Application deadline: 6/1. *Unit head:* Dr. Alan Christensen, Chair, E-mail: christensenal19@ecu.edu. *Application contact:* Graduate School Admissions, 252-328-6012, Fax: 252-328-6071, E-mail: gradschool@ecu.edu.
Website: https://psychology.ecu.edu/

Georgian Court University, School of Arts and Sciences, Lakewood, NJ 08701. Offers applied behavior analysis (MA); autism spectrum disorders (Certificate); clinical mental health counseling (MA); criminal justice and human rights (MS); holistic health studies (MA); homeland security (Certificate); instructional technology (CPC); integrative health (Certificate); mercy spirituality (Certificate); parish business management (Certificate); professional counselor (Certificate); school psychology (MA, Certificate); theology (MA, Certificate). *Program availability:* Part-time, evening/weekend. *Faculty:* 19 full-time (11 women), 7 part-time/adjunct (3 women). *Students:* 90 full-time (80 women), 71 part-time (59 women); includes 26 minority (8 Black or African American, non-Hispanic/Latino; 2 Asian, non-Hispanic/Latino; 14 Hispanic/Latino; 2 Two or more races, non-Hispanic/Latino), 1 international. Average age 32. 138 applicants, 58% accepted, 57 enrolled. In 2019, 68 master's, 19 other advanced degrees awarded. *Degree requirements:* For master's, comprehensive exam (for some programs), thesis (for some programs); for other advanced degree, comprehensive exam (for some programs). *Entrance requirements:* Additional exam requirements/recommendations for international students: required—TOEFL (minimum score 550 paper-based; 79 iBT). *Application deadline:* For fall admission, 8/15 for domestic students, 5/1 for international students; for spring admission, 1/15 for domestic students, 10/1 for international students. Applications are processed on a rolling basis. Application fee: $40. Electronic applications accepted. *Financial support:* Scholarships/grants, health care benefits, and unspecified assistantships available. Financial award application deadline: 4/15; financial award applicants required to submit FAFSA. *Unit head:* Dr. Mary Chinery, Dean, 732-987-2493, Fax: 732-987-2007, E-mail: mchinery@georgian.edu. *Application contact:* Dr. Mary Chinery, Dean, 732-987-2493, Fax: 732-987-2007, E-mail: mchinery@georgian.edu.
Website: https://georgian.edu/academics/school-of-arts-sciences/

John F. Kennedy University, College of Psychology, Program in Holistic Psychology, Pleasant Hill, CA 94523-4817. Offers depth and transpersonal psychotherapy (MA); expressive arts (MA); holistic studies (MA); somatic psychology (MA). *Program availability:* Part-time, evening/weekend. *Degree requirements:* For master's, thesis or alternative. *Entrance requirements:* For master's, interview. Additional exam requirements/recommendations for international students: required—TOEFL.

La Salle University, School of Arts and Sciences, Program in Clinical Psychology, Philadelphia, PA 19141-1199. Offers child clinical psychology (Psy D); clinical health psychology (Psy D); clinical psychology (MA); general practice psychology (Psy D). *Accreditation:* AAMFT/COAMFTE. *Program availability:* Part-time, evening/weekend. Terminal master's awarded for partial completion of doctoral program. *Degree requirements:* For doctorate, comprehensive exam, thesis/dissertation. *Entrance*

requirements: For doctorate, GRE (minimum scores of 148 on both the Verbal Reasoning and Quantitative Reasoning sections strongly recommended); GRE Subject Test in psychology (for those entering with bachelor's degree), baccalaureate degree from accredited institution with major in psychology or related discipline; minimum undergraduate GPA of 3.0, 3.2 graduate; three letters of recommendation; statement of interest and intent; curriculum vitae or resume; personal interview. Additional exam requirements/recommendations for international students: required—TOEFL. Electronic applications accepted. Application fee is waived when completed online. *Expenses:* Contact institution.

Lesley University, Graduate School of Arts and Social Sciences, Cambridge, MA 02138-2790. Offers clinical mental health counseling (MA), including holistic counseling, school and community counseling, trauma studies; counseling psychology (MA, CAGS), including professional counseling (MA), school counseling (MA); creative writing (MFA); expressive therapies (MA, PhD, CAGS), including art (MA), clinical mental health counseling (MA), dance (MA), expressive therapies (MA), music (MA); independent studies (CAGS); independent study (MA); intercultural relations (MA, CAGS); interdisciplinary studies (MA), including individualized studies, integrative holistic health, mindfulness studies, peace and conflict transformation, trauma sensitive assessment, intervention, and consultation, women's studies; urban environmental leadership (MA). *Program availability:* Part-time, online learning. *Degree requirements:* For master's, internship, practicum, thesis (for expressive therapies); for doctorate, thesis/dissertation, arts apprenticeship, field placement; for CAGS, thesis, internship (for counseling psychology, expressive therapies). *Entrance requirements:* For master's, MAT (counseling psychology), interview, writing samples, art portfolio; for doctorate, GRE or MAT, interview, master's degree; for CAGS, interview, master's degree. Additional exam requirements/recommendations for international students: required—TOEFL (minimum score 550 paper-based; 80 iBT). Electronic applications accepted.

North Dakota State University, College of Graduate and Interdisciplinary Studies, College of Science and Mathematics, Department of Psychology, Fargo, ND 58102. Offers clinical psychology (MS); health and social psychology (PhD); psychological clinical science (PhD); psychology (MS); visual and cognitive neuroscience (PhD). *Entrance requirements:* Additional exam requirements/recommendations for international students: required—TOEFL. Electronic applications accepted. Tuition and fees vary according to program and reciprocity agreements.

Northern Kentucky University, Office of Graduate Programs, College of Arts and Sciences, Program in Industrial-Organizational Psychology, Highland Heights, KY 41099. Offers industrial psychology (Certificate); industrial-organizational psychology (MS); occupational health psychology (Certificate); organizational psychology (Certificate). *Program availability:* Part-time, evening/weekend. *Degree requirements:* For master's, thesis optional, capstone. *Entrance requirements:* For master's, GRE General Test (minimum scores of 141 verbal, 144 quantitative, and 3.5 writing), bachelor's degree with minimum GPA of 3.0, nine semester hours of psychology coursework, at least one undergraduate course in statistics with minimum B grade, official transcripts, current resume or vita, statement of personal interest, three letters of recommendation; for Certificate, official transcripts, bachelor's degree, minimum undergraduate GPA of 3.0, no grade lower than B on all graduate coursework previously taken that may apply. Additional exam requirements/recommendations for international students: required—TOEFL (minimum score 79 iBT); recommended—IELTS (minimum score 6.5). Electronic applications accepted.

Oregon State University, College of Liberal Arts, Program in Psychology, Corvallis, OR 97331. Offers applied cognition (MS, PhD); engineering psychology (MS, PhD); health psychology (MS, PhD).

Penn State Harrisburg, Graduate School, School of Behavioral Sciences and Education, Middletown, PA 17057. Offers adult education in the health and medical professions (Certificate); applied behavior analysis (MA); applied clinical psychology (MA); applied psychological research (MA); community psychology and social change (MA); English as a second language (ESL) program specialist and leadership (Certificate); health education (M Ed); lifelong learning and adult education (M Ed, D Ed); literacy education (M Ed); literacy leadership (Certificate); psychology: applications in clinical psychology (Certificate); psychology: health psychology (Certificate); teaching and curriculum (M Ed); training and development (M Ed, Certificate). *Program availability:* Part-time, evening/weekend.

Prescott College, Graduate Programs, Program in Counseling and Psychology, Prescott, AZ 86301. Offers adventure-based psychotherapy (MA); counseling psychology (MA); ecopsychology (MA); ecotherapy (MA); equine-assisted mental health (MA); expressive arts therapy (MA); somatic psychology (MA); student-directed independent study (MA). *Program availability:* Part-time, online learning. Terminal master's awarded for partial completion of doctoral program. *Degree requirements:* For master's, thesis, fieldwork or internship, practicum. *Entrance requirements:* For master's, 2 letters of recommendation, resume. Additional exam requirements/recommendations for international students: required—TOEFL (minimum score 500 paper-based). Electronic applications accepted.

Rhode Island College, School of Graduate Studies, Faculty of Arts and Sciences, Department of Psychology, Providence, RI 02908-1991. Offers health psychology (CGS); psychology (MA). *Program availability:* Part-time, evening/weekend. *Faculty:* 5 full-time (all women). *Students:* 6 full-time (4 women), 2 part-time (1 woman); includes 1 minority (Hispanic/Latino). Average age 26. In 2019, 6 master's awarded. *Degree requirements:* For master's, comprehensive exam. *Entrance requirements:* For master's, GRE, 3 letters of recommendation. Additional exam requirements/recommendations for international students: required—TOEFL (minimum score 550 paper-based; 80 iBT). *Application deadline:* For fall admission, 3/1 for domestic students; for spring admission, 11/1 for domestic students. Applications are processed on a rolling basis. Application fee: $50. Electronic applications accepted. *Expenses: Tuition, area resident:* Part-time $462 per credit hour. *Tuition, state resident:* part-time $462 per credit hour. *Required fees:* $720. One-time fee: $140. *Financial support:* Teaching assistantships, Federal Work-Study, scholarships/grants, health care benefits, and unspecified assistantships available. Support available to part-time students. Financial award application deadline: 5/15; financial award applicants required to submit FAFSA. *Unit head:* Bethany Lewis, Chair, 401-456-8015. *Application contact:* Bethany Lewis, Chair, 401-456-8015.
Website: http://www.ric.edu/psychology/Pages/Graduate-Studies-in-Psychology.aspx

Rutgers University - New Brunswick, Graduate School-New Brunswick, Program in Psychology, Piscataway, NJ 08854-8097. Offers behavioral neuroscience (PhD); clinical psychology (PhD); cognitive psychology (PhD); interdisciplinary health psychology (PhD); social psychology (PhD). *Accreditation:* APA. *Degree requirements:* For doctorate, comprehensive exam, thesis/dissertation. *Entrance requirements:* For doctorate, GRE General Test, 3 letters of recommendation. Additional exam requirements/recommendations for international students: required—TOEFL (minimum score 577 paper-based). Electronic applications accepted.

San Diego State University, Graduate and Research Affairs, College of Health and Human Services, School of Public Health, San Diego, CA 92182. Offers environmental health (MPH); epidemiology (MPH, PhD), including biostatistics (MPH); global emergency preparedness and response (MS); global health (PhD); health behavior (PhD); health promotion (MPH); health services administration (MPH); toxicology (MS); MPH/MA; MSW/MPH. *Accreditation:* CAHME (one or more programs are accredited); CEPH. *Program availability:* Part-time. *Degree requirements:* For master's, comprehensive exam (for some programs), thesis (for some programs); for doctorate, thesis/dissertation. *Entrance requirements:* For master's, GMAT (MPH in health services administration), GRE General Test; for doctorate, GRE General Test. Additional exam requirements/recommendations for international students: required—TOEFL.

Saybrook University, School of Psychology and Interdisciplinary Inquiry, San Francisco, CA 94612. Offers human science (MA, PhD), including consciousness and spirituality, humanistic and transpersonal psychology, integrative health studies, organizational systems, social transformation; organizational systems (MA, PhD), including consciousness and spirituality, humanistic and transpersonal psychology, integrative health studies, leadership of sustainable systems (MA), organizational systems, social transformation; psychology (MA, PhD), including consciousness and spirituality, creativity studies (MA), humanistic and transpersonal psychology, integrative health studies, Jungian studies, marriage and family therapy (MA), organizational systems, social transformation. *Program availability:* Online learning. Terminal master's awarded for partial completion of doctoral program. *Degree requirements:* For master's, thesis or alternative; for doctorate, thesis/dissertation. *Entrance requirements:* Additional exam requirements/recommendations for international students: required—TOEFL (minimum score 580 paper-based; 93 iBT). Electronic applications accepted.

Southwestern College, Program in Integral Somatic Psychology, Santa Fe, NM 87502-4788. Offers Certificate.

Stony Brook University, State University of New York, Graduate School, College of Arts and Sciences, Department of Psychology, Program in Social and Health Psychology, Stony Brook, NY 11794. Offers PhD. *Students:* 15 full-time (14 women); includes 5 minority (2 Black or African American, non-Hispanic/Latino; 1 Asian, non-Hispanic/Latino; 2 Hispanic/Latino). Average age 27. 59 applicants, 14% accepted, 4 enrolled. In 2019, 6 doctorates awarded. *Entrance requirements:* For doctorate, GRE General Test, GRE Subject Test. Additional exam requirements/recommendations for international students: required—TOEFL (minimum score 90 iBT). *Application deadline:* For fall admission, 1/15 for domestic students; for spring admission, 10/1 for domestic students. Application fee: $100. Electronic applications accepted. *Expenses:* Contact institution. *Financial support:* In 2019–20, 1 research assistantship, 11 teaching assistantships were awarded; fellowships also available. *Unit head:* Dr. Sheri Levy, Chair, 631-632-4355, E-mail: sheri.levy@stonybrook.edu. *Application contact:* Marilynn Wollmuth, Coordinator, 631-632-7855, Fax: 631-632-7876, E-mail: marilyn.wollmuth@stonybrook.edu.
Website: http://www.stonybrook.edu/commcms/psychology/social_health/overview.html

United States International University–Africa, School of Arts and Sciences, Nairobi, Kenya. Offers counseling psychology (MA), including chemical dependency, health psychology; international relations (MA), including development studies, diplomacy and foreign policy, peace and conflict studies. *Program availability:* Part-time, evening/weekend. *Degree requirements:* For master's, thesis, practicum. *Entrance requirements:* For master's, GRE General Test, 2 letters of recommendation, resume. Additional exam requirements/recommendations for international students: required—TOEFL.

The University of Alabama at Birmingham, School of Public Health, Program in Health Care Organization and Policy, Birmingham, AL 35294. Offers applied epidemiology and pharmacoepidemiology (MSPH); biostatistics (MPH); clinical and translational science (MSPH); environmental health (MPH); environmental health and toxicology (MSPH); epidemiology (MPH); general theory and practice (MPH); health behavior (MPH); health care organization (MPH, Dr PH); health policy (MPH); industrial hygiene (MPH, MSPH); maternal and child health policy (Dr PH); maternal and child health policy and leadership (MPH); occupational health and safety (MPH); outcomes research (MSPH, Dr PH); public health (PhD); public health preparedness management (MPH). *Accreditation:* CEPH. *Program availability:* Part-time, 100% online, blended/hybrid learning. *Faculty:* 14 full-time (6 women). *Students:* 53 full-time (37 women), 61 part-time (45 women); includes 37 minority (12 Black or African American, non-Hispanic/Latino; 20 Asian, non-Hispanic/Latino; 1 Hispanic/Latino; 4 Two or more races, non-Hispanic/Latino), 17 international. Average age 31. 136 applicants, 59% accepted, 44 enrolled. In 2019, 36 master's, 4 doctorates awarded. *Degree requirements:* For master's, comprehensive exam (for some programs), thesis (for some programs); for doctorate, comprehensive exam, thesis/dissertation. *Entrance requirements:* For doctorate, GRE. Additional exam requirements/recommendations for international students: required—TOEFL (minimum score 80 iBT), IELTS (minimum score 6.5). *Application deadline:* For fall admission, 4/1 priority date for domestic students, 4/1 for international students; for spring admission, 11/1 for domestic students; for summer admission, 4/1 for domestic students. Application fee: $50 ($60 for international students). Electronic applications accepted. *Financial support:* Fellowships, research assistantships, teaching assistantships, scholarships/grants, traineeships, and unspecified assistantships available. Financial award application deadline: 3/1; financial award applicants required to submit FAFSA. *Unit head:* Dr. Martha Wingate, Program Director, 205-934-6783, Fax: 205-975-5484, E-mail: mslay@uab.edu. *Application contact:* Dustin Shaw, Coordinator, Student Admissions and Record, 205-934-3939, E-mail: bcampbel@uab.edu.
Website: http://www.soph.uab.edu

The University of British Columbia, Faculty of Arts, Department of Psychology, Vancouver, BC V6T 1Z4, Canada. Offers behavioral neuroscience (MA, PhD); clinical psychology (MA, PhD); cognitive science (MA, PhD); developmental psychology (MA, PhD); health psychology (MA, PhD); quantitative methods (MA, PhD); social/personality psychology (MA, PhD). *Accreditation:* APA (one or more programs are accredited). Terminal master's awarded for partial completion of doctoral program. *Degree requirements:* For master's, thesis; for doctorate, comprehensive exam, thesis/dissertation. *Entrance requirements:* For master's and doctorate, GRE General Test. Additional exam requirements/recommendations for international students: required—TOEFL. Electronic applications accepted. *Expenses:* Contact institution.

University of Colorado Denver, College of Liberal Arts and Sciences, Department of Psychology, Denver, CO 80217. Offers clinical health psychology (PhD). *Program availability:* Part-time, evening/weekend. *Degree requirements:* For doctorate, comprehensive exam, thesis/dissertation, 69 credits of coursework, minimum of 12 clinical practicum hours, 30 dissertation hours, three credits of pre-doctoral internship. *Entrance requirements:* For doctorate, GRE General Test; GRE Subject Test (recommended), minimum GPA of 3.5; undergraduate courses in introductory psychology, psychological statistics, research methods and abnormal psychology; letters of recommendation; personal statement; resume. Additional exam requirements/recommendations for international students: required—TOEFL (minimum score 537 paper-based; 75 iBT); recommended—IELTS (minimum score 6.5). Electronic applications accepted. Tuition and fees vary according to course load, program and reciprocity agreements.

University of Florida, Graduate School, College of Public Health and Health Professions, Department of Clinical and Health Psychology, Gainesville, FL 32611. Offers clinical and translational science (PhD); psychology (MS). *Accreditation:* APA (one or more programs are accredited). *Degree requirements:* For doctorate, comprehensive exam, thesis/dissertation, pre-doctoral internship. *Entrance requirements:* For master's and doctorate, GRE General Test, minimum GPA of 3.0. Additional exam requirements/recommendations for international students: required—TOEFL (minimum score 550 paper-based; 80 iBT), IELTS (minimum score 6). Electronic applications accepted.

University of Michigan–Dearborn, College of Arts, Sciences, and Letters, Master of Science in Psychology Program, Dearborn, MI 48128. Offers clinical health psychology (MS); health psychology (MS). *Program availability:* Part-time. *Faculty:* 17 full-time (9 women). *Students:* 19 full-time (16 women), 8 part-time (4 women); includes 6 minority (1 Black or African American, non-Hispanic/Latino; 3 Asian, non-Hispanic/Latino; 2 Hispanic/Latino). Average age 27. 54 applicants, 50% accepted, 10 enrolled. In 2019, 11 master's awarded. *Degree requirements:* For master's, thesis optional. *Entrance requirements:* For master's, GRE, 3 letters of recommendation. Additional exam requirements/recommendations for international students: required—TOEFL (minimum score 560 paper-based; 84 iBT), IELTS (minimum score 6.5). *Application deadline:* For fall admission, 3/15 for domestic and international students. Application fee: $60. Electronic applications accepted. *Financial support:* Career-related internships or fieldwork, scholarships/grants, and non-resident tuition scholarships available. Financial award application deadline: 3/1; financial award applicants required to submit FAFSA. *Unit head:* Dr. Michelle Leonard, Program Director, 313-593-5608, E-mail: mtleon@umich.edu. *Application contact:* Office of Graduate Studies, 313-583-6321, E-mail: umd-graduatestudies@umich.edu.
Website: http://umdearborn.edu/casl/psychology/

University of New Mexico, Graduate Studies, College of Arts and Sciences, Program in Psychology, Albuquerque, NM 87131-2039. Offers behavioral neuroscience (PhD); clinical psychology (PhD); cognitive neuroimaging (PhD); developmental psychology (PhD); evolution (PhD); health psychology (PhD); quantitative methodology (PhD). *Accreditation:* APA. *Degree requirements:* For doctorate, comprehensive exam, thesis/dissertation. *Entrance requirements:* For doctorate, GRE General Test, GRE Subject Test (psychology), minimum GPA of 3.0. Additional exam requirements/recommendations for international students: required—TOEFL (minimum score 550 paper-based; 79 iBT), IELTS (minimum score 6.5). Electronic applications accepted. *Expenses:* Tuition, state resident: full-time $7633; part-time $972 per year. Tuition, nonresident: full-time $22,586; part-time $3840 per year. *International tuition:* $23,292 full-time. *Required fees:* $8608. Tuition and fees vary according to course level, course load, degree level, program and student level.

The University of North Carolina at Chapel Hill, Graduate School, Gillings School of Global Public Health, Department of Health Behavior, Chapel Hill, NC 27599. Offers MPH, PhD, MPH/MCRP, MSPH/PhD. *Accreditation:* CEPH (one or more programs are accredited). *Faculty:* 25 full-time (19 women), 55 part-time/adjunct (39 women). *Students:* 87 full-time (79 women), 4 part-time (2 women); includes 26 minority (8 Black or African American, non-Hispanic/Latino; 5 Asian, non-Hispanic/Latino; 7 Hispanic/Latino; 6 Two or more races, non-Hispanic/Latino), 5 international. Average age 29. 73 applicants, 34% accepted, 9 enrolled. In 2019, 45 master's, 12 doctorates awarded. *Degree requirements:* For master's, comprehensive exam, thesis or alternative, major paper, capstone, practicum; for doctorate, comprehensive exam, thesis/dissertation, practicum. *Entrance requirements:* For master's, GRE General Test or MCAT, three letters of recommendation (academic and/or professional); for doctorate, GRE General Test, master's degree, three letters of recommendation (academic and/or professional). Additional exam requirements/recommendations for international students: required—TOEFL (minimum score 90 iBT), IELTS (minimum score 7). *Application deadline:* For fall admission, 12/1 for domestic and international students. Application fee: $90. Electronic applications accepted. *Financial support:* Fellowships with tuition reimbursements, research assistantships with tuition reimbursements, teaching assistantships with tuition reimbursements, career-related internships or fieldwork, Federal Work-Study, institutionally sponsored loans, scholarships/grants, traineeships, health care benefits, and unspecified assistantships available. Financial award application deadline: 12/10; financial award applicants required to submit FAFSA. *Unit head:* Dr. Kurt M. Ribisl, Chair, 919-843-8042, E-mail: kurt_ribisl@unc.edu. *Application contact:* Cindy Reilly, Academic Coordinator, 919-843-2385, Fax: 919-966-2921, E-mail: cindy_reilly@email.unc.edu.
Website: https://sph.unc.edu/hb/health-behavior-home/

The University of North Carolina at Charlotte, College of Liberal Arts and Sciences, Department of Psychology, Charlotte, NC 28223-0001. Offers cognitive science (Graduate Certificate); health psychology (PhD), including general; community; clinical; interdisciplinary; industrial/organizational psychology (MA); psychology (MA). *Accreditation:* APA. *Program availability:* Part-time. *Faculty:* 29 full-time (19 women), 2 part-time/adjunct (both women). *Students:* 42 full-time (35 women), 32 part-time (24 women); includes 18 minority (6 Black or African American, non-Hispanic/Latino; 4 Asian, non-Hispanic/Latino; 3 Hispanic/Latino; 5 Two or more races, non-Hispanic/Latino), 2 international. Average age 27. 164 applicants, 15% accepted, 14 enrolled. In 2019, 31 master's, 5 doctorates, 3 other advanced degrees awarded. *Degree requirements:* For master's, thesis (for some programs); for doctorate, comprehensive exam, thesis/dissertation. *Entrance requirements:* For master's, GRE, GMAT, MAT, bachelor's degree; statement of purpose addressing motivation for degree, preparation for graduate studies and impact of the degree; 2 letters of recommendation; (MA, Psychology) minimum 3.0 GPA in psychology courses; 18 credit hours of undergraduate psychology courses, undergraduate course in statistics; for doctorate, GRE and/or GMAT (Org. Science), at least 18 hours of coursework in psychology including introductory psychology and research methods, undergraduate course in statistics, transcripts of all academic work attempted since high school including evidence of the completion of a bachelor's degree, at least three references, personal statement, resume or curriculum vitae; for Graduate Certificate, enrolled and in good standing in a graduate degree program at UNC Charlotte, or have minimum GPA of 3.0 for undergraduate courses. Additional exam requirements/recommendations for international students: required—TOEFL (minimum score 557 paper-based; 83 iBT), IELTS (minimum score 6.5), TOEFL (minimum score 557 paper-based, 83 iBT) or IELTS (6.5). *Application deadline:* Applications are processed on a rolling basis. Application fee: $75. Electronic applications accepted. *Expenses:* Contact institution. *Financial support:* In 2019–20, 15 students received support, including 9 research assistantships (averaging $10,659 per year), 6 teaching assistantships (averaging $9,454 per year); fellowships, career-related internships or fieldwork, Federal Work-Study, institutionally sponsored loans, scholarships/grants, and unspecified assistantships also available. Support available to part-time students. Financial award applicants required to submit FAFSA. *Unit head:* Dr. Eric Heggestad, Chair & Associate Professor, 704-687-1338, E-mail: edhegges@uncc.edu. *Application contact:* Kathy B. Giddings, Director of Graduate Admissions, 704-687-5503, Fax: 704-687-1668, E-mail: gradadm@uncc.edu.
Website: http://psych.uncc.edu

University of Pittsburgh, Kenneth P. Dietrich School of Arts and Sciences, Department of Psychology, Pittsburgh, PA 15260. Offers biological and health psychology (PhD); clinical psychology (PhD); cognitive psychology (PhD); developmental psychology (PhD); social psychology (PhD). *Accreditation:* APA. *Faculty:* 33 full-time (18 women), 10 part-time/adjunct (3 women). *Students:* 90 full-time (73 women); includes 25 minority (4 Black or African American, non-Hispanic/Latino; 2 American Indian or Alaska Native, non-Hispanic/Latino; 10 Asian, non-Hispanic/Latino; 2 Hispanic/Latino; 7 Two or more races, non-Hispanic/Latino). Average age 25. 580 applicants, 6% accepted, 18 enrolled. In 2019, 16 doctorates awarded. Terminal master's awarded for partial completion of doctoral program. *Degree requirements:* For doctorate, comprehensive exam, thesis/dissertation. *Entrance requirements:* For doctorate, GRE General Test, minimum GPA of 3.0. Additional exam requirements/recommendations for international students: required—TOEFL (minimum score 550 paper-based; 90 iBT). *Application deadline:* For fall admission, 12/1 for domestic and international students. Application fee: $75. Electronic applications accepted. *Financial support:* In 2019–20, 90 students received support, including 38 fellowships with full tuition reimbursements available (averaging $30,378 per year), 19 research assistantships with full tuition reimbursements available (averaging $29,220 per year), 33 teaching assistantships with full tuition reimbursements available (averaging $29,220 per year); career-related internships or fieldwork, scholarships/grants, health care benefits, and unspecified assistantships also available. Financial award application deadline: 12/1. *Unit head:* Dr. Julie Fiez, Chair, 412-624-7078, Fax: 412-422-9149, E-mail: fiez@pitt.edu. *Application contact:* Francesca Sirianni, Graduate Administrator, 412-624-4502, Fax: 412-624-4428, E-mail: psygrad@pitt.edu.
Website: http://www.psychology.pitt.edu/

The University of Texas at Arlington, Graduate School, College of Science, Department of Psychology, Arlington, TX 76019. Offers experimental health psychology (PhD); experimental psychology (MS, PhD); health/neuroscience psychology (MS, PhD); industrial and organizational psychology (MS). *Program availability:* Part-time. Terminal master's awarded for partial completion of doctoral program. *Degree requirements:* For master's, comprehensive exam or thesis; for doctorate, thesis/dissertation (for some programs). *Entrance requirements:* For master's and doctorate, GRE General Test, minimum GPA of 3.0 in last 60 hours of course work. Additional exam requirements/recommendations for international students: required—TOEFL (minimum score 550 paper-based).

University of the Sciences, Program in Health Psychology, Philadelphia, PA 19104-4495. Offers MS. *Entrance requirements:* For master's, bachelor's degree in related field, minimum GPA of 3.0 in major. Additional exam requirements/recommendations for international students: required—TOEFL, TWE. *Expenses:* Contact institution.

Virginia Commonwealth University, Graduate School, College of Humanities and Sciences, Department of Psychology, Richmond, VA 23284-9005. Offers clinical psychology (PhD), including behavioral medicine, clinical child psychology; counseling psychology (PhD); health psychology (PhD). *Accreditation:* APA. *Degree requirements:* For doctorate, thesis/dissertation. *Entrance requirements:* For doctorate, GRE General Test. Additional exam requirements/recommendations for international students: required—TOEFL (minimum score 600 paper-based; 100 iBT); recommended—IELTS (minimum score 6.5). Electronic applications accepted.

Virginia State University, College of Graduate Studies, College of Natural and Health Sciences, Department of Psychology, Petersburg, VA 23806-0001. Offers behavioral

and community health sciences (PhD); clinical health psychology (PhD); clinical psychology (MS); general psychology (MS). *Degree requirements:* For master's, one foreign language, thesis. *Entrance requirements:* For master's, GRE General Test.

Viterbo University, Master of Science in Mental Health Counseling Program, La Crosse, WI 54601-4797. Offers addiction counseling (MS); child and adolescent counseling (MS); complementary health and wellness counseling (MS). *Accreditation:* ACA. *Program availability:* Part-time, evening/weekend. *Degree requirements:* For master's, comprehensive exam, thesis, 54 credits of core program courses; 6 elective credits; minimum GPA of 3.0; action research project; practicum/internship experience. *Entrance requirements:* For master's, MAT, BS in a human service or social science discipline; prerequisite coursework in general psychology, behavior disorders/abnormal psychology, and research methods/statistics; minimum undergraduate cumulative GPA of 3.0; background check; personal statement; undergraduate transcripts; interview. Additional exam requirements/recommendations for international students: required—TOEFL (minimum score 525 paper-based). Electronic applications accepted. Application fee is waived when completed online. *Expenses:* Contact institution.

Walden University, Graduate Programs, School of Psychology, Minneapolis, MN 55401. Offers clinical psychology (MS), including counseling, general program; forensic psychology (MS), including forensic psychology in the community, general program, mental health applications, program planning and evaluation in forensic settings, psychology and legal systems; industrial organizational (MS, PhD), including consulting psychology, forensic (MS), forensic psychology (PhD), general practice, leadership development and coaching (MS), organizational diversity and social change, research evaluation (PhD); online teaching in psychology (Post-Master's Certificate); organizational psychology and development (Postbaccalaureate Certificate); psychology (MS, PhD), including applied psychology (MS), clinical psychology (PhD), crisis management and response (MS), educational psychology, forensic psychology (PhD), general psychology (MS), general psychology research (PhD), general psychology teaching (PhD), health psychology, leadership development and coaching (MS), psychology of culture (MS), psychology, public administration, and social change (MS), social psychology, terrorism and security (MS); psychology respecialization (Post-Doctoral Certificate). *Program availability:* Part-time, evening/weekend, online only, 100% online. Terminal master's awarded for partial completion of doctoral program. *Degree requirements:* For master's, thesis optional; for doctorate, thesis/dissertation, residency. *Entrance requirements:* For master's, bachelor's degree or higher; minimum GPA of 2.5; official transcripts; goal statement (for some programs); access to computer and Internet; for doctorate, master's degree or higher; three years of related professional or academic experience (preferred); minimum GPA of 3.0; goal statement and current resume (for select programs); official transcripts; access to computer and Internet; for other advanced degree, relevant work experience; access to computer and Internet. Additional exam requirements/recommendations for international students: required—TOEFL (minimum score 550 paper-based, 79 iBT), IELTS (minimum score 6.5), Michigan English Language Assessment Battery (minimum score 82), or PTE (minimum score 53). Electronic applications accepted.

Yeshiva University, Ferkauf Graduate School of Psychology, Program in Clinical Health Psychology, New York, NY 10033-3201. Offers PhD. *Accreditation:* APA. *Program availability:* Part-time. *Degree requirements:* For doctorate, comprehensive exam, thesis/dissertation. *Entrance requirements:* For doctorate, GRE General Test.

Human Development

Alabama Agricultural and Mechanical University, School of Graduate Studies, College of Agricultural, Life and Natural Sciences, Department of Family and Consumer Sciences, Huntsville, AL 35811. Offers apparel, merchandising and design (MS); family and consumer sciences (MS); human development and family studies (MS); nutrition and hospitality management (MS). *Program availability:* Part-time, evening/weekend. *Degree requirements:* For master's, comprehensive exam, thesis optional. *Entrance requirements:* For master's, GRE General Test. Additional exam requirements/recommendations for international students: required—TOEFL (minimum score 500 paper-based; 61 iBT). Electronic applications accepted.

Argosy University, Chicago, Illinois School of Professional Psychology, Doctoral Program in Clinical Psychology, Chicago, IL 60601. Offers child and adolescent psychology (Psy D); client-centered and experiential psychotherapies (Psy D); diversity and multicultural psychology (Psy D); family psychology (Psy D); forensic psychology (Psy D); health psychology (Psy D); neuropsychology (Psy D); organizational consulting (Psy D); psychoanalytic psychology (Psy D); psychology and spirituality (Psy D). *Accreditation:* APA.

Arizona State University at Tempe, College of Liberal Arts and Sciences, School of Social and Family Dynamics, Tempe, AZ 85287-3701. Offers family and human development (MS, PhD); infant-family practice (MAS); marriage and family therapy (MAS); sociology (MA, PhD). Terminal master's awarded for partial completion of doctoral program. *Degree requirements:* For master's, thesis or alternative, interactive Program of Study (iPOS) submitted before completing 50 percent of required credit hours; for doctorate, thesis/dissertation, interactive Program of Study (iPOS) submitted before completing 50 percent of required credit hours. *Entrance requirements:* For master's and doctorate, GRE, minimum GPA of 3.0 or equivalent in last 2 years of work leading to bachelor's degree. Additional exam requirements/recommendations for international students: required—TOEFL, IELTS, or PTE. Electronic applications accepted. *Expenses:* Contact institution.

Auburn University, Graduate School, College of Human Sciences, Department of Human Development and Family Studies, Auburn, AL 36849. Offers MS, PhD. *Accreditation:* AAMFT/COAMFTE (one or more programs are accredited). *Program availability:* Part-time. *Faculty:* 26 full-time (17 women), 1 (woman) part-time/adjunct. *Students:* 26 full-time (15 women), 16 part-time (15 women); includes 9 minority (4 Black or African American, non-Hispanic/Latino; 2 Asian, non-Hispanic/Latino; 2 Hispanic/Latino; 1 Native Hawaiian or other Pacific Islander, non-Hispanic/Latino), 2 international. Average age 28. 50 applicants, 22% accepted, 11 enrolled. In 2019, 8 master's awarded. *Degree requirements:* For master's, thesis, oral exam; for doctorate, thesis/dissertation. *Entrance requirements:* For master's, GRE General Test; for doctorate, GRE General Test, master's degree. Additional exam requirements/recommendations for international students: required—iTEP; recommended—TOEFL (minimum score 550 paper-based; 79 iBT), IELTS (minimum score 6.5). *Application deadline:* Applications are processed on a rolling basis. Application fee: $60 ($70 for international students). Electronic applications accepted. *Expenses: Tuition, area resident:* Full-time $9828;

part-time $546 per credit hour. Tuition, state resident: full-time $9828; part-time $546 per credit hour. Tuition, nonresident: full-time $29,484; part-time $1638 per credit hour. *International tuition:* $29,744 full-time. Tuition and fees vary according to course load, program and reciprocity agreements. *Financial support:* In 2019–20, 46 fellowships with tuition reimbursements, 39 research assistantships with tuition reimbursements (averaging $18,077 per year), 9 teaching assistantships with tuition reimbursements (averaging $14,893 per year) were awarded; Federal Work-Study also available. Support available to part-time students. Financial award application deadline: 3/15; financial award applicants required to submit FAFSA. *Unit head:* Dr. Angela Wiley, Head, 334-844-3242, E-mail: arw0044@auburn.edu. *Application contact:* Dr. George Flowers, Dean of the Graduate School, 334-844-2125.
Website: http://www.humsci.auburn.edu/hdfs/

Ball State University, Graduate School, Teachers College, Department of Educational Psychology, Muncie, IN 47306. Offers educational psychology (MA, MS), including educational psychology (MA, MS, PhD); educational psychology (PhD), including educational psychology (MA, MS, PhD); gifted and talented education (Certificate); human development and learning (Certificate); instructional design and assessment (Certificate); neuropsychology (Certificate); quantitative psychology (MS); response to intervention (Certificate); school psychology (MA, PhD), including school psychology (MA, PhD, Ed S); school psychology (Ed S), including school psychology (MA, PhD, Ed S). *Program availability:* 100% online. *Degree requirements:* For doctorate, thesis/dissertation; for other advanced degree, thesis. *Entrance requirements:* For master's, GRE General Test, minimum baccalaureate GPA of 2.75 or 3.0 in latter half of baccalaureate, professional goals and self-assessment; for doctorate, GRE General Test, minimum graduate GPA of 3.2; for other advanced degree, GRE General Test. Additional exam requirements/recommendations for international students: required—TOEFL (minimum score 550 paper-based; 79 iBT), IELTS (minimum score 6.5). Electronic applications accepted. *Expenses: Tuition, area resident:* Full-time $7506; part-time $417 per credit hour. Tuition, nonresident: full-time $20,610; part-time $1145 per credit hour. *Required fees:* $2126. Tuition and fees vary according to course load, campus/location and program.

Bradley University, The Graduate School, College of Education and Health Sciences, Education, Counseling and Leadership Department, Peoria, IL 61625-0002. Offers counseling (MA), including clinical mental health counseling, professional school counseling; leadership in educational administration (MA); nonprofit leadership (MA). *Accreditation:* ACA; NCATE. *Program availability:* Part-time, evening/weekend, blended/hybrid learning. *Faculty:* 24 full-time (15 women), 10 part-time/adjunct (6 women). *Students:* 48 full-time (43 women), 246 part-time (197 women); includes 62 minority (35 Black or African American, non-Hispanic/Latino; 3 American Indian or Alaska Native, non-Hispanic/Latino; 4 Asian, non-Hispanic/Latino; 17 Hispanic/Latino; 3 Two or more races, non-Hispanic/Latino), 3 international. Average age 33. 125 applicants, 74% accepted, 68 enrolled. In 2019, 67 master's awarded. *Degree requirements:* For master's, comprehensive exam, thesis optional. *Entrance requirements:* For master's, GRE General Test or MAT, interview, 3 letters of recommendation. Additional exam

requirements/recommendations for international students: required—TOEFL (minimum score 550 paper-based; 79 iBT), IELTS (minimum score 6.5), PTE (minimum score 58). *Application deadline:* For fall admission, 5/15 priority date for domestic and international students; for spring admission, 10/15 priority date for domestic and international students. Applications are processed on a rolling basis. Application fee: $40 ($50 for international students). Electronic applications accepted. *Expenses: Tuition:* Part-time $930 per credit hour. *Financial support:* In 2019–20, 40 students received support, including 13 research assistantships with full tuition reimbursements available (averaging $11,040 per year); fellowships, career-related internships or fieldwork, scholarships/grants, tuition waivers (full), and unspecified assistantships also available. Support available to part-time students. Financial award application deadline: 4/1. *Unit head:* Dean Cantu, Associate Dean and Director, Professor, 309-677-3190, E-mail: dcantu@bradley.edu. *Application contact:* Rachel Webb, Director of On-Campus Graduate Admissions and International Student and Scholar Services, 309-677-2375, E-mail: rkwebb@bradley.edu.
Website: https://www.bradley.edu/academic/departments/ecl/

Brigham Young University, Graduate Studies, College of Family, Home, and Social Sciences, Program in Marriage, Family and Human Development, Provo, UT 84602. Offers MS, PhD. *Accreditation:* AAMFT/COAMFTE. *Faculty:* 24 full-time (5 women). *Students:* 20 full-time (17 women); includes 1 minority (Asian, non-Hispanic/Latino), 1 international. Average age 28. 25 applicants, 56% accepted, 8 enrolled. In 2019, 9 master's awarded. *Degree requirements:* For master's, thesis; for doctorate, comprehensive exam, thesis/dissertation. *Entrance requirements:* For master's and doctorate, GRE General Test, minimum GPA of 3.0 in last 60 semester hours, letters of recommendation. Additional exam requirements/recommendations for international students: required—TOEFL (minimum score 580 paper-based; 85 iBT), IELTS (minimum score 7). *Application deadline:* For fall admission, 1/10 for domestic and international students. Application fee: $50. Electronic applications accepted. *Expenses:* LDS: 2-year masters degree: $14,580 tuition/fees, per credit $430, per course $1,290; 3-year doctorate degree: $21,870 tuition/fees, per credit $430, per course $1,290. NonLDS: 2-year masters degree: $29,160 tuition/fees, per credit $860, per course $2,580; 3-year doctorate degree: $43,740 tuition/fees, per credit $860, per course $2,580. *Financial support:* In 2019–20, 20 students received support, including 20 research assistantships with full and partial tuition reimbursements available (averaging $8,944 per year), 8 teaching assistantships with tuition reimbursements available (averaging $2,800 per year); scholarships/grants and unspecified assistantships also available. Financial award application deadline: 3/20. *Unit head:* Dr. Alan J. Hawkins, Director, School of Life, 801-422-7088, Fax: 801-422-0230, E-mail: alan_hawkins@byu.edu. *Application contact:* Graduate Secretary, 801-422-2060, E-mail: mfhdgrad@byu.edu.
Website: http://mfhd.byu.edu

Brock University, Faculty of Graduate Studies, Faculty of Social Sciences, Program in Psychology, St. Catharines, ON L2S 3A1, Canada. Offers behavioral neuroscience (MA, PhD); life span development (MA, PhD); social personality (MA, PhD). *Program availability:* Part-time. *Degree requirements:* For master's, thesis; for doctorate, thesis/dissertation. *Entrance requirements:* For master's, GRE, honors degree; for doctorate, GRE, master's degree. Additional exam requirements/recommendations for international students: required—TOEFL (minimum score 550 paper-based; 80 iBT), IELTS (minimum score 6.5), TWE (minimum score 4). Electronic applications accepted.

California State University, Fresno, Division of Research and Graduate Studies, Kremen School of Education and Human Development, Fresno, CA 93740-8027. Offers MA, MS, Ed D. *Accreditation:* NCATE. *Program availability:* Part-time, evening/weekend. *Degree requirements:* For master's, thesis or alternative; for doctorate, thesis/dissertation. *Entrance requirements:* For master's, GRE General Test, MAT; for doctorate, GRE or MAT, minimum GPA of 3.2, master's degree. Additional exam requirements/recommendations for international students: required—TOEFL. Electronic applications accepted. *Expenses:* Tuition, state resident: full-time $4012; part-time $2506 per semester.

Central Michigan University, College of Graduate Studies, College of Education and Human Services, Department of Human Environmental Studies, Mount Pleasant, MI 48859. Offers apparel product development and merchandising technology (MS); gerontology (Graduate Certificate); human development and family studies (MA); nutrition and dietetics (MS). *Program availability:* Part-time, evening/weekend. *Degree requirements:* For master's, thesis or alternative. Electronic applications accepted. *Expenses: Tuition, area resident:* Full-time $12,267; part-time $8178 per year. Tuition, state resident: full-time $12,267; part-time $8178 per year. Tuition, nonresident: full-time $12,267; part-time $8178 per year. *International tuition:* $16,110 full-time. *Required fees:* $225 per semester. Tuition and fees vary according to degree level and program.

Claremont Graduate University, Graduate Programs, School of Educational Studies, Claremont, CA 91711-6160. Offers Africana education (Certificate); education and policy (MA, PhD); higher education/student affairs (MA, PhD); human development (MA, PhD); public school administration (MA, PhD); quantitative evaluation (MA, PhD); special education (MA, PhD); teacher education (MA); teaching and learning (MA, PhD); urban leadership (PhD); MBA/PhD. *Program availability:* Part-time. Terminal master's awarded for partial completion of doctoral program. *Entrance requirements:* For master's and doctorate, GRE General Test. Additional exam requirements/recommendations for international students: required—TOEFL (minimum score 75 iBT). Electronic applications accepted.

Colorado State University, College of Health and Human Sciences, Department of Human Development and Family Studies, Fort Collins, CO 80523-1570. Offers applied developmental science (PhD); family and developmental studies (MS); marriage and family therapy (MS). *Accreditation:* AAMFT/COAMFTE. *Faculty:* 22 full-time (20 women), 2 part-time/adjunct (0 women). *Students:* 32 full-time (28 women), 4 part-time (all women); includes 9 minority (4 Asian, non-Hispanic/Latino; 4 Hispanic/Latino; 1 Two or more races, non-Hispanic/Latino), 2 international. Average age 27. 74 applicants, 42% accepted, 12 enrolled. In 2019, 9 master's, 2 doctorates awarded. Terminal master's awarded for partial completion of doctoral program. *Degree requirements:* For master's, thesis; for doctorate, comprehensive exam, thesis/dissertation. *Entrance requirements:* For master's, GRE General Test, 3 letters of recommendation; minimum GPA of 3.0; bachelor's degree; curriculum vitae/resume. Additional exam requirements/recommendations for international students: required—TOEFL (minimum score 550 paper-based; 80 iBT), IELTS (minimum score 6.5), PTE (minimum score 58). *Application deadline:* For fall admission, 1/2 priority date for domestic and international students. Electronic applications accepted. *Expenses:* Tuition, state resident: full-time $10,520; part-time $5844 per credit hour. Tuition, nonresident: full-time $25,791; part-time $14,328 per credit hour. *International tuition:* $25,791 full-time. *Required fees:* $2512.80. Part-time tuition and fees vary according to course level, course load, degree level, program and student level. *Financial support:* In 2019–20, 31 students received support, including 1 fellowship with full and partial tuition reimbursement available (averaging $7,605 per year), 15 research assistantships with full and partial tuition reimbursements available (averaging $13,182 per year), 15 teaching assistantships with full and partial tuition reimbursements available (averaging $9,633 per year); Federal Work-Study and unspecified assistantships also available. Financial award application

deadline: 3/1; financial award applicants required to submit FAFSA. *Unit head:* Dr. Julia Braungart-Rieker, Department Head, 970-491-3581, Fax: 970-491-7975, E-mail: JulieBraungart.Rieker@colostate.edu. *Application contact:* Mary Daughtrey, Administrative Assistant III, 970-491-2872, Fax: 970-491-7975, E-mail: mary.daughtrey@colostate.edu.
Website: https://www.chhs.colostate.edu/hdfs

Cornell University, Graduate School, Graduate Fields of Human Ecology, Field of Human Development, Ithaca, NY 14853. Offers developmental psychology (MA, PhD), including cognitive development, developmental psychopathology, ecology of human development, social and personality development; human development and family studies (MA, PhD), including ecology of human development, family studies and the life course. *Degree requirements:* For doctorate, comprehensive exam, thesis/dissertation, pre-doctoral research project, teaching experience. *Entrance requirements:* For doctorate, GRE General Test, 2 letters of recommendation. Additional exam requirements/recommendations for international students: required—TOEFL (minimum score 550 paper-based; 77 iBT). Electronic applications accepted.

Duke University, Graduate School, Department of Psychology and Neuroscience, Durham, NC 27708. Offers biological psychology (PhD); clinical psychology (PhD); cognitive psychology (PhD); developmental psychology (PhD); experimental psychology (PhD); health psychology (PhD); human social development (PhD); JD/MA. *Accreditation:* APA (one or more programs are accredited). *Degree requirements:* For doctorate, thesis/dissertation. *Entrance requirements:* For doctorate, GRE General Test. Additional exam requirements/recommendations for international students: required—TOEFL (minimum score 577 paper-based; 90 iBT) or IELTS (minimum score 7). Electronic applications accepted.

Eastern Illinois University, Graduate School, College of Health and Human Services, Department of Human Services and Community Leadership, Charleston, IL 61920. Offers MHS. *Program availability:* Part-time, evening/weekend, online learning. *Degree requirements:* For master's, comprehensive exam (for some programs), thesis (for some programs). *Entrance requirements:* For master's, GMAT or GRE. Additional exam requirements/recommendations for international students: required—TOEFL (minimum score 500 paper-based; 61 iBT), IELTS (minimum score 6). Electronic applications accepted.

Erikson Institute, Academic Programs, Chicago, IL 60654. Offers administration (Certificate); bilingual/ESL (Certificate); child development (MS); early childhood education (MS); infant mental health (Certificate); infant studies (Certificate); social work (MSW); MS/MSW. *Program availability:* Part-time, evening/weekend. *Degree requirements:* For master's, comprehensive exam, internship; for Certificate, internship. *Entrance requirements:* For master's and Certificate, minimum GPA of 2.75. Additional exam requirements/recommendations for international students: required—TOEFL.

Fielding Graduate University, Graduate Programs, School of Leadership, Human and Organizational Development, Santa Barbara, CA 93105-3814. Offers human development (PhD); organizational consulting (Graduate Certificate); organizational development and change (PhD); organizational development and leadership (MA, Graduate Certificate). *Program availability:* Part-time, evening/weekend, 100% online, blended/hybrid learning. *Faculty:* 15 full-time (8 women), 16 part-time/adjunct (7 women). *Students:* 137 full-time (95 women), 45 part-time (31 women); includes 77 minority (35 Black or African American, non-Hispanic/Latino; 1 American Indian or Alaska Native, non-Hispanic/Latino; 12 Asian, non-Hispanic/Latino; 17 Hispanic/Latino; 1 Native Hawaiian or other Pacific Islander, non-Hispanic/Latino; 11 Two or more races, non-Hispanic/Latino). Average age 51. 36 applicants, 94% accepted, 19 enrolled. In 2019, 28 doctorates awarded. Terminal master's awarded for partial completion of doctoral program. *Degree requirements:* For master's, thesis or alternative, Master's Project; for doctorate, comprehensive exam, thesis/dissertation. *Entrance requirements:* For master's and Graduate Certificate, bachelor's or master's degree, resume, statement of purpose, official transcript; for doctorate, bachelor's or master's degree, resume, statement of purpose, reflexive essay, official transcript. *Application deadline:* For fall admission, 7/16 for domestic and international students; for spring admission, 11/21 for domestic and international students; for summer admission, 3/25 for domestic and international students. Application fee: $75. Electronic applications accepted. *Expenses:* Contact institution. *Financial support:* In 2019–20, 31 students received support. Research assistantships, teaching assistantships, scholarships/grants, and tuition waivers available. Support available to part-time students. Financial award applicants required to submit FAFSA. *Unit head:* Dr. Barbara Mink, Program Director, E-mail: bmink@fielding.edu. *Application contact:* Enrollment Coordinator, 800-340-1099 Ext. 4098, Fax: 805-687-9793, E-mail: admissions@fielding.edu.
Website: http://www.fielding.edu/our-programs/school-of-leadership-studies/

Florida State University, The Graduate School, College of Human Sciences, Department of Family and Child Sciences, Tallahassee, FL 32306. Offers family and child sciences (MS); human development and family sciences (PhD); marriage and family therapy (PhD). *Accreditation:* AAMFT/COAMFTE. *Program availability:* Part-time. *Faculty:* 17 full-time (11 women). *Students:* 28 full-time (22 women), 4 part-time (2 women); includes 12 minority (7 Black or African American, non-Hispanic/Latino; 1 Asian, non-Hispanic/Latino; 1 Hispanic/Latino; 3 Two or more races, non-Hispanic/Latino), 2 international. 39 applicants, 46% accepted, 5 enrolled. In 2019, 9 doctorates awarded. Terminal master's awarded for partial completion of doctoral program. *Degree requirements:* For master's, thesis optional, special project for non-thesis students; for doctorate, thesis/dissertation, preliminary examination; clinical examination (for marriage and family therapy). *Entrance requirements:* For master's, GRE General Test, minimum upper division GPA of 3.0; for doctorate, GRE General Test, writing assessment, minimum upper division GPA of 3.0 or master's degree. Additional exam requirements/recommendations for international students: required—TOEFL (minimum score 550 paper-based; 80 iBT). *Application deadline:* For fall admission, 12/1 for domestic and international students. Applications are processed on a rolling basis. Application fee: $30. Electronic applications accepted. *Financial support:* In 2019–20, 34 students received support, including 5 research assistantships with full tuition reimbursements available (averaging $21,020 per year), 29 teaching assistantships with full tuition reimbursements available (averaging $21,020 per year); fellowships with partial tuition reimbursements available, career-related internships or fieldwork, Federal Work-Study, institutionally sponsored loans, scholarships/grants, health care benefits, and unspecified assistantships also available. Financial award application deadline: 1/5; financial award applicants required to submit FAFSA. *Unit head:* Dr. Chester Ray, Interim Department Chair, 850-644-3217, E-mail: caray@fsu.edu. *Application contact:* Mary-Sue McLemore, Academic Support Assistant, 850-644-1117, E-mail: mmclemore@fsu.edu.
Website: https://humansciences.fsu.edu/family-child-sciences/students/graduate-programs/

Georgetown University, Graduate School of Arts and Sciences, Department of Psychology, Washington, DC 20005. Offers human development and public policy (PhD); lifespan cognitive neuroscience (PhD); PhD/MPP. *Faculty:* 14 full-time (9 women). *Students:* 16 full-time (9 women); includes 3 minority (1 Asian, non-Hispanic/Latino; 2 Hispanic/Latino). Average age 25. 101 applicants, 5 enrolled. In 2019, 4 doctorates awarded. *Degree requirements:* For doctorate, thesis/dissertation, area

paper. *Entrance requirements:* For doctorate, GRE General Test, GRE Subject Test. Additional exam requirements/recommendations for international students: required—TOEFL. *Application deadline:* For fall admission, 12/1 for domestic and international students. Application fee: $51 ($50 for international students). Electronic applications accepted. *Financial support:* In 2019–20, 16 students received support, including 16 teaching assistantships with full tuition reimbursements available (averaging $28,000 per year); research assistantships also available. Financial award application deadline: 2/1; financial award applicants required to submit FAFSA. *Unit head:* Dr. Jennifer Woolard, Interim Chair, 202-687-9258, Fax: 202-687-6050, E-mail: jlw47@georgetown.edu. *Application contact:* Graduate School Admissions Office, 202-687-5568, E-mail: gradmail@georgetown.edu.
Website: https://psychology.georgetown.edu

Georgetown University, Graduate School of Arts and Sciences, Walsh School of Foreign Service, Program in Global Human Development, Washington, DC 20057. Offers MA.

The George Washington University, Graduate School of Education and Human Development, Department of Educational Leadership, Individualized Master's Program, Washington, DC 20052. Offers MA Ed. *Entrance requirements:* For master's, GRE General Test or MAT, minimum GPA of 2.75.

Georgia State University, College of Education and Human Development, Atlanta, GA 30302-3083. Offers M Ed, MAT, MS, Ed D, PhD, Ed S. *Accreditation:* NCATE. *Program availability:* Part-time, evening/weekend, online learning. *Faculty:* 111 full-time (70 women), 47 part-time/adjunct (38 women). *Students:* 830 full-time (614 women), 582 part-time (164 women); includes 778 minority (560 Black or African American, non-Hispanic/Latino; 1 American Indian or Alaska Native, non-Hispanic/Latino; 65 Asian, non-Hispanic/Latino; 94 Hispanic/Latino; 58 Two or more races, non-Hispanic/Latino), 38 international. Average age 32. 1,059 applicants, 48% accepted, 354 enrolled. In 2019, 433 master's, 63 doctorates, 13 other advanced degrees awarded. Terminal master's awarded for partial completion of doctoral program. *Degree requirements:* For master's, comprehensive exam (for some programs), thesis (for some programs), minimum GPA of 3.0; for doctorate, comprehensive exam, thesis/dissertation, minimum GPA of 3.5; for Ed S, thesis or alternative, minimum GPA of 3.0. *Entrance requirements:* For master's, GRE, MAT (for some programs), minimum GPA of 2.5 on all undergraduate work attempted in which letter grades were awarded; for doctorate, GRE, MAT (for some programs), minimum GPA of 3.3 on all graduate coursework for which letter grades were awarded (for PhD); for Ed S, GRE, MAT (for some programs), graduate degree from regionally-accredited college or university unless specified otherwise by the program with minimum GPA of 3.25 on all graduate coursework for which letter grades were awarded. Application fee: $50. Electronic applications accepted. *Expenses: Tuition, area resident:* Full-time $7164; part-time $398 per credit hour. Tuition, state resident: full-time $7164; part-time $398 per credit hour. Tuition, nonresident: full-time $22,662; part-time $1259 per credit hour. *International tuition:* $22,662 full-time. *Required fees:* $2128; $312 per credit hour. Tuition and fees vary according to course load and program. *Financial support:* In 2019–20, fellowships with full tuition reimbursements (averaging $25,000 per year), research assistantships with tuition reimbursements (averaging $4,867 per year), teaching assistantships with tuition reimbursements (averaging $4,683 per year) were awarded; career-related internships or fieldwork, Federal Work-Study, scholarships/grants, tuition waivers (partial), and unspecified assistantships also available. Support available to part-time students. Financial award applicants required to submit FAFSA. *Unit head:* Dr. Paul A. Alberto, Dean, 404-413-8100, Fax: 404-413-8103, E-mail: palberto@gsu.edu. *Application contact:* Nancy Keita, Assistant Dean for Student Services, 404-413-8001, E-mail: nkeita@gsu.edu.
Website: https://education.gsu.edu/

Harvard University, Harvard Graduate School of Education, Master's Programs in Education, Cambridge, MA 02138. Offers arts in education (Ed M); education policy and management (Ed M); higher education (Ed M); human development and psychology (Ed M); international education policy (Ed M); language and literacy (Ed M); learning and teaching (Ed M); mind, brain, and education (Ed M); prevention science and practice (Ed M); school leadership (Ed M); special studies (Ed M); teacher education (Ed M); technology, innovation, and education (Ed M). *Program availability:* Part-time. *Entrance requirements:* For master's, GRE General Test, statement of purpose, 3 letters of recommendation, resume, official transcripts. Additional exam requirements/recommendations for international students: required—TOEFL (minimum score 613 paper-based; 104 iBT), TWE (minimum score 5). Electronic applications accepted.

Iowa State University of Science and Technology, Department of Human Development and Family Studies, Ames, IA 50011. Offers human development and family studies (MFCS, MS, PhD). *Degree requirements:* For master's, thesis; for doctorate, thesis/dissertation. *Entrance requirements:* For master's and doctorate, GRE General Test. Additional exam requirements/recommendations for international students: required—TOEFL (minimum score 550 paper-based; 79 iBT), IELTS (minimum score 6.5). Electronic applications accepted.

Kansas State University, Graduate School, College of Human Ecology, Doctorate in Human Ecology Program, Manhattan, KS 66506-1407. Offers apparel and textiles (PhD); applied family sciences (PhD); couple and family therapy (PhD); hospitality administration (PhD); kinesiology (PhD); life-span human development (PhD). *Program availability:* Part-time. *Degree requirements:* For doctorate, thesis/dissertation. *Entrance requirements:* Additional exam requirements/recommendations for international students: required—TOEFL. Electronic applications accepted.

Kansas State University, Graduate School, College of Human Ecology, School of Family Studies and Human Services, Manhattan, KS 66506-1403. Offers applied family sciences (MS); communication sciences and disorders (MS); conflict resolution (Graduate Certificate); couple and family therapy (MS); early childhood education (MS); family and community service (MS); life-span human development (MS); personal financial planning (MS, PhD, Graduate Certificate); youth development (MS, Graduate Certificate). *Accreditation:* AAMFT/COAMFTE; ASHA. *Program availability:* Part-time, online learning. *Degree requirements:* For master's, comprehensive exam (for some programs), thesis optional. *Entrance requirements:* For master's, GRE, minimum GPA of 3.0 in last 2 years (60 semester hours) of undergraduate study; for doctorate, GRE. Additional exam requirements/recommendations for international students: required—TOEFL (minimum score 600 paper-based). Electronic applications accepted.

Kent State University, College of Education, Health and Human Services, School of Lifespan Development and Educational Sciences, Counselor Education and Supervision, Kent, OH 44242-0001. Offers PhD. *Accreditation:* ACA; NCATE. *Degree requirements:* For doctorate, comprehensive exam, thesis/dissertation. *Entrance requirements:* For doctorate, GRE General Test, preliminary written exam, 2 letters of reference, resume, interview. Additional exam requirements/recommendations for international students: required—TOEFL (minimum score 550 paper-based; 80 iBT). Electronic applications accepted.

Kent State University, College of Education, Health and Human Services, School of Lifespan Development and Educational Sciences, Program in Human Development and Family Studies, Kent, OH 44242-0001. Offers MA. *Degree requirements:* For master's,

thesis optional. *Entrance requirements:* For master's, minimum undergraduate GPA of 3.0, 3 letters of reference, goals statement. Additional exam requirements/recommendations for international students: required—TOEFL (minimum score 550 paper-based; 80 iBT).

Laurentian University, School of Graduate Studies and Research, Programme in Human Development, Sudbury, ON P3E 2C6, Canada. Offers M Sc, MA. *Program availability:* Part-time. *Degree requirements:* For master's, thesis or alternative. *Entrance requirements:* For master's, honors degree with second class or better.

Lindsey Wilson College, School of Professional Counseling, Columbia, KY 42728. Offers counseling and human development (M Ed); counselor education and supervision (PhD). *Accreditation:* ACA (one or more programs are accredited). *Program availability:* Part-time, evening/weekend, online learning.

Marywood University, Academic Affairs, Center for Interdisciplinary Studies, Scranton, PA 18509-1598. Offers human development (PhD), including educational administration, health promotion, higher education administration, instructional leadership, social work. *Program availability:* Part-time. Electronic applications accepted. *Expenses:* Contact institution.

Michigan State University, The Graduate School, College of Social Science, Department of Human Development and Family Studies, East Lansing, MI 48824. Offers child development (MS); family and community services (MA); human development and family studies (MS, PhD); youth development (MA). *Accreditation:* AAMFT/COAMFTE (one or more programs are accredited). *Entrance requirements:* For master's, GRE General Test, minimum GPA of 3.0 in last 2 years of undergraduate course work, 3 letters of recommendation; for doctorate, GRE General Test, minimum GPA of 3.0, 3 letters of recommendation, background in behavioral sciences. Additional exam requirements/recommendations for international students: required—TOEFL. Electronic applications accepted.

Mississippi State University, College of Agriculture and Life Sciences, School of Human Sciences, Mississippi State, MS 39762. Offers agriculture and extension education (MS), including communication, leadership; agriculture science (PhD), including agriculture and extension education; fashion design and merchandising (MS), including design and product development, merchandising; human development and family studies (MS, PhD). *Accreditation:* NCATE (one or more programs are accredited). *Program availability:* Part-time. *Faculty:* 21 full-time (11 women). *Students:* 26 full-time (21 women), 62 part-time (46 women); includes 16 minority (12 Black or African American, non-Hispanic/Latino; 1 American Indian or Alaska Native, non-Hispanic/Latino; 1 Hispanic/Latino; 2 Two or more races, non-Hispanic/Latino), 4 international. Average age 34. 26 applicants, 69% accepted, 16 enrolled. In 2019, 12 master's, 4 doctorates awarded. *Degree requirements:* For master's, thesis optional, comprehensive oral or written exam. *Entrance requirements:* For master's, GRE, minimum GPA of 2.75 in last 4 semesters of course work; for doctorate, minimum GPA of 3.0 on prior graduate work. Additional exam requirements/recommendations for international students: required—TOEFL (minimum score 477 paper-based; 53 iBT); recommended—IELTS (minimum score 4.5). *Application deadline:* For fall admission, 7/1 for domestic students, 5/1 for international students; for spring admission, 11/1 for domestic students, 9/1 for international students. Applications are processed on a rolling basis. Application fee: $60 ($80 for international students). Electronic applications accepted. *Expenses: Tuition, area resident:* Full-time $8880; part-time $456 per credit hour. Tuition, state resident: full-time $8880. Tuition, nonresident: full-time $23,840; part-time $1236 per credit hour. *Required fees:* $110; $11.12 per credit hour. Tuition and fees vary according to course load. *Financial support:* In 2019–20, 15 research assistantships (averaging $12,541 per year) were awarded; Federal Work-Study, institutionally sponsored loans, and unspecified assistantships also available. Financial award application deadline: 4/1; financial award applicants required to submit FAFSA. *Unit head:* Dr. Michael Newman, Professor and Director, 662-325-2950, E-mail: mnewman@humansci.msstate.edu. *Application contact:* Ryan King, Admissions and Enrollment Assistant, 662-325-8951, E-mail: rjk101@grad.msstate.edu.
Website: http://www.humansci.msstate.edu

Montana State University, The Graduate School, College of Education, Health, and Human Development, Department of Health and Human Development, Bozeman, MT 59717. Offers family and consumer sciences (MS). *Accreditation:* ACA. *Program availability:* Part-time, online learning. *Degree requirements:* For master's, comprehensive exam. *Entrance requirements:* For master's, GRE (minimum scores: verbal 480; quantitative 480). Additional exam requirements/recommendations for international students: required—TOEFL (minimum score 550 paper-based). Electronic applications accepted.

Murray State University, College of Education and Human Services, Department of Community Leadership and Human Services, Murray, KY 42071. Offers nonprofit leadership studies (MS, Certificate). *Program availability:* Part-time, evening/weekend, 100% online, blended/hybrid learning. *Entrance requirements:* For master's, GRE or GMAT, minimum university GPA of 2.75. Additional exam requirements/recommendations for international students: required—TOEFL (minimum score 527 paper-based; 71 iBT). Electronic applications accepted.

Murray State University, College of Education and Human Services, Department of Educational Studies, Leadership and Counseling, Murray, KY 42071. Offers college advising (Certificate); education administration (MA Ed); human development and leadership (MS, Certificate); library media (MA Ed); middle school teacher leader (MA Ed); P-20 and community leadership (Ed D); postsecondary education administration (MA Ed); school counseling (MA Ed); school guidance and counseling (Ed S); secondary teacher leader (MA Ed). *Program availability:* Part-time, evening/weekend, 100% online, blended/hybrid learning. *Entrance requirements:* For master's and other advanced degree, GRE or GMAT, minimum university GPA of 2.75. Additional exam requirements/recommendations for international students: required—TOEFL (minimum score 527 paper-based; 71 iBT). Electronic applications accepted.

National Louis University, National College of Education, Chicago, IL 60603. Offers administration and supervision (M Ed, Ed D, CAS, Ed S); curriculum and instruction (M Ed, MS Ed, CAS); early childhood administration (M Ed, CAS); early childhood education (M Ed, MAT, MS Ed, CAS); education (Ed D); educational psychology/human learning and development (M Ed, MS Ed, CAS, Ed S); elementary education (MAT); interdisciplinary curriculum and instruction (M Ed); mathematics education (M Ed, MS Ed, CAS); middle grades education (MAT); reading and language (M Ed, MS Ed, CAS); school psychology (M Ed, Ed S); science education (M Ed, MS Ed, CAS); secondary education (MAT); special education (M Ed, MAT, CAS); technology in education (M Ed, CAS). *Accreditation:* NCATE. *Program availability:* Part-time, evening/weekend. *Degree requirements:* For doctorate, comprehensive exam, thesis/dissertation. *Entrance requirements:* For master's, MAT or GRE, minimum GPA of 3.0; for doctorate, GRE General Test, minimum GPA of 3.25, interview, resume, writing sample, 4 recommendations. Additional exam requirements/recommendations for international students: required—TOEFL (minimum score 550 paper-based; 79 iBT).

New York University, Steinhardt School of Culture, Education, and Human Development, New York, NY 10003. Offers MA, MFA, MM, MPH, MS, DPS, DPT, Ed D, PhD, Advanced Certificate, Post Master's Certificate, Postbaccalaureate Certificate,

Advanced Certificate/MPH, MA/Advanced Certificate, MA/MA, MA/MS, MLIS/MA. *Accreditation:* TEAC. *Program availability:* Part-time. *Entrance requirements:* For doctorate, GRE General Test, interview. Additional exam requirements/recommendations for international students: required—TOEFL (minimum score 100 iBT). Electronic applications accepted. *Expenses:* Contact institution.

New York University, Steinhardt School of Culture, Education, and Human Development, Department of Applied Psychology, Programs in Educational and Developmental Psychology, New York, NY 10012. Offers developmental psychology (PhD); human development and social intervention (MA); psychology and social intervention (PhD). *Accreditation:* APA (one or more programs are accredited). *Program availability:* Part-time. *Entrance requirements:* For doctorate, GRE General Test, interview. Additional exam requirements/recommendations for international students: required—TOEFL. Electronic applications accepted.

Northern Arizona University, College of Social and Behavioral Sciences, Institute for Human Development, Flagstaff, AZ 86011. Offers assistive technology (Graduate Certificate). *Program availability:* Part-time. *Degree requirements:* For Graduate Certificate, comprehensive exam (for some programs). *Entrance requirements:* For degree, undergraduate degree from regionally-accredited institution with minimum GPA of 3.0, or the equivalent. Additional exam requirements/recommendations for international students: required—TOEFL (minimum score 80 iBT), IELTS (minimum score 6.5). Electronic applications accepted.

Northwestern University, The Graduate School, School of Education and Social Policy, Program in Human Development and Social Policy, Evanston, IL 60208. Offers PhD. *Degree requirements:* For doctorate, comprehensive exam, thesis/dissertation. *Entrance requirements:* For doctorate, GRE General Test. Additional exam requirements/recommendations for international students: required—TOEFL (minimum score 600 paper-based; 100 iBT). Electronic applications accepted.

The Ohio State University, Graduate School, College of Education and Human Ecology, Department of Human Sciences, Columbus, OH 43210. Offers consumer sciences (MS, PhD); human development and family science (PhD); human nutrition (MS, PhD); kinesiology (MA, Ed D, PhD). *Program availability:* Part-time. *Degree requirements:* For master's, thesis optional; for doctorate, thesis/dissertation. *Entrance requirements:* For master's and doctorate, GRE. Additional exam requirements/recommendations for international students: required—TOEFL (minimum score 550 paper-based; 79 iBT), Michigan English Language Assessment Battery (minimum score 82); recommended—IELTS (minimum score 7). Electronic applications accepted.

Oregon State University, College of Public Health and Human Sciences, Program in Human Development and Family Studies, Corvallis, OR 97331. Offers MS, PhD. *Entrance requirements:* For master's, GRE; for doctorate, GRE, master's degree (including thesis). Additional exam requirements/recommendations for international students: required—TOEFL (minimum score 80 iBT), IELTS (minimum score 6.5).

Pacific Oaks College, Graduate School, Program in Human Development, Pasadena, CA 91103. Offers MA. *Program availability:* Part-time, evening/weekend, online learning. *Degree requirements:* For master's, thesis. *Entrance requirements:* Additional exam requirements/recommendations for international students: required—TOEFL (minimum score 550 paper-based).

Penn State University Park, Graduate School, College of Health and Human Development, Department of Human Development and Family Studies, University Park, PA 16802. Offers MS, PhD.

Purdue University, Graduate School, College of Health and Human Sciences, Department of Child Development and Family Studies, West Lafayette, IN 47907. Offers developmental studies (MS, PhD); family studies (MS, PhD); marriage and family therapy (MS, PhD). *Program availability:* Part-time. *Faculty:* 22 full-time (16 women), 2 part-time/adjunct (1 woman). *Students:* 22 full-time (21 women), 1 (woman) part-time; includes 3 minority (1 Black or African American, non-Hispanic/Latino; 1 Asian, non-Hispanic/Latino; 1 Two or more races, non-Hispanic/Latino), 8 international. Average age 26. 51 applicants, 25% accepted, 4 enrolled. In 2019, 2 master's, 3 doctorates awarded. Terminal master's awarded for partial completion of doctoral program. *Degree requirements:* For master's, thesis; for doctorate, thesis/dissertation. *Entrance requirements:* For master's and doctorate, GRE General Test (minimum score 1000 combined verbal and quantitative), minimum undergraduate GPA of 3.0 or equivalent. Additional exam requirements/recommendations for international students: required—TOEFL (minimum score 600 paper-based; 90 iBT), TWE (minimum score 4). *Application deadline:* For fall admission, 1/4 for domestic and international students. Applications are processed on a rolling basis. Application fee: $60 ($75 for international students). Electronic applications accepted. *Financial support:* Fellowships with full tuition reimbursements, research assistantships with full tuition reimbursements, teaching assistantships with full tuition reimbursements, and career-related internships or fieldwork available. Support available to part-time students. Financial award application deadline: 1/15; financial award applicants required to submit FAFSA. *Unit head:* Dr. Doran C. French, Head, 765-494-9511, E-mail: dcfrench@purdue.edu. *Application contact:* Tina Putz, Graduate Contact, 765-496-3816, E-mail: tputz@purdue.edu.
Website: http://www.purdue.edu/hhs/hdfs/

Saint Mary's University of Minnesota, Schools of Graduate and Professional Programs, Graduate School of Business and Technology, Integrated Studies Program, Winona, MN 55987-1399. Offers MA. *Unit head:* John Ebert, Director, 507-457-6961, E-mail: jebert@smumn.edu. *Application contact:* Laurie Roy, Director of Admission of Schools of Graduate and Professional Programs, 507-457-8606, Fax: 612-728-5121, E-mail: lroy@smumn.edu.
Website: https://www.smumn.edu/academics/graduate/business-technology/m.a.-in-integrated-studies

Syracuse University, David B. Falk College of Sport and Human Dynamics, Programs in Human Development and Family Science, Syracuse, NY 13244. Offers MA, MS, PhD. *Accreditation:* AAMFT/COAMFTE (one or more programs are accredited). *Program availability:* Part-time. *Degree requirements:* For master's, comprehensive exam (for some programs), thesis; for doctorate, comprehensive exam, thesis/dissertation. *Entrance requirements:* For master's and doctorate, GRE General Test, personal statement, official transcripts, three letters of recommendation, resume. Additional exam requirements/recommendations for international students: required—TOEFL (minimum score 100 iBT). Electronic applications accepted.

Texas A&M University–Corpus Christi, College of Graduate Studies, College of Education and Human Development, Corpus Christi, TX 78412. Offers counseling (MS), including counseling; counselor education (PhD); curriculum and instruction (MS, PhD); early childhood education (MS); educational administration (MS); educational leadership (Ed D); elementary education (MS); instructional design and educational technology (MS); kinesiology (MS); reading (MS); secondary education (MS); special education (MS). *Program availability:* Part-time, evening/weekend, blended/hybrid learning. *Degree requirements:* For master's, comprehensive exam, capstone; for doctorate, thesis/dissertation. *Entrance requirements:* For master's, GRE General Test, essay (300 words); for doctorate, GRE, essay, resume, 3-4 reference forms. Electronic applications accepted.

Texas Tech University, Graduate School, College of Human Sciences, Department of Human Development and Family Studies, Lubbock, TX 79409-1230. Offers human development and family studies (MS, PhD), including gerontology (MS). *Accreditation:* AAMFT/COAMFTE (one or more programs are accredited). *Program availability:* 100% online. *Faculty:* 26 full-time (22 women), 2 part-time/adjunct (both women). *Students:* 23 full-time (17 women), 22 part-time (17 women); includes 12 minority (2 Black or African American, non-Hispanic/Latino; 3 Asian, non-Hispanic/Latino; 6 Hispanic/Latino; 1 Two or more races, non-Hispanic/Latino), 3 international. Average age 29. 29 applicants, 59% accepted, 13 enrolled. In 2019, 4 master's, 4 doctorates awarded. *Degree requirements:* For master's, thesis; for doctorate, comprehensive exam, thesis/dissertation. *Entrance requirements:* For master's and doctorate, GRE General Test. Additional exam requirements/recommendations for international students: required—TOEFL (minimum score 550 paper-based; 79 iBT). *Application deadline:* For fall admission, 6/1 priority date for domestic students, 1/15 priority date for international students; for spring admission, 9/1 priority date for domestic students, 6/15 priority date for international students. Applications are processed on a rolling basis. Application fee: $65. Electronic applications accepted. *Expenses:* Contact institution. *Financial support:* In 2019–20, 29 students received support, including 28 fellowships (averaging $6,779 per year), 16 research assistantships (averaging $18,338 per year), 8 teaching assistantships (averaging $14,356 per year); scholarships/grants and unspecified assistantships also available. Financial award application deadline: 12/1; financial award applicants required to submit FAFSA. *Unit head:* Dr. Ann M. Mastergeorge, Chairperson, Rockwell Endowed Child and Family Professor, 806-834-7162, Fax: 806-742-3042, E-mail: ann.mastergeorge@ttu.edu. *Application contact:* Dr. Elizabeth Trejos-Castillo, Graduate Program Director, 806-834-6080, Fax: 806-742-0285, E-mail: elizabeth.trejos@ttu.edu.
Website: www.hdfs.ttu.edu

Tufts University, Graduate School of Arts and Sciences, Eliot-Pearson Department of Child Study and Human Development, Medford, MA 02155. Offers child study and human development (MA, PhD). *Program availability:* Part-time. *Degree requirements:* For master's, thesis (for some programs); for doctorate, comprehensive exam, thesis/dissertation. *Entrance requirements:* For master's and doctorate, GRE General Test. Additional exam requirements/recommendations for international students: required—TOEFL (minimum score 550 paper-based; 80 iBT), IELTS (minimum score 6.5). Electronic applications accepted. *Expenses:* Contact institution.

The University of Alabama, Graduate School, College of Human Environmental Sciences, Department of Human Development and Family Studies, Tuscaloosa, AL 35487. Offers human development and family studies (MSHES); marriage and family therapy (MSHES); parent and family life education (MSHES). *Program availability:* Part-time. *Faculty:* 10 full-time (7 women). *Students:* 17 full-time (12 women), 2 part-time (both women); includes 7 minority (3 Black or African American, non-Hispanic/Latino; 3 Hispanic/Latino; 1 Two or more races, non-Hispanic/Latino). Average age 28. 13 applicants, 69% accepted, 7 enrolled. In 2019, 12 master's awarded. Terminal master's awarded for partial completion of doctoral program. *Degree requirements:* For master's, comprehensive exam (for some programs), thesis optional. *Entrance requirements:* For master's, GRE General Test or MAT, minimum GPA of 3.0. Additional exam requirements/recommendations for international students: required—TOEFL (minimum score 79 iBT), IELTS (minimum score 6.5). *Application deadline:* For fall admission, 12/15 priority date for domestic and international students. Applications are processed on a rolling basis. Application fee: $50 ($60 for international students). Electronic applications accepted. *Expenses: Tuition, area resident:* Full-time $10,780; part-time $440 per credit hour. Tuition, nonresident: full-time $30,250; part-time $1550 per credit hour. *Financial support:* In 2019–20, 15 students received support. Fellowships, research assistantships with full tuition reimbursements available, teaching assistantships, career-related internships or fieldwork, Federal Work-Study, scholarships/grants, health care benefits, and unspecified assistantships available. Financial award application deadline: 3/15. *Unit head:* Dr. Robert Laird, 205-348-9277, E-mail: rdlaird@ches.ua.edu. *Application contact:* Patrick Fuller, Admissions Officer, 205-348-5932, Fax: 205-348-0400, E-mail: patrick.d.fuller@ua.edu.
Website: http://www.hdfs.ches.ua.edu/

The University of Arizona, College of Education, Department of Disability and Psychoeducational Studies, Tucson, AZ 85721. Offers counseling and mental health (MA), including rehabilitation counseling, school counseling; family studies and human development (M Ed); rehabilitation counseling (PhD); school counseling (MA); school psychology (PhD, Ed S); special education (MA, PhD), including cross-categorical special education (MA), deaf and hard of hearing (MA), learning disabilities (MA), severe and multiple disabilities (MA), special education (PhD), visual impairment (MA). *Accreditation:* CORE. *Program availability:* Part-time. Terminal master's awarded for partial completion of doctoral program. *Degree requirements:* For master's, comprehensive exam, thesis optional; for doctorate, comprehensive exam, thesis/dissertation. *Entrance requirements:* For master's, statement of purpose; for doctorate, GRE General Test (minimum score 1100) or MAT, 3 letters of recommendation. Additional exam requirements/recommendations for international students: required—TOEFL (minimum score 550 paper-based; 79 iBT).

The University of British Columbia, Faculty of Education, Department of Educational and Counseling Psychology, and Special Education, Vancouver, BC V6T 1Z4, Canada. Offers counseling psychology (M Ed, MA, PhD); guidance studies (Diploma); human development, learning and culture (M Ed, MA, PhD); measurement, evaluation, and research methodology (M Ed, MA, PhD); school psychology (M Ed, MA, PhD); special education (M Ed, MA, PhD, Diploma). *Program availability:* Part-time. *Degree requirements:* For master's, thesis (for some programs); for doctorate, comprehensive exam, thesis/dissertation. *Entrance requirements:* For master's, GRE General Test (for MA in counseling psychology); for doctorate, GRE General Test. Additional exam requirements/recommendations for international students: required—TOEFL. Electronic applications accepted. *Expenses:* Contact institution.

University of California, Berkeley, Graduate Division, School of Education, Programs in Education, Berkeley, CA 94720. Offers development in mathematics and science (MA); education in mathematics, science, and technology (MA, PhD); human development and education (MA, PhD); leadership education (MA); special education (PhD); teacher education (MA); MA/Credential; PhD/Credential; PhD/MA. Terminal master's awarded for partial completion of doctoral program. *Degree requirements:* For master's, exam or thesis; for doctorate, thesis/dissertation, oral qualifying exam. *Entrance requirements:* For master's and doctorate, GRE General Test, minimum GPA of 3.0 during last 2 years of undergraduate course work. Electronic applications accepted.

University of California, Davis, Graduate Studies, Graduate Group in Human Development, Davis, CA 95616. Offers PhD. *Degree requirements:* For doctorate, thesis/dissertation. *Entrance requirements:* For doctorate, GRE General Test, GRE Subject Test, minimum GPA of 3.0. Additional exam requirements/recommendations for international students: required—TOEFL (minimum score 550 paper-based). Electronic applications accepted.

University of Central Oklahoma, The Jackson College of Graduate Studies, College of Education and Professional Studies, Department of Human Environmental Sciences,

Edmond, OK 73034-5209. Offers family and child studies (MS), including family life education, infant/child specialist, marriage and family therapy; nutrition-food science (MS). *Program availability:* Part-time. *Degree requirements:* For master's, comprehensive exam (for some programs), thesis (for some programs). *Entrance requirements:* For master's, GRE, essay, physical, CPR and First Aid training. Additional exam requirements/recommendations for international students: required—TOEFL (minimum score 550 paper-based; 79 iBT), IELTS (minimum score 6.5). Electronic applications accepted.

University of Chicago, Division of the Social Sciences, Department of Comparative Human Development, Chicago, IL 60637. Offers PhD. *Degree requirements:* For doctorate, one foreign language, thesis/dissertation, trial research project. *Entrance requirements:* For doctorate, GRE General Test, 3 letters of recommendation, statement of purpose, transcripts, resume or curriculum vitae, writing sample (dependent on department). Additional exam requirements/recommendations for international students: required—TOEFL (minimum score 104 iBT), IELTS (minimum score 7). Electronic applications accepted.

University of Colorado Denver, School of Education and Human Development, Program in Education and Human Development, Denver, CO 80217. Offers administrative leadership and policy (PhD); assessment (MA); early childhood special education/early childhood education (PhD); family science and human development (PhD); human development and family relations (MA); learning (MA); mathematics education (PhD); research and evaluation methods (MA); research, assessment and evaluation (PhD); science education (PhD); urban ecologies (PhD). *Program availability:* Part-time, evening/weekend. *Degree requirements:* For master's, comprehensive exam, 9 hours of core courses embedded within a minimum of 36 to 38 hours of relevant coursework, including an educational psychology practicum, independent study project or thesis (recommended). *Entrance requirements:* For master's, GRE if undergraduate GPA below 2.75, resume, three letters of recommendation, transcripts. Additional exam requirements/recommendations for international students: required—TOEFL (minimum score 537 paper-based; 75 iBT); recommended—IELTS (minimum score 6.5). Electronic applications accepted. *Expenses:* Contact institution.

University of Connecticut, Graduate School, College of Liberal Arts and Sciences, Department of Human Development and Family Studies, Storrs, CT 06269. Offers MA, PhD. *Accreditation:* AAMFT/COAMFTE (one or more programs are accredited). Terminal master's awarded for partial completion of doctoral program. *Degree requirements:* For master's, comprehensive exam; for doctorate, thesis/dissertation. *Entrance requirements:* For doctorate, GRE General Test. Additional exam requirements/recommendations for international students: required—TOEFL (minimum score 550 paper-based). Electronic applications accepted.

University of Dayton, Department of Counselor Education and Human Services, Dayton, OH 45469. Offers clinical mental health counseling (MS Ed); college student personnel (MS Ed); higher education administration (MS Ed); human services (MS Ed); school counseling (MS Ed); school psychology (MS Ed, Ed S). *Accreditation:* ACA; NCATE. *Program availability:* Part-time. *Degree requirements:* For master's, thesis (for some programs); for Ed S, thesis (for some programs), professional portfolio. *Entrance requirements:* For master's, MAT or GRE (if GPA less than 2.75), essays (for some programs). Additional exam requirements/recommendations for international students: required—TOEFL (minimum score 550 paper-based; 80 iBT). Electronic applications accepted. *Expenses:* Contact institution.

University of Delaware, College of Education and Human Development, Department of Human Development and Family Studies, Newark, DE 19716. Offers MS, PhD. *Program availability:* Part-time. Terminal master's awarded for partial completion of doctoral program. *Degree requirements:* For master's, thesis or alternative; for doctorate, comprehensive exam, thesis/dissertation. *Entrance requirements:* For master's and doctorate, GRE General Test, 3 letters of recommendation. Additional exam requirements/recommendations for international students: required—TOEFL. Electronic applications accepted.

University of Guelph, Office of Graduate and Postdoctoral Studies, College of Social and Applied Human Sciences, Department of Family Relations and Applied Nutrition, Guelph, ON N1G 2W1, Canada. Offers applied nutrition (MAN); family relations and human development (M Sc, PhD), including applied human nutrition, couple and family therapy (M Sc), family relations and human development. *Accreditation:* AAMFT/COAMFTE (one or more programs are accredited). *Program availability:* Part-time. *Degree requirements:* For master's, thesis (for some programs); for doctorate, comprehensive exam, thesis/dissertation. *Entrance requirements:* For master's, minimum B+ average; for doctorate, master's degree in family relations and human development or related field with a minimum B+ average or master's degree in applied human nutrition. Additional exam requirements/recommendations for international students: required—TOEFL (minimum score 600 paper-based). Electronic applications accepted.

University of Illinois at Chicago, College of Applied Health Sciences, Department of Disability and Human Development, Chicago, IL 60607-7128. Offers MS, PhD. *Accreditation:* AOTA. *Program availability:* Part-time. *Degree requirements:* For master's, thesis optional; for doctorate, thesis/dissertation. *Entrance requirements:* For master's and doctorate, GRE General Test. Additional exam requirements/recommendations for international students: required—TOEFL. Electronic applications accepted.

University of Illinois at Springfield, Graduate Programs, College of Education and Human Services, Program in Human Development Counseling, Springfield, IL 62703-5407. Offers MA. *Accreditation:* ACA. *Program availability:* Part-time. *Faculty:* 5 full-time (4 women), 1 (woman) part-time/adjunct. *Students:* 57 full-time (54 women), 28 part-time (22 women); includes 20 minority (14 Black or African American, non-Hispanic/Latino; 3 Hispanic/Latino; 3 Two or more races, non-Hispanic/Latino), 4 international. Average age 31. 62 applicants, 52% accepted, 22 enrolled. In 2019, 32 master's awarded. *Degree requirements:* For master's, comprehensive exam, Students who do not pass both the multiple choice and clinical case presentation portion of the exam must register each term until the exam is passed. Students who do not pass the clinical case presentation portion must also enroll again and provide added counseling services. *Entrance requirements:* For master's, minimum undergraduate GPA of 3.0 in last 60 hours of coursework or cumulative; essay; personal references; group interview. Additional exam requirements/recommendations for international students: required—TOEFL (minimum score 500 paper-based; 61 iBT). *Application deadline:* Applications are processed on a rolling basis. Application fee: $60 ($75 for international students). Electronic applications accepted. *Expenses: Tuition, area resident:* Full-time $7896; part-time $329 per credit hour. Tuition, nonresident: full-time $16,200; part-time $675 per credit hour. *Required fees:* $2735.60; $130.65 per credit hour. *Financial support:* In 2019–20, research assistantships with full tuition reimbursements (averaging $10,562 per year), teaching assistantships with full tuition reimbursements (averaging $10,652 per year) were awarded; fellowships, career-related internships or fieldwork, Federal Work-Study, scholarships/grants, health care benefits, and unspecified assistantships also available. Support available to part-time students. Financial award application deadline: 11/15; financial award applicants required to submit FAFSA. *Unit head:* Dr. Ann McCaughan, Program Administrator, 217-206-6504, Fax: 217-206-6775, E-mail: amcca7@uis.edu. *Application contact:* Dr. Ann McCaughan, Program Administrator, 217-206-6504, Fax: 217-206-6775, E-mail: amcca7@uis.edu.
Website: http://www.uis.edu/hdc

University of Illinois at Urbana-Champaign, Graduate College, College of Agricultural, Consumer and Environmental Sciences, Department of Human and Community Development, Champaign, IL 61820. Offers MS, PhD.

University of Maine, Graduate School, College of Education and Human Development, School of Educational Leadership, Higher Education, and Human Development, Orono, ME 04469. Offers educational leadership (M Ed, CAS); higher education (CAS); human development (MS). *Program availability:* Part-time. *Faculty:* 11 full-time (7 women), 10 part-time/adjunct (5 women). *Students:* 81 full-time (59 women), 102 part-time (72 women); includes 13 minority (2 Black or African American, non-Hispanic/Latino; 3 American Indian or Alaska Native, non-Hispanic/Latino; 5 Asian, non-Hispanic/Latino; 3 Hispanic/Latino), 1 international. Average age 37. 128 applicants, 91% accepted, 85 enrolled. In 2019, 17 master's, 3 doctorates, 1 other advanced degree awarded. *Degree requirements:* For master's, thesis (for some programs); for doctorate, comprehensive exam, thesis/dissertation. *Entrance requirements:* For master's, GRE General Test, MAT; for doctorate, GRE. Additional exam requirements/recommendations for international students: required—TOEFL (minimum score 550 paper-based; 80 iBT), IELTS (minimum score 6.5). *Application deadline:* For fall admission, 2/1 priority date for domestic students. Applications are processed on a rolling basis. Application fee: $65. Electronic applications accepted. *Expenses: Tuition, area resident:* Full-time $8100; part-time $450 per credit hour. Tuition, state resident: full-time $8100; part-time $450 per credit hour. Tuition, nonresident: full-time $26,388; part-time $1466 per credit hour. *International tuition:* $26,388 full-time. *Required fees:* $1257; $278 per semester. Tuition and fees vary according to course load. *Financial support:* In 2019–20, 56 students received support, including 15 teaching assistantships with full tuition reimbursements available (averaging $15,825 per year); career-related internships or fieldwork, Federal Work-Study, institutionally sponsored loans, tuition waivers (full and partial), and unspecified assistantships also available. Financial award application deadline: 3/1; financial award applicants required to submit FAFSA. *Unit head:* Dr. Jim Artesani, Associate Dean of Accreditation and Graduate Affairs, 207-581-4061, Fax: 207-581-2423, E-mail: arthur.artesani@maine.edu. *Application contact:* Scott G. Delcourt, Senior Associate Dean of the Graduate School, 207-581-3291, Fax: 207-581-3232, E-mail: graduate@maine.edu.
Website: http://www.umaine.edu/edhd/

University of Maryland, College Park, Academic Affairs, College of Education, Department of Human Development and Quantitative Methodology, College Park, MD 20742. Offers MA, Ed D, PhD. *Entrance requirements:* Additional exam requirements/recommendations for international students: required—TOEFL.

University of Missouri, Office of Research and Graduate Studies, College of Human Environmental Sciences, Department of Human Development and Family Studies, Columbia, MO 65211. Offers MA, MS, PhD. *Entrance requirements:* For master's, GRE General Test, minimum GPA of 3.0. Additional exam requirements/recommendations for international students: required—TOEFL.

University of Nebraska–Lincoln, Graduate College, College of Education and Human Sciences, Department of Child, Youth and Family Studies, Lincoln, NE 68588. Offers child development/early childhood education (MS, PhD); child, youth and family studies (MS); family and consumer sciences education (MS, PhD); family financial planning (MS); family science (MS, PhD); gerontology (PhD); human sciences (PhD), including child, youth and family studies, gerontology, medical family therapy; marriage and family therapy (MS); medical family therapy (PhD); youth development (MS). *Accreditation:* AAMFT/COAMFTE (one or more programs are accredited). *Program availability:* Online learning. *Degree requirements:* For master's, thesis optional. *Entrance requirements:* For master's, GRE. Additional exam requirements/recommendations for international students: required—TOEFL (minimum score 550 paper-based). Electronic applications accepted.

University of Nebraska–Lincoln, Graduate College, College of Education and Human Sciences, Department of Special Education and Communication Disorders, Lincoln, NE 68588. Offers audiology research (PhD); clinical audiology (Au D); educational studies (PhD); human sciences (PhD), including communication disorders; special education (M Ed, MA, Ed S), including special education (M Ed, MA), special education and communication disorders (Ed S); speech-language pathology and audiology (MS, Au D), including audiology and hearing science (Au D), speech-language pathology (Au D), speech-language pathology and audiology (MS). *Accreditation:* ASHA (one or more programs are accredited); NCATE. *Degree requirements:* For master's, thesis optional. *Entrance requirements:* For master's, GRE General Test. Additional exam requirements/recommendations for international students: required—TOEFL. Electronic applications accepted.

University of Nebraska–Lincoln, Graduate College, College of Education and Human Sciences, Department of Textiles, Clothing and Design, Lincoln, NE 68588. Offers human sciences (PhD), including textiles, clothing and design (MS, PhD); merchandising (MS); textile history/quilt studies (MA); textile science (MS); textile-apparel (MA); textiles, clothing and design (MA, MS), including textiles, clothing and design (MS, PhD). *Program availability:* Part-time, online learning. *Degree requirements:* For master's, thesis optional. *Entrance requirements:* For master's, GRE General Test. Additional exam requirements/recommendations for international students: required—TOEFL (minimum score 550 paper-based). Electronic applications accepted.

University of Nevada, Reno, Graduate School, College of Education, Department of Human Development and Family Studies, Reno, NV 89557. Offers MS. *Degree requirements:* For master's, thesis optional. *Entrance requirements:* For master's, GRE General Test, minimum GPA of 2.75. Additional exam requirements/recommendations for international students: required—TOEFL (minimum score 500 paper-based; 61 iBT), IELTS (minimum score 6). Electronic applications accepted.

University of New Mexico, Graduate Studies, College of Education and Human Sciences, Program in Family Studies, Albuquerque, NM 87131-2039. Offers family life education (MA); family relations (MA); family studies (PhD); human development in families (MA). *Program availability:* Part-time, evening/weekend. *Degree requirements:* For master's, comprehensive exam, thesis (for some programs); for doctorate, comprehensive exam, thesis/dissertation. *Entrance requirements:* For master's, written paper, 3 letters of recommendation, personal statement; for doctorate, GRE General Test, written paper, 3 letters of recommendation, personal statement, interview. Additional exam requirements/recommendations for international students: required—TOEFL (minimum score 550 paper-based). Electronic applications accepted. *Expenses:* Tuition, state resident: full-time $7633; part-time $972 per year. Tuition, nonresident: full-time $22,586; part-time $3840 per year. *International tuition:* $23,292 full-time. *Required fees:* $8608. Tuition and fees vary according to course level, course load, degree level, program and student level.

The University of North Carolina at Greensboro, Graduate School, School of Health and Human Sciences, Department of Human Development and Family Studies, Greensboro, NC 27412-5001. Offers M Ed, MS, PhD. *Degree requirements:* For

Human Development

master's, one foreign language; for doctorate, one foreign language, thesis/dissertation. *Entrance requirements:* For master's and doctorate, GRE General Test. Additional exam requirements/recommendations for international students: required—TOEFL. Electronic applications accepted. *Expenses:* Contact institution.

University of North Texas, Toulouse Graduate School, Denton, TX 76203-5459. Offers accounting (MS); applied anthropology (MA, MS); applied behavior analysis (Certificate); applied geography (MA); applied technology and performance improvement (M Ed, MS); art education (MA); art history (MA); arts leadership (Certificate); audiology (Au D); behavior analysis (MS); behavioral science (PhD); biochemistry and molecular biology (MS); biology (MA, MS); biomedical engineering (MS); business analysis (MS); chemistry (MS); clinical health psychology (PhD); communication studies (MA, MS); computer engineering (MS); computer science (MS); counseling (M Ed, MS), including clinical mental health counseling (MS), college and university counseling, elementary school counseling, secondary school counseling; creative writing (MA); criminal justice (MS); curriculum and instruction (M Ed); decision sciences (MBA); design (MA, MFA), including fashion design (MFA), innovation studies, interior design (MFA); early childhood studies (MS); economics (MS); educational leadership (M Ed, Ed D); educational psychology (MS, PhD), including family studies (MS), gifted and talented (MS), human development (MS), learning and cognition (MS), research, measurement and evaluation (MS); electrical engineering (MS); emergency management (MPA); engineering technology (MS); English (MA); English as a second language (MA); environmental science (MS); finance (MBA, MS); financial management (MPA); French (MA); health services management (MBA); higher education (M Ed, Ed D); history (MA, MS); hospitality management (MS); human resources management (MPA); information science (MS); information systems (PhD); information technologies (MBA); interdisciplinary studies (MA, MS); international studies (MA); international sustainable tourism (MS); jazz studies (MM); journalism (MA, MJ, Graduate Certificate), including interactive and virtual digital communication (Graduate Certificate), narrative journalism (Graduate Certificate), public relations (Graduate Certificate); kinesiology (MS); linguistics (MA); local government management (MPA); logistics (PhD); logistics and supply chain management (MBA); long-term care, senior housing, and aging services (MA); management (PhD); marketing (MBA); mathematics (MA, MS); mechanical and energy engineering (MS, PhD); music (MA), including ethnomusicology, music theory, musicology, performance; music composition (PhD); music education (MM Ed, PhD); nonprofit management (MPA); operations and supply chain management (MBA); performance (MM, DMA); philosophy (MA); political science (MA); professional and technical communication (MA); radio, television and film (MA, MFA); rehabilitation counseling (Certificate); sociology (MA); Spanish (MA); special education (M Ed); speech-language pathology (MA); strategic management (MBA); studio art (MFA); teaching (M Ed); MBA/MS. *Program availability:* Part-time, evening/weekend, online learning. Terminal master's awarded for partial completion of doctoral program. *Degree requirements:* For master's, variable foreign language requirement, comprehensive exam (for some programs), thesis (for some programs); for doctorate, variable foreign language requirement, comprehensive exam (for some programs), thesis/dissertation; for other advanced degree, variable foreign language requirement, comprehensive exam (for some programs). *Entrance requirements:* For master's and doctorate, GRE, GMAT. Additional exam requirements/recommendations for international students: required—TOEFL (minimum score 550 paper-based; 79 iBT). Electronic applications accepted.

University of Pennsylvania, Graduate School of Education, Division of Human Development and Quantitative Methods, Program in Interdisciplinary Studies in Human Development, Philadelphia, PA 19104. Offers MS Ed, PhD. *Program availability:* Part-time. *Students:* 57 full-time (51 women), 9 part-time (8 women); includes 9 minority (6 Black or African American, non-Hispanic/Latino; 2 Hispanic/Latino; 1 Two or more races, non-Hispanic/Latino), 51 international. Average age 27. 179 applicants, 53% accepted, 31 enrolled. In 2019, 22 master's, 4 doctorates awarded. Terminal master's awarded for partial completion of doctoral program. Application fee: $75.
Website: http://www.gse.upenn.edu/aphd/ishd/msed

University of Rhode Island, Graduate School, College of Health Sciences, Department of Human Development and Family Studies, Kingston, RI 02881. Offers college student personnel (MS); human development and family studies (MS); marriage and family therapy (MS). *Accreditation:* AAMFT/COAMFTE. *Program availability:* Part-time. *Faculty:* 16 full-time (12 women). *Students:* 50 full-time (40 women), 12 part-time (11 women); includes 14 minority (4 Black or African American, non-Hispanic/Latino; 2 Asian, non-Hispanic/Latino; 5 Hispanic/Latino; 3 Two or more races, non-Hispanic/Latino), 2 international. In 2019, 25 master's awarded. *Entrance requirements:* Additional exam requirements/recommendations for international students: required—TOEFL. *Application deadline:* For fall admission, 1/15 for domestic and international students. Application fee: $65. Electronic applications accepted. *Expenses: Tuition, area resident:* Full-time $13,734; part-time $763 per credit. Tuition, state resident: full-time $13,734; part-time $763 per credit. Tuition, nonresident: full-time $26,512; part-time $1473 per credit. *International tuition:* $26,512 full-time. *Required fees:* $1780; $52 per credit. $35 per term. One-time fee: $165. *Financial support:* In 2019–20, 2 research assistantships with tuition reimbursements (averaging $4,746 per year), 5 teaching assistantships with tuition reimbursements (averaging $11,866 per year) were awarded. Financial award application deadline: 1/15; financial award applicants required to submit FAFSA. *Unit head:* Dr. Sue Adam, Chair, 401-874-5958, E-mail: suekadams@uri.edu. *Application contact:* Dr. Sue Adam, Chair, 401-874-5958, E-mail: suekadams@uri.edu. Website: http://www.uri.edu/hss/hdf/

University of Rochester, Margaret Warner Graduate School of Education and Human Development, Doctoral Programs in Education, Rochester, NY 14627. Offers counseling (Ed D); educational administration (Ed D); educational policy and theory (PhD); higher education (PhD); human development in educational context (PhD); teaching, curriculum, and change (PhD).

University of Rochester, Margaret Warner Graduate School of Education and Human Development, Master's Program in Human Development, Rochester, NY 14627. Offers MS.

University of St. Thomas, College of Education, Leadership and Counseling, Department of Organization Learning and Development, St. Paul, MN 55105-1096. Offers organization development and change (Ed D). *Program availability:* Part-time, evening/weekend. *Degree requirements:* For doctorate, comprehensive exam, thesis/dissertation. *Entrance requirements:* For doctorate, minimum GPA of 3.5, interview, 5-7 years of organization development or leadership experience. Additional exam requirements/recommendations for international students: required—TOEFL (minimum score 550 paper-based). Electronic applications accepted. *Expenses:* Contact institution.

University of South Africa, College of Human Sciences, Pretoria, South Africa. Offers adult education (M Ed); African languages (MA, PhD); African politics (MA, PhD); Afrikaans (MA, PhD); ancient history (MA, PhD); ancient Near Eastern studies (MA, PhD); anthropology (MA, PhD); applied linguistics (MA); Arabic (MA, PhD); archaeology (MA); art history (MA); Biblical archaeology (MA); Biblical studies (M Th, D Th, PhD); Christian spirituality (M Th, D Th); church history (M Th, D Th); classical studies (MA, PhD); clinical psychology (MA); communication (MA, PhD); comparative education

(M Ed, Ed D); consulting psychology (D Admin, D Com, PhD); curriculum studies (M Ed, Ed D); development studies (M Admin, MA, D Admin, PhD); didactics (M Ed, Ed D); education (M Tech); education management (M Ed, Ed D); educational psychology (M Ed); English (MA); environmental education (M Ed); French (MA, PhD); German (MA, PhD); Greek (MA); guidance and counseling (M Ed); health studies (MA, PhD), including health sciences education (MA), health services management (MA), medical and surgical nursing science (critical care general) (MA), midwifery and neonatal nursing science (MA), trauma and emergency care (MA); history (MA, PhD); history of education (Ed D); inclusive education (M Ed, Ed D); information and communications technology policy and regulation (MA); information science (MA, MIS, PhD); international politics (MA, PhD); Islamic studies (MA, PhD); Italian (MA, PhD); Judaica (MA, PhD); linguistics (MA, PhD); mathematical education (M Ed); mathematics education (MA); missiology (M Th, D Th); modern Hebrew (MA, PhD); musicology (MA, MMus, D Mus, PhD); natural science education (M Ed); New Testament (M Th, D Th); Old Testament (D Th); pastoral therapy (M Th, D Th); philosophy (MA); philosophy of education (M Ed, Ed D); politics (MA, PhD); Portuguese (MA, PhD); practical theology (M Th, D Th); psychology (MA, MS, PhD); psychology of education (M Ed, Ed D); public health (MA); religious studies (MA, D Th, PhD); Romance languages (MA); Russian (MA, PhD); Semitic languages (MA, PhD); social behavior studies in HIV/AIDS (MA); social science (mental health) (MA); social science in development studies (MA); social science in psychology (MA); social science in social work (MA); social science in sociology (MA); social work (MSW, DSW, PhD); socio-education (M Ed, Ed D); sociolinguistics (MA); sociology (MA, PhD); Spanish (MA, PhD); systematic theology (M Th, D Th); TESOL (teaching English to speakers of other languages) (MA); theological ethics (M Th, D Th); theory of literature (MA, PhD); urban ministries (D Th); urban ministry (M Th).

University of South Dakota, Graduate School, School of Education, Division of Counseling and Psychology in Education, Vermillion, SD 57069. Offers counseling (MA, PhD, Ed S); human development and educational psychology (MA, PhD, Ed S); mental health counseling (Certificate); school psychology (PhD, Ed S). *Accreditation:* ACA (one or more programs are accredited); NCATE. *Program availability:* Part-time. *Degree requirements:* For master's and other advanced degree, comprehensive exam, thesis or alternative; for doctorate, comprehensive exam, thesis/dissertation. *Entrance requirements:* For master's and doctorate, GRE General Test, minimum GPA of 3.0. Additional exam requirements/recommendations for international students: required—TOEFL (minimum score 550 paper-based; 79 iBT). Electronic applications accepted.

The University of Texas at Austin, Graduate School, College of Education, Department of Educational Psychology, Austin, TX 78712-1111. Offers academic educational psychology (M Ed, MA); counseling psychology (PhD); counselor education (M Ed); human development, culture and learning sciences (PhD); program evaluation (MA); quantitative methods (M Ed, MA, PhD); school psychology (MA, PhD). *Accreditation:* APA (one or more programs are accredited). *Degree requirements:* For master's, thesis optional; for doctorate, thesis/dissertation. *Entrance requirements:* For master's and doctorate, GRE General Test, 3 letters of recommendation. Additional exam requirements/recommendations for international students: required—TOEFL.

The University of Texas at Austin, Graduate School, College of Fine Arts, Sarah and Ernest Butler School of Music, Austin, TX 78712-1111. Offers band and wind conducting (M Music, DMA); brass/woodwind/percussion (MM, DMA); chamber music (MM); choral conducting (MM, DMA); collaborative piano (MM, DMA); composition (MM, DMA), including composition, jazz, jazz (DMA); ethnomusicology (MM, PhD); literature and pedagogy (MM); music and human learning (MM, PhD); music and human learning (DMA), including jazz (MM, DMA), piano pedagogy; musicology (MM, PhD); opera performance (MM, DMA); orchestral conducting (MM, DMA); organ (MM), including sacred music; organ performance (MM, DMA); performance (MM), including jazz (MM, DMA); performance (DMA), including jazz (MM, DMA), piano (DMA), including jazz (MM, DMA); piano literature and pedagogy (MM); piano performance (MM, DMA); string performance (MM, DMA); theory (MM, PhD); vocal performance (MM, DMA); voice (DMA), including opera; voice performance pedagogy (DMA); woodwind, brass, percussion performance (MM). *Accreditation:* NASM. *Program availability:* Part-time. *Degree requirements:* For master's, one foreign language, comprehensive exam, thesis (for some programs), recital (performance or composition majors); for doctorate, one foreign language, comprehensive exam, thesis/dissertation (for some programs), recital (for performance or composition majors). *Entrance requirements:* For master's and doctorate, GRE General Test (except for performance or composition majors), audition (performance majors). Electronic applications accepted.

University of Utah, Graduate School, College of Social and Behavioral Science, Department of Family and Consumer Studies, Salt Lake City, UT 84112-0080. Offers human development and social policy (MS). *Program availability:* Part-time. *Faculty:* 8 full-time (6 women), 1 part-time/adjunct (0 women). *Students:* 12 full-time (11 women), 3 part-time (2 women); includes 4 minority (1 Asian, non-Hispanic/Latino; 1 Hispanic/Latino; 2 Two or more races, non-Hispanic/Latino). Average age 31. In 2019, 7 master's awarded. Terminal master's awarded for partial completion of doctoral program. *Application deadline:* For fall admission, 2/1 priority date for domestic and international students. Applications are processed on a rolling basis. Electronic applications accepted. *Expenses:* Tuition, state resident: full-time $7085; part-time $272.51 per credit hour. Tuition, nonresident: full-time $24,937; part-time $959.12 per credit hour. *Required fees:* $880.52; $880.52 per semester. Tuition and fees vary according to degree level, program and student level. *Financial support:* In 2019–20, 10 teaching assistantships (averaging $11,700 per year) were awarded. *Unit head:* Prof. Lori Kowaleski-Jones, PhD, Chair, 801-585-0074, Fax: 801-581-5156, E-mail: lk2700@fcs.utah.edu. *Application contact:* Prof. Jessie Fan, PhD, Graduate Director, 801-581-4170, E-mail: jessie.fan@fcs.utah.edu.
Website: http://fcs.utah.edu/

University of Victoria, Faculty of Graduate Studies, Faculty of Education, Department of Educational Psychology and Leadership Studies, Victoria, BC V8W 2Y2, Canada. Offers aboriginal communities counseling (M Ed); counseling (M Ed, MA); educational psychology (M Ed, MA, PhD), including counseling psychology (M Ed, MA), leadership studies (PhD), learning and development (MA, PhD), measurement and evaluation, special education (M Ed, MA); leadership studies (M Ed, MA). *Program availability:* Part-time. *Degree requirements:* For master's, thesis (for some programs), comprehensive exam (M Ed); for doctorate, comprehensive exam, thesis/dissertation, candidacy exam. *Entrance requirements:* For master's, 2 years of work experience in a relevant field; for doctorate, GRE, 2 years of work experience in a relevant field, minimum B average. Additional exam requirements/recommendations for international students: required—TOEFL (minimum score 575 paper-based), IELTS (minimum score 7).

University of Victoria, Faculty of Graduate Studies, Faculty of Human and Social Development, Studies in Policy and Practice Program, Victoria, BC V8W 2Y2, Canada. Offers MA. *Program availability:* Part-time. *Degree requirements:* For master's, thesis. *Entrance requirements:* For master's, resume. Additional exam requirements/recommendations for international students: required—TOEFL (minimum score 575 paper-based), IELTS (minimum score 7). Electronic applications accepted.

University of Washington, Graduate School, College of Education, Program in Educational Psychology, Seattle, WA 98195. Offers educational psychology (PhD); human development and cognition (M Ed); learning sciences (M Ed, PhD);

measurement, statistics and research design (M Ed); school psychology (M Ed). *Accreditation:* APA. *Degree requirements:* For master's, thesis optional; for doctorate, thesis/dissertation. *Entrance requirements:* For master's and doctorate, GRE General Test, minimum GPA of 3.0. Additional exam requirements/recommendations for international students: required—TOEFL.

University of Wisconsin–Madison, Graduate School, School of Human Ecology, Program in Human Development and Family Studies, Madison, WI 53706-1380. Offers MS, PhD. *Program availability:* Part-time. Terminal master's awarded for partial completion of doctoral program. *Degree requirements:* For master's, thesis; for doctorate, comprehensive exam, thesis/dissertation. *Entrance requirements:* For master's, GRE General Test, 3 letters of recommendation; for doctorate, GRE General Test, MS or MA, 3 letters of recommendation. Additional exam requirements/recommendations for international students: required—TOEFL (minimum score 580 paper-based; 92 iBT). Electronic applications accepted.

Utah State University, School of Graduate Studies, Emma Eccles Jones College of Education and Human Services, Department of Family, Consumer, and Human Development, Logan, UT 84322. Offers family and human development (MFHD); family, consumer, and human development (MS, PhD), including adolescence/youth (MS); adult development/aging (MS), consumer science (MS), infancy/childhood (MS), marriage and family relations (MS), marriage and family therapy (MS). *Accreditation:* AAMFT/COAMFTE (one or more programs are accredited). *Program availability:* Part-time, evening/weekend, online learning. *Degree requirements:* For master's, thesis; for doctorate, comprehensive exam, thesis/dissertation, competencies. *Entrance requirements:* For master's, GRE General Test or MAT, minimum GPA of 3.0, 3 letters of recommendation; for doctorate, GRE, minimum GPA of 3.0, 3 letters of recommendation. Additional exam requirements/recommendations for international students: required—TOEFL. Electronic applications accepted.

Vanderbilt University, Peabody College, Department of Human and Organizational Development, Nashville, TN 37240-1001. Offers community development and action (M Ed); human development counseling (M Ed), including clinical mental health counseling. *Accreditation:* ACA; NCATE. *Program availability:* Part-time, evening/weekend, blended/hybrid learning, on-campus immersion once every semester. *Degree requirements:* For master's, comprehensive exam, thesis optional. *Entrance requirements:* For master's, GRE General Test. Additional exam requirements/recommendations for international students: required—TOEFL (minimum score 550 paper-based; 80 iBT). Electronic applications accepted. *Expenses: Tuition:* Full-time $51,018; part-time $2087 per hour. *Required fees:* $542. Tuition and fees vary according to program.

Washington State University, College of Agricultural, Human, and Natural Resource Sciences, Department of Human Development, Pullman, WA 99164-4852. Offers prevention science (PhD). *Program availability:* Part-time. *Degree requirements:* For doctorate, comprehensive exam, thesis/dissertation. *Entrance requirements:* For doctorate, GRE General Test, bachelor's or master's degree in prevention science related field (e.g., communication, educational psychology, human development, nursing, psychology, sociology); written statement specifying qualifications, educational goals, and career objectives; official copies of all college transcripts; three letters of reference. Additional exam requirements/recommendations for international students: required—TOEFL, IELTS. Electronic applications accepted.

Wright Graduate University for the Realization of Human Potential, Graduate Programs, Elkhorn, WI 53121. Offers emotional intelligence for leadership and coaching (Graduate Certificate); social intelligence for leadership and coaching (Graduate Certificate); transformational coaching (Graduate Certificate); transformational leadership (Graduate Certificate); transformational leadership and coaching (MA, Ed D).

Industrial and Organizational Psychology

Adler University, Master's Degrees in Industrial and Organizational Psychology, Vancouver, BC V6B 3J5, Canada. Offers MA. *Program availability:* Part-time, evening/weekend. In 2019, 2 master's awarded. *Degree requirements:* For master's, thesis optional, Thesis and Non-Thesis options; Social Justice Practicum. *Unit head:* Michelle Brice, Associate Vice President of Admissions, 236-521-2409, E-mail: vanadmissions@adler.edu. *Application contact:* Michelle Brice, Associate Vice President of Admissions, 236-521-2409, E-mail: vanadmissions@adler.edu.

Albizu University - Miami, Graduate Programs, Doral, FL 33172. Offers clinical psychology (PhD, Psy D); entrepreneurship (MBA); exceptional student education (MS); human services (PhD); industrial/organizational psychology (MS); marriage and family therapy (MS); mental health counseling (MS); nonprofit management (MBA); organizational management (MBA); school counseling (MS); speech and language pathology (MS); teaching English for speakers of other languages (MS). *Accreditation:* APA. *Program availability:* Part-time, 100% online, blended/hybrid learning. *Faculty:* 28 full-time (21 women), 27 part-time/adjunct (15 women). *Students:* 410 full-time (351 women), 190 part-time (163 women); includes 519 minority (33 Black or African American, non-Hispanic/Latino; 3 Asian, non-Hispanic/Latino; 477 Hispanic/Latino; 6 Two or more races, non-Hispanic/Latino), 21 international. Average age 33. 286 applicants, 66% accepted, 127 enrolled. In 2019, 96 master's, 54 doctorates awarded. Terminal master's awarded for partial completion of doctoral program. *Degree requirements:* For master's, comprehensive exam (for some programs), integrative project (for MBA); research project (for exceptional student education, teaching English as a second language); comprehensive examination for Speech and Language Pathology; for doctorate, comprehensive exam, thesis/dissertation, comprehensive examinations, internship, project/dissertation. *Entrance requirements:* For master's, GRE/EXADEP, bachelor's degree from accredited institution, minimum GPA of 3.0, 3 letters of recommendation, interview, resume, statement of purpose, official transcripts; for doctorate, GRE (for Psy D), 3 letters of recommendation, resume, interview, statement of purpose, official transcripts; bachelor's degree and minimum GPA of 3.25 (for Psy D); master's degree and minimum GPA of 3.0 (for PhD). Additional exam requirements/recommendations for international students: required—Michigan Test of English Language Proficiency. *Application deadline:* For fall admission, 4/1 priority date for domestic students, 5/1 priority date for international students; for spring admission, 11/1 priority date for domestic students, 9/1 priority date for international students. Applications are processed on a rolling basis. Application fee: $50. Electronic applications accepted. Application fee is waived when completed online. *Expenses:* $600 per credit or $620 per credit or $650 per credit (for master's depending on field); $800 per credit or $1,050 per credit (for doctoral depending on program). *Financial support:* In 2019–20, 158 students received support. Federal Work-Study, scholarships/grants, unspecified assistantships, and tuition discounts available. Financial award application deadline: 6/1; financial award applicants required to submit FAFSA. *Unit head:* Dr. Tilokie Depoo, PhD, Chancellor, 305-593-1223 Ext. 3138, Fax: 305-477-8983, E-mail: tdepoo@albizu.edu. *Application contact:* Nancy Alvarez, Director of Enrollment Management, 305-593-1223 Ext. 3136, Fax: 305-593-1854, E-mail: nalvarez@albizu.edu
Website: www.albizu.edu

Albizu University - San Juan, Graduate Programs, San Juan, PR 00901. Offers clinical psychology (MS, PhD, Psy D); general psychology (PhD); industrial/organizational psychology (MS, PhD); speech and language pathology (MS). *Accreditation:* APA (one or more programs are accredited). *Program availability:* Part-time, evening/weekend. Terminal master's awarded for partial completion of doctoral program. *Degree requirements:* For master's, one foreign language, comprehensive exam, thesis; for doctorate, one foreign language, comprehensive exam, thesis/dissertation, written qualifying exams. *Entrance requirements:* For master's, GRE General Test or EXADEP, interview; minimum GPA of 2.8 (industrial/organizational psychology); for doctorate, GRE General Test or EXADEP, interview; minimum GPA of 3.0 (PhD in industrial/organizational psychology and clinical psychology), 3.25 (Psy D).

Alliant International University–Fresno, California School of Professional Psychology, Organizational Psychology Programs, Fresno, CA 93727. Offers organizational behavior (MA); organizational development (Psy D); MA/PhD; Psy D/MA. *Program availability:* Part-time, evening/weekend. *Degree requirements:* For doctorate, thesis/dissertation. *Entrance requirements:* For doctorate, interview, minimum GPA of 3.0. Additional exam requirements/recommendations for international students: required—TOEFL (minimum score 550 paper-based; 80 iBT), TWE (minimum score 5). Electronic applications accepted.

Alliant International University - Los Angeles, California School of Professional Psychology, Organizational Psychology Division, Alhambra, CA 91803. Offers MA, PhD. *Accreditation:* APA. *Program availability:* Part-time. Terminal master's awarded for partial completion of doctoral program. *Degree requirements:* For doctorate, comprehensive exam, thesis/dissertation. *Entrance requirements:* For master's and doctorate, interview, minimum GPA of 3.0 in both psychology and overall. Additional exam requirements/recommendations for international students: required—TOEFL (minimum score 600 paper-based), TWE (minimum score 5). Electronic applications accepted.

Alliant International University - San Diego, California School of Professional Psychology, Organizational Psychology Division, San Diego, CA 92131. Offers clinical/industrial organizational psychology (PhD); consulting psychology (PhD); industrial/organizational psychology (MA, MS, PhD); leadership (PhD). *Program availability:* Part-time, evening/weekend. Terminal master's awarded for partial completion of doctoral program. *Degree requirements:* For doctorate, comprehensive exam, thesis/dissertation, internship/practicum. *Entrance requirements:* For master's and doctorate, minimum GPA of 3.0, recommendations, essay, interview. Additional exam requirements/recommendations for international students: required—TOEFL (minimum score 550 paper-based; 80 iBT), TWE (minimum score 5). Electronic applications accepted.

Alliant International University–San Francisco, California School of Professional Psychology, Organizational Psychology Division, San Francisco, CA 94133. Offers MA, PhD. *Accreditation:* APA. *Program availability:* Part-time, evening/weekend. Terminal master's awarded for partial completion of doctoral program. *Degree requirements:* For doctorate, comprehensive exam, thesis/dissertation, field placement. *Entrance requirements:* For master's and doctorate, minimum GPA of 3.0, interview. Additional exam requirements/recommendations for international students: required—TOEFL (minimum score 550 paper-based; 80 iBT), TWE (minimum score 5). Electronic applications accepted.

American InterContinental University Online, Program in Business Administration, Schaumburg, IL 60173. Offers accounting and finance (MBA); finance (MBA); healthcare management (MBA); human resource management (MBA); international business (MBA); management (MBA); marketing (MBA); operations management (MBA); organizational psychology and development (MBA); project management (MBA). *Accreditation:* ACBSP. *Program availability:* Evening/weekend, online learning. *Entrance requirements:* Additional exam requirements/recommendations for international students: required—TOEFL (minimum score 550 paper-based). Electronic applications accepted.

Angelo State University, College of Graduate Studies and Research, Archer College of Health and Human Services, Department of Psychology and Sociology, San Angelo, TX 76909. Offers industrial-organizational psychology (MS). *Program availability:* Part-time, evening/weekend. *Degree requirements:* For master's, comprehensive exam, thesis optional. *Entrance requirements:* For master's, GRE General Test (for industrial and organizational psychology only), essay, letters of recommendation (for industrial and organizational psychology only). Additional exam requirements/recommendations for international students: required—TOEFL or IELTS. Electronic applications accepted.

Anna Maria College, Graduate Division, Program in Industrial/Organizational Psychology, Paxton, MA 01612. Offers MS.

Argosy University, Atlanta, Georgia School of Professional Psychology, Atlanta, GA 30328. Offers clinical psychology (MA, Psy D, Postdoctoral Respecialization Certificate), including child and family psychology (Psy D); general adult clinical (Psy D), health psychology (Psy D), neuropsychology/geropsychology (Psy D); community counseling (MA), including marriage and family therapy; counselor education and supervision (Ed D); forensic psychology (MA); industrial organizational psychology (MA); marriage and family therapy (Certificate); sport-exercise psychology (MA). *Accreditation:* APA.

Argosy University, Chicago, Illinois School of Professional Psychology, Chicago, IL 60601. Offers clinical psychology (MA, Psy D), including child and adolescent psychology (Psy D), client-centered and experiential psychotherapies (Psy D), diversity and multicultural psychology (Psy D), family psychology (Psy D), forensic psychology (Psy D), health psychology (Psy D), neuropsychology (Psy D), organizational consulting (Psy D), psychoanalytic psychology (Psy D), psychology and spirituality (Psy D); community counseling (MA); counseling psychology (Ed D), including counselor education and supervision; counselor education and supervision (Ed D); industrial organizational psychology (MA). *Accreditation:* APA (one or more programs are accredited). *Program availability:* Online learning.

Industrial and Organizational Psychology

Argosy University, Phoenix, Arizona School of Professional Psychology, Program in Industrial Organizational Psychology, Phoenix, AZ 85021. Offers MA.

Argosy University, Tampa, Florida School of Professional Psychology, Tampa, FL 33607. Offers clinical psychology (MA, Psy D), including clinical psychology; counselor education and supervision (Ed D); industrial organizational psychology (MA); marriage and family therapy (MA); mental health counseling (MA).

Argosy University, Twin Cities, Minnesota School of Professional Psychology, Eagan, MN 55121. Offers clinical psychology (MA, Psy D), including child and family psychology (Psy D), forensic psychology (Psy D), health and neuropsychology (Psy D), trauma (Psy D); forensic counseling (Post-Graduate Certificate); forensic psychology (MA); industrial organizational psychology (MA); marriage and family therapy (MA, DMFT), including forensic counseling (MA). *Accreditation:* AAMFT; AAMFT/COAMFTE; APA.

Austin Peay State University, College of Graduate Studies, College of Behavioral and Health Sciences, Department of Psychological Science and Counseling, Clarksville, TN 37044. Offers industrial-organizational psychology (MS); mental health counseling (MS), including clinical mental health, school counseling; school counseling (MS). *Program availability:* Part-time, online learning. *Faculty:* 9 full-time (6 women), 5 part-time/adjunct (4 women). *Students:* 64 full-time (46 women), 27 part-time (24 women); includes 30 minority (16 Black or African American, non-Hispanic/Latino; 1 Asian, non-Hispanic/Latino; 5 Hispanic/Latino; 8 Two or more races, non-Hispanic/Latino), 1 international. Average age 29. 34 applicants, 68% accepted, 19 enrolled. In 2019, 28 master's awarded. *Degree requirements:* For master's, comprehensive exam, thesis (for some programs). *Entrance requirements:* For master's, GRE General Test, minimum undergraduate GPA of 2.5, 3 letters of recommendation, bachelor's degree. Additional exam requirements/recommendations for international students: required—TOEFL (minimum score 500 paper-based). *Application deadline:* For fall admission, 8/5 priority date for domestic students. Applications are processed on a rolling basis. Application fee: $45 ($55 for international students). Electronic applications accepted. *Financial support:* Research assistantships with full tuition reimbursements, career-related internships or fieldwork, Federal Work-Study, institutionally sponsored loans, scholarships/grants, and unspecified assistantships available. Support available to part-time students. Financial award application deadline: 7/1; financial award applicants required to submit FAFSA. *Unit head:* Dr. Nicole Knickmeyer, Chair, 931-221-7232, Fax: 931-221-6267, E-mail: knickmeyer@apsu.edu. *Application contact:* Megan Mitchell, Coordinator of Graduate Admissions, 800-859-4723, Fax: 931-221-7641, E-mail: gradadmissions@apsu.edu.
Website: http://www.apsu.edu/psychology/index.php

Azusa Pacific University, School of Behavioral and Applied Sciences, Department of Leadership and Organizational Psychology, Program in Organizational Psychology, Azusa, CA 91702-7000. Offers MS. *Expenses:* Contact institution.

Baruch College of the City University of New York, Weissman School of Arts and Sciences, Program in Industrial/Organizational Psychology, New York, NY 10010-5585. Offers MS. *Program availability:* Part-time, evening/weekend. Terminal master's awarded for partial completion of doctoral program. *Degree requirements:* For master's, thesis or alternative. *Entrance requirements:* For master's, GRE, 2 letters of recommendation, personal essay, resume. Additional exam requirements/recommendations for international students: required—TOEFL. Electronic applications accepted.

Baruch College of the City University of New York, Zicklin School of Business, Program in Industrial and Organizational Psychology, New York, NY 10010-5585. Offers MBA, MS, PhD. *Program availability:* Part-time, evening/weekend. *Degree requirements:* For master's, thesis or alternative; for doctorate, comprehensive exam, thesis/dissertation. *Entrance requirements:* For master's, GMAT or GRE General Test, 2 letters of recommendation, resumé, 2 years of work experience; for doctorate, GMAT or GRE General Test. Additional exam requirements/recommendations for international students: required—TOEFL (minimum score 590 paper-based), TWE.

Bayamón Central University, Graduate Programs, Program in Organizational Psychology, Bayamón, PR 00960-1725. Offers MA. *Program availability:* Part-time, evening/weekend. *Degree requirements:* For master's, comprehensive exam. *Entrance requirements:* For master's, EXADEP, bachelor's degree in psychology or related field.

Bowling Green State University, Graduate College, College of Arts and Sciences, Department of Psychology, Bowling Green, OH 43403. Offers clinical psychology (MA, PhD); developmental psychology (MA, PhD); experimental psychology (MA, PhD); industrial/organizational psychology (MA, PhD); quantitative psychology (MA, PhD). *Accreditation:* APA (one or more programs are accredited). *Degree requirements:* For doctorate, thesis/dissertation. *Entrance requirements:* For doctorate, GRE General Test, GRE Subject Test. Additional exam requirements/recommendations for international students: required—TOEFL. Electronic applications accepted.

Brooklyn College of the City University of New York, School of Natural and Behavioral Sciences, Department of Psychology, Brooklyn, NY 11210-2889. Offers experimental psychology (MA); industrial and organizational psychology (MA), including human relations, organizational behavior; mental health counseling (MA); psychology (PhD). *Program availability:* Part-time. *Degree requirements:* For master's, comprehensive exam, thesis (for some programs). *Entrance requirements:* For master's, minimum GPA of 3.0, 2 letters of recommendation, essay; for doctorate, GRE. Additional exam requirements/recommendations for international students: required—TOEFL (minimum score 520 paper-based; 69 iBT). Electronic applications accepted.

California State University, Long Beach, Graduate Studies, College of Liberal Arts, Department of Psychology, Long Beach, CA 90840. Offers human factors (MS); industrial/organizational psychology (MS); psychology (MA). *Program availability:* Part-time, evening/weekend. *Degree requirements:* For master's, comprehensive exam, thesis. *Entrance requirements:* For master's, GRE General Test, GRE Subject Test. Electronic applications accepted.

California State University, Sacramento, College of Social Sciences and Interdisciplinary Studies, Department of Psychology, Sacramento, CA 95819. Offers applied behavior analysis (MA); industrial/organizational psychology (MA). *Program availability:* Part-time. *Students:* 26 full-time (22 women), 30 part-time (21 women); includes 22 minority (1 Black or African American, non-Hispanic/Latino; 2 American Indian or Alaska Native, non-Hispanic/Latino; 4 Asian, non-Hispanic/Latino; 14 Hispanic/Latino; 1 Native Hawaiian or other Pacific Islander, non-Hispanic/Latino), 3 international. Average age 27. 86 applicants, 23% accepted, 16 enrolled. In 2019, 7 master's awarded. *Degree requirements:* For master's, thesis, project; writing proficiency exam. *Entrance requirements:* For master's, GRE, minimum GPA of 3.0 during previous 2 years. Additional exam requirements/recommendations for international students: required—TOEFL (minimum score 550 paper-based; 80 iBT); recommended—IELTS (minimum score 7). *Application deadline:* For fall admission, 3/1 for domestic students, 2/1 for international students. Applications are processed on a rolling basis. Application fee: $70. Electronic applications accepted. *Expenses:* Contact institution. *Financial support:* Teaching assistantships, career-related internships or fieldwork, Federal Work-Study, and scholarships/grants available. Support available to part-time students. Financial award application deadline: 3/1; financial award applicants required to submit FAFSA. *Unit head:* Dr. Rebecca Cameron, Interim Department Chair, 916-278-6254, E-mail: cameron@csus.edu. *Application contact:* Jose Martinez, Graduate Admissions Supervisor, 916-278-7871, E-mail: martinj@skymail.csus.edu.
Website: http://www.csus.edu/psyc

California State University, San Bernardino, Graduate Studies, College of Social and Behavioral Sciences, Department of Psychology, San Bernardino, CA 92407. Offers child development (MA); clinical/counseling psychology (MS); industrial/organizational psychology (MS); psychological science (MA). *Faculty:* 15 full-time (7 women). *Students:* 62 full-time (43 women), 13 part-time (7 women); includes 44 minority (3 Black or African American, non-Hispanic/Latino; 3 Asian, non-Hispanic/Latino; 31 Hispanic/Latino; 7 Two or more races, non-Hispanic/Latino), 5 international. Average age 27. 163 applicants, 24% accepted, 25 enrolled. In 2019, 32 master's awarded. *Degree requirements:* For master's, comprehensive exam, thesis (for some programs). *Entrance requirements:* Additional exam requirements/recommendations for international students: required—TOEFL. Application fee: $55. *Financial support:* Fellowships, research assistantships, and teaching assistantships available. *Unit head:* Dr. Robert Ricco, Chair, 909-537-5485, Fax: 909-537-7003, E-mail: rricco@csusb.edu. *Application contact:* Dr. Dorota Huizinga, Dean of Graduate Studies, 909-537-3064, E-mail: dorota.huizinga@csusb.edu.
Website: https://csbs.csusb.edu/psychology

Capella University, Harold Abel School of Social and Behavioral Science, Doctoral Programs in Psychology, Minneapolis, MN 55402. Offers addiction psychology (PhD); clinical psychology (Psy D); educational psychology (PhD); general advanced studies in human behavior (PhD); general psychology (PhD); industrial/organizational psychology (PhD); school psychology (Psy D).

Capella University, Harold Abel School of Social and Behavioral Science, Master's Programs in Psychology, Minneapolis, MN 55402. Offers applied behavior analysis (MS); clinical psychology (MS); counseling psychology (MS); educational psychology (MS); evaluation, research, and measurement (MS); general advanced studies in human behavior (MS); general psychology (MS); industrial/organizational psychology (MS); leadership coaching psychology (MS); school psychology (MS); sport psychology (MS).

Central Michigan University, College of Graduate Studies, College of Liberal Arts and Social Sciences, Department of Psychology, Program in Industrial and Organizational Psychology, Mount Pleasant, MI 48859. Offers industrial and organizational psychology (MA, PhD); occupational health psychology (PhD). *Degree requirements:* For master's, thesis; for doctorate, comprehensive exam, thesis/dissertation. *Entrance requirements:* For master's and doctorate, GRE. Electronic applications accepted. *Expenses: Tuition, area resident:* Full-time $12,267; part-time $8178 per year. Tuition, state resident: full-time $12,267; part-time $8178 per year. Tuition, nonresident: full-time $12,267; part-time $8178 per year. *International tuition:* $16,110 full-time. *Required fees:* $225 per semester. Tuition and fees vary according to degree level and program.

Chatham University, Program in Counseling Psychology, Pittsburgh, PA 15232-2826. Offers child, adolescent and family (MSCP); counseling psychology (Psy D); health and holistic (MSCP); organization and supervision (MSCP); sport and exercise (MSCP). *Accreditation:* APA. *Program availability:* Part-time, evening/weekend. *Faculty:* 13 full-time (8 women), 21 part-time/adjunct (17 women). *Students:* 93 full-time (79 women), 56 part-time (44 women); includes 29 minority (16 Black or African American, non-Hispanic/Latino; 4 Asian, non-Hispanic/Latino; 6 Hispanic/Latino; 3 Two or more races, non-Hispanic/Latino), 2 international. Average age 29. 172 applicants, 46% accepted, 54 enrolled. In 2019, 30 master's, 7 doctorates awarded. *Degree requirements:* For master's, thesis optional, supervised internship; for doctorate, thesis/dissertation, internship. *Entrance requirements:* For master's, minimum GPA of 3.0; 2 letters of recommendation; resume; prerequisite coursework in statistics, biology, and psychology; for doctorate, GRE. Additional exam requirements/recommendations for international students: required—TOEFL (minimum score 600 paper-based; 100 iBT), IELTS (minimum score 7), TWE. *Application deadline:* For fall admission, 4/1 priority date for domestic and international students; for spring admission, 11/1 for domestic students, 10/1 for international students. Applications are processed on a rolling basis. Application fee: $45. Electronic applications accepted. Application fee is waived when completed online. *Expenses:* $1,017 per credit hour. *Financial support:* Career-related internships or fieldwork available. Financial award applicants required to submit FAFSA. *Unit head:* Dr. Mary Jo Loughran, Director, 412-365-2783, Fax: 412-365-1505, E-mail: mloughran@chatham.edu. *Application contact:* Melanie Elmer, Assistant Director of Graduate Admission, 412-365-1394, Fax: 412-365-1609, E-mail: gradadmissions@chatham.edu.
Website: http://www.chatham.edu/mscp

The Chicago School of Professional Psychology, Program in Business Psychology, Chicago, IL 60610. Offers business psychology (PhD); industrial and organizational business psychology (Psy D); industrial and organizational psychology (MA); organizational leadership (MA, PhD). *Degree requirements:* For doctorate, thesis/dissertation optional. *Entrance requirements:* For doctorate, GRE. Additional exam requirements/recommendations for international students: required—TOEFL.

The Chicago School of Professional Psychology, Program in Industrial and Organizational Psychology, Chicago, IL 60610. Offers business psychology (Psy D); industrial and organizational psychology (MA). *Program availability:* Part-time, evening/weekend. *Degree requirements:* For master's, internship; for doctorate, thesis/dissertation, internship. *Entrance requirements:* For master's, 1 course each in psychology, statistics, and research methods. Additional exam requirements/recommendations for international students: required—TOEFL (minimum score 550 paper-based; 79 iBT).

The Chicago School of Professional Psychology at Downtown Los Angeles, Program in Industrial and Organizational Psychology, Los Angeles, CA 90017. Offers MA.

The Chicago School of Professional Psychology at San Diego, Graduate Programs, San Diego, CA 92101. Offers applied behavior analysis (MS, PhD); applied clinical psychology (Psy D); clinical psychology (MA); industrial and organizational psychology (MA).

The Chicago School of Professional Psychology: Online, PhD Program in Organizational Leadership, Chicago, IL 60654. Offers PhD.

The Chicago School of Professional Psychology: Online, Program in Applied Industrial and Organizational Psychology, Chicago, IL 60654. Offers MA, Certificate.

Claremont Graduate University, Graduate Programs, School of Social Science, Policy and Evaluation, Department of Psychology, Claremont, CA 91711-6160. Offers advanced study in evaluation (Certificate); cognitive psychology (MA, PhD); developmental psychology (MA, PhD); evaluation and applied research methods (MA, PhD); health behavior research and evaluation (MA, PhD); human resource development and evaluation (MA); industrial/organizational psychology (MA, PhD); organizational behavior (MA, PhD); organizational psychology (MA, PhD); social psychology (MA, PhD); MBA/PhD. *Program availability:* Part-time. Terminal master's awarded for partial completion of doctoral program. *Entrance requirements:* For master's and doctorate, GRE General Test. Additional exam requirements/recommendations for international students: required—TOEFL (minimum score 75 iBT). Electronic applications accepted.

Clemson University, Graduate School, College of Behavioral, Social and Health Sciences, Department of Psychology, Clemson, SC 29634. Offers applied psychology (MS); human factors psychology (PhD); industrial-organizational psychology (PhD). *Faculty:* 32 full-time (15 women). *Students:* 40 full-time (28 women), 4 part-time (2 women); includes 8 minority (2 Black or African American, non-Hispanic/Latino; 1 Asian, non-Hispanic/Latino; 5 Hispanic/Latino), 1 international. Average age 26. 168 applicants, 11% accepted, 14 enrolled. In 2019, 13 master's, 6 doctorates awarded. *Expenses:* Full-Time Student per Semester: Tuition: $6225 (in-state), $13425 (out-of-state), Fees: $598; Graduate Assistant Per Semester: $1144; Part-Time Student Per Credit Hour: $833 (in-state), $1731 (out-of-state), Fees: $617. Doctoral Base Fee per Semester: $4938 (in-state), $10405 (out-of-state). *Financial support:* In 2019–20, 43 students received support, including 5 fellowships with full and partial tuition reimbursements available (averaging $12,800 per year), 9 research assistantships with full and partial tuition reimbursements available (averaging $14,408 per year), 28 teaching assistantships with full and partial tuition reimbursements available (averaging $15,268 per year); career-related internships or fieldwork and unspecified assistantships also available. *Application contact:* Dr. Robert Sinclair, Graduate Program Coordinator, 864-656-3931, E-mail: RSINCLA@clemson.edu.
Website: http://www.clemson.edu/cbshs/departments/psychology/index.html

East Carolina University, Graduate School, Thomas Harriot College of Arts and Sciences, Department of Psychology, Greenville, NC 27858-4353. Offers health psychology (PhD), including clinical health psychology, occupational health psychology, pediatric school psychology; industrial and organizational psychology (MA); quantitative methods for the social and behavioral sciences (Certificate); MA/CAS. *Program availability:* Part-time, evening/weekend. *Application deadline:* For fall admission, 12/1 priority date for domestic and international students. *Expenses: Tuition, area resident:* Full-time $4749; part-time $185 per credit hour. Tuition, state resident: full-time $4749; part-time $185 per credit hour. Tuition, nonresident: full-time $17,898; part-time $864 per credit hour. *International tuition:* $17,898 full-time. *Required fees:* $2787. *Financial support:* Application deadline: 6/1. *Unit head:* Dr. Alan Christensen, Chair, E-mail: christensenal19@ecu.edu. *Application contact:* Graduate School Admissions, 252-328-6012, Fax: 252-328-6071, E-mail: gradschool@ecu.edu.
Website: https://psychology.ecu.edu/

Eastern Kentucky University, The Graduate School, College of Arts and Sciences, Department of Psychology, Richmond, KY 40475-3102. Offers clinical psychology (MS); industrial/organizational psychology (MS); school psychology (Psy S). *Program availability:* Part-time. *Entrance requirements:* For master's and Psy S, GRE General Test, minimum GPA of 2.5.

Elmhurst University, Graduate Programs, Program in Industrial/Organizational Psychology, Elmhurst, IL 60126-3296. Offers MA. *Program availability:* Part-time, evening/weekend. *Faculty:* 4 full-time (2 women), 2 part-time/adjunct (both women). *Students:* 8 full-time (5 women), 47 part-time (32 women); includes 10 minority (2 Black or African American, non-Hispanic/Latino; 2 Asian, non-Hispanic/Latino; 6 Hispanic/Latino). Average age 25. 91 applicants, 33% accepted, 30 enrolled. In 2019, 32 master's awarded. *Degree requirements:* For master's, thesis optional. *Entrance requirements:* For master's, GRE General Test, 3 recommendations, resume, statement of purpose. Additional exam requirements/recommendations for international students: required—TOEFL (minimum score 550 paper-based; 79 iBT), IELTS (minimum score 6.5). *Application deadline:* Applications are processed on a rolling basis. Application fee: $0. Electronic applications accepted. *Expenses:* $795 per semester hour. *Financial support:* In 2019–20, 38 students received support. Fellowships, scholarships/grants, and unspecified assistantships available. Support available to part-time students. Financial award applicants required to submit FAFSA. *Unit head:* Carrie Hewitt, Director, 630-617-3735, E-mail: hewittc@elmhurst.edu. *Application contact:* Timothy J. Panfil, Senior Director of Graduate Admission and Enrollment Management, 630-617-3300 Ext. 3256, Fax: 630-617-6471, E-mail: panfilt@elmhurst.edu.
Website: http://www.elmhurst.edu/iop

Emporia State University, Program in Psychology, Emporia, KS 66801-5415. Offers general psychology (MS); industrial/organizational psychology (MS). *Program availability:* Part-time. *Degree requirements:* For master's, comprehensive exam or thesis, internship. *Entrance requirements:* For master's, GRE General Test or MAT, essay exam, appropriate bachelor's degree, letters of recommendation. Additional exam requirements/recommendations for international students: required—TOEFL (minimum score 520 paper-based; 68 iBT). Electronic applications accepted. *Expenses: Tuition, area resident:* Full-time $6394; part-time $266.41 per credit hour. Tuition, state resident: full-time $6394; part-time $266.41 per credit hour. Tuition, nonresident: full-time $20,128; part-time $828.66 per credit hour. *International tuition:* $20,128 full-time. *Required fees:* $2183; $90.95 per credit hour. Tuition and fees vary according to campus/location and program.

Fairleigh Dickinson University, Florham Campus, Maxwell Becton College of Arts and Sciences, Department of Psychology, Program in Industrial/Organizational Psychology, Madison, NJ 07940-1099. Offers MA, MA/MBA. *Entrance requirements:* For master's, GRE General Test.

Florida Institute of Technology, College of Psychology and Liberal Arts, Program in Industrial/Organizational Psychology, Melbourne, FL 32901-6975. Offers industrial/organizational psychology (MS). *Program availability:* Part-time. Terminal master's awarded for partial completion of doctoral program. *Degree requirements:* For master's, comprehensive exam (for some programs), thesis (for some programs), minimum of 45 credit hours; for doctorate, thesis/dissertation, minimum of 90 credit hours beyond bachelor's degree. *Entrance requirements:* For master's, GRE General Test, minimum GPA of 3.0, 3 letters of recommendation, resume, statement of objectives, bachelor's degree in psychology (recommended); for doctorate, GRE General Test, minimum GPA of 3.2, 3 letters of recommendation, statement of objectives, resume. Additional exam requirements/recommendations for international students: required—TOEFL (minimum score 550 paper-based; 79 iBT). Electronic applications accepted.

Florida International University, College of Arts, Sciences, and Education, Department of Psychology, Miami, FL 33199. Offers behavioral analysis (MS); clinical science (PhD); cognitive neuroscience (PhD); counseling psychology (MS); developmental science (MS, PhD); legal psychology (MS, PhD); organizational psychology (MS, PhD). *Accreditation:* APA. *Program availability:* Part-time, evening/weekend. *Faculty:* 52 full-time (33 women), 50 part-time/adjunct (37 women). *Students:* 203 full-time (159 women), 2 part-time (both women); includes 117 minority (15 Black or African American, non-Hispanic/Latino; 8 Asian, non-Hispanic/Latino; 86 Hispanic/Latino; 8 Two or more races, non-Hispanic/Latino), 15 international. Average age 26. 410 applicants, 19% accepted, 60 enrolled. In 2019, 57 master's, 7 doctorates awarded. Terminal master's awarded for partial completion of doctoral program. *Degree requirements:* For master's, thesis; for doctorate, comprehensive exam, thesis/dissertation. *Entrance requirements:* For master's, GRE General Test, minimum GPA of 3.0, resume, 3 letters of recommendation; for doctorate, GRE General Test, 3 letters of

recommendation, resume, letter of intent, two writing samples, minimum GPA of 3.0. Additional exam requirements/recommendations for international students: required—TOEFL (minimum score 550 paper-based; 80 iBT). *Application deadline:* For fall admission, 12/15 for domestic and international students. Application fee: $30. Electronic applications accepted. *Expenses: Tuition, area resident:* Full-time $8912; part-time $446 per credit hour. Tuition, state resident: full-time $8912; part-time $446 per credit hour. Tuition, nonresident: full-time $21,393; part-time $992 per credit hour. *Required fees:* $2194. *Financial support:* Institutionally sponsored loans and scholarships/grants available. Financial award application deadline: 3/1. *Unit head:* Dr. Jeremy Pettit, Interim Chair, 305-348-1671, Fax: 305-348-2880, E-mail: jeremy.pettit@fiu.edu. *Application contact:* Nanett Rojas, Manager, Admissions Operations, 305-348-7464, Fax: 305-348-7441, E-mail: gradadm@fiu.edu.

George Mason University, College of Humanities and Social Sciences, Department of Psychology, Fairfax, VA 22030. Offers applied developmental psychology (MA, PhD); clinical psychology (PhD); cognitive and behavioral neuroscience (MA, PhD); cognitive neuroscience (Certificate); human factors/applied cognition (MA, PhD, Certificate), including transportation human factors (Certificate), usability (Certificate); industrial/organizational psychology (MA, PhD). *Accreditation:* APA. *Degree requirements:* For master's, comprehensive exam, thesis or practicum research; for doctorate, comprehensive exam, thesis/dissertation, 2nd-year project. *Entrance requirements:* For master's, GRE, 2 official transcripts; goals statement; 15 undergraduate credits in concentration for which the applicant is applying; for doctorate, GRE, 3 letters of recommendation; resume; goals statement; minimum GPA of 3.0 overall for last 60 undergraduate credits, 3.25 in psychology courses; 15 undergraduate credits in concentration for which the applicant is applying; 2 official transcripts; for Certificate, GRE, 2 official transcripts; expanded goals statement; 3 letters of recommendation. Additional exam requirements/recommendations for international students: required—TOEFL (minimum score 575 paper-based; 88 iBT), IELTS (minimum score 6.5), PTE (minimum score 59). Electronic applications accepted.

The Graduate Center, City University of New York, Graduate Studies, Program in Psychology, New York, NY 10016-4039. Offers basic applied neurocognition (PhD); biopsychology (PhD); clinical psychology (PhD); developmental psychology (PhD); environmental psychology (PhD); experimental psychology (PhD); industrial psychology (PhD); learning processes (PhD); neuropsychology (PhD); psychology (PhD); social personality (PhD). *Degree requirements:* For doctorate, one foreign language, thesis/dissertation. *Entrance requirements:* For doctorate, GRE General Test. Additional exam requirements/recommendations for international students: required—TOEFL. Electronic applications accepted.

Grand Canyon University, College of Doctoral Studies, Phoenix, AZ 85017-1097. Offers data analytics (DBA); general psychology (PhD), including cognition and instruction, industrial and organizational psychology, integrating technology, learning, and psychology, performance psychology; management (DBA); marketing (DBA); organizational leadership (Ed D), including behavioral health, Christian ministry, health care administration, organizational development. *Degree requirements:* For doctorate, comprehensive exam, thesis/dissertation. *Entrance requirements:* For doctorate, minimum GPA of 3.4 on earned advanced degree from regionally-accredited institution; transcripts; goals statement.

Hofstra University, College of Liberal Arts and Sciences, Programs in Psychology, Hempstead, NY 11549. Offers applied organizational psychology (PhD); clinical psychology (PhD); industrial/organizational psychology (MA); school-community psychology (Psy D). *Accreditation:* APA. *Program availability:* Part-time, evening/weekend. *Students:* 193 full-time (138 women), 22 part-time (10 women); includes 42 minority (6 Black or African American, non-Hispanic/Latino; 1 American Indian or Alaska Native, non-Hispanic/Latino; 9 Asian, non-Hispanic/Latino; 23 Hispanic/Latino; 3 Two or more races, non-Hispanic/Latino), 21 international. Average age 26. 338 applicants, 36% accepted, 61 enrolled. In 2019, 60 master's, 33 doctorates awarded. Terminal master's awarded for partial completion of doctoral program. *Degree requirements:* For master's, comprehensive exam, thesis optional, internship, minimum GPA of 3.0; for doctorate, comprehensive exam, thesis/dissertation, 1st year qualifying examination, 2nd year research project, successful practicum/externship placements, written presentation and successful oral defense of dissertation, completion of full-time internship. *Entrance requirements:* For master's, GRE General Test, minimum GPA of 3.0, essay, interview; for doctorate, GRE General Test, GRE Subject Test (psychology), 3 letters of recommendation, interview, essay, curriculum vitae. Additional exam requirements/recommendations for international students: required—TOEFL (minimum score 550 paper-based; 80 iBT); recommended—IELTS (minimum score 6.5). *Application deadline:* For fall admission, 12/31 for domestic and international students. Application fee: $75. Electronic applications accepted. *Expenses: Tuition:* Full-time $25,164; part-time $1398 per credit. *Required fees:* $580; $165 per semester. Tuition and fees vary according to course load, degree level and program. *Financial support:* In 2019–20, 152 students received support, including 125 fellowships with full and partial tuition reimbursements available (averaging $8,256 per year), 4 research assistantships with full and partial tuition reimbursements available (averaging $5,531 per year); career-related internships or fieldwork, Federal Work-Study, institutionally sponsored loans, scholarships/grants, traineeships, tuition waivers (full and partial), unspecified assistantships, and scholarships and endowed scholarships also available. Support available to part-time students. Financial award applicants required to submit FAFSA. *Unit head:* Dr. Craig Johnson, Chairperson, 516-463-5636, E-mail: craig.a.johnson@hofstra.edu. *Application contact:* Sunil Samuel, Assistant Vice President of Admissions, 516-463-4723, Fax: 516-463-4664, E-mail: graduateadmission@hofstra.edu.
Website: http://www.hofstra.edu/hclas

Illinois Institute of Technology, Graduate College, Lewis College of Human Sciences, Department of Psychology, Chicago, IL 60616. Offers clinical psychology (PhD); industrial and organizational psychology (PhD); personnel and human resource development (MS); rehabilitation and mental health counseling (MS); rehabilitation counseling education (PhD). *Accreditation:* APA (one or more programs are accredited); CORE. *Program availability:* Part-time, evening/weekend. Terminal master's awarded for partial completion of doctoral program. *Degree requirements:* For master's, thesis (for some programs); for doctorate, comprehensive exam, thesis/dissertation, minimum of 107 credit hours, 1-year full-time internship. *Entrance requirements:* For master's, GRE General Test (minimum score 298 Quantitative and Verbal, 3.0 Analytical Writing), minimum GPA of 3.0; 3 letters of recommendation; bachelor's degree from accredited institution (for personnel and human resource development); for doctorate, GRE General Test (minimum score 298 Quantitative and Verbal, 3.0 Analytical Writing), bachelor's or master's degree from accredited institution, recommendations. Additional exam requirements/recommendations for international students: required—TOEFL (minimum score 550 paper-based; 80 iBT). Electronic applications accepted.

Illinois State University, Graduate School, College of Arts and Sciences, Department of Psychology, Normal, IL 61790. Offers psychology (MA, MS), including clinical-counseling psychology, cognitive and behavioral sciences, developmental psychology, industrial/organizational-social psychology; school psychology (PhD, SSP). *Accreditation:* APA. *Faculty:* 32 full-time (14 women), 6 part-time/adjunct (5 women).

Industrial and Organizational Psychology

Students: 92 full-time (77 women), 18 part-time (14 women). Average age 25. 154 applicants, 32% accepted, 37 enrolled. In 2019, 27 master's, 3 doctorates, 5 other advanced degrees awarded. *Degree requirements:* For master's, thesis or alternative; for doctorate, variable foreign language requirement, thesis/dissertation, 2 terms of residency, internship, practicum. *Entrance requirements:* For master's, GRE General Test, GRE Subject Test, minimum GPA of 3.0 in last 60 hours of course work; for doctorate, GRE General Test. *Application deadline:* Applications are processed on a rolling basis. Application fee: $50. *Expenses: Tuition, area resident:* Full-time $7956; part-time $9767 per year. Tuition, nonresident: full-time $9233; part-time $17,592 per year. *Required fees:* $1797. *Financial support:* In 2019–20, 26 research assistantships, 34 teaching assistantships were awarded; tuition waivers (full) and unspecified assistantships also available. Financial award application deadline: 4/1. *Unit head:* Dr. J Scott Jordan, Department Chair, 309-438-2484, E-mail: jsjorda@illinoisState.edu. *Application contact:* Dr. Karen Mark, Graduate Coordinator, 309-438-8130, E-mail: kimark@ilstu.edu.
Website: http://psychology.illinoisstate.edu/

Indiana University-Purdue University Indianapolis, School of Science, Department of Psychology, Indianapolis, IN 46202-3275. Offers addiction neuroscience (PhD); applied social and organizational psychology (PhD); clinical psychology (PhD); industrial/organizational psychology (MS). *Accreditation:* APA (one or more programs are accredited). Terminal master's awarded for partial completion of doctoral program. *Degree requirements:* For master's, thesis; for doctorate, thesis/dissertation. *Entrance requirements:* For master's, GRE General Test, minimum undergraduate GPA of 3.0; for doctorate, GRE General Test, GRE Subject Test (clinical psychology), minimum undergraduate GPA of 3.2. Additional exam requirements/recommendations for international students: required—TOEFL (minimum score 567 paper-based; 86 iBT), IELTS (minimum score 6.5). Electronic applications accepted.

Inter American University of Puerto Rico, Metropolitan Campus, Graduate Programs, Program in Psychology, San Juan, PR 00919-1293. Offers counseling psychology (MA, PhD); industrial/organizational psychology (MA, PhD); labor relations (MA); school psychology (MA, PhD). *Degree requirements:* For master's, comprehensive exam. *Entrance requirements:* For master's, GRE or EXADEP, interview. Electronic applications accepted.

Iona College, School of Arts and Science, Department of Psychology, New Rochelle, NY 10801-1890. Offers general-experimental psychology (MA); human resources (Certificate); industrial-organizational psychology (MA); mental health counseling (MA); organizational behavior (Certificate); psychology (MA); school psychology (MA). *Program availability:* Part-time. *Faculty:* 8 full-time (4 women), 12 part-time/adjunct (8 women). *Students:* 71 full-time (64 women), 41 part-time (34 women); includes 51 minority (12 Black or African American, non-Hispanic/Latino; 5 Asian, non-Hispanic/Latino; 28 Hispanic/Latino; 1 Native Hawaiian or other Pacific Islander, non-Hispanic/Latino; 5 Two or more races, non-Hispanic/Latino), 3 international. Average age 25. 104 applicants, 85% accepted, 34 enrolled. In 2019, 29 master's, 15 other advanced degrees awarded. *Degree requirements:* For master's, thesis (for some programs), literature review (for some programs). *Entrance requirements:* For master's, BA in psychology including 3 credits each in psychology statistics and experimental research methods, or 9 credits in psychology including 3 credits each in psychology statistics, psychology research methods and upper-level coursework. Additional exam requirements/recommendations for international students: required—TOEFL (minimum score 550 paper-based), IELTS (minimum score 6.5). *Application deadline:* For fall admission, 8/15 for domestic students, 5/1 for international students; for spring admission, 1/15 for domestic students, 9/1 for international students. Applications are processed on a rolling basis. Electronic applications accepted. *Financial support:* In 2019–20, 51 students received support, including 4 research assistantships with partial tuition reimbursements available (averaging $10,143 per year); scholarships/grants, tuition waivers (partial), and unspecified assistantships also available. Support available to part-time students. Financial award application deadline: 4/15; financial award applicants required to submit FAFSA. *Unit head:* Colleen Jacobsen, PhD, Chair, 914-637-2770, E-mail: cjacobsen@iona.edu. *Application contact:* Shantell Smith, Associate Director of Graduate Admissions, Arts and Science, 914-633-2440, Fax: 914-633-2277, E-mail: ssmith@iona.edu.
Website: http://www.iona.edu/Academics/School-of-Arts-Science/Departments/Psychology/Graduate-Programs.aspx

Kean University, College of Liberal Arts, Program in Psychology, Union, NJ 07083. Offers human behavior and organizational psychology (MA); psychological services (MA). *Program availability:* Part-time. *Faculty:* 18 full-time (14 women). *Students:* 68 full-time (56 women), 52 part-time (40 women); includes 70 minority (32 Black or African American, non-Hispanic/Latino; 5 Asian, non-Hispanic/Latino; 32 Hispanic/Latino; 1 Two or more races, non-Hispanic/Latino), 4 international. Average age 28. 68 applicants, 84% accepted, 42 enrolled. In 2019, 52 master's awarded. *Degree requirements:* For master's, comprehensive exam, research component, two semesters of advanced seminar. *Entrance requirements:* For master's, GRE General Test, minimum GPA of 3.0; official transcripts from all institutions attended; two letters of recommendation; professional resume/curriculum vitae; 12 credits in behavioral sciences on the undergraduate level. Additional exam requirements/recommendations for international students: required—TOEFL (minimum score 550 paper-based; 79 iBT), IELTS (minimum score 6.5). *Application deadline:* For fall admission, 6/30 for domestic and international students; for spring admission, 12/1 for domestic and international students. Applications are processed on a rolling basis. Application fee: $75. Electronic applications accepted. *Expenses:* Tuition, state resident: full-time $15,326; part-time $748 per credit. Tuition, nonresident: full-time $20,288; part-time $902 per credit. *Required fees:* $2149.50; $91.25 per credit. Tuition and fees vary according to course level, course load, degree level and program. *Financial support:* Scholarships/grants and unspecified assistantships available. Financial award applicants required to submit FAFSA. *Unit head:* Dr. Zandra Gratz, Program Coordinator, 908-737-5881, E-mail: zgratz@kean.edu. *Application contact:* Amy Clark, Program Assistant, 908-737-7100, E-mail: gradadmissions@kean.edu.
Website: http://grad.kean.edu/masters-programs/psychological-services

Keiser University, MS in Organizational Psychology Program, Fort Lauderdale, FL 33309. Offers MS.

Keiser University, PhD in Industrial and Organizational Psychology Program, Fort Lauderdale, FL 33309. Offers PhD.

La Salle University, School of Arts and Sciences, Program in Counseling and Family Therapy, Philadelphia, PA 19141-1199. Offers industrial/organizational psychology (MA); marriage and family therapy (MA); professional clinical counseling (MA). *Accreditation:* ACA; APA. *Program availability:* Part-time, evening/weekend. *Degree requirements:* For master's, comprehensive exam. *Entrance requirements:* For master's, GRE or MAT (waived for applicants that already possess a master's degree in any field or for applicants that have a cumulative GPA of 3.5 or higher), minimum of 15 hours in psychology, counseling, or marriage and family studies; minimum GPA of 3.0; three letters of recommendation; personal statement; work experience (paid or volunteer). Additional exam requirements/recommendations for international students: required—TOEFL. Electronic applications accepted. Application fee is waived when completed online. *Expenses:* Contact institution.

Liberty University, School of Behavioral Sciences, Lynchburg, VA 24515. Offers applied psychology (MA), including developmental psychology (MA, MS), industrial/organizational psychology (MA, MS); clinical mental health counseling (MA); community care and counseling (Ed D), including marriage and family counseling, pastoral care and counseling, traumatology; counselor education and supervision (PhD); human services counseling (MA), including addictions and recovery, business, child and family law, Christian ministries, criminal justice, crisis response and trauma, executive leadership, health and wellness, life coaching, marriage and family, military resilience; marriage and family counseling (MA); marriage and family therapy (MA); military resilience (Certificate); pastoral counseling (MA), including addictions and recovery, community chaplaincy, crisis response and trauma, discipleship and church ministry, leadership, life coaching, marriage and family, marriage and family studies, military resilience, parenting and child/adolescent, pastoral counseling, theology; professional counseling (MA); psychology (MS), including developmental psychology (MA, MS), industrial/organizational psychology (MA, MS); school counseling (M Ed). *Program availability:* Part-time, online learning. *Students:* 3,786 full-time (3,065 women), 5,193 part-time (4,081 women); includes 2,733 minority (1,967 Black or African American, non-Hispanic/Latino; 48 American Indian or Alaska Native, non-Hispanic/Latino; 103 Asian, non-Hispanic/Latino; 349 Hispanic/Latino; 19 Native Hawaiian or other Pacific Islander, non-Hispanic/Latino; 247 Two or more races, non-Hispanic/Latino), 133 international. Average age 38. 13,324 applicants, 28% accepted, 2,163 enrolled. In 2019, 2,322 master's, 19 doctorates, 112 other advanced degrees awarded. *Entrance requirements:* For master's, Official bachelor's degree transcripts with a 2.0 GPA or higher. *Application deadline:* Applications are processed on a rolling basis. Application fee: $50. Electronic applications accepted. *Expenses: Tuition:* Full-time $545; part-time $410 per credit hour. One-time fee: $50. *Financial support:* In 2019–20, 1,003 students received support. Teaching assistantships and Federal Work-Study available. Financial award applicants required to submit FAFSA. *Unit head:* Dr. Kenyon Knapp, Dean, School of Behavioral Services, E-mail: kcknapp@liberty.edu. *Application contact:* Jay Bridge, Director of Admissions, 800-424-9595, Fax: 800-628-7977, E-mail: gradadmissions@liberty.edu.
Website: https://www.liberty.edu/behavioral-sciences/

London Metropolitan University, Graduate Programs, London, United Kingdom. Offers applied psychology (M Sc); architecture (MA); biomedical science (M Sc); blood science (M Sc); cancer pharmacology (M Sc); computer networking and cyber security (M Sc); computing and information systems (M Sc); conference interpreting (MA); counter-terrorism studies (M Sc); creative, digital and professional writing (MA); crime, violence and prevention (M Sc); criminology (M Sc); curating contemporary art (MA); data analytics (M Sc); digital media (MA); early childhood studies (MA); education (MA, Ed D); financial services law, regulation and compliance (LL M); food science (M Sc); forensic psychology (M Sc); health and social care management and policy (M Sc); human nutrition (M Sc); human resource management (MA); human rights and international conflict (MA); information technology (M Sc); intelligence and security studies (M Sc); international oil, gas and energy law (LL M); international relations (MA); interpreting (MA); learning and teaching in higher education (MA); legal practice (LL M); media and entertainment law (LL M); organizational and consumer psychology (M Sc); psychological therapy (M Sc); psychology of mental health (M Sc); public health (M Sc); public policy and management (MPA); security studies (M Sc); social work (M Sc); spatial planning and urban design (MA); sports therapy (M Sc); supporting older children and young people with dyslexia (MA); teaching languages (MA), including Arabic, English; translation (MA); woman and child abuse (MA).

Louisiana Tech University, Graduate School, College of Education, Ruston, LA 71272. Offers counseling and guidance (MA), including clinical mental health counseling, human services, orientation and mobility; counseling psychology (PhD); curriculum and instruction (M Ed); cyber education (Graduate Certificate); dynamics of domestic and family violence (Graduate Certificate); early childhood education - PreK-3 (MAT); educational leadership (M Ed, Ed D); elementary education and special education mild/moderate grades 1-5 (MAT); higher education administration (Graduate Certificate); industrial/organizational psychology (MA, PhD); kinesiology (MS); middle school education (MAT), including mathematics; orientation and mobility (Graduate Certificate); rehabilitation teaching for the blind (Graduate Certificate); secondary education (MAT), including agriculture, biology, business, chemistry, English; special education: visually impaired (MAT); teacher leader education (Graduate Certificate); visual impairments - blind education (Graduate Certificate). *Accreditation:* NCATE. *Program availability:* Part-time. *Degree requirements:* For master's, thesis; for doctorate, thesis/dissertation. *Entrance requirements:* For master's and doctorate, GRE General Test. Additional exam requirements/recommendations for international students: required—TOEFL (minimum score 550 paper-based; 80 iBT), IELTS (minimum score 6.5). Electronic applications accepted. *Expenses: Tuition, area resident:* Full-time $6592; part-time $400 per credit. Tuition, state resident: full-time $6592; part-time $400 per credit. Tuition, nonresident: full-time $13,333; part-time $681 per credit. *International tuition:* $13,333 full-time. *Required fees:* $3011; $3011 per unit.

Meredith College, School of Education, Health and Human Sciences, Master of Arts in Psychology Program, Raleigh, NC 27607-5298. Offers industrial/organizational psychology (MA). *Students:* 20 full-time (17 women), 7 part-time (6 women); includes 8 minority (4 Black or African American, non-Hispanic/Latino; 1 Asian, non-Hispanic/Latino; 3 Hispanic/Latino). Average age 30. *Degree requirements:* For master's, internship. *Entrance requirements:* For master's, GRE, official transcripts, two recommendation forms, resume or curriculum vitae, essay. *Application deadline:* Applications are processed on a rolling basis. Application fee: $60. *Unit head:* Lori Kelley, Program Manager/Admissions Counselor, 919-760-8723, E-mail: lrkelley@meredith.edu. *Application contact:* Lori Kelley, Program Manager/Admissions Counselor, 919-760-8723, E-mail: lrkelley@meredith.edu.
Website: https://www.meredith.edu/master-of-psychology

Middle Tennessee State University, College of Graduate Studies, College of Behavioral and Health Sciences, Department of Psychology, Murfreesboro, TN 37132. Offers clinical psychology (MA); experimental psychology (MA); industrial/organizational psychology (MA); psychology (MA, Ed S); quantitative psychology (MA); school psychology (MA). *Program availability:* Part-time, evening/weekend, online learning. *Degree requirements:* For master's, comprehensive exam, thesis. *Entrance requirements:* For master's, GRE. Additional exam requirements/recommendations for international students: required—TOEFL (minimum score 525 paper-based; 71 iBT) or IELTS (minimum score 6). Electronic applications accepted.

Minnesota State University Mankato, College of Graduate Studies and Research, College of Social and Behavioral Sciences, Department of Psychology, Mankato, MN 56001. Offers clinical psychology (MA); industrial/organizational psychology (MA); school psychology (Psy D). *Program availability:* Part-time. *Degree requirements:* For master's, one foreign language, comprehensive exam, thesis (for some programs). *Entrance requirements:* For master's, GRE General Test, GRE Subject Test (clinical psychology), minimum GPA of 3.0 during previous 2 years, 3 letters of reference. Additional exam requirements/recommendations for international students: required—TOEFL. Electronic applications accepted.

Missouri State University, Graduate College, College of Health and Human Services, Department of Psychology, Springfield, MO 65897. Offers applied behavior analysis (MS); clinical psychology (MS); experimental psychology (MS); forensic child psychology (Certificate); industrial/organizational psychology (MS). *Degree requirements:* For master's, comprehensive exam, thesis. *Entrance requirements:* For master's, GRE General Test, GRE Subject Test, minimum GPA of 3.25 in major, 3.0 overall; 20 hours of course work in psychology. Additional exam requirements/recommendations for international students: required—TOEFL (minimum score 550 paper-based; 79 iBT), IELTS (minimum score 6). Electronic applications accepted. *Expenses: Tuition, area resident:* Full-time $2600; part-time $1735 per credit hour. Tuition, nonresident: full-time $5240; part-time $3495 per credit hour. *International tuition:* $5240 full-time. *Required fees:* $530; $438 per credit hour. Tuition and fees vary according to class time, course level, course load, degree level, campus/location and program.

Missouri University of Science and Technology, Department of Psychological Science, Rolla, MO 65409. Offers industrial-organizational psychology (MS). *Expenses:* Tuition, state resident: full-time $7839; part-time $435.50 per credit hour. Tuition, nonresident: full-time $22,169; part-time $1231.60 per credit hour. *International tuition:* $22,169 full-time. *Required fees:* $649.76. One-time fee: $119. Tuition and fees vary according to course load and program.

Montclair State University, The Graduate School, College of Humanities and Social Sciences, Program in Industrial and Organizational Psychology, Montclair, NJ 07043-1624. Offers MA. *Program availability:* Part-time, evening/weekend. *Degree requirements:* For master's, thesis. *Entrance requirements:* For master's, GRE General Test, 2 letters of recommendation, essay. Additional exam requirements/recommendations for international students: required—TOEFL (minimum score 83 iBT), IELTS (minimum score 6.5). Electronic applications accepted.

New York University, Graduate School of Arts and Science, Department of Psychology, New York, NY 10012-1019. Offers cognition and perception (PhD); general psychology (MA); industrial/organizational psychology (MA); psychotherapy and psychoanalysis (Advanced Certificate); social psychology (PhD). *Program availability:* Part-time. Terminal master's awarded for partial completion of doctoral program. *Degree requirements:* For master's, comprehensive exam, thesis or alternative; for doctorate, thesis/dissertation. *Entrance requirements:* For master's and doctorate, GRE General Test. Additional exam requirements/recommendations for international students: required—TOEFL, IELTS.

North Carolina State University, Graduate School, College of Humanities and Social Sciences, Department of Psychology, Raleigh, NC 27695. Offers applied social and community psychology (PhD); human factors and applied cognition (PhD); industrial/organizational psychology (PhD); lifespan developmental psychology (PhD); school psychology (PhD). *Accreditation:* APA. *Degree requirements:* For doctorate, comprehensive exam, thesis/dissertation. *Entrance requirements:* For doctorate, GRE General Test, GRE Subject Test (industrial/organizational psychology), MAT (recommended), minimum GPA of 3.0 in major. Electronic applications accepted.

Northern Kentucky University, Office of Graduate Programs, College of Arts and Sciences, Program in Industrial-Organizational Psychology, Highland Heights, KY 41099. Offers industrial psychology (Certificate); industrial-organizational psychology (MS); occupational health psychology (Certificate); organizational psychology (Certificate). *Program availability:* Part-time, evening/weekend. *Degree requirements:* For master's, thesis optional, capstone. *Entrance requirements:* For master's, GRE General Test (minimum scores of 141 verbal, 144 quantitative, and 3.5 writing), bachelor's degree with minimum GPA of 3.0, nine semester hours of psychology coursework, at least one undergraduate course in statistics with minimum B grade, official transcripts, current resume or vita, statement of personal interest, three letters of recommendation; for Certificate, official transcripts, bachelor's degree, minimum undergraduate GPA of 3.0, no grade lower than B on all graduate coursework previously taken that may apply. Additional exam requirements/recommendations for international students: required—TOEFL (minimum score 79 iBT); recommended—IELTS (minimum score 6.5). Electronic applications accepted.

Ohio University, Graduate College, College of Arts and Sciences, Department of Psychology, Program in Organizational Psychology, Athens, OH 45701-2979. Offers PhD. *Degree requirements:* For doctorate, one foreign language, comprehensive exam, thesis/dissertation. *Entrance requirements:* For doctorate, GRE General Test, GRE Subject Test. Additional exam requirements/recommendations for international students: required—TOEFL.

Old Dominion University, College of Sciences, Doctoral Program in Psychology, Norfolk, VA 23529. Offers applied psychological sciences (PhD); human factors psychology (PhD); industrial/organizational psychology (PhD). *Degree requirements:* For doctorate, comprehensive exam, thesis/dissertation, candidacy exam. *Entrance requirements:* For doctorate, GRE General Test, GRE Subject Test, 3 recommendation letters. Additional exam requirements/recommendations for international students: required—TOEFL. Electronic applications accepted. *Expenses:* Contact institution.

Philadelphia College of Osteopathic Medicine, Graduate and Professional Programs, School of Professional and Applied Psychology, Philadelphia, PA 19131. Offers applied behavior analysis (Certificate); clinical health psychology (Post-Doctoral Certificate); clinical neuropsychology (Post-Doctoral Certificate); clinical psychology (Psy D); educational psychology (PhD); mental health counseling (MS); organizational development and leadership (MS); psychology (Certificate); public health management and administration (MS); school psychology (MS, Psy D, Ed S). *Accreditation:* APA. *Faculty:* 19 full-time (11 women), 122 part-time/adjunct (58 women). *Students:* 342 (285 women); includes 108 minority (65 Black or African American, non-Hispanic/Latino; 1 American Indian or Alaska Native, non-Hispanic/Latino; 10 Asian, non-Hispanic/Latino; 14 Hispanic/Latino; 18 Two or more races, non-Hispanic/Latino). Average age 25. 357 applicants, 51% accepted, 113 enrolled. In 2019, 79 master's, 38 doctorates, 16 other advanced degrees awarded. Terminal master's awarded for partial completion of doctoral program. *Degree requirements:* For master's, comprehensive exam (for some programs), thesis (for some programs); for doctorate, comprehensive exam, thesis/dissertation. *Entrance requirements:* For master's, GRE or MAT, minimum GPA of 3.0; bachelor's degree from regionally-accredited college or university; for doctorate, PRAXIS II (for Psy D in school psychology), minimum undergraduate GPA of 3.0; for other advanced degree, GRE (for Ed S). Additional exam requirements/recommendations for international students: required—TOEFL (minimum score 79 iBT). *Application deadline:* Applications are processed on a rolling basis. Application fee: $50. Electronic applications accepted. *Financial support:* In 2019–20, 28 teaching assistantships were awarded; Federal Work-Study, institutionally sponsored loans, and scholarships/grants also available. Financial award application deadline: 3/15; financial award applicants required to submit FAFSA. *Unit head:* Dr. Robert DiTomasso, Chairman, 215-871-6442, Fax: 215-871-6458, E-mail: robertd@pcom.edu. *Application contact:* Johnathan Cox, Associate Director of Admissions, 215-871-6700, Fax: 215-871-6719, E-mail: johnathancox@pcom.edu. Website: pcom.edu

Pontifical Catholic University of Puerto Rico, College of Graduate Studies in Behavioral Science and Community Affairs, Program in Industrial Psychology (Doctorate), Ponce, PR 00717-0777. Offers PhD. *Program availability:* Part-time, evening/weekend. *Entrance requirements:* For doctorate, EXADEP, minimum GPA of 2.75.

Purdue University, Graduate School, College of Health and Human Sciences, Department of Psychological Sciences, West Lafayette, IN 47907. Offers behavioral neuroscience (PhD); clinical psychology (PhD); cognitive psychology (PhD); industrial/organizational psychology (PhD); mathematical and computational cognitive science (PhD). *Accreditation:* APA. *Faculty:* 43 full-time (17 women), 2 part-time/adjunct (both women). *Students:* 69 full-time (55 women), 4 part-time (2 women); includes 18 minority (2 Black or African American, non-Hispanic/Latino; 2 Asian, non-Hispanic/Latino; 11 Hispanic/Latino; 3 Two or more races, non-Hispanic/Latino), 19 international. Average age 28. 314 applicants, 15% accepted, 28 enrolled. In 2019, 12 doctorates awarded. Terminal master's awarded for partial completion of doctoral program. *Degree requirements:* For doctorate, thesis/dissertation. *Entrance requirements:* For doctorate, GRE General Test, minimum undergraduate GPA of 3.0 or equivalent. Additional exam requirements/recommendations for international students: required—TOEFL (minimum score 550 paper-based; 77 iBT); recommended—TWE. *Application deadline:* For fall admission, 12/3 for domestic and international students. Applications are processed on a rolling basis. Application fee: $60 ($75 for international students). Electronic applications accepted. *Financial support:* Fellowships with partial tuition reimbursements, research assistantships with partial tuition reimbursements, teaching assistantships with partial tuition reimbursements, and career-related internships or fieldwork available. Support available to part-time students. Financial award applicants required to submit FAFSA. *Unit head:* Dr. Jefferey D. Karpicke, Head, 765-494-6061, E-mail: karpicke@purdue.edu. *Application contact:* Nancy A. O'Brien, Graduate Contact, 765-494-6067, E-mail: nobrien@psych.pardue.edu. Website: http://www.psych.purdue.edu/

Radford University, College of Graduate Studies and Research, Psychology, MA/MS, Radford, VA 24142. Offers clinical-counseling psychology (MA, MS); experimental psychology (MA); industrial-organizational psychology (MA, MS). *Program availability:* Part-time. *Degree requirements:* For master's, comprehensive exam, thesis (for some programs). *Entrance requirements:* For master's, GRE, minimum GPA of 3.0, 3 letters of reference, essay, resume, official transcripts. Additional exam requirements/recommendations for international students: required—TOEFL (minimum score 550 paper-based; 79 iBT), IELTS (minimum score 6.5). Electronic applications accepted.

Rice University, Graduate Programs, School of Social Sciences, Department of Psychology, Houston, TX 77251-1892. Offers cognitive sciences (MA, PhD); industrial-organizational/social psychology (MA, PhD); psychology (MA, PhD). Terminal master's awarded for partial completion of doctoral program. *Degree requirements:* For master's, thesis; for doctorate, thesis/dissertation. *Entrance requirements:* For doctorate, GRE General Test, minimum GPA of 3.0. Additional exam requirements/recommendations for international students: required—TOEFL. Electronic applications accepted.

Roosevelt University, Graduate Division, College of Arts and Sciences, Department of Psychology, Program in Industrial/Organizational Psychology, Chicago, IL 60605. Offers MA, PhD. Electronic applications accepted.

Sacred Heart University, Graduate Programs, College of Arts and Sciences, Department of Psychology, Fairfield, CT 06825. Offers applied psychology (MS), including community psychology, general applied psychology, industrial-organizational psychology. *Program availability:* Part-time, evening/weekend, online learning. *Degree requirements:* For master's, comprehensive exam, thesis optional. *Entrance requirements:* For master's, minimum overall GPA of 3.0, bachelor's degree from accredited college or university. Additional exam requirements/recommendations for international students: required—TOEFL (minimum score 570 paper-based, 80 iBT), TWE, or IELTS (6.5). Electronic applications accepted. *Expenses:* Contact institution.

St. Cloud State University, School of Graduate Studies, College of Liberal Arts, Program in Industrial-Organizational Psychology, St. Cloud, MN 56301-4498. Offers MS. *Degree requirements:* For master's, thesis or portfolio. *Entrance requirements:* For master's, GRE General Test, minimum GPA of 2.75. Additional exam requirements/recommendations for international students: required—TOEFL (minimum score 550 paper-based) or IELTS (minimum score 6.5). Electronic applications accepted.

Saint Louis University, Graduate Programs, College of Arts and Sciences, Department of Psychology, St. Louis, MO 63103. Offers clinical psychology (MS-R, PhD); experimental psychology (MS-R, PhD); industrial-organizational psychology (PhD); psychology (PhD). *Accreditation:* APA (one or more programs are accredited). *Program availability:* Part-time. *Degree requirements:* For master's, comprehensive exam, thesis; for doctorate, thesis/dissertation, clinical internship (for clinical psychology PhD). *Entrance requirements:* For master's, GRE General Test, interview, letters of recommendation, resume; for doctorate, GRE General Test, interview, letters of recommendation, resumé, transcripts, goal statement. Additional exam requirements/recommendations for international students: required—TOEFL (minimum score 550 paper-based). Electronic applications accepted.

Saint Mary's University, Faculty of Science, Department of Psychology, Halifax, NS B3H 3C3, Canada. Offers applied psychology (M Sc, PhD), including industrial/organizational psychology (M Sc). *Program availability:* Part-time. *Degree requirements:* For master's, thesis, 500-hour internship; for doctorate, comprehensive exam, thesis/dissertation, research project. *Entrance requirements:* For master's and doctorate, GRE General Test.

St. Mary's University, Graduate Studies, Program in Industrial/Organizational Psychology, San Antonio, TX 78228. Offers MA, MS. *Program availability:* Part-time, evening/weekend. *Degree requirements:* For master's, comprehensive exam, thesis optional. *Entrance requirements:* For master's, GRE (minimum combined score on verbal and quantitative sections of 294; no less than 146 on the verbal section or 140 on the quantitative section), bachelor's degree from accredited institution; satisfactory completion of the following prerequisite courses or their equivalent (12 credit hours): general psychology, introductory statistics, research methods or experimental psychology, or upper-level psychology course. Additional exam requirements/recommendations for international students: required—TOEFL (minimum score 550 paper-based; 80 iBT), IELTS (minimum score 6). Electronic applications accepted.

San Diego State University, Graduate and Research Affairs, College of Sciences, Department of Psychology, San Diego, CA 92182. Offers clinical psychology (MS, PhD); industrial and organizational psychology (MS); program evaluation (MS); psychology (MA). *Accreditation:* APA (one or more programs are accredited). Terminal master's awarded for partial completion of doctoral program. *Degree requirements:* For master's, thesis, oral exam; for doctorate, thesis/dissertation. *Entrance requirements:* For master's, GRE General Test, GRE Subject Test, 3 letters of recommendation; for doctorate, GRE General Test, GRE Subject Test, minimum GPA of 3.0, 3 letters of recommendation. Additional exam requirements/recommendations for international students: required—TOEFL. Electronic applications accepted.

Industrial and Organizational Psychology

San Francisco State University, Division of Graduate Studies, College of Science and Engineering, Department of Psychology, San Francisco, CA 94132-1722. Offers clinical psychology (MS); developmental psychology (MA); industrial/organizational psychology (MS); mind, brain, and behavior (MA); school psychology (MS, Credential); social, personality, and affective science psychology (MA). *Expenses: Tuition, area resident:* Full-time $7176; part-time $4164 per year. Tuition, state resident: full-time $7176; part-time $4164 per year. Tuition, nonresident: full-time $16,680; part-time $396 per unit. *International tuition:* $16,680 full-time. *Required fees:* $1524; $1524 per unit. $762 per semester. Tuition and fees vary according to degree level and program. *Financial support:* Teaching assistantships available. Financial award application deadline: 3/1. *Unit head:* Dr. Chris Wright, Chair, 415-338-7555, Fax: 415-338-2398, E-mail: cwright@sfsu.edu. *Application contact:* Dr. Ryan Howell, Department Graduate Program Coordinator, 415-405-2140, Fax: 415-338-2398, E-mail: rhowell@sfsu.edu. Website: http://psychology.sfsu.edu/graduate/application.html

San Jose State University, Program in Psychology, San Jose, CA 95192-0120. Offers clinical psychology (MS); experimental psychology (MA); industrial/organizational psychology (MS); psychology (MA). *Faculty:* 19 full-time (12 women), 2 part-time/adjunct (1 woman). *Students:* 51 full-time (44 women), 30 part-time (21 women); includes 37 minority (2 Black or African American, non-Hispanic/Latino; 14 Asian, non-Hispanic/Latino; 21 Hispanic/Latino), 4 international. Average age 27. 184 applicants, 23% accepted, 31 enrolled. In 2019, 35 master's awarded. *Application deadline:* For fall admission, 2/1 for domestic and international students. Application fee: $70. Electronic applications accepted. *Expenses: Tuition, area resident:* Full-time $7176; part-time $4164 per credit hour. Tuition, state resident: full-time $7176; part-time $4164 per credit hour. Tuition, nonresident: full-time $7176; part-time $4165 per credit hour. *International tuition:* $7176 full-time. *Required fees:* $2110; $2110. *Financial support:* In 2019–20, 22 students received support, including 1 research assistantship (averaging $500 per year); scholarships/grants also available. Financial award application deadline: 5/1; financial award applicants required to submit FAFSA. *Unit head:* Clifton Oyamot, Professor and Chair, 408-924-5650, E-mail: clifton.oyamot@sjsu.edu. *Application contact:* Psychology Department, 408-408-924-5600, E-mail: psychology@sjsu.edu. Website: http://www.sjsu.edu/psych/

Seattle Pacific University, Industrial-Organizational Psychology Program, Seattle, WA 98119-1997. Offers MA, PhD. *Students:* 53 full-time (39 women), 23 part-time (16 women); includes 24 minority (4 Black or African American, non-Hispanic/Latino; 1 American Indian or Alaska Native, non-Hispanic/Latino; 9 Asian, non-Hispanic/Latino; 6 Hispanic/Latino; 4 Two or more races, non-Hispanic/Latino), 2 international. Average age 28. 67 applicants, 43% accepted, 29 enrolled. In 2019, 28 master's, 3 doctorates awarded. *Degree requirements:* For master's, research project; for doctorate, thesis/dissertation, field placement. *Entrance requirements:* For master's, GRE (administered within five years of application to program, with minimum combined score of 950/295 new scoring on verbal and quantitative sections preferred), personal statement; recommendations; language competency; statement of financial support; for doctorate, GRE (administered within five years of application to program, with minimum combined score of 1100/300 new scoring on verbal and quantitative sections preferred), personal statement; recommendations; language competency; statement of financial support. Additional exam requirements/recommendations for international students: required—TOEFL (minimum score 550 paper-based). *Application deadline:* For fall admission, 12/15 for domestic and international students. Application fee: $50. Electronic applications accepted. *Financial support:* Applicants required to submit FAFSA. *Unit head:* Dr. Robert B. McKenna, Chair, 206-281-2629, E-mail: rmckenna@spu.edu. *Application contact:* The Graduate Center, 206-281-2091. Website: http://spu.edu/academics/school-of-psychology-family-community/graduate-programs/industrial-organizational-psychology

South Dakota State University, Graduate School, College of Arts, Humanities and Social Sciences, Department of Psychology, Brookings, SD 57007. Offers industrial/organizational psychology (MS). *Degree requirements:* For master's, thesis, internship.

Southeastern Louisiana University, College of Arts, Humanities and Social Sciences, Department of Psychology, Hammond, LA 70402. Offers psychology (MA), including industrial/organizational psychology. *Program availability:* Part-time. *Faculty:* 7 full-time (5 women). *Students:* 18 full-time (11 women), 7 part-time (4 women); includes 6 minority (1 Black or African American, non-Hispanic/Latino; 2 Asian, non-Hispanic/Latino; 1 Native Hawaiian or other Pacific Islander, non-Hispanic/Latino; 2 Two or more races, non-Hispanic/Latino). Average age 26. 11 applicants, 100% accepted, 5 enrolled. In 2019, 9 master's awarded. *Degree requirements:* For master's, comprehensive exam, thesis optional, 38 hours of psychology course work; either a thesis or non-thesis project. *Entrance requirements:* For master's, GRE; for regular admission status a combined score of 294, for provisional admission status a combined score of 289, 3 letters of reference; 3.0 undergraduate GPA; 18 semester hours of undergraduate credit in psychology and/or educational psychology, including at least 3 semester hours each in a statistics course and in a general experimental (laboratory) course. Additional exam requirements/recommendations for international students: required—TOEFL (minimum score 500 paper-based; 61 iBT). *Application deadline:* For fall admission, 3/15 priority date for domestic and international students; for spring admission, 10/15 priority date for domestic students, 10/1 priority date for international students. Applications are processed on a rolling basis. Application fee: $20 ($30 for international students). Electronic applications accepted. *Expenses: Tuition, area resident:* Full-time $6684; part-time $489 per credit hour. Tuition, state resident: full-time $6684; part-time $489 per credit hour. Tuition, nonresident: full-time $19,162; part-time $1183 per credit hour. *International tuition:* $19,162 full-time. *Required fees:* $2124. *Financial support:* In 2019–20, 15 students received support, including 11 research assistantships with tuition reimbursements available (averaging $9,300 per year); career-related internships or fieldwork, institutionally sponsored loans, traineeships, and unspecified assistantships also available. Financial award application deadline: 5/1; financial award applicants required to submit FAFSA. *Unit head:* Dr. Susan Coats, Department Head, 985-549-2154, Fax: 985-549-6892, E-mail: scoats@southeastern.edu. *Application contact:* Dr. Susan Coats, Department Head, 985-549-2154, Fax: 985-549-6892, E-mail: scoats@southeastern.edu. Website: http://www.southeastern.edu/acad_research/depts/psyc/index.html

Southern Illinois University Edwardsville, Graduate School, School of Education, Health, and Human Behavior, Department of Psychology, Program in Industrial-Organizational Psychology, Edwardsville, IL 62026. Offers MA. *Program availability:* Part-time. *Degree requirements:* For master's, thesis. *Entrance requirements:* For master's, GRE. Additional exam requirements/recommendations for international students: required—TOEFL (minimum score 550 paper-based, 79 iBT), IELTS (minimum score 6.5), Michigan Test of English Language Proficiency or PTE. Electronic applications accepted.

Springfield College, Graduate Programs, Programs in Psychology, Springfield, MA 01109-3797. Offers athletic counseling (MS, CAGS); clinical mental health counseling (M Ed, CAGS); counseling psychology (Psy D); general counseling (M Ed); industrial/organizational psychology (M Ed, CAGS); school counseling (M Ed, CAGS); student personnel administration in higher education (M Ed, CAGS). *Accreditation:* APA. *Program availability:* Part-time. *Degree requirements:* For master's, research project,

portfolio; for doctorate, dissertation project, 1500 hours of counseling psychology practicum, full-year internship. *Entrance requirements:* For doctorate, GRE. Additional exam requirements/recommendations for international students: required—TOEFL (minimum score 550 paper-based); recommended—IELTS (minimum score 7). Electronic applications accepted.

Teachers College, Columbia University, Department of Organization and Leadership, New York, NY 10027-6696. Offers adult education guided intensive study (Ed D); adult learning and leadership (Ed M, MA, Ed D); educational leadership (Ed D); higher and postsecondary education (MA, Ed D); leadership, policy and politics (Ed D); nurse executive (MA, Ed D), including administration studies (MA), professorial studies (MA); private school leadership (Ed M, MA); public school building leadership (Ed M, MA); social and organizational psychology (MA); urban education leaders (Ed D); MA/MBA. *Faculty:* 24 full-time (12 women). *Students:* 272 full-time (178 women), 321 part-time (222 women); includes 239 minority (78 Black or African American, non-Hispanic/Latino; 70 Asian, non-Hispanic/Latino; 71 Hispanic/Latino; 1 Native Hawaiian or other Pacific Islander, non-Hispanic/Latino; 19 Two or more races, non-Hispanic/Latino), 73 international. 761 applicants, 65% accepted, 330 enrolled. *Unit head:* Prof. Bill Baldwin, Chair, 212-678-3043, E-mail: wjb12@tc.columbia.edu. *Application contact:* Kelly Sutton-Skinner, Director of Admission and New Student Enrollment, 212-678-3710, E-mail: kms2237@tc.columbia.edu.

Thomas Edison State University, Heavin School of Arts and Sciences, Program in Liberal Studies, Trenton, NJ 08608. Offers digital humanities (MALS, Graduate Certificate); geropsychology (MALS, Graduate Certificate); industrial-organizational psychology (MALS, Graduate Certificate); learner-designed area of study (MALS); professional communications (MALS, Graduate Certificate). *Program availability:* Part-time, online learning. *Degree requirements:* For master's, final project. *Entrance requirements:* For master's, bachelor's degree from a regionally-accredited college or university; minimum 2 letters of recommendation; 3-5 years of related working experience; current resume. Additional exam requirements/recommendations for international students: required—TOEFL (minimum score 550 paper-based; 79 iBT). Electronic applications accepted.

University at Albany, State University of New York, College of Arts and Sciences, Department of Psychology, Albany, NY 12222-0001. Offers behavioral neuroscience (PhD); clinical psychology (PhD); cognitive psychology (PhD); industrial/organizational psychology (MA, PhD); social-personality psychology (PhD). *Accreditation:* APA (one or more programs are accredited). *Program availability:* Blended/hybrid learning. *Faculty:* 31 full-time (14 women), 6 part-time/adjunct (4 women). *Students:* 68 full-time (44 women), 53 part-time (35 women); includes 30 minority (3 Black or African American, non-Hispanic/Latino; 10 Asian, non-Hispanic/Latino; 11 Hispanic/Latino; 6 Two or more races, non-Hispanic/Latino), 9 international. 253 applicants, 21% accepted, 28 enrolled. In 2019, 22 master's, 11 doctorates awarded. *Degree requirements:* For doctorate, thesis/dissertation. *Entrance requirements:* For master's, transcripts of all schools attended, statement of background and goals, departmental questionnaire, resume, names and contact information for 3 recommenders; for doctorate, GRE General Test, GRE Subject Test, transcripts of all schools attended, statement of background and goals, departmental questionnaire, resume, names and contact information for 3 recommenders. Additional exam requirements/recommendations for international students: required—TOEFL (minimum score 550 paper-based). *Application deadline:* For fall admission, 1/15 for domestic and international students; for spring admission, 11/15 for domestic students. Application fee: $75. Electronic applications accepted. *Expenses: Tuition, area resident:* Full-time $11,530; part-time $480 per credit hour. Tuition, nonresident: full-time $23,530; part-time $980 per credit hour. *International tuition:* $23,530 full-time. *Required fees:* $2185; $96 per credit hour. Part-time tuition and fees vary according to course load and program. *Financial support:* Fellowships, research assistantships, teaching assistantships, and career-related internships or fieldwork available. Financial award application deadline: 2/1. *Unit head:* Christine K. Wagner, Chair, 518-442-4820, Fax: 518-442-4867, E-mail: cwagner@albany.edu. *Application contact:* Michael DeRensis, Director, Graduate Admissions, 518-442-3980, Fax: 518-442-3922, E-mail: graduate@albany.edu. Website: https://www.albany.edu/psychology/

The University of Akron, Graduate School, Buchtel College of Arts and Sciences, Department of Psychology, Program in Industrial/Organizational Psychology, Akron, OH 44325. Offers MA, PhD. Terminal master's awarded for partial completion of doctoral program. *Degree requirements:* For master's, thesis or specialty exam; for doctorate, one foreign language, comprehensive exam, thesis/dissertation. *Entrance requirements:* For master's, GRE General Test, minimum GPA of 2.75, three letters of recommendation, personal statement, curriculum vitae; for doctorate, GRE General Test, minimum graduate GPA of 3.25, three letters of recommendation, personal statement, curriculum vitae. Additional exam requirements/recommendations for international students: required—TOEFL (minimum score 79 iBT), IELTS (minimum score 6.5). Electronic applications accepted.

The University of Alabama in Huntsville, School of Graduate Studies, College of Arts, Humanities, and Social Sciences, Department of Psychology, Huntsville, AL 35899. Offers industrial/organizational psychology (MA); psychology (MA). *Program availability:* Part-time. *Degree requirements:* For master's, comprehensive exam, thesis or alternative, oral and written exams. *Entrance requirements:* For master's, GRE General Test, 15 hours of course work in psychology, minimum GPA of 3.25, sample of written work. Additional exam requirements/recommendations for international students: required—TOEFL (minimum score 500 paper-based; 80 iBT), IELTS (minimum score 6.5). Electronic applications accepted.

University of Central Florida, College of Sciences, Department of Psychology, Program in Industrial/Organizational Psychology, Orlando, FL 32816. Offers MS, PhD. *Students:* 59 full-time (36 women), 4 part-time (3 women); includes 20 minority (3 Black or African American, non-Hispanic/Latino; 4 Asian, non-Hispanic/Latino; 11 Hispanic/Latino; 2 Two or more races, non-Hispanic/Latino), 8 international. Average age 26. 208 applicants, 19% accepted, 23 enrolled. In 2019, 19 master's awarded. *Degree requirements:* For master's, comprehensive exam, thesis, practicum; for doctorate, thesis/dissertation, candidacy examination. *Entrance requirements:* For master's, GRE General Test, bachelor's degree with major in psychology or allied area, or baccalaureate degree with completion of undergraduate courses in statistics and research methods, and preference of four additional upper-division psychology courses (12 credit hours); resume; goal statement; letters of recommendation; for doctorate, GRE General Test, bachelor's or master's degree in psychology or another allied area, resume, personal statement, letters of recommendation. Additional exam requirements/recommendations for international students: required—TOEFL. *Application deadline:* For fall admission, 12/15 for domestic students. Application fee: $30. Electronic applications accepted. *Financial support:* In 2019–20, 38 students received support, including 7 fellowships (averaging $6,457 per year), 11 research assistantships with partial tuition reimbursements available (averaging $6,600 per year), 24 teaching assistantships with partial tuition reimbursements available (averaging $8,191 per year); career-related internships or fieldwork, Federal Work-Study, institutionally sponsored loans, health care benefits, tuition waivers (partial), and unspecified assistantships also available. Financial award application deadline: 3/1; financial award applicants required to submit FAFSA. *Unit head:* Dr. Barbara Fritzsche, Program Director, 407-823-0674, E-mail: barbara.fritzsche@ucf.edu. *Application contact:* Associate Director, Graduate Admissions, 407-823-2766, Fax: 407-823-6442, E-mail: gradadmissions@ucf.edu. Website: http://psychology.cos.ucf.edu/graduate/

University of Connecticut, Graduate School, College of Liberal Arts and Sciences, Department of Psychological Sciences, Storrs, CT 06269. Offers behavioral neuroscience (PhD); biopsychology (PhD); clinical psychology (MA, PhD); cognition and instruction (PhD); developmental psychology (MA, PhD); ecological psychology (PhD); experimental psychology (PhD); general psychology (MA, PhD); industrial/ organizational psychology (PhD); language and cognition (PhD); neuroscience (PhD); social psychology (MA, PhD). *Accreditation:* APA. Terminal master's awarded for partial completion of doctoral program. *Degree requirements:* For master's, comprehensive exam; for doctorate, thesis/dissertation. *Entrance requirements:* For master's and doctorate, GRE General Test, GRE Subject Test. Additional exam requirements/ recommendations for international students: required—TOEFL (minimum score 550 paper-based). Electronic applications accepted.

University of Detroit Mercy, College of Liberal Arts and Education, Detroit, MI 48221. Offers addiction counseling (MA); addiction studies (Certificate); clinical mental health counseling (MA); clinical psychology (MA, PhD); computer and information systems (MS); criminal justice (MA); curriculum and instruction (MA); economics (MA); educational administration (MA); financial economics (MA); industrial/organizational psychology (MA); information assurance (MS); intelligence analysis (MA); liberal studies (MALS); religious studies (MA); school counseling (MA, Certificate); school psychology (Spec); security administration (MS); special education: emotionally impaired/ behaviorally disordered (MA); special education: learning disabilities (MA). *Program availability:* Part-time, evening/weekend. *Degree requirements:* For doctorate, departmental qualifying exam.

University of Guelph, Office of Graduate and Postdoctoral Studies, College of Social and Applied Human Sciences, Department of Psychology, Guelph, ON N1G 2W1, Canada. Offers applied social psychology (MA, PhD); clinical psychology: applied development emphasis (PhD); clinical psychology: applied developmental emphasis (MA); industrial/organizational psychology (MA, PhD); neuroscience and applied cognitive science (MA, PhD). *Degree requirements:* For master's, thesis; for doctorate, comprehensive exam, thesis/dissertation. *Entrance requirements:* For master's, GRE General Test, GRE Subject Test, minimum B+ average during previous 2 years of course work; for doctorate, GRE General Test, GRE Subject Test, minimum A- average. Additional exam requirements/recommendations for international students: required— TOEFL (minimum score 89 iBT). Electronic applications accepted.

University of Houston, College of Liberal Arts and Social Sciences, Department of Psychology, Houston, TX 77204. Offers clinical psychology (PhD); developmental psychology (PhD); industrial/organizational psychology (PhD); psychology (MA); social psychology (PhD). *Accreditation:* APA (one or more programs are accredited). *Degree requirements:* For master's, comprehensive exam, thesis; for doctorate, comprehensive exam, thesis/dissertation. *Entrance requirements:* For master's, GRE General Test, career statement, 3 letters of recommendation; for doctorate, GRE General Test, 3 letters of recommendation. Additional exam requirements/recommendations for international students: required—TOEFL (minimum score 550 paper-based; 79 iBT). Electronic applications accepted.

The University of Manchester, The University of Manchester - Grad School Programmes, Manchester, United Kingdom. Offers accounting and finance (M Sc); business (M Ent); business analysis and strategic management (M Sc); business analytics: operational research and risk analysis (M Sc); business psychology (M Sc); corporate communications and reputation management (M Sc); finance (M Sc); finance and business economics (M Sc); human resource management and industrial relations (M Sc); innovation management and entrepreneurship (M Sc); international business and management (M Sc); international human resource management and comparative industrial relations (M Sc); management (M Sc); marketing (M Sc); operations, project and supply chain management (M Sc); organizational psychology (M Sc); quantitative finance (M Sc). *Program availability:* Blended/hybrid learning. *Students:* 13,395. *Degree requirements:* For master's, variable foreign language requirement, comprehensive exam (for some programs), thesis. *Entrance requirements:* For master's, GMAT/GRE only required for a small number of programmes, US Bachelor's degree with GPA of 3.0- 3.3, depending on the major applied to. Additional exam requirements/recommendations for international students: required—students are required to complete a Secure English Language Test if their first language is not English (some exceptions do apply); recommended—TOEFL (minimum score 100 iBT), IELTS (minimum score 7), TSE. *Application deadline:* For summer admission, 6/30 for domestic and international students. Applications are processed on a rolling basis. Application fee: 50 British pounds. Electronic applications accepted. *Financial support:* Scholarships/grants available. *Application contact:* Daniel Annoot, International Officer, 44 161 306 1634, E-mail: international@manchester.ac.uk. Website: http://www.manchester.ac.uk/usa

University of Maryland, Baltimore County, The Graduate School, College of Arts, Humanities and Social Sciences, Department of Psychology, Program in Industrial/ Organizational Psychology, Rockville, MD 20850. Offers MPS. *Program availability:* Part-time, evening/weekend. *Faculty:* 2 full-time (1 woman), 13 part-time/adjunct (4 women). *Students:* 15 full-time (11 women), 83 part-time (56 women); includes 53 minority (26 Black or African American, non-Hispanic/Latino; 9 Asian, non-Hispanic/ Latino; 12 Hispanic/Latino; 6 Two or more races, non-Hispanic/Latino), 3 international. Average age 27. 78 applicants, 63% accepted, 31 enrolled. In 2019, 39 master's awarded. *Entrance requirements:* Additional exam requirements/recommendations for international students: required—TOEFL (minimum score 99 iBT), IELTS (minimum score 7). *Application deadline:* For fall admission, 4/1 for domestic students, 1/1 for international students. Applications are processed on a rolling basis. Application fee: $50. Electronic applications accepted. *Expenses:* $14,382 per year. *Financial support:* In 2019–20, 4 students received support, including 4 teaching assistantships with full tuition reimbursements available (averaging $14,000 per year); unspecified assistantships also available. *Unit head:* Dr. Elliot Lasson, Program Director, 301-738- 6171, E-mail: elasson@umbc.edu. *Application contact:* Rickeysha Jones, Program Coordinator, 301-738-6285, E-mail: rcjones@umbc.edu. Website: http://www.umbc.edu/shadygrove/io/

University of Maryland, College Park, Academic Affairs, College of Behavioral and Social Sciences, Department of Psychology, College Park, MD 20742. Offers clinical psychology (PhD); developmental psychology (PhD); experimental psychology (PhD); industrial psychology (MA, MS, PhD); social psychology (PhD). *Accreditation:* APA (one or more programs are accredited). *Degree requirements:* For master's, thesis; for doctorate, variable foreign language requirement, comprehensive exam, thesis/ dissertation. *Entrance requirements:* For master's and doctorate, GRE General Test, GRE Subject Test, minimum GPA of 3.5, research and/or work experience, 3 letters of recommendation. Electronic applications accepted.

University of Minnesota, Twin Cities Campus, Graduate School, College of Liberal Arts, Department of Psychology, Program in Industrial/Organizational Psychology, Minneapolis, MN 55455-0213. Offers PhD. *Degree requirements:* For doctorate, comprehensive exam, thesis/dissertation. *Entrance requirements:* For doctorate, GRE General Test, GRE Subject Test (recommended), 12 credits of upper-level psychology courses, including a course in statistics or psychological measurement. Additional exam requirements/recommendations for international students: required—TOEFL (minimum score 550 paper-based; 79 iBT).

University of Nebraska at Omaha, Graduate Studies, College of Arts and Sciences, Department of Psychology, Omaha, NE 68182. Offers applied behavior analysis (Certificate); human resources and training (Certificate); industrial/organizational psychology (MS); psychology (MA, PhD); school psychology (MS, Ed S). *Program availability:* Part-time. *Degree requirements:* For master's, comprehensive exam, thesis (for some programs); for doctorate, comprehensive exam, thesis/dissertation. *Entrance requirements:* For master's and doctorate, GRE, minimum GPA of 3.0, official transcripts, 3 letters of recommendation, statement of purpose, writing sample, resume. Additional exam requirements/recommendations for international students: required— TOEFL, IELTS, PTE. Electronic applications accepted.

University of New Haven, Graduate School, College of Arts and Sciences, Program in Industrial and Organizational Psychology, West Haven, CT 06516. Offers conflict management (MA); industrial organizational psychology (MA); industrial-human resources psychology (MA); organizational development and consultation (MA); psychology of conflict management (Graduate Certificate). *Program availability:* Part-time, evening/weekend. *Students:* 63 full-time (37 women), 3 part-time (2 women); includes 15 minority (8 Black or African American, non-Hispanic/Latino; 2 Asian, non-Hispanic/Latino; 5 Hispanic/Latino), 9 international. Average age 27. 80 applicants, 78% accepted, 31 enrolled. In 2019, 41 master's awarded. *Degree requirements:* For master's, thesis or alternative, internship or practicum. *Entrance requirements:* Additional exam requirements/recommendations for international students: required— TOEFL (minimum score 80 iBT), IELTS, PTE. *Application deadline:* Applications are processed on a rolling basis. Application fee: $50. Electronic applications accepted. Application fee is waived when completed online. *Expenses:* Contact institution. *Financial support:* Research assistantships with partial tuition reimbursements, teaching assistantships with partial tuition reimbursements, career-related internships or fieldwork, Federal Work-Study, scholarships/grants, and unspecified assistantships available. Support available to part-time students. Financial award applicants required to submit FAFSA. *Unit head:* Dr. Eric Marcus, Distinguished Lecturer, 203-932-1242, E-mail: emarcus@newhaven.edu. *Application contact:* Selina O'Toole, Senior Associate Director of Graduate Admissions, 203-932-7337, E-mail: SOToole@newhaven.edu. Website: https://www.newhaven.edu/arts-sciences/graduate-programs/industrial- organizational-psychology/

The University of North Carolina at Charlotte, College of Liberal Arts and Sciences, Department of Psychology, Charlotte, NC 28223-0001. Offers cognitive science (Graduate Certificate); health psychology (PhD), including general; community; clinical; interdisciplinary; industrial/organizational psychology (MA); psychology (MA). *Accreditation:* APA. *Program availability:* Part-time. *Faculty:* 29 full-time (19 women), 2 part-time/adjunct (both women). *Students:* 42 full-time (35 women), 32 part-time (24 women); includes 18 minority (6 Black or African American, non-Hispanic/Latino; 4 Asian, non-Hispanic/Latino; 3 Hispanic/Latino; 5 Two or more races, non-Hispanic/ Latino), 2 international. Average age 27. 164 applicants, 15% accepted, 14 enrolled. In 2019, 31 master's, 5 doctorates, 3 other advanced degrees awarded. *Degree requirements:* For master's, thesis (for some programs); for doctorate, comprehensive exam, thesis/dissertation. *Entrance requirements:* For master's, GRE, GMAT, MAT, bachelor's degree; statement of purpose addressing motivation for degree, preparation for graduate studies and impact of the degree; 2 letters of recommendation; (MA, Psychology) minimum 3.0 GPA in psychology courses; 18 credit hours of undergraduate psychology courses, undergraduate course in statistics; for doctorate, GRE and/or GMAT (Org. Science), at least 18 hours of coursework in psychology including introductory psychology and research methods, undergraduate course in statistics, transcripts of all academic work attempted since high school including evidence of the completion of a bachelor's degree, at least three references, personal statement, resume or curriculum vitae; for Graduate Certificate, enrolled and in good standing in a graduate degree program at UNC Charlotte, or have minimum GPA of 3.0 for undergraduate courses. Additional exam requirements/recommendations for international students: required—TOEFL (minimum score 557 paper-based; 83 iBT), IELTS (minimum score 6.5), TOEFL (minimum score 557 paper-based, 83 iBT) or IELTS (6.5). *Application deadline:* Applications are processed on a rolling basis. Application fee: $75. Electronic applications accepted. *Expenses:* Contact institution. *Financial support:* In 2019–20, 15 students received support, including 9 research assistantships (averaging $10,659 per year), 6 teaching assistantships (averaging $9,454 per year); fellowships, career-related internships or fieldwork, Federal Work-Study, institutionally sponsored loans, scholarships/grants, and unspecified assistantships also available. Support available to part-time students. Financial award applicants required to submit FAFSA. *Unit head:* Dr. Eric Heggestad, Chair & Associate Professor, 704-687-1338, E-mail: edhegges@uncc.edu. *Application contact:* Kathy B. Giddings, Director of Graduate Admissions, 704-687-5503, Fax: 704-687-1668, E-mail: gradadm@uncc.edu. Website: http://psych.uncc.edu

University of Phoenix–Online Campus, College of Social Science, Phoenix, AZ 85034-7209. Offers mediation (Certificate); psychology (MS), including behavioral health, industrial-organizational, psychology. *Program availability:* Evening/weekend, online learning. *Entrance requirements:* Additional exam requirements/ recommendations for international students: required—TOEFL, TOEIC (Test of English as an International Communication), Berlitz Online English Proficiency Exam, PTE, or IELTS. Electronic applications accepted. *Expenses:* Contact institution.

University of Phoenix–Online Campus, School of Advanced Studies, Phoenix, AZ 85034-7209. Offers business administration (DBA); education (Ed S); educational leadership (Ed D), including curriculum and instruction, education technology, educational leadership; health administration (DHA); higher education administration (PhD); industrial/organizational psychology (PhD); nursing (PhD); organizational leadership (DM), including information systems and technology, organizational leadership. *Program availability:* Evening/weekend, online learning. *Degree requirements:* For doctorate, thesis/dissertation. *Entrance requirements:* Additional exam requirements/recommendations for international students: required—TOEFL, TOEIC (Test of English as an International Communication), Berlitz Online English Proficiency Exam, PTE, or IELTS. Electronic applications accepted. *Expenses:* Contact institution.

University of Puerto Rico at Rio Piedras, College of Social Sciences, Department of Psychology, San Juan, PR 00931-3300. Offers clinical psychology (MA); industrial organizational psychology (MA); investigative academic psychology (MA); psychology (PhD); social-community psychology (MA). *Program availability:* Part-time. *Degree requirements:* For master's, comprehensive exam, thesis; for doctorate, comprehensive exam, thesis/dissertation, internship. *Entrance requirements:* For master's, GRE or PAEG, interview, minimum GPA of 3.0; for doctorate, GRE or PAEG, interview, master's degree, minimum GPA of 3.0.

Industrial and Organizational Psychology

University of South Africa, College of Economic and Management Sciences, Pretoria, South Africa. Offers accounting (D Admin, D Com); accounting science (DA); auditing (D Admin, D Com); business administration (M Tech); business economics (D Admin); business leadership (DBL); business management (D Admin, D Com); economic management analysis (M Tech); economics (D Admin, D Com, PhD); human resource development (M Tech); industrial psychology (D Admin, D Com, PhD); logistics (D Com); marketing (M Tech); public administration (D Admin, D Com, DPA, PhD); public management (M Tech); quantitative management (D Admin, D Com); real estate (M Tech); statistics (D Admin, PhD); tourism management (D Admin, D Com); transport economics (D Admin, D Com).

University of South Africa, College of Human Sciences, Pretoria, South Africa. Offers adult education (M Ed); African languages (MA, PhD); African politics (MA, PhD); Afrikaans (MA, PhD); ancient history (MA, PhD); ancient Near Eastern studies (MA, PhD); anthropology (MA, PhD); applied linguistics (MA); Arabic (MA, PhD); archaeology (MA); art history (MA); Biblical archaeology (MA); Biblical studies (M Th, D Th, PhD); Christian spirituality (M Th, D Th); church history (M Th, D Th); classical studies (MA, PhD); clinical psychology (MA); communication (MA, PhD); comparative education (M Ed, Ed D); consulting psychology (D Admin, D Com, PhD); curriculum studies (M Ed, Ed D); development studies (M Admin, MA, D Admin, PhD); didactics (M Ed, Ed D); education (M Tech); education management (M Ed, Ed D); educational psychology (M Ed); English (MA); environmental education (M Ed); French (MA, PhD); German (MA, PhD); Greek (MA); guidance and counseling (M Ed); health studies (MA, PhD), including health sciences education (MA), health services management (MA), medical and surgical nursing science (critical care general) (MA); midwifery and neonatal nursing science (MA), trauma and emergency care (MA); history (MA, PhD); history of education (Ed D); inclusive education (M Ed, Ed D); information and communications technology policy and regulation (MA); information science (MA, MIS, PhD); international politics (MA, PhD); Islamic studies (MA, PhD); Italian (MA, PhD); Judaica (MA, PhD); linguistics (MA, PhD); mathematical education (M Ed); mathematics education (MA); missiology (M Th, D Th); modern Hebrew (MA, PhD); musicology (MA, MMus, D Mus, PhD); natural science education (M Ed); New Testament (M Th, D Th); Old Testament (D Th); pastoral therapy (M Th, D Th); philosophy (MA); philosophy of education (M Ed, Ed D); politics (MA, PhD); Portuguese (MA, PhD); practical theology (M Th, D Th); psychology (MA, MS, PhD); psychology of education (M Ed, Ed D); public health (MA); religious studies (MA, D Th, PhD); Romance languages (MA); Russian (MA, PhD); Semitic languages (MA, PhD); social behavior studies in HIV/AIDS (MA); social science (mental health) (MA); social science in development studies (MA); social science in psychology (MA); social science in social work (MA); social science in sociology (MA); social work (MSW, DSW, PhD); socio-education (M Ed, Ed D); sociolinguistics (MA); sociology (MA, PhD); Spanish (MA, PhD); systematic theology (M Th, D Th); TESOL (teaching English to speakers of other languages) (MA); theological ethics (M Th, D Th); theory of literature (MA, PhD); urban ministries (D Th); urban ministry (M Th).

University of South Florida, College of Arts and Sciences, Department of Psychology, Tampa, FL 33620-9951. Offers psychology (PhD), including clinical psychology, cognition, neuroscience and social psychology, industrial-organizational psychology. *Accreditation:* APA. *Faculty:* 30 full-time (11 women). *Students:* 79 full-time (55 women), 12 part-time (8 women); includes 16 minority (2 Black or African American, non-Hispanic/Latino; 6 Asian, non-Hispanic/Latino; 6 Hispanic/Latino; 2 Two or more races, non-Hispanic/Latino), 8 international. Average age 28. 355 applicants, 5% accepted, 19 enrolled. In 2019, 17 doctorates awarded. *Degree requirements:* For doctorate, comprehensive exam, thesis/dissertation, internship. *Entrance requirements:* For doctorate, a GRE Score Report with a strong preference for GRE V and Q scores each at the 50th percentile or better, statement of purpose; Research Interests and Faculty Matches Form (http://psychology.usf.edu/forms/ResearchInterest.aspx); 3 letters of recommendation; GPA worksheet (http://www.grad.usf.edu/inc/linked-files/gpa.pdf). Additional exam requirements/recommendations for international students: required—TOEFL, TOEFL (minimum score 550 paper-based; 79 iBT) or IELTS (minimum score 6.5). *Application deadline:* For fall admission, 12/1 priority date for domestic and international students. Application fee: $30. Electronic applications accepted. *Expenses:* Contact institution. *Financial support:* In 2019–20, 44 students received support, including 18 research assistantships with tuition reimbursements available (averaging $14,727 per year), 57 teaching assistantships with tuition reimbursements available (averaging $14,543 per year); tuition waivers (partial) and unspecified assistantships also available. Financial award applicants required to submit FAFSA. *Unit head:* Dr. Toru Shimizu, Chairperson, 813-974-0352, Fax: 813-974-4617, E-mail: shimizu@usf.edu. *Application contact:* Dr. Sandra Schneider, Professor and Graduate Program Director, 813-974-0928, E-mail: sandra@usf.edu.
Website: http://psychology.usf.edu/

The University of Tennessee, Graduate School, College of Business Administration, Program in Industrial and Organizational Psychology, Knoxville, TN 37996. Offers PhD. *Degree requirements:* For doctorate, thesis/dissertation. *Entrance requirements:* For doctorate, GRE General Test, minimum GPA of 2.7. Additional exam requirements/recommendations for international students: required—TOEFL. Electronic applications accepted.

The University of Tennessee at Chattanooga, Program in Psychology, Chattanooga, TN 37403. Offers industrial/organizational psychology (MS); research psychology (MS). *Program availability:* Part-time. *Faculty:* 17 full-time (10 women), 4 part-time/adjunct (2 women). *Students:* 44 full-time (35 women), 4 part-time (3 women); includes 6 minority (1 Black or African American, non-Hispanic/Latino; 3 Hispanic/Latino; 2 Two or more races, non-Hispanic/Latino), 1 international. Average age 25. 98 applicants, 24% accepted, 20 enrolled. In 2019, 26 master's awarded. *Degree requirements:* For master's, comprehensive exam (for some programs), thesis (for some programs). *Entrance requirements:* For master's, GRE General Test. Additional exam requirements/recommendations for international students: required—TOEFL (minimum score 550 paper-based; 79 iBT), IELTS (minimum score 6). *Application deadline:* For fall admission, 6/15 priority date for domestic students, 7/1 for international students; for spring admission, 11/1 priority date for domestic students, 11/1 for international students. Applications are processed on a rolling basis. Application fee: $35 ($40 for international students). Electronic applications accepted. *Financial support:* Research assistantships, teaching assistantships, career-related internships or fieldwork, scholarships/grants, and unspecified assistantships available. Support available to part-time students. Financial award application deadline: 7/1; financial award applicants required to submit FAFSA. *Unit head:* Dr. Brian O'Leary, Department Head, 423-425-4283, Fax: 423-425-4284, E-mail: Boleary@utc.edu. *Application contact:* Dr. Joanne Romagni, Dean of the Graduate School, 423-425-4478, Fax: 423-425-5223, E-mail: joanne-romagni@utc.edu.
Website: http://www.utc.edu/psychology/

The University of Texas at Arlington, Graduate School, College of Science, Department of Psychology, Arlington, TX 76019. Offers experimental health psychology (PhD); experimental psychology (MS, PhD); health/neuroscience psychology (MS, PhD); industrial and organizational psychology (MS). *Program availability:* Part-time. Terminal master's awarded for partial completion of doctoral program. *Degree requirements:* For master's, comprehensive exam or thesis; for doctorate, thesis/

dissertation (for some programs). *Entrance requirements:* For master's and doctorate, GRE General Test, minimum GPA of 3.0 in last 60 hours of course work. Additional exam requirements/recommendations for international students: required—TOEFL (minimum score 550 paper-based).

University of the Incarnate Word, School of Professional Studies, San Antonio, TX 78209-6397. Offers communication arts (MAA), including applied administration, communication arts, healthcare administration, industrial and organizational psychology, organizational development; organizational development and leadership (MS); professional studies (DBA). *Program availability:* Part-time, evening/weekend, 100% online, blended/hybrid learning. *Faculty:* 16 full-time (12 women), 41 part-time/adjunct (18 women). *Students:* 503 full-time (236 women), 385 part-time (175 women); includes 571 minority (124 Black or African American, non-Hispanic/Latino; 5 American Indian or Alaska Native, non-Hispanic/Latino; 35 Asian, non-Hispanic/Latino; 382 Hispanic/Latino; 3 Native Hawaiian or other Pacific Islander, non-Hispanic/Latino; 22 Two or more races, non-Hispanic/Latino), 1 international. 670 applicants, 99% accepted, 296 enrolled. In 2019, 429 master's, 5 doctorates awarded. *Degree requirements:* For master's, comprehensive exam (for some programs), thesis or alternative. *Entrance requirements:* For master's, GMAT, GRE, official transcripts from all other colleges attended. Additional exam requirements/recommendations for international students: required—TOEFL (minimum score 560 paper-based; 83 iBT). *Application deadline:* Applications are processed on a rolling basis. Electronic applications accepted. *Expenses:* Tuition: Full-time $11,520; part-time $960 per credit hour. *Required fees:* $1128; $94 per credit hour. Tuition and fees vary according to degree level, campus/location, program and student level. *Financial support:* Scholarships/grants and unspecified assistantships available. Financial award applicants required to submit FAFSA. *Unit head:* Vincent Porter, Dean, 210-8292770, E-mail: porterv@uiwtx.edu. *Application contact:* Julie Weber, Director of Marketing and Recruitment, 210-318-1876, Fax: 210-829-2756, E-mail: eapadmission@uiwtx.edu.
Website: https://sps.uiw.edu/

The University of Tulsa, Graduate School, Kendall College of Arts and Sciences, Department of Psychology, Program in Industrial/Organizational Psychology, Tulsa, OK 74104-3189. Offers MA, PhD, JD/MA. *Program availability:* Part-time. Terminal master's awarded for partial completion of doctoral program. *Degree requirements:* For master's, comprehensive exam, thesis (for some programs), 100-hour internship; for doctorate, comprehensive exam, thesis/dissertation, 100-hour internship. *Entrance requirements:* For master's and doctorate, GRE General Test. Additional exam requirements/recommendations for international students: required—TOEFL (minimum score 577 paper-based; 91 iBT), IELTS (minimum score 6.5). Electronic applications accepted. *Expenses: Tuition:* Full-time $22,896; part-time $1272 per credit hour. *Required fees:* $6 per credit hour. Tuition and fees vary according to course load and program.

University of West Florida, Usha Kundu, MD College of Health, Department of Psychology, Pensacola, FL 32514-5750. Offers applied experimental (MA); counseling (MA); industrial-organizational (MA). *Program availability:* Part-time. *Degree requirements:* For master's, thesis (for some programs). *Entrance requirements:* For master's, GRE, official transcripts; minimum GPA of 3.0; writing sample; three letters of reference; field experience or skill sets; oral interview (for counseling specialization). Additional exam requirements/recommendations for international students: required—TOEFL (minimum score 550 paper-based).

University of Wisconsin–Oshkosh, Graduate Studies, College of Letters and Science, Department of Psychology, Oshkosh, WI 54901. Offers experimental psychology (MS); industrial/organizational psychology (MS). *Degree requirements:* For master's, thesis. *Entrance requirements:* For master's, GRE, 10 semester hours of undergraduate course work in psychology. Additional exam requirements/recommendations for international students: required—TOEFL (minimum score 550 paper-based; 79 iBT). Electronic applications accepted.

Valdosta State University, Department of Psychology, Counseling, and Family Therapy, Valdosta, GA 31698. Offers industrial/organizational psychology (MS); marriage and family therapy (MS); school counseling (M Ed, Ed S). *Accreditation:* AAMFT/COAMFTE. *Program availability:* Part-time, evening/weekend, 100% online, blended/hybrid learning. *Degree requirements:* For master's, thesis or alternative, comprehensive written and/or oral exams; for Ed S, thesis. *Entrance requirements:* For master's, GRE General Test or MAT, GACE; for Ed S, GRE General Test or MAT. Additional exam requirements/recommendations for international students: required—TOEFL (minimum score 523 paper-based); recommended—IELTS. Electronic applications accepted. *Expenses:* Contact institution.

Vanguard University of Southern California, Graduate Program in Organizational Psychology, Costa Mesa, CA 92626. Offers intercultural studies (MS); training and development in organizations (MS).

Walden University, Graduate Programs, School of Psychology, Minneapolis, MN 55401. Offers clinical psychology (MS), including counseling, general program; forensic psychology (MS), including forensic psychology in the community, general program, mental health applications, program planning and evaluation in forensic settings, psychology and legal systems; industrial organizational (MS, PhD), including consulting psychology, forensic (MS), forensic psychology (PhD), general practice, leadership development and coaching (MS), organizational diversity and social change, research evaluation (PhD); online teaching in psychology (Post-Master's Certificate); organizational psychology and development (Postbaccalaureate Certificate); psychology (MS, PhD), including applied psychology (MS), clinical psychology (PhD), crisis management and response (MS), educational psychology, forensic psychology (PhD), general psychology (MS), general psychology research (PhD), general psychology teaching (PhD), health psychology, leadership development and coaching (MS), psychology of culture (MS), psychology, public administration, and social change (MS), social psychology, terrorism and security (MS); psychology respecialization (Post-Doctoral Certificate). *Program availability:* Part-time, evening/weekend, online only, 100% online. Terminal master's awarded for partial completion of doctoral program. *Degree requirements:* For master's, thesis optional; for doctorate, thesis/dissertation, residency. *Entrance requirements:* For master's, bachelor's degree or higher; minimum GPA of 2.5; official transcripts; goal statement (for some programs); access to computer and Internet; for doctorate, master's degree or higher; three years of related professional or academic experience (preferred); minimum GPA of 3.0; goal statement and current resume (for select programs); official transcripts; access to computer and Internet; for other advanced degree, relevant work experience; access to computer and Internet. Additional exam requirements/recommendations for international students: required—TOEFL (minimum score 550 paper-based, 79 iBT), IELTS (minimum score 6.5), Michigan English Language Assessment Battery (minimum score 82), or PTE (minimum score 53). Electronic applications accepted.

Wayne State University, College of Liberal Arts and Sciences, Department of Psychology, Detroit, MI 48202. Offers behavioral and cognitive neuroscience (PhD); clinical psychology (PhD); developmental science (PhD); industrial/organizational psychology (MA, PhD); social personality (PhD). *Accreditation:* APA (one or more programs are accredited). *Faculty:* 40. *Students:* 92 full-time (66 women), 42 part-time (27 women); includes 23 minority (4 Black or African American, non-Hispanic/Latino; 2

Asian, non-Hispanic/Latino; 9 Hispanic/Latino; 8 Two or more races, non-Hispanic/Latino), 10 international. Average age 27. 433 applicants, 15% accepted, 36 enrolled. In 2019, 28 master's, 13 doctorates awarded. Terminal master's awarded for partial completion of doctoral program. *Degree requirements:* For master's, thesis (for some programs); for doctorate, comprehensive exam, thesis/dissertation, training assignments. *Entrance requirements:* For master's, GRE General Test, minimum undergraduate upper-division cumulative GPA of 3.0, courses in psychology and statistics; for doctorate, GRE General Test, bachelor's, master's, or other advanced degree; at least twelve credits in psychology with minimum GPA of 3.0; courses in laboratory psychology and statistical methods in psychology; at least three letters of recommendation; statement of purpose. Additional exam requirements/recommendations for international students: required—TOEFL (minimum score 550 paper-based; 79 iBT), TWE (minimum score 5.5), Michigan English Language Assessment Battery (minimum score 85); recommended—IELTS (minimum score 6.5). Application fee: $50. Electronic applications accepted. *Expenses: Tuition:* Full-time $34,567. *Financial support:* In 2019–20, 93 students received support, including 11 fellowships with tuition reimbursements available (averaging $21,181 per year), 8 research assistantships with tuition reimbursements available (averaging $20,965 per year), 48 teaching assistantships with tuition reimbursements available (averaging $19,952 per year); scholarships/grants, health care benefits, and unspecified assistantships also available. Financial award applicants required to submit FAFSA. *Unit head:* Scott Bowen, PhD, Chair/Professor, 313-577-2803, E-mail: ad4771@wayne.edu. *Application contact:* Alia Allen, Academic Services Officer III, 313-577-2823, E-mail: aallen@wayne.edu.
Website: http://clas.wayne.edu/psychology/

Western Kentucky University, Graduate School, College of Education and Behavioral Sciences, Department of Psychology, Bowling Green, KY 42101. Offers clinical psychology (MA); experimental psychology (MA); general psychology (MA); industrial/organizational psychology (MA); school psychology (Ed S). *Degree requirements:* For master's, comprehensive exam, thesis (for some programs); for Ed S, thesis, oral exam. *Entrance requirements:* For master's, GRE General Test; for Ed S, GRE General Test, minimum GPA of 3.5. Additional exam requirements/recommendations for international students: required—TOEFL (minimum score 555 paper-based; 79 iBT).

Western Michigan University, Graduate College, College of Arts and Sciences, Department of Psychology, Kalamazoo, MI 49008. Offers behavior analysis (MA, PhD); clinical psychology (PhD); industrial/organizational behavior management (MA). *Accreditation:* APA (one or more programs are accredited). *Degree requirements:* For master's, variable foreign language requirement, thesis; for doctorate, 2 foreign languages, comprehensive exam, thesis/dissertation.

William James College, Graduate Programs, Newton, MA 02459. Offers applied psychology in higher education student personnel administration (MA); clinical psychology (Psy D); counseling psychology (MA); counseling psychology and community mental health (MA); counseling psychology and global mental health (MA); executive coaching (Graduate Certificate); forensic and counseling psychology (MA); leadership psychology (Psy D); organizational psychology (MA); primary care psychology (MA); respecialization in clinical psychology (Certificate); school psychology (Psy D); MA/CAGS. *Accreditation:* APA. *Degree requirements:* For master's, comprehensive exam (for some programs); for doctorate, thesis/dissertation (for some programs). Electronic applications accepted.

Wright State University, Graduate School, College of Science and Mathematics, Department of Psychology, Program in Human Factors and Industrial/Organizational Psychology, Dayton, OH 45435. Offers MS, PhD. *Degree requirements:* For master's, thesis; for doctorate, thesis/dissertation.

Xavier University, College of Professional Sciences, Department of Psychology, Cincinnati, OH 45207. Offers clinical psychology (Psy D); industrial-organizational psychology (MA). *Accreditation:* APA (one or more programs are accredited). *Degree requirements:* For master's, one foreign language, comprehensive exam, thesis, internship; for doctorate, one foreign language, comprehensive exam, thesis/dissertation, internship. *Entrance requirements:* For master's, GRE, official transcript; 3 letters of recommendation; for doctorate, GRE General Test; GRE Subject Test in psychology (if no undergraduate degree in psychology), bachelor's or master's degree; 18 semester hours of psychology coursework; minimum GPA of 3.0; work and research experience; official transcript; 3 letters of recommendation; statement of purpose. Additional exam requirements/recommendations for international students: required—TOEFL (minimum score 550 paper-based; 79 iBT), IELTS (minimum score 6.5). Electronic applications accepted. *Expenses:* Contact institution.

Marriage and Family Therapy

Abilene Christian University, College of Graduate and Professional Studies, School of Health and Human Services, Addison, TX 75001. Offers child and adolescent therapy (MMFT); medical family therapy (MMFT); therapy with military families (MMFT); treatment of trauma (MMFT). *Program availability:* Part-time, online only. *Faculty:* 3 full-time (1 woman), 16 part-time/adjunct (11 women). *Students:* 155 full-time (132 women), 63 part-time (53 women); includes 101 minority (56 Black or African American, non-Hispanic/Latino; 3 Asian, non-Hispanic/Latino; 35 Hispanic/Latino; 1 Native Hawaiian or other Pacific Islander, non-Hispanic/Latino; 6 Two or more races, non-Hispanic/Latino), 2 international. 68 applicants, 99% accepted, 45 enrolled. In 2019, 28 master's awarded. *Entrance requirements:* For master's, application; earned bachelor's degree from a regionally accredited college or university or equivalent; official transcript(s) in English of all previous colleges attended; minimum cumulative undergraduate GPA of 3.0 on a 4-point scale; departmental requirements; statement of purpose, 3 letters of recommendation. Additional exam requirements/recommendations for international students: required—TOEFL (minimum score 80 iBT), IELTS (minimum score 6). *Application deadline:* For fall admission, 10/7 for domestic students; for winter admission, 12/20 for domestic students; for spring admission, 2/24 for domestic students; for summer admission, 4/20 for domestic students. Applications are processed on a rolling basis. Application fee: $50. *Expenses:* $825 per hour. *Financial support:* In 2019–20, 56 students received support. Scholarships/grants available. Financial award application deadline: 7/1; financial award applicants required to submit FAFSA. *Unit head:* Dr. Sara Salkil, Program Director, 214-305-9459, Fax: 214-602-5307, E-mail: seb04b@acu.edu. *Application contact:* Graduate Advisor, 855-219-7300, E-mail: onlineadmissions@acu.edu.
Website: https://www.acu.edu/online/graduate/school-of-health-human-services.html

Abilene Christian University, Office of Graduate Programs, College of Biblical Studies, Marriage and Family Studies Department, Abilene, TX 79699. Offers MMFT. *Accreditation:* AAMFT/COAMFTE. *Faculty:* 5 full-time (4 women), 6 part-time/adjunct (4 women). *Students:* 22 full-time (17 women), 1 part-time (0 women); includes 6 minority (3 Black or African American, non-Hispanic/Latino; 3 Hispanic/Latino), 1 international. 44 applicants, 39% accepted, 13 enrolled. In 2019, 18 master's awarded. *Degree requirements:* For master's, comprehensive exam, thesis or alternative, internship. *Entrance requirements:* For master's, GRE General Test, interview, writing sample, official transcripts, recommendations, purpose statement, psychosocial history. Additional exam requirements/recommendations for international students: required—TOEFL (minimum score 80 iBT), IELTS (minimum score 6), PTE (minimum score 51). *Application deadline:* For fall admission, 2/15 priority date for domestic students. Applications are processed on a rolling basis. Application fee: $65. Electronic applications accepted. *Expenses:* $1169 per hour. *Financial support:* In 2019–20, 22 students received support. Research assistantships, career-related internships or fieldwork, and scholarships/grants available. Support available to part-time students. Financial award application deadline: 4/1; financial award applicants required to submit FAFSA. *Unit head:* Dr. Lisa Merchant, Program Director, 325-674-3778, Fax: 325-674-3749, E-mail: lisa.merchant@acu.edu. *Application contact:* Graduate Admissions, 325-674-6911, E-mail: gradinfo@acu.edu.
Website: http://www.acu.edu/on-campus/graduate/college-of-biblical-studies/marriage-and-family-studies.html

Adler University, Doctor of Philosophy (Ph.D.) in Couple and Family Therapy, Chicago, IL 60602. Offers PhD. In 2019, 1 doctorate awarded. *Degree requirements:* For doctorate, Dissertation Required, Practicum; Internship. *Unit head:* Phyllis Horton, Director of Admissions, 312-662-4100, E-mail: admissions@adler.edu. *Application contact:* Phyllis Horton, Director of Admissions, 312-662-4100, E-mail: admissions@adler.edu.

Adler University, Master of Arts (M.A.) in Couple and Family Therapy, Chicago, IL 60602. Offers MA. In 2019, 1 master's awarded. *Degree requirements:* For master's, thesis, Social Justice Practicum during first year; Clinical Practicum during second year. *Unit head:* Phyllis Horton, Director of Admissions, 312-662-4100, E-mail: admissions@adler.edu. *Application contact:* Phyllis Horton, Director of Admissions, 312-662-4100, E-mail: admissions@adler.edu.

Albizu University - Miami, Graduate Programs, Doral, FL 33172. Offers clinical psychology (PhD, Psy D); entrepreneurship (MBA); exceptional student education (MS); human services (PhD); industrial/organizational psychology (MS); marriage and family therapy (MS); mental health counseling (MS); nonprofit management (MBA); organizational management (MBA); school counseling (MS); speech and language pathology (MS); teaching English for speakers of other languages (MS). *Accreditation:* APA. *Program availability:* Part-time, 100% online, blended/hybrid learning. *Faculty:* 28 full-time (21 women), 27 part-time/adjunct (15 women). *Students:* 410 full-time (351 women), 190 part-time (163 women); includes 519 minority (33 Black or African American, non-Hispanic/Latino; 3 Asian, non-Hispanic/Latino; 477 Hispanic/Latino; 6 Two or more races, non-Hispanic/Latino), 21 international. Average age 33. 286 applicants, 66% accepted, 127 enrolled. In 2019, 96 master's, 54 doctorates awarded. Terminal master's awarded for partial completion of doctoral program. *Degree requirements:* For master's, comprehensive exam (for some programs), integrative project (for MBA); research project (for exceptional student education, teaching English as a second language); comprehensive examination for Speech and Language Pathology; for doctorate, comprehensive exam, thesis/dissertation, comprehensive examinations, internship, project/dissertation. *Entrance requirements:* For master's, GRE/EXADEP, bachelor's degree from accredited institution, minimum GPA of 3.0, 3 letters of recommendation, interview, resume, statement of purpose, official transcripts; for doctorate, GRE (for Psy D), 3 letters of recommendation, resume, interview, statement of purpose, official transcripts; bachelor's degree and minimum GPA of 3.25 (for Psy D); master's degree and minimum GPA of 3.0 (for PhD). Additional exam requirements/recommendations for international students: required—Michigan Test of English Language Proficiency. *Application deadline:* For fall admission, 4/1 priority date for domestic students, 5/1 priority date for international students; for spring admission, 11/1 priority date for domestic students, 9/1 priority date for international students. Applications are processed on a rolling basis. Application fee: $50. Electronic applications accepted. Application fee is waived when completed online. *Expenses:* $600 per credit or $620 per credit or $650 per credit (for master's depending on field); $800 per credit or $1,050 per credit (for doctoral depending on program). *Financial support:* In 2019–20, 158 students received support. Federal Work-Study, scholarships/grants, unspecified assistantships, and tuition discounts available. Financial award application deadline: 6/1; financial award applicants required to submit FAFSA. *Unit head:* Dr. Tilokie Depoo, PhD, Chancellor, 305-593-1223 Ext. 3138, Fax: 305-477-8983, E-mail: tdepoo@albizu.edu. *Application contact:* Nancy Alvarez, Director of Enrollment Management, 305-593-1223 Ext. 3136, Fax: 305-593-1854, E-mail: nalvarez@albizu.edu.
Website: www.albizu.edu

Alliant International University–Irvine, California School of Professional Psychology, Program in Couple and Family Therapy, Irvine, CA 92606. Offers MA, Psy D. *Accreditation:* AAMFT/COAMFTE. *Program availability:* Part-time. *Degree requirements:* For doctorate, thesis/dissertation. *Entrance requirements:* For master's, minimum GPA of 3.0, letters of recommendation, interview; for doctorate, letters of recommendation, minimum GPA of 3.0, interview. Additional exam requirements/recommendations for international students: required—TOEFL (minimum score 550 paper-based; 80 iBT), TWE (minimum score 5). Electronic applications accepted.

Alliant International University - Los Angeles, California School of Professional Psychology, Program in Couple and Family Therapy, Alhambra, CA 91803. Offers chemical dependency (MA); gerontology (MA); Latin American family therapy (MA). *Accreditation:* AAMFT/COAMFTE. *Program availability:* Part-time, evening/weekend. Terminal master's awarded for partial completion of doctoral program. *Degree requirements:* For master's, comprehensive exam, 50 hours of professional development activities. *Entrance requirements:* Additional exam requirements/recommendations for international students: required—TOEFL (minimum score 550 paper-based). Electronic applications accepted.

Alliant International University - Los Angeles, California School of Professional Psychology, Psy D Program in Clinical Psychology, Alhambra, CA 91803. Offers clinical health psychology (Psy D); family/child and couple clinical psychology (Psy D); multi-interest option (Psy D); multicultural community-clinical psychology (Psy D).

Accreditation: APA. *Degree requirements:* For doctorate, comprehensive exam, thesis/dissertation. *Entrance requirements:* For doctorate, interview, minimum GPA of 3.0 in both psychology and overall. Additional exam requirements/recommendations for international students: required—TOEFL (minimum score 600 paper-based), TWE. Electronic applications accepted.

Alliant International University–Sacramento, California School of Professional Psychology, Program in Couple and Family Therapy, Sacramento, CA 95833. Offers MA, Psy D. *Accreditation:* AAMFT/COAMFTE. *Degree requirements:* For master's, practicum; for doctorate, thesis/dissertation, practicum. *Entrance requirements:* For master's and doctorate, minimum GPA of 3.0, letters of recommendation, interview. Additional exam requirements/recommendations for international students: required—TOEFL (minimum score 600 paper-based), TWE (minimum score 5). Electronic applications accepted.

Alliant International University - San Diego, California School of Professional Psychology, Program in Couple and Family Therapy, San Diego, CA 92131. Offers marital and family therapy (MA, Psy D). *Accreditation:* AAMFT/COAMFTE. *Program availability:* Part-time. *Degree requirements:* For doctorate, thesis/dissertation. *Entrance requirements:* For master's and doctorate, minimum GPA of 3.0, letters of recommendation, interview. Additional exam requirements/recommendations for international students: required—TOEFL (minimum score 550 paper-based; 80 iBT), TWE (minimum score 5). Electronic applications accepted.

Amberton University, Graduate School, Programs in Counseling, Garland, TX 75041-5595. Offers marriage and family therapy (MA); professional counseling (MA); school counseling (MA). *Entrance requirements:* For master's, minimum GPA of 3.0.

Amridge University, Graduate and Professional Programs, Montgomery, AL 36117. Offers Biblical studies (MA, PhD); Christian ministry (MS); family therapy (D Min); human services (MS); leadership and management (MS); marriage and family therapy (M Div, MA, PhD); ministerial leadership (M Div, MS); New Testament studies (MA); Old Testament studies (MA); professional counseling (M Div, MA, PhD); theology (M Div, D Min). *Program availability:* Part-time, evening/weekend, online learning. *Degree requirements:* For master's, one foreign language, comprehensive exam (for some programs), thesis (for some programs); for doctorate, one foreign language, comprehensive exam (for some programs), thesis/dissertation (for some programs). *Entrance requirements:* For master's, official transcript showing an earned 4-year BA or BS from regionally- or nationally-accredited institution; for doctorate, official transcript showing earned graduate degree from regionally- or nationally-accredited institution; writing sample (e.g. career monograph, published journal article, term paper from master's degree or doctoral dissertation); interview. Additional exam requirements/recommendations for international students: required—TOEFL (minimum score 79 iBT). Electronic applications accepted.

Antioch University New England, Graduate School, Department of Applied Psychology, Keene, NH 03431-3552. Offers autism spectrum disorders (Certificate), including applied behavioral analysis internship, autism spectrum disorders; clinical mental health counseling (MA), including clinical mental health counseling, substance abuse counseling; dance/movement therapy and counseling (M Ed, MA, PMC); marriage and family therapy (MA, PhD, Certificate). *Faculty:* 15 full-time (12 women), 30 part-time/adjunct (25 women). *Students:* 264 full-time (217 women), 79 part-time (64 women); includes 67 minority (25 Black or African American, non-Hispanic/Latino; 2 American Indian or Alaska Native, non-Hispanic/Latino; 8 Asian, non-Hispanic/Latino; 27 Hispanic/Latino; 5 Two or more races, non-Hispanic/Latino), 5 international. Average age 35. 149 applicants, 52% accepted, 77 enrolled. In 2019, 49 master's awarded. *Degree requirements:* For master's, internship, practicum. *Entrance requirements:* For master's, previous course work and work experience in psychology. Additional exam requirements/recommendations for international students: required—TOEFL (minimum score 550 paper-based). *Application deadline:* For fall admission, 7/15 for domestic and international students; for spring admission, 12/1 for domestic and international students. Applications are processed on a rolling basis. Application fee: $50. Electronic applications accepted. *Expenses:* Contact institution. *Financial support:* In 2019–20, 56 students received support. Fellowships, research assistantships, career-related internships or fieldwork, Federal Work-Study, and scholarships/grants available. Financial award application deadline: 6/1; financial award applicants required to submit FAFSA. *Unit head:* Dr. Kevin Lyness, Department Chair, 603-283-2149, E-mail: klyness@antioch.edu. *Application contact:* Admissions, 800-552-8380, Fax: 603-357-0718, E-mail: admissions.ane@antioch.edu.
Website: https://www.antioch.edu/new-england/degrees-programs/counseling-wellness/

Antioch University Seattle, Program in Counseling, Therapy and Wellness, Seattle, WA 98121. Offers clinical mental health counseling (MA); counselor education and supervision (PhD); couple and family therapy (MA). *Program availability:* Part-time, evening/weekend. *Faculty:* 34 full-time (23 women), 26 part-time/adjunct (21 women). *Students:* 150 full-time (129 women), 56 part-time (47 women); includes 37 minority (6 Black or African American, non-Hispanic/Latino; 10 Asian, non-Hispanic/Latino; 13 Hispanic/Latino; 8 Two or more races, non-Hispanic/Latino). Average age 35. 223 applicants, 32% accepted, 69 enrolled. In 2019, 88 master's awarded. *Application deadline:* For fall admission, 9/1 for domestic students; for winter admission, 12/1 for domestic students; for spring admission, 3/1 for domestic students; for summer admission, 6/1 for domestic students. Applications are processed on a rolling basis. Application fee: $50. Electronic applications accepted. *Expenses: Tuition:* Full-time $18,604. *Required fees:* $75. *Unit head:* Kathrine Fort, Chair & Core Faculty, Clinical Mental Health CounselingChair & Core F, 206-268-4875, E-mail: kfort@antioch.edu. *Application contact:* Kathrine Fort, Chair & Core Faculty, Clinical Mental Health CounselingChair & Core F, 206-268-4875, E-mail: kfort@antioch.edu.

Appalachian State University, Cratis D. Williams School of Graduate Studies, Department of Human Development and Psychological Counseling, Boone, NC 28608. Offers clinical mental health counseling (MA); college student development (MA); marriage and family therapy (MA); school counseling (MA). *Accreditation:* AAMFT/COAMFTE; ACA; NCATE. *Program availability:* Part-time. *Degree requirements:* For master's, comprehensive exam (for some programs), thesis optional, internships. *Entrance requirements:* For master's, GRE General Test, 3 letters of recommendation. Additional exam requirements/recommendations for international students: required—TOEFL (minimum score 570 paper-based; 79 iBT), IELTS (minimum score 6.5). Electronic applications accepted.

Arcadia University, College of Arts and Sciences, Department of Psychology, Glenside, PA 19038-3295. Offers applied behavior analysis (MAC); autism (MAC); child/family therapy (MAC); community public health (MAC); counseling/international peace and conflict resolution dual degree (MAC); mental health counseling (MAC); trauma (MAC). *Program availability:* Part-time. *Faculty:* 13 full-time (8 women). *Students:* 30 full-time (27 women), 31 part-time (26 women); includes 17 minority (11 Black or African American, non-Hispanic/Latino; 2 Asian, non-Hispanic/Latino; 1 Hispanic/Latino; 3 Two or more races, non-Hispanic/Latino). In 2019, 18 master's awarded. *Degree requirements:* For master's, practicum. *Entrance requirements:* For master's, test scores are not required of applicants with an earned master's degree or who have a GPA greater than a 3.0. Test scores from the Graduate Record Examination (GRE) or the Miller Analogies Test (MAT), taken within the past five years are required for all other applicants. Additional exam requirements/recommendations for international students: required—TOEFL. *Application deadline:* Applications are processed on a rolling basis. Application fee: $25. Electronic applications accepted. *Expenses:* Contact institution. *Financial support:* Research assistantships, career-related internships or fieldwork, and unspecified assistantships available. Support available to part-time students. Financial award application deadline: 8/15. *Unit head:* Dr. Marianne Miserandino, Chair, 215-572-2183. *Application contact:* 215-572-2925, Fax: 215-572-2126, E-mail: grad@arcadia.edu.

Argosy University, Atlanta, Georgia School of Professional Psychology, Atlanta, GA 30328. Offers clinical psychology (MA, Psy D, Postdoctoral Respecialization Certificate), including child and family psychology (Psy D), general adult clinical (Psy D), health psychology (Psy D), neuropsychology/geropsychology (Psy D); community counseling (MA), including marriage and family therapy; counselor education and supervision (Ed D); forensic psychology (MA); industrial organizational psychology (MA); marriage and family therapy (Certificate); sport-exercise psychology (MA). *Accreditation:* APA.

Argosy University, Chicago, Illinois School of Professional Psychology, Doctoral Program in Clinical Psychology, Chicago, IL 60601. Offers child and adolescent psychology (Psy D); client-centered and experiential psychotherapies (Psy D); diversity and multicultural psychology (Psy D); family psychology (Psy D); forensic psychology (Psy D); health psychology (Psy D); neuropsychology (Psy D); organizational consulting (Psy D); psychoanalytic psychology (Psy D); psychology and spirituality (Psy D). *Accreditation:* APA.

Argosy University, Hawaii, Hawai'i School of Professional Psychology, Program in Marriage and Family Therapy, Honolulu, HI 96813. Offers MA.

Argosy University, Los Angeles, College of Psychology and Behavioral Sciences, Los Angeles, CA 90045. Offers clinical psychology/marriage and family therapy (MA); counseling psychology (Ed D); counseling psychology/marriage and family therapy (MA); forensic psychology (MA).

Argosy University, Northern Virginia, American School of Professional Psychology, Arlington, VA 22209. Offers clinical psychology (MA, Psy D), including child and family psychology (Psy D), diversity and multicultural psychology (Psy D), forensic psychology (Psy D), health and neuropsychology (Psy D); community counseling (MA); counseling psychology (Ed D), including counselor education and supervision; counselor education and supervision (Ed D); forensic psychology (MA).

Argosy University, Orange County, American School of Professional Psychology, Program in Clinical Psychology, Orange, CA 92868. Offers child and adolescent psychology (Psy D); forensic psychology (Psy D); marriage and family therapy (MA).

Argosy University, Orange County, American School of Professional Psychology, Program in Counseling Psychology, Orange, CA 92868. Offers counseling psychology (Ed D); marriage and family therapy (MA).

Argosy University, Tampa, Florida School of Professional Psychology, Program in Clinical Psychology, Tampa, FL 33607. Offers clinical psychology (MA, Psy D), including child and adolescent psychology (Psy D), geropsychology (Psy D), marriage/couples and family therapy (Psy D), neuropsychology (Psy D). *Accreditation:* APA.

Argosy University, Twin Cities, Minnesota School of Professional Psychology, Eagan, MN 55121. Offers clinical psychology (MA, Psy D), including child and family psychology (Psy D), forensic psychology (Psy D), health and neuropsychology (Psy D), trauma (Psy D); forensic counseling (Post-Graduate Certificate); forensic psychology (MA); industrial organizational psychology (MA); marriage and family therapy (MA, DMFT), including forensic counseling (MA). *Accreditation:* AAMFT; AAMFT/COAMFTE; APA.

Arizona State University at Tempe, College of Liberal Arts and Sciences, School of Social and Family Dynamics, Tempe, AZ 85287-3701. Offers family and human development (MS, PhD); infant-family practice (MAS); marriage and family therapy (MAS); sociology (MA, PhD). Terminal master's awarded for partial completion of doctoral program. *Degree requirements:* For master's, thesis or alternative, interactive Program of Study (iPOS) submitted before completing 50 percent of required credit hours; for doctorate, thesis/dissertation, interactive Program of Study (iPOS) submitted before completing 50 percent of required credit hours. *Entrance requirements:* For master's and doctorate, GRE, minimum GPA of 3.0 or equivalent in last 2 years of work leading to bachelor's degree. Additional exam requirements/recommendations for international students: required—TOEFL, IELTS, or PTE. Electronic applications accepted. *Expenses:* Contact institution.

Azusa Pacific University, School of Behavioral and Applied Sciences, Department of Clinical Psychology, Azusa, CA 91702-7000. Offers family psychology (Psy D). *Accreditation:* APA. *Program availability:* Part-time, evening/weekend. *Degree requirements:* For doctorate, comprehensive exam. *Entrance requirements:* Additional exam requirements/recommendations for international students: required—TOEFL (minimum score 600 paper-based). *Expenses:* Contact institution.

Barry University, School of Education, Program in Marital, Couple and Family Counseling/Therapy, Miami Shores, FL 33161-6695. Offers MS, Ed S. *Program availability:* Part-time, evening/weekend. *Degree requirements:* For master's, comprehensive exam, scholarly paper; for Ed S, comprehensive exam. *Entrance requirements:* For master's, GRE General Test or MAT, minimum GPA of 3.0; for Ed S, GRE General Test, minimum GPA of 3.0. Electronic applications accepted.

Bayamón Central University, Graduate Programs, Program in Education, Bayamón, PR 00960-1725. Offers administration and supervision (MA Ed); commercial education (MA Ed); elementary education (K–3) (MA Ed); family counseling (Graduate Certificate); guidance and counseling (MA Ed); pre-elementary teacher (MA Ed); rehabilitation counseling (MA Ed); special education (MA Ed), including attention deficit disorder, education of the autistic, learning disabilities. *Program availability:* Part-time, evening/weekend. *Degree requirements:* For master's, comprehensive exam. *Entrance requirements:* For master's, EXADEP, bachelor's degree in education or related field.

Bethel Seminary, Graduate and Professional Programs, St. Paul, MN 55112-6998. Offers Anglican studies (Certificate); children's and family ministry (MA); Christian studies (Certificate); Christian thought (MA); church planting (Certificate); Greek and Hebrew language (M Div); Greek language (M Div); Hebrew language (M Div); marriage and family therapy (MA, Certificate); mental health counseling (MA); ministry (MA, D Min); ministry practice (Certificate); theological studies (MA, Certificate); transformational leadership (MA); young life youth ministry (Certificate). *Accreditation:* ACIPE. *Program availability:* Part-time, evening/weekend, 100% online, blended/hybrid learning. *Degree requirements:* For master's, variable foreign language requirement, thesis (for some programs); for doctorate, thesis/dissertation. *Entrance requirements:* For master's, letters of reference, transcripts, personal statement; for doctorate, M Div, letters of reference, organizational support; for Certificate, letters of reference, family essay, personal statement, and family of origin paper (for marriage and family therapy). Additional exam requirements/recommendations for international students: required—TOEFL (minimum score 550 paper-based; 87 iBT). Electronic applications accepted. *Expenses:* Contact institution.

Brandman University, School of Arts and Sciences, Irvine, CA 92618. Offers psychology (MA), including counseling, marriage and family therapy, professional clinical counseling; social work (MSW).

Briercrest Seminary, Graduate Programs, Program in Christian Ministries, Caronport, SK S0H 0S0, Canada. Offers leadership (MA); marriage and family counseling (MA); missions (MA); pastoral counseling (MA); worship (MA); youth and family ministry (MA). *Program availability:* Part-time. *Degree requirements:* For master's, comprehensive exam, thesis optional. *Entrance requirements:* Additional exam requirements/ recommendations for international students: required—TOEFL (minimum score 550 paper-based).

Brigham Young University, Graduate Studies, College of Family, Home, and Social Sciences, Marriage and Family Therapy Program, Provo, UT 84602. Offers MS, PhD. *Accreditation:* AAMFT/COAMFTE. *Faculty:* 10 full-time (4 women), 4 part-time/adjunct (2 women). *Students:* 31 full-time (22 women); includes 6 minority (1 Asian, non-Hispanic/Latino; 2 Hispanic/Latino; 3 Two or more races, non-Hispanic/Latino). Average age 23. 102 applicants, 14% accepted, 13 enrolled. In 2019, 9 master's, 2 doctorates awarded. *Degree requirements:* For master's, thesis (for some programs), 500 clinical hours; for doctorate, thesis/dissertation, 500 clinical hours, portfolio. *Entrance requirements:* For master's and doctorate, GRE General Test, minimum GPA of 3.0 in last 60 hours of course work. Additional exam requirements/recommendations for international students: required—TOEFL (minimum score 85 paper-based). *Application deadline:* For fall admission, 12/1 for domestic and international students. Application fee: $50. Electronic applications accepted. *Expenses:* Contact institution. *Financial support:* In 2019–20, 20 research assistantships with partial tuition reimbursements (averaging $8,300 per year), 8 teaching assistantships with partial tuition reimbursements (averaging $21,000 per year) were awarded; career-related internships or fieldwork, scholarships/grants, and tuition waivers (full and partial) also available. Financial award application deadline: 12/1. *Unit head:* Jason Whiting, Program Director, 801-422-0163, Fax: 801-422-0163, E-mail: jason.whiting@byu.edu. *Application contact:* Dr. Lauren A. Barnes, Director of Clinical Training, 801-422-3889, Fax: 801-422-0163, E-mail: lauren_barnes@byu.edu. Website: http://mft.byu.edu

California Lutheran University, Graduate Studies, Department of Psychology, Thousand Oaks, CA 91360-2787. Offers clinical psychology (MS, Psy D); marital and family therapy (MS). *Accreditation:* APA. *Program availability:* Part-time. *Degree requirements:* For master's, thesis or comprehensive exams; for doctorate, thesis/ dissertation, internship. *Entrance requirements:* For master's, GRE General Test, interview, minimum GPA of 3.0; for doctorate, GRE General Test. Electronic applications accepted.

California State University, Chico, Office of Graduate Studies, College of Behavioral and Social Sciences, Department of Psychology, Program in Marriage and Family Therapy, Chico, CA 95929-0722. Offers MS. *Degree requirements:* For master's, oral exam and thesis or analytical review and written exam. *Entrance requirements:* For master's, GRE General Test or MAT, fall admissions only, deadline February 17th. 3 letters of recommendation, 3 departmental recommendation forms, statement of purpose, departmental application. Additional exam requirements/recommendations for international students: required—TOEFL (minimum score 550 paper-based; 80 iBT), IELTS (minimum score 6.5), PTE. Electronic applications accepted.

California State University, Dominguez Hills, College of Health, Human Services and Nursing, Program in Marital and Family Therapy, Carson, CA 90747-0001. Offers MS. *Program availability:* Part-time, evening/weekend. *Degree requirements:* For master's, comprehensive exam. *Entrance requirements:* For master's, minimum GPA of 3.0. Additional exam requirements/recommendations for international students: required— TOEFL (minimum score 550 paper-based). Electronic applications accepted.

California State University, East Bay, Office of Graduate Studies, College of Education and Allied Studies, Department of Educational Psychology, Hayward, CA 94542-3000. Offers counseling (MS), including marriage and family therapy; special education (MS), including mild-moderate disabilities, moderate-severe disabilities. *Program availability:* Part-time. *Degree requirements:* For master's, comprehensive exam, project or thesis. *Entrance requirements:* For master's, GRE or MAT, interview; minimum GPA of 3.0 during previous 2 years of course work; 3 letters of recommendation; valid teaching credential; negative TB test. Additional exam requirements/recommendations for international students: required—TOEFL (minimum score 550 paper-based). Electronic applications accepted.

California State University, Fresno, Division of Research and Graduate Studies, Kremen School of Education and Human Development, Department of Counselor Education and Rehabilitation, Program in Marriage, Family and Child Counseling, Fresno, CA 93740-8027. Offers MS. *Accreditation:* ACA. *Program availability:* Part-time, evening/weekend. *Degree requirements:* For master's, thesis or alternative. *Entrance requirements:* For master's, GRE General Test, MAT, minimum GPA of 3.0. Additional exam requirements/recommendations for international students: required—TOEFL. Electronic applications accepted. *Expenses:* Tuition, state resident: full-time $4012; part-time $2506 per semester.

California State University, Long Beach, Graduate Studies, College of Education, Department of Advanced Studies in Education and Counseling, Long Beach, CA 90840. Offers counseling (MS), including marriage and family therapy, school counseling, student development in higher education; education (MA, Ed D); educational administration (MA, Ed D); educational psychology (MA); special education (MS). *Program availability:* Part-time, evening/weekend. *Entrance requirements:* For master's, GRE General Test, minimum GPA of 2.75. Electronic applications accepted.

California State University, Northridge, Graduate Studies, Michael D. Eisner College of Education, Department of Educational Psychology and Counseling, Northridge, CA 91330. Offers counseling (MS), including career counseling, college counseling and student services, marriage and family therapy, school counseling, school psychology; educational psychology (MA Ed), including development, learning, and instruction, early childhood education. *Accreditation:* ACA (one or more programs are accredited); NCATE. *Program availability:* Part-time, evening/weekend. *Entrance requirements:* For master's, GRE General Test or minimum GPA of 3.0. Additional exam requirements/ recommendations for international students: required—TOEFL.

Cambridge College, School of Psychology and Counseling, Boston, MA 02129. Offers alcohol and drug counseling (Certificate); behavioral health care management (CAGS); marriage and family therapy (M Ed); mental health and school counseling (M Ed); mental health counseling (M Ed); psychological studies (M Ed); rehabilitation counseling (Certificate); school adjustment and mental health counseling (M Ed); school adjustment counseling for mental health counselors (Certificate); school counseling (M Ed); trauma studies (Certificate). *Program availability:* Part-time, evening/weekend. *Degree requirements:* For master's and other advanced degree, thesis, practicum/internship. *Entrance requirements:* For master's, resume, 2 professional references; for other advanced degree, official transcripts, documents for transfer credit evaluation, resume, written personal statement/essay, 2 professional references, health insurance, immunizations form. Additional exam requirements/recommendations for international students: required—TOEFL (minimum score 550 paper-based; 79 iBT), Michigan English Language Assessment Battery (minimum score 85); recommended—IELTS (minimum score 6). Electronic applications accepted. *Expenses:* Contact institution.

Campbellsville University, School of Theology, Campbellsville, KY 42718-2799. Offers marriage and family therapy (MMFT); theology (M Th). *Program availability:* Part-time, evening/weekend, 100% online, blended/hybrid learning. *Degree requirements:* For master's, comprehensive exam, thesis optional. *Entrance requirements:* For master's, GRE General Test, minimum GPA of 3.0 in major, 2.75 overall; 18 hours of undergraduate coursework in Christian studies; college transcripts; letters of recommendation. Additional exam requirements/recommendations for international students: recommended—TOEFL (minimum score 550 paper-based; 79 iBT), IELTS (minimum score 6). Electronic applications accepted. Application fee is waived when completed online. *Expenses:* Contact institution.

Capella University, Harold Abel School of Social and Behavioral Science, Master's Programs in Counseling, Minneapolis, MN 55402. Offers child and adolescent development (MS); general addiction counseling (MS); general marriage and family counseling/therapy (MS); general mental health counseling (MS); general school counseling (MS).

Central Connecticut State University, School of Graduate Studies, School of Education and Professional Studies, Department of Counselor Education and Family Therapy, New Britain, CT 06050-4010. Offers marriage and family therapy (MS); professional counseling (MS, AC, Certificate); school counseling (MS); student development in higher education (MS). *Accreditation:* AAMFT/COAMFTE; ACA. *Program availability:* Part-time, evening/weekend. *Degree requirements:* For master's, comprehensive exam, thesis or alternative; for other advanced degree, qualifying exam. *Entrance requirements:* For master's, minimum undergraduate GPA of 2.7, essay, interview, letters of recommendation. Additional exam requirements/recommendations for international students: required—TOEFL (minimum score 550 paper-based; 79 iBT); recommended—IELTS (minimum score 6.5). Electronic applications accepted.

Chapman University, Crean College of Health and Behavioral Sciences, Marriage and Family Therapy Program, Orange, CA 92866. Offers MA. *Accreditation:* AAMFT/ COAMFTE. *Program availability:* Part-time, evening/weekend. *Faculty:* 2 full-time (1 woman), 9 part-time/adjunct (8 women). *Students:* 39 full-time (36 women), 31 part-time (24 women); includes 39 minority (10 Asian, non-Hispanic/Latino; 24 Hispanic/Latino; 5 Two or more races, non-Hispanic/Latino), 1 international. Average age 27. 89 applicants, 60% accepted, 20 enrolled. In 2019, 21 master's awarded. *Degree requirements:* For master's, comprehensive exam, clinical practicum, capstone project. *Entrance requirements:* For master's, GRE (if undergraduate GPA less than 3.3). Additional exam requirements/recommendations for international students: required— TOEFL (minimum score 80 iBT), IELTS (minimum score 6.5), PTE (minimum score 53). *Application deadline:* For fall admission, 2/1 priority date for domestic students. Applications are processed on a rolling basis. Application fee: $60. Electronic applications accepted. *Expenses:* $1,240 per unit. *Financial support:* Fellowships, Federal Work-Study, scholarships/grants, and unspecified assistantships available. Financial award applicants required to submit FAFSA. *Unit head:* Dr. Naveen Jonathan, Chair, 714-997-6932, E-mail: jonathan@chapman.edu. *Application contact:* Melissa Liberman, Graduate Admission Counselor, 714-628-2847, E-mail: mft@chapman.edu.

Chatham University, Program in Counseling Psychology, Pittsburgh, PA 15232-2826. Offers child, adolescent and family (MSCP); counseling psychology (Psy D); health and holistic (MSCP); organization and supervision (MSCP); sport and exercise (MSCP). *Accreditation:* APA. *Program availability:* Part-time, evening/weekend. *Faculty:* 13 full-time (8 women), 21 part-time/adjunct (17 women). *Students:* 93 full-time (79 women), 56 part-time (44 women); includes 29 minority (16 Black or African American, non-Hispanic/ Latino; 4 Asian, non-Hispanic/Latino; 6 Hispanic/Latino; 3 Two or more races, non-Hispanic/Latino), 2 international. Average age 29. 172 applicants, 46% accepted, 54 enrolled. In 2019, 30 master's, 7 doctorates awarded. *Degree requirements:* For master's, thesis optional, supervised internship; for doctorate, thesis/dissertation, internship. *Entrance requirements:* For master's, minimum GPA of 3.0; 2 letters of recommendation; resume; prerequisite coursework in statistics, biology, and psychology; for doctorate, GRE. Additional exam requirements/recommendations for international students: required—TOEFL (minimum score 600 paper-based; 100 iBT), IELTS (minimum score 7), TWE. *Application deadline:* For fall admission, 4/1 priority date for domestic and international students; for spring admission, 11/1 for domestic students, 10/1 for international students. Applications are processed on a rolling basis. Application fee: $45. Electronic applications accepted. Application fee is waived when completed online. *Expenses:* $1,017 per credit hour. *Financial support:* Career-related internships or fieldwork available. Financial award applicants required to submit FAFSA. *Unit head:* Dr. Mary Jo Loughran, Director, 412-365-2783, Fax: 412-365-1505, E-mail: mloughran@chatham.edu. *Application contact:* Melanie Elmer, Assistant Director of Graduate Admission, 412-365-1394, Fax: 412-365-1609, E-mail: gradadmissions@chatham.edu.
Website: http://www.chatham.edu/mscp

Chestnut Hill College, School of Graduate Studies, Division of Psychology, Program in Clinical and Counseling Psychology, Philadelphia, PA 19118-2693. Offers clinical and counseling psychology (MS, CAS), including child and adolescent therapy, child and adolescent therapy with autism spectrum disorders, co-occurring disorders, couple and family therapy, diverse and underserved communities, generalist (MS), trauma studies. *Program availability:* Part-time, evening/weekend. *Degree requirements:* For master's, thesis optional, practica. *Entrance requirements:* For master's, GRE General Test, writing sample, letters of recommendation. Additional exam requirements/ recommendations for international students: required—TOEFL (minimum score 500 paper-based), IELTS (minimum score 6.0), or TWE (minimum score 22). Electronic applications accepted. *Expenses:* Contact institution.

Chestnut Hill College, School of Graduate Studies, Division of Psychology, Program in Clinical Psychology, Philadelphia, PA 19118-2693. Offers clinical psychology (Psy D), including clinical psychology, couple and family therapy, psychological assessment. *Accreditation:* APA. *Program availability:* Part-time, evening/weekend. *Degree requirements:* For doctorate, comprehensive exam, thesis/dissertation, internship, practica, clinical competency exam. *Entrance requirements:* For doctorate, GRE General Test, letters of recommendation, writing sample, master's degree in clinical/ counseling psychology or closely-related field. Additional exam requirements/ recommendations for international students: required—TOEFL (minimum score 500 paper-based), IELTS (minimum score 6.0), or TWE (minimum score 22). Electronic applications accepted. *Expenses:* Contact institution.

The Chicago School of Professional Psychology at Downtown Los Angeles, Program in Clinical Psychology, Los Angeles, CA 90017. Offers applied behavior analysis (MA); clinical psychology (Psy D); marital and family therapy (MA).

The Chicago School of Professional Psychology at Irvine, Program in Marital and Family Therapy, Irvine, CA 92612. Offers clinical psychology (MA), including marital and family therapy; management practice (Psy D); psychodynamic psychotherapy (Psy D).

Christian Theological Seminary, Graduate and Professional Programs, Indianapolis, IN 46208-3301. Offers educational and arts ministries (MA); marriage and family therapy (MA); pastoral care and counseling (D Min); psychotherapy and faith (MA); theological studies (MTS); theology (M Div). *Accreditation:* AAMFT/COAMFTE (one or more programs are accredited); ACIPE; ATS. *Program availability:* Part-time. Terminal master's awarded for partial completion of doctoral program. *Degree requirements:* For master's, comprehensive exam (for some programs), thesis (for some programs), missionary and cross-cultural experience (for M Div); for doctorate, comprehensive exam, thesis/dissertation. *Entrance requirements:* For doctorate, M Div. Additional exam requirements/recommendations for international students: recommended—TOEFL. Electronic applications accepted.

The College of New Jersey, Office of Graduate and Advancing Education, School of Education, Department of Counselor Education, Ewing, NJ 08628. Offers community counseling: human services (MA); community counseling: substance abuse and addiction (MA, Certificate); marriage and family therapy (Ed S); school counseling (MA). *Accreditation:* NCATE. *Program availability:* Part-time. *Degree requirements:* For master's, comprehensive exam. *Entrance requirements:* For master's, GRE General Test, minimum GPA of 3.0 in field or 2.75 overall, interview; for other advanced degree, previous master's degree or higher. Additional exam requirements/recommendations for international students: required—TOEFL. Electronic applications accepted.

The College of New Rochelle, Graduate School, Division of Human Services, Program in Marriage and Family Therapy, New Rochelle, NY 10805-2308. Offers MMFT. *Degree requirements:* For master's, practica. *Entrance requirements:* For master's, minimum GPA of 3.0 in baccalaureate or other graduate-level work (overall and major field); undergraduate major in psychology, social work, or related field; personal statement; two letters of recommendation; official transcripts from all colleges/universities attended; proof of immunizations.

Colorado State University, College of Health and Human Sciences, Department of Human Development and Family Studies, Fort Collins, CO 80523-1570. Offers applied developmental science (PhD); family and developmental studies (MS); marriage and family therapy (MS). *Accreditation:* AAMFT/COAMFTE. *Faculty:* 22 full-time (20 women), 2 part-time/adjunct (0 women). *Students:* 32 full-time (28 women), 4 part-time (all women); includes 9 minority (4 Asian, non-Hispanic/Latino; 4 Hispanic/Latino; 1 Two or more races, non-Hispanic/Latino), 2 international. Average age 27. 74 applicants, 42% accepted, 12 enrolled. In 2019, 9 master's, 2 doctorates awarded. Terminal master's awarded for partial completion of doctoral program. *Degree requirements:* For master's, thesis; for doctorate, comprehensive exam, thesis/dissertation. *Entrance requirements:* For master's, GRE General Test, 3 letters of recommendation; minimum GPA of 3.0; bachelor's degree; curriculum vitae/resume. Additional exam requirements/recommendations for international students: required—TOEFL (minimum score 550 paper-based; 80 iBT), IELTS (minimum score 6.5), PTE (minimum score 58). *Application deadline:* For fall admission, 1/2 priority date for domestic and international students. Electronic applications accepted. *Expenses:* Tuition, state resident: full-time $10,520; part-time $5844 per credit hour. Tuition, nonresident: full-time $25,791; part-time $14,328 per credit hour. *International tuition:* $25,791 full-time. *Required fees:* $2512.80. Part-time tuition and fees vary according to course level, course load, degree level, program and student level. *Financial support:* In 2019–20, 31 students received support, including 1 fellowship with full and partial tuition reimbursement available (averaging $7,605 per year), 15 research assistantships with full and partial tuition reimbursements available (averaging $13,182 per year), 15 teaching assistantships with full and partial tuition reimbursements available (averaging $9,633 per year); Federal Work-Study and unspecified assistantships also available. Financial award application deadline: 3/1; financial award applicants required to submit FAFSA. *Unit head:* Dr. Julia Braungart-Rieker, Department Head, 970-491-3581, Fax: 970-491-7975, E-mail: JulieBraungart.Rieker@colostate.edu. *Application contact:* Mary Daughtrey, Administrative Assistant III, 970-491-2872, Fax: 970-491-7975, E-mail: mary.daughtrey@colostate.edu.
Website: https://www.chhs.colostate.edu/hdfs

Converse College, Program in Marriage and Family Therapy, Spartanburg, SC 29302. Offers MMFT. *Accreditation:* AAMFT/COAMFTE.

Denver Seminary, Graduate and Professional Programs, Littleton, CO 80120. Offers apologetics (Certificate); biblical studies (MA); Christian formation and soul care (MA, Certificate); Christian studies (MA, Certificate); church and parachurch leadership (D Min); counseling licensure (MA); counseling ministry (MA); intercultural ministry (Certificate); leadership (MA, Certificate); marriage and family counseling (D Min); pastoral ministry (D Min); philosophy of religion (MA); spiritual guidance (Certificate); theology (M Div, Certificate); worship (Certificate); youth and family ministry (MA). *Accreditation:* ACA; ACIPE; ATS (one or more programs are accredited). *Program availability:* Part-time, evening/weekend, online learning. *Degree requirements:* For master's, 2 foreign languages, thesis (for some programs); for doctorate, 2 foreign languages, thesis/dissertation. *Entrance requirements:* For doctorate, M Div, 3 years of ministry experience. Additional exam requirements/recommendations for international students: required—TOEFL (minimum score 575 paper-based; 90 iBT). Electronic applications accepted.

Drexel University, College of Nursing and Health Professions, Department of Couple and Family Therapy, Philadelphia, PA 19104-2875. Offers MFT, PhD. *Accreditation:* AAMFT/COAMFTE (one or more programs are accredited). *Program availability:* Part-time. Terminal master's awarded for partial completion of doctoral program. *Degree requirements:* For master's, comprehensive exam, thesis; for doctorate, thesis/dissertation, qualifying exam. *Entrance requirements:* For master's, GRE General Test or MAT, minimum GPA of 2.75; for doctorate, GRE General Test, minimum GPA of 3.0. Electronic applications accepted.

Duquesne University, School of Education, Department of Counseling, Psychology, and Special Education, Program in Counselor Education, Pittsburgh, PA 15282-0001. Offers clinical mental health counseling (MS Ed, Post-Master's Certificate); counselor education and supervision (Ed D); counselor licensure (Post-Master's Certificate); marriage and family counseling (MS Ed); school counseling (MS Ed). *Accreditation:* ACA (one or more programs are accredited). *Program availability:* Part-time, evening/weekend. *Degree requirements:* For master's, thesis optional; for doctorate, thesis/dissertation. *Entrance requirements:* For master's, letters of recommendation, essay, interview, bachelor's degree; for doctorate, GRE, letters of recommendation, essay, interview, master's degree; for Post-Master's Certificate, GRE, letters of recommendation, essay, interview, bachelor's/master's degree. Additional exam requirements/recommendations for international students: required—TOEFL (minimum score 550 paper-based), IELTS (minimum score 6.5). Electronic applications accepted.

East Carolina University, Graduate School, College of Health and Human Performance, Department of Human Development and Family Science, Greenville, NC 27858-4353. Offers birth through kindergarten education (MA Ed); human development and family science (MS); marriage and family therapy (MS); medical family therapy (PhD). *Accreditation:* AAMFT/COAMFTE. *Program availability:* Part-time. *Application deadline:* For fall admission, 1/15 for domestic students; for spring admission, 10/15 for domestic students. *Expenses: Tuition, area resident:* Full-time $4749; part-time $185 per credit hour. Tuition, state resident: full-time $4749; part-time $185 per credit hour. Tuition, nonresident: full-time $17,898; part-time $864 per credit hour. *International tuition:* $17,898 full-time. *Required fees:* $2787. *Financial support:* Application deadline: 6/1. *Unit head:* Dr. Sharon Ballard, Chair, 252-328-4220, E-mail: ballards@ecu.edu. *Application contact:* Graduate School Admissions, 252-328-6012, Fax: 252-328-6071, E-mail: gradschool@ecu.edu.
Website: https://hhp.ecu.edu/hdfs/

Eastern Nazarene College, Adult and Graduate Studies, Program in Marriage and Family Therapy, Quincy, MA 02170. Offers MS. *Program availability:* Part-time, evening/weekend. *Entrance requirements:* For master's, 3 letters of recommendation, resume. Additional exam requirements/recommendations for international students: required—TOEFL (minimum score 550 paper-based).

East Tennessee State University, College of Graduate and Continuing Studies, Clemmer College, Department of Counseling and Human Services, Johnson City, TN 37614. Offers clinical mental health counseling (MA); college counseling/student affairs higher education (MA); couples and family therapy (MA); human services (MS); school counseling (MA). *Accreditation:* ACA; NCATE. *Program availability:* Part-time. *Degree requirements:* For master's, comprehensive exam, thesis optional, internship, student teaching, culminating experience. *Entrance requirements:* For master's, GRE General Test, minimum GPA of 3.0, three letters of recommendation, interview, 2-3 page essay detailing experiences that have shaped pursuit of degree, resume. Additional exam requirements/recommendations for international students: required—TOEFL (minimum score 550 paper-based; 79 iBT). Electronic applications accepted.

Evangelical Seminary, Graduate and Professional Programs, Myerstown, PA 17067-1212. Offers Biblical studies (MAR); congregational ministry (M Div); global and contextual studies (M Div, MAR); historical and theological studies (MAR); interdisciplinary studies (MAR); marriage and family counseling (M Div); marriage and family therapy (MA); New Testament (MAR); Old Testament (MAR); spiritual formation (MAR); teaching ministry (M Div); youth ministry (M Div). *Accreditation:* ATS (one or more programs are accredited). *Program availability:* Part-time, online learning. *Degree requirements:* For master's, 2 foreign languages. *Entrance requirements:* For master's, minimum GPA of 2.5. Additional exam requirements/recommendations for international students: required—TOEFL (minimum score 550 paper-based).

Fairfield University, Graduate School of Education and Allied Professions, Fairfield, CT 06824. Offers applied behavior analysis (ATC); applied psychology (MA); clinical mental health counseling (MA, CAS); educational technology (MA); elementary education (MA, CAS); family studies (MA); integration of spirituality and religion in counseling (ATC); marriage and family therapy (MA); reading and language development (Sixth Year Certificate); school counseling (MA, CAS); school psychology (MA, CAS); school-based marriage and family therapy (ATC); secondary education (MA); special education (MA, CAS); substance abuse counseling (ATC); teaching (Certificate); teaching and foundations (MA, CAS); TESOL, world languages, and bilingual education (MA, CAS). *Accreditation:* NCATE. *Program availability:* Part-time, evening/weekend. *Faculty:* 24 full-time (18 women), 28 part-time/adjunct (20 women). *Students:* 169 full-time (149 women), 227 part-time (187 women); includes 96 minority (21 Black or African American, non-Hispanic/Latino; 8 Asian, non-Hispanic/Latino; 60 Hispanic/Latino; 7 Two or more races, non-Hispanic/Latino), 1 international. Average age 31. 194 applicants, 60% accepted, 101 enrolled. In 2019, 136 master's, 28 other advanced degrees awarded. *Degree requirements:* For master's, comprehensive exam. *Entrance requirements:* For master's, One of the following for certification programs: Praxis Core, SAT, ACT, or GRE, minimum GPA of 3.0, 2 recommendations, resume. Additional exam requirements/recommendations for international students: required—TOEFL (minimum score 550 paper-based; 84 iBT), IELTS (minimum score 7.5), TOEFL (minimum score 550 paper-based; 84 iBT) or IELTS (minimum score 7.5). *Application deadline:* For fall admission, 2/15 for international students; for spring admission, 10/1 for international students. Application fee: $60. Electronic applications accepted. *Expenses:* Tuition $815/credit hour; Lab Fee (ED598) $300/semester; Lab Fee (CN457,CN467, PY538, PY540) $70/course; Wilson Reading Course Fee $141/credit hour; Registration Fee $50/semester; Graduate Student Activity Fee (Fall and Spring) $65/semester. *Financial support:* In 2019–20, 34 students received support. Career-related internships or fieldwork and unspecified assistantships available. Support available to part-time students. Financial award applicants required to submit FAFSA. *Unit head:* Dr. Laurie Grupp, Dean, 203-254-4250, Fax: 203-254-4241, E-mail: lgrupp@fairfield.edu. *Application contact:* Melanie Rogers, Director of Graduate Admission, 203-254-4184, Fax: 203-254-4073, E-mail: gradadmis@fairfield.edu.
Website: http://www.fairfield.edu/gseap

Florida State University, The Graduate School, College of Human Sciences, Department of Family and Child Sciences, Tallahassee, FL 32306. Offers family and child sciences (MS); human development and family sciences (PhD); marriage and family therapy (PhD). *Accreditation:* AAMFT/COAMFTE. *Program availability:* Part-time. *Faculty:* 17 full-time (11 women). *Students:* 28 full-time (22 women), 4 part-time (2 women); includes 12 minority (7 Black or African American, non-Hispanic/Latino; 1 Asian, non-Hispanic/Latino; 1 Hispanic/Latino; 3 Two or more races, non-Hispanic/Latino), 2 international. 39 applicants, 46% accepted, 5 enrolled. In 2019, 9 doctorates awarded. Terminal master's awarded for partial completion of doctoral program. *Degree requirements:* For master's, thesis optional, special project for non-thesis students; for doctorate, thesis/dissertation, preliminary examination; clinical examination (for marriage and family therapy). *Entrance requirements:* For master's, GRE General Test, minimum upper division GPA of 3.0; for doctorate, GRE General Test, writing assessment, minimum upper division GPA of 3.0 or master's degree. Additional exam requirements/recommendations for international students: required—TOEFL (minimum score 550 paper-based; 80 iBT). *Application deadline:* For fall admission, 12/1 for domestic and international students. Applications are processed on a rolling basis. Application fee: $30. Electronic applications accepted. *Financial support:* In 2019–20, 34 students received support, including 5 research assistantships with full tuition reimbursements available (averaging $21,020 per year), 29 teaching assistantships with full tuition reimbursements available (averaging $21,020 per year); fellowships with partial tuition reimbursements available, career-related internships or fieldwork, Federal Work-Study, institutionally sponsored loans, scholarships/grants, health care benefits, and unspecified assistantships also available. Financial award application deadline: 1/5; financial award applicants required to submit FAFSA. *Unit head:* Dr. Chester Ray, Interim Department Chair, 850-644-3217, E-mail: caray@fsu.edu. *Application contact:* Mary-Sue McLemore, Academic Support Assistant, 850-644-1117, E-mail: mmclemore@fsu.edu.
Website: https://humansciences.fsu.edu/family-child-sciences/students/graduate-programs/

Fresno Pacific University, Biblical Seminary, Program in Marriage and Family Therapy, Fresno, CA 93702-4709. Offers MA. *Degree requirements:* For master's, thesis or alternative. *Entrance requirements:* For master's, minimum GPA of 3.0. Additional exam requirements/recommendations for international students: required—TOEFL (minimum score 550 paper-based). *Expenses:* Contact institution.

Friends University, Graduate School, Wichita, KS 67213. Offers family therapy (MSFT); global business administration (MBA), including accounting, business law, change management, health care leadership, management information systems, supply chain management and logistics; health care leadership (MHCL); management information systems (MMIS); professional business administration (MBA), including accounting, business law, change management, health care leadership, management information systems, supply chain management and logistics. *Program availability:* Part-time, evening/weekend, online learning. *Degree requirements:* For master's, research project. *Entrance requirements:* For master's, bachelor's degree from accredited institution, official transcripts, interview with program director, letter(s) of recommendation. Additional exam requirements/recommendations for international students: required—TOEFL (minimum score 560 paper-based). Electronic applications accepted.

Fuller Theological Seminary, Graduate Programs, Pasadena, CA 91182. Offers Christian leadership (MACL); clinical psychology (PhD, Psy D); family studies (MA); global leadership (MA); global ministries (D Min); global ministries (Korean language) (D Min); intercultural studies (MA, Th M, PhD); intercultural studies (Korean language) (MA); marital and family therapy (MS); marriage and family enrichment (Certificate); ministry (M Div, D Min); missiology (D Miss); missiology (Korean language) (Th M); theology (MA, Th M, PhD), including evangelism (MA), family life education (MA), pastoral ministry (MA), recovery ministry (MA), worship music ministry (MA), worship, theology, and the arts (MA); youth, family, and culture (MA); theology and ministry (MA).

Geneva College, Master of Arts in Counseling Program, Beaver Falls, PA 15010. Offers clinical mental health counseling (MA); marriage and family counseling (MA); school counseling (MA). *Accreditation:* ACA. *Program availability:* Part-time, evening/weekend, online only, 100% online, blended/hybrid learning. *Faculty:* 4 full-time (1 woman), 5 part-time/adjunct (2 women). *Students:* 26 full-time (20 women), 22 part-time (17 women); includes 11 minority (9 Black or African American, non-Hispanic/Latino; 1 Asian, non-Hispanic/Latino; 1 Two or more races, non-Hispanic/Latino), 1 international. Average age 33. 24 applicants, 63% accepted, 14 enrolled. In 2019, 34 master's awarded. *Degree requirements:* For master's, comprehensive exam, 60 credits including practicum and internship. *Entrance requirements:* For master's, minimum GPA of 3.0 (preferred), 3 letters of recommendation, essay on career goals, resume of educational and professional experiences. Additional exam requirements/recommendations for international students: required—TOEFL. *Application deadline:* For fall admission, 9/1 for domestic students; for spring admission, 1/10 for domestic students. Applications are processed on a rolling basis. Electronic applications accepted. *Expenses:* $680 per credit. 60 credits required for graduation. *Financial support:* Research assistantships, teaching assistantships, career-related internships or fieldwork, and unspecified assistantships available. Financial award application deadline: 8/1; financial award applicants required to submit FAFSA. *Unit head:* Dr. Shannan Shiderly, Program Director, 724-847-6649, Fax: 724-847-6101, E-mail: slshider@geneva.edu. *Application contact:* Marina Frazier, Graduate Program Manager, 724-847-6697, E-mail: counseling@geneva.edu.
Website: https://www.geneva.edu/graduate/counseling/

George Fox University, College of Education, Graduate Department of Counseling, Newberg, OR 97132-2697. Offers clinical mental health counseling (MA); marriage, couple and family counseling (MA, Certificate); school counseling (MA, Certificate); school psychology (Ed S). *Program availability:* Part-time. *Degree requirements:* For master's, clinical project. *Entrance requirements:* For master's, MAT or GRE, bachelor's degree from regionally-accredited college or university, minimum cumulative GPA of 3.0, 1 professional and 1 academic reference, resume, on-campus interview, official transcripts. Additional exam requirements/recommendations for international students: required—TOEFL (minimum score 577 paper-based; 90 iBT), IELTS (minimum score 7). Electronic applications accepted. *Expenses:* Contact institution.

Gonzaga University, School of Education, Spokane, WA 99258. Offers clinical mental health counseling (MA); educational leadership (M Ed, Ed D); elementary education (MIT); marriage and family counseling (MA); school counseling (MA); secondary education (MIT); special education (M Ed, MIT); sport and athletic administration (MA). *Accreditation:* NCATE. *Program availability:* Part-time, evening/weekend, 100% online, blended/hybrid learning. *Degree requirements:* For master's, comprehensive exam. *Entrance requirements:* For master's, GRE, MAT, and/or Washington Educator Skills Test-Basic (WEST-B), Washington Educator Skills Test-Endorsements (WEST-E), official transcripts from all colleges or universities attended, interview, two letters of recommendation, resume, essay, minimum GPA of 3.0. Additional exam requirements/recommendations for international students: required—TOEFL (minimum score 580 paper-based, 88 iBT) or IELTS (minimum score 6.5). Electronic applications accepted. *Expenses:* Contact institution.

Hampton University, School of Liberal Arts and Education, Program in Psychology, Hampton, VA 23668. Offers marriage and family studies (MS); psychology (MS). *Program availability:* Part-time. *Students:* 4 part-time (all women); all minorities (all Black or African American, non-Hispanic/Latino). Average age 26. 9 applicants. In 2019, 1 master's awarded. *Degree requirements:* For master's, thesis. *Entrance requirements:* For master's, GRE. Additional exam requirements/recommendations for international students: required—TOEFL (minimum score 525 paper-based) or IELTS (6.5). *Application deadline:* For fall admission, 6/1 priority date for domestic students, 4/1 priority date for international students; for spring admission, 11/1 priority date for domestic students, 9/1 priority date for international students; for summer admission, 4/1 priority date for domestic and international students. Application fee: $35. Electronic applications accepted. *Expenses:* Contact institution. *Financial support:* Unspecified assistantships available. Financial award application deadline: 6/30; financial award applicants required to submit FAFSA. *Unit head:* Dr. Tamara Williams, Interim Chairperson, 757-727-5301. *Application contact:* Dr. Tamara Williams, Interim Chairperson, 757-727-5301.

Hardin-Simmons University, Graduate School, Cynthia Ann Parker College of Liberal Arts, Department of Psychology, Abilene, TX 79698-0001. Offers clinical counseling and marriage and family therapy (MA). *Program availability:* Part-time. *Degree requirements:* For master's, comprehensive exam, clinical experience, project. *Entrance requirements:* For master's, 21 semester hours of course work in psychology (18 in upper-division classes); minimum undergraduate GPA of 3.0 in major, 2.7 overall; writing sample; letters of recommendation. Additional exam requirements/recommendations for international students: required—TOEFL (minimum score 550 paper-based; 79 iBT). Electronic applications accepted.

Hofstra University, School of Health Professions and Human Services, Programs in Counseling, Hempstead, NY 11549. Offers counseling (MS Ed, PD); creative arts therapy (MA); interdisciplinary transition specialist (Advanced Certificate); marriage and family therapy (MA); mental health counseling (MA, Advanced Certificate); rehabilitation administration (PD); rehabilitation counseling (MS Ed, Advanced Certificate); rehabilitation counseling in mental health (MS Ed, Advanced Certificate). *Accreditation:* ACA. *Program availability:* Part-time, evening/weekend. *Students:* 124 full-time (105 women), 69 part-time (64 women); includes 68 minority (23 Black or African American, non-Hispanic/Latino; 10 Asian, non-Hispanic/Latino; 32 Hispanic/Latino; 3 Native Hawaiian or other Pacific Islander, non-Hispanic/Latino), 4 international. Average age 28. 188 applicants, 77% accepted, 75 enrolled. In 2019, 58 master's, 3 other advanced degrees awarded. *Degree requirements:* For master's, comprehensive exam (for some programs), thesis (for some programs), internship, practicum, student teaching, seminars, minimum GPA of 3.0. *Entrance requirements:* For master's, GRE, interview, letters of recommendation, portfolio, essay, professional experience, certification; for

other advanced degree, GRE, interview, letters of recommendation, essay, professional experience, resume, master's degree. Additional exam requirements/recommendations for international students: required—TOEFL (minimum score 550 paper-based; 80 iBT); recommended—IELTS (minimum score 6.5). *Application deadline:* Applications are processed on a rolling basis. Application fee: $75. Electronic applications accepted. *Expenses:* Tuition: Full-time $25,164; part-time $1398 per credit. *Required fees:* $580; $165 per semester. Tuition and fees vary according to course load, degree level and program. *Financial support:* In 2019–20, 77 students received support, including 44 fellowships with full and partial tuition reimbursements available (averaging $3,811 per year), 9 research assistantships with full and partial tuition reimbursements available (averaging $6,586 per year); career-related internships or fieldwork, Federal Work-Study, institutionally sponsored loans, scholarships/grants, traineeships, tuition waivers (full and partial), unspecified assistantships, and scholarships and endowed scholarships also available. Support available to part-time students. Financial award applicants required to submit FAFSA. *Unit head:* Dr. Jamie Mitus, Chairperson, 516-463-5759, E-mail: jamie.s.mitus@hofstra.edu. *Application contact:* Sunil Samuel, Assistant Vice President of Admissions, 516-463-4723, Fax: 516-463-4664, E-mail: graduateadmission@hofstra.edu.
Website: http://www.hofstra.edu/academics/colleges/healthscienceshumanservices/

Hope International University, School of Graduate and Professional Studies, Program in Marriage and Family Therapy, Fullerton, CA 92831-3138. Offers MA, MFT. *Accreditation:* AAMFT/COAMFTE. *Degree requirements:* For master's, comprehensive exam, thesis (for some programs), final exam, practicum. *Entrance requirements:* For master's, minimum GPA of 3.0, interview, bachelor's degree, 2 references. Additional exam requirements/recommendations for international students: required—TOEFL (minimum score 550 paper-based; 86 iBT); recommended—IELTS (minimum score 6.5). Electronic applications accepted. *Expenses:* Contact institution.

Idaho State University, Graduate School, College of Health Professions, Department of Counseling, Pocatello, ID 83209-8120. Offers counseling (M Coun, Ed S), including marriage and family counseling (M Coun), mental health counseling (M Coun), school counseling (M Coun), student affairs and college counseling (M Coun); counselor education and counseling (PhD). *Accreditation:* ACA (one or more programs are accredited). *Program availability:* Part-time. *Degree requirements:* For master's, comprehensive exam, thesis, 4 semesters resident graduate study, practicum/internship; for doctorate, comprehensive exam, thesis/dissertation, 3 semesters internship, 4 consecutive semesters doctoral-level study on campus; for Ed S, comprehensive exam, thesis, case studies, oral exam. *Entrance requirements:* For master's, GRE General Test, MAT, minimum GPA of 3.0, bachelors degree, interview, 3 letters of recommendation; for doctorate, GRE General Test, MAT, minimum graduate GPA of 3.0, resume, interview, counseling license, master's degree; for Ed S, GRE General Test, minimum graduate GPA of 3.0, master's degree in counseling, 3 letters of recommendation, 2 years work experience. Additional exam requirements/recommendations for international students: required—TOEFL (minimum score 600 paper-based; 80 iBT). Electronic applications accepted.

Indiana University South Bend, School of Education, South Bend, IN 46615. Offers addiction counseling (MS Ed); alcohol and drug counseling (Graduate Certificate); clinical mental health counseling (MS Ed); educational leadership (MS Ed); elementary education (MS Ed); marriage, couple, and family counseling (MS Ed); school counseling (MS Ed); secondary education (MS Ed); special education (MAT, MS Ed), including intense intervention (MS Ed), mild intervention (MS Ed). *Accreditation:* NCATE. *Program availability:* Part-time, evening/weekend. *Degree requirements:* For master's, thesis or alternative, exit project. *Entrance requirements:* For master's, letters of recommendation, GRE or minimum GPA of 3.0. Additional exam requirements/recommendations for international students: required—TOEFL. Electronic applications accepted. *Expenses:* Contact institution.

Indiana Wesleyan University, Graduate School, College of Arts and Sciences, Marion, IN 46953. Offers addictions counseling (MS); clinical mental health counseling (MS); community counseling (MS); marriage and family therapy (MS); school counseling (MS); student development counseling and administration (MS). *Accreditation:* ACA. *Program availability:* Part-time. *Degree requirements:* For master's, thesis or alternative. *Entrance requirements:* For master's, GRE General Test. Additional exam requirements/recommendations for international students: required—TOEFL. Electronic applications accepted. *Expenses:* Contact institution.

Instituto Tecnologico de Santo Domingo, Graduate School, Area of Humanities and Social Sciences, Santo Domingo, Dominican Republic. Offers accounting (Certificate); adult education (Certificate); applied linguistics (MA); economics (MA); education (M Ed); educational psychology (MA, Certificate); gender and development (MA, Certificate); humanistic studies (MA); international marketing management (Certificate); international relations in the Caribbean basin (Certificate); intervention systems in family therapy (MA); linguistic and literary communication (Certificate); pedagogical support (MA); social science education (M Ed); sustainable human development (MA); terminal illness and death psychology (Certificate); youth and adult education (M Ed).

Iona College, School of Arts and Science, Marriage and Family Therapy Program, New Rochelle, NY 10801-1890. Offers MS. *Accreditation:* AAMFT/COAMFTE. *Program availability:* Part-time. *Faculty:* 3 full-time (all women), 3 part-time/adjunct (1 woman). *Students:* 35 full-time (32 women), 6 part-time (5 women); includes 26 minority (10 Black or African American, non-Hispanic/Latino; 3 Asian, non-Hispanic/Latino; 13 Hispanic/Latino). Average age 30. 22 applicants, 100% accepted, 13 enrolled. In 2019, 15 master's awarded. *Degree requirements:* For master's, thesis, project. *Entrance requirements:* For master's, interview, minimum GPA of 3.0. *Application deadline:* For fall admission, 8/1 priority date for domestic students, 7/1 for international students. Applications are processed on a rolling basis. Application fee: $50. Electronic applications accepted. *Expenses:* Contact institution. *Financial support:* In 2019–20, 11 students received support. Career-related internships or fieldwork, scholarships/grants, tuition waivers (partial), and unspecified assistantships available. Support available to part-time students. Financial award application deadline: 4/15; financial award applicants required to submit FAFSA. *Unit head:* Lisa Reynolds, PhD, Program Director, Marriage and Family Therapy, 914-633-4471, E-mail: lreynolds@iona.edu. *Application contact:* Shantell Smith, Associate Director of Graduate Admissions, 914-633-2440, Fax: 914-633-2277, E-mail: ssmith@iona.edu.
Website: http://www.iona.edu/Academics/School-of-Arts-Science/Departments/Marriage-and-Family-Therapy/Graduate-Programs.aspx

Jacksonville University, Brooks Rehabilitation College of Healthcare Sciences, School of Applied Health Sciences, Program in Clinical Mental Health Counseling, Jacksonville, FL 32211. Offers clinical mental health counseling (MS), including marriage and family therapy. *Program availability:* Part-time, blended/hybrid learning. *Students:* 39 full-time (35 women); includes 9 minority (6 Black or African American, non-Hispanic/Latino; 1 Asian, non-Hispanic/Latino; 2 Hispanic/Latino), 3 international. Average age 40. 63 applicants, 59% accepted, 22 enrolled. *Entrance requirements:* For master's, baccalaureate degree from accredited college or university with minimum GPA of 3.0; background check; 1-2 page essay stating intent; resume (education, work experience); 3 letters of recommendation; interview. Additional exam requirements/recommendations for international students: required—TOEFL (minimum score 650 paper-based; 114

iBT), IELTS (minimum score 8). *Application deadline:* Applications are processed on a rolling basis. Application fee: $50. Electronic applications accepted. *Expenses:* Contact institution. *Financial support:* Federal Work-Study, institutionally sponsored loans, scholarships/grants, and health care benefits available. Support available to part-time students. Financial award application deadline: 3/15; financial award applicants required to submit FAFSA. *Unit head:* Dr. Whitney George, Department Chair, Clinical Mental Health Counseling, 904-256-7620, E-mail: wgeorge@ju.edu. *Application contact:* Pamela Adrian, Assistant Director, Graduate Admissions, 904-256-7245, E-mail: padrian@ju.edu.
Website: https://www.ju.edu/mentalhealth/

John Brown University, Graduate Counseling Programs, Siloam Springs, AR 72761-2121. Offers clinical mental health counseling (MS); marriage and family therapy (MS); play therapy (Graduate Certificate); school counseling (MS). *Accreditation:* NCATE. *Program availability:* Part-time, evening/weekend. *Degree requirements:* For master's, practica or internships. *Entrance requirements:* For master's, GRE (minimum score of 300), recommendation forms from three people, 200-word essay describing professional plans and reason for seeking acceptance. Additional exam requirements/recommendations for international students: required—TOEFL (minimum score 550 paper-based; 79 iBT). Electronic applications accepted. *Expenses:* Contact institution.

Kansas State University, Graduate School, College of Human Ecology, Doctorate in Human Ecology Program, Manhattan, KS 66506-1407. Offers apparel and textiles (PhD); applied family sciences (PhD); couple and family therapy (PhD); hospitality administration (PhD); kinesiology (PhD); life-span human development (PhD). *Program availability:* Part-time. *Degree requirements:* For doctorate, thesis/dissertation. *Entrance requirements:* Additional exam requirements/recommendations for international students: required—TOEFL. Electronic applications accepted.

Kansas State University, Graduate School, College of Human Ecology, School of Family Studies and Human Services, Manhattan, KS 66506-1403. Offers applied family sciences (MS); communication sciences and disorders (MS); conflict resolution (Graduate Certificate); couple and family therapy (MS); early childhood education (MS); family and community service (MS); life-span human development (MS); personal financial planning (MS, PhD, Graduate Certificate); youth development (MS, Graduate Certificate). *Accreditation:* AAMFT/COAMFTE; ASHA. *Program availability:* Part-time, online learning. *Degree requirements:* For master's, comprehensive exam (for some programs), thesis optional. *Entrance requirements:* For master's, GRE, minimum GPA of 3.0 in last 2 years (60 semester hours) of undergraduate study; for doctorate, GRE. Additional exam requirements/recommendations for international students: required—TOEFL (minimum score 600 paper-based). Electronic applications accepted.

Kean University, College of Liberal Arts, Program in Marriage and Family Therapy, Union, NJ 07083. Offers MA. *Program availability:* Part-time. *Faculty:* 18 full-time (14 women). *Students:* 39 full-time (37 women), 12 part-time (11 women); includes 33 minority (15 Black or African American, non-Hispanic/Latino; 4 Asian, non-Hispanic/Latino; 14 Hispanic/Latino). Average age 31. 19 applicants, 95% accepted, 16 enrolled. In 2019, 5 master's awarded. *Entrance requirements:* Additional exam requirements/recommendations for international students: required—TOEFL (minimum score 550 paper-based; 79 iBT), IELTS (minimum score 6.5). *Application deadline:* For fall admission, 6/30 for domestic and international students; for spring admission, 12/1 for domestic and international students. Applications are processed on a rolling basis. Application fee: $75. Electronic applications accepted. *Expenses:* Tuition, state resident: full-time $15,326; part-time $748 per credit. Tuition, nonresident: full-time $20,288; part-time $902 per credit. *Required fees:* $2149.50; $91.25 per credit. Tuition and fees vary according to course level, course load, degree level and program. *Financial support:* Scholarships/grants and unspecified assistantships available. Financial award applicants required to submit FAFSA. *Unit head:* Dr. Zandra Gratz, Program Coordinator, 908-737-5881, E-mail: zgratz@kean.edu. *Application contact:* Amy Clark, Program Assistant, 908-737-7100, E-mail: gradadmissions@kean.edu.
Website: http://grad.kean.edu/professional-diploma-programs/marriage-family-therapy

Lancaster Bible College, Graduate School, Lancaster, PA 17601-5036. Offers adult ministries (MA); Bible (MA); children and family ministry (MA); church planting (MA); consulting resource teacher (M Ed); elementary school counseling (M Ed); leadership (PhD); leadership studies (MA); marriage and family counseling (MA); mental health counseling (MA); pastoral studies (MA); secondary school counseling (M Ed); sports ministry (MA); student ministry (MA); town and country ministry (MA). *Program availability:* Part-time, evening/weekend. *Degree requirements:* For master's, comprehensive exam (for some programs), thesis (for some programs). *Entrance requirements:* For master's, bachelor's degree with a minimum of 30 credits of course work in Bible, minimum undergraduate GPA of 3.0, interview. Additional exam requirements/recommendations for international students: required—TOEFL.

La Salle University, School of Arts and Sciences, Program in Counseling and Family Therapy, Philadelphia, PA 19141-1199. Offers industrial/organizational psychology (MA); marriage and family therapy (MA); professional clinical counseling (MA). *Accreditation:* ACA; APA. *Program availability:* Part-time, evening/weekend. *Degree requirements:* For master's, comprehensive exam. *Entrance requirements:* For master's, GRE or MAT (waived for applicants that already possess a master's degree in any field or for applicants that have a cumulative GPA of 3.5 or higher), minimum of 15 hours in psychology, counseling, or marriage and family studies; minimum GPA of 3.0; three letters of recommendation; personal statement; work experience (paid or volunteer). Additional exam requirements/recommendations for international students: required—TOEFL. Electronic applications accepted. Application fee is waived when completed online. *Expenses:* Contact institution.

LeTourneau University, Graduate Programs, Longview, TX 75607-7001. Offers business administration (MBA); counseling (MA); curriculum and instruction (M Ed); educational administration (M Ed); engineering (ME, MS); engineering management (MEM); health care administration (MS); marriage and family therapy (MA); psychology (MA); strategic leadership (MSL); teacher leadership (M Ed); teaching and learning (M Ed). *Program availability:* Part-time, 100% online, blended/hybrid learning. *Students:* 45 full-time (34 women), 243 part-time (186 women); includes 142 minority (89 Black or African American, non-Hispanic/Latino; 1 Asian, non-Hispanic/Latino; 26 Hispanic/Latino; 26 Two or more races, non-Hispanic/Latino), 2 international. Average age 37. In 2019, 143 master's awarded. *Entrance requirements:* Additional exam requirements/recommendations for international students: required—TOEFL (minimum score 525 paper-based; 80 iBT), IELTS (minimum score 6), Either a TOEFL or IELTS is required for graduate students. One or the other. *Application deadline:* Applications are processed on a rolling basis. Application fee: $0. Electronic applications accepted. *Financial support:* Unspecified assistantships and employee tuition waivers and institutionally sponsored loans available. Financial award applicants required to submit FAFSA.
Website: http://www.letu.edu

Lewis & Clark College, Graduate School of Education and Counseling, Department of Counseling Psychology, Program in Marriage, Couple, and Family Therapy, Portland, OR 97219-7899. Offers MA, MS. *Accreditation:* AAMFT/COAMFTE. *Program availability:* Part-time, evening/weekend. *Degree requirements:* For master's, thesis (MS). *Entrance requirements:* For master's, GRE General Test, minimum undergraduate GPA of 2.75. Additional exam requirements/recommendations for international students: required—TOEFL (minimum score 575 paper-based). Electronic applications accepted.

Liberty University, School of Behavioral Sciences, Lynchburg, VA 24515. Offers applied psychology (MA), including developmental psychology (MA, MS), industrial/organizational psychology (MA, MS); clinical mental health counseling (MA); community care and counseling (Ed D), including marriage and family counseling, pastoral care and counseling, traumatology; counselor education and supervision (PhD); human services counseling (MA), including addictions and recovery, business, child and family law, Christian ministries, criminal justice, crisis response and trauma, executive leadership, health and wellness, life coaching, marriage and family, military resilience; marriage and family counseling (MA); marriage and family therapy (MA); military resilience (Certificate); pastoral counseling (MA), including addictions and recovery, community chaplaincy, crisis response and trauma, discipleship and church ministry, leadership, life coaching, marriage and family, marriage and family studies, military resilience, parenting and child/adolescent, pastoral counseling, theology; professional counseling (MA); psychology (MS), including developmental psychology (MA, MS), industrial/organizational psychology (MA, MS); school counseling (M Ed). *Program availability:* Part-time, online learning. *Students:* 3,786 full-time (3,065 women), 5,193 part-time (4,081 women); includes 2,733 minority (1,967 Black or African American, non-Hispanic/Latino; 48 American Indian or Alaska Native, non-Hispanic/Latino; 103 Asian, non-Hispanic/Latino; 349 Hispanic/Latino; 19 Native Hawaiian or other Pacific Islander, non-Hispanic/Latino; 247 Two or more races, non-Hispanic/Latino), 133 international. Average age 38. 13,324 applicants, 28% accepted, 2,163 enrolled. In 2019, 2,322 master's, 19 doctorates, 112 other advanced degrees awarded. *Entrance requirements:* For master's, Official bachelor's degree transcripts with a 2.0 GPA or higher. *Application deadline:* Applications are processed on a rolling basis. Application fee: $50. Electronic applications accepted. *Expenses: Tuition:* Full-time $545; part-time $410 per credit hour. One-time fee: $50. *Financial support:* In 2019–20, 1,003 students received support. Teaching assistantships and Federal Work-Study available. Financial award applicants required to submit FAFSA. *Unit head:* Dr. Kenyon Knapp, Dean, School of Behavioral Services, E-mail: kcknapp@liberty.edu. *Application contact:* Jay Bridge, Director of Admissions, 800-424-9595, Fax: 800-628-7977, E-mail: gradadmissions@liberty.edu.
Website: https://www.liberty.edu/behavioral-sciences/

Liberty University, School of Divinity, Lynchburg, VA 24515. Offers Biblical exposition (MA); Biblical languages (M Div); Biblical studies (M Div, MA, MAR, Th M, D Min); chaplaincy (M Div, D Min); Christian apologetics (M Div, MA, MAR, Th M); Christian leadership and church ministries (M Div); Christian ministries (M Div); Christian ministry (MA); Christian thought (M Div); church history (M Div, MAR, Th M); community chaplaincy (M Div, MAR); discipleship (D Min); discipleship and church ministry (M Div, MAR, MCM); evangelism and church planting (MAR, MCM, D Min); expository preaching (D Min); global ministry (MA); global studies (M Div, MAR, MCM, MGS, Th M); healthcare chaplaincy (M Div); homiletics (M Div, MAR, Th M); leadership (M Div, MAR); marketplace chaplaincy (M Div, MCM); ministry leadership (Ed D); pastoral counseling (M Div, MA, MAR, D Min), including addictions and recovery (MA), crisis response and trauma (MA), discipleship and church ministries (MA), leadership (MA), life coaching (MA), marketplace chaplaincy (MA), marriage and family (MA), military resilience (MA), pastoral counseling (MA); pastoral leadership (D Min); pastoral ministries (M Div, M Serv Soc, MCM); religious education (MRE); sports chaplaincy (MA); theology (M Div, MAR, MTS, Th M); theology and apologetics (D Min, PhD); worship (M Div, MAR, MCM, D Min); youth and family ministries (M Div). *Program availability:* Part-time, online learning. *Students:* 2,691 full-time (814 women), 2,570 part-time (732 women); includes 1,484 minority (1,046 Black or African American, non-Hispanic/Latino; 33 American Indian or Alaska Native, non-Hispanic/Latino; 120 Asian, non-Hispanic/Latino; 167 Hispanic/Latino; 8 Native Hawaiian or other Pacific Islander, non-Hispanic/Latino; 110 Two or more races, non-Hispanic/Latino), 101 international. Average age 43. 4,508 applicants, 34% accepted, 952 enrolled. In 2019, 1,251 master's, 71 doctorates awarded. *Degree requirements:* For master's, 2 foreign languages, thesis (for some programs); for doctorate, 2 foreign languages, thesis/dissertation. *Entrance requirements:* For master's, minimum undergraduate GPA of 2.0; for doctorate, GRE General Test or MAT, minimum graduate GPA of 3.0. Additional exam requirements/recommendations for international students: required—TOEFL (minimum score 600 paper-based; 100 iBT). *Application deadline:* For fall admission, 6/1 for domestic students; for spring admission, 11/1 for domestic students. Applications are processed on a rolling basis. Application fee: $50. Electronic applications accepted. *Expenses:* Contact institution. *Financial support:* Teaching assistantships with tuition reimbursements, career-related internships or fieldwork, and Federal Work-Study available. Financial award applicants required to submit FAFSA. *Unit head:* Dr. Troy Temple, Interim Dean, School of Divinity, E-mail: divinity@liberty.edu. *Application contact:* Jay Bridge, Director of Graduate Admissions, 800-424-9595, Fax: 800-628-7977, E-mail: gradadmissions@liberty.edu.
Website: https://www.liberty.edu/divinity/

Lipscomb University, Department of Psychology, Counseling, and Family Science, Nashville, TN 37204-3951. Offers clinical mental health counseling (MS); counseling psychology (Certificate); marriage and family therapy (MMFT); psychology (MS). *Program availability:* Part-time, evening/weekend. *Degree requirements:* For master's, thesis (for some programs), practicum, internship, capstone. *Entrance requirements:* For master's, GRE, resume, 3 reference letters, transcripts, goals statement. Additional exam requirements/recommendations for international students: required—TOEFL (minimum score 570 paper-based; 80 iBT). Electronic applications accepted. *Expenses:* Contact institution.

Loma Linda University, School of Behavioral Health, Department of Counseling and Family Sciences, Loma Linda, CA 92350. Offers child life specialist (MS); clinical mediation (Certificate); counseling (MS); drug and alcohol counseling (Certificate); family life education (Certificate); marital and family therapy (DMFT); school counseling (Certificate). *Degree requirements:* For master's, comprehensive exam, thesis optional; for doctorate, comprehensive exam, thesis/dissertation (for some programs). *Entrance requirements:* For master's, minimum GPA of 3.0; for doctorate, GRE. Additional exam requirements/recommendations for international students: required—TOEFL (minimum score 550 paper-based). Electronic applications accepted.

Long Island University - Brooklyn, School of Education, Brooklyn, NY 11201-8423. Offers adolescence urban education (MS Ed); applied behavior analysis (Advanced Certificate); bilingual education (Advanced Certificate); bilingual education in urban setting (MS Ed); bilingual school counselor (MS Ed, Advanced Certificate); childhood urban education (MS Ed); childhood/early childhood education (MS Ed); childhood/early childhood urban education (MS Ed); early childhood urban education (MS Ed, Advanced Certificate); educational leadership (Advanced Certificate); marriage and family therapy (MS, Advanced Certificate); mental health counseling (MS, Advanced Certificate); school building district leader (Advanced Certificate); school counselor (MS Ed, Advanced Certificate); school psychologist (MS Ed); teaching students with disabilities (MS Ed); teaching urban children with disabilities (MS Ed); TESOL (MS Ed, Advanced Certificate). *Accreditation:* TEAC. *Program availability:* Part-time, evening/weekend,

100% online. *Entrance requirements:* For master's, GRE. Additional exam requirements/recommendations for international students: required—TOEFL (minimum score 527 paper-based, 75 iBT), IELTS, or PTE. Electronic applications accepted.

Long Island University - Hudson, Graduate School, Purchase, NY 10577. Offers autism (Advanced Certificate); bilingual education (Advanced Certificate); childhood education (MS Ed); crisis management (Advanced Certificate); early childhood education (MS Ed); educational leadership (MS Ed); health administration (MPA); literacy (MS Ed); marriage and family therapy (MS); mental health counseling (MS, Advanced Certificate, including credentialed alcoholism and substance abuse counselor (MS); middle childhood and adolescence education (MS Ed); pharmaceutics (MS), including cosmetic science, industrial pharmacy; public administration (MPA); school counseling (MS Ed, Advanced Certificate); school psychology (MS Ed); special education (MS Ed); TESOL (MS Ed); TESOL (all grades) (Advanced Certificate). *Program availability:* Part-time, evening/weekend. *Entrance requirements:* Additional exam requirements/recommendations for international students: required—TOEFL. Electronic applications accepted. *Expenses:* Contact institution.

Loyola Marymount University, College of Communication and Fine Arts, Program in Marital and Family Therapy, Los Angeles, CA 90045-. Offers MA. *Students:* 49 full-time (48 women); includes 27 minority (1 Black or African American, non-Hispanic/Latino; 9 Asian, non-Hispanic/Latino; 16 Hispanic/Latino; 1 Two or more races, non-Hispanic/Latino), 2 international. Average age 31. 93 applicants, 31% accepted, 25 enrolled. In 2019, 23 master's awarded. *Entrance requirements:* For master's, GRE or Miller Analogies Test, bachelor's degree; undergrad GPA 3.0+; 2 letters of recommendation; psychology and studio art prerequisites; art portfolio; personal autobiography; graduate application; official transcript; online interview; on campus interview; prerequisite checklist form. *Application deadline:* For fall admission, 11/25 for domestic students. Application fee: $50. Electronic applications accepted. *Financial support:* Research assistantships, teaching assistantships, and scholarships/grants available. Financial award applicants required to submit FAFSA. *Unit head:* Anthony Bodlovic, Program Director, Marital and Family Therapy, 310-258-5448, E-mail: anthony.bodlovic@lmu.edu. *Application contact:* Ammar Dalal, Assistant Vice Provost for Graduate Enrollment, 310-338-2721, Fax: 310-338-6086, E-mail: graduateadmission@lmu.edu.
Website: http://cfa.lmu.edu/programs/mft

Loyola University New Orleans, College of Nursing and Health, Department of Counseling, New Orleans, LA 70118. Offers counseling (MS), including marriage and family. *Program availability:* Part-time, evening/weekend. *Faculty:* 5 full-time (3 women), 3 part-time/adjunct (2 women). *Students:* 42 full-time (33 women), 40 part-time (36 women); includes 18 minority (9 Black or African American, non-Hispanic/Latino; 8 Hispanic/Latino; 1 Two or more races, non-Hispanic/Latino), 3 international. Average age 29. 50 applicants, 68% accepted, 27 enrolled. In 2019, 19 master's awarded. *Degree requirements:* For master's, comprehensive exam, minimum GPA of 3.0 in counseling coursework. *Entrance requirements:* For master's, GRE if undergraduate GPA is below 3.0, resume, transcripts, 3 letters of recommendation, statement of objectives (1-3 pgs), bachelors degree from regionally-accredited institution, interview, writing sample. Additional exam requirements/recommendations for international students: required—TOEFL (minimum score 550 paper-based; 79 iBT). *Application deadline:* For fall admission, 12/1 priority date for domestic and international students. Applications are processed on a rolling basis. Electronic applications accepted. *Expenses:* Contact institution. *Financial support:* In 2019–20, 58 students received support. Research assistantships, career-related internships or fieldwork, and tuition waivers (partial) available. Support available to part-time students. Financial award application deadline: 5/1; financial award applicants required to submit FAFSA. *Unit head:* Dr. John Dewell, Chair, 504-864-7858, Fax: 504-864-7844, E-mail: counselingdept@loyno.edu. *Application contact:* Dianna Whitfield, Department Assistant, 504-864-7848, Fax: 504-864-7844, E-mail: counselingdept@loyno.edu.
Website: http://css.loyno.edu/counseling

Manhattan College, Graduate Programs, School of Education and Health, Program in Marriage and Family Therapy, Riverdale, NY 10471. Offers MS.

Maryville University of Saint Louis, Myrtle E. and Earl E. Walker College of Health Professions, Program in Rehabilitation Counseling, St. Louis, MO 63141-7299. Offers marriage and family therapy (MARC); music therapy (MARC); substance abuse (MARC). *Accreditation:* CORE. *Program availability:* Part-time. *Faculty:* 3 full-time (1 woman). *Students:* 18 full-time (16 women), 16 part-time (12 women); includes 9 minority (7 Black or African American, non-Hispanic/Latino; 2 Two or more races, non-Hispanic/Latino). Average age 31. In 2019, 7 master's awarded. *Degree requirements:* For master's, internship, seminar. *Entrance requirements:* For master's, Bachelors degree from regionally accredited institution. minimum cumulative GPA of 3.0, 2 letters of recommendation, interview, essay, transcripts, resume. Additional exam requirements/recommendations for international students: required—TOEFL (minimum score 563 paper-based; 92 iBT). *Application deadline:* For fall admission, 1/15 for domestic students; for spring admission, 10/1 for domestic students. Applications are processed on a rolling basis. Electronic applications accepted. *Expenses:* Contact institution. *Financial support:* Career-related internships or fieldwork, Federal Work-Study, and campus employment available. Financial award application deadline: 4/1; financial award applicants required to submit FAFSA. *Unit head:* Dr. Michael Kiener, Director, 314-529-9443, Fax: 314-529-9495, E-mail: mkiener@maryville.edu. *Application contact:* Jeannie DeLuca, Director, Admissions and Advising, 314-529-9355, Fax: 314-529-9927, E-mail: jdeluca@maryville.edu.
Website: http://www.maryville.edu/hp/rehabilitation-counseling/

Medaille College, Programs in Psychology, Buffalo, NY 14214-2695. Offers clinical psychology (Psy D); marriage and family therapy (MA); mental health counseling (MA); psychology (MA). *Accreditation:* ACA. *Program availability:* Part-time, evening/weekend. *Degree requirements:* For master's, comprehensive exam (for some programs), thesis (for some programs). *Entrance requirements:* For master's, GRE General Test (psychology), minimum GPA of 2.75 (psychology). Additional exam requirements/recommendations for international students: required—TOEFL (minimum score 550 paper-based). Electronic applications accepted.

Mercy College, School of Social and Behavioral Sciences, Program in Counseling, Dobbs Ferry, NY 10522-1189. Offers counseling (MS); family counseling (Certificate). *Program availability:* Part-time, evening/weekend, blended/hybrid learning. *Students:* 53 full-time (48 women), 112 part-time (95 women); includes 125 minority (59 Black or African American, non-Hispanic/Latino; 1 Asian, non-Hispanic/Latino; 62 Hispanic/Latino; 1 Native Hawaiian or other Pacific Islander, non-Hispanic/Latino; 2 Two or more races, non-Hispanic/Latino). Average age 33. 216 applicants, 71% accepted, 63 enrolled. In 2019, 65 master's awarded. *Degree requirements:* For master's, comprehensive exam, Internship. *Entrance requirements:* For master's, transcript(s); two letters of recommendation; resume; essay; interview. Additional exam requirements/recommendations for international students: required—TOEFL (minimum score 80 iBT), IELTS (minimum score 6.5). *Application deadline:* Applications are processed on a rolling basis. Application fee: $40. Electronic applications accepted. *Expenses: Tuition:* Full-time $16,146; part-time $897 per credit. *Required fees:* $332; $166 per semester. Tuition and fees vary according to course load and program. *Financial support:* Career-

related internships or fieldwork, Federal Work-Study, scholarships/grants, and unspecified assistantships available. Support available to part-time students. Financial award applicants required to submit FAFSA. *Unit head:* Dr. Diana Juettner, Interim Dean, School of Social and Behavioral Sciences, 914-674-7546, E-mail: djuettner@mercy.edu. *Application contact:* Allison Gurdineer, Executive Director of Admissions, 877-637-2946, Fax: 914-674-7382, E-mail: admissions@mercy.edu.
Website: https://www.mercy.edu/degrees-programs/ms-counseling

Mercy College, School of Social and Behavioral Sciences, Program in Marriage and Family Therapy, Dobbs Ferry, NY 10522-1189. Offers MS. *Program availability:* Part-time, evening/weekend. *Students:* 14 full-time (11 women), 17 part-time (13 women); includes 19 minority (10 Black or African American, non-Hispanic/Latino; 9 Hispanic/Latino), 1 international. Average age 34. 39 applicants, 64% accepted, 12 enrolled. In 2019, 14 master's awarded. *Degree requirements:* For master's, Capstone project; clinical practicum. *Entrance requirements:* For master's, transcript(s); two letters of recommendation; resume; essay; interview. Additional exam requirements/recommendations for international students: required—TOEFL (minimum score 80 iBT), IELTS (minimum score 6.5). *Application deadline:* Applications are processed on a rolling basis. Application fee: $40. Electronic applications accepted. *Expenses: Tuition:* Full-time $16,146; part-time $897 per credit. *Required fees:* $332; $166 per semester. Tuition and fees vary according to course load and program. *Financial support:* Career-related internships or fieldwork, Federal Work-Study, scholarships/grants, and unspecified assistantships available. Support available to part-time students. Financial award applicants required to submit FAFSA. *Unit head:* Dr. Diana Juettner, Interim Dean, School of Social and Behavioral Sciences, 914-674-7546, E-mail: djuettner@mercy.edu. *Application contact:* Allison Gurdineer, Executive Director of Admissions, 877-637-2946, Fax: 914-674-7382, E-mail: admissions@mercy.edu.
Website: https://www.mercy.edu/degrees-programs/ms-marriage-and-family-therapy

Messiah University, Program in Counseling, Mechanicsburg, PA 17055. Offers clinical mental health counseling (MAC); counseling (CAGS); marriage, couple, and family counseling (MAC); school counseling (MAC). *Accreditation:* ACA. *Program availability:* Part-time, online learning. *Entrance requirements:* For master's, minimum undergraduate cumulative GPA of 3.0, 2 recommendations, resume or curriculum vitae, interview; for CAGS, bachelor's degree, minimum undergraduate cumulative GPA of 3.0, essay, two recommendations, resume or curriculum vitae, interview. Electronic applications accepted.

Mid-America Christian University, Program in Counseling, Oklahoma City, OK 73170-4504. Offers marital and family therapy (MS); pastoral/spiritual direction (MS); professional counselor (MS). *Entrance requirements:* For master's, MAT, bachelor's degree from a regionally accredited college or university, minimum overall cumulative GPA of 2.75 of bachelor course work. Additional exam requirements/recommendations for international students: required—TOEFL (minimum score 550 paper-based).

MidAmerica Nazarene University, School of Behavioral Sciences and Counseling, Olathe, KS 66062-1899. Offers counseling (MA), including clinical mental health, marriage, couple and family, school counseling, spiritual formation in counseling. *Accreditation:* ACA. *Program availability:* 100% online. *Faculty:* 7 full-time (2 women), 14 part-time/adjunct (9 women). *Students:* 64 full-time (52 women), 143 part-time (113 women); includes 33 minority (20 Black or African American, non-Hispanic/Latino; 2 American Indian or Alaska Native, non-Hispanic/Latino; 2 Asian, non-Hispanic/Latino; 8 Hispanic/Latino; 1 Two or more races, non-Hispanic/Latino), 1 international. Average age 34. 131 applicants, 73% accepted, 84 enrolled. In 2019, 50 master's awarded. *Degree requirements:* For master's, comprehensive exam. *Entrance requirements:* For master's, on-site writing assessment, official transcript, three recommendations, personal interview, background check. Additional exam requirements/recommendations for international students: required—TOEFL (minimum score 81 iBT). *Application deadline:* For winter admission, 2/15 for domestic and international students; for spring admission, 4/1 for domestic and international students. Electronic applications accepted. *Expenses:* Technology fee ($2,040), Graduation fee ($100), carrying fee ($286), professional fee($811), lab fee ($325), other fee ($1,068). *Financial support:* Applicants required to submit FAFSA. *Unit head:* Dr. Todd Frye, Dean, School of Behavioral Sciences and Counseling, 913-971-3449, Fax: 913-971-3402, E-mail: tmfrye@mnu.edu. *Application contact:* Jeanne Blades, Administrative Assistant, 913-971-3730, E-mail: jmblades@mnu.edu.

Midwest University, Graduate Programs, Wentzville, MO 63385. Offers asset management/investment/real estate (MBA); Christian counseling (D Min); Christian education (D Min); counseling (MA), including marriage and family counseling, school counseling; divinity (M Div); education (MA), including brain and gifted education, Christian education; global business management (MBA); global leadership (MBA); leadership (PhD), including brain and gifted educational leadership, entrepreneurial leadership, international aviation leadership, organizational leadership, political leadership; mission studies (D Min); music (MM, DMA); pastoral theology (D Min); public policy/administration (MBA); teaching English to speakers of other languages (MA). *Program availability:* Part-time, online learning. *Degree requirements:* For master's, thesis (for some programs); for doctorate, thesis/dissertation. *Entrance requirements:* Additional exam requirements/recommendations for international students: recommended—TOEFL (minimum score 550 paper-based).

Mississippi College, Graduate School, School of Education, Department of Psychology and Counseling, Clinton, MS 39058. Offers counseling (Ed S); marriage and family counseling (MS); mental health counseling (MS); school counseling (M Ed). *Program availability:* Part-time. *Degree requirements:* For master's and Ed S, comprehensive exam, thesis optional. *Entrance requirements:* For master's, GRE or NTE. Additional exam requirements/recommendations for international students: recommended—TOEFL, IELTS. Electronic applications accepted.

Mount Mercy University, Program in Marriage and Family Therapy, Cedar Rapids, IA 52402-4797. Offers MA. *Accreditation:* AAMFT/COAMFTE. *Program availability:* Evening/weekend.

National University, College of Letters and Sciences, La Jolla, CA 92037-1011. Offers biology (MS); counseling psychology (MA), including licensed professional clinical counseling, marriage and family therapy; creative writing (MFA); English (MA); film studies (MA); forensic and crime scene investigations (Certificate); forensic sciences (MFS); human behavior (MA); mathematics for educators (MS); performance psychology (MA); strategic communications (MA). *Program availability:* Part-time, evening/weekend, 100% online, blended/hybrid learning. *Degree requirements:* For master's, thesis (for some programs). *Entrance requirements:* For master's, interview, minimum GPA of 2.5. Additional exam requirements/recommendations for international students: required—TOEFL (minimum score 550 paper-based; 79 iBT), IELTS (minimum score 6). Electronic applications accepted. *Expenses: Tuition:* Full-time $442; part-time $442 per unit.

Northcentral University, Graduate Studies, San Diego, CA 92106. Offers business (MBA, DBA, PhD, Postbaccalaureate Certificate); education (M Ed, Ed D, PhD, Ed S, Post-Master's Certificate, Postbaccalaureate Certificate); marriage and family therapy (MA, DMFT, PhD, Post-Master's Certificate, Postbaccalaureate Certificate); psychology (MA, PhD, Post-Master's Certificate, Postbaccalaureate Certificate); technology (MS,

PhD), including computer science, cybersecurity (MS), data science, technology and innovation management (PhD). *Program availability:* Part-time, evening/weekend, online only, 100% online. *Degree requirements:* For doctorate, comprehensive exam, thesis/dissertation. *Entrance requirements:* For master's, bachelor's degree from regionally- or nationally-accredited institution, current resume or curriculum vitae, statement of intent, interview, and background check (for marriage and family therapy); for doctorate, post-baccalaureate master's degree and/or doctoral degree from nationally- or regionally-accredited academic institution; for other advanced degree, bachelor's-level or higher degree from accredited institution or university (for Post-Baccalaureate Certificate); master's and/or doctoral degree from regionally- or nationally-accredited academic institution (for Post-Master's Certificate). Additional exam requirements/recommendations for international students: required—TOEFL (minimum score 550 paper-based; 79 iBT), IELTS (minimum score 6.5), PTE (minimum score 53). Electronic applications accepted. *Expenses: Tuition:* Part-time $1053 per credit. *Required fees:* $95 per course. Full-time tuition and fees vary according to degree level and program.

Northeastern Illinois University, College of Graduate Studies and Research, Daniel L. Goodwin College of Education, Program in Family Counseling, Chicago, IL 60625. Offers MA.

Northern Kentucky University, Office of Graduate Programs, College of Informatics, Program in Communication, Highland Heights, KY 41099. Offers communication (MA); communication teaching (Certificate); documentary studies (Certificate); public relations (Certificate); relationships (Certificate). *Program availability:* Part-time, evening/weekend. Terminal master's awarded for partial completion of doctoral program. *Degree requirements:* For master's, comprehensive exams, thesis or applied capstone project. *Entrance requirements:* For master's, GRE, minimum GPA of 3.0, 3 letters of recommendation, letter of intent. Additional exam requirements/recommendations for international students: required—TOEFL (minimum score 79 iBT); recommended—IELTS (minimum score 6.5). Electronic applications accepted.

Northwestern University, The Graduate School, Program in Marital and Family Therapy, Evanston, IL 60208. Offers MS. *Entrance requirements:* For master's, GRE General Test.

Northwest Nazarene University, Program in Counselor Education, Nampa, ID 83686-5897. Offers clinical counseling (MS); marriage and family counseling (MS); school counseling (MS). *Program availability:* Part-time, evening/weekend. *Degree requirements:* For master's, comprehensive exam. *Entrance requirements:* For master's, GRE (if GPA less than 3.0), minimum GPA of 3.0, BA, 2 letters of recommendation, definition of counseling writing sample, background check, group evaluation, role play, dispositions rubric score. Additional exam requirements/recommendations for international students: required—TOEFL (minimum score 85 paper-based), WES. Electronic applications accepted.

Notre Dame de Namur University, Division of Academic Affairs, School of Education and Psychology, Program in Clinical Psychology: Marital and Family Therapy, Belmont, CA 94002-1908. Offers MS. *Program availability:* Part-time, evening/weekend. *Degree requirements:* For master's, thesis. *Entrance requirements:* Additional exam requirements/recommendations for international students: required—TOEFL (minimum score 550 paper-based; 79 iBT). Electronic applications accepted.

Nova Southeastern University, College of Arts, Humanities, and Social Sciences, Fort Lauderdale, FL 33314-7796. Offers advanced conflict resolution practice (Graduate Certificate); child protection (MHS); college student affairs (MS); conflict analysis and resolution (MS, PhD); criminal justice (MS, PhD); cross-disciplinary studies (MA); developmental disabilities (MS); family studies (Graduate Certificate); family systems health care (Graduate Certificate); family therapy (MS, PhD); marriage and family therapy (DMFT); peace studies (Graduate Certificate); qualitative research (Graduate Certificate); solution focused coaching (Graduate Certificate). *Accreditation:* AAMFT/COAMFTE (one or more programs are accredited). *Program availability:* Part-time, evening/weekend, 100% online, blended/hybrid learning. *Faculty:* 60 full-time (37 women), 88 part-time/adjunct (65 women). *Students:* 201 full-time (157 women), 418 part-time (297 women); includes 365 minority (180 Black or African American, non-Hispanic/Latino; 4 American Indian or Alaska Native, non-Hispanic/Latino; 15 Asian, non-Hispanic/Latino; 141 Hispanic/Latino; 25 Two or more races, non-Hispanic/Latino), 49 international. Average age 37. 303 applicants, 84% accepted, 197 enrolled. In 2019, 125 master's, 63 doctorates, 24 other advanced degrees awarded. *Degree requirements:* For master's, comprehensive exam (for some programs), thesis optional, comprehensive exams, portfolios (for some programs), table-top exams (for some programs); for doctorate, comprehensive exam, thesis/dissertation, qualifying exams, portfolios (for some programs). *Entrance requirements:* For master's, interview, minimum GPA of 3.0, writing sample; for doctorate, interview, minimum GPA of 3.5, master's degree in related field, writing sample; for Graduate Certificate, minimum GPA of 3.0. Additional exam requirements/recommendations for international students: required—TOEFL (minimum score 79 paper-based). *Application deadline:* Applications are processed on a rolling basis. Application fee: $50. Electronic applications accepted. *Expenses:* Contact institution. *Financial support:* In 2019–20, 170 students received support. Career-related internships or fieldwork, Federal Work-Study, scholarships/grants, and unspecified assistantships available. Financial award application deadline: 4/1; financial award applicants required to submit FAFSA. *Unit head:* Dr. Honggang Yang, Dean, 954-262-3016, Fax: 954-262-3968, E-mail: yangh@nova.edu. *Application contact:* Marcia Arango, Student Recruitment Coordinator, 954-262-3006, Fax: 954-262-3968, E-mail: marango@nsu.nova.edu.
Website: http://cahss.nova.edu/

Nyack College, Alliance Graduate School of Counseling, New York, NY 10004. Offers marriage and family therapy (MA); mental health counseling (MA). *Program availability:* Part-time, evening/weekend, 100% online, blended/hybrid learning. *Students:* 62 full-time (56 women), 128 part-time (102 women); includes 157 minority (62 Black or African American, non-Hispanic/Latino; 1 American Indian or Alaska Native, non-Hispanic/Latino; 40 Asian, non-Hispanic/Latino; 48 Hispanic/Latino; 6 Two or more races, non-Hispanic/Latino), 4 international. Average age 37. In 2019, 60 master's awarded. *Degree requirements:* For master's, comprehensive exam, counselor-in-training therapy, internship, CPCE exam. *Entrance requirements:* For master's, Millon Clinical Multiaxial Inventory-3, Minnesota Multiphasic Personality Inventory-2, transcripts, statement of Christian life and experience, statement of support systems. Additional exam requirements/recommendations for international students: required—TOEFL (minimum score 550 paper-based; 80 iBT). *Application deadline:* For fall admission, 8/1 for domestic students, 2/15 for international students; for spring admission, 12/15 for domestic students, 7/15 for international students. Applications are processed on a rolling basis. Application fee: $30. Electronic applications accepted. *Expenses:* $800 per credit. *Financial support:* Career-related internships or fieldwork and scholarships/grants available. Financial award applicants required to submit FAFSA. *Unit head:* Dr. Antoinette Gines-Rivera, Director, 646-378-6160. *Application contact:* Dr. Antoinette Gines-Rivera, Director, 646-378-6160.
Website: http://www.nyack.edu/agsc

Oklahoma Baptist University, Program in Marriage and Family Therapy, Shawnee, OK 74804. Offers MS. *Program availability:* Part-time, evening/weekend. *Degree requirements:* For master's, thesis optional, practicum. *Entrance requirements:* For master's, GRE General Test. Additional exam requirements/recommendations for international students: required—TOEFL. Electronic applications accepted.

Oral Roberts University, School of Theology and Missions, Tulsa, OK 74171. Offers biblical literature (MA), including advanced languages, Judaic-Christian studies; church ministries and leadership (D Min); clinical pastoral education (M Div); missions (MA); pastoral care and chaplaincy (M Div, D Min); practical theology (MA), including teaching ministries, urban ministries; professional counseling (MA), including addiction studies, marriage and family therapy; theological/historical studies (MA). *Accreditation:* ATS. *Program availability:* Part-time, online learning. *Faculty:* 17 full-time (2 women). *Students:* 268 full-time (146 women), 96 part-time (52 women); includes 66 minority (48 Black or African American, non-Hispanic/Latino; 9 American Indian or Alaska Native, non-Hispanic/Latino; 8 Asian, non-Hispanic/Latino; 1 Native Hawaiian or other Pacific Islander, non-Hispanic/Latino), 65 international. Average age 40. 661 applicants, 24% accepted, 136 enrolled. In 2019, 113 master's, 19 doctorates awarded. *Degree requirements:* For master's, thesis (for some programs), practicum/internship; for doctorate, thesis/dissertation, applied research project. *Entrance requirements:* For master's, GRE General Test or MAT (waived for those with undergraduate degree from regionally accredited institution and 3.0 or higher GPA), minimum GPA of 2.5 (professional) or 3.0 (academic); for doctorate, M Div, minimum GPA of 3.0, 3 years of full-time ministry experience. Additional exam requirements/recommendations for international students: recommended—TOEFL (minimum score 550 paper-based; 79 iBT), IELTS (minimum score 7). *Application deadline:* Applications are processed on a rolling basis. Application fee: $35. Electronic applications accepted. Application fee is waived when completed online. *Expenses: Tuition:* Full-time $11,052; part-time $5526 per year. *Required fees:* $1230; $615 per unit. Tuition and fees vary according to program. *Financial support:* Fellowships and scholarships/grants available. Financial award application deadline: 6/1. *Unit head:* Dr. Bill Buker, Chair, 918-495-6493, E-mail: bbuker@oru.edu. *Application contact:* Joe Sims, Enrollment Counselor, 918-495-6618, E-mail: jsims@oru.edu.
Website: http://www.gradtheology.oru.edu/

Ottawa University, Graduate Studies-Arizona, Program in Professional Counseling, Ottawa, KS 66067-3399. Offers Christian counseling (MA); expressive arts therapy (MA); marriage and family therapy (MA); treatment of trauma, abuse and deprivation (MA). *Program availability:* Part-time, evening/weekend, online learning. *Degree requirements:* For master's, comprehensive exam, thesis or alternative, field experience, practicum. *Entrance requirements:* For master's, minimum undergraduate GPA of 3.0; course work in theories of personality, abnormal psychology, and human growth and development. Additional exam requirements/recommendations for international students: required—TOEFL (minimum score 550 paper-based).

Our Lady of the Lake University, College of Professional Studies, Program in Psychology, San Antonio, TX 78207-4689. Offers marriage and family therapy (MS); school psychology (MS). *Accreditation:* APA. *Program availability:* Part-time. *Degree requirements:* For master's, comprehensive exam, practicum. *Entrance requirements:* For master's, GRE General Test or MAT, bachelor's degree with at least 12 undergraduate semester hours in psychology including one course in statistics and minimum cumulative GPA of 3.0; criminal background check; personal statement addressing background in psychology, expectations of the MS program, and professional goals; statement of purpose; 2 letters of recommendation. Additional exam requirements/recommendations for international students: required—TOEFL. Electronic applications accepted. Application fee is waived when completed online.

Pacific Lutheran University, Division of Social Sciences, Program in Marriage and Family Therapy, Tacoma, WA 98447. Offers MA. *Accreditation:* AAMFT/COAMFTE. *Program availability:* Part-time. *Degree requirements:* For master's, thesis optional, clinical competency. *Entrance requirements:* Additional exam requirements/recommendations for international students: required—TOEFL (minimum score 550 paper-based; 88 iBT). Electronic applications accepted.

Pacific Oaks College, Graduate School, Program in Marriage and Family Therapy, Pasadena, CA 91103. Offers marriage, family and child counseling (MA). *Program availability:* Part-time, evening/weekend. *Degree requirements:* For master's, thesis. *Entrance requirements:* For master's, interview. Additional exam requirements/recommendations for international students: required—TOEFL (minimum score 550 paper-based).

Palm Beach Atlantic University, School of Education and Behavioral Studies, West Palm Beach, FL 33416-4708. Offers counseling psychology (MS), including addictions/mental health, general counseling, marriage and family therapy, mental health counseling, school guidance counseling. *Program availability:* Part-time, evening/weekend. *Entrance requirements:* For master's, GRE or MAT, minimum GPA of 3.0; essay. Additional exam requirements/recommendations for international students: required—TOEFL (minimum score 550 paper-based; 79 iBT). Electronic applications accepted. *Expenses: Tuition:* Part-time $570 per credit hour. *Required fees:* $580 per unit. Tuition and fees vary according to degree level, campus/location and program.

Palo Alto University, MA in Counseling Program, Palo Alto, CA 94304. Offers clinical mental health (MA); marriage, family and child (MA). *Program availability:* Part-time, 100% online, blended/hybrid learning. *Degree requirements:* For master's, capstone project. *Entrance requirements:* For master's, undergraduate degree in psychology with minimum GPA of 3.3. Additional exam requirements/recommendations for international students: required—TOEFL. Electronic applications accepted. *Expenses:* Contact institution.

Phillips Graduate University, Master's Program in Psychology, Chatsworth, CA 91311. Offers art therapy (MA); marriage and family therapy (MA); school counseling (MA); school psychology (MA). *Program availability:* Evening/weekend. *Degree requirements:* For master's, comprehensive exam, thesis. *Entrance requirements:* For master's, minimum GPA of 2.5. Electronic applications accepted.

Pillar College, Program in Counseling, Newark, NJ 07102. Offers MA.

Plymouth State University, College of Graduate Studies, Graduate Studies in Education, Programs in Counseling, Plymouth, NH 03264-1595. Offers addictions treatment (MS); couples and family therapy (MS); play therapy (MS). *Accreditation:* ACA; NCATE. *Program availability:* Part-time, evening/weekend. *Entrance requirements:* For master's, MAT, minimum GPA of 3.0.

Point Loma Nazarene University, College of Extended Learning, Program in Clinical Counseling, San Diego, CA 92108. Offers marriage and family therapy (MA); professional clinical counselor (MA). *Faculty:* 1 (woman) full-time, 12 part-time/adjunct (6 women). *Students:* 81 full-time (70 women), 10 part-time (all women); includes 45 minority (4 Black or African American, non-Hispanic/Latino; 4 Asian, non-Hispanic/Latino; 31 Hispanic/Latino; 6 Two or more races, non-Hispanic/Latino). Average age 29. 32 applicants, 91% accepted, 28 enrolled. In 2019, 19 master's awarded. *Degree requirements:* For master's, comprehensive exam. Application fee: $50. *Expenses:* $790 per unit. *Financial support:* In 2019–20, 18 students received support. Scholarships/grants available. Financial award applicants required to submit FAFSA. *Unit head:* Dr. Daniel Lee Jenkins, Ph.D, Program Director, 619-849-7850, E-mail:

DanJenkins@pointloma.edu. *Application contact:* Dana Barger, Director of Recruitment and Admissions, Graduate and Professional Students, 619-329-6799, E-mail: gradinfo@pointloma.edu.
Website: https://www.pointloma.edu/graduate-studies/programs/clinical-counseling-ma

Pontifical John Paul II Institute for Studies on Marriage and Family, Graduate Programs, Washington, DC 20064. Offers biotechnology and ethics (MTS); marriage and family (MTS, STD, STL); theology (PhD).

Purdue University, Graduate School, College of Health and Human Sciences, Department of Child Development and Family Studies, West Lafayette, IN 47907. Offers developmental studies (MS, PhD); family studies (MS, PhD); marriage and family therapy (MS, PhD). *Program availability:* Part-time. *Faculty:* 22 full-time (16 women), 2 part-time/adjunct (1 woman). *Students:* 22 full-time (21 women), 1 (woman) part-time; includes 3 minority (1 Black or African American, non-Hispanic/Latino; 1 Asian, non-Hispanic/Latino; 1 Two or more races, non-Hispanic/Latino), 8 international. Average age 26. 51 applicants, 25% accepted, 4 enrolled. In 2019, 2 master's, 3 doctorates awarded. Terminal master's awarded for partial completion of doctoral program. *Degree requirements:* For master's, thesis; for doctorate, thesis/dissertation. *Entrance requirements:* For master's and doctorate, GRE General Test (minimum score 1000 combined verbal and quantitative), minimum undergraduate GPA of 3.0 or equivalent. Additional exam requirements/recommendations for international students: required—TOEFL (minimum score 600 paper-based; 90 iBT), TWE (minimum score 4). *Application deadline:* For fall admission, 1/4 for domestic and international students. Applications are processed on a rolling basis. Application fee: $60 ($75 for international students). Electronic applications accepted. *Financial support:* Fellowships with full tuition reimbursements, research assistantships with full tuition reimbursements, teaching assistantships with full tuition reimbursements, and career-related internships or fieldwork available. Support available to part-time students. Financial award application deadline: 1/15; financial award applicants required to submit FAFSA. *Unit head:* Dr. Doran C. French, Head, 765-494-9511, E-mail: dcfrench@purdue.edu. *Application contact:* Tina Putz, Graduate Contact, 765-496-3816, E-mail: tputz@purdue.edu.
Website: http://www.purdue.edu/hhs/hdfs/

Purdue University Fort Wayne, College of Professional Studies, School of Education, Fort Wayne, IN 46805-1499. Offers couple and family counseling (MS Ed); educational leadership (MS Ed); elementary education (MS Ed); school counseling (MS Ed); secondary education (MS Ed); special education (MS Ed, Certificate). *Accreditation:* NCATE. *Program availability:* Part-time. *Entrance requirements:* For master's, minimum GPA of 2.5, three professional letters of recommendation. Additional exam requirements/recommendations for international students: required—TOEFL (minimum score 550 paper-based; 79 iBT).

Purdue University Northwest, Graduate Studies Office, School of Liberal Arts and Social Sciences, Department of Behavioral Sciences, Hammond, IN 46323-2094. Offers child development and family studies (MS); marriage and family therapy (MS). *Accreditation:* AAMFT/COAMFTE. *Program availability:* Part-time. *Degree requirements:* For master's, thesis. *Entrance requirements:* For master's, GRE, interview. Additional exam requirements/recommendations for international students: required—TOEFL.

Reformed Theological Seminary–Jackson Campus, Graduate and Professional Programs, Jackson, MS 39209-3004. Offers Bible, theology, and missions (Certificate); Biblical exegesis (M Div); biblical studies (MA); Christian education (MA); counseling (M Div); marriage and family therapy (MA); ministry (D Min); missions (M Div, MA, D Min); theological studies (MA). *Accreditation:* AAMFT/COAMFTE (one or more programs are accredited); ATS (one or more programs are accredited). *Degree requirements:* For master's, thesis (for some programs), fieldwork; for doctorate, 2 foreign languages, thesis/dissertation. *Entrance requirements:* For master's, minimum GPA of 2.6; for doctorate, minimum GPA of 3.0. Additional exam requirements/recommendations for international students: required—TOEFL.

Regent University, Graduate School, School of Psychology and Counseling, Virginia Beach, VA 23464-9800. Offers clinical mental health counseling (MA); clinical psychology (Psy D); counseling and psychological studies - clinical (PhD); counseling and psychological studies - research (PhD); counseling studies (CAGS); counselor education and supervision (PhD); general psychology (MS); human services (MA), including addictions counseling, Biblical counseling, Christian counseling, conflict and mediation ministry, criminal justice and ministry, grief counseling, human services counseling, human services for student affairs, life coaching, marriage and family ministry, trauma and crisis counseling; marriage, couple, and family counseling (MA); pastoral counseling (MA); school counseling (MA); M Div/MA; M Ed/MA; MBA/MA. *Accreditation:* ACA; APA (one or more programs are accredited). *Program availability:* Part-time, evening/weekend, 100% online, blended/hybrid learning. *Degree requirements:* For master's, thesis or alternative, internship, practicum, written competency exam; for doctorate, thesis/dissertation or alternative. *Entrance requirements:* For master's, GRE General Test (including writing exam) or MAT, minimum undergraduate GPA of 3.0, resume, transcripts, writing sample, personal goals statement; for doctorate, GRE General Test (including writing exam), minimum undergraduate GPA of 3.0, graduate 3.5; writing sample; 3 recommendations; resume; college transcripts; personal goals statement. Additional exam requirements/recommendations for international students: required—TOEFL (minimum score 577 paper-based). Electronic applications accepted. *Expenses:* Contact institution.

Regis University, Rueckert-Hartman College for Health Professions, Denver, CO 80221-1099. Offers advanced practice nurse (DNP); counseling (MA); counseling children and adolescents (Post-Graduate Certificate); counseling military families (Post-Graduate Certificate); depth psychotherapy (Post-Graduate Certificate); fellowship in orthopedic manual physical therapy (Certificate); health care business management (Certificate); health care quality and patient safety (Certificate); health industry leadership (MBA); health services administration (MS); marriage and family therapy (MA, Post-Graduate Certificate); neonatal nurse practitioner (MSN); nursing education (MSN); nursing leadership (MSN); occupational therapy (OTD); pharmacy (Pharm D); physical therapy (DPT). *Accreditation:* ACPE. *Program availability:* Part-time, evening/weekend, 100% online, blended/hybrid learning. *Degree requirements:* For master's, thesis (for some programs), internship. *Entrance requirements:* For master's, official transcript reflecting baccalaureate degree awarded from regionally-accredited college or university. Additional exam requirements/recommendations for international students: required—TOEFL (minimum score 550 paper-based; 82 iBT). Electronic applications accepted. *Expenses:* Contact institution.

Richmont Graduate University, School of Counseling, Atlanta, GA 30339. Offers clinical mental health counseling (MA); marriage and family therapy (MA). *Accreditation:* ACA. *Program availability:* Part-time, evening/weekend. *Degree requirements:* For master's, comprehensive exam, thesis optional. *Entrance requirements:* For master's, GRE or MAT. Electronic applications accepted.

St. Cloud State University, School of Graduate Studies, School of Health and Human Services, Department of Counseling and Community Psychology, Program in Marriage and Family Therapy, St. Cloud, MN 56301-4498. Offers MS. *Accreditation:* AAMFT/COAMFTE. *Entrance requirements:* Additional exam requirements/recommendations

for international students: required—Michigan English Language Assessment Battery; recommended—TOEFL (minimum score 550 paper-based), IELTS (minimum score 6.5). Electronic applications accepted.

Saint Mary's College of California, Kalmanovitz School of Education, Program in Counseling, Moraga, CA 94575. Offers career counseling (MA); college student services (Credential); general counseling (MA); marriage and family therapy (MA); pupil personnel services (Credential), including school counseling, school psychology; school counseling (MA); school psychology (MA). *Program availability:* Part-time, evening/weekend. *Degree requirements:* For master's, thesis or alternative. *Entrance requirements:* For master's, interview, minimum GPA of 3.0.

Saint Mary's University of Minnesota, Schools of Graduate and Professional Programs, Graduate School of Health and Human Services, Marriage and Family Therapy Program, Winona, MN 55987-1399. Offers MA. *Unit head:* Dr. Samantha Zaid, Program Director, 612-728-5140, Fax: 612-728-5121, E-mail: szaid@smumn.edu. *Application contact:* Laurie Roy, Director of Admission of Schools of Graduate and Professional Programs, 507-457-8606, Fax: 612-728-5121, E-mail: lroy@smumn.edu.
Website: http://www.smumn.edu/graduate-home/areas-of-study/graduate-school-of-health-human-services/ma-in-marriage-family-therapy

Saint Paul University, Faculty of Human Sciences, Program in Counseling and Spirituality, Ottawa, ON K1S 1C4, Canada. Offers individual or marital/couple counseling (MA); spiritual care (MA). *Program availability:* Part-time. *Degree requirements:* For master's, research project or thesis. *Entrance requirements:* For master's, honors BA in human sciences, minimum B average, 12 theology credits.

St. Thomas University - Florida, Biscayne College, Department of Social Sciences and Counseling, Program in Marriage and Family Therapy, Miami Gardens, FL 33054-6459. Offers MS, Post-Master's Certificate. *Program availability:* Part-time, evening/weekend. *Degree requirements:* For master's, comprehensive exam. *Entrance requirements:* For master's, interview, minimum GPA of 3.0 or GRE. Additional exam requirements/recommendations for international students: required—TOEFL. Electronic applications accepted.

San Francisco State University, Division of Graduate Studies, College of Health and Social Sciences, Department of Counseling, San Francisco, CA 94132-1722. Offers clinical mental health counseling (MS); marriage, family and child counseling (MS). *Accreditation:* ACA. *Program availability:* Part-time. *Application deadline:* Applications are processed on a rolling basis. *Expenses: Tuition, area resident:* Full-time $7176; part-time $4164 per year. Tuition, state resident: full-time $7176; part-time $4164 per year. Tuition, nonresident: full-time $16,680; part-time $396 per unit. *International tuition:* $16,680 full-time. *Required fees:* $1524; $1524 per unit. $762 per semester. Tuition and fees vary according to degree level and program. *Unit head:* Dr. Rebecca Toporek, Chair, 415-338-2005, Fax: 415-338-0594, E-mail: counsel@sfsu.edu. *Application contact:* Dr. Graciela Orozco, College Counseling Coordinator, 415-338-1064, Fax: 415-338-0594, E-mail: orozco@sfsu.edu.
Website: http://counseling.sfsu.edu

Saybrook University, School of Psychology and Interdisciplinary Inquiry, San Francisco, CA 94612. Offers human science (MA, PhD), including consciousness and spirituality, humanistic and transpersonal psychology, integrative health studies, organizational systems, social transformation; organizational systems (MA, PhD), including consciousness and spirituality, humanistic and transpersonal psychology, integrative health studies, leadership of sustainable systems (MA), organizational systems, social transformation; psychology (MA, PhD), including consciousness and spirituality, creativity studies (MA), humanistic and transpersonal psychology, integrative health studies, Jungian studies, marriage and family therapy (MA), organizational systems, social transformation. *Program availability:* Online learning. Terminal master's awarded for partial completion of doctoral program. *Degree requirements:* For master's, thesis or alternative; for doctorate, thesis/dissertation. *Entrance requirements:* Additional exam requirements/recommendations for international students: required—TOEFL (minimum score 580 paper-based; 93 iBT). Electronic applications accepted.

Seattle Pacific University, MS in Marriage and Family Therapy Program, Seattle, WA 98119-1997. Offers marriage and family therapy (MS); medical family therapy (Certificate). *Accreditation:* AAMFT/COAMFTE. *Program availability:* Part-time. *Students:* 51 full-time (44 women), 12 part-time (9 women); includes 16 minority (3 Black or African American, non-Hispanic/Latino; 6 Asian, non-Hispanic/Latino; 3 Hispanic/Latino; 4 Two or more races, non-Hispanic/Latino), 3 international. Average age 31. 60 applicants, 47% accepted, 27 enrolled. In 2019, 22 master's awarded. *Degree requirements:* For master's, thesis optional, internship, clinical portfolio. *Entrance requirements:* For master's, GRE General Test or MAT, interview. Additional exam requirements/recommendations for international students: required—TOEFL (minimum score 550 paper-based). *Application deadline:* For fall admission, 1/23 for domestic students, 2/1 for international students. Applications are processed on a rolling basis. Application fee: $50. Electronic applications accepted. *Expenses:* Contact institution. *Financial support:* Fellowships and Federal Work-Study available. Financial award applicants required to submit FAFSA. *Unit head:* Dr. Scott Edwards, Chair, 206-281-2681, E-mail: sedwards@spu.edu. *Application contact:* Dr. Scott Edwards, Chair, 206-281-2681, E-mail: sedwards@spu.edu.
Website: http://spu.edu/academics/school-of-psychology-family-community/graduate-programs/marriage-and-family-therapy

Seattle University, School of Theology and Ministry, Program in Couples and Family Therapy, Seattle, WA 98122-1090. Offers MA. *Program availability:* Part-time, evening/weekend. *Faculty:* 22 full-time (12 women), 22 part-time/adjunct (14 women). *Students:* 27 full-time (24 women), 22 part-time (21 women); includes 17 minority (4 Black or African American, non-Hispanic/Latino; 5 Asian, non-Hispanic/Latino; 3 Hispanic/Latino; 5 Two or more races, non-Hispanic/Latino). Average age 32. 23 applicants, 87% accepted, 12 enrolled. In 2019, 5 master's awarded. *Entrance requirements:* For master's, minimum GPA of 2.75 (3.0 for international students); two years of experience in some form of education, ministry, or service as a profession or volunteer; recommendations; interview with admissions committee. *Application deadline:* For fall admission, 7/1 for domestic students. *Expenses:* Contact institution. *Financial support:* In 2019–20, 28 students received support. Scholarships/grants available. *Unit head:* Rev. Clinton McNair, Director, 206-296-6968. *Application contact:* Catherine Kehoe Fallon, Admissions Coordinator, 206-296-5333, Fax: 206-296-5329, E-mail: fallon@seattleu.edu.
Website: https://www.seattleu.edu/stm/degrees/macft/

Sioux Falls Seminary, Graduate and Professional Programs, Master of Divinity Program, Sioux Falls, SD 57105-1599. Offers marriage and family therapy (M Div); pastoral care and counseling (M Div). *Accreditation:* ACIPE. *Program availability:* Part-time, online learning.

Southeastern University, College of Behavioral & Social Sciences, Lakeland, FL 33801. Offers human services (MA); international community development (MA); pastoral care and counseling (MS); professional counseling (MS); school counseling (MS); social work (MSW). *Program availability:* Evening/weekend. *Faculty:* 17 full-time (12 women). *Students:* 95 full-time (80 women), 9 part-time (6 women); includes 49 minority (18 Black or African American, non-Hispanic/Latino; 3 Asian, non-Hispanic/

Latino; 25 Hispanic/Latino; 1 Native Hawaiian or other Pacific Islander, non-Hispanic/ Latino; 2 Two or more races, non-Hispanic/Latino), 1 international. Average age 28. In 2019, 50 master's awarded. *Entrance requirements:* Additional exam requirements/ recommendations for international students: required—TOEFL (minimum score 76 iBT), IELTS (minimum score 6). Application fee: $50. Electronic applications accepted. *Unit head:* Dr. Erica H. Sirrine, Dean, 863-667-5341, E-mail: ehsirrine@seu.edu. *Application contact:* Dr. Erica H. Sirrine, Dean, 863-667-5341, E-mail: ehsirrine@seu.edu.
Website: http://www.seu.edu/behavior/

Southern California Seminary, Graduate and Professional Programs, El Cajon, CA 92019. Offers Biblical studies (MABS); counseling psychology (MACP); marriage and family therapy (MAMFT); psychology (Psy D); religious studies (MRS); theology (M Div). *Program availability:* Part-time, evening/weekend, online learning. *Degree requirements:* For master's, thesis (for some programs); for doctorate, thesis/dissertation. *Entrance requirements:* For doctorate, master's degree in psychology. Additional exam requirements/recommendations for international students: required—TOEFL (minimum score 550 paper-based). Electronic applications accepted.

Southern Nazarene University, College of Professional and Graduate Studies, Department of Psychology and Counseling, Bethany, OK 73008. Offers counseling psychology (MA, MSCP); marital and family therapy (MA). *Degree requirements:* For master's, thesis optional. *Entrance requirements:* For master's, English proficiency exam, minimum GPA of 3.0 in last 60 hours/major, 2.7 overall.

Syracuse University, David B. Falk College of Sport and Human Dynamics, Dual Master's Program in Social Work and Marriage and Family Therapy (MSW/MA), Syracuse, NY 13244. Offers MSW/MA. *Accreditation:* AAMFT/COAMFTE. *Entrance requirements:* Additional exam requirements/recommendations for international students: required—TOEFL or IELTS. Electronic applications accepted.

Syracuse University, David B. Falk College of Sport and Human Dynamics, Programs in Marriage and Family Therapy, Syracuse, NY 13244. Offers MA, PhD. *Accreditation:* AAMFT/COAMFTE. *Program availability:* Part-time. *Degree requirements:* For master's, thesis or alternative, internship; for doctorate, comprehensive exam, thesis/dissertation. *Entrance requirements:* For master's and doctorate, GRE, personal statement, three letters of recommendation, official transcripts, resume. Additional exam requirements/ recommendations for international students: required—TOEFL (minimum score 100 iBT). Electronic applications accepted.

Texas A&M University–Central Texas, Graduate Studies and Research, Killeen, TX 76549. Offers accounting (MS); business administration (MBA); clinical mental health counseling (MS); criminal justice (MCJ); curriculum and instruction (M Ed); educational administration (M Ed); educational psychology - experimental psychology (MS); history (MA); human resource management (MS); information systems (MS); liberal studies (MS); management and leadership (MS); marriage and family therapy (MS); mathematics (MS); political science (MA); school counseling (M Ed); school psychology (Ed S).

Texas A&M University–San Antonio, Department of Counseling, Health and Kinesiology, San Antonio, TX 78224. Offers clinical mental health counseling (MA); counseling and guidance (MA); kinesiology (MS); marriage and family counseling (MA). *Program availability:* Part-time, evening/weekend, online learning. *Degree requirements:* For master's, comprehensive exam, thesis or alternative. *Entrance requirements:* For master's, MAT or GRE (composite quantitative and verbal). Additional exam requirements/recommendations for international students: required—TOEFL (minimum score 550 paper-based; 79 iBT), IELTS (minimum score 6). Electronic applications accepted. *Expenses: Tuition, area resident:* Full-time $3822; part-time $1068 per semester. *Required fees:* $2146; $1412 per unit. $706 per semester.

Texas State University, The Graduate College, College of Education, Program in Professional Counseling, San Marcos, TX 78666. Offers clinical mental health counseling (MA); marriage and family counseling (MA); school counseling (MA). *Accreditation:* ACA. *Program availability:* Part-time. *Degree requirements:* For master's, comprehensive exam, thesis optional, internship. *Entrance requirements:* For master's, Official GRE (general test only) required with competitive scores in the verbal and quantitative reasoning sections, baccalaureate degree from regionally-accredited institution with minimum GPA of 3.0 in last 60 hours of undergraduate work; resume; statement of purpose addressing professional goals, reasoning for specified emphasis (i.e., community, school, marital), strengths and weaknesses, and perspective on diversity; 3 references. Additional exam requirements/recommendations for international students: required—TOEFL (minimum iBT scores: 22 listening, 22 reading, 24 speaking, 21 writing). Electronic applications accepted.

Texas Tech University, Graduate School, College of Human Sciences, Department of Community, Family, and Addiction Sciences, Lubbock, TX 79409-1250. Offers couple, marriage, & family therapy (MS, PhD). *Accreditation:* AAMFT/COAMFTE. *Faculty:* 16 full-time (5 women), 3 part-time/adjunct (2 women). *Students:* 50 full-time (32 women), 11 part-time (6 women); includes 20 minority (3 Black or African American, non-Hispanic/Latino; 14 Hispanic/Latino; 3 Two or more races, non-Hispanic/Latino), 2 international. Average age 29. 76 applicants, 29% accepted, 21 enrolled. In 2019, 15 master's, 10 doctorates awarded. *Degree requirements:* For master's, comprehensive exam, thesis optional; for doctorate, thesis/dissertation. *Entrance requirements:* For master's and doctorate, GRE. Additional exam requirements/recommendations for international students: required—TOEFL (minimum score 550 paper-based; 79 iBT). *Application deadline:* For fall admission, 6/1 priority date for domestic students, 1/15 priority date for international students; for spring admission, 9/1 priority date for domestic students, 6/15 priority date for international students. Applications are processed on a rolling basis. Application fee: $65. Electronic applications accepted. *Expenses:* Contact institution. *Financial support:* In 2019–20, 65 students received support, including 55 fellowships (averaging $4,411 per year), 18 research assistantships (averaging $13,288 per year), 17 teaching assistantships (averaging $14,931 per year); career-related internships or fieldwork, Federal Work-Study, scholarships/grants, health care benefits, and unspecified assistantships also available. Financial award application deadline: 2/1; financial award applicants required to submit FAFSA. *Unit head:* Dr. Sterling T. Shumway, Chairperson, Evelyn M. Davies Regent's Professor, 806-742-3060, Fax: 806-742-0053, E-mail: sterling.shumway@ttu.edu. *Application contact:* Lori Minner, Coordinator, 806-742-3060, Fax: 806-742-0053, E-mail: lori.minner@ttu.edu.
Website: www.cfas.ttu.edu

Texas Woman's University, Graduate School, College of Professional Education, Department of Human Development, Family Studies, and Counseling, Denton, TX 76204. Offers child development (MS); child life (MS); counseling and development (MS); early childhood development and education (PhD); early childhood education (M Ed); family studies (MS, PhD); family therapy (MS, PhD). *Accreditation:* ACA (one or more programs are accredited). *Program availability:* Part-time, evening/weekend, 100% online, blended/hybrid learning. *Faculty:* 27 full-time (22 women), 11 part-time/ adjunct (10 women). *Students:* 187 full-time (180 women), 245 part-time (230 women); includes 177 minority (83 Black or African American, non-Hispanic/Latino; 17 Asian, non-Hispanic/Latino; 62 Hispanic/Latino; 15 Two or more races, non-Hispanic/Latino), 8 international. Average age 31. 234 applicants, 49% accepted, 80 enrolled. In 2019, 89 master's, 24 doctorates awarded. *Degree requirements:* For master's, comprehensive exam (for some programs), thesis (for some programs), thesis, professional paper, portfolio, or coursework; practicums (for some programs); for doctorate, comprehensive exam, thesis/dissertation, seminars, qualifying exam, dissertation. *Entrance requirements:* For master's, minimum GPA of 3.0 (3.25 for family therapy), letter of intent, curriculum vitae/resume, interview, writing sample, 2 letters of recommendation, interview (counseling and development); for doctorate, GRE scores (147 verbal, 144 quantitative, 4 analytical), minimum GPA of 3.5 (3.35 for family studies) on all prior graduate work, curriculum vitae/resume, letter of intent, 3 letters of recommendation, master's degree or prerequisite equivalents in core area. Additional exam requirements/ recommendations for international students: required—TOEFL (minimum score 79 iBT); recommended—IELTS (minimum score 6.5), TSE (minimum score 53). *Application deadline:* For fall admission, 3/15 for domestic students, 3/1 priority date for international students; for spring admission, 10/1 for domestic students, 7/1 priority date for international students; for summer admission, 2/1 for domestic and international students. Application fee: $50 ($75 for international students). Electronic applications accepted. *Expenses: Tuition, area resident:* Full-time $4973.40; part-time $276.30 per semester hour. Tuition, state resident: full-time $4973.40; part-time $276.30 per semester hour. Tuition, nonresident: full-time $12,569; part-time $698.30 per semester hour. *International tuition:* $12,569.40 full-time. *Required fees:* $2524.30. Tuition and fees vary according to course level, course load, degree level and program. *Financial support:* In 2019–20, 141 students received support, including 2 research assistantships, 17 teaching assistantships (averaging $10,532 per year); career-related internships or fieldwork, scholarships/grants, health care benefits, and unspecified assistantships also available. Support available to part-time students. Financial award application deadline: 3/1; financial award applicants required to submit FAFSA. *Unit head:* Dr. Holly Hansen-Thomas, Interim Chair, 940-898-2685, Fax: 940-898-2676, E-mail: HDFSC@twu.edu. *Application contact:* Korie Hawkins, Associate Director of Admissions, Graduate Recruitment, 940-898-3188, Fax: 940-898-3081, E-mail: admissions@twu.edu.
Website: http://www.twu.edu/family-sciences/

Thomas Jefferson University, Jefferson College of Health Professions, Department of Couple and Family Therapy, Philadelphia, PA 19107. Offers MFT. *Accreditation:* AAMFT/COAMFTE. *Entrance requirements:* Additional exam requirements/ recommendations for international students: required—TOEFL (minimum score 87 iBT). Electronic applications accepted.

Trevecca Nazarene University, Graduate Counseling Program, Nashville, TN 37210-2877. Offers clinical counseling: teaching and supervision (PhD); clinical mental health counseling (MA); marriage and family counseling/therapy (MMFC/T). *Accreditation:* ACA. *Program availability:* Part-time, evening/weekend. *Degree requirements:* For master's, comprehensive exam; for doctorate, comprehensive exam, thesis/dissertation. *Entrance requirements:* For master's, MAT (minimum score of 380) or GRE (minimum score of 290 combined verbal and quantitative), minimum GPA of 2.7, official transcript from regionally accredited institution, 2 reference assessment forms; for doctorate, GRE (minimum scores: 300 combined verbal and quantitative, 3.5 analytical writing), minimum GPA of 3.25, official transcript of master's degree from regionally accredited institution, 3 recommendation forms, 400-word letter of intent, professional vita, interview. Additional exam requirements/recommendations for international students: required—TOEFL (minimum score 600 paper-based; 100 iBT). Electronic applications accepted. *Expenses:* Contact institution.

Universidad de las Americas, A.C., Program in Psychology, Mexico City, Mexico. Offers family therapy (MA).

The University of Akron, Graduate School, College of Health Professions, School of Counseling, Program in Marriage and Family Counseling/Therapy, Akron, OH 44325. Offers MA, MS. *Accreditation:* AAMFT/COAMFTE; ACA. *Degree requirements:* For master's, comprehensive exam. *Entrance requirements:* For master's, minimum GPA of 2.75, three letters of recommendation. Additional exam requirements/recommendations for international students: required—TOEFL (minimum score 79 iBT), IELTS (minimum score 6.5). Electronic applications accepted.

The University of Alabama, Graduate School, College of Human Environmental Sciences, Department of Human Development and Family Studies, Tuscaloosa, AL 35487. Offers human development and family studies (MSHES); marriage and family therapy (MSHES); parent and family life education (MSHES). *Program availability:* Part-time. *Faculty:* 10 full-time (7 women). *Students:* 17 full-time (12 women), 2 part-time (both women); includes 7 minority (3 Black or African American, non-Hispanic/Latino; 3 Hispanic/Latino; 1 Two or more races, non-Hispanic/Latino). Average age 28. 13 applicants, 69% accepted, 7 enrolled. In 2019, 12 master's awarded. Terminal master's awarded for partial completion of doctoral program. *Degree requirements:* For master's, comprehensive exam (for some programs), thesis optional. *Entrance requirements:* For master's, GRE General Test or MAT, minimum GPA of 3.0. Additional exam requirements/recommendations for international students: required—TOEFL (minimum score 79 iBT), IELTS (minimum score 6.5). *Application deadline:* For fall admission, 12/ 15 priority date for domestic and international students. Applications are processed on a rolling basis. Application fee: $50 ($60 for international students). Electronic applications accepted. *Expenses: Tuition, area resident:* Full-time $10,780; part-time $440 per credit hour. Tuition, nonresident: full-time $30,250; part-time $1550 per credit hour. *Financial support:* In 2019–20, 15 students received support. Fellowships, research assistantships with full tuition reimbursements available, teaching assistantships, career-related internships or fieldwork, Federal Work-Study, scholarships/grants, health care benefits, and unspecified assistantships available. Financial award application deadline: 3/15. *Unit head:* Dr. Robert Laird, 205-348-9277, E-mail: rdlaird@ches.ua.edu. *Application contact:* Patrick Fuller, Admissions Officer, 205-348-5932, Fax: 205-348-0400, E-mail: patrick.d.fuller@ua.edu.
Website: http://www.hdfs.ches.ua.edu/

University of Central Florida, College of Community Innovation and Education, Department of Counselor Education and School Psychology, Program in Marriage, Couple, and Family Therapy, Orlando, FL 32816. Offers MA, Certificate. *Students:* 55 full-time (49 women), 3 part-time (all women); includes 28 minority (13 Black or African American, non-Hispanic/Latino; 1 Asian, non-Hispanic/Latino; 13 Hispanic/Latino; 1 Two or more races, non-Hispanic/Latino), 2 international. Average age 27. 51 applicants, 63% accepted, 28 enrolled. In 2019, 14 master's, 11 other advanced degrees awarded. *Degree requirements:* For master's, thesis or alternative. *Entrance requirements:* For master's, GRE, letters of recommendation, resume, goal statement. Additional exam requirements/recommendations for international students: required—TOEFL. *Application deadline:* For fall admission, 2/15 for domestic students. Application fee: $30. Electronic applications accepted. *Financial support:* In 2019–20, 8 students received support, including 1 fellowship with partial tuition reimbursement available (averaging $5,000 per year), 7 research assistantships with partial tuition reimbursements available (averaging $5,355 per year); tuition waivers also available. Financial award application deadline: 3/1; financial award applicants required to submit FAFSA. *Unit head:* Dr. Sejal Barden, Program Coordinator, 407-823-6106, E-mail: sejal.barden@ucf.edu. *Application contact:* Associate Director, Graduate Admissions, 407-823-2766, Fax: 407-823-6442, E-mail: gradadmissions@ucf.edu.
Website: http://education.ucf.edu/counselored/progDetail.cfm?pid-ma#1

University of Central Oklahoma, The Jackson College of Graduate Studies, College of Education and Professional Studies, Department of Human Environmental Sciences, Edmond, OK 73034-5209. Offers family and child studies (MS), including family life education, infant/child specialist, marriage and family therapy; nutrition-food science (MS). *Program availability:* Part-time. *Degree requirements:* For master's, comprehensive exam (for some programs), thesis (for some programs). *Entrance requirements:* For master's, GRE, essay, physical, CPR and First Aid training. Additional exam requirements/recommendations for international students: required—TOEFL (minimum score 550 paper-based; 79 iBT), IELTS (minimum score 6.5). Electronic applications accepted.

University of Colorado Denver, School of Education and Human Development, Program in Counseling Psychology and Counselor Education, Denver, CO 80217. Offers counseling (MA), including clinical mental health counseling, couple and family counseling, multicultural counseling, school counseling; school counseling (MA). *Accreditation:* ACA; NCATE. *Program availability:* Part-time, evening/weekend. *Entrance requirements:* For master's, GRE or MAT (unless applicant already holds a graduate degree), letters of recommendation, interview, resume, transcripts from all colleges/universities attended. Tuition and fees vary according to course load, program and reciprocity agreements.

University of Denver, Graduate School of Social Work, Denver, CO 80208. Offers animal-assisted social work (Certificate); couples and family therapy (Certificate); social work (MSW, PhD); social work with Latinos/as (Certificate). *Accreditation:* CSWE (one or more programs are accredited). *Program availability:* Part-time, evening/weekend, online learning. *Faculty:* 44 full-time (33 women), 80 part-time/adjunct (70 women). *Students:* 887 full-time (806 women), 212 part-time (191 women); includes 343 minority (85 Black or African American, non-Hispanic/Latino; 13 American Indian or Alaska Native, non-Hispanic/Latino; 26 Asian, non-Hispanic/Latino; 174 Hispanic/Latino; 3 Native Hawaiian or other Pacific Islander, non-Hispanic/Latino; 42 Two or more races, non-Hispanic/Latino), 5 international. Average age 29. 1,439 applicants, 86% accepted, 494 enrolled. In 2019, 294 master's, 5 doctorates, 75 other advanced degrees awarded. *Degree requirements:* For doctorate, comprehensive exam, thesis/dissertation, research methods and statistics qualifying exam. *Entrance requirements:* For master's, 20 semester hours or 30 quarter hours in undergraduate course work in the arts and humanities, social/behavioral sciences, and biological sciences; completed at least one course in English composition or present evidence of testing out of the English composition requirement; transcripts; two letters of recommendation; essays; resume; for doctorate, GRE, master's degree in social work or in one of the social sciences with substantial professional experience in the social work field; basic proficiency in descriptive and inferential statistics; two years of post-master's practice experience (preferred); transcripts; three letters of recommendation; personal statement; resume; writing sample. Additional exam requirements/recommendations for international students: required—TOEFL (minimum score 587 paper-based; 95 iBT). *Application deadline:* For fall admission, 1/15 priority date for domestic and international students. Applications are processed on a rolling basis. Application fee: $65. Electronic applications accepted. *Expenses:* Contact institution. *Financial support:* In 2019–20, 504 students received support. Research assistantships, teaching assistantships, scholarships/grants, and unspecified assistantships available. Support available to part-time students. Financial award application deadline: 2/15; financial award applicants required to submit FAFSA. *Unit head:* Dr. Amanda Moore McBride, Morris Endowed Dean and Professor, 303-871-2203, E-mail: gssw.communications@du.edu. *Application contact:* Roberto Garcia, Executive Director, Enrollment, 303-871-2602, E-mail: gsswadmission@du.edu.
Website: https://socialwork.du.edu/

University of Florida, Graduate School, College of Education, School of Human Development and Organizational Studies in Education, Gainesville, FL 32611. Offers counseling and counselor education (Ed D, PhD), including counseling and counselor education, marriage and family counseling, mental health counseling, school counseling and guidance; educational leadership (M Ed, MAE, Ed D, PhD, Ed S), including educational leadership (Ed D, PhD), educational policy (Ed D, PhD); higher education administration (Ed D, PhD), including education policy (Ed D), educational policy, higher education administration; marriage and family counseling (M Ed, MAE, Ed D, PhD, Ed S); mental health counseling (M Ed, MAE, Ed D, PhD, Ed S); research and evaluation methodology (M Ed, MAE, Ed D, PhD); school counseling and guidance (M Ed, MAE, Ed D, PhD, Ed S); student personnel in higher education (M Ed, MAE). *Accreditation:* ACA (one or more programs are accredited); NCATE. *Program availability:* Part-time, online learning. Terminal master's awarded for partial completion of doctoral program. *Degree requirements:* For master's, thesis optional; for doctorate, comprehensive exam, thesis/dissertation. *Entrance requirements:* For master's and doctorate, GRE General Test, minimum GPA of 3.0 (undergraduate), 3.5 (graduate); for Ed S, GRE General Test. Additional exam requirements/recommendations for international students: required—TOEFL (minimum score 550 paper-based; 80 iBT), IELTS (minimum score 6). Electronic applications accepted.

University of Guelph, Office of Graduate and Postdoctoral Studies, College of Social and Applied Human Sciences, Department of Family Relations and Applied Nutrition, Guelph, ON N1G 2W1, Canada. Offers applied nutrition (MAN); family relations and human development (M Sc, PhD), including applied human nutrition, couple and family therapy (M Sc), family relations and human development. *Accreditation:* AAMFT/COAMFTE (one or more programs are accredited). *Program availability:* Part-time. *Degree requirements:* For master's, thesis (for some programs); for doctorate, comprehensive exam, thesis/dissertation. *Entrance requirements:* For master's, minimum B+ average; for doctorate, master's degree in family relations and human development or related field with a minimum B+ average or master's degree in applied human nutrition. Additional exam requirements/recommendations for international students: required—TOEFL (minimum score 600 paper-based). Electronic applications accepted.

University of Holy Cross, Graduate Programs, New Orleans, LA 70131-7399. Offers biomedical sciences (MS); Catholic theology (MA); counseling (MA, PhD), including community counseling (MA), marriage and family counseling (MA), school counseling (MA); educational leadership (M Ed); executive leadership (Ed D); management (MS), including healthcare management, operations management; teaching and learning (M Ed). *Accreditation:* ACA; NCATE. *Program availability:* Part-time, evening/weekend, online learning. *Degree requirements:* For master's, thesis. *Entrance requirements:* For master's, GRE General Test, minimum GPA of 2.7.

University of Houston–Clear Lake, School of Human Sciences and Humanities, Programs in Human Sciences, Houston, TX 77058-1002. Offers behavioral sciences (MA), including criminology, cross cultural studies, general psychology, sociology; clinical psychology (MA); criminology (MA); cross cultural studies (MA); family therapy (MA); fitness and human performance (MA); school psychology (MA). *Accreditation:* AAMFT/COAMFTE. *Program availability:* Part-time, evening/weekend, online learning. *Degree requirements:* For master's, thesis or alternative. *Entrance requirements:* For master's, GRE General Test. Additional exam requirements/recommendations for international students: required—TOEFL (minimum score 550 paper-based). Electronic applications accepted.

The University of Iowa, Graduate College, College of Education, Department of Rehabilitation and Counselor Education, Iowa City, IA 52242-1316. Offers counselor education and supervision (PhD); couple and family therapy (PhD); rehabilitation and mental health counseling (MA); rehabilitation counselor education (PhD); school counseling (MA). *Accreditation:* ACA (one or more programs are accredited); CORE (one or more programs are accredited). *Degree requirements:* For master's, thesis optional, exam; for doctorate, comprehensive exam, thesis/dissertation. *Entrance requirements:* For master's and doctorate, GRE General Test, minimum GPA of 3.0. Additional exam requirements/recommendations for international students: required—TOEFL (minimum score 550 paper-based; 81 iBT). Electronic applications accepted.

University of La Verne, College of Arts and Sciences, Department of Psychology, Program in Marriage and Family Therapy, La Verne, CA 91750-4443. Offers MFT. *Program availability:* Part-time. *Degree requirements:* For master's, thesis, competency exam, fieldwork, culminating project. *Entrance requirements:* For master's, minimum undergraduate GPA of 3.0, 5- to 7-page statement of purpose and autobiography, 3 letters of recommendation, interview, curriculum vitae. Additional exam requirements/recommendations for international students: required—TOEFL (minimum score 600 paper-based; 100 iBT), IELTS (minimum score 6.5). *Expenses:* Contact institution.

University of Louisiana at Monroe, Graduate School, College of Health Sciences, Program in Marriage and Family Therapy, Monroe, LA 71209-0001. Offers MA, PhD. *Accreditation:* AAMFT/COAMFTE (one or more programs are accredited); ACA. *Program availability:* Part-time, evening/weekend, online learning. *Faculty:* 7 full-time (2 women), 2 part-time/adjunct (1 woman). *Students:* 51 full-time (40 women), 36 part-time (24 women); includes 25 minority (19 Black or African American, non-Hispanic/Latino; 1 American Indian or Alaska Native, non-Hispanic/Latino; 2 Asian, non-Hispanic/Latino; 1 Hispanic/Latino; 1 Native Hawaiian or other Pacific Islander, non-Hispanic/Latino; 1 Two or more races, non-Hispanic/Latino), 1 international. Average age 34. 43 applicants, 63% accepted, 25 enrolled. In 2019, 12 master's, 2 doctorates awarded. *Degree requirements:* For master's, thesis optional, internship; client contact hours; for doctorate, comprehensive exam (for some programs), thesis/dissertation, clinical experience. *Entrance requirements:* For master's, GRE General Test, Bachelor's degree; minimum undergraduate GPA of 2.5; for doctorate, GRE General Test, Master's degree in related discipline; minimum GPA of 3.5. Additional exam requirements/recommendations for international students: required—TOEFL (minimum score 500 paper-based; 61 iBT); recommended—IELTS (minimum score 5.5). *Application deadline:* For fall admission, 2/1 for domestic and international students. Applications are processed on a rolling basis. Application fee: $55. Electronic applications accepted. *Expenses: Tuition, area resident:* Full-time $6489. Tuition, state resident: full-time $6489. Tuition, nonresident: full-time $18,989. *Required fees:* $2748. Tuition and fees vary according to course load and program. *Financial support:* In 2019–20, 30 students received support. Teaching assistantships with full tuition reimbursements available, career-related internships or fieldwork, Federal Work-Study, scholarships/grants, and unspecified assistantships available. Financial award application deadline: 2/15; financial award applicants required to submit FAFSA. *Unit head:* Dr. David Hale, Graduate Coordinator and Interim Program Director, 318-342-1349, E-mail: dhale@ulm.edu. *Application contact:* Dr. David Hale, Graduate Coordinator and Interim Program Director, 318-342-1349, E-mail: dhale@ulm.edu.
Website: http://www.ulm.edu/mft/

University of Louisville, Graduate School, Kent School of Social Work, Louisville, KY 40292-0001. Offers marriage and family therapy (PMC), including mental health; social work (MSSW, PhD), including alcohol and drug counseling (MSSW), gerontology (MSSW), marriage and family (PhD), school social work (MSSW). *Accreditation:* AAMFT/COAMFTE; CSWE (one or more programs are accredited). *Program availability:* Part-time, evening/weekend, 100% online, blended/hybrid learning. *Faculty:* 33 full-time (22 women), 90 part-time/adjunct (73 women). *Students:* 385 full-time (333 women), 96 part-time (73 women); includes 143 minority (75 Black or African American, non-Hispanic/Latino; 2 American Indian or Alaska Native, non-Hispanic/Latino; 8 Asian, non-Hispanic/Latino; 26 Hispanic/Latino; 2 Native Hawaiian or other Pacific Islander, non-Hispanic/Latino; 30 Two or more races, non-Hispanic/Latino), 7 international. Average age 32. 313 applicants, 77% accepted, 176 enrolled. In 2019, 243 master's, 4 doctorates awarded. *Degree requirements:* For doctorate, comprehensive exam, thesis/dissertation. *Entrance requirements:* For master's, 3 letters of recommendation, admissions essay, resume, transcripts; for doctorate, GRE scores, TOFEL scores or equivalent for international students, transcripts (undergraduate and graduate), 3 letters of recommendation, writing sample, personal statement, interview. Additional exam requirements/recommendations for international students: required—TOEFL (minimum score 550 paper-based; 79 iBT), IELTS (minimum score 6.5). *Application deadline:* For fall admission, 5/30 for domestic and international students; for spring admission, 9/30 for domestic and international students; for summer admission, 2/28 for domestic and international students. Applications are processed on a rolling basis. Application fee: $65. Electronic applications accepted. *Expenses: Tuition, area resident:* Full-time $13,000; part-time $723 per credit hour. Tuition, state resident: full-time $13,000; part-time $723 per credit hour. Tuition, nonresident: full-time $27,114; part-time $1507 per credit hour. *International tuition:* $27,114 full-time. *Required fees:* $196. Tuition and fees vary according to program and reciprocity agreements. *Financial support:* In 2019–20, 53 students received support, including 1 fellowship with full tuition reimbursement available (averaging $20,000 per year), 7 research assistantships with full tuition reimbursements available (averaging $20,000 per year), 1 teaching assistantship with full tuition reimbursement available (averaging $20,000 per year); scholarships/grants, health care benefits, and unspecified assistantships also available. Financial award application deadline: 5/15; financial award applicants required to submit FAFSA. *Unit head:* Dr. David Jenkins, Dean, 502-852-3944, Fax: 502-852-0422, E-mail: d.jenkins@louisville.edu. *Application contact:* Sarah Caragianis, Program Manager, MSSW Admissions, 502-852-0414, Fax: 502-852-0422, E-mail: sarah.caragianis@louisville.edu.
Website: http://www.louisville.edu/kent

University of Mary Hardin-Baylor, Graduate Studies in Counseling, Belton, TX 76513. Offers clinical and mental health counseling (MA); marriage, family and child counseling (MA); non-clinical professional studies (MA). *Accreditation:* ACA. *Program availability:* Part-time, evening/weekend. *Faculty:* 6 full-time (3 women), 4 part-time/adjunct (2 women). *Students:* 54 full-time (41 women), 23 part-time (19 women); includes 36 minority (13 Black or African American, non-Hispanic/Latino; 1 American Indian or Alaska Native, non-Hispanic/Latino; 1 Asian, non-Hispanic/Latino; 18 Hispanic/Latino; 3 Two or more races, non-Hispanic/Latino). Average age 31. 57 applicants, 75% accepted, 25 enrolled. In 2019, 32 master's awarded. *Degree requirements:* For master's, comprehensive exam. *Entrance requirements:* For master's, GRE General Test with minimum cumulative score of 300 on verbal and quantitative portions and 3.0 on analytical section (if overall undergraduate GPA is below a 3.0), minimum cumulative undergraduate GPA of 2.75 or 3.0 on last 60 hours of course work; three letters of recommendation; interview with departmental graduate admissions committee. Additional exam requirements/recommendations for international students: required—TOEFL (minimum score 60 iBT), IELTS (minimum score 4.5). *Application deadline:* For fall admission, 6/1 for domestic students, 4/30 priority date for international students; for spring admission, 11/1 for domestic students, 9/30 priority date for international

students. Applications are processed on a rolling basis. Application fee: $35 ($135 for international students). Electronic applications accepted. *Expenses: Tuition:* Full-time $16,200; part-time $10,800 per credit hour. *Required fees:* $1350; $75 per credit hour. $50 per term. Tuition and fees vary according to course load and degree level. *Financial support:* In 2019–20, 58 students received support. Federal Work-Study, unspecified assistantships, and scholarships for some active duty military personnel available. Support available to part-time students. Financial award applicants required to submit FAFSA. *Unit head:* Dr. Ty Leonard, Interim Director, Graduate Counseling, 254-295-5532, E-mail: hleonard@umhb.edu. *Application contact:* Katherine Moore, Assistant Director, Graduate Admissions, 254-295-4924, E-mail: kmoore@umhb.edu.
Website: https://go.umhb.edu/graduate/counseling/home

University of Maryland, College Park, Academic Affairs, School of Public Health, Department of Family Science, College Park, MD 20742. Offers family studies (PhD); marriage and family therapy (MS); maternal and child health (PhD). *Accreditation:* AAMFT/COAMFTE. *Program availability:* Part-time, evening/weekend. *Degree requirements:* For master's, thesis or alternative; for doctorate, comprehensive exam, thesis/dissertation, oral defense. *Entrance requirements:* For master's, GRE General Test, minimum GPA of 3.0, 3 letters of recommendation; for doctorate, GRE General Test, minimum GPA of 3.0, 3 letters of recommendation, research sample. Electronic applications accepted.

University of Massachusetts Boston, College of Education and Human Development, Program in Family Therapy, Boston, MA 02125-3393. Offers MS. Electronic applications accepted.

University of Miami, Graduate School, School of Education and Human Development, Department of Educational and Psychological Studies, Program in Counseling, Coral Gables, FL 33124. Offers counseling and research (MS Ed); Latino mental health (Certificate); marriage and family therapy (MS Ed); mental health counseling (MS Ed). *Program availability:* Part-time, evening/weekend. *Students:* 20 full-time (18 women), 7 part-time (5 women); includes 10 minority (1 Black or African American, non-Hispanic/Latino; 9 Hispanic/Latino), 6 international. Average age 26. 53 applicants, 55% accepted, 11 enrolled. In 2019, 12 master's awarded. *Degree requirements:* For master's, comprehensive exam, personal growth experience, 15-practicum credit hours. *Entrance requirements:* For master's, GRE General Test. Additional exam requirements/recommendations for international students: required—TOEFL (minimum score 550 paper-based; 80 iBT); recommended—IELTS (minimum score 6.5). *Application deadline:* For fall admission, 5/1 priority date for domestic students, 10/1 priority date for international students. Application fee: $85. Electronic applications accepted. *Financial support:* Tuition waivers (partial) available. Financial award application deadline: 3/1; financial award applicants required to submit FAFSA. *Unit head:* Dr. Guerda Nicolas, Professor and Program Director, 305-284-3001, Fax: 305-284-3003, E-mail: nguerda@miami.edu. *Application contact:* Dr. Guerda Nicolas, Professor and Program Director, 305-284-3001, Fax: 305-284-3003, E-mail: nguerda@miami.edu.
Website: https://sites.education.miami.edu/counseling-therapy/

University of Minnesota, Twin Cities Campus, Graduate School, College of Education and Human Development, Department of Family Social Science, Minneapolis, MN 55455-0213. Offers family education (M Ed); marriage and family therapy (MA, PhD); prevention science (MA). *Accreditation:* AAMFT/COAMFTE (one or more programs are accredited). *Faculty:* 18 full-time (12 women). *Students:* 62 full-time (57 women), 19 part-time (17 women); includes 15 minority (7 Black or African American, non-Hispanic/Latino; 5 Asian, non-Hispanic/Latino; 2 Hispanic/Latino; 1 Two or more races, non-Hispanic/Latino), 14 international. Average age 34. 79 applicants, 67% accepted, 44 enrolled. In 2019, 21 master's, 5 doctorates awarded. *Degree requirements:* For master's, thesis; for doctorate, thesis/dissertation. *Entrance requirements:* For master's and doctorate, GRE General Test, minimum undergraduate GPA of 3.0 (preferred). Additional exam requirements/recommendations for international students: required—TOEFL. *Application deadline:* For fall admission, 12/15 for domestic students. Application fee: $75 ($95 for international students). *Financial support:* In 2019–20, 3 fellowships, 27 research assistantships (averaging $10,086 per year), 19 teaching assistantships (averaging $9,129 per year) were awarded; career-related internships or fieldwork, Federal Work-Study, institutionally sponsored loans, and tuition waivers (partial) also available. Financial award application deadline: 6/30; financial award applicants required to submit FAFSA. *Unit head:* Dr. Jodi Dworkin, Head, 612-625-1900, Fax: 612-625-4227, E-mail: jdworkin@umn.edu. *Application contact:* Dr. Catherine Solheim, Director of Graduate Studies, 612-625-1201, E-mail: csolheim@umn.edu.
Website: http://www.cehd.umn.edu/fsos/

University of Mobile, Graduate Studies, Program in Marriage and Family Counseling, Mobile, AL 36613. Offers MA. *Program availability:* Part-time, evening/weekend. *Degree requirements:* For master's, comprehensive exam, thesis optional. *Entrance requirements:* For master's, GRE, official transcripts, essay, 2 letters of recommendation, interview. Additional exam requirements/recommendations for international students: required—TOEFL (minimum score 550 paper-based; 80 iBT). Electronic applications accepted. *Expenses:* Contact institution.

University of Nebraska–Lincoln, Graduate College, College of Education and Human Sciences, Department of Child, Youth and Family Studies, Lincoln, NE 68588. Offers child development/early childhood education (MS, PhD); child, youth and family studies (MS); family and consumer sciences education (MS, PhD); family financial planning (MS); family science (MS, PhD); gerontology (PhD); human sciences (PhD), including child, youth and family studies, gerontology, medical family therapy; marriage and family therapy (MS); medical family therapy (PhD); youth development (MS). *Accreditation:* AAMFT/COAMFTE (one or more programs are accredited). *Program availability:* Online learning. *Degree requirements:* For master's, thesis optional. *Entrance requirements:* For master's, GRE. Additional exam requirements/recommendations for international students: required—TOEFL (minimum score 550 paper-based). Electronic applications accepted.

University of New Hampshire, Graduate School, College of Health and Human Services, Department of Human Development and Family Studies, Durham, NH 03824. Offers adolescent development (Postbaccalaureate Certificate); human development and family studies (MS), including adolescent development, child development; marriage and family therapy (MS). *Accreditation:* AAMFT/COAMFTE. *Program availability:* Part-time. *Faculty:* 2 full-time (1 woman), 2 part-time/adjunct (1 woman). *Students:* 17 full-time (13 women), 2 part-time (both women); includes 4 minority (2 Black or African American, non-Hispanic/Latino; 1 Hispanic/Latino; 1 Two or more races, non-Hispanic/Latino). Average age 29. 18 applicants, 72% accepted, 7 enrolled. In 2019, 8 master's awarded. *Entrance requirements:* Additional exam requirements/recommendations for international students: required—TOEFL (minimum score 550 paper-based; 80 iBT), IELTS (minimum score 6.5), PTE (minimum score 59), Duolingo. *Application deadline:* For fall admission, 1/15 for domestic and international students. Application fee: $65. Electronic applications accepted. *Financial support:* In 2019–20, 12 students received support, including 4 teaching assistantships; fellowships, research assistantships, Federal Work-Study, scholarships/grants, tuition waivers (full and partial), and unspecified assistantships also available. Support available to part-time students. Financial award application deadline: 1/15. *Unit head:* Kerry Kazura, Chair, 603-862-2135. *Application contact:* Barbara Frankel, Graduate Program Coordinator, 603-862-2153, E-mail: barbara.frankel@unh.edu.
Website: http://www.chhs.unh.edu/hdfs

The University of North Carolina at Greensboro, Graduate School, School of Education, Department of Counseling and Educational Development, Greensboro, NC 27412-5001. Offers advanced school counseling (PMC); counseling and counselor education (PhD); counseling and educational development (MS); couple and family counseling (PMC); school counseling (PMC); MS/Ed S. *Accreditation:* ACA (one or more programs are accredited); NCATE. *Degree requirements:* For master's, comprehensive exam, practicum, internship; for doctorate, comprehensive exam, thesis/dissertation. *Entrance requirements:* For master's, doctorate, and PMC, GRE General Test. Additional exam requirements/recommendations for international students: required—TOEFL. Electronic applications accepted.

University of Oregon, Graduate School, College of Education, Eugene, OR 97403. Offers communication disorders and sciences (MA, MS, PhD); counseling psychology (PhD); couples and family therapy (MS); critical and sociocultural studies in education (PhD); curriculum and teacher education (MA, MS); educational leadership (MS, D Ed, PhD); prevention science (M Ed, MS, PhD); school psychology (MS, PhD); special education (M Ed, MA, MS, PhD). *Accreditation:* ASHA. *Program availability:* Part-time. Terminal master's awarded for partial completion of doctoral program. *Degree requirements:* For master's, exam, paper, or project; for doctorate, comprehensive exam, thesis/dissertation. *Entrance requirements:* Additional exam requirements/recommendations for international students: required—TOEFL.

University of Phoenix - Bay Area Campus, College of Social Sciences, San Jose, CA 95134-1805. Offers marriage, family, and child therapy (MSC). *Program availability:* Evening/weekend. *Degree requirements:* For master's, thesis or alternative. *Entrance requirements:* For master's, Comprehensive Cognitive Assessment, minimum undergraduate GPA of 2.5, 3 years of work experience.

University of Phoenix - Central Valley Campus, College of Human Services, Fresno, CA 93720-1552. Offers marriage, family and child therapy (MSC).

University of Phoenix - Las Vegas Campus, College of Human Services, Las Vegas, NV 89135. Offers marriage, family, and child therapy (MSC); mental health counseling (MSC); school counseling (MSC). *Program availability:* Online learning. *Entrance requirements:* For master's, minimum undergraduate GPA of 2.5, 3 years of work experience. Additional exam requirements/recommendations for international students: required—TOEFL (minimum score 550 paper-based; 79 iBT). Electronic applications accepted.

University of Phoenix - Phoenix Campus, College of Social Sciences, Tempe, AZ 85282-2371. Offers counseling (MS), including clinical mental health counseling, community counseling, counseling, marriage, family and child therapy; psychology (MS). *Program availability:* Evening/weekend, online learning. *Entrance requirements:* Additional exam requirements/recommendations for international students: required—TOEFL, TOEIC (Test of English as an International Communication), Berlitz Online English Proficiency Exam, PTE, or IELTS. Electronic applications accepted. *Expenses:* Contact institution.

University of Rhode Island, Graduate School, College of Health Sciences, Department of Human Development and Family Studies, Kingston, RI 02881. Offers college student personnel (MS); human development and family studies (MS); marriage and family therapy (MS). *Accreditation:* AAMFT/COAMFTE. *Program availability:* Part-time. *Faculty:* 16 full-time (12 women). *Students:* 50 full-time (40 women), 12 part-time (11 women); includes 14 minority (4 Black or African American, non-Hispanic/Latino; 2 Asian, non-Hispanic/Latino; 5 Hispanic/Latino; 3 Two or more races, non-Hispanic/Latino), 2 international. In 2019, 25 master's awarded. *Entrance requirements:* Additional exam requirements/recommendations for international students: required—TOEFL. *Application deadline:* For fall admission, 1/15 for domestic and international students. Application fee: $65. Electronic applications accepted. *Expenses: Tuition, area resident:* Full-time $13,734; part-time $763 per credit. Tuition, state resident: full-time $13,734; part-time $763 per credit. Tuition, nonresident: full-time $26,512; part-time $1473 per credit. *International tuition:* $26,512 full-time. *Required fees:* $1780; $52 per credit. $35 per term. One-time fee: $165. *Financial support:* In 2019–20, 2 research assistantships with tuition reimbursements (averaging $4,746 per year), 5 teaching assistantships with tuition reimbursements (averaging $11,866 per year) were awarded. Financial award application deadline: 1/15; financial award applicants required to submit FAFSA. *Unit head:* Dr. Sue Adam, Chair, 401-874-5958, E-mail: suekadams@uri.edu. *Application contact:* Dr. Sue Adam, Chair, 401-874-5958, E-mail: suekadams@uri.edu.
Website: http://www.uri.edu/hss/hdf/

University of Rochester, School of Medicine and Dentistry, Graduate Programs in Medicine and Dentistry, Department of Psychiatry, Rochester, NY 14627. Offers marriage and family therapy (MS). *Accreditation:* AAMFT/COAMFTE. *Program availability:* Part-time. *Degree requirements:* For master's, projects. *Entrance requirements:* For master's, GRE General Test.

University of Saint Joseph, Program in Marriage and Family Therapy, West Hartford, CT 06117-2700. Offers MA. *Accreditation:* AAMFT/COAMFTE. *Program availability:* Part-time, evening/weekend. *Degree requirements:* For master's, comprehensive exam, thesis or alternative, practicum, internship. *Entrance requirements:* For master's, 2 letters of recommendation. Electronic applications accepted. Application fee is waived when completed online.

University of San Diego, School of Leadership and Education Sciences, Department of Counseling and Marital and Family Therapy, San Diego, CA 92110-2492. Offers clinical mental health counseling (MA); marital and family therapy (MA); school counseling (MA). *Accreditation:* ACA. *Program availability:* Part-time, evening/weekend. *Faculty:* 14 full-time (8 women), 24 part-time/adjunct (14 women). *Students:* 178 full-time (160 women), 47 part-time (41 women); includes 106 minority (9 Black or African American, non-Hispanic/Latino; 21 Asian, non-Hispanic/Latino; 59 Hispanic/Latino; 17 Two or more races, non-Hispanic/Latino), 5 international. Average age 27. 391 applicants, 42% accepted, 88 enrolled. In 2019, 96 master's awarded. *Degree requirements:* For master's, comprehensive exam, international experience. *Entrance requirements:* For master's, GRE or GMAT (minimum overall score in 50th percentile), group interview with faculty. Additional exam requirements/recommendations for international students: required—TOEFL (minimum score 580 paper-based; 83 iBT), TWE. *Application deadline:* For fall admission, 2/10 for domestic and international students. Applications are processed on a rolling basis. Application fee: $45. Electronic applications accepted. *Financial support:* In 2019–20, 199 students received support. Career-related internships or fieldwork, Federal Work-Study, institutionally sponsored loans, scholarships/grants, unspecified assistantships, and stipends available. Support available to part-time students. Financial award application deadline: 4/1; financial award applicants required to submit FAFSA. *Unit head:* Dr. Wendell Callahan, Director, 619-260-7988, E-mail: wcallahan@sandiego.edu. *Application contact:* Erika Garwood, Director of Admissions and Enrollment, 619-260-4524, Fax: 619-260-4158, E-mail: grads@sandiego.edu.
Website: http://www.sandiego.edu/soles/counseling-and-marital-and-family-therapy//

University of San Francisco, School of Education, Department of Counseling Psychology, San Francisco, CA 94117. Offers counseling (MA), including educational counseling, life transitions counseling, marital and family therapy. *Program availability:* Part-time. *Faculty:* 8 full-time (all women), 30 part-time/adjunct (18 women). *Students:* 364 full-time (302 women), 6 part-time (3 women); includes 215 minority (22 Black or African American, non-Hispanic/Latino; 2 American Indian or Alaska Native, non-Hispanic/Latino; 48 Asian, non-Hispanic/Latino; 123 Hispanic/Latino; 1 Native Hawaiian or other Pacific Islander, non-Hispanic/Latino; 19 Two or more races, non-Hispanic/Latino), 3 international. Average age 29. 351 applicants, 66% accepted, 137 enrolled. In 2019, 119 master's awarded. *Entrance requirements:* Additional exam requirements/recommendations for international students: required—TOEFL, IELTS, PTE. *Application deadline:* For fall admission, 3/1 priority date for domestic students, 3/1 for international students; for spring admission, 10/15 priority date for domestic students, 10/15 for international students. Applications are processed on a rolling basis. Application fee: $55 ($65 for international students). Electronic applications accepted. *Financial support:* Fellowships, research assistantships, and teaching assistantships available. Financial award application deadline: 3/2; financial award applicants required to submit FAFSA. *Unit head:* Dr. Christine Yeh, Chair, 415-422-6868. *Application contact:* Peter Cole, Admission Coordinator, 415-422-5467, E-mail: schoolofeducation@usfca.edu.

University of Southern California, Graduate School, Rossier School of Education, Master's Programs in Education, Los Angeles, CA 90089-4038. Offers educational counseling (ME); marriage, family and child counseling (MMFT); postsecondary administration and student affairs [PASA] (ME); school counseling (ME); teaching (online) (MAT); teaching and teaching credential (MAT); teaching English to speakers of other languages (MAT). *Program availability:* Part-time, evening/weekend, online learning. *Degree requirements:* For master's, thesis optional. *Entrance requirements:* For master's, GRE (for all programs except MAT). Additional exam requirements/recommendations for international students: required—TOEFL (minimum score 100 iBT). Electronic applications accepted.

University of Southern Mississippi, College of Education and Human Sciences, School of Child and Family Sciences, Hattiesburg, MS 39406-0001. Offers child and family studies (MS); marriage and family therapy (MS); school counseling (M Ed). *Accreditation:* AAMFT/COAMFTE (one or more programs are accredited). *Program availability:* Part-time, online learning. *Students:* 35 full-time (27 women), 57 part-time (all women); includes 33 minority (22 Black or African American, non-Hispanic/Latino; 3 American Indian or Alaska Native, non-Hispanic/Latino; 7 Hispanic/Latino; 1 Two or more races, non-Hispanic/Latino), 1 international. 130 applicants, 21% accepted, 25 enrolled. In 2019, 32 master's awarded. *Degree requirements:* For master's, comprehensive exam, thesis optional. *Entrance requirements:* For master's, GRE General Test, minimum GPA of 2.75 on last 60 hours. Additional exam requirements/recommendations for international students: required—TOEFL. *Application deadline:* For fall admission, 3/1 priority date for domestic students, 3/1 for international students; for spring admission, 1/1 priority date for domestic and international students. Applications are processed on a rolling basis. Application fee: $60. Electronic applications accepted. *Expenses:* Tuition, area resident: Full-time $4393; part-time $488 per credit hour. Tuition, nonresident: full-time $5393; part-time $600 per credit hour. *Required fees:* $6 per semester. *Financial support:* Fellowships, research assistantships with full tuition reimbursements, career-related internships or fieldwork, Federal Work-Study, institutionally sponsored loans, scholarships/grants, health care benefits, and unspecified assistantships available. Financial award application deadline: 3/15; financial award applicants required to submit FAFSA. *Unit head:* Pat Sims, Director, 601-266-6990, Fax: 601-266-4680. *Application contact:* Pat Sims, Director, 601-266-6990, Fax: 601-266-4680.
Website: https://www.usm.edu/family-studies-child-development

University of South Florida, College of Behavioral and Community Sciences, Department of Child and Family Studies, Tampa, FL 33620-9951. Offers applied behavior analysis (MA, MS, PhD); behavioral and community sciences (PhD); child and adolescent behavioral health (MS), including developmental disabilities, leadership in child and adolescent health, translational research and evaluation, youth and behavioral health; rehabilitation and mental health counseling (MA), including addictions and substance abuse counseling, marriage and family therapy. *Accreditation:* ACA. *Faculty:* 21 full-time (13 women), 3 part-time/adjunct (all women). *Students:* 184 full-time (157 women), 104 part-time (88 women); includes 113 minority (42 Black or African American, non-Hispanic/Latino; 4 Asian, non-Hispanic/Latino; 54 Hispanic/Latino; 1 Native Hawaiian or other Pacific Islander, non-Hispanic/Latino; 12 Two or more races, non-Hispanic/Latino), 7 international. Average age 27. 310 applicants, 51% accepted, 92 enrolled. In 2019, 127 master's, 8 doctorates awarded. *Degree requirements:* For master's, comprehensive exam, thesis (for some programs); for doctorate, comprehensive exam, thesis/dissertation, Behavior Analyst Board Certification Exam. *Entrance requirements:* For master's, GRE General Test, 3.00 GPA; 3 letters of reference; resume or CV; statement of purpose; writing sample; undergraduate statistics or research methods course (for Rehab and Mental Health Counseling); for doctorate, GRE General Test, master's degree in behavioral analysis or closely-related field; minimum GPA of 3.5 in graduate course work; three letters of recommendation; campus visit with faculty interview; personal statement; curriculum vitae; evidence of research experiences and expertise; campus visit and interview. Additional exam requirements/recommendations for international students: required—TOEFL, TOEFL (minimum score 550 paper-based; 79 iBT) or IELTS (minimum score 6.5). *Application deadline:* For fall admission, 12/5 for domestic and international students. Application fee: $30. *Financial support:* In 2019–20, 57 students received support. Unspecified assistantships available. *Unit head:* Jason Anthony, Professor and Director, Rightpath Research and Innovation Center, 813-974-6009, E-mail: jasonanthony@usf.edu. *Application contact:* Dr. Raymond G. Miltenberger, Professor/Director of Master's Program, 813-974-5079, Fax: 813-974-6115, E-mail: miltenbe@usf.edu.
Website: http://cfs.cbcs.usf.edu/

University of South Florida, Innovative Education, Tampa, FL 33620-9951. Offers adult, career and higher education (Graduate Certificate), including college teaching, leadership in developing human resources, leadership in higher education; Africana studies (Graduate Certificate), including diasporas and health disparities, genocide and human rights; aging studies (Graduate Certificate), including gerontology; art research (Graduate Certificate), including museum studies; business foundations (Graduate Certificate); chemical and biomedical engineering (Graduate Certificate), including materials science and engineering, water, health and sustainability; child and family studies (Graduate Certificate), including positive behavior support; civil and industrial engineering (Graduate Certificate), including transportation systems analysis; community and family health (Graduate Certificate), including maternal and child health, social marketing and public health, violence and injury: prevention and intervention, women's health; criminology (Graduate Certificate), including criminal justice administration; data science for public administration (Graduate Certificate); digital humanities (Graduate Certificate); educational measurement and research (Graduate Certificate), including evaluation; English (Graduate Certificate), including comparative literary studies, creative writing, professional and technical communication; entrepreneurship (Graduate Certificate); environmental health (Graduate Certificate), including safety management; epidemiology and biostatistics (Graduate Certificate),

including applied biostatistics, biostatistics, concepts and tools of epidemiology, epidemiology, epidemiology of infectious diseases; geography, environment and planning (Graduate Certificate), including community development, environmental policy and management, geographical information systems; geology (Graduate Certificate), including hydrogeology; global health (Graduate Certificate), including disaster management, global health and Latin American and Caribbean studies, global health practice, humanitarian assistance, infection control; government and international affairs (Graduate Certificate), including Cuban studies, globalization studies; health policy and management (Graduate Certificate), including health management and leadership, public health policy and programs; hearing specialist: early intervention (Graduate Certificate); industrial and management systems engineering (Graduate Certificate), including systems engineering, technology management; information studies (Graduate Certificate), including school library media specialist; information systems/decision sciences (Graduate Certificate), including analytics and business intelligence; instructional technology (Graduate Certificate), including distance education, Florida digital/virtual educator, instructional design, multimedia design, Web design; internal medicine, bioethics and medical humanities (Graduate Certificate), including biomedical ethics; Latin American and Caribbean studies (Graduate Certificate); leadership for coastal resiliency planning (Graduate Certificate); mass communications (Graduate Certificate), including multimedia journalism; mathematics and statistics (Graduate Certificate), including mathematics; medicine (Graduate Certificate), including aging and neuroscience, bioinformatics, biotechnology, brain fitness and memory management, clinical investigation, hand and upper limb rehabilitation, health informatics, health sciences, integrative weight management, intellectual property, medicine and gender, metabolic and nutritional medicine, metabolic cardiology, pharmacy sciences; national and competitive intelligence (Graduate Certificate); nursing (Graduate Certificate), including simulation based academic fellowship in advanced pain management; psychological and social foundations (Graduate Certificate), including career counseling, college teaching, diversity in education, mental health counseling, school counseling; public affairs (Graduate Certificate), including nonprofit management, public management, research administration; public health (Graduate Certificate), including assessing chemical toxicity and public health risks, health equity, pharmacoepidemiology, public health generalist, toxicology, translational research in adolescent behavioral health; public health practices (Graduate Certificate), including planning for healthy communities; rehabilitation and mental health counseling (Graduate Certificate), including integrative mental health care, marriage and family therapy, rehabilitation technology; secondary education (Graduate Certificate), including ESOL, foreign language education: culture and content, foreign language education: professional; social work (Graduate Certificate), including geriatric social work/clinical gerontology; special education (Graduate Certificate), including autism spectrum disorder, disabilities education: severe/profound; world languages (Graduate Certificate), including teaching English as a second language (TESL) or foreign language. *Unit head:* Dr. Cynthia DeLuca, Associate Vice President and Assistant Vice Provost, 813-974-3077, Fax: 813-974-7061, E-mail: deluca@usf.edu. *Application contact:* Owen Hooper, Director, Summer and Alternative Calendar Programs, 813-974-6917, E-mail: hooper@usf.edu.
Website: http://www.usf.edu/innovative-education/

The University of Texas at Tyler, College of Education and Psychology, Department of Psychology and Counseling, Tyler, TX 75799-0001. Offers clinical psychology (MS), including neuropsychology, school psychology; counseling psychology (MA), including general, marriage and family; interdisciplinary studies (MSIS); school counseling (MA). *Program availability:* Part-time, evening/weekend. *Faculty:* 12 full-time (5 women), 6 part-time/adjunct (3 women). *Students:* 131 full-time (103 women), 83 part-time (67 women); includes 67 minority (10 Black or African American, non-Hispanic/Latino; 1 American Indian or Alaska Native, non-Hispanic/Latino; 7 Asian, non-Hispanic/Latino; 41 Hispanic/Latino; 8 Two or more races, non-Hispanic/Latino), 8 international. Average age 30. 130 applicants, 65% accepted, 47 enrolled. In 2019, 94 master's awarded. *Degree requirements:* For master's, comprehensive exam, thesis optional. *Entrance requirements:* For master's, GRE General Test, minimum GPA of 3.0. Additional exam requirements/recommendations for international students: required—TOEFL. *Application deadline:* For fall admission, 8/17 priority date for domestic students, 7/1 priority date for international students; for spring admission, 12/21 priority date for domestic students, 11/1 priority date for international students. Application fee: $25 ($50 for international students). Electronic applications accepted. *Financial support:* In 2019–20, fellowships with partial tuition reimbursements (averaging $3,000 per year) were awarded; research assistantships, teaching assistantships, career-related internships or fieldwork, Federal Work-Study, and institutionally sponsored loans also available. Support available to part-time students. Financial award application deadline: 7/1. *Unit head:* Dr. Charles B. Barke, Chair, 903-565-5875, E-mail: cbarke@uttyler.edu. *Application contact:* Dr. Charles B. Barke, Chair, 903-565-5875, E-mail: cbarke@uttyler.edu.
Website: http://www.uttyler.edu/psychology/

The University of West Alabama, School of Graduate Studies, College of Education, Program in Family Counseling, Livingston, AL 35470. Offers MS. *Program availability:* Part-time, evening/weekend, 100% online. *Faculty:* 9 full-time (7 women), 21 part-time/adjunct (12 women). *Students:* 55 full-time (46 women); includes 47 minority (43 Black or African American, non-Hispanic/Latino; 2 American Indian or Alaska Native, non-Hispanic/Latino; 1 Native Hawaiian or other Pacific Islander, non-Hispanic/Latino; 1 Two or more races, non-Hispanic/Latino). Average age 36. 12 applicants, 100% accepted, 10 enrolled. In 2019, 4 master's awarded. *Degree requirements:* For master's, comprehensive exam. *Entrance requirements:* For master's, GRE, minimum GPA of 2.75. Additional exam requirements/recommendations for international students: required—TOEFL (minimum score 500 paper-based; 61 iBT). *Application deadline:* Applications are processed on a rolling basis. Application fee: $40. Electronic applications accepted. *Expenses:* Required fees: $380; $130. *Financial support:* Teaching assistantships, Federal Work-Study, scholarships/grants, and unspecified assistantships available. Support available to part-time students. Financial award application deadline: 3/1; financial award applicants required to submit FAFSA. *Unit head:* Dr. Jodie Winship, Chair of College of Education, 205-652-5415, Fax: 205-652-3706, E-mail: jwinship@uwa.edu. *Application contact:* Dr. Jodie Winship, Chair of College of Education, 205-652-5415, Fax: 205-652-3706, E-mail: jwinship@uwa.edu.

The University of Winnipeg, Faculty of Theology, Winnipeg, MB R3B 2E9, Canada. Offers marriage and family therapy (MMFT, Certificate); sacred theology (STM); theology (M Div). *Accreditation:* AAMFT/COAMFTE. *Program availability:* Part-time.

University of Wisconsin–Stout, Graduate School, College of Education, Health and Human Sciences, Program in Marriage and Family Therapy, Menomonie, WI 54751. Offers MS. *Accreditation:* AAMFT/COAMFTE. *Program availability:* Part-time. *Degree requirements:* For master's, thesis or alternative. *Entrance requirements:* For master's, minimum GPA of 2.75. Additional exam requirements/recommendations for international students: required—TOEFL (minimum score 500 paper-based; 61 iBT). Electronic applications accepted.

Utah State University, School of Graduate Studies, Emma Eccles Jones College of Education and Human Services, Department of Family, Consumer, and Human

Development, Logan, UT 84322. Offers family and human development (MFHD); family, consumer, and human development (MS, PhD), including adolescence/youth (MS), adult development/aging (MS), consumer science (MS), infancy/childhood (MS), marriage and family relations (MS), marriage and family therapy (MS). *Accreditation:* AAMFT/COAMFTE (one or more programs are accredited). *Program availability:* Part-time, evening/weekend, online learning. *Degree requirements:* For master's, thesis; for doctorate, comprehensive exam, thesis/dissertation, competencies. *Entrance requirements:* For master's, GRE General Test or MAT, minimum GPA of 3.0, 3 letters of recommendation; for doctorate, GRE, minimum GPA of 3.0, 3 letters of recommendation. Additional exam requirements/recommendations for international students: required—TOEFL. Electronic applications accepted.

Valdosta State University, Department of Psychology, Counseling, and Family Therapy, Valdosta, GA 31698. Offers industrial/organizational psychology (MS); marriage and family therapy (MS); school counseling (M Ed, Ed S). *Accreditation:* AAMFT/COAMFTE. *Program availability:* Part-time, evening/weekend, 100% online, blended/hybrid learning. *Degree requirements:* For master's, thesis or alternative, comprehensive written and/or oral exams; for Ed S, thesis. *Entrance requirements:* For master's, GRE General Test or MAT, GACE; for Ed S, GRE General Test or MAT. Additional exam requirements/recommendations for international students: required—TOEFL (minimum score 523 paper-based); recommended—IELTS. Electronic applications accepted. *Expenses:* Contact institution.

Walden University, Graduate Programs, School of Counseling, Minneapolis, MN 55401. Offers addiction counseling (MS), including addictions and public health, child and adolescent counseling, family studies and interventions, forensic counseling, general program, military families and culture, trauma and crisis counseling; clinical mental health counseling (MS), including addiction counseling, forensic counseling, military families and culture, trauma and crisis counseling; counselor education and supervision (PhD), including consultation, counseling and social change, forensic mental health counseling, leadership and program evaluation, trauma and crisis; marriage, couple, and family counseling (MS), including addiction counseling, career counseling, forensic counseling, military families and culture, trauma and crisis counseling; school counseling (MS), including addiction counseling, career counseling, crisis and trauma, military families and culture. *Accreditation:* ACA. *Program availability:* Part-time, evening/weekend, online only, 100% online. *Degree requirements:* For master's, residency, field experience, professional development plan, licensure plan; for doctorate, thesis/dissertation, residency, practicum, internship. *Entrance requirements:* For master's, bachelor's degree or higher; minimum GPA of 2.5; official transcripts; goal statement (for some programs); access to computer and Internet; for doctorate, master's degree or higher; three years of related professional or academic experience (preferred); minimum GPA of 3.0; goal statement and current resume (for select programs); official transcripts; access to computer and Internet. Additional exam requirements/recommendations for international students: required—TOEFL (minimum score 550 paper-based, 79 iBT), IELTS (minimum score 6.5), Michigan English Language Assessment Battery (minimum score 82), or PTE (minimum score 53). Electronic applications accepted.

Western Kentucky University, Graduate School, College of Education and Behavioral Sciences, Department of Counseling and Student Affairs, Bowling Green, KY 42101. Offers counseling (MA Ed), including marriage and family therapy, mental health counseling; school counseling (P-12) (MA Ed); student affairs in higher education (MA Ed). *Accreditation:* ACA; NCATE. *Program availability:* Part-time, evening/weekend. *Degree requirements:* For master's, comprehensive exam, thesis optional. *Entrance requirements:* For master's, GRE General Test. Additional exam requirements/recommendations for international students: required—TOEFL (minimum score 555 paper-based; 79 iBT).

Western Seminary–Sacramento Campus, Program in Marital and Family Therapy, Rocklin, CA 95765. Offers MA. *Entrance requirements:* For master's, essays, undergraduate transcripts, 4 recommendations. Additional exam requirements/recommendations for international students: required—TOEFL.

Western Seminary - San Jose Campus, Graduate Programs, Milpitas, CA 95035. Offers Bible and theology (Graduate Diploma); Bible, camp and conference ministry (CGS); Biblical and theological studies (MA), including exegetical track, theological track; coaching (CGS); expositional ministry (M Div); marital and family therapy (MA); ministry (Graduate Diploma); ministry and leadership (MA), including camp and conference ministry, coaching, pastoral care to women, youth ministry; pastoral care to women (CGS, Graduate Diploma); pastoral ministry (M Div); theology (CGS); youth and family (CGS). *Program availability:* Part-time, evening/weekend, online learning. *Entrance requirements:* For master's, minimum GPA of 3.0. Electronic applications accepted.

Wheaton College, Graduate School, School of Psychology Counseling and Family Therapy, Wheaton, IL 60187-5593. Offers clinical mental health counseling (MA); clinical psychology (Psy D); marriage and family therapy (MA). *Accreditation:* APA (one or more programs are accredited). Terminal master's awarded for partial completion of doctoral program. *Degree requirements:* For master's, thesis or alternative; for doctorate, thesis/dissertation, internship. *Entrance requirements:* For master's, GRE General Test, 18 hours of course work in psychology; for doctorate, GRE General Test. Additional exam requirements/recommendations for international students: required—TOEFL (minimum score 550 paper-based; 80 iBT), IELTS (minimum score 6.5). *Expenses: Tuition:* Full-time $16,800; part-time $700 per credit hour. Tuition and fees vary according to degree level and program.

William & Mary, School of Education, Program in Counselor Education, Williamsburg, VA 23187-8795. Offers family counseling (M Ed); school counseling (M Ed). *Accreditation:* ACA; NCATE. *Program availability:* Part-time, evening/weekend, 100% online with required residency. *Faculty:* 11 full-time (3 women), 9 part-time/adjunct (6 women). *Students:* 39 full-time (21 women), 119 part-time (43 women); includes 29 minority (6 Black or African American, non-Hispanic/Latino; 6 Asian, non-Hispanic/Latino; 10 Hispanic/Latino; 7 Two or more races, non-Hispanic/Latino), 9 international. Average age 33. 240 applicants, 46% accepted, 64 enrolled. In 2019, 27 master's, 2 doctorates awarded. *Degree requirements:* For doctorate, comprehensive exam, thesis/dissertation. *Entrance requirements:* For master's, GRE, minimum GPA of 3.0; for doctorate, GRE, minimum GPA of 3.5. Additional exam requirements/recommendations for international students: required—TOEFL (minimum score 100 iBT), IELTS (minimum score 7). *Application deadline:* For fall admission, 1/15 for domestic and international students. Application fee: $50. Electronic applications accepted. *Expenses:* Tuition and fees for on-ground students per year in-state $16440; Tuition and fees for on-ground students per year out of state $34800; Tuition and fees for on-line students per credit hour $665. *Financial support:* In 2019–20, 31 students received support, including 26 research assistantships with full tuition reimbursements available (averaging $23,773 per year); teaching assistantships, scholarships/grants, and unspecified assistantships also available. Financial award application deadline: 1/15; financial award applicants required to submit FAFSA. *Unit head:* Dr. Patrick R. Mullen, Department Chair, 757-221-6071, E-mail: prmullen@wm.edu. *Application contact:* Dorothy Smith Osborne, Assistant Dean for Academic Programs and Student Services, 757-221-2317, E-mail: dsosbo@wm.edu.
Website: http://education.wm.edu

Psychoanalysis and Psychotherapy

Argosy University, Chicago, Illinois School of Professional Psychology, Doctoral Program in Clinical Psychology, Chicago, IL 60601. Offers child and adolescent psychology (Psy D); client-centered and experiential psychotherapies (Psy D); diversity and multicultural psychology (Psy D); family psychology (Psy D); forensic psychology (Psy D); health psychology (Psy D); neuropsychology (Psy D); organizational consulting (Psy D); psychoanalytic psychology (Psy D); psychology and spirituality (Psy D). *Accreditation:* APA.

Atlantic University, Program in Integrated Imagery: Regression Hypnosis, Virginia Beach, VA 23451-2061. Offers Graduate Certificate. *Program availability:* Blended/hybrid learning. *Entrance requirements:* For degree, bachelor's degree, minimum undergraduate GPA of 3.0, official transcripts, 1000-word essay. Electronic applications accepted. *Expenses:* Contact institution.

Boston Graduate School of Psychoanalysis, BGSP-New Jersey, Brookline, MA 02446-4602. Offers psychoanalysis (MA); psychoanalytic counseling (MA).

Boston Graduate School of Psychoanalysis, CAGS and Certificate Programs, Brookline, MA 02446-4602. Offers child and adolescent intervention (CAGS); psychoanalysis (Certificate); psychoanalytic psychotherapy (CAGS). *Program availability:* Part-time. *Degree requirements:* For other advanced degree, thesis. *Entrance requirements:* For degree, interview, BA, writing sample, 3 letters of reference, transcripts. Additional exam requirements/recommendations for international students: required—TOEFL (minimum score 550 paper-based; 79 iBT).

Boston Graduate School of Psychoanalysis, Doctoral Programs, Brookline, MA 02446-4602. Offers psychoanalysis (Psya D); psychoanalysis, society and culture (Psya D). *Program availability:* Part-time. *Degree requirements:* For doctorate, thesis/dissertation. *Entrance requirements:* For doctorate, interview, BA, personal statement, writing sample, 3 letters of recommendation. Additional exam requirements/recommendations for international students: required—TOEFL (minimum score 550 paper-based; 79 iBT).

Boston Graduate School of Psychoanalysis, Master's Programs, Brookline, MA 02446-4602. Offers mental health counseling (MA); psychoanalysis (MA); psychoanalysis, society and culture (MA). *Program availability:* Part-time. Terminal master's awarded for partial completion of doctoral program. *Degree requirements:* For master's, thesis. *Entrance requirements:* For master's, interview, BA, personal statement, writing sample, 3 letters of recommendation. Additional exam requirements/recommendations for international students: required—TOEFL (minimum score 550 paper-based; 79 iBT).

Boston Graduate School of Psychoanalysis, New York Graduate School of Psychoanalysis, New York, NY 10011. Offers MA. *Program availability:* Part-time. *Degree requirements:* For master's, thesis. *Entrance requirements:* For master's, interview, BA, writing sample, letters of recommendation. Additional exam requirements/recommendations for international students: required—TOEFL.

Immaculata University, College of Graduate Studies, Department of Psychology, Immaculata, PA 19345. Offers clinical mental health counseling (MA); clinical psychology (Psy D); forensic psychology (Graduate Certificate); integrative psychotherapy (Graduate Certificate); neuropsychology (Graduate Certificate); psychodynamic psychotherapy (Graduate Certificate); psychological testing (Graduate Certificate); school counseling (MA, Graduate Certificate); school psychology (MA). *Accreditation:* APA. *Program availability:* Part-time, evening/weekend. Terminal master's awarded for partial completion of doctoral program. *Degree requirements:* For master's, comprehensive exam, thesis optional; for doctorate, comprehensive exam, thesis/dissertation. *Entrance requirements:* For master's, GRE General Test or MAT, minimum GPA of 3.0; for doctorate, GRE General Test or MAT, minimum GPA of 3.5. Additional exam requirements/recommendations for international students: required—TOEFL, IELTS. Electronic applications accepted.

Naropa University, Graduate Programs, Program in Clinical Mental Health Counseling, Concentration in Contemplative Psychotherapy and Buddhist Psychology, Boulder, CO 80302-6697. Offers MA. *Degree requirements:* For master's, thesis, internship. *Entrance requirements:* For master's, interview; curriculum vitae/resume with pertinent academic, employment and volunteer activities; 2 letters of recommendation; statement of interest essay; transcripts; paid or volunteer experience in a clinical setting (recommended). Additional exam requirements/recommendations for international students: required—TOEFL (minimum score 550 paper-based; 80 iBT). Electronic applications accepted. *Expenses:* Contact institution.

Naropa University, Graduate Programs, Program in Clinical Mental Health Counseling, Concentration in Somatic Counseling: Body Psychotherapy, Boulder, CO 80302-6697. Offers MA. *Degree requirements:* For master's, thesis, internship, clinical practicum. *Entrance requirements:* For master's, BA (preferably in field related to the helping professions); minimum of 100 hours of paid or volunteer experience in mental health field or community facility/service organization; interview; state of interest essay; supplemental essays; 2 letters of recommendation; transcripts. Additional exam requirements/recommendations for international students: required—TOEFL (minimum score 550 paper-based; 80 iBT). Electronic applications accepted. *Expenses:* Contact institution.

The New School, The New School for Social Research, Department of Philosophy, New York, NY 10003. Offers philosophy (MA); psychoanalysis (PhD). *Program availability:* Part-time. *Faculty:* 12 full-time (4 women), 5 part-time/adjunct (0 women). *Students:* 125 full-time (37 women), 8 part-time (2 women); includes 23 minority (2 Black or African American, non-Hispanic/Latino; 3 Asian, non-Hispanic/Latino; 12 Hispanic/Latino; 6 Two or more races, non-Hispanic/Latino), 46 international. Average age 33.

146 applicants, 53% accepted, 19 enrolled. In 2019, 37 master's, 5 doctorates awarded. Terminal master's awarded for partial completion of doctoral program. *Degree requirements:* For master's, one foreign language, comprehensive exam, thesis; for doctorate, one foreign language, comprehensive exam, thesis/dissertation. *Entrance requirements:* For master's, GRE, letters of recommendation, writing sample, essays, transcript; for doctorate, letters of recommendation, writing sample, essays, transcript. Additional exam requirements/recommendations for international students: required—TOEFL (minimum score 100 iBT), IELTS (minimum score 7), PTE (minimum score 68). *Application deadline:* For fall admission, 1/5 priority date for domestic and international students; for spring admission, 10/15 priority date for domestic and international students. Applications are processed on a rolling basis. Application fee: $50. Electronic applications accepted. *Expenses:* 2260 per credit. *Financial support:* In 2019–20, 86 students received support, including 14 fellowships (averaging $5,268 per year), 20 research assistantships (averaging $4,088 per year), 25 teaching assistantships with full and partial tuition reimbursements available (averaging $9,914 per year); Federal Work-Study and scholarships/grants also available. Support available to part-time students. Financial award application deadline: 2/1; financial award applicants required to submit FAFSA. *Unit head:* Dr. Zed Adams, Department Chair, 212-229-5777, E-mail: adamsz@newschool.edu. *Application contact:* Merida Gasbarro, Director of Graduate Admission, 212-229-5150 Ext. 2300, E-mail: escandom@newschool.edu. Website: http://www.newschool.edu/nssr/philosophy/

New York University, Graduate School of Arts and Science, Department of Psychology, New York, NY 10012-1019. Offers cognition and perception (PhD); general psychology (MA); industrial/organizational psychology (MA); psychotherapy and psychoanalysis (Advanced Certificate); social psychology (PhD). *Program availability:* Part-time. Terminal master's awarded for partial completion of doctoral program. *Degree requirements:* For master's, comprehensive exam, thesis or alternative; for doctorate, thesis/dissertation. *Entrance requirements:* For master's and doctorate, GRE General Test. Additional exam requirements/recommendations for international students: required—TOEFL, IELTS.

Prescott College, Graduate Programs, Program in Counseling and Psychology, Prescott, AZ 86301. Offers adventure-based psychotherapy (MA); counseling psychology (MA); ecopsychology (MA); ecotherapy (MA); equine-assisted mental health (MA); expressive arts therapy (MA); somatic psychology (MA); student-directed independent study (MA). *Program availability:* Part-time, online learning. Terminal master's awarded for partial completion of doctoral program. *Degree requirements:* For master's, thesis, fieldwork or internship, practicum. *Entrance requirements:* For master's, 2 letters of recommendation, resume. Additional exam requirements/recommendations for international students: required—TOEFL (minimum score 500 paper-based). Electronic applications accepted.

University of Manitoba, Max Rady College of Medicine and Faculty of Graduate Studies, Graduate Programs in Medicine, Department of Psychiatry, Winnipeg, MB R3T 2N2, Canada. Offers M Sc. *Degree requirements:* For master's, thesis (for some programs).

Rehabilitation Counseling

Adler University, Master of Arts (M.A.) in Counseling: Specialization in Rehabilitation Counseling, Chicago, IL 60602. Offers MAC. *Program availability:* Part-time. In 2019, 1 master's awarded. *Degree requirements:* For master's, comprehensive exam, thesis optional, Social Justice Practicum; Internship. *Unit head:* Phyllis Horton, Director of Admissions, 312-662-4100, E-mail: admissions@adler.edu. *Application contact:* Michelle Brice, 312-662-4113, Fax: 312-662-4199.

Alabama Agricultural and Mechanical University, School of Graduate Studies, College of Education, Humanities, and Behavioral Sciences, Department of Social Work, Psychology and Counseling, Huntsville, AL 35811. Offers psychology and counseling (MS, Ed S), including clinical psychology (MS), counseling psychology (MS), guidance and counseling, rehabilitation counseling (MS), school counseling (MS), school psychology (MS), school psychometry (MS); social work (MSW). *Accreditation:* CORE; NCATE. *Program availability:* Part-time, evening/weekend. *Degree requirements:* For master's, comprehensive exam. *Entrance requirements:* For master's, GRE General Test. Additional exam requirements/recommendations for international students: required—TOEFL (minimum score 500 paper-based; 61 iBT).

Alabama State University, College of Health Sciences, Department of Rehabilitation Studies, Montgomery, AL 36101-0271. Offers rehabilitation counseling (MRC). *Accreditation:* CORE. *Faculty:* 4 full-time (2 women). *Students:* 27 full-time (22 women); all minorities (all Black or African American, non-Hispanic/Latino). Average age 25. 29 applicants, 59% accepted, 15 enrolled. In 2019, 10 master's awarded. *Degree requirements:* For master's, comprehensive exam. *Entrance requirements:* For master's, bachelor's degree from an accredited institution with a cumulative GPA of 2.5 or higher on a 4.0 scale (GPA requirement for scholarships and grant traineeships may be higher than admission requirements); recent GRE or MAT scores submitted to Graduate Studies with completed application, 3 letters of recommendation from persons qualified to evaluate the application's academic abilities and character. Additional exam requirements/recommendations for international students: required—TOEFL (minimum score 500 paper-based). *Application deadline:* For fall admission, 4/15 priority date for domestic students, 4/15 for international students; for spring admission, 11/15 for domestic and international students; for summer admission, 3/15 for domestic and international students. Applications are processed on a rolling basis. Application fee: $25. Electronic applications accepted. *Financial support:* Fellowships, research assistantships, scholarships/grants, tuition waivers (partial), and unspecified assistantships available. Financial award application deadline: 6/30; financial award applicants required to submit FAFSA. *Unit head:* Dr. Danita H. Stapleton, Chair/Program Coordinator, 334-229-4865, E-mail: dstapleton@alasu.edu. *Application contact:* Dr. Ed Brown, Dean of Graduate Studies, 334-229-4274, Fax: 334-229-4928, E-mail: ebrown@alasu.edu. Website: http://www.alasu.edu/academics/colleges—departments/health-sciences/rehabilitation-studies/master-of-rehabilitation-counseling/index.aspx

Arkansas State University, Graduate School, College of Education and Behavioral Science, Department of Psychology and Counseling, State University, AR 72467. Offers clinical mental health counseling (Graduate Certificate); college student personnel services (MS); dyslexia therapy (Graduate Certificate); psychological science (MS); psychology and counseling (Ed S); rehabilitation counseling (MRC); school counseling (MSE); student affairs (Graduate Certificate). *Accreditation:* ACA (one or more programs are accredited); CORE (one or more programs are accredited); NCATE. *Program availability:* Part-time. *Degree requirements:* For master's and other advanced degree, comprehensive exam, thesis or alternative. *Entrance requirements:* For master's, GRE General Test or MAT (for MSE), appropriate bachelor's degree, interview, letters of reference, official transcripts, immunization records, written statement, 2-3 page autobiography; for other advanced degree, GRE General Test, interview, master's degree, letters of reference, official transcript, personal statement, immunization records. Additional exam requirements/recommendations for international students: required—TOEFL (minimum score 550 paper-based; 79 iBT), IELTS (minimum score 6), PTE (minimum score 56). Electronic applications accepted.

Assumption University, Rehabilitation Counseling Program, Worcester, MA 01609-1296. Offers MA, CAGS. *Accreditation:* CORE. *Program availability:* Part-time, evening/weekend, blended/hybrid learning. *Degree requirements:* For master's, comprehensive exam, internship, practicum. *Entrance requirements:* For master's, bachelor's degree with at least 15 semester hours of undergraduate course work in the behavioral and social sciences and minimum GPA of 2.75; three letters of recommendation; official transcripts; personal statement; current resume; interview; for CAGS, master's degree in human service, counseling, education, social work or related field; three letters of recommendation; official transcripts; personal statement; current resume; interview. Additional exam requirements/recommendations for international students: required—TOEFL (minimum score 540 paper-based; 76 iBT), IELTS (minimum score 6). Electronic applications accepted. *Expenses:* Tuition: Full-time $12,690; part-time $705 per credit. *Required fees:* $70 per term.

Ball State University, Graduate School, College of Health, Department of Counseling Psychology, Social Psychology, and Counseling, Program in Counseling Psychology, Muncie, IN 47306. Offers counseling (MA), including clinical mental health counseling, mental health counseling, rehabilitation counseling, school counseling; counseling psychology (PhD). *Accreditation:* ACA; APA. *Program availability:* Part-time. *Degree requirements:* For doctorate, thesis/dissertation. *Entrance requirements:* For master's, GRE General Test (minimum scores 144 quantitative, 153 verbal), minimum baccalaureate GPA of 2.75 or 3.0 in latter half of baccalaureate, minimum GPA of 3.0 in psychology coursework, three letters of recommendation; for doctorate, GRE General Test, interview, minimum graduate GPA of 3.2, resume. Additional exam requirements/recommendations for international students: required—TOEFL (minimum score 550 paper-based; 79 iBT), IELTS (minimum score 6.5). Electronic applications accepted. *Expenses: Tuition, area resident:* Full-time $7506; part-time $417 per credit hour. Tuition, nonresident: full-time $20,610; part-time $1145 per credit hour. *Required fees:* $2126. Tuition and fees vary according to course load, campus/location and program.

Barry University, School of Education, Program in Rehabilitation Counseling, Miami Shores, FL 33161-6695. Offers MS, Ed S. *Program availability:* Part-time, evening/weekend. *Degree requirements:* For master's, comprehensive exam, scholarly paper; for Ed S, comprehensive exam. *Entrance requirements:* For master's, GRE General Test or MAT, minimum GPA of 3.0; for Ed S, GRE General Test, minimum GPA of 3.0. Electronic applications accepted.

Bayamón Central University, Graduate Programs, Program in Education, Bayamón, PR 00960-1725. Offers administration and supervision (MA Ed); commercial education (MA Ed); elementary education (K–3) (MA Ed); family counseling (Graduate Certificate); guidance and counseling (MA Ed); pre-elementary teacher (MA Ed); rehabilitation counseling (MA Ed); special education (MA Ed), including attention deficit disorder, education of the autistic, learning disabilities. *Program availability:* Part-time, evening/weekend. *Degree requirements:* For master's, comprehensive exam. *Entrance requirements:* For master's, EXADEP, bachelor's degree in education or related field.

California State University, Fresno, Division of Research and Graduate Studies, Kremen School of Education and Human Development, Department of Counselor Education and Rehabilitation, Program in Clinical Rehabilitation and Mental Health Counseling, Fresno, CA 93740-8027. Offers MS. *Accreditation:* ACA; CORE. *Program availability:* Part-time, evening/weekend. *Degree requirements:* For master's, internship; project, thesis, or comprehensive exam. *Entrance requirements:* For master's, GRE General Test, MAT, minimum GPA of 3.0, official transcripts. Additional exam requirements/recommendations for international students: required—TOEFL. Electronic applications accepted. *Expenses:* Tuition, state resident: full-time $4012; part-time $2506 per semester.

California State University, Los Angeles, Graduate Studies, Charter College of Education, Division of Special Education and Counseling, Los Angeles, CA 90032-8530. Offers counseling (MS), including applied behavior analysis, community college counseling, rehabilitation counseling, school counseling, school psychology; special education (MA, PhD). *Accreditation:* ACA. *Program availability:* Part-time, evening/weekend. *Entrance requirements:* For master's, minimum GPA of 2.75 in last 90 units of course work, teaching certificate. Additional exam requirements/recommendations for international students: required—TOEFL (minimum score 500 paper-based). Electronic applications accepted. *Expenses: Tuition, area resident:* Full-time $7176; part-time $4164 per year. Tuition, state resident: full-time $7176; part-time $4164 per year. Tuition, nonresident: full-time $14,304; part-time $8916 per year. *International tuition:* $14,304 full-time. *Required fees:* $1037.76; $1037.76 per unit. Tuition and fees vary according to degree level and program.

California State University, San Bernardino, Graduate Studies, College of Education, Program in Counseling and Guidance, San Bernardino, CA 92407. Offers counseling and guidance (MS); rehabilitation counseling (MA). *Accreditation:* NCATE. *Program availability:* Part-time, evening/weekend. *Students:* 154 full-time (130 women), 8 part-time (7 women); includes 124 minority (9 Black or African American, non-Hispanic/Latino; 1 American Indian or Alaska Native, non-Hispanic/Latino; 8 Asian, non-Hispanic/Latino; 104 Hispanic/Latino; 1 Native Hawaiian or other Pacific Islander, non-Hispanic/Latino; 1 Two or more races, non-Hispanic/Latino), 5 international. Average age 29. 107 applicants, 69% accepted, 68 enrolled. In 2019, 35 master's awarded. *Degree requirements:* For master's, comprehensive exam, thesis or alternative. *Entrance requirements:* Additional exam requirements/recommendations for international students: required—TOEFL. *Application deadline:* For fall admission, 7/16 for domestic students. Application fee: $55. *Unit head:* Dr. Lorraine Hedtke, Program Coordinator, 909-537-7640, E-mail: lhedtke@csusb.edu. *Application contact:* Dr. Dorota Huizinga, Dean of Graduate Studies, 909-537-3064, E-mail: dorota.huizinga@csusb.edu.

California State University, San Bernardino, Graduate Studies, College of Education, Program in Rehabilitation Counseling, San Bernardino, CA 92407. Offers MA.

Accreditation: CORE; NCATE. *Program availability:* Part-time, evening/weekend. *Students:* 1 full-time (0 women), 39 part-time (10 women); includes 32 minority (2 Black or African American, non-Hispanic/Latino; 4 Asian, non-Hispanic/Latino; 24 Hispanic/Latino; 2 Two or more races, non-Hispanic/Latino), 1 international. Average age 35. 26 applicants, 88% accepted, 18 enrolled. In 2019, 17 master's awarded. *Degree requirements:* For master's, thesis or alternative. *Entrance requirements:* Additional exam requirements/recommendations for international students: required—TOEFL. *Application deadline:* For fall admission, 7/16 for domestic students. Application fee: $55. *Financial support:* Career-related internships or fieldwork and Federal Work-Study available. Support available to part-time students. *Unit head:* Dr. Connie McReynolds, Program Coordinator, 909-537-5453, E-mail: cmcreyno@csusb.edu. *Application contact:* Dr. Dorota Huizinga, Dean of Graduate Studies, 909-537-3064, E-mail: dorota.huizinga@csusb.edu.

Cambridge College, School of Psychology and Counseling, Boston, MA 02129. Offers alcohol and drug counseling (Certificate); behavioral health care management (CAGS); marriage and family therapy (M Ed); mental health and school counseling (M Ed); mental health counseling (M Ed); psychological studies (M Ed); rehabilitation counseling (Certificate); school adjustment and mental health counseling (M Ed); school adjustment counseling for mental health counselors (Certificate); school counseling (M Ed); trauma studies (Certificate). *Program availability:* Part-time, evening/weekend. *Degree requirements:* For master's and other advanced degree, thesis, practicum/internship. *Entrance requirements:* For master's, resume, 2 professional references; for other advanced degree, official transcripts, documents for transfer credit evaluation, resume, written personal statement/essay, 2 professional references, health insurance, immunizations form. Additional exam requirements/recommendations for international students: required—TOEFL (minimum score 550 paper-based; 79 iBT), Michigan English Language Assessment Battery (minimum score 85); recommended—IELTS (minimum score 6). Electronic applications accepted. *Expenses:* Contact institution.

Central Connecticut State University, School of Graduate Studies, School of Education and Professional Studies, Department of Counselor Education and Family Therapy, New Britain, CT 06050-4010. Offers marriage and family therapy (MS); professional counseling (MS, AC, Certificate); school counseling (MS); student development in higher education (MS). *Accreditation:* AAMFT/COAMFTE; ACA. *Program availability:* Part-time, evening/weekend. *Degree requirements:* For master's, comprehensive exam, thesis or alternative; for other advanced degree, qualifying exam. *Entrance requirements:* For master's, minimum undergraduate GPA of 2.7, essay, interview, letters of recommendation. Additional exam requirements/recommendations for international students: required—TOEFL (minimum score 550 paper-based; 79 iBT); recommended—IELTS (minimum score 6.5). Electronic applications accepted.

Coppin State University, School of Graduate Studies, College of Behavioral and Social Sciences, Department of Applied Psychology and Rehabilitation Counseling, Program in Rehabilitation Counseling, Baltimore, MD 21216-3698. Offers M Ed. *Accreditation:* CORE. *Program availability:* Part-time. *Degree requirements:* For master's, comprehensive exam (for some programs), thesis optional, internship, clinical requirements. *Entrance requirements:* For master's, GRE General Test, interview, minimum GPA of 3.0.

East Carolina University, Graduate School, College of Allied Health Sciences, Department of Addictions and Rehabilitation Studies, Greenville, NC 27858-4353. Offers clinical counseling (MS); military and trauma counseling (Certificate); rehabilitation and career counseling (MS); rehabilitation counseling (Certificate); rehabilitation counseling and administration (PhD); substance abuse counseling (Certificate); vocational evaluation (Certificate). *Accreditation:* CORE. *Program availability:* Part-time, evening/weekend. *Students:* Average age 33. 51 applicants, 73% accepted, 31 enrolled. In 2019, 19 master's, 5 doctorates, 34 other advanced degrees awarded. *Degree requirements:* For master's, comprehensive exam, thesis or alternative, internship; for doctorate, thesis/dissertation, internship. *Entrance requirements:* For master's and doctorate, GRE General Test or MAT. Additional exam requirements/recommendations for international students: recommended—TOEFL (minimum score 78 iBT), IELTS (minimum score 6.5). *Application deadline:* For fall admission, 3/1 priority date for domestic students; for spring admission, 10/1 priority date for domestic students. Applications are processed on a rolling basis. Application fee: $75. Electronic applications accepted. *Expenses: Tuition, area resident:* Full-time $4749; part-time $185 per credit hour. Tuition, state resident: full-time $4749; part-time $185 per credit hour. Tuition, nonresident: full-time $17,898; part-time $864 per credit hour. *International tuition:* $17,898 full-time. *Required fees:* $2787. *Financial support:* Research assistantships with partial tuition reimbursements, teaching assistantships with partial tuition reimbursements, Federal Work-Study, scholarships/grants, and unspecified assistantships available. Support available to part-time students. Financial award application deadline: 3/1; financial award applicants required to submit FAFSA. *Unit head:* Dr. Paul Toriello, Chair, 252-744-6292, E-mail: toriellop@ecu.edu. *Application contact:* Graduate School Admissions, 252-328-6013, Fax: 252-328-6071, E-mail: gradschool@ecu.edu.
Website: http://www.ecu.edu/rehb/

East Central University, School of Graduate Studies, Department of Professional Programs in Human Services, Ada, OK 74820. Offers clinical rehabilitation and clinical mental health counseling (MSHR); criminal justice (MSHR); human resources (MSHR). *Accreditation:* CORE. *Program availability:* Part-time, evening/weekend. *Degree requirements:* For master's, thesis optional. *Entrance requirements:* For master's, GRE General Test, MAT, minimum GPA of 2.5. Electronic applications accepted.

Edinboro University of Pennsylvania, Department of Counseling, School Psychology and Special Education, Edinboro, PA 16444. Offers counseling (MA), including art therapy, clinical mental health counseling, college counseling, rehabilitation counseling, school counseling; educational psychology (M Ed); school psychology (Ed S); special education (M Ed), including autism, behavior management. *Accreditation:* ACA. *Program availability:* Part-time, evening/weekend. *Faculty:* 19 full-time (13 women), 2 part-time/adjunct (1 woman). *Students:* 180 full-time (146 women), 215 part-time (186 women); includes 42 minority (18 Black or African American, non-Hispanic/Latino; 2 American Indian or Alaska Native, non-Hispanic/Latino; 4 Asian, non-Hispanic/Latino; 12 Hispanic/Latino; 1 Native Hawaiian or other Pacific Islander, non-Hispanic/Latino; 5 Two or more races, non-Hispanic/Latino), 3 international. Average age 31. 197 applicants, 63% accepted, 71 enrolled. In 2019, 87 master's, 8 other advanced degrees awarded. *Degree requirements:* For master's, thesis or alternative, competency exam; for Ed S, thesis or alternative. *Entrance requirements:* For master's and Ed S, GRE or MAT, minimum QPA of 2.5. Additional exam requirements/recommendations for international students: required—TOEFL (minimum score 550 paper-based; 213 iBT), IELTS (minimum score 6.5). *Application deadline:* Applications are processed on a rolling basis. Application fee: $30. Electronic applications accepted. *Expenses: Tuition, area resident:* Full-time $11,261; part-time $625.60 per credit. Tuition, state resident: full-time $11,261; part-time $625.60 per credit. Tuition, nonresident: full-time $16,850; part-time $936.10 per credit. *International tuition:* $16,850 full-time. *Required fees:* $57.75 per credit. *Financial support:* In 2019–20, 35 students received support. Research assistantships with tuition reimbursements available, career-related internships or fieldwork, Federal Work-Study, scholarships/grants, and unspecified assistantships available. Support available to part-time students. Financial award application deadline: 2/15; financial award applicants required to submit FAFSA. *Unit head:* Dr. Penelope Orr, Chairperson, 814-732-1684, E-mail: porr@edinboro.edu. *Application contact:* Dr. Penelope Orr, Chairperson, 814-732-1684, E-mail: porr@edinboro.edu.
Website: https://www.edinboro.edu/academics/schools-and-departments/soe/departments/cspe/

Emporia State University, Program in Rehabilitation Counseling, Emporia, KS 66801-5415. Offers MS. *Accreditation:* CORE. *Program availability:* Part-time. *Degree requirements:* For master's, comprehensive exam or thesis, practicum. *Entrance requirements:* For master's, GRE or MAT, essay exam, appropriate bachelor's degree, interview, letters of recommendation. Electronic applications accepted. *Expenses: Tuition, area resident:* Full-time $6394; part-time $266.41 per credit hour. Tuition, state resident: full-time $6394; part-time $266.41 per credit hour. Tuition, nonresident: full-time $20,128; part-time $828.66 per credit hour. *International tuition:* $20,128 full-time. *Required fees:* $2183; $90.95 per credit hour. Tuition and fees vary according to campus/location and program.

Fort Valley State University, College of Graduate Studies and Extended Education, Department of Counseling Psychology, Program in Rehabilitation Counseling, Fort Valley, GA 31030. Offers MS. *Accreditation:* CORE. *Program availability:* Part-time. *Degree requirements:* For master's, comprehensive exam (for some programs), thesis optional. *Entrance requirements:* For master's, GRE General Test or MAT. Additional exam requirements/recommendations for international students: recommended—TOEFL.

The George Washington University, Graduate School of Education and Human Development, Department of Counseling and Human Development, Program in Rehabilitation Counseling, Washington, DC 20052. Offers autism spectrum disorder (MA Ed/HD); substance abuse and psychiatric disabilities (MA Ed/HD); traumatic brain injury (MA Ed/HD). *Accreditation:* CORE. *Program availability:* Online learning. *Entrance requirements:* For master's, GRE or MAT, two letters of recommendation, 1- to 2-page statement of purpose, official transcripts from all institutions attended, resume. Additional exam requirements/recommendations for international students: required—TOEFL or IELTS. Electronic applications accepted.

Georgia State University, College of Education and Human Development, Department of Counseling and Psychological Services, Program in Rehabilitation Counseling, Atlanta, GA 30302-3083. Offers MS. *Accreditation:* CORE. *Program availability:* Online learning. *Entrance requirements:* For master's, GRE, goal statement, resume, 3 letters of recommendation, transcripts. Additional exam requirements/recommendations for international students: required—TOEFL. Application fee: $50. Electronic applications accepted. *Expenses: Tuition, area resident:* Full-time $7164; part-time $398 per credit hour. Tuition, state resident: full-time $7164; part-time $398 per credit hour. Tuition, nonresident: full-time $22,662; part-time $1259 per credit hour. *International tuition:* $22,662 full-time. *Required fees:* $2128; $312 per credit hour. Tuition and fees vary according to course load and program. *Financial support:* Research assistantships, teaching assistantships, career-related internships or fieldwork, institutionally sponsored loans, scholarships/grants, health care benefits, tuition waivers, and unspecified assistantships available. Financial award application deadline: 4/1. *Unit head:* Dr. Brian Dew, Department Chair, 404-413-8168, Fax: 404-413-8013, E-mail: bdew@gsu.edu. *Application contact:* CPS Admissions Office, 404-413-8200.
Website: https://education.gsu.edu/cps/

Hofstra University, School of Health Professions and Human Services, Programs in Counseling, Hempstead, NY 11549. Offers counseling (MS Ed, PD); creative arts therapy (MA); interdisciplinary transition specialist (Advanced Certificate); marriage and family therapy (MA); mental health counseling (MA, Advanced Certificate); rehabilitation administration (PD); rehabilitation counseling (MS Ed, Advanced Certificate); rehabilitation counseling in mental health (MS Ed, Advanced Certificate). *Accreditation:* ACA. *Program availability:* Part-time, evening/weekend. *Students:* 124 full-time (105 women), 69 part-time (64 women); includes 68 minority (23 Black or African American, non-Hispanic/Latino; 10 Asian, non-Hispanic/Latino; 32 Hispanic/Latino; 3 Native Hawaiian or other Pacific Islander, non-Hispanic/Latino), 4 international. Average age 28. 188 applicants, 77% accepted, 75 enrolled. In 2019, 58 master's, 3 other advanced degrees awarded. *Degree requirements:* For master's, comprehensive exam (for some programs), thesis (for some programs), internship, practicum, student teaching, seminars, minimum GPA of 3.0. *Entrance requirements:* For master's, GRE, interview, letters of recommendation, portfolio, essay, professional experience, certification; for other advanced degree, GRE, interview, letters of recommendation, essay, professional experience, resume, master's degree. Additional exam requirements/recommendations for international students: required—TOEFL (minimum score 550 paper-based; 80 iBT); recommended—IELTS (minimum score 6.5). *Application deadline:* Applications are processed on a rolling basis. Application fee: $75. Electronic applications accepted. *Expenses: Tuition:* Full-time $25,164; part-time $1398 per credit. *Required fees:* $580; $165 per semester. Tuition and fees vary according to course load, degree level and program. *Financial support:* In 2019–20, 77 students received support, including 44 fellowships with full and partial tuition reimbursements available (averaging $3,811 per year), 9 research assistantships with full and partial tuition reimbursements available (averaging $6,586 per year); career-related internships or fieldwork, Federal Work-Study, institutionally sponsored loans, scholarships/grants, traineeships, tuition waivers (full and partial), unspecified assistantships, and scholarships and endowed scholarships also available. Support available to part-time students. Financial award applicants required to submit FAFSA. *Unit head:* Dr. Jamie Mitus, Chairperson, 516-463-5759, E-mail: jamie.s.mitus@hofstra.edu. *Application contact:* Sunil Samuel, Assistant Vice President of Admissions, 516-463-4723, Fax: 516-463-4664, E-mail: graduateadmission@hofstra.edu.
Website: http://www.hofstra.edu/academics/colleges/healthscienceshumanservices/

Hunter College of the City University of New York, Graduate School, School of Education, Department of Educational Foundations and Counseling, Program in Rehabilitation Counseling, New York, NY 10065-5085. Offers MS Ed. *Accreditation:* CORE. *Degree requirements:* For master's, thesis, seminar. *Entrance requirements:* For master's, interview, minimum GPA of 2.7, recommendations. Additional exam requirements/recommendations for international students: required—TOEFL, TWE.

Illinois Institute of Technology, Graduate College, Lewis College of Human Sciences, Department of Psychology, Chicago, IL 60616. Offers clinical psychology (PhD); industrial and organizational psychology (PhD); personnel and human resource development (MS); rehabilitation and mental health counseling (MS); rehabilitation counseling education (PhD). *Accreditation:* APA (one or more programs are accredited); CORE. *Program availability:* Part-time, evening/weekend. Terminal master's awarded for partial completion of doctoral program. *Degree requirements:* For master's, thesis (for some programs); for doctorate, comprehensive exam, thesis/dissertation, minimum of 107 credit hours, 1-year full-time internship. *Entrance requirements:* For master's, GRE General Test (minimum score 298 Quantitative and Verbal, 3.0 Analytical Writing), minimum GPA of 3.0; 3 letters of recommendation; bachelor's degree from accredited institution (for personnel and human resource development); for doctorate, GRE General Test (minimum score 298 Quantitative and Verbal, 3.0 Analytical Writing), bachelor's or master's degree from accredited institution, recommendations. Additional exam requirements/recommendations for international students: required—TOEFL (minimum score 550 paper-based; 80 iBT). Electronic applications accepted.

Kent State University, College of Education, Health and Human Services, School of Lifespan Development and Educational Sciences, Program in Rehabilitation Counseling, Kent, OH 44242-0001. Offers M Ed. *Accreditation:* CORE. *Entrance requirements:* For master's, 2 letters of reference, goals statement, minimum undergraduate GPA of 2.75, interview. Additional exam requirements/recommendations for international students: required—TOEFL (minimum score 550 paper-based; 80 iBT). Electronic applications accepted.

Langston University, School of Education and Behavioral Sciences, Langston, OK 73050. Offers bilingual/multicultural (M Ed); elementary education (M Ed); English as a second language (M Ed); rehabilitation counseling (M Sc); urban education (M Ed). *Accreditation:* CORE; NCATE (one or more programs are accredited). *Program availability:* Part-time. *Degree requirements:* For master's, comprehensive exam, thesis optional. *Entrance requirements:* For master's, GRE, writing skills test, minimum GPA of 2.5, 3 letters of recommendation. Additional exam requirements/recommendations for international students: required—TOEFL, TWE.

Louisiana State University Health Sciences Center, School of Allied Health Professions, Department of Clinical Rehabilitation and Counseling, New Orleans, LA 70112-2262. Offers MHS. *Accreditation:* CORE. *Faculty:* 6 full-time (5 women). *Students:* 25 full-time (22 women), 1 part-time; includes 11 minority (9 Black or African American, non-Hispanic/Latino; 1 Hispanic/Latino; 1 Two or more races, non-Hispanic/Latino). Average age 25. 40 applicants, 28% accepted, 11 enrolled. In 2019, 6 master's awarded. *Entrance requirements:* For master's, GRE General Test, minimum GPA of 2.5, 2 letters of recommendation. Additional exam requirements/recommendations for international students: required—TOEFL (minimum score 550 paper-based; 79 iBT). *Application deadline:* For fall admission, 7/6 priority date for domestic students. Application fee: $95. Electronic applications accepted. *Expenses:* Contact institution. *Financial support:* Application deadline: 4/15; applicants required to submit FAFSA. *Unit head:* Dr. Erin M. Dugan, Interim Head, 504-556-3403, Fax: 504-556-7540, E-mail: emart3@lsuhsc.edu. *Application contact:* Yudialys D. Cazanas, Student Affairs Director, 504-568-4253, Fax: 504-568-3185, E-mail: ydelga@lsuhsc.edu.
Website: http://alliedhealth.lsuhsc.edu/crc/default.aspx

Maryville University of Saint Louis, Myrtle E. and Earl E. Walker College of Health Professions, Program in Rehabilitation Counseling, St. Louis, MO 63141-7299. Offers marriage and family therapy (MARC); music therapy (MARC); substance abuse (MARC). *Accreditation:* CORE. *Program availability:* Part-time. *Faculty:* 3 full-time (1 woman). *Students:* 18 full-time (16 women), 16 part-time (12 women); includes 9 minority (7 Black or African American, non-Hispanic/Latino; 2 Two or more races, non-Hispanic/Latino). Average age 31. In 2019, 7 master's awarded. *Degree requirements:* For master's, internship, seminar. *Entrance requirements:* For master's, Bachelors degree from regionally accredited institution. minimum cumulative GPA of 3.0, 2 letters of recommendation, interview, essay, transcripts, resume. Additional exam requirements/recommendations for international students: required—TOEFL (minimum score 563 paper-based; 92 iBT). *Application deadline:* For fall admission, 1/15 for domestic students; for spring admission, 10/1 for domestic students. Applications are processed on a rolling basis. Electronic applications accepted. *Expenses:* Contact institution. *Financial support:* Career-related internships or fieldwork, Federal Work-Study, and campus employment available. Financial award application deadline: 4/1; financial award applicants required to submit FAFSA. *Unit head:* Dr. Michael Kiener, Director, 314-529-9443, Fax: 314-529-9495, E-mail: mkiener@maryville.edu. *Application contact:* Jeannie DeLuca, Director, Admissions and Advising, 314-529-9355, Fax: 314-529-9927, E-mail: jdeluca@maryville.edu.
Website: http://www.maryville.edu/hp/rehabilitation-counseling/

Mercer University, Graduate Studies, Cecil B. Day Campus, College of Professional Advancement, Atlanta, GA 31207. Offers certified rehabilitation counseling (MS); clinical mental health (MS); counselor education and supervision (PhD); criminal justice and public safety leadership (MS); health informatics (MS); human services (MS), including child and adolescent services, gerontology services; organizational leadership (MS), including leadership for the health care professional, leadership for the nonprofit organization, organizational development and change; school counseling (MS). *Program availability:* Part-time, evening/weekend, 100% online, blended/hybrid learning. *Faculty:* 19 full-time (11 women), 34 part-time/adjunct (30 women). *Students:* 193 full-time (156 women), 277 part-time (225 women); includes 260 minority (211 Black or African American, non-Hispanic/Latino; 2 American Indian or Alaska Native, non-Hispanic/Latino; 23 Asian, non-Hispanic/Latino; 19 Hispanic/Latino; 5 Two or more races, non-Hispanic/Latino), 3 international. Average age 32. 300 applicants, 45% accepted, 114 enrolled. In 2019, 183 master's, 7 doctorates awarded. *Degree requirements:* For master's, comprehensive exam (for some programs), thesis (for some programs); for doctorate, thesis/dissertation. *Entrance requirements:* For master's, GRE or MAT, Georgia Professional Standards Commission (GPSC) Certification at the SC-5 level; for doctorate, GRE or MAT. Additional exam requirements/recommendations for international students: recommended—TOEFL (minimum score 550 paper-based; 80 iBT), IELTS (minimum score 6.5). *Application deadline:* For fall admission, 7/1 priority date for domestic and international students; for spring admission, 11/1 priority date for domestic and international students; for summer admission, 4/1 priority date for domestic and international students. Application fee: $35. Electronic applications accepted. Application fee is waived when completed online. *Expenses:* Contact institution. *Financial support:* In 2019–20, 32 students received support. Federal Work-Study, scholarships/grants, and unspecified assistantships available. Financial award applicants required to submit FAFSA. *Unit head:* Dr. Priscilla R. Danheiser, Dean, 678-547-6028, Fax: 678-547-6008, E-mail: danheiser_p@mercer.edu. *Application contact:* Theatis Anderson, Asst VP for Enrollment Management, 678-547-6421, E-mail: anderson_t@mercer.edu.
Website: https://professionaladvancement.mercer.edu/

Michigan State University, The Graduate School, College of Education, Department of Counseling, Educational Psychology and Special Education, East Lansing, MI 48824. Offers counseling (MA); educational psychology and educational technology (PhD); educational technology (MA); measurement and quantitative methods (PhD); rehabilitation counseling (MA); rehabilitation counselor education (PhD); school psychology (MA, PhD, Ed S); special education (MA, PhD). *Accreditation:* APA (one or more programs are accredited); CORE (one or more programs are accredited). *Program availability:* Part-time. *Entrance requirements:* Additional exam requirements/recommendations for international students: required—TOEFL. Electronic applications accepted.

Minnesota State University Mankato, College of Graduate Studies and Research, College of Allied Health and Nursing, Program in Rehabilitation Counseling, Mankato, MN 56001. Offers MS. *Accreditation:* CORE. *Degree requirements:* For master's, comprehensive exam. *Entrance requirements:* For master's, GRE General Test, minimum GPA of 3.0 during previous 2 years, references.

Mississippi State University, College of Education, Department of Counseling, Educational Psychology, and Foundations, Mississippi State, MS 39762. Offers clinical mental health (MS); college counseling (MS); counseling/mental health (PhD); counseling/school psychology (PhD); counselor education (Ed S); educational psychology/general educational psychology (PhD); educational psychology/school psychology (PhD); general educational psychology (MS); psychometry (MS); rehabilitation counseling (MS); school counseling (MS); school psychology (Ed S); student affairs (MS). *Accreditation:* ACA (one or more programs are accredited); APA; CORE (one or more programs are accredited); NCATE. *Program availability:* Part-time, blended/hybrid learning. *Faculty:* 15 full-time (10 women), 3 part-time/adjunct (all women). *Students:* 105 full-time (87 women), 47 part-time (37 women); includes 58 minority (49 Black or African American, non-Hispanic/Latino; 1 Asian, non-Hispanic/Latino; 6 Hispanic/Latino; 2 Two or more races, non-Hispanic/Latino), 7 international. Average age 30. 83 applicants, 69% accepted, 40 enrolled. In 2019, 39 master's, 3 doctorates, 7 other advanced degrees awarded. Terminal master's awarded for partial completion of doctoral program. *Degree requirements:* For master's, comprehensive exam, thesis optional; for doctorate, thesis/dissertation, comprehensive oral and written exam. *Entrance requirements:* For master's, GRE (taken within the last five years), BS with minimum GPA of 2.75 on last 60 hours; for doctorate, GRE, MS from CACREP- or CORE-accredited program in counseling; for Ed S, GRE, MS in counseling or related field, minimum GPA of 3.3 on all graduate work. Additional exam requirements/recommendations for international students: required—TOEFL (minimum score 550 paper-based; 79 iBT); recommended—IELTS (minimum score 6.5). *Application deadline:* For fall admission, 2/1 priority date for domestic and international students. Applications are processed on a rolling basis. Application fee: $60 ($80 for international students). Electronic applications accepted. *Expenses: Tuition, area resident:* Full-time $8880; part-time $456 per credit hour. Tuition, state resident: full-time $8880. Tuition, nonresident: full-time $23,840; part-time $1236 per credit hour. *Required fees:* $110; $11.12 per credit hour. Tuition and fees vary according to course load. *Financial support:* In 2019–20, 3 research assistantships (averaging $9,000 per year), 7 teaching assistantships with full tuition reimbursements (averaging $8,401 per year) were awarded; career-related internships or fieldwork, Federal Work-Study, institutionally sponsored loans, and unspecified assistantships also available. Financial award application deadline: 2/1; financial award applicants required to submit FAFSA. *Unit head:* Dr. Daniel Gadke, Professor and Interim Head, 662-325-3426, Fax: 662-325-3263, E-mail: dgadke@colled.msstate.edu. *Application contact:* Ryan King, Admissions and Enrollment Assistant, 662-325-8951, E-mail: rjk101@grad.msstate.edu.
Website: http://www.cep.msstate.edu/

Montana State University Billings, College of Allied Health Professions, Program in Clinical Rehabilitation and Mental Health Counseling, Billings, MT 59101. Offers MS. *Accreditation:* ACA; CORE. *Program availability:* Part-time. *Degree requirements:* For master's, thesis or professional paper and/or field experience. *Entrance requirements:* For master's, GRE General Test or MAT, minimum GPA of 3.0, letters of recommendation, letter of intent. Additional exam requirements/recommendations for international students: required—TOEFL (minimum score 79 iBT), IELTS (minimum score 6.5). Electronic applications accepted.

Mount Mary University, Graduate Programs, Program in Counseling, Milwaukee, WI 53222-4597. Offers clinical mental health counseling (MS, Certificate); clinical rehabilitation counseling (MS, Certificate); school counseling (MS, Certificate); vocational rehabilitation counseling (MS, Certificate). *Accreditation:* ACA. *Program availability:* Part-time, evening/weekend. *Degree requirements:* For master's, comprehensive exam, thesis or alternative. *Entrance requirements:* For master's, minimum GPA of 3.0. Additional exam requirements/recommendations for international students: required—TOEFL (minimum score 550 paper-based; 80 iBT); recommended—IELTS (minimum score 6.5). Electronic applications accepted. *Expenses:* Contact institution.

North Carolina Agricultural and Technical State University, The Graduate College, College of Education, Department of Counseling, Greensboro, NC 27411. Offers mental health counseling (MS); rehabilitation counseling and rehabilitation counselor education (PhD); school counseling (MS). *Accreditation:* ACA. *Program availability:* Part-time, evening/weekend. *Degree requirements:* For master's, comprehensive exam, thesis, qualifying exam. *Entrance requirements:* For master's, GRE General Test, minimum GPA of 3.0.

Northeastern Illinois University, College of Graduate Studies and Research, Daniel L. Goodwin College of Education, Program in Rehabilitation Counseling, Chicago, IL 60625. Offers MA. *Accreditation:* CORE.

Ohio University, Graduate College, Gladys W. and David H. Patton College of Education and Human Services, Department of Counseling and Higher Education, Athens, OH 45701-2979. Offers college student personnel (M Ed); community/agency counseling (M Ed); counselor education (PhD); higher education (PhD); rehabilitation counseling (M Ed); school counseling (M Ed). *Accreditation:* ACA; CORE. *Program availability:* Part-time, evening/weekend. *Degree requirements:* For master's, comprehensive exam (for some programs), thesis or alternative; for doctorate, comprehensive exam, thesis/dissertation. *Entrance requirements:* For master's, GRE General Test or MAT (if GPA less than 2.9), 3 letters of reference; for doctorate, GRE General Test, work experience, minimum GPA of 3.4. Additional exam requirements/recommendations for international students: required—TOEFL (minimum score 550 paper-based; 80 iBT) or IELTS (minimum score 6.5). Electronic applications accepted.

Pontifical Catholic University of Puerto Rico, College of Graduate Studies in Behavioral Science and Community Affairs, Program in Rehabilitation Counseling, Ponce, PR 00717-0777. Offers MA. *Accreditation:* CORE. *Program availability:* Part-time. *Degree requirements:* For master's, thesis. *Entrance requirements:* For master's, EXADEP, GRE General Test, 3 letters of recommendation, interview, minimum GPA of 2.75.

Rutgers University - Newark, School of Health Related Professions, Department of Psychiatric Rehabilitation and Counseling Professions, Program in Psychiatric Rehabilitation, Newark, NJ 07102. Offers MS, PhD. *Accreditation:* CORE. *Program availability:* Part-time, evening/weekend, online learning. *Degree requirements:* For doctorate, comprehensive exam, thesis/dissertation. *Entrance requirements:* For master's, all transcripts, interview, statement of interest, bachelor's degree, 2 reference letters; for doctorate, GRE General Test, all transcripts, bachelor's degree, personal statement, 3 reference letters. Additional exam requirements/recommendations for international students: required—TOEFL (minimum score 500 paper-based; 79 iBT). Electronic applications accepted.

Rutgers University - Newark, School of Health Related Professions, Department of Psychiatric Rehabilitation and Counseling Professions, Program in Rehabilitation Counseling, Newark, NJ 07102. Offers community counseling (MS). *Accreditation:* CORE. *Program availability:* Part-time, evening/weekend. *Degree requirements:* For master's, internship, practicum. *Entrance requirements:* For master's, bachelor's degree with transcript, interview, personal goals statement, 2 reference letters. Additional exam requirements/recommendations for international students: required—TOEFL (minimum score 500 paper-based; 79 iBT). Electronic applications accepted.

St. Bonaventure University, School of Graduate Studies, School of Education, Program in Counselor Education, St. Bonaventure, NY 14778-2284. Offers community

mental health counseling (MS Ed); rehabilitation counseling (MS Ed); school counseling (MS Ed); school counselor (Adv C). *Accreditation:* ACA. *Program availability:* Part-time, 100% online. *Faculty:* 7 full-time (4 women), 10 part-time/adjunct (7 women). *Students:* 43 full-time (37 women), 213 part-time (175 women); includes 39 minority (2 Black or African American, non-Hispanic/Latino; 2 American Indian or Alaska Native, non-Hispanic/Latino; 7 Asian, non-Hispanic/Latino; 18 Hispanic/Latino; 1 Native Hawaiian or other Pacific Islander, non-Hispanic/Latino; 9 Two or more races, non-Hispanic/Latino). Average age 32. 167 applicants, 85% accepted, 64 enrolled. In 2019, 17 master's, 7 Adv Cs awarded. *Degree requirements:* For master's, comprehensive exam, thesis optional, internship, portfolio, two consecutive summer residencies; for Adv C, internship. *Entrance requirements:* For master's, statement of intent/writing sample; transcripts from all colleges previously attended; two references; interview; minimum undergraduate GPA of 3.0; for Adv C, interview, writing sample, minimum undergraduate GPA of 3.0, two letters of recommendation, master's degree, transcripts from all colleges previously attended. Additional exam requirements/recommendations for international students: required—TOEFL (minimum score 550 paper-based; 79 iBT). *Application deadline:* For fall admission, 3/15 priority date for domestic students, 2/1 priority date for international students; for spring admission, 10/15 priority date for domestic students, 7/1 priority date for international students. Applications are processed on a rolling basis. Electronic applications accepted. *Expenses: Tuition:* Full-time $770; part-time $770 per credit hour. *Required fees:* $35; $35 per credit hour. Tuition and fees vary according to course load. *Financial support:* Scholarships/grants, health care benefits, and unspecified assistantships available. Financial award application deadline: 4/15; financial award applicants required to submit FAFSA. *Unit head:* Dr. LaToya Pierce, Director, 716-375-2038, Fax: 716-375-2360, E-mail: lpierce@sbu.edu. *Application contact:* Matthew Retchless, Director of Graduate Admissions, 716-375-2021, Fax: 716-375-4015, E-mail: gradsch@sbu.edu.
Website: http://www.sbu.edu/academics/msed-in-school-counseling

Salve Regina University, Program in Rehabilitation Counseling, Newport, RI 02840-4192. Offers clinical rehabilitation and mental health counseling (MA); mental health (CAGS), including rehabilitation counseling; rehabilitation (CAGS), including substance abuse counseling; rehabilitation counseling (MA); substance abuse and treatment (CAGS). *Accreditation:* CORE. *Program availability:* Part-time, evening/weekend. *Entrance requirements:* For master's, GMAT, GRE General Test or MAT. Additional exam requirements/recommendations for international students: required—TOEFL (minimum score 600 paper-based; 100 iBT) or IELTS. Electronic applications accepted.

San Diego State University, Graduate and Research Affairs, College of Education, Department of Administration, Rehabilitation and Post-Secondary Education, San Diego, CA 92182. Offers educational leadership in post-secondary education (MA); rehabilitation counseling (MS), including deafness. *Program availability:* Evening/weekend, online learning. *Degree requirements:* For master's, comprehensive exam (for some programs), thesis (for some programs). *Entrance requirements:* For master's, GRE General Test, letters of reference. Additional exam requirements/recommendations for international students: required—TOEFL. Electronic applications accepted.

South Carolina State University, College of Graduate and Professional Studies, Department of Human Services, Orangeburg, SC 29117-0001. Offers counselor education (M Ed); rehabilitation counseling (MA). *Accreditation:* CORE. *Program availability:* Part-time, evening/weekend. *Degree requirements:* For master's, comprehensive exam (for some programs), departmental qualifying exam, internship. *Entrance requirements:* For master's, GRE, MAT, minimum GPA of 2.7. Electronic applications accepted.

Southern University and Agricultural and Mechanical College, Graduate School, Nelson Mandela College of Government and Social Sciences, Department of Psychology, Program in Rehabilitation Counseling, Baton Rouge, LA 70813. Offers MS. *Accreditation:* CORE. *Degree requirements:* For master's, comprehensive exam, thesis optional. *Entrance requirements:* For master's, GMAT or GRE General Test. Additional exam requirements/recommendations for international students: required—TOEFL.

Springfield College, Graduate Programs, Programs in Rehabilitation Counseling, Springfield, MA 01109-3797. Offers rehabilitation counseling (M Ed, MS). *Accreditation:* CORE (one or more programs are accredited). *Program availability:* Part-time. *Degree requirements:* For master's, comprehensive exam. *Entrance requirements:* Additional exam requirements/recommendations for international students: required—TOEFL (minimum score 550 paper-based); recommended—IELTS (minimum score 7). Electronic applications accepted.

Texas Tech University Health Sciences Center, School of Health Professions, Program in Clinical Rehabilitation Counseling, Lubbock, TX 79430. Offers MRC. *Accreditation:* CORE. *Program availability:* Part-time, online only. *Faculty:* 9 full-time (4 women), 3 part-time/adjunct (1 woman). *Students:* 21 full-time (12 women), 38 part-time (28 women); includes 32 minority (11 Black or African American, non-Hispanic/Latino; 1 American Indian or Alaska Native, non-Hispanic/Latino; 3 Asian, non-Hispanic/Latino; 15 Hispanic/Latino; 2 Two or more races, non-Hispanic/Latino), 1 international. Average age 36. 32 applicants, 56% accepted, 15 enrolled. In 2019, 14 master's awarded. *Entrance requirements:* Additional exam requirements/recommendations for international students: required—TOEFL (minimum score 550 paper-based; 79 iBT). *Application deadline:* For fall admission, 6/1 for domestic students; for spring admission, 11/1 for domestic students. Applications are processed on a rolling basis. Application fee: $75. Electronic applications accepted. *Financial support:* In 2019–20, 16 students received support. Career-related internships or fieldwork available. Support available to part-time students. Financial award application deadline: 9/1; financial award applicants required to submit FAFSA. *Unit head:* Dr. Rebecca Sametz, Program Director, 806-743-2590, Fax: 806-743-3244, E-mail: health.professions@ttuhsc.edu. *Application contact:* Lindsay Johnson, Associate Dean for Admissions and Student Affairs, 806-743-3220, Fax: 806-743-2994, E-mail: health.professions@ttuhsc.edu.
Website: http://www.ttuhsc.edu/health-professions/master-of-science-clinical-rehabilitation-counseling/

Thomas University, Department of Human Services, Thomasville, GA 31792-7499. Offers community counseling (MSCC); rehabilitation counseling (MRC). *Accreditation:* CORE. *Program availability:* Part-time. *Entrance requirements:* For master's, resume, 3 academic/professional references. Additional exam requirements/recommendations for international students: required—TOEFL (minimum score 600 paper-based). Electronic applications accepted.

University at Buffalo, the State University of New York, Graduate School, Graduate School of Education, Department of Counseling, School, and Educational Psychology, Buffalo, NY 14260. Offers applied statistical analysis (Advanced Certificate); counseling/school psychology (PhD); counselor education (PhD); education studies (Ed M); educational psychology (MA, PhD); mental health counseling (MS, Certificate); mindful counseling for wellness and engagement (Advanced Certificate); rehabilitation counseling (MS, Advanced Certificate); school counseling (Ed M, Certificate). *Accreditation:* CORE (one or more programs are accredited). *Program availability:* Part-time, 100% online. *Faculty:* 23 full-time (12 women), 23 part-time/adjunct (16 women). *Students:* 147 full-time (117 women), 125 part-time (109 women); includes 52 minority (24 Black or African American, non-Hispanic/Latino; 8 Asian, non-Hispanic/Latino; 14 Hispanic/Latino; 6 Two or more races, non-Hispanic/Latino), 18 international. Average age 32. 349 applicants, 52% accepted, 125 enrolled. In 2019, 77 master's, 9 doctorates, 59 other advanced degrees awarded. Terminal master's awarded for partial completion of doctoral program. *Degree requirements:* For master's, comprehensive exam (for some programs), thesis (for some programs); for doctorate, comprehensive exam, thesis/dissertation. *Entrance requirements:* For master's, GRE General Test, interview, letters of reference, personal statement; for doctorate, GRE General Test, interview, letters of reference, writing sample, personal statement; for other advanced degree, proof of previous degrees for specific counseling certificates. Additional exam requirements/recommendations for international students: required—TOEFL (minimum score 600 paper-based; 79 iBT), IELTS (minimum score 6.5), PTE (minimum score 55), The Graduate School of Education requires international students to submit test scores for at least one of the exams (TOEFL, IELTS, PTE). *Application deadline:* For fall admission, 2/1 priority date for domestic and international students. Applications are processed on a rolling basis. Application fee: $50. Electronic applications accepted. *Expenses: Tuition, area resident:* Full-time $11,310; part-time $471 per credit hour. Tuition, state resident: full-time $11,310; part-time $471 per credit hour. Tuition, nonresident: full-time $23,100; part-time $963 per credit hour. *International tuition:* $23,100 full-time. *Required fees:* $2820. *Financial support:* In 2019–20, 10 fellowships (averaging $20,000 per year), 14 research assistantships with tuition reimbursements (averaging $26,000 per year) were awarded; teaching assistantships, career-related internships or fieldwork, Federal Work-Study, institutionally sponsored loans, scholarships/grants, tuition waivers (full and partial), and unspecified assistantships also available. Financial award application deadline: 2/1; financial award applicants required to submit FAFSA. *Unit head:* Dr. Myles Faith, Department Chair, 716-645-2484, Fax: 716-645-6616, E-mail: mfaith@buffalo.edu. *Application contact:* Renad Aref, Assistant Director of Admission Recruitment, 716-645-2110, Fax: 716-645-7937, E-mail: gseinfo@buffalo.edu.
Website: http://ed.buffalo.edu/counseling

The University of Arizona, College of Education, Department of Disability and Psychoeducational Studies, Program in Counseling and Mental Health, Tucson, AZ 85721. Offers rehabilitation counseling (MA); school counseling (MA). *Accreditation:* ACA. *Entrance requirements:* Additional exam requirements/recommendations for international students: required—TOEFL (minimum score 550 paper-based; 80 iBT).

The University of Arizona, College of Education, Department of Disability and Psychoeducational Studies, Program in Rehabilitation Counseling, Tucson, AZ 85721. Offers PhD. *Accreditation:* CORE. *Entrance requirements:* For doctorate, GMAT, 3 letters of recommendation. Additional exam requirements/recommendations for international students: required—TOEFL (minimum score 550 paper-based; 79 iBT). Electronic applications accepted.

University of Arkansas, Graduate School, College of Education and Health Professions, Department of Rehabilitation, Human Resources and Communication Disorders, Program in Rehabilitation, Fayetteville, AR 72701. Offers MS, PhD. *Accreditation:* CORE (one or more programs are accredited). *Program availability:* Part-time. *Students:* 5 full-time (4 women), 3 part-time (2 women); includes 2 minority (both Black or African American, non-Hispanic/Latino). In 2019, 15 master's, 1 doctorate awarded. *Entrance requirements:* For doctorate, GRE General Test. *Application deadline:* For fall admission, 8/1 for domestic students, 4/1 for international students; for spring admission, 12/1 for domestic students, 10/1 for international students; for summer admission, 4/15 for domestic students, 3/1 for international students. Applications are processed on a rolling basis. Application fee: $60. Electronic applications accepted. *Financial support:* In 2019–20, 6 research assistantships were awarded; fellowships with tuition reimbursements, teaching assistantships, career-related internships or fieldwork, and Federal Work-Study also available. Support available to part-time students. Financial award application deadline: 4/1; financial award applicants required to submit FAFSA. *Unit head:* Dr. Michael Hevel, Department Head, 479-575-4924, Fax: 479-575-3319, E-mail: hevel@uark.edu. *Application contact:* Dr. Sandra Ward, 479-575-4188, E-mail: sdward@uark.edu.
Website: http://rhrc.uark.edu

University of Arkansas at Little Rock, Graduate School, College of Education and Health Professions, Department of Counseling, Adult and Rehabilitation Education, Little Rock, AR 72204-1099. Offers adult education (M Ed); counselor education (M Ed); rehabilitation counseling (MA, Graduate Certificate); rehabilitation for the blind: orientation and mobility (MA). *Accreditation:* CORE; NCATE. *Program availability:* Part-time. *Entrance requirements:* For master's, interview, minimum GPA of 2.75.

University of Idaho, College of Graduate Studies, College of Education, Health and Human Sciences, Department of Leadership and Counseling, Boise, ID 83844-2282. Offers adult/organizational learning and leadership (Ed S); educational leadership (Ed S); rehabilitation counseling and human services (M Ed); school counseling (M Ed, MS). *Faculty:* 14. *Students:* 37 full-time (23 women), 112 part-time (68 women). Average age 37. In 2019, 53 master's, 22 other advanced degrees awarded. *Entrance requirements:* For master's, minimum GPA of 3.0, writing sample. Additional exam requirements/recommendations for international students: required—TOEFL (minimum score 79 iBT). *Application deadline:* For fall admission, 7/30 for domestic students; for spring admission, 12/1 for domestic students. Applications are processed on a rolling basis. Application fee: $60. Electronic applications accepted. *Expenses:* Tuition, state resident: full-time $7753.80; part-time $502 per credit hour. Tuition, nonresident: full-time $26,990; part-time $1571 per credit hour. *Required fees:* $2122.20; $47 per credit hour. *Financial support:* Applicants required to submit FAFSA.
Website: https://www.uidaho.edu/ed/lc

The University of Iowa, Graduate College, College of Education, Department of Rehabilitation and Counselor Education, Iowa City, IA 52242-1316. Offers counselor education and supervision (PhD); couple and family therapy (PhD); rehabilitation and mental health counseling (MA); rehabilitation counselor education (PhD); school counseling (MA). *Accreditation:* ACA (one or more programs are accredited); CORE (one or more programs are accredited). *Degree requirements:* For master's, thesis optional, exam; for doctorate, comprehensive exam, thesis/dissertation. *Entrance requirements:* For master's and doctorate, GRE General Test, minimum GPA of 3.0. Additional exam requirements/recommendations for international students: required—TOEFL (minimum score 550 paper-based; 81 iBT). Electronic applications accepted.

University of Kentucky, Graduate School, College of Education, Program in Special Education, Lexington, KY 40506-0032. Offers early childhood (MS Ed); rehabilitation counseling (MRC, PhD); special education (MS Ed, PhD). *Accreditation:* CORE; NCATE. Terminal master's awarded for partial completion of doctoral program. *Degree requirements:* For master's, comprehensive exam, thesis optional; for doctorate, comprehensive exam, thesis/dissertation. *Entrance requirements:* For master's, GRE General Test, minimum undergraduate GPA of 2.75; for doctorate, GRE General Test, minimum graduate GPA of 3.0. Additional exam requirements/recommendations for international students: required—TOEFL (minimum score 550 paper-based). Electronic applications accepted.

University of Maryland, College Park, Academic Affairs, College of Education, Department of Counseling, Higher Education and Special Education, College Park, MD 20742. Offers college student personnel (M Ed, MA); college student personnel administration (PhD); community counseling (CAGS); community/career counseling (M Ed, MA); counseling and personnel services (M Ed, MA, PhD), including art therapy (M Ed), college student personnel (M Ed), counseling and personnel services (PhD), counseling psychology (M Ed), mental health counseling (M Ed), school counseling (M Ed); counseling psychology (PhD); counselor education (PhD); rehabilitation counseling (M Ed, MA, AGSC); school counseling (M Ed, MA); school psychology (M Ed, MA, PhD). *Accreditation:* APA (one or more programs are accredited); NCATE. *Program availability:* Part-time, evening/weekend, online learning. *Degree requirements:* For master's, thesis (for some programs); for doctorate, thesis/dissertation. *Entrance requirements:* For master's, GRE General Test or MAT, minimum GPA of 3.0, 3 letters of recommendation; for doctorate, GRE General Test or MAT, minimum GPA of 3.5, 3 letters of recommendation. Additional exam requirements/recommendations for international students: required—TOEFL. Electronic applications accepted.

University of Maryland Eastern Shore, Graduate Programs, Department of Rehabilitation Services, Princess Anne, MD 21853. Offers rehabilitation counseling (MS). *Accreditation:* CORE. *Program availability:* Part-time, evening/weekend. *Degree requirements:* For master's, internship. *Entrance requirements:* For master's, interview. Additional exam requirements/recommendations for international students: required—TOEFL (minimum score 80 iBT). Electronic applications accepted.

University of Massachusetts Boston, Graduate School of Global Inclusion and Social Development, Program in Rehabilitation Counseling, Boston, MA 02125-3393. Offers MS. *Accreditation:* CORE.

University of Memphis, Graduate School, College of Education, Department of Counseling, Educational Psychology and Research, Memphis, TN 38152. Offers counseling (MS, Ed D), including clinical mental health counseling (MS), clinical rehabilitation counseling (MS), rehabilitation counseling (MS), school counseling (MS); counseling psychology (PhD); educational psychology and research (MS, PhD), including educational psychology, educational research. *Accreditation:* ACA (one or more programs are accredited); APA (one or more programs are accredited); CORE (one or more programs are accredited); NCATE. *Program availability:* 100% online, blended/hybrid learning. *Students:* 136 full-time (110 women), 145 part-time (117 women); includes 107 minority (81 Black or African American, non-Hispanic/Latino; 10 Asian, non-Hispanic/Latino; 11 Hispanic/Latino; 5 Two or more races, non-Hispanic/Latino), 4 international. Average age 32. 149 applicants, 53% accepted, 61 enrolled. In 2019, 30 master's, 19 doctorates awarded. *Degree requirements:* For master's, comprehensive exam, thesis or alternative, internship; for doctorate, comprehensive exam, thesis/dissertation, practicum, internship, residency, scholarly work. *Entrance requirements:* For master's, GRE General Test or MAT, minimum GPA of 2.5, letters of reference, interview; for doctorate, GRE General Test, master's degree or equivalent, letters of reference, interview, curriculum vitae, personal statement. Additional exam requirements/recommendations for international students: required—TOEFL (minimum score 550 paper-based; 79 iBT). *Application deadline:* For fall admission, 10/1 priority date for domestic students; for spring admission, 4/1 priority date for domestic students. Applications are processed on a rolling basis. Application fee: $35 ($60 for international students). Electronic applications accepted. *Expenses: Tuition, area resident:* Full-time $9216; part-time $512 per credit hour. Tuition, state resident: full-time $9216; part-time $512 per credit hour. Tuition, nonresident: full-time $12,672; part-time $704 per credit hour. *International tuition:* $16,128 full-time. *Required fees:* $1530; $85 per credit hour. Tuition and fees vary according to program. *Financial support:* Fellowships with full tuition reimbursements, research assistantships with full tuition reimbursements, teaching assistantships with full tuition reimbursements, career-related internships or fieldwork, Federal Work-Study, scholarships/grants, and unspecified assistantships available. Financial award application deadline: 2/1; financial award applicants required to submit FAFSA. *Unit head:* Dr. Steve West, Chair, 901-678-2841, Fax: 901-678-5114, E-mail: slwest@memphis.edu. *Application contact:* Stormey Warren, Graduate Programs, 901-678-2363, Fax: 901-678-4778, E-mail: shutsell@memphis.edu.
Website: http://www.memphis.edu/cepr/

University of Northern Colorado, Graduate School, College of Natural and Health Sciences, School of Human Sciences, Program in Rehabilitation Counseling and Sciences, Greeley, CO 80639. Offers rehabilitation counseling (MA); rehabilitation sciences (PhD). *Accreditation:* CORE (one or more programs are accredited). *Program availability:* Part-time. *Degree requirements:* For master's, comprehensive exam, thesis or alternative; for doctorate, comprehensive exam, thesis/dissertation. *Entrance requirements:* For master's, GRE General Test or MAT, 2 letters of recommendation; for doctorate, GRE General Test, 2 letters of recommendation. Electronic applications accepted.

University of North Texas, Toulouse Graduate School, Denton, TX 76203-5459. Offers accounting (MS); applied anthropology (MA, MS); applied behavior analysis (Certificate); applied geography (MA); applied technology and performance improvement (M Ed, MS); art education (MA); art history (MA); arts leadership (Certificate); audiology (Au D); behavior analysis (MS); behavioral science (PhD); biochemistry and molecular biology (MS); biology (MA, MS); biomedical engineering (MS); business analysis (MS); chemistry (MS); clinical health psychology (PhD); communication studies (MA, MS); computer engineering (MS); computer science (MS); counseling (M Ed, MS), including clinical mental health counseling (MS), college and university counseling, elementary school counseling, secondary school counseling; creative writing (MA); criminal justice (MS); curriculum and instruction (M Ed); decision sciences (MBA); design (MA, MFA), including fashion design (MFA), innovation studies, interior design (MFA); early childhood studies (MS); economics (MS); educational leadership (M Ed, Ed D); educational psychology (MS, PhD), including family studies (MS), gifted and talented (MS), human development (MS), learning and cognition (MS), research, measurement and evaluation (MS); electrical engineering (MS); emergency management (MPA); engineering technology (MS); English (MA); English as a second language (MA); environmental science (MS); finance (MBA, MS); financial management (MPA); French (MA); health services management (MBA); higher education (M Ed, Ed D); history (MA, MS); hospitality management (MS); human resources management (MPA); information science (MS); information systems (PhD); information technologies (MBA); interdisciplinary studies (MA, MS); international studies (MA); international sustainable tourism (MS); jazz studies (MM); journalism (MA, MJ, Graduate Certificate), including interactive and virtual digital communication (Graduate Certificate), narrative journalism (Graduate Certificate), public relations (Graduate Certificate); kinesiology (MS); linguistics (MA); local government management (MPA); logistics (PhD); logistics and supply chain management (MBA); long-term care, senior housing, and aging services (MA); management (PhD); marketing (MBA); mathematics (MA, MS); mechanical and energy engineering (MS, PhD); music (MA), including ethnomusicology, music theory, musicology, performance; music composition (PhD); music education (MM Ed, PhD); nonprofit management (MPA); operations and supply chain management (MBA); performance (MM, DMA); philosophy (MA); political science (MA); professional and technical communication (MA); radio, television and film (MA, MFA); rehabilitation counseling (Certificate); sociology (MA); Spanish (MA); special education (M Ed); speech-language pathology (MA); strategic management (MBA); studio art (MFA); teaching (M Ed); MBA/MS. *Program availability:* Part-time, evening/weekend, online learning. Terminal master's awarded for partial completion of doctoral program. *Degree requirements:* For master's, variable foreign language requirement, comprehensive exam (for some programs), thesis (for some programs); for doctorate, variable foreign language requirement, comprehensive exam (for some programs), thesis/dissertation; for other advanced degree, variable foreign language requirement, comprehensive exam (for some programs). *Entrance requirements:* For master's and doctorate, GRE, GMAT. Additional exam requirements/recommendations for international students: required—TOEFL (minimum score 550 paper-based; 79 iBT). Electronic applications accepted.

University of Pittsburgh, School of Health and Rehabilitation Sciences, Department of Rehabilitation Science and Technology, Pittsburgh, PA 15260. Offers clinical rehabilitation and mental health counseling (MS); physician assistant studies (MS); prosthetics and orthotics (DPT); rehabilitation technology (MS). *Program availability:* Part-time, blended/hybrid learning. *Faculty:* 26 full-time (15 women), 6 part-time/adjunct (3 women). *Students:* 97 full-time (57 women), 16 part-time (13 women); includes 19 minority (3 Black or African American, non-Hispanic/Latino; 5 Asian, non-Hispanic/Latino; 3 Hispanic/Latino; 8 Two or more races, non-Hispanic/Latino), 9 international. Average age 26. 187 applicants, 58% accepted, 49 enrolled. In 2019, 50 master's awarded. *Degree requirements:* For master's, comprehensive exam (for some programs), thesis (for some programs). *Entrance requirements:* For master's, Varies by program, Varies by program. Additional exam requirements/recommendations for international students: required—International applicants may provide Duolingo English Test, IELTS or TOEFL scores to verify English language proficiency. Electronic applications accepted. *Financial support:* In 2019–20, 14 students received support, including 1 fellowship with full tuition reimbursement available (averaging $30,000 per year), 9 research assistantships with full tuition reimbursements available (averaging $30,000 per year); scholarships/grants also available. *Unit head:* Dr. Jonathan Pearlman, Chair and Associate Professor, Department of Rehabilitation Science and Technology, 412-383-3955, E-mail: jpearlman@pitt.edu. *Application contact:* Jessica Maguire, Director of Admissions, 412-383-6557, Fax: 412-383-6535, E-mail: maguire@pitt.edu.
Website: http://www.shrs.pitt.edu/rst

University of Puerto Rico at Rio Piedras, College of Social Sciences, Graduate School of Rehabilitation Counseling, San Juan, PR 00931-3300. Offers MRC. *Accreditation:* CORE. *Program availability:* Part-time. *Degree requirements:* For master's, comprehensive exam, thesis, internship. *Entrance requirements:* For master's, GRE or PAEG, interview, minimum GPA of 3.0, letter of recommendation.

The University of Scranton, Panuska College of Professional Studies, Department of Counseling and Human Services, Program in Rehabilitation Counseling, Scranton, PA 18510. Offers MS. *Accreditation:* CORE. *Program availability:* Part-time, evening/weekend. *Degree requirements:* For master's, comprehensive exam (for some programs), thesis (for some programs), capstone experience. *Entrance requirements:* For master's, minimum GPA of 3.0, three letters of reference. Additional exam requirements/recommendations for international students: required—TOEFL (minimum score 500 paper-based; 80 iBT), IELTS (minimum score 6.5). Electronic applications accepted.

University of South Carolina, School of Medicine and The Graduate School, Graduate Programs in Medicine, Program in Rehabilitation Counseling, Columbia, SC 29208. Offers psychiatric rehabilitation (Certificate); rehabilitation counseling (MRC). *Accreditation:* CORE. *Program availability:* Part-time, evening/weekend. *Degree requirements:* For master's, comprehensive exam, internship, practicum. *Entrance requirements:* For master's and Certificate, GRE General Test or GMAT. Electronic applications accepted. *Expenses:* Contact institution.

University of Southern Maine, College of Management and Human Service, School of Education and Human Development, Program in Counselor Education, Portland, ME 04103. Offers clinical mental health counseling (MS); counseling (CAS); culturally responsive practices in education and human development (CGS); mental health rehabilitation technician/community (CGS); rehabilitation counseling (MS); school counseling (MS); substance abuse counseling (CGS). *Accreditation:* ACA (one or more programs are accredited); CORE; TEAC. *Program availability:* Part-time, evening/weekend. *Degree requirements:* For master's, comprehensive exam, thesis or alternative; for other advanced degree, thesis or alternative. *Entrance requirements:* For master's, GRE General Test or MAT, interview; for other advanced degree, master's degree. Additional exam requirements/recommendations for international students: required—TOEFL (minimum score 550 paper-based; 79 iBT). Electronic applications accepted. *Expenses: Tuition, area resident:* Full-time $864; part-time $432 per credit hour. Tuition, state resident: full-time $864; part-time $432 per credit hour. Tuition, nonresident: full-time $2372; part-time $1186 per credit hour. *Required fees:* $141; $108 per credit hour. Tuition and fees vary according to course load.

University of South Florida, College of Behavioral and Community Sciences, Department of Child and Family Studies, Tampa, FL 33620-9951. Offers applied behavior analysis (MA, MS, PhD); behavioral and community sciences (PhD); child and adolescent behavioral health (MS), including developmental disabilities, leadership in child and adolescent health, translational research and evaluation, youth and behavioral health; rehabilitation and mental health counseling (MA), including addictions and substance abuse counseling, marriage and family therapy. *Accreditation:* ACA. *Faculty:* 21 full-time (13 women), 3 part-time/adjunct (all women). *Students:* 184 full-time (157 women), 104 part-time (88 women); includes 113 minority (42 Black or African American, non-Hispanic/Latino; 4 Asian, non-Hispanic/Latino; 54 Hispanic/Latino; 1 Native Hawaiian or other Pacific Islander, non-Hispanic/Latino; 12 Two or more races, non-Hispanic/Latino), 7 international. Average age 27. 310 applicants, 51% accepted, 92 enrolled. In 2019, 127 master's, 8 doctorates awarded. *Degree requirements:* For master's, comprehensive exam, thesis (for some programs); for doctorate, comprehensive exam, thesis/dissertation, Behavior Analyst Board Certification Exam. *Entrance requirements:* For master's, GRE General Test, 3.00 GPA; 3 letters of reference; resume or CV; statement of purpose; writing sample; undergraduate statistics or research methods course (for Rehab and Mental Health Counseling); for doctorate, GRE General Test, master's degree in behavioral analysis or closely-related field; minimum GPA of 3.5 in graduate course work; three letters of recommendation; campus visit with faculty interview; personal statement; curriculum vitae; evidence of research experiences and expertise; campus visit and interview. Additional exam requirements/recommendations for international students: required—TOEFL, TOEFL (minimum score 550 paper-based; 79 iBT) or IELTS (minimum score 6.5). *Application deadline:* For fall admission, 12/5 for domestic and international students. Application fee: $30. *Financial support:* In 2019–20, 57 students received support. Unspecified assistantships available. *Unit head:* Jason Anthony, Professor and Director, Rightpath Research and Innovation Center, 813-974-6009, E-mail: jasonanthony@usf.edu. *Application contact:* Dr. Raymond G. Miltenberger, Professor/Director of Master's Program, 813-974-5079, Fax: 813-974-6115, E-mail: miltenbe@usf.edu.
Website: http://cfs.cbcs.usf.edu/

Rehabilitation Counseling

University of South Florida, Innovative Education, Tampa, FL 33620-9951. Offers adult, career and higher education (Graduate Certificate), including college teaching, leadership in developing human resources, leadership in higher education; Africana studies (Graduate Certificate), including diasporas and health disparities, genocide and human rights; aging studies (Graduate Certificate), including gerontology; art research (Graduate Certificate), including museum studies; business foundations (Graduate Certificate); chemical and biomedical engineering (Graduate Certificate), including materials science and engineering, water, health and sustainability; child and family studies (Graduate Certificate), including positive behavior support; civil and industrial engineering (Graduate Certificate), including transportation systems analysis; community and family health (Graduate Certificate), including maternal and child health, social marketing and public health, violence and injury: prevention and intervention, women's health; criminology (Graduate Certificate), including criminal justice administration; data science for public administration (Graduate Certificate); digital humanities (Graduate Certificate); educational measurement and research (Graduate Certificate), including evaluation; English (Graduate Certificate), including comparative literary studies, creative writing, professional and technical communication; entrepreneurship (Graduate Certificate); environmental health (Graduate Certificate), including safety management; epidemiology and biostatistics (Graduate Certificate), including applied biostatistics, biostatistics, concepts and tools of epidemiology, epidemiology, epidemiology of infectious diseases; geography, environment and planning (Graduate Certificate), including community development, environmental policy and management, geographical information systems; geology (Graduate Certificate), including hydrogeology; global health (Graduate Certificate), including disaster management, global health and Latin American and Caribbean studies, global health practice, humanitarian assistance, infection control; government and international affairs (Graduate Certificate), including Cuban studies, globalization studies; health policy and management (Graduate Certificate), including health management and leadership, public health policy and programs; hearing specialist: early intervention (Graduate Certificate); industrial and management systems engineering (Graduate Certificate), including systems engineering, technology management; information studies (Graduate Certificate), including school library media specialist; information systems/decision sciences (Graduate Certificate), including analytics and business intelligence; instructional technology (Graduate Certificate), including distance education, Florida digital/virtual educator, instructional design, multimedia design, Web design; internal medicine, bioethics and medical humanities (Graduate Certificate), including biomedical ethics; Latin American and Caribbean studies (Graduate Certificate); leadership for coastal resiliency planning (Graduate Certificate); mass communications (Graduate Certificate), including multimedia journalism; mathematics and statistics (Graduate Certificate), including mathematics; medicine (Graduate Certificate), including aging and neuroscience, bioinformatics, biotechnology, brain fitness and memory management, clinical investigation, hand and upper limb rehabilitation, health informatics, health sciences, integrative weight management, intellectual property, medicine and gender, metabolic and nutritional medicine, metabolic cardiology, pharmacy sciences; national and competitive intelligence (Graduate Certificate); nursing (Graduate Certificate), including simulation based academic fellowship in advanced pain management; psychological and social foundations (Graduate Certificate), including career counseling, college teaching, diversity in education, mental health counseling, school counseling; public affairs (Graduate Certificate), including nonprofit management, public management, research administration; public health (Graduate Certificate), including assessing chemical toxicity and public health risks, health equity, pharmacoepidemiology, public health generalist, toxicology, translational research in adolescent behavioral health; public health practices (Graduate Certificate), including planning for healthy communities; rehabilitation and mental health counseling (Graduate Certificate), including integrative mental health care, marriage and family therapy, rehabilitation technology; secondary education (Graduate Certificate), including ESOL, foreign language education: culture and content, foreign language education: professional; social work (Graduate Certificate), including geriatric social work/clinical gerontology; special education (Graduate Certificate), including autism spectrum disorder, disabilities education: severe/profound; world languages (Graduate Certificate), including teaching English as a second language (TESL) or foreign language. *Unit head:* Dr. Cynthia DeLuca, Associate Vice President and Assistant Vice Provost, 813-974-3077, Fax: 813-974-7061, E-mail: deluca@usf.edu. *Application contact:* Owen Hooper, Director, Summer and Alternative Calendar Programs, 813-974-6917, E-mail: hooper@usf.edu.
Website: http://www.usf.edu/innovative-education/

The University of Tennessee, Graduate School, College of Education, Health and Human Sciences, Department of Educational Psychology and Counseling, Knoxville, TN 37996. Offers adult education (MS); applied educational psychology (MS); collaborative learning (Ed D); college student personnel (MS); mental health counseling (MS); rehabilitation counseling (MS); school counseling (MS). *Accreditation:* ACA (one or more programs are accredited); CORE (one or more programs are accredited); NCATE. *Program availability:* Part-time, evening/weekend. *Degree requirements:* For master's, thesis optional. *Entrance requirements:* For master's, GRE General Test, minimum GPA of 2.7. Additional exam requirements/recommendations for international students: required—TOEFL. Electronic applications accepted.

The University of Texas at Austin, Graduate School, College of Education, Department of Special Education, Austin, TX 78712-1111. Offers autism and developmental disabilities (Ed D, PhD); autism and developmental disability (M Ed, MA); early childhood special education (M Ed, MA, Ed D, PhD); learning disabilities (Ed D, PhD); learning disabilities/behavior disorders (M Ed, MA); multicultural special education (M Ed, MA, Ed D, PhD); rehabilitation counselor (M Ed); rehabilitation counselor education (Ed D, PhD); special education administration (Ed D, PhD). *Accreditation:* CORE. *Program availability:* Part-time, evening/weekend, online learning. *Degree requirements:* For master's, thesis or alternative; for doctorate, thesis/dissertation. *Entrance requirements:* For master's and doctorate, GRE General Test.

The University of Texas at El Paso, Graduate School, College of Health Sciences, Rehabilitation Counseling Program, El Paso, TX 79968-0001. Offers MRC. *Accreditation:* CORE. *Program availability:* Part-time, evening/weekend. *Degree requirements:* For master's, comprehensive exam, thesis optional. *Entrance requirements:* For master's, GRE, minimum GPA of 3.0, statement of professional goals, letters of recommendation. Additional exam requirements/recommendations for international students: required—TOEFL; recommended—IELTS. Electronic applications accepted.

The University of Texas Rio Grande Valley, College of Health Affairs, School of Rehabilitation Services and Counseling, Edinburg, TX 78539. Offers MS, PhD. *Accreditation:* CORE. *Program availability:* Part-time, evening/weekend. *Faculty:* 16 full-time (10 women), 2 part-time/adjunct (both women). *Students:* 99 full-time (80 women), 113 part-time (93 women); includes 192 minority (1 Black or African American, non-Hispanic/Latino; 2 Asian, non-Hispanic/Latino; 189 Hispanic/Latino; 3 international. Average age 31. 41 applicants, 93% accepted, 34 enrolled. In 2019, 39 master's, 7 doctorates awarded. *Degree requirements:* For master's, comprehensive exam; for doctorate, comprehensive exam, thesis/dissertation. *Entrance requirements:* For master's, minimum GPA 3.0; for doctorate, master's degree related counseling field.

minimum GPA of 3.25. Additional exam requirements/recommendations for international students: required—TOEFL, we follow university/college on which exams are required of int'l students. *Application deadline:* For fall admission, 3/15 for domestic and international students; for spring admission, 10/15 for domestic and international students; for summer admission, 3/15 for domestic and international students. Application fee: $50. Electronic applications accepted. *Expenses:* Contact institution. *Financial support:* In 2019–20, 60 students received support, including 12 research assistantships (averaging $25,500 per year), 10 teaching assistantships (averaging $12,600 per year); career-related internships or fieldwork, Federal Work-Study, institutionally sponsored loans, scholarships/grants, traineeships, and unspecified assistantships also available. *Unit head:* Dr. Bruce Reed, Director/Professor, 956-665-7036, Fax: 956-665-5237, E-mail: bruce.reed@utrgv.edu. *Application contact:* Dr. Elizabeth Chavez-Palacios, Clinical Assistant Professor/Graduate Coordinator, 956-665-3734, Fax: 956-665-5237, E-mail: elizabeth.palacios@utrgv.edu.
Website: http://www.utrgv.edu/rehab-counseling/index.htm

The University of Texas Southwestern Medical Center, Southwestern School of Health Professions, Rehabilitation Counseling Psychology Program, Dallas, TX 75390. Offers MRC. *Accreditation:* CORE. *Degree requirements:* For master's, thesis. *Entrance requirements:* For master's, GRE General Test, minimum GPA of 3.0. Electronic applications accepted.

University of the District of Columbia, College of Arts and Sciences, Program in Rehabilitation Counseling, Washington, DC 20008-1175. Offers MA.

University of Wisconsin–Madison, Graduate School, School of Education, Department of Rehabilitation Psychology and Special Education, Program in Rehabilitation Psychology, Madison, WI 53706-1380. Offers MA, MS, PhD. *Accreditation:* CORE (one or more programs are accredited). *Degree requirements:* For doctorate, thesis/dissertation.

University of Wisconsin–Stout, Graduate School, College of Education, Health and Human Sciences, Program in Vocational Rehabilitation, Menomonie, WI 54751. Offers MS. *Accreditation:* CORE. *Program availability:* Part-time, online learning. *Degree requirements:* For master's, comprehensive exam or thesis. *Entrance requirements:* For master's, minimum GPA of 2.75. Additional exam requirements/recommendations for international students: required—TOEFL (minimum score 500 paper-based; 61 iBT). Electronic applications accepted.

Utah State University, School of Graduate Studies, Emma Eccles Jones College of Education and Human Services, Department of Special Education and Rehabilitation, Program in Rehabilitation Counseling, Logan, UT 84322. Offers MRC. *Accreditation:* CORE. *Program availability:* Part-time, online learning. *Degree requirements:* For master's, internship. *Entrance requirements:* For master's, GRE General Test, minimum GPA of 3.0. Additional exam requirements/recommendations for international students: required—TOEFL (minimum score 550 paper-based). Electronic applications accepted. *Expenses:* Contact institution.

Virginia Commonwealth University, Graduate School, School of Allied Health Professions, Department of Rehabilitation Counseling, Richmond, VA 23284-9005. Offers MS. *Accreditation:* CORE. *Entrance requirements:* For master's, GRE General Test or MAT. Additional exam requirements/recommendations for international students: required—TOEFL (minimum score 600 paper-based; 100 iBT). Electronic applications accepted.

Wayne State University, College of Education, Division of Theoretical and Behavioral Foundations, Detroit, MI 48202. Offers applied behavior analysis (Certificate); counseling (M Ed, MA, Ed D, Ed S); counseling psychology (MA, PhD); education evaluation and research (M Ed, Ed D); educational psychology (M Ed, PhD), including learning and instruction sciences (PhD); rehabilitation counseling and community inclusion (MA); school and community psychology (MA, Certificate). *Accreditation:* ACA (one or more programs are accredited); CORE (one or more programs are accredited). *Program availability:* Part-time, evening/weekend. *Faculty:* 10. *Students:* 199 full-time (171 women), 142 part-time (107 women); includes 135 minority (90 Black or African American, non-Hispanic/Latino; 2 American Indian or Alaska Native, non-Hispanic/Latino; 6 Asian, non-Hispanic/Latino; 16 Hispanic/Latino; 21 Two or more races, non-Hispanic/Latino), 10 international. Average age 32. 364 applicants, 25% accepted, 72 enrolled. In 2019, 101 master's, 11 doctorates, 19 other advanced degrees awarded. *Degree requirements:* For master's, thesis (for some programs); for doctorate, comprehensive exam, thesis/dissertation. *Entrance requirements:* For master's, GRE, interview, personal statement, portfolio (only art therapy); references; program application; for doctorate, GRE, departmental writing exam, interview, curriculum vitae, references, master's degree in closely-related field with minimum GPA of 3.5, demonstration of counseling skills (for Ed D in counseling); autobiographical statement; letter of application; personal statement; for other advanced degree, education specialist certificate: master's degree in counseling or closely related field and licensure; personal statement; recommendations; autobiographical statement; interview. Additional exam requirements/recommendations for international students: required—TOEFL (minimum score 550 paper-based; 79 iBT); recommended—IELTS (minimum score 6.5), TWE (minimum score 5.5), TSE (minimum score 58). *Application deadline:* Applications are processed on a rolling basis. Application fee: $50. Electronic applications accepted. *Expenses:* Tuition: Full-time $34,567. *Financial support:* In 2019–20, 92 students received support, including 1 fellowship (averaging $20,000 per year), 1 research assistantship with tuition reimbursement available (averaging $19,967 per year); teaching assistantships, Federal Work-Study, scholarships/grants, health care benefits, and unspecified assistantships also available. Support available to part-time students. Financial award applicants required to submit FAFSA. *Unit head:* Dr. William Hill, Assistant Dean, 313-577-9316, E-mail: ad2107@wayne.edu. *Application contact:* Dr. Mary L Waker, Graduate Admissions Officer, 313-577-1601, Fax: 313-577-7904, E-mail: m.waker@wayne.edu.
Website: https://education.wayne.edu/counseling-educational-psychology

Western Oregon University, Graduate Programs, College of Education, Division of Special Education, Program in Rehabilitation Counseling, Monmouth, OR 97361. Offers MS. *Accreditation:* CORE. *Degree requirements:* For master's, thesis optional, oral exam, portfolio. *Entrance requirements:* For master's, interview, minimum GPA of 3.0. Additional exam requirements/recommendations for international students: required—TOEFL (minimum score 550 paper-based; 79 iBT), IELTS (minimum score 6.5).

Western Washington University, Graduate School, Woodring College of Education, Program in Rehabilitation Counseling, Bellingham, WA 98225-5996. Offers MA. *Accreditation:* CORE. *Program availability:* Part-time, evening/weekend, online learning. *Degree requirements:* For master's, research project. *Entrance requirements:* For master's, GRE General Test or MAT, minimum GPA of 3.0 in last 60 semester hours or last 90 quarter hours of course work. Additional exam requirements/recommendations for international students: required—TOEFL (minimum score 567 paper-based). Electronic applications accepted.

West Virginia University, College of Education and Human Services, Morgantown, WV 26506. Offers audiology (Au D); autism spectrum disorder (MA); clinical rehabilitation and mental health counseling (MS); communication science and disorders (PhD); counseling (MA); counseling psychology (PhD); curriculum and instruction (Ed D); early childhood education (MA); early intervention/ early childhood special education (MA); education (PhD); educational leadership (MA); educational leadership/ public school administration (Ed D); educational leadership/public school administration (MA); educational psychology (MA, Ed D); elementary education (MA); gifted education (MA); higher education administration (MA, Ed D); higher education curriculum and teaching (MA); institutional design and technology (MA); instructional design and technology (Ed D); literacy education (MA); secondary education (MA); secondary education/ English (MA); special education (Ed D); speech pathology (MS). *Accreditation:* ASHA; NCATE. *Program availability:* Part-time, evening/weekend, online learning. *Degree requirements:* For master's, content exams; for doctorate, comprehensive exam, thesis/ dissertation. *Entrance requirements:* Additional exam requirements/recommendations for international students: required—TOEFL (minimum score 500 paper-based; 61 iBT). Electronic applications accepted.

Wilberforce University, Program in Rehabilitation Counseling, Wilberforce, OH 45384. Offers MS. *Entrance requirements:* For master's, bachelor's degree, 3 letters of recommendation, interview. Additional exam requirements/recommendations for international students: required—TOEFL.

Winston-Salem State University, Program in Rehabilitation Counseling, Winston-Salem, NC 27110-0003. Offers MRC. *Program availability:* Part-time, online learning. *Degree requirements:* For master's, thesis optional. *Entrance requirements:* For master's, GRE, 3 letters of recommendation. Electronic applications accepted.

Wright State University, Graduate School, College of Education and Human Services, Department of Human Services, Program in Rehabilitation Counseling, Dayton, OH 45435. Offers chemical dependency (MRC). *Accreditation:* CORE. *Degree requirements:* For master's, comprehensive exam. *Entrance requirements:* For master's, GRE General Test, MAT, interview. Additional exam requirements/ recommendations for international students: required—TOEFL.

School Psychology

Abilene Christian University, Office of Graduate Programs, College of Arts and Sciences, Department of Psychology, Abilene, TX 79699. Offers clinical psychology (MS); counseling psychology (MS); psychology (MS); school psychology (Specialist). *Program availability:* Part-time. *Faculty:* 11 part-time/adjunct (3 women). *Students:* 24 full-time (19 women), 8 part-time (7 women); includes 8 minority (3 Black or African American, non-Hispanic/Latino; 5 Hispanic/Latino), 2 international. 99 applicants, 27% accepted, 10 enrolled. In 2019, 23 master's awarded. *Degree requirements:* For master's, comprehensive exam, thesis (for some programs), practicum; internship. *Entrance requirements:* For master's, official transcripts, purpose statement, Recommendations. Additional exam requirements/recommendations for international students: required—TOEFL (minimum score 80 iBT), IELTS (minimum score 6), PTE (minimum score 51). *Application deadline:* For fall admission, 3/30 priority date for domestic students, 2/15 for international students. Applications are processed on a rolling basis. Application fee: $65. Electronic applications accepted. *Expenses: Tuition:* Full-time $22,356; part-time $1242 per credit hour. Tuition and fees vary according to program. *Financial support:* In 2019–20, 25 students received support, including 28 research assistantships with partial tuition reimbursements available; career-related internships or fieldwork, Federal Work-Study, and scholarships/grants also available. Support available to part-time students. Financial award application deadline: 4/1; financial award applicants required to submit FAFSA. *Unit head:* Dr. Cherisse Flanagan, Graduate Program Director, 325-674-2282, Fax: 325-674-6968, E-mail: cyf07a@acu.edu. *Application contact:* Graduate Admissions, 325-674-6911, E-mail: gradinfo@acu.edu.
Website: http://www.acu.edu/on-campus/graduate/college-of-arts-and-sciences/psychology-department.html

Adelphi University, Gordon F. Derner School of Psychology, Program in School Psychology, Garden City, NY 11530-0701. Offers MA. *Program availability:* Part-time. *Degree requirements:* For master's, comprehensive exam. *Entrance requirements:* For master's, minimum GPA of 3.0; 15 credits of course work in psychology including general psychology, developmental child or adolescent psychology, abnormal personality in school psychology, tests and measurements, statistics; 3 letters of recommendation. Additional exam requirements/recommendations for international students: required—TOEFL (minimum score 550 paper-based; 80 iBT), IELTS (minimum score 6.5). Electronic applications accepted. *Expenses:* Contact institution.

Adler University, Master's Degrees in Counselling Psychology, Vancouver, BC V6B 3J5, Canada. Offers MCP. In 2019, 2 master's awarded. *Degree requirements:* For master's, thesis optional, Thesis and Non-Thesis options; Dual Practicum. *Unit head:* Michelle Brice, Associate Vice President of Admissions, 236-521-2409, E-mail: vanadmissions@adler.edu. *Application contact:* Michelle Brice, Associate Vice President of Admissions, 236-521-2409, E-mail: vanadmissions@adler.edu.

Adler University, Master's Degrees in Counselling Psychology; School & Youth Concentration, Vancouver, BC V6B 3J5, Canada. Offers MACP. In 2019, 2 master's awarded. *Degree requirements:* For master's, thesis optional, Thesis and Non-Thesis options; Social Justice Practicum. *Unit head:* Michelle Brice, Associate Vice President of Admissions, 236-521-2409, E-mail: vanadmissions@adler.edu. *Application contact:* Michelle Brice, Associate Vice President of Admissions, 236-521-2409, E-mail: vanadmissions@adler.edu.

Alabama Agricultural and Mechanical University, School of Graduate Studies, College of Education, Humanities, and Behavioral Sciences, Department of Social Work, Psychology and Counseling, Huntsville, AL 35811. Offers psychology and counseling (MS, Ed S), including clinical psychology (MS), counseling psychology (MS), guidance and counseling, rehabilitation counseling (MS), school counseling (MS), school psychology (MS), school psychometry (MS); social work (MSW). *Accreditation:* CORE; NCATE. *Program availability:* Part-time, evening/weekend. *Degree requirements:* For master's, comprehensive exam. *Entrance requirements:* For master's, GRE General Test. Additional exam requirements/recommendations for international students: required—TOEFL (minimum score 500 paper-based; 61 iBT).

Alfred University, Graduate School, Counseling and School Psychology Program, Alfred, NY 14802-1205. Offers mental health counseling (MS Ed); school counseling (MS Ed, CAS); school psychology (MA, Psy D, CAS). *Accreditation:* APA. *Program availability:* Part-time, evening/weekend. *Faculty:* 14 full-time (7 women), 24 part-time/ adjunct (12 women). *Students:* 56 full-time (41 women), 394 part-time (317 women); includes 256 minority (120 Black or African American, non-Hispanic/Latino; 2 American Indian or Alaska Native, non-Hispanic/Latino; 7 Asian, non-Hispanic/Latino; 127 Hispanic/Latino), 2 international. Average age 33. 249 applicants, 98% accepted, 224 enrolled. In 2019, 172 master's, 5 doctorates, 111 other advanced degrees awarded. *Degree requirements:* For master's, thesis (for some programs), internship; for doctorate, thesis/dissertation, internship. *Entrance requirements:* For master's and doctorate, GRE General Test. Additional exam requirements/recommendations for international students: required—TOEFL (minimum score 590 paper-based; 90 iBT), IELTS (minimum score 6.5). *Application deadline:* For fall admission, 1/15 priority date for domestic and international students. Applications are processed on a rolling basis. Application fee: $60. Electronic applications accepted. Application fee is waived when completed online. *Expenses:* $7,580 per year. *Financial support:* Research assistantships with partial tuition reimbursements, career-related internships or fieldwork, and unspecified assistantships available. Financial award application deadline: 3/15; financial award applicants required to submit FAFSA. *Unit head:* Dr. Jay Cerio, Dean, 607-871-2757, E-mail: fcerio@alfred.edu. *Application contact:* Lindsey Gertin, Assistant Director of Graduate Admissions, 607-871-2017, Fax: 607-871-2198, E-mail: gradinquiry@alfred.edu.

Alliant International University–Irvine, Shirley M. Hufstedler School of Education, Educational Psychology Programs, Irvine, CA 92606. Offers educational psychology (Psy D); pupil personnel services (Credential); school psychology (MA). *Program availability:* Part-time. *Degree requirements:* For doctorate, thesis/dissertation. *Entrance requirements:* For master's, minimum GPA of 2.5, letters of recommendation; for doctorate, interview, minimum GPA of 3.0, letters of recommendation. Additional exam requirements/recommendations for international students: required—TOEFL (minimum score 550 paper-based; 80 iBT), TWE (minimum score 5).

Alliant International University - Los Angeles, Shirley M. Hufstedler School of Education, Educational Psychology Programs, Alhambra, CA 91803. Offers educational psychology (Psy D); pupil personnel services (Credential); school psychology (MA). *Program availability:* Part-time. *Degree requirements:* For doctorate, comprehensive exam, thesis/dissertation. *Entrance requirements:* For master's, minimum GPA of 2.5, letters of recommendation; for doctorate, interview, minimum GPA of 3.0, letters of recommendation. Additional exam requirements/recommendations for international students: required—TOEFL (minimum score 550 paper-based), TWE (minimum score 5). Electronic applications accepted.

Alliant International University - San Diego, Shirley M. Hufstedler School of Education, Educational Psychology Programs, San Diego, CA 92131. Offers educational psychology (Psy D); pupil personnel services (Credential); school neuropsychology (Certificate); school psychology (MA); school-based mental health (Certificate). *Program availability:* Part-time. *Degree requirements:* For doctorate, comprehensive exam, thesis/dissertation, internship. *Entrance requirements:* For master's, minimum GPA of 2.5, letters of recommendation; for doctorate, minimum GPA of 3.0, letters of recommendation. Additional exam requirements/recommendations for international students: required—TOEFL (minimum score 550 paper-based; 80 iBT), TWE (minimum score 5). Electronic applications accepted.

Alliant International University–San Francisco, Shirley M. Hufstedler School of Education, Educational Psychology Programs, San Francisco, CA 94133. Offers educational psychology (Psy D); pupil personnel services (Credential); school psychology (MA). *Program availability:* Part-time. Terminal master's awarded for partial completion of doctoral program. *Degree requirements:* For doctorate, thesis/ dissertation. *Entrance requirements:* For master's, minimum GPA of 3.0, letters of recommendation; for doctorate, interview, minimum GPA of 3.0, letters of recommendation. Additional exam requirements/recommendations for international students: required—TOEFL (minimum score 550 paper-based), TWE (minimum score 5). Electronic applications accepted.

Andrews University, School of Graduate Studies, College of Education and International Services, Department of Graduate Psychology and Counseling, Program in School Counseling, Berrien Springs, MI 49104. Offers MA. *Students:* 5 full-time (all women), 1 part-time (0 women); includes 4 minority (1 Black or African American, non-Hispanic/Latino; 3 Hispanic/Latino), 2 international. Average age 29. In 2019, 1 master's awarded. *Degree requirements:* For master's, thesis optional. *Entrance requirements:* For master's, GRE. Additional exam requirements/recommendations for international students: required—TOEFL (minimum score 550 paper-based). *Application deadline:* Applications are processed on a rolling basis. Application fee: $60. Electronic applications accepted. *Unit head:* Dr. Brad Hinman, 269-471-3466. *Application contact:* Jillian Clayburn, Director, University Admissions, 800-253-2874, Fax: 269-471-6321, E-mail: graduate@andrews.edu.

Andrews University, School of Graduate Studies, College of Education and International Services, Department of Graduate Psychology and Counseling, Program in School Psychology, Berrien Springs, MI 49104. Offers Ed S. *Program availability:* Part-time. *Students:* 13 full-time (9 women), 1 (woman) part-time; includes 4 minority (all Black or African American, non-Hispanic/Latino), 6 international. Average age 32. In 2019, 4 Ed Ss awarded. *Entrance requirements:* Additional exam requirements/ recommendations for international students: required—TOEFL (minimum score 550 paper-based). *Application deadline:* Applications are processed on a rolling basis. Application fee: $60. *Application contact:* Jillian Panigot, Director, University Admissions, 800-253-2874, Fax: 269-471-6321, E-mail: graduate@andrews.edu.

Appalachian State University, Cratis D. Williams School of Graduate Studies, Department of Human Development and Psychological Counseling, Boone, NC 28608. Offers clinical mental health counseling (MA); college student development (MA); marriage and family therapy (MA); school counseling (MA). *Accreditation:* AAMFT/ COAMFTE; ACA; NCATE. *Program availability:* Part-time. *Degree requirements:* For master's, comprehensive exam (for some programs), thesis optional, internships. *Entrance requirements:* For master's, GRE General Test, 3 letters of recommendation. Additional exam requirements/recommendations for international students: required—TOEFL (minimum score 570 paper-based; 79 iBT), IELTS (minimum score 6.5). Electronic applications accepted.

Argosy University, Hawaii, College of Education, Program in School Psychology, Honolulu, HI 96813. Offers MA.

Argosy University, Phoenix, College of Education, Program in School Psychology, Phoenix, AZ 85021. Offers MA, Psy D.

Arkansas State University, Graduate School, College of Education and Behavioral Science, Department of Psychology and Counseling, State University, AR 72467. Offers clinical mental health counseling (Graduate Certificate); college student personnel services (MS); dyslexia therapy (Graduate Certificate); psychological science (MS); psychology and counseling (Ed S); rehabilitation counseling (MRC); school counseling (MSE); student affairs (Graduate Certificate). *Accreditation:* ACA (one or more programs are accredited); CORE (one or more programs are accredited); NCATE. *Program availability:* Part-time. *Degree requirements:* For master's and other advanced degree, comprehensive exam, thesis or alternative. *Entrance requirements:* For master's, GRE General Test or MAT (for MSE), appropriate bachelor's degree, interview, letters of reference, official transcripts, immunization records, written statement, 2-3 page autobiography; for other advanced degree, GRE General Test, interview, master's degree, letters of reference, official transcript, personal statement, immunization records. Additional exam requirements/recommendations for international students: required—TOEFL (minimum score 550 paper-based; 79 iBT), IELTS (minimum score 6), PTE (minimum score 56). Electronic applications accepted.

Assumption University, School Counseling Program, Worcester, MA 01609-1296. Offers school counseling (MA, CAGS). *Program availability:* Part-time, evening/weekend. *Degree requirements:* For master's, comprehensive exam, internship, practicum; for CAGS, comprehensive exam, practicum. *Entrance requirements:* For master's, bachelor's degree with minimum GPA of 3.0, three letters of recommendation, official transcripts, personal statement, current resume, interview; for CAGS, master's degree in counseling or closely-related field, three letters of recommendation, official transcripts, personal statement, current resume, interview. Additional exam requirements/recommendations for international students: required—TOEFL (minimum score 540 paper-based; 76 iBT), IELTS (minimum score 6). Electronic applications accepted. *Expenses: Tuition:* Full-time $12,690; part-time $705 per credit. *Required fees:* $70 per term.

Auburn University at Montgomery, College of Education, Department of Counselor, Leadership, and Special Education, Montgomery, AL 36124. Offers counselor education (M Ed, Ed S), including clinical mental health counseling, school counseling; early childhood special education (M Ed); instructional leadership (M Ed, Ed S); special education/collaborative teacher (M Ed, Ed S). *Accreditation:* ACA; NCATE. *Program availability:* Part-time, evening/weekend. *Faculty:* 6 full-time (3 women), 4 part-time/adjunct (2 women). *Students:* 64 full-time (45 women), 53 part-time (42 women); includes 59 minority (56 Black or African American, non-Hispanic/Latino; 1 Asian, non-Hispanic/Latino; 2 Hispanic/Latino), 1 international. Average age 36. 90 applicants, 79% accepted, 71 enrolled. In 2019, 34 master's awarded. *Degree requirements:* For master's, 3 letters of recommendation from company/school. *Entrance requirements:* For master's, GRE General Test or MAT, certification, BS in teaching; for Ed S, GRE General Test or MAT, certification. Additional exam requirements/recommendations for international students: recommended—TOEFL (minimum score 500 paper-based; 61 iBT), IELTS (minimum score 5.5), TSE (minimum score 44). *Application deadline:* For fall admission, 7/15 for international students; for spring admission, 11/15 for international students; for summer admission, 4/15 for international students. Applications are processed on a rolling basis. Application fee: $25. Electronic applications accepted. *Expenses: Tuition, area resident:* Full-time $7578; part-time $421 per credit hour. Tuition, state resident: full-time $7578; part-time $421 per credit hour. Tuition, nonresident: full-time $17,046; part-time $947 per credit hour. *International tuition:* $17,046 full-time. *Required fees:* $868. *Financial support:* Career-related internships or fieldwork and scholarships/grants available. Support available to part-time students. Financial award application deadline: 3/1; financial award applicants required to submit FAFSA. *Unit head:* Dr. Alan Miller, Department Head, 334-244-3036, E-mail: sflynt@aum.edu. *Application contact:* Lessie Garcia-Latimore, Administrative Associate, 334-244-3879, E-mail: lgarcia@aum.edu.
Website: http://education.aum.edu/academic-departments/counselor-leadership-and-special-education

Augusta University, College of Education, Department of Counselor Education, Leadership, and Research, Augusta, GA 30912. Offers counselor education (M Ed, Ed S), including clinical mental health counseling (M Ed), school counselor (M Ed). *Accreditation:* ACA; NCATE. *Program availability:* Part-time, evening/weekend. *Degree requirements:* For master's, comprehensive exam; for Ed S, comprehensive exam, thesis. *Entrance requirements:* For master's, GRE, MAT, minimum GPA of 2.5; for Ed S, GRE, MAT.

Azusa Pacific University, School of Behavioral and Applied Sciences, Department of Higher Education, Azusa, CA 91702-7000. Offers college counseling and student development (MS); higher education (PhD); higher education leadership (Ed D).

Azusa Pacific University, School of Education, Department of School Counseling and School Psychology, Program in Educational Psychology, Azusa, CA 91702-7000. Offers MA Ed. *Accreditation:* APA.

Ball State University, Graduate School, Teachers College, Department of Educational Psychology, Program in School Psychology, Muncie, IN 47306. Offers MA, PhD, Ed S. *Accreditation:* APA (one or more programs are accredited); NCATE. *Program availability:* Part-time. *Degree requirements:* For doctorate, thesis/dissertation; for Ed S, thesis. *Entrance requirements:* For doctorate, GRE General Test, interview, minimum graduate GPA of 3.2; for Ed S, GRE General Test. Additional exam requirements/recommendations for international students: required—TOEFL (minimum score 550 paper-based; 79 iBT), IELTS (minimum score 6.5). Electronic applications accepted. *Expenses: Tuition, area resident:* Full-time $7506; part-time $417 per credit hour. Tuition, nonresident: full-time $20,610; part-time $1145 per credit hour. *Required fees:* $2126. Tuition and fees vary according to course load, campus/location and program.

Barry University, College of Arts and Sciences, Department of Psychology, Miami Shores, FL 33161-6695. Offers clinical psychology (MS); school psychology (MS, SSP). *Program availability:* Part-time, evening/weekend. *Degree requirements:* For master's, thesis, practicum. *Entrance requirements:* For master's, GRE General Test, minimum GPA of 3.0, course work in psychology. Electronic applications accepted.

Baylor University, Graduate School, School of Education, Department of Educational Psychology, Waco, TX 76798. Offers educational psychology (MS Ed); exceptionalities (PhD); learning and development (PhD); quantitative methods (MA); school psychology (Ed S). *Accreditation:* NCATE. *Program availability:* Part-time. *Faculty:* 11 full-time (6 women), 1 (woman) part-time/adjunct. *Students:* 55 full-time (48 women), 10 part-time (all women); includes 25 minority (2 Black or African American, non-Hispanic/Latino; 3 Asian, non-Hispanic/Latino; 17 Hispanic/Latino; 3 Two or more races, non-Hispanic/Latino), 3 international. 22 applicants, 59% accepted, 11 enrolled. In 2019, 17 master's, 3 doctorates, 3 other advanced degrees awarded. *Degree requirements:* For master's, comprehensive exam, thesis (for some programs); for doctorate, comprehensive exam, thesis/dissertation; for Ed S, comprehensive exam. *Entrance requirements:* For master's, GRE, transcripts, resume, personal statement, 3 letters of recommendation; for doctorate, GRE, transcripts, resume, personal statement, 3 letters of recommendation; for Ed S, GRE for the EdS in School Psychology, transcripts, resume, personal statement, 2 letters of recommendation. Additional exam requirements/recommendations for international students: required—TOEFL (minimum score 550 paper-based), IELTS (minimum score 6.5), PTE, International graduate applicants must demonstrate English-language proficiency by submitting either TOEFL or IELTS scores. *Application deadline:* For fall admission, 12/1 for domestic and international students. Application fee: $50. Electronic applications accepted. *Financial support:* In 2019–20, 52 students received support, including 18 research assistantships with full tuition reimbursements available (averaging $22,000 per year); scholarships/grants, health care benefits, tuition waivers (full), and unspecified assistantships also available. Financial award applicants required to submit CSS PROFILE or FAFSA. *Unit head:* Dr. Grant B. Morgan, PhD, Department Chair, 254-710-7231, E-mail: Grant_Morgan@baylor.edu. *Application contact:* Dr. Nicholas Frank Benson, PhD, Graduate Program Director, 254-710-4234, E-mail: Nicholas_Benson@baylor.edu.
Website: http://www.baylor.edu/soe/EDP/

Brigham Young University, Graduate Studies, David O. McKay School of Education, Department of Counseling Psychology and Special Education, Provo, UT 84602-1001. Offers counseling psychology (PhD); school psychology (Ed S); special education (MS). *Program availability:* Part-time, evening/weekend. *Faculty:* 14 full-time (4 women), 6 part-time/adjunct (2 women). *Students:* 71 full-time (46 women), 18 part-time (17 women); includes 16 minority (1 Black or African American, non-Hispanic/Latino; 4 American Indian or Alaska Native, non-Hispanic/Latino; 6 Asian, non-Hispanic/Latino; 4 Hispanic/Latino; 1 Native Hawaiian or other Pacific Islander, non-Hispanic/Latino), 7 international. Average age 31. 86 applicants, 29% accepted, 25 enrolled. In 2019, 7 master's, 6 doctorates, 14 other advanced degrees awarded. *Degree requirements:* For master's and Ed S, comprehensive exam, thesis; for doctorate, comprehensive exam, thesis/dissertation. *Entrance requirements:* For master's, doctorate, and Ed S, GRE General Test, application & application fee; unofficial transcripts; honor code commitment; 3 letters of recommendation. Additional exam requirements/recommendations for international students: required—TOEFL (minimum score 580 paper-based; 85 iBT), IELTS (minimum score 7), E3PT. *Application deadline:* For fall admission, 12/15 for domestic and international students. Application fee: $50. Electronic applications accepted. *Financial support:* In 2019–20, 91 students received support, including 87 fellowships (averaging $7,100 per year), 57 research assistantships (averaging $6,400 per year), 10 teaching assistantships (averaging $5,250 per year); institutionally sponsored loans also available. Financial award application deadline: 5/1. *Unit head:* Dr. Lane Fischer, Department Chair, 801-422-8293, E-mail: lane_fischer@byu.edu. *Application contact:* Diane Hancock, Executive Secretary, 801-422-3859, E-mail: diane_hancock@byu.edu.
Website: https://education.byu.edu/cpse

Brooklyn College of the City University of New York, School of Education, Program in School Psychologist, Brooklyn, NY 11210-2889. Offers play therapy (AC); school psychologist (MS Ed). *Program availability:* Part-time, evening/weekend. *Degree requirements:* For master's, internship. *Entrance requirements:* For master's, interview, previous course work in education and psychology, teaching certificate, resume, 2 letters of recommendation. Additional exam requirements/recommendations for international students: required—TOEFL (minimum score 500 paper-based; 61 iBT). Electronic applications accepted.

California Baptist University, Program in School Psychology, Riverside, CA 92504-3206. Offers MS. *Program availability:* Part-time. *Degree requirements:* For master's, 450 hours of introductory fieldwork, 1200 hours of field experience/internship, PRAXIS. *Entrance requirements:* For master's, CBEST, minimum GPA of 3.0, completion of prerequisites with minimum C grade, three letters of recommendation, 500-word essay. Additional exam requirements/recommendations for international students: required—TOEFL (minimum score 80 iBT). Electronic applications accepted. *Expenses:* Contact institution.

California State University, Chico, Office of Graduate Studies, College of Behavioral and Social Sciences, Department of Psychology, Program in Applied/School Psychology, Chico, CA 95929-0722. Offers MA. *Degree requirements:* For master's, thesis or comprehensive exam. *Entrance requirements:* For master's, GRE General Test or MAT, fall admissions only, deadline February 17th. 3 letters of recommendation, 3 departmental recommendation forms, statement of purpose, departmental application. Additional exam requirements/recommendations for international students: required—TOEFL (minimum score 550 paper-based; 80 iBT), IELTS (minimum score 6.5), PTE. Electronic applications accepted.

California State University, Dominguez Hills, College of Education, Division of Graduate Education, Program in Counseling, Carson, CA 90747-0001. Offers college counseling (MS); school counseling (MS). *Program availability:* Part-time, evening/weekend. *Degree requirements:* For master's, comprehensive exam. *Entrance requirements:* For master's, minimum GPA of 3.0. Additional exam requirements/recommendations for international students: required—TOEFL.

California State University, Fresno, Division of Research and Graduate Studies, College of Science and Mathematics, Department of Psychology, Fresno, CA 93740-8027. Offers applied behavior analysis (MA); general/experimental psychology (MA); school psychology (Ed S). *Degree requirements:* For master's, thesis. *Entrance requirements:* For master's, GRE General Test, GRE Subject Test, minimum GPA of 3.0. Additional exam requirements/recommendations for international students: required—TOEFL. Electronic applications accepted. *Expenses:* Tuition, state resident: full-time $4012; part-time $2506 per semester.

California State University, Los Angeles, Graduate Studies, Charter College of Education, Division of Special Education and Counseling, Los Angeles, CA 90032-8530. Offers counseling (MS), including applied behavior analysis, community college counseling, rehabilitation counseling, school counseling, school psychology; special education (MA, PhD). *Accreditation:* ACA. *Program availability:* Part-time, evening/weekend. *Entrance requirements:* For master's, minimum GPA of 2.75 in last 90 units of course work, teaching certificate. Additional exam requirements/recommendations for international students: required—TOEFL (minimum score 500 paper-based). Electronic applications accepted. *Expenses: Tuition, area resident:* Full-time $7176; part-time $4164 per year. Tuition, state resident: full-time $7176; part-time $4164 per year. Tuition, nonresident: full-time $14,304; part-time $8916 per year. *International tuition:* $14,304 full-time. *Required fees:* $1037.76; $1037.76 per unit. Tuition and fees vary according to degree level and program.

California State University, Northridge, Graduate Studies, Michael D. Eisner College of Education, Department of Educational Psychology and Counseling, Northridge, CA 91330. Offers counseling (MS), including career counseling, college counseling and student services, marriage and family therapy, school counseling, school psychology; educational psychology (MA Ed), including development, learning, and instruction, early childhood education. *Accreditation:* ACA (one or more programs are accredited); NCATE. *Program availability:* Part-time, evening/weekend. *Entrance requirements:* For master's, GRE General Test or minimum GPA of 3.0. Additional exam requirements/recommendations for international students: required—TOEFL.

California State University, Sacramento, College of Education, Graduate and Professional Studies in Education, Sacramento, CA 95819. Offers behavioral science and gender equity (MA); child development (MA); counseling (MS); curriculum and instruction (MA); education (Ed D), including K-12 and community college; education leadership and policy studies (MA), including higher education, PreK-12; education specialist (Ed S), including school psychology; educational technology (MA); language

and literacy (MA); multicultural education (MA); school psychology (MA); special education (MA); workforce development advocacy (MA). *Program availability:* Part-time, evening/weekend, blended/hybrid learning. *Students:* 469 full-time (369 women), 155 part-time (124 women); includes 342 minority (58 Black or African American, non-Hispanic/Latino; 12 American Indian or Alaska Native, non-Hispanic/Latino; 92 Asian, non-Hispanic/Latino; 177 Hispanic/Latino; 3 Native Hawaiian or other Pacific Islander, non-Hispanic/Latino), 8 international. Average age 32. 704 applicants, 49% accepted, 265 enrolled. In 2019, 128 master's, 18 other advanced degrees awarded. *Degree requirements:* For master's, comprehensive exam (for some programs), thesis (for some programs), thesis or project; writing proficiency exam. *Entrance requirements:* For master's and doctorate, GRE. Additional exam requirements/recommendations for international students: required—TOEFL (minimum score 550 paper-based; 80 iBT); recommended—IELTS (minimum score 7). *Application deadline:* For fall admission, 3/1 for domestic students, 2/1 for international students. Applications are processed on a rolling basis. Application fee: $70. Electronic applications accepted. *Expenses:* Contact institution. *Financial support:* Career-related internships or fieldwork, Federal Work-Study, and scholarships/grants available. Support available to part-time students. Financial award application deadline: 3/1; financial award applicants required to submit FAFSA. *Unit head:* Dr. Carlos Nevarez, Chair, E-mail: nevarezc@csus.edu. *Application contact:* Jose Martinez, Graduate Admissions Supervisor, 916-278-6470, E-mail: martinj@skymail.csus.edu.
Website: http://www.csus.edu/coe/academics/graduate/index.html

California University of Pennsylvania, School of Graduate Studies and Research, College of Liberal Arts, Program in School Psychology, California, PA 15419-1394. Offers MS. *Accreditation:* NCATE. *Program availability:* Part-time, evening/weekend. *Degree requirements:* For master's, comprehensive exam, thesis optional, internship. *Entrance requirements:* For master's, MAT or GRE, minimum GPA of 3.0, work experience in psychology, letters of reference. Additional exam requirements/recommendations for international students: required—TOEFL (minimum score 550 paper-based; 80 iBT). Electronic applications accepted. *Expenses: Tuition, area resident:* Full-time $9288; part-time $516 per credit. Tuition, state resident: full-time $9288; part-time $516 per credit. Tuition, nonresident: full-time $13,932; part-time $774 per credit. *Required fees:* $3631; $291.13 per credit. Part-time tuition and fees vary according to course load.

Cambridge College, School of Psychology and Counseling, Boston, MA 02129. Offers alcohol and drug counseling (Certificate); behavioral health care management (CAGS); marriage and family therapy (M Ed); mental health and school counseling (M Ed); mental health counseling (M Ed); psychological studies (M Ed); rehabilitation counseling (Certificate); school adjustment and mental health counseling (M Ed); school adjustment counseling for mental health counselors (Certificate); school counseling (M Ed); trauma studies (Certificate). *Program availability:* Part-time, evening/weekend. *Degree requirements:* For master's and other advanced degree, thesis, practicum/internship. *Entrance requirements:* For master's, resume, 2 professional references; for other advanced degree, official transcripts, documents for transfer credit evaluation, resume, written personal statement/essay, 2 professional references, health insurance, immunizations form. Additional exam requirements/recommendations for international students: required—TOEFL (minimum score 550 paper-based; 79 iBT), Michigan English Language Assessment Battery (minimum score 85); recommended—IELTS (minimum score 6). Electronic applications accepted. *Expenses:* Contact institution.

Campbellsville University, School of Education, Campbellsville, KY 42718. Offers education (MA); school counseling (MA); school improvement (MA); special education (MASE); special education-teacher leader (MA); teacher leader (MA); teaching (MAT), including middle grades biology, middle grades chemistry, middle grades English. *Accreditation:* NCATE. *Program availability:* Part-time, evening/weekend, 100% online, blended/hybrid learning. *Faculty:* 22 full-time (16 women), 11 part-time/adjunct (4 women). *Students:* 181 full-time (144 women), 66 part-time (54 women); includes 21 minority (16 Black or African American, non-Hispanic/Latino; 1 American Indian or Alaska Native, non-Hispanic/Latino; 3 Hispanic/Latino; 1 Two or more races, non-Hispanic/Latino). Average age 34. 295 applicants, 37% accepted, 90 enrolled. In 2019, 67 master's awarded. *Degree requirements:* For master's, comprehensive exam (for some programs), thesis, research paper. *Entrance requirements:* For master's, GRE or PRAXIS, minimum undergraduate GPA of 2.75, teaching certificate, professional growth plan, letters of recommendation, interview. Additional exam requirements/recommendations for international students: recommended—TOEFL (minimum score 550 paper-based; 79 iBT), IELTS (minimum score 6). *Application deadline:* For fall admission, 8/15 for domestic students; for spring admission, 12/15 for domestic students; for summer admission, 4/15 for domestic students. Applications are processed on a rolling basis. Application fee: $25. Electronic applications accepted. Application fee is waived when completed online. *Expenses:* All of the School of Education graduate programs are $299 per credit hour. *Financial support:* Unspecified assistantships available. Financial award applicants required to submit FAFSA. *Unit head:* Dr. Lisa Allen, Dean of School of Education, 270-789-5344, Fax: 270-789-5206, E-mail: lsallen@campbellsville.edu. *Application contact:* Monica Bamwine, Director of Graduate Admissions, 270-789-5221, Fax: 270-789-5071, E-mail: mkbamwine@campbellsville.edu.
Website: https://www.campbellsville.edu/academics/schools-and-colleges/school-of-education/

Capella University, Harold Abel School of Social and Behavioral Science, Doctoral Programs in Psychology, Minneapolis, MN 55402. Offers addiction psychology (PhD); clinical psychology (Psy D); educational psychology (PhD); general advanced studies in human behavior (PhD); general psychology (PhD); industrial/organizational psychology (PhD); school psychology (Psy D).

Capella University, Harold Abel School of Social and Behavioral Science, Master's Programs in Psychology, Minneapolis, MN 55402. Offers applied behavior analysis (MS); clinical psychology (MS); counseling psychology (MS); educational psychology (MS); evaluation, research, and measurement (MS); general advanced studies in human behavior (MS); general psychology (MS); industrial/organizational psychology (MS); leadership coaching psychology (MS); school psychology (MS); sport psychology (MS).

Central Connecticut State University, School of Graduate Studies, School of Education and Professional Studies, Department of Counselor Education and Family Therapy, New Britain, CT 06050-4010. Offers marriage and family therapy (MS); professional counseling (MS, AC, Certificate); school counseling (MS); student development in higher education (MS). *Accreditation:* AAMFT/COAMFTE; ACA. *Program availability:* Part-time, evening/weekend. *Degree requirements:* For master's, comprehensive exam, thesis or alternative; for other advanced degree, qualifying exam. *Entrance requirements:* For master's, minimum undergraduate GPA of 2.7, essay, interview, letters of recommendation. Additional exam requirements/recommendations for international students: required—TOEFL (minimum score 550 paper-based; 79 iBT); recommended—IELTS (minimum score 6.5). Electronic applications accepted.

Central Michigan University, College of Graduate Studies, College of Liberal Arts and Social Sciences, Department of Psychology, Program in School Psychology, Mount Pleasant, MI 48859. Offers PhD, S Psy S. *Accreditation:* APA. *Degree requirements:* For doctorate, thesis/dissertation; for S Psy S, thesis. *Entrance requirements:* For doctorate, GRE. Electronic applications accepted. *Expenses: Tuition, area resident:* Full-time $12,267; part-time $8178 per year. Tuition, state resident: full-time $12,267; part-time $8178 per year. Tuition, nonresident: full-time $12,267; part-time $8178 per year. *International tuition:* $16,110 full-time. *Required fees:* $225 per semester. Tuition and fees vary according to degree level and program.

Central Washington University, School of Graduate Studies and Research, College of the Sciences, Department of Psychology, Program in School Psychology, Ellensburg, WA 98926. Offers Ed S. *Entrance requirements:* Additional exam requirements/recommendations for international students: required—TOEFL (minimum score 550 paper-based; 79 iBT). Electronic applications accepted.

Chapman University, Donna Ford Attallah College of Educational Studies, Orange, CA 92866. Offers counseling (MA), including school counseling (MA, Credential); curriculum and instruction (MA), including elementary education, secondary education; education (PhD), including cultural and curricular studies, disability studies, leadership studies, school psychology (PhD, Credential); educational psychology (MA); leadership development (MA); multiple subjects (Credential), including Spanish/English bilingual; pupil personnel services (Credential), including school counseling (MA, Credential), school psychology (PhD, Credential); school psychology (Ed S); single subject (Credential); special education (MA, Credential), including mild/moderate (Credential), moderate/severe (Credential); teaching (MA), including elementary education, secondary education, secondary music education. *Accreditation:* TEAC. *Program availability:* Part-time, evening/weekend. *Faculty:* 33 full-time (19 women), 49 part-time/adjunct (36 women). *Students:* 145 full-time (127 women), 179 part-time (136 women); includes 178 minority (8 Black or African American, non-Hispanic/Latino; 1 American Indian or Alaska Native, non-Hispanic/Latino; 41 Asian, non-Hispanic/Latino; 117 Hispanic/Latino; 11 Two or more races, non-Hispanic/Latino), 16 international. Average age 28. 333 applicants, 61% accepted, 143 enrolled. In 2019, 153 master's, 11 doctorates awarded. *Entrance requirements:* Additional exam requirements/recommendations for international students: required—TOEFL (minimum score 80 iBT), IELTS (minimum score 6.5), PTE (minimum score 53). *Application deadline:* Applications are processed on a rolling basis. Application fee: $60. Electronic applications accepted. *Expenses:* Contact institution. *Financial support:* Fellowships and scholarships/grants available. Financial award applicants required to submit FAFSA. *Unit head:* Dr. Roxanne Greitz Miller, Interim Dean, 714-997-6781, E-mail: rgmiller@chapman.edu. *Application contact:* Shannon McCance, Graduate Admission Counselor, 714-516-5236, E-mail: smccance@chapman.edu.
Website: http://www.chapman.edu/CES/

The Chicago School of Professional Psychology, Program in School Psychology, Chicago, IL 60610. Offers Ed D, Psy D, Ed S. *Program availability:* Part-time. *Entrance requirements:* For degree, GRE (recommended), minimum GPA of 3.2 (recommended); completion of one course in statistics or research methods and one course in psychology. Additional exam requirements/recommendations for international students: required—TOEFL (minimum score 550 paper-based; 79 iBT).

The Chicago School of Professional Psychology at Washington DC, Program in School Psychology, Washington, DC 20005. Offers Ed S. *Program availability:* Part-time.

The Citadel, The Military College of South Carolina, Citadel Graduate College, School of Humanities and Social Sciences, Department of Psychology, Charleston, SC 29409. Offers psychology (MA), including clinical counseling; school psychology (Ed S). *Program availability:* Part-time, evening/weekend. *Degree requirements:* For master's, comprehensive exam, practicum; internship (written and oral presentation of a case study as part of internship); for Ed S, comprehensive exam, thesis (for some programs), practicum, internship. *Entrance requirements:* For master's, GRE (minimum combined score of 297, 150 on verbal reasoning and 141 on quantitative reasoning) or MAT (minimum score of 410), minimum undergraduate GPA of 3.0; 12 credit hours in psychology or minimum score on GRE Subject Test in psychology of 600; 2 letters of recommendation; for Ed S, GRE (minimum combined score of 297, 150 on verbal reasoning and 147 on quantitative reasoning) or MAT (minimum score of 410), minimum undergraduate or graduate GPA of 3.0; 2 letters of recommendation. Additional exam requirements/recommendations for international students: required—TOEFL (minimum score 550 paper-based; 79 iBT). Electronic applications accepted.

The Citadel, The Military College of South Carolina, Citadel Graduate College, Zucker Family School of Education, Charleston, SC 29409. Offers elementary/secondary school administration and supervision (M Ed); elementary/secondary school counseling (M Ed); interdisciplinary STEM education (M Ed); literacy education (M Ed, Graduate Certificate); middle grades (MAT), including English, mathematics, science, social studies; physical education (grades K-12) (MAT); school superintendency (Ed S); secondary education (MAT), including biology, English, mathematics, social studies; student affairs (Graduate Certificate); student affairs and college counseling (M Ed). *Accreditation:* NCATE. *Program availability:* Part-time, evening/weekend, 100% online, blended/hybrid learning. *Faculty:* 16 full-time (10 women), 10 part-time/adjunct (7 women). *Students:* 37 full-time (27 women), 166 part-time (128 women); includes 55 minority (42 Black or African American, non-Hispanic/Latino; 1 Asian, non-Hispanic/Latino; 8 Hispanic/Latino; 4 Two or more races, non-Hispanic/Latino). In 2019, 120 master's, 27 other advanced degrees awarded. *Entrance requirements:* For master's, GRE or MAT for MAT Secondary Education, MAT Middle Grades, MAT Physical Education, MEd Counselor Education - Elementary and Secondary, MEd Counselor Education - Student Affairs and College and MEd Higher Education Leadership, MAT Secondary Education: Submission of an official transcript of the baccalaureate degree and all other undergraduate or graduate work directly from each regionally accredited college and university, 3.0 cum GPA. MAT Middle Grades: Submission of official transcript of the baccalaureate degree and all other undergraduate or graduate work directly fr; for other advanced degree, Certificate Higher Education Leadership: Submission of an official transcript reflecting the highest degree earned from a regionally accredited college or university. Certificate Literacy Education: Submission of an official transcript directly from each regionally accredited college or university from which a degree has been conferred, 2.5 cum GPA. Additional exam requirements/recommendations for international students: required—TOEFL (minimum score 550 paper-based; 79 iBT). *Application deadline:* Applications are processed on a rolling basis. Application fee: $40. Electronic applications accepted. *Expenses:* MEd Higher Education Leadership, MEd Interdisciplinary STEM Education, MS Instructional Systems Design and Performance Improvement, Certificate Higher Education Leadership: $695 per credit hour. $165 per semester in fees ($75 Technology Fee + $75 Infrastructure Fee + $15 Registration Fee). *Financial support:* In 2019–20, 21,283 students received support. Federal Work-Study, scholarships/grants, tuition waivers (partial), and Athletics available. Financial award applicants required to submit FAFSA. *Unit head:* Evan Ortlieb, Zucker Family School of Education Dean, 843-953-5097, Fax: 843-953-7258, E-mail: eortlieb@citadel.edu. *Application contact:* Carl Hill, Assistant Director of Enrollment Management, 843-953-6808, Fax: 843-953-7630, E-mail: chill9@citadel.edu.
Website: http://www.citadel.edu/root/education-graduate-programs

School Psychology

The College of New Rochelle, Graduate School, Division of Human Services, Program in School Psychology, New Rochelle, NY 10805-2308. Offers MS. *Degree requirements:* For master's, comprehensive exam, clinical fieldwork journal. *Entrance requirements:* For master's, interview, minimum GPA of 3.0, course work in psychology, sample of written work.

College of Saint Elizabeth, Department of Psychology, Morristown, NJ 07960-6989. Offers counseling psychology (MA, Psy D), including mental health counseling (MA), school counseling (MA). *Program availability:* Part-time. *Degree requirements:* For master's, thesis or alternative; for doctorate, thesis/dissertation. *Entrance requirements:* For master's, minimum GPA of 3.0, BA in psychology (preferred), 12 credits of course work in psychology; for doctorate, GRE, 3 letters of recommendation from professionals who can comment on the applicant's qualifications for doctoral study; master's degree in counseling psychology, forensic psychology and counseling, or its equivalent. Additional exam requirements/recommendations for international students: required—TOEFL (minimum score 550 paper-based; 79 iBT), IELTS (minimum score 6.5). Electronic applications accepted. Application fee is waived when completed online. *Expenses:* Contact institution.

College of St. Joseph, Graduate Programs, Division of Psychology and Human Services, Program in School Guidance Counseling, Rutland, VT 05701-3899. Offers MS. *Program availability:* Part-time, evening/weekend. *Degree requirements:* For master's, comprehensive exam, thesis optional. *Entrance requirements:* For master's, PRAXIS I, official college transcripts; 2 letters of reference. Additional exam requirements/recommendations for international students: required—TOEFL (minimum score 550 paper-based). Electronic applications accepted.

The College of Saint Rose, Graduate Studies, Thelma P. Lally School of Education, Educational and School Psychology Programs, Albany, NY 12203-1419. Offers educational psychology (MS Ed, Certificate); school psychology (MS Ed). *Students:* 44 full-time (41 women), 28 part-time (27 women); includes 5 minority (1 Black or African American, non-Hispanic/Latino; 1 Asian, non-Hispanic/Latino; 1 Hispanic/Latino; 2 Two or more races, non-Hispanic/Latino), 2 international. Average age 25. 57 applicants, 68% accepted, 25 enrolled. In 2019, 17 master's, 16 Certificates awarded. *Entrance requirements:* For master's, minimum undergraduate GPA of 3.0. Additional exam requirements/recommendations for international students: required—TOEFL (minimum score 550 paper-based; 80 iBT), IELTS (minimum score 6), PTE (minimum score 56). *Application deadline:* For fall admission, 2/15 priority date for domestic and international students. Applications are processed on a rolling basis. Application fee: $40. Electronic applications accepted. *Expenses: Tuition:* Full-time $14,382; part-time $799 per credit hour. *Required fees:* $954; $698. Tuition and fees vary according to course load. *Financial support:* Career-related internships or fieldwork, scholarships/grants, tuition waivers (partial), and unspecified assistantships available. Support available to part-time students. Financial award application deadline: 4/15. *Unit head:* Dr. Andrew Shanock, Chair, 518-337-5694, E-mail: shanocka@strose.edu. *Application contact:* Daniel Gallagher, Assistant Vice President for Graduate Recruitment and Enrollment, 518-485-3390, Fax: 518-458-5479, E-mail: grad@strose.edu.
Website: https://www.strose.edu/school-psychology/

Creighton University, Graduate School, College of Arts and Sciences, Department of Education, Program in School Counseling and Preventive Mental Health, Omaha, NE 68178-0001. Offers elementary school guidance (MS); secondary school guidance (MS). *Program availability:* Part-time, online only, 100% online, blended/hybrid learning. *Degree requirements:* For master's, comprehensive exam. *Entrance requirements:* For master's, resume, 3 letters of recommendation, personal statement, background check. Additional exam requirements/recommendations for international students: required—TOEFL (minimum score 90 iBT). Electronic applications accepted.

DePaul University, College of Education, Chicago, IL 60614. Offers bilingual-bicultural education (M Ed, MA); counseling (M Ed, MA), including clinical mental health counseling, college student development, school counseling; curriculum studies (M Ed, MA, Ed D); early childhood education (M Ed, MA, Ed D); educational leadership (M Ed, MA, Ed D), including Catholic leadership (M Ed, MA), general (M Ed, MA), higher education (M Ed, MA), physical education (M Ed, MA), principal preparation (M Ed), teacher preparation (M Ed); elementary education (M Ed, MA); middle grades education (M Ed); middle school mathematics education (MS); reading specialist (M Ed, MA); secondary education (M Ed, MA); social and cultural foundations in education (M Ed, MA); special education (M Ed); sport, fitness and recreation leadership (MS); value-creating education for global citizenship (M Ed); world languages education (M Ed, MA). *Program availability:* Part-time, evening/weekend, online learning. *Degree requirements:* For doctorate, thesis/dissertation. Electronic applications accepted.

Doane University, Program in Education, Crete, NE 68333-2430. Offers curriculum and instruction (M Ed); education (Ed D); education specialist (Ed S); educational leadership (M Ed); school counseling (M Ed). *Accreditation:* NCATE. *Program availability:* Part-time, evening/weekend. *Degree requirements:* For master's, thesis; for doctorate, thesis/dissertation. *Entrance requirements:* For master's, minimum GPA of 2.5. Additional exam requirements/recommendations for international students: required—TOEFL. Electronic applications accepted. *Expenses:* Contact institution.

Duquesne University, School of Education, Department of Counseling, Psychology, and Special Education, Program in School Psychology, Pittsburgh, PA 15282-0001. Offers child psychology (MS Ed). *Program availability:* Part-time, evening/weekend. *Degree requirements:* For doctorate, comprehensive exam. *Entrance requirements:* For master's, bachelor's degree; for doctorate, GRE, letters of reference, letter of intent, interview, master's degree. Additional exam requirements/recommendations for international students: required—TOEFL (minimum score 550 paper-based), IELTS (minimum score 6.5). Electronic applications accepted.

Eastern Illinois University, Graduate School, College of Liberal Arts and Sciences, Department of Psychology, Charleston, IL 61920. Offers clinical psychology (MA); school psychology (SSP). *Program availability:* Part-time, evening/weekend. *Degree requirements:* For master's, comprehensive exam, thesis; for SSP, thesis. *Entrance requirements:* For master's and SSP, GMAT or GRE. Additional exam requirements/recommendations for international students: required—TOEFL (minimum score 500 paper-based; 61 iBT), IELTS (minimum score 6). Electronic applications accepted.

Eastern Kentucky University, The Graduate School, College of Arts and Sciences, Department of Psychology, Richmond, KY 40475-3102. Offers clinical psychology (MS); industrial/organizational psychology (MS); school psychology (Psy S). *Program availability:* Part-time. *Entrance requirements:* For master's and Psy S, GRE General Test, minimum GPA of 2.5.

Eastern University, Graduate Education Programs, St. Davids, PA 19087-3696. Offers ESL program specialist (K-12) (Certificate); general supervisor (PreK-12) (Certificate); health and physical education (K-12) (Certificate); middle level (4-8) (Certificate); multicultural education (M Ed); music (K-12) (Certificate); Pre K-4 (Certificate); Pre K-4 with special education (Certificate); reading (M Ed); reading specialist (K-12) (Certificate); reading supervisor (K-12) (Certificate); school counseling (MA, CAGS); school principalship (preK-12) (Certificate); school psychology (MS, CAGS); secondary biology education (7-12) (Certificate); secondary chemistry education (7-12) (Certificate); secondary communication education (7-12) (Certificate); secondary

English education (7-12) (Certificate); secondary math education (7-12) (Certificate); secondary social studies education (7-12) (Certificate); special education (M Ed); special education (7-12) (Certificate); special education (Pre K-8) (Certificate); special education supervisor (K-12) (Certificate); TESOL (M Ed); world language (Certificate), including Spanish. *Program availability:* Part-time, evening/weekend, online learning. *Students:* 54 full-time (45 women), 149 part-time (134 women); includes 75 minority (54 Black or African American, non-Hispanic/Latino; 3 Asian, non-Hispanic/Latino; 15 Hispanic/Latino; 3 Two or more races, non-Hispanic/Latino). Average age 33. In 2019, 89 master's, 10 other advanced degrees awarded. *Entrance requirements:* Additional exam requirements/recommendations for international students: required—TOEFL. *Application deadline:* Applications are processed on a rolling basis. Application fee: $35. Electronic applications accepted. Application fee is waived when completed online. *Expenses:* Contact institution. *Unit head:* Michael Dziedziak, Executive Director of Enrollment, 800-452-0996, E-mail: gpsadmissions@eastern.edu. *Application contact:* Michael Dziedziak, Executive Director of Enrollment, 800-452-0996, E-mail: gpsadmissions@eastern.edu.
Website: https://www.eastern.edu/academics/programs/education-department-graduate-programs/graduate-programs

Eastern Washington University, Graduate Studies, College of Social Sciences, Department of Psychology, Cheney, WA 99004-2431. Offers clinical psychology (MS); experimental psychology (MS); mental health counseling (MS), including applied psychology, mental health counseling; school counseling (MS), including applied psychology, school counseling; school psychology respecialization (Ed S). *Faculty:* 22 full-time (15 women). *Students:* 119 full-time (94 women), 13 part-time (10 women); includes 3 minority (all Hispanic/Latino), 6 international. Average age 34. 83 applicants, 42% accepted, 31 enrolled. In 2019, 49 master's awarded. *Degree requirements:* For master's, comprehensive exam, thesis or alternative. *Entrance requirements:* For master's, GRE General Test, minimum GPA of 3.0. Additional exam requirements/recommendations for international students: required—TOEFL (minimum score 580 paper-based; 92 iBT), IELTS (minimum score 7), PTE (minimum score 63). *Application deadline:* For fall admission, 3/1 for domestic students. Applications are processed on a rolling basis. Application fee: $75. Electronic applications accepted. *Financial support:* Teaching assistantships with partial tuition reimbursements, career-related internships or fieldwork, Federal Work-Study, institutionally sponsored loans, scholarships/grants, health care benefits, tuition waivers (partial), and unspecified assistantships available. Support available to part-time students. Financial award application deadline: 2/1; financial award applicants required to submit FAFSA. *Unit head:* Dennis Anderson, 509-359-2087, E-mail: danderson2@ewu.edu. *Application contact:* Kathy White, Advisor/Recruiter for Graduate Studies, 509-359-6297, Fax: 509-359-6044, E-mail: gradprograms@ewu.edu.

East Tennessee State University, College of Graduate and Continuing Studies, Clemmer College, Department of Counseling and Human Services, Johnson City, TN 37614. Offers clinical mental health counseling (MA); college counseling/student affairs higher education (MA); couples and family therapy (MA); human services (MS); school counseling (MA). *Accreditation:* ACA; NCATE. *Program availability:* Part-time. *Degree requirements:* For master's, comprehensive exam, thesis optional, internship, student teaching, culminating experience. *Entrance requirements:* For master's, GRE General Test, minimum GPA of 3.0, three letters of recommendation, interview, 2-3 page essay detailing experiences that have shaped pursuit of degree, resume. Additional exam requirements/recommendations for international students: required—TOEFL (minimum score 550 paper-based; 79 iBT). Electronic applications accepted.

Edinboro University of Pennsylvania, Department of Counseling, School Psychology and Special Education, Edinboro, PA 16444. Offers counseling (MA), including art therapy, clinical mental health counseling, college counseling, rehabilitation counseling, school counseling; educational psychology (M Ed); school psychology (Ed S); special education (M Ed), including autism, behavior management. *Accreditation:* ACA. *Program availability:* Part-time, evening/weekend. *Faculty:* 19 full-time (13 women), 2 part-time/adjunct (1 woman). *Students:* 180 full-time (146 women), 215 part-time (186 women); includes 42 minority (18 Black or African American, non-Hispanic/Latino; 2 American Indian or Alaska Native, non-Hispanic/Latino; 4 Asian, non-Hispanic/Latino; 12 Hispanic/Latino; 1 Native Hawaiian or other Pacific Islander, non-Hispanic/Latino; 5 Two or more races, non-Hispanic/Latino), 3 international. Average age 31. 197 applicants, 63% accepted, 71 enrolled. In 2019, 87 master's, 8 other advanced degrees awarded. *Degree requirements:* For master's, thesis or alternative, competency exam; for Ed S, thesis or alternative. *Entrance requirements:* For master's and Ed S, GRE or MAT, minimum QPA of 2.5. Additional exam requirements/recommendations for international students: required—TOEFL (minimum score 550 paper-based; 213 iBT), IELTS (minimum score 6.5). *Application deadline:* Applications are processed on a rolling basis. Application fee: $30. Electronic applications accepted. *Expenses: Tuition, area resident:* Full-time $11,261; part-time $625.60 per credit. Tuition, state resident: full-time $11,261; part-time $625.60 per credit. Tuition, nonresident: full-time $16,850; part-time $936.10 per credit. *International tuition:* $16,850 full-time. *Required fees:* $57.75 per credit. *Financial support:* In 2019-20, 35 students received support. Research assistantships with tuition reimbursements available, career-related internships or fieldwork, Federal Work-Study, scholarships/grants, and unspecified assistantships available. Support available to part-time students. Financial award application deadline: 2/15; financial award applicants required to submit FAFSA. *Unit head:* Dr. Penelope Orr, Chairperson, 814-732-1684, E-mail: porr@edinboro.edu. *Application contact:* Dr. Penelope Orr, Chairperson, 814-732-1684, E-mail: porr@edinboro.edu.
Website: https://www.edinboro.edu/academics/schools-and-departments/soe/departments/cspe/

Emporia State University, Program in School Psychology, Emporia, KS 66801-5415. Offers MS, Ed S. *Accreditation:* NCATE. *Program availability:* Part-time. *Degree requirements:* For master's, comprehensive exam or thesis, internship; for Ed S, comprehensive exam, thesis or alternative, internship. *Entrance requirements:* For master's, GRE General Test or MAT, essay exam, appropriate bachelor's degree, teacher certification, letters of recommendation; for Ed S, GRE, essay exam, letters of recommendation, teacher certification. Additional exam requirements/recommendations for international students: required—TOEFL (minimum score 520 paper-based; 68 iBT). Electronic applications accepted. *Expenses: Tuition, area resident:* Full-time $6394; part-time $266.41 per credit hour. Tuition, state resident: full-time $6394; part-time $266.41 per credit hour. Tuition, nonresident: full-time $20,128; part-time $828.66 per credit hour. *International tuition:* $20,128 full-time. *Required fees:* $2183; $90.95 per credit hour. Tuition and fees vary according to campus/location and program.

Evangel University, School Counseling Program, Springfield, MO 65802. Offers MS. *Program availability:* Part-time, evening/weekend. *Degree requirements:* For master's, comprehensive exam. *Entrance requirements:* For master's, MAT (preferred) or GRE. Additional exam requirements/recommendations for international students: required—TOEFL (minimum score 550 paper-based). Electronic applications accepted.

Fairfield University, Graduate School of Education and Allied Professions, Fairfield, CT 06824. Offers applied behavior analysis (ATC); applied psychology (MA); clinical mental health counseling (MA, CAS); educational technology (MA); elementary education (MA,

CAS); family studies (MA); integration of spirituality and religion in counseling (ATC); marriage and family therapy (MA); reading and language development (Sixth Year Certificate); school counseling (MA, CAS); school psychology (MA, CAS); school-based marriage and family therapy (ATC); secondary education (MA); special education (MA, CAS); substance abuse counseling (ATC); teaching (Certificate); teaching and foundations (MA, CAS); TESOL, world languages, and bilingual education (MA, CAS). *Accreditation:* NCATE. *Program availability:* Part-time, evening/weekend. *Faculty:* 24 full-time (18 women), 28 part-time/adjunct (20 women). *Students:* 169 full-time (149 women), 227 part-time (187 women); includes 96 minority (21 Black or African American, non-Hispanic/Latino; 8 Asian, non-Hispanic/Latino; 60 Hispanic/Latino; 7 Two or more races, non-Hispanic/Latino), 1 international. Average age 31. 194 applicants, 60% accepted, 101 enrolled. In 2019, 136 master's, 28 other advanced degrees awarded. *Degree requirements:* For master's, comprehensive exam. *Entrance requirements:* For master's, One of the following for certification programs: Praxis Core, SAT, ACT, or GRE, minimum GPA of 3.0, 2 recommendations, resume. Additional exam requirements/recommendations for international students: required—TOEFL (minimum score 550 paper-based; 84 iBT), IELTS (minimum score 7.5), TOEFL (minimum score 550 paper-based; 84 iBT) or IELTS (minimum score 7.5). *Application deadline:* For fall admission, 2/15 for international students; for spring admission, 10/1 for international students. Application fee: $60. Electronic applications accepted. *Expenses:* Tuition $815/credit hour; Lab Fee (ED598) $300/semester; Lab Fee (CN457,CN467, PY538, PY540) $70/course; Wilson Reading Course Fee $141/credit hour; Registration Fee $50/semester; Graduate Student Activity Fee (Fall and Spring) $65/semester. *Financial support:* In 2019–20, 34 students received support. Career-related internships or fieldwork and unspecified assistantships available. Support available to part-time students. Financial award applicants required to submit FAFSA. *Unit head:* Dr. Laurie Grupp, Dean, 203-254-4250, Fax: 203-254-4241, E-mail: lgrupp@fairfield.edu. *Application contact:* Melanie Rogers, Director of Graduate Admission, 203-254-4184, Fax: 203-254-4073, E-mail: gradadmis@fairfield.edu.
Website: http://www.fairfield.edu/gseap

Fairleigh Dickinson University, Metropolitan Campus, University College: Arts, Sciences, and Professional Studies, School of Psychology, Program in School Psychology, Teaneck, NJ 07666-1914. Offers MA, Psy D.

Florida Gulf Coast University, Elaine Nicpon Marieb College of Health and Human Services, Program in School Counseling, Fort Myers, FL 33965-6565. Offers clinical mental health counseling (MA); school counseling (MA). *Accreditation:* ACA. *Program availability:* Part-time, evening/weekend. *Degree requirements:* For master's, thesis or alternative. *Entrance requirements:* For master's, GRE General Test, MAT, minimum GPA of 3.0. Additional exam requirements/recommendations for international students: required—TOEFL (minimum score 550 paper-based). Electronic applications accepted. *Expenses: Tuition, area resident:* Full-time $6974; part-time $4350 per credit hour. Tuition, state resident: full-time $6974; part-time $4350 per credit hour. Tuition, nonresident: full-time $28,169; part-time $17,595 per credit hour. *International tuition:* $28,169 full-time. *Required fees:* $2027; $1267 per credit hour. $507 per semester. Tuition and fees vary according to course load.

Fordham University, Graduate School of Education, Division of Psychological and Educational Services, New York, NY 10023. Offers counseling and personnel services (MSE); counseling psychology (PhD); school psychology (PhD). *Accreditation:* APA (one or more programs are accredited); NCATE. *Program availability:* Part-time, evening/weekend. Terminal master's awarded for partial completion of doctoral program. *Degree requirements:* For master's, comprehensive exam (for some programs); for doctorate, comprehensive exam (for some programs), thesis/dissertation. *Entrance requirements:* For doctorate, GRE General Test. Additional exam requirements/recommendations for international students: required—TOEFL (minimum score 577 paper-based; 90 iBT), IELTS (minimum score 7). Electronic applications accepted.

Fort Hays State University, Graduate School, College of Health and Behavioral Sciences, Department of Psychology, Program in School Psychology, Hays, KS 67601-4099. Offers Ed S. *Accreditation:* NCATE. *Degree requirements:* For Ed S, comprehensive exam, thesis. *Entrance requirements:* Additional exam requirements/recommendations for international students: required—TOEFL (minimum score 550 paper-based). Electronic applications accepted.

Francis Marion University, Graduate Programs, Department of Psychology, Florence, SC 29502-0547. Offers applied psychology (MS), including clinical/counseling psychology, school psychology; school psychology (SSP). *Program availability:* Part-time, evening/weekend. *Degree requirements:* For master's, internship. *Entrance requirements:* For master's, GRE General Test, official transcripts, two letters of recommendation. Additional exam requirements/recommendations for international students: required—TOEFL (minimum score 550 paper-based; 79 iBT). *Expenses: Tuition, area resident:* Full-time $10,612; part-time $530.60 per credit hour. Tuition, state resident: full-time $10,612; part-time $530.60 per credit hour. Tuition, nonresident: full-time $21,224; part-time $1061.20 per credit hour. *International tuition:* $21,224 full-time. *Required fees:* $312; $156 per credit hour. $332 per semester. Tuition and fees vary according to program.

Fresno Pacific University, Graduate Programs, School of Education, Division of Pupil Personnel Services, Program in School Psychology, Fresno, CA 93702-4709. Offers MA. *Program availability:* Part-time, evening/weekend. *Degree requirements:* For master's, thesis or alternative. *Entrance requirements:* Additional exam requirements/recommendations for international students: required—TOEFL (minimum score 550 paper-based). *Expenses:* Contact institution.

Gallaudet University, The Graduate School, Washington, DC 20002. Offers American Sign Language/English bilingual early childhood deaf education: birth to 5 (Certificate); audiology (Au D); clinical psychology (PhD); deaf and hard of hearing infants, toddlers, and their families (Certificate); deaf education (MA, Ed S); deaf history (Certificate); deaf studies (Certificate); educating deaf students with disabilities (Certificate); education: teacher preparation (MA), including deaf education, early childhood education and deaf education, elementary education and deaf education, secondary education and deaf education; educational neuroscience (PhD); hearing, speech and language sciences (MS, PhD); international development (MA); interpretation (MA, PhD), including combined interpreting practice and research (MA), interpreting research (MA); linguistics (MA, PhD); mental health counseling (MA); peer mentoring (Certificate); public administration (MPA); school counseling (MA); school psychology (Psy S); sign language teaching (MA); social work (MSW); speech-language pathology (MS). *Program availability:* Part-time. *Faculty:* 101 full-time (70 women). *Students:* 267 full-time (208 women), 139 part-time (95 women); includes 120 minority (38 Black or African American, non-Hispanic/Latino; 20 Asian, non-Hispanic/Latino; 44 Hispanic/Latino; 18 Two or more races, non-Hispanic/Latino), 19 international. Average age 30. 484 applicants, 50% accepted, 162 enrolled. In 2019, 138 master's, 25 doctorates, 14 other advanced degrees awarded. Terminal master's awarded for partial completion of doctoral program. *Degree requirements:* For master's, comprehensive exam (for some programs), thesis optional; for doctorate, comprehensive exam, thesis/dissertation. *Entrance requirements:* For master's and doctorate, GRE General Test or MAT, letters of recommendation, interviews, goals statement, American Sign Language proficiency interview, written English competency. Additional exam requirements/recommendations for international students: required—TOEFL. *Application deadline:* For fall admission, 2/15 for domestic students. Applications are processed on a rolling basis. Application fee: $75. Electronic applications accepted. *Expenses: Tuition:* Full-time $18,180; part-time $688 per credit. *Required fees:* $526; $526. Tuition and fees vary according to course load. *Financial support:* In 2019–20, 50 students received support. Fellowships, research assistantships, teaching assistantships, career-related internships or fieldwork, Federal Work-Study, scholarships/grants, tuition waivers (partial), and unspecified assistantships available. Support available to part-time students. Financial award application deadline: 7/1; financial award applicants required to submit FAFSA. *Unit head:* Dr. Gaurav Mathur, Dean, Graduate School and Continuing Studies, 202-250-2380, Fax: 202-651-5027, E-mail: gaurav.mathur@gallaudet.edu. *Application contact:* Heidi Zornes-Foster, Senior Graduate Admissions Counselor, 202-650-5436, Fax: 202-651-5295, E-mail: graduate.school@gallaudet.edu.
Website: www.gallaudet.edu

Gardner-Webb University, Graduate School, School of Psychology, Boiling Springs, NC 28017. Offers mental health counseling (MA); school counseling (MA). *Program availability:* Part-time, evening/weekend. *Degree requirements:* For master's, comprehensive exam. *Entrance requirements:* For master's, GRE General Test, MAT, minimum GPA of 2.7. Electronic applications accepted. *Expenses:* Contact institution.

George Fox University, College of Education, Graduate Department of Counseling, Newberg, OR 97132-2697. Offers clinical mental health counseling (MA); marriage, couple and family counseling (MA, Certificate); school counseling (MA, Certificate); school psychology (Ed S). *Program availability:* Part-time. *Degree requirements:* For master's, clinical project. *Entrance requirements:* For master's, MAT or GRE, bachelor's degree from regionally-accredited college or university, minimum cumulative GPA of 3.0, 1 professional and 1 academic reference, resume, on-campus interview, official transcripts. Additional exam requirements/recommendations for international students: required—TOEFL (minimum score 577 paper-based; 90 iBT), IELTS (minimum score 7). Electronic applications accepted. *Expenses:* Contact institution.

Georgian Court University, School of Arts and Sciences, Lakewood, NJ 08701. Offers applied behavior analysis (MA); autism spectrum disorders (Certificate); clinical mental health counseling (MA); criminal justice and human rights (MS); holistic health studies (MA); homeland security (Certificate); instructional technology (CPC); integrative health (Certificate); mercy spirituality (Certificate); parish business management (Certificate); professional counselor (Certificate); school psychology (MA, Certificate); theology (MA, Certificate). *Program availability:* Part-time, evening/weekend. *Faculty:* 19 full-time (11 women), 7 part-time/adjunct (3 women). *Students:* 90 full-time (80 women), 71 part-time (59 women); includes 26 minority (8 Black or African American, non-Hispanic/Latino; 2 Asian, non-Hispanic/Latino; 14 Hispanic/Latino; 2 Two or more races, non-Hispanic/Latino), 1 international. Average age 32. 138 applicants, 58% accepted, 57 enrolled. In 2019, 68 master's, 19 other advanced degrees awarded. *Degree requirements:* For master's, comprehensive exam (for some programs), thesis (for some programs); for other advanced degree, comprehensive exam (for some programs). *Entrance requirements:* Additional exam requirements/recommendations for international students: required—TOEFL (minimum score 550 paper-based; 79 iBT). *Application deadline:* For fall admission, 8/15 for domestic students, 5/1 for international students; for spring admission, 1/15 for domestic students, 10/1 for international students. Applications are processed on a rolling basis. Application fee: $40. Electronic applications accepted. *Financial support:* Scholarships/grants, health care benefits, and unspecified assistantships available. Financial award application deadline: 4/15; financial award applicants required to submit FAFSA. *Unit head:* Dr. Mary Chinery, Dean, 732-987-2493, Fax: 732-987-2007, E-mail: mchinery@georgian.edu. *Application contact:* Dr. Mary Chinery, Dean, 732-987-2493, Fax: 732-987-2007, E-mail: mchinery@georgian.edu.
Website: https://georgian.edu/academics/school-of-arts-sciences/

Georgia Southern University, Jack N. Averitt College of Graduate Studies, College of Education, Department of Leadership, Technology, and Human Development, Program in Counselor Education, Statesboro, GA 30460. Offers mental health counseling (M Ed); school counseling (M Ed). *Accreditation:* ACA; NCATE. *Program availability:* Part-time, evening/weekend. *Students:* 46 full-time (39 women), 2 part-time (1 woman); includes 18 minority (13 Black or African American, non-Hispanic/Latino; 4 Hispanic/Latino; 1 Two or more races, non-Hispanic/Latino). Average age 27. 52 applicants, 48% accepted, 13 enrolled. In 2019, 16 master's awarded. *Degree requirements:* For master's, comprehensive exam, transition point assessments. *Entrance requirements:* For master's, minimum GPA of 2.5, letters of recommendation, interview. Additional exam requirements/recommendations for international students: required—TOEFL (minimum score 550 paper-based; 80 iBT), IELTS (minimum score 6). *Application deadline:* For fall admission, 3/2 for domestic students, 3/15 for international students; for spring admission, 3/2 for domestic students, 10/1 for international students. Application fee: $50. Electronic applications accepted. *Expenses: Tuition, area resident:* Full-time $4986; part-time $277 per credit hour. Tuition, nonresident: full-time $19,890; part-time $1105 per credit hour. *International tuition:* $19,890 full-time. *Required fees:* $2114; $1057 per semester. $1057 per semester. Tuition and fees vary according to course load, campus/location and program. *Financial support:* In 2019–20, 27 students received support, including 3 research assistantships with full tuition reimbursements available (averaging $7,750 per year); career-related internships or fieldwork, scholarships/grants, and unspecified assistantships also available. Financial award application deadline: 4/15; financial award applicants required to submit FAFSA. *Unit head:* Dr. Brandon Hunt, Program Director, 912-478-0502, Fax: 912-478-7104, E-mail: bhunt@georgiasouthern.edu. *Application contact:* Dr. Lydia Cross, Graduate Academic Services Center, 912-478-8664, E-mail: lcross@georgiasouthern.edu.
Website: http://coe.georgiasouthern.edu/coun/

Georgia Southern University, Jack N. Averitt College of Graduate Studies, College of Education, Department of Leadership, Technology, and Human Development, Program in School Psychology, Statesboro, GA 30460. Offers M Ed, Ed S. *Accreditation:* NCATE. *Program availability:* Part-time, evening/weekend. *Students:* 46 full-time (42 women), 20 part-time (19 women); includes 21 minority (16 Black or African American, non-Hispanic/Latino; 1 Hispanic/Latino; 4 Two or more races, non-Hispanic/Latino). Average age 27. 42 applicants, 52% accepted, 16 enrolled. In 2019, 20 master's, 12 Ed Ss awarded. *Degree requirements:* For Ed S, comprehensive exam, field-based research project. *Entrance requirements:* For degree, minimum graduate GPA of 3.25, letters of reference, interview. Additional exam requirements/recommendations for international students: required—TOEFL (minimum score 550 paper-based; 80 iBT), IELTS (minimum score 6). *Application deadline:* For fall admission, 4/10 for domestic students, 3/1 priority date for international students; for spring admission, 11/10 for domestic students, 10/1 for international students. Application fee: $50. Electronic applications accepted. *Expenses: Tuition, area resident:* Full-time $4986; part-time $277 per credit hour. Tuition, nonresident: full-time $19,890; part-time $1105 per credit hour. *International tuition:* $19,890 full-time. *Required fees:* $2114; $1057 per semester. $1057 per semester. Tuition and fees vary according to course load, campus/location and program. *Financial support:* In 2019–20, 31 students received support, including 3 fellowships with full tuition reimbursements available (averaging $7,750 per year);

research assistantships with partial tuition reimbursements available, teaching assistantships with partial tuition reimbursements available, career-related internships or fieldwork, Federal Work-Study, scholarships/grants, tuition waivers (full), and unspecified assistantships also available. Support available to part-time students. Financial award application deadline: 4/15; financial award applicants required to submit FAFSA. *Unit head:* Dr. Dawn Tysinger, Director, 912-478-5792, Fax: 912-478-7104, E-mail: dtysinger@georgiasouthern.edu. *Application contact:* Dr. Lydia Cross, Coordinator for Graduate Student Recruitment, 912-478-8664, E-mail: lcross@georgiasouthern.edu.
Website: http://coe.georgiasouthern.edu/espy/

Georgia State University, College of Education and Human Development, Department of Counseling and Psychological Services, Program in School Psychology, Atlanta, GA 30302-3083. Offers M Ed, PhD, Ed S. *Accreditation:* APA (one or more programs are accredited); NCATE. Terminal master's awarded for partial completion of doctoral program. *Entrance requirements:* For master's and doctorate, GRE, writing sample, resume, 3 letters of recommendation, goal statement, transcripts. Additional exam requirements/recommendations for international students: required—TOEFL. Application fee: $50. Electronic applications accepted. *Expenses: Tuition, area resident:* Full-time $7164; part-time $398 per credit hour. Tuition, state resident: full-time $7164; part-time $398 per credit hour. Tuition, nonresident: full-time $22,662; part-time $1259 per credit hour. *International tuition:* $22,662 full-time. *Required fees:* $2128; $312 per credit hour. Tuition and fees vary according to course load and program. *Financial support:* Fellowships, research assistantships, teaching assistantships, career-related internships or fieldwork, institutionally sponsored loans, scholarships/grants, health care benefits, and unspecified assistantships available. Financial award application deadline: 4/1. *Unit head:* Dr. Brian Dew, Chairperson, 404-413-8168, Fax: 404-413-8013, E-mail: bdew@gsu.edu. *Application contact:* Nancy Keita, Director, Office of Academic Assistance and Graduate Admissions, 404-413-8001, E-mail: nkeita@gsu.edu.
Website: https://education.gsu.edu/cps/

Grand Valley State University, College of Education, Program in School Counseling, Allendale, MI 49401-9403. Offers M Ed. *Program availability:* Part-time. *Students:* 13 full-time (8 women), 44 part-time (38 women); includes 6 minority (1 Black or African American, non-Hispanic/Latino; 2 Asian, non-Hispanic/Latino; 3 Hispanic/Latino). Average age 29. 32 applicants, 94% accepted, 16 enrolled. In 2019, 19 master's awarded. *Degree requirements:* For master's, thesis optional, thesis or project. *Entrance requirements:* For master's, GRE General Test or minimum GPA of 3.0; last 60 credits from regionally-accredited college/university; 3 letters of recommendation. Additional exam requirements/recommendations for international students: required—TOEFL (minimum iBT score of 80), IELTS (6.5), or Michigan English Language Assessment Battery (77). *Application deadline:* Applications are processed on a rolling basis. Application fee: $30. Electronic applications accepted. *Expenses:* $697 per credit hour, 36 credit hours. *Financial support:* In 2019–20, 11 students received support, including 8 fellowships, 3 research assistantships with full and partial tuition reimbursements available (averaging $8,000 per year); career-related internships or fieldwork and unspecified assistantships also available. *Unit head:* Dr. Catherine Meyer-Looze, Department Chair, 616-331-6250, Fax: 616-331-6515, E-mail: meyerlca@gvsu.edu. *Application contact:* Dr. Shawn Bultsma, Graduate Program Director, 616-331-6648, Fax: 616-331-6422, E-mail: bultsmas@gvsu.edu.

Grand Valley State University, College of Liberal Arts and Sciences, Program in School Psychology, Allendale, MI 49401-9403. Offers MS, Psy S. *Program availability:* Part-time. *Faculty:* 6 full-time (all women). *Students:* 24 full-time (20 women), 14 part-time (12 women); includes 2 minority (1 Black or African American, non-Hispanic/Latino; 1 Two or more races, non-Hispanic/Latino), 1 international. Average age 25. 35 applicants, 49% accepted, 12 enrolled. In 2019, 12 master's, 12 other advanced degrees awarded. *Degree requirements:* For master's, project and internship. *Entrance requirements:* For master's, GRE, bachelor's degree in psychology, special education, or related field with minimum GPA of 3.0; completion of prerequisite courses in child development, statistics, and research methods; professional vitae or resume; 3 letters of recommendation; personal statement. Additional exam requirements/recommendations for international students: required—TOEFL (minimum iBT score of 80), IELTS (6.5), or Michigan English Language Assessment Battery (77). *Application deadline:* For fall admission, 12/15 for domestic and international students. Applications are processed on a rolling basis. Application fee: $30. Electronic applications accepted. *Expenses:* $697 per credit hour, 66 credit hours. *Financial support:* In 2019–20, 12 students received support, including 3 fellowships, 2 research assistantships with full and partial tuition reimbursements available (averaging $8,000 per year); unspecified assistantships also available. *Unit head:* Dr. Michael Wolfe, Director, 616-331-2989, Fax: 616-331-2480, E-mail: wolfem@gvsu.edu. *Application contact:* Dr. Amy Campbell, Graduate Program Director, 616-331-2409, Fax: 616-331-2480, E-mail: campbeam@gvsu.edu.
Website: http://www.gvsu.edu/grad/schoolpsy/

Hofstra University, College of Liberal Arts and Sciences, Programs in Psychology, Hempstead, NY 11549. Offers applied organizational psychology (PhD); clinical psychology (PhD); industrial/organizational psychology (MA); school-community psychology (Psy D). *Accreditation:* APA. *Program availability:* Part-time, evening/weekend. *Students:* 193 full-time (138 women), 22 part-time (10 women); includes 42 minority (6 Black or African American, non-Hispanic/Latino; 1 American Indian or Alaska Native, non-Hispanic/Latino; 9 Asian, non-Hispanic/Latino; 23 Hispanic/Latino; 3 Two or more races, non-Hispanic/Latino), 21 international. Average age 26. 338 applicants, 36% accepted, 61 enrolled. In 2019, 60 master's, 33 doctorates awarded. Terminal master's awarded for partial completion of doctoral program. *Degree requirements:* For master's, comprehensive exam, thesis optional, internship, minimum GPA of 3.0; for doctorate, comprehensive exam, thesis/dissertation, 1st year qualifying examination, 2nd year research project, successful practicum/externship placements, written presentation and successful oral defense of dissertation, completion of full-time internship. *Entrance requirements:* For master's, GRE General Test, minimum GPA of 3.0, essay, interview; for doctorate, GRE General Test, GRE Subject Test (psychology), 3 letters of recommendation, interview, essay, curriculum vitae. Additional exam requirements/recommendations for international students: required—TOEFL (minimum score 550 paper-based; 80 iBT); recommended—IELTS (minimum score 6.5). *Application deadline:* For fall admission, 12/31 for domestic and international students. Application fee: $75. Electronic applications accepted. *Expenses: Tuition:* Full-time $25,164; part-time $1398 per credit. *Required fees:* $580; $165 per semester. Tuition and fees vary according to course load, degree level and program. *Financial support:* In 2019–20, 152 students received support, including 125 fellowships with full and partial tuition reimbursements available (averaging $8,256 per year), 4 research assistantships with full and partial tuition reimbursements available (averaging $5,531 per year); career-related internships or fieldwork, Federal Work-Study, institutionally sponsored loans, scholarships/grants, traineeships, tuition waivers (full and partial), unspecified assistantships, and scholarships and endowed scholarships also available. Support available to part-time students. Financial award applicants required to submit FAFSA. *Unit head:* Dr. Craig Johnson, Chairperson, 516-463-5636, E-mail: craig.a.johnson@hofstra.edu. *Application contact:* Sunil Samuel, Assistant Vice President of Admissions, 516-463-4723, Fax: 516-463-4664, E-mail: graduateadmission@hofstra.edu.
Website: http://www.hofstra.edu/hclas

Hood College, Graduate School, Program in Counseling, Frederick, MD 21701-8575. Offers clinical mental health counseling (MS); school counseling (MS). *Program availability:* Part-time, evening/weekend. *Degree requirements:* For master's, 700 hour practicum and internship (R). *Entrance requirements:* For master's, minimum GPA of 3.0 (or if below 3.0 applicant may submit GRE scores for possible consideration), official transcripts, personal statement, essay, resume, two letters of recommendation. Additional exam requirements/recommendations for international students: required—TOEFL (minimum score 575 paper-based; 89 iBT), IELTS (minimum score 6.5). Electronic applications accepted. *Expenses:* Contact institution.

Howard University, School of Education, Department of Human Development and Psychoeducational Studies, Program in School Psychology, Washington, DC 20059-0002. Offers M Ed, PhD. *Accreditation:* NCATE. *Degree requirements:* For doctorate, one foreign language, comprehensive exam, thesis/dissertation, expository writing exam, internship. *Entrance requirements:* For doctorate, GRE General Test, minimum GPA of 3.4. Additional exam requirements/recommendations for international students: required—TOEFL (minimum score 550 paper-based; 79 iBT). Electronic applications accepted.

Humboldt State University, Academic Programs, College of Professional Studies, Department of Psychology, Arcata, CA 95521-8299. Offers psychology (MA), including biological psychology, counseling, developmental psychopathology, school psychology, social and environmental psychology. *Program availability:* Part-time. *Faculty:* 14 full-time (9 women), 13 part-time/adjunct (8 women). *Students:* 76 full-time (54 women), 11 part-time (4 women); includes 37 minority (1 Black or African American, non-Hispanic/Latino; 3 American Indian or Alaska Native, non-Hispanic/Latino; 4 Asian, non-Hispanic/Latino; 22 Hispanic/Latino; 7 Two or more races, non-Hispanic/Latino), 1 international. Average age 28. 89 applicants, 42% accepted, 31 enrolled. In 2019, 38 master's awarded. *Degree requirements:* For master's, thesis. *Entrance requirements:* For master's, appropriate bachelor's degree, minimum GPA of 2.5. Additional exam requirements/recommendations for international students: required—TOEFL (minimum score 500 paper-based). *Application deadline:* For fall admission, 2/1 for domestic students, 2/15 for international students. Applications are processed on a rolling basis. Application fee: $55. *Expenses:* Tuition, state resident: full-time $7176; part-time $4164 per term. *Required fees:* $2120; $1672 per term. *Financial support:* Career-related internships or fieldwork available. Financial award application deadline: 3/1; financial award applicants required to submit FAFSA. *Unit head:* Dr. Carrie Aigner, Graduate Program Coordinator, 707-826-3757, E-mail: carrie.aigner@humboldt.edu. *Application contact:* Dr. Carrie Aigner, Graduate Program Coordinator, 707-826-3757, E-mail: carrie.aigner@humboldt.edu.
Website: http://www2.humboldt.edu/psychology/programs-child/graduate-programs-psychology

Husson University, Graduate Programs in Counseling and Human Relations, Bangor, ME 04401-2999. Offers clinical mental health counseling (MS); human relations (MS); school counseling (MS). *Accreditation:* ACA. *Program availability:* Part-time, evening/weekend. *Degree requirements:* For master's, comprehensive exam (for some programs), thesis optional. *Entrance requirements:* For master's, BS with minimum GPA of 3.0, letters of recommendation, interview. Additional exam requirements/recommendations for international students: required—TOEFL (minimum score 550 paper-based; 80 iBT), IELTS (minimum score 6.5). Electronic applications accepted. *Expenses:* Contact institution.

Idaho State University, Graduate School, College of Education, Department of School Psychology and Educational Leadership, Pocatello, ID 83209-8059. Offers educational administration (M Ed, 6th Year Certificate, Ed S); educational leadership (Ed D), including higher education administration, K-12 school administration; school psychology (M Ed, Ed S). *Program availability:* Part-time. *Degree requirements:* For master's, comprehensive exam, thesis optional, internship, oral exam or deferred thesis; for doctorate, comprehensive exam, thesis/dissertation, written exam; for other advanced degree, comprehensive exam, thesis (for some programs), written and oral exam. *Entrance requirements:* For master's, MAT, bachelor's degree, minimum GPA of 3.0, 1 year of training experience; for doctorate, GRE General Test or MAT, minimum GPA of 3.0 (undergraduate), 3.5 (graduate); departmental interview; for other advanced degree, GRE General Test, minimum GPA of 3.0, master's degree. Additional exam requirements/recommendations for international students: required—TOEFL (minimum score 550 paper-based; 80 iBT). Electronic applications accepted.

Idaho State University, Graduate School, College of Health Professions, Department of Counseling, Pocatello, ID 83209-8120. Offers counseling (M Coun, Ed S), including marriage and family counseling (M Coun), mental health counseling (M Coun), school counseling (M Coun), student affairs and college counseling (M Coun); counselor education and counseling (PhD). *Accreditation:* ACA (one or more programs are accredited). *Program availability:* Part-time. *Degree requirements:* For master's, comprehensive exam, thesis, 4 semesters resident graduate study, practicum/internship; for doctorate, comprehensive exam, thesis/dissertation, 3 semesters internship, 4 consecutive semesters doctoral-level study on campus; for Ed S, comprehensive exam, thesis, case studies, oral exam. *Entrance requirements:* For master's, GRE General Test, MAT, minimum GPA of 3.0, bachelors degree, interview, 3 letters of recommendation; for doctorate, GRE General Test, MAT, minimum graduate GPA of 3.0, resume, interview, counseling license, master's degree; for Ed S, GRE General Test, minimum graduate GPA of 3.0, master's degree in counseling, 3 letters of recommendation, 2 years work experience. Additional exam requirements/recommendations for international students: required—TOEFL (minimum score 600 paper-based; 80 iBT). Electronic applications accepted.

Illinois State University, Graduate School, College of Arts and Sciences, Department of Psychology, Normal, IL 61790. Offers psychology (MA, MS), including clinical-counseling psychology, cognitive and behavioral sciences, developmental psychology, industrial/organizational-social psychology; school psychology (PhD, SSP). *Accreditation:* APA. *Faculty:* 32 full-time (14 women), 6 part-time/adjunct (5 women). *Students:* 92 full-time (77 women), 18 part-time (14 women). Average age 25. 154 applicants, 32% accepted, 37 enrolled. In 2019, 27 master's, 3 doctorates, 5 other advanced degrees awarded. *Degree requirements:* For master's, thesis or alternative; for doctorate, variable foreign language requirement, thesis/dissertation, 2 terms of residency, internship, practicum. *Entrance requirements:* For master's, GRE General Test, GRE Subject Test, minimum GPA of 3.0 in last 60 hours of course work; for doctorate, GRE General Test. *Application deadline:* Applications are processed on a rolling basis. Application fee: $50. *Expenses: Tuition, area resident:* Full-time $7956; part-time $9767 per year. Tuition, nonresident: full-time $9233; part-time $17,592 per year. *Required fees:* $1797. *Financial support:* In 2019–20, 26 research assistantships, 34 teaching assistantships were awarded; tuition waivers (full) and unspecified assistantships also available. Financial award application deadline: 4/1. *Unit head:* Dr. J Scott Jordan, Department Chair, 309-438-2484, E-mail: jsjorda@illinoisState.edu. *Application contact:* Dr. Karen Mark, Graduate Coordinator, 309-438-8130, E-mail: kimark@ilstu.edu.
Website: http://psychology.illinoisstate.edu/

Immaculata University, College of Graduate Studies, Department of Psychology, Immaculata, PA 19345. Offers clinical mental health counseling (MA); clinical psychology (Psy D); forensic psychology (Graduate Certificate); integrative psychotherapy (Graduate Certificate); neuropsychology (Graduate Certificate); psychodynamic psychotherapy (Graduate Certificate); psychological testing (Graduate Certificate); school counseling (MA, Graduate Certificate); school psychology (MA). *Accreditation:* APA. *Program availability:* Part-time, evening/weekend. Terminal master's awarded for partial completion of doctoral program. *Degree requirements:* For master's, comprehensive exam, thesis optional; for doctorate, comprehensive exam, thesis/dissertation. *Entrance requirements:* For master's, GRE General Test or MAT, minimum GPA of 3.0; for doctorate, GRE General Test or MAT, minimum GPA of 3.5. Additional exam requirements/recommendations for international students: required—TOEFL, IELTS. Electronic applications accepted.

Indiana State University, College of Graduate and Professional Studies, Bayh College of Education, Department of Communication Disorders and Counseling, School, and Educational Psychology, Terre Haute, IN 47809. Offers clinical mental health counseling (MS); communication disorders (MS); school counseling (M Ed); school psychology (PhD, Ed S); MA/MS. *Accreditation:* ACA; ASHA; NCATE. *Program availability:* Part-time, evening/weekend. *Degree requirements:* For master's, thesis optional; for doctorate, thesis/dissertation, research tools proficiency tests. *Entrance requirements:* For master's, GRE General Test or MAT, minimum undergraduate GPA of 2.75; for doctorate, GRE General Test, master's degree, minimum undergraduate GPA of 3.5. Electronic applications accepted.

Indiana University Bloomington, School of Education, Department of Counseling and Educational Psychology, Bloomington, IN 47405-1006. Offers counseling (MS, PhD, Ed S); counselor education (MS, Ed S); educational psychology (MS, PhD); inquiry methodology (PhD); learning and developmental sciences (MS, PhD); school psychology (PhD, Ed S). *Accreditation:* ACA (one or more programs are accredited); APA (one or more programs are accredited); NCATE. Terminal master's awarded for partial completion of doctoral program. *Degree requirements:* For master's, thesis optional; for doctorate, thesis/dissertation; for Ed S, comprehensive exam or project. *Entrance requirements:* For master's, doctorate, and Ed S, GRE General Test. Additional exam requirements/recommendations for international students: required—TOEFL. Electronic applications accepted.

Indiana University of Pennsylvania, School of Graduate Studies and Research, College of Education and Communications, Department of Educational and School Psychology, Program in School Psychology, Indiana, PA 15705. Offers D Ed, Certificate. *Accreditation:* NCATE. *Program availability:* Part-time, evening/weekend. *Faculty:* 6 full-time (2 women). *Students:* 23 full-time (16 women), 31 part-time (24 women); includes 7 minority (2 Black or African American, non-Hispanic/Latino; 1 Asian, non-Hispanic/Latino; 2 Hispanic/Latino; 2 Two or more races, non-Hispanic/Latino). Average age 33. 27 applicants, 81% accepted, 14 enrolled. In 2019, 3 doctorates, 8 Certificates awarded. *Degree requirements:* For doctorate, comprehensive exam, thesis/dissertation. *Entrance requirements:* For doctorate, GRE General Test, PRAXIS II School Psychology Exam, 3 letters of recommendation, official transcription, goal statement. Additional exam requirements/recommendations for international students: required—TOEFL (minimum score 540 paper-based; 76 iBT), recommended—IELTS (minimum score 6). *Application deadline:* For fall admission, 1/15 priority date for domestic students. Applications are processed on a rolling basis. Application fee: $50. Electronic applications accepted. *Expenses: Tuition, area resident:* Full-time $9288; part-time $516 per credit. Tuition, nonresident: full-time $13,932; part-time $774 per credit. *Required fees:* $4454. One-time fee: $115 full-time. Tuition and fees vary according to course load and program. *Financial support:* In 2019–20, 4 fellowships with tuition reimbursements (averaging $675 per year), 10 research assistantships with tuition reimbursements (averaging $5,215 per year), 3 teaching assistantships with partial tuition reimbursements (averaging $25,035 per year) were awarded; career-related internships or fieldwork, Federal Work-Study, scholarships/grants, and unspecified assistantships also available. Support available to part-time students. Financial award application deadline: 4/15; financial award applicants required to submit FAFSA. *Unit head:* Dr. Courtney L. McLaughlin, Graduate Coordinator, 724-357-2299, E-mail: cmc@iup.edu. *Application contact:* Amber Dworek, Director of Graduate Admissions, 724-357-2222, E-mail: a.m.dworek@iup.edu. Website: http://www.iup.edu/schoolpsychology/grad/school-psychology-ded/default.aspx

Indiana University South Bend, School of Education, South Bend, IN 46615. Offers addiction counseling (MS Ed); alcohol and drug counseling (Graduate Certificate); clinical mental health counseling (MS Ed); educational leadership (MS Ed); elementary education (MS Ed); marriage, couple, and family counseling (MS Ed); school counseling (MS Ed); secondary education (MS Ed); special education (MAT, MS Ed), including intense intervention (MS Ed), mild intervention (MS Ed). *Accreditation:* NCATE. *Program availability:* Part-time, evening/weekend. *Degree requirements:* For master's, thesis or alternative, exit project. *Entrance requirements:* For master's, letters of recommendation, GRE or minimum GPA of 3.0. Additional exam requirements/recommendations for international students: required—TOEFL. Electronic applications accepted. *Expenses:* Contact institution.

Inter American University of Puerto Rico, Metropolitan Campus, Graduate Programs, Program in Psychology, San Juan, PR 00919-1293. Offers counseling psychology (MA, PhD); industrial/organizational psychology (MA, PhD); labor relations (MA); school psychology (MA, PhD). *Degree requirements:* For master's, comprehensive exam. *Entrance requirements:* For master's, GRE or EXADEP, interview. Electronic applications accepted.

Inter American University of Puerto Rico, San Germán Campus, Graduate Studies Center, Program in Psychology, San Germán, PR 00683-5008. Offers counseling psychology (MA, PhD); school psychology (MA, PhD). *Program availability:* Part-time, evening/weekend. *Degree requirements:* For master's, comprehensive exam, thesis; for doctorate, comprehensive exam, thesis/dissertation. *Entrance requirements:* For master's, GRE General Test or EXADEP, minimum GPA of 3.0; for doctorate, GRE, EXADEP or MAT, minimum GPA of 3.0.

Iona College, School of Arts and Science, Department of Psychology, New Rochelle, NY 10801-1890. Offers general-experimental psychology (MA); human resources (Certificate); industrial-organizational psychology (MA); mental health counseling (MA); organizational behavior (Certificate); psychology (MA); school psychology (MA). *Program availability:* Part-time. *Faculty:* 8 full-time (4 women), 12 part-time/adjunct (8 women). *Students:* 71 full-time (64 women), 41 part-time (34 women); includes 51 minority (12 Black or African American, non-Hispanic/Latino; 5 Asian, non-Hispanic/Latino; 28 Hispanic/Latino; 1 Native Hawaiian or other Pacific Islander, non-Hispanic/Latino; 5 Two or more races, non-Hispanic/Latino), 3 international. Average age 25. 104 applicants, 85% accepted, 34 enrolled. In 2019, 29 master's, 15 other advanced degrees awarded. *Degree requirements:* For master's, thesis (for some programs), literature review (for some programs). *Entrance requirements:* For master's, BA in psychology including 3 credits each in psychology statistics and experimental research methods, or 9 credits in psychology including 3 credits each in psychology statistics, psychology research methods and upper-level coursework. Additional exam

requirements/recommendations for international students: required—TOEFL (minimum score 550 paper-based), IELTS (minimum score 6.5). *Application deadline:* For fall admission, 8/15 for domestic students, 5/1 for international students; for spring admission, 1/15 for domestic students, 9/1 for international students. Applications are processed on a rolling basis. Electronic applications accepted. *Financial support:* In 2019–20, 51 students received support, including 4 research assistantships with partial tuition reimbursements available (averaging $10,143 per year); scholarships/grants, tuition waivers (partial), and unspecified assistantships also available. Support available to part-time students. Financial award application deadline: 4/15; financial award applicants required to submit FAFSA. *Unit head:* Colleen Jacobsen, PhD, Chair, 914-637-2770, E-mail: cjacobsen@iona.edu. *Application contact:* Shantell Smith, Associate Director of Graduate Admissions, Arts and Science, 914-633-2440, Fax: 914-633-2277, E-mail: ssmith@iona.edu. Website: http://www.iona.edu/Academics/School-of-Arts-Science/Departments/Psychology/Graduate-Programs.aspx

Jackson State University, Graduate School, College of Education and Human Development, Department of Counseling, Rehabilitation and Psychometric Services, Jackson, MS 39217. Offers clinical mental health (MS); rehabilitation counseling (MS); school counseling (MS Ed). *Accreditation:* ACA; CORE (one or more programs are accredited); NCATE. *Program availability:* Part-time, evening/weekend, 100% online, blended/hybrid learning. *Degree requirements:* For master's, comprehensive exam, thesis. *Entrance requirements:* For master's, GRE General Test. Additional exam requirements/recommendations for international students: required—TOEFL (minimum score 520 paper-based; 67 iBT). Electronic applications accepted. *Expenses:* Contact institution.

James Madison University, The Graduate School, College of Health and Behavioral Studies, Program in Combined-Integrated Clinical and School Psychology, Harrisonburg, VA 22807. Offers Psy D. *Program availability:* Part-time, evening/weekend. *Students:* 23 full-time (20 women), 3 part-time (all women); includes 6 minority (2 Black or African American, non-Hispanic/Latino; 1 Asian, non-Hispanic/Latino; 2 Hispanic/Latino; 1 Two or more races, non-Hispanic/Latino), 3 international. Average age 30. In 2019, 4 doctorates awarded. Application fee: $60. Electronic applications accepted. *Financial support:* In 2019–20, 18 students received support. Fellowships, teaching assistantships, Federal Work-Study, unspecified assistantships, and 17 doctoral assistantships (stipend varies) available. Financial award application deadline: 3/1; financial award applicants required to submit FAFSA. *Unit head:* Dr. Gregg R. Henriques, Graduate Program Director, 540-568-7857, E-mail: henrigg@jmu.edu. *Application contact:* Lynette D. Michael, Director of Graduate Admissions, 540-568-6131 Ext. 6395, Fax: 540-568-7860, E-mail: michaeld@jmu.edu. Website: http://www.psyc.jmu.edu/cipsyd/

James Madison University, The Graduate School, College of Health and Behavioral Studies, Program in School Psychology, Harrisonburg, VA 22807. Offers MA, Ed S. *Accreditation:* APA (one or more programs are accredited); NCATE (one or more programs are accredited). *Program availability:* Part-time, evening/weekend. *Students:* 10 full-time (8 women); includes 5 minority (2 Black or African American, non-Hispanic/Latino; 2 Hispanic/Latino; 1 Two or more races, non-Hispanic/Latino). Average age 30. In 2019, 9 master's awarded. Application fee: $60. Electronic applications accepted. *Financial support:* In 2019–20, 10 students received support, including teaching assistantships with full tuition reimbursements available (averaging $9,284 per year); fellowships, career-related internships or fieldwork, Federal Work-Study, and assistantships (averaging $7911) also available. Financial award application deadline: 3/1; financial award applicants required to submit FAFSA. *Unit head:* Dr. Tammy D. Gilligan, Graduate Program Director, 540-568-6564, E-mail: gilligtd@jmu.edu. *Application contact:* Lynette D. Michael, Director of Graduate Admissions, 540-568-6131 Ext. 6395, Fax: 540-568-7860, E-mail: michaeld@jmu.edu. Website: http://psyc.jmu.edu/school/

Kean University, Nathan Weiss Graduate College, Doctorate Program in Combined School and Clinical Psychology, Union, NJ 07083. Offers Psy D. *Program availability:* Part-time. *Faculty:* 7 full-time (4 women). *Students:* 43 full-time (30 women), 12 part-time (8 women); includes 13 minority (4 Black or African American, non-Hispanic/Latino; 4 Asian, non-Hispanic/Latino; 5 Hispanic/Latino), 1 international. Average age 28. 117 applicants, 23% accepted, 12 enrolled. In 2019, 7 doctorates awarded. *Degree requirements:* For doctorate, comprehensive exam, thesis/dissertation, externship. *Entrance requirements:* For doctorate, GRE General Test, GRE Subject Test in psychology (taken within last 5 years), minimum undergraduate GPA of 3.3, graduate 3.5; 3 letters of recommendation; personal interview; prerequisite coursework in theories of personality, abnormal psychology, tests and measurements, statistics, and experimental psychology; personal statement. Additional exam requirements/recommendations for international students: required—TOEFL (minimum score 550 paper-based; 79 iBT), IELTS (minimum score 6.5). *Application deadline:* For fall admission, 1/1 for domestic and international students. Applications are processed on a rolling basis. Application fee: $75. Electronic applications accepted. *Expenses:* Contact institution. *Financial support:* Scholarships/grants and unspecified assistantships available. Financial award applicants required to submit FAFSA. *Unit head:* Dr. Jennifer Block-Lerner, Program Coordinator, 908-737-5864, E-mail: jlerner@kean.edu. *Application contact:* Pedro Lopes, Admissions Counselor, 908-737-7100, E-mail: gradadmissions@kean.edu. Website: http://grad.kean.edu/doctoral-programs/combined-school-and-clinical-psychology

Kean University, Nathan Weiss Graduate College, Program in School Psychology, Union, NJ 07083. Offers Diploma. *Accreditation:* APA. *Program availability:* Part-time. *Faculty:* 7 full-time (4 women). *Students:* 23 full-time (19 women), 15 part-time (14 women); includes 12 minority (1 Black or African American, non-Hispanic/Latino; 1 Asian, non-Hispanic/Latino; 10 Hispanic/Latino). Average age 24. 18 applicants, 78% accepted, 11 enrolled. In 2019, 10 Diplomas awarded. *Degree requirements:* For Diploma, comprehensive exam, practicum, externship. *Entrance requirements:* For degree, GRE General Test, minimum GPA of 3.0, interview, 3 letters of recommendation, prerequisites in psychology, official transcripts from all institutions attended, resume. Additional exam requirements/recommendations for international students: required—TOEFL (minimum score 550 paper-based; 79 iBT), IELTS. *Application deadline:* For fall admission, 2/5 for domestic and international students. Application fee: $75. Electronic applications accepted. *Expenses:* Tuition, state resident: full-time $15,326; part-time $748 per credit. Tuition, nonresident: full-time $20,288; part-time $902 per credit. *Required fees:* $2149.50; $91.25 per credit. Tuition and fees vary according to course level, course load, degree level and program. *Financial support:* Scholarships/grants and unspecified assistantships available. Financial award applicants required to submit FAFSA. *Unit head:* Dr. Adrienne Garro, Program Coordinator, 908-737-5863, E-mail: agarro@kean.edu. *Application contact:* Pedro Lopes, Admissions Counselor, 908-737-7100, E-mail: gradadmissions@kean.edu. Website: http://grad.kean.edu/professional-diploma-programs/school-psychology

Kent State University, College of Education, Health and Human Services, School of Lifespan Development and Educational Sciences, Program in School Psychology, Kent,

OH 44242-0001. Offers M Ed, PhD, Ed S. *Accreditation:* APA; NCATE. *Degree requirements:* For doctorate, comprehensive exam, thesis/dissertation. *Entrance requirements:* For master's, doctorate, and Ed S, GRE General Test, 2 letters of reference, goals statement, moral character form, sample of written work, resume, interview. Additional exam requirements/recommendations for international students: required—TOEFL (minimum score 550 paper-based; 80 iBT). Electronic applications accepted.

La Sierra University, School of Education, Department of School Psychology and Counseling, Riverside, CA 92505. Offers counseling (MA); educational psychology (Ed S); school psychology (Ed S). *Program availability:* Part-time, evening/weekend. *Degree requirements:* For master's, thesis optional; for Ed S, practicum (educational psychology). *Entrance requirements:* For master's, California Basic Educational Skills Test, NTE, minimum GPA of 3.0; for Ed S, minimum GPA of 3.3.

Lehigh University, College of Education, Program in School Psychology, Bethlehem, PA 18015. Offers PhD, Ed S. *Accreditation:* APA (one or more programs are accredited). *Faculty:* 6 full-time (4 women), 1 part-time/adjunct (0 women). *Students:* 34 full-time (33 women), 8 part-time (7 women); includes 9 minority (4 Black or African American, non-Hispanic/Latino; 3 Asian, non-Hispanic/Latino; 2 Hispanic/Latino), 2 international. Average age 26. 52 applicants, 35% accepted, 8 enrolled. In 2019, 4 doctorates, 4 other advanced degrees awarded. *Degree requirements:* For doctorate, comprehensive exam, thesis/dissertation, internship, research qualifying exam; for Ed S, comprehensive exam, internship. *Entrance requirements:* For doctorate and Ed S, GRE General Test, minimum GPA of 3.0, 2 letters of recommendation (at least one academic), transcripts, vitae. Additional exam requirements/recommendations for international students: required—TOEFL (minimum score 93 iBT); recommended—IELTS. *Application deadline:* For fall admission, 12/1 for domestic and international students. Application fee: $65. Electronic applications accepted. Application fee is waived when completed online. *Expenses:* $565 per credit; $125 internship fee. *Financial support:* In 2019–20, 36 students received support, including 2 fellowships with full tuition reimbursements available (averaging $23,000 per year), 21 research assistantships with full and partial tuition reimbursements available (averaging $12,015 per year); scholarships/grants and unspecified assistantships also available. Financial award application deadline: 1/15; financial award applicants required to submit FAFSA. *Unit head:* Bridget V Devers, Program Director/Associate Professor, 610-758-3210, Fax: 610-758-6223, E-mail: bdever@lehigh.edu. *Application contact:* Lori J Anderson, Coordinator, 610-758-3250, Fax: 610-758-6223, E-mail: lja320@lehigh.edu.
Website: https://ed.lehigh.edu/academics/programs/school-psychology

Lesley University, Graduate School of Arts and Social Sciences, Cambridge, MA 02138-2790. Offers clinical mental health counseling (MA), including holistic counseling, school and community counseling, trauma studies; counseling psychology (MA, CAGS), including professional counseling (MA), school counseling (MA); creative writing (MFA); expressive therapies (MA, PhD, CAGS), including art (MA), clinical mental health counseling (MA), dance (MA), expressive therapies (MA), music (MA); independent studies (CAGS); independent study (MA); intercultural relations (MA, CAGS); interdisciplinary studies (MA), including individualized studies, integrative holistic health, mindfulness studies, peace and conflict transformation, trauma sensitive assessment, intervention, and consultation, women's studies; urban environmental leadership (MA). *Program availability:* Part-time, online learning. *Degree requirements:* For master's, internship, practicum, thesis (for expressive therapies); for doctorate, thesis/dissertation, arts apprenticeship, field placement; for CAGS, thesis, internship (for counseling psychology, expressive therapies). *Entrance requirements:* For master's, MAT (counseling psychology), interview, writing samples, art portfolio; for doctorate, GRE or MAT, interview, master's degree; for CAGS, interview, master's degree. Additional exam requirements/recommendations for international students: required—TOEFL (minimum score 550 paper-based; 80 iBT). Electronic applications accepted.

Lewis & Clark College, Graduate School of Education and Counseling, Department of Counseling Psychology, Program in School Psychology, Portland, OR 97219-7899. Offers Ed S. *Program availability:* Part-time, evening/weekend. *Entrance requirements:* Additional exam requirements/recommendations for international students: required—TOEFL (minimum score 575 paper-based). Electronic applications accepted.

Lewis & Clark College, Graduate School of Education and Counseling, Department of Educational Leadership, Program in School Counseling, Portland, OR 97219-7899. Offers M Ed. *Program availability:* Part-time, evening/weekend. *Entrance requirements:* For master's, minimum undergraduate GPA of 2.75. Additional exam requirements/recommendations for international students: required—TOEFL (minimum score 575 paper-based). Electronic applications accepted.

Liberty University, School of Behavioral Sciences, Lynchburg, VA 24515. Offers applied psychology (MA), including developmental psychology (MA, MS), industrial/organizational psychology (MA, MS); clinical mental health counseling (MA); community care and counseling (Ed D), including marriage and family counseling, pastoral care and counseling, traumatology; counselor education and supervision (PhD); human services counseling (MA), including addictions and recovery, business, child and family law, Christian ministries, criminal justice, crisis response and trauma, executive leadership, health and wellness, life coaching, marriage and family, military resilience; marriage and family counseling (MA); marriage and family therapy (MA); military resilience (Certificate); pastoral counseling (MA), including addictions and recovery, community chaplaincy, crisis response and trauma, discipleship and church ministry, leadership, life coaching, marriage and family, marriage and family studies, military resilience, parenting and child/adolescent, pastoral counseling, theology; professional counseling (MA); psychology (MS), including developmental psychology (MA, MS), industrial/organizational psychology (MA, MS); school counseling (M Ed). *Program availability:* Part-time, online learning. *Students:* 3,786 full-time (3,065 women), 5,193 part-time (4,081 women); includes 2,733 minority (1,967 Black or African American, non-Hispanic/Latino; 48 American Indian or Alaska Native, non-Hispanic/Latino; 103 Asian, non-Hispanic/Latino; 349 Hispanic/Latino; 19 Native Hawaiian or other Pacific Islander, non-Hispanic/Latino; 247 Two or more races, non-Hispanic/Latino), 133 international. Average age 38. 13,324 applicants, 28% accepted, 2,163 enrolled. In 2019, 2,322 master's, 19 doctorates, 112 other advanced degrees awarded. *Entrance requirements:* For master's, Official bachelor's degree transcripts with a 2.0 GPA or higher. *Application deadline:* Applications are processed on a rolling basis. Application fee: $50. Electronic applications accepted. *Expenses: Tuition:* Full-time $545; part-time $410 per credit hour. One-time fee: $50. *Financial support:* In 2019–20, 1,003 students received support. Teaching assistantships and Federal Work-Study available. Financial award applicants required to submit FAFSA. *Unit head:* Dr. Kenyon Knapp, Dean, School of Behavioral Services, E-mail: kcknapp@liberty.edu. *Application contact:* Jay Bridge, Director of Admissions, 800-424-9595, Fax: 800-628-7977, E-mail: gradadmissions@liberty.edu.
Website: https://www.liberty.edu/behavioral-sciences/

Lindenwood University, Graduate Programs, School of Education, St. Charles, MO 63301-1695. Offers behavioral analysis (MA); education (MA), including autism spectrum disorders, character education, early intervention in autism and sensory impairment, gifted, technology; educational administration (MA, Ed D, Ed S); English to speakers of other languages (MA); instructional leadership (Ed D, Ed S); library media (MA); professional counseling (MA); school administration (MA, Ed S); school counseling (MA); teaching (MA). *Program availability:* Part-time, evening/weekend, 100% online, blended/hybrid learning. *Faculty:* 39 full-time (28 women), 133 part-time/adjunct (83 women). *Students:* 391 full-time (287 women), 1,149 part-time (889 women); includes 358 minority (284 Black or African American, non-Hispanic/Latino; 8 American Indian or Alaska Native, non-Hispanic/Latino; 6 Asian, non-Hispanic/Latino; 32 Hispanic/Latino; 28 Two or more races, non-Hispanic/Latino), 11 international. Average age 35. 465 applicants, 71% accepted, 229 enrolled. In 2019, 432 master's, 60 doctorates, 77 other advanced degrees awarded. *Degree requirements:* For master's, thesis (for some programs), minimum GPA of 3.0; for doctorate, thesis/dissertation, minimum GPA of 3.0; for Ed S, comprehensive exam, project, minimum GPA of 3.0. *Entrance requirements:* For master's, interview, minimum undergraduate cumulative GPA of 3.0, writing sample, letter of recommendation; for doctorate, minimum graduate GPA of 3.4, resume, interview, writing sample, 4 letters of recommendation; for Ed S, master's degree in education, relevant work experience. Additional exam requirements/recommendations for international students: required—TOEFL (minimum score 553 paper-based; 81 iBT); recommended—IELTS (minimum score 6.5). *Application deadline:* For fall admission, 8/9 priority date for domestic students, 6/1 priority date for international students; for spring admission, 12/20 priority date for domestic students, 11/1 priority date for international students; for summer admission, 5/15 priority date for domestic students, 3/27 priority date for international students. Applications are processed on a rolling basis. Application fee: $0 ($100 for international students). Electronic applications accepted. *Expenses: Tuition:* Full-time $8910; part-time $495 per credit. Tuition and fees vary according to course load, degree level and program. *Financial support:* In 2019–20, 198 students received support. Career-related internships or fieldwork, Federal Work-Study, institutionally sponsored loans, scholarships/grants, tuition waivers (partial), and unspecified assistantships available. Financial award application deadline: 6/30; financial award applicants required to submit FAFSA. *Unit head:* Dr. Anthony Scheffler, Dean, School of Education, 636-949-4618, Fax: 636-949-4197, E-mail: ascheffler@lindenwood.edu. *Application contact:* Kara Schilli, Assistant Vice President, University Admissions, 636-949-4349, Fax: 636-949-4109, E-mail: adultadmissions@lindenwood.edu.
Website: https://www.lindenwood.edu/academics/academic-schools/school-of-education/

Lipscomb University, College of Education, Nashville, TN 37204-3951. Offers applied behavior analysis (MS, Certificate); coaching for learning (M Ed, Certificate, Ed S); educational leadership (M Ed, Ed S); English language learning (M Ed, Ed S); instructional coaching (M Ed, Certificate, Ed S); instructional practice (M Ed); learning organizations and strategic change (Ed D); literacy coaching (Certificate, Ed S); reading specialty (M Ed, Ed S); school counseling (M Ed, Ed S); special education (M Ed); teaching, learning, and leading (M Ed); technology integration (M Ed, Ed S); technology integration specialist (Certificate). *Accreditation:* NCATE. *Program availability:* Part-time, evening/weekend, 100% online. *Degree requirements:* For master's, comprehensive exam, portfolio, research project and presentation; for doctorate, practical capstone project in experiential setting. *Entrance requirements:* For master's, MAT (minimum score 31) or GRE General Test (minimum score 294), 2 reference letters, goals statement, writing sample, interview; for doctorate, MAT or GRE General Test, 3 reference letters, artifact of demonstrated academic excellence, written personal statements, interview. Additional exam requirements/recommendations for international students: required—TOEFL (minimum score 570 paper-based; 80 iBT). Electronic applications accepted. *Expenses:* Contact institution.

Long Island University - Hudson, Graduate School, Purchase, NY 10577. Offers autism (Advanced Certificate); bilingual education (Advanced Certificate); childhood education (MS Ed); crisis management (Advanced Certificate); early childhood education (MS Ed); educational leadership (MS Ed); health administration (MPA); literacy (MS Ed); marriage and family therapy (MS); mental health counseling (MS, Advanced Certificate), including credentialed alcoholism and substance abuse counselor (MS); middle childhood and adolescence education (MS Ed); pharmaceutics (MS), including cosmetic science, industrial pharmacy; public administration (MPA); school counseling (MS Ed, Advanced Certificate); school psychology (MS Ed); special education (MS Ed); TESOL (MS Ed); TESOL (all grades) (Advanced Certificate). *Program availability:* Part-time, evening/weekend. *Entrance requirements:* Additional exam requirements/recommendations for international students: required—TOEFL. Electronic applications accepted. *Expenses:* Contact institution.

Long Island University - Post, College of Education, Information and Technology, Brookville, NY 11548-1300. Offers adolescence education (MS); adolescence education 7-12 (MS); archives and records management (AC); art education (MS); childhood education (MS); childhood education/literacy B-6 (MS); childhood education/special education (MS); clinical mental health counseling (MS, AC); early childhood education (MS); early childhood education/childhood education (MS); educational leadership (AC); educational technology (MS); information studies (PhD); interdisciplinary educational studies (Ed D); middle childhood education (MS); music education (MS); public library administration (AC); school counselor (MS); special education (MS Ed); speech-language pathology (MA); students with disabilities, 7-12 generalist (AC); TESOL (MA). *Accreditation:* ASHA; TEAC. *Program availability:* Part-time, 100% online, blended/hybrid learning. Terminal master's awarded for partial completion of doctoral program. *Degree requirements:* For master's, variable foreign language requirement, comprehensive exam (for some programs), thesis optional; for doctorate, comprehensive exam, thesis/dissertation. *Entrance requirements:* For master's and AC, GRE (for some programs). Additional exam requirements/recommendations for international students: required—TOEFL (minimum score 550 paper-based, 75 iBT), IELTS, or PTE. Electronic applications accepted.

Louisiana State University and Agricultural & Mechanical College, Graduate School, College of Humanities and Social Sciences, Department of Psychology, Baton Rouge, LA 70803. Offers biological psychology (MA, PhD); clinical psychology (MA, PhD); cognitive psychology (MA, PhD); developmental psychology (MA, PhD); school psychology (MA, PhD). *Accreditation:* APA (one or more programs are accredited).

Louisiana State University in Shreveport, College of Business, Education, and Human Development, Program in School Psychology, Shreveport, LA 71115-2399. Offers SSP. *Entrance requirements:* For degree, GRE General Test, minimum GPA of 2.75, references, letter of intent, interview. Additional exam requirements/recommendations for international students: required—TOEFL (minimum score 550 paper-based; 61 iBT). Electronic applications accepted.

Loyola Marymount University, School of Education, Program in School Psychology, Los Angeles, CA 90045. Offers MA. *Students:* 20 full-time (all women); includes 14 minority (1 Black or African American, non-Hispanic/Latino; 1 Asian, non-Hispanic/Latino; 12 Hispanic/Latino), 1 international. Average age 29. In 2019, 20 master's awarded. *Entrance requirements:* For master's, GRE, graduate admissions application, undergrad major or minor in psychology, 3 letters of recommendation (1 from psychology-related professional), undergrad GPA of at least 3.0, technology requirement form, CBEST by end of fall semester, statement of intent, official transcript. Additional exam requirements/recommendations for international students: required—TOEFL, IELTS. *Application deadline:* For summer admission, 2/15 for domestic students. Application fee: $50. Electronic applications accepted. *Financial support:*

Federal Work-Study and scholarships/grants available. Financial award applicants required to submit FAFSA. *Unit head:* Dr. Brian P. Leung, Director, School Psychology, 310-338-7313, E-mail: bleung@lmu.edu. *Application contact:* Ammar Dalal, Assistant Vice Provost for Graduate Enrollment, 310-338-2721, Fax: 310-338-6086, E-mail: graduateadmission@lmu.edu.
Website: http://soe.lmu.edu/academics/schoolpsychology

Loyola University Chicago, School of Education, Program in School Psychology, Chicago, IL 60660. Offers Ed D, PhD, Ed S. *Program availability:* Blended/hybrid learning. *Faculty:* 6 full-time (5 women), 8 part-time/adjunct (4 women). *Students:* 72 full-time (66 women), 27 part-time (22 women); includes 37 minority (14 Black or African American, non-Hispanic/Latino; 5 Asian, non-Hispanic/Latino; 16 Hispanic/Latino; 2 Two or more races, non-Hispanic/Latino), 3 international. Average age 30. 161 applicants, 61% accepted, 50 enrolled. In 2019, 10 doctorates awarded. Terminal master's awarded for partial completion of doctoral program. *Degree requirements:* For doctorate, comprehensive exam, thesis/dissertation; for Ed S, comprehensive exam. *Entrance requirements:* For doctorate, GRE, interview, letters of recommendation, minimum GPA of 3.0. Additional exam requirements/recommendations for international students: required—TOEFL (minimum score 550 paper-based; 79 iBT). *Application deadline:* For fall admission, 12/1 for domestic and international students. Application fee: $50. Electronic applications accepted. Application fee is waived when completed online. *Expenses:* 17642. *Financial support:* In 2019–20, 31 fellowships with partial tuition reimbursements, 11 research assistantships with full tuition reimbursements (averaging $14,000 per year), 20 teaching assistantships (averaging $4,000 per year) were awarded; career-related internships or fieldwork, institutionally sponsored loans, scholarships/grants, health care benefits, and unspecified assistantships also available. Support available to part-time students. Financial award application deadline: 2/1; financial award applicants required to submit FAFSA. *Unit head:* Dr. Pamela Fenning, Program Chair, 312-915-6800, E-mail: pfennin@luc.edu. *Application contact:* Dr. Pamela Fenning, Program Chair, 312-915-6800, E-mail: pfennin@luc.edu.

Marist College, Graduate Programs, School of Social and Behavioral Sciences, Poughkeepsie, NY 12601-1387. Offers education (M Ed, MA); mental health counseling (MA); school psychology (MA, Adv C). *Program availability:* Part-time, evening/weekend. *Degree requirements:* For master's, thesis optional. *Entrance requirements:* For master's, GRE General Test, letters of recommendation, minimum undergraduate GPA of 3.0, interview. Additional exam requirements/recommendations for international students: required—TOEFL (minimum score 550 paper-based; 80 iBT); recommended—IELTS (minimum score 6.5). Electronic applications accepted.

Marshall University, Academic Affairs Division, College of Education and Professional Development, Program in School Psychology, Huntington, WV 25755. Offers Ed S. *Accreditation:* NCATE. *Program availability:* Part-time, evening/weekend. *Entrance requirements:* For degree, master's degree in psychology.

McGill University, Faculty of Graduate and Postdoctoral Studies, Faculty of Education, Department of Educational and Counseling Psychology, Montréal, QC H3A 2T5, Canada. Offers counseling psychology (MA, PhD); educational psychology (M Ed, MA, PhD); school/applied child psychology and applied developmental psychology (M Ed, MA, PhD, Diploma), including school psychology. *Accreditation:* APA.

McNeese State University, Doré School of Graduate Studies, Burton College of Education, Department of Education Professions, Lake Charles, LA 70609. Offers curriculum and instruction (M Ed), including academically gifted education, elementary education, reading, secondary education, special education; early childhood education grades PK-3 (Postbaccalaureate Certificate); educational leadership (M Ed, Ed S), including educational leadership, educational technology (Ed S); educational technology leadership (M Ed); elementary education (MAT); elementary education grades 1-5 (Postbaccalaureate Certificate); instructional technology (MS); middle school education grades 4-8 (Postbaccalaureate Certificate), including middle school education grades 4-8; multiple levels grades K-12 (Postbaccalaureate Certificate), including multiple levels grades K-12; school counseling (M Ed); school librarian (Postbaccalaureate Certificate); secondary education (MAT); secondary education grades 6-12 (Postbaccalaureate Certificate); special education (M Ed), including advanced professional, autism, educational diagnostician; special education - mild/moderate grades 1-12 (MAT); special education, mild/moderate for elementary education grades 1-5 (Postbaccalaureate Certificate). *Program availability:* Evening/weekend. *Entrance requirements:* For master's, GRE.

Mercer University, Graduate Studies, Cecil B. Day Campus, College of Professional Advancement, Atlanta, GA 31207. Offers certified rehabilitation counseling (MS); clinical mental health (MS); counselor education and supervision (PhD); criminal justice and public safety leadership (MS); health informatics (MS); human services (MS), including child and adolescent services, gerontology services; organizational leadership (MS), including leadership for the health care professional, leadership for the nonprofit organization, organizational development and change; school counseling (MS). *Program availability:* Part-time, evening/weekend, 100% online, blended/hybrid learning. *Faculty:* 19 full-time (11 women), 34 part-time/adjunct (30 women). *Students:* 193 full-time (156 women), 277 part-time (225 women); includes 260 minority (211 Black or African American, non-Hispanic/Latino; 2 American Indian or Alaska Native, non-Hispanic/Latino; 23 Asian, non-Hispanic/Latino; 19 Hispanic/Latino; 5 Two or more races, non-Hispanic/Latino), 3 international. Average age 32. 300 applicants, 45% accepted, 114 enrolled. In 2019, 183 master's, 7 doctorates awarded. *Degree requirements:* For master's, comprehensive exam (for some programs), thesis (for some programs); for doctorate, thesis/dissertation. *Entrance requirements:* For master's, GRE or MAT, Georgia Professional Standards Commission (GPSC) Certification at the SC-5 level; for doctorate, GRE or MAT. Additional exam requirements/recommendations for international students: recommended—TOEFL (minimum score 550 paper-based; 80 iBT), IELTS (minimum score 6.5). *Application deadline:* For fall admission, 7/1 priority date for domestic and international students; for spring admission, 11/1 priority date for domestic and international students; for summer admission, 4/1 priority date for domestic and international students. Application fee: $35. Electronic applications accepted. Application fee is waived when completed online. *Expenses:* Contact institution. *Financial support:* In 2019–20, 32 students received support. Federal Work-Study, scholarships/grants, and unspecified assistantships available. Financial award applicants required to submit FAFSA. *Unit head:* Dr. Priscilla R. Danheiser, Dean, 678-547-6028, Fax: 678-547-6008, E-mail: danheiser_p@mercer.edu. *Application contact:* Theatis Anderson, Asst VP for Enrollment Management, 678-547-6421, E-mail: anderson_t@mercer.edu.
Website: https://professionaladvancement.mercer.edu/

Mercy College, School of Social and Behavioral Sciences, Program in School Psychology, Dobbs Ferry, NY 10522-1189. Offers MS. *Program availability:* Part-time, evening/weekend. *Students:* 38 full-time (37 women), 17 part-time (15 women); includes 34 minority (9 Black or African American, non-Hispanic/Latino; 25 Hispanic/Latino), 1 international. Average age 28. 125 applicants, 41% accepted, 32 enrolled. In 2019, 12 master's awarded. *Degree requirements:* For master's, Fieldwork; internship; passing grade on the PRAXIS II. *Entrance requirements:* For master's, transcript(s); two letters of recommendation; resume; interview. Additional exam requirements/recommendations for international students: required—TOEFL (minimum score 80 iBT), IELTS (minimum

score 6.5). *Application deadline:* Applications are processed on a rolling basis. Application fee: $40. Electronic applications accepted. *Expenses: Tuition:* Full-time $16,146; part-time $897 per credit. *Required fees:* $332; $166 per semester. Tuition and fees vary according to course load and program. *Financial support:* Career-related internships or fieldwork, Federal Work-Study, scholarships/grants, and unspecified assistantships available. Support available to part-time students. Financial award applicants required to submit FAFSA. *Unit head:* Dr. Diana Juettner, Interim Dean, School of Social and Behavioral Sciences, 914-674-7546, E-mail: djuettner@mercy.edu. *Application contact:* Allison Gurdineer, Executive Director of Admissions, 877-637-2946, Fax: 914-674-7382, E-mail: admissions@mercy.edu.
Website: https://www.mercy.edu/degrees-programs/ms-school-psychology

Michigan State University, The Graduate School, College of Education, Department of Counseling, Educational Psychology and Special Education, East Lansing, MI 48824. Offers counseling (MA); educational psychology and educational technology (PhD); educational technology (MA); measurement and quantitative methods (PhD); rehabilitation counseling (MA); rehabilitation counselor education (PhD); school psychology (MA, PhD, Ed S); special education (MA, PhD). *Accreditation:* APA (one or more programs are accredited); CORE (one or more programs are accredited). *Program availability:* Part-time. *Entrance requirements:* Additional exam requirements/recommendations for international students: required—TOEFL. Electronic applications accepted.

MidAmerica Nazarene University, School of Behavioral Sciences and Counseling, Olathe, KS 66062-1899. Offers counseling (MA), including clinical mental health, marriage, couple and family, school counseling, spiritual formation in counseling. *Accreditation:* ACA. *Program availability:* 100% online. *Faculty:* 7 full-time (2 women), 14 part-time/adjunct (9 women). *Students:* 64 full-time (52 women), 143 part-time (113 women); includes 33 minority (20 Black or African American, non-Hispanic/Latino; 2 American Indian or Alaska Native, non-Hispanic/Latino; 2 Asian, non-Hispanic/Latino; 8 Hispanic/Latino; 1 Two or more races, non-Hispanic/Latino), 1 international. Average age 34. 131 applicants, 73% accepted, 84 enrolled. In 2019, 50 master's awarded. *Degree requirements:* For master's, comprehensive exam. *Entrance requirements:* For master's, on-site writing assessment, official transcript, three recommendations, personal interview, background check. Additional exam requirements/recommendations for international students: required—TOEFL (minimum score 81 iBT). *Application deadline:* For winter admission, 2/15 for domestic and international students; for spring admission, 4/1 for domestic and international students. Electronic applications accepted. *Expenses:* Technology fee ($2,040), Graduation fee ($100), carrying fee ($286), professional fee($811), lab fee ($325), other fee ($1,068). *Financial support:* Applicants required to submit FAFSA. *Unit head:* Dr. Todd Frye, Dean, School of Behavioral Sciences and Counseling, 913-971-3449, Fax: 913-971-3402, E-mail: tmfrye@mnu.edu. *Application contact:* Jeanne Blades, Administrative Assistant, 913-971-3730, E-mail: jmblades@mnu.edu.

Middle Tennessee State University, College of Graduate Studies, College of Behavioral and Health Sciences, Department of Psychology, Murfreesboro, TN 37132. Offers clinical psychology (MA); experimental psychology (MA); industrial/organizational psychology (MA); psychology (MA, Ed S); quantitative psychology (MA); school psychology (MA). *Program availability:* Part-time, evening/weekend, online learning. *Degree requirements:* For master's, comprehensive exam, thesis. *Entrance requirements:* For master's, GRE. Additional exam requirements/recommendations for international students: required—TOEFL (minimum score 525 paper-based; 71 iBT) or IELTS (minimum score 6). Electronic applications accepted.

Millersville University of Pennsylvania, College of Graduate Studies and Adult Learning, College of Education and Human Services, Department of Psychology, Millersville, PA 17551-0302. Offers psychology (MS), including clinical psychology, school psychology; school counseling (M Ed). *Program availability:* Part-time. *Faculty:* 11 full-time (6 women), 3 part-time/adjunct (0 women). *Students:* 63 full-time (52 women), 84 part-time (65 women); includes 19 minority (3 Black or African American, non-Hispanic/Latino; 3 Asian, non-Hispanic/Latino; 11 Hispanic/Latino; 2 Two or more races, non-Hispanic/Latino), 2 international. Average age 27. 77 applicants, 75% accepted, 43 enrolled. In 2019, 42 master's awarded. *Degree requirements:* For master's, comprehensive exam (for some programs), thesis optional, internship, practicum, portfolio. *Entrance requirements:* For master's, GRE required only if cumulative GPA is lower than 3.0, At least 1 academic reference, interview, 18 undergraduate credits in Psychology (Clinical and School), 6 undergraduate credits in Psychology (school counseling). Additional exam requirements/recommendations for international students: required—TOEFL, IELTS (minimum score 6), PTE (minimum score 60). *Application deadline:* For fall admission, 1/15 for domestic students; for winter admission, 4/15 for domestic students; for spring admission, 10/1 for domestic students. Application fee: $40. Electronic applications accepted. *Expenses: Tuition, area resident:* Part-time $516 per credit. Tuition, state resident: part-time $516 per credit. Tuition, nonresident: part-time $774 per credit. *Required fees:* $118.75 per credit. Tuition and fees vary according to course load, degree level and program. *Financial support:* In 2019–20, 55 students received support. Scholarships/grants and unspecified assistantships available. Financial award application deadline: 3/15; financial award applicants required to submit FAFSA. *Unit head:* Dr. Debra S. Vredenburg-Rudy, Chair, 717-871-7279, Fax: 717-871-7946, E-mail: debra.vredenburg@millersville.edu. *Application contact:* Dr. James A. Delle, Acting Dean of College of Graduate Studies and Adult Learning/Associate Provost, Academic Administration, 717-871-7462, E-mail: James.Delle@millersville.edu.
Website: https://www.millersville.edu/psychology/index.php

Millersville University of Pennsylvania, College of Graduate Studies and Adult Learning, College of Education and Human Services, Department of Psychology, Program in School Counseling, Millersville, PA 17551-0302. Offers school counseling (M Ed). *Accreditation:* NCATE. *Program availability:* Part-time. *Students:* 18 full-time (15 women), 35 part-time (29 women); includes 5 minority (1 Black or African American, non-Hispanic/Latino; 1 Asian, non-Hispanic/Latino; 2 Hispanic/Latino; 1 Two or more races, non-Hispanic/Latino). Average age 29. 17 applicants, 88% accepted, 13 enrolled. In 2019, 8 master's awarded. *Degree requirements:* For master's, thesis optional, internship, practicum, portfolio. *Entrance requirements:* For master's, GRE required only if cumulative GPA is lower than 3.0, at least 1 academic reference; interview; 6 undergraduate credits in psychology. Additional exam requirements/recommendations for international students: required—TOEFL, IELTS (minimum score 6), PTE (minimum score 60). *Application deadline:* For fall admission, 1/15 for domestic students; for winter admission, 4/15 for domestic students; for spring admission, 10/1 for domestic students. Application fee: $40. Electronic applications accepted. *Expenses: Tuition, area resident:* Part-time $516 per credit. Tuition, state resident: part-time $516 per credit. Tuition, nonresident: part-time $774 per credit. *Required fees:* $118.75 per credit. Tuition and fees vary according to course load, degree level and program. *Financial support:* In 2019–20, 12 students received support. Scholarships/grants and unspecified assistantships available. Financial award application deadline: 3/15; financial award applicants required to submit FAFSA. *Unit head:* Dr. Jason B. Baker, Coordinator, 717-871-7267, Fax: 717-871-7946, E-mail: jason.baker@millersville.edu. *Application contact:* Dr. James A. Delle, Acting Dean of College of Graduate Studies and Adult

Learning/Associate Provost, Academic Administration, 717-871-7462, E-mail: James.Delle@millersville.edu.
Website: https://www.millersville.edu/psychology/graduate-programs-webpages/school-counseling/index.php

Millersville University of Pennsylvania, College of Graduate Studies and Adult Learning, College of Education and Human Services, Department of Psychology, Program in School Psychology, Millersville, PA 17551-0302. Offers psychology (MS). *Program availability:* Part-time. *Students:* 20 full-time (17 women), 19 part-time (17 women); includes 6 minority (1 Black or African American, non-Hispanic/Latino; 1 Asian, non-Hispanic/Latino; 4 Hispanic/Latino). Average age 26. 23 applicants, 83% accepted, 11 enrolled. In 2019, 18 master's awarded. *Degree requirements:* For master's, comprehensive exam, thesis optional, practicum, internship, portfolio. *Entrance requirements:* For master's, GRE required only if cumulative GPA is lower than 3.0, at least 1 academic reference; interview; 18 undergraduate credits in psychology. Additional exam requirements/recommendations for international students: required—TOEFL, IELTS (minimum score 6), PTE (minimum score 60). *Application deadline:* For fall admission, 1/15 for domestic students; for winter admission, 4/15 for domestic students; for spring admission, 10/1 for domestic students. Application fee: $40. Electronic applications accepted. *Expenses: Tuition, area resident:* Part-time $516 per credit. Tuition, state resident: part-time $516 per credit. Tuition, nonresident: part-time $774 per credit. *Required fees:* $118.75 per credit. Tuition and fees vary according to course load, degree level and program. *Financial support:* In 2019–20, 24 students received support. Scholarships/grants and unspecified assistantships available. Financial award application deadline: 3/15; financial award applicants required to submit FAFSA. *Unit head:* Dr. Helena Tuleya-Payne, Coordinator, 717-871-4420, Fax: 717-871-7946, E-mail: helena.tuleya-payne@millersville.edu. *Application contact:* Dr. James A. Delle, Acting Dean of College of Graduate Studies and Adult Learning/Associate Provost, Academic Administration, 717-871-7462, E-mail: James.Delle@millersville.edu.
Website: https://www.millersville.edu/programs/school-psychology.php

Minnesota State University Mankato, College of Graduate Studies and Research, College of Social and Behavioral Sciences, Department of Psychology, Mankato, MN 56001. Offers clinical psychology (MA); industrial/organizational psychology (MA); school psychology (Psy D). *Program availability:* Part-time. *Degree requirements:* For master's, one foreign language, comprehensive exam, thesis (for some programs). *Entrance requirements:* For master's, GRE General Test, GRE Subject Test (clinical psychology), minimum GPA of 3.0 during previous 2 years, 3 letters of reference. Additional exam requirements/recommendations for international students: required—TOEFL. Electronic applications accepted.

Minnesota State University Moorhead, Graduate and Extended Learning, College of Science, Health and the Environment, Moorhead, MN 56563. Offers healthcare administration (MHA); nursing (MS); school psychology (MS, Psy S). *Program availability:* Part-time, evening/weekend, 100% online, blended/hybrid learning. *Students:* 30 full-time (26 women), 120 part-time (91 women). Average age 33. 77 applicants, 57% accepted. In 2019, 40 master's, 11 other advanced degrees awarded. *Degree requirements:* For master's, comprehensive exam (for some programs), thesis, final oral defense. *Entrance requirements:* For master's, GRE (for school psychology program), minimum GPA of 3.0, essay, letters of reference, RN license (for nursing program). Additional exam requirements/recommendations for international students: required—TOEFL (minimum score 550 paper-based; 80 iBT); recommended—IELTS (minimum score 6.5). *Application deadline:* Applications are processed on a rolling basis. Application fee: $35. Electronic applications accepted. *Financial support:* Federal Work-Study and unspecified assistantships available. Financial award application deadline: 10/1; financial award applicants required to submit FAFSA. *Unit head:* Dr. Elizabeth Nawrot, Interim Dean, 218-477-5892, E-mail: nawrot@mnstate.edu. *Application contact:* Karla Wenger, Office Manager, 218-477-2344, Fax: 218-477-2482, E-mail: wengerk@mnstate.edu.
Website: http://www.mnstate.edu/cshe/

Minot State University, Graduate School, Program in School Psychology, Minot, ND 58707-0002. Offers Ed Sp. *Degree requirements:* For Ed Sp, comprehensive exam, thesis optional. *Entrance requirements:* For degree, GRE General Test, minimum GPA of 3.0. Additional exam requirements/recommendations for international students: required—TOEFL (minimum score 79 iBT), IELTS (minimum score 6).

Mississippi State University, College of Education, Department of Counseling, Educational Psychology, and Foundations, Mississippi State, MS 39762. Offers clinical mental health (MS); college counseling (MS); counseling/mental health (PhD); counseling/school psychology (PhD); counselor education (Ed S); educational psychology/general educational psychology (PhD); educational psychology/school psychology (PhD); general educational psychology (MS); psychometry (MS); rehabilitation counseling (MS); school counseling (MS); school psychology (Ed S); student affairs (MS). *Accreditation:* ACA (one or more programs are accredited); APA; CORE (one or more programs are accredited); NCATE. *Program availability:* Part-time, blended/hybrid learning. *Faculty:* 15 full-time (10 women), 3 part-time/adjunct (all women). *Students:* 105 full-time (87 women), 47 part-time (37 women); includes 58 minority (49 Black or African American, non-Hispanic/Latino; 1 Asian, non-Hispanic/Latino; 6 Hispanic/Latino; 2 Two or more races, non-Hispanic/Latino), 7 international. Average age 30. 83 applicants, 69% accepted, 40 enrolled. In 2019, 39 master's, 3 doctorates, 7 other advanced degrees awarded. Terminal master's awarded for partial completion of doctoral program. *Degree requirements:* For master's, comprehensive exam, thesis optional; for doctorate, thesis/dissertation, comprehensive oral and written exam. *Entrance requirements:* For master's, GRE (taken within the last five years), BS with minimum GPA of 2.75 on last 60 hours; for doctorate, GRE, MS from CACREP- or CORE-accredited program in counseling; for Ed S, GRE, MS in counseling or related field, minimum GPA of 3.3 on all graduate work. Additional exam requirements/recommendations for international students: required—TOEFL (minimum score 550 paper-based; 79 iBT); recommended—IELTS (minimum score 6.5). *Application deadline:* For fall admission, 2/1 priority date for domestic and international students. Applications are processed on a rolling basis. Application fee: $60 ($80 for international students). Electronic applications accepted. *Expenses: Tuition, area resident:* Full-time $8880; part-time $456 per credit hour. Tuition, state resident: full-time $8880. Tuition, nonresident: full-time $23,840; part-time $1236 per credit hour. *Required fees:* $110; $11.12 per credit hour. Tuition and fees vary according to course load. *Financial support:* In 2019–20, 3 research assistantships (averaging $9,000 per year), 7 teaching assistantships with full tuition reimbursements (averaging $8,401 per year) were awarded; career-related internships or fieldwork, Federal Work-Study, institutionally sponsored loans, and unspecified assistantships also available. Financial award application deadline: 2/1; financial award applicants required to submit FAFSA. *Unit head:* Dr. Daniel Gadke, Professor and Interim Head, 662-325-3426, Fax: 662-325-3263, E-mail: dgadke@colled.msstate.edu. *Application contact:* Ryan King, Admissions and Enrollment Assistant, 662-325-8951, E-mail: rjk101@grad.msstate.edu.
Website: http://www.cep.msstate.edu/

Monmouth University, Graduate Studies, School of Education, West Long Branch, NJ 07764-1898. Offers applied behavior analysis (Certificate); autism (Certificate); director of school counseling services (Post-Master's Certificate); early childhood (M Ed); educational leadership (Ed D); elementary education (MAT), including elementary level, secondary level; English as a second language (M Ed); learning disabilities teacher-consultant (Post-Master's Certificate); literacy (MS Ed); school counseling (MS Ed); special education (MS Ed), including autism, learning disabilities teacher-consultant, teacher of students with disabilities, teaching in inclusive settings; speech-language pathology (MS Ed); student affairs and college counseling (MS Ed); supervisor (Post-Master's Certificate); teaching English to speakers of other languages (Certificate). *Accreditation:* NCATE. *Program availability:* Part-time, evening/weekend, 100% online, blended/hybrid learning. *Faculty:* 28 full-time (19 women), 34 part-time/adjunct (25 women). *Students:* 168 full-time (144 women), 225 part-time (197 women); includes 66 minority (20 Black or African American, non-Hispanic/Latino; 6 Asian, non-Hispanic/Latino; 37 Hispanic/Latino; 3 Two or more races, non-Hispanic/Latino), 2 international. Average age 30. In 2019, 108 master's, 9 other advanced degrees awarded. *Degree requirements:* For master's, thesis (for some programs); for doctorate, thesis/dissertation, Project. *Entrance requirements:* For master's, GRE taken within last 5 years (for MS Ed in speech-language pathology); SAT (minimum combined score of 1660 in 3 sections), ACT (23), GRE (minimum score of 4.0 on analytical writing section and minimum combined score of 310 on quantitative and verbal sections), or passing scores on 3 parts of Core Academic Skills Educators, minimum GPA of 3.0 in major; 2 letters of recommendation (for some programs); resume, personal statement or essay (depending on program). Additional exam requirements/recommendations for international students: required—TOEFL (minimum score 550 paper-based; 79 iBT), IELTS (minimum score 6), Michigan English Language Assessment Battery (minimum score 77) or Certificate of Advanced English (minimum score 160). *Application deadline:* For fall admission, 7/15 priority date for domestic students, 7/1 for international students; for spring admission, 12/1 priority date for domestic students, 11/1 for international students; for summer admission, 5/1 for domestic students. Applications are processed on a rolling basis. Application fee: $50. Electronic applications accepted. *Expenses: Tuition:* Full-time $22,194; part-time $14,796 per credit. *Required fees:* $712; $178 per semester. $178 per semester. Tuition and fees vary according to course load. *Financial support:* In 2019–20, 337 students received support. Research assistantships, teaching assistantships, scholarships/grants, and unspecified assistantships available. Support available to part-time students. Financial award applicants required to submit FAFSA. *Unit head:* Dr. John E. Henning, Dean, 732-263-5513, Fax: 732-263-5277, E-mail: kodonnel@monmouth.edu. *Application contact:* Kirsten Sneeringer, Graduate Admission Counselor, 732-571-3452, Fax: 732-263-5123, E-mail: gradadm@monmouth.edu.
Website: http://www.monmouth.edu/academics/schools/education/default.asp

Montana State University, The Graduate School, College of Education, Health, and Human Development, Department of Education, Bozeman, MT 59717. Offers adult and higher education (Ed D); curriculum and instruction (M Ed, Ed D), including professional educator (M Ed), technology education (M Ed); education (M Ed), including adult and higher education, educational leadership, school counseling; educational leadership (Ed D, Ed S). *Accreditation:* TEAC. *Program availability:* Part-time, online learning. *Degree requirements:* For master's, comprehensive exam; for doctorate, comprehensive exam, thesis/dissertation. *Entrance requirements:* For master's, GRE, 3 letters of reference, essays, BA transcripts; for doctorate, GRE, MAT, 3 letters of reference, essay, BA and M Ed transcripts; for Ed S, PRAXIS. Additional exam requirements/recommendations for international students: required—TOEFL (minimum score 550 paper-based). Electronic applications accepted.

Mount Saint Vincent University, Graduate Programs, Faculty of Education, Program in School Psychology, Halifax, NS B3M 2J6, Canada. Offers MA. *Degree requirements:* For master's, thesis, 500-hour practicum. *Entrance requirements:* For master's, bachelor's degree in psychology or equivalent, related work experience. Electronic applications accepted.

Murray State University, College of Education and Human Services, Department of Educational Studies, Leadership and Counseling, Murray, KY 42071. Offers college advising (Certificate); education administration (MA Ed); human development and leadership (MS, Certificate); library media (MA Ed); middle school teacher leader (MA Ed); P-20 and community leadership (Ed D); postsecondary education administration (MA Ed); school counseling (MA Ed); school guidance and counseling (Ed S); secondary teacher leader (MA Ed). *Program availability:* Part-time, evening/weekend, 100% online, blended/hybrid learning. *Entrance requirements:* For master's and other advanced degree, GRE or GMAT, minimum university GPA of 2.75. Additional exam requirements/recommendations for international students: required—TOEFL (minimum score 527 paper-based; 71 iBT). Electronic applications accepted.

National Louis University, National College of Education, Chicago, IL 60603. Offers administration and supervision (M Ed, Ed D, CAS, Ed S); curriculum and instruction (M Ed, MS Ed, CAS); early childhood administration (M Ed, CAS); early childhood education (M Ed, MAT, MS Ed, CAS); education (Ed D); educational psychology/human learning and development (M Ed, MS Ed, CAS, Ed S); elementary education (MAT); interdisciplinary curriculum and instruction (M Ed); mathematics education (M Ed, MS Ed, CAS); middle grades education (MAT); reading and language (M Ed, MS Ed, CAS); school psychology (M Ed, Ed S); science education (M Ed, MS Ed, CAS); secondary education (MAT); special education (M Ed, MAT, CAS); technology in education (M Ed, CAS). *Accreditation:* NCATE. *Program availability:* Part-time, evening/weekend. *Degree requirements:* For doctorate, comprehensive exam, thesis/dissertation. *Entrance requirements:* For master's, MAT or GRE, minimum GPA of 3.0; for doctorate, GRE General Test, minimum GPA of 3.25, interview, resume, writing sample, 4 recommendations. Additional exam requirements/recommendations for international students: required—TOEFL (minimum score 550 paper-based; 79 iBT).

National University, Sanford College of Education, La Jolla, CA 92037-1011. Offers advanced teaching practices (MS); applied behavior analysis (MS); applied school leadership (MS); e-teaching and learning (Certificate); education (MA); educational administration (MS); educational and instructional technology (MS); educational counseling (MS); higher education administration (MS); inspired teaching and learning (M Ed); school psychology (MS); special education (MA, MS). *Program availability:* Part-time, evening/weekend, 100% online, blended/hybrid learning. *Degree requirements:* For master's, thesis (for some programs). *Entrance requirements:* For master's, interview, minimum GPA of 2.5. Additional exam requirements/recommendations for international students: required—TOEFL (minimum score 550 paper-based; 79 iBT), IELTS (minimum score 6). Electronic applications accepted. *Expenses: Tuition:* Full-time $442; part-time $442 per unit.

New Mexico State University, College of Education, Department of Counseling and Educational Psychology, Las Cruces, NM 88003-8001. Offers counseling psychology (PhD); educational diagnostics (MA), including clinical mental health counseling, educational diagnostics; school psychology (Ed S). *Accreditation:* ACA; APA (one or more programs are accredited); NCATE. *Program availability:* Part-time, evening/weekend. *Faculty:* 12 full-time (9 women), 4 part-time/adjunct (all women). *Students:* 90 full-time (71 women), 59 part-time (43 women); includes 82 minority (6 Black or African American, non-Hispanic/Latino; 4 American Indian or Alaska Native, non-Hispanic/Latino; 3 Asian, non-Hispanic/Latino; 63 Hispanic/Latino; 6 Two or more races, non-

Hispanic/Latino), 5 international. Average age 33. 140 applicants, 51% accepted, 54 enrolled. In 2019, 21 master's, 8 doctorates, 6 other advanced degrees awarded. *Degree requirements:* For master's, comprehensive exam, thesis optional, internship; for doctorate, comprehensive exam, thesis/dissertation, internship; for Ed S, comprehensive exam, thesis or alternative, internship as alternate. *Entrance requirements:* For master's, doctorate, and Ed S, GRE General Test, minimum GPA of 3.0. Additional exam requirements/recommendations for international students: required—TOEFL (minimum score 550 paper-based; 79 iBT), IELTS (minimum score 6.5). *Application deadline:* For fall admission, 12/15 for domestic and international students; for spring admission, 2/1 priority date for domestic students, 2/1 for international students. Application fee: $40 ($50 for international students). Electronic applications accepted. *Financial support:* In 2019–20, 87 students received support, including 10 fellowships (averaging $4,844 per year), 3 research assistantships (averaging $9,959 per year), 25 teaching assistantships (averaging $15,189 per year); career-related internships or fieldwork, Federal Work-Study, scholarships/grants, traineeships, health care benefits, and unspecified assistantships also available. Support available to part-time students. Financial award application deadline: 3/1. *Unit head:* Dr. Barbara Gormley, Department Head, 575-646-2121, Fax: 575-646-8035, E-mail: bgormley@nmsu.edu. *Application contact:* Norma Arrieta, Student Program Coordinator, 575-646-2121, Fax: 575-646-8035, E-mail: cep@nmsu.edu. Website: http://cep.education.nmsu.edu

Niagara University, Graduate Division of Education, Concentration in School Psychology, Niagara University, NY 14109. Offers MS. *Program availability:* Part-time. *Entrance requirements:* For master's, GRE. Additional exam requirements/recommendations for international students: required—TOEFL (minimum score 550 paper-based; 79 iBT), IELTS (minimum score 6). Electronic applications accepted. *Expenses:* Contact institution.

Nicholls State University, Graduate Studies, College of Education, Department of Psychology, Counseling and Family Studies, Thibodaux, LA 70310. Offers clinical mental health counseling (MA); school counseling (M Ed); school psychology (SSP). *Accreditation:* NCATE. *Program availability:* Part-time, evening/weekend. *Degree requirements:* For master's, comprehensive exam; for SSP, comprehensive exam, internship. *Entrance requirements:* For master's, GRE General Test. Electronic applications accepted.

North Carolina State University, Graduate School, College of Humanities and Social Sciences, Department of Psychology, Raleigh, NC 27695. Offers applied social and community psychology (PhD); human factors and applied cognition (PhD); industrial/organizational psychology (PhD); lifespan developmental psychology (PhD); school psychology (PhD). *Accreditation:* APA. *Degree requirements:* For doctorate, comprehensive exam, thesis/dissertation. *Entrance requirements:* For doctorate, GRE General Test, GRE Subject Test (industrial/organizational psychology), MAT (recommended), minimum GPA of 3.0 in major. Electronic applications accepted.

North Dakota State University, College of Graduate and Interdisciplinary Studies, College of Human Development and Education, School of Education, Program in Counselor Education, Fargo, ND 58102. Offers clinical mental health counseling (M Ed, MS); counselor education and supervision (PhD); school counseling (M Ed, MS). *Accreditation:* ACA; NCATE. *Program availability:* Part-time, online learning. *Degree requirements:* For master's, comprehensive exam, thesis or alternative; for doctorate, comprehensive exam, thesis/dissertation. *Entrance requirements:* For master's, GRE, MAT, interview. Additional exam requirements/recommendations for international students: required—TOEFL. Tuition and fees vary according to program and reciprocity agreements.

Northeastern University, Bouvé College of Health Sciences, Boston, MA 02115-5096. Offers applied behavior analysis (MS); audiology (Au D); counseling psychology (MS, PhD, CAGS); exercise science (MS); nursing (MS, PhD, CAGS), including administration (MS), adult-gerontology acute care nurse practitioner (MS, CAGS), adult-gerontology primary care nurse practitioner (MS, CAGS), anesthesia (MS), family nurse practitioner (MS, CAGS), neonatal nurse practitioner (MS, CAGS), pediatric nurse practitioner (MS, CAGS), psychiatric mental health nurse practitioner (MS, CAGS); nursing practice (DNP); pharmaceutical sciences (MS, PhD), including interdisciplinary concentration, pharmaceutics and drug delivery systems; pharmacology (MS); pharmacy (Pharm D); school psychology (PhD); speech-language pathology (MS); urban health (MPH); MS/MBA. *Accreditation:* AANA/CANAEP; ACPE (one or more programs are accredited); ASHA; CEPH. *Program availability:* Part-time, evening/weekend, online learning. *Degree requirements:* For doctorate, thesis/dissertation (for some programs); for CAGS, comprehensive exam. Electronic applications accepted. *Expenses:* Contact institution.

Northern Arizona University, College of Education, Department of Educational Psychology, Flagstaff, AZ 86011. Offers clinical mental health counseling (MA); combined counseling/school psychology (PhD), including counseling psychology; counseling (M Ed), including school counseling, student affairs; human relations (M Ed); psychology of human development and learning (Graduate Certificate); school psychology (Ed S). *Program availability:* Part-time, 100% online, blended/hybrid learning. Terminal master's awarded for partial completion of doctoral program. *Degree requirements:* For master's, variable foreign language requirement, comprehensive exam (for some programs), thesis (for some programs); for doctorate, variable foreign language requirement, comprehensive exam (for some programs), thesis/dissertation (for some programs); for other advanced degree, comprehensive exam (for some programs). *Entrance requirements:* Additional exam requirements/recommendations for international students: required—TOEFL (minimum score 80 iBT), IELTS (minimum score 6.5). Electronic applications accepted.

Northern Vermont University–Johnson, Program in Counseling, Johnson, VT 05656. Offers addictions counseling (MA); clinical mental health counseling (MA); general counseling (MA); school counseling (MA). *Program availability:* Part-time. *Degree requirements:* For master's, comprehensive exam. *Entrance requirements:* For master's, interview. Additional exam requirements/recommendations for international students: required—TOEFL. Electronic applications accepted.

Northwest Nazarene University, Program in Counselor Education, Nampa, ID 83686-5897. Offers clinical counseling (MS); marriage and family counseling (MS); school counseling (MS). *Program availability:* Part-time, evening/weekend. *Degree requirements:* For master's, comprehensive exam. *Entrance requirements:* For master's, GRE (if GPA less than 3.0), minimum GPA of 3.0, BA, 2 letters of recommendation, definition of counseling writing sample, background check, group evaluation, role play, dispositions rubric score. Additional exam requirements/recommendations for international students: required—TOEFL (minimum score 85 paper-based), WES. Electronic applications accepted.

Nova Southeastern University, College of Psychology, Fort Lauderdale, FL 33314-7796. Offers clinical mental health counseling (MS); clinical psychology (PhD, Psy D); counseling (MS); experimental psychology (MS); forensic psychology (MS); general psychology (MS); school counseling (MS); school psychology (Psy D, Psy S); substance abuse counseling (MS); substance abuse counseling and education (MS). *Accreditation:* APA (one or more programs are accredited). *Program availability:* Part-time, 100%

online, blended/hybrid learning. *Faculty:* 72 full-time (34 women), 111 part-time/adjunct (76 women). *Students:* 1,263 full-time (1,068 women), 868 part-time (761 women); includes 1,221 minority (368 Black or African American, non-Hispanic/Latino; 3 American Indian or Alaska Native, non-Hispanic/Latino; 111 Asian, non-Hispanic/Latino; 668 Hispanic/Latino; 1 Native Hawaiian or other Pacific Islander, non-Hispanic/Latino; 70 Two or more races, non-Hispanic/Latino), 59 international. Average age 31. 935 applicants, 56% accepted, 375 enrolled. In 2019, 400 master's, 72 doctorates, 13 other advanced degrees awarded. Terminal master's awarded for partial completion of doctoral program. *Degree requirements:* For master's, comprehensive exam, 3 practica; for doctorate, thesis/dissertation, clinical internship, competency exam; for Psy S, comprehensive exam, internship. *Entrance requirements:* For master's and Psy S, GRE General Test, letters of recommendation, research/personal statement, interview; for doctorate, GRE General Test, GRE Subject Test (recommended), minimum undergraduate GPA of 3.0, letters of recommendation, research/personal statement, interview, curriculum vitae/resume. Additional exam requirements/recommendations for international students: required—TOEFL (minimum score 550 paper-based). *Application deadline:* Applications are processed on a rolling basis. Application fee: $50. Electronic applications accepted. *Expenses:* Contact institution. *Financial support:* In 2019–20, 197 students received support, including 15 research assistantships (averaging $5,600 per year), 68 teaching assistantships (averaging $2,000 per year); career-related internships or fieldwork, Federal Work-Study, institutionally sponsored loans, scholarships/grants, and unspecified assistantships also available. Support available to part-time students. Financial award application deadline: 4/15; financial award applicants required to submit FAFSA. *Unit head:* Dr. Karen Grosby, Dean, 954-262-5712, Fax: 954-262-3859, E-mail: grosby@nova.edu. *Application contact:* Gregory Gayle, Director, Recruitment and Admissions, 954-262-5903, Fax: 954-262-3893, E-mail: ggayle1@nova.edu. Website: http://psychology.nova.edu/

Old Dominion University, Darden College of Education, Counseling Program, Norfolk, VA 23529. Offers clinical mental health counseling (MS Ed); college counseling (MS Ed); counseling (Ed S); counselor education (PhD); school counseling (MS Ed). *Accreditation:* ACA. *Program availability:* Part-time, evening/weekend. *Degree requirements:* For master's and Ed S, comprehensive exam; for doctorate, comprehensive exam, thesis/dissertation. *Entrance requirements:* For master's and Ed S, GRE General Test, resume, essay, transcripts, recommendations; for doctorate, GRE General Test, resume, interview, essay, transcripts, recommendations. Additional exam requirements/recommendations for international students: required—TOEFL. Electronic applications accepted. *Expenses:* Contact institution.

Oregon State University, College of Education, Program in Counseling, Corvallis, OR 97331. Offers clinical mental health counseling (M Coun); counseling (PhD); school counseling (M Coun). *Accreditation:* ACA (one or more programs are accredited); NCATE. *Program availability:* Part-time, blended/hybrid learning. *Degree requirements:* For master's, thesis or alternative; for doctorate, one foreign language, thesis/dissertation. *Entrance requirements:* For master's, minimum GPA of 3.0 in last 90 hours; for doctorate, GRE or MAT, master's degree, minimum GPA of 3.0 in last 90 hours of course work, 2 years of teaching experience. Additional exam requirements/recommendations for international students: required—TOEFL (minimum score 575 paper-based).

Oregon State University–Cascades, Program in Counseling, Bend, OR 97701. Offers community counseling (MS); school counseling (MS).

Ottawa University, Graduate Studies-Arizona, Program in Education, Ottawa, KS 66067-3399. Offers community college counseling (MA); curriculum and instruction (MA); early childhood (MA); education intervention (MA); education leadership (MA); education technology (MA); Montessori early childhood education (MA); Montessori elementary education (MA); professional development (MA); school guidance counseling (MA); special education - cross categorical (MA). *Accreditation:* NCATE. *Program availability:* Part-time. *Degree requirements:* For master's, thesis or alternative. *Entrance requirements:* For master's, minimum undergraduate GPA of 3.0, copy of current state certification or teaching license. Additional exam requirements/recommendations for international students: required—TOEFL (minimum score 550 paper-based). Electronic applications accepted. *Expenses:* Contact institution.

Our Lady of the Lake University, College of Professional Studies, Program in Psychology, San Antonio, TX 78207-4689. Offers marriage and family therapy (MS); school psychology (MS). *Accreditation:* APA. *Program availability:* Part-time. *Degree requirements:* For master's, comprehensive exam, practicum. *Entrance requirements:* For master's, GRE General Test or MAT, bachelor's degree with at least 12 undergraduate semester hours in psychology including one course in statistics and minimum cumulative GPA of 3.0; criminal background check; personal statement addressing background in psychology, expectations of the MS program, and professional goals; statement of purpose; 2 letters of recommendation. Additional exam requirements/recommendations for international students: required—TOEFL. Electronic applications accepted. Application fee is waived when completed online.

Pace University, Dyson College of Arts and Sciences, Department of Psychology, Program in School-Clinical Child Psychology, New York, NY 10038. Offers school psychology (MS Ed); school-clinical child psychology (Psy D). *Accreditation:* APA (one or more programs are accredited). Terminal master's awarded for partial completion of doctoral program. *Degree requirements:* For master's, qualifying exams, internship; for doctorate, comprehensive exam, thesis/dissertation, qualifying exams, externship, internship. *Entrance requirements:* For master's, GRE General Test, GRE Subject Test in psychology (recommended), interview, 3 letters of recommendation, resume, personal statement; for doctorate, GRE General Test, GRE Subject Test in psychology (recommended), interview, transcripts, 3 letters of recommendation. Additional exam requirements/recommendations for international students: required—TOEFL (minimum score 88 iBT), IELTS (minimum score 7) or PTE (minimum score 60). Electronic applications accepted.

Penn State University Park, Graduate School, College of Education, Department of Educational Psychology, Counseling, and Special Education, University Park, PA 16802. Offers counselor education (M Ed, D Ed, PhD, Certificate); educational psychology (MS, PhD, Certificate); school psychology (M Ed, MS, PhD, Certificate); special education (M Ed, MS, PhD).

Philadelphia College of Osteopathic Medicine, Graduate and Professional Programs, School of Professional and Applied Psychology, Philadelphia, PA 19131. Offers applied behavior analysis (Certificate); clinical health psychology (Post-Doctoral Certificate); clinical neuropsychology (Post-Doctoral Certificate); clinical psychology (Psy D); educational psychology (PhD); mental health counseling (MS); organizational development and leadership (MS); psychology (Certificate); public health management and administration (MS); school psychology (MS, Psy D, Ed S). *Accreditation:* APA. *Faculty:* 19 full-time (11 women), 122 part-time/adjunct (58 women). *Students:* 342 (285 women); includes 108 minority (65 Black or African American, non-Hispanic/Latino; 1 American Indian or Alaska Native, non-Hispanic/Latino; 10 Asian, non-Hispanic/Latino; 14 Hispanic/Latino; 18 Two or more races, non-Hispanic/Latino). Average age 25. 357 applicants, 51% accepted, 113 enrolled. In 2019, 79 master's, 38 doctorates, 16 other advanced degrees awarded. Terminal master's awarded for partial completion of

doctoral program. *Degree requirements:* For master's, comprehensive exam (for some programs), thesis (for some programs); for doctorate, comprehensive exam, thesis/dissertation. *Entrance requirements:* For master's, GRE or MAT, minimum GPA of 3.0; bachelor's degree from regionally-accredited college or university; for doctorate, PRAXIS II (for Psy D in school psychology), minimum undergraduate GPA of 3.0; for other advanced degree, GRE (for Ed S). Additional exam requirements/recommendations for international students: required—TOEFL (minimum score 79 iBT). *Application deadline:* Applications are processed on a rolling basis. Application fee: $50. Electronic applications accepted. *Financial support:* In 2019–20, 28 teaching assistantships were awarded; Federal Work-Study, institutionally sponsored loans, and scholarships/grants also available. Financial award application deadline: 3/15; financial award applicants required to submit FAFSA. *Unit head:* Dr. Robert DiTomasso, Chairman, 215-871-6442, Fax: 215-871-6458, E-mail: robertd@pcom.edu. *Application contact:* Johnathan Cox, Associate Director of Admissions, 215-871-6700, Fax: 215-871-6719, E-mail: johnathancox@pcom.edu.
Website: pcom.edu

Phillips Graduate University, Master's Program in Psychology, Chatsworth, CA 91311. Offers art therapy (MA); marriage and family therapy (MA); school counseling (MA); school psychology (MA). *Program availability:* Evening/weekend. *Degree requirements:* For master's, comprehensive exam, thesis. *Entrance requirements:* For master's, minimum GPA of 2.5. Electronic applications accepted.

Pittsburg State University, Graduate School, College of Education, Department of Psychology and Counseling, Program in School Psychology, Pittsburg, KS 66762. Offers Ed S. *Accreditation:* NCATE. *Program availability:* Part-time. *Degree requirements:* For Ed S, thesis or alternative. *Entrance requirements:* For degree, GRE General Test, minimum GPA of 3.0. Additional exam requirements/recommendations for international students: required—TOEFL (minimum score 550 paper-based; 79 iBT), IELTS (minimum score 6.5), PTE (minimum score 53). Electronic applications accepted. *Expenses:* Contact institution.

Plymouth State University, College of Graduate Studies, Graduate Studies in Education, Certificate of Advanced Graduate Studies Programs, Plymouth, NH 03264-1595. Offers clinical mental health counseling (CAGS); educational leadership (CAGS); higher education (CAGS); school psychology (CAGS). *Program availability:* Part-time, evening/weekend.

Purdue University Northwest, Graduate Studies Office, School of Education, Program in Counseling, Hammond, IN 46323-2094. Offers human services (MS Ed); mental health counseling (MS Ed); school counseling (MS Ed). *Accreditation:* ACA. *Entrance requirements:* Additional exam requirements/recommendations for international students: required—TOEFL.

Queens College of the City University of New York, Division of Education, Department of Educational and Community Programs, Queens, NY 11367-1597. Offers bilingual pupil personnel (AC); counselor education (MS Ed); mental health counseling (MS); school building leader (AC); school district leader (AC); school psychologist (MS Ed); special education-childhood education (AC); special education-early childhood (MS Ed); teacher of special education 1-6 (MS Ed); teacher of special education birth-2 (MS Ed); teaching students with disabilities, grades 7-12 (MS Ed, AC). *Program availability:* Part-time. *Degree requirements:* For master's, research project; for AC, internship, research project. *Entrance requirements:* For master's, minimum GPA of 3.0. Additional exam requirements/recommendations for international students: required—TOEFL, IELTS. Electronic applications accepted.

Quincy University, Master of Science in Education Counseling Program, Quincy, IL 62301-2699. Offers clinical mental health counseling (MS Ed); college student personnel (MS Ed); school counseling (MS Ed). *Program availability:* Part-time, evening/weekend. *Degree requirements:* For master's, comprehensive exam, practicum, internship. *Entrance requirements:* For master's, MAT or GRE. Additional exam requirements/recommendations for international students: required—TOEFL (minimum score 550 paper-based; 79 iBT). Electronic applications accepted.

Radford University, College of Graduate Studies and Research, School Psychology, Ed.S., Radford, VA 24142. Offers Ed S. *Accreditation:* NCATE. *Degree requirements:* For Ed S, comprehensive exam. *Entrance requirements:* For degree, GRE, minimum GPA of 3.0, 2 letters of reference, essay, resume, official transcripts. Additional exam requirements/recommendations for international students: required—TOEFL (minimum score 550 paper-based; 79 iBT), IELTS (minimum score 6.5). Electronic applications accepted.

Rhode Island College, School of Graduate Studies, Feinstein School of Education and Human Development, Department of Counseling, Educational Leadership, and School Psychology, Providence, RI 02908-1991. Offers advanced counseling (CGS); agency counseling (MA); clinical mental health counseling (MS); co-occurring disorders (MA, CGS); educational leadership (M Ed); mental health counseling (CAGS); school counseling (MA); school psychology (CAGS); teacher leadership (CGS). *Accreditation:* ACA; NCATE. *Program availability:* Part-time, evening/weekend. *Faculty:* 10 full-time (7 women), 5 part-time/adjunct (4 women). *Students:* 51 full-time (37 women), 73 part-time (57 women); includes 21 minority (8 Black or African American, non-Hispanic/Latino; 11 Hispanic/Latino; 2 Two or more races, non-Hispanic/Latino). Average age 33. In 2019, 13 master's, 27 other advanced degrees awarded. *Degree requirements:* For master's and other advanced degree, comprehensive exam (for some programs), thesis (for some programs). *Entrance requirements:* For master's, GRE General Test or MAT, undergraduate transcripts; minimum undergraduate GPA of 3.0; for other advanced degree, GRE or MAT (for most programs), undergraduate transcripts; minimum undergraduate GPA of 3.0; 3 letters of recommendation; current resume. Additional exam requirements/recommendations for international students: required—TOEFL (minimum score 550 paper-based; 80 iBT). *Application deadline:* For fall admission, 3/1 for domestic students; for spring admission, 11/1 for domestic students. Applications are processed on a rolling basis. Application fee: $50. Electronic applications accepted. *Expenses: Tuition, area resident:* Part-time $462 per credit hour. Tuition, state resident: part-time $462 per credit hour. *Required fees:* $720. One-time fee: $140. *Financial support:* Teaching assistantships, career-related internships or fieldwork, Federal Work-Study, scholarships/grants, health care benefits, and unspecified assistantships available. Support available to part-time students. Financial award application deadline: 5/15; financial award applicants required to submit FAFSA. *Unit head:* Charles Boisvert, Chair, 401-456-8023. *Application contact:* Charles Boisvert, Chair, 401-456-8023.
Website: http://www.ric.edu/counselingEducationalLeadershipSchoolPsychology/index.php

Rider University, College of Education and Human Services, Program in School Psychology, Lawrenceville, NJ 08648-3001. Offers Certificate, Ed S. *Entrance requirements:* Additional exam requirements/recommendations for international students: required—TOEFL (minimum score 540 paper-based; 79 iBT). Electronic applications accepted.

Roberts Wesleyan College, Graduate Psychology Programs, Rochester, NY 14624-1997. Offers clinical/school psychology (Psy D); school counseling (MS); school psychology (MS). *Program availability:* Part-time, evening/weekend. *Degree requirements:* For master's, comprehensive exam, PRAXIS II (for school psychology). *Entrance requirements:* For master's, GRE. Electronic applications accepted. Application fee is waived when completed online.

Rochester Institute of Technology, Graduate Enrollment Services, College of Liberal Arts, Psychology Department, Advanced Certificate Program in School Psychology, Rochester, NY 14623-5603. Offers Advanced Certificate. *Program availability:* Part-time. *Entrance requirements:* For degree, minimum GPA of 3.0 (recommended). Additional exam requirements/recommendations for international students: required—TOEFL (minimum score 600 paper-based; 100 iBT), IELTS (minimum score 7), PTE (minimum score 68). Electronic applications accepted.

Rochester Institute of Technology, Graduate Enrollment Services, College of Liberal Arts, Psychology Department, MS Program in School Psychology, Rochester, NY 14623-5603. Offers MS. *Program availability:* Part-time. *Degree requirements:* For master's, internship, portfolio. *Entrance requirements:* For master's, GRE, minimum GPA of 3.0, minimum of 18 semester hours of behavioral science courses with a B or better, complete prerequisite courses, personal statement, personal interview, two letters of recommendation. Additional exam requirements/recommendations for international students: required—TOEFL (minimum score 600 paper-based; 100 iBT), IELTS (minimum score 7), PTE (minimum score 68). Electronic applications accepted.

Roosevelt University, Graduate Division, College of Education, Program in Clinical Mental Health Counseling and School Counseling, Chicago, IL 60605. Offers clinical mental health counseling (MA); school counseling (MA). *Accreditation:* ACA.

Rowan University, Graduate School, College of Education, Department of Educational Services and Leadership, Ed S in School Psychology Program, Glassboro, NJ 08028-1701. Offers Ed S. *Degree requirements:* For Ed S, practicum, internship. *Entrance requirements:* For degree, master's degree, official transcripts, current professional resume, statement of professional objectives, two letters of recommendation, interview. Electronic applications accepted. *Expenses: Tuition, area resident:* Part-time $715.50 per semester hour. Tuition, state resident: part-time $715.50 per semester hour. Tuition, nonresident: part-time $715.50 per semester hour. *Required fees:* $161.55 per semester hour.

Rowan University, Graduate School, College of Education, Department of Educational Services and Leadership, MA in School Psychology Program, Glassboro, NJ 08028-1701. Offers MA. *Accreditation:* NCATE. *Program availability:* Part-time, evening/weekend. *Degree requirements:* For master's, comprehensive exam, thesis. *Entrance requirements:* For master's, GRE General Test, GRE Subject Test, interview, minimum GPA of 3.0. Additional exam requirements/recommendations for international students: required—TOEFL. *Expenses: Tuition, area resident:* Part-time $715.50 per semester hour. Tuition, state resident: part-time $715.50 per semester hour. Tuition, nonresident: part-time $715.50 per semester hour. *Required fees:* $161.55 per semester hour.

Rutgers University - New Brunswick, Graduate School of Applied and Professional Psychology, Program in School Psychology, Piscataway, NJ 08854-8097. Offers Psy M, Psy D. *Accreditation:* APA (one or more programs are accredited). *Degree requirements:* For doctorate, comprehensive exam, thesis/dissertation, 1 year internship. *Entrance requirements:* For doctorate, GRE General Test, GRE Subject Test, bachelor's degree in psychology or equivalent. Additional exam requirements/recommendations for international students: required—TOEFL. Electronic applications accepted. *Expenses:* Contact institution.

St. John's University, St. John's College of Liberal Arts and Sciences, Department of Psychology, Program in School Psychology, Queens, NY 11439. Offers MS, Psy D. Terminal master's awarded for partial completion of doctoral program. *Degree requirements:* For master's, comprehensive exam, internship; for doctorate, comprehensive exam, thesis/dissertation, 105 credits, 2 practica, 2 externships, internship. *Entrance requirements:* For master's and doctorate, GRE General Test, letters of recommendation, transcripts, resume, personal statement, 24 credits of psychology prerequisites, lab paper, term paper. Additional exam requirements/recommendations for international students: required—TOEFL (minimum score 80 iBT), IELTS (minimum score 6.5). Electronic applications accepted. *Expenses:* Contact institution.

Saint Mary's College of California, Kalmanovitz School of Education, Program in Counseling, Moraga, CA 94575. Offers career counseling (MA); college student services (Credential); general counseling (MA); marriage and family therapy (MA); pupil personnel services (Credential), including school counseling, school psychology; school counseling (MA); school psychology (MA). *Program availability:* Part-time, evening/weekend. *Degree requirements:* For master's, thesis or alternative. *Entrance requirements:* For master's, interview, minimum GPA of 3.0.

Sam Houston State University, College of Humanities and Social Sciences, Department of Psychology and Philosophy, Huntsville, TX 77341. Offers psychology (MA, PhD, SSP), including clinical psychology (MA, PhD), psychology (MA), school psychology (SSP). *Accreditation:* APA. *Program availability:* Part-time. Terminal master's awarded for partial completion of doctoral program. *Degree requirements:* For master's, comprehensive exam, thesis optional; for doctorate, comprehensive exam, thesis/dissertation. *Entrance requirements:* For master's, GRE General Test, personal statement, letters of recommendation; for doctorate, GRE General Test, GRE Subject Test (advanced psychology), personal essay, letters of recommendation, resume. Additional exam requirements/recommendations for international students: required—TOEFL (minimum score 550 paper-based; 79 iBT), IELTS (minimum score 6.5). Electronic applications accepted.

San Diego State University, Graduate and Research Affairs, College of Education, Department of Counseling and School Psychology, San Diego, CA 92182. Offers MS. *Accreditation:* NCATE. *Program availability:* Evening/weekend. *Degree requirements:* For master's, comprehensive exam (for some programs), thesis (for some programs). *Entrance requirements:* For master's, GRE General Test, interview, letters of reference. Additional exam requirements/recommendations for international students: required—TOEFL. Electronic applications accepted.

San Francisco State University, Division of Graduate Studies, College of Science and Engineering, Department of Psychology, San Francisco, CA 94132-1722. Offers clinical psychology (MS); developmental psychology (MA); industrial/organizational psychology (MS); mind, brain, and behavior (MA); school psychology (MS, Credential); social, personality, and affective science psychology (MA). *Expenses: Tuition, area resident:* Full-time $7176; part-time $4164 per year. Tuition, state resident: full-time $7176; part-time $4164 per year. Tuition, nonresident: full-time $16,680; part-time $396 per unit. *International tuition:* $16,680 full-time. *Required fees:* $1524; $1524 per unit. $762 per semester. Tuition and fees vary according to degree level and program. *Financial support:* Teaching assistantships available. Financial award application deadline: 3/1. *Unit head:* Dr. Chris Wright, Chair, 415-338-7555, Fax: 415-338-2398, E-mail: cwright@sfsu.edu. *Application contact:* Dr. Ryan Howell, Department Graduate Program Coordinator, 415-405-2140, Fax: 415-338-2398, E-mail: rhowell@sfsu.edu.
Website: http://psychology.sfsu.edu/graduate/application.html

Seattle University, College of Education, Program in Counseling and School Psychology, Seattle, WA 98122-1090. Offers MA, Certificate, Ed S. *Accreditation:* ACA; NCATE. *Program availability:* Part-time, evening/weekend. *Faculty:* 15 full-time (8

women), 13 part-time/adjunct (8 women). *Students:* 106 full-time (89 women), 105 part-time (90 women); includes 78 minority (12 Black or African American, non-Hispanic/Latino; 2 American Indian or Alaska Native, non-Hispanic/Latino; 29 Asian, non-Hispanic/Latino; 27 Hispanic/Latino; 8 Two or more races, non-Hispanic/Latino), 1 international. Average age 29. 239 applicants, 42% accepted, 60 enrolled. In 2019, 47 master's, 25 other advanced degrees awarded. *Entrance requirements:* For master's, interview; GRE, MAT, or minimum GPA of 3.0; related work experience. Additional exam requirements/recommendations for international students: required—TOEFL. *Application deadline:* For fall admission, 7/1 for domestic students; for winter admission, 10/20 for domestic students; for spring admission, 1/20 for domestic students. Application fee: $55. *Financial support:* In 2019–20, 52 students received support. *Unit head:* Hutch Haney, Director, 206-296-5750, E-mail: schpsy@seattleu.edu. *Application contact:* Janet Shandley, Associate Dean of Graduate Admissions, 206-296-5900, Fax: 206-298-5656, E-mail: grad_admissions@seattleu.edu.
Website: https://www.seattleu.edu/education/psychology/

Seton Hall University, College of Education and Human Services, Department of Professional Psychology and Family Therapy, Program in School Psychology, South Orange, NJ 07079-2697. Offers MA. *Faculty:* 2 full-time (1 woman), 8 part-time/adjunct (2 women). *Students:* 4 full-time (all women), 102 part-time (90 women); includes 22 minority (12 Black or African American, non-Hispanic/Latino; 1 American Indian or Alaska Native, non-Hispanic/Latino; 2 Asian, non-Hispanic/Latino; 6 Hispanic/Latino; 1 Two or more races, non-Hispanic/Latino). Average age 27. 25 applicants, 40% accepted, 7 enrolled. In 2019, 27 master's awarded. *Degree requirements:* For master's, comprehensive exam, thesis, internship. *Entrance requirements:* For master's, GRE or MAT, interview. *Application deadline:* For fall admission, 2/1 priority date for domestic and international students. Applications are processed on a rolling basis. Application fee: $75. Electronic applications accepted. *Financial support:* In 2019–20, 5 students received support. Unspecified assistantships available. Financial award application deadline: 2/1; financial award applicants required to submit CSS PROFILE. *Unit head:* Dr. Thomas Massarelli, Director, 973-313-6129, Fax: 973-275-2188, E-mail: massarth@shu.edu. *Application contact:* Diana Minakakis, Director of Graduate Admissions, 973-275-2824.
Website: http://www.shu.edu/academics/ma-eds-school-psychology.cfm

Sonoma State University, School of Social Sciences, Department of Counseling, Rohnert Park, CA 94928-3609. Offers clinical mental health counseling (MA); school counseling (MA). *Accreditation:* ACA. *Program availability:* Part-time. *Entrance requirements:* For master's, minimum GPA of 3.0. Additional exam requirements/recommendations for international students: required—TOEFL (minimum score 500 paper-based).

Southern Connecticut State University, School of Graduate Studies, School of Education, Department of Counseling and School Psychology, New Haven, CT 06515-1355. Offers community counseling (MS); counseling (Diploma); school counseling (MS); school psychology (MS, Diploma). *Accreditation:* ACA (one or more programs are accredited); NCATE. *Program availability:* Part-time, evening/weekend. *Degree requirements:* For master's, comprehensive exam. *Entrance requirements:* For master's, interview, previous course work in behavioral sciences, minimum QPA of 2.7. Electronic applications accepted.

Southern Illinois University Edwardsville, Graduate School, School of Education, Health, and Human Behavior, Department of Psychology, Program in School Psychology, Edwardsville, IL 62026. Offers SD. *Accreditation:* NCATE. *Program availability:* Part-time, evening/weekend. *Degree requirements:* For SD, thesis. *Entrance requirements:* For degree, GRE. Additional exam requirements/recommendations for international students: required—TOEFL (minimum score 550 paper-based; 79 iBT), IELTS (minimum score 6.5). Electronic applications accepted.

Southwestern Oklahoma State University, College of Professional and Graduate Studies, School of Behavioral Sciences and Education, Specialization in School Psychology, Weatherford, OK 73096-3098. Offers Ed S. *Entrance requirements:* Additional exam requirements/recommendations for international students: required—TOEFL (minimum score 550 paper-based), IELTS (minimum score 6.5).

State University of New York at Plattsburgh, School of Arts and Sciences, Department of Psychology, Plattsburgh, NY 12901-2681. Offers school psychology (MA, CAS). *Program availability:* Part-time. *Entrance requirements:* For master's, GRE General Test, minimum GPA of 3.0. Additional exam requirements/recommendations for international students: required—TOEFL.

Stephen F. Austin State University, Graduate School, James I. Perkins College of Education, Department of Human Services, Nacogdoches, TX 75962. Offers counseling (MA); school psychology (MA); special education (M Ed); speech-language pathology (MS). *Accreditation:* ACA (one or more programs are accredited); ASHA (one or more programs are accredited); CORE; NCATE. *Degree requirements:* For master's, comprehensive exam, thesis (for some programs). *Entrance requirements:* For master's, GRE General Test, minimum GPA of 2.8. Additional exam requirements/recommendations for international students: required—TOEFL.

Syracuse University, College of Arts and Sciences, Department of Psychology, Syracuse, NY 13244. Offers clinical psychology (PhD); cognition, brain, and behavior (PhD); school psychology (PhD); social psychology (PhD). *Accreditation:* APA. Terminal master's awarded for partial completion of doctoral program. *Degree requirements:* For doctorate, comprehensive exam, thesis/dissertation. *Entrance requirements:* For doctorate, GRE General Test, GRE Subject Test, resume, personal statement, three letters of recommendation. Additional exam requirements/recommendations for international students: required—TOEFL (minimum score 100 iBT). Electronic applications accepted.

Syracuse University, School of Education, Programs in School Counseling, Syracuse, NY 13244. Offers MS, CAS. *Accreditation:* APA. *Program availability:* Part-time. *Entrance requirements:* For master's, GRE or MAT, baccalaureate degree from regionally-accredited college/university, three letters of recommendation, transcripts, personal statement, interview; for CAS, master's degree in counseling; minimum of 60 credits beyond the baccalaureate, of which 30 credits must be taken at Syracuse University. Additional exam requirements/recommendations for international students: required—TOEFL (minimum score 100 iBT). Electronic applications accepted.

Teachers College, Columbia University, Department of Counseling and Clinical Psychology, New York, NY 10027-6696. Offers clinical psychology (PhD); counseling psychology (Ed M, Ed D, PhD); mental health counseling (ME); psychological counseling (ME, ND); psychology in education (MA, ND); school counselor (ME). *Accreditation:* APA (one or more programs are accredited). *Program availability:* Part-time.

Teachers College, Columbia University, Department of Health and Behavior Studies, New York, NY 10027-6696. Offers applied behavior analysis (MA, PhD); applied educational psychology: school psychology (Ed M, PhD); behavioral nutrition (PhD), including nutrition (Ed D, PhD); community health education (MS); community nutrition education (Ed M), including community nutrition education; education of deaf and hard of hearing (MA, PhD); health education (MA, Ed D); hearing impairment (Ed D); intellectual disability/autism (MA, Ed D, PhD); nursing education (Ed D, Advanced Certificate); nutrition and education (MS); nutrition and exercise physiology (MS); nutrition and public health (MS); nutrition education (Ed D), including nutrition (Ed D, PhD); physical disabilities (Ed D); reading specialist (MA); severe or multiple disabilities (MA); special education (Ed M, MA, Ed D); teaching of sign language (MA). *Faculty:* 17 full-time (11 women). *Students:* 243 full-time (225 women), 246 part-time (211 women); includes 172 minority (33 Black or African American, non-Hispanic/Latino; 2 American Indian or Alaska Native, non-Hispanic/Latino; 63 Asian, non-Hispanic/Latino; 63 Hispanic/Latino; 11 Two or more races, non-Hispanic/Latino), 67 international. 515 applicants, 68% accepted, 170 enrolled. *Unit head:* Dr. Dolores Perin, Chair, 212-678-3091, E-mail: dp111@tc.columbia.edu. *Application contact:* Kelly Sutton-Skinner, Director of Admission and New Student Enrollment, E-mail: kms2237@tc.columbia.edu.
Website: http://www.tc.columbia.edu/health-and-behavior-studies/

Temple University, College of Education and Human Development, Department of Psychological Studies in Education, Philadelphia, PA 19122-6096. Offers applied behavior analysis (MS Ed); counseling psychology (Ed M), including agency counseling, school counseling; educational psychology (Ed M); school psychology (PhD, Ed S). *Accreditation:* APA (one or more programs are accredited). *Program availability:* Part-time, evening/weekend. *Faculty:* 19 full-time (10 women), 19 part-time/adjunct (9 women). *Students:* 165 full-time (122 women), 49 part-time (37 women); includes 74 minority (39 Black or African American, non-Hispanic/Latino; 13 Asian, non-Hispanic/Latino; 17 Hispanic/Latino; 5 Two or more races, non-Hispanic/Latino), 11 international. 374 applicants, 49% accepted, 100 enrolled. In 2019, 73 master's, 5 doctorates, 16 other advanced degrees awarded. *Degree requirements:* For master's, comprehensive exam (for some programs); for doctorate, thesis/dissertation. *Entrance requirements:* For master's, statement of goals, 2 recommendation letters; for doctorate, GRE, statement of goals, academic writing sample, 2 recommendation letters. Additional exam requirements/recommendations for international students: required—TOEFL (minimum score 79 iBT), IELTS, PTE, one of three is required. Application fee: $60. Electronic applications accepted. *Financial support:* Fellowships, research assistantships, teaching assistantships, career-related internships or fieldwork, Federal Work-Study, health care benefits, and unspecified assistantships available. Financial award applicants required to submit FAFSA. *Unit head:* Renee Tobin, Prof. of Counseling Psychology and Dept. Chairperson, 215-204-7884, E-mail: renee.tobin@temple.edu. *Application contact:* Remy Van Wyk, Academic Coordinator, 215-204-1474, E-mail: remy.van.wyk@temple.edu.
Website: http://education.temple.edu/pse

Texas A&M University, College of Education and Human Development, Department of Educational Psychology, College Station, TX 77843. Offers bilingual education (M Ed, MS); counseling psychology (PhD); educational psychology (M Ed, MS, PhD); educational technology (M Ed); school psychology (PhD); special education (M Ed, MS). *Accreditation:* APA (one or more programs are accredited). *Program availability:* Part-time, evening/weekend, blended/hybrid learning. *Faculty:* 47. *Students:* 162 full-time (135 women), 248 part-time (205 women); includes 154 minority (26 Black or African American, non-Hispanic/Latino; 1 American Indian or Alaska Native, non-Hispanic/Latino; 20 Asian, non-Hispanic/Latino; 97 Hispanic/Latino; 1 Native Hawaiian or other Pacific Islander, non-Hispanic/Latino; 9 Two or more races, non-Hispanic/Latino), 49 international. Average age 33. 174 applicants, 51% accepted, 61 enrolled. In 2019, 107 master's, 21 doctorates awarded. *Degree requirements:* For master's, thesis optional; for doctorate, thesis/dissertation. *Entrance requirements:* For master's and doctorate, GRE General Test. Additional exam requirements/recommendations for international students: required—TOEFL (minimum score 550 paper-based; 80 iBT), IELTS (minimum score 6), PTE (minimum score 53). Application fee: $65 ($90 for international students). Electronic applications accepted. *Expenses:* Contact institution. *Financial support:* In 2019–20, 272 students received support, including 16 fellowships with tuition reimbursements available (averaging $13,000 per year), 122 research assistantships with tuition reimbursements available (averaging $14,333 per year), 23 teaching assistantships with tuition reimbursements available (averaging $9,052 per year); career-related internships or fieldwork, institutionally sponsored loans, scholarships/grants, traineeships, health care benefits, tuition waivers (full and partial), and unspecified assistantships also available. Support available to part-time students. Financial award application deadline: 3/15; financial award applicants required to submit FAFSA. *Unit head:* Dr. Fuhui Tong, Interim Department Head, E-mail: fuhuitong@tamu.edu. *Application contact:* Sally Kallina, Academic Advisor IV, E-mail: skallina@tamu.edu.
Website: http://epsy.tamu.edu

Texas A&M University–Central Texas, Graduate Studies and Research, Killeen, TX 76549. Offers accounting (MS); business administration (MBA); clinical mental health counseling (MS); criminal justice (MCJ); curriculum and instruction (M Ed); educational administration (M Ed); educational psychology - experimental psychology (MS); history (MA); human resource management (MS); information systems (MS); liberal studies (MS); management and leadership (MS); marriage and family therapy (MS); mathematics (MS); political science (MA); school counseling (M Ed); school psychology (Ed S).

Texas State University, The Graduate College, College of Education, Program in School Psychology, San Marcos, TX 78666. Offers SSP. *Program availability:* Part-time. *Entrance requirements:* Additional exam requirements/recommendations for international students: required—TOEFL (minimum score 550 paper-based; 78 iBT), IELTS (minimum score 6.5). Electronic applications accepted.

Texas Woman's University, Graduate School, College of Arts and Sciences, Department of Psychology and Philosophy, Denton, TX 76204. Offers counseling psychology (MA, PhD); psychological science (MS); school psychology (PhD, SSP). *Accreditation:* APA (one or more programs are accredited). *Faculty:* 16 full-time (12 women), 5 part-time/adjunct (3 women). *Students:* 88 full-time (81 women), 50 part-time (42 women); includes 65 minority (16 Black or African American, non-Hispanic/Latino; 14 Asian, non-Hispanic/Latino; 33 Hispanic/Latino; 2 Two or more races, non-Hispanic/Latino). Average age 28. 132 applicants, 33% accepted, 33 enrolled. In 2019, 20 master's, 6 doctorates awarded. Terminal master's awarded for partial completion of doctoral program. *Degree requirements:* For master's, comprehensive exam (for some programs), thesis or alternative, practica (for MA); thesis or coursework; written exam required for those who do not complete a thesis; for doctorate, comprehensive exam, thesis/dissertation, internship, residency; for SSP, comprehensive exam, SSP-internship, capstone evaluation. *Entrance requirements:* For master's, GRE (preferred minimum score 153 Verbal, 144 Quantitative), BA/BS or 18 hours in psychology; minimum GPA of 3.0, 3.5 in psychology classes; 3 letters of reference; curriculum vitae/resume; essay, interview; for doctorate, GRE (preferred minimum score 153 [500 old version] Verbal, 144 [500 old version] Quantitative, 4 Analytical), 3 letters of reference, minimum GPA of 3.0 overall and 3.5 in psychology classes, MA in psychology or related discipline with thesis, curriculum vitae, essays; for SSP, GRE (preferred minimum score 153 [500 old version] Verbal, 144 [500 old version] Quantitative, 4 Analytical), BA/BS or 18 hours in psychology; minimum GPA of 3.0, 3.5 in psychology classes; 3 letters of reference; curriculum vitae; personal essay. Additional exam requirements/recommendations for international students: required—TOEFL (minimum score 550

paper-based; 79 iBT); recommended—IELTS (minimum score 6.5), TSE (minimum score 53). *Application deadline:* For fall admission, 2/1 for domestic and international students. Application fee: $50 ($75 for international students). Electronic applications accepted. *Expenses: Tuition, area resident:* Full-time $4973.40; part-time $276.30 per semester hour. Tuition, state resident: full-time $4973.40; part-time $276.30 per semester hour. Tuition, nonresident: full-time $12,569; part-time $698.30 per semester hour. *International tuition:* $12,569.40 full-time. *Required fees:* $2524.30. Tuition and fees vary according to course level, course load, degree level and program. *Financial support:* In 2019–20, 93 students received support, including 53 teaching assistantships (averaging $6,217 per year); career-related internships or fieldwork, scholarships/grants, health care benefits, and unspecified assistantships also available. Support available to part-time students. Financial award application deadline: 3/1; financial award applicants required to submit FAFSA. *Unit head:* Dr. Brian Harding, Acting Chair, 940-898-2303, Fax: 940-898-2301, E-mail: psychology@twu.edu. *Application contact:* Korie Hawkins, Associate Director of Admissions, Graduate Recruitment, 940-898-3188, Fax: 940-898-3081, E-mail: admissions@twu.edu.
Website: http://www.twu.edu/psychology-philosophy/

Towson University, College of Liberal Arts, Program in Psychology, Towson, MD 21252-0001. Offers clinical psychology (MA); counseling psychology (MA); experimental psychology (MA); school psychology (MA). *Program availability:* Part-time, evening/weekend. *Students:* 97 full-time (79 women), 25 part-time (20 women); includes 27 minority (15 Black or African American, non-Hispanic/Latino; 3 Asian, non-Hispanic/Latino; 2 Hispanic/Latino; 7 Two or more races, non-Hispanic/Latino), 3 international. *Entrance requirements:* For master's, GRE, minimum GPA of 3.0, letters of recommendation. *Application deadline:* For fall admission, 1/17 for domestic students, 5/15 for international students; for spring admission, 10/15 for domestic students, 12/1 for international students. Applications are processed on a rolling basis. Application fee: $45. Electronic applications accepted. *Expenses: Tuition, area resident:* Full-time $7920; part-time $439 per credit. Tuition, nonresident: full-time $16,344; part-time $908 per credit. *International tuition:* $16,344 full-time. *Required fees:* $2628; $146 per credit. $876 per term. *Financial support:* Application deadline: 4/1. *Unit head:* Dr. Geoffrey Munro, Department Chair, 410-704-2634, E-mail: psycdept@towson.edu. *Application contact:* Coverley Beidleman, Assistant Director of Graduate Admissions, 410-704-5630, Fax: 410-704-3030, E-mail: grads@towson.edu.
Website: https://www.towson.edu/cla/departments/psychology/grad/

Trinity University, Department of Education, San Antonio, TX 78212-7200. Offers school leadership (M Ed); school psychology (MA); teaching (MAT). *Accreditation:* NCATE. *Program availability:* Part-time, evening/weekend. *Faculty:* 1 (woman) full-time, 14 part-time/adjunct (6 women). *Students:* 57 full-time (44 women), 4 part-time (2 women); includes 38 minority (6 Black or African American, non-Hispanic/Latino; 1 Asian, non-Hispanic/Latino; 26 Hispanic/Latino; 5 Two or more races, non-Hispanic/Latino), 2 international. Average age 36. In 2019, 42 master's awarded. *Financial support:* Application deadline: 5/1; applicants required to submit FAFSA. *Unit head:* Norvella Carter, Interim Chair, 210-999-7506, Fax: 210-999-7592, E-mail: ncarter1@trinity.edu. *Application contact:* Office of Admissions, 210-999-7207, Fax: 210-999-8164, E-mail: admissions@trinity.edu.

Trinity University, Department of Education, Master of Arts in School Psychology Program, San Antonio, TX 78212-7200. Offers school psychology (MA). *Accreditation:* NCATE. *Students:* 13 full-time (11 women), 4 part-time (2 women); includes 11 minority (1 Black or African American, non-Hispanic/Latino; 1 Asian, non-Hispanic/Latino; 8 Hispanic/Latino; 1 Two or more races, non-Hispanic/Latino). Average age 26. In 2019, 6 master's awarded. *Entrance requirements:* For master's, GRE or master's degree, minimum GPA of 3.0, academic and professional references, interview with program director, written statement, resume. *Application deadline:* For fall admission, 2/1 for domestic and international students. Application fee: $50. Electronic applications accepted. *Financial support:* Institutionally sponsored loans, scholarships/grants, and unspecified assistantships available. Support available to part-time students. Financial award application deadline: 5/1; financial award applicants required to submit FAFSA. *Unit head:* Dr. Laurie Klose, Director, 210-999-7595, E-mail: lklose@trinity.edu. *Application contact:* Sonia Mireles, Academic Office Manager, 210-999-8835, E-mail: smireles@trinity.edu.
Website: https://new.trinity.edu/academics/departments/education/master-arts-school-psychology

Tufts University, Graduate School of Arts and Sciences, Department of Education, Program in School Psychology, Medford, MA 02155. Offers MA, Ed S. *Degree requirements:* For master's, internship. *Entrance requirements:* For master's, GRE General Test. Additional exam requirements/recommendations for international students: required—TOEFL (minimum score 550 paper-based; 80 iBT), IELTS (minimum score 6.5). Electronic applications accepted. *Expenses:* Contact institution.

Union College, Graduate Programs, Department of Psychology, Barbourville, KY 40906-1499. Offers clinical psychology (MA); counseling psychology (MA); school psychology (MA).

University of Alberta, Faculty of Graduate Studies and Research, Department of Educational Psychology, Edmonton, AB T6G 2E1, Canada. Offers counseling psychology (M Ed, PhD); educational psychology (M Ed, PhD); instructional technology (M Ed); school counseling (M Ed); school psychology (M Ed, PhD); special education (M Ed, PhD); special education-deafness studies (M Ed); teaching English as a second language (M Ed). *Program availability:* Part-time. *Degree requirements:* For master's, thesis optional; for doctorate, comprehensive exam, thesis/dissertation. *Entrance requirements:* For master's and doctorate, minimum GPA of 3.0. Additional exam requirements/recommendations for international students: required—TOEFL.

The University of Arizona, College of Education, Department of Disability and Psychoeducational Studies, Program in School Psychology, Tucson, AZ 85721. Offers PhD, Ed S. *Program availability:* Part-time. *Entrance requirements:* For doctorate, GRE General Test; for Ed S, minimum GPA of 3.5, 3 letters of recommendation, curriculum vitae, writing sample. Additional exam requirements/recommendations for international students: required—TOEFL (minimum score 550 paper-based; 79 iBT). Electronic applications accepted.

The University of British Columbia, Faculty of Education, Department of Educational and Counseling Psychology, and Special Education, Vancouver, BC V6T 1Z4, Canada. Offers counseling psychology (M Ed, MA, PhD); guidance studies (Diploma); human development, learning and culture (M Ed, MA, PhD); measurement, evaluation, and research methodology (M Ed, MA, PhD); school psychology (M Ed, MA, PhD); special education (M Ed, MA, PhD, Diploma). *Program availability:* Part-time. *Degree requirements:* For master's, thesis (for some programs); for doctorate, comprehensive exam, thesis/dissertation. *Entrance requirements:* For master's, GRE General Test (for MA in counseling psychology); for doctorate, GRE General Test. Additional exam requirements/recommendations for international students: required—TOEFL. Electronic applications accepted. *Expenses:* Contact institution.

University of Calgary, Faculty of Graduate Studies, Werklund School of Education, Program in School of Applied Child Psychology, Calgary, AB T2N 1N4, Canada. Offers counseling psychology (M Sc, MC, PhD); school and applied child psychology (M Ed, M Sc, PhD). *Program availability:* Part-time. *Degree requirements:* For master's, thesis (for some programs), final oral exam; for doctorate, thesis/dissertation, candidacy exam, final oral exam. *Entrance requirements:* For master's, minimum GPA of 3.0, 3 letters of reference; for doctorate, minimum GPA of 3.5, 3 letters of reference.

University of California, Riverside, Graduate Division, Graduate School of Education, Riverside, CA 92521. Offers applied behavior analysis (M Ed); diversity and equity (M Ed); education policy analysis and leadership (PhD); education specialist (Credential); education, society, and culture (MA, PhD); educational psychology (MA, PhD); general education (M Ed); higher education administration and policy (M Ed, PhD); multiple subject (Credential); research, evaluation, measurement and statistics (MA); school psychology (PhD); single subject (Credential); special education (M Ed, PhD); special education and autism (MA); TESOL (M Ed). Terminal master's awarded for partial completion of doctoral program. *Degree requirements:* For master's, comprehensive exams or thesis (MA), case study or analytical report (M Ed); for doctorate, comprehensive exam, thesis/dissertation, written and oral qualifying exams, college teaching practicum. *Entrance requirements:* For master's, GRE General Test (for MA); CBEST and CSET (for M Ed in general education only), UCR Extension TESOL certificate (for M Ed with TESOL emphasis only); for doctorate, GRE General Test, writing sample; for Credential, CBEST, CSET. Additional exam requirements/recommendations for international students: required—TOEFL (minimum score 550 paper-based; 80 iBT), IELTS (minimum score 7). Electronic applications accepted.

University of California, Santa Barbara, Graduate Division, Gevirtz Graduate School of Education, Santa Barbara, CA 93106-9490. Offers counseling, clinical and school psychology (MA, PhD, Credential), including clinical psychology (PhD), counseling psychology (MA, PhD), pupil personnel services (Credential), school psychology (PhD); education (MA, PhD); teacher education (M Ed, Credential), including multiple subject teaching (Credential), single subject teaching (Credential), special education (Credential), teaching (M Ed); MA/PhD. *Accreditation:* APA (one or more programs are accredited). Terminal master's awarded for partial completion of doctoral program. *Degree requirements:* For master's, comprehensive exam (for some programs), thesis (for some programs); for doctorate, comprehensive exam (for some programs), thesis/dissertation. *Entrance requirements:* For master's and doctorate, GRE; for Credential, GRE or MAT, CSET, CBEST. Additional exam requirements/recommendations for international students: required—TOEFL (minimum score 550 paper-based; 80 iBT), IELTS (minimum score 7). Electronic applications accepted.

University of Central Arkansas, Graduate School, College of Health and Behavioral Sciences, Department of Counseling and Psychology, Program in School Psychology, Conway, AR 72035-0001. Offers MS, PhD, PMC. *Accreditation:* APA; NCATE. Terminal master's awarded for partial completion of doctoral program. *Degree requirements:* For master's, comprehensive exam, thesis optional; for doctorate, comprehensive exam, thesis/dissertation. *Entrance requirements:* For master's, GRE General Test, minimum GPA of 2.7; for doctorate, GRE General Test. Additional exam requirements/recommendations for international students: required—TOEFL (minimum score 550 paper-based). Electronic applications accepted.

University of Central Florida, College of Community Innovation and Education, Department of Counselor Education and School Psychology, Program in School Psychology, Orlando, FL 32816. Offers Ed S. *Program availability:* Part-time, evening/weekend. *Students:* 35 full-time (32 women); includes 9 minority (3 Black or African American, non-Hispanic/Latino; 1 Asian, non-Hispanic/Latino; 4 Hispanic/Latino; 1 Two or more races, non-Hispanic/Latino). Average age 27. 71 applicants, 25% accepted, 17 enrolled. In 2019, 16 Ed Ss awarded. *Degree requirements:* For Ed S, thesis or alternative, practicum, internship. *Entrance requirements:* For degree, GRE General Test, minimum GPA of 3.0, resume, letters of recommendation, goal statement, interview. Additional exam requirements/recommendations for international students: required—TOEFL. *Application deadline:* For fall admission, 3/1 for domestic students. Application fee: $30. Electronic applications accepted. *Financial support:* In 2019–20, 6 students received support, including 1 fellowship (averaging $5,000 per year), 2 research assistantships with partial tuition reimbursements available (averaging $6,395 per year), 3 teaching assistantships with partial tuition reimbursements available (averaging $5,478 per year); career-related internships or fieldwork, Federal Work-Study, institutionally sponsored loans, health care benefits, and tuition waivers (partial) also available. Financial award application deadline: 3/1; financial award applicants required to submit FAFSA. *Unit head:* Dr. Oliver Edwards, Program Coordinator, 407-823-2401, E-mail: oliver.edwards@ucf.edu. *Application contact:* Associate Director, Graduate Admissions, 407-823-2766, Fax: 407-823-6442, E-mail: gradadmissions@ucf.edu.
Website: http://education.ucf.edu/schpsy/

University of Central Oklahoma, The Jackson College of Graduate Studies, College of Education and Professional Studies, Department of Psychology, Edmond, OK 73034-5209. Offers psychology (MA), including counseling psychology, experimental psychology, forensic psychology, general psychology, school psychology. *Degree requirements:* For master's, thesis (for some programs). *Entrance requirements:* For master's, GRE. Additional exam requirements/recommendations for international students: required—TOEFL (minimum score 550 paper-based; 79 iBT), IELTS (minimum score 6.5). Electronic applications accepted.

University of Cincinnati, Graduate School, College of Education, Criminal Justice, and Human Services, School of Human Services, School Psychology Program, Cincinnati, OH 45221. Offers PhD, Ed S. *Accreditation:* NCATE. *Program availability:* Online only, 100% online. Terminal master's awarded for partial completion of doctoral program. *Degree requirements:* For doctorate, comprehensive exam, thesis/dissertation. *Entrance requirements:* For doctorate, GRE General Test, GRE Subject Test. Additional exam requirements/recommendations for international students: required—TOEFL (minimum score 520 paper-based; 68 iBT). Electronic applications accepted.

University of Colorado Denver, School of Education and Human Development, Program in Counseling Psychology and Counselor Education, Denver, CO 80217. Offers counseling (MA), including clinical mental health counseling, couple and family counseling, multicultural counseling, school counseling; school counseling (MA). *Accreditation:* ACA; NCATE. *Program availability:* Part-time, evening/weekend. *Entrance requirements:* For master's, GRE or MAT (unless applicant already holds a graduate degree), letters of recommendation, interview, resume, transcripts from all colleges/universities attended. Tuition and fees vary according to course load, program and reciprocity agreements.

University of Colorado Denver, School of Education and Human Development, Program in School Psychology, Denver, CO 80217-3364. Offers Psy D. Tuition and fees vary according to course load, program and reciprocity agreements.

University of Dayton, Department of Counselor Education and Human Services, Dayton, OH 45469. Offers clinical mental health counseling (MS Ed); college student personnel (MS Ed); higher education administration (MS Ed); human services (MS Ed); school counseling (MS Ed); school psychology (MS Ed, Ed S). *Accreditation:* ACA; NCATE. *Program availability:* Part-time. *Degree requirements:* For master's, thesis (for some programs); for Ed S, thesis (for some programs), professional portfolio. *Entrance requirements:* For master's, MAT or GRE (if GPA less than 2.75), essays (for some programs). Additional exam requirements/recommendations for international students: required—TOEFL (minimum score 550 paper-based; 80 iBT). Electronic applications accepted. *Expenses:* Contact institution.

University of Delaware, College of Education and Human Development, School of Education, Newark, DE 19716. Offers education (PhD); educational leadership (Ed D); higher education (M Ed); instruction (MI); reading (M Ed); school leadership (M Ed); school psychology (MA, Ed S); teaching English as a second language (TESL) (MA). *Accreditation:* NCATE. *Program availability:* Part-time, evening/weekend. Terminal master's awarded for partial completion of doctoral program. *Degree requirements:* For master's, comprehensive exam (for some programs), thesis (for some programs); for doctorate, comprehensive exam (for some programs), thesis/dissertation. *Entrance requirements:* For master's and doctorate, GRE, 3 letters of recommendation. Additional exam requirements/recommendations for international students: required—TOEFL (minimum score 600 paper-based). Electronic applications accepted.

University of Denver, Morgridge College of Education, Denver, CO 80208. Offers child, family and school psychology (MA, PhD, Ed S); counseling psychology (MA, PhD); curriculum and instruction (MA, Ed D, PhD); curriculum instruction and teaching (Certificate); early childhood special education (MA, Certificate); educational leadership and policy studies (MA, Ed D, PhD, Certificate); higher education (Ed D, PhD); library and information science (MLIS); research methods and statistics (MA, PhD). *Accreditation:* ALA; APA (one or more programs are accredited). *Program availability:* Part-time, evening/weekend, online learning. *Faculty:* 54 full-time (38 women), 28 part-time/adjunct (16 women). *Students:* 477 full-time (385 women), 492 part-time (378 women); includes 266 minority (59 Black or African American, non-Hispanic/Latino; 7 American Indian or Alaska Native, non-Hispanic/Latino; 36 Asian, non-Hispanic/Latino; 128 Hispanic/Latino; 2 Native Hawaiian or other Pacific Islander, non-Hispanic/Latino; 34 Two or more races, non-Hispanic/Latino), 58 international. Average age 31. 1,252 applicants, 68% accepted, 420 enrolled. In 2019, 222 master's, 46 doctorates, 129 other advanced degrees awarded. Terminal master's awarded for partial completion of doctoral program. *Degree requirements:* For master's, comprehensive exam (for some programs); for doctorate, comprehensive exam (for some programs), thesis/dissertation. *Entrance requirements:* For master's, GRE General Test or GMAT, bachelors degree; transcripts; two letters of recommendation; personal statement; resume; for doctorate, GRE General Test or GMAT, Masters degree; transcripts; two letters of recommendation; personal statement(s); resume. Additional exam requirements/recommendations for international students: required—TOEFL (minimum score 550 paper-based; 80 iBT). *Application deadline:* Applications are processed on a rolling basis. Application fee: $65. Electronic applications accepted. *Expenses:* Contact institution. *Financial support:* In 2019–20, 698 students received support, including 19 research assistantships with tuition reimbursements available (averaging $11,372 per year), 3 teaching assistantships with tuition reimbursements available (averaging $4,333 per year); career-related internships or fieldwork, Federal Work-Study, institutionally sponsored loans, scholarships/grants, and unspecified assistantships also available. Support available to part-time students. Financial award application deadline: 2/15; financial award applicants required to submit FAFSA. *Unit head:* Dr. Karen Riley, Dean, 303-871-3665, E-mail: karen.riley@du.edu. *Application contact:* Jodi Dye, Director of Admissions, 303-871-2510, E-mail: jodi.dye@du.edu.
Website: http://morgridge.du.edu

University of Detroit Mercy, College of Liberal Arts and Education, Detroit, MI 48221. Offers addiction counseling (MA); addiction studies (Certificate); clinical mental health counseling (MA); clinical psychology (MA, PhD); computer and information systems (MS); criminal justice (MA); curriculum and instruction (MA); economics (MA); educational administration (MA); financial economics (MA); industrial/organizational psychology (MA); information assurance (MS); intelligence analysis (MA); liberal studies (MALS); religious studies (MA); school counseling (MA, Certificate); school psychology (Spec); security administration (MS); special education: emotionally impaired/behaviorally disordered (MA); special education: learning disabilities (MA). *Program availability:* Part-time, evening/weekend. *Degree requirements:* For doctorate, departmental qualifying exam.

University of Florida, Graduate School, College of Education, School of Special Education, School Psychology and Early Childhood Studies, Gainesville, FL 32611. Offers early childhood education (M Ed, MAE); school psychology (M Ed, MAE, Ed D, PhD, Ed S); special education (M Ed, MAE, Ed D, PhD, Ed S). *Accreditation:* NCATE. *Program availability:* Part-time, evening/weekend, online learning. *Degree requirements:* For master's, comprehensive exam (for some programs), thesis (MAE); for doctorate, comprehensive exam, thesis/dissertation. *Entrance requirements:* For master's and doctorate, GRE General Test, minimum GPA of 3.0; for Ed S, GRE General Test. Additional exam requirements/recommendations for international students: required—TOEFL (minimum score 550 paper-based; 80 iBT), IELTS (minimum score 6). Electronic applications accepted.

University of Hartford, College of Arts and Sciences, Department of Psychology, Program in School Psychology, West Hartford, CT 06117-1599. Offers MS. *Accreditation:* NCATE. *Program availability:* Part-time. *Faculty:* 2 full-time (1 woman). *Students:* 19 full-time (17 women), 13 part-time (10 women); includes 5 minority (1 Black or African American, non-Hispanic/Latino; 3 Hispanic/Latino; 1 Two or more races, non-Hispanic/Latino). Average age 24. 37 applicants, 65% accepted, 23 enrolled. In 2019, 7 master's awarded. *Entrance requirements:* For master's, GRE General Test, GRE Subject Test, minimum GPA of 3.0, 3 letters of recommendation. Additional exam requirements/recommendations for international students: required—TOEFL (minimum score 550 paper-based). *Application deadline:* For fall admission, 2/15 priority date for domestic students. Application fee: $45. Electronic applications accepted. *Expenses: Tuition:* Full-time $23,700; part-time $645 per credit. *Required fees:* $510; $510 per unit. Tuition and fees vary according to course load, degree level and program. *Financial support:* In 2019–20, 1 research assistantship (averaging $2,000 per year), 5 teaching assistantships (averaging $2,600 per year) were awarded; Federal Work-Study also available. Support available to part-time students. Financial award application deadline: 6/1; financial award applicants required to submit FAFSA. *Unit head:* Dr. Tony Crespi, Director, 860-768-5081, Fax: 860-768-5292, E-mail: crespi@hartford.edu. *Application contact:* Renee Murphy, Assistant Director of Graduate Admissions, 860-768-4371, Fax: 860-768-5160, E-mail: gettoknow@hartford.edu.
Website: http://whaweb.hartford.edu/psych/

University of Houston–Clear Lake, School of Human Sciences and Humanities, Programs in Human Sciences, Houston, TX 77058-1002. Offers behavioral sciences (MA), including criminology, cross cultural studies, general psychology, sociology; clinical psychology (MA); criminology (MA); cross cultural studies (MA); family therapy (MA); fitness and human performance (MA); school psychology (MA). *Accreditation:* AAMFT/COAMFTE. *Program availability:* Part-time, evening/weekend, online learning. *Degree requirements:* For master's, thesis or alternative. *Entrance requirements:* For master's, GRE General Test. Additional exam requirements/recommendations for international students: required—TOEFL (minimum score 550 paper-based). Electronic applications accepted.

University of Houston–Victoria, School of Arts and Sciences, Program in Psychology, Victoria, TX 77901-4450. Offers counseling psychology (MA); forensic psychology (MA); school psychology (MA). *Program availability:* Part-time, evening/weekend, online learning. *Degree requirements:* For master's, project or thesis. *Entrance requirements:* For master's, GRE General Test. Additional exam requirements/recommendations for international students: required—TOEFL (minimum score 550 paper-based). Electronic applications accepted.

The University of Iowa, Graduate College, College of Education, Department of Psychological and Quantitative Foundations, Iowa City, IA 52242-1316. Offers counseling psychology (PhD); educational measurement and statistics (MA, PhD); educational psychology (MA, PhD); school psychology (PhD, Ed S). *Accreditation:* APA. *Degree requirements:* For master's, thesis optional, exam; for doctorate, comprehensive exam, thesis/dissertation; for Ed S, exam. *Entrance requirements:* For master's, doctorate, and Ed S, GRE General Test, minimum GPA of 3.0. Additional exam requirements/recommendations for international students: required—TOEFL (minimum score 550 paper-based; 81 iBT). Electronic applications accepted.

The University of Kansas, Graduate Studies, School of Education, Department of Educational Psychology, Program in School Psychology, Lawrence, KS 66045. Offers PhD, Ed S. *Accreditation:* APA (one or more programs are accredited); NCATE. *Students:* 25 full-time (22 women), 1 (woman) part-time; includes 5 minority (all Hispanic/Latino), 2 international. Average age 28. 37 applicants, 70% accepted, 10 enrolled. In 2019, 7 other advanced degrees awarded. *Entrance requirements:* For doctorate and Ed S, GRE General Test, minimum GPA of 3.0, resume, statement of purpose, official transcript, three letters of recommendation. Additional exam requirements/recommendations for international students: required—TOEFL, IELTS. *Application deadline:* For fall admission, 12/15 for domestic and international students. Application fee: $65 ($85 for international students). Electronic applications accepted. *Expenses:* Tuition, state resident: full-time $9989. Tuition, nonresident: full-time $23,950. *International tuition:* $23,950 full-time. *Required fees:* $984; $81.99 per credit hour. Tuition and fees vary according to course load, campus/location and program. *Financial support:* Fellowships, research assistantships, teaching assistantships, scholarships/grants, and unspecified assistantships available. Financial award application deadline: 12/15. *Unit head:* David M Hansen, Chair, 785-864-1874, Fax: 785-864-3820, E-mail: dhansen1@ku.edu. *Application contact:* Penny Fritts, Admissions Coordinator, 785-864-9645, E-mail: fritts@ku.edu.
Website: http://epsy.ku.edu/

University of Kentucky, Graduate School, College of Education, Program in Educational and Counseling Psychology, Lexington, KY 40506-0032. Offers counseling psychology (MS, PhD, Ed S); educational psychology (MS, PhD); school psychology (PhD, Ed S). *Accreditation:* APA (one or more programs are accredited); NCATE. *Degree requirements:* For doctorate, comprehensive exam, thesis/dissertation; for Ed S, comprehensive exam. *Entrance requirements:* For doctorate, GRE General Test, minimum graduate GPA of 3.0; for Ed S, GRE General Test. Additional exam requirements/recommendations for international students: required—TOEFL (minimum score 550 paper-based). Electronic applications accepted.

University of La Verne, LaFetra College of Education, Program in Educational Counseling, La Verne, CA 91750-4443. Offers educational counseling (MS); pupil personnel services (Credential); school psychology (MS). *Program availability:* Part-time. *Entrance requirements:* For master's, California Basic Educational Skills Test, minimum undergraduate GPA of 2.75, graduate 3.0; interview; 1 year's experience working with children; 3 letters of reference. Additional exam requirements/recommendations for international students: required—TOEFL (minimum score 550 paper-based). *Expenses:* Contact institution.

University of Louisville, Graduate School, College of Education and Human Development, Department of Counseling and Human Development, Louisville, KY 40292-0001. Offers counseling and personnel services (M Ed, PhD), including art therapy (M Ed), college student personnel, counseling psychology, counselor education and supervision (PhD), educational psychology, measurement, and evaluation (PhD), mental health counseling (M Ed), school counseling (M Ed). *Accreditation:* APA; NCATE. *Program availability:* Part-time. *Faculty:* 11 full-time (7 women), 10 part-time/adjunct (6 women). *Students:* 118 full-time (95 women), 60 part-time (45 women); includes 54 minority (32 Black or African American, non-Hispanic/Latino; 1 American Indian or Alaska Native, non-Hispanic/Latino; 2 Asian, non-Hispanic/Latino; 12 Hispanic/Latino; 1 Native Hawaiian or other Pacific Islander, non-Hispanic/Latino; 6 Two or more races, non-Hispanic/Latino), 3 international. Average age 29. 118 applicants, 52% accepted, 43 enrolled. In 2019, 61 master's, 11 doctorates awarded. Terminal master's awarded for partial completion of doctoral program. *Degree requirements:* For master's, thesis optional; for doctorate, comprehensive exam, thesis/dissertation. *Entrance requirements:* For master's, professional statement, recommendation letters, resume, transcripts; for doctorate, GRE, professional statement, recommendation letters, resume, transcripts. Additional exam requirements/recommendations for international students: required—TOEFL (minimum score 550 paper-based; 79 iBT); recommended—IELTS (minimum score 6.5). *Application deadline:* For fall admission, 3/1 priority date for domestic and international students; for spring admission, 10/1 priority date for domestic and international students; for summer admission, 3/1 priority date for domestic and international students. Application fee: $65. Electronic applications accepted. *Expenses: Tuition, area resident:* Full-time $13,000; part-time $723 per credit hour. Tuition, state resident: full-time $13,000; part-time $723 per credit hour. Tuition, nonresident: full-time $27,114; part-time $1507 per credit hour. *International tuition:* $27,114 full-time. *Required fees:* $196. Tuition and fees vary according to program and reciprocity agreements. *Financial support:* In 2019–20, 73 students received support, including 3 fellowships with full tuition reimbursements available (averaging $21,024 per year), 5 research assistantships with full tuition reimbursements available (averaging $21,024 per year), 3 teaching assistantships with full tuition reimbursements available (averaging $21,024 per year); scholarships/grants, health care benefits, and unspecified assistantships also available. Financial award application deadline: 3/1; financial award applicants required to submit FAFSA. *Unit head:* Dr. Mark M. Leach, Department Chair, 502-852-0588, Fax: 502-852-0629, E-mail: m.leach@louisville.edu. *Application contact:* Dr. Margaret Pentecost, Assistant Dean for Graduate Student Success, 502-852-2628, Fax: 502-852-1417, E-mail: gedadm@louisville.edu.
Website: http://www.louisville.edu/education/departments/ecpy

University of Lynchburg, Graduate Studies, M Ed Program in School Counseling, Lynchburg, VA 24501-3199. Offers M Ed. *Accreditation:* ACA. *Program availability:* Part-time, evening/weekend. *Degree requirements:* For master's, counseling internship. *Entrance requirements:* For master's, GRE, minimum GPA of 3.0 (preferred), official transcripts (bachelor's, others as relevant), three letters of recommendation, career goals statement, personal interview. Additional exam requirements/recommendations for international students: required—TOEFL (minimum score 550 paper-based; 80 iBT), IELTS (minimum score 6). Electronic applications accepted. Application fee is waived when completed online. *Expenses:* Contact institution.

University of Manitoba, Faculty of Graduate Studies, Faculty of Arts, Department of Psychology, Winnipeg, MB R3T 2N2, Canada. Offers clinical psychology (PhD); psychology (MA, PhD); school psychology (MA). *Degree requirements:* For master's, thesis; for doctorate, one foreign language, thesis/dissertation. *Entrance requirements:* For master's and doctorate, GRE General Test.

School Psychology

University of Maryland, College Park, Academic Affairs, College of Education, Department of Counseling, Higher Education and Special Education, College Park, MD 20742. Offers college student personnel (M Ed, MA); college student personnel administration (PhD); community counseling (CAGS); community/career counseling (M Ed, MA); counseling and personnel services (M Ed, MA, PhD), including art therapy (M Ed), college student personnel (M Ed), counseling and personnel services (PhD), counseling psychology (M Ed); mental health counseling (M Ed), school counseling (M Ed); counseling psychology (PhD); counselor education (PhD); rehabilitation counseling (M Ed, MA, AGSC); school counseling (M Ed, MA); school psychology (M Ed, MA, PhD). *Accreditation:* APA (one or more programs are accredited); NCATE. *Program availability:* Part-time, evening/weekend, online learning. *Degree requirements:* For master's, thesis (for some programs); for doctorate, thesis/dissertation. *Entrance requirements:* For master's, GRE General Test or MAT, minimum GPA of 3.0, 3 letters of recommendation; for doctorate, GRE General Test or MAT, minimum GPA of 3.5, 3 letters of recommendation. Additional exam requirements/recommendations for international students: required—TOEFL. Electronic applications accepted.

University of Massachusetts Amherst, Graduate School, College of Education, Program in Education, Amherst, MA 01003. Offers bilingual, English as a second language, and multicultural education (M Ed, Ed S); child study and early education (M Ed); children, families and schools (Ed D, Ed S); early childhood and elementary teacher education (M Ed); educational leadership (M Ed); educational policy and leadership (Ed D); higher education (M Ed); international education (M Ed); language, literacy and culture (Ed D); learning, media and technology (M Ed, Ed S); mathematics, science, and learning technologies (Ed D); reading and writing (M Ed); research, educational measurement and psychometrics (Ed D); school counselor education (M Ed, Ed S); school psychology (Ed S); science education (Ed S); secondary teacher education (M Ed); social justice education (M Ed, Ed D, Ed S); special education (M Ed, Ed D, Ed S); teacher education and school improvement (Ed D, Ed S). *Accreditation:* NCATE. *Program availability:* Part-time, online learning. Terminal master's awarded for partial completion of doctoral program. *Degree requirements:* For doctorate, comprehensive exam, thesis/dissertation. *Entrance requirements:* Additional exam requirements/recommendations for international students: required—TOEFL (minimum score 550 paper-based; 80 iBT), IELTS (minimum score 6.5). Electronic applications accepted.

University of Massachusetts Amherst, Graduate School, College of Education, Program in School Psychology, Amherst, MA 01003. Offers M Ed, PhD, Ed S. *Accreditation:* APA; NCATE. *Program availability:* Part-time. Terminal master's awarded for partial completion of doctoral program. *Degree requirements:* For doctorate, comprehensive exam, thesis/dissertation. *Entrance requirements:* For doctorate, 3 letters of recommendation. Additional exam requirements/recommendations for international students: required—TOEFL (minimum score 550 paper-based; 80 iBT), IELTS (minimum score 6.5). Electronic applications accepted.

University of Massachusetts Boston, College of Education and Human Development, Program in Counseling and School Psychology, Boston, MA 02125-3393. Offers PhD. *Accreditation:* ACA; CORE. *Program availability:* Part-time, evening/weekend. Electronic applications accepted.

University of Massachusetts Boston, College of Education and Human Development, Program in School Psychology, Boston, MA 02125-3393. Offers M Ed. *Program availability:* Part-time, evening/weekend. *Entrance requirements:* For master's, GRE General Test or MAT, minimum GPA of 3.0.

University of Memphis, Graduate School, College of Arts and Sciences, Department of Psychology, Memphis, TN 38152-3230. Offers clinical psychology (PhD); experimental psychology (PhD); general psychology (MS); school psychology (MA, PhD, Ed S). *Accreditation:* APA. *Students:* 102 full-time (74 women), 24 part-time (18 women); includes 31 minority (13 Black or African American, non-Hispanic/Latino; 6 Asian, non-Hispanic/Latino; 6 Hispanic/Latino; 6 Two or more races, non-Hispanic/Latino), 6 international. Average age 28. 57 applicants, 84% accepted, 32 enrolled. In 2019, 21 master's, 12 doctorates, 6 other advanced degrees awarded. *Degree requirements:* For master's, comprehensive exam (for some programs), thesis (for some programs), 37 credit hours (for MA); 33 credit hours with thesis or 36 with exam (for MS); for doctorate, comprehensive exam, thesis/dissertation, 80 semester hours, major area paper; 1-year placement and 1-year internship (for clinical psychology); internship (for school psychology); for Ed S, 30 credit hours. *Entrance requirements:* For master's, GRE, 3 letters of recommendation, 18 undergraduate hours in psychology; for doctorate, GRE, minimum GPA of 2.75, 18 hours of undergraduate psychology courses, transcripts, personal statement, 3 letters of recommendation, interview; for Ed S, GRE, minimum GPA of 2.75, 18 hours of undergraduate psychology courses, 3 letters of recommendation. Additional exam requirements/recommendations for international students: required—TOEFL (minimum score 550 paper-based; 79 iBT). *Application deadline:* For fall admission, 12/5 for domestic students. Applications are processed on a rolling basis. Application fee: $35 ($60 for international students). Electronic applications accepted. *Expenses: Tuition, area resident:* Full-time $9216; part-time $512 per credit hour. Tuition, state resident: full-time $9216; part-time $512 per credit hour. Tuition, nonresident: full-time $12,672; part-time $704 per credit hour. *International tuition:* $16,128 full-time. *Required fees:* $1530; $85 per credit hour. Tuition and fees vary according to program. *Financial support:* Fellowships with full tuition reimbursements, research assistantships with full tuition reimbursements, teaching assistantships with full tuition reimbursements, Federal Work-Study, scholarships/grants, tuition waivers (partial), and unspecified assistantships available. Financial award application deadline: 2/1; financial award applicants required to submit FAFSA. *Unit head:* Dr. Randy Floyd, Chair, 901-678-2146, Fax: 901-678-2579, E-mail: rgfloyd@memphis.edu. *Application contact:* Dr. Robert Cohen, Graduate Programs Coordinator, 901-678-4679, Fax: 901-678-2579, E-mail: rcohen@memphis.edu. Website: http://www.memphis.edu/psychology

University of Minnesota, Twin Cities Campus, Graduate School, College of Education and Human Development, Department of Educational Psychology, Program in School Psychology, Minneapolis, MN 55455-0213. Offers MA, PhD, Ed S. *Accreditation:* APA. *Students:* 34 full-time (28 women), 14 part-time (9 women); includes 9 minority (2 Black or African American, non-Hispanic/Latino; 1 Asian, non-Hispanic/Latino; 1 Hispanic/Latino; 5 Two or more races, non-Hispanic/Latino), 5 international. Average age 28. 30 applicants, 17% accepted, 3 enrolled. In 2019, 9 master's, 4 doctorates, 3 other advanced degrees awarded. Application fee: $75 ($95 for international students). *Unit head:* Dr. Kristen McMaster, Chair, 612-624-6083, Fax: 612-624-8241, E-mail: mcmas004@umn.edu. *Application contact:* Dr. Panayiota Kendeou, Director of Graduate Studies, 612-626-7814, E-mail: kend0040@umn.edu. Website: http://www.cehd.umn.edu/EdPsych/programs/SchoolPsych/

University of Minnesota, Twin Cities Campus, Graduate School, College of Liberal Arts, Department of Psychology, Minneapolis, MN 55455-0213. Offers biological psychopathology (PhD); clinical psychology (PhD); cognitive and biological psychology (PhD); counseling psychology (PhD); industrial/organizational psychology (PhD); personality, individual differences, and behavior genetics (PhD); quantitative/psychometric methods (PhD); school psychology (PhD); social psychology (PhD). *Accreditation:* APA. *Degree requirements:* For doctorate, comprehensive exam, thesis/

dissertation. *Entrance requirements:* For doctorate, GRE General Test, GRE Subject Test (recommended), 12 credits of upper-level psychology courses, including a course in statistics or psychological measurement. Additional exam requirements/recommendations for international students: required—TOEFL (minimum score 79 iBT).

University of Missouri, Office of Research and Graduate Studies, College of Education, Department of Educational, School, and Counseling Psychology, Columbia, MO 65211. Offers counseling psychology (M Ed, MA, PhD, Ed S); educational psychology (M Ed, MA, PhD, Ed S); learning and instruction (M Ed); school psychology (M Ed, MA, PhD, Ed S). *Accreditation:* APA (one or more programs are accredited). *Program availability:* Part-time. *Entrance requirements:* For master's, doctorate, and Ed S, GRE General Test, minimum GPA of 3.0. Additional exam requirements/recommendations for international students: required—TOEFL.

University of Missouri–St. Louis, College of Education, Department of Education Sciences and Professional Programs, St. Louis, MO 63121. Offers adult and higher education (M Ed); educational psychology (M Ed), including character and citizenship education, research and program evaluation; program evaluation (Certificate); school psychology (Ed S). *Degree requirements:* For other advanced degree, comprehensive exam, thesis or alternative, internship. *Entrance requirements:* For degree, GRE General Test, 2-4 letters of recommendation, personal interview. Additional exam requirements/recommendations for international students: required—IELTS (minimum score 6.5); recommended—TOEFL (minimum score 550 paper-based; 79 iBT). Electronic applications accepted. *Expenses: Tuition, area resident:* Full-time $9005.40; part-time $6003.60 per credit hour. Tuition, state resident: full-time $9005.40; part-time $6003.60 per credit hour. Tuition, nonresident: full-time $22,108; part-time $14,738.40 per credit hour. *International tuition:* $22,108 full-time. Tuition and fees vary according to course load.

University of Montana, Graduate School, College of Humanities and Sciences, Department of Psychology, Program in School Psychology, Missoula, MT 59812. Offers MA, PhD, Ed S. *Degree requirements:* For master's, oral exam, professional paper; for Ed S, thesis. *Entrance requirements:* For master's, GRE General Test, GRE Subject Test, minimum GPA of 3.25 during previous 2 years; for Ed S, GRE General Test. Additional exam requirements/recommendations for international students: required—TOEFL.

University of Nebraska at Kearney, College of Education, Department of Counseling and School Psychology, Kearney, NE 68849. Offers clinical mental health counseling (MS Ed); school counseling (MS Ed), including elementary, secondary; school psychology (Ed S); student affairs (MS Ed). *Accreditation:* ACA; NCATE. *Program availability:* Part-time, evening/weekend, 100% online, blended/hybrid learning. *Faculty:* 7 full-time (4 women). *Students:* 76 full-time (63 women), 124 part-time (91 women); includes 25 minority (1 Black or African American, non-Hispanic/Latino; 3 Asian, non-Hispanic/Latino; 17 Hispanic/Latino; 4 Two or more races, non-Hispanic/Latino), 6 international. Average age 30. 61 applicants, 85% accepted, 44 enrolled. In 2019, 38 master's, 15 Ed Ss awarded. *Degree requirements:* For master's, comprehensive exam, thesis optional; for Ed S, comprehensive exam. *Entrance requirements:* For master's and Ed S, personal statement, recommendations, resume, interview. Additional exam requirements/recommendations for international students: required—TOEFL (minimum score 550 paper-based; 79 iBT), IELTS (minimum score 6.5). *Application deadline:* For fall admission, 6/15 for domestic students, 5/15 for international students; for spring admission, 10/15 for domestic students, 9/15 for international students; for summer admission, 4/15 for domestic students, 1/15 for international students. Application fee: $45. Electronic applications accepted. *Expenses: Tuition, area resident:* Full-time $4662; part-time $259 per credit hour. Tuition, nonresident: full-time $10,242; part-time $569 per credit hour. *International tuition:* $10,242 full-time. *Required fees:* $1222; $381.50 per term. Full-time tuition and fees vary according to course load, campus/location and program. *Financial support:* In 2019–20, 8 students received support, including 7 research assistantships with full tuition reimbursements available (averaging $10,980 per year), 1 teaching assistantship with full tuition reimbursement available (averaging $10,980 per year); career-related internships or fieldwork, scholarships/grants, health care benefits, and unspecified assistantships also available. Support available to part-time students. Financial award application deadline: 2/28; financial award applicants required to submit FAFSA. *Unit head:* Dr. David Hof, Chair, Counseling & School Psychology, 308-865-8320, E-mail: hofdd@unk.edu. *Application contact:* Linda Johnson, Director, Graduate Admissions and Programs, 800-717-7881, Fax: 308-865-8837, E-mail: gradstudies@unk.edu. Website: http://www.unk.edu/academics/csp/

University of Nebraska at Omaha, Graduate Studies, College of Arts and Sciences, Department of Psychology, Omaha, NE 68182. Offers applied behavior analysis (Certificate); human resources and training (Certificate); industrial/organizational psychology (MS); psychology (MA, PhD); school psychology (MS, Ed S). *Program availability:* Part-time. *Degree requirements:* For master's, comprehensive exam, thesis (for some programs); for doctorate, comprehensive exam, thesis/dissertation. *Entrance requirements:* For master's and doctorate, GRE, minimum GPA of 3.0, official transcripts, 3 letters of recommendation, statement of purpose, writing sample, resume. Additional exam requirements/recommendations for international students: required—TOEFL, IELTS, PTE. Electronic applications accepted.

University of Nebraska–Lincoln, Graduate College, College of Education and Human Sciences, Department of Educational Psychology, Lincoln, NE 68588. Offers cognition, learning and development (MA); counseling psychology (MA); educational psychology (MA, Ed S); psychological studies in education (PhD), including cognition, learning and development, counseling psychology, quantitative, qualitative, and psychometric methods, school psychology; quantitative, qualitative, and psychometric methods (MA); school psychology (MA, Ed S). *Accreditation:* APA (one or more programs are accredited); NCATE. *Degree requirements:* For master's, thesis optional. *Entrance requirements:* For master's, GRE General Test. Additional exam requirements/recommendations for international students: required—TOEFL (minimum score 500 paper-based). Electronic applications accepted.

The University of North Carolina at Chapel Hill, Graduate School, School of Education, Program in School Psychology, Chapel Hill, NC 27599. Offers M Ed, MA, PhD. *Accreditation:* APA (one or more programs are accredited); NCATE. *Degree requirements:* For master's, comprehensive exam, thesis (for some programs); for doctorate, comprehensive exam, thesis/dissertation. *Entrance requirements:* For master's and doctorate, GRE General Test, minimum GPA of 3.0 during last 2 years of undergraduate course work. Additional exam requirements/recommendations for international students: required—TOEFL (minimum score 550 paper-based). Electronic applications accepted.

The University of North Carolina at Greensboro, Graduate School, School of Education, Department of Counseling and Educational Development, Greensboro, NC 27412-5001. Offers advanced school counseling (PMC); counseling and counselor education (PhD); counseling and educational development (MS); couple and family counseling (PMC); school counseling (PMC); MS/Ed S. *Accreditation:* ACA (one or more programs are accredited); NCATE. *Degree requirements:* For master's, comprehensive exam, practicum, internship; for doctorate, comprehensive exam, thesis/dissertation.

Entrance requirements: For master's, doctorate, and PMC, GRE General Test. Additional exam requirements/recommendations for international students: required—TOEFL. Electronic applications accepted.

University of Northern Colorado, Graduate School, College of Education and Behavioral Sciences, Department of School Psychology, Greeley, CO 80639. Offers Ed S. *Accreditation:* APA; NCATE. *Program availability:* Part-time, evening/weekend. *Degree requirements:* For Ed S, comprehensive exam. Electronic applications accepted.

University of Northern Iowa, Graduate College, College of Education, Department of Educational Psychology and Foundations, Ed S Program in School Psychology, Cedar Falls, IA 50614. Offers Ed S.

University of Northern Iowa, Graduate College, College of Social and Behavioral Sciences, School of Applied Human Sciences, Cedar Falls, IA 50614. Offers counseling (MA), including mental health counseling, school counseling; mental health counseling (MA); school counseling (MA). *Program availability:* Part-time. *Degree requirements:* For master's, comprehensive exam, thesis (for some programs). *Entrance requirements:* Additional exam requirements/recommendations for international students: required—TOEFL (minimum score 550 paper-based; 79 iBT). Electronic applications accepted.

University of Oregon, Graduate School, College of Education, Eugene, OR 97403. Offers communication disorders and sciences (MA, MS, PhD); counseling psychology (PhD); couples and family therapy (MS); critical and sociocultural studies in education (PhD); curriculum and teacher education (MA, MS); educational leadership (MS, D Ed, PhD); prevention science (M Ed, MS, PhD); school psychology (MS, PhD); special education (M Ed, MA, MS, PhD). *Accreditation:* ASHA. *Program availability:* Part-time. Terminal master's awarded for partial completion of doctoral program. *Degree requirements:* For master's, exam, paper, or project; for doctorate, comprehensive exam, thesis/dissertation. *Entrance requirements:* Additional exam requirements/recommendations for international students: required—TOEFL.

University of Phoenix - Las Vegas Campus, College of Education, Las Vegas, NV 89135. Offers administration and supervision (MA Ed); curriculum and instruction (MA Ed); school counseling (MSC); teacher education-elementary licensure (MA Ed). *Program availability:* Evening/weekend. *Degree requirements:* For master's, thesis (for some programs). *Entrance requirements:* For master's, minimum undergraduate GPA of 2.5, 3 years of work experience. Additional exam requirements/recommendations for international students: required—TOEFL (minimum score 550 paper-based; 79 iBT). Electronic applications accepted.

University of Rhode Island, Graduate School, College of Health Sciences, Department of Psychology, Kingston, RI 02881. Offers behavioral science (PhD); clinical psychology (PhD); school psychology (MS, PhD). *Accreditation:* APA (one or more programs are accredited). *Program availability:* Part-time. *Faculty:* 23 full-time (13 women), 1 part-time/adjunct (0 women). *Students:* 59 full-time (50 women), 5 part-time (2 women); includes 10 minority (5 Black or African American, non-Hispanic/Latino; 2 Asian, non-Hispanic/Latino; 3 Hispanic/Latino), 4 international. 353 applicants, 11% accepted, 11 enrolled. In 2019, 11 master's, 15 doctorates awarded. *Entrance requirements:* Additional exam requirements/recommendations for international students: required—TOEFL. *Application deadline:* For fall admission, 12/1 for domestic and international students. Application fee: $65. Electronic applications accepted. *Expenses: Tuition, area resident:* Full-time $13,734; part-time $763 per credit. Tuition, state resident: full-time $13,734; part-time $763 per credit. Tuition, nonresident: full-time $26,512; part-time $1473 per credit. *International tuition:* $26,512 full-time. *Required fees:* $1780; $52 per credit. $35 per term. One-time fee: $165. *Financial support:* In 2019–20, 9 research assistantships with tuition reimbursements (averaging $10,024 per year), 20 teaching assistantships with tuition reimbursements (averaging $17,045 per year) were awarded. Financial award application deadline: 12/1; financial award applicants required to submit FAFSA. *Unit head:* Dr. Mark Robbins, Chair, 401-874-5082, E-mail: markrobb@uri.edu. *Application contact:* Dr. Mark Robbins, Chair, 401-874-5082, E-mail: markrobb@uri.edu. Website: http://www.uri.edu/artsci/psy/

University of San Diego, School of Leadership and Education Sciences, Department of Counseling and Marital and Family Therapy, San Diego, CA 92110-2492. Offers clinical mental health counseling (MA); marital and family therapy (MA); school counseling (MA). *Accreditation:* ACA. *Program availability:* Part-time, evening/weekend. *Faculty:* 14 full-time (8 women), 24 part-time/adjunct (14 women). *Students:* 178 full-time (160 women), 47 part-time (41 women); includes 106 minority (9 Black or African American, non-Hispanic/Latino; 21 Asian, non-Hispanic/Latino; 59 Hispanic/Latino; 17 Two or more races, non-Hispanic/Latino), 5 international. Average age 27. 391 applicants, 42% accepted, 88 enrolled. In 2019, 96 master's awarded. *Degree requirements:* For master's, comprehensive exam, international experience. *Entrance requirements:* For master's, GRE or GMAT (minimum overall score in 50th percentile), group interview with faculty. Additional exam requirements/recommendations for international students: required—TOEFL (minimum score 580 paper-based; 83 iBT), TWE. *Application deadline:* For fall admission, 2/10 for domestic and international students. Applications are processed on a rolling basis. Application fee: $45. Electronic applications accepted. *Financial support:* In 2019–20, 199 students received support. Career-related internships or fieldwork, Federal Work-Study, institutionally sponsored loans, scholarships/grants, unspecified assistantships, and stipends available. Support available to part-time students. Financial award application deadline: 4/1; financial award applicants required to submit FAFSA. *Unit head:* Dr. Wendell Callahan, Director, 619-260-7988, E-mail: wcallahan@sandiego.edu. *Application contact:* Erika Garwood, Director of Admissions and Enrollment, 619-260-4524, Fax: 619-260-4158, E-mail: grads@sandiego.edu. Website: http://www.sandiego.edu/soles/counseling-and-marital-and-family-therapy//

University of Saskatchewan, College of Graduate and Postdoctoral Studies, College of Education, Department of Educational Psychology and Special Education, Saskatoon, SK S7N 5A2, Canada. Offers measurement and evaluation (M Ed, PhD); school and counseling psychology (M Ed, PhD); special education (M Ed, PhD). *Degree requirements:* For master's, thesis (for some programs); for doctorate, comprehensive exam (for some programs), thesis/dissertation. *Entrance requirements:* Additional exam requirements/recommendations for international students: required—TOEFL (minimum score 80 iBT); recommended—IELTS (minimum score 6.5). Electronic applications accepted.

University of South Carolina, The Graduate School, College of Arts and Sciences, Department of Psychology, Program in School Psychology, Columbia, SC 29208. Offers PhD. *Accreditation:* APA; NCATE. *Degree requirements:* For doctorate, thesis/dissertation. *Entrance requirements:* For doctorate, GRE General Test, minimum GPA of 3.0. Additional exam requirements/recommendations for international students: required—TOEFL. Electronic applications accepted.

University of South Dakota, Graduate School, School of Education, Division of Counseling and Psychology in Education, Vermillion, SD 57069. Offers counseling (MA, PhD, Ed S); human development and educational psychology (MA, PhD, Ed S); mental health counseling (Certificate); school psychology (PhD, Ed S). *Accreditation:* ACA (one or more programs are accredited); NCATE. *Program availability:* Part-time. *Degree requirements:* For master's and other advanced degree, comprehensive exam, thesis or

alternative; for doctorate, comprehensive exam, thesis/dissertation. *Entrance requirements:* For master's and doctorate, GRE General Test, minimum GPA of 3.0. Additional exam requirements/recommendations for international students: required—TOEFL (minimum score 550 paper-based; 79 iBT). Electronic applications accepted.

University of Southern Maine, College of Management and Human Service, School of Education and Human Development, Program in School Psychology, Portland, ME 04103. Offers MS, Psy D. *Program availability:* Part-time, evening/weekend. *Degree requirements:* For doctorate, comprehensive exam, thesis/dissertation, dissertation defense. *Entrance requirements:* For doctorate, GRE General Test, interview. Additional exam requirements/recommendations for international students: required—TOEFL (minimum score 550 paper-based; 79 iBT). Electronic applications accepted. *Expenses: Tuition, area resident:* Full-time $864; part-time $432 per credit hour. Tuition, state resident: full-time $864; part-time $432 per credit hour. Tuition, nonresident: full-time $2372; part-time $1186 per credit hour. *Required fees:* $141; $108 per credit hour. Tuition and fees vary according to course load.

The University of Tennessee, Graduate School, College of Education, Health and Human Sciences, Program in Education, Knoxville, TN 37996. Offers art education (MS); counseling education (PhD); cultural studies in education (PhD); curriculum (MS, Ed S); curriculum, educational research and evaluation (Ed D, PhD); early childhood education (PhD); early childhood special education (MS); education of deaf and hard of hearing (MS); educational administration and policy studies (Ed D, PhD); educational administration and supervision (Ed S); educational psychology (Ed D, PhD); elementary education (MS, Ed S); elementary teaching (MS); English education (MS, Ed S); exercise science (PhD); foreign language/ESL education (MS, Ed S); instructional technology (MS, Ed D, PhD, Ed S); literacy, language and ESL education (PhD); literacy, language education, and ESL education (Ed D); mathematics education (MS, Ed S); modified and comprehensive special education (MS); reading education (MS, Ed S); school counseling (Ed S); school psychology (PhD, Ed S); science education (MS, Ed S); secondary teaching (MS); social foundations (MS); social science education (MS, Ed S); socio-cultural foundations of sports and education (PhD); special education (Ed S); teacher education (Ed D, PhD). *Accreditation:* NCATE. *Program availability:* Part-time, evening/weekend. *Degree requirements:* For master's and Ed S, thesis optional; for doctorate, variable foreign language requirement, thesis/dissertation. *Entrance requirements:* For master's, minimum GPA of 2.7; for doctorate and Ed S, GRE General Test, minimum GPA of 2.7. Additional exam requirements/recommendations for international students: required—TOEFL. Electronic applications accepted.

The University of Tennessee at Chattanooga, Program in Counseling, Chattanooga, TN 37403. Offers mental health (M Ed); school counseling (M Ed, Post Master's Certificate). *Faculty:* 3 full-time (2 women), 2 part-time/adjunct (both women). *Students:* 37 full-time (29 women), 16 part-time (12 women); includes 10 minority (4 Black or African American, non-Hispanic/Latino; 1 Asian, non-Hispanic/Latino; 3 Hispanic/Latino; 2 Two or more races, non-Hispanic/Latino). Average age 29. 41 applicants, 63% accepted, 12 enrolled. In 2019, 21 master's awarded. *Degree requirements:* For master's, comprehensive exam, internship. *Entrance requirements:* For master's, MAT or GRE, 2 letters of reference, interview; for Post Master's Certificate, graduate degree in counseling, 2 letters of reference. Additional exam requirements/recommendations for international students: required—TOEFL (minimum score 550 paper-based; 79 iBT), IELTS (minimum score 6). *Application deadline:* For fall admission, 6/15 priority date for domestic students, 7/1 for international students; for spring admission, 11/1 priority date for domestic students, 11/1 for international students. Applications are processed on a rolling basis. Application fee: $35 ($40 for international students). Electronic applications accepted. *Financial support:* Research assistantships, career-related internships or fieldwork, scholarships/grants, and unspecified assistantships available. Support available to part-time students. Financial award application deadline: 7/1; financial award applicants required to submit FAFSA. *Unit head:* Dr. Elizabeth O'Brien, Director, 423-425-4544, E-mail: elizabeth-o'brien@utc.edu. *Application contact:* Dr. Joanne Romagni, Dean of the Graduate School, 423-425-4478, Fax: 423-425-4052, E-mail: joanne-romagni@utc.edu. Website: https://www.utc.edu/counselor-education-program/

The University of Tennessee at Chattanooga, School of Education, Chattanooga, TN 37403. Offers counseling (M Ed), including community counseling, school counseling; education (M Ed, Post-Master's Certificate), including elementary education (M Ed), school leadership (Post-Master's Certificate); elementary education (M Ed); learning and leadership (Ed D), including educational leadership; school leadership (Post-Master's Certificate); school leadership: principal licensure (Ed S); secondary education (M Ed); special education (M Ed). *Accreditation:* ACA; NCATE. *Program availability:* Part-time. *Faculty:* 21 full-time (14 women), 16 part-time/adjunct (15 women). *Students:* 28 full-time (18 women), 63 part-time (44 women); includes 20 minority (10 Black or African American, non-Hispanic/Latino; 1 American Indian or Alaska Native, non-Hispanic/Latino; 1 Asian, non-Hispanic/Latino; 3 Hispanic/Latino; 5 Two or more races, non-Hispanic/Latino). Average age 32. 59 applicants, 78% accepted, 24 enrolled. In 2019, 42 master's, 7 other advanced degrees awarded. *Degree requirements:* For master's, comprehensive exam, thesis optional, culminating experience; for other advanced degree, practicum. *Entrance requirements:* For master's, GRE General Test, PPST 1 if student is not already licensed to teach; for other advanced degree, two letters of recommendation, graduate degree in education, teaching certificate with three years of experience. Additional exam requirements/recommendations for international students: required—TOEFL (minimum score 550 paper-based; 79 iBT), IELTS (minimum score 6). *Application deadline:* For fall admission, 6/15 for domestic students, 7/1 for international students; for spring admission, 11/1 for domestic and international students. Applications are processed on a rolling basis. Application fee: $35 ($40 for international students). Electronic applications accepted. *Financial support:* Research assistantships, teaching assistantships, career-related internships or fieldwork, institutionally sponsored loans, scholarships/grants, and unspecified assistantships available. Support available to part-time students. Financial award application deadline: 7/1; financial award applicants required to submit FAFSA. *Unit head:* Dr. Renee Murley, Director, 423-425-4684, Fax: 423-425-5380, E-mail: renee-murley@utc.edu. *Application contact:* Dr. Joanne Romagni, Dean of the Graduate School, 423-425-4478, Fax: 423-425-5223, E-mail: joanne-romagni@utc.edu. Website: https://www.utc.edu/school-education/

The University of Texas at Austin, Graduate School, College of Education, Department of Educational Psychology, Austin, TX 78712-1111. Offers academic educational psychology (M Ed, MA); counseling psychology (PhD); counselor education (M Ed); human development, culture and learning sciences (PhD); program evaluation (MA); quantitative methods (M Ed, MA, PhD); school psychology (MA, PhD). *Accreditation:* APA (one or more programs are accredited). *Degree requirements:* For master's, thesis optional; for doctorate, thesis/dissertation. *Entrance requirements:* For master's and doctorate, GRE General Test, 3 letters of recommendation. Additional exam requirements/recommendations for international students: required—TOEFL.

The University of Texas at San Antonio, College of Education and Human Development, Department of Educational Psychology, San Antonio, TX 78207. Offers applied behavior analysis (Certificate); educational psychology (MA), including applied educational psychology, behavior assessment and intervention, general educational psychology, program evaluation; language acquisition and bilingual psychoeducational assessment (Certificate); school psychology (MA). *Program availability:* Part-time. *Degree requirements:* For master's, comprehensive exam, thesis (for some programs). *Entrance requirements:* For master's, GRE, bachelor's degree with 18 credit hours in field of study or in another appropriate field of study, two letters of recommendation, statement of purpose; for Certificate, 18 hours in psychology, sociology, education, or anything related (for applied behavioral analysis); minimum GPA of 2.7 in last 30 hours (for language acquisition and bilingual psychoeducational assessment). Additional exam requirements/recommendations for international students: required—TOEFL (minimum score 550 paper-based; 79 iBT), IELTS (minimum score 6.5). Electronic applications accepted.

The University of Texas at Tyler, College of Education and Psychology, Department of Psychology and Counseling, Tyler, TX 75799-0001. Offers clinical psychology (MS), including neuropsychology, school psychology; counseling psychology (MA), including general, marriage and family; interdisciplinary studies (MSIS); school counseling (MA). *Program availability:* Part-time, evening/weekend. *Faculty:* 12 full-time (5 women), 6 part-time/adjunct (3 women). *Students:* 131 full-time (103 women), 83 part-time (67 women); includes 67 minority (10 Black or African American, non-Hispanic/Latino; 1 American Indian or Alaska Native, non-Hispanic/Latino; 7 Asian, non-Hispanic/Latino; 41 Hispanic/Latino; 8 Two or more races, non-Hispanic/Latino), 8 international. Average age 30. 130 applicants, 65% accepted, 47 enrolled. In 2019, 94 master's awarded. *Degree requirements:* For master's, comprehensive exam, thesis optional. *Entrance requirements:* For master's, GRE General Test, minimum GPA of 3.0. Additional exam requirements/recommendations for international students: required—TOEFL. *Application deadline:* For fall admission, 8/17 priority date for domestic students, 7/1 priority date for international students; for spring admission, 12/21 priority date for domestic students, 11/1 priority date for international students. Application fee: $25 ($50 for international students). Electronic applications accepted. *Financial support:* In 2019–20, fellowships with partial tuition reimbursements (averaging $3,000 per year) were awarded; research assistantships, teaching assistantships, career-related internships or fieldwork, Federal Work-Study, and institutionally sponsored loans also available. Support available to part-time students. Financial award application deadline: 7/1. *Unit head:* Dr. Charles B. Barke, Chair, 903-565-5875, E-mail: cbarke@uttyler.edu. *Application contact:* Dr. Charles B. Barke, Chair, 903-565-5875, E-mail: cbarke@uttyler.edu.
Website: http://www.uttyler.edu/psychology/

The University of Texas Rio Grande Valley, College of Education and P-16 Integration, Department of Human Development and School Services, Edinburg, TX 78539. Offers early childhood education (M Ed); early childhood special education (M Ed); school psychology (MA); special education (M Ed). *Faculty:* 11 full-time (7 women), 2 part-time/adjunct (1 woman). *Students:* 43 full-time (40 women), 138 part-time (126 women); includes 162 minority (2 Black or African American, non-Hispanic/Latino; 160 Hispanic/Latino), 3 international. Average age 32. 68 applicants, 94% accepted, 50 enrolled. In 2019, 129 master's awarded. *Expenses: Tuition, area resident:* Full-time $5959; part-time $440 per credit hour. Tuition, state resident: full-time $5959. Tuition, nonresident: full-time $5959. *International tuition:* $13,321 full-time. *Required fees:* $1169; $185 per credit hour.
Website: utrgv.edu/hdss/

University of the Pacific, Gladys L. Benerd School of Education, Stockton, CA 95211-0197. Offers curriculum and instruction (MA, Ed D); education (M Ed); educational administration and leadership (MA, Ed D); educational and school psychology (MA, Ed D); educational entrepreneurship (MA); school psychology (Ed S); special education (MA); teacher education (MA). *Accreditation:* NCATE. *Degree requirements:* For doctorate, thesis/dissertation. *Entrance requirements:* For master's, GRE General Test; for doctorate, GRE General Test, GRE Subject Test. Additional exam requirements/recommendations for international students: required—TOEFL.

University of the Virgin Islands, School of Education, St. Thomas, VI 00802. Offers creative leadership for innovation and change (PhD); educational leadership (MA); school counseling (MA); school psychology (Ed S). *Program availability:* Part-time, evening/weekend. *Faculty:* 2 full-time, 10 part-time/adjunct (6 women). *Students:* 13 full-time (10 women), 110 part-time (84 women); includes 79 minority (75 Black or African American, non-Hispanic/Latino; 3 Hispanic/Latino; 1 Native Hawaiian or other Pacific Islander, non-Hispanic/Latino), 19 international. Average age 46. 42 applicants, 98% accepted, 24 enrolled. In 2019, 6 master's, 6 doctorates awarded. *Degree requirements:* For master's, comprehensive exam, thesis or alternative; for doctorate, comprehensive exam, thesis/dissertation, qualifying examination; for Ed S, comprehensive exam. *Entrance requirements:* For master's, GRE, minimum GPA of 2.5, BA degree from accredited institution; for doctorate, Minimum GPA of 3.50, master's degree from an accredited institution. Personal statement regarding motivation for attaining the doctoral degree. 3 letters of recommendations, with 2 from former teachers. Additional exam requirements/recommendations for international students: required—TOEFL (minimum score 550 paper-based). *Application deadline:* For fall admission, 4/30 for domestic and international students; for spring admission, 10/30 for domestic and international students. Application fee: $25. Electronic applications accepted. *Expenses: Tuition, area resident:* Full-time $6948; part-time $386 per credit hour. Tuition, state resident: part-time $386 per credit hour. Tuition, nonresident: full-time $13,230; part-time $735 per credit hour. *Required fees:* $508; $254 per semester. *Financial support:* In 2019–20, 1 student received support. Fellowships, research assistantships, teaching assistantships, and scholarships/grants available. Financial award application deadline: 4/15; financial award applicants required to submit FAFSA. *Unit head:* Dr. Karen Brown, Dean, 340-693-1321, Fax: 340-693-1335, E-mail: karen.brown@uvi.edu. *Application contact:* Charmaine M. Smith, Director of Admissions, 340-692-4070, E-mail: csmith@uvi.edu.

The University of Toledo, College of Graduate Studies, College of Health and Human Services, School of Intervention and Wellness, Toledo, OH 43606-3390. Offers counselor education (MA, PhD); school psychology (Ed S); speech-language pathology (MA). *Accreditation:* ACA (one or more programs are accredited); NCATE. *Degree requirements:* For master's, seminar paper. *Entrance requirements:* For master's, GRE General Test, interview, minimum GPA of 3.0. Electronic applications accepted.

The University of Toledo, College of Graduate Studies, College of Social Justice and Human Service, Department of School Psychology, Higher Education and Counselor Education, Toledo, OH 43606-3390. Offers counselor education (MA, PhD); higher education (ME, PhD, Certificate); school psychology (MA, Ed S). *Program availability:* Part-time. *Degree requirements:* For master's, comprehensive exam, thesis or alternative; for doctorate, comprehensive exam, thesis/dissertation; for other advanced degree, thesis optional. *Entrance requirements:* For master's, doctorate, and other advanced degree, minimum cumulative GPA of 2.7 for all previous academic work, letters of recommendation. Additional exam requirements/recommendations for international students: required—TOEFL (minimum score 550 paper-based; 80 iBT). Electronic applications accepted.

University of Utah, Graduate School, College of Education, Department of Educational Psychology, Salt Lake City, UT 84112. Offers clinical mental health counseling (M Ed); counseling psychology (PhD); elementary education (M Ed); instructional design and educational technology (M Ed); instructional design and technology (MS); learning and cognition (MS, PhD); reading and literacy (M Ed, PhD); school counseling (M Ed); school psychology (M Ed, PhD, Ed S); statistics (M Stat). *Accreditation:* APA (one or more programs are accredited). *Faculty:* 25 full-time (15 women), 7 part-time/adjunct (4 women). *Students:* 237 full-time (159 women); includes 37 minority (19 Asian, non-Hispanic/Latino; 9 Hispanic/Latino; 9 Two or more races, non-Hispanic/Latino). Average age 27. 262 applicants, 24% accepted, 54 enrolled. In 2019, 62 master's, 8 doctorates awarded. Terminal master's awarded for partial completion of doctoral program. *Degree requirements:* For master's, comprehensive exam, thesis (for some programs); for doctorate, comprehensive exam, thesis/dissertation. *Entrance requirements:* For master's and doctorate, graduation application, transcripts, GRE scores, CV/resume, personal statement, letters of recommendation. Additional exam requirements/recommendations for international students: required—TOEFL (minimum score 80 paper-based; 80 iBT), IELTS (minimum score 6.5). *Application deadline:* For fall admission, 12/15 for domestic and international students; for spring admission, 7/15 for domestic and international students; for summer admission, 3/15 for domestic and international students. Application fee: $55 ($75 for international students). Electronic applications accepted. *Expenses:* Tuition, state resident: full-time $7085; part-time $272.51 per credit hour. Tuition, nonresident: full-time $24,937; part-time $959.12 per credit hour. *Required fees:* $880.52; $880.52 per semester. Tuition and fees vary according to degree level, program and student level. *Financial support:* In 2019–20, 86 students received support, including 5 fellowships with full and partial tuition reimbursements available (averaging $11,500 per year), 14 research assistantships with full and partial tuition reimbursements available (averaging $15,900 per year), 2 teaching assistantships with full and partial tuition reimbursements available (averaging $12,560 per year); scholarships/grants, health care benefits, and unspecified assistantships also available. Financial award application deadline: 3/30. *Unit head:* Dr. Jason Burrow-Sanchez, Chair, Educational Psychology, 801-581-7148, Fax: 801-581-5566, E-mail: jason.burrow-sanchez@utah.edu. *Application contact:* JoLynn N. Yates, Academic Coordinator, 801-581-6811, Fax: 801-581-5566, E-mail: jo.yates@utah.edu.
Website: http://www.ed.utah.edu/edps/

University of Vermont, Graduate College, College of Education and Social Services, Counseling Program, Burlington, VT 05405. Offers counseling (MS), including clinical mental health, school counseling. *Accreditation:* ACA; NCATE. *Entrance requirements:* For master's, resume. Additional exam requirements/recommendations for international students: required—TOEFL (minimum score 550 paper-based, 90 iBT) or IELTS (6.5). Electronic applications accepted.

University of Virginia, Curry School of Education, Department of Human Services, Program in Clinical and School Psychology, Charlottesville, VA 22903. Offers PhD.

University of Virginia, Curry School of Education, Program in Education, Charlottesville, VA 22903. Offers administration and supervision (PhD); applied developmental science (PhD); counselor education (PhD); curriculum and instruction (PhD); early childhood special education (MT); education evaluation (PhD); educational psychology (PhD); educational research (PhD); elementary education (MT); English education (MT, PhD); foreign language education (MT); higher education (PhD); instructional technology (PhD); kinesiology (MT, PhD); math education (PhD); reading education (PhD); research, statistics and evaluation (PhD); school psychology (PhD); science education (PhD); social studies education (MT, PhD); special education (PhD); world languages education (MT). *Degree requirements:* For master's, comprehensive exam (for some programs), field project; for doctorate, comprehensive exam, thesis/dissertation. *Entrance requirements:* For doctorate, GRE General Test. Additional exam requirements/recommendations for international students: required—TOEFL (minimum score 600 paper-based; 90 iBT), IELTS (minimum score 7). Electronic applications accepted.

University of Washington, Graduate School, College of Education, Program in Educational Psychology, Seattle, WA 98195. Offers educational psychology (PhD); human development and cognition (M Ed); learning sciences (M Ed, PhD); measurement, statistics and research design (M Ed); school psychology (M Ed). *Accreditation:* APA. *Degree requirements:* For master's, thesis optional; for doctorate, thesis/dissertation. *Entrance requirements:* For master's and doctorate, GRE General Test, minimum GPA of 3.0. Additional exam requirements/recommendations for international students: required—TOEFL.

University of Wisconsin–Eau Claire, College of Arts and Sciences, Department of Psychology, Eau Claire, WI 54702-4004. Offers school psychology (MSE, Ed S). *Program availability:* Part-time. *Degree requirements:* For master's, comprehensive exam, thesis, National Certified School Psychologist Professional Exam, written exam, externship. *Entrance requirements:* For master's, GRE, minimum undergraduate GPA of 3.0; courses in exceptional children and youth, statistics, psychopathology, and theories of counseling. Additional exam requirements/recommendations for international students: required—TOEFL (minimum score 79 iBT).

University of Wisconsin–La Crosse, College of Arts, Social Sciences, and Humanities, Department of Psychology, La Crosse, WI 54601-3742. Offers school psychology (MS Ed, Ed S). *Faculty:* 4 full-time (2 women), 1 (woman) part-time/adjunct. *Students:* 24 full-time (20 women), 12 part-time (11 women). Average age 24. 57 applicants, 32% accepted, 13 enrolled. In 2019, 28 master's, 28 Ed Ss awarded. *Degree requirements:* For master's, thesis, seminar, or comprehensive exams. *Entrance requirements:* For master's and Ed S, GRE. Additional exam requirements/recommendations for international students: required—TOEFL (minimum score 550 paper-based; 79 iBT). *Application deadline:* For fall admission, 1/31 for domestic and international students. Electronic applications accepted. *Financial support:* Research assistantships, Federal Work-Study, scholarships/grants, and health care benefits available. Support available to part-time students. *Unit head:* Dr. Robert Dixon, Director of School Psychology, 608-785-6893, E-mail: rdixon@uwlax.edu. *Application contact:* Jennifer Weber, Senior Student Services Coordinator Graduate Admissions, 608-785-8939, E-mail: admissions@uwlax.edu.
Website: https://www.uwlax.edu/Psychology/Graduate-program/

University of Wisconsin–Milwaukee, Graduate School, School of Education, Department of Educational Psychology, Milwaukee, WI 53201-0413. Offers children's mental health for school professionals (Graduate Certificate); counseling psychology (PhD); educational statistics and measurement (MS, PhD); learning and development (MS, PhD); multicultural knowledge of mental health practices (Graduate Certificate); school counseling (MS, Graduate Certificate); school psychology (MS, PhD, Ed S). *Accreditation:* APA. *Program availability:* Part-time. *Degree requirements:* For master's, comprehensive exam, thesis; for doctorate, thesis/dissertation. *Entrance requirements:* For master's, minimum GPA of 3.0; for doctorate, GRE General Test, minimum GPA of 3.0. Additional exam requirements/recommendations for international students: required—TOEFL (minimum score 550 paper-based; 79 iBT), IELTS (minimum score 6.5). Electronic applications accepted.

University of Wisconsin–River Falls, Outreach and Graduate Studies, College of Education and Professional Studies, Department of Counseling and School Psychology, River Falls, WI 54022. Offers counseling (MSE); school psychology (MSE, Ed S). *Accreditation:* ACA. *Program availability:* Part-time. *Entrance requirements:* For master's, minimum GPA of 2.75, resume, 3 letters of reference, vita. Additional exam requirements/recommendations for international students: required—TOEFL (minimum score 500 paper-based; 65 iBT), IELTS (minimum score 5.5). Electronic applications accepted.

University of Wisconsin–Stout, Graduate School, College of Education, Health and Human Sciences, School of Education, Program in School Psychology, Menomonie, WI 54751. Offers MS Ed, Ed S. *Program availability:* Part-time. *Degree requirements:* For master's and Ed S, thesis. *Entrance requirements:* For master's, minimum GPA of 3.0; for Ed S, minimum GPA of 3.25. Additional exam requirements/recommendations for international students: required—TOEFL (minimum score 500 paper-based; 61 iBT). Electronic applications accepted.

University of Wisconsin–Superior, Graduate Division, Department of Counseling and Psychological Professions, Superior, WI 54880-4500. Offers community counseling (MSE); human relations (MSE); school counseling (MSE). *Program availability:* Part-time, evening/weekend. *Degree requirements:* For master's, position paper, practicum. *Entrance requirements:* For master's, GRE and/or MAT, minimum GPA of 2.75. Electronic applications accepted.

University of Wisconsin–Whitewater, School of Graduate Studies, College of Letters and Sciences, Department of Psychology, Program in School Psychology, Whitewater, WI 53190-1790. Offers MSE, Ed S. *Program availability:* Evening/weekend, online learning. *Degree requirements:* For Ed S, project. *Entrance requirements:* For degree, master's degree in school psychology from an accredited school. Additional exam requirements/recommendations for international students: required—TOEFL (minimum score 550 paper-based; 80 iBT), IELTS (minimum score 6). Electronic applications accepted.

Utah State University, School of Graduate Studies, Emma Eccles Jones College of Education and Human Services, Department of Psychology, Logan, UT 84322. Offers clinical/counseling/school psychology (PhD); research and evaluation methodology (PhD); school counseling (MS); school psychology (MS). *Accreditation:* APA (one or more programs are accredited). *Program availability:* Part-time, evening/weekend, online learning. Terminal master's awarded for partial completion of doctoral program. *Degree requirements:* For master's, thesis (for some programs); for doctorate, thesis/dissertation. *Entrance requirements:* For master's, GRE General Test (school psychology), MAT (school counseling), minimum GPA of 3.5; for doctorate, GRE General Test, minimum GPA of 3.5. Additional exam requirements/recommendations for international students: required—TOEFL.

Valparaiso University, Graduate School and Continuing Education, Programs in Education, Valparaiso, IN 46383. Offers initial licensure (M Ed), including Chinese teaching, elementary education, secondary education; instructional leadership (M Ed); school psychology (Ed S); secondary education (M Ed); M Ed/Ed S. *Accreditation:* NCATE. *Program availability:* Part-time, evening/weekend, online learning. *Entrance requirements:* For master's, GRE General Test, minimum GPA of 3.0. Additional exam requirements/recommendations for international students: required—TOEFL (minimum score 550 paper-based; 80 iBT), IELTS (minimum score 6). Electronic applications accepted.

Wayne State University, College of Education, Division of Theoretical and Behavioral Foundations, Detroit, MI 48202. Offers applied behavior analysis (Certificate); counseling (M Ed, MA, Ed D, Ed S); counseling psychology (MA, PhD); education evaluation and research (M Ed, Ed D); educational psychology (M Ed, PhD), including learning and instruction sciences (PhD); rehabilitation counseling and community inclusion (MA); school and community psychology (MA, Certificate). *Accreditation:* ACA (one or more programs are accredited); CORE (one or more programs are accredited). *Program availability:* Part-time, evening/weekend. *Faculty:* 10. *Students:* 199 full-time (171 women), 142 part-time (107 women); includes 135 minority (90 Black or African American, non-Hispanic/Latino; 2 American Indian or Alaska Native, non-Hispanic/Latino; 6 Asian, non-Hispanic/Latino; 16 Hispanic/Latino; 21 Two or more races, non-Hispanic/Latino), 10 international. Average age 32. 364 applicants, 25% accepted, 72 enrolled. In 2019, 101 master's, 11 doctorates, 19 other advanced degrees awarded. *Degree requirements:* For master's, thesis (for some programs); for doctorate, comprehensive exam, thesis/dissertation. *Entrance requirements:* For master's, GRE, interview, personal statement, portfolio (only art therapy); references; program application; for doctorate, GRE, departmental writing exam, interview, curriculum vitae, references, master's degree in closely-related field with minimum GPA of 3.5, demonstration of counseling skills (for Ed D in counseling); autobiographical statement; letter of application; personal statement; for other advanced degree, education specialist certificate: master's degree in counseling or closely related field and licensure; personal statement; recommendations; autobiographical statement; interview. Additional exam requirements/recommendations for international students: required—TOEFL (minimum score 550 paper-based; 79 iBT); recommended—IELTS (minimum score 6.5), TWE (minimum score 5.5), TSE (minimum score 58). *Application deadline:* Applications are processed on a rolling basis. *Application fee:* $50. Electronic applications accepted. *Expenses:* Tuition: Full-time $34,567. *Financial support:* In 2019–20, 92 students received support, including 1 fellowship (averaging $20,000 per year), 1 research assistantship with tuition reimbursement available (averaging $19,967 per year); teaching assistantships, Federal Work-Study, scholarships/grants, health care benefits, and unspecified assistantships also available. Support available to part-time students. Financial award applicants required to submit FAFSA. *Unit head:* Dr. William Hill, Assistant Dean, 313-577-9316, E-mail: ad2107@wayne.edu. *Application contact:* Dr. Mary L Waker, Graduate Admissions Officer, 313-577-1601, Fax: 313-577-7904, E-mail: m.waker@wayne.edu.
Website: https://education.wayne.edu/counseling-educational-psychology

Western Illinois University, School of Graduate Studies, College of Arts and Sciences, Department of Psychology, Macomb, IL 61455-1390. Offers clinical/community mental health (MS); general experimental psychology (MS); school psychology (SSP). *Program availability:* Part-time. *Degree requirements:* For master's, comprehensive exam (for some programs), thesis or alternative. *Entrance requirements:* For master's and SSP, GRE General Test. Additional exam requirements/recommendations for international

students: required—TOEFL (minimum score 550 paper-based; 80 iBT). Electronic applications accepted.

Western Kentucky University, Graduate School, College of Education and Behavioral Sciences, Department of Psychology, Bowling Green, KY 42101. Offers clinical psychology (MA); experimental psychology (MA); general psychology (MA); industrial/organizational psychology (MA); school psychology (Ed S). *Degree requirements:* For master's, comprehensive exam, thesis (for some programs); for Ed S, thesis, oral exam. *Entrance requirements:* For master's, GRE General Test; for Ed S, GRE General Test, minimum GPA of 3.5. Additional exam requirements/recommendations for international students: required—TOEFL (minimum score 555 paper-based; 79 iBT).

Wichita State University, Graduate School, College of Applied Studies, Department of Counseling, Educational Leadership, Educational and School Psychology, Wichita, KS 67260. Offers counseling (M Ed); educational leadership (M Ed, Ed D); educational psychology (M Ed); school psychology (Ed S). *Accreditation:* NCATE. *Program availability:* Part-time, evening/weekend.

William & Mary, School of Education, Program in School Psychology, Williamsburg, VA 23187-8795. Offers M Ed, Ed S. *Accreditation:* NCATE. *Faculty:* 3 full-time (2 women), 1 part-time/adjunct (0 women). *Students:* 25 full-time (23 women), 7 part-time (6 women); includes 4 minority (1 Black or African American, non-Hispanic/Latino; 1 Asian, non-Hispanic/Latino; 1 Hispanic/Latino; 1 Two or more races, non-Hispanic/Latino), 1 international. Average age 26. 62 applicants, 58% accepted, 26 enrolled. In 2019, 19 Ed Ss awarded. *Degree requirements:* For Ed S, internship. *Entrance requirements:* For master's and Ed S, GRE, minimum GPA of 3.5. Additional exam requirements/recommendations for international students: required—TOEFL (minimum score 100 iBT), IELTS (minimum score 7). *Application deadline:* For fall admission, 1/15 for domestic and international students. Application fee: $50. Electronic applications accepted. *Expenses:* In State Tuition per year $16440; Out of state Tuition per year $34800. *Financial support:* In 2019–20, 18 students received support, including 18 research assistantships with full tuition reimbursements available (averaging $11,859 per year); unspecified assistantships also available. Financial award application deadline: 1/15; financial award applicants required to submit FAFSA. *Unit head:* Dr. Leandra Parris, Assistant Professor, 757-221-2341, E-mail: lparris@wm.edu. *Application contact:* Dorothy Smith Osborne, Assistant Dean for Academic Programs and Student Services, 757-221-2317, E-mail: dsosbo@wm.edu.
Website: http://education.wm.edu

William James College, Graduate Programs, Newton, MA 02459. Offers applied psychology in higher education student personnel administration (MA); clinical psychology (Psy D); counseling psychology (MA); counseling psychology and community mental health (MA); counseling psychology and global mental health (MA); executive coaching (Graduate Certificate); forensic and counseling psychology (MA); leadership psychology (Psy D); organizational psychology (MA); primary care psychology (MA); respecialization in clinical psychology (Certificate); school psychology (Psy D); MA/CAGS. *Accreditation:* APA. *Degree requirements:* For master's, comprehensive exam (for some programs); for doctorate, thesis/dissertation (for some programs). Electronic applications accepted.

Worcester State University, Graduate School, Department of Education, Program in School Psychology, Worcester, MA 01602-2597. Offers M Ed, Ed S. *Faculty:* 6 full-time (all women), 24 part-time/adjunct (11 women). *Students:* 28 full-time (27 women), 13 part-time (12 women); includes 5 minority (1 Black or African American, non-Hispanic/Latino; 1 Hispanic/Latino; 3 Two or more races, non-Hispanic/Latino). Average age 26. In 2019, 17 master's, 12 Ed Ss awarded. *Degree requirements:* For master's, comprehensive exam, thesis optional, practicum; internship. For a detail list in Degree Completion requirements please see the graduate catalog at catalog.worcester.edu. *Entrance requirements:* For master's, For a detail list of entrance requirements please see the graduate catalog at catalog.worcester.edu; for Ed S, MTEL Communication and Literacy Skills test (strongly recommended), undergraduate major or concentration in psychology. Additional exam requirements/recommendations for international students: required—TOEFL (minimum score 550 paper-based; 79 iBT), IELTS (minimum score 6). *Application deadline:* For fall admission, 3/1 priority date for domestic and international students; for spring admission, 11/1 for domestic and international students; for summer admission, 3/1 for domestic and international students. Applications are processed on a rolling basis. Application fee: $50. Electronic applications accepted. *Expenses:* Tuition, area resident: Full-time $3042; part-time $169 per credit hour. Tuition, state resident: full-time $3042; part-time $169 per credit hour. Tuition, nonresident: full-time $3042; part-time $169 per credit hour. *International tuition:* $3042 full-time. *Required fees:* $2754; $153 per credit hour. *Financial support:* Career-related internships or fieldwork, scholarships/grants, and unspecified assistantships available. Financial award application deadline: 3/1; financial award applicants required to submit FAFSA. *Unit head:* Dr. Diane Tighe Cooke, School Psychology Graduate Program Coordinator, 508-929-8673, Fax: 508-929-8164, E-mail: dcooke@worcester.edu. *Application contact:* Sara Grady, Associate Dean for Graduate Studies and Professional Development, 508-929-8130, Fax: 508-929-8100, E-mail: sara.grady@worcester.edu.

Yeshiva University, Ferkauf Graduate School of Psychology, Program in School/Clinical-Child Psychology, New York, NY 10033-3201. Offers Psy D. *Accreditation:* APA. *Program availability:* Part-time. *Degree requirements:* For doctorate, comprehensive exam, thesis/dissertation. *Entrance requirements:* For doctorate, GRE General Test.

Youngstown State University, College of Graduate Studies, Beeghly College of Education, Department of Counseling, School Psychology and Educational Leadership, Youngstown, OH 44555-0001. Offers counseling (MS Ed); educational administration (MS Ed); educational leadership (Ed D); school psychology (Ed S). *Accreditation:* NCATE. *Program availability:* Part-time, evening/weekend. *Degree requirements:* For master's, comprehensive exam; for doctorate, comprehensive exam, thesis/dissertation. *Entrance requirements:* For master's, GRE, MAT, or teaching certificate; minimum GPA of 2.7; for doctorate, GRE General Test, GRE Subject Test, interview, minimum GPA of 3.5. Additional exam requirements/recommendations for international students: required—TOEFL.

Social Psychology

Adler University, Master of Public Policy and Administration Program: Social Change Leadership, Vancouver, BC V6B 3J5, Canada. Offers MPPA. *Program availability:* Part-time, evening/weekend. In 2019, 1 master's awarded. *Degree requirements:* For master's, In-Field Practicum; Capstone Project. *Unit head:* Michelle Brice, Associate Vice President of Admissions, 236-521-2409, E-mail: vanadmissions@adler.edu.

Application contact: Michelle Brice, Associate Vice President of Admissions, 236-521-2409, E-mail: vanadmissions@adler.edu.

Alliant International University - Los Angeles, California School of Professional Psychology, Psy D Program in Clinical Psychology, Alhambra, CA 91803. Offers clinical health psychology (Psy D); family/child and couple clinical psychology (Psy D); multi-interest option (Psy D); multicultural community-clinical psychology (Psy D). *Accreditation:* APA. *Degree requirements:* For doctorate, comprehensive exam, thesis/dissertation. *Entrance requirements:* For doctorate, interview, minimum GPA of 3.0 in both psychology and overall. Additional exam requirements/recommendations for international students: required—TOEFL (minimum score 600 paper-based), TWE. Electronic applications accepted.

Alvernia University, School of Graduate Studies, Department of Psychology and Counseling, Reading, PA 19607-1799. Offers community counseling (MA). *Entrance requirements:* For master's, GRE or MAT.

Alverno College, School of Professional Studies - Psychology, Milwaukee, WI 53234-3922. Offers community-based research and consultation (MSCP); professional counselor (MSCP). *Program availability:* Part-time, evening/weekend. *Faculty:* 4 full-time (all women). *Students:* 113 full-time (102 women), 10 part-time (9 women); includes 45 minority (23 Black or African American, non-Hispanic/Latino; 2 Asian, non-Hispanic/Latino; 17 Hispanic/Latino; 3 Two or more races, non-Hispanic/Latino), 1 international. Average age 33. 65 applicants, 89% accepted, 39 enrolled. In 2019, 25 master's awarded. *Degree requirements:* For master's, 700 hours of internship/practicum for community psychology; 1800 hours of internship/practicum (two 300 hour semesters plus two 600 hour semesters) for school psychology. *Entrance requirements:* For master's, bachelor's degree in any discipline; admission requirements vary by program. Additional exam requirements/recommendations for international students: required—TOEFL. *Application deadline:* For fall admission, 7/15 priority date for domestic and international students; for spring admission, 12/15 priority date for domestic and international students. Applications are processed on a rolling basis. Application fee: $0. Electronic applications accepted. *Expenses:* $866 per credit hour. *Financial support:* Federal Work-Study and scholarships/grants available. Support available to part-time students. Financial award applicants required to submit FAFSA. *Unit head:* Dr. Patricia Luebke, Dean, School of Professional Studies, 414-382-6368, Fax: 414-382-6354, E-mail: patricia.luebke@alverno.edu. *Application contact:* Annie Barrett, Graduate, Adult, and Transfer Admissions Counselor, 414-382-6113, Fax: 414-382-6354, E-mail: annie.barrett@alverno.edu.

Andrews University, School of Graduate Studies, College of Education and International Services, Department of Graduate Psychology and Counseling, Program in Community Counseling, Berrien Springs, MI 49104. Offers clinical mental health counseling (MA); community counseling (MA). *Students:* 25 full-time (19 women), 4 part-time (3 women); includes 14 minority (4 Black or African American, non-Hispanic/Latino; 1 Asian, non-Hispanic/Latino; 9 Hispanic/Latino), 9 international. Average age 32. In 2019, 10 master's awarded. *Degree requirements:* For master's, thesis optional. *Entrance requirements:* For master's, GRE. Additional exam requirements/recommendations for international students: required—TOEFL (minimum score 550 paper-based). *Application deadline:* Applications are processed on a rolling basis. Application fee: $60. Electronic applications accepted. *Unit head:* Dr. Nancy Carbonell, Coordinator, 269-471-3472. *Application contact:* Jillian Panigot, Director, University Admissions, 800-253-2874, Fax: 269-471-6321, E-mail: graduate@andrews.edu.

Argosy University, Atlanta, Georgia School of Professional Psychology, Atlanta, GA 30328. Offers clinical psychology (MA, Psy D, Postdoctoral Respecialization Certificate), including child and family psychology (Psy D), general adult clinical (Psy D), health psychology (Psy D), neuropsychology/geropsychology (Psy D); community counseling (MA), including marriage and family therapy; counselor education and supervision (Ed D); forensic psychology (MA); industrial organizational psychology (MA); marriage and family therapy (Certificate); sport-exercise psychology (MA). *Accreditation:* APA.

Argosy University, Chicago, Illinois School of Professional Psychology, Chicago, IL 60601. Offers clinical psychology (MA, Psy D), including child and adolescent psychology (Psy D), client-centered and experiential psychotherapies (Psy D), diversity and multicultural psychology (Psy D), family psychology (Psy D), forensic psychology (Psy D), health psychology (Psy D), neuropsychology (Psy D), organizational consulting (Psy D), psychoanalytic psychology (Psy D), psychology and spirituality (Psy D); community counseling (MA); counseling psychology (Ed D), including counselor education and supervision; counselor education and supervision (Ed D); industrial organizational psychology (MA). *Accreditation:* APA (one or more programs are accredited). *Program availability:* Online learning.

Argosy University, Northern Virginia, American School of Professional Psychology, Arlington, VA 22209. Offers clinical psychology (MA, Psy D), including child and family psychology (Psy D), diversity and multicultural psychology (Psy D), forensic psychology (Psy D), health and neuropsychology (Psy D); community counseling (MA); counseling psychology (Ed D), including counselor education and supervision; counselor education and supervision (Ed D); forensic psychology (MA).

Arizona State University at Tempe, College of Liberal Arts and Sciences, Department of Psychology, Tempe, AZ 85287-1104. Offers applied behavior analysis (MS); behavioral neuroscience (PhD); clinical psychology (PhD); cognitive science (PhD); developmental psychology (PhD); quantitative psychology (PhD); social psychology (PhD). *Accreditation:* APA. *Degree requirements:* For doctorate, comprehensive exam, thesis/dissertation, interactive Program of Study (iPOS) submitted before completing 50 percent of required credit hours. *Entrance requirements:* For doctorate, GRE General Test, GRE Subject Test, minimum GPA of 3.0 or equivalent in last 2 years of work leading to bachelor's degree. Additional exam requirements/recommendations for international students: required—TOEFL, IELTS, or PTE. Electronic applications accepted.

Ball State University, Graduate School, College of Health, Department of Counseling Psychology, Social Psychology, and Counseling, Program in Social Psychology, Muncie, IN 47306. Offers social psychology (MA); social psychology and clinical mental health counseling (MA). *Entrance requirements:* For master's, GRE General Test (minimum scores 144 quantitative, 153 verbal), minimum baccalaureate GPA of 2.75 or 3.0 in latter half of baccalaureate, minimum GPA of 3.0 in psychology coursework, three letters of recommendation. Additional exam requirements/recommendations for international students: required—TOEFL (minimum score 550 paper-based; 79 iBT), IELTS (minimum score 6.5). Electronic applications accepted. *Expenses: Tuition, area resident:* Full-time $7506; part-time $417 per credit hour. Tuition, nonresident: full-time $20,610; part-time $1145 per credit hour. *Required fees:* $2126. Tuition and fees vary according to course load, campus/location and program.

Becker College, Program in Mental Health Counseling, Worcester, MA 01609. Offers community mental health (MA); school consultation (MA). *Entrance requirements:* For master's, GRE, interview, official transcript, three letters of recommendation, essay. Electronic applications accepted.

Bowling Green State University, Graduate College, College of Arts and Sciences, Department of Sociology, Bowling Green, OH 43403. Offers demography and population studies (MA); social psychology (MA); sociology (PhD). *Program availability:* Part-time. *Degree requirements:* For master's, thesis or alternative; for doctorate, comprehensive exam, thesis/dissertation. *Entrance requirements:* For master's and doctorate, GRE General Test. Additional exam requirements/recommendations for international students: required—TOEFL. Electronic applications accepted.

Brandeis University, Graduate School of Arts and Sciences, Department of Psychology, Waltham, MA 02454-9110. Offers brain, body and behavior (PhD); cognitive neuroscience (PhD); general psychology (MA); social/developmental psychology (PhD). *Program availability:* Part-time. *Faculty:* 14 full-time (7 women), 3 part-time/adjunct (all women). *Students:* 31 full-time (21 women), 1 (woman) part-time; includes 6 minority (4 Asian, non-Hispanic/Latino; 2 Hispanic/Latino), 8 international. Average age 26. 157 applicants, 14% accepted, 12 enrolled. In 2019, 18 master's, 2 doctorates awarded. Terminal master's awarded for partial completion of doctoral program. *Degree requirements:* For master's, thesis (for some programs); for doctorate, thesis/dissertation. *Entrance requirements:* For master's and doctorate, GRE General required; GRE Subject recommended, transcripts, letters of recommendation, resume, and statement of purpose. Additional exam requirements/recommendations for international students: required—TOEFL, IELTS, PTE. *Application deadline:* For fall admission, 12/1 priority date for domestic and international students. Applications are processed on a rolling basis. Application fee: $75. Electronic applications accepted. *Financial support:* In 2019–20, 23 fellowships with full tuition reimbursements (averaging $25,000 per year), 16 teaching assistantships (averaging $3,550 per year) were awarded; research assistantships, scholarships/grants, traineeships, health care benefits, and tuition waivers also available. Support available to part-time students. *Unit head:* Dr. Angela Gutchess, Director of Graduate Studies, 781-736-3247, E-mail: gutchess@brandeis.edu. *Application contact:* Sarah Lupis, Administrator, 781-736-3303, E-mail: slupis@brandeis.edu.
Website: http://www.brandeis.edu/gsas/programs/psychology.html

Brock University, Faculty of Graduate Studies, Faculty of Social Sciences, Program in Psychology, St. Catharines, ON L2S 3A1, Canada. Offers behavioral neuroscience (MA, PhD); life span development (MA, PhD); social personality (MA, PhD). *Program availability:* Part-time. *Degree requirements:* For master's, thesis; for doctorate, thesis/dissertation. *Entrance requirements:* For master's, GRE, honors degree; for doctorate, GRE, master's degree. Additional exam requirements/recommendations for international students: required—TOEFL (minimum score 550 paper-based; 80 iBT), IELTS (minimum score 6.5), TWE (minimum score 4). Electronic applications accepted.

Brooklyn College of the City University of New York, School of Natural and Behavioral Sciences, Department of Psychology, Brooklyn, NY 11210-2889. Offers experimental psychology (MA); industrial and organizational psychology (MA), including human relations, organizational behavior; mental health counseling (MA); psychology (PhD). *Program availability:* Part-time. *Degree requirements:* For master's, comprehensive exam, thesis (for some programs). *Entrance requirements:* For master's, minimum GPA of 3.0, 2 letters of recommendation, essay; for doctorate, GRE. Additional exam requirements/recommendations for international students: required—TOEFL (minimum score 520 paper-based; 69 iBT). Electronic applications accepted.

California State University, East Bay, Office of Graduate Studies, College of Letters, Arts, and Social Sciences, Department of Social Work, Hayward, CA 94542-3000. Offers children, youth, and family services (MSW); community mental health services (MSW). *Accreditation:* CSWE. *Degree requirements:* For master's, comprehensive exam. *Entrance requirements:* For master's, minimum GPA of 2.8; courses in statistics and either human biology, physiology, or anatomy; liberal arts or social science baccalaureate degree; 3 letters of recommendation; personal statement; criminal background check; student professional liability insurance. Additional exam requirements/recommendations for international students: required—TOEFL (minimum score 550 paper-based). Electronic applications accepted.

California State University, Fullerton, Graduate Studies, College of Health and Human Development, Department of Social Work, Fullerton, CA 92831-3599. Offers aging (MSW); child welfare (MSW); community mental health (MSW). *Accreditation:* CSWE. *Program availability:* Part-time. *Entrance requirements:* For master's, minimum GPA of 3.0 for last 60 semester or 90 quarter units.

Carnegie Mellon University, Dietrich College of Humanities and Social Sciences, Department of Psychology, Program in Social/Personality/Health Psychology, Pittsburgh, PA 15213-3891. Offers PhD. *Degree requirements:* For doctorate, comprehensive exam, thesis/dissertation. *Entrance requirements:* For doctorate, GRE General Test. Additional exam requirements/recommendations for international students: required—TOEFL.

Claremont Graduate University, Graduate Programs, School of Social Science, Policy and Evaluation, Department of Psychology, Claremont, CA 91711-6160. Offers advanced study in evaluation (Certificate); cognitive psychology (MA, PhD); developmental psychology (MA, PhD); evaluation and applied research methods (MA, PhD); health behavior research and evaluation (MA, PhD); human resource development and evaluation (MA); industrial/organizational psychology (MA, PhD); organizational behavior (MA, PhD); organizational psychology (MA, PhD); social psychology (MA, PhD); MBA/PhD. *Program availability:* Part-time. Terminal master's awarded for partial completion of doctoral program. *Entrance requirements:* For master's and doctorate, GRE General Test. Additional exam requirements/recommendations for international students: required—TOEFL (minimum score 75 iBT). Electronic applications accepted.

Clark University, Graduate School, Hiatt School of Psychology, Program in Social Psychology, Worcester, MA 01610-1477. Offers PhD. *Entrance requirements:* For doctorate, GRE General Test. Additional exam requirements/recommendations for international students: required—TOEFL. *Expenses: Tuition:* Full-time $47,650; part-time $4765 per course. *Required fees:* $1850.

College of St. Joseph, Graduate Programs, Division of Psychology and Human Services, Program in Community Counseling, Rutland, VT 05701-3899. Offers MS. *Program availability:* Part-time, evening/weekend. *Degree requirements:* For master's, comprehensive exam, thesis optional. *Entrance requirements:* For master's, official college transcripts; 2 letters of reference. Additional exam requirements/recommendations for international students: required—TOEFL (minimum score 550 paper-based). Electronic applications accepted.

Concordia University, College of Arts and Sciences, Portland, OR 97211-6099. Offers community psychology (MA); teaching English to speakers of other languages (MA).

Cornell University, Graduate School, Graduate Fields of Arts and Sciences, Field of Psychology, Ithaca, NY 14853. Offers biopsychology (PhD); human experimental psychology (PhD); personality and social psychology (PhD). *Degree requirements:* For doctorate, comprehensive exam, thesis/dissertation, 2 semesters of teaching experience. *Entrance requirements:* For doctorate, GRE General Test, 3 letters of recommendation. Additional exam requirements/recommendations for international students: required—TOEFL (minimum score 550 paper-based; 77 iBT). Electronic applications accepted.

Cornell University, Graduate School, Graduate Fields of Arts and Sciences, Field of Sociology, Ithaca, NY 14853. Offers economy and society (MA, PhD); gender and life course (MA, PhD); methodology (MA, PhD); organizations (MA, PhD); policy analysis (MA, PhD); political sociology/social movements (MA, PhD); racial and ethnic relations (MA, PhD); social networks (MA, PhD); social psychology (MA, PhD); social stratification (MA, PhD). Terminal master's awarded for partial completion of doctoral program.

Degree requirements: For master's, thesis; for doctorate, thesis/dissertation, 1 year of teaching experience. *Entrance requirements:* For master's and doctorate, GRE General Test, 2 letters of recommendation, writing sample. Additional exam requirements/recommendations for international students: required—TOEFL (minimum score 550 paper-based; 77 iBT). Electronic applications accepted.

Delaware Valley University, Program in Counseling Psychology, Doylestown, PA 18901-2697. Offers child and adolescent therapy (MA); social justice community counseling (MA).

Florida Agricultural and Mechanical University, Division of Graduate Studies, Research, and Continuing Education, College of Social Sciences, Arts and Humanities, Department of Psychology, Program in Community Psychology, Tallahassee, FL 32307-3200. Offers MS. *Degree requirements:* For master's, thesis, internship. *Entrance requirements:* For master's, GRE General Test, minimum GPA of 3.0, letters of recommendation (3). Additional exam requirements/recommendations for international students: required—TOEFL.

Florida State University, The Graduate School, Department of Anthropology, Department of Psychology, Program in Social Psychology, Tallahassee, FL 32306-4301. Offers PhD. *Faculty:* 6 full-time (2 women). *Students:* 16 full-time (13 women); includes 4 minority (1 Asian, non-Hispanic/Latino; 2 Hispanic/Latino; 1 Two or more races, non-Hispanic/Latino). Average age 26. 49 applicants, 10% accepted, 4 enrolled. In 2019, 1 doctorate awarded. Terminal master's awarded for partial completion of doctoral program. *Degree requirements:* For doctorate, comprehensive exam, thesis/dissertation. *Entrance requirements:* For doctorate, GRE General Test, minimum GPA of 3.0, research experience, letters of recommendation. Additional exam requirements/recommendations for international students: required—TOEFL (minimum score 80 iBT). *Application deadline:* For fall admission, 12/1 for domestic and international students. Application fee: $30. Electronic applications accepted. *Financial support:* In 2019–20, 15 students received support, including 1 fellowship with full tuition reimbursement available, 1 research assistantship with full tuition reimbursement available, 14 teaching assistantships with full tuition reimbursements available; health care benefits also available. Financial award application deadline: 12/1; financial award applicants required to submit FAFSA. *Unit head:* Dr. James McNulty, Director of Social Psychology, 850-645-0023, Fax: 850-644-7739, E-mail: mcnulty@psy.fsu.edu. *Application contact:* Lynda L. Gibson, Graduate Program Associate, 850-644-2499, Fax: 850-644-7739, E-mail: grad-info@psy.fsu.edu.
Website: http://www.psy.fsu.edu/

Future Generations University, Program in Applied Community Change, Franklin, WV 26807. Offers conservation (MA). *Program availability:* Blended/hybrid learning. *Degree requirements:* For master's, portfolio. *Entrance requirements:* For master's, bachelor's degree, community involvement. Additional exam requirements/recommendations for international students: recommended—TOEFL. Electronic applications accepted.

The George Washington University, Columbian College of Arts and Sciences, Department of Psychology, Washington, DC 20052. Offers applied social psychology (PhD); clinical psychology (PhD); cognitive neuroscience (PhD). *Accreditation:* APA. *Program availability:* Part-time, evening/weekend. *Degree requirements:* For doctorate, thesis/dissertation or alternative, general exam. *Entrance requirements:* For doctorate, GRE General Test, minimum GPA of 3.0. Additional exam requirements/recommendations for international students: required—TOEFL (minimum score 550 paper-based; 80 iBT).

Georgia State University, College of Arts and Sciences, Department of Psychology, Atlanta, GA 30302-3083. Offers clinical psychology (PhD); cognitive sciences (PhD); community psychology (PhD); developmental psychology (PhD); neuropsychology and behavioral neuroscience (PhD). *Accreditation:* APA. *Faculty:* 29 full-time (17 women). *Students:* 107 full-time (85 women), 2 part-time (both women); includes 23 minority (9 Black or African American, non-Hispanic/Latino; 6 Asian, non-Hispanic/Latino; 7 Hispanic/Latino; 1 Two or more races, non-Hispanic/Latino), 13 international. Average age 28. 498 applicants, 5% accepted, 17 enrolled. In 2019, 18 doctorates awarded. *Entrance requirements:* For doctorate, GRE. Additional exam requirements/recommendations for international students: required—TOEFL (minimum score 550 paper-based; 80 iBT). *Application deadline:* For fall admission, 12/1 for domestic and international students. Application fee: $50. Electronic applications accepted. *Expenses: Tuition, area resident:* Full-time $7164; part-time $398 per credit hour. Tuition, state resident: full-time $7164; part-time $398 per credit hour. Tuition, nonresident: full-time $22,662; part-time $1259 per credit hour. *International tuition:* $22,662 full-time. *Required fees:* $2128; $312 per credit hour. Tuition and fees vary according to course load and program. *Financial support:* In 2019–20, fellowships with full tuition reimbursements (averaging $19,282 per year), research assistantships with full tuition reimbursements (averaging $5,173 per year), teaching assistantships with full tuition reimbursements (averaging $6,389 per year) were awarded; scholarships/grants, traineeships, health care benefits, and unspecified assistantships also available. Financial award applicants required to submit FAFSA. *Unit head:* Dr. Lisa Armistead, Professor, Associate Provost for Graduate Programs, 404-413-2091, Fax: 404-413-6207, E-mail: lparmistead@gsu.edu. *Application contact:* Dr. Lindsey Cohen, Director of Graduate Studies, 404-413-6263, Fax: 404-413-6207, E-mail: llcohen@gsu.edu.
Website: https://psychology.gsu.edu/

The Graduate Center, City University of New York, Graduate Studies, Program in Psychology, New York, NY 10016-4039. Offers basic applied neurocognition (PhD); biopsychology (PhD); clinical psychology (PhD); developmental psychology (PhD); environmental psychology (PhD); experimental psychology (PhD); industrial psychology (PhD); learning processes (PhD); neuropsychology (PhD); psychology (PhD); social personality (PhD). *Degree requirements:* For doctorate, one foreign language, thesis/dissertation. *Entrance requirements:* For doctorate, GRE General Test. Additional exam requirements/recommendations for international students: required—TOEFL. Electronic applications accepted.

Harvard University, Graduate School of Arts and Sciences, Department of Psychology, Cambridge, MA 02138. Offers psychology (PhD), including behavior and decision analysis, cognition, developmental psychology, experimental psychology, personality, psychobiology, psychopathology; social psychology (PhD). *Accreditation:* APA. *Degree requirements:* For doctorate, thesis/dissertation, general exams. *Entrance requirements:* For doctorate, GRE General Test. Additional exam requirements/recommendations for international students: required—TOEFL.

Hofstra University, College of Liberal Arts and Sciences, Programs in Psychology, Hempstead, NY 11549. Offers applied organizational psychology (PhD); clinical psychology (PhD); industrial/organizational psychology (MA); school-community psychology (Psy D). *Accreditation:* APA. *Program availability:* Part-time, evening/weekend. *Students:* 193 full-time (138 women), 22 part-time (10 women); includes 42 minority (6 Black or African American, non-Hispanic/Latino; 1 American Indian or Alaska Native, non-Hispanic/Latino; 9 Asian, non-Hispanic/Latino; 23 Hispanic/Latino; 3 Two or more races, non-Hispanic/Latino), 21 international. Average age 26. 338 applicants, 36% accepted, 61 enrolled. In 2019, 60 master's, 33 doctorates awarded. Terminal master's awarded for partial completion of doctoral program. *Degree requirements:* For master's, comprehensive exam, thesis optional, internship, minimum GPA of 3.0; for doctorate, comprehensive exam, thesis/dissertation, 1st year qualifying examination, 2nd year research project, successful practicum/externship placements, written presentation and successful oral defense of dissertation, completion of full-time internship. *Entrance requirements:* For master's, GRE General Test, minimum GPA of 3.0, essay, interview; for doctorate, GRE General Test, GRE Subject Test (psychology), 3 letters of recommendation, interview, essay, curriculum vitae. Additional exam requirements/recommendations for international students: required—TOEFL (minimum score 550 paper-based; 80 iBT); recommended—IELTS (minimum score 6.5). *Application deadline:* For fall admission, 12/31 for domestic and international students. Application fee: $75. Electronic applications accepted. *Expenses: Tuition:* Full-time $25,164; part-time $1398 per credit. *Required fees:* $580; $165 per semester. Tuition and fees vary according to course load, degree level and program. *Financial support:* In 2019–20, 152 students received support, including 125 fellowships with full and partial tuition reimbursements available (averaging $8,256 per year), 4 research assistantships with full and partial tuition reimbursements available (averaging $5,531 per year); career-related internships or fieldwork, Federal Work-Study, institutionally sponsored loans, scholarships/grants, traineeships, tuition waivers (full and partial), unspecified assistantships, and scholarships and endowed scholarships also available. Support available to part-time students. Financial award applicants required to submit FAFSA. *Unit head:* Dr. Craig Johnson, Chairperson, 516-463-5636, E-mail: craig.a.johnson@hofstra.edu. *Application contact:* Sunil Samuel, Assistant Vice President of Admissions, 516-463-4723, Fax: 516-463-4664, E-mail: graduateadmission@hofstra.edu.
Website: http://www.hofstra.edu/hclas

Howard University, Graduate School, Department of Psychology, Washington, DC 20059-0002. Offers clinical psychology (PhD); developmental psychology (PhD); experimental psychology (PhD); neuropsychology (PhD); personality psychology (PhD); psychology (MS); social psychology (PhD). *Accreditation:* APA (one or more programs are accredited). *Program availability:* Part-time. *Degree requirements:* For master's, thesis; for doctorate, comprehensive exam, thesis/dissertation, qualifying exam. *Entrance requirements:* For master's, GRE General Test, minimum GPA of 2.5, bachelor's degree in psychology or related field; for doctorate, GRE General Test, minimum GPA of 3.0.

Humboldt State University, Academic Programs, College of Professional Studies, Department of Psychology, Arcata, CA 95521-8299. Offers psychology (MA), including biological psychology, counseling, developmental psychopathology, school psychology, social and environmental psychology. *Program availability:* Part-time. *Faculty:* 14 full-time (9 women), 13 part-time/adjunct (8 women). *Students:* 76 full-time (54 women), 11 part-time (4 women); includes 37 minority (1 Black or African American, non-Hispanic/Latino; 3 American Indian or Alaska Native, non-Hispanic/Latino; 4 Asian, non-Hispanic/Latino; 22 Hispanic/Latino; 7 Two or more races, non-Hispanic/Latino), 1 international. Average age 28. 89 applicants, 42% accepted, 31 enrolled. In 2019, 38 master's awarded. *Degree requirements:* For master's, thesis. *Entrance requirements:* For master's, appropriate bachelor's degree, minimum GPA of 2.5. Additional exam requirements/recommendations for international students: required—TOEFL (minimum score 500 paper-based). *Application deadline:* For fall admission, 2/1 for domestic students, 2/15 for international students. Applications are processed on a rolling basis. Application fee: $55. *Expenses:* Tuition, state resident: full-time $7176; part-time $4164 per term. *Required fees:* $2120; $1672 per term. *Financial support:* Career-related internships or fieldwork available. Financial award application deadline: 3/1; financial award applicants required to submit FAFSA. *Unit head:* Dr. Carrie Aigner, Graduate Program Coordinator, 707-826-3757, E-mail: carrie.aigner@humboldt.edu. *Application contact:* Dr. Carrie Aigner, Graduate Program Coordinator, 707-826-3757, E-mail: carrie.aigner@humboldt.edu.
Website: http://www2.humboldt.edu/psychology/programs-child/graduate-programs-psychology

Husson University, Graduate Programs in Counseling and Human Relations, Bangor, ME 04401-2999. Offers clinical mental health counseling (MS); human relations (MS); school counseling (MS). *Accreditation:* ACA. *Program availability:* Part-time, evening/weekend. *Degree requirements:* For master's, comprehensive exam (for some programs), thesis optional. *Entrance requirements:* For master's, BS with minimum GPA of 3.0, letters of recommendation, interview. Additional exam requirements/recommendations for international students: required—TOEFL (minimum score 550 paper-based; 80 iBT), IELTS (minimum score 6.5). Electronic applications accepted. *Expenses:* Contact institution.

Indiana University Bloomington, University Graduate School, College of Arts and Sciences, Department of Psychological and Brain Sciences, Bloomington, IN 47405. Offers clinical science (PhD); cognitive neuroscience (PhD); cognitive psychology (PhD); developmental psychology (PhD); methods of behavior (PhD); molecular systems neuroscience (PhD); social psychology (PhD). *Accreditation:* APA. *Degree requirements:* For doctorate, comprehensive exam, 90 credit hours, 2 advanced statistics/methods courses, 2 written research projects, the teaching of psychology course, teaching 1 semester of undergraduate methods course, qualifying examination, minor or a second major, first-year research seminar course, dissertation defense, written dissertation. *Entrance requirements:* For doctorate, GRE. Additional exam requirements/recommendations for international students: required—TOEFL (minimum score 550 paper-based; 79 iBT). Electronic applications accepted.

Indiana University of Pennsylvania, School of Graduate Studies and Research, College of Education and Communications, Department of Counseling, Indiana, PA 15705. Offers clinical mental health counseling (MA); community counseling (MA); school counseling (M Ed). *Accreditation:* ACA; NCATE. *Program availability:* Part-time, evening/weekend. *Faculty:* 10 full-time (9 women), 5 part-time/adjunct (4 women). *Students:* 96 full-time (75 women), 77 part-time (63 women); includes 23 minority (12 Black or African American, non-Hispanic/Latino; 2 Hispanic/Latino; 9 Two or more races, non-Hispanic/Latino), 3 international. Average age 30. 124 applicants, 72% accepted, 69 enrolled. In 2019, 47 master's awarded. *Degree requirements:* For master's, thesis optional. *Entrance requirements:* For master's, 2 letters of recommendation, goal statement, official transcripts. Additional exam requirements/recommendations for international students: required—TOEFL (minimum score 540 paper-based; 76 iBT); recommended—IELTS (minimum score 6). *Application deadline:* Applications are processed on a rolling basis. Application fee: $50. Electronic applications accepted. *Expenses: Tuition, area resident:* Full-time $9288; part-time $516 per credit. Tuition, nonresident: full-time $13,932; part-time $774 per credit. *Required fees:* $4454. One-time fee: $115 full-time. Tuition and fees vary according to course load and program. *Financial support:* In 2019–20, 11 fellowships (averaging $818 per year), 36 research assistantships with tuition reimbursements (averaging $4,832 per year) were awarded; teaching assistantships with partial tuition reimbursements, career-related internships or fieldwork, Federal Work-Study, scholarships/grants, and unspecified assistantships also available. Support available to part-time students. Financial award application deadline: 4/15; financial award applicants required to submit FAFSA. *Unit head:* Dr. Claire Dandeneau, Chairperson/Graduate Coordinator, 724-357-4534, E-mail: claire.dandeneau@iup.edu. *Application contact:* Dr. Brittany Pollard, Graduate

Social Psychology

Coordinator for the Pittsburgh Area Program, 412-824-1999, E-mail: bpollard@iup.edu. Website: http://www.iup.edu/counseling

Indiana University–Purdue University Indianapolis, School of Science, Department of Psychology, Indianapolis, IN 46202-3275. Offers addiction neuroscience (PhD); applied social and organizational psychology (PhD); clinical psychology (PhD); industrial/organizational psychology (MS). *Accreditation:* APA (one or more programs are accredited). Terminal master's awarded for partial completion of doctoral program. *Degree requirements:* For master's, thesis; for doctorate, thesis/dissertation. *Entrance requirements:* For master's, GRE General Test, minimum undergraduate GPA of 3.0; for doctorate, GRE General Test, GRE Subject Test (clinical psychology), minimum undergraduate GPA of 3.2. Additional exam requirements/recommendations for international students: required—TOEFL (minimum score 567 paper-based; 86 iBT), IELTS (minimum score 6.5). Electronic applications accepted.

Indiana Wesleyan University, Graduate School, College of Arts and Sciences, Marion, IN 46953. Offers addictions counseling (MS); clinical mental health counseling (MS); community counseling (MS); marriage and family therapy (MS); school counseling (MS); student development counseling and administration (MS). *Accreditation:* ACA. *Program availability:* Part-time. *Degree requirements:* For master's, thesis or alternative. *Entrance requirements:* For master's, GRE General Test. Additional exam requirements/ recommendations for international students: required—TOEFL. Electronic applications accepted. *Expenses:* Contact institution.

Iowa State University of Science and Technology, Department of Psychology, Ames, IA 50011. Offers cognitive psychology (PhD); counseling psychology (PhD); psychology (MS, PhD); social psychology (PhD). *Accreditation:* APA (one or more programs are accredited). *Entrance requirements:* For doctorate, GRE General Test, GRE Subject Test (psychology), 3 letters of recommendation. Additional exam requirements/ recommendations for international students: required—TOEFL (minimum score 560 paper-based; 79 iBT), IELTS (minimum score 6.5). Electronic applications accepted.

Lesley University, Graduate School of Arts and Social Sciences, Cambridge, MA 02138-2790. Offers clinical mental health counseling (MA), including holistic counseling, school and community counseling, trauma studies; counseling psychology (MA, CAGS), including professional counseling (MA), school counseling (MA); creative writing (MFA); expressive therapies (MA, PhD, CAGS), including art (MA), clinical mental health counseling (MA), dance (MA), expressive therapies (MA), music (MA); independent studies (CAGS); independent study (MA); intercultural relations (MA, CAGS); interdisciplinary studies (MA), including individualized studies, integrative holistic health, mindfulness studies, peace and conflict transformation, trauma sensitive assessment, intervention, and consultation, women's studies; urban environmental leadership (MA). *Program availability:* Part-time, online learning. *Degree requirements:* For master's, internship, practicum, thesis (for expressive therapies); for doctorate, thesis/dissertation, arts apprenticeship, field placement; for CAGS, thesis, internship (for counseling psychology, expressive therapies). *Entrance requirements:* For master's, MAT (counseling psychology), interview, writing samples, art portfolio; for doctorate, GRE or MAT, interview, master's degree; for CAGS, interview, master's degree. Additional exam requirements/recommendations for international students: required—TOEFL (minimum score 550 paper-based; 80 iBT). Electronic applications accepted.

Loyola University Chicago, School of Education, Program in Community Counseling, Chicago, IL 60660. Offers clinical mental health counseling (Ed S); community counseling (M Ed, MA). *Program availability:* Part-time. *Faculty:* 5 full-time (2 women), 5 part-time/adjunct (4 women). *Students:* 24 full-time (21 women), 4 part-time (0 women); includes 7 minority (3 Black or African American, non-Hispanic/Latino; 3 Hispanic/Latino; 1 Two or more races, non-Hispanic/Latino), 1 international. Average age 28. 60 applicants, 72% accepted, 13 enrolled. In 2019, 9 master's awarded. *Degree requirements:* For master's, comprehensive exam (for some programs), thesis (for some programs). *Entrance requirements:* For master's, GRE General Test, minimum GPA of 3.0, letters of recommendation, resume. Additional exam requirements/ recommendations for international students: required—TOEFL (minimum score 550 paper-based; 79 iBT). *Application deadline:* For fall admission, 1/1 for domestic and international students. Application fee: $50. Electronic applications accepted. Application fee is waived when completed online. *Expenses:* 17082. *Financial support:* Career-related internships or fieldwork, institutionally sponsored loans, scholarships/ grants, and unspecified assistantships available. Support available to part-time students. Financial award application deadline: 2/1; financial award applicants required to submit FAFSA. *Unit head:* Dr. Matt Miller, Director, 312-915-6800, E-mail: mmill11@luc.edu. *Application contact:* Dr. Matt Miller, Director, 312-915-6800, E-mail: mmill11@luc.edu.

Marquette University, Graduate School, College of Education, Department of Counselor Education and Counseling Psychology, Milwaukee, WI 53201-1881. Offers clinical mental health counseling (MS); community counseling (MA); counseling psychology (PhD); school counseling (MA). *Accreditation:* ACA. *Program availability:* Part-time. Terminal master's awarded for partial completion of doctoral program. *Degree requirements:* For master's, comprehensive exam, thesis (for some programs); for doctorate, thesis/dissertation, qualifying exam. *Entrance requirements:* For master's, GRE General Test or MAT, official transcripts from all current and previous colleges/ universities except Marquette, three letters of recommendation, statement of purpose; for doctorate, GRE General Test, MAT, sample of written work, official transcripts from all current and previous colleges/universities except Marquette, three letters of recommendation, statement of purpose, resume/curriculum vitae. Additional exam requirements/recommendations for international students: required—TOEFL (minimum score 530 paper-based).

Martin University, Division of Psychology, Indianapolis, IN 46218-3867. Offers community psychology (MS). *Program availability:* Part-time, evening/weekend. *Degree requirements:* For master's, thesis. *Entrance requirements:* For master's, GRE General Test, GRE Subject Test.

Marymount California University, Program in Community Psychology, Rancho Palos Verdes, CA 90275-6299. Offers MS.

Missouri Valley College, Graduate Studies, Marshall, MO 65340-3197. Offers community counseling (MA).

Mount Aloysius College, Program in Community Counseling, Cresson, PA 16630-1999. Offers MS. *Program availability:* Evening/weekend. *Entrance requirements:* Additional exam requirements/recommendations for international students: required—IELTS (minimum score 5.5); recommended—TOEFL. *Application deadline:* For fall admission, 8/1 for domestic students; for spring admission, 12/1 for domestic students. Applications are processed on a rolling basis. Application fee: $30. Electronic applications accepted. Application fee is waived when completed online. *Financial support:* Unspecified assistantships available. Financial award applicants required to submit FAFSA. *Application contact:* Matthew P. Bodenschatz, Director of Graduate and Continuing Education Admissions, 814-886-6556, Fax: 814-886-6441, E-mail: mbodenschatz@mtaloy.edu.

The New School, The New School for Social Research, Department of Psychology, New York, NY 10011. Offers clinical psychology (PhD); cognitive, social, and developmental psychology (PhD); psychology (MA). *Accreditation:* APA (one or more programs are accredited). *Program availability:* Part-time. *Faculty:* 17 full-time (9 women), 8 part-time/adjunct (2 women). *Students:* 173 full-time (135 women), 32 part-time (28 women); includes 36 minority (8 Black or African American, non-Hispanic/Latino; 8 Asian, non-Hispanic/Latino; 17 Hispanic/Latino; 1 Native Hawaiian or other Pacific Islander, non-Hispanic/Latino; 2 Two or more races, non-Hispanic/Latino), 42 international. Average age 29. 217 applicants, 85% accepted, 58 enrolled. In 2019, 75 master's, 14 doctorates awarded. Terminal master's awarded for partial completion of doctoral program. *Degree requirements:* For master's, comprehensive exam, thesis (for some programs); for doctorate, comprehensive exam, thesis/dissertation. *Entrance requirements:* For master's, GRE, letters of recommendation, writing sample, essays, transcripts; for doctorate, letters of recommendation, writing sample, essays, transcripts. Additional exam requirements/recommendations for international students: required—TOEFL (minimum score 100 iBT), IELTS (minimum score 7), PTE (minimum score 68). *Application deadline:* For fall admission, 1/5 priority date for domestic and international students; for spring admission, 10/15 priority date for domestic and international students. Applications are processed on a rolling basis. Application fee: $50. Electronic applications accepted. *Expenses:* 2260 per credit. *Financial support:* In 2019–20, 191 students received support, including 21 fellowships with full and partial tuition reimbursements available (averaging $6,560 per year), 43 research assistantships (averaging $5,556 per year), 52 teaching assistantships with full and partial tuition reimbursements available (averaging $7,423 per year); career-related internships or fieldwork, Federal Work-Study, scholarships/grants, and tuition waivers (full and partial) also available. Support available to part-time students. Financial award application deadline: 2/1; financial award applicants required to submit FAFSA. *Unit head:* Dr. Howard Steele, Department Chair, 212-2295727 Ext. 3118, E-mail: steeleh@newschool.edu. *Application contact:* Merida Gasbarro, Director of Graduate Admission, 212-229-5600 Ext. 1108, E-mail: escandom@newschool.edu. Website: https://www.newschool.edu/nssr/psychology/

New York University, Graduate School of Arts and Science, Department of Psychology, New York, NY 10012-1019. Offers cognition and perception (PhD); general psychology (MA); industrial/organizational psychology (MA); psychotherapy and psychoanalysis (Advanced Certificate); social psychology (PhD). *Program availability:* Part-time. Terminal master's awarded for partial completion of doctoral program. *Degree requirements:* For master's, comprehensive exam, thesis or alternative; for doctorate, thesis/dissertation. *Entrance requirements:* For master's and doctorate, GRE General Test. Additional exam requirements/recommendations for international students: required—TOEFL, IELTS.

Norfolk State University, School of Graduate Studies, School of Liberal Arts, Department of Psychology, Program in Community/Clinical Psychology, Norfolk, VA 23504. Offers MA. *Degree requirements:* For master's, comprehensive exam, thesis or alternative. *Entrance requirements:* For master's, minimum GPA of 2.7.

North Carolina State University, Graduate School, College of Education, Department of Teacher Education and Learning Sciences, Program in Agency Counseling, Raleigh, NC 27695. Offers M Ed, MS. *Accreditation:* APA. *Degree requirements:* For master's, thesis optional. *Entrance requirements:* For master's, GRE General Test or MAT, minimum GPA of 3.0 in major. Electronic applications accepted.

North Carolina State University, Graduate School, College of Humanities and Social Sciences, Department of Psychology, Raleigh, NC 27695. Offers applied social and community psychology (PhD); human factors and applied cognition (PhD); industrial/ organizational psychology (PhD); lifespan developmental psychology (PhD); school psychology (PhD). *Accreditation:* APA. *Degree requirements:* For doctorate, comprehensive exam, thesis/dissertation. *Entrance requirements:* For doctorate, GRE General Test, GRE Subject Test (industrial/organizational psychology), MAT (recommended), minimum GPA of 3.0 in major. Electronic applications accepted.

North Dakota State University, College of Graduate and Interdisciplinary Studies, College of Science and Mathematics, Department of Psychology, Fargo, ND 58102. Offers clinical psychology (MS); health and social psychology (PhD); psychological clinical science (PhD); psychology (MS); visual and cognitive neuroscience (PhD). *Entrance requirements:* Additional exam requirements/recommendations for international students: required—TOEFL. Electronic applications accepted. Tuition and fees vary according to program and reciprocity agreements.

Northwestern University, The Graduate School, Judd A. and Marjorie Weinberg College of Arts and Sciences, Department of Psychology, Evanston, IL 60208. Offers brain, behavior and cognition (PhD); clinical psychology (PhD); cognitive psychology (PhD); personality psychology (PhD); social psychology (PhD); JD/PhD. *Accreditation:* APA (one or more programs are accredited). *Program availability:* Part-time. *Degree requirements:* For doctorate, thesis/dissertation. *Entrance requirements:* For doctorate, GRE General Test, GRE Subject Test. Additional exam requirements/recommendations for international students: required—TOEFL. Electronic applications accepted.

The Ohio State University, Graduate School, College of Arts and Sciences, Division of Social and Behavioral Sciences, Department of Psychology, Columbus, OH 43210. Offers behavioral neuroscience (PhD); clinical psychology (PhD); cognitive psychology (PhD); developmental psychology (PhD); intellectual and developmental disabilities psychology (PhD); quantitative psychology (PhD); social psychology (PhD). *Accreditation:* APA. *Entrance requirements:* For doctorate, GRE General Test. Additional exam requirements/recommendations for international students: required—TOEFL (minimum score 600 paper-based; 100 iBT); recommended—IELTS (minimum score 8). Electronic applications accepted.

Oregon State University–Cascades, Program in Counseling, Bend, OR 97701. Offers community counseling (MS); school counseling (MS).

Penn State Harrisburg, Graduate School, School of Behavioral Sciences and Education, Middletown, PA 17057. Offers adult education in the health and medical professions (Certificate); applied behavior analysis (MA); applied clinical psychology (MA); applied psychological research (MA); community psychology and social change (MA); English as a second language (ESL) program specialist and leadership (Certificate); health education (M Ed); lifelong learning and adult education (M Ed, D Ed); literacy education (M Ed); literacy leadership (Certificate); psychology: applications in clinical psychology (Certificate); psychology: health psychology (Certificate); teaching and curriculum (M Ed); training and development (M Ed, Certificate). *Program availability:* Part-time, evening/weekend.

Queen's University at Kingston, School of Graduate Studies, Faculty of Arts and Science, Department of Psychology, Kingston, ON K7L 3N6, Canada. Offers brain behavior and cognitive science (MA, PhD); clinical psychology (MA, PhD); developmental psychology (MA, PhD); social personality psychology (MA, PhD). *Degree requirements:* For master's, thesis; for doctorate, comprehensive exam, thesis/ dissertation. *Entrance requirements:* For master's and doctorate, GRE General Test. Additional exam requirements/recommendations for international students: required—TOEFL.

Rutgers University - Newark, Graduate School, Program in Psychology, Newark, NJ 07102. Offers cognitive neuroscience (PhD); cognitive science (PhD); perception (PhD); psychobiology (PhD); social cognition (PhD). *Degree requirements:* For doctorate, comprehensive exam, thesis/dissertation. *Entrance requirements:* For doctorate, GRE General Test, GRE Subject Test, minimum undergraduate B average. Electronic applications accepted.

Rutgers University - New Brunswick, Graduate School-New Brunswick, Program in Psychology, Piscataway, NJ 08854-8097. Offers behavioral neuroscience (PhD); clinical psychology (PhD); cognitive psychology (PhD); interdisciplinary health psychology (PhD); social psychology (PhD). *Accreditation:* APA. *Degree requirements:* For doctorate, comprehensive exam, thesis/dissertation. *Entrance requirements:* For doctorate, GRE General Test, 3 letters of recommendation. Additional exam requirements/recommendations for international students: required—TOEFL (minimum score 577 paper-based). Electronic applications accepted.

Sacred Heart University, Graduate Programs, College of Arts and Sciences, Department of Psychology, Fairfield, CT 06825. Offers applied psychology (MS), including community psychology, general applied psychology, industrial-organizational psychology. *Program availability:* Part-time, evening/weekend, online learning. *Degree requirements:* For master's, comprehensive exam, thesis optional. *Entrance requirements:* For master's, minimum overall GPA of 3.0, bachelor's degree from accredited college or university. Additional exam requirements/recommendations for international students: required—TOEFL (minimum score 570 paper-based, 80 iBT), TWE, or IELTS (6.5). Electronic applications accepted. *Expenses:* Contact institution.

Sage Graduate School, School of Health Sciences, Department of Psychology, Program in Community Psychology, Troy, NY 12180-4115. Offers MA. *Program availability:* Part-time, evening/weekend. *Students:* 1 applicant. In 2019, 1 master's awarded. *Degree requirements:* For master's, thesis or alternative. *Entrance requirements:* For master's, official transcripts of all previous undergraduate study; 2 letters of reference (academic or professional); undergraduate courses in statistics, history and systems of psychology; 3 other courses in behavioral science; personal prospectus statement; current resume. Additional exam requirements/recommendations for international students: required—TOEFL (minimum score 550 paper-based). *Application deadline:* Applications are processed on a rolling basis. Application fee: $30. Electronic applications accepted. *Expenses: Tuition:* Part-time $730 per credit hour. Tuition and fees vary according to course load, degree level and program. *Financial support:* Fellowships, research assistantships, scholarships/grants, and unspecified assistantships available. Financial award application deadline: 3/1; financial award applicants required to submit FAFSA. *Unit head:* Dr. Kathleen Kelly, Dean, School of Health Sciences, 518-244-2030, Fax: 518-244-4571, E-mail: kellyk5@sage.edu. *Application contact:* Dr. Gayle Morse, Graduate Program Director, 518-292-1819, E-mail: morseg@sage.edu.

Sage Graduate School, School of Health Sciences, Department of Psychology, Program in Counseling and Community Psychology, Troy, NY 12180-4115. Offers MA. *Program availability:* Part-time, evening/weekend. *Faculty:* 4 full-time (all women), 2 part-time/adjunct (both women). *Students:* 39 full-time (36 women), 35 part-time (27 women); includes 16 minority (3 Black or African American, non-Hispanic/Latino; 2 Asian, non-Hispanic/Latino; 9 Hispanic/Latino; 2 Two or more races, non-Hispanic/Latino). Average age 27. 77 applicants, 65% accepted, 30 enrolled. In 2019, 11 master's awarded. *Degree requirements:* For master's, externship, internship, thesis or research seminar. *Entrance requirements:* For master's, Completed application; minimum GPA of 3.0 or higher; official transcripts of all previous undergraduate study; 2 letters of reference (academic or professional); undergraduate courses in statistics, history and systems of psychology; 3 other courses in behavioral science; personal prospectus statement; current resume. Additional exam requirements/recommendations for international students: required—TOEFL (minimum score 550 paper-based). *Application deadline:* Applications are processed on a rolling basis. Application fee: $30. Electronic applications accepted. *Expenses: Tuition:* Part-time $730 per credit hour. Tuition and fees vary according to course load, degree level and program. *Financial support:* Fellowships, research assistantships, scholarships/grants, and unspecified assistantships available. Financial award applicants required to submit FAFSA. *Unit head:* Dr. Kathleen Kelly, Dean, School of Health Sciences, 518-244-2030, Fax: 518-244-4571, E-mail: kellyk5@sage.edu. *Application contact:* Dr. Gayle Morse, Graduate Program Director, 518-292-1819, E-mail: morseg@sage.edu.
Website: http://www.sage.edu/academics/psychology/programs/counseling/

St. Bonaventure University, School of Graduate Studies, School of Education, Program in Counselor Education, St. Bonaventure, NY 14778-2284. Offers community mental health counseling (MS Ed); rehabilitation counseling (MS Ed); school counseling (MS Ed); school counselor (Adv C). *Accreditation:* ACA. *Program availability:* Part-time, 100% online. *Faculty:* 7 full-time (4 women), 10 part-time/adjunct (7 women). *Students:* 43 full-time (37 women), 213 part-time (175 women); includes 39 minority (2 Black or African American, non-Hispanic/Latino; 2 American Indian or Alaska Native, non-Hispanic/Latino; 7 Asian, non-Hispanic/Latino; 18 Hispanic/Latino; 1 Native Hawaiian or other Pacific Islander, non-Hispanic/Latino; 9 Two or more races, non-Hispanic/Latino). Average age 32. 167 applicants, 85% accepted, 64 enrolled. In 2019, 17 master's, 7 Adv Cs awarded. *Degree requirements:* For master's, comprehensive exam, thesis optional, internship, portfolio, two consecutive summer residencies; for Adv C, internship. *Entrance requirements:* For master's, statement of intent/writing sample; transcripts from all colleges previously attended; two references; interview; minimum undergraduate GPA of 3.0; for Adv C, interview, writing sample, minimum undergraduate GPA of 3.0, two letters of recommendation, master's degree, transcripts from all colleges previously attended. Additional exam requirements/recommendations for international students: required—TOEFL (minimum score 550 paper-based; 79 iBT). *Application deadline:* For fall admission, 3/15 priority date for domestic students, 2/1 priority date for international students; for spring admission, 10/15 priority date for domestic students, 7/1 priority date for international students. Applications are processed on a rolling basis. Electronic applications accepted. *Expenses: Tuition:* Full-time $770; part-time $770 per credit hour. *Required fees:* $35; $35 per credit hour. Tuition and fees vary according to course load. *Financial support:* Scholarships/grants, health care benefits, and unspecified assistantships available. Financial award application deadline: 4/15; financial award applicants required to submit FAFSA. *Unit head:* Dr. LaToya Pierce, Director, 716-375-2038, Fax: 716-375-2360, E-mail: lpierce@sbu.edu. *Application contact:* Matthew Retchless, Director of Graduate Admissions, 716-375-2021, Fax: 716-375-4015, E-mail: gradsch@sbu.edu.
Website: http://www.sbu.edu/academics/msed-in-school-counseling

Saint Martin's University, Office of Graduate Studies, Program in Counseling, Lacey, WA 98503. Offers MAC. *Program availability:* Part-time. *Students:* 73 full-time (54 women), 21 part-time (17 women); includes 26 minority (10 Black or African American, non-Hispanic/Latino; 3 American Indian or Alaska Native, non-Hispanic/Latino; 2 Asian, non-Hispanic/Latino; 7 Hispanic/Latino; 4 Two or more races, non-Hispanic/Latino), 3 international. Average age 36. In 2019, 33 master's awarded. *Degree requirements:* For master's, clinical experience, interview. *Entrance requirements:* For master's, clinical experience. Additional exam requirements/recommendations for international students: required—TOEFL (minimum score 550 paper-based; 79 iBT); recommended—IELTS (minimum score 6.5). *Application deadline:* For fall admission, 4/1 priority date for domestic and international students; for spring admission, 11/1 priority date for domestic and international students. Applications are processed on a rolling basis. Application fee: $50. Electronic applications accepted. *Expenses: Tuition:* Full-time $22,950; part-time $15,300 per year. Tuition and fees vary according to course level, course load, degree level, campus/location and program. *Financial support:* Career-related internships or fieldwork, Federal Work-Study, and institutionally sponsored loans available. Support available to part-time students. Financial award application deadline: 3/1; financial award applicants required to submit FAFSA. *Unit head:* Dr. Alexandra Onno, Chair, 360-438-4560, E-mail: aonno@stmartin.edu. *Application contact:* Timothy Greer, Graduate Admissions Counselor, 360-412-6128, E-mail: tgreer@stmartin.edu.
Website: https://www.stmartin.edu

San Francisco State University, Division of Graduate Studies, College of Science and Engineering, Department of Psychology, San Francisco, CA 94132-1722. Offers clinical psychology (MS); developmental psychology (MA); industrial/organizational psychology (MS); mind, brain, and behavior (MA); school psychology (MS, Credential); social, personality, and affective science psychology (MA). *Expenses: Tuition, area resident:* Full-time $7176; part-time $4164 per year. Tuition, state resident: full-time $7176; part-time $4164 per year. Tuition, nonresident: full-time $16,680; part-time $396 per unit. *International tuition:* $16,680 full-time. *Required fees:* $1524; $1524 per unit. $762 per semester. Tuition and fees vary according to degree level and program. *Financial support:* Teaching assistantships available. Financial award application deadline: 3/1. *Unit head:* Dr. Chris Wright, Chair, 415-338-7555, Fax: 415-338-2398, E-mail: cwright@sfsu.edu. *Application contact:* Dr. Ryan Howell, Department Graduate Program Coordinator, 415-405-2140, Fax: 415-338-2398, E-mail: rhowell@sfsu.edu.
Website: http://psychology.sfsu.edu/graduate/application.html

Southwestern College, Program in Transformational Ecopsychology, Santa Fe, NM 87502-4788. Offers Certificate. *Entrance requirements:* For degree, 3 letters of reference, interview.

Stony Brook University, State University of New York, Graduate School, College of Arts and Sciences, Department of Psychology, Program in Social and Health Psychology, Stony Brook, NY 11794. Offers PhD. *Students:* 15 full-time (14 women); includes 5 minority (2 Black or African American, non-Hispanic/Latino; 1 Asian, non-Hispanic/Latino; 2 Hispanic/Latino). Average age 27. 59 applicants, 14% accepted, 4 enrolled. In 2019, 6 doctorates awarded. *Entrance requirements:* For doctorate, GRE General Test, GRE Subject Test. Additional exam requirements/recommendations for international students: required—TOEFL (minimum score 90 iBT). *Application deadline:* For fall admission, 1/15 for domestic students; for spring admission, 10/1 for domestic students. Application fee: $100. Electronic applications accepted. *Expenses:* Contact institution. *Financial support:* In 2019–20, 1 research assistantship, 11 teaching assistantships were awarded; fellowships also available. *Unit head:* Dr. Sheri Levy, Chair, 631-632-4355, E-mail: sheri.levy@stonybrook.edu. *Application contact:* Marilynn Wollmuth, Coordinator, 631-632-7855, Fax: 631-632-7876, E-mail: marilyn.wollmuth@stonybrook.edu.
Website: http://www.stonybrook.edu/commcms/psychology/social_health/overview.html

Syracuse University, College of Arts and Sciences, Department of Psychology, Syracuse, NY 13244. Offers clinical psychology (PhD); cognition, brain, and behavior (PhD); school psychology (PhD); social psychology (PhD). *Accreditation:* APA. Terminal master's awarded for partial completion of doctoral program. *Degree requirements:* For doctorate, comprehensive exam, thesis/dissertation. *Entrance requirements:* For doctorate, GRE General Test, GRE Subject Test, resume, personal statement, three letters of recommendation. Additional exam requirements/recommendations for international students: required—TOEFL (minimum score 100 iBT). Electronic applications accepted.

Teachers College, Columbia University, Department of Organization and Leadership, New York, NY 10027-6696. Offers adult education guided intensive study (Ed D); adult learning and leadership (Ed M, MA, Ed D); educational leadership (Ed D); higher and postsecondary education (MA, Ed D); leadership, policy and politics (Ed D); nurse executive (MA, Ed D), including administration studies (MA), professorial studies (MA); private school leadership (Ed M, MA); public school building leadership (Ed M, MA); social and organizational psychology (MA); urban education leaders (Ed D); MA/MBA. *Faculty:* 24 full-time (12 women). *Students:* 272 full-time (178 women), 321 part-time (222 women); includes 239 minority (78 Black or African American, non-Hispanic/Latino; 70 Asian, non-Hispanic/Latino; 71 Hispanic/Latino; 1 Native Hawaiian or other Pacific Islander, non-Hispanic/Latino; 19 Two or more races, non-Hispanic/Latino), 73 international. 761 applicants, 65% accepted, 330 enrolled. *Unit head:* Prof. Bill Baldwin, Chair, 212-678-3043, E-mail: wjb12@tc.columbia.edu. *Application contact:* Kelly Sutton-Skinner, Director of Admission and New Student Enrollment, 212-678-3710, E-mail: kms2237@tc.columbia.edu.

Temple University, College of Education and Human Development, Department of Psychological Studies in Education, Philadelphia, PA 19122-6096. Offers applied behavior analysis (MS Ed); counseling psychology (Ed M), including agency counseling, school counseling; educational psychology (Ed M); school psychology (PhD, Ed S). *Accreditation:* APA (one or more programs are accredited). *Program availability:* Part-time, evening/weekend. *Faculty:* 19 full-time (10 women), 19 part-time/adjunct (9 women). *Students:* 165 full-time (122 women), 49 part-time (37 women); includes 74 minority (39 Black or African American, non-Hispanic/Latino; 13 Asian, non-Hispanic/Latino; 17 Hispanic/Latino; 5 Two or more races, non-Hispanic/Latino), 11 international. 374 applicants, 49% accepted, 100 enrolled. In 2019, 73 master's, 5 doctorates, 16 other advanced degrees awarded. *Degree requirements:* For master's, comprehensive exam (for some programs); for doctorate, thesis/dissertation. *Entrance requirements:* For master's, statement of goals, 2 recommendation letters; for doctorate, GRE, statement of goals, academic writing sample, 2 recommendation letters. Additional exam requirements/recommendations for international students: required—TOEFL (minimum score 79 iBT), IELTS, PTE, one of three is required. Application fee: $60. Electronic applications accepted. *Financial support:* Fellowships, research assistantships, teaching assistantships, career-related internships or fieldwork, Federal Work-Study, health care benefits, and unspecified assistantships available. Financial award applicants required to submit FAFSA. *Unit head:* Renee Tobin, Prof. of Counseling Psychology and Dept. Chairperson, 215-204-7884, E-mail: renee.tobin@temple.edu. *Application contact:* Remy Van Wyk, Academic Coordinator, 215-204-1474, E-mail: remy.van.wyk@temple.edu.
Website: http://education.temple.edu/pse

Texas Christian University, College of Science and Engineering, Department of Psychology, Fort Worth, TX 76129-0002. Offers developmental trauma (MS); experimental psychology (PhD), including cognition/developmental, learning, neuroscience, social. *Faculty:* 14 full-time (7 women), 1 part-time/adjunct (0 women). *Students:* 31 full-time (26 women); includes 2 minority (both Asian, non-Hispanic/Latino), 2 international. Average age 25. 52 applicants, 35% accepted, 13 enrolled. In 2019, 10 master's, 4 doctorates awarded. Terminal master's awarded for partial completion of doctoral program. *Entrance requirements:* For doctorate, GRE General Test. Additional exam requirements/recommendations for international students: required—TOEFL (minimum score 550 paper-based; 80 iBT). *Application deadline:* For fall admission, 1/1 for domestic and international students. Application fee: $60 ($0 for international students). Electronic applications accepted. Full-time tuition and fees vary according to program. *Financial support:* In 2019–20, 23 students received support,

including 23 teaching assistantships with full tuition reimbursements available (averaging $19,750 per year); scholarships/grants also available. Financial award application deadline: 1/1; financial award applicants required to submit FAFSA. *Unit head:* Dr. Anna I. Petursdottir, Chair, 817-257-7410, Fax: 817-257-7681, E-mail: a.petursdottir@tcu.edu. *Application contact:* Cindy Hayes, Administrative Assistant, 817-257-7410, Fax: 817-257-7681, E-mail: c.hayes@tcu.edu.
Website: https://psychology.tcu.edu/

Thomas Jefferson University, Jefferson College of Health Professions, Program in Community and Trauma Counseling, Philadelphia, PA 19107. Offers MS.

Thomas University, Department of Human Services, Thomasville, GA 31792-7499. Offers community counseling (MSCC); rehabilitation counseling (MRC). *Accreditation:* CORE. *Program availability:* Part-time. *Entrance requirements:* For master's, resume, 3 academic/professional references. Additional exam requirements/recommendations for international students: required—TOEFL (minimum score 600 paper-based). Electronic applications accepted.

Université du Québec à Rimouski, Graduate Programs, Program in Psychosocial Studies, Rimouski, QC G5L 3A1, Canada. Offers MA.

University at Albany, State University of New York, College of Arts and Sciences, Department of Psychology, Albany, NY 12222-0001. Offers behavioral neuroscience (PhD); clinical psychology (PhD); cognitive psychology (PhD); industrial/organizational psychology (MA, PhD); social-personality psychology (PhD). *Accreditation:* APA (one or more programs are accredited). *Program availability:* Blended/hybrid learning. *Faculty:* 31 full-time (14 women), 6 part-time/adjunct (4 women). *Students:* 68 full-time (44 women), 53 part-time (35 women); includes 30 minority (3 Black or African American, non-Hispanic/Latino; 10 Asian, non-Hispanic/Latino; 11 Hispanic/Latino; 6 Two or more races, non-Hispanic/Latino), 9 international. 253 applicants, 21% accepted, 28 enrolled. In 2019, 22 master's, 11 doctorates awarded. *Degree requirements:* For doctorate, thesis/dissertation. *Entrance requirements:* For master's, transcripts of all schools attended, statement of background and goals, departmental questionnaire, resume, names and contact information for 3 recommenders; for doctorate, GRE General Test, GRE Subject Test, transcripts of all schools attended, statement of background and goals, departmental questionnaire, resume, names and contact information for 3 recommenders. Additional exam requirements/recommendations for international students: required—TOEFL (minimum score 550 paper-based). *Application deadline:* For fall admission, 1/15 for domestic and international students; for spring admission, 11/15 for domestic students. Application fee: $75. Electronic applications accepted. *Expenses: Tuition, area resident:* Full-time $11,530; part-time $480 per credit hour. Tuition, nonresident: full-time $23,530; part-time $980 per credit hour. *International tuition:* $23,530 full-time. *Required fees:* $2185; $96 per credit hour. Part-time tuition and fees vary according to course load and program. *Financial support:* Fellowships, research assistantships, teaching assistantships, and career-related internships or fieldwork available. Financial award application deadline: 2/1. *Unit head:* Christine K. Wagner, Chair, 518-442-4820, Fax: 518-442-4867, E-mail: cwagner@albany.edu. *Application contact:* Michael DeRensis, Director, Graduate Admissions, 518-442-3980, Fax: 518-442-3922, E-mail: graduate@albany.edu.
Website: https://www.albany.edu/psychology/

University of Alaska Anchorage, College of Arts and Sciences, Department of Psychology, Anchorage, AK 99508. Offers clinical psychology (MS); clinical-community psychology with rural and indigenous emphasis (PhD). *Accreditation:* APA. *Program availability:* Part-time. *Degree requirements:* For master's, thesis. *Entrance requirements:* For master's, GRE General Test, GRE Subject Test, interview, references; for doctorate, interview, bachelor's or master's degree in psychology. Additional exam requirements/recommendations for international students: required—TOEFL (minimum score 550 paper-based).

University of Alaska Fairbanks, School of Education, Program in Counseling, Fairbanks, AK 99775-7520. Offers community counseling (M Ed). *Program availability:* Part-time, evening/weekend, 100% online, blended/hybrid learning. Terminal master's awarded for partial completion of doctoral program. *Degree requirements:* For master's, comprehensive exam, oral defense of project or thesis. *Entrance requirements:* For master's, bachelor's degree from accredited institution with minimum cumulative undergraduate and major GPA of 3.0, 3 letters of recommendation, statement of academic goals, resume, interview; for Graduate Certificate, master's degree from accredited institution with minimum GPA of 3.0. Additional exam requirements/recommendations for international students: required—TOEFL (minimum score 550 paper-based; 79 iBT), IELTS (minimum score 6.5). Electronic applications accepted.

University of Bridgeport, School of Arts and Sciences, Department of Counseling, Bridgeport, CT 06604. Offers clinical mental health counseling (MS); college student personnel (MS); community counseling (MS); human resource development (MS); human service (MS). *Program availability:* Part-time, evening/weekend. *Degree requirements:* For master's, thesis, project. *Entrance requirements:* Additional exam requirements/recommendations for international students: recommended—TOEFL (minimum score 550 paper-based; 80 iBT), IELTS (minimum score 6.5). Electronic applications accepted. *Expenses:* Contact institution.

The University of British Columbia, Faculty of Arts, Department of Psychology, Vancouver, BC V6T 1Z4, Canada. Offers behavioral neuroscience (MA, PhD); clinical psychology (MA, PhD); cognitive science (MA, PhD); developmental psychology (MA, PhD); health psychology (MA, PhD); quantitative methods (MA, PhD); social/personality psychology (MA, PhD). *Accreditation:* APA (one or more programs are accredited). Terminal master's awarded for partial completion of doctoral program. *Degree requirements:* For master's, thesis; for doctorate, comprehensive exam, thesis/dissertation. *Entrance requirements:* For master's and doctorate, GRE General Test. Additional exam requirements/recommendations for international students: required—TOEFL. Electronic applications accepted. *Expenses:* Contact institution.

University of Central Arkansas, Graduate School, College of Health and Behavioral Sciences, Department of Counseling and Psychology, Program in Community Counseling, Conway, AR 72035-0001. Offers MS. *Degree requirements:* For master's, comprehensive exam, thesis optional. *Entrance requirements:* For master's, GRE General Test, minimum GPA of 2.7. Additional exam requirements/recommendations for international students: required—TOEFL (minimum score 550 paper-based). Electronic applications accepted.

University of Connecticut, Graduate School, College of Liberal Arts and Sciences, Department of Psychological Sciences, Storrs, CT 06269. Offers behavioral neuroscience (PhD); biopsychology (PhD); clinical psychology (MA, PhD); cognition and instruction (PhD); developmental psychology (MA, PhD); ecological psychology (PhD); experimental psychology (PhD); general psychology (MA, PhD); industrial/organizational psychology (PhD); language and cognition (PhD); neuroscience (PhD); social psychology (MA, PhD). *Accreditation:* APA. Terminal master's awarded for partial completion of doctoral program. *Degree requirements:* For master's, comprehensive exam; for doctorate, thesis/dissertation. *Entrance requirements:* For master's and doctorate, GRE General Test, GRE Subject Test. Additional exam requirements/recommendations for international students: required—TOEFL (minimum score 550 paper-based). Electronic applications accepted.

University of Delaware, College of Arts and Sciences, Department of Psychology, Newark, DE 19716. Offers behavioral neuroscience (PhD); clinical psychology (PhD); cognitive psychology (PhD); social psychology (PhD). *Accreditation:* APA. *Degree requirements:* For doctorate, thesis/dissertation. *Entrance requirements:* For doctorate, GRE General Test. Additional exam requirements/recommendations for international students: required—TOEFL (minimum score 600 paper-based). Electronic applications accepted.

University of Denver, Division of Arts, Humanities and Social Sciences, Department of Psychology, Denver, CO 80208. Offers affective/cognitive/social psychology (PhD); clinical child psychology (PhD); developmental psychology (PhD). *Accreditation:* APA. *Faculty:* 29 full-time (20 women). *Students:* 30 full-time (24 women); includes 8 minority (2 Asian, non-Hispanic/Latino; 5 Hispanic/Latino; 1 Two or more races, non-Hispanic/Latino), 2 international. Average age 27. 457 applicants, 4% accepted, 10 enrolled. In 2019, 5 doctorates awarded. Terminal master's awarded for partial completion of doctoral program. *Degree requirements:* For doctorate, comprehensive exam (for some programs), thesis/dissertation. *Entrance requirements:* For doctorate, GRE General Test, master's degree, transcripts, biographical statement, three letters of recommendation, resume, essay on diversity (for clinical child program only). Additional exam requirements/recommendations for international students: required—TOEFL (minimum score 550 paper-based; 80 iBT). *Application deadline:* For fall admission, 12/21 for domestic and international students. Application fee: $65. Electronic applications accepted. *Expenses:* Contact institution. *Financial support:* In 2019–20, 30 students received support, including 13 research assistantships with tuition reimbursements available (averaging $15,392 per year), 15 teaching assistantships with tuition reimbursements available (averaging $13,800 per year); Federal Work-Study, institutionally sponsored loans, scholarships/grants, and unspecified assistantships also available. Support available to part-time students. Financial award application deadline: 2/15; financial award applicants required to submit FAFSA. *Unit head:* Dr. Sarah Watamura, Associate Professor and Chair, 303-871-4130, E-mail: sarah.watamura@du.edu. *Application contact:* Paula Plank-Houghtaling, Graduate Program Administrator, 303-871-3803, E-mail: phoughta@du.edu.
Website: http://www.du.edu/ahss/psychology

University of Guelph, Office of Graduate and Postdoctoral Studies, College of Social and Applied Human Sciences, Department of Psychology, Guelph, ON N1G 2W1, Canada. Offers applied social psychology (MA, PhD); clinical psychology: applied development emphasis (PhD); clinical psychology: applied developmental emphasis (MA); industrial/organizational psychology (MA, PhD); neuroscience and applied cognitive science (MA, PhD). *Degree requirements:* For master's, thesis; for doctorate, comprehensive exam, thesis/dissertation. *Entrance requirements:* For master's, GRE General Test, GRE Subject Test, minimum B+ average during previous 2 years of course work; for doctorate, GRE General Test, GRE Subject Test, minimum A- average. Additional exam requirements/recommendations for international students: required—TOEFL (minimum score 89 iBT). Electronic applications accepted.

University of Hawaii at Manoa, Office of Graduate Education, College of Social Sciences, Department of Psychology, Honolulu, HI 96822. Offers clinical psychology (PhD); community and cultural psychology (PhD); community and culture (MA); psychology (MA, PhD, Graduate Certificate). *Accreditation:* APA (one or more programs are accredited). *Program availability:* Part-time. Terminal master's awarded for partial completion of doctoral program. *Degree requirements:* For master's, comprehensive exam, thesis; for doctorate, comprehensive exam, thesis/dissertation. *Entrance requirements:* For master's and doctorate, GRE General Test, GRE Subject Test. Additional exam requirements/recommendations for international students: required—TOEFL (minimum score 600 paper-based; 100 iBT), IELTS (minimum score 7).

University of Houston, College of Liberal Arts and Social Sciences, Department of Psychology, Houston, TX 77204. Offers clinical psychology (PhD); developmental psychology (PhD); industrial/organizational psychology (PhD); psychology (MA); social psychology (PhD). *Accreditation:* APA (one or more programs are accredited). *Degree requirements:* For master's, comprehensive exam, thesis; for doctorate, comprehensive exam, thesis/dissertation. *Entrance requirements:* For master's, GRE General Test, career statement, 3 letters of recommendation; for doctorate, GRE General Test, 3 letters of recommendation. Additional exam requirements/recommendations for international students: required—TOEFL (minimum score 550 paper-based; 79 iBT). Electronic applications accepted.

The University of Kansas, Graduate Studies, College of Liberal Arts and Sciences, Department of Psychology, Lawrence, KS 66045. Offers clinical psychology (MA, PhD); cognitive and brain sciences (MA, PhD); developmental psychology (MA, PhD); quantitative psychology (PhD); social psychology (MA, PhD). *Accreditation:* APA (one or more programs are accredited). *Program availability:* Part-time. *Students:* 72 full-time (51 women), 1 (woman) part-time; includes 16 minority (6 Black or African American, non-Hispanic/Latino; 3 Asian, non-Hispanic/Latino; 1 Hispanic/Latino; 6 Two or more races, non-Hispanic/Latino), 9 international. Average age 27. 343 applicants, 9% accepted, 17 enrolled. In 2019, 15 master's, 14 doctorates awarded. Terminal master's awarded for partial completion of doctoral program. *Entrance requirements:* For doctorate, GRE General Test, three letters of recommendation, resume/curriculum vitae, statement of purpose/personal statement, writing sample. Additional exam requirements/recommendations for international students: required—TOEFL, IELTS. *Application deadline:* For fall admission, 12/1 for domestic and international students. Application fee: $65 ($85 for international students). Electronic applications accepted. *Expenses:* Tuition, state resident: full-time $9989. Tuition, nonresident: full-time $23,950. *International tuition:* $23,950 full-time. *Required fees:* $984; $81.99 per credit hour. Tuition and fees vary according to course load, campus/location and program. *Financial support:* Fellowships, research assistantships, teaching assistantships, career-related internships or fieldwork, Federal Work-Study, scholarships/grants, health care benefits, and unspecified assistantships available. Financial award application deadline: 12/1; financial award applicants required to submit FAFSA. *Unit head:* Michael Vitevitch, Chair, 785-864-9312, E-mail: mvitevit@ku.edu. *Application contact:* Kirsten Hermreck, Graduate Admissions Contact, 785-864-4195, E-mail: psycgrad@ku.edu.
Website: http://www.psych.ku.edu/

University of Maryland, Baltimore County, The Graduate School, College of Arts, Humanities and Social Sciences, Department of Psychology, Program in Human Services Psychology, Baltimore, MD 21250. Offers applied behavioral analysis (MA); human services psychology (PhD), including behavioral medicine, clinical psychology, community psychology. *Faculty:* 17 full-time (9 women), 11 part-time/adjunct (4 women). *Students:* 58 full-time (47 women), 17 part-time (12 women); includes 19 minority (8 Black or African American, non-Hispanic/Latino; 5 Asian, non-Hispanic/Latino; 5 Hispanic/Latino; 1 Two or more races, non-Hispanic/Latino), 3 international. Average age 27. 212 applicants, 18% accepted, 17 enrolled. In 2019, 15 master's, 9 doctorates awarded. *Degree requirements:* For master's, thesis; for doctorate, comprehensive exam, thesis/dissertation. *Entrance requirements:* For master's, GRE General Test, minimum GPA of 3.0; for doctorate, GRE General Test, GRE Subject Test, minimum GPA of 3.0. Additional exam requirements/recommendations for international students: required—TOEFL. *Application deadline:* For fall admission, 12/1 for domestic and international students. Application fee: $50. Electronic applications accepted. *Expenses:*

$14,382 per year. *Financial support:* In 2019–20, 34 students received support, including 4 fellowships with full tuition reimbursements available (averaging $26,000 per year), 20 research assistantships with full tuition reimbursements available (averaging $20,400 per year), 10 teaching assistantships with full tuition reimbursements available (averaging $17,250 per year); career-related internships or fieldwork, Federal Work-Study, scholarships/grants, health care benefits, tuition waivers, and unspecified assistantships also available. Financial award application deadline: 3/1; financial award applicants required to submit FAFSA. *Unit head:* Dr. Steve Pitts, Program Director, 410-455-2362, Fax: 410-455-1055, E-mail: spitts@umbc.edu. *Application contact:* Beverly McDougall, Program Management Specialist, 410-455-2613, Fax: 410-455-1055, E-mail: psycdept@umbc.edu.
Website: http://psychology.umbc.edu/

University of Maryland, College Park, Academic Affairs, College of Behavioral and Social Sciences, Department of Psychology, College Park, MD 20742. Offers clinical psychology (PhD); developmental psychology (PhD); experimental psychology (PhD); industrial psychology (MA, MS, PhD); social psychology (PhD). *Accreditation:* APA (one or more programs are accredited). *Degree requirements:* For master's, thesis; for doctorate, variable foreign language requirement, comprehensive exam, thesis/dissertation. *Entrance requirements:* For master's and doctorate, GRE General Test, GRE Subject Test, minimum GPA of 3.5, research and/or work experience, 3 letters of recommendation. Electronic applications accepted.

University of Massachusetts Amherst, Graduate School, College of Natural Sciences, Department of Psychological and Brain Sciences, Amherst, MA 01003. Offers clinical psychology (MS, PhD); cognitive psychology (MS, PhD); developmental science (MS, PhD); psychology of peace and violence (MS, PhD); social psychology (MS, PhD). *Accreditation:* APA (one or more programs are accredited). Terminal master's awarded for partial completion of doctoral program. *Degree requirements:* For master's, thesis; for doctorate, comprehensive exam, thesis/dissertation. *Entrance requirements:* For master's and doctorate, GRE General Test, 3 letters of recommendation. Additional exam requirements/recommendations for international students: required—TOEFL (minimum score 550 paper-based; 80 iBT), IELTS (minimum score 6.5). Electronic applications accepted.

University of Massachusetts Lowell, College of Fine Arts, Humanities and Social Sciences, Department of Psychology, Lowell, MA 01854. Offers community social psychology (MA). *Program availability:* Part-time. *Degree requirements:* For master's, thesis optional. *Entrance requirements:* For master's, GRE General Test or MAT. Electronic applications accepted.

University of Michigan, Rackham Graduate School, College of Literature, Science, and the Arts, Department of Psychology, Ann Arbor, MI 48109. Offers biopsychology (PhD); clinical science (PhD); cognition and cognitive neuroscience (PhD); developmental psychology (PhD); personality and social contexts (PhD); social psychology (PhD). *Accreditation:* APA. Terminal master's awarded for partial completion of doctoral program. *Degree requirements:* For doctorate, comprehensive exam, thesis/dissertation, oral defense of dissertation, preliminary exam. *Entrance requirements:* For doctorate, GRE (Biopsychology, Cognition and Cognitive Neuroscience, Developmental, Social, and Clinical); GRE Subject Test also strongly recommended (Clinical); GRE not required (Personality and Social Contexts). Additional exam requirements/recommendations for international students: required—TOEFL. Electronic applications accepted.

University of Minnesota, Twin Cities Campus, Graduate School, College of Liberal Arts, Department of Psychology, Program in Social Psychology, Minneapolis, MN 55455-0213. Offers PhD. *Degree requirements:* For doctorate, comprehensive exam, thesis/dissertation. *Entrance requirements:* For doctorate, GRE General Test, GRE Subject Test (recommended), 12 credits of upper-level psychology courses, including a course in statistics or psychological measurement. Additional exam requirements/recommendations for international students: required—TOEFL (minimum score 550 paper-based; 79 iBT).

University of Missouri–Kansas City, College of Arts and Sciences, Department of Psychology, Kansas City, MO 64110-2499. Offers community psychology (PhD). *Accreditation:* APA. Terminal master's awarded for partial completion of doctoral program. *Degree requirements:* For master's, thesis; for doctorate, comprehensive exam, thesis/dissertation, residency. *Entrance requirements:* For master's, GRE, minimum GPA of 3.5, letter of recommendation; for doctorate, GRE, minimum GPA of 3.25. Additional exam requirements/recommendations for international students: required—TOEFL (minimum score 550 paper-based; 80 iBT). Electronic applications accepted.

University of Nebraska–Lincoln, Graduate College, College of Arts and Sciences, Department of Psychology, Lincoln, NE 68588. Offers biopsychology (PhD); clinical psychology (PhD); cognitive psychology (PhD); developmental psychology (PhD); psychology (MA); social/personality psychology (PhD); JD/MA; JD/PhD. *Accreditation:* APA (one or more programs are accredited). *Degree requirements:* For master's, thesis optional; for doctorate, comprehensive exam, thesis/dissertation. *Entrance requirements:* For master's and doctorate, GRE General Test. Additional exam requirements/recommendations for international students: required—TOEFL (minimum score 550 paper-based). Electronic applications accepted.

University of Nevada, Reno, Graduate School, Interdisciplinary Program in Social Psychology, Reno, NV 89557. Offers PhD. *Degree requirements:* For doctorate, one foreign language, thesis/dissertation. *Entrance requirements:* For doctorate, GRE General Test, GRE Subject Test (psychology or sociology), minimum GPA of 3.0. Additional exam requirements/recommendations for international students: required—TOEFL (minimum score 500 paper-based; 61 iBT), IELTS (minimum score 6). Electronic applications accepted.

University of New Haven, Graduate School, College of Arts and Sciences, Program in Community Psychology, West Haven, CT 06516. Offers applications of psychology (Graduate Certificate); community clinical services (MA); community psychology (MA); forensic psychology (MA); program development (MA). *Program availability:* Part-time, evening/weekend. *Students:* 24 full-time (20 women), 9 part-time (8 women); includes 11 minority (7 Black or African American, non-Hispanic/Latino; 2 Asian, non-Hispanic/Latino; 2 Hispanic/Latino), 6 international. Average age 28. 28 applicants, 79% accepted, 10 enrolled. In 2019, 10 master's awarded. *Degree requirements:* For master's, thesis or alternative, fieldwork. *Entrance requirements:* Additional exam requirements/recommendations for international students: required—TOEFL (minimum score 80 iBT), IELTS, PTE. *Application deadline:* Applications are processed on a rolling basis. Application fee: $50. Electronic applications accepted. Application fee is waived when completed online. *Financial support:* Research assistantships with partial tuition reimbursements, teaching assistantships with partial tuition reimbursements, Federal Work-Study, scholarships/grants, and unspecified assistantships available. Support available to part-time students. Financial award application deadline: 5/1; financial award applicants required to submit FAFSA. *Unit head:* Dr. Melissa Whitson, Associate Professor, 203-479-4589, E-mail: mwhitson@newhaven.edu. *Application contact:* Selina O'Toole, Senior Associate Director of Graduate Admissions, 203-932-7337, E-mail: SOToole@newhaven.edu.
Website: http://www.newhaven.edu/4725/

The University of North Carolina at Chapel Hill, Graduate School, College of Arts and Sciences, Department of Psychology, Chapel Hill, NC 27599-3270. Offers behavioral neuroscience psychology (PhD); clinical psychology (PhD); cognitive psychology (PhD); developmental psychology (PhD); quantitative psychology (PhD); social psychology (PhD). *Accreditation:* APA. *Degree requirements:* For doctorate, comprehensive exam, thesis/dissertation. *Entrance requirements:* For doctorate, GRE General Test, minimum GPA of 3.0. Additional exam requirements/recommendations for international students: required—TOEFL (minimum score 550 paper-based; 79 iBT), IELTS (minimum score 7). Electronic applications accepted.

The University of North Carolina at Greensboro, Graduate School, College of Arts and Sciences, Department of Psychology, Greensboro, NC 27412-5001. Offers clinical psychology (MA, PhD); cognitive psychology (MA, PhD); developmental psychology (MA, PhD); social psychology (MA, PhD). *Accreditation:* APA (one or more programs are accredited). Terminal master's awarded for partial completion of doctoral program. *Degree requirements:* For master's, comprehensive exam, thesis; for doctorate, one foreign language, thesis/dissertation, preliminary exam. *Entrance requirements:* For master's and doctorate, GRE General Test. Additional exam requirements/recommendations for international students: required—TOEFL. Electronic applications accepted.

University of Oregon, Graduate School, College of Arts and Sciences, Department of Psychology, Eugene, OR 97403. Offers clinical psychology (PhD); cognitive psychology (MA, MS, PhD); developmental psychology (MA, MS, PhD); physiological psychology (MA, MS, PhD); psychology (MA, MS, PhD); social/personality psychology (MA, MS, PhD). *Accreditation:* APA (one or more programs are accredited). Terminal master's awarded for partial completion of doctoral program. *Degree requirements:* For doctorate, thesis/dissertation. *Entrance requirements:* For master's, GRE General Test, minimum GPA of 3.0; for doctorate, GRE General Test. Additional exam requirements/recommendations for international students: required—TOEFL.

University of Phoenix - Phoenix Campus, College of Social Sciences, Tempe, AZ 85282-2371. Offers counseling (MS), including clinical mental health counseling, community counseling, counseling, marriage, family and child therapy; psychology (MS). *Program availability:* Evening/weekend, online learning. *Entrance requirements:* Additional exam requirements/recommendations for international students: required—TOEFL, TOEIC (Test of English as an International Communication), Berlitz Online English Proficiency Exam, PTE, or IELTS. Electronic applications accepted. *Expenses:* Contact institution.

University of Pittsburgh, Kenneth P. Dietrich School of Arts and Sciences, Department of Psychology, Pittsburgh, PA 15260. Offers biological and health psychology (PhD); clinical psychology (PhD); cognitive psychology (PhD); developmental psychology (PhD); social psychology (PhD). *Accreditation:* APA. *Faculty:* 33 full-time (18 women), 10 part-time/adjunct (3 women). *Students:* 90 full-time (73 women); includes 25 minority (4 Black or African American, non-Hispanic/Latino; 2 American Indian or Alaska Native, non-Hispanic/Latino; 10 Asian, non-Hispanic/Latino; 2 Hispanic/Latino; 7 Two or more races, non-Hispanic/Latino). Average age 25. 580 applicants, 6% accepted, 18 enrolled. In 2019, 16 doctorates awarded. Terminal master's awarded for partial completion of doctoral program. *Degree requirements:* For doctorate, comprehensive exam, thesis/dissertation. *Entrance requirements:* For doctorate, GRE General Test, minimum GPA of 3.0. Additional exam requirements/recommendations for international students: required—TOEFL (minimum score 550 paper-based; 90 iBT). *Application deadline:* For fall admission, 12/1 for domestic and international students. Application fee: $75. Electronic applications accepted. *Financial support:* In 2019–20, 90 students received support, including 38 fellowships with full tuition reimbursements available (averaging $30,378 per year), 19 research assistantships with full tuition reimbursements available (averaging $29,220 per year), 33 teaching assistantships with full tuition reimbursements available (averaging $29,220 per year); career-related internships or fieldwork, scholarships/grants, health care benefits, and unspecified assistantships also available. Financial award application deadline: 12/1. *Unit head:* Dr. Julie Fiez, Chair, 412-624-7078, Fax: 412-422-9149, E-mail: fiez@pitt.edu. *Application contact:* Francesca Sirianni, Graduate Administrator, 412-624-4502, Fax: 412-624-4428, E-mail: psygrad@pitt.edu.
Website: http://www.psychology.pitt.edu/

University of Puerto Rico at Rio Piedras, College of Social Sciences, Department of Psychology, San Juan, PR 00931-3300. Offers clinical psychology (MA); industrial organizational psychology (MA); investigative academic psychology (MA); psychology (PhD); social-community psychology (MA). *Program availability:* Part-time. *Degree requirements:* For master's, comprehensive exam, thesis; for doctorate, comprehensive exam, thesis/dissertation, internship. *Entrance requirements:* For master's, GRE or PAEG, interview, minimum GPA of 3.0; for doctorate, GRE or PAEG, interview, master's degree, minimum GPA of 3.0.

University of Rochester, Margaret Warner Graduate School of Education and Human Development, Master's Program in Counseling, Rochester, NY 14627. Offers school and community counseling (MS); school counseling (MS).

University of Rochester, School of Arts and Sciences, Psychology, Rochester, NY 14627. Offers clinical psychology (PhD); developmental psychology (PhD); social-personality psychology (PhD). *Accreditation:* APA. *Faculty:* 16 full-time (9 women). *Students:* 42 full-time (35 women); includes 10 minority (1 Black or African American, non-Hispanic/Latino; 5 Asian, non-Hispanic/Latino; 3 Hispanic/Latino; 1 Two or more races, non-Hispanic/Latino), 5 international. Average age 28. 240 applicants, 6% accepted, 9 enrolled. In 2019, 10 doctorates awarded. Terminal master's awarded for partial completion of doctoral program. *Degree requirements:* For doctorate, thesis/dissertation. *Entrance requirements:* For doctorate, GRE General Test (optional for Fall 2021 admission cycle), personal statement, official transcripts, three letters of recommendation, curriculum vitae or resume. Additional exam requirements/recommendations for international students: required—TOEFL. *Application deadline:* For fall admission, 12/1 for domestic and international students. Application fee: $20. Electronic applications accepted. *Financial support:* In 2019–20, 35 students received support, including 5 fellowships with full tuition reimbursements available, 8 research assistantships with full tuition reimbursements available (averaging $24,000 per year), 22 teaching assistantships with full tuition reimbursements available (averaging $24,000 per year); career-related internships or fieldwork, scholarships/grants, and tuition waivers (full) also available. Financial award application deadline: 4/15. *Unit head:* Loisa Bennetto, Chair, 585-275-8712, E-mail: loisa.bennetto@rochester.edu. *Application contact:* Loisa Bennetto, Chair, 585-275-8712, E-mail: loisa.bennetto@rochester.edu.
Website: http://www.sas.rochester.edu/psy/graduate/index.html

University of South Carolina, The Graduate School, College of Arts and Sciences, Department of Psychology, Program in Clinical/Community Psychology, Columbia, SC 29208. Offers clinical/community psychology (PhD); general psychology (MA). *Accreditation:* APA. *Degree requirements:* For master's, comprehensive exam, thesis; for doctorate, comprehensive exam, thesis/dissertation. *Entrance requirements:* For doctorate, GRE General Test, minimum GPA of 3.2. Additional exam requirements/

recommendations for international students: required—TOEFL. Electronic applications accepted.

University of Southern California, Graduate School, Dana and David Dornsife College of Letters, Arts and Sciences, Department of Psychology, Los Angeles, CA 90089. Offers brain and cognitive science (PhD); clinical science (PhD); developmental psychology (PhD); human behavior (MHB); quantitative methods (PhD); social psychology (PhD). *Accreditation:* APA. *Degree requirements:* For doctorate, comprehensive exam, thesis/dissertation, one-year internship (for clinical science students). *Entrance requirements:* For doctorate, GRE. Additional exam requirements/recommendations for international students: recommended—TOEFL (minimum score 600 paper-based; 100 iBT). Electronic applications accepted.

The University of Tennessee at Chattanooga, School of Education, Chattanooga, TN 37403. Offers counseling (M Ed), including community counseling, school counseling; education (M Ed, Post-Master's Certificate), including elementary education (M Ed), school leadership (Post-Master's Certificate); elementary education (M Ed); learning and leadership (Ed D), including educational leadership; school leadership (Post-Master's Certificate); school leadership: principal licensure (Ed S); secondary education (M Ed); special education (M Ed). *Accreditation:* ACA; NCATE. *Program availability:* Part-time. *Faculty:* 21 full-time (14 women), 16 part-time/adjunct (15 women). *Students:* 28 full-time (18 women), 63 part-time (44 women); includes 20 minority (10 Black or African American, non-Hispanic/Latino; 1 American Indian or Alaska Native, non-Hispanic/Latino; 1 Asian, non-Hispanic/Latino; 3 Hispanic/Latino; 5 Two or more races, non-Hispanic/Latino). Average age 32. 59 applicants, 78% accepted, 24 enrolled. In 2019, 42 master's, 7 other advanced degrees awarded. *Degree requirements:* For master's, comprehensive exam, thesis optional, culminating experience; for other advanced degree, practicum. *Entrance requirements:* For master's, GRE General Test, PPST 1 if student is not already licensed to teach; for other advanced degree, two letters of recommendation, graduate degree in education, teaching certificate with three years of experience. Additional exam requirements/recommendations for international students: required—TOEFL (minimum score 550 paper-based; 79 iBT), IELTS (minimum score 6). *Application deadline:* For fall admission, 6/15 for domestic students, 7/1 for international students; for spring admission, 11/1 for domestic and international students. Applications are processed on a rolling basis. Application fee: $35 ($40 for international students). Electronic applications accepted. *Financial support:* Research assistantships, teaching assistantships, career-related internships or fieldwork, institutionally sponsored loans, scholarships/grants, and unspecified assistantships available. Support available to part-time students. Financial award application deadline: 7/1; financial award applicants required to submit FAFSA. *Unit head:* Dr. Renee Murley, Director, 423-425-4684, Fax: 423-425-5380, E-mail: renee-murley@utc.edu. *Application contact:* Dr. Joanne Romagni, Dean of the Graduate School, 423-425-4478, Fax: 423-425-5223, E-mail: joanne-romagni@utc.edu. Website: https://www.utc.edu/school-education/

The University of Tennessee at Martin, Graduate Programs, College of Education, Health and Behavioral Sciences, Program in Counseling, Martin, TN 38238. Offers addictions counseling (MS Ed); clinical mental health counseling (MS Ed); school counseling (MS Ed); student affairs and college counseling (MS Ed). *Accreditation:* NCATE. *Program availability:* Part-time, online only, 100% online. *Students:* 26 full-time (24 women), 53 part-time (47 women); includes 9 minority (all Black or African American, non-Hispanic/Latino). Average age 32. 101 applicants, 38% accepted, 28 enrolled. In 2019, 16 master's awarded. *Degree requirements:* For master's, comprehensive exam. *Entrance requirements:* For master's, minimum GPA of 2.5, resume, letters of reference. Additional exam requirements/recommendations for international students: required—TOEFL (minimum score 525 paper-based; 71 iBT). *Application deadline:* For fall admission, 7/28 priority date for domestic and international students; for spring admission, 12/17 priority date for domestic and international students; for summer admission, 5/10 priority date for domestic and international students. Applications are processed on a rolling basis. Application fee: $30 ($130 for international students). Electronic applications accepted. *Expenses: Tuition, area resident:* Full-time $9096; part-time $505 per credit hour. Tuition, state resident: full-time $9096; part-time $505 per credit hour. Tuition, nonresident: full-time $15,136; part-time $841 per credit hour. *International tuition:* $23,040 full-time. *Required fees:* $1520; $85 per credit hour. Part-time tuition and fees vary according to course load. *Financial support:* In 2019–20, 12 students received support, including 1 teaching assistantship with full tuition reimbursement available (averaging $6,283 per year); research assistantships with full tuition reimbursements available, scholarships/grants, and tuition waivers (full and partial) also available. Financial award application deadline: 2/1; financial award applicants required to submit FAFSA. *Unit head:* Cynthia West, Dean, 731-881-7125, Fax: 731-881-7975, E-mail: cwest@utm.edu. *Application contact:* Jolene L. Cunningham, Student Services Specialist, 731-881-7012, Fax: 731-881-7499, E-mail: jcunningham@utm.edu.

University of Utah, Graduate School, College of Social and Behavioral Science, Department of Psychology, Salt Lake City, UT 84112. Offers clinical psychology (PhD); psychology (PhD), including cognitive neuroscience, developmental psychology, social psychology. *Accreditation:* APA. *Faculty:* 27 full-time (14 women), 1 (woman) part-time/adjunct. *Students:* 53 full-time (40 women); includes 8 minority (1 Black or African American, non-Hispanic/Latino; 4 Hispanic/Latino; 3 Two or more races, non-Hispanic/Latino), 6 international. Average age 28. 295 applicants, 8% accepted, 13 enrolled. In 2019, 11 doctorates awarded. *Degree requirements:* For doctorate, thesis/dissertation. *Entrance requirements:* For doctorate, GRE General Test. Additional exam requirements/recommendations for international students: required—TOEFL (minimum score 500 paper-based). *Application deadline:* For fall admission, 12/1 for domestic and international students. Application fee: $55 ($65 for international students). Electronic applications accepted. *Expenses:* Tuition, state resident: full-time $7085; part-time $272.51 per credit hour. Tuition, nonresident: full-time $24,937; part-time $959.12 per credit hour. *Required fees:* $880.52; $880.52 per semester. Tuition and fees vary according to degree level, program and student level. *Financial support:* In 2019–20, 5 fellowships (averaging $13,400 per year), 22 research assistantships (averaging $15,000 per year), 33 teaching assistantships (averaging $14,909 per year) were awarded; unspecified assistantships also available. Financial award applicants required to submit FAFSA. *Unit head:* Dr. Bert N. Uchino, Chair, 801-581-8925, Fax: 801-581-5841, E-mail: bert.uchino@psych.utah.edu. *Application contact:* Nancy Seegmiller, Program Manager, 801-581-8925, Fax: 801-581-5841, E-mail: nancy.seegmiller@psych.utah.edu. Website: http://www.psych.utah.edu/

University of Vermont, Graduate College, College of Arts and Sciences, Program in General/Experimental Psychology, Burlington, VT 05405-0134. Offers psychology (PhD), including biobehavioral psychology, developmental psychology, human behavioral pharmacology, social psychology. *Accreditation:* APA. *Degree requirements:* For doctorate, thesis/dissertation. *Entrance requirements:* For doctorate, GRE General Test. Additional exam requirements/recommendations for international students: required—TOEFL (minimum score 550 paper-based, 100 iBT) or IELTS (7). Electronic applications accepted.

University of Victoria, Faculty of Graduate Studies, Faculty of Education, Department of Educational Psychology and Leadership Studies, Victoria, BC V8W 2Y2, Canada. Offers aboriginal communities counseling (M Ed); counseling (M Ed, MA); educational psychology (M Ed, MA, PhD), including counseling psychology (M Ed, MA), leadership studies (PhD), learning and development (MA, PhD), measurement and evaluation, special education (M Ed, MA); leadership studies (M Ed, MA). *Program availability:* Part-time. *Degree requirements:* For master's, thesis (for some programs), comprehensive exam (M Ed); for doctorate, comprehensive exam, thesis/dissertation, candidacy exam. *Entrance requirements:* For master's, 2 years of work experience in a relevant field; for doctorate, GRE, 2 years of work experience in a relevant field, minimum B average. Additional exam requirements/recommendations for international students: required—TOEFL (minimum score 575 paper-based), IELTS (minimum score 7).

University of Victoria, Faculty of Graduate Studies, Faculty of Social Sciences, Department of Psychology, Victoria, BC V8W 2Y2, Canada. Offers clinical psychology (PhD); clinical psychology (neuropsychology) (M Sc); cognition and brain science (M Sc, PhD); experimental neuropsychology (M Sc, PhD); individualized study (M Sc, PhD); life span development psychology (PhD); life span developmental psychology (M Sc); social psychology (M Sc, PhD). *Degree requirements:* For master's, thesis; for doctorate, thesis/dissertation, candidacy exam. *Entrance requirements:* For master's and doctorate, GRE General Test. Additional exam requirements/recommendations for international students: required—TOEFL (minimum score 600 paper-based). Electronic applications accepted.

University of Washington, Graduate School, College of Arts and Sciences, Department of Psychology, Seattle, WA 98195. Offers animal behavior (PhD); applied child and adolescent psychology: prevention and treatment (MA); behavioral neuroscience (PhD); clinical psychology (PhD); cognition and perception (PhD); developmental psychology (PhD); quantitative psychology (PhD); social psychology and personality (PhD). *Accreditation:* APA (one or more programs are accredited). *Degree requirements:* For doctorate, thesis/dissertation. *Entrance requirements:* For doctorate, GRE General Test, minimum GPA of 3.0. Electronic applications accepted.

University of Windsor, Faculty of Graduate Studies, Faculty of Arts and Social Sciences, Department of Psychology, Windsor, ON N9B 3P4, Canada. Offers adult clinical (MA, PhD); applied social psychology (MA, PhD); child clinical (MA, PhD); clinical neuropsychology (MA, PhD). *Degree requirements:* For master's, thesis; for doctorate, comprehensive exam, thesis/dissertation. *Entrance requirements:* For master's, GRE General Test, GRE Subject Test in psychology, minimum B average; for doctorate, GRE General Test, GRE Subject Test in psychology, master's degree. Additional exam requirements/recommendations for international students: required—TOEFL (minimum score 600 paper-based). Electronic applications accepted.

University of Wisconsin–Madison, Graduate School, College of Letters and Science, Department of Psychology, Program in Social and Personality Psychology, Madison, WI 53706-1380. Offers PhD. *Degree requirements:* For doctorate, comprehensive exam, thesis/dissertation. *Entrance requirements:* For doctorate, GRE General Test, minimum undergraduate GPA of 3.0. Additional exam requirements/recommendations for international students: required—TOEFL. Electronic applications accepted.

University of Wisconsin–Superior, Graduate Division, Department of Counseling and Psychological Professions, Superior, WI 54880-4500. Offers community counseling (MSE); human relations (MSE); school counseling (MSE). *Program availability:* Part-time, evening/weekend. *Degree requirements:* For master's, position paper, practicum. *Entrance requirements:* For master's, GRE and/or MAT, minimum GPA of 2.75. Electronic applications accepted.

Université Laval, Faculty of Social Sciences, School of Psychology, Programs in Psychology, Québec, QC G1K 7P4, Canada. Offers clinical psychology (PhD); community psychology (PhD); psychology (PhD, Psy D). *Degree requirements:* For doctorate, comprehensive exam, thesis/dissertation. *Entrance requirements:* For doctorate, comprehension of written English, knowledge of French, interview. Electronic applications accepted.

Walden University, Graduate Programs, School of Psychology, Minneapolis, MN 55401. Offers clinical psychology (MS), including counseling, general program; forensic psychology (MS), including forensic psychology in the community, general program, mental health applications, program planning and evaluation in forensic settings, psychology and legal systems; industrial organizational (MS, PhD), including consulting psychology, forensic (MS), forensic psychology (PhD), general practice, leadership development and coaching (MS), organizational diversity and social change, research evaluation (PhD); online teaching in psychology (Post-Master's Certificate); organizational psychology and development (Postbaccalaureate Certificate); psychology (MS, PhD), including applied psychology (MS), clinical psychology (PhD), crisis management and response (MS), educational psychology, forensic psychology (PhD), general psychology (MS), general psychology research (PhD), general psychology teaching (PhD), health psychology, leadership development and coaching (MS), psychology of culture (MS), psychology, public administration, and social change (MS), social psychology, terrorism and security (MS); psychology respecialization (Post-Doctoral Certificate). *Program availability:* Part-time, evening/weekend, online only, 100% online. Terminal master's awarded for partial completion of doctoral program. *Degree requirements:* For master's, thesis optional; for doctorate, thesis/dissertation, residency. *Entrance requirements:* For master's, bachelor's degree or higher; minimum GPA of 2.5; official transcripts; goal statement (for some programs); access to computer and Internet; for doctorate, master's degree or higher; three years of related professional or academic experience (preferred); minimum GPA of 3.0; goal statement and current resume (for select programs); official transcripts; access to computer and Internet; for other advanced degree, relevant work experience; access to computer and Internet. Additional exam requirements/recommendations for international students: required—TOEFL (minimum score 550 paper-based, 79 iBT), IELTS (minimum score 6.5), Michigan English Language Assessment Battery (minimum score 82), or PTE (minimum score 53). Electronic applications accepted.

Wayne State University, College of Education, Division of Theoretical and Behavioral Foundations, Detroit, MI 48202. Offers applied behavior analysis (Certificate); counseling (M Ed, MA, Ed D, Ed S); counseling psychology (MA, PhD); education evaluation and research (M Ed, Ed D); educational psychology (M Ed, PhD), including learning and instruction sciences (PhD); rehabilitation counseling and community inclusion (MA); school and community psychology (MA, Certificate). *Accreditation:* ACA (one or more programs are accredited); CORE (one or more programs are accredited). *Program availability:* Part-time, evening/weekend. *Faculty:* 10. *Students:* 199 full-time (171 women), 142 part-time (107 women); includes 135 minority (90 Black or African American, non-Hispanic/Latino; 2 American Indian or Alaska Native, non-Hispanic/Latino; 6 Asian, non-Hispanic/Latino; 16 Hispanic/Latino; 21 Two or more races, non-Hispanic/Latino), 10 international. Average age 32. 364 applicants, 25% accepted, 72 enrolled. In 2019, 101 master's, 11 doctorates, 19 other advanced degrees awarded. *Degree requirements:* For master's, thesis (for some programs); for doctorate, comprehensive exam, thesis/dissertation. *Entrance requirements:* For master's, GRE, interview, personal statement, portfolio (only art therapy); references; program application; for doctorate, GRE, departmental writing exam, interview, curriculum vitae,

references, master's degree in closely-related field with minimum GPA of 3.5, demonstration of counseling skills (for Ed D in counseling); autobiographical statement; letter of application; personal statement; for other advanced degree, education specialist certificate: master's degree in counseling or closely related field and licensure; personal statement; recommendations; autobiographical statement; interview. Additional exam requirements/recommendations for international students: required—TOEFL (minimum score 550 paper-based; 79 iBT); recommended—IELTS (minimum score 6.5), TWE (minimum score 5.5), TSE (minimum score 58). *Application deadline:* Applications are processed on a rolling basis. Application fee: $50. Electronic applications accepted. *Expenses: Tuition:* Full-time $34,567. *Financial support:* In 2019–20, 92 students received support, including 1 fellowship (averaging $20,000 per year), 1 research assistantship with tuition reimbursement available (averaging $19,967 per year); teaching assistantships, Federal Work-Study, scholarships/grants, health care benefits, and unspecified assistantships also available. Support available to part-time students. Financial award applicants required to submit FAFSA. *Unit head:* Dr. William Hill, Assistant Dean, 313-577-9316, E-mail: ad2107@wayne.edu. *Application contact:* Dr. Mary L Waker, Graduate Admissions Officer, 313-577-1601, Fax: 313-577-7904, E-mail: m.waker@wayne.edu.
Website: https://education.wayne.edu/counseling-educational-psychology

Western Illinois University, School of Graduate Studies, College of Arts and Sciences, Department of Psychology, Macomb, IL 61455-1390. Offers clinical/community mental health (MS); general experimental psychology (MS); school psychology (SSP). *Program availability:* Part-time. *Degree requirements:* For master's, comprehensive exam (for some programs), thesis or alternative. *Entrance requirements:* For master's and SSP,

GRE General Test. Additional exam requirements/recommendations for international students: required—TOEFL (minimum score 550 paper-based; 80 iBT). Electronic applications accepted.

Wichita State University, Graduate School, Fairmount College of Liberal Arts and Sciences, Department of Psychology, Wichita, KS 67260. Offers clinical (PhD); community (PhD); human factors (PhD). *Accreditation:* APA. *Program availability:* Part-time.

Wilfrid Laurier University, Faculty of Graduate and Postdoctoral Studies, Faculty of Science, Department of Psychology, Waterloo, ON N2L 3C5, Canada. Offers behavioral neuroscience (M Sc, PhD); cognitive neuroscience (M Sc, PhD); community psychology (MA, PhD); social and developmental psychology (MA, PhD). *Program availability:* Part-time. *Degree requirements:* For master's, thesis; for doctorate, thesis/dissertation. *Entrance requirements:* For master's, GRE General Test, honors BA or the equivalent in psychology, minimum B average in undergraduate course work; for doctorate, GRE General Test, master's degree, minimum A- average. Additional exam requirements/recommendations for international students: required—TOEFL (minimum score 89 iBT). Electronic applications accepted.

Yale University, Graduate School of Arts and Sciences, Department of Psychology, New Haven, CT 06520. Offers behavioral neuroscience (PhD); clinical psychology (PhD); cognitive psychology (PhD); developmental psychology (PhD); social/personality psychology (PhD). *Accreditation:* APA. *Degree requirements:* For doctorate, thesis/dissertation. *Entrance requirements:* For doctorate, GRE General Test.

Sport Psychology

Adams State University, Office of Graduate Studies, Department of Kinesiology, Alamosa, CO 81101. Offers human performance and physical education (MA, MS), including applied sport psychology, coaching (MA), exercise science (MA), sport management (MA). *Program availability:* Part-time. *Entrance requirements:* For master's, GRE General Test or MAT, minimum undergraduate GPA of 2.75. *Application deadline:* For fall admission, 5/15 priority date for domestic students; for spring admission, 10/15 for domestic students. Applications are processed on a rolling basis. Application fee: $30. *Financial support:* In 2019–20, fellowships with partial tuition reimbursements (averaging $4,000 per year) were awarded; career-related internships or fieldwork, Federal Work-Study, institutionally sponsored loans, and unspecified assistantships also available. Support available to part-time students. Financial award application deadline: 4/15; financial award applicants required to submit FAFSA. *Application contact:* Caryn Chavez, Administrative Assistant III, 719-587-7208, Fax: 719-587-8230, E-mail: hppe@adams.edu.
Website: https://www.adams.edu/academics/graduate/kinesiology/

Adler University, Master of Science (M.S.) in Sport and Human Performance, Chicago, IL 60602. Offers MAC. In 2019, 1 master's awarded. *Degree requirements:* For master's, Social Justice Practicum; Sports Externship. *Unit head:* Phyllis Horton, Director of Admissions, 312-662-4100, E-mail: admissions@adler.edu. *Application contact:* Phyllis Horton, Director of Admissions, 312-662-4100, E-mail: admissions@adler.edu.

Argosy University, Atlanta, Georgia School of Professional Psychology, Atlanta, GA 30328. Offers clinical psychology (MA, Psy D, Postdoctoral Respecialization Certificate), including child and family psychology (Psy D), general adult clinical (Psy D), health psychology (Psy D), neuropsychology/geropsychology (Psy D); community counseling (MA), including marriage and family therapy; counselor education and supervision (Ed D); forensic psychology (MA); industrial organizational psychology (MA); marriage and family therapy (Certificate); sport-exercise psychology (MA). *Accreditation:* APA.

Argosy University, Orange County, American School of Professional Psychology, Program in Sport-Exercise Psychology, Orange, CA 92868. Offers MA.

Argosy University, Phoenix, Arizona School of Professional Psychology, Program in Clinical Psychology, Phoenix, AZ 85021. Offers clinical psychology (MA); neuropsychology (Psy D); sports-exercise psychology (Psy D).

Argosy University, Phoenix, Arizona School of Professional Psychology, Program in Sport–Exercise Psychology, Phoenix, AZ 85021. Offers MA.

A.T. Still University, College of Graduate Health Studies, Kirksville, MO 63501. Offers dental public health (MPH); exercise and sport psychology (Certificate); fundamentals of education (Certificate); geriatric exercise science (Certificate); global health (Certificate); health administration (MHA, DHA); health professions (Ed D); health sciences (DH Sc); kinesiology (MS); leadership and organizational behavior (Certificate); public health (MPH); sports conditioning (Certificate). *Accreditation:* CEPH. *Program availability:* Part-time, evening/weekend, online only, 100% online, blended/hybrid learning. *Faculty:* 49 full-time (36 women), 109 part-time/adjunct (66 women). *Students:* 601 full-time (406 women), 532 part-time (331 women); includes 457 minority (197 Black or African American, non-Hispanic/Latino; 15 American Indian or Alaska Native, non-Hispanic/Latino; 114 Asian, non-Hispanic/Latino; 105 Hispanic/Latino; 3 Native Hawaiian or other Pacific Islander, non-Hispanic/Latino; 23 Two or more races, non-Hispanic/Latino), 30 international. Average age 36. 339 applicants, 73% accepted, 217 enrolled. In 2019, 175 master's, 100 doctorates, 118 other advanced degrees awarded. *Degree requirements:* For master's, thesis, integrated terminal project, practicum; for doctorate, thesis/dissertation. *Entrance requirements:* For master's, minimum GPA of 2.5, bachelor's degree or equivalent, essay, resume, English proficiency; for doctorate, minimum GPA of 2.5, master's or terminal degree, essay, past experience in relevant field, resume, English proficiency. Additional exam requirements/recommendations for international students: required—TOEFL (minimum score 550 paper-based; 80 iBT). *Application deadline:* For fall admission, 6/24 for domestic and international students; for winter admission, 9/9 for domestic and international students; for spring admission, 12/9 for domestic and international students; for summer admission, 3/2 for domestic and international students. Applications are processed on a rolling basis. Application fee: $70. Electronic applications accepted. *Financial support:* In 2019–20, 13 students received support. Scholarships/grants available. Financial award applicants required to submit FAFSA. *Unit head:* Dr. Donald Altman, Dean, 480-219-6008, Fax: 660-626-2826, E-mail: daltman@atsu.edu. *Application contact:* Amie Waldemer, Associate Director, Online Admissions, 480-219-6146, E-mail: awaldemer@atsu.edu.
Website: http://www.atsu.edu/college-of-graduate-health-studies

Ball State University, Graduate School, College of Health, School of Kinesiology, Program in Physical Education and Sport, Muncie, IN 47306. Offers physical education and sport (MA, MS), including athletic coaching education, sport administration, sport

and exercise psychology. *Program availability:* Part-time, 100% online. *Entrance requirements:* For master's, GRE General Test, minimum baccalaureate GPA of 2.75 or 3.0 in latter half of baccalaureate, curriculum vitae, three letters of recommendation; campus visit to meet faculty and see facilities (strongly encouraged). Additional exam requirements/recommendations for international students: required—TOEFL (minimum score 550 paper-based; 79 iBT), IELTS (minimum score 6.5). Electronic applications accepted. *Expenses: Tuition, area resident:* Full-time $7506; part-time $417 per credit hour. Tuition, nonresident: full-time $20,610; part-time $1145 per credit hour. *Required fees:* $2126. Tuition and fees vary according to course load, campus/location and program.

Barry University, School of Human Performance and Leisure Sciences, Programs in Movement Science, Specialization in Sport and Exercise Psychology, Miami Shores, FL 33161-6695. Offers MS. *Entrance requirements:* For master's, GRE.

California State University, Fresno, Division of Research and Graduate Studies, College of Health and Human Services, Department of Kinesiology, Fresno, CA 93740-8027. Offers exercise science (MA); general kinesiology (MA); sport administration (MA); sport psychology (MA). *Program availability:* Part-time, evening/weekend. *Degree requirements:* For master's, thesis or alternative. *Entrance requirements:* For master's, GRE General Test, minimum GPA of 2.7. Additional exam requirements/recommendations for international students: required—TOEFL. Electronic applications accepted. *Expenses:* Tuition, state resident: full-time $4012; part-time $2506 per semester.

California State University, Long Beach, Graduate Studies, College of Health and Human Services, Department of Kinesiology, Long Beach, CA 90840. Offers adapted physical education (MA); coaching and student athlete development (MA); exercise physiology and nutrition (MS); exercise science (MS); individualized studies (MA); kinesiology (MA); pedagogical studies (MA); sport and exercise psychology (MS); sport management (MA); sports medicine and injury studies (MS). *Program availability:* Part-time. *Degree requirements:* For master's, oral and written comprehensive exams or thesis. *Entrance requirements:* For master's, GRE General Test, minimum GPA of 2.75 during previous 2 years of course work. Electronic applications accepted.

California University of Pennsylvania, School of Graduate Studies and Research, College of Education and Human Services, Department of Exercise Science and Sport Studies, California, PA 15419-1394. Offers applied sport science (MS); exercise science (MS), including group fitness leadership, nutrition, performance enhancement and injury prevention, rehabilitation science; group fitness leadership (MS); nutrition (MS); wellness coaching (MS). *Program availability:* Part-time, evening/weekend, online learning. *Degree requirements:* For master's, comprehensive exam, thesis optional. *Entrance requirements:* For master's, minimum GPA of 3.0. Additional exam requirements/recommendations for international students: required—TOEFL (minimum score 550 paper-based; 80 iBT). Electronic applications accepted. *Expenses:* Contact institution.

Capella University, Harold Abel School of Social and Behavioral Science, Master's Programs in Psychology, Minneapolis, MN 55402. Offers applied behavior analysis (MS); clinical psychology (MS); counseling psychology (MS); educational psychology (MS); evaluation, research, and measurement (MS); general advanced studies in human behavior (MS); general psychology (MS); industrial/organizational psychology (MS); leadership coaching psychology (MS); school psychology (MS); sport psychology (MS).

Chatham University, Program in Counseling Psychology, Pittsburgh, PA 15232-2826. Offers child, adolescent and family (MSCP); counseling psychology (Psy D); health and holistic (MSCP); organization and supervision (MSCP); sport and exercise (MSCP). *Accreditation:* APA. *Program availability:* Part-time, evening/weekend. *Faculty:* 13 full-time (8 women), 21 part-time/adjunct (17 women). *Students:* 93 full-time (79 women), 56 part-time (44 women); includes 29 minority (16 Black or African American, non-Hispanic/Latino; 4 Asian, non-Hispanic/Latino; 6 Hispanic/Latino; 3 Two or more races, non-Hispanic/Latino), 2 international. Average age 29. 172 applicants, 46% accepted, 54 enrolled. In 2019, 30 master's, 7 doctorates awarded. *Degree requirements:* For master's, thesis optional, supervised internship; for doctorate, thesis/dissertation, internship. *Entrance requirements:* For master's, minimum GPA of 3.0; 2 letters of recommendation; resume; prerequisite coursework in statistics, biology, and psychology; for doctorate, GRE. Additional exam requirements/recommendations for international students: required—TOEFL (minimum score 600 paper-based; 100 iBT), IELTS (minimum score 7), TWE. *Application deadline:* For fall admission, 4/1 priority date for domestic and international students; for spring admission, 11/1 for domestic students, 10/1 for international students. Applications are processed on a rolling basis. Application fee: $45. Electronic applications accepted. Application fee is waived when completed online. *Expenses:* $1,017 per credit hour. *Financial support:* Career-related

internships or fieldwork available. Financial award applicants required to submit FAFSA. *Unit head:* Dr. Mary Jo Loughran, Director, 412-365-2783, Fax: 412-365-1505, E-mail: mloughran@chatham.edu. *Application contact:* Melanie Elmer, Assistant Director of Graduate Admission, 412-365-1394, Fax: 412-365-1609, E-mail: gradadmissions@chatham.edu.
Website: http://www.chatham.edu/mscp

John F. Kennedy University, College of Psychology, Program in Sport Psychology, Pleasant Hill, CA 94523-4817. Offers MA, Graduate Certificate. *Program availability:* Part-time, evening/weekend. *Degree requirements:* For master's, thesis or alternative. *Entrance requirements:* For master's, interview. Additional exam requirements/ recommendations for international students: required—TOEFL.

Lock Haven University of Pennsylvania, The Stephen Poorman College of Business, Information Systems, and Human Services, Lock Haven, PA 17745-2390. Offers clinical mental health counseling (MS); sport science (MS). *Program availability:* Online learning. *Degree requirements:* For master's, thesis. *Entrance requirements:* For master's, minimum undergraduate GPA of 3.0. Additional exam requirements/ recommendations for international students: required—TOEFL. Electronic applications accepted.

Purdue University, Graduate School, College of Health and Human Sciences, Department of Health and Kinesiology, West Lafayette, IN 47907. Offers athletic training education administration (MS, PhD); biomechanics (MS, PhD); exercise physiology (MS, PhD); health education (MS, PhD); history/philosophy of sport (MS, PhD); motor control and development (MS, PhD); physical education pedagogy (PhD); physical education teacher education (MS); recreation and sport management (MS, PhD); sport and exercise psychology (MS, PhD). *Program availability:* Part-time. *Faculty:* 18 full-time (7 women). *Students:* 27 full-time (10 women), 13 part-time (10 women); includes 4 minority (3 Asian, non-Hispanic/Latino; 1 Two or more races, non-Hispanic/Latino), 8 international. Average age 26. 81 applicants, 19% accepted, 12 enrolled. In 2019, 10 master's, 1 doctorate awarded. *Degree requirements:* For master's, thesis optional; for doctorate, comprehensive exam, thesis/dissertation, qualifying examination, preliminary examination. *Entrance requirements:* For master's, GRE General Test (minimum score 1000 combined verbal and quantitative), minimum undergraduate GPA of 3.0 or equivalent; for doctorate, GRE General Test (minimum score 1100 combined verbal and quantitative), minimum undergraduate GPA of 3.0 or equivalent; master's degree with minimum GPA of 3.25 (recommended). Additional exam requirements/ recommendations for international students: required—TOEFL (minimum score 77 iBT); recommended—TWE. *Application deadline:* For fall admission, 4/30 for domestic and international students; for spring admission, 10/15 for domestic and international students. Applications are processed on a rolling basis. Application fee: $60 ($75 for international students). Electronic applications accepted. *Financial support:* Fellowships with partial tuition reimbursements, research assistantships with partial tuition reimbursements, teaching assistantships with partial tuition reimbursements, and Federal Work-Study available. Support available to part-time students. Financial award applicants required to submit FAFSA. *Unit head:* Dr. Timothy P. Gavin, Head of the Graduate Program, 765-494-3178, E-mail: gavin1@purdue.edu. *Application contact:* David B. Klenosky, Graduate Contact, 765-494-0865, E-mail: klenosky@purdue.edu.
Website: http://www.purdue.edu/hhs/hk/

Queen's University at Kingston, School of Graduate Studies, School of Kinesiology and Health Studies, Kingston, ON K7L 3N6, Canada. Offers biomechanics and ergonomics (M Sc, PhD); exercise physiology (M Sc, PhD); health promotion (M Sc, PhD); physical activity epidemiology (M Sc, PhD); sociocultural studies of sport, health and the body (MA, PhD); sport psychology (M Sc, PhD). *Program availability:* Part-time. *Degree requirements:* For master's, thesis (for some programs); for doctorate, comprehensive exam, thesis/dissertation. *Entrance requirements:* For master's and doctorate, minimum B+ average. Additional exam requirements/recommendations for international students: required—TOEFL. Electronic applications accepted.

Southern Illinois University Edwardsville, Graduate School, School of Education, Health, and Human Behavior, Department of Kinesiology and Health Education, Program in Exercise and Sport Psychology, Edwardsville, IL 62026. Offers MS. *Program availability:* Part-time, evening/weekend. *Degree requirements:* For master's, comprehensive exam (for some programs), thesis (for some programs). *Entrance requirements:* Additional exam requirements/recommendations for international students: required—TOEFL (minimum score 550 paper-based, 79 iBT), IELTS (minimum score 6.5), Michigan Test of English Language Proficiency or PTE. Electronic applications accepted.

Springfield College, Graduate Programs, Programs in Exercise Science and Sport Studies, Springfield, MA 01109-3797. Offers athletic training (MS); clinical exercise physiology (MS); exercise physiology (MS); sport and exercise psychology (MS); strength and conditioning (MS). *Program availability:* Part-time. Terminal master's awarded for partial completion of doctoral program. *Degree requirements:* For master's, comprehensive exam, research project or thesis. *Entrance requirements:* For master's, GRE General Test. Additional exam requirements/recommendations for international students: required—TOEFL (minimum score 550 paper-based); recommended—IELTS (minimum score 7). Electronic applications accepted.

Springfield College, Graduate Programs, Programs in Psychology, Springfield, MA 01109-3797. Offers athletic counseling (MS, CAGS); clinical mental health counseling (M Ed, CAGS); counseling psychology (Psy D); general counseling (M Ed); industrial/organizational psychology (M Ed, CAGS); school counseling (M Ed, CAGS); student personnel administration in higher education (M Ed, CAGS). *Accreditation:* APA. *Program availability:* Part-time. *Degree requirements:* For master's, research project, portfolio; for doctorate, dissertation project, 1500 hours of counseling psychology practicum, full-year internship. *Entrance requirements:* For doctorate, GRE. Additional exam requirements/recommendations for international students: required—TOEFL (minimum score 550 paper-based); recommended—IELTS (minimum score 7). Electronic applications accepted.

University of Denver, Graduate School of Professional Psychology, Denver, CO 80208. Offers clinical psychology (Psy D); forensic psychology (MA); international disaster psychology (MA); sport and performance psychology (MA); sport coaching (MA); strength and conditioning and fitness coaching (Certificate). *Accreditation:* APA. *Faculty:* 23 full-time (15 women), 16 part-time/adjunct (9 women). *Students:* 243 full-time (192 women), 84 part-time (44 women); includes 95 minority (18 Black or African American, non-Hispanic/Latino; 1 American Indian or Alaska Native, non-Hispanic/ Latino; 18 Asian, non-Hispanic/Latino; 46 Hispanic/Latino; 1 Native Hawaiian or other Pacific Islander, non-Hispanic/Latino; 11 Two or more races, non-Hispanic/Latino), 9 international. Average age 27. 953 applicants, 27% accepted, 137 enrolled. In 2019, 117 master's, 35 doctorates, 152 other advanced degrees awarded. *Degree requirements:* For master's, comprehensive exam (for some programs); for doctorate, comprehensive exam, community field placement, paper, clinical internship, complete 4 assessments, professional psychology clinic. *Entrance requirements:* For master's and doctorate, GRE General Test, psychology major/minor or 660 or higher on psychology subject GRE exam, transcripts, resume, two letters of recommendation, essay. Additional exam requirements/recommendations for international students: required—TOEFL (minimum score 550 paper-based; 80 iBT). *Application deadline:* For fall admission, 1/11 for domestic and international students. Application fee: $65. Electronic applications accepted. *Expenses:* Contact institution. *Financial support:* In 2019–20, 249 students received support, including 20 teaching assistantships with tuition reimbursements available (averaging $2,835 per year); career-related internships or fieldwork, Federal Work-Study, institutionally sponsored loans, scholarships/grants, unspecified assistantships, and clinical assistantships also available. Support available to part-time students. Financial award application deadline: 2/15; financial award applicants required to submit FAFSA. *Unit head:* Dr. Shelly Smith-Acuna, Dean, 303-871-3880, Fax: 303-871-4220, E-mail: shelly.smith-acuna@du.edu. *Application contact:* Julie Schellman, Director of Enrollment, 303-871-2908, E-mail: Julie.Schellman@du.edu.
Website: http://www.du.edu/gspp

University of Rhode Island, Graduate School, College of Health Sciences, Department of Kinesiology, Kingston, RI 02881. Offers cultural studies of sport and physical culture (MS); exercise science (MS); psychosocial/behavioral aspects of physical activity (MS). *Accreditation:* NCATE. *Program availability:* Part-time. *Faculty:* 14 full-time (11 women). *Students:* 17 full-time (8 women), 1 part-time (0 women); includes 1 minority (Two or more races, non-Hispanic/Latino). 16 applicants, 94% accepted, 10 enrolled. In 2019, 6 master's awarded. *Entrance requirements:* Additional exam requirements/ recommendations for international students: required—TOEFL. *Application deadline:* For fall admission, 7/15 for domestic students, 2/1 for international students; for spring admission, 11/15 for domestic students, 7/15 for international students. Application fee: $65. Electronic applications accepted. *Expenses: Tuition, area resident:* Full-time $13,734; part-time $763 per credit. Tuition, state resident: full-time $13,734; part-time $763 per credit. Tuition, nonresident: full-time $26,512; part-time $1473 per credit. *International tuition:* $26,512 full-time. *Required fees:* $1780; $52 per credit. $35 per term. One-time fee: $165. *Financial support:* In 2019–20, 6 teaching assistantships with tuition reimbursements (averaging $14,240 per year) were awarded. Financial award application deadline: 2/1; financial award applicants required to submit FAFSA. *Unit head:* Dr. Disa Hatfield, Interim Chair, 401-874-5183, E-mail: doch@uri.edu. *Application contact:* Dr. Matthew Delmonico, Graduate Program Director, 401-874-5440, E-mail: delmonico@uri.edu.
Website: http://web.uri.edu/kinesiology/

The University of Texas at Austin, Graduate School, College of Education, Department of Kinesiology and Health Education, Austin, TX 78712-1111. Offers behavioral health (PhD); exercise and sport psychology (M Ed, MA); exercise science (M Ed, MS, PhD); health education (M Ed, MS, Ed D, PhD). *Program availability:* Part-time. Terminal master's awarded for partial completion of doctoral program. *Degree requirements:* For master's, thesis (for some programs); for doctorate, thesis/ dissertation. *Entrance requirements:* For master's and doctorate, GRE General Test. Additional exam requirements/recommendations for international students: required—TOEFL. Electronic applications accepted.

West Virginia University, College of Physical Activity and Sport Sciences, Morgantown, WV 26506. Offers athletic training (MS); coaching and sport education (MS); coaching and teaching studies (Ed D, PhD), including curriculum and instruction (PhD); physical education/teacher education (MS); sport coaching (MS); sport management (MS); sport, exercise & performance psychology (MS). *Degree requirements:* For doctorate, comprehensive exam, thesis/dissertation, oral exam. *Entrance requirements:* For master's, GRE or MAT, minimum GPA of 3.0; for doctorate, GRE General Test or MAT, minimum GPA of 3.5. Additional exam requirements/ recommendations for international students: required—TOEFL (minimum score 550 paper-based). Electronic applications accepted.

Thanatology

Brooklyn College of the City University of New York, School of Natural and Behavioral Sciences, Department of Health and Nutrition Sciences, Program in Community Health, Brooklyn, NY 11210-2889. Offers community health education (MA); thanatology (MA). *Accreditation:* CEPH. *Degree requirements:* For master's, thesis or alternative. *Entrance requirements:* For master's, 2 letters of recommendation, essay. Additional exam requirements/recommendations for international students: required—TOEFL. Electronic applications accepted.

The College of New Rochelle, Graduate School, Division of Human Services, Program in Mental Health Counseling, New Rochelle, NY 10805-2308. Offers mental health counseling (MS); thanatology (Certificate). *Degree requirements:* For Certificate, internship.

Marian University, School of Nursing and Health Professions, Fond du Lac, WI 54935-4699. Offers adult nurse practitioner (MSN); nurse educator (MSN); thanatology (MS). *Accreditation:* AACN. *Program availability:* Part-time, evening/weekend. *Degree requirements:* For master's, thesis, 675 clinical practicum hours. *Entrance requirements:* For master's, 3 letters of professional recommendation; undergraduate work in nursing research, statistics, health assessment. Additional exam requirements/ recommendations for international students: required—TOEFL (minimum score 525 paper-based; 70 iBT). Electronic applications accepted. *Expenses:* Contact institution.

Southwestern College, Program in Grief, Loss and Trauma Counseling, Santa Fe, NM 87502-4788. Offers MA, Certificate. *Program availability:* Part-time, evening/weekend, online learning. *Entrance requirements:* For master's, interview, references, resume; for Certificate, 3 letters of reference, interview.

University of Maryland, Baltimore, Graduate School, Program in Thanatology, Baltimore, MD 21201. Offers Certificate. *Entrance requirements:* For degree, minimum GPA of 3.0, curriculum vitae, essay. Additional exam requirements/recommendations for international students: required—TOEFL (minimum score 80 iBT); recommended—IELTS (minimum score 7). Electronic applications accepted. *Expenses:* Contact institution.

Washington & Jefferson College, Graduate and Continuing Studies, Washington, PA 15301. Offers applied health care economics and outcomes management (MS); professional accounting (MAC); professional writing (Graduate Certificate); thanatology (Graduate Certificate).

Transpersonal and Humanistic Psychology

Atlantic University, Program in Transpersonal Psychology, Virginia Beach, VA 23451-2061. Offers applied spirituality (MA); consciousness (MA); creativity (MA); general studies (MA); leadership and conflict transformation (MA). *Program availability:* Part-time, evening/weekend, online learning. *Degree requirements:* For master's, culminating project. *Entrance requirements:* For master's, official transcripts, 1000-word essay, interview. Additional exam requirements/recommendations for international students: required—TOEFL (minimum score 550 paper-based). Electronic applications accepted. *Expenses:* Contact institution.

John F. Kennedy University, College of Psychology, Program in Consciousness and Transformative Studies, Pleasant Hill, CA 94523-4817. Offers MA. *Program availability:* Part-time, evening/weekend, 100% online, blended/hybrid learning. *Degree requirements:* For master's, thesis or alternative. *Entrance requirements:* For master's, interview. Additional exam requirements/recommendations for international students: required—TOEFL.

John F. Kennedy University, College of Psychology, Program in Holistic Psychology, Pleasant Hill, CA 94523-4817. Offers depth and transpersonal psychotherapy (MA); expressive arts (MA); holistic studies (MA); somatic psychology (MA). *Program availability:* Part-time, evening/weekend. *Degree requirements:* For master's, thesis or alternative. *Entrance requirements:* For master's, interview. Additional exam requirements/recommendations for international students: required—TOEFL.

Michigan School of Psychology, MA and Psy D Programs in Clinical Psychology, Farmington Hills, MI 48334. Offers MA, Psy D. *Accreditation:* APA. *Program availability:* Part-time, evening/weekend. *Faculty:* 14 full-time (7 women), 16 part-time/adjunct (11 women). *Students:* 125 full-time (97 women), 60 part-time (43 women); includes 47 minority (29 Black or African American, non-Hispanic/Latino; 3 Asian, non-Hispanic/Latino; 6 Hispanic/Latino; 9 Two or more races, non-Hispanic/Latino). Average age 30. 205 applicants, 54% accepted, 86 enrolled. In 2019, 61 master's, 13 doctorates awarded. *Degree requirements:* For master's, practicum; for doctorate, comprehensive exam, thesis/dissertation, internship, practicum. *Entrance requirements:* For master's, undergraduate degree from accredited institution with minimum GPA of 2.5; major in psychology, social work, or counseling (prerequisites apply without one of these degrees); for doctorate, GRE General Test, undergraduate degree from accredited institution with minimum GPA of 2.5; graduate degree in psychology, social work, or counseling from accredited institution with minimum GPA of 3.25; graduate-level practicum. Additional exam requirements/recommendations for international students: required—TOEFL (minimum score 550 paper-based; 79 iBT). *Application deadline:* For fall admission, 2/15 for domestic students. Application fee: $75. Electronic applications accepted. *Expenses:* Tuition: Full-time $40,000; part-time $15,000 per year. *Required fees:* $2265; $780 per semester. $260 per semester. One-time fee: $75. Tuition and fees vary according to course load, degree level and program. *Financial support:* In 2019–20, 12 students received support, including 1 research assistantship (averaging $8,566 per year), 5 teaching assistantships (averaging $14,436 per year); institutionally sponsored loans, scholarships/grants, and unspecified assistantships also available. Financial award application deadline: 8/30; financial award applicants required to submit FAFSA. *Unit head:* Dr. Shannon Chavez-Korell, Program Director, 248-476-1122, Fax: 248-476-1125. *Application contact:* Carrie Pyeatt, Coordinator of Admissions and Student Engagement, 248-476-1122 Ext. 117, Fax: 248-476-1125, E-mail: cpyeatt@msp.edu.
Website: msp.edu

Naropa University, Graduate Programs, Program in Clinical Mental Health Counseling, Concentration in Mindfulness-based Transpersonal Counseling, Boulder, CO 80302-6697. Offers MA. *Degree requirements:* For master's, internship, counseling practicum.

Entrance requirements: For master's, interview, statement of interest, essay, professional experience, resume, 2 letters of recommendation, transcripts. Additional exam requirements/recommendations for international students: required—TOEFL (minimum score 550 paper-based; 80 iBT). Electronic applications accepted. *Expenses:* Contact institution.

Saybrook University, School of Psychology and Interdisciplinary Inquiry, San Francisco, CA 94612. Offers human science (MA, PhD), including consciousness and spirituality, humanistic and transpersonal psychology, integrative health studies, organizational systems, social transformation; organizational systems (MA, PhD), including consciousness and spirituality, humanistic and transpersonal psychology, integrative health studies, leadership of sustainable systems (MA), organizational systems, social transformation; psychology (MA, PhD), including consciousness and spirituality, creativity studies (MA), humanistic and transpersonal psychology, integrative health studies, Jungian studies, marriage and family therapy (MA), organizational systems, social transformation. *Program availability:* Online learning. Terminal master's awarded for partial completion of doctoral program. *Degree requirements:* For master's, thesis or alternative; for doctorate, thesis/dissertation. *Entrance requirements:* Additional exam requirements/recommendations for international students: required—TOEFL (minimum score 580 paper-based; 93 iBT). Electronic applications accepted.

Seattle University, College of Arts and Sciences, Department of Psychology, Seattle, WA 98122-1090. Offers existential and phenomenological therapeutic psychology (MA Psych). *Faculty:* 13 full-time (10 women), 12 part-time/adjunct (10 women). *Students:* 39 full-time (22 women), 2 part-time (both women); includes 11 minority (3 Black or African American, non-Hispanic/Latino; 1 American Indian or Alaska Native, non-Hispanic/Latino; 2 Asian, non-Hispanic/Latino; 3 Hispanic/Latino; 2 Two or more races, non-Hispanic/Latino), 2 international. Average age 30. 56 applicants, 45% accepted, 24 enrolled. In 2019, 10 master's awarded. *Entrance requirements:* For master's, interview, minimum GPA of 3.0, previous undergraduate course work in psychology, experience (paid or volunteer) in counseling or human services. *Application deadline:* For fall admission, 1/15 for domestic and international students. Application fee: $55. Electronic applications accepted. *Financial support:* In 2019–20, 30 students received support. Career-related internships or fieldwork and Federal Work-Study available. Support available to part-time students. Financial award applicants required to submit FAFSA. *Unit head:* Dr. Kevin Krycka, Director of Graduate Programs, 206-296-5398, Fax: 206-296-2141, E-mail: krycka@seattleu.edu. *Application contact:* Janet Shandley, Associate Dean of Graduate Admissions, 206-296-5900, Fax: 206-298-5656, E-mail: grad_admissions@seattleu.edu.
Website: http://www.seattleu.edu/artsci/departments/psychology/

Sofia University, Hybrid: Face-to-Face/Online Programs, Palo Alto, CA 94303. Offers transpersonal psychology (MA, PhD), including transpersonal psychology (PhD). *Program availability:* Online learning. *Entrance requirements:* For master's, bachelor's degree; for doctorate, bachelor's degree; master's degree. Electronic applications accepted.

Sofia University, Residential Programs, Palo Alto, CA 94303. Offers clinical psychology (Psy D); computer science (MS); counseling psychology (MA); transpersonal psychology (MA, PhD). *Program availability:* Part-time, evening/weekend. Terminal master's awarded for partial completion of doctoral program. *Degree requirements:* For doctorate, thesis/dissertation. *Entrance requirements:* For master's, bachelor's degree; for doctorate, bachelor's degree; master's degree (for some programs). Electronic applications accepted.

Section 25
Public, Regional, and Industrial Affairs

This section contains a directory of institutions offering graduate work in public, regional, and industrial affairs, followed by in-depth entries submitted by institutions that chose to prepare detailed program descriptions. Additional information about programs listed in the directory but not augmented by an in-depth entry may be obtained by writing directly to the dean of a graduate school or chair of a department at the address given in the directory.

For programs offering related work, see also in this book *Architecture, Area and Cultural Studies, Criminology and Forensics, Economics, Humanities, Political Science and International Affairs,* and *Sociology, Anthropology, and Archaeology.* In the other guides in this series:

Graduate Programs in the Biological/Biomedical Sciences & Health-Related Medical Professions
See *Public Health*

Graduate Programs in the Physical Sciences, Mathematics, Agricultural Sciences, the Environment & Natural Resources
See *Environmental Sciences and Management*

Graduate Programs in Engineering & Applied Sciences
See *Management of Engineering and Technology*

Graduate Programs in Business, Education, Information Studies, Law & Social Work
See *Business Administration and Management* and *Law*

CONTENTS

Program Directories

Disability Studies

Brandeis University, The Heller School for Social Policy and Management, Program in Social Policy, Waltham, MA 02454-9110. Offers assets and inequalities (PhD); children, youth and families (PhD); global health and development (PhD); health and behavioral health (PhD). *Degree requirements:* For doctorate, comprehensive exam, thesis/dissertation, qualifying paper, 2-year residency. *Entrance requirements:* For doctorate, GRE General Test, 3 letters of recommendation, statement of purpose, writing sample, at least 3-5 years of professional experience. Additional exam requirements/recommendations for international students: required—TOEFL (minimum score 600 paper-based; 100 iBT). Electronic applications accepted.

Brock University, Faculty of Graduate Studies, Faculty of Social Sciences, Program in Applied Disability Studies, St. Catharines, ON L2S 3A1, Canada. Offers MA, MADS, Diploma. *Program availability:* Part-time. *Degree requirements:* For master's, thesis (for some programs). *Entrance requirements:* For master's, honors degree. Additional exam requirements/recommendations for international students: required—TOEFL (minimum score 550 paper-based; 80 iBT), IELTS (minimum score 6.5). Electronic applications accepted.

Chapman University, Donna Ford Attallah College of Educational Studies, Orange, CA 92866. Offers counseling (MA), including school counseling (MA, Credential); curriculum and instruction (MA), including elementary education, secondary education; education (PhD), including cultural and curricular studies, disability studies, leadership studies, school psychology (PhD, Credential); educational psychology (MA); leadership development (MA); multiple subjects (Credential), including Spanish/English bilingual; pupil personnel services (Credential), including school counseling (MA, Credential), school psychology (PhD, Credential); school psychology (Ed S); single subject (Credential); special education (MA, Credential), including mild/moderate (Credential), moderate/severe (Credential); teaching (MA), including elementary education, secondary education, secondary music education. *Accreditation:* TEAC. *Program availability:* Part-time, evening/weekend. *Faculty:* 33 full-time (19 women), 49 part-time/adjunct (36 women). *Students:* 145 full-time (127 women), 179 part-time (136 women); includes 178 minority (8 Black or African American, non-Hispanic/Latino; 1 American Indian or Alaska Native, non-Hispanic/Latino; 41 Asian, non-Hispanic/Latino; 117 Hispanic/Latino; 11 Two or more races, non-Hispanic/Latino), 16 international. Average age 28. 333 applicants, 61% accepted, 143 enrolled. In 2019, 153 master's, 11 doctorates awarded. *Entrance requirements:* Additional exam requirements/recommendations for international students: required—TOEFL (minimum score 80 iBT), IELTS (minimum score 6.5), PTE (minimum score 53). *Application deadline:* Applications are processed on a rolling basis. Application fee: $60. Electronic applications accepted. *Expenses:* Contact institution. *Financial support:* Fellowships and scholarships/grants available. Financial award applicants required to submit FAFSA. *Unit head:* Dr. Roxanne Greitz Miller, Interim Dean, 714-997-6781, E-mail: rgmiller@chapman.edu. *Application contact:* Shannon McCance, Graduate Admission Counselor, 714-516-5236, E-mail: smccance@chapman.edu. Website: http://www.chapman.edu/CES/

Montclair State University, The Graduate School, College of Education and Human Services, Developmental Models of Autism Intervention Certificate Program, Montclair, NJ 07043-1624. Offers Certificate. *Program availability:* Part-time, evening/weekend. *Entrance requirements:* Additional exam requirements/recommendations for international students: required—TOEFL (minimum score 83 iBT), IELTS (minimum score 6.5). Electronic applications accepted.

Montclair State University, The Graduate School, College of Education and Human Services, Program in Learning Disabilities, Montclair, NJ 07043-1624. Offers M Ed. *Program availability:* Part-time, evening/weekend. *Degree requirements:* For master's, comprehensive exam, thesis or alternative. *Entrance requirements:* For master's, GRE General Test, interview, 2 letters of recommendation. Additional exam requirements/

recommendations for international students: required—TOEFL (minimum score 83 iBT), IELTS (minimum score 6.5). Electronic applications accepted.

Syracuse University, School of Education, CAS Program in Disability Studies, Syracuse, NY 13244. Offers CAS. *Program availability:* Part-time. *Entrance requirements:* For degree, baccalaureate degree from regionally-accredited college/university, two letters of recommendation. Additional exam requirements/recommendations for international students: required—TOEFL (minimum score 100 iBT). Electronic applications accepted.

University of Hawaii at Manoa, Office of Graduate Education, College of Education, Program in Disability and Diversity Studies, Honolulu, HI 96822. Offers Graduate Certificate. *Program availability:* Part-time. *Entrance requirements:* Additional exam requirements/recommendations for international students: required—TOEFL (minimum score 500 paper-based; 61 iBT), IELTS (minimum score 5).

University of Illinois at Chicago, College of Applied Health Sciences, Department of Disability and Human Development, Chicago, IL 60607-7128. Offers MS, PhD. *Accreditation:* AOTA. *Program availability:* Part-time. *Degree requirements:* For master's, thesis optional; for doctorate, thesis/dissertation. *Entrance requirements:* For master's and doctorate, GRE General Test. Additional exam requirements/recommendations for international students: required—TOEFL. Electronic applications accepted.

University of Manitoba, Faculty of Graduate Studies, Interdisciplinary Programs, Program in Disability Studies, Winnipeg, MB R3T 2N2, Canada. Offers M Sc, MA.

University of Northern British Columbia, Office of Graduate Studies, Prince George, BC V2N 4Z9, Canada. Offers business administration (Diploma); community health science (M Sc); disability management (MA); education (M Ed); first nations studies (MA); gender studies (MA); history (MA); interdisciplinary studies (MA); international studies (MA); mathematical, computer and physical sciences (M Sc); natural resources and environmental studies (M Sc, MA, MNRES, PhD); political science (MA); psychology (M Sc, PhD); social work (MSW). *Program availability:* Part-time, evening/weekend, online learning. *Degree requirements:* For master's, thesis; for doctorate, thesis/dissertation. *Entrance requirements:* For master's, GRE, minimum B average in undergraduate course work; for doctorate, candidacy exam, minimum A average in graduate course work.

University of Pittsburgh, School of Law, Certificate Program in Disability Legal Studies, Pittsburgh, PA 15260. Offers Certificate. *Entrance requirements:* For degree, official transcript, two letters of recommendation, essay. Additional exam requirements/recommendations for international students: required—TOEFL.

Utah State University, School of Graduate Studies, Emma Eccles Jones College of Education and Human Services, Department of Special Education and Rehabilitation, Logan, UT 84322. Offers disability disciplines (PhD); rehabilitation counseling (MRC); special education (M Ed, MS, Ed S). *Program availability:* Part-time, online learning. *Degree requirements:* For master's, thesis (for some programs), internships (for some programs); for doctorate, comprehensive exam, thesis/dissertation. *Entrance requirements:* For master's and doctorate, GRE General Test, minimum GPA of 3.0. Additional exam requirements/recommendations for international students: required—TOEFL (minimum score 550 paper-based). Electronic applications accepted.

York University, Faculty of Graduate Studies, Faculty of Health, Program in Critical Disability Studies, Toronto, ON M3J 1P3, Canada. Offers MA, PhD. *Degree requirements:* For master's, thesis or alternative. *Entrance requirements:* Additional exam requirements/recommendations for international students: required—TOEFL (minimum score 600 paper-based). Electronic applications accepted.

Emergency Management

Adelphi University, College of Professional and Continuing Studies, Graduate Certificate in Emergency Management Program, Garden City, NY 11530-0701. Offers Certificate. *Program availability:* Part-time, evening/weekend. *Entrance requirements:* Additional exam requirements/recommendations for international students: required—TOEFL (minimum score 550 paper-based; 80 iBT), IELTS (minimum score 6.5). Electronic applications accepted.

Anna Maria College, Graduate Division, Program in Health Emergency Management, Paxton, MA 01612. Offers MS, Graduate Certificate. *Program availability:* Part-time, evening/weekend. *Degree requirements:* For master's, thesis. *Entrance requirements:* For master's, minimum GPA of 2.7. Additional exam requirements/recommendations for international students: required—TOEFL (minimum score 500 paper-based). Electronic applications accepted.

Arizona State University at Tempe, College of Public Programs, School of Public Affairs, Phoenix, AZ 85004-0687. Offers emergency management and homeland security (MA); program evaluation (MS); public administration (MPA, PhD), including nonprofit administration (MPA), urban management (MPA); public policy (MPP); MPA/MSW. *Accreditation:* NASPAA (one or more programs are accredited). *Program availability:* Part-time, evening/weekend. Terminal master's awarded for partial completion of doctoral program. *Degree requirements:* For master's, thesis or alternative, policy analysis or capstone project; interactive Program of Study (iPOS) submitted before completing 50 percent of required credit hours; for doctorate, comprehensive exam, thesis/dissertation, interactive Program of Study (iPOS) submitted before completing 50 percent of required credit hours. *Entrance requirements:* For master's, GRE, minimum GPA of 3.0 or equivalent in last 2 years of work leading to bachelor's degree; for doctorate, GRE, minimum GPA of 3.0 or equivalent in last 2 years of work leading to bachelor's degree, 3 letters of recommendation, resume, statement of goals, samples of research reports. Additional exam requirements/recommendations for international students: required—TOEFL (minimum score 600 paper-based; 100 iBT), IELTS (minimum score 6.5). Electronic applications accepted. *Expenses:* Contact institution.

Arkansas State University, Graduate School, College of Nursing and Health Professions, Disaster Preparedness Program, State University, AR 72467. Offers

disaster preparedness and emergency management (MS); healthcare emergency management (Graduate Certificate). *Program availability:* Part-time. *Degree requirements:* For master's and Graduate Certificate, comprehensive exam, thesis or alternative. *Entrance requirements:* For master's, GRE General Test or MAT, appropriate bachelor's degree, TB skin test, TB mask fit test, CPR certification, liability insurance; for Graduate Certificate, bachelor's degree, TB skin test, TB mask fit test, CPR certification, liability insurance. Additional exam requirements/recommendations for international students: required—TOEFL (minimum score 550 paper-based; 79 iBT), IELTS (minimum score 6), PTE (minimum score 56). Electronic applications accepted. *Expenses:* Contact institution.

Arkansas Tech University, College of Engineering and Applied Sciences, Russellville, AR 72801. Offers electrical engineering (M Engr); emergency management (MS); information technology (MS); mechanical engineering (M Engr). *Program availability:* Part-time, evening/weekend, 100% online, blended/hybrid learning. *Students:* 38 full-time (11 women), 45 part-time (22 women); includes 13 minority (10 Black or African American, non-Hispanic/Latino; 1 Asian, non-Hispanic/Latino; 1 Hispanic/Latino; 1 Two or more races, non-Hispanic/Latino), 24 international. Average age 32. In 2019, 26 master's awarded. *Degree requirements:* For master's, comprehensive exam (for some programs), thesis (for some programs). *Entrance requirements:* Additional exam requirements/recommendations for international students: required—TOEFL (minimum score 550 paper-based; 79 iBT), IELTS (minimum score 6.5), PTE (minimum score 58). *Application deadline:* For fall admission, 3/1 priority date for domestic students, 5/1 priority date for international students; for spring admission, 10/1 priority date for domestic and international students. Applications are processed on a rolling basis. Application fee: $40 ($90 for international students). Electronic applications accepted. *Expenses: Tuition, area resident:* Full-time $7008; part-time $292 per credit hour. *Tuition, state resident:* full-time $7008; part-time $292 per credit hour. *Tuition, nonresident:* full-time $14,016; part-time $584 per credit hour. *International tuition:* $14,016 full-time. *Required fees:* $343 per term. *Financial support:* In 2019–20, research assistantships with full and partial tuition reimbursements (averaging $4,800 per year), teaching assistantships with full and partial tuition reimbursements (averaging $4,800 per year) were awarded; career-related internships or fieldwork, Federal Work-Study,

scholarships/grants, health care benefits, and unspecified assistantships also available. Support available to part-time students. Financial award application deadline: 4/15; financial award applicants required to submit FAFSA. *Unit head:* Dr. Judy Cezeaux, Dean, 479-968-0353, E-mail: jcezeaux@atu.edu. *Application contact:* Dr. Richard Schoephoerster, Dean of Graduate College and Research, 479-968-0398, Fax: 479-964-0542, E-mail: gradcollege@atu.edu.
Website: http://www.atu.edu/appliedsci/

Ball State University, Graduate School, College of Sciences and Humanities, Department of Natural Resources and Environmental Management, Muncie, IN 47306. Offers emergency management and homeland security (Certificate); natural resources and environmental management (MA, MS). *Program availability:* Part-time. *Degree requirements:* For master's, thesis (for some programs). *Entrance requirements:* For master's, GRE General Test, minimum baccalaureate GPA of 2.75 or 3.0 in latter half of baccalaureate, two letters of reference. Additional exam requirements/recommendations for international students: required—TOEFL (minimum score 550 paper-based; 79 iBT), IELTS (minimum score 6.5). Electronic applications accepted. *Expenses: Tuition, area resident:* Full-time $7506; part-time $417 per credit hour. Tuition, nonresident: full-time $20,610; part-time $1145 per credit hour. *Required fees:* $2126. Tuition and fees vary according to course load, campus/location and program.

Ball State University, Graduate School, College of Sciences and Humanities, Department of Political Science, Program in Public Administration, Muncie, IN 47306. Offers public administration (MPA, Certificate), including community and economic development (MPA), criminal justice (MPA), emergency management and homeland security (MPA), information and communication technology (MPA). *Program availability:* Part-time. *Degree requirements:* For master's, comprehensive exam. *Entrance requirements:* For master's, GRE General Test, minimum baccalaureate GPA of 2.8, two letters of recommendation. Additional exam requirements/recommendations for international students: required—TOEFL (minimum score 550 paper-based; 79 iBT), IELTS (minimum score 6.5). Electronic applications accepted. *Expenses: Tuition, area resident:* Full-time $7506; part-time $417 per credit hour. Tuition, nonresident: full-time $20,610; part-time $1145 per credit hour. *Required fees:* $2126. Tuition and fees vary according to course load, campus/location and program.

Benedictine University, Graduate Programs, Program in Public Health, Lisle, IL 60532. Offers administration of health care institutions (MPH); dietetics (MPH); disaster management (MPH); health education (MPH); health information systems (MPH); management information systems (MPH/MS); MBA/MPH; MPH/MS. *Accreditation:* CEPH. *Program availability:* Part-time, evening/weekend, 100% online. *Entrance requirements:* For master's, GRE, MAT, GMAT, LSAT, DAT or other graduate professional exams, official transcript; 2 letters of recommendation from individuals familiar with the applicant's professional or academic work, excluding family or personal friends; essay describing the candidate's career path. Additional exam requirements/recommendations for international students: required—TOEFL (minimum score 600 paper-based; 79 iBT), IELTS (minimum score 6.5). Electronic applications accepted.

Boston University, School of Medicine, Graduate Medical Sciences, Program in Healthcare Emergency Management, Boston, MA 02215. Offers MS. *Financial support:* Applicants required to submit FAFSA. *Unit head:* Dr. Kevin Thomas, Director, 617-414-2316, Fax: 617-414-2332, E-mail: kipthoma@bu.edu. *Application contact:* Patricia Jones, E-mail: psterlin@bu.edu.
Website: http://www.bumc.bu.edu/gms/hem/

California State University, Long Beach, Graduate Studies, College of Health and Human Services, Department of Criminology and Criminal Justice, Long Beach, CA 90840. Offers criminal justice (MS); emergency services administration (MS). *Program availability:* Part-time. *Degree requirements:* For master's, comprehensive course or thesis. *Entrance requirements:* For master's, minimum GPA of 3.0. Electronic applications accepted.

California State University Maritime Academy, Graduate Studies, Vallejo, CA 94590. Offers transportation and engineering management (MS), including engineering management, humanitarian disaster management, transportation. *Program availability:* Evening/weekend, online only, 100% online. *Degree requirements:* For master's, comprehensive exam (for some programs), thesis, Minimum GPA of 3.0 in 10 required courses including capstone course and project, demonstrated proficiency in graduate-level writing. *Entrance requirements:* For master's, GMAT/GRE (for applicants with fewer than five years of post-baccalaureate professional experience), Equivalent of four-year U.S. bachelor's degree with minimum GPA of 2.5 during last two years (60 semester units or 90 quarter units) of coursework in degree program. Additional exam requirements/recommendations for international students: required—TOEFL (minimum score 550 paper-based). Electronic applications accepted.

Capella University, School of Public Service Leadership, Doctoral Programs in Healthcare, Minneapolis, MN 55402. Offers criminal justice (PhD); emergency management (PhD); epidemiology (Dr PH); general health administration (DHA); general public administration (DPA); health advocacy and leadership (Dr PH); health care administration (PhD); health care leadership (DHA); health policy advocacy (DHA); multidisciplinary human services (PhD); nonprofit management and leadership (PhD); public safety leadership (PhD); social and community services (PhD).

Capella University, School of Public Service Leadership, Master's Programs in Healthcare, Minneapolis, MN 55402. Offers criminal justice (MS); emergency management (MS); general public health (MPH); gerontology (MS); health administration (MHA); health care operations (MHA); health management policy (MPH); health policy (MHA); homeland security (MS); multidisciplinary human services (MS); public administration (MPA); public safety leadership (MS); social and community services (MS); social behavioral sciences (MPH); MS/MPA.

Columbia Southern University, College of Safety and Emergency Services, Orange Beach, AL 36561. Offers criminal justice administration (MS); emergency services management (MS); occupational safety and health (MS), including environmental management. *Program availability:* Part-time, evening/weekend, online learning. *Entrance requirements:* For master's, bachelor's degree from accredited/approved institution. Additional exam requirements/recommendations for international students: required—TOEFL. Electronic applications accepted.

Drexel University, College of Nursing and Health Professions, Emergency and Public Safety Services Program, Philadelphia, PA 19104-2875. Offers MS. *Program availability:* Part-time, evening/weekend. *Degree requirements:* For master's, comprehensive exam. *Entrance requirements:* For master's, GRE General Test, minimum GPA of 2.75.

Endicott College, Endicott College School of Arts and Sciences, Program in Homeland Security, Beverly, MA 01915. Offers cybersecurity (MS, Postbaccalaureate Certificate); emergency management (MS). *Program availability:* Part-time, evening/weekend, 100% online. *Faculty:* 2 full-time (1 woman), 17 part-time/adjunct (4 women). *Students:* 16 full-time (7 women), 14 part-time (4 women); includes 5 minority (3 Black or African American, non-Hispanic/Latino; 2 Hispanic/Latino). Average age 29. 23 applicants, 74% accepted, 14 enrolled. In 2019, 18 master's, 2 other advanced degrees awarded. *Degree requirements:* For master's, Capstone project. *Entrance requirements:* For

master's, Updated resume; Official transcript of all post-secondary academic work; 250-500 word essay on specified topic; 2 letters of recommendation; interview with program director; for Postbaccalaureate Certificate, Same as Master's. Additional exam requirements/recommendations for international students: required—TOEFL. *Application deadline:* Applications are processed on a rolling basis. Application fee: $50. Electronic applications accepted. *Expenses:* Tuition varies by program. *Financial support:* Applicants required to submit FAFSA. *Unit head:* Dr. Joshua McCabe, Assistant Dean, Social Sciences, 978-232-2380, E-mail: gwong@endicott.edu. *Application contact:* Ian Menchini, Director, Graduate Enrollment and Advising, 978-232-5292, Fax: 978-232-3000, E-mail: imenchin@endicott.edu.
Website: https://www.endicott.edu/academics/schools/arts-sciences/graduate-programs/homeland-security-studies-program

Florida International University, Steven J. Green School of International and Public Affairs, Department of Emergency Management, Miami, FL 33199. Offers disaster management (MA). *Accreditation:* AACSB. *Program availability:* Part-time, evening/weekend. *Faculty:* 3 part-time/adjunct (all women). *Students:* 42 full-time (13 women), 3 part-time (all women); includes 35 minority (8 Black or African American, non-Hispanic/Latino; 26 Hispanic/Latino; 1 Two or more races, non-Hispanic/Latino). Average age 39. 70 applicants, 86% accepted, 39 enrolled. In 2019, 38 master's awarded. *Entrance requirements:* For master's, minimum GPA of 3.0 in upper-level coursework; resume. *Application deadline:* For fall admission, 6/1 for domestic and international students; for spring admission, 10/1 for domestic students, 9/1 for international students. Applications are processed on a rolling basis. Application fee: $30. Electronic applications accepted. *Expenses: Tuition, area resident:* Full-time $8912; part-time $446 per credit hour. Tuition, state resident: full-time $8912; part-time $446 per credit hour. Tuition, nonresident: full-time $21,393; part-time $992 per credit hour. *Required fees:* $2194. *Financial support:* Institutionally sponsored loans and scholarships/grants available. Financial award application deadline: 3/1; financial award applicants required to submit FAFSA. *Unit head:* Dulce Suarez, Director, 305-348-0451, E-mail: dulce.boza1@fiu.edu. *Application contact:* Nanett Rojas, Manager, Admissions Operations, 305-348-7464, Fax: 305-348-7441, E-mail: gradadm@fiu.edu.

Fordham University, Graduate School of Arts and Sciences, Program in International Humanitarian Action, New York, NY 10458. Offers MA. *Students:* Average age 37. 16 applicants. *Entrance requirements:* For master's, official transcripts, 3 letters of recommendation, resume, statement of interest. Application fee: $70. Electronic applications accepted. *Unit head:* Dr. Brendan Cahill, Executive Director, 212-636-6294, Fax: 212-636-7060, E-mail: iiha@fordham.edu. *Application contact:* Garrett Marino, Director of Graduate Admissions, 718-817-4419, Fax: 718-817-3566, E-mail: gmarino10@fordham.edu.
Website: http://www.fordham.edu/academics/programs_at_fordham_/international_humani/index.asp

Georgetown University, Graduate School of Arts and Sciences, School of Continuing Studies, Washington, DC 20057. Offers American studies (MALS); applied intelligence (MPS); Catholic studies (MALS); classical civilizations (MALS); emergency and disaster management (MPS); ethics and the professions (MALS); global strategic communications (MPS); hospitality management (MPS); human resources management (MPS); humanities (MALS); individualized study (MALS); integrated marketing communications (MPS); international affairs (MALS); Islam and Muslim-Christian relations (MALS); journalism (MPS); liberal studies (DLS); literature and society (MALS); medieval and early modern European studies (MALS); public relations and corporate communications (MPS); real estate (MPS); religious studies (MALS); social and public policy (MALS); sports industry management (MPS); systems engineering management (MPS); technology management (MPS); the theory and practice of American democracy (MALS); urban and regional planning (MPS); visual culture (MALS). *Entrance requirements:* Additional exam requirements/recommendations for international students: required—TOEFL.

The George Washington University, School of Medicine and Health Sciences, Health Sciences Programs, Washington, DC 20052. Offers clinical practice management (MSHS); clinical research administration (MSHS); emergency services management (MSHS); end-of-life care (MSHS); immunohematology (MSHS); immunohematology and biotechnology (MSHS); physical therapy (DPT); physician assistant (MSHS). *Program availability:* Online learning. *Entrance requirements:* Additional exam requirements/recommendations for international students: required—TOEFL (minimum score 550 paper-based). *Expenses:* Contact institution.

Georgia State University, Andrew Young School of Policy Studies, Department of Public Management and Policy, Atlanta, GA 30303. Offers criminal justice (MPA); disaster management (Certificate); disaster policy (MPA); environmental policy (PhD); health policy (PhD); management and finance (MPA); nonprofit management (MPA, Certificate); nonprofit policy (MPA); planning and economic development (MPP, Certificate); policy analysis and evaluation (MPA), including planning and economic development; public and nonprofit management (PhD); public finance and budgeting (PhD), including science and technology policy, urban and regional economic development; public finance policy (MPA), including social policy; public health (MPA). *Accreditation:* NASPAA (one or more programs are accredited). *Program availability:* Part-time. *Faculty:* 13 full-time (7 women), 3 part-time/adjunct (1 woman). *Students:* 125 full-time (81 women), 91 part-time (66 women); includes 103 minority (78 Black or African American, non-Hispanic/Latino; 3 Asian, non-Hispanic/Latino; 14 Hispanic/Latino; 8 Two or more races, non-Hispanic/Latino), 31 international. Average age 32. 298 applicants, 60% accepted, 82 enrolled. In 2019, 70 master's, 8 other advanced degrees awarded. Terminal master's awarded for partial completion of doctoral program. *Degree requirements:* For master's, thesis optional; for doctorate, comprehensive exam, thesis/dissertation. *Entrance requirements:* For master's and doctorate, GRE. Additional exam requirements/recommendations for international students: required—TOEFL (minimum score 603 paper-based; 100 iBT) or IELTS (minimum score 7). *Application deadline:* For fall admission, 1/15 for domestic and international students. Application fee: $50. Electronic applications accepted. *Expenses: Tuition, area resident:* Full-time $7164; part-time $398 per credit hour. Tuition, state resident: full-time $7164; part-time $398 per credit hour. Tuition, nonresident: full-time $22,662; part-time $1259 per credit hour. *International tuition:* $22,662 full-time. *Required fees:* $2128; $312 per credit hour. Tuition and fees vary according to course load and program. *Financial support:* In 2019–20, fellowships (averaging $8,194 per year), research assistantships (averaging $8,068 per year), teaching assistantships (averaging $3,600 per year) were awarded; institutionally sponsored loans, scholarships/grants, health care benefits, and unspecified assistantships also available. Financial award application deadline: 2/1. *Unit head:* Dr. Cathy Yang Liu, Chair and Professor, 404-413-0102, Fax: 404-413-0104, E-mail: cyliu@gsu.edu. *Application contact:* Dr. Cathy Yang Liu, Chair and Professor, 404-413-0102, Fax: 404-413-0104, E-mail: cyliu@gsu.edu.
Website: https://aysps.gsu.edu/public-management-policy/

Grand Canyon University, Colangelo College of Business, Phoenix, AZ 85017-1097. Offers accounting (MBA, MS); business analytics (MS); disaster preparedness and executive fire service leadership (MS); finance (MBA); general management (MBA); health systems management (MBA); information technology management (MS);

leadership (MBA, MS); marketing (MBA); organizational leadership and entrepreneurship (MS); project management (MBA); sports business (MBA); strategic human resource management (MBA). *Accreditation:* ACBSP. *Program availability:* Part-time, evening/weekend, online learning. *Entrance requirements:* For master's, equivalent of two years' full-time professional work experience. Additional exam requirements/recommendations for international students: required—TOEFL (minimum score 575 paper-based; 90 iBT), IELTS (minimum score 7). Electronic applications accepted.

Indiana University-Purdue University Indianapolis, School of Public and Environmental Affairs, Indianapolis, IN 46202. Offers criminal justice and public safety (MS); homeland security and emergency management (Graduate Certificate); library management (Graduate Certificate); nonprofit management (Graduate Certificate); public affairs (MPA); public management (Graduate Certificate); social entrepreneurship: nonprofit and public benefit organizations (Graduate Certificate); JD/MPA; MLS/NMC; MLS/PMC; MPA/MA. *Accreditation:* CAHME (one or more programs are accredited); NASPAA. *Program availability:* Part-time, evening/weekend, online learning. *Entrance requirements:* For master's, GRE General Test, GMAT or LSAT, minimum GPA of 3.0 (preferred). Additional exam requirements/recommendations for international students: required—TOEFL (minimum score 93 iBT), IELTS (minimum score 6.5). Electronic applications accepted.

Jacksonville State University, Graduate Studies, School of Human Services and Social Sciences, Department of Emergency Management, Jacksonville, AL 36265-1602. Offers MS, D Sc. *Program availability:* Part-time, evening/weekend. *Degree requirements:* For master's, comprehensive exam, thesis (for some programs); for doctorate, comprehensive exam, thesis/dissertation. *Entrance requirements:* Additional exam requirements/recommendations for international students: required—TOEFL (minimum score 500 paper-based; 61 iBT). Electronic applications accepted.

Lander University, Graduate Studies, Greenwood, SC 29649-2099. Offers clinical nurse leader (MSN); emergency management (MS); Montessori education (M Ed); teaching and learning (M Ed). *Accreditation:* NCATE. *Program availability:* Part-time, online learning. *Degree requirements:* For master's, comprehensive exam, thesis or alternative. *Entrance requirements:* For master's, GRE General Test. Additional exam requirements/recommendations for international students: required—TOEFL (minimum score 550 paper-based). Electronic applications accepted.

Lasell College, Graduate and Professional Studies in Criminal Justice, Newton, MA 02466-2709. Offers emergency and crisis management (MS, Certificate); homeland security and global justice (MS, Certificate); violence prevention and advocacy (MS, Certificate). *Program availability:* Part-time, evening/weekend, online only, 100% online. *Faculty:* 6 full-time (3 women), 1 part-time/adjunct (0 women). *Students:* 28 full-time (5 women), 71 part-time (21 women); includes 27 minority (9 Black or African American, non-Hispanic/Latino; 2 Asian, non-Hispanic/Latino; 13 Hispanic/Latino; 3 Two or more races, non-Hispanic/Latino). Average age 33. 38 applicants, 63% accepted, 17 enrolled. In 2019, 33 master's awarded. *Degree requirements:* For master's, minimum GPA of 3.0; internship or research paper. *Entrance requirements:* For master's, one-page personal statement, 2 letters of recommendation, resume, bachelor's degree transcript; for Certificate, bachelor's transcript, 2 letters of recommendation, 1-page statement, resume. Additional exam requirements/recommendations for international students: required—TOEFL (minimum score 550 paper-based, 79 iBT) or IELTS (minimum score 6). *Application deadline:* For fall admission, 8/31 priority date for domestic students, 6/30 priority date for international students; for spring admission, 12/31 priority date for domestic students, 10/31 priority date for international students. Applications are processed on a rolling basis. Electronic applications accepted. *Expenses: Tuition:* Part-time $600 per credit. *Required fees:* $40 per semester. *Financial support:* Federal Work-Study, scholarships/grants, and tuition discounts available. Support available to part-time students. Financial award application deadline: 8/31; financial award applicants required to submit FAFSA. *Unit head:* Chrystal Porter, Vice President of Graduate and Professional Studies, 617-243-2083, Fax: 617-243-2450, E-mail: gradinfo@lasell.edu. *Application contact:* Adrienne Franciosi, Assistant Vice President of Graduate and Professional Studies, 617-243-2214, Fax: 617-243-2450, E-mail: gradinfo@lasell.edu.
Website: http://www.lasell.edu/academics/graduate-and-professional-studies/programs-of-study/master-of-science-in-criminal-justice-.html

Liberty University, School of Behavioral Sciences, Lynchburg, VA 24515. Offers applied psychology (MA), including developmental psychology (MA, MS), industrial/organizational psychology (MA, MS); clinical mental health counseling (MA); community care and counseling (Ed D), including marriage and family counseling, pastoral care and counseling, traumatology; counselor education and supervision (PhD); human services counseling (MA), including addictions and recovery, business, child and family law, Christian ministries, criminal justice, crisis response and trauma, executive leadership, health and wellness, life coaching, marriage and family, military resilience; marriage and family counseling (MA); marriage and family therapy (MA); military resilience (Certificate); pastoral counseling (MA), including addictions and recovery, community chaplaincy, crisis response and trauma, discipleship and church ministry, leadership, life coaching, marriage and family, marriage and family studies, military resilience, parenting and child/adolescent, pastoral counseling, theology; professional counseling (MA); psychology (MS), including developmental psychology (MA, MS), industrial/organizational psychology (MA, MS); school counseling (M Ed). *Program availability:* Part-time, online learning. *Students:* 3,786 full-time (3,065 women), 5,193 part-time (4,081 women); includes 2,733 minority (1,967 Black or African American, non-Hispanic/Latino; 48 American Indian or Alaska Native, non-Hispanic/Latino; 103 Asian, non-Hispanic/Latino; 349 Hispanic/Latino; 19 Native Hawaiian or other Pacific Islander, non-Hispanic/Latino; 247 Two or more races, non-Hispanic/Latino), 133 international. Average age 38. 13,324 applicants, 28% accepted, 2,163 enrolled. In 2019, 2,322 master's, 19 doctorates, 112 other advanced degrees awarded. *Entrance requirements:* For master's, Official bachelor's degree transcripts with a 2.0 GPA or higher. *Application deadline:* Applications are processed on a rolling basis. Application fee: $50. Electronic applications accepted. *Expenses: Tuition:* Full-time $545; part-time $410 per credit hour. One-time fee: $50. *Financial support:* In 2019–20, 1,003 students received support. Teaching assistantships and Federal Work-Study available. Financial award applicants required to submit FAFSA. *Unit head:* Dr. Kenyon Knapp, Dean, School of Behavioral Services, E-mail: kcknapp@liberty.edu. *Application contact:* Jay Bridge, Director of Admissions, 800-424-9595, Fax: 800-628-7977, E-mail: gradadmissions@liberty.edu.
Website: https://www.liberty.edu/behavioral-sciences/

London Metropolitan University, Graduate Programs, London, United Kingdom. Offers applied psychology (M Sc); architecture (MA); biomedical science (M Sc); blood science (M Sc); cancer pharmacology (M Sc); computer networking and cyber security (M Sc); computing and information systems (M Sc); conference interpreting (MA); counter-terrorism studies (M Sc); creative, digital and professional writing (MA); crime, violence and prevention (M Sc); criminology (M Sc); curating contemporary art (MA); data analytics (M Sc); digital media (MA); early childhood studies (MA); education (MA, Ed D); financial services law, regulation and compliance (LL M); food science (M Sc); forensic psychology (M Sc); health and social care management and policy (M Sc); human nutrition (M Sc); human resource management (MA); human rights and international conflict (MA); information technology (M Sc); intelligence and security studies (M Sc); international oil, gas and energy law (LL M); international relations (MA); interpreting (MA); learning and teaching in higher education (MA); legal practice (LL M); media and entertainment law (LL M); organizational and consumer psychology (M Sc); psychological therapy (M Sc); psychology of mental health (M Sc); public health (M Sc); public policy and management (MPA); security studies (M Sc); social work (M Sc); spatial planning and urban design (MA); sports therapy (M Sc); supporting older children and young people with dyslexia (MA); teaching languages (MA), including Arabic, English; translation (MA); woman and child abuse (MA).

Massachusetts Maritime Academy, Program in Emergency Management, Buzzards Bay, MA 02532-1803. Offers MS. *Program availability:* Evening/weekend. Electronic applications accepted. *Expenses:* Contact institution.

Metropolitan College of New York, Program in Public Administration, New York, NY 10006. Offers emergency and disaster management (MPA); public affairs and administration (MPA). *Program availability:* Evening/weekend. *Degree requirements:* For master's, thesis. *Entrance requirements:* For master's, appropriate work experience, interview, minimum GPA of 2.7, internship or job in administrative setting. Additional exam requirements/recommendations for international students: required—TOEFL (minimum score 600 paper-based). Electronic applications accepted. *Expenses:* Contact institution.

Millersville University of Pennsylvania, College of Graduate Studies and Adult Learning, College of Science and Technology, Emergency Management, Millersville, PA 17551-0302. Offers emergency management (MS). *Program availability:* Part-time, online only, 100% online. *Students:* 10 full-time (3 women), 47 part-time (12 women); includes 13 minority (3 Black or African American, non-Hispanic/Latino; 1 Asian, non-Hispanic/Latino; 5 Hispanic/Latino; 4 Two or more races, non-Hispanic/Latino). Average age 32. 25 applicants, 100% accepted, 18 enrolled. In 2019, 17 master's awarded. *Entrance requirements:* For master's, GRE or MAT (if undergraduate cumulative GPA is lower than 2.8, resume. Additional exam requirements/recommendations for international students: required—TOEFL, IELTS (minimum score 6), PTE (minimum score 60). *Application deadline:* Applications are processed on a rolling basis. Application fee: $40. Electronic applications accepted. *Expenses:* Master of Science in Emergency Management: $516 per credit resident tuition, $601.75 per credit non-resident tuition, $61 per credit academic support fee (resident and non-resident), $28 per credit resident tech fee, $40 per credit non-resident tech fee. *Financial support:* In 2019–20, 3 students received support. Scholarships/grants and unspecified assistantships available. Financial award application deadline: 3/15; financial award applicants required to submit FAFSA. *Unit head:* Dr. Sepideh Yalda, Director and Graduate Program Coordinator, 717-871-7433, Fax: 717-871-2429, E-mail: sepi.yalda@millersville.edu. *Application contact:* Dr. James A. Delle, Acting Dean of College of Graduate Studies and Adult Learning/Associate Provost, Academic Administration, 717-871-7462, E-mail: James.Delle@millersville.edu.
Website: https://www.millersville.edu/cdre/msem/index.php

National University, School of Professional Studies, La Jolla, CA 92037-1011. Offers criminal justice (MCJ); digital cinema production (MFA); digital journalism (MA); homeland security and emergency management (MS); juvenile justice (MS); professional screenwriting (MFA); public administration (MPA), including human resource management, organizational leadership. *Program availability:* Part-time, evening/weekend, 100% online, blended/hybrid learning. *Degree requirements:* For master's, thesis (for some programs). *Entrance requirements:* For master's, interview, minimum GPA of 2.5. Additional exam requirements/recommendations for international students: required—TOEFL (minimum score 550 paper-based; 79 iBT), IELTS (minimum score 6). Electronic applications accepted. *Expenses: Tuition:* Full-time $442; part-time $442 per unit.

New York Medical College, School of Health Sciences and Practice, Valhalla, NY 10595. Offers behavioral sciences and health promotion (MPH); biostatistics (MS); children with special health care (Graduate Certificate); emergency preparedness (Graduate Certificate); environmental health science (MPH); epidemiology (MPH, MS); global health (Graduate Certificate); health education (Graduate Certificate); health policy and management (MPH, Dr PH); industrial hygiene (Graduate Certificate); pediatric dysphagia (Post-Graduate Certificate); physical therapy (DPT); public health (Graduate Certificate); speech-language pathology (MS). *Accreditation:* ASHA; CEPH. *Program availability:* Part-time, evening/weekend, 100% online, blended/hybrid learning. *Faculty:* 47 full-time (34 women), 203 part-time/adjunct (125 women). *Students:* 230 full-time (171 women), 292 part-time (207 women); includes 204 minority (73 Black or African American, non-Hispanic/Latino; 4 American Indian or Alaska Native, non-Hispanic/Latino; 59 Asian, non-Hispanic/Latino; 54 Hispanic/Latino; 1 Native Hawaiian or other Pacific Islander, non-Hispanic/Latino; 13 Two or more races, non-Hispanic/Latino), 35 international. Average age 29. 790 applicants, 61% accepted, 162 enrolled. In 2019, 113 master's, 47 doctorates awarded. *Degree requirements:* For master's, comprehensive exam (for some programs), thesis (for some programs); for doctorate, thesis/dissertation. *Entrance requirements:* For master's, GRE (for MS in speech-language pathology); for doctorate, GRE (for Doctor of Physical Therapy and Doctor of Public Health). Additional exam requirements/recommendations for international students: required—TOEFL (minimum score 96 paper-based; 24 iBT), IELTS (minimum score 7). *Application deadline:* For fall admission, 8/1 for domestic students, 4/15 for international students; for spring admission, 12/1 for domestic students; for summer admission, 5/1 for domestic students, 4/15 for international students. Applications are processed on a rolling basis. Application fee: $128 ($120 for international students). Electronic applications accepted. *Expenses:* $1195 credit fee, academic support fee $200, Student activities fee $140 per year, technology fee $150. *Financial support:* In 2019–20, 18 students received support. Federal Work-Study, scholarships/grants, unspecified assistantships, and Federal student loans available. Financial award application deadline: 4/30; financial award applicants required to submit FAFSA. *Unit head:* Ben Johnson, PhD, Vice Dean, 914-594-4531, E-mail: bjohnson23@nymc.edu. *Application contact:* Irene Bundziak, Assistant to Director of Admissions, 914-594-4905, E-mail: irene_bundziak@nymc.edu.
Website: http://www.nymc.edu/school-of-health-sciences-and-practice-shsp/

Norwich University, College of Graduate and Continuing Studies, Master of Public Administration Program, Northfield, VT 05663. Offers criminal justice and public safety (MPA); fiscal management (MPA); international development and influence (MPA); municipal governance (MPA); nonprofit management (MPA); policy analysis and analytics (MPA); public administration leadership and crisis management (MPA); public works and sustainability (MPA). *Program availability:* Evening/weekend, online only, mostly all online with a week-long residency requirement. *Degree requirements:* For master's, capstone. *Entrance requirements:* For master's, minimum undergraduate GPA of 2.75. Additional exam requirements/recommendations for international students: required—TOEFL (minimum score 550 paper-based; 80 iBT), IELTS (minimum score 6.5). Electronic applications accepted. *Expenses:* Contact institution.

Nova Southeastern University, Dr. Kiran C. Patel College of Osteopathic Medicine, Fort Lauderdale, FL 33314-7796. Offers biomedical informatics (MS, Graduate Certificate), including biomedical informatics (MS), clinical informatics (Graduate Certificate), public health informatics (Graduate Certificate); disaster and emergency management (MS); medical education (MS); nutrition (MS, Graduate Certificate),

including functional nutrition and herbal therapy (Graduate Certificate); osteopathic medicine (DO); public health (MPH, Graduate Certificate), including health education (Graduate Certificate); social medicine (Graduate Certificate); DO/DMD. *Accreditation:* AOsA; CEPH. *Program availability:* Part-time, 100% online, blended/hybrid learning. *Faculty:* 73 full-time (43 women), 35 part-time/adjunct (14 women). *Students:* 1,410 full-time (740 women), 182 part-time (118 women); includes 895 minority (126 Black or African American, non-Hispanic/Latino; 1 American Indian or Alaska Native, non-Hispanic/Latino; 416 Asian, non-Hispanic/Latino; 309 Hispanic/Latino; 1 Native Hawaiian or other Pacific Islander, non-Hispanic/Latino; 42 Two or more races, non-Hispanic/Latino), 70 international. Average age 26. 5,078 applicants, 10% accepted, 495 enrolled. In 2019, 117 master's, 233 doctorates, 3 other advanced degrees awarded. *Degree requirements:* For master's, comprehensive exam (for MPH); field/special projects; for doctorate, comprehensive exam, COMLEX Board Exams; for Graduate Certificate, thesis or alternative. *Entrance requirements:* For master's, GRE; for doctorate, MCAT, coursework in biology, chemistry, organic chemistry, physics (all with labs), biochemistry, and English. *Application deadline:* For fall admission, 1/15 for domestic students. Applications are processed on a rolling basis. Application fee: $50. Electronic applications accepted. *Expenses:* Contact institution. *Financial support:* In 2019–20, 83 students received support, including 24 fellowships with tuition reimbursements available; Federal Work-Study and scholarships/grants also available. Financial award application deadline: 6/1; financial award applicants required to submit FAFSA. *Unit head:* Elaine M. Wallace, Dean, 954-262-1457, Fax: 954-262-2250, E-mail: ewallace@nova.edu. *Application contact:* HPD Admissions, 877-640-0218, E-mail: hpdinfo@nova.edu.
Website: https://www.osteopathic.nova.edu/

Oklahoma State University, College of Arts and Sciences, Department of Political Science, Stillwater, OK 74078. Offers fire and emergency management administration (MS, PhD); political science (MA). *Faculty:* 9 full-time (5 women). *Students:* 9 full-time (1 woman), 4 part-time (3 women); includes 3 minority (2 Black or African American, non-Hispanic/Latino; 1 Asian, non-Hispanic/Latino), 1 international. Average age 25. 12 applicants, 67% accepted, 6 enrolled. In 2019, 11 master's awarded. *Entrance requirements:* For master's and doctorate, GRE. Additional exam requirements/recommendations for international students: required—TOEFL (minimum score 550 paper-based; 79 iBT). *Application deadline:* For fall admission, 3/1 priority date for international students; for spring admission, 8/1 priority date for international students. Applications are processed on a rolling basis. Application fee: $50 ($75 for international students). Electronic applications accepted. *Expenses: Tuition, area resident:* Full-time $4148.10; part-time $2765.40 per credit hour. Tuition, state resident: full-time $4148.10; part-time $2765.40 per credit hour. Tuition, nonresident: full-time $15,775; part-time $10,516.80 per credit hour. *International tuition:* $15,775.20 full-time. *Required fees:* $2196.90; $122.05 per credit hour. Tuition and fees vary according to course load, campus/location and program. *Financial support:* In 2019–20, 9 teaching assistantships (averaging $1,625 per year) were awarded; research assistantships, career-related internships or fieldwork, Federal Work-Study, scholarships/grants, health care benefits, tuition waivers (partial), and unspecified assistantships also available. Support available to part-time students. Financial award application deadline: 3/1; financial award applicants required to submit FAFSA. *Unit head:* Dr. Rebekah Herrick, Interim Department Head, 405-744-8437, E-mail: rebekah.herrick@okstate.edu. *Application contact:* Dr. Sheryl Tucker, Dean, 405-744-6368, Fax: 405-744-0355, E-mail: gradi@okstate.edu.
Website: http://polsci.okstate.edu

Pace University, Dyson College of Arts and Sciences, MA Program in Management for Public Safety and Homeland Security Professionals, New York, NY 10038. Offers MA. *Program availability:* Evening/weekend, blended/hybrid learning. *Degree requirements:* For master's, project. *Entrance requirements:* For master's, 2 letters of recommendation, resume, personal statement, official transcripts. Additional exam requirements/recommendations for international students: required—TOEFL. Electronic applications accepted.

Park University, School of Graduate and Professional Studies, Kansas City, MO 54105. Offers adult education (M Ed); business and government leadership (Graduate Certificate); business, government, and global society (MPA); communication and leadership (MA); creative and life writing (Graduate Certificate); disaster and emergency management (MPA, Graduate Certificate); educational leadership (M Ed); finance (MBA, Graduate Certificate); general business (MBA); global business (Graduate Certificate); healthcare administration (MHA); healthcare services management and leadership (Graduate Certificate); international business (MBA); language and literacy (M Ed), including English for speakers of other languages, special reading teacher/literacy coach; leadership of international healthcare organizations (Graduate Certificate); management information systems (MBA, Graduate Certificate); music performance (ADP, Graduate Certificate), including cello (MM, ADP), piano (MM, ADP), viola (MM, ADP), violin (MM, ADP); nonprofit and community services management (MPA); nonprofit leadership (Graduate Certificate); performance (MM), including cello (MM, ADP), piano (MM, ADP), viola (MM, ADP), violin (MM, ADP); public management (MPA); social work (MSW); teacher leadership (M Ed), including curriculum and assessment, instructional leader. *Program availability:* Part-time, evening/weekend, online learning. *Degree requirements:* For master's, comprehensive exam (for some programs), thesis (for some programs), internship (for some programs); exam (for some programs). *Entrance requirements:* For master's, GRE or GMAT (for some programs), teacher certification (for some M Ed programs), letters of recommendation, essay, resume (for some programs). Additional exam requirements/recommendations for international students: required—TOEFL (minimum score 550 paper-based; 79 iBT), IELTS (minimum score 6). Electronic applications accepted.

Post University, Program in Public Administration, Waterbury, CT 06723-2540. Offers emergency management and homeland security (MPA). *Program availability:* Online learning. *Degree requirements:* For master's, capstone project. *Entrance requirements:* For master's, resume.

Regent University, Graduate School, Robertson School of Government, Virginia Beach, VA 23464. Offers government (MA), including American government, healthcare policy and ethics (MA, MPA), international relations, law and public policy, national security studies, political communication, political theory, religion and politics; national security studies (MA), including cybersecurity, homeland security, international security, Middle East politics; public administration (MPA), including emergency management and homeland security, federal government, general public administration, healthcare policy and ethics (MA, MPA), law, nonprofit administration and faith-based organizations, public leadership and management, servant leadership. *Program availability:* Part-time, evening/weekend, 100% online, blended/hybrid learning. *Faculty:* 5 full-time (1 woman), 19 part-time/adjunct (2 women). *Students:* 36 full-time (22 women), 159 part-time (89 women); includes 82 minority (52 Black or African American, non-Hispanic/Latino; 2 American Indian or Alaska Native, non-Hispanic/Latino; 2 Asian, non-Hispanic/Latino; 23 Hispanic/Latino; 3 Two or more races, non-Hispanic/Latino), 4 international. Average age 36. 181 applicants, 70% accepted, 75 enrolled. In 2019, 58 master's awarded. *Degree requirements:* For master's, thesis optional, internship. *Entrance requirements:* For master's, GRE General Test or LSAT, personal essay,

writing sample, resume, college transcripts. Additional exam requirements/recommendations for international students: required—TOEFL (minimum score 577 paper-based). *Application deadline:* For fall admission, 5/1 priority date for domestic students; for spring admission, 11/1 priority date for domestic students. Applications are processed on a rolling basis. Application fee: $50. Electronic applications accepted. *Expenses:* Contact institution. *Financial support:* In 2019–20, 132 students received support. Career-related internships or fieldwork, scholarships/grants, and unspecified assistantships available. Support available to part-time students. Financial award applicants required to submit FAFSA. *Unit head:* Dr. Stephen Perry, Interim Dean, 757-352-4082, E-mail: sperry@regent.edu. *Application contact:* Heidi Cece, Assistant Vice President for Enrollment Management, 800-373-5504, Fax: 757-352-4381, E-mail: admissions@regent.edu.
Website: https://www.regent.edu/robertson-school-of-government/

Royal Roads University, Graduate Studies, Peace and Conflict Studies Program, Victoria, BC V9B 5Y2, Canada. Offers conflict analysis (G Dip); conflict analysis and management (MA); disaster and emergency management (MA, G Dip); human security and peacebuilding (MA, G Dip); justice studies (G Dip); peace and conflict studies (MAIS). *Program availability:* Blended/hybrid learning. *Degree requirements:* For master's, thesis. *Entrance requirements:* For master's, 5-7 years of related work experience. Additional exam requirements/recommendations for international students: required—TOEFL (minimum score 570 paper-based) or IELTS (7) recommended. Electronic applications accepted.

Rutgers University - New Brunswick, School of Public Health, Piscataway, NJ 08854. Offers biostatistics (MPH, MS, Dr PH, PhD); clinical epidemiology (Certificate); environmental and occupational health (MPH, Dr PH, PhD, Certificate); epidemiology (MPH, Dr PH, PhD); general public health (Certificate); health education and behavioral science (MPH, Dr PH, PhD); health systems and policy (MPH, PhD); public health (MPH, Dr PH, PhD); public health preparedness (Certificate); DO/MPH; JD/MPH; MBA/MPH; MD/MPH; MPH/MBA; MPH/MSPA; MS/MPH; Psy D/MPH. *Accreditation:* CEPH. *Program availability:* Part-time, evening/weekend. *Degree requirements:* For master's, thesis, internship; for doctorate, comprehensive exam, thesis/dissertation. *Entrance requirements:* For master's, GRE General Test; for doctorate, GRE General Test, MPH (Dr PH); MA, MPH, or MS (PhD). Additional exam requirements/recommendations for international students: required—TOEFL. Electronic applications accepted.

Saint Leo University, Graduate Studies in Public Safety Administration, Saint Leo, FL 33574-6665. Offers criminal justice (MS, DCJ), including behavioral studies (MS), corrections (MS), criminal investigation (MS), criminal justice (MS), emergency and disaster management (MS), forensic science (MS), legal studies (MS); emergency and disaster management (MS), including emergency and disaster management, fire science. *Program availability:* Part-time, evening/weekend, 100% online, blended/hybrid learning. *Faculty:* 10 full-time (4 women), 26 part-time/adjunct (6 women). *Students:* 1 (woman) full-time, 761 part-time (490 women); includes 466 minority (252 Black or African American, non-Hispanic/Latino; 4 American Indian or Alaska Native, non-Hispanic/Latino; 5 Asian, non-Hispanic/Latino; 94 Hispanic/Latino; 111 Two or more races, non-Hispanic/Latino). Average age 37. 314 applicants, 82% accepted, 173 enrolled. In 2019, 236 master's, 2 doctorates awarded. *Degree requirements:* For master's, comprehensive project; for doctorate, thesis/dissertation. *Entrance requirements:* For master's, official transcripts, bachelor's degree from regionally-accredited university with minimum GPA of 3.0, statement of professional goals; for doctorate, Official transcript showing completion of Master's degree with a minimum graduate gpa of 3.25, statement of professional goals, two letter of reference (professional or personal). Additional exam requirements/recommendations for international students: required—TOEFL (minimum score 550 paper-based; 78 iBT). *Application deadline:* For fall admission, 7/1 priority date for domestic and international students; for spring admission, 11/1 priority date for domestic and international students. Applications are processed on a rolling basis. Electronic applications accepted. *Expenses:* MS in Criminal Justice $10,770 per FT yr., DCJ $14,101 per FT yr. *Financial support:* In 2019–20, 62 students received support. Scholarships/grants, health care benefits, and tuition remission for Saint Leo employees and their dependents available. Financial award application deadline: 3/1; financial award applicants required to submit FAFSA. *Unit head:* Dr. Robert Diemer, Director of Graduate Studies in Public Safety Administration, 352-588-8974, Fax: 352-588-8660, E-mail: graduatepublicsafety@saintleo.edu. *Application contact:* Saint Leo University Office of Graduate Admissions, 800-707-8846, Fax: 352-588-7873, E-mail: grad.admissions@saintleo.edu.
Website: https://www.saintleo.edu/criminal-justice-master-degree

Saint Louis University, Graduate Programs, College for Public Health and Social Justice, Program in Criminology and Criminal Justice, St. Louis, MO 63103. Offers administration of justice (MA); emergency management (MA); treatment and rehabilitation (MA). *Program availability:* Part-time. *Degree requirements:* For master's, comprehensive exam. *Entrance requirements:* For master's, GRE General Test, two letters of recommendation, resume, transcripts. Additional exam requirements/recommendations for international students: required—TOEFL (minimum score 525 paper-based).

San Diego State University, Graduate and Research Affairs, College of Health and Human Services, School of Public Health, San Diego, CA 92182. Offers environmental health (MPH); epidemiology (MPH, PhD), including biostatistics (MPH); global emergency preparedness and response (MS); global health (PhD); health behavior (PhD); health promotion (MPH); health services administration (MPH); toxicology (MS); MPH/MA; MSW/MPH. *Accreditation:* CAHME (one or more programs are accredited); CEPH. *Program availability:* Part-time. *Degree requirements:* For master's, comprehensive exam (for some programs), thesis (for some programs); for doctorate, thesis/dissertation. *Entrance requirements:* For master's, GMAT (MPH in health services administration), GRE General Test; for doctorate, GRE General Test. Additional exam requirements/recommendations for international students: required—TOEFL.

Sul Ross State University, College of Professional Studies, Department of Criminal Justice, Alpine, TX 79832. Offers criminal justice (MS); homeland security (MS); MS/MA. *Entrance requirements:* For master's, GRE General Test, minimum GPA of 2.5 in last 60 hours of undergraduate work.

Syracuse University, David B. Falk College of Sport and Human Dynamics, CAS Program in Trauma-Informed Practice, Syracuse, NY 13244. Offers CAS. *Program availability:* Part-time. *Entrance requirements:* For degree, three letters of recommendation, transcripts, personal statement, resume. Additional exam requirements/recommendations for international students: required—TOEFL or IELTS. Electronic applications accepted.

Thomas Jefferson University, Jefferson College of Health Professions, Program in Disaster Medicine and Management, Philadelphia, PA 19107. Offers MS. *Program availability:* Online learning.

Trident University International, College of Health Sciences, Program in Health Sciences, Cypress, CA 90630. Offers clinical research administration (MS, Certificate); emergency and disaster management (MS, Certificate); environmental health science (Certificate); health care administration (PhD); health care management (MS), including health informatics; health education (MS, Certificate); health informatics (Certificate); health sciences (PhD); international health (MS); international health: educator or researcher option (PhD); international health: practitioner option (PhD); law and expert witness studies (MS, Certificate); public health (MS); quality assurance (Certificate). *Program availability:* Part-time, evening/weekend, online learning. *Degree requirements:* For doctorate, comprehensive exam, thesis/dissertation, defense of dissertation. *Entrance requirements:* For master's, minimum GPA of 2.5 (students with GPA 3.0 or greater may transfer up to 30% of graduate level credits); for doctorate, minimum GPA of 3.4, curriculum vitae, course work in research methods or statistics. Additional exam requirements/recommendations for international students: required—TOEFL. Electronic applications accepted.

Trine University, Program in Criminal Justice, Angola, IN 46703-1764. Offers emergency management (MS). *Program availability:* Part-time, evening/weekend, online only, 100% online, blended/hybrid learning. *Entrance requirements:* Additional exam requirements/recommendations for international students: required—TOEFL. Electronic applications accepted. *Expenses:* Contact institution.

Tulane University, School of Social Work, New Orleans, LA 70118-5669. Offers city, culture and community (PhD); disaster resilience leadership (MS); social work (MSW, DSW). *Accreditation:* CSWE (one or more programs are accredited). *Program availability:* Part-time. *Degree requirements:* For master's, thesis. *Entrance requirements:* Additional exam requirements/recommendations for international students: required—TOEFL. Electronic applications accepted. *Expenses: Tuition:* Full-time $57,004; part-time $3167 per credit hour. *Required fees:* $2086; $44.50 per credit hour. $80 per term. Tuition and fees vary according to course load, degree level and program.

Université de Montréal, Faculty of Medicine, Programs in Environment and Prevention, Montréal, QC H3C 3J7, Canada. Offers environment, health and disaster management (DESS). Electronic applications accepted.

University at Albany, State University of New York, College of Emergency Preparedness, Homeland Security and Cybersecurity, Albany, NY 12222-0001. Offers cybersecurity (Certificate); emergency preparedness (Certificate); homeland security (Certificate); information science (MS, PhD). *Program availability:* 100% online, blended/hybrid learning. *Faculty:* 25 full-time (9 women), 35 part-time/adjunct (11 women). *Students:* 63 full-time (44 women), 127 part-time (93 women); includes 31 minority (9 Black or African American, non-Hispanic/Latino; 3 Asian, non-Hispanic/Latino; 18 Hispanic/Latino; 1 Two or more races, non-Hispanic/Latino), 22 international. Average age 27. 173 applicants, 77% accepted, 76 enrolled. In 2019, 35 master's, 2 doctorates, 24 other advanced degrees awarded. *Degree requirements:* For doctorate, thesis/dissertation optional. *Entrance requirements:* For master's and doctorate, GRE, transcripts from all schools attended, 3 letters of recommendation, resume, personal statement. Additional exam requirements/recommendations for international students: required—TOEFL (minimum score 550 paper-based). *Application deadline:* For fall admission, 1/15 for domestic students; for spring admission, 11/15 for domestic students. Application fee: $75. Electronic applications accepted. *Expenses: Tuition, area resident:* Full-time $11,530; part-time $480 per credit hour. Tuition, nonresident: full-time $23,530; part-time $980 per credit hour. International tuition: $23,530 full-time. *Required fees:* $2185; $96 per credit hour. Part-time tuition and fees vary according to course load and program. *Financial support:* Research assistantships, teaching assistantships, career-related internships or fieldwork, traineeships, and unspecified assistantships available. *Unit head:* Dr. Robert Griffin, Dean, 518-442-5258, E-mail: rpgriffin@albany.edu. *Application contact:* Jennifer J Goodall, Vice Dean, 518-949-3283, E-mail: jgoodall@albany.edu.
Website: http://www.albany.edu/cehc/

University of Alaska Fairbanks, School of Management, Program in Security and Disaster Management, Fairbanks, AK 99775-7520. Offers MSDM. *Program availability:* Part-time, evening/weekend, 100% online, blended/hybrid learning. *Entrance requirements:* For master's, Watson-Glaser Critical Thinking Appraisal, bachelor's degree from accredited institution with minimum cumulative undergraduate and major GPA of 2.75. Additional exam requirements/recommendations for international students: required—TOEFL (minimum score 79 iBT), IELTS (minimum score 6.5). Electronic applications accepted. *Expenses:* Contact institution.

University of Central Florida, College of Community Innovation and Education, School of Public Administration, Orlando, FL 32816. Offers emergency management and homeland security (Certificate); fundraising (Certificate); nonprofit management (MNM, Certificate); public administration (MPA); research administration (MRA); urban and regional planning (MS). *Accreditation:* NASPAA. *Program availability:* Part-time, evening/weekend. *Students:* 149 full-time (95 women), 497 part-time (347 women); includes 277 minority (128 Black or African American, non-Hispanic/Latino; 1 American Indian or Alaska Native, non-Hispanic/Latino; 13 Asian, non-Hispanic/Latino; 118 Hispanic/Latino; 1 Native Hawaiian or other Pacific Islander, non-Hispanic/Latino; 16 Two or more races, non-Hispanic/Latino), 9 international. Average age 33. 430 applicants, 79% accepted, 226 enrolled. In 2019, 106 master's, 26 other advanced degrees awarded. *Degree requirements:* For master's, comprehensive exam, thesis or alternative, research report. *Entrance requirements:* For master's, letters of recommendation, goal statement, resume. Additional exam requirements/recommendations for international students: required—TOEFL. *Application deadline:* For fall admission, 6/15 for domestic students; for spring admission, 11/1 for domestic students. Application fee: $30. Electronic applications accepted. *Financial support:* In 2019–20, 6 students received support, including 1 fellowship with partial tuition reimbursement available (averaging $5,000 per year), 4 research assistantships with partial tuition reimbursements available (averaging $6,049 per year), 1 teaching assistantship with partial tuition reimbursement available (averaging $5,478 per year); career-related internships or fieldwork, Federal Work-Study, institutionally sponsored loans, health care benefits, tuition waivers (partial), and unspecified assistantships also available. Financial award application deadline: 3/1; financial award applicants required to submit FAFSA. *Unit head:* Dr. Naim Kapucu, Director, 407-823-6096, Fax: 407-823-5651, E-mail: kapucu@ucf.edu. *Application contact:* Associate Director, Graduate Admissions, 407-823-2766, Fax: 407-823-6442, E-mail: gradadmissions@ucf.edu.
Website: https://www.cohpa.ucf.edu/publicadmin/

University of Chicago, Graham School of Continuing Liberal and Professional Studies, Program in Threat and Response Management, Chicago, IL 60637. Offers M Sc. *Program availability:* Part-time-only, evening/weekend. *Entrance requirements:* For master's, 3 letters of recommendation, statement of purpose, transcripts, resume or curriculum vitae, U.S. citizen or permanent resident. Additional exam requirements/recommendations for international students: required—TOEFL (minimum score 104 iBT), IELTS (minimum score 7). Electronic applications accepted.

University of Colorado Denver, School of Public Affairs, Program in Criminology and Criminal Justice, Denver, CO 80217. Offers criminal justice (MCJ), including criminal justice, domestic violence, emergency management and homeland security. *Program availability:* Part-time, evening/weekend. Tuition and fees vary according to course load, program and reciprocity agreements.

University of Colorado Denver, School of Public Affairs, Program in Public Affairs and Administration, Denver, CO 80127. Offers public administration (MPA), including domestic violence, emergency management and homeland security, environmental policy, management and law, homeland security and defense, local government, nonprofit management, public administration; public affairs (PhD). *Accreditation:* NASPAA. *Program availability:* Part-time, evening/weekend, online learning. Tuition and fees vary according to course load, program and reciprocity agreements.

University of Delaware, College of Arts and Sciences, School of Public Policy and Administration, Program in Disaster Science and Management, Newark, DE 19716. Offers MS, PhD.

University of Denver, University College, Denver, CO 80208. Offers arts and culture (MA, Certificate); communication management (MS, Certificate), including translation studies (Certificate), world history and culture (Certificate); environmental policy and management (MS); geographic information systems (MS); global affairs (MA, Certificate), including human capital in organizations (Certificate), philanthropic leadership (Certificate), project management (Certificate), strategic innovation and change (Certificate); healthcare leadership (MS); information communications and technology (MS); leadership and organizations (MS); professional creative writing (MA, Certificate), including emergency planning and response (Certificate), organizational security (Certificate); security management (MS, Certificate); strategic human resources (Certificate). *Program availability:* Part-time, evening/weekend, 100% online, blended/hybrid learning. *Faculty:* 104 part-time/adjunct (52 women). *Students:* 59 full-time (33 women), 1,893 part-time (1,210 women); includes 545 minority (133 Black or African American, non-Hispanic/Latino; 16 American Indian or Alaska Native, non-Hispanic/Latino; 64 Asian, non-Hispanic/Latino; 252 Hispanic/Latino; 4 Native Hawaiian or other Pacific Islander, non-Hispanic/Latino; 76 Two or more races, non-Hispanic/Latino), 78 international. Average age 32. 1,290 applicants, 91% accepted, 752 enrolled. In 2019, 457 master's, 181 other advanced degrees awarded. *Degree requirements:* For master's, capstone project. *Entrance requirements:* For master's, baccalaureate degree, transcripts, two letters of recommendation, personal statement, resume, writing sample (Master of Arts in Professional Creative Writing). Additional exam requirements/recommendations for international students: required—TOEFL (minimum score 550 paper-based; 80 iBT). *Application deadline:* For fall admission, 6/19 priority date for domestic students, 6/14 priority date for international students; for winter admission, 10/25 priority date for domestic students, 9/27 priority date for international students; for spring admission, 2/7 priority date for domestic students, 1/10 priority date for international students; for summer admission, 4/24 priority date for domestic students, 3/27 priority date for international students. Applications are processed on a rolling basis. Application fee: $75. Electronic applications accepted. *Expenses:* Contact institution. *Financial support:* In 2019–20, 56 students received support. Teaching assistantships available. Financial award applicants required to submit FAFSA. *Unit head:* Dr. Michael McGuire, Dean, 303-871-3518, E-mail: michael.mcguire@du.edu. *Application contact:* Admission Team, 303-871-2291, E-mail: ucoladm@du.edu.
Website: http://universitycollege.du.edu/

University of Florida, Graduate School, College of Design, Construction and Planning, M.E. Rinker, Sr. School of Construction Management, Gainesville, FL 32611. Offers construction management (MSCM); fire and emergency services (MFES); historic preservation (MSCM); international construction (MICM), including historic preservation; sustainable construction (MSCM); sustainable design (MSCM). *Program availability:* Part-time, online learning. *Degree requirements:* For master's, thesis. *Entrance requirements:* For master's, GRE General Test, minimum GPA of 3.0. Additional exam requirements/recommendations for international students: required—TOEFL (minimum score 550 paper-based; 80 iBT), IELTS (minimum score 6). Electronic applications accepted.

University of Hawaii at Manoa, Office of Graduate Education, College of Social Sciences, Department of Urban and Regional Planning, Program in Disaster Preparedness and Emergency Management, Honolulu, HI 96822. Offers Graduate Certificate. *Program availability:* Part-time. *Entrance requirements:* Additional exam requirements/recommendations for international students: required—TOEFL (minimum score 500 paper-based; 61 iBT), IELTS (minimum score 5).

University of Illinois at Springfield, Graduate Programs, College of Public Affairs and Administration, Program in Public Health, Springfield, IL 62703-5407. Offers community health education (Graduate Certificate); emergency preparedness and homeland security (Graduate Certificate); environmental health (MPH, Graduate Certificate); environmental risk assessment (Graduate Certificate); epidemiology (Graduate Certificate); public health (MPH). *Program availability:* Part-time, 100% online. *Faculty:* 7 full-time (5 women). *Students:* 31 full-time (24 women), 36 part-time (27 women); includes 13 minority (9 Black or African American, non-Hispanic/Latino; 1 Asian, non-Hispanic/Latino; 1 Hispanic/Latino; 2 Two or more races, non-Hispanic/Latino), 27 international. Average age 30. 90 applicants, 54% accepted, 12 enrolled. In 2019, 13 master's, 10 other advanced degrees awarded. *Degree requirements:* For master's, comprehensive exam, internship. *Entrance requirements:* For master's, GRE, minimum undergraduate GPA of 3.0, 3 letters of recommendation, essay addressing the areas outlined on the department application form. Additional exam requirements/recommendations for international students: required—TOEFL (minimum score 500 paper-based; 61 iBT). *Application deadline:* Applications are processed on a rolling basis. Application fee: $60 ($75 for international students). Electronic applications accepted. *Expenses:* $33.25 per credit hour (online fee). *Financial support:* In 2019–20, research assistantships with full tuition reimbursements (averaging $10,562 per year), teaching assistantships with full tuition reimbursements (averaging $10,652 per year) were awarded; fellowships, career-related internships or fieldwork, Federal Work-Study, scholarships/grants, health care benefits, and unspecified assistantships also available. Support available to part-time students. Financial award application deadline: 11/15; financial award applicants required to submit FAFSA. *Unit head:* Dr. Josiah Alamu, Program Administrator, 217-206-7874, Fax: 217-206-7279, E-mail: jalam3@uis.edu. *Application contact:* Dr. Josiah Alamu, Program Administrator, 217-206-7874, Fax: 217-206-7279, E-mail: jalam3@uis.edu.
Website: http://www.uis.edu/publichealth/

University of Maryland, Baltimore County, The Graduate School, College of Arts, Humanities and Social Sciences, Department of Emergency Health Services, Baltimore, MD 21250. Offers emergency health services (MS), including administration, planning, and policy, preventive medicine and epidemiology; emergency management (Postbaccalaureate Certificate); public policy (PhD), including emergency health, emergency management. *Program availability:* Part-time, evening/weekend, 100% online, blended/hybrid learning. *Faculty:* 4 full-time (2 women), 8 part-time/adjunct (3 women). *Students:* 5 full-time (4 women), 9 part-time (5 women); includes 5 minority (2 Black or African American, non-Hispanic/Latino; 1 Asian, non-Hispanic/Latino; 2 Hispanic/Latino), 2 international. Average age 37. 19 applicants, 68% accepted, 3 enrolled. In 2019, 5 master's, 2 other advanced degrees awarded. Terminal master's awarded for partial completion of doctoral program. *Degree requirements:* For master's, comprehensive exam (for some programs), capstone project or thesis. *Entrance requirements:* For master's, GRE General Test if GPA is below 3.2, minimum GPA of 3.2. Additional exam requirements/recommendations for international students:

required—TOEFL (minimum score 80 iBT), IELTS, or PTE. *Application deadline:* For fall admission, 6/15 for domestic students, 3/1 for international students; for spring admission, 12/1 for domestic students, 10/1 for international students. Applications are processed on a rolling basis. Application fee: $50. Electronic applications accepted. *Expenses:* $14,382 per year. *Financial support:* In 2019–20, 1 student received support, including 1 research assistantship with full tuition reimbursement available (averaging $16,875 per year); career-related internships or fieldwork, Federal Work-Study, health care benefits, and unspecified assistantships also available. Financial award application deadline: 5/30; financial award applicants required to submit FAFSA. *Unit head:* Dr. J. Lee Jenkins, Department Chair, 410-455-3216, Fax: 410-455-3045, E-mail: jleejenkins@umbc.edu. *Application contact:* Dr. Rick Bissell, Program Director, 410-455-3776, Fax: 410-455-3045, E-mail: bissell@umbc.edu.
Website: http://ehs.umbc.edu/

University of Nebraska Medical Center, Program in Emergency Preparedness, Omaha, NE 68198. Offers MS. *Program availability:* Part-time, 100% online, blended/ hybrid learning. *Degree requirements:* For master's, thesis. *Entrance requirements:* For master's, GRE. Additional exam requirements/recommendations for international students: required—TOEFL (minimum score 550 paper-based; 80 iBT). Electronic applications accepted.

University of Nevada, Las Vegas, Graduate College, Greenspun College of Urban Affairs, School of Public Policy and Leadership, Las Vegas, NV 89154-4030. Offers crisis and emergency management (MS); emergency crisis management cybersecurity (Certificate); environmental science (MS, PhD); non-profit management (Certificate); public administration (MPA); public affairs (PhD); public management (Certificate); urban leadership (MA). *Program availability:* Part-time. *Faculty:* 12 full-time (5 women), 6 part-time/adjunct (1 woman). *Students:* 106 full-time (61 women), 96 part-time (71 women); includes 118 minority (34 Black or African American, non-Hispanic/Latino; 1 American Indian or Alaska Native, non-Hispanic/Latino; 11 Asian, non-Hispanic/Latino; 49 Hispanic/Latino; 2 Native Hawaiian or other Pacific Islander, non-Hispanic/Latino; 21 Two or more races, non-Hispanic/Latino), 5 international. Average age 36. 115 applicants, 77% accepted, 73 enrolled. In 2019, 49 master's, 13 doctorates, 16 other advanced degrees awarded. *Degree requirements:* For master's, comprehensive exam (for some programs), thesis (for some programs), oral exam; for doctorate, comprehensive exam, thesis/dissertation; for Certificate, portfolio. *Entrance requirements:* For master's, GRE General Test or GMAT, bachelor's degree with minimum GPA 2.75; statement of purpose; 3 letters of recommendation; for doctorate, GRE General Test, master's degree with minimum GPA of 3.5; 3 letters of recommendation; statement of purpose; writing sample; personal interview; for Certificate, bachelor's degree; 2 letters of recommendation; writing sample. Additional exam requirements/recommendations for international students: required—TOEFL (minimum score 550 paper-based; 80 iBT), IELTS (minimum score 7). *Application deadline:* For fall admission, 6/1 for domestic and international students; for spring admission, 11/1 for domestic and international students; for summer admission, 3/1 for domestic students. Application fee: $60 ($95 for international students). Electronic applications accepted. *Expenses:* Contact institution. *Financial support:* In 2019–20, 25 students received support, including 15 research assistantships with full tuition reimbursements available (averaging $15,700 per year), 10 teaching assistantships with full tuition reimbursements available (averaging $16,625 per year); institutionally sponsored loans, scholarships/grants, health care benefits, and unspecified assistantships also available. Financial award application deadline: 3/15; financial award applicants required to submit FAFSA. *Unit head:* Dr. Christopher Stream, Director, 702-895-5120, Fax: 702-895-4436, E-mail: sppl.chair@unlv.edu. *Application contact:* Dr. Jayce Farmer, Graduate Coordinator, 702-895-4828, E-mail: sppl.gradcoord@unlv.edu. Website: https://www.unlv.edu/publicpolicy

University of New Haven, Graduate School, Henry C. Lee College of Criminal Justice and Forensic Sciences, Program in Emergency Management, West Haven, CT 06516. Offers MS, Graduate Certificate. *Program availability:* Part-time, 100% online. *Students:* 35 full-time (10 women), 29 part-time (4 women); includes 6 minority (3 Black or African American, non-Hispanic/Latino; 2 Asian, non-Hispanic/Latino; 1 Hispanic/Latino), 20 international. Average age 34. 46 applicants, 100% accepted, 18 enrolled. In 2019, 36 master's, 4 other advanced degrees awarded. Application fee: $50. *Unit head:* Wayne Sandford, Lecturer, 203-479-4891, E-mail: wsandford@newhaven.edu. *Application contact:* Selina O'Toole, Senior Associate Director of Graduate Admissions, 203-932-7337, E-mail: SOToole@newhaven.edu.
Website: https://www.newhaven.edu/lee-college/graduate-programs/emergency-management/

The University of North Carolina at Charlotte, College of Liberal Arts and Sciences, Department of Political Science and Public Administration, Charlotte, NC 28223-0001. Offers emergency management (Graduate Certificate); non-profit management (Graduate Certificate); public administration (MPA), including arts administration, emergency management, non-profit management, public budgeting and finance, urban management and policy; public budgeting and finance (Graduate Certificate); urban management and policy (Graduate Certificate). *Accreditation:* NASPAA. *Program availability:* Part-time, evening/weekend. *Faculty:* 20 full-time (10 women), 5 part-time/adjunct (1 woman). *Students:* 30 full-time (21 women), 45 part-time (29 women); includes 23 minority (15 Black or African American, non-Hispanic/Latino; 1 American Indian or Alaska Native, non-Hispanic/Latino; 5 Hispanic/Latino; 2 Two or more races, non-Hispanic/Latino), 2 international. Average age 30. 38 applicants, 68% accepted, 21 enrolled. In 2019, 18 master's, 13 other advanced degrees awarded. *Degree requirements:* For master's, thesis or alternative. *Entrance requirements:* For master's, GRE General Test, bachelor's degree, or its equivalent, from accredited college or university; minimum undergraduate GPA of 3.0; 3 letters of recommendation; statement of purpose; for Graduate Certificate, one official transcript from each post-secondary institution; three letters of recommendation from academic or professional sources; overall undergraduate GPA of 3.0 on a 4.0 scale; statement of purpose (1-2 pages in length) in which the applicant explains his/her career goals, how the Certificate fits into achieving those goals, and any relevant w. Additional exam requirements/ recommendations for international students: required—TOEFL (minimum score 557 paper-based; 83 iBT), IELTS (minimum score 6.5), TOEFL (minimum score 557paper-based, 83 iBT) or IELTS (6.5). *Application deadline:* For fall admission, 8/15 for domestic students; for spring admission, 12/1 for domestic students; for summer admission, 5/11 for domestic students. Applications are processed on a rolling basis. Application fee: $75. Electronic applications accepted. *Expenses:* Tuition, state resident: full-time $4337. Tuition, nonresident: full-time $17,771. *Required fees:* $3093. Tuition and fees vary according to course load, degree level and program. *Financial support:* In 2019–20, 16 students received support, including 1 fellowship (averaging $55,000 per year), 15 research assistantships (averaging $8,583 per year); teaching assistantships, career-related internships or fieldwork, institutionally sponsored loans, scholarships/grants, and unspecified assistantships also available. Support available to part-time students. Financial award applicants required to submit FAFSA. *Unit head:* Dr. Cheryl L. Brown, Interim Chair, Undergraduate Coordinator, & Associate Professor, 704-687-7574, E-mail: cbrown@uncc.edu. *Application contact:* Kathy B. Giddings, Director of Graduate Admissions, 704-687-5503, Fax: 704-687-1668, E-mail: gradadm@uncc.edu.
Website: http://politicalscience.uncc.edu/

The University of North Carolina at Pembroke, The Graduate School, Department of Political Science and Public Administration, Pembroke, NC 28372-1510. Offers criminal justice (MPA); emergency management (MPA); health administration (MPA); public management (MPA). *Program availability:* Part-time, evening/weekend, online learning. *Degree requirements:* For master's, comprehensive exam, thesis optional. *Entrance requirements:* For master's, GRE General Test or MAT, minimum GPA of 3.0 in major, 2.5 overall; interview. Additional exam requirements/recommendations for international students: required—TOEFL.

University of North Texas, Toulouse Graduate School, Denton, TX 76203-5459. Offers accounting (MS); applied anthropology (MA, MS); applied behavior analysis (Certificate); applied geography (MA); applied technology and performance improvement (M Ed, MS); art education (MA); art history (MA); arts leadership (Certificate); audiology (Au D); behavior analysis (MS); behavioral science (PhD); biochemistry and molecular biology (MS); biology (MA, MS); biomedical engineering (MS); business analysis (MS); chemistry (MS); clinical health psychology (PhD); communication studies (MA, MS); computer engineering (MS); computer science (MS); counseling (M Ed, MS), including clinical mental health counseling (MS), college and university counseling, elementary school counseling, secondary school counseling; creative writing (MA); criminal justice (MS); curriculum and instruction (M Ed); decision sciences (MBA); design (MA, MFA), including fashion design (MFA), innovation studies, interior design (MFA); early childhood studies (MS); economics (MS); educational leadership (M Ed, Ed D); educational psychology (MS, PhD), including family studies (MS), gifted and talented (MS), human development (MS), learning and cognition (MS), research, measurement and evaluation (MS); electrical engineering (MS); emergency management (MPA); engineering technology (MS); English (MA); English as a second language (MA); environmental science (MS); finance (MBA, MS); financial management (MPA); French (MA); health services management (MBA); higher education (M Ed, Ed D); history (MA, MS); hospitality management (MS); human resources management (MPA); information science (MS); information systems (PhD); information technologies (MBA); interdisciplinary studies (MA, MS); international studies (MA); international sustainable tourism (MS); jazz studies (MM); journalism (MA, MJ, Graduate Certificate), including interactive and virtual digital communication (Graduate Certificate), narrative journalism (Graduate Certificate), public relations (Graduate Certificate); kinesiology (MS); linguistics (MA); local government management (MPA); logistics (PhD); logistics and supply chain management (MBA); long-term care, senior housing, and aging services (MA); management (PhD); marketing (MBA); mathematics (MA, MS); mechanical and energy engineering (MS, PhD); music (MA), including ethnomusicology, music theory, musicology, performance; music composition (PhD); music education (MM Ed, PhD); nonprofit management (MPA); operations and supply chain management (MBA); performance (MM, DMA); philosophy (MA); political science (MA); professional and technical communication (MA); radio, television and film (MA, MFA); rehabilitation counseling (Certificate); sociology (MA); Spanish (MA); special education (M Ed); speech-language pathology (MA); strategic management (MBA); studio art (MFA); teaching (M Ed); MBA/MS. *Program availability:* Part-time, evening/weekend, online learning. Terminal master's awarded for partial completion of doctoral program. *Degree requirements:* For master's, variable foreign language requirement, comprehensive exam (for some programs), thesis (for some programs); for doctorate, variable foreign language requirement, comprehensive exam (for some programs), thesis/dissertation; for other advanced degree, variable foreign language requirement, comprehensive exam (for some programs). *Entrance requirements:* For master's and doctorate, GRE, GMAT. Additional exam requirements/recommendations for international students: required—TOEFL (minimum score 550 paper-based; 79 iBT). Electronic applications accepted.

University of South Florida, Innovative Education, Tampa, FL 33620-9951. Offers adult, career and higher education (Graduate Certificate), including college teaching, leadership in developing human resources, leadership in higher education; Africana studies (Graduate Certificate), including diasporas and health disparities, genocide and human rights; aging studies (Graduate Certificate), including gerontology; art research (Graduate Certificate), including museum studies; business foundations (Graduate Certificate); chemical and biomedical engineering (Graduate Certificate), including materials science and engineering, water, health and sustainability; child and family studies (Graduate Certificate), including positive behavior support; civil and industrial engineering (Graduate Certificate), including transportation systems analysis; community and family health (Graduate Certificate), including maternal and child health, social marketing and public health, violence and injury: prevention and intervention, women's health; criminology (Graduate Certificate), including criminal justice administration; data science for public administration (Graduate Certificate); digital humanities (Graduate Certificate); educational measurement and research (Graduate Certificate), including evaluation; English (Graduate Certificate), including comparative literary studies, creative writing, professional and technical communication; entrepreneurship (Graduate Certificate); environmental health (Graduate Certificate), including safety management; epidemiology and biostatistics (Graduate Certificate), including applied biostatistics, biostatistics, concepts and tools of epidemiology, epidemiology, epidemiology of infectious diseases; geography, environment and planning (Graduate Certificate), including community development, environmental policy and management, geographical information systems; geology (Graduate Certificate), including hydrogeology; global health (Graduate Certificate), including disaster management, global health and Latin American and Caribbean studies, global health practice, humanitarian assistance, infection control; government and international affairs (Graduate Certificate), including Cuban studies, globalization studies; health policy and management (Graduate Certificate), including health management and leadership, public health policy and programs; hearing specialist: early intervention (Graduate Certificate); industrial and management systems engineering (Graduate Certificate), including systems engineering, technology management; information studies (Graduate Certificate), including school library media specialist; information systems/decision sciences (Graduate Certificate), including analytics and business intelligence; instructional technology (Graduate Certificate), including distance education, Florida digital/virtual educator, instructional design, multimedia design, Web design; internal medicine, bioethics and medical humanities (Graduate Certificate), including biomedical ethics; Latin American and Caribbean studies (Graduate Certificate); leadership for coastal resiliency planning (Graduate Certificate); mass communications (Graduate Certificate), including multimedia journalism; mathematics and statistics (Graduate Certificate), including mathematics; medicine (Graduate Certificate), including aging and neuroscience, bioinformatics, biotechnology, brain fitness and memory management, clinical investigation, hand and upper limb rehabilitation, health informatics, health sciences, integrative weight management, intellectual property, medicine and gender, metabolic and nutritional medicine, metabolic cardiology, pharmacy sciences; national and competitive intelligence (Graduate Certificate); nursing (Graduate Certificate), including simulation based academic fellowship in advanced pain management; psychological and social foundations (Graduate Certificate), including career counseling, college teaching, diversity in education, mental health counseling, school counseling; public affairs (Graduate Certificate), including nonprofit management, public management, research administration; public health (Graduate Certificate), including assessing chemical toxicity and public health risks, health equity,

pharmacoepidemiology, public health generalist, toxicology, translational research in adolescent behavioral health; public health practices (Graduate Certificate), including planning for healthy communities; rehabilitation and mental health counseling (Graduate Certificate), including integrative mental health care, marriage and family therapy, rehabilitation technology; secondary education (Graduate Certificate), including ESOL, foreign language education: culture and content, foreign language education: professional; social work (Graduate Certificate), including geriatric social work/clinical gerontology; special education (Graduate Certificate), including autism spectrum disorder, disabilities education: severe/profound; world languages (Graduate Certificate), including teaching English as a second language (TESL) or foreign language. *Unit head:* Dr. Cynthia DeLuca, Associate Vice President and Assistant Vice Provost, 813-974-3077, Fax: 813-974-7061, E-mail: deluca@usf.edu. *Application contact:* Owen Hooper, Director, Summer and Alternative Calendar Programs, 813-974-6917, E-mail: hooper@usf.edu.
Website: http://www.usf.edu/innovative-education/

The University of Texas Rio Grande Valley, College of Liberal Arts, Department of Sociology and Anthropology, Edinburg, TX 78539. Offers disaster studies (MA); sociology (MS). *Faculty:* 9 full-time (3 women). *Students:* 28 full-time (16 women), 19 part-time (14 women); includes 40 minority (1 Black or African American, non-Hispanic/Latino; 1 Asian, non-Hispanic/Latino; 38 Hispanic/Latino), 6 international. Average age 32. 21 applicants, 86% accepted, 12 enrolled. In 2019, 12 master's awarded. *Entrance requirements:* Additional exam requirements/recommendations for international students: required—TOEFL or IELTS. *Expenses: Tuition, area resident:* Full-time $5959; part-time $440 per credit hour. Tuition, state resident: full-time $5959. Tuition, nonresident: full-time $5959. *International tuition:* $13,321 full-time. *Required fees:* $1169; $185 per credit hour.
Website: utrgv.edu/sociology/index.htm

The University of Toledo, College of Graduate Studies, College of Medicine and Life Sciences, Department of Public Health and Preventative Medicine, Toledo, OH 43606-3390. Offers biostatistics and epidemiology (Certificate); contemporary gerontological practice (Certificate); environmental and occupational health and safety (MPH); epidemiology (Certificate); global public health (Certificate); health promotion and education (MPH); industrial hygiene (MSOH); medical and health science teaching and learning (Certificate); occupational health (Certificate); public health administration (MPH); public health and emergency response (Certificate); public health epidemiology (MPH); public health nutrition (MPH); MD/MPH. *Program availability:* Part-time, evening/weekend. *Degree requirements:* For master's, thesis or alternative. *Entrance requirements:* For master's, GRE, minimum undergraduate GPA of 3.0, three letters of recommendation, statement of purpose, transcripts from all prior institutions attended, resume; for Certificate, minimum undergraduate GPA of 3.0, three letters of recommendation, statement of purpose, transcripts from all prior institutions attended, resume. Additional exam requirements/recommendations for international students: required—TOEFL (minimum score 550 paper-based; 80 iBT), IELTS (minimum score 6.5). Electronic applications accepted.

Upper Iowa University, Online Master's Programs, Fayette, IA 52142-1857. Offers accounting (MBA); corporate financial management (MBA); emergency management and homeland security (MPA); general management (MBA); general studies (MPA); government administration (MPA); health and human services (MPA); human resources management (MBA); nonprofit organizational management (MPA); organizational development (MBA); public management (MPA); sport administration (MSA). *Program availability:* Part-time, online learning. *Degree requirements:* For master's, research project. *Entrance requirements:* For master's, GMAT, GRE, or minimum GPA of 2.7 during last 60 hours. Additional exam requirements/recommendations for international students: required—TOEFL (minimum score 570 paper-based). Electronic applications accepted.

Virginia Commonwealth University, Graduate School, L. Douglas Wilder School of Government and Public Affairs, Program in Homeland Security and Emergency Preparedness, Richmond, VA 23284-9005. Offers MA, Graduate Certificate. *Program availability:* Part-time, online learning. *Entrance requirements:* For master's, GRE, GMAT, MAT or LSAT, minimum GPA of 2.7; for Graduate Certificate, minimum GPA of 2.7. Additional exam requirements/recommendations for international students: required—TOEFL (minimum score 600 paper-based; 100 iBT); recommended—IELTS (minimum score 6.5). Electronic applications accepted.

Walden University, Graduate Programs, School of Health Sciences, Minneapolis, MN 55401. Offers clinical research administration (MS, Graduate Certificate); health education and promotion (MS, PhD), including behavioral health (PhD), disease surveillance (PhD), emergency preparedness (MS), general (MHA, MS), global health (PhD), health policy (PhD), health policy and advocacy (MS), population health (PhD); health informatics (MS); health services (PhD), including community health, healthcare administration, leadership, public health policy, self-designed; healthcare administration (MHA, DHA), including general (MHA, MS); leadership and organizational development (MHA); public health (MPH, Dr PH, PhD, Graduate Certificate), including community health education (PhD), epidemiology (PhD); systems policy (MHA). *Program availability:* Part-time, evening/weekend, online only, 100% online. *Degree requirements:* For doctorate, thesis/dissertation, residency. *Entrance requirements:* For master's, bachelor's degree or higher; minimum GPA of 2.5; official transcripts; goal statement (for some programs); access to computer and Internet; for doctorate, master's degree or higher; three years of related professional or academic experience (preferred); minimum GPA of 3.0; goal statement and current resume (for select programs); official transcripts; access to computer and Internet; for Graduate Certificate, relevant work experience; access to computer and Internet. Additional exam requirements/recommendations for international students: required—TOEFL (minimum score 550 paper-based, 79 iBT), IELTS (minimum score 6.5), Michigan English Language Assessment Battery (minimum score 82), or PTE (minimum score 53). Electronic applications accepted.

Walden University, Graduate Programs, School of Public Policy and Administration, Minneapolis, MN 55401. Offers criminal justice (MPA, MPP, MS, Graduate Certificate), including emergency management (MS, PhD), general program (MS), global leadership (MS, PhD), homeland security and policy coordination (MS, PhD), law and public policy (MS, PhD), policy analysis (MS, PhD), public management and leadership (MS, PhD), self-designed (MS), terrorism, mediation, and peace (MS, PhD); criminal justice and executive management (MS), including global leadership (MS, PhD); criminal justice leadership and executive management (MS), including emergency management (MS, PhD), general program, homeland security and policy coordination (MS, PhD), law and public policy (MS, PhD), policy analysis (MS, PhD), public management and leadership (MS, PhD), self-designed, terrorism, mediation, and peace (MS, PhD); emergency management (MPA, MPP, MS), including criminal justice (MS, PhD), general program (MS), homeland security (MS), public management and leadership (MS, PhD), terrorism and emergency management (MS); general program (MPA, MPP); global leadership (MPA, MPP); government management (Graduate Certificate); health policy (MPA, MPP); homeland security (Graduate Certificate); homeland security and policy coordination (MPA, MPP); international nongovernmental organizations (MPA, MPP); law and public policy (MPA, MPP); local government management for sustainable communities (MPA, MPP); nonprofit management (Graduate Certificate); nonprofit management and leadership (MPA, MPP, MS), including global leadership (MS, PhD), international nongovernmental organization (MS), local government for sustainable communities (MS), self-designed (MS); online teaching in higher education (Post-Master's Certificate); policy analysis (MPA); public management and leadership (MPA, MPP, Graduate Certificate); public policy (Graduate Certificate); public policy and administration (PhD), including criminal justice (MS, PhD), emergency management (MS, PhD), global leadership (MS, PhD), health policy, homeland security and policy coordination (MS, PhD), international nongovernmental organizations, law and public policy (MS, PhD), local government management for sustainable communities, nonprofit management and leadership, policy analysis (MS, PhD), public management and leadership (MS, PhD), terrorism, mediation, and peace (MS, PhD); strategic planning and public policy (Graduate Certificate); terrorism, mediation, and peace (MPA, MPP). *Program availability:* Part-time, evening/weekend, online only, 100% online. *Degree requirements:* For doctorate, thesis/dissertation, residency. *Entrance requirements:* For master's, bachelor's degree or higher; minimum GPA of 2.5; official transcripts; goal statement (for some programs); access to computer and Internet; for doctorate, master's degree or higher; three years of related professional or academic experience (preferred); minimum. GPA of 3.0; goal statement and current resume (for select programs); official transcripts; access to computer and Internet; for other advanced degree, relevant work experience; access to computer and Internet. Additional exam requirements/recommendations for international students: required—TOEFL (minimum score 550 paper-based, 79 iBT), IELTS (minimum score 6.5), Michigan English Language Assessment Battery (minimum score 82), or PTE (minimum score 53). Electronic applications accepted.

Waldorf University, Program in Organizational Leadership, Forest City, IA 50436. Offers criminal justice leadership (MA); emergency management leadership (MA); fire/rescue executive leadership (MA); human resource development (MA); public administration (MA); sport management (MA); teacher leader (MA).

Wheaton College, Graduate School, Humanitarian and Disaster Leadership Program, Wheaton, IL 60187-5593. Offers humanitarian and disaster leadership (MA). *Program availability:* Part-time. *Degree requirements:* For master's, thesis or alternative. *Entrance requirements:* Additional exam requirements/recommendations for international students: required—TOEFL (minimum score 550 paper-based; 80 iBT), IELTS (minimum score 6.5). Electronic applications accepted. *Expenses: Tuition:* Full-time $16,800; part-time $700 per credit hour. Tuition and fees vary according to degree level and program.

York University, Faculty of Graduate Studies, Faculty of Liberal Arts and Professional Studies, Program in Disaster and Emergency Management, Toronto, ON M3J 1P3, Canada. Offers MA.

Homeland Security

Angelo State University, College of Graduate Studies and Research, College of Arts and Humanities, Department of Security Studies and Criminal Justice, San Angelo, TX 76909. Offers criminal justice (MS); homeland security (MS); intelligence, security studies, and analysis (MSS); security studies (MSS). *Program availability:* Part-time, evening/weekend, online learning. *Entrance requirements:* For master's, essay, letters of recommendation. Additional exam requirements/recommendations for international students: required—TOEFL or IELTS. Electronic applications accepted.

Arizona State University at Tempe, College of Public Programs, School of Public Affairs, Phoenix, AZ 85004-0687. Offers emergency management and homeland security (MA); program evaluation (MS); public administration (MPA, PhD), including nonprofit administration (MPA), urban management (MPA); public policy (MPP); MPA/MSW. *Accreditation:* NASPAA (one or more programs are accredited). *Program availability:* Part-time, evening/weekend. Terminal master's awarded for partial completion of doctoral program. *Degree requirements:* For master's, thesis or alternative, policy analysis or capstone project; interactive Program of Study (iPOS) submitted before completing 50 percent of required credit hours; for doctorate, comprehensive exam, thesis/dissertation, interactive Program of Study (iPOS) submitted before completing 50 percent of required credit hours. *Entrance requirements:* For master's, GRE, minimum GPA of 3.0 or equivalent in last 2 years of work leading to bachelor's degree; for doctorate, GRE, minimum GPA of 3.0 or equivalent in last 2 years of work leading to bachelor's degree, 3 letters of recommendation, resume, statement of goals, samples of research reports. Additional exam requirements/recommendations for international students: required—TOEFL (minimum score 600 paper-based; 100 iBT), IELTS (minimum score 6.5). Electronic applications accepted. *Expenses:* Contact institution.

Aurora University, School of Arts and Sciences, Aurora, IL 60506-4892. Offers homeland security (MS); mathematics (MS); mathematics and science education for elementary teachers (MA); mathematics education (MA); science education (MA). *Program availability:* Part-time, evening/weekend, 100% online. *Faculty:* 2 full-time (1 woman), 8 part-time/adjunct (4 women). *Students:* 7 full-time (2 women), 48 part-time (32 women); includes 6 minority (1 Black or African American, non-Hispanic/Latino; 1 Asian, non-Hispanic/Latino; 3 Hispanic/Latino; 1 Two or more races, non-Hispanic/Latino). Average age 35. 21 applicants, 100% accepted, 12 enrolled. In 2019, 30 master's awarded. *Degree requirements:* For master's, research seminars. *Entrance requirements:* For master's, bachelor's degree in mathematics or in some other field with extensive course work in mathematics (for MS in mathematics). Additional exam requirements/recommendations for international students: required—TOEFL (minimum score 550 paper-based; 79 iBT). *Application deadline:* For fall admission, 6/1 for international students; for spring admission, 10/1 for international students. Applications are processed on a rolling basis. Application fee: $0. Electronic applications accepted. *Expenses:* The tuition listed is for the program with the greatest enrollment, the online MA in Mathematics Education. *Financial support:* Federal Work-Study, scholarships/

grants, and unspecified assistantships available. Financial award applicants required to submit FAFSA. *Unit head:* Dr. Karol Dean, Dean, School of Arts and Sciences, 630-8447585, E-mail: kdean@aurora.edu. *Application contact:* Jason Harmon, Dean of Adult and Graduate Studies, 630-947-8955, E-mail: AUadmission@aurora.edu.
Website: https://aurora.edu/academics/colleges-schools/liberal-arts

Ball State University, Graduate School, College of Sciences and Humanities, Department of Natural Resources and Environmental Management, Muncie, IN 47306. Offers emergency management and homeland security (Certificate); natural resources and environmental management (MA, MS). *Program availability:* Part-time. *Degree requirements:* For master's, thesis (for some programs). *Entrance requirements:* For master's, GRE General Test, minimum baccalaureate GPA of 2.75 or 3.0 in latter half of baccalaureate, two letters of reference. Additional exam requirements/recommendations for international students: required—TOEFL (minimum score 550 paper-based; 79 iBT), IELTS (minimum score 6.5). Electronic applications accepted. *Expenses: Tuition, area resident:* Full-time $7506; part-time $417 per credit hour. Tuition, nonresident: full-time $20,610; part-time $1145 per credit hour. *Required fees:* $2126. Tuition and fees vary according to course load, campus/location and program.

Ball State University, Graduate School, College of Sciences and Humanities, Department of Political Science, Program in Public Administration, Muncie, IN 47306. Offers public administration (MPA, Certificate), including community and economic development (MPA), criminal justice (MPA), emergency management and homeland security (MPA), information and communication technology (MPA). *Program availability:* Part-time. *Degree requirements:* For master's, comprehensive exam. *Entrance requirements:* For master's, GRE General Test, minimum baccalaureate GPA of 2.8, two letters of recommendation. Additional exam requirements/recommendations for international students: required—TOEFL (minimum score 550 paper-based; 79 iBT), IELTS (minimum score 6.5). Electronic applications accepted. *Expenses: Tuition, area resident:* Full-time $7506; part-time $417 per credit hour. Tuition, nonresident: full-time $20,610; part-time $1145 per credit hour. *Required fees:* $2126. Tuition and fees vary according to course load, campus/location and program.

Capella University, School of Public Service Leadership, Master's Programs in Healthcare, Minneapolis, MN 55402. Offers criminal justice (MS); emergency management (MS); general public health (MPH); gerontology (MS); health administration (MHA); health care operations (MHA); health management policy (MPH); health policy (MHA); homeland security (MS); multidisciplinary human services (MS); public administration (MPA); public safety leadership (MS); social and community services (MS); social behavioral sciences (MPH); MS/MPA.

The Citadel, The Military College of South Carolina, Citadel Graduate College, School of Humanities and Social Sciences, Department of Criminal Justice, Charleston, SC 29409. Offers homeland security (Graduate Certificate); intelligence analysis (Graduate Certificate); intelligence and security studies (MA). *Program availability:* Part-time, evening/weekend, 100% online, blended/hybrid learning. *Entrance requirements:* For master's, GRE or MAT, writing sample that demonstrates strong critical thinking and communication skills. Additional exam requirements/recommendations for international students: required—TOEFL (minimum score 550 paper-based; 79 iBT). Electronic applications accepted.

Columbus State University, Graduate Studies, College of Letters and Sciences, Program in Public Safety Administration, Columbus, GA 31907-5645. Offers MPSA. *Program availability:* Part-time. *Entrance requirements:* For master's, baccalaureate degree, employment in a public safety profession. Additional exam requirements/recommendations for international students: required—TOEFL (minimum score 550 paper-based; 79 iBT). Electronic applications accepted. *Expenses: Tuition, area resident:* Full-time $210; part-time $210 per credit hour. Tuition, state resident: full-time $210; part-time $210 per credit hour. Tuition, nonresident: full-time $817; part-time $817 per credit hour. *International tuition:* $817 full-time. *Required fees:* $802.50. Tuition and fees vary according to course load, degree level and program.

Drexel University, Goodwin College of Professional Studies, School of Technology and Professional Studies, Philadelphia, PA 19104-2875. Offers construction management (MS); creativity and innovation (MS); engineering technology (MS); food science (MS); hospitality management (MS); professional studies: creativity studies (MS); professional studies: e-learning leadership (MS); professional studies: homeland security management (MS); project management (MS); property management (MS); sport management (MS). *Program availability:* Part-time, evening/weekend. *Entrance requirements:* Additional exam requirements/recommendations for international students: required—TOEFL, IELTS. Electronic applications accepted. Application fee is waived when completed online.

Endicott College, Endicott College School of Arts and Sciences, Program in Homeland Security, Beverly, MA 01915. Offers cybersecurity (MS, Postbaccalaureate Certificate); emergency management (MS). *Program availability:* Part-time, evening/weekend, 100% online. *Faculty:* 2 full-time (1 woman), 17 part-time/adjunct (4 women). *Students:* 16 full-time (7 women), 14 part-time (4 women); includes 5 minority (3 Black or African American, non-Hispanic/Latino; 2 Hispanic/Latino). Average age 29. 23 applicants, 74% accepted, 14 enrolled. In 2019, 18 master's, 2 other advanced degrees awarded. *Degree requirements:* For master's, Capstone project. *Entrance requirements:* For master's, Updated resume; Official transcript of all post-secondary academic work; 250-500 word essay on specified topic; 2 letters of recommendation; interview with program director; for Postbaccalaureate Certificate, Same as Master's. Additional exam requirements/recommendations for international students: required—TOEFL. *Application deadline:* Applications are processed on a rolling basis. Application fee: $50. Electronic applications accepted. *Expenses:* Tuition varies by program. *Financial support:* Applicants required to submit FAFSA. *Unit head:* Dr. Joshua McCabe, Assistant Dean, Social Sciences, 978-232-2380, E-mail: gwong@endicott.edu. *Application contact:* Ian Menchini, Director, Graduate Enrollment and Advising, 978-232-5292, Fax: 978-232-3000, E-mail: imenchin@endicott.edu.
Website: https://www.endicott.edu/academics/schools/arts-sciences/graduate-programs/homeland-security-studies-program

Fairleigh Dickinson University, Metropolitan Campus, Anthony J. Petrocelli College of Continuing Studies, School of Administrative Science, Program in Homeland Security, Teaneck, NJ 07666-1914. Offers MSHS.

Georgian Court University, School of Arts and Sciences, Lakewood, NJ 08701. Offers applied behavior analysis (MA); autism spectrum disorders (Certificate); clinical mental health counseling (MA); criminal justice and human rights (MS); holistic health studies (MA); homeland security (Certificate); instructional technology (CPC); integrative health (Certificate); mercy spirituality (Certificate); parish business management (Certificate); professional counselor (Certificate); school psychology (MA, Certificate); theology (MA, Certificate). *Program availability:* Part-time, evening/weekend. *Faculty:* 19 full-time (11 women), 7 part-time/adjunct (3 women). *Students:* 90 full-time (80 women), 71 part-time (59 women); includes 26 minority (8 Black or African American, non-Hispanic/Latino; 2 Asian, non-Hispanic/Latino; 14 Hispanic/Latino; 2 Two or more races, non-Hispanic/Latino), 1 international. Average age 32. 138 applicants, 58% accepted, 57 enrolled. In 2019, 68 master's, 19 other advanced degrees awarded. *Degree requirements:* For master's, comprehensive exam (for some programs), thesis (for some programs); for other advanced degree, comprehensive exam (for some programs). *Entrance requirements:* Additional exam requirements/recommendations for international students: required—TOEFL (minimum score 550 paper-based; 79 iBT). *Application deadline:* For fall admission, 8/15 for domestic students, 5/1 for international students; for spring admission, 1/15 for domestic students, 10/1 for international students. Applications are processed on a rolling basis. Application fee: $40. Electronic applications accepted. *Financial support:* Scholarships/grants, health care benefits, and unspecified assistantships available. Financial award application deadline: 4/15; financial award applicants required to submit FAFSA. *Unit head:* Dr. Mary Chinery, Dean, 732-987-2493, Fax: 732-987-2007, E-mail: mchinery@georgian.edu. *Application contact:* Dr. Mary Chinery, Dean, 732-987-2493, Fax: 732-987-2007, E-mail: mchinery@georgian.edu.
Website: https://georgian.edu/academics/school-of-arts-sciences/

Henley-Putnam School of Strategic Security, Master of Science Program in Intelligence Management, Rapid City, SD 57701. Offers MS. *Program availability:* Part-time, online learning. *Degree requirements:* For master's, thesis. *Entrance requirements:* For master's, bachelor's degree from an institution accredited by an agency recognized by the U.S. Department of Education and/or the Council for Higher Education Accreditation; background check. Additional exam requirements/recommendations for international students: required—TOEFL (minimum score 650 paper-based; 79 iBT); recommended—IELTS (minimum score 7). *Expenses:* Contact institution.

Henley-Putnam School of Strategic Security, Master of Science Program in Strategic Security and Protection Management, Rapid City, SD 57701. Offers extremist organizations (MS). *Program availability:* Part-time, online learning. *Degree requirements:* For master's, comprehensive exam, thesis. *Entrance requirements:* For master's, bachelor's degree from institution accredited by an agency recognized by the U.S. Department of Education and/or the Council for Higher Education Accreditation, background check. Additional exam requirements/recommendations for international students: required—TOEFL (minimum score 650 paper-based; 79 iBT); recommended—IELTS. *Expenses:* Contact institution.

Henley-Putnam School of Strategic Security, Master of Science Program in Terrorism and Counterterrorism Studies, Rapid City, SD 57701. Offers intelligence operations (MS); protective intelligence (MS). *Program availability:* Part-time, online learning. *Degree requirements:* For master's, thesis. *Entrance requirements:* For master's, bachelor's degree from institution accredited by an agency recognized by the U.S. Department of Education and/or the Council for Higher Education Accreditation, background check. Additional exam requirements/recommendations for international students: required—TOEFL (minimum score 650 paper-based; 79 iBT); recommended—IELTS (minimum score 7). *Expenses:* Contact institution.

Indiana University-Purdue University Indianapolis, School of Public and Environmental Affairs, Indianapolis, IN 46202. Offers criminal justice and public safety (MS); homeland security and emergency management (Graduate Certificate); library management (Graduate Certificate); nonprofit management (Graduate Certificate); public affairs (MPA); public management (Graduate Certificate); social entrepreneurship: nonprofit and public benefit organizations (Graduate Certificate); JD/MPA; MLS/NMC; MLS/PMC; MPA/MA. *Accreditation:* CAHME (one or more programs are accredited); NASPAA. *Program availability:* Part-time, evening/weekend, online learning. *Entrance requirements:* For master's, GRE General Test, GMAT or LSAT, minimum GPA of 3.0 (preferred). Additional exam requirements/recommendations for international students: required—TOEFL (minimum score 93 iBT), IELTS (minimum score 6.5). Electronic applications accepted.

The Institute of World Politics, Graduate Programs in National Security, Intelligence, and International Affairs, Washington, DC 20036. Offers American foreign policy (Certificate); comparative political culture (Certificate); conflict prevention (Certificate); counterintelligence (Certificate); counterterrorism (Certificate); cyber statecraft (Certificate); economic statecraft (Certificate); homeland security (Certificate); intelligence (Certificate); international politics (Certificate); national security affairs (Executive MA, Certificate); nonviolent conflict (Certificate); peace building, stabilization, and humanitarian affairs (Certificate); public diplomacy and strategic influence (Certificate); statecraft and international affairs (MA); statecraft and national security (MA, DSNS); strategic communication (Certificate); strategic intelligence studies (MA, Professional MA); strategic soft power (Certificate). *Program availability:* Part-time, evening/weekend. *Degree requirements:* For master's, 52 credit hours, comprehensive written and oral exam (for MA); proficiency in critical language (for MA in statecraft and international affairs); 28 credit hours (for Executive MA); 36 credit hours (for Professional MA); for doctorate, comprehensive exam, thesis/dissertation; for Certificate, 20 credit hours. *Entrance requirements:* For master's, resume, personal statement, 3 references, essay; 7-10 years of professional experience (for Executive MA); 5-7 years of professional experience (for Professional MA); for doctorate, MA. Additional exam requirements/recommendations for international students: required—TOEFL. Electronic applications accepted.

Johns Hopkins University, Advanced Academic Programs, Program in Government, Washington, DC 21218. Offers global security studies (MA); government (MA); national securities study (Certificate); nonprofit management (Certificate); public management (MA); research administration (MS); MA/MBA. *Program availability:* Part-time, evening/weekend, online learning. *Entrance requirements:* For master's, minimum GPA of 3.0. Additional exam requirements/recommendations for international students: required—TOEFL (minimum score 100 iBT). Electronic applications accepted.

Keiser University, MA in Homeland Security Program, Fort Lauderdale, FL 33309. Offers MA.

Lasell College, Graduate and Professional Studies in Criminal Justice, Newton, MA 02466-2709. Offers emergency and crisis management (MS, Certificate); homeland security and global justice (MS, Certificate); violence prevention and advocacy (MS, Certificate). *Program availability:* Part-time, evening/weekend, online only, 100% online. *Faculty:* 6 full-time (3 women), 1 part-time/adjunct (0 women). *Students:* 28 full-time (5 women), 71 part-time (21 women); includes 27 minority (9 Black or African American, non-Hispanic/Latino; 2 Asian, non-Hispanic/Latino; 13 Hispanic/Latino; 3 Two or more races, non-Hispanic/Latino). Average age 33. 38 applicants, 63% accepted, 17 enrolled. In 2019, 33 master's awarded. *Degree requirements:* For master's, minimum GPA of 3.0; internship or research paper. *Entrance requirements:* For master's, one-page personal statement, 2 letters of recommendation, resume, bachelor's degree transcript; for Certificate, bachelor's transcript, 2 letters of recommendation, 1-page statement, resume. Additional exam requirements/recommendations for international students: required—TOEFL (minimum score 550 paper-based, 79 iBT) or IELTS (minimum score 6). *Application deadline:* For fall admission, 8/31 priority date for domestic students, 6/30 priority date for international students; for spring admission, 12/31 priority date for domestic students, 10/31 priority date for international students. Applications are processed on a rolling basis. Electronic applications accepted. *Expenses: Tuition:* Part-time $600 per credit. *Required fees:* $40 per semester. *Financial support:* Federal Work-Study, scholarships/grants, and tuition discounts available. Support available to part-time students. Financial award application deadline: 8/31; financial award applicants

required to submit FAFSA. *Unit head:* Chrystal Porter, Vice President of Graduate and Professional Studies, 617-243-2083, Fax: 617-243-2450, E-mail: gradinfo@lasell.edu. *Application contact:* Adrienne Franciosi, Assistant Vice President of Graduate and Professional Studies, 617-243-2214, Fax: 617-243-2450, E-mail: gradinfo@lasell.edu.
Website: http://www.lasell.edu/academics/graduate-and-professional-studies/programs-of-study/master-of-science-in-criminal-justice-.html

Liberty University, Helms School of Government, Lynchburg, VA 24515. Offers criminal justice (MS), including forensic psychology, homeland security, public administration (MA, MS); international relations (MS); political science (MS); public administration (MPA), including business and government, healthcare, law and public policy, public and non-profit management; public policy (MA), including campaigns and elections, international affairs, Middle East affairs, public administration (MA, MS). *Program availability:* Part-time, online learning. *Students:* 1,143 full-time (565 women), 572 part-time (408 women); includes 795 minority (499 Black or African American, non-Hispanic/Latino; 16 American Indian or Alaska Native, non-Hispanic/Latino; 23 Asian, non-Hispanic/Latino; 162 Hispanic/Latino; 7 Native Hawaiian or other Pacific Islander, non-Hispanic/Latino; 88 Two or more races, non-Hispanic/Latino), 27 international. Average age 35. 3,017 applicants, 44% accepted, 728 enrolled. In 2019, 415 master's awarded. *Entrance requirements:* For master's, minimum undergraduate GPA of 3.0. Additional exam requirements/recommendations for international students: required—TOEFL (minimum score 600 paper-based; 100 iBT). *Application deadline:* Applications are processed on a rolling basis. Application fee: $50. Electronic applications accepted. *Expenses: Tuition:* Full-time $545; part-time $410 per credit hour. One-time fee: $50. *Financial support:* In 2019–20, 808 students received support. Teaching assistantships and Federal Work-Study available. *Unit head:* Ron Miller, Dean, 434-592-4986, E-mail: govtdean@liberty.edu. *Application contact:* Jay Bridge, Director of Admissions, 800-424-9595, Fax: 800-628-7977, E-mail: gradadmissions@liberty.edu.
Website: https://www.liberty.edu/government/

London Metropolitan University, Graduate Programs, London, United Kingdom. Offers applied psychology (M Sc); architecture (MA); biomedical science (M Sc); blood science (M Sc); cancer pharmacology (M Sc); computer networking and cyber security (M Sc); computing and information systems (M Sc); conference interpreting (MA); counter-terrorism studies (M Sc); creative, digital and professional writing (MA); crime, violence and prevention (M Sc); criminology (M Sc); curating contemporary art (MA); data analytics (M Sc); digital media (MA); early childhood studies (MA); education (MA, Ed D); financial services law, regulation and compliance (LL M); food science (M Sc); forensic psychology (M Sc); health and social care management and policy (M Sc); human nutrition (M Sc); human resource management (MA); human rights and international conflict (MA); information technology (M Sc); intelligence and security studies (M Sc); international oil, gas and energy law (LL M); international relations (MA); interpreting (MA); learning and teaching in higher education (MA); legal practice (LL M); media and entertainment law (LL M); organizational and consumer psychology (M Sc); psychological therapy (M Sc); psychology of mental health (M Sc); public health (M Sc); public policy and management (MPA); security studies (M Sc); social work (M Sc); spatial planning and urban design (MA); sports therapy (M Sc); supporting older children and young people with dyslexia (MA); teaching languages (MA), including Arabic, English; translation (MA); woman and child abuse (MA).

Long Island University - Riverhead, Graduate Programs, Riverhead, NY 11901. Offers applied behavior analysis (Advanced Certificate); childhood education (MS), including grades 1-6; cybersecurity policy (Advanced Certificate); homeland security management (MS, Advanced Certificate); literacy education (MS); literacy education B-6 (MS); teaching students with disabilities (MS), including grades 1-6; TESOL (Advanced Certificate). *Accreditation:* TEAC. *Program availability:* Part-time. *Entrance requirements:* Additional exam requirements/recommendations for international students: required—TOEFL or IELTS. Electronic applications accepted. *Expenses:* Contact institution.

Missouri State University, Graduate College, College of Humanities and Public Affairs, Department of Criminology and Criminal Justice, Springfield, MO 65897. Offers community corrections (Certificate); criminology and criminal justice (MS); homeland security and defense (Certificate). *Program availability:* Part-time, 100% online, blended/hybrid learning. *Degree requirements:* For master's, comprehensive exam, thesis or alternative. *Entrance requirements:* For master's, bachelor's degree in criminology, criminal justice, or sociology; minimum undergraduate GPA of 3.0. Additional exam requirements/recommendations for international students: required—TOEFL (minimum score 550 paper-based; 79 iBT), IELTS (minimum score 6). Electronic applications accepted. *Expenses: Tuition, area resident:* Full-time $2600; part-time $1735 per credit hour. Tuition, nonresident: full-time $5240; part-time $3495 per credit hour. *International tuition:* $5240 full-time. *Required fees:* $530; $438 per credit hour. Tuition and fees vary according to class time, course level, course load, degree level, campus/location and program.

Missouri State University, Graduate College, Interdisciplinary Program in Professional Studies, Springfield, MO 65897. Offers administrative studies (Certificate); applied communication (MS); criminal justice (MS); environmental management (MS); homeland security (MS); individualized (MS); professional studies (MS); screenwriting and producing (MS); sports management (MS). *Program availability:* Part-time, evening/weekend, 100% online, blended/hybrid learning. *Degree requirements:* For master's, comprehensive exam, thesis or alternative. *Entrance requirements:* For master's, GRE, GMAT (if GPA less than 3.0). Additional exam requirements/recommendations for international students: required—TOEFL (minimum score 550 paper-based; 79 iBT), IELTS (minimum score 6). Electronic applications accepted. *Expenses: Tuition, area resident:* Full-time $2600; part-time $1735 per credit hour. Tuition, nonresident: full-time $5240; part-time $3495 per credit hour. *International tuition:* $5240 full-time. *Required fees:* $530; $438 per credit hour. Tuition and fees vary according to class time, course level, course load, degree level, campus/location and program.

Monmouth University, Graduate Studies, Department of Criminal Justice, West Long Branch, NJ 07764-1898. Offers criminal justice (MA), including homeland security; criminal justice administration (Certificate). *Program availability:* Part-time, evening/weekend, 100% online. *Faculty:* 4 full-time (2 women), 1 part-time/adjunct (0 women). *Students:* 20 full-time (7 women), 17 part-time (14 women); includes 7 minority (1 Black or African American, non-Hispanic/Latino; 6 Hispanic/Latino). Average age 26. In 2019, 14 master's, 1 other advanced degree awarded. *Degree requirements:* For master's, comprehensive exam (for some programs), thesis (for some programs). *Entrance requirements:* For master's and Certificate, baccalaureate degree with minimum GPA of 3.0 in major, 2.5 overall; two letters of recommendation; personal essay. Additional exam requirements/recommendations for international students: required—TOEFL (minimum score 550 paper-based; 79 iBT), IELTS (minimum score 6), Michigan English Language Assessment Battery (minimum score 77) or Certificate of Advanced English (minimum score 160). *Application deadline:* For fall admission, 7/15 priority date for domestic students, 6/1 for international students; for spring admission, 12/1 priority date for domestic students, 11/1 for international students; for summer admission, 5/1 for domestic students. Applications are processed on a rolling basis. Application fee: $50. Electronic applications accepted. *Expenses: Tuition:* Full-time $22,194; part-time $14,796 per credit. *Required fees:* $712; $178 per semester. $178 per semester. Tuition and fees vary according to course load. *Financial support:* In 2019–20, 14 students received support. Research assistantships, teaching assistantships, scholarships/grants, and unspecified assistantships available. Support available to part-time students. Financial award applicants required to submit FAFSA. *Unit head:* Dr. Brian Lockwood, Program Director, 732-571-7567, Fax: 732-263-5148, E-mail: blockwoo@monmouth.edu. *Application contact:* Kevin New, Graduate Admission Counselor, 732-571-3452, Fax: 732-263-5123, E-mail: gradadm@monmouth.edu.
Website: http://www.monmouth.edu/academics/criminal_justice/default.asp

National Defense University, College of International Security Affairs, Washington, DC 20319-5066. Offers strategic security studies (MA), including counterterrorism, homeland defense, international security studies. *Program availability:* Part-time, evening/weekend. *Degree requirements:* For master's, thesis. *Entrance requirements:* Additional exam requirements/recommendations for international students: required—TOEFL.

National University, School of Professional Studies, La Jolla, CA 92037-1011. Offers criminal justice (MCJ); digital cinema production (MFA); digital journalism (MA); homeland security and emergency management (MS); juvenile justice (MS); professional screenwriting (MFA); public administration (MPA), including human resource management, organizational leadership. *Program availability:* Part-time, evening/weekend, 100% online, blended/hybrid learning. *Degree requirements:* For master's, thesis (for some programs). *Entrance requirements:* For master's, interview, minimum GPA of 2.5. Additional exam requirements/recommendations for international students: required—TOEFL (minimum score 550 paper-based; 79 iBT), IELTS (minimum score 6). Electronic applications accepted. *Expenses: Tuition:* Full-time $442; part-time $442 per unit.

Naval Postgraduate School, Departments and Academic Groups, Department of National Security Affairs, Monterey, CA 93943. Offers security studies (MA, PhD), including civil-military relations (MA), combating terrorism: policy and strategy (MA), defense decision-making and planning (MA), Europe and Eurasia (MA), Far East, Southeast Asia, and the Pacific (MA), homeland security and defense (MA), Middle East, South Asia, Sub-Saharan Africa (MA), stabilization and reconstruction (MA), western hemisphere (MA). *Program availability:* Part-time. *Degree requirements:* For master's, thesis (for some programs).

Nichols College, Graduate and Professional Studies, Dudley, MA 01571-5000. Offers business administration (MBA); counterterrorism (MS); organizational leadership (MSOL). *Program availability:* Part-time, evening/weekend, online learning. *Degree requirements:* For master's, project (for MOL). *Entrance requirements:* For master's, 2 letters of recommendation, current resume, official transcripts, 800-word personal statement. Additional exam requirements/recommendations for international students: required—TOEFL (minimum score 500 paper-based). Electronic applications accepted.

Northeastern University, College of Professional Studies, Boston, MA 02115-5096. Offers applied nutrition (MS); college athletics administration (MSL); commerce and economic development (MS); corporate and organizational communication (MS); criminal justice (MS); digital media (MPS); elearning and instructional design (M Ed); elementary education (MAT); geographic information technology (MPS); global studies and international relations (MS); higher education administration (M Ed); homeland security (MA); human services (MS); informatics (MPS); leadership (MS); learning analytics (M Ed); learning and instruction (M Ed); nonprofit management (MS); professional sports administration (MSL); project management (MS); regulatory affairs for drugs, biologics, and medical devices (MS); respiratory care leadership (MS); special education (M Ed); technical communication (MS). *Program availability:* Part-time, evening/weekend, 100% online, blended/hybrid learning. *Faculty:* 85 full-time (53 women), 892 part-time/adjunct (379 women). *Students:* 5,699 part-time (3,305 women). In 2019, 1,787 master's awarded. *Application deadline:* Applications are processed on a rolling basis. Application fee: $0. Electronic applications accepted. *Expenses:* Contact institution. *Financial support:* Applicants required to submit FAFSA. *Unit head:* Dr. Mary Loeffelholz, Dean of the College of Professional Studies, 617-373-6060. *Application contact:* Dr. Mary Loeffelholz, Dean of the College of Professional Studies, 617-373-6060.
Website: https://cps.northeastern.edu/

Northeastern University, College of Social Sciences and Humanities, Boston, MA 02115. Offers criminology and criminal justice (MSCJ); criminology and justice policy (PhD); economics (MA, PhD); English (MA, PhD); international affairs (MA); law and public policy (PhD); political science (MA, PhD); public administration (MPA); public policy (MPP); security and resilience studies (MS); sociology (MA, PhD); urban and regional policy (MS); urban informatics (MS); world history (MA, PhD). *Program availability:* Online learning. *Degree requirements:* For doctorate, variable foreign language requirement, comprehensive exam, thesis/dissertation. *Entrance requirements:* For master's and doctorate, GRE. Additional exam requirements/recommendations for international students: required—TOEFL, IELTS. Electronic applications accepted. *Expenses:* Contact institution.

Northwestern State University of Louisiana, Graduate Studies and Research, Department of Criminal Justice, History and Social Sciences, Program in Homeland Security, Natchitoches, LA 71497. Offers MS. *Degree requirements:* For master's, comprehensive exam, thesis or alternative. *Entrance requirements:* For master's, GRE General Test. Additional exam requirements/recommendations for international students: required—TOEFL. Electronic applications accepted.

Notre Dame College, Graduate Programs, South Euclid, OH 44121. Offers mild/moderate needs (M Ed); reading (M Ed); security policy studies (MA, Graduate Certificate); technology (M Ed). *Program availability:* Part-time, evening/weekend, online only, 100% online. *Faculty:* 11 full-time (8 women), 8 part-time/adjunct (5 women). *Students:* 20 full-time (17 women), 83 part-time (59 women); includes 28 minority (12 Black or African American, non-Hispanic/Latino; 2 Hispanic/Latino; 1 Native Hawaiian or other Pacific Islander, non-Hispanic/Latino; 13 Two or more races, non-Hispanic/Latino). Average age 35. In 2019, 5 master's awarded. *Degree requirements:* For master's, thesis. *Entrance requirements:* For master's, GRE General Test, MAT, minimum undergraduate GPA of 2.75, valid teaching certificate, bachelor's degree in an education-related field from accredited college or university, official transcripts of most recent college work. *Application deadline:* For fall admission, 8/1 priority date for domestic students; for spring admission, 1/1 for domestic students. Applications are processed on a rolling basis. Application fee: $40. *Expenses: Tuition:* Full-time $590; part-time $590 per credit hour. *Financial support:* Tuition waivers (full) available. Support available to part-time students. Financial award application deadline: 4/15; financial award applicants required to submit FAFSA. *Unit head:* Florentine Hoelker, Dean of Online and Graduate Programs, 215-373-6469, E-mail: fhoelker@ndc.edu. *Application contact:* Brandy Viol, Assistant Dean of Enrollment, 216-373-5350, Fax: 216-373-6330, E-mail: bviol@ndc.edu.
Website: https://online.notredamecollege.edu/online-degrees/#master

Pace University, Dyson College of Arts and Sciences, MA Program in Management for Public Safety and Homeland Security Professionals, New York, NY 10038. Offers MA. *Program availability:* Evening/weekend, blended/hybrid learning. *Degree requirements:* For master's, project. *Entrance requirements:* For master's, 2 letters of recommendation, resume, personal statement, official transcripts. Additional exam requirements/recommendations for international students: required—TOEFL. Electronic applications accepted.

Penn State Harrisburg, Graduate School, School of Public Affairs, Middletown, PA 17057. Offers criminal justice (MA); health administration (MHA); health administration: long term care (Certificate); homeland security (MPS, Certificate); public administration (MPA, PhD); public administration: non-profit administration (Certificate); public budgeting and financial management (Certificate); public sector human resource management (Certificate). *Accreditation:* NASPAA.

Post University, Program in Public Administration, Waterbury, CT 06723-2540. Offers emergency management and homeland security (MPA). *Program availability:* Online learning. *Degree requirements:* For master's, capstone project. *Entrance requirements:* For master's, resume.

Regent University, Graduate School, Robertson School of Government, Virginia Beach, VA 23464. Offers government (MA), including American government, healthcare policy and ethics (MA, MPA), international relations, law and public policy, national security studies, political communication, political theory, religion and politics; national security studies (MA), including cybersecurity, homeland security, international security, Middle East politics; public administration (MPA), including emergency management and homeland security, federal government, general public administration, healthcare policy and ethics (MA, MPA), law, nonprofit administration and faith-based organizations, public leadership and management, servant leadership. *Program availability:* Part-time, evening/weekend, 100% online, blended/hybrid learning. *Faculty:* 5 full-time (1 woman), 19 part-time/adjunct (2 women). *Students:* 36 full-time (22 women), 159 part-time (89 women); includes 82 minority (52 Black or African American, non-Hispanic/Latino; 2 American Indian or Alaska Native, non-Hispanic/Latino; 2 Asian, non-Hispanic/Latino; 23 Hispanic/Latino; 3 Two or more races, non-Hispanic/Latino), 4 international. Average age 36. 181 applicants, 70% accepted, 75 enrolled. In 2019, 58 master's awarded. *Degree requirements:* For master's, thesis optional, internship. *Entrance requirements:* For master's, GRE General Test or LSAT, personal essay, writing sample, resume, college transcripts. Additional exam requirements/recommendations for international students: required—TOEFL (minimum score 577 paper-based). *Application deadline:* For fall admission, 5/1 priority date for domestic students; for spring admission, 11/1 priority date for domestic students. Applications are processed on a rolling basis. Application fee: $50. Electronic applications accepted. *Expenses:* Contact institution. *Financial support:* In 2019–20, 132 students received support. Career-related internships or fieldwork, scholarships/grants, and unspecified assistantships available. Support available to part-time students. Financial award applicants required to submit FAFSA. *Unit head:* Dr. Stephen Perry, Interim Dean, 757-352-4082, E-mail: sperry@regent.edu. *Application contact:* Heidi Cece, Assistant Vice President for Enrollment Management, 800-373-5504, Fax: 757-352-4381, E-mail: admissions@regent.edu.
Website: https://www.regent.edu/robertson-school-of-government/

Rider University, College of Liberal Arts and Sciences, Program in Homeland Security, Lawrenceville, NJ 08648-3001. Offers domestic security (MA); global security (MA). *Program availability:* Evening/weekend, online only, 100% online. *Entrance requirements:* For master's, bachelor's degree with minimum cumulative GPA of 2.7. Additional exam requirements/recommendations for international students: required—TOEFL (minimum score 540 paper-based; 79 iBT). Electronic applications accepted.

St. John's University, College of Professional Studies, Department of Criminal Justice, Legal Studies, and Homeland Security, Queens, NY 11439. Offers homeland security and criminal justice leadership (MPS). *Entrance requirements:* For master's, letters of recommendation, transcripts, resume, personal statement, proficiency in a foreign language. Additional exam requirements/recommendations for international students: required—TOEFL (minimum score 90 iBT), IELTS (minimum score 6.5). Electronic applications accepted.

St. Mary's University, Graduate Studies, Program in International Relations, San Antonio, TX 78228. Offers conflict transformation (Certificate); international conflict resolution (MA); international development (MA); international relations (MA); security policy (MA); JD/MA. *Program availability:* Part-time, evening/weekend, 100% online. *Degree requirements:* For master's, one foreign language, comprehensive exam (for some programs), thesis (for some programs), thesis or comprehensive exam. *Entrance requirements:* For master's, minimum undergraduate cumulative GPA of 3.0. Additional exam requirements/recommendations for international students: required—TOEFL (minimum score 550 paper-based; 80 iBT), IELTS (minimum score 6). Electronic applications accepted.

Salve Regina University, Program in Administration of Justice and Homeland Security, Newport, RI 02840. Offers administration of justice and homeland security (MS); cybersecurity and intelligence (CGS); digital forensics (CGS); leadership in justice (CGS). *Program availability:* Part-time, evening/weekend, some in-person. *Entrance requirements:* Additional exam requirements/recommendations for international students: required—TOEFL (minimum score 600 paper-based; 100 iBT). *Application deadline:* For fall admission, 7/1 priority date for domestic students, 3/15 priority date for international students; for spring admission, 11/1 priority date for domestic students, 9/5 priority date for international students. Applications are processed on a rolling basis. Application fee: $0. Electronic applications accepted. *Financial support:* Application deadline: 3/1; applicants required to submit FAFSA. *Unit head:* Jeffrey Mace, Director, 401-341-2338, E-mail: jeffrey.mac@salve.edu. *Application contact:* Laurie Reilly, Graduate Admissions Manager, 401-341-2153, Fax: 401-341-2973, E-mail: laurie.reilly@salve.edu.
Website: http://www.salve.edu/graduate-studies/administration-of-justice-and-homeland-security

Sam Houston State University, College of Criminal Justice, Department of Security Studies, Huntsville, TX 77341. Offers homeland security studies (MS). *Program availability:* Part-time, online learning. *Degree requirements:* For master's, thesis optional. *Entrance requirements:* For master's, undergraduate degree, official transcripts, three letters of recommendation, current resume, personal essay. Additional exam requirements/recommendations for international students: required—TOEFL (minimum score 550 paper-based; 79 iBT); recommended—IELTS (minimum score 6.5). Electronic applications accepted.

Southern Illinois University Carbondale, Graduate School, College of Applied Science, Program in Fire Service and Homeland Security, Carbondale, IL 62901-4701. Offers MS. *Program availability:* Part-time, evening/weekend, online learning. *Entrance requirements:* Additional exam requirements/recommendations for international students: required—TOEFL. Electronic applications accepted.

Texas A&M University–Commerce, College of Humanities, Social Sciences and Arts, Commerce, TX 75429. Offers applied criminology (MS); applied linguistics (MA, MS); art (MA, MFA); christianity in history (Graduate Certificate); computational linguistics (Graduate Certificate); creative writing (Graduate Certificate); criminal justice management (Graduate Certificate); criminal justice studies (Graduate Certificate); English (MA, MS, PhD); film studies (Graduate Certificate); history (MA, MS); Holocaust studies (Graduate Certificate); homeland security (Graduate Certificate); music (MM);

music performance (MM); political science (MA, MS); public history (Graduate Certificate); sociology (MS); Spanish (MA); studies in children's and adolescent literature and culture (Graduate Certificate); teaching English to speakers of other languages (Graduate Certificate); theater (MA, MS); world history (Graduate Certificate). *Program availability:* Part-time. *Faculty:* 49 full-time (28 women), 8 part-time/adjunct (2 women). *Students:* 34 full-time (21 women), 427 part-time (302 women); includes 175 minority (66 Black or African American, non-Hispanic/Latino; 1 American Indian or Alaska Native, non-Hispanic/Latino; 13 Asian, non-Hispanic/Latino; 79 Hispanic/Latino; 16 Two or more races, non-Hispanic/Latino), 15 international. Average age 38. 193 applicants, 49% accepted, 78 enrolled. In 2019, 122 master's, 6 doctorates awarded. *Degree requirements:* For master's, one foreign language, comprehensive exam, thesis (for some programs); for doctorate, one foreign language, comprehensive exam, thesis/dissertation, departmental qualifying exam. *Entrance requirements:* For master's, GRE General Test, official transcripts, letters of recommendation, resume, statement of goals; for doctorate, GRE General Test, official transcripts, letters of recommendation, statement of goals, writing samples, writing sessions, resumes. Additional exam requirements/recommendations for international students: required—TOEFL (minimum score 550 paper-based; 79 iBT), IELTS (minimum score 6), PTE (minimum score 53). *Application deadline:* For fall admission, 6/1 priority date for international students; for spring admission, 10/15 priority date for international students; for summer admission, 3/15 priority date for international students. Applications are processed on a rolling basis. Application fee: $50 ($75 for international students). Electronic applications accepted. *Expenses: Tuition, area resident:* Full-time $3630; part-time $202 per credit hour. Tuition, state resident: full-time $3630; part-time $202 per credit hour. Tuition, nonresident: full-time $11,232; part-time $624 per credit hour. *International tuition:* $11,232 full-time. *Required fees:* $2948. *Financial support:* In 2019–20, 30 students received support, including 18 research assistantships with partial tuition reimbursements available (averaging $3,231 per year), 136 teaching assistantships with partial tuition reimbursements available (averaging $4,053 per year); Federal Work-Study, institutionally sponsored loans, scholarships/grants, health care benefits, and unspecified assistantships also available. Financial award application deadline: 5/1; financial award applicants required to submit FAFSA. *Unit head:* Dr. William F. Kuracina, Interim Dean, 903-886-5166, Fax: 903-886-5774, E-mail: william.kuracina@tamuc.edu. *Application contact:* Rebecca Stevens, Graduate Student Services Coordinator, 903-468-6049, E-mail: rebecca.stevens@tamuc.edu.
Website: http://www.tamuc.edu/academics/colleges/humanitiesSocialSciencesArts/

Thomas Edison State University, John S. Watson School of Public Service and Continuing Studies, Trenton, NJ 08608. Offers community and economic development (MSM); environmental policy/environmental justice (MSM); homeland security (MSHS, MSM); information and technology for public service (MSM); nonprofit management (MSM); public and municipal finance (MSM); public health (MSM); public service administration and leadership (MSM); public service leadership (MPSL). *Program availability:* Part-time, online learning. *Entrance requirements:* Additional exam requirements/recommendations for international students: required—TOEFL (minimum score 550 paper-based; 79 iBT). Electronic applications accepted.

Tiffin University, Program in Criminal Justice, Tiffin, OH 44883-2161. Offers criminal justice (MS), including crime analysis, criminal behavior, forensic psychology, homeland security administration, justice administration. *Program availability:* Part-time, evening/weekend, 100% online, blended/hybrid learning. *Degree requirements:* For master's, thesis optional. *Entrance requirements:* For master's, minimum undergraduate GPA of 2.5, work experience. Additional exam requirements/recommendations for international students: required—TOEFL (minimum score 550 paper-based; 79 iBT). Electronic applications accepted. *Expenses:* Contact institution.

Towson University, College of Liberal Arts, Program in Integrated Homeland Security Management, Towson, MD 21252-0001. Offers integrated homeland security management (MS); security assessment and management (Postbaccalaureate Certificate). *Program availability:* Part-time, evening/weekend. *Students:* 3 full-time (all women), 13 part-time (2 women); includes 3 minority (2 Black or African American, non-Hispanic/Latino; 1 Two or more races, non-Hispanic/Latino). *Entrance requirements:* For master's and Postbaccalaureate Certificate, BA in related field, 3 years of related work experience, resume, 2 letters of reference, minimum GPA of 3.0. *Application deadline:* For fall admission, 1/17 for domestic students, 5/15 for international students; for spring admission, 10/15 for domestic students, 12/1 for international students. Applications are processed on a rolling basis. Application fee: $45. Electronic applications accepted. *Expenses: Tuition, area resident:* Full-time $7920; part-time $439 per credit. Tuition, nonresident: full-time $16,344; part-time $908 per credit. *International tuition:* $16,344 full-time. *Required fees:* $2628; $146 per credit. $876 per term. *Financial support:* Application deadline: 4/1. *Unit head:* Dr. Joseph Clark, Graduate Program Director, 410-704-4490, E-mail: jrclark@towson.edu. *Application contact:* Coverley Beidleman, Assistant Director of Graduate Admissions, 410-704-5630, Fax: 410-704-3030, E-mail: grads@towson.edu.
Website: https://www.towson.edu/cla/departments/interdisciplinary/grad/homelandsecurity/

Tulane University, School of Professional Advancement, New Orleans, LA 70118-5669. Offers health and wellness management (MPS); homeland security studies (MPS); information technology management (MPS); liberal arts (MLA). *Program availability:* Part-time. *Degree requirements:* For master's, thesis. *Entrance requirements:* For master's, GRE General Test, minimum B average in undergraduate course work. Additional exam requirements/recommendations for international students: required—TOEFL. *Expenses: Tuition:* Full-time $57,004; part-time $3167 per credit hour. *Required fees:* $2086; $44.50 per credit hour. $80 per term. Tuition and fees vary according to course load, degree level and program.

University at Albany, State University of New York, College of Emergency Preparedness, Homeland Security and Cybersecurity, Albany, NY 12222-0001. Offers cybersecurity (Certificate); emergency preparedness (Certificate); homeland security (Certificate); information science (MS, PhD). *Program availability:* 100% online, blended/hybrid learning. *Faculty:* 25 full-time (9 women), 35 part-time/adjunct (11 women). *Students:* 63 full-time (44 women), 127 part-time (93 women); includes 31 minority (9 Black or African American, non-Hispanic/Latino; 3 Asian, non-Hispanic/Latino; 18 Hispanic/Latino; 1 Two or more races, non-Hispanic/Latino), 22 international. Average age 27. 173 applicants, 77% accepted, 76 enrolled. In 2019, 35 master's, 2 doctorates, 24 other advanced degrees awarded. *Degree requirements:* For doctorate, thesis/dissertation optional. *Entrance requirements:* For master's and doctorate, GRE, transcripts from all schools attended, 3 letters of recommendation, resume, personal statement. Additional exam requirements/recommendations for international students: required—TOEFL (minimum score 550 paper-based). *Application deadline:* For fall admission, 1/15 for domestic students; for spring admission, 11/15 for domestic students. Application fee: $75. Electronic applications accepted. *Expenses: Tuition, area resident:* Full-time $11,530; part-time $480 per credit hour. Tuition, nonresident: full-time $23,530; part-time $980 per credit hour. *International tuition:* $23,530 full-time. *Required fees:* $2185; $96 per credit hour. Part-time tuition and fees vary according to course load and program. *Financial support:* Research assistantships, teaching assistantships, career-related internships or fieldwork, traineeships, and unspecified

assistantships available. *Unit head:* Dr. Robert Griffin, Dean, 518-442-5258, E-mail: rpgriffin@albany.edu. *Application contact:* Jennifer J Goodall, Vice Dean, 518-949-3283, E-mail: jgoodall@albany.edu.
Website: http://www.albany.edu/cehc/

University at Albany, State University of New York, Nelson A. Rockefeller College of Public Affairs and Policy, Department of Public Administration and Policy, Albany, NY 12222-0001. Offers financial management and public economics (MPA); financial market regulation (MPA); health policy (MPA); healthcare management (MPA); homeland security (MPA); human resources management (MPA); information strategy and management (MPA); local government management (MPA); nonprofit management (MPA); nonprofit management and leadership (Certificate); organizational behavior and theory (MPA, PhD); planning and policy analysis (CAS); policy analysis (MPA); politics and administration (PhD); public finance (PhD); public management (PhD); public policy (PhD); public sector management (Certificate); women and public policy (Certificate); JD/MPA. *Accreditation:* NASPAA (one or more programs are accredited). *Program availability:* Blended/hybrid learning. *Faculty:* 19 full-time (8 women), 12 part-time/adjunct (4 women). *Students:* 119 full-time (71 women), 41 part-time (4 women); includes 45 minority (18 Black or African American, non-Hispanic/Latino; 7 Asian, non-Hispanic/Latino; 14 Hispanic/Latino; 6 Two or more races, non-Hispanic/Latino), 28 international. Average age 29. 172 applicants, 81% accepted, 85 enrolled. In 2019, 57 master's, 6 doctorates, 11 other advanced degrees awarded. *Degree requirements:* For doctorate, one foreign language, thesis/dissertation. *Entrance requirements:* For doctorate, GRE General Test. Additional exam requirements/recommendations for international students: required—TOEFL (minimum score 550 paper-based). *Application deadline:* For fall admission, 1/15 priority date for domestic students, 5/1 for international students; for spring admission, 11/15 for domestic students. Applications are processed on a rolling basis. Application fee: $75. Electronic applications accepted. *Expenses: Tuition, area resident:* Full-time $11,530; part-time $480 per credit hour. Tuition, nonresident: full-time $23,530; part-time $980 per credit hour. *International tuition:* $23,530 full-time. *Required fees:* $2185; $96 per credit hour. Part-time tuition and fees vary according to course load and program. *Financial support:* Research assistantships, teaching assistantships, and Federal Work-Study available. Financial award application deadline: 2/1. *Unit head:* Edmund Stazyk, Chair, 518-591-8723, E-mail: estazyk@albany.edu. *Application contact:* Luis Felipe Luna-Reyes, 518-442-5297, E-mail: llunareyes@albany.edu.
Website: http://www.albany.edu/rockefeller/pad.shtml

University of Alaska Fairbanks, School of Management, Program in Security and Disaster Management, Fairbanks, AK 99775-7520. Offers MSDM. *Program availability:* Part-time, evening/weekend, 100% online, blended/hybrid learning. *Entrance requirements:* For master's, Watson-Glaser Critical Thinking Appraisal, bachelor's degree from accredited institution with minimum cumulative undergraduate and major GPA of 2.75. Additional exam requirements/recommendations for international students: required—TOEFL (minimum score 79 iBT), IELTS (minimum score 6.5). Electronic applications accepted. *Expenses:* Contact institution.

University of Central Florida, College of Community Innovation and Education, School of Public Administration, Orlando, FL 32816. Offers emergency management and homeland security (Certificate); fundraising (Certificate); nonprofit management (MNM, Certificate); public administration (MPA); research administration (MRA); urban and regional planning (MS). *Accreditation:* NASPAA. *Program availability:* Part-time, evening/weekend. *Students:* 149 full-time (95 women), 497 part-time (347 women); includes 277 minority (128 Black or African American, non-Hispanic/Latino; 1 American Indian or Alaska Native, non-Hispanic/Latino; 13 Asian, non-Hispanic/Latino; 118 Hispanic/Latino; 1 Native Hawaiian or other Pacific Islander, non-Hispanic/Latino; 16 Two or more races, non-Hispanic/Latino), 9 international. Average age 33. 430 applicants, 79% accepted, 226 enrolled. In 2019, 106 master's, 26 other advanced degrees awarded. *Degree requirements:* For master's, comprehensive exam, thesis or alternative, research report. *Entrance requirements:* For master's, letters of recommendation, goal statement, resume. Additional exam requirements/recommendations for international students: required—TOEFL. *Application deadline:* For fall admission, 6/15 for domestic students; for spring admission, 11/1 for domestic students. Application fee: $30. Electronic applications accepted. *Financial support:* In 2019–20, 6 students received support, including 1 fellowship with partial tuition reimbursement available (averaging $5,000 per year), 4 research assistantships with partial tuition reimbursements available (averaging $6,049 per year), 1 teaching assistantship with partial tuition reimbursement available (averaging $5,478 per year); career-related internships or fieldwork, Federal Work-Study, institutionally sponsored loans, health care benefits, tuition waivers (partial), and unspecified assistantships also available. Financial award application deadline: 3/1; financial award applicants required to submit FAFSA. *Unit head:* Dr. Naim Kapucu, Director, 407-823-6096, Fax: 407-823-5651, E-mail: kapucu@ucf.edu. *Application contact:* Associate Director, Graduate Admissions, 407-823-2766, Fax: 407-823-6442, E-mail: gradadmissions@ucf.edu.
Website: https://www.cohpa.ucf.edu/publicadmin/

University of Colorado Denver, School of Public Affairs, Program in Public Affairs and Administration, Denver, CO 80127. Offers public administration (MPA), including domestic violence, emergency management and homeland security, environmental policy, management and law, homeland security and defense, local government, nonprofit management, public administration; public affairs (PhD). *Accreditation:* NASPAA. *Program availability:* Part-time, evening/weekend, online learning. Tuition and fees vary according to course load, program and reciprocity agreements.

University of Denver, Josef Korbel School of International Studies, Denver, CO 80208. Offers conflict resolution (MA); global business and corporate social responsibility (Certificate); global finance, trade and economic integration (MA); global health affairs (Certificate); homeland security (Certificate); humanitarian assistance (Certificate); international administration (MA); international development (MA); international human rights (MA); international security (MA); international studies (MA, PhD); public policy studies (MPP); religion and international affairs (Certificate). *Program availability:* Part-time. *Faculty:* 41 full-time (15 women), 14 part-time/adjunct (2 women). *Students:* 208 full-time (112 women), 24 part-time (13 women); includes 50 minority (11 Black or African American, non-Hispanic/Latino; 10 Asian, non-Hispanic/Latino; 15 Hispanic/Latino; 14 Two or more races, non-Hispanic/Latino), 20 international. Average age 27. 718 applicants, 70% accepted, 88 enrolled. In 2019, 134 master's, 2 doctorates, 26 other advanced degrees awarded. *Degree requirements:* For master's, variable foreign language requirement, thesis (for some programs); for doctorate, one foreign language, comprehensive exam, thesis/dissertation, one extended research paper. *Entrance requirements:* For master's, GRE General Test, bachelor's degree, transcripts, two letters of recommendation, personal statement, resume or curriculum vitae; for doctorate, GRE General Test, bachelor's degree (most have a master's degree), transcripts, personal statement, resume or curriculum vitae, writing sample. Additional exam requirements/recommendations for international students: required—TOEFL (minimum score 587 paper-based; 95 iBT). *Application deadline:* For fall admission, 1/23 priority date for domestic and international students; for winter admission, 11/1 for domestic and international students. Applications are processed on a rolling basis. Application fee: $65. Electronic applications accepted. *Expenses:* Contact institution. *Financial support:* In 2019–20, 161 students received support, including 4 teaching assistantships with tuition reimbursements available (averaging $16,875 per year); research assistantships with tuition reimbursements available, career-related internships or fieldwork, Federal Work-Study, institutionally sponsored loans, scholarships/grants, and unspecified assistantships also available. Support available to part-time students. Financial award application deadline: 2/15; financial award applicants required to submit FAFSA. *Unit head:* Dr. Fritz Mayer, Dean, 303-871-6338, E-mail: frederick.mayer@du.edu. *Application contact:* Admissions Contact, 303-871-2324, E-mail: korbeladm@du.edu.
Website: http://www.du.edu/korbel

University of Illinois at Springfield, Graduate Programs, College of Public Affairs and Administration, Program in Public Health, Springfield, IL 62703-5407. Offers community health education (Graduate Certificate); emergency preparedness and homeland security (Graduate Certificate); environmental health (MPH, Graduate Certificate); environmental risk assessment (Graduate Certificate); epidemiology (Graduate Certificate); public health (MPH). *Program availability:* Part-time, 100% online. *Faculty:* 7 full-time (5 women). *Students:* 31 full-time (24 women), 36 part-time (27 women); includes 13 minority (9 Black or African American, non-Hispanic/Latino; 1 Asian, non-Hispanic/Latino; 1 Hispanic/Latino; 2 Two or more races, non-Hispanic/Latino), 27 international. Average age 30. 90 applicants, 54% accepted, 12 enrolled. In 2019, 13 master's, 10 other advanced degrees awarded. *Degree requirements:* For master's, comprehensive exam, internship. *Entrance requirements:* For master's, GRE, minimum undergraduate GPA of 3.0, 3 letters of recommendation, essay addressing the areas outlined on the department application form. Additional exam requirements/recommendations for international students: required—TOEFL (minimum score 500 paper-based; 61 iBT). *Application deadline:* Applications are processed on a rolling basis. Application fee: $60 ($75 for international students). Electronic applications accepted. *Expenses:* $33.25 per credit hour (online fee). *Financial support:* In 2019–20, research assistantships with full tuition reimbursements (averaging $10,562 per year), teaching assistantships with full tuition reimbursements (averaging $10,652 per year) were awarded; fellowships, career-related internships or fieldwork, Federal Work-Study, scholarships/grants, health care benefits, and unspecified assistantships also available. Support available to part-time students. Financial award application deadline: 11/15; financial award applicants required to submit FAFSA. *Unit head:* Dr. Josiah Alamu, Program Administrator, 217-206-7874, Fax: 217-206-7279, E-mail: jalam3@uis.edu. *Application contact:* Dr. Josiah Alamu, Program Administrator, 217-206-7874, Fax: 217-206-7279, E-mail: jalam3@uis.edu.
Website: http://www.uis.edu/publichealth/

University of Management and Technology, Program in Criminal Justice, Arlington, VA 22209-1609. Offers homeland security (MS). *Program availability:* Part-time, evening/weekend, online learning. *Entrance requirements:* Additional exam requirements/recommendations for international students: required—TOEFL (minimum score 530 paper-based; 71 iBT). *Expenses: Tuition:* Full-time $7020; part-time $390 per credit hour. *Required fees:* $90; $30 per semester.

University of Management and Technology, Program in Homeland Security, Arlington, VA 22209-1609. Offers MS. *Degree requirements:* For master's, capstone course. *Expenses: Tuition:* Full-time $7020; part-time $390 per credit hour. *Required fees:* $90; $30 per semester.

University of Oklahoma Health Sciences Center, Graduate College, Hudson College of Public Health, Program in Preparedness and Terrorism, Oklahoma City, OK 73190. Offers MPH.

University of Phoenix–Online Campus, College of Justice and Security, Phoenix, AZ 85034-7209. Offers administration of justice and security (MS), including administration of justice and security, global and homeland security, law enforcement organizations; public administration (MPA). *Program availability:* Evening/weekend, online learning. *Entrance requirements:* Additional exam requirements/recommendations for international students: required—TOEFL, TOEIC (Test of English as an International Communication), Berlitz Online English Proficiency Exam, PTE, or IELTS. Electronic applications accepted. *Expenses:* Contact institution.

University of Phoenix - Phoenix Campus, College of Criminal Justice and Security, Tempe, AZ 85282-2371. Offers administration of justice and security (MS); global and homeland security (MS); law enforcement organizations (MS); public administration (MPA). *Program availability:* Evening/weekend, online learning. *Entrance requirements:* Additional exam requirements/recommendations for international students: required—TOEFL, TOEIC (Test of English as an International Communication), Berlitz Online English Proficiency Exam, PTE, or IELTS. Electronic applications accepted. *Expenses:* Contact institution.

University of Southern California, Graduate School, Sol Price School of Public Policy, Public Policy Programs, Los Angeles, CA 90089. Offers homeland security and public policy (Graduate Certificate); public policy (MPP, Graduate Certificate); M Pl/MPP; MPP/JD. *Program availability:* Part-time. Terminal master's awarded for partial completion of doctoral program. *Degree requirements:* For master's, practicum. *Entrance requirements:* For master's, GRE. Additional exam requirements/recommendations for international students: required—TOEFL (minimum score 600 paper-based; 100 iBT). Electronic applications accepted.

University of the District of Columbia, College of Arts and Sciences, Program in Homeland Security, Washington, DC 20008-1175. Offers MS. *Degree requirements:* For master's, thesis or public policy paper.

Upper Iowa University, Online Master's Programs, Fayette, IA 52142-1857. Offers accounting (MBA); corporate financial management (MBA); emergency management and homeland security (MPA); general management (MBA); general studies (MPA); government administration (MPA); health and human services (MPA); human resources management (MBA); nonprofit organizational management (MPA); organizational development (MBA); public management (MPA); sport administration (MSA). *Program availability:* Part-time, online learning. *Degree requirements:* For master's, research project. *Entrance requirements:* For master's, GMAT, GRE, or minimum GPA of 2.7 during last 60 hours. Additional exam requirements/recommendations for international students: required—TOEFL (minimum score 570 paper-based). Electronic applications accepted.

Virginia Commonwealth University, Graduate School, L. Douglas Wilder School of Government and Public Affairs, Program in Homeland Security and Emergency Preparedness, Richmond, VA 23284-9005. Offers MA, Graduate Certificate. *Program availability:* Part-time, online learning. *Entrance requirements:* For master's, GRE, GMAT, MAT or LSAT, minimum GPA of 2.7; for Graduate Certificate, minimum GPA of 2.7. Additional exam requirements/recommendations for international students: required—TOEFL (minimum score 600 paper-based; 100 iBT); recommended—IELTS (minimum score 6.5). Electronic applications accepted.

Walden University, Graduate Programs, School of Psychology, Minneapolis, MN 55401. Offers clinical psychology (MS), including counseling, general program; forensic psychology (MS), including forensic psychology in the community, general program, mental health applications, program planning and evaluation in forensic settings, psychology and legal systems; industrial organizational (MS, PhD), including consulting psychology, forensic (MS), forensic psychology (PhD), general practice, leadership development and coaching (MS), organizational diversity and social change, research evaluation (PhD); online teaching in psychology (Post-Master's Certificate); organizational psychology and development (Postbaccalaureate Certificate); psychology (MS, PhD), including applied psychology (MS), clinical psychology (PhD), crisis management and response (MS), educational psychology, forensic psychology (PhD), general psychology (MS), general psychology research (PhD), general psychology teaching (PhD), health psychology, leadership development and coaching (MS), psychology of culture (MS), psychology, public administration, and social change (MS), social psychology, terrorism and security (MS); psychology respecialization (Post-Doctoral Certificate). *Program availability:* Part-time, evening/weekend, online only, 100% online. Terminal master's awarded for partial completion of doctoral program. *Degree requirements:* For master's, thesis optional; for doctorate, thesis/dissertation, residency. *Entrance requirements:* For master's, bachelor's degree or higher; minimum GPA of 2.5; official transcripts; goal statement (for some programs); access to computer and Internet; for doctorate, master's degree or higher; three years of related professional or academic experience (preferred); minimum GPA of 3.0; goal statement and current resume (for select programs); official transcripts; access to computer and Internet; for other advanced degree, relevant work experience; access to computer and Internet. Additional exam requirements/recommendations for international students: required—TOEFL (minimum score 550 paper-based, 79 iBT), IELTS (minimum score 6.5), Michigan English Language Assessment Battery (minimum score 82), or PTE (minimum score 53). Electronic applications accepted.

Walden University, Graduate Programs, School of Public Policy and Administration, Minneapolis, MN 55401. Offers criminal justice (MPA, MPP, MS, Graduate Certificate), including emergency management (MS, PhD), general program (MS), global leadership (MS, PhD), homeland security and policy coordination (MS, PhD), law and public policy (MS, PhD), policy analysis (MS, PhD), public management and leadership (MS, PhD), self-designed (MS), terrorism, mediation, and peace (MS, PhD); criminal justice and executive management (MS), including global leadership (MS, PhD); criminal justice leadership and executive management (MS), including emergency management (MS, PhD), general program, homeland security and policy coordination (MS, PhD), law and public policy (MS, PhD), policy analysis (MS, PhD), public management and leadership (MS, PhD), self-designed, terrorism, mediation, and peace (MS, PhD); emergency management (MPA, MPP, MS), including criminal justice (MS, PhD), general program (MS), homeland security (MS), public management and leadership (MS, PhD), terrorism and emergency management (MS); general program (MPA, MPP), global leadership (MPA, MPP); government management (Graduate Certificate); health policy (MPA, MPP); homeland security (Graduate Certificate); homeland security and policy coordination (MPA, MPP); international nongovernmental organizations (MPA, MPP); law and public policy (MPA, MPP); local government management for sustainable communities (MPA, MPP); nonprofit management (Graduate Certificate); nonprofit management and leadership (MPA, MPP, MS), including global leadership (MS, PhD), international nongovernmental organization (MS), local government for sustainable communities (MS), self-designed (MS); online teaching in higher education (Post-Master's Certificate); policy analysis (MPA); public management and leadership (MPA, MPP, Graduate Certificate); public policy (Graduate Certificate); public policy and administration (PhD), including criminal justice (MS, PhD), emergency management (MS, PhD), global leadership (MS, PhD), health policy, homeland security and policy coordination (MS, PhD), international nongovernmental organizations, law and public policy (MS, PhD), local government management for sustainable communities, nonprofit management and leadership, policy analysis (MS, PhD), public management and leadership (MS, PhD), terrorism, mediation, and peace (MS, PhD); strategic planning and public policy (Graduate Certificate); terrorism, mediation, and peace (MPA, MPP). *Program availability:* Part-time, evening/weekend, online only, 100% online. *Degree*

requirements: For doctorate, thesis/dissertation, residency. *Entrance requirements:* For master's, bachelor's degree or higher; minimum GPA of 2.5; official transcripts; goal statement (for some programs); access to computer and Internet; for doctorate, master's degree or higher; three years of related professional or academic experience (preferred); minimum GPA of 3.0; goal statement and current resume (for select programs); official transcripts; access to computer and Internet; for other advanced degree, relevant work experience; access to computer and Internet. Additional exam requirements/recommendations for international students: required—TOEFL (minimum score 550 paper-based, 79 iBT), IELTS (minimum score 6.5), Michigan English Language Assessment Battery (minimum score 82), or PTE (minimum score 53). Electronic applications accepted.

Wayland Baptist University, Graduate Programs, Programs in Behavioral and Social Sciences, Plainview, TX 79072-6998. Offers counseling (MA); criminal justice (MACJ); government administration (MPA); history (MA); homeland security (MPA); humanities (MAH); justice administration (MPA). *Program availability:* Part-time, evening/weekend, 100% online, blended/hybrid learning. *Degree requirements:* For master's, comprehensive exam. *Entrance requirements:* For master's, GRE, MAT. Additional exam requirements/recommendations for international students: required—TOEFL (minimum score 500 paper-based; 61 iBT). Electronic applications accepted. *Expenses: Tuition:* Full-time $728; part-time $728 per semester. *Required fees:* $1218. Tuition and fees vary according to degree level, campus/location and program.

Western Kentucky University, Graduate School, Ogden College of Science and Engineering, Department of Physics and Astronomy, Bowling Green, KY 42101. Offers homeland security sciences (MS); physics (MA Ed).

Western Michigan University Cooley Law School, Graduate Programs, Lansing, MI 48901-3038. Offers administrative law (public law) (JD); business transactions (JD); Canadian law practice (JD); corporate law and finance (LL M); environmental law (public law) (JD); general practice (JD), including solo and small firm; general studies (LL M); homeland and national security law (LL M); insurance law (LL M); intellectual property (JD); intellectual property law (LL M); international law (JD); litigation (JD); taxation (LL M); U.S. legal studies for foreign attorneys (LL M); JD/LL M; JD/MBA; JD/MHA; JD/MPA; JD/MSW. *Accreditation:* ABA. *Program availability:* Part-time, evening/weekend, 100% online, blended/hybrid learning. *Degree requirements:* For master's, thesis (for some programs); for doctorate, minimum of 3 credits of clinical experience. *Entrance requirements:* For master's, JD or LL B; for doctorate, LSAT. Additional exam requirements/recommendations for international students: required—TOEFL (for U.S. legal studies for foreign attorneys LL M program); recommended—TOEFL. Electronic applications accepted. *Expenses:* Contact institution.

Wilmington University, College of Business, New Castle, DE 19720-6491. Offers accounting (MBA, MS); business administration (MBA, DBA); environmental stewardship (MBA); finance (MBA); health care administration (MBA, MSM); homeland security (MBA, MSM); human resource management (MSM); management information systems (MBA, MSN); marketing (MSM); marketing management (MBA); military leadership (MSM); organizational leadership (MBA, MSM); public administration (MSM). *Program availability:* Part-time, evening/weekend. *Entrance requirements:* Additional exam requirements/recommendations for international students: required—TOEFL (minimum score 500 paper-based). Electronic applications accepted.

Wilmington University, College of Social and Behavioral Sciences, New Castle, DE 19720-6491. Offers administration of human services (MS); administration of justice (MS); clinical mental health counseling (MS); homeland security (MS). *Accreditation:* ACA. *Program availability:* Part-time, evening/weekend. *Entrance requirements:* Additional exam requirements/recommendations for international students: required—TOEFL (minimum score 500 paper-based). Electronic applications accepted.

Industrial and Labor Relations

Baruch College of the City University of New York, Zicklin School of Business, Zicklin Executive Programs, Baruch Executive Master of Science in Industrial and Labor Relations Program, New York, NY 10010-5585. Offers MS. *Program availability:* Part-time, evening/weekend. *Entrance requirements:* For master's, professional experience in HR or labor relations. Additional exam requirements/recommendations for international students: required—TOEFL. *Expenses:* Contact institution.

Carnegie Mellon University, Dietrich College of Humanities and Social Sciences, Department of History, Pittsburgh, PA 15213-3891. Offers African and African-American diaspora (PhD); culture and power (PhD); labor, politics and social movements (PhD); technology, environment, science and health (PhD); women, gender and the family (PhD). *Program availability:* Part-time. *Degree requirements:* For doctorate, oral and written comprehensive exams, dissertation defense. *Entrance requirements:* For doctorate, GRE General Test. Additional exam requirements/recommendations for international students: required—TOEFL. Electronic applications accepted.

Cleveland State University, College of Graduate Studies, Monte Ahuja College of Business, Department of Management, Cleveland, OH 44115. Offers health care administration (MBA); labor relations and human resources (MLRHR). *Program availability:* Part-time, evening/weekend. *Faculty:* 6 full-time (3 women), 8 part-time/adjunct (1 woman). *Students:* 9 full-time (7 women), 15 part-time (14 women); includes 6 minority (3 Black or African American, non-Hispanic/Latino; 1 Asian, non-Hispanic/Latino; 1 Hispanic/Latino; 1 Two or more races, non-Hispanic/Latino), 1 international. Average age 28. In 2019, 14 master's awarded. *Entrance requirements:* For master's, GMAT or GRE, minimum GPA of 3.0. Additional exam requirements/recommendations for international students: required—TOEFL (minimum score 550 paper-based; 78 iBT). *Application deadline:* For fall admission, 7/15 for domestic students; for spring admission, 12/15 for domestic students. Applications are processed on a rolling basis. Application fee: $40. Electronic applications accepted. *Expenses:* Tuition, state resident: full-time $10,215; part-time $6810 per credit hour. Tuition, nonresident: full-time $17,496; part-time $11,664 per credit hour. *International tuition:* $19,316 full-time. Tuition and fees vary according to degree level and program. *Financial support:* In 2019–20, 3 students received support. Career-related internships or fieldwork, scholarships/grants, and unspecified assistantships available. Financial award application deadline: 5/1; financial award applicants required to submit FAFSA. *Unit head:* Dr. Kenneth J. Dunegan, Chairperson, 216-687-4747, Fax: 216-687-4708, E-mail: t.degroot@csuohio.edu. *Application contact:* Lisa Marie Sample, Administrative Assistant, 216-687-4726, Fax: 216-687-6888, E-mail: l.m.sample@csuohio.edu. Website: https://www.csuohio.edu/business/management/management

Cornell University, Graduate School, Graduate Fields of Industrial and Labor Relations, Ithaca, NY 14853. Offers collective bargaining, labor law and labor history (MILR, MPS, MS, PhD); economic and social statistics (MILR); human resource studies (MILR, MPS, MS, PhD); industrial and labor relations problems (MILR, MPS, MS, PhD); international and comparative labor (MILR, MPS, MS, PhD); labor economics (MILR, MPS, MS, PhD); organizational behavior (MILR, MPS, MS, PhD). *Degree requirements:* For master's, thesis (MS); for doctorate, comprehensive exam, thesis/dissertation, teaching experience. *Entrance requirements:* For master's and doctorate, GMAT or GRE General Test, 2 academic recommendations. Additional exam requirements/recommendations for international students: required—TOEFL (minimum score 550 paper-based; 77 iBT). Electronic applications accepted. *Expenses:* Contact institution.

Georgetown University, Graduate School of Arts and Sciences, Department of Economics, Washington, DC 20057. Offers econometrics (PhD); economic development (PhD); economic theory (PhD); industrial organization (PhD); international macro and finance (PhD); international trade (PhD); labor economics (PhD); macroeconomics (PhD); public economics and political economy (PhD); MA/PhD; MS/MA. *Degree requirements:* For doctorate, comprehensive exam, thesis/dissertation. *Entrance requirements:* For doctorate, GRE General Test. Additional exam requirements/recommendations for international students: required—TOEFL.

Georgia State University, Andrew Young School of Policy Studies, Department of Economics, Atlanta, GA 30302-3083. Offers economics (MA); environmental economics (PhD); experimental economics (PhD); labor economics (PhD); policy (MA); public finance (PhD); urban and regional economics (PhD). *Program availability:* Part-time. *Faculty:* 22 full-time (4 women). *Students:* 113 full-time (49 women), 14 part-time (6 women); includes 27 minority (11 Black or African American, non-Hispanic/Latino; 10 Asian, non-Hispanic/Latino; 5 Hispanic/Latino; 1 Two or more races, non-Hispanic/Latino), 60 international. Average age 29. 250 applicants, 48% accepted, 31 enrolled. In 2019, 29 master's, 10 doctorates awarded. Terminal master's awarded for partial completion of doctoral program. *Degree requirements:* For master's, thesis optional; for doctorate, comprehensive exam, thesis/dissertation. *Entrance requirements:* For master's and doctorate, GRE. Additional exam requirements/recommendations for international students: required—TOEFL (minimum score 603 paper-based; 100 iBT) or IELTS (minimum score 7). *Application deadline:* For fall admission, 1/15 for domestic and international students. Application fee: $50. Electronic applications accepted. *Expenses: Tuition, area resident:* Full-time $7164; part-time $398 per credit hour. Tuition, state resident: full-time $7164; part-time $398 per credit hour. Tuition, nonresident: full-time $22,662; part-time $1259 per credit hour. *International tuition:* $22,662 full-time. *Required fees:* $2128; $312 per credit hour. Tuition and fees vary

according to course load and program. *Financial support:* In 2019–20, fellowships with full tuition reimbursements (averaging $11,333 per year), research assistantships with full tuition reimbursements (averaging $9,788 per year), teaching assistantships with full tuition reimbursements (averaging $3,000 per year) were awarded; career-related internships or fieldwork also available. Financial award application deadline: 2/15; financial award applicants required to submit FAFSA. *Unit head:* Dr. Rusty Tchernis, Director of the Doctoral Program, 404-413-0154, Fax: 404-413-0145, E-mail: rtchernis@gsu.edu. *Application contact:* Dr. Rusty Tchernis, Director of the Doctoral Program, 404-413-0154, Fax: 404-413-0145, E-mail: rtchernis@gsu.edu.
Website: http://economics.gsu.edu/

Indiana University of Pennsylvania, School of Graduate Studies and Research, College of Health and Human Services, Department of Employment and Labor Relations, Human Resources and Employment Relations, Indiana, PA 15705. Offers MA. *Program availability:* Part-time, evening/weekend, 100% online, blended/hybrid learning. *Faculty:* 4 full-time (0 women). *Students:* 21 full-time (13 women), 19 part-time (13 women); includes 5 minority (4 Black or African American, non-Hispanic/Latino; 1 American Indian or Alaska Native, non-Hispanic/Latino), 5 international. Average age 31. 49 applicants, 90% accepted, 24 enrolled. In 2019, 23 master's awarded. *Entrance requirements:* For master's, 1 letter of recommendation, goal statement, official transcripts. Additional exam requirements/recommendations for international students: required—TOEFL (minimum score 550 paper-based; 80 iBT); recommended—IELTS (minimum score 6.5). *Application deadline:* Applications are processed on a rolling basis. Application fee: $50. Electronic applications accepted. *Expenses: Tuition, area resident:* Full-time $9288; part-time $516 per credit. Tuition, nonresident: full-time $13,932; part-time $774 per credit. *Required fees:* $4454. One-time fee: $115 full-time. Tuition and fees vary according to course load and program. *Financial support:* In 2019–20, 16 research assistantships with full and partial tuition reimbursements (averaging $2,096 per year) were awarded; fellowships with full tuition reimbursements, career-related internships or fieldwork, Federal Work-Study, scholarships/grants, and unspecified assistantships also available. Financial award application deadline: 4/15; financial award applicants required to submit FAFSA. *Unit head:* Dr. David M. Piper, Coordinator, 724-357-4470, E-mail: david.piper@iup.edu. *Application contact:* Dr. David M. Piper, Coordinator, 724-357-4470, E-mail: david.piper@iup.edu.
Website: http://www.iup.edu/elr/programs/ma/

Inter American University of Puerto Rico, Metropolitan Campus, Graduate Programs, Program in Labor Relations, San Juan, PR 00919-1293. Offers MA. *Degree requirements:* For master's, comprehensive exam. *Entrance requirements:* For master's, GRE or EXADEP, interview. Electronic applications accepted.

Inter American University of Puerto Rico, Metropolitan Campus, Graduate Programs, Program in Psychology, San Juan, PR 00919-1293. Offers counseling psychology (MA, PhD); industrial/organizational psychology (MA, PhD); labor relations (MA); school psychology (MA, PhD). *Degree requirements:* For master's, comprehensive exam. *Entrance requirements:* For master's, GRE or EXADEP, interview. Electronic applications accepted.

McMaster University, School of Graduate Studies, Faculty of Social Sciences, Program in Labour Studies, Hamilton, ON L8S 4M2, Canada. Offers work and society (MA).

Memorial University of Newfoundland, School of Graduate Studies, Interdisciplinary Program in Employment Relations, St. John's, NL A1C 5S7, Canada. Offers MER. *Program availability:* Part-time. *Degree requirements:* For master's, major supervised paper. *Entrance requirements:* For master's, undergraduate degree in related field, minimum B average. Electronic applications accepted.

Michigan State University, The Graduate School, College of Social Science, School of Human Resources and Labor Relations, East Lansing, MI 48824. Offers MLRHR, PhD. *Entrance requirements:* Additional exam requirements/recommendations for international students: required—TOEFL.

New York Institute of Technology, School of Management, Department of Human Resource Studies, Old Westbury, NY 11568-8000. Offers human resource management (Advanced Certificate); human resource management and labor relations (MS). *Program availability:* Part-time. *Degree requirements:* For master's, thesis or alternative, seminar and comprehensive exam, or thesis. *Entrance requirements:* For master's, bachelor's degree; minimum undergraduate GPA of 3.0; interview; for Advanced Certificate, bachelor's degree; minimum undergraduate GPA of 3.0. Additional exam requirements/recommendations for international students: required—TOEFL (minimum score 79 iBT), IELTS (minimum score 6), PTE (minimum score 53). Electronic applications accepted. *Expenses: Tuition:* Full-time $23,760; part-time $1320 per credit. *Required fees:* $260; $220 per unit. Full-time tuition and fees vary according to degree level and program. Part-time tuition and fees vary according to course load and program.

The Ohio State University, Graduate School, Max M. Fisher College of Business, Program in Human Resource Management, Columbus, OH 43210. Offers human resource management (MHRM, PhD); labor and human resources (PhD). *Program availability:* Part-time. *Degree requirements:* For doctorate, thesis/dissertation. *Entrance requirements:* For master's and doctorate, GRE General Test or GMAT. Additional exam requirements/recommendations for international students: required—Michigan English Language Assessment Battery (minimum score 86); recommended—TOEFL (minimum score 600 paper-based; 100 iBT), IELTS (minimum score 7). Electronic applications accepted.

Penn State University Park, Graduate School, College of the Liberal Arts, School of Labor and Employment Relations, University Park, PA 16802. Offers human resources and employment relations (MS); labor and global workers' rights (MPS).

Queen's University at Kingston, School of Graduate Studies, Program in Industrial Relations, Kingston, ON K7L 3N6, Canada. Offers MIR. *Program availability:* Part-time. *Degree requirements:* For master's, research essay, skill seminars and modules. *Entrance requirements:* For master's, course work in micro-economics, macro-economics, and quantitative statistics. Additional exam requirements/recommendations for international students: required—TOEFL (minimum score 600 paper-based).

Rutgers University - New Brunswick, School of Management and Labor Relations, Program in Industrial Relations and Human Resources, Piscataway, NJ 08854-8097. Offers PhD. *Program availability:* Part-time. *Degree requirements:* For doctorate, comprehensive exam, thesis/dissertation. *Entrance requirements:* For doctorate, GRE or GMAT, 3 letters of recommendation. Additional exam requirements/recommendations for international students: required—TOEFL (minimum score 575 paper-based; 91 iBT). Electronic applications accepted.

Rutgers University - New Brunswick, School of Management and Labor Relations, Program in Labor and Employment Relations, Piscataway, NJ 08854-8097. Offers MLER. *Program availability:* Part-time, online learning. *Degree requirements:* For master's, thesis optional. *Entrance requirements:* For master's, GRE General Test. Additional exam requirements/recommendations for international students: required—TOEFL. Electronic applications accepted. *Expenses:* Contact institution.

State University of New York Empire State College, School for Graduate Studies, Program in Labor and Policy Studies, Saratoga Springs, NY 12866-4391. Offers MA. *Program availability:* Part-time, evening/weekend, online learning. *Degree requirements:* For master's, thesis, exam, final project. *Entrance requirements:* Additional exam requirements/recommendations for international students: required—TOEFL (minimum score 600 paper-based). Electronic applications accepted.

Temple University, Beasley School of Law, Master's and Certificate Programs, Philadelphia, PA 19122-6096. Offers Asian law (LL M); business law (Certificate); employee benefits (Certificate); estate planning (Certificate); trial advocacy (LL M); trial advocacy and litigation (Certificate).

Université de Montréal, Faculty of Arts and Sciences, School of Industrial Relations, Montréal, QC H3C 3J7, Canada. Offers M Sc, PhD, DESS. *Program availability:* Part-time. *Degree requirements:* For master's, thesis; for doctorate, thesis/dissertation, general exam. *Entrance requirements:* For master's, BS in industrial relations. Electronic applications accepted.

Université du Québec à Trois-Rivières, Graduate Programs, Program in Labor Relations, Trois-Rivières, QC G9A 5H7, Canada. Offers DESS.

Université du Québec en Outaouais, Graduate Programs, Department of Industrial Relations, Gatineau, QC J8X 3X7, Canada. Offers M Sc, MA, PhD, Diploma. *Program availability:* Part-time. *Degree requirements:* For master's, thesis (for some programs), internship (for some programs); for doctorate, thesis/dissertation. *Entrance requirements:* For master's, appropriate bachelor's degree, proficiency in French; for doctorate, appropriate master's degree, proficiency in French.

University of Alberta, Faculty of Graduate Studies and Research, Doctoral Program in Business, Edmonton, AB T6G 2E1, Canada. Offers accounting (PhD); finance (PhD); human resources/industrial relations (PhD); management science (PhD); marketing (PhD); organizational analysis (PhD); MBA/PhD. *Accreditation:* AACSB. *Program availability:* Part-time. *Degree requirements:* For doctorate, comprehensive exam, thesis/dissertation. *Entrance requirements:* For doctorate, GMAT. Additional exam requirements/recommendations for international students: required—TOEFL (minimum score 550 paper-based). Electronic applications accepted.

University of California, Berkeley, Graduate Division, Haas School of Business, PhD in Business Administration Program, Berkeley, CA 94720. Offers accounting (PhD); business and public policy (PhD); finance (PhD); management of organizations (PhD); marketing (PhD); real estate (PhD). *Accreditation:* AACSB. *Degree requirements:* For doctorate, comprehensive exam, thesis/dissertation, written preliminary exams, oral qualifying exam. *Entrance requirements:* For doctorate, GMAT or GRE, minimum GPA of 3.0 in undergraduate and graduate coursework. Additional exam requirements/recommendations for international students: required—TOEFL (minimum score 570 paper-based; 70 iBT), IELTS (minimum score 7). Electronic applications accepted. *Expenses:* Contact institution.

University of Cincinnati, Graduate School, McMicken College of Arts and Sciences, Center for Organizational Leadership, Program in Labor and Employment Relations, Cincinnati, OH 45221. Offers MALER. *Program availability:* Part-time, evening/weekend. *Degree requirements:* For master's, thesis or alternative, final experience project. *Entrance requirements:* For master's, minimum undergraduate GPA of 3.0. Additional exam requirements/recommendations for international students: required—TOEFL (minimum score 560 paper-based). Electronic applications accepted.

University of Illinois at Urbana-Champaign, Graduate College, School of Labor and Employment Relations, Champaign, IL 61820. Offers human resources and industrial relations (MHRIR, PhD); MHRIR/JD; MHRIR/MBA. Terminal master's awarded for partial completion of doctoral program.

The University of Manchester, The University of Manchester - Grad School Programmes, Manchester, United Kingdom. Offers accounting and finance (M Sc); business (M Ent); business analysis and strategic management (M Sc); business analytics: operational research and risk analysis (M Sc); business psychology (M Sc); corporate communications and reputation management (M Sc); finance (M Sc); finance and business economics (M Sc); human resource management and industrial relations (M Sc); innovation management and entrepreneurship (M Sc); international business and management (M Sc); international human resource management and comparative industrial relations (M Sc); management (M Sc); marketing (M Sc); operations, project and supply chain management (M Sc); organizational psychology (M Sc); quantitative finance (M Sc). *Program availability:* Blended/hybrid learning. *Students:* 13,395. *Degree requirements:* For master's, variable foreign language requirement, comprehensive exam (for some programs), thesis. *Entrance requirements:* For master's, GMAT/GRE only required for a small number of programmes, US Bachelor's degree with GPA of 3.0-3.3, depending on the major applied to. Additional exam requirements/recommendations for international students: required—students are required to complete a Secure English Language Test if their first language is not English (some exceptions do apply); recommended—TOEFL (minimum score 100 iBT), IELTS (minimum score 7), TSE. *Application deadline:* For summer admission, 6/30 for domestic and international students. Applications are processed on a rolling basis. Application fee: 50 British pounds. Electronic applications accepted. *Financial support:* Scholarships/grants available. *Application contact:* Daniel Annoot, International Officer, 44 161 306 1634, E-mail: international@manchester.ac.uk.
Website: http://www.manchester.ac.uk/usa

University of Massachusetts Amherst, Graduate School, College of Social and Behavioral Sciences, The Labor Center, Amherst, MA 01003. Offers labor studies (MS); union leadership and administration (MS). *Program availability:* Part-time, online learning. *Degree requirements:* For master's, thesis or alternative. *Entrance requirements:* Additional exam requirements/recommendations for international students: required—TOEFL (minimum score 550 paper-based; 80 iBT), IELTS (minimum score 6.5). Electronic applications accepted.

University of Minnesota, Twin Cities Campus, Carlson School of Management, Master of Human Resources & Industrial Relations, Minneapolis, MN 55455-0213. Offers MA. *Accreditation:* AACSB. *Program availability:* Part-time, evening/weekend. *Degree requirements:* For master's, thesis or alternative, 48 course credits. *Entrance requirements:* For master's, GMAT or GRE General Test, undergraduate degree from accredited institution, course in microeconomics. Additional exam requirements/recommendations for international students: required—TOEFL (minimum score 550 paper-based; 79 iBT), IELTS (minimum score 6.5). Electronic applications accepted. *Expenses:* Contact institution.

University of Rhode Island, Graduate School, College of Business, Schmidt Labor Research Center, Kingston, RI 02881. Offers labor relations and human resources (MS, Graduate Certificate); MS/JD. *Program availability:* Part-time, evening/weekend. *Faculty:* 1 part-time/adjunct (0 women). *Students:* 6 full-time (4 women), 18 part-time (14 women); includes 2 minority (1 Black or African American, non-Hispanic/Latino; 1 Two or more races, non-Hispanic/Latino). 28 applicants, 96% accepted, 8 enrolled. In 2019, 11 master's, 14 other advanced degrees awarded. *Entrance requirements:* Additional exam requirements/recommendations for international students: required—TOEFL. *Application deadline:* For fall admission, 7/15 for domestic students, 2/1 for international

students; for spring admission, 11/15 for domestic students, 7/15 for international students; for summer admission, 4/15 for domestic students. Application fee: $65. Electronic applications accepted. *Expenses: Tuition, area resident:* Full-time $13,734; part-time $763 per credit. Tuition, state resident: full-time $13,734; part-time $763 per credit. Tuition, nonresident: full-time $26,512; part-time $1473 per credit. *International tuition:* $26,512 full-time. *Required fees:* $1780; $52 per credit. $35 per term. One-time fee: $165. *Financial support:* In 2019–20, 2 teaching assistantships with tuition reimbursements (averaging $18,986 per year) were awarded. Financial award application deadline: 2/1; financial award applicants required to submit FAFSA. *Unit head:* Dr. Aimee Phelps, Acting Director, 401-874-4693, E-mail: aimee@uri.edu. *Application contact:* Dr. Aimee Phelps, Acting Director, 401-874-4693, E-mail: aimee@uri.edu.
Website: https://web.uri.edu/lrc/

University of Toronto, School of Graduate Studies, Faculty of Arts and Science, Centre for Industrial Relations and Human Resources, Toronto, ON M5S 1A1, Canada. Offers MIRHR, PhD. *Program availability:* Part-time. *Degree requirements:* For doctorate, thesis/dissertation. *Entrance requirements:* For master's, GRE or GMAT (for applicants who completed degree outside of Canada), minimum B+ in final 2 years of bachelor's degree completion, 2 letters of reference, resume; for doctorate, GRE or GMAT, MIR or equivalent, minimum B+ average, 3 letters of reference, resume. Additional exam requirements/recommendations for international students: required—TOEFL (minimum score 600 paper-based; 100 iBT), IELTS, TWE (minimum score 5), Michigan English Language Assessment Battery, or COPE. Electronic applications accepted. *Expenses:* Contact institution.

University of Wisconsin–Milwaukee, Graduate School, College of Letters and Science, Interdepartmental Program in Human Resources and Labor Relations, Milwaukee, WI 53201-0413. Offers human resources and labor relations (MHRLR); international human resources and labor relations (Graduate Certificate); mediation and negotiation (Graduate Certificate). *Program availability:* Part-time. *Entrance requirements:* For master's, GMAT or GRE General Test. Additional exam requirements/recommendations for international students: required—TOEFL (minimum score 80 iBT), IELTS (minimum score 6.5). Electronic applications accepted.

Université Laval, Faculty of Social Sciences, Department of Industrial Relations, Programs in Industrial Relations, Québec, QC G1K 7P4, Canada. Offers MA, PhD. Terminal master's awarded for partial completion of doctoral program. *Degree requirements:* For master's, thesis (for some programs); for doctorate, comprehensive exam, thesis/dissertation. *Entrance requirements:* For master's and doctorate, knowledge of French, comprehension of written English. Electronic applications accepted.

Wayne State University, College of Liberal Arts and Sciences, Department of Economics, Detroit, MI 48202. Offers applied macroeconomics (MA, PhD); health economics (MA, PhD); industrial organization (MA, PhD); international economics (MA, PhD); labor and human resources (MA, PhD); JD/MA. *Faculty:* 10. *Students:* 47 full-time (13 women), 6 part-time (2 women); includes 8 minority (4 Black or African American, non-Hispanic/Latino; 2 Asian, non-Hispanic/Latino; 2 Hispanic/Latino), 18 international. Average age 31. 67 applicants, 37% accepted, 8 enrolled. In 2019, 4 master's, 2 doctorates awarded. *Degree requirements:* For master's, comprehensive exam; for doctorate, comprehensive exam, thesis/dissertation, oral examination on research, completion of course work in quantitative methods, final lecture. *Entrance requirements:* For master's, minimum upper-division GPA of 3.0; prior coursework in intermediate microeconomic and macroeconomic theory, statistics, and elementary calculus; for doctorate, GRE, minimum upper-division GPA of 3.0, prior coursework in intermediate microeconomic and macroeconomic theory, statistics, two courses in calculus, three letters of recommendation from officials or teaching staff at institution(s) most recently attended, statement of purpose. Additional exam requirements/recommendations for international students: required—TOEFL (minimum score 550 paper-based; 79 iBT), TWE (minimum score 5.5), Michigan English Language Assessment Battery (minimum score 85); recommended—IELTS (minimum score 6.5). *Application deadline:* For fall admission, 5/1 for domestic and international students; for winter admission, 10/1 priority date for domestic students, 9/1 priority date for international students; for spring admission, 1/1 priority date for domestic and international students. Applications are processed on a rolling basis. Application fee: $50. Electronic applications accepted. *Expenses: Tuition:* Full-time $34,567. *Financial support:* In 2019–20, 30 students received support, including 2 fellowships with tuition reimbursements available (averaging $20,000 per year), 17 teaching assistantships with tuition reimbursements available (averaging $19,883 per year); research assistantships, scholarships/grants, health care benefits, and unspecified assistantships also available. Support available to part-time students. Financial award applicants required to submit FAFSA. *Unit head:* Dr. Kevin Cotter, Department Chair, 313-577-3345, E-mail: kevin.cotter@wayne.edu. *Application contact:* Dr. Allen Charles Goodman, Professor and Director of Graduate Studies, 313-577-3235, E-mail: aa1313@wayne.edu.
Website: http://clas.wayne.edu/economics/

Wayne State University, Law School, Detroit, MI 48202. Offers corporate and finance law (LL M); labor and employment law (LL M); law (JD); taxation (LL M); United States law (LL M); JD/MA; JD/MADR; JD/MBA; JD/MS. *Accreditation:* ABA. *Program availability:* Part-time, evening/weekend. *Faculty:* 40 full-time (17 women), 52 part-time/adjunct (23 women). *Students:* 393 full-time (197 women), 41 part-time (20 women); includes 63 minority (38 Black or African American, non-Hispanic/Latino; 6 American Indian or Alaska Native, non-Hispanic/Latino; 9 Asian, non-Hispanic/Latino; 5 Hispanic/Latino; 5 Two or more races, non-Hispanic/Latino), 8 international. Average age 26. 741 applicants, 44% accepted, 119 enrolled. In 2019, 4 master's awarded. *Degree requirements:* For master's, thesis (for some programs). *Entrance requirements:* For master's, JD or LL B from ABA-accredited institution and member institution of the AALS; for doctorate, LSAT, LDAS report, bachelor's degree from accredited institution, personal statement, transcripts from all U.S. undergraduate schools attended and an analysis and summary of the transcripts; letter of recommendation (up to two are accepted). Additional exam requirements/recommendations for international students: required—TOEFL (minimum score 600 paper-based; 100 iBT), Michigan English Language Assessment Battery (minimum score 85); recommended—IELTS (minimum score 7). *Application deadline:* For fall admission, 7/1 for domestic students. Applications are processed on a rolling basis. Application fee: $0. Electronic applications accepted. *Expenses:* Resident tuition: $1,055.56 per credit hour, $315.70 per semester registration fee, $54.56 per credit hour student service fee. Non-resident tuition: $1,158 per credit hour, $315.70 per semester registration fee, $54.56 per credit hour student service fee. *Financial support:* In 2019–20, 326 students received support. Federal Work-Study and scholarships/grants available. Support available to part-time students. Financial award application deadline: 6/30; financial award applicants required to submit FAFSA. *Unit head:* Richard A. Bierschbach, Dean and Professor of Law, 313-577-3933, E-mail: rbierschbach@wayne.edu. *Application contact:* Kathy Fox, Assistant Dean of Admissions, 313-577-3937, Fax: 313-993-8129, E-mail: lawinquire@wayne.edu.
Website: http://law.wayne.edu/

West Virginia University, College of Business and Economics, Morgantown, WV 26506. Offers accountancy (M Acc); accounting (PhD); business administration (MBA); business cyber security management (MS); business data analytics (MS); economics (MA, PhD); finance (MS, PhD); forensic and fraud examination (MS); industrial relations (MS); management (PhD); marketing (PhD). *Program availability:* Part-time, online learning. Terminal master's awarded for partial completion of doctoral program. *Degree requirements:* For master's, thesis optional; for doctorate, comprehensive exam, thesis/dissertation. *Entrance requirements:* For doctorate, GRE General Test, minimum GPA of 3.0. Additional exam requirements/recommendations for international students: required—TOEFL (minimum score 550 paper-based; 92 iBT). Electronic applications accepted. *Expenses:* Contact institution.

Philanthropic Studies

Central Michigan University, Central Michigan University Global Campus, Program in Administration, Mount Pleasant, MI 48859. Offers acquisitions administration (MSA, Certificate); engineering management administration (MSA, Certificate); general administration (MSA, Certificate); health services administration (MSA, Certificate); human resources administration (MSA, Certificate); information resource management (MSA); information resource management administration (Certificate); international administration (MSA, Certificate); leadership (MSA, Certificate); philanthropy and fundraising administration (MSA, Certificate); public administration (MSA, Certificate); recreation and park administration (MSA); research administration (MSA, Certificate). *Program availability:* Part-time, evening/weekend, online learning. *Entrance requirements:* For master's, minimum GPA of 2.7 in major. Electronic applications accepted. *Expenses: Tuition, area resident:* Full-time $12,267; part-time $8178 per year. Tuition, state resident: full-time $12,267; part-time $8178 per year. Tuition, nonresident: full-time $12,267; part-time $8178 per year. *International tuition:* $16,110 full-time. *Required fees:* $225 per semester. Tuition and fees vary according to degree level and program.

Indiana University-Purdue University Indianapolis, Lilly Family School of Philanthropy, Indianapolis, IN 46202. Offers MA, XMA, PhD. *Degree requirements:* For master's, thesis optional; for doctorate, thesis/dissertation. *Entrance requirements:* For master's, GRE General Test (minimum score 500 quantitative, 500 verbal, 4.5 analytical writing), minimum undergraduate GPA of 3.0; for doctorate, GRE General Test (minimum score 500 quantitative, 500 verbal, 4.5 analytical writing), minimum GPA of 3.0, master's degree.

Saint Mary's University of Minnesota, Schools of Graduate and Professional Programs, Graduate School of Business and Technology, Philanthropy and Development Program, Winona, MN 55987-1399. Offers MA. *Unit head:* Cheryl Pray, Executive Director, 612-728-5137, E-mail: cpray@smumn.edu. *Application contact:* Jami Spitzer, Information Contact, 507-457-7500, E-mail: jspitzer@smumn.edu.
Website: http://www.smumn.edu/graduate-home/areas-of-study/graduate-school-of-business-technology/ma-in-philanthropy-development

University of Denver, University College, Denver, CO 80208. Offers arts and culture (MA, Certificate); communication management (MS, Certificate), including translation studies (Certificate), world history and culture (Certificate); environmental policy and management (MS); geographic information systems (MS); global affairs (MA, Certificate), including human capital in organizations (Certificate), philanthropic leadership (Certificate), project management (Certificate), strategic innovation and change (Certificate); healthcare leadership (MS); information communications and technology (MS); leadership and organizations (MS); professional creative writing (MA, Certificate), including emergency planning and response (Certificate), organizational security (Certificate); security management (MS, Certificate); strategic human resources (Certificate). *Program availability:* Part-time, evening/weekend, 100% online, blended/hybrid learning. *Faculty:* 104 part-time/adjunct (52 women). *Students:* 59 full-time (33 women), 1,893 part-time (1,210 women); includes 545 minority (133 Black or African American, non-Hispanic/Latino; 16 American Indian or Alaska Native, non-Hispanic/Latino; 64 Asian, non-Hispanic/Latino; 252 Hispanic/Latino; 4 Native Hawaiian or other Pacific Islander, non-Hispanic/Latino; 76 Two or more races, non-Hispanic/Latino), 78 international. Average age 32. 1,290 applicants, 91% accepted, 752 enrolled. In 2019, 457 master's, 181 other advanced degrees awarded. *Degree requirements:* For master's, capstone project. *Entrance requirements:* For master's, baccalaureate degree, transcripts, two letters of recommendation, personal statement, resume, writing sample (Master of Arts in Professional Creative Writing). Additional exam requirements/recommendations for international students: required—TOEFL (minimum score 550 paper-based; 80 iBT). *Application deadline:* For fall admission, 6/19 priority date for domestic students, 6/14 priority date for international students; for winter admission, 10/25 priority date for domestic students, 9/27 priority date for international students; for spring admission, 2/7 priority date for domestic students, 1/10 priority date for international students; for summer admission, 4/24 priority date for domestic students, 3/27 priority date for international students. Applications are processed on a rolling basis. Application fee: $75. Electronic applications accepted. *Expenses:* Contact institution. *Financial support:* In 2019–20, 56 students received support. Teaching assistantships available. Financial award applicants required to submit FAFSA. *Unit head:* Dr. Michael McGuire, Dean, 303-871-3518, E-mail: michael.mcguire@du.edu. *Application contact:* Admission Team, 303-871-2291, E-mail: ucoladm@du.edu.
Website: http://universitycollege.du.edu/

University of Memphis, Graduate School, College of Arts and Sciences, Division of Public and Nonprofit Administration, Memphis, TN 38152. Offers local government management (Graduate Certificate); philanthropy and nonprofit leadership (Graduate Certificate). *Accreditation:* NASPAA. *Program availability:* Part-time, evening/weekend, blended/hybrid learning. *Students:* 20 full-time (10 women), 30 part-time (21 women); includes 20 minority (17 Black or African American, non-Hispanic/Latino; 1 Asian, non-Hispanic/Latino; 2 Two or more races, non-Hispanic/Latino). Average age 36. 15 applicants, 87% accepted, 6 enrolled. In 2019, 8 master's, 11 other advanced degrees awarded. *Degree requirements:* For master's, comprehensive exam, thesis or alternative, internship. *Entrance requirements:* For master's, GRE General Test, GMAT, MAT, or LSAT, minimum GPA of 3.0, resume, two references, statement of interest. Additional exam requirements/recommendations for international students: required—TOEFL. *Application deadline:* For fall admission, 7/1 for domestic students, 5/1 for international students; for spring admission, 12/1 for domestic students, 9/15 for international students; for summer admission, 5/1 for domestic students, 2/1 for international students. Applications are processed on a rolling basis. Application fee: $35 ($60 for international students). Electronic applications accepted. *Expenses: Tuition, area resident:* Full-time $9216; part-time $512 per credit hour. *Tuition, state resident:* full-time $9216; part-time $512 per credit hour. *Tuition, nonresident:* full-time $12,672; part-time $704 per credit hour. *International tuition:* $16,128 full-time. *Required fees:* $1530; $85 per credit hour. Tuition and fees vary according to program. *Financial support:* Fellowships, research assistantships with full tuition reimbursements, career-related internships or fieldwork, Federal Work-Study, scholarships/grants, health care benefits, and unspecified assistantships available. Support available to part-time students. Financial award application deadline: 2/1; financial award applicants required to submit FAFSA. *Unit head:* Dr. Sharon Wrobel, Chair, 901-678-4720, Fax: 901-678-2981, E-mail: swrobel@memphis.edu. *Application contact:* Dr. Sharon Wrobel, Chair, 901-678-4720, Fax: 901-678-2981, E-mail: swrobel@memphis.edu. Website: http://www.memphis.edu/padm/

Public Administration

Adams State University, Office of Graduate Studies, Department of History, Government and Philosophy, Alamosa, CO 81101. Offers humanities (MA), including cultural resource management, public administration, U.S. history. *Degree requirements:* For master's, thesis. Application fee: $30. *Unit head:* Chair, 719-587-7771, Fax: 719-587-7176. *Application contact:* Chair, 719-587-7771, Fax: 719-587-7176.
Website: https://www.adams.edu/academics/graduate/humanities/

Adler University, Master of Public Administration Program, Chicago, IL 60602. Offers criminal justice (MPA); sustainable communities (MPA). *Program availability:* Part-time, evening/weekend. In 2019, 1 master's awarded. *Degree requirements:* For master's, Social Justice Practicum; Capstone Project. *Unit head:* Phyllis Horton, Director of Admissions, 312-662-4100, E-mail: admissions@adler.edu. *Application contact:* Phyllis Horton, Director of Admissions, 312-662-4100, E-mail: admissions@adler.edu.

Albany State University, College of Arts and Humanities, Albany, GA 31705-2717. Offers criminal justice (MS); English education (M Ed); public administration (MPA), including community and economic development, criminal justice administration, health administration and policy, human resources management, public management, public policy, water resources management and policy; social work (MSW). *Accreditation:* NASPAA. *Program availability:* Part-time. *Degree requirements:* For master's, comprehensive exam, professional portfolio (for MPA), internship, capstone report. *Entrance requirements:* For master's, GRE, MAT, minimum GPA of 3.0, official transcript, pre-medical record/certificate of immunization, letters of reference. Electronic applications accepted.

Albany State University, College of Business, Albany, GA 31705-2717. Offers accounting (MBA); general business administration (MBA); healthcare (MBA); public administration (MBA); supply chain and logistics (MBA). *Accreditation:* ACBSP. *Program availability:* Part-time, evening/weekend. *Degree requirements:* For master's, comprehensive exam, internship, 3 hours of physical education. *Entrance requirements:* For master's, GMAT (minimum score of 450)/GRE (minimum score of 800) for those without earned master's degree or higher, minimum undergraduate GPA of 2.5, 2 letters of reference, official transcript, pre-entrance medical record and certificate of immunization. Electronic applications accepted.

Alfred University, Graduate School, Public Administration Program, Alfred, NY 14802-1205. Offers MPA. *Program availability:* Part-time-only, evening/weekend. *Faculty:* 5 full-time (2 women), 8 part-time/adjunct (2 women). *Students:* 57 part-time (44 women); includes 47 minority (33 Black or African American, non-Hispanic/Latino; 2 Asian, non-Hispanic/Latino; 12 Hispanic/Latino). Average age 38. 41 applicants, 98% accepted, 38 enrolled. In 2019, 18 master's awarded. *Degree requirements:* For master's, thesis or alternative. *Entrance requirements:* Additional exam requirements/recommendations for international students: required—TOEFL; recommended—IELTS. *Application deadline:* Applications are processed on a rolling basis. Application fee: $60. Electronic applications accepted. Application fee is waived when completed online. *Expenses:* $7,665 per year. *Financial support:* Application deadline: 3/15; applicants required to submit FAFSA. *Unit head:* Dr. John D. Cerio, Dean Graduate/Continued Studies AUNY, 607-871-2757, E-mail: fcerio@alfred.edu. *Application contact:* Dr. John D. Cerio, Dean Graduate/Continued Studies AUNY, 607-871-2757, E-mail: fcerio@alfred.edu.

American University, School of Public Affairs, Department of Public Administration and Policy, Washington, DC 20016-8070. Offers organization development (MSOD, Certificate), including leadership for organizational change (Certificate), organization development (MSOD); public administration (MPA, PhD, Certificate), including nonprofit management (Certificate), public financial management (Certificate), public management (Certificate); public administration and policy (MPAP), including public administration policy; public policy (MPP, Certificate), including public policy (MPP), public policy analysis (Certificate); LL M/MPA; MPA/JD; MPP/JD; MPP/LL M. *Program availability:* Part-time, evening/weekend, 100% online, blended/hybrid learning. *Degree requirements:* For master's, comprehensive exam; for doctorate, comprehensive exam, thesis/dissertation. *Entrance requirements:* For master's, GRE; Please see website: https://www.american.edu/spa/jlc/, statement of purpose, 2 recommendations, resume, transcript; for doctorate, GRE; Please see website: https://www.american.edu/spa/jlc/, 3 recommendations, statement of purpose, resume, writing sample, transcript; for Certificate, bachelor's degree. Additional exam requirements/recommendations for international students: required—TOEFL. *Expenses:* Contact institution.

The American University in Cairo, School of Global Affairs and Public Policy, Cairo, Egypt. Offers gender and women's studies (MA); global affairs (MGA); international and comparative law (LL M); international human rights law (MA); journalism and mass communication (MA); Middle East studies (MA); migration and refugee studies (MA, Diploma); public administration (MPA); public policy (MPP); television and digital journalism (MA). *Program availability:* Part-time, evening/weekend. *Degree requirements:* For master's, comprehensive exam (for some programs), thesis (for some programs). *Entrance requirements:* Additional exam requirements/recommendations for international students: required—TOEFL (minimum score 450 paper-based; 45 iBT), IELTS (minimum score 5). Electronic applications accepted. *Expenses:* Contact institution.

Anabaptist Mennonite Biblical Seminary, Graduate and Professional Programs, Elkhart, IN 46517-1999. Offers chaplaincy (M Div); Christian faith formation (M Div); Christian formation (MA); Christian spiritual formation (Certificate); divinity (M Div); pastoral ministry (M Div); pastoral theology for financial professionals (Certificate); peace studies (M Div), including environmental sustainability leadership (M Div, MA), theological studies (M Div, Certificate), including peace studies (M Div), theology and ethics (M Div); theology and peace studies (MA), including conflict transformation, environmental sustainability leadership (M Div, MA), international development administration; United Methodist leadership (M Div). *Accreditation:* ACIPE; ATS.

Program availability: Part-time, 100% online, blended/hybrid learning. *Degree requirements:* For master's, variable foreign language requirement, comprehensive exam (for some programs), thesis optional, senior interview. *Entrance requirements:* For master's, undergraduate degree transcripts, 3 letters of reference, essay. Additional exam requirements/recommendations for international students: required—TOEFL (minimum score 90 iBT); recommended—IELTS (minimum score 7). Electronic applications accepted.

Anna Maria College, Graduate Division, Program in Public Administration, Paxton, MA 01612. Offers MPA.

Appalachian State University, Cratis D. Williams School of Graduate Studies, Department of Government and Justice Studies, Boone, NC 28608. Offers political science (MA), including American government; public administration (MPA), including public management. *Accreditation:* NASPAA. *Program availability:* Part-time, online learning. *Degree requirements:* For master's, variable foreign language requirement, comprehensive exam, thesis optional. *Entrance requirements:* For master's, GRE General Test, 3 letters of recommendation. Additional exam requirements/recommendations for international students: required—TOEFL (minimum score 570 paper-based; 79 iBT), IELTS (minimum score 6.5). Electronic applications accepted.

Argosy University, Chicago, College of Business, Chicago, IL 60601. Offers accounting (DBA); customized professional concentration (MBA, DBA); finance (MBA); fraud examination (MBA); global business sustainability (DBA); healthcare administration (MBA); information systems (DBA); information systems management (MBA); international business (MBA, DBA); management (MBA, MSM, DBA); marketing (MBA, DBA); organizational leadership (Ed D); public administration (MBA); sustainable management (MBA). *Accreditation:* ACBSP. *Program availability:* Online learning.

Argosy University, Los Angeles, College of Business, Los Angeles, CA 90045. Offers accounting (DBA); corporate compliance (MBA); customized professional concentration (MBA, DBA); finance (MBA); fraud examination (MBA); global business sustainability (DBA); healthcare administration (MBA); information systems (DBA); information systems management (MBA); international business (MBA, DBA); management (MBA, MSM, DBA); marketing (MBA, DBA); organizational leadership (Ed D); public administration (MBA); sustainable management (MBA).

Argosy University, Northern Virginia, College of Business, Arlington, VA 22209. Offers accounting (DBA); customized professional concentration (MBA, DBA); finance (MBA); fraud examination (MBA); global business sustainability (DBA); healthcare administration (MBA); information systems (DBA); information systems management (MBA); international business (MBA, DBA, Certificate); management (MBA, MSM, DBA); marketing (MBA, DBA, Certificate); organizational leadership (Ed D); public administration (MBA); sustainable management (MBA).

Argosy University, Orange County, College of Business, Orange, CA 92868. Offers accounting (DBA, Adv C); corporate compliance (MBA); customized professional concentration (MBA, DBA); finance (MBA, Certificate); fraud examination (MBA); global business sustainability (DBA); healthcare administration (MBA, Certificate); information systems (DBA, Adv C, Certificate); information systems management (MBA); international business (MBA, DBA, Adv C, Certificate); management (MBA, MSM, DBA, Adv C); marketing (MBA, DBA, Adv C, Certificate); organizational leadership (Ed D); public administration (MBA, Certificate); sustainable management (MBA).

Argosy University, Phoenix, College of Business, Phoenix, AZ 85021. Offers accounting (DBA); corporate compliance (MBA); customized professional concentration (MBA, DBA); finance (MBA); fraud examination (MBA); global business sustainability (DBA); healthcare administration (MBA); information systems (DBA); information systems management (MBA); international business (MBA, DBA); management (MBA, DBA); marketing (MBA, DBA); public administration (MBA); sustainable management (MBA).

Argosy University, Seattle, College of Business, Seattle, WA 98121. Offers accounting (DBA); corporate compliance (MBA); customized professional concentration (MBA, DBA); finance (MBA); fraud examination (MBA); global business sustainability (DBA); healthcare administration (MBA); information systems (DBA); information systems management (MBA); international business (MBA, DBA); management (MBA, MSM, DBA); marketing (MBA, DBA); organizational leadership (Ed D); public administration (MBA); sustainable management (MBA).

Argosy University, Tampa, College of Business, Tampa, FL 33607. Offers accounting (DBA); corporate compliance (MBA); customized professional concentration (MBA, DBA); finance (MBA); fraud examination (MBA); global business sustainability (DBA); healthcare administration (MBA); information systems (DBA); information systems management (MBA); international business (MBA, DBA); management (MBA, MSM, DBA); marketing (MBA, DBA); organizational leadership (Ed D); public administration (MBA); sustainable management (MBA).

Argosy University, Twin Cities, College of Business, Eagan, MN 55121. Offers accounting (DBA); customized professional concentration (MBA, DBA); finance (MBA); fraud examination (MBA); global business sustainability (DBA); healthcare administration (MBA); information systems (DBA); information systems management (MBA); international business (MBA, DBA); management (MBA, MSM, DBA); marketing (MBA, DBA); organizational leadership (Ed D); public administration (MBA); sustainable management (MBA).

Arizona State University at Tempe, College of Public Programs, School of Public Affairs, Phoenix, AZ 85004-0687. Offers emergency management and homeland security (MA); program evaluation (MS); public administration (MPA, PhD), including nonprofit administration (MPA); urban management (MPA); public policy (MPP); MPA/MSW. *Accreditation:* NASPAA (one or more programs are accredited). *Program availability:* Part-time, evening/weekend. Terminal master's awarded for partial completion of doctoral program. *Degree requirements:* For master's, thesis or alternative, policy analysis or capstone project; interactive Program of Study (iPOS) submitted before completing 50 percent of required credit hours; for doctorate, comprehensive exam, thesis/dissertation, interactive Program of Study (iPOS) submitted before completing 50 percent of required credit hours. *Entrance requirements:* For master's, GRE, minimum GPA of 3.0 or equivalent in last 2 years of work leading to bachelor's degree; for doctorate, GRE, minimum GPA of 3.0 or equivalent in last 2 years of work leading to bachelor's degree, 3 letters of recommendation, resume, statement of goals, samples of research reports. Additional exam requirements/recommendations for international students: required—TOEFL (minimum score 600 paper-based; 100 iBT), IELTS (minimum score 6.5). Electronic applications accepted. *Expenses:* Contact institution.

Arkansas State University, Graduate School, College of Humanities and Social Sciences, Department of Political Science, State University, AR 72467. Offers political science (MA); political science education (SCCT); public administration (MPA). *Accreditation:* NASPAA (one or more programs are accredited). *Program availability:* Part-time. *Degree requirements:* For master's, comprehensive exam, thesis or alternative; for SCCT, comprehensive exam. *Entrance requirements:* For master's, GRE General Test or MAT, GMAT, appropriate bachelor's degree, letters of recommendation, official transcripts, immunization records, statement of purpose; for SCCT, GRE General Test or MAT, GMAT, interview, master's degree, official transcript, letters of recommendation, immunization records. Additional exam requirements/recommendations for international students: required—TOEFL (minimum score 550 paper-based; 79 iBT), IELTS (minimum score 6), PTE (minimum score 56). Electronic applications accepted.

Auburn University, Graduate School, College of Liberal Arts, Department of Political Science, Program in Public Administration, Auburn, AL 36849. Offers MPA, PhD, Graduate Certificate, MPA/MCP. *Accreditation:* NASPAA (one or more programs are accredited). *Program availability:* Part-time. *Faculty:* 30 full-time (14 women), 5 part-time/adjunct (4 women). *Students:* 59 full-time (30 women), 43 part-time (22 women); includes 21 minority (19 Black or African American, non-Hispanic/Latino; 1 American Indian or Alaska Native, non-Hispanic/Latino; 1 Asian, non-Hispanic/Latino), 37 international. Average age 34. 36 applicants, 69% accepted, 19 enrolled. In 2019, 49 master's, 2 doctorates awarded. *Degree requirements:* For master's, internship or research project; for doctorate, thesis/dissertation. *Entrance requirements:* For master's, GRE General Test, sample of written work; for doctorate, GRE General Test. Additional exam requirements/recommendations for international students: required—iTEP; recommended—TOEFL (minimum score 550 paper-based; 79 iBT), IELTS (minimum score 6.5). *Application deadline:* Applications are processed on a rolling basis. Application fee: $60 ($70 for international students). Electronic applications accepted. *Expenses: Tuition, area resident:* Full-time $9828; part-time $546 per credit hour. Tuition, state resident: full-time $9828; part-time $546 per credit hour. Tuition, nonresident: full-time $29,484; part-time $1638 per credit hour. *International tuition:* $29,744 full-time. Tuition and fees vary according to course load, program and reciprocity agreements. *Financial support:* Fellowships, research assistantships, teaching assistantships, career-related internships or fieldwork, and Federal Work-Study available. Support available to part-time students. Financial award application deadline: 3/15; financial award applicants required to submit FAFSA. *Unit head:* Dr. Kathleen Hale, Head, 334-844-6155, E-mail: halekat@auburn.edu. *Application contact:* Dr. George Flowers, Dean of the Graduate School, 334-844-2125.
Website: http://www.cla.auburn.edu/polisci/

Auburn University at Montgomery, College of Liberal Arts & Social Sciences, Department of Political Science and Public Administration, Montgomery, AL 36124. Offers political science (MPS); public administration (MPA); public administration and public policy (PhD). *Accreditation:* NASPAA (one or more programs are accredited). *Program availability:* Part-time, evening/weekend. *Faculty:* 5 full-time (1 woman). *Students:* 8 full-time (3 women), 43 part-time (22 women); includes 18 minority (17 Black or African American, non-Hispanic/Latino; 1 Asian, non-Hispanic/Latino), 6 international. Average age 35. 22 applicants, 95% accepted, 20 enrolled. In 2019, 16 master's awarded. Terminal master's awarded for partial completion of doctoral program. *Degree requirements:* For master's, comprehensive exam; for doctorate, thesis/dissertation. *Entrance requirements:* For master's, GRE General Test or MAT; for doctorate, GRE General Test. Additional exam requirements/recommendations for international students: recommended—TOEFL (minimum score 500 paper-based; 61 iBT), IELTS (minimum score 5.5), TSE (minimum score 44). *Application deadline:* For fall admission, 7/15 for international students; for spring admission, 11/15 for international students; for summer admission, 4/15 for international students. Applications are processed on a rolling basis. Application fee: $25. Electronic applications accepted. *Expenses: Tuition, area resident:* Full-time $7578; part-time $421 per credit hour. Tuition, state resident: full-time $7578; part-time $421 per credit hour. Tuition, nonresident: full-time $17,046; part-time $947 per credit hour. *International tuition:* $17,046 full-time. *Required fees:* $868. *Financial support:* Research assistantships, teaching assistantships, career-related internships or fieldwork, and scholarships/grants available. Support available to part-time students. Financial award application deadline: 3/1; financial award applicants required to submit FAFSA. *Unit head:* Dr. Andrew Cortell, Department Head, 334-244-3622, E-mail: acortell@aum.edu. *Application contact:* Shannon Richardson, Administrative Associate, 244-244-3698, E-mail: sricha17@aum.edu.
Website: http://www.cas.aum.edu/academic-programs/graduate-programs/master-of-science-in-political-science

Ball State University, Graduate School, College of Sciences and Humanities, Department of Political Science, Program in Public Administration, Muncie, IN 47306. Offers public administration (MPA, Certificate), including community and economic development (MPA), criminal justice (MPA), emergency management and homeland security (MPA), information and communication technology (MPA). *Program availability:* Part-time. *Degree requirements:* For master's, comprehensive exam. *Entrance requirements:* For master's, GRE General Test, minimum baccalaureate GPA of 2.8, two letters of recommendation. Additional exam requirements/recommendations for international students: required—TOEFL (minimum score 550 paper-based; 79 iBT), IELTS (minimum score 6.5). Electronic applications accepted. *Expenses: Tuition, area resident:* Full-time $7506; part-time $417 per credit hour. Tuition, nonresident: full-time $20,610; part-time $1145 per credit hour. *Required fees:* $2126. Tuition and fees vary according to course load, campus/location and program.

Barry University, School of Adult and Continuing Education, Program in Public Administration, Miami Shores, FL 33161-6695. Offers MPA. *Program availability:* Part-time, evening/weekend. *Entrance requirements:* For master's, GMAT, GRE or MAT, recommendations. Electronic applications accepted.

Baruch College of the City University of New York, Austin W. Marxe School of Public and International Affairs, Program in Public Administration, New York, NY 10010-5585. Offers general public administration (MPA); health care policy (MPA); nonprofit administration (MPA); policy analysis and evaluation (MPA); public management (MPA); urban development and sustainability (MPA); MS/MPA. *Accreditation:* NASPAA. *Program availability:* Part-time, evening/weekend. *Degree requirements:* For master's, thesis, capstone. *Entrance requirements:* For master's, GRE General Test. Additional exam requirements/recommendations for international students: required—TOEFL. Electronic applications accepted. *Expenses:* Contact institution.

Bellevue University, Graduate School, College of Professional Studies, Bellevue, NE 68005-3098. Offers instructional design and development (MS); justice administration and criminal management (MS); leadership (MA); organizational performance (MS); public administration (MPA); security management (MS).

Binghamton University, State University of New York, Graduate School, College of Community and Public Affairs, Department of Public Administration, Binghamton, NY 13902-6000. Offers MPA. *Accreditation:* NASPAA. *Program availability:* Part-time. *Degree requirements:* For master's, thesis. *Entrance requirements:* Additional exam requirements/recommendations for international students: required—TOEFL (minimum score 80 iBT). Electronic applications accepted.

Boise State University, School of Public Service, Department of Public Policy and Administration, Boise, ID 83725-0399. Offers public policy and administration (MPA, PhD, Graduate Certificate), including environmental, natural resource and energy policy and administration (MPA), general public administration (MPA), state and local government policy and administration (MPA). *Accreditation:* NASPAA. *Students:* 29 full-time (20 women), 81 part-time (54 women); includes 16 minority (2 Black or African American, non-Hispanic/Latino; 2 Asian, non-Hispanic/Latino; 10 Hispanic/Latino; 2 Two or more races, non-Hispanic/Latino), 5 international. *Degree requirements:* For master's, comprehensive exam, thesis optional, directed research project, internship; for doctorate, thesis/dissertation. *Application deadline:* For fall admission, 2/1 for domestic and international students; for spring admission, 10/1 for domestic and international students. Electronic applications accepted. *Expenses: Tuition, area resident:* Full-time $7110; part-time $470 per credit hour. Tuition, state resident: full-time $7110; part-time $470 per credit hour. Tuition, nonresident: full-time $24,030; part-time $827 per credit hour. *International tuition:* $24,030 full-time. *Required fees:* $2536. Tuition and fees vary according to course load and program. *Financial support:* Application deadline: 2/1; applicants required to submit FAFSA. *Unit head:* Luke Fowler, MPA Director, 208-426-5527, E-mail: lukefowler@boisestate.edu. *Application contact:* Luke Fowler, MPA Director, 208-426-5527, E-mail: lukefowler@boisestate.edu.
Website: https://www.boisestate.edu/sps-publicpolicy/

Bowie State University, Graduate Programs, Program in Public Administration, Bowie, MD 20715-9465. Offers MPA. *Accreditation:* NASPAA. *Program availability:* Part-time, evening/weekend. *Degree requirements:* For master's, comprehensive exam. *Entrance requirements:* For master's, minimum undergraduate GPA of 2.5. Electronic applications accepted. *Expenses: Tuition, area resident:* Full-time $11,942; part-time $423 per credit hour. Tuition, state resident: full-time $11,942; part-time $423 per credit hour. Tuition, nonresident: full-time $18,806; part-time $709 per credit hour. *International tuition:* $18,806 full-time. *Required fees:* $1106; $1106 per semester. $553 per semester.

Bowling Green State University, Graduate College, College of Arts and Sciences, Department of Political Science, Bowling Green, OH 43403. Offers public administration (MPA). *Degree requirements:* For master's, comprehensive exam or thesis. *Entrance requirements:* For master's, GRE General Test. Additional exam requirements/recommendations for international students: required—TOEFL. Electronic applications accepted.

Brandman University, School of Business and Professional Studies, Irvine, CA 92618. Offers accounting (MBA); business administration (MBA); business intelligence and data analytics (MBA); e-business strategic management (MBA); entrepreneurship (MBA); finance (MBA); health administration (MBA); human resources (MBA, MS); international business (MBA); marketing (MBA); organizational leadership (MA, MBA, MPA); public administration (MPA).

Bridgewater State University, College of Graduate Studies, College of Humanities and Social Sciences, Department of Political Science, Program in Public Administration, Bridgewater, MA 02325. Offers MPA. *Accreditation:* NASPAA. *Entrance requirements:* For master's, GRE General Test.

Brigham Young University, Graduate Studies, BYU Marriott School of Business, Executive Master of Public Administration Program, Provo, UT 84602. Offers MPA. *Program availability:* Part-time-only, evening/weekend. *Faculty:* 14 full-time (2 women), 5 part-time/adjunct (0 women). *Students:* 118 part-time (62 women); includes 13 minority (1 Black or African American, non-Hispanic/Latino; 1 Asian, non-Hispanic/Latino; 4 Hispanic/Latino; 7 Native Hawaiian or other Pacific Islander, non-Hispanic/Latino). Average age 35. 51 applicants, 80% accepted, 37 enrolled. In 2019, 35 master's awarded. *Entrance requirements:* For master's, GRE or GMAT, 4 years of work experience, 3 letters of recommendation, statement of intent, resume. Additional exam requirements/recommendations for international students: required—TOEFL (minimum score 580 paper-based; 79 iBT). *Application deadline:* For fall admission, 5/1 for domestic and international students. Application fee: $50. Electronic applications accepted. *Expenses:* Tuition is paid per credit hour ($810 a credit hour with yearly increases) for 45 credits is almost $35,000. *Financial support:* In 2019–20, 12 students received support. Scholarships/grants available. Financial award applicants required to submit FAFSA. *Unit head:* Dr. Lori Wadsworth, Director, 801-422-5956, Fax: 801-422-0311, E-mail: Lori_Wadsworth@byu.edu. *Application contact:* Catherine Cooper, Associate Director, 801-422-4221, Fax: 801-422-0311, E-mail: clc@byu.edu.
Website: http://empa.byu.edu

Brigham Young University, Graduate Studies, BYU Marriott School of Business, Master of Public Administration Program, Provo, UT 84602. Offers healthcare (MPA); local government (MPA); nonprofit management (MPA); state and federal government (MPA); JD/MPA. *Accreditation:* NASPAA. *Faculty:* 10 full-time (2 women), 10 part-time/adjunct (2 women). *Students:* 95 full-time (52 women); includes 10 minority (4 Black or African American, non-Hispanic/Latino; 1 American Indian or Alaska Native, non-Hispanic/Latino; 1 Asian, non-Hispanic/Latino; 2 Hispanic/Latino; 2 Native Hawaiian or other Pacific Islander, non-Hispanic/Latino). Average age 26. 81 applicants, 85% accepted, 57 enrolled. In 2019, 45 master's awarded. *Entrance requirements:* For master's, GMAT or GRE, statement of intent, resume, bachelor's degree, 3 letters or recommendation, ecclesiastical endorsement. Additional exam requirements/recommendations for international students: required—TOEFL (minimum score 580 paper-based; 85 iBT). *Application deadline:* For fall admission, 1/15 for domestic and international students. Application fee: $50. Electronic applications accepted. *Expenses:* Full-time LDS tuition $6,725 a semester in 2019, books, health insurance. *Financial support:* In 2019–20, 93 students received support. Scholarships/grants available. Financial award application deadline: 4/15; financial award applicants required to submit FAFSA. *Unit head:* Dr. Lori Wadsworth, Director, 801-422-5956, E-mail: lori_wadsworth@byu.edu. *Application contact:* Catherine Cooper, Associate Director, 801-422-9173, E-mail: clc@byu.edu.
Website: https://marriottschool.byu.edu/mpa/

California Baptist University, Program in Public Administration, Riverside, CA 92504-3206. Offers public administration (MPA). *Program availability:* Part-time, evening/weekend, online only, 100% online, blended/hybrid learning. *Degree requirements:* For master's, comprehensive exam or thesis. *Entrance requirements:* For master's, minimum GPA of 2.75; bachelor's degree in applicable field or any field with five years of managerial experience; three recommendations; resume; 500-word essay. Additional exam requirements/recommendations for international students: required—TOEFL (minimum score 80 iBT). Electronic applications accepted. *Expenses:* Contact institution.

California State Polytechnic University, Pomona, Program in Public Administration, Pomona, CA 91768-2557. Offers MPA. *Accreditation:* NASPAA. *Program availability:* Part-time, evening/weekend. *Entrance requirements:* Additional exam requirements/ recommendations for international students: required—TOEFL (minimum score 550 paper-based). Electronic applications accepted. *Expenses:* Contact institution.

California State University, Chico, Office of Graduate Studies, College of Behavioral and Social Sciences, Department of Political Science and Criminal Justice, Program in Public Administration, Chico, CA 95929-0722. Offers health administration (MPA); local government management (MPA). *Accreditation:* NASPAA. *Program availability:* Part-time. *Degree requirements:* For master's, thesis or culminating practicum. *Entrance requirements:* For master's, 2 letters of recommendation and statement of purpose. Additional exam requirements/recommendations for international students: required—TOEFL (minimum score 550 paper-based; 80 iBT), IELTS (minimum score 6.5), PTE. Electronic applications accepted.

California State University, Dominguez Hills, College of Business Administration and Public Policy, Program in Public Administration, Carson, CA 90747-0001. Offers MPA. *Accreditation:* NASPAA. *Program availability:* Part-time, evening/weekend, online learning. *Degree requirements:* For master's, thesis or alternative, capstone project. *Entrance requirements:* For master's, GRE, minimum GPA of 2.75. Additional exam requirements/recommendations for international students: required—TOEFL (minimum score 550 paper-based; 79 iBT).

California State University, East Bay, Office of Graduate Studies, College of Letters, Arts, and Social Sciences, Department of Public Affairs and Administration, Program in Public Administration, Hayward, CA 94542-3000. Offers health care administration (MPA); public management and policy analysis (MPA). *Program availability:* Part-time, evening/weekend. *Degree requirements:* For master's, comprehensive exam (for some programs), comprehensive exam or thesis. *Entrance requirements:* For master's, minimum GPA of 2.5; statement of purpose; 2 letters of recommendation; professional resume/curriculum vitae. Additional exam requirements/recommendations for international students: required—TOEFL (minimum score 550 paper-based; 79 iBT). Electronic applications accepted.

California State University, Fresno, Division of Research and Graduate Studies, College of Social Sciences, Department of Political Science, Program in Public Administration, Fresno, CA 93740-8027. Offers MPA. *Accreditation:* NASPAA. *Program availability:* Part-time, evening/weekend. *Degree requirements:* For master's, thesis or alternative. *Entrance requirements:* For master's, GRE General Test or GMAT, minimum GPA of 3.0. Additional exam requirements/recommendations for international students: required—TOEFL. Electronic applications accepted. *Expenses:* Tuition, state resident: full-time $4012; part-time $2506 per semester.

California State University, Fullerton, Graduate Studies, College of Humanities and Social Sciences, Division of Politics, Administration, and Justice, Fullerton, CA 92831-3599. Offers political science (MA); public administration (MPA). *Accreditation:* NASPAA (one or more programs are accredited). *Program availability:* Part-time. *Degree requirements:* For master's, comprehensive exam, project or thesis. *Entrance requirements:* For master's, minimum GPA of 2.5 in last 60 units of course work, 12 units of course work in social sciences.

California State University, Long Beach, Graduate Studies, College of Health and Human Services, Graduate Center for Public Policy and Administration, Long Beach, CA 90840. Offers MPA, Graduate Certificate. *Accreditation:* NASPAA (one or more programs are accredited). *Program availability:* Part-time, evening/weekend. *Degree requirements:* For master's, comprehensive exam. *Entrance requirements:* For master's, minimum GPA of 2.75. Electronic applications accepted.

California State University, Los Angeles, Graduate Studies, College of Natural and Social Sciences, Department of Political Science, Los Angeles, CA 90032-8530. Offers political science (MA); public administration (MS). *Program availability:* Part-time, evening/weekend. *Degree requirements:* For master's, comprehensive exam or thesis. *Entrance requirements:* Additional exam requirements/recommendations for international students: required—TOEFL (minimum score 500 paper-based). Electronic applications accepted. *Expenses: Tuition, area resident:* Full-time $7176; part-time $4164 per year. Tuition, state resident: full-time $7176; part-time $4164 per year. Tuition, nonresident: full-time $14,304; part-time $8916 per year. *International tuition:* $14,304 full-time. *Required fees:* $1037.76; $1037.76 per unit. Tuition and fees vary according to degree level and program.

California State University, Northridge, Graduate Studies, Tseng College, Northridge, CA 91330. Offers business administration (Graduate Certificate); health administration (MPA); health education (MPH); knowledge management (MKM); music industry administration (MA); nonprofit-sector management (Graduate Certificate); public administration (MPA); public sector management and leadership (MPA); social work (MSW); taxation (MS); tourism, hospitality and recreation management (MS). *Entrance requirements:* For master's, GRE (if cumulative undergraduate GPA less than 3.0).

California State University, Sacramento, College of Social Sciences and Interdisciplinary Studies, Program in Public Policy and Administration, Sacramento, CA 95819. Offers MPPA. *Program availability:* Part-time. *Students:* 26 full-time (12 women), 30 part-time (17 women); includes 18 minority (2 Black or African American, non-Hispanic/Latino; 7 Asian, non-Hispanic/Latino; 9 Hispanic/Latino). Average age 31. 40 applicants, 73% accepted, 16 enrolled. In 2019, 8 master's awarded. *Degree requirements:* For master's, thesis, thesis or writing proficiency exam. *Entrance requirements:* For master's, GRE, minimum GPA of 3.0 for all undergraduate coursework and in last 60 units. Additional exam requirements/recommendations for international students: required—TOEFL (minimum score 560 paper-based; 83 iBT); recommended—IELTS (minimum score 7). *Application deadline:* For fall admission, 3/1 for domestic students, 2/1 for international students. Applications are processed on a rolling basis. Application fee: $70. Electronic applications accepted. *Expenses:* Contact institution. *Financial support:* Teaching assistantships, career-related internships or fieldwork, Federal Work-Study, and scholarships/grants available. Support available to part-time students. Financial award application deadline: 3/1; financial award applicants required to submit FAFSA. *Unit head:* Dr. Ted Lascher, Chair, 916-278-6557, E-mail: tedl@csus.edu. *Application contact:* Jose Martinez, Graduate Admissions Supervisor, 916-278-7871, E-mail: martinj@skymail.csus.edu.
Website: http://www.csus.edu/ppa

California State University, San Bernardino, Graduate Studies, College of Business and Public Administration, Program in Public Administration, San Bernardino, CA 92407. Offers MPA. *Accreditation:* NASPAA. *Program availability:* Part-time, evening/ weekend. *Faculty:* 5 full-time (2 women), 8 part-time/adjunct (2 women). *Students:* 40 full-time (22 women), 205 part-time (138 women); includes 169 minority (29 Black or African American, non-Hispanic/Latino; 2 American Indian or Alaska Native, non-Hispanic/Latino; 8 Asian, non-Hispanic/Latino; 123 Hispanic/Latino; 2 Native Hawaiian or other Pacific Islander, non-Hispanic/Latino; 5 Two or more races, non-Hispanic/ Latino), 6 international. Average age 34. 164 applicants, 86% accepted, 99 enrolled. In 2019, 76 master's awarded. *Degree requirements:* For master's, comprehensive exam. *Entrance requirements:* Additional exam requirements/recommendations for international students: required—TOEFL. *Application deadline:* For fall admission, 7/16 for domestic students; for winter admission, 10/23 for domestic students; for spring admission, 1/22 for domestic students. Application fee: $55. *Financial support:* Institutionally sponsored loans available. Financial award application deadline: 3/1. *Unit head:* Dr. Jonathan Anderson, Chair, 909-537-5759, E-mail: jfanders@csusb.edu. *Application contact:* Dr. Dorota Huizinga, Dean of Graduate Studies, 909-537-3064, E-mail: dorota.huizinga@csusb.edu.

California State University, Stanislaus, College of the Arts, Humanities and Social Sciences, Master of Public Administration Program, Turlock, CA 95382. Offers MPA. *Accreditation:* NASPAA. *Program availability:* Part-time, evening/weekend. *Degree requirements:* For master's, comprehensive exam, thesis or alternative. *Entrance requirements:* For master's, minimum GPA of 2.7, 3 letters of reference, personal statement. Additional exam requirements/recommendations for international students: required—TOEFL (minimum score 550 paper-based), ELPT (minimum score 954). Electronic applications accepted.

Capella University, School of Public Service Leadership, Doctoral Programs in Healthcare, Minneapolis, MN 55402. Offers criminal justice (PhD); emergency management (PhD); epidemiology (Dr PH); general health administration (DHA); general public administration (DPA); health advocacy and leadership (Dr PH); health care administration (PhD); health care leadership (DHA); health policy advocacy (DHA); multidisciplinary human services (PhD); nonprofit management and leadership (PhD); public safety leadership (PhD); social and community services (PhD).

Capella University, School of Public Service Leadership, Master's Programs in Healthcare, Minneapolis, MN 55402. Offers criminal justice (MS); emergency management (MS); general public health (MPH); gerontology (MS); health administration (MHA); health care operations (MHA); health management policy (MPH); health policy (MHA); homeland security (MS); multidisciplinary human services (MS); public administration (MPA); public safety leadership (MS); social and community services (MS); social behavioral sciences (MPH); MS/MPA.

Carleton University, Faculty of Graduate Studies, Faculty of Public Affairs and Management, School of Public Policy and Administration, Ottawa, ON K1S 5B6, Canada. Offers public administration (MA, DPA); public policy (PhD). *Program availability:* Part-time. *Degree requirements:* For master's, thesis optional; for doctorate, one foreign language, comprehensive exam, thesis/dissertation. *Entrance requirements:* For master's, GRE, honors degree; for doctorate, master's degree. Additional exam requirements/recommendations for international students: required—TOEFL.

Carnegie Mellon University, Heinz College, School of Public Policy and Management, Master of Public Management Program, Pittsburgh, PA 15213-3891. Offers MPM. *Accreditation:* NASPAA. *Program availability:* Part-time, evening/weekend. *Degree requirements:* For master's, internship. *Entrance requirements:* For master's, undergraduate degree; five years of full-time, relevant work experience.

Central European University, School of Public Policy, 1051, Hungary. Offers public administration (MPA); public policy (MA, PhD). *Degree requirements:* For master's, one foreign language, thesis; for doctorate, one foreign language, comprehensive exam, thesis/dissertation. *Entrance requirements:* For master's and doctorate, interview. Additional exam requirements/recommendations for international students: required—TOEFL (minimum score 570 paper-based); recommended—IELTS (minimum score 6.5). Electronic applications accepted.

Central Michigan University, Central Michigan University Global Campus, Program in Administration, Mount Pleasant, MI 48859. Offers acquisitions administration (MSA, Certificate); engineering management administration (MSA, Certificate); general administration (MSA, Certificate); health services administration (MSA, Certificate); human resources administration (MSA, Certificate); information resource management (MSA); information resource management administration (Certificate); international administration (MSA, Certificate); leadership (MSA, Certificate); philanthropy and fundraising administration (MSA, Certificate); public administration (MSA, Certificate); recreation and park administration (MSA); research administration (MSA, Certificate). *Program availability:* Part-time, evening/weekend, online learning. *Entrance requirements:* For master's, minimum GPA of 2.7 in major. Electronic applications accepted. *Expenses: Tuition, area resident:* Full-time $12,267; part-time $8178 per year. Tuition, state resident: full-time $12,267; part-time $8178 per year. Tuition, nonresident: full-time $12,267; part-time $8178 per year. *International tuition:* $16,110 full-time. *Required fees:* $225 per semester. Tuition and fees vary according to degree level and program.

Central Michigan University, Central Michigan University Global Campus, Program in Public Administration, Mount Pleasant, MI 48859. Offers general public administration (MPA); public management (MPA); state and local government (MPA). *Accreditation:* NASPAA. *Program availability:* Part-time, evening/weekend. *Entrance requirements:* For master's, minimum GPA of 2.8. Additional exam requirements/recommendations for international students: required—TOEFL. Electronic applications accepted. *Expenses: Tuition, area resident:* Full-time $12,267; part-time $8178 per year. Tuition, state resident: full-time $12,267; part-time $8178 per year. Tuition, nonresident: full-time $12,267; part-time $8178 per year. *International tuition:* $16,110 full-time. *Required fees:* $225 per semester. Tuition and fees vary according to degree level and program.

Central Michigan University, College of Graduate Studies, College of Liberal Arts and Social Sciences, Department of Political Science and Public Administration, Program in Public Administration, Mount Pleasant, MI 48859. Offers professional development in public administration (Graduate Certificate); public administration (MPA); public management (MPA); state and local government (MPA). *Accreditation:* NASPAA. *Program availability:* Part-time. *Degree requirements:* For master's, thesis or alternative. Electronic applications accepted. *Expenses: Tuition, area resident:* Full-time $12,267; part-time $8178 per year. Tuition, state resident: full-time $12,267; part-time $8178 per year. Tuition, nonresident: full-time $12,267; part-time $8178 per year. *International tuition:* $16,110 full-time. *Required fees:* $225 per semester. Tuition and fees vary according to degree level and program.

Central Michigan University, College of Graduate Studies, Interdisciplinary Administration Programs, Mount Pleasant, MI 48859. Offers acquisitions administration (MSA, Graduate Certificate); general administration (MSA, Graduate Certificate); health services administration (MSA, Graduate Certificate); human resource administration (Graduate Certificate); human resources administration (MSA); information resource management (MSA, Graduate Certificate); international administration (MSA, Graduate Certificate); leadership (MSA, Graduate Certificate); public administration (MSA, Graduate Certificate); research administration (Graduate Certificate); sport administration (MSA). *Accreditation:* AACSB. *Program availability:* Part-time, evening/ weekend, online learning. *Degree requirements:* For master's, thesis or alternative. *Entrance requirements:* For master's, bachelor's degree with minimum GPA of 2.7. Electronic applications accepted. *Expenses: Tuition, area resident:* Full-time $12,267; part-time $8178 per year. Tuition, state resident: full-time $12,267; part-time $8178 per year. Tuition, nonresident: full-time $12,267; part-time $8178 per year. *International* *tuition:* $16,110 full-time. *Required fees:* $225 per semester. Tuition and fees vary according to degree level and program.

Cheyney University of Pennsylvania, Graduate Programs, Program in Public Administration, Cheyney, PA 19319. Offers MPA.

City College of the City University of New York, Graduate School, Colin Powell School for Civic and Global Leadership, New York, NY 10031-9198. Offers economics and business (MA), including economics; international relations (MA); psychology (MA, PhD), including clinical psychology (PhD), general psychology (MA), mental health counseling (MA); public service management (MPA); sociology (MA). *Program availability:* Part-time. *Entrance requirements:* For master's, GRE. Additional exam requirements/recommendations for international students: required—TOEFL (minimum score 500 paper-based; 61 iBT). Electronic applications accepted.

Clark Atlanta University, School of Arts and Sciences, Department of Public Administration, Atlanta, GA 30314. Offers MPA. *Accreditation:* NASPAA. *Program availability:* Part-time. *Degree requirements:* For master's, one foreign language, thesis or alternative. *Entrance requirements:* For master's, GRE General Test, minimum GPA of 2.5. Additional exam requirements/recommendations for international students: required—TOEFL (minimum score 500 paper-based; 61 iBT).

Clark University, Graduate School, School of Professional Studies, Program in Public Administration, Worcester, MA 01610-1477. Offers MPA, Certificate. *Program availability:* Part-time, evening/weekend. *Students:* 32 full-time (13 women), 45 part-time (28 women); includes 12 minority (3 Black or African American, non-Hispanic/Latino; 7 Hispanic/Latino; 2 Two or more races, non-Hispanic/Latino), 21 international. Average age 31. 107 applicants, 60% accepted, 41 enrolled. In 2019, 21 master's awarded. *Entrance requirements:* For master's, 2 references, resume or curriculum vitae, personal statement. Additional exam requirements/recommendations for international students: required—TOEFL (minimum score 575 paper-based; 90 iBT), IELTS (minimum score 6.5). *Application deadline:* Applications are processed on a rolling basis. Application fee: $75. Electronic applications accepted. *Expenses:* Contact institution. *Financial support:* Career-related internships or fieldwork available. Support available to part-time students. *Unit head:* Mary Piecewicz, Assistant Dean, 508-793-7212, E-mail: mpiecewicz@clarku.edu. *Application contact:* Mary Piecewicz, Assistant Dean, 508-793-7212, E-mail: mpiecewicz@clarku.edu.
Website: http://www.clarku.edu/programs/masters-public-administration

Clemson University, Graduate School, College of Behavioral, Social and Health Sciences, Department of Parks, Recreation, and Tourism Management, Clemson, SC 29634. Offers international parks and tourism (Certificate); parks, recreation and tourism management (MS, PhD), including recreational therapy (PhD); public administration (MPA, Certificate); recreational therapy (MS); youth development leadership (MS, Certificate). *Program availability:* Part-time, evening/weekend, 100% online. *Faculty:* 39 full-time (15 women), 4 part-time/adjunct (1 woman). *Students:* 72 full-time (50 women), 230 part-time (150 women); includes 51 minority (35 Black or African American, non-Hispanic/Latino; 10 Hispanic/Latino; 2 Native Hawaiian or other Pacific Islander, non-Hispanic/Latino; 4 Two or more races, non-Hispanic/Latino), 19 international. Average age 32. 251 applicants, 86% accepted, 125 enrolled. In 2019, 91 master's, 8 doctorates, 32 other advanced degrees awarded. *Degree requirements:* For master's, comprehensive exam (for some programs), thesis (for some programs); for doctorate, comprehensive exam, thesis/dissertation; for Certificate, portfolio. *Entrance requirements:* For master's and doctorate, GRE General Test, unofficial transcripts, letter of intent, letters of reference; for Certificate, letter of recommendation, unofficial transcripts, personal statement, resume. Additional exam requirements/recommendations for international students: required—TOEFL (minimum score 80 paper-based; 80 iBT); recommended—IELTS (minimum score 6.5), TSE (minimum score 54). *Application deadline:* For fall admission, 4/15 priority date for international students; for spring admission, 10/15 priority date for international students. Applications are processed on a rolling basis. Application fee: $80 ($90 for international students). Electronic applications accepted. *Expenses: Tuition, area resident:* Full-time $10,600; part-time $8688 per semester. Tuition, state resident: full-time $10,600; part-time $8688 per semester. Tuition, nonresident: full-time $22,050; part-time $17,412 per semester. *International tuition:* $22,050 full-time. *Required fees:* $1196; $617 per semester. $617 per semester. Tuition and fees vary according to course load, degree level, campus/location and program. *Financial support:* In 2019–20, 77 students received support, including 5 fellowships with full and partial tuition reimbursements available (averaging $8,000 per year), 1 research assistantship with full and partial tuition reimbursement available (averaging $4,324 per year), 9 teaching assistantships with full and partial tuition reimbursements available (averaging $14,556 per year); career-related internships or fieldwork and unspecified assistantships also available. *Unit head:* Dr. Fran McGuire, Interim Chair, 864-656-3036, E-mail: lefty@clemson.edu. *Application contact:* Dr. Jeff Hallo, Graduate Coordinator, 864-656-3237, E-mail: jhallo@clemson.edu.
Website: http://www.clemson.edu/hehd/departments/prtm/

Cleveland State University, College of Graduate Studies, Maxine Goodman Levin College of Urban Affairs, Program in Public Administration, Cleveland, OH 44115. Offers economic development (MPA); non-profit management (MPA); public management (MPA); JD/MPA. *Accreditation:* NASPAA. *Program availability:* Part-time, evening/weekend. *Students:* Average age 32. 79 applicants, 77% accepted, 12 enrolled. In 2019, 28 master's awarded. *Degree requirements:* For master's, thesis or alternative, exit project. *Entrance requirements:* For master's, GRE General Test (minimum scores in 40th percentile verbal and quantitative, 4.0 writing), minimum GPA of 3.0. Additional exam requirements/recommendations for international students: required—TOEFL (minimum score 550 paper-based; 78 iBT), IELTS (6.0), or International Test of English Proficiency (iTEP). *Application deadline:* For fall admission, 7/1 priority date for domestic students, 5/15 for international students; for spring admission, 11/15 for domestic students, 11/1 for international students; for summer admission, 4/1 for domestic students, 3/15 for international students. Applications are processed on a rolling basis. Application fee: $40. Electronic applications accepted. *Expenses:* Contact institution. *Financial support:* In 2019–20, 16 students received support, including 5 research assistantships with full tuition reimbursements available (averaging $7,200 per year), 1 teaching assistantship with partial tuition reimbursement available (averaging $2,400 per year); scholarships/grants, tuition waivers (full and partial), and unspecified assistantships also available. Support available to part-time students. Financial award application deadline: 3/1; financial award applicants required to submit FAFSA. *Unit head:* Dr. Nicholas Zingale, Director, 216-802-3389, Fax: 216-687-9342, E-mail: n.zingale@csuohio.edu. *Application contact:* David Arrighi, Graduate Academic Advisor, 216-523-7522, Fax: 216-687-5398, E-mail: d.arrighi@csuohio.edu.
Website: http://urban.csuohio.edu/academics/graduate/mpa/

Cleveland State University, College of Graduate Studies, Maxine Goodman Levin College of Urban Affairs, Program in Urban Studies and Public Affairs, Cleveland, OH 44115. Offers communication (PhD); public administration (PhD); urban policy and development (PhD). *Program availability:* Part-time, evening/weekend. *Degree requirements:* For doctorate, comprehensive exam, thesis/dissertation. *Entrance requirements:* For doctorate, GRE General Test (minimum score: verbal and quantitative 50th percentile, analytical writing 4.0), minimum GPA of 3.5. Additional exam requirements/recommendations for international students: required—TOEFL (minimum score 550 paper-based; 78 iBT), IELTS (6.0), or International Test of English Proficiency (iTEP). Electronic applications accepted. *Expenses:* Contact institution.

College of Charleston, Graduate School, School of Humanities and Social Sciences, Program in Public Administration, Charleston, SC 29424-0001. Offers MPA. *Accreditation:* NASPAA. *Program availability:* Part-time, evening/weekend. *Degree requirements:* For master's, thesis optional, internship, capstone seminar. *Entrance requirements:* For master's, GRE General Test, previous course work in statistics, 3 letters of recommendation, minimum GPA of 3.0. Additional exam requirements/recommendations for international students: required—TOEFL (minimum score 81 iBT). Electronic applications accepted.

The College of New Rochelle, Graduate School, Division of Human Services, Program in Public Administration, New Rochelle, NY 10805-2308. Offers long term care administration (MPA); public administration (MPA). *Degree requirements:* For master's, comprehensive exam, internship. *Entrance requirements:* For master's, minimum GPA of 3.0, personal statement, two letters of recommendation, official transcripts of all colleges/universities attended, proof of immunizations.

College of Saint Elizabeth, Program in Justice Administration and Public Service, Morristown, NJ 07960-6989. Offers counter terrorism (Certificate); cyber security investigation (Certificate); justice administration and public service (MA); leadership in community policing (Certificate). *Program availability:* Part-time, 100% online, blended/hybrid learning. *Degree requirements:* For master's, thesis. *Entrance requirements:* Additional exam requirements/recommendations for international students: required—TOEFL (minimum score 550 paper-based; 79 iBT), IELTS (minimum score 6.5). Electronic applications accepted. Application fee is waived when completed online. *Expenses:* Contact institution.

Columbia University, School of International and Public Affairs, Program in Public Policy and Administration, New York, NY 10027. Offers MPA, JD/MPA, MPA/MS, MPH/MPA. *Accreditation:* NASPAA. *Entrance requirements:* For master's, GRE General Test. Additional exam requirements/recommendations for international students: required—TOEFL (minimum score 600 paper-based; 100 iBT), IELTS (minimum score 7), PTE (minimum score 68). Electronic applications accepted. *Expenses: Tuition:* Full-time $47,600; part-time $1880 per credit. One-time fee: $105.

Columbus State University, Graduate Studies, College of Letters and Sciences, Department of Political Science and Public Administration, Columbus, GA 31907-5645. Offers public administration (MPA), including criminal justice, environmental policy, government administration, health services administration, political campaigning, urban policy. *Program availability:* Part-time, evening/weekend, 100% online, blended/hybrid learning. *Degree requirements:* For master's, comprehensive exam. *Entrance requirements:* For master's, GRE General Test, minimum GPA of 2.75, three letters of recommendation. Additional exam requirements/recommendations for international students: required—TOEFL (minimum score 550 paper-based; 79 iBT). Electronic applications accepted. *Expenses: Tuition, area resident:* Full-time $210; part-time $210 per credit hour. Tuition, state resident: full-time $210; part-time $210 per credit hour. Tuition, nonresident: full-time $817; part-time $817 per credit hour. *International tuition:* $817 full-time. *Required fees:* $802.50. Tuition and fees vary according to course load, degree level and program.

Concordia University, School of Graduate Studies, Faculty of Arts and Science, Department of Political Science, Montréal, QC H3G 1M8, Canada. Offers political science (PhD); public policy and public administration (MA), including geography. *Degree requirements:* For master's, one foreign language, comprehensive exam, thesis optional, internship. *Entrance requirements:* For master's, honors degree or equivalent. Additional exam requirements/recommendations for international students: required—TOEFL.

Concordia University Wisconsin, Graduate Programs, Batterman School of Business, MBA Program, Mequon, WI 53097-2402. Offers finance (MBA); health care administration (MBA); human resource management (MBA); international business (MBA); international business-bilingual English/Chinese (MBA); management (MBA); management information systems (MBA); managerial communications (MBA); marketing (MBA); public administration (MBA); risk management (MBA). *Program availability:* Online learning. *Degree requirements:* For master's, comprehensive exam, thesis or alternative. *Entrance requirements:* Additional exam requirements/recommendations for international students: required—TOEFL. *Expenses:* Contact institution.

Copenhagen Business School, Graduate Programs, Copenhagen, Denmark. Offers business administration (Exec MBA, MBA, PhD); business administration and information systems (M Sc); business, language and culture (M Sc); economics and business administration (M Sc); health management (MHM); international business and politics (M Sc); public administration (MPA); shipping and logistics (Exec MBA); technology, market and organization (MBA).

Cumberland University, Program in Public Service Administration, Lebanon, TN 37087. Offers MS. *Program availability:* Part-time, evening/weekend. *Degree requirements:* For master's, comprehensive exam. *Entrance requirements:* For master's, MAT, 3 letters of recommendation. Additional exam requirements/recommendations for international students: required—TOEFL (minimum score 500 paper-based).

Dalhousie University, Faculty of Management, School of Public Administration, Halifax, NS B3H 3J5, Canada. Offers management (MPA); public administration (MPA, GDPA); LL B/MPA; MLIS/MPA. *Program availability:* Part-time. *Entrance requirements:* For master's, GMAT. Additional exam requirements/recommendations for international students: required—TOEFL, IELTS, CANTEST, CAEL, or Michigan English Language Assessment Battery. Electronic applications accepted. *Expenses:* Contact institution.

DePaul University, College of Liberal Arts and Social Sciences, Chicago, IL 60614. Offers Arabic (MA); Chinese (MA); critical ethnic studies (MA); English (MA); French (MA); German (MA); history (MA); interdisciplinary studies (MA, MS); international public service (MS); international studies (MA); Italian (MA); Japanese (MA); liberal studies (MA); nonprofit management (MNM); public administration (MPA); public health (MPH); public policy (MPP); public service management (MS); refugee and forced migration studies (MS); social work (MSW); sociology (MA); Spanish (MA); sustainable urban development (MA); women's and gender studies (MA); writing and publishing (MA); writing, rhetoric and discourse (MA); MA/PhD. *Accreditation:* CEPH. *Program availability:* Part-time, evening/weekend, online learning. Terminal master's awarded for partial completion of doctoral program. *Degree requirements:* For master's, variable foreign language requirement, comprehensive exam (for some programs), thesis (for some programs). Electronic applications accepted.

DeVry University–Folsom Campus, Graduate Programs, Folsom, CA 95630. Offers accounting (M Acc); accounting and financial management (MAFM); business administration (MBA); curriculum leadership (M Ed); educational leadership (M Ed); educational technology (M Ed); higher education leadership (M Ed); human resource management (MHRM); information systems management (MISM); network and communications management (MNCM); project management (MPM); public administration (MPA).

Drake University, College of Business and Public Administration, Des Moines, IA 50311-4516. Offers accounting (M Acc); business administration (MBA); public administration (MPA); JD/MBA; JD/MPA; Pharm D/MBA; Pharm D/MPA. *Program availability:* Part-time, evening/weekend, 100% online, blended/hybrid learning. *Students:* 29 full-time (18 women), 217 part-time (126 women); includes 33 minority (7 Black or African American, non-Hispanic/Latino; 1 American Indian or Alaska Native, non-Hispanic/Latino; 4 Asian, non-Hispanic/Latino; 15 Hispanic/Latino; 6 Two or more races, non-Hispanic/Latino), 13 international. Average age 33. In 2019, 123 master's awarded. *Degree requirements:* For master's, comprehensive exam (for some programs), thesis (for some programs), internships. *Entrance requirements:* For master's, GMAT, letters of recommendation, resume. Additional exam requirements/recommendations for international students: required—TOEFL (minimum score 550 paper-based). *Application deadline:* For fall admission, 8/15 priority date for domestic students; for winter admission, 12/20 priority date for domestic students; for spring admission, 12/1 priority date for domestic students. Applications are processed on a rolling basis. Application fee: $25. Electronic applications accepted. *Expenses:* Contact institution. *Financial support:* Fellowships with tuition reimbursements, teaching assistantships, career-related internships or fieldwork, and institutionally sponsored loans available. Support available to part-time students. Financial award application deadline: 3/1; financial award applicants required to submit FAFSA. *Unit head:* Dr. Daniel J. Connolly, Dean, 515-271-2872, Fax: 515-271-4518, E-mail: daniel.connolly@drake.edu. *Application contact:* Danette Kenne, Assistant Dean, 515-271-2188, Fax: 515-271-4518, E-mail: cbpa.gradprograms@drake.edu. Website: http://www.drake.edu/cbpa/

East Carolina University, Graduate School, Thomas Harriot College of Arts and Sciences, Department of Political Science, Greenville, NC 27858-4353. Offers public administration (MPA); security studies (MS, Certificate). *Accreditation:* NASPAA. *Program availability:* Part-time, evening/weekend, online learning. *Application deadline:* For fall admission, 6/1 priority date for domestic students; for spring admission, 10/15 for domestic students. *Expenses: Tuition, area resident:* Full-time $4749; part-time $185 per credit hour. Tuition, state resident: full-time $4749; part-time $185 per credit hour. Tuition, nonresident: full-time $17,898; part-time $864 per credit hour. *International tuition:* $17,898 full-time. *Required fees:* $2787. *Financial support:* Application deadline: 3/1. *Unit head:* Dr. Alethia Cook, Chair, 252-328-5869, E-mail: cooka@ecu.edu. *Application contact:* Graduate School Admissions, 252-328-6012, Fax: 252-328-6071, E-mail: gradschool@ecu.edu. Website: https://politicalscience.ecu.edu/

Eastern Kentucky University, The Graduate School, College of Arts and Sciences, Department of Government, Program in General Public Administration, Richmond, KY 40475-3102. Offers community development (MPA); community health administration (MPA); general public administration (MPA). *Accreditation:* NASPAA. *Program availability:* Part-time, evening/weekend. *Entrance requirements:* For master's, GRE General Test, minimum GPA of 2.5.

Eastern Michigan University, Graduate School, College of Arts and Sciences, Department of Political Science, Programs in Public Administration, Ypsilanti, MI 48197. Offers general public management (Graduate Certificate); local government management (Graduate Certificate); management of public healthcare services (Graduate Certificate); nonprofit management (Graduate Certificate); public administration (MPA); public budget management (Graduate Certificate); public land planning and development management (Graduate Certificate); public personnel management (Graduate Certificate); public policy analysis (Graduate Certificate). *Accreditation:* NASPAA. *Students:* 12 full-time (7 women), 31 part-time (14 women); includes 13 minority (11 Black or African American, non-Hispanic/Latino; 1 Hispanic/Latino; 1 Two or more races, non-Hispanic/Latino), 2 international. Average age 35. 38 applicants, 82% accepted, 13 enrolled. In 2019, 16 master's, 9 other advanced degrees awarded. Application fee: $45. *Application contact:* Dr. Rose Jindal, MPA Coordinator, 734-487-3113, Fax: 734-487-3340, E-mail: rsoliven@emich.edu. Website: http://www.emich.edu/polisci/

Eastern Washington University, Graduate Studies, College of Business and Public Administration, Program in Public Administration, Cheney, WA 99004-2431. Offers MPA, MPA/MURP. *Accreditation:* NASPAA. *Program availability:* Part-time, evening/weekend. *Students:* 31 full-time (18 women), 11 part-time (8 women); includes 6 minority (1 Black or African American, non-Hispanic/Latino; 1 American Indian or Alaska Native, non-Hispanic/Latino; 4 Hispanic/Latino), 1 international. Average age 34. 2 applicants. In 2019, 19 master's awarded. *Degree requirements:* For master's, comprehensive exam, thesis optional. *Entrance requirements:* For master's, minimum GPA of 3.0. Additional exam requirements/recommendations for international students: required—TOEFL (minimum score 580 paper-based; 92 iBT), IELTS (minimum score 7), PTE (minimum score 63). *Application deadline:* For fall admission, 4/1 priority date for domestic students; for spring admission, 1/15 for domestic students. Applications are processed on a rolling basis. Application fee: $75. Electronic applications accepted. *Financial support:* Teaching assistantships with partial tuition reimbursements, career-related internships or fieldwork, Federal Work-Study, institutionally sponsored loans, scholarships/grants, health care benefits, tuition waivers (partial), and unspecified assistantships available. Support available to part-time students. Financial award application deadline: 2/1; financial award applicants required to submit FAFSA. *Unit head:* Dr. Kerry Brooks, Interim Dean, 509-828-1230, E-mail: kbrooks@ewu.edu. *Application contact:* Kathy White, Student Application Contact, 509-359-7870, E-mail: gradprograms@ewu.edu. Website: http://www.ewu.edu/CBPA/Programs/Public-Administration.xml

East Stroudsburg University of Pennsylvania, Graduate and Extended Studies, College of Arts and Sciences, Department of Political Science and Economics, East Stroudsburg, PA 18301-2999. Offers management and leadership in public administration (MS); political science (MA). *Program availability:* Part-time, evening/weekend. *Degree requirements:* For master's, variable foreign language requirement, comprehensive exam, thesis or alternative. *Entrance requirements:* For master's, Goals statement, letters of recommendation. Additional exam requirements/recommendations for international students: recommended—TOEFL (minimum score 560 paper-based; 83 iBT), IELTS. Electronic applications accepted.

East Tennessee State University, College of Graduate and Continuing Studies, College of Arts and Sciences, Department of Political Science, International Affairs and Public Administration, Johnson City, TN 37614. Offers economic development (Postbaccalaureate Certificate); economic development and planning (MPA); local government management (MPA); nonprofit and public financial management (MPA); urban planning (Postbaccalaureate Certificate). *Program availability:* Part-time. *Degree requirements:* For master's, internship, capstone. *Entrance requirements:* For master's, GRE General Test, three letters of recommendation. Additional exam requirements/recommendations for international students: required—TOEFL (minimum score 550 paper-based; 79 iBT). Electronic applications accepted.

The Evergreen State College, Graduate Programs, Program in Public Administration, Olympia, WA 98505. Offers MPA. *Program availability:* Part-time, evening/weekend. *Faculty:* 6 full-time (3 women), 6 part-time/adjunct (5 women). *Students:* 73 full-time (49 women), 69 part-time (54 women); includes 52 minority (15 Black or African American, non-Hispanic/Latino; 15 American Indian or Alaska Native, non-Hispanic/Latino; 2 Asian, non-Hispanic/Latino; 18 Hispanic/Latino; 1 Native Hawaiian or other Pacific Islander, non-Hispanic/Latino; 1 Two or more races, non-Hispanic/Latino). Average age 36. 113 applicants, 82% accepted, 73 enrolled. In 2019, 58 master's awarded. *Degree requirements:* For master's, 6-credit capstone course or 8-credit thesis. *Entrance requirements:* For master's, minimum GPA of 3.0 in last 90 quarter hours toward BA/BS; 4 quarter credits in statistics within past 3 years; evidence of writing, analytical, and general communication skills at appropriate level for graduate study. Additional exam requirements/recommendations for international students: required—TOEFL (minimum score 600 paper-based; 100 iBT). *Application deadline:* For fall admission, 2/1 priority date for domestic and international students. Application fee: $50. Electronic applications accepted. *Expenses:* Contact institution. *Financial support:* In 2019–20, 54 students received support, including 14 fellowships with partial tuition reimbursements available (averaging $1,590 per year); career-related internships or fieldwork, Federal Work-Study, scholarships/grants, and tuition waivers (partial) also available. Support available to part-time students. Financial award application deadline: 2/1; financial award applicants required to submit FAFSA. *Unit head:* Dr. Michael Craw, MPA Program Director, 360-867-6820, E-mail: crawm@evergreen.edu. *Application contact:* Marcia Zitzelman, Associate MPA Program Director, 360-867-6554, E-mail: zitzelmm@evergreen.edu. Website: http://www.evergreen.edu/mpa/

Fairfield University, College of Arts and Sciences, Fairfield, CT 06824. Offers American studies (MA); communication (MA); creative writing (MFA); mathematics (MS); public administration (MPA). *Program availability:* Part-time, evening/weekend, online learning. *Faculty:* 35 full-time (19 women), 19 part-time/adjunct (10 women). *Students:* 64 full-time (44 women), 84 part-time (48 women); includes 35 minority (9 Black or African American, non-Hispanic/Latino; 1 American Indian or Alaska Native, non-Hispanic/Latino; 1 Asian, non-Hispanic/Latino; 21 Hispanic/Latino; 3 Two or more races, non-Hispanic/Latino), 7 international. Average age 36. 98 applicants, 68% accepted, 64 enrolled. In 2019, 38 master's awarded. *Degree requirements:* For master's, capstone research course. *Entrance requirements:* For master's, minimum GPA of 3.0, 2 letters of recommendation, resume, personal statement. Additional exam requirements/recommendations for international students: required—TOEFL (minimum score 550 paper-based; 80 iBT) or IELTS (minimum score 6.5). *Application deadline:* For fall admission, 5/15 for international students; for spring admission, 10/15 for international students. Applications are processed on a rolling basis. Application fee: $60. Electronic applications accepted. *Expenses:* Tuition $850/credit hour; Registration Fee $50/semester; Graduate Student Activity Fee (Fall and Spring) $65/semester. *Financial support:* In 2019–20, 11 students received support. Scholarships/grants and unspecified assistantships available. Financial award applicants required to submit FAFSA. *Unit head:* Dr. Richard Greenwald, Dean, 203-254-4000 Ext. 2221, Fax: 203-254-4119, E-mail: rgreenwald@fairfield.edu. *Application contact:* Melanie Rogers, Director of Graduate Admission, 203-254-4184, Fax: 203-254-4073, E-mail: gradadmis@fairfield.edu. Website: http://www.fairfield.edu/cas

Fairleigh Dickinson University, Florham Campus, Anthony J. Petrocelli College of Continuing Studies, Public Administration Institute, Program in Public Administration, Madison, NJ 07940-1099. Offers MPA.

Fairleigh Dickinson University, Metropolitan Campus, Anthony J. Petrocelli College of Continuing Studies, Public Administration Institute, Program in Public Administration, Teaneck, NJ 07666-1914. Offers MPA, Certificate.

Florida Agricultural and Mechanical University, Division of Graduate Studies, Research, and Continuing Education, College of Social Sciences, Arts and Humanities, Department of History and Political Science, Program in Applied Social Science, Tallahassee, FL 32307-3200. Offers criminal justice (MASS); history (MASS); political science (MASS); public administration (MASS). *Program availability:* Part-time. *Degree requirements:* For master's, thesis optional. *Entrance requirements:* For master's, GRE General Test, minimum GPA of 3.0.

Florida Atlantic University, College for Design and Social Inquiry, School of Public Administration, Boca Raton, FL 33431-0991. Offers MPA, PhD. *Accreditation:* NASPAA (one or more programs are accredited). *Program availability:* Part-time, evening/weekend. *Faculty:* 11 full-time (4 women), 1 part-time/adjunct (0 women). *Students:* 14 full-time (9 women), 56 part-time (32 women); includes 36 minority (16 Black or African American, non-Hispanic/Latino; 4 Asian, non-Hispanic/Latino; 13 Hispanic/Latino; 3 Two or more races, non-Hispanic/Latino), 5 international. Average age 36. 51 applicants, 45% accepted, 17 enrolled. In 2019, 27 master's, 3 doctorates awarded. *Degree requirements:* For master's, thesis optional; for doctorate, comprehensive exam, thesis/dissertation. *Entrance requirements:* For master's, GRE General Test, minimum GPA of 3.0; for doctorate, GRE General Test, faculty reference, scholarly writing samples, letters of recommendation. Additional exam requirements/recommendations for international students: required—TOEFL (minimum score 500 paper-based; 61 iBT), IELTS (minimum score 6). *Application deadline:* For fall admission, 5/1 priority date for domestic students, 2/15 for international students; for spring admission, 11/1 for domestic students, 7/15 for international students. Applications are processed on a rolling basis. Application fee: $30. *Expenses: Tuition:* Full-time $20,536; part-time $371.82 per credit hour. Tuition and fees vary according to program. *Financial support:* Fellowships with full tuition reimbursements, research assistantships with partial tuition reimbursements, teaching assistantships with partial tuition reimbursements, career-related internships or fieldwork, Federal Work-Study, institutionally sponsored loans, and tuition waivers (partial) available. Support available to part-time students. Financial award application deadline: 4/1. *Unit head:* Leslie Leip, Program Coordinator, 561-297-4153, E-mail: lleip@fau.edu. *Application contact:* Leslie Leip, Program Coordinator, 561-297-4153, E-mail: lleip@fau.edu. Website: http://www.fau.edu/spa/

Florida Gulf Coast University, College of Arts and Sciences, Program in Public Administration, Fort Myers, FL 33965-6565. Offers environmental policy (MPA); management (MPA). *Accreditation:* NASPAA. *Program availability:* Part-time. *Degree requirements:* For master's, thesis. *Entrance requirements:* For master's, GRE General Test, MAT, minimum GPA of 3.0. Additional exam requirements/recommendations for international students: required—TOEFL (minimum score 550 paper-based). Electronic applications accepted. *Expenses: Tuition, area resident:* Full-time $6974; part-time $4350 per credit hour. Tuition, state resident: full-time $6974; part-time $4350 per credit hour. Tuition, nonresident: full-time $28,169; part-time $17,595 per credit hour. *International tuition:* $28,169 full-time. *Required fees:* $2027; $1267 per credit hour. $507 per semester. Tuition and fees vary according to course load.

Florida Institute of Technology, Aberdeen Education Center (Maryland), Program in Management, Melbourne, FL 32901-6975. Offers acquisition and contract management (MS, PMBA); business administration (MS, PMBA); contracts management (PMBA); financial management (MPA); global management (PMBA); health management (MS);

human resources management (MS, PMBA); information systems (PMBA); logistics management (MS); management (MS), including information systems, operations research; materials acquisition management (MS); operations research (MS); public administration (MPA); research (PMBA); space systems (MS); space systems management (MS).

Florida Institute of Technology, Hampton Roads Education Center (Virginia), Program in Public Administration, Melbourne, FL 32901-6975. Offers financial management (MPA); public administration (MPA). *Program availability:* Part-time, evening/weekend, online learning. Electronic applications accepted.

Florida International University, Steven J. Green School of International and Public Affairs, Department of Public Administration, Miami, FL 33199. Offers public administration (MPA); public affairs (PhD); JD/MPA; MS/MPA. *Accreditation:* NASPAA (one or more programs are accredited). *Program availability:* Part-time, evening/weekend. *Faculty:* 14 full-time (5 women), 16 part-time/adjunct (8 women). *Students:* 96 full-time (60 women), 125 part-time (88 women); includes 182 minority (54 Black or African American, non-Hispanic/Latino; 2 Asian, non-Hispanic/Latino; 120 Hispanic/Latino; 6 Two or more races, non-Hispanic/Latino), 18 international. Average age 31. 115 applicants, 71% accepted, 64 enrolled. In 2019, 92 master's, 9 doctorates awarded. *Degree requirements:* For doctorate, comprehensive exam, thesis/dissertation. *Entrance requirements:* For master's, minimum undergraduate GPA of 3.0 in upper-level coursework, letter of recommendation, letter of intent; for doctorate, GRE, minimum undergraduate GPA of 3.0 in upper-level coursework, 3 letters of recommendation, samples of scholarly written work, interview (when student lives within 50 miles of campus). Additional exam requirements/recommendations for international students: required—TOEFL (minimum score 550 paper-based; 80 iBT). *Application deadline:* For fall admission, 6/1 for domestic students, 4/1 for international students; for spring admission, 10/1 for domestic students, 9/1 for international students. Applications are processed on a rolling basis. Application fee: $30. Electronic applications accepted. *Expenses: Tuition, area resident:* Full-time $8912; part-time $446 per credit hour. Tuition, state resident: full-time $8912; part-time $446 per credit hour. Tuition, nonresident: full-time $21,393; part-time $992 per credit hour. *Required fees:* $2194. *Financial support:* Institutionally sponsored loans and scholarships/grants available. Financial award application deadline: 3/1; financial award applicants required to submit FAFSA. *Unit head:* Dr. Howard Frank, Chair, 305-348-0410, E-mail: howard.frank@fiu.edu. *Application contact:* Nanett Rojas, Manager, Admissions Operations, 305-348-7464, Fax: 305-348-7441, E-mail: gradadm@fiu.edu.

Florida National University, Program in Business Administration, Hialeah, FL 33139. Offers accounting (MBA); finance (MBA); general management (MBA); health services administration (MBA); marketing (MBA); public management and leadership (MBA). *Program availability:* Part-time, online only, blended/hybrid learning. *Faculty:* 3 full-time (1 woman), 5 part-time/adjunct (2 women). *Students:* 23 full-time (15 women), 18 part-time (7 women); includes 37 minority (4 Black or African American, non-Hispanic/Latino; 1 American Indian or Alaska Native, non-Hispanic/Latino; 32 Hispanic/Latino), 1 international. Average age 35. 14 applicants, 100% accepted, 14 enrolled. In 2019, 13 master's awarded. *Degree requirements:* For master's, capstone. *Entrance requirements:* For master's, writing assessment, bachelor's degree from accredited institution; official undergraduate transcripts; minimum undergraduate GPA of 2.5, GMAT (minimum score of 400), or GRE (minimum score of 900); two letters of recommendation; resume. Additional exam requirements/recommendations for international students: required—TOEFL (minimum score 500 paper-based; 62 iBT), IELTS (minimum score 5.5). *Application deadline:* Applications are processed on a rolling basis. Electronic applications accepted. *Expenses:* Contact institution. *Financial support:* Federal Work-Study, institutionally sponsored loans, scholarships/grants, and tuition waivers (full and partial) available. Financial award applicants required to submit FAFSA. *Unit head:* Dr. James Bullen, Business and Economics Division Head, 305-821-3333 Ext. 1163, Fax: 305-362-0595, E-mail: jbullen@fnu.edu. *Application contact:* Dr. Ernesto Gonzalez, Business and Economics Department Head, 305-821- 3333 Ext. 1170, Fax: 305-362-0595, E-mail: egonzalez@fnu.edu.
Website: https://www.fnu.edu/prospective-students/our-programs/select-a-program/master-of-business-administration/business-administration-mba-masters/

Florida State University, The Graduate School, College of Social Sciences and Public Policy, Reubin O'D. Askew School of Public Administration and Policy, Tallahassee, FL 32306-2250. Offers public administration (MPA, PhD); public administration and policy (Certificate); JD/MPA; MPA/MSC; MPA/MSP; MPA/MSW. *Accreditation:* NASPAA (one or more programs are accredited). *Program availability:* Part-time, evening/weekend. *Faculty:* 10 full-time (2 women), 10 part-time/adjunct (3 women). *Students:* 74 full-time (37 women), 75 part-time (47 women); includes 47 minority (17 Black or African American, non-Hispanic/Latino; 3 Asian, non-Hispanic/Latino; 18 Hispanic/Latino; 9 Two or more races, non-Hispanic/Latino), 46 international. Average age 32. 190 applicants, 54% accepted, 55 enrolled. In 2019, 35 master's, 7 doctorates awarded. *Degree requirements:* For master's, action report; for doctorate, comprehensive exam, thesis/dissertation. *Entrance requirements:* For master's, GRE General Test, GMAT, MAT, LSAT, minimum undergraduate upper-division GPA of 3.0; for doctorate, GRE General Test (minimum score of 1100 or equivalent on current grading scale); GMAT; MAT; LSAT, minimum undergraduate GPA of 3.0, graduate 3.5. Additional exam requirements/recommendations for international students: required—TOEFL (minimum score 550 paper-based; 80 iBT), IELTS (minimum score 6.5), PTE (minimum score 55), Michigan English Language Assessment Battery (minimum score 77). *Application deadline:* For fall admission, 7/1 for domestic students, 5/1 for international students; for spring admission, 11/1 for domestic students, 9/1 for international students; for summer admission, 3/1 for domestic students, 1/1 for international students. Applications are processed on a rolling basis. Application fee: $30. Electronic applications accepted. *Financial support:* In 2019–20, 6 students received support, including fellowships with full tuition reimbursements available (averaging $18,000 per year), 4 research assistantships with full tuition reimbursements available (averaging $15,000 per year), 2 teaching assistantships with full tuition reimbursements available (averaging $15,000 per year); career-related internships or fieldwork, Federal Work-Study, institutionally sponsored loans, scholarships/grants, tuition waivers (full and partial), and unspecified assistantships also available. Support available to part-time students. Financial award application deadline: 2/1; financial award applicants required to submit FAFSA. *Unit head:* Dr. Keon-Hyung Lee, Director, 850-645-8210, Fax: 850-644-7617, E-mail: klee2@fsu.edu. *Application contact:* Christina Havlicek, Academic Program Specialist, 850-644-3060, Fax: 850-644-7617, E-mail: chavlicek@fsu.edu.
Website: http://askew.fsu.edu/

Framingham State University, Graduate Studies, Program in Public Administration, Framingham, MA 01701-9101. Offers MPA. *Program availability:* Part-time, evening/weekend.

Gallaudet University, The Graduate School, Washington, DC 20002. Offers American Sign Language/English bilingual early childhood deaf education: birth to 5 (Certificate); audiology (Au D); clinical psychology (PhD); deaf and hard of hearing infants, toddlers, and their families (Certificate); deaf education (MA, Ed S); deaf history (Certificate); deaf studies (Certificate); educating deaf students with disabilities (Certificate); education: teacher preparation (MA), including deaf education, early childhood education and deaf education, elementary education and deaf education, secondary education and deaf education; educational neuroscience (PhD); hearing, speech and language sciences (MS, PhD); international development (MA); interpretation (MA, PhD), including combined interpreting practice and research (MA), interpreting research (MA); linguistics (MA, PhD); mental health counseling (MA); peer mentoring (Certificate); public administration (MPA); school counseling (MA); school psychology (Psy S); sign language teaching (MA); social work (MSW); speech-language pathology (MS). *Program availability:* Part-time. *Faculty:* 101 full-time (70 women). *Students:* 267 full-time (208 women), 139 part-time (95 women); includes 120 minority (38 Black or African American, non-Hispanic/Latino; 20 Asian, non-Hispanic/Latino; 44 Hispanic/Latino; 18 Two or more races, non-Hispanic/Latino), 19 international. Average age 30. 484 applicants, 50% accepted, 162 enrolled. In 2019, 138 master's, 25 doctorates, 14 other advanced degrees awarded. Terminal master's awarded for partial completion of doctoral program. *Degree requirements:* For master's, comprehensive exam (for some programs), thesis optional; for doctorate, comprehensive exam, thesis/dissertation. *Entrance requirements:* For master's and doctorate, GRE General Test or MAT, letters of recommendation, interviews, goals statement, American Sign Language proficiency interview, written English competency. Additional exam requirements/recommendations for international students: required—TOEFL. *Application deadline:* For fall admission, 2/15 for domestic students. Applications are processed on a rolling basis. Application fee: $75. Electronic applications accepted. *Expenses: Tuition:* Full-time $18,180; part-time $688 per credit. *Required fees:* $526; $526. Tuition and fees vary according to course load. *Financial support:* In 2019–20, 50 students received support. Fellowships, research assistantships, teaching assistantships, career-related internships or fieldwork, Federal Work-Study, scholarships/grants, tuition waivers (partial), and unspecified assistantships available. Support available to part-time students. Financial award application deadline: 7/1; financial award applicants required to submit FAFSA. *Unit head:* Dr. Gaurav Mathur, Dean, Graduate School and Continuing Studies, 202-250-2380, Fax: 202-651-5027, E-mail: gaurav.mathur@gallaudet.edu. *Application contact:* Heidi Zornes-Foster, Senior Graduate Admissions Counselor, 202-650-5436, Fax: 202-651-5295, E-mail: graduate.school@gallaudet.edu.
Website: www.gallaudet.edu

Gannon University, School of Graduate Studies, College of Engineering and Business, Dahlkemper School of Business, Program in Public Administration, Erie, PA 16541-0001. Offers MPA. *Program availability:* Part-time, evening/weekend, 100% online, blended/hybrid learning. *Degree requirements:* For master's, thesis or alternative, research project. *Entrance requirements:* For master's, GRE, bachelor's degree in any discipline from accredited college or university, transcripts, 3 letters of recommendation. Additional exam requirements/recommendations for international students: required—TOEFL (minimum score 79 iBT). Electronic applications accepted. Application fee is waived when completed online.

George Mason University, Schar School of Policy and Government, Program in Public Administration, Arlington, VA 22030. Offers MPA. *Accreditation:* NASPAA. *Degree requirements:* For master's, thesis or alternative, professional experience. *Entrance requirements:* Additional exam requirements/recommendations for international students: required—TOEFL (minimum score 575 paper-based; 88 iBT), IELTS (minimum score 6.5), PTE (minimum score 59). Electronic applications accepted. *Expenses:* Contact institution.

The George Washington University, Columbian College of Arts and Sciences, Trachtenberg School of Public Policy and Public Administration, Washington, DC 20052. Offers environmental resource policy (MA); public administration (MPA); public policy (MPP); public policy and administration (PhD); JD/MPP; MPA/JD; PhD/MPP. *Program availability:* Part-time, evening/weekend, online learning. *Faculty:* 13 full-time (7 women), 20 part-time/adjunct (8 women). *Students:* 184 full-time (104 women), 235 part-time (150 women); includes 127 minority (50 Black or African American, non-Hispanic/Latino; 2 American Indian or Alaska Native, non-Hispanic/Latino; 22 Asian, non-Hispanic/Latino; 42 Hispanic/Latino; 11 Two or more races, non-Hispanic/Latino), 45 international. Average age 26. 1,015 applicants, 63% accepted, 164 enrolled. In 2019, 135 master's, 16 doctorates awarded. *Degree requirements:* For master's, capstone project; for doctorate, comprehensive exam, thesis/dissertation. *Entrance requirements:* For master's, minimum GPA of 3.0; for doctorate, GRE, minimum GPA of 3.0. Additional exam requirements/recommendations for international students: required—TOEFL (minimum score 600 paper-based; 100 iBT), IELTS (minimum score 7). *Application deadline:* For fall admission, 1/15 priority date for domestic and international students; for spring admission, 10/1 priority date for domestic students, 10/1 for international students. Application fee: $80. Electronic applications accepted. *Expenses:* Contact institution. *Financial support:* In 2019–20, 57 students received support. Fellowships, research assistantships, teaching assistantships, Federal Work-Study, scholarships/grants, health care benefits, and unspecified assistantships available. Support available to part-time students. Financial award application deadline: 1/15; financial award applicants required to submit FAFSA. *Unit head:* Dr. Mary Tschirhart, Director, 202-994-2006, Fax: 202-994-6792, E-mail: marytschirhart@gwu.edu. *Application contact:* Lindsey A. Duble-Dice, Director of Graduate Admissions and Recruitment, 202-994-8569, Fax: 202-994-6792, E-mail: ldubledice@gwu.edu.
Website: http://www.tspppa.gwu.edu/

Georgia College & State University, The Graduate School, College of Arts and Sciences, Department of Government and Sociology, Program in Public Administration, Milledgeville, GA 31061. Offers MPA. *Accreditation:* NASPAA. *Program availability:* Part-time, evening/weekend. *Students:* 15 full-time (10 women), 74 part-time (51 women); includes 30 minority (29 Black or African American, non-Hispanic/Latino; 1 Hispanic/Latino). Average age 33. 36 applicants, 97% accepted, 27 enrolled. In 2019, 7 master's awarded. *Degree requirements:* For master's, capstone project or thesis, minimum GPA of 3.0. *Entrance requirements:* For master's, Applicants with an undergraduate GPA 2.75 - 2.99 must submit official test scores on either the Graduate Record Exam (290), Miller Analogies Test (395) or Graduate Management Aptitude Test (450) scores. Scores must be within the last five years, transcript of all undergraduate and graduate work, current resume, minimum undergraduate GPA of 3.0. Additional exam requirements/recommendations for international students: required—English proficiency: TOEFL score with a minimum score of 79 on the Internet test or 550 on the paper-based test OR 6.5 on IELTS. *Application deadline:* For fall admission, 7/1 priority date for domestic students, 4/1 priority date for international students; for spring admission, 11/1 priority date for domestic students, 9/1 priority date for international students; for summer admission, 4/1 priority date for domestic students. Applications are processed on a rolling basis. Application fee: $40. Electronic applications accepted. *Expenses:* For full time students - tuition $3042 & fees $338 per semester. *Financial support:* In 2019–20, 2 students received support. Unspecified assistantships available. Financial award application deadline: 3/1; financial award applicants required to submit FAFSA. *Unit head:* Dr. Min Kim, Graduate Coordinator for MPA Program, 478-445-0938, E-mail: min.kim@gcsu.edu. *Application contact:* Kate Marshall, Graduate Admissions Coordinator, 478-445-1184, E-mail: kate.marshall@gcsu.edu.
Website: http://www.gcsu.edu/artsandsciences/gov/public-administration-mpa

Georgia Southern University, Jack N. Averitt College of Graduate Studies, College of Behavioral and Social Sciences, Department of Public and Nonprofit Studies,

Statesboro, GA 30460. Offers public administration (MPA, Graduate Certificate). *Program availability:* Part-time, evening/weekend. *Faculty:* 7 full-time (5 women). *Students:* 25 full-time (9 women), 12 part-time (8 women); includes 16 minority (14 Black or African American, non-Hispanic/Latino; 1 Asian, non-Hispanic/Latino; 1 Two or more races, non-Hispanic/Latino), 4 international. Average age 27. 22 applicants, 95% accepted, 14 enrolled. *Degree requirements:* For master's, comprehensive exam. *Entrance requirements:* For master's, GRE General Test and/or GMAT, letters of reference, resume. Additional exam requirements/recommendations for international students: required—TOEFL (minimum score 550 paper-based; 80 iBT), IELTS (minimum score 6). *Application deadline:* For fall admission, 3/1 priority date for domestic and international students; for spring admission, 10/1 priority date for domestic students, 10/1 for international students. Applications are processed on a rolling basis. Application fee: $50. Electronic applications accepted. *Expenses: Tuition, area resident:* Full-time $4986; part-time $277 per credit hour. Tuition, nonresident: full-time $19,890; part-time $1105 per credit hour. *International tuition:* $19,890 full-time. *Required fees:* $2114; $1057 per semester. $1057 per semester. Tuition and fees vary according to course load, campus/location and program. *Financial support:* In 2019–20, 19 students received support, including 4 fellowships with full tuition reimbursements available (averaging $8,000 per year); Federal Work-Study, scholarships/grants, tuition waivers (full), and unspecified assistantships also available. Support available to part-time students. Financial award application deadline: 4/15; financial award applicants required to submit FAFSA. *Unit head:* Dr. Trenton Davis, Professor and Chair, 912-478-5430, Fax: 912-478-5348, E-mail: tjdavis@georgiasouthern.edu. *Application contact:* Dr. Trenton Davis, Professor and Chair, 912-467-5430, Fax: 912-478-5348, E-mail: publicadmin@georgiasouthern.edu.
Website: http://cbss.georgiasouthern.edu/publicadmin

Georgia Southern University, Jack N. Averitt College of Graduate Studies, College of Behavioral and Social Sciences, Department of Public and Nonprofit Studies, Master of Public Administration, Statesboro, GA 30460. Offers public and nonprofit management (MPA). *Program availability:* Part-time, evening/weekend. *Faculty:* 7 full-time (5 women). *Students:* 25 full-time (9 women), 12 part-time (8 women); includes 16 minority (14 Black or African American, non-Hispanic/Latino; 1 Asian, non-Hispanic/Latino; 1 Native Hawaiian or other Pacific Islander, non-Hispanic/Latino), 4 international. Average age 27. 22 applicants, 95% accepted, 14 enrolled. In 2019, 11 master's awarded. *Degree requirements:* For master's, comprehensive exam, internship (if pre-service). *Entrance requirements:* For master's, GRE General Test and/or GMAT, minimum GPA of 2.75, resume, undergraduate major appropriate to field, letters of reference. Additional exam requirements/recommendations for international students: required—TOEFL (minimum score 550 paper-based; 80 iBT), IELTS (minimum score 6). *Application deadline:* For fall admission, 3/1 priority date for domestic and international students; for spring admission, 10/1 priority date for domestic students, 10/1 for international students. Applications are processed on a rolling basis. Application fee: $50. Electronic applications accepted. *Expenses: Tuition, area resident:* Full-time $4986; part-time $277 per credit hour. Tuition, nonresident: full-time $19,890; part-time $1105 per credit hour. *International tuition:* $19,890 full-time. *Required fees:* $2114; $1057 per semester. $1057 per semester. Tuition and fees vary according to course load, campus/location and program. *Financial support:* In 2019–20, 19 students received support, including 4 fellowships with full tuition reimbursements available (averaging $8,000 per year); career-related internships or fieldwork, Federal Work-Study, scholarships/grants, tuition waivers (full), and unspecified assistantships also available. Support available to part-time students. Financial award application deadline: 4/15; financial award applicants required to submit FAFSA. *Unit head:* Dr. Trenton Davis, Chair and Professor, 912-478-5430, Fax: 912-478-8029, E-mail: tjdavis@georgiasouthern.edu.
Website: http://cbss.georgiasouthern.edu/publicadmin

Georgia State University, Andrew Young School of Policy Studies, Department of Public Management and Policy, Atlanta, GA 30303. Offers criminal justice (MPA); disaster management (Certificate); disaster policy (MPA); environmental policy (PhD); health policy (PhD); management and finance (MPA); nonprofit management (MPA, Certificate); nonprofit policy (MPA); planning and economic development (MPP, Certificate); policy analysis and evaluation (MPA), including planning and economic development; public and nonprofit management (PhD); public finance and budgeting (PhD), including science and technology policy, urban and regional economic development; public finance policy (MPA), including social policy; public health (MPA). *Accreditation:* NASPAA (one or more programs are accredited). *Program availability:* Part-time. *Faculty:* 13 full-time (7 women), 3 part-time/adjunct (1 woman). *Students:* 125 full-time (81 women), 91 part-time (66 women); includes 103 minority (78 Black or African American, non-Hispanic/Latino; 3 Asian, non-Hispanic/Latino; 14 Hispanic/Latino; 8 Two or more races, non-Hispanic/Latino), 31 international. Average age 32. 298 applicants, 60% accepted, 82 enrolled. In 2019, 70 master's, 8 other advanced degrees awarded. Terminal master's awarded for partial completion of doctoral program. *Degree requirements:* For master's, thesis optional; for doctorate, comprehensive exam, thesis/dissertation. *Entrance requirements:* For master's and doctorate, GRE. Additional exam requirements/recommendations for international students: required—TOEFL (minimum score 603 paper-based; 100 iBT) or IELTS (minimum score 7). *Application deadline:* For fall admission, 1/15 for domestic and international students. Application fee: $50. Electronic applications accepted. *Expenses: Tuition, area resident:* Full-time $7164; part-time $398 per credit hour. Tuition, state resident: full-time $7164; part-time $398 per credit hour. Tuition, nonresident: full-time $22,662; part-time $1259 per credit hour. *International tuition:* $22,662 full-time. *Required fees:* $2128; $312 per credit hour. Tuition and fees vary according to course load and program. *Financial support:* In 2019–20, fellowships (averaging $8,194 per year), research assistantships (averaging $8,068 per year), teaching assistantships (averaging $3,600 per year) were awarded; institutionally sponsored loans, scholarships/grants, health care benefits, and unspecified assistantships also available. Financial award application deadline: 2/1. *Unit head:* Dr. Cathy Yang Liu, Chair and Professor, 404-413-0102, Fax: 404-413-0104, E-mail: cyliu@gsu.edu. *Application contact:* Dr. Cathy Yang Liu, Chair and Professor, 404-413-0102, Fax: 404-413-0104, E-mail: cyliu@gsu.edu.
Website: https://aysps.gsu.edu/public-management-policy/

Golden Gate University, Ageno School of Business, San Francisco, CA 94105-2968. Offers accounting (MBA); adaptive leadership (MBA); advanced financial planning (MS); business administration (EMBA, MBA, DBA); business analytics (MBA, MS); entrepreneurship (MBA); finance (MBA, MS, Certificate); financial life planning (Certificate); financial planning (MS, Certificate); global supply chain management (MBA, Certificate); human resource management (MBA, MS, Certificate); information technology management (MBA, MS, Certificate); international business (MBA); marketing (MBA, MS, Certificate); project management (MBA, MS, Certificate); psychology (MA, Certificate); public administration (EMPA, MBA); public administration leadership (Certificate); JD/MBA. *Program availability:* Part-time, evening/weekend. *Degree requirements:* For doctorate, thesis/dissertation, qualifying examination. *Entrance requirements:* For master's, GMAT (for MBA), minimum GPA of 2.5 (MS). Additional exam requirements/recommendations for international students: required—TOEFL (minimum score 550 paper-based; 79 iBT). Electronic applications accepted. *Expenses:* Contact institution.

Governors State University, College of Arts and Sciences, Program in Public Administration, University Park, IL 60484. Offers MPA. *Accreditation:* NASPAA. *Program availability:* Part-time. *Faculty:* 57 full-time (33 women), 72 part-time/adjunct (40 women). *Students:* 3 full-time (2 women), 58 part-time (36 women); includes 46 minority (37 Black or African American, non-Hispanic/Latino; 8 Hispanic/Latino; 1 Two or more races, non-Hispanic/Latino). Average age 40. 31 applicants, 45% accepted, 12 enrolled. In 2019, 3 master's awarded. *Application deadline:* For fall admission, 4/1 for domestic students. Applications are processed on a rolling basis. Application fee: $50. Electronic applications accepted. *Expenses: Tuition, area resident:* Full-time $8472; part-time $353 per credit hour. Tuition, state resident: full-time $8472; part-time $353 per credit hour. Tuition, nonresident: full-time $16,944; part-time $706 per credit hour. *International tuition:* $16,944 full-time. *Required fees:* $2520; $105 per credit hour. $38 per term. Tuition and fees vary according to course load, degree level and program. *Financial support:* Application deadline: 5/1; applicants required to submit FAFSA. *Unit head:* Jason Zingsheim, Chair, Division of Arts and Letters, 708-534-5000 Ext. 7493, E-mail: jzingsheim@govst.edu. *Application contact:* Jason Zingsheim, Chair, Division of Arts and Letters, 708-534-5000 Ext. 7493, E-mail: jzingsheim@govst.edu.

Grambling State University, School of Graduate Studies and Research, College of Arts and Sciences, Department of Political Science and Public Administration, Grambling, LA 71270. Offers health services administration (MPA); human resource management (MPA); public management (MPA); state and local government (MPA). *Accreditation:* NASPAA. *Program availability:* Part-time. *Degree requirements:* For master's, comprehensive exam (for some programs), thesis optional. *Entrance requirements:* For master's, GRE, minimum GPA of 2.75 on last degree. Additional exam requirements/recommendations for international students: required—TOEFL (minimum score 500 paper-based; 62 iBT). Electronic applications accepted.

Grand Valley State University, College of Community and Public Service, School of Public, Nonprofit and Health Administration, Allendale, MI 49401-9403. Offers MHA, MPA, MPNL. *Accreditation:* NASPAA. *Program availability:* Part-time, evening/weekend. *Faculty:* 9 full-time (3 women), 6 part-time/adjunct (2 women). *Students:* 29 full-time (20 women), 72 part-time (47 women); includes 11 minority (6 Black or African American, non-Hispanic/Latino; 2 American Indian or Alaska Native, non-Hispanic/Latino; 2 Asian, non-Hispanic/Latino; 1 Hispanic/Latino), 5 international. Average age 29. 68 applicants, 88% accepted, 23 enrolled. In 2019, 40 master's awarded. *Degree requirements:* For master's, thesis optional, capstone course. *Entrance requirements:* For master's, three references from informed sources; essay on career and educational objectives (250 to 750 words); resume. Additional exam requirements/recommendations for international students: required—TOEFL (minimum iBT score of 80), IELTS (6.5), or Michigan English Language Assessment Battery (77). *Application deadline:* For fall admission, 6/1 priority date for domestic students; for winter admission, 11/1 priority date for domestic students; for spring admission, 4/1 priority date for domestic students. Applications are processed on a rolling basis. Application fee: $30. Electronic applications accepted. *Expenses:* $671 per credit hour, 39-42 credit hours. *Financial support:* In 2019–20, 26 students received support, including 16 fellowships, 8 research assistantships with full and partial tuition reimbursements available (averaging $4,000 per year); career-related internships or fieldwork, Federal Work-Study, scholarships/grants, and unspecified assistantships also available. Financial award application deadline: 5/1. *Unit head:* Dr. Richard Jelier, Director, 616-331-6575, Fax: 616-331-7120, E-mail: jelierr@gvsu.edu. *Application contact:* Dr. Davia Downey, Graduate Program Director/Recruiting Contact, 616-331-6681, Fax: 616-331-7120, E-mail: downeyd@gvsu.edu.
Website: http://www.gvsu.edu/spnha/

Hamline University, School of Business, St. Paul, MN 55104-1284. Offers business administration (MBA); nonprofit management (MNM); public administration (MPA, DPA); MBA/MNM; MBA/MPA; MPA/MNM. *Program availability:* Part-time, evening/weekend, blended/hybrid learning. *Degree requirements:* For master's, thesis (for some programs); for doctorate, comprehensive exam, thesis/dissertation. *Entrance requirements:* For master's and doctorate, personal statement, official transcripts, resume or curriculum vitae, letters of recommendation, writing sample. Additional exam requirements/recommendations for international students: required—TOEFL (minimum score 550 paper-based; 80 iBT), IELTS (minimum score 6.5). Electronic applications accepted. *Expenses:* Contact institution.

Harvard University, John F. Kennedy School of Government, Master in Public Administration in International Development Program, Cambridge, MA 02138. Offers MPAID. *Entrance requirements:* For master's, one course each in microeconomics and macroeconomics; two college-level calculus courses (one must contain multivariable calculus); bachelor's degree; 2-3 years of professional experience in development (strongly encouraged). Additional exam requirements/recommendations for international students: required—TOEFL (minimum score 600 paper-based; 100 iBT). Electronic applications accepted.

Harvard University, John F. Kennedy School of Government, Mid-Career Program in Public Administration, Cambridge, MA 02138. Offers MPA. *Entrance requirements:* For master's, GMAT or GRE General Test, minimum 7 years of professional experience. Additional exam requirements/recommendations for international students: required—TOEFL (minimum score 600 paper-based; 100 iBT), TWE. Electronic applications accepted. *Expenses:* Contact institution.

Harvard University, John F. Kennedy School of Government, Program in Public Administration, Cambridge, MA 02138. Offers MPA. *Entrance requirements:* For master's, GMAT or GRE General Test, minimum of 3 years of work experience. Additional exam requirements/recommendations for international students: required—TOEFL (minimum score 600 paper-based; 100 iBT), TWE. Electronic applications accepted.

Hawaii Pacific University, College of Professional Studies, Program in Public Administration, Honolulu, HI 96813. Offers MPA. *Program availability:* Part-time, evening/weekend, 100% online, blended/hybrid learning. *Entrance requirements:* For master's, official transcript reflecting conferred bachelor's degree, resume, statement of purpose/essay. Additional exam requirements/recommendations for international students: recommended—TOEFL (minimum score 550 paper-based; 80 iBT), IELTS (minimum score 6), TWE (minimum score 5). Electronic applications accepted. *Expenses: Tuition:* Full-time $18,000; part-time $1125 per credit. *Required fees:* $213; $38 per semester.

Hilbert College, Program in Public Administration, Hamburg, NY 14075-1597. Offers health administration (MPA); public administration (MPA). *Program availability:* Evening/weekend. *Degree requirements:* For master's, final capstone project. *Entrance requirements:* For master's, essay, official transcripts from all prior colleges, two letters of recommendation, current resume, relevant work experience, baccalaureate degree from accredited college or university with minimum cumulative GPA of 3.0, personal interview. Additional exam requirements/recommendations for international students: recommended—TOEFL. Electronic applications accepted. Application fee is waived when completed online. *Expenses:* Contact institution.

Howard University, Graduate School, Department of Political Science, Program in Public Administration, Washington, DC 20059-0002. Offers MAPA. *Program availability:*

Part-time. *Degree requirements:* For master's, comprehensive exam. *Entrance requirements:* For master's, GRE General Test, minimum GPA of 3.0.

Idaho State University, Graduate School, College of Arts and Letters, Department of Political Science, Program in Public Administration, Pocatello, ID 83209-8073. Offers MPA. *Program availability:* Part-time. *Degree requirements:* For master's, comprehensive exam, thesis optional, public service internship. *Entrance requirements:* For master's, GRE General Test, course work in humanities and social sciences, 3 letters of recommendation. Additional exam requirements/recommendations for international students: required—TOEFL (minimum score 550 paper-based; 80 iBT). Electronic applications accepted.

IGlobal University, Graduate Programs, Vienna, VA 22182. Offers accounting (MBA); data management and analytics (MSIT); entrepreneurship (MBA); finance (MBA); global business management (MBA); health care management (MBA); hospitality and tourism management (MBA); human resources management (MBA); information technology (MBA); information technology systems and management (MSIT); leadership and management (MBA); project management (MBA); public service and administration (MBA); software design and management (MSIT).

Illinois Institute of Technology, Stuart School of Business, Program in Public Administration, Chicago, IL 60661. Offers MPA, JD/MPA, MBA/MPA. *Program availability:* Part-time, evening/weekend. *Entrance requirements:* For master's, minimum cumulative undergraduate GPA of 3.0. Additional exam requirements/recommendations for international students: required—TOEFL (minimum score 575 paper-based; 90 iBT); recommended—IELTS (minimum score 7). Electronic applications accepted.

Indiana State University, College of Graduate and Professional Studies, College of Arts and Sciences, Department of Political Science, Terre Haute, IN 47809. Offers public administration (MPA). *Degree requirements:* For master's, thesis (for some programs), capstone project. *Entrance requirements:* For master's, GRE or minimum undergraduate GPA of 2.75, 18 semester hours of course work in political science. Additional exam requirements/recommendations for international students: required—TOEFL (minimum score 550 paper-based). Electronic applications accepted.

Indiana University Bloomington, School of Public and Environmental Affairs, Public Affairs Programs, Bloomington, IN 47405. Offers economic development (MPA); energy (MPA); environmental policy (PhD); environmental policy and natural resource management (MPA); information systems (MPA); international development (MPA); local government management (MPA); nonprofit management (MPA, Certificate); policy analysis (MPA); public budgeting and financial management (Certificate); public finance (PhD); public financial administration (MPA); public management (MPA, PhD, Certificate); public policy analysis (PhD); social entrepreneurship (Certificate); specialized public affairs (MPA); sustainability and sustainable development (MPA); JD/MPA; MPA/MA; MPA/MIS; MPA/MLS; MSES/MPA. *Accreditation:* NASPAA (one or more programs are accredited). *Program availability:* Part-time. *Degree requirements:* For master's, capstone, internship; for doctorate, comprehensive exam, thesis/dissertation. *Entrance requirements:* For master's, GRE General Test or GMAT, official transcripts, 3 letters of recommendation, resume, personal statement; for doctorate, GRE General Test, official transcripts, 3 letters of recommendation, statement of purpose. Additional exam requirements/recommendations for international students: required—TOEFL (minimum score 600 paper-based; 96 iBT); recommended—IELTS (minimum score 7). Electronic applications accepted.

Indiana University Kokomo, Department of Public Administration and Health Management, Kokomo, IN 46904. Offers health management (MPM, Graduate Certificate); public management (Graduate Certificate); public management and policy (MPM). *Program availability:* Part-time, evening/weekend. *Entrance requirements:* For master's, GRE/GMAT for GPAs lower than 3.0, letters of recommendation. Additional exam requirements/recommendations for international students: required—TOEFL (minimum score 550 paper-based; 73 iBT). Electronic applications accepted. *Expenses:* Contact institution.

Indiana University Northwest, School of Public and Environmental Affairs, Gary, IN 46408. Offers criminal justice (MPA); environmental affairs (Graduate Certificate); health services (MPA); nonprofit management (Certificate); public management (MPA, Graduate Certificate). *Accreditation:* NASPAA (one or more programs are accredited). *Program availability:* Part-time. *Entrance requirements:* For master's, GRE General Test (minimum combined verbal and quantitative score of 280), GMAT, or LSAT, letters of recommendation. Electronic applications accepted.

Indiana University-Purdue University Indianapolis, School of Public and Environmental Affairs, Indianapolis, IN 46202. Offers criminal justice and public safety (MS); homeland security and emergency management (Graduate Certificate); library management (Graduate Certificate); nonprofit management (Graduate Certificate); public affairs (MPA); public management (Graduate Certificate); social entrepreneurship: nonprofit and public benefit organizations (Graduate Certificate); JD/MPA; MLS/NMC; MLS/PMC; MPA/MA. *Accreditation:* CAHME (one or more programs are accredited); NASPAA. *Program availability:* Part-time, evening/weekend, online learning. *Entrance requirements:* For master's, GRE General Test, GMAT or LSAT, minimum GPA of 3.0 (preferred). Additional exam requirements/recommendations for international students: required—TOEFL (minimum score 93 iBT), IELTS (minimum score 6.5). Electronic applications accepted.

Indiana University South Bend, College of Liberal Arts and Sciences, South Bend, IN 46615. Offers advanced computer programming (Graduate Certificate); applied informatics (Graduate Certificate); applied mathematics and computer science (MS); behavior modification (Graduate Certificate); computer applications (Graduate Certificate); computer programming (Graduate Certificate); correctional management and supervision (Graduate Certificate); English (MA); health systems management (Graduate Certificate); international studies (Graduate Certificate); liberal studies (MLS); nonprofit management (Graduate Certificate); paralegal studies (Graduate Certificate); professional writing (Graduate Certificate); public affairs (MPA); public management (Graduate Certificate); social and cultural diversity (Graduate Certificate); strategic sustainability leadership (Graduate Certificate); technology for administration (Graduate Certificate). *Program availability:* Part-time, evening/weekend. *Degree requirements:* For master's, variable foreign language requirement, thesis (for some programs). *Entrance requirements:* For master's, minimum GPA of 3.0. Additional exam requirements/recommendations for international students: required—TOEFL (minimum score 550 paper-based; 80 iBT). *Expenses:* Contact institution.

Institute of Public Administration, Programs in Public Administration, Dublin, Ireland. Offers healthcare management (MA); local government management (MA); public management (MA, Diploma).

Instituto Tecnológico y de Estudios Superiores de Monterrey, Campus Ciudad Juárez, Program in Applied Public Management, Ciudad Juárez, Mexico. Offers MPM.

International University in Geneva, Leadership Programs, Geneva, Switzerland. Offers international relations and diplomacy (MIRD); media and communication (MA); public administration (DPA). *Degree requirements:* For master's, comprehensive exam. *Entrance requirements:* Additional exam requirements/recommendations for international students: required—TOEFL. Electronic applications accepted.

Iowa State University of Science and Technology, Department of Political Science, Ames, IA 50011. Offers political science (MA); public administration (MPA); JD/MA. *Degree requirements:* For master's, thesis (for some programs). *Entrance requirements:* For master's, GRE General Test, GMAT or LSAT. Additional exam requirements/recommendations for international students: required—TOEFL (minimum score 570 paper-based; 80 iBT), IELTS (minimum score 6.5). Electronic applications accepted.

Jackson State University, Graduate School, College of Public Service, Department of Public Policy and Administration, Jackson, MS 39217. Offers public administration (PhD); public policy and administration (MPPA). *Accreditation:* NASPAA (one or more programs are accredited). *Program availability:* Evening/weekend. *Degree requirements:* For master's, comprehensive exam, thesis optional; for doctorate, comprehensive exam, thesis/dissertation. *Entrance requirements:* For master's, GRE General Test; for doctorate, GRE, GMAT, MAT. Additional exam requirements/recommendations for international students: required—TOEFL (minimum score 520 paper-based; 67 iBT).

Jacksonville State University, Graduate Studies, School of Human Services and Social Sciences, Department of Political Science and Public Administration, Jacksonville, AL 36265-1602. Offers public administration (MPA). *Program availability:* Part-time, evening/weekend. *Degree requirements:* For master's, comprehensive exam, thesis (for some programs). *Entrance requirements:* For master's, GRE General Test or MAT. Additional exam requirements/recommendations for international students: required—TOEFL (minimum score 61 iBT). Electronic applications accepted.

James Madison University, The Graduate School, College of Arts and Letters, Program in Public Administration, Harrisonburg, VA 22807. Offers individualized (MPA); public management (MPA), including international stabilization and recovery, management in international non-governmental organizations, nonprofit management, public management. *Accreditation:* NASPAA. *Program availability:* Part-time. *Students:* 21 full-time (11 women), 15 part-time (8 women); includes 7 minority (4 Black or African American, non-Hispanic/Latino; 3 Two or more races, non-Hispanic/Latino). Average age 30. In 2019, 12 master's awarded. Application fee: $60. Electronic applications accepted. *Financial support:* In 2019–20, 16 students received support. Fellowships, Federal Work-Study, and assistantships (averaging $7911) available. Financial award application deadline: 3/1; financial award applicants required to submit FAFSA. *Unit head:* Dr. Charles Blake, Department Head, 540-568-6149, E-mail: blakech@jmu.edu. *Application contact:* Lynette D. Michael, Director of Graduate Admissions, 540-568-6131, Fax: 540-568-7860, E-mail: michaeld@jmu.edu.
Website: http://www.jmu.edu/mpa

John Jay College of Criminal Justice of the City University of New York, Graduate Studies, Program in Public Administration, New York, NY 10019. Offers MPA. *Accreditation:* NASPAA. *Program availability:* Part-time, evening/weekend. *Degree requirements:* For master's, thesis or alternative. *Entrance requirements:* For master's, minimum B average. Additional exam requirements/recommendations for international students: required—TOEFL (minimum score 500 paper-based).

Johns Hopkins University, Advanced Academic Programs, Program in Government, Washington, DC 21218. Offers global security studies (MA); government (MA); national securities study (Certificate); nonprofit management (Certificate); public management (MA); research administration (MS); MA/MBA. *Program availability:* Part-time, evening/weekend, online learning. *Entrance requirements:* For master's, minimum GPA of 3.0. Additional exam requirements/recommendations for international students: required—TOEFL (minimum score 100 iBT). Electronic applications accepted.

Kansas State University, Graduate School, College of Arts and Sciences, Department of Political Science, Manhattan, KS 66506. Offers political science (MA); public administration (MPA). *Accreditation:* NASPAA. *Program availability:* Part-time. *Degree requirements:* For master's, comprehensive exam, thesis or alternative. *Entrance requirements:* For master's, GRE (recommended), minimum GPA of 3.0. Additional exam requirements/recommendations for international students: required—TOEFL (minimum score 550 paper-based; 79 iBT); recommended—IELTS (minimum score 6.5), TSE (minimum score 58). Electronic applications accepted.

Kean University, College of Business and Public Management, Program in Public Administration, Union, NJ 07083. Offers health services administration (MPA); non-profit management (MPA); public administration (MPA). *Accreditation:* NASPAA. *Program availability:* Part-time. *Faculty:* 15 full-time (5 women). *Students:* 44 full-time (32 women), 56 part-time (33 women); includes 77 minority (45 Black or African American, non-Hispanic/Latino; 6 Asian, non-Hispanic/Latino; 25 Hispanic/Latino; 1 Two or more races, non-Hispanic/Latino), 2 international. Average age 31. 45 applicants, 93% accepted, 28 enrolled. In 2019, 31 master's awarded. *Degree requirements:* For master's, thesis, internship, research seminar. *Entrance requirements:* For master's, minimum cumulative GPA of 3.0, official transcripts from all institutions attended, two letters of recommendation, personal statement, writing sample, professional resume/curriculum vitae. Additional exam requirements/recommendations for international students: required—TOEFL (minimum score 550 paper-based; 79 iBT), IELTS (minimum score 6.5). *Application deadline:* For fall admission, 6/30 for domestic and international students; for spring admission, 12/1 for domestic and international students. Applications are processed on a rolling basis. Application fee: $75. Electronic applications accepted. *Expenses:* Tuition, state resident: full-time $15,326; part-time $748 per credit. Tuition, nonresident: full-time $20,288; part-time $902 per credit. *Required fees:* $2149.50; $91.25 per credit. Tuition and fees vary according to course level, course load, degree level and program. *Financial support:* Scholarships/grants and unspecified assistantships available. Financial award applicants required to submit FAFSA. *Unit head:* Dr. Deborah Mohammed-Spigner, Program Coordinator, 908-737-4037, E-mail: demohamm@kean.edu. *Application contact:* Pedro Lopes, Admissions Counselor, 908-737-7100, E-mail: gradadmissions@kean.edu.
Website: http://grad.kean.edu/masters-programs/public-administration

Kennesaw State University, College of Humanities and Social Sciences, Program in Public Administration, Kennesaw, GA 30144. Offers MPA. *Accreditation:* NASPAA. *Program availability:* Part-time, evening/weekend. *Students:* 26 full-time (19 women), 57 part-time (39 women); includes 50 minority (31 Black or African American, non-Hispanic/Latino; 5 Asian, non-Hispanic/Latino; 9 Hispanic/Latino; 5 Two or more races, non-Hispanic/Latino). Average age 29. 32 applicants, 84% accepted, 21 enrolled. In 2019, 25 master's awarded. *Degree requirements:* For master's, thesis optional. *Entrance requirements:* For master's, minimum GPA of 2.75. Additional exam requirements/recommendations for international students: required—TOEFL (minimum score 80 iBT), IELTS (minimum score 6.5). *Application deadline:* For fall admission, 7/1 for domestic and international students; for spring admission, 11/1 for domestic and international students; for summer admission, 4/1 for domestic and international students. Applications are processed on a rolling basis. Application fee: $60. Electronic applications accepted. *Expenses: Tuition, area resident:* Full-time $7104; part-time $296 per credit hour. Tuition, state resident: full-time $7104; part-time $296 per credit hour. Tuition, nonresident: full-time $25,584; part-time $1066 per credit hour. *International tuition:* $25,584 full-time. *Required fees:* $2006; $1706 per unit. $853 per semester. *Financial support:* Applicants required to submit FAFSA. *Unit head:* Dr. Jerry Herbel, Program Director, 470-578-7869. *Application contact:* Maureen Wilson, Coordinator,

470-578-7869, Fax: 470-578-9172, E-mail: mwils152@kennesaw.edu.
Website: http://chss.kennesaw.edu/mpa/

Kent State University, College of Arts and Sciences, Department of Political Science, Kent, OH 44242-0001. Offers political science (MA, PhD), including American politics and policy, conflict analysis and management, transnational and comparative politics and policy; public administration (MPA). *Accreditation:* NASPAA. *Program availability:* Part-time, 100% online. *Faculty:* 15 full-time (5 women), 2 part-time/adjunct (1 woman). *Students:* 39 full-time (19 women), 66 part-time (44 women); includes 14 minority (9 Black or African American, non-Hispanic/Latino; 2 Asian, non-Hispanic/Latino; 3 Two or more races, non-Hispanic/Latino), 12 international. Average age 36. 40 applicants, 90% accepted, 25 enrolled. In 2019, 26 master's, 2 doctorates awarded. *Degree requirements:* For master's, thesis, Capstone for non-thesis option; for doctorate, comprehensive exam, thesis/dissertation. *Entrance requirements:* For master's, GRE -combined verbal and quantitative GRE score above 300, goal statement, transcripts, writing sample, 3 letters of recommendation, minimum GPA of 3.0, resume; for doctorate, GRE -combined verbal and quantitative GRE score above 300, goal statement, transcripts, writing sample, 3 letters of recommendation, minimum GPA of 3.0, resume. Additional exam requirements/recommendations for international students: required—TOEFL (minimum score 79 iBT), IELTS (minimum score 6.5), Michigan English Language Assessment Battery (minimum score 77). *Application deadline:* For fall admission, 1/31 for domestic and international students. Applications are processed on a rolling basis. Application fee: $45 ($70 for international students). Electronic applications accepted. *Financial support:* Research assistantships with full tuition reimbursements, teaching assistantships with full tuition reimbursements, and unspecified assistantships available. Financial award application deadline: 1/31. *Unit head:* Dr. Anthony Molina, Chairperson and Assistant Professor, 330-672-2060, E-mail: amolina4@kent.edu. *Application contact:* Julie Mazzei, Associate Professor and Graduate Coordinator, 330-672-8934, E-mail: jmazzei@kent.edu.
Website: http://www.kent.edu/polisci

Kutztown University of Pennsylvania, College of Liberal Arts and Sciences, Program in Public Administration, Kutztown, PA 19530-0730. Offers MPA. *Program availability:* Part-time, evening/weekend. *Faculty:* 4 full-time (2 women). *Students:* 12 full-time (7 women), 13 part-time (9 women); includes 5 minority (3 Black or African American, non-Hispanic/Latino; 2 Hispanic/Latino). Average age 30. 17 applicants, 88% accepted, 8 enrolled. In 2019, 13 master's awarded. *Degree requirements:* For master's, comprehensive exam, thesis optional. *Entrance requirements:* For master's, GRE, GMAT, MAT, or LSAT, 3 letters of recommendation. Additional exam requirements/recommendations for international students: required—TOEFL (minimum score 550 paper-based, 79 iBT), IELTS (minimum score 6.5), or PTE (minimum score 53). *Application deadline:* For fall admission, 8/1 for domestic and international students; for spring admission, 12/1 for domestic and international students. Application fee: $35. Electronic applications accepted. *Expenses: Tuition, area resident:* Full-time $9288; part-time $515 per credit. Tuition, state resident: full-time $9288. Tuition, nonresident: full-time $13,932; part-time $774 per credit. *Required fees:* $1688; $94 per credit. *Financial support:* Career-related internships or fieldwork, Federal Work-Study, and unspecified assistantships available. Financial award application deadline: 3/1; financial award applicants required to submit FAFSA. *Unit head:* Dr. Robert A. Portada, Department Chair, 610-683-4469, Fax: 610-683-4603, E-mail: portada@kutztown.edu. *Application contact:* Stacy Kushner, Academic Department Secretary, 610-683-4449, E-mail: kushner@kutztown.edu.
Website: https://www.kutztown.edu/academics/graduate-programs/public-administration.htm

Liberty University, Helms School of Government, Lynchburg, VA 24515. Offers criminal justice (MS), including forensic psychology, homeland security, public administration (MA, MS); international relations (MS); political science (MS); public administration (MPA), including business and government, healthcare, law and public policy, public and non-profit management; public policy (MA), including campaigns and elections, international affairs, Middle East affairs, public administration (MA, MS). *Program availability:* Part-time, online learning. *Students:* 1,143 full-time (565 women), 572 part-time (408 women); includes 795 minority (499 Black or African American, non-Hispanic/Latino; 16 American Indian or Alaska Native, non-Hispanic/Latino; 23 Asian, non-Hispanic/Latino; 162 Hispanic/Latino; 7 Native Hawaiian or other Pacific Islander, non-Hispanic/Latino; 88 Two or more races, non-Hispanic/Latino), 27 international. Average age 35. 3,017 applicants, 44% accepted, 728 enrolled. In 2019, 415 master's awarded. *Entrance requirements:* For master's, minimum undergraduate GPA of 3.0. Additional exam requirements/recommendations for international students: required—TOEFL (minimum score 600 paper-based; 100 iBT). *Application deadline:* Applications are processed on a rolling basis. Application fee: $50. Electronic applications accepted. *Expenses: Tuition:* Full-time $545; part-time $410 per credit hour. One-time fee: $50. *Financial support:* In 2019–20, 808 students received support. Teaching assistantships and Federal Work-Study available. *Unit head:* Ron Miller, Dean, 434-592-4986, E-mail: govtdean@liberty.edu. *Application contact:* Jay Bridge, Director of Admissions, 800-424-9595, Fax: 800-628-7977, E-mail: gradadmissions@liberty.edu.
Website: https://www.liberty.edu/government/

Lipscomb University, School of Public Policy, Nashville, TN 37204-3951. Offers leadership and public service (MA). *Entrance requirements:* For master's, GRE or GMAT, references, resume, goals statement. Additional exam requirements/recommendations for international students: required—TOEFL (minimum score 550 paper-based). Electronic applications accepted. *Expenses:* Contact institution.

London Metropolitan University, Graduate Programs, London, United Kingdom. Offers applied psychology (M Sc); architecture (MA); biomedical science (M Sc); blood science (M Sc); cancer pharmacology (M Sc); computer networking and cyber security (M Sc); computing and information systems (M Sc); conference interpreting (MA); counter-terrorism studies (M Sc); creative, digital and professional writing (MA); crime, violence and prevention (M Sc); criminology (M Sc); curating contemporary art (MA); data analytics (M Sc); digital media (MA); early childhood studies (MA); education (MA, Ed D); financial services law, regulation and compliance (LL M); food science (M Sc); forensic psychology (M Sc); health and social care management and policy (M Sc); human nutrition (M Sc); human resource management (MA); human rights and international conflict (MA); information technology (M Sc); intelligence and security studies (M Sc); international oil, gas and energy law (LL M); international relations (MA); interpreting (MA); learning and teaching in higher education (MA); legal practice (LL M); media and entertainment law (LL M); organizational and consumer psychology (M Sc); psychological therapy (M Sc); psychology of mental health (M Sc); public health (M Sc); public policy and management (MPA); security studies (M Sc); social work (M Sc); spatial planning and urban design (MA); sports therapy (M Sc); supporting older children and young people with dyslexia (MA); teaching languages (MA), including Arabic, English; translation (MA); woman and child abuse (MA).

Long Island University - Brooklyn, School of Business, Public Administration and Information Sciences, Brooklyn, NY 11201-8423. Offers accounting (MBA); accounting (MS); business administration (MBA); computer science (MS); gerontology (Advanced Certificate); health administration (MPA); human resources management (MS); not-for-profit management (Advanced Certificate); public administration (MPA); taxation (MS). *Program availability:* Part-time, evening/weekend. *Entrance requirements:* Additional exam requirements/recommendations for international students: required—TOEFL (minimum score 550 paper-based; 75 iBT). Electronic applications accepted.

Long Island University - Hudson, Graduate School, Purchase, NY 10577. Offers autism (Advanced Certificate); bilingual education (Advanced Certificate); childhood education (MS Ed); crisis management (Advanced Certificate); early childhood education (MS Ed); educational leadership (MS Ed); health administration (MPA); literacy (MS Ed); marriage and family therapy (MS); mental health counseling (MS, Advanced Certificate), including credentialed alcoholism and substance abuse counselor (MS); middle childhood and adolescence education (MS Ed); pharmaceutics (MS), including cosmetic science, industrial pharmacy; public administration (MPA); school counseling (MS Ed, Advanced Certificate); school psychology (MS Ed); special education (MS Ed); TESOL (MS Ed); TESOL (all grades) (Advanced Certificate). *Program availability:* Part-time, evening/weekend. *Entrance requirements:* Additional exam requirements/recommendations for international students: required—TOEFL. Electronic applications accepted. *Expenses:* Contact institution.

Long Island University - Post, School of Health Professions and Nursing, Brookville, NY 11548-1300. Offers biomedical science (MS); cardiovascular perfusion (MS); clinical lab sciences (MS); clinical laboratory management (MS); dietetic internship (Advanced Certificate); family nurse practitioner (MS, Advanced Certificate); forensic social work (Advanced Certificate); gerontology (Advanced Certificate); health administration (MPA); non-profit management (Advanced Certificate); nursing education (MS); nutrition (MS); public administration (MPA); social work (MSW). *Program availability:* Part-time, blended/hybrid learning. *Degree requirements:* For master's, comprehensive exam (for some programs), thesis (for some programs). *Entrance requirements:* Additional exam requirements/recommendations for international students: required—TOEFL (minimum score 85 iBT) or IELTS (7.5). Electronic applications accepted.

Louisiana State University and Agricultural & Mechanical College, Graduate School, E. J. Ourso College of Business, Public Administration Institute, Baton Rouge, LA 70803. Offers MPA, JD/MPA. *Accreditation:* NASPAA.

Louisiana State University and Agricultural & Mechanical College, Graduate School, Manship School of Mass Communication, Baton Rouge, LA 70803. Offers MMC, PhD, JD/MMC. *Accreditation:* ACEJMC.

Marist College, Graduate Programs, School of Management, Program in Public Administration, Poughkeepsie, NY 12601-1387. Offers MPA. *Accreditation:* NASPAA. *Program availability:* Part-time, evening/weekend, online learning. *Entrance requirements:* For master's, GRE General Test, resume. Additional exam requirements/recommendations for international students: required—TOEFL (minimum score 550 paper-based; 80 iBT); recommended—IELTS (minimum score 6.5). Electronic applications accepted.

Marshall University, Academic Affairs Division, College of Liberal Arts, Department of Political Science, Huntington, WV 25755. Offers MA, MPA. *Degree requirements:* For master's, thesis optional. *Entrance requirements:* For master's, GRE General Test.

Marywood University, Academic Affairs, College of Health and Human Services, School of Social Work, Program in Public Administration, Scranton, PA 18509-1598. Offers MPA. *Program availability:* Part-time. Electronic applications accepted.

McMaster University, School of Graduate Studies, Faculty of Social Sciences, Department of Political Science, Hamilton, ON L8S 4M2, Canada. Offers international relations (PhD); political science (MA); public and the global economy (MA); public policy (PhD); public policy and administration (MA). *Program availability:* Part-time. *Degree requirements:* For master's, thesis or alternative. *Entrance requirements:* For master's, minimum B+ average. Additional exam requirements/recommendations for international students: required—TOEFL (minimum score 580 paper-based).

Metropolitan College of New York, Program in Public Administration, New York, NY 10006. Offers emergency and disaster management (MPA); public affairs and administration (MPA). *Program availability:* Evening/weekend. *Degree requirements:* For master's, thesis. *Entrance requirements:* For master's, appropriate work experience, interview, minimum GPA of 2.7, internship or job in administrative setting. Additional exam requirements/recommendations for international students: required—TOEFL (minimum score 600 paper-based). Electronic applications accepted. *Expenses:* Contact institution.

Metropolitan State University, College of Community Studies and Public Affairs, St. Paul, MN 55106-5000. Offers alcohol and drug counseling (MS); co-occurring disorders recovery counseling (MS); public administration (MPA); public and nonprofit administration (MPNA).

Mid-America Christian University, Program in Public Administration, Oklahoma City, OK 73170-4504. Offers MA. *Entrance requirements:* For master's, bachelor's degree from a regionally accredited college or university, minimum overall cumulative GPA of 2.75 of bachelor course work. Additional exam requirements/recommendations for international students: required—TOEFL (minimum score 550 paper-based).

Middlebury Institute of International Studies at Monterey, Graduate School of International Policy and Management, Program in Public Administration, Monterey, CA 93940-2691. Offers MPA. *Degree requirements:* For master's, one foreign language. *Entrance requirements:* For master's, minimum GPA of 3.0, proficiency in a foreign language. Additional exam requirements/recommendations for international students: required—TOEFL (minimum score 550 paper-based; 80 iBT). Electronic applications accepted.

Midwest University, Graduate Programs, Wentzville, MO 63385. Offers asset management/investment/real estate (MBA); Christian counseling (D Min); Christian education (D Min); counseling (MA), including marriage and family counseling, school counseling; divinity (M Div); education (MA), including brain and gifted education, Christian education; global business management (MBA); global leadership (MBA); leadership (PhD), including brain and gifted educational leadership, entrepreneurial leadership, international aviation leadership, organizational leadership, political leadership; mission studies (D Min); music (MM, DMA); pastoral theology (D Min); public policy/administration (MBA); teaching English to speakers of other languages (MA). *Program availability:* Part-time, online learning. *Degree requirements:* For master's, thesis (for some programs); for doctorate, thesis/dissertation. *Entrance requirements:* Additional exam requirements/recommendations for international students: recommended—TOEFL (minimum score 550 paper-based).

Minnesota State University Mankato, College of Graduate Studies and Research, College of Social and Behavioral Sciences, Department of Government, Program in Public Administration, Mankato, MN 56001. Offers MPA. *Accreditation:* NASPAA. *Degree requirements:* For master's, one foreign language, comprehensive exam, thesis or alternative. *Entrance requirements:* For master's, minimum GPA of 3.0 during previous 2 years. Additional exam requirements/recommendations for international students: required—TOEFL. Electronic applications accepted.

Mississippi State University, College of Arts and Sciences, Department of Political Science and Public Administration, Mississippi State, MS 39762. Offers political science (MA); public policy and administration (MPPA, PhD). *Accreditation:* NASPAA (one or

more programs are accredited). *Program availability:* Evening/weekend, blended/hybrid learning. *Faculty:* 15 full-time (6 women). *Students:* 24 full-time (13 women), 39 part-time (19 women); includes 18 minority (15 Black or African American, non-Hispanic/Latino; 1 American Indian or Alaska Native, non-Hispanic/Latino; 1 Asian, non-Hispanic/Latino; 1 Hispanic/Latino), 5 international. Average age 32. 29 applicants, 90% accepted, 19 enrolled. In 2019, 11 master's, 1 doctorate awarded. *Degree requirements:* For master's, thesis optional, comprehensive oral or written exam; for doctorate, thesis/dissertation, comprehensive oral and written exam. *Entrance requirements:* For master's, GRE, minimum GPA of 3.0 on the last two years of undergraduate courses or graduate work; for doctorate, GRE General Test, minimum graduate GPA of 3.35. Additional exam requirements/recommendations for international students: required—TOEFL (minimum score 600 paper-based; 100 iBT); recommended—IELTS (minimum score 7.5). *Application deadline:* For fall admission, 8/1 priority date for domestic students, 5/1 for international students; for spring admission, 12/1 priority date for domestic students, 9/1 for international students. Applications are processed on a rolling basis. Application fee: $60 ($80 for international students). Electronic applications accepted. *Expenses: Tuition, area resident:* Full-time $8880; part-time $456 per credit hour. Tuition, state resident: full-time $8880. Tuition, nonresident: full-time $23,840; part-time $1236 per credit hour. *Required fees:* $110; $11.12 per credit hour. Tuition and fees vary according to course load. *Financial support:* In 2019–20, 9 teaching assistantships with full tuition reimbursements (averaging $11,083 per year) were awarded; Federal Work-Study, institutionally sponsored loans, scholarships/grants, and unspecified assistantships also available. Financial award application deadline: 4/1; financial award applicants required to submit FAFSA. *Unit head:* Dr. P. Edward French, Professor and Head, 662-325-2711, Fax: 662-325-2716, E-mail: efrench@pspa.msstate.edu. *Application contact:* Nathan Drake, Manager, Graduate Programs, 662-325-7394, E-mail: ndrake@grad.msstate.edu.
Website: http://www.pspa.msstate.edu/

Missouri State University, Graduate College, College of Humanities and Public Affairs, Department of Political Science, Program in Public Administration, Springfield, MO 65897. Offers MPA. *Accreditation:* NASPAA. *Program availability:* Part-time. *Degree requirements:* For master's, comprehensive exam, thesis or alternative, internship. *Entrance requirements:* For master's, GRE, minimum GPA of 3.0. Additional exam requirements/recommendations for international students: required—TOEFL (minimum score 550 paper-based; 79 iBT), IELTS (minimum score 6). Electronic applications accepted. *Expenses: Tuition, area resident:* Full-time $2600; part-time $1735 per credit hour. Tuition, nonresident: full-time $5240; part-time $3495 per credit hour. *International tuition:* $5240 full-time. *Required fees:* $530; $438 per credit hour. Tuition and fees vary according to class time, course level, course load, degree level, campus/location and program.

Missouri State University, Graduate College, Interdisciplinary Program in Professional Studies, Springfield, MO 65897. Offers administrative studies (Certificate); applied communication (MS); criminal justice (MS); environmental management (MS); homeland security (MS); individualized (MS); professional studies (MS); screenwriting and producing (MS); sports management (MS). *Program availability:* Part-time, evening/weekend, 100% online, blended/hybrid learning. *Degree requirements:* For master's, comprehensive exam, thesis or alternative. *Entrance requirements:* For master's, GRE, GMAT (if GPA less than 3.0). Additional exam requirements/recommendations for international students: required—TOEFL (minimum score 550 paper-based; 79 iBT), IELTS (minimum score 6). Electronic applications accepted. *Expenses: Tuition, area resident:* Full-time $2600; part-time $1735 per credit hour. Tuition, nonresident: full-time $5240; part-time $3495 per credit hour. *International tuition:* $5240 full-time. *Required fees:* $530; $438 per credit hour. Tuition and fees vary according to class time, course level, course load, degree level, campus/location and program.

Montana State University, The Graduate School, College of Letters and Science, Department of Political Science, Bozeman, MT 59717. Offers public administration (MPA). *Program availability:* Part-time. *Degree requirements:* For master's, comprehensive exam, thesis (for some programs). *Entrance requirements:* For master's, GRE General Test. Additional exam requirements/recommendations for international students: required—TOEFL (minimum score 550 paper-based). Electronic applications accepted.

National University, School of Professional Studies, La Jolla, CA 92037-1011. Offers criminal justice (MCJ); digital cinema production (MFA); digital journalism (MA); homeland security and emergency management (MS); juvenile justice (MS); professional screenwriting (MFA); public administration (MPA), including human resource management, organizational leadership. *Program availability:* Part-time, evening/weekend, 100% online, blended/hybrid learning. *Degree requirements:* For master's, thesis (for some programs). *Entrance requirements:* For master's, interview, minimum GPA of 2.5. Additional exam requirements/recommendations for international students: required—TOEFL (minimum score 550 paper-based; 79 iBT), IELTS (minimum score 6). Electronic applications accepted. *Expenses: Tuition:* Full-time $442; part-time $442 per unit.

New Mexico State University, College of Arts and Sciences, Department of Government, Las Cruces, NM 88003-8001. Offers government (MA); public administration (MPA). *Accreditation:* NASPAA (one or more programs are accredited). *Program availability:* Part-time. *Faculty:* 8 full-time (3 women), 1 (woman) part-time/adjunct. *Students:* 13 full-time (5 women), 18 part-time (6 women); includes 20 minority (3 Black or African American, non-Hispanic/Latino; 17 Hispanic/Latino), 1 international. Average age 33. 12 applicants, 83% accepted, 7 enrolled. In 2019, 14 master's awarded. *Degree requirements:* For master's, comprehensive exam (for some programs), thesis optional. *Entrance requirements:* For master's, GRE (if GPA less than 3.0), writing sample, 3 letters of recommendation, resume. Additional exam requirements/recommendations for international students: required—TOEFL (minimum score 550 paper-based; 79 iBT), IELTS (minimum score 6.5). *Application deadline:* For fall admission, 10/1 for domestic and international students; for spring admission, 3/1 for domestic and international students; for summer admission, 3/1 for domestic and international students. Application fee: $40 ($50 for international students). Electronic applications accepted. *Financial support:* In 2019–20, 13 students received support, including 9 teaching assistantships (averaging $14,126 per year); career-related internships or fieldwork, Federal Work-Study, scholarships/grants, traineeships, health care benefits, and unspecified assistantships also available. Support available to part-time students. Financial award application deadline: 3/1. *Unit head:* Dr. Neil Harvey, Head, 575-646-4935, Fax: 575-646-2052, E-mail: nharvey@nmsu.edu. *Application contact:* Dr. Neil Harvey, Director, Master of Arts in Government Program, 575-646-4935, Fax: 575-646-2052, E-mail: nharvey@nmsu.edu.
Website: http://deptofgov.nmsu.edu

New York University, Wagner Graduate School of Public Service, Executive Master of Public Administration Program, New York, NY 10012. Offers global public policy and management (EMPA); MSW/EMPA. *Accreditation:* AACSB. *Program availability:* Part-time. *Entrance requirements:* Additional exam requirements/recommendations for international students: required—TOEFL (minimum score 100 iBT), IELTS (minimum score 7.5), TWE. Electronic applications accepted. *Expenses:* Contact institution.

New York University, Wagner Graduate School of Public Service, Program in Public Administration, New York, NY 10012. Offers public administration (PhD); public and nonprofit management and policy (MPA, Advanced Certificate), including financial management and public finance (MPA), international policy and management (MPA), management for public and nonprofit organizations, public policy analysis, social impact, innovation, and investment (MPA); JD/MPA; MBA/MPA; MPA/MA. *Accreditation:* NASPAA (one or more programs are accredited). *Program availability:* Part-time. *Degree requirements:* For master's, thesis or alternative, capstone end event; for doctorate, one foreign language, comprehensive exam, thesis/dissertation, preliminary qualifying examination. *Entrance requirements:* Additional exam requirements/recommendations for international students: required—TOEFL (minimum score 100 iBT), IELTS (minimum score 7.5), TWE. Electronic applications accepted. *Expenses:* Contact institution.

North Carolina Central University, College of Behavioral and Social Sciences, Department of Public Administration, Durham, NC 27707-3129. Offers MPA. *Program availability:* Part-time, evening/weekend. *Degree requirements:* For master's, one foreign language, comprehensive exam, thesis or alternative. *Entrance requirements:* For master's, GRE, minimum GPA of 3.0 in major, 2.5 overall. Additional exam requirements/recommendations for international students: required—TOEFL.

North Carolina State University, Graduate School, College of Humanities and Social Sciences, School of Public and International Affairs, Program in Public Administration, Raleigh, NC 27695. Offers MPA, PhD. *Accreditation:* NASPAA. *Degree requirements:* For master's, thesis optional; for doctorate, thesis/dissertation. *Entrance requirements:* For master's, GRE General Test, minimum GPA of 3.0 during previous 2 years; for doctorate, GRE General Test. Electronic applications accepted.

Northeastern University, College of Social Sciences and Humanities, Boston, MA 02115. Offers criminology and criminal justice (MSCJ); criminology and justice policy (PhD); economics (MA, PhD); English (MA, PhD); international affairs (MA); law and public policy (PhD); political science (MA, PhD); public administration (MPA); public policy (MPP); security and resilience studies (MS); sociology (MA, PhD); urban and regional policy (MS); urban informatics (MS); world history (MA, PhD). *Program availability:* Online learning. *Degree requirements:* For doctorate, variable foreign language requirement, comprehensive exam, thesis/dissertation. *Entrance requirements:* For master's and doctorate, GRE. Additional exam requirements/recommendations for international students: required—TOEFL, IELTS. Electronic applications accepted. *Expenses:* Contact institution.

Northern Arizona University, College of Social and Behavioral Sciences, Department of Politics and International Affairs, Flagstaff, AZ 86011. Offers political science (MA, PhD, Graduate Certificate); public administration (MPA); public management (Graduate Certificate). *Program availability:* Part-time, 100% online, blended/hybrid learning. *Degree requirements:* For master's, variable foreign language requirement, comprehensive exam (for some programs), thesis (for some programs); for doctorate, variable foreign language requirement, comprehensive exam (for some programs), thesis/dissertation (for some programs); for Graduate Certificate, comprehensive exam (for some programs). *Entrance requirements:* For master's and doctorate, GRE General Test. Additional exam requirements/recommendations for international students: required—TOEFL (minimum score 93 iBT), IELTS (minimum score 6.5). Electronic applications accepted.

Northern Illinois University, Graduate School, College of Liberal Arts and Sciences, Department of Public Administration, De Kalb, IL 60115-2854. Offers MPA. *Accreditation:* NASPAA. *Program availability:* Part-time, evening/weekend. *Faculty:* 5 full-time (1 woman), 3 part-time/adjunct (1 woman). *Students:* 43 full-time (14 women), 43 part-time (23 women); includes 22 minority (5 Black or African American, non-Hispanic/Latino; 2 Asian, non-Hispanic/Latino; 14 Hispanic/Latino; 1 Two or more races, non-Hispanic/Latino), 1 international. Average age 30. 65 applicants, 72% accepted, 26 enrolled. In 2019, 45 master's awarded. *Degree requirements:* For master's, comprehensive exam, internship, research paper. *Entrance requirements:* For master's, GRE General Test, minimum GPA of 2.75, 9 hours in social science. Additional exam requirements/recommendations for international students: required—TOEFL (minimum score 550 paper-based). *Application deadline:* For fall admission, 3/1 priority date for domestic students, 5/1 for international students; for spring admission, 10/1 priority date for domestic students, 10/1 for international students. Applications are processed on a rolling basis. Application fee: $40. Electronic applications accepted. *Financial support:* In 2019–20, 17 research assistantships with full tuition reimbursements, 1 teaching assistantship were awarded; fellowships with full tuition reimbursements, career-related internships or fieldwork, Federal Work-Study, scholarships/grants, tuition waivers (full), and unspecified assistantships also available. Support available to part-time students. Financial award applicants required to submit FAFSA. *Unit head:* Dr. Kurt Thurmaier, Chair, 815-753-0311, Fax: 815-753-2539, E-mail: kthur@niu.edu. *Application contact:* Graduate School Office, 815-753-0395, E-mail: gradsch@niu.edu.
Website: http://www.niu.edu/pub_ad/

Northern Kentucky University, Office of Graduate Programs, College of Arts and Sciences, Program in Public Administration, Highland Heights, KY 41099. Offers nonprofit management (Certificate); public administration (MPA). *Accreditation:* NASPAA. *Program availability:* Part-time. *Degree requirements:* For master's, 39 semester hours, including completion of the capstone course. *Entrance requirements:* For master's, GRE, minimum GPA of 2.5, letters of references, portfolios; for Certificate, minimum GPA of 2.0. Additional exam requirements/recommendations for international students: required—TOEFL (minimum score 79 iBT); recommended—IELTS (minimum score 6.5). Electronic applications accepted.

Northwestern University, School of Professional Studies, Program in Public Policy and Administration, Evanston, IL 60208. Offers global policy (MA); health services policy (MA); public administration (MA); public policy (MA). *Program availability:* Part-time, evening/weekend, online learning.

Norwich University, College of Graduate and Continuing Studies, Master of Public Administration Program, Northfield, VT 05663. Offers criminal justice and public safety (MPA); fiscal management (MPA); international development and influence (MPA); municipal governance (MPA); nonprofit management (MPA); policy analysis and analytics (MPA); public administration leadership and crisis management (MPA); public works and sustainability (MPA). *Program availability:* Evening/weekend, online only, mostly all online with a week-long residency requirement. *Degree requirements:* For master's, capstone. *Entrance requirements:* For master's, minimum undergraduate GPA of 2.75. Additional exam requirements/recommendations for international students: required—TOEFL (minimum score 550 paper-based; 80 iBT), IELTS (minimum score 6.5). Electronic applications accepted. *Expenses:* Contact institution.

Notre Dame de Namur University, Division of Academic Affairs, School of Business and Management, Program in Public Administration, Belmont, CA 94002-1908. Offers MPA. *Program availability:* Part-time, evening/weekend, 100% online. *Entrance requirements:* For master's, interview, minimum GPA of 2.5. Additional exam requirements/recommendations for international students: required—TOEFL (minimum score 550 paper-based; 79 iBT). Electronic applications accepted.

Public Administration

Nova Southeastern University, H. Wayne Huizenga College of Business and Entrepreneurship, Fort Lauderdale, FL 33314-7796. Offers accounting (M Acc); business (MBA); business intelligence/analytics (MBA); complex health systems (MBA); enterprise informatics (MBA); entrepreneurship (MBA); finance (MBA); human resource management (MBA); international business (MBA); management (MBA); marketing (MBA); process improvement (MBA); public administration (MPA); real estate development (MS); sport revenue generation (MBA); supply chain management (MBA). *Accreditation:* NASPAA. *Program availability:* Part-time, evening/weekend, 100% online, blended/hybrid learning. *Faculty:* 54 full-time (23 women), 38 part-time/adjunct (11 women). *Students:* 1,988 full-time (1,145 women), 316 part-time (195 women); includes 1,484 minority (554 Black or African American, non-Hispanic/Latino; 3 American Indian or Alaska Native, non-Hispanic/Latino; 117 Asian, non-Hispanic/Latino; 747 Hispanic/Latino; 4 Native Hawaiian or other Pacific Islander, non-Hispanic/Latino; 59 Two or more races, non-Hispanic/Latino), 254 international. Average age 33. 877 applicants, 57% accepted, 352 enrolled. In 2019, 828 master's awarded. *Entrance requirements:* For master's, GMAT or GRE (depending on undergraduate GPA), official transcripts from all schools attended while in pursuit of bachelor's degree; minimum GPA of 2.5 from regionally-accredited institution. Additional exam requirements/recommendations for international students: required—TOEFL (minimum score 550 paper-based; 79 iBT), IELTS (minimum score 6), PTE (minimum score 54). *Application deadline:* For fall admission, 8/5 priority date for domestic students, 7/29 priority date for international students; for winter admission, 12/16 priority date for domestic students, 12/9 priority date for international students; for summer admission, 4/21 priority date for domestic and international students. Applications are processed on a rolling basis. Application fee: $50. Electronic applications accepted. *Expenses:* Contact institution. *Financial support:* In 2019–20, 325 students received support. Federal Work-Study and scholarships/grants available. Support available to part-time students. Financial award application deadline: 4/15; financial award applicants required to submit FAFSA. *Unit head:* Dr. Andrew Rosman, Dean, 954-262-5127, E-mail: arosman1@nova.edu. *Application contact:* Liza Sumulong, Executive Director, 954-262-5119, Fax: 954-262-3822, E-mail: sumulong@nova.edu.
Website: http://www.huizenga.nova.edu

Oakland University, Graduate Study and Lifelong Learning, College of Arts and Sciences, Department of Political Science, Rochester, MI 48309-4401. Offers local government management (Graduate Certificate); non-profit and organizational management (PMC); public administration (MPA). *Accreditation:* NASPAA. *Program availability:* Part-time, 100% online, blended/hybrid learning. *Entrance requirements:* Additional exam requirements/recommendations for international students: required—TOEFL (minimum score 550 paper-based; 79 iBT), IELTS (minimum score 6.5). Electronic applications accepted. *Expenses: Tuition, area resident:* Full-time $12,328; part-time $770.50 per credit hour. Tuition, state resident: full-time $12,328; part-time $770.50 per credit hour. Tuition, nonresident: full-time $16,432; part-time $1027 per credit hour. *International tuition:* $16,432 full-time. Tuition and fees vary according to degree level and program.

The Ohio State University, Graduate School, John Glenn College of Public Affairs, Columbus, OH 43210. Offers public administration (MA, MPA); public policy and management (PhD). *Accreditation:* NASPAA (one or more programs are accredited). *Program availability:* Part-time. *Degree requirements:* For doctorate, thesis/dissertation. *Entrance requirements:* For master's, GRE General Test (for MPA), minimum GPA of 3.0 (for MA); for doctorate, GRE General Test. Additional exam requirements/recommendations for international students: required—TOEFL (minimum score 600 paper-based; 100 iBT); recommended—IELTS (minimum score 7.5). Electronic applications accepted.

Ohio University, Graduate College, Voinovich School of Leadership and Public Affairs, Athens, OH 45701-2979. Offers environmental studies (MS, Certificate); public administration (MPA). Electronic applications accepted.

Old Dominion University, Strome College of Business, Master of Public Administration Program, Norfolk, VA 23529. Offers multi-sector public service (MPA); public administration (MPA). *Accreditation:* NASPAA. *Program availability:* Part-time, evening/weekend, 100% online, blended/hybrid learning. *Degree requirements:* For master's, capstone seminar. *Entrance requirements:* For master's, GRE (waived for work experience or undergraduate GPA greater than or equal to 3.5). Additional exam requirements/recommendations for international students: required—TOEFL (minimum score 550 paper-based; 79 iBT), IELTS (minimum score 6.5). Electronic applications accepted. *Expenses:* Contact institution.

Old Dominion University, Strome College of Business, Program in Public Administration and Policy, Norfolk, VA 23529. Offers PhD. *Program availability:* Part-time, evening/weekend. *Degree requirements:* For doctorate, comprehensive exam, thesis/dissertation. *Entrance requirements:* For doctorate, GMAT, GRE General Test, LSAT, master's degree, minimum graduate GPA of 3.25. Additional exam requirements/recommendations for international students: required—TOEFL (minimum score 550 paper-based; 79 iBT). Electronic applications accepted. *Expenses:* Contact institution.

Pace University, Dyson College of Arts and Sciences, Department of Public Administration, New York, NY 10038. Offers government management (MPA); health care administration (MPA); not-for-profit management (MPA); JD/MPA. *Program availability:* Part-time, evening/weekend. *Degree requirements:* For master's, comprehensive exam, thesis (for some programs), capstone project. *Entrance requirements:* For master's, 2 letters of recommendation, resume, personal statement, official transcripts, essay. Additional exam requirements/recommendations for international students: required—TOEFL (minimum score 88 iBT), IELTS (minimum score 7) or PTE (minimum score 60). Electronic applications accepted.

Park University, School of Graduate and Professional Studies, Kansas City, MO 54105. Offers adult education (M Ed); business and government leadership (Graduate Certificate); business, government, and global society (MPA); communication and leadership (MA); creative and life writing (Graduate Certificate); disaster and emergency management (MPA, Graduate Certificate); educational leadership (M Ed); finance (MBA, Graduate Certificate); general business (MBA); global business (Graduate Certificate); healthcare administration (MHA); healthcare services management and leadership (Graduate Certificate); international business (MBA); language and literacy (M Ed), including English for speakers of other languages, special reading teacher/literacy coach; leadership of international healthcare organizations (Graduate Certificate); management information systems (MBA, Graduate Certificate); music performance (ADP, Graduate Certificate), including cello (MM, ADP), piano (MM, ADP), viola (MM, ADP), violin (MM, ADP); nonprofit and community services management (MPA); nonprofit leadership (Graduate Certificate); performance (MM), including cello (MM, ADP), piano (MM, ADP), viola (MM, ADP), violin (MM, ADP); public management (MPA); social work (MSW); teacher leadership (M Ed), including curriculum and assessment, instructional leader. *Program availability:* Part-time, evening/weekend, online learning. *Degree requirements:* For master's, comprehensive exam (for some programs), thesis (for some programs), internship (for some programs); exam (for some programs). *Entrance requirements:* For master's, GRE or GMAT (for some programs), teacher certification (for some M Ed programs), letters of recommendation, essay, resume (for some programs). Additional exam requirements/recommendations for international students: required—TOEFL (minimum score 550 paper-based; 79 iBT), IELTS (minimum score 6). Electronic applications accepted.

Penn State Harrisburg, Graduate School, School of Public Affairs, Middletown, PA 17057. Offers criminal justice (MA); health administration (MHA); health administration: long term care (Certificate); homeland security (MPS, Certificate); public administration (MPA, PhD); public administration: non-profit administration (Certificate); public budgeting and financial management (Certificate); public sector human resource management (Certificate). *Accreditation:* NASPAA.

Pontifical Catholic University of Puerto Rico, College of Graduate Studies in Behavioral Science and Community Affairs, Program in Public Administration, Ponce, PR 00717-0777. Offers MSS. *Program availability:* Part-time, evening/weekend. *Degree requirements:* For master's, thesis. *Entrance requirements:* For master's, EXADEP, 3 letters of recommendation, interview, minimum GPA of 2.75.

Portland State University, Graduate Studies, College of Urban and Public Affairs, Hatfield School of Government, Department of Public Administration, Portland, OR 97207-0751. Offers collaborative governance (Certificate); energy policy and management (Certificate); global management and leadership (MPA); health administration (MPA); human resource management (MPA); local government (MPA); natural resource policy and administration (MPA); nonprofit and public management (Certificate); nonprofit management (MPA); public administration (EMPA); public affairs and policy (PhD); sustainable food systems (Certificate). *Accreditation:* CAHME; NASPAA (one or more programs are accredited). *Program availability:* Part-time, evening/weekend. *Faculty:* 14 full-time (6 women), 9 part-time/adjunct (5 women). *Students:* 86 full-time (55 women), 119 part-time (73 women); includes 46 minority (3 Black or African American, non-Hispanic/Latino; 4 American Indian or Alaska Native, non-Hispanic/Latino; 8 Asian, non-Hispanic/Latino; 18 Hispanic/Latino; 2 Native Hawaiian or other Pacific Islander, non-Hispanic/Latino; 11 Two or more races, non-Hispanic/Latino), 17 international. Average age 35. 138 applicants, 82% accepted, 67 enrolled. In 2019, 64 master's, 2 doctorates awarded. *Degree requirements:* For master's, integrative field experience (MPA), practicum (MPH); for doctorate, comprehensive exam, thesis/dissertation. *Entrance requirements:* For master's, GRE (minimum scores: verbal 150, quantitative 149, and analytic writing 4.5), minimum GPA of 3.0, 3 recommendation letters, resume, 500-word statement of intent; for doctorate, GRE, 3 recommendation letters, resume, 500-word personal essay. Additional exam requirements/recommendations for international students: required—TOEFL (minimum score 550 paper-based; 80 iBT), IELTS (minimum score 7). *Application deadline:* For fall admission, 8/15 for domestic and international students; for winter admission, 10/31 for domestic and international students; for spring admission, 1/31 for domestic and international students. Applications are processed on a rolling basis. Application fee: $65. Electronic applications accepted. *Expenses: Tuition, area resident:* Full-time $13,020; part-time $6510 per year. Tuition, state resident: full-time $13,020; part-time $6510 per year. Tuition, nonresident: full-time $19,830; part-time $9915 per year. *International tuition:* $19,830 full-time. *Required fees:* $1226. One-time fee: $350. Tuition and fees vary according to course load, program and reciprocity agreements. *Financial support:* In 2019–20, 1 research assistantship with full and partial tuition reimbursement (averaging $8,500 per year), 3 teaching assistantships (averaging $7,840 per year) were awarded; career-related internships or fieldwork, Federal Work-Study, scholarships/grants, and unspecified assistantships also available. Support available to part-time students. Financial award application deadline: 3/1; financial award applicants required to submit FAFSA. *Unit head:* Dr. Masami Nishishiba, Chair, 503-725-5151, E-mail: nishism@pdx.edu. *Application contact:* Megan Heljeson, Office Coordinator, 503-725-3921, Fax: 503-725-8250, E-mail: publicad@pdx.edu.
Website: https://www.pdx.edu/hatfieldschool/public-administration

Post University, Program in Public Administration, Waterbury, CT 06723-2540. Offers emergency management and homeland security (MPA). *Program availability:* Online learning. *Degree requirements:* For master's, capstone project. *Entrance requirements:* For master's, resume.

Queen's University at Kingston, School of Graduate Studies, School of Policy Studies, Kingston, ON K7L 3N6, Canada. Offers MPA. *Program availability:* Part-time. *Entrance requirements:* For master's, minimum B+ average. Additional exam requirements/recommendations for international students: required—TOEFL.

Regent University, Graduate School, Robertson School of Government, Virginia Beach, VA 23464. Offers government (MA), including American government, healthcare policy and ethics (MA, MPA), international relations, law and public policy, national security studies, political communication, political theory, religion and politics; national security studies (MA), including cybersecurity, homeland security, international security, Middle East politics; public administration (MPA), including emergency management and homeland security, federal government, general public administration, healthcare policy and ethics (MA, MPA), law, nonprofit administration and faith-based organizations, public leadership and management, servant leadership. *Program availability:* Part-time, evening/weekend, 100% online, blended/hybrid learning. *Faculty:* 5 full-time (1 woman), 19 part-time/adjunct (2 women). *Students:* 36 full-time (22 women), 159 part-time (89 women); includes 82 minority (52 Black or African American, non-Hispanic/Latino; 2 American Indian or Alaska Native, non-Hispanic/Latino; 2 Asian, non-Hispanic/Latino; 23 Hispanic/Latino; 3 Two or more races, non-Hispanic/Latino), 4 international. Average age 36. 181 applicants, 70% accepted, 75 enrolled. In 2019, 58 master's awarded. *Degree requirements:* For master's, thesis optional, internship. *Entrance requirements:* For master's, GRE General Test or LSAT, personal essay, writing sample, resume, college transcripts. Additional exam requirements/recommendations for international students: required—TOEFL (minimum score 577 paper-based). *Application deadline:* For fall admission, 5/1 priority date for domestic students; for spring admission, 11/1 priority date for domestic students. Applications are processed on a rolling basis. Application fee: $50. Electronic applications accepted. *Expenses:* Contact institution. *Financial support:* In 2019–20, 132 students received support. Career-related internships or fieldwork, scholarships/grants, and unspecified assistantships available. Support available to part-time students. Financial award applicants required to submit FAFSA. *Unit head:* Dr. Stephen Perry, Interim Dean, 757-352-4082, E-mail: sperry@regent.edu. *Application contact:* Heidi Cece, Assistant Vice President for Enrollment Management, 800-373-5504, Fax: 757-352-4381, E-mail: admissions@regent.edu.
Website: https://www.regent.edu/robertson-school-of-government/

Reinhardt University, School of Professional Studies, Waleska, GA 30183-2981. Offers MPA. *Program availability:* Part-time-only, blended/hybrid learning. *Entrance requirements:* Additional exam requirements/recommendations for international students: required—TOEFL (minimum score 500 paper-based). Electronic applications accepted.

Roger Williams University, School of Justice Studies, Bristol, RI 02809. Offers criminal justice (MS); cybersecurity (MS); leadership (MS), including health care administration (MPA, MS), public management (MPA, MS); public administration (MPA), including health care administration (MPA, MS), public management (MPA, MS); MS/JD. *Program availability:* Part-time, evening/weekend, 100% online, blended/hybrid learning. *Faculty:* 1 (woman) full-time, 5 part-time/adjunct (0 women). *Students:* 24 full-time (15 women),

109 part-time (59 women); includes 31 minority (9 Black or African American, non-Hispanic/Latino; 1 Asian, non-Hispanic/Latino; 17 Hispanic/Latino; 4 Two or more races, non-Hispanic/Latino), 2 international. Average age 34. 94 applicants, 83% accepted, 46 enrolled. In 2019, 46 master's awarded. *Degree requirements:* For master's, thesis. *Entrance requirements:* For master's, No, Letter of intent, transcripts, two letters of recommendation, resume, background check (cybersecurity). Additional exam requirements/recommendations for international students: required—TOEFL (minimum score 85 paper-based), IELTS (minimum score 6.5). *Application deadline:* Applications are processed on a rolling basis. Application fee: $50. Electronic applications accepted. Application fee is waived when completed online. *Expenses: Tuition:* Full-time $15,768. *Required fees:* $900; $450. *Financial support:* In 2019–20, 8 students received support. Scholarships/grants and unspecified assistantships available. Financial award application deadline: 3/15; financial award applicants required to submit FAFSA. *Unit head:* Dr. Eric Bronson, Dean and Professor of Criminal Justice, 401-254-3336, E-mail: ebronson@rwu.edu. *Application contact:* Marcus Hanscom, Director of Graduate Admission, 401-254-3345, Fax: 401-254-3557, E-mail: gradadmit@rwu.edu. Website: http://www.rwu.edu/academics/departments/criminaljustice.htm#graduate

Roosevelt University, Graduate Division, College of Arts and Sciences, Department of Justice, Chicago, IL 60605. Offers public administration (MPA). *Program availability:* Part-time, evening/weekend. *Degree requirements:* For master's, thesis optional. Electronic applications accepted.

Rutgers University - Camden, Graduate School of Arts and Sciences, Department of Public Policy and Administration, Camden, NJ 08102. Offers education policy and leadership (MPA); international public service and development (MPA); public management (MPA); JD/MPA; MPA/MA. *Accreditation:* NASPAA. *Program availability:* Part-time, evening/weekend. *Degree requirements:* For master's, directed study, research workshop, 42 credits. *Entrance requirements:* For master's, GRE General Test, GMAT or LSAT, 3 letters of recommendation; resume. Additional exam requirements/recommendations for international students: required—TOEFL (minimum score 550 paper-based), IELTS. Electronic applications accepted.

Rutgers University - Newark, Graduate School, Program in Public Administration, Newark, NJ 07102. Offers health care administration (MPA); human resources administration (MPA); public administration (PhD); public management (MPA); public policy analysis (MPA); urban systems and issues (MPA). *Accreditation:* NASPAA (one or more programs are accredited). *Program availability:* Part-time, evening/weekend. *Degree requirements:* For master's, comprehensive exam, thesis or alternative; for doctorate, thesis/dissertation. *Entrance requirements:* For master's, GRE, minimum undergraduate B average; for doctorate, GRE, MPA, minimum B average. Electronic applications accepted.

Sacred Heart University, Graduate Programs, College of Arts and Sciences, Department of Government, Politics and Global Studies, Fairfield, CT 06825. Offers public administration (MPA). *Program availability:* Part-time, online learning. *Entrance requirements:* For master's, BA or BS, minimum GPA of 3.0.

Saginaw Valley State University, College of Arts and Behavioral Sciences, Program in Public Administration, University Center, MI 48710. Offers MA. *Program availability:* Part-time, evening/weekend. *Students:* 13 full-time (10 women), 27 part-time (18 women); includes 9 minority (4 Black or African American, non-Hispanic/Latino; 3 Hispanic/Latino; 2 Two or more races, non-Hispanic/Latino). Average age 29. 30 applicants, 67% accepted, 17 enrolled. In 2019, 10 master's awarded. *Degree requirements:* For master's, thesis optional. *Entrance requirements:* For master's, minimum GPA of 2.75. Additional exam requirements/recommendations for international students: required—TOEFL (minimum score 580 paper-based; 92 iBT). *Application deadline:* For fall admission, 7/15 for international students; for winter admission, 11/15 for international students; for spring admission, 4/15 for international students. Applications are processed on a rolling basis. Application fee: $30 ($90 for international students). Electronic applications accepted. *Expenses: Tuition, area resident:* Full-time $11,212; part-time $622.90 per credit hour. Tuition, state resident: full-time $11,212; part-time $622.90 per credit hour. Tuition, nonresident: full-time $11,212; part-time $1253 per credit hour. *Required fees:* $263; $14.60 per credit hour. Tuition and fees vary according to course load, degree level and program. *Financial support:* Federal Work-Study and scholarships/grants available. Support available to part-time students. Financial award application deadline: 4/1; financial award applicants required to submit FAFSA. *Unit head:* Dr. Joseph Jaksa, Program Coordinator, 989-964-2178, E-mail: jjjaksa@svsu.edu. *Application contact:* Jenna Briggs, Director, Graduate and International Admissions, 989-964-6096, Fax: 989-964-2788, E-mail: gradadm@svsu.edu.

St. John's University, St. John's College of Liberal Arts and Sciences, Department of Government and Politics, Program in Government and Politics, Queens, NY 11439. Offers government and politics (MA); international law and diplomacy (Adv C); public administration (Adv C); JD/MA. *Program availability:* Part-time, evening/weekend. *Degree requirements:* For master's, comprehensive exam, thesis optional. *Entrance requirements:* For master's, letters of recommendation, transcripts, resume, personal statement. Additional exam requirements/recommendations for international students: required—TOEFL (minimum score 80 iBT), IELTS (minimum score 6.5). Electronic applications accepted.

St. Mary's University, Graduate Studies, Program in Public Administration, San Antonio, TX 78228. Offers public administration (MPA); public communication, public policy and public leadership (Certificate); JD/MPA. *Program availability:* Part-time, evening/weekend, online learning. *Degree requirements:* For master's, comprehensive exam, 6-hour internship or applied public service. *Entrance requirements:* For master's, GRE General Test, letters of recommendation, writing sample, essay. Additional exam requirements/recommendations for international students: required—TOEFL (minimum score 550 paper-based; 80 iBT), IELTS (minimum score 6). Electronic applications accepted.

Saint Mary's University of Minnesota, Schools of Graduate and Professional Programs, Graduate School of Business and Technology, Public Administration Program, Winona, MN 55987-1399. Offers MA. *Unit head:* George Diaz, Director, 612-238-4510, E-mail: gdiaz@smumn.edu. *Application contact:* Laurie Roy, Director of Admission of Schools of Graduate and Professional Programs, 507-457-8606, Fax: 612-728-5121, E-mail: lroy@smumn.edu.
Website: https://onlineprograms.smumn.edu/mpa/masters-in-public-administration?_ga-2.254655304.1736907137.1523547391-1359115499.1515170921

Saint Peter's University, Program in Public Administration, Jersey City, NJ 07306-5997. Offers MPA. *Degree requirements:* For master's, capstone project.

St. Thomas University - Florida, School of Business, Department of Management, Miami Gardens, FL 33054-6459. Offers accounting (MBA); general management (MSM, Certificate); health management (MBA, MSM, Certificate); human resource management (MBA, MSM, Certificate); international business (MBA, MIB, MSM, Certificate); justice administration (MSM, Certificate); management accounting (MSM, Certificate); public management (MSM, Certificate); sports administration (MS). *Program availability:* Part-time, evening/weekend. *Degree requirements:* For master's, comprehensive exam. *Entrance requirements:* For master's, interview, minimum GPA of

3.0 or GMAT. Additional exam requirements/recommendations for international students: required—TOEFL (minimum score 550 paper-based; 79 iBT). Electronic applications accepted.

Sam Houston State University, College of Humanities and Social Sciences, Department of Political Science, Huntsville, TX 77341. Offers political science (MA); public administration (MPA). *Program availability:* Part-time, online learning. *Degree requirements:* For master's, comprehensive exam, thesis optional, internship. *Entrance requirements:* For master's, GRE General Test, GMAT, writing sample of scholarly work, letters of recommendation, statement of purpose, resume. Additional exam requirements/recommendations for international students: required—TOEFL (minimum score 550 paper-based; 79 iBT), IELTS (minimum score 6.5). Electronic applications accepted.

San Diego State University, Graduate and Research Affairs, College of Professional Studies and Fine Arts, School of Public Affairs, Program in Public Administration, San Diego, CA 92182. Offers MPA. *Accreditation:* NASPAA. *Program availability:* Part-time. *Entrance requirements:* For master's, GRE General Test, 2 letters of reference. Additional exam requirements/recommendations for international students: required—TOEFL. Electronic applications accepted.

San Francisco State University, Division of Graduate Studies, College of Health and Social Sciences, Public Administration Program, San Francisco, CA 94132-1722. Offers criminal justice administration (MPA); environmental administration and policy (MPA); gerontology (MPA); nonprofit administration (MPA); public management (MPA); public policy (MPA); urban administration (MPA). *Accreditation:* NASPAA. *Expenses: Tuition, area resident:* Full-time $7176; part-time $4164 per year. Tuition, state resident: full-time $7176; part-time $4164 per year. Tuition, nonresident: full-time $16,680; part-time $396 per unit. *International tuition:* $16,680 full-time. *Required fees:* $1524; $1524 per unit. $762 per semester. Tuition and fees vary according to degree level and program. *Unit head:* Dr. Janey Wang, Graduate Coordinator, 415-817-4456, Fax: 415-338-0586, E-mail: jqwang@sfsu.edu. *Application contact:* Dr. Janey Wang, Graduate Coordinator, 415-817-4456, Fax: 415-338-0586, E-mail: jqwang@sfsu.edu.
Website: http://mpa.sfsu.edu/

San Jose State University, Program in Political Science, San Jose, CA 95192-0030. Offers public administration (MPA). *Accreditation:* NASPAA. *Program availability:* Part-time, evening/weekend. *Faculty:* 5 full-time (1 woman), 4 part-time/adjunct (0 women). *Students:* 23 full-time (14 women), 70 part-time (46 women); includes 59 minority (5 Black or African American, non-Hispanic/Latino; 23 Asian, non-Hispanic/Latino; 29 Hispanic/Latino; 2 Native Hawaiian or other Pacific Islander, non-Hispanic/Latino), 5 international. Average age 31. 56 applicants, 64% accepted, 19 enrolled. In 2019, 16 master's awarded. *Degree requirements:* For master's, Project. *Entrance requirements:* For master's, Prerequisites: American government, mirco economics, statistics; proof of Excel competency. GPA of 3.0. *Application deadline:* For fall admission, 4/1 for domestic students; for spring admission, 10/1 for domestic students. Application fee: $70. Electronic applications accepted. *Expenses: Tuition, area resident:* Full-time $7176; part-time $4164 per credit hour. Tuition, state resident: full-time $7176; part-time $4164 per credit hour. Tuition, nonresident: full-time $7176; part-time $4165 per credit hour. *International tuition:* $7176 full-time. *Required fees:* $2110; $2110. *Financial support:* In 2019–20, 15 students received support, including 2 research assistantships (averaging $1,500 per year); scholarships/grants also available. Financial award application deadline: 5/1; financial award applicants required to submit FAFSA. *Unit head:* Dr. Garrick Percival, Department Chair, 408-924-5553, E-mail: garrick.percival@sjsu.edu. *Application contact:* Dr. Frances Edwards, MPA Director, 408-806-7937, E-mail: frances.edwards@sjsu.edu.
Website: http://www.sjsu.edu/polisci/

Savannah State University, Master of Public Administration Program, Savannah, GA 31404. Offers city management (MPA); human resources (MPA). *Accreditation:* NASPAA. *Program availability:* Part-time. *Degree requirements:* For master's, comprehensive exam, thesis, public service internship, capstone seminar. *Entrance requirements:* For master's, GRE General Test, GMAT, or MAT, minimum cumulative GPA of 2.5, 3 letters of recommendation, essay, official transcripts, resume, essay of 500-1000 words detailing reasons for pursuing degree. Additional exam requirements/recommendations for international students: required—TOEFL. Electronic applications accepted. *Expenses:* Contact institution.

Seattle University, College of Arts and Sciences, Institute of Public Service, Seattle, WA 98122-1090. Offers MNPL, MPA. *Accreditation:* NASPAA. *Program availability:* Part-time, evening/weekend. *Faculty:* 7 full-time (4 women), 3 part-time/adjunct (2 women). *Students:* 11 full-time (6 women), 111 part-time (69 women); includes 59 minority (17 Black or African American, non-Hispanic/Latino; 1 American Indian or Alaska Native, non-Hispanic/Latino; 9 Asian, non-Hispanic/Latino; 22 Hispanic/Latino; 1 Native Hawaiian or other Pacific Islander, non-Hispanic/Latino; 9 Two or more races, non-Hispanic/Latino), 1 international. Average age 31. 53 applicants, 91% accepted, 35 enrolled. In 2019, 50 master's awarded. *Entrance requirements:* For master's, minimum GPA of 3.0, letters of recommendation, current resume reflecting two years of relevant professional experience in nonprofit organization (preferred). Additional exam requirements/recommendations for international students: required—TOEFL, IELTS. *Application deadline:* For fall admission, 7/20 priority date for domestic students, 7/20 for international students; for winter admission, 10/20 priority date for domestic students, 10/20 for international students; for spring admission, 2/20 priority date for domestic students, 2/20 for international students. Applications are processed on a rolling basis. Application fee: $55. Electronic applications accepted. *Financial support:* In 2019–20, 23 students received support. Career-related internships or fieldwork, Federal Work-Study, and unspecified assistantships available. Support available to part-time students. Financial award applicants required to submit FAFSA. *Unit head:* Dr. John Collins, Interim Director, Institute of Public Service, 206-296-5442, Fax: 206-296-5997, E-mail: collinsj@seattleu.edu. *Application contact:* Janet Shandley, Associate Dean of Graduate Admissions, 206-296-5900, Fax: 206-298-5656, E-mail: grad_admissions@seattleu.edu.
Website: http://www.seattleu.edu/artsci/departments/ips/

Seton Hall University, College of Arts and Sciences, Department of Political Science and Public Affairs, South Orange, NJ 07079-2697. Offers nonprofit organization management (Graduate Certificate); public administration (MPA), including data visualization and analytics, health policy and management, nonprofit organization management, public service: leadership, governance, and policy. *Accreditation:* CAHME; NASPAA. *Program availability:* Part-time, evening/weekend. *Degree requirements:* For master's, thesis or alternative, internship or practicum. *Entrance requirements:* Additional exam requirements/recommendations for international students: required—TOEFL. Electronic applications accepted.

Shippensburg University of Pennsylvania, School of Graduate Studies, College of Arts and Sciences, Department of Political Science, Shippensburg, PA 17257-2299. Offers public administration (MPA). *Program availability:* Part-time, evening/weekend. *Faculty:* 5 full-time (2 women). *Students:* 7 full-time (2 women), 19 part-time (10 women); includes 5 minority (2 Black or African American, non-Hispanic/Latino; 2 Hispanic/Latino; 1 Two or more races, non-Hispanic/Latino). Average age 34. 22

applicants, 91% accepted, 7 enrolled. In 2019, 14 master's awarded. *Degree requirements:* For master's, thesis, thesis or internship. *Entrance requirements:* For master's, current resume, official transcript showing minimum cumulative GPA of 2.75 or sufficient work experience, personal goals statement, and track selection form. Additional exam requirements/recommendations for international students: required—TOEFL (minimum score 550 paper-based; 68 iBT), IELTS (minimum score 6), TOEFL (minimum score 550 paper-based, 68 iBT or IELTS (minimum score 6). *Application deadline:* For fall admission, 4/30 for international students; for spring admission, 9/30 for international students. Applications are processed on a rolling basis. Application fee: $45. Electronic applications accepted. *Expenses:* Tuition, state resident: part-time $516 per credit. Tuition, nonresident: part-time $774 per credit. *Required fees:* $149 per credit. *Financial support:* In 2019–20, 7 students received support. Career-related internships or fieldwork, scholarships/grants, unspecified assistantships, and resident hall director and student payroll positions available. Support available to part-time students. Financial award application deadline: 3/1; financial award applicants required to submit FAFSA. *Unit head:* Dr. C. Niel Brasher, Department Chair and Program Coordinator, 717-477-1718, Fax: 717-477-4030, E-mail: cnbras@ship.edu. *Application contact:* Maya T. Mapp, Director of Admissions, 717-477-1231, Fax: 717-477-4016, E-mail: mtmapp@ship.edu.
Website: http://www.ship.edu/political_science/

Sonoma State University, School of Social Sciences, Department of Political Science, Rohnert Park, CA 94928. Offers public administration (MPA). *Program availability:* Part-time, evening/weekend. *Entrance requirements:* For master's, GRE General Test, minimum GPA of 3.0. Additional exam requirements/recommendations for international students: required—TOEFL (minimum score 500 paper-based).

Southeast Missouri State University, School of Graduate Studies, Department of Political Science, Philosophy and Religion, Cape Girardeau, MO 63701. Offers MPA. *Program availability:* Part-time, evening/weekend, 100% online, blended/hybrid learning. *Faculty:* 5 full-time (2 women). *Students:* 17 full-time (11 women), 15 part-time (8 women); includes 6 minority (4 Black or African American, non-Hispanic/Latino; 1 Hispanic/Latino; 1 Two or more races, non-Hispanic/Latino), 7 international. Average age 29. 24 applicants, 83% accepted, 13 enrolled. In 2019, 8 master's awarded. *Degree requirements:* For master's, thesis or alternative, internship paper. *Entrance requirements:* For master's, statement of interest, minimum GPA of 2.7. Additional exam requirements/recommendations for international students: required—TOEFL (minimum score 550 paper-based; 79 iBT), IELTS (minimum score 6), PTE (minimum score 53). *Application deadline:* For fall admission, 8/1 for domestic students, 7/1 priority date for international students; for spring admission, 11/21 for domestic students, 11/1 priority date for international students; for summer admission, 5/15 for domestic students. Applications are processed on a rolling basis. Application fee: $30 ($40 for international students). Electronic applications accepted. *Expenses:* Tuition, state resident: full-time $6989; part-time $291.20 per credit hour. Tuition, nonresident: full-time $13,061; part-time $544.20 per credit hour. *International tuition:* $13,061 full-time. *Required fees:* $955; $39.80 per credit hour. Tuition and fees vary according to degree level. *Financial support:* In 2019–20, 7 students received support, including 1 teaching assistantship with full tuition reimbursement available; career-related internships or fieldwork, Federal Work-Study, scholarships/grants, traineeships, tuition waivers (full), and unspecified assistantships also available. Financial award application deadline: 2/1; financial award applicants required to submit FAFSA. *Unit head:* Dr. Hamner Hill, Chairperson, 573-651-2816, Fax: 573-651-2695, E-mail: hhill@semo.edu. *Application contact:* Dr. Jeremy Walling, Graduate Coordinator, 573-651-2691, Fax: 573-651-2695, E-mail: jwalling@semo.edu.
Website: http://www.semo.edu/polisci/

Southern Arkansas University–Magnolia, School of Graduate Studies, Magnolia, AR 71753. Offers agriculture (MS); business administration (MBA), including agribusiness, social entrepreneurship, supply chain management; clinical and mental health counseling (MS); computer and information sciences (MS), including cyber security and privacy, data science, information technology; gifted and talented (M Ed), including curriculum and instruction, educational administration and supervision, gifted and talented P-8/7-12, instructional specialist P-4; higher, adult and lifelong education (M Ed); kinesiology (M Ed), including coaching; library media and information specialist (M Ed); public administration (MPA); school counseling K-12 (M Ed); student affairs and college counseling (M Ed); teaching (MAT). *Accreditation:* NCATE. *Program availability:* Part-time, 100% online, blended/hybrid learning. *Faculty:* 33 full-time (18 women), 29 part-time/adjunct (17 women). *Students:* 134 full-time (80 women), 704 part-time (471 women); includes 223 minority (158 Black or African American, non-Hispanic/Latino; 5 American Indian or Alaska Native, non-Hispanic/Latino; 19 Asian, non-Hispanic/Latino; 6 Hispanic/Latino; 1 Native Hawaiian or other Pacific Islander, non-Hispanic/Latino; 34 Two or more races, non-Hispanic/Latino), 135 international. Average age 28. 290 applicants, 99% accepted, 149 enrolled. In 2019, 177 master's awarded. *Degree requirements:* For master's, comprehensive exam (for some programs), thesis optional. *Entrance requirements:* For master's, GRE, MAT or GMAT, minimum GPA of 2.5. Additional exam requirements/recommendations for international students: required—TOEFL (minimum score 550 paper-based), IELTS (minimum score 6). *Application deadline:* For fall admission, 8/1 for domestic and international students; for spring admission, 12/1 for domestic students, 11/15 for international students; for summer admission, 5/1 for domestic students, 5/10 for international students. Applications are processed on a rolling basis. Application fee: $25 ($90 for international students). Electronic applications accepted. *Expenses:* Tuition, area resident: Full-time $6720; part-time $3360 per semester. Tuition, state resident: full-time $6720; part-time $3360 per semester. Tuition, nonresident: full-time $10,560; part-time $5280 per semester. *International tuition:* $10,560 full-time. *Required fees:* $2046; $1023 $267. One-time fee: $25. Tuition and fees vary according to course load. *Financial support:* Career-related internships or fieldwork, Federal Work-Study, scholarships/grants, tuition waivers (full), and unspecified assistantships available. Financial award applicants required to submit FAFSA. *Unit head:* Dr. Kim Bloss, Dean, School of Graduate Studies, 870-235-4150, Fax: 870-235-5227, E-mail: kkbloss@saumag.edu. *Application contact:* Talia Jett, Admissions Coordinator, 870-2355450, Fax: 870-235-5227, E-mail: taliajett@saumag.edu.
Website: http://www.saumag.edu/graduate

Southern Illinois University Carbondale, Graduate School, College of Liberal Arts, Department of Political Science, Public Administration Program, Carbondale, IL 62901-4701. Offers MPA, JD/MPA. *Accreditation:* NASPAA. *Program availability:* Part-time. *Degree requirements:* For master's, thesis or alternative. *Entrance requirements:* For master's, minimum GPA of 3.0. Additional exam requirements/recommendations for international students: required—TOEFL (minimum score 600 paper-based; 100 iBT).

Southern Illinois University Edwardsville, Graduate School, College of Arts and Sciences, Department of Public Administration and Policy Analysis, Edwardsville, IL 62026. Offers public administration (MPA). *Accreditation:* NASPAA. *Program availability:* Part-time, evening/weekend. *Degree requirements:* For master's, comprehensive exam. *Entrance requirements:* Additional exam requirements/recommendations for international students: required—TOEFL (minimum score 550 paper-based; 79 iBT), IELTS (minimum score 6.5). Electronic applications accepted.

Southern New Hampshire University, School of Business, Manchester, NH 03106-1045. Offers accounting (MBA, Graduate Certificate); accounting finance (MS); accounting/auditing (MS); accounting/forensic accounting (MS); accounting/management accounting (MS); accounting/taxation (MS); applied economics (MS); athletic administration (MBA, Graduate Certificate); business administration (IMBA, Certificate), including business information systems (Certificate), human resource management (Certificate); business analytics (MBA); business intelligence (MBA); communication (MA), including new media and marketing, public relations; community economic development (MBA); criminal justice (MBA); data analytics (MS); economics (MBA); engineering management (MBA); entrepreneurship (MBA); finance (MBA, MS, Graduate Certificate); finance/corporate finance (MS); finance/investments (MS); forensic accounting (MBA); forensic accounting and fraud examination (Graduate Certificate); healthcare informatics (MBA); healthcare management (MBA); human resource management (MS); human resources (MBA); information technology (MS); information technology management (MBA); international business (PhD); Internet marketing (MBA); leadership (MBA); leadership of nonprofit organizations (Graduate Certificate); management (MS); marketing (MBA, MS, Graduate Certificate); music business (MBA); operations and project management (MS); operations and supply chain management (MBA, Graduate Certificate); organizational leadership (MS); project management (MBA, Graduate Certificate); public administration (MBA, Graduate Certificate); quantitative analysis (MBA); Six Sigma (Graduate Certificate); Six Sigma quality (MBA); social media marketing (MBA, Graduate Certificate); sport management (MBA, MS, Graduate Certificate); sustainability and environmental compliance (MBA); MBA/Certificate. *Accreditation:* ACBSP. *Program availability:* Part-time, evening/weekend, online learning. Terminal master's awarded for partial completion of doctoral program. *Degree requirements:* For master's, one foreign language, comprehensive exam (for some programs), thesis or alternative; for doctorate, one foreign language, comprehensive exam, thesis/dissertation. *Entrance requirements:* For master's, minimum GPA of 2.5; for doctorate, GMAT. Additional exam requirements/recommendations for international students: required—TOEFL (minimum score 500 paper-based). Electronic applications accepted.

Southern University and Agricultural and Mechanical College, Graduate School, Nelson Mandela College of Government and Social Sciences, Department of Public Administration, Baton Rouge, LA 70813. Offers MPA. *Accreditation:* NASPAA. *Program availability:* Part-time, evening/weekend. *Degree requirements:* For master's, thesis. *Entrance requirements:* For master's, GRE General Test. Additional exam requirements/recommendations for international students: required—TOEFL (minimum score 525 paper-based).

Southern Utah University, Program in Public Administration, Cedar City, UT 84720-2498. Offers MPA. *Accreditation:* NASPAA. *Program availability:* Part-time, evening/weekend, 100% online. *Entrance requirements:* Additional exam requirements/recommendations for international students: required—TOEFL (minimum score 550 paper-based; 79 iBT), IELTS (minimum score 6), TOEFL (minimum score 550 paper-based, 213 Computer based test, 79 iBT) or IELTS (minimum score 6). Electronic applications accepted. *Expenses:* Contact institution.

South University - Montgomery, Program in Public Administration, Montgomery, AL 36116-1120. Offers MPA.

South University - Savannah, Graduate Programs, College of Business, Program in Public Administration, Savannah, GA 31406. Offers MPA.

South University - West Palm Beach, Program in Public Administration, Royal Palm Beach, FL 33411. Offers MPA.

Stephen F. Austin State University, Graduate School, College of Liberal and Applied Arts, Department of Government, Nacogdoches, TX 75962. Offers public administration (MPA). *Degree requirements:* For master's, thesis optional. *Entrance requirements:* For master's, GRE General Test. Additional exam requirements/recommendations for international students: required—TOEFL.

Strayer University, Graduate Studies, Washington, DC 20005-2603. Offers accounting (MS); acquisition (MBA); business administration (MBA); communications technology (MS); educational management (M Ed); finance (MBA); health services administration (MHSA); hospitality and tourism management (MBA); human resource management (MBA); information systems (MS), including computer security management, decision support system management, enterprise resource management, network management, software engineering management, systems development management; management (MBA); management information systems (MS); marketing (MBA); professional accounting (MS), including accounting information systems, controllership, taxation; public administration (MPA); supply chain management (MBA); technology in education (M Ed). *Accreditation:* ACBSP. *Program availability:* Part-time, evening/weekend, online learning. *Degree requirements:* For master's, thesis. *Entrance requirements:* For master's, GMAT, GRE General Test, bachelor's degree from an accredited college or university, minimum undergraduate GPA of 2.75. Electronic applications accepted.

Suffolk University, Sawyer Business School, Department of Public Administration, Boston, MA 02108-2770. Offers community health (MPA); information systems, performance management, and big data analytics (MPA); nonprofit management (MPA); state and local government (MPA); JD/MPA; MPA/MS; MPA/MSCJ; MPA/MSMHC; MPA/MSPS. *Accreditation:* NASPAA (one or more programs are accredited). *Program availability:* Part-time, evening/weekend. *Faculty:* 12 full-time (7 women), 4 part-time/adjunct (3 women). *Students:* 13 full-time (5 women), 72 part-time (55 women); includes 35 minority (21 Black or African American, non-Hispanic/Latino; 3 Asian, non-Hispanic/Latino; 9 Hispanic/Latino; 2 Two or more races, non-Hispanic/Latino), 2 international. Average age 35. 89 applicants, 85% accepted, 30 enrolled. In 2019, 40 master's awarded. *Entrance requirements:* Additional exam requirements/recommendations for international students: required—TOEFL (minimum score 550 paper-based; 80 iBT). *Application deadline:* For fall admission, 3/15 priority date for domestic and international students; for spring admission, 10/15 priority date for domestic and international students. Applications are processed on a rolling basis. Application fee: $50. Electronic applications accepted. *Expenses:* Contact institution. *Financial support:* In 2019–20, 47 students received support, including 2 fellowships (averaging $2,657 per year); career-related internships or fieldwork, Federal Work-Study, institutionally sponsored loans, and scholarships/grants also available. Support available to part-time students. Financial award application deadline: 4/1; financial award applicants required to submit FAFSA. *Unit head:* Brenda Bond, Director/Department Chair, 617-305-1768, E-mail: bbond@suffolk.edu. *Application contact:* Mara Marzocchi, Associate Director of Graduate Admissions, 617-573-8302, Fax: 617-305-1733, E-mail: grad.admission@suffolk.edu.
Website: http://www.suffolk.edu/mpa

SUNY Brockport, School of Business and Management, Department of Public Administration, Brockport, NY 14420-2997. Offers arts administration (AGC); nonprofit management (AGC); public administration (MPA), including health care management, nonprofit management, poverty studies, public management, public safety. *Accreditation:* NASPAA. *Program availability:* Part-time, evening/weekend. *Faculty:* 5 full-time (3 women), 7 part-time/adjunct (0 women). *Students:* 35 full-time (23 women), 92 part-time (56 women); includes 15 minority (10 Black or African American, non-

Hispanic/Latino; 1 Asian, non-Hispanic/Latino; 3 Hispanic/Latino; 1 Native Hawaiian or other Pacific Islander, non-Hispanic/Latino). 41 applicants, 78% accepted, 23 enrolled. In 2019, 104 master's, 6 other advanced degrees awarded. *Degree requirements:* For master's, thesis or alternative. *Entrance requirements:* For master's, GRE or minimum GPA of 3.0, letters of recommendation, statement of objectives, current resume. Additional exam requirements/recommendations for international students: required—TOEFL (minimum score 550 paper-based; 79 iBT), IELTS (minimum score 6.5). *Application deadline:* For fall admission, 8/15 priority date for domestic and international students; for spring admission, 1/15 priority date for domestic and international students; for summer admission, 4/15 priority date for domestic and international students. Application fee: $50. Electronic applications accepted. *Expenses: Tuition, area resident:* Part-time $471 per credit hour. Tuition, nonresident: part-time $963 per credit hour. *Financial support:* In 2019–20, 1 fellowship with full tuition reimbursement (averaging $7,500 per year), 1 teaching assistantship with full tuition reimbursement (averaging $6,000 per year) were awarded; Federal Work-Study, scholarships/grants, and unspecified assistantships also available. Support available to part-time students. Financial award application deadline: 3/15; financial award applicants required to submit FAFSA. *Unit head:* Dr. Wendy Wright, Graduate Director, 585-395-5570, Fax: 585-395-2172, E-mail: wwright@brockport.edu. *Application contact:* Danielle A. Welch, Graduate Admissions Counselor, 585-395-2525, Fax: 585-395-2515.
Website: https://www.brockport.edu/academics/public_administration/graduate/masters.html

Syracuse University, Maxwell School of Citizenship and Public Affairs, Dual MPA/IR Program in Public Administration and International Relations, Syracuse, NY 13244. Offers MPA/MA. *Entrance requirements:* Additional exam requirements/recommendations for international students: required—TOEFL (minimum score 100 iBT). Electronic applications accepted.

Syracuse University, Maxwell School of Citizenship and Public Affairs, EMPA Program of Public Administration, Syracuse, NY 13244. Offers EMPA. *Program availability:* Part-time. *Entrance requirements:* For master's, 7 years of mid-level professional experience, resume, personal statement, official transcripts, three letters of recommendation. Additional exam requirements/recommendations for international students: required—TOEFL (minimum score 100 iBT). Electronic applications accepted.

Syracuse University, Maxwell School of Citizenship and Public Affairs, Programs in Public Administration, Syracuse, NY 13244. Offers MPA, PhD, JD/MPA, MPA/MA. *Accreditation:* NASPAA (one or more programs are accredited). *Program availability:* Part-time. *Degree requirements:* For doctorate, comprehensive exam, thesis/dissertation. *Entrance requirements:* For master's and doctorate, GRE General Test, resume, three letters of recommendation, personal statement, official transcripts. Additional exam requirements/recommendations for international students: required—TOEFL (minimum score 100 iBT). Electronic applications accepted.

Tennessee State University, The School of Graduate Studies and Research, College of Public Service, Nashville, TN 37209-1561. Offers human resource management (MPS); public administration (MPA, PhD); social work (MSW); strategic leadership (MPS); training and development (MPS). *Accreditation:* NASPAA (one or more programs are accredited). *Program availability:* Part-time, evening/weekend. *Degree requirements:* For master's, comprehensive exam, thesis optional; for doctorate, comprehensive exam, thesis/dissertation. *Entrance requirements:* For master's, GRE General Test, minimum GPA of 2.5, writing sample; for doctorate, GRE General Test, minimum GPA of 3.25, writing sample.

Texas A&M International University, Office of Graduate Studies and Research, College of Arts and Sciences, Department of Social Sciences, Laredo, TX 78041. Offers criminal justice (MS); history and political thought (MA); public administration (MPA); sociology (MA). *Degree requirements:* For master's, comprehensive exam (for some programs), thesis (for some programs). *Entrance requirements:* For master's, GRE General Test. Additional exam requirements/recommendations for international students: required—TOEFL (minimum score 550 paper-based; 79 iBT).

Texas A&M University–Corpus Christi, College of Graduate Studies, College of Liberal Arts, Corpus Christi, TX 78412. Offers communication (MA); English (MA); history (MA); psychology (MA), including clinical psychology, general psychology; public administration (MPA); studio art (MFA). *Program availability:* Part-time, evening/weekend. *Degree requirements:* For master's, comprehensive exam (for some programs). *Entrance requirements:* For master's, portfolio. Additional exam requirements/recommendations for international students: required—TOEFL (minimum score 550 paper-based; 79 iBT), IELTS (minimum score 6.5). Electronic applications accepted.

Texas Southern University, Barbara Jordan-Mickey Leland School of Public Affairs, Program in Public Administration, Houston, TX 77004-4584. Offers MPA. *Accreditation:* NASPAA. *Degree requirements:* For master's, comprehensive exam, thesis optional. *Entrance requirements:* For master's, GRE General Test, minimum GPA of 2.5. Additional exam requirements/recommendations for international students: required—TOEFL. Electronic applications accepted.

Texas State University, The Graduate College, College of Liberal Arts, Program in Public Administration, San Marcos, TX 78666. Offers international relations (MPA); legal and judicial administration (MPA). *Accreditation:* NASPAA. *Program availability:* Part-time, evening/weekend. *Degree requirements:* For master's, comprehensive exam, applied research project. *Entrance requirements:* For master's, baccalaureate degree from regionally-accredited university with minimum GPA of 3.0 on last 60 undergraduate semester hours, statement of purpose, 2 letters of recommendation. Additional exam requirements/recommendations for international students: required—TOEFL (minimum score 550 paper-based; 78 iBT), IELTS (minimum score 6.5). Electronic applications accepted.

Texas Tech University, Graduate School, College of Arts and Sciences, Department of Political Science, Lubbock, TX 79409-1015. Offers political science (MA, PhD); public administration (MPA); JD/MPA. *Accreditation:* NASPAA (one or more programs are accredited). *Program availability:* 100% online, blended/hybrid learning, Regional sites. *Faculty:* 26 full-time (6 women), 5 part-time/adjunct (3 women). *Students:* 43 full-time (21 women), 28 part-time (15 women); includes 18 minority (4 Black or African American, non-Hispanic/Latino; 2 Asian, non-Hispanic/Latino; 10 Hispanic/Latino; 2 Two or more races, non-Hispanic/Latino), 16 international. Average age 32. 46 applicants, 74% accepted, 27 enrolled. In 2019, 22 master's awarded. *Degree requirements:* For master's, thesis or alternative; for doctorate, thesis/dissertation. *Entrance requirements:* For master's and doctorate, GRE General Test, 3 letters of reference. Additional exam requirements/recommendations for international students: required—TOEFL (minimum score 550 paper-based; 79 iBT). *Application deadline:* For fall admission, 6/1 priority date for domestic students, 1/15 priority date for international students; for spring admission, 9/1 priority date for domestic students, 6/15 priority date for international students. Applications are processed on a rolling basis. Application fee: $65. Electronic applications accepted. *Expenses:* Contact institution. *Financial support:* In 2019–20, 47 students received support, including 38 fellowships (averaging $2,581 per year), 44 teaching assistantships (averaging $12,978 per year); research assistantships, scholarships/grants, tuition waivers, and grader positions also available. Financial award

application deadline: 4/15; financial award applicants required to submit FAFSA. *Unit head:* Dr. Timothy Nokken, Associate Professor and Department Chairperson, 806-834-2988, Fax: 806-742-0850, E-mail: timothy.nokken@ttu.edu. *Application contact:* Dr. Toby Rider, Graduate Director, 806-834-8640, Fax: 806-742-0850, E-mail: toby.rider@ttu.edu.
Website: www.depts.ttu.edu/politicalscience/

Thomas Edison State University, John S. Watson School of Public Service and Continuing Studies, Trenton, NJ 08608. Offers community and economic development (MSM); environmental policy/environmental justice (MSM); homeland security (MSHS, MSM); information and technology for public service (MSM); nonprofit management (MSM); public and municipal finance (MSM); public health (MSM); public service administration and leadership (MSM); public service leadership (MPSL). *Program availability:* Part-time, online learning. *Entrance requirements:* Additional exam requirements/recommendations for international students: required—TOEFL (minimum score 550 paper-based; 79 iBT). Electronic applications accepted.

Trident University International, College of Business Administration, Program in Business Administration, Cypress, CA 90630. Offers business administration (PhD); conflict and negotiation management (MBA); criminal justice administration (MBA); entrepreneurship (MBA); finance (MBA); general management (MBA); government accounting (MBA); human resource management (MBA); information security and digital assurance management (MBA); information technology management (MBA); international business (MBA); logistics management (MBA); marketing (MBA); project management (MBA); public management (MBA); quality management (MBA); strategic leadership (MBA). *Program availability:* Part-time, evening/weekend, online learning. *Degree requirements:* For doctorate, comprehensive exam, thesis/dissertation, defense of dissertation. *Entrance requirements:* For master's, minimum GPA of 2.5 (students with GPA 3.0 or greater may transfer up to 30% of graduate level credits); for doctorate, minimum GPA of 3.4, curriculum vitae, course work in research methods or statistics. Additional exam requirements/recommendations for international students: required—TOEFL. Electronic applications accepted.

Troy University, Graduate School, College of Arts and Sciences, Program in Public Administration, Troy, AL 36082. Offers government contracting (MPA). *Accreditation:* NASPAA. *Program availability:* Part-time, evening/weekend, 100% online, blended/hybrid learning. *Faculty:* 10 full-time (6 women), 1 part-time/adjunct (0 women). *Students:* 49 full-time (35 women), 251 part-time (162 women); includes 140 minority (125 Black or African American, non-Hispanic/Latino; 2 American Indian or Alaska Native, non-Hispanic/Latino; 1 Asian, non-Hispanic/Latino; 5 Hispanic/Latino; 7 Two or more races, non-Hispanic/Latino), 5 international. Average age 35. 225 applicants, 94% accepted, 110 enrolled. In 2019, 62 master's awarded. *Degree requirements:* For master's, capstone course with minimum B grade, minimum GPA of 3.0, admission to candidacy. *Entrance requirements:* For master's, GRE 290 (recommended:150 verbal, 140 quantitative) and GRE writing score. If student has taken the MCAT (recommended: 487), DAT (recommended: 16) or equivalent professional exam, then this may be substituted for the GRE, bachelor's degree, minimum undergraduate GPA of 2.5 or 3.0 on last 30 semester hours, letter of recommendation, essay, resume. Additional exam requirements/recommendations for international students: required—TOEFL (minimum score 523 paper-based; 70 iBT), IELTS (minimum score 6). *Application deadline:* Applications are processed on a rolling basis. Application fee: $50. Electronic applications accepted. *Expenses: Tuition, area resident:* Full-time $7650; part-time $2550 per semester hour. Tuition, state resident: full-time $7650; part-time $2550 per semester hour. Tuition, nonresident: full-time $15,300; part-time $5100 per semester hour. *International tuition:* $15,300 full-time. *Required fees:* $856; $352 per semester hour. $176 per semester. *Financial support:* In 2019–20, 114 students received support. Fellowships, research assistantships, teaching assistantships, career-related internships or fieldwork, Federal Work-Study, scholarships/grants, traineeships, tuition waivers, and unspecified assistantships available. Support available to part-time students. Financial award application deadline: 3/1; financial award applicants required to submit FAFSA. *Unit head:* Dr. Terry Anderson, Associate Professor, MPA Program Director, 850-301-2144, E-mail: tanderson@troy.edu. *Application contact:* Haley McKinnon, Director of Graduate Admissions, 334-670-3178, Fax: 334-670-3733, E-mail: hmckinnon@troy.edu.
Website: https://www.troy.edu/academics/academic-programs/political-science-american-politics-public-administration.html

Tufts University, Graduate School of Arts and Sciences, Graduate Certificate Programs, Program Evaluation Program, Medford, MA 02155. Offers Certificate. *Program availability:* Part-time, evening/weekend. Electronic applications accepted. *Expenses:* Contact institution.

UNB Fredericton, School of Graduate Studies, Faculty of Business Administration, Fredericton, NB E3B 5A3, Canada. Offers business administration (MBA); engineering management (MBA); entrepreneurship (MBA); sports and recreation management (MBA); MBA/LL B. *Program availability:* Part-time. *Faculty:* 32 full-time (11 women), 7 part-time/adjunct (3 women). *Students:* 73 full-time (27 women), 23 part-time (10 women), 40 international. Average age 32. In 2019, 31 master's awarded. *Degree requirements:* For master's, thesis optional. *Entrance requirements:* For master's, GMAT (minimum score 550), minimum GPA of 3.0; 3-5 years of work experience; 3 letters of reference with at least one academic reference. Additional exam requirements/recommendations for international students: required—TOEFL (minimum score 580 paper-based; 92 iBT), IELTS (minimum score 7), TOEFL (minimum score 580 paper-based; 92 iBT) or IELTS (minimum score 7). *Application deadline:* For fall admission, 10/31 priority date for domestic and international students; for spring admission, 3/31 priority date for domestic and international students. Application fee: $50 Canadian dollars. Electronic applications accepted. *Expenses: Tuition, area resident:* Full-time $6975 Canadian dollars; part-time $3423 Canadian dollars per year. Tuition, state resident: full-time $6975 Canadian dollars; part-time $3423 Canadian dollars per year. Tuition, Canadian resident: full-time $6975 Canadian dollars; part-time $3423 Canadian dollars per year. *International tuition:* $12,435 Canadian dollars full-time. *Required fees:* $92.25 Canadian dollars per term. Full-time tuition and fees vary according to degree level, campus/location, program, reciprocity agreements and student level. *Financial support:* Fellowships, research assistantships, and teaching assistantships available. Financial award application deadline: 1/15. *Unit head:* Dr. Donglei Du, Director of Graduate Studies, 506-458-7353, Fax: 506-453-3561, E-mail: ddu@unb.ca. *Application contact:* Marilyn Davis, Acting Graduate Secretary, 506-453-4766, Fax: 506-453-3561, E-mail: mbacontact@unb.ca.
Website: http://go.unb.ca/gradprograms

Université de Moncton, Faculty of Arts and Social Sciences, Department of Public Administration, Moncton, NB E1A 3E9, Canada. Offers MPA, LL B/MPA. *Program availability:* Part-time, evening/weekend. *Degree requirements:* For master's, one foreign language. *Entrance requirements:* For master's, minimum GPA of 3.0.

Université de Sherbrooke, Faculty of Administration, Program in Public Management, Sherbrooke, QC J1K 2R1, Canada. Offers M Adm. *Degree requirements:* For master's, one foreign language, thesis. *Entrance requirements:* For master's, bachelor's degree in related field, minimum GPA of 3.0 (on 4.3 scale). Electronic applications accepted.

Public Administration

Université du Québec à Montréal, Graduate Programs, Program in Urban Analysis and Management, Montréal, QC H3C 3P8, Canada. Offers MA. *Program availability:* Part-time. *Entrance requirements:* For master's, appropriate bachelor's degree or equivalent and proficiency in French.

Université du Québec, École nationale d'administration publique, Graduate Programs in Public Administration, Diploma Program in Public Administration, Quebec, QC G1K 9E5, Canada. Offers Diploma.

Université du Québec, École nationale d'administration publique, Graduate Programs in Public Administration, Doctorate Program in Public Administration, Quebec, QC G1K 9E5, Canada. Offers PhD.

University at Albany, State University of New York, Nelson A. Rockefeller College of Public Affairs and Policy, Department of Public Administration and Policy, Albany, NY 12222-0001. Offers financial management and public economics (MPA); financial market regulation (MPA); health policy (MPA); healthcare management (MPA); homeland security (MPA); human resources management (MPA); information strategy and management (MPA); local government management (MPA); nonprofit management (MPA); nonprofit management and leadership (Certificate); organizational behavior and theory (MPA, PhD); planning and policy analysis (CAS); policy analysis (MPA); politics and administration (PhD); public finance (PhD); public management (PhD); public policy (PhD); public sector management (Certificate); women and public policy (Certificate); JD/MPA. *Accreditation:* NASPAA (one or more programs are accredited). *Program availability:* Blended/hybrid learning. *Faculty:* 19 full-time (8 women), 12 part-time/adjunct (4 women). *Students:* 119 full-time (71 women), 41 part-time (4 women); includes 45 minority (18 Black or African American, non-Hispanic/Latino; 7 Asian, non-Hispanic/Latino; 14 Hispanic/Latino; 6 Two or more races, non-Hispanic/Latino), 28 international. Average age 29. 172 applicants, 81% accepted, 85 enrolled. In 2019, 57 master's, 6 doctorates, 11 other advanced degrees awarded. *Degree requirements:* For doctorate, one foreign language, thesis/dissertation. *Entrance requirements:* For doctorate, GRE General Test. Additional exam requirements/recommendations for international students: required—TOEFL (minimum score 550 paper-based). *Application deadline:* For fall admission, 1/15 priority date for domestic students, 5/1 for international students; for spring admission, 11/15 for domestic students. Applications are processed on a rolling basis. Application fee: $75. Electronic applications accepted. *Expenses: Tuition, area resident:* Full-time $11,530; part-time $480 per credit hour. *Tuition, nonresident:* full-time $23,530; part-time $980 per credit hour. *International tuition:* $23,530 full-time. *Required fees:* $2185; $96 per credit hour. Part-time tuition and fees vary according to course load and program. *Financial support:* Research assistantships, teaching assistantships, and Federal Work-Study available. Financial award application deadline: 2/1. *Unit head:* Edmund Stazyk, Chair, 518-591-8723, E-mail: estazyk@albany.edu. *Application contact:* Luis Felipe Luna-Reyes, 518-442-5297, E-mail: llunareyes@albany.edu.
Website: http://www.albany.edu/rockefeller/pad.shtml

The University of Akron, Graduate School, Buchtel College of Arts and Sciences, Department of Public Administration and Urban Studies, Program in Public Administration, Akron, OH 44325. Offers MPA, JD/MPA. *Entrance requirements:* For master's, GRE, GMAT, LSAT, MAT (if undergraduate cumulative GPA less than 3.0), minimum GPA of 3.0, resume, one-page personal essay, three letters of recommendation. Additional exam requirements/recommendations for international students: required—TOEFL (minimum score 79 iBT). Electronic applications accepted.

The University of Alabama, Graduate School, College of Arts and Sciences, Department of Political Science, Tuscaloosa, AL 35487. Offers political science (MA, PhD); public administration (MPA). *Program availability:* Part-time. *Faculty:* 20 full-time (5 women). *Students:* 50 full-time (20 women), 4 part-time (3 women); includes 14 minority (10 Black or African American, non-Hispanic/Latino; 2 American Indian or Alaska Native, non-Hispanic/Latino; 1 Asian, non-Hispanic/Latino; 1 Two or more races, non-Hispanic/Latino), 7 international. Average age 29. 37 applicants, 73% accepted, 15 enrolled. In 2019, 21 master's, 5 doctorates awarded. Terminal master's awarded for partial completion of doctoral program. *Degree requirements:* For master's, comprehensive exam, thesis optional; for doctorate, comprehensive exam, thesis/dissertation. *Entrance requirements:* For master's and doctorate, GRE, minimum undergraduate GPA of 3.0. Additional exam requirements/recommendations for international students: required—TOEFL. *Application deadline:* For fall admission, 6/30 for domestic and international students; for spring admission, 10/15 for domestic and international students. Applications are processed on a rolling basis. Application fee: $50 ($60 for international students). Electronic applications accepted. *Expenses: Tuition, area resident:* Full-time $10,780; part-time $440 per credit hour. *Tuition, nonresident:* full-time $30,250; part-time $1550 per credit hour. *Financial support:* In 2019–20, 19 students received support, including fellowships with full tuition reimbursements available (averaging $15,000 per year), teaching assistantships with full tuition reimbursements available (averaging $12,500 per year); career-related internships or fieldwork and Federal Work-Study also available. Financial award application deadline: 2/15; financial award applicants required to submit FAFSA. *Unit head:* Dr. Joseph Smith, Chair and Professor, 205-348-5981, E-mail: josmith@bama.ua.edu. *Application contact:* Dr. Holger Albrecht, Associate Professor and Director of Graduate Studies, 205-348-5528, Fax: 205-348-5298, E-mail: halbrecht@ua.edu.
Website: http://www.as.ua.edu/psc/

The University of Alabama at Birmingham, College of Arts and Sciences, Master of Public Administration Program, Birmingham, AL 35294. Offers MPA, MPA/JD, MPA/MPH, MPA/MSCJ. *Accreditation:* NASPAA (one or more programs are accredited). *Program availability:* Part-time, evening/weekend, 100% online, blended/hybrid learning. *Faculty:* 7 full-time (3 women), 1 (woman) part-time/adjunct. *Students:* 46 full-time (28 women), 19 part-time (11 women); includes 21 minority (16 Black or African American, non-Hispanic/Latino; 1 American Indian or Alaska Native, non-Hispanic/Latino; 1 Asian, non-Hispanic/Latino; 1 Hispanic/Latino; 2 Two or more races, non-Hispanic/Latino), 5 international. Average age 32. 36 applicants, 69% accepted, 13 enrolled. In 2019, 50 master's awarded. *Degree requirements:* For master's, portfolio or thesis. *Entrance requirements:* For master's, GRE General Test (preferred), references. Additional exam requirements/recommendations for international students: required—TOEFL (minimum score 500 paper-based; 70 iBT), IELTS (minimum score 6.5). *Application deadline:* For fall admission, 7/1 for domestic students; for spring admission, 11/1 for domestic students. Applications are processed on a rolling basis. Application fee: $45 ($60 for international students). Electronic applications accepted. *Expenses:* Contact institution. *Financial support:* In 2019–20, 4 students received support, including 4 research assistantships with partial tuition reimbursements available (averaging $12,000 per year); career-related internships or fieldwork, scholarships/grants, and unspecified assistantships also available. Financial award application deadline: 4/15. *Unit head:* Dr. Akhlaque Haque, Program Director, 205-934-4653, Fax: 205-975-5712, E-mail: mpa@uab.edu. *Application contact:* Carin C. Mayo, MPA Program Coordinator, 205-975-3413, Fax: 205-975-5712, E-mail: mpa@uab.edu.
Website: http://www.uab.edu/cas/government/graduate-program

University of Alaska Anchorage, College of Business and Public Policy, Program in Public Administration, Anchorage, AK 99508. Offers MPA. *Program availability:* Part-

time. *Degree requirements:* For master's, comprehensive exam, thesis or alternative, capstone project. *Entrance requirements:* For master's, GRE General Test. Additional exam requirements/recommendations for international students: required—TOEFL (minimum score 550 paper-based).

University of Alaska Southeast, Graduate Programs, Program in Public Administration, Juneau, AK 99801. Offers MPA. *Program availability:* Part-time, evening/weekend, online learning. *Degree requirements:* For master's, capstone course or thesis. *Entrance requirements:* For master's, minimum GPA of 3.0, resume or curriculum vitae, three letters of reference. Additional exam requirements/recommendations for international students: recommended—TOEFL. Electronic applications accepted.

The University of Arizona, College of Social and Behavioral Sciences, Program in Public Administration, Tucson, AZ 85721. Offers public administration (MPA); public administration and policy (PhD). *Accreditation:* NASPAA. *Degree requirements:* For master's, internship of 400 hours; for doctorate, comprehensive exam, thesis/dissertation. *Entrance requirements:* For doctorate, GMAT or GRE, minimum graduate GPA of 3.5, letter of interest, 3 letters of recommendation, resume. Additional exam requirements/recommendations for international students: required—TOEFL (minimum score 650 paper-based; 115 iBT). Electronic applications accepted. *Expenses:* Contact institution.

University of Arkansas, Graduate School, J. William Fulbright College of Arts and Sciences, Department of Political Science, Program in Public Administration, Fayetteville, AR 72701. Offers MPA. *Students:* 11 full-time (8 women), 4 part-time (all women); includes 3 minority (1 Black or African American, non-Hispanic/Latino; 1 Hispanic/Latino; 1 Two or more races, non-Hispanic/Latino), 2 international. 12 applicants, 100% accepted. In 2019, 4 master's awarded. *Degree requirements:* For master's, comprehensive exam, thesis or alternative. *Entrance requirements:* For master's, GRE General Test. *Application deadline:* For fall admission, 8/1 for domestic students, 4/1 for international students; for spring admission, 12/1 for domestic students, 10/1 for international students; for summer admission, 4/15 for domestic students, 3/1 for international students. Applications are processed on a rolling basis. Application fee: $60. Electronic applications accepted. *Financial support:* In 2019–20, 2 research assistantships, 1 teaching assistantship were awarded; fellowships with tuition reimbursements, career-related internships or fieldwork, and Federal Work-Study also available. Support available to part-time students. Financial award application deadline: 4/1; financial award applicants required to submit FAFSA. *Unit head:* Dr. William Schreckhise, Department Chair, 479-575-7695, E-mail: schreckw@uark.edu. *Application contact:* Dr. Patrick Conge, Graduate Coordinator, 479-575-6443, E-mail: pconge@uark.edu.
Website: https://fulbright.uark.edu/departments/political-science/

University of Arkansas at Little Rock, Graduate School, College of Social Sciences and Communication, Program in Public Administration, Little Rock, AR 72204-1099. Offers MPA. *Accreditation:* NASPAA. *Program availability:* Part-time, evening/weekend. *Degree requirements:* For master's, comprehensive exam. *Entrance requirements:* For master's, GRE General Test or MAT, minimum GPA of 2.7.

University of Baltimore, Graduate School, College of Public Affairs, Doctoral Program in Public Administration, Baltimore, MD 21201-5779. Offers DPA. *Program availability:* Part-time, evening/weekend. *Degree requirements:* For doctorate, thesis/dissertation. *Entrance requirements:* For doctorate, GRE. Additional exam requirements/recommendations for international students: required—TOEFL.

University of Baltimore, Graduate School, College of Public Affairs, Master's Program in Public Administration, Baltimore, MD 21201-5779. Offers MPA, JD/MPA. *Accreditation:* NASPAA. *Program availability:* Part-time, evening/weekend, online learning. *Entrance requirements:* For master's, interview, minimum GPA of 3.0. Additional exam requirements/recommendations for international students: required—TOEFL (minimum score 550 paper-based). Electronic applications accepted. *Expenses:* Contact institution.

University of Central Florida, College of Community Innovation and Education, School of Public Administration, Orlando, FL 32816. Offers emergency management and homeland security (Certificate); fundraising (Certificate); nonprofit management (MNM, Certificate); public administration (MPA); research administration (MRA); urban and regional planning (MS). *Accreditation:* NASPAA. *Program availability:* Part-time, evening/weekend. *Students:* 149 full-time (95 women), 497 part-time (347 women); includes 277 minority (128 Black or African American, non-Hispanic/Latino; 1 American Indian or Alaska Native, non-Hispanic/Latino; 13 Asian, non-Hispanic/Latino; 118 Hispanic/Latino; 1 Native Hawaiian or other Pacific Islander, non-Hispanic/Latino; 16 Two or more races, non-Hispanic/Latino), 9 international. Average age 33. 430 applicants, 79% accepted, 226 enrolled. In 2019, 106 master's, 26 other advanced degrees awarded. *Degree requirements:* For master's, comprehensive exam, thesis or alternative, research report. *Entrance requirements:* For master's, letters of recommendation, goal statement, resume. Additional exam requirements/recommendations for international students: required—TOEFL. *Application deadline:* For fall admission, 6/15 for domestic students; for spring admission, 11/1 for domestic students. Application fee: $30. Electronic applications accepted. *Financial support:* In 2019–20, 6 students received support, including 1 fellowship with partial tuition reimbursement available (averaging $5,000 per year), 4 research assistantships with partial tuition reimbursements available (averaging $6,049 per year), 1 teaching assistantship with partial tuition reimbursement available (averaging $5,478 per year); career-related internships or fieldwork, Federal Work-Study, institutionally sponsored loans, health care benefits, tuition waivers (partial), and unspecified assistantships also available. Financial award application deadline: 3/1; financial award applicants required to submit FAFSA. *Unit head:* Dr. Naim Kapucu, Director, 407-823-6096, Fax: 407-823-5651, E-mail: kapucu@ucf.edu. *Application contact:* Associate Director, Graduate Admissions, 407-823-2766, Fax: 407-823-6442, E-mail: gradadmissions@ucf.edu.
Website: https://www.cohpa.ucf.edu/publicadmin/

University of Central Oklahoma, The Jackson College of Graduate Studies, College of Liberal Arts, Department of Political Science, Edmond, OK 73034-5209. Offers political science (MA), including international affairs; public administration (MPA), including public and nonprofit management, urban management. *Program availability:* Part-time. *Degree requirements:* For master's, comprehensive exam (for some programs), thesis (for some programs). *Entrance requirements:* For master's, 18 undergraduate hours in political science. Additional exam requirements/recommendations for international students: required—TOEFL (minimum score 550 paper-based; 79 iBT), IELTS (minimum score 6.5). Electronic applications accepted.

University of Colorado Colorado Springs, School of Public Affairs, Colorado Springs, CO 80918. Offers criminal justice (MCJ); public administration (MPA). *Accreditation:* NASPAA. *Program availability:* Part-time, evening/weekend, 100% online, blended/hybrid learning. *Faculty:* 22 full-time (12 women), 20 part-time/adjunct (10 women). *Students:* 28 full-time (18 women), 194 part-time (127 women); includes 87 minority (19 Black or African American, non-Hispanic/Latino; 4 American Indian or Alaska Native, non-Hispanic/Latino; 6 Asian, non-Hispanic/Latino; 48 Hispanic/Latino; 10 Two or more races, non-Hispanic/Latino), 4 international. Average age 34. 89 applicants, 83% accepted, 58 enrolled. In 2019, 38 master's awarded. *Degree requirements:* For master's, internship, capstone project, or thesis. *Entrance requirements:* For master's, 2 professional and/or academic recommendations by qualified references that establish the applicant's personal qualifications for graduate work; 3.00 (or better) undergraduate GPA for regular admission into the MPA program; current resume; statement of goals (prompts given within the application). Additional exam requirements/recommendations for international students: recommended—TOEFL (minimum score 80 iBT), IELTS (minimum score 6.5). *Application deadline:* Applications are processed on a rolling basis. Application fee: $60 ($100 for international students). Electronic applications accepted. *Expenses:* Contact institution. *Financial support:* In 2019–20, 35 students received support. Career-related internships or fieldwork, Federal Work-Study, scholarships/grants, and tuition waivers available. Support available to part-time students. Financial award application deadline: 3/1; financial award applicants required to submit FAFSA. *Unit head:* Dr. George Reed, Dean, 719-255-4109, E-mail: george.reed@uccs.edu. *Application contact:* Stephani Hosain, Graduate Student Services Specialist, 719-255-4993, E-mail: shosain@uccs.edu. Website: https://www.uccs.edu/spa/

University of Colorado Denver, School of Public Affairs, Program in Public Affairs and Administration, Denver, CO 80127. Offers public administration (MPA), including domestic violence, emergency management and homeland security, environmental policy, management and law, homeland security and defense, local government, nonprofit management, public administration; public affairs (PhD). *Accreditation:* NASPAA. *Program availability:* Part-time, evening/weekend, online learning. Tuition and fees vary according to course load, program and reciprocity agreements.

University of Connecticut, Graduate School, College of Liberal Arts and Sciences, Department of Public Policy, Field of Public Administration, Storrs, CT 06269. Offers MPA. *Accreditation:* NASPAA. *Degree requirements:* For master's, comprehensive exam, internship. *Entrance requirements:* For master's, GRE General Test. Additional exam requirements/recommendations for international students: required—TOEFL (minimum score 550 paper-based). Electronic applications accepted.

University of Dayton, Master of Public Administration Program, Dayton, OH 45469. Offers MPA. *Accreditation:* NASPAA. *Program availability:* Part-time, evening/weekend. *Degree requirements:* For master's, internship or public service project. *Entrance requirements:* For master's, GRE. Additional exam requirements/recommendations for international students: required—TOEFL (minimum score 550 paper-based; 80 iBT). Electronic applications accepted. *Expenses:* Contact institution.

University of Delaware, College of Arts and Sciences, School of Public Policy and Administration, Program in Public Administration, Newark, DE 19716. Offers MPA. *Accreditation:* NASPAA. *Program availability:* Part-time, evening/weekend. *Degree requirements:* For master's, internship or thesis. *Entrance requirements:* For master's, GRE General Test. Additional exam requirements/recommendations for international students: required—TOEFL. Electronic applications accepted.

University of Evansville, Center for Adult Education, Evansville, IN 47722. Offers public service administration (MS). *Program availability:* Part-time, evening/weekend. *Entrance requirements:* For master's, GRE or MAT, minimum undergraduate GPA of 3.0, resume, minimum of 3 years' work experience, 2 letters of reference. Additional exam requirements/recommendations for international students: required—TOEFL (minimum score 79 iBT), IELTS (minimum score 6.5). *Expenses:* Contact institution.

The University of Findlay, Office of Graduate Admissions, Findlay, OH 45840. Offers applied security and analytics (MSAS); athletic training (MAT); business (MBA), including certified management accountant, certified public accountant, health care management, hospitality management; education (MA Ed, Ed D), including children's literature (MA Ed), curriculum and teaching (MA Ed), education (MA Ed), educational administration (MA Ed), human resource development (MA Ed), mathematics (MA Ed), reading (MA Ed), science education (MA Ed), superintendent (Ed D), teaching (Ed D), technology (MA Ed); environmental, safety, and health management (MSEM); health informatics (MS); occupational therapy (MOT); pharmacy (Pharm D); physical therapy (DPT); physician assistant (MPA); rhetoric and writing (MA); teaching English to speakers of other languages (TESOL) and applied linguistics (MA). *Program availability:* Part-time, evening/weekend, 100% online, blended/hybrid learning. *Students:* 688 full-time (430 women), 553 part-time (308 women), 170 international. Average age 28. 865 applicants, 31% accepted, 235 enrolled. In 2019, 363 master's, 141 doctorates awarded. *Degree requirements:* For master's, comprehensive exam (for some programs), thesis (for some programs), cumulative project, capstone project; for doctorate, thesis/dissertation (for some programs). *Entrance requirements:* For master's, GRE/GMAT, bachelor's degree from accredited institution, minimum undergraduate GPA of 2.5 in last 64 hours of course work; for doctorate, GRE, MAT, minimum cumulative GPA of 3.0. Additional exam requirements/recommendations for international students: required—TOEFL (minimum score 79 iBT), IELTS (minimum score 7), PTE (minimum score 61). *Application deadline:* Applications are processed on a rolling basis. Electronic applications accepted. *Financial support:* In 2019–20, 10 research assistantships with partial tuition reimbursements (averaging $7,200 per year), 35 teaching assistantships with partial tuition reimbursements (averaging $7,200 per year) were awarded; Federal Work-Study, institutionally sponsored loans, and unspecified assistantships also available. Financial award applicants required to submit FAFSA. *Unit head:* Dave M. Emsweller, Director of Admissions, Interim, 419-434-4578, E-mail: emsweller@findlay.edu. *Application contact:* Amber Feehan, Graduate Admissions Counselor, 419-434-6933, Fax: 419-434-4898, E-mail: feehan@findlay.edu. Website: http://www.findlay.edu/admissions/graduate/Pages/default.aspx

University of Georgia, School of Public and International Affairs, Department of Public Administration and Policy, Athens, GA 30602. Offers public administration (MPA, PhD). *Accreditation:* NASPAA (one or more programs are accredited). *Degree requirements:* For master's, internship; for doctorate, thesis/dissertation. *Entrance requirements:* For master's and doctorate, GRE General Test. Electronic applications accepted.

University of Guam, Office of Graduate Studies, School of Business and Public Administration, Public Administration Program, Mangilao, GU 96923. Offers MPA. *Entrance requirements:* For master's, GRE General Test. Additional exam requirements/recommendations for international students: required—TOEFL.

University of Guelph, Office of Graduate and Postdoctoral Studies, College of Social and Applied Human Sciences, Department of Political Science, Guelph, ON N1G 2W1, Canada. Offers comparative politics (MA); international development (MA); political science (MA); public policy and public administration (MA); the Americas (Canada emphasis) (MA). *Degree requirements:* For master's, thesis or paper. *Entrance requirements:* For master's, minimum B average during previous 2 years of course work, 4 year Honours Degree in Political Science. Additional exam requirements/recommendations for international students: required—TOEFL. Electronic applications accepted.

University of Hawaii at Manoa, Office of Graduate Education, College of Social Sciences, Department of Public Administration, Honolulu, HI 96822. Offers MPA, Graduate Certificate. *Program availability:* Part-time. *Degree requirements:* For master's, thesis optional, practicum. *Entrance requirements:* Additional exam requirements/recommendations for international students: required—TOEFL (minimum score 540 paper-based; 76 iBT), IELTS (minimum score 5).

University of Houston, College of Liberal Arts and Social Sciences, Department of Political Science, Houston, TX 77204. Offers political science (MA, PhD); public administration (MA). *Program availability:* Part-time. Terminal master's awarded for partial completion of doctoral program. *Degree requirements:* For master's, thesis optional; for doctorate, thesis/dissertation. *Entrance requirements:* For master's and doctorate, GRE. Additional exam requirements/recommendations for international students: required—TOEFL (minimum score 550 paper-based; 79 iBT).

University of Idaho, College of Graduate Studies, College of Letters, Arts and Social Sciences, Department of Politics and Philosophy, Moscow, ID 83844-2282. Offers political science (MA, PhD); public administration (MPA). *Faculty:* 5 full-time. *Students:* 25 full-time (13 women), 21 part-time (12 women). Average age 32. In 2019, 10 master's awarded. *Entrance requirements:* For master's, minimum GPA of 3.0. Additional exam requirements/recommendations for international students: required—TOEFL (minimum score 96 iBT). *Expenses:* Tuition, state resident: full-time $7753.80; part-time $502 per credit hour. Tuition, nonresident: full-time $26,990; part-time $1571 per credit hour. *Required fees:* $2122.20; $47 per credit hour. *Unit head:* Dr. Graham Hubbs, Chair, 208-885-6328, E-mail: politics-and-philosophy@uidaho.edu. *Application contact:* Dr. Graham Hubbs, Chair, 208-885-6328, E-mail: politics-and-philosophy@uidaho.edu. Website: https://www.uidaho.edu/class/politics-and-philosophy

University of Illinois at Chicago, College of Urban Planning and Public Affairs, Department of Public Administration, Chicago, IL 60607-7128. Offers MPA, PhD. *Accreditation:* NASPAA (one or more programs are accredited). *Program availability:* Part-time, evening/weekend. Terminal master's awarded for partial completion of doctoral program. *Degree requirements:* For master's, internship/project. *Entrance requirements:* For master's, GRE General Test, minimum GPA of 3.0. Additional exam requirements/recommendations for international students: required—TOEFL. Electronic applications accepted. *Expenses:* Contact institution.

University of Illinois at Springfield, Graduate Programs, College of Public Affairs and Administration, Program in Public Administration, Springfield, IL 62703-5407. Offers MPA, DPA, Graduate Certificate. *Accreditation:* NASPAA. *Program availability:* Part-time, 100% online, blended/hybrid learning. *Faculty:* 11 full-time (3 women), 6 part-time/adjunct (2 women). *Students:* 56 full-time (30 women), 176 part-time (85 women); includes 66 minority (49 Black or African American, non-Hispanic/Latino; 5 Asian, non-Hispanic/Latino; 11 Hispanic/Latino; 1 Two or more races, non-Hispanic/Latino), 7 international. Average age 37. 146 applicants, 56% accepted, 36 enrolled. In 2019, 71 master's, 13 other advanced degrees awarded. *Degree requirements:* For master's, capstone seminar; for doctorate, comprehensive exam, thesis/dissertation. *Entrance requirements:* For master's, minimum undergraduate GPA of 2.5; completion of prerequisites that include undergraduate coursework in political science in American national government, microeconomics or a market-based economics survey course, basic statistics, and competence in one computer spreadsheet application package; resume; career goals statement; writing skills; for doctorate, GRE, master's degree with minimum GPA of 3.25; educational and professional goals statement of at least 600 words, including possible research interest; evidence of significant work experience in public affairs field; at least one sample of professional writing sample; current vitae; 3 letters of recommendation. Additional exam requirements/recommendations for international students: required—TOEFL (minimum score 550 paper-based). *Application deadline:* Applications are processed on a rolling basis. Application fee: $60 ($75 for international students). Electronic applications accepted. *Expenses:* $90.75 per credit hour for online MPA students and $80.75 per credit hour for onground DPA students (online DPA program is not offered) (differential tuitions on top of the $33.25 per credit hour online fee). *Financial support:* In 2019–20, research assistantships with full tuition reimbursements (averaging $10,562 per year), teaching assistantships with full tuition reimbursements (averaging $10,652 per year) were awarded; fellowships, career-related internships or fieldwork, Federal Work-Study, scholarships/grants, health care benefits, and unspecified assistantships also available. Support available to part-time students. Financial award application deadline: 11/15; financial award applicants required to submit FAFSA. *Unit head:* Dr. Robert Blankenberger, Program Administrator, 217-206-8327, E-mail: rblan2@uis.edu. *Application contact:* Dr. Robert Blankenberger, Program Administrator, 217-206-8327, E-mail: rblan2@uis.edu. Website: http://www.uis.edu/publicadministration/

University of Kentucky, Graduate School, Martin School of Public Policy and Administration, Lexington, KY 40506-0027. Offers public administration (MPA); public financial management (MPFM, Graduate Certificate); public policy (MPP); public policy and administration (PhD). *Accreditation:* NASPAA (one or more programs are accredited). *Program availability:* Part-time, evening/weekend, 100% online. Terminal master's awarded for partial completion of doctoral program. *Degree requirements:* For master's, thesis; for doctorate, comprehensive exam, thesis/dissertation. *Entrance requirements:* For master's, GMAT or GRE General Test, minimum undergraduate GPA of 2.75; for doctorate, GMAT or GRE General Test, minimum graduate GPA of 3.0. Additional exam requirements/recommendations for international students: required—TOEFL (minimum score 550 paper-based; 79 iBT); recommended—IELTS (minimum score 6.5). Electronic applications accepted. *Expenses:* Contact institution.

University of La Verne, College of Business and Public Management, Doctoral Program in Public Administration, La Verne, CA 91750-4443. Offers DPA. *Program availability:* Part-time. *Degree requirements:* For doctorate, thesis/dissertation. *Entrance requirements:* For doctorate, MAT, GMAT or GRE, minimum undergraduate GPA of 3.25, interview, 3 letters of recommendation, statement of purpose. Additional exam requirements/recommendations for international students: required—TOEFL (minimum score 550 paper-based). *Expenses:* Contact institution.

University of La Verne, College of Business and Public Management, Master's Program in Public Administration, La Verne, CA 91750-4443. Offers gerontology (MPA); nonprofit (MPA); public health (MPA); urban management and affairs (MPA). *Accreditation:* NASPAA. *Program availability:* Part-time. *Entrance requirements:* For master's, minimum undergraduate GPA of 3.0, statement of purpose, 2 letters of recommendation, resume. Additional exam requirements/recommendations for international students: required—TOEFL (minimum score 550 paper-based). *Expenses:* Contact institution.

University of Louisiana at Monroe, Graduate School, College of Business and Social Sciences, Program in Public Administration, Monroe, LA 71209-0001. Offers MPA. *Program availability:* Part-time, evening/weekend, online learning. *Faculty:* 4 full-time (1 woman), 1 part-time/adjunct (0 women). *Students:* 17 full-time (8 women), 56 part-time (35 women); includes 37 minority (29 Black or African American, non-Hispanic/Latino; 3 Asian, non-Hispanic/Latino; 3 Hispanic/Latino; 2 Two or more races, non-Hispanic/Latino), 1 international. Average age 29. 42 applicants, 71% accepted, 23 enrolled. In 2019, 22 master's awarded. *Entrance requirements:* For master's, GRE General Test, minimum undergraduate GPA of 2.5. Additional exam requirements/recommendations for international students: required—TOEFL (minimum score 500 paper-based; 61 iBT); recommended—IELTS (minimum score 5.5). *Application deadline:* For fall admission, 8/1 for domestic students, 6/1 for international students; for spring admission, 1/1 for domestic students, 11/1 for international students; for summer admission, 6/1 for domestic students, 3/1 for international students. Applications are processed on a rolling basis. Application fee: $40. Electronic applications accepted. *Expenses:* Tuition, area

resident: Full-time $6489. Tuition, state resident: full-time $6489. Tuition, nonresident: full-time $18,989. *Required fees:* $2748. Tuition and fees vary according to course load and program. *Financial support:* In 2019–20, 46 students received support. Career-related internships or fieldwork, Federal Work-Study, scholarships/grants, and unspecified assistantships available. Financial award application deadline: 2/15; financial award applicants required to submit FAFSA. *Unit head:* Dr. Leigh Hersey, Program Coordinator, 318-342-1332, E-mail: hersey@ulm.edu. *Application contact:* Dr. Leigh Hersey, Program Coordinator, 318-342-1332, E-mail: hersey@ulm.edu.
Website: http://www.ulm.edu/onlinedegrees/m_pa.html

University of Louisville, Graduate School, College of Arts and Sciences, Department of Urban and Public Affairs, Louisville, KY 40208. Offers public administration (MPA), including human resources management, non-profit management, public policy and administration; urban and public affairs (PhD), including urban planning and development, urban policy and administration; urban planning (MUP), including administration of planning organizations, housing and community development, land use and environmental planning, spatial analysis. *Program availability:* Part-time, evening/weekend. *Faculty:* 13 full-time (6 women), 2 part-time/adjunct (1 woman). *Students:* 44 full-time (24 women), 24 part-time (14 women); includes 12 minority (6 Black or African American, non-Hispanic/Latino; 2 Hispanic/Latino; 4 Two or more races, non-Hispanic/Latino), 7 international. Average age 34. 51 applicants, 67% accepted, 25 enrolled. In 2019, 14 master's, 3 doctorates awarded. Terminal master's awarded for partial completion of doctoral program. *Degree requirements:* For master's, internship; for doctorate, comprehensive exam, thesis/dissertation. *Entrance requirements:* For master's, GRE General Test, 2 letters of reference, official transcripts. Minimum GPA of 3.0; for doctorate, GRE General Test, Two letters of reference, official transcripts. Masters degree in appropriate field. Additional exam requirements/recommendations for international students: required—TOEFL (minimum score 550 paper-based; 79 iBT), IELTS can be used in place of the TOEFL; recommended—IELTS (minimum score 6.5). *Application deadline:* For fall admission, 2/1 for domestic and international students. Applications are processed on a rolling basis. Application fee: $65. Electronic applications accepted. *Expenses: Tuition, area resident:* Full-time $13,000; part-time $723 per credit hour. Tuition, state resident: full-time $13,000; part-time $723 per credit hour. Tuition, nonresident: full-time $27,114; part-time $1507 per credit hour. *International tuition:* $27,114 full-time. *Required fees:* $196. Tuition and fees vary according to program and reciprocity agreements. *Financial support:* In 2019–20, 29 students received support, including 11 research assistantships with full tuition reimbursements available (averaging $19,000 per year); fellowships, teaching assistantships, health care benefits, and unspecified assistantships also available. Financial award application deadline: 2/1. *Unit head:* Dr. David Simpson, Professor/Chair, 502-852-8019, Fax: 502-852-4558, E-mail: dave.simpson@louisville.edu.
Website: http://supa.louisville.edu

University of Management and Technology, Program in Public Administration, Arlington, VA 22209-1609. Offers MPA, Advanced Certificate. *Expenses: Tuition:* Full-time $7020; part-time $390 per credit hour. *Required fees:* $90; $30 per semester.

University of Manitoba, Faculty of Graduate Studies, Faculty of Arts, Department of Political Studies, Program in Public Administration, Winnipeg, MB R3T 2N2, Canada. Offers MPA. *Degree requirements:* For master's, thesis or alternative.

University of Maryland, College Park, Academic Affairs, Joint Program in Business and Management/Public Policy, College Park, MD 20742. Offers MBA/MPM. *Accreditation:* AACSB. Electronic applications accepted.

University of Maryland, College Park, Academic Affairs, School of Public Policy, Joint Program in Public Policy/Law, College Park, MD 20742. Offers JD/MPM. Electronic applications accepted.

University of Maryland, College Park, Academic Affairs, School of Public Policy, Public Management Program, College Park, MD 20742. Offers MPM. *Degree requirements:* For master's, internship. *Entrance requirements:* For master's, GRE General Test, minimum GPA of 3.0. Additional exam requirements/recommendations for international students: required—TOEFL. Electronic applications accepted.

University of Massachusetts Amherst, Graduate School, College of Social and Behavioral Sciences, Center for Public Policy and Administration, Amherst, MA 01003. Offers MPP, MPPA, MPH/MPPA, MPPA/M Ed, MPPA/MBA, MRP/MPPA. *Program availability:* Part-time. *Degree requirements:* For master's, thesis or alternative. *Entrance requirements:* For master's, GRE General Test. Additional exam requirements/recommendations for international students: required—TOEFL (minimum score 550 paper-based; 80 iBT), IELTS (minimum score 6.5). Electronic applications accepted.

University of Massachusetts Amherst, Graduate School, Interdisciplinary Programs, Dual Degree Program in Education and Public Policy and Administration, Amherst, MA 01003. Offers MPPA/M Ed. *Entrance requirements:* Additional exam requirements/recommendations for international students: required—TOEFL (minimum score 550 paper-based; 80 iBT), IELTS (minimum score 6.5). Electronic applications accepted.

University of Massachusetts Amherst, Graduate School, Interdisciplinary Programs, Dual Degree Program in Management and Public Policy and Administration, Amherst, MA 01003. Offers MPPA/MBA. *Accreditation:* AACSB. *Program availability:* Part-time. *Entrance requirements:* Additional exam requirements/recommendations for international students: required—TOEFL (minimum score 600 paper-based; 100 iBT), IELTS (minimum score 7). Electronic applications accepted.

University of Massachusetts Amherst, Graduate School, Interdisciplinary Programs, Dual Degree Program in Public Policy and Administration and Public Health, Amherst, MA 01003. Offers MPH/MPPA. *Entrance requirements:* Additional exam requirements/recommendations for international students: required—TOEFL (minimum score 550 paper-based; 80 iBT), IELTS (minimum score 6.5). Electronic applications accepted.

University of Massachusetts Amherst, Graduate School, Interdisciplinary Programs, Dual Degree Program in Regional Planning and Public Policy and Administration, Amherst, MA 01003. Offers MPPA/MRP. *Entrance requirements:* Additional exam requirements/recommendations for international students: required—TOEFL (minimum score 550 paper-based; 80 iBT), IELTS (minimum score 6.5). Electronic applications accepted.

University of Massachusetts Boston, McCormack Graduate School of Policy and Global Studies, Program in Global Comparative Public Administration, Boston, MA 02125-3393. Offers MPA. *Program availability:* Online learning.

University of Massachusetts Boston, McCormack Graduate School of Policy and Global Studies, Program in Public Administration, Boston, MA 02125-3393. Offers MPA. *Program availability:* Part-time, evening/weekend. *Entrance requirements:* For master's, GRE General Test or MAT, minimum GPA of 2.75.

University of Massachusetts Dartmouth, Graduate School, College of Arts and Sciences, Department of Public Policy, North Dartmouth, MA 02747-2300. Offers educational policy (Graduate Certificate); environmental policy (Graduate Certificate); public management (Graduate Certificate); public policy (MPP). *Program availability:* Part-time, 100% online, blended/hybrid learning. *Faculty:* 4 full-time (0 women), 1 part-time/adjunct (0 women). *Students:* 6 full-time (4 women), 77 part-time (44 women); includes 17 minority (5 Black or African American, non-Hispanic/Latino; 1 Asian, non-Hispanic/Latino; 9 Hispanic/Latino; 2 Two or more races, non-Hispanic/Latino). Average age 36. 53 applicants, 100% accepted, 41 enrolled. In 2019, 18 master's, 20 other advanced degrees awarded. *Degree requirements:* For master's, e-portfolio. *Entrance requirements:* For master's, GRE or GMAT or waiver, statement of purpose (600-900 words), resume, 2 letters of recommendation, official transcripts; for Graduate Certificate, statement of purpose (minimum of 300 words), resume, official transcripts. Additional exam requirements/recommendations for international students: required—TOEFL (minimum score 600 paper-based). *Application deadline:* Applications are processed on a rolling basis. Application fee: $60. Electronic applications accepted. *Expenses: Tuition, area resident:* Full-time $16,390; part-time $682.92 per credit. Tuition, state resident: full-time $16,390; part-time $682.92 per credit. Tuition, nonresident: full-time $29,578; part-time $1232.42 per credit. *Required fees:* $575. *Financial support:* Application deadline: 3/1; applicants required to submit FAFSA. *Unit head:* Chad McGuire, Graduate Program Director, Public Policy, 508-999-8520, E-mail: chad.mcguire@umassd.edu. *Application contact:* Scott Webster, Director of Graduate Studies and Admissions, 508-999-8604, Fax: 508-999-8183, E-mail: graduate@umassd.edu.
Website: http://www.umassd.edu/cas/departmentsanddegreeprograms/publicpolicy/

University of Memphis, Graduate School, College of Arts and Sciences, Division of Public and Nonprofit Administration, Memphis, TN 38152. Offers local government management (Graduate Certificate); philanthropy and nonprofit leadership (Graduate Certificate). *Accreditation:* NASPAA. *Program availability:* Part-time, evening/weekend, blended/hybrid learning. *Students:* 20 full-time (10 women), 30 part-time (21 women); includes 20 minority (17 Black or African American, non-Hispanic/Latino; 1 Asian, non-Hispanic/Latino; 2 Two or more races, non-Hispanic/Latino). Average age 36. 15 applicants, 87% accepted, 6 enrolled. In 2019, 8 master's, 11 other advanced degrees awarded. *Degree requirements:* For master's, comprehensive exam, thesis or alternative, internship. *Entrance requirements:* For master's, GRE General Test, GMAT, MAT, or LSAT, minimum GPA of 3.0, resume, two references, statement of interest. Additional exam requirements/recommendations for international students: required—TOEFL. *Application deadline:* For fall admission, 7/1 for domestic students, 5/1 for international students; for spring admission, 12/1 for domestic students, 9/15 for international students; for summer admission, 5/1 for domestic students, 2/1 for international students. Applications are processed on a rolling basis. Application fee: $35 ($60 for international students). Electronic applications accepted. *Expenses: Tuition, area resident:* Full-time $9216; part-time $512 per credit hour. Tuition, state resident: full-time $9216; part-time $512 per credit hour. Tuition, nonresident: full-time $12,672; part-time $704 per credit hour. *International tuition:* $16,128 full-time. *Required fees:* $1530; $85 per credit hour. Tuition and fees vary according to program. *Financial support:* Fellowships, research assistantships with full tuition reimbursements, career-related internships or fieldwork, Federal Work-Study, scholarships/grants, health care benefits, and unspecified assistantships available. Support available to part-time students. Financial award application deadline: 2/1; financial award applicants required to submit FAFSA. *Unit head:* Dr. Sharon Wrobel, Chair, 901-678-4720, Fax: 901-678-2981, E-mail: swrobel@memphis.edu. *Application contact:* Dr. Sharon Wrobel, Chair, 901-678-4720, Fax: 901-678-2981, E-mail: swrobel@memphis.edu.
Website: http://www.memphis.edu/padm/

University of Michigan–Dearborn, College of Arts, Sciences, and Letters, Master of Public Administration and Policy (MPAP) Program, Dearborn, MI 48128. Offers MPA. *Program availability:* Part-time, evening/weekend. *Faculty:* 6 full-time (3 women), 10 part-time/adjunct (5 women). *Students:* 6 full-time (5 women), 13 part-time (9 women); includes 8 minority (5 Black or African American, non-Hispanic/Latino; 1 Asian, non-Hispanic/Latino; 2 Hispanic/Latino). Average age 31. 23 applicants, 70% accepted, 5 enrolled. In 2019, 13 master's awarded. *Entrance requirements:* Additional exam requirements/recommendations for international students: required—TOEFL (minimum score 560 paper-based; 84 iBT), IELTS (minimum score 6.5). *Application deadline:* For fall admission, 8/1 priority date for domestic students, 5/1 priority date for international students; for winter admission, 12/1 priority date for domestic students, 9/1 priority date for international students; for spring admission, 4/1 priority date for domestic students, 1/1 priority date for international students. Applications are processed on a rolling basis. Application fee: $60. Electronic applications accepted. *Financial support:* Career-related internships or fieldwork, scholarships/grants, and non-resident tuition scholarships available. Financial award application deadline: 3/1; financial award applicants required to submit FAFSA. *Unit head:* Dr. Vadym Pyrozhenko, Director, E-mail: vpyrozhe@umich.edu. *Application contact:* Office of Graduate Studies, 313-583-6321, E-mail: umd-graduatestudies@umich.edu.
Website: http://umdearborn.edu/casl/mpad/

University of Michigan–Flint, Graduate Programs, Program in Public Administration, Flint, MI 48502-1950. Offers administration of non-profit agencies (MPA); criminal justice administration (MPA); educational administration (MPA); general public administration (MPA); healthcare administration (MPA). *Program availability:* Part-time. *Faculty:* 2 part-time/adjunct (1 woman). *Students:* 7 full-time (4 women), 79 part-time (54 women); includes 31 minority (27 Black or African American, non-Hispanic/Latino; 1 American Indian or Alaska Native, non-Hispanic/Latino; 2 Hispanic/Latino; 1 Two or more races, non-Hispanic/Latino), 2 international. Average age 38. 54 applicants, 72% accepted, 19 enrolled. In 2019, 40 master's awarded. *Degree requirements:* For master's, thesis or alternative, internship. *Entrance requirements:* For master's, bachelor's degree from regionally-accredited institution, minimum overall undergraduate GPA of 3.0 on 4.0 scale. Additional exam requirements/recommendations for international students: required—TOEFL (minimum score 84 iBT), IELTS (minimum score 6.5). *Application deadline:* For fall admission, 8/1 for domestic students, 5/1 for international students; for winter admission, 11/15 for domestic students, 10/1 for international students; for spring admission, 3/15 for domestic students, 1/1 for international students; for summer admission, 5/15 for domestic students. Applications are processed on a rolling basis. Application fee: $55. Electronic applications accepted. *Expenses:* Contact institution. *Financial support:* Career-related internships or fieldwork, Federal Work-Study, and scholarships/grants available. Support available to part-time students. Financial award application deadline: 3/1; financial award applicants required to submit FAFSA. *Unit head:* Dr. Kim Sacks McManaway, Director, 810-766-6628, E-mail: kimsaks@umflint.edu. *Application contact:* Matt Bohlen, Associate Director of Graduate Admissions, 810-762-3171, Fax: 810-766-6789, E-mail: mbohlen@umflint.edu.
Website: http://www.umflint.edu/graduateprograms/public-administration-mpa

University of Missouri, Office of Research and Graduate Studies, Harry S Truman School of Public Affairs, Columbia, MO 65211. Offers grantsmanship (Graduate Certificate); nonprofit management (Graduate Certificate); organizational change (Graduate Certificate); public affairs (MPA, PhD); public management (Graduate Certificate); science and public policy (Graduate Certificate). *Accreditation:* NASPAA. *Entrance requirements:* For master's, GRE General Test, minimum GPA of 3.0. Additional exam requirements/recommendations for international students: required—TOEFL, IELTS. Electronic applications accepted.

University of Missouri–Kansas City, Henry W. Bloch School of Management, Kansas City, MO 64110-2499. Offers accounting (MS); finance (MS); public affairs (MPA, PhD);

JD/MBA; LL M/MPA. *Accreditation:* AACSB; NASPAA. *Program availability:* Part-time, evening/weekend. Terminal master's awarded for partial completion of doctoral program. *Entrance requirements:* For master's, GMAT, GRE, 2 essays, 2 references, support of employer; for doctorate, GRE, minimum GPA of 3.0. Additional exam requirements/recommendations for international students: required—TOEFL (minimum score 550 paper-based; 80 iBT). Electronic applications accepted.

University of Missouri–St. Louis, College of Arts and Sciences, Department of Political Science, St. Louis, MO 63121. Offers American politics (MA); comparative politics (MA); international politics (MA); political process and behavior (MA); political science (PhD); public administration and public policy (MA); urban and regional politics (MA). *Program availability:* Part-time, evening/weekend. Terminal master's awarded for partial completion of doctoral program. *Degree requirements:* For master's, thesis optional; for doctorate, thesis/dissertation. *Entrance requirements:* For master's, GRE General Test, 2 letters of recommendation, statement of purpose; for doctorate, GRE General Test, 3 letters of recommendation, statement of purpose. Additional exam requirements/recommendations for international students: required—TOEFL (minimum score 550 paper-based; 79 iBT), IELTS (minimum score 6.5). Electronic applications accepted. *Expenses: Tuition, area resident:* Full-time $9005.40; part-time $6003.60 per credit hour. Tuition, state resident: full-time $9005.40; part-time $6003.60 per credit hour. Tuition, nonresident: full-time $22,108; part-time $14,738.40 per credit hour. *International tuition:* $22,108 full-time. Tuition and fees vary according to course load.

University of Missouri–St. Louis, College of Arts and Sciences, Department of Sociology, St. Louis, MO 63121. Offers advanced social perspective (MA); community conflict intervention (MA); program design and evaluation research (MA); social policy planning and administration (MA). *Program availability:* Part-time, evening/weekend. *Degree requirements:* For master's, thesis optional. *Entrance requirements:* For master's, 2 letters of recommendation. Additional exam requirements/recommendations for international students: required—TOEFL (minimum score 550 paper-based). Electronic applications accepted. *Expenses: Tuition, area resident:* Full-time $9005.40; part-time $6003.60 per credit hour. Tuition, state resident: full-time $9005.40; part-time $6003.60 per credit hour. Tuition, nonresident: full-time $22,108; part-time $14,738.40 per credit hour. *International tuition:* $22,108 full-time. Tuition and fees vary according to course load.

University of Montana, Graduate School, College of Humanities and Sciences, Department of Political Science, Program in Public Administration, Missoula, MT 59812. Offers MPA, JD/MPA. *Degree requirements:* For master's, professional paper. *Entrance requirements:* For master's, GRE General Test.

University of Nebraska at Omaha, Graduate Studies, College of Public Affairs and Community Service, School of Public Administration, Omaha, NE 68182. Offers public administration (MPA, PhD); public management (Certificate); urban studies (MS). *Accreditation:* NASPAA (one or more programs are accredited). *Program availability:* Part-time, evening/weekend, online learning. *Degree requirements:* For master's, comprehensive exam (for some programs), thesis (for some programs); for doctorate, comprehensive exam, thesis/dissertation. *Entrance requirements:* For master's, GRE General Test, minimum GPA of 3.0, 2 letters of recommendation, statement of purpose, resume, official transcripts; for doctorate, GRE General Test, master's degree, minimum GPA of 3.2, 3 letters of recommendation, statement of purpose, resume, official transcripts; for Certificate, 3 years of work experience in the public sector, official transcripts, resume, statement of purpose, minimum undergraduate GPA of 3.0. Additional exam requirements/recommendations for international students: required—TOEFL (minimum score 550 paper-based; 80 iBT), IELTS (minimum score 5.5), PTE (minimum score 44). Electronic applications accepted.

University of Nevada, Las Vegas, Graduate College, Greenspun College of Urban Affairs, School of Public Policy and Leadership, Las Vegas, NV 89154-4030. Offers crisis and emergency management (MS); emergency crisis management cybersecurity (Certificate); environmental science (MS, PhD); non-profit management (Certificate); public administration (MPA); public affairs (PhD); public management (Certificate); urban leadership (MA). *Program availability:* Part-time. *Faculty:* 12 full-time (5 women), 6 part-time/adjunct (1 woman). *Students:* 106 full-time (61 women), 96 part-time (71 women); includes 118 minority (34 Black or African American, non-Hispanic/Latino; 1 American Indian or Alaska Native, non-Hispanic/Latino; 11 Asian, non-Hispanic/Latino; 49 Hispanic/Latino; 2 Native Hawaiian or other Pacific Islander, non-Hispanic/Latino; 21 Two or more races, non-Hispanic/Latino), 5 international. Average age 36. 115 applicants, 77% accepted, 73 enrolled. In 2019, 49 master's, 13 doctorates, 16 other advanced degrees awarded. *Degree requirements:* For master's, comprehensive exam (for some programs), thesis (for some programs), oral exam; for doctorate, comprehensive exam, thesis/dissertation; for Certificate, portfolio. *Entrance requirements:* For master's, GRE General Test or GMAT, bachelor's degree with minimum GPA 2.75; statement of purpose; 3 letters of recommendation; for doctorate, GRE General Test, master's degree with minimum GPA of 3.5; 3 letters of recommendation; statement of purpose; writing sample; personal interview; for Certificate, bachelor's degree; 2 letters of recommendation; writing sample. Additional exam requirements/recommendations for international students: required—TOEFL (minimum score 550 paper-based; 80 iBT), IELTS (minimum score 7). *Application deadline:* For fall admission, 6/1 for domestic and international students; for spring admission, 11/1 for domestic and international students; for summer admission, 3/1 for domestic students. Application fee: $60 ($95 for international students). Electronic applications accepted. *Expenses:* Contact institution. *Financial support:* In 2019–20, 25 students received support, including 15 research assistantships with full tuition reimbursements available (averaging $15,700 per year), 10 teaching assistantships with full tuition reimbursements available (averaging $16,625 per year); institutionally sponsored loans, scholarships/grants, health care benefits, and unspecified assistantships also available. Financial award application deadline: 3/15; financial award applicants required to submit FAFSA. *Unit head:* Dr. Christopher Stream, Director, 702-895-5120, Fax: 702-895-4436, E-mail: sppl.chair@unlv.edu. *Application contact:* Dr. Jayce Farmer, Graduate Coordinator, 702-895-4828, E-mail: sppl.gradcoord@unlv.edu. Website: https://www.unlv.edu/publicpolicy

University of Nevada, Reno, Graduate School, College of Liberal Arts, Department of Political Science, Program in Public Administration and Policy, Reno, NV 89557. Offers public administration (MPA). *Degree requirements:* For master's, comprehensive exam, oral exam/thesis or professional paper. *Entrance requirements:* For master's, GRE General Test, GMAT, or LSAT, minimum GPA of 2.75. Additional exam requirements/recommendations for international students: required—TOEFL (minimum score 500 paper-based; 61 iBT), IELTS (minimum score 6). Electronic applications accepted.

University of New Hampshire, Graduate School, Carsey School of Public Policy, Program in Public Administration, Durham, NH 03824. Offers MPA. *Program availability:* Part-time. *Students:* 26 part-time (15 women); includes 4 minority (1 Black or African American, non-Hispanic/Latino; 2 Hispanic/Latino; 1 Two or more races, non-Hispanic/Latino). Average age 35. 14 applicants, 64% accepted, 4 enrolled. In 2019, 14 master's awarded. *Entrance requirements:* For master's, If you are requesting a graduate assistantship or tuition assistance from the department then they require that you also submit GRE test scores. Additional exam requirements/recommendations for international students: required—TOEFL (minimum score 550 paper-based; 80 iBT),

IELTS, PTE. *Application deadline:* For fall admission, 8/15 for domestic students; for spring admission, 12/15 for domestic students; for summer admission, 4/15 for domestic students. Application fee: $65. Electronic applications accepted. *Financial support:* In 2019–20, 1 student received support. Fellowships, research assistantships, teaching assistantships, career-related internships or fieldwork, Federal Work-Study, scholarships/grants, and tuition waivers (full and partial) available. Support available to part-time students. Financial award application deadline: 2/15. *Unit head:* Michael Swack, Chair, 603-862-2821. *Application contact:* Robin Husslage, Administrative Assistant, 603-862-2338, E-mail: robin.husslage@unh.edu. Website: https://carsey.unh.edu/master-public-administration

University of New Hampshire, Graduate School Manchester Campus, Manchester, NH 03101. Offers business administration (MBA); cybersecurity policy and risk management (MS); educational administration and supervision (Ed S); educational studies (M Ed); elementary education (M Ed); information technology (MS); public administration (MPA); public health (MPH, Certificate); secondary education (M Ed, MAT); social work (MSW); substance use disorders (Certificate). *Program availability:* Part-time, evening/weekend. *Students:* 118 full-time (56 women), 110 part-time (47 women); includes 23 minority (4 Black or African American, non-Hispanic/Latino; 5 Asian, non-Hispanic/Latino; 13 Hispanic/Latino; 1 Two or more races, non-Hispanic/Latino), 39 international. Average age 32. 231 applicants, 78% accepted, 64 enrolled. In 2019, 47 master's, 3 other advanced degrees awarded. *Entrance requirements:* Additional exam requirements/recommendations for international students: required—TOEFL (minimum score 550 paper-based; 80 iBT), IELTS, PTE. *Application deadline:* For fall admission, 6/1 for domestic students, 4/1 for international students; for spring admission, 12/1 for domestic students. Application fee: $65. Electronic applications accepted. *Financial support:* In 2019–20, 11 students received support, including 1 teaching assistantship; fellowships, research assistantships, Federal Work-Study, scholarships/grants, health care benefits, and unspecified assistantships also available. Support available to part-time students. Financial award application deadline: 2/15; financial award applicants required to submit FAFSA. *Unit head:* Candice Morey, Educational Programs Coordinator, 603-641-4313, E-mail: unhm.gradcenter@unh.edu. *Application contact:* Candice Morey, Educational Programs Coordinator, 603-641-4313, E-mail: unhm.gradcenter@unh.edu. Website: http://www.gradschool.unh.edu/manchester/

University of New Haven, Graduate School, Henry C. Lee College of Criminal Justice and Forensic Sciences, Program in National Security, West Haven, CT 06516. Offers national security (MS, Graduate Certificate); national security administration (Graduate Certificate). *Program availability:* Part-time, evening/weekend. *Students:* 35 full-time (19 women), 18 part-time (7 women); includes 16 minority (5 Black or African American, non-Hispanic/Latino; 1 Asian, non-Hispanic/Latino; 9 Hispanic/Latino; 1 Native Hawaiian or other Pacific Islander, non-Hispanic/Latino), 2 international. Average age 30. 45 applicants, 87% accepted, 22 enrolled. In 2019, 28 master's awarded. *Entrance requirements:* Additional exam requirements/recommendations for international students: required—TOEFL (minimum score 70 iBT), IELTS, or PTE (minimum score of 53). *Application deadline:* Applications are processed on a rolling basis. Application fee: $50. Electronic applications accepted. Application fee is waived when completed online. *Financial support:* Research assistantships with partial tuition reimbursements, teaching assistantships with partial tuition reimbursements, Federal Work-Study, scholarships/grants, and unspecified assistantships available. Support available to part-time students. Financial award applicants required to submit FAFSA. *Unit head:* Dr. Jeffrey Treistman, Assistant Professor, 203-479-4567, E-mail: JTreistman@newhaven.edu. *Application contact:* Selina O'Toole, Senior Associate Director of Graduate Admissions, 203-932-7337, E-mail: SOToole@newhaven.edu. Website: https://www.newhaven.edu/lee-college/graduate-programs/national-security/

University of New Haven, Graduate School, Henry C. Lee College of Criminal Justice and Forensic Sciences, Program in Public Administration, West Haven, CT 06516. Offers fire and emergency medical services (MPA); municipal management (MPA); nonprofit organization management (MPA); public administration (MPA, Graduate Certificate); public finance (MPA); public safety (MPA). *Program availability:* Part-time, evening/weekend. *Students:* 20 full-time (10 women), 34 part-time (10 women); includes 14 minority (9 Black or African American, non-Hispanic/Latino; 1 Asian, non-Hispanic/Latino; 4 Hispanic/Latino), 5 international. Average age 33. 53 applicants, 85% accepted, 21 enrolled. In 2019, 21 master's, 1 other advanced degree awarded. *Entrance requirements:* Additional exam requirements/recommendations for international students: required—TOEFL (minimum score 80 iBT), IELTS, PTE. *Application deadline:* Applications are processed on a rolling basis. Application fee: $50. Electronic applications accepted. Application fee is waived when completed online. *Financial support:* Research assistantships with partial tuition reimbursements, teaching assistantships with partial tuition reimbursements, career-related internships or fieldwork, Federal Work-Study, scholarships/grants, and unspecified assistantships available. Support available to part-time students. Financial award application deadline: 5/1; financial award applicants required to submit FAFSA. *Unit head:* Dr. Christy Smith, Associate Professor, 203-479-4193, E-mail: cdsmith@newhaven.edu. *Application contact:* Selina O'Toole, Senior Associate Director of Graduate Admissions, 203-932-7337, E-mail: SOToole@newhaven.edu. Website: http://www.newhaven.edu/lee-college/graduate-programs/public-administration/

University of New Mexico, Graduate Studies, School of Public Administration, Program in Public Administration, Albuquerque, NM 87131-2039. Offers MPA. *Accreditation:* NASPAA. *Entrance requirements:* For master's, baccalaureate degree from accredited college or university with minimum undergraduate GPA of 3.0 for last 60 hours or overall major; letter of intent; three letters of recommendation; resume; official transcripts. Electronic applications accepted. *Expenses: Tuition, state resident:* full-time $7633; part-time $972 per year. Tuition, nonresident: full-time $22,586; part-time $3840 per year. *International tuition:* $23,292 full-time. *Required fees:* $8608. Tuition and fees vary according to course level, course load, degree level, program and student level.

University of New Orleans, Graduate School, College of Liberal Arts, Education and Human Development, Department of Political Science, Program in Public Administration, New Orleans, LA 70148. Offers MPA. *Accreditation:* NASPAA. *Degree requirements:* For master's, thesis. *Entrance requirements:* For master's, GRE General Test. Additional exam requirements/recommendations for international students: required—TOEFL (minimum score 550 paper-based; 79 iBT), IELTS (minimum score 6.5). Electronic applications accepted.

The University of North Carolina at Chapel Hill, Graduate School, School of Government, Chapel Hill, NC 27599. Offers MPA, JD/MPA, MPA/MRP, MPA/MSW. *Accreditation:* NASPAA. *Degree requirements:* For master's, comprehensive exam. *Entrance requirements:* For master's, GRE General Test, minimum GPA of 3.0. Additional exam requirements/recommendations for international students: required—TOEFL. Electronic applications accepted.

The University of North Carolina at Charlotte, College of Liberal Arts and Sciences, Department of Political Science and Public Administration, Charlotte, NC 28223-0001. Offers emergency management (Graduate Certificate); non-profit management (Graduate Certificate); public administration (MPA), including arts administration,

emergency management, non-profit management, public budgeting and finance, urban management and policy; public budgeting and finance (Graduate Certificate); urban management and policy (Graduate Certificate). *Accreditation:* NASPAA. *Program availability:* Part-time, evening/weekend. *Faculty:* 20 full-time (10 women), 5 part-time/adjunct (1 woman). *Students:* 30 full-time (21 women), 45 part-time (29 women); includes 23 minority (15 Black or African American, non-Hispanic/Latino; 1 American Indian or Alaska Native, non-Hispanic/Latino; 5 Hispanic/Latino; 2 Two or more races, non-Hispanic/Latino), 2 international. Average age 30. 38 applicants, 68% accepted, 21 enrolled. In 2019, 18 master's, 13 other advanced degrees awarded. *Degree requirements:* For master's, thesis or alternative. *Entrance requirements:* For master's, GRE General Test, bachelor's degree, or its equivalent, from accredited college or university; minimum undergraduate GPA of 3.0; 3 letters of recommendation; statement of purpose; for Graduate Certificate, one official transcript from each post-secondary institution; three letters of recommendation from academic or professional sources; overall undergraduate GPA of 3.0 on a 4.0 scale; statement of purpose (1-2 pages in length) in which the applicant explains his/her career goals, how the Certificate fits into achieving those goals, and any relevant w. Additional exam requirements/recommendations for international students: required—TOEFL (minimum score 557 paper-based; 83 iBT), IELTS (minimum score 6.5), TOEFL (minimum score 557paper-based, 83 iBT) or IELTS (6.5). *Application deadline:* For fall admission, 8/15 for domestic students; for spring admission, 12/1 for domestic students; for summer admission, 5/11 for domestic students. Applications are processed on a rolling basis. Application fee: $75. Electronic applications accepted. *Expenses:* Tuition, state resident: full-time $4337. Tuition, nonresident: full-time $17,771. *Required fees:* $3093. Tuition and fees vary according to course load, degree level and program. *Financial support:* In 2019–20, 16 students received support, including 1 fellowship (averaging $55,000 per year), 15 research assistantships (averaging $8,583 per year); teaching assistantships, career-related internships or fieldwork, institutionally sponsored loans, scholarships/grants, and unspecified assistantships also available. Support available to part-time students. Financial award applicants required to submit FAFSA. *Unit head:* Dr. Cheryl L. Brown, Interim Chair, Undergraduate Coordinator, & Associate Professor, 704-687-7574, E-mail: cbrown@uncc.edu. *Application contact:* Kathy B. Giddings, Director of Graduate Admissions, 704-687-5503, Fax: 704-687-1668, E-mail: gradadm@uncc.edu.
Website: http://politicalscience.uncc.edu/

The University of North Carolina at Pembroke, The Graduate School, Department of Political Science and Public Administration, Pembroke, NC 28372-1510. Offers criminal justice (MPA); emergency management (MPA); health administration (MPA); public management (MPA). *Program availability:* Part-time, evening/weekend, online learning. *Degree requirements:* For master's, comprehensive exam, thesis optional. *Entrance requirements:* For master's, GRE General Test or MAT, minimum GPA of 3.0 in major, 2.5 overall; interview. Additional exam requirements/recommendations for international students: required—TOEFL.

The University of North Carolina Wilmington, College of Arts and Sciences, Department of Public and International Affairs, Wilmington, NC 28403-3297. Offers coastal and ocean policy (MS); conflict management and resolution (MA); public administration (MPA), including coastal management. *Accreditation:* NASPAA. *Program availability:* Blended/hybrid learning. *Faculty:* 12 full-time (5 women). *Students:* 51 full-time (32 women), 49 part-time (32 women); includes 21 minority (7 Black or African American, non-Hispanic/Latino; 10 Hispanic/Latino; 4 Two or more races, non-Hispanic/Latino), 1 international. Average age 30. 60 applicants, 93% accepted, 36 enrolled. In 2019, 45 master's awarded. *Degree requirements:* For master's, thesis (for some programs), internship, practicum, capstone project. *Entrance requirements:* For master's, GRE General Test (Coastal and Ocean Policy, or MCOP, degree), 3 letters of recommendation (all degrees); minimum of 3 years of professional work experience, personal statement, resume (for MPA degree); personal statement & resume (MCOP degree); essay and resume (Conflict & Resolution Management degree). Additional exam requirements/recommendations for international students: required—TOEFL (minimum score 79 iBT), IELTS (minimum score 6.5). *Application deadline:* For fall admission, 7/1 for domestic students; for spring admission, 11/15 for domestic students; for summer admission, 4/15 for domestic students. Applications are processed on a rolling basis. Application fee: $75. Electronic applications accepted. *Expenses:* $4,717.97 per year in-state (for Public Administration main campus students), $11,632.47 per year out-of-state (for Public Administration main campus students), $259.01 per credit hour in-state (for online students), $936.91 per credit hour out-of-state (for online students), $3,728.47 per year for the remaining in-state main campus students, $10,642.97 per year for the remaining out-of-state main campus students. *Financial support:* Teaching assistantships and scholarships/grants available. Financial award application deadline: 1/1; financial award applicants required to submit FAFSA. *Unit head:* Dr. Raymonde Kleinberg, Chair, 910-962-4254, Fax: 910-962-3286, E-mail: kleinbergr@uncw.edu. *Application contact:* Dr. Chris Prentice, MPA Program Director, 910-962-2135, E-mail: prenticecr@uncw.edu.
Website: http://www.uncw.edu/pia/graduate/index.html

University of North Dakota, Graduate School, College of Business and Public Administration, Program in Public Administration, Grand Forks, ND 58202. Offers MPA, MPA/JD. *Accreditation:* NASPAA. *Program availability:* Part-time, online learning. *Degree requirements:* For master's, comprehensive exam, thesis or alternative, final exam. *Entrance requirements:* For master's, GRE General Test, GMAT or LSAT, minimum GPA of 3.0. Additional exam requirements/recommendations for international students: required—TOEFL (minimum score 550 paper-based; 79 iBT), IELTS (minimum score 6.5). Electronic applications accepted.

University of North Florida, College of Arts and Sciences, Department of Political Science and Public Administration, Jacksonville, FL 32224. Offers nonprofit management (Graduate Certificate); public administration (MPA). *Accreditation:* NASPAA. *Program availability:* Part-time. *Degree requirements:* For master's, thesis or alternative, internship. *Entrance requirements:* For master's, GRE General Test, minimum GPA of 3.0 in last 60 hours, 2 letters of recommendation, interview. Additional exam requirements/recommendations for international students: required—TOEFL (minimum score 500 paper-based; 61 iBT). Electronic applications accepted.

University of North Georgia, Program in Public Administration, Dahlonega, GA 30597. Offers MPA.
Website: https://ung.edu/graduate-admissions/programs/master-of-public-administration.php

University of North Texas, Toulouse Graduate School, Denton, TX 76203-5459. Offers accounting (MS); applied anthropology (MA, MS); applied behavior analysis (Certificate); applied geography (MA); applied technology and performance improvement (M Ed, MS); art education (MA); art history (MA); arts leadership (Certificate); audiology (Au D); behavior analysis (MS); behavioral science (PhD); biochemistry and molecular biology (MS); biology (MA, MS); biomedical engineering (MS); business analysis (MS); chemistry (MS); clinical health psychology (PhD); communication studies (MA, MS); computer engineering (MS); computer science (MS); counseling (M Ed, MS), including clinical mental health counseling (MS), college and university counseling, elementary school counseling, secondary school counseling; creative writing (MA); criminal justice (MS); curriculum and instruction (M Ed); decision sciences (MBA); design (MA, MFA), including fashion design (MFA), innovation studies, interior design (MFA); early childhood studies (MS); economics (MS); educational leadership (M Ed, Ed D); educational psychology (MS, PhD), including family studies (MS), gifted and talented (MS), human development (MS), learning and cognition (MS), research, measurement and evaluation (MS); electrical engineering (MS); emergency management (MPA); engineering technology (MS); English (MA); English as a second language (MA); environmental science (MS); finance (MBA, MS); financial management (MPA); French (MA); health services management (MBA); higher education (M Ed, Ed D); history (MA, MS); hospitality management (MS); human resources management (MPA); information science (MS); information systems (PhD); information technologies (MBA); interdisciplinary studies (MA, MS); international studies (MA); international sustainable tourism (MS); jazz studies (MM); journalism (MA, MJ, Graduate Certificate), including interactive and virtual digital communication (Graduate Certificate), narrative journalism (Graduate Certificate), public relations (Graduate Certificate); kinesiology (MS); linguistics (MA); local government management (MPA); logistics (PhD); logistics and supply chain management (MBA); long-term care, senior housing, and aging services (MA); management (PhD); marketing (MBA); mathematics (MA, MS); mechanical and energy engineering (MS, PhD); music (MA), including ethnomusicology, music theory, musicology, performance; music composition (PhD); music education (MM Ed, PhD); nonprofit management (MPA); operations and supply chain management (MBA); performance (MM, DMA); philosophy (MA); political science (MA); professional and technical communication (MA); radio, television and film (MA, MFA); rehabilitation counseling (Certificate); sociology (MA); Spanish (MA); special education (M Ed); speech-language pathology (MA); strategic management (MBA); studio art (MFA); teaching (M Ed); MBA/MS. *Program availability:* Part-time, evening/weekend, online learning. Terminal master's awarded for partial completion of doctoral program. *Degree requirements:* For master's, variable foreign language requirement, comprehensive exam (for some programs), thesis (for some programs); for doctorate, variable foreign language requirement, comprehensive exam (for some programs), thesis/dissertation; for other advanced degree, variable foreign language requirement, comprehensive exam (for some programs). *Entrance requirements:* For master's and doctorate, GRE, GMAT. Additional exam requirements/recommendations for international students: required—TOEFL (minimum score 550 paper-based; 79 iBT). Electronic applications accepted.

University of North Texas at Dallas, Graduate School, Dallas, TX 75241. Offers accounting (MBA); counseling (M Ed, MS); criminal justice (MS); curriculum and instruction (M Ed); educational administration (M Ed); human resources and organizational behavior (MBA); public leadership (MS); strategic management (MBA).

University of Oklahoma, College of Arts and Sciences, Department of Political Science, Norman, OK 73019-0390. Offers political science (MA, PhD); public administration (MPA), including general, nonprofit management, public management, public policy. Terminal master's awarded for partial completion of doctoral program. *Degree requirements:* For master's, comprehensive exam, thesis optional, 36 hours; for doctorate, comprehensive exam, thesis/dissertation, 90 hours. *Entrance requirements:* For master's, GRE, purpose statement, writing sample, and three letters of recommendation (for MA); for doctorate, GRE, purpose statement, writing sample, three letters of recommendation. Additional exam requirements/recommendations for international students: required—TOEFL (minimum score 100 iBT) or IELTS (minimum score 7.0). Electronic applications accepted. *Expenses:* Tuition, state resident: full-time $6583.20; part-time $274.30 per credit hour. Tuition, nonresident: full-time $21,242; part-time $885.10 per credit hour. *International tuition:* $21,242.40 full-time. *Required fees:* $1994.20; $72.55 per credit hour. $126.50 per semester. Tuition and fees vary according to course load and degree level.

University of Oregon, Graduate School, College of Design, School of Planning, Public Policy and Management, Program in Public Administration, Eugene, OR 97403. Offers MPA. *Accreditation:* NASPAA. *Program availability:* Part-time, evening/weekend. *Degree requirements:* For master's, thesis. *Entrance requirements:* For master's, minimum GPA of 3.0. Additional exam requirements/recommendations for international students: required—TOEFL.

University of Ottawa, Faculty of Graduate and Postdoctoral Studies, Interdisciplinary Programs, Ottawa, ON K1N 6N5, Canada. Offers e-business (Certificate); e-commerce (Certificate); finance (Certificate); health services and policies research (Diploma); population health (PhD); population health risk assessment and management (Certificate); public management and governance (Certificate); systems science (Certificate).

University of Pennsylvania, School of Arts and Sciences, Fels Institute of Government, Philadelphia, PA 19104. Offers economic development and growth (Certificate); government administration (MGA); nonprofit administration (Certificate); organization dynamics (MS); politics (Certificate); public administration (MPA); public finance (Certificate). *Program availability:* Part-time, evening/weekend. *Students:* 15 full-time (9 women), 49 part-time (24 women); includes 19 minority (8 Black or African American, non-Hispanic/Latino; 6 Asian, non-Hispanic/Latino; 5 Hispanic/Latino), 3 international. Average age 33. 664 applicants, 44% accepted, 130 enrolled. In 2019, 67 master's, 3 other advanced degrees awarded. *Financial support:* Application deadline: 1/1.
Website: http://www.fels.upenn.edu/

University of Phoenix - Bay Area Campus, School of Business, San Jose, CA 95134-1805. Offers accountancy (MS); accounting (MBA); business administration (MBA, DBA); energy management (MBA); global management (MBA); health care management (MBA); human resource management (MBA); human resources management (MM); management (MM); marketing (MBA); organizational leadership (DM); project management (MBA); public administration (MPA); technology management (MBA). *Accreditation:* ACBSP. *Program availability:* Evening/weekend, online learning. *Degree requirements:* For master's, thesis (for some programs). *Entrance requirements:* For master's, minimum undergraduate GPA of 3.0, 3 years of work experience. Additional exam requirements/recommendations for international students: required—TOEFL (minimum score 550 paper-based; 79 iBT). Electronic applications accepted.

University of Phoenix - Central Valley Campus, School of Business, Fresno, CA 93720-1552. Offers accounting (MBA); business administration (MBA); global management (MBA); human resources management (MBA, MM); management (MM); marketing (MBA); public administration (MBA, MM). *Accreditation:* ACBSP.

University of Phoenix - Dallas Campus, School of Business, Dallas, TX 75251. Offers accounting (MBA); business administration (MBA); global management (MBA); human resources management (MBA, MM); management (MM); marketing (MBA); public administration (MBA, MM). *Accreditation:* ACBSP. *Program availability:* Evening/weekend, online learning. *Degree requirements:* For master's, thesis (for some programs). *Entrance requirements:* For master's, 3 years of work experience, minimum undergraduate GPA of 3.0. Additional exam requirements/recommendations for international students: required—TOEFL (minimum score 550 paper-based; 79 iBT). Electronic applications accepted.

University of Phoenix - Hawaii Campus, School of Business, Honolulu, HI 96813-3800. Offers accounting (MBA); business administration (MBA); global management (MBA); human resources management (MBA, MM); management (MM); marketing (MBA); public administration (MBA, MM). *Accreditation:* ACBSP. *Program availability:* Evening/weekend. *Degree requirements:* For master's, thesis (for some programs). *Entrance requirements:* For master's, minimum undergraduate GPA of 3.0, 3 years of work experience. Additional exam requirements/recommendations for international students: required—TOEFL (minimum score 550 paper-based; 79 iBT). Electronic applications accepted.

University of Phoenix - Houston Campus, School of Business, Houston, TX 77079-2004. Offers accounting (MBA); business administration (MBA); global management (MBA); human resources management (MBA, MM); management (MM); marketing (MBA); public administration (MBA, MM). *Accreditation:* ACBSP. *Program availability:* Evening/weekend, online learning. *Degree requirements:* For master's, thesis (for some programs). *Entrance requirements:* For master's, 3 years of work experience, minimum undergraduate GPA of 3.0. Additional exam requirements/recommendations for international students: required—TOEFL (minimum score 550 paper-based; 79 iBT). Electronic applications accepted.

University of Phoenix - Las Vegas Campus, School of Business, Las Vegas, NV 89135. Offers accounting (MBA); business administration (MBA); global management (MBA); human resources management (MBA, MM); management (MM); marketing (MBA); public administration (MM). *Accreditation:* ACBSP. *Program availability:* Evening/weekend, online learning. *Degree requirements:* For master's, thesis (for some programs). *Entrance requirements:* For master's, minimum undergraduate GPA of 3.0, 3 years of work experience. Additional exam requirements/recommendations for international students: required—TOEFL (minimum score 550 paper-based; 79 iBT). Electronic applications accepted.

University of Phoenix–Online Campus, College of Justice and Security, Phoenix, AZ 85034-7209. Offers administration of justice and security (MS), including administration of justice and security, global and homeland security, law enforcement organizations; public administration (MPA). *Program availability:* Evening/weekend, online learning. *Entrance requirements:* Additional exam requirements/recommendations for international students: required—TOEFL, TOEIC (Test of English as an International Communication), Berlitz Online English Proficiency Exam, PTE, or IELTS. Electronic applications accepted. *Expenses:* Contact institution.

University of Phoenix–Online Campus, School of Business, Phoenix, AZ 85034-7209. Offers accountancy (MS); accounting (MBA, Certificate); business administration (MBA); energy management (MBA); global management (MBA); health care management (MBA); human resource management (MBA, Certificate); human resources management (MM); management (MM); marketing (MBA, Certificate); project management (MBA, Certificate); public administration (MBA, MM); technology management (MBA). *Program availability:* Evening/weekend, online learning. *Entrance requirements:* Additional exam requirements/recommendations for international students: required—TOEFL, TOEIC (Test of English as an International Communication), Berlitz Online English Proficiency Exam, PTE, or IELTS. Electronic applications accepted. *Expenses:* Contact institution.

University of Phoenix - Phoenix Campus, College of Criminal Justice and Security, Tempe, AZ 85282-2371. Offers administration of justice and security (MS); global and homeland security (MS); law enforcement organizations (MS); public administration (MPA). *Program availability:* Evening/weekend, online learning. *Entrance requirements:* Additional exam requirements/recommendations for international students: required—TOEFL, TOEIC (Test of English as an International Communication), Berlitz Online English Proficiency Exam, PTE, or IELTS. Electronic applications accepted. *Expenses:* Contact institution.

University of Phoenix - Sacramento Valley Campus, School of Business, Sacramento, CA 95833-4334. Offers accounting (MBA); business administration (MBA); global management (MBA); human resources management (MBA, MM); management (MM); marketing (MBA); public administration (MBA, MM). *Accreditation:* ACBSP. *Program availability:* Evening/weekend. *Degree requirements:* For master's, thesis (for some programs). *Entrance requirements:* For master's, minimum undergraduate GPA of 3.0, 3 years work experience. Additional exam requirements/recommendations for international students: required—TOEFL (minimum score 550 paper-based; 79 iBT). Electronic applications accepted.

University of Phoenix - San Antonio Campus, School of Business, San Antonio, TX 78230. Offers accounting (MBA); business administration (MBA); e-business (MBA); global management (MBA); human resources management (MBA, MM); management (MM); marketing (MBA); public administration (MBA, MM). *Accreditation:* ACBSP.

University of Phoenix - San Diego Campus, School of Business, San Diego, CA 92123. Offers accounting (MBA); business administration (MBA); global management (MBA); human resources management (MBA, MM); management (MM); marketing (MBA); public administration (MBA). *Accreditation:* ACBSP. *Program availability:* Evening/weekend. *Degree requirements:* For master's, thesis (for some programs). *Entrance requirements:* For master's, 3 years of work experience, minimum undergraduate GPA of 3.0. Additional exam requirements/recommendations for international students: required—TOEFL (minimum score 550 paper-based; 79 iBT). Electronic applications accepted.

University of Pittsburgh, Graduate School of Public and International Affairs, Master of Public Administration Program, Pittsburgh, PA 15260. Offers energy and environment (MPA); governance and international public management (MPA); policy research and analysis (MPA); public and nonprofit management (MPA); urban affairs and planning (MPA); JD/MPA; MPH/MPA; MSIS/MPA; MSW/MPA. *Accreditation:* NASPAA. *Program availability:* Part-time, evening/weekend. *Faculty:* 33 full-time (11 women), 10 part-time/adjunct (5 women). *Students:* 76 full-time (51 women), 17 part-time (10 women); includes 9 minority (5 Black or African American, non-Hispanic/Latino; 1 Asian, non-Hispanic/Latino; 3 Hispanic/Latino), 37 international. Average age 26. 167 applicants, 91% accepted, 44 enrolled. In 2019, 49 master's awarded. *Degree requirements:* For master's, thesis optional, capstone seminar. *Entrance requirements:* For master's, Personal essay, resume, two letters of recommendation, transcripts. Additional exam requirements/recommendations for international students: required—TOEFL (minimum score 80 iBT), Duolingo English Test; recommended—IELTS (minimum score 6.5). *Application deadline:* For fall admission, 2/1 for domestic students, 1/15 priority date for international students; for spring admission, 11/1 for domestic students, 8/1 priority date for international students. Application fee: $50. Electronic applications accepted. *Expenses:* $24,480 in-state, $40,848 out-of-state. *Financial support:* In 2019–20, 30 students received support, including 2 fellowships with full tuition reimbursements available (averaging $16,060 per year); scholarships/grants also available. Financial award application deadline: 2/1; financial award applicants required to submit FAFSA. *Unit head:* Dr. John Keeler, Dean, 412-648-7605, Fax: 412-648-7601, E-mail: gspia@pitt.edu. *Application contact:* Dr. Michael Rizzi, Director of Student Services, 412-648-7643, Fax: 412-648-7641, E-mail: rizzim@pitt.edu.
Website: http://www.gspia.pitt.edu/

University of Pittsburgh, Graduate School of Public and International Affairs, PhD Program in Public and International Affairs, Pittsburgh, PA 15260. Offers international affairs (PhD); international development (PhD); public administration (PhD); public policy (PhD). *Faculty:* 33 full-time (11 women), 10 part-time/adjunct (5 women). *Students:* 28 full-time (12 women), 4 part-time (2 women); includes 4 minority (1 Black or African American, non-Hispanic/Latino; 3 Hispanic/Latino), 14 international. Average age 36. 65 applicants, 3% accepted, 2 enrolled. In 2019, 1 doctorate awarded. *Degree requirements:* For doctorate, comprehensive exam, thesis/dissertation. *Entrance requirements:* For doctorate, GRE or GMAT, Personal essay, research proposal essay, two letters of recommendation, transcripts, resume. Additional exam requirements/recommendations for international students: required—TOEFL (minimum score 80 iBT), Duolingo English Test; recommended—IELTS (minimum score 6.5). *Application deadline:* For fall admission, 1/15 for domestic and international students. Application fee: $50. Electronic applications accepted. *Expenses:* $24,480 in-state, $40,848 out-of-state. *Financial support:* In 2019–20, 15 students received support, including 15 research assistantships with full tuition reimbursements available (averaging $16,060 per year). Financial award application deadline: 1/15. *Unit head:* Dr. John Keeler, Dean, 412-648-7605, Fax: 412-648-7601, E-mail: gspia@pitt.edu. *Application contact:* Dr. Michael Rizzi, Director of Student Services, 412-648-7640, Fax: 412-648-7641, E-mail: rizzim@pitt.edu.
Website: http://www.gspia.pitt.edu/

University of Puerto Rico at Rio Piedras, College of Social Sciences, School of Public Administration, San Juan, PR 00931-3300. Offers MPA. *Accreditation:* NASPAA. *Program availability:* Part-time. *Degree requirements:* For master's, comprehensive exam, thesis. *Entrance requirements:* For master's, GRE or PAEG, interview, minimum GPA of 3.0, letter of recommendation.

University of Regina, Faculty of Graduate Studies and Research, Johnson-Shoyama Graduate School of Public Policy, Regina, SK S4S 0A2, Canada. Offers economic analysis for public policy (Master's Certificate); health administration (MHA); health systems management (Master's Certificate); public management (MPA, Master's Certificate); public policy (MPA, MPP, PhD); public policy analysis (Master's Certificate). *Program availability:* Part-time. *Faculty:* 9 full-time (4 women), 19 part-time/adjunct (8 women). *Students:* 116 full-time (71 women), 202 part-time (155 women). Average age 30. 328 applicants, 50% accepted. In 2019, 67 master's, 12 other advanced degrees awarded. Terminal master's awarded for partial completion of doctoral program. *Degree requirements:* For master's, thesis (for some programs), course work, in person residencies; for doctorate, comprehensive exam, thesis/dissertation, seminar. *Entrance requirements:* For master's, 4 year undergraduate degree in any area, transcript, 2 letters of recommendation, authorization of release. Students without a background in economics may be required to complete introductory courses in micro and macro economics; for doctorate, master's degree, intended research program in an area of public policy, proposal. Additional exam requirements/recommendations for international students: required—TOEFL (minimum score 585 paper-based; 86 iBT), IELTS (minimum score 6.5), PTE (minimum score 63), Could be one of the listed above. Other options are MELAB, CANTEST, CAEl, and UR ESL. *Application deadline:* For fall admission, 5/1 for domestic and international students; for winter admission, 10/1 for domestic and international students. Application fee: $100. Electronic applications accepted. *Expenses:* Tuition fee is different for each program. See tuition and fees details on each program. *Financial support:* In 2019–20, 78 students received support, including 33 fellowships, 15 teaching assistantships (averaging $2,552 per year); research assistantships, career-related internships or fieldwork, Federal Work-Study, scholarships/grants, unspecified assistantships, and travel award and Graduate Scholarship Base funds also available. Support available to part-time students. Financial award application deadline: 9/30. *Unit head:* Dr. Doug Moen, Executive Director, 306-585-4921, Fax: 306-585-5461, E-mail: doeg.moen@uregina.ca. *Application contact:* John Bird, Academic Advisor, 306-585-5469, Fax: 306-585-5461, E-mail: john.bird@uregina.ca.
Website: http://www.schoolofpublicpolicy.sk.ca/

University of Rhode Island, Graduate School, College of Arts and Sciences, Department of Political Science, Kingston, RI 02881. Offers international relations (MA), including American politics; public policy and administration (MPA). *Program availability:* Part-time. *Faculty:* 12 full-time (6 women). *Students:* 25 full-time (15 women), 33 part-time (21 women); includes 12 minority (2 Black or African American, non-Hispanic/Latino; 1 American Indian or Alaska Native, non-Hispanic/Latino; 1 Asian, non-Hispanic/Latino; 6 Hispanic/Latino; 2 Two or more races, non-Hispanic/Latino), 2 international. 36 applicants, 94% accepted, 26 enrolled. In 2019, 18 master's awarded. *Entrance requirements:* For master's, GRE, GMAT, or MAT if undergraduate GPA below 3.0, 2 letters of recommendation. Additional exam requirements/recommendations for international students: required—TOEFL. *Application deadline:* For fall admission, 11/15 for domestic students, 2/1 for international students; for spring admission, 7/15 for domestic students, 7/15 priority date for international students. Application fee: $65. Electronic applications accepted. *Expenses: Tuition, area resident:* Full-time $13,734; part-time $763 per credit. Tuition, state resident: full-time $13,734; part-time $763 per credit. Tuition, nonresident: full-time $26,512; part-time $1473 per credit. *International tuition:* $26,512 full-time. *Required fees:* $1780; $52 per credit. $35 per term. One-time fee: $165. *Financial support:* In 2019–20, 1 research assistantship with full tuition reimbursement (averaging $19,368 per year), 4 teaching assistantships with full tuition reimbursements (averaging $15,189 per year) were awarded; health care benefits also available. Financial award application deadline: 2/1; financial award applicants required to submit FAFSA. *Unit head:* Dr. Marc Hutchison, Department Chair, 401-874-4051, Fax: 401-874-4072, E-mail: mlhutch@uri.edu. *Application contact:* Dr. Kristin Johnson, Director/Associate Professor, 401-874-5495, E-mail: kristin_johnson@uri.edu.
Website: http://www.uri.edu/artsci/psc/

University of St. Thomas, School of Arts and Sciences, Houston, TX 77006-4696. Offers public policy administration (MPPA); sacred music (MSM). *Program availability:* Part-time-only, evening/weekend. *Faculty:* 44 full-time (14 women), 49 part-time/adjunct (15 women). *Students:* 8 full-time (4 women), 94 part-time (67 women); includes 87 minority (1 Black or African American, non-Hispanic/Latino; 2 Asian, non-Hispanic/Latino; 84 Hispanic/Latino), 9 international. Average age 44. 164 applicants, 70% accepted, 58 enrolled. In 2019, 35 master's awarded. *Degree requirements:* For master's, Number of Foreign Languages-S, Comprehensive Exam -S, Thesis/Dissertation -A. *Entrance requirements:* For master's, Letters of recommendation required, undergraduate GPA of 3.0, essay requirement, transcripts from all undergraduate and graduate institutions, GRE/GMAT recommended but not required for most programs. Additional exam requirements/recommendations for international students: recommended—TOEFL, IELTS. *Application deadline:* For fall admission, 7/15 priority date for domestic and international students; for spring admission, 12/15 priority date for domestic and international students; for summer admission, 4/15 priority date for domestic and international students. Applications are processed on a rolling basis. Application fee: $35. Electronic applications accepted. Application fee is waived when completed online. *Expenses: Tuition:* Full-time $30,800; part-time $1163 per credit hour. *Required fees:* $250; $210 per semester. One-time fee: $660. Tuition and fees vary according to degree level and program. *Financial support:* Fellowships, research assistantships, teaching assistantships, career-related internships or fieldwork, Federal

Work-Study, institutionally sponsored loans, scholarships/grants, tuition waivers, and unspecified assistantships available. Support available to part-time students. Financial award application deadline: 7/15; financial award applicants required to submit FAFSA. *Unit head:* George A. Harne, PhD, Executive Dean of the School of Arts and Sciences, 713-942-3419, E-mail: harneg@stthom.edu. *Application contact:* Christopher S Cheek, Graduate Admissions Manager, 713-525-3817, E-mail: cheekc@stthom.edu.
Website: http://www.stthom.edu/Academics/School_of_Arts_and_Sciences/Index.aqf

University of San Francisco, School of Management, Master of Public Administration Program, San Francisco, CA 94117. Offers health services administration (MPA); public administration (MPA). *Program availability:* Part-time, evening/weekend, online learning. *Faculty:* 6 full-time (2 women), 2 part-time/adjunct (0 women). *Students:* 99 full-time (72 women), 4 part-time (3 women); includes 68 minority (8 Black or African American, non-Hispanic/Latino; 1 American Indian or Alaska Native, non-Hispanic/Latino; 25 Asian, non-Hispanic/Latino; 30 Hispanic/Latino; 4 Two or more races, non-Hispanic/Latino). Average age 33. 95 applicants, 80% accepted, 37 enrolled. In 2019, 65 master's awarded. *Entrance requirements:* For master's, resume demonstrating minimum of two years of professional work experience, transcripts from each college or university attended, two letters of recommendation, personal statement. Additional exam requirements/recommendations for international students: required—TOEFL (minimum score 600 paper-based, 100 iBT), IELTS (minimum score 7) or PTE (minimum score 68). *Application deadline:* For fall admission, 6/15 for domestic students, 5/15 for international students. Application fee: $55. Electronic applications accepted. *Expenses:* Contact institution. *Financial support:* Scholarships/grants available. Financial award application deadline: 3/2; financial award applicants required to submit FAFSA. *Unit head:* Dr. Catherine Horiuchi, Director, 415-422-2221, E-mail: management@usfca.edu. *Application contact:* Office of Graduate Recruiting and Admissions, 415-422-2221, E-mail: management@usfca.edu.
Website: http://www.usfca.edu/mpa

University of South Africa, College of Economic and Management Sciences, Pretoria, South Africa. Offers accounting (D Admin, D Com); accounting science (DA); auditing (D Admin, D Com); business administration (M Tech); business economics (D Admin); business leadership (DBL); business management (D Admin, D Com); economic management analysis (M Tech); economics (D Admin, D Com, PhD); human resource development (M Tech); industrial psychology (D Admin, D Com, PhD); logistics (D Com); marketing (M Tech); public administration (D Admin, D Com, DPA, PhD); public management (M Tech); quantitative management (D Admin, D Com); real estate (M Tech); statistics (D Admin, PhD); tourism management (D Admin, D Com); transport economics (D Admin, D Com).

University of South Alabama, College of Arts and Sciences, Department of Political Science and Criminal Justice, Mobile, AL 36688-0002. Offers public administration (MPA). *Program availability:* Part-time, evening/weekend. *Faculty:* 5 full-time (2 women). *Students:* 52 full-time (37 women), 7 part-time (4 women); includes 32 minority (28 Black or African American, non-Hispanic/Latino; 2 Asian, non-Hispanic/Latino; 2 Two or more races, non-Hispanic/Latino), 2 international. Average age 27. 45 applicants, 96% accepted, 28 enrolled. In 2019, 12 master's awarded. *Degree requirements:* For master's, comprehensive exam, thesis optional. *Entrance requirements:* For master's, GRE. Additional exam requirements/recommendations for international students: required—TOEFL (minimum score 71 iBT). *Application deadline:* For fall admission, 7/1 priority date for domestic students, 6/1 priority date for international students; for spring admission, 12/1 priority date for domestic students, 11/1 priority date for international students; for summer admission, 5/1 priority date for domestic students, 4/1 for international students. Applications are processed on a rolling basis. Application fee: $35. Electronic applications accepted. *Expenses: Tuition, area resident:* Part-time $442 per credit hour. Tuition, state resident: full-time $10,608; part-time $442 per credit hour. Tuition, nonresident: full-time $21,216; part-time $884 per credit hour. *Financial support:* Fellowships, research assistantships, teaching assistantships, career-related internships or fieldwork, Federal Work-Study, institutionally sponsored loans, scholarships/grants, and unspecified assistantships available. Support available to part-time students. Financial award application deadline: 3/31; financial award applicants required to submit FAFSA. *Unit head:* Dr. Philip Habel, Chair, Political Science/Criminal Justice, 251-460-7161, E-mail: habel@southalabama.edu. *Application contact:* Dr. Philip Habel, Chair, Political Science/Criminal Justice, 251-460-7161, E-mail: habel@southalabama.edu.
Website: http://www.southalabama.edu/colleges/artsandsci/pscj/

University of South Carolina, The Graduate School, College of Arts and Sciences, Department of Political Science, Program in Public Administration, Columbia, SC 29208. Offers MPA, JD/MPA, MSW/MPA. *Accreditation:* NASPAA. *Program availability:* Part-time, evening/weekend. *Degree requirements:* For master's, capstone seminar. *Entrance requirements:* For master's, GRE General Test, minimum GPA of 3.0. Additional exam requirements/recommendations for international students: required—TOEFL. Electronic applications accepted.

University of Southern California, Graduate School, Sol Price School of Public Policy, Master of Public Administration Program, Los Angeles, CA 90089. Offers nonprofit management and policy (Graduate Certificate); political management (Graduate Certificate); public administration (MPA); public management (Graduate Certificate); MPA/JD; MPA/M Pl; MPA/MA; MPA/MAJCS; MPA/MS; MPA/MSW. *Accreditation:* NASPAA (one or more programs are accredited). *Program availability:* Part-time, evening/weekend, online learning. Terminal master's awarded for partial completion of doctoral program. *Degree requirements:* For master's, capstone, internship. *Entrance requirements:* For master's, GRE, GMAT. Additional exam requirements/recommendations for international students: required—TOEFL (minimum score 600 paper-based; 100 iBT). Electronic applications accepted.

University of Southern Indiana, Graduate Studies, College of Liberal Arts, Program in Public Administration, Evansville, IN 47712-3590. Offers nonprofit administration (MPA); public sector administration (MPA). *Program availability:* Part-time, evening/weekend. *Entrance requirements:* For master's, resume, 2 letters of reference, personal statement, minimum GPA of 3.0. Additional exam requirements/recommendations for international students: required—TOEFL (minimum score 550 paper-based; 79 iBT), IELTS (minimum score 6). Electronic applications accepted.

University of South Florida, Innovative Education, Tampa, FL 33620-9951. Offers adult, career and higher education (Graduate Certificate), including college teaching, leadership in developing human resources, leadership in higher education; Africana studies (Graduate Certificate), including diasporas and health disparities, genocide and human rights; aging studies (Graduate Certificate), including gerontology; art research (Graduate Certificate), including museum studies; business foundations (Graduate Certificate); chemical and biomedical engineering (Graduate Certificate), including materials science and engineering, water, health and sustainability; child and family studies (Graduate Certificate), including positive behavior support; civil and industrial engineering (Graduate Certificate), including transportation systems analysis; community and family health (Graduate Certificate), including maternal and child health, social marketing and public health, violence and injury: prevention and intervention, women's health; criminology (Graduate Certificate), including criminal justice administration; data science for public administration (Graduate Certificate); digital humanities (Graduate Certificate); educational measurement and research (Graduate Certificate), including evaluation; English (Graduate Certificate), including comparative literary studies, creative writing, professional and technical communication; entrepreneurship (Graduate Certificate); environmental health (Graduate Certificate), including safety management; epidemiology and biostatistics (Graduate Certificate), including applied biostatistics, biostatistics, concepts and tools of epidemiology, epidemiology, epidemiology of infectious diseases; geography, environment and planning (Graduate Certificate), including community development, environmental policy and management, geographical information systems; geology (Graduate Certificate), including hydrogeology; global health (Graduate Certificate), including disaster management, global health and Latin American and Caribbean studies, global health practice, humanitarian assistance, infection control; government and international affairs (Graduate Certificate), including Cuban studies, globalization studies; health policy and management (Graduate Certificate), including health management and leadership, public health policy and programs; hearing specialist: early intervention (Graduate Certificate); industrial and management systems engineering (Graduate Certificate), including systems engineering, technology management; information studies (Graduate Certificate), including school library media specialist; information systems/decision sciences (Graduate Certificate), including analytics and business intelligence; instructional technology (Graduate Certificate), including distance education, Florida digital/virtual educator, instructional design, multimedia design, Web design; internal medicine, bioethics and medical humanities (Graduate Certificate), including biomedical ethics; Latin American and Caribbean studies (Graduate Certificate); leadership for coastal resiliency planning (Graduate Certificate); mass communications (Graduate Certificate), including multimedia journalism; mathematics and statistics (Graduate Certificate), including mathematics; medicine (Graduate Certificate), including aging and neuroscience, bioinformatics, biotechnology, brain fitness and memory management, clinical investigation, hand and upper limb rehabilitation, health informatics, health sciences, integrative weight management, intellectual property, medicine and gender, metabolic and nutritional medicine, metabolic cardiology, pharmacy sciences; national and competitive intelligence (Graduate Certificate); nursing (Graduate Certificate), including simulation based academic fellowship in advanced pain management; psychological and social foundations (Graduate Certificate), including career counseling, college teaching, diversity in education, mental health counseling, school counseling; public affairs (Graduate Certificate), including nonprofit management, public management, research administration; public health (Graduate Certificate), including assessing chemical toxicity and public health risks, health equity, pharmacoepidemiology, public health generalist, toxicology, translational research in adolescent behavioral health; public health practices (Graduate Certificate), including planning for healthy communities; rehabilitation and mental health counseling (Graduate Certificate), including integrative mental health care, marriage and family therapy, rehabilitation technology; secondary education (Graduate Certificate), including ESOL, foreign language education: culture and content, foreign language education: professional; social work (Graduate Certificate), including geriatric social work/clinical gerontology; special education (Graduate Certificate), including autism spectrum disorder, disabilities education: severe/profound; world languages (Graduate Certificate), including teaching English as a second language (TESL) or foreign language. *Unit head:* Dr. Cynthia DeLuca, Associate Vice President and Assistant Vice Provost, 813-974-3077, Fax: 813-974-7061, E-mail: deluca@usf.edu. *Application contact:* Owen Hooper, Director, Summer and Alternative Calendar Programs, 813-974-6917, E-mail: hooper@usf.edu.
Website: http://www.usf.edu/innovative-education/

The University of Tennessee, Graduate School, College of Arts and Sciences, Department of Political Science, Program in Public Administration, Knoxville, TN 37996. Offers MPA, JD/MPA. *Accreditation:* NASPAA. *Program availability:* Part-time. *Degree requirements:* For master's, thesis or alternative. *Entrance requirements:* For master's, GRE General Test, minimum GPA of 2.7. Additional exam requirements/recommendations for international students: required—TOEFL. Electronic applications accepted.

The University of Tennessee at Chattanooga, Department of Political Science and Public Service, Chattanooga, TN 37403. Offers local government management (MPA); non-profit management (MPA); public administration (MPA); public administration and non-profit management (Postbaccalaureate Certificate). *Program availability:* Part-time, evening/weekend. *Faculty:* 12 full-time (5 women), 4 part-time/adjunct (0 women). *Students:* 21 full-time (15 women), 12 part-time (7 women); includes 5 minority (4 Black or African American, non-Hispanic/Latino; 1 Asian, non-Hispanic/Latino). Average age 30. 17 applicants, 82% accepted, 13 enrolled. In 2019, 12 master's, 1 other advanced degree awarded. *Degree requirements:* For master's, internship. *Entrance requirements:* For master's, GRE General Test if applicant's undergraduate GPA is less than 3.25, three letters of recommendation; for Postbaccalaureate Certificate, bachelor's degree with related experience or master's degree. Additional exam requirements/recommendations for international students: required—TOEFL (minimum score 550 paper-based; 79 iBT), IELTS (minimum score 6). *Application deadline:* For fall admission, 6/15 priority date for domestic students, 7/1 for international students; for spring admission, 11/1 priority date for domestic students, 11/1 for international students. Applications are processed on a rolling basis. Application fee: $35 ($40 for international students). Electronic applications accepted. *Financial support:* Research assistantships, career-related internships or fieldwork, scholarships/grants, and unspecified assistantships available. Support available to part-time students. Financial award application deadline: 7/1; financial award applicants required to submit FAFSA. *Unit head:* Dr. Michelle D. Deardorf, Department Head, 423-425-4231, Fax: 423-425-2373, E-mail: michelle-deardorff@utc.edu. *Application contact:* Dr. Joanne Romagni, Dean of the Graduate School, 423-425-4478, Fax: 423-425-5223, E-mail: joanne-romagni@utc.edu.
Website: http://www.utc.edu/political-science-public-service/

The University of Texas at Arlington, Graduate School, College of Architecture, Planning and Public Affairs, Program in Public Administration, Arlington, TX 76019. Offers MPA. *Accreditation:* NASPAA. *Program availability:* Part-time, evening/weekend, online learning. *Degree requirements:* For master's, comprehensive exam, thesis or alternative. *Entrance requirements:* For master's, GRE General Test, three letters of recommendation, essay (approximately 250 words), minimum GPA of 3.0. Additional exam requirements/recommendations for international students: required—TOEFL (minimum score 550 paper-based). Electronic applications accepted.

The University of Texas at Austin, Graduate School, Lyndon B. Johnson School of Public Affairs, Austin, TX 78712-1111. Offers global policy studies (MGPS); public affairs (MP Aff); public leadership (EMPL); public policy (PhD); JD/MP Aff; MBA/MP Aff; MP Aff/MA; MP Aff/MSE. *Accreditation:* NASPAA (one or more programs are accredited). *Program availability:* Part-time. *Degree requirements:* For master's, thesis, summer internship; for doctorate, thesis/dissertation. *Entrance requirements:* For master's, GRE General Test (for MP Aff and MGPS), minimum GPA of 3.0 in upper-division classes, seven years of experience in the public sector, and interview (for EMPL); for doctorate, GRE General Test, master's degree in policy-related field. Additional exam requirements/recommendations for international students: required—TOEFL. Electronic applications accepted.

The University of Texas at Dallas, School of Economic, Political and Policy Sciences, Program in Public and Nonprofit Management, Richardson, TX 75080. Offers applied sociology (MS); public affairs (MPA, PhD). *Accreditation:* NASPAA. *Program availability:* Part-time, evening/weekend. *Faculty:* 11 full-time (4 women), 3 part-time/adjunct (0 women). *Students:* 40 full-time (25 women), 58 part-time (35 women); includes 41 minority (16 Black or African American, non-Hispanic/Latino; 4 Asian, non-Hispanic/Latino; 18 Hispanic/Latino; 3 Two or more races, non-Hispanic/Latino), 14 international. Average age 37. 97 applicants, 49% accepted, 28 enrolled. In 2019, 29 master's, 4 doctorates awarded. *Degree requirements:* For master's, internship; for doctorate, thesis/dissertation. *Entrance requirements:* For master's and doctorate, GRE (minimum combined score of 1000 on verbal and quantitative), minimum GPA of 3.0 in upper-level course work in field. Additional exam requirements/recommendations for international students: required—TOEFL (minimum score 550 paper-based). *Application deadline:* For fall admission, 7/15 for domestic students, 5/1 priority date for international students; for spring admission, 11/15 for domestic students, 9/1 priority date for international students. Applications are processed on a rolling basis. Application fee: $50 ($100 for international students). Electronic applications accepted. *Expenses: Tuition, area resident:* Full-time $16,504. Tuition, state resident: full-time $16,504. Tuition, nonresident: full-time $34,266. Tuition and fees vary according to course load. *Financial support:* In 2019–20, 10 students received support, including 1 research assistantship with partial tuition reimbursement available (averaging $18,000 per year), 9 teaching assistantships with partial tuition reimbursements available (averaging $13,500 per year); career-related internships or fieldwork, Federal Work-Study, institutionally sponsored loans, and scholarships/grants also available. Support available to part-time students. Financial award application deadline: 4/30; financial award applicants required to submit FAFSA. *Unit head:* Dr. Meghna Sabharwal, Program Head, 972-883-6473, Fax: 972-883-2735, E-mail: ph.pnm@utdallas.edu. *Application contact:* Rita Medford, Graduate Program Administrator, 972-883-4932, Fax: 972-883-2735, E-mail: gpa.pnm@utdallas.edu.
Website: https://epps.utdallas.edu/about/programs/public-and-nonprofit-management/

The University of Texas at San Antonio, College of Public Policy, Department of Public Administration, San Antonio, TX 78207. Offers MPA. *Accreditation:* NASPAA. *Program availability:* Part-time, evening/weekend. *Degree requirements:* For master's, comprehensive exam, final exit paper. *Entrance requirements:* For master's, bachelor's degree with 18 credit hours in field of study or in another appropriate field of study, two letters of recommendation, statement of purpose. Additional exam requirements/recommendations for international students: required—TOEFL (minimum score 550 paper-based; 79 iBT), IELTS (minimum score 6.5). Electronic applications accepted.

The University of Texas at Tyler, College of Arts and Sciences, Department of Social Sciences, Tyler, TX 75799-0001. Offers criminal justice (MS); public administration (MPA); sociology (MS). *Program availability:* Part-time, evening/weekend. *Faculty:* 5 full-time (2 women), 5 part-time/adjunct (1 woman). *Students:* 17 full-time (12 women), 36 part-time (25 women); includes 22 minority (7 Black or African American, non-Hispanic/Latino; 1 Asian, non-Hispanic/Latino; 12 Hispanic/Latino; 2 Two or more races, non-Hispanic/Latino), 2 international. Average age 36. 27 applicants, 89% accepted, 16 enrolled. In 2019, 19 master's awarded. *Degree requirements:* For master's, comprehensive exam, thesis optional. *Entrance requirements:* For master's, GRE General Test, minimum GPA of 3.0. Additional exam requirements/recommendations for international students: required—TOEFL. *Application deadline:* For fall admission, 8/17 priority date for domestic students, 7/1 priority date for international students; for spring admission, 12/21 priority date for domestic students, 11/1 priority date for international students. Applications are processed on a rolling basis. Application fee: $25 ($50 for international students). *Financial support:* In 2019–20, 1 fellowship (averaging $1,000 per year) was awarded; research assistantships, teaching assistantships, career-related internships or fieldwork, Federal Work-Study, and scholarships/grants also available. Support available to part-time students. Financial award application deadline: 7/1; financial award applicants required to submit FAFSA. *Unit head:* Dr. Thomas Guderjan, Chair, 903-566-7418, E-mail: tguderjan@uttyler.edu. *Application contact:* Dr. Thomas Guderjan, Chair, 903-566-7418, E-mail: tguderjan@uttyler.edu.
Website: https://www.uttyler.edu/socialsciences/

The University of Texas Rio Grande Valley, College of Liberal Arts, Department of Public Affairs and Security Studies, Edinburg, TX 78539. Offers global security studies and leadership (MPA); public administration (MPA); public policy and management (MPA). *Faculty:* 4 full-time (1 woman), 2 part-time/adjunct (1 woman). *Students:* 14 full-time (8 women), 135 part-time (75 women); includes 126 minority (3 Black or African American, non-Hispanic/Latino; 123 Hispanic/Latino), 2 international. Average age 33. 67 applicants, 93% accepted, 40 enrolled. In 2019, 56 master's awarded. *Expenses: Tuition, area resident:* Full-time $5959; part-time $440 per credit hour. Tuition, state resident: full-time $5959. Tuition, nonresident: full-time $5959. *International tuition:* $13,321 full-time. *Required fees:* $1169; $185 per credit hour.
Website: utrgv.edu/pass/index.htm

University of the District of Columbia, School of Business and Public Administration, Program in Public Administration, Washington, DC 20008-1175. Offers MPA. *Program availability:* Part-time, evening/weekend. *Degree requirements:* For master's, comprehensive exam, thesis optional. *Entrance requirements:* For master's, GMAT or GRE General Test, writing proficiency exam. Additional exam requirements/recommendations for international students: required—TOEFL.

The University of Toledo, College of Graduate Studies, College of Languages, Literature and Social Sciences, Department of Political Science and Public Administration, Toledo, OH 43606-3390. Offers health care policy and administration (Certificate); management of non-profit organizations (Certificate); municipal administration (Certificate); political science (MA); public administration (MPA); JD/MPA. *Program availability:* Part-time. *Degree requirements:* For master's, comprehensive exam (for some programs), thesis. *Entrance requirements:* For master's, GRE General Test, minimum cumulative point-hour ratio of 2.7 (3.0 for MPA) for all previous academic work, three letters of recommendation, statement of purpose, transcripts from all prior institutions attended; for Certificate, minimum cumulative point-hour ratio of 2.7 for all previous academic work, three letters of recommendation, statement of purpose, transcripts from all prior institutions attended. Additional exam requirements/recommendations for international students: required—TOEFL (minimum score 550 paper-based; 80 iBT). Electronic applications accepted.

University of Utah, Graduate School, College of Social and Behavioral Science, Department of Political Science, Program in Political Science, Salt Lake City, UT 84112-1107. Offers American politics (MA, MS, PhD); comparative politics (MA, MS, PhD); international relations (MA, MS, PhD); political theory (MA, MS, PhD); public administration (MA, MS, PhD). *Program availability:* Part-time. *Faculty:* 21 full-time (6 women), 2 part-time/adjunct (0 women). *Students:* 100 full-time (55 women), 97 part-time (52 women); includes 36 minority (2 Black or African American, non-Hispanic/Latino; 4 Asian, non-Hispanic/Latino; 20 Hispanic/Latino; 1 Native Hawaiian or other Pacific Islander, non-Hispanic/Latino; 9 Two or more races, non-Hispanic/Latino), 6 international. Average age 32. 47 applicants, 66% accepted, 14 enrolled. In 2019, 84 master's, 5 doctorates awarded. Terminal master's awarded for partial completion of doctoral program. *Degree requirements:* For master's, final project, defense; for

doctorate, comprehensive exam, thesis/dissertation. *Entrance requirements:* For master's and doctorate, GRE General Test, minimum GPA of 3.2. Additional exam requirements/recommendations for international students: required—TOEFL (minimum score 580 paper-based; 80 iBT), IELTS (minimum score 6.5). *Application deadline:* For fall admission, 1/15 priority date for domestic and international students. Application fee: $55 ($65 for international students). Electronic applications accepted. *Expenses:* General graduate tuition charged by the university. *Financial support:* In 2019–20, 2 students received support, including 1 fellowship (averaging $24,000 per year), 23 teaching assistantships (averaging $11,043 per year); research assistantships and unspecified assistantships also available. Financial award application deadline: 4/1; financial award applicants required to submit CSS PROFILE or FAFSA. *Unit head:* Dr. Brent J. Steele, Department Chair and Professor, 801-581-7031, Fax: 801-585-6492, E-mail: brent.steele@utah.edu. *Application contact:* Sandy Hiskey, Graduate Academic Advisor, 801-581-8608, Fax: 801-585-6492, E-mail: sandy.hiskey@utah.edu. Website: http://www.poli-sci.utah.edu/

University of Vermont, Graduate College, College of Agriculture and Life Sciences, Program in Public Administration, Burlington, VT 05405. Offers MPA. *Accreditation:* NASPAA. *Entrance requirements:* For master's, GRE General Test. Additional exam requirements/recommendations for international students: required—TOEFL (minimum score 550 paper-based, 90 iBT) or IELTS (6.5). Electronic applications accepted. *Expenses:* Contact institution.

University of Victoria, Faculty of Graduate Studies, Faculty of Human and Social Development, School of Public Administration, Victoria, BC V8W 2Y2, Canada. Offers dispute resolution (MADR); public administration (MPA, PhD); MPA/LL B. *Program availability:* Part-time, evening/weekend, online learning. *Degree requirements:* For master's, thesis (for some programs), report; for doctorate, thesis/dissertation, candidacy exam. *Entrance requirements:* For master's, GMAT or GRE General Test, professional resume; for doctorate, GMAT or GRE General Test. Additional exam requirements/recommendations for international students: required—TOEFL (minimum score 610 paper-based). Electronic applications accepted.

University of Washington, Graduate School, Evans School of Public Policy and Governance, Seattle, WA 98195. Offers public administration (MPA); public policy and management (PhD); JD/MPA; MPA/MAIS; MPA/MPH; MPA/MS; MPA/MUP. *Accreditation:* NASPAA. *Program availability:* Part-time, evening/weekend. *Degree requirements:* For master's, thesis, internship or cooperative experience. *Entrance requirements:* For master's and doctorate, GRE General Test, minimum GPA of 3.0. Additional exam requirements/recommendations for international students: required—TOEFL (minimum score 580 paper-based; 92 iBT). Electronic applications accepted.

University of West Florida, College of Education and Professional Studies, Department of Legal Studies, Public Administration and Sport Management, Pensacola, FL 32514-5750. Offers MSA. *Program availability:* Part-time, evening/weekend. *Degree requirements:* For master's, thesis or alternative. *Entrance requirements:* For master's, GRE General Test, minimum GPA of 3.0. Additional exam requirements/recommendations for international students: required—TOEFL (minimum score 550 paper-based).

The University of Winnipeg, Faculty of Graduate Studies, Program in Public Administration, Winnipeg, MB R3B 2E9, Canada. Offers MPA. *Program availability:* Part-time. *Degree requirements:* For master's, comprehensive exam, thesis optional. *Entrance requirements:* For master's, minimum GPA of 3.0 in last 60 credit hours.

University of Wisconsin–Milwaukee, Graduate School, College of Letters and Science, Department of Public and Nonprofit Administration, Milwaukee, WI 53201-0413. Offers public administration (MPA), including general public administration, municipal management, non-profit management. *Program availability:* Part-time. *Entrance requirements:* For master's, GRE General Test, minimum GPA of 3.0. Additional exam requirements/recommendations for international students: required—TOEFL (minimum score 550 paper-based; 79 iBT), IELTS (minimum score 6.5). Electronic applications accepted.

University of Wisconsin–Oshkosh, Graduate Studies, College of Letters and Science, Department of Public Administration, Oshkosh, WI 54901. Offers general agency (MPA); health care (MPA). *Program availability:* Part-time, evening/weekend. *Degree requirements:* For master's, thesis or alternative. *Entrance requirements:* For master's, public service-related experience, resume, sample of written work. Additional exam requirements/recommendations for international students: required—TOEFL (minimum score 550 paper-based; 79 iBT). Electronic applications accepted.

University of Wyoming, College of Arts and Sciences, School of Politics, Public Affairs and International Studies, Program in Public Administration, Laramie, WY 82071. Offers MPA. *Program availability:* Part-time, online learning. *Degree requirements:* For master's, comprehensive exam (for some programs), thesis (for some programs). *Entrance requirements:* For master's, GRE General Test, minimum GPA of 3.0. Additional exam requirements/recommendations for international students: required—TOEFL (minimum score 525 paper-based). Electronic applications accepted.

Upper Iowa University, Online Master's Programs, Fayette, IA 52142-1857. Offers accounting (MBA); corporate financial management (MBA); emergency management and homeland security (MPA); general management (MBA); general studies (MPA); government administration (MPA); health and human services (MPA); human resources management (MBA); nonprofit organizational management (MPA); organizational development (MBA); public management (MPA); sport administration (MSA). *Program availability:* Part-time, online learning. *Degree requirements:* For master's, research project. *Entrance requirements:* For master's, GMAT, GRE, or minimum GPA of 2.7 during last 60 hours. Additional exam requirements/recommendations for international students: required—TOEFL (minimum score 570 paper-based). Electronic applications accepted.

Valdosta State University, Department of Political Science, Valdosta, GA 31698. Offers public administration (MPA, DPA). *Accreditation:* NASPAA. *Program availability:* Part-time, evening/weekend, online learning. *Degree requirements:* For master's, comprehensive written and/or oral exams, internship; for doctorate, portfolio/dissertation. *Entrance requirements:* For master's, GMAT, GRE General Test, or MAT, minimum GPA of 2.5; for doctorate, GRE, recommendations. Additional exam requirements/recommendations for international students: required—TOEFL (minimum score 523 paper-based). Electronic applications accepted.

Villanova University, Graduate School of Liberal Arts and Sciences, Department of Public Administration, Villanova, PA 19085-1699. Offers city management (Certificate); nonprofit management (Certificate); public administration (MPA, Certificate). *Accreditation:* NASPAA. *Program availability:* Part-time, evening/weekend, 100% online. *Degree requirements:* For master's, comprehensive exam. *Entrance requirements:* For master's, GRE General Test, minimum GPA of 3.0, statement of goals, 3 letters of recommendation. Additional exam requirements/recommendations for international students: required—TOEFL. Electronic applications accepted.

Virginia Commonwealth University, Graduate School, L. Douglas Wilder School of Government and Public Affairs, Program in Public Administration, Richmond, VA 23284-9005. Offers financial management (MPA); human resource management (MPA); state and local government management (MPA). *Accreditation:* NASPAA. *Program availability:* Part-time. *Entrance requirements:* For master's, GRE, GMAT or LSAT. Additional exam requirements/recommendations for international students: required—TOEFL (minimum score 600 paper-based; 100 iBT); recommended—IELTS (minimum score 6.5). Electronic applications accepted.

Virginia International University, School of Public and International Affairs, Fairfax, VA 22030. Offers international relations (MS); public administration (MPA).

Virginia Polytechnic Institute and State University, Graduate School, College of Architecture and Urban Studies, Blacksburg, VA 24061. Offers architecture (M Arch, MS); architecture and design research (PhD); building construction science management (MS); creative technologies (MFA); environmental design and planning (PhD); government and international affairs (MPIA); landscape architecture (MLA, PhD); planning, governance, and globalization (PhD); public administration and public affairs (MPA, PhD); urban and regional planning (MURPL). *Accreditation:* ASLA (one or more programs are accredited). *Faculty:* 145 full-time (58 women), 2 part-time/adjunct (1 woman). *Students:* 304 full-time (156 women), 180 part-time (77 women); includes 90 minority (40 Black or African American, non-Hispanic/Latino; 19 Asian, non-Hispanic/Latino; 24 Hispanic/Latino; 7 Two or more races, non-Hispanic/Latino), 130 international. Average age 33. 475 applicants, 72% accepted, 126 enrolled. In 2019, 130 master's, 23 doctorates awarded. *Degree requirements:* For master's, comprehensive exam (for some programs), thesis (for some programs); for doctorate, comprehensive exam (for some programs), thesis/dissertation (for some programs). *Entrance requirements:* For master's and doctorate, GRE/GMAT. Additional exam requirements/recommendations for international students: required—TOEFL (minimum score 90 iBT). *Application deadline:* For fall admission, 8/1 for domestic students, 4/1 for international students; for spring admission, 1/1 for domestic students, 9/1 for international students. Applications are processed on a rolling basis. Application fee: $75. Electronic applications accepted. *Expenses:* Tuition, state resident: full-time $13,700; part-time $761.25 per credit hour. Tuition, nonresident: full-time $27,614; part-time $1534 per credit hour. *Required fees:* $886.50 per term. Tuition and fees vary according to campus/location and program. *Financial support:* In 2019–20, 2 fellowships with full tuition reimbursements (averaging $24,875 per year), 35 research assistantships with full tuition reimbursements (averaging $16,344 per year), 126 teaching assistantships with full tuition reimbursements (averaging $11,525 per year) were awarded; scholarships/grants and unspecified assistantships also available. Financial award application deadline: 3/1; financial award applicants required to submit FAFSA. *Unit head:* Dr. Richard Blythe, Dean, 540-231-6416, Fax: 540-231-6332, E-mail: richbl1@vt.edu. *Application contact:* Christine Mattsson-Coon, Executive Assistant, 540-231-6416, Fax: 540-231-6332, E-mail: cmattsso@vt.edu.
Website: http://www.caus.vt.edu/

Walden University, Graduate Programs, School of Public Policy and Administration, Minneapolis, MN 55401. Offers criminal justice (MPA, MPP, MS, Graduate Certificate), including emergency management (MS, PhD), general program (MS), global leadership (MS, PhD), homeland security and policy coordination (MS, PhD), law and public policy (MS, PhD), policy analysis (MS, PhD), public management and leadership (MS, PhD), self-designed (MS), terrorism, mediation, and peace (MS, PhD); criminal justice and executive management (MS), including global leadership (MS, PhD); criminal justice leadership and executive management (MS), including emergency management (MS, PhD), general program, homeland security and policy coordination (MS, PhD), law and public policy (MS, PhD), policy analysis (MS, PhD), public management and leadership (MS, PhD), self-designed, terrorism, mediation, and peace (MS, PhD); emergency management (MPA, MPP, MS), including criminal justice (MS, PhD), general program (MS), homeland security (MS), public management and leadership (MS, PhD), terrorism and emergency management (MS); general program (MPA, MPP); global leadership (MPA, MPP); government management (Graduate Certificate); health policy (MPA, MPP); homeland security (Graduate Certificate); homeland security and policy coordination (MPA, MPP); international nongovernmental organizations (MPA, MPP); law and public policy (MPA, MPP); local government management for sustainable communities (MPA, MPP); nonprofit management (Graduate Certificate); nonprofit management and leadership (MPA, MPP, MS), including global leadership (MS, PhD), international nongovernmental organization (MS), local government for sustainable communities (MS), self-designed (MS); online teaching in higher education (Post-Master's Certificate); policy analysis (MPA); public management and leadership (MPA, MPP, Graduate Certificate); public policy (Graduate Certificate); public policy and administration (PhD), including criminal justice (MS, PhD), emergency management (MS, PhD), global leadership (MS, PhD), health policy, homeland security and policy coordination (MS, PhD), international nongovernmental organizations, law and public policy (MS, PhD), local government management for sustainable communities, nonprofit management and leadership, policy analysis (MS, PhD), public management and leadership (MS, PhD), terrorism, mediation, and peace (MS, PhD); strategic planning and public policy (Graduate Certificate); terrorism, mediation, and peace (MPA, MPP). *Program availability:* Part-time, evening/weekend, online only, 100% online. *Degree requirements:* For doctorate, thesis/dissertation, residency. *Entrance requirements:* For master's, bachelor's degree or higher; minimum GPA of 2.5; official transcripts; goal statement (for some programs); access to computer and Internet; for doctorate, master's degree or higher; three years of related professional or academic experience (preferred); minimum GPA of 3.0; goal statement and current resume (for select programs); official transcripts; access to computer and Internet; for other advanced degree, relevant work experience; access to computer and Internet. Additional exam requirements/recommendations for international students: required—TOEFL (minimum score 550 paper-based, 79 iBT), IELTS (minimum score 6.5), Michigan English Language Assessment Battery (minimum score 82), or PTE (minimum score 53). Electronic applications accepted.

Waldorf University, Program in Organizational Leadership, Forest City, IA 50436. Offers criminal justice leadership (MA); emergency management leadership (MA); fire/rescue executive leadership (MA); human resource development (MA); public administration (MA); sport management (MA); teacher leader (MA).

Washington Adventist University, Program in Public Administration, Takoma Park, MD 20912. Offers MPA. *Program availability:* Part-time. *Entrance requirements:* Additional exam requirements/recommendations for international students: required—TOEFL (minimum score 550 paper-based), IELTS (minimum score 5).

Wayne State University, College of Liberal Arts and Sciences, Department of Political Science, Detroit, MI 48202. Offers political science (MA, PhD); public administration (MPA), including economic development policy and management, health and human services policy and management, human and fiscal resource management, nonprofit policy and management, organizational behavior and management, urban and metropolitan policy and management; JD/MA. *Accreditation:* NASPAA. *Program availability:* Part-time, evening/weekend. *Faculty:* 22 full-time (9 women). *Students:* 50 full-time (22 women), 64 part-time (32 women); includes 28 minority (20 Black or African American, non-Hispanic/Latino; 2 Asian, non-Hispanic/Latino; 1 Hispanic/Latino; 5 Two or more races, non-Hispanic/Latino), 10 international. Average age 34. 105 applicants, 40% accepted, 24 enrolled. In 2019, 21 master's, 7 doctorates awarded. Terminal master's awarded for partial completion of doctoral program. *Degree requirements:* For master's, comprehensive exam (for some programs), thesis (for some programs); for doctorate, thesis/dissertation. *Entrance requirements:* For master's, GRE General Test, substantial undergraduate preparation in the social sciences, minimum upper-division undergraduate GPA of 3.0, two letters of recommendation, personal statement; for doctorate, GRE General Test, 3 letters of recommendation; personal statement; interview. Additional exam requirements/recommendations for international students: required—TOEFL (minimum score 550 paper-based; 79 iBT), TWE (minimum score 5.5), Michigan English Language Assessment Battery (minimum score 85); recommended—IELTS (minimum score 6.5). *Application deadline:* For fall admission, 5/15 for domestic students, 5/1 priority date for international students; for winter admission, 10/15 for domestic students, 9/1 priority date for international students. Applications are processed on a rolling basis. Application fee: $50. Electronic applications accepted. *Expenses:* $678.55 per credit in-state tuition, $1,469.75 per credit out-of-state tuition, $54.56 per credit hour student service fee, $315.70 registration fee. *Financial support:* In 2019–20, 48 students received support, including 4 fellowships with partial tuition reimbursements available (averaging $57,000 per year), 1 research assistantship with partial tuition reimbursement available (averaging $45,000 per year), 13 teaching assistantships with partial tuition reimbursements available (averaging $58,000 per year); scholarships/grants, health care benefits, and unspecified assistantships also available. Financial award applicants required to submit FAFSA. *Unit head:* Dr. Daniel Geller, Professor and Chair, 313-577-6328, E-mail: dgeller@wayne.edu. *Application contact:* Dr. Jeffrey Grynaviski, Graduate Director, 313-577-2620, E-mail: gradpolisci@wayne.edu.
Website: http://clas.wayne.edu/politicalscience/

Webster University, George Herbert Walker School of Business and Technology, Department of Management, St. Louis, MO 63119-3194. Offers business and organizational security management (MA); digital marketing management (Graduate Certificate); government contracting (Graduate Certificate); health administration (MHA); health care management (MA); health services management (MA); human resources development (MA); human resources management (MA); information technology management (MA, MS); management (D Mgt); management and leadership (MA); marketing (MA); nonprofit leadership (MA); nonprofit revenue development (Graduate Certificate); organizational development (Graduate Certificate); procurement and acquisitions management (MA); public administration (MPA); space systems operations management (MS). *Program availability:* Part-time, evening/weekend, online learning. *Degree requirements:* For master's, thesis (for some programs); for doctorate, thesis/dissertation, written exam. *Entrance requirements:* For doctorate, GMAT, 3 years of work experience, MBA. Additional exam requirements/recommendations for international students: required—TOEFL.

Western Kentucky University, Graduate School, Potter College of Arts and Letters, Department of Political Science, Bowling Green, KY 42101. Offers MPA. *Accreditation:* NASPAA. *Program availability:* Part-time, evening/weekend. *Degree requirements:* For master's, comprehensive exam, final exam. *Entrance requirements:* For master's, GRE General Test, minimum GPA of 2.75. Additional exam requirements/recommendations for international students: required—TOEFL (minimum score 555 paper-based; 79 iBT).

Western Michigan University, Graduate College, College of Arts and Sciences, Department of Political Science, Kalamazoo, MI 49008. Offers international development administration (MIDA), including Peace Corps; political science (MA, PhD). *Degree requirements:* For master's, thesis optional; for doctorate, thesis/dissertation.

Western Michigan University, Graduate College, College of Arts and Sciences, School of Public Affairs and Administration, Kalamazoo, MI 49008. Offers health care administration (MPA, Graduate Certificate); nonprofit leadership and administration (Graduate Certificate); public administration (PhD). *Accreditation:* NASPAA (one or more programs are accredited). *Degree requirements:* For doctorate, thesis/dissertation.

Westfield State University, College of Graduate and Continuing Education, Department of Political Science, Westfield, MA 01086. Offers criminal justice administration (MPA); non-profit management (MPA); public management (MPA). *Program availability:* Part-time, evening/weekend. *Degree requirements:* For master's, comprehensive exam, thesis (for some programs). *Entrance requirements:* For master's, GRE General Test or MAT, minimum undergraduate GPA of 2.8. Additional exam requirements/recommendations for international students: recommended—TOEFL (minimum score 550 paper-based; 79 iBT).

West Virginia University, Eberly College of Arts and Sciences, Morgantown, WV 26506. Offers biology (MS, PhD); chemistry (MS, PhD); communication studies (MA, PhD); computational statistics (PhD); creative writing (MFA); English (MA, PhD); forensic and investigative science (MS); forensic science (PhD); geography (MA); geology (MA, PhD); history (MA, PhD); legal studies (MLS); mathematics (MS); physics (MS, PhD); political science (MA, PhD); professional writing and editing (MA); psychology (MA); public administration (MPA); social work (MSW); sociology (MA, PhD); statistics (MS). *Program availability:* Part-time, evening/weekend, online learning. Terminal master's awarded for partial completion of doctoral program. *Degree requirements:* For master's, thesis (for some programs); for doctorate, comprehensive exam, thesis/dissertation. *Entrance requirements:* For master's and doctorate, GRE. Additional exam requirements/recommendations for international students: required—TOEFL (minimum score 600 paper-based); recommended—TWE. Electronic applications accepted.

Wichita State University, Graduate School, Fairmount College of Liberal Arts and Sciences, Hugo Wall School of Public Affairs, Wichita, KS 67260. Offers public administration (MPA). *Accreditation:* NASPAA. *Program availability:* Part-time, 100% online, blended/hybrid learning.

Widener University, College of Arts and Sciences, Program in Public Administration, Chester, PA 19013-5792. Offers MPA, Psy D/MPA. *Program availability:* Part-time, evening/weekend. *Degree requirements:* For master's, thesis or comprehensive exam. *Entrance requirements:* For master's, minimum undergraduate GPA of 3.0. Electronic applications accepted. *Expenses:* Contact institution.

Wilmington University, College of Business, New Castle, DE 19720-6491. Offers accounting (MBA, MS); business administration (MBA, DBA); environmental stewardship (MBA); finance (MBA); health care administration (MBA, MSM); homeland security (MBA, MSM); human resource management (MSM); management information systems (MBA, MSN); marketing (MSM); marketing management (MBA); military leadership (MSM); organizational leadership (MBA, MSM); public administration (MSM). *Program availability:* Part-time, evening/weekend. *Entrance requirements:* Additional exam requirements/recommendations for international students: required—TOEFL (minimum score 500 paper-based). Electronic applications accepted.

Wright State University, Graduate School, College of Liberal Arts, Department of Urban Affairs and Geography, Dayton, OH 45435. Offers public administration (MPA). *Accreditation:* NASPAA. *Degree requirements:* For master's, thesis optional. *Entrance requirements:* For master's, interview, minimum GPA of 2.7. Additional exam requirements/recommendations for international students: required—TOEFL.

York University, Faculty of Graduate Studies, Faculty of Liberal Arts and Professional Studies, Program in Public Policy, Administration and Law, Toronto, ON M3J 1P3, Canada. Offers MPPAL.

Public Affairs

Arizona State University at Tempe, College of Public Programs, School of Public Affairs, Phoenix, AZ 85004-0687. Offers emergency management and homeland security (MA); program evaluation (MS); public administration (MPA, PhD), including nonprofit administration (MPA), urban management (MPA); public policy (MPP); MPA/MSW. *Accreditation:* NASPAA (one or more programs are accredited). *Program availability:* Part-time, evening/weekend. Terminal master's awarded for partial completion of doctoral program. *Degree requirements:* For master's, thesis or alternative, policy analysis or capstone project; interactive Program of Study (iPOS) submitted before completing 50 percent of required credit hours; for doctorate, comprehensive exam, thesis/dissertation, interactive Program of Study (iPOS) submitted before completing 50 percent of required credit hours. *Entrance requirements:* For master's, GRE, minimum GPA of 3.0 or equivalent in last 2 years of work leading to bachelor's degree; for doctorate, GRE, minimum GPA of 3.0 or equivalent in last 2 years of work leading to bachelor's degree, 3 letters of recommendation, resume, statement of goals, samples of research reports. Additional exam requirements/recommendations for international students: required—TOEFL (minimum score 600 paper-based; 100 iBT), IELTS (minimum score 6.5). Electronic applications accepted. *Expenses:* Contact institution.

Binghamton University, State University of New York, Graduate School, College of Community and Public Affairs, Program in Community Research and Action, Binghamton, NY 13902-6000. Offers PhD. *Entrance requirements:* For doctorate, undergraduate and graduate transcripts, minimum undergraduate and graduate GPA of 3.0, personal statement, resume or curriculum vitae, three letters of recommendation, writing sample. Additional exam requirements/recommendations for international students: required—TOEFL (minimum score 100 iBT), IELTS (minimum score 7).

Cleveland State University, College of Graduate Studies, Maxine Goodman Levin College of Urban Affairs, Program in Urban Studies and Public Affairs, Cleveland, OH 44115. Offers communication (PhD); public administration (PhD); urban policy and development (PhD). *Program availability:* Part-time, evening/weekend. *Degree requirements:* For doctorate, comprehensive exam, thesis/dissertation. *Entrance requirements:* For doctorate, GRE General Test (minimum score: verbal and quantitative 50th percentile, analytical writing 4.0), minimum GPA of 3.5. Additional exam requirements/recommendations for international students: required—TOEFL (minimum score 550 paper-based; 78 iBT), IELTS (6.0), or International Test of English Proficiency (iTEP). Electronic applications accepted. *Expenses:* Contact institution.

Concordia University, School of Graduate Studies, Faculty of Arts and Science, School of Community and Public Affairs, Montréal, QC H3G 1M8, Canada. Offers community economic development (Diploma).

Cornell University, Graduate School, Graduate Fields of Human Ecology, Field of Public Affairs, Ithaca, NY 14853. Offers MPA. *Degree requirements:* For master's, thesis, research project, paper. *Entrance requirements:* For master's, GRE General Test, 2 letters of recommendation. Additional exam requirements/recommendations for international students: required—TOEFL (minimum score 550 paper-based; 77 iBT). Electronic applications accepted.

Drake University, School of Journalism and Mass Communication, Des Moines, IA 50311-4516. Offers brand communication (MCL); communication leadership (MCL); public affairs and advocacy (MCL). *Program availability:* Part-time, evening/weekend, 100% online, blended/hybrid learning. *Expenses: Tuition:* Full-time $19,300; part-time $625 per credit hour. Tuition and fees vary according to degree level, program and student level.

Florida International University, Steven J. Green School of International and Public Affairs, Department of Public Administration, Miami, FL 33199. Offers public administration (MPA); public affairs (PhD); JD/MPA; MS/MPA. *Accreditation:* NASPAA (one or more programs are accredited). *Program availability:* Part-time, evening/weekend. *Faculty:* 14 full-time (5 women), 16 part-time/adjunct (8 women). *Students:* 96 full-time (60 women), 125 part-time (88 women); includes 182 minority (54 Black or African American, non-Hispanic/Latino; 2 Asian, non-Hispanic/Latino; 120 Hispanic/Latino; 6 Two or more races, non-Hispanic/Latino), 18 international. Average age 31. 115 applicants, 71% accepted, 64 enrolled. In 2019, 92 master's, 9 doctorates awarded. *Degree requirements:* For doctorate, comprehensive exam, thesis/dissertation. *Entrance requirements:* For master's, minimum undergraduate GPA of 3.0 in upper-level coursework, letter of recommendation, letter of intent; for doctorate, GRE, minimum undergraduate GPA of 3.0 in upper-level coursework, 3 letters of recommendation, samples of scholarly written work, interview (when student lives within 50 miles of campus). Additional exam requirements/recommendations for international students: required—TOEFL (minimum score 550 paper-based; 80 iBT). *Application deadline:* For fall admission, 6/1 for domestic students, 4/1 for international students; for spring admission, 10/1 for domestic students, 9/1 for international students. Applications are processed on a rolling basis. Application fee: $30. Electronic applications accepted. *Expenses: Tuition, area resident:* Full-time $8912; part-time $446 per credit hour. Tuition, state resident: full-time $8912; part-time $446 per credit hour. Tuition, nonresident: full-time $21,393; part-time $992 per credit hour. *Required fees:* $2194. *Financial support:* Institutionally sponsored loans and scholarships/grants available. Financial award application deadline: 3/1; financial award applicants required to submit FAFSA. *Unit head:* Dr. Howard Frank, Chair, 305-348-0410, E-mail: howard.frank@fiu.edu. *Application contact:* Nanett Rojas, Manager, Admissions Operations, 305-348-7464, Fax: 305-348-7441, E-mail: gradadm@fiu.edu.

George Mason University, College of Humanities and Social Sciences, Department of Philosophy, Fairfax, VA 22030. Offers ethics and public affairs (MA); philosophy and cultural theory (MA). *Entrance requirements:* For master's, college transcripts, goals statement, 2 letters of recommendation, resume, writing sample; completion of certain undergraduate preparation coursework with grades of B or higher in each course (for philosophy and cultural theory). Additional exam requirements/recommendations for international students: required—TOEFL (minimum score 575 paper-based, 88 iBT), IELTS (6.5), or PTE (59). Electronic applications accepted.

The George Washington University, Columbian College of Arts and Sciences, School of Media and Public Affairs, Washington, DC 20052. Offers MA, Graduate Certificate. *Entrance requirements:* For master's, GRE General Test. Additional exam requirements/recommendations for international students: required—TOEFL (minimum score 550 paper-based; 80 iBT). Electronic applications accepted.

Indiana University Bloomington, School of Public and Environmental Affairs, Public Affairs Programs, Bloomington, IN 47405. Offers economic development (MPA); energy (MPA); environmental policy (PhD); environmental policy and natural resource management (MPA); information systems (MPA); international development (MPA); local government management (MPA); nonprofit management (MPA, Certificate); policy analysis (MPA); public budgeting and financial management (Certificate); public finance (PhD); public financial administration (MPA); public management (MPA, PhD, Certificate); public policy analysis (PhD); social entrepreneurship (Certificate); specialized public affairs (MPA); sustainability and sustainable development (MPA); JD/MPA; MPA/MA; MPA/MIS; MPA/MLS; MSES/MPA. *Accreditation:* NASPAA (one or more programs are accredited). *Program availability:* Part-time. *Degree requirements:* For master's, capstone, internship; for doctorate, comprehensive exam, thesis/dissertation. *Entrance requirements:* For master's, GRE General Test or GMAT, official transcripts, 3 letters of recommendation, resume, personal statement; for doctorate, GRE General Test, official transcripts, 3 letters of recommendation, statement of purpose. Additional exam requirements/recommendations for international students: required—TOEFL (minimum score 600 paper-based; 96 iBT); recommended—IELTS (minimum score 7). Electronic applications accepted.

Indiana University Northwest, School of Public and Environmental Affairs, Gary, IN 46408. Offers criminal justice (MPA); environmental affairs (Graduate Certificate); health services (MPA); nonprofit management (Certificate); public management (MPA, Graduate Certificate). *Accreditation:* NASPAA (one or more programs are accredited). *Program availability:* Part-time. *Entrance requirements:* For master's, GRE General Test (minimum combined verbal and quantitative score of 280), GMAT, or LSAT, letters of recommendation. Electronic applications accepted.

Indiana University of Pennsylvania, School of Graduate Studies and Research, College of Humanities and Social Sciences, Department of Political Science, Program in Public Affairs, Indiana, PA 15705. Offers MA. *Program availability:* Part-time. *Faculty:* 4 full-time (3 women), 1 part-time/adjunct (0 women). *Students:* 6 full-time (4 women), 4 part-time (2 women); includes 3 minority (2 Black or African American, non-Hispanic/Latino; 1 Hispanic/Latino), 2 international. Average age 29. 17 applicants, 100% accepted, 8 enrolled. In 2019, 11 master's awarded. *Degree requirements:* For master's, thesis optional. *Entrance requirements:* For master's, 2 letters of recommendation, official transcripts, goal statement. Additional exam requirements/recommendations for international students: required—TOEFL (minimum score 550 paper-based; 80 iBT), IELTS (minimum score 6.5). *Application deadline:* Applications are processed on a rolling basis. Application fee: $50. Electronic applications accepted. *Expenses: Tuition, area resident:* Full-time $9288; part-time $516 per credit. Tuition, nonresident: full-time $13,932; part-time $774 per credit. *Required fees:* $4454. One-time fee: $115 full-time. Tuition and fees vary according to course load and program. *Financial support:* In 2019–20, 1 fellowship (averaging $600 per year), 8 research assistantships with tuition reimbursements (averaging $2,975 per year) were awarded; career-related internships or fieldwork, Federal Work-Study, scholarships/grants, and unspecified assistantships also available. Support available to part-time students. Financial award application deadline: 4/15; financial award applicants required to submit FAFSA. *Unit head:* Dr. Sarah Wheeler, Graduate Coordinator, 724-357-2683, E-mail: SarahM.Wheeler@iup.edu. *Application contact:* Dr. Sarah Wheeler, Graduate Coordinator, 724-357-2683, E-mail: SarahM.Wheeler@iup.edu. Website: http://www.iup.edu/grad/publicaffairs/default.aspx

Indiana University-Purdue University Indianapolis, School of Public and Environmental Affairs, Indianapolis, IN 46202. Offers criminal justice and public safety (MS); homeland security and emergency management (Graduate Certificate); library management (Graduate Certificate); nonprofit management (Graduate Certificate); public affairs (MPA); public management (Graduate Certificate); social entrepreneurship: nonprofit and public benefit organizations (Graduate Certificate); JD/MPA; MLS/NMC; MLS/PMC; MPA/MA. *Accreditation:* CAHME (one or more programs are accredited); NASPAA. *Program availability:* Part-time, evening/weekend, online learning. *Entrance requirements:* For master's, GRE General Test, GMAT or LSAT, minimum GPA of 3.0 (preferred). Additional exam requirements/recommendations for international students: required—TOEFL (minimum score 93 iBT), IELTS (minimum score 6.5). Electronic applications accepted.

Indiana University South Bend, College of Liberal Arts and Sciences, South Bend, IN 46615. Offers advanced computer programming (Graduate Certificate); applied informatics (Graduate Certificate); applied mathematics and computer science (MS); behavior modification (Graduate Certificate); computer applications (Graduate Certificate); computer programming (Graduate Certificate); correctional management and supervision (Graduate Certificate); English (MA); health systems management (Graduate Certificate); international studies (Graduate Certificate); liberal studies (MLS); nonprofit management (Graduate Certificate); paralegal studies (Graduate Certificate); professional writing (Graduate Certificate); public affairs (MPA); public management (Graduate Certificate); social and cultural diversity (Graduate Certificate); strategic sustainability leadership (Graduate Certificate); technology for administration (Graduate Certificate). *Program availability:* Part-time, evening/weekend. *Degree requirements:* For master's, variable foreign language requirement, thesis (for some programs). *Entrance requirements:* For master's, minimum GPA of 3.0. Additional exam requirements/recommendations for international students: required—TOEFL (minimum score 550 paper-based; 80 iBT). *Expenses:* Contact institution.

The Institute of World Politics, Graduate Programs in National Security, Intelligence, and International Affairs, Washington, DC 20036. Offers American foreign policy (Certificate); comparative political culture (Certificate); conflict prevention (Certificate); counterintelligence (Certificate); counterterrorism (Certificate); cyber statecraft (Certificate); economic statecraft (Certificate); homeland security (Certificate); intelligence (Certificate); international politics (Certificate); national security affairs (Executive MA, Certificate); nonviolent conflict (Certificate); peace building, stabilization, and humanitarian affairs (Certificate); public diplomacy and strategic influence (Certificate); statecraft and international affairs (MA); statecraft and national security (MA, DSNS); strategic communication (Certificate); strategic intelligence studies (MA, Professional MA); strategic soft power (Certificate). *Program availability:* Part-time, evening/weekend. *Degree requirements:* For master's, 52 credit hours, comprehensive written and oral exam (for MA); proficiency in critical language (for MA in statecraft and international affairs); 28 credit hours (for Executive MA); 36 credit hours (for Professional MA); for doctorate, comprehensive exam, thesis/dissertation; for Certificate, 20 credit hours. *Entrance requirements:* For master's, resume, personal statement, 3 references, essay; 7-10 years of professional experience (for Executive MA); 5-7 years of professional experience (for Professional MA); for doctorate, MA. Additional exam requirements/recommendations for international students: required—TOEFL. Electronic applications accepted.

Jackson State University, Graduate School, College of Public Service, Jackson, MS 39217. Offers MA, MPPA, MSW, PhD. *Degree requirements:* For master's, comprehensive exam. *Entrance requirements:* For master's, GRE General Test. Additional exam requirements/recommendations for international students: required—TOEFL.

McMaster University, School of Graduate Studies, Faculty of Social Sciences, Department of Political Science, Hamilton, ON L8S 4M2, Canada. Offers international relations (PhD); political science (MA); public and the global economy (MA); public policy (PhD); public policy and administration (MA). *Program availability:* Part-time. *Degree requirements:* For master's, thesis or alternative. *Entrance requirements:* For master's, minimum B+ average. Additional exam requirements/recommendations for international students: required—TOEFL (minimum score 580 paper-based).

Merrimack College, School of Liberal Arts, North Andover, MA 01845-5800. Offers clinical mental health counseling (MS); interfaith spirituality (Certificate); public affairs (MPA); spiritual direction (MA, Certificate); spirituality (MA). *Program availability:* Part-time, evening/weekend. *Degree requirements:* For master's, internship/strategic capstone (for MPA); 700-hour fieldwork placement (for MS); practicum (for MA in spiritual direction); for Certificate, practicum (for spiritual direction). *Entrance requirements:* For master's, official college transcripts, resume, personal statement, 2 recommendations (3 for MS in clinical mental health counseling); interview (for MA in spirituality). Additional exam requirements/recommendations for international students: required—TOEFL (minimum score 84 iBT), IELTS (minimum score 6.5), PTE (minimum score 56). Electronic applications accepted. Application fee is waived when completed online. *Expenses:* Contact institution.

Metropolitan College of New York, Program in Public Administration, New York, NY 10006. Offers emergency and disaster management (MPA); public affairs and administration (MPA). *Program availability:* Evening/weekend. *Degree requirements:* For master's, thesis. *Entrance requirements:* For master's, appropriate work experience, interview, minimum GPA of 2.7, internship or job in administrative setting. Additional exam requirements/recommendations for international students: required—TOEFL (minimum score 600 paper-based). Electronic applications accepted. *Expenses:* Contact institution.

Metropolitan State University, College of Community Studies and Public Affairs, St. Paul, MN 55106-5000. Offers alcohol and drug counseling (MS); co-occurring disorders recovery counseling (MS); public administration (MPA); public and nonprofit administration (MPNA).

New Mexico Highlands University, Graduate Studies, College of Arts and Sciences, Department of History, Political Science, and Languages and Culture, Las Vegas, NM 87701. Offers public affairs (MA), including historical and cross-cultural perspectives, history/political science, political and governmental processes. *Degree requirements:* For master's, comprehensive exam, thesis or alternative. *Entrance requirements:* Additional exam requirements/recommendations for international students: required—TOEFL (minimum score 540 paper-based).

New Mexico Highlands University, Graduate Studies, College of Arts and Sciences, Department of Social and Behavioral Sciences, Las Vegas, NM 87701. Offers psychology (MS), including clinical psychology/counseling, general psychology; public affairs (MA), including applied sociology; Southwest studies (MA), including anthropology. *Program availability:* Part-time. *Degree requirements:* For master's, comprehensive exam, thesis or alternative. *Entrance requirements:* For master's, minimum undergraduate GPA of 3.0. Additional exam requirements/recommendations for international students: required—TOEFL (minimum score 540 paper-based).

The Ohio State University, Graduate School, John Glenn College of Public Affairs, Columbus, OH 43210. Offers public administration (MA, MPA); public policy and management (PhD). *Accreditation:* NASPAA (one or more programs are accredited). *Program availability:* Part-time. *Degree requirements:* For doctorate, thesis/dissertation. *Entrance requirements:* For master's, GRE General Test (for MPA), minimum GPA of 3.0 (for MA); for doctorate, GRE General Test. Additional exam requirements/recommendations for international students: required—TOEFL (minimum score 600 paper-based; 100 iBT); recommended—IELTS (minimum score 7.5). Electronic applications accepted.

Park University, School of Graduate and Professional Studies, Kansas City, MO 54105. Offers adult education (M Ed); business and government leadership (Graduate Certificate); business, government, and global society (MPA); communication and leadership (MA); creative and life writing (Graduate Certificate); disaster and emergency management (MPA, Graduate Certificate); educational leadership (M Ed); finance (MBA, Graduate Certificate); general business (MBA); global business (Graduate Certificate); healthcare administration (MHA); healthcare services management and leadership (Graduate Certificate); international business (MBA); language and literacy (M Ed), including English for speakers of other languages, special reading teacher/literacy coach; leadership of international healthcare organizations (Graduate Certificate); management information systems (MBA, Graduate Certificate); music performance (ADP, Graduate Certificate), including cello (MM, ADP), piano (MM, ADP), viola (MM, ADP), violin (MM, ADP); nonprofit and community services management (MPA); nonprofit leadership (Graduate Certificate); performance (MM), including cello (MM, ADP), piano (MM, ADP), viola (MM, ADP), violin (MM, ADP); public management (MPA); social work (MSW); teacher leadership (M Ed), including curriculum and assessment, instructional leader. *Program availability:* Part-time, evening/weekend, online learning. *Degree requirements:* For master's, comprehensive exam (for some programs), thesis (for some programs), internship (for some programs); exam (for some programs). *Entrance requirements:* For master's, GRE or GMAT (for some programs), teacher certification (for some M Ed programs), letters of recommendation, essay, resume (for some programs). Additional exam requirements/recommendations for international students: required—TOEFL (minimum score 550 paper-based; 79 iBT), IELTS (minimum score 6). Electronic applications accepted.

Penn State Harrisburg, Graduate School, School of Public Affairs, Middletown, PA 17057. Offers criminal justice (MA); health administration (MHA); health administration: long term care (Certificate); homeland security (MPS, Certificate); public administration (MPA, PhD); public administration: non-profit administration (Certificate); public budgeting and financial management (Certificate); public sector human resource management (Certificate). *Accreditation:* NASPAA.

Portland State University, Graduate Studies, College of Urban and Public Affairs, Hatfield School of Government, Department of Public Administration, Portland, OR 97207-0751. Offers collaborative governance (Certificate); energy policy and management (Certificate); global management and leadership (MPA); health administration (MPA); human resource management (MPA); local government (MPA); natural resource policy and administration (MPA); nonprofit and public management (Certificate); nonprofit management (MPA); public administration (EMPA); public affairs and policy (PhD); sustainable food systems (Certificate). *Accreditation:* CAHME; NASPAA (one or more programs are accredited). *Program availability:* Part-time, evening/weekend. *Faculty:* 14 full-time (6 women), 9 part-time/adjunct (5 women). *Students:* 86 full-time (55 women), 119 part-time (73 women); includes 46 minority (3 Black or African American, non-Hispanic/Latino; 4 American Indian or Alaska Native, non-Hispanic/Latino; 8 Asian, non-Hispanic/Latino; 18 Hispanic/Latino; 2 Native Hawaiian or other Pacific Islander, non-Hispanic/Latino; 11 Two or more races, non-Hispanic/Latino), 17 international. Average age 35. 138 applicants, 82% accepted, 67 enrolled. In 2019, 64 master's, 2 doctorates awarded. *Degree requirements:* For master's, integrative field experience (MPA), practicum (MPH); for doctorate, comprehensive exam, thesis/dissertation. *Entrance requirements:* For master's, GRE (minimum scores: verbal 150, quantitative 149, and analytic writing 4.5), minimum GPA of 3.0, 3 recommendation letters, resume, 500-word statement of intent; for doctorate, GRE, 3 recommendation letters, resume, 500-word personal essay. Additional exam requirements/recommendations for international students: required—TOEFL (minimum score 550 paper-based; 80 iBT), IELTS (minimum score 7). *Application deadline:* For fall admission, 8/15 for domestic and international students; for winter admission, 10/31 for domestic and international students; for spring admission, 1/31 for domestic and international students. Applications are processed on a rolling basis. Application fee: $65. Electronic applications accepted. *Expenses: Tuition, area resident:* Full-time $13,020; part-time $6510 per year. Tuition, state resident: full-time $13,020; part-time $6510 per year. Tuition, nonresident: full-time $19,830; part-time $9915 per year. *International tuition:* $19,830 full-time. *Required fees:* $1226. One-time fee: $350. Tuition and fees vary according to course load, program and reciprocity agreements. *Financial support:* In 2019–20, 1 research assistantship with full and partial tuition reimbursement (averaging $8,500 per year), 3 teaching assistantships (averaging $7,840 per year) were awarded; career-related internships or fieldwork, Federal Work-Study, scholarships/grants, and unspecified assistantships also available. Support available to part-time students. Financial award application deadline: 3/1; financial award applicants required to submit FAFSA. *Unit head:* Dr. Masami Nishishiba, Chair, 503-725-5151, E-mail: nishism@pdx.edu. *Application contact:* Megan Heljeson, Office Coordinator, 503-725-3921, Fax: 503-725-8250, E-mail: publicad@pdx.edu.
Website: https://www.pdx.edu/hatfieldschool/public-administration

Princeton University, Graduate School, Program in Population Studies, Princeton, NJ 08544-1019. Offers demography (PhD, Certificate); economics and demography (PhD); public affairs and demography (PhD); sociology and demography (PhD). *Degree requirements:* For doctorate, thesis/dissertation. *Entrance requirements:* For doctorate, GRE General Test. Additional exam requirements/recommendations for international students: required—TOEFL (minimum score 600 paper-based). Electronic applications accepted.

Princeton University, Graduate School, Woodrow Wilson School of Public and International Affairs, Princeton, NJ 08544-1019. Offers public affairs (MPA, PhD); public policy (MPP); JD/MPA. Terminal master's awarded for partial completion of doctoral program. *Degree requirements:* For master's, internship; for doctorate, one foreign language, thesis/dissertation. *Entrance requirements:* For master's, GRE General Test, original policy memo; for doctorate, GRE General Test. Additional exam requirements/recommendations for international students: required—TOEFL (minimum score 600 paper-based). Electronic applications accepted.

Syracuse University, Maxwell School of Citizenship and Public Affairs, MA/MS Program in Public Diplomacy, Syracuse, NY 13244. Offers MS/MA. *Entrance requirements:* Additional exam requirements/recommendations for international students: required—TOEFL (minimum score 100 iBT). Electronic applications accepted.

Syracuse University, S. I. Newhouse School of Public Communications, MS/MA in Public Diplomacy Program, Syracuse, NY 13244. Offers MS/MA. *Entrance requirements:* Additional exam requirements/recommendations for international students: required—TOEFL (minimum score 100 iBT). Electronic applications accepted.

Texas A&M University, Bush School of Government and Public Service, College Station, TX 77843. Offers international affairs (MIA). *Accreditation:* NASPAA. *Degree requirements:* For master's, summer internship. *Entrance requirements:* For master's, GRE (preferred) or GMAT. Additional exam requirements/recommendations for international students: required—TOEFL (minimum score 550 paper-based; 80 iBT), IELTS (minimum score 6), PTE (minimum score 53). Electronic applications accepted. *Expenses:* Contact institution.

The University of Alabama in Huntsville, School of Graduate Studies, College of Arts, Humanities, and Social Sciences, Program in Public Affairs, Huntsville, AL 35899. Offers MA. *Program availability:* Part-time. *Degree requirements:* For master's, comprehensive exam, thesis or alternative, oral and written exams. *Entrance requirements:* For master's, GRE General Test, minimum GPA of 3.0. Additional exam requirements/recommendations for international students: required—TOEFL (minimum score 500 paper-based; 80 iBT), IELTS (minimum score 6.5). Electronic applications accepted.

University of Arkansas at Little Rock, Graduate School, Clinton School of Public Service, Little Rock, AR 72204-1099. Offers MPS, Graduate Certificate.

University of Baltimore, Graduate School, College of Public Affairs, Baltimore, MD 21201-5779. Offers MPA, MS, DPA, JD/MPA, JD/MS.

University of California, Berkeley, Graduate Division, Graduate School of Public Policy, Program in Public Affairs, Berkeley, CA 94720. Offers MPA. *Program availability:* Part-time-only.

University of California, Los Angeles, Graduate Division, Luskin School of Public Affairs, Los Angeles, CA 90095. Offers MA, MPP, MSW, PhD, JD/MA, JD/MSW, MA/MA, MBA/MA, MD/PhD. *Accreditation:* CSWE. *Degree requirements:* For doctorate, thesis/dissertation, oral and written qualifying exams. *Entrance requirements:* For master's, minimum GPA of 3.0; for doctorate, minimum undergraduate GPA of 3.0. Additional exam requirements/recommendations for international students: required—TOEFL. Electronic applications accepted.

University of Central Florida, College of Community Innovation and Education, Program in Public Affairs, Orlando, FL 32816. Offers PhD. *Program availability:* Part-time, evening/weekend. *Students:* 36 full-time (20 women), 21 part-time (15 women); includes 24 minority (11 Black or African American, non-Hispanic/Latino; 3 Asian, non-Hispanic/Latino; 8 Hispanic/Latino; 2 Two or more races, non-Hispanic/Latino), 11 international. Average age 33. 50 applicants, 50% accepted, 13 enrolled. In 2019, 11 doctorates awarded. *Degree requirements:* For doctorate, comprehensive exam, thesis/dissertation, candidacy and qualifying exams. *Entrance requirements:* For doctorate, GRE General Test, letters of recommendation, resume, writing sample. Additional exam requirements/recommendations for international students: required—TOEFL. *Application deadline:* For fall admission, 3/1 for domestic students. Application fee: $30. Electronic applications accepted. *Financial support:* In 2019–20, 28 students received support, including 8 fellowships with partial tuition reimbursements available (averaging $5,068 per year), 10 research assistantships with partial tuition reimbursements available (averaging $6,343 per year), 31 teaching assistantships with partial tuition reimbursements available (averaging $5,019 per year); career-related internships or fieldwork, Federal Work-Study, institutionally sponsored loans, health care benefits, tuition waivers (partial), and unspecified assistantships also available. Financial award application deadline: 3/1; financial award applicants required to submit FAFSA. *Unit head:* Dr. Robyne Stevenson, Program Director, 407-823-3459, Fax: 407-823-0822, E-mail: robyne.stevenson@ucf.edu. *Application contact:* Associate Director, Graduate Admissions, 407-823-2766, Fax: 407-823-6442, E-mail: gradadmissions@ucf.edu. Website: https://www.cohpa.ucf.edu/publicaffairs/

University of Colorado Colorado Springs, School of Public Affairs, Colorado Springs, CO 80918. Offers criminal justice (MCJ); public administration (MPA). *Accreditation:* NASPAA. *Program availability:* Part-time, evening/weekend, 100% online, blended/hybrid learning. *Faculty:* 22 full-time (12 women), 20 part-time/adjunct (10 women). *Students:* 28 full-time (18 women), 194 part-time (127 women); includes 87 minority (19 Black or African American, non-Hispanic/Latino; 4 American Indian or Alaska Native, non-Hispanic/Latino; 6 Asian, non-Hispanic/Latino; 48 Hispanic/Latino; 10 Two or more races, non-Hispanic/Latino), 4 international. Average age 34. 89 applicants, 83% accepted, 58 enrolled. In 2019, 38 master's awarded. *Degree requirements:* For master's, internship, capstone project, or thesis. *Entrance requirements:* For master's, 2 professional and/or academic recommendations by qualified references that establish the applicant's personal qualifications for graduate work; 3.00 (or better) undergraduate GPA for regular admission into the MPA program; current resume; statement of goals (prompts given within the application). Additional exam requirements/recommendations for international students: recommended—TOEFL (minimum score 80 iBT), IELTS (minimum score 6.5). *Application deadline:* Applications are processed on a rolling basis. Application fee: $60 ($100 for international students). Electronic applications accepted. *Expenses:* Contact institution. *Financial support:* In 2019–20, 35 students received support. Career-related internships or fieldwork, Federal Work-Study, scholarships/grants, and tuition waivers available. Support available to part-time students. Financial award application deadline: 3/1; financial award applicants required to submit FAFSA. *Unit head:* Dr. George Reed, Dean, 719-255-4109, E-mail: george.reed@uccs.edu. *Application contact:* Stephani Hosain, Graduate Student Services Specialist, 719-255-4993, E-mail: shosain@uccs.edu. Website: https://www.uccs.edu/spa/

University of Colorado Denver, School of Public Affairs, Program in Public Affairs and Administration, Denver, CO 80127. Offers public administration (MPA), including domestic violence, emergency management and homeland security, environmental policy, management and law, homeland security and defense, local government, nonprofit management, public administration; public affairs (PhD). *Accreditation:* NASPAA. *Program availability:* Part-time, evening/weekend, online learning. Tuition and fees vary according to course load, program and reciprocity agreements.

University of Florida, Graduate School, College of Liberal Arts and Sciences, Department of Political Science, Gainesville, FL 32611. Offers educational policy (PhD); international development policy and administration (MA, Certificate); international relations (MA, MAT); political campaigning (MA, Certificate); political science (MA, PhD); public affairs (MA, Certificate); tropical conservation and development (MA, PhD); JD/MA. Terminal master's awarded for partial completion of doctoral program. *Degree requirements:* For master's, variable foreign language requirement, comprehensive exam (for some programs), thesis or alternative, internship (for some programs); for doctorate, variable foreign language requirement, comprehensive exam, thesis/dissertation. *Entrance requirements:* For master's and doctorate, GRE General Test (minimum score: 308 combined verbal/quantitative), minimum GPA of 3.5. Additional exam requirements/recommendations for international students: required—TOEFL (minimum score 550 paper-based; 80 iBT), IELTS (minimum score 6). Electronic applications accepted.

University of Louisville, Graduate School, College of Arts and Sciences, Department of Urban and Public Affairs, Louisville, KY 40208. Offers public administration (MPA), including human resources management, non-profit management, public policy and administration; urban and public affairs (PhD), including urban planning and development, urban policy and administration; urban planning (MUP), including administration of planning organizations, housing and community development, land use and environmental planning, spatial analysis. *Program availability:* Part-time, evening/weekend. *Faculty:* 13 full-time (6 women), 2 part-time/adjunct (1 woman). *Students:* 44 full-time (24 women), 24 part-time (14 women); includes 12 minority (6 Black or African American, non-Hispanic/Latino; 2 Hispanic/Latino; 4 Two or more races, non-Hispanic/Latino), 7 international. Average age 34. 51 applicants, 67% accepted, 25 enrolled. In 2019, 14 master's, 3 doctorates awarded. Terminal master's awarded for partial completion of doctoral program. *Degree requirements:* For master's, internship; for doctorate, comprehensive exam, thesis/dissertation. *Entrance requirements:* For master's, GRE General Test, 2 letters of reference, official transcripts. Minimum GPA of 3.0; for doctorate, GRE General Test, Two letters of reference, official transcripts. Masters degree in appropriate field. Additional exam requirements/recommendations for international students: required—TOEFL (minimum score 550 paper-based; 79 iBT), IELTS can be used in place of the TOEFL; recommended—IELTS (minimum score 6.5). *Application deadline:* For fall admission, 2/1 for domestic and international students. Applications are processed on a rolling basis. Application fee: $65. Electronic applications accepted. *Expenses: Tuition, area resident:* Full-time $13,000; part-time $723 per credit hour. *Tuition, state resident:* full-time $13,000; part-time $723 per credit hour. *Tuition, nonresident:* full-time $27,114; part-time $1507 per credit hour. *International tuition:* $27,114 full-time. *Required fees:* $196. Tuition and fees vary according to program and reciprocity agreements. *Financial support:* In 2019–20, 29 students received support, including 11 research assistantships with full tuition reimbursements available (averaging $19,000 per year); fellowships, teaching assistantships, health care benefits, and unspecified assistantships also available. Financial award application deadline: 2/1. *Unit head:* Dr. David Simpson, Professor/Chair, 502-852-8019, Fax: 502-852-4558, E-mail: dave.simpson@louisville.edu. Website: http://supa.louisville.edu

University of Minnesota, Twin Cities Campus, Graduate School, Humphrey School of Public Affairs, PhD Program in Public Affairs, Minneapolis, MN 55455. Offers management and governance (PhD); public policy (PhD); science, technology, and environmental policy (PhD); urban planning (PhD). *Program availability:* Part-time. *Degree requirements:* For doctorate, comprehensive exam, thesis/dissertation. *Entrance requirements:* For doctorate, GRE General Test. Additional exam requirements/recommendations for international students: required—TOEFL (minimum score 650 paper-based; 100 iBT), IELTS (minimum score 7). Electronic applications accepted. *Expenses:* Contact institution.

University of Minnesota, Twin Cities Campus, Graduate School, Humphrey School of Public Affairs, Program in Public Affairs, Minneapolis, MN 55455-0213. Offers MPA. *Program availability:* Part-time-only, evening/weekend. *Students:* 69 part-time (39 women); includes 22 minority (13 Black or African American, non-Hispanic/Latino; 3 American Indian or Alaska Native, non-Hispanic/Latino; 2 Asian, non-Hispanic/Latino; 4 Hispanic/Latino). Average age 41. 105 applicants, 43% accepted, 36 enrolled. In 2019, 26 master's awarded. *Entrance requirements:* For master's, 10 years of work experience. Additional exam requirements/recommendations for international students: required—TOEFL (minimum score 600 paper-based; 100 iBT), IELTS (minimum score 7). *Application deadline:* For fall admission, 4/1 priority date for domestic students, 4/1 for international students. Application fee: $75 ($95 for international students). Electronic applications accepted. *Expenses:* Contact institution. *Financial support:* In 2019–20, 11 students received support. Fellowships, career-related internships or fieldwork, Federal Work-Study, scholarships/grants, health care benefits, tuition waivers (full and partial), and unspecified assistantships available. Support available to part-time students. Financial award application deadline: 4/1; financial award applicants required to submit FAFSA. *Unit head:* Laura Bloomberg, Associate Dean, 612-625-0608, Fax: 612-626-0002, E-mail: bloom004@umn.edu. *Application contact:* Jacob Merrifield, Admissions Program Manager, 612-624-3800, Fax: 612-626-0002, E-mail: jmerrifi@umn.edu. Website: http://www.hhh.umn.edu/degrees/mpa/

University of Missouri, Office of Research and Graduate Studies, Harry S Truman School of Public Affairs, Columbia, MO 65211. Offers grantsmanship (Graduate Certificate); nonprofit management (Graduate Certificate); organizational change (Graduate Certificate); public affairs (MPA, PhD); public management (Graduate Certificate); science and public policy (Graduate Certificate). *Accreditation:* NASPAA. *Entrance requirements:* For master's, GRE General Test, minimum GPA of 3.0. Additional exam requirements/recommendations for international students: required—TOEFL, IELTS. Electronic applications accepted.

University of Missouri–Kansas City, Henry W. Bloch School of Management, Kansas City, MO 64110-2499. Offers accounting (MS); finance (MS); public affairs (MPA, PhD); JD/MBA; LL M/MPA. *Accreditation:* AACSB; NASPAA. *Program availability:* Part-time, evening/weekend. Terminal master's awarded for partial completion of doctoral program. *Entrance requirements:* For master's, GMAT, GRE, 2 essays, 2 references, support of employer; for doctorate, GRE, minimum GPA of 3.0. Additional exam requirements/recommendations for international students: required—TOEFL (minimum score 550 paper-based; 80 iBT). Electronic applications accepted.

University of Nevada, Las Vegas, Graduate College, Greenspun College of Urban Affairs, School of Public Policy and Leadership, Las Vegas, NV 89154-4030. Offers crisis and emergency management (MS); emergency crisis management cybersecurity (Certificate); environmental science (MS, PhD); non-profit management (Certificate); public administration (MPA); public affairs (PhD); public management (Certificate); urban leadership (MA). *Program availability:* Part-time. *Faculty:* 12 full-time (5 women), 6 part-time/adjunct (1 woman). *Students:* 106 full-time (61 women), 96 part-time (71 women); includes 118 minority (34 Black or African American, non-Hispanic/Latino; 1 American Indian or Alaska Native, non-Hispanic/Latino; 11 Asian, non-Hispanic/Latino; 49 Hispanic/Latino; 2 Native Hawaiian or other Pacific Islander, non-Hispanic/Latino; 21 Two or more races, non-Hispanic/Latino), 5 international. Average age 36. 115 applicants, 77% accepted, 73 enrolled. In 2019, 49 master's, 13 doctorates, 16 other advanced degrees awarded. *Degree requirements:* For master's, comprehensive exam (for some programs), thesis (for some programs), oral exam; for doctorate, comprehensive exam, thesis/dissertation; for Certificate, portfolio. *Entrance requirements:* For master's, GRE General Test or GMAT, bachelor's degree with minimum GPA 2.75; statement of purpose; 3 letters of recommendation; for doctorate, GRE General Test, master's degree with minimum GPA of 3.5; 3 letters of recommendation; statement of purpose; writing sample; personal interview; for Certificate, bachelor's degree; 2 letters of recommendation; writing sample. Additional exam requirements/recommendations for international students: required—TOEFL (minimum score 550 paper-based; 80 iBT), IELTS (minimum score 7). *Application deadline:* For fall admission, 6/1 for domestic and international students; for spring admission, 11/1 for domestic and international students; for summer admission, 3/1 for domestic students. Application fee: $60 ($95 for international students). Electronic applications accepted. *Expenses:* Contact institution. *Financial support:* In 2019–20, 25 students received support, including 15 research assistantships with full tuition reimbursements available (averaging $15,700 per year), 10 teaching assistantships with full tuition reimbursements available (averaging $16,625 per year); institutionally sponsored loans, scholarships/grants, health care benefits, and unspecified assistantships also available. Financial award application deadline: 3/15; financial award applicants required to submit FAFSA. *Unit head:* Dr. Christopher Stream, Director, 702-895-5120, Fax: 702-895-4436, E-mail: sppl.chair@unlv.edu. *Application contact:* Dr. Jayce Farmer, Graduate Coordinator, 702-895-4828, E-mail: sppl.gradcoord@unlv.edu. Website: https://www.unlv.edu/publicpolicy

The University of North Carolina at Greensboro, Graduate School, College of Arts and Sciences, Department of Political Science, Greensboro, NC 27412-5001. Offers nonprofit management (Certificate); public affairs (MPA); urban and economic development (Certificate). *Accreditation:* NASPAA. *Degree requirements:* For master's, comprehensive exam. *Entrance requirements:* For master's, GRE General Test. Additional exam requirements/recommendations for international students: required—TOEFL. Electronic applications accepted.

University of South Florida, Innovative Education, Tampa, FL 33620-9951. Offers adult, career and higher education (Graduate Certificate), including college teaching, leadership in developing human resources, leadership in higher education; Africana studies (Graduate Certificate), including diasporas and health disparities, genocide and human rights; aging studies (Graduate Certificate), including gerontology; art research (Graduate Certificate), including museum studies; business foundations (Graduate Certificate); chemical and biomedical engineering (Graduate Certificate), including materials science and engineering, water, health and sustainability; child and family studies (Graduate Certificate), including positive behavior support; civil and industrial engineering (Graduate Certificate), including transportation systems analysis; community and family health (Graduate Certificate), including maternal and child health, social marketing and public health, violence and injury: prevention and intervention, women's health; criminology (Graduate Certificate), including criminal justice administration; data science for public administration (Graduate Certificate); digital humanities (Graduate Certificate); educational measurement and research (Graduate Certificate), including evaluation; English (Graduate Certificate), including comparative literary studies, creative writing, professional and technical communication; entrepreneurship (Graduate Certificate); environmental health (Graduate Certificate), including safety management; epidemiology and biostatistics (Graduate Certificate), including applied biostatistics, biostatistics, concepts and tools of epidemiology, epidemiology, epidemiology of infectious diseases; geography, environment and planning (Graduate Certificate), including community development, environmental policy and management, geographical information systems; geology (Graduate Certificate), including hydrogeology; global health (Graduate Certificate), including disaster management, global health and Latin American and Caribbean studies, global health practice, humanitarian assistance, infection control; government and international affairs (Graduate Certificate), including Cuban studies, globalization studies; health policy and management (Graduate Certificate), including health management and leadership, public health policy and programs; hearing specialist: early intervention (Graduate Certificate); industrial and management systems engineering (Graduate Certificate),

including systems engineering, technology management; information studies (Graduate Certificate), including school library media specialist; information systems/decision sciences (Graduate Certificate), including analytics and business intelligence; instructional technology (Graduate Certificate), including distance education, Florida digital/virtual educator, instructional design, multimedia design, Web design; internal medicine, bioethics and medical humanities (Graduate Certificate), including biomedical ethics; Latin American and Caribbean studies (Graduate Certificate); leadership for coastal resiliency planning (Graduate Certificate); mass communications (Graduate Certificate), including multimedia journalism; mathematics and statistics (Graduate Certificate), including mathematics; medicine (Graduate Certificate), including aging and neuroscience, bioinformatics, biotechnology, brain fitness and memory management, clinical investigation, hand and upper limb rehabilitation, health informatics, health sciences, integrative weight management, intellectual property, medicine and gender, metabolic and nutritional medicine, metabolic cardiology, pharmacy sciences; national and competitive intelligence (Graduate Certificate); nursing (Graduate Certificate), including simulation based academic fellowship in advanced pain management; psychological and social foundations (Graduate Certificate), including career counseling, college teaching, diversity in education, mental health counseling, school counseling; public affairs (Graduate Certificate), including nonprofit management, public management, research administration; public health (Graduate Certificate), including assessing chemical toxicity and public health risks, health equity, pharmacoepidemiology, public health generalist, toxicology, translational research in adolescent behavioral health; public health practices (Graduate Certificate), including planning for healthy communities; rehabilitation and mental health counseling (Graduate Certificate), including integrative mental health care, marriage and family therapy, rehabilitation technology; secondary education (Graduate Certificate), including ESOL, foreign language education: culture and content, foreign language education: professional; social work (Graduate Certificate), including geriatric social work/clinical gerontology; special education (Graduate Certificate), including autism spectrum disorder, disabilities education: severe/profound; world languages (Graduate Certificate), including teaching English as a second language (TESL) or foreign language. *Unit head:* Dr. Cynthia DeLuca, Associate Vice President and Assistant Vice Provost, 813-974-3077, Fax: 813-974-7061, E-mail: deluca@usf.edu. *Application contact:* Owen Hooper, Director, Summer and Alternative Calendar Programs, 813-974-6917, E-mail: hooper@usf.edu.
Website: http://www.usf.edu/innovative-education/

The University of Texas at Austin, Graduate School, Lyndon B. Johnson School of Public Affairs, Austin, TX 78712-1111. Offers global policy studies (MGPS); public affairs (MP Aff); public leadership (EMPL); public policy (PhD); JD/MP Aff; MBA/MP Aff; MP Aff/MA; MP Aff/MSE. *Accreditation:* NASPAA (one or more programs are accredited). *Program availability:* Part-time. *Degree requirements:* For master's, thesis, summer internship; for doctorate, thesis/dissertation. *Entrance requirements:* For master's, GRE General Test (for MP Aff and MGPS), minimum GPA of 3.0 in upper-division classes, seven years of experience in the public sector, and interview (for EMPL); for doctorate, GRE General Test, master's degree in policy-related field. Additional exam requirements/recommendations for international students: required—TOEFL. Electronic applications accepted.

The University of Texas Rio Grande Valley, College of Liberal Arts, Department of Public Affairs and Security Studies, Edinburg, TX 78539. Offers global security studies and leadership (MPA); public administration (MPA); public policy and management (MPA). *Faculty:* 4 full-time (1 woman), 2 part-time/adjunct (1 woman). *Students:* 14 full-time (8 women), 135 part-time (75 women); includes 126 minority (3 Black or African American, non-Hispanic/Latino; 123 Hispanic/Latino), 2 international. Average age 33. 67 applicants, 93% accepted, 40 enrolled. In 2019, 56 master's awarded. *Expenses: Tuition, area resident:* Full-time $5959; part-time $440 per credit hour. Tuition, state resident: full-time $5959. Tuition, nonresident: full-time $5959. *International tuition:* $13,321 full-time. *Required fees:* $1169; $185 per credit hour.
Website: utrgv.edu/pass/index.htm

University of Washington, Graduate School, Evans School of Public Policy and Governance, Seattle, WA 98195. Offers public administration (MPA); public policy and management (PhD); JD/MPA; MPA/MAIS; MPA/MPH; MPA/MS; MPA/MUP. *Accreditation:* NASPAA. *Program availability:* Part-time, evening/weekend. *Degree requirements:* For master's, thesis, internship or cooperative experience. *Entrance requirements:* For master's and doctorate, GRE General Test, minimum GPA of 3.0. Additional exam requirements/recommendations for international students: required—TOEFL (minimum score 580 paper-based; 92 iBT). Electronic applications accepted.

University of Waterloo, Graduate Studies and Postdoctoral Affairs, Faculty of Arts, Department of Anthropology, Waterloo, ON N2L 3G1, Canada. Offers anthropology (MA); public issues (MA). *Entrance requirements:* Additional exam requirements/recommendations for international students: required—TOEFL, IELTS, PTE. Electronic applications accepted.

University of Wisconsin–Madison, Graduate School, College of Letters and Science, Robert M. La Follette School of Public Affairs, Public Policy and Administration Program, Madison, WI 53706-1380. Offers MIPA, MPA. *Program availability:* Part-time. Electronic applications accepted.

Virginia Commonwealth University, Graduate School, L. Douglas Wilder School of Government and Public Affairs, Richmond, VA 23284-9005. Offers MA, MPA, MS, MURP, PhD, Certificate, Graduate Certificate, Postbaccalaureate Certificate.

Virginia Polytechnic Institute and State University, Graduate School, College of Architecture and Urban Studies, Blacksburg, VA 24061. Offers architecture (M Arch, MS); architecture and design research (PhD); building construction science management (MS); creative technologies (MFA); environmental design and planning (PhD); government and international affairs (MPIA); landscape architecture (MLA, PhD); planning, governance, and globalization (PhD); public administration and public affairs (MPA, PhD); urban and regional planning (MURPL). *Accreditation:* ASLA (one or more programs are accredited). *Faculty:* 145 full-time (58 women), 2 part-time/adjunct (1 woman). *Students:* 304 full-time (156 women), 180 part-time (77 women); includes 90 minority (40 Black or African American, non-Hispanic/Latino; 19 Asian, non-Hispanic/Latino; 24 Hispanic/Latino; 7 Two or more races, non-Hispanic/Latino), 130 international. Average age 33. 475 applicants, 72% accepted, 126 enrolled. In 2019, 130 master's, 23 doctorates awarded. *Degree requirements:* For master's, comprehensive exam (for some programs), thesis (for some programs); for doctorate, comprehensive exam (for some programs), thesis/dissertation (for some programs). *Entrance requirements:* For master's and doctorate, GRE/GMAT. Additional exam requirements/recommendations for international students: required—TOEFL (minimum score 90 iBT). *Application deadline:* For fall admission, 8/1 for domestic students, 4/1 for international students; for spring admission, 1/1 for domestic students, 9/1 for international students. Applications are processed on a rolling basis. Application fee: $75. Electronic applications accepted. *Expenses:* Tuition, state resident: full-time $13,700; part-time $761.25 per credit hour. Tuition, nonresident: full-time $27,614; part-time $1534 per credit hour. *Required fees:* $886.50 per term. Tuition and fees vary according to campus/location and program. *Financial support:* In 2019–20, 2 fellowships with full tuition reimbursements (averaging $24,875 per year), 35 research assistantships with full tuition reimbursements (averaging $16,344 per year), 126 teaching assistantships with full tuition reimbursements (averaging $11,525 per year) were awarded; scholarships/grants and unspecified assistantships also available. Financial award application deadline: 3/1; financial award applicants required to submit FAFSA. *Unit head:* Dr. Richard Blythe, Dean, 540-231-6416, Fax: 540-231-6332, E-mail: richbl1@vt.edu. *Application contact:* Christine Mattsson-Coon, Executive Assistant, 540-231-6416, Fax: 540-231-6332, E-mail: cmattsso@vt.edu.
Website: http://www.caus.vt.edu/

Washington State University, College of Arts and Sciences, School of Politics, Philosophy and Public Affairs, Pullman, WA 99164-4880. Offers bioethics (Graduate Certificate); political science (MA, PhD); public affairs (MPA). *Accreditation:* NASPAA. *Program availability:* Online learning. Terminal master's awarded for partial completion of doctoral program. *Degree requirements:* For master's, comprehensive exam (for some programs), thesis, oral exam; for doctorate, comprehensive exam, thesis/dissertation, oral exam, written exam. *Entrance requirements:* For master's, GRE General Test, minimum GPA of 3.0; for doctorate, GRE General Test, minimum GPA of 3.5. Additional exam requirements/recommendations for international students: required—TOEFL. Electronic applications accepted.

Western Carolina University, Graduate School, College of Arts and Sciences, Department of Political Science and Public Affairs, Cullowhee, NC 28723. Offers MPA. *Accreditation:* NASPAA. *Program availability:* Part-time, evening/weekend. *Degree requirements:* For master's, comprehensive exam. *Entrance requirements:* For master's, GRE General Test, appropriate undergraduate degree, 3 letters of recommendation, resume, 1-2 page essay. Additional exam requirements/recommendations for international students: required—TOEFL (minimum score 550 paper-based, 79 iBT) or IELTS (6.5). Electronic applications accepted. *Expenses:* Contact institution.

Western Michigan University, Graduate College, College of Arts and Sciences, School of Public Affairs and Administration, Kalamazoo, MI 49008. Offers health care administration (MPA, Graduate Certificate); nonprofit leadership and administration (Graduate Certificate); public administration (PhD). *Accreditation:* NASPAA (one or more programs are accredited). *Degree requirements:* For doctorate, thesis/dissertation.

York University, Faculty of Graduate Studies, Glendon Campus, Program in Public and International Affairs, Toronto, ON M3J 1P3, Canada. Offers MA.

Public Policy

Adler University, Master of Public Policy Program, Chicago, IL 60602. Offers community health (MPP); human rights advocacy (MPP). *Program availability:* Part-time, evening/weekend. In 2019, 1 master's awarded. *Degree requirements:* For master's, Social Justice Practicum; Capstone Project. *Unit head:* Phyllis Horton, Director of Admissions, 312-662-4100, E-mail: admissions@adler.edu. *Application contact:* Phyllis Horton, Director of Admissions, 312-662-4100, E-mail: admissions@adler.edu.

Albany State University, College of Arts and Humanities, Albany, GA 31705-2717. Offers criminal justice (MS); English education (M Ed); public administration (MPA), including community and economic development, criminal justice administration, health administration and policy, human resources management, public management, public policy, water resources management and policy; social work (MSW). *Accreditation:* NASPAA. *Program availability:* Part-time. *Degree requirements:* For master's, comprehensive exam, professional portfolio (for MPA), internship, capstone report. *Entrance requirements:* For master's, GRE, MAT, minimum GPA of 3.0, official transcript, pre-medical record/certificate of immunization, letters of reference. Electronic applications accepted.

American Public University System, AMU/APU Graduate Programs, Charles Town, WV 25414. Offers accounting (MS); applied business analytics (MS); business administration (MBA); criminal justice (MA); cybersecurity studies (MS); educational leadership (M Ed); environmental policy and management (MS); global security (DGS); health information management (MS); history (MA), including American military history, American Revolution, civil war, war since 1945, World War II; information technology (MS); international relations and conflict resolution (MA), including American politics and government, comparative government and development, general, international relations, public policy; national security studies (MA); nursing (MSN); political science (MA); public policy (MPP); reverse logistics management (MA), including comparative and security issues, conflict resolution, international and transnational security issues, peacekeeping; space studies (MS); sports management (MS); strategic intelligence (DSI); teaching (M Ed), including secondary social studies; transportation and logistics management (MA). *Program availability:* Part-time, evening/weekend, online only, 100% online. *Students:* 461 full-time (193 women), 7,322 part-time (3,127 women); includes 3,089 minority (1,404 Black or African American, non-Hispanic/Latino; 30 American Indian or Alaska Native, non-Hispanic/Latino; 210 Asian, non-Hispanic/Latino; 753 Hispanic/Latino; 445 Native Hawaiian or other Pacific Islander, non-Hispanic/Latino; 247 Two or more races, non-Hispanic/Latino), 117 international. Average age 37. In 2019, 2,681 master's awarded. *Degree requirements:* For master's, comprehensive exam or practicum; for doctorate, practicum. *Entrance requirements:* For master's, official transcript showing earned bachelor's degree from institution accredited by recognized accrediting body. Additional exam requirements/recommendations for international students: required—TOEFL (minimum score 550 paper-based), IELTS (minimum score 6.5). *Application deadline:* Applications are processed on a rolling basis. Application fee: $0. Electronic applications accepted. *Financial support:* Scholarships/grants available. Financial award applicants required to submit FAFSA. *Unit head:* Dr. Wallace Boston, President, 877-468-6268, Fax: 304-728-2348, E-mail: president@apus.edu. *Application contact:* Yoci Deal, Associate Vice President, Graduate and International Admissions, 877-468-6268, Fax: 304-724-3764, E-mail: info@apus.edu.
Website: http://www.apus.edu

American University, School of Public Affairs, Department of Public Administration and Policy, Washington, DC 20016-8070. Offers organization development (MSOD, Certificate), including leadership for organizational change (Certificate), organization development (MSOD); public administration (MPA, PhD, Certificate), including nonprofit management (Certificate), public financial management (Certificate), public management (Certificate); public administration and policy (MPAP), including public administration policy; public policy (MPP, Certificate), including public policy (MPP), public policy analysis (Certificate); LL M/MPA; MPA/JD; MPP/JD; MPP/LL M. *Program availability:* Part-time, evening/weekend, 100% online, blended/hybrid learning. *Degree requirements:* For master's, comprehensive exam; for doctorate, comprehensive exam, thesis/dissertation. *Entrance requirements:* For master's, GRE; Please see website: https://www.american.edu/spa/jlc/, statement of purpose, 2 recommendations, resume, transcript; for doctorate, GRE; Please see website: https://www.american.edu/spa/jlc/, 3 recommendations, statement of purpose, resume, writing sample, transcript; for Certificate, bachelor's degree. Additional exam requirements/recommendations for international students: required—TOEFL. *Expenses:* Contact institution.

The American University in Cairo, School of Global Affairs and Public Policy, Cairo, Egypt. Offers gender and women's studies (MA); global affairs (MGA); international and comparative law (LL M); international human rights law (MA); journalism and mass communication (MA); Middle East studies (MA); migration and refugee studies (MA, Diploma); public administration (MPA); public policy (MPP); television and digital journalism (MA). *Program availability:* Part-time, evening/weekend. *Degree requirements:* For master's, comprehensive exam (for some programs), thesis (for some programs). *Entrance requirements:* Additional exam requirements/recommendations for international students: required—TOEFL (minimum score 450 paper-based; 45 iBT), IELTS (minimum score 5). Electronic applications accepted. *Expenses:* Contact institution.

The American University of Paris, Graduate Programs, Paris, France. Offers cross-cultural and sustainable business management (MA); cultural translation (MA); global communications (MA); global communications and civil society (MA); international affairs (MA); international affairs, conflict resolution and civil society development (MA); Middle East and Islamic studies (MA); Middle East and Islamic studies and international affairs (MA); public policy and international affairs (MA); public policy and international law (MA). *Degree requirements:* For master's, thesis (for some programs). *Entrance requirements:* For master's, minimum undergraduate GPA of 3.0. Additional exam requirements/recommendations for international students: recommended—TOEFL, IELTS. Electronic applications accepted.

Arizona State University at Tempe, College of Public Programs, School of Public Affairs, Phoenix, AZ 85004-0687. Offers emergency management and homeland security (MA); program evaluation (MS); public administration (MPA, PhD), including nonprofit administration (MPA), urban management (MPA); public policy (MPP); MPA/MSW. *Accreditation:* NASPAA (one or more programs are accredited). *Program availability:* Part-time, evening/weekend. Terminal master's awarded for partial completion of doctoral program. *Degree requirements:* For master's, thesis or alternative, policy analysis or capstone project; interactive Program of Study (iPOS) submitted before completing 50 percent of required credit hours; for doctorate, comprehensive exam, thesis/dissertation, interactive Program of Study (iPOS) submitted before completing 50 percent of required credit hours. *Entrance requirements:* For master's, GRE, minimum GPA of 3.0 or equivalent in last 2 years of work leading to bachelor's degree; for doctorate, GRE, minimum GPA of 3.0 or equivalent in last 2 years of work leading to bachelor's degree, 3 letters of recommendation, resume, statement of goals, samples of research reports. Additional exam requirements/recommendations for international students: required—TOEFL (minimum score 600 paper-based; 100 iBT), IELTS (minimum score 6.5). Electronic applications accepted. *Expenses:* Contact institution.

Arizona State University at Tempe, Sandra Day O'Connor College of Law, Phoenix, AZ 85287-7906. Offers biotechnology and genomics (LL M); law (JD); legal studies (MLS); patent practice (MLS); sports law and business (MSLB); tribal policy, law and government (LL M); JD/MBA; JD/MD; JD/MSW; JD/PhD. *Accreditation:* ABA. *Faculty:* 67 full-time (27 women), 138 part-time/adjunct (37 women). *Students:* 811 full-time (396 women); includes 197 minority (16 Black or African American, non-Hispanic/Latino; 19 American Indian or Alaska Native, non-Hispanic/Latino; 35 Asian, non-Hispanic/Latino; 87 Hispanic/Latino; 2 Native Hawaiian or other Pacific Islander, non-Hispanic/Latino; 38 Two or more races, non-Hispanic/Latino), 22 international. 3,710 applicants, 29% accepted, 272 enrolled. In 2019, 282 doctorates awarded. *Degree requirements:* For doctorate, See www.law.asu.edu for Juris Doctor degree requirements. *Entrance requirements:* For doctorate, LSAT, bachelor's degree. Additional exam requirements/recommendations for international students: required—TOEFL (minimum score 550 paper-based; 80 iBT). *Application deadline:* For fall admission, 3/1 priority date for domestic and international students. Applications are processed on a rolling basis. Application fee: $0. Electronic applications accepted. *Expenses:* Contact institution. *Financial support:* In 2019–20, 648 students received support. Institutionally sponsored loans and scholarships/grants available. Financial award application deadline: 3/15; financial award applicants required to submit FAFSA. *Unit head:* Douglas Sylvester, Dean/Professor, 480-965-6188, Fax: 480-965-6521, E-mail: douglas.sylvester@asu.edu. *Application contact:* Chitra Damania, Director, 480-965-1474, Fax: 480-727-7930, E-mail: law.admissions@asu.edu.
Website: http://www.law.asu.edu/

Arizona State University at Tempe, School of Letters and Sciences, Program in Applied Ethics, Tempe, AZ 85287-4503. Offers biomedical and health ethics (MA); ethics and emerging technologies (MA); public administration, policy and ethics (MA); science, technology and ethics (MA). *Program availability:* Part-time, evening/weekend. *Degree requirements:* For master's, thesis or alternative, applied project, interactive Program of Study (iPOS) submitted before completing 50 percent of required credit hours. *Entrance requirements:* For master's, GRE (for ethics and emerging technologies concentration), minimum GPA of 3.0 or equivalent in last 2 years of work leading to bachelor's degree, 2 letters of recommendation, resume, personal statement of interest and qualifications. Additional exam requirements/recommendations for international students: required—TOEFL (minimum score 550 paper-based; 80 iBT). Electronic applications accepted.

Auburn University at Montgomery, College of Liberal Arts & Social Sciences, Department of Political Science and Public Administration, Montgomery, AL 36124. Offers political science (MPS); public administration (MPA); public administration and public policy (PhD). *Accreditation:* NASPAA (one or more programs are accredited). *Program availability:* Part-time, evening/weekend. *Faculty:* 5 full-time (1 woman). *Students:* 8 full-time (3 women), 43 part-time (22 women); includes 18 minority (17 Black or African American, non-Hispanic/Latino; 1 Asian, non-Hispanic/Latino), 6 international. Average age 35. 22 applicants, 95% accepted, 20 enrolled. In 2019, 16 master's awarded. Terminal master's awarded for partial completion of doctoral program. *Degree requirements:* For master's, comprehensive exam; for doctorate, thesis/dissertation. *Entrance requirements:* For master's, GRE General Test or MAT; for doctorate, GRE General Test. Additional exam requirements/recommendations for international students: recommended—TOEFL (minimum score 500 paper-based; 61 iBT), IELTS

(minimum score 5.5), TSE (minimum score 44). *Application deadline:* For fall admission, 7/15 for international students; for spring admission, 11/15 for international students; for summer admission, 4/15 for international students. Applications are processed on a rolling basis. Application fee: $25. Electronic applications accepted. *Expenses:* Tuition, area resident: Full-time $7578; part-time $421 per credit hour. Tuition, state resident: full-time $7578; part-time $421 per credit hour. Tuition, nonresident: full-time $17,046; part-time $947 per credit hour. *International tuition:* $17,046 full-time. *Required fees:* $868. *Financial support:* Research assistantships, teaching assistantships, career-related internships or fieldwork, and scholarships/grants available. Support available to part-time students. Financial award application deadline: 3/1; financial award applicants required to submit FAFSA. *Unit head:* Dr. Andrew Cortell, Department Head, 334-244-3622, E-mail: acortell@aum.edu. *Application contact:* Shannon Richardson, Administrative Associate, 244-244-3698, E-mail: sricha17@aum.edu.
Website: http://www.cas.aum.edu/academic-programs/graduate-programs/master-of-science-in-political-science

Aurora University, Dunham School of Business and Public Policy, Aurora, IL 60506-4892. Offers accountancy (MS); business (MBA). *Program availability:* Part-time, 100% online, blended/hybrid learning. *Faculty:* 11 full-time (3 women), 30 part-time/adjunct (15 women). *Students:* 160 full-time (98 women), 182 part-time (119 women); includes 134 minority (56 Black or African American, non-Hispanic/Latino; 9 Asian, non-Hispanic/Latino; 64 Hispanic/Latino; 5 Two or more races, non-Hispanic/Latino). Average age 31. 277 applicants, 95% accepted, 134 enrolled. In 2019, 162 master's awarded. *Degree requirements:* For master's, Capstone project and internship. *Entrance requirements:* For master's, minimum GPA of 3.0, 2 years of work experience, resume. Additional exam requirements/recommendations for international students: required—TOEFL (minimum score 550 paper-based; 79 iBT). *Application deadline:* For fall admission, 6/1 for international students; for spring admission, 10/1 for international students. Applications are processed on a rolling basis. Application fee: $0. Electronic applications accepted. *Expenses:* The listed tuition and fees is for the MBA, MS, and MPA on-ground programs. Costs vary for online and plus one programs. The Dual MBA/MSW and MPA/MSW programs are roughly double the cost of the MBA. *Financial support:* In 2019–20, 66 students received support. Federal Work-Study, scholarships/grants, and unspecified assistantships available. Financial award applicants required to submit FAFSA. *Unit head:* Dr. Toby Arquette, Dean, School of Business and Policy, 630-844-5614, E-mail: tarquett@aurora.edu. *Application contact:* Jason Harmon, Dean of Adult and Graduate Studies, 630-9478955, E-mail: AUadmission@aurora.edu.
Website: https://aurora.edu/academics/colleges-schools/dsb

Baruch College of the City University of New York, Austin W. Marxe School of Public and International Affairs, Program in Public Administration, New York, NY 10010-5585. Offers general public administration (MPA); health care policy (MPA); nonprofit administration (MPA); policy analysis and evaluation (MPA); public management (MPA); urban development and sustainability (MPA); MS/MPA. *Accreditation:* NASPAA. *Program availability:* Part-time, evening/weekend. *Degree requirements:* For master's, thesis, capstone. *Entrance requirements:* For master's, GRE General Test. Additional exam requirements/recommendations for international students: required—TOEFL. Electronic applications accepted. *Expenses:* Contact institution.

Boise State University, School of Public Service, Department of Public Policy and Administration, Boise, ID 83725-0399. Offers public policy and administration (MPA, PhD, Graduate Certificate), including environmental, natural resource and energy policy and administration (MPA), general public administration (MPA), state and local government policy and administration (MPA). *Accreditation:* NASPAA. *Students:* 29 full-time (20 women), 81 part-time (54 women); includes 16 minority (2 Black or African American, non-Hispanic/Latino; 2 Asian, non-Hispanic/Latino; 10 Hispanic/Latino; 2 Two or more races, non-Hispanic/Latino), 5 international. *Degree requirements:* For master's, comprehensive exam, thesis optional, directed research project, internship; for doctorate, thesis/dissertation. *Application deadline:* For fall admission, 2/1 for domestic and international students; for spring admission, 10/1 for domestic and international students. Electronic applications accepted. *Expenses:* Tuition, area resident: Full-time $7110; part-time $470 per credit hour. Tuition, state resident: full-time $7110; part-time $470 per credit hour. Tuition, nonresident: full-time $24,030; part-time $827 per credit hour. *International tuition:* $24,030 full-time. *Required fees:* $2536. Tuition and fees vary according to course load and program. *Financial support:* Application deadline: 2/1; applicants required to submit FAFSA. *Unit head:* Luke Fowler, MPA Director, 208-426-5527, E-mail: lukefowler@boisestate.edu. *Application contact:* Luke Fowler, MPA Director, 208-426-5527, E-mail: lukefowler@boisestate.edu.
Website: https://www.boisestate.edu/sps-publicpolicy/

Brandeis University, Graduate School of Arts and Sciences, Program in Women's, Gender, and Sexuality Studies, Waltham, MA 02454-9110. Offers anthropology/women's, gender, and sexuality studies (MA); English/women's, gender, and sexuality studies (MA); near Eastern and Judaic studies /women's, gender, and sexuality studies (MA); public policy/women's, gender, and sexuality studies (MA); sociology/women's, gender, and sexuality studies (MA); sustainable international development/women's, gender, and sexuality studies (MA); women's, gender, and sexuality studies (MA). *Program availability:* Part-time. *Faculty:* 19 full-time (16 women), 2 part-time/adjunct (both women). *Students:* 6 full-time (all women); includes 2 minority (both Hispanic/Latino). Average age 27. 41 applicants, 54% accepted, 8 enrolled. In 2019, 4 master's awarded. *Degree requirements:* For master's, thesis or alternative. *Entrance requirements:* For master's, GRE General, transcripts, letters of recommendation, resume, statement of purpose, and writing sample. Additional exam requirements/recommendations for international students: required—TOEFL, IELTS, PTE. *Application deadline:* For fall admission, 1/15 for domestic and international students. Application fee: $75. Electronic applications accepted. *Financial support:* Fellowships, scholarships/grants, health care benefits, and tuition waivers available. Support available to part-time students. *Unit head:* Dr. Ellen Schattschneider, Director of Graduate Studies, 781-736-2219, E-mail: eschatt@brandeis.edu. *Application contact:* Alexandra Brandon, Administrator, 781-736-3045, E-mail: abrandon@brandeis.edu.
Website: http://www.brandeis.edu/gsas/programs/wgs.html

Brandeis University, The Heller School for Social Policy and Management, Program in Public Policy, Waltham, MA 02454-9110. Offers aging (MPP); behavioral health (MPP); children, youth and families (MPP); general social policy (MPP); health (MPP); poverty alleviation and development (MPP); MPP/MA. *Degree requirements:* For master's, thesis. *Entrance requirements:* For master's, GRE, 3 letters of recommendation, statement of purpose, 3 to 5 years of professional experience. Additional exam requirements/recommendations for international students: required—TOEFL (minimum score 600 paper-based; 100 iBT). Electronic applications accepted.

Brock University, Faculty of Graduate Studies, Faculty of Social Sciences, Program in Political Science, St. Catharines, ON L2S 3A1, Canada. Offers Canadian politics (MA); comparative politics (MA); international relations (MA); political theory or philosophy (MA); public policy (MA). *Program availability:* Part-time. *Degree requirements:* For master's, thesis optional. *Entrance requirements:* For master's, honors degree. Additional exam requirements/recommendations for international students: required—TOEFL (minimum score 550 paper-based; 80 iBT), IELTS (minimum score 6.5), TWE (minimum score 4). Electronic applications accepted.

Public Policy

Brooklyn College of the City University of New York, School of Humanities and Social Sciences, Department of Political Science, Brooklyn, NY 11210-2889. Offers international affairs (MA); political science (MA); urban policy and administration (MA). *Program availability:* Part-time, evening/weekend. *Degree requirements:* For master's, comprehensive exam (for some programs), thesis or alternative, foreign language exam (for international affairs program). *Entrance requirements:* For master's, 2 letters of recommendation, personal statement. Additional exam requirements/recommendations for international students: required—TOEFL (minimum score 500 paper-based; 61 iBT).

Brown University, Graduate School, A. Alfred Taubman Center for Public Policy and American Institutions, Providence, RI 02912. Offers MPA, MPP, MD/MPP. *Entrance requirements:* For master's, GRE, 3 letters of recommendation. Additional exam requirements/recommendations for international students: required—TOEFL.

California Lutheran University, Graduate Studies, School of Management, Thousand Oaks, CA 91360-2787. Offers business (IMBA); entrepreneurship (MBA, Certificate); finance (MBA, Certificate); financial planning (MBA, MS, Certificate); human capital management (MBA, Certificate); information technology (MS); information technology management (MBA, Certificate); international business (MBA, Certificate); management (MS); marketing (MBA, Certificate); public policy and administration (MPPA); quantitative economics (MS). *Program availability:* Part-time, evening/weekend, 100% online, blended/hybrid learning. *Degree requirements:* For master's, comprehensive exam (for some programs). *Entrance requirements:* For master's, GMAT, interview, minimum GPA of 3.0. Electronic applications accepted. *Expenses:* Contact institution.

California State University, East Bay, Office of Graduate Studies, College of Letters, Arts, and Social Sciences, Department of Public Affairs and Administration, Program in Public Administration, Hayward, CA 94542-3000. Offers health care administration (MPA); public management and policy analysis (MPA). *Program availability:* Part-time, evening/weekend. *Degree requirements:* For master's, comprehensive exam (for some programs), comprehensive exam or thesis. *Entrance requirements:* For master's, minimum GPA of 2.5; statement of purpose; 2 letters of recommendation; professional resume/curriculum vitae. Additional exam requirements/recommendations for international students: required—TOEFL (minimum score 550 paper-based; 79 iBT). Electronic applications accepted.

California State University, Long Beach, Graduate Studies, College of Health and Human Services, Graduate Center for Public Policy and Administration, Long Beach, CA 90840. Offers MPA, Graduate Certificate. *Accreditation:* NASPAA (one or more programs are accredited). *Program availability:* Part-time, evening/weekend. *Degree requirements:* For master's, comprehensive exam. *Entrance requirements:* For master's, minimum GPA of 2.75. Electronic applications accepted.

California State University, Sacramento, College of Social Sciences and Interdisciplinary Studies, Program in Public Policy and Administration, Sacramento, CA 95819. Offers MPPA. *Program availability:* Part-time. *Students:* 26 full-time (12 women), 30 part-time (17 women); includes 18 minority (2 Black or African American, non-Hispanic/Latino; 7 Asian, non-Hispanic/Latino; 9 Hispanic/Latino). Average age 31. 40 applicants, 73% accepted, 16 enrolled. In 2019, 8 master's awarded. *Degree requirements:* For master's, thesis, thesis or writing proficiency exam. *Entrance requirements:* For master's, GRE, minimum GPA of 3.0 for all undergraduate coursework and in last 60 units. Additional exam requirements/recommendations for international students: required—TOEFL (minimum score 560 paper-based; 83 iBT); recommended—IELTS (minimum score 7). *Application deadline:* For fall admission, 3/1 for domestic students, 2/1 for international students. Applications are processed on a rolling basis. Application fee: $70. Electronic applications accepted. *Expenses:* Contact institution. *Financial support:* Teaching assistantships, career-related internships or fieldwork, Federal Work-Study, and scholarships/grants available. Support available to part-time students. Financial award application deadline: 3/1; financial award applicants required to submit FAFSA. *Unit head:* Dr. Ted Lascher, Chair, 916-278-6557, E-mail: tedl@csus.edu. *Application contact:* Jose Martinez, Graduate Admissions Supervisor, 916-278-7871, E-mail: martinj@skymail.csus.edu.
Website: http://www.csus.edu/ppa

Carleton University, Faculty of Graduate Studies, Faculty of Public Affairs and Management, School of Public Policy and Administration, Ottawa, ON K1S 5B6, Canada. Offers public administration (MA, DPA); public policy (PhD). *Program availability:* Part-time. *Degree requirements:* For master's, thesis optional; for doctorate, one foreign language, comprehensive exam, thesis/dissertation. *Entrance requirements:* For master's, GRE, honors degree; for doctorate, master's degree. Additional exam requirements/recommendations for international students: required—TOEFL.

Carnegie Mellon University, Dietrich College of Humanities and Social Sciences, Department of Statistics, Pittsburgh, PA 15213-3891. Offers machine learning and statistics (PhD); mathematical finance (PhD); statistics (MS, PhD), including applied statistics (PhD), computational statistics (PhD), theoretical statistics (PhD); statistics and public policy (PhD). Terminal master's awarded for partial completion of doctoral program. *Degree requirements:* For doctorate, comprehensive exam, thesis/dissertation. *Entrance requirements:* For master's and doctorate, GRE General Test. Additional exam requirements/recommendations for international students: required—TOEFL.

Carnegie Mellon University, Heinz College Australia, Master of Science in Public Policy and Management Program (Adelaide, South Australia), Adelaide SA 5000, Australia. Offers MS. *Entrance requirements:* For master's, GRE or GMAT, college-level course in advanced algebra/pre-calculus; college-level courses in economics and statistics (recommended). Additional exam requirements/recommendations for international students: required—TOEFL or IELTS.

Carnegie Mellon University, Heinz College, School of Public Policy and Management, Master of Science in Public Policy and Management Program, Pittsburgh, PA 15213-3891. Offers MS. *Accreditation:* NASPAA. *Degree requirements:* For master's, internship. *Entrance requirements:* For master's, GRE or GMAT, college-level course in advanced algebra/pre-calculus; college-level courses in economics and statistics (recommended). Additional exam requirements/recommendations for international students: required—TOEFL or IELTS. Electronic applications accepted.

Carnegie Mellon University, Heinz College, School of Public Policy and Management, PhD in Public Policy and Management Program, Pittsburgh, PA 15213-3891. Offers PhD. *Entrance requirements:* For doctorate, GRE or GMAT. Additional exam requirements/recommendations for international students: required—TOEFL or IELTS.

The Catholic University of America, School of Arts and Sciences, Department of Sociology, Washington, DC 20064. Offers crime and justice studies (MA); global and comparative sociology (MA); public policy (MA). *Program availability:* Part-time. *Faculty:* 3 full-time (2 women), 2 part-time/adjunct (both women). *Students:* 1 (woman) full-time. Average age 23. 1 applicant, 100% accepted, 1 enrolled. In 2019, 1 master's awarded. *Degree requirements:* For master's, comprehensive exam, thesis or alternative, two seminar papers. *Entrance requirements:* For master's, GRE General Test, statement of purpose, official copies of academic transcripts, three letters of recommendation. Additional exam requirements/recommendations for international students: required—TOEFL (minimum score 550 paper-based; 80 iBT). *Application deadline:* For fall admission, 7/15 priority date for domestic students, 7/1 for international students; for spring admission, 11/15 priority date for domestic students, 11/1 for international students. Applications are processed on a rolling basis. Application fee: $55. Electronic applications accepted. *Financial support:* Fellowships, research assistantships, teaching assistantships, Federal Work-Study, scholarships/grants, tuition waivers (full and partial), and unspecified assistantships available. Financial award application deadline: 2/1; financial award applicants required to submit FAFSA. *Unit head:* Dr. Brandon Vaidyanathan, Chair, 202-319-5941, Fax: 202-319-4980, E-mail: brandonv@cua.edu. *Application contact:* Dr. Steven Brown, Director of Graduate Admissions, 202-319-5057, Fax: 202-319-6533, E-mail: cua-admissions@cua.edu.
Website: http://sociology.cua.edu/

Central European University, School of Public Policy, 1051, Hungary. Offers public administration (MPA); public policy (MA, PhD). *Degree requirements:* For master's, one foreign language, thesis; for doctorate, one foreign language, comprehensive exam, thesis/dissertation. *Entrance requirements:* For master's and doctorate, interview. Additional exam requirements/recommendations for international students: required—TOEFL (minimum score 570 paper-based); recommended—IELTS (minimum score 6.5). Electronic applications accepted.

Claremont Graduate University, Graduate Programs, School of Social Science, Policy and Evaluation, Department of Economics, Claremont, CA 91711-6160. Offers behavioral economics and neuroeconomics (PhD); business and financial economics (MA, PhD); economic development (Certificate); international economic and development policy (PhD); international economics policy and development (MA); international money and finance (PhD); political economy and public economics (PhD); political economy and public policy (MA); MBA/PhD. *Program availability:* Part-time. *Entrance requirements:* For master's and doctorate, GRE General Test or GMAT. Additional exam requirements/recommendations for international students: required—TOEFL (minimum score 75 iBT). Electronic applications accepted.

Claremont Graduate University, Graduate Programs, School of Social Science, Policy and Evaluation, Department of Politics and Policy, Claremont, CA 91711-6160. Offers American politics (MA, PhD); comparative politics (PhD); international political economy (MA); international studies (MA); political philosophy (PhD); political science (PhD); politics, economics and business (MA); public policy (MA, PhD); world politics (PhD); MBA/PhD. *Program availability:* Part-time. Terminal master's awarded for partial completion of doctoral program. *Entrance requirements:* For master's and doctorate, GRE General Test. Additional exam requirements/recommendations for international students: required—TOEFL (minimum score 75 iBT). Electronic applications accepted.

Claremont Graduate University, Graduate Programs, School of Social Science, Policy and Evaluation, Program in Public Policy and Evaluation, Claremont, CA 91711-6160. Offers MA. *Entrance requirements:* For master's, GRE General Test. Additional exam requirements/recommendations for international students: required—TOEFL (minimum score 75 iBT). Electronic applications accepted.

Clemson University, Graduate School, College of Behavioral, Social and Health Sciences, PhD Program in Policy Studies, Clemson, SC 29634. Offers PhD, Certificate. *Faculty:* 2 full-time (1 woman). *Students:* 6 full-time (3 women), 7 part-time (3 women); includes 2 minority (1 Black or African American, non-Hispanic/Latino; 1 Native Hawaiian or other Pacific Islander, non-Hispanic/Latino), 3 international. Average age 38. 17 applicants, 65% accepted, 4 enrolled. In 2019, 3 doctorates awarded. *Expenses: Tuition, area resident:* Full-time $10,600; part-time $8688 per semester. Tuition, state resident: full-time $10,600; part-time $8688 per semester. Tuition, nonresident: full-time $22,050; part-time $17,412 per semester. *International tuition:* $22,050 full-time. *Required fees:* $1196; $617 per semester. $617 per semester. Tuition and fees vary according to course load, degree level, campus/location and program. *Financial support:* In 2019–20, 6 students received support, including 2 research assistantships with full and partial tuition reimbursements available (averaging $19,500 per year), 4 teaching assistantships with full and partial tuition reimbursements available (averaging $15,000 per year); career-related internships or fieldwork also available. *Unit head:* Dr. Laura Olson, Director, 864-656-1457, E-mail: LAURAO@clemson.edu. *Application contact:* Angie Newell, Administrative Assistant, 864-656-0690, E-mail: NANGELA@clemson.edu.
Website: https://www.clemson.edu/cbshs/departments/political-science/academics/policy-studies/index.html

Columbia University, School of International and Public Affairs, Program in Public Policy and Administration, New York, NY 10027. Offers MPA, JD/MPA, MPA/MS, MPH/MPA. *Accreditation:* NASPAA. *Entrance requirements:* For master's, GRE General Test. Additional exam requirements/recommendations for international students: required—TOEFL (minimum score 600 paper-based; 100 iBT), IELTS (minimum score 7), PTE (minimum score 68). Electronic applications accepted. *Expenses: Tuition:* Full-time $47,600; part-time $1880 per credit. One-time fee: $105.

Concordia University, School of Graduate Studies, Faculty of Arts and Science, Department of Political Science, Montréal, QC H3G 1M8, Canada. Offers political science (PhD); public policy and public administration (MA), including geography. *Degree requirements:* For master's, one foreign language, comprehensive exam, thesis optional, internship. *Entrance requirements:* For master's, honors degree or equivalent. Additional exam requirements/recommendations for international students: required—TOEFL.

Cornell University, Graduate School, Graduate Fields of Arts and Sciences, Field of Government, Ithaca, NY 14853. Offers American politics (PhD); comparative politics (PhD); international relations (PhD); political methodology (PhD); political thought (PhD); public policy (PhD). *Degree requirements:* For doctorate, comprehensive exam, thesis/dissertation. *Entrance requirements:* For doctorate, GRE General Test, sample of written work, 3 letters of recommendation. Additional exam requirements/recommendations for international students: required—TOEFL (minimum score 550 paper-based; 77 iBT). Electronic applications accepted.

Cornell University, Graduate School, Graduate Fields of Human Ecology, Field of Policy Analysis and Management, Ithaca, NY 14853. Offers consumer policy (PhD); family and social welfare policy (PhD); health administration (MHA); health management and policy (PhD); public policy (PhD). *Degree requirements:* For master's, thesis; for doctorate, thesis/dissertation. *Entrance requirements:* For master's, GRE General Test or GMAT, 2 letters of recommendation; for doctorate, GRE General Test, 2 letters of recommendation. Additional exam requirements/recommendations for international students: required—TOEFL (minimum score 550 paper-based; 77 iBT). Electronic applications accepted.

DePaul University, College of Liberal Arts and Social Sciences, Chicago, IL 60614. Offers Arabic (MA); Chinese (MA); critical ethnic studies (MA); English (MA); French (MA); German (MA); history (MA); interdisciplinary studies (MA, MS); international public service (MS); international studies (MA); Italian (MA); Japanese (MA); liberal studies (MA); nonprofit management (MNM); public administration (MPA); public health (MPH); public policy (MPP); public service management (MS); refugee and forced migration studies (MS); social work (MSW); sociology (MA); Spanish (MA); sustainable urban development (MA); women's and gender studies (MA); writing and publishing (MA); writing, rhetoric and discourse (MA); MA/PhD. *Accreditation:* CEPH. *Program* *availability:* Part-time, evening/weekend, online learning. Terminal master's awarded for partial completion of doctoral program. *Degree requirements:* For master's, variable foreign language requirement, comprehensive exam (for some programs), thesis (for some programs). Electronic applications accepted.

Duke University, Graduate School, PhD Program in Public Policy, Durham, NC 27708. Offers PhD. *Entrance requirements:* For doctorate, GRE General Test. Additional exam requirements/recommendations for international students: required—TOEFL (minimum score 577 paper-based; 90 iBT) or IELTS. Electronic applications accepted.

Duke University, Sanford School of Public Policy, MPP Program, Durham, NC 27708. Offers MPP, MBA/MPP, MD/MPP, MEM/MPP, MPP/JD, MPP/M Div. Terminal master's awarded for partial completion of doctoral program. *Degree requirements:* For master's, thesis, internship. *Entrance requirements:* For master's, GRE. Additional exam requirements/recommendations for international students: required—TOEFL (minimum score 100 iBT), IELTS. Electronic applications accepted. *Expenses:* Contact institution.

Eastern Michigan University, Graduate School, College of Arts and Sciences, Department of Political Science, Programs in Public Administration, Ypsilanti, MI 48197. Offers general public management (Graduate Certificate); local government management (Graduate Certificate); management of public healthcare services (Graduate Certificate); nonprofit management (Graduate Certificate); public administration (MPA); public budget management (Graduate Certificate); public land planning and development management (Graduate Certificate); public personnel management (Graduate Certificate); public policy analysis (Graduate Certificate). *Accreditation:* NASPAA. *Students:* 12 full-time (7 women), 31 part-time (14 women); includes 13 minority (11 Black or African American, non-Hispanic/Latino; 1 Hispanic/Latino; 1 Two or more races, non-Hispanic/Latino), 2 international. Average age 35. 38 applicants, 82% accepted, 13 enrolled. In 2019, 16 master's, 9 other advanced degrees awarded. Application fee: $45. *Application contact:* Dr. Rose Jindal, MPA Coordinator, 734-487-3113, Fax: 734-487-3340, E-mail: rsoliven@emich.edu. Website: http://www.emich.edu/polisci/

Florida State University, The Graduate School, College of Social Sciences and Public Policy, Reubin O'D. Askew School of Public Administration and Policy, Tallahassee, FL 32306-2250. Offers public administration (MPA, PhD); public administration and policy (Certificate); JD/MPA; MPA/MSC; MPA/MSP; MPA/MSW. *Accreditation:* NASPAA (one or more programs are accredited). *Program availability:* Part-time, evening/weekend. *Faculty:* 10 full-time (2 women), 10 part-time/adjunct (3 women). *Students:* 74 full-time (37 women), 75 part-time (47 women); includes 47 minority (17 Black or African American, non-Hispanic/Latino; 3 Asian, non-Hispanic/Latino; 18 Hispanic/Latino; 9 Two or more races, non-Hispanic/Latino), 46 international. Average age 32. 190 applicants, 54% accepted, 55 enrolled. In 2019, 35 master's, 7 doctorates awarded. *Degree requirements:* For master's, action report; for doctorate, comprehensive exam, thesis/dissertation. *Entrance requirements:* For master's, GRE General Test, GMAT, MAT, LSAT, minimum undergraduate upper-division GPA of 3.0; for doctorate, GRE General Test (minimum score of 1100 or equivalent on current grading scale); GMAT; MAT; LSAT, minimum undergraduate GPA of 3.0, graduate 3.5. Additional exam requirements/recommendations for international students: required—TOEFL (minimum score 550 paper-based; 80 iBT), IELTS (minimum score 6.5), PTE (minimum score 55), Michigan English Language Assessment Battery (minimum score 77). *Application deadline:* For fall admission, 7/1 for domestic students, 5/1 for international students; for spring admission, 11/1 for domestic students, 9/1 for international students; for summer admission, 3/1 for domestic students, 1/1 for international students. Applications are processed on a rolling basis. Application fee: $30. Electronic applications accepted. *Financial support:* In 2019–20, 6 students received support, including fellowships with full tuition reimbursements available (averaging $18,000 per year), 4 research assistantships with full tuition reimbursements available (averaging $15,000 per year), 2 teaching assistantships with full tuition reimbursements available (averaging $15,000 per year); career-related internships or fieldwork, Federal Work-Study, institutionally sponsored loans, scholarships/grants, tuition waivers (full and partial), and unspecified assistantships also available. Support available to part-time students. Financial award application deadline: 2/1; financial award applicants required to submit FAFSA. *Unit head:* Dr. Keon-Hyung Lee, Director, 850-645-8210, Fax: 850-644-7617, E-mail: klee2@fsu.edu. *Application contact:* Christina Havlicek, Academic Program Specialist, 850-644-3060, Fax: 850-644-7617, E-mail: chavlicek@fsu.edu. Website: http://askew.fsu.edu/

Frederick S. Pardee RAND Graduate School, Program in Policy Analysis, Santa Monica, CA 90407-2138. Offers PhD. *Degree requirements:* For doctorate, comprehensive exam, thesis/dissertation. *Entrance requirements:* For doctorate, GMAT or GRE General Test, resume or curriculum vitae, three essays, three letters of recommendation. Additional exam requirements/recommendations for international students: required—TOEFL (minimum score 100 iBT). Electronic applications accepted. *Expenses:* Contact institution.

George Mason University, Schar School of Policy and Government, Program in Public Policy, Arlington, VA 22201. Offers MPP, PhD. *Degree requirements:* For master's, thesis or alternative, professional experience; for doctorate, comprehensive exam, thesis/dissertation, field studies. *Entrance requirements:* For master's, GRE/GMAT (for students seeking merit-based scholarships), bachelor's degree with minimum GPA of 3.0, current resume, 2 letters of recommendation, expanded goals statement, 2 copies of official transcripts; for doctorate, GMAT or GRE General Test, master's degree with minimum GPA of 3.0; current resume; expanded goals statement; 2 official copies of transcripts; writing sample. Additional exam requirements/recommendations for international students: required—TOEFL (minimum score 575 paper-based; 88 iBT), IELTS (minimum score 6.5), PTE (minimum score 59). Electronic applications accepted. *Expenses:* Contact institution.

Georgetown University, Graduate School of Arts and Sciences, Department of Government, Washington, DC 20057. Offers American government (MA); conflict resolution (MA); democracy and governance (MA); development, management and policy (MA); government (PhD); MA/PhD. Terminal master's awarded for partial completion of doctoral program. *Degree requirements:* For master's, one foreign language, comprehensive exam; for doctorate, one foreign language, comprehensive exam, thesis/dissertation. *Entrance requirements:* For master's, GRE General Test, minimum B average; for doctorate, GRE General Test, MA. Additional exam requirements/recommendations for international students: required—TOEFL.

Georgetown University, Graduate School of Arts and Sciences, School of Continuing Studies, Washington, DC 20057. Offers American studies (MALS); applied intelligence (MPS); Catholic studies (MALS); classical civilizations (MALS); emergency and disaster management (MPS); ethics and the professions (MALS); global strategic communications (MPS); hospitality management (MPS); human resources management (MPS); humanities (MALS); individualized study (MALS); integrated marketing communications (MPS); international affairs (MALS); Islam and Muslim-Christian relations (MALS); journalism (MPS); liberal studies (DLS); literature and society (MALS); medieval and early modern European studies (MALS); public relations and corporate communications (MPS); real estate (MPS); religious studies (MALS); social and public policy (MALS); sports industry management (MPS); systems engineering management (MPS); technology management (MPS); the theory and practice of American democracy (MALS); urban and regional planning (MPS); visual culture (MALS). *Entrance requirements:* Additional exam requirements/recommendations for international students: required—TOEFL.

Georgetown University, McCourt School of Public Policy, Washington, DC, DC 20057. Offers data science for public policy (MDSPP); international development policy (MIDP); policy leadership (EMPL); policy management (MPM); public policy (MPP); MBA/MPP; MPP/JD; MPP/MA; MPP/MSFS; MPP/PhD. *Program availability:* Part-time. *Faculty:* 35 full-time (14 women), 35 part-time/adjunct (16 women). *Students:* 243 full-time (148 women), 25 part-time (16 women); includes 65 minority (24 Black or African American, non-Hispanic/Latino; 16 Asian, non-Hispanic/Latino; 15 Hispanic/Latino; 10 Two or more races, non-Hispanic/Latino), 78 international. 1,353 applicants, 78% accepted, 268 enrolled. *Degree requirements:* For master's, thesis or alternative. *Entrance requirements:* For master's, GRE General Test or GMAT required for MPP, MIDP and MS-DSPP applicants; LSAT accepted for applicants to dual JD/MPP program, minimum B average (3.0 GPA). Additional exam requirements/recommendations for international students: required—TOEFL (minimum score 600 paper-based; 100 iBT), IELTS (minimum score 7), If an applicant did not earn a degree from an institution where English is the primary language of instruction, a TOEFL or IELTS score is required. *Application deadline:* For fall admission, 1/15 priority date for domestic and international students; for summer admission, 1/15 priority date for domestic students, 1/17 priority date for international students. Application fee: $90. Electronic applications accepted. *Financial support:* In 2019–20, 230 students received support, including 5 fellowships with full tuition reimbursements available (averaging $10,000 per year), 40 research assistantships, 60 teaching assistantships; career-related internships or fieldwork, scholarships/grants, and unspecified assistantships also available. Support available to part-time students. Financial award application deadline: 1/15; financial award applicants required to submit FAFSA. *Unit head:* Dr. Maria Cancian, Dean, McCourt School of Public Policy, 202-687-6163, E-mail: mcancian@georgetown.edu. *Application contact:* Julie Ito, Director of Admissions, 202-687-0678, E-mail: mccourtadmissions@georgetown.edu. Website: https://mccourt.georgetown.edu/

The George Washington University, Columbian College of Arts and Sciences, Department of Philosophy, Washington, DC 20052. Offers philosophy and social policy (MA). *Degree requirements:* For master's, comprehensive exam, thesis or alternative. *Entrance requirements:* For master's, GRE General Test, interview, minimum GPA of 3.0. Additional exam requirements/recommendations for international students: required—TOEFL (minimum score 600 paper-based; 100 iBT). Electronic applications accepted.

The George Washington University, Columbian College of Arts and Sciences, Trachtenberg School of Public Policy and Public Administration, Washington, DC 20052. Offers environmental resource policy (MA); public administration (MPA); public policy (MPP); public policy and administration (PhD); JD/MPP; MPA/JD; PhD/MPP. *Program availability:* Part-time, evening/weekend, online learning. *Faculty:* 13 full-time (7 women), 20 part-time/adjunct (8 women). *Students:* 184 full-time (104 women), 235 part-time (150 women); includes 127 minority (50 Black or African American, non-Hispanic/Latino; 2 American Indian or Alaska Native, non-Hispanic/Latino; 22 Asian, non-Hispanic/Latino; 42 Hispanic/Latino; 11 Two or more races, non-Hispanic/Latino), 45 international. Average age 26. 1,015 applicants, 63% accepted, 164 enrolled. In 2019, 135 master's, 16 doctorates awarded. *Degree requirements:* For master's, capstone project; for doctorate, comprehensive exam, thesis/dissertation. *Entrance requirements:* For master's, minimum GPA of 3.0; for doctorate, GRE, minimum GPA of 3.0. Additional exam requirements/recommendations for international students: required—TOEFL (minimum score 600 paper-based; 100 iBT), IELTS (minimum score 7). *Application deadline:* For fall admission, 1/15 priority date for domestic and international students; for spring admission, 10/1 priority date for domestic students, 10/1 for international students. Application fee: $80. Electronic applications accepted. *Expenses:* Contact institution. *Financial support:* In 2019–20, 57 students received support. Fellowships, research assistantships, teaching assistantships, Federal Work-Study, scholarships/grants, health care benefits, and unspecified assistantships available. Support available to part-time students. Financial award application deadline: 1/15; financial award applicants required to submit FAFSA. *Unit head:* Dr. Mary Tschirhart, Director, 202-994-2006, Fax: 202-994-6792, E-mail: marytschirhart@gwu.edu. *Application contact:* Lindsey A. Duble-Dice, Director of Graduate Admissions and Recruitment, 202-994-8569, Fax: 202-994-6792, E-mail: ldubledice@gwu.edu. Website: http://www.tspppa.gwu.edu/

The George Washington University, School of Business, Department of Strategic Management and Public Policy, Washington, DC 20052. Offers MBA, PhD. *Accreditation:* NASPAA. *Program availability:* Part-time, evening/weekend. *Entrance requirements:* For master's, GMAT; for doctorate, GMAT or GRE. Additional exam requirements/recommendations for international students: required—TOEFL.

Georgia Institute of Technology, Graduate Studies, Ivan Allen College of Liberal Arts, School of Public Policy, Atlanta, GA 30332. Offers MS, PhD. *Program availability:* Part-time, 100% online. *Faculty:* 22 full-time (7 women), 4 part-time/adjunct (2 women). *Students:* 68 full-time (35 women), 18 part-time (5 women); includes 19 minority (7 Black or African American, non-Hispanic/Latino; 7 Asian, non-Hispanic/Latino; 3 Hispanic/Latino; 2 Two or more races, non-Hispanic/Latino), 20 international. Average age 31. 156 applicants, 46% accepted, 38 enrolled. In 2019, 13 master's, 3 doctorates awarded. Terminal master's awarded for partial completion of doctoral program. *Degree requirements:* For master's, professional paper, public policy workshop or thesis; internship; minimum overall GPA of 3.0; for doctorate, comprehensive exam, thesis/dissertation, minimum overall GPA of 3.0, one year of full-time residency. *Entrance requirements:* For master's and doctorate, GRE, three letters of recommendation, transcripts from each college/university attended, essays. Additional exam requirements/recommendations for international students: required—TOEFL (minimum score 600 paper-based; 100 iBT), IELTS (minimum score 7), TOEFL is the preferred method with the requirements shown on the programs. *Application deadline:* For fall admission, 2/15 priority date for domestic students; for spring admission, 10/31 for domestic students. Applications are processed on a rolling basis. Application fee: $75 ($85 for international students). Electronic applications accepted. *Expenses:* Tuition, area resident: Full-time $14,064; part-time $586 per credit hour. Tuition, state resident: full-time $14,064; part-time $586 per credit hour. Tuition, nonresident: full-time $29,140; part-time $1215 per credit hour. *International tuition:* $29,140 full-time. *Required fees:* $2024; $840 per semester. $2096. Tuition and fees vary according to course load. *Financial support:* In 2019–20, 7 fellowships, 24 research assistantships, 20 teaching assistantships were awarded; career-related internships or fieldwork, Federal Work-Study, institutionally sponsored loans, tuition waivers (full and partial), and unspecified assistantships also available. Support available to part-time students. Financial award application deadline: 7/1; financial award applicants required to submit FAFSA. *Unit head:* Marilyn Brown, School Chair, 404-385-8577, Fax: 404-894-0504, E-mail: marilyn.brown@pubpolicy.gatech.edu. *Application contact:* Marla Bruner, Director of Graduate Studies, 404-894-1610, Fax: 404-894-1609, E-mail:

gradinfo@mail.gatech.edu.
Website: http://www.spp.gatech.edu

Georgia State University, Andrew Young School of Policy Studies, Department of Public Management and Policy, Atlanta, GA 30303. Offers criminal justice (MPA); disaster management (Certificate); disaster policy (MPA); environmental policy (PhD); health policy (PhD); management and finance (MPA); nonprofit management (MPA, Certificate); nonprofit policy (MPA); planning and economic development (MPP, Certificate); policy analysis and evaluation (MPA), including planning and economic development; public and nonprofit management (PhD); public finance and budgeting (PhD), including science and technology policy, urban and regional economic development; public finance policy (MPA), including social policy; public health (MPA). *Accreditation:* NASPAA (one or more programs are accredited). *Program availability:* Part-time. *Faculty:* 13 full-time (7 women), 3 part-time/adjunct (1 woman). *Students:* 125 full-time (81 women), 91 part-time (66 women); includes 103 minority (78 Black or African American, non-Hispanic/Latino; 3 Asian, non-Hispanic/Latino; 14 Hispanic/Latino; 8 Two or more races, non-Hispanic/Latino), 31 international. Average age 32. 298 applicants, 60% accepted, 82 enrolled. In 2019, 70 master's, 8 other advanced degrees awarded. Terminal master's awarded for partial completion of doctoral program. *Degree requirements:* For master's, thesis optional; for doctorate, comprehensive exam, thesis/dissertation. *Entrance requirements:* For master's and doctorate, GRE. Additional exam requirements/recommendations for international students: required—TOEFL (minimum score 603 paper-based; 100 iBT) or IELTS (minimum score 7). *Application deadline:* For fall admission, 1/15 for domestic and international students. Application fee: $50. Electronic applications accepted. *Expenses: Tuition, area resident:* Full-time $7164; part-time $398 per credit hour. Tuition, state resident: full-time $7164; part-time $398 per credit hour. Tuition, nonresident: full-time $22,662; part-time $1259 per credit hour. *International tuition:* $22,662 full-time. *Required fees:* $2128; $312 per credit hour. Tuition and fees vary according to course load and program. *Financial support:* In 2019–20, fellowships (averaging $8,194 per year), research assistantships (averaging $8,068 per year), teaching assistantships (averaging $3,600 per year) were awarded; institutionally sponsored loans, scholarships/grants, health care benefits, and unspecified assistantships also available. Financial award application deadline: 2/1. *Unit head:* Dr. Cathy Yang Liu, Chair and Professor, 404-413-0102, Fax: 404-413-0104, E-mail: cyliu@gsu.edu. *Application contact:* Dr. Cathy Yang Liu, Chair and Professor, 404-413-0102, Fax: 404-413-0104, E-mail: cyliu@gsu.edu.
Website: https://aysps.gsu.edu/public-management-policy/

Harvard University, Graduate School of Arts and Sciences and John F. Kennedy School of Government, Committee on Public Policy, Cambridge, MA 02138. Offers PhD. *Degree requirements:* For doctorate, thesis/dissertation, exams. *Entrance requirements:* For doctorate, GRE General Test or GMAT, Harvard MPP degree. Additional exam requirements/recommendations for international students: required—TOEFL.

Harvard University, Graduate School of Arts and Sciences, Program in Social Policy, Cambridge, MA 02138. Offers PhD.

Harvard University, John F. Kennedy School of Government, Doctoral Programs in Government, Cambridge, MA 02138. Offers political economy and government (PhD); public policy (PhD). *Degree requirements:* For doctorate, comprehensive exam, thesis/dissertation. *Entrance requirements:* For doctorate, GRE General Test, course work in macroeconomics, multi-variable calculus. Additional exam requirements/recommendations for international students: required—TOEFL (minimum score 600 paper-based; 100 iBT), TWE. Electronic applications accepted.

Harvard University, John F. Kennedy School of Government, Program in Public Policy, Cambridge, MA 02138. Offers MPP, JD/MPP, MBA/MPP, MD/MPP. *Entrance requirements:* For master's, GMAT or GRE General Test. Additional exam requirements/recommendations for international students: required—TOEFL (minimum score 600 paper-based; 100 iBT), TWE. Electronic applications accepted.

Indiana University Bloomington, School of Public and Environmental Affairs, Public Affairs Programs, Bloomington, IN 47405. Offers economic development (MPA); energy (MPA); environmental policy (PhD); environmental policy and natural resource management (MPA); information systems (MPA); international development (MPA); local government management (MPA); nonprofit management (MPA, Certificate); policy analysis (MPA); public budgeting and financial management (Certificate); public finance (PhD); public financial administration (MPA); public management (MPA, PhD, Certificate); public policy analysis (PhD); social entrepreneurship (Certificate); specialized public affairs (MPA); sustainability and sustainable development (MPA); JD/MPA; MPA/MA; MPA/MIS; MPA/MLS; MSES/MPA. *Accreditation:* NASPAA (one or more programs are accredited). *Program availability:* Part-time. *Degree requirements:* For master's, capstone, internship; for doctorate, comprehensive exam, thesis/dissertation. *Entrance requirements:* For master's, GRE General Test or GMAT, official transcripts, 3 letters of recommendation, resume, personal statement; for doctorate, GRE General Test, official transcripts, 3 letters of recommendation, statement of purpose. Additional exam requirements/recommendations for international students: required—TOEFL (minimum score 600 paper-based; 96 iBT); recommended—IELTS (minimum score 7). Electronic applications accepted.

Indiana University Kokomo, Department of Public Administration and Health Management, Kokomo, IN 46904. Offers health management (MPM, Graduate Certificate); public management (Graduate Certificate); public management and policy (MPM). *Program availability:* Part-time, evening/weekend. *Entrance requirements:* For master's, GRE/GMAT for GPAs lower than 3.0, letters of recommendation. Additional exam requirements/recommendations for international students: required—TOEFL (minimum score 550 paper-based; 73 iBT). Electronic applications accepted. *Expenses:* Contact institution.

The Institute of World Politics, Graduate Programs in National Security, Intelligence, and International Affairs, Washington, DC 20036. Offers American foreign policy (Certificate); comparative political culture (Certificate); conflict prevention (Certificate); counterintelligence (Certificate); counterterrorism (Certificate); cyber statecraft (Certificate); economic statecraft (Certificate); homeland security (Certificate); intelligence (Certificate); international politics (Certificate); national security affairs (Executive MA, Certificate); nonviolent conflict (Certificate); peace building, stabilization, and humanitarian affairs (Certificate); public diplomacy and strategic influence (Certificate); statecraft and international affairs (MA); statecraft and national security (MA, DSNS); strategic communication (Certificate); strategic intelligence studies (MA, Professional MA); strategic soft power (Certificate). *Program availability:* Part-time, evening/weekend. *Degree requirements:* For master's, 52 credit hours, comprehensive written and oral exam (for MA); proficiency in critical language (for MA in statecraft and international affairs); 28 credit hours (for Executive MA); 36 credit hours (for Professional MA); for doctorate, comprehensive exam, thesis/dissertation; for Certificate, 20 credit hours. *Entrance requirements:* For master's, resume, personal statement, 3 references, essay; 7-10 years of professional experience (for Executive MA); 5-7 years of professional experience (for Professional MA); for doctorate, MA. Additional exam requirements/recommendations for international students: required—TOEFL. Electronic applications accepted.

Jackson State University, Graduate School, College of Public Service, Department of Public Policy and Administration, Jackson, MS 39217. Offers public administration (PhD); public policy and administration (MPPA). *Accreditation:* NASPAA (one or more programs are accredited). *Program availability:* Evening/weekend. *Degree requirements:* For master's, comprehensive exam, thesis optional; for doctorate, comprehensive exam, thesis/dissertation. *Entrance requirements:* For master's, GRE General Test; for doctorate, GRE, GMAT, MAT. Additional exam requirements/recommendations for international students: required—TOEFL (minimum score 520 paper-based; 67 iBT).

Jacksonville University, Public Policy Institute, Jacksonville, FL 32211. Offers MPP, MBA/MPP, MPP/JD, MPP/MS. *Program availability:* Part-time, evening/weekend. *Faculty:* 6 full-time (1 woman), 15 part-time/adjunct (3 women). *Students:* 13 full-time (9 women), 39 part-time (24 women); includes 22 minority (15 Black or African American, non-Hispanic/Latino; 1 Asian, non-Hispanic/Latino; 3 Hispanic/Latino; 3 Two or more races, non-Hispanic/Latino). Average age 36. 40 applicants, 68% accepted, 22 enrolled. In 2019, 14 master's awarded. *Degree requirements:* For master's, thesis, internship, capstone project. *Entrance requirements:* For master's, GRE, GMAT, LSAT, resume, essay, statement of intent, two current references, official transcripts of academic work. Additional exam requirements/recommendations for international students: recommended—TOEFL (minimum score 540 paper-based; 76 iBT). *Application deadline:* For fall admission, 2/15 priority date for domestic students, 2/15 for international students. Applications are processed on a rolling basis. Application fee: $50. Electronic applications accepted. *Expenses:* Contact institution. *Financial support:* Fellowships, career-related internships or fieldwork, Federal Work-Study, scholarships/grants, and unspecified assistantships available. Support available to part-time students. Financial award application deadline: 4/1; financial award applicants required to submit FAFSA. *Unit head:* Dr. Richard A. Mullaney, Director of Public Policy Institute, 904-256-7342, E-mail: rmullan1@ju.edu. *Application contact:* Fowler Martens, Administrative Associate, 904-256-7053, E-mail: fmarten@ju.edu.
Website: https://www.ju.edu/publicpolicy/

John Jay College of Criminal Justice of the City University of New York, Graduate Studies, Programs in Criminal Justice, New York, NY 10019. Offers criminal justice (MA, PhD); criminology and deviance (PhD); forensic psychology (PhD); forensic science (PhD); international crime and justice (MA); law and philosophy (PhD); organizational behavior (PhD); public policy (PhD). *Program availability:* Part-time, evening/weekend. Terminal master's awarded for partial completion of doctoral program. *Degree requirements:* For master's, thesis or alternative; for doctorate, one foreign language, thesis/dissertation. *Entrance requirements:* For master's, GRE General Test, minimum B average; for doctorate, GRE General Test. Additional exam requirements/recommendations for international students: required—TOEFL (minimum score 500 paper-based).

Johns Hopkins University, Bloomberg School of Public Health, Department of Health Policy and Management, Baltimore, MD 21205-1996. Offers bioethics and policy (PhD); health administration (MHA); health and public policy (PhD); health economics (MHS); health economics and policy (PhD); health finance and management (MHS); health policy (MSPH); health policy and management (Dr PH); health services research and policy (PhD); public policy (MPP). *Accreditation:* CAHME (one or more programs are accredited). *Program availability:* Part-time. *Degree requirements:* For master's, thesis (for some programs), internship (for some programs); for doctorate, comprehensive exam, thesis/dissertation, 1-year full-time residency (for some programs), oral and written exams. *Entrance requirements:* For master's, GRE General Test or GMAT, 3 letters of recommendation, curriculum vitae/resume; for doctorate, GRE General Test or GMAT, 3 letters of recommendation, curriculum vitae, transcripts. Additional exam requirements/recommendations for international students: required—TOEFL (minimum score 100 iBT), IELTS (minimum score 7). Electronic applications accepted.

Liberty University, Helms School of Government, Lynchburg, VA 24515. Offers criminal justice (MS), including forensic psychology, homeland security, public administration (MA, MS); international relations (MS); political science (MS); public administration (MPA), including business and government, healthcare, law and public policy, public and non-profit management; public policy (MA), including campaigns and elections, international affairs, Middle East affairs, public administration (MA, MS). *Program availability:* Part-time, online learning. *Students:* 1,143 full-time (565 women), 572 part-time (408 women); includes 795 minority (499 Black or African American, non-Hispanic/Latino; 16 American Indian or Alaska Native, non-Hispanic/Latino; 23 Asian, non-Hispanic/Latino; 162 Hispanic/Latino; 7 Native Hawaiian or other Pacific Islander, non-Hispanic/Latino; 88 Two or more races, non-Hispanic/Latino), 27 international. Average age 35. 3,017 applicants, 44% accepted, 728 enrolled. In 2019, 415 master's awarded. *Entrance requirements:* For master's, minimum undergraduate GPA of 3.0. Additional exam requirements/recommendations for international students: required—TOEFL (minimum score 600 paper-based; 100 iBT). *Application deadline:* Applications are processed on a rolling basis. Application fee: $50. Electronic applications accepted. *Expenses: Tuition:* Full-time $545; part-time $410 per credit hour. One-time fee: $50. *Financial support:* In 2019–20, 808 students received support. Teaching assistantships and Federal Work-Study available. *Unit head:* Ron Miller, Dean, 434-592-4986, E-mail: govtdean@liberty.edu. *Application contact:* Jay Bridge, Director of Admissions, 800-424-9595, Fax: 800-628-7977, E-mail: gradadmissions@liberty.edu.
Website: https://www.liberty.edu/government/

Lipscomb University, School of Public Policy, Nashville, TN 37204-3951. Offers leadership and public service (MA). *Entrance requirements:* For master's, GRE or GMAT, references, resume, goals statement. Additional exam requirements/recommendations for international students: required—TOEFL (minimum score 550 paper-based). Electronic applications accepted. *Expenses:* Contact institution.

London Metropolitan University, Graduate Programs, London, United Kingdom. Offers applied psychology (M Sc); architecture (MA); biomedical science (M Sc); blood science (M Sc); cancer pharmacology (M Sc); computer networking and cyber security (M Sc); computing and information systems (M Sc); conference interpreting (MA); counter-terrorism studies (M Sc); creative, digital and professional writing (MA); crime, violence and prevention (M Sc); criminology (M Sc); curating contemporary art (MA); data analytics (M Sc); digital media (MA); early childhood studies (MA); education (MA, Ed D); financial services law, regulation and compliance (LL M); food science (M Sc); forensic psychology (M Sc); health and social care management and policy (M Sc); human nutrition (M Sc); human resource management (MA); human rights and international conflict (MA); information technology (M Sc); intelligence and security studies (M Sc); international oil, gas and energy law (LL M); international relations (MA); interpreting (MA); learning and teaching in higher education (MA); legal practice (LL M); media and entertainment law (LL M); organizational and consumer psychology (M Sc); psychological therapy (M Sc); psychology of mental health (M Sc); public health (M Sc); public policy and management (MPA); security studies (M Sc); social work (M Sc); spatial planning and urban design (MA); sports therapy (M Sc); supporting older children and young people with dyslexia (MA); teaching languages (MA), including Arabic, English; translation (MA); woman and child abuse (MA).

Loyola University Chicago, Graduate School, Program in Public Policy, Chicago, IL 60660. Offers MPP. *Program availability:* Part-time, evening/weekend. *Faculty:* 2 full-time (both women), 3 part-time/adjunct (1 woman). *Students:* 9 full-time (5 women), 5 part-time (3 women); includes 5 minority (3 Black or African American, non-Hispanic/Latino; 1 Hispanic/Latino; 1 Two or more races, non-Hispanic/Latino). Average age 25. 32 applicants, 75% accepted, 6 enrolled. In 2019, 16 master's awarded. *Entrance requirements:* For master's, GRE, three letters of recommendation, transcripts, statement of purpose. Additional exam requirements/recommendations for international students: required—TOEFL (minimum score 550 paper-based). *Application deadline:* For fall admission, 6/30 for domestic students. Applications are processed on a rolling basis. Application fee: $0. Electronic applications accepted. Application fee is waived when completed online. *Expenses: Tuition:* Full-time $18,540; part-time $1033 per credit hour. *Required fees:* $904; $230 per credit hour. *Financial support:* In 2019–20, 5 students received support, including 1 fellowship with full tuition reimbursement available (averaging $18,000 per year), 3 research assistantships with partial tuition reimbursements available (averaging $14,000 per year); unspecified assistantships also available. Financial award application deadline: 2/15; financial award applicants required to submit FAFSA. *Unit head:* Dr. Annette Steinacker, Director, 773-508-3396. *Application contact:* Jill Schur, Director, Graduate Enrollment Management, 312-915-8902, E-mail: gradinfo@luc.edu.

McMaster University, School of Graduate Studies, Faculty of Social Sciences, Department of Political Science, Hamilton, ON L8S 4M2, Canada. Offers international relations (PhD); political science (MA); public and the global economy (MA); public policy (PhD); public policy and administration (MA). *Program availability:* Part-time. *Degree requirements:* For master's, thesis or alternative. *Entrance requirements:* For master's, minimum B+ average. Additional exam requirements/recommendations for international students: required—TOEFL (minimum score 580 paper-based).

Midwest University, Graduate Programs, Wentzville, MO 63385. Offers asset management/investment/real estate (MBA); Christian counseling (D Min); Christian education (D Min); counseling (MA), including marriage and family counseling, school counseling; divinity (M Div); education (MA), including brain and gifted education, Christian education; global business management (MBA); global leadership (MBA); leadership (PhD), including brain and gifted educational leadership, entrepreneurial leadership, international aviation leadership, organizational leadership, political leadership; mission studies (D Min); music (MM, DMA); pastoral theology (D Min); public policy/administration (MBA); teaching English to speakers of other languages (MA). *Program availability:* Part-time, online learning. *Degree requirements:* For master's, thesis (for some programs); for doctorate, thesis/dissertation. *Entrance requirements:* Additional exam requirements/recommendations for international students: recommended—TOEFL (minimum score 550 paper-based).

Mills College, Graduate Studies, Joint MBA/MPP Program, Oakland, CA 94613-1000. Offers MBA/MPP. *Entrance requirements:* Additional exam requirements/recommendations for international students: required—TOEFL (minimum score 550 paper-based; 80 iBT) or IELTS (minimum score 6). Electronic applications accepted. *Expenses:* Contact institution.

Mills College, Graduate Studies, Program in Public Policy, Oakland, CA 94613-1000. Offers MPP. *Degree requirements:* For master's, thesis. *Entrance requirements:* For master's, GRE, SAT, or ACT, statement of purpose, resume. Additional exam requirements/recommendations for international students: required—TOEFL (minimum score 550 paper-based; 80 iBT) or IELTS (minimum score 6). Electronic applications accepted. *Expenses:* Contact institution.

Mississippi State University, College of Arts and Sciences, Department of Political Science and Public Administration, Mississippi State, MS 39762. Offers political science (MA); public policy and administration (MPPA, PhD). *Accreditation:* NASPAA (one or more programs are accredited). *Program availability:* Evening/weekend, blended/hybrid learning. *Faculty:* 15 full-time (6 women). *Students:* 24 full-time (13 women), 39 part-time (19 women); includes 18 minority (15 Black or African American, non-Hispanic/Latino; 1 American Indian or Alaska Native, non-Hispanic/Latino; 1 Asian, non-Hispanic/Latino; 1 Hispanic/Latino), 5 international. Average age 32. 29 applicants, 90% accepted, 19 enrolled. In 2019, 11 master's, 1 doctorate awarded. *Degree requirements:* For master's, thesis optional, comprehensive oral or written exam; for doctorate, thesis/dissertation, comprehensive oral and written exam. *Entrance requirements:* For master's, GRE, minimum GPA of 3.0 on the last two years of undergraduate courses or graduate work; for doctorate, GRE General Test, minimum graduate GPA of 3.35. Additional exam requirements/recommendations for international students: required—TOEFL (minimum score 600 paper-based; 100 iBT); recommended—IELTS (minimum score 7.5). *Application deadline:* For fall admission, 8/1 priority date for domestic students, 5/1 for international students; for spring admission, 12/1 priority date for domestic students, 9/1 for international students. Applications are processed on a rolling basis. Application fee: $60 ($80 for international students). Electronic applications accepted. *Expenses: Tuition, area resident:* Full-time $8880; part-time $456 per credit hour. Tuition, state resident: full-time $8880. Tuition, nonresident: full-time $23,840; part-time $1236 per credit hour. *Required fees:* $110; $11.12 per credit hour. Tuition and fees vary according to course load. *Financial support:* In 2019–20, 9 teaching assistantships with full tuition reimbursements (averaging $11,083 per year) were awarded; Federal Work-Study, institutionally sponsored loans, scholarships/grants, and unspecified assistantships also available. Financial award application deadline: 4/1; financial award applicants required to submit FAFSA. *Unit head:* Dr. P. Edward French, Professor and Head, 662-325-2711, Fax: 662-325-2716, E-mail: efrench@pspa.msstate.edu. *Application contact:* Nathan Drake, Manager, Graduate Programs, 662-325-7394, E-mail: ndrake@grad.msstate.edu.
Website: http://www.pspa.msstate.edu/

National Louis University, College of Arts and Sciences, Chicago, IL 60603. Offers adult education (Ed D); counseling and human services (MS); language and academic development (M Ed, Certificate); psychology (MA, PhD, Certificate); public policy (MA); written communication (MS, Certificate). *Program availability:* Part-time, evening/weekend, online learning. *Degree requirements:* For master's and Certificate, comprehensive exam (for some programs), thesis (for some programs); for doctorate, thesis/dissertation. *Entrance requirements:* For master's, MAT or GRE, 3 professional or academic references, interview, minimum GPA of 3.0; for doctorate, GRE General Test, MAT, or Watson-Glaser Critical Thinking Appraisal, three professional or academic references, statement of academic and professional goals, 3 years of experience in field, interview, master's degree, resume, writing sample; for Certificate, GRE, MAT, or Watson-Glaser Critical Thinking Appraisal, three professional or academic references, statement of academic and professional goals, interview, minimum GPA of 3.0. Additional exam requirements/recommendations for international students: required—Department of Language Studies Assessment or TOEFL (minimum score 550 paper-based; 79 iBT). Electronic applications accepted.

New England College, Program in Public Policy, Henniker, NH 03242-3293. Offers MA. *Program availability:* Part-time, evening/weekend, online learning. *Degree requirements:* For master's, thesis. *Entrance requirements:* Additional exam requirements/recommendations for international students: recommended—TOEFL (minimum score 600 paper-based). Electronic applications accepted.

The New School, Schools of Public Engagement, Program in Public and Urban Policy, New York, NY 10011. Offers public and urban policy (PhD). *Accreditation:* NASPAA. *Program availability:* Part-time, evening/weekend. *Faculty:* 7 full-time (3 women), 17 part-time/adjunct. *Students:* 77 full-time (51 women), 35 part-time (25 women); includes 42 minority (17 Black or African American, non-Hispanic/Latino; 6 Asian, non-Hispanic/Latino; 16 Hispanic/Latino; 3 Two or more races, non-Hispanic/Latino), 30 international. Average age 33. 106 applicants, 72% accepted, 21 enrolled. In 2019, 21 master's, 4 doctorates awarded. Terminal master's awarded for partial completion of doctoral program. *Degree requirements:* For master's, thesis; for doctorate, comprehensive exam, thesis/dissertation. *Entrance requirements:* For master's, transcripts, recommendation letters, resume, statement of goals and purpose; for doctorate, transcripts, recommendation letters, resume, statement of goals and purpose, example of scholarly work. Additional exam requirements/recommendations for international students: required—TOEFL (minimum score 92 iBT), IELTS (minimum score 7), PTE (minimum score 68). *Application deadline:* For fall admission, 1/15 priority date for domestic and international students. Applications are processed on a rolling basis. Application fee: $50. Electronic applications accepted. *Expenses:* 1710 per credit. *Financial support:* In 2019–20, 78 students received support, including 9 fellowships (averaging $5,572 per year), 24 research assistantships (averaging $5,268 per year), 17 teaching assistantships (averaging $6,119 per year); career-related internships or fieldwork, Federal Work-Study, scholarships/grants, and unspecified assistantships also available. Support available to part-time students. Financial award application deadline: 2/1; financial award applicants required to submit FAFSA. *Unit head:* Michael A Cohen, Director, 212-206-3524 Ext. 2413, E-mail: cohenm2@newschool.edu. *Application contact:* Merida Gasbarro, Director of Graduate Admission, 212-229-5600 Ext. 1108, E-mail: escandom@newschool.edu.
Website: https://www.newschool.edu/public-engagement/ms-public-urban-policy/

New York University, Wagner Graduate School of Public Service, Executive Master of Public Administration Program, New York, NY 10012. Offers global public policy and management (EMPA); MSW/EMPA. *Accreditation:* AACSB. *Program availability:* Part-time. *Entrance requirements:* Additional exam requirements/recommendations for international students: required—TOEFL (minimum score 100 iBT), IELTS (minimum score 7.5), TWE. Electronic applications accepted. *Expenses:* Contact institution.

Northeastern University, College of Engineering, Boston, MA 02115-5096. Offers bioengineering (MS, PhD); chemical engineering (MS, PhD); civil engineering (MS, PhD); computer engineering (PhD); computer systems engineering (MS); electrical and computer engineering (MS); electrical and computer engineering leadership (MS); electrical engineering (PhD); energy systems (MS); engineering and public policy (MS); engineering management (MS, Certificate); environmental engineering (MS); industrial engineering (MS, PhD); information assurance (PhD); information systems (MS); interdisciplinary engineering (PhD); mechanical engineering (PhD); operations research (MS); telecommunication systems management (MS). *Program availability:* Part-time, online learning. Electronic applications accepted. *Expenses:* Contact institution.

Northeastern University, College of Social Sciences and Humanities, Boston, MA 02115. Offers criminology and criminal justice (MSCJ); criminology and justice policy (PhD); economics (MA, PhD); English (MA, PhD); international affairs (MA); law and public policy (PhD); political science (MA, PhD); public administration (MPA); public policy (MPP); security and resilience studies (MS); sociology (MA, PhD); urban and regional policy (MS); urban informatics (MS); world history (MA, PhD). *Program availability:* Online learning. *Degree requirements:* For doctorate, variable foreign language requirement, comprehensive exam, thesis/dissertation. *Entrance requirements:* For master's and doctorate, GRE. Additional exam requirements/recommendations for international students: required—TOEFL, IELTS. Electronic applications accepted. *Expenses:* Contact institution.

Northwestern University, The Graduate School, School of Education and Social Policy, Program in Human Development and Social Policy, Evanston, IL 60208. Offers PhD. *Degree requirements:* For doctorate, comprehensive exam, thesis/dissertation. *Entrance requirements:* For doctorate, GRE General Test. Additional exam requirements/recommendations for international students: required—TOEFL (minimum score 600 paper-based; 100 iBT). Electronic applications accepted.

Northwestern University, School of Professional Studies, Program in Public Policy and Administration, Evanston, IL 60208. Offers global policy (MA); health services policy (MA); public administration (MA); public policy (MA). *Program availability:* Part-time, evening/weekend, online learning.

Norwich University, College of Graduate and Continuing Studies, Master of Public Administration Program, Northfield, VT 05663. Offers criminal justice and public safety (MPA); fiscal management (MPA); international development and influence (MPA); municipal governance (MPA); nonprofit management (MPA); policy analysis and analytics (MPA); public administration leadership and crisis management (MPA); public works and sustainability (MPA). *Program availability:* Evening/weekend, online only, mostly all online with a week-long residency requirement. *Degree requirements:* For master's, capstone. *Entrance requirements:* For master's, minimum undergraduate GPA of 2.75. Additional exam requirements/recommendations for international students: required—TOEFL (minimum score 550 paper-based; 80 iBT), IELTS (minimum score 6.5). Electronic applications accepted. *Expenses:* Contact institution.

The Ohio State University, Graduate School, John Glenn College of Public Affairs, Columbus, OH 43210. Offers public administration (MA, MPA); public policy and management (PhD). *Accreditation:* NASPAA (one or more programs are accredited). *Program availability:* Part-time. *Degree requirements:* For doctorate, thesis/dissertation. *Entrance requirements:* For master's, GRE General Test (for MPA), minimum GPA of 3.0 (for MA); for doctorate, GRE General Test. Additional exam requirements/recommendations for international students: required—TOEFL (minimum score 600 paper-based; 100 iBT); recommended—IELTS (minimum score 7.5). Electronic applications accepted.

Old Dominion University, Strome College of Business, Program in Public Administration and Policy, Norfolk, VA 23529. Offers PhD. *Program availability:* Part-time, evening/weekend. *Degree requirements:* For doctorate, comprehensive exam, thesis/dissertation. *Entrance requirements:* For doctorate, GMAT, GRE General Test, LSAT, master's degree, minimum graduate GPA of 3.25. Additional exam requirements/recommendations for international students: required—TOEFL (minimum score 550 paper-based; 79 iBT). Electronic applications accepted. *Expenses:* Contact institution.

Oregon State University, College of Liberal Arts, Program in Public Policy, Corvallis, OR 97331. Offers energy policy (MPP, PhD); environmental policy (MPP, PhD); international policy (MPP, PhD); law, crime and policy (MPP, PhD); rural policy (MPP, PhD); science and technology policy (MPP, PhD); social policy (MPP, PhD). *Accreditation:* NASPAA. *Program availability:* Part-time, 100% online. *Entrance requirements:* For master's and doctorate, GRE. Additional exam requirements/recommendations for international students: required—TOEFL, IELTS (minimum score 6.5).

Pepperdine University, School of Public Policy, Malibu, CA 90263. Offers American politics (MPP); economics (MPP); international relations (MPP); state and local policy (MPP); JD/MPP; MBA/MPP; MDR/MPP. *Entrance requirements:* For master's, GRE or

GMAT or LSAT, transcripts, 2 letters of recommendation, resume, two essays. Additional exam requirements/recommendations for international students: required—TOEFL (minimum score 95 iBT), IELTS (minimum score 7). Electronic applications accepted. *Expenses:* Contact institution.

Portland State University, Graduate Studies, College of Urban and Public Affairs, Hatfield School of Government, Department of Public Administration, Portland, OR 97207-0751. Offers collaborative governance (Certificate); energy policy and management (Certificate); global management and leadership (MPA); health administration (MPA); human resource management (MPA); local government (MPA); natural resource policy and administration (MPA); nonprofit and public management (Certificate); nonprofit management (MPA); public administration (EMPA); public affairs and policy (PhD); sustainable food systems (Certificate). *Accreditation:* CAHME; NASPAA (one or more programs are accredited). *Program availability:* Part-time, evening/weekend. *Faculty:* 14 full-time (6 women), 9 part-time/adjunct (5 women). *Students:* 86 full-time (55 women), 119 part-time (73 women); includes 46 minority (3 Black or African American, non-Hispanic/Latino; 4 American Indian or Alaska Native, non-Hispanic/Latino; 8 Asian, non-Hispanic/Latino; 18 Hispanic/Latino; 2 Native Hawaiian or other Pacific Islander, non-Hispanic/Latino; 11 Two or more races, non-Hispanic/Latino), 17 international. Average age 35. 138 applicants, 82% accepted, 67 enrolled. In 2019, 64 master's, 2 doctorates awarded. *Degree requirements:* For master's, integrative field experience (MPA), practicum (MPH); for doctorate, comprehensive exam, thesis/dissertation. *Entrance requirements:* For master's, GRE (minimum scores: verbal 150, quantitative 149, and analytic writing 4.5), minimum GPA of 3.0, 3 recommendation letters, resume, 500-word statement of intent; for doctorate, GRE, 3 recommendation letters, resume, 500-word personal essay. Additional exam requirements/recommendations for international students: required—TOEFL (minimum score 550 paper-based; 80 iBT), IELTS (minimum score 7). *Application deadline:* For fall admission, 8/15 for domestic and international students; for winter admission, 10/31 for domestic and international students; for spring admission, 1/31 for domestic and international students. Applications are processed on a rolling basis. Application fee: $65. Electronic applications accepted. *Expenses: Tuition, area resident:* Full-time $13,020; part-time $6510 per year. Tuition, state resident: full-time $13,020; part-time $6510 per year. Tuition, nonresident: full-time $19,830; part-time $9915 per year. *International tuition:* $19,830 full-time. *Required fees:* $1226. One-time fee: $350. Tuition and fees vary according to course load, program and reciprocity agreements. *Financial support:* In 2019–20, 1 research assistantship with full and partial tuition reimbursement (averaging $8,500 per year), 3 teaching assistantships (averaging $7,840 per year) were awarded; career-related internships or fieldwork, Federal Work-Study, scholarships/grants, and unspecified assistantships also available. Support available to part-time students. Financial award application deadline: 3/1; financial award applicants required to submit FAFSA. *Unit head:* Dr. Masami Nishishiba, Chair, 503-725-5151, E-mail: nishism@pdx.edu. *Application contact:* Megan Heljeson, Office Coordinator, 503-725-3921, Fax: 503-725-8250, E-mail: publicad@pdx.edu. Website: https://www.pdx.edu/hatfieldschool/public-administration

Princeton University, Graduate School, Woodrow Wilson School of Public and International Affairs, Princeton, NJ 08544-1019. Offers public affairs (MPA, PhD); public policy (MPP); JD/MPA. Terminal master's awarded for partial completion of doctoral program. *Degree requirements:* For master's, internship; for doctorate, one foreign language, thesis/dissertation. *Entrance requirements:* For master's, GRE General Test, original policy memo; for doctorate, GRE General Test. Additional exam requirements/recommendations for international students: required—TOEFL (minimum score 600 paper-based). Electronic applications accepted.

Purdue University Fort Wayne, College of Professional Studies, Department of Public Policy, Fort Wayne, IN 46805-1499. Offers public management (MPM, Certificate). *Program availability:* Part-time. *Degree requirements:* For master's, internship. *Entrance requirements:* For master's, GRE General Test or GMAT, minimum GPA of 3.0, 3 letters of reference. Additional exam requirements/recommendations for international students: required—TOEFL (minimum score 550 paper-based; 79 iBT).

Regent University, Graduate School, Robertson School of Government, Virginia Beach, VA 23464. Offers government (MA), including American government, healthcare policy and ethics (MA, MPA), international relations, law and public policy, national security studies, political communication, political theory, religion and politics; national security studies (MA), including cybersecurity, homeland security, international security, Middle East politics; public administration (MPA), including emergency management and homeland security, federal government, general public administration, healthcare policy and ethics (MA, MPA), law, nonprofit administration and faith-based organizations, public leadership and management, servant leadership. *Program availability:* Part-time, evening/weekend, 100% online, blended/hybrid learning. *Faculty:* 5 full-time (1 woman), 19 part-time/adjunct (2 women). *Students:* 36 full-time (22 women), 159 part-time (89 women); includes 82 minority (52 Black or African American, non-Hispanic/Latino; 2 American Indian or Alaska Native, non-Hispanic/Latino; 2 Asian, non-Hispanic/Latino; 23 Hispanic/Latino; 3 Two or more races, non-Hispanic/Latino), 4 international. Average age 36. 181 applicants, 70% accepted, 75 enrolled. In 2019, 58 master's awarded. *Degree requirements:* For master's, thesis optional, internship. *Entrance requirements:* For master's, GRE General Test or LSAT, personal essay, writing sample, resume, college transcripts. Additional exam requirements/recommendations for international students: required—TOEFL (minimum score 577 paper-based). *Application deadline:* For fall admission, 5/1 priority date for domestic students; for spring admission, 11/1 priority date for domestic students. Applications are processed on a rolling basis. Application fee: $50. Electronic applications accepted. *Expenses:* Contact institution. *Financial support:* In 2019–20, 132 students received support. Career-related internships or fieldwork, scholarships/grants, and unspecified assistantships available. Support available to part-time students. Financial award applicants required to submit FAFSA. *Unit head:* Dr. Stephen Perry, Interim Dean, 757-352-4082, E-mail: sperry@regent.edu. *Application contact:* Heidi Cece, Assistant Vice President for Enrollment Management, 800-373-5504, Fax: 757-352-4381, E-mail: admissions@regent.edu.
Website: https://www.regent.edu/robertson-school-of-government/

Rochester Institute of Technology, Graduate Enrollment Services, College of Liberal Arts, Department of Public Policy, MS Program in Science, Technology and Public Policy, Rochester, NY 14623-5603. Offers MS. *Program availability:* Part-time. *Degree requirements:* For master's, thesis or alternative, thesis or comprehensive exam plus 2 graduate electives. *Entrance requirements:* For master's, GRE, minimum GPA of 3.0 (recommended), completed course work in calculus and statistics, two writing samples, two letters of recommendation. Additional exam requirements/recommendations for international students: required—TOEFL (minimum score 570 paper-based; 88 iBT), IELTS (minimum score 6.5), PTE (minimum score 61). Electronic applications accepted. *Expenses:* Contact institution.

Rutgers University - Camden, Graduate School of Arts and Sciences, Department of Public Policy and Administration, Camden, NJ 08102. Offers education policy and leadership (MPA); international public service and development (MPA); public management (MPA); JD/MPA; MPA/MA. *Accreditation:* NASPAA. *Program availability:* Part-time, evening/weekend. *Degree requirements:* For master's, directed study,

research workshop, 42 credits. *Entrance requirements:* For master's, GRE General Test, GMAT or LSAT, 3 letters of recommendation; resume. Additional exam requirements/recommendations for international students: required—TOEFL (minimum score 550 paper-based), IELTS. Electronic applications accepted.

Rutgers University - Newark, Graduate School, Program in Public Administration, Newark, NJ 07102. Offers health care administration (MPA); human resources administration (MPA); public administration (PhD); public management (MPA); public policy analysis (MPA); urban systems and issues (MPA). *Accreditation:* NASPAA (one or more programs are accredited). *Program availability:* Part-time, evening/weekend. *Degree requirements:* For master's, comprehensive exam, thesis or alternative; for doctorate, thesis/dissertation. *Entrance requirements:* For master's, GRE, minimum undergraduate B average; for doctorate, GRE, MPA, minimum B average. Electronic applications accepted.

Rutgers University - Newark, School of Public Health, Newark, NJ 07107-1709. Offers clinical epidemiology (Certificate); dental public health (MPH); general public health (Certificate); public policy and oral health services administration (Certificate); quantitative methods (MPH); urban health (MPH); DMD/MPH; MD/MPH; MS/MPH. *Program availability:* Part-time, evening/weekend. *Degree requirements:* For master's, thesis, internship. *Entrance requirements:* For master's, GRE General Test. Additional exam requirements/recommendations for international students: required—TOEFL. Electronic applications accepted.

Rutgers University - New Brunswick, Edward J. Bloustein School of Planning and Public Policy, Doctoral Program in Planning and Public Policy, New Brunswick, NJ 08901. Offers PhD. *Program availability:* Part-time. *Degree requirements:* For doctorate, comprehensive exam, thesis/dissertation. *Entrance requirements:* For doctorate, GRE, master's degree. Additional exam requirements/recommendations for international students: required—TOEFL (minimum score 575 paper-based; 88 iBT). Electronic applications accepted.

Rutgers University - New Brunswick, Edward J. Bloustein School of Planning and Public Policy, Program in Public Policy, New Brunswick, NJ 08901. Offers MPAP, MPP, JD/MPAP, MBA/MPP, MCRP/MPP. *Accreditation:* NASPAA. *Program availability:* Part-time, evening/weekend. *Entrance requirements:* For master's, GRE General Test. Additional exam requirements/recommendations for international students: required—TOEFL (minimum score 575 paper-based; 88 iBT). Electronic applications accepted.

San Francisco State University, Division of Graduate Studies, College of Health and Social Sciences, Public Administration Program, San Francisco, CA 94132-1722. Offers criminal justice administration (MPA); environmental administration and policy (MPA); gerontology (MPA); nonprofit administration (MPA); public management (MPA); public policy (MPA); urban administration (MPA). *Accreditation:* NASPAA. *Expenses: Tuition, area resident:* Full-time $7176; part-time $4164 per year. Tuition, state resident: full-time $7176; part-time $4164 per year. Tuition, nonresident: full-time $16,680; part-time $396 per unit. *International tuition:* $16,680 full-time. *Required fees:* $1524; $1524 per unit. $762 per semester. Tuition and fees vary according to degree level and program. *Unit head:* Dr. Janey Wang, Graduate Coordinator, 415-817-4456, Fax: 415-338-0586, E-mail: jqwang@sfsu.edu. *Application contact:* Dr. Janey Wang, Graduate Coordinator, 415-817-4456, Fax: 415-338-0586, E-mail: jqwang@sfsu.edu.
Website: http://mpa.sfsu.edu

Seton Hall University, College of Arts and Sciences, Department of Political Science and Public Affairs, South Orange, NJ 07079-2697. Offers nonprofit organization management (Graduate Certificate); public administration (MPA), including data visualization and analytics, health policy and management, nonprofit organization management, public service: leadership, governance, and policy. *Accreditation:* CAHME; NASPAA. *Program availability:* Part-time, evening/weekend. *Degree requirements:* For master's, thesis or alternative, internship or practicum. *Entrance requirements:* Additional exam requirements/recommendations for international students: required—TOEFL. Electronic applications accepted.

Simmons University, Gwen Ifill College of Media, Arts, and Humanities, Boston, MA 02115. Offers behavior analysis (MS, PhD, Ed S); children's literature (MA); dietetics (Certificate); elementary education (MAT); English (MA); gender/cultural studies (MA); history (MA); nutrition and health promotion (MS); physical therapy (DPT); public health (MPH); public policy (MPP); special education: moderate and severe disabilities (MS Ed); sports nutrition (Certificate); writing for children (MFA). *Program availability:* Part-time. *Faculty:* 10 full-time (9 women), 7 part-time/adjunct (6 women). *Students:* 2 full-time (both women), 67 part-time (57 women); includes 13 minority (3 Black or African American, non-Hispanic/Latino; 4 Asian, non-Hispanic/Latino; 3 Hispanic/Latino; 3 Two or more races, non-Hispanic/Latino), 1 international. Average age 31. 42 applicants, 62% accepted, 23 enrolled. In 2019, 24 master's awarded. *Degree requirements:* For master's, thesis optional. *Entrance requirements:* For master's, GRE, bachelor's degree from accredited college or university; minimum B average (preferred). Additional exam requirements/recommendations for international students: required—TOEFL (minimum score 600 paper-based; 100 iBT). *Application deadline:* For fall admission, 8/1 for domestic and international students; for spring admission, 12/15 for domestic and international students; for summer admission, 5/1 for domestic and international students. Applications are processed on a rolling basis. Application fee: $35. Electronic applications accepted. *Expenses:* Contact institution. *Financial support:* In 2019–20, 14 students received support, including 1 fellowship (averaging $15,360 per year), 13 teaching assistantships (averaging $2,000 per year); scholarships/grants also available. Financial award applicants required to submit FAFSA. *Unit head:* Dr. Brian Norman, Dean, 617-521-2472, E-mail: brian.norman@simmons.edu. *Application contact:* Patricia Flaherty, Director, Graduate Studies Admission, 617-521-3902, Fax: 617-521-3058, E-mail: gsa@simmons.edu.
Website: https://www.simmons.edu/academics/colleges-schools-departments/ifill

Simon Fraser University, Office of Graduate Studies and Postdoctoral Fellows, Faculty of Arts and Social Sciences, School of Public Policy, Vancouver, BC V6B 5K3, Canada. Offers MPP. *Degree requirements:* For master's, thesis or alternative, internship. *Entrance requirements:* For master's, GRE (for applicants with non-Canadian degrees), minimum GPA of 3.0 (on scale of 4.33) or 3.33 based on last 60 credits of undergraduate courses. Additional exam requirements/recommendations for international students: recommended—TOEFL (minimum score 580 paper-based; 93 iBT), IELTS (minimum score 7), TWE (minimum score 5). Electronic applications accepted. *Expenses:* Contact institution.

Southern University and Agricultural and Mechanical College, Graduate School, Nelson Mandela College of Government and Social Sciences, Program in Public Policy, Baton Rouge, LA 70813. Offers PhD. *Degree requirements:* For doctorate, comprehensive exam, thesis/dissertation. *Entrance requirements:* For doctorate, GRE General Test. Additional exam requirements/recommendations for international students: required—TOEFL (minimum score 525 paper-based).

State University of New York Empire State College, School for Graduate Studies, Program in Social Policy, Saratoga Springs, NY 12866-4391. Offers MA. *Program availability:* Part-time, evening/weekend, online learning. *Degree requirements:* For master's, thesis, exam, final project. *Entrance requirements:* Additional exam requirements/recommendations for international students: required—TOEFL (minimum score 600 paper-based). Electronic applications accepted.

Stony Brook University, State University of New York, Graduate School, College of Arts and Sciences, Department of Political Science, Program in Public Policy and Urban Development, Stony Brook, NY 11794. Offers MA. *Students:* 17 full-time (10 women), 8 part-time (5 women); includes 10 minority (2 Black or African American, non-Hispanic/Latino; 4 Asian, non-Hispanic/Latino; 3 Hispanic/Latino; 1 Two or more races, non-Hispanic/Latino), 2 international. 23 applicants, 87% accepted, 14 enrolled. In 2019, 31 master's awarded. *Entrance requirements:* For master's, GRE, three letters of recommendation, statement of purpose. Additional exam requirements/recommendations for international students: required—TOEFL (minimum score 85 iBT). *Application deadline:* For fall admission, 7/1 for domestic students, 5/15 for international students; for spring admission, 12/5 for domestic students, 10/15 for international students. Application fee: $100. Electronic applications accepted. *Expenses:* Contact institution. *Unit head:* Dr. Leonie Huddy, Chair, 631-632-7639, Fax: 631-632-4116, E-mail: leonie.huddy@stonybrook.edu. *Application contact:* Carri Ann Horner, Graduate Program Coordinator, 631-632-7667, Fax: 631-632-4116, E-mail: carri.horner@stonybrook.edu.

Suffolk University, College of Arts and Sciences, Department of Philosophy, Boston, MA 02108-2770. Offers administration of higher education (M Ed, CAGS); disability services (Certificate); ethics and public policy (MS). *Program availability:* Part-time, evening/weekend. *Faculty:* 3 full-time (2 women), 5 part-time/adjunct (0 women). *Students:* 11 full-time (6 women), 23 part-time (20 women); includes 5 minority (2 Black or African American, non-Hispanic/Latino; 2 Hispanic/Latino; 1 Two or more races, non-Hispanic/Latino), 2 international. Average age 31. 35 applicants, 91% accepted, 14 enrolled. In 2019, 24 master's awarded. *Degree requirements:* For master's, internship or thesis; practicum (for M Ed). *Entrance requirements:* For master's, GRE General Test, MAT, GMAT, statement of professional goals, official transcripts, 2 letters of recommendation, resume. Additional exam requirements/recommendations for international students: required—TOEFL (minimum score 550 paper-based; 80 iBT). *Application deadline:* For fall admission, 3/15 priority date for domestic and international students; for spring admission, 10/15 priority date for domestic and international students. Applications are processed on a rolling basis. Application fee: $50. Electronic applications accepted. *Expenses:* Contact institution. *Financial support:* In 2019–20, 10 students received support, including 6 fellowships (averaging $3,600 per year); career-related internships or fieldwork, Federal Work-Study, institutionally sponsored loans, and unspecified assistantships also available. Support available to part-time students. Financial award application deadline: 4/1; financial award applicants required to submit FAFSA. *Unit head:* Dr. Evgenia Cherkasova, Chair of Philosophy Department, 617-573-1970, E-mail: echerkasova@suffolk.edu. *Application contact:* Mara Marzocchi, Associate Director of Graduate Admissions, 617-573-8302, Fax: 617-305-1733, E-mail: grad.admission@suffolk.edu.
Website: http://www.suffolk.edu/college/graduate/69296.php

Trinity College, Graduate Programs, Program in Public Policy, Hartford, CT 06106-3100. Offers health care policy (MA); public policy studies (MA). *Program availability:* Part-time, evening/weekend. *Degree requirements:* For master's, thesis optional, departmental qualifying exam. *Entrance requirements:* For master's, minimum GPA of 3.0, two letters of recommendation, statement of purpose.

Tufts University, The Fletcher School of Law and Diplomacy, Medford, MA 02155. Offers economics and public policy (PhD); international affairs (PhD); international business (MIB); international law (LL M); law and diplomacy (MA, MALD); transatlantic affairs (MA); DVM/MA; JD/MALD; MALD/MA; MALD/MBA; MALD/MS; MD/MA. *Program availability:* Online learning. *Degree requirements:* For master's, one foreign language, thesis; for doctorate, one foreign language, comprehensive exam, thesis/dissertation, dissertation defense. *Entrance requirements:* For master's and doctorate, GMAT or GRE General Test. Additional exam requirements/recommendations for international students: required—TOEFL (minimum score 600 paper-based; 100 iBT), IELTS (minimum score 7). Electronic applications accepted. *Expenses:* Contact institution.

Tufts University, Graduate School of Arts and Sciences, Department of Urban and Environmental Policy and Planning, Medford, MA 02155. Offers community development (MA); environmental policy (MA); health and human welfare (MA); housing policy (MA); international environment/development policy (MA); public policy (MPP); MA/JD; MA/MBA; MA/MPH; MA/MS; MALD/MA. *Accreditation:* ACSP (one or more programs are accredited). *Program availability:* Part-time. *Degree requirements:* For master's, thesis or alternative, internship. *Entrance requirements:* For master's, GRE General Test. Additional exam requirements/recommendations for international students: required—TOEFL (minimum score 550 paper-based; 80 iBT), IELTS (minimum score 6.5). Electronic applications accepted. *Expenses:* Contact institution.

Union Institute & University, Master of Arts Program, Cincinnati, OH 45206-1925. Offers creativity studies (MA); health and wellness (MA); history and culture (MA); leadership, public policy, and social issues (MA); literature and writing (MA). *Program availability:* Part-time, online only, 100% online. *Degree requirements:* For master's, thesis. *Entrance requirements:* For master's, transcript, essay, 3 letters of recommendation, resume. Additional exam requirements/recommendations for international students: recommended—TOEFL. Electronic applications accepted. *Expenses:* Contact institution.

Union Institute & University, PhD Program in Interdisciplinary Studies, Cincinnati, OH 45206-1925. Offers educational studies (PhD), including Martin Luther King studies; ethical and creative leadership (PhD); humanities and culture (PhD); public policy and social change (PhD). *Program availability:* Part-time, online only, blended/hybrid learning. *Degree requirements:* For doctorate, comprehensive exam, thesis/dissertation. *Entrance requirements:* For doctorate, master's degree, three letters of recommendation, statement of purpose. Additional exam requirements/recommendations for international students: required—TOEFL. Electronic applications accepted. *Expenses:* Contact institution.

Universidad Autonoma de Guadalajara, Graduate Programs, Guadalajara, Mexico. Offers administrative law and justice (LL M); advertising and corporate communications (MA); architecture (M Arch); business (MBA); computational science (MCC); education (Ed M, Ed D); English-Spanish translation (MA); entrepreneurship and management (MBA); integrated management of digital animation (MA); international business (MIB); international corporate law (LL M); Internet technologies (MS); manufacturing systems (MMS); occupational health (MS); philosophy (MA, PhD); power electronics (MS); quality systems (MQS); renewable energy (MS); social evaluation of projects (MBA); strategic market research (MBA); tax law (MA); teaching mathematics (MA).

Universidad del Este, Graduate School, Carolina, PR 00984. Offers accounting (MBA); adult education (M Ed); agribusiness (MBA); criminal justice and criminology (MA); curriculum and instruction - early education (M Ed); curriculum and instruction - elementary (M Ed); curriculum and instruction - English (M Ed); curriculum and instruction - Spanish (M Ed); human resources (MBA); information security management (MBA); information technology and Web business development (MBA); management (MBA); public policy (MPA); social work (MA), including clinical social work; special education (M Ed); strategic leadership (MBA).

Université de Montréal, Faculty of Arts and Sciences, Program in Societies, Public Policies and Health, Montréal, QC H3C 3J7, Canada. Offers DESS.

University at Albany, State University of New York, Nelson A. Rockefeller College of Public Affairs and Policy, Department of Public Administration and Policy, Albany, NY 12222-0001. Offers financial management and public economics (MPA); financial market regulation (MPA); health policy (MPA); healthcare management (MPA); homeland security (MPA); human resources management (MPA); information strategy and management (MPA); local government management (MPA); nonprofit management (MPA); nonprofit management and leadership (Certificate); organizational behavior and theory (MPA, PhD); planning and policy analysis (CAS); policy analysis (MPA); politics and administration (PhD); public finance (PhD); public management (PhD); public policy (PhD); public sector management (Certificate); women and public policy (Certificate); JD/MPA. *Accreditation:* NASPAA (one or more programs are accredited). *Program availability:* Blended/hybrid learning. *Faculty:* 19 full-time (8 women), 12 part-time/adjunct (4 women). *Students:* 119 full-time (71 women), 41 part-time (4 women); includes 45 minority (18 Black or African American, non-Hispanic/Latino; 7 Asian, non-Hispanic/Latino; 14 Hispanic/Latino; 6 Two or more races, non-Hispanic/Latino), 28 international. Average age 29. 172 applicants, 81% accepted, 85 enrolled. In 2019, 57 master's, 6 doctorates, 11 other advanced degrees awarded. *Degree requirements:* For doctorate, one foreign language, thesis/dissertation. *Entrance requirements:* For doctorate, GRE General Test. Additional exam requirements/recommendations for international students: required—TOEFL (minimum score 550 paper-based). *Application deadline:* For fall admission, 1/15 priority date for domestic students, 5/1 for international students; for spring admission, 11/15 for domestic students. Applications are processed on a rolling basis. Application fee: $75. Electronic applications accepted. *Expenses: Tuition, area resident:* Full-time $11,530; part-time $480 per credit hour. Tuition, nonresident: full-time $23,530; part-time $980 per credit hour. *International tuition:* $23,530 full-time. *Required fees:* $2185; $96 per credit hour. Part-time tuition and fees vary according to course load and program. *Financial support:* Research assistantships, teaching assistantships, and Federal Work-Study available. Financial award application deadline: 2/1. *Unit head:* Edmund Stazyk, Chair, 518-591-8723, E-mail: estazyk@albany.edu. *Application contact:* Luis Felipe Luna-Reyes, 518-442-5297, E-mail: llunareyes@albany.edu.
Website: http://www.albany.edu/rockefeller/pad.shtml

The University of Arizona, College of Social and Behavioral Sciences, Program in Public Administration, Tucson, AZ 85721. Offers public administration (MPA); public administration and policy (PhD). *Accreditation:* NASPAA. *Degree requirements:* For master's, internship of 400 hours; for doctorate, comprehensive exam, thesis/dissertation. *Entrance requirements:* For doctorate, GMAT or GRE, minimum graduate GPA of 3.5, letter of interest, 3 letters of recommendation, resume. Additional exam requirements/recommendations for international students: required—TOEFL (minimum score 650 paper-based; 115 iBT). Electronic applications accepted. *Expenses:* Contact institution.

University of Arkansas, Graduate School, Interdisciplinary Program in Public Policy, Fayetteville, AR 72701. Offers PhD. *Students:* 11 full-time (9 women), 36 part-time (24 women); includes 14 minority (9 Black or African American, non-Hispanic/Latino; 2 American Indian or Alaska Native, non-Hispanic/Latino; 1 Asian, non-Hispanic/Latino; 2 Hispanic/Latino), 4 international. 23 applicants, 87% accepted. In 2019, 4 doctorates awarded. *Application deadline:* For fall admission, 8/1 for domestic students, 4/1 for international students; for spring admission, 12/1 for domestic students, 10/1 for international students; for summer admission, 4/15 for domestic students, 3/1 for international students. Applications are processed on a rolling basis. Application fee: $60. Electronic applications accepted. *Financial support:* In 2019–20, 10 research assistantships, 1 teaching assistantship were awarded; fellowships with tuition reimbursements also available. Financial award application deadline: 4/1; financial award applicants required to submit FAFSA. *Unit head:* Dr. Brinck Kerr, Director, 479-575-3356, Fax: 479-575-5908, E-mail: jbkerr@uark.edu. *Application contact:* Dr. Valerie H. Hunt, Associate Director, 479-575-4401, Fax: 479-575-5908, E-mail: vhunt@uark.edu.
Website: https://policy.uark.edu

The University of British Columbia, Institute of Asian Research, Vancouver, BC V6T 1Z2, Canada. Offers Asia Pacific policy studies (MAAPPS); public policy and global affairs (MPPGA). *Degree requirements:* For master's, thesis optional. *Entrance requirements:* Additional exam requirements/recommendations for international students: required—TOEFL. Electronic applications accepted. *Expenses:* Contact institution.

University of Calgary, Faculty of Graduate Studies, The School of Public Policy, Calgary, AB T2N 1N4, Canada. Offers MPP. *Program availability:* Part-time. *Degree requirements:* For master's, capstone project. *Entrance requirements:* For master's, minimum GPA of 3.3 in last two years of undergraduate program or over last 60 units; baccalaureate degree; personal statement; current resume/curriculum vitae; official transcripts; two reference letters. Additional exam requirements/recommendations for international students: required—TOEFL (minimum score 600 paper-based; 105 iBT), IELTS (minimum score 7.5).

University of California, Berkeley, Graduate Division, Graduate School of Public Policy, Program in Public Policy, Berkeley, CA 94720. Offers MPP, PhD. Electronic applications accepted.

University of California, Berkeley, Graduate Division, Haas School of Business, PhD in Business Administration Program, Berkeley, CA 94720. Offers accounting (PhD); business and public policy (PhD); finance (PhD); management of organizations (PhD); marketing (PhD); real estate (PhD). *Accreditation:* AACSB. *Degree requirements:* For doctorate, comprehensive exam, thesis/dissertation, written preliminary exams, oral qualifying exam. *Entrance requirements:* For doctorate, GMAT or GRE, minimum GPA of 3.0 in undergraduate and graduate coursework. Additional exam requirements/recommendations for international students: required—TOEFL (minimum score 570 paper-based; 70 iBT), IELTS (minimum score 7). Electronic applications accepted. *Expenses:* Contact institution.

University of California, Los Angeles, Graduate Division, Luskin School of Public Affairs, Program in Public Policy, Los Angeles, CA 90095. Offers MPP. *Accreditation:* NASPAA. *Entrance requirements:* For master's, GRE General Test, minimum GPA of 3.0. Additional exam requirements/recommendations for international students: required—TOEFL. Electronic applications accepted.

University of California, Riverside, Graduate Division, School of Public Policy, Riverside, CA 92521-0102. Offers global health (MS); public policy (MPP, PhD); MD/MPP.

University of California, San Diego, Graduate Division, School of Global Policy and Strategy, Master of Public Policy Program, La Jolla, CA 92093. Offers American policy in global context (MPP); business, government and regulation (MPP); energy and environmental policy (MPP); health policy (MPP); program design and evaluation (MPP); security policy (MPP). *Entrance requirements:* For master's, GMAT or GRE General Test. Additional exam requirements/recommendations for international students: required—TOEFL (minimum score 90 iBT), IELTS (minimum score 7). Electronic applications accepted. *Expenses:* Contact institution.

University of Chicago, Harris School of Public Policy, Master of Arts in Public Policy Program, Chicago, IL 60637. Offers public policy studies (AM). *Program availability:* Part-time, evening/weekend. *Entrance requirements:* For master's, GRE General Test, graduate degree; transcripts; resume or curriculum vitae; letters of recommendation. Additional exam requirements/recommendations for international students: required—TOEFL (minimum score 600 paper-based; 104 iBT), IELTS (minimum score 7). Electronic applications accepted.

University of Chicago, Harris School of Public Policy, Master of Public Policy Program, Chicago, IL 60637. Offers MPP. *Entrance requirements:* For master's, GRE General Test, transcripts, resume, 3 letters of recommendation. Additional exam requirements/recommendations for international students: required—TOEFL (minimum score 600 paper-based; 104 iBT), IELTS (minimum score 7). Electronic applications accepted.

University of Chicago, Harris School of Public Policy, PhD Program in Public Policy, Chicago, IL 60637. Offers PhD. *Degree requirements:* For doctorate, comprehensive exam, thesis/dissertation. *Entrance requirements:* For doctorate, GRE General Test, transcripts, resume, 3 letters of recommendation, writing sample. Additional exam requirements/recommendations for international students: required—TOEFL (minimum score 600 paper-based; 104 iBT), IELTS (minimum score 7). Electronic applications accepted.

University of Delaware, Center for Energy and Environmental Policy, Newark, DE 19716. Offers energy and environmental policy (MA, MEEP, PhD); urban affairs and public policy (PhD), including technology, environment, and society. *Degree requirements:* For master's, analytical paper or thesis; for doctorate, comprehensive exam, thesis/dissertation. *Entrance requirements:* For master's, GRE General Test, minimum GPA of 3.0; for doctorate, GRE General Test, minimum GPA of 3.5. Additional exam requirements/recommendations for international students: required—TOEFL. Electronic applications accepted.

University of Delaware, College of Arts and Sciences, School of Public Policy and Administration, Program in Urban Affairs and Public Policy, Newark, DE 19716. Offers governance planning and management (PhD); historic preservation (MA); social and urban policy (PhD); technology, environment and society (PhD); urban affairs and public policy (MA). *Program availability:* Part-time. Terminal master's awarded for partial completion of doctoral program. *Degree requirements:* For master's, analytical paper or thesis; for doctorate, thesis/dissertation. *Entrance requirements:* For master's, GRE General Test, minimum GPA of 3.0; for doctorate, GRE General Test, minimum GPA of 3.5. Additional exam requirements/recommendations for international students: required—TOEFL. Electronic applications accepted.

University of Denver, Josef Korbel School of International Studies, Institute for Public Policy Studies, Denver, CO 80208. Offers MPP. *Faculty:* 2 full-time (0 women), 1 part-time/adjunct (0 women). *Students:* 13 full-time (8 women), 1 (woman) part-time; includes 4 minority (2 Black or African American, non-Hispanic/Latino; 2 Hispanic/Latino), 2 international. Average age 27. 70 applicants, 70% accepted, 8 enrolled. In 2019, 10 master's awarded. *Degree requirements:* For master's, thesis or alternative, policy memorandum capstone. *Entrance requirements:* For master's, GRE General Test, bachelor's degree, transcripts, personal statement, two letters of recommendation, resume. Additional exam requirements/recommendations for international students: required—TOEFL (minimum score 587 paper-based; 95 iBT). *Application deadline:* For fall admission, 1/23 priority date for domestic and international students; for winter admission, 11/1 priority date for domestic and international students. Applications are processed on a rolling basis. Application fee: $65. Electronic applications accepted. *Expenses:* Contact institution. *Financial support:* In 2019–20, 11 students received support, including 1 teaching assistantship with tuition reimbursement available (averaging $7,500 per year); Federal Work-Study, scholarships/grants, and unspecified assistantships also available. Financial award application deadline: 2/15; financial award applicants required to submit FAFSA. *Unit head:* Dr. Richard Caldwell, Director, 303-871-2468, Fax: 303-871-3066, E-mail: richard.caldwell@du.edu. *Application contact:* Institute for Public Policy Studies, E-mail: ipps@du.edu.
Website: http://www.du.edu/korbel/ipps/index.html

University of Georgia, School of Public and International Affairs, Department of Public Administration and Policy, Athens, GA 30602. Offers public administration (MPA, PhD). *Accreditation:* NASPAA (one or more programs are accredited). *Degree requirements:* For master's, internship; for doctorate, thesis/dissertation. *Entrance requirements:* For master's and doctorate, GRE General Test. Electronic applications accepted.

University of Guelph, Office of Graduate and Postdoctoral Studies, College of Social and Applied Human Sciences, Department of Political Science, Guelph, ON N1G 2W1, Canada. Offers comparative politics (MA); international development (MA); political science (MA); public policy and public administration (MA); the Americas (Canada emphasis) (MA). *Degree requirements:* For master's, thesis or paper. *Entrance requirements:* For master's, minimum B average during previous 2 years of course work, 4 year Honours Degree in Political Science. Additional exam requirements/recommendations for international students: required—TOEFL. Electronic applications accepted.

University of Hawaii at Manoa, Office of Graduate Education, College of Social Sciences, Public Policy Center, Honolulu, HI 96822. Offers Graduate Certificate. *Program availability:* Part-time. *Entrance requirements:* Additional exam requirements/recommendations for international students: required—TOEFL (minimum score 500 paper-based; 61 iBT), IELTS (minimum score 5).

University of Houston, Hobby School of Public Affairs, Houston, TX 77204-5021. Offers public policy (MPP). *Program availability:* Part-time. *Faculty:* 5 full-time (0 women), 4 part-time/adjunct (2 women). *Students:* 36 full-time (25 women), 6 part-time (2 women); includes 19 minority (5 Black or African American, non-Hispanic/Latino; 3 Asian, non-Hispanic/Latino; 11 Hispanic/Latino), 4 international. Average age 25. 43 applicants, 79% accepted, 23 enrolled. In 2019, 14 master's awarded. *Entrance requirements:* For master's, GRE General Test. Additional exam requirements/recommendations for international students: required—TOEFL (minimum score 550 paper-based; 79 iBT), IELTS (minimum score 6.5). *Application deadline:* For fall admission, 6/15 for domestic and international students; for spring admission, 12/1 for domestic and international students. Applications are processed on a rolling basis. Application fee: $75 ($125 for international students). Electronic applications accepted. *Financial support:* In 2019–20, 53 students received support. Fellowships, research assistantships, teaching assistantships, career-related internships or fieldwork, Federal Work-Study, institutionally sponsored loans, scholarships/grants, traineeships, and unspecified assistantships available. Support available to part-time students. Financial award application deadline: 6/15; financial award applicants required to submit FAFSA. *Unit head:* Kirk Watson, Founding Dean, Fax: 713-743-3978, E-mail: kpwatson@uh.edu. *Application contact:* Scott Mason, Program Manager 2, 713-743-5572, Fax: 713-743-3978, E-mail: smason@uh.edu.
Website: http://www.uh.edu/hobby/

University of Kentucky, Graduate School, Martin School of Public Policy and Administration, Lexington, KY 40506-0027. Offers public administration (MPA); public financial management (MPFM, Graduate Certificate); public policy (MPP); public policy and administration (PhD). *Accreditation:* NASPAA (one or more programs are accredited). *Program availability:* Part-time, evening/weekend, 100% online. Terminal master's awarded for partial completion of doctoral program. *Degree requirements:* For master's, thesis; for doctorate, comprehensive exam, thesis/dissertation. *Entrance requirements:* For master's, GMAT or GRE General Test, minimum undergraduate GPA of 2.75; for doctorate, GMAT or GRE General Test, minimum graduate GPA of 3.0. Additional exam requirements/recommendations for international students: required—TOEFL (minimum score 550 paper-based; 79 iBT); recommended—IELTS (minimum score 6.5). Electronic applications accepted. *Expenses:* Contact institution.

University of Louisville, Graduate School, College of Arts and Sciences, Department of Urban and Public Affairs, Louisville, KY 40208. Offers public administration (MPA), including human resources management, non-profit management, public policy and administration; urban and public affairs (PhD), including urban planning and development, urban policy and administration; urban planning (MUP), including administration of planning organizations, housing and community development, land use and environmental planning, spatial analysis. *Program availability:* Part-time, evening/weekend. *Faculty:* 13 full-time (6 women), 2 part-time/adjunct (1 woman). *Students:* 44 full-time (24 women), 24 part-time (14 women); includes 12 minority (6 Black or African American, non-Hispanic/Latino; 2 Hispanic/Latino; 4 Two or more races, non-Hispanic/Latino), 7 international. Average age 34. 51 applicants, 67% accepted, 25 enrolled. In 2019, 14 master's, 3 doctorates awarded. Terminal master's awarded for partial completion of doctoral program. *Degree requirements:* For master's, internship; for doctorate, comprehensive exam, thesis/dissertation. *Entrance requirements:* For master's, GRE General Test, 2 letters of reference, official transcripts. Minimum GPA of 3.0; for doctorate, GRE General Test, Two letters of reference, official transcripts. Masters degree in appropriate field. Additional exam requirements/recommendations for international students: required—TOEFL (minimum score 550 paper-based; 79 iBT), IELTS can be used in place of the TOEFL; recommended—IELTS (minimum score 6.5). *Application deadline:* For fall admission, 2/1 for domestic and international students. Applications are processed on a rolling basis. Application fee: $65. Electronic applications accepted. *Expenses:* Tuition, area resident: Full-time $13,000; part-time $723 per credit hour. Tuition, state resident: full-time $13,000; part-time $723 per credit hour. Tuition, nonresident: full-time $27,114; part-time $1507 per credit hour. *International tuition:* $27,114 full-time. *Required fees:* $196. Tuition and fees vary according to program and reciprocity agreements. *Financial support:* In 2019–20, 29 students received support, including 11 research assistantships with full tuition reimbursements available (averaging $19,000 per year); fellowships, teaching assistantships, health care benefits, and unspecified assistantships also available. Financial award application deadline: 2/1. *Unit head:* Dr. David Simpson, Professor/Chair, 502-852-8019, Fax: 502-852-4558, E-mail: dave.simpson@louisville.edu.
Website: http://supa.louisville.edu

University of Maryland, Baltimore County, The Graduate School, College of Arts, Humanities and Social Sciences, Department of Emergency Health Services, Baltimore, MD 21250. Offers emergency health services (MS), including administration, planning, and policy, preventive medicine and epidemiology; emergency management (Postbaccalaureate Certificate); public policy (PhD), including emergency health, emergency management. *Program availability:* Part-time, evening/weekend, 100% online, blended/hybrid learning. *Faculty:* 4 full-time (2 women), 8 part-time/adjunct (3 women). *Students:* 5 full-time (4 women), 9 part-time (5 women); includes 5 minority (2 Black or African American, non-Hispanic/Latino; 1 Asian, non-Hispanic/Latino; 2 Hispanic/Latino), 2 international. Average age 37. 19 applicants, 68% accepted, 3 enrolled. In 2019, 5 master's, 2 other advanced degrees awarded. Terminal master's awarded for partial completion of doctoral program. *Degree requirements:* For master's, comprehensive exam (for some programs), capstone project or thesis. *Entrance requirements:* For master's, GRE General Test if GPA is below 3.2, minimum GPA of 3.2. Additional exam requirements/recommendations for international students: required—TOEFL (minimum score 80 iBT), IELTS, or PTE. *Application deadline:* For fall admission, 6/15 for domestic students, 3/1 for international students; for spring admission, 12/1 for domestic students, 10/1 for international students. Applications are processed on a rolling basis. Application fee: $50. Electronic applications accepted. *Expenses:* $14,382 per year. *Financial support:* In 2019–20, 1 student received support, including 1 research assistantship with full tuition reimbursement available (averaging $16,875 per year); career-related internships or fieldwork, Federal Work-Study, health care benefits, and unspecified assistantships also available. Financial award application deadline: 5/30; financial award applicants required to submit FAFSA. *Unit head:* Dr. J. Lee Jenkins, Department Chair, 410-455-3216, Fax: 410-455-3045, E-mail: jleejenkins@umbc.edu. *Application contact:* Dr. Rick Bissell, Program Director, 410-455-3776, Fax: 410-455-3045, E-mail: bissell@umbc.edu.
Website: http://ehs.umbc.edu/

University of Maryland, Baltimore County, The Graduate School, College of Arts, Humanities and Social Sciences, Program in Economic Policy Analysis, Baltimore, MD 21250. Offers MA. *Program availability:* Part-time. *Faculty:* 17 full-time (6 women), 4 part-time/adjunct (2 women). *Students:* 5 full-time (1 woman), 7 part-time (3 women); includes 2 minority (1 Black or African American, non-Hispanic/Latino; 1 Hispanic/Latino), 3 international. Average age 29. 14 applicants, 64% accepted, 4 enrolled. In 2019, 4 master's awarded. *Degree requirements:* For master's, comprehensive exam, capstone research project. *Entrance requirements:* For master's, GRE General Test, undergraduate coursework in economic theory, econometrics, and calculus; letters of reference; statement of purpose; transcripts. Additional exam requirements/recommendations for international students: required—TOEFL (minimum score 80 iBT). *Application deadline:* For fall admission, 7/1 priority date for domestic students, 3/1 priority date for international students; for spring admission, 1/1 priority date for domestic students, 9/15 priority date for international students. Applications are processed on a rolling basis. Application fee: $45. Electronic applications accepted. *Expenses:* $14,382 per year. *Financial support:* In 2019–20, 5 students received support, including 5 research assistantships with tuition reimbursements available (averaging $12,560 per year), teaching assistantships with partial tuition reimbursements available (averaging $6,500 per year); Federal Work-Study, health care benefits, tuition waivers (full and partial), and unspecified assistantships also available. Support available to part-time students. Financial award application deadline: 4/15; financial award applicants required to submit FAFSA. *Unit head:* Dr. David F. Mitch, Chair, 410-455-2157, Fax: 410-455-1054, E-mail: mitch@umbc.edu. *Application contact:* Dr. Tim H. Gindling, Graduate Program Director, 410-455-3629, Fax: 410-455-1054, E-mail: econmasters@umbc.edu.
Website: http://www.umbc.edu/economics/grad_intro.html

University of Maryland, Baltimore County, The Graduate School, College of Arts, Humanities and Social Sciences, School of Public Policy, Baltimore, MD 21250. Offers public policy (MPP, PhD), including economics (PhD), educational policy, emergency services (PhD), environmental policy (MPP), evaluation and analytical methods, health policy, policy history (PhD), public management, urban policy. *Program availability:* Part-time, evening/weekend. *Faculty:* 10 full-time (5 women). *Students:* 49 full-time (29 women), 63 part-time (31 women); includes 39 minority (18 Black or African American, non-Hispanic/Latino; 1 American Indian or Alaska Native, non-Hispanic/Latino; 9 Asian, non-Hispanic/Latino; 9 Hispanic/Latino; 2 Two or more races, non-Hispanic/Latino), 10 international. Average age 36. 73 applicants, 74% accepted, 31 enrolled. In 2019, 17 master's, 8 doctorates awarded. Terminal master's awarded for partial completion of doctoral program. *Degree requirements:* For master's, thesis, policy analysis paper, internship for pre-service; for doctorate, comprehensive exam, thesis/dissertation, comprehensive and field qualifying exams. *Entrance requirements:* For master's, GRE General Test, 3 academic letters of reference, resume, official transcripts; for doctorate, GRE General Test, 3 academic letters of reference, resume, research paper, official transcripts. Additional exam requirements/recommendations for international students: required—TOEFL (minimum score 550 paper-based; 80 iBT), IELTS (minimum score 6.5). *Application deadline:* For fall admission, 1/15 priority date for domestic students, 1/1 priority date for international students; for spring admission, 11/1 priority date for domestic students, 5/1 priority date for international students. Applications are processed on a rolling basis. Application fee: $50. Electronic applications accepted. *Expenses:* $14,382 per year. *Financial support:* In 2019–20, 26 students received support, including 23 research assistantships with full tuition reimbursements available (averaging $20,000 per year), 3 teaching assistantships; Federal Work-Study, scholarships/grants, health care benefits, and unspecified assistantships also available. Financial award application deadline: 1/1; financial award applicants required to submit FAFSA. *Unit head:* Dr. Susan Sterett, Director, 410-455-2140, Fax: 410-455-1172, E-mail: ssterett@umbc.edu. *Application contact:* Shelley Morris, Administrator of Academic Affairs, 410-455-3202, Fax: 410-455-1172, E-mail: shelleym@umbc.edu. Website: http://publicpolicy.umbc.edu/

University of Maryland, College Park, Academic Affairs, A. James Clark School of Engineering and School of Public Policy, Program in Engineering and Public Policy, College Park, MD 20742. Offers MS.

University of Maryland, College Park, Academic Affairs, School of Public Policy, Policy Studies Program, College Park, MD 20742. Offers PhD. *Degree requirements:* For doctorate, comprehensive exam, thesis/dissertation, written and oral exams. *Entrance requirements:* For doctorate, GRE General Test, writing sample. Electronic applications accepted.

University of Maryland, College Park, Academic Affairs, School of Public Policy, Programs in Public Policy, College Park, MD 20742. Offers MPP. *Accreditation:* NASPAA. *Entrance requirements:* Additional exam requirements/recommendations for international students: required—TOEFL. Electronic applications accepted.

University of Massachusetts Amherst, Graduate School, College of Social and Behavioral Sciences, Center for Public Policy and Administration, Amherst, MA 01003. Offers MPP, MPPA, MPH/MPPA, MPPA/M Ed, MPPA/MBA, MRP/MPPA. *Program availability:* Part-time. *Degree requirements:* For master's, thesis or alternative. *Entrance requirements:* For master's, GRE General Test. Additional exam requirements/recommendations for international students: required—TOEFL (minimum score 550 paper-based; 80 iBT), IELTS (minimum score 6.5). Electronic applications accepted.

University of Massachusetts Amherst, Graduate School, Interdisciplinary Programs, Dual Degree Program in Education and Public Policy and Administration, Amherst, MA 01003. Offers MPPA/M Ed. *Entrance requirements:* Additional exam requirements/recommendations for international students: required—TOEFL (minimum score 550 paper-based; 80 iBT), IELTS (minimum score 6.5). Electronic applications accepted.

University of Massachusetts Amherst, Graduate School, Interdisciplinary Programs, Dual Degree Program in Management and Public Policy and Administration, Amherst, MA 01003. Offers MPPA/MBA. *Accreditation:* AACSB. *Program availability:* Part-time. *Entrance requirements:* Additional exam requirements/recommendations for international students: required—TOEFL (minimum score 600 paper-based; 100 iBT), IELTS (minimum score 7). Electronic applications accepted.

University of Massachusetts Amherst, Graduate School, Interdisciplinary Programs, Dual Degree Program in Public Policy and Administration and Public Health, Amherst, MA 01003. Offers MPH/MPPA. *Entrance requirements:* Additional exam requirements/recommendations for international students: required—TOEFL (minimum score 550 paper-based; 80 iBT), IELTS (minimum score 6.5). Electronic applications accepted.

University of Massachusetts Amherst, Graduate School, Interdisciplinary Programs, Dual Degree Program in Regional Planning and Public Policy and Administration, Amherst, MA 01003. Offers MPPA/MRP. *Entrance requirements:* Additional exam requirements/recommendations for international students: required—TOEFL (minimum score 550 paper-based; 80 iBT), IELTS (minimum score 6.5). Electronic applications accepted.

University of Massachusetts Boston, McCormack Graduate School of Policy and Global Studies, Program in Public Policy, Boston, MA 02125-3393. Offers MS, PhD. *Program availability:* Evening/weekend. *Entrance requirements:* For doctorate, GRE General Test.

University of Massachusetts Dartmouth, Graduate School, College of Arts and Sciences, Department of Public Policy, North Dartmouth, MA 02747-2300. Offers educational policy (Graduate Certificate); environmental policy (Graduate Certificate); public management (Graduate Certificate); public policy (MPP). *Program availability:* Part-time, 100% online, blended/hybrid learning. *Faculty:* 4 full-time (0 women), 1 part-time/adjunct (0 women). *Students:* 6 full-time (4 women), 77 part-time (44 women); includes 17 minority (5 Black or African American, non-Hispanic/Latino; 1 Asian, non-Hispanic/Latino; 9 Hispanic/Latino; 2 Two or more races, non-Hispanic/Latino). Average age 36. 53 applicants, 100% accepted, 41 enrolled. In 2019, 18 master's, 20 other advanced degrees awarded. *Degree requirements:* For master's, e-portfolio. *Entrance requirements:* For master's, GRE or GMAT or waiver, statement of purpose (600-900 words), resume, 2 letters of recommendation, official transcripts; for Graduate Certificate, statement of purpose (minimum of 300 words), resume, official transcripts. Additional exam requirements/recommendations for international students: required—TOEFL (minimum score 600 paper-based). *Application deadline:* Applications are processed on a rolling basis. Application fee: $60. Electronic applications accepted. *Expenses:* Tuition, area resident: Full-time $16,390; part-time $682.92 per credit. Tuition, state resident: full-time $16,390; part-time $682.92 per credit. Tuition, nonresident: full-time $29,578; part-time $1232.42 per credit. *Required fees:* $575. *Financial support:* Application deadline: 3/1; applicants required to submit FAFSA. *Unit head:* Chad McGuire, Graduate Program Director, Public Policy, 508-999-8520, E-mail: chad.mcguire@umassd.edu. *Application contact:* Scott Webster, Director of Graduate Studies and Admissions, 508-999-8604, Fax: 508-999-8183, E-mail: graduate@umassd.edu. Website: http://www.umassd.edu/cas/departmentsanddegreeprograms/publicpolicy/

University of Memphis, Graduate School, College of Arts and Sciences, Division of Public and Nonprofit Administration, Memphis, TN 38152. Offers local government management (Graduate Certificate); philanthropy and nonprofit leadership (Graduate Certificate). *Accreditation:* NASPAA. *Program availability:* Part-time, evening/weekend, blended/hybrid learning. *Students:* 20 full-time (10 women), 30 part-time (21 women); includes 20 minority (17 Black or African American, non-Hispanic/Latino; 1 Asian, non-

Hispanic/Latino; 2 Two or more races, non-Hispanic/Latino). Average age 36. 15 applicants, 87% accepted, 6 enrolled. In 2019, 8 master's, 11 other advanced degrees awarded. *Degree requirements:* For master's, comprehensive exam, thesis or alternative, internship. *Entrance requirements:* For master's, GRE General Test, GMAT, MAT, or LSAT, minimum GPA of 3.0, resume, two references, statement of interest. Additional exam requirements/recommendations for international students: required—TOEFL. *Application deadline:* For fall admission, 7/1 for domestic students, 5/1 for international students; for spring admission, 12/1 for domestic students, 9/15 for international students; for summer admission, 5/1 for domestic students, 2/1 for international students. Applications are processed on a rolling basis. Application fee: $35 ($60 for international students). Electronic applications accepted. *Expenses: Tuition, area resident:* Full-time $9216; part-time $512 per credit hour. Tuition, state resident: full-time $9216; part-time $512 per credit hour. Tuition, nonresident: full-time $12,672; part-time $704 per credit hour. *International tuition:* $16,128 full-time. *Required fees:* $1530; $85 per credit hour. Tuition and fees vary according to program. *Financial support:* Fellowships, research assistantships with full tuition reimbursements, career-related internships or fieldwork, Federal Work-Study, scholarships/grants, health care benefits, and unspecified assistantships available. Support available to part-time students. Financial award application deadline: 2/1; financial award applicants required to submit FAFSA. *Unit head:* Dr. Sharon Wrobel, Chair, 901-678-4720, Fax: 901-678-2981, E-mail: swrobel@memphis.edu. *Application contact:* Dr. Sharon Wrobel, Chair, 901-678-4720, Fax: 901-678-2981, E-mail: swrobel@memphis.edu. Website: http://www.memphis.edu/padm/

University of Michigan, Gerald R. Ford School of Public Policy, Ann Arbor, MI 48109. Offers MPA, MPP, PhD, JD/MPP, MBA/MPP, MD/MPP, MHSA/MPP, MPH/MPP, MPP/AM, MPP/MA, MPP/MIS, MPP/MS, MPP/MUP, MSW/MPP. *Faculty:* 43 full-time (17 women), 36 part-time/adjunct (14 women). *Students:* 282 full-time (149 women); includes 91 minority (23 Black or African American, non-Hispanic/Latino; 1 American Indian or Alaska Native, non-Hispanic/Latino; 26 Asian, non-Hispanic/Latino; 30 Hispanic/Latino; 11 Two or more races, non-Hispanic/Latino), 38 international. Average age 27. 663 applicants, 65% accepted, 114 enrolled. In 2019, 116 master's, 3 doctorates awarded. *Degree requirements:* For doctorate, comprehensive exam, thesis/dissertation. *Entrance requirements:* For master's and doctorate, GRE. Additional exam requirements/recommendations for international students: required—TOEFL (minimum score 560 paper-based; 84 iBT). *Application deadline:* For fall admission, 1/15 priority date for domestic students, 1/15 for international students. Application fee: $75 ($90 for international students). Electronic applications accepted. *Expenses:* Contact institution. *Financial support:* In 2019–20, 203 students received support, including 169 fellowships with tuition reimbursements available, 33 teaching assistantships with tuition reimbursements available; research assistantships, career-related internships or fieldwork, traineeships, health care benefits, and unspecified assistantships also available. Financial award application deadline: 1/15; financial award applicants required to submit FAFSA. *Unit head:* Michael S. Barr, Dean of Public Policy, 734-764-2258, E-mail: ford.school.dean@umich.edu. *Application contact:* Beth Soboleski, Director, Admissions and Recruiting, 734-764-0453, Fax: 734-647-7486, E-mail: fspp-admissions@umich.edu. Website: http://fordschool.umich.edu/

University of Michigan, Rackham Graduate School, College of Literature, Science, and the Arts, Department of Economics, Ann Arbor, MI 48109. Offers applied economics (AM); economics (AM, PhD); public policy and economics (PhD); social work and economics (PhD); JD/PhD; MPP/AM. Terminal master's awarded for partial completion of doctoral program. *Degree requirements:* For doctorate, comprehensive exam, thesis/dissertation, oral defense of dissertation; preliminary exams in microeconomics, macroeconomics, and 2 fields. *Entrance requirements:* For master's and doctorate, GRE General Test. Additional exam requirements/recommendations for international students: required—TOEFL (minimum score 600 paper-based; 100 iBT). Electronic applications accepted.

University of Michigan, Rackham Graduate School, College of Literature, Science, and the Arts, Department of Political Science, Ann Arbor, MI 48109. Offers political science (PhD); political science and public policy (PhD); social work and political science (PhD). Terminal master's awarded for partial completion of doctoral program. *Degree requirements:* For doctorate, comprehensive exam, thesis/dissertation, oral defense of dissertation, preliminary exams. *Entrance requirements:* For doctorate, GRE General Test. Additional exam requirements/recommendations for international students: required—TOEFL. Electronic applications accepted. *Expenses:* Contact institution.

University of Michigan, Rackham Graduate School, College of Literature, Science, and the Arts, Department of Sociology, Ann Arbor, MI 48109. Offers public policy and sociology (PhD); social work and sociology (PhD); sociology (PhD). *Degree requirements:* For doctorate, comprehensive exam, thesis/dissertation, oral defense of dissertation, preliminary exam, dissertation prospectus. *Entrance requirements:* For doctorate, GRE General Test, letters of recommendation, writing sample, academic statement of purpose, personal statement, transcript. Additional exam requirements/recommendations for international students: required—TOEFL (minimum score 560 paper-based; 84 iBT), IELTS (minimum score 6.5). Electronic applications accepted.

University of Minnesota, Twin Cities Campus, Graduate School, Humphrey School of Public Affairs, PhD Program in Public Affairs, Minneapolis, MN 55455. Offers management and governance (PhD); public policy (PhD); science, technology, and environmental policy (PhD); urban planning (PhD). *Program availability:* Part-time. *Degree requirements:* For doctorate, comprehensive exam, thesis/dissertation. *Entrance requirements:* For doctorate, GRE General Test. Additional exam requirements/recommendations for international students: required—TOEFL (minimum score 650 paper-based; 100 iBT), IELTS (minimum score 7). Electronic applications accepted. *Expenses:* Contact institution.

University of Minnesota, Twin Cities Campus, Graduate School, Humphrey School of Public Affairs, Program in Public Policy, Minneapolis, MN 55455-0213. Offers MPP, JD/MPP, MBA/MPP, MPP/MPH, MSW/MPP. *Accreditation:* NASPAA. *Program availability:* Part-time. *Students:* 158 full-time (90 women), 11 part-time (10 women); includes 37 minority (11 Black or African American, non-Hispanic/Latino; 6 American Indian or Alaska Native, non-Hispanic/Latino; 10 Asian, non-Hispanic/Latino; 10 Hispanic/Latino), 11 international. Average age 26. 189 applicants, 90% accepted, 72 enrolled. In 2019, 75 master's awarded. *Degree requirements:* For master's, thesis or alternative, internship or equivalent work experience. *Entrance requirements:* For master's, GRE General Test. Additional exam requirements/recommendations for international students: required—TOEFL (minimum score 600 paper-based; 100 iBT), IELTS (minimum score 7). *Application deadline:* For fall admission, 4/1 for domestic and international students. Application fee: $75 ($95 for international students). Electronic applications accepted. *Expenses:* Contact institution. *Financial support:* In 2019–20, 80 students received support, including fellowships with tuition reimbursements available (averaging $9,000 per year), research assistantships with tuition reimbursements available (averaging $26,000 per year), teaching assistantships with tuition reimbursements available (averaging $18,000 per year); career-related internships or fieldwork, Federal Work-Study, scholarships/grants, health care benefits, tuition waivers (full and partial), and unspecified assistantships also available. Financial award

application deadline: 1/15; financial award applicants required to submit FAFSA. *Unit head:* Laura Bloomberg, Associate Dean, 612-625-0608, Fax: 612-626-0002, E-mail: bloom004@umn.edu. *Application contact:* Jacob Merrifield, Admissions Program Manager, 612-624-3800, Fax: 612-626-0002, E-mail: jmerrifi@umn.edu.
Website: http://www.hhh.umn.edu/degrees/mpp/

University of Missouri, Office of Research and Graduate Studies, Harry S Truman School of Public Affairs, Columbia, MO 65211. Offers grantsmanship (Graduate Certificate); nonprofit management (Graduate Certificate); organizational change (Graduate Certificate); public affairs (MPA, PhD); public management (Graduate Certificate); science and public policy (Graduate Certificate). *Accreditation:* NASPAA. *Entrance requirements:* For master's, GRE General Test, minimum GPA of 3.0. Additional exam requirements/recommendations for international students: required—TOEFL, IELTS. Electronic applications accepted.

University of Missouri–St. Louis, College of Arts and Sciences, Department of Political Science, St. Louis, MO 63121. Offers American politics (MA); comparative politics (MA); international politics (MA); political process and behavior (MA); political science (PhD); public administration and public policy (MA); urban and regional politics (MA). *Program availability:* Part-time, evening/weekend. Terminal master's awarded for partial completion of doctoral program. *Degree requirements:* For master's, thesis optional; for doctorate, thesis/dissertation. *Entrance requirements:* For master's, GRE General Test, 2 letters of recommendation, statement of purpose; for doctorate, GRE General Test, 3 letters of recommendation, statement of purpose. Additional exam requirements/recommendations for international students: required—TOEFL (minimum score 550 paper-based; 79 iBT), IELTS (minimum score 6.5). Electronic applications accepted. *Expenses: Tuition, area resident:* Full-time $9005.40; part-time $6003.60 per credit hour. Tuition, state resident: full-time $9005.40; part-time $6003.60 per credit hour. Tuition, nonresident: full-time $22,108; part-time $14,738.40 per credit hour. *International tuition:* $22,108 full-time. Tuition and fees vary according to course load.

University of Nebraska–Lincoln, Graduate College, College of Arts and Sciences, Department of Political Science, Lincoln, NE 68588. Offers political science (MA, PhD); public policy analysis (Graduate Certificate). *Degree requirements:* For master's, thesis optional; for doctorate, variable foreign language requirement, comprehensive exam, thesis/dissertation. *Entrance requirements:* For master's and doctorate, GRE General Test, writing sample. Additional exam requirements/recommendations for international students: required—TOEFL (minimum score 600 paper-based). Electronic applications accepted.

University of Nevada, Las Vegas, Graduate College, Greenspun College of Urban Affairs, School of Public Policy and Leadership, Las Vegas, NV 89154-4030. Offers crisis and emergency management (MS); emergency crisis management cybersecurity (Certificate); environmental science (MS, PhD); non-profit management (Certificate); public administration (MPA); public affairs (PhD); public management (Certificate); urban leadership (MA). *Program availability:* Part-time. *Faculty:* 12 full-time (5 women), 6 part-time/adjunct (1 woman). *Students:* 106 full-time (61 women), 96 part-time (71 women); includes 118 minority (34 Black or African American, non-Hispanic/Latino; 1 American Indian or Alaska Native, non-Hispanic/Latino; 11 Asian, non-Hispanic/Latino; 49 Hispanic/Latino; 2 Native Hawaiian or other Pacific Islander, non-Hispanic/Latino; 21 Two or more races, non-Hispanic/Latino), 5 international. Average age 36. 115 applicants, 77% accepted, 73 enrolled. In 2019, 49 master's, 13 doctorates, 16 other advanced degrees awarded. *Degree requirements:* For master's, comprehensive exam (for some programs), thesis (for some programs), oral exam; for doctorate, comprehensive exam, thesis/dissertation; for Certificate, portfolio. *Entrance requirements:* For master's, GRE General Test or GMAT, bachelor's degree with minimum GPA 2.75; statement of purpose; 3 letters of recommendation; for doctorate, GRE General Test, master's degree with minimum GPA of 3.5; 3 letters of recommendation; statement of purpose; writing sample; personal interview; for Certificate, bachelor's degree; 2 letters of recommendation; writing sample. Additional exam requirements/recommendations for international students: required—TOEFL (minimum score 550 paper-based; 80 iBT), IELTS (minimum score 7). *Application deadline:* For fall admission, 6/1 for domestic and international students; for spring admission, 11/1 for domestic and international students; for summer admission, 3/1 for domestic students. Application fee: $60 ($95 for international students). Electronic applications accepted. *Expenses:* Contact institution. *Financial support:* In 2019–20, 25 students received support, including 15 research assistantships with full tuition reimbursements available (averaging $15,700 per year), 10 teaching assistantships with full tuition reimbursements available (averaging $16,625 per year); institutionally sponsored loans, scholarships/grants, health care benefits, and unspecified assistantships also available. Financial award application deadline: 3/15; financial award applicants required to submit FAFSA. *Unit head:* Dr. Christopher Stream, Director, 702-895-5120, Fax: 702-895-4436, E-mail: sppl.chair@unlv.edu. *Application contact:* Dr. Jayce Farmer, Graduate Coordinator, 702-895-4828, E-mail: sppl.gradcoord@unlv.edu.
Website: https://www.unlv.edu/publicpolicy

University of New Hampshire, Graduate School, Carsey School of Public Policy, Program in Public Policy, Durham, NH 03824. Offers MPP. *Faculty:* 11 full-time (7 women). *Students:* 11 full-time (7 women), 8 part-time (3 women); includes 1 minority (Two or more races, non-Hispanic/Latino), 1 international. Average age 26. 27 applicants, 70% accepted, 6 enrolled. In 2019, 7 master's awarded. *Entrance requirements:* For master's, GRE. Additional exam requirements/recommendations for international students: required—TOEFL (minimum score 550 paper-based; 80 iBT), IELTS (minimum score 6.5), PTE. *Application deadline:* For fall admission, 8/15 for domestic students; for spring admission, 12/15 for domestic students; for summer admission, 4/15 for domestic students. Application fee: $65. Electronic applications accepted. *Financial support:* In 2019–20, 7 students received support. Fellowships and scholarships/grants available. Financial award application deadline: 2/15; financial award applicants required to submit FAFSA. *Unit head:* Michael Swack, Chair, 603-862-2821, Fax: 603-862-0275, E-mail: michael.swack@unh.edu. *Application contact:* Robin Husslage, Administrative Assistant, 603-862-2338, E-mail: robin.husslage@unh.edu.
Website: https://carsey.unh.edu/mpp

The University of North Carolina at Chapel Hill, Graduate School, College of Arts and Sciences, Department of Public Policy, Chapel Hill, NC 27599. Offers PhD. *Degree requirements:* For doctorate, thesis/dissertation. *Entrance requirements:* For doctorate, GRE General Test. Electronic applications accepted.

The University of North Carolina at Charlotte, College of Liberal Arts and Sciences, Department of Political Science and Public Administration, Charlotte, NC 28223-0001. Offers emergency management (Graduate Certificate); non-profit management (Graduate Certificate); public administration (MPA), including arts administration, emergency management, non-profit management, public budgeting and finance, urban management and policy; public budgeting and finance (Graduate Certificate); urban management and policy (Graduate Certificate). *Accreditation:* NASPAA. *Program availability:* Part-time, evening/weekend. *Faculty:* 20 full-time (10 women), 5 part-time/adjunct (1 woman). *Students:* 30 full-time (21 women), 45 part-time (29 women); includes 23 minority (15 Black or African American, non-Hispanic/Latino; 1 American Indian or Alaska Native, non-Hispanic/Latino; 5 Hispanic/Latino; 2 Two or more races, non-Hispanic/Latino), 2 international. Average age 30. 38 applicants, 68% accepted, 21 enrolled. In 2019, 18 master's, 13 other advanced degrees awarded. *Degree requirements:* For master's, thesis or alternative. *Entrance requirements:* For master's, GRE General Test, bachelor's degree, or its equivalent, from accredited college or university; minimum undergraduate GPA of 3.0; 3 letters of recommendation; statement of purpose; for Graduate Certificate, one official transcript from each post-secondary institution; three letters of recommendation from academic or professional sources; overall undergraduate GPA of 3.0 on a 4.0 scale; statement of purpose (1-2 pages in length) in which the applicant explains his/her career goals, how the Certificate fits into achieving those goals, and any relevant w. Additional exam requirements/recommendations for international students: required—TOEFL (minimum score 557 paper-based; 83 iBT), IELTS (minimum score 6.5), TOEFL (minimum score 557paper-based, 83 iBT) or IELTS (6.5). *Application deadline:* For fall admission, 8/15 for domestic students; for spring admission, 12/1 for domestic students; for summer admission, 5/11 for domestic students. Applications are processed on a rolling basis. Application fee: $75. Electronic applications accepted. *Expenses:* Tuition, state resident: full-time $4337. Tuition, nonresident: full-time $17,771. *Required fees:* $3093. Tuition and fees vary according to course load, degree level and program. *Financial support:* In 2019–20, 16 students received support, including 1 fellowship (averaging $55,000 per year), 15 research assistantships (averaging $8,583 per year); teaching assistantships, career-related internships or fieldwork, institutionally sponsored loans, scholarships/grants, and unspecified assistantships also available. Support available to part-time students. Financial award applicants required to submit FAFSA. *Unit head:* Dr. Cheryl L. Brown, Interim Chair, Undergraduate Coordinator, & Associate Professor, 704-687-7574, E-mail: cbrown@uncc.edu. *Application contact:* Kathy B. Giddings, Director of Graduate Admissions, 704-687-5503, Fax: 704-687-1668, E-mail: gradadm@uncc.edu.
Website: http://politicalscience.uncc.edu/

The University of North Carolina at Charlotte, College of Liberal Arts and Sciences, Interdisciplinary Liberal Arts and Sciences Programs, Charlotte, NC 28223-0001. Offers gender, sexuality and women's studies (Graduate Certificate); gerontology (MA, Graduate Certificate); Latin American studies (MA); liberal studies (MA); organizational science (PhD); public policy (PhD). *Program availability:* Part-time, evening/weekend. *Students:* 74 full-time (50 women), 56 part-time (43 women); includes 41 minority (16 Black or African American, non-Hispanic/Latino; 3 Asian, non-Hispanic/Latino; 16 Hispanic/Latino; 6 Two or more races, non-Hispanic/Latino), 16 international. Average age 33. 101 applicants, 51% accepted, 37 enrolled. In 2019, 21 master's, 5 doctorates, 8 other advanced degrees awarded. *Entrance requirements:* For master's, GRE General Test or MAT, bachelor's degree from accredited college or university; official transcripts of all previous academic work attempted beyond high school with minimum overall GPA of 3.0; statement of purpose; recommendation letters; for doctorate, GRE or GMAT, statement of purpose discussing interest in program and objectives for pursuing degree, current resume or curriculum vitae, unofficial transcripts; for Graduate Certificate, bachelor's degree from accredited university and either enrolled and in good standing in a graduate degree program at UNC Charlotte or have a minimum undergraduate GPA of 3.0. Additional exam requirements/recommendations for international students: required—TOEFL (minimum score 557 paper-based; 83 iBT), IELTS (minimum score 6.5), TOEFL (minimum score 557 paper-based, 83 iBT) or IELTS (6.5). *Application deadline:* Applications are processed on a rolling basis. Application fee: $75. Electronic applications accepted. *Expenses:* Tuition, state resident: full-time $4337. Tuition, nonresident: full-time $17,771. *Required fees:* $3093. Tuition and fees vary according to course load, degree level and program. *Financial support:* In 2019–20, 3 students received support, including 2 research assistantships (averaging $6,750 per year), 1 teaching assistantship (averaging $21,000 per year); career-related internships or fieldwork, institutionally sponsored loans, scholarships/grants, unspecified assistantships, and administrative assistantships also available. Support available to part-time students. Financial award applicants required to submit FAFSA. *Unit head:* Dr. Nancy A. Gutierrez, Dean, 704-687-0081, E-mail: ngutierr@uncc.edu. *Application contact:* Kathy B. Giddings, Director of Graduate Admissions, 704-687-5503, Fax: 704-687-3279, E-mail: gradadm@uncc.edu.
Website: http://clas.uncc.edu/academics

University of Northern Iowa, Graduate College, College of Social and Behavioral Sciences, MPP Program in Public Policy, Cedar Falls, IA 50614. Offers MPP. *Program availability:* Part-time. *Degree requirements:* For master's, comprehensive exam (for some programs). *Entrance requirements:* For master's, minimum GPA of 3.0. Additional exam requirements/recommendations for international students: required—TOEFL (minimum score 500 paper-based; 61 iBT). Electronic applications accepted.

University of Oklahoma, College of Arts and Sciences, Department of Political Science, Norman, OK 73019-0390. Offers political science (MA, PhD); public administration (MPA), including general, nonprofit management, public management, public policy. Terminal master's awarded for partial completion of doctoral program. *Degree requirements:* For master's, comprehensive exam, thesis optional, 36 hours; for doctorate, comprehensive exam, thesis/dissertation, 90 hours. *Entrance requirements:* For master's, GRE, purpose statement, writing sample, and three letters of recommendation (for MA); for doctorate, GRE, purpose statement, writing sample, three letters of recommendation. Additional exam requirements/recommendations for international students: required—TOEFL (minimum score 100 iBT) or IELTS (minimum score 7.0). Electronic applications accepted. *Expenses:* Tuition, state resident: full-time $6583.20; part-time $274.30 per credit hour. Tuition, nonresident: full-time $21,242; part-time $885.10 per credit hour. *International tuition:* $21,242.40 full-time. *Required fees:* $1994.20; $72.55 per credit hour. $126.50 per semester. Tuition and fees vary according to course load and degree level.

University of Pennsylvania, Wharton School, Department of Business and Public Policy, Philadelphia, PA 19104. Offers MBA, PhD. *Degree requirements:* For doctorate, thesis/dissertation. *Entrance requirements:* For doctorate, GRE General Test.

University of Pittsburgh, Graduate School of Public and International Affairs, Master of Public Administration Program, Pittsburgh, PA 15260. Offers energy and environment (MPA); governance and international public management (MPA); policy research and analysis (MPA); public and nonprofit management (MPA); urban affairs and planning (MPA); JD/MPA; MPH/MPA; MSIS/MPA; MSW/MPA. *Accreditation:* NASPAA. *Program availability:* Part-time, evening/weekend. *Faculty:* 33 full-time (11 women), 10 part-time/adjunct (5 women). *Students:* 76 full-time (51 women), 17 part-time (10 women); includes 9 minority (5 Black or African American, non-Hispanic/Latino; 1 Asian, non-Hispanic/Latino; 3 Hispanic/Latino), 37 international. Average age 26. 167 applicants, 91% accepted, 44 enrolled. In 2019, 49 master's awarded. *Degree requirements:* For master's, thesis optional, capstone seminar. *Entrance requirements:* For master's, Personal essay, resume, two letters of recommendation, transcripts. Additional exam requirements/recommendations for international students: required—TOEFL (minimum score 80 iBT), Duolingo English Test; recommended—IELTS (minimum score 6.5). *Application deadline:* For fall admission, 2/1 for domestic students, 1/15 priority date for international students; for spring admission, 11/1 for domestic students, 8/1 priority date for international students. Application fee: $50. Electronic applications accepted. *Expenses:* $24,480 in-state, $40,848 out-of-state. *Financial support:* In 2019–20, 30 students received support, including 2 fellowships with full tuition reimbursements available (averaging $16,060 per year); scholarships/grants also available. Financial

award application deadline: 2/1; financial award applicants required to submit FAFSA. *Unit head:* Dr. John Keeler, Dean, 412-648-7605, Fax: 412-648-7601, E-mail: gspia@pitt.edu. *Application contact:* Dr. Michael Rizzi, Director of Student Services, 412-648-7643, Fax: 412-648-7641, E-mail: rizzim@pitt.edu.
Website: http://www.gspia.pitt.edu/

University of Pittsburgh, Graduate School of Public and International Affairs, Master of Public Policy and Management Program, Pittsburgh, PA 15260. Offers MPPM. *Program availability:* Part-time, evening/weekend, 100% online. *Faculty:* 33 full-time (11 women), 10 part-time/adjunct (5 women). *Students:* 8 full-time (2 women), 113 part-time (69 women); includes 12 minority (8 Black or African American, non-Hispanic/Latino; 2 Asian, non-Hispanic/Latino; 1 Hispanic/Latino; 1 Two or more races, non-Hispanic/Latino), 6 international. Average age 41. 67 applicants, 84% accepted, 42 enrolled. In 2019, 44 master's awarded. *Entrance requirements:* For master's, Personal essay, resume, two letters of recommendation, transcripts. Additional exam requirements/recommendations for international students: required—TOEFL (minimum score 80 iBT), Duolingo English Test; recommended—IELTS (minimum score 6.5). *Application deadline:* For fall admission, 2/1 priority date for domestic students, 1/15 priority date for international students; for spring admission, 11/1 priority date for domestic students, 8/1 priority date for international students; for summer admission, 3/1 priority date for domestic students, 1/15 priority date for international students. Application fee: $50. Electronic applications accepted. *Financial support:* In 2019–20, 13 students received support. Scholarships/grants available. Financial award application deadline: 2/1. *Unit head:* Dr. John Keeler, Dean, 412-648-7605, Fax: 412-648-7601, E-mail: gspia@pitt.edu. *Application contact:* Dr. Michael Rizzi, Director of Student Services, 412-648-7643, Fax: 412-648-7641, E-mail: rizzim@pitt.edu.
Website: http://www.gspia.pitt.edu/

University of Pittsburgh, Graduate School of Public and International Affairs, PhD Program in Public and International Affairs, Pittsburgh, PA 15260. Offers international affairs (PhD); international development (PhD); public administration (PhD); public policy (PhD). *Faculty:* 33 full-time (11 women), 10 part-time/adjunct (5 women). *Students:* 28 full-time (12 women), 4 part-time (2 women); includes 4 minority (1 Black or African American, non-Hispanic/Latino; 3 Hispanic/Latino), 14 international. Average age 36. 65 applicants, 3% accepted, 2 enrolled. In 2019, 1 doctorate awarded. *Degree requirements:* For doctorate, comprehensive exam, thesis/dissertation. *Entrance requirements:* For doctorate, GRE or GMAT, Personal essay, research proposal essay, two letters of recommendation, transcripts, resume. Additional exam requirements/recommendations for international students: required—TOEFL (minimum score 80 iBT), Duolingo English Test; recommended—IELTS (minimum score 6.5). *Application deadline:* For fall admission, 1/15 for domestic and international students. Application fee: $50. Electronic applications accepted. *Expenses:* $24,480 in-state, $40,848 out-of-state. *Financial support:* In 2019–20, 15 students received support, including 15 research assistantships with full tuition reimbursements available (averaging $16,060 per year). Financial award application deadline: 1/15. *Unit head:* Dr. John Keeler, Dean, 412-648-7605, Fax: 412-648-7601, E-mail: gspia@pitt.edu. *Application contact:* Dr. Michael Rizzi, Director of Student Services, 412-648-7640, Fax: 412-648-7641, E-mail: rizzim@pitt.edu.
Website: http://www.gspia.pitt.edu/

University of Puerto Rico at Rio Piedras, Graduate School of Planning, San Juan, PR 00931-3300. Offers economic planning systems (MP); environmental planning (MP); social policy and planning (MP); urban and territorial planning (MP). *Accreditation:* ACSP. *Program availability:* Part-time. *Degree requirements:* For master's, comprehensive exam, thesis, planning project defense. *Entrance requirements:* For master's, PAEG, GRE, minimum GPA of 3.0, 2 letters of recommendation.

University of Regina, Faculty of Graduate Studies and Research, Johnson-Shoyama Graduate School of Public Policy, Regina, SK S4S 0A2, Canada. Offers economic analysis for public policy (Master's Certificate); health administration (MHA); health systems management (Master's Certificate); public management (MPA, Master's Certificate); public policy (MPA, MPP, PhD); public policy analysis (Master's Certificate). *Program availability:* Part-time. *Faculty:* 9 full-time (4 women), 19 part-time/adjunct (8 women). *Students:* 116 full-time (71 women), 202 part-time (155 women). Average age 30. 328 applicants, 50% accepted. In 2019, 67 master's, 12 other advanced degrees awarded. Terminal master's awarded for partial completion of doctoral program. *Degree requirements:* For master's, thesis (for some programs), course work, in person residencies; for doctorate, comprehensive exam, thesis/dissertation, seminar. *Entrance requirements:* For master's, 4 year undergraduate degree in any area, transcript, 2 letters of recommendation, authorization of release. Students without a background in economics may be required to complete introductory courses in micro and macro economics; for doctorate, master's degree, intended research program in an area of public policy, proposal. Additional exam requirements/recommendations for international students: required—TOEFL (minimum score 585 paper-based; 86 iBT), IELTS (minimum score 6.5), PTE (minimum score 63), Could be one of the listed above. Other options are MELAB, CANTEST, CAEl, and UR ESL. *Application deadline:* For fall admission, 5/1 for domestic and international students; for winter admission, 10/1 for domestic and international students. Application fee: $100. Electronic applications accepted. *Expenses:* Tuition fee is different for each program. See tuition and fees details on each program. *Financial support:* In 2019–20, 78 students received support, including 33 fellowships, 15 teaching assistantships (averaging $2,552 per year); research assistantships, career-related internships or fieldwork, Federal Work-Study, scholarships/grants, unspecified assistantships, and travel award and Graduate Scholarship Base funds also available. Support available to part-time students. Financial award application deadline: 9/30. *Unit head:* Dr. Doug Moen, Executive Director, 306-585-4921, Fax: 306-585-5461, E-mail: doeg.moen@uregina.ca. *Application contact:* John Bird, Academic Advisor, 306-585-5469, Fax: 306-585-5461, E-mail: john.bird@uregina.ca.
Website: http://www.schoolofpublicpolicy.sk.ca/

University of Rhode Island, Graduate School, College of Arts and Sciences, Department of Political Science, Kingston, RI 02881. Offers international relations (MA), including American politics; public policy and administration (MPA). *Program availability:* Part-time. *Faculty:* 12 full-time (6 women). *Students:* 25 full-time (15 women), 33 part-time (21 women); includes 12 minority (2 Black or African American, non-Hispanic/Latino; 1 American Indian or Alaska Native, non-Hispanic/Latino; 1 Asian, non-Hispanic/Latino; 6 Hispanic/Latino; 2 Two or more races, non-Hispanic/Latino), 2 international. 36 applicants, 94% accepted, 26 enrolled. In 2019, 18 master's awarded. *Entrance requirements:* For master's, GRE, GMAT, or MAT if undergraduate GPA below 3.0, 2 letters of recommendation. Additional exam requirements/recommendations for international students: required—TOEFL. *Application deadline:* For fall admission, 11/15 for domestic students, 2/1 for international students; for spring admission, 7/15 for domestic students, 7/15 priority date for international students. Application fee: $65. Electronic applications accepted. *Expenses: Tuition, area resident:* Full-time $13,734; part-time $763 per credit. Tuition, state resident: full-time $13,734; part-time $763 per credit. Tuition, nonresident: full-time $26,512; part-time $1473 per credit. *International tuition:* $26,512 full-time. *Required fees:* $1780; $52 per credit. $35 per term. One-time fee: $165. *Financial support:* In 2019–20, 1 research assistantship with full tuition reimbursement (averaging $19,368 per year), 4 teaching assistantships with full tuition reimbursements (averaging $15,189 per year) were awarded; health care benefits also available. Financial award application deadline: 2/1; financial award applicants required to submit FAFSA. *Unit head:* Dr. Marc Hutchison, Department Chair, 401-874-4051, Fax: 401-874-4072, E-mail: mlhutch@uri.edu. *Application contact:* Dr. Kristin Johnson, Director/Associate Professor, 401-874-5495, E-mail: kristin_johnson@uri.edu.
Website: http://www.uri.edu/artsci/psc/

University of St. Thomas, School of Arts and Sciences, Houston, TX 77006-4696. Offers public policy administration (MPPA); sacred music (MSM). *Program availability:* Part-time-only, evening/weekend. *Faculty:* 44 full-time (14 women), 49 part-time/adjunct (15 women). *Students:* 8 full-time (4 women), 94 part-time (67 women); includes 87 minority (1 Black or African American, non-Hispanic/Latino; 2 Asian, non-Hispanic/Latino; 84 Hispanic/Latino), 9 international. Average age 44. 164 applicants, 70% accepted, 58 enrolled. In 2019, 35 master's awarded. *Degree requirements:* For master's, Number of Foreign Languages-S, Comprehensive Exam -S, Thesis/Dissertation -A. *Entrance requirements:* For master's, Letters of recommendation required, undergraduate GPA of 3.0, essay requirement, transcripts from all undergraduate and graduate institutions, GRE/GMAT recommended but not required for most programs. Additional exam requirements/recommendations for international students: recommended—TOEFL, IELTS. *Application deadline:* For fall admission, 7/15 priority date for domestic and international students; for spring admission, 12/15 priority date for domestic and international students; for summer admission, 4/15 priority date for domestic and international students. Applications are processed on a rolling basis. Application fee: $35. Electronic applications accepted. Application fee is waived when completed online. *Expenses: Tuition:* Full-time $30,800; part-time $1163 per credit hour. *Required fees:* $250; $210 per semester. One-time fee: $660. Tuition and fees vary according to degree level and program. *Financial support:* Fellowships, research assistantships, teaching assistantships, career-related internships or fieldwork, Federal Work-Study, institutionally sponsored loans, scholarships/grants, tuition waivers, and unspecified assistantships available. Support available to part-time students. Financial award application deadline: 7/15; financial award applicants required to submit FAFSA. *Unit head:* George A. Harne, PhD, Executive Dean of the School of Arts and Sciences, 713-942-3419, E-mail: harneg@stthom.edu. *Application contact:* Christopher S Cheek, Graduate Admissions Manager, 713-525-3817, E-mail: cheekc@stthom.edu.
Website: http://www.stthom.edu/Academics/School_of_Arts_and_Sciences/Index.aqf

University of Saskatchewan, College of Graduate and Postdoctoral Studies, School of Public Policy, Saskatoon, SK S7N 5A2, Canada. Offers MPP, PhD.

University of Southern California, Graduate School, Sol Price School of Public Policy, Doctor of Philosophy in Public Policy and Management Program, Los Angeles, CA 90089. Offers PhD. *Degree requirements:* For doctorate, thesis/dissertation. *Entrance requirements:* For doctorate, GRE. Additional exam requirements/recommendations for international students: required—TOEFL (minimum score 600 paper-based; 100 iBT). Electronic applications accepted.

University of Southern California, Graduate School, Sol Price School of Public Policy, Public Policy Programs, Los Angeles, CA 90089. Offers homeland security and public policy (Graduate Certificate); public policy (MPP, Graduate Certificate); M Pl/MPP; MPP/JD. *Program availability:* Part-time. Terminal master's awarded for partial completion of doctoral program. *Degree requirements:* For master's, practicum. *Entrance requirements:* For master's, GRE. Additional exam requirements/recommendations for international students: required—TOEFL (minimum score 600 paper-based; 100 iBT). Electronic applications accepted.

University of Southern Maine, College of Management and Human Service, Muskie School of Public Service, Program in Public Policy and Management, Portland, ME 04103. Offers MPPM, JD/MPPM. *Program availability:* Part-time, evening/weekend, online learning. *Degree requirements:* For master's, thesis, capstone project, field experience. *Entrance requirements:* For master's, GRE General Test or LSAT. Additional exam requirements/recommendations for international students: required—TOEFL. Electronic applications accepted. *Expenses: Tuition, area resident:* Full-time $864; part-time $432 per credit hour. Tuition, state resident: full-time $864; part-time $432 per credit hour. Tuition, nonresident: full-time $2372; part-time $1186 per credit hour. *Required fees:* $141; $108 per credit hour. Tuition and fees vary according to course load.

The University of Texas at Arlington, Graduate School, College of Architecture, Planning and Public Affairs, Program in Public Policy, Arlington, TX 76019. Offers MPP. *Accreditation:* NASPAA. *Program availability:* Part-time, evening/weekend. Electronic applications accepted.

The University of Texas at Arlington, Graduate School, College of Architecture, Planning and Public Affairs, Program in Urban Planning and Public Policy, Arlington, TX 76019. Offers PhD. *Accreditation:* ACSP. *Program availability:* Part-time, evening/weekend. *Entrance requirements:* Additional exam requirements/recommendations for international students: required—TOEFL (minimum score 550 paper-based). Electronic applications accepted.

The University of Texas at Austin, Graduate School, Lyndon B. Johnson School of Public Affairs, Austin, TX 78712-1111. Offers global policy studies (MGPS); public affairs (MP Aff); public leadership (EMPL); public policy (PhD); JD/MP Aff; MBA/MP Aff; MP Aff/MA; MP Aff/MSE. *Accreditation:* NASPAA (one or more programs are accredited). *Program availability:* Part-time. *Degree requirements:* For master's, thesis, summer internship; for doctorate, thesis/dissertation. *Entrance requirements:* For master's, GRE General Test (for MP Aff and MGPS), minimum GPA of 3.0 in upper-division classes, seven years of experience in the public sector, and interview (for EMPL); for doctorate, GRE General Test, master's degree in policy-related field. Additional exam requirements/recommendations for international students: required—TOEFL. Electronic applications accepted.

The University of Texas at Dallas, School of Economic, Political and Policy Sciences, Program in Public Policy and Political Economy, Richardson, TX 75080. Offers international political economy (MS); public policy (MPP); public policy and political economy (PhD); social data analytics and research (MS). *Program availability:* Part-time, evening/weekend. *Faculty:* 26 full-time (4 women), 3 part-time/adjunct (0 women). *Students:* 51 full-time (25 women), 28 part-time (18 women); includes 29 minority (7 Black or African American, non-Hispanic/Latino; 5 Asian, non-Hispanic/Latino; 14 Hispanic/Latino; 3 Two or more races, non-Hispanic/Latino), 17 international. Average age 34. 48 applicants, 38% accepted, 18 enrolled. In 2019, 22 master's, 7 doctorates awarded. *Degree requirements:* For doctorate, thesis/dissertation. *Entrance requirements:* For master's and doctorate, GRE General Test, minimum GPA of 3.0 in upper-level course work in field. Additional exam requirements/recommendations for international students: required—TOEFL (minimum score 550 paper-based). *Application deadline:* For fall admission, 7/15 for domestic students, 5/1 priority date for international students; for spring admission, 11/15 for domestic students, 9/1 priority date for international students. Applications are processed on a rolling basis. Application fee: $50 ($100 for international students). Electronic applications accepted. *Expenses: Tuition, area resident:* Full-time $16,504. Tuition, state resident: full-time $16,504. Tuition, nonresident: full-time $34,266. Tuition and fees vary according to course load.

Financial support: In 2019–20, 22 students received support, including 1 fellowship (averaging $2,000 per year), 2 research assistantships with partial tuition reimbursements available (averaging $18,000 per year), 17 teaching assistantships with partial tuition reimbursements available (averaging $13,500 per year); career-related internships or fieldwork, Federal Work-Study, institutionally sponsored loans, scholarships/grants, and unspecified assistantships also available. Support available to part-time students. Financial award application deadline: 4/30; financial award applicants required to submit FAFSA. *Unit head:* Dr. Thomas Brunell, Program Head, 972-883-4963, Fax: 972-883-6297, E-mail: ph.pppe@utdallas.edu. *Application contact:* Marjorie McDonald, Graduate Program Administrator, 972-883-6406, Fax: 972-883-6297, E-mail: pppe@utdallas.edu.
Website: https://epps.utdallas.edu/about/programs/public-policy-and-political-economy/

The University of Texas Rio Grande Valley, College of Liberal Arts, Department of Public Affairs and Security Studies, Edinburg, TX 78539. Offers global security studies and leadership (MPA); public administration (MPA); public policy and management (MPA). *Faculty:* 4 full-time (1 woman), 2 part-time/adjunct (1 woman). *Students:* 14 full-time (8 women), 135 part-time (75 women); includes 126 minority (3 Black or African American, non-Hispanic/Latino; 123 Hispanic/Latino), 2 international. Average age 33. 67 applicants, 93% accepted, 40 enrolled. In 2019, 56 master's awarded. *Expenses: Tuition, area resident:* Full-time $5959; part-time $440 per credit hour. Tuition, state resident: full-time $5959. Tuition, nonresident: full-time $5959. *International tuition:* $13,321 full-time. *Required fees:* $1169; $185 per credit hour.
Website: utrgv.edu/pass/index.htm

University of the Pacific, McGeorge School of Law, Sacramento, CA 95817. Offers advocacy (JD); international water resources law (JSD); public policy and law (LL M); JD/MBA; JD/MPPA. *Accreditation:* ABA. *Program availability:* Part-time, evening/weekend. *Degree requirements:* For master's, thesis (for some programs); for doctorate, thesis/dissertation (for some programs). *Entrance requirements:* For master's, JD; for doctorate, LSAT (for JD), LL M (for JSD). Additional exam requirements/recommendations for international students: required—TOEFL (minimum score 600 paper-based; 100 iBT). Electronic applications accepted. *Expenses:* Contact institution.

University of Virginia, Frank Batten Sr. School of Leadership and Public Policy, Charlottesville, VA 22903. Offers MPP, JD/MPP, MBA/MPP, MPP/MPH, MPP/MUEP, MPP/PhD. *Entrance requirements:* Additional exam requirements/recommendations for international students: required—TOEFL, IELTS. Electronic applications accepted. *Expenses:* Contact institution.

University of Washington, Graduate School, Evans School of Public Policy and Governance, Seattle, WA 98195. Offers public administration (MPA); public policy and management (PhD); JD/MPA; MPA/MAIS; MPA/MPH; MPA/MS; MPA/MUP. *Accreditation:* NASPAA. *Program availability:* Part-time, evening/weekend. *Degree requirements:* For master's, thesis, internship or cooperative experience. *Entrance requirements:* For master's and doctorate, GRE General Test, minimum GPA of 3.0. Additional exam requirements/recommendations for international students: required—TOEFL (minimum score 580 paper-based; 92 iBT). Electronic applications accepted.

University of Washington, Bothell, Master of Arts in Policy Studies Program, Bothell, WA 98011. Offers MA. *Program availability:* Evening/weekend. *Degree requirements:* For master's, thesis. *Entrance requirements:* For master's, GRE, statistics and micro-economics courses. Additional exam requirements/recommendations for international students: required—TOEFL. Electronic applications accepted.

Vanderbilt University, Program in Community Research and Action, Nashville, TN 37240-1001. Offers PhD. *Students:* 31 full-time (24 women); includes 14 minority (7 Black or African American, non-Hispanic/Latino; 2 Asian, non-Hispanic/Latino; 2 Hispanic/Latino; 3 Two or more races, non-Hispanic/Latino), 4 international. Average age 30. 84 applicants, 11% accepted, 5 enrolled. In 2019, 2 doctorates awarded. *Degree requirements:* For doctorate, thesis/dissertation, internship, fundable grant proposal. *Entrance requirements:* For doctorate, GRE General Test. Additional exam requirements/recommendations for international students: required—TOEFL (minimum score 570 paper-based; 88 iBT). *Application deadline:* For fall admission, 12/1 for domestic and international students. Application fee: $0. Electronic applications accepted. *Expenses:* Contact institution. *Financial support:* In 2019–20, 16 students received support. Fellowships, research assistantships with full tuition reimbursements available, teaching assistantships with full tuition reimbursements available, Federal Work-Study, scholarships/grants, health care benefits, tuition waivers, and unspecified assistantships available. Financial award application deadline: 1/15; financial award applicants required to submit FAFSA. *Unit head:* Paul Speer, Chair, 615-322-3117, Fax: 615-322-1769, E-mail: paul.w.speer@vanderbilt.edu. *Application contact:* Brian Christens, Director of Graduate Studies, 615-322-6881, Fax: 615-322-1141, E-mail: b.christens@vanderbilt.edu.
Website: http://peabody.vanderbilt.edu/departments/hod/graduate-programs/phd_in_community_research_and_action/community_research_and_action_program.php

Virginia Commonwealth University, Graduate School, L. Douglas Wilder School of Government and Public Affairs, Center for Public Policy, Richmond, VA 23284-9005. Offers public policy and administration (PhD). *Degree requirements:* For doctorate, thesis/dissertation. *Entrance requirements:* For doctorate, GMAT, GRE General Test, LSAT, or MAT. Additional exam requirements/recommendations for international students: required—TOEFL (minimum score 600 paper-based; 100 iBT); recommended—IELTS (minimum score 6.5). Electronic applications accepted.

Virginia Polytechnic Institute and State University, Graduate School, College of Science, Blacksburg, VA 24061. Offers biological sciences (MS, PhD); biomedical technology development and management (MS); chemistry (MS, PhD); data analysis and applied statistics (MA); economics (PhD); geosciences (MS, PhD); mathematics (MS, PhD); physics (MS, PhD); psychology (MS, PhD); statistics (MS, PhD). *Faculty:* 375 full-time (118 women), 2 part-time/adjunct (1 woman). *Students:* 544 full-time (221 women), 37 part-time (15 women); includes 75 minority (14 Black or African American, non-Hispanic/Latino; 1 American Indian or Alaska Native, non-Hispanic/Latino; 20 Asian, non-Hispanic/Latino; 31 Hispanic/Latino; 9 Two or more races, non-Hispanic/Latino), 216 international. Average age 27. 962 applicants, 33% accepted, 138 enrolled. In 2019, 75 master's, 69 doctorates awarded. *Degree requirements:* For master's, comprehensive exam (for some programs), thesis (for some programs); for doctorate, comprehensive exam (for some programs), thesis/dissertation (for some programs). *Entrance requirements:* For master's and doctorate, GRE/GMAT. Additional exam requirements/recommendations for international students: required—TOEFL (minimum score 90 iBT). *Application deadline:* For fall admission, 8/1 for domestic students, 4/1 for international students; for spring admission, 1/1 for domestic students, 9/1 for international students. Applications are processed on a rolling basis. Application fee: $75. Electronic applications accepted. *Expenses:* Tuition, state resident: full-time $13,700; part-time $761.25 per credit hour. Tuition, nonresident: full-time $27,614; part-time $1534 per credit hour. *Required fees:* $886.50 per term. Tuition and fees vary according to campus/location and program. *Financial support:* In 2019–20, 5 fellowships with full tuition reimbursements (averaging $25,988 per year), 281 research assistantships with full tuition reimbursements (averaging $15,597 per year), 370 teaching assistantships with full tuition reimbursements (averaging $18,225 per year) were awarded; unspecified assistantships also available. Financial award application deadline: 3/1; financial award applicants required to submit FAFSA. *Unit head:* Dr. Sally C. Morton, Dean, 540-231-5422, Fax: 540-231-3380, E-mail: scmorton@vt.edu. *Application contact:* Allison Craft, Executive Assistant, 540-231-6394, Fax: 540-231-3380, E-mail: crafta@vt.edu.
Website: http://www.science.vt.edu/

Walden University, Graduate Programs, Richard W. Riley College of Education and Leadership, Minneapolis, MN 55401. Offers adult education (Post-Master's Certificate); adult learning (Graduate Certificate); college teaching and learning (Graduate Certificate); community college leadership (Ed D); curriculum, instruction and assessment (Ed D, Ed S, Graduate Certificate); developmental education (Graduate Certificate); early childhood administration, management, and leadership (Graduate Certificate); early childhood education (Ed D, Ed S); early childhood public policy and advocacy (Graduate Certificate); early childhood studies (MS), including administration, management and leadership, early childhood public policy and advocacy, teaching adults in the early childhood field, teaching and diversity in early childhood education; education (MS, PhD), including adolescent literacy and learning (MS), curriculum, instruction, and assessment (grades K-12) (MS), curriculum, instruction, assessment, and evaluation (PhD), early childhood leadership and advocacy (PhD), early childhood special education (PhD), educational leadership (MS), educational leadership and administration (principal preparation) (MS), educational technology and design (PhD), elementary reading and literacy (PreK-6) (MS), elementary reading and mathematics (grades K-6) (MS), global and comparative education (PhD), higher education leadership management and policy (PhD), integrating technology in the classroom (grades K-12) (MS), learning, instruction and innovation (PhD), mathematics (grades 5-8) (MS), mathematics (grades K-6) (MS), mathematics and science (grades K-8) (MS), organizational research, assessment, and evaluation (PhD), reading and literacy with a reading K-12 endorsement (MS), reading literacy assessment and evaluation (PhD), science (grades K-8) (MS), special education (non-licensure) (grades K-12) (MS), teacher leadership (grades K-12) (MS), teaching English language learners (grades K-12) (MS); educational administration and leadership (Ed D); educational leadership and administration (principal preparation) (Ed S); educational technology (Ed D, Ed S, Post Master's Certificate); elementary reading and literacy (Graduate Certificate); engaging culturally diverse learners (Graduate Certificate); enrollment management and institutional marketing (Graduate Certificate); higher education (MS), including adult learning, college teaching and learning, enrollment management and institutional marketing, global higher education, leadership for student success, online and distance learning; higher education and adult learning (Ed D); higher education leadership and management (Ed D); higher education leadership for student success (Graduate Certificate); instructional design and technology (MS, Postbaccalaureate Certificate), including general program (MS), online learning (MS), training and performance improvement (MS); integrating technology in the classroom (Graduate Certificate); mathematics 5-8 (Graduate Certificate); mathematics K-6 (Graduate Certificate); online teaching for adult educators (Graduate Certificate); reading, literacy, and assessment (Ed D, Ed S); science K-8 (Graduate Certificate); special education (Ed D, Ed S, Graduate Certificate); special education (K-age 21) (MAT); teacher leadership (Graduate Certificate); teaching adults English as a second language (Graduate Certificate); teaching adults in the early childhood field (Graduate Certificate); teaching and diversity in early childhood education (Graduate Certificate); teaching English language learners (grades K-12) (Graduate Certificate); teaching K-12 students online (Graduate Certificate). *Accreditation:* NCATE. *Program availability:* Part-time, evening/weekend, online only, 100% online. *Degree requirements:* For doctorate, thesis/dissertation (for some programs), residency; for other advanced degree, residency (for some programs). *Entrance requirements:* For master's, bachelor's degree or higher; minimum GPA of 2.5; official transcripts; goal statement (for some programs); access to computer and Internet; for doctorate, master's degree or higher; three years of related professional or academic experience (preferred); minimum GPA of 3.0; goal statement and current resume (for select programs); official transcripts; access to computer and Internet; for other advanced degree, relevant work experience; access to computer and Internet. Additional exam requirements/recommendations for international students: required—TOEFL (minimum score 550 paper-based, 79 iBT), IELTS (minimum score 6.5), Michigan English Language Assessment Battery (minimum score 82), or PTE (minimum score 53). Electronic applications accepted.

Walden University, Graduate Programs, School of Public Policy and Administration, Minneapolis, MN 55401. Offers criminal justice (MPA, MPP, MS, Graduate Certificate), including emergency management (MS, PhD), general program (MS), global leadership (MS, PhD), homeland security and policy coordination (MS, PhD), law and public policy (MS, PhD), policy analysis (MS, PhD), public management and leadership (MS, PhD), self-designed (MS), terrorism, mediation, and peace (MS, PhD); criminal justice and executive management (MS), including global leadership (MS, PhD); criminal justice leadership and executive management (MS), including emergency management (MS, PhD), general program, homeland security and policy coordination (MS, PhD), law and public policy (MS, PhD), policy analysis (MS, PhD), public management and leadership (MS, PhD), self-designed, terrorism, mediation, and peace (MS, PhD); emergency management (MPA, MPP, MS), including criminal justice (MS, PhD), general program (MS), homeland security (MS), public management and leadership (MS, PhD), terrorism and emergency management (MS); general program (MPA, MPP); global leadership (MPA, MPP); government management (Graduate Certificate); health policy (MPA, MPP); homeland security (Graduate Certificate); homeland security and policy coordination (MPA, MPP); international nongovernmental organizations (MPA, MPP); law and public policy (MPA, MPP); local government management for sustainable communities (MPA, MPP); nonprofit management (Graduate Certificate); nonprofit management and leadership (MPA, MPP, MS), including global leadership (MS, PhD), international nongovernmental organization (MS), local government for sustainable communities (MS), self-designed (MS); online teaching in higher education (Post-Master's Certificate); policy analysis (MPA); public management and leadership (MPA, MPP, Graduate Certificate); public policy (Graduate Certificate); public policy and administration (PhD), including criminal justice (MS, PhD), emergency management (MS, PhD), global leadership (MS, PhD), health policy, homeland security and policy coordination (MS, PhD), international nongovernmental organizations, law and public policy (MS, PhD), local government management for sustainable communities, nonprofit management and leadership, policy analysis (MS, PhD), public management and leadership (MS, PhD), terrorism, mediation, and peace (MS, PhD); strategic planning and public policy (Graduate Certificate); terrorism, mediation, and peace (MPA, MPP). *Program availability:* Part-time, evening/weekend, online only, 100% online. *Degree requirements:* For doctorate, thesis/dissertation, residency. *Entrance requirements:* For master's, bachelor's degree or higher; minimum GPA of 2.5; official transcripts; goal statement (for some programs); access to computer and Internet; for doctorate, master's degree or higher; three years of related professional or academic experience (preferred); minimum GPA of 3.0; goal statement and current resume (for select programs); official transcripts; access to computer and Internet; for other advanced degree, relevant work experience; access to computer and Internet. Additional exam requirements/recommendations for international students: required—TOEFL (minimum score 550 paper-based, 79 iBT), IELTS (minimum score 6.5), Michigan English Language Assessment Battery (minimum score 82), or PTE (minimum score 53). Electronic applications accepted.

Walden University, Graduate Programs, School of Social Work and Human Services, Minneapolis, MN 55401. Offers addictions and social work (DSW); advanced clinical practice (MSW); clinical expertise (DSW); criminal justice (DSW); disaster, crisis, and intervention (DSW); family studies and interventions (DSW); human and social services (PhD), including advanced research, community and social services, community intervention and leadership, conflict management, criminal justice, disaster crisis and intervention, family studies and intervention, gerontology, global social services, higher education, human services and nonprofit administration, mental health facilitation; medical social work (DSW); military social work (MSW); policy practice (DSW); social work (PhD), including addictions and social work, clinical expertise, criminal justice, disaster, crisis and intervention, family studies and interventions, medical social work, policy practice, social work administration; social work administration (DSW); social work in healthcare (MSW); social work with children and families (MSW). *Accreditation:* CSWE. *Program availability:* Part-time, evening/weekend, online only, 100% online. *Degree requirements:* For master's, residency (for some programs); for doctorate, thesis/dissertation, residency. *Entrance requirements:* For master's, bachelor's degree or higher; minimum GPA of 2.5; official transcripts; goal statement (for some programs); access to computer and Internet; for doctorate, master's degree or higher; three years of related professional or academic experience (preferred); minimum GPA of 3.0; goal statement and current resume (for select programs); official transcripts; access to computer and Internet. Additional exam requirements/recommendations for international students: required—TOEFL (minimum score 550 paper-based, 79 iBT), IELTS (minimum score 6.5), Michigan English Language Assessment Battery (minimum score 82), or PTE (minimum score 53). Electronic applications accepted.

Wayne State University, College of Liberal Arts and Sciences, Department of Political Science, Detroit, MI 48202. Offers political science (MA, PhD); public administration (MPA), including economic development policy and management, health and human services policy and management, human and fiscal resource management, nonprofit policy and management, organizational behavior and management, urban and metropolitan policy and management; JD/MA. *Accreditation:* NASPAA. *Program availability:* Part-time, evening/weekend. *Faculty:* 22 full-time (9 women). *Students:* 50 full-time (22 women), 64 part-time (32 women); includes 28 minority (20 Black or African American, non-Hispanic/Latino; 2 Asian, non-Hispanic/Latino; 1 Hispanic/Latino; 5 Two or more races, non-Hispanic/Latino), 10 international. Average age 34. 105 applicants, 40% accepted, 24 enrolled. In 2019, 21 master's, 7 doctorates awarded. Terminal master's awarded for partial completion of doctoral program. *Degree requirements:* For master's, comprehensive exam (for some programs), thesis (for some programs); for doctorate, thesis/dissertation. *Entrance requirements:* For master's, GRE General Test, substantial undergraduate preparation in the social sciences, minimum upper-division undergraduate GPA of 3.0, two letters of recommendation, personal statement; for doctorate, GRE General Test, 3 letters of recommendation; personal statement; interview. Additional exam requirements/recommendations for international students: required—TOEFL (minimum score 550 paper-based; 79 iBT), TWE (minimum score 5.5), Michigan English Language Assessment Battery (minimum score 85); recommended—IELTS (minimum score 6.5). *Application deadline:* For fall admission, 5/15 for domestic students, 5/1 priority date for international students; for winter admission, 10/15 for domestic students, 9/1 priority date for international students. Applications are processed on a rolling basis. Application fee: $50. Electronic applications accepted. *Expenses:* $678.55 per credit in-state tuition, $1,469.75 per credit out-of-state tuition, $54.56 per credit hour student service fee, $315.70 registration fee. *Financial support:* In 2019–20, 48 students received support, including 4 fellowships with partial tuition reimbursements available (averaging $57,000 per year), 1 research assistantship with partial tuition reimbursement available (averaging $45,000 per year), 13 teaching assistantships with partial tuition reimbursements available (averaging $58,000 per year); scholarships/grants, health care benefits, and unspecified assistantships also available. Financial award applicants required to submit FAFSA. *Unit head:* Dr. Daniel Geller, Professor and Chair, 313-577-6328, E-mail: dgeller@wayne.edu. *Application contact:* Dr. Jeffrey Grynaviski, Graduate Director, 313-577-2620, E-mail: gradpolisci@wayne.edu.
Website: http://clas.wayne.edu/politicalscience/

Wayne State University, College of Liberal Arts and Sciences, Tracy Neumann, Detroit, MI 48202. Offers history (MA, PhD); public history (MA), including African American history and culture, cultural resource management, gender, sexuality, and women's studies, labor and urban history, museum studies, public policy; world history (Graduate Certificate); JD/MA; M Ed/MA; MLIS/MA. *Program availability:* Evening/weekend. *Faculty:* 23 full-time (11 women). *Students:* 18 full-time (7 women), 16 part-time (7 women); includes 4 minority (2 Black or African American, non-Hispanic/Latino; 2 Two or more races, non-Hispanic/Latino). Average age 37. 38 applicants, 34% accepted, 13 enrolled. In 2019, 7 master's, 3 doctorates awarded. *Degree requirements:* For master's, thesis (for some programs), final oral exam on thesis or essay and seminar; internship and project (for public history); for doctorate, variable foreign language requirement, comprehensive exam, thesis/dissertation, qualifying exam in 4 fields of history. *Entrance requirements:* For master's, GRE General Test, minimum undergraduate GPA of 3.25 in history, 3.0 overall; at least 18 credits in history and related subjects at the advanced undergraduate level; foreign language; letter of intent; research paper; at least two letters of recommendation from former instructors; for doctorate, GRE General Test, minimum GPA of 3.0, 3.25 in minimum of 18 semester credits in history and related subjects; letter of intent; research paper; at least three letters of recommendation from former professors; for Graduate Certificate, baccalaureate degree from accredited college or university; minimum GPA of 3.0, 3.25 in a minimum of eighteen semester credits in history and related subjects at the advanced undergraduate level. Additional exam requirements/recommendations for international students: required—TOEFL (minimum score 550 paper-based; 79 iBT), TWE (minimum score 5.5), Michigan English Language Assessment Battery (minimum score 85); recommended—IELTS (minimum score 6.5). *Application deadline:* For fall admission, 1/15 priority date for domestic and international students; for winter admission, 4/15 for domestic students, 4/15 priority date for international students; for spring admission, 10/15 for domestic students, 10/15 priority date for international students. Application fee: $50. Electronic applications accepted. *Expenses: Tuition:* Full-time $34,567. *Financial support:* In 2019–20, 18 students received support, including 2 fellowships with tuition reimbursements available (averaging $20,797 per year), 2 research assistantships with tuition reimbursements available (averaging $23,960 per year), 7 teaching assistantships with tuition reimbursements available (averaging $19,967 per year); scholarships/grants, health care benefits, and unspecified assistantships also available. Financial award applicants required to submit FAFSA. *Unit head:* Dr. Elizabeth V. Faue, Professor/Chair, 313-577-2525, E-mail: evfaue@wayne.edu. *Application contact:* Dr. Tracy Neumann, Associate Professor and Director of Graduate Studies, 313-577-2525, E-mail: tracyneumann@wayne.edu.
Website: http://clas.wayne.edu/history/

Wilfrid Laurier University, Faculty of Graduate and Postdoctoral Studies, School of International Policy and Governance, International Public Policy Program, Waterloo, ON N2L 3C5, Canada. Offers global governance (MIPP); human security (MIPP); international economic relations (MIPP); international environmental policy (MIPP). *Entrance requirements:* For master's, honours BA with minimum B average. Additional exam requirements/recommendations for international students: required—TOEFL (minimum score 89 iBT). Electronic applications accepted.

York University, Faculty of Graduate Studies, Faculty of Liberal Arts and Professional Studies, Program in Public Policy, Administration and Law, Toronto, ON M3J 1P3, Canada. Offers MPPAL.

Rural Planning and Studies

Brandon University, Department of Rural Development, Brandon, MB R7A 6A9, Canada. Offers MRD, Diploma. *Degree requirements:* For master's, thesis. *Entrance requirements:* For master's, minimum GPA of 3.0, 2 letters of reference. Additional exam requirements/recommendations for international students: required—TOEFL (minimum score 580 paper-based). Electronic applications accepted.

Dalhousie University, Faculty of Architecture and Planning, School of Planning, Halifax, NS B3J 2X4, Canada. Offers M Eng, M Plan, MPS. *Degree requirements:* For master's, thesis. *Entrance requirements:* Additional exam requirements/recommendations for international students: required—TOEFL, IELTS, CANTEST, CAEL, or Michigan English Language Assessment Battery. Electronic applications accepted.

East Carolina University, Graduate School, Thomas Harriot College of Arts and Sciences, Department of Geography, Planning, and Environment, Greenville, NC 27858-4353. Offers development and environmental planning (Certificate); economic development (Certificate); geographic information science and technology (Certificate); geography (MA), including geography, planning, rural development. *Program availability:* Part-time, evening/weekend, online learning. *Degree requirements:* For master's, comprehensive exam, thesis optional. *Entrance requirements:* For master's, GRE General Test. *Application deadline:* For fall admission, 4/1 priority date for domestic and international students. Applications are processed on a rolling basis. Electronic applications accepted. *Expenses: Tuition, area resident:* Full-time $4749; part-time $185 per credit hour. Tuition, state resident: full-time $4749; part-time $185 per credit hour. Tuition, nonresident: full-time $17,898; part-time $864 per credit hour. *International tuition:* $17,898 full-time. *Required fees:* $2787. *Financial support:* Research assistantships with partial tuition reimbursements, teaching assistantships with partial tuition reimbursements, and Federal Work-Study available. Support available to part-time students. Financial award application deadline: 3/1. *Unit head:* Dr. Thad Wasklewicz, Chair, 252-328-6230, E-mail: wasklewiczt@ecu.edu. *Application contact:* Graduate Admissions, 252-328-6012, Fax: 252-328-6071, E-mail: gradschool@ecu.edu.
Website: https://geography.ecu.edu/

Iowa State University of Science and Technology, Rural, Agricultural, Technological, and Environmental History Program, Ames, IA 50011-1054. Offers PhD. *Entrance requirements:* Additional exam requirements/recommendations for international students: required—TOEFL (minimum score 600 paper-based; 79 iBT), IELTS (minimum score 7). Electronic applications accepted.

University of Alaska Fairbanks, College of Rural and Community Development, Department of Alaska Native Studies and Rural Development, Fairbanks, AK 99775. Offers rural development (MA). *Program availability:* Part-time, evening/weekend, online only, blended/hybrid learning. *Degree requirements:* For master's, comprehensive exam, thesis, oral defense of project or thesis. *Entrance requirements:* For master's, bachelor's degree from accredited institution with minimum cumulative undergraduate and major GPA of 3.0. Additional exam requirements/recommendations for international students: required—TOEFL (minimum score 550 paper-based; 79 iBT). Electronic applications accepted.

University of Guelph, Office of Graduate and Postdoctoral Studies, Ontario Agricultural College, School of Environmental Design and Rural Development, Interdisciplinary Program in Rural Studies, Guelph, ON N1G 2W1, Canada. Offers PhD. *Program availability:* Part-time. *Degree requirements:* For doctorate, thesis/dissertation, qualifying exam. *Entrance requirements:* Additional exam requirements/recommendations for international students: required—TOEFL (minimum score 600 paper-based), IELTS (minimum score 7). Electronic applications accepted.

University of Guelph, Office of Graduate and Postdoctoral Studies, Ontario Agricultural College, School of Environmental Design and Rural Development, Program in Capacity Development and Extension, Guelph, ON N1G 2W1, Canada. Offers M Sc. *Program availability:* Part-time. *Degree requirements:* For master's, thesis optional. *Entrance requirements:* For master's, minimum B- average in previous 2 years of course work. Additional exam requirements/recommendations for international students: required—TOEFL (minimum score 550 paper-based; 89 iBT), IELTS (minimum score 6.5). Electronic applications accepted.

University of Guelph, Office of Graduate and Postdoctoral Studies, Ontario Agricultural College, School of Environmental Design and Rural Development, Program in Rural Planning and Development, Guelph, ON N1G 2W1, Canada. Offers international rural planning and development (M Sc); rural planning and development in Canada (M Sc). *Program availability:* Part-time. *Degree requirements:* For master's, thesis or alternative. *Entrance requirements:* For master's, minimum B- average during previous 2 years of course work. Additional exam requirements/recommendations for international students: required—TOEFL (minimum score 550 paper-based), IELTS (minimum score 6.5). Electronic applications accepted.

University of Montana, Graduate School, College of Humanities and Sciences, Department of Geography, Missoula, MT 59812. Offers community and environmental planning (MA); geography (MA, MS). *Entrance requirements:* For master's, GRE

General Test. Additional exam requirements/recommendations for international students: required—TOEFL.

University of Wyoming, College of Arts and Sciences, Department of Geography, Program in Rural Planning and Natural Resources, Laramie, WY 82071. Offers community and regional planning and natural resources (MP). *Degree requirements:* For master's, thesis or alternative. *Entrance requirements:* For master's, GRE General Test, minimum GPA of 3.0. Additional exam requirements/recommendations for international students: required—TOEFL.

Université Laval, Faculty of Agricultural and Food Sciences, Program in Integrated Rural Development, Québec, QC G1K 7P4, Canada. Offers Diploma. *Entrance requirements:* For degree, good knowledge of French. Electronic applications accepted.

Sustainable Development

American University, School of International Service, Washington, DC 20016-8071. Offers comparative and regional studies (Certificate); cross-cultural communication (Certificate); development management (MS); ethics, peace, and global affairs (MA); European studies (Certificate); global environmental policy (MA, Certificate); global information technology (Certificate); global media (MA); international affairs (MA), including comparative and regional studies, global governance, politics, and security, international economic relations, natural resources and sustainable development, U.S. foreign policy and national security; international arts management (Certificate); international communication (MA, Certificate); international development (MA); international economic policy (Certificate); international economic relations (Certificate); international economics (MA); international peace and conflict resolution (MA, Certificate); international politics (Certificate); international relations (MA, PhD); international service (MIS); peacebuilding (Certificate); social enterprise (MA); the Americas (Certificate); United States foreign policy (Certificate); JD/MA. *Program availability:* Part-time, evening/weekend, 100% online, blended/hybrid learning. Terminal master's awarded for partial completion of doctoral program. *Degree requirements:* For master's, one foreign language, comprehensive exam, thesis or alternative; for doctorate, one foreign language, comprehensive exam, thesis/dissertation. *Entrance requirements:* For master's, transcripts, resume, 2 letters of recommendation, statement of purpose; for doctorate, GRE, transcripts, resume, 3 letters of recommendation, statement of purpose. Additional exam requirements/recommendations for international students: required—TOEFL. Electronic applications accepted. *Expenses:* Contact institution.

The American University in Cairo, School of Sciences and Engineering, Cairo, Egypt. Offers biotechnology (MS); chemistry (MS); computer science (MS); computing (M Comp); construction engineering (M Eng, MS); electronics and communications engineering (M Eng); environmental engineering (MS); environmental system design (M Eng); mechanical engineering (M Eng, MS); nanotechnology (MS); physics (MS); robotics, control and smart systems (MS); sciences and engineering (PhD); sustainable development (MS, Graduate Diploma). *Program availability:* Part-time, evening/weekend. *Degree requirements:* For master's, comprehensive exam (for some programs), thesis (for some programs); for doctorate, comprehensive exam (for some programs), thesis/dissertation. *Entrance requirements:* Additional exam requirements/recommendations for international students: required—TOEFL (minimum score 450 paper-based; 45 iBT), IELTS (minimum score 5). Electronic applications accepted.

Antioch University Los Angeles, Program in Urban Sustainability, Culver City, CA 90230. Offers MA. *Faculty:* 2 full-time (1 woman), 4 part-time/adjunct (2 women). *Students:* 17 full-time (14 women), 4 part-time (3 women); includes 7 minority (3 Black or African American, non-Hispanic/Latino; 1 Asian, non-Hispanic/Latino; 3 Hispanic/Latino). Average age 43. 9 applicants, 67% accepted, 6 enrolled. In 2019, 9 master's awarded. *Expenses: Tuition:* Full-time $29,992; part-time $17,996 per credit hour. *Unit head:* Dr. Adonia Lugo, Chair, 310-578-1080 Ext. 287, E-mail: alugo@antioch.edu. *Application contact:* Information Contact, 310-578-1090, Fax: 310-822-4824, E-mail: admissions@antiochla.edu.
Website: https://www.antioch.edu/los-angeles/degrees-programs/environmental-community-studies/urban-sustainability-ma/

Antioch University New England, Graduate School, Department of Environmental Studies, Keene, NH 03431-3552. Offers advocacy for social justice and sustainability (MS); conservation biology (MS); environmental education (MS); environmental studies (PhD); resource management and conservation (MS); science teacher certification (MS); self-designed studies (MS); sustainable development and climate change (MS). *Faculty:* 3 full-time (1 woman), 6 part-time/adjunct (3 women). *Students:* 120 full-time (88 women), 75 part-time (49 women); includes 21 minority (3 Black or African American, non-Hispanic/Latino; 6 Asian, non-Hispanic/Latino; 10 Hispanic/Latino; 1 Native Hawaiian or other Pacific Islander, non-Hispanic/Latino; 1 Two or more races, non-Hispanic/Latino), 7 international. Average age 36. 81 applicants, 98% accepted, 54 enrolled. In 2019, 108 master's, 10 doctorates awarded. *Degree requirements:* For master's, practicum; for doctorate, thesis/dissertation, practicum. *Entrance requirements:* Additional exam requirements/recommendations for international students: required—TOEFL (minimum score 550 paper-based). *Application deadline:* For fall admission, 7/1 for domestic students, 6/1 for international students; for spring admission, 12/1 for domestic and international students. Applications are processed on a rolling basis. Application fee: $50. Electronic applications accepted. *Expenses:* Contact institution. *Financial support:* Applicants required to submit FAFSA. *Unit head:* Dr. Michael Simpson, Chairperson, 603-283-2331, Fax: 603-357-0718, E-mail: msimpson@antioch.edu. *Application contact:* Jennifer Fritz, Director of Admissions, 800-552-8380, Fax: 603-357-0718, E-mail: admissions.ane@antioch.edu.
Website: http://www.antiochne.edu/environmental-studies/

Arizona State University at Tempe, School of Sustainability, Tempe, AZ 85287-5502. Offers sustainability (MA, MS, PhD); sustainable technology and management (Graduate Certificate). *Program availability:* Part-time, evening/weekend. Terminal master's awarded for partial completion of doctoral program. *Degree requirements:* For master's, thesis, interactive Program of Study (iPOS) submitted before completing 50 percent of required credit hours; for doctorate, comprehensive exam, thesis/dissertation, interactive Program of Study (iPOS) submitted before completing 50 percent of required credit hours. *Entrance requirements:* For master's, GRE; for doctorate, GRE, minimum GPA of 3.0 or equivalent in last 2 years of work leading to bachelor's degree. Additional exam requirements/recommendations for international students: required—TOEFL, IELTS, or PTE. Electronic applications accepted.

Baruch College of the City University of New York, Austin W. Marxe School of Public and International Affairs, Program in Public Administration, New York, NY 10010-5585. Offers general public administration (MPA); health care policy (MPA); nonprofit administration (MPA); policy analysis and evaluation (MPA); public management (MPA); urban development and sustainability (MPA); MS/MPA. *Accreditation:* NASPAA. *Program availability:* Part-time, evening/weekend. *Degree requirements:* For master's, thesis, capstone. *Entrance requirements:* For master's, GRE General Test. Additional exam requirements/recommendations for international students: required—TOEFL. Electronic applications accepted. *Expenses:* Contact institution.

Binghamton University, State University of New York, Graduate School, Program in Sustainable Communities, Binghamton, NY 13902-6000. Offers MA, MS. *Program availability:* Part-time. *Entrance requirements:* For master's, undergraduate transcripts, minimum GPA of 3.0, personal statement, resume or curriculum vitae, two letters of recommendation, professional writing sample or essay. Additional exam requirements/recommendations for international students: required—TOEFL, IELTS, or PTE.

Boston Architectural College, Graduate Programs, Boston, MA 02115-2795. Offers architecture (M Arch); historic preservation (MDS); interior design (MID); landscape architecture (MLA); sustainable design (MDS). *Accreditation:* CIDA. *Degree requirements:* For master's, thesis. *Entrance requirements:* For master's, portfolio (recommended). Electronic applications accepted.

Brandeis University, The Heller School for Social Policy and Management, Program in Nonprofit Management, Waltham, MA 02454-9110. Offers child, youth, and family management (MBA); health care management (MBA); social impact management (MBA); social policy and management (MBA); sustainable development (MBA); MBA/MA; MBA/MD. *Accreditation:* AACSB. *Program availability:* Part-time. *Degree requirements:* For master's, team consulting project. *Entrance requirements:* For master's, GMAT (preferred) or GRE, 2 letters of recommendation, problem statement analysis, 3-5 years of professional experience. Additional exam requirements/recommendations for international students: required—TOEFL (minimum score 600 paper-based; 100 iBT). Electronic applications accepted. *Expenses:* Contact institution.

Brandeis University, The Heller School for Social Policy and Management, Program in Sustainable International Development, Waltham, MA 02454-9110. Offers international development (MA); MA/JD; MA/MA; MBA/MA. *Degree requirements:* For master's, 2nd year fieldwork or internship; capstone paper and presentation. *Entrance requirements:* For master's, 3 letters of recommendation, curriculum vitae or resume, 3 years of development experience (international experience preferred). Additional exam requirements/recommendations for international students: required—TOEFL (minimum score 600 paper-based; 100 iBT). Electronic applications accepted.

California State University, Stanislaus, College of Natural Sciences, MS Program in Ecology and Sustainability, Turlock, CA 95382. Offers ecological conservation (MS). *Program availability:* Part-time. *Degree requirements:* For master's, thesis. *Entrance requirements:* For master's, GRE, minimum GPA of 3.0, 3 letters of recommendation, personal statement. Additional exam requirements/recommendations for international students: required—TOEFL (minimum score 550 paper-based). Electronic applications accepted.

Carnegie Mellon University, Carnegie Institute of Technology, Department of Civil and Environmental Engineering, Pittsburgh, PA 15213. Offers advanced infrastructure systems (MS, PhD); advanced infrastructure systems technology development and application (MS); air quality engineering and science (MS); civil and environmental engineering (MS, PhD); civil and environmental engineering/engineering and public policy (PhD); civil engineering (MS, PhD); computational mechanics (MS, PhD); computational modeling and monitoring for resilient structural and material systems (MS); energy infrastructure systems (MS); environmental engineering (MS, PhD); environmental management and science (MS, PhD); IT-based sustainable global infrastructure and construction management (MS); sustainability and green design (MS); water quality engineering and science (MS). *Program availability:* Part-time. *Faculty:* 23 full-time (5 women), 12 part-time/adjunct (3 women). *Students:* 261 full-time (109 women); includes 19 minority (7 Black or African American, non-Hispanic/Latino; 8 Asian, non-Hispanic/Latino; 4 Hispanic/Latino), 214 international. Average age 25. 649 applicants, 57% accepted, 106 enrolled. In 2019, 80 master's, 12 doctorates awarded. Terminal master's awarded for partial completion of doctoral program. *Degree requirements:* For master's, thesis optional; for doctorate, comprehensive exam, thesis/dissertation, two-part qualifying exam, public defense of dissertation. *Entrance requirements:* For master's, GRE General Test, BS in engineering, science, or mathematics; for doctorate, GRE General Test, BS or MS in engineering, science, or mathematics. Additional exam requirements/recommendations for international students: required—TOEFL (minimum score 84 iBT), TOEFL (minimum score 84 iBT) or IELTS (7.0). *Application deadline:* For fall admission, 1/5 priority date for domestic and international students; for spring admission, 9/15 priority date for domestic and international students. Applications are processed on a rolling basis. Application fee: $75. Electronic applications accepted. *Financial support:* In 2019–20, 113 students received support. Fellowships with tuition reimbursements available, research assistantships with tuition reimbursements available, teaching assistantships, scholarships/grants, health care benefits, tuition waivers (full and partial), and unspecified assistantships available. Financial award application deadline: 1/5. *Unit head:* Dr. David A. Dzombak, Professor and Department Head, 412-268-2941, Fax: 412-268-7813, E-mail: dzombak@cmu.edu. *Application contact:* David A. Vey, Director of Graduate Programs, 412-268-2292, Fax: 412-268-7813, E-mail: dvey@andrew.cmu.edu.
Website: http://www.cmu.edu/cee/

The Catholic University of America, School of Architecture and Planning, Washington, DC 20064. Offers architecture and planning (M Arch, MS Arch St); city and regional planning (M Arch); facilities management (MS Arch); regional development (Certificate); sustainable design (M Arch, Certificate). *Program availability:* Part-time. *Degree requirements:* For master's, thesis. *Entrance requirements:* For master's, GRE (minimum score: 1000), minimum GPA of 2.8, portfolio, statement of purpose, official copies of academic transcripts, three letters of recommendation. Additional exam requirements/recommendations for international students: required—TOEFL (minimum score 550 paper-based; 80 iBT). Electronic applications accepted. *Expenses:* Contact institution.

City College of the City University of New York, Graduate School, Program in Sustainability in the Urban Environment, New York, NY 10031-9198. Offers MS. *Degree requirements:* For master's, capstone project.

Clarkson University, Institute for a Sustainable Environment, Potsdam, NY 13699. Offers MS, PhD. *Faculty:* 1 full-time (0 women), 9 part-time/adjunct (5 women). *Students:* 22 full-time (12 women); includes 1 minority (Hispanic/Latino), 8 international. In 2019, 5 master's, 1 doctorate awarded. *Expenses: Tuition:* Full-time $24,984; part-time $1388 per credit hour. *Required fees:* $225. Tuition and fees vary according to campus/location and program. *Unit head:* Dr. Susan Powers, Director of the Institute for a Sustainable Environment, 315-268-6542, E-mail: spowers@clarkson.edu. *Application contact:* Daniel Capogna, Director of Graduate Admissions & Recruitment, 518-631-9910, E-mail: graduate@clarkson.edu.

Clark University, Graduate School, Department of International Development, Community, and Environment, Worcester, MA 01610-1477. Offers community and global health (MHS); community development and planning (MA); environmental science and policy (MS); geographic information science for development and environment (MS); international development and social change (MA); MA/MBA; MBA/MS. *Faculty:* 19 full-time (10 women), 4 part-time/adjunct (3 women). *Students:* 152 full-time (89 women), 7 part-time (6 women); includes 26 minority (11 Black or African American, non-Hispanic/Latino; 8 Asian, non-Hispanic/Latino; 5 Hispanic/Latino; 2 Two or more races, non-Hispanic/Latino, 55 international. Average age 27. 364 applicants, 86% accepted, 113 enrolled. In 2019, 85 master's awarded. *Entrance requirements:* For master's, 3 references, resume or curriculum vitae. Additional exam requirements/recommendations for international students: required—TOEFL (minimum score 575 paper-based; 90 iBT) or IELTS (minimum score 6.5). *Application deadline:* For fall admission, 1/15 for domestic students. Application fee: $75. *Expenses: Tuition:* Full-time $47,650; part-time $4765 per course. *Required fees:* $1850. *Financial support:* Fellowships, research assistantships, teaching assistantships, institutionally sponsored loans, and scholarships/grants available. *Unit head:* Dr. Ed Carr, Director, 508-421-3895, Fax: 508-793-8820, E-mail: edcarr@clarku.edu. *Application contact:* Erika Paradis, Student and Academic Services Director, 508-793-7201, Fax: 508-793-8820, E-mail: eparadis@clarku.edu.
Website: http://www2.clarku.edu/departments/international-development-community-environment/

Cleveland State University, College of Graduate Studies, Maxine Goodman Levin College of Urban Affairs, Program in Urban Planning and Development, Cleveland, OH 44115. Offers economic development (MUPD); environmental sustainability (MUPD); historic preservation (MUPD); housing and neighborhood development (MUPD); real estate development and finance (MUPD); urban economic development (Certificate); urban geographic information systems (MUPD); JD/MUPDD. *Accreditation:* ACSP. *Program availability:* Part-time, evening/weekend. *Degree requirements:* For master's, thesis or alternative, exit project. *Entrance requirements:* For master's, GRE General Test (minimum score: 50th percentile combined verbal and quantitative, 4.0 analytical writing), minimum GPA of 3.0. Additional exam requirements/recommendations for international students: required—TOEFL (minimum score 550 paper-based; 78 iBT), IELTS (6.0), or International Test of English Proficiency (iTEP). Electronic applications accepted. *Expenses:* Contact institution.

Colorado State University, Interdisciplinary College, School of Global Environmental Sustainability, Fort Collins, CO 80523. Offers applied global stability: agriculture (Graduate Certificate). *Program availability:* Part-time-only, online only, 100% online. *Entrance requirements:* For degree, bachelor's degree; transcripts. Additional exam requirements/recommendations for international students: required—TOEFL (minimum score 550 paper-based), IELTS. Electronic applications accepted. *Expenses:* Contact institution.

Colorado State University, Warner College of Natural Resources, Department of Ecosystem Science and Sustainability, Fort Collins, CO 80523-1476. Offers greenhouse gas management and accounting (MGMA); watershed science (MS). *Degree requirements:* For master's, thesis (for some programs). *Entrance requirements:* For master's, GRE (70th percentile or higher), minimum GPA of 3.0; resume; transcript; letters of recommendation; statement of purpose; undergraduate degree in a related field. Additional exam requirements/recommendations for international students: required—TOEFL (minimum score 550 paper-based; 80 iBT), IELTS (minimum score 6.5). Electronic applications accepted. *Expenses:* Contact institution.

Columbia University, Graduate School of Arts and Sciences, New York, NY 10027. Offers African-American studies (MA); American studies (MA); anthropology (MA, PhD); art history and archaeology (MA, PhD); astronomy (PhD); biological sciences (PhD); biotechnology (MA); chemical physics (PhD); chemistry (PhD); classical studies (MA, PhD); classics (MA, PhD); climate and society (MA); conservation biology (MA); earth and environmental sciences (PhD); East Asia: regional studies (MA); East Asian languages and cultures (MA, PhD); ecology, evolution and environmental biology (MA), including conservation biology; ecology, evolution, and environmental biology (PhD), including ecology and evolutionary biology, evolutionary primatology; economics (MA, PhD); English and comparative literature (MA, PhD); French and Romance philology (MA, PhD); Germanic languages (MA, PhD); global French studies (MA); global thought (MA); Hispanic cultural studies (MA); history (PhD); history and literature (MA); human rights studies (MA); Islamic studies (MA); Italian (MA, PhD); Japanese pedagogy (MA); Jewish studies (MA); Latin America and the Caribbean: regional studies (MA); Latin American and Iberian cultures (PhD); mathematics (MA, PhD), including finance (MA); medieval and Renaissance studies (MA); Middle Eastern, South Asian, and African studies (MA, PhD); modern art: critical and curatorial studies (MA); modern European studies (MA); museum anthropology (MA); music (DMA, PhD); oral history (MA); philosophical foundations of physics (MA); philosophy (MA, PhD); physics (PhD); political science (MA, PhD); psychology (PhD); quantitative methods in the social sciences (MA); religion (MA, PhD); Russia, Eurasia and East Europe: regional studies (MA); Russian translation (MA); Slavic cultures (MA); Slavic languages (MA, PhD); sociology (MA, PhD); South Asian studies (MA); statistics (MA, PhD); theatre (PhD). *Program availability:* Part-time. *Students:* 3,506 full-time (1,844 women), 208 part-time (121 women); includes 864 minority (110 Black or African American, non-Hispanic/Latino; 5 American Indian or Alaska Native, non-Hispanic/Latino; 416 Asian, non-Hispanic/Latino; 147 Hispanic/Latino; 6 Native Hawaiian or other Pacific Islander, non-Hispanic/Latino; 180 Two or more races, non-Hispanic/Latino, 2,065 international. 14,545 applicants, 25% accepted, 1,429 enrolled. In 2019, 1,262 master's, 363 doctorates awarded. Terminal master's awarded for partial completion of doctoral program. *Degree requirements:* For master's, variable foreign language requirement, comprehensive exam (for some programs), thesis (for some programs); for doctorate, variable foreign language requirement, comprehensive exam (for some programs), thesis/dissertation. *Entrance requirements:* For master's and doctorate, GRE General Test, GRE Subject Test (for some programs). Additional exam requirements/recommendations for international students: required—TOEFL (minimum score 600 paper-based; 100 iBT), IELTS (minimum score 7.5). Application fee: $115. Electronic applications accepted. *Expenses: Tuition:* Full-time $47,600; part-time $1880 per credit. One-time fee: $105. *Financial support:* Fellowships, research assistantships, teaching assistantships, career-related internships or fieldwork, Federal Work-Study, institutionally sponsored loans, scholarships/grants, traineeships, health care benefits, tuition waivers, and unspecified assistantships available. Support available to part-time students. Financial award application deadline: 12/15. *Unit head:* Dr. Carlos J. Alonso,

Dean of the Graduate School of Arts and Sciences and Vice President for Graduate Education, 212-854-2861, E-mail: gsas-dean@columbia.edu. *Application contact:* GSAS Office of Admissions, 212-854-6729, E-mail: gsas-admissions@columbia.edu. Website: http://gsas.columbia.edu/

Columbia University, School of International and Public Affairs, Program in Development Practice, New York, NY 10027. Offers MPA. *Entrance requirements:* For master's, GRE. Additional exam requirements/recommendations for international students: required—TOEFL (minimum score 100 iBT), IELTS (minimum score 7), PTE (minimum score 68). *Expenses: Tuition:* Full-time $47,600; part-time $1880 per credit. One-time fee: $105.

Cornell University, Graduate School, Graduate Fields of Agriculture and Life Sciences and Graduate Fields of Engineering, Field of Biological and Environmental Engineering, Ithaca, NY 14853. Offers bioenergy and integrated energy systems (M Eng, MPS, MS, PhD); biological engineering (M Eng, MPS, MS, PhD); bioprocess engineering (M Eng, MPS, MS, PhD); ecohydrology (M Eng, MPS, MS, PhD); environmental engineering (M Eng, MPS, MS, PhD); environmental management (MPS); food engineering (M Eng, MPS, MS, PhD); industrial biotechnology (M Eng, MPS, MS, PhD); nanobiotechnology (M Eng, MPS, MS, PhD); sustainable systems (M Eng, MPS, MS, PhD); synthetic biology (MS); synthetic biology (M Eng, MPS, PhD). Terminal master's awarded for partial completion of doctoral program. *Degree requirements:* For master's, thesis (MS); for doctorate, comprehensive exam, thesis/dissertation. *Entrance requirements:* For master's, letters of recommendation (3 for MS, 2 for M Eng and MPS); for doctorate, GRE General Test, 3 letters of recommendation. Additional exam requirements/recommendations for international students: required—TOEFL (minimum score 550 paper-based; 77 iBT). Electronic applications accepted.

Dartmouth College, Guarini School of Graduate and Advanced Studies, Graduate Programs in Biological Sciences, Program in Ecology, Evolution, Ecosystems, and Society, Hanover, NH 03755. Offers ecology and evolutionary biology (PhD); sustainability, ecosystems, and environment (PhD). *Entrance requirements:* For doctorate, GRE General Test, GRE Subject Test in biology (highly recommended). Additional exam requirements/recommendations for international students: required—TOEFL. Electronic applications accepted.

DePaul University, College of Liberal Arts and Social Sciences, Chicago, IL 60614. Offers Arabic (MA); Chinese (MA); critical ethnic studies (MA); English (MA); French (MA); German (MA); history (MA); interdisciplinary studies (MA, MS); international public service (MS); international studies (MA); Italian (MA); Japanese (MA); liberal studies (MA); nonprofit management (MNM); public administration (MPA); public health (MPH); public policy (MPP); public service management (MS); refugee and forced migration studies (MS); social work (MSW); sociology (MA); Spanish (MA); sustainable urban development (MA); women's and gender studies (MA); writing and publishing (MA); writing, rhetoric and discourse (MA); MA/PhD. *Accreditation:* CEPH. *Program availability:* Part-time, evening/weekend, online learning. Terminal master's awarded for partial completion of doctoral program. *Degree requirements:* For master's, variable foreign language requirement, comprehensive exam (for some programs), thesis (for some programs). Electronic applications accepted.

Eastern Illinois University, Graduate School, Lumpkin College of Business and Technology, School of Technology, Program in Sustainable Energy, Charleston, IL 61920. Offers MS, MS/MBA, MS/MS. *Program availability:* Part-time, evening/weekend. *Degree requirements:* For master's, comprehensive exam. *Entrance requirements:* For master's, GMAT or GRE. Additional exam requirements/recommendations for international students: required—TOEFL (minimum score 500 paper-based; 61 iBT), IELTS (minimum score 6). Electronic applications accepted.

Eastern Michigan University, Graduate School, College of Engineering and Technology, School of Visual and Built Environments, Programs in Construction Management, Ypsilanti, MI 48197. Offers construction (Certificate); construction management (MS); project leadership (Certificate); sustainable construction (Certificate). *Program availability:* Part-time, evening/weekend, online learning. *Students:* 12 full-time (4 women), 9 part-time (3 women); includes 5 minority (1 Black or African American, non-Hispanic/Latino; 2 Asian, non-Hispanic/Latino; 2 Two or more races, non-Hispanic/Latino), 9 international. Average age 31. 47 applicants, 38% accepted, 4 enrolled. In 2019, 13 master's awarded. *Entrance requirements:* Additional exam requirements/recommendations for international students: required—TOEFL. *Application deadline:* Applications are processed on a rolling basis. Application fee: $45. *Financial support:* Fellowships, research assistantships with full tuition reimbursements, teaching assistantships with full tuition reimbursements, career-related internships or fieldwork, Federal Work-Study, institutionally sponsored loans, scholarships/grants, tuition waivers (partial), and unspecified assistantships available. Support available to part-time students. Financial award applicants required to submit FAFSA. *Application contact:* Dr. Armagan Korkmaz, Advisor, 734-487-2492, Fax: 734-487-8755, E-mail: kkorkmaz@emich.edu.

Emory University, Laney Graduate School, Program in Development Practice, Atlanta, GA 30322-1100. Offers MDP. *Entrance requirements:* Additional exam requirements/recommendations for international students: recommended—TOEFL.

Future Generations University, Program in Applied Community Change, Franklin, WV 26807. Offers conservation (MA). *Program availability:* Blended/hybrid learning. *Degree requirements:* For master's, portfolio. *Entrance requirements:* For master's, bachelor's degree, community involvement. Additional exam requirements/recommendations for international students: recommended—TOEFL. Electronic applications accepted.

Hawaii Pacific University, College of Liberal Arts, Program in Global Leadership and Sustainable Development, Honolulu, HI 96813. Offers MA. *Program availability:* Part-time, evening/weekend. *Entrance requirements:* Additional exam requirements/recommendations for international students: recommended—TOEFL (minimum score 550 paper-based; 80 iBT), IELTS (minimum score 6), TWE (minimum score 5). Electronic applications accepted. *Expenses: Tuition:* Full-time $18,000; part-time $1125 per credit. *Required fees:* $213; $38 per semester.

HEC Montreal, School of Business Administration, Graduate Diploma Programs in Administration, Program in Management and Sustainable Development, Montréal, QC H3T 2A7, Canada. Offers Graduate Diploma. *Entrance requirements:* For degree, bachelor's degree. Electronic applications accepted.

Hofstra University, College of Liberal Arts and Sciences, Program in Sustainability Studies, Hempstead, NY 11549. Offers sustainability studies (MA). *Accreditation:* APA; NCATE. *Program availability:* Part-time, evening/weekend. *Students:* 4 full-time (2 women), 10 part-time (all women); includes 2 minority (1 Black or African American, non-Hispanic/Latino; 1 Hispanic/Latino), 3 international. Average age 39. 19 applicants, 74% accepted, 3 enrolled. In 2019, 2 master's awarded. *Entrance requirements:* For master's, minimum GPA of 3.0, essay, 3 letters of recommendation. Additional exam requirements/recommendations for international students: required—TOEFL (minimum score 550 paper-based; 80 iBT); recommended—IELTS (minimum score 6.5). *Application deadline:* Applications are processed on a rolling basis. Application fee: $75. Electronic applications accepted. *Expenses: Tuition:* Full-time $25,164; part-time $1398 per credit. *Required fees:* $580; $165 per semester. Tuition and fees vary according to

course load, degree level and program. *Financial support:* In 2019–20, 6 students received support, including 3 fellowships with full and partial tuition reimbursements available (averaging $4,667 per year); research assistantships with full and partial tuition reimbursements available, career-related internships or fieldwork, Federal Work-Study, institutionally sponsored loans, scholarships/grants, tuition waivers (full and partial), unspecified assistantships, and scholarships and endowed scholarships also available. Support available to part-time students. Financial award applicants required to submit FAFSA. *Unit head:* Dr. Bret Bennington, Chairperson, 516-463-5568, E-mail: j.b.bennington@hofstra.edu. *Application contact:* Sunil Samuel, Assistant Vice President of Admissions, 516-463-4723, Fax: 516-463-4664, E-mail: graduateadmission@hofstra.edu.
Website: http://www.hofstra.edu/hclas

Hunter College of the City University of New York, Graduate School, School of Arts and Sciences, Department of Psychology, New York, NY 10065-5085. Offers animal behavior and conservation (MA, Certificate); general psychology (MA). *Program availability:* Part-time, evening/weekend. *Degree requirements:* For master's, comprehensive exam, thesis. *Entrance requirements:* For master's, GRE General Test, minimum 12 credits of course work in psychology, including statistics and experimental psychology; 2 letters of recommendation. Additional exam requirements/recommendations for international students: required—TOEFL.

Instituto Centroamericano de Administracion de Empresas, Graduate Programs, La Garita, Costa Rica. Offers agribusiness management (MIAM); business administration (EMBA); finance (MBA); real estate management (MGREM); sustainable development (MBA); technology (MBA). *Degree requirements:* For master's, comprehensive exam, essay. *Entrance requirements:* For master's, GMAT or GRE General Test, fluency in Spanish, interview, letters of recommendation, minimum 1 year of work experience. Additional exam requirements/recommendations for international students: recommended—TOEFL. Electronic applications accepted.

Instituto Tecnologico de Santo Domingo, Graduate School, Area of Humanities and Social Sciences, Santo Domingo, Dominican Republic. Offers accounting (Certificate); adult education (Certificate); applied linguistics (MA); economics (MA); education (M Ed); educational psychology (MA, Certificate); gender and development (MA, Certificate); humanistic studies (MA); international marketing management (Certificate); international relations in the Caribbean basin (Certificate); intervention systems in family therapy (MA); linguistic and literary communication (Certificate); pedagogical support (MA); social science education (M Ed); sustainable human development (MA); terminal illness and death psychology (Certificate); youth and adult education (M Ed).

Iowa State University of Science and Technology, Program in Sustainable Agriculture, Ames, IA 50011. Offers MS, PhD. *Entrance requirements:* For master's and doctorate, GRE General Test. Additional exam requirements/recommendations for international students: required—TOEFL (minimum score 570 paper-based; 80 iBT), IELTS (minimum score 6.5). Electronic applications accepted.

Johnson & Wales University, Graduate Studies, MS Program in Global Tourism and Sustainable Economic Development, Providence, RI 02903-3703. Offers MS. *Program availability:* Online learning.

Judson University, Master of Architecture Program, Elgin, IL 60123. Offers architecture (M Arch); sustainable design (M Arch); traditional architecture and urbanism (M Arch). *Program availability:* Part-time. *Faculty:* 4 full-time (0 women), 2 part-time/adjunct (0 women). *Students:* 11 full-time (4 women), 1 part-time (0 women); includes 10 minority (all Hispanic/Latino). Average age 24. 12 applicants, 100% accepted, 12 enrolled. In 2019, 18 master's awarded. *Degree requirements:* For master's, thesis optional, 1600-hour practicum/preceptorship completed prior to enrollment. *Entrance requirements:* For master's, GRE, BA in Architecture or equivalent; transcripts, 1600 hours under a licensed architect, portfolio, minimum cumulative undergraduate GPA of 2.75, 3.0 in architecture; 3 letters of recommendation, letter of intent. Additional exam requirements/recommendations for international students: required—TOEFL (minimum score 550 paper-based), IELTS (minimum score 6.5). *Application deadline:* For fall admission, 2/15 priority date for domestic and international students; for winter admission, 11/15 for domestic students; for spring admission, 11/15 for domestic and international students. Applications are processed on a rolling basis. Application fee: $100. Electronic applications accepted. *Expenses:* Contact institution. *Financial support:* In 2019–20, 9 students received support. Fellowships, research assistantships, teaching assistantships, scholarships/grants, and 8 assistantships available. Financial award application deadline: 5/1; financial award applicants required to submit FAFSA. *Unit head:* Dr. Curtis Sartor, Interim Chair, 847-628-1017, E-mail: csartor@judsonu.edu. *Application contact:* Annelise Pollard, Admissions Representative, 847-628-2519, E-mail: annelise.pollard@judsonu.edu.
Website: http://www.judsonu.edu/ArchMaster/

Lehigh University, College of Arts and Sciences, Environmental Policy Program, Bethlehem, PA 18015. Offers environmental health (Graduate Certificate); environmental justice (Graduate Certificate); environmental policy and law (Graduate Certificate); environmental policy design (MA); sustainable development (Graduate Certificate); urban environmental policy (Graduate Certificate). *Faculty:* 8 full-time (3 women). *Students:* 12 full-time (10 women), 4 part-time (3 women); includes 3 minority (1 Asian, non-Hispanic/Latino; 1 Hispanic/Latino; 1 Two or more races, non-Hispanic/Latino), 2 international. Average age 26. 10 applicants, 80% accepted, 6 enrolled. In 2019, 5 master's awarded. *Degree requirements:* For master's, thesis or additional course work. *Entrance requirements:* For master's, GRE, minimum GPA of 2.75, 3.0 for last two undergraduate semesters; essay; 2 letters of recommendation. Additional exam requirements/recommendations for international students: required—TOEFL (minimum score 85 iBT), IELTS (minimum score 6.5). *Application deadline:* For fall admission, 1/1 for domestic and international students; for spring admission, 12/1 for domestic and international students. Application fee: $75. *Financial support:* In 2019–20, 6 students received support. Fellowships, teaching assistantships, career-related internships or fieldwork, scholarships/grants, health care benefits, and unspecified assistantships available. Financial award application deadline: 1/1. *Unit head:* Dr. Karen B. Pooley, Director, 610-758-2637, E-mail: kbp312@lehigh.edu. *Application contact:* Mandy Fraley, Academic Coordinator, 610-758-5837, Fax: 610-758-6232, E-mail: amf518@lehigh.edu.
Website: http://ei.cas2.lehigh.edu/

Lenoir-Rhyne University, Graduate Programs, School of Natural Sciences, Program in Sustainability Studies, Hickory, NC 28601. Offers MS. *Program availability:* Part-time, evening/weekend, online learning. *Entrance requirements:* For master's, GRE General Test or MAT, official transcripts, essay. Additional exam requirements/recommendations for international students: required—TOEFL (minimum score 600 paper-based). Electronic applications accepted. *Expenses:* Contact institution.

Lesley University, Graduate School of Arts and Social Sciences, Cambridge, MA 02138-2790. Offers clinical mental health counseling (MA), including holistic counseling, school and community counseling, trauma studies; counseling psychology (MA, CAGS), including professional counseling (MA), school counseling (MA); creative writing (MFA); expressive therapies (MA, PhD, CAGS), including art (MA), clinical mental health counseling (MA), dance (MA), expressive therapies (MA), music (MA); independent studies (CAGS); independent study (MA); intercultural relations (MA, CAGS); interdisciplinary studies (MA), including individualized studies, integrative holistic health, mindfulness studies, peace and conflict transformation, trauma sensitive assessment, intervention, and consultation, women's studies; urban environmental leadership (MA). *Program availability:* Part-time, online learning. *Degree requirements:* For master's, internship, practicum, thesis (for expressive therapies); for doctorate, thesis/dissertation, arts apprenticeship, field placement; for CAGS, thesis, internship (for counseling psychology, expressive therapies). *Entrance requirements:* For master's, MAT (counseling psychology), interview, writing samples, art portfolio; for doctorate, GRE or MAT, interview, master's degree; for CAGS, interview, master's degree. Additional exam requirements/recommendations for international students: required—TOEFL (minimum score 550 paper-based; 80 iBT). Electronic applications accepted.

Lipscomb University, Institute for Sustainable Practice, Nashville, TN 37204-3951. Offers MS, Certificate. *Program availability:* Part-time, evening/weekend, online learning. *Degree requirements:* For master's, capstone project. *Entrance requirements:* For master's, GRE or GMAT, 2 references, interview. Additional exam requirements/recommendations for international students: required—TOEFL (minimum score 570 paper-based; 80 iBT). Electronic applications accepted. *Expenses:* Contact institution.

Long Island University - Post, College of Liberal Arts and Sciences, Brookville, NY 11548-1300. Offers applied mathematics (MS); behavior analysis (MA); biology (MS); criminal justice (MS); earth science (MS); English (MA); environmental sustainability (MS); genetic counseling (MS); history (MA); interdisciplinary studies (MA, MS); political science (MA); psychology (MA). *Program availability:* Part-time, evening/weekend, blended/hybrid learning. Terminal master's awarded for partial completion of doctoral program. *Degree requirements:* For master's, comprehensive exam (for some programs), thesis (for some programs). *Entrance requirements:* Additional exam requirements/recommendations for international students: required—TOEFL, IELTS, or PTE. Electronic applications accepted.

Manhattanville College, School of Education, Program in Middle Childhood/Adolescence Education (Grades 5-12), Purchase, NY 10577-2132. Offers biology and special education (MPS); chemistry and special education (MPS); education for sustainability (Advanced Certificate); English and special education (MPS); literacy and special education (MPS); literacy specialist (MPS); math and special education (MPS); mathematics (Advanced Certificate); middle childhood/adolescence ed science (biology or chemistry grades 5-12) or (physics grades 7-12) (MAT); middle childhood/adolescence education (grades 5-12) English (MAT, Advanced Certificate); middle childhood/adolescence education (grades 5-12) mathematics (MAT, Advanced Certificate); middle childhood/adolescence education (grades 5-12) science (biology chemistry, physics, earth science) (Advanced Certificate); middle childhood/adolescence education (grades 5-12) social studies (MAT, Advanced Certificate); physics (MAT, Advanced Certificate); social studies (MAT); social studies and special education (MPS); special education generalist (MPS). *Program availability:* Part-time, evening/weekend. *Faculty:* 3 full-time (2 women), 17 part-time/adjunct (11 women). *Students:* 21 full-time (13 women), 25 part-time (16 women); includes 9 minority (4 Black or African American, non-Hispanic/Latino; 1 Asian, non-Hispanic/Latino; 4 Hispanic/Latino). Average age 29. 10 applicants, 80% accepted, 5 enrolled. In 2019, 15 master's, 4 other advanced degrees awarded. *Degree requirements:* For master's, comprehensive exam (for some programs), thesis (for some programs), student teaching, research seminars, portfolios, internships, writing assessment; for Advanced Certificate, comprehensive exam (for some programs). *Entrance requirements:* For master's, for programs leading to certification, candidates must submit scores from GRE or MAT(Miller Analogies Test), minimum undergraduate GPA of 3.0, all transcripts from all colleges and universities attended, 2 letters of recommendation, interview, essay (2-3 page personal statement that describes reasons for choosing education as profession and personal philosophy of education), proof of immunization (for those born after 1957). Additional exam requirements/recommendations for international students: required—TOEFL or IELTS are required. Manhattanville College now accepts the Duolingo English Test with a required score of 105; recommended—TOEFL (minimum score 600 paper-based; 110 iBT), IELTS (minimum score 8). *Application deadline:* Applications are processed on a rolling basis. Application fee: $75. Electronic applications accepted. *Expenses:* $935 per credit, $45 technology fee, and $60 registration fee. *Financial support:* In 2019–20, 18 students received support. Teaching assistantships, scholarships/grants, tuition waivers, and unspecified assistantships available. Support available to part-time students. Financial award application deadline: 3/15; financial award applicants required to submit FAFSA. *Unit head:* Dr. Shelley Wepner, Dean, 914-323-3153, Fax: 914-323-5493, E-mail: Shelley.Wepner@mville.edu. *Application contact:* Alissa Wilson, Director, Graduate Admissions, 914-323-3150, Fax: 914-694-1732, E-mail: Alissa.Wilson@mville.edu.
Website: http://www.mville.edu/programs#/search/19

Michigan State University, The Graduate School, College of Agriculture and Natural Resources, Department of Community Sustainability, East Lansing, MI 48824. Offers MS, PhD. *Entrance requirements:* Additional exam requirements/recommendations for international students: required—TOEFL. Electronic applications accepted.

Minneapolis College of Art and Design, Master of Arts in Sustainable Design, Minneapolis, MN 55404-4347. Offers MA. *Program availability:* Part-time, evening/weekend. *Students:* 11 applicants, 82% accepted, 6 enrolled. *Degree requirements:* For master's, thesis. *Entrance requirements:* For master's, No exams are required for the MA in Sustainable Design, Application requirements for the MA in Sustainable Design can be found online here: https://mcad.edu/admissions-and-aid/master-of-arts/application-checklist. Additional exam requirements/recommendations for international students: required—TOEFL (minimum score 550 paper-based; 79 iBT), IELTS (minimum score 6.5), MCAD accepts the Duolingo English Test. Minimum score: 100. *Application deadline:* For fall admission, 4/1 priority date for domestic and international students; for spring admission, 11/1 priority date for domestic and international students. Applications are processed on a rolling basis. Application fee: $50. Electronic applications accepted. *Expenses: Tuition:* Full-time $41,344. *Required fees:* $450. One-time fee: $300 full-time. *Financial support:* Career-related internships or fieldwork available. Support available to part-time students. Financial award application deadline: 3/15; financial award applicants required to submit FAFSA. *Unit head:* Denise DeLuca, Director, Sustainable Design Program, 612-8722915, E-mail: denise_deluca@mcad.edu. *Application contact:* Mary Kazura, Director of Admissions, 612-8743668, E-mail: mkazura@mcad.edu.
Website: https://mcad.edu/academic-programs/sustainable-design

Mississippi State University, College of Forest Resources, Department of Sustainable Bioproducts, Mississippi State, MS 39762. Offers forest resources (PhD), including sustainable biproducts; sustainable bioproducts (MS). *Faculty:* 13 full-time (2 women), 1 part-time/adjunct (0 women). *Students:* 19 full-time (10 women); includes 3 minority (2 Black or African American, non-Hispanic/Latino; 1 Two or more races, non-Hispanic/Latino), 12 international. Average age 28. 10 applicants, 40% accepted, 3 enrolled. In 2019, 6 master's, 11 doctorates awarded. *Degree requirements:* For master's, thesis optional; for doctorate, comprehensive exam, thesis/dissertation. *Entrance requirements:* For master's, GRE (if undergraduate GPA of last two years less than 3.0); for doctorate, GRE if undergraduate GPA of last two years is below 3.0. Additional exam requirements/recommendations for international students: required—TOEFL (minimum

score 550 paper-based; 79 iBT); recommended—IELTS (minimum score 6.5). *Application deadline:* For fall admission, 7/1 for domestic students, 5/1 for international students; for spring admission, 11/1 for domestic students, 9/1 for international students. Applications are processed on a rolling basis. Application fee: $60 ($80 for international students). Electronic applications accepted. *Expenses: Tuition, area resident:* Full-time $8880; part-time $456 per credit hour. Tuition, state resident: full-time $8880. Tuition, nonresident: full-time $23,840; part-time $1236 per credit hour. *Required fees:* $110; $11.12 per credit hour. Tuition and fees vary according to course load. *Financial support:* In 2019–20, 100 students received support, including 19 research assistantships with full tuition reimbursements available (averaging $18,065 per year); Federal Work-Study, institutionally sponsored loans, and unspecified assistantships also available. Financial award application deadline: 4/1; financial award applicants required to submit FAFSA. *Unit head:* Dr. Rubin Shmulsky, Department Head and Graduate Coordinator, 662-325-2116, Fax: 662-325-8126, E-mail: rshmulsky@cfr.msstate.edu. *Application contact:* Nathan Drake, Manager, Graduate Programs, 662-325-7394, E-mail: ndrake@grad.msstate.edu.
Website: http://www.cfr.msstate.edu/forestp/index.asp

Montclair State University, The Graduate School, College of Science and Mathematics, Program in Sustainability Science, Montclair, NJ 07043-1624. Offers MS.

New Jersey Institute of Technology, College of Science and Liberal Arts, Newark, NJ 07102. Offers applied mathematics (MS); applied physics (MS, PhD); applied statistics (MS, Certificate); biology (MS, PhD); biostatistics (MS); chemistry (MS, PhD); environmental and sustainability policy (MS); environmental science (MS, PhD); history (MA, MAT); materials science and engineering (MS, PhD); mathematical and computational finance (MS); mathematical sciences (PhD); pharmaceutical chemistry (MS); professional and technical communications (MS); technical communication essentials (Certificate). *Program availability:* Part-time, evening/weekend. *Faculty:* 159 full-time (42 women), 156 part-time/adjunct (61 women). *Students:* 197 full-time (80 women), 58 part-time (14 women); includes 58 minority (18 Black or African American, non-Hispanic/Latino; 22 Asian, non-Hispanic/Latino; 16 Hispanic/Latino; 2 Two or more races, non-Hispanic/Latino), 130 international. Average age 29. 401 applicants, 63% accepted, 73 enrolled. In 2019, 54 master's, 10 doctorates, 1 other advanced degree awarded. Terminal master's awarded for partial completion of doctoral program. *Degree requirements:* For master's, thesis (for some programs); for doctorate, thesis/dissertation. *Entrance requirements:* For master's and doctorate, GRE General Test, Minimum GPA of 3.0, personal statement, 3 letters of recommendation, and transcripts. Additional exam requirements/recommendations for international students: required—TOEFL (minimum score 550 paper-based; 79 iBT), IELTS (minimum score 6.5). *Application deadline:* For fall admission, 6/1 priority date for domestic students, 5/1 priority date for international students; for spring admission, 11/15 priority date for domestic and international students. Applications are processed on a rolling basis. Application fee: $75. Electronic applications accepted. *Expenses:* $23,828 per year (in-state), $33,744 per year (out-of-state). *Financial support:* In 2019–20, 147 students received support, including 13 fellowships with full tuition reimbursements available (averaging $24,000 per year), 41 research assistantships with full tuition reimbursements available (averaging $24,000 per year), 87 teaching assistantships with full tuition reimbursements available (averaging $24,000 per year); scholarships/grants, traineeships, health care benefits, and unspecified assistantships also available. Financial award application deadline: 1/15. *Unit head:* Dr. Kevin Belfield, Dean, 973-596-3676, Fax: 973-565-0586, E-mail: kevin.d.belfield@njit.edu. *Application contact:* Stephen Eck, Director of Admissions, 973-596-3300, Fax: 973-596-3461, E-mail: admissions@njit.edu.
Website: http://csla.njit.edu/

New York School of Interior Design, Program in Sustainable Interior Environments, New York, NY 10021-5110. Offers MPS. *Entrance requirements:* For master's, degree in interior design, architecture, or closely-related field; portfolio. Additional exam requirements/recommendations for international students: required—TOEFL (minimum score 550 paper-based; 79 iBT). Electronic applications accepted.

New York University, Graduate School of Arts and Science, Program in Historical and Sustainable Architecture, New York, NY 10012-1019. Offers MA. *Entrance requirements:* For master's, GRE, writing sample. Additional exam requirements/recommendations for international students: required—TOEFL, IELTS.

New York University, School of Professional Studies, Schack Institute of Real Estate, Program in Real Estate Development, New York, NY 10012-1019. Offers real estate development (MS), including global real estate, sustainable development, the business of development. *Program availability:* Part-time, evening/weekend. *Degree requirements:* For master's, thesis, capstone project. *Entrance requirements:* For master's, GRE or GMAT (only upon request), bachelor's degree, resume with relevant professional work, internship or volunteer experience, 2 letters of recommendation, personal statement. Additional exam requirements/recommendations for international students: required—TOEFL (minimum score 600 paper-based; 100 iBT), IELTS (minimum score 7). Electronic applications accepted. *Expenses:* Contact institution.

Northern Arizona University, College of Social and Behavioral Sciences, Sustainable Communities Program, Flagstaff, AZ 86011. Offers MA. *Program availability:* Part-time. *Degree requirements:* For master's, variable foreign language requirement, comprehensive exam (for some programs), thesis, fieldwork experience/internship, oral defense. *Entrance requirements:* Additional exam requirements/recommendations for international students: required—TOEFL (minimum score 80 iBT), IELTS (minimum score 6.5). Electronic applications accepted.

Penn State University Park, Graduate School, Intercollege Graduate Programs, Intercollege Program in Renewable Energy and Sustainability Systems, University Park, PA 16802. Offers MPS.

Pratt Institute, School of Architecture, Program in Sustainable Environmental Systems, Brooklyn, NY 11205-3899. Offers MS. *Program availability:* Part-time. *Students:* 16 full-time (9 women), 4 part-time (3 women); includes 3 minority (1 Black or African American, non-Hispanic/Latino; 1 Hispanic/Latino; 1 Two or more races, non-Hispanic/Latino), 9 international. Average age 27. 61 applicants, 61% accepted, 7 enrolled. In 2019, 13 master's awarded. *Degree requirements:* For master's, thesis. *Entrance requirements:* For master's, portfolio or writing sample, letters of recommendation. Additional exam requirements/recommendations for international students: required—TOEFL (minimum score 550 paper-based; 79 iBT). *Application deadline:* For fall admission, 1/5 for domestic and international students; for spring admission, 10/1 for domestic and international students. Application fee: $50 ($90 for international students). Electronic applications accepted. *Expenses: Tuition:* Full-time $33,246; part-time $1847 per credit. *Required fees:* $1980. *Financial support:* Career-related internships or fieldwork, Federal Work-Study, institutionally sponsored loans, scholarships/grants, health care benefits, and unspecified assistantships available. Support available to part-time students. Financial award application deadline: 2/1; financial award applicants required to submit FAFSA. *Unit head:* Leonel Ponce, Acting Director, 718-399-4328, E-mail: lponce@pratt.edu. *Application contact:* Natalie Capannelli, Director of Graduate Admissions, 718-636-3551, Fax: 718-399-4242, E-mail: ncapanne@pratt.edu.

Website: https://www.pratt.edu/academics/architecture/sustainable-environmental-systems/

Rochester Institute of Technology, Graduate Enrollment Services, Golisano Institute for Sustainability, Architecture and Sustainability Department, MS Program in Sustainable Systems, Rochester, NY 14623-5603. Offers MS. *Program availability:* Part-time. *Degree requirements:* For master's, thesis or alternative, Thesis or Capstone. *Entrance requirements:* For master's, GRE, minimum GPA of 3.0 (recommended), one year of college science and one year of college mathematics, personal statement of educational objectives, resume, interview with the academic department, two letters of recommendation. Additional exam requirements/recommendations for international students: required—TOEFL (minimum score 600 paper-based; 100 iBT), IELTS (minimum score 7), PTE (minimum score 68). Electronic applications accepted.

Rochester Institute of Technology, Graduate Enrollment Services, Golisano Institute for Sustainability, Architecture and Sustainability Department, PhD Program in Sustainability, Rochester, NY 14623-5603. Offers PhD. *Degree requirements:* For doctorate, thesis/dissertation. *Entrance requirements:* For doctorate, GRE, minimum GPA of 3.0 (recommended); one year of college science and one year of college mathematics, including calculus and statistics; personal statement of educational objectives; resume; at least two letters of recommendation. Additional exam requirements/recommendations for international students: required—TOEFL (minimum score 600 paper-based; 100 iBT), IELTS (minimum score 7), PTE (minimum score 68). Electronic applications accepted. *Expenses:* Contact institution.

Rochester Institute of Technology, Graduate Enrollment Services, Kate Gleason College of Engineering, Industrial and Systems Engineering Department, ME Program in Sustainable Engineering, Rochester, NY 14623-5603. Offers ME. *Program availability:* Part-time. *Degree requirements:* For master's, capstone project. *Entrance requirements:* For master's, GRE, minimum GPA of 3.0 (recommended), statement of purpose, 3 letters of recommendation. Additional exam requirements/recommendations for international students: required—TOEFL (minimum score 550 paper-based; 79 iBT), IELTS (minimum score 6.5), PTE (minimum score 58). Electronic applications accepted.

Rochester Institute of Technology, Graduate Enrollment Services, Kate Gleason College of Engineering, Industrial and Systems Engineering Department, MS Program in Sustainable Engineering, Rochester, NY 14623-5603. Offers MS. *Program availability:* Part-time. *Degree requirements:* For master's, thesis. *Entrance requirements:* For master's, GRE, minimum GPA of 3.0 (recommended), statement of purpose, 3 letters of recommendation. Additional exam requirements/recommendations for international students: required—TOEFL (minimum score 550 paper-based; 79 iBT), IELTS (minimum score 6.5), PTE (minimum score 58). Electronic applications accepted.

St. Edward's University, School of Behavioral and Social Sciences, Austin, TX 78704. Offers environmental management and sustainability (PSM). *Entrance requirements:* Additional exam requirements/recommendations for international students: required—TOEFL, IELTS. Electronic applications accepted.

Savannah College of Art and Design, Program in Design for Sustainability, Savannah, GA 31402-3146. Offers built environment (MFA); management (MFA); packaging and print media (MFA); products (MFA). *Program availability:* Part-time. *Degree requirements:* For master's, final project (for MA); thesis (for MFA). *Entrance requirements:* For master's, GRE (recommended), portfolio (submitted in digital format), audition or writing submission, resume, statement of purpose, two letters of recommendation. Additional exam requirements/recommendations for international students: recommended—TOEFL (minimum score 550 paper-based; 85 iBT), IELTS (minimum score 6.5). Electronic applications accepted.

Saybrook University, School of Psychology and Interdisciplinary Inquiry, San Francisco, CA 94612. Offers human science (MA, PhD), including consciousness and spirituality, humanistic and transpersonal psychology, integrative health studies, organizational systems, social transformation; organizational systems (MA, PhD), including consciousness and spirituality, humanistic and transpersonal psychology, integrative health studies, leadership of sustainable systems (MA), organizational systems, social transformation; psychology (MA, PhD), including consciousness and spirituality, creativity studies (MA), humanistic and transpersonal psychology, integrative health studies, Jungian studies, marriage and family therapy (MA), organizational systems, social transformation. *Program availability:* Online learning. Terminal master's awarded for partial completion of doctoral program. *Degree requirements:* For master's, thesis or alternative; for doctorate, thesis/dissertation. *Entrance requirements:* Additional exam requirements/recommendations for international students: required—TOEFL (minimum score 580 paper-based; 93 iBT). Electronic applications accepted.

SIT Graduate Institute, Graduate Programs, Master's Programs in Intercultural Service, Leadership, and Management, Master's Program in Sustainable Development, Washington, DC 20005. Offers MA. *Expenses: Tuition:* Full-time $43,500; part-time $21,750 per credit.

Southern Illinois University Edwardsville, Graduate School, Program in Integrative Studies, Edwardsville, IL 62026. Offers cultural heritage and resources management (MA, MS); diversity training (MA, MS); organizational design thinking (MS); sustainability (MS). *Program availability:* Part-time, evening/weekend. *Degree requirements:* For master's, variable foreign language requirement, comprehensive exam (for some programs), thesis (for some programs). *Entrance requirements:* Additional exam requirements/recommendations for international students: required—TOEFL (minimum score 550 paper-based; 79 iBT), IELTS (minimum score 6.5). Electronic applications accepted.

Southern Methodist University, Lyle School of Engineering, Department of Civil and Environmental Engineering, Dallas, TX 75275-0340. Offers civil and environmental engineering (PhD); civil engineering (MS), including geotechnical engineering, structural engineering, transportation systems; environmental engineering (MS); sustainability and development (MA). *Program availability:* Part-time, evening/weekend, online learning. Terminal master's awarded for partial completion of doctoral program. *Degree requirements:* For master's, thesis optional; for doctorate, thesis/dissertation, oral and written qualifying exams. *Entrance requirements:* For master's, GRE General Test, minimum GPA of 3.0 in last 2 years; bachelor's degree in engineering, mathematics, or sciences; for doctorate, GRE, BS and MS in related field, minimum GPA of 3.3. Additional exam requirements/recommendations for international students: required—TOEFL. Electronic applications accepted.

Stanford University, School of Engineering, Department of Civil and Environmental Engineering, Stanford, CA 94305-2004. Offers atmosphere and energy (MS, PhD); construction (MS), including construction engineering and management, design-construction integration, sustainable design and construction; environmental engineering and science (MS, PhD); environmental fluid mechanics and hydrology (PhD); structural engineering (MS). *Expenses: Tuition:* Full-time $52,479; part-time $34,110 per unit. *Required fees:* $672; $224 per quarter. Tuition and fees vary according to program and student level.
Website: http://www-ce.stanford.edu/

State University of New York College of Environmental Science and Forestry, Department of Paper and Bioprocess Engineering, Syracuse, NY 13210-2779. Offers

biomaterials engineering (MS, PhD); bioprocess engineering (MPS, MS, PhD); bioprocessing (Advanced Certificate); paper science and engineering (MPS, MS, PhD); sustainable engineering management (MPS). *Program availability:* Part-time. *Faculty:* 13 full-time (2 women), 1 part-time/adjunct (0 women). *Students:* 28 full-time (13 women), 3 part-time (0 women); includes 1 minority (Hispanic/Latino), 22 international. Average age 29. 19 applicants, 89% accepted, 10 enrolled. In 2019, 5 master's, 2 doctorates awarded. Terminal master's awarded for partial completion of doctoral program. *Degree requirements:* For master's, thesis; for doctorate, comprehensive exam, thesis/dissertation; for Advanced Certificate, 15 credit hours. *Entrance requirements:* For master's and doctorate, GRE General Test, minimum GPA of 3.0; for Advanced Certificate, BS, calculus plus science major. Additional exam requirements/recommendations for international students: required—TOEFL (minimum score 550 paper-based; 80 iBT), IELTS (minimum score 6). *Application deadline:* For fall admission, 2/1 priority date for domestic and international students; for spring admission, 11/1 priority date for domestic and international students. Applications are processed on a rolling basis. Application fee: $60. Electronic applications accepted. *Expenses:* Tuition, state resident: full-time $11,310; part-time $472 per credit hour. Tuition, nonresident: full-time $23,100; part-time $963 per credit hour. *Required fees:* $1890; $95.21 per credit hour. *Financial support:* In 2019–20, 17 students received support. Unspecified assistantships available. Financial award application deadline: 6/30; financial award applicants required to submit FAFSA. *Unit head:* Dr. Bandaru Ramarao, Chair, 315-470-6502, Fax: 315-470-6945, E-mail: bvramara@esf.edu. *Application contact:* Laura Payne, Office of Instruction and Graduate Studies, 315-470-6599, Fax: 315-470-6978, E-mail: esfgrad@esf.edu.
Website: http://www.esf.edu/pbe/

Texas A&M University–Kingsville, College of Graduate Studies, Frank H. Dotterweich College of Engineering, Program in Sustainable Energy Systems Engineering, Kingsville, TX 78363. Offers PhD. *Degree requirements:* For doctorate, variable foreign language requirement, comprehensive exam, thesis/dissertation (for some programs). *Entrance requirements:* For doctorate, GRE, MAT, GMAT, bachelor's or master's degree in engineering or science, curriculum vitae, official transcripts, statement of purpose, three letters of recommendation. Additional exam requirements/recommendations for international students: required—TOEFL (minimum score 550 paper-based; 79 iBT). Electronic applications accepted.

Texas State University, The Graduate College, College of Liberal Arts, Program in Sustainability Studies, San Marcos, TX 78666. Offers MA, MS. *Program availability:* Part-time. *Degree requirements:* For master's, comprehensive exam, thesis optional. *Entrance requirements:* For master's, bachelor's degree from accredited institution, minimum GPA of 3.0 on last 60 hours of undergraduate work, statement of personal goals, 3 letters of recommendation, letter of intent to mentor from faculty member who will serve as research advisor and chair the master's committee. Additional exam requirements/recommendations for international students: required—TOEFL (minimum score 550 paper-based; 78 iBT), IELTS (minimum score 6). Electronic applications accepted.

Texas Tech University, Graduate School, Interdisciplinary Programs, Lubbock, TX 79409-1030. Offers arid land studies (MS); biotechnology (MS); heritage and museum sciences (MA); interdisciplinary studies (MA, MS); wind science and engineering (PhD); JD/MS. *Program availability:* Part-time, 100% online, blended/hybrid learning. *Faculty:* 5 full-time (3 women). *Students:* 114 full-time (46 women), 94 part-time (59 women); includes 72 minority (30 Black or African American, non-Hispanic/Latino; 3 Asian, non-Hispanic/Latino; 31 Hispanic/Latino; 8 Two or more races, non-Hispanic/Latino), 34 international. Average age 31. 118 applicants, 85% accepted, 66 enrolled. In 2019, 57 master's, 4 doctorates awarded. Terminal master's awarded for partial completion of doctoral program. *Degree requirements:* For master's, comprehensive exam (for some programs), thesis (for some programs); for doctorate, comprehensive exam, thesis/dissertation (for some programs). *Entrance requirements:* Additional exam requirements/recommendations for international students: required—TOEFL (minimum score 550 paper-based; 79 iBT), IELTS (minimum score 6.5), PTE (minimum score 60), Cambridge Advanced (B), Cambridge Proficiency (C), ELS English for Academic Purposes (Level 112), Duolingo English Test (100). *Application deadline:* For fall admission, 6/1 priority date for domestic students, 1/15 priority date for international students; for spring admission, 9/1 priority date for domestic students, 6/15 priority date for international students. Applications are processed on a rolling basis. Application fee: $65. Electronic applications accepted. *Expenses:* Tuition, state resident: full-time $7944; part-time $331 per credit hour. Tuition, nonresident: full-time $17,904; part-time $746 per credit hour. *Required fees:* $2556; $55.50 per credit hour. $612 per semester. Tuition and fees vary according to program. *Financial support:* In 2019–20, 150 students received support, including 138 fellowships (averaging $5,639 per year), 26 research assistantships (averaging $18,634 per year), 16 teaching assistantships (averaging $13,404 per year); scholarships/grants and unspecified assistantships also available. Financial award application deadline: 4/15; financial award applicants required to submit FAFSA. *Unit head:* Dr. Mark A. Sheridan, Vice Provost for Graduate and Postdoctoral Affairs/Dean of the Graduate School, 806-834-5537, Fax: 806-742-1746, E-mail: mark.sheridan@ttu.edu. *Application contact:* Dr. David Doerfert, Associate Dean, 806-834-4477, Fax: 806-742-4038, E-mail: david.doerfert@ttu.edu.
Website: www.gradschool.ttu.edu

Thomas Jefferson University, College of Architecture and the Built Environment, Program in Sustainable Design, Philadelphia, PA 19107. Offers MS. *Program availability:* Part-time, online learning.

Unity College, Program in Professional Science, Unity, ME 04988. Offers sustainability science (MS); sustainable natural resource management (MS). *Program availability:* Online learning.

University at Buffalo, the State University of New York, Graduate School, School of Engineering and Applied Sciences, Department of Civil, Structural, and Environmental Engineering, Buffalo, NY 14260. Offers civil engineering (MS, PhD); engineering science (MS), including data sciences, green energy, Internet of Things, nanoelectronics; environmental and water resources engineering (MS). *Program availability:* Part-time, online learning. Terminal master's awarded for partial completion of doctoral program. *Degree requirements:* For master's, project, thesis, or comprehensive exam; for doctorate, thesis/dissertation. *Entrance requirements:* For master's and doctorate, GRE General Test, letters of reference. Additional exam requirements/recommendations for international students: required—TOEFL (minimum score 550 paper-based; 79 iBT). Electronic applications accepted. *Expenses: Tuition, area resident:* Full-time $11,310; part-time $471 per credit hour. Tuition, state resident: full-time $11,310; part-time $471 per credit hour. Tuition, nonresident: full-time $23,100; part-time $963 per credit hour. *International tuition:* $23,100 full-time. *Required fees:* $2820.

The University of Alabama at Birmingham, School of Engineering, Professional Engineering Degrees, Birmingham, AL 35294. Offers advanced safety engineering and management (M Eng); construction engineering management (M Eng); design and commercialization (M Eng); information engineering management (M Eng); structural engineering (M Eng); sustainable smart cities (M Eng). *Program availability:* Part-time, evening/weekend, online only, 100% online. *Faculty:* 5 full-time (1 woman), 15 part-time/adjunct (3 women). *Students:* 13 full-time (4 women), 315 part-time (70 women); includes 83 minority (64 Black or African American, non-Hispanic/Latino; 3 American Indian or Alaska Native, non-Hispanic/Latino; 9 Asian, non-Hispanic/Latino; 7 Hispanic/Latino), 8 international. 126 applicants, 84% accepted, 90 enrolled. In 2019, 123 master's awarded. *Entrance requirements:* For master's, 3.0 GPA on 4.0 scale, undergraduate degree from a nationally accredited school. Additional exam requirements/recommendations for international students: required—TOEFL (minimum score 80 iBT); recommended—IELTS (minimum score 6.5). *Application deadline:* For fall admission, 8/1 for domestic and international students; for spring admission, 12/1 for domestic and international students; for summer admission, 5/1 for domestic and international students. Applications are processed on a rolling basis. Application fee: $50 ($60 for international students). Electronic applications accepted. *Expenses:* Contact institution. *Unit head:* Dr. Gregg Janowski, Associate Dean for Graduate Programs and Assessment, E-mail: janowski@uab.edu. *Application contact:* Jesse Kepply, Director of Student and Academic Services, 205-996-5696, E-mail: gradschool@uab.edu.

University of Alaska Fairbanks, School of Natural Resources and Extension, Fairbanks, AK 99775-7140. Offers natural resources and sustainability (PhD); natural resources management (MS). *Program availability:* Part-time. *Degree requirements:* For master's, comprehensive exam, thesis (for some programs), oral defense of project or thesis; for doctorate, comprehensive exam, thesis/dissertation, defense of the dissertation. *Entrance requirements:* For master's, GRE General Test, bachelor's degree from accredited institution with minimum cumulative undergraduate and major GPA of 3.0; for doctorate, minimum cumulative GPA of 3.0. Additional exam requirements/recommendations for international students: required—TOEFL (minimum score 550 paper-based; 89 iBT), IELTS (minimum score 6.5). Electronic applications accepted.

The University of British Columbia, Faculty of Applied Science, Clean Energy Research Center, Vancouver, BC V6T 1Z1, Canada. Offers MEL. *Entrance requirements:* For master's, undergraduate degree in engineering or BS in environmental science; undergraduate thermodynamics course; three or more years of relevant work experience.

University of Calgary, School of Architecture, Planning and Landscaping, Program in Environmental Design, Calgary, AB T2N 1N4, Canada. Offers architecture (M Arch); environmental design (M Env Des, PhD); landscape architecture (MLA); planning (M Plan). *Degree requirements:* For master's, thesis; for doctorate, thesis/dissertation. *Entrance requirements:* For master's, minimum GPA of 3.0; for doctorate, minimum GPA of 3.5. Additional exam requirements/recommendations for international students: required—TOEFL (minimum score 550 paper-based).

University of California, Berkeley, Graduate Division, College of Natural Resources, Master of Development Practice Program, Berkeley, CA 94720. Offers MDP.

University of California, Berkeley, UC Berkeley Extension, Certificate Programs in Sustainability Studies, Berkeley, CA 94720. Offers leadership in sustainability and environmental management (Professional Certificate); solar energy and green building (Professional Certificate); sustainable design (Professional Certificate).

University of California, Santa Barbara, Graduate Division, College of Letters and Sciences, Division of Social Sciences, Department of Global Studies, Santa Barbara, CA 93106-7065. Offers global culture, ideology, and religion (MA, PhD); global government, human rights, and civil society (MA, PhD); political economy, sustainable development, and the environment (MA, PhD). *Degree requirements:* For master's, one foreign language, thesis, 2 years of a second language; for doctorate, one foreign language, thesis/dissertation, reading proficiency in at least one language other than English. *Entrance requirements:* For master's, GRE, 2 years of a second language with minimum B grade in the final term, statement of purpose, resume or curriculum vitae, 3 letters of recommendation, transcripts (from all post-secondary institutions attended), writing sample (15-20 pages); for doctorate, GRE, statement of purpose, personal achievements/contributions statement, resume or curriculum vitae, 3 letters of recommendation, transcripts from all post-secondary institutions attended, writing sample (15-20 pages). Additional exam requirements/recommendations for international students: required—TOEFL (minimum score 600 paper-based; 94 iBT), IELTS (minimum score 7). Electronic applications accepted.

University of Colorado Denver, College of Architecture and Planning, Program in Design and Planning, Denver, CO 80217. Offers history of architecture, landscape and urbanism (PhD); sustainable and healthy environments (PhD). *Program availability:* Part-time. *Degree requirements:* For doctorate, comprehensive exam, thesis/dissertation. *Entrance requirements:* For doctorate, GRE (minimum score of 158 for both verbal and quantitative; writing 4.0), minimum undergraduate GPA of 3.0, graduate 3.5; writing sample; three letters of recommendation; statement of personal and professional goals. Additional exam requirements/recommendations for international students: required—TOEFL (minimum score 80 iBT); recommended—IELTS (minimum score 6.8). Electronic applications accepted. *Expenses:* Contact institution.

University of Colorado Denver, College of Engineering, Design and Computing, Department of Civil Engineering, Denver, CO 80217. Offers civil engineering (EASPh D); civil engineering systems (PhD); environmental and sustainability engineering (MS, PhD); geographic information systems (MS); geotechnical engineering (MS, PhD); hydrology and hydraulics (MS, PhD); structural engineering (MS, PhD); transportation engineering (MS, PhD). *Program availability:* Part-time, evening/weekend. *Degree requirements:* For master's, comprehensive exam, 30 credit hours, project or thesis; for doctorate, comprehensive exam, thesis/dissertation, 60 credit hours (30 of which are dissertation research). *Entrance requirements:* For master's, GRE, statement of purpose, transcripts, three references; for doctorate, GRE, statement of purpose, transcripts, references, letter of support from faculty stating willingness to serve as dissertation advisor and outlining plan for financial support. Additional exam requirements/recommendations for international students: required—TOEFL (minimum score 537 paper-based; 75 iBT); recommended—IELTS (minimum score 6.5). Electronic applications accepted. Tuition and fees vary according to course load, program and reciprocity agreements.

University of Colorado Denver, College of Liberal Arts and Sciences, Department of Anthropology, Denver, CO 80217. Offers archaeological studies (MA); biological anthropology (MA); medical anthropology (MA); sustainable development and political ecology (MA). *Program availability:* Part-time, evening/weekend. *Degree requirements:* For master's, comprehensive exam, thesis or alternative, 30-36 credit hours. *Entrance requirements:* For master's, GRE General Test, minimum GPA of 3.0 for all undergraduate studies, transcripts from all undergraduate/graduate institutions attended, prior training in anthropology, three letters of recommendation, statement of purpose. Additional exam requirements/recommendations for international students: required—TOEFL (minimum score 537 paper-based; 75 iBT); recommended—IELTS (minimum score 6.5). Tuition and fees vary according to course load, program and reciprocity agreements.

University of Florida, Graduate School, College of Liberal Arts and Sciences, Center for Latin American Studies, Gainesville, FL 32611. Offers Latin American studies (MA, Certificate); sustainable development practice (MDP); tropical conservation and development (MA); JD/MA. *Program availability:* Part-time. *Degree requirements:* For master's, thesis. *Entrance requirements:* For master's, GRE General Test, minimum GPA of 3.0. Additional exam requirements/recommendations for international students: required—TOEFL (minimum score 550 paper-based; 80 iBT), IELTS (minimum score 6). Electronic applications accepted.

University of Georgia, Eugene P. Odum School of Ecology, Athens, GA 30602. Offers conservation ecology and sustainable development (MS); ecology (PhD). *Degree requirements:* For master's, thesis; for doctorate, one foreign language, thesis/dissertation. *Entrance requirements:* For master's and doctorate, GRE General Test. Electronic applications accepted.

University of Hawaii at Manoa, Office of Graduate Education, College of Social Sciences, Department of Urban and Regional Planning, Honolulu, HI 96822. Offers community planning (MURP); disaster management and humanitarian assistance (Graduate Certificate); environmental planning and sustainability (MURP); international development planning (MURP); land use, transportation and infrastructure planning (MURP); planning studies (Graduate Certificate); urban and regional planning (PhD, Graduate Certificate). *Accreditation:* ACSP. *Program availability:* Part-time. *Entrance requirements:* For master's, GRE General Test, minimum GPA of 3.0; for doctorate, GRE General Test. Additional exam requirements/recommendations for international students: required—TOEFL (minimum score 500 paper-based; 61 iBT), IELTS (minimum score 5).

University of Houston, Gerald D. Hines College of Architecture and Design, Houston, TX 77204. Offers architectural studies (MA); architecture (M Arch, MS), including media and fabrication (MS), sustainable design (MS), sustainable urban systems (MS), urban design (MS); industrial design (MS). *Faculty:* 15 full-time (4 women), 13 part-time/adjunct (3 women). *Students:* 92 full-time (40 women), 6 part-time (2 women); includes 23 minority (1 Black or African American, non-Hispanic/Latino; 1 American Indian or Alaska Native, non-Hispanic/Latino; 9 Asian, non-Hispanic/Latino; 9 Hispanic/Latino; 3 Two or more races, non-Hispanic/Latino), 20 international. Average age 28. 192 applicants, 45% accepted, 47 enrolled. In 2019, 21 master's awarded. *Degree requirements:* For master's, thesis (for some programs). *Entrance requirements:* For master's, GRE General Test, digital portfolio. Additional exam requirements/recommendations for international students: required—TOEFL (minimum score 550 paper-based; 79 iBT), IELTS (minimum score 6.5). *Application deadline:* For fall admission, 2/1 priority date for domestic students, 2/1 for international students. Applications are processed on a rolling basis. Application fee: $50. Electronic applications accepted. *Expenses:* M.Arch + 3 is $50,825.70; M.Arch + 2 is $33,883.80. *Financial support:* In 2019–20, 8 students received support, including 8 research assistantships with tuition reimbursements available (averaging $1,358 per year), 5 teaching assistantships (averaging $3,487 per year); career-related internships or fieldwork, institutionally sponsored loans, scholarships/grants, and unspecified assistantships also available. Financial award application deadline: 1/1; financial award applicants required to submit FAFSA. *Unit head:* Patricia Belton Oliver, Dean, 713-743-2400, Fax: 713-743-2358, E-mail: poliver@central.uh.edu. *Application contact:* Trang Phan, Assistant Dean, 713-743-2400, Fax: 713-743-2358, E-mail: tphan@uh.edu. Website: http://www.uh.edu/architecture/

The University of Iowa, Graduate College, College of Engineering, Department of Civil and Environmental Engineering, Iowa City, IA 52242-1316. Offers environmental engineering and science (MS, PhD); hydraulics and water resources (MS, PhD); structures, mechanics and materials (MS, PhD); sustainable water development (MS, PhD); transportation engineering (MS, PhD). *Program availability:* Part-time. Terminal master's awarded for partial completion of doctoral program. *Degree requirements:* For master's, thesis optional, exam; for doctorate, comprehensive exam, thesis/dissertation, exam. *Entrance requirements:* For master's, GRE (minimum combined score of 301 on verbal and quantitative), minimum undergraduate GPA of 3.0; for doctorate, GRE (minimum combined score of 301 on verbal and quantitative), minimum graduate GPA of 3.0. Additional exam requirements/recommendations for international students: required—TOEFL (minimum score 550 paper-based; 81 iBT), IELTS (minimum score 7). Electronic applications accepted.

University of Maryland, College Park, Academic Affairs, College of Computer, Mathematical and Natural Sciences, Department of Biology, Program in Sustainable Development and Conservation Biology, College Park, MD 20742. Offers MS. *Program availability:* Part-time, evening/weekend. *Degree requirements:* For master's, internship, scholarly paper. *Entrance requirements:* For master's, GRE General Test, minimum GPA of 3.0, 3 letters of recommendation. Electronic applications accepted.

University of Massachusetts Amherst, Graduate School, College of Natural Sciences, Department of Environmental Conservation, Program in Sustainability Science, Amherst, MA 01003. Offers MS. *Program availability:* Part-time. *Degree requirements:* For master's, internship. *Entrance requirements:* Additional exam requirements/recommendations for international students: required—TOEFL (minimum score 550 paper-based; 80 iBT), IELTS (minimum score 6.5). Electronic applications accepted.

University of Michigan, School for Environment and Sustainability, Program in Environment and Sustainability, Ann Arbor, MI 48109. Offers behavior, education and communication (MS); conservation ecology (MS); environment and sustainability (PhD); environmental informatics (MS); environmental justice (MS); environmental policy and planning (MS); sustainable systems (MS); MS/JD; MS/MBA; MS/MPH; MS/MPP; MS/MSE; MS/MURP. Terminal master's awarded for partial completion of doctoral program. *Degree requirements:* For master's, thesis, practicum, or group project; for doctorate, comprehensive exam, thesis/dissertation, oral defense of dissertation, preliminary exam. *Entrance requirements:* For master's, GRE General Test (must be taken within 5 years of application submission); for doctorate, GRE General Test (must be taken within 5 years of application submission), Master's Degree. Additional exam requirements/recommendations for international students: required—TOEFL (minimum score 560 paper-based; 84 iBT). Electronic applications accepted.

University of Notre Dame, The Graduate School, Keough School of Global Affairs, Notre Dame, IN 46556. Offers global affairs (MGA); sustainable development (MGA).

University of Oklahoma, College of Atmospheric and Geographic Sciences, School of Geosciences, Norman, OK 73019. Offers environmental sustainability (MS); geography (MA, MS, PhD), including geospatial technologies (MS), physical geography (MS). *Program availability:* Part-time. *Degree requirements:* For master's, comprehensive exam (for some programs), thesis (for some programs); for doctorate, comprehensive exam (for some programs), thesis/dissertation (for some programs). *Entrance requirements:* For master's and doctorate, GRE, personal statement, transcripts, two letters of recommendation, writing sample. Additional exam requirements/recommendations for international students: required—TOEFL (minimum score 79 iBT) or IELTS (minimum score 6.5). Electronic applications accepted. *Expenses:* Tuition, state resident: full-time $6583.20; part-time $274.30 per credit hour. Tuition, nonresident: full-time $21,242; part-time $885.10 per credit hour. *International tuition:* $21,242.40 full-time. *Required fees:* $1994.20; $72.55 per credit hour. $126.50 per semester. Tuition and fees vary according to course load and degree level.

University of South Dakota, Graduate School, College of Arts and Sciences, Department of Sustainability and Environment, Vermillion, SD 57069. Offers

sustainability (MS, PhD). Terminal master's awarded for partial completion of doctoral program. *Degree requirements:* For master's, thesis optional; for doctorate, thesis/dissertation. *Entrance requirements:* Additional exam requirements/recommendations for international students: required—TOEFL (minimum score 550 paper-based; 79 iBT).

University of Southern California, Graduate School, Sol Price School of Public Policy, Master of Planning Program, Los Angeles, CA 90089. Offers sustainable cities (Graduate Certificate); transportation systems (Graduate Certificate); urban planning (M Pl); M Arch/M Pl; M Pl/MA; M Pl/MPP; M Pl/MRED; M Pl/MS; M Pl/MSW; MBA/M Pl; ML Arch/M Pl; MPA/M Pl. *Accreditation:* ACSP. *Program availability:* Part-time. *Degree requirements:* For master's, comprehensive exam, internship. *Entrance requirements:* For master's, GRE, GMAT. Additional exam requirements/recommendations for international students: required—TOEFL (minimum score 600 paper-based; 100 iBT). Electronic applications accepted.

University of Southern California, Graduate School, Viterbi School of Engineering, Sonny Astani Department of Civil and Environmental Engineering, Los Angeles, CA 90089. Offers applied mechanics (MS); civil engineering (MS, PhD); computer-aided engineering (ME, Graduate Certificate); construction management (MCM); engineering technology commercialization (Graduate Certificate); environmental engineering (MS, PhD); environmental quality management (ME); structural design (ME); sustainable cities (Graduate Certificate); transportation systems (MS, Graduate Certificate); water and waste management (MS). *Program availability:* Part-time, evening/weekend. Terminal master's awarded for partial completion of doctoral program. *Degree requirements:* For master's, thesis optional; for doctorate, thesis/dissertation. *Entrance requirements:* For master's and doctorate, GRE General Test. Additional exam requirements/recommendations for international students: recommended—TOEFL. Electronic applications accepted.

University of South Florida, Innovative Education, Tampa, FL 33620-9951. Offers adult, career and higher education (Graduate Certificate), including college teaching, leadership in developing human resources, leadership in higher education; Africana studies (Graduate Certificate), including diasporas and health disparities, genocide and human rights; aging studies (Graduate Certificate), including gerontology; art research (Graduate Certificate), including museum studies; business foundations (Graduate Certificate); chemical and biomedical engineering (Graduate Certificate), including materials science and engineering, water, health and sustainability; child and family studies (Graduate Certificate), including positive behavior support; civil and industrial engineering (Graduate Certificate), including transportation systems analysis; community and family health (Graduate Certificate), including maternal and child health, social marketing and public health, violence and injury: prevention and intervention, women's health; criminology (Graduate Certificate), including criminal justice administration; data science for public administration (Graduate Certificate); digital humanities (Graduate Certificate); educational measurement and research (Graduate Certificate), including evaluation; English (Graduate Certificate), including comparative literary studies, creative writing, professional and technical communication; entrepreneurship (Graduate Certificate); environmental health (Graduate Certificate), including safety management; epidemiology and biostatistics (Graduate Certificate), including applied biostatistics, biostatistics, concepts and tools of epidemiology, epidemiology, epidemiology of infectious diseases; geography, environment and planning (Graduate Certificate), including community development, environmental policy and management, geographical information systems; geology (Graduate Certificate), including hydrogeology; global health (Graduate Certificate), including disaster management, global health and Latin American and Caribbean studies, global health practice, humanitarian assistance, infection control; government and international affairs (Graduate Certificate), including Cuban studies, globalization studies; health policy and management (Graduate Certificate), including health management and leadership, public health policy and programs; hearing specialist: early intervention (Graduate Certificate); industrial and management systems engineering (Graduate Certificate), including systems engineering, technology management; information studies (Graduate Certificate), including school library media specialist; information systems/decision sciences (Graduate Certificate), including analytics and business intelligence; instructional technology (Graduate Certificate), including distance education, Florida digital/virtual educator, instructional design, multimedia design, Web design; internal medicine, bioethics and medical humanities (Graduate Certificate), including biomedical ethics; Latin American and Caribbean studies (Graduate Certificate); leadership for coastal resiliency planning (Graduate Certificate); mass communications (Graduate Certificate), including multimedia journalism; mathematics and statistics (Graduate Certificate), including mathematics; medicine (Graduate Certificate), including aging and neuroscience, bioinformatics, biotechnology, brain fitness and memory management, clinical investigation, hand and upper limb rehabilitation, health informatics, health sciences, integrative weight management, intellectual property, medicine and gender, metabolic and nutritional medicine, metabolic cardiology, pharmacy sciences; national and competitive intelligence (Graduate Certificate); nursing (Graduate Certificate), including simulation based academic fellowship in advanced pain management; psychological and social foundations (Graduate Certificate), including career counseling, college teaching, diversity in education, mental health counseling, school counseling; public affairs (Graduate Certificate), including nonprofit management, public management, research administration; public health (Graduate Certificate), including assessing chemical toxicity and public health risks, health equity, pharmacoepidemiology, public health generalist, toxicology, translational research in adolescent behavioral health; public health practices (Graduate Certificate), including planning for healthy communities; rehabilitation and mental health counseling (Graduate Certificate), including integrative mental health care, marriage and family therapy, rehabilitation technology; secondary education (Graduate Certificate), including ESOL, foreign language education: culture and content, foreign language education: professional; social work (Graduate Certificate), including geriatric social work/clinical gerontology; special education (Graduate Certificate), including autism spectrum disorder, disabilities education: severe/profound; world languages (Graduate Certificate), including teaching English as a second language (TESL) or foreign language. *Unit head:* Dr. Cynthia DeLuca, Associate Vice President and Assistant Vice Provost, 813-974-3077, Fax: 813-974-7061, E-mail: deluca@usf.edu. *Application contact:* Owen Hooper, Director, Summer and Alternative Calendar Programs, 813-974-6917, E-mail: hooper@usf.edu. Website: http://www.usf.edu/innovative-education/

University of South Florida, Patel College of Global Sustainability, Tampa, FL 33620-9951. Offers energy, global, water and sustainable tourism (Graduate Certificate); global sustainability (MA), including building sustainable enterprise, climate change and sustainability, coastal sustainability, entrepreneurship, food sustainability and security, sustainability policy, sustainable energy, sustainable tourism, water. *Faculty:* 1 full-time (0 women). *Students:* 82 full-time (56 women), 75 part-time (49 women); includes 34 minority (8 Black or African American, non-Hispanic/Latino; 4 Asian, non-Hispanic/Latino; 17 Hispanic/Latino; 5 Two or more races, non-Hispanic/Latino), 43 international. Average age 29. 121 applicants, 79% accepted, 65 enrolled. In 2019, 93 master's awarded. *Degree requirements:* For master's, comprehensive exam (for some programs), thesis or alternative, internship. *Entrance requirements:* For master's, GPA of at least 3.25 or greater; alternatively a GPA of at least 3.00 along with a GRE Verbal

score of 153 (61 percentile) or higher, Quantitative of 153 (51 percentile) or higher and Analytical Writing of 3.5 or higher, all taken within 5 years of application; at least 2 letters of recommendation from professors or supervisors. Additional exam requirements/recommendations for international students: required—TOEFL (minimum score 550 paper-based; 79 iBT). *Application deadline:* For fall admission, 6/1 for domestic students, 5/1 for international students; for spring admission, 10/15 for domestic students, 9/15 for international students. Electronic applications accepted. *Financial support:* In 2019–20, 35 students received support. *Unit head:* Dr. Govindan Parayil, Dean, 813-974-9694, E-mail: gparayil@usf.edu. *Application contact:* Dr. Govindan Parayil, Dean, 813-974-9694, E-mail: gparayil@usf.edu.
Website: http://psgs.usf.edu/

The University of Texas at Austin, Graduate School, School of Architecture, Program in Sustainable Design, Austin, TX 78712-1111. Offers M Arch I, M Arch II, MSSD.

The University of Texas Rio Grande Valley, College of Sciences, School of Earth, Environmental, and Marine Sciences, Edinburg, TX 78539. Offers agricultural, environmental, and sustainability sciences (MS); ocean, coastal, and earth sciences (MS). *Faculty:* 7 full-time (2 women). *Students:* 48 full-time (25 women), 20 part-time (10 women); includes 33 minority (1 Asian, non-Hispanic/Latino; 32 Hispanic/Latino), 15 international. Average age 27. 22 applicants, 82% accepted, 14 enrolled. In 2019, 14 master's awarded. *Expenses: Tuition, area resident:* Full-time $5959; part-time $440 per credit hour. Tuition, state resident: full-time $5959. Tuition, nonresident: full-time $5959. *International tuition:* $13,321 full-time. *Required fees:* $1169; $185 per credit hour.
Website: https://www.utrgv.edu/seems/

University of Vermont, Graduate College, The Rubenstein School of Environment and Natural Resources, Program in Leadership for Sustainability, Burlington, VT 05405. Offers MPS. *Program availability:* Part-time. *Entrance requirements:* Additional exam requirements/recommendations for international students: required—TOEFL (minimum iBT score of 90) or IELTS (6.5). Electronic applications accepted. *Expenses:* Contact institution.

University of Washington, Graduate School, College of the Environment, School of Environmental and Forest Sciences, Seattle, WA 98195. Offers bioresource science and engineering (MS, PhD); environmental horticulture (MEH); forest ecology (MS, PhD); forest management (MFR); forest soils (MS, PhD); restoration ecology (MS, PhD); restoration ecology and environmental horticulture (MS, PhD); social sciences (MS, PhD); sustainable resource management (MS, PhD); wildlife science (MS, PhD); MFR/MAIS; MPA/MS. *Accreditation:* SAF. *Program availability:* Part-time. *Degree requirements:* For master's, thesis; for doctorate, comprehensive exam, thesis/dissertation. *Entrance requirements:* For master's and doctorate, GRE, minimum GPA of 3.0. Additional exam requirements/recommendations for international students: required—TOEFL. Electronic applications accepted.

University of Washington, Graduate School, School of Law, Seattle, WA 98195-3020. Offers Asian law (LL M, PhD); intellectual property law and policy (LL M); law (JD); law of sustainable international development (LL M); taxation (LL M); JD/LL M; JD/MA; JD/MAIS; JD/MBA; JD/MPA; JD/MS; JD/PhD. *Accreditation:* ABA. *Degree requirements:* For master's, thesis; for doctorate, thesis/dissertation (for some programs). *Entrance requirements:* For master's, language proficiency (LL M in Asian law); for doctorate, LSAT (for JD). Additional exam requirements/recommendations for international students: required—TOEFL. *Expenses:* Contact institution.

The University of Western Ontario, School of Graduate and Postdoctoral Studies, Faculty of Science, Department of Earth Sciences, London, ON N6A 3K7, Canada. Offers environment and sustainability (MES); geology (M Sc, PhD); geology and environmental science (M Sc, PhD); geophysics (M Sc, PhD); geophysics and environmental science (M Sc, PhD). *Degree requirements:* For master's, thesis; for doctorate, thesis/dissertation, qualifying exam. *Entrance requirements:* For master's, honors in B Sc; for doctorate, M Sc. Additional exam requirements/recommendations for international students: required—TOEFL.

University of Wisconsin–Madison, Graduate School, Gaylord Nelson Institute for Environmental Studies, Environmental Conservation Program, Madison, WI 53706-

1380. Offers MS. *Degree requirements:* For master's, thesis or alternative, spring/summer leadership (internship) experience. *Entrance requirements:* For master's, GRE General Test (recommended for potential scholarship consideration). Additional exam requirements/recommendations for international students: required—TOEFL (minimum score 550 paper-based, 80 iBT) or IELTS (6.5). Electronic applications accepted. *Expenses:* Contact institution.

University of Wisconsin–Stevens Point, College of Professional Studies, School of Education, Program in Educational Sustainability, Stevens Point, WI 54481-3897. Offers Ed D. *Program availability:* Online learning.

Walden University, Graduate Programs, School of Public Policy and Administration, Minneapolis, MN 55401. Offers criminal justice (MPA, MPP, MS, Graduate Certificate), including emergency management (MS, PhD), general program (MS), global leadership (MS, PhD), homeland security and policy coordination (MS, PhD), law and public policy (MS, PhD), policy analysis (MS, PhD), public management and leadership (MS, PhD), self-designed (MS), terrorism, mediation, and peace (MS, PhD); criminal justice and executive management (MS), including global leadership (MS, PhD); criminal justice leadership and executive management (MS), including emergency management (MS, PhD), general program, homeland security and policy coordination (MS, PhD), law and public policy (MS, PhD), policy analysis (MS, PhD), public management and leadership (MS, PhD), self-designed, terrorism, mediation, and peace (MS, PhD); emergency management (MPA, MPP, MS), including criminal justice (MS, PhD), general program (MS), homeland security (MS), public management and leadership (MS, PhD), terrorism and emergency management (MS); general program (MPA, MPP); global leadership (MPA, MPP); government management (Graduate Certificate); health policy (MPA, MPP); homeland security (Graduate Certificate); homeland security and policy coordination (MPA, MPP); international nongovernmental organizations (MPA, MPP); law and public policy (MPA, MPP); local government management for sustainable communities (MPA, MPP); nonprofit management (Graduate Certificate); nonprofit management and leadership (MPA, MPP, MS), including global leadership (MS, PhD), international nongovernmental organization (MS), local government for sustainable communities (MS), self-designed (MS); online teaching in higher education (Post-Master's Certificate); policy analysis (MPA); public management and leadership (MPA, MPP, Graduate Certificate); public policy (Graduate Certificate); public policy and administration (PhD), including criminal justice (MS, PhD), emergency management (MS, PhD), global leadership (MS, PhD), health policy, homeland security and policy coordination (MS, PhD), international nongovernmental organizations, law and public policy (MS, PhD), local government management for sustainable communities, nonprofit management and leadership, policy analysis (MS, PhD), public management and leadership (MS, PhD), terrorism, mediation, and peace (MS, PhD); strategic planning and public policy (Graduate Certificate); terrorism, mediation, and peace (MPA, MPP). *Program availability:* Part-time, evening/weekend, online only, 100% online. *Degree requirements:* For doctorate, thesis/dissertation, residency. *Entrance requirements:* For master's, bachelor's degree or higher; minimum GPA of 2.5; official transcripts; goal statement (for some programs); access to computer and Internet; for doctorate, master's degree or higher; three years of related professional or academic experience (preferred); minimum GPA of 3.0; goal statement and current resume (for select programs); official transcripts; access to computer and Internet; for other advanced degree, relevant work experience; access to computer and Internet. Additional exam requirements/recommendations for international students: required—TOEFL (minimum score 550 paper-based, 79 iBT), IELTS (minimum score 6.5), Michigan English Language Assessment Battery (minimum score 82), or PTE (minimum score 53). Electronic applications accepted.

Xavier University, College of Arts and Sciences, Department of Interdisciplinary Studies, Cincinnati, OH 45207. Offers urban sustainability and resilience (MA). *Degree requirements:* For master's, thesis (for some programs), internship. *Entrance requirements:* For master's, MAT or GRE, official transcript, resume, 500-word statement of purpose, two letters of reference. Additional exam requirements/recommendations for international students: required—TOEFL (minimum score 550 paper-based; 79 iBT). Electronic applications accepted. Application fee is waived when completed online. *Expenses:* Contact institution.

Urban and Regional Planning

Alabama Agricultural and Mechanical University, School of Graduate Studies, College of Agricultural, Life and Natural Sciences, Department of Community and Regional Planning, Huntsville, AL 35811. Offers urban and regional planning (MURP). *Accreditation:* ACSP. *Program availability:* Part-time, evening/weekend. *Degree requirements:* For master's, comprehensive exam. *Entrance requirements:* For master's, GRE General Test. Additional exam requirements/recommendations for international students: required—TOEFL (minimum score 500 paper-based; 61 iBT). Electronic applications accepted.

American University of Sharjah, Graduate Programs, Sharjah, United Arab Emirates. Offers accounting (MS); biomedical engineering (MSBME); business administration (MBA); chemical engineering (MS Ch E); civil engineering (MSCE); computer engineering (MS); electrical engineering (MSEE); engineering systems management (MS, PhD); mathematics (MS); mechanical engineering (MSME); mechatronics engineering (MS); teaching English to speakers of other languages (MA); translation and interpreting (MA); urban planning (MUP). *Program availability:* Part-time, evening/weekend. *Degree requirements:* For master's, thesis (for some programs). *Entrance requirements:* For master's, GMAT (for MBA). Additional exam requirements/recommendations for international students: required—TOEFL (minimum score 550 paper-based; 80 iBT), TWE (minimum score 5); recommended—IELTS (minimum score 6.5). Electronic applications accepted.

Andrews University, School of Graduate Studies, College of Arts and Sciences, Department of Behavioral Science, Program in International Development, Berrien Springs, MI 49104. Offers community and international development (MSCID). *Program availability:* Online learning. *Faculty:* 10 full-time (2 women), 1 part-time/adjunct (0 women). *Students:* 14 full-time (8 women), 13 part-time (6 women); includes 7 minority (5 Black or African American, non-Hispanic/Latino; 1 Asian, non-Hispanic/Latino; 1 Hispanic/Latino), 19 international. Average age 33. In 2019, 8 master's awarded. *Entrance requirements:* For master's, GRE General Test. Additional exam requirements/recommendations for international students: required—TOEFL (minimum score 550 paper-based). *Application deadline:* Applications are processed on a rolling basis. Application fee: $60. Electronic applications accepted. *Unit head:* Dr. Harvey Burnett, Director, 269-471-3152. *Application contact:* Jillian Panigot, Director, University Admissions, 800-253-2874, Fax: 269-471-6321, E-mail: graduate@andrews.edu.

Website: http://www.andrews.edu/grad/programs/community-and-international-development-off-campus.html

Arizona State University at Tempe, College of Liberal Arts and Sciences, School of Geographical Sciences and Urban Planning, Tempe, AZ 85287-5302. Offers geographic information systems (MAS); geographical information science (Graduate Certificate); geography (MA, PhD); transportation systems (Graduate Certificate); urban and environmental planning (MUEP); urban planning (PhD). *Accreditation:* ACSP. Terminal master's awarded for partial completion of doctoral program. *Degree requirements:* For master's, thesis, interactive Program of Study (iPOS) submitted before completing 50 percent of required credit hours; for doctorate, comprehensive exam, thesis/dissertation, interactive Program of Study (iPOS) submitted before completing 50 percent of required credit hours. *Entrance requirements:* For master's and doctorate, GRE, minimum GPA of 3.0 or equivalent in last 2 years of work leading to bachelor's degree. Additional exam requirements/recommendations for international students: required—TOEFL, IELTS, or PTE. Electronic applications accepted. *Expenses:* Contact institution.

Arizona State University at Tempe, College of Public Programs, School of Community Resources and Development, Phoenix, AZ 85004-0685. Offers community resources and development (MS, PhD); nonprofit leadership and management (Graduate Certificate); nonprofit studies (MNpS); sustainable tourism (MAS). *Program availability:* Part-time, evening/weekend. Terminal master's awarded for partial completion of doctoral program. *Degree requirements:* For master's, thesis or alternative, interactive Program of Study (iPOS) submitted before completing 50 percent of required credit hours; for doctorate, comprehensive exam, thesis/dissertation, interactive Program of Study (iPOS) submitted before completing 50 percent of required credit hours. *Entrance requirements:* For master's and doctorate, GRE, minimum GPA of 3.0 or equivalent in last 2 years of work leading to bachelor's degree. Additional exam requirements/recommendations for international students: required—TOEFL, IELTS, or PTE. Electronic applications accepted. *Expenses:* Contact institution.

Arizona State University at Tempe, College of Public Programs, School of Public Affairs, Phoenix, AZ 85004-0687. Offers emergency management and homeland security (MA); program evaluation (MS); public administration (MPA, PhD), including nonprofit administration (MPA), urban management (MPA); public policy (MPP); MPA/

MSW. *Accreditation:* NASPAA (one or more programs are accredited). *Program availability:* Part-time, evening/weekend. Terminal master's awarded for partial completion of doctoral program. *Degree requirements:* For master's, thesis or alternative, policy analysis or capstone project; interactive Program of Study (iPOS) submitted before completing 50 percent of required credit hours; for doctorate, comprehensive exam, thesis/dissertation, interactive Program of Study (iPOS) submitted before completing 50 percent of required credit hours. *Entrance requirements:* For master's, GRE, minimum GPA of 3.0 or equivalent in last 2 years of work leading to bachelor's degree; for doctorate, GRE, minimum GPA of 3.0 or equivalent in last 2 years of work leading to bachelor's degree, 3 letters of recommendation, resume, statement of goals, samples of research reports. Additional exam requirements/recommendations for international students: required—TOEFL (minimum score 600 paper-based; 100 iBT), IELTS (minimum score 6.5). Electronic applications accepted. *Expenses:* Contact institution.

Auburn University, Graduate School, College of Architecture, Design, and Construction, Program in Community Planning, Auburn University, AL 36849. Offers MCP, MPA/MCP. *Program availability:* Part-time. *Faculty:* 4 full-time (3 women), 2 part-time/adjunct (both women). *Students:* 34 full-time (21 women), 3 part-time (0 women); includes 9 minority (4 Black or African American, non-Hispanic/Latino; 1 Asian, non-Hispanic/Latino; 4 Hispanic/Latino), 13 international. Average age 28. 17 applicants, 82% accepted, 6 enrolled. In 2019, 15 master's awarded. *Degree requirements:* For master's, oral exam, project. *Entrance requirements:* For master's, GRE General Test. Additional exam requirements/recommendations for international students: required—TOEFL (minimum score 550 paper-based; 79 iBT), iTEP; recommended—IELTS (minimum score 6.5). *Application deadline:* Applications are processed on a rolling basis. Application fee: $60 ($70 for international students). Electronic applications accepted. *Expenses: Tuition, area resident:* Full-time $9828; part-time $546 per credit hour. Tuition, state resident: full-time $9828; part-time $546 per credit hour. Tuition, nonresident: full-time $29,484; part-time $1638 per credit hour. *International tuition:* $29,744 full-time. Tuition and fees vary according to course load, program and reciprocity agreements. *Financial support:* Federal Work-Study available. Support available to part-time students. Financial award application deadline: 3/15; financial award applicants required to submit FAFSA. *Unit head:* Dr. Jay Mittal, Director, 334-844-8409, E-mail: jzm0029@auburn.edu. *Application contact:* Dr. George Flowers, Dean of the Graduate School, 334-844-2125.
Website: https://cla.auburn.edu/polisci/graduate-programs/master-of-community-planning/

Ball State University, Graduate School, College of Architecture and Planning, Department of Urban Planning, Muncie, IN 47306. Offers urban and regional planning (MURP). *Accreditation:* ACSP. *Program availability:* Part-time. *Degree requirements:* For master's, thesis. *Entrance requirements:* For master's, minimum baccalaureate GPA of 2.75 or 3.0 in latter half of baccalaureate; at least three letters of recommendation (minimum of two from instructors); two-page personal statement (if GPA is below 3.0). Additional exam requirements/recommendations for international students: required—TOEFL (minimum score 550 paper-based; 79 iBT), IELTS (minimum score 6.5). Electronic applications accepted. *Expenses:* Contact institution.

Ball State University, Graduate School, Miller College of Business, Interdepartmental Program in Business Administration, Muncie, IN 47306. Offers business administration (MBA); business essentials (Graduate Certificate); community and economic development (Certificate). *Accreditation:* AACSB. *Program availability:* Part-time, 100% online, blended/hybrid learning. *Entrance requirements:* For master's, GMAT or GRE, minimum baccalaureate GPA of 2.75 or 3.0 in latter half of baccalaureate, resume or curriculum vitae, four professional letters of recommendation. Additional exam requirements/recommendations for international students: required—TOEFL (minimum score 550 paper-based; 79 iBT), IELTS (minimum score 6.5). Electronic applications accepted. *Expenses:* Contact institution.

Boston University, Metropolitan College, Program in City Planning, Boston, MA 02215. Offers MCP. *Program availability:* Part-time, evening/weekend. *Faculty:* 2 full-time (both women), 8 part-time/adjunct (2 women). *Students:* 13 full-time (6 women), 21 part-time (10 women); includes 8 minority (3 Black or African American, non-Hispanic/Latino; 2 Asian, non-Hispanic/Latino; 3 Hispanic/Latino), 10 international. Average age 26. In 2019, 19 master's awarded. *Entrance requirements:* Additional exam requirements/recommendations for international students: required—TOEFL (minimum score 84 iBT). *Application deadline:* For fall admission, 7/15 priority date for international students; for spring admission, 11/15 priority date for international students. Applications are processed on a rolling basis. Application fee: $85. Electronic applications accepted. *Expenses:* Contact institution. *Financial support:* In 2019–20, 3 research assistantships (averaging $8,400 per year), 3 teaching assistantships (averaging $2,500 per year) were awarded; career-related internships or fieldwork and unspecified assistantships also available. Support available to part-time students. Financial award applicants required to submit FAFSA. *Unit head:* Dr. Mary Ellen Mastrorilli, Chair, 617-353-3025, E-mail: memastro@bu.edu. *Application contact:* Dr. Madhu Dutta-Koehler, Assistant Professor and Director, 617-358-3264, Fax: 617-358-3595, E-mail: duttam@bu.edu.
Website: http://www.bu.edu/cityplanning/

California Polytechnic State University, San Luis Obispo, College of Architecture and Environmental Design, Department of City and Regional Planning, San Luis Obispo, CA 93407. Offers MCRP, MCRP/MS. *Accreditation:* ACSP. *Program availability:* Part-time. *Faculty:* 5 full-time (3 women), 2 part-time/adjunct (0 women). *Students:* 24 full-time (9 women), 1 (woman) part-time; includes 7 minority (2 Asian, non-Hispanic/Latino; 4 Hispanic/Latino; 1 Two or more races, non-Hispanic/Latino). Average age 26. 43 applicants, 74% accepted, 15 enrolled. In 2019, 19 master's awarded. *Degree requirements:* For master's, comprehensive exam (for some programs), thesis. *Entrance requirements:* For master's, GRE. Additional exam requirements/recommendations for international students: required—TOEFL (minimum score 80 iBT). *Application deadline:* For fall admission, 4/1 for domestic and international students. Applications are processed on a rolling basis. Application fee: $55. Electronic applications accepted. *Expenses:* Tuition, state resident: full-time $7176; part-time $4164 per year. Tuition, nonresident: full-time $18,690; part-time $8916 per year. *Required fees:* $4206; $3185 per unit. $1061 per term. *Financial support:* Fellowships, research assistantships, career-related internships or fieldwork, institutionally sponsored loans, and unspecified assistantships available. Financial award application deadline: 3/2; financial award applicants required to submit FAFSA. *Unit head:* Kelly Main, Graduate Coordinator, 805-756-2285, E-mail: kdmain@calpoly.edu. *Application contact:* Kelly Main, Graduate Coordinator, 805-756-2285, E-mail: kdmain@calpoly.edu.
Website: http://www.planning.calpoly.edu/

California State Polytechnic University, Pomona, Program in Urban and Regional Planning, Pomona, CA 91768-2557. Offers MURP. *Accreditation:* ACSP. *Program availability:* Part-time, evening/weekend. *Entrance requirements:* Additional exam requirements/recommendations for international students: required—TOEFL (minimum score 580 paper-based). Electronic applications accepted. *Expenses:* Contact institution.

The Catholic University of America, School of Architecture and Planning, Washington, DC 20064. Offers architecture and planning (M Arch, MS Arch St); city and regional planning (M Arch); facilities management (MS Arch); regional development (Certificate); sustainable design (M Arch, Certificate). *Program availability:* Part-time. *Degree requirements:* For master's, thesis. *Entrance requirements:* For master's, GRE (minimum score: 1000), minimum GPA of 2.8, portfolio, statement of purpose, official copies of academic transcripts, three letters of recommendation. Additional exam requirements/recommendations for international students: required—TOEFL (minimum score 550 paper-based; 80 iBT). Electronic applications accepted. *Expenses:* Contact institution.

Clark University, Graduate School, Department of International Development, Community, and Environment, Program in Community Development and Planning, Worcester, MA 01610-1477. Offers MA, MA/MBA. *Degree requirements:* For master's, thesis. *Entrance requirements:* For master's, 2 references, resume or curriculum vitae, personal statement. Additional exam requirements/recommendations for international students: required—TOEFL (minimum score 575 paper-based; 90 iBT), IELTS (minimum score 6.5). Electronic applications accepted. *Expenses:* Contact institution.

Cleveland State University, College of Graduate Studies, Maxine Goodman Levin College of Urban Affairs, Program in Urban Planning and Development, Cleveland, OH 44115. Offers economic development (MUPD); environmental sustainability (MUPD); historic preservation (MUPD); housing and neighborhood development (MUPD); real estate development and finance (MUPD); urban economic development (Certificate); urban geographic information systems (MUPD); JD/MUPDD. *Accreditation:* ACSP. *Program availability:* Part-time, evening/weekend. *Degree requirements:* For master's, thesis or alternative, exit project. *Entrance requirements:* For master's, GRE General Test (minimum score: 50th percentile combined verbal and quantitative, 4.0 analytical writing), minimum GPA of 3.0. Additional exam requirements/recommendations for international students: required—TOEFL (minimum score 550 paper-based; 78 iBT), IELTS (6.0), or International Test of English Proficiency (iTEP). Electronic applications accepted. *Expenses:* Contact institution.

College of Charleston, Graduate School, School of Humanities and Social Sciences, Program in Urban and Regional Planning, Charleston, SC 29424-0001. Offers Certificate. *Program availability:* Part-time, evening/weekend. *Entrance requirements:* Additional exam requirements/recommendations for international students: required—TOEFL (minimum score 81 iBT). Electronic applications accepted.

Columbia University, Graduate School of Architecture, Planning, and Preservation, Program in Urban Planning, New York, NY 10027. Offers MS, PhD, JD/MS, M Arch/MS, MBA/MS, MIA/MS, MPH/MS, MS/MS. *Accreditation:* ACSP (one or more programs are accredited). *Faculty:* 4 full-time (0 women), 12 part-time/adjunct (2 women). *Students:* 64 full-time (38 women). In 2019, 50 master's, 2 doctorates awarded. *Degree requirements:* For master's, thesis. *Entrance requirements:* For master's, GRE General Test. Additional exam requirements/recommendations for international students: required—TOEFL. *Application deadline:* For fall admission, 1/15 for domestic students. Application fee: $75. *Expenses: Tuition:* Full-time $47,600; part-time $1880 per credit. One-time fee: $105. *Financial support:* Fellowships and teaching assistantships available. Financial award application deadline: 1/15. *Unit head:* Weiping Wu, Director, 212-854-0004. *Application contact:* Kevin Smith, Office of Admissions, 212-854-0246.
Website: http://www.arch.columbia.edu/up/

Concordia University, School of Graduate Studies, Faculty of Arts and Science, School of Community and Public Affairs, Montréal, QC H3G 1M8, Canada. Offers community economic development (Diploma).

Cornell University, Graduate School, Graduate Fields of Architecture, Art and Planning, Field of City and Regional Planning, Ithaca, NY 14853. Offers city and regional planning (MRP, PhD); environmental planning and design (MRP, PhD); historic preservation planning (MA); international development planning (MRP, PhD); planning theory and systems analysis (MRP, PhD); regional economics and development planning (MRP, PhD); regional science (MRP, PhD); social and health systems planning (MRP, PhD); urban and regional theory (MRP, PhD); urban planning history (MRP, PhD). *Accreditation:* ACSP (one or more programs are accredited). *Degree requirements:* For master's, thesis (MA); for doctorate, comprehensive exam, thesis/dissertation. *Entrance requirements:* For master's and doctorate, GRE General Test, 2 letters of recommendation. Additional exam requirements/recommendations for international students: required—TOEFL (minimum score 600 paper-based; 77 iBT). Electronic applications accepted.

Cornell University, Graduate School, Graduate Fields of Architecture, Art and Planning, Field of Regional Science, Ithaca, NY 14853. Offers environmental studies (MA, MS, PhD); international spatial problems (MA, MS, PhD); location theory (MA, MS, PhD); multiregional economic analysis (MA, MS, PhD); peace science (MA, MS, PhD); planning methods (MA, MS, PhD); urban and regional economics (MA, MS, PhD). Terminal master's awarded for partial completion of doctoral program. *Degree requirements:* For master's, thesis; for doctorate, comprehensive exam, thesis/dissertation. *Entrance requirements:* For master's and doctorate, GRE General Test, 2 letters of recommendation. Additional exam requirements/recommendations for international students: required—TOEFL (minimum score 600 paper-based; 77 iBT). Electronic applications accepted.

Dalhousie University, Faculty of Architecture and Planning, School of Planning, Halifax, NS B3J 2X4, Canada. Offers M Eng, M Plan, MPS. *Degree requirements:* For master's, thesis. *Entrance requirements:* Additional exam requirements/recommendations for international students: required—TOEFL, IELTS, CANTEST, CAEL, or Michigan English Language Assessment Battery. Electronic applications accepted.

Delta State University, Graduate Programs, College of Arts and Sciences, Division of Social Sciences and History, Program in Community Development, Cleveland, MS 38733-0001. Offers MS. *Program availability:* Part-time. *Degree requirements:* For master's, thesis or alternative. *Expenses: Tuition, area resident:* Full-time $7501; part-time $417 per credit hour. Tuition, state resident: full-time $7501; part-time $417 per credit hour. Tuition, nonresident: full-time $7501; part-time $417 per credit hour. *International tuition:* $7501 full-time. *Required fees:* $170; $9.45 per credit hour. $9.45 per semester.

East Carolina University, Graduate School, Thomas Harriot College of Arts and Sciences, Department of Geography, Planning, and Environment, Greenville, NC 27858-4353. Offers development and environmental planning (Certificate); economic development (Certificate); geographic information science and technology (Certificate); geography (MA), including geography, planning, rural development. *Program availability:* Part-time, evening/weekend, online learning. *Degree requirements:* For master's, comprehensive exam, thesis optional. *Entrance requirements:* For master's, GRE General Test. *Application deadline:* For fall admission, 4/1 priority date for domestic and international students. Applications are processed on a rolling basis. Electronic applications accepted. *Expenses: Tuition, area resident:* Full-time $4749; part-time $185 per credit hour. Tuition, state resident: full-time $4749; part-time $185 per credit hour. Tuition, nonresident: full-time $17,898; part-time $864 per credit hour. *International tuition:* $17,898 full-time. *Required fees:* $2787. *Financial support:* Research assistantships with partial tuition reimbursements, teaching assistantships with partial tuition reimbursements, and Federal Work-Study available. Support available

to part-time students. Financial award application deadline: 3/1. *Unit head:* Dr. Thad Wasklewicz, Chair, 252-328-6230, E-mail: wasklewiczt@ecu.edu. *Application contact:* Graduate Admissions, 252-328-6012, Fax: 252-328-6071, E-mail: gradschool@ecu.edu.
Website: https://geography.ecu.edu/

Eastern Kentucky University, The Graduate School, College of Arts and Sciences, Department of Government, Program in General Public Administration, Richmond, KY 40475-3102. Offers community development (MPA); community health administration (MPA); general public administration (MPA). *Accreditation:* NASPAA. *Program availability:* Part-time, evening/weekend. *Entrance requirements:* For master's, GRE General Test, minimum GPA of 2.5.

Eastern Michigan University, Graduate School, College of Arts and Sciences, Department of Geography and Geology, Programs in Urban and Regional Planning, Ypsilanti, MI 48197. Offers transportation planning and modeling (Graduate Certificate); urban and regional planning (MS). *Students:* 1 full-time (0 women), 5 part-time (3 women); includes 2 minority (both Black or African American, non-Hispanic/Latino). Average age 33. 10 applicants, 50% accepted, 2 enrolled. In 2019, 4 master's awarded. Application fee: $45. *Application contact:* Dr. Heather Khan, Program Advisor, 734-487-8021, Fax: 734-487-6979, E-mail: hkhan3@emich.edu.

East Tennessee State University, College of Graduate and Continuing Studies, College of Arts and Sciences, Department of Political Science, International Affairs and Public Administration, Johnson City, TN 37614. Offers economic development (Postbaccalaureate Certificate); economic development and planning (MPA); local government management (MPA); nonprofit and public financial management (MPA); urban planning (Postbaccalaureate Certificate). *Program availability:* Part-time. *Degree requirements:* For master's, internship, capstone. *Entrance requirements:* For master's, GRE General Test, three letters of recommendation. Additional exam requirements/recommendations for international students: required—TOEFL (minimum score 550 paper-based; 79 iBT). Electronic applications accepted.

Florida Atlantic University, College for Design and Social Inquiry, School of Urban and Regional Planning, Boca Raton, FL 33431-0991. Offers MURP. *Accreditation:* ACSP. *Program availability:* Part-time, evening/weekend. *Faculty:* 5 full-time (1 woman). *Students:* 22 full-time (13 women), 19 part-time (5 women); includes 19 minority (10 Black or African American, non-Hispanic/Latino; 1 Asian, non-Hispanic/Latino; 7 Hispanic/Latino; 1 Two or more races, non-Hispanic/Latino), 3 international. Average age 27. 39 applicants, 64% accepted, 20 enrolled. In 2019, 9 master's awarded. *Entrance requirements:* For master's, GRE General Test, minimum GPA of 3.0. Additional exam requirements/recommendations for international students: required—TOEFL (minimum score 500 paper-based; 61 iBT), IELTS (minimum score 6). *Application deadline:* For fall admission, 5/1 priority date for domestic students, 2/15 for international students; for spring admission, 11/1 priority date for domestic students, 7/15 for international students. Applications are processed on a rolling basis. Application fee: $30. *Expenses: Tuition:* Full-time $20,536; part-time $371.82 per credit hour. Tuition and fees vary according to program. *Financial support:* Fellowships with full tuition reimbursements, research assistantships, career-related internships or fieldwork, Federal Work-Study, institutionally sponsored loans, and tuition waivers (partial) available. Financial award application deadline: 4/1.
Website: http://www.fau.edu/durp/

Florida State University, The Graduate School, College of Social Sciences and Public Policy, Department of Urban and Regional Planning, Tallahassee, FL 32306. Offers planning (MSP); urban and regional planning (PhD); JD/MSP; MA/MSP; MPH/MSP; MSP/MS. *Accreditation:* ACSP (one or more programs are accredited). *Program availability:* Part-time. *Faculty:* 10 full-time (4 women), 16 part-time/adjunct (4 women). *Students:* 75 full-time (32 women), 9 part-time (7 women); includes 30 minority (10 Black or African American, non-Hispanic/Latino; 1 Asian, non-Hispanic/Latino; 11 Hispanic/Latino; 8 Two or more races, non-Hispanic/Latino), 11 international. Average age 29. 111 applicants, 48% accepted, 34 enrolled. In 2019, 37 master's, 4 doctorates awarded. *Degree requirements:* For master's, capstone project, internship; for doctorate, thesis/dissertation. *Entrance requirements:* For master's and doctorate, GRE General Test, minimum GPA of 3.0. Additional exam requirements/recommendations for international students: required—TOEFL (minimum score 600 paper-based; 100 iBT); recommended—IELTS (minimum score 7). *Application deadline:* For fall admission, 2/15 priority date for domestic students, 11/15 priority date for international students; for spring admission, 11/1 for domestic students, 9/1 for international students. Applications are processed on a rolling basis. Application fee: $30. Electronic applications accepted. *Financial support:* In 2019–20, 32 students received support, including fellowships with full tuition reimbursements available (averaging $18,000 per year), 3 research assistantships with full tuition reimbursements available (averaging $9,600 per year), 1 teaching assistantship with full tuition reimbursement available (averaging $18,000 per year); career-related internships or fieldwork, Federal Work-Study, institutionally sponsored loans, and tuition waivers (partial) also available. Financial award application deadline: 2/15; financial award applicants required to submit FAFSA. *Unit head:* Dr. Jeffrey R. Brown, Professor and Chairperson, 850-644-4510, Fax: 850-645-4841, E-mail: jrbrown3@fsu.edu. *Application contact:* Susan A. Taylor, Admissions Coordinator, 850-644-4510, Fax: 850-644-4841, E-mail: durp@coss.fsu.edu.
Website: http://www.coss.fsu.edu/durp/

Future Generations University, Program in Applied Community Change, Franklin, WV 26807. Offers conservation (MA). *Program availability:* Blended/hybrid learning. *Degree requirements:* For master's, portfolio. *Entrance requirements:* For master's, bachelor's degree, community involvement. Additional exam requirements/recommendations for international students: recommended—TOEFL. Electronic applications accepted.

Georgetown University, Graduate School of Arts and Sciences, School of Continuing Studies, Washington, DC 20057. Offers American studies (MALS); applied intelligence (MPS); Catholic studies (MALS); classical civilizations (MALS); emergency and disaster management (MPS); ethics and the professions (MALS); global strategic communications (MPS); hospitality management (MPS); human resources management (MPS); humanities (MALS); individualized study (MALS); integrated marketing communications (MPS); international affairs (MALS); Islam and Muslim-Christian relations (MALS); journalism (MPS); liberal studies (DLS); literature and society (MALS); medieval and early modern European studies (MALS); public relations and corporate communications (MPS); real estate (MPS); religious studies (MALS); social and public policy (MALS); sports industry management (MPS); systems engineering management (MPS); technology management (MPS); the theory and practice of American democracy (MALS); urban and regional planning (MPS); visual culture (MALS). *Entrance requirements:* Additional exam requirements/recommendations for international students: required—TOEFL.

Georgia Institute of Technology, Graduate Studies, College of Design, School of City and Regional Planning, Atlanta, GA 30332-0001. Offers city and regional planning (PhD); economic development (MCRP); environmental planning and management (MCRP); geographic information systems (MCRP); land and community development (MCRP); land use planning (MCRP); transportation (MCRP); urban design (MCRP); MCP/MSCE. *Accreditation:* ACSP. *Degree requirements:* For master's, thesis, internship. *Entrance requirements:* For master's, GRE General Test, minimum GPA of 2.7. Additional exam requirements/recommendations for international students: required—TOEFL. Electronic applications accepted. *Expenses: Tuition, area resident:* Full-time $14,064; part-time $586 per credit hour. Tuition, state resident: full-time $14,064; part-time $586 per credit hour. Tuition, nonresident: full-time $29,140; part-time $1215 per credit hour. *International tuition:* $29,140 full-time. *Required fees:* $2024; $840 per semester. $2096. Tuition and fees vary according to course load.

Georgia State University, Andrew Young School of Policy Studies, Department of Public Management and Policy, Atlanta, GA 30303. Offers criminal justice (MPA); disaster management (Certificate); disaster policy (MPA); environmental policy (PhD); health policy (PhD); management and finance (MPA); nonprofit management (MPA, Certificate); nonprofit policy (MPA); planning and economic development (MPP, Certificate); policy analysis and evaluation (MPA), including planning and economic development; public and nonprofit management (PhD); public finance and budgeting (PhD), including science and technology policy, urban and regional economic development; public finance policy (MPA), including social policy; public health (MPA). *Accreditation:* NASPAA (one or more programs are accredited). *Program availability:* Part-time. *Faculty:* 13 full-time (7 women), 3 part-time/adjunct (1 woman). *Students:* 125 full-time (81 women), 91 part-time (66 women); includes 103 minority (78 Black or African American, non-Hispanic/Latino; 3 Asian, non-Hispanic/Latino; 14 Hispanic/Latino; 8 Two or more races, non-Hispanic/Latino), 31 international. Average age 32. 298 applicants, 60% accepted, 82 enrolled. In 2019, 70 master's, 8 other advanced degrees awarded. Terminal master's awarded for partial completion of doctoral program. *Degree requirements:* For master's, thesis optional; for doctorate, comprehensive exam, thesis/dissertation. *Entrance requirements:* For master's and doctorate, GRE. Additional exam requirements/recommendations for international students: required—TOEFL (minimum score 603 paper-based; 100 iBT) or IELTS (minimum score 7). *Application deadline:* For fall admission, 1/15 for domestic and international students. Application fee: $50. Electronic applications accepted. *Expenses: Tuition, area resident:* Full-time $7164; part-time $398 per credit hour. Tuition, state resident: full-time $7164; part-time $398 per credit hour. Tuition, nonresident: full-time $22,662; part-time $1259 per credit hour. *International tuition:* $22,662 full-time. *Required fees:* $2128; $312 per credit hour. Tuition and fees vary according to course load and program. *Financial support:* In 2019–20, fellowships (averaging $8,194 per year), research assistantships (averaging $8,068 per year), teaching assistantships (averaging $3,600 per year) were awarded; institutionally sponsored loans, scholarships/grants, health care benefits, and unspecified assistantships also available. Financial award application deadline: 2/1. *Unit head:* Dr. Cathy Yang Liu, Chair and Professor, 404-413-0102, Fax: 404-413-0104, E-mail: cyliu@gsu.edu. *Application contact:* Dr. Cathy Yang Liu, Chair and Professor, 404-413-0102, Fax: 404-413-0104, E-mail: cyliu@gsu.edu.
Website: https://aysps.gsu.edu/public-management-policy/

Harvard University, Graduate School of Arts and Sciences, Committee on Architecture, Landscape Architecture, and Urban Planning, Cambridge, MA 02138. Offers architecture (PhD); landscape architecture (PhD); urban planning (PhD). *Accreditation:* ACSP. *Degree requirements:* For doctorate, one foreign language, thesis/dissertation, oral exam. *Entrance requirements:* For doctorate, GRE General Test. Additional exam requirements/recommendations for international students: required—TOEFL.

Harvard University, Graduate School of Design, Department of Urban Planning and Design, Cambridge, MA 02138. Offers urban planning (MUP); urban planning and design (MAUD, MLAUD). *Accreditation:* ACSP (one or more programs are accredited). *Entrance requirements:* For master's, GRE General Test. Additional exam requirements/recommendations for international students: required—TOEFL (minimum score 600 paper-based; 104 iBT). Electronic applications accepted.

Hunter College of the City University of New York, Graduate School, School of Arts and Sciences, Department of Urban Policy and Planning, Program in Urban Planning, New York, NY 10065-5085. Offers MUP, JD/MUP. *Accreditation:* ACSP. *Program availability:* Part-time. *Degree requirements:* For master's, planning studio and internship. *Entrance requirements:* For master's, minimum 12 credits of course work in social sciences, 2 letters of recommendation. Additional exam requirements/recommendations for international students: required—TOEFL.

Indiana University of Pennsylvania, School of Graduate Studies and Research, College of Humanities and Social Sciences, Department of Geography and Regional Planning, Regional Planning Track, Indiana, PA 15705. Offers MS. *Program availability:* Part-time. *Faculty:* 8 full-time (2 women). *Students:* 4 full-time (1 woman); includes 1 minority (Black or African American, non-Hispanic/Latino). Average age 24. 3 applicants, 100% accepted, 2 enrolled. In 2019, 1 master's awarded. *Degree requirements:* For master's, thesis optional. *Entrance requirements:* For master's, goal statement, letters of recommendation, official transcripts. Additional exam requirements/recommendations for international students: required—TOEFL (minimum score 550 paper-based; 80 iBT), IELTS (minimum score 6.5), TOEFL or IELTS. *Application deadline:* Applications are processed on a rolling basis. Application fee: $50. Electronic applications accepted. *Expenses: Tuition, area resident:* Full-time $9288; part-time $516 per credit. Tuition, nonresident: full-time $13,932; part-time $774 per credit. *Required fees:* $4454. One-time fee: $115 full-time. Tuition and fees vary according to course load and program. *Financial support:* In 2019–20, 3 research assistantships with tuition reimbursements (averaging $3,500 per year) were awarded; fellowships with full tuition reimbursements, career-related internships or fieldwork, Federal Work-Study, scholarships/grants, and unspecified assistantships also available. Financial award application deadline: 4/15; financial award applicants required to submit FAFSA. *Unit head:* Dr. Jennifer Smith, Graduate Coordinator, 724-357-2250, E-mail: jsmith@iup.edu. *Application contact:* Dr. Jennifer Smith, Graduate Coordinator, 724-357-2250, E-mail: jsmith@iup.edu.
Website: http://www.iup.edu/georegionalplan/grad/default.aspx

Iowa State University of Science and Technology, Department of Community and Regional Planning, Ames, IA 50011. Offers community and regional planning (MCRP); transportation (MS); M Arch/MCRP; MBA/MCRP; MCRP/MLA; MCRP/MPA. *Accreditation:* ACSP (one or more programs are accredited). *Degree requirements:* For master's, thesis or alternative. *Entrance requirements:* For master's, GRE General Test. Additional exam requirements/recommendations for international students: required—TOEFL (minimum score 550 paper-based; 79 iBT), IELTS (minimum score 6.5). Electronic applications accepted.

Jackson State University, Graduate School, College of Public Service, Department of Urban and Regional Planning, Jackson, MS 39217. Offers MA, PhD. *Accreditation:* ACSP. *Degree requirements:* For master's, comprehensive exam. *Entrance requirements:* For master's, GRE General Test. Additional exam requirements/recommendations for international students: required—TOEFL (minimum score 520 paper-based; 67 iBT).

Kansas State University, Graduate School, College of Architecture, Planning and Design, Department of Landscape Architecture and Regional and Community Planning, Manhattan, KS 66506. Offers community development (MS); landscape architecture (MLA); regional and community planning (MRCP). *Accreditation:* ACSP; ASLA. *Program* availability: Part-time, 100% online. Terminal master's awarded for partial completion of doctoral program. *Degree requirements:* For master's, thesis, oral exam. *Entrance requirements:* Additional exam requirements/recommendations for international students: required—TOEFL (minimum score 600 paper-based), IELTS (minimum score 6.5). Electronic applications accepted.

Lesley University, Graduate School of Arts and Social Sciences, Cambridge, MA 02138-2790. Offers clinical mental health counseling (MA), including holistic counseling, school and community counseling, trauma studies; counseling psychology (MA, CAGS), including professional counseling (MA), school counseling (MA); creative writing (MFA); expressive therapies (MA, PhD, CAGS), including art (MA), clinical mental health counseling (MA), dance (MA), expressive therapies (MA), music (MA); independent studies (CAGS); independent study (MA); intercultural relations (MA, CAGS); interdisciplinary studies (MA), including individualized studies, integrative holistic health, mindfulness studies, peace and conflict transformation, trauma sensitive assessment, intervention, and consultation, women's studies; urban environmental leadership (MA). *Program availability:* Part-time, online learning. *Degree requirements:* For master's, internship, practicum, thesis (for expressive therapies); for doctorate, thesis/dissertation, arts apprenticeship, field placement; for CAGS, thesis, internship (for counseling psychology, expressive therapies). *Entrance requirements:* For master's, MAT (counseling psychology), interview, writing samples, art portfolio; for doctorate, GRE or MAT, interview, master's degree; for CAGS, interview, master's degree. Additional exam requirements/recommendations for international students: required—TOEFL (minimum score 550 paper-based; 80 iBT). Electronic applications accepted.

Massachusetts Institute of Technology, School of Architecture and Planning, Department of Urban Studies and Planning, Cambridge, MA 02139. Offers city planning (MCP); urban and regional planning (PhD); urban and regional studies (PhD); urban studies and planning (SM). *Accreditation:* ACSP (one or more programs are accredited). *Degree requirements:* For master's, thesis; for doctorate, comprehensive exam, thesis/ dissertation. *Entrance requirements:* For master's and doctorate, GRE General Test. Additional exam requirements/recommendations for international students: required—TOEFL, IELTS. Electronic applications accepted.

McGill University, Faculty of Graduate and Postdoctoral Studies, Faculty of Engineering, School of Urban Planning, Montréal, QC H3A 2T5, Canada. Offers environmental planning (MUP); housing (MUP); transportation (MUP); urban design (MUP); urban planning, policy and design (PhD).

Michigan State University, The Graduate School, College of Agriculture and Natural Resources and College of Social Science, School of Planning, Design and Construction, East Lansing, MI 48824. Offers construction management (MS, PhD); environmental design (MA); interior design and facilities management (MA); international planning studies (MIPS); urban and regional planning (MURP). *Degree requirements:* For master's, thesis or alternative. *Entrance requirements:* Additional exam requirements/ recommendations for international students: required—TOEFL. Electronic applications accepted.

Minnesota State University Mankato, College of Graduate Studies and Research, College of Social and Behavioral Sciences, Urban and Regional Studies Institute, Mankato, MN 56001. Offers local government management (Certificate); non-profit leadership (Certificate); urban and regional studies (MA); urban planning (MA, Certificate). *Degree requirements:* For master's, one foreign language, comprehensive exam, thesis or alternative. *Entrance requirements:* For master's, minimum GPA of 3.0 during previous 2 years, 2 letters of recommendation. Additional exam requirements/ recommendations for international students: required—TOEFL. Electronic applications accepted.

Missouri State University, Graduate College, College of Natural and Applied Sciences, Department of Geography, Geology, and Planning, Springfield, MO 65897. Offers geography, geology, and planning (Certificate); natural and applied science (MNAS), including geography, geology and planning; secondary education (MS Ed), including earth science, physical geography. *Program availability:* Part-time, evening/weekend. *Degree requirements:* For master's, comprehensive exam, thesis (for some programs). *Entrance requirements:* For master's, GRE General Test (MS, MNAS), minimum undergraduate GPA of 3.0 (MS, MNAS), 9-12 teacher certification (MS Ed). Additional exam requirements/recommendations for international students: required—TOEFL (minimum score 550 paper-based; 79 iBT), IELTS (minimum score 6). Electronic applications accepted. *Expenses:* Tuition, area resident: Full-time $2600; part-time $1735 per credit hour. Tuition, nonresident: full-time $5240; part-time $3495 per credit hour. *International tuition:* $5240 full-time. *Required fees:* $530; $438 per credit hour. Tuition and fees vary according to class time, course level, course load, degree level, campus/location and program.

Morgan State University, School of Graduate Studies, School of Architecture and Planning, Program in City and Regional Planning, Baltimore, MD 21251. Offers MCRP. *Accreditation:* ACSP. *Program availability:* Part-time, evening/weekend. *Faculty:* 3 full-time (1 woman), 1 part-time/adjunct (0 women). *Students:* 17 full-time (14 women), 14 part-time (11 women); includes 25 minority (21 Black or African American, non-Hispanic/ Latino; 2 Asian, non-Hispanic/Latino; 1 Hispanic/Latino; 1 Two or more races, non-Hispanic/Latino), 1 international. Average age 33. 12 applicants, 92% accepted, 6 enrolled. In 2019, 4 master's awarded. *Degree requirements:* For master's, thesis. *Entrance requirements:* For master's, GRE, Minimum GPA 3.0. Additional exam requirements/recommendations for international students: required—TOEFL (minimum score 550 paper-based; 70 iBT), IELTS (minimum score 6). *Application deadline:* For fall admission, 6/15 for domestic students, 4/1 for international students; for spring admission, 11/15 priority date for domestic students, 10/1 for international students. Applications are processed on a rolling basis. Application fee: $50 ($70 for international students). Electronic applications accepted. *Expenses:* Tuition, state resident: full-time $455; part-time $455 per credit hour. Tuition, nonresident: full-time $894; part-time $894 per credit hour. *Required fees:* $82; $82 per credit hour. *Financial support:* In 2019–20, 2 students received support. Fellowships with full tuition reimbursements available, research assistantships with full tuition reimbursements available, teaching assistantships with full tuition reimbursements available, career-related internships or fieldwork, Federal Work-Study, scholarships/grants, tuition waivers (full and partial), and unspecified assistantships available. Support available to part-time students. Financial award application deadline: 2/1. *Unit head:* Dr. Daniel Campo, Program Director of Graduate Program, 443-885-3514, E-mail: daniel.campo@morgan.edu. *Application contact:* Dr. Jahmaine Smith, Director of Admissions, 443-885-3185, Fax: 443-885-8226, E-mail: gradapply@morgan.edu.
Website: https://morgan.edu/sap/crep

New York University, Tandon School of Engineering, Department of Civil and Urban Engineering, Major in Urban Systems Engineering and Management, New York, NY 10012-1019. Offers urban systems engineering and management (MS). *Entrance requirements:* Additional exam requirements/recommendations for international students: required—TOEFL (minimum score 550 paper-based; 90 iBT); recommended—IELTS (minimum score 7).

New York University, Wagner Graduate School of Public Service, Program in Urban Planning, New York, NY 10012-1019. Offers MUP, JD/MUP. *Accreditation:* ACSP (one

or more programs are accredited). *Program availability:* Part-time. *Degree requirements:* For master's, thesis or alternative, end event capstone program. *Entrance requirements:* Additional exam requirements/recommendations for international students: required— TOEFL (minimum score 100 iBT), IELTS (minimum score 7.5), TWE. Electronic applications accepted.

North Dakota State University, College of Graduate and Interdisciplinary Studies, College of Arts, Humanities and Social Sciences, Department of Sociology and Anthropology, Program in Community Development, Fargo, ND 58102. Offers MA, MS. Electronic applications accepted. Tuition and fees vary according to program and reciprocity agreements.

Northern Arizona University, College of Social and Behavioral Sciences, Department of Geography, Planning, and Recreation, Flagstaff, AZ 86011. Offers applied geospatial sciences (MS); community planning (Certificate); geographic information systems (Certificate); parks and recreation management (MS). *Program availability:* Part-time, 100% online, blended/hybrid learning. *Degree requirements:* For master's, variable foreign language requirement, comprehensive exam (for some programs), thesis (for some programs); for Certificate, comprehensive exam (for some programs). *Entrance requirements:* Additional exam requirements/recommendations for international students: required—TOEFL (minimum score 80 iBT), IELTS (minimum score 6.5). Electronic applications accepted.

Northwest University, College of Social and Behavioral Sciences, Kirkland, WA 98033. Offers counseling psychology (MA, Psy D); international community development (MA). *Program availability:* Evening/weekend. *Entrance requirements:* For master's, 3 character references. Additional exam requirements/recommendations for international students: required—TOEFL (minimum score 580 paper-based). *Expenses:* Contact institution.

The Ohio State University, Graduate School, College of Engineering, Austin E. Knowlton School of Architecture, Columbus, OH 43210. Offers architecture (M Arch); city and regional planning (MCRP, PhD); landscape architecture (M Land Arch). *Accreditation:* ACSP; ASLA. *Entrance requirements:* For master's, GRE or GMAT (city and regional planning), portfolio (for architecture and landscape architecture); for doctorate, GRE or GMAT (city and regional planning), example of research or written work. Additional exam requirements/recommendations for international students: required—TOEFL (minimum score 600 paper-based; 100 iBT), Michigan English Language Assessment Battery (minimum score 86); recommended—IELTS (minimum score 8). Electronic applications accepted.

Pratt Institute, School of Architecture, Program in City and Regional Planning, Brooklyn, NY 11205-3899. Offers MSCRP. *Accreditation:* ACSP. *Program availability:* Part-time. *Students:* 34 full-time (18 women), 14 part-time (9 women); includes 20 minority (6 Black or African American, non-Hispanic/Latino; 4 Asian, non-Hispanic/ Latino; 8 Hispanic/Latino; 2 Two or more races, non-Hispanic/Latino), 9 international. Average age 28. 78 applicants, 94% accepted, 8 enrolled. In 2019, 15 master's awarded. *Degree requirements:* For master's, thesis. *Entrance requirements:* For master's, writing sample, bachelor's degree, transcripts, letters of recommendation, portfolio. Additional exam requirements/recommendations for international students: required—TOEFL (minimum score 575 paper-based; 90 iBT). *Application deadline:* For fall admission, 1/5 for domestic and international students; for spring admission, 10/1 for domestic and international students. Application fee: $50 ($90 for international students). Electronic applications accepted. *Expenses:* Tuition: Full-time $33,246; part-time $1847 per credit. *Required fees:* $1980. *Financial support:* Career-related internships or fieldwork, Federal Work-Study, institutionally sponsored loans, scholarships/grants, health care benefits, and unspecified assistantships available. Support available to part-time students. Financial award application deadline: 2/1; financial award applicants required to submit FAFSA. *Unit head:* Eve Baron, Chairperson, 718-687-5641, Fax: 718-636-3709, E-mail: ebaron@pratt.edu. *Application contact:* Natalie Capannelli, Director of Graduate Admissions, 718-636-3551, Fax: 718-399-4242, E-mail: ncapanne@pratt.edu.
Website: https://www.pratt.edu/academics/architecture/city-and-regional-planning/

Pratt Institute, School of Architecture, Program in Urban Placemaking and Management, Brooklyn, NY 11205-3899. Offers MS. *Students:* 15 full-time (14 women); includes 2 minority (1 Hispanic/Latino; 1 Two or more races, non-Hispanic/Latino), 5 international. Average age 27. 24 applicants, 92% accepted, 7 enrolled. In 2019, 15 master's awarded. *Degree requirements:* For master's, thesis. *Entrance requirements:* For master's, resume, writing sample, work sample or portfolio. Additional exam requirements/recommendations for international students: required—TOEFL (minimum score 575 paper-based; 90 iBT). *Application deadline:* For fall admission, 1/5 for domestic and international students; for spring admission, 10/1 for domestic and international students. Application fee: $50 ($90 for international students). Electronic applications accepted. *Expenses:* Tuition: Full-time $33,246; part-time $1847 per credit. *Required fees:* $1980. *Financial support:* Career-related internships or fieldwork, Federal Work-Study, institutionally sponsored loans, scholarships/grants, health care benefits, and unspecified assistantships available. Support available to part-time students. Financial award application deadline: 2/1; financial award applicants required to submit FAFSA. *Unit head:* David Burney, Coordinator, 718-399-4323, E-mail: dburn153@pratt.edu. *Application contact:* Natalie Capannelli, Director of Graduate Admissions, 718-636-3551, Fax: 718-399-4242, E-mail: ncapanne@pratt.edu.
Website: https://www.pratt.edu/academics/architecture/urban-placemaking-and-management/

Queen's University at Kingston, School of Graduate Studies, Faculty of Arts and Science, School of Urban and Regional Planning, Kingston, ON K7L 3N6, Canada. Offers M Pl. *Program availability:* Part-time. *Degree requirements:* For master's, thesis optional. *Entrance requirements:* Additional exam requirements/recommendations for international students: required—TOEFL (minimum score 580 paper-based).

Roger Williams University, School of Architecture, Art and Historic Preservation, Bristol, RI 02809. Offers architecture (M Arch); art and architectural history (MA); historical preservation (MS, Certificate); urban and regional planning (Certificate). *Program availability:* Part-time. *Faculty:* 8 full-time (4 women), 6 part-time/adjunct (1 woman). *Students:* 97 full-time (46 women), 10 part-time (0 women); includes 15 minority (1 Black or African American, non-Hispanic/Latino; 1 American Indian or Alaska Native, non-Hispanic/Latino; 1 Asian, non-Hispanic/Latino; 8 Hispanic/Latino; 4 Two or more races, non-Hispanic/Latino), 5 international. Average age 23. 97 applicants, 92% accepted, 54 enrolled. In 2019, 48 master's awarded. *Degree requirements:* For master's, thesis. *Entrance requirements:* For master's, letter of intent, transcripts, 2 letters of recommendation, portfolio (Architecture only), writing sample (Preservation only); for Certificate, transcripts. Additional exam requirements/recommendations for international students: required—TOEFL (minimum score 85 paper-based), IELTS (minimum score 6.5). *Application deadline:* For fall admission, 1/15 for domestic students, 5/1 for international students. Application fee: $50. Electronic applications accepted. *Expenses:* Tuition per credit hour: Architecture: $1579, Preservation: $951. *Financial support:* In 2019–20, 103 students received support. Scholarships/grants and unspecified assistantships available. Financial award application deadline: 3/15; financial award applicants required to submit FAFSA. *Unit head:* Stephen White, Dean,

401-254-3607, E-mail: swhite@rwu.edu. *Application contact:* Gregory Laramie, Associate Dean, 401-254-3743, E-mail: glaramie@rwu.edu.
Website: https://www.rwu.edu/academics/schools-and-colleges/saahp

Rutgers University - New Brunswick, Edward J. Bloustein School of Planning and Public Policy, Doctoral Program in Planning and Public Policy, New Brunswick, NJ 08901. Offers PhD. *Program availability:* Part-time. *Degree requirements:* For doctorate, comprehensive exam, thesis/dissertation. *Entrance requirements:* For doctorate, GRE, master's degree. Additional exam requirements/recommendations for international students: required—TOEFL (minimum score 575 paper-based; 88 iBT). Electronic applications accepted.

Rutgers University - New Brunswick, Edward J. Bloustein School of Planning and Public Policy, Program in Urban Planning and Policy Development, New Brunswick, NJ 08901. Offers MCRP, MCRS, JD/MCRP, MBA/MCRP. *Accreditation:* ACSP (one or more programs are accredited). *Program availability:* Part-time, evening/weekend. *Entrance requirements:* For master's, GRE General Test. Additional exam requirements/recommendations for international students: required—TOEFL (minimum score 575 paper-based; 88 iBT). Electronic applications accepted.

St. Francis Xavier University, Graduate Studies, Department of Adult Education, Antigonish, NS B2G 2W5, Canada. Offers adult education (M Ad Ed); community development (M Ad Ed). *Program availability:* Part-time, online learning. *Degree requirements:* For master's, thesis. *Entrance requirements:* For master's, minimum undergraduate B average, 2 years of work experience in field. Additional exam requirements/recommendations for international students: required—TOEFL (minimum score 580 paper-based). *Expenses: Tuition, area resident:* Part-time $1731 Canadian dollars per course. Tuition, state resident: part-time $1731 Canadian dollars per course. Tuition, nonresident: part-time $1988 Canadian dollars per course. *International tuition:* $3976 Canadian dollars full-time. *Required fees:* $185 Canadian dollars per course. Tuition and fees vary according to course level, course load, degree level and program.

Saint Louis University, Graduate Programs, College for Public Health and Social Justice, Program in Urban Planning, St. Louis, MO 63103. Offers urban planning and development (MS). *Program availability:* Part-time. *Degree requirements:* For master's, comprehensive exam (for some programs), thesis (for some programs). *Entrance requirements:* For master's, GMAT, GRE General Test, or LSAT, three letters of recommendation, resume, professional goal statement, minimum GPA of 3.0. Additional exam requirements/recommendations for international students: required—TOEFL (minimum score 525 paper-based). Electronic applications accepted.

San Diego State University, Graduate and Research Affairs, College of Professional Studies and Fine Arts, School of Public Affairs, Program in City Planning, San Diego, CA 92182. Offers MCP. *Program availability:* Part-time. *Entrance requirements:* For master's, GRE General Test. Additional exam requirements/recommendations for international students: required—TOEFL. Electronic applications accepted.

Savannah State University, Master of Public Administration Program, Savannah, GA 31404. Offers city management (MPA); human resources (MPA). *Accreditation:* NASPAA. *Program availability:* Part-time. *Degree requirements:* For master's, comprehensive exam, thesis, public service internship, capstone seminar. *Entrance requirements:* For master's, GRE General Test, GMAT, or MAT, minimum cumulative GPA of 2.5, 3 letters of recommendation, essay, official transcripts, resume, essay of 500-1000 words detailing reasons for pursuing degree. Additional exam requirements/recommendations for international students: required—TOEFL. Electronic applications accepted. *Expenses:* Contact institution.

Southeastern University, College of Behavioral & Social Sciences, Lakeland, FL 33801. Offers human services (MA); international community development (MA); pastoral care and counseling (MS); professional counseling (MS); school counseling (MS); social work (MSW). *Program availability:* Evening/weekend. *Faculty:* 17 full-time (12 women). *Students:* 95 full-time (80 women), 9 part-time (6 women); includes 49 minority (18 Black or African American, non-Hispanic/Latino; 3 Asian, non-Hispanic/Latino; 25 Hispanic/Latino; 1 Native Hawaiian or other Pacific Islander, non-Hispanic/Latino; 2 Two or more races, non-Hispanic/Latino), 1 international. Average age 28. In 2019, 50 master's awarded. *Entrance requirements:* Additional exam requirements/recommendations for international students: required—TOEFL (minimum score 76 iBT), IELTS (minimum score 6). Application fee: $50. Electronic applications accepted. *Unit head:* Dr. Erica H. Sirrine, Dean, 863-667-5341, E-mail: ehsirrine@seu.edu. *Application contact:* Dr. Erica H. Sirrine, Dean, 863-667-5341, E-mail: ehsirrine@seu.edu.
Website: http://www.seu.edu/behavior/

Southern California Institute of Architecture, Center for Advanced Studies, Los Angeles, CA 90013. Offers architectural technologies (MS); design of cities (MS); design theory and pedagogy (MS); fiction and entertainment (MS).

State University of New York College of Environmental Science and Forestry, Department of Landscape Architecture, Syracuse, NY 13210-2779. Offers community design and planning (MLA, MS); cultural landscape studies and conservation (MLA, MS); landscape and urban ecology (MLA, MS). *Accreditation:* ASLA (one or more programs are accredited). *Program availability:* Part-time. *Faculty:* 10 full-time (4 women), 7 part-time/adjunct (5 women). *Students:* 19 full-time (13 women), 5 international. Average age 27. 21 applicants, 95% accepted, 7 enrolled. In 2019, 9 master's awarded. *Degree requirements:* For master's, comprehensive exam (for some programs), thesis (for some programs). *Entrance requirements:* For master's, GRE General Test, minimum GPA of 3.0. Additional exam requirements/recommendations for international students: required—TOEFL (minimum score 550 paper-based; 80 iBT), IELTS (minimum score 6), or STEP Eiken (grade 1). *Application deadline:* For fall admission, 2/1 priority date for domestic and international students; for spring admission, 11/1 priority date for domestic and international students. Applications are processed on a rolling basis. Application fee: $60. Electronic applications accepted. *Expenses:* Tuition, state resident: full-time $11,310; part-time $472 per credit hour. Tuition, nonresident: full-time $23,100; part-time $963 per credit hour. *Required fees:* $1890; $95.21 per credit hour. *Financial support:* In 2019–20, 10 students received support. Unspecified assistantships available. Financial award application deadline: 6/30; financial award applicants required to submit FAFSA. *Unit head:* Dr. Douglas Johnston, Chair, 315-470-6544, Fax: 315-470-6540, E-mail: dmjohnst@esf.edu. *Application contact:* Scott Shannon, Associate Provost for Instruction/Dean of the Graduate School, 315-470-6599, Fax: 315-470-6978, E-mail: esfgrad@esf.edu.
Website: http://www.esf.edu/la/

State University of New York College of Environmental Science and Forestry, Program in Environmental Science, Syracuse, NY 13210-2779. Offers biophysical and ecological economics (MPS); coupled natural and human systems (MPS); ecosystem restoration (MPS); environmental and community land planning (MPS, MS); environmental and natural resources policy (PhD); environmental communication and participatory processes (PhD); environmental monitoring and modeling (MPS); water and wetland resource studies (MPS, MS). *Program availability:* Part-time. *Faculty:* 1 full-time (0 women), 1 (woman) part-time/adjunct. *Students:* 62 full-time (40 women), 12 part-time (9 women); includes 8 minority (1 Black or African American, non-Hispanic/Latino; 4 American Indian or Alaska Native, non-Hispanic/Latino; 2 Asian, non-Hispanic/Latino; 1 Hispanic/Latino), 28 international. Average age 31. 68 applicants, 84% accepted, 26 enrolled. In 2019, 10 master's, 2 doctorates awarded. Terminal master's awarded for partial completion of doctoral program. *Degree requirements:* For master's, thesis (for some programs); for doctorate, comprehensive exam, thesis/dissertation. *Entrance requirements:* For master's and doctorate, GRE General Test, minimum GPA of 3.0. Additional exam requirements/recommendations for international students: required—TOEFL (minimum score 550 paper-based; 80 iBT), IELTS (minimum score 6). *Application deadline:* For fall admission, 2/1 priority date for domestic and international students; for spring admission, 11/1 priority date for domestic and international students. Applications are processed on a rolling basis. Application fee: $60. Electronic applications accepted. *Expenses:* Tuition, state resident: full-time $11,310; part-time $472 per credit hour. Tuition, nonresident: full-time $23,100; part-time $963 per credit hour. *Required fees:* $1890; $95.21 per credit hour. *Financial support:* In 2019–20, 15 students received support. Unspecified assistantships available. Financial award application deadline: 6/30; financial award applicants required to submit FAFSA. *Unit head:* Dr. Russell Briggs, Director of the Division of Environmental Science, 315-470-6989, Fax: 315-470-6700, E-mail: rdbriggs@esf.edu. *Application contact:* Laura Payne, Office of Instruction and Graduate Studies, 315-470-6599, E-mail: esfgrad@esf.edu.
Website: http://www.esf.edu/environmentalscience/graduate/

Syracuse University, Maxwell School of Citizenship and Public Affairs, CAS Program in Public Infrastructure Management and Leadership, Syracuse, NY 13244. Offers CAS. *Program availability:* Part-time. *Entrance requirements:* For degree, personal statement, resume, three letters of recommendation, official transcripts. Additional exam requirements/recommendations for international students: required—TOEFL.

Texas A&M University, College of Architecture, Department of Landscape Architecture and Urban Planning, College Station, TX 77843. Offers land and property development (MLPD); landscape architecture (MLA); urban and regional planning (MUP); urban and regional science (PhD). *Accreditation:* ACSP (one or more programs are accredited); ASLA (one or more programs are accredited). *Faculty:* 33. *Students:* 151 full-time (75 women), 14 part-time (6 women); includes 33 minority (6 Black or African American, non-Hispanic/Latino; 1 American Indian or Alaska Native, non-Hispanic/Latino; 8 Asian, non-Hispanic/Latino; 18 Hispanic/Latino), 70 international. Average age 28. 179 applicants, 64% accepted, 49 enrolled. In 2019, 68 master's, 5 doctorates awarded. Terminal master's awarded for partial completion of doctoral program. *Degree requirements:* For master's, comprehensive exam (for some programs), thesis (for some programs), professional internship; for doctorate, comprehensive exam, thesis/dissertation, seminar. *Entrance requirements:* For master's, GRE General Test, portfolio (MLA), letters of recommendation; for doctorate, GRE General Test, writing sample (URSC), letters of recommendation. Additional exam requirements/recommendations for international students: required—TOEFL (minimum score 550 paper-based; 80 iBT), IELTS (minimum score 6), PTE (minimum score 53). *Application deadline:* For fall admission, 12/1 priority date for domestic and international students. Applications are processed on a rolling basis. Application fee: $65 ($90 for international students). Electronic applications accepted. *Expenses:* Contact institution. *Financial support:* In 2019–20, 125 students received support, including 3 fellowships with tuition reimbursements available (averaging $21,706 per year), 38 research assistantships with tuition reimbursements available (averaging $10,851 per year), 14 teaching assistantships with tuition reimbursements available (averaging $12,905 per year); career-related internships or fieldwork, institutionally sponsored loans, scholarships/grants, traineeships, health care benefits, tuition waivers (full and partial), and unspecified assistantships also available. Support available to part-time students. Financial award application deadline: 12/1; financial award applicants required to submit FAFSA. *Unit head:* Dr. Shannon Van Zandt, Head, 979-458-1223, E-mail: svanzandt@tamu.edu. *Application contact:* Brandi Blankenship, Administrative Coordinator & Graduate Advisor, E-mail: bblankenship@arch.tamu.edu.
Website: http://laup.arch.tamu.edu/

Texas Southern University, Barbara Jordan-Mickey Leland School of Public Affairs, Program in Urban Planning and Environmental Policy, Houston, TX 77004-4584. Offers MS, PhD. *Accreditation:* ACSP. *Program availability:* Part-time, evening/weekend. *Degree requirements:* For master's, comprehensive exam, thesis optional. *Entrance requirements:* For master's, GRE General Test, minimum GPA of 2.5. Additional exam requirements/recommendations for international students: required—TOEFL. Electronic applications accepted.

Thomas Edison State University, John S. Watson School of Public Service and Continuing Studies, Trenton, NJ 08608. Offers community and economic development (MSM); environmental policy/environmental justice (MSM); homeland security (MSHS, MSM); information and technology for public service (MSM); nonprofit management (MSM); public and municipal finance (MSM); public health (MSM); public service administration and leadership (MSM); public service leadership (MPSL). *Program availability:* Part-time, online learning. *Entrance requirements:* Additional exam requirements/recommendations for international students: required—TOEFL (minimum score 550 paper-based; 79 iBT). Electronic applications accepted.

Thomas Jefferson University, College of Architecture and the Built Environment, Program in Geospatial Technology for Geodesign, Philadelphia, PA 19107. Offers MS. *Program availability:* Part-time.

Tufts University, Graduate School of Arts and Sciences, Department of Urban and Environmental Policy and Planning, Medford, MA 02155. Offers community development (MA); environmental policy (MA); health and human welfare (MA); housing policy (MA); international environment/development policy (MA); public policy (MPP); MA/JD; MA/MBA; MA/MPH; MA/MS; MALD/MA. *Accreditation:* ACSP (one or more programs are accredited). *Program availability:* Part-time. *Degree requirements:* For master's, thesis or alternative, internship. *Entrance requirements:* For master's, GRE General Test. Additional exam requirements/recommendations for international students: required—TOEFL (minimum score 550 paper-based; 80 iBT), IELTS (minimum score 6.5). Electronic applications accepted. *Expenses:* Contact institution.

Université de Montréal, Faculty of Environmental Design and Planning, Montréal, QC H3C 3J7, Canada. Offers environmental design and planning (M Sc A, PhD); environmental planning and design projects (DESS); game design (DESS); urban management for developing countries (DESS); urban planning (M Urb). *Accreditation:* ACSP. *Degree requirements:* For doctorate, thesis/dissertation, general exam. Electronic applications accepted. *Expenses:* Contact institution.

Université du Québec à Rimouski, Graduate Programs, Program in Regional Development, Rimouski, QC G5L 3A1, Canada. Offers MA, PhD, Diploma. *Program availability:* Part-time. *Degree requirements:* For master's, thesis. *Entrance requirements:* For master's, appropriate bachelor's degree, proficiency in French.

Université du Québec en Outaouais, Graduate Programs, Program in Regional Development, Gatineau, QC J8X 3X7, Canada. Offers MA. *Program availability:* Part-time. *Degree requirements:* For master's, thesis (for some programs).

University at Albany, State University of New York, College of Arts and Sciences, Department of Geography and Planning, Albany, NY 12222-0001. Offers geographic information science (Certificate); geography (MA); regional planning (MRP); urban policy (Certificate). *Program availability:* Part-time, blended/hybrid learning. *Faculty:* 12 full-time (3 women), 10 part-time/adjunct (3 women). *Students:* 46 full-time (19 women), 23 part-time (10 women); includes 13 minority (6 Black or African American, non-Hispanic/Latino; 2 Asian, non-Hispanic/Latino; 5 Hispanic/Latino), 9 international. 20 applicants, 100% accepted, 12 enrolled. In 2019, 20 master's, 9 other advanced degrees awarded. *Entrance requirements:* For master's, transcripts of all schools attended, statement of background and goals, departmental questionnaire, resume, names and contact information for 3 recommenders. Additional exam requirements/recommendations for international students: required—TOEFL (minimum score 550 paper-based). *Application deadline:* For fall admission, 7/15 for domestic students, 5/1 for international students; for spring admission, 11/15 for domestic and international students. Applications are processed on a rolling basis. Application fee: $75. Electronic applications accepted. *Expenses:* Tuition, area resident: Full-time $11,530; part-time $480 per credit hour. Tuition, nonresident: full-time $23,530; part-time $980 per credit hour. *International tuition:* $23,530 full-time. *Required fees:* $2185; $96 per credit hour. Part-time tuition and fees vary according to course load and program. *Financial support:* Fellowships, teaching assistantships, career-related internships or fieldwork, Federal Work-Study, and institutionally sponsored loans available. Financial award application deadline: 3/1. *Unit head:* Catherine Lawson, Chair, 518-442-4636, Fax: 518-442-4742, E-mail: lawsonc@albany.edu. *Application contact:* Michael DeRensis, Director, Graduate Admissions, 518-442-3980, Fax: 518-442-3922, E-mail: graduate@albany.edu. Website: https://www.albany.edu/gp/

University at Buffalo, the State University of New York, Graduate School, School of Architecture and Planning, Department of Urban and Regional Planning, Buffalo, NY 14214. Offers economic development (MUP); environment/land use (MUP); health and food systems (MUP); historic preservation (MUP, Certificate); neighborhood/community development (MUP); real estate development (MSRED); urban and regional planning (PhD); urban design (MUP); JD/MUP; M Arch/MUP. *Accreditation:* ACSP. *Program availability:* Part-time. *Faculty:* 11 full-time (4 women), 15 part-time/adjunct (6 women). *Students:* 88 full-time (40 women), 25 part-time (10 women); includes 32 minority (16 Black or African American, non-Hispanic/Latino; 2 Asian, non-Hispanic/Latino; 7 Hispanic/Latino; 7 Two or more races, non-Hispanic/Latino), 13 international. Average age 26. 146 applicants, 40% accepted, 40 enrolled. In 2019, 31 master's, 1 doctorate, 4 other advanced degrees awarded. *Degree requirements:* For master's, thesis or alternative, project; for doctorate, comprehensive exam, thesis/dissertation, dissertation. *Entrance requirements:* For master's, resume, two letters of recommendation, personal statement, transcripts; for doctorate, GRE, transcripts, three letters of recommendation, resume, research statement, writing sample. Additional exam requirements/recommendations for international students: required—TOEFL (minimum score 79 iBT), IELTS (minimum score 6.5). *Application deadline:* For fall admission, 3/1 priority date for domestic and international students; for spring admission, 10/31 priority date for domestic students, 10/1 priority date for international students. Applications are processed on a rolling basis. Application fee: $75. Electronic applications accepted. *Expenses:* Tuition, area resident: Full-time $11,310; part-time $471 per credit hour. Tuition, state resident: full-time $11,310; part-time $471 per credit hour. Tuition, nonresident: full-time $23,100; part-time $963 per credit hour. *International tuition:* $23,100 full-time. *Required fees:* $2820. *Financial support:* In 2019–20, 54 students received support, including 5 fellowships with full tuition reimbursements available (averaging $22,560 per year), 1 research assistantship with partial tuition reimbursement available (averaging $16,027 per year), 20 teaching assistantships with partial tuition reimbursements available (averaging $6,912 per year); career-related internships or fieldwork, Federal Work-Study, institutionally sponsored loans, scholarships/grants, health care benefits, tuition waivers (full and partial), and unspecified assistantships also available. Financial award application deadline: 3/1; financial award applicants required to submit FAFSA. *Unit head:* Dr. Daniel B. Hess, Professor and Chair, 716-829-5326, Fax: 716-829-3256, E-mail: dbhess@buffalo.edu. *Application contact:* Norma Everett, Graduate Programs Coordinator, 716-829-3283, Fax: 716-829-3256, E-mail: norma.everett@buffalo.edu. Website: http://www.ap.buffalo.edu/planning/

The University of Arizona, College of Architecture, Planning, and Landscape Architecture, Planning Program, Tucson, AZ 85721. Offers MS. *Accreditation:* ACSP. *Entrance requirements:* For master's, GRE, 3 letters of recommendation, letter of intent. Additional exam requirements/recommendations for international students: required—TOEFL (minimum score 573 paper-based; 80 iBT). Electronic applications accepted.

The University of British Columbia, Faculty of Applied Science, School of Community and Regional Planning, Vancouver, BC V6T 1Z2, Canada. Offers M Sc P, MAP, MCRP, PhD. *Accreditation:* ACSP. *Degree requirements:* For master's, thesis; for doctorate, thesis/dissertation, oral exam. *Entrance requirements:* For master's, GRE (recommended); for doctorate, MCRP or equivalent. Additional exam requirements/recommendations for international students: required—TOEFL. Electronic applications accepted. *Expenses:* Contact institution.

University of California, Berkeley, Graduate Division, College of Environmental Design, Department of City and Regional Planning, Berkeley, CA 94720. Offers MCP, PhD; JD/MCP, M Arch/MCP, MCP/MPH, MCP/MS, MLA/MCP. *Accreditation:* ACSP. *Degree requirements:* For master's, comprehensive exam (for some programs), thesis (for some programs), professional project or thesis; for doctorate, thesis/dissertation, qualifying exam. *Entrance requirements:* For master's and doctorate, GRE General Test, minimum GPA of 3.0, 3 letters of recommendation. Additional exam requirements/recommendations for international students: required—TOEFL (minimum score 570 paper-based; 90 iBT). Electronic applications accepted.

University of California, Davis, Graduate Studies, Graduate Group in Community Development, Davis, CA 95616. Offers MS. *Degree requirements:* For master's, comprehensive exam (for some programs), thesis (for some programs). *Entrance requirements:* For master's, GRE General Test, minimum GPA of 3.0. Additional exam requirements/recommendations for international students: required—TOEFL (minimum score 550 paper-based). Electronic applications accepted.

University of California, Irvine, School of Social Ecology, Department of Urban Planning and Public Policy, Irvine, CA 92697. Offers planning, policy and design (PhD); urban and regional planning (MURP). *Accreditation:* ACSP (one or more programs are accredited). *Students:* 122 full-time (85 women); includes 65 minority (6 Black or African American, non-Hispanic/Latino; 15 Asian, non-Hispanic/Latino; 38 Hispanic/Latino; 1 Native Hawaiian or other Pacific Islander, non-Hispanic/Latino; 5 Two or more races, non-Hispanic/Latino), 31 international. Average age 28. 306 applicants, 64% accepted, 55 enrolled. In 2019, 50 master's, 1 doctorate awarded. *Degree requirements:* For doctorate, thesis/dissertation, research project. *Entrance requirements:* For master's and doctorate, GRE General Test, minimum GPA of 3.0. Additional exam requirements/recommendations for international students: required—TOEFL (minimum score 550 paper-based). *Application deadline:* For fall admission, 1/15 priority date for domestic and international students. Application fee: $120 ($140 for international students). Electronic applications accepted. *Financial support:* Fellowships, research assistantships with full tuition reimbursements, teaching assistantships, institutionally sponsored loans, traineeships, health care benefits, and unspecified assistantships available. Financial award application deadline: 1/15; financial award applicants required to submit FAFSA. *Unit head:* David L. Feldman, Chair, 949-824-4384, Fax: 949-824-3056, E-mail: feldmand@uci.edu. *Application contact:* Janet Gallagher, Graduate Coordinator, 949-824-9849, Fax: 949-824-8566, E-mail: janetg@uci.edu. Website: http://uppp.soceco.uci.edu/

University of California, Los Angeles, Graduate Division, Luskin School of Public Affairs, Department of Urban Planning, Los Angeles, CA 90095. Offers MA, PhD, JD/MA, MA/MA, MBA/MA. *Accreditation:* ACSP (one or more programs are accredited). *Degree requirements:* For master's, comprehensive exam or thesis; for doctorate, thesis/dissertation, oral and written qualifying exams. *Entrance requirements:* For master's, GRE General Test (recommended); for doctorate, GRE General Test, master's degree in urban planning or related field. Additional exam requirements/recommendations for international students: required—TOEFL. Electronic applications accepted.

University of Central Arkansas, Graduate School, College of Natural Sciences and Math, Department of Geography, Conway, AR 72035-0001. Offers community and economic development (MS); geographic information systems (MGIS, Certificate). *Program availability:* Part-time, online learning. *Entrance requirements:* Additional exam requirements/recommendations for international students: required—TOEFL (minimum score 550 paper-based). Electronic applications accepted.

University of Central Florida, College of Community Innovation and Education, School of Public Administration, Orlando, FL 32816. Offers emergency management and homeland security (Certificate); fundraising (Certificate); nonprofit management (MNM, Certificate); public administration (MPA); research administration (MRA); urban and regional planning (MS). *Accreditation:* NASPAA. *Program availability:* Part-time, evening/weekend. *Students:* 149 full-time (95 women), 497 part-time (347 women); includes 277 minority (128 Black or African American, non-Hispanic/Latino; 1 American Indian or Alaska Native, non-Hispanic/Latino; 13 Asian, non-Hispanic/Latino; 118 Hispanic/Latino; 1 Native Hawaiian or other Pacific Islander, non-Hispanic/Latino; 16 Two or more races, non-Hispanic/Latino), 9 international. Average age 33. 430 applicants, 79% accepted, 226 enrolled. In 2019, 106 master's, 26 other advanced degrees awarded. *Degree requirements:* For master's, comprehensive exam, thesis or alternative, research report. *Entrance requirements:* For master's, letters of recommendation, goal statement, resume. Additional exam requirements/recommendations for international students: required—TOEFL. *Application deadline:* For fall admission, 6/15 for domestic students; for spring admission, 11/1 for domestic students. Application fee: $30. Electronic applications accepted. *Financial support:* In 2019–20, 6 students received support, including 1 fellowship with partial tuition reimbursement available (averaging $5,000 per year), 4 research assistantships with partial tuition reimbursements available (averaging $6,049 per year), 1 teaching assistantship with partial tuition reimbursement available (averaging $5,478 per year); career-related internships or fieldwork, Federal Work-Study, institutionally sponsored loans, health care benefits, tuition waivers (partial), and unspecified assistantships also available. Financial award application deadline: 3/1; financial award applicants required to submit FAFSA. *Unit head:* Dr. Naim Kapucu, Director, 407-823-6096, Fax: 407-823-5651, E-mail: kapucu@ucf.edu. *Application contact:* Associate Director, Graduate Admissions, 407-823-2766, Fax: 407-823-6442, E-mail: gradadmissions@ucf.edu. Website: https://www.cohpa.ucf.edu/publicadmin/

University of Central Oklahoma, The Jackson College of Graduate Studies, College of Liberal Arts, Department of Political Science, Edmond, OK 73034-5209. Offers political science (MA), including international affairs; public administration (MPA), including public and nonprofit management, urban management. *Program availability:* Part-time. *Degree requirements:* For master's, comprehensive exam (for some programs), thesis (for some programs). *Entrance requirements:* For master's, 18 undergraduate hours in political science. Additional exam requirements/recommendations for international students: required—TOEFL (minimum score 550 paper-based; 79 iBT), IELTS (minimum score 6.5). Electronic applications accepted.

University of Cincinnati, Graduate School, College of Design, Architecture, Art, and Planning, School of Planning, Program in Community Planning, Cincinnati, OH 45221. Offers MCP, JD/MCP. *Accreditation:* ACSP. *Degree requirements:* For master's, thesis. *Entrance requirements:* For master's, GRE General Test. Additional exam requirements/recommendations for international students: required—TOEFL.

University of Colorado Denver, College of Architecture and Planning, Program in Design and Planning, Denver, CO 80217. Offers history of architecture, landscape and urbanism (PhD); sustainable and healthy environments (PhD). *Program availability:* Part-time. *Degree requirements:* For doctorate, comprehensive exam, thesis/dissertation. *Entrance requirements:* For doctorate, GRE (minimum score of 158 for both verbal and quantitative; writing 4.0), minimum undergraduate GPA of 3.0, graduate 3.5; writing sample; three letters of recommendation; statement of personal and professional goals. Additional exam requirements/recommendations for international students: required—TOEFL (minimum score 80 iBT); recommended—IELTS (minimum score 6.8). Electronic applications accepted. *Expenses:* Contact institution.

University of Colorado Denver, College of Architecture and Planning, Program in Urban and Regional Planning, Denver, CO 80217. Offers economic and community development planning (MURP); land use and environmental planning (MURP); urban place making (MURP). *Accreditation:* ACSP. *Program availability:* Part-time. *Degree requirements:* For master's, thesis, minimum of 51 semester hours. *Entrance requirements:* For master's, GRE (for students with an undergraduate GPA below 3.0), sample of writing or work project; statement of interest; resume; three letters of recommendation. Additional exam requirements/recommendations for international students: required—TOEFL (minimum score 75 iBT). Electronic applications accepted. *Expenses:* Contact institution.

University of Detroit Mercy, School of Architecture, Detroit, MI 48221. Offers architecture (M Arch); community development (MA). *Entrance requirements:* For master's, BS in architecture, minimum GPA of 3.0, portfolio.

University of Florida, Graduate School, College of Design, Construction and Planning, Department of Urban and Regional Planning, Gainesville, FL 32611. Offers geographic information systems (MAURP); historic preservation (MAURP); sustainable design (MAURP); tropical conservation and development (MAURP); urban and regional planning (MAURP, MURP); wetland sciences (MAURP); JD/MAURP. *Accreditation:* ACSP (one or more programs are accredited). *Program availability:* Online learning. *Entrance requirements:* For master's, GRE General Test, minimum GPA of 3.0. Additional exam requirements/recommendations for international students: required—TOEFL (minimum score 550 paper-based; 80 iBT), IELTS (minimum score 6). Electronic applications accepted.

University of Florida, Graduate School, College of Design, Construction and Planning, Doctoral Program in Design, Construction and Planning, Gainesville, FL 32611. Offers construction management (PhD); design, construction and planning (PhD); geographic information systems (PhD); historic preservation (PhD); interior design (PhD); landscape architecture (PhD); urban and regional planning (PhD). *Degree requirements:* For doctorate, thesis/dissertation. *Entrance requirements:* For doctorate, GRE General Test, minimum GPA of 3.0. Additional exam requirements/recommendations for international students: required—TOEFL (minimum score 550 paper-based; 80 iBT), IELTS (minimum score 6). Electronic applications accepted.

Urban and Regional Planning

University of Hawaii at Manoa, Office of Graduate Education, College of Social Sciences, Department of Urban and Regional Planning, Honolulu, HI 96822. Offers community planning (MURP); disaster management and humanitarian assistance (Graduate Certificate); environmental planning and sustainability (MURP); international development planning (MURP); land use, transportation and infrastructure planning (MURP); planning studies (Graduate Certificate); urban and regional planning (PhD, Graduate Certificate). *Accreditation:* ACSP. *Program availability:* Part-time. *Entrance requirements:* For master's, GRE General Test, minimum GPA of 3.0; for doctorate, GRE General Test. Additional exam requirements/recommendations for international students: required—TOEFL (minimum score 500 paper-based; 61 iBT), IELTS (minimum score 5).

University of Idaho, College of Graduate Studies, College of Art and Architecture, Program in Bioregional Planning and Community Design, Moscow, ID 83844-2282. Offers MS. *Students:* 7. Average age 29. *Entrance requirements:* For master's, GRE or LSAT, minimum GPA of 3.0. Additional exam requirements/recommendations for international students: required—TOEFL (minimum score 550 paper-based; 79 iBT), IELTS (minimum score 6.5), Michigan English Language Assessment Battery (minimum score of 77). *Application deadline:* Applications are processed on a rolling basis. Application fee: $60. Electronic applications accepted. *Expenses:* Tuition, state resident: full-time $7753.80; part-time $502 per credit hour. Tuition, nonresident: full-time $26,990; part-time $1571 per credit hour. *Required fees:* $2122.20; $47 per credit hour. *Financial support:* Applicants required to submit FAFSA. *Unit head:* Dr. Rula Awwad-Rafferty, Program Head, 208-364-4595, E-mail: caa@uidaho.edu. *Application contact:* Dr. Rula Awwad-Rafferty, Program Head, 208-364-4595, E-mail: caa@uidaho.edu.
Website: http://www.uidaho.edu/caa/programs/biop

University of Illinois at Chicago, College of Urban Planning and Public Affairs, Department of Urban Planning and Policy, Chicago, IL 60607-7128. Offers MUPP, PhD. *Accreditation:* ACSP (one or more programs are accredited). *Program availability:* Part-time. *Degree requirements:* For master's, thesis or alternative, internship; for doctorate, thesis/dissertation. *Entrance requirements:* For master's and doctorate, GRE General Test, minimum GPA of 2.75, writing sample. Additional exam requirements/recommendations for international students: required—TOEFL. Electronic applications accepted. *Expenses:* Contact institution.

University of Illinois at Urbana-Champaign, Graduate College, College of Fine and Applied Arts, Department of Urban and Regional Planning, Champaign, IL 61820. Offers regional planning (PhD); urban planning (MUP); JD/MUP; M Arch/MUP; MLA/MUP. *Accreditation:* ACSP (one or more programs are accredited).

The University of Iowa, Graduate College, Program in Urban and Regional Planning, Iowa City, IA 52242-1316. Offers MA, MS, JD/MA, MHA/MA, MHA/MS, MS/MA, MS/MS, MSW/MA, MSW/MS. *Accreditation:* ACSP. *Degree requirements:* For master's, thesis optional, portfolio. *Entrance requirements:* For master's, GRE General Test, minimum GPA of 3.0. Additional exam requirements/recommendations for international students: required—TOEFL (minimum score 600 paper-based; 100 iBT). Electronic applications accepted.

The University of Kansas, Graduate Studies, College of Liberal Arts and Sciences, School of Public Affairs and Administration, Urban Planning Program, Lawrence, KS 66045. Offers MUP. *Accreditation:* ACSP. *Program availability:* Part-time. *Students:* 31 full-time (14 women), 4 part-time (2 women); includes 6 minority (1 Black or African American, non-Hispanic/Latino; 2 American Indian or Alaska Native, non-Hispanic/Latino; 1 Hispanic/Latino; 2 Two or more races, non-Hispanic/Latino), 4 international. Average age 27. 31 applicants, 77% accepted, 12 enrolled. In 2019, 20 master's awarded. *Entrance requirements:* For master's, GRE, three letters of reference, resume, statement of career goals and substantive interests in urban planning, official transcripts. Additional exam requirements/recommendations for international students: required—TOEFL, IELTS. *Application deadline:* For fall admission, 7/1 for domestic students, 6/1 for international students; for spring admission, 12/1 for domestic students, 11/1 for international students; for summer admission, 5/1 for domestic students, 4/1 for international students. Application fee: $65 ($85 for international students). Electronic applications accepted. *Expenses:* Tuition, state resident: full-time $9989. Tuition, nonresident: full-time $23,950. *International tuition:* $23,950 full-time. *Required fees:* $984; $81.99 per credit hour. Tuition and fees vary according to course load, campus/location and program. *Financial support:* Fellowships, research assistantships, teaching assistantships, career-related internships or fieldwork, scholarships/grants, and unspecified assistantships available. Financial award application deadline: 7/1; financial award applicants required to submit FAFSA. *Unit head:* Bonnie Johnson, Acting Director, 785-864-7147, E-mail: bojojohn@ku.edu. *Application contact:* Anya Waters, Graduate Admission Contact, 785-864-9113, E-mail: anyawaters@ku.edu.
Website: http://urbanplanning.ku.edu/

University of Louisville, Graduate School, College of Arts and Sciences, Department of Urban and Public Affairs, Louisville, KY 40208. Offers public administration (MPA), including human resources management, non-profit management, public policy and administration; urban and public affairs (PhD), including urban planning and development, urban policy and administration; urban planning (MUP), including administration of planning organizations, housing and community development, land use and environmental planning, spatial analysis. *Program availability:* Part-time, evening/weekend. *Faculty:* 13 full-time (6 women), 2 part-time/adjunct (1 woman). *Students:* 44 full-time (24 women), 24 part-time (14 women); includes 12 minority (6 Black or African American, non-Hispanic/Latino; 2 Hispanic/Latino; 4 Two or more races, non-Hispanic/Latino), 7 international. Average age 34. 51 applicants, 67% accepted, 25 enrolled. In 2019, 14 master's, 3 doctorates awarded. Terminal master's awarded for partial completion of doctoral program. *Degree requirements:* For master's, internship; for doctorate, comprehensive exam, thesis/dissertation. *Entrance requirements:* For master's, GRE General Test, 2 letters of reference, official transcripts. Minimum GPA of 3.0; for doctorate, GRE General Test, Two letters of reference, official transcripts. Masters degree in appropriate field. Additional exam requirements/recommendations for international students: required—TOEFL (minimum score 550 paper-based; 79 iBT), IELTS can be used in place of the TOEFL; recommended—IELTS (minimum score 6.5). *Application deadline:* For fall admission, 2/1 for domestic and international students. Applications are processed on a rolling basis. Application fee: $65. Electronic applications accepted. *Expenses: Tuition, area resident:* Full-time $13,000; part-time $723 per credit hour. Tuition, state resident: full-time $13,000; part-time $723 per credit hour. Tuition, nonresident: full-time $27,114; part-time $1507 per credit hour. *International tuition:* $27,114 full-time. *Required fees:* $196. Tuition and fees vary according to program and reciprocity agreements. *Financial support:* In 2019–20, 29 students received support, including 11 research assistantships with full tuition reimbursements available (averaging $19,000 per year); fellowships, teaching assistantships, health care benefits, and unspecified assistantships also available. Financial award application deadline: 2/1. *Unit head:* Dr. David Simpson, Professor/Chair, 502-852-8019, Fax: 502-852-4558, E-mail: dave.simpson@louisville.edu.
Website: http://supa.louisville.edu

University of Manitoba, Faculty of Graduate Studies, Faculty of Architecture, Department of City Planning, Winnipeg, MB R3T 2N2, Canada. Offers MCP. *Degree requirements:* For master's, thesis.

University of Maryland, College Park, Academic Affairs, School of Architecture, Planning and Preservation, Program in Urban Studies and Planning, College Park, MD 20742. Offers urban and regional planning/design (PhD); urban studies and planning (MCP). *Accreditation:* ACSP. *Program availability:* Part-time, evening/weekend. *Entrance requirements:* For master's and doctorate, GRE General Test, minimum GPA of 3.0, 3 letters of recommendation. Additional exam requirements/recommendations for international students: required—TOEFL. Electronic applications accepted.

University of Massachusetts Amherst, Graduate School, College of Social and Behavioral Sciences, Department of Landscape Architecture and Regional Planning, Dual Degree Program in Landscape Architecture and Regional Planning, Amherst, MA 01003. Offers MLA/MRP. *Accreditation:* ACSP; ASLA. *Program availability:* Part-time. *Entrance requirements:* Additional exam requirements/recommendations for international students: required—TOEFL (minimum score 550 paper-based; 80 iBT), IELTS (minimum score 6.5). Electronic applications accepted.

University of Massachusetts Amherst, Graduate School, College of Social and Behavioral Sciences, Department of Landscape Architecture and Regional Planning, Program in Regional Planning, Amherst, MA 01003. Offers MRP, PhD, M Arch/MRP, MRP/MPPA. *Accreditation:* ACSP (one or more programs are accredited). *Program availability:* Part-time. Terminal master's awarded for partial completion of doctoral program. *Degree requirements:* For master's, thesis or alternative; for doctorate, comprehensive exam, thesis/dissertation. *Entrance requirements:* For master's and doctorate, GRE General Test. Additional exam requirements/recommendations for international students: required—TOEFL (minimum score 550 paper-based; 80 iBT), IELTS (minimum score 6.5). Electronic applications accepted.

University of Massachusetts Amherst, Graduate School, Interdisciplinary Programs, Dual Degree Program in Regional Planning and Public Policy and Administration, Amherst, MA 01003. Offers MPPA/MRP. *Entrance requirements:* Additional exam requirements/recommendations for international students: required—TOEFL (minimum score 550 paper-based; 80 iBT), IELTS (minimum score 6.5). Electronic applications accepted.

University of Massachusetts Boston, School for the Environment, Program in Urban Planning and Community Development, Boston, MA 02125-3393. Offers MS.

University of Massachusetts Lowell, College of Fine Arts, Humanities and Social Sciences, Program in Regional Economic and Social Development, Lowell, MA 01854. Offers MA, Graduate Certificate. *Program availability:* Part-time. *Entrance requirements:* For master's, GRE. Electronic applications accepted.

University of Memphis, Graduate School, College of Arts and Sciences, Department of City and Regional Planning, Memphis, TN 38152. Offers MCRP. *Accreditation:* ACSP. *Students:* 15 full-time (5 women), 7 part-time (5 women); includes 6 minority (4 Black or African American, non-Hispanic/Latino; 2 Two or more races, non-Hispanic/Latino), 3 international. Average age 27. 17 applicants, 100% accepted, 11 enrolled. In 2019, 10 master's awarded. *Degree requirements:* For master's, comprehensive exam, Terminal Project. *Entrance requirements:* For master's, GRE General Test or MAT, personal statement, resume. Additional exam requirements/recommendations for international students: required—TOEFL (minimum score 550 paper-based; 79 iBT). *Application deadline:* For fall admission, 4/15 priority date for domestic students; for spring admission, 12/1 for domestic students. Applications are processed on a rolling basis. Application fee: $35 ($60 for international students). Electronic applications accepted. *Expenses: Tuition, area resident:* Full-time $9216; part-time $512 per credit hour. Tuition, state resident: full-time $9216; part-time $512 per credit hour. Tuition, nonresident: full-time $12,672; part-time $704 per credit hour. *International tuition:* $16,128 full-time. *Required fees:* $1530; $85 per credit hour. Tuition and fees vary according to program. *Financial support:* Research assistantships, career-related internships or fieldwork, Federal Work-Study, scholarships/grants, and unspecified assistantships available. Financial award application deadline: 2/1; financial award applicants required to submit FAFSA. *Unit head:* Dr. Charlie Santo, Chair, 901-678-2161, Fax: 901-678-4162, E-mail: casanto@memphis.edu. *Application contact:* Dr. Charlie Santo, Chair, 901-678-2161, Fax: 901-678-4162, E-mail: casanto@memphis.edu.
Website: http://www.memphis.edu/planning/

University of Michigan, Taubman College of Architecture and Urban Planning, Master of Urban and Regional Planning Program, Ann Arbor, MI 48109. Offers MURP. *Accreditation:* ACSP. *Degree requirements:* For master's, thesis or alternative. *Entrance requirements:* Additional exam requirements/recommendations for international students: required—TOEFL (minimum score 83 iBT), GRE. Electronic applications accepted. *Expenses:* Contact institution.

University of Michigan, Taubman College of Architecture and Urban Planning, Urban and Regional Planning PhD Program, Ann Arbor, MI 48109. Offers PhD. *Accreditation:* ACSP. *Degree requirements:* For doctorate, comprehensive exam, thesis/dissertation. *Entrance requirements:* Additional exam requirements/recommendations for international students: required—TOEFL (minimum score 83 iBT), GRE. Electronic applications accepted.

University of Minnesota, Twin Cities Campus, Graduate School, Humphrey School of Public Affairs, PhD Program in Public Affairs, Minneapolis, MN 55455. Offers management and governance (PhD); public policy (PhD); science, technology, and environmental policy (PhD); urban planning (PhD). *Program availability:* Part-time. *Degree requirements:* For doctorate, comprehensive exam, thesis/dissertation. *Entrance requirements:* For doctorate, GRE General Test. Additional exam requirements/recommendations for international students: required—TOEFL (minimum score 650 paper-based; 100 iBT), IELTS (minimum score 7). Electronic applications accepted. *Expenses:* Contact institution.

University of Minnesota, Twin Cities Campus, Graduate School, Humphrey School of Public Affairs, Program in Urban and Regional Planning, Minneapolis, MN 55455-0213. Offers MURP, JD/MURP, MURP/MPH, MURP/MS, MURP/MSW. *Accreditation:* ACSP (one or more programs are accredited). *Program availability:* Part-time. *Students:* 69 full-time (37 women), 2 part-time (1 woman); includes 17 minority (4 Black or African American, non-Hispanic/Latino; 5 Asian, non-Hispanic/Latino; 8 Hispanic/Latino), 5 international. Average age 26. 92 applicants, 95% accepted, 41 enrolled. In 2019, 25 master's awarded. *Degree requirements:* For master's, thesis or alternative, internship or equivalent work experience. *Entrance requirements:* For master's, GRE General Test. Additional exam requirements/recommendations for international students: required—TOEFL (minimum score 600 paper-based; 100 iBT), IELTS (minimum score 7). *Application deadline:* For fall admission, 4/1 for domestic and international students. Application fee: $75 ($95 for international students). Electronic applications accepted. *Expenses:* Contact institution. *Financial support:* In 2019–20, 34 students received support, including fellowships with tuition reimbursements available (averaging $8,000 per year), research assistantships with tuition reimbursements available (averaging $25,000 per year); career-related internships or fieldwork, Federal Work-Study,

scholarships/grants, health care benefits, tuition waivers (full and partial), and unspecified assistantships also available. Financial award application deadline: 1/15; financial award applicants required to submit FAFSA. *Unit head:* Laura Bloomberg, Associate Dean, 612-625-0608, Fax: 612-626-0002, E-mail: bloom004@umn.edu. *Application contact:* Jacob Merrifield, Admissions Program Manager, 612-624-3800, Fax: 612-626-0002, E-mail: jmerrifi@umn.edu.
Website: http://www.hhh.umn.edu/degrees/murp/

University of Nebraska–Lincoln, Graduate College, College of Agricultural Sciences and Natural Resources, Department of Agricultural Economics, Lincoln, NE 68588. Offers agribusiness (MBA); agricultural economics (MS, PhD); community development (M Ag). *Degree requirements:* For master's, thesis optional; for doctorate, comprehensive exam, thesis/dissertation. *Entrance requirements:* For master's and doctorate, GRE General Test. Additional exam requirements/recommendations for international students: required—TOEFL (minimum score 550 paper-based). Electronic applications accepted.

University of Nebraska–Lincoln, Graduate College, College of Architecture, Department of Community and Regional Planning, Lincoln, NE 68588. Offers MCRP, JD/MCRP, M Arch/MCRP, MCRP/MSCE. *Accreditation:* ACSP. *Degree requirements:* For master's, thesis optional. *Entrance requirements:* For master's, GRE General Test. Additional exam requirements/recommendations for international students: required—TOEFL (minimum score 550 paper-based). Electronic applications accepted.

University of New Mexico, Graduate Studies, School of Architecture and Planning, Program in Community and Regional Planning, Albuquerque, NM 87131-2039. Offers MCRP, MCRP/MA, MPA/MCRP. *Accreditation:* ACSP. *Program availability:* Part-time. *Entrance requirements:* For master's, minimum GPA of 3.0 in last two years of graduate study, 3 letters of recommendation, letter of intent, resume, copies of all official transcripts. Additional exam requirements/recommendations for international students: required—TOEFL (minimum score 550 paper-based; 79 iBT). Electronic applications accepted. *Expenses:* Tuition, state resident: full-time $7633; part-time $972 per year. Tuition, nonresident: full-time $22,586; part-time $3840 per year. *International tuition:* $23,292 full-time. *Required fees:* $8608. Tuition and fees vary according to course level, course load, degree level, program and student level.

University of New Orleans, Graduate School, College of Liberal Arts, Education and Human Development, Department of Planning and Urban Studies, Program in Urban and Regional Planning, New Orleans, LA 70148. Offers MURP. *Accreditation:* ACSP. *Degree requirements:* For master's, thesis. *Entrance requirements:* For master's, GRE General Test. Additional exam requirements/recommendations for international students: required—TOEFL (minimum score 550 paper-based; 79 iBT), IELTS (minimum score 6.5). Electronic applications accepted.

The University of North Carolina at Chapel Hill, Graduate School, College of Arts and Sciences, Department of City and Regional Planning, Chapel Hill, NC 27599-3140. Offers city and regional planning (MCRP); planning (PhD); public policy analysis (PhD); JD/MCRP; MBA/MCRP; MPA/MCRP. *Accreditation:* ACSP (one or more programs are accredited). *Degree requirements:* For master's, project; for doctorate, comprehensive exam, thesis/dissertation. *Entrance requirements:* For master's and doctorate, GRE General Test. Additional exam requirements/recommendations for international students: required—TOEFL (minimum score 550 paper-based). Electronic applications accepted.

The University of North Carolina at Charlotte, College of Liberal Arts and Sciences, Department of Political Science and Public Administration, Charlotte, NC 28223-0001. Offers emergency management (Graduate Certificate); non-profit management (Graduate Certificate); public administration (MPA), including arts administration, emergency management, non-profit management, public budgeting and finance, urban management and policy; public budgeting and finance (Graduate Certificate); urban management and policy (Graduate Certificate). *Accreditation:* NASPAA. *Program availability:* Part-time, evening/weekend. *Faculty:* 20 full-time (10 women), 5 part-time/adjunct (1 woman). *Students:* 30 full-time (21 women), 45 part-time (29 women); includes 23 minority (15 Black or African American, non-Hispanic/Latino; 1 American Indian or Alaska Native, non-Hispanic/Latino; 5 Hispanic/Latino; 2 Two or more races, non-Hispanic/Latino), 2 international. Average age 30. 38 applicants, 68% accepted, 21 enrolled. In 2019, 18 master's, 13 other advanced degrees awarded. *Degree requirements:* For master's, thesis or alternative. *Entrance requirements:* For master's, GRE General Test, bachelor's degree, or its equivalent, from accredited college or university; minimum undergraduate GPA of 3.0; 3 letters of recommendation; statement of purpose; for Graduate Certificate, one official transcript from each post-secondary institution; three letters of recommendation from academic or professional sources; overall undergraduate GPA of 3.0 on a 4.0 scale; statement of purpose (1-2 pages in length) in which the applicant explains his/her career goals, how the Certificate fits into achieving those goals, and any relevant w. Additional exam requirements/recommendations for international students: required—TOEFL (minimum score 557 paper-based; 83 iBT), IELTS (minimum score 6.5), TOEFL (minimum score 557paper-based, 83 iBT) or IELTS (6.5). *Application deadline:* For fall admission, 8/15 for domestic students; for spring admission, 12/1 for domestic students; for summer admission, 5/11 for domestic students. Applications are processed on a rolling basis. Application fee: $75. Electronic applications accepted. *Expenses:* Tuition, state resident: full-time $4337. Tuition, nonresident: full-time $17,771. *Required fees:* $3093. Tuition and fees vary according to course load, degree level and program. *Financial support:* In 2019–20, 16 students received support, including 1 fellowship (averaging $55,000 per year), 15 research assistantships (averaging $8,583 per year); teaching assistantships, career-related internships or fieldwork, institutionally sponsored loans, scholarships/grants, and unspecified assistantships also available. Support available to part-time students. Financial award applicants required to submit FAFSA. *Unit head:* Dr. Cheryl L. Brown, Interim Chair, Undergraduate Coordinator, & Associate Professor, 704-687-7574, E-mail: cbrown@uncc.edu. *Application contact:* Kathy B. Giddings, Director of Graduate Admissions, 704-687-5503, Fax: 704-687-1668, E-mail: gradadm@uncc.edu.
Website: http://politicalscience.uncc.edu/

University of Oklahoma, Christopher C. Gibbs College of Architecture, Division of Architecture, Norman, OK 73019-0390. Offers architecture (MS); data and digital representation (M Arch); design entrepreneurship and real estate (M Arch); planning, design and construction (PhD); resilient planning, design, and construction (M Arch). *Program availability:* Part-time. Terminal master's awarded for partial completion of doctoral program. *Degree requirements:* For master's, variable foreign language requirement; for doctorate, variable foreign language requirement, comprehensive exam, thesis/dissertation. *Entrance requirements:* Additional exam requirements/recommendations for international students: required—TOEFL (minimum score 79 iBT) or IELTS (minimum score 6.5). Electronic applications accepted. *Expenses:* Tuition, state resident: full-time $6583.20; part-time $274.30 per credit hour. Tuition, nonresident: full-time $21,242; part-time $885.10 per credit hour. *International tuition:* $21,242.40 full-time. *Required fees:* $1994.20; $72.55 per credit hour. $126.50 per semester. Tuition and fees vary according to course load and degree level.

University of Oklahoma, Christopher C. Gibbs College of Architecture, Division of Regional and City Planning, Norman, OK 73019-0390. Offers community development (MRCP); physical planning (MRCP); MRCP/MLA. *Accreditation:* ACSP. *Program availability:* Part-time. Terminal master's awarded for partial completion of doctoral program. *Degree requirements:* For master's, comprehensive exam or thesis. *Entrance requirements:* Additional exam requirements/recommendations for international students: required—TOEFL (minimum score 79 iBT) or IELTS (minimum score 6.5). Electronic applications accepted. *Expenses:* Tuition, state resident: full-time $6583.20; part-time $274.30 per credit hour. Tuition, nonresident: full-time $21,242; part-time $885.10 per credit hour. *International tuition:* $21,242.40 full-time. *Required fees:* $1994.20; $72.55 per credit hour. $126.50 per semester. Tuition and fees vary according to course load and degree level.

University of Oklahoma, Christopher C. Gibbs College of Architecture, Haskell and Irene Lemon Division of Construction Science, Norman, OK 73019-0390. Offers construction management (MS); construction science (MCM); planning, design, and construction (PhD), including construction. *Program availability:* Part-time. Terminal master's awarded for partial completion of doctoral program. *Degree requirements:* For master's, thesis optional, special project; for doctorate, thesis/dissertation. *Entrance requirements:* For master's, minimum GPA of 3.5. Additional exam requirements/recommendations for international students: required—TOEFL (minimum score 79 iBT) or IELTS (minimum score 6.5). Electronic applications accepted. *Expenses:* Tuition, state resident: full-time $6583.20; part-time $274.30 per credit hour. Tuition, nonresident: full-time $21,242; part-time $885.10 per credit hour. *International tuition:* $21,242.40 full-time. *Required fees:* $1994.20; $72.55 per credit hour. $126.50 per semester. Tuition and fees vary according to course load and degree level.

University of Oregon, Graduate School, College of Design, School of Planning, Public Policy and Management, Program in Community and Regional Planning, Eugene, OR 97403. Offers MCRP. *Accreditation:* ACSP. *Program availability:* Part-time. *Degree requirements:* For master's, thesis or alternative. *Entrance requirements:* For master's, minimum GPA of 3.0. Additional exam requirements/recommendations for international students: required—TOEFL.

University of Pennsylvania, Stuart Weitzman School of Design, Department of City and Regional Planning, Philadelphia, PA 19104. Offers city and regional planning (PhD); city planning (MCP); GIS and spatial analysis (Certificate); land preservation (Certificate); urban design (Certificate); urban redevelopment (Certificate); urban spatial analytics (MUSA). *Accreditation:* ACSP (one or more programs are accredited). *Program availability:* Part-time. *Faculty:* 24 full-time (10 women), 4 part-time/adjunct (0 women). *Students:* 191 full-time (120 women), 6 part-time (3 women); includes 40 minority (14 Black or African American, non-Hispanic/Latino; 13 Asian, non-Hispanic/Latino; 8 Hispanic/Latino; 5 Two or more races, non-Hispanic/Latino), 94 international. Average age 26. 433 applicants, 59% accepted, 119 enrolled. In 2019, 92 master's, 1 doctorate, 7 other advanced degrees awarded. *Entrance requirements:* Additional exam requirements/recommendations for international students: required—TOEFL (minimum score 100 iBT); recommended—IELTS (minimum score 7), TSE (minimum score 68). *Application deadline:* For spring admission, 1/12 for domestic students. Application fee: $80. Electronic applications accepted. *Financial support:* In 2019–20, 39 teaching assistantships (averaging $2,000 per year) were awarded; fellowships, research assistantships, and Federal Work-Study also available. Financial award application deadline: 2/15; financial award applicants required to submit FAFSA. *Application contact:* Lauren Hoover, Admissions & Recruitment Coordinator, 215-898-6520, E-mail: lhoover@design.upenn.edu.
Website: https://www.design.upenn.edu/city-regional-planning

University of Pittsburgh, Graduate School of Public and International Affairs, Master of International Development Program, Pittsburgh, PA 15260. Offers energy and environment (MID); governance and international public management (MID); human security (MID); nongovernmental organizations and civil society (MID); urban affairs and planning (MID); MID/JD; MID/MBA; MID/MPH; MID/MSIS; MID/MSW. *Program availability:* Part-time, evening/weekend. *Faculty:* 33 full-time (11 women), 10 part-time/adjunct (5 women). *Students:* 61 full-time (42 women), 10 part-time (8 women); includes 11 minority (5 Black or African American, non-Hispanic/Latino; 4 Asian, non-Hispanic/Latino; 1 Hispanic/Latino; 1 Two or more races, non-Hispanic/Latino), 10 international. Average age 27. 89 applicants, 91% accepted, 26 enrolled. In 2019, 20 master's awarded. *Degree requirements:* For master's, thesis optional, capstone seminar. *Entrance requirements:* For master's, Personal essay, resume, two letters of recommendation, transcripts. Additional exam requirements/recommendations for international students: required—TOEFL (minimum score 80 iBT), Duolingo English Test; recommended—IELTS (minimum score 6.5). *Application deadline:* For fall admission, 2/1 for domestic students, 1/15 for international students; for spring admission, 11/1 for domestic students, 8/1 for international students. Application fee: $50. Electronic applications accepted. *Financial support:* In 2019–20, 41 students received support, including 6 fellowships with full tuition reimbursements available (averaging $16,060 per year); scholarships/grants also available. Financial award application deadline: 2/1. *Unit head:* Dr. John Keeler, Dean, 412-648-7605, Fax: 412-648-7601, E-mail: gspia@pitt.edu. *Application contact:* Dr. Michael Rizzi, Director of Student Services, 412-648-7640, Fax: 412-648-7641, E-mail: rizzim@pitt.edu.
Website: http://www.gspia.pitt.edu/

University of Pittsburgh, Graduate School of Public and International Affairs, Master of Public Administration Program, Pittsburgh, PA 15260. Offers energy and environment (MPA); governance and international public management (MPA); policy research and analysis (MPA); public and nonprofit management (MPA); urban affairs and planning (MPA); JD/MPA; MPH/MPA; MSIS/MPA; MSW/MPA. *Accreditation:* NASPAA. *Program availability:* Part-time, evening/weekend. *Faculty:* 33 full-time (11 women), 10 part-time/adjunct (5 women). *Students:* 76 full-time (51 women), 17 part-time (10 women); includes 9 minority (5 Black or African American, non-Hispanic/Latino; 1 Asian, non-Hispanic/Latino; 3 Hispanic/Latino), 37 international. Average age 26. 167 applicants, 91% accepted, 44 enrolled. In 2019, 49 master's awarded. *Degree requirements:* For master's, thesis optional, capstone seminar. *Entrance requirements:* For master's, Personal essay, resume, two letters of recommendation, transcripts. Additional exam requirements/recommendations for international students: required—TOEFL (minimum score 80 iBT), Duolingo English Test; recommended—IELTS (minimum score 6.5). *Application deadline:* For fall admission, 2/1 for domestic students, 1/15 priority date for international students; for spring admission, 11/1 for domestic students, 8/1 priority date for international students. Application fee: $50. Electronic applications accepted. *Expenses:* $24,480 in-state, $40,848 out-of-state. *Financial support:* In 2019–20, 30 students received support, including 2 fellowships with full tuition reimbursements available (averaging $16,060 per year); scholarships/grants also available. Financial award application deadline: 2/1; financial award applicants required to submit FAFSA. *Unit head:* Dr. John Keeler, Dean, 412-648-7605, Fax: 412-648-7601, E-mail: gspia@pitt.edu. *Application contact:* Dr. Michael Rizzi, Director of Student Services, 412-648-7643, Fax: 412-648-7641, E-mail: rizzim@pitt.edu.
Website: http://www.gspia.pitt.edu/

University of Puerto Rico at Rio Piedras, Graduate School of Planning, San Juan, PR 00931-3300. Offers economic planning systems (MP); environmental planning (MP); social policy and planning (MP); urban and territorial planning (MP). *Accreditation:* ACSP. *Program availability:* Part-time. *Degree requirements:* For master's, comprehensive exam, thesis, planning project defense. *Entrance requirements:* For master's, PAEG, GRE, minimum GPA of 3.0, 2 letters of recommendation.

University of Southern California, Graduate School, Sol Price School of Public Policy, Doctor of Philosophy in Urban Planning and Development Program, Los Angeles, CA 90089. Offers PhD. *Accreditation:* ACSP. *Degree requirements:* For doctorate, thesis/dissertation. *Entrance requirements:* For doctorate, GRE. Additional exam requirements/recommendations for international students: required—TOEFL (minimum score 600 paper-based; 100 iBT). Electronic applications accepted.

University of Southern California, Graduate School, Sol Price School of Public Policy, Doctor of Policy, Planning, and Development Program, Los Angeles, CA 90089. Offers DPPD. *Accreditation:* ACSP. *Program availability:* Part-time. *Degree requirements:* For doctorate, project. *Entrance requirements:* Additional exam requirements/recommendations for international students: required—TOEFL (minimum score 600 paper-based; 100 iBT). Electronic applications accepted.

University of Southern California, Graduate School, Sol Price School of Public Policy, Master of Planning Program, Los Angeles, CA 90089. Offers sustainable cities (Graduate Certificate); transportation systems (Graduate Certificate); urban planning (M Pl); M Arch/M Pl; M Pl/MA; M Pl/MPP; M Pl/MRED; M Pl/MS; M Pl/MSW; MBA/M Pl; ML Arch/M Pl; MPA/M Pl. *Accreditation:* ACSP. *Program availability:* Part-time. *Degree requirements:* For master's, comprehensive exam, internship. *Entrance requirements:* For master's, GRE, GMAT. Additional exam requirements/recommendations for international students: required—TOEFL (minimum score 600 paper-based; 100 iBT). Electronic applications accepted.

University of Southern Maine, College of Management and Human Service, Muskie School of Public Service, Program in Community Planning and Development, Portland, ME 04103. Offers MCPD, CGS, JD/MCPD. *Program availability:* Part-time, evening/weekend. *Degree requirements:* For master's, thesis, capstone project, field experience. *Entrance requirements:* For master's, GRE General Test or LSAT. Additional exam requirements/recommendations for international students: required—TOEFL. Electronic applications accepted. *Expenses: Tuition, area resident:* Full-time $864; part-time $432 per credit hour. Tuition, state resident: full-time $864; part-time $432 per credit hour. Tuition, nonresident: full-time $2372; part-time $1186 per credit hour. *Required fees:* $141; $108 per credit hour. Tuition and fees vary according to course load.

University of South Florida, Innovative Education, Tampa, FL 33620-9951. Offers adult, career and higher education (Graduate Certificate), including college teaching, leadership in developing human resources, leadership in higher education; Africana studies (Graduate Certificate), including diasporas and health disparities, genocide and human rights; aging studies (Graduate Certificate), including gerontology; art research (Graduate Certificate), including museum studies; business foundations (Graduate Certificate); chemical and biomedical engineering (Graduate Certificate), including materials science and engineering, water, health and sustainability; child and family studies (Graduate Certificate), including positive behavior support; civil and industrial engineering (Graduate Certificate), including transportation systems analysis; community and family health (Graduate Certificate), including maternal and child health, social marketing and public health, violence and injury: prevention and intervention, women's health; criminology (Graduate Certificate), including criminal justice administration; data science for public administration (Graduate Certificate); digital humanities (Graduate Certificate); educational measurement and research (Graduate Certificate), including evaluation; English (Graduate Certificate), including comparative literary studies, creative writing, professional and technical communication; entrepreneurship (Graduate Certificate); environmental health (Graduate Certificate), including safety management; epidemiology and biostatistics (Graduate Certificate), including applied biostatistics, biostatistics, concepts and tools of epidemiology, epidemiology, epidemiology of infectious diseases; geography, environment and planning (Graduate Certificate), including community development, environmental policy and management, geographical information systems; geology (Graduate Certificate), including hydrogeology; global health (Graduate Certificate), including disaster management, global health and Latin American and Caribbean studies, global health practice, humanitarian assistance, infection control; government and international affairs (Graduate Certificate), including Cuban studies, globalization studies; health policy and management (Graduate Certificate), including health management and leadership, public health policy and programs; hearing specialist: early intervention (Graduate Certificate); industrial and management systems engineering (Graduate Certificate), including systems engineering, technology management; information studies (Graduate Certificate), including school library media specialist; information systems/decision sciences (Graduate Certificate), including analytics and business intelligence; instructional technology (Graduate Certificate), including distance education, Florida digital/virtual educator, instructional design, multimedia design, Web design; internal medicine, bioethics and medical humanities (Graduate Certificate), including biomedical ethics; Latin American and Caribbean studies (Graduate Certificate); leadership for coastal resiliency planning (Graduate Certificate); mass communications (Graduate Certificate), including multimedia journalism; mathematics and statistics (Graduate Certificate), including mathematics; medicine (Graduate Certificate), including aging and neuroscience, bioinformatics, biotechnology, brain fitness and memory management, clinical investigation, hand and upper limb rehabilitation, health informatics, health sciences, integrative weight management, intellectual property, medicine and gender, metabolic and nutritional medicine, metabolic cardiology, pharmacy sciences; national and competitive intelligence (Graduate Certificate); nursing (Graduate Certificate), including simulation based academic fellowship in advanced pain management; psychological and social foundations (Graduate Certificate), including career counseling, college teaching, diversity in education, mental health counseling, school counseling; public affairs (Graduate Certificate), including nonprofit management, public management, research administration; public health (Graduate Certificate), including assessing chemical toxicity and public health risks, health equity, pharmacoepidemiology, public health generalist, toxicology, translational research in adolescent behavioral health; public health practices (Graduate Certificate), including planning for healthy communities; rehabilitation and mental health counseling (Graduate Certificate), including integrative mental health care, marriage and family therapy, rehabilitation technology; secondary education (Graduate Certificate), including ESOL, foreign language education: culture and content, foreign language education: professional; social work (Graduate Certificate), including geriatric social work/clinical gerontology; special education (Graduate Certificate), including autism spectrum disorder, disabilities education: severe/profound; world languages (Graduate Certificate), including teaching English as a second language (TESL) or foreign language. *Unit head:* Dr. Cynthia DeLuca, Associate Vice President and Assistant Vice Provost, 813-974-3077, Fax: 813-974-7061, E-mail: deluca@usf.edu. *Application contact:* Owen Hooper, Director, Summer and Alternative Calendar Programs, 813-974-6917, E-mail: hooper@usf.edu.
Website: http://www.usf.edu/innovative-education/

The University of Texas at Arlington, Graduate School, College of Architecture, Planning and Public Affairs, Program in Public and Urban Administration, Arlington, TX 76019. Offers PhD. *Program availability:* Part-time, evening/weekend. *Entrance requirements:* Additional exam requirements/recommendations for international students: required—TOEFL (minimum score 550 paper-based).

The University of Texas at Arlington, Graduate School, College of Architecture, Planning and Public Affairs, Program in Urban Planning and Public Policy, Arlington, TX 76019. Offers PhD. *Accreditation:* ACSP. *Program availability:* Part-time, evening/weekend. *Entrance requirements:* Additional exam requirements/recommendations for international students: required—TOEFL (minimum score 550 paper-based). Electronic applications accepted.

The University of Texas at Austin, Graduate School, School of Architecture, Program in Community and Regional Planning, Austin, TX 78712-1111. Offers MSCRP, PhD, JD/MSCRP, MSCRP/MA. *Accreditation:* ACSP. *Degree requirements:* For master's, thesis; for doctorate, thesis/dissertation. *Entrance requirements:* For master's and doctorate, GRE General Test. Electronic applications accepted.

The University of Texas at San Antonio, College of Architecture, Construction and Planning, Program in Urban and Regional Planning, San Antonio, TX 78249-0617. Offers MS. *Program availability:* Part-time. *Entrance requirements:* For master's, GRE, transcripts, two letters of recommendation, letter of intent. Additional exam requirements/recommendations for international students: required—TOEFL (minimum score 550 paper-based; 79 iBT), IELTS (minimum score 6.5). Electronic applications accepted.

The University of Toledo, College of Graduate Studies, College of Languages, Literature and Social Sciences, Department of Geography and Planning, Toledo, OH 43606-3390. Offers geographic information science and applied geographics (Certificate); geography and planning (MA); spatially-integrated social science (PhD). *Program availability:* Part-time. *Degree requirements:* For master's, comprehensive exam, thesis; for doctorate, thesis/dissertation. *Entrance requirements:* For master's and doctorate, GRE General Test, minimum cumulative point-hour ratio of 2.7 for all previous academic work, three letters of recommendation; for Certificate, minimum cumulative point-hour ratio of 2.7 for all previous academic work, three letters of recommendation. Additional exam requirements/recommendations for international students: required—TOEFL (minimum score 550 paper-based; 80 iBT). Electronic applications accepted.

University of Toronto, School of Graduate Studies, Faculty of Arts and Science, Department of Geography, Program in Planning, Toronto, ON M5S 1A1, Canada. Offers M Sc Pl, MUDS, PhD. *Program availability:* Part-time. *Degree requirements:* For master's, summer internship. *Entrance requirements:* For master's, bachelor's degree in planning, geography, social science or a closely related professional field, minimum B+ average in final year, 3 letters of reference; for doctorate, minimum A- or equivalent standing in previous master's program. Additional exam requirements/recommendations for international students: required—TOEFL (minimum score 580 paper-based; 93 iBT), TWE (minimum score 5). Electronic applications accepted. *Expenses:* Contact institution.

University of Utah, Graduate School, College of Architecture and Planning, Department of City and Metropolitan Planning, Salt Lake City, UT 84112. Offers city and metropolitan planning (MCMP), including ecological planning, small town and resort planning, smart growth and transportation, urban design; metropolitan planning, policy and design (PhD). *Accreditation:* ACSP. *Program availability:* Part-time. *Faculty:* 7 full-time (5 women), 6 part-time/adjunct (1 woman). *Students:* 40 full-time (23 women), 10 part-time (5 women); includes 8 minority (2 Asian, non-Hispanic/Latino; 4 Hispanic/Latino; 2 Two or more races, non-Hispanic/Latino), 16 international. Average age 31. In 2019, 21 master's awarded. *Degree requirements:* For master's, thesis or alternative, comprehensive project; for doctorate, thesis/dissertation. *Entrance requirements:* For master's, GRE, minimum undergraduate GPA of 3.0; for doctorate, GRE, minimum GPA of 3.5. Additional exam requirements/recommendations for international students: required—TOEFL (minimum score 500 paper-based; 61 iBT); recommended—IELTS (minimum score 6). *Application deadline:* For fall admission, 1/15 priority date for domestic and international students; for spring admission, 11/1 for domestic and international students. Applications are processed on a rolling basis. Electronic applications accepted. *Expenses:* Contact institution. *Financial support:* In 2019–20, 25 students received support, including 11 fellowships (averaging $14,273 per year), 6 research assistantships (averaging $19,500 per year), 17 teaching assistantships (averaging $17,765 per year); career-related internships or fieldwork, Federal Work-Study, scholarships/grants, health care benefits, and unspecified assistantships also available. Financial award application deadline: 1/15; financial award applicants required to submit FAFSA. *Unit head:* Reid Ewing, Chair, 801-585-3745, Fax: 801-581-8217, E-mail: ewing@arch.utah.edu. *Application contact:* Saolo Utu, Recruitment and Admissions Advisor, 801-581-2361, Fax: 801-581-8217, E-mail: recruitment@arch.utah.edu.
Website: http://www.plan.utah.edu/

University of Virginia, School of Architecture, Department of Urban and Environmental Planning, Charlottesville, VA 22903. Offers MUEP, JD/MUEP, MPP/MUEP. *Accreditation:* ACSP (one or more programs are accredited). *Entrance requirements:* For master's, GRE General Test, previous course work in statistics, 3 letters of recommendation. Additional exam requirements/recommendations for international students: required—TOEFL (minimum score 600 paper-based; 90 iBT). Electronic applications accepted.

University of Washington, Graduate School, College of Built Environments, Department of Urban Design and Planning, Seattle, WA 98195. Offers urban design and planning (PhD); urban planning (MUP). *Accreditation:* ACSP (one or more programs are accredited). *Degree requirements:* For master's, thesis or alternative; for doctorate, thesis/dissertation. *Entrance requirements:* For master's and doctorate, GRE General Test, minimum GPA of 3.0. Additional exam requirements/recommendations for international students: required—TOEFL.

University of Waterloo, Graduate Studies and Postdoctoral Affairs, Faculty of Environment, School of Planning, Waterloo, ON N2L 3G1, Canada. Offers M Plan, MA, MAES, MES, PhD. *Program availability:* Part-time. *Degree requirements:* For master's, thesis (for some programs); for doctorate, comprehensive exam, thesis/dissertation. *Entrance requirements:* For master's, honors degree, minimum B+ average; for doctorate, master's degree, minimum A- average, resume. Additional exam requirements/recommendations for international students: required—TOEFL, IELTS, PTE. Electronic applications accepted.

University of Wisconsin–Madison, Graduate School, College of Letters and Science, Department of Planning and Landscape Architecture, Madison, WI 53706-1380. Offers landscape architecture (MS); urban and regional planning (MS, PhD). *Accreditation:* ACSP (one or more programs are accredited). *Program availability:* Part-time. *Degree requirements:* For master's, thesis optional, internship; for doctorate, thesis/dissertation, 3 preliminary exams. *Entrance requirements:* For master's, GRE, minimum GPA of 3.0, previous course work in statistics; for doctorate, 1 year of experience, master's degree in related field. Electronic applications accepted.

University of Wisconsin–Milwaukee, Graduate School, School of Architecture and Urban Planning, Department of Urban Planning, Milwaukee, WI 53201-0413. Offers

MUP. *Accreditation:* ACSP. *Program availability:* Part-time. *Degree requirements:* For master's, comprehensive exam, thesis or alternative. *Entrance requirements:* For master's, GRE General Test. Additional exam requirements/recommendations for international students: required—TOEFL (minimum score 550 paper-based; 79 iBT), IELTS (minimum score 6.5). Electronic applications accepted.

Université Laval, Faculty of Architecture, Planning and Visual Arts, Department of Regional Planning, Programs in Planning and Regional Development, Québec, QC G1K 7P4, Canada. Offers MATDR, PhD. Terminal master's awarded for partial completion of doctoral program. *Degree requirements:* For master's, thesis (for some programs); for doctorate, comprehensive exam, thesis/dissertation. *Entrance requirements:* For master's and doctorate, knowledge of French and English. Electronic applications accepted.

Utah State University, School of Graduate Studies, College of Agriculture and Applied Sciences, Department of Landscape Architecture and Environmental Planning, Logan, UT 84322. Offers bioregional planning (MS); landscape architecture (MLA). *Accreditation:* ASLA (one or more programs are accredited). *Degree requirements:* For master's, thesis. *Entrance requirements:* For master's, GRE General Test, minimum GPA of 3.0. Additional exam requirements/recommendations for international students: required—TOEFL.

Utah State University, School of Graduate Studies, S.J. and Jessie E. Quinney College of Natural Resources, Department of Environment and Society, Logan, UT 84322. Offers bioregional planning (MS); geography (MA, MS); human dimensions of ecosystem science and management (MS, PhD); recreation resource management (MS, PhD). *Degree requirements:* For master's, comprehensive exam, thesis (for some programs). *Entrance requirements:* For master's and doctorate, GRE General Test, minimum GPA of 3.0. Additional exam requirements/recommendations for international students: required—TOEFL. Electronic applications accepted.

Vanderbilt University, Peabody College, Department of Human and Organizational Development, Nashville, TN 37240-1001. Offers community development and action (M Ed); human development counseling (M Ed), including clinical mental health counseling. *Accreditation:* ACA; NCATE. *Program availability:* Part-time, evening/weekend, blended/hybrid learning, on-campus immersion once every semester. *Degree requirements:* For master's, comprehensive exam, thesis optional. *Entrance requirements:* For master's, GRE General Test. Additional exam requirements/recommendations for international students: required—TOEFL (minimum score 550 paper-based; 80 iBT). Electronic applications accepted. *Expenses:* Tuition: Full-time $51,018; part-time $2087 per hour. *Required fees:* $542. Tuition and fees vary according to program.

Virginia Commonwealth University, Graduate School, L. Douglas Wilder School of Government and Public Affairs, Program in Urban and Regional Studies and Planning, Richmond, VA 23284-9005. Offers MURP. *Degree requirements:* For master's, thesis optional, internship. *Entrance requirements:* For master's, GRE General Test, GMAT, or LSAT, minimum GPA of 2.7. Additional exam requirements/recommendations for international students: required—TOEFL (minimum score 600 paper-based; 100 iBT); recommended—IELTS (minimum score 6.5). Electronic applications accepted.

Virginia Polytechnic Institute and State University, Graduate School, College of Architecture and Urban Studies, Blacksburg, VA 24061. Offers architecture (M Arch, MS); architecture and design research (PhD); building construction science management (MS); creative technologies (MFA); environmental design and planning (PhD); government and international affairs (MPIA); landscape architecture (MLA, PhD); planning, governance, and globalization (PhD); public administration and public affairs (MPA, PhD); urban and regional planning (MURPL). *Accreditation:* ASLA (one or more programs are accredited). *Faculty:* 145 full-time (58 women), 2 part-time/adjunct (1

woman). *Students:* 304 full-time (156 women), 180 part-time (77 women); includes 90 minority (40 Black or African American, non-Hispanic/Latino; 19 Asian, non-Hispanic/Latino; 24 Hispanic/Latino; 7 Two or more races, non-Hispanic/Latino), 130 international. Average age 33. 475 applicants, 72% accepted, 126 enrolled. In 2019, 130 master's, 23 doctorates awarded. *Degree requirements:* For master's, comprehensive exam (for some programs), thesis (for some programs); for doctorate, comprehensive exam (for some programs), thesis/dissertation (for some programs). *Entrance requirements:* For master's and doctorate, GRE/GMAT. Additional exam requirements/recommendations for international students: required—TOEFL (minimum score 90 iBT). *Application deadline:* For fall admission, 8/1 for domestic students, 4/1 for international students; for spring admission, 1/1 for domestic students, 9/1 for international students. Applications are processed on a rolling basis. Application fee: $75. Electronic applications accepted. *Expenses:* Tuition, state resident: full-time $13,700; part-time $761.25 per credit hour. Tuition, nonresident: full-time $27,614; part-time $1534 per credit hour. *Required fees:* $886.50 per term. Tuition and fees vary according to campus/location and program. *Financial support:* In 2019–20, 2 fellowships with full tuition reimbursements (averaging $24,875 per year), 35 research assistantships with full tuition reimbursements (averaging $16,344 per year), 126 teaching assistantships with full tuition reimbursements (averaging $11,525 per year) were awarded; scholarships/grants and unspecified assistantships also available. Financial award application deadline: 3/1; financial award applicants required to submit FAFSA. *Unit head:* Dr. Richard Blythe, Dean, 540-231-6416, Fax: 540-231-6332, E-mail: richbl1@vt.edu. *Application contact:* Christine Mattsson-Coon, Executive Assistant, 540-231-6416, Fax: 540-231-6332, E-mail: cmattsso@vt.edu. Website: http://www.caus.vt.edu/

Wayne State University, College of Liberal Arts and Sciences, Department of Urban Studies and Planning, Detroit, MI 48202. Offers economic development (Graduate Certificate); urban studies and planning (MUP). *Accreditation:* ACSP. *Program availability:* Part-time, evening/weekend. *Faculty:* 6 full-time (2 women), 7 part-time/adjunct (2 women). *Students:* 9 full-time (5 women), 53 part-time (32 women); includes 29 minority (24 Black or African American, non-Hispanic/Latino; 1 American Indian or Alaska Native, non-Hispanic/Latino; 1 Hispanic/Latino; 3 Two or more races, non-Hispanic/Latino), 2 international. Average age 30. 84 applicants, 42% accepted, 25 enrolled. In 2019, 8 master's awarded. *Degree requirements:* For master's, 48 credits of coursework; for Graduate Certificate, 12 credits of coursework, at least three of which must be outside of the student's Master's degree. *Entrance requirements:* For master's, transcripts, two letters of recommendation, and personal statement; for Graduate Certificate, graduate degree or actively pursuing a graduate degree at WSU; personal statement of interest. Additional exam requirements/recommendations for international students: required—TOEFL (minimum score 550 paper-based; 79 iBT), TWE (minimum score 5.5), Michigan English Language Assessment Battery (minimum score 85); recommended—IELTS (minimum score 6.5). *Application deadline:* For fall admission, 6/1 priority date for domestic students, 5/1 priority date for international students; for winter admission, 10/1 priority date for domestic students, 9/1 priority date for international students; for spring admission, 2/1 priority date for domestic students, 1/1 priority date for international students. Applications are processed on a rolling basis. Application fee: $50. Electronic applications accepted. *Expenses:* Tuition: Full-time $34,567. *Financial support:* In 2019–20, 19 students received support. Scholarships/grants available. Financial award application deadline: 6/30; financial award applicants required to submit FAFSA. *Unit head:* Dr. Rayman Mohamed, Chair, 313-577-3356, E-mail: rayman.mohamed@wayne.edu. *Application contact:* Dr. Rayman Mohamed, Chair, 313-577-3356, E-mail: rayman.mohamed@wayne.edu. Website: http://clas.wayne.edu/dusp/

Urban Studies

Arizona State University at Tempe, College of Liberal Arts and Sciences, School of Human Evolution and Social Change, Tempe, AZ 85287-2402. Offers anthropology (MA, PhD), including anthropology (PhD), archaeology (PhD), bioarchaeology (PhD), evolutionary (PhD), museum studies (MA), sociocultural (PhD); applied mathematics for the life and social sciences (PhD); environmental social science (PhD), including environmental social science, urbanism; global health (MA, PhD), including complex adaptive systems science (PhD), evolutionary global health sciences (PhD), health and culture (PhD), urbanism (PhD); immigration studies (Graduate Certificate). Terminal master's awarded for partial completion of doctoral program. *Degree requirements:* For master's, thesis or alternative, interactive Program of Study (iPOS) submitted before completing 50 percent of required credit hours; for doctorate, comprehensive exam, thesis/dissertation, interactive Program of Study (iPOS) submitted before completing 50 percent of required credit hours. *Entrance requirements:* For master's and doctorate, GRE, minimum GPA of 3.0 or equivalent in last 2 years of work leading to bachelor's degree. Additional exam requirements/recommendations for international students: required—TOEFL, IELTS, or PTE. Electronic applications accepted.

Azusa Pacific University, Azusa Pacific Seminary, Program in Pastoral Studies, Concentration in Urban Studies, Azusa, CA 91702-7000. Offers MAPS. *Degree requirements:* For master's, project.

Boston University, Metropolitan College, Program in Urban Affairs, Boston, MA 02215. Offers MUA. *Program availability:* Part-time, evening/weekend. *Faculty:* 2 full-time (both women), 8 part-time/adjunct (2 women). *Students:* 2 full-time (0 women), 11 part-time (5 women); includes 5 minority (3 Black or African American, non-Hispanic/Latino; 2 Hispanic/Latino), 3 international. Average age 27. 18 applicants, 83% accepted, 4 enrolled. In 2019, 14 master's awarded. *Entrance requirements:* Additional exam requirements/recommendations for international students: required—TOEFL. *Application deadline:* For fall admission, 7/15 priority date for domestic and international students; for spring admission, 12/15 for domestic students, 11/15 priority date for international students. Applications are processed on a rolling basis. Application fee: $85. Electronic applications accepted. *Expenses:* Contact institution. *Financial support:* In 2019–20, 3 research assistantships (averaging $8,400 per year), 3 teaching assistantships (averaging $2,500 per year) were awarded; career-related internships or fieldwork, Federal Work-Study, and unspecified assistantships also available. Support available to part-time students. Financial award applicants required to submit FAFSA. *Unit head:* Dr. Mary Ellen Mastrorilli, Chair, 617-353-3025, Fax: 617-358-3595, E-mail: memastro@bu.edu. *Application contact:* Dr. Madhu Dutta-Koehler, Director, 617-358-2364, E-mail: duttam@bu.edu. Website: https://www.bu.edu/met/programs/graduate/urban-affairs/

Brooklyn College of the City University of New York, School of Humanities and Social Sciences, Department of Political Science, Brooklyn, NY 11210-2889. Offers international affairs (MA); political science (MA); urban policy and administration (MA). *Program availability:* Part-time, evening/weekend. *Degree requirements:* For master's, comprehensive exam (for some programs), thesis or alternative, foreign language exam (for international affairs program). *Entrance requirements:* For master's, 2 letters of recommendation, personal statement. Additional exam requirements/recommendations for international students: required—TOEFL (minimum score 500 paper-based; 61 iBT).

Cleveland State University, College of Graduate Studies, Maxine Goodman Levin College of Urban Affairs, Program in Urban Studies, Cleveland, OH 44115. Offers MS, Certificate. *Program availability:* Part-time, evening/weekend. *Faculty:* 23 full-time (11 women), 23 part-time/adjunct (6 women). *Students:* 7 full-time (4 women), 27 part-time (15 women); includes 9 minority (8 Black or African American, non-Hispanic/Latino; 1 Hispanic/Latino), 4 international. Average age 34. 21 applicants, 29% accepted, 4 enrolled. In 2019, 3 master's awarded. *Degree requirements:* For master's, thesis or alternative, exit project. *Entrance requirements:* For master's, GRE General Test (minimum score: verbal and quantitative combined 40th percentile, analytical writing 4.0), minimum GPA of 3.0. Additional exam requirements/recommendations for international students: required—TOEFL (minimum score 550 paper-based; 78 iBT), IELTS (6.0), or International Test of English Proficiency (iTEP). *Application deadline:* For fall admission, 7/1 priority date for domestic students, 5/15 for international students; for spring admission, 11/15 for domestic students, 11/1 for international students; for summer admission, 4/1 for domestic students, 3/15 for international students. Applications are processed on a rolling basis. Application fee: $40. Electronic applications accepted. *Expenses:* Tuition, state resident: full-time $10,215; part-time $6810 per credit hour. Tuition, nonresident: full-time $17,496; part-time $11,664 per credit hour. *International tuition:* $19,316 full-time. Tuition and fees vary according to degree level and program. *Financial support:* In 2019–20, 4 students received support, including 1 research assistantship with full tuition reimbursement available (averaging $6,960 per year), 1 teaching assistantship with tuition reimbursement available (averaging $6,960 per year); scholarships/grants, tuition waivers (full and partial), and unspecified assistantships also available. Support available to part-time students. Financial award application deadline: 3/1; financial award applicants required to submit FAFSA. *Unit head:* Dr. Brian Mikelbank, Associate Professor/Program Director, 216-875-9980, Fax: 216-687-9342, E-mail: b.mikelbank@csuohio.edu. *Application contact:* David Arrighi, Graduate Academic Advisor, 216-523-7522, Fax: 216-687-5398, E-mail: d.arrighi@csuohio.edu. Website: http://urban.csuohio.edu/academics/graduate/msus/

Urban Studies

Cleveland State University, College of Graduate Studies, Maxine Goodman Levin College of Urban Affairs, Program in Urban Studies and Public Affairs, Cleveland, OH 44115. Offers communication (PhD); public administration (PhD); urban policy and development (PhD). *Program availability:* Part-time, evening/weekend. *Degree requirements:* For doctorate, comprehensive exam, thesis/dissertation. *Entrance requirements:* For doctorate, GRE General Test (minimum score: verbal and quantitative 50th percentile, analytical writing 4.0), minimum GPA of 3.5. Additional exam requirements/recommendations for international students: required—TOEFL (minimum score 550 paper-based; 78 iBT), IELTS (6.0), or International Test of English Proficiency (iTEP). Electronic applications accepted. *Expenses:* Contact institution.

Columbus State University, Graduate Studies, College of Letters and Sciences, Department of Political Science and Public Administration, Columbus, GA 31907-5645. Offers public administration (MPA), including criminal justice, environmental policy, government administration, health services administration, political campaigning, urban policy. *Program availability:* Part-time, evening/weekend, 100% online, blended/hybrid learning. *Degree requirements:* For master's, comprehensive exam. *Entrance requirements:* For master's, GRE General Test, minimum GPA of 2.75, three letters of recommendation. Additional exam requirements/recommendations for international students: required—TOEFL (minimum score 550 paper-based; 79 iBT). Electronic applications accepted. *Expenses:* Tuition, area resident: Full-time $210; part-time $210 per credit hour. Tuition, state resident: full-time $210; part-time $210 per credit hour. Tuition, nonresident: full-time $817; part-time $817 per credit hour. *International tuition:* $817 full-time. *Required fees:* $802.50. Tuition and fees vary according to course load, degree level and program.

Concordia University, School of Graduate Studies, Faculty of Arts and Science, Department of Geography, Planning and Environment, Montréal, QC H3G 1M8, Canada. Offers environmental assessment (M Env, Diploma); geography, urban and environmental studies (M Sc, PhD).

Fordham University, Graduate School of Arts and Sciences, Program in Urban Studies, New York, NY 10458. Offers MA. *Students:* Average age 28. 14 applicants, 86% accepted, 4 enrolled. In 2019, 1 master's awarded. *Entrance requirements:* Additional exam requirements/recommendations for international students: required—TOEFL. Application fee: $70. *Financial support:* Tuition waivers (partial) available. *Unit head:* Dr. Annika Hinze, Director, 718-817-3960, E-mail: rwakeman@fordham.edu. *Application contact:* Garrett Marino, Director of Graduate Admissions, 718-817-4419, Fax: 718-817-3566, E-mail: gmarino10@fordham.edu.

Fresno Pacific University, Biblical Seminary, Program in Community Leadership and Transformation, Fresno, CA 93702-4709. Offers MA. *Entrance requirements:* For master's, bachelor's degree, minimum GPA of 2.5, personal profile statement, three letters of references, writing sample.

Hunter College of the City University of New York, Graduate School, School of Arts and Sciences, Department of Urban Policy and Planning, Program in Urban Affairs, New York, NY 10065-5085. Offers MS. *Program availability:* Part-time. *Degree requirements:* For master's, thesis or alternative, 2 formal reports, internship. *Entrance requirements:* For master's, minimum 12 credits of course work in social sciences. Additional exam requirements/recommendations for international students: required—TOEFL.

Indiana University Northwest, College of Arts and Sciences, Gary, IN 46408. Offers clinical counseling (MS), including drug and alcohol counseling; community development/urban studies (Graduate Certificate); computer information systems (Graduate Certificate); liberal studies (MLS); race-ethnic studies (Graduate Certificate); women's and gender studies (Graduate Certificate). *Program availability:* Part-time, evening/weekend. *Entrance requirements:* For master's, GRE (recommended for MS), minimum undergraduate GPA of 3.0, bachelor's degree from accredited university (for MS). Electronic applications accepted. *Expenses:* Contact institution.

Le Moyne College, Department of Education, Syracuse, NY 13214. Offers adolescent education (MS Ed, MST); adolescent education/special education (MS Ed, MST); adolescent English (MST), including grades 7-12; adolescent English/special education (MST), including grades 7-12; adolescent foreign language (MST), including grades 7-12; adolescent history (MST), including grades 7-12; childhood education (MS Ed); childhood education/special education (MS Ed); elementary education (MS Ed); general education (MS Ed); inclusive childhood education (MST); literacy education (MS Ed), including birth to grade 6, grades 5-12; school building leader (MS Ed); school building leadership (CAS); school district business leader (MS Ed, CAS); school district leader (MS Ed); school district leadership (CAS); secondary education (MS Ed); special education (MS Ed); teaching English to speakers of other languages (MS Ed); urban studies (MS Ed). *Accreditation:* TEAC. *Program availability:* Part-time, evening/weekend. *Faculty:* 8 full-time (5 women), 15 part-time/adjunct (10 women). *Students:* 27 full-time (21 women), 127 part-time (83 women); includes 16 minority (6 Black or African American, non-Hispanic/Latino; 1 American Indian or Alaska Native, non-Hispanic/Latino; 2 Asian, non-Hispanic/Latino; 6 Hispanic/Latino; 1 Two or more races, non-Hispanic/Latino), 1 international. Average age 34. 155 applicants, 88% accepted, 117 enrolled. In 2019, 66 master's, 39 CASs awarded. *Degree requirements:* For master's, thesis, 30 credit hours; for CAS, varies by program. *Entrance requirements:* For master's, GRE or MAT, bachelor's degree with minimum undergraduate GPA of 3.0, 2 letters of recommendation, official transcripts; personal statement; for CAS, bachelor's degree with minimum undergraduate GPA of 3.0, 2 letters of recommendation; resume; official transcripts; personal statement; gainful employment disclosure. Additional exam requirements/recommendations for international students: required—TOEFL (minimum score 79 iBT), GRE; recommended—IELTS (minimum score 6.5). *Application deadline:* For fall admission, 4/1 priority date for domestic and international students; for spring admission, 10/1 priority date for domestic and international students; for summer admission, 3/1 priority date for domestic and international students. Applications are processed on a rolling basis. Electronic applications accepted. *Expenses:* $764 per credit hour; $75 per semester fee. *Financial support:* In 2019–20, 37 students received support. Career-related internships or fieldwork, Federal Work-Study, scholarships/grants, and health care benefits available. Support available to part-time students. Financial award applicants required to submit FAFSA. *Unit head:* Dr. Stephen C. Fleury, Chair, Department of Education, 315-445-4376, Fax: 315-445-4744, E-mail: fleurysc@lemoyne.edu. *Application contact:* Teresa M. Renn, Director of Graduate Admission, 315-445-5444, Fax: 315-445-6092, E-mail: GradEducation@lemoyne.edu. Website: http://www.lemoyne.edu/education

Long Island University - Brooklyn, Richard L. Conolly College of Liberal Arts and Sciences, Brooklyn, NY 11201-8423. Offers biology (MS); chemistry (MS); clinical psychology (PhD); creative writing (MFA); English (MA); media arts (MA, MFA); political science (MA); psychology (MA); social science (MS); United Nations (Advanced Certificate); urban studies (MA); writing and production for television (MFA). *Program availability:* Part-time. Terminal master's awarded for partial completion of doctoral program. *Degree requirements:* For master's, comprehensive exam (for some programs), thesis (for some programs); for doctorate, thesis/dissertation. *Entrance requirements:* For doctorate, GRE. Additional exam requirements/recommendations for international students: required—TOEFL (minimum score 550 paper-based, 79 iBT) or IELTS. Electronic applications accepted.

Loyola University Chicago, Graduate School, Program in Urban Affairs, Chicago, IL 60611. Offers MA. *Program availability:* Part-time, evening/weekend. *Students:* 5 applicants, 20% accepted. *Application deadline:* For fall admission, 6/30 for domestic students. Applications are processed on a rolling basis. Application fee: $0. Electronic applications accepted. *Expenses:* Tuition: Full-time $18,540; part-time $1033 per credit hour. *Required fees:* $904; $230 per credit hour. *Unit head:* Dr. Annette Steinacker, Director, 312-518-8611, E-mail: muapp@luc.edu. *Application contact:* Jill Schur, Director, Graduate Enrollment Management, 312-915-8902, E-mail: gradinfo@luc.edu. Website: https://www.luc.edu/muapp/

Massachusetts Institute of Technology, School of Architecture and Planning, Department of Urban Studies and Planning, Cambridge, MA 02139. Offers city planning (MCP); urban and regional planning (PhD); urban and regional studies (PhD); urban studies and planning (SM). *Accreditation:* ACSP (one or more programs are accredited). *Degree requirements:* For master's, thesis; for doctorate, comprehensive exam, thesis/dissertation. *Entrance requirements:* For master's and doctorate, GRE General Test. Additional exam requirements/recommendations for international students: required—TOEFL, IELTS. Electronic applications accepted.

Minnesota State University Mankato, College of Graduate Studies and Research, College of Social and Behavioral Sciences, Urban and Regional Studies Institute, Mankato, MN 56001. Offers local government management (Certificate); non-profit leadership (Certificate); urban and regional studies (MA); urban planning (MA, Certificate). *Degree requirements:* For master's, one foreign language, comprehensive exam, thesis or alternative. *Entrance requirements:* For master's, minimum GPA of 3.0 during previous 2 years, 2 letters of recommendation. Additional exam requirements/recommendations for international students: required—TOEFL. Electronic applications accepted.

Moody Bible Institute, Graduate School, Chicago, IL 60610-3284. Offers biblical studies (MABS, Graduate Certificate); intercultural studies (MAIS, Graduate Certificate); ministry (M Div, M Min); spiritual formation and discipleship (MASF, Graduate Certificate); urban studies (MA, Graduate Certificate). *Program availability:* Part-time. *Degree requirements:* For master's, 2 foreign languages, fieldwork (MABS); colloquium, field research project (MA Min). *Entrance requirements:* For master's, 30 hours in Bible/theology, 2 years of ministry experience (MA Min).

New Jersey City University, Debra Cannon Partridge Wolfe College of Education, Department of Educational Leadership and Counseling, Jersey City, NJ 07305-1597. Offers counselor education (MA); educational administration and supervision (MA); urban education (MA). *Accreditation:* TEAC. *Program availability:* Part-time, evening/weekend. *Entrance requirements:* Additional exam requirements/recommendations for international students: required—TOEFL (minimum score 79 iBT).

New York University, Tandon School of Engineering, Department of Civil and Urban Engineering, Major in Urban Systems Engineering and Management, New York, NY 10012-1019. Offers urban systems engineering and management (MS). *Entrance requirements:* Additional exam requirements/recommendations for international students: required—TOEFL (minimum score 550 paper-based; 90 iBT); recommended—IELTS (minimum score 7).

Norfolk State University, School of Graduate Studies, School of Liberal Arts, Department of Sociology, Program in Urban Affairs, Norfolk, VA 23504. Offers MA. *Program availability:* Part-time. *Degree requirements:* For master's, thesis. *Entrance requirements:* For master's, minimum GPA of 2.5.

North Dakota State University, College of Graduate and Interdisciplinary Studies, Interdisciplinary Program in Transportation and Logistics, Fargo, ND 58102. Offers managerial logistics (MML); transportation and logistics (PhD); transportation and urban systems (MS). *Entrance requirements:* Additional exam requirements/recommendations for international students: required—TOEFL. Tuition and fees vary according to program and reciprocity agreements.

Northeastern University, College of Social Sciences and Humanities, Boston, MA 02115. Offers criminology and criminal justice (MSCJ); criminology and justice policy (PhD); economics (MA, PhD); English (MA, PhD); international affairs (MA); law and public policy (PhD); political science (MA, PhD); public administration (MPA); public policy (MPP); security and resilience studies (MS); sociology (MA, PhD); urban and regional policy (MS); urban informatics (MS); world history (MA, PhD). *Program availability:* Online learning. *Degree requirements:* For doctorate, variable foreign language requirement, comprehensive exam, thesis/dissertation. *Entrance requirements:* For master's and doctorate, GRE. Additional exam requirements/recommendations for international students: required—TOEFL, IELTS. Electronic applications accepted. *Expenses:* Contact institution.

Queens College of the City University of New York, School of Social Sciences, Department of Urban Studies, Queens, NY 11367-1597. Offers urban affairs (MA). *Program availability:* Part-time, evening/weekend. *Degree requirements:* For master's, thesis. *Entrance requirements:* For master's, minimum GPA of 3.0. Additional exam requirements/recommendations for international students: required—TOEFL (minimum score 61 iBT), IELTS (minimum score 5). Electronic applications accepted.

Rutgers University - Newark, Graduate School, Program in Public Administration, Newark, NJ 07102. Offers health care administration (MPA); human resources administration (MPA); public administration (PhD); public management (MPA); public policy analysis (MPA); urban systems and issues (MPA). *Accreditation:* NASPAA (one or more programs are accredited). *Program availability:* Part-time, evening/weekend. *Degree requirements:* For master's, comprehensive exam, thesis or alternative; for doctorate, thesis/dissertation. *Entrance requirements:* For master's, GRE, minimum undergraduate B average; for doctorate, GRE, MPA, minimum B average. Electronic applications accepted.

Rutgers University - Newark, Graduate School, Program in Urban Systems, Newark, NJ 07102. Offers PhD.

Savannah State University, Master of Science in Urban Studies and Planning Program, Savannah, GA 31404. Offers MSUS. *Program availability:* Part-time. *Degree requirements:* For master's, thesis or capstone project. *Entrance requirements:* For master's, GRE or MAT, minimum cumulative GPA of 2.6, 3 letters of recommendation, statement of interest, official transcripts, curriculum vitae. Additional exam requirements/recommendations for international students: required—TOEFL. Electronic applications accepted. *Expenses:* Contact institution.

Simon Fraser University, Office of Graduate Studies and Postdoctoral Fellows, Faculty of Arts and Social Sciences, Urban Studies Program, Vancouver, BC V6B 5K3, Canada. Offers M Urb, Graduate Diploma. *Program availability:* Part-time. *Degree requirements:* For master's, project. *Entrance requirements:* For master's, minimum GPA of 3.0 (on scale of 4.33) or 3.33 based on last 60 credits of undergraduate courses; for Graduate Diploma, minimum GPA of 2.5 (on scale of 4.33) or 2.67 based on last 60 credits of undergraduate courses. Additional exam requirements/recommendations for international students: recommended—TOEFL (minimum score 580 paper-based; 93 iBT), IELTS (minimum score 7), TWE (minimum score 5). Electronic applications accepted.

Temple University, College of Liberal Arts, Department of Geography and Urban Studies, Philadelphia, PA 19122-6096. Offers geographic information systems (PSM, Graduate Certificate); geography and urban studies (MA, PhD). *Program availability:* Part-time, evening/weekend. *Faculty:* 17 full-time (5 women), 3 part-time/adjunct (all women). *Students:* 31 full-time (16 women), 36 part-time (19 women); includes 17 minority (8 Black or African American, non-Hispanic/Latino; 2 Asian, non-Hispanic/Latino; 6 Hispanic/Latino; 1 Two or more races, non-Hispanic/Latino), 8 international. 63 applicants, 33% accepted, 15 enrolled. In 2019, 12 master's, 3 doctorates, 3 other advanced degrees awarded. *Entrance requirements:* For master's, GRE (M.A.), 3 letters of recommendation, statement of goals; for doctorate, GRE, 3 letters of recommendation, statement of goals, writing sample. Additional exam requirements/recommendations for international students: required—TOEFL (minimum score 88 iBT), IELTS, PTE, one of three is required. *Application deadline:* Applications are processed on a rolling basis. Application fee: $60. Electronic applications accepted. *Financial support:* Fellowships, research assistantships, teaching assistantships, Federal Work-Study, health care benefits, tuition waivers, and unspecified assistantships available. Financial award applicants required to submit FAFSA. *Unit head:* Melissa Gilbert, Chairperson, 215-204-7692, E-mail: mgilbert@temple.edu. *Application contact:* Liz Janczewski, Coordinator, 215-204-3386, E-mail: liz.janczewski@temple.edu. Website: http://www.cla.temple.edu/gus/

Tufts University, Graduate School of Arts and Sciences, Department of Urban and Environmental Policy and Planning, Medford, MA 02155. Offers community development (MA); environmental policy (MA); health and human welfare (MA); housing policy (MA); international environment/development policy (MA); public policy (MPP); MA/JD; MA/MBA; MA/MPH; MA/MS; MALD/MA. *Accreditation:* ACSP (one or more programs are accredited). *Program availability:* Part-time. *Degree requirements:* For master's, thesis or alternative, internship. *Entrance requirements:* For master's, GRE General Test. Additional exam requirements/recommendations for international students: required—TOEFL (minimum score 550 paper-based; 80 iBT), IELTS (minimum score 6.5). Electronic applications accepted. *Expenses:* Contact institution.

Université du Québec à Montréal, Graduate Programs, Program in Urban Analysis and Management, Montréal, QC H3C 3P8, Canada. Offers MA. *Program availability:* Part-time. *Entrance requirements:* For master's, appropriate bachelor's degree or equivalent and proficiency in French.

Université du Québec à Montréal, Graduate Programs, Program in Urban Studies, Montréal, QC H3C 3P8, Canada. Offers MA, PhD. *Program availability:* Part-time. *Degree requirements:* For doctorate, thesis/dissertation. *Entrance requirements:* For doctorate, appropriate master's degree or equivalent, proficiency in French.

Université du Québec, École nationale d'administration publique, Graduate Programs in Public Administration, Program in Urban Analysis and Management, Quebec, QC G1K 9E5, Canada. Offers MAGU. *Program availability:* Part-time. *Entrance requirements:* For master's, appropriate bachelor's degree, proficiency in French.

Université du Québec, Institut National de la Recherche Scientifique, Graduate Programs, Centre for Urbanisation Culture Societe, Montreal, QC H2X 1E3, Canada. Offers population studies (M Sc, PhD); urban studies (MA). *Program availability:* Part-time. *Faculty:* 32 full-time. *Students:* 77 full-time (43 women), 24 part-time (11 women), 22 international. Average age 33. 27 applicants, 93% accepted, 20 enrolled. In 2019, 9 master's, 4 doctorates awarded. *Degree requirements:* For master's, thesis (for some programs); for doctorate, thesis/dissertation; for DESS, thesis or alternative. *Entrance requirements:* For master's, appropriate bachelor's degree, proficiency in French; for doctorate, appropriate master's degree, proficiency in French; for DESS, proficiency in French. *Application deadline:* For fall admission, 3/30 for domestic and international students; for winter admission, 11/1 for domestic and international students; for spring admission, 3/1 for domestic and international students. Application fee: $45. Electronic applications accepted. *Financial support:* In 2019–20, fellowships (averaging $16,500 per year) were awarded; research assistantships also available. *Unit head:* Helene Belleau, Director, 514-499-4001, Fax: 514-499-4065, E-mail: helene.belleau@ucs.inrs.ca. *Application contact:* Sean Otto, Registrar, 418-654-2518, Fax: 418-654-3858, E-mail: sean.otto@inrs.ca. Website: http://www.ucs.inrs.ca

University at Albany, State University of New York, College of Arts and Sciences, Department of Sociology, Albany, NY 12222-0001. Offers demography (Certificate); sociology (MA, PhD); urban policy (Certificate). *Program availability:* Blended/hybrid learning. *Faculty:* 23 full-time (10 women), 11 part-time/adjunct (8 women). *Students:* 31 full-time (26 women), 52 part-time (38 women); includes 17 minority (6 Black or African American, non-Hispanic/Latino; 1 American Indian or Alaska Native, non-Hispanic/Latino; 5 Asian, non-Hispanic/Latino; 3 Hispanic/Latino; 2 Two or more races, non-Hispanic/Latino), 35 international. 77 applicants, 49% accepted, 16 enrolled. In 2019, 6 master's, 8 doctorates awarded. Terminal master's awarded for partial completion of doctoral program. *Degree requirements:* For master's, thesis; for doctorate, thesis/dissertation, 2 specialization exams, research tool. *Entrance requirements:* For master's, GRE General Test, transcripts of all schools attended, statement of background and goals, departmental questionnaire, resume, names and contact information for 3 recommenders; for doctorate, GRE General Test. Additional exam requirements/recommendations for international students: required—TOEFL (minimum score 550 paper-based). *Application deadline:* For fall admission, 1/15 for domestic students, 5/1 for international students; for spring admission, 11/15 for domestic students. Applications are processed on a rolling basis. Application fee: $75. Electronic applications accepted. *Expenses: Tuition, area resident:* Full-time $11,530; part-time $480 per credit hour. Tuition, nonresident: full-time $23,530; part-time $980 per credit hour. *International tuition:* $23,530 full-time. *Required fees:* $2185; $96 per credit hour. Part-time tuition and fees vary according to course load and program. *Financial support:* Fellowships, research assistantships, teaching assistantships, career-related internships or fieldwork, and Federal Work-Study available. Financial award application deadline: 3/15. *Unit head:* Glenn Deane, Chair, 518-442-4666, Fax: 518-442-4936, E-mail: gdeane@albany.edu. *Application contact:* Michael DeRensis, Director, Graduate Admissions, 518-442-3980, Fax: 518-442-3922, E-mail: graduate@albany.edu. Website: https://www.albany.edu/sociology/index.html

University of California, Irvine, School of Social Ecology, Department of Urban Planning and Public Policy, Irvine, CA 92697. Offers planning, policy and design (PhD); urban and regional planning (MURP). *Accreditation:* ACSP (one or more programs are accredited). *Students:* 122 full-time (85 women); includes 65 minority (6 Black or African American, non-Hispanic/Latino; 15 Asian, non-Hispanic/Latino; 38 Hispanic/Latino; 1 Native Hawaiian or other Pacific Islander, non-Hispanic/Latino; 5 Two or more races, non-Hispanic/Latino), 31 international. Average age 28. 306 applicants, 64% accepted, 55 enrolled. In 2019, 50 master's, 1 doctorate awarded. *Degree requirements:* For doctorate, thesis/dissertation, research project. *Entrance requirements:* For master's and doctorate, GRE General Test, minimum GPA of 3.0. Additional exam requirements/recommendations for international students: required—TOEFL (minimum score 550 paper-based). *Application deadline:* For fall admission, 1/15 priority date for domestic and international students. Application fee: $120 ($140 for international students). Electronic applications accepted. *Financial support:* Fellowships, research assistantships with full tuition reimbursements, teaching assistantships, institutionally

sponsored loans, traineeships, health care benefits, and unspecified assistantships available. Financial award application deadline: 1/15; financial award applicants required to submit FAFSA. *Unit head:* David L. Feldman, Chair, 949-824-4384, Fax: 949-824-3056, E-mail: feldmand@uci.edu. *Application contact:* Janet Gallagher, Graduate Coordinator, 949-824-9849, Fax: 949-824-8566, E-mail: janetg@uci.edu. Website: http://uppp.soceco.uci.edu/

University of Delaware, Center for Energy and Environmental Policy, Newark, DE 19716. Offers energy and environmental policy (MA, MEEP, PhD); urban affairs and public policy (PhD), including technology, environment, and society. *Degree requirements:* For master's, analytical paper or thesis; for doctorate, comprehensive exam, thesis/dissertation. *Entrance requirements:* For master's, GRE General Test, minimum GPA of 3.0; for doctorate, GRE General Test, minimum GPA of 3.5. Additional exam requirements/recommendations for international students: required—TOEFL. Electronic applications accepted.

University of Delaware, College of Arts and Sciences, School of Public Policy and Administration, Program in Urban Affairs and Public Policy, Newark, DE 19716. Offers governance planning and management (PhD); historic preservation (MA); social and urban policy (PhD); technology, environment and society (PhD); urban affairs and public policy (MA). *Program availability:* Part-time. Terminal master's awarded for partial completion of doctoral program. *Degree requirements:* For master's, analytical paper or thesis; for doctorate, thesis/dissertation. *Entrance requirements:* For master's, GRE General Test, minimum GPA of 3.0; for doctorate, GRE General Test, minimum GPA of 3.5. Additional exam requirements/recommendations for international students: required—TOEFL. Electronic applications accepted.

University of Lethbridge, School of Graduate Studies, Lethbridge, AB T1K 3M4, Canada. Offers addictions counseling (M Sc); agricultural biotechnology (M Sc); agricultural studies (M Sc, MA); anthropology (MA); archaeology (M Sc, MA); art (MA, MFA); biochemistry (M Sc); biological sciences (M Sc); biomolecular science (PhD); biosystems and biodiversity (PhD); Canadian studies (MA); chemistry (M Sc); computer science (M Sc); computer science and geographical information science (M Sc); counseling (MC); counseling psychology (M Ed); dramatic arts (MA); earth, space, and physical science (PhD); economics (MA); education (MA, PhD); educational leadership (M Ed); English (MA); environmental science (M Sc); evolution and behavior (PhD); exercise science (M Sc); French (MA); French/German (MA); French/Spanish (MA); general education (M Ed); geography (M Sc, MA); German (MA); health sciences (M Sc); individualized multidisciplinary (M Sc, MA); kinesiology (M Sc, MA); management (M Sc), including accounting, finance, human resource management and labor relations, information systems, international management, marketing, policy and strategy; mathematics (M Sc); music (M Mus, MA); Native American studies (MA); neuroscience (M Sc, PhD); new media (MA, MFA); nursing (M Sc, MN); philosophy (MA); physics (M Sc); political science (MA); psychology (M Sc, MA); religious studies (MA); sociology (MA); theatre and dramatic arts (MFA); theoretical and computational science (PhD); urban and regional studies (MA); women and gender studies (MA). *Program availability:* Part-time, evening/weekend. *Degree requirements:* For master's, thesis (for some programs); for doctorate, comprehensive exam, thesis/dissertation. *Entrance requirements:* For master's, GMAT (for M Sc in management), bachelor's degree in related field, minimum GPA of 3.0 during previous 20 graded semester courses, 2 years' teaching or related experience (M Ed); for doctorate, master's degree, minimum graduate GPA of 3.5. Additional exam requirements/recommendations for international students: required—TOEFL (minimum score 580 paper-based; 93 iBT). Electronic applications accepted.

University of Louisville, Graduate School, College of Arts and Sciences, Department of Urban and Public Affairs, Louisville, KY 40208. Offers public administration (MPA), including human resources management, non-profit management, public policy and administration; urban and public affairs (PhD), including urban planning and development, urban policy and administration; urban planning (MUP), including administration of planning organizations, housing and community development, land use and environmental planning, spatial analysis. *Program availability:* Part-time, evening/weekend. *Faculty:* 13 full-time (6 women), 2 part-time/adjunct (1 woman). *Students:* 44 full-time (24 women), 24 part-time (14 women); includes 12 minority (6 Black or African American, non-Hispanic/Latino; 2 Hispanic/Latino; 4 Two or more races, non-Hispanic/Latino), 7 international. Average age 34. 51 applicants, 67% accepted, 25 enrolled. In 2019, 14 master's, 3 doctorates awarded. Terminal master's awarded for partial completion of doctoral program. *Degree requirements:* For master's, internship; for doctorate, comprehensive exam, thesis/dissertation. *Entrance requirements:* For master's, GRE General Test, 2 letters of reference, official transcripts. Minimum GPA of 3.0; for doctorate, GRE General Test, Two letters of reference, official transcripts. Masters degree in appropriate field. Additional exam requirements/recommendations for international students: required—TOEFL (minimum score 550 paper-based; 79 iBT), IELTS can be used in place of the TOEFL; recommended—IELTS (minimum score 6.5). *Application deadline:* For fall admission, 2/1 for domestic and international students. Applications are processed on a rolling basis. Application fee: $65. Electronic applications accepted. *Expenses: Tuition, area resident:* Full-time $13,000; part-time $723 per credit hour. Tuition, state resident: full-time $13,000; part-time $723 per credit hour. Tuition, nonresident: full-time $27,114; part-time $1507 per credit hour. *International tuition:* $27,114 full-time. *Required fees:* $196. Tuition and fees vary according to program and reciprocity agreements. *Financial support:* In 2019–20, 29 students received support, including 11 research assistantships with full tuition reimbursements available (averaging $19,000 per year); fellowships, teaching assistantships, health care benefits, and unspecified assistantships also available. Financial award application deadline: 2/1. *Unit head:* Dr. David Simpson, Professor/Chair, 502-852-8019, Fax: 502-852-4558, E-mail: dave.simpson@louisville.edu. Website: http://supa.louisville.edu

University of Maryland, Baltimore County, The Graduate School, College of Arts, Humanities and Social Sciences, School of Public Policy, Baltimore, MD 21250. Offers public policy (MPP, PhD), including economics (PhD), educational policy, emergency services (PhD), environmental policy (MPP), evaluation and analytical methods, health policy, policy history (PhD), public management, urban policy. *Program availability:* Part-time, evening/weekend. *Faculty:* 10 full-time (5 women). *Students:* 49 full-time (29 women), 63 part-time (31 women); includes 39 minority (18 Black or African American, non-Hispanic/Latino; 1 American Indian or Alaska Native, non-Hispanic/Latino; 9 Asian, non-Hispanic/Latino; 9 Hispanic/Latino; 2 Two or more races, non-Hispanic/Latino), 10 international. Average age 36. 73 applicants, 74% accepted, 31 enrolled. In 2019, 17 master's, 8 doctorates awarded. Terminal master's awarded for partial completion of doctoral program. *Degree requirements:* For master's, thesis, policy analysis paper, internship for pre-service; for doctorate, comprehensive exam, thesis/dissertation, comprehensive and field qualifying exams. *Entrance requirements:* For master's, GRE General Test, 3 academic letters of reference, resume, official transcripts; for doctorate, GRE General Test, 3 academic letters of reference, resume, research paper, official transcripts. Additional exam requirements/recommendations for international students: required—TOEFL (minimum score 550 paper-based; 80 iBT), IELTS (minimum score 6.5). *Application deadline:* For fall admission, 1/15 priority date for domestic students, 1/1 priority date for international students; for spring admission, 11/1 priority date for

Urban Studies

domestic students, 5/1 priority date for international students. Applications are processed on a rolling basis. Application fee: $50. Electronic applications accepted. *Expenses:* $14,382 per year. *Financial support:* In 2019–20, 26 students received support, including 23 research assistantships with full tuition reimbursements available (averaging $20,000 per year), 3 teaching assistantships; Federal Work-Study, scholarships/grants, health care benefits, and unspecified assistantships also available. Financial award application deadline: 1/1; financial award applicants required to submit FAFSA. *Unit head:* Dr. Susan Sterett, Director, 410-455-2140, Fax: 410-455-1172, E-mail: ssterett@umbc.edu. *Application contact:* Shelley Morris, Administrator of Academic Affairs, 410-455-3202, Fax: 410-455-1172, E-mail: shelleym@umbc.edu. Website: http://publicpolicy.umbc.edu/

University of New Orleans, Graduate School, College of Liberal Arts, Education and Human Development, Department of Planning and Urban Studies, Program in Urban Studies, New Orleans, LA 70148. Offers MS, PhD. *Degree requirements:* For master's, thesis; for doctorate, thesis/dissertation. *Entrance requirements:* For master's, GRE General Test. Additional exam requirements/recommendations for international students: required—TOEFL (minimum score 550 paper-based; 79 iBT), IELTS (minimum score 6.5). Electronic applications accepted.

University of San Francisco, College of Arts and Sciences, Urban and Public Affairs Program, San Francisco, CA 94117. Offers MA. *Program availability:* Part-time, evening/weekend. *Faculty:* 3 full-time (2 women), 3 part-time/adjunct (1 woman). *Students:* 40 full-time (19 women); includes 20 minority (6 Black or African American, non-Hispanic/Latino; 3 Asian, non-Hispanic/Latino; 11 Hispanic/Latino), 3 international. Average age 26. 61 applicants, 77% accepted, 18 enrolled. In 2019, 12 master's awarded. *Entrance requirements:* Additional exam requirements/recommendations for international students: required—TOEFL (minimum score 100 iBT), IELTS (minimum score 7), PTE (minimum score 65). *Application deadline:* For fall admission, 3/1 for domestic and international students. Applications are processed on a rolling basis. Application fee: $55. Electronic applications accepted. Application fee is waived when completed online. *Financial support:* Career-related internships or fieldwork and scholarships/grants available. Financial award applicants required to submit FAFSA. *Unit head:* Kresten Froistad-Martin, Graduate Director, 415-422-5683, E-mail: upa@usfca.edu. *Application contact:* Kresten Froistad-Martin, Graduate Director, 415-422-5683, E-mail: upa@usfca.edu. Website: https://www.usfca.edu/arts-sciences/graduate-programs/urban-public-affairs

University of Wisconsin–Milwaukee, Graduate School, College of Letters and Science, Program in Urban Studies, Milwaukee, WI 53201-0413. Offers MS, PhD.

Virginia Polytechnic Institute and State University, Graduate School, College of Architecture and Urban Studies, Blacksburg, VA 24061. Offers architecture (M Arch, MS); architecture and design research (PhD); building construction science management (MS); creative technologies (MFA); environmental design and planning (PhD); government and international affairs (MPIA); landscape architecture (MLA, PhD); planning, governance, and globalization (PhD); public administration and public affairs (MPA, PhD); urban and regional planning (MURPL). *Accreditation:* ASLA (one or more programs are accredited). *Faculty:* 145 full-time (58 women), 2 part-time/adjunct (1 woman). *Students:* 304 full-time (156 women), 180 part-time (77 women); includes 90 minority (40 Black or African American, non-Hispanic/Latino; 19 Asian, non-Hispanic/Latino; 24 Hispanic/Latino; 7 Two or more races, non-Hispanic/Latino), 130 international. Average age 33. 475 applicants, 72% accepted, 126 enrolled. In 2019, 130 master's, 23 doctorates awarded. *Degree requirements:* For master's, comprehensive exam (for some programs), thesis (for some programs); for doctorate, comprehensive exam (for some programs), thesis/dissertation (for some programs). *Entrance requirements:* For master's and doctorate, GRE/GMAT. Additional exam requirements/recommendations for international students: required—TOEFL (minimum score 90 iBT). *Application deadline:* For fall admission, 8/1 for domestic students, 4/1 for international students; for spring admission, 1/1 for domestic students, 9/1 for international students. Applications are processed on a rolling basis. Application fee: $75. Electronic applications accepted. *Expenses:* Tuition, state resident: full-time $13,700; part-time $761.25 per credit hour. Tuition, nonresident: full-time $27,614; part-time $1534 per credit hour. *Required fees:* $886.50 per term. Tuition and fees vary according to campus/location and program. *Financial support:* In 2019–20, 2 fellowships with full tuition reimbursements (averaging $24,875 per year), 35 research assistantships with full tuition reimbursements (averaging $16,344 per year), 126 teaching assistantships with full tuition reimbursements (averaging $11,525 per year) were awarded; scholarships/grants and unspecified assistantships also available. Financial award

application deadline: 3/1; financial award applicants required to submit FAFSA. *Unit head:* Dr. Richard Blythe, Dean, 540-231-6416, Fax: 540-231-6332, E-mail: richbl1@vt.edu. *Application contact:* Christine Mattsson-Coon, Executive Assistant, 540-231-6416, Fax: 540-231-6332, E-mail: cmattsso@vt.edu. Website: http://www.caus.vt.edu/

Wayne State University, College of Fine, Performing and Communication Arts, Department of Communication, Detroit, MI 48202. Offers communication (PhD), including democratic participation and culture, identity and representation, media, society and culture, risk, crisis and conflict, wellness, work life and relationships; communication and new media (Graduate Certificate); communication studies (MA); dispute resolution (MADR, Graduate Certificate), including community and urban studies (MADR), conflict area studies (MADR), health and family (MADR), international conflict and cooperation (MADR), professional practice (MADR), theory of conflict (MADR), workplace (MADR); health communication (Graduate Certificate); journalism (MA); media arts (MA); media studies (MA); public relations and organizational communication (MA); JD/MADR. *Program availability:* Online learning. *Degree requirements:* For master's, thesis (for some programs), thesis or essay; for doctorate, thesis/dissertation. *Entrance requirements:* For master's, GRE (for MA if undergraduate GPA less than 3.2), personal statement; BA or BS in communication or related field with minimum upper-division GPA of 3.2 and minimum upper-division undergraduate GPA of 3.0, and sample of academic writing (for MA); undergraduate degree with minimum upper-division GPA of 3.0 and three letters of recommendation (for MADR); for doctorate, GRE, undergraduate degree in communication or related field; master's degree in communication or related field with minimum GPA of 3.5; letters of recommendation; personal statement; sample of written scholarship. Additional exam requirements/recommendations for international students: required—TOEFL (minimum score 100 iBT), IELTS, TWE. Electronic applications accepted. *Expenses:* Contact institution.

Wayne State University, College of Liberal Arts and Sciences, Department of Political Science, Detroit, MI 48202. Offers political science (MA, PhD); public administration (MPA), including economic development policy and management, health and human services policy and management, human and fiscal resource management, nonprofit policy and management, organizational behavior and management, urban and metropolitan policy and management; JD/MA. *Accreditation:* NASPAA. *Program availability:* Part-time, evening/weekend. *Faculty:* 22 full-time (9 women). *Students:* 50 full-time (22 women), 64 part-time (32 women); includes 28 minority (20 Black or African American, non-Hispanic/Latino; 2 Asian, non-Hispanic/Latino; 1 Hispanic/Latino; 5 Two or more races, non-Hispanic/Latino), 10 international. Average age 34. 105 applicants, 40% accepted, 24 enrolled. In 2019, 21 master's, 7 doctorates awarded. Terminal master's awarded for partial completion of doctoral program. *Degree requirements:* For master's, comprehensive exam (for some programs), thesis (for some programs); for doctorate, thesis/dissertation. *Entrance requirements:* For master's, GRE General Test, substantial undergraduate preparation in the social sciences, minimum upper-division undergraduate GPA of 3.0, two letters of recommendation, personal statement; for doctorate, GRE General Test, 3 letters of recommendation, personal statement; interview. Additional exam requirements/recommendations for international students: required—TOEFL (minimum score 550 paper-based; 79 iBT), TWE (minimum score 5.5), Michigan English Language Assessment Battery (minimum score 85); recommended—IELTS (minimum score 6.5). *Application deadline:* For fall admission, 5/15 for domestic students, 5/1 priority date for international students; for winter admission, 10/15 for domestic students, 9/1 priority date for international students. Applications are processed on a rolling basis. Application fee: $50. Electronic applications accepted. *Expenses:* $678.55 per credit in-state tuition, $1,469.75 per credit out-of-state tuition, $54.56 per credit hour student service fee, $315.70 registration fee. *Financial support:* In 2019–20, 48 students received support, including 4 fellowships with partial tuition reimbursements available (averaging $57,000 per year), 1 research assistantship with partial tuition reimbursement available (averaging $45,000 per year), 13 teaching assistantships with partial tuition reimbursements available (averaging $58,000 per year); scholarships/grants, health care benefits, and unspecified assistantships also available. Financial award applicants required to submit FAFSA. *Unit head:* Dr. Daniel Geller, Professor and Chair, 313-577-6328, E-mail: dgeller@wayne.edu. *Application contact:* Dr. Jeffrey Grynaviski, Graduate Director, 313-577-2620, E-mail: gradpolisci@wayne.edu. Website: http://clas.wayne.edu/politicalscience/

Section 26
Social Sciences

This section contains a directory of institutions offering graduate work in social sciences. Additional information about programs listed in the directory may be obtained by writing directly to the dean of a graduate school or chair of a department at the address given in the directory.

For programs offering related work, see also in this book *Area and Cultural Studies, Communication and Media, Criminology and Forensics, Economics, Geography, Family and Consumer Sciences,* *Political Science and International Affairs, Psychology and Counseling,* and *Sociology, Anthropology, and Archaeology.*

CONTENTS

Program Directory

Social Sciences

Assumption University, Resiliency in the Helping Professions Program, Worcester, MA 01609-1296. Offers CAGS, CGS. *Program availability:* Part-time, evening/weekend. *Entrance requirements:* For degree, bachelor's degree with minimum GPA of 3.0 (for CGS); master's degree (for CAGS); two letters of recommendation, official transcripts, personal statement, current resume. Additional exam requirements/recommendations for international students: required—TOEFL (minimum score 540 paper-based; 76 iBT), IELTS (minimum score 6). *Expenses: Tuition:* Full-time $12,690; part-time $705 per credit. *Required fees:* $70 per term.

Augusta University, College of Allied Health Sciences, Program in Public Health, Augusta, GA 30912. Offers environmental health (MPH); health informatics (MPH); health management (MPH); social and behavioral sciences (MPH). *Accreditation:* CEPH. *Program availability:* Part-time. *Degree requirements:* For master's, thesis (for some programs). *Entrance requirements:* For master's, GRE General Test, three letters of recommendation. Additional exam requirements/recommendations for international students: required—TOEFL. Electronic applications accepted.

California Institute of Technology, Division of the Humanities and Social Sciences, Social Science Program, Pasadena, CA 91125-0001. Offers MS, PhD. Terminal master's awarded for partial completion of doctoral program. *Degree requirements:* For doctorate, thesis/dissertation. *Entrance requirements:* For doctorate, GRE General Test. Additional exam requirements/recommendations for international students: required— TOEFL (minimum score 90 iBT); recommended—TWE. Electronic applications accepted.

California State University, Chico, Office of Graduate Studies, College of Behavioral and Social Sciences, Social Science Program, Chico, CA 95929-0722. Offers MA. *Degree requirements:* For master's, thesis or project. *Entrance requirements:* For master's, GRE General Test or MAT, two letters of recommendation, statement of purpose. Additional exam requirements/recommendations for international students: required—TOEFL (minimum score 550 paper-based; 80 iBT), IELTS (minimum score 6.5), PTE (minimum score 59). Electronic applications accepted.

California State University, San Bernardino, Graduate Studies, College of Social and Behavioral Sciences, Program in Social Sciences and Globalization, San Bernardino, CA 92407. Offers MA. *Faculty:* 8 full-time (3 women), 14 part-time/adjunct (13 women). *Students:* 3 full-time (2 women), 13 part-time (9 women); includes 9 minority (1 Black or African American, non-Hispanic/Latino; 8 Hispanic/Latino). Average age 35. 18 applicants, 50% accepted, 4 enrolled. In 2019, 8 master's awarded. *Entrance requirements:* Additional exam requirements/recommendations for international students: required—TOEFL. *Application deadline:* For fall admission, 5/15 for domestic students. Application fee: $55. *Financial support:* Fellowships, research assistantships, teaching assistantships, and institutionally sponsored loans available. Financial award application deadline: 5/1. *Unit head:* Dr. Jose Munoz, Coordinator, 909-537-5524, E-mail: munoz@csusb.edu. *Application contact:* Dr. Dorota Huizinga, Dean of Graduate Studies, 909-537-3064, E-mail: dorota.huizinga@csusb.edu.

Campbellsville University, College of Arts and Sciences, Campbellsville, KY 42718-2799. Offers justice studies (MS); sport management (MA). *Program availability:* Part-time, evening/weekend, 100% online, blended/hybrid learning. *Degree requirements:* For master's, comprehensive exam, thesis optional. *Entrance requirements:* For master's, GRE General Test, minimum GPA of 2.9, letters of recommendation, college transcripts. Additional exam requirements/recommendations for international students: recommended—TOEFL, IELTS. Electronic applications accepted. Application fee is waived when completed online. *Expenses:* Contact institution.

Carnegie Mellon University, Dietrich College of Humanities and Social Sciences, Department of Social and Decision Sciences, Pittsburgh, PA 15213-3891. Offers behavioral decision research (PhD); social and decision science (PhD); strategy, entrepreneurship, and technological change (PhD). Terminal master's awarded for partial completion of doctoral program. *Degree requirements:* For doctorate, comprehensive exam, thesis/dissertation, research paper. *Entrance requirements:* For doctorate, GRE General Test. Additional exam requirements/recommendations for international students: required—TOEFL. Electronic applications accepted.

The Citadel, The Military College of South Carolina, Citadel Graduate College, School of Humanities and Social Sciences, Department of Political Science, Charleston, SC 29409. Offers international politics and military affairs (MA); social science (MA). *Program availability:* Part-time, evening/weekend, 100% online, blended/hybrid learning. *Entrance requirements:* For master's, GRE (minimum combined score of 290 verbal and quantitative), MAT (minimum raw score of 396), written statement of purpose setting forth intentions, goals, and preparation for graduate study; at least 2 academic letters of recommendation addressing ability to undertake coursework at graduate level. Additional exam requirements/recommendations for international students: required— TOEFL (minimum score 550 paper-based; 79 iBT). Electronic applications accepted.

Colorado School of Mines, Office of Graduate Studies, Division of Humanities, Arts and Social Sciences, Golden, CO 80401. Offers international political economy (Graduate Certificate); science and technology policy (Graduate Certificate). *Program availability:* Part-time. *Entrance requirements:* Additional exam requirements/ recommendations for international students: required—TOEFL (minimum score 550 paper-based; 79 iBT). Electronic applications accepted. *Expenses:* Tuition, state resident: full-time $16,650; part-time $925 per credit hour. Tuition, nonresident: full-time $37,350; part-time $2075 per credit hour. *International tuition:* $37,350 full-time. *Required fees:* $2412.

Columbia University, Graduate School of Arts and Sciences, New York, NY 10027. Offers African-American studies (MA); American studies (MA); anthropology (MA, PhD); art history and archaeology (MA, PhD); astronomy (PhD); biological sciences (PhD); biotechnology (MA); chemical physics (PhD); chemistry (PhD); classical studies (MA, PhD); classics (MA, PhD); climate and society (MA); conservation biology (MA); earth and environmental sciences (PhD); East Asia: regional studies (MA); East Asian languages and cultures (MA, PhD); ecology, evolution and environmental biology (MA), including conservation biology; ecology, evolution, and environmental biology (PhD), including ecology and evolutionary biology, evolutionary primatology; economics (MA, PhD); English and comparative literature (MA, PhD); French and Romance philology (MA, PhD); Germanic languages (MA, PhD); global French studies (MA); global thought (MA); Hispanic cultural studies (MA); history (PhD); history and literature (MA); human rights studies (MA); Islamic studies (MA); Italian (MA, PhD); Japanese pedagogy (MA); Jewish studies (MA); Latin America and the Caribbean: regional studies (MA); Latin American and Iberian cultures (PhD); mathematics (MA, PhD), including finance (MA); medieval and Renaissance studies (MA); Middle Eastern, South Asian, and African studies (MA, PhD); modern art: critical and curatorial studies (MA); modern European studies (MA); museum anthropology (MA); music (DMA, PhD); oral history (MA);

philosophical foundations of physics (MA); philosophy (MA, PhD); physics (PhD); political science (MA, PhD); psychology (PhD); quantitative methods in the social sciences (MA); religion (MA, PhD); Russia, Eurasia and East Europe: regional studies (MA); Russian translation (MA); Slavic cultures (MA); Slavic languages (MA, PhD); sociology (MA, PhD); South Asian studies (MA); statistics (MA, PhD); theatre (PhD). *Program availability:* Part-time. *Students:* 3,506 full-time (1,844 women), 208 part-time (121 women); includes 864 minority (110 Black or African American, non-Hispanic/ Latino; 5 American Indian or Alaska Native, non-Hispanic/Latino; 416 Asian, non-Hispanic/Latino; 147 Hispanic/Latino; 6 Native Hawaiian or other Pacific Islander, non-Hispanic/Latino; 180 Two or more races, non-Hispanic/Latino); 2,065 international. 14,545 applicants, 25% accepted, 1,429 enrolled. In 2019, 1,262 master's, 363 doctorates awarded. Terminal master's awarded for partial completion of doctoral program. *Degree requirements:* For master's, variable foreign language requirement, comprehensive exam (for some programs), thesis (for some programs); for doctorate, variable foreign language requirement, comprehensive exam (for some programs), thesis/dissertation. *Entrance requirements:* For master's and doctorate, GRE General Test, GRE Subject Test (for some programs). Additional exam requirements/ recommendations for international students: required—TOEFL (minimum score 600 paper-based; 100 iBT), IELTS (minimum score 7.5). Application fee: $115. Electronic applications accepted. *Expenses: Tuition:* Full-time $47,600; part-time $1880 per credit. One-time fee: $105. *Financial support:* Fellowships, research assistantships, teaching assistantships, career-related internships or fieldwork, Federal Work-Study, institutionally sponsored loans, scholarships/grants, traineeships, health care benefits, tuition waivers, and unspecified assistantships available. Support available to part-time students. Financial award application deadline: 12/15. *Unit head:* Dr. Carlos J. Alonso, Dean of the Graduate School of Arts and Sciences and Vice President for Graduate Education, 212-854-2861, E-mail: gsas-dean@columbia.edu. *Application contact:* GSAS Office of Admissions, 212-854-6729, E-mail: gsas-admissions@columbia.edu. Website: http://gsas.columbia.edu/

East Carolina University, Graduate School, Thomas Harriot College of Arts and Sciences, Department of Psychology, Greenville, NC 27858-4353. Offers health psychology (PhD), including clinical health psychology, occupational health psychology, pediatric school psychology; industrial and organizational psychology (MA); quantitative methods for the social and behavioral sciences (Certificate); MA/CAS. *Program availability:* Part-time, evening/weekend. *Application deadline:* For fall admission, 12/1 priority date for domestic and international students. *Expenses: Tuition, area resident:* Full-time $4749; part-time $185 per credit hour. Tuition, state resident: full-time $4749; part-time $185 per credit hour. Tuition, nonresident: full-time $17,898; part-time $864 per credit hour. *International tuition:* $17,898 full-time. *Required fees:* $2787. *Financial support:* Application deadline: 6/1. *Unit head:* Dr. Alan Christensen, Chair, E-mail: christensenal19@ecu.edu. *Application contact:* Graduate School Admissions, 252-328-6012, Fax: 252-328-6071, E-mail: gradschool@ecu.edu. Website: https://psychology.ecu.edu/

Eastern Michigan University, Graduate School, College of Arts and Sciences, Department of History and Philosophy, Program in Social Science, Ypsilanti, MI 48197. Offers MA. *Program availability:* Part-time, evening/weekend, online learning. *Students:* 4 part-time (3 women); includes 2 minority (1 Black or African American, non-Hispanic/ Latino; 1 Hispanic/Latino). Average age 33. 7 applicants, 43% accepted. In 2019, 3 master's awarded. *Entrance requirements:* Additional exam requirements/ recommendations for international students: required—TOEFL. *Application deadline:* Applications are processed on a rolling basis. Application fee: $45. *Financial support:* Fellowships, research assistantships with full tuition reimbursements, teaching assistantships with full tuition reimbursements, career-related internships or fieldwork, Federal Work-Study, institutionally sponsored loans, scholarships/grants, tuition waivers (partial), and unspecified assistantships available. Support available to part-time students. Financial award applicants required to submit FAFSA. *Application contact:* Dr. John McCurdy, Graduate Coordinator, 734-487-1018, Fax: 734-487-6835, E-mail: jmccurdy@emich.edu.

Elms College, Division of Social Sciences, Chicopee, MA 01013-2839. Offers applied behavior analysis (MS); autism spectrum disorders (MS, CAGS); communication sciences and disorders (CAGS). *Program availability:* Part-time. *Faculty:* 2 full-time (1 woman), 3 part-time/adjunct (2 women). *Students:* 12 part-time (11 women); includes 1 minority (Hispanic/Latino). Average age 30. 13 applicants, 85% accepted, 11 enrolled. In 2019, 8 master's, 1 other advanced degree awarded. *Entrance requirements:* For degree, minimum GPA of 3.0. Additional exam requirements/recommendations for international students: required—TOEFL (minimum score 80 iBT). *Application deadline:* Applications are processed on a rolling basis. Application fee: $0. Electronic applications accepted. *Financial support:* Applicants required to submit FAFSA. *Unit head:* Dr. Jennifer Rivers, Chair, Division of Social Sciences, 413-265-2422, E-mail: riversj@elms.edu. *Application contact:* Nancy Davis, Director, Office of Graduate and Continuing Education Admissions, 413-265-2456, E-mail: grad@elms.edu.

Evangel University, Department of Behavioral and Social Sciences, Springfield, MO 65802. Offers clinical mental health counseling (MS). *Program availability:* Part-time. *Degree requirements:* For master's, comprehensive exam. *Entrance requirements:* For master's, GRE General Test, minimum undergraduate GPA of 3.0. Additional exam requirements/recommendations for international students: required—TOEFL (minimum score 550 paper-based). Electronic applications accepted. Application fee is waived when completed online.

Florida Agricultural and Mechanical University, Division of Graduate Studies, Research, and Continuing Education, College of Social Sciences, Arts and Humanities, Department of History and Political Science, Program in Applied Social Science, Tallahassee, FL 32307-3200. Offers criminal justice (MASS); history (MASS); political science (MASS); public administration (MASS). *Program availability:* Part-time. *Degree requirements:* For master's, thesis optional. *Entrance requirements:* For master's, GRE General Test, minimum GPA of 3.0.

The Graduate Center, City University of New York, Graduate Studies, Program in Quantitative Methods in the Social Sciences, New York, NY 10016-4039. Offers MS.

Graduate Theological Union, Graduate Programs, Berkeley, CA 94709-1212. Offers art and religion (MA, PhD, Th D); biblical languages (MA); Biblical studies (PhD, Th D); biblical studies (MA); Buddhist studies (MA); Christian spirituality (MA, PhD, Th D); cultural and historical studies of religions (MA, PhD, Th D); ethics and social theory (PhD, Th D); history (MA, PhD, Th D); homiletics (MA, PhD, Th D); interdisciplinary studies (PhD, Th D); Jewish studies (MA, PhD, Th D, Certificate); liturgical studies (MA, PhD, Th D); Near Eastern religions (PhD, Th D); Orthodox Christian studies (MA); religion and psychology (MA, PhD, Th D); religion and society/ethics and social theory (MA); systematic and philosophical theology (MA, PhD, Th D). *Accreditation:* ATS.

Terminal master's awarded for partial completion of doctoral program. *Degree requirements:* For master's, one foreign language, thesis; for doctorate, one foreign language, comprehensive exam, thesis/dissertation. *Entrance requirements:* For master's, GRE General Test; for doctorate, GRE General Test, MA or M Div. Additional exam requirements/recommendations for international students: required—TOEFL. Electronic applications accepted.

Harrison Middleton University, Graduate Program, Tempe, AZ 85282. Offers education (MA, Ed D); humanities (MA); imaginative literature (MA); interdisciplinary studies (DA); jurisprudence (MA); natural science (MA); philosophy and religion (MA); social science (MA). *Program availability:* Part-time, evening/weekend, online learning. *Degree requirements:* For master's and doctorate, capstone project. *Entrance requirements:* For master's, interview; for doctorate, 2 academic letters of reference, interview, essay. Additional exam requirements/recommendations for international students: required—TOEFL (minimum score 550 paper-based; 80 iBT). Electronic applications accepted.

Hollins University, Graduate Programs, Program in Liberal Studies, Roanoke, VA 24020. Offers humanities (MALS); interdisciplinary studies (MALS); leadership (MALS); social sciences (MALS); visual and performing arts (MALS). *Program availability:* Part-time, evening/weekend, 100% online, blended/hybrid learning. *Degree requirements:* For master's, thesis. *Entrance requirements:* For master's, three letters of recommendation, interview, bachelor's degree, undergraduate transcripts, statement of educational objectives. Additional exam requirements/recommendations for international students: required—TOEFL (minimum score 550 paper-based; 80 iBT), IELTS (minimum score 6.5). Electronic applications accepted. *Expenses:* Contact institution.

Humboldt State University, Academic Programs, College of Arts, Humanities, and Social Sciences, Program in Environment and Community, Arcata, CA 95521-8299. Offers MA. *Program availability:* Part-time. *Faculty:* 6 full-time (3 women), 5 part-time/ adjunct (1 woman). *Students:* 20 full-time (16 women), 11 part-time (8 women); includes 12 minority (3 American Indian or Alaska Native, non-Hispanic/Latino; 1 Asian, non-Hispanic/Latino; 5 Hispanic/Latino; 3 Two or more races, non-Hispanic/Latino). Average age 32. 23 applicants, 74% accepted, 13 enrolled. In 2019, 11 master's awarded. *Degree requirements:* For master's, thesis or alternative, qualifying exam. *Entrance requirements:* For master's, minimum GPA of 2.5, 3 letters of recommendation. Additional exam requirements/recommendations for international students: required—TOEFL (minimum score 500 paper-based). *Application deadline:* For fall admission, 3/1 for domestic students, 3/15 for international students. Applications are processed on a rolling basis. Application fee: $55. *Expenses:* Tuition, state resident: full-time $7176; part-time $4164 per term. *Required fees:* $2120; $1672 per term. *Financial support:* Application deadline: 3/1; applicants required to submit FAFSA. *Unit head:* Dr. Mark Baker, Graduate Program Coordinator, 707-826-3907, E-mail: j.mark.baker@humboldt.edu. *Application contact:* Dr. Mark Baker, Graduate Program Coordinator, 707-826-3907, E-mail: j.mark.baker@humboldt.edu. Website: http://www.humboldt.edu/envcomm/

Indiana University Bloomington, Maurer School of Law, Bloomington, IN 47405-7000. Offers comparative law (MCL); juridical science (SJD); law (LL M, JD); law and social sciences (PhD); legal studies (Certificate); JD/MA; JD/MBA; JD/MLS; JD/MPA; JD/MS; JD/MSES. *Accreditation:* ABA. *Degree requirements:* For master's, thesis or practicum; for doctorate, thesis/dissertation (for some programs), research seminar (for JD). *Entrance requirements:* For master's, LSAT, 3 letters of recommendation, law degree or license to practice; for doctorate, LSAT. Additional exam requirements/ recommendations for international students: required—TOEFL (minimum score 560 paper-based; 80 iBT). Electronic applications accepted.

Indiana University-Purdue University Indianapolis, Richard M. Fairbanks School of Public Health, Indianapolis, IN 46202. Offers biostatistics (MS, PhD); environmental health (MPH); epidemiology (MPH, PhD); global health leadership (Dr PH); health administration (MHA); health policy (Graduate Certificate); health policy and management (MPH, PhD); health systems management (Graduate Certificate); product stewardship (MS); public health (Graduate Certificate); social and behavioral sciences (MPH). *Accreditation:* CAHME; CEPH. *Expenses:* Contact institution.

Massachusetts Institute of Technology, School of Humanities, Arts, and Social Sciences, Program in Science, Technology, and Society, Cambridge, MA 02139. Offers history, anthropology, and science, technology and society (PhD). *Degree requirements:* For doctorate, one foreign language, comprehensive exam, thesis/dissertation. *Entrance requirements:* For doctorate, GRE General Test. Additional exam requirements/recommendations for international students: required—TOEFL, IELTS. Electronic applications accepted.

Mississippi College, Graduate School, College of Arts and Sciences, School of Humanities and Social Sciences, Department of History and Political Science, Clinton, MS 39058. Offers administration of justice (MSS); history (M Ed, MA, MSS); paralegal studies (Certificate); political science (MSS); social sciences (M Ed, MSS). *Program availability:* Part-time. *Degree requirements:* For master's, one foreign language, comprehensive exam, thesis (for some programs). *Entrance requirements:* For master's, GRE or NTE, minimum GPA of 2.5. Additional exam requirements/recommendations for international students: recommended—TOEFL, IELTS. Electronic applications accepted.

Montclair State University, The Graduate School, College of Education and Human Services, MAT Program in Teaching, Montclair, NJ 07043-1624. Offers art (MAT); biology (MAT); chemistry (MAT); earth science (MAT); English (MAT); French (MAT); health and physical education (MAT); health education (MAT); mathematics (MAT); music (MAT); physical education (MAT); physical science (MAT); social studies (MAT); Spanish (MAT); teacher of English as a second language (MAT). *Degree requirements:* For master's, comprehensive exam, thesis or alternative. *Entrance requirements:* For master's, interview, 2 letters of recommendation. Additional exam requirements/ recommendations for international students: required—TOEFL (minimum score 83 iBT), IELTS (minimum score 6.5). Electronic applications accepted.

The New School, The New School for Social Research, New York, NY 10003. Offers M Phil, MA, MS, PhD. *Program availability:* Part-time. *Faculty:* 99 full-time (58 women). *Students:* 637 full-time (344 women), 105 part-time (67 women); includes 123 minority (26 Black or African American, non-Hispanic/Latino; 25 Asian, non-Hispanic/Latino; 56 Hispanic/Latino; 1 Native Hawaiian or other Pacific Islander, non-Hispanic/Latino; 15 Two or more races, non-Hispanic/Latino), 283 international. Average age 31. 832 applicants, 72% accepted, 166 enrolled. In 2019, 247 master's, 53 doctorates awarded. Terminal master's awarded for partial completion of doctoral program. *Degree requirements:* For master's, comprehensive exam (for some programs), thesis (for some programs); for doctorate, variable foreign language requirement, comprehensive exam (for some programs), thesis/dissertation. *Entrance requirements:* For master's, letters of recommendation, writing sample, essays, official transcripts. Additional exam requirements/recommendations for international students: required—TOEFL (minimum score 100 iBT), IELTS (minimum score 7), PTE (minimum score 68). *Application deadline:* For fall admission, 6/15 priority date for domestic and international students; for spring admission, 10/15 priority date for domestic and international students.

Applications are processed on a rolling basis. Application fee: $50. Electronic applications accepted. *Expenses:* 2260 per credit. *Financial support:* In 2019–20, 587 students received support, including 79 fellowships (averaging $6,866 per year), 157 research assistantships (averaging $5,006 per year), 150 teaching assistantships with full and partial tuition reimbursements available (averaging $7,736 per year); career-related internships or fieldwork, Federal Work-Study, scholarships/grants, and tuition waivers (full and partial) also available. Support available to part-time students. Financial award application deadline: 2/1; financial award applicants required to submit FAFSA. *Unit head:* Dr. William Milberg, Dean, The New School for Social Research, 212-229-5777, E-mail: milbergw@newschool.edu. *Application contact:* Merida Gasbarro, Director of Graduate Admission, 212-229-5600 Ext. 1108, E-mail: escandom@newschool.edu. Website: http://www.newschool.edu/nssr

New York University, College of Global Public Health, New York, NY 10012. Offers biological basis of public health (PhD); community and international health (MPH); global health leadership (MPH); health systems and health services research (PhD); population and community health (PhD); public health nutrition (MPH); social and behavioral sciences (MPH); socio-behavioral health (PhD). *Accreditation:* CEPH. *Program availability:* Part-time, online learning. *Degree requirements:* For master's, thesis (for some programs); for doctorate, thesis/dissertation. *Entrance requirements:* For master's and doctorate, GRE. Additional exam requirements/recommendations for international students: required—TOEFL. Electronic applications accepted. *Expenses:* Contact institution.

Nova Southeastern University, College of Arts, Humanities, and Social Sciences, Fort Lauderdale, FL 33314-7796. Offers advanced conflict resolution practice (Graduate Certificate); child protection (MHS); college student affairs (MS); conflict analysis and resolution (MS, PhD); criminal justice (MS, PhD); cross-disciplinary studies (MA); developmental disabilities (MS); family studies (Graduate Certificate); family systems health care (Graduate Certificate); family therapy (MS, PhD); marriage and family therapy (DMFT); peace studies (Graduate Certificate); qualitative research (Graduate Certificate); solution focused coaching (Graduate Certificate). *Accreditation:* AAMFT/ COAMFTE (one or more programs are accredited). *Program availability:* Part-time, evening/weekend, 100% online, blended/hybrid learning. *Faculty:* 60 full-time (37 women), 88 part-time/adjunct (65 women). *Students:* 201 full-time (157 women), 418 part-time (297 women); includes 365 minority (180 Black or African American, non-Hispanic/Latino; 4 American Indian or Alaska Native, non-Hispanic/Latino; 15 Asian, non-Hispanic/Latino; 141 Hispanic/Latino; 25 Two or more races, non-Hispanic/Latino), 49 international. Average age 37. 303 applicants, 84% accepted, 197 enrolled. In 2019, 125 master's, 63 doctorates, 24 other advanced degrees awarded. *Degree requirements:* For master's, comprehensive exam (for some programs), thesis optional, comprehensive exams, portfolios (for some programs), table-top exams (for some programs); for doctorate, comprehensive exam, thesis/dissertation, qualifying exams, portfolios (for some programs). *Entrance requirements:* For master's, interview, minimum GPA of 3.0, writing sample; for doctorate, interview, minimum GPA of 3.5, master's degree in related field, writing sample; for Graduate Certificate, minimum GPA of 3.0. Additional exam requirements/recommendations for international students: required—TOEFL (minimum score 79 paper-based). *Application deadline:* Applications are processed on a rolling basis. Application fee: $50. Electronic applications accepted. *Expenses:* Contact institution. *Financial support:* In 2019–20, 170 students received support. Career-related internships or fieldwork, Federal Work-Study, scholarships/ grants, and unspecified assistantships available. Financial award application deadline: 4/1; financial award applicants required to submit FAFSA. *Unit head:* Dr. Honggang Yang, Dean, 954-262-3016, Fax: 954-262-3968, E-mail: yangh@nova.edu. *Application contact:* Marcia Arango, Student Recruitment Coordinator, 954-262-3006, Fax: 954-262-3968, E-mail: marango@nsu.nova.edu. Website: http://cahss.nova.edu/

The Ohio State University, Graduate School, College of Food, Agricultural, and Environmental Sciences, School of Environment and Natural Resources, Columbus, OH 43210. Offers ecological restoration (MS, PhD); ecosystem science (MS, PhD); environment and natural resources (MENR); environmental social sciences (MS, PhD); fisheries and wildlife science (MS, PhD); forest science (MS, PhD); rural sociology (MS, PhD); soil science (MS, PhD). *Entrance requirements:* For master's and doctorate, GRE. Additional exam requirements/recommendations for international students: required— TOEFL (minimum score 550 paper-based; 79 iBT), Michigan English Language Assessment Battery (minimum score 82); recommended—IELTS (minimum score 7). Electronic applications accepted.

Ohio University, Graduate College, College of Arts and Sciences, Program in Social Sciences, Athens, OH 45701-2979. Offers MSS. *Program availability:* Online learning. *Degree requirements:* For master's, oral exam. *Entrance requirements:* For master's, minimum GPA of 2.75. Additional exam requirements/recommendations for international students: required—TOEFL (minimum score 600 paper-based). Electronic applications accepted.

Oregon State University, Interdisciplinary/Institutional Programs, Program in Environmental Sciences, Corvallis, OR 97331. Offers biogeochemistry (MA, MS, PSM, PhD); ecology (MA, MS, PSM, PhD); environmental education (MA, MS, PhD); quantitative analysis (PSM); social science (MA, MS, PSM, PhD); water resources (MA, MS, PhD). *Program availability:* Part-time. *Degree requirements:* For master's, variable foreign language requirement, thesis; for doctorate, thesis/dissertation. *Entrance requirements:* For master's and doctorate, GRE. Additional exam requirements/ recommendations for international students: required—TOEFL (minimum score 80 iBT), IELTS (minimum score 6.5).

Southern University and Agricultural and Mechanical College, Graduate School, Nelson Mandela College of Government and Social Sciences, Department of History, Baton Rouge, LA 70813. Offers social sciences (MA). *Program availability:* Part-time. *Degree requirements:* For master's, thesis. *Entrance requirements:* For master's, GRE General Test. Additional exam requirements/recommendations for international students: required—TOEFL (minimum score 525 paper-based).

Syracuse University, Maxwell School of Citizenship and Public Affairs, Programs in Social Sciences, Syracuse, NY 13244. Offers MA, PhD. *Program availability:* Part-time, evening/weekend, online learning. *Degree requirements:* For doctorate, comprehensive exam, thesis/dissertation. *Entrance requirements:* For master's, resume, personal statement, official transcripts, three letters of recommendation; for doctorate, GRE General Test, resume, personal statement, official transcripts, three letters of recommendation. Additional exam requirements/recommendations for international students: required—TOEFL (minimum score 100 iBT). Electronic applications accepted.

Texas A&M International University, Office of Graduate Studies and Research, College of Arts and Sciences, Department of Social Sciences, Laredo, TX 78041. Offers criminal justice (MS); history and political thought (MA); public administration (MPA); sociology (MA). *Degree requirements:* For master's, comprehensive exam (for some programs), thesis (for some programs). *Entrance requirements:* For master's, GRE General Test. Additional exam requirements/recommendations for international students: required—TOEFL (minimum score 550 paper-based; 79 iBT).

Social Sciences

Towson University, College of Liberal Arts, Program in Social Science, Towson, MD 21252-0001. Offers MS. *Program availability:* Part-time, evening/weekend. *Students:* 4 full-time (2 women), 10 part-time (5 women); includes 5 minority (3 Black or African American, non-Hispanic/Latino; 2 Two or more races, non-Hispanic/Latino). *Entrance requirements:* For master's, minimum GPA of 3.0, 3 letters of recommendation, statement of intent. *Application deadline:* For fall admission, 1/17 for domestic students, 5/15 for international students; for spring admission, 10/15 for domestic students, 12/1 for international students. Applications are processed on a rolling basis. Application fee: $45. Electronic applications accepted. *Expenses: Tuition, area resident:* Full-time $7920; part-time $439 per credit. Tuition, nonresident: full-time $16,344; part-time $908 per credit. *International tuition:* $16,344 full-time. *Required fees:* $2628; $146 per credit. $876 per term. *Financial support:* Application deadline: 4/1. *Unit head:* Dr. Paul McCartney, Program Director, 410-704-5218, E-mail: pmccartney@towson.edu. *Application contact:* Coverley Beidleman, Assistant Director of Graduate Admissions, 410-704-5630, Fax: 410-704-3030, E-mail: grads@towson.edu. *Website:* https://www.towson.edu/cla/departments/interdisciplinary/grad/socialscience/

Troy University, Graduate School, College of Arts and Sciences, Program in Social Science, Troy, AL 36082. Offers MS Sc. *Program availability:* Part-time, evening/weekend, online learning. *Faculty:* 2 full-time (1 woman), 3 part-time/adjunct (2 women). *Students:* 15 full-time (11 women), 66 part-time (47 women); includes 36 minority (30 Black or African American, non-Hispanic/Latino; 1 American Indian or Alaska Native, non-Hispanic/Latino; 1 Asian, non-Hispanic/Latino; 4 Hispanic/Latino), 1 international. Average age 37. 50 applicants, 100% accepted, 32 enrolled. In 2019, 26 master's awarded. *Degree requirements:* For master's, comprehensive exam, thesis optional. *Entrance requirements:* For master's, GRE 290 (recommended:150 verbal, 140 quantitative) and GRE writing score. If student has taken the MCAT (recommended: 487), DAT (recommended: 16) or equivalent professional exam, then this may be substituted for the GRE, bachelor's degree, minimum undergraduate GPA of 2.5 or 3.0 on last 30 semester hours, letter of recommendation. Additional exam requirements/recommendations for international students: required—TOEFL (minimum score 523 paper-based; 70 iBT), IELTS (minimum score 6). *Application deadline:* For fall admission, 6/1 for international students; for spring admission, 10/15 for international students. Applications are processed on a rolling basis. Application fee: $50. Electronic applications accepted. *Expenses: Tuition, area resident:* Full-time $7650; part-time $2550 per semester hour. Tuition, state resident: full-time $7650; part-time $2550 per semester hour. Tuition, nonresident: full-time $15,300; part-time $5100 per semester hour. *International tuition:* $15,300 full-time. *Required fees:* $856; $352 per semester hour. $176 per semester. *Financial support:* In 2019–20, 23 students received support. Fellowships, research assistantships, teaching assistantships, career-related internships or fieldwork, Federal Work-Study, scholarships/grants, traineeships, tuition waivers, and unspecified assistantships available. Support available to part-time students. Financial award application deadline: 3/1; financial award applicants required to submit FAFSA. *Unit head:* Dr. Sharon Everhardt, Associate Professor, Chair, Social Science, 334-832-7287, Fax: 334-670-3753, E-mail: severhardt@troy.edu. *Application contact:* Haley McKinnon, Director of Graduate Admissions, 334-670-3178, Fax: 334-670-3733, E-mail: hmckinnon@troy.edu. *Website:* https://www.troy.edu/academics/academic-programs/social-science.html

University at Buffalo, the State University of New York, Graduate School, College of Arts and Sciences, Program in Interdisciplinary Studies, Buffalo, NY 14260. Offers humanities (MA); natural sciences (MS); social sciences (MS). *Program availability:* Part-time. *Degree requirements:* For master's, thesis or alternative. *Entrance requirements:* Additional exam requirements/recommendations for international students: required—TOEFL (minimum score 550 paper-based; 79 iBT). Electronic applications accepted. *Expenses: Tuition, area resident:* Full-time $11,310; part-time $471 per credit hour. Tuition, state resident: full-time $11,310; part-time $471 per credit hour. Tuition, nonresident: full-time $23,100; part-time $963 per credit hour. *International tuition:* $23,100 full-time. *Required fees:* $2820.

University of California, Merced, Graduate Division, School of Social Sciences, Humanities and Arts, Merced, CA 95343. Offers cognitive and information sciences (PhD); interdisciplinary humanities (MA, PhD); psychological sciences (MA, PhD); social sciences (MA, PhD); sociology (MA, PhD). *Faculty:* 113 full-time (57 women), 2 part-time/adjunct (0 women). *Students:* 194 full-time (128 women), 1 (woman) part-time; includes 81 minority (5 Black or African American, non-Hispanic/Latino; 18 Asian, non-Hispanic/Latino; 54 Hispanic/Latino; 4 Two or more races, non-Hispanic/Latino), 39 international. Average age 31. 218 applicants, 48% accepted, 36 enrolled. In 2019, 12 master's, 23 doctorates awarded. Terminal master's awarded for partial completion of doctoral program. *Degree requirements:* For master's, variable foreign language requirement, comprehensive exam, thesis or alternative, oral defense; for doctorate, variable foreign language requirement, comprehensive exam, thesis/dissertation, oral defense. *Entrance requirements:* For master's and doctorate, GRE. Additional exam requirements/recommendations for international students: required—TOEFL (minimum score 550 paper-based; 80 iBT); recommended—IELTS (minimum score 6.5). *Application deadline:* For fall admission, 1/15 for domestic and international students. Application fee: $105 ($125 for international students). Electronic applications accepted. *Expenses: Tuition, area resident:* Full-time $11,442; part-time $5721 per semester. Tuition, state resident: full-time $11,442; part-time $5721 per semester. Tuition, nonresident: full-time $26,544; part-time $13,272 per semester. *International tuition:* $26,544 full-time. *Required fees:* $564 per semester. *Financial support:* In 2019–20, 183 students received support, including 7 fellowships with full tuition reimbursements available (averaging $22,005 per year), 5 research assistantships with full tuition reimbursements available (averaging $21,420 per year), 171 teaching assistantships with full tuition reimbursements available (averaging $21,911 per year); scholarships/grants, traineeships, and health care benefits also available. *Unit head:* Dr. Jeffrey Gilger, Dean, 209-228-4343, E-mail: jgilger@ucmerced.edu. *Application contact:* Tsu Ya, Director of Admissions and Academic Services, 209-228-4521, Fax: 209-228-6906, E-mail: tya@ucmerced.edu.

University of California, Santa Barbara, Graduate Division, College of Letters and Sciences, Division of Mathematics, Life, and Physical Sciences, Department of Psychological and Brain Sciences, Santa Barbara, CA 93106-9660. Offers cognitive science (PhD); psychology (PhD); quantitative methods in the social sciences (PhD); technology and society (PhD). Terminal master's awarded for partial completion of doctoral program. *Degree requirements:* For doctorate, comprehensive exam, thesis/dissertation, teaching assistant training, progress report, papers, mini-convention presentation, 1 quarter of student teaching or teaching assistant class with section lab, continued participation in research and weekly area meetings. *Entrance requirements:* For doctorate, GRE General Test. Additional exam requirements/recommendations for international students: required—TOEFL (minimum score 550 paper-based; 80 iBT) or IELTS (minimum score 7). Electronic applications accepted.

University of California, Santa Barbara, Graduate Division, College of Letters and Sciences, Division of Social Sciences, Department of Communication, Santa Barbara, CA 93106-4020. Offers cognitive science (PhD); communication (PhD); feminist studies (PhD); language, interaction and social organization (PhD); quantitative methods in the social sciences (PhD); society and technology (PhD); MA/PhD. Terminal master's

awarded for partial completion of doctoral program. *Degree requirements:* For doctorate, comprehensive exam, thesis/dissertation. *Entrance requirements:* For doctorate, GRE. Additional exam requirements/recommendations for international students: required—TOEFL (minimum score 80 iBT), IELTS (minimum score 7). Electronic applications accepted.

University of California, Santa Cruz, Division of Graduate Studies, Division of Humanities, Program in the History of Consciousness, Santa Cruz, CA 95064. Offers PhD. *Degree requirements:* For doctorate, one foreign language, thesis/dissertation, qualifying exam. *Entrance requirements:* For doctorate, GRE General Test. Additional exam requirements/recommendations for international students: required—TOEFL (minimum score 550 paper-based; 83 iBT); recommended—IELTS (minimum score 8). Electronic applications accepted.

University of Chicago, Division of the Social Sciences, The John U. Nef Committee on Social Thought, Chicago, IL 60637. Offers PhD. *Degree requirements:* For doctorate, one foreign language, thesis/dissertation. *Entrance requirements:* For doctorate, GRE General Test, 3 letters of recommendation, statement of purpose, transcripts, resume or curriculum vitae, writing sample (dependent on department). Additional exam requirements/recommendations for international students: required—TOEFL (minimum score 104 iBT), IELTS (minimum score 7). Electronic applications accepted. *Expenses:* Contact institution.

University of Chicago, Division of the Social Sciences, Master of Arts Program in Computational Social Science, Chicago, IL 60637. Offers MA. *Degree requirements:* For master's, thesis. *Entrance requirements:* For master's, GRE General Test, 3 letters of recommendation, statement of purpose, transcripts, resume or curriculum vitae, writing sample (dependent on department). Additional exam requirements/recommendations for international students: required—TOEFL (minimum score 104 iBT), IELTS (minimum score 7). Electronic applications accepted. *Expenses:* Contact institution.

University of Chicago, Division of the Social Sciences, Master of Arts Program in the Social Sciences, Chicago, IL 60637. Offers MA. *Program availability:* Part-time. *Degree requirements:* For master's, thesis. *Entrance requirements:* For master's, GRE General Test, 3 letters of recommendation, statement of purpose, transcripts, resume or curriculum vitae, writing sample (dependent on department). Additional exam requirements/recommendations for international students: required—TOEFL (minimum score 104 iBT), IELTS (minimum score 7). Electronic applications accepted. *Expenses:* Contact institution.

University of Florida, Graduate School, College of Public Health and Health Professions, Programs in Public Health, Gainesville, FL 32611. Offers biostatistics (MPH); clinical and translational science (PhD); environmental health (MPH); epidemiology (MPH); health management and policy (MPH); public health (MPH, PhD, Certificate); public health practice (MPH); rehabilitation science (PhD); social and behavioral sciences (MPH); DPT/MPH; DVM/MPH; JD/MPH; MD/MPH; Pharm D/MPH. *Accreditation:* CEPH. *Program availability:* Online learning. *Degree requirements:* For master's, internship. *Entrance requirements:* For master's, GRE General Test, minimum GPA of 3.0. Additional exam requirements/recommendations for international students: required—TOEFL (minimum score 550 paper-based; 80 iBT), IELTS (minimum score 6).

University of Illinois at Springfield, Graduate Programs, College of Education and Human Services, Program in Human Services, Springfield, IL 62703-5407. Offers alcohol and substance abuse (Graduate Certificate); alcoholism and substance abuse (MA); child and family studies (MA); gerontology (MA); social services administration (MA). *Program availability:* Part-time, 100% online, blended/hybrid learning. *Faculty:* 3 full-time (all women), 3 part-time/adjunct (2 women). *Students:* 12 full-time (all women), 49 part-time (47 women); includes 27 minority (19 Black or African American, non-Hispanic/Latino; 6 Hispanic/Latino; 2 Two or more races, non-Hispanic/Latino), 1 international. Average age 33. 29 applicants, 69% accepted, 12 enrolled. In 2019, 24 master's, 1 other advanced degree awarded. *Degree requirements:* For master's, internship; capstone project. *Entrance requirements:* For master's, minimum undergraduate GPA of 3.0, 2 letters of recommendation from professional or academic sources, statement of intent, interview. Additional exam requirements/recommendations for international students: required—TOEFL (minimum score 500 paper-based; 61 iBT). *Application deadline:* Applications are processed on a rolling basis. Application fee: $60 ($75 for international students). Electronic applications accepted. *Expenses:* $33.25 per credit hour (online fee). *Financial support:* In 2019–20, research assistantships with full tuition reimbursements (averaging $10,562 per year), teaching assistantships with full tuition reimbursements (averaging $10,652 per year) were awarded; fellowships, career-related internships or fieldwork, Federal Work-Study, scholarships/grants, health care benefits, and unspecified assistantships also available. Support available to part-time students. Financial award application deadline: 11/15; financial award applicants required to submit FAFSA. *Unit head:* Dr. Denise Bockmier-Sommers, Program Administrator, 217-206-6908, Fax: 217-206-6775, E-mail: dsomm2@uis.edu. *Application contact:* Dr. Denise Bockmier-Sommers, Program Administrator, 217-206-6908, Fax: 217-206-6775, E-mail: dsomm2@uis.edu. *Website:* http://www.uis.edu/humanservices

The University of Manchester, School of Social Sciences, Manchester, United Kingdom. Offers ethnographic documentary (M Phil); interdisciplinary study of culture (PhD); philosophy (PhD); politics (PhD); social anthropology (PhD); social anthropology with visual media (PhD); social change (PhD); social statistics (PhD); sociology (PhD); visual anthropology (M Phil).

University of Maryland, Baltimore County, The Graduate School, College of Arts, Humanities and Social Sciences, PhD Program in Gerontology at UMB/UMBC, Baltimore, MD 21201. Offers aging policy issues (PhD); epidemiology of aging (PhD); social, cultural, and behavioral sciences (PhD); MA/PhD; MS/PhD. *Program availability:* Part-time. *Faculty:* 15 part-time/adjunct (10 women). *Students:* 8 full-time (6 women); includes 4 minority (1 Black or African American, non-Hispanic/Latino; 2 Asian, non-Hispanic/Latino; 1 Hispanic/Latino). Average age 48. 15 applicants, 27% accepted, 1 enrolled. In 2019, 2 doctorates awarded. *Degree requirements:* For doctorate, comprehensive exam, thesis/dissertation. *Entrance requirements:* For doctorate, GRE General Test. Additional exam requirements/recommendations for international students: required—TOEFL, TWE. *Application deadline:* For spring admission, 1/15 for domestic and international students. Application fee: $45. Electronic applications accepted. *Expenses: Tuition, area resident:* Full-time $659. Tuition, state resident: full-time $659. Tuition, nonresident: full-time $1132. *International tuition:* $1132 full-time. *Required fees:* $140; $140 per credit hour. *Financial support:* In 2019–20, 4 students received support, including fellowships with full tuition reimbursements available (averaging $23,844 per year), 3 research assistantships with full tuition reimbursements available (averaging $20,000 per year), 1 teaching assistantship; health care benefits and dissertation awards also available. Financial award application deadline: 2/1; financial award applicants required to submit FAFSA. *Unit head:* Dr. John Schumacher, Co-Director, UMBC Campus, 410-455-3184, Fax: 410-455-2074, E-mail: jschuma@umbc.edu. *Application contact:* Justine Golden, Academic Coordinator, 410-706-4926, Fax: 410-706-4433, E-mail: jgold002@umaryland.edu. *Website:* http://lifesciences.umaryland.edu/gerontologyphd/

University of Memphis, Graduate School, School of Public Health, Memphis, TN 38152. Offers biostatistics (MPH); environmental health (MPH); epidemiology (MPH, PhD); health systems and policy (PhD); health systems management (MPH); public health (MHA); social and behavioral sciences (MPH, PhD). *Accreditation:* CAHME; CEPH. *Program availability:* Part-time, evening/weekend, online learning. *Faculty:* 20 full-time (7 women), 10 part-time/adjunct (4 women). *Students:* 126 full-time (80 women), 77 part-time (60 women); includes 70 minority (40 Black or African American, non-Hispanic/Latino; 17 Asian, non-Hispanic/Latino; 9 Hispanic/Latino; 4 Two or more races, non-Hispanic/Latino), 29 international. Average age 30. 105 applicants, 97% accepted, 67 enrolled. In 2019, 47 master's, 9 doctorates awarded. *Degree requirements:* For master's, comprehensive exam, thesis (for some programs), practicum/field experience; for doctorate, comprehensive exam, thesis/dissertation, residency. *Entrance requirements:* For master's, GRE or GMAT, letters of recommendation; letter of intent; for doctorate, GRE, letters of recommendation; personal statement. Additional exam requirements/recommendations for international students: required—TOEFL (minimum score 550 paper-based; 79 iBT). *Application deadline:* For fall admission, 4/1 for domestic students; for spring admission, 11/1 for domestic students. Application fee: $35 ($60 for international students). Electronic applications accepted. *Expenses:* Tuition, area resident: Full-time $9216; part-time $512 per credit hour. Tuition, state resident: full-time $9216; part-time $512 per credit hour. Tuition, nonresident: full-time $12,672; part-time $704 per credit hour. *International tuition:* $16,128 full-time. *Required fees:* $1530; $85 per credit hour. Tuition and fees vary according to program. *Financial support:* Research assistantships with full tuition reimbursements, Federal Work-Study, scholarships/grants, and unspecified assistantships available. Financial award application deadline: 2/1; financial award applicants required to submit FAFSA. *Unit head:* Dr. James Gurney, Dean, 901-678-1673, E-mail: jggurney@memphis.edu. *Application contact:* Dr. Marian Levy, Associate Dean, 901-678-4514, E-mail: mlevy@memphis.edu.
Website: http://www.memphis.edu/sph/

University of Michigan, School of Social Work, Interdisciplinary PhD Program in Social Work and Social Science, Ann Arbor, MI 48109. Offers social work and anthropology (PhD); social work and economics (PhD); social work and political science (PhD); social work and psychology (PhD); social work and sociology (PhD). *Degree requirements:* For doctorate, thesis/dissertation, oral defense of dissertation, preliminary exam. *Entrance requirements:* For doctorate, GRE General Test. Additional exam requirements/recommendations for international students: required—TOEFL (minimum score 620 paper-based, 88 iBT) or IELTS. Electronic applications accepted. *Expenses:* Contact institution.

University of Michigan–Flint, College of Arts and Sciences, Program in Social Sciences, Flint, MI 48502-1950. Offers gender studies (MA); global studies (MA); U.S. history and politics (MA). *Program availability:* Part-time. *Faculty:* 11 full-time (6 women), 4 part-time/adjunct (all women). *Students:* 3 full-time (2 women), 7 part-time (5 women); includes 4 minority (3 Black or African American, non-Hispanic/Latino; 1 Two or more races, non-Hispanic/Latino). Average age 43. 15 applicants, 60% accepted, 2 enrolled. In 2019, 4 master's awarded. *Entrance requirements:* For master's, bachelor's degree from regionally-accredited institution, minimum overall undergraduate GPA of 3.0 on 4.0 scale. Additional exam requirements/recommendations for international students: required—TOEFL (minimum score 84 iBT), IELTS (minimum score 6.5). *Application deadline:* For fall admission, 8/1 for domestic students, 5/1 for international students; for winter admission, 11/15 for domestic students, 10/1 for international students; for spring admission, 3/15 for domestic students, 1/1 for international students; for summer admission, 5/15 for domestic students. Applications are processed on a rolling basis. Application fee: $55. Electronic applications accepted. *Expenses:* Contact institution. *Financial support:* Federal Work-Study, scholarships/grants, and unspecified assistantships available. Financial award application deadline: 3/1; financial award applicants required to submit FAFSA. *Unit head:* Dr. Adam Lutzker, Director, 810-762-3470, Fax: 810-762-3281, E-mail: alutzker@umflint.edu. *Application contact:* Matt Bohlen, Associate Director of Graduate Programs, 810-762-3171, Fax: 810-766-6789, E-mail: mbohlen@umflint.edu.
Website: http://www.umflint.edu/graduateprograms/social-sciences-ma

University of Northern Iowa, Graduate College, College of Social and Behavioral Sciences, MA Program in Social Science, Cedar Falls, IA 50614. Offers MA. *Entrance requirements:* For master's, minimum GPA of 3.0. Additional exam requirements/recommendations for international students: required—TOEFL (minimum score 500 paper-based; 61 iBT).

University of Regina, Faculty of Graduate Studies and Research, Faculty of Arts, Department of Sociology and Social Studies, Regina, SK S4S 0A2, Canada. Offers social studies (MA); sociology (MA). *Program availability:* Part-time. *Faculty:* 8 full-time (4 women), 4 part-time/adjunct (1 woman). *Students:* 4 full-time (3 women), 3 part-time (all women). Average age 30. 26 applicants, 35% accepted. In 2019, 4 master's awarded. *Degree requirements:* For master's, thesis. *Entrance requirements:* For master's, post secondary transcripts and 2 letters of recommendation; BA Honours degree or equivalent in sociology. Additional exam requirements/recommendations for international students: required—TOEFL (minimum score 580 paper-based; 80 iBT), IELTS (minimum score 6.5), PTE (minimum score 59), other options are CAEL, MELAB, Cantest and U of R ESL. *Application deadline:* Applications are processed on a rolling basis. Application fee: $100. Electronic applications accepted. *Expenses:* Tuition: Full-time $6684 Canadian dollars. *Required fees:* $100 Canadian dollars; $3351.45 Canadian dollars per trimester. $1117.15 Canadian dollars per semester. Tuition and fees vary according to course level, course load, degree level and program. *Financial support:* Fellowships, research assistantships, teaching assistantships, career-related internships or fieldwork, Federal Work-Study, scholarships/grants, unspecified assistantships, and travel award and Graduate Scholarship and Base funds available. Support available to part-time students. Financial award application deadline: 9/30. *Unit head:* Dr. Rozzete Jurdi-Hage, Department Head, 306-585-4196, Fax: 306-585-4815, E-mail: Rozzet.Jurdi@uregina.ca. *Application contact:* Dr. JoAnn Jaffe, Graduate Coordinator, 306-585-4198, Fax: 306-585-4815, E-mail: JoAnn.Jaffe@uregina.ca.
Website: http://www.uregina.ca/arts/sociology-social-studies

University of South Florida Sarasota-Manatee, College of Liberal Arts and Social Sciences, Sarasota, FL 34243. Offers criminal justice (MA); education (MA); educational leadership (M Ed), including curriculum leadership, K-12 public school leadership, non-public/charter school leadership; elementary education (MAT); English education (MA); social work (MSW). *Program availability:* Part-time, 100% online, blended/hybrid learning. *Degree requirements:* For master's, comprehensive exam (for some programs). *Entrance requirements:* For master's, GRE. Additional exam requirements/recommendations for international students: required—TOEFL (minimum score 550 paper-based; 79 iBT), IELTS (minimum score 6.5). Electronic applications accepted.

The University of Texas at Tyler, College of Arts and Sciences, Department of Social Sciences, Tyler, TX 75799-0001. Offers criminal justice (MS); public administration (MPA); sociology (MS). *Program availability:* Part-time, evening/weekend. *Faculty:* 5 full-time (2 women), 5 part-time/adjunct (1 woman). *Students:* 17 full-time (12 women), 36 part-time (25 women); includes 22 minority (7 Black or African American, non-Hispanic/Latino; 1 Asian, non-Hispanic/Latino; 12 Hispanic/Latino; 2 Two or more races, non-Hispanic/Latino), 2 international. Average age 36. 27 applicants, 89% accepted, 16 enrolled. In 2019, 19 master's awarded. *Degree requirements:* For master's, comprehensive exam, thesis optional. *Entrance requirements:* For master's, GRE General Test, minimum GPA of 3.0. Additional exam requirements/recommendations for international students: required—TOEFL. *Application deadline:* For fall admission, 8/17 priority date for domestic students, 7/1 priority date for international students; for spring admission, 12/21 priority date for domestic students, 11/1 priority date for international students. Applications are processed on a rolling basis. Application fee: $25 ($50 for international students). *Financial support:* In 2019–20, 1 fellowship (averaging $1,000 per year) was awarded; research assistantships, teaching assistantships, career-related internships or fieldwork, Federal Work-Study, and scholarships/grants also available. Support available to part-time students. Financial award application deadline: 7/1; financial award applicants required to submit FAFSA. *Unit head:* Dr. Thomas Guderjan, Chair, 903-566-7418, E-mail: tguderjan@uttyler.edu. *Application contact:* Dr. Thomas Guderjan, Chair, 903-566-7418, E-mail: tguderjan@uttyler.edu.
Website: https://www.uttyler.edu/socialsciences/

University of the Virgin Islands, College of Liberal Arts and Social Sciences, St. Thomas, VI 00802. Offers M Psych, MPA. *Program availability:* Part-time, evening/weekend. *Degree requirements:* For master's, comprehensive exam, thesis or alternative. *Entrance requirements:* For master's, GRE, minimum GPA of 2.5. Additional exam requirements/recommendations for international students: required—TOEFL (minimum score 550 paper-based). Electronic applications accepted. *Expenses:* Contact institution.

University of Toronto, School of Graduate Studies, Department of Public Health Sciences, Toronto, ON M5S 1A1, Canada. Offers biostatistics (M Sc, PhD); community health (M Sc); community nutrition (MPH), including nutrition and dietetics; epidemiology (MPH, PhD); family and community medicine (MPH); occupational and environmental health (MPH); social and behavioral health science (PhD); social and behavioral health sciences (MPH), including health promotion. *Accreditation:* CAHME (one or more programs are accredited). *Program availability:* Part-time. *Degree requirements:* For master's, thesis (for some programs), practicum; for doctorate, comprehensive exam, thesis/dissertation, oral thesis defense. *Entrance requirements:* For master's, 2 letters of reference, relevant professional/research experience, minimum B average in final year; for doctorate, 2 letters of reference, relevant professional/research experience, minimum B+ average. Additional exam requirements/recommendations for international students: required—TOEFL (minimum score 580 paper-based; 93 iBT), TWE (minimum score 5). Electronic applications accepted. *Expenses:* Contact institution.

University of Washington, Graduate School, School of Public Health, Department of Health Services, Seattle, WA 98195. Offers community-oriented public health practice (MPH); health services (MPH, MS, PhD); health systems and policy (MPH); maternal and child health (MPH); social and behavioral sciences (MPH); MPH/JD; MPH/MD; MPH/MN; MPH/MPA; MPH/MS; MPH/MSD; MPH/MSW; MPH/PhD. *Program availability:* Blended/hybrid learning. *Faculty:* 50 full-time (26 women), 71 part-time/adjunct (36 women). *Students:* 136 full-time (109 women), 16 part-time (all women); includes 62 minority (12 Black or African American, non-Hispanic/Latino; 6 American Indian or Alaska Native, non-Hispanic/Latino; 28 Asian, non-Hispanic/Latino; 14 Hispanic/Latino; 2 Native Hawaiian or other Pacific Islander, non-Hispanic/Latino), 9 international. Average age 31. 236 applicants, 62% accepted, 56 enrolled. In 2019, 63 master's, 10 doctorates awarded. Terminal master's awarded for partial completion of doctoral program. *Degree requirements:* For doctorate, comprehensive exam, thesis/dissertation. *Entrance requirements:* Additional exam requirements/recommendations for international students: required—TOEFL (minimum score 80 iBT). Application fee: $85. Electronic applications accepted. *Expenses:* MPH resident $22,476, MPH non-resident $38,316, resident MS & PhD $19,389, non-resident MS & PhD $32,775. *Financial support:* Fellowships, research assistantships, teaching assistantships, Federal Work-Study, institutionally sponsored loans, scholarships/grants, traineeships, health care benefits, and unspecified assistantships available. Financial award applicants required to submit FAFSA. *Unit head:* Dr. Jeffrey Harris, Chair, 206-616-2930, E-mail: hschair@uw.edu. *Application contact:* Marketing & Recruitment Specialist, 206-616-1397, E-mail: hservask@uw.edu.
Website: http://depts.washington.edu/hserv/

Wilfrid Laurier University, Faculty of Graduate and Postdoctoral Studies, Faculty of Arts, Cultural Analysis and Social Theory Program, Waterloo, ON N2L 3C5, Canada. Offers body politics (MA); cultural representation and social theory (MA); gender, sexuality and embodiment (MA); globalization, identity and social movements (MA). *Program availability:* Part-time. *Entrance requirements:* For master's, honours BA in humanities, social science or interdisciplinary program with social theory, minimum B+ in final year of full-time study. Additional exam requirements/recommendations for international students: required—TOEFL (minimum score 89 iBT). Electronic applications accepted.

Worcester Polytechnic Institute, Graduate Admissions, Department of Social Science and Policy Studies, Worcester, MA 01609-2280. Offers interdisciplinary social science (PhD); system dynamics (MS, Graduate Certificate). *Program availability:* Part-time, evening/weekend, 100% online. *Entrance requirements:* For master's and doctorate, GRE General Test, 3 letters of recommendation, statement of purpose. Additional exam requirements/recommendations for international students: required—TOEFL (minimum score 563 paper-based; 84 iBT), IELTS (minimum score 7). Electronic applications accepted.

Worcester Polytechnic Institute, Graduate Admissions, Programs in Interdisciplinary Studies, Worcester, MA 01609-2280. Offers bioscience administration (MS); nuclear science and engineering (Graduate Certificate); power systems management (MS); social science (PhD); system dynamics and innovation management (MS, Graduate Certificate); systems modeling (MS). *Program availability:* Part-time, evening/weekend, 100% online. Terminal master's awarded for partial completion of doctoral program. *Degree requirements:* For master's, thesis; for doctorate, comprehensive exam, thesis/dissertation. *Entrance requirements:* For master's and doctorate, 3 letters of recommendation. Additional exam requirements/recommendations for international students: required—TOEFL (minimum score 563 paper-based; 84 iBT), IELTS (minimum score 7). Electronic applications accepted.

Yale University, Yale School of Medicine, Yale School of Public Health, New Haven, CT 06520. Offers applied biostatistics and epidemiology (APMPH); biostatistics (MPH, MS, PhD), including global health (MPH); chronic disease epidemiology (MPH, PhD), including global health (MPH); environmental health sciences (MPH, PhD), including global health (MPH); epidemiology of microbial diseases (MPH, PhD), including global health (MPH); global health (APMPH); health management (MPH), including global health; health policy (MPH), including global health; health policy and administration (APMPH, PhD); occupational and environmental medicine (APMPH); preventive medicine (APMPH); social and behavioral sciences (APMPH, MPH), including global health (MPH); JD/MPH; M Div/MPH; MBA/MPH; MD/MPH; MEM/MPH; MFS/MPH; MM Sc/MPH; MPH/MA; MSN/MPH. *Accreditation:* CEPH. *Faculty:* 161 full-time (71 women), 121 part-time/adjunct (57 women). *Students:* 534 full-time (386 women); includes 156 minority (24 Black or African American, non-Hispanic/Latino; 83 Asian, non-Hispanic/Latino; 30 Hispanic/Latino; 19 Two or more races, non-Hispanic/Latino),

Social Sciences

220 international. Average age 25. 1,300 applicants, 220 enrolled. In 2019, 250 master's, 12 doctorates awarded. *Degree requirements:* For master's, thesis; for doctorate, comprehensive exam, thesis/dissertation. *Entrance requirements:* For master's, GMAT, GRE, or MCAT; for doctorate, GRE General Test. Additional exam requirements/recommendations for international students: required—TOEFL (minimum score 100 iBT). *Application deadline:* For fall admission, 12/15 for domestic and international students; for summer admission, 12/15 for domestic and international students. Applications are processed on a rolling basis. Application fee: $135. Electronic applications accepted. *Expenses:* Contact institution. *Financial support:* Fellowships with full tuition reimbursements, research assistantships with full tuition reimbursements, teaching assistantships with full tuition reimbursements, career-related internships or fieldwork, institutionally sponsored loans, scholarships/grants, and tuition waivers available. Support available to part-time students. Financial award application deadline: 3/1; financial award applicants required to submit FAFSA. *Unit head:* Dr. Sten Vermund, Dean and Anna M.R. Lauder Professor of Public Health, E-mail: sten.vermund@yale.edu. *Application contact:* Mary Keefe, Director of Admissions, 203-785-2844, E-mail: ysph.admissions@yale.edu.
Website: http://publichealth.yale.edu/

Section 27
Sociology, Anthropology, and Archaeology

This section contains a directory of institutions offering graduate work in sociology, anthropology, and archaeology. Additional information about programs listed in the directory may be obtained by writing directly to the dean of a graduate school or chair of a department at the address given in the directory.

For programs offering related work, see also in this book *Area and Cultural Studies, Art and Art History, History, Humanities, Language and Literature,* and *Psychology and Counseling.*

CONTENTS

Program Directories

Anthropology

American University, College of Arts and Sciences, Department of Anthropology, Washington, DC 20016-8003. Offers anthropology (PhD, Certificate); public anthropology (MA). *Program availability:* Part-time, evening/weekend. Terminal master's awarded for partial completion of doctoral program. *Degree requirements:* For master's, comprehensive exam, thesis or alternative; for doctorate, comprehensive exam, thesis/dissertation. *Entrance requirements:* For master's, sample of written work, personal statement, 2 letters of recommendation, transcripts, resume; for doctorate, GRE, sample of written work, personal statement, 3 letters of recommendation, resume, transcripts; for Certificate, statement of purpose, transcripts. Additional exam requirements/recommendations for international students: required—TOEFL. *Expenses:* Contact institution.

Arizona State University at Tempe, College of Liberal Arts and Sciences, School of Human Evolution and Social Change, Tempe, AZ 85287-2402. Offers anthropology (MA, PhD), including anthropology (PhD), archaeology (PhD), bioarchaeology (PhD), evolutionary (PhD), museum studies (MA), sociocultural (PhD); applied mathematics for the life and social sciences (PhD); environmental social science (PhD), including environmental social science, urbanism; global health (MA, PhD), including complex adaptive systems science (PhD), evolutionary global health sciences (PhD), health and culture (PhD), urbanism (PhD); immigration studies (Graduate Certificate). Terminal master's awarded for partial completion of doctoral program. *Degree requirements:* For master's, thesis or alternative, interactive Program of Study (iPOS) submitted before completing 50 percent of required credit hours; for doctorate, comprehensive exam, thesis/dissertation, interactive Program of Study (iPOS) submitted before completing 50 percent of required credit hours. *Entrance requirements:* For master's and doctorate, GRE, minimum GPA of 3.0 or equivalent in last 2 years of work leading to bachelor's degree. Additional exam requirements/recommendations for international students: required—TOEFL, IELTS, or PTE. Electronic applications accepted.

Ball State University, Graduate School, College of Sciences and Humanities, Department of Anthropology, Muncie, IN 47306. Offers anthropology (MA); interpretive ethnography (Certificate). *Program availability:* Part-time. *Entrance requirements:* For master's, GRE General Test, minimum baccalaureate GPA of 2.75 or 3.0 in latter half of baccalaureate, official transcripts, goals statement, resume, three letters of recommendation. Additional exam requirements/recommendations for international students: required—TOEFL (minimum score 550 paper-based; 79 iBT), IELTS (minimum score 6.5). Electronic applications accepted. *Expenses:* Tuition, area resident: Full-time $7506; part-time $417 per credit hour. Tuition, nonresident: full-time $20,610; part-time $1145 per credit hour. *Required fees:* $2126. Tuition and fees vary according to course load, campus/location and program.

Binghamton University, State University of New York, Graduate School, Harpur College of Arts and Sciences, Department of Anthropology, Binghamton, NY 13902-6000. Offers anthropology (MA, PhD); biomedical anthropology (MS). *Program availability:* Part-time. Terminal master's awarded for partial completion of doctoral program. *Degree requirements:* For master's, variable foreign language requirement, comprehensive exam (for some programs), thesis (for some programs); for doctorate, variable foreign language requirement, comprehensive exam, thesis/dissertation. *Entrance requirements:* For master's and doctorate, GRE General Test. Additional exam requirements/recommendations for international students: required—TOEFL (minimum score 550 paper-based; 80 iBT). Electronic applications accepted.

Biola University, Cook School of Intercultural Studies, La Mirada, CA 90639-0001. Offers anthropology (MA); applied linguistics (MA); intercultural education (PhD); intercultural studies (MA, PhD); linguistics (Certificate); linguistics and Biblical languages (MA); missiology (D Miss); missions (MA); teaching English to speakers of other languages (MA, Certificate). *Program availability:* Part-time, 100% online. *Faculty:* 19. *Students:* 108 full-time (55 women), 154 part-time (86 women); includes 77 minority (11 Black or African American, non-Hispanic/Latino; 1 American Indian or Alaska Native, non-Hispanic/Latino; 43 Asian, non-Hispanic/Latino; 19 Hispanic/Latino; 3 Two or more races, non-Hispanic/Latino), 67 international. Average age 35. 142 applicants, 63% accepted, 52 enrolled. In 2019, 37 master's, 14 doctorates awarded. *Degree requirements:* For master's, comprehensive exam (for some programs), thesis or alternative, All students must successfully complete all required coursework with a minimum GPA of 3.0; for doctorate, thesis/dissertation, All students must present an acceptable dissertation, have satisfactorily passed their qualifying exam and completed all required course work with a minimum 3.3 GPA; for Certificate, All students musts successfully complete all required coursework with a minimum GPA of 3.0. *Entrance requirements:* For master's, minimum undergraduate GPA of 3.0; for doctorate, master's degree or equivalent, 3 years of cross-cultural experience, minimum graduate GPA of 3.3. Additional exam requirements/recommendations for international students: required—TOEFL. *Application deadline:* For fall admission, 7/1 for domestic students, 6/1 for international students; for spring admission, 11/1 for domestic students; for summer admission, 5/1 for domestic students. Applications are processed on a rolling basis. Application fee: $65. Electronic applications accepted. *Financial support:* Scholarships/grants available. Support available to part-time students. Financial award applicants required to submit FAFSA. *Unit head:* Dr. Bulus Y. Galadima, Dean, 562-903-4844. *Application contact:* Graduate Admissions Office, 562-903-4752, E-mail: graduate.admissions@biola.edu.
Website: http://cook.biola.edu

Boise State University, College of Arts and Sciences, Department of Anthropology, Boise, ID 83725-0399. Offers anthropology (MA); applied anthropology (MAA). *Program availability:* Part-time. *Students:* 12 full-time (10 women), 4 part-time (3 women); includes 2 minority (both Hispanic/Latino). *Entrance requirements:* For master's, GRE General Test. Additional exam requirements/recommendations for international students: required—TOEFL, IELTS. Electronic applications accepted. *Expenses:* Tuition, area resident: Full-time $7110; part-time $470 per credit hour. Tuition, state resident: full-time $7110; part-time $470 per credit hour. Tuition, nonresident: full-time $24,030; part-time $827 per credit hour. International tuition: $24,030 full-time. *Required fees:* $2536. Tuition and fees vary according to course load and program. *Financial support:* Scholarships/grants and unspecified assistantships available. Financial award application deadline: 2/15; financial award applicants required to submit FAFSA. *Unit head:* Dr. John Ziker, Department Chair, 208-426-2121, E-mail: jziker@boisestate.edu. *Application contact:* Dr. Mark Plew, Graduate Program Coordinator, 208-426-3444, E-mail: mplew@boisestate.edu.
Website: https://www.boisestate.edu/anthropology/

Boston University, Graduate School of Arts and Sciences, Department of Anthropology, Boston, MA 02215. Offers anthropology (PhD); applied anthropology (MA). *Students:* 50 full-time (34 women), 2 part-time (both women); includes 7 minority (1 Black or African American, non-Hispanic/Latino; 3 Asian, non-Hispanic/Latino; 1

Hispanic/Latino; 2 Two or more races, non-Hispanic/Latino), 19 international. Average age 27. 104 applicants, 15% accepted, 8 enrolled. In 2019, 1 master's, 9 doctorates awarded. Terminal master's awarded for partial completion of doctoral program. *Degree requirements:* For master's, one foreign language, comprehensive exam, thesis or alternative, Research paper; for doctorate, one foreign language, comprehensive exam, thesis/dissertation. *Entrance requirements:* For master's, 3 letters of recommendation, transcripts, personal statement; for doctorate, 3 letters of recommendation, transcripts, personal statement, writing sample, resume/CV. Additional exam requirements/recommendations for international students: required—TOEFL (minimum score 550 paper-based; 84 iBT). *Application deadline:* For fall admission, 1/15 for domestic and international students. Application fee: $95. Electronic applications accepted. *Financial support:* In 2019–20, 48 students received support, including 19 fellowships with full tuition reimbursements available (averaging $23,340 per year), research assistantships with full tuition reimbursements available (averaging $23,340 per year), 22 teaching assistantships with full tuition reimbursements available (averaging $22,660 per year); Federal Work-Study, scholarships/grants, health care benefits, and unspecified assistantships also available. Support available to part-time students. Financial award application deadline: 1/15. *Unit head:* Nancy Smith-Hefner, Chair, 617-353-2198, Fax: 617-353-2610, E-mail: smhefner@bu.edu. *Application contact:* Veronica Little, Administrator, 617-353-2195, Fax: 617-353-2610, E-mail: vclittle@bu.edu.
Website: http://www.bu.edu/ANTHROP/

Boston University, School of Medicine, Graduate Medical Sciences, Program in Forensic Anthropology, Boston, MA 02215. Offers MS. *Financial support:* Applicants required to submit FAFSA. *Unit head:* Dr. Tara L. Moore, Program Director, E-mail: tlmoore@bu.edu. *Application contact:* GMS Admissions Office, 617-358-9518, Fax: 617-358-2913, E-mail: gmsbusm@bu.edu.
Website: http://www.bumc.bu.edu/gms/forensicanthropology/

Boston University, School of Medicine, Graduate Medical Sciences, Program in Medical Anthropology and Cross Cultural Practice, Boston, MA 02215. Offers MS. *Unit head:* Dr. Linda Barnes, Director, 617-414-4534, Fax: 617-414-5511, E-mail: linda.barnes@bmc.org. *Application contact:* GMS Admissions Office, 617-358-9518, Fax: 617-358-2913, E-mail: gmsbusm@bu.edu.
Website: http://www.bumc.bu.edu/gms/maccp/

Brandeis University, Graduate School of Arts and Sciences, Department of Anthropology, Waltham, MA 02454. Offers anthropology/women's, gender, and sexuality studies (MA); Mesoamerican archaeology (MA, PhD); sociocultural anthropology (MA, PhD). *Program availability:* Part-time. *Faculty:* 13 full-time (6 women), 1 (woman) part-time/adjunct. *Students:* 28 full-time (19 women), 1 (woman) part-time; includes 6 minority (1 Black or African American, non-Hispanic/Latino; 3 Asian, non-Hispanic/Latino; 2 Two or more races, non-Hispanic/Latino), 3 international. Average age 27. 50 applicants, 60% accepted, 9 enrolled. In 2019, 6 master's, 2 doctorates awarded. Terminal master's awarded for partial completion of doctoral program. *Degree requirements:* For master's, thesis or alternative, paper; for doctorate, one foreign language, comprehensive exam, thesis/dissertation. *Entrance requirements:* For master's and doctorate, General GRE, transcripts, letters of recommendation, resume, statement of purpose, and writing sample. Additional exam requirements/recommendations for international students: required—TOEFL, IELTS, PTE. *Application deadline:* For fall admission, 1/15 priority date for domestic and international students. Applications are processed on a rolling basis. Application fee: $75. Electronic applications accepted. *Financial support:* In 2019–20, 8 fellowships with full tuition reimbursements (averaging $25,000 per year), 8 teaching assistantships (averaging $3,550 per year) were awarded; scholarships/grants and health care benefits also available. Support available to part-time students. *Unit head:* Dr. Charles Golden, Director of Graduate Studies, 781-736-2217, E-mail: cgolden@brandeis.edu. *Application contact:* Laurel Woolf, Administrator, 781-736-4873, E-mail: lwoolf@brandeis.edu.
Website: http://www.brandeis.edu/gsas/programs/anthropology.html

Brigham Young University, Graduate Studies, College of Family, Home, and Social Sciences, Department of Anthropology, Provo, UT 84602-1001. Offers MA. *Faculty:* 11 full-time (1 woman). *Students:* 19 full-time (12 women); includes 1 minority (Asian, non-Hispanic/Latino), 1 international. Average age 28. 10 applicants, 80% accepted, 5 enrolled. In 2019, 2 master's awarded. *Degree requirements:* For master's, comprehensive exam, thesis. *Entrance requirements:* For master's, GRE General Test, minimum GPA of 3.0 in last 60 hours. Additional exam requirements/recommendations for international students: required—TOEFL (minimum score 580 paper-based). *Application deadline:* For fall admission, 2/1 for domestic and international students. Application fee: $50. Electronic applications accepted. *Financial support:* In 2019–20, 16 students received support, including 17 fellowships (averaging $1,000 per year), 13 research assistantships (averaging $13,000 per year), 9 teaching assistantships (averaging $8,000 per year); career-related internships or fieldwork, institutionally sponsored loans, and tuition waivers (partial) also available. Financial award application deadline: 3/1; financial award applicants required to submit FAFSA. *Unit head:* Dr. James R. Allison, Chair/Graduate Coordinator, 801-422-3059, Fax: 801-422-7942, E-mail: jallison@byu.edu. *Application contact:* Dr. James R. Allison, Chair/Graduate Coordinator, 801-422-3059, Fax: 801-422-7942, E-mail: jallison@byu.edu.
Website: http://anthropology.byu.edu/

Brown University, Graduate School, Department of Anthropology, Providence, RI 02912. Offers MA, PhD. *Degree requirements:* For doctorate, one foreign language, thesis/dissertation, preliminary exam.

California State University, Chico, Office of Graduate Studies, College of Behavioral and Social Sciences, Department of Anthropology, Chico, CA 95929-0722. Offers anthropology (MA); museum studies (MA). *Degree requirements:* For master's, comprehensive exam, thesis, Thesis, project or oral examination. *Entrance requirements:* For master's, GRE General Test, Deadline for January 10th. Fall admission only. Two letters of recommendation, statement of purpose, curriculum vitae, writing sample, and department letter of recommendation to access waiver form. Additional exam requirements/recommendations for international students: required—TOEFL (minimum score 550 paper-based; 80 iBT), IELTS (minimum score 6.5), PTE (minimum score 59). Electronic applications accepted.

California State University, East Bay, Office of Graduate Studies, College of Letters, Arts, and Social Sciences, Department of Anthropology, Geography and Environmental Studies, Hayward, CA 94542-3000. Offers anthropology (MA); geography (MA). *Program availability:* Part-time. *Degree requirements:* For master's, variable foreign language requirement, project or thesis. *Entrance requirements:* For master's, minimum GPA of 3.0 in field. Additional exam requirements/recommendations for international students: required—TOEFL (minimum score 550 paper-based). Electronic applications accepted.

California State University, Fullerton, Graduate Studies, College of Humanities and Social Sciences, Department of Anthropology, Fullerton, CA 92831-3599. Offers MA. *Program availability:* Part-time. *Entrance requirements:* For master's, minimum GPA of 2.5 in last 60 hours of course work.

California State University, Long Beach, Graduate Studies, College of Liberal Arts, Department of Anthropology, Long Beach, CA 90840. Offers anthropology (MA); applied anthropology (MA). *Program availability:* Part-time. *Degree requirements:* For master's, one foreign language, comprehensive exam or thesis. Electronic applications accepted.

California State University, Los Angeles, Graduate Studies, College of Natural and Social Sciences, Department of Anthropology, Los Angeles, CA 90032-8530. Offers MA. *Program availability:* Part-time, evening/weekend. *Degree requirements:* For master's, one foreign language, comprehensive exam or thesis. *Entrance requirements:* Additional exam requirements/recommendations for international students: required— TOEFL (minimum score 500 paper-based). *Expenses: Tuition, area resident:* Full-time $7176; part-time $4164 per year. Tuition, state resident: full-time $7176; part-time $4164 per year. Tuition, nonresident: full-time $14,304; part-time $8916 per year. *International tuition:* $14,304 full-time. *Required fees:* $1037.76; $1037.76 per unit. Tuition and fees vary according to degree level and program.

California State University, Northridge, Graduate Studies, College of Social and Behavioral Sciences, Department of Anthropology, Northridge, CA 91330. Offers general anthropology (MA); public archaeology (MA). *Degree requirements:* For master's, thesis or alternative. *Entrance requirements:* For master's, GRE General Test or minimum GPA of 3.0. Additional exam requirements/recommendations for international students: required—TOEFL.

California State University, Sacramento, College of Social Sciences and Interdisciplinary Studies, Department of Anthropology, Sacramento, CA 95819. Offers MA. *Program availability:* Part-time. *Degree requirements:* For master's, project or thesis; writing proficiency exam. *Entrance requirements:* For master's, minimum GPA of 3.0 during previous 2 years. Additional exam requirements/recommendations for international students: required—TOEFL (minimum score 550 paper-based; 80 iBT); recommended—IELTS, TSE. Electronic applications accepted. *Expenses:* Contact institution.

Carleton University, Faculty of Graduate Studies, Faculty of Arts and Social Sciences, Department of Sociology and Anthropology, Program in Anthropology, Ottawa, ON K1S 5B6, Canada. Offers MA. *Degree requirements:* For master's, comprehensive exam, thesis optional. *Entrance requirements:* For master's, honors degree. Additional exam requirements/recommendations for international students: required—TOEFL.

Case Western Reserve University, School of Graduate Studies, Department of Anthropology, Cleveland, OH 44106. Offers MA, PhD, MD/MA, MD/PhD, MPH/MA, MSN/MA, PhD/MPH. *Program availability:* Part-time. Terminal master's awarded for partial completion of doctoral program. *Degree requirements:* For master's, comprehensive exam, thesis optional; for doctorate, thesis/dissertation. *Entrance requirements:* For master's and doctorate, GRE General Test, statement of purpose; 3 letters of recommendation; official transcripts. Additional exam requirements/ recommendations for international students: required—TOEFL (minimum score 577 paper-based; 90 iBT), IELTS (minimum score 7). Electronic applications accepted.

The Catholic University of America, School of Arts and Sciences, Department of Anthropology, Washington, DC 20064. Offers MA. *Program availability:* Part-time. *Faculty:* 3 full-time (2 women), 4 part-time/adjunct (2 women). *Students:* 2 applicants. *Degree requirements:* For master's, one foreign language, comprehensive exam, thesis or alternative. *Entrance requirements:* For master's, GRE General Test, statement of purpose, official copies of academic transcripts, three letters of recommendation. Additional exam requirements/recommendations for international students: required— TOEFL (minimum score 550 paper-based; 80 iBT). *Application deadline:* For fall admission, 2/1 priority date for domestic students, 7/1 for international students; for spring admission, 11/15 priority date for domestic students, 11/1 for international students. Applications are processed on a rolling basis. Application fee: $55. Electronic applications accepted. *Expenses:* Contact institution. *Financial support:* Fellowships, research assistantships, teaching assistantships, Federal Work-Study, scholarships/ grants, tuition waivers (full and partial), and unspecified assistantships available. Financial award application deadline: 2/1; financial award applicants required to submit FAFSA. *Unit head:* Dr. Anita Cook, Chair, 202-319-5080, Fax: 202-319-4782, E-mail: cook@cua.edu. *Application contact:* Dr. Steven Brown, Director of Graduate Admissions, 202-319-5057, Fax: 202-319-6533, E-mail: cua-admissions@cua.edu. Website: http://anthropology.cua.edu/

Central European University, Department of Sociology and Social Anthropology, Budapest, Hungary. Offers MA, PhD. *Degree requirements:* For master's, one foreign language, thesis; for doctorate, one foreign language, comprehensive exam, thesis/ dissertation. *Entrance requirements:* For master's and doctorate, interview. Additional exam requirements/recommendations for international students: required—TOEFL (minimum score 570 paper-based); recommended—IELTS (minimum score 6.5). Electronic applications accepted.

Central Washington University, School of Graduate Studies and Research, College of the Sciences, Program in Cultural and Environmental Resource Management, Ellensburg, WA 98926. Offers anthropology (MS); geography (MS). *Entrance requirements:* For master's, GRE, minimum GPA of 3.0. Additional exam requirements/ recommendations for international students: required—TOEFL (minimum score 550 paper-based; 79 iBT). Electronic applications accepted.

Clemson University, Graduate School, College of Behavioral, Social and Health Sciences, Department of Sociology, Anthropology and Criminal Justice, Clemson, SC 29634. Offers applied sociology (MS). *Program availability:* Part-time. *Faculty:* 21 full-time (11 women). *Students:* 7 full-time (3 women); includes 1 minority (Black or African American, non-Hispanic/Latino), 1 international. Average age 23. 12 applicants, 75% accepted. In 2019, 4 master's awarded. *Degree requirements:* For master's, thesis optional. *Entrance requirements:* For master's, GRE General Test, unofficial transcripts, letters of recommendation. Additional exam requirements/recommendations for international students: required—TOEFL (minimum score 80 paper-based; 80 iBT); recommended—IELTS (minimum score 6.5), TSE (minimum score 54). *Application deadline:* For fall admission, 4/15 priority date for international students; for spring admission, 10/15 priority date for international students. Applications are processed on a rolling basis. Application fee: $80 ($90 for international students). Electronic applications accepted. *Expenses:* Full-Time Student per Semester: Tuition: $4600 (in-state), $9525 (out-of-state), Fees: $598; Graduate Assistant Per Semester: $1144; Part-Time Student Per Credit Hour: $556 (in-state), $1106 (out-of-state), Fees: $617; other fees apply depending on program, credit hours, campus & residency. *Financial support:* In 2019– 20, 7 teaching assistantships with full and partial tuition reimbursements (averaging $11,000 per year) were awarded; career-related internships or fieldwork also available. *Unit head:* Dr. Catherine Weisensee, Department Chair, 864-656-3238, E-mail: kweisen@clemson.edu. *Application contact:* Dr. Bryan Miller, Graduate Program

Coordinator, 864-656-3818, E-mail: BLM2@clemson.edu. Website: http://www.clemson.edu/cbshs/departments/sociology/

Colorado State University, College of Liberal Arts, Department of Anthropology and Geography, Fort Collins, CO 80523-1787. Offers anthropology (MA, PhD). *Program availability:* Part-time. *Faculty:* 8 full-time (3 women), 2 part-time/adjunct (1 woman). *Students:* 19 full-time (10 women), 15 part-time (10 women); includes 3 minority (1 Hispanic/Latino; 2 Two or more races, non-Hispanic/Latino), 2 international. Average age 29. 61 applicants, 30% accepted, 10 enrolled. In 2019, 8 master's awarded. *Degree requirements:* For master's, thesis (for some programs); for doctorate, thesis/ dissertation. *Entrance requirements:* For master's, GRE General Test, minimum GPA of 3.0, BA/BS, transcripts, statement of purpose, writing sample, 3 letters of recommendation; for doctorate, GRE General Test, master's degree in anthropology or geography, transcripts, statement of purpose, writing sample, 3 letters of recommendation. Additional exam requirements/recommendations for international students: required—TOEFL (minimum score 550 paper-based; 80 iBT). *Application deadline:* For fall admission, 2/1 for domestic and international students. Application fee: $60 ($70 for international students). Electronic applications accepted. *Expenses:* Tuition, state resident: full-time $10,520; part-time $5844 per credit hour. Tuition, nonresident: full-time $25,791; part-time $14,328 per credit hour. *International tuition:* $25,791 full-time. *Required fees:* $2512.80. Part-time tuition and fees vary according to course level, course load, degree level, program and student level. *Financial support:* In 2019–20, 17 teaching assistantships with full and partial tuition reimbursements (averaging $17,624 per year) were awarded; scholarships/grants and unspecified assistantships also available. *Unit head:* Dr. Michelle M. Glantz, Professor and Chair, 970-491-4635, Fax: 970-491-7597, E-mail: mica.glantz@colostate.edu. *Application contact:* Dr. Mary Van Buren, Graduate Program Coordinator, 970-491-3781, Fax: 970-491-7597, E-mail: mary.vanburen@colostate.edu. Website: https://anthgr.colostate.edu/

Columbia University, Graduate School of Arts and Sciences, New York, NY 10027. Offers African-American studies (MA); American studies (MA); anthropology (MA, PhD); art history and archaeology (MA, PhD); astronomy (PhD); biological sciences (PhD); biotechnology (MA); chemical physics (PhD); chemistry (PhD); classical studies (MA, PhD); classics (MA, PhD); climate and society (MA); conservation biology (MA); earth and environmental sciences (PhD); East Asia: regional studies (MA); East Asian languages and cultures (MA, PhD); ecology, evolution and environmental biology (MA), including conservation biology; ecology, evolution, and environmental biology (PhD), including ecology and evolutionary biology, evolutionary primatology; economics (MA, PhD); English and comparative literature (MA, PhD); French and Romance philology (MA, PhD); Germanic languages (MA, PhD); global French studies (MA); global thought (MA); Hispanic cultural studies (MA); history (PhD); history and literature (MA); human rights studies (MA); Islamic studies (MA); Italian (MA, PhD); Japanese pedagogy (MA); Jewish studies (MA); Latin America and the Caribbean: regional studies (MA); Latin American and Iberian cultures (PhD); mathematics (MA, PhD), including finance (MA); medieval and Renaissance studies (MA); Middle Eastern, South Asian, and African studies (MA, PhD); modern art: critical and curatorial studies (MA); modern European studies (MA); museum anthropology (MA); music (DMA, PhD); oral history (MA); philosophical foundations of physics (MA); philosophy (MA, PhD); physics (PhD); political science (MA, PhD); psychology (PhD); quantitative methods in the social sciences (MA); religion (MA, PhD); Russia, Eurasia and East Europe: regional studies (MA); Russian translation (MA); Slavic cultures (MA); Slavic languages (MA, PhD); sociology (MA, PhD); South Asian studies (MA); statistics (MA, PhD); theatre (PhD). *Program availability:* Part-time. *Students:* 3,506 full-time (1,844 women), 208 part-time (121 women); includes 864 minority (110 Black or African American, non-Hispanic/ Latino; 5 American Indian or Alaska Native, non-Hispanic/Latino; 416 Asian, non-Hispanic/Latino; 147 Hispanic/Latino; 6 Native Hawaiian or other Pacific Islander, non-Hispanic/Latino; 180 Two or more races, non-Hispanic/Latino), 2,065 international. 14,545 applicants, 25% accepted, 1,429 enrolled. In 2019, 1,262 master's, 363 doctorates awarded. Terminal master's awarded for partial completion of doctoral program. *Degree requirements:* For master's, variable foreign language requirement, comprehensive exam (for some programs), thesis (for some programs); for doctorate, variable foreign language requirement, comprehensive exam (for some programs), thesis/dissertation. *Entrance requirements:* For master's and doctorate, GRE General Test, GRE Subject Test (for some programs). Additional exam requirements/ recommendations for international students: required—TOEFL (minimum score 600 paper-based; 100 iBT), IELTS (minimum score 7.5). Application fee: $115. Electronic applications accepted. *Expenses: Tuition:* Full-time $47,600; part-time $1880 per credit. One-time fee: $105. *Financial support:* Fellowships, research assistantships, teaching assistantships, career-related internships or fieldwork, Federal Work-Study, institutionally sponsored loans, scholarships/grants, traineeships, health care benefits, tuition waivers, and unspecified assistantships available. Support available to part-time students. Financial award application deadline: 12/15. *Unit head:* Dr. Carlos J. Alonso, Dean of the Graduate School of Arts and Sciences and Vice President for Graduate Education, 212-854-2861, E-mail: gsas-dean@columbia.edu. *Application contact:* GSAS Office of Admissions, 212-854-6729, E-mail: gsas-admissions@columbia.edu. Website: http://gsas.columbia.edu/

Concordia University, School of Graduate Studies, Faculty of Arts and Science, Department of Sociology and Anthropology, Montréal, QC H3G 1M8, Canada. Offers social and cultural analysis (PhD); social and cultural anthropology (MA); sociology (MA). *Degree requirements:* For master's, comprehensive exam or thesis. *Entrance requirements:* For master's, honors degree in sociology or equivalent.

Cornell University, Graduate School, Graduate Fields of Arts and Sciences, Field of Anthropology, Ithaca, NY 14853. Offers archaeological anthropology (PhD); biological anthropology (PhD); sociocultural anthropology (PhD). *Degree requirements:* For doctorate, one foreign language, comprehensive exam, thesis/dissertation, teaching experience. *Entrance requirements:* For doctorate, GRE General Test, 3 letters of recommendation, sample of written work. Additional exam requirements/ recommendations for international students: required—TOEFL (minimum score 550 paper-based; 77 iBT). Electronic applications accepted.

Dalhousie University, Faculty of Arts and Social Sciences, Department of Sociology and Social Anthropology, Halifax, NS B3H 4R2, Canada. Offers social anthropology (MA, PhD); sociology (MA, PhD). *Entrance requirements:* Additional exam requirements/ recommendations for international students: required—TOEFL, IELTS, CANTEST, CAEL, or Michigan English Language Assessment Battery. Electronic applications accepted.

East Carolina University, Graduate School, Thomas Harriot College of Arts and Sciences, Department of Anthropology, Greenville, NC 27858-4353. Offers MA. *Program availability:* Part-time. *Application deadline:* For fall admission, 3/1 priority date for domestic and international students. *Expenses: Tuition, area resident:* Full-time $4749; part-time $185 per credit hour. Tuition, state resident: full-time $4749; part-time $185 per credit hour. Tuition, nonresident: full-time $17,898; part-time $864 per credit hour. *International tuition:* $17,898 full-time. *Required fees:* $2787. *Financial support:* Application deadline: 3/1. *Unit head:* Dr. I Randolph Daniel, Jr., Chair, 252-328-9455, E-mail: danieli@ecu.edu. *Application contact:* Graduate School Admissions, 252-328-

6012, E-mail: gradschool@ecu.edu.
Website: https://anthropology.ecu.edu/

Eastern New Mexico University, Graduate School, College of Liberal Arts and Sciences, Department of Anthropology and Applied Archaeology, Portales, NM 88130. Offers anthropology (MA). *Program availability:* Part-time. *Degree requirements:* For master's, variable foreign language requirement, comprehensive exam, thesis. *Entrance requirements:* For master's, minimum GPA of 3.0, letters of recommendation, curriculum vitae, writing sample. Additional exam requirements/recommendations for international students: required—TOEFL (minimum score 550 paper-based; 79 iBT), IELTS (minimum score 6). Electronic applications accepted. *Expenses: Tuition, area resident:* Full-time $5283; part-time $389.25 per credit hour. Tuition, state resident: full-time $5283; part-time $389.25 per credit hour. Tuition, nonresident: full-time $7007; part-time $389.25 per credit hour. *International tuition:* $7007 full-time. *Required fees:* $36; $35 per semester. One-time fee: $25.

Emory University, Laney Graduate School, Department of Anthropology, Atlanta, GA 30322-1100. Offers PhD. *Degree requirements:* For doctorate, thesis/dissertation, qualifying exams. *Entrance requirements:* For doctorate, GRE General Test. Additional exam requirements/recommendations for international students: required—TOEFL. Electronic applications accepted.

Florida Atlantic University, Dorothy F. Schmidt College of Arts and Letters, Department of Anthropology, Boca Raton, FL 33431-0991. Offers MA, MAT. *Program availability:* Part-time. *Faculty:* 7 full-time (4 women), 1 (woman) part-time/adjunct. *Students:* 20 full-time (13 women), 11 part-time (4 women); includes 12 minority (3 Black or African American, non-Hispanic/Latino; 8 Hispanic/Latino; 1 Two or more races, non-Hispanic/Latino), 2 international. Average age 30. 19 applicants, 74% accepted, 12 enrolled. In 2019, 7 master's awarded. *Degree requirements:* For master's, one foreign language, thesis. *Entrance requirements:* For master's, GRE General Test, minimum GPA of 3.0. Additional exam requirements/recommendations for international students: required—TOEFL (minimum score 500 paper-based; 61 iBT), IELTS (minimum score 6). *Application deadline:* For fall admission, 7/1 priority date for domestic students, 2/15 for international students; for spring admission, 11/1 for domestic students, 7/15 for international students. Applications are processed on a rolling basis. Application fee: $30. Electronic applications accepted. *Expenses: Tuition:* Full-time $20,536; part-time $371.82 per credit hour. Tuition and fees vary according to program. *Financial support:* Fellowships, research assistantships, teaching assistantships, Federal Work-Study, and unspecified assistantships available. *Unit head:* Dr. Michael S. Harris, Chairman, 561-297-3233, Fax: 561-297-0084, E-mail: mharris@fau.edu. *Application contact:* Dr. Michael S. Harris, Chairman, 561-297-3233, Fax: 561-297-0084, E-mail: mharris@fau.edu.
Website: http://www.fau.edu/anthro/

Florida State University, The Graduate School, Department of Anthropology, Department of Anthropology, Tallahassee, FL 32306. Offers MA, MS, PhD. *Program availability:* Part-time. Terminal master's awarded for partial completion of doctoral program. *Degree requirements:* For master's, one foreign language, comprehensive exam, thesis optional; for doctorate, one foreign language, comprehensive exam, thesis/dissertation. *Entrance requirements:* For master's, GRE General Test, minimum GPA of 3.0; for doctorate, GRE General Test, minimum GPA of 3.5 (recommended). Additional exam requirements/recommendations for international students: required—TOEFL. Electronic applications accepted.

George Mason University, College of Humanities and Social Sciences, Department of Sociology and Anthropology, Fairfax, VA 22030. Offers anthropology (MA); sociology (MA, PhD). *Degree requirements:* For master's, thesis; for doctorate, comprehensive exam, thesis/dissertation. *Entrance requirements:* For master's, official transcript; expanded goals statement; 3 letters of recommendation; writing sample; resume; 3 credits in undergraduate sociology theory, statistics and research methods (for sociology); 3 credits of sociocultural anthropology (for anthropology); for doctorate, GRE General Test, expanded goals statement; 3 letters of recommendation; writing sample; official transcript. Additional exam requirements/recommendations for international students: required—TOEFL (minimum score 575 paper-based; 88 iBT), IELTS (minimum score 6.5), PTE (minimum score 59). Electronic applications accepted.

The George Washington University, Columbian College of Arts and Sciences, Department of Anthropology, Washington, DC 20052. Offers anthropology (MA, PhD); international development (MA); medical anthropology (MA); museum training (MA). *Program availability:* Part-time, evening/weekend. *Degree requirements:* For master's, one foreign language, comprehensive exam, thesis or alternative. *Entrance requirements:* For master's, GRE General Test, minimum GPA of 3.0. Additional exam requirements/recommendations for international students: required—TOEFL (minimum score 550 paper-based; 80 iBT). Electronic applications accepted.

Georgia State University, College of Arts and Sciences, Department of Anthropology, Atlanta, GA 30302. Offers MA. *Program availability:* Part-time. *Faculty:* 11 full-time (6 women). *Students:* 44 full-time (30 women), 8 part-time (6 women); includes 21 minority (9 Black or African American, non-Hispanic/Latino; 4 Asian, non-Hispanic/Latino; 5 Hispanic/Latino; 3 Two or more races, non-Hispanic/Latino), 2 international. Average age 30. 49 applicants, 73% accepted, 25 enrolled. In 2019, 19 master's awarded. *Degree requirements:* For master's, one foreign language, comprehensive exam, 33 to 36 credit hours, thesis/practicum defense. *Entrance requirements:* For master's, GRE, statement of purpose, writing sample, official transcripts, two letters of recommendation, curriculum vitae. Additional exam requirements/recommendations for international students: required—TOEFL (minimum score 550 paper-based; 80 iBT), IELTS (minimum score 6.5). *Application deadline:* For fall admission, 3/15 for domestic and international students; for spring admission, 10/15 for domestic and international students. Applications are processed on a rolling basis. Application fee: $50. Electronic applications accepted. *Expenses: Tuition, area resident:* Full-time $7164; part-time $398 per credit hour. Tuition, state resident: full-time $7164; part-time $398 per credit hour. Tuition, nonresident: full-time $22,662; part-time $1259 per credit hour. *International tuition:* $22,662 full-time. *Required fees:* $2128; $312 per credit hour. Tuition and fees vary according to course load and program. *Financial support:* In 2019–20, research assistantships with full tuition reimbursements (averaging $4,000 per year) were awarded. Financial award applicants required to submit FAFSA. *Unit head:* Dr. Kathryn Kozaitas, Chair and Associate Professor, 404-413-5151, Fax: 404-413-5159, E-mail: kozaitis@gsu.edu. *Application contact:* Dr. Emanuela Guano, Professor, 404-413-5152, Fax: 404-413-5159, E-mail: eguano@gsu.edu.
Website: https://anthropology.gsu.edu/

The Graduate Center, City University of New York, Graduate Studies, Program in Anthropology, New York, NY 10016-4039. Offers anthropological linguistics (PhD); archaeology (PhD); cultural anthropology (PhD); physical anthropology (PhD). *Degree requirements:* For doctorate, one foreign language, thesis/dissertation. *Entrance requirements:* For doctorate, GRE General Test. Additional exam requirements/recommendations for international students: required—TOEFL. Electronic applications accepted.

Harvard University, Graduate School of Arts and Sciences, Committee on Middle Eastern Studies, Cambridge, MA 02138. Offers anthropology and Middle Eastern studies (PhD); economics and Middle Eastern studies (PhD); fine arts and Middle Eastern studies (PhD); history and Middle Eastern studies (PhD); regional studies–Middle East (AM). Terminal master's awarded for partial completion of doctoral program. *Degree requirements:* For master's, one foreign language; for doctorate, 2 foreign languages, thesis/dissertation. *Entrance requirements:* For master's, GRE General Test; for doctorate, GRE General Test, 1 year of course work in Middle Eastern regional studies, proficiency in a related language. Additional exam requirements/recommendations for international students: required—TOEFL.

Harvard University, Graduate School of Arts and Sciences, Department of Anthropology, Cambridge, MA 02138. Offers archaeology (PhD); biological anthropology (PhD); legal anthropology (AM); medical anthropology (AM); social anthropology (AM, PhD); social change and development (AM). Terminal master's awarded for partial completion of doctoral program. *Degree requirements:* For master's, 2 foreign languages, thesis (for some programs); for doctorate, 2 foreign languages, thesis/dissertation, laboratory and/or fieldwork; general, qualifying, or special exams. *Entrance requirements:* For master's and doctorate, GRE General Test. Additional exam requirements/recommendations for international students: required—TOEFL.

Humboldt State University, Academic Programs, College of Arts, Humanities, and Social Sciences, Department of Anthropology, Arcata, CA 95521-8299. Offers applied anthropology (MA). *Program availability:* Part-time, blended/hybrid learning. *Faculty:* 6 full-time (5 women), 3 part-time/adjunct (all women). *Students:* 32 part-time (27 women); includes 8 minority (2 American Indian or Alaska Native, non-Hispanic/Latino; 1 Asian, non-Hispanic/Latino; 3 Hispanic/Latino; 2 Two or more races, non-Hispanic/Latino). Average age 33. 2 applicants, 100% accepted, 2 enrolled. In 2019, 8 master's awarded. *Degree requirements:* For master's, comprehensive exam, thesis, 180 hours of field placement/internship. *Entrance requirements:* For master's, three letters of recommendation. *Application deadline:* For fall admission, 2/15 priority date for domestic students. Applications are processed on a rolling basis. Application fee: $55. Electronic applications accepted. *Expenses:* $375 per unit. *Financial support:* Application deadline: 3/1; applicants required to submit FAFSA. *Unit head:* Dr. Rebecca Robertson, Graduate Program Coordinator, 707-826-4372, E-mail: rebecca.robertson@humboldt.edu. *Application contact:* Dr. Rebecca Robertson, Graduate Program Coordinator, 707-826-4372, E-mail: rebecca.robertson@humboldt.edu.
Website: http://www2.humboldt.edu/anthropology/

Hunter College of the City University of New York, Graduate School, School of Arts and Sciences, Department of Anthropology, New York, NY 10065-5085. Offers MA. *Program availability:* Part-time, evening/weekend. *Degree requirements:* For master's, comprehensive exam, thesis, language or statistics exam. *Entrance requirements:* For master's, GRE General Test, minimum 9 credits of course work in anthropology or a related field. Additional exam requirements/recommendations for international students: required—TOEFL.

Idaho State University, Graduate School, College of Arts and Letters, Department of Anthropology, Pocatello, ID 83209-8005. Offers MA, MS. *Program availability:* Part-time. *Degree requirements:* For master's, one foreign language, comprehensive exam, thesis, 4 semesters foreign language, oral defense. *Entrance requirements:* For master's, GRE General Test, GMAT or MAT, minimum GPA of 3.0 in all upper-division classes, 3 letters of recommendation. Additional exam requirements/recommendations for international students: required—TOEFL (minimum score 550 paper-based; 80 iBT). Electronic applications accepted.

Indiana University Bloomington, University Graduate School, College of Arts and Sciences, Department of Anthropology, Bloomington, IN 47405. Offers anthropology (MA, PhD), including archaeology (PhD), bioanthropology (PhD), linguistic anthropology (PhD), social-cultural anthropology (PhD). *Degree requirements:* For master's, comprehensive exam (for some programs), thesis or alternative; for doctorate, 2 foreign languages, comprehensive exam, thesis/dissertation. *Entrance requirements:* For master's and doctorate, GRE General Test, minimum GPA of 3.0. Additional exam requirements/recommendations for international students: required—TOEFL (minimum score 550 paper-based, 79 iBT) or IELTS. Electronic applications accepted. *Expenses:* Contact institution.

Iowa State University of Science and Technology, Department of Anthropology, Ames, IA 50011. Offers MA. *Degree requirements:* For master's, thesis. *Entrance requirements:* For master's, GRE General Test. Additional exam requirements/recommendations for international students: required—TOEFL (minimum score 550 paper-based; 79 iBT), IELTS (minimum score 6.5). Electronic applications accepted.

Johns Hopkins University, Zanvyl Krieger School of Arts and Sciences, Department of Anthropology, Baltimore, MD 21218. Offers PhD. *Degree requirements:* For doctorate, one foreign language, thesis/dissertation. *Entrance requirements:* For doctorate, GRE General Test. Additional exam requirements/recommendations for international students: required—TOEFL, IELTS. Electronic applications accepted.

Kent State University, College of Arts and Sciences, Department of Anthropology, Kent, OH 44242. Offers MA. *Program availability:* Part-time. *Faculty:* 7 full-time (3 women), 1 part-time/adjunct. *Students:* 12 full-time (8 women), 8 part-time (3 women); includes 1 minority (Black or African American, non-Hispanic/Latino). Average age 31. 17 applicants, 47% accepted, 4 enrolled. In 2019, 7 master's awarded. *Degree requirements:* For master's, thesis. *Entrance requirements:* For master's, GRE, statement of goals, three letters of recommendation, official transcript,m bachelor's degree from accredited college or university, minimum 3.0 undergraduate GPA on a 4.0 scale. Additional exam requirements/recommendations for international students: required—TOEFL (minimum score 71 iBT), IELTS (minimum score 6), PTE (minimum score 50), MELAB minimum score 74. *Application deadline:* For fall admission, 2/1 for domestic and international students. Application fee: $45 ($70 for international students). Electronic applications accepted. *Financial support:* Research assistantships with full tuition reimbursements, teaching assistantships with full tuition reimbursements, career-related internships or fieldwork, Federal Work-Study, scholarships/grants, and unspecified assistantships available. Financial award application deadline: 2/1; financial award applicants required to submit FAFSA. *Unit head:* Dr. Mary Ann Raghanti, Chairperson, 330-672-9354, E-mail: mraghant@kent.edu. *Application contact:* Dr. Richard S. Meindl, Professor, 330-672-7998, E-mail: rmeindl@kent.edu.
Website: https://www.kent.edu/anthropology

Louisiana State University and Agricultural & Mechanical College, Graduate School, College of Humanities and Social Sciences, Department of Geography and Anthropology, Baton Rouge, LA 70803. Offers geography (MA, MS); geography and anthropology (PhD).

McGill University, Faculty of Graduate and Postdoctoral Studies, Faculty of Arts, Department of Anthropology, Montréal, QC H3A 2T5, Canada. Offers anthropology (MA, PhD); medical anthropology (MA).

McGill University, Faculty of Graduate and Postdoctoral Studies, Faculty of Medicine, Department of Social Studies of Medicine, Montréal, QC H3A 2T5, Canada. Offers medical anthropology (MA, PhD); medical history (MA, PhD); medical sociology (MA, PhD).

McMaster University, School of Graduate Studies, Faculty of Social Sciences, Department of Anthropology, Hamilton, ON L8S 4M2, Canada. Offers MA, PhD. *Program availability:* Part-time. *Degree requirements:* For master's, thesis or alternative; for doctorate, one foreign language, comprehensive exam, thesis/dissertation, fieldwork. *Entrance requirements:* Additional exam requirements/recommendations for international students: required—TOEFL (minimum score 580 paper-based).

Memorial University of Newfoundland, School of Graduate Studies, Department of Anthropology, St. John's, NL A1C 5S7, Canada. Offers archaeology and physical anthropology (MA, PhD); social and cultural anthropology (MA, PhD). *Program availability:* Part-time. *Degree requirements:* For master's, comprehensive exam (for some programs), thesis (for some programs); for doctorate, comprehensive exam, thesis/dissertation, oral defense of thesis. *Entrance requirements:* For master's, 2nd class degree in related field. Electronic applications accepted.

Mercyhurst University, Graduate Studies, Program in Anthropology, Erie, PA 16546. Offers archaeology and geological archaeology (MS); forensic and biological anthropology (MS). *Entrance requirements:* For master's, GRE or MAT, undergraduate degree in related field, interview, resume, essay, three professional references, transcripts. Additional exam requirements/recommendations for international students: required—TOEFL.

Michigan State University, The Graduate School, College of Social Science, Department of Anthropology, East Lansing, MI 48824. Offers anthropology (MA, PhD); professional applications in anthropology (MA). Terminal master's awarded for partial completion of doctoral program. *Degree requirements:* For master's, comprehensive exam (for some programs); for doctorate, annual evaluation. *Entrance requirements:* Additional exam requirements/recommendations for international students: required—TOEFL. Electronic applications accepted.

Minnesota State University Mankato, College of Graduate Studies and Research, College of Social and Behavioral Sciences, Department of Anthropology, Mankato, MN 56001. Offers applied anthropology (MS). *Program availability:* Part-time. *Degree requirements:* For master's, comprehensive exam, thesis. *Entrance requirements:* For master's, GRE. Additional exam requirements/recommendations for international students: required—TOEFL. Electronic applications accepted.

Mississippi State University, College of Arts and Sciences, Department of Anthropology and Middle Eastern Cultures, Mississippi State, MS 39762. Offers MA. *Program availability:* Part-time. *Faculty:* 9 full-time (4 women). *Students:* 22 full-time (16 women), 12 part-time (7 women); includes 4 minority (1 Black or African American, non-Hispanic/Latino; 3 Hispanic/Latino), 1 international. Average age 28. 21 applicants, 76% accepted, 7 enrolled. In 2019, 6 master's awarded. *Degree requirements:* For master's, thesis. *Entrance requirements:* For master's, GRE, minimum GPA of 3.0 on last 60 hours of undergraduate courses. Additional exam requirements/recommendations for international students: required—TOEFL (minimum score 477 paper-based; 53 iBT); recommended—IELTS (minimum score 4.5). *Application deadline:* For fall admission, 7/15 priority date for domestic students, 4/15 for international students; for spring admission, 11/1 priority date for domestic students, 9/1 for international students. Applications are processed on a rolling basis. Application fee: $60 ($80 for international students). Electronic applications accepted. *Expenses: Tuition, area resident:* Full-time $8880; part-time $456 per credit hour. *Tuition, state resident:* full-time $8880. *Tuition, nonresident:* full-time $23,840; part-time $1236 per credit hour. *Required fees:* $110; $11.12 per credit hour. Tuition and fees vary according to course load. *Financial support:* In 2019–20, 9 teaching assistantships with partial tuition reimbursements (averaging $9,400 per year) were awarded; Federal Work-Study, institutionally sponsored loans, scholarships/grants, and unspecified assistantships also available. Financial award application deadline: 3/15; financial award applicants required to submit FAFSA. *Unit head:* Dr. Hsain Ilahiane, Professor and Department Head, 662-325-0136, Fax: 662-325-8690, E-mail: hsain.ilahiane@anthro.msstate.edu. *Application contact:* Robbie Salters, Admissions and Enrollment Management Assistant Coordinator, 662-325-7400, E-mail: rks139@msstate.edu.
Website: http://www.amec.msstate.edu

Monmouth University, Graduate Studies, Program in Anthropology, West Long Branch, NJ 07764-1898. Offers MA. *Program availability:* Part-time, evening/weekend. *Faculty:* 9 full-time (2 women). *Students:* 8 full-time (5 women), 24 part-time (15 women); includes 4 minority (3 Hispanic/Latino; 1 Two or more races, non-Hispanic/Latino), 1 international. Average age 31. In 2019, 12 master's awarded. *Degree requirements:* For master's, comprehensive exam (for some programs), thesis (for some programs). *Entrance requirements:* For master's, minimum undergraduate GPA of 3.0, 500-word essay highlighting personal and/or professional goals and objectives for graduate anthropology study, two professional letters of recommendation. Additional exam requirements/recommendations for international students: required—TOEFL (minimum score 550 paper-based; 79 iBT), IELTS (minimum score 6), Michigan English Language Assessment Battery (minimum score 77) or Certificate of Advanced English (minimum score 160). *Application deadline:* For fall admission, 7/15 for domestic students, 6/1 for international students; for spring admission, 12/1 for domestic students, 11/1 for international students; for summer admission, 5/1 for domestic students. Applications are processed on a rolling basis. Application fee: $50. Electronic applications accepted. *Expenses: Tuition:* Full-time $22,194; part-time $14,796 per credit. *Required fees:* $712; $178 per semester. $178 per semester. Tuition and fees vary according to course load. *Financial support:* In 2019–20, 33 students received support. Research assistantships, teaching assistantships, institutionally sponsored loans, scholarships/grants, and unspecified assistantships available. Support available to part-time students. Financial award applicants required to submit FAFSA. *Unit head:* Dr. Veronica Davidov, Program Director, 732-571-7502, Fax: 732-263-5320, E-mail: vdavidov@monmouth.edu. *Application contact:* Kevin New, Graduate Admission Counselor, 732-571-3452, Fax: 732-263-5123, E-mail: gradadm@monmouth.edu.
Website: https://www.monmouth.edu/graduate/ma-anthropology/

New Mexico Highlands University, Graduate Studies, College of Arts and Sciences, Department of Social and Behavioral Sciences, Las Vegas, NM 87701. Offers psychology (MS), including clinical psychology/counseling, general psychology; public affairs (MA), including applied sociology; Southwest studies (MA), including anthropology. *Program availability:* Part-time. *Degree requirements:* For master's, comprehensive exam, thesis or alternative. *Entrance requirements:* For master's, minimum undergraduate GPA of 3.0. Additional exam requirements/recommendations for international students: required—TOEFL (minimum score 540 paper-based).

New Mexico State University, College of Arts and Sciences, Department of Anthropology, Las Cruces, NM 88003-8001. Offers anthropology (MA); cultural resource management (Graduate Certificate); museum studies (Graduate Certificate). *Program availability:* Part-time. *Faculty:* 9 full-time (6 women), 1 part-time/adjunct (0 women). *Students:* 24 full-time (15 women), 21 part-time (15 women); includes 20 minority (1 Black or African American, non-Hispanic/Latino; 2 American Indian or Alaska Native, non-Hispanic/Latino; 1 Asian, non-Hispanic/Latino; 13 Hispanic/Latino; 3 Two or more races, non-Hispanic/Latino), 2 international. Average age 32. 19 applicants, 79% accepted, 12 enrolled. In 2019, 15 master's, 21 other advanced degrees awarded. *Degree requirements:* For master's, thesis optional, non-theses option will complete an internship or special research project; for Graduate Certificate, graduate certificate in cultural resource management; graduate certificate in museum studies-available via secondary application. *Entrance requirements:* For master's and Graduate Certificate, minimum undergraduate GPA of 3.0. Additional exam requirements/recommendations for international students: required—TOEFL (minimum score 550 paper-based; 79 iBT), IELTS (minimum score 6.5). *Application deadline:* For fall admission, 2/1 priority date for domestic and international students; for spring admission, 10/1 priority date for domestic and international students. Applications are processed on a rolling basis. Application fee: $40 ($50 for international students). Electronic applications accepted. *Financial support:* In 2019–20, 24 students received support, including 2 research assistantships (averaging $9,081 per year), 10 teaching assistantships (averaging $11,274 per year); career-related internships or fieldwork, Federal Work-Study, scholarships/grants, traineeships, health care benefits, and unspecified assistantships also available. Support available to part-time students. Financial award application deadline: 3/1. *Unit head:* Dr. Rani Alexander, Department Head, 575-646-5809, E-mail: raalexan@nmsu.edu. *Application contact:* Dr. Lois Stanford, Graduate Advisor, 575-646-6092, E-mail: lstanfor@nmsu.edu.
Website: http://anthropology.nmsu.edu

The New School, The New School for Social Research, Department of Anthropology, New York, NY 10003. Offers MA, PhD. *Program availability:* Part-time. *Faculty:* 8 full-time (4 women). *Students:* 44 full-time (31 women), 9 part-time (7 women); includes 8 minority (1 Black or African American, non-Hispanic/Latino; 1 Asian, non-Hispanic/Latino; 6 Hispanic/Latino), 27 international. Average age 31. 49 applicants, 88% accepted, 12 enrolled. In 2019, 15 master's, 5 doctorates awarded. Terminal master's awarded for partial completion of doctoral program. *Degree requirements:* For master's, variable foreign language requirement, comprehensive exam; for doctorate, one foreign language, comprehensive exam, thesis/dissertation. *Entrance requirements:* For master's, GRE, letters of recommendation, writing sample, essays, transcript; for doctorate, letters of recommendation, writing sample, essays, transcript. Additional exam requirements/recommendations for international students: required—TOEFL (minimum score 100 iBT), IELTS (minimum score 7), PTE (minimum score 68). *Application deadline:* For fall admission, 1/5 priority date for domestic and international students; for spring admission, 10/15 priority date for domestic and international students. Applications are processed on a rolling basis. Application fee: $50. Electronic applications accepted. *Expenses:* 2260 per credit. *Financial support:* In 2019–20, 45 students received support, including 6 fellowships (averaging $6,243 per year), 16 research assistantships (averaging $5,282 per year), 8 teaching assistantships with full and partial tuition reimbursements available (averaging $5,852 per year); Federal Work-Study, scholarships/grants, and tuition waivers (full and partial) also available. Support available to part-time students. Financial award application deadline: 2/1; financial award applicants required to submit FAFSA. *Unit head:* Nicolas Langlitz, Department Chair, 212-229-5757 Ext. 2443, E-mail: langlitn@newschool.edu. *Application contact:* Merida Gasbarro, Director of Graduate Admission, 212-229-5600 Ext. 1108, E-mail: escandom@newschool.edu.
Website: https://www.newschool.edu/nssr/anthropology/

New York University, Graduate School of Arts and Science, Department of Anthropology, New York, NY 10012-1019. Offers anthropology (MA, PhD), including archaeological anthropology, linguistic anthropology, physical anthropology, socio-cultural anthropology; anthropology and French studies (PhD); MA/Advanced Certificate; PhD/Advanced Certificate. *Program availability:* Part-time. *Degree requirements:* For master's, thesis; for doctorate, one foreign language, comprehensive exam, thesis/dissertation. *Entrance requirements:* For master's and doctorate, GRE General Test. Additional exam requirements/recommendations for international students: required—TOEFL, IELTS.

North Carolina State University, Graduate School, College of Humanities and Social Sciences, Department of Sociology and Anthropology, Program in Anthropology, Raleigh, NC 27695. Offers MA.

North Dakota State University, College of Graduate and Interdisciplinary Studies, College of Arts, Humanities and Social Sciences, Department of Sociology and Anthropology, Fargo, ND 58102. Offers anthropology (MA, MS); community development (MA, MS); sociology (MS). *Program availability:* Part-time. *Entrance requirements:* For master's, GRE (for emergency management), course work in sociology, minimum GPA of 3.2. Additional exam requirements/recommendations for international students: required—TOEFL. Electronic applications accepted. Tuition and fees vary according to program and reciprocity agreements.

Northern Arizona University, College of Social and Behavioral Sciences, Department of Anthropology, Flagstaff, AZ 86011. Offers anthropology (MA), including applied anthropology, research anthropology. *Degree requirements:* For master's, variable foreign language requirement, comprehensive exam (for some programs), thesis, fieldwork experience/internship, oral defense. *Entrance requirements:* For master's, minimum GPA of 3.0 overall and in all anthropology courses taken, with no grade below a C; 12 hours of required anthropology courses. Additional exam requirements/recommendations for international students: required—TOEFL (minimum score 80 iBT), IELTS (minimum score 6.5). Electronic applications accepted.

Northern Illinois University, Graduate School, College of Liberal Arts and Sciences, Department of Anthropology, De Kalb, IL 60115-2854. Offers MA. *Program availability:* Part-time. *Faculty:* 12 full-time (6 women). *Students:* 5 full-time (4 women), 5 part-time (2 women), 1 international. Average age 30. 11 applicants, 36% accepted, 2 enrolled. In 2019, 12 master's awarded. *Degree requirements:* For master's, one foreign language, comprehensive exam, thesis optional. *Entrance requirements:* For master's, GRE General Test, minimum GPA of 2.75, 15 hours of course work in anthropology, course work in statistics. Additional exam requirements/recommendations for international students: required—TOEFL (minimum score 550 paper-based). *Application deadline:* For fall admission, 6/1 for domestic students, 5/1 for international students; for spring admission, 11/1 for domestic students, 10/1 for international students. Applications are processed on a rolling basis. Application fee: $40. Electronic applications accepted. *Financial support:* In 2019–20, 4 research assistantships with full tuition reimbursements, 8 teaching assistantships with full tuition reimbursements were awarded; fellowships with full tuition reimbursements, career-related internships or fieldwork, Federal Work-Study, scholarships/grants, tuition waivers (full), and unspecified assistantships also available. Support available to part-time students. Financial award applicants required to submit FAFSA. *Unit head:* Dr. Leila Porter, Chair, 815-753-0479, Fax: 815-753-7027. *Application contact:* Graduate School Office, 815-753-0395, E-mail: gradsch@niu.edu.
Website: http://www.niu.edu/anthro/

Northwestern University, The Graduate School, Judd A. and Marjorie Weinberg College of Arts and Sciences, Department of Anthropology, Evanston, IL 60208. Offers PhD, JD/PhD. *Degree requirements:* For doctorate, thesis/dissertation. *Entrance requirements:* For doctorate, GRE General Test. Additional exam requirements/recommendations for international students: required—TOEFL. Electronic applications accepted.

Anthropology

The Ohio State University, Graduate School, College of Arts and Sciences, Division of Social and Behavioral Sciences, Department of Anthropology, Columbus, OH 43210. Offers MA, PhD. *Degree requirements:* For master's, thesis optional; for doctorate, one foreign language, thesis/dissertation. *Entrance requirements:* For master's and doctorate, GRE General Test, minimum GPA of 3.3 in undergraduate work, 3.5 in all previous graduate work (recommended). Additional exam requirements/recommendations for international students: required—TOEFL (minimum score 550 paper-based; 79 iBT), Michigan English Language Assessment Battery (minimum score 82); recommended—IELTS (minimum score 7). Electronic applications accepted.

Oregon State University, College of Liberal Arts, Program in Applied Anthropology, Corvallis, OR 97331. Offers MA. *Degree requirements:* For master's, one foreign language, thesis. *Entrance requirements:* Additional exam requirements/recommendations for international students: required—TOEFL (minimum score 80 iBT), IELTS (minimum score 6.5).

Penn State University Park, Graduate School, College of the Liberal Arts, Department of Anthropology, University Park, PA 16802. Offers MA, PhD.

Portland State University, Graduate Studies, College of Liberal Arts and Sciences, Department of Anthropology, Portland, OR 97207-0751. Offers MA, MS. *Program availability:* Part-time. *Faculty:* 10 full-time (7 women), 5 part-time/adjunct (3 women). *Students:* 9 full-time (7 women), 15 part-time (10 women); includes 6 minority (1 Black or African American, non-Hispanic/Latino; 3 Hispanic/Latino; 2 Two or more races, non-Hispanic/Latino). Average age 32. 19 applicants, 63% accepted, 5 enrolled. In 2019, 4 master's awarded. *Degree requirements:* For master's, one foreign language, thesis. *Entrance requirements:* For master's, GRE General Test, minimum GPA of 3.25 in upper-division anthropology course work, 3.0 overall; 3 letters of recommendation; writing sample. Additional exam requirements/recommendations for international students: required—TOEFL (minimum score 550 paper-based; 80 iBT), IELTS (minimum score 6.5). *Application deadline:* For fall admission, 2/1 for domestic and international students. Application fee: $65. Electronic applications accepted. *Expenses: Tuition, area resident:* Full-time $13,020; part-time $6510 per year. Tuition, state resident: full-time $13,020; part-time $6510 per year. Tuition, nonresident: full-time $19,830; part-time $9915 per year. *International tuition:* $19,830 full-time. *Required fees:* $1226. One-time fee: $350. Tuition and fees vary according to course load, program and reciprocity agreements. *Financial support:* In 2019–20, 2 research assistantships with full tuition reimbursements (averaging $13,722 per year), 4 teaching assistantships with full tuition reimbursements (averaging $10,200 per year) were awarded; fellowships, career-related internships or fieldwork, Federal Work-Study, and unspecified assistantships also available. Support available to part-time students. Financial award application deadline: 3/1; financial award applicants required to submit FAFSA. *Unit head:* Dr. Virginia Butler, Chair, 503-725-3303, E-mail: virginia@pdx.edu. *Application contact:* Michele R Gamburd, Graduate Program Coordinator, 503-725-3317, Fax: 503-725-3905, E-mail: gamburdm@pdx.edu.
Website: http://www.pdx.edu/anthropology/

Portland State University, Graduate Studies, College of Liberal Arts and Sciences, Systems Science Program, Portland, OR 97207-0751. Offers computational intelligence (Certificate); computer modeling and simulation (Certificate); systems science (MS); systems science/anthropology (PhD); systems science/business administration (PhD); systems science/civil engineering (PhD); systems science/economics (PhD); systems science/engineering management (PhD); systems science/general (PhD); systems science/mathematical sciences (PhD); systems science/mechanical engineering (PhD); systems science/psychology (PhD); systems science/sociology (PhD). *Program availability:* Part-time. *Faculty:* 2 full-time (0 women), 6 part-time/adjunct (1 woman). *Students:* 6 full-time (3 women), 25 part-time (8 women); includes 7 minority (2 Asian, non-Hispanic/Latino; 4 Hispanic/Latino; 1 Two or more races, non-Hispanic/Latino), 2 international. Average age 39. 25 applicants, 80% accepted, 15 enrolled. In 2019, 7 master's, 2 doctorates awarded. Terminal master's awarded for partial completion of doctoral program. *Degree requirements:* For master's, comprehensive exam (for some programs), thesis optional; for doctorate, variable foreign language requirement, comprehensive exam (for some programs), thesis/dissertation. *Entrance requirements:* For master's, GRE/GMAT (recommended), minimum GPA of 3.0 on undergraduate or graduate work, 2 letters of recommendation, statement of interest; for doctorate, GRE required, minimum GPA of 3.0 undergraduate, 3.25 graduate; 3 letters of recommendation; statement of interest. Additional exam requirements/recommendations for international students: required—TOEFL (minimum score 550 paper-based; 80 iBT). *Application deadline:* For fall admission, 3/15 priority date for domestic and international students. Application fee: $65. Electronic applications accepted. *Expenses: Tuition, area resident:* Full-time $13,020; part-time $6510 per year. Tuition, state resident: full-time $13,020; part-time $6510 per year. Tuition, nonresident: full-time $19,830; part-time $9915 per year. *International tuition:* $19,830 full-time. *Required fees:* $1226. One-time fee: $350. Tuition and fees vary according to course load, program and reciprocity agreements. *Financial support:* Research assistantships, teaching assistantships, career-related internships or fieldwork, Federal Work-Study, scholarships/grants, and unspecified assistantships available. Support available to part-time students. Financial award application deadline: 3/1; financial award applicants required to submit FAFSA. *Unit head:* Dr. Wayne Wakeland, Chair, 503-725-4975, E-mail: wakeland@pdx.edu. *Application contact:* Dr. Wayne Wakeland, Chair, 503-725-4975, E-mail: wakeland@pdx.edu.
Website: http://www.pdx.edu/sysc/

Princeton University, Graduate School, Department of Anthropology, Princeton, NJ 08544-1019. Offers PhD. *Degree requirements:* For doctorate, variable foreign language requirement, thesis/dissertation. *Entrance requirements:* For doctorate, GRE General Test, sample of written work. Additional exam requirements/recommendations for international students: required—TOEFL (minimum score 600 paper-based). Electronic applications accepted.

Purdue University, Graduate School, College of Liberal Arts, Department of Anthropology, West Lafayette, IN 47907. Offers MS, PhD. *Faculty:* 17 full-time (13 women). *Students:* 23 full-time (19 women), 5 part-time (4 women); includes 8 minority (1 Black or African American, non-Hispanic/Latino; 1 Asian, non-Hispanic/Latino; 5 Hispanic/Latino; 1 Two or more races, non-Hispanic/Latino), 3 international. Average age 28. 44 applicants, 32% accepted, 10 enrolled. In 2019, 4 master's awarded. Terminal master's awarded for partial completion of doctoral program. *Degree requirements:* For master's, thesis; for doctorate, comprehensive exam, thesis/dissertation. *Entrance requirements:* For master's, GRE General Test, minimum undergraduate GPA of 3.0 or equivalent; for doctorate, GRE General Test, minimum undergraduate GPA of 3.0 or equivalent; master's degree. Additional exam requirements/recommendations for international students: required—TOEFL (minimum score 550 paper-based; 77 iBT), TWE. *Application deadline:* For fall admission, 12/1 for domestic and international students. Applications are processed on a rolling basis. Application fee: $60 ($75 for international students). Electronic applications accepted. *Financial support:* In 2019–20, 27 students received support. Fellowships, research assistantships, teaching assistantships, and tuition waivers (full) available. Support available to part-time students. Financial award application deadline: 2/15; financial award applicants required to submit FAFSA. *Unit head:* Melissa J. Remis, Head, 765-

496-1514, E-mail: remism@purdue.edu. *Application contact:* Graduate School Admissions, 765-494-2600, Fax: 765-494-0136, E-mail: gradinfo@purdue.edu.
Website: http://www.cla.purdue.edu/anthropology/

Rice University, Graduate Programs, School of Social Sciences, Department of Anthropology, Houston, TX 77251-1892. Offers archaeology (MA, PhD); social-cultural anthropology (MA, PhD). Terminal master's awarded for partial completion of doctoral program. *Degree requirements:* For master's, one foreign language, 3 major papers, dissertation proposal and language exam or thesis; for doctorate, one foreign language, thesis/dissertation. *Entrance requirements:* For master's and doctorate, research proposal. Additional exam requirements/recommendations for international students: required—TOEFL (minimum score 90 iBT). Electronic applications accepted.

Rutgers University - New Brunswick, Graduate School-New Brunswick, Program in Anthropology, Piscataway, NJ 08854-8097. Offers MA, PhD. Terminal master's awarded for partial completion of doctoral program. *Degree requirements:* For master's, thesis or alternative; for doctorate, comprehensive exam, thesis/dissertation. *Entrance requirements:* For master's and doctorate, GRE General Test, writing sample. Additional exam requirements/recommendations for international students: required—TOEFL. Electronic applications accepted.

San Diego State University, Graduate and Research Affairs, College of Arts and Letters, Department of Anthropology, San Diego, CA 92182. Offers MA. *Degree requirements:* For master's, one foreign language, thesis. *Entrance requirements:* For master's, GRE General Test, 3 letters of recommendation, typed writing sample. Additional exam requirements/recommendations for international students: required—TOEFL. Electronic applications accepted.

San Francisco State University, Division of Graduate Studies, College of Liberal and Creative Arts, Department of Anthropology, San Francisco, CA 94132-1722. Offers archaeology (MA); biological anthropology (MA); cultural anthropology (MA); visual anthropology (MA). *Expenses: Tuition, area resident:* Full-time $7176; part-time $4164 per year. Tuition, state resident: full-time $7176; part-time $4164 per year. Tuition, nonresident: full-time $16,680; part-time $396 per unit. *International tuition:* $16,680 full-time. *Required fees:* $1524; $1524 per unit. $762 per semester. Tuition and fees vary according to degree level and program. *Unit head:* Dr. Cynthia Wilczak, Chair, 415-338-2046, Fax: 415-338-6159, E-mail: anthro@sfsu.edu. *Application contact:* Dr. Peter Biella, MA Graduate Coordinator, 415-405-0536, Fax: 415-338-6159, E-mail: biella@sfsu.edu.
Website: http://anthropology.sfsu.edu/

San Jose State University, Program in Anthropology, San Jose, CA 95192-0113. Offers applied anthropology (MA). *Program availability:* Part-time, evening/weekend. *Faculty:* 4 full-time (2 women). *Students:* 15 full-time (9 women), 12 part-time (6 women); includes 16 minority (3 Black or African American, non-Hispanic/Latino; 3 Asian, non-Hispanic/Latino; 10 Hispanic/Latino), 2 international. Average age 30. 16 applicants, 69% accepted, 7 enrolled. In 2019, 9 master's awarded. *Application deadline:* For fall admission, 7/1 for domestic students, 5/1 for international students. Applications are processed on a rolling basis. Application fee: $70. Electronic applications accepted. *Expenses: Tuition, area resident:* Full-time $7176; part-time $4164 per credit hour. Tuition, state resident: full-time $7176; part-time $4164 per credit hour. Tuition, nonresident: full-time $7176; part-time $4165 per credit hour. *International tuition:* $7176 full-time. *Required fees:* $2110; $2110. *Financial support:* In 2019–20, 12 students received support. Scholarships/grants available. Financial award application deadline: 5/15; financial award applicants required to submit FAFSA. *Unit head:* Roberto Gonzalez, Department Chair, 408-924-5715, E-mail: roberto.gonzalez@sjsu.edu. *Application contact:* Roberto Gonzalez, Department Chair, 408-924-5715, E-mail: roberto.gonzalez@sjsu.edu.
Website: http://www.sjsu.edu/anthropology/

Simon Fraser University, Office of Graduate Studies and Postdoctoral Fellows, Faculty of Arts and Social Sciences, Department of Sociology and Anthropology, Burnaby, BC V5A 1S6, Canada. Offers anthropology (MA, PhD); sociology (MA, PhD). *Degree requirements:* For master's, thesis; for doctorate, comprehensive exam, thesis/dissertation, cooperative education. *Entrance requirements:* For master's, minimum GPA of 3.0 (on scale of 4.33) or 3.33 based on last 60 credits of undergraduate courses; for doctorate, minimum GPA of 3.5 (on scale of 4.33). Additional exam requirements/recommendations for international students: recommended—TOEFL (minimum score 580 paper-based; 93 iBT), IELTS (minimum score 7), TWE (minimum score 5). Electronic applications accepted.

Sonoma State University, School of Social Sciences, Program in Cultural Resources Management, Rohnert Park, CA 94928. Offers MA. *Program availability:* Part-time. *Entrance requirements:* For master's, minimum GPA of 3.0. Additional exam requirements/recommendations for international students: required—TOEFL (minimum score 500 paper-based).

Southern Illinois University Carbondale, Graduate School, College of Liberal Arts, Department of Anthropology, Carbondale, IL 62901-4701. Offers MA, PhD. *Degree requirements:* For master's, one foreign language, thesis; for doctorate, one foreign language, thesis/dissertation. *Entrance requirements:* For master's, GRE General Test, minimum GPA of 2.7; for doctorate, GRE General Test, minimum GPA of 3.25. Additional exam requirements/recommendations for international students: required—TOEFL (minimum score 600 paper-based; 100 iBT).

Southern Methodist University, Dedman College of Humanities and Sciences, Department of Anthropology, Dallas, TX 75205. Offers applied medical anthropology (MA); archaeology (PhD); cultural anthropology (PhD); medical anthropology (PhD). Terminal master's awarded for partial completion of doctoral program. *Degree requirements:* For master's, one foreign language, comprehensive exam, thesis or alternative; for doctorate, one foreign language, comprehensive exam, thesis/dissertation, qualifying exam, defense of dissertation. *Entrance requirements:* For master's and doctorate, GRE General Test, minimum GPA of 3.0. Additional exam requirements/recommendations for international students: required—TOEFL (minimum score 550 paper-based).

Stanford University, School of Humanities and Sciences, Department of Anthropology, Stanford, CA 94305-2004. Offers anthropology (MA); archaeology (PhD); culture and society (PhD); ecology and environment (PhD). *Expenses: Tuition:* Full-time $52,479; part-time $34,110 per unit. *Required fees:* $672; $224 per quarter. Tuition and fees vary according to program and student level.
Website: http://www.stanford.edu/dept/anthsci/

Stony Brook University, State University of New York, Graduate School, College of Arts and Sciences, Department of Anthropology, Stony Brook, NY 11794. Offers MA, PhD. *Program availability:* Part-time. *Faculty:* 13 full-time (6 women), 1 (woman) part-time/adjunct. *Students:* 30 full-time (20 women); includes 4 minority (2 Hispanic/Latino; 2 Two or more races, non-Hispanic/Latino), 5 international. Average age 29. 43 applicants, 19% accepted, 4 enrolled. In 2019, 5 master's, 1 doctorate awarded. *Degree requirements:* For master's, fieldwork; for doctorate, thesis/dissertation. *Entrance requirements:* For master's and doctorate, GRE General Test. Additional exam requirements/recommendations for international students: required—TOEFL (minimum

score 90 iBT). *Application deadline:* For fall admission, 1/15 for domestic students; for spring admission, 10/1 for domestic students. Application fee: $100. *Expenses:* Contact institution. *Financial support:* In 2019–20, 2 fellowships, 4 research assistantships, 18 teaching assistantships were awarded; career-related internships or fieldwork also available. *Unit head:* Dr. Frederick E Grine, Chair, 631-632-7622, E-mail: frederick.grine@stonybrook.edu. *Application contact:* Tara J. Powers, Coordinator, 631-632-7606, E-mail: tara.powers@stonybrook.edu.
Website: http://www.stonybrook.edu/commcms/anthropology/

Stony Brook University, State University of New York, Graduate School, College of Arts and Sciences, Interdepartmental Doctoral Program in Anthropological Sciences (IDPAS), Stony Brook, NY 11794. Offers PhD. *Students:* 29 full-time (19 women); includes 4 minority (2 Hispanic/Latino; 2 Two or more races, non-Hispanic/Latino), 5 international. Average age 29. 43 applicants, 19% accepted, 4 enrolled. In 2019, 1 doctorate awarded. *Degree requirements:* For doctorate, one foreign language, thesis/dissertation, fieldwork. *Entrance requirements:* For doctorate, GRE General Test. Additional exam requirements/recommendations for international students: required—TOEFL (minimum score 90 iBT). *Application deadline:* For fall admission, 1/15 for domestic students; for spring admission, 10/1 for domestic students. Application fee: $100. Electronic applications accepted. *Expenses: Tuition, area resident:* Full-time $11,310; part-time $471 per credit. Tuition, state resident: full-time $11,310; part-time $471 per credit. Tuition, nonresident: full-time $23,100; part-time $963 per credit. *International tuition:* $23,100 full-time. *Required fees:* $2247.50. *Financial support:* In 2019–20, 2 fellowships, 4 research assistantships, 18 teaching assistantships were awarded. *Unit head:* Prof. Katheryn Twiss, Director of the Ph.D. Program (IDPAS Director), 631-632-1539, E-mail: idpas_director@stonybrook.edu. *Application contact:* Tara J. Powers, Coordinator, 631-632-7606, Fax: 631-632-9165, E-mail: tara.powers@stonybrook.edu.
Website: https://www.stonybrook.edu/commcms/idpas/

Syracuse University, Maxwell School of Citizenship and Public Affairs, Programs in Anthropology, Syracuse, NY 13244. Offers MA, PhD. *Degree requirements:* For master's, thesis or alternative; for doctorate, one foreign language, comprehensive exam, thesis/dissertation. *Entrance requirements:* For master's and doctorate, GRE General Test, resume, three letters of recommendation, personal statement, official transcripts. Additional exam requirements/recommendations for international students: required—TOEFL (minimum score 100 iBT). Electronic applications accepted.

Teachers College, Columbia University, Department of International and Transcultural Studies, New York, NY 10027-6696. Offers anthropology and education (MA, Ed D, PhD); applied anthropology (PhD); comparative and international education (MA, Ed D, PhD); international educational development (Ed M, MA, Ed D, PhD). *Faculty:* 11 full-time (7 women). *Students:* 94 full-time (75 women), 142 part-time (123 women); includes 79 minority (19 Black or African American, non-Hispanic/Latino; 31 Asian, non-Hispanic/Latino; 25 Hispanic/Latino; 4 Two or more races, non-Hispanic/Latino), 102 international. 312 applicants, 69% accepted, 105 enrolled. *Unit head:* Prof. Herve Varenne, Chair, 212-678-3190, E-mail: varenne@tc.columbia.edu. *Application contact:* Kelly Sutton Skinner, Director of Admission and New Student Enrollment, E-mail: kms2237@tc.columbia.edu.

Temple University, College of Liberal Arts, Department of Anthropology, Philadelphia, PA 19122-6096. Offers PhD. *Program availability:* Part-time. *Faculty:* 13 full-time (7 women). *Students:* 23 full-time (18 women); includes 6 minority (1 Black or African American, non-Hispanic/Latino; 3 Hispanic/Latino; 2 Two or more races, non-Hispanic/Latino), 1 international. 10 applicants, 40% accepted, 2 enrolled. In 2019, 4 doctorates awarded. *Degree requirements:* For doctorate, one foreign language, thesis/dissertation. *Entrance requirements:* For doctorate, GRE, minimum GPA of 3.0; 3 letters of recommendation, statement of goals. Additional exam requirements/recommendations for international students: required—TOEFL (minimum score 79 iBT), IELTS, PTE, one of three is required. *Application deadline:* For fall admission, 1/5 for domestic students, 12/10 for international students. Application fee: $60. Electronic applications accepted. *Financial support:* Fellowships, research assistantships, teaching assistantships, Federal Work-Study, and health care benefits available. Financial award application deadline: 1/15; financial award applicants required to submit FAFSA. *Unit head:* Paul Farnsworth, Chairperson, 215-204-1424, E-mail: paul.farnsworth@temple.edu. *Application contact:* Yvonne Davis, Department Coordinator, 215-204-7775, Fax: 215-204-1410, E-mail: yvonne.davis@temple.edu.
Website: https://www.cla.temple.edu/anthropology/

Texas A&M University, College of Liberal Arts, Department of Anthropology, College Station, TX 77843. Offers anthropology (MA, PhD); maritime archaeology and conservation (MS). *Faculty:* 23. *Students:* 49 full-time (28 women), 38 part-time (18 women); includes 19 minority (3 Black or African American, non-Hispanic/Latino; 1 American Indian or Alaska Native, non-Hispanic/Latino; 3 Asian, non-Hispanic/Latino; 6 Hispanic/Latino; 6 Two or more races, non-Hispanic/Latino), 12 international. Average age 33. 48 applicants, 38% accepted, 13 enrolled. In 2019, 9 master's, 9 doctorates awarded. *Degree requirements:* For master's, comprehensive exam, thesis optional; for doctorate, comprehensive exam, thesis/dissertation. *Entrance requirements:* For master's and doctorate, GRE General Test, Three letters of recommendation, letter of intent, writing sample, curriculum vitae. Additional exam requirements/recommendations for international students: required—TOEFL (minimum score 550 paper-based; 80 iBT), IELTS (minimum score 6), PTE (minimum score 53). *Application deadline:* For fall admission, 12/1 for domestic students. Application fee: $65 ($90 for international students). Electronic applications accepted. *Expenses:* Contact institution. *Financial support:* In 2019–20, 65 students received support, including 8 fellowships with tuition reimbursements available (averaging $15,095 per year), 16 research assistantships with tuition reimbursements available (averaging $13,394 per year), 29 teaching assistantships with tuition reimbursements available (averaging $13,598 per year); career-related internships or fieldwork, institutionally sponsored loans, scholarships/grants, traineeships, health care benefits, tuition waivers (full and partial), and unspecified assistantships also available. Support available to part-time students. Financial award application deadline: 3/15; financial award applicants required to submit FAFSA. *Unit head:* Dr. Darryl de Ruiter, Department Head, 979-4584037, E-mail: deruiter@tamu.edu. *Application contact:* Marco Valadez, Academic Advisor, 979-845-9333, Fax: 979-845-4070, E-mail: mlvaladez@tamu.edu.
Website: https://liberalarts.tamu.edu/anthropology/

Texas State University, The Graduate College, College of Liberal Arts, Program in Anthropology, San Marcos, TX 78666. Offers MA. *Program availability:* Part-time. *Degree requirements:* For master's, comprehensive exam, thesis. *Entrance requirements:* For master's, official GRE (general test only) required with competitive scores in the verbal reasoning and quantitative reasoning sections, baccalaureate degree from regionally-accredited university with minimum GPA of 3.0 on last 60 undergraduate semester hours, resume, statement of purpose detailing academic interest identifying possible areas of anthropological research, three letters of recommendation. Additional exam requirements/recommendations for international students: required—TOEFL (minimum score 550 paper-based; 78 iBT), IELTS (minimum score 6.5). Electronic applications accepted.

Texas Tech University, Graduate School, College of Arts and Sciences, Department of Sociology, Anthropology and Social Work, Lubbock, TX 79409-1012. Offers anthropology (MA); social work (MSW); sociology (MA). *Accreditation:* CSWE. *Program availability:* Part-time. *Faculty:* 28 full-time (17 women), 6 part-time/adjunct (5 women). *Students:* 43 full-time (30 women), 10 part-time (6 women); includes 14 minority (1 Black or African American, non-Hispanic/Latino; 1 Asian, non-Hispanic/Latino; 7 Hispanic/Latino; 5 Two or more races, non-Hispanic/Latino), 7 international. Average age 31. 43 applicants, 51% accepted, 18 enrolled. In 2019, 29 master's awarded. *Degree requirements:* For master's, one foreign language, comprehensive exam (for some programs), thesis (for some programs). *Entrance requirements:* For master's, two letters of recommendation, statement of purpose, writing sample, curriculum vitae; minimum GPA of 3.0 and coursework in sociology or closely-related fields (for MA in sociology); coursework in anthropology (for MA in anthropology). Additional exam requirements/recommendations for international students: required—TOEFL (minimum score 550 paper-based; 79 iBT). *Application deadline:* For fall admission, 6/1 priority date for domestic students, 1/15 priority date for international students; for spring admission, 9/1 priority date for domestic students, 6/15 priority date for international students. Applications are processed on a rolling basis. Application fee: $65. Electronic applications accepted. *Expenses:* Contact institution. *Financial support:* In 2019–20, 46 students received support, including 40 fellowships (averaging $4,359 per year), 28 teaching assistantships (averaging $12,255 per year); research assistantships, Federal Work-Study, scholarships/grants, tuition waivers (partial), and unspecified assistantships also available. Financial award application deadline: 2/1; financial award applicants required to submit FAFSA. *Unit head:* Dr. Cristina Bradatan, Associate Professor and Chair, 806-834-1796, Fax: 806-742-1088, E-mail: cristina.bradatan@ttu.edu. *Application contact:* Dr. Martha Smithey, Associate Professor/Sociology Graduate Program Director, 806-834-1995, E-mail: martha.smithey@ttu.edu.
Website: www.sasw.ttu.edu

Trent University, Graduate Studies, Program in Anthropology, Peterborough, ON K9J 7B8, Canada. Offers MA. *Program availability:* Part-time. *Degree requirements:* For master's, thesis. *Entrance requirements:* For master's, honors degree.

Tulane University, School of Liberal Arts, Department of Anthropology, New Orleans, LA 70118-5669. Offers PhD. Terminal master's awarded for partial completion of doctoral program. *Degree requirements:* For doctorate, 2 foreign languages, thesis/dissertation. *Entrance requirements:* For doctorate, GRE General Test. Additional exam requirements/recommendations for international students: required—TOEFL. Electronic applications accepted. *Expenses: Tuition:* Full-time $57,004; part-time $3167 per credit hour. *Required fees:* $2086; $44.50 per credit hour. $80 per term. Tuition and fees vary according to course load, degree level and program.

UNB Fredericton, School of Graduate Studies, Faculty of Arts - Saint John, Department of Anthropology, Fredericton, NB E3B 5A3, Canada. Offers MA. *Program availability:* Part-time. *Faculty:* 6 full-time (4 women). *Students:* 8 full-time (5 women), 1 part-time (0 women), 6 international. Average age 27. In 2019, 4 master's awarded. *Degree requirements:* For master's, thesis. *Entrance requirements:* For master's, minimum GPA of 3.0. Additional exam requirements/recommendations for international students: required—TOEFL. *Application deadline:* For fall admission, 1/31 for domestic and international students; for winter admission, 1/31 priority date for domestic and international students; for spring admission, 1/31 for domestic and international students. Applications are processed on a rolling basis. Application fee: $50 Canadian dollars. Electronic applications accepted. *Expenses: Tuition, area resident:* Full-time $6975 Canadian dollars; part-time $3423 Canadian dollars per year. Tuition, state resident: full-time $6975 Canadian dollars; part-time $3423 Canadian dollars per year. Tuition, Canadian resident: full-time $6975 Canadian dollars; part-time $3423 Canadian dollars per year. *International tuition:* $12,435 Canadian dollars full-time. *Required fees:* $92.25 Canadian dollars per term. Full-time tuition and fees vary according to degree level, campus/location, program, reciprocity agreements and student level. *Financial support:* Fellowships, research assistantships, teaching assistantships, scholarships/grants, and unspecified assistantships available. *Unit head:* Dr. Koumari Mitra, Chairperson, 506-458-7997, Fax: 506-453-5071, E-mail: kmitra@unb.ca. *Application contact:* Judy Babin, Graduate Secretary, 506-453-4975, Fax: 506-453-5071, E-mail: judy.babin@unb.ca.
Website: http://go.unb.ca/gradprograms

Universidad de las Américas Puebla, Division of Graduate Studies, School of Social Sciences, Program in Anthropology, Puebla, Mexico. Offers anthropology (MA); archaeology (MA). *Program availability:* Part-time, evening/weekend. *Degree requirements:* For master's, one foreign language, thesis. *Entrance requirements:* For master's, bachelor's degree in anthropology or equivalent.

Université de Montréal, Faculty of Arts and Sciences, Department of Anthropology, Montréal, QC H3C 3J7, Canada. Offers M Sc, PhD. *Program availability:* Part-time. *Degree requirements:* For master's, thesis; for doctorate, thesis/dissertation, general exam. Electronic applications accepted.

University at Albany, State University of New York, College of Arts and Sciences, Department of Anthropology, Albany, NY 12222-0001. Offers MA, PhD. *Program availability:* Part-time, blended/hybrid learning. *Faculty:* 19 full-time (9 women), 2 part-time/adjunct (1 woman). *Students:* 20 full-time (15 women), 35 part-time (20 women); includes 13 minority (3 Black or African American, non-Hispanic/Latino; 5 Asian, non-Hispanic/Latino; 4 Hispanic/Latino; 1 Two or more races, non-Hispanic/Latino), 6 international. Average age 28. 12 applicants, 100% accepted, 4 enrolled. In 2019, 6 master's, 6 doctorates awarded. Terminal master's awarded for partial completion of doctoral program. *Degree requirements:* For master's, comprehensive exam, thesis; for doctorate, 2 foreign languages, thesis/dissertation, field exams. *Entrance requirements:* For master's and doctorate, GRE, transcripts of all schools attended, statement of background and goals, departmental questionnaire, resume, names and contact information for 3 recommenders. Additional exam requirements/recommendations for international students: required—TOEFL (minimum score 550 paper-based). *Application deadline:* For fall admission, 1/15 for domestic students, 4/1 for international students; for spring admission, 11/15 for domestic students, 11/16 for international students. Applications are processed on a rolling basis. Application fee: $75. Electronic applications accepted. *Expenses: Tuition, area resident:* Full-time $11,530; part-time $480 per credit hour. Tuition, nonresident: full-time $23,530; part-time $980 per credit hour. *International tuition:* $23,530 full-time. *Required fees:* $2185; $96 per credit hour. Part-time tuition and fees vary according to course load and program. *Financial support:* Fellowships, research assistantships, teaching assistantships, and career-related internships or fieldwork available. Financial award application deadline: 3/15. *Unit head:* Louise Burkhart, Chair, 518-442-4700, Fax: 518-442-5710, E-mail: lburkhart@albany.edu. *Application contact:* Michael DeRensis, Director, Graduate Studies, 518-442-3980, Fax: 518-442-3922, E-mail: graduate@albany.edu.
Website: http://www.albany.edu/anthro/

University at Buffalo, the State University of New York, Graduate School, College of Arts and Sciences, Department of Anthropology, Amherst, NY 14261. Offers MA, PhD. *Faculty:* 15 full-time (6 women), 2 part-time/adjunct (both women). *Students:* 66 full-time (39 women), 1 part-time (0 women); includes 9 minority (2 Black or African American,

non-Hispanic/Latino; 2 American Indian or Alaska Native, non-Hispanic/Latino; 3 Asian, non-Hispanic/Latino; 2 Hispanic/Latino), 1 international. Average age 29. 52 applicants, 54% accepted, 18 enrolled. In 2019, 8 master's, 7 doctorates awarded. Terminal master's awarded for partial completion of doctoral program. *Degree requirements:* For master's, project; for doctorate, one foreign language, comprehensive exam, thesis/dissertation, exam. *Entrance requirements:* For master's, GRE General Test, minimum GPA of 3.0; for doctorate, GRE General Test, minimum GPA of 3.2. Additional exam requirements/recommendations for international students: required—TOEFL (minimum score 79 iBT). *Application deadline:* For fall admission, 12/15 priority date for domestic and international students; for winter admission, 5/1 for domestic students, 3/15 for international students. Applications are processed on a rolling basis. Application fee: $75. Electronic applications accepted. *Expenses: Tuition, area resident:* Full-time $11,310; part-time $471 per credit hour. Tuition, state resident: full-time $11,310; part-time $471 per credit hour. Tuition, nonresident: full-time $23,100; part-time $963 per credit hour. *International tuition:* $23,100 full-time. *Required fees:* $2820. *Unit head:* Dr. Donald Pollock, Chair, 716-645-3080, Fax: 716-645-3808. *Application contact:* Maria Portera, Graduate Coordinator, 716-645-2414, Fax: 716-645-3808, E-mail: mportera@buffalo.edu.
Website: http://www.buffalo.edu/cas/anthropology

The University of Alabama, Graduate School, College of Arts and Sciences, Department of Anthropology, Tuscaloosa, AL 35487. Offers MA, PhD. *Faculty:* 11 full-time (4 women). *Students:* 29 full-time (21 women), 5 part-time (3 women); includes 3 minority (2 Asian, non-Hispanic/Latino; 1 Two or more races, non-Hispanic/Latino), 2 international. Average age 31. 26 applicants, 58% accepted, 7 enrolled. In 2019, 3 master's, 1 doctorate awarded. *Degree requirements:* For master's, one foreign language, comprehensive exam, thesis optional; for doctorate, one foreign language, comprehensive exam, thesis/dissertation. *Entrance requirements:* For master's, GRE, bachelor's degree in anthropology or closely-related discipline, undergraduate coursework in at least three of four anthropology subdisciplines; for doctorate, master's degree in anthropology or closely-related discipline, undergraduate or graduate coursework in at least three of four anthropology subdisciplines. Additional exam requirements/recommendations for international students: required—TOEFL. *Application deadline:* For fall admission, 1/31 for domestic and international students. Application fee: $50 ($60 for international students). Electronic applications accepted. *Expenses: Tuition, area resident:* Full-time $10,780; part-time $440 per credit hour. Tuition, nonresident: full-time $30,250; part-time $1550 per credit hour. *Financial support:* In 2019–20, 25 students received support, including 4 fellowships with full tuition reimbursements available (averaging $15,000 per year), 1 research assistantship with full tuition reimbursement available (averaging $13,500 per year), 21 teaching assistantships with full tuition reimbursements available (averaging $14,720 per year); Federal Work-Study and health care benefits also available. Financial award application deadline: 1/15. *Unit head:* Dr. Keith P. Jacobi, Chair and Professor, 205-348-1960, Fax: 205-348-7937, E-mail: kjacobi@ua.edu. *Application contact:* Dr. Christopher D. Lynn, Associate Professor and Director of Graduate Studies, 205-348-4162, Fax: 205-348-7937, E-mail: cdlynn@ua.edu.
Website: http://anthropology.ua.edu

The University of Alabama at Birmingham, College of Arts and Sciences, Program in Anthropology, Birmingham, AL 35294. Offers MA. *Faculty:* 7 full-time (3 women). *Students:* 12 full-time (6 women), 6 part-time (5 women); includes 3 minority (2 Black or African American, non-Hispanic/Latino; 1 Hispanic/Latino), 177 international. Average age 34. 10 applicants, 80% accepted, 6 enrolled. *Degree requirements:* For master's, one foreign language, thesis (for some programs). *Entrance requirements:* For master's, GRE General Test. Additional exam requirements/recommendations for international students: required—TOEFL, TWE. *Application deadline:* For fall admission, 1/31 for domestic students. Electronic applications accepted. *Financial support:* Career-related internships or fieldwork, Federal Work-Study, and institutionally sponsored loans available. *Unit head:* Dr. Loretta Cormier, Program Director, 205-934-6526, Fax: 205-975-8360, E-mail: lcormier@uab.edu. *Application contact:* Susan Noblitt Banks, Director of Graduate School Operations, 205-934-8227, Fax: 205-934-8413, E-mail: gradschool@uab.edu.
Website: http://www.uab.edu/cas/anthropology/graduate-program

University of Alaska Anchorage, College of Arts and Sciences, Department of Anthropology, Anchorage, AK 99508. Offers MA. *Degree requirements:* For master's, comprehensive exam, thesis (for some programs), practicum. *Entrance requirements:* For master's, GRE General Test. Additional exam requirements/recommendations for international students: required—TOEFL (minimum score 550 paper-based).

University of Alaska Fairbanks, College of Liberal Arts, Department of Anthropology, Fairbanks, AK 99775-7720. Offers MA, PhD. *Program availability:* Part-time. *Degree requirements:* For master's, one foreign language, comprehensive exam, thesis, oral defense of project or thesis, 4 semesters of a foreign language or proficiency in a research tool; for doctorate, one foreign language, comprehensive exam, thesis/dissertation, oral defense of thesis, two foreign languages or one foreign language and research tool. *Entrance requirements:* For master's, GRE general test, bachelor's degree in anthropology with minimum cumulative undergraduate and major GPA of 3.0, application packet which includes letters of recommendation and a statement of goals; for doctorate, GRE general test, master's degree in anthropology, application packet which includes letters of recommendation and a statement of goals. Additional exam requirements/recommendations for international students: required—TOEFL (minimum score 550 paper-based; 79 iBT), IELTS (minimum score 6.5). Electronic applications accepted.

University of Alberta, Faculty of Graduate Studies and Research, Department of Anthropology, Edmonton, AB T6G 2E1, Canada. Offers MA, PhD. *Degree requirements:* For master's, thesis; for doctorate, one foreign language, thesis/dissertation. *Entrance requirements:* For master's and doctorate, minimum GPA of 7.0 on a 9.0 scale in last 2 years. Additional exam requirements/recommendations for international students: required—TOEFL.

The University of Arizona, College of Social and Behavioral Sciences, School of Anthropology, Tucson, AZ 85721. Offers MA, MS, PhD, Graduate Certificate. *Program availability:* Part-time. Terminal master's awarded for partial completion of doctoral program. *Degree requirements:* For master's, thesis or alternative; for doctorate, one foreign language, thesis/dissertation. *Entrance requirements:* For master's and doctorate, GRE General Test, minimum GPA of 3.5, 2 letters of recommendation. Additional exam requirements/recommendations for international students: required—TOEFL (minimum score 550 paper-based; 79 iBT). Electronic applications accepted.

University of Arkansas, Graduate School, J. William Fulbright College of Arts and Sciences, Department of Anthropology, Fayetteville, AR 72701. Offers MA, PhD. *Program availability:* Part-time, evening/weekend. *Students:* 21 full-time (11 women), 11 part-time (8 women); includes 4 minority (1 Asian, non-Hispanic/Latino; 2 Hispanic/Latino; 1 Two or more races, non-Hispanic/Latino), 2 international. 25 applicants, 56% accepted. In 2019, 5 master's, 3 doctorates awarded. *Entrance requirements:* For master's, GRE General Test, minimum GPA of 3.0; for doctorate, GRE General Test. *Application deadline:* For fall admission, 8/1 for domestic students, 4/1 for international students; for spring admission, 12/1 for domestic students, 10/1 for international students; for summer admission, 4/15 for domestic students, 3/1 for international students. Applications are processed on a rolling basis. Application fee: $60. Electronic applications accepted. *Financial support:* In 2019–20, 6 research assistantships, 21 teaching assistantships were awarded; fellowships with tuition reimbursements, career-related internships or fieldwork, and Federal Work-Study also available. Support available to part-time students. Financial award application deadline: 4/1; financial award applicants required to submit FAFSA. *Unit head:* Dr. JoAnn D'Alisera, Interim Department Chair, 479-575-4460, E-mail: dalisera@uark.edu. *Application contact:* Dr. JoAnn D'Alisera, Interim Department Chair, 479-575-4460, E-mail: dalisera@uark.edu.
Website: https://fulbright.uark.edu/departments/anthropology/

The University of British Columbia, Faculty of Arts, Department of Anthropology, Vancouver, BC V6T 1Z1, Canada. Offers MA, PhD. *Program availability:* Part-time. *Degree requirements:* For master's, thesis; for doctorate, comprehensive exam, thesis/dissertation. *Entrance requirements:* For master's, BA in anthropology or equivalent with minimum B+ average in upper-level courses; for doctorate, MA in anthropology or equivalent. Additional exam requirements/recommendations for international students: required—TOEFL. Electronic applications accepted. *Expenses:* Contact institution.

University of California, Berkeley, Graduate Division, College of Letters and Science, Department of Anthropology, Program in Anthropology, Berkeley, CA 94720. Offers PhD. *Degree requirements:* For doctorate, thesis/dissertation. *Entrance requirements:* For doctorate, GRE General Test, minimum GPA of 3.0, 3 letters of recommendation. Additional exam requirements/recommendations for international students: required—TOEFL (minimum score 570 paper-based; 90 iBT). Electronic applications accepted.

University of California, Berkeley, Graduate Division, College of Letters and Science, Department of Anthropology, Program in Medical Anthropology, Berkeley, CA 94720. Offers PhD. *Degree requirements:* For doctorate, thesis/dissertation. *Entrance requirements:* For doctorate, GRE General Test, minimum GPA of 3.0, 3 letters of recommendation. Additional exam requirements/recommendations for international students: required—TOEFL (minimum score 570 paper-based; 90 iBT). Electronic applications accepted.

University of California, Davis, Graduate Studies, Program in Anthropology, Davis, CA 95616. Offers MA, PhD. Terminal master's awarded for partial completion of doctoral program. *Degree requirements:* For master's, one foreign language; for doctorate, one foreign language, thesis/dissertation. *Entrance requirements:* For master's and doctorate, GRE General Test, minimum GPA of 3.0. Additional exam requirements/recommendations for international students: required—TOEFL (minimum score 550 paper-based). Electronic applications accepted.

University of California, Irvine, School of Social Sciences, Department of Anthropology, Irvine, CA 92697. Offers MA, PhD. *Students:* 64 full-time (42 women); includes 27 minority (3 Black or African American, non-Hispanic/Latino; 2 American Indian or Alaska Native, non-Hispanic/Latino; 4 Asian, non-Hispanic/Latino; 15 Hispanic/Latino; 3 Two or more races, non-Hispanic/Latino), 11 international. Average age 30. 86 applicants, 27% accepted, 13 enrolled. In 2019, 8 master's, 8 doctorates awarded. *Entrance requirements:* For master's, GRE, minimum GPA of 3.0; for doctorate, GRE General Test, minimum GPA of 3.0. Additional exam requirements/recommendations for international students: required—TOEFL (minimum score 550 paper-based). *Application deadline:* For fall admission, 1/15 priority date for domestic and international students. Applications are processed on a rolling basis. Application fee: $120 ($140 for international students). Electronic applications accepted. *Financial support:* Fellowships, research assistantships with full tuition reimbursements, teaching assistantships, institutionally sponsored loans, traineeships, health care benefits, and unspecified assistantships available. Financial award application deadline: 3/1; financial award applicants required to submit FAFSA. *Unit head:* Kim Fortun, Chair, 949-824-0376, E-mail: kfortun@uci.edu. *Application contact:* Damien Sojoyner, Admissions Director, 949-824-3230, E-mail: dsojoyne@uci.edu.
Website: http://www.anthropology.uci.edu/

University of California, Los Angeles, Graduate Division, College of Letters and Science, Department of Anthropology, Los Angeles, CA 90095. Offers MA, PhD. Terminal master's awarded for partial completion of doctoral program. *Degree requirements:* For master's, thesis; for doctorate, thesis/dissertation, oral and written qualifying exams. *Entrance requirements:* For master's and doctorate, GRE General Test, bachelor's degree; minimum undergraduate GPA of 3.0 (or its equivalent if letter grade system not used); writing sample. Additional exam requirements/recommendations for international students: required—TOEFL. Electronic applications accepted.

University of California, Riverside, Graduate Division, Department of Anthropology, Riverside, CA 92521-0102. Offers MA, MS, PhD. *Program availability:* Part-time. Terminal master's awarded for partial completion of doctoral program. *Degree requirements:* For master's, comprehensive exams or thesis; for doctorate, one foreign language, comprehensive exam, thesis/dissertation, qualifying exams. *Entrance requirements:* For master's and doctorate, GRE General Test, sample of written work, minimum GPA of 3.2, 3 letters of recommendation. Additional exam requirements/recommendations for international students: required—TOEFL (minimum score 550 paper-based; 80 iBT). Electronic applications accepted.

University of California, San Diego, Graduate Division, Department of Anthropology, La Jolla, CA 92093. Offers PhD. *Students:* 53 full-time (34 women). 84 applicants, 14% accepted, 8 enrolled. In 2019, 5 doctorates awarded. *Degree requirements:* For doctorate, variable foreign language requirement, comprehensive exam, thesis/dissertation, 1-quarter teaching assistantship. *Entrance requirements:* For doctorate, GRE General Test, 3 letters of recommendation, statement of purpose. Additional exam requirements/recommendations for international students: required—TOEFL (minimum score 550 paper-based; 80 iBT), IELTS (minimum score 7), PTE. *Application deadline:* For fall admission, 1/18 for domestic students. Application fee: $105 ($125 for international students). Electronic applications accepted. *Financial support:* Fellowships, research assistantships, teaching assistantships, and scholarships/grants available. Financial award applicants required to submit FAFSA. *Unit head:* Steve Parish, Department Chair, 858-534-8880, E-mail: sparish@ucsd.edu. *Application contact:* Laura Jimenez, Graduate Coordinator, 858-534-0107, E-mail: lajimenez@ucsd.edu.
Website: http://anthropology.ucsd.edu/

University of California, San Francisco, Graduate Division, Program in Medical Anthropology, San Francisco, CA 94143. Offers PhD. *Degree requirements:* For doctorate, one foreign language, thesis/dissertation, 3 field statements. *Entrance requirements:* For doctorate, GRE General Test, master's degree in anthropology or a related social or health science.

University of California, Santa Barbara, Graduate Division, College of Letters and Sciences, Division of Social Sciences, Department of Anthropology, Santa Barbara, CA 93106-2014. Offers sociocultural anthropology (PhD); MA/PhD. Terminal master's awarded for partial completion of doctoral program. *Degree requirements:* For master's, comprehensive exam (for some programs), thesis (for some programs); for doctorate, comprehensive exam (for some programs), thesis/dissertation. *Entrance requirements:* For master's and doctorate, GRE General Test, statement of purpose, personal achievements statement, transcripts, writing sample, curriculum vitae, letters of recommendation. Additional exam requirements/recommendations for international students: required—TOEFL (minimum score 550 paper-based; 80 iBT), IELTS (minimum score 7). Electronic applications accepted.

University of California, Santa Cruz, Division of Graduate Studies, Division of Social Sciences, Department of Anthropology, Santa Cruz, CA 95064. Offers cultural anthropology (PhD). *Degree requirements:* For doctorate, thesis/dissertation, qualifying exam. *Entrance requirements:* For doctorate, GRE General Test. Additional exam requirements/recommendations for international students: required—TOEFL (minimum score 550 paper-based; 83 iBT); recommended—IELTS (minimum score 8). Electronic applications accepted.

University of Central Florida, College of Sciences, Department of Anthropology, Orlando, FL 32816. Offers MA. *Students:* 44 full-time (31 women), 7 part-time (all women); includes 12 minority (1 Black or African American, non-Hispanic/Latino; 1 Asian, non-Hispanic/Latino; 6 Hispanic/Latino; 4 Two or more races, non-Hispanic/Latino), 3 international. Average age 30. 47 applicants, 74% accepted, 20 enrolled. In 2019, 14 master's awarded. *Entrance requirements:* For master's, GRE General Test, letters of recommendation, personal statement. Additional exam requirements/recommendations for international students: required—TOEFL. *Application deadline:* For fall admission, 2/15 for domestic students; for spring admission, 11/1 for domestic students. Application fee: $30. Electronic applications accepted. *Financial support:* In 2019–20, 27 students received support, including 2 fellowships with partial tuition reimbursements available (averaging $10,733 per year), 4 research assistantships (averaging $7,113 per year), 22 teaching assistantships with partial tuition reimbursements available (averaging $8,027 per year); institutionally sponsored loans, scholarships/grants, and health care benefits also available. Financial award application deadline: 3/1; financial award applicants required to submit FAFSA. *Unit head:* Dr. Toshas Dupras, Chair, 407-823-6568, Fax: 407-823-3498, E-mail: tosha.dupras@ucf.edu. *Application contact:* Associate Director, Graduate Admissions, 407-823-2766, Fax: 407-823-6442, E-mail: gradadmissions@ucf.edu. Website: http://anthropology.cos.ucf.edu/

University of Chicago, Division of the Humanities, Department of Linguistics, Chicago, IL 60637. Offers anthropology and linguistics (PhD); linguistics (PhD). Terminal master's awarded for partial completion of doctoral program. *Degree requirements:* For doctorate, 2 foreign languages, thesis/dissertation. *Entrance requirements:* For doctorate, GRE General Test, 15-20 page writing sample, statement of purpose, 3 letters of recommendation, transcripts for all previous degrees and institutions attended. Additional exam requirements/recommendations for international students: required—TOEFL (minimum score 104 iBT), IELTS (minimum score 7). Electronic applications accepted.

University of Chicago, Division of the Social Sciences, Department of Anthropology, Chicago, IL 60637. Offers archaeology (PhD); sociocultural and linguistic anthropology (PhD). *Degree requirements:* For doctorate, one foreign language, thesis/dissertation. *Entrance requirements:* For doctorate, GRE General Test, 3 letters of recommendation, statement of purpose, transcripts, resume or curriculum vitae, writing sample (dependent on department). Additional exam requirements/recommendations for international students: required—TOEFL (minimum score 104 iBT), IELTS (minimum score 7). Electronic applications accepted.

University of Cincinnati, Graduate School, McMicken College of Arts and Sciences, Department of Anthropology, Cincinnati, OH 45221. Offers MA. *Program availability:* Part-time. *Degree requirements:* For master's, thesis or alternative. *Entrance requirements:* For master's, GRE General Test. Additional exam requirements/recommendations for international students: required—TOEFL; recommended—TWE. Electronic applications accepted.

University of Colorado Boulder, Graduate School, College of Arts and Sciences, Department of Anthropology, Boulder, CO 80309. Offers MA, PhD. Terminal master's awarded for partial completion of doctoral program. *Degree requirements:* For master's, comprehensive exam, thesis or alternative; for doctorate, one foreign language, thesis/dissertation. *Entrance requirements:* For master's, GRE General Test, minimum undergraduate GPA of 3.0; for doctorate, GRE General Test, minimum undergraduate GPA of 3.0, master's degree in anthropology. Electronic applications accepted. Application fee is waived when completed online.

University of Colorado Denver, College of Liberal Arts and Sciences, Department of Anthropology, Denver, CO 80217. Offers archaeological studies (MA); biological anthropology (MA); medical anthropology (MA); sustainable development and political ecology (MA). *Program availability:* Part-time, evening/weekend. *Degree requirements:* For master's, comprehensive exam, thesis or alternative, 30-36 credit hours. *Entrance requirements:* For master's, GRE General Test, minimum GPA of 3.0 for all undergraduate studies, transcripts from all undergraduate/graduate institutions attended, prior training in anthropology, three letters of recommendation, statement of purpose. Additional exam requirements/recommendations for international students: required—TOEFL (minimum score 537 paper-based; 75 iBT); recommended—IELTS (minimum score 6.5). Tuition and fees vary according to course load, program and reciprocity agreements.

University of Connecticut, Graduate School, College of Liberal Arts and Sciences, Department of Anthropology, Storrs, CT 06269. Offers MA, PhD. Terminal master's awarded for partial completion of doctoral program. *Degree requirements:* For master's, comprehensive exam; for doctorate, thesis/dissertation. *Entrance requirements:* For master's and doctorate, GRE General Test. Additional exam requirements/recommendations for international students: required—TOEFL (minimum score 550 paper-based). Electronic applications accepted.

University of Denver, Division of Arts, Humanities and Social Sciences, Department of Anthropology, Denver, CO 80208. Offers archaeology (MA); cultural anthropology (MA); museum and heritage studies (MA). *Program availability:* Part-time. *Faculty:* 8 full-time (4 women), 1 part-time/adjunct (0 women). *Students:* 2 full-time (both women), 21 part-time (16 women); includes 7 minority (2 Black or African American, non-Hispanic/Latino; 1 Asian, non-Hispanic/Latino; 3 Hispanic/Latino; 1 Two or more races, non-Hispanic/Latino). Average age 27. 35 applicants, 57% accepted, 11 enrolled. In 2019, 12 master's awarded. *Degree requirements:* For master's, comprehensive exam, thesis (for some programs). *Entrance requirements:* For master's, GRE General Test, bachelor's degree, transcripts, personal statement, two letters of recommendation. Additional exam requirements/recommendations for international students: required—TOEFL (minimum score 550 paper-based; 80 iBT). *Application deadline:* For fall admission, 2/28 for domestic and international students. Applications are processed on a rolling basis. Application fee: $65. Electronic applications accepted. *Expenses:* Contact institution. *Financial support:* In 2019–20, 22 students received support, including 12 teaching assistantships with tuition reimbursements available (averaging $5,233 per year); career-related internships or fieldwork, Federal Work-Study, institutionally sponsored loans, scholarships/grants, and unspecified assistantships also available. Support available to part-time students. Financial award application deadline: 2/15; financial award applicants required to submit FAFSA. *Unit head:* Dr. Larry Conyers, Professor, Director of Graduate Program, 303-871-2684, E-mail: lconyers@du.edu. *Application contact:* Dr. Larry Conyers, Professor, Director of Graduate Program, 303-871-2684,

E-mail: lconyers@du.edu.
Website: http://www.du.edu/ahss/anthropology

University of Florida, Graduate School, College of Liberal Arts and Sciences, Department of Anthropology, Gainesville, FL 32611. Offers anthropology (MA, MAT, PhD), including historic preservation (MA, PhD), tropical conservation and development, women's and gender studies (PhD). *Program availability:* Part-time. *Degree requirements:* For master's, thesis optional; for doctorate, comprehensive exam, thesis/dissertation. *Entrance requirements:* For master's and doctorate, GRE General Test, minimum GPA of 3.2. Additional exam requirements/recommendations for international students: required—TOEFL (minimum score 550 paper-based; 80 iBT), IELTS (minimum score 6). Electronic applications accepted.

University of Georgia, Franklin College of Arts and Sciences, Department of Anthropology, Athens, GA 30602. Offers anthropology (MA, PhD). *Degree requirements:* For master's, one foreign language, thesis; for doctorate, one foreign language, thesis/dissertation. *Entrance requirements:* For master's and doctorate, GRE General Test. Electronic applications accepted.

University of Guelph, Office of Graduate and Postdoctoral Studies, College of Social and Applied Human Sciences, Department of Sociology and Anthropology, Guelph, ON N1G 2W1, Canada. Offers anthropology (MA); crime and criminal justice policy (MA); sociology (MA, PhD). *Degree requirements:* For master's, thesis or major paper; for doctorate, comprehensive exam, thesis/dissertation. *Entrance requirements:* For master's, minimum B+ average during previous 2 years of course work, honors BA or equivalent; for doctorate, must have an MA in Sociology, must have 80% or higher in graduate level studies. Additional exam requirements/recommendations for international students: required—TOEFL (minimum score 550 paper-based; 89 iBT) or IELTS (minimum score 6.5). Electronic applications accepted.

University of Hawaii at Manoa, Office of Graduate Education, College of Social Sciences, Department of Anthropology, Honolulu, HI 96822. Offers MA, PhD. *Program availability:* Part-time. *Degree requirements:* For master's, thesis optional; for doctorate, comprehensive exam, thesis/dissertation. *Entrance requirements:* For master's and doctorate, GRE General Test. Additional exam requirements/recommendations for international students: required—TOEFL (minimum score 560 paper-based; 83 iBT), IELTS (minimum score 5).

University of Houston, College of Liberal Arts and Social Sciences, Department of Comparative Cultural Studies, Houston, TX 77204. Offers anthropology (MA). *Program availability:* Part-time. *Degree requirements:* For master's, comprehensive exam, thesis. *Entrance requirements:* For master's, GRE General Test (minimum 500 verbal, 500 quantitative), minimum GPA of 3.0 in last 60 undergraduate hours. Additional exam requirements/recommendations for international students: required—TOEFL (minimum score 550 paper-based; 79 iBT). Electronic applications accepted.

University of Idaho, College of Graduate Studies, College of Letters, Arts and Social Sciences, Department of Sociology and Anthropology, Moscow, ID 83844-2282. Offers anthropology (MA). *Faculty:* 6. *Students:* 11 full-time, 6 part-time. Average age 32. In 2019, 7 master's awarded. *Degree requirements:* For master's, variable foreign language requirement. *Entrance requirements:* For master's, minimum GPA of 3.0. Additional exam requirements/recommendations for international students: required—TOEFL (minimum score 79 iBT). *Application deadline:* For fall admission, 4/15 for domestic students; for spring admission, 11/1 for domestic students. Applications are processed on a rolling basis. Application fee: $60. Electronic applications accepted. *Expenses:* Tuition, state resident: full-time $7753.80; part-time $502 per credit hour. Tuition, nonresident: full-time $26,990; part-time $1571 per credit hour. *Required fees:* $2122.20; $47 per credit hour. *Financial support:* Research assistantships and teaching assistantships available. Financial award applicants required to submit FAFSA. *Unit head:* Dr. Brian Wolf, Chair, 208-885-6751, E-mail: socanth@uidaho.edu. *Application contact:* Dr. Brian Wolf, Chair, 208-885-6751, E-mail: socanth@uidaho.edu. Website: https://www.uidaho.edu/class/soc-anthro

University of Illinois at Chicago, College of Liberal Arts and Sciences, Department of Anthropology, Chicago, IL 60607-7128. Offers anthropology (MA, PhD); environmental and urban geography (MA), including environmental studies, urban geography. *Program availability:* Part-time. *Degree requirements:* For doctorate, comprehensive exam. *Entrance requirements:* For master's and doctorate, minimum GPA of 2.75. Additional exam requirements/recommendations for international students: required—TOEFL. Electronic applications accepted.

University of Illinois at Urbana-Champaign, Graduate College, College of Liberal Arts and Sciences, Department of Anthropology, Champaign, IL 61820. Offers MA, PhD. Terminal master's awarded for partial completion of doctoral program.

University of Indianapolis, Graduate Programs, Shaheen College of Arts and Sciences, Department of Anthropology, Indianapolis, IN 46227-3697. Offers MS. *Entrance requirements:* For master's, GRE General Test (minimum score of 500 on both the verbal and quantitative sections), bachelor's degree with major or minor in anthropology or closely-related field; undergraduate or graduate coursework in anthropology and the natural sciences with minimum C grade (ideally, semester in cultural anthropology, biological anthropology, archeology, statistics, and geology); minimum cumulative undergraduate GPA of 3.2. Additional exam requirements/recommendations for international students: required—TOEFL (minimum score 550 paper-based; 79 iBT).

The University of Iowa, Graduate College, College of Liberal Arts and Sciences, Department of Anthropology, Iowa City, IA 52242-1316. Offers MA, PhD. *Degree requirements:* For master's, thesis optional, exam; for doctorate, comprehensive exam, thesis/dissertation. *Entrance requirements:* For master's and doctorate, GRE General Test, minimum GPA of 3.0. Additional exam requirements/recommendations for international students: required—TOEFL (minimum score 550 paper-based; 81 iBT). Electronic applications accepted.

The University of Kansas, Graduate Studies, College of Liberal Arts and Sciences, Department of Anthropology, Lawrence, KS 66045. Offers MA, PhD. *Students:* 22 full-time (13 women), 3 part-time (1 woman); includes 1 minority (Hispanic/Latino), 3 international. Average age 33. 10 applicants, 30% accepted, 3 enrolled. In 2019, 6 master's, 2 doctorates awarded. *Entrance requirements:* For master's, GRE (for university fellowship), letter stating academic objectives and clearly indicating disciplinary track of interest; copy of curriculum vitae; transcripts of undergraduate and graduate study completed; three letters of recommendation; for doctorate, GRE (for university fellowship), letter stating academic objectives and clearly indicating disciplinary track of interest; copy of curriculum vitae; transcripts of undergraduate and graduate study completed; three letters of recommendation; professional writing sample. Additional exam requirements/recommendations for international students: required—TOEFL, IELTS. *Application deadline:* For fall admission, 1/12 for domestic students, 1/5 for international students. Application fee: $65 ($85 for international students). Electronic applications accepted. *Expenses:* Tuition, state resident: full-time $9989. Tuition, nonresident: full-time $23,950. *International tuition:* $23,950 full-time. *Required fees:* $984; $81.99 per credit hour. Tuition and fees vary according to course load, campus/location and program. *Financial support:* Fellowships, research assistantships, teaching

assistantships, career-related internships or fieldwork, institutionally sponsored loans, and unspecified assistantships available. Financial award application deadline: 1/12; financial award applicants required to submit FAFSA. *Unit head:* Joane P. Nagel, Chair, 785-864-4114, E-mail: nagel@ku.edu. *Application contact:* Corinne Butler, Graduate Officer, 785-864-9419, E-mail: cebutler@ku.edu.
Website: http://anthropology.ku.edu/

University of Kentucky, Graduate School, College of Arts and Sciences, Program in Anthropology, Lexington, KY 40506-0032. Offers MA, PhD. *Program availability:* Part-time. *Degree requirements:* For master's, comprehensive exam, thesis optional; for doctorate, one foreign language, comprehensive exam, thesis/dissertation. *Entrance requirements:* For master's, GRE General Test, minimum undergraduate GPA of 2.75; for doctorate, GRE General Test, minimum graduate GPA of 3.0. Additional exam requirements/recommendations for international students: required—TOEFL (minimum score 550 paper-based). Electronic applications accepted.

University of Lethbridge, School of Graduate Studies, Lethbridge, AB T1K 3M4, Canada. Offers addictions counseling (M Sc); agricultural biotechnology (M Sc); agricultural studies (M Sc, MA); anthropology (MA); archaeology (M Sc, MA); art (MA, MFA); biochemistry (M Sc); biological sciences (M Sc); biomolecular science (PhD); biosystems and biodiversity (PhD); Canadian studies (MA); chemistry (M Sc); computer science (M Sc); computer science and geographical information science (M Sc); counseling (MC); counseling psychology (M Ed); dramatic arts (MA); earth, space, and physical science (PhD); economics (MA); education (MA, PhD); educational leadership (M Ed); English (MA); environmental science (M Sc); evolution and behavior (PhD); exercise science (M Sc); French (MA); French/German (MA); French/Spanish (MA); general education (M Ed); geography (M Sc, MA); German (MA); health sciences (M Sc); individualized multidisciplinary (M Sc, MA); kinesiology (M Sc, MA); management (M Sc), including accounting, finance, human resource management and labor relations, information systems, international management, marketing, policy and strategy; mathematics (M Sc); music (M Mus, MA); Native American studies (MA); neuroscience (M Sc, PhD); new media (MA, MFA); nursing (M Sc, MN); philosophy (MA); physics (M Sc); political science (MA); psychology (M Sc, MA); religious studies (MA); sociology (MA); theatre and dramatic arts (MFA); theoretical and computational science (PhD); urban and regional studies (MA); women and gender studies (MA). *Program availability:* Part-time, evening/weekend. *Degree requirements:* For master's, thesis (for some programs); for doctorate, comprehensive exam, thesis/dissertation. *Entrance requirements:* For master's, GMAT (for M Sc in management), bachelor's degree in related field, minimum GPA of 3.0 during previous 20 graded semester courses, 2 years' teaching or related experience (M Ed); for doctorate, master's degree, minimum graduate GPA of 3.5. Additional exam requirements/recommendations for international students: required—TOEFL (minimum score 580 paper-based; 93 iBT). Electronic applications accepted.

University of Louisville, Graduate School, College of Arts and Sciences, Department of Anthropology, Louisville, KY 40292-0001. Offers anthropology (MA). *Program availability:* Part-time, evening/weekend. *Faculty:* 14 full-time (7 women), 6 part-time/adjunct (3 women). *Students:* 12 full-time (5 women), 5 part-time (2 women); includes 2 minority (1 Black or African American, non-Hispanic/Latino; 1 Two or more races, non-Hispanic/Latino). Average age 31. 10 applicants, 90% accepted, 7 enrolled. In 2019, 8 master's awarded. *Degree requirements:* For master's, variable foreign language requirement, thesis or alternative. *Entrance requirements:* For master's, transcripts, statement of purpose, references. Additional exam requirements/recommendations for international students: required—TOEFL (minimum score 550 paper-based; 79 iBT), IELTS can be used in place of TOEFL; recommended—IELTS (minimum score 6.5). *Application deadline:* For fall admission, 3/1 priority date for domestic and international students; for spring admission, 11/1 for domestic and international students. Applications are processed on a rolling basis. Application fee: $65. Electronic applications accepted. *Expenses: Tuition, area resident:* Full-time $13,000; part-time $723 per credit hour. Tuition, state resident: full-time $13,000; part-time $723 per credit hour. Tuition, nonresident: full-time $27,114; part-time $1507 per credit hour. *International tuition:* $27,114 full-time. *Required fees:* $196. Tuition and fees vary according to program and reciprocity agreements. *Financial support:* In 2019–20, 7 students received support, including 3 teaching assistantships with full tuition reimbursements available (averaging $12,000 per year); fellowships, scholarships/grants, health care benefits, and unspecified assistantships also available. Financial award application deadline: 3/1. *Unit head:* Dr. Jonathan Haws, Chair and Professor, 502-852-2423, E-mail: johnathan.haws@louisville.edu. *Application contact:* Dr. Lisa Markowitz, Associate Professor, 502-852-2426, E-mail: lisa.markowitz@louisville.edu.
Website: http://louisville.edu/anthropology

University of Maine, Graduate School, College of Liberal Arts and Sciences, Department of Anthropology, Orono, ME 04469. Offers anthropology and environmental policy (PhD). *Faculty:* 10 full-time (5 women). *Students:* 12 full-time (6 women), 1 part-time (0 women); includes 2 minority (both American Indian or Alaska Native, non-Hispanic/Latino), 2 international. Average age 33. 28 applicants, 79% accepted, 6 enrolled. In 2019, 1 doctorate awarded. *Degree requirements:* For doctorate, comprehensive exam, thesis/dissertation. *Entrance requirements:* For doctorate, GRE General Test. Additional exam requirements/recommendations for international students: required—TOEFL (minimum score 80 iBT), IELTS (minimum score 6.5). *Application deadline:* For fall admission, 1/15 for domestic and international students. Application fee: $65. Electronic applications accepted. *Expenses: Tuition, area resident:* Full-time $8100; part-time $450 per credit hour. Tuition, state resident: full-time $8100; part-time $450 per credit hour. Tuition, nonresident: full-time $26,388; part-time $1466 per credit hour. *International tuition:* $26,388 full-time. *Required fees:* $1257; $278 per semester. Tuition and fees vary according to course load. *Financial support:* In 2019–20, 12 students received support, including 3 research assistantships with full tuition reimbursements available (averaging $15,825 per year), 3 teaching assistantships with full tuition reimbursements available (averaging $15,825 per year); scholarships/grants and unspecified assistantships also available. Financial award application deadline: 3/1; financial award applicants required to submit FAFSA. *Unit head:* Darren Ranco, Chair, 207-581-1801, E-mail: aep.grad@maine.edu. *Application contact:* Scott G. Delcourt, Assistant Vice President for Graduate Studies and Senior Associate Dean, 207-581-3291, Fax: 207-581-3232, E-mail: graduate@maine.edu.
Website: http://www.umaine.edu/anthropology/graduate-programs/

The University of Manchester, School of Arts, Languages and Cultures, Manchester, United Kingdom. Offers anthropology, media and performance (PhD); applied theatre (PhD); Arab world studies (PhD); archaeology (PhD); art history and visual studies (PhD); arts and cultural management (PhD); arts management and cultural policy (PhD); Chinese studies (PhD); classics and ancient history (PhD); composition (PhD); creative writing (PhD); drama (PhD); East Asian studies (PhD); electroacoustic composition (PhD); English and American studies (PhD); English language (PhD); French studies (PhD); German studies (PhD); history (PhD); humanitarianism and conflict response (PhD); interpreting studies (PhD); Japanese studies (PhD); Latin American cultural studies (PhD); linguistics (PhD); Middle Eastern studies (PhD); museology (PhD); museum practice (PhD); music (PhD); musicology (PhD); Polish studies (PhD); Portuguese studies (PhD); religions and theology (PhD); Russian studies (PhD); Spanish studies (PhD); translation and intercultural studies (PhD).

The University of Manchester, School of Social Sciences, Manchester, United Kingdom. Offers ethnographic documentary (M Phil); interdisciplinary study of culture (PhD); philosophy (PhD); politics (PhD); social anthropology (PhD); social anthropology with visual media (PhD); social change (PhD); social statistics (PhD); sociology (PhD); visual anthropology (M Phil).

University of Manitoba, Faculty of Graduate Studies, Faculty of Arts, Department of Anthropology, Winnipeg, MB R3T 2N2, Canada. Offers MA, PhD. *Degree requirements:* For master's, thesis or alternative.

University of Maryland, College Park, Academic Affairs, College of Behavioral and Social Sciences, Department of Anthropology, College Park, MD 20742. Offers applied anthropology (MAA). *Program availability:* Part-time, evening/weekend. *Degree requirements:* For master's, internship. *Entrance requirements:* For master's, GRE General Test, minimum GPA of 3.0, 3 letters of recommendation. Additional exam requirements/recommendations for international students: required—TOEFL. Electronic applications accepted.

University of Massachusetts Amherst, Graduate School, College of Social and Behavioral Sciences, Department of Anthropology, Amherst, MA 01003. Offers MA, PhD. *Program availability:* Part-time. Terminal master's awarded for partial completion of doctoral program. *Degree requirements:* For master's, thesis or alternative; for doctorate, comprehensive exam, thesis/dissertation. *Entrance requirements:* Additional exam requirements/recommendations for international students: required—TOEFL (minimum score 550 paper-based; 80 iBT), IELTS (minimum score 6.5). Electronic applications accepted.

University of Memphis, Graduate School, College of Arts and Sciences, Department of Anthropology, Memphis, TN 38152. Offers medical anthropology (MA). *Program availability:* Part-time. *Students:* 16 full-time (12 women), 2 part-time (1 woman); includes 5 minority (4 Black or African American, non-Hispanic/Latino; 1 Hispanic/Latino). Average age 27. 12 applicants, 100% accepted, 5 enrolled. In 2019, 4 master's awarded. *Degree requirements:* For master's, comprehensive exam, practicum. *Entrance requirements:* For master's, GRE General Test, minimum GPA of 3.0, letter of intent, 3 letters of recommendation. *Application deadline:* For fall admission, 1/31 priority date for domestic students; for spring admission, 9/1 priority date for domestic students. Applications are processed on a rolling basis. Application fee: $35 ($60 for international students). Electronic applications accepted. *Expenses: Tuition, area resident:* Full-time $9216; part-time $512 per credit hour. Tuition, state resident: full-time $9216; part-time $512 per credit hour. Tuition, nonresident: full-time $12,672; part-time $704 per credit hour. *International tuition:* $16,128 full-time. *Required fees:* $1530; $85 per credit hour. Tuition and fees vary according to program. *Financial support:* Fellowships, research assistantships with full tuition reimbursements, teaching assistantships with full tuition reimbursements, career-related internships or fieldwork, Federal Work-Study, scholarships/grants, and unspecified assistantships available. Financial award application deadline: 2/1; financial award applicants required to submit FAFSA. *Unit head:* Dr. Keri Brondo, Chair, 901-678-2080, Fax: 901-678-2069, E-mail: kbrondo@memphis.edu. *Application contact:* Dr. Micah Trapp, Coordinator of Graduate Studies, 901-678-2080, Fax: 901-678-2069, E-mail: mmtrapp@memphis.edu.
Website: http://www.memphis.edu/anthropology

University of Michigan, Rackham Graduate School, College of Literature, Science, and the Arts, Department of Anthropology, Ann Arbor, MI 48109. Offers anthropological archaeology (PhD); biological anthropology (PhD); linguistic anthropology (PhD); sociocultural anthropology (PhD). *Degree requirements:* For doctorate, one foreign language, comprehensive exam, thesis/dissertation, preliminary examination, oral defense of dissertation. *Entrance requirements:* For doctorate, GRE General Test. Additional exam requirements/recommendations for international students: required—TOEFL (minimum score 560 paper-based; 84 iBT). Electronic applications accepted.

University of Michigan, Rackham Graduate School, College of Literature, Science, and the Arts, Doctoral Program in Anthropology and History, Ann Arbor, MI 48109. Offers PhD. *Degree requirements:* For doctorate, 2 foreign languages, thesis/dissertation, oral defense of dissertation, preliminary exam. *Entrance requirements:* For doctorate, GRE General Test, writing sample. Additional exam requirements/recommendations for international students: required—TOEFL. Electronic applications accepted.

University of Michigan, School of Social Work, Interdisciplinary PhD Program in Social Work and Social Science, Ann Arbor, MI 48109. Offers social work and anthropology (PhD); social work and economics (PhD); social work and political science (PhD); social work and psychology (PhD); social work and sociology (PhD). *Degree requirements:* For doctorate, thesis/dissertation, oral defense of dissertation, preliminary exam. *Entrance requirements:* For doctorate, GRE General Test. Additional exam requirements/recommendations for international students: required—TOEFL (minimum score 620 paper-based, 88 iBT) or IELTS. Electronic applications accepted. *Expenses:* Contact institution.

University of Minnesota, Duluth, Graduate School, College of Liberal Arts, Department of Sociology/Anthropology, Duluth, MN 55812-2496. Offers criminology (MA); liberal studies (MLS). *Program availability:* Part-time. *Degree requirements:* For master's, thesis or alternative. *Entrance requirements:* For master's, interview, minimum GPA of 3.0, letters of recommendation. Additional exam requirements/recommendations for international students: required—TOEFL.

University of Minnesota, Twin Cities Campus, Graduate School, College of Liberal Arts, Department of Anthropology, Minneapolis, MN 55455-0213. Offers MA, PhD. Terminal master's awarded for partial completion of doctoral program. *Degree requirements:* For master's, thesis optional; for doctorate, comprehensive exam, thesis/dissertation. *Entrance requirements:* For master's and doctorate, GRE. Additional exam requirements/recommendations for international students: recommended—TOEFL. Electronic applications accepted.

University of Mississippi, Graduate School, College of Liberal Arts, University, MS 38677. Offers anthropology (MA); biology (MS, PhD); chemistry (MS, DA, PhD); creative writing (MFA); documentary expression (MFA); economics (MA, PhD); English (MA, PhD); experimental psychology (PhD); history (MA, PhD); mathematics (MS, PhD); modern languages (MA); music (MM); philosophy (MA); physics (MA, MS, PhD); political science (MA, PhD); Southern studies (MA); studio art (MFA). *Program availability:* Part-time. *Faculty:* 481 full-time (215 women), 71 part-time/adjunct (40 women). *Students:* 509 full-time (258 women), 55 part-time (21 women); includes 89 minority (40 Black or African American, non-Hispanic/Latino; 13 Asian, non-Hispanic/Latino; 25 Hispanic/Latino; 11 Two or more races, non-Hispanic/Latino), 157 international. Average age 29. In 2019, 119 master's, 51 doctorates awarded. *Degree requirements:* For doctorate, thesis/dissertation. *Entrance requirements:* For master's, GRE General Test, minimum GPA of 3.0; for doctorate, GRE General Test. Additional exam requirements/recommendations for international students: required—TOEFL. *Application deadline:* Applications are processed on a rolling basis. Application fee: $50. Electronic applications accepted. *Expenses:* Tuition, state resident: full-time $8718; part-time

$484.25 per credit hour. Tuition, nonresident: full-time $24,990; part-time $1388.25 per credit hour. *Required fees:* $100; $4.16 per credit hour. *Financial support:* Fellowships, research assistantships, teaching assistantships, career-related internships or fieldwork, Federal Work-Study, institutionally sponsored loans, scholarships/grants, and unspecified assistantships available. Financial award application deadline: 3/1; financial award applicants required to submit FAFSA. *Unit head:* Dr. Lee Michael Cohen, Dean, 662-915-7177, Fax: 662-915-5792, E-mail: libarts@olemiss.edu. *Application contact:* Tameka Smith, Graduate Activities Specialist for Admissions, 662-915-7474, Fax: 662-915-7577, E-mail: gschool@olemiss.edu.
Website: ventress@olemiss.edu

University of Missouri, Office of Research and Graduate Studies, College of Arts and Science, Department of Anthropology, Columbia, MO 65211. Offers MA, PhD. *Entrance requirements:* For master's, GRE General Test (minimum score 1000 verbal and quantitative), minimum GPA of 3.25 in last 60 hours and in all anthropology courses; for doctorate, GRE General Test (minimum score 1000 verbal and quantitative), minimum GPA of 3.5 in previous graduate work.

University of Montana, Graduate School, College of Humanities and Sciences, Department of Anthropology, Missoula, MT 59812. Offers anthropology (MA, PhD); applied anthropology (PhD); applied medical anthropology (MA); cultural heritage (MA, PhD); forensic anthropology (MA); linguistic anthropology (MA). *Degree requirements:* For master's, thesis (for some programs). *Entrance requirements:* For master's, GRE General Test. Additional exam requirements/recommendations for international students: required—TOEFL.

University of Nebraska–Lincoln, Graduate College, College of Arts and Sciences, Department of Anthropology and Geography, Program in Anthropology, Lincoln, NE 68588. Offers MA. *Degree requirements:* For master's, thesis optional. *Entrance requirements:* For master's, GRE General Test. Additional exam requirements/recommendations for international students: required—TOEFL (minimum score 500 paper-based). Electronic applications accepted.

University of Nevada, Las Vegas, Graduate College, College of Liberal Arts, Department of Anthropology, Las Vegas, NV 89154-5003. Offers MA, PhD. *Program availability:* Part-time. *Faculty:* 14 full-time (5 women), 1 part-time/adjunct (0 women). *Students:* 30 full-time (20 women), 11 part-time (6 women); includes 14 minority (1 American Indian or Alaska Native, non-Hispanic/Latino; 3 Asian, non-Hispanic/Latino; 7 Hispanic/Latino; 3 Two or more races, non-Hispanic/Latino), 1 international. Average age 32. 47 applicants, 49% accepted, 11 enrolled. In 2019, 3 master's, 2 doctorates awarded. *Degree requirements:* For master's, thesis, oral defense of thesis; for doctorate, comprehensive exam, thesis/dissertation, oral defense of dissertation. *Entrance requirements:* For master's, GRE General Test, 18 semester credit hours in anthropology with minimum GPA of 3.0; research paper; letter of intent; 3 letters of recommendation; for doctorate, GRE General Test, minimum GPA of 3.5 for previous graduate work; example of previous work; statement of intent; 3 letters of recommendation. Additional exam requirements/recommendations for international students: required—TOEFL (minimum score 550 paper-based; 80 iBT), IELTS (minimum score 7). *Application deadline:* For fall admission, 2/1 for domestic and international students. Application fee: $60 ($95 for international students). Electronic applications accepted. *Expenses:* Contact institution. *Financial support:* In 2019–20, 28 students received support, including 1 fellowship with full tuition reimbursement available (averaging $20,000 per year), 5 research assistantships with full tuition reimbursements available (averaging $16,250 per year), 22 teaching assistantships with full tuition reimbursements available (averaging $15,727 per year); institutionally sponsored loans, scholarships/grants, health care benefits, and unspecified assistantships also available. Financial award application deadline: 3/15; financial award applicants required to submit FAFSA. *Unit head:* Dr. Daniel Benyshek, Chair/Professor, 702-895-2070, Fax: 702-895-4823, E-mail: anthropology.chair@unlv.edu. *Application contact:* Dr. Alyssa Crittenden, Graduate Coordinator, 702-895-3590, Fax: 702-895-4823, E-mail: anthropology.gradcoord@unlv.edu.
Website: http://anthro.unlv.edu/

University of Nevada, Reno, Graduate School, College of Liberal Arts, Department of Anthropology, Reno, NV 89557. Offers MA, PhD. Terminal master's awarded for partial completion of doctoral program. *Degree requirements:* For master's, thesis; for doctorate, thesis/dissertation. *Entrance requirements:* For master's, GRE, minimum GPA of 2.75; for doctorate, GRE, minimum GPA of 3.0. Additional exam requirements/recommendations for international students: required—TOEFL (minimum score 500 paper-based; 61 iBT), IELTS (minimum score 6). Electronic applications accepted.

University of New Mexico, Graduate Studies, College of Arts and Sciences, Program in Anthropology, Albuquerque, NM 87131-2039. Offers archaeology (MA, MS, PhD); ethnology (MA, MS, PhD); evolutionary anthropology (PhD); public archaeology (MA, MS, PhD). Terminal master's awarded for partial completion of doctoral program. *Degree requirements:* For master's, comprehensive exam (for some programs), thesis or alternative, 1-2 exams; for doctorate, one foreign language, comprehensive exam, thesis/dissertation, exam, proposal, oral defense, skill and/or second language. *Entrance requirements:* For master's and doctorate, GRE General Test, 3 letters of recommendation, letter of interest, transcripts. Additional exam requirements/recommendations for international students: required—TOEFL (minimum score 550 paper-based), IELTS (minimum score 7). Electronic applications accepted. *Expenses:* Tuition, state resident: full-time $7633; part-time $972 per year. Tuition, nonresident: full-time $22,586; part-time $3840 per year. *International tuition:* $23,292 full-time. *Required fees:* $8608. Tuition and fees vary according to course level, course load, degree level, program and student level.

The University of North Carolina at Chapel Hill, Graduate School, College of Arts and Sciences, Department of Anthropology, Chapel Hill, NC 27599-3115. Offers MA, PhD. Terminal master's awarded for partial completion of doctoral program. *Degree requirements:* For master's, variable foreign language requirement, thesis; for doctorate, variable foreign language requirement, comprehensive exam, thesis/dissertation. *Entrance requirements:* For master's and doctorate, GRE General Test, minimum GPA of 3.0. Additional exam requirements/recommendations for international students: required—TOEFL. Electronic applications accepted.

The University of North Carolina at Charlotte, College of Liberal Arts and Sciences, Department of Anthropology, Charlotte, NC 28223-0001. Offers anthropology (MA), including applied anthropology, medical anthropology. *Program availability:* Part-time. *Faculty:* 11 full-time (7 women), 1 part-time/adjunct (0 women). *Students:* 13 full-time (10 women), 4 part-time (3 women); includes 3 minority (1 Black or African American, non-Hispanic/Latino; 1 Asian, non-Hispanic/Latino; 1 Two or more races, non-Hispanic/Latino). Average age 28. 16 applicants, 75% accepted, 5 enrolled. In 2019, 8 master's awarded. *Degree requirements:* For master's, thesis or alternative, capstone (thesis/practicum). *Entrance requirements:* For master's, three letters of recommendation from individuals who can comment on candidate's academic and professional promise, at least two from academic referees; statement of purpose that discusses applicant's specific interests in anthropology and professional goals; transcripts from all colleges or universities attended, undergraduate GPA of at least 3.0. Additional exam requirements/recommendations for international students: required—TOEFL (minimum score 557 paper-based; 83 iBT), IELTS (minimum score 6.5), TOEFL (minimum score 557 paper-based, 83 iBT) or IELTS (6.5). *Application deadline:* For fall admission, 1/15 priority date for domestic students. Applications are processed on a rolling basis. Application fee: $75. Electronic applications accepted. *Expenses:* Tuition, state resident: full-time $4337. Tuition, nonresident: full-time $17,771. *Required fees:* $3093. Tuition and fees vary according to course load, degree level and program. *Financial support:* In 2019–20, 3 students received support, including 2 research assistantships (averaging $11,000 per year), 1 teaching assistantship (averaging $11,000 per year); institutionally sponsored loans, scholarships/grants, and unspecified assistantships also available. Support available to part-time students. Financial award application deadline: 1/15. *Unit head:* Dr. Steven Falconer, Professor and Chair, 704-687-7459, E-mail: sfalcon1@uncc.edu. *Application contact:* Kathy B. Giddings, Director of Graduate Admissions, 704-687-5503, Fax: 704-687-1668, E-mail: gradadm@uncc.edu.
Website: http://anthropology.uncc.edu/

University of North Georgia, Department of History, Anthropology and Philosophy, Dahlonega, GA 30597. Offers history (MA), including American history, military history, world history. *Unit head:* Dr. Jeff Pardue, Department Head, 678-717-3867. *Application contact:* Cory Thornton, Director of Graduate Admissions, 706-867-2077, E-mail: cory.thornton@ung.edu.
Website: http://ung.edu/history-anthropology-philosophy/

University of North Texas, Toulouse Graduate School, Denton, TX 76203-5459. Offers accounting (MS); applied anthropology (MA, MS); applied behavior analysis (Certificate); applied geography (MA); applied technology and performance improvement (M Ed, MS); art education (MA); art history (MA); arts leadership (Certificate); audiology (Au D); behavior analysis (MS); behavioral science (PhD); biochemistry and molecular biology (MS); biology (MA, MS); biomedical engineering (MS); business analysis (MS); chemistry (MS); clinical health psychology (PhD); communication studies (MA, MS); computer engineering (MS); computer science (MS); counseling (M Ed, MS), including clinical mental health counseling (MS), college and university counseling, elementary school counseling, secondary school counseling; creative writing (MA); criminal justice (MS); curriculum and instruction (M Ed); decision sciences (MBA); design (MA, MFA), including fashion design (MFA), innovation studies, interior design (MFA); early childhood studies (MS); economics (MS); educational leadership (M Ed, Ed D); educational psychology (MS, PhD), including family studies (MS), gifted and talented (MS), human development (MS), learning and cognition (MS), research, measurement and evaluation (MS); electrical engineering (MS); emergency management (MPA); engineering technology (MS); English (MA); English as a second language (MA); environmental science (MS); finance (MBA, MS); financial management (MPA); French (MA); health services management (MBA); higher education (M Ed, Ed D); history (MA, MS); hospitality management (MS); human resources management (MPA); information science (MS); information systems (PhD); information technologies (MBA); interdisciplinary studies (MA, MS); international studies (MA); international sustainable tourism (MS); jazz studies (MM); journalism (MA, MJ, Graduate Certificate), including interactive and virtual digital communication (Graduate Certificate), narrative journalism (Graduate Certificate), public relations (Graduate Certificate); kinesiology (MS); linguistics (MA); local government management (MPA); logistics (PhD); logistics and supply chain management (MBA); long-term care, senior housing, and aging services (MA); management (PhD); marketing (MBA); mathematics (MA, MS); mechanical and energy engineering (MS, PhD); music (MA), including ethnomusicology, music theory, musicology, performance; music composition (PhD); music education (MM Ed, PhD); nonprofit management (MPA); operations and supply chain management (MBA); performance (MM, DMA); philosophy (MA); political science (MA); professional and technical communication (MA); radio, television and film (MA, MFA); rehabilitation counseling (Certificate); sociology (MA); Spanish (MA); special education (M Ed); speech-language pathology (MA); strategic management (MBA); studio art (MFA); teaching (M Ed); MBA/MS. *Program availability:* Part-time, evening/weekend, online learning. Terminal master's awarded for partial completion of doctoral program. *Degree requirements:* For master's, variable foreign language requirement, comprehensive exam (for some programs), thesis (for some programs); for doctorate, variable foreign language requirement, comprehensive exam (for some programs), thesis/dissertation; for other advanced degree, variable foreign language requirement, comprehensive exam (for some programs). *Entrance requirements:* For master's and doctorate, GRE, GMAT. Additional exam requirements/recommendations for international students: required—TOEFL (minimum score 550 paper-based; 79 iBT). Electronic applications accepted.

University of Oklahoma, College of Arts and Sciences, Department of Anthropology, Norman, OK 73019. Offers anthropology (MA, PhD); applied linguistic anthropology (MA); archaeology (PhD); health and human biology (PhD); socio-cultural and linguistics (PhD); socio-cultural anthropology (MA). *Degree requirements:* For master's, thesis; for doctorate, comprehensive exam, thesis/dissertation. *Entrance requirements:* For master's and doctorate, GRE, minimum undergraduate GPA of 3.0; statement of purpose; 2 letters of recommendation. Additional exam requirements/recommendations for international students: required—TOEFL (minimum score 79 iBT) or IELTS (minimum score 6.5). Electronic applications accepted. *Expenses:* Tuition, state resident: full-time $6583.20; part-time $274.30 per credit hour. Tuition, nonresident: full-time $21,242; part-time $885.10 per credit hour. *International tuition:* $21,242.40 full-time. *Required fees:* $1994.20; $72.55 per credit hour. $126.50 per semester. Tuition and fees vary according to course load and degree level.

University of Oregon, Graduate School, College of Arts and Sciences, Department of Anthropology, Eugene, OR 97403. Offers MA, MS, PhD. Terminal master's awarded for partial completion of doctoral program. *Degree requirements:* For master's, one foreign language; for doctorate, 2 foreign languages, thesis/dissertation. *Entrance requirements:* For master's and doctorate, GRE General Test. Additional exam requirements/recommendations for international students: required—TOEFL.

University of Ottawa, Faculty of Graduate and Postdoctoral Studies, Faculty of Social Sciences, Department of Sociology and Anthropology, Ottawa, ON K1N 6N5, Canada. Offers MA. *Degree requirements:* For master's, thesis or alternative. *Entrance requirements:* For master's, honors bachelor's degree or equivalent, minimum B average. Electronic applications accepted.

University of Pennsylvania, School of Arts and Sciences, Graduate Group in Anthropology, Philadelphia, PA 19104. Offers AM, MS, PhD. *Faculty:* 18 full-time (9 women), 12 part-time/adjunct (7 women). *Students:* 68 full-time (47 women), 3 part-time (all women); includes 13 minority (4 Black or African American, non-Hispanic/Latino; 3 Asian, non-Hispanic/Latino; 4 Hispanic/Latino; 2 Two or more races, non-Hispanic/Latino), 10 international. Average age 30. 205 applicants, 7% accepted, 10 enrolled. In 2019, 3 master's, 8 doctorates awarded. Terminal master's awarded for partial completion of doctoral program. Application fee: $90.
Website: http://www.sas.upenn.edu/graduate-division

University of Pittsburgh, Kenneth P. Dietrich School of Arts and Sciences, Department of Anthropology, Pittsburgh, PA 15260. Offers MA, PhD. *Faculty:* 16 full-time (7 women). *Students:* 61 full-time (38 women); includes 4 minority (2 Black or African American, non-Hispanic/Latino; 2 Hispanic/Latino), 34 international. Average age 26. 67 applicants, 12% accepted, 4 enrolled. In 2019, 4 master's, 8 doctorates awarded.

Anthropology

Terminal master's awarded for partial completion of doctoral program. *Degree requirements:* For master's, one foreign language, thesis; for doctorate, one foreign language, comprehensive exam, thesis/dissertation, exam. *Entrance requirements:* For master's and doctorate, BA degree. Additional exam requirements/recommendations for international students: required—TOEFL (minimum score 550 paper-based; 90 iBT), IELTS (minimum score 6.5). *Application deadline:* For fall admission, 1/15 for domestic and international students. Application fee: $75. Electronic applications accepted. *Financial support:* In 2019–20, 57 students received support, including 25 fellowships with full tuition reimbursements available (averaging $24,240 per year), 6 research assistantships (averaging $15,540 per year), 26 teaching assistantships with full tuition reimbursements available (averaging $19,960 per year); health care benefits also available. Financial award application deadline: 1/15. *Unit head:* Nicole Constable, Professor, 412-648-7530, E-mail: ncgrad@pitt.edu. *Application contact:* Brian Deutsch, Academic Support Manager, 412-648-7270, E-mail: briandeutsch@pitt.edu.
Website: http://www.anthropology.pitt.edu

University of Regina, Faculty of Graduate Studies and Research, Faculty of Arts, Department of Anthropology, Regina, SK S4S 0A2, Canada. Offers MA. *Program availability:* Part-time. *Faculty:* 5 full-time (2 women), 1 part-time/adjunct (0 women). *Students:* 1 (woman) part-time. Average age 30. In 2019, 1 master's awarded. *Degree requirements:* For master's, thesis (for some programs). *Entrance requirements:* For master's, Special Case program. For all requirements please see our website at https://www.uregina.ca/gradstudies/current-students/grad-calendar/appendix-d.html. Additional exam requirements/recommendations for international students: required—TOEFL (minimum score 580 paper-based; 80 iBT), IELTS (minimum score 6.5), PTE (minimum score 59), CAEL, CANTEST, MELAB and U of R ESL. *Application deadline:* For fall admission, 1/31 for domestic and international students; for winter admission, 9/30 for domestic and international students. Applications are processed on a rolling basis. Application fee: $100. *Expenses: Tuition:* Full-time $6684 Canadian dollars. *Required fees:* $100 Canadian dollars; $3351.45 Canadian dollars per trimester. $1117.15 Canadian dollars per semester. Tuition and fees vary according to course level, course load, degree level and program. *Financial support:* Fellowships, research assistantships, teaching assistantships, Federal Work-Study, scholarships/grants, unspecified assistantships, and travel award and Graduate Scholarship Base funds available. Support available to part-time students. Financial award application deadline: 9/30. *Unit head:* Dr. Tobias Sperlich, Department Head, 306-585-4773, E-mail: tobias.sperlich@uregina.ca. *Application contact:* Dr. Gediminas Lankauskas, 306-585-4181, E-mail: gediminas.lankauskas@uregina.ca.
Website: http://www.uregina.ca/arts/anthropology/

University of Rhode Island, Graduate School, College of Arts and Sciences, Department of History, Kingston, RI 02881. Offers archaeology and anthropology (MA); European history (MA), including European history, United States history; MLIS/MA. *Program availability:* Part-time. *Faculty:* 16 full-time (7 women). *Students:* 7 full-time (2 women), 10 part-time (5 women). 11 applicants, 91% accepted, 4 enrolled. In 2019, 5 master's awarded. *Entrance requirements:* Additional exam requirements/recommendations for international students: required—TOEFL. *Application deadline:* For fall admission, 7/15 for domestic students; for spring admission, 11/15 for domestic students. Application fee: $65. Electronic applications accepted. *Expenses: Tuition, area resident:* Full-time $13,734; part-time $763 per credit. Tuition, state resident: full-time $13,734; part-time $763 per credit. Tuition, nonresident: full-time $26,512; part-time $1473 per credit. *International tuition:* $26,512 full-time. *Required fees:* $1780; $52 per credit. $35 per term. One-time fee: $165. *Financial support:* In 2019–20, 4 teaching assistantships with tuition reimbursements (averaging $18,986 per year) were awarded. Financial award application deadline: 2/1; financial award applicants required to submit FAFSA. *Unit head:* Dr. Rod Mather, Chair, 401-874-4093, E-mail: rodmather@uri.edu. *Application contact:* Dr. Evelyn Sterne, Director of Graduate Studies, 401-874-4074, E-mail: sterne@uri.edu.
Website: http://www.uri.edu/artsci/his/

University of Saskatchewan, College of Graduate and Postdoctoral Studies, College of Arts and Science, Department of Archaeology and Anthropology, Saskatoon, SK S7N 5A2, Canada. Offers MA. *Program availability:* Part-time. *Degree requirements:* For master's, thesis. *Entrance requirements:* Additional exam requirements/recommendations for international students: required—TOEFL (minimum score 80 iBT); recommended—IELTS (minimum score 6.5).

University of South Africa, College of Human Sciences, Pretoria, South Africa. Offers adult education (M Ed); African languages (MA, PhD); African politics (MA, PhD); Afrikaans (MA, PhD); ancient history (MA, PhD); ancient Near Eastern studies (MA, PhD); anthropology (MA, PhD); applied linguistics (MA); Arabic (MA, PhD); archaeology (MA); art history (MA); Biblical archaeology (MA); Biblical studies (M Th, D Th, PhD); Christian spirituality (M Th, D Th); church history (M Th, D Th); classical studies (MA, PhD); clinical psychology (MA); communication (MA, PhD); comparative education (M Ed, Ed D); consulting psychology (D Admin, D Com, PhD); curriculum studies (M Ed, Ed D); development studies (M Admin, MA, D Admin, PhD); didactics (M Ed, Ed D); education (M Tech); education management (M Ed, Ed D); educational psychology (M Ed); English (MA); environmental education (M Ed); French (MA, PhD); German (MA, PhD); Greek (MA); guidance and counseling (M Ed); health studies (MA, PhD), including health sciences education (MA), health services management (MA), medical and surgical nursing science (critical care general) (MA), midwifery and neonatal nursing science (MA), trauma and emergency care (MA); history (MA, PhD); history of education (Ed D); inclusive education (M Ed, Ed D); information and communications technology policy and regulation (MA); information science (MA, MIS, PhD); international politics (MA, PhD); Islamic studies (MA, PhD); Italian (MA, PhD); Judaica (MA, PhD); linguistics (MA, PhD); mathematical education (M Ed); mathematics education (MA); missiology (M Th, D Th); modern Hebrew (MA, PhD); musicology (MA, MMus, D Mus, PhD); natural science education (M Ed); New Testament (M Th, D Th); Old Testament (D Th); pastoral therapy (M Th, D Th); philosophy (MA); philosophy of education (M Ed, Ed D); politics (MA, PhD); Portuguese (MA, PhD); practical theology (M Th, D Th); psychology (MA, MS, PhD); psychology of education (M Ed, Ed D); public health (MA); religious studies (MA, D Th, PhD); Romance languages (MA); Russian (MA, PhD); Semitic languages (MA, PhD); social behavior studies in HIV/AIDS (MA); social science (mental health) (MA); social science in development studies (MA); social science in psychology (MA); social science in social work (MA); social science in sociology (MA); social work (MSW, DSW, PhD); socio-education (M Ed, Ed D); sociolinguistics (MA); sociology (MA, PhD); Spanish (MA, PhD); systematic theology (M Th, D Th); TESOL (teaching English to speakers of other languages) (MA); theological ethics (M Th, D Th); theory of literature (MA, PhD); urban ministries (D Th); urban ministry (M Th).

University of South Carolina, The Graduate School, College of Arts and Sciences, Department of Anthropology, Columbia, SC 29208. Offers MA, PhD. Terminal master's awarded for partial completion of doctoral program. *Degree requirements:* For master's, comprehensive exam, thesis; for doctorate, comprehensive exam, thesis/dissertation. *Entrance requirements:* For master's and doctorate, GRE General Test, letters of reference. Additional exam requirements/recommendations for international students: required—TOEFL. Electronic applications accepted.

University of South Florida, College of Arts and Sciences, Department of Anthropology, Tampa, FL 33620-9951. Offers applied anthropology (MA), including archaeological and forensic sciences, biocultural medical anthropology, cultural resource management, heritage studies; medical anthropology (Graduate Certificate). *Program availability:* Part-time. *Faculty:* 22 full-time (13 women). *Students:* 67 full-time (51 women), 47 part-time (32 women); includes 30 minority (5 Black or African American, non-Hispanic/Latino; 1 Asian, non-Hispanic/Latino; 23 Hispanic/Latino; 1 Two or more races, non-Hispanic/Latino), 9 international. Average age 32. 152 applicants, 37% accepted, 26 enrolled. In 2019, 11 master's, 11 doctorates awarded. *Degree requirements:* For master's, one foreign language, comprehensive exam, thesis; for doctorate, one foreign language, comprehensive exam, thesis/dissertation. *Entrance requirements:* For master's, GRE (no minimum score requirement), minimum GPA of 3.0, 3 letters of recommendation, statement of purpose, signed research ethics statement, resume or curriculum vitae, writing sample (optional), GA Application (optional); for doctorate, GRE required, minimum GPA of 3.0, 3 letters of recommendation, statement of purpose, signed research ethics statement, resume or curriculum vitae, writing sample (optional), GA Application (optional); for Graduate Certificate, bachelor's degree with minimum GPA of 3.0. Additional exam requirements/recommendations for international students: required—TOEFL, TOEFL (minimum score 550 paper-based; 79 iBT) or IELTS (minimum score 6.5). *Application deadline:* For fall admission, 12/15 priority date for domestic and international students. Application fee: $30. Electronic applications accepted. *Financial support:* In 2019–20, 17 students received support, including 14 research assistantships with tuition reimbursements available (averaging $14,475 per year), 52 teaching assistantships with partial tuition reimbursements available (averaging $12,540 per year); scholarships/grants and tuition waivers (partial) also available. Financial award application deadline: 1/15; financial award applicants required to submit FAFSA. *Unit head:* Dr. David Himmelgreen, Professor/Chair, 813-974-5455, E-mail: dhimmelg@usf.edu. *Application contact:* Dr. Rebecca Zarger, Associate Professor and Graduate Director, 813-974-0069, E-mail: rzarger@usf.edu.
Website: http://anthropology.usf.edu/graduate/

The University of Tennessee, Graduate School, College of Arts and Sciences, Department of Anthropology, Knoxville, TN 37996. Offers archaeology (MA, PhD); biological anthropology (MA, PhD); cultural anthropology (MA, PhD); zoo-archaeology (MA, PhD). *Degree requirements:* For master's, thesis; for doctorate, one foreign language, thesis/dissertation. *Entrance requirements:* For master's and doctorate, GRE General Test, minimum GPA of 2.7. Additional exam requirements/recommendations for international students: required—TOEFL. Electronic applications accepted.

The University of Texas at Arlington, Graduate School, College of Liberal Arts, Department of Sociology and Anthropology, Program in Anthropology, Arlington, TX 79019. Offers MA. *Program availability:* Part-time, evening/weekend. *Degree requirements:* For master's, comprehensive exam, thesis or alternative. *Entrance requirements:* For master's, GRE General Test, minimum GPA of 3.0, 3 letters of recommendation. Additional exam requirements/recommendations for international students: required—TOEFL (minimum score 550 paper-based). Electronic applications accepted.

The University of Texas at Austin, Graduate School, College of Liberal Arts, Department of Anthropology, Austin, TX 78712-1111. Offers archaeology (MA, PhD); cultural forms (MA, PhD); linguistic anthropology (MA, PhD); physical anthropology (MA, PhD); social anthropology (MA, PhD). *Program availability:* Part-time. Terminal master's awarded for partial completion of doctoral program. *Degree requirements:* For master's, thesis; for doctorate, one foreign language, thesis/dissertation. *Entrance requirements:* For master's and doctorate, GRE General Test. Additional exam requirements/recommendations for international students: required—TOEFL. Electronic applications accepted.

The University of Texas at El Paso, Graduate School, College of Liberal Arts, Department of Sociology and Anthropology, El Paso, TX 79968-0001. Offers applied anthropology (Certificate); applied social sciences (Certificate); sociology (MA). *Program availability:* Part-time, evening/weekend. *Degree requirements:* For master's, thesis. *Entrance requirements:* For master's, GRE General Test, minimum GPA of 3.0. Additional exam requirements/recommendations for international students: required—TOEFL. Electronic applications accepted.

The University of Texas at San Antonio, College of Liberal and Fine Arts, Department of Anthropology, San Antonio, TX 78249-0617. Offers MA, PhD. *Program availability:* Part-time. Terminal master's awarded for partial completion of doctoral program. *Degree requirements:* For master's, comprehensive exam, thesis; for doctorate, comprehensive exam, thesis/dissertation, proficiency in foreign language, statistics, or computer programming. *Entrance requirements:* For master's, GRE General Test, minimum GPA of 3.3 during last 60 hours (preferred), 18 hours in major field, three letters of recommendation, statement of purpose, writing sample; for doctorate, GRE General Test, minimum GPA of 3.3 (preferred), transcripts from all colleges and universities attended, 3 letters of recommendation, statement of purpose, writing sample. Additional exam requirements/recommendations for international students: required—TOEFL (minimum score 550 paper-based; 79 iBT), IELTS (minimum score 6.5). Electronic applications accepted. *Expenses:* Contact institution.

University of Toronto, School of Graduate Studies, Faculty of Arts and Science, Department of Anthropology, Toronto, ON M5S 1A1, Canada. Offers M Sc, MA, PhD. *Program availability:* Part-time. *Degree requirements:* For master's, research paper; for doctorate, one foreign language, thesis/dissertation, language exam, thesis defense. *Entrance requirements:* For master's, minimum B+ average, 5 full-year anthropology courses, 2 letters of reference, statement of interest; for doctorate, minimum B+ average, master's degree in relevant area, resume, 2 letters of reference, statement of interest. Additional exam requirements/recommendations for international students: required—TOEFL (minimum score 580 paper-based; 93 iBT), IELTS (minimum score 7), TWE (minimum score 5), Michigan English Language Assessment Battery (minimum score 85), or COPE (minimum score 4). Electronic applications accepted.

The University of Tulsa, Graduate School, Kendall College of Arts and Sciences, Department of Anthropology, Tulsa, OK 74104-3189. Offers MA, PhD, JD/MA. *Program availability:* Part-time. Terminal master's awarded for partial completion of doctoral program. *Degree requirements:* For master's, thesis (for some programs); for doctorate, comprehensive exam, thesis/dissertation. *Entrance requirements:* For master's, GRE General Test. Additional exam requirements/recommendations for international students: required—TOEFL (minimum score 577 paper-based; 91 iBT), IELTS (minimum score 6.5). Electronic applications accepted. *Expenses: Tuition:* Full-time $22,896; part-time $1272 per credit hour. *Required fees:* $6 per credit hour. Tuition and fees vary according to course load and program.

University of Utah, Graduate School, College of Social and Behavioral Science, Department of Anthropology, Salt Lake City, UT 84112. Offers MA, MS, PhD. *Program availability:* Part-time. *Faculty:* 15 full-time (6 women), 5 part-time/adjunct (3 women). *Students:* 19 full-time (11 women), 5 part-time (3 women); includes 1 minority (Hispanic/Latino), 1 international. Average age 37. 25 applicants, 28% accepted, 6 enrolled. In 2019, 2 master's, 4 doctorates awarded. *Degree requirements:* For master's, variable

foreign language requirement, comprehensive exam, thesis or alternative, MA requires language, MS no language requirement; for doctorate, comprehensive exam, thesis/dissertation. *Entrance requirements:* For master's, GRE - 70th percentile and above preferred, personal statement, writing sample, 3 letters of recommendation, bachelor's degree; for doctorate, GRE General Test, GRE - 70th percentile and above preferred. Additional exam requirements/recommendations for international students: recommended—TOEFL (minimum score 80 paper-based), IELTS (minimum score 6.5). *Application deadline:* For fall admission, 12/29 for domestic and international students. Application fee: $50. Electronic applications accepted. *Expenses:* Tuition, state resident: full-time $7085; part-time $272.51 per credit hour. Tuition, nonresident: full-time $24,937; part-time $959.12 per credit hour. *Required fees:* $880.52; $880.52 per semester. Tuition and fees vary according to degree level, program and student level. *Financial support:* In 2019–20, 20 students received support, including 4 fellowships with full tuition reimbursements available (averaging $20,000 per year), 3 research assistantships with full tuition reimbursements available (averaging $20,000 per year), 9 teaching assistantships with full tuition reimbursements available (averaging $20,000 per year); career-related internships or fieldwork, scholarships/grants, health care benefits, and unspecified assistantships also available. Financial award application deadline: 2/28. *Unit head:* Jack Broughton, Department Chair, 801-581-0885, Fax: 801-581-6252, E-mail: jack.broughton@anthro.utah.edu. *Application contact:* Kyla Welch, Programs Manager, 801-581-0885, Fax: 801-581-6252, E-mail: kyla.welch@anthro.utah.edu.
Website: http://www.anthro.utah.edu/

University of Victoria, Faculty of Graduate Studies, Faculty of Social Sciences, Department of Anthropology, Victoria, BC V8W 2Y2, Canada. Offers MA. *Program availability:* Part-time. *Degree requirements:* For master's, comprehensive exam (for some programs), thesis (for some programs). *Entrance requirements:* For master's, minimum B+ average in last 2 years of undergraduate course work, writing sample. Additional exam requirements/recommendations for international students: required—TOEFL (minimum score 575 paper-based), IELTS (minimum score 7).

University of Virginia, College and Graduate School of Arts and Sciences, Department of Anthropology, Charlottesville, VA 22903. Offers MA, PhD. *Degree requirements:* For master's, one foreign language, thesis; for doctorate, 2 foreign languages, thesis/dissertation. *Entrance requirements:* For master's and doctorate, GRE General Test, GRE Subject Test, 3 letters of recommendation. Additional exam requirements/recommendations for international students: required—TOEFL (minimum score 600 paper-based; 90 iBT), IELTS (minimum score 7). Electronic applications accepted.

University of Washington, Graduate School, College of Arts and Sciences, Department of Anthropology, Seattle, WA 98195. Offers MA, PhD. *Faculty:* 32 full-time (16 women), 5 part-time/adjunct (3 women). *Students:* 55 full-time (33 women), 6 part-time (1 woman); includes 25 minority (3 Black or African American, non-Hispanic/Latino; 5 American Indian or Alaska Native, non-Hispanic/Latino; 5 Asian, non-Hispanic/Latino; 9 Hispanic/Latino; 1 Native Hawaiian or other Pacific Islander, non-Hispanic/Latino; 2 Two or more races, non-Hispanic/Latino), 12 international. Average age 32. 121 applicants, 12% accepted, 4 enrolled. In 2019, 2 master's, 15 doctorates awarded. Terminal master's awarded for partial completion of doctoral program. *Degree requirements:* For master's, comprehensive exam, thesis or alternative; for doctorate, variable foreign language requirement, comprehensive exam, thesis/dissertation. *Entrance requirements:* For doctorate, GRE General Test, minimum GPA of 3.6. Additional exam requirements/recommendations for international students: recommended—TOEFL (minimum score 500 paper-based; 61 iBT). *Application deadline:* For fall admission, 12/15 for domestic and international students. Application fee: $85. Electronic applications accepted. *Financial support:* In 2019–20, 45 students received support, including 3 fellowships with full tuition reimbursements available (averaging $20,000 per year), 6 research assistantships with full tuition reimbursements available (averaging $21,000 per year), 23 teaching assistantships with full tuition reimbursements available (averaging $21,000 per year); institutionally sponsored loans, scholarships/grants, traineeships, health care benefits, tuition waivers (full and partial), and unspecified assistantships also available. Financial award application deadline: 1/15; financial award applicants required to submit FAFSA. *Unit head:* Dr. Patricia Ann Kramer, Chair, 206-543-5240, Fax: 206-543-3285, E-mail: pakramer@uw.edu. *Application contact:* Catherine M. Zeigler, Graduate Program Advisor, 206-685-1562, Fax: 206-543-3285, E-mail: gradanth@uw.edu.
Website: https://anthropology.washington.edu.

University of Waterloo, Graduate Studies and Postdoctoral Affairs, Faculty of Arts, Department of Anthropology, Waterloo, ON N2L 3G1, Canada. Offers anthropology (MA); public issues (MA). *Entrance requirements:* Additional exam requirements/recommendations for international students: required—TOEFL, IELTS, PTE. Electronic applications accepted.

The University of Western Ontario, School of Graduate and Postdoctoral Studies, Faculty of Social Science, Department of Anthropology, London, ON N6A 3K7, Canada. Offers MA, PhD. *Degree requirements:* For master's, thesis; for doctorate, thesis/dissertation. *Entrance requirements:* For master's, minimum B average, honors BA. Additional exam requirements/recommendations for international students: required—TOEFL. Electronic applications accepted.

University of West Florida, College of Arts, Social Sciences, and Humanities, Division of Anthropology and Archaeology, Pensacola, FL 32514-5750. Offers anthropology (MA); historical archaeology (MA). *Degree requirements:* For master's, internship or thesis. *Entrance requirements:* For master's, GRE, transcripts; minimum GPA of 3.0; 3 letters of recommendation; writing sample; letter of intent describing background, study interests, and professional goals. Additional exam requirements/recommendations for international students: required—TOEFL (minimum score 550 paper-based).

University of Wisconsin–Madison, Graduate School, College of Letters and Science, Department of Anthropology, Madison, WI 53706-1380. Offers archaeology (PhD); biological anthropology (PhD); cultural anthropology (PhD). Terminal master's awarded for partial completion of doctoral program. *Degree requirements:* For doctorate, thesis/dissertation. *Entrance requirements:* For doctorate, qualifying exam. Electronic applications accepted.

University of Wisconsin–Milwaukee, Graduate School, College of Letters and Science, Department of Anthropology, Milwaukee, WI 53201-0413. Offers anthropology (MS, PhD); museum studies (Graduate Certificate). *Degree requirements:* For master's, thesis or alternative; for doctorate, one foreign language, thesis/dissertation, departmental qualifying exam. *Entrance requirements:* For master's, GRE; for doctorate, GRE, minimum GPA of 3.0, master's degree. Additional exam requirements/recommendations for international students: required—TOEFL (minimum score 550 paper-based; 79 iBT), IELTS (minimum score 6.5). Electronic applications accepted.

University of Wyoming, College of Arts and Sciences, Department of Anthropology, Laramie, WY 82071. Offers MA, PhD. *Program availability:* Part-time. Terminal master's awarded for partial completion of doctoral program. *Degree requirements:* For master's,

one foreign language, comprehensive exam, thesis optional; for doctorate, one foreign language, comprehensive exam, thesis/dissertation. *Entrance requirements:* For master's and doctorate, GRE General Test, minimum GPA of 3.0. Electronic applications accepted.

Université Laval, Faculty of Social Sciences, Department of Anthropology, Programs in Anthropology, Québec, QC G1K 7P4, Canada. Offers MA, PhD. Terminal master's awarded for partial completion of doctoral program. *Degree requirements:* For master's, thesis; for doctorate, thesis/dissertation. *Entrance requirements:* For master's, knowledge of French, interview; for doctorate, knowledge of French, comprehensive of written English, knowledge of a third language. Electronic applications accepted.

Utah State University, School of Graduate Studies, College of Humanities and Social Sciences, Department of Sociology, Social Work, and Anthropology, Logan, UT 84322. Offers anthropology (MS); social work (MSW); sociology (MS, PhD). *Accreditation:* CSWE. *Degree requirements:* For master's, thesis; for doctorate, comprehensive exam, thesis/dissertation. *Entrance requirements:* For master's, GRE General Test, minimum GPA of 3.0, recommendation letters; for doctorate, GRE General Test, minimum GPA of 3.0, recommendation letters, transcripts, personal statement, MS degree. Additional exam requirements/recommendations for international students: required—TOEFL; recommended—TWE.

Vanderbilt University, Department of Anthropology, Nashville, TN 37240-1001. Offers MA, PhD. *Faculty:* 13 full-time (4 women). *Students:* 25 full-time (16 women); includes 4 minority (1 Black or African American, non-Hispanic/Latino; 3 Hispanic/Latino), 9 international. Average age 32. 48 applicants, 8% accepted, 3 enrolled. In 2019, 5 master's, 2 doctorates awarded. *Degree requirements:* For master's, comprehensive exam, thesis or alternative; for doctorate, one foreign language, comprehensive exam, thesis/dissertation, general, qualifying, and final exams. *Entrance requirements:* For master's and doctorate, GRE General Test. Additional exam requirements/recommendations for international students: required—TOEFL (minimum score 570 paper-based; 88 iBT). *Application deadline:* For fall admission, 1/15 for domestic and international students. Application fee: $0. Electronic applications accepted. *Expenses:* Tuition: Full-time $51,018; part-time $2087 per hour. *Required fees:* $542. Tuition and fees vary according to program. *Financial support:* Fellowships with tuition reimbursements, research assistantships with full tuition reimbursements, teaching assistantships with full tuition reimbursements, career-related internships or fieldwork, Federal Work-Study, institutionally sponsored loans, scholarships/grants, and health care benefits available. Financial award application deadline: 1/15; financial award applicants required to submit CSS PROFILE or FAFSA. *Unit head:* Dr. Beth Conklin, Chair, 615-343-6120, Fax: 615-343-0230, E-mail: beth.a.conklin@vanderbilt.edu. *Application contact:* John Janusek, Director of Graduate Studies, 615-343-6120, E-mail: john.w.janusek@vanderbilt.edu.
Website: http://as.vanderbilt.edu/anthropology/

Washington State University, College of Arts and Sciences, Department of Anthropology, Pullman, WA 99164. Offers archaeology (MA, PhD); cultural anthropology (PhD); evolutionary anthropology (MA, PhD). *Degree requirements:* For master's, one foreign language, comprehensive exam (for some programs), thesis; for doctorate, one foreign language, comprehensive exam, thesis/dissertation, written and oral preliminary exam. *Entrance requirements:* For master's and doctorate, GRE General Test, curriculum vitae, statement of intent, official transcripts, 3 letters of recommendation, one or two undergraduate papers (from BA/BS applicants), minimum GPA of 3.0. Additional exam requirements/recommendations for international students: required—TOEFL (minimum score 550 paper-based), IELTS. Electronic applications accepted.

Washington University in St. Louis, The Graduate School, Department of Anthropology, St. Louis, MO 63130-4899. Offers PhD. Terminal master's awarded for partial completion of doctoral program. *Degree requirements:* For doctorate, thesis/dissertation. *Entrance requirements:* Additional exam requirements/recommendations for international students: required—TOEFL. Electronic applications accepted.

Wayne State University, College of Liberal Arts and Sciences, Department of Anthropology, Detroit, MI 48202. Offers anthropology (MA, PhD); social work (PhD). *Program availability:* Part-time. *Degree requirements:* For master's, thesis (for some programs); for doctorate, one foreign language, thesis/dissertation. *Entrance requirements:* For master's, three letters of recommendation, completion of introduction to anthropology, letter of intent, writing sample, minimum undergraduate GPA of 3.2; for doctorate, GRE, bachelor's degree in anthropology or a related field, three letters of recommendation, completion of introduction to anthropology, letter of intent, writing sample, minimum undergraduate GPA of 3.2. Additional exam requirements/recommendations for international students: required—TOEFL (minimum score 550 paper-based; 79 iBT), TWE (minimum score 5.5), Michigan English Language Assessment Battery (minimum score 85); recommended—IELTS (minimum score 6.5). Electronic applications accepted. *Expenses: Tuition:* Full-time $34,567.

Western Kentucky University, Graduate School, Potter College of Arts and Letters, Department of Folk Studies and Anthropology, Bowling Green, KY 42101. Offers folk studies (MA). *Degree requirements:* For master's, comprehensive exam, thesis optional, written exam. *Entrance requirements:* For master's, GRE General Test, minimum GPA of 3.0. Additional exam requirements/recommendations for international students: required—TOEFL (minimum score 555 paper-based; 79 iBT).

Western Michigan University, Graduate College, College of Arts and Sciences, Department of Anthropology, Kalamazoo, MI 49008. Offers MA. *Degree requirements:* For master's, comprehensive exam, thesis.

Western Washington University, Graduate School, College of Humanities and Social Sciences, Department of Anthropology, Bellingham, WA 98225-5996. Offers MA. *Program availability:* Part-time. *Degree requirements:* For master's, thesis. *Entrance requirements:* For master's, GRE General Test, minimum GPA of 3.0 in last 60 semester hours or last 90 quarter hours. Additional exam requirements/recommendations for international students: required—TOEFL (minimum score 567 paper-based). Electronic applications accepted.

Wichita State University, Graduate School, Fairmount College of Liberal Arts and Sciences, Department of Anthropology, Wichita, KS 67260. Offers MA. *Program availability:* Part-time. *Entrance requirements:* For master's, minimum GPA of 2.75 in last 60 hours, 3.0 in anthropology.

Yale University, Graduate School of Arts and Sciences, Department of Anthropology, New Haven, CT 06520. Offers M Phil, MA, PhD. *Degree requirements:* For doctorate, thesis/dissertation. *Entrance requirements:* For master's and doctorate, GRE General Test.

York University, Faculty of Graduate Studies, Faculty of Liberal Arts and Professional Studies, Program in Social Anthropology, Toronto, ON M3J 1P3, Canada. Offers MA, PhD. *Program availability:* Part-time. *Degree requirements:* For master's, thesis or alternative; for doctorate, comprehensive exam, thesis/dissertation. Electronic applications accepted.

Applied Social Research

American University, College of Arts and Sciences, Department of Sociology, Washington, DC 22016-8072. Offers public sociology (Certificate); social research (Certificate); sociology (MA). *Program availability:* Part-time, evening/weekend. *Degree requirements:* For master's, comprehensive exam, thesis or alternative. *Entrance requirements:* For master's, GRE; Please see website: https://www.american.edu/cas/psychology/, statement of purpose, transcripts, 2 letters of recommendation, resume; for Certificate, bachelor's degree, statement of purpose, transcripts, resume. Additional exam requirements/recommendations for international students: required—TOEFL (minimum score 600 paper-based; 100 iBT). *Expenses:* Contact institution.

California State University, Dominguez Hills, College of Natural and Behavioral Sciences, Program in Sociology, Carson, CA 90747-0001. Offers social research (MA); sociology (MA). *Program availability:* Part-time, evening/weekend. *Degree requirements:* For master's, comprehensive exam, thesis. *Entrance requirements:* For master's, minimum GPA of 2.85.

Concordia University Irvine, School of Theology, Irvine, CA 92612-3299. Offers Christian leadership (MA); research in theology (MA); theology and culture (MA). *Program availability:* Part-time, evening/weekend. *Degree requirements:* For master's, project/thesis or vicarage. *Entrance requirements:* For master's, official college transcript(s), statement of intent, 2 references, interview. Additional exam requirements/recommendations for international students: required—TOEFL. Electronic applications accepted. *Expenses:* Contact institution.

Florida State University, The Graduate School, College of Social Sciences and Public Policy, Department of Sociology, Tallahassee, FL 32306. Offers applied social research (MS); sociology (MS, PhD); sociology of health and aging (MS). *Faculty:* 21 full-time (15 women). *Students:* 44 full-time (28 women), 1 part-time (0 women); includes 16 minority (6 Black or African American, non-Hispanic/Latino; 5 Hispanic/Latino; 5 Two or more races, non-Hispanic/Latino), 2 international. Average age 30. 64 applicants, 33% accepted, 11 enrolled. In 2019, 8 master's, 7 doctorates awarded. *Degree requirements:* For doctorate, comprehensive exam, thesis/dissertation. *Entrance requirements:* For master's and doctorate, GRE General Test, minimum GPA of 3.0. Additional exam requirements/recommendations for international students: required—TOEFL (minimum score 550 paper-based; 80 iBT). *Application deadline:* For fall admission, 12/15 priority date for domestic students, 12/15 for international students. Applications are processed on a rolling basis. Application fee: $30. Electronic applications accepted. *Financial support:* In 2019–20, 35 students received support, including 2 fellowships with full tuition reimbursements available (averaging $25,115 per year), 25 research assistantships with full tuition reimbursements available (averaging $21,150 per year), 8 teaching assistantships with full tuition reimbursements available (averaging $21,150 per year); institutionally sponsored loans, scholarships/grants, health care benefits, and unspecified assistantships also available. Financial award application deadline: 12/15; financial award applicants required to submit FAFSA. *Unit head:* Dr. Kathryn Harker Tillman, Chair, 850-644-6416, E-mail: ktillman@fsu.edu. *Application contact:* Kimberly McClellan, Academic Specialist/Graduate Program Coordinator, 850-644-8329, E-mail: kmcclellan@fsu.edu.
Website: http://coss.fsu.edu/sociology/

Hunter College of the City University of New York, Graduate School, School of Arts and Sciences, Department of Sociology, Program in Applied Social Research, New York, NY 10065-5085. Offers MS. *Program availability:* Part-time, evening/weekend. *Degree requirements:* For master's, internship, research reports. *Entrance requirements:* For master's, GRE General Test or GMAT, 3 credits of course work in statistics, research methods, background in sociology or related social science. Additional exam requirements/recommendations for international students: required—TOEFL.

Laurentian University, School of Graduate Studies and Research, Programme in Sociology, Sudbury, ON P3E 2C6, Canada. Offers applied social research (MA). *Program availability:* Part-time. *Entrance requirements:* For master's, honors degree in sociology or equivalent.

Loma Linda University, School of Behavioral Health, Department of Social Work and Social Ecology, Loma Linda, CA 92350. Offers criminal justice (MS); gerontology (MS); social policy and social research (PhD); social work (MSW). *Accreditation:* CSWE. *Degree requirements:* For master's, comprehensive exam, thesis optional; for doctorate, comprehensive exam, thesis/dissertation. *Entrance requirements:* For master's and doctorate, GRE General Test. Additional exam requirements/recommendations for international students: required—TOEFL, Michigan English Language Assessment Battery. Electronic applications accepted.

The New School, The New School for Social Research, New York, NY 10003. Offers M Phil, MA, MS, PhD. *Program availability:* Part-time. *Faculty:* 99 full-time (58 women). *Students:* 637 full-time (344 women), 105 part-time (67 women); includes 123 minority (26 Black or African American, non-Hispanic/Latino; 25 Asian, non-Hispanic/Latino; 56 Hispanic/Latino; 1 Native Hawaiian or other Pacific Islander, non-Hispanic/Latino; 15 Two or more races, non-Hispanic/Latino), 283 international. Average age 31. 832 applicants, 72% accepted, 166 enrolled. In 2019, 247 master's, 53 doctorates awarded. Terminal master's awarded for partial completion of doctoral program. *Degree requirements:* For master's, comprehensive exam (for some programs), thesis (for some programs); for doctorate, variable foreign language requirement, comprehensive exam (for some programs), thesis/dissertation. *Entrance requirements:* For master's, letters of recommendation, writing sample, essays, official transcripts. Additional exam requirements/recommendations for international students: required—TOEFL (minimum score 100 iBT), IELTS (minimum score 7), PTE (minimum score 68). *Application deadline:* For fall admission, 6/15 priority date for domestic and international students; for spring admission, 10/15 priority date for domestic and international students. Applications are processed on a rolling basis. Application fee: $50. Electronic applications accepted. *Expenses:* 2260 per credit. *Financial support:* In 2019–20, 587 students received support, including 79 fellowships (averaging $6,866 per year), 157 research assistantships (averaging $5,006 per year), 150 teaching assistantships with full and partial tuition reimbursements available (averaging $7,736 per year); career-related internships or fieldwork, Federal Work-Study, scholarships/grants, and tuition waivers (full and partial) also available. Support available to part-time students. Financial award application deadline: 2/1; financial award applicants required to submit FAFSA. *Unit head:* Dr. William Milberg, Dean, The New School for Social Research, 212-229-5777, E-mail: milbergw@newschool.edu. *Application contact:* Merida Gasbarro, Director of Graduate Admission, 212-229-5600 Ext. 1108, E-mail: escandom@newschool.edu. Website: http://www.newschool.edu/nssr

New York University, Steinhardt School of Culture, Education, and Human Development, Applied Statistics, Social Science, and Humanities, Program in Applied Statistics for Social Science Research, New York, NY 10012-1019. Offers MS. *Entrance requirements:* For master's, GRE, statement of purpose, resume/curriculum vitae, two letters of recommendation, transcripts. Additional exam requirements/recommendations for international students: required—TOEFL. Electronic applications accepted.

Portland State University, Graduate Studies, School of Social Work, Portland, OR 97207-0751. Offers social work (MSW); social work and social research (PhD). *Accreditation:* CSWE (one or more programs are accredited). *Program availability:* Part-time, 100% online, blended/hybrid learning. *Faculty:* 71 full-time (59 women), 75 part-time/adjunct (64 women). *Students:* 369 full-time (303 women), 288 part-time (242 women); includes 179 minority (30 Black or African American, non-Hispanic/Latino; 12 American Indian or Alaska Native, non-Hispanic/Latino; 19 Asian, non-Hispanic/Latino; 86 Hispanic/Latino; 2 Native Hawaiian or other Pacific Islander, non-Hispanic/Latino; 30 Two or more races, non-Hispanic/Latino), 7 international. Average age 34. 599 applicants, 64% accepted, 253 enrolled. In 2019, 235 master's, 6 doctorates awarded. Terminal master's awarded for partial completion of doctoral program. *Degree requirements:* For master's, two 500-hour field placements; for doctorate, comprehensive exam, thesis/dissertation, residency. *Entrance requirements:* For master's, minimum GPA of 3.0 in upper-division course work or 2.75 overall, resume, 3 letters of reference, 3-4 page statement of purpose; for doctorate, GRE General Test, Three letters of recommendation (two letters for references should address your ability to do doctoral-level academic work. Additional exam requirements/recommendations for international students: required—TOEFL (minimum score 550 paper-based; 80 iBT). Application fee: $65. Electronic applications accepted. *Expenses: Tuition, area resident:* Full-time $13,020; part-time $6510 per year. Tuition, state resident: full-time $13,020; part-time $6510 per year. Tuition, nonresident: full-time $19,830; part-time $9915 per year. *International tuition:* $19,830 full-time. *Required fees:* $1226. One-time fee: $350. Tuition and fees vary according to course load, program and reciprocity agreements. *Financial support:* In 2019–20, 12 research assistantships with full and partial tuition reimbursements (averaging $11,761 per year), 4 teaching assistantships with full and partial tuition reimbursements (averaging $6,613 per year) were awarded; career-related internships or fieldwork, Federal Work-Study, scholarships/grants, tuition waivers (full and partial), and unspecified assistantships also available. Support available to part-time students. Financial award application deadline: 3/1; financial award applicants required to submit FAFSA. *Unit head:* Dr. Jose Coll, Dean, 503-725-3997, Fax: 503-725-5545, E-mail: Coll@pdx.edu. *Application contact:* Sarah Bradley, Director of MSW Program, 503-725-8028, E-mail: bradles@pdx.edu.
Website: https://www.pdx.edu/ssw/

Queens College of the City University of New York, School of Social Sciences, Department of Sociology, Queens, NY 11367-1597. Offers data analytics and applied social research (MA). *Program availability:* Part-time, evening/weekend. *Entrance requirements:* For master's, minimum GPA of 3.0. Additional exam requirements/recommendations for international students: required—TOEFL (minimum score 100 iBT), IELTS (minimum score 7). Electronic applications accepted.

Archaeology

Arizona State University at Tempe, College of Liberal Arts and Sciences, School of Human Evolution and Social Change, Tempe, AZ 85287-2402. Offers anthropology (MA, PhD), including anthropology (PhD), archaeology (PhD), bioarchaeology (PhD), evolutionary (PhD), museum studies (MA), sociocultural (PhD); applied mathematics for the life and social sciences (PhD); environmental social science (PhD), including environmental social science, urbanism; global health (MA, PhD), including complex adaptive systems science (PhD), evolutionary global health sciences (PhD), health and culture (PhD), urbanism (PhD); immigration studies (Graduate Certificate). Terminal master's awarded for partial completion of doctoral program. *Degree requirements:* For master's, thesis or alternative, interactive Program of Study (iPOS) submitted before completing 50 percent of required credit hours; for doctorate, comprehensive exam, thesis/dissertation, interactive Program of Study (iPOS) submitted before completing 50 percent of required credit hours. *Entrance requirements:* For master's and doctorate, GRE, minimum GPA of 3.0 or equivalent in last 2 years of work leading to bachelor's degree. Additional exam requirements/recommendations for international students: required—TOEFL, IELTS, or PTE. Electronic applications accepted.

Boston University, Graduate School of Arts and Sciences, Archaeology Program, Boston, MA 02215. Offers MA, PhD. *Students:* 10 full-time (8 women), 3 international. Average age 28. 12 applicants, 25% accepted. In 2019, 2 master's, 2 doctorates awarded. Terminal master's awarded for partial completion of doctoral program. *Degree requirements:* For master's, one foreign language, comprehensive exam, thesis or alternative. *Entrance requirements:* For master's, GRE General Test, transcripts, three letters of recommendation, personal statement. Additional exam requirements/recommendations for international students: required—TOEFL (minimum score 550 paper-based; 84 iBT). *Application deadline:* For fall admission, 3/1 for domestic and international students. Application fee: $95. Electronic applications accepted. *Financial support:* In 2019–20, 5 students received support, including 2 teaching assistantships with full tuition reimbursements available (averaging $23,340 per year); career-related internships or fieldwork, Federal Work-Study, scholarships/grants, and health care benefits also available. Support available to part-time students. *Unit head:* John Marston, Director, 617-353-2357, Fax: 617-353-6800, E-mail: marston@bu.edu. *Application contact:* Maria Sousa, Administrator, 617-358-1641, Fax: 617-353-6800,

E-mail: mhsousa@bu.edu.
Website: http://www.bu.edu/ARCHAEOLOGY/

Brown University, Graduate School, Department of Egyptology and Assyriology, Providence, RI 02912. Offers ancient western Asian studies (PhD); Egyptology (PhD); history of the exact sciences in antiquity (PhD). *Degree requirements:* For doctorate, 2 foreign languages, comprehensive exam, thesis/dissertation. *Entrance requirements:* For doctorate, GRE General Test.

Brown University, Graduate School, Joukowsky Institute for Archaeology and the Ancient World, Providence, RI 02912. Offers PhD. *Degree requirements:* For doctorate, thesis/dissertation.

Bryn Mawr College, Graduate School of Arts and Sciences, Department of Classical and Near Eastern Archaeology, Bryn Mawr, PA 19010-2899. Offers MA, PhD. *Program availability:* Part-time. *Degree requirements:* For master's, 2 foreign languages, thesis; for doctorate, 3 foreign languages, comprehensive exam, thesis/dissertation. *Entrance requirements:* For master's and doctorate, GRE General Test, transcripts, three letters of recommendation, statement of interest, resume or curriculum vitae, writing sample. Additional exam requirements/recommendations for international students: required—TOEFL (minimum score 600 paper-based; 100 iBT), IELTS (minimum score 7). Electronic applications accepted.

California State University, Northridge, Graduate Studies, College of Social and Behavioral Sciences, Department of Anthropology, Northridge, CA 91330. Offers general anthropology (MA); public archaeology (MA). *Degree requirements:* For master's, thesis or alternative. *Entrance requirements:* For master's, GRE General Test or minimum GPA of 3.0. Additional exam requirements/recommendations for international students: required—TOEFL.

California State University, San Bernardino, Graduate Studies, College of Social and Behavioral Sciences, Program in Applied Archaeology, San Bernardino, CA 92407. Offers clinical psychology (MS). *Faculty:* 3 full-time (0 women). *Students:* 14 part-time (all women); includes 4 minority (all Hispanic/Latino). Average age 34. 15 applicants, 47% accepted, 7 enrolled. In 2019, 1 master's awarded. *Entrance requirements:* Additional exam requirements/recommendations for international students: required—TOEFL. *Application deadline:* For fall admission, 5/20 for domestic students. Application fee: $55. *Financial support:* Application deadline: 3/1. *Unit head:* Dr. Nicholas P Jew, Program Director, 909-537-5551, E-mail: nicholas.jew@csusb.edu. *Application contact:* Dr. Nicholas P Jew, Program Director, 909-537-5551, E-mail: nicholas.jew@csusb.edu.

Columbia University, Graduate School of Arts and Sciences, New York, NY 10027. Offers African-American studies (MA); American studies (MA); anthropology (MA, PhD); art history and archaeology (MA, PhD); astronomy (PhD); biological sciences (PhD); biotechnology (MA); chemical physics (PhD); chemistry (PhD); classical studies (MA, PhD); classics (MA, PhD); climate and society (MA); conservation biology (MA); earth and environmental sciences (PhD); East Asia: regional studies (MA); East Asian languages and cultures (MA, PhD); ecology, evolution and environmental biology (MA), including conservation biology; ecology, evolution, and environmental biology (PhD), including ecology and evolutionary biology, evolutionary primatology; economics (MA, PhD); English and comparative literature (MA, PhD); French and Romance philology (MA, PhD); Germanic languages (MA, PhD); global French studies (MA); global thought (MA); Hispanic cultural studies (MA); history (PhD); history and literature (MA); human rights studies (MA); Islamic studies (MA); Italian (MA, PhD); Japanese pedagogy (MA); Jewish studies (MA); Latin America and the Caribbean: regional studies (MA); Latin American and Iberian cultures (PhD); mathematics (MA, PhD), including finance (MA); medieval and Renaissance studies (MA); Middle Eastern, South Asian, and African studies (MA, PhD); modern art: critical and curatorial studies (MA); modern European studies (MA); museum anthropology (MA); music (DMA, PhD); oral history (MA); philosophical foundations of physics (MA); philosophy (MA, PhD); physics (PhD); political science (MA, PhD); psychology (PhD); quantitative methods in the social sciences (MA); religion (MA, PhD); Russia, Eurasia and East Europe: regional studies (MA); Russian translation (MA); Slavic cultures (MA); Slavic languages (MA, PhD); sociology (MA, PhD); South Asian studies (MA); statistics (MA, PhD); theatre (PhD). *Program availability:* Part-time. *Students:* 3,506 full-time (1,844 women), 208 part-time (121 women); includes 864 minority (110 Black or African American, non-Hispanic/Latino; 5 American Indian or Alaska Native, non-Hispanic/Latino; 416 Asian, non-Hispanic/Latino; 147 Hispanic/Latino; 6 Native Hawaiian or other Pacific Islander, non-Hispanic/Latino; 180 Two or more races, non-Hispanic/Latino), 2,065 international. 14,545 applicants, 25% accepted, 1,429 enrolled. In 2019, 1,262 master's, 363 doctorates awarded. Terminal master's awarded for partial completion of doctoral program. *Degree requirements:* For master's, variable foreign language requirement, comprehensive exam (for some programs), thesis (for some programs); for doctorate, variable foreign language requirement, comprehensive exam (for some programs), thesis/dissertation. *Entrance requirements:* For master's and doctorate, GRE General Test, GRE Subject Test (for some programs). Additional exam requirements/recommendations for international students: required—TOEFL (minimum score 600 paper-based; 100 iBT), IELTS (minimum score 7.5). Application fee: $115. Electronic applications accepted. *Expenses: Tuition:* Full-time $47,600; part-time $1880 per credit. One-time fee: $105. *Financial support:* Fellowships, research assistantships, teaching assistantships, career-related internships or fieldwork, Federal Work-Study, institutionally sponsored loans, scholarships/grants, traineeships, health care benefits, tuition waivers, and unspecified assistantships available. Support available to part-time students. Financial award application deadline: 12/15. *Unit head:* Dr. Carlos J. Alonso, Dean of the Graduate School of Arts and Sciences and Vice President for Graduate Education, 212-854-2861, E-mail: gsas-dean@columbia.edu. *Application contact:* GSAS Office of Admissions, 212-854-6729, E-mail: gsas-admissions@columbia.edu. Website: http://gsas.columbia.edu/

Cornell University, Graduate School, Graduate Fields of Arts and Sciences, Field of Archaeology, Ithaca, NY 14853. Offers environmental archaeology (MA); historical archaeology (MA); Latin American archaeology (MA); medieval archaeology (MA); Mediterranean and Near Eastern archaeology (MA); Stone Age archaeology (MA). *Degree requirements:* For master's, one foreign language, thesis. *Entrance requirements:* For master's, GRE General Test, 3 letters of recommendation, sample of written work. Additional exam requirements/recommendations for international students: required—TOEFL (minimum score 550 paper-based; 77 iBT). Electronic applications accepted.

Cornell University, Graduate School, Graduate Fields of Arts and Sciences, Field of History of Art, Archaeology and Visual Studies, Ithaca, NY 14853. Offers 19th century art (PhD); African, African American and African diaspora (PhD); American art (PhD); ancient art and archaeology (PhD); Asian American art (PhD); Baroque art (PhD); Comparative Modernities (PhD); digital art (PhD); East Asian art (PhD); history of photography (PhD); Islamic art (PhD); Latin American art (PhD); medieval art (PhD); modern art (PhD); Renaissance art (PhD); Southeast Asian art (PhD); theory and criticism (PhD); visual studies (PhD). *Degree requirements:* For doctorate, one foreign language, comprehensive exam, thesis/dissertation, general exams in 3 areas. *Entrance requirements:* For doctorate, GRE General Test, sample of written work, 3 letters of recommendation. Additional exam requirements/recommendations for international

students: required—TOEFL (minimum score 550 paper-based; 77 iBT). Electronic applications accepted.

Florida State University, The Graduate School, Department of Anthropology, Department of Classics, Tallahassee, FL 32306-1510. Offers ancient history (MA); classical archaeology (MA); classical civilization (MA); classics (PhD), including classical archaeology, classics; Greek (MA); Greek and Latin (MA); Latin (MA). *Faculty:* 18 full-time (8 women), 1 (woman) part-time/adjunct. *Students:* 31 full-time (22 women); includes 4 minority (1 Asian, non-Hispanic/Latino; 3 Two or more races, non-Hispanic/Latino). Average age 27. 41 applicants, 32% accepted, 13 enrolled. In 2019, 16 master's, 4 doctorates awarded. Terminal master's awarded for partial completion of doctoral program. *Degree requirements:* For master's, 2 foreign languages, comprehensive exam, thesis or alternative; for doctorate, 4 foreign languages, comprehensive exam, thesis/dissertation. *Entrance requirements:* For master's and doctorate, GRE General Test, minimum GPA of 3.0, official transcripts, resume/CV, statement of purpose, writing sample. Additional exam requirements/recommendations for international students: required—TOEFL (minimum score 550 paper-based; 80 iBT). *Application deadline:* For fall admission, 12/15 priority date for domestic students, 12/15 for international students. Applications are processed on a rolling basis. Application fee: $30. Electronic applications accepted. *Financial support:* In 2019–20, 39 students received support, including 1 fellowship with full tuition reimbursement available (averaging $18,000 per year), 2 research assistantships with full tuition reimbursements available (averaging $12,000 per year), 24 teaching assistantships with full tuition reimbursements available (averaging $12,400 per year); Federal Work-Study, scholarships/grants, tuition waivers (full), and unspecified assistantships also available. Financial award application deadline: 1/15; financial award applicants required to submit FAFSA. *Unit head:* Dr. John Marincola, Chair, 850-644-0304, Fax: 850-644-4073, E-mail: jmarinco@fsu.edu. *Application contact:* Dr. Jessica Clark, Admissions Director, 850-644-4259, Fax: 850-644-4073, E-mail: jhclark@fsu.edu. Website: http://classics.fsu.edu/

Gordon-Conwell Theological Seminary, Graduate and Professional Programs, South Hamilton, MA 01982. Offers Biblical languages (MABL); church history (MACH); counseling (MACO); ministry (D Min); missions/evangelism (MAME); New Testament (MANT); Old Testament (MAOT); religion (MAR); theology (M Div, MATH, Th M, Th D). *Accreditation:* ACIPE; ATS (one or more programs are accredited). *Program availability:* Part-time, evening/weekend. *Degree requirements:* For master's, one foreign language, thesis optional; for doctorate, 2 foreign languages, thesis/dissertation. *Entrance requirements:* For master's, minimum GPA of 2.5; for doctorate, minimum GPA of 3.0.

The Graduate Center, City University of New York, Graduate Studies, Program in Anthropology, New York, NY 10016-4039. Offers anthropological linguistics (PhD); archaeology (PhD); cultural anthropology (PhD); physical anthropology (PhD). *Degree requirements:* For doctorate, one foreign language, thesis/dissertation. *Entrance requirements:* For doctorate, GRE General Test. Additional exam requirements/recommendations for international students: required—TOEFL. Electronic applications accepted.

Harvard University, Graduate School of Arts and Sciences, Department of Anthropology, Cambridge, MA 02138. Offers archaeology (PhD); biological anthropology (PhD); legal anthropology (AM); medical anthropology (AM); social anthropology (AM, PhD); social change and development (AM). Terminal master's awarded for partial completion of doctoral program. *Degree requirements:* For master's, 2 foreign languages, thesis (for some programs); for doctorate, 2 foreign languages, thesis/dissertation, laboratory and/or fieldwork; general, qualifying, or special exams. *Entrance requirements:* For master's and doctorate, GRE General Test. Additional exam requirements/recommendations for international students: required—TOEFL.

Harvard University, Graduate School of Arts and Sciences, Department of Near Eastern Languages and Civilizations, Cambridge, MA 02138. Offers Akkadian and Sumerian (AM, PhD); Arabic (AM, PhD); Armenian (AM, PhD); biblical history (AM, PhD); Hebrew (AM, PhD); Indo-Muslim culture (AM, PhD); Iranian (AM, PhD); Jewish history and literature (AM, PhD); Persian (AM, PhD); Semitic philology (AM, PhD); Syro-Palestinian archaeology (AM, PhD); Turkish (AM, PhD). *Degree requirements:* For doctorate, variable foreign language requirement, thesis/dissertation, general exams. *Entrance requirements:* For master's, GRE General Test; for doctorate, GRE General Test, proficiency in a Near Eastern language. Additional exam requirements/recommendations for international students: required—TOEFL.

Harvard University, Graduate School of Arts and Sciences, Department of the Classics, Cambridge, MA 02138. Offers Byzantine Greek (PhD); classical archaeology (PhD); classical philology (PhD); classical philosophy (PhD); medieval Latin (PhD). *Degree requirements:* For doctorate, 4 foreign languages, thesis/dissertation, preliminary and special exams. *Entrance requirements:* For doctorate, GRE General Test. Additional exam requirements/recommendations for international students: required—TOEFL.

Illinois State University, Graduate School, College of Arts and Sciences, Department of Sociology, Normal, IL 61790. Offers historical archaeology (MA, MS); sociology (MA, MS). *Faculty:* 24 full-time (11 women), 3 part-time/adjunct (2 women). *Students:* 29 full-time (11 women), 12 part-time (8 women). Average age 29. 40 applicants, 68% accepted, 17 enrolled. In 2019, 13 master's awarded. *Degree requirements:* For master's, thesis. *Entrance requirements:* For master's, GRE General Test, GRE Subject Test, minimum GPA of 2.4 in last 60 hours of course work. *Application deadline:* Applications are processed on a rolling basis. Application fee: $50. *Expenses: Tuition, area resident:* Full-time $7956; part-time $9767 per year. Tuition, nonresident: full-time $9233; part-time $17,592 per year. *Required fees:* $1797. *Financial support:* In 2019–20, 9 research assistantships, 14 teaching assistantships were awarded; career-related internships or fieldwork, Federal Work-Study, tuition waivers (full and partial), and unspecified assistantships also available. Financial award application deadline: 4/1. *Unit head:* Dr. Joan Brehm, Department Chair, 309-438-7177, E-mail: jmbrehm@ilstu.edu. *Application contact:* Dr. Gina Hunter, Graduate Coordinator (ANT), 309-438-5713, E-mail: glhunt2@ilstu.edu. Website: http://lilt.ilstu.edu/SOA/

Indiana University Bloomington, University Graduate School, College of Arts and Sciences, Department of Anthropology, Bloomington, IN 47405. Offers anthropology (MA, PhD), including archaeology (PhD), bioanthropology (PhD), linguistic anthropology (PhD), social-cultural anthropology (PhD). *Degree requirements:* For master's, comprehensive exam (for some programs), thesis or alternative; for doctorate, 2 foreign languages, comprehensive exam, thesis/dissertation. *Entrance requirements:* For master's and doctorate, GRE General Test, minimum GPA of 3.0. Additional exam requirements/recommendations for international students: required—TOEFL (minimum score 550 paper-based, 79 iBT) or IELTS. Electronic applications accepted. *Expenses:* Contact institution.

Indiana University of Pennsylvania, School of Graduate Studies and Research, College of Humanities and Social Sciences, Department of Anthropology, Indiana, PA 15705. Offers applied archaeology (MA). *Program availability:* Part-time. *Faculty:* 5 full-time (2 women). *Students:* 15 full-time (8 women), 4 part-time (0 women); includes 2 minority (1 Asian, non-Hispanic/Latino; 1 Two or more races, non-Hispanic/Latino).

Average age 26. 18 applicants, 94% accepted, 9 enrolled. In 2019, 5 master's awarded. *Degree requirements:* For master's, thesis and/or internship. *Entrance requirements:* For master's, GRE, 2 letters of recommendation, goal statement, official transcripts. Additional exam requirements/recommendations for international students: required—TOEFL (minimum score 540 paper-based), IELTS. *Application deadline:* Applications are processed on a rolling basis. Application fee: $50. Electronic applications accepted. *Expenses: Tuition, area resident:* Full-time $9288; part-time $516 per credit. Tuition, nonresident: full-time $13,932; part-time $774 per credit. *Required fees:* $4454. One-time fee: $115 full-time. Tuition and fees vary according to course load and program. *Financial support:* In 2019–20, 1 fellowship with tuition reimbursement (averaging $600 per year), 12 research assistantships with tuition reimbursements (averaging $3,370 per year) were awarded; Federal Work-Study, scholarships/grants, and unspecified assistantships also available. Financial award application deadline: 4/15; financial award applicants required to submit FAFSA. *Unit head:* Dr. Ben Ford, Chair, 724-357-2733, Fax: 724-357-7637, E-mail: ben.ford@iup.edu. *Application contact:* Dr. Ben Ford, Chair, 724-357-2733, Fax: 724-357-7637, E-mail: ben.ford@iup.edu.
Website: http://www.iup.edu/anthropology/

Johns Hopkins University, Zanvyl Krieger School of Arts and Sciences, Department of Near Eastern Studies, Baltimore, MD 21218. Offers archaeology (PhD); Assyriology (PhD); Egyptology (PhD); Hebrew Bible/Northwest Semitics (PhD). *Degree requirements:* For doctorate, 2 foreign languages, comprehensive exam, thesis/dissertation. *Entrance requirements:* For doctorate, GRE. Additional exam requirements/recommendations for international students: required—TOEFL (minimum score 600 paper-based; 100 iBT); recommended—IELTS. Electronic applications accepted. *Expenses:* Contact institution.

Massachusetts Institute of Technology, School of Engineering, Department of Materials Science and Engineering, Cambridge, MA 02139. Offers archaeological materials (PhD, Sc D); materials engineering (Mat E); materials science and engineering (SM, PhD, Sc D). *Degree requirements:* For master's, thesis; for doctorate, comprehensive exam, thesis/dissertation; for Mat E, comprehensive exam, thesis. *Entrance requirements:* For master's and doctorate, GRE General Test. Additional exam requirements/recommendations for international students: required—IELTS. Electronic applications accepted.

Memorial University of Newfoundland, School of Graduate Studies, Department of Anthropology, St. John's, NL A1C 5S7, Canada. Offers archaeology and physical anthropology (MA, PhD); social and cultural anthropology (MA, PhD). *Program availability:* Part-time. *Degree requirements:* For master's, comprehensive exam (for some programs), thesis (for some programs); for doctorate, comprehensive exam, thesis/dissertation, oral defense of thesis. *Entrance requirements:* For master's, 2nd class degree in related field. Electronic applications accepted.

Mercyhurst University, Graduate Studies, Program in Anthropology, Erie, PA 16546. Offers archaeology and geological archaeology (MS); forensic and biological anthropology (MS). *Entrance requirements:* For master's, GRE or MAT, undergraduate degree in related field, interview, resume, essay, three professional references, transcripts. Additional exam requirements/recommendations for international students: required—TOEFL.

New York University, Graduate School of Arts and Science, Institute of Fine Arts, Program in Art History and Archaeology, New York, NY 10012-1019. Offers architectural studies (PhD); art history and archaeology (MA, PhD); classical art and archaeology (PhD); curatorial studies (PhD); East and South Asian art (PhD); Near Eastern art and archaeology (PhD); MA/Diploma; PhD/Certificate. *Program availability:* Part-time. Terminal master's awarded for partial completion of doctoral program. *Degree requirements:* For master's, 2 foreign languages, thesis or alternative, 2 qualifying papers; for doctorate, 2 foreign languages, thesis/dissertation. *Entrance requirements:* For master's, GRE General Test; for doctorate, GRE General Test, MA. Additional exam requirements/recommendations for international students: required—TOEFL, IELTS.

Princeton University, Graduate School, Department of Art and Archaeology, Princeton, NJ 08544-1019. Offers classical art and archaeology (PhD); East Asian art and archaeology (PhD). *Degree requirements:* For doctorate, 2 foreign languages, thesis/dissertation. *Entrance requirements:* For doctorate, GRE General Test. Additional exam requirements/recommendations for international students: required—TOEFL (minimum score 600 paper-based). Electronic applications accepted.

Rice University, Graduate Programs, School of Social Sciences, Department of Anthropology, Houston, TX 77251-1892. Offers archaeology (MA, PhD); social-cultural anthropology (MA, PhD). Terminal master's awarded for partial completion of doctoral program. *Degree requirements:* For master's, one foreign language, 3 major papers, dissertation proposal and language exam or thesis; for doctorate, one foreign language, thesis/dissertation. *Entrance requirements:* For master's and doctorate, research proposal. Additional exam requirements/recommendations for international students: required—TOEFL (minimum score 90 iBT). Electronic applications accepted.

St. Cloud State University, School of Graduate Studies, College of Social Sciences, Program in Cultural Resource Management Archeology, St. Cloud, MN 56301-4498. Offers MS, Graduate Certificate. *Entrance requirements:* For master's, GRE General Test, minimum GPA of 2.75. Additional exam requirements/recommendations for international students: required—Michigan English Language Assessment Battery; recommended—TOEFL (minimum score 550 paper-based).

San Francisco State University, Division of Graduate Studies, College of Liberal and Creative Arts, Department of Anthropology, San Francisco, CA 94132-1722. Offers archaeology (MA); biological anthropology (MA); cultural anthropology (MA); visual anthropology (MA). *Expenses: Tuition, area resident:* Full-time $7176; part-time $4164 per year. Tuition, state resident: full-time $7176; part-time $4164 per year. Tuition, nonresident: full-time $16,680; part-time $396 per unit. *International tuition:* $16,680 full-time. *Required fees:* $1524; $1524 per unit. $762 per semester. Tuition and fees vary according to degree level and program. *Unit head:* Dr. Cynthia Wilczak, Chair, 415-338-2046, Fax: 415-338-6159, E-mail: anthro@sfsu.edu. *Application contact:* Dr. Peter Biella, MA Graduate Coordinator, 415-405-0536, Fax: 415-338-6159, E-mail: biella@sfsu.edu.
Website: http://anthropology.sfsu.edu/

Simon Fraser University, Office of Graduate Studies and Postdoctoral Fellows, Faculty of Environment, Department of Archaeology, Burnaby, BC V5A 1S6, Canada. Offers MA, PhD. *Degree requirements:* For master's, one foreign language, thesis; for doctorate, one foreign language, comprehensive exam, thesis/dissertation. *Entrance requirements:* For master's, minimum GPA of 3.0 (on scale of 4.33) or 3.33 based on last 60 credits of undergraduate courses; for doctorate, minimum GPA of 3.5 (on scale of 4.33). Additional exam requirements/recommendations for international students: recommended—TOEFL (minimum score 580 paper-based; 93 iBT), IELTS (minimum score 7), TWE (minimum score 5). Electronic applications accepted.

Southern Methodist University, Dedman College of Humanities and Sciences, Department of Anthropology, Dallas, TX 75205. Offers applied medical anthropology (MA); archaeology (PhD); cultural anthropology (PhD); medical anthropology (PhD). Terminal master's awarded for partial completion of doctoral program. *Degree requirements:* For master's, one foreign language, comprehensive exam, thesis or alternative; for doctorate, one foreign language, comprehensive exam, thesis/dissertation, qualifying exam, defense of dissertation. *Entrance requirements:* For master's and doctorate, GRE General Test, minimum GPA of 3.0. Additional exam requirements/recommendations for international students: required—TOEFL (minimum score 550 paper-based).

Stanford University, School of Humanities and Sciences, Department of Anthropology, Stanford, CA 94305-2004. Offers anthropology (MA); archaeology (PhD); culture and society (PhD); ecology and environment (PhD). *Expenses: Tuition:* Full-time $52,479; part-time $34,110 per unit. *Required fees:* $672; $224 per quarter. Tuition and fees vary according to program and student level.
Website: http://www.stanford.edu/dept/anthsci/

Trinity International University, Trinity Evangelical Divinity School, Deerfield, IL 60015-1284. Offers academic ministry (M Div); Biblical and Near Eastern archaeology and languages (MA); chaplaincy and ministry care (MA); Christian studies (Certificate); church and parachurch ministry (M Div); church history (MA, Th M); counseling (Th M); educational ministries (MA); educational ministry (Th M); educational studies (PhD); intercultural studies (MA, PhD); leadership and management (D Min); mental health counseling (MA); military chaplaincy (D Min); ministry (MA); missions (Th M); missions and evangelism (D Min); New Testament (MA, Th M); Old Testament (Th M); Old Testament and Semitic languages (MA); pastoral ministry and care (D Min); pastoral theology (Th M); preaching and teaching (D Min); spiritual formation and education (D Min); systematic theology (MA, Th M); theological studies (MA, PhD); urban ministry (MA). *Program availability:* Part-time, online learning. *Degree requirements:* For master's, comprehensive exam, thesis, fieldwork; for doctorate, comprehensive exam (for some programs), thesis/dissertation; for Certificate, comprehensive exam, integrative papers. *Entrance requirements:* For master's, GRE, MAT, minimum cumulative undergraduate GPA of 3.0; for doctorate, GRE, minimum cumulative graduate GPA of 3.2; for Certificate, GRE, MAT, minimum undergraduate GPA of 2.5. Additional exam requirements/recommendations for international students: required—TOEFL (minimum score 580 paper-based), TWE (minimum score 4). Electronic applications accepted.

Universidad de las Américas Puebla, Division of Graduate Studies, School of Social Sciences, Program in Anthropology, Puebla, Mexico. Offers anthropology (MA); archaeology (MA). *Program availability:* Part-time, evening/weekend. *Degree requirements:* For master's, one foreign language, thesis. *Entrance requirements:* For master's, bachelor's degree in anthropology or equivalent.

University of Alberta, Faculty of Graduate Studies and Research, Department of History and Classics, Edmonton, AB T6G 2E1, Canada. Offers ancient history (PhD); classical archaeology (MA, PhD); classical literature (PhD); classics (MA); history (MA, PhD). *Program availability:* Part-time, evening/weekend. *Degree requirements:* For master's, one foreign language, thesis (for some programs); for doctorate, one foreign language, thesis/dissertation. *Entrance requirements:* For master's, minimum B+ average; for doctorate, minimum A- average. Additional exam requirements/recommendations for international students: required—TOEFL (minimum score 580 paper-based). Electronic applications accepted.

The University of British Columbia, Faculty of Arts, Department of Classical, Near Eastern and Religious Studies, Program in Classical and Near Eastern Archaeology, Vancouver, BC V6T 1Z1, Canada. Offers MA. *Degree requirements:* For master's, thesis.

University of California, Berkeley, Graduate Division, College of Letters and Science, Department of Classics, Berkeley, CA 94720. Offers classical archaeology (MA, PhD); classics (MA, PhD); Greek (MA); Latin (MA). Terminal master's awarded for partial completion of doctoral program. *Degree requirements:* For master's, one foreign language, exams; for doctorate, 2 foreign languages, thesis/dissertation, qualifying exam. *Entrance requirements:* For master's and doctorate, GRE General Test, minimum GPA of 3.0, 3 letters of recommendation. Additional exam requirements/recommendations for international students: required—TOEFL (minimum score 570 paper-based; 90 iBT), TWE. Electronic applications accepted.

University of California, Berkeley, Graduate Division, College of Letters and Science, Group in Ancient History and Mediterranean Archaeology, Berkeley, CA 94720. Offers MA, PhD. Terminal master's awarded for partial completion of doctoral program. *Degree requirements:* For master's, one foreign language, exam or thesis; for doctorate, 2 foreign languages, thesis/dissertation, qualifying exam. *Entrance requirements:* For master's and doctorate, GRE General Test, minimum GPA of 3.0, 3 letters of recommendation. Additional exam requirements/recommendations for international students: required—TOEFL (minimum score 570 paper-based; 90 iBT), TWE. Electronic applications accepted.

University of California, Los Angeles, Graduate Division, College of Letters and Science, Interdepartmental Program in Archaeology, Los Angeles, CA 90095. Offers MA, PhD. Terminal master's awarded for partial completion of doctoral program. *Degree requirements:* For master's, one foreign language, comprehensive exam, field experience; for doctorate, 2 foreign languages, thesis/dissertation, oral and written qualifying exams. *Entrance requirements:* For doctorate, GRE General Test, bachelor's degree; minimum undergraduate GPA of 3.0 (or its equivalent if letter grade system not used); writing sample. Additional exam requirements/recommendations for international students: required—TOEFL. Electronic applications accepted.

University of California, Los Angeles, Graduate Division, College of Letters and Science, Interdepartmental Program in Conservation of Archaeological and Ethnographic Materials, Los Angeles, CA 90095. Offers MA. *Degree requirements:* For master's, one foreign language, thesis, eleven-month internship. *Entrance requirements:* For master's, GRE General Test, bachelor's degree; minimum undergraduate GPA of 3.0 (or its equivalent if letter grade system not used); proficiency in one foreign language; portfolio; writing sample; documented practical experience; interview. Additional exam requirements/recommendations for international students: required—TOEFL.

University of Chicago, Division of the Social Sciences, Department of Anthropology, Chicago, IL 60637. Offers archaeology (PhD); sociocultural and linguistic anthropology (PhD). *Degree requirements:* For doctorate, one foreign language, thesis/dissertation. *Entrance requirements:* For doctorate, GRE General Test, 3 letters of recommendation, statement of purpose, transcripts, resume or curriculum vitae, writing sample (dependent on department). Additional exam requirements/recommendations for international students: required—TOEFL (minimum score 104 iBT), IELTS (minimum score 7). Electronic applications accepted.

University of Colorado Denver, College of Liberal Arts and Sciences, Department of Anthropology, Denver, CO 80217. Offers archaeological studies (MA); biological anthropology (MA); medical anthropology (MA); sustainable development and political ecology (MA). *Program availability:* Part-time, evening/weekend. *Degree requirements:* For master's, comprehensive exam, thesis or alternative, 30-36 credit hours. *Entrance requirements:* For master's, GRE General Test, minimum GPA of 3.0 for all undergraduate studies, transcripts from all undergraduate/graduate institutions attended, prior training in anthropology, three letters of recommendation, statement of purpose. Additional exam requirements/recommendations for international students: required—TOEFL (minimum score 537 paper-based; 75 iBT); recommended—IELTS (minimum score 6.5). Tuition and fees vary according to course load, program and reciprocity agreements.

University of Denver, Division of Arts, Humanities and Social Sciences, Department of Anthropology, Denver, CO 80208. Offers archaeology (MA); cultural anthropology (MA); museum and heritage studies (MA). *Program availability:* Part-time. *Faculty:* 8 full-time (4 women), 1 part-time/adjunct (0 women). *Students:* 2 full-time (both women), 21 part-time (16 women); includes 7 minority (2 Black or African American, non-Hispanic/Latino; 1 Asian, non-Hispanic/Latino; 3 Hispanic/Latino; 1 Two or more races, non-Hispanic/Latino). Average age 27. 35 applicants, 57% accepted, 11 enrolled. In 2019, 12 master's awarded. *Degree requirements:* For master's, comprehensive exam, thesis (for some programs). *Entrance requirements:* For master's, GRE General Test, bachelor's degree, transcripts, personal statement, two letters of recommendation. Additional exam requirements/recommendations for international students: required—TOEFL (minimum score 550 paper-based; 80 iBT). *Application deadline:* For fall admission, 2/28 for domestic and international students. Applications are processed on a rolling basis. Application fee: $65. Electronic applications accepted. *Expenses:* Contact institution. *Financial support:* In 2019–20, 22 students received support, including 12 teaching assistantships with tuition reimbursements available (averaging $5,233 per year); career-related internships or fieldwork, Federal Work-Study, institutionally sponsored loans, scholarships/grants, and unspecified assistantships also available. Support available to part-time students. Financial award application deadline: 2/15; financial award applicants required to submit FAFSA. *Unit head:* Dr. Larry Conyers, Professor, Director of Graduate Program, 303-871-2684, E-mail: lconyers@du.edu. *Application contact:* Dr. Larry Conyers, Professor, Director of Graduate Program, 303-871-2684, E-mail: lconyers@du.edu.
Website: http://www.du.edu/ahss/anthropology

University of Lethbridge, School of Graduate Studies, Lethbridge, AB T1K 3M4, Canada. Offers addictions counseling (M Sc); agricultural biotechnology (M Sc); agricultural studies (M Sc, MA); anthropology (MA); archaeology (M Sc, MA); art (MA, MFA); biochemistry (M Sc); biological sciences (M Sc); biomolecular science (PhD); biosystems and biodiversity (PhD); Canadian studies (MA); chemistry (M Sc); computer science (M Sc); computer science and geographical information science (M Sc); counseling (MC); counseling psychology (M Ed); dramatic arts (MA); earth, space, and physical science (PhD); economics (MA); education (MA, PhD); educational leadership (M Ed); English (MA); environmental science (M Sc); evolution and behavior (PhD); exercise science (M Sc); French (MA); French/German (MA); French/Spanish (MA); general education (M Ed); geography (M Sc, MA); German (MA); health sciences (M Sc); individualized multidisciplinary (M Sc, MA); kinesiology (M Sc, MA); management (M Sc), including accounting, finance, human resource management and labor relations, information systems, international management, marketing, policy and strategy; mathematics (M Sc); music (M Mus, MA); Native American studies (MA); neuroscience (M Sc, PhD); new media (MA, MFA); nursing (M Sc, MN); philosophy (MA); physics (M Sc); political science (MA); psychology (M Sc, MA); religious studies (MA); sociology (MA); theatre and dramatic arts (MFA); theoretical and computational science (PhD); urban and regional studies (MA); women and gender studies (MA). *Program availability:* Part-time, evening/weekend. *Degree requirements:* For master's, thesis (for some programs); for doctorate, comprehensive exam, thesis/dissertation. *Entrance requirements:* For master's, GMAT (for M Sc in management), bachelor's degree in related field, minimum GPA of 3.0 during previous 20 graded semester courses, 2 years' teaching or related experience (M Ed); for doctorate, master's degree, minimum graduate GPA of 3.5. Additional exam requirements/recommendations for international students: required—TOEFL (minimum score 580 paper-based; 93 iBT). Electronic applications accepted.

The University of Manchester, School of Arts, Languages and Cultures, Manchester, United Kingdom. Offers anthropology, media and performance (PhD); applied theatre (PhD); Arab world studies (PhD); archaeology (PhD); art history and visual studies (PhD); arts and cultural management (PhD); arts management and cultural policy (PhD); Chinese studies (PhD); classics and ancient history (PhD); composition (PhD); creative writing (PhD); drama (PhD); East Asian studies (PhD); electroacoustic composition (PhD); English and American studies (PhD); English language (PhD); French studies (PhD); German studies (PhD); history (PhD); humanitarianism and conflict response (PhD); interpreting studies (PhD); Japanese studies (PhD); Latin American cultural studies (PhD); linguistics (PhD); Middle Eastern studies (PhD); museology (PhD); museum practice (PhD); music (PhD); musicology (PhD); Polish studies (PhD); Portuguese studies (PhD); religions and theology (PhD); Russian studies (PhD); Spanish studies (PhD); translation and intercultural studies (PhD).

University of Massachusetts Boston, College of Liberal Arts, Program in Historical Archaeology, Boston, MA 02125-3393. Offers MA. *Program availability:* Part-time, evening/weekend. *Entrance requirements:* For master's, GRE General Test, minimum GPA of 2.75. Electronic applications accepted.

University of Memphis, Graduate School, College of Arts and Sciences, Department of Earth Sciences, Memphis, TN 38152. Offers earth sciences (MA, MS, PhD), including archaeology (MS), geography (MS), geology (MS), geophysics (MS), interdisciplinary studies (MS); geographic information systems (Graduate Certificate), including geographic information systems, GIS educator, GIS planning, GIS professional. *Program availability:* Part-time, evening/weekend. *Students:* 40 full-time (17 women), 22 part-time (7 women); includes 12 minority (2 Black or African American, non-Hispanic/Latino; 8 Asian, non-Hispanic/Latino; 2 Hispanic/Latino), 18 international. Average age 31. 23 applicants, 91% accepted, 18 enrolled. In 2019, 13 master's, 5 doctorates, 8 other advanced degrees awarded. Terminal master's awarded for partial completion of doctoral program. *Degree requirements:* For master's, comprehensive exam, thesis, seminar presentation; for doctorate, comprehensive exam, thesis/dissertation, qualifying exam, submission of two manuscripts for publication in peer-reviewed journal or books. *Entrance requirements:* For master's, GRE General Test, 3 letters of recommendation, statement of research interests; for doctorate, GRE General Test, 2 letters of recommendation, resume, personal statement. Additional exam requirements/recommendations for international students: required—TOEFL (minimum score 550 paper-based; 79 iBT). *Application deadline:* For fall admission, 1/15 for domestic students; for spring admission, 11/1 for domestic students. Applications are processed on a rolling basis. Application fee: $35 ($60 for international students). Electronic applications accepted. *Expenses: Tuition, area resident:* Full-time $9216; part-time $512 per credit hour. Tuition, state resident: full-time $9216; part-time $512 per credit hour. Tuition, nonresident: full-time $12,672; part-time $704 per credit hour. *International tuition:* $16,128 full-time. *Required fees:* $1530; $85 per credit hour. Tuition and fees vary according to program. *Financial support:* Fellowships with full tuition reimbursements, research assistantships with full tuition reimbursements, teaching assistantships with full tuition reimbursements, Federal Work-Study, scholarships/grants, and unspecified assistantships available. Financial award application deadline: 2/1; financial award applicants required to submit FAFSA. *Unit head:* Dr. Daniel Larsen, Chair, 901-678-4358, Fax: 901-678-2178, E-mail: dlarsen@memphis.edu. *Application contact:* Dr. Daniel Larsen, Chair, 901-678-4358, Fax: 901-678-2178, E-mail: dlarsen@memphis.edu.
Website: http://www.memphis.edu/earthsciences/

University of Michigan, Rackham Graduate School, College of Literature, Science, and the Arts, Department of Anthropology, Ann Arbor, MI 48109. Offers anthropological archaeology (PhD); biological anthropology (PhD); linguistic anthropology (PhD); sociocultural anthropology (PhD). *Degree requirements:* For doctorate, one foreign language, comprehensive exam, thesis/dissertation, preliminary examination, oral defense of dissertation. *Entrance requirements:* For doctorate, GRE General Test. Additional exam requirements/recommendations for international students: required—TOEFL (minimum score 560 paper-based; 84 iBT). Electronic applications accepted.

University of Michigan, Rackham Graduate School, College of Literature, Science, and the Arts, Interdepartmental Program in Classical Art and Archaeology, Ann Arbor, MI 48109-1390. Offers MA, PhD. *Degree requirements:* For doctorate, 4 foreign languages, comprehensive exam, thesis/dissertation, ancient history exam, qualifying exam, preliminary exam. *Entrance requirements:* For doctorate, GRE General Test. Additional exam requirements/recommendations for international students: required—TOEFL (minimum score 560 paper-based; 84 iBT). Electronic applications accepted.

University of Minnesota, Twin Cities Campus, Graduate School, College of Liberal Arts, Department of Classical and Near Eastern Studies, Minneapolis, MN 55455-0213. Offers ancient and medieval art and archaeology (MA, PhD); classics (MA, PhD); Greek (MA, PhD); Latin (MA, PhD); religions in antiquity (MA). *Program availability:* Part-time. Terminal master's awarded for partial completion of doctoral program. *Degree requirements:* For master's, 2 foreign languages, comprehensive exam, thesis or alternative; for doctorate, variable foreign language requirement, comprehensive exam, thesis/dissertation. *Entrance requirements:* For master's and doctorate, GRE, 3 letters of recommendation, writing sample, copies of transcripts, personal statement. Additional exam requirements/recommendations for international students: required—TOEFL. Electronic applications accepted.

University of Nebraska–Lincoln, Graduate College, College of Arts and Sciences, Department of Anthropology and Geography, Lincoln, NE 68588. Offers anthropology (MA); geography (MA, PhD); professional archaeology (MA). *Degree requirements:* For master's, thesis optional. *Entrance requirements:* For master's, GRE General Test. Additional exam requirements/recommendations for international students: required—TOEFL. Electronic applications accepted.

University of New Mexico, Graduate Studies, College of Arts and Sciences, Program in Anthropology, Albuquerque, NM 87131-2039. Offers archaeology (MA, MS, PhD); ethnology (MA, MS, PhD); evolutionary anthropology (PhD); public archaeology (MA, MS, PhD). Terminal master's awarded for partial completion of doctoral program. *Degree requirements:* For master's, comprehensive exam (for some programs), thesis or alternative, 1-2 exams; for doctorate, one foreign language, comprehensive exam, thesis/dissertation, exam, proposal, oral defense, skill and/or second language. *Entrance requirements:* For master's and doctorate, GRE General Test, 3 letters of recommendation, letter of interest, transcripts. Additional exam requirements/recommendations for international students: required—TOEFL (minimum score 550 paper-based), IELTS (minimum score 7). Electronic applications accepted. *Expenses:* Tuition, state resident: full-time $7633; part-time $972 per year. Tuition, nonresident: full-time $22,586; part-time $3840 per year. *International tuition:* $23,292 full-time. *Required fees:* $8608. Tuition and fees vary according to course level, course load, degree level, program and student level.

The University of North Carolina at Chapel Hill, Graduate School, College of Arts and Sciences, Department of Classics, Chapel Hill, NC 27599. Offers classical archaeology (MA, PhD); classics (MA, PhD). Terminal master's awarded for partial completion of doctoral program. *Degree requirements:* For master's, one foreign language, comprehensive exam, thesis; for doctorate, 2 foreign languages, comprehensive exam, thesis/dissertation. *Entrance requirements:* For master's and doctorate, GRE General Test, minimum GPA of 3.0. Electronic applications accepted.

University of Oklahoma, College of Arts and Sciences, Department of Anthropology, Norman, OK 73019. Offers anthropology (MA, PhD); applied linguistic anthropology (MA); archaeology (PhD); health and human biology (PhD); socio-cultural and linguistics (PhD); socio-cultural anthropology (MA). *Degree requirements:* For master's, thesis; for doctorate, comprehensive exam, thesis/dissertation. *Entrance requirements:* For master's and doctorate, GRE, minimum undergraduate GPA of 3.0; statement of purpose; 2 letters of recommendation. Additional exam requirements/recommendations for international students: required—TOEFL (minimum score 79 iBT) or IELTS (minimum score 6.5). Electronic applications accepted. *Expenses:* Tuition, state resident: full-time $6583.20; part-time $274.30 per credit hour. Tuition, nonresident: full-time $21,242; part-time $885.10 per credit hour. *International tuition:* $21,242.40 full-time. *Required fees:* $1994.20; $72.55 per credit hour. $126.50 per semester. Tuition and fees vary according to course load and degree level.

University of Pennsylvania, School of Arts and Sciences, Graduate Group in Art and Archaeology of the Mediterranean World, Philadelphia, PA 19104. Offers AM, PhD. *Program availability:* Part-time. *Faculty:* 15 full-time (10 women), 6 part-time/adjunct (5 women). *Students:* 13 full-time (7 women); includes 1 minority (Two or more races, non-Hispanic/Latino). Average age 32. 62 applicants, 15% accepted, 3 enrolled. In 2019, 1 master's, 6 doctorates awarded. Terminal master's awarded for partial completion of doctoral program. Application fee: $90.
Website: http://www.sas.upenn.edu/graduate-division

University of Rhode Island, Graduate School, College of Arts and Sciences, Department of History, Kingston, RI 02881. Offers archaeology and anthropology (MA); European history (MA), including European history, United States history; MLIS/MA. *Program availability:* Part-time. *Faculty:* 16 full-time (7 women). *Students:* 7 full-time (2 women), 10 part-time (5 women). 11 applicants, 91% accepted, 4 enrolled. In 2019, 5 master's awarded. *Entrance requirements:* Additional exam requirements/recommendations for international students: required—TOEFL. *Application deadline:* For fall admission, 7/15 for domestic students; for spring admission, 11/15 for domestic students. Application fee: $65. Electronic applications accepted. *Expenses: Tuition, area resident:* Full-time $13,734; part-time $763 per credit. Tuition, state resident: full-time $13,734; part-time $763 per credit. Tuition, nonresident: full-time $26,512; part-time $1473 per credit. *International tuition:* $26,512 full-time. *Required fees:* $1780; $52 per credit. $35 per term. One-time fee: $165. *Financial support:* In 2019–20, 4 teaching assistantships with tuition reimbursements (averaging $18,986 per year) were awarded. Financial award application deadline: 2/1; financial award applicants required to submit FAFSA. *Unit head:* Dr. Rod Mather, Chair, 401-874-4093, E-mail: rodmather@uri.edu. *Application contact:* Dr. Evelyn Sterne, Director of Graduate Studies, 401-874-4074, E-mail: sterne@uri.edu.
Website: http://www.uri.edu/artsci/his/

University of Saskatchewan, College of Graduate and Postdoctoral Studies, College of Arts and Science, Department of Archaeology and Anthropology, Saskatoon, SK S7N 5A2, Canada. Offers MA. *Program availability:* Part-time. *Degree requirements:* For master's, thesis. *Entrance requirements:* Additional exam requirements/

recommendations for international students: required—TOEFL (minimum score 80 iBT); recommended—IELTS (minimum score 6.5).

University of South Africa, College of Human Sciences, Pretoria, South Africa. Offers adult education (M Ed); African languages (MA, PhD); African politics (MA, PhD); Afrikaans (MA, PhD); ancient history (MA, PhD); ancient Near Eastern studies (MA, PhD); anthropology (MA, PhD); applied linguistics (MA); Arabic (MA, PhD); archaeology (MA); art history (MA); Biblical archaeology (MA); Biblical studies (M Th, D Th, PhD); Christian spirituality (M Th, D Th); church history (M Th, D Th); classical studies (MA, PhD); clinical psychology (MA); communication (MA, PhD); comparative education (M Ed, Ed D); consulting psychology (D Admin, D Com, PhD); curriculum studies (M Ed, Ed D); development studies (M Admin, MA, D Admin, PhD); didactics (M Ed, Ed D); education (M Tech); education management (M Ed, Ed D); educational psychology (M Ed); English (MA); environmental education (M Ed); French (MA, PhD); German (MA, PhD); Greek (MA); guidance and counseling (M Ed); health studies (MA, PhD), including health sciences education (MA), health services management (MA), medical and surgical nursing science (critical care general) (MA), midwifery and neonatal nursing science (MA), trauma and emergency care (MA); history (MA, PhD); history of education (Ed D); inclusive education (M Ed, Ed D); information and communications technology policy and regulation (MA); information science (MA, MIS, PhD); international politics (MA, PhD); Islamic studies (MA, PhD); Italian (MA, PhD); Judaica (MA, PhD); linguistics (MA, PhD); mathematical education (M Ed); mathematics education (MA); missiology (M Th, D Th); modern Hebrew (MA, PhD); musicology (MA, MMus, D Mus, PhD); natural science education (M Ed); New Testament (M Th, D Th); Old Testament (D Th); pastoral therapy (M Th, D Th); philosophy (MA); philosophy of education (M Ed, Ed D); politics (MA, PhD); Portuguese (MA, PhD); practical theology (M Th, D Th); psychology (MA, MS, PhD); psychology of education (M Ed, Ed D); public health (MA); religious studies (MA, D Th, PhD); Romance languages (MA); Russian (MA, PhD); Semitic languages (MA, PhD); social behavior studies in HIV/AIDS (MA); social science (mental health) (MA); social science in development studies (MA); social science in psychology (MA); social science in social work (MA); social science in sociology (MA); social work (MSW, DSW, PhD); socio-education (M Ed, Ed D); sociolinguistics (MA); sociology (MA, PhD); Spanish (MA, PhD); systematic theology (M Th, D Th); TESOL (teaching English to speakers of other languages) (MA); theological ethics (M Th, D Th); theory of literature (MA, PhD); urban ministries (D Th); urban ministry (M Th).

University of South Florida, College of Arts and Sciences, Department of Anthropology, Tampa, FL 33620-9951. Offers applied anthropology (MA), including archaeological and forensic sciences, biocultural medical anthropology, cultural resource management, heritage studies; medical anthropology (Graduate Certificate). *Program availability:* Part-time. *Faculty:* 22 full-time (13 women). *Students:* 67 full-time (51 women), 47 part-time (32 women); includes 30 minority (5 Black or African American, non-Hispanic/Latino; 1 Asian, non-Hispanic/Latino; 23 Hispanic/Latino; 1 Two or more races, non-Hispanic/Latino), 9 international. Average age 32. 152 applicants, 37% accepted, 26 enrolled. In 2019, 11 master's, 11 doctorates awarded. *Degree requirements:* For master's, one foreign language, comprehensive exam, thesis; for doctorate, one foreign language, comprehensive exam, thesis/dissertation. *Entrance requirements:* For master's, GRE (no minimum score requirement), minimum GPA of 3.0, 3 letters of recommendation, statement of purpose, signed research ethics statement, resume or curriculum vitae, writing sample (optional), GA Application (optional); for doctorate, GRE required, minimum GPA of 3.0, 3 letters of recommendation, statement of purpose, signed research ethics statement, resume or curriculum vitae, writing sample (optional), GA Application (optional); for Graduate Certificate, bachelor's degree with minimum GPA of 3.0. Additional exam requirements/recommendations for international students: required—TOEFL, TOEFL (minimum score 550 paper-based; 79 iBT) or IELTS (minimum score 6.5). *Application deadline:* For fall admission, 12/15 priority date for domestic and international students. Application fee: $30. Electronic applications accepted. *Financial support:* In 2019–20, 17 students received support, including 14 research assistantships with tuition reimbursements available (averaging $14,475 per year), 52 teaching assistantships with partial tuition reimbursements available (averaging $12,540 per year); scholarships/grants and tuition waivers (partial) also available. Financial award application deadline: 1/15; financial award applicants required to submit FAFSA. *Unit head:* Dr. David Himmelgreen, Professor/Chair, 813-974-5455, E-mail: dhimmelg@usf.edu. *Application contact:* Dr. Rebecca Zarger, Associate Professor and Graduate Director, 813-974-0069, E-mail: rzarger@usf.edu.
Website: http://anthropology.usf.edu/graduate/

The University of Tennessee, Graduate School, College of Arts and Sciences, Department of Anthropology, Knoxville, TN 37996. Offers archaeology (MA, PhD); biological anthropology (MA, PhD); cultural anthropology (MA, PhD); zoo-archaeology (MA, PhD). *Degree requirements:* For master's, thesis; for doctorate, one foreign language, thesis/dissertation. *Entrance requirements:* For master's and doctorate, GRE General Test, minimum GPA of 2.7. Additional exam requirements/recommendations for international students: required—TOEFL. Electronic applications accepted.

The University of Texas at Austin, Graduate School, College of Liberal Arts, Department of Anthropology, Austin, TX 78712-1111. Offers archaeology (MA, PhD); cultural forms (MA, PhD); linguistic anthropology (MA, PhD); physical anthropology (MA, PhD); social anthropology (MA, PhD). *Program availability:* Part-time. Terminal master's awarded for partial completion of doctoral program. *Degree requirements:* For master's, thesis; for doctorate, one foreign language, thesis/dissertation. *Entrance requirements:* For master's and doctorate, GRE General Test. Additional exam requirements/recommendations for international students: required—TOEFL. Electronic applications accepted.

University of West Florida, College of Arts, Social Sciences, and Humanities, Division of Anthropology and Archaeology, Pensacola, FL 32514-5750. Offers anthropology (MA); historical archaeology (MA). *Degree requirements:* For master's, internship or thesis. *Entrance requirements:* For master's, GRE, transcripts; minimum GPA of 3.0; 3 letters of recommendation; writing sample; letter of intent describing background, study interests, and professional goals. Additional exam requirements/recommendations for international students: required—TOEFL (minimum score 550 paper-based).

University of Wisconsin–Madison, Graduate School, College of Letters and Science, Department of Anthropology, Madison, WI 53706-1380. Offers archaeology (PhD); biological anthropology (PhD); cultural anthropology (PhD). Terminal master's awarded for partial completion of doctoral program. *Degree requirements:* For doctorate, thesis/dissertation. *Entrance requirements:* For doctorate, qualifying exam. Electronic applications accepted.

Université Laval, Faculty of Letters, Department of History, Programs in Archaeology, Québec, QC G1K 7P4, Canada. Offers MA, PhD. Terminal master's awarded for partial completion of doctoral program. *Degree requirements:* For master's, thesis; for doctorate, comprehensive exam, thesis/dissertation. *Entrance requirements:* For master's and doctorate, English test, knowledge of French. Electronic applications accepted.

Washington State University, College of Arts and Sciences, Department of Anthropology, Pullman, WA 99164. Offers archaeology (MA, PhD); cultural anthropology (PhD); evolutionary anthropology (MA, PhD). *Degree requirements:* For master's, one foreign language, comprehensive exam (for some programs), thesis; for doctorate, one foreign language, comprehensive exam, thesis/dissertation, written and oral preliminary exam. *Entrance requirements:* For master's and doctorate, GRE General Test, curriculum vitae, statement of intent, official transcripts, 3 letters of recommendation, one or two undergraduate papers (from BA/BS applicants), minimum GPA of 3.0. Additional exam requirements/recommendations for international students: required—TOEFL (minimum score 550 paper-based), IELTS. Electronic applications accepted.

Washington University in St. Louis, The Graduate School, Department of Art History and Archaeology, St. Louis, MO 63130-4899. Offers AM, PhD. *Degree requirements:* For doctorate, 2 foreign languages, comprehensive exam, thesis/dissertation. *Entrance requirements:* For master's and doctorate, GRE General Test, sample of written work. Electronic applications accepted.

Wheaton College, Graduate School, School of Biblical and Theological Studies, Wheaton, IL 60187-5593. Offers Biblical and theological studies (PhD); Biblical archaeology (MA); Biblical exegesis (MA); Biblical studies (MA); general theological studies (MA); historical and systematic theology (MA), including Biblical and theological studies; history of Christianity (MA), including Biblical and theological studies. *Program availability:* Part-time. *Degree requirements:* For doctorate, thesis/dissertation. *Entrance requirements:* For master's, GRE General Test. Additional exam requirements/recommendations for international students: required—TOEFL (minimum score 550 paper-based; 80 iBT), IELTS (minimum score 6.5). Electronic applications accepted. *Expenses:* Tuition: Full-time $16,800; part-time $700 per credit hour. Tuition and fees vary according to degree level and program.

Yale University, Graduate School of Arts and Sciences, Interdisciplinary Program in Archaeological Studies, New Haven, CT 06520. Offers MA. *Degree requirements:* For master's, thesis. *Entrance requirements:* For master's, GRE General Test.

Biological Anthropology

Cornell University, Graduate School, Graduate Fields of Arts and Sciences, Field of Anthropology, Ithaca, NY 14853. Offers archaeological anthropology (PhD); biological anthropology (PhD); sociocultural anthropology (PhD). *Degree requirements:* For doctorate, one foreign language, comprehensive exam, thesis/dissertation, teaching experience. *Entrance requirements:* For doctorate, GRE General Test, 3 letters of recommendation, sample of written work. Additional exam requirements/recommendations for international students: required—TOEFL (minimum score 550 paper-based; 77 iBT). Electronic applications accepted.

Duke University, Graduate School, Department of Evolutionary Anthropology, Durham, NC 27708. Offers cellular and molecular biology (PhD); gross anatomy and physical anthropology (PhD), including comparative morphology of human and non-human primates, primate social behavior, vertebrate paleontology; neuroanatomy (PhD). *Degree requirements:* For doctorate, one foreign language, thesis/dissertation. *Entrance requirements:* For doctorate, GRE General Test. Additional exam requirements/recommendations for international students: required—TOEFL (minimum score 577 paper-based; 90 iBT) or IELTS (minimum score 7). Electronic applications accepted.

Harvard University, Graduate School of Arts and Sciences, Department of Anthropology, Cambridge, MA 02138. Offers archaeology (PhD); biological anthropology (PhD); legal anthropology (AM); medical anthropology (AM); social anthropology (AM, PhD); social change and development (AM). Terminal master's awarded for partial completion of doctoral program. *Degree requirements:* For master's, 2 foreign languages, thesis (for some programs); for doctorate, 2 foreign languages, thesis/dissertation, laboratory and/or fieldwork; general, qualifying, or special exams. *Entrance requirements:* For master's and doctorate, GRE General Test. Additional exam requirements/recommendations for international students: required—TOEFL.

Kent State University, College of Arts and Sciences, School of Biomedical Sciences, Kent, OH 44242-0001. Offers biological anthropology (PhD); biomedical mathematics (MS, PhD); cellular and molecular biology (MS, PhD), including cellular biology and structures, molecular biology and genetics; neurosciences (MS, PhD); pharmacology (MS, PhD); physiology (MS, PhD). *Faculty:* 17 full-time (8 women). *Students:* 73 full-time (48 women), 2 part-time (1 woman); includes 9 minority (2 Black or African American, non-Hispanic/Latino; 1 Asian, non-Hispanic/Latino; 3 Hispanic/Latino; 3 Two or more races, non-Hispanic/Latino), 53 international. Average age 29. 78 applicants, 17% accepted, 9 enrolled. In 2019, 2 master's, 5 doctorates awarded. *Degree requirements:* For master's, thesis; for doctorate, comprehensive exam, thesis/dissertation. *Entrance requirements:* For master's, GRE, bachelor's degree, transcripts, minimum GPA of 3.0 undergraduate GPA, goal statement, three letters of recommendation, academic preparation adequate to perform graduate work in the desired field (typically two years of chemistry, one year of mathematics, one year of physics and courses in anthropology, biology and psychology); for doctorate, GRE, master's degree, minimum GPA of 3.0, transcripts, goal statement, three letters of recommendation. Additional exam requirements/recommendations for international students: required—TOEFL (minimum score 100 iBT), IELTS (minimum score 7), PTE (minimum score 68), Michigan English Language Assessment Battery (minimum score 85). *Application deadline:* For fall admission, 1/1 for domestic students, 12/15 for international students. Applications are processed on a rolling basis. Application fee: $45 ($70 for international students). Electronic applications accepted. *Financial support:* Research assistantships with full tuition reimbursements, teaching assistantships, health care benefits, and unspecified assistantships available. Financial award application deadline: 1/1. *Unit head:* Dr. Ernest J. Freeman, Director, School of Biomedical Sciences, 330-672-2363, E-mail: efreema2@kent.edu. *Application contact:* School of Biomedical Sciences, 330-6722263, Fax: 330-6729391.
Website: http://www.kent.edu/biomedical/

Mercyhurst University, Graduate Studies, Program in Anthropology, Erie, PA 16546. Offers archaeology and geological archaeology (MS); forensic and biological anthropology (MS). *Entrance requirements:* For master's, GRE or MAT, undergraduate degree in related field, interview, resume, essay, three professional references, transcripts. Additional exam requirements/recommendations for international students: required—TOEFL.

San Francisco State University, Division of Graduate Studies, College of Liberal and Creative Arts, Department of Anthropology, San Francisco, CA 94132-1722. Offers archaeology (MA); biological anthropology (MA); cultural anthropology (MA); visual anthropology (MA). *Expenses: Tuition, area resident:* Full-time $7176; part-time $4164 per year. Tuition, state resident: full-time $7176; part-time $4164 per year. Tuition, nonresident: full-time $16,680; part-time $396 per unit. *International tuition:* $16,680 full-time. *Required fees:* $1524; $1524 per unit. $762 per semester. Tuition and fees vary according to degree level and program. *Unit head:* Dr. Cynthia Wilczak, Chair, 415-338-2046, Fax: 415-338-6159, E-mail: anthro@sfsu.edu. *Application contact:* Dr. Peter Biella, MA Graduate Coordinator, 415-405-0536, Fax: 415-338-6159, E-mail: biella@sfsu.edu.
Website: http://anthropology.sfsu.edu/

University of Colorado Denver, College of Liberal Arts and Sciences, Department of Anthropology, Denver, CO 80217. Offers archaeological studies (MA); biological anthropology (MA); medical anthropology (MA); sustainable development and political ecology (MA). *Program availability:* Part-time, evening/weekend. *Degree requirements:* For master's, comprehensive exam, thesis or alternative, 30-36 credit hours. *Entrance requirements:* For master's, GRE General Test, minimum GPA of 3.0 for all undergraduate studies, transcripts from all undergraduate/graduate institutions attended, prior training in anthropology, three letters of recommendation, statement of purpose. Additional exam requirements/recommendations for international students: required—TOEFL (minimum score 537 paper-based; 75 iBT); recommended—IELTS (minimum score 6.5). Tuition and fees vary according to course load, program and reciprocity agreements.

University of Michigan, Rackham Graduate School, College of Literature, Science, and the Arts, Department of Anthropology, Ann Arbor, MI 48109. Offers anthropological archaeology (PhD); biological anthropology (PhD); linguistic anthropology (PhD); sociocultural anthropology (PhD). *Degree requirements:* For doctorate, one foreign language, comprehensive exam, thesis/dissertation, preliminary examination, oral defense of dissertation. *Entrance requirements:* For doctorate, GRE General Test. Additional exam requirements/recommendations for international students: required—TOEFL (minimum score 560 paper-based; 84 iBT). Electronic applications accepted.

The University of Tennessee, Graduate School, College of Arts and Sciences, Department of Anthropology, Knoxville, TN 37996. Offers archaeology (MA, PhD); biological anthropology (MA, PhD); cultural anthropology (MA, PhD); zoo-archaeology (MA, PhD). *Degree requirements:* For master's, thesis; for doctorate, one foreign language, thesis/dissertation. *Entrance requirements:* For master's and doctorate, GRE General Test, minimum GPA of 2.7. Additional exam requirements/recommendations for international students: required—TOEFL. Electronic applications accepted.

University of Wisconsin–Madison, Graduate School, College of Letters and Science, Department of Anthropology, Madison, WI 53706-1380. Offers archaeology (PhD); biological anthropology (PhD); cultural anthropology (PhD). Terminal master's awarded for partial completion of doctoral program. *Degree requirements:* For doctorate, thesis/dissertation. *Entrance requirements:* For doctorate, qualifying exam. Electronic applications accepted.

Cultural Anthropology

Brandeis University, Graduate School of Arts and Sciences, Department of Anthropology, Waltham, MA 02454. Offers anthropology/women's, gender, and sexuality studies (MA); Mesoamerican archaeology (MA, PhD); sociocultural anthropology (MA, PhD). *Program availability:* Part-time. *Faculty:* 13 full-time (6 women), 1 (woman) part-time/adjunct. *Students:* 28 full-time (19 women), 1 (woman) part-time; includes 6 minority (1 Black or African American, non-Hispanic/Latino; 3 Asian, non-Hispanic/Latino; 2 Two or more races, non-Hispanic/Latino), 3 international. Average age 27. 50 applicants, 60% accepted, 9 enrolled. In 2019, 6 master's, 2 doctorates awarded. Terminal master's awarded for partial completion of doctoral program. *Degree requirements:* For master's, thesis or alternative, paper; for doctorate, one foreign language, comprehensive exam, thesis/dissertation. *Entrance requirements:* For master's and doctorate, General GRE, transcripts, letters of recommendation, resume, statement of purpose, and writing sample. Additional exam requirements/recommendations for international students: required—TOEFL, IELTS, PTE. *Application deadline:* For fall admission, 1/15 priority date for domestic and international students. Applications are processed on a rolling basis. Application fee: $75. Electronic applications accepted. *Financial support:* In 2019–20, 8 fellowships with full tuition reimbursements (averaging $25,000 per year), 8 teaching assistantships (averaging $3,550 per year) were awarded; scholarships/grants and health care benefits also available. Support available to part-time students. *Unit head:* Dr. Charles Golden, Director of Graduate Studies, 781-736-2217, E-mail: cgolden@brandeis.edu. *Application contact:* Laurel Woolf, Administrator, 781-736-4873, E-mail: lwoolf@brandeis.edu.
Website: http://www.brandeis.edu/gsas/programs/anthropology.html

Concordia University, School of Graduate Studies, Faculty of Arts and Science, Department of Sociology and Anthropology, Montréal, QC H3G 1M8, Canada. Offers social and cultural analysis (PhD); social and cultural anthropology (MA); sociology (MA). *Degree requirements:* For master's, comprehensive exam or thesis. *Entrance requirements:* For master's, honors degree in sociology or equivalent.

Cornell University, Graduate School, Graduate Fields of Arts and Sciences, Field of Anthropology, Ithaca, NY 14853. Offers archaeological anthropology (PhD); biological anthropology (PhD); sociocultural anthropology (PhD). *Degree requirements:* For doctorate, one foreign language, comprehensive exam, thesis/dissertation, teaching experience. *Entrance requirements:* For doctorate, GRE General Test, 3 letters of recommendation, sample of written work. Additional exam requirements/recommendations for international students: required—TOEFL (minimum score 550 paper-based; 77 iBT). Electronic applications accepted.

Duke University, Graduate School, Department of Cultural Anthropology, Durham, NC 27708. Offers physical anthropology (PhD), including comparative morphology of human and non-human primates, primate social behavior; social/cultural anthropology (PhD); JD/AM. *Degree requirements:* For doctorate, one foreign language, thesis/dissertation. *Entrance requirements:* For doctorate, GRE General Test. Additional exam requirements/recommendations for international students: required—TOEFL (minimum score 577 paper-based; 90 iBT) or IELTS (minimum score 7).

The Graduate Center, City University of New York, Graduate Studies, Program in Anthropology, New York, NY 10016-4039. Offers anthropological linguistics (PhD); archaeology (PhD); cultural anthropology (PhD); physical anthropology (PhD). *Degree requirements:* For doctorate, one foreign language, thesis/dissertation. *Entrance requirements:* For doctorate, GRE General Test. Additional exam requirements/recommendations for international students: required—TOEFL. Electronic applications accepted.

Memorial University of Newfoundland, School of Graduate Studies, Department of Anthropology, St. John's, NL A1C 5S7, Canada. Offers archaeology and physical anthropology (MA, PhD); social and cultural anthropology (MA, PhD). *Program availability:* Part-time. *Degree requirements:* For master's, comprehensive exam (for some programs), thesis (for some programs); for doctorate, comprehensive exam, thesis/dissertation, oral defense of thesis. *Entrance requirements:* For master's, 2nd class degree in related field. Electronic applications accepted.

Rice University, Graduate Programs, School of Social Sciences, Department of Anthropology, Houston, TX 77251-1892. Offers archaeology (MA, PhD); social-cultural anthropology (MA, PhD). Terminal master's awarded for partial completion of doctoral program. *Degree requirements:* For master's, one foreign language, 3 major papers, dissertation proposal and language exam or thesis; for doctorate, one foreign language, thesis/dissertation. *Entrance requirements:* For master's and doctorate, research proposal. Additional exam requirements/recommendations for international students: required—TOEFL (minimum score 90 iBT). Electronic applications accepted.

San Francisco State University, Division of Graduate Studies, College of Liberal and Creative Arts, Department of Anthropology, San Francisco, CA 94132-1722. Offers archaeology (MA); biological anthropology (MA); cultural anthropology (MA); visual anthropology (MA). *Expenses: Tuition, area resident:* Full-time $7176; part-time $4164 per year. Tuition, state resident: full-time $7176; part-time $4164 per year. Tuition, nonresident: full-time $16,680; part-time $396 per unit. *International tuition:* $16,680 full-time. *Required fees:* $1524; $1524 per unit. $762 per semester. Tuition and fees vary according to degree level and program. *Unit head:* Dr. Cynthia Wilczak, Chair, 415-338-2046, Fax: 415-338-6159, E-mail: anthro@sfsu.edu. *Application contact:* Dr. Peter Biella, MA Graduate Coordinator, 415-405-0536, Fax: 415-338-6159, E-mail: biella@sfsu.edu.
Website: http://anthropology.sfsu.edu/

Southern Illinois University Edwardsville, Graduate School, Program in Integrative Studies, Edwardsville, IL 62026. Offers cultural heritage and resources management (MA, MS); diversity training (MA, MS); organizational design thinking (MS); sustainability (MS). *Program availability:* Part-time, evening/weekend. *Degree requirements:* For master's, variable foreign language requirement, comprehensive exam (for some programs), thesis (for some programs). *Entrance requirements:* Additional exam requirements/recommendations for international students: required—TOEFL (minimum score 550 paper-based; 79 iBT), IELTS (minimum score 6.5). Electronic applications accepted.

Southern Methodist University, Dedman College of Humanities and Sciences, Department of Anthropology, Dallas, TX 75205. Offers applied medical anthropology (MA); archaeology (PhD); cultural anthropology (PhD); medical anthropology (PhD). Terminal master's awarded for partial completion of doctoral program. *Degree requirements:* For master's, one foreign language, comprehensive exam, thesis or alternative; for doctorate, one foreign language, comprehensive exam, thesis/dissertation, qualifying exam, defense of dissertation. *Entrance requirements:* For master's and doctorate, GRE General Test, minimum GPA of 3.0. Additional exam requirements/recommendations for international students: required—TOEFL (minimum score 550 paper-based).

University of California, Santa Barbara, Graduate Division, College of Letters and Sciences, Division of Social Sciences, Department of Anthropology, Santa Barbara, CA 93106-2014. Offers sociocultural anthropology (PhD); MA/PhD. Terminal master's awarded for partial completion of doctoral program. *Degree requirements:* For master's, comprehensive exam (for some programs), thesis (for some programs); for doctorate, comprehensive exam (for some programs), thesis/dissertation. *Entrance requirements:* For master's and doctorate, GRE General Test, statement of purpose, personal achievements statement, transcripts, writing sample, curriculum vitae, letters of recommendation. Additional exam requirements/recommendations for international students: required—TOEFL (minimum score 550 paper-based; 80 iBT), IELTS (minimum score 7). Electronic applications accepted.

University of California, Santa Cruz, Division of Graduate Studies, Division of Social Sciences, Department of Anthropology, Santa Cruz, CA 95064. Offers cultural anthropology (PhD). *Degree requirements:* For doctorate, thesis/dissertation, qualifying exam. *Entrance requirements:* For doctorate, GRE General Test. Additional exam requirements/recommendations for international students: required—TOEFL (minimum score 550 paper-based; 83 iBT); recommended—IELTS (minimum score 8). Electronic applications accepted.

University of Denver, Division of Arts, Humanities and Social Sciences, Department of Anthropology, Denver, CO 80208. Offers archaeology (MA); cultural anthropology (MA); museum and heritage studies (MA). *Program availability:* Part-time. *Faculty:* 8 full-time (4 women), 1 part-time/adjunct (0 women). *Students:* 2 full-time (both women), 21 part-time (16 women); includes 7 minority (2 Black or African American, non-Hispanic/Latino; 1 Asian, non-Hispanic/Latino; 3 Hispanic/Latino; 1 Two or more races, non-Hispanic/Latino). Average age 27. 35 applicants, 57% accepted, 11 enrolled. In 2019, 12 master's awarded. *Degree requirements:* For master's, comprehensive exam, thesis (for some programs). *Entrance requirements:* For master's, GRE General Test, bachelor's degree, transcripts, personal statement, two letters of recommendation. Additional exam requirements/recommendations for international students: required—TOEFL (minimum score 550 paper-based; 80 iBT). *Application deadline:* For fall admission, 2/28 for domestic and international students. Applications are processed on a rolling basis. Application fee: $65. Electronic applications accepted. *Expenses:* Contact institution. *Financial support:* In 2019–20, 22 students received support, including 12 teaching assistantships with tuition reimbursements available (averaging $5,233 per year); career-related internships or fieldwork, Federal Work-Study, institutionally sponsored loans, scholarships/grants, and unspecified assistantships also available. Support

available to part-time students. Financial award application deadline: 2/15; financial award applicants required to submit FAFSA. *Unit head:* Dr. Larry Conyers, Professor, Director of Graduate Program, 303-871-2684, E-mail: lconyers@du.edu. *Application contact:* Dr. Larry Conyers, Professor, Director of Graduate Program, 303-871-2684, E-mail: lconyers@du.edu.
Website: http://www.du.edu/ahss/anthropology

University of Michigan, Rackham Graduate School, College of Literature, Science, and the Arts, Department of Anthropology, Ann Arbor, MI 48109. Offers anthropological archaeology (PhD); biological anthropology (PhD); linguistic anthropology (PhD); sociocultural anthropology (PhD). *Degree requirements:* For doctorate, one foreign language, comprehensive exam, thesis/dissertation, preliminary examination, oral defense of dissertation. *Entrance requirements:* For doctorate, GRE General Test. Additional exam requirements/recommendations for international students: required—TOEFL (minimum score 560 paper-based; 84 iBT). Electronic applications accepted.

The University of Tennessee, Graduate School, College of Arts and Sciences, Department of Anthropology, Knoxville, TN 37996. Offers archaeology (MA, PhD); biological anthropology (MA, PhD); cultural anthropology (MA, PhD); zoo-archaeology (MA, PhD). *Degree requirements:* For master's, thesis; for doctorate, one foreign language, thesis/dissertation. *Entrance requirements:* For master's and doctorate, GRE

General Test, minimum GPA of 2.7. Additional exam requirements/recommendations for international students: required—TOEFL. Electronic applications accepted.

University of Wisconsin–Madison, Graduate School, College of Letters and Science, Department of Anthropology, Madison, WI 53706-1380. Offers archaeology (PhD); biological anthropology (PhD); cultural anthropology (PhD). Terminal master's awarded for partial completion of doctoral program. *Degree requirements:* For doctorate, thesis/dissertation. *Entrance requirements:* For doctorate, qualifying exam. Electronic applications accepted.

Washington State University, College of Arts and Sciences, Department of Anthropology, Pullman, WA 99164. Offers archaeology (MA, PhD); cultural anthropology (PhD); evolutionary anthropology (MA, PhD). *Degree requirements:* For master's, one foreign language, comprehensive exam (for some programs), thesis; for doctorate, one foreign language, comprehensive exam, thesis/dissertation, written and oral preliminary exam. *Entrance requirements:* For master's and doctorate, GRE General Test, curriculum vitae, statement of intent, official transcripts, 3 letters of recommendation, one or two undergraduate papers (from BA/BS applicants), minimum GPA of 3.0. Additional exam requirements/recommendations for international students: required—TOEFL (minimum score 550 paper-based), IELTS. Electronic applications accepted.

Demography and Population Studies

Bowling Green State University, Graduate College, College of Arts and Sciences, Department of Sociology, Bowling Green, OH 43403. Offers demography and population studies (MA); social psychology (MA); sociology (PhD). *Program availability:* Part-time. *Degree requirements:* For master's, thesis or alternative; for doctorate, comprehensive exam, thesis/dissertation. *Entrance requirements:* For master's and doctorate, GRE General Test. Additional exam requirements/recommendations for international students: required—TOEFL. Electronic applications accepted.

Cornell University, Graduate School, Graduate Fields of Agriculture and Life Sciences, Field of Development Sociology, Ithaca, NY 14853. Offers population and development (MS, PhD); rural and environmental sociology (MS, PhD); state, economy, and society (MS, PhD). *Degree requirements:* For doctorate, comprehensive exam, thesis/dissertation. *Entrance requirements:* For master's and doctorate, GRE General Test, 3 letters of recommendation. Additional exam requirements/recommendations for international students: required—TOEFL (minimum score 550 paper-based; 77 iBT). Electronic applications accepted.

Cornell University, Graduate School, Graduate Fields of Agriculture and Life Sciences, Field of Global Development, Ithaca, NY 14853. Offers development policy (MPS); international agriculture and development (MPS); international development (MPS); international nutrition (MPS); international planning (MPS); international population (MPS); science and technology policy (MPS). *Degree requirements:* For master's, project paper. *Entrance requirements:* For master's, GRE General Test (recommended), 2 years of development experience, 2 letters of recommendation. Additional exam requirements/recommendations for international students: required—TOEFL (minimum score 550 paper-based; 77 iBT). Electronic applications accepted.

Florida State University, The Graduate School, College of Social Sciences and Public Policy, Center for Demography and Population Health, Tallahassee, FL 32306-2240. Offers demography (MS). *Program availability:* Part-time. *Faculty:* 10 full-time (6 women). *Students:* 6 full-time (2 women), 1 (woman) part-time; includes 3 minority (2 Black or African American, non-Hispanic/Latino; 1 Hispanic/Latino). Average age 26. 10 applicants, 70% accepted, 6 enrolled. In 2019, 6 master's awarded. *Degree requirements:* For master's, thesis, minimum 27 hours' course work (including 18 hours of statistics and data analysis). *Entrance requirements:* For master's, GRE General Test, minimum upper-division GPA of 3.0. Additional exam requirements/recommendations for international students: required—TOEFL (minimum score 550 paper-based; 80 iBT). *Application deadline:* For fall admission, 6/1 for domestic and international students; for spring admission, 11/1 for domestic and international students. Application fee: $30. Electronic applications accepted. *Financial support:* Career-related internships or fieldwork, institutionally sponsored loans, scholarships/grants, and tuition waivers (full and partial) available. Financial award application deadline: 6/1. *Unit head:* Dr. Carl Schmertmann, Director, 850-644-7100, Fax: 850-644-8818, E-mail: Schmertmann@fsu.edu. *Application contact:* Lynn Peacock, Program Assistant, 850-644-1762, Fax: 850-644-8818, E-mail: lpeacock@fsu.edu. Website: http://popcenter.fsu.edu

Harvard University, Harvard T.H. Chan School of Public Health, Department of Global Health and Population, Boston, MA 02115-6096. Offers global health and population (SM); population health sciences (PhD). *Program availability:* Part-time. *Faculty:* 48 full-time (18 women), 16 part-time/adjunct (5 women). *Students:* 39 full-time (30 women); includes 17 minority (8 Asian, non-Hispanic/Latino; 4 Hispanic/Latino; 1 Native Hawaiian or other Pacific Islander, non-Hispanic/Latino; 4 Two or more races, non-Hispanic/Latino), 15 international. Average age 29. 66 applicants, 48% accepted, 18 enrolled. In 2019, 17 master's, 8 doctorates awarded. *Degree requirements:* For master's, thesis; for doctorate, thesis/dissertation, qualifying exam. *Entrance requirements:* For master's, GRE, MCAT; for doctorate, GRE. Additional exam requirements/recommendations for international students: recommended—TOEFL (minimum score 600 paper-based; 100 iBT), IELTS (minimum score 7). *Application deadline:* For fall admission, 12/1 for domestic and international students. Application fee: $140. Electronic applications accepted. *Financial support:* Fellowships, research assistantships, teaching assistantships, Federal Work-Study, scholarships/grants, traineeships, and unspecified assistantships available. Support available to part-time students. Financial award application deadline: 2/15; financial award applicants required to submit FAFSA. *Unit head:* Dr. Marcia Castro, Chair, E-mail: mcastro@hsph.harvard.edu. *Application contact:* Vincent W. James, Director of Admissions, 617-432-1031, Fax: 617-432-7080, E-mail: admissions@hsph.harvard.edu.
Website: http://www.hsph.harvard.edu/global-health-and-population/

Harvard University, Harvard T.H. Chan School of Public Health, PhD Program in Population Health Sciences, Boston, MA 02138. Offers environmental health (PhD); epidemiology (PhD); global health and population (PhD); nutrition (PhD); social and behavioral sciences (PhD). *Students:* 159 full-time (0 women). Average age 29. In 2019, 5 doctorates awarded. *Entrance requirements:* Additional exam requirements/recommendations for international students: recommended—TOEFL, IELTS. *Application deadline:* For fall admission, 12/1 for domestic and international students. Electronic applications accepted. *Financial support:* Application deadline: 2/15; applicants required to submit FAFSA. *Unit head:* Bruce Villineau, Assistant Director,

617-432-6076, E-mail: phdphs@hsph.harvard.edu. *Application contact:* Bruce Villineau, Assistant Director, 617-432-6076, E-mail: phdphs@hsph.harvard.edu.

Johns Hopkins University, Bloomberg School of Public Health, Department of Population, Family and Reproductive Health, Baltimore, MD 21205. Offers demography (MHS); population, family and reproductive health (MHS, MSPH, PhD). *Degree requirements:* For master's, essay, fieldwork; for doctorate, thesis/dissertation, 1-year full-time residency, oral and written exams. *Entrance requirements:* For master's and doctorate, GRE General Test, 3 letters of recommendation, curriculum vitae. Additional exam requirements/recommendations for international students: required—TOEFL (minimum score 600 paper-based), IELTS. Electronic applications accepted.

Miami University, College of Arts and Science, Department of Sociology and Gerontology, Oxford, OH 45056. Offers gerontology (MGS); population and social gerontology (MPSG); social gerontology (PhD).

New York University, College of Global Public Health, New York, NY 10012. Offers biological basis of public health (PhD); community and international health (MPH); global health leadership (MPH); health systems and health services research (PhD); population and community health (PhD); public health nutrition (MPH); social and behavioral sciences (MPH); socio-behavioral health (PhD). *Accreditation:* CEPH. *Program availability:* Part-time, online learning. *Degree requirements:* For master's, thesis (for some programs); for doctorate, thesis/dissertation. *Entrance requirements:* For master's and doctorate, GRE. Additional exam requirements/recommendations for international students: required—TOEFL. Electronic applications accepted. *Expenses:* Contact institution.

Princeton University, Graduate School, Department of Sociology, Princeton, NJ 08544-1019. Offers sociology (PhD); sociology and demography (PhD). *Degree requirements:* For doctorate, variable foreign language requirement, thesis/dissertation. *Entrance requirements:* For doctorate, GRE General Test, GRE Subject Test (recommended), sample of written work. Additional exam requirements/recommendations for international students: required—TOEFL (minimum score 600 paper-based). Electronic applications accepted.

Princeton University, Graduate School, Program in Population Studies, Princeton, NJ 08544-1019. Offers demography (PhD, Certificate); economics and demography (PhD); public affairs and demography (PhD); sociology and demography (PhD). *Degree requirements:* For doctorate, thesis/dissertation. *Entrance requirements:* For doctorate, GRE General Test. Additional exam requirements/recommendations for international students: required—TOEFL (minimum score 600 paper-based). Electronic applications accepted.

Université de Montréal, Faculty of Arts and Sciences, Department of Demography, Montréal, QC H3C 3J7, Canada. Offers M Sc, PhD. Terminal master's awarded for partial completion of doctoral program. *Degree requirements:* For master's, one foreign language, thesis; for doctorate, one foreign language, thesis/dissertation, general exam. *Entrance requirements:* For master's, minimum GPA of 2.7. Electronic applications accepted.

Université du Québec, Institut National de la Recherche Scientifique, Graduate Programs, Centre for Urbanisation Culture Societe, Montreal, QC H2X 1E3, Canada. Offers population studies (M Sc, PhD); urban studies (MA). *Program availability:* Part-time. *Faculty:* 32 full-time. *Students:* 77 full-time (43 women), 24 part-time (11 women), 22 international. Average age 33. 27 applicants, 93% accepted, 20 enrolled. In 2019, 9 master's, 4 doctorates awarded. *Degree requirements:* For master's, thesis (for some programs); for doctorate, thesis/dissertation; for DESS, thesis or alternative. *Entrance requirements:* For master's, appropriate bachelor's degree, proficiency in French; for doctorate, appropriate master's degree, proficiency in French; for DESS, proficiency in French. *Application deadline:* For fall admission, 3/30 for domestic and international students; for winter admission, 11/1 for domestic and international students; for spring admission, 3/1 for domestic and international students. Application fee: $45. Electronic applications accepted. *Financial support:* In 2019–20, fellowships (averaging $16,500 per year) were awarded; research assistantships also available. *Unit head:* Helene Belleau, Director, 514-499-4001, Fax: 514-499-4065, E-mail: helene.belleau@ucs.inrs.ca. *Application contact:* Sean Otto, Registrar, 418-654-2518, Fax: 418-654-3858, E-mail: sean.otto@inrs.ca.
Website: http://www.ucs.inrs.ca

University at Albany, State University of New York, College of Arts and Sciences, Department of Sociology, Albany, NY 12222-0001. Offers demography (Certificate); sociology (MA, PhD); urban policy (Certificate). *Program availability:* Blended/hybrid learning. *Faculty:* 23 full-time (10 women), 11 part-time/adjunct (8 women). *Students:* 31 full-time (26 women), 52 part-time (38 women); includes 17 minority (6 Black or African American, non-Hispanic/Latino; 1 American Indian or Alaska Native, non-Hispanic/Latino; 5 Asian, non-Hispanic/Latino; 3 Hispanic/Latino; 2 Two or more races, non-Hispanic/Latino), 35 international. 77 applicants, 49% accepted, 16 enrolled. In 2019, 6 master's, 8 doctorates awarded. Terminal master's awarded for partial completion of doctoral program. *Degree requirements:* For master's, thesis; for doctorate, thesis/dissertation, 2 specialization exams, research tool. *Entrance requirements:* For master's, GRE General Test, transcripts of all schools attended, statement of background and goals, departmental questionnaire, resume, names and contact information for 3 recommenders; for doctorate, GRE General Test. Additional exam requirements/recommendations for international students: required—TOEFL (minimum score 550 paper-based). *Application deadline:* For fall admission, 1/15 for domestic students, 5/1 for international students; for spring admission, 11/15 for domestic students. Applications are processed on a rolling basis. Application fee: $75. Electronic applications accepted. *Expenses: Tuition, area resident:* Full-time $11,530; part-time $480 per credit hour. Tuition, nonresident: full-time $23,530; part-time $980 per credit hour. *International tuition:* $23,530 full-time. *Required fees:* $2185; $96 per credit hour. Part-time tuition and fees vary according to course load and program. *Financial support:* Fellowships, research assistantships, teaching assistantships, career-related internships or fieldwork, and Federal Work-Study available. Financial award application deadline: 3/15. *Unit head:* Glenn Deane, Chair, 518-442-4666, Fax: 518-442-4936, E-mail: gdeane@albany.edu. *Application contact:* Michael DeRensis, Director, Graduate Admissions, 518-442-3980, Fax: 518-442-3922, E-mail: graduate@albany.edu. Website: https://www.albany.edu/sociology/index.html

University of Alberta, Faculty of Graduate Studies and Research, Department of Sociology, Edmonton, AB T6G 2E1, Canada. Offers criminal justice (MA); demography (MA, PhD); sociology (MA, PhD). *Program availability:* Part-time. *Degree requirements:* For master's, thesis (for some programs); for doctorate, thesis/dissertation.

University of California, Berkeley, Graduate Division, College of Letters and Science, Department of Demography, Berkeley, CA 94720. Offers PhD. *Degree requirements:* For doctorate, thesis/dissertation, qualifying exam. *Entrance requirements:* For doctorate, GRE General Test, minimum GPA of 3.0, 3 letters of recommendation. Additional exam requirements/recommendations for international students: required—TOEFL (minimum score 570 paper-based; 90 iBT). Electronic applications accepted.

University of California, Berkeley, Graduate Division, College of Letters and Science, Group in Sociology and Demography, Berkeley, CA 94720. Offers MA, PhD. *Degree requirements:* For doctorate, thesis/dissertation, qualifying exam. *Entrance requirements:* For master's and doctorate, GRE General Test, minimum GPA of 3.0, 3 letters of recommendation. Electronic applications accepted.

University of California, Irvine, School of Social Sciences and School of Social Ecology, Program in Demographic and Social Analysis, Irvine, CA 92697. Offers MA. *Students:* 12 full-time (8 women), 1 part-time (0 women); includes 7 minority (4 Asian, non-Hispanic/Latino; 3 Hispanic/Latino), 2 international. Average age 27. 29 applicants, 83% accepted, 13 enrolled. In 2019, 14 master's awarded. *Entrance requirements:* For master's, GRE, minimum GPA of 3.0. Additional exam requirements/recommendations for international students: required—TOEFL (minimum score 550 paper-based). *Application deadline:* For fall admission, 1/15 priority date for domestic and international students. Application fee: $120 ($140 for international students). *Financial support:* Application deadline: 3/1. *Unit head:* Susan Brown, Graduate Director, 949-824-9382, Fax: 949-824-4717, E-mail: skbrown@uci.edu. *Application contact:* John Sommerhauser, Director of Graduate Affairs, 949-824-4074, E-mail: john.sommerhauser@uci.edu. Website: http://www.demography.uci.edu/

University of Colorado Denver, College of Liberal Arts and Sciences, Program in Health and Behavioral Sciences, Denver, CO 80217. Offers PhD. *Program availability:* Part-time, evening/weekend. *Degree requirements:* For doctorate, comprehensive exam, thesis/dissertation, minimum of 62 credit hours of course work. *Entrance requirements:* For doctorate, GRE (minimum scores in the top 30th percentile), master's or equivalent graduate degree; prior coursework or experience in social or behavioral sciences (minimum 15 semester hours), human biology or physiology (minimum six semester hours), and statistics and epidemiology (minimum three semester hours each); minimum undergraduate GPA of 3.25, graduate 3.5; three letters of recommendation; essay. Additional exam requirements/recommendations for

international students: required—TOEFL (minimum score 525 paper-based; 71 iBT). Electronic applications accepted. Tuition and fees vary according to course load, program and reciprocity agreements.

University of Guelph, Ontario Veterinary College and Office of Graduate and Postdoctoral Studies, Graduate Programs in Veterinary Sciences, Department of Population Medicine, Guelph, ON N1G 2W1, Canada. Offers epidemiology (M Sc, DV Sc, PhD); health management (DV Sc); population medicine and health management (M Sc); swine health management (M Sc); theriogenology (M Sc, DV Sc). *Degree requirements:* For master's, thesis; for doctorate, comprehensive exam, thesis/dissertation. *Entrance requirements:* Additional exam requirements/recommendations for international students: required—TOEFL.

University of Hawaii at Manoa, John A. Burns School of Medicine, Department of Public Health Sciences and Epidemiology, Global Health and Population Studies Program, Honolulu, HI 96822. Offers Graduate Certificate. *Program availability:* Part-time. *Entrance requirements:* For degree, GRE General Test. Additional exam requirements/recommendations for international students: required—TOEFL (minimum score 550 paper-based; 79 iBT), IELTS (minimum score 5).

University of Pennsylvania, School of Arts and Sciences, Graduate Group in Demography, Philadelphia, PA 19104. Offers AM, PhD. *Faculty:* 35 full-time (17 women), 10 part-time/adjunct (4 women). *Students:* 13 full-time (6 women); includes 3 minority (1 Black or African American, non-Hispanic/Latino; 1 Asian, non-Hispanic/Latino; 1 Hispanic/Latino), 6 international. Average age 30. 27 applicants, 19% accepted, 2 enrolled. In 2019, 2 doctorates awarded. Terminal master's awarded for partial completion of doctoral program. Application fee: $90. *Unit head:* Dr. Beth S. Wenger, Associate Dean for Graduate Studies, 215-898-7156, Fax: 215-573-8068, E-mail: grad-dean@sas.upenn.edu. *Application contact:* Arts and Sciences Graduate Admissions, 215-573-5816, Fax: 215-573-8068, E-mail: gdasadmis@sas.upenn.edu. Website: http://demog.pop.upenn.edu

University of Puerto Rico - Medical Sciences Campus, Graduate School of Public Health, Department of Social Sciences, Program in Demography, San Juan, PR 00936-5067. Offers MS. *Program availability:* Part-time. *Degree requirements:* For master's, thesis. *Entrance requirements:* For master's, GRE, previous course work in algebra and statistics.

The University of Texas at San Antonio, College of Public Policy, Department of Demography, San Antonio, TX 78207. Offers applied demography (PhD). *Program availability:* Part-time, evening/weekend. *Degree requirements:* For doctorate, comprehensive exam, thesis/dissertation, dissertation proposal defense. *Entrance requirements:* For doctorate, GRE, three letters of recommendation, statement of purpose, MA/MS. Additional exam requirements/recommendations for international students: required—TOEFL (minimum score 550 paper-based; 79 iBT), IELTS (minimum score 6.5). Electronic applications accepted.

The University of Texas Medical Branch, Graduate School of Biomedical Sciences, Program in Population Health Sciences, Galveston, TX 77555. Offers PhD.

University of Wisconsin–Madison, School of Medicine and Public Health, Population Health and Epidemiology Graduate Program, Madison, WI 53726. Offers epidemiology (MS, PhD); population health (MS, PhD), including epidemiology. *Program availability:* Part-time. Terminal master's awarded for partial completion of doctoral program. *Degree requirements:* For master's, thesis, thesis defense; for doctorate, comprehensive exam, thesis/dissertation, qualifying exam, preliminary exam, dissertation defense. *Entrance requirements:* For master's and doctorate, GRE taken within the last 5 years (MCAT or LSAT acceptable for those with doctoral degrees), minimum GPA of 3.0, quantitative preparation (calculus, statistics, or other) with minimum B average. Additional exam requirements/recommendations for international students: required—TOEFL (minimum score 580 paper-based; 92 iBT). Electronic applications accepted. *Expenses:* Contact institution.

Rural Sociology

Auburn University, Graduate School, Interdepartmental Programs, Graduate Programs in Sociology and Rural Sociology, Auburn, AL 36849. Offers MA, MS. *Program availability:* Part-time. *Faculty:* 25 full-time (17 women), 4 part-time/adjunct (2 women). *Students:* 7 full-time (5 women), 6 part-time (4 women); includes 1 minority (Hispanic/Latino), 2 international. Average age 31. 8 applicants, 63% accepted, 4 enrolled. In 2019, 10 master's awarded. *Degree requirements:* For master's, thesis, computer language (MS), foreign language (MA). *Entrance requirements:* For master's, GRE General Test. Additional exam requirements/recommendations for international students: required—TOEFL (minimum score 550 paper-based; 79 iBT). *Application deadline:* Applications are processed on a rolling basis. Application fee: $60 ($70 for international students). *Expenses: Tuition, area resident:* Full-time $9828; part-time $546 per credit hour. Tuition, state resident: full-time $9828; part-time $546 per credit hour. Tuition, nonresident: full-time $29,484; part-time $1638 per credit hour. *International tuition:* $29,744 full-time. Tuition and fees vary according to course load, program and reciprocity agreements. *Financial support:* In 2019–20, 18 research assistantships with partial tuition reimbursements (averaging $15,628 per year) were awarded; teaching assistantships also available. Financial award application deadline: 3/15; financial award applicants required to submit FAFSA. *Unit head:* Dr. Joshua Duke, Chair, 334-844-4800, E-mail: duke@auburn.edu. *Application contact:* Dr. George Flowers, Dean of the Graduate School, 334-844-4700. Website: https://agriculture.auburn.edu/academics/graduate-degrees/rural-sociology/

Cornell University, Graduate School, Graduate Fields of Agriculture and Life Sciences, Field of Development Sociology, Ithaca, NY 14853. Offers population and development (MS, PhD); rural and environmental sociology (MS, PhD); state, economy, and society (MS, PhD). *Degree requirements:* For doctorate, comprehensive exam, thesis/ dissertation. *Entrance requirements:* For master's and doctorate, GRE General Test, 3 letters of recommendation. Additional exam requirements/recommendations for international students: required—TOEFL (minimum score 550 paper-based; 77 iBT). Electronic applications accepted.

Iowa State University of Science and Technology, Department of Sociology, Ames, IA 50011. Offers rural sociology (MS, PhD); sociology (MS, PhD). *Degree requirements:* For master's, thesis; for doctorate, thesis/dissertation. *Entrance requirements:* For master's and doctorate, GRE General Test. Additional exam requirements/ recommendations for international students: required—TOEFL (minimum score 550 paper-based; 79 iBT), IELTS (minimum score 6.5). Electronic applications accepted.

Iowa State University of Science and Technology, Program in Rural Sociology, Ames, IA 50011. Offers MS, PhD. *Degree requirements:* For master's, thesis; for doctorate, thesis/dissertation. *Entrance requirements:* For master's, GRE General Test; for doctorate, GRE General Test, master's degree. Additional exam requirements/ recommendations for international students: required—TOEFL (minimum score 550 paper-based; 79 iBT), IELTS (minimum score 6.5). Electronic applications accepted.

The Ohio State University, Graduate School, College of Food, Agricultural, and Environmental Sciences, School of Environment and Natural Resources, Columbus, OH 43210. Offers ecological restoration (MS, PhD); ecosystem science (MS, PhD); environment and natural resources (MENR); environmental social sciences (MS, PhD); fisheries and wildlife science (MS, PhD); forest science (MS, PhD); rural sociology (MS, PhD); soil science (MS, PhD). *Entrance requirements:* For master's and doctorate, GRE. Additional exam requirements/recommendations for international students: required—TOEFL (minimum score 550 paper-based; 79 iBT), Michigan English Language Assessment Battery (minimum score 82); recommended—IELTS (minimum score 7). Electronic applications accepted.

Penn State University Park, Graduate School, College of Agricultural Sciences, Department of Agricultural Economics, Sociology, and Education, University Park, PA 16802. Offers agricultural and extension education (M Ed, MS, PhD, Certificate); applied youth, family and community education (M Ed); energy, environmental, and food economics (MS, PhD); rural sociology (MS, PhD).

University of Alberta, Faculty of Graduate Studies and Research, Department of Rural Economy, Edmonton, AB T6G 2E1, Canada. Offers agricultural economics (M Ag, M Sc, PhD); forest economics (M Ag, M Sc, PhD); rural sociology (M Ag, M Sc); MBA/M Ag. *Program availability:* Part-time. *Degree requirements:* For doctorate, thesis/dissertation. *Entrance requirements:* Additional exam requirements/recommendations for international students: required—TOEFL.

University of Missouri, Office of Research and Graduate Studies, College of Agriculture, Food and Natural Resources, Department of Rural Sociology, Columbia, MO 65211. Offers MS, PhD. *Program availability:* Part-time. *Entrance requirements:* For master's and doctorate, GRE General Test, minimum GPA of 3.0. Additional exam requirements/recommendations for international students: required—TOEFL.

University of Montana, Graduate School, College of Humanities and Sciences, Department of Sociology, Missoula, MT 59812. Offers criminology (MA); inequality and social justice (MA); rural and environmental change (MA); sociology (MA). *Entrance*

requirements: For master's, GRE General Test. Additional exam requirements/recommendations for international students: required—TOEFL.

University of Puerto Rico at Mayagüez, Graduate Studies, College of Agricultural Sciences, Department of Agricultural Economics and Rural Sociology, Mayagüez, PR 00681-9000. Offers MS. *Program availability:* Part-time. *Degree requirements:* For master's, comprehensive exam, thesis. *Entrance requirements:* For master's, bachelor's degree in agricultural economics or its equivalent. Electronic applications accepted.

University of Wisconsin–Madison, Graduate School, College of Letters and Science, Department of Sociology, Madison, WI 53706-1380. Offers rural sociology (MS); sociology (MS, PhD). *Program availability:* Part-time. Terminal master's awarded for partial completion of doctoral program. *Degree requirements:* For master's, thesis, oral exam; for doctorate, thesis/dissertation, preliminary and final oral exams, 4 seminars. *Entrance requirements:* For master's and doctorate, GRE General Test. Additional exam requirements/recommendations for international students: required—TOEFL. Electronic applications accepted.

Sociology

Acadia University, Faculty of Arts, Department of Sociology, Wolfville, NS B4P 2R6, Canada. Offers MA. *Entrance requirements:* For master's, honors degree, minimum GPA of 3.25. Additional exam requirements/recommendations for international students: required—TOEFL (minimum score 630 paper-based; 93 iBT), IELTS (minimum score 6.5).

American University, College of Arts and Sciences, Department of Sociology, Washington, DC 22016-8072. Offers public sociology (Certificate); social research (Certificate); sociology (MA). *Program availability:* Part-time, evening/weekend. *Degree requirements:* For master's, comprehensive exam, thesis or alternative. *Entrance requirements:* For master's, GRE; Please see website: https://www.american.edu/cas/psychology/, statement of purpose, transcripts, 2 letters of recommendation, resume; for Certificate, bachelor's degree, statement of purpose, transcripts, resume. Additional exam requirements/recommendations for international students: required—TOEFL (minimum score 600 paper-based; 100 iBT). *Expenses:* Contact institution.

Angelo State University, College of Graduate Studies and Research, Archer College of Health and Human Services, Department of Psychology and Sociology, San Angelo, TX 76909. Offers industrial-organizational psychology (MS). *Program availability:* Part-time, evening/weekend. *Degree requirements:* For master's, comprehensive exam, thesis optional. *Entrance requirements:* For master's, GRE General Test (for industrial and organizational psychology only), essay, letters of recommendation (for industrial and organizational psychology only). Additional exam requirements/recommendations for international students: required—TOEFL or IELTS. Electronic applications accepted.

Arizona State University at Tempe, College of Liberal Arts and Sciences, School of Social and Family Dynamics, Tempe, AZ 85287-3701. Offers family and human development (MS, PhD); infant-family practice (MAS); marriage and family therapy (MAS); sociology (MA, PhD). Terminal master's awarded for partial completion of doctoral program. *Degree requirements:* For master's, thesis or alternative, interactive Program of Study (iPOS) submitted before completing 50 percent of required credit hours; for doctorate, thesis/dissertation, interactive Program of Study (iPOS) submitted before completing 50 percent of required credit hours. *Entrance requirements:* For master's and doctorate, GRE, minimum GPA of 3.0 or equivalent in last 2 years of work leading to bachelor's degree. Additional exam requirements/recommendations for international students: required—TOEFL, IELTS, or PTE. Electronic applications accepted. *Expenses:* Contact institution.

Arkansas State University, Graduate School, College of Humanities and Social Sciences, Department of Criminology, Sociology, and Geography, State University, AR 72467. Offers criminal justice (MA); sociology (MA); sociology education (SCCT). *Program availability:* Part-time. *Degree requirements:* For master's, one foreign language, comprehensive exam, thesis or alternative; for SCCT, comprehensive exam. *Entrance requirements:* For master's, GRE General Test or MAT, appropriate bachelor's degree, letters of recommendation, official transcripts, immunization records; for SCCT, GRE General Test or MAT, interview, master's degree, official transcript, immunization records. Additional exam requirements/recommendations for international students: required—TOEFL (minimum score 550 paper-based; 79 iBT), IELTS (minimum score 6), PTE (minimum score 56). Electronic applications accepted.

Arkansas Tech University, College of Arts and Humanities, Russellville, AR 72801. Offers applied sociology (MS); English (M Ed, MA); history (MA); liberal arts (MLA); multi-media journalism (MA); psychology (MS); teaching English as a second language (MA). *Program availability:* Part-time, 100% online, blended/hybrid learning. *Students:* 32 full-time (19 women), 102 part-time (70 women); includes 22 minority (5 Black or African American, non-Hispanic/Latino; 1 American Indian or Alaska Native, non-Hispanic/Latino; 1 Asian, non-Hispanic/Latino; 12 Hispanic/Latino; 3 Two or more races, non-Hispanic/Latino), 9 international. Average age 32. In 2019, 89 master's awarded. *Degree requirements:* For master's, comprehensive exam (for some programs), thesis (for some programs), project. *Entrance requirements:* Additional exam requirements/recommendations for international students: required—TOEFL (minimum score 550 paper-based; 79 iBT), IELTS (minimum score 6.5), PTE (minimum score 58). *Application deadline:* For fall admission, 3/1 priority date for domestic students, 5/1 priority date for international students; for spring admission, 10/1 priority date for domestic and international students. Applications are processed on a rolling basis. Application fee: $40 ($90 for international students). Electronic applications accepted. *Expenses: Tuition, area resident:* Full-time $7008; part-time $292 per credit hour. Tuition, state resident: full-time $7008; part-time $292 per credit hour. Tuition, nonresident: full-time $14,016; part-time $584 per credit hour. *International tuition:* $14,016 full-time. *Required fees:* $343 per term. *Financial support:* In 2019–20, research assistantships with full and partial tuition reimbursements (averaging $4,800 per year), teaching assistantships with full and partial tuition reimbursements (averaging $4,800 per year) were awarded; career-related internships or fieldwork, Federal Work-Study, scholarships/grants, health care benefits, and unspecified assistantships also available. Support available to part-time students. Financial award application deadline: 4/15; financial award applicants required to submit FAFSA. *Unit head:* Dr. Jeffrey Cass, Dean of College of Arts and Humanities, 479-968-0274, Fax: 479-964-0812, E-mail: jcass@atu.edu. *Application contact:* Dr. Richard Schoephoerster, Dean of Graduate College and Research, 479-968-0398, Fax: 479-964-0542, E-mail: gradcollege@atu.edu.
Website: http://www.atu.edu/humanities/

Auburn University, Graduate School, Interdepartmental Programs, Graduate Programs in Sociology and Rural Sociology, Auburn, AL 36849. Offers MA, MS. *Program availability:* Part-time. *Faculty:* 25 full-time (17 women), 4 part-time/adjunct (2 women). *Students:* 7 full-time (5 women), 6 part-time (4 women); includes 1 minority (Hispanic/Latino), 2 international. Average age 31. 8 applicants, 63% accepted, 4 enrolled. In 2019, 10 master's awarded. *Degree requirements:* For master's, thesis, computer language (MS), foreign language (MA). *Entrance requirements:* For master's, GRE General Test. Additional exam requirements/recommendations for international students: required—TOEFL (minimum score 550 paper-based; 79 iBT). *Application deadline:* Applications are processed on a rolling basis. Application fee: $60 ($70 for international students). *Expenses: Tuition, area resident:* Full-time $9828; part-time $546 per credit hour. Tuition, state resident: full-time $9828; part-time $546 per credit hour. Tuition, nonresident: full-time $29,484; part-time $1638 per credit hour. *International tuition:* $29,744 full-time. Tuition and fees vary according to course load, program and reciprocity agreements. *Financial support:* In 2019–20, 18 research assistantships with partial tuition reimbursements (averaging $15,628 per year) were awarded; teaching assistantships also available. Financial award application deadline: 3/15; financial award applicants required to submit FAFSA. *Unit head:* Dr. Joshua Duke, Chair, 334-844-4800, E-mail: duke@auburn.edu. *Application contact:* Dr. George Flowers, Dean of the Graduate School, 334-844-4700.
Website: https://agriculture.auburn.edu/academics/graduate-degrees/rural-sociology/

Ball State University, Graduate School, College of Sciences and Humanities, Department of Sociology, Muncie, IN 47306. Offers MA. *Program availability:* Part-time. *Entrance requirements:* For master's, GRE General Test, minimum baccalaureate GPA of 2.75 or 3.0 in latter half of baccalaureate, three letters of recommendation. Additional exam requirements/recommendations for international students: required—TOEFL (minimum score 550 paper-based; 79 iBT), IELTS (minimum score 6.5). Electronic applications accepted. *Expenses: Tuition, area resident:* Full-time $7506; part-time $417 per credit hour. Tuition, nonresident: full-time $20,610; part-time $1145 per credit hour. *Required fees:* $2126. Tuition and fees vary according to course load, campus/location and program.

Baylor University, Graduate School, College of Arts and Sciences, Department of Sociology, Waco, TX 76798. Offers community analytics (PhD); health and society (PhD); sociology (MA); sociology of religion (PhD). *Faculty:* 12 full-time (3 women). *Students:* 23 full-time (12 women); includes 3 minority (1 Asian, non-Hispanic/Latino; 2 Hispanic/Latino), 5 international. In 2019, 7 master's, 3 doctorates awarded. *Degree requirements:* For master's, thesis; for doctorate, comprehensive exam, thesis/dissertation. *Entrance requirements:* For doctorate, GRE, application, personal statement, CV, 3 letters of recommendation, official transcripts from all universities attended. Additional exam requirements/recommendations for international students: required—TOEFL (minimum score 550 paper-based; 80 iBT), IELTS (minimum score 6.5), PTE (minimum score 58), GRE. *Application deadline:* For fall admission, 1/15 for domestic and international students. Application fee: $50. Electronic applications accepted. *Financial support:* In 2019–20, 23 students received support, including 23 teaching assistantships (averaging $22,000 per year); research assistantships, institutionally sponsored loans, scholarships/grants, health care benefits, tuition waivers (full), and unspecified assistantships also available. Financial award application deadline: 1/15. *Unit head:* Carson Mencken, Professor of Sociology and Chair of Sociology, 254-710-4863, Fax: 254-710-1175, E-mail: Carson_Mencken@Baylor.edu. *Application contact:* Kevin D. Dougherty, Associate Professor of Sociology and Graduate Program Director of Sociology, 254-710-6232, Fax: 254-710-1175, E-mail: Kevin_Dougherty@Baylor.edu.
Website: http://www.baylor.edu/sociology/

Binghamton University, State University of New York, Graduate School, Harpur College of Arts and Sciences, Department of Sociology, Binghamton, NY 13902-6000. Offers MA, PhD. *Program availability:* Part-time. Terminal master's awarded for partial completion of doctoral program. *Degree requirements:* For doctorate, comprehensive exam, thesis/dissertation. *Entrance requirements:* For master's and doctorate, GRE General Test, writing sample. Additional exam requirements/recommendations for international students: required—TOEFL (minimum score 550 paper-based; 80 iBT). Electronic applications accepted.

Boston College, Morrissey Graduate School of Arts and Sciences, Department of Sociology, Chestnut Hill, MA 02467-3800. Offers MA, PhD, MBA/MA, MBA/PhD. Terminal master's awarded for partial completion of doctoral program. *Degree requirements:* For master's, thesis optional; for doctorate, thesis/dissertation. *Entrance requirements:* For master's and doctorate, GRE General Test. Additional exam requirements/recommendations for international students: required—TOEFL (minimum score 600 paper-based; 100 iBT), IELTS (minimum score 8). Electronic applications accepted.

Boston University, Graduate School of Arts and Sciences, Department of Sociology, Boston, MA 02215. Offers MA, PhD. *Students:* 33 full-time (25 women); includes 5 minority (2 Black or African American, non-Hispanic/Latino; 3 Hispanic/Latino), 13 international. Average age 28. 176 applicants, 11% accepted, 5 enrolled. In 2019, 2 master's, 5 doctorates awarded. Terminal master's awarded for partial completion of doctoral program. *Degree requirements:* For master's, thesis; for doctorate, comprehensive exam, thesis/dissertation. *Entrance requirements:* For master's and doctorate, GRE General Test, 3 letters of recommendation, transcripts, personal statement, academic writing sample. Additional exam requirements/recommendations for international students: required—TOEFL (minimum score 550 paper-based; 84 iBT). *Application deadline:* For fall admission, 1/15 for domestic and international students. Application fee: $95. Electronic applications accepted. *Financial support:* In 2019–20, 32 students received support, including 14 fellowships with full tuition reimbursements available (averaging $23,340 per year), 2 research assistantships with full tuition reimbursements available (averaging $23,340 per year), 11 teaching assistantships with full tuition reimbursements available (averaging $23,340 per year); career-related internships or fieldwork, Federal Work-Study, scholarships/grants, and health care benefits also available. Financial award application deadline: 1/15. *Unit head:* Deborah Carr, Chair, 617-353-3308, Fax: 617-353-4837, E-mail: carrds@bu.edu. *Application contact:* Ashley Mears, Director of Graduate Studies, 617-358-0637, Fax: 617-353-4837, E-mail: mears@bu.edu.
Website: http://www.bu.edu/sociology/

Bowling Green State University, Graduate College, College of Arts and Sciences, Department of Sociology, Bowling Green, OH 43403. Offers demography and population studies (MA); social psychology (MA); sociology (PhD). *Program availability:*

Part-time. *Degree requirements:* For master's, thesis or alternative; for doctorate, comprehensive exam, thesis/dissertation. *Entrance requirements:* For master's and doctorate, GRE General Test. Additional exam requirements/recommendations for international students: required—TOEFL. Electronic applications accepted.

Brandeis University, Graduate School of Arts and Sciences, Department of Sociology, Waltham, MA 02454-9110. Offers social policy and sociology (PhD); sociology (PhD); sociology/women's, gender, and sexuality studies (MA). *Program availability:* Part-time. *Faculty:* 8 full-time (5 women), 1 (woman) part-time/adjunct. *Students:* 20 full-time (17 women); includes 5 minority (1 Black or African American, non-Hispanic/Latino; 3 Asian, non-Hispanic/Latino; 1 Hispanic/Latino), 2 international. Average age 29. 76 applicants, 17% accepted, 8 enrolled. In 2019, 2 master's, 4 doctorates awarded. Terminal master's awarded for partial completion of doctoral program. *Degree requirements:* For master's, thesis or alternative; for doctorate, comprehensive exam, thesis/dissertation. *Entrance requirements:* For master's and doctorate, GRE General, transcripts, letters of recommendation, resume, writing sample, and statement of purpose. Additional exam requirements/recommendations for international students: required—TOEFL, IELTS, PTE. *Application deadline:* For fall admission, 12/15 for domestic and international students. Application fee: $75. Electronic applications accepted. *Financial support:* In 2019–20, 9 fellowships with full tuition reimbursements (averaging $25,000 per year), 13 teaching assistantships (averaging $3,550 per year) were awarded; scholarships/grants and health care benefits also available. *Unit head:* Dr. Karen Hansen, Director of Graduate Studies, 781-736-2651, E-mail: khansen@brandeis.edu. *Application contact:* Lauren Jordahl, Administrator, 781-736-2644, E-mail: ljordahl@brandeis.edu. Website: http://www.brandeis.edu/gsas/programs/sociology.html

Brigham Young University, Graduate Studies, College of Family, Home, and Social Sciences, Department of Sociology, Provo, UT 84602. Offers MS. *Faculty:* 19 full-time (5 women). *Students:* 13 full-time (8 women); includes 3 minority (1 Black or African American, non-Hispanic/Latino; 2 Hispanic/Latino). Average age 26. 24 applicants, 58% accepted, 7 enrolled. In 2019, 2 master's awarded. Terminal master's awarded for partial completion of doctoral program. *Degree requirements:* For master's, thesis. *Entrance requirements:* For master's, GRE General Test, minimum GPA of 3.0 in last 60 hours, writing sample, bachelor's degree in sociology or related field, 3 letters of recommendation, Honor Code commitment. Additional exam requirements/recommendations for international students: required—TOEFL (minimum score 580 paper-based; 85 iBT), IELTS (minimum score 7). *Application deadline:* For fall admission, 1/15 for domestic and international students. Application fee: $50. Electronic applications accepted. *Financial support:* In 2019–20, 13 students received support, including 13 research assistantships (averaging $18,400 per year); institutionally sponsored loans and unspecified assistantships also available. Financial award application deadline: 4/15. *Unit head:* Dr. Richard B. Miller, Department Chair, 801-422-2860, Fax: 801-422-0625, E-mail: rick_miller@byu.edu. *Application contact:* Dr. Richard B. Miller, Department Chair, 801-422-2860, Fax: 801-422-0625, E-mail: rick_miller@byu.edu. Website: http://sociology.byu.edu/

Brock University, Faculty of Graduate Studies, Faculty of Social Sciences, Program in Critical Sociology, St. Catharines, ON L2S 3A1, Canada. Offers MA.

Brooklyn College of the City University of New York, School of Humanities and Social Sciences, Department of Sociology, Brooklyn, NY 11210-2889. Offers MA, PhD. *Program availability:* Part-time, evening/weekend. *Degree requirements:* For master's, comprehensive exam or research essay. *Entrance requirements:* For master's, 12 upper-level credits in sociology, 2 letters of recommendation, essay. Additional exam requirements/recommendations for international students: required—TOEFL (minimum score 500 paper-based; 61 iBT). Electronic applications accepted.

Brown University, Graduate School, Department of Sociology, Providence, RI 02912. Offers MA, PhD. *Degree requirements:* For master's, thesis; for doctorate, thesis/dissertation, oral exam. *Entrance requirements:* For master's and doctorate, GRE General Test.

California State University, Dominguez Hills, College of Natural and Behavioral Sciences, Program in Sociology, Carson, CA 90747-0001. Offers social research (MA); sociology (MA). *Program availability:* Part-time, evening/weekend. *Degree requirements:* For master's, comprehensive exam, thesis. *Entrance requirements:* For master's, minimum GPA of 2.85.

California State University, Fullerton, Graduate Studies, College of Humanities and Social Sciences, Department of Sociology, Fullerton, CA 92831-3599. Offers MA. *Program availability:* Part-time. *Entrance requirements:* For master's, minimum GPA of 3.0 in sociology, 2.5 in last 60 units.

California State University, Los Angeles, Graduate Studies, College of Natural and Social Sciences, Department of Sociology, Los Angeles, CA 90032-8530. Offers MA. *Program availability:* Part-time, evening/weekend. *Degree requirements:* For master's, comprehensive exam or thesis. *Entrance requirements:* For master's, minimum GPA of 2.5 in last 90 units of course work. Additional exam requirements/recommendations for international students: required—TOEFL (minimum score 500 paper-based). Electronic applications accepted. *Expenses:* Tuition, area resident: Full-time $7176; part-time $4164 per year. Tuition, state resident: full-time $7176; part-time $4164 per year. Tuition, nonresident: full-time $14,304; part-time $8916 per year. International tuition: $14,304 full-time. *Required fees:* $1037.76; $1037.76 per unit. Tuition and fees vary according to degree level and program.

California State University, Northridge, Graduate Studies, College of Social and Behavioral Sciences, Department of Sociology, Northridge, CA 91330. Offers MA. *Accreditation:* CSWE. *Program availability:* Part-time, evening/weekend. *Degree requirements:* For master's, thesis or alternative. *Entrance requirements:* For master's, GRE General Test. Additional exam requirements/recommendations for international students: required—TOEFL.

California State University, Sacramento, College of Social Sciences and Interdisciplinary Studies, Department of Sociology, Sacramento, CA 95819. Offers MA. *Program availability:* Part-time. *Degree requirements:* For master's, thesis or project; writing proficiency exam. *Entrance requirements:* For master's, minimum GPA of 3.0 during previous 2 years; completion of 18 undergraduate units in sociology. Additional exam requirements/recommendations for international students: required—TOEFL (minimum score 550 paper-based; 80 iBT); recommended—IELTS, TSE. Electronic applications accepted. *Expenses:* Contact institution.

California State University, San Marcos, College of Humanities, Arts, Behavioral and Social Sciences, Program in Sociological Practice, San Marcos, CA 92096-0001. Offers MA. *Program availability:* Part-time, evening/weekend. *Entrance requirements:* For master's, minimum GPA of 3.0, statement of purpose, writing sample, official transcripts, three letters of recommendation. *Application deadline:* For fall admission, 2/15 for domestic students. Applications are processed on a rolling basis. Application fee: $55. Electronic applications accepted. *Expenses:* Tuition, area resident: Full-time $7176. Tuition, state resident: full-time $7176. Tuition, nonresident: full-time $18,640. International tuition: $18,640 full-time. *Required fees:* $1960. *Financial support:* Fellowships, research assistantships, teaching assistantships, and tuition waivers

available. *Unit head:* Dr. Richelle Swan, Graduate Coordinator, 760-750-4633, E-mail: rswan@csusm.edu. *Application contact:* Dr. Charles De Leone, Interim Dean of Office of Graduate Studies and Research, 760-750-8045, Fax: 760-750-8045, E-mail: apply@csusm.edu. Website: https://www.csusm.edu/sociology/graduateprogramprospective/index.html

Carleton University, Faculty of Graduate Studies, Faculty of Arts and Social Sciences, Department of Sociology and Anthropology, Program in Sociology, Ottawa, ON K1S 5B6, Canada. Offers MA, PhD. *Degree requirements:* For master's, thesis optional; for doctorate, one foreign language, comprehensive exam, thesis/dissertation. *Entrance requirements:* For master's, honors degree; for doctorate, master's degree. Additional exam requirements/recommendations for international students: required—TOEFL.

Case Western Reserve University, School of Graduate Studies, Department of Sociology, Cleveland, OH 44106. Offers MA, PhD. *Faculty:* 10 full-time (6 women), 1 part-time/adjunct (0 women). *Students:* 32 full-time (24 women), 1 (woman) part-time; includes 8 minority (5 Black or African American, non-Hispanic/Latino; 1 Hispanic/Latino; 2 Two or more races, non-Hispanic/Latino), 10 international. Average age 34. 15 applicants, 40% accepted, 3 enrolled. In 2019, 2 master's, 1 doctorate awarded. Terminal master's awarded for partial completion of doctoral program. *Degree requirements:* For master's, comprehensive exam; for doctorate, comprehensive exam, thesis/dissertation. *Entrance requirements:* For master's and doctorate, GRE, curriculum vitae, writing sample, letter of intent, three letters of recommendation. Additional exam requirements/recommendations for international students: required—TOEFL (minimum score 577 paper-based; 90 iBT); recommended—IELTS (minimum score 7). *Application deadline:* For fall admission, 2/1 priority date for domestic students. Applications are processed on a rolling basis. Application fee: $50. Electronic applications accepted. *Financial support:* Research assistantships, health care benefits, tuition waivers (full and partial), and student employment available. Financial award application deadline: 2/1; financial award applicants required to submit FAFSA. *Unit head:* Dr. Dale Dannefer, Professor and Chair, Department of Sociology, 216-368-2703, Fax: 216-368-2676, E-mail: dale.dannefer@case.edu. *Application contact:* Michelle Rizzuto, Department Administrator, 216-368-2214, Fax: 216-368-2676, E-mail: michelle.rizzuto@case.edu. Website: http://sociology.case.edu/

The Catholic University of America, School of Arts and Sciences, Department of Sociology, Washington, DC 20064. Offers crime and justice studies (MA); global and comparative sociology (MA); public policy (MA). *Program availability:* Part-time. *Faculty:* 3 full-time (2 women), 2 part-time/adjunct (both women). *Students:* 1 (woman) full-time. Average age 23. 1 applicant, 100% accepted, 1 enrolled. In 2019, 1 master's awarded. *Degree requirements:* For master's, comprehensive exam, thesis or alternative, two seminar papers. *Entrance requirements:* For master's, GRE General Test, statement of purpose, official copies of academic transcripts, three letters of recommendation. Additional exam requirements/recommendations for international students: required—TOEFL (minimum score 550 paper-based; 80 iBT). *Application deadline:* For fall admission, 7/15 priority date for domestic students, 7/1 for international students; for spring admission, 11/15 priority date for domestic students, 11/1 for international students. Applications are processed on a rolling basis. Application fee: $55. Electronic applications accepted. *Financial support:* Fellowships, research assistantships, teaching assistantships, Federal Work-Study, scholarships/grants, tuition waivers (full and partial), and unspecified assistantships available. Financial award application deadline: 2/1; financial award applicants required to submit FAFSA. *Unit head:* Dr. Brandon Vaidyanathan, Chair, 202-319-5941, Fax: 202-319-4980, E-mail: brandonv@cua.edu. *Application contact:* Dr. Steven Brown, Director of Graduate Admissions, 202-319-5057, Fax: 202-319-6533, E-mail: cua-admissions@cua.edu. Website: http://sociology.cua.edu/

Central European University, Department of Sociology and Social Anthropology, Budapest, Hungary. Offers MA, PhD. *Degree requirements:* For master's, one foreign language, thesis; for doctorate, one foreign language, comprehensive exam, thesis/dissertation. *Entrance requirements:* For master's and doctorate, interview. Additional exam requirements/recommendations for international students: required—TOEFL (minimum score 570 paper-based); recommended—IELTS (minimum score 6.5). Electronic applications accepted.

City College of the City University of New York, Graduate School, Colin Powell School for Civic and Global Leadership, Department of Sociology, New York, NY 10031-9198. Offers MA. *Degree requirements:* For master's, one foreign language, comprehensive exam, thesis. *Entrance requirements:* Additional exam requirements/recommendations for international students: required—TOEFL (minimum score 500 paper-based; 61 iBT). Electronic applications accepted.

Clark Atlanta University, School of Arts and Sciences, Department of Sociology and Criminal Justice, Atlanta, GA 30314. Offers MA. *Program availability:* Part-time. *Degree requirements:* For master's, one foreign language, comprehensive exam, thesis. *Entrance requirements:* For master's, GRE General Test, minimum GPA of 2.5. Additional exam requirements/recommendations for international students: required—TOEFL (minimum score 500 paper-based; 61 iBT). Electronic applications accepted.

Clemson University, Graduate School, College of Behavioral, Social and Health Sciences, Department of Sociology, Anthropology and Criminal Justice, Clemson, SC 29634. Offers applied sociology (MS). *Program availability:* Part-time. *Faculty:* 21 full-time (11 women). *Students:* 7 full-time (3 women); includes 1 minority (Black or African American, non-Hispanic/Latino), 1 international. Average age 23. 12 applicants, 75% accepted. In 2019, 4 master's awarded. *Degree requirements:* For master's, thesis optional. *Entrance requirements:* For master's, GRE General Test, unofficial transcripts, letters of recommendation. Additional exam requirements/recommendations for international students: required—TOEFL (minimum score 80 paper-based; 80 iBT); recommended—IELTS (minimum score 6.5), TSE (minimum score 54). *Application deadline:* For fall admission, 4/15 priority date for international students; for spring admission, 10/15 priority date for international students. Applications are processed on a rolling basis. Application fee: $80 ($90 for international students). Electronic applications accepted. *Expenses:* Full-Time Student per Semester: Tuition: $4600 (in-state), $9525 (out-of-state), Fees: $598; Graduate Assistant Per Semester: $1144; Part-Time Student Per Credit Hour: $556 (in-state), $1106 (out-of-state), Fees: $617; other fees apply depending on program, credit hours, campus & residency. *Financial support:* In 2019–20, 7 teaching assistantships with full and partial tuition reimbursements (averaging $11,000 per year) were awarded; career-related internships or fieldwork also available. *Unit head:* Dr. Catherine Weisensee, Department Chair, 864-656-3238, E-mail: kweisen@clemson.edu. *Application contact:* Dr. Bryan Miller, Graduate Program Coordinator, 864-656-3818, E-mail: BLM2@clemson.edu. Website: http://www.clemson.edu/cbshs/departments/sociology/

Colorado State University, College of Liberal Arts, Department of Sociology, Fort Collins, CO 80523-1784. Offers MA, PhD. Terminal master's awarded for partial completion of doctoral program. *Degree requirements:* For master's, thesis (for some programs), practicum, professional paper; for doctorate, comprehensive exam, thesis/dissertation. *Entrance requirements:* For master's, GRE General Test, minimum GPA of 3.0, BA coursework in sociology, three letters of recommendation, official transcripts, statement of purpose; for doctorate, GRE General Test, minimum GPA of 3.0, BA and MA coursework in sociology, three letters of recommendation, official transcripts, statement of purpose. Additional exam requirements/recommendations for international students: required—TOEFL (minimum score 550 paper-based; 80 iBT), IELTS (minimum score 6.5). Electronic applications accepted. *Expenses:* Tuition, state resident: full-time $10,520; part-time $5844 per credit hour. Tuition, nonresident: full-time $25,791; part-time $14,328 per credit hour. *International tuition:* $25,791 full-time. *Required fees:* $2512.80. Part-time tuition and fees vary according to course level, course load, degree level, program and student level.

Columbia University, Graduate School of Arts and Sciences, New York, NY 10027. Offers African-American studies (MA); American studies (MA); anthropology (MA, PhD); art history and archaeology (MA, PhD); astronomy (PhD); biological sciences (PhD); biotechnology (MA); chemical physics (PhD); chemistry (PhD); classical studies (MA, PhD); classics (MA, PhD); climate and society (MA); conservation biology (MA); earth and environmental sciences (PhD); East Asia: regional studies (MA); East Asian languages and cultures (MA, PhD); ecology, evolution and environmental biology (MA), including conservation biology; ecology, evolution, and environmental biology (PhD), including ecology and evolutionary biology, evolutionary primatology; economics (MA, PhD); English and comparative literature (MA, PhD); French and Romance philology (MA, PhD); Germanic languages (MA, PhD); global French studies (MA); global thought (MA); Hispanic cultural studies (MA); history (PhD); history and literature (MA); human rights studies (MA); Islamic studies (MA); Italian (MA, PhD); Japanese pedagogy (MA); Jewish studies (MA); Latin America and the Caribbean: regional studies (MA); Latin American and Iberian cultures (PhD); mathematics (MA, PhD), including finance (MA); medieval and Renaissance studies (MA); Middle Eastern, South Asian, and African studies (MA, PhD); modern art: critical and curatorial studies (MA); modern European studies (MA); museum anthropology (MA); music (DMA, PhD); oral history (MA); philosophical foundations of physics (MA); philosophy (MA, PhD); physics (PhD); political science (MA, PhD); psychology (PhD); quantitative methods in the social sciences (MA); religion (MA, PhD); Russia, Eurasia and East Europe: regional studies (MA); Russian translation (MA); Slavic cultures (MA); Slavic languages (MA, PhD); sociology (MA, PhD); South Asian studies (MA); statistics (MA, PhD); theatre (PhD). *Program availability:* Part-time. *Students:* 3,506 full-time (1,844 women), 208 part-time (121 women); includes 864 minority (110 Black or African American, non-Hispanic/Latino; 5 American Indian or Alaska Native, non-Hispanic/Latino; 416 Asian, non-Hispanic/Latino; 147 Hispanic/Latino; 6 Native Hawaiian or other Pacific Islander, non-Hispanic/Latino; 180 Two or more races, non-Hispanic/Latino), 2,065 international. 14,545 applicants, 25% accepted, 1,429 enrolled. In 2019, 1,262 master's, 363 doctorates awarded. Terminal master's awarded for partial completion of doctoral program. *Degree requirements:* For master's, variable foreign language requirement, comprehensive exam (for some programs), thesis (for some programs); for doctorate, variable foreign language requirement, comprehensive exam (for some programs), thesis/dissertation. *Entrance requirements:* For master's and doctorate, GRE General Test, GRE Subject Test (for some programs). Additional exam requirements/recommendations for international students: required—TOEFL (minimum score 600 paper-based; 100 iBT), IELTS (minimum score 7.5). Application fee: $115. Electronic applications accepted. *Expenses: Tuition:* Full-time $47,600; part-time $1880 per credit. One-time fee: $105. *Financial support:* Fellowships, research assistantships, teaching assistantships, career-related internships or fieldwork, Federal Work-Study, institutionally sponsored loans, scholarships/grants, traineeships, health care benefits, tuition waivers, and unspecified assistantships available. Support available to part-time students. Financial award application deadline: 12/15. *Unit head:* Dr. Carlos J. Alonso, Dean of the Graduate School of Arts and Sciences and Vice President for Graduate Education, 212-854-2861, E-mail: gsas-dean@columbia.edu. *Application contact:* GSAS Office of Admissions, 212-854-6729, E-mail: gsas-admissions@columbia.edu.
Website: http://gsas.columbia.edu/

Concordia University, School of Graduate Studies, Faculty of Arts and Science, Department of Sociology and Anthropology, Montréal, QC H3G 1M8, Canada. Offers social and cultural analysis (PhD); social and cultural anthropology (MA); sociology (MA). *Degree requirements:* For master's, comprehensive exam or thesis. *Entrance requirements:* For master's, honors degree in sociology or equivalent.

Cornell University, Graduate School, Graduate Fields of Agriculture and Life Sciences, Field of Development Sociology, Ithaca, NY 14853. Offers population and development (MS, PhD); rural and environmental sociology (MS, PhD); state, economy, and society (MS, PhD). *Degree requirements:* For doctorate, comprehensive exam, thesis/dissertation. *Entrance requirements:* For master's and doctorate, GRE General Test, 3 letters of recommendation. Additional exam requirements/recommendations for international students: required—TOEFL (minimum score 550 paper-based; 77 iBT). Electronic applications accepted.

Cornell University, Graduate School, Graduate Fields of Arts and Sciences, Field of Sociology, Ithaca, NY 14853. Offers economy and society (MA, PhD); gender and life course (MA, PhD); methodology (MA, PhD); organizations (MA, PhD); policy analysis (MA, PhD); political sociology/social movements (MA, PhD); racial and ethnic relations (MA, PhD); social networks (MA, PhD); social psychology (MA, PhD); social stratification (MA, PhD). Terminal master's awarded for partial completion of doctoral program. *Degree requirements:* For master's, thesis; for doctorate, thesis/dissertation, 1 year of teaching experience. *Entrance requirements:* For master's and doctorate, GRE General Test, 2 letters of recommendation, writing sample. Additional exam requirements/recommendations for international students: required—TOEFL (minimum score 550 paper-based; 77 iBT). Electronic applications accepted.

Dalhousie University, Faculty of Arts and Social Sciences, Department of Sociology and Social Anthropology, Halifax, NS B3H 4R2, Canada. Offers social anthropology (MA, PhD); sociology (MA, PhD). *Entrance requirements:* Additional exam requirements/recommendations for international students: required—TOEFL, IELTS, CANTEST, CAEL, or Michigan English Language Assessment Battery. Electronic applications accepted.

DePaul University, College of Liberal Arts and Social Sciences, Chicago, IL 60614. Offers Arabic (MA); Chinese (MA); critical ethnic studies (MA); English (MA); French (MA); German (MA); history (MA); interdisciplinary studies (MA, MS); international public service (MS); international studies (MA); Italian (MA); Japanese (MA); liberal studies (MA); nonprofit management (MNM); public administration (MPA); public health (MPH); public policy (MPP); public service management (MS); refugee and forced migration studies (MS); social work (MSW); sociology (MA); Spanish (MA); sustainable urban development (MA); women's and gender studies (MA); writing and publishing (MA); writing, rhetoric and discourse (MA); MA/PhD. *Accreditation:* CEPH. *Program availability:* Part-time, evening/weekend, online learning. Terminal master's awarded for partial completion of doctoral program. *Degree requirements:* For master's, variable foreign language requirement, comprehensive exam (for some programs), thesis (for some programs). Electronic applications accepted.

Duke University, Graduate School, Department of Sociology, Durham, NC 27708. Offers AM, PhD. Terminal master's awarded for partial completion of doctoral program. *Degree requirements:* For doctorate, thesis/dissertation. *Entrance requirements:* For master's and doctorate, GRE General Test. Additional exam requirements/recommendations for international students: required—TOEFL (minimum score 577 paper-based; 90 iBT) or IELTS (minimum score 7). Electronic applications accepted.

East Carolina University, Graduate School, Thomas Harriot College of Arts and Sciences, Department of Sociology, Greenville, NC 27858-4353. Offers MA. *Program availability:* Part-time, evening/weekend. *Application deadline:* For fall admission, 6/15 priority date for domestic and international students; for spring admission, 11/15 priority date for domestic and international students. *Expenses: Tuition, area resident:* Full-time $4749; part-time $185 per credit hour. Tuition, state resident: full-time $4749; part-time $185 per credit hour. Tuition, nonresident: full-time $17,898; part-time $864 per credit hour. *International tuition:* $17,898 full-time. *Required fees:* $2787. *Financial support:* Application deadline: 3/1. *Unit head:* Dr. Susan Pearce, Interim Chair, 252-328-2544, E-mail: pearces@ecu.edu. *Application contact:* Graduate School Admissions, 252-328-6012, Fax: 252-328-6071, E-mail: gradschool@ecu.edu.
Website: http://www.ecu.edu/soci/

Eastern Michigan University, Graduate School, College of Arts and Sciences, Department of Sociology, Anthropology and Criminology, Programs in Sociology, Ypsilanti, MI 48197. Offers sociology (MA); sociology - applied research specialty (MA). *Students:* 4 full-time (3 women), 8 part-time (5 women); includes 4 minority (2 Black or African American, non-Hispanic/Latino; 1 Hispanic/Latino; 1 Two or more races, non-Hispanic/Latino), 1 international. Average age 30. 8 applicants, 50% accepted, 3 enrolled. In 2019, 6 master's awarded. Application fee: $45. *Application contact:* Dr. Solage Simoes, Graduate Coordinator, 734-487-0012, Fax: 734-487-9666, E-mail: ssimoes@emich.edu.
Website: http://www.emich.edu/sac/

East Tennessee State University, College of Graduate and Continuing Studies, College of Arts and Sciences, Department of Sociology and Anthropology, Johnson City, TN 37614-1701. Offers applied sociology (MA); general sociology (MA). *Program availability:* Part-time, evening/weekend. *Degree requirements:* For master's, comprehensive exam, internship or thesis. *Entrance requirements:* For master's, GRE General Test, minimum GPA of 3.0 in sociology major, three letters of recommendation. Additional exam requirements/recommendations for international students: required—TOEFL (minimum score 550 paper-based; 79 iBT). Electronic applications accepted.

Emory University, Laney Graduate School, Department of Sociology, Atlanta, GA 30322-1100. Offers PhD. Terminal master's awarded for partial completion of doctoral program. *Degree requirements:* For doctorate, comprehensive exam, thesis/dissertation, 2 preliminary exams, research paper, paper presentation. *Entrance requirements:* For doctorate, GRE General Test, minimum GPA of 3.0. Additional exam requirements/recommendations for international students: required—TOEFL. Electronic applications accepted.

Fayetteville State University, Graduate School, Program in Sociology, Fayetteville, NC 28301. Offers MA. *Program availability:* Part-time, evening/weekend, online learning. *Faculty:* 3 full-time (1 woman). *Students:* 15 full-time (14 women), 25 part-time (19 women); includes 23 minority (22 Black or African American, non-Hispanic/Latino; 1 Two or more races, non-Hispanic/Latino). Average age 37. 33 applicants, 82% accepted, 22 enrolled. In 2019, 7 master's awarded. *Degree requirements:* For master's, comprehensive exam (for some programs), thesis (for some programs). *Entrance requirements:* For master's, No GRE. Additional exam requirements/recommendations for international students: required—TOEFL (minimum score 61 paper-based). *Application deadline:* Applications are processed on a rolling basis. Application fee: $50. Electronic applications accepted. *Financial support:* Application deadline: 3/1; applicants required to submit FAFSA. *Unit head:* Dr. Hideki Morooka, Interim Department Chair, 910-672-2402, E-mail: hmorooka@uncfsu.edu. *Application contact:* Dr. Akbar Aghajanian, Graduate Program Coordinator, 910-672-2927, E-mail: aaghajanian@uncfsu.edu.
Website: https://www.uncfsu.edu/academics/colleges-schools-and-departments/college-of-humanities-and-social-sciences/department-of-sociology-and-interdisciplin

Florida Atlantic University, Dorothy F. Schmidt College of Arts and Letters, Department of Sociology, Boca Raton, FL 33431-0991. Offers MA. *Program availability:* Part-time, evening/weekend. *Faculty:* 7 full-time (3 women). *Students:* 16 full-time (10 women), 2 part-time (1 woman); includes 11 minority (7 Black or African American, non-Hispanic/Latino; 3 Hispanic/Latino; 1 Two or more races, non-Hispanic/Latino), 1 international. Average age 29. 8 applicants, 88% accepted, 6 enrolled. In 2019, 11 master's awarded. *Entrance requirements:* For master's, GRE General Test, minimum GPA of 3.0. Additional exam requirements/recommendations for international students: required—TOEFL, IELTS. *Application deadline:* For fall admission, 5/1 priority date for domestic and international students. Applications are processed on a rolling basis. Application fee: $30. Electronic applications accepted. *Expenses: Tuition:* Full-time $20,536; part-time $371.82 per credit hour. Tuition and fees vary according to program. *Financial support:* Teaching assistantships and Federal Work-Study available. *Unit head:* Cathy King, Program Administrator, 561-297-3270, E-mail: cking11@fau.edu. *Application contact:* Cathy King, Program Administrator, 561-297-3270, E-mail: cking11@fau.edu.
Website: http://www.fau.edu/sociology/

Florida International University, Steven J. Green School of International and Public Affairs, Department of Global and Sociocultural Studies, Miami, FL 33199. Offers MA, PhD. *Program availability:* Part-time, evening/weekend. *Faculty:* 28 full-time (11 women), 16 part-time/adjunct (6 women). *Students:* 187 full-time (112 women), 13 part-time (11 women); includes 153 minority (34 Black or African American, non-Hispanic/Latino; 8 Asian, non-Hispanic/Latino; 106 Hispanic/Latino; 5 Two or more races, non-Hispanic/Latino), 16 international. Average age 30. 214 applicants, 68% accepted, 99 enrolled. In 2019, 50 master's, 8 doctorates awarded. *Degree requirements:* For master's, thesis; for doctorate, comprehensive exam, thesis/dissertation. *Entrance requirements:* For master's, GRE General Test, 3 letters of recommendation; minimum undergraduate GPA of 3.25, 3.5 on any previous graduate work; written examples of academic or other relevant professional work; for doctorate, GRE General Test, letter of intent; 3 letters of recommendation; minimum undergraduate GPA of 3.25, 3.5 on any previous graduate work; written examples of academic or other relevant professional work. Additional exam requirements/recommendations for international students: required—TOEFL (minimum score 550 paper-based; 80 iBT). *Application deadline:* For fall admission, 6/1 for domestic students, 4/1 for international students; for spring admission, 10/1 for domestic students, 9/1 for international students. Applications are processed on a rolling basis. Application fee: $30. Electronic applications accepted. *Expenses: Tuition, area resident:* Full-time $8912; part-time $446 per credit hour. Tuition, state resident: full-time $8912; part-time $446 per credit hour. Tuition, nonresident: full-time $21,393; part-time $992 per credit hour. *Required fees:* $2194. *Financial support:* Institutionally sponsored loans and scholarships/grants available. Financial award application deadline: 3/1; financial award applicants required to submit FAFSA. *Unit head:* Dr. Guillermo Grenier, Chair, 305-348-3217, Fax: 305-348-3605, E-mail: Guillermo.Grenier@fiu.edu. *Application contact:* Nanett Rojas, Manager, Admissions Operations, 305-348-7464, Fax: 305-348-7441, E-mail: gradadm@fiu.edu.

Florida State University, The Graduate School, College of Social Sciences and Public Policy, Department of Sociology, Tallahassee, FL 32306. Offers applied social research

(MS); sociology (MS, PhD); sociology of health and aging (MS). *Faculty:* 21 full-time (15 women). *Students:* 44 full-time (28 women), 1 part-time (0 women); includes 16 minority (6 Black or African American, non-Hispanic/Latino; 5 Hispanic/Latino; 5 Two or more races, non-Hispanic/Latino), 2 international. Average age 30. 64 applicants, 33% accepted, 11 enrolled. In 2019, 8 master's, 7 doctorates awarded. *Degree requirements:* For doctorate, comprehensive exam, thesis/dissertation. *Entrance requirements:* For master's and doctorate, GRE General Test, minimum GPA of 3.0. Additional exam requirements/recommendations for international students: required—TOEFL (minimum score 550 paper-based; 80 iBT). *Application deadline:* For fall admission, 12/15 priority date for domestic students, 12/15 for international students. Applications are processed on a rolling basis. Application fee: $30. Electronic applications accepted. *Financial support:* In 2019–20, 35 students received support, including 2 fellowships with full tuition reimbursements available (averaging $25,115 per year), 25 research assistantships with full tuition reimbursements available (averaging $21,150 per year), 8 teaching assistantships with full tuition reimbursements available (averaging $21,150 per year); institutionally sponsored loans, scholarships/grants, health care benefits, and unspecified assistantships also available. Financial award application deadline: 12/15; financial award applicants required to submit FAFSA. *Unit head:* Dr. Kathryn Harker Tillman, Chair, 850-644-6416, E-mail: ktillman@fsu.edu. *Application contact:* Kimberly McClellan, Academic Specialist/Graduate Program Coordinator, 850-644-8329, E-mail: kmcclellan@fsu.edu.
Website: http://coss.fsu.edu/sociology/

George Mason University, College of Humanities and Social Sciences, Department of Sociology and Anthropology, Fairfax, VA 22030. Offers anthropology (MA); sociology (MA, PhD). *Degree requirements:* For master's, thesis; for doctorate, comprehensive exam, thesis/dissertation. *Entrance requirements:* For master's, official transcript; expanded goals statement; 3 letters of recommendation; writing sample; resume; 3 credits in undergraduate sociology theory, statistics and research methods (for sociology); 3 credits of sociocultural anthropology (for anthropology); for doctorate, GRE General Test, expanded goals statement; 3 letters of recommendation; writing sample; official transcript. Additional exam requirements/recommendations for international students: required—TOEFL (minimum score 575 paper-based; 88 iBT), IELTS (minimum score 6.5), PTE (minimum score 59). Electronic applications accepted.

The George Washington University, Columbian College of Arts and Sciences, Department of Sociology, Washington, DC 20052. Offers criminology (MA); sociology (MA). *Program availability:* Part-time, evening/weekend. *Degree requirements:* For master's, comprehensive exam, thesis or alternative. *Entrance requirements:* For master's, GRE General Test, minimum GPA of 3.0. Additional exam requirements/recommendations for international students: required—TOEFL (minimum score 550 paper-based; 80 iBT). Electronic applications accepted.

Georgia Southern University, Jack N. Averitt College of Graduate Studies, College of Behavioral and Social Sciences, Master of Arts in Social Science, Statesboro, GA 30460. Offers MA. *Program availability:* Part-time, evening/weekend. *Faculty:* 21 full-time (12 women), 1 (woman) part-time/adjunct. *Students:* 21 full-time (15 women), 8 part-time (3 women); includes 10 minority (4 Black or African American, non-Hispanic/Latino; 1 Asian, non-Hispanic/Latino; 4 Hispanic/Latino; 1 Two or more races, non-Hispanic/Latino), 1 international. Average age 29. 16 applicants, 100% accepted, 10 enrolled. In 2019, 6 master's awarded. *Degree requirements:* For master's, thesis optional. *Entrance requirements:* For master's, GRE General Test. Additional exam requirements/recommendations for international students: required—TOEFL (minimum score 550 paper-based; 80 iBT), IELTS (minimum score 6). *Application deadline:* For fall admission, 3/1 priority date for domestic and international students; for spring admission, 10/1 priority date for domestic students, 10/1 for international students. Applications are processed on a rolling basis. Application fee: $50. Electronic applications accepted. *Expenses: Tuition,* area resident: Full-time $4986; part-time $277 per credit hour. Tuition, nonresident: full-time $19,890; part-time $1105 per credit hour. *International tuition:* $19,890 full-time. *Required fees:* $2114; $1057 per semester. $1057 per semester. Tuition and fees vary according to course load, campus/location and program. *Financial support:* In 2019–20, 14 students received support, including 7 fellowships with full tuition reimbursements available (averaging $7,750 per year); career-related internships or fieldwork, Federal Work-Study, scholarships/grants, tuition waivers (full), and unspecified assistantships also available. Support available to part-time students. Financial award application deadline: 4/15; financial award applicants required to submit FAFSA. *Unit head:* Dr. Ted Brimeyer, Department Chair, 912-4785621, Fax: 912-478-0703, E-mail: tbrimeyer@georgiasouthern.edu.
Website: http://class.georgiasouthern.edu/socianth/

Georgia State University, College of Arts and Sciences, Department of Sociology, Atlanta, GA 30302-3083. Offers MA, PhD, MA/PhD. *Program availability:* Part-time, evening/weekend. *Faculty:* 12 full-time (8 women). *Students:* 64 full-time (46 women), 19 part-time (9 women); includes 45 minority (30 Black or African American, non-Hispanic/Latino; 4 Asian, non-Hispanic/Latino; 5 Hispanic/Latino; 6 Two or more races, non-Hispanic/Latino), 5 international. Average age 33. 67 applicants, 55% accepted, 16 enrolled. In 2019, 16 master's, 5 doctorates awarded. Terminal master's awarded for partial completion of doctoral program. *Entrance requirements:* For master's and doctorate, GRE. Additional exam requirements/recommendations for international students: required—TOEFL (minimum score 600 paper-based; 100 iBT). *Application deadline:* For fall admission, 4/15 for domestic students, 2/1 for international students; for spring admission, 4/15 for domestic and international students. Applications are processed on a rolling basis. Application fee: $50. Electronic applications accepted. *Expenses: Tuition,* area resident: Full-time $7164; part-time $398 per credit hour. Tuition, state resident: full-time $7164; part-time $398 per credit hour. Tuition, nonresident: full-time $22,662; part-time $1259 per credit hour. *International tuition:* $22,662 full-time. *Required fees:* $2128; $312 per credit hour. Tuition and fees vary according to course load and program. *Financial support:* In 2019–20, fellowships with tuition reimbursements (averaging $5,000 per year), research assistantships with tuition reimbursements (averaging $17,500 per year), teaching assistantships with tuition reimbursements (averaging $13,000 per year) were awarded; scholarships/grants and unspecified assistantships also available. Financial award application deadline: 2/1; financial award applicants required to submit FAFSA. *Unit head:* Dr. Eric Wright, Professor, Chair, 404-413-6527, Fax: 404-413-6505, E-mail: ewright28@gsu.edu. *Application contact:* Dr. Eric Wright, Professor, Chair, 404-413-6527, Fax: 404-413-6505, E-mail: ewright28@gsu.edu.
Website: https://sociology.gsu.edu/

The Graduate Center, City University of New York, Graduate Studies, Program in Sociology, New York, NY 10016-4039. Offers PhD. *Degree requirements:* For doctorate, one foreign language, thesis/dissertation. *Entrance requirements:* For doctorate, GRE General Test, writing sample. Additional exam requirements/recommendations for international students: required—TOEFL. Electronic applications accepted.

Harvard University, Graduate School of Arts and Sciences, Department of Sociology, Cambridge, MA 02138. Offers PhD. *Degree requirements:* For doctorate, thesis/dissertation, oral exams in 2 subfields. *Entrance requirements:* For doctorate, GRE General Test. Additional exam requirements/recommendations for international students: required—TOEFL.

Howard University, Graduate School, Department of Health, Human Performance and Leisure Studies, Washington, DC 20059-0002. Offers exercise physiology (MS); health education (MS); sports studies (MS), including sociology of sports, sports management; urban recreation (MS), including leisure studies. *Program availability:* Part-time, evening/weekend. *Degree requirements:* For master's, comprehensive exam, thesis. *Entrance requirements:* For master's, BS in human performance or related field. Additional exam requirements/recommendations for international students: recommended—TOEFL. Electronic applications accepted.

Howard University, Graduate School, Department of Sociology and Anthropology, Washington, DC 20059-0002. Offers sociology (MA, PhD). *Program availability:* Part-time, evening/weekend. *Degree requirements:* For master's, thesis; for doctorate, one foreign language, comprehensive exam, thesis/dissertation, RCR, writing exam. *Entrance requirements:* For master's, GRE General Test, minimum GPA of 3.0; for doctorate, GRE General Test, minimum GPA of 3.5. Additional exam requirements/recommendations for international students: required—TOEFL. Electronic applications accepted.

Humboldt State University, Academic Programs, College of Arts, Humanities, and Social Sciences, Department of Sociology, Arcata, CA 95521-8299. Offers MA. *Program availability:* Part-time. *Faculty:* 6 full-time (3 women), 8 part-time/adjunct (6 women). *Students:* 10 full-time (1 woman), 10 part-time (4 women); includes 7 minority (1 American Indian or Alaska Native, non-Hispanic/Latino; 1 Asian, non-Hispanic/Latino; 5 Hispanic/Latino). Average age 31. 18 applicants, 83% accepted, 6 enrolled. In 2019, 7 master's awarded. *Degree requirements:* For master's, thesis or alternative, qualifying exam. *Entrance requirements:* For master's, minimum GPA of 2.5, 3 letters of recommendation. Additional exam requirements/recommendations for international students: required—TOEFL (minimum score 500 paper-based). *Application deadline:* For fall admission, 3/15 for domestic students; for spring admission, 12/1 for domestic students. Applications are processed on a rolling basis. Application fee: $55. Electronic applications accepted. *Expenses:* Tuition, state resident: full-time $7176; part-time $4164 per term. *Required fees:* $2120; $1672 per term. *Financial support:* Application deadline: 3/1; applicants required to submit FAFSA. *Unit head:* Dr. Jennifer Eichstedt, Graduate Program Coordinator, 707-826-4949, E-mail: jennifer.eichstedt@humboldt.edu. *Application contact:* Dr. Jennifer Eichstedt, Graduate Program Coordinator, 707-826-4949, E-mail: jennifer.eichstedt@humboldt.edu.

Hunter College of the City University of New York, Graduate School, School of Arts and Sciences, Department of Sociology, New York, NY 10065-5085. Offers applied social research (MS). *Degree requirements:* For master's, internship. *Entrance requirements:* For master's, GRE General Test or GMAT, 3 credits of course work in statistics, 2 letters of recommendation. Additional exam requirements/recommendations for international students: required—TOEFL.

Idaho State University, Graduate School, College of Arts and Letters, Department of Sociology, Social Work and Criminology, Pocatello, ID 83209-8114. Offers sociology (MA). *Program availability:* Part-time. *Degree requirements:* For master's, comprehensive exam, thesis, oral defense of thesis. *Entrance requirements:* For master's, GRE General Test (minimum 40th percentile in one of 3 sections), minimum undergraduate GPA of 3.0, 3 letters of recommendation. Additional exam requirements/recommendations for international students: required—TOEFL (minimum score 550 paper-based; 80 iBT). Electronic applications accepted.

Illinois State University, Graduate School, College of Arts and Sciences, Department of Sociology, Normal, IL 61790. Offers historical archaeology (MA, MS); sociology (MA, MS). *Faculty:* 24 full-time (11 women), 3 part-time/adjunct (2 women). *Students:* 29 full-time (11 women), 12 part-time (8 women). Average age 29. 40 applicants, 68% accepted, 17 enrolled. In 2019, 13 master's awarded. *Degree requirements:* For master's, thesis. *Entrance requirements:* For master's, GRE General Test, GRE Subject Test, minimum GPA of 2.4 in last 60 hours of course work. *Application deadline:* Applications are processed on a rolling basis. Application fee: $50. *Expenses: Tuition,* area resident: Full-time $7956; part-time $9767 per year. Tuition, nonresident: full-time $9233; part-time $17,592 per year. *Required fees:* $1797. *Financial support:* In 2019–20, 9 research assistantships, 14 teaching assistantships were awarded; career-related internships or fieldwork, Federal Work-Study, tuition waivers (full and partial), and unspecified assistantships also available. Financial award application deadline: 4/1. *Unit head:* Dr. Joan Brehm, Department Chair, 309-438-7177, E-mail: jmbrehm@ilstu.edu. *Application contact:* Dr. Gina Hunter, Graduate Coordinator (ANT), 309-438-5713, E-mail: glhunt2@ilstu.edu.
Website: http://lilt.ilstu.edu/SOA/

Indiana University Bloomington, University Graduate School, College of Arts and Sciences, Department of Sociology, Bloomington, IN 47405-7000. Offers MA, PhD. Terminal master's awarded for partial completion of doctoral program. *Degree requirements:* For master's, thesis; for doctorate, comprehensive exam, thesis/dissertation. *Entrance requirements:* For master's and doctorate, GRE General Test. Additional exam requirements/recommendations for international students: required—TOEFL. Electronic applications accepted.

Indiana University of Pennsylvania, School of Graduate Studies and Research, College of Humanities and Social Sciences, Department of Sociology, Program in Sociology, Indiana, PA 15705. Offers MA. *Program availability:* Part-time. *Faculty:* 8 full-time (5 women). *Students:* 10 full-time (7 women), 7 part-time (all women); includes 6 minority (5 Black or African American, non-Hispanic/Latino; 1 Two or more races, non-Hispanic/Latino). Average age 24. 14 applicants, 100% accepted, 8 enrolled. In 2019, 2 master's awarded. *Degree requirements:* For master's, thesis optional. *Entrance requirements:* For master's, GRE, 2 letters of recommendation, official transcripts, goal statement. Additional exam requirements/recommendations for international students: required—TOEFL (minimum score 550 paper-based; 80 iBT), IELTS (minimum score 6.5), TOEFL or IELTS. *Application deadline:* Applications are processed on a rolling basis. Application fee: $50. Electronic applications accepted. *Expenses: Tuition, area resident:* Full-time $9288; part-time $516 per credit. Tuition, nonresident: full-time $13,932; part-time $774 per credit. *Required fees:* $4454. One-time fee: $115 full-time. Tuition and fees vary according to course load and program. *Financial support:* In 2019–20, 1 fellowship (averaging $300 per year), 10 research assistantships with tuition reimbursements (averaging $3,840 per year) were awarded; career-related internships or fieldwork, Federal Work-Study, scholarships/grants, and unspecified assistantships also available. Financial award application deadline: 4/15; financial award applicants required to submit FAFSA. *Unit head:* Dr. Melanie Duncan, Coordinator, 724-357-3931, E-mail: mduncan@iup.edu. *Application contact:* Dr. Melanie Duncan, Coordinator, 724-357-3931, E-mail: mduncan@iup.edu.
Website: http://www.iup.edu/grad/sociology/default.aspx

Indiana University-Purdue University Indianapolis, School of Liberal Arts, Department of Sociology, Indianapolis, IN 46202. Offers general sociology (MA); medical sociology (MA).

Iowa State University of Science and Technology, Department of Sociology, Ames, IA 50011. Offers rural sociology (MS, PhD); sociology (MS, PhD). *Degree requirements:* For master's, thesis; for doctorate, thesis/dissertation. *Entrance requirements:* For master's and doctorate, GRE General Test. Additional exam requirements/

recommendations for international students: required—TOEFL (minimum score 550 paper-based; 79 iBT), IELTS (minimum score 6.5). Electronic applications accepted.

Jackson State University, Graduate School, College of Liberal Arts, Department of Criminal Justice and Sociology, Jackson, MS 39217. Offers criminology and justice services (MA); sociology (MA). *Program availability:* Part-time, evening/weekend. *Degree requirements:* For master's, comprehensive exam, thesis or alternative. *Entrance requirements:* For master's, GRE General Test. Additional exam requirements/recommendations for international students: required—TOEFL (minimum score 520 paper-based; 67 iBT).

Johns Hopkins University, Zanvyl Krieger School of Arts and Sciences, Department of Sociology, Baltimore, MD 21218. Offers PhD. *Entrance requirements:* For doctorate, GRE General Test. Additional exam requirements/recommendations for international students: required—TOEFL (minimum score 600 paper-based; 100 iBT), IELTS; recommended—TWE. Electronic applications accepted.

Kansas State University, Graduate School, College of Arts and Sciences, Department of Sociology, Anthropology and Social Work, Manhattan, KS 66506. Offers sociology (MA, PhD). *Program availability:* Part-time. *Degree requirements:* For master's, thesis or alternative; for doctorate, comprehensive exam, thesis/dissertation. *Entrance requirements:* For master's, GRE, minimum undergraduate GPA of 3.0; for doctorate, GRE, master's degree in sociology or related field. Additional exam requirements/recommendations for international students: required—TOEFL (minimum score 550 paper-based; 79 iBT), IELTS (minimum score 6.5). Electronic applications accepted.

Kent State University, College of Arts and Sciences, Department of Sociology, Kent, OH 44242-0001. Offers criminology and criminal justice (MA), including corrections, global security, policing, victimology; sociology (MA, PhD). *Program availability:* Part-time, 100% online. *Faculty:* 18 full-time (10 women), 2 part-time/adjunct (1 woman). *Students:* 37 full-time (25 women), 37 part-time (30 women); includes 13 minority (5 Black or African American, non-Hispanic/Latino; 1 Asian, non-Hispanic/Latino; 3 Hispanic/Latino; 4 Two or more races, non-Hispanic/Latino), 3 international. Average age 31. 40 applicants, 65% accepted, 17 enrolled. In 2019, 27 master's, 4 doctorates awarded. *Degree requirements:* For master's, thesis, project, or internship; for doctorate, comprehensive exam, thesis/dissertation. *Entrance requirements:* For master's, GRE scores from within the last 5 years (not required for fall 2020 and fall 2021 admissions), three letters of recommendation, official transcript(s), goal statement, resume or vita; for doctorate, GRE scores from within the last 5 years (not required for fall 2020 and fall 2021), minimum undergraduate GPA of 3.0, transcripts, personal statement of 2-4 pages, 3 letters of recommendation, writing samples can be included but are not required. Additional exam requirements/recommendations for international students: required—TOEFL (minimum score 94 iBT), IELTS (minimum score 7), PTE (minimum score 65), Michigan English Language Assessment Battery (minimum score 82). *Application deadline:* For fall admission, 12/1 for domestic and international students. Applications are processed on a rolling basis. Application fee: $45 ($70 for international students). Electronic applications accepted. *Financial support:* Research assistantships with full tuition reimbursements, teaching assistantships with full tuition reimbursements, scholarships/grants, and unspecified assistantships available. Financial award application deadline: 12/1. *Unit head:* Dr. Richard E. Adams, Chair and Full Professor, 330-672-2721, E-mail: radams12@kent.edu. *Application contact:* Dr. William Kalkhoff, Professor and Graduate Coordinator, 330-672-3712, E-mail: wkalkhof@kent.edu. Website: http://www.kent.edu/sociology/

Lakehead University, Graduate Studies, Faculty of Social Sciences and Humanities, Department of Sociology, Thunder Bay, ON P7B 5E1, Canada. Offers gerontology (MA); health services and policy research (MA); sociology (MA); women's studies (MA). *Program availability:* Part-time, evening/weekend. *Degree requirements:* For master's, research project or thesis. *Entrance requirements:* For master's, minimum B average. Additional exam requirements/recommendations for international students: required—TOEFL.

Laurentian University, School of Graduate Studies and Research, Programme in Sociology, Sudbury, ON P3E 2C6, Canada. Offers applied social research (MA). *Program availability:* Part-time. *Entrance requirements:* For master's, honors degree in sociology or equivalent.

Lincoln University, Graduate Studies, Jefferson City, MO 65101. Offers accounting (MBA); counseling (M Ed), including addictions counseling; environmental science (MS); higher education (MA), including hbcu; history (MA); natural sciences (MS); school teaching middle school with certification (M Ed); school teaching-elementary (M Ed); school teaching-secondary (M Ed); sociology (MA); sociology/criminal justice (MA); sustainable agriculture (MS). *Program availability:* Part-time, evening/weekend, 100% online, blended/hybrid learning. *Students:* 47 full-time (33 women), 62 part-time (35 women); includes 42 minority (39 Black or African American, non-Hispanic/Latino; 1 American Indian or Alaska Native, non-Hispanic/Latino; 1 Asian, non-Hispanic/Latino; 1 Native Hawaiian or other Pacific Islander, non-Hispanic/Latino), 13 international. Average age 33. In 2019, 32 master's awarded. *Degree requirements:* For master's, comprehensive exam, thesis optional. *Entrance requirements:* For master's, GRE, MAT, or GMAT, minimum GPA of 2.75 overall, 3.0 in courses related to specialization; 3 letters of recommendation; minimum C average in English composition; personal statement of purpose. Additional exam requirements/recommendations for international students: required—TOEFL (minimum score 500 paper-based; 61 iBT), IELTS (minimum score 5.5), Michigan English Language Assessment Battery (minimum score 80). *Application deadline:* For fall admission, 7/1 priority date for domestic students, 5/1 priority date for international students; for spring admission, 11/1 priority date for domestic students, 10/1 priority date for international students; for summer admission, 6/1 priority date for domestic students. Applications are processed on a rolling basis. Application fee: $30. Electronic applications accepted. *Expenses: Tuition, area resident:* Full-time $511; part-time $511 per credit hour. *Tuition, state resident:* full-time $511; part-time $511 per credit hour. *Tuition, nonresident:* full-time $886; part-time $886 per credit hour. *International tuition:* $886 full-time. *Required fees:* $20; $20 per credit hour. $381.10 per semester. *Financial support:* In 2019–20, 8 fellowships (averaging $4,017 per year), 6 research assistantships (averaging $18,500 per year) were awarded; Federal Work-Study, scholarships/grants, and unspecified assistantships also available. Support available to part-time students. Financial award application deadline: 3/1; financial award applicants required to submit FAFSA. *Unit head:* Dr. Benjamin Arnold, Assistant Vice President of Academic Affairs, 573-681-5247, Fax: 573-681-5106, E-mail: gradschool@lincolnu.edu. *Application contact:* James Kendall, Graduate Admission Coordinator/Recruiter, 573-681-5150, Fax: 573-681-5106, E-mail: gradschool@lincolnu.edu.
Website: http://www.lincolnu.edu/web/graduate-studies/graduate-studies

Louisiana State University and Agricultural & Mechanical College, Graduate School, College of Humanities and Social Sciences, Department of Sociology, Baton Rouge, LA 70803. Offers MA, PhD.

Loyola University Chicago, Graduate School, Department of Sociology, Chicago, IL 60660. Offers sociology (MA, PhD). *Program availability:* Part-time, evening/weekend. *Faculty:* 13 full-time (8 women). *Students:* 29 full-time (17 women), 8 part-time (5 women); includes 16 minority (7 Black or African American, non-Hispanic/Latino; 5 Asian, non-Hispanic/Latino; 4 Hispanic/Latino), 4 international. Average age 31. 56 applicants, 70% accepted, 17 enrolled. In 2019, 7 master's, 3 doctorates awarded. Terminal master's awarded for partial completion of doctoral program. *Degree requirements:* For master's, thesis or alternative; for doctorate, comprehensive exam, thesis/dissertation. *Entrance requirements:* For master's, GRE General Test (recommended); for doctorate, GRE General Test. Additional exam requirements/recommendations for international students: required—TOEFL (minimum score 550 paper-based; 79 iBT), IELTS (minimum score 6.5). *Application deadline:* For fall admission, 1/5 for domestic and international students; for winter admission, 1/5 for domestic students, 1/4 for international students. Electronic applications accepted. *Expenses:* Contact institution. *Financial support:* In 2019–20, 14 students received support, including 4 fellowships with full tuition reimbursements available (averaging $18,000 per year), 6 research assistantships with full tuition reimbursements available (averaging $18,000 per year), 4 teaching assistantships with full tuition reimbursements available (averaging $18,000 per year); Federal Work-Study, health care benefits, and tuition waivers (full and partial) also available. Financial award application deadline: 2/1; financial award applicants required to submit FAFSA. *Unit head:* Dr. Marilyn Krogh, Graduate Program Director, 773-508-3471, Fax: 773-508-7099, E-mail: mkrogh@luc.edu. *Application contact:* Dr. Marilyn Krogh, Graduate Program Director, 773-508-3471, Fax: 773-508-7099, E-mail: mkrogh@luc.edu.
Website: https://www.luc.edu/sociology/index.shtml

Marshall University, Academic Affairs Division, College of Liberal Arts, Department of Sociology and Anthropology, Huntington, WV 25755. Offers sociology (MA). *Degree requirements:* For master's, thesis optional. *Entrance requirements:* For master's, GRE.

McGill University, Faculty of Graduate and Postdoctoral Studies, Faculty of Arts, Department of Sociology, Montréal, QC H3A 2T5, Canada. Offers medical sociology (MA); neo-tropical environment (MA); social statistics (MA); sociology (MA, PhD, Diploma).

McGill University, Faculty of Graduate and Postdoctoral Studies, Faculty of Medicine, Department of Social Studies of Medicine, Montréal, QC H3A 2T5, Canada. Offers medical anthropology (MA, PhD); medical history (MA, PhD); medical sociology (MA, PhD).

McMaster University, School of Graduate Studies, Faculty of Social Sciences, Department of Sociology, Hamilton, ON L8S 4M2, Canada. Offers MA, PhD. *Program availability:* Part-time. *Degree requirements:* For master's, thesis; for doctorate, comprehensive exam, thesis/dissertation. *Entrance requirements:* For master's and doctorate, minimum B+ average. Additional exam requirements/recommendations for international students: required—TOEFL (minimum score 580 paper-based).

Memorial University of Newfoundland, School of Graduate Studies, Department of Sociology, St. John's, NL A1C 5S7, Canada. Offers gender (PhD); maritime sociology (PhD); sociology (M Phil, MA); work and development (PhD). *Program availability:* Part-time. *Degree requirements:* For master's, comprehensive exam, thesis optional, program journal (M Phil); for doctorate, one foreign language, comprehensive exam, thesis/dissertation, oral defense of thesis. *Entrance requirements:* For master's, 2nd class degree from university of recognized standing in area of study; for doctorate, MA, M Phil, or equivalent. Electronic applications accepted.

Michigan State University, The Graduate School, College of Social Science, Department of Sociology, East Lansing, MI 48824. Offers MA, PhD. *Program availability:* Part-time. *Entrance requirements:* Additional exam requirements/recommendations for international students: required—TOEFL (minimum score 550 paper-based), Michigan State University ELT (minimum score 85), Michigan English Language Assessment Battery (minimum score 83). Electronic applications accepted.

Middle Tennessee State University, College of Graduate Studies, College of Liberal Arts, Department of Sociology and Anthropology, Murfreesboro, TN 37132. Offers sociology (MA). *Program availability:* Part-time, evening/weekend, online learning. *Degree requirements:* For master's, comprehensive exam, thesis. *Entrance requirements:* For master's, GRE. Additional exam requirements/recommendations for international students: required—TOEFL (minimum score 525 paper-based; 71 iBT) or IELTS (minimum score 6). Electronic applications accepted.

Minnesota State University Mankato, College of Graduate Studies and Research, College of Social and Behavioral Sciences, Department of Sociology and Corrections, Mankato, MN 56001. Offers sociology (MA); sociology: college teaching (MA); sociology: corrections (MS); sociology: human services planning and administration (MS). *Program availability:* Part-time. *Degree requirements:* For master's, comprehensive exam, thesis or alternative. *Entrance requirements:* For master's, minimum GPA of 3.0 during previous 2 years, 3 letters of reference, resume. Additional exam requirements/recommendations for international students: required—TOEFL. Electronic applications accepted.

Mississippi State University, College of Arts and Sciences, Department of Sociology, Mississippi State, MS 39762. Offers MS, PhD. *Program availability:* Part-time. *Faculty:* 20 full-time (14 women). *Students:* 22 full-time (16 women), 15 part-time (10 women); includes 7 minority (3 Black or African American, non-Hispanic/Latino; 1 Asian, non-Hispanic/Latino; 2 Hispanic/Latino; 1 Two or more races, non-Hispanic/Latino), 5 international. Average age 30. 28 applicants, 61% accepted, 12 enrolled. In 2019, 4 master's, 1 doctorate awarded. *Degree requirements:* For master's, thesis optional, comprehensive oral or written exam; for doctorate, thesis/dissertation, comprehensive oral and written exam. *Entrance requirements:* For master's, minimum GPA of 3.0 on last two years of undergraduate courses or GRE; academic writing sample in English (student's choice); for doctorate, GRE, academic writing sample in English (student's choice). Additional exam requirements/recommendations for international students: required—TOEFL (minimum score 477 paper-based; 53 iBT); recommended—IELTS (minimum score 4.5). *Application deadline:* For fall admission, 4/15 priority date for domestic students, 5/1 for international students; for spring admission, 10/15 priority date for domestic students, 9/1 for international students. Applications are processed on a rolling basis. Application fee: $60 ($80 for international students). Electronic applications accepted. *Expenses: Tuition, area resident:* Full-time $8880; part-time $456 per credit hour. *Tuition, state resident:* full-time $8880. *Tuition, nonresident:* full-time $23,840; part-time $1236 per credit hour. *Required fees:* $110; $11.12 per credit hour. Tuition and fees vary according to course load. *Financial support:* In 2019–20, 1 research assistantship with full tuition reimbursement (averaging $17,045 per year), 13 teaching assistantships with partial tuition reimbursements (averaging $13,082 per year) were awarded; Federal Work-Study, institutionally sponsored loans, scholarships/grants, and unspecified assistantships also available. Financial award application deadline: 2/15; financial award applicants required to submit FAFSA. *Unit head:* Dr. Nicole Rader, Professor and Head, 662-325-7880, Fax: 662-325-4564, E-mail: NRader@soc.msstate.edu. *Application contact:* Robbie Salters, Admissions and Enrollment Management Assistant and Coordinator, 662-325-5188, E-mail: rsalters@grad.msstate.edu.
Website: http://www.sociology.msstate.edu/

Morehead State University, Graduate School, Caudill College of Arts, Humanities and Social Sciences, School of Humanities and Social Sciences, Morehead, KY 40351.

Offers criminology (MA); general sociology (MA); gerontology (MA); sociology regional analysis (MA); sociology/chemical dependency (MA). *Program availability:* Part-time, evening/weekend. *Faculty:* 20 full-time (10 women), 3 part-time/adjunct (2 women). *Students:* 27 full-time (19 women), 15 part-time (9 women); includes 3 minority (2 Black or African American, non-Hispanic/Latino; 1 Hispanic/Latino), 1 international. 53 applicants, 60% accepted, 23 enrolled. In 2019, 8 master's awarded. *Degree requirements:* For master's, comprehensive exam (for some programs), thesis (for some programs), min 3.0 GPA, complete 40 credit hours, option 3 is approved practicum in chemical dependency, written or oral exam, public presentation of thesis or research query or practicum experience (for MPA); demonstration of mastery of skills through individual courses and examinations and taped videos displaying skills (for MA Sociology). *Entrance requirements:* For master's, GRE, 3.0 UG GPA in 18 hours of PA courses; 3.0 UG GPA in all Sociology courses;MA Sociology: UG GPA of 2.75 or higher; submission of 2-page statement of educational and career goals relative to program. Additional exam requirements/recommendations for international students: required—TOEFL (minimum score 525 paper-based). *Application deadline:* Applications are processed on a rolling basis. Application fee: $30. Electronic applications accepted. *Expenses: Tuition, area resident:* Part-time $570 per credit hour. Tuition, state resident: part-time $570 per credit hour. Tuition, nonresident: part-time $570 per credit hour. *Required fees:* $14 per credit hour. *Financial support:* Teaching assistantships, career-related internships or fieldwork, and unspecified assistantships available. Financial award applicants required to submit FAFSA. *Unit head:* Dr. Dianna D. Murphy, Associate Dean/Professor Legal Studies, 606-7832720, E-mail: d.murphy@moreheadstate.edu. *Application contact:* Dr. Dianna D. Murphy, Associate Dean/Professor Legal Studies, 606-7832720, E-mail: d.murphy@moreheadstate.edu.

Morgan State University, School of Graduate Studies, James H. Gilliam Jr College of Liberal Arts, Department of Sociology and Anthropology, Baltimore, MD 21251. Offers sociology (MA, MS). *Program availability:* Part-time, evening/weekend. *Faculty:* 9 full-time (7 women), 3 part-time/adjunct (1 woman). *Students:* 11 full-time (6 women), 2 part-time (both women); includes 10 minority (all Black or African American, non-Hispanic/Latino), 3 international. Average age 28. 7 applicants, 71% accepted, 4 enrolled. In 2019, 9 master's awarded. *Degree requirements:* For master's, comprehensive exam, thesis. *Entrance requirements:* For master's, GRE, Minimum GPA 3.0. Additional exam requirements/recommendations for international students: required—TOEFL (minimum score 550 paper-based; 70 iBT); recommended—IELTS (minimum score 6). *Application deadline:* For fall admission, 2/1 priority date for domestic students, 4/1 for international students; for spring admission, 11/15 priority date for domestic students, 10/1 for international students. Applications are processed on a rolling basis. Application fee: $50 ($70 for international students). Electronic applications accepted. *Expenses:* Tuition, state resident: full-time $455; part-time $455 per credit hour. Tuition, nonresident: full-time $894; part-time $894 per credit hour. *Required fees:* $82; $82 per credit hour. *Financial support:* In 2019–20, 2 students received support. Fellowships with full and partial tuition reimbursements available, research assistantships with full and partial tuition reimbursements available, teaching assistantships with full and partial tuition reimbursements available, career-related internships or fieldwork, Federal Work-Study, scholarships/grants, tuition waivers (full and partial), and unspecified assistantships available. Support available to part-time students. Financial award application deadline: 2/1. *Unit head:* Dr. Stella Hargett, Interim Chairperson, 443-885-3518, Fax: 443-885-8242, E-mail: stella.hargett@morgan.edu. *Application contact:* Dr. Jahmaine Smith, Director of Admissions, 443-885-3185, Fax: 443-885-8226, E-mail: gradapply@morgan.edu.
Website: https://morgan.edu/college_of_liberal_arts/departments/sociology_and_anthropology/master_of_arts/science_in_sociology.html

Murray State University, College of Humanities and Fine Arts, Department of Political Science and Sociology, Murray, KY 42071. Offers MPA. *Program availability:* Part-time, evening/weekend. *Entrance requirements:* For master's, GRE or GMAT, minimum university GPA of 2.75. Additional exam requirements/recommendations for international students: required—TOEFL (minimum score 527 paper-based; 71 iBT). Electronic applications accepted.

New Mexico Highlands University, Graduate Studies, College of Arts and Sciences, Department of Social and Behavioral Sciences, Las Vegas, NM 87701. Offers psychology (MS), including clinical psychology/counseling, general psychology; public affairs (MA), including applied sociology; Southwest studies (MA), including anthropology. *Program availability:* Part-time. *Degree requirements:* For master's, comprehensive exam, thesis or alternative. *Entrance requirements:* For master's, minimum undergraduate GPA of 3.0. Additional exam requirements/recommendations for international students: required—TOEFL (minimum score 540 paper-based).

New Mexico State University, College of Arts and Sciences, Department of Sociology, Las Cruces, NM 88003-8001. Offers MA. *Program availability:* Part-time, 100% online. *Faculty:* 9 full-time (5 women), 2 part-time/adjunct (both women). *Students:* 9 full-time (5 women), 27 part-time (18 women); includes 11 minority (4 Black or African American, non-Hispanic/Latino; 2 Asian, non-Hispanic/Latino; 4 Hispanic/Latino; 1 Two or more races, non-Hispanic/Latino), 2 international. Average age 36. 50 applicants, 58% accepted, 6 enrolled. In 2019, 9 master's awarded. *Degree requirements:* For master's, thesis optional, options are comprehensive exam or thesis. *Entrance requirements:* Additional exam requirements/recommendations for international students: required—TOEFL (minimum score 550 paper-based; 79 iBT), IELTS (minimum score 6.5). *Application deadline:* For fall admission, 3/15 for domestic and international students. Application fee: $40 ($50 for international students). Electronic applications accepted. *Financial support:* In 2019–20, 10 students received support, including 1 fellowship (averaging $4,844 per year), 1 research assistantship (averaging $18,162 per year), 6 teaching assistantships (averaging $10,595 per year); career-related internships or fieldwork, Federal Work-Study, scholarships/grants, traineeships, health care benefits, and unspecified assistantships also available. Support available to part-time students. Financial award application deadline: 3/1. *Unit head:* Dr. David G. LoConto, Department Head, 575-646-3448, Fax: 575-646-7601, E-mail: dloconto@nmsu.edu. *Application contact:* Dr. Sandra M. Way, Director of Graduate Studies, 575-646-3448, Fax: 575-646-7601, E-mail: sway@nmsu.edu.
Website: http://sociology.nmsu.edu/

The New School, The New School for Social Research, Department of Historical Studies, New York, NY 10003. Offers historical studies (MA); politics (PhD), including historical studies; sociology (PhD), including historical studies. *Program availability:* Part-time, evening/weekend. *Faculty:* 1 (woman) full-time, 2 part-time/adjunct (both women). *Students:* 10 full-time (3 women), 4 part-time (2 women); includes 1 minority (Asian, non-Hispanic/Latino), 4 international. Average age 28. 8 applicants, 100% accepted, 6 enrolled. In 2019, 7 master's awarded. *Degree requirements:* For master's, thesis. *Entrance requirements:* For master's, GRE, two letters of recommendation, writing sample, essays, transcripts. Additional exam requirements/recommendations for international students: required—TOEFL (minimum score 100 iBT), IELTS (minimum score 7), PTE (minimum score 68). *Application deadline:* For fall admission, 1/15 priority date for domestic and international students; for spring admission, 10/15 priority date for domestic and international students. Applications are processed on a rolling basis. Application fee: $50. Electronic applications accepted. *Expenses:* 2260 per credit.

Financial support: In 2019–20, 11 students received support, including 6 research assistantships (averaging $5,723 per year), 4 teaching assistantships (averaging $7,022 per year); Federal Work-Study, scholarships/grants, traineeships, health care benefits, and tuition waivers (full and partial) also available. Support available to part-time students. Financial award application deadline: 2/1; financial award applicants required to submit FAFSA. *Unit head:* Dr. Oz Frankel, Department Chair, 212-229-5376 Ext. 4924, E-mail: frankelo@newschool.edu. *Application contact:* Merida Gasbarro, Director of Graduate Admission, 212-229-5600 Ext. 1108, E-mail: escandom@newschool.edu. Website: http://www.newschool.edu/nssr/historical-studies/

The New School, The New School for Social Research, Department of Sociology, New York, NY 10003. Offers historical studies (PhD); sociology (M Phil, MA). *Program availability:* Part-time. *Faculty:* 11 full-time (5 women), 1 (woman) part-time/adjunct. *Students:* 76 full-time (43 women), 7 part-time (4 women); includes 13 minority (4 Black or African American, non-Hispanic/Latino; 2 Asian, non-Hispanic/Latino; 6 Hispanic/Latino; 1 Two or more races, non-Hispanic/Latino), 45 international. Average age 34. 68 applicants, 65% accepted, 21 enrolled. In 2019, 25 master's, 10 doctorates awarded. Terminal master's awarded for partial completion of doctoral program. *Degree requirements:* For master's, comprehensive exam; for doctorate, one foreign language, thesis/dissertation. *Entrance requirements:* For master's and doctorate, GRE, letters of recommendation, writing sample, essays, transcripts. Additional exam requirements/recommendations for international students: required—TOEFL (minimum score 92 iBT), IELTS (minimum score 7), PTE (minimum score 68). *Application deadline:* For fall admission, 5/5 priority date for domestic students, 6/15 priority date for international students; for spring admission, 10/15 priority date for domestic and international students. Applications are processed on a rolling basis. Application fee: $50. Electronic applications accepted. *Expenses:* 2260. *Financial support:* In 2019–20, 62 students received support, including 8 fellowships (averaging $7,023 per year), 24 research assistantships (averaging $4,958 per year), 16 teaching assistantships (averaging $10,026 per year); Federal Work-Study, scholarships/grants, and tuition waivers (full and partial) also available. Support available to part-time students. Financial award application deadline: 2/1; financial award applicants required to submit FAFSA. *Unit head:* Dr. Benoit Challand, 212-229-5747 Ext. 3034, E-mail: challanb@newschool.edu. *Application contact:* Merida Gasbarro, Director of Graduate Admission, 212-229-5600 Ext. 1108, E-mail: escandom@newschool.edu.
Website: https://www.newschool.edu/nssr/sociology/

New York University, Graduate School of Arts and Science, Department of Sociology, New York, NY 10012-1019. Offers MA, PhD, JD/MA. *Program availability:* Part-time. Terminal master's awarded for partial completion of doctoral program. *Degree requirements:* For master's, thesis or alternative; for doctorate, comprehensive exam, thesis/dissertation. *Entrance requirements:* For master's and doctorate, GRE General Test. Additional exam requirements/recommendations for international students: required—TOEFL, IELTS.

New York University, Steinhardt School of Culture, Education, and Human Development, Applied Statistics, Social Science, and Humanities, Program in Sociology of Education, New York, NY 10012. Offers education policy (MA); social and cultural studies of education (MA); sociology of education (PhD). *Program availability:* Part-time. *Entrance requirements:* For master's, letters of recommendation; for doctorate, GRE General Test, interview. Additional exam requirements/recommendations for international students: required—TOEFL (minimum score 100 iBT). Electronic applications accepted.

North Carolina State University, Graduate School, College of Humanities and Social Sciences, Department of Sociology and Anthropology, Program in Sociology, Raleigh, NC 27695. Offers PhD. *Program availability:* Part-time. *Degree requirements:* For doctorate, comprehensive exam, thesis/dissertation. *Entrance requirements:* For doctorate, GRE General Test, sample of written work. Electronic applications accepted.

North Dakota State University, College of Graduate and Interdisciplinary Studies, College of Arts, Humanities and Social Sciences, Department of Sociology and Anthropology, Fargo, ND 58102. Offers anthropology (MA, MS); community development (MA, MS); sociology (MS). *Program availability:* Part-time. *Entrance requirements:* For master's, GRE (for emergency management), course work in sociology, minimum GPA of 3.2. Additional exam requirements/recommendations for international students: required—TOEFL. Electronic applications accepted. Tuition and fees vary according to program and reciprocity agreements.

Northeastern University, College of Social Sciences and Humanities, Boston, MA 02115. Offers criminology and criminal justice (MSCJ); criminology and justice policy (PhD); economics (MA, PhD); English (MA, PhD); international affairs (MA); law and public policy (PhD); political science (MA, PhD); public administration (MPA); public policy (MPP); security and resilience studies (MS); sociology (MA, PhD); urban and regional policy (MS); urban informatics (MS); world history (MA, PhD). *Program availability:* Online learning. *Degree requirements:* For doctorate, variable foreign language requirement, comprehensive exam, thesis/dissertation. *Entrance requirements:* For master's and doctorate, GRE. Additional exam requirements/recommendations for international students: required—TOEFL, IELTS. Electronic applications accepted. *Expenses:* Contact institution.

Northern Arizona University, College of Social and Behavioral Sciences, Department of Sociology, Flagstaff, AZ 86011. Offers applied sociology (MA). *Program availability:* Part-time, 100% online, blended/hybrid learning. *Degree requirements:* For master's, variable foreign language requirement, comprehensive exam (for some programs), thesis (for some programs). *Entrance requirements:* For master's, minimum undergraduate GPA of 3.0, minimum of 250 volunteer and/or relevant paid human service work experience. Additional exam requirements/recommendations for international students: required—TOEFL (minimum score 80 iBT), IELTS (minimum score 6.5). Electronic applications accepted.

Northern Illinois University, Graduate School, College of Liberal Arts and Sciences, Department of Sociology, De Kalb, IL 60115-2854. Offers MA. *Program availability:* Part-time. *Faculty:* 14 full-time (3 women). *Students:* 16 full-time (10 women), 2 part-time (both women); includes 9 minority (3 Black or African American, non-Hispanic/Latino; 1 Asian, non-Hispanic/Latino; 5 Hispanic/Latino), 1 international. Average age 26. 16 applicants, 94% accepted, 7 enrolled. In 2019, 7 master's awarded. *Degree requirements:* For master's, comprehensive exam, thesis optional. *Entrance requirements:* For master's, GRE General Test, minimum GPA of 2.75; course work in social theory, social methods, and statistics. Additional exam requirements/recommendations for international students: required—TOEFL (minimum score 550 paper-based). *Application deadline:* For fall admission, 6/1 for domestic students, 5/1 for international students; for spring admission, 11/1 for domestic students, 10/1 for international students. Applications are processed on a rolling basis. Application fee: $40. Electronic applications accepted. *Financial support:* In 2019–20, 2 research assistantships with full tuition reimbursements, 12 teaching assistantships with full tuition reimbursements were awarded; fellowships with full tuition reimbursements, career-related internships or fieldwork, Federal Work-Study, scholarships/grants, tuition waivers (full), and unspecified assistantships also available. Support available to part-time students. Financial award applicants required to submit FAFSA. *Unit head:* Dr.

Mike Ezell, Chair, 815-753-1194, Fax: 815-753-6302, E-mail: mezell@niu.edu. *Application contact:* Dr. Diane Rodgers, Graduate Advising, 815-753-1984, E-mail: drodgers@niu.edu.
Website: http://www.sociology.niu.edu/

Northwestern University, The Graduate School, Judd A. and Marjorie Weinberg College of Arts and Sciences, Department of Sociology, Evanston, IL 60208. Offers PhD, JD/PhD. *Degree requirements:* For doctorate, thesis/dissertation. *Entrance requirements:* For doctorate, GRE General Test. Additional exam requirements/recommendations for international students: required—TOEFL. Electronic applications accepted.

The Ohio State University, Graduate School, College of Arts and Sciences, Division of Social and Behavioral Sciences, Department of Sociology, Columbus, OH 43210. Offers PhD. *Entrance requirements:* For doctorate, GRE General Test. Additional exam requirements/recommendations for international students: required—TOEFL (minimum score 600 paper-based; 100 iBT); recommended—IELTS (minimum score 7). Electronic applications accepted.

Ohio University, Graduate College, College of Arts and Sciences, Department of Sociology and Anthropology, Athens, OH 45701-2979. Offers sociology (MA). *Program availability:* Part-time. *Degree requirements:* For master's, thesis or alternative. *Entrance requirements:* For master's, minimum GPA of 3.0; minimum of 20 hours in sociology including statistics, theory, and research methods. Additional exam requirements/recommendations for international students: required—TOEFL (minimum score 550 paper-based; 80 iBT) or IELTS (minimum score 6.5). Electronic applications accepted.

Oklahoma City University, Petree College of Arts and Sciences, Oklahoma City, OK 73106-1402. Offers applied behavioral studies (M Ed); applied sociology: nonprofit leadership (MA); creative writing (MFA); criminology (MS); early childhood education (M Ed); elementary education (M Ed); general studies (MLA); leadership/management (MLA); moving image arts (MFA); professional counseling (M Ed); teaching (MA); teaching English to speakers of other languages (MA). *Program availability:* Part-time, evening/weekend. *Degree requirements:* For master's, capstone/practicum. *Entrance requirements:* For master's, bachelor's degree from accredited institution with minimum GPA of 3.0, essay, recommendation letters. Additional exam requirements/recommendations for international students: required—TOEFL (minimum score 550 paper-based; 80 iBT). Electronic applications accepted. *Expenses:* Contact institution.

Oklahoma State University, College of Arts and Sciences, Department of Sociology, Stillwater, OK 74078. Offers MS, PhD. *Faculty:* 14 full-time (7 women), 1 (woman) part-time/adjunct. *Students:* 9 full-time (6 women), 16 part-time (10 women); includes 4 minority (1 Black or African American, non-Hispanic/Latino; 1 Asian, non-Hispanic/Latino; 2 Hispanic/Latino), 4 international. Average age 31. 19 applicants, 58% accepted, 8 enrolled. In 2019, 2 master's, 4 doctorates awarded. *Entrance requirements:* For master's and doctorate, GRE General Test. Additional exam requirements/recommendations for international students: required—TOEFL (minimum score 550 paper-based; 79 iBT). *Application deadline:* For fall admission, 3/1 priority date for international students; for spring admission, 8/1 priority date for international students. Applications are processed on a rolling basis. Application fee: $50 ($75 for international students). Electronic applications accepted. *Expenses: Tuition, area resident:* Full-time $4148.10; part-time $2765.40 per credit hour. Tuition, state resident: full-time $4148.10; part-time $2765.40 per credit hour. Tuition, nonresident: full-time $15,775; part-time $10,516.80 per credit hour. *International tuition:* $15,775.20 full-time. *Required fees:* $2196.90; $122.05 per credit hour. Tuition and fees vary according to course load, campus/location and program. *Financial support:* In 2019–20, 1 research assistantship (averaging $1,862 per year), 21 teaching assistantships (averaging $1,657 per year) were awarded; career-related internships or fieldwork, Federal Work-Study, scholarships/grants, health care benefits, tuition waivers (partial), and unspecified assistantships also available. Support available to part-time students. Financial award application deadline: 3/1; financial award applicants required to submit FAFSA. *Unit head:* Dr. Tamara Mix, Department Head, 405-744-6104, Fax: 405-744-5780, E-mail: tamara.mix@okstate.edu. *Application contact:* Dr. Sheryl Tucker, Dean, 405-744-6368, Fax: 405-744-0355, E-mail: gradi@okstate.edu.
Website: http://sociology.okstate.edu

Old Dominion University, College of Arts and Letters, Program in Applied Sociology, Norfolk, VA 23529. Offers criminal justice (MA); general sociology (MA); women's studies (MA). *Program availability:* Part-time, evening/weekend. *Degree requirements:* For master's, thesis. *Entrance requirements:* For master's, GRE General Test, minimum GPA of 3.0; 12 credits in criminal justice, sociology, or women's studies. Additional exam requirements/recommendations for international students: required—TOEFL. Electronic applications accepted. *Expenses:* Contact institution.

Omega Graduate School, Graduate Programs, Dayton, TN 37321-6736. Offers family life education (M Litt); integration of religion and society (D Phil); organizational leadership (M Litt). *Entrance requirements:* For master's, official transcripts, three letters of recommendation, bachelor's degree or its equivalent, minimum undergraduate GPA of 3.0, minimum of 3 years of professional experience; for doctorate, official transcripts, three letters of recommendation, master's degree with minimum GPA of 3.0, minimum of 5 years of professional experience. *Expenses:* Contact institution.

Our Lady of the Lake University, College of Professional Studies, Program in Sociology, San Antonio, TX 78207-4689. Offers MA. *Program availability:* Part-time, evening/weekend, online learning. *Entrance requirements:* For master's, official transcripts showing minimum B grade in undergraduate statistics course, personal statement, two letters of recommendation, interview. Additional exam requirements/recommendations for international students: required—TOEFL. Electronic applications accepted.

Penn State University Park, Graduate School, College of the Liberal Arts, Department of Sociology and Criminology, University Park, PA 16802. Offers criminology (MA, PhD); sociology (MA, PhD).

Portland State University, Graduate Studies, College of Liberal Arts and Sciences, Department of Sociology, Portland, OR 97207-0751. Offers MA, MS, PhD. *Program availability:* Part-time. *Faculty:* 14 full-time (9 women), 6 part-time/adjunct (3 women). *Students:* 20 full-time (15 women), 11 part-time (8 women); includes 4 minority (1 Black or African American, non-Hispanic/Latino; 2 Hispanic/Latino; 1 Two or more races, non-Hispanic/Latino), 4 international. Average age 36. 26 applicants, 77% accepted, 6 enrolled. In 2019, 7 master's, 4 doctorates awarded. Terminal master's awarded for partial completion of doctoral program. *Degree requirements:* For master's, variable foreign language requirement, thesis, oral defense of thesis; for doctorate, comprehensive exam, thesis/dissertation, proposal, research project. *Entrance requirements:* For master's, GRE General Test, GRE Subject Test, minimum GPA of 3.0 in upper-division course work or 2.75 overall, 3 letters of recommendation, personal statement, curriculum vitae/resume, writing sample. Additional exam requirements/recommendations for international students: required—TOEFL (minimum score 550 paper-based; 80 iBT), IELTS (minimum score 6.5). *Application deadline:* For fall admission, 1/15 for domestic and international students. Application fee: $65. Electronic applications accepted. *Expenses:* $429 per credit hour resident, $645 per credit hour non-resident. *Financial support:* In 2019–20, 2 research assistantships with full tuition reimbursements (averaging $15,301 per year), 10 teaching assistantships with full and partial tuition reimbursements (averaging $10,200 per year) were awarded; fellowships, career-related internships or fieldwork, Federal Work-Study, and unspecified assistantships also available. Support available to part-time students. Financial award application deadline: 3/1; financial award applicants required to submit FAFSA. *Unit head:* Dr. Lindsey Wilkinson, Chair, 503-725-3975, E-mail: lindsw@pdx.edu. *Application contact:* Dr. Amy Lubitow, Graduate Director/Associate Professor, 503-725-3989, E-mail: alubitow@pdx.edu.
Website: https://www.pdx.edu/sociology/

Portland State University, Graduate Studies, College of Liberal Arts and Sciences, Systems Science Program, Portland, OR 97207-0751. Offers computational intelligence (Certificate); computer modeling and simulation (Certificate); systems science (MS); systems science/anthropology (PhD); systems science/business administration (PhD); systems science/civil engineering (PhD); systems science/economics (PhD); systems science/engineering management (PhD); systems science/general (PhD); systems science/mathematical sciences (PhD); systems science/mechanical engineering (PhD); systems science/psychology (PhD); systems science/sociology (PhD). *Program availability:* Part-time. *Faculty:* 2 full-time (0 women), 6 part-time/adjunct (1 woman). *Students:* 6 full-time (3 women), 25 part-time (8 women); includes 7 minority (2 Asian, non-Hispanic/Latino; 4 Hispanic/Latino; 1 Two or more races, non-Hispanic/Latino), 2 international. Average age 39. 25 applicants, 80% accepted, 15 enrolled. In 2019, 7 master's, 2 doctorates awarded. Terminal master's awarded for partial completion of doctoral program. *Degree requirements:* For master's, comprehensive exam (for some programs), thesis optional; for doctorate, variable foreign language requirement, comprehensive exam (for some programs), thesis/dissertation. *Entrance requirements:* For master's, GRE/GMAT (recommended), minimum GPA of 3.0 on undergraduate or graduate work, 2 letters of recommendation, statement of interest; for doctorate, GRE required, minimum GPA of 3.0 undergraduate, 3.25 graduate; 3 letters of recommendation; statement of interest. Additional exam requirements/recommendations for international students: required—TOEFL (minimum score 550 paper-based; 80 iBT). *Application deadline:* For fall admission, 3/15 priority date for domestic and international students. Application fee: $65. Electronic applications accepted. *Expenses: Tuition, area resident:* Full-time $13,020; part-time $6510 per year. Tuition, state resident: full-time $13,020; part-time $6510 per year. Tuition, nonresident: full-time $19,830; part-time $9915 per year. *International tuition:* $19,830 full-time. *Required fees:* $1226. One-time fee: $350. Tuition and fees vary according to course load, program and reciprocity agreements. *Financial support:* Research assistantships, teaching assistantships, career-related internships or fieldwork, Federal Work-Study, scholarships/grants, and unspecified assistantships available. Support available to part-time students. Financial award application deadline: 3/1; financial award applicants required to submit FAFSA. *Unit head:* Dr. Wayne Wakeland, Chair, 503-725-4975, E-mail: wakeland@pdx.edu. *Application contact:* Dr. Wayne Wakeland, Chair, 503-725-4975, E-mail: wakeland@pdx.edu.
Website: http://www.pdx.edu/sysc/

Prairie View A&M University, College of Arts and Sciences, Division of Social Work, Behavioral and Political Sciences, Prairie View, TX 77446. Offers sociology (MA). *Program availability:* Part-time, evening/weekend. *Faculty:* 3 full-time (1 woman). *Students:* 15 full-time (12 women), 6 part-time (all women); includes 19 minority (all Black or African American, non-Hispanic/Latino), 1 international. Average age 33. 13 applicants, 85% accepted, 10 enrolled. In 2019, 12 master's awarded. *Degree requirements:* For master's, comprehensive exam, thesis (for some programs). *Entrance requirements:* For master's, GRE General Test. Additional exam requirements/recommendations for international students: required—TOEFL (minimum score 550 paper-based; 79 iBT). *Application deadline:* For fall admission, 5/1 priority date for domestic and international students; for spring admission, 10/1 priority date for domestic students, 9/1 priority date for international students; for summer admission, 3/1 priority date for domestic students, 2/1 priority date for international students. Applications are processed on a rolling basis. Application fee: $50. Electronic applications accepted. *Expenses: Tuition, area resident:* Full-time $5479.68. Tuition, state resident: full-time $5479.68. Tuition, nonresident: full-time $15,439. *International tuition:* $15,439 full-time. *Required fees:* $2149.32. *Financial support:* Application deadline: 4/1; applicants required to submit FAFSA. *Unit head:* Dr. Walle Engedayehu, Division Head, 936-261-3202, Fax: 936-261-3229, E-mail: waengedayehu@pvamu.edu. *Application contact:* Pauline Walker, Administrative Assistant II, Research and Graduate Studies, 936-261-3521, Fax: 936-261-3529, E-mail: gradadmissions@pvamu.edu.
Website: http://www.pvamu.edu/swbps/

Princeton University, Graduate School, Department of Sociology, Princeton, NJ 08544-1019. Offers sociology (PhD); sociology and demography (PhD). *Degree requirements:* For doctorate, variable foreign language requirement, thesis/dissertation. *Entrance requirements:* For doctorate, GRE General Test, GRE Subject Test (recommended), sample of written work. Additional exam requirements/recommendations for international students: required—TOEFL (minimum score 600 paper-based). Electronic applications accepted.

Princeton University, Graduate School, Program in Population Studies, Princeton, NJ 08544-1019. Offers demography (PhD, Certificate); economics and demography (PhD); public affairs and demography (PhD); sociology and demography (PhD). *Degree requirements:* For doctorate, thesis/dissertation. *Entrance requirements:* For doctorate, GRE General Test. Additional exam requirements/recommendations for international students: required—TOEFL (minimum score 600 paper-based). Electronic applications accepted.

Purdue University, Graduate School, College of Liberal Arts, Department of Sociology, West Lafayette, IN 47907. Offers MS, PhD. *Faculty:* 23 full-time (9 women), 1 (woman) part-time/adjunct. *Students:* 27 full-time (19 women), 1 (woman) part-time; includes 3 minority (all Hispanic/Latino), 7 international. Average age 28. 46 applicants, 20% accepted, 6 enrolled. In 2019, 5 master's, 6 doctorates awarded. *Degree requirements:* For master's, thesis; for doctorate, comprehensive exam, thesis/dissertation. *Entrance requirements:* For master's, GRE General Test, minimum undergraduate GPA of 3.0 or equivalent; for doctorate, GRE General Test, minimum undergraduate GPA of 3.0 or equivalent; master's degree in sociology with minimum GPA of 3.25 or equivalent. Additional exam requirements/recommendations for international students: required—TOEFL (minimum score 78 iBT). *Application deadline:* For fall admission, 12/15 for domestic and international students. Application fee: $60 ($75 for international students). *Unit head:* Shawn G. Bauldry, Head, 765-496-3200, E-mail: sbauldry@purdue.edu. *Application contact:* Shawn G. Bauldry, Graduate Contact, 765-494-3200, E-mail: sbauldry@purdue.edu.
Website: http://www.cla.purdue.edu/sociology/

Queens College of the City University of New York, School of Social Sciences, Department of Sociology, Queens, NY 11367-1597. Offers data analytics and applied social research (MA). *Program availability:* Part-time, evening/weekend. *Entrance requirements:* For master's, minimum GPA of 3.0. Additional exam requirements/recommendations for international students: required—TOEFL (minimum score 100 iBT), IELTS (minimum score 7). Electronic applications accepted.

Queen's University at Kingston, School of Graduate Studies, Faculty of Arts and Science, Department of Sociology, Kingston, ON K7L 3N6, Canada. Offers communication and information technology (MA, PhD); feminist sociology (MA, PhD); socio-legal studies (MA, PhD); sociological theory (MA, PhD). *Program availability:* Part-time. *Degree requirements:* For master's, thesis; for doctorate, comprehensive exam, thesis/dissertation. *Entrance requirements:* For master's, honors bachelor's degree in sociology; for doctorate, honors bachelor's degree, master's degree in sociology. Additional exam requirements/recommendations for international students: required—TOEFL.

Rice University, Graduate Programs, School of Social Sciences, Department of Sociology, Houston, TX 77251-1892. Offers PhD.

Roosevelt University, Graduate Division, College of Arts and Sciences, Department of Sociology and Sustainability Studies, Chicago, IL 60605. Offers community development and action (MA). *Program availability:* Part-time, evening/weekend.

Rutgers University - New Brunswick, Graduate School-New Brunswick, Program in Sociology, Piscataway, NJ 08854-8097. Offers MA, PhD. Terminal master's awarded for partial completion of doctoral program. *Degree requirements:* For master's, qualifying paper; for doctorate, thesis/dissertation, qualifying exam, qualifying papers. *Entrance requirements:* For master's, GRE General Test; for doctorate, GRE General Test, sample of written work. Additional exam requirements/recommendations for international students: required—TOEFL. Electronic applications accepted.

St. John's University, St. John's College of Liberal Arts and Sciences, Department of Sociology and Anthropology, Queens, NY 11439. Offers criminology and justice (MA); sociology (MA). *Program availability:* Part-time, evening/weekend. *Degree requirements:* For master's, comprehensive exam, thesis optional. *Entrance requirements:* For master's, letters of recommendation, transcripts, resume, personal statement. Additional exam requirements/recommendations for international students: required—TOEFL (minimum score 80 iBT), IELTS (minimum score 6.5). Electronic applications accepted.

Sam Houston State University, College of Humanities and Social Sciences, Department of Sociology, Huntsville, TX 77341. Offers MA. *Program availability:* Part-time, evening/weekend, online learning. *Degree requirements:* For master's, comprehensive exam, thesis optional, professional paper. *Entrance requirements:* For master's, GRE General Test, minimum GPA of 3.0, letter of intent, letters of recommendation. Additional exam requirements/recommendations for international students: required—TOEFL (minimum score 550 paper-based; 79 iBT), IELTS (minimum score 6.5). Electronic applications accepted.

San Diego State University, Graduate and Research Affairs, College of Arts and Letters, Department of Sociology, San Diego, CA 92182. Offers MA. *Degree requirements:* For master's, thesis. *Entrance requirements:* For master's, GRE General Test, 3 letters of recommendation, writing sample. Additional exam requirements/recommendations for international students: required—TOEFL. Electronic applications accepted.

Shippensburg University of Pennsylvania, School of Graduate Studies, College of Arts and Sciences, Department of Sociology and Anthropology, Shippensburg, PA 17257-2299. Offers organizational development and leadership (MS), including business. *Program availability:* Part-time, evening/weekend. *Faculty:* 3 full-time (1 woman). *Students:* 13 full-time (9 women), 23 part-time (14 women); includes 11 minority (8 Black or African American, non-Hispanic/Latino; 1 Asian, non-Hispanic/Latino; 2 Hispanic/Latino), 1 international. Average age 30. 54 applicants, 65% accepted, 15 enrolled. In 2019, 15 master's awarded. *Degree requirements:* For master's, thesis, capstone experience including internship. *Entrance requirements:* For master's, interview (if GPA less than 2.75), current resume, personal goals statement, track selection form. Additional exam requirements/recommendations for international students: required—TOEFL (minimum score 550 paper-based; 68 iBT), IELTS (minimum score 6), TOEFL (minimum score 550 paper-based, 68 iBT) or IELTS (minimum score 6). *Application deadline:* For fall admission, 4/30 for international students; for spring admission, 9/30 for international students. Applications are processed on a rolling basis. Application fee: $45. Electronic applications accepted. *Expenses:* Tuition, state resident: part-time $516 per credit. Tuition, nonresident: part-time $774 per credit. *Required fees:* $149 per credit. *Financial support:* In 2019–20, 17 students received support. Career-related internships or fieldwork, scholarships/grants, unspecified assistantships, and resident hall director and student payroll positions available. Support available to part-time students. Financial award application deadline: 3/1; financial award applicants required to submit FAFSA. *Unit head:* Dr. Barbara J. Denison, Departmental Chair and Program Coordinator, 717-477-1735, Fax: 717-477-4011, E-mail: bjdeni@ship.edu. *Application contact:* Maya T. Mapp, Director of Admissions, 717-477-1231, Fax: 717-477-4016, E-mail: mtmapp@ship.edu.
Website: http://www.ship.edu/odl/

Simon Fraser University, Office of Graduate Studies and Postdoctoral Fellows, Faculty of Arts and Social Sciences, Department of Sociology and Anthropology, Burnaby, BC V5A 1S6, Canada. Offers anthropology (MA, PhD); sociology (MA, PhD). *Degree requirements:* For master's, thesis; for doctorate, comprehensive exam, thesis/dissertation, cooperative education. *Entrance requirements:* For master's, minimum GPA of 3.0 (on scale of 4.33) or 3.33 based on last 60 credits of undergraduate courses; for doctorate, minimum GPA of 3.5 (on scale of 4.33). Additional exam requirements/recommendations for international students: recommended—TOEFL (minimum score 580 paper-based; 93 iBT), IELTS (minimum score 7), TWE (minimum score 5). Electronic applications accepted.

South Dakota State University, Graduate School, College of Arts, Humanities and Social Sciences, Department of Sociology and Rural Studies, Brookings, SD 57007. Offers sociology (MS, PhD). *Program availability:* Part-time, online learning. *Degree requirements:* For master's, comprehensive exam (for some programs), thesis, oral and written exams; for doctorate, comprehensive exam, thesis/dissertation, preliminary oral and written exams. *Entrance requirements:* Additional exam requirements/recommendations for international students: required—TOEFL (minimum score 550 paper-based; 79 iBT).

Southeastern Louisiana University, College of Arts, Humanities and Social Sciences, Department of Communication and Media Studies, Hammond, LA 70402. Offers health communications (MA); journalism (MA); marketing (MA); public relations (MA); sociology (MA). *Program availability:* Part-time. *Faculty:* 7 full-time (5 women). *Students:* 10 full-time (6 women), 11 part-time (6 women); includes 7 minority (5 Black or African American, non-Hispanic/Latino; 2 Hispanic/Latino). Average age 30. 9 applicants, 100% accepted, 6 enrolled. In 2019, 3 master's awarded. *Degree requirements:* For master's, comprehensive exam. *Entrance requirements:* For master's, GRE (minimum score 148 on Verbal section, 3.5 Written), Minimum 2.5 undergraduate GPA. Additional exam requirements/recommendations for international students: required—TOEFL (minimum score 525 paper-based; 75 iBT). *Application deadline:* For fall admission, 7/15 priority date for domestic students, 6/1 priority date for international students; for spring admission, 12/1 priority date for domestic students, 10/1 priority date for international students. Applications are processed on a rolling basis. Application fee: $20 ($30 for international students). Electronic applications accepted. *Expenses: Tuition, area resident:* Full-time $6684; part-time $489 per credit hour. Tuition, state resident: full-time $6684; part-time $489 per credit hour. Tuition, nonresident: full-time $19,162; part-time $1183 per credit hour. *International tuition:* $19,162 full-time. *Required fees:* $2124. *Financial support:* In 2019–20, 11 students received support, including 3 research assistantships with tuition reimbursements available (averaging $10,100 per year); career-related internships or fieldwork, institutionally sponsored loans, and unspecified assistantships also available. Financial award application deadline: 5/1; financial award applicants required to submit FAFSA. *Unit head:* Dr. James O'Connor, Department Head, 985-549-5060, Fax: 985-549-3088, E-mail: james.oconnor@selu.edu. *Application contact:* Office of Admissions, 985-549-5637, Fax: 985-549-5632, E-mail: admissions@southeastern.edu.
Website: http://www.southeastern.edu/acad_research/depts/comm/index.html

Southeastern Louisiana University, College of Arts, Humanities and Social Sciences, Department of Sociology and Criminal Justice, Hammond, LA 70402. Offers criminal justice (MS); globalization and sustainability (MS). *Program availability:* Part-time. *Faculty:* 9 full-time (3 women). *Students:* 18 full-time (9 women), 6 part-time (4 women); includes 10 minority (6 Black or African American, non-Hispanic/Latino; 3 Hispanic/Latino; 1 Two or more races, non-Hispanic/Latino), 1 international. Average age 27. 6 applicants, 83% accepted, 3 enrolled. In 2019, 3 master's awarded. *Degree requirements:* For master's, comprehensive exam, thesis. *Entrance requirements:* For master's, GRE, A Bachelor's degree from an accredited institution in Sociology, Criminal Justice, Social Work or a related social science field. Satisfactory completion of prerequisite courses: sociological theory, social research methods and elementary social statistics. Two letters of recommendation. A personal/autobiographical statement. Additional exam requirements/recommendations for international students: required—TOEFL (minimum score 500 paper-based; 61 iBT). *Application deadline:* For fall admission, 7/15 priority date for domestic students, 6/1 priority date for international students; for spring admission, 12/1 priority date for domestic students, 10/1 priority date for international students. Applications are processed on a rolling basis. Application fee: $20 ($30 for international students). Electronic applications accepted. *Expenses: Tuition, area resident:* Full-time $6684; part-time $489 per credit hour. Tuition, state resident: full-time $6684; part-time $489 per credit hour. Tuition, nonresident: full-time $19,162; part-time $1183 per credit hour. *International tuition:* $19,162 full-time. *Required fees:* $2124. *Financial support:* In 2019–20, 16 students received support, including 1 fellowship with tuition reimbursement available (averaging $2,500 per year), 5 research assistantships with tuition reimbursements available (averaging $10,100 per year); career-related internships or fieldwork, institutionally sponsored loans, and unspecified assistantships also available. Financial award application deadline: 5/1; financial award applicants required to submit FAFSA. *Unit head:* Dr. Kenneth Bolton, Department Head, 985-549-2110, Fax: 985-549-5961, E-mail: kbolton@southeastern.edu. *Application contact:* Office of Admissions, 985-549-5637, Fax: 985-549-5632, E-mail: admissions@southeastern.edu.
Website: http://www.southeastern.edu/acad_research/depts/soc_cj/grad_degree/index.html

Southern Connecticut State University, School of Graduate Studies, School of Arts and Sciences, Department of Sociology, New Haven, CT 06515-1355. Offers MS. *Program availability:* Part-time, evening/weekend. *Degree requirements:* For master's, thesis or alternative. *Entrance requirements:* For master's, interview. Electronic applications accepted.

Southern Illinois University Carbondale, Graduate School, College of Liberal Arts, Department of Sociology, Carbondale, IL 62901-4701. Offers MA, PhD. *Program availability:* Part-time. *Degree requirements:* For master's, thesis; for doctorate, thesis/dissertation. *Entrance requirements:* For master's, GRE, minimum GPA of 2.7; for doctorate, GRE, minimum GPA of 3.25. Additional exam requirements/recommendations for international students: required—TOEFL.

Southern Illinois University Edwardsville, Graduate School, College of Arts and Sciences, Department of Sociology and Criminal Justice Studies, Edwardsville, IL 62026. Offers sociology (MA). *Program availability:* Part-time. *Degree requirements:* For master's, thesis (for some programs), internship. *Entrance requirements:* Additional exam requirements/recommendations for international students: required—TOEFL (minimum score 550 paper-based; 79 iBT), IELTS (minimum score 6.5). Electronic applications accepted.

Stanford University, School of Humanities and Sciences, Department of Sociology, Stanford, CA 94305-2004. Offers PhD. *Expenses: Tuition:* Full-time $52,479; part-time $34,110 per unit. *Required fees:* $672; $224 per quarter. Tuition and fees vary according to program and student level.
Website: http://www.stanford.edu/dept/soc/

Stony Brook University, State University of New York, Graduate School, College of Arts and Sciences, Department of Sociology, Stony Brook, NY 11794. Offers MA, PhD. *Faculty:* 16 full-time (7 women), 1 (woman) part-time/adjunct. *Students:* 36 full-time (21 women), 1 (woman) part-time; includes 10 minority (2 Black or African American, non-Hispanic/Latino; 5 Asian, non-Hispanic/Latino; 1 Hispanic/Latino; 2 Two or more races, non-Hispanic/Latino), 11 international. Average age 32. 40 applicants, 15% accepted, 4 enrolled. In 2019, 6 master's, 6 doctorates awarded. *Degree requirements:* For doctorate, thesis/dissertation, comprehensive exam or professional papers, field exam, teaching practicum. *Entrance requirements:* For doctorate, GRE General Test, minimum GPA of 3.0. Additional exam requirements/recommendations for international students: required—TOEFL (minimum score 90 iBT). *Application deadline:* For fall admission, 1/15 for domestic students; for spring admission, 10/1 for domestic students. Application fee: $100. *Expenses:* Contact institution. *Financial support:* In 2019–20, 21 teaching assistantships were awarded; fellowships and research assistantships also available. *Unit head:* Dr. Kathleen M Fallon, Chair, 631-632-7581, E-mail: Kathleen.Fallon@stonybrook.edu. *Application contact:* Wanda Vega, Coordinator, 631-632-7730, Fax: 631-632-8203, E-mail: wanda.olivera@stonybrook.edu.
Website: http://www.sunysb.edu/sociology/

Syracuse University, Maxwell School of Citizenship and Public Affairs, Programs in Sociology, Syracuse, NY 13244. Offers MA, PhD. *Degree requirements:* For master's, thesis; for doctorate, comprehensive exam, thesis/dissertation. *Entrance requirements:* For master's and doctorate, GRE General Test, three letters of recommendation, resume, personal statement, official transcripts. Additional exam requirements/recommendations for international students: required—TOEFL (minimum score 100 iBT). Electronic applications accepted.

Teachers College, Columbia University, Department of Education Policy and Social Analysis, New York, NY 10027-6696. Offers economics and education (Ed M, MA, PhD); education policy (Ed M, MA, Ed D, PhD); politics and education (Ed M, MA, Ed D, PhD); sociology and education (Ed M, MA, Ed D, PhD). *Faculty:* 11 full-time (4 women). *Students:* 89 full-time (71 women), 154 part-time (113 women); includes 91 minority (36 Black or African American, non-Hispanic/Latino; 19 Asian, non-Hispanic/Latino; 29 Hispanic/Latino; 7 Two or more races, non-Hispanic/Latino), 73 international. 433 applicants, 60% accepted, 107 enrolled. *Unit head:* Dr. Aaron Pallas, Chair, 212-678-8119, E-mail: amp155@tc.columbia.edu. *Application contact:* Kelly Sutton-Skinner, Director of Admission and New Student Enrollment, 212-678-3710, E-mail:

kms2237@tc.columbia.edu.
Website: http://www.tc.columbia.edu/education-policy-and-social-analysis/

Temple University, College of Liberal Arts, Department of Sociology, Philadelphia, PA 19122-6096. Offers MA, PhD. *Program availability:* Part-time. *Faculty:* 15 full-time (6 women), 2 part-time/adjunct (1 woman). *Students:* 29 full-time (17 women), 3 part-time (2 women); includes 10 minority (5 Black or African American, non-Hispanic/Latino; 3 Hispanic/Latino; 2 Two or more races, non-Hispanic/Latino), 4 international. 59 applicants, 19% accepted, 5 enrolled. In 2019, 1 master's, 1 doctorate awarded. Terminal master's awarded for partial completion of doctoral program. *Entrance requirements:* For master's and doctorate, GRE, 3 letters of recommendation, statement of goals, writing sample. Additional exam requirements/recommendations for international students: required—TOEFL (minimum score 100 iBT), IELTS (minimum score 7), PTE (minimum score 68), one of three is required. Application fee: $60. Electronic applications accepted. *Financial support:* Fellowships, teaching assistantships, Federal Work-Study, and health care benefits available. Financial award applicants required to submit FAFSA. *Unit head:* Kimberly Goyette, Chair, 215-204-0134, E-mail: kgoyette@temple.edu. *Application contact:* Pamela Smallwood, Coordinator, 215-204-7750, E-mail: poppy@temple.edu.
Website: http://www.cla.temple.edu/sociology/

Texas A&M International University, Office of Graduate Studies and Research, College of Arts and Sciences, Department of Social Sciences, Laredo, TX 78041. Offers criminal justice (MS); history and political thought (MA); public administration (MPA); sociology (MA). *Degree requirements:* For master's, comprehensive exam (for some programs), thesis (for some programs). *Entrance requirements:* For master's, GRE General Test. Additional exam requirements/recommendations for international students: required—TOEFL (minimum score 550 paper-based; 79 iBT).

Texas A&M University, College of Liberal Arts, Department of Sociology, College Station, TX 77843. Offers sociology (MS, PhD). *Faculty:* 24. *Students:* 50 full-time (31 women), 21 part-time (14 women); includes 32 minority (9 Black or African American, non-Hispanic/Latino; 3 Asian, non-Hispanic/Latino; 19 Hispanic/Latino; 1 Two or more races, non-Hispanic/Latino), 8 international. Average age 32. 32 applicants, 94% accepted, 11 enrolled. In 2019, 1 master's, 10 doctorates awarded. *Degree requirements:* For master's, comprehensive exam (for some programs), thesis optional; for doctorate, comprehensive exam, thesis/dissertation. *Entrance requirements:* For master's and doctorate, GRE General Test, statement of purpose, letters of recommendation, curriculum vitae, writing sample. Additional exam requirements/recommendations for international students: required—TOEFL (minimum score 550 paper-based; 80 iBT), IELTS (minimum score 6), PTE. *Application deadline:* For fall admission, 1/5 for domestic students. Applications are processed on a rolling basis. Application fee: $65 ($90 for international students). Electronic applications accepted. *Expenses:* Contact institution. *Financial support:* In 2019–20, 60 students received support, including 16 fellowships with tuition reimbursements available (averaging $9,996 per year), 9 research assistantships with tuition reimbursements available (averaging $11,183 per year), 39 teaching assistantships with tuition reimbursements available (averaging $14,102 per year); career-related internships or fieldwork, institutionally sponsored loans, scholarships/grants, traineeships, health care benefits, tuition waivers (full and partial), and unspecified assistantships also available. Support available to part-time students. Financial award application deadline: 3/15; financial award applicants required to submit FAFSA. *Unit head:* Dr. Jane Sell, Interim Department Head, 979-845-6120, Fax: 979-862-4057, E-mail: j-sell@tamu.edu. *Application contact:* Dr. Pat Rubio Goldsmith, Director of Graduate Admissions, E-mail: pgoldsmith@tamu.edu.
Website: http://sociology.tamu.edu/

Texas A&M University–Commerce, College of Humanities, Social Sciences and Arts, Commerce, TX 75429. Offers applied criminology (MS); applied linguistics (MA, MS); art (MA, MFA); christianity in history (Graduate Certificate); computational linguistics (Graduate Certificate); creative writing (Graduate Certificate); criminal justice management (Graduate Certificate); criminal justice studies (Graduate Certificate); English (MA, MS, PhD); film studies (Graduate Certificate); history (MA, MS); Holocaust studies (Graduate Certificate); homeland security (Graduate Certificate); music (MM); music performance (MM); political science (MA, MS); public history (Graduate Certificate); sociology (MS); Spanish (MA); studies in children's and adolescent literature and culture (Graduate Certificate); teaching English to speakers of other languages (Graduate Certificate); theater (MA, MS); world history (Graduate Certificate). *Program availability:* Part-time. *Faculty:* 49 full-time (28 women), 8 part-time/adjunct (2 women). *Students:* 34 full-time (21 women), 427 part-time (302 women); includes 175 minority (66 Black or African American, non-Hispanic/Latino; 1 American Indian or Alaska Native, non-Hispanic/Latino; 13 Asian, non-Hispanic/Latino; 79 Hispanic/Latino; 16 Two or more races, non-Hispanic/Latino), 15 international. Average age 38. 193 applicants, 49% accepted, 78 enrolled. In 2019, 122 master's, 6 doctorates awarded. *Degree requirements:* For master's, one foreign language, comprehensive exam, thesis (for some programs); for doctorate, one foreign language, comprehensive exam, thesis/dissertation, departmental qualifying exam. *Entrance requirements:* For master's, GRE General Test, official transcripts, letters of recommendation, resume, statement of goals; for doctorate, GRE General Test, official transcripts, letters of recommendation, statement of goals, writing samples, writing sessions, resumes. Additional exam requirements/recommendations for international students: required—TOEFL (minimum score 550 paper-based; 79 iBT), IELTS (minimum score 6), PTE (minimum score 53). *Application deadline:* For fall admission, 6/1 priority date for international students; for spring admission, 10/15 priority date for international students; for summer admission, 3/15 priority date for international students. Applications are processed on a rolling basis. Application fee: $50 ($75 for international students). Electronic applications accepted. *Expenses: Tuition, area resident:* Full-time $3630; part-time $202 per credit hour. Tuition, state resident: full-time $3630; part-time $202 per credit hour. Tuition, nonresident: full-time $11,232; part-time $624 per credit hour. *International tuition:* $11,232 full-time. *Required fees:* $2948. *Financial support:* In 2019–20, 30 students received support, including 18 research assistantships with partial tuition reimbursements available (averaging $3,231 per year), 136 teaching assistantships with partial tuition reimbursements available (averaging $4,053 per year); Federal Work-Study, institutionally sponsored loans, scholarships/grants, health care benefits, and unspecified assistantships also available. Financial award application deadline: 5/1; financial award applicants required to submit FAFSA. *Unit head:* Dr. William F. Kuracina, Interim Dean, 903-886-5166, Fax: 903-886-5774, E-mail: william.kuracina@tamuc.edu. *Application contact:* Rebecca Stevens, Graduate Student Services Coordinator, 903-468-6049, E-mail: rebecca.stevens@tamuc.edu.
Website: http://www.tamuc.edu/academics/colleges/humanitiesSocialSciencesArts/

Texas A&M University–Kingsville, College of Graduate Studies, College of Arts and Sciences, Department of Psychology and Sociology, Program in Sociology, Kingsville, TX 78363. Offers MA, MS. *Entrance requirements:* Additional exam requirements/recommendations for international students: required—TOEFL (minimum score 550 paper-based; 79 iBT); recommended—IELTS. Electronic applications accepted.

Texas Southern University, College of Liberal Arts and Behavioral Sciences, Department of Sociology, Houston, TX 77004-4584. Offers MA. *Program availability:* Part-time, evening/weekend. *Degree requirements:* For master's, comprehensive exam, thesis. *Entrance requirements:* For master's, GRE General Test, minimum GPA of 2.5. Additional exam requirements/recommendations for international students: required—TOEFL. Electronic applications accepted.

Texas State University, The Graduate College, College of Liberal Arts, Program in Applied Sociology, San Marcos, TX 78666. Offers MS. *Program availability:* Part-time, evening/weekend. *Degree requirements:* For master's, comprehensive exam. *Entrance requirements:* For master's, baccalaureate degree from regionally-accredited university with minimum GPA of 3.0 on last 60 undergraduate semester hours; background course work in sociological theory, statistics, and social research; statement of purpose describing personal goals and academic interest in relation to personal goals; three letters of recommendation. Additional exam requirements/recommendations for international students: required—TOEFL (minimum score 550 paper-based; 78 iBT), IELTS (minimum score 6.5). Electronic applications accepted.

Texas State University, The Graduate College, College of Liberal Arts, Program in Sociology, San Marcos, TX 78666. Offers MA. *Program availability:* Part-time, evening/weekend. *Degree requirements:* For master's, comprehensive exam, thesis optional. *Entrance requirements:* For master's, baccalaureate degree from regionally-accredited university with minimum GPA of 3.0 on last 60 undergraduate semester hours; background course work in sociological theory, statistics, and social research; statement of purpose describing personal goals, academic interest and career goals; 3 letters of recommendation. Additional exam requirements/recommendations for international students: required—TOEFL (minimum score 550 paper-based; 78 iBT), IELTS (minimum score 6.5). Electronic applications accepted.

Texas Tech University, Graduate School, College of Arts and Sciences, Department of Sociology, Anthropology and Social Work, Lubbock, TX 79409-1012. Offers anthropology (MA); social work (MSW); sociology (MA). *Accreditation:* CSWE. *Program availability:* Part-time. *Faculty:* 28 full-time (17 women), 6 part-time/adjunct (5 women). *Students:* 43 full-time (30 women), 10 part-time (6 women); includes 14 minority (1 Black or African American, non-Hispanic/Latino; 1 Asian, non-Hispanic/Latino; 7 Hispanic/Latino; 5 Two or more races, non-Hispanic/Latino), 7 international. Average age 31. 43 applicants, 51% accepted, 18 enrolled. In 2019, 29 master's awarded. *Degree requirements:* For master's, one foreign language, comprehensive exam (for some programs), thesis (for some programs). *Entrance requirements:* For master's, two letters of recommendation, statement of purpose, writing sample, curriculum vitae; minimum GPA of 3.0 and coursework in sociology or closely-related fields (for MA in sociology); coursework in anthropology (for MA in anthropology). Additional exam requirements/recommendations for international students: required—TOEFL (minimum score 550 paper-based; 79 iBT). *Application deadline:* For fall admission, 6/1 priority date for domestic students, 1/15 priority date for international students; for spring admission, 9/1 priority date for domestic students, 6/15 priority date for international students. Applications are processed on a rolling basis. Application fee: $65. Electronic applications accepted. *Expenses:* Contact institution. *Financial support:* In 2019–20, 46 students received support, including 40 fellowships (averaging $4,359 per year), 28 teaching assistantships (averaging $12,255 per year); research assistantships, Federal Work-Study, scholarships/grants, tuition waivers (partial), and unspecified assistantships also available. Financial award application deadline: 2/1; financial award applicants required to submit FAFSA. *Unit head:* Dr. Cristina Bradatan, Associate Professor and Chair, 806-834-1796, Fax: 806-742-1088, E-mail: cristina.bradatan@ttu.edu. *Application contact:* Dr. Martha Smithey, Associate Professor/Sociology Graduate Program Director, 806-834-1995, E-mail: martha.smithey@ttu.edu.
Website: www.sasw.ttu.edu

Texas Woman's University, Graduate School, College of Arts and Sciences, Department of Sociology, Denton, TX 76204. Offers social work (MSW); sociology (MA, PhD). *Program availability:* Evening/weekend. *Faculty:* 6 full-time (2 women). *Students:* 2 full-time (both women), 51 part-time (40 women); includes 23 minority (11 Black or African American, non-Hispanic/Latino; 2 Asian, non-Hispanic/Latino; 7 Hispanic/Latino; 3 Two or more races, non-Hispanic/Latino), 3 international. Average age 39. 14 applicants, 57% accepted, 3 enrolled. In 2019, 7 master's, 4 doctorates awarded. *Degree requirements:* For master's, comprehensive exam, thesis or alternative, written comprehensive exam, thesis or non-thesis options; for doctorate, comprehensive exam, thesis/dissertation, 2 written exams. *Entrance requirements:* For master's, 2 letters of reference, 2-3 page statement of interest, minimum GPA of 3.0 in last 60 hours of undergraduate work and all graduate work; for doctorate, GRE General Test, minimum GPA of 3.5 on last 60 undergraduate hours and all graduate coursework, graduate statistics and social sciences research methods, 3 letters of reference, writing sample. Additional exam requirements/recommendations for international students: required—TOEFL (minimum score 550 paper-based; 79 iBT); recommended—IELTS (minimum score 6.5), TSE (minimum score 53). *Application deadline:* For fall admission, 3/1 priority date for domestic students, 3/1 for international students; for spring admission, 11/1 priority date for domestic students, 7/1 for international students; for summer admission, 5/1 priority date for domestic students, 2/1 for international students. Applications are processed on a rolling basis. Application fee: $50 ($75 for international students). Electronic applications accepted. *Expenses: Tuition, area resident:* Full-time $4973.40; part-time $276.30 per semester hour. Tuition, state resident: full-time $4973.40; part-time $276.30 per semester hour. Tuition, nonresident: full-time $12,569; part-time $698.30 per semester hour. *International tuition:* $12,569.40 full-time. *Required fees:* $2524.30. Tuition and fees vary according to course level, course load, degree level and program. *Financial support:* In 2019–20, 27 students received support, including 18 teaching assistantships (averaging $13,239 per year); career-related internships or fieldwork, scholarships/grants, health care benefits, and unspecified assistantships also available. Support available to part-time students. Financial award application deadline: 3/1; financial award applicants required to submit FAFSA. *Unit head:* Dr. Celia Lo, Chair, 940-898-2052, Fax: 940-898-2067, E-mail: sociology@twu.edu. *Application contact:* Korie Hawkins, Associate Director of Admissions, Graduate Recruitment, 940-898-3188, Fax: 940-898-3081, E-mail: admissions@twu.edu.
Website: http://www.twu.edu/sociology/

Tulane University, School of Liberal Arts, Department of Sociology, New Orleans, LA 70118-5669. Offers MA. Terminal master's awarded for partial completion of doctoral program. *Degree requirements:* For master's, thesis. *Entrance requirements:* For master's, GRE General Test, minimum B average in undergraduate course work. Additional exam requirements/recommendations for international students: required—TOEFL. Electronic applications accepted. *Expenses: Tuition:* Full-time $57,004; part-time $3167 per credit hour. *Required fees:* $2086; $44.50 per credit hour. $80 per term. Tuition and fees vary according to course load, degree level and program.

UNB Fredericton, School of Graduate Studies, Faculty of Arts - Saint John, Sociology, Fredericton, NB E3B 5A3, Canada. Offers MA, PhD. *Program availability:* Part-time. *Faculty:* 11 full-time (7 women), 3 part-time/adjunct (2 women). *Students:* 21 full-time (18 women), 3 part-time (all women), 2 international. Average age 31. In 2019, 2 doctorates awarded. *Degree requirements:* For master's, thesis; for doctorate, comprehensive exam, thesis/dissertation, 6 courses. *Entrance requirements:* For

master's, minimum GPA of 3.5; for doctorate, MA in sociology with thesis or equivalent, curriculum vitae, statement of interest about intended research and why UNB was selected. Additional exam requirements/recommendations for international students: required—TOEFL. *Application deadline:* For fall admission, 3/1 for domestic students; for winter admission, 1/15 priority date for domestic and international students. Applications are processed on a rolling basis. Application fee: $50 Canadian dollars. Electronic applications accepted. *Expenses: Tuition, area resident:* Full-time $6975 Canadian dollars; part-time $3423 Canadian dollars per year. Tuition, state resident: full-time $6975 Canadian dollars; part-time $3423 Canadian dollars per year. Tuition, Canadian resident: full-time $6975 Canadian dollars; part-time $3423 Canadian dollars per year. *International tuition:* $12,435 Canadian dollars full-time. *Required fees:* $92.25 Canadian dollars per term. Full-time tuition and fees vary according to degree level, campus/location, program, reciprocity agreements and student level. *Financial support:* Fellowships, research assistantships, and teaching assistantships with tuition reimbursements available. Financial award application deadline: 1/15. *Unit head:* Dr. Nick Hardy, Director of Graduate Studies, 506-458-7444, Fax: 506-453-4659, E-mail: nhardy@unb.ca. *Application contact:* Wanda Birch, Acting Graduate Secretary, 506-458-7474, Fax: 506-453-4659, E-mail: wanda.birch@unb.ca.
Website: http://go.unb.ca/gradprograms

Université de Montréal, Faculty of Arts and Sciences, Department of Sociology, Montréal, QC H3C 3J7, Canada. Offers M Sc, PhD. *Degree requirements:* For master's, thesis; for doctorate, thesis/dissertation, general exam. *Entrance requirements:* For master's, minimum GPA of 3.0; for doctorate, minimum GPA of 3.5, proficiency in French. Electronic applications accepted.

Université du Québec à Montréal, Graduate Programs, Program in Social Intervention, Montréal, QC H3C 3P8, Canada. Offers MA. *Program availability:* Part-time. *Degree requirements:* For master's, thesis. *Entrance requirements:* For master's, appropriate bachelor's degree or equivalent, proficiency in French.

Université du Québec à Montréal, Graduate Programs, Program in Sociology, Montréal, QC H3C 3P8, Canada. Offers MA, PhD. *Program availability:* Part-time. *Degree requirements:* For master's, thesis optional; for doctorate, thesis/dissertation. *Entrance requirements:* For master's, appropriate bachelor's degree or equivalent, proficiency in French; for doctorate, appropriate master's degree or equivalent, proficiency in French.

University at Albany, State University of New York, College of Arts and Sciences, Department of Communication, Albany, NY 12222-0001. Offers communication (MA); sociology and communication (PhD). *Program availability:* Part-time, blended/hybrid learning. *Faculty:* 17 full-time (9 women), 21 part-time/adjunct (13 women). *Students:* 39 full-time (28 women), 36 part-time (32 women); includes 18 minority (9 Black or African American, non-Hispanic/Latino; 4 Asian, non-Hispanic/Latino; 4 Hispanic/Latino; 1 Two or more races, non-Hispanic/Latino), 14 international. 49 applicants, 71% accepted, 19 enrolled. In 2019, 18 master's, 1 doctorate awarded. *Degree requirements:* For master's, comprehensive exam, thesis or alternative; for doctorate, comprehensive exam, thesis/dissertation. *Entrance requirements:* For master's, minimum GPA of 3.0, transcripts of all schools attended, statement of background and goals, departmental questionnaire, resume, names and contact information for 3 recommenders; for doctorate, GRE, minimum GPA of 3.0, transcripts of all schools attended, statement of background and goals, departmental questionnaire, resume, names and contact information for 3 recommenders. Additional exam requirements/recommendations for international students: required—TOEFL (minimum score 550 paper-based). *Application deadline:* For fall admission, 1/15 priority date for domestic students, 5/1 for international students. Applications are processed on a rolling basis. Application fee: $75. Electronic applications accepted. *Expenses: Tuition, area resident:* Full-time $11,530; part-time $480 per credit hour. Tuition, nonresident: full-time $23,530; part-time $980 per credit hour. *International tuition:* $23,530 full-time. *Required fees:* $2185; $96 per credit hour. Part-time tuition and fees vary according to course load and program. *Financial support:* Fellowships, teaching assistantships, career-related internships or fieldwork, and institutionally sponsored loans available. Financial award application deadline: 3/1. *Unit head:* Annis Golden, Chair, 518-442-4871, Fax: 518-442-3884, E-mail: agolden@albany.edu. *Application contact:* Michael DeRensis, Director, Graduate Admissions, 518-442-3980, Fax: 518-442-3922, E-mail: graduate@albany.edu.
Website: https://www.albany.edu/communication/

University at Albany, State University of New York, College of Arts and Sciences, Department of Sociology, Albany, NY 12222-0001. Offers demography (Certificate); sociology (MA, PhD); urban policy (Certificate). *Program availability:* Blended/hybrid learning. *Faculty:* 23 full-time (10 women), 11 part-time/adjunct (8 women). *Students:* 31 full-time (26 women), 52 part-time (38 women); includes 17 minority (6 Black or African American, non-Hispanic/Latino; 1 American Indian or Alaska Native, non-Hispanic/Latino; 5 Asian, non-Hispanic/Latino; 3 Hispanic/Latino; 2 Two or more races, non-Hispanic/Latino), 35 international. 77 applicants, 49% accepted, 16 enrolled. In 2019, 6 master's, 8 doctorates awarded. Terminal master's awarded for partial completion of doctoral program. *Degree requirements:* For master's, thesis; for doctorate, thesis/dissertation, 2 specialization exams, research tool. *Entrance requirements:* For master's, GRE General Test, transcripts of all schools attended, statement of background and goals, departmental questionnaire, resume, names and contact information for 3 recommenders; for doctorate, GRE General Test. Additional exam requirements/recommendations for international students: required—TOEFL (minimum score 550 paper-based). *Application deadline:* For fall admission, 1/15 for domestic students, 5/1 for international students; for spring admission, 11/15 for domestic students. Applications are processed on a rolling basis. Application fee: $75. Electronic applications accepted. *Expenses: Tuition, area resident:* Full-time $11,530; part-time $480 per credit hour. Tuition, nonresident: full-time $23,530; part-time $980 per credit hour. *International tuition:* $23,530 full-time. *Required fees:* $2185; $96 per credit hour. Part-time tuition and fees vary according to course load and program. *Financial support:* Fellowships, research assistantships, teaching assistantships, career-related internships or fieldwork, and Federal Work-Study available. Financial award application deadline: 3/15. *Unit head:* Glenn Deane, Chair, 518-442-4666, Fax: 518-442-4936, E-mail: gdeane@albany.edu. *Application contact:* Michael DeRensis, Director, Graduate Admissions, 518-442-3980, Fax: 518-442-3922, E-mail: graduate@albany.edu.
Website: https://www.albany.edu/sociology/index.html

University at Buffalo, the State University of New York, Graduate School, College of Arts and Sciences, Department of Sociology, Buffalo, NY 14260. Offers MA, PhD. *Program availability:* Part-time. *Faculty:* 18 full-time (9 women). *Students:* 59 full-time (44 women), 2 part-time (0 women); includes 28 minority (5 Black or African American, non-Hispanic/Latino; 21 Asian, non-Hispanic/Latino; 2 Hispanic/Latino). Average age 30. 58 applicants, 72% accepted, 19 enrolled. In 2019, 18 master's, 4 doctorates awarded. Terminal master's awarded for partial completion of doctoral program. *Degree requirements:* For master's, project (paper) or portfolio; for doctorate, thesis/dissertation, qualifying paper. *Entrance requirements:* For master's and doctorate, GRE General Test. Additional exam requirements/recommendations for international students: required—TOEFL (minimum score 550 paper-based; 79 iBT), IELTS (minimum score 6.5). *Application deadline:* For fall admission, 8/1 priority date for domestic students, 4/1 priority date for international students. Applications are processed on a rolling basis.

Application fee: $75. Electronic applications accepted. *Expenses: Tuition, area resident:* Full-time $11,310; part-time $471 per credit hour. Tuition, state resident: full-time $11,310; part-time $471 per credit hour. Tuition, nonresident: full-time $23,100; part-time $963 per credit hour. *International tuition:* $23,100 full-time. *Required fees:* $2820. *Financial support:* In 2019–20, 14 students received support, including 4 fellowships with full tuition reimbursements available (averaging $4,250 per year), 14 teaching assistantships with full tuition reimbursements available (averaging $17,250 per year); scholarships/grants, health care benefits, and tuition waivers (full) also available. Financial award application deadline: 1/15; financial award applicants required to submit FAFSA. *Unit head:* Dr. Robert Adelman, Chair, 716-645-8478, Fax: 716-645-3934, E-mail: adelman4@buffalo.edu. *Application contact:* Dr. Mary Nell Trautner, Director of Graduate Studies, 716-645-8477, Fax: 716-645-3934, E-mail: trautner@buffalo.edu.
Website: http://arts-sciences.buffalo.edu/sociology.html

The University of Alabama at Birmingham, College of Arts and Sciences, Program in Medical Sociology, Birmingham, AL 35294. Offers PhD. *Program availability:* Part-time. *Faculty:* 12 full-time (7 women), 1 part-time/adjunct (0 women). *Students:* 16 full-time (9 women), 3 part-time (2 women); includes 5 minority (3 Black or African American, non-Hispanic/Latino; 1 Asian, non-Hispanic/Latino; 1 Two or more races, non-Hispanic/Latino), 3 international. Average age 34. 10 applicants, 60% accepted, 2 enrolled. In 2019, 5 doctorates awarded. Terminal master's awarded for partial completion of doctoral program. *Degree requirements:* For doctorate, comprehensive exam, thesis/dissertation, student teaching, manuscript submitted. *Entrance requirements:* For doctorate, GRE, minimum GPA of 3.0 overall and in all previous graduate coursework, 3.2 on last 60 semester hours of baccalaureate work. Additional exam requirements/recommendations for international students: required—TOEFL (minimum score 80 iBT), IELTS (minimum score 6.5). *Application deadline:* For fall admission, 8/1 for domestic students; for spring admission, 12/1 for domestic students; for summer admission, 5/1 for domestic students. Applications are processed on a rolling basis. Application fee: $60. Electronic applications accepted. *Financial support:* In 2019–20, 19 students received support, including fellowships with full tuition reimbursements available (averaging $34,000 per year), 1 research assistantship with full tuition reimbursement available (averaging $18,000 per year), 11 teaching assistantships with full tuition reimbursements available (averaging $18,000 per year); traineeships, health care benefits, and unspecified assistantships also available. *Unit head:* Dr. Verna Keith, Department Chair, 205-934-3307, Fax: 205-975-5614, E-mail: vmkeith@uab.edu. *Application contact:* Jesse Keppley, Director of Student and Academic Services, 205-934-8227, Fax: 205-934-8413, E-mail: gradschool@uab.edu.
Website: http://www.uab.edu/cas/sociology/graduate-programs

University of Alberta, Faculty of Graduate Studies and Research, Department of Sociology, Edmonton, AB T6G 2E1, Canada. Offers criminal justice (MA); demography (MA, PhD); sociology (MA, PhD). *Program availability:* Part-time. *Degree requirements:* For master's, thesis (for some programs); for doctorate, thesis/dissertation.

The University of Arizona, College of Social and Behavioral Sciences, Department of Sociology, Tucson, AZ 85721. Offers MA, PhD. *Degree requirements:* For master's, publishable paper/oral; for doctorate, thesis/dissertation, 2 preliminary exams. *Entrance requirements:* For doctorate, GRE General Test, 3 letters of recommendation, writing samples. Additional exam requirements/recommendations for international students: required—TOEFL (minimum score 630 paper-based). Electronic applications accepted.

University of Arkansas, Graduate School, J. William Fulbright College of Arts and Sciences, Department of Sociology, Fayetteville, AR 72701. Offers MA. *Program availability:* Part-time. *Students:* 9 full-time (7 women), 13 part-time (8 women); includes 5 minority (1 Black or African American, non-Hispanic/Latino; 1 Hispanic/Latino; 3 Two or more races, non-Hispanic/Latino), 2 international. 12 applicants, 83% accepted. In 2019, 2 master's awarded. *Application deadline:* For fall admission, 8/1 for domestic students, 4/1 for international students; for spring admission, 12/1 for domestic students, 10/1 for international students; for summer admission, 4/15 for domestic students, 3/1 for international students. Applications are processed on a rolling basis. Application fee: $60. Electronic applications accepted. *Financial support:* In 2019–20, 5 research assistantships, 10 teaching assistantships were awarded; fellowships with tuition reimbursements, career-related internships or fieldwork, and Federal Work-Study also available. Support available to part-time students. Financial award application deadline: 4/1; financial award applicants required to submit FAFSA. *Unit head:* Dr. Anna Zajicek, Department Chair, 479-575-3205, E-mail: azajicek@uark.edu. *Application contact:* Dr. Shauna Morimoto, Vice-Chair/Director of Graduate Studies, 479-575-3205, E-mail: smorimot@uark.edu.
Website: https://fulbright.uark.edu/departments/sociology/

The University of British Columbia, Faculty of Arts, Department of Sociology, Vancouver, BC V6T 1Z1, Canada. Offers MA, PhD. *Degree requirements:* For master's, thesis; for doctorate, comprehensive exam, thesis/dissertation. *Entrance requirements:* For master's, BA in sociology or equivalent with minimum B+ average in upper-level courses; for doctorate, master's degree in sociology or equivalent. Additional exam requirements/recommendations for international students: required—TOEFL. Electronic applications accepted. *Expenses:* Contact institution.

University of Calgary, Faculty of Graduate Studies, Faculty of Arts, Program in Sociology, Calgary, AB T2N 1N4, Canada. Offers MA, PhD. Terminal master's awarded for partial completion of doctoral program. *Degree requirements:* For master's, thesis, prospectus; for doctorate, comprehensive exam, thesis/dissertation, oral and written candidacy exams, prospectus, qualifying paper. *Entrance requirements:* For master's, minimum GPA of 3.2; for doctorate, minimum GPA of 3.5. Additional exam requirements/recommendations for international students: required—TOEFL or IELTS. Electronic applications accepted.

University of California, Berkeley, Graduate Division, College of Letters and Science, Department of Sociology, Berkeley, CA 94720. Offers PhD. *Degree requirements:* For doctorate, thesis/dissertation, qualifying exam. *Entrance requirements:* For doctorate, GRE General Test, minimum GPA of 3.0, sample of academic written work, 3 letters of recommendation. Additional exam requirements/recommendations for international students: required—TOEFL (minimum score 570 paper-based) or IELTS. Electronic applications accepted.

University of California, Davis, Graduate Studies, Program in Sociology, Davis, CA 95616. Offers MA, PhD. Terminal master's awarded for partial completion of doctoral program. *Degree requirements:* For master's, written exam; for doctorate, thesis/dissertation, professional paper, qualifying exam. *Entrance requirements:* For master's and doctorate, GRE General Test, minimum GPA of 3.0, writing sample. Additional exam requirements/recommendations for international students: required—TOEFL (minimum score 550 paper-based). Electronic applications accepted.

University of California, Irvine, School of Social Sciences, Department of Sociology, Irvine, CA 92697. Offers social networks (PhD); social science (PhD); sociology and social relations (PhD). *Students:* 90 full-time (48 women), 2 part-time (1 woman); includes 47 minority (8 Black or African American, non-Hispanic/Latino; 10 Asian, non-Hispanic/Latino; 22 Hispanic/Latino; 1 Native Hawaiian or other Pacific Islander, non-Hispanic/Latino; 6 Two or more races, non-Hispanic/Latino), 8 international. Average age 29. 149 applicants, 21% accepted, 11 enrolled. In 2019, 12 doctorates awarded.

Sociology

Entrance requirements: For doctorate, GRE General Test, minimum GPA of 3.0. *Application deadline:* For fall admission, 1/15 priority date for domestic students, 1/15 for international students. Applications are processed on a rolling basis. Application fee: $120 ($140 for international students). Electronic applications accepted. *Financial support:* Fellowships, research assistantships with full tuition reimbursements, teaching assistantships, institutionally sponsored loans, traineeships, health care benefits, and unspecified assistantships available. Financial award application deadline: 3/1; financial award applicants required to submit FAFSA. *Unit head:* Prof. Matt Huffman, Chair, 949-824-5341, E-mail: mhuffman@uci.edu. *Application contact:* David Smith, Graduate Program Director, 949-824-7292, E-mail: dasmith@uci.edu.
Website: http://www.sociology.uci.edu/

University of California, Los Angeles, Graduate Division, College of Letters and Science, Department of Sociology, Los Angeles, CA 90095. Offers MA, PhD. Terminal master's awarded for partial completion of doctoral program. *Degree requirements:* For master's, thesis or alternative, paper; for doctorate, thesis/dissertation, oral and written qualifying exams. *Entrance requirements:* For doctorate, GRE General Test, bachelor's degree; minimum undergraduate GPA of 3.0 (or its equivalent if letter grade system not used); writing sample. Additional exam requirements/recommendations for international students: required—TOEFL. Electronic applications accepted.

University of California, Merced, Graduate Division, School of Social Sciences, Humanities and Arts, Merced, CA 95343. Offers cognitive and information sciences (PhD); interdisciplinary humanities (MA, PhD); psychological sciences (MA, PhD); social sciences (MA, PhD); sociology (MA, PhD). *Faculty:* 113 full-time (57 women), 2 part-time/adjunct (0 women). *Students:* 194 full-time (128 women), 1 (woman) part-time; includes 81 minority (5 Black or African American, non-Hispanic/Latino; 18 Asian, non-Hispanic/Latino; 54 Hispanic/Latino; 4 Two or more races, non-Hispanic/Latino), 39 international. Average age 31. 218 applicants, 48% accepted, 36 enrolled. In 2019, 12 master's, 23 doctorates awarded. Terminal master's awarded for partial completion of doctoral program. *Degree requirements:* For master's, variable foreign language requirement, comprehensive exam, thesis or alternative, oral defense; for doctorate, variable foreign language requirement, comprehensive exam, thesis/dissertation, oral defense. *Entrance requirements:* For master's and doctorate, GRE. Additional exam requirements/recommendations for international students: required—TOEFL (minimum score 550 paper-based; 80 iBT); recommended—IELTS (minimum score 6.5). *Application deadline:* For fall admission, 1/15 for domestic and international students. Application fee: $105 ($125 for international students). Electronic applications accepted. *Expenses: Tuition, area resident:* Full-time $11,442; part-time $5721 per semester. Tuition, state resident: full-time $11,442; part-time $5721 per semester. Tuition, nonresident: full-time $26,544; part-time $13,272 per semester. *International tuition:* $26,544 full-time. *Required fees:* $564 per semester. *Financial support:* In 2019–20, 183 students received support, including 7 fellowships with full tuition reimbursements available (averaging $22,005 per year), 5 research assistantships with full tuition reimbursements available (averaging $21,420 per year), 171 teaching assistantships with full tuition reimbursements available (averaging $21,911 per year); scholarships/grants, traineeships, and health care benefits also available. *Unit head:* Dr. Jeffrey Gilger, Dean, 209-228-4343, E-mail: jgilger@ucmerced.edu. *Application contact:* Tsu Ya, Director of Admissions and Academic Services, 209-228-4521, Fax: 209-228-6906, E-mail: tya@ucmerced.edu.

University of California, Riverside, Graduate Division, Department of Sociology, Riverside, CA 92521. Offers MA, PhD. *Degree requirements:* For doctorate, thesis/dissertation, 1 quarter of teaching experience, professional paper. *Entrance requirements:* For doctorate, GRE General Test, minimum GPA of 3.2. Additional exam requirements/recommendations for international students: required—TOEFL (minimum score 550 paper-based; 80 iBT). Electronic applications accepted.

University of California, San Diego, Graduate Division, Department of Sociology, La Jolla, CA 92093. Offers PhD. *Students:* 54 full-time (28 women), 1 (woman) part-time. 143 applicants, 20% accepted, 8 enrolled. In 2019, 8 doctorates awarded. *Degree requirements:* For doctorate, comprehensive exam, thesis/dissertation. *Entrance requirements:* For doctorate, GRE General Test, minimum GPA of 3.0, writing sample, statement of purpose, 3 letters of recommendation. Additional exam requirements/recommendations for international students: required—TOEFL (minimum score 550 paper-based; 80 iBT), IELTS (minimum score 7). *Application deadline:* For fall admission, 1/9 for domestic students. Application fee: $105 ($125 for international students). Electronic applications accepted. *Financial support:* Fellowships, teaching assistantships, scholarships/grants, and readerships, research and travel funds available. Financial award applicants required to submit FAFSA. *Unit head:* Amy Binder, Chair, 858- 534-0483, E-mail: abinder@ucsd.edu. *Application contact:* Teresa Eckert, Graduate Coordinator, 858-534-4627, E-mail: socphd@ucsd.edu.
Website: http://sociology.ucsd.edu/

University of California, San Francisco, Graduate Division, School of Nursing, Department of Social and Behavioral Sciences, San Francisco, CA 94143. Offers sociology (PhD). *Degree requirements:* For doctorate, one foreign language, thesis/dissertation. *Entrance requirements:* For doctorate, GRE General Test, statement of purpose, official transcripts, two letters of recommendation, scholarly writing example, curriculum vitae or resume. Additional exam requirements/recommendations for international students: required—TOEFL (minimum score 84 iBT).

University of California, Santa Barbara, Graduate Division, College of Letters and Sciences, Division of Social Sciences, Department of Sociology, Santa Barbara, CA 93106-9430. Offers interdisciplinary emphasis: Black studies (PhD); interdisciplinary emphasis: environment and society (PhD); interdisciplinary emphasis: feminist studies (PhD); interdisciplinary emphasis: global studies (PhD); interdisciplinary emphasis: language, interaction and social organization (PhD); interdisciplinary emphasis: quantitative methods in the social sciences (PhD); interdisciplinary emphasis: technology and society (PhD); sociology (PhD); MA/PhD. Terminal master's awarded for partial completion of doctoral program. *Degree requirements:* For doctorate, comprehensive exam, thesis/dissertation. *Entrance requirements:* For doctorate, GRE General Test. Additional exam requirements/recommendations for international students: required—TOEFL (minimum score 550 paper-based; 80 iBT), IELTS (minimum score 7). Electronic applications accepted.

University of California, Santa Cruz, Division of Graduate Studies, Division of Social Sciences, Department of Sociology, Santa Cruz, CA 95064. Offers PhD. *Degree requirements:* For doctorate, thesis/dissertation, qualifying exam. *Entrance requirements:* For doctorate, GRE General Test. Additional exam requirements/recommendations for international students: required—TOEFL (minimum score 550 paper-based; 83 iBT); recommended—IELTS (minimum score 8). Electronic applications accepted.

University of Central Florida, College of Sciences, Department of Sociology, Orlando, FL 32816. Offers MA, PhD. *Program availability:* Part-time, evening/weekend. *Students:* 39 full-time (29 women), 23 part-time (16 women); includes 30 minority (9 Black or African American, non-Hispanic/Latino; 2 Asian, non-Hispanic/Latino; 18 Hispanic/Latino; 1 Two or more races, non-Hispanic/Latino), 2 international. Average age 32. 40 applicants, 78% accepted, 14 enrolled. In 2019, 9 master's, 3 doctorates awarded. *Degree requirements:* For master's, thesis or alternative; for doctorate, comprehensive exam, thesis/dissertation. *Entrance requirements:* For master's, GRE General Test, minimum GPA of 3.0 in last 60 hours of course work, letters of recommendation, personal statement; for doctorate, GRE General Test, master's degree in related field from accredited institution, letters of recommendation, personal statement, resume, writing sample. Additional exam requirements/recommendations for international students: required—TOEFL. Application fee: $30. Electronic applications accepted. *Financial support:* In 2019–20, 31 students received support, including 10 fellowships with partial tuition reimbursements available (averaging $3,756 per year), 6 research assistantships with partial tuition reimbursements available (averaging $5,837 per year), 25 teaching assistantships with partial tuition reimbursements available (averaging $7,607 per year); career-related internships or fieldwork, Federal Work-Study, institutionally sponsored loans, health care benefits, tuition waivers (partial), and unspecified assistantships also available. Financial award application deadline: 3/1; financial award applicants required to submit FAFSA. *Unit head:* Dr. Elizabeth Mustaine, Chair, 407-823-6568, E-mail: elizabeth.mustaine@ucf.edu. *Application contact:* Associate Director, Graduate Admissions, 407-823-2766, Fax: 407-823-6442, E-mail: gradadmissions@ucf.edu.
Website: http://sociology.cos.ucf.edu/

University of Central Missouri, The Graduate School, Warrensburg, MO 64093. Offers accountancy (MA); accounting (MBA); applied mathematics (MS); aviation safety (MA); biology (MS); business administration (MBA); career and technology education (MS); college student personnel administration (MS); communication (MA); computer information systems and information technology (MS); computer science (MS); counseling (MS); criminal justice and criminology (MS); educational leadership (Ed S); educational leadership and policy analysis (Ed D); educational technology (MS, Ed S); elementary and early childhood education (MSE); English (MA); english language learners - teaching english as a second language (MA); environmental studies (MA); finance (MBA); history (MA); industrial hygiene (MS); industrial management (MS); information systems (MBA); kinesiology (MS); library science and information services (MS); literacy education (MSE); marketing (MBA); mathematics (MS); music (MA); occupational safety management (MS); professional leadership - adult, career, and technical education (Ed S); professional leadership - counseling (Ed S); psychology (MS); rural family nursing (MS); school administration (MSE); social gerontology (MS); sociology (MA); special education (MSE); speech language pathology (MS); teaching (MAT); technology (MS); technology management (PhD); theatre (MA). *Accreditation:* ASHA. *Program availability:* Part-time, 100% online, blended/hybrid learning. *Faculty:* 236 full-time (113 women), 97 part-time/adjunct (61 women). *Students:* 787 full-time (448 women), 1,459 part-time (997 women); includes 213 minority (72 Black or African American, non-Hispanic/Latino; 5 American Indian or Alaska Native, non-Hispanic/Latino; 27 Asian, non-Hispanic/Latino; 59 Hispanic/Latino; 50 Two or more races, non-Hispanic/Latino), 574 international. Average age 30. 1,477 applicants, 68% accepted, 664 enrolled. In 2019, 831 master's, 93 other advanced degrees awarded. *Degree requirements:* For master's and Ed S, comprehensive exam (for some programs), thesis (for some programs). *Entrance requirements:* For master's, A GRE or GMAT test score may be required by some of the programs, A minimum GPA, letters of recommendation, a statement of purpose may be required by some of the programs; for Ed S, A master's degree is required for the application of an Education Specialist's degree program. Additional exam requirements/recommendations for international students: required—TOEFL (minimum score 550 paper-based; 79 iBT). *Application deadline:* For fall admission, 6/1 priority date for domestic and international students; for spring admission, 10/15 priority date for domestic and international students; for summer admission, 4/1 priority date for domestic and international students. Applications are processed on a rolling basis. Application fee: $30 ($75 for international students). Electronic applications accepted. *Expenses: Tuition, area resident:* Full-time $7524; part-time $313.50 per credit hour. Tuition, state resident: full-time $7524; part-time $313.50 per credit hour. Tuition, nonresident: full-time $15,048; part-time $627 per credit hour. *International tuition:* $15,048 full-time. *Required fees:* $915; $30.50 per credit hour. *Financial support:* In 2019–20, 89 students received support. Research assistantships, teaching assistantships, career-related internships or fieldwork, Federal Work-Study, scholarships/grants, unspecified assistantships, and administrative and laboratory assistantships available. Support available to part-time students. Financial award application deadline: 4/1; financial award applicants required to submit FAFSA. *Unit head:* Shellie Hewitt, Director of Graduate and International Student Services, 660-543-4621, Fax: 660-543-4778, E-mail: hewitt@ucmo.edu. *Application contact:* Shellie Hewitt, Director of Graduate and International Student Services, 660-543-4621, Fax: 660-543-4778, E-mail: hewitt@ucmo.edu.
Website: http://www.ucmo.edu/graduate/

University of Central Oklahoma, The Jackson College of Graduate Studies, College of Liberal Arts, Department of Sociology, Gerontology, and Substance Abuse Studies, Edmond, OK 73034-5209. Offers gerontology (MA); substance abuse studies (MA), including substance abuse studies. *Program availability:* Part-time. *Degree requirements:* For master's, variable foreign language requirement, comprehensive exam (for some programs), thesis (for some programs). *Entrance requirements:* Additional exam requirements/recommendations for international students: required—TOEFL (minimum score 550 paper-based; 79 iBT), IELTS (minimum score 6.5). Electronic applications accepted.

University of Chicago, Division of the Social Sciences, Department of Sociology, Chicago, IL 60637. Offers PhD. *Degree requirements:* For doctorate, one foreign language, comprehensive exam, thesis/dissertation, 2 field exams. *Entrance requirements:* For doctorate, GRE General Test, 3 letters of recommendation, statement of purpose, transcripts, resume or curriculum vitae, writing sample (dependent on department). Additional exam requirements/recommendations for international students: required—TOEFL (minimum score 104 iBT), IELTS (minimum score 7). Electronic applications accepted.

University of Cincinnati, Graduate School, McMicken College of Arts and Sciences, Department of Sociology, Cincinnati, OH 45221-. Offers MA, PhD. *Program availability:* Part-time. Terminal master's awarded for partial completion of doctoral program. *Degree requirements:* For master's, comprehensive exam (for some programs), thesis (for some programs); for doctorate, comprehensive exam, thesis/dissertation. *Entrance requirements:* For master's and doctorate, GRE General Test or LSAT or MCAT or GMAT. Additional exam requirements/recommendations for international students: required—TOEFL (minimum score 600 paper-based; 100 iBT), IELTS (minimum score 7). Electronic applications accepted. *Expenses:* Contact institution.

University of Colorado Boulder, Graduate School, College of Arts and Sciences, Department of Sociology, Boulder, CO 80309. Offers PhD. *Degree requirements:* For doctorate, comprehensive exam, thesis/dissertation. *Entrance requirements:* For doctorate, GRE General Test, GRE Subject Test, minimum undergraduate GPA of 2.75. Electronic applications accepted. Application fee is waived when completed online.

University of Colorado Colorado Springs, College of Letters, Arts and Sciences, Department of Sociology, Colorado Springs, CO 80918. Offers sociology (MA). *Program availability:* Blended/hybrid learning. *Faculty:* 13 full-time (7 women), 6 part-time/adjunct (5 women). *Students:* 6 full-time (all women), 33 part-time (27 women); includes 15

minority (2 Black or African American, non-Hispanic/Latino; 10 Hispanic/Latino; 3 Two or more races, non-Hispanic/Latino). Average age 32. 22 applicants, 77% accepted, 12 enrolled. In 2019, 4 master's awarded. *Degree requirements:* For master's, thesis optional. *Entrance requirements:* For master's, minimum GPA of 3.0 or applicants with lower GPA may be considered with strong GRE scores (GRE exam not required otherwise). Additional exam requirements/recommendations for international students: recommended—TOEFL (minimum score 600 paper-based; 100 iBT), IELTS (minimum score 7). *Application deadline:* For fall admission, 2/1 priority date for domestic and international students; for spring admission, 4/15 priority date for domestic and international students; for summer admission, 11/15 for domestic and international students. Applications are processed on a rolling basis. Application fee: $60 ($100 for international students). Electronic applications accepted. *Expenses:* Contact institution. *Financial support:* In 2019–20, 17 students received support, including 10 teaching assistantships (averaging $2,000 per year); career-related internships or fieldwork, Federal Work-Study, scholarships/grants, and unspecified assistantships also available. Support available to part-time students. Financial award application deadline: 3/1; financial award applicants required to submit FAFSA. *Unit head:* Dr. Jeffrey Montez de Oca, Associate Professor/Director, Graduate Studies, 719-255-4138, Fax: 719-255-4450, E-mail: jmontezd@uccs.edu. *Application contact:* Rosemary Kelbel, Program Assistant, 719-255-4153, Fax: 719-255-4450, E-mail: rkelbel@uccs.edu.
Website: https://www.uccs.edu/soc/graduate

University of Colorado Denver, College of Liberal Arts and Sciences, Department of Sociology, Denver, CO 80217. Offers MA. *Program availability:* Part-time, evening/weekend. *Degree requirements:* For master's, 36 credit hours, project or thesis. *Entrance requirements:* For master's, GRE (recommended), minimum combined GPA of 3.3 for all courses taken at undergraduate or graduate level, 3.5 for all sociology courses; writing sample; statement of intent; three letters of recommendation. Additional exam requirements/recommendations for international students: required—TOEFL (minimum score 537 paper-based; 75 iBT); recommended—IELTS (minimum score 6.5). Electronic applications accepted. Tuition and fees vary according to course load, program and reciprocity agreements.

University of Colorado Denver, College of Liberal Arts and Sciences, Program in Humanities, Denver, CO 80217. Offers community health (MSS); ethnic studies (MH, MSS); humanities (MH, Graduate Certificate); international studies (MSS); philosophy and theory (MH); social justice (MH, MSS); society and the environment (MSS); visual studies (MH); women's and gender studies (MH, MSS). *Program availability:* Part-time, evening/weekend. *Degree requirements:* For master's, 36 credit hours, project or thesis. *Entrance requirements:* For master's, writing sample, statement of purpose/letter of intent, three letters of recommendation. Additional exam requirements/recommendations for international students: required—TOEFL (minimum score 537 paper-based; 75 iBT); recommended—IELTS (minimum score 6.5). Electronic applications accepted. Tuition and fees vary according to course load, program and reciprocity agreements.

University of Connecticut, Graduate School, College of Liberal Arts and Sciences, Department of Sociology, Storrs, CT 06269. Offers MA, PhD. Terminal master's awarded for partial completion of doctoral program. *Degree requirements:* For master's, comprehensive exam; for doctorate, thesis/dissertation. *Entrance requirements:* For master's and doctorate, GRE General Test. Additional exam requirements/recommendations for international students: required—TOEFL (minimum score 550 paper-based). Electronic applications accepted.

University of Delaware, College of Arts and Sciences, Department of Sociology and Criminal Justice, Newark, DE 19716. Offers criminology (MA, PhD); sociology (MA, PhD). *Degree requirements:* For master's, thesis; for doctorate, comprehensive exam, thesis/dissertation. *Entrance requirements:* For master's and doctorate, GRE, 3 letters of recommendation. Additional exam requirements/recommendations for international students: required—TOEFL. Electronic applications accepted.

University of Florida, Graduate School, College of Liberal Arts and Sciences, Department of Sociology and Criminology and Law, Gainesville, FL 32611. Offers criminology, law, and society (MA, PhD); sociology (MA, PhD), including sociology, tropical conservation and development, women's and gender studies (PhD); MA/JD. *Program availability:* Part-time. Terminal master's awarded for partial completion of doctoral program. *Degree requirements:* For master's, thesis optional; for doctorate, comprehensive exam, thesis/dissertation. *Entrance requirements:* For master's and doctorate, GRE, minimum GPA of 3.0. Additional exam requirements/recommendations for international students: required—TOEFL (minimum score 550 paper-based; 80 iBT), IELTS (minimum score 6). Electronic applications accepted.

University of Georgia, Franklin College of Arts and Sciences, Department of Sociology, Athens, GA 30602. Offers MA, PhD. *Degree requirements:* For master's, thesis; for doctorate, thesis/dissertation. *Entrance requirements:* For master's and doctorate, GRE General Test. Additional exam requirements/recommendations for international students: required—TOEFL. Electronic applications accepted.

University of Guelph, Office of Graduate and Postdoctoral Studies, College of Social and Applied Human Sciences, Department of Sociology and Anthropology, Guelph, ON N1G 2W1, Canada. Offers anthropology (MA); crime and criminal justice policy (MA); sociology (MA, PhD). *Degree requirements:* For master's, thesis or major paper; for doctorate, comprehensive exam, thesis/dissertation. *Entrance requirements:* For master's, minimum B+ average during previous 2 years of course work, honors BA or equivalent; for doctorate, must have an MA in Sociology, must have 80% or higher in graduate level studies. Additional exam requirements/recommendations for international students: required—TOEFL (minimum score 550 paper-based; 89 iBT) or IELTS (minimum score 6.5). Electronic applications accepted.

University of Hawaii at Manoa, Office of Graduate Education, College of Social Sciences, Department of Sociology, Honolulu, HI 96822. Offers MA, PhD. *Program availability:* Part-time. *Degree requirements:* For master's, thesis optional; for doctorate, comprehensive exam, thesis/dissertation. *Entrance requirements:* For master's and doctorate, GRE General Test. Additional exam requirements/recommendations for international students: required—TOEFL (minimum score 500 paper-based; 61 iBT), IELTS (minimum score 5).

University of Houston, College of Liberal Arts and Social Sciences, Department of Sociology, Houston, TX 77204. Offers MA. *Program availability:* Part-time. *Degree requirements:* For master's, thesis, 4 core courses, 36 hours. *Entrance requirements:* For master's, GRE (minimum score 1000), minimum GPA of 3.0; letters of recommendation, resume. Additional exam requirements/recommendations for international students: required—TOEFL (minimum score 550 paper-based; 79 iBT). Electronic applications accepted.

University of Houston–Clear Lake, School of Human Sciences and Humanities, Programs in Human Sciences, Houston, TX 77058-1002. Offers behavioral sciences (MA), including criminology, cross cultural studies, general psychology, sociology; clinical psychology (MA); criminology (MA); cross cultural studies (MA); family therapy (MA); fitness and human performance (MA); school psychology (MA). *Accreditation:* AAMFT/COAMFTE. *Program availability:* Part-time, evening/weekend, online learning. *Degree requirements:* For master's, thesis or alternative. *Entrance requirements:* For master's, GRE General Test. Additional exam requirements/recommendations for international students: required—TOEFL (minimum score 550 paper-based). Electronic applications accepted.

University of Illinois at Chicago, College of Liberal Arts and Sciences, Department of Sociology, Chicago, IL 60607-7128. Offers MA, PhD. Terminal master's awarded for partial completion of doctoral program. *Degree requirements:* For master's, comprehensive exam, thesis; for doctorate, thesis/dissertation, qualifying exam. *Entrance requirements:* For master's and doctorate, GRE General Test, minimum GPA of 3.0. Additional exam requirements/recommendations for international students: required—TOEFL. Electronic applications accepted.

University of Illinois at Urbana-Champaign, Graduate College, College of Liberal Arts and Sciences, Department of Sociology, Champaign, IL 61820. Offers MA, PhD.

University of Indianapolis, Graduate Programs, Shaheen College of Arts and Sciences, Department of Social Sciences, Indianapolis, IN 46227-3697. Offers applied sociology (MA). *Program availability:* Part-time, evening/weekend. *Degree requirements:* For master's, thesis optional. *Entrance requirements:* For master's, GRE Subject Test, minimum GPA of 3.0, letter of intent, 3 letters of recommendation. Additional exam requirements/recommendations for international students: required—TOEFL (minimum score 550 paper-based). Electronic applications accepted.

The University of Iowa, Graduate College, College of Liberal Arts and Sciences, Department of Sociology, Iowa City, IA 52242-1316. Offers MA, PhD. *Degree requirements:* For master's, thesis optional, exam; for doctorate, comprehensive exam, thesis/dissertation. *Entrance requirements:* For master's and doctorate, GRE General Test, minimum GPA of 3.0. Additional exam requirements/recommendations for international students: required—TOEFL (minimum score 600 paper-based; 100 iBT). Electronic applications accepted.

The University of Kansas, Graduate Studies, College of Liberal Arts and Sciences, Department of Sociology, Lawrence, KS 66045. Offers PhD. *Program availability:* Part-time. *Students:* 39 full-time (19 women), 1 (woman) part-time; includes 5 minority (1 Asian, non-Hispanic/Latino; 3 Hispanic/Latino; 1 Two or more races, non-Hispanic/Latino), 6 international. Average age 33. 19 applicants, 58% accepted, 5 enrolled. In 2019, 4 doctorates awarded. *Entrance requirements:* For doctorate, GRE General Test, current resume, statement of academic interests and professional goals, writing sample of academic work, three recommendation letters, official transcripts. Additional exam requirements/recommendations for international students: required—TOEFL, IELTS, TOEFL or IELTS. *Application deadline:* For fall admission, 1/13 for domestic and international students. Application fee: $65 ($85 for international students). Electronic applications accepted. *Expenses:* Tuition, state resident: full-time $9989. Tuition, nonresident: full-time $23,950. *International tuition:* $23,950 full-time. *Required fees:* $984; $81.99 per credit hour. Tuition and fees vary according to course load, campus/location and program. *Financial support:* Fellowships, research assistantships, teaching assistantships, scholarships/grants, and unspecified assistantships available. Financial award application deadline: 1/13. *Unit head:* Kelly H. Chong, Director, 785-864-9415, Fax: 785-864-5280, E-mail: kchong@ku.edu. *Application contact:* Corinne Butler, Graduate Secretary, 785-864-9419, Fax: 785-864-5280, E-mail: cleg@ku.edu.
Website: http://www.sociology.ku.edu/

University of Kentucky, Graduate School, College of Arts and Sciences, Program in Sociology, Lexington, KY 40506-0032. Offers MA, MS, PhD. *Program availability:* Part-time. *Degree requirements:* For master's, comprehensive exam, thesis optional; for doctorate, comprehensive exam, thesis/dissertation. *Entrance requirements:* For master's, GRE General Test, minimum undergraduate GPA of 2.75; for doctorate, GRE General Test, minimum graduate GPA of 3.0. Additional exam requirements/recommendations for international students: required—TOEFL (minimum score 550 paper-based). Electronic applications accepted.

University of Lethbridge, School of Graduate Studies, Lethbridge, AB T1K 3M4, Canada. Offers addictions counseling (M Sc); agricultural biotechnology (M Sc); agricultural studies (M Sc, MA); anthropology (MA); archaeology (M Sc, MA); art (MA, MFA); biochemistry (M Sc); biological sciences (M Sc); biomolecular science (PhD); biosystems and biodiversity (PhD); Canadian studies (MA); chemistry (M Sc); computer science (M Sc); computer science and geographical information science (M Sc); counseling (MC); counseling psychology (M Ed); dramatic arts (MA); earth, space, and physical science (PhD); economics (MA); education (MA, PhD); educational leadership (M Ed); English (MA); environmental science (M Sc); evolution and behavior (PhD); exercise science (M Sc); French (MA); French/German (MA); French/Spanish (MA); general education (M Ed); geography (M Sc, MA); German (MA); health sciences (M Sc); individualized multidisciplinary (M Sc, MA); kinesiology (M Sc, MA); management (M Sc), including accounting, finance, human resource management and labor relations, information systems, international management, marketing, policy and strategy; mathematics (M Sc); music (M Mus, MA); Native American studies (MA); neuroscience (M Sc, PhD); new media (MA, MFA); nursing (M Sc, MN); philosophy (MA); physics (M Sc); political science (MA); psychology (M Sc, MA); religious studies (MA); sociology (MA); theatre and dramatic arts (MFA); theoretical and computational science (PhD); urban and regional studies (MA); women and gender studies (MA). *Program availability:* Part-time, evening/weekend. *Degree requirements:* For master's, thesis (for some programs); for doctorate, comprehensive exam, thesis/dissertation. *Entrance requirements:* For master's, GMAT (for M Sc in management), bachelor's degree in related field, minimum GPA of 3.0 during previous 20 graded semester courses, 2 years' teaching or related experience (M Ed); for doctorate, master's degree, minimum graduate GPA of 3.5. Additional exam requirements/recommendations for international students: required—TOEFL (minimum score 580 paper-based; 93 iBT). Electronic applications accepted.

University of Louisiana at Lafayette, College of Liberal Arts, Department of English, Lafayette, LA 70504. Offers American culture (MA, PhD), including history, sociology; American literature and language (PhD); creative writing (MA, PhD), including creative writing (MA), folklore (MA), rhetoric (MA); folklore (MA, PhD); linguistic studies (MA, PhD); professional writing (PhD); rhetoric (MA, PhD); TESOL studies (MA, PhD). *Program availability:* Part-time. Terminal master's awarded for partial completion of doctoral program. *Degree requirements:* For master's, one foreign language, thesis or alternative; for doctorate, 2 foreign languages, comprehensive exam, thesis/dissertation. *Entrance requirements:* For master's, GRE General Test, minimum GPA of 2.75; for doctorate, GRE General Test, minimum GPA of 3.0. Additional exam requirements/recommendations for international students: required—TOEFL (minimum score 550 paper-based). Electronic applications accepted. *Expenses: Tuition, area resident:* Full-time $5511; part-time $1630 per credit hour. Tuition, state resident: full-time $5511; part-time $1630 per credit hour. Tuition, nonresident: full-time $19,239; part-time $2409 per credit hour. *Required fees:* $46,637.

University of Louisville, Graduate School, College of Arts and Sciences, Department of Sociology, Louisville, KY 40292. Offers applied sociology (PhD); sociology (MA). *Program availability:* Part-time, evening/weekend, 100% online. *Faculty:* 16 full-time (10 women), 5 part-time/adjunct (4 women). *Students:* 23 full-time (12 women), 4 part-time (2 women); includes 3 minority (2 Black or African American, non-Hispanic/Latino; 1 Hispanic/Latino). Average age 33. 12 applicants, 75% accepted, 6 enrolled. In 2019, 2

master's, 2 doctorates awarded. Terminal master's awarded for partial completion of doctoral program. *Degree requirements:* For master's, thesis (for some programs), may do practicum instead of thesis; for doctorate, comprehensive exam, thesis/dissertation. *Entrance requirements:* For master's and doctorate, Quantitative and verbal GRE scores, official transcripts, two references, CV. Additional exam requirements/recommendations for international students: required—TOEFL (minimum score 550 paper-based; 79 iBT), IELTS can be used in place of the TOEFL; recommended—IELTS (minimum score 6.5). *Application deadline:* For fall admission, 6/1 for domestic and international students; for spring admission, 11/1 for domestic and international students. Applications are processed on a rolling basis. Application fee: $65. Electronic applications accepted. *Expenses: Tuition, area resident:* Full-time $13,000; part-time $723 per credit hour. Tuition, state resident: full-time $13,000; part-time $723 per credit hour. Tuition, nonresident: full-time $27,114; part-time $1507 per credit hour. *International tuition:* $27,114 full-time. *Required fees:* $196. Tuition and fees vary according to program and reciprocity agreements. *Financial support:* In 2019–20, 14 students received support, including 2 research assistantships with full tuition reimbursements available (averaging $18,000 per year), 9 teaching assistantships with full tuition reimbursements available (averaging $18,000 per year); fellowships, scholarships/grants, health care benefits, tuition waivers (full), and unspecified assistantships also available. Financial award application deadline: 1/5. *Unit head:* Dr. Gul Marshall, Professor and Chair, 502-852-8027, Fax: 502-852-0099, E-mail: gamars01@louisville.edu. *Application contact:* Dr. Jonetta D. Weber, Director of Academic Services, 502-852-8028, Fax: 502-852-0099, E-mail: jonettaweber@louisville.edu.
Website: http://louisville.edu/sociology

The University of Manchester, School of Social Sciences, Manchester, United Kingdom. Offers ethnographic documentary (M Phil); interdisciplinary study of culture (PhD); philosophy (PhD); politics (PhD); social anthropology (PhD); social anthropology with visual media (PhD); social change (PhD); social statistics (PhD); sociology (PhD); visual anthropology (M Phil).

University of Manitoba, Faculty of Graduate Studies, Faculty of Arts, Department of Sociology, Winnipeg, MB R3T 2N2, Canada. Offers MA, PhD. *Degree requirements:* For master's, thesis.

University of Maryland, Baltimore County, The Graduate School, College of Arts, Humanities and Social Sciences, Department of Sociology, Anthropology, and Health Administration and Policy, Program in Applied Sociology, Baltimore, MD 21250. Offers MA. *Program availability:* Part-time, evening/weekend. *Faculty:* 18 full-time (13 women), 1 (woman) part-time/adjunct. *Students:* 15 full-time (12 women), 13 part-time (11 women); includes 15 minority (5 Black or African American, non-Hispanic/Latino; 6 Asian, non-Hispanic/Latino; 2 Hispanic/Latino; 2 Two or more races, non-Hispanic/Latino), 1 international. Average age 28. 13 applicants, 85% accepted, 10 enrolled. In 2019, 8 master's awarded. *Degree requirements:* For master's, thesis or alternative. *Entrance requirements:* For master's, minimum GPA of 3.0. Additional exam requirements/recommendations for international students: required—TOEFL. *Application deadline:* For fall admission, 3/15 for domestic students, 1/1 for international students; for spring admission, 11/15 for domestic students, 9/1 for international students. Application fee: $70. Electronic applications accepted. *Expenses: Tuition, area resident:* Full-time $659. Tuition, state resident: full-time $659. Tuition, nonresident: full-time $1132. *International tuition:* $1132 full-time. *Required fees:* $140; $140 per credit hour. *Financial support:* In 2019–20, 12 students received support, including 3 research assistantships with tuition reimbursements available, 9 teaching assistantships with tuition reimbursements available; health care benefits, unspecified assistantships, and tuition remission also available. *Unit head:* Dr. Marina Adler, Graduate Program Director, 410-455-3155, Fax: 410-455-1154, E-mail: adler@umbc.edu. *Application contact:* Emily Byrne, Graduate Program Coordinator, 410-455-3365, Fax: 410-455-1154, E-mail: ebyrme@umbc.edu.
Website: http://sociology.umbc.edu/ma-in-applied-sociology/

University of Maryland, College Park, Academic Affairs, College of Behavioral and Social Sciences, Department of Sociology, College Park, MD 20742. Offers MA, PhD. *Degree requirements:* For master's, thesis; for doctorate, thesis/dissertation, 2 qualifying exams. *Entrance requirements:* For master's, GRE General Test, minimum GPA of 3.0, 3 letters of recommendation; for doctorate, GRE General Test, 3 letters of recommendation. Additional exam requirements/recommendations for international students: required—TOEFL. Electronic applications accepted.

University of Massachusetts Amherst, Graduate School, College of Social and Behavioral Sciences, Department of Sociology, Amherst, MA 01003. Offers MA, PhD. *Program availability:* Part-time. Terminal master's awarded for partial completion of doctoral program. *Degree requirements:* For master's, thesis or alternative; for doctorate, comprehensive exam, thesis/dissertation. *Entrance requirements:* For master's and doctorate, GRE General Test, writing sample, 3 letters of recommendation. Additional exam requirements/recommendations for international students: required—TOEFL (minimum score 550 paper-based; 80 iBT), IELTS (minimum score 6.5). Electronic applications accepted.

University of Massachusetts Boston, College of Liberal Arts, Program in Applied Sociology, Boston, MA 02125-3393. Offers MA. *Program availability:* Part-time, evening/weekend. *Entrance requirements:* For master's, GRE or MAT, minimum GPA of 2.75. Electronic applications accepted.

University of Massachusetts Boston, College of Liberal Arts, Program in Sociology, Boston, MA 02125-3393. Offers PhD. Electronic applications accepted.

University of Massachusetts Lowell, College of Fine Arts, Humanities and Social Sciences, Program in Regional Economic and Social Development, Lowell, MA 01854. Offers MA, Graduate Certificate. *Program availability:* Part-time. *Entrance requirements:* For master's, GRE. Electronic applications accepted.

University of Memphis, Graduate School, College of Arts and Sciences, Department of Sociology, Memphis, TN 38152. Offers MA. *Program availability:* Part-time. *Students:* 13 full-time (8 women); includes 6 minority (5 Black or African American, non-Hispanic/Latino; 1 Two or more races, non-Hispanic/Latino), 1 international. Average age 26. 7 applicants, 100% accepted, 6 enrolled. In 2019, 9 master's awarded. *Degree requirements:* For master's, comprehensive exam, thesis (for some programs). *Entrance requirements:* For master's, GRE General Test, 12 undergraduate hours in sociology, letters of reference, writing sample. Additional exam requirements/recommendations for international students: required—TOEFL (minimum score 550 paper-based; 79 iBT). *Application deadline:* For fall admission, 7/1 for domestic students, 5/1 for international students; for spring admission, 12/1 for domestic students, 9/15 for international students. Applications are processed on a rolling basis. Application fee: $35 ($60 for international students). Electronic applications accepted. *Expenses: Tuition, area resident:* Full-time $9216; part-time $512 per credit hour. Tuition, state resident: full-time $9216; part-time $512 per credit hour. Tuition, nonresident: full-time $12,672; part-time $704 per credit hour. *International tuition:* $16,128 full-time. *Required fees:* $1530; $85 per credit hour. Tuition and fees vary according to program. *Financial support:* Research assistantships with full tuition reimbursements, teaching assistantships with full tuition reimbursements, Federal Work-Study, scholarships/grants, and unspecified assistantships available. Financial award application deadline: 2/1; financial award applicants required to submit FAFSA. *Unit head:* Dr. Gretchen Peterson, Chair, 901-678-2241, Fax: 901-678-2525, E-mail: gpterson@memphis.edu. *Application contact:* Dr. Wesley James, Coordinator of Graduate Studies, 901-678-1631, Fax: 901-678-2525, E-mail: wes.james@memphis.edu.
Website: https://www.memphis.edu/sociology

University of Miami, Graduate School, College of Arts and Sciences, Department of Sociology, Coral Gables, FL 33124. Offers MA, PhD. *Program availability:* Part-time. Terminal master's awarded for partial completion of doctoral program. *Degree requirements:* For master's, thesis; for doctorate, comprehensive exam, thesis/dissertation. *Entrance requirements:* For master's and doctorate, GRE General Test. Additional exam requirements/recommendations for international students: required—TOEFL (minimum score 515 paper-based). Electronic applications accepted.

University of Miami, Graduate School, School of Education and Human Development, Department of Educational and Psychological Studies, Program in Community and Social Change, Coral Gables, FL 33124. Offers MS Ed. *Program availability:* Part-time, evening/weekend. *Students:* 8 full-time (6 women), 10 part-time (8 women); includes 13 minority (3 Black or African American, non-Hispanic/Latino; 1 Asian, non-Hispanic/Latino; 9 Hispanic/Latino). Average age 30. 14 applicants, 93% accepted, 11 enrolled. In 2019, 13 master's awarded. *Degree requirements:* For master's, comprehensive exam, thesis optional, capstone project or comprehensive exam. *Entrance requirements:* For master's, GRE General Test. Additional exam requirements/recommendations for international students: required—TOEFL (minimum score 550 paper-based; 80 iBT); recommended—IELTS (minimum score 6.5). *Application deadline:* For fall admission, 5/31 priority date for domestic students, 10/1 priority date for international students. Application fee: $85. Electronic applications accepted. *Financial support:* Tuition waivers (partial) available. Financial award application deadline: 3/1; financial award applicants required to submit FAFSA. *Unit head:* Dr. Ashmeet Oberoi, Clinical Assistant Professor and Program Director, 305-284-5956, E-mail: a.oberoi@miami.edu. *Application contact:* Dr. Ashmeet Oberoi, Clinical Assistant Professor and Program Director, 305-284-5956, E-mail: a.oberoi@miami.edu.
Website: https://sites.education.miami.edu/community-social-change/

University of Miami, Graduate School, School of Education and Human Development, Department of Teaching and Learning, Program in Education and Social Change, Coral Gables, FL 33124. Offers MS Ed. *Program availability:* Part-time, evening/weekend. *Students:* 101 part-time (78 women); includes 77 minority (22 Black or African American, non-Hispanic/Latino; 1 Asian, non-Hispanic/Latino; 53 Hispanic/Latino; 1 Two or more races, non-Hispanic/Latino). Average age 35. 13 applicants, 38% accepted, 4 enrolled. In 2019, 10 master's awarded. *Entrance requirements:* For master's, GRE General Test. Additional exam requirements/recommendations for international students: required—TOEFL (minimum score 550 paper-based; 80 iBT); recommended—IELTS (minimum score 6.5). *Application deadline:* For fall admission, 6/1 priority date for domestic students, 10/1 priority date for international students. Application fee: $85. Electronic applications accepted. *Financial support:* Scholarships/grants and tuition waivers (partial) available. Financial award application deadline: 3/1; financial award applicants required to submit FAFSA. *Unit head:* Dr. Mary Avalos, Research Associate Professor and Program Director, 305-284-6467, Fax: 305-284-3003, E-mail: mavalos@miami.edu. *Application contact:* Dr. Mary Avalos, Research Associate Professor and Program Director, 305-284-6467, Fax: 305-284-3003, E-mail: mavalos@miami.edu.
Website: http://www.education.miami.edu/education-social-change-m-s-ed

University of Michigan, Rackham Graduate School, College of Literature, Science, and the Arts, Department of Sociology, Ann Arbor, MI 48109. Offers public policy and sociology (PhD); social work and sociology (PhD); sociology (PhD). *Degree requirements:* For doctorate, comprehensive exam, thesis/dissertation, oral defense of dissertation, preliminary exam, dissertation prospectus. *Entrance requirements:* For doctorate, GRE General Test, letters of recommendation, writing sample, academic statement of purpose, personal statement, transcript. Additional exam requirements/recommendations for international students: required—TOEFL (minimum score 560 paper-based; 84 iBT), IELTS (minimum score 6.5). Electronic applications accepted.

University of Michigan, School of Social Work, Interdisciplinary PhD Program in Social Work and Social Science, Ann Arbor, MI 48109. Offers social work and anthropology (PhD); social work and economics (PhD); social work and political science (PhD); social work and psychology (PhD); social work and sociology (PhD). *Degree requirements:* For doctorate, thesis/dissertation, oral defense of dissertation, preliminary exam. *Entrance requirements:* For doctorate, GRE General Test. Additional exam requirements/recommendations for international students: required—TOEFL (minimum score 620 paper-based, 88 iBT) or IELTS. Electronic applications accepted. *Expenses:* Contact institution.

University of Minnesota, Duluth, Graduate School, College of Liberal Arts, Department of Sociology/Anthropology, Duluth, MN 55812-2496. Offers criminology (MA); liberal studies (MLS). *Program availability:* Part-time. *Degree requirements:* For master's, thesis or alternative. *Entrance requirements:* For master's, interview, minimum GPA of 3.0, letters of recommendation. Additional exam requirements/recommendations for international students: required—TOEFL.

University of Minnesota, Twin Cities Campus, Graduate School, College of Liberal Arts, Department of Sociology, Minneapolis, MN 55455. Offers MA, PhD. Terminal master's awarded for partial completion of doctoral program. *Degree requirements:* For master's, thesis optional; for doctorate, comprehensive exam, thesis/dissertation, preliminary written and oral exam, prospectus hearing, final oral defense and dissertation. *Entrance requirements:* For doctorate, GRE General Test, bachelor's degree, transcripts, minimum GPA of 3.0, personal statement, three letters of recommendation, writing sample. Additional exam requirements/recommendations for international students: required—TOEFL (minimum score 587 paper-based; 95 iBT). Electronic applications accepted.

University of Missouri, Office of Research and Graduate Studies, College of Arts and Science, Department of Sociology, Columbia, MO 65211. Offers MA, PhD. *Entrance requirements:* For master's and doctorate, GRE General Test, minimum GPA of 3.0; 15 hours of undergraduate sociology with minimum B average, including one course each in sociological theory and basic statistics. Additional exam requirements/recommendations for international students: required—TOEFL.

University of Missouri–Kansas City, College of Arts and Sciences, Department of Sociology, Kansas City, MO 64110-2499. Offers MA. *Program availability:* Part-time, evening/weekend. *Degree requirements:* For master's, thesis optional. *Entrance requirements:* For master's, GRE, minimum GPA of 3.0 in major, 2.7 overall. Additional exam requirements/recommendations for international students: required—TOEFL (minimum score 550 paper-based; 80 iBT). Electronic applications accepted.

University of Missouri–St. Louis, College of Arts and Sciences, Department of Sociology, St. Louis, MO 63121. Offers advanced social perspective (MA); community conflict intervention (MA); program design and evaluation research (MA); social policy planning and administration (MA). *Program availability:* Part-time, evening/weekend. *Degree requirements:* For master's, thesis optional. *Entrance requirements:* For master's, 2 letters of recommendation. Additional exam requirements/recommendations for international students: required—TOEFL (minimum score 550 paper-based). Electronic applications accepted. *Expenses: Tuition, area resident:* Full-time $9005.40; part-time $6003.60 per credit hour. Tuition, state resident: full-time $9005.40; part-time $6003.60 per credit hour. Tuition, nonresident: full-time $22,108; part-time $14,738.40 per credit hour. *International tuition:* $22,108 full-time. Tuition and fees vary according to course load.

University of Montana, Graduate School, College of Humanities and Sciences, Department of Sociology, Missoula, MT 59812. Offers criminology (MA); inequality and social justice (MA); rural and environmental change (MA); sociology (MA). *Entrance requirements:* For master's, GRE General Test. Additional exam requirements/recommendations for international students: required—TOEFL.

University of Nebraska at Omaha, Graduate Studies, College of Arts and Sciences, Department of Sociology and Anthropology, Omaha, NE 68182. Offers sociology (MA). *Program availability:* Part-time. *Degree requirements:* For master's, comprehensive exam (for some programs), thesis optional. *Entrance requirements:* For master's, 3 letters of recommendation, resume, statement of purpose, writing sample, minimum GPA of 3.0, official transcripts. Additional exam requirements/recommendations for international students: required—TOEFL, IELTS, PTE. Electronic applications accepted.

University of Nebraska–Lincoln, Graduate College, College of Arts and Sciences, Department of Sociology, Lincoln, NE 68588. Offers MA, PhD. *Degree requirements:* For master's, thesis optional; for doctorate, comprehensive exam, thesis/dissertation. *Entrance requirements:* For master's and doctorate, GRE General Test, writing sample. Additional exam requirements/recommendations for international students: required—TOEFL (minimum score 550 paper-based). Electronic applications accepted.

University of Nevada, Las Vegas, Graduate College, College of Liberal Arts. Department of Sociology, Las Vegas, NV 89154-5003. Offers MA, PhD. *Program availability:* Part-time. *Faculty:* 15 full-time (8 women), 1 (woman) part-time/adjunct. *Students:* 32 full-time (23 women), 16 part-time (9 women); includes 23 minority (5 Black or African American, non-Hispanic/Latino; 2 Asian, non-Hispanic/Latino; 11 Hispanic/Latino; 5 Two or more races, non-Hispanic/Latino), 1 international. Average age 33. 26 applicants, 50% accepted, 7 enrolled. In 2019, 5 master's, 4 doctorates awarded. Terminal master's awarded for partial completion of doctoral program. *Degree requirements:* For doctorate, comprehensive exam, thesis/dissertation, oral defense. *Entrance requirements:* For doctorate, GRE General Test, 3 letters of recommendation; statement of purpose; writing samples. Additional exam requirements/recommendations for international students: required—TOEFL (minimum score 550 paper-based; 80 iBT), IELTS (minimum score 7). *Application deadline:* For fall admission, 2/1 for domestic and international students. Application fee: $60 ($95 for international students). Electronic applications accepted. *Expenses:* Contact institution. *Financial support:* In 2019–20, 29 students received support, including 14 research assistantships with full tuition reimbursements available (averaging $16,750 per year), 15 teaching assistantships with full tuition reimbursements available (averaging $16,500 per year); institutionally sponsored loans, scholarships/grants, health care benefits, and unspecified assistantships also available. Financial award application deadline: 3/15; financial award applicants required to submit FAFSA. *Unit head:* Dr. Robert Futrell, Chair/Professor, 702-895-0270, Fax: 702-895-4800, E-mail: sociology.chair@unlv.edu. *Application contact:* Michael Borer, Graduate Coordinator, 702-895-0266, Fax: 702-895-4800, E-mail: sociology.gradcoord@unlv.edu.
Website: http://www.unlv.edu/sociology

University of Nevada, Reno, Graduate School, College of Liberal Arts, School of Social Research and Justice Studies, Department of Sociology, Reno, NV 89557. Offers MA. *Degree requirements:* For master's, thesis optional. *Entrance requirements:* For master's, GRE General Test, minimum GPA of 2.75. Additional exam requirements/recommendations for international students: required—TOEFL (minimum score 500 paper-based; 61 iBT), IELTS (minimum score 6). Electronic applications accepted.

University of New Hampshire, Graduate School, College of Liberal Arts, Department of Sociology, Durham, NH 03824. Offers MA, PhD. *Program availability:* Part-time. *Students:* 23 full-time (14 women), 3 part-time (all women); includes 3 minority (1 Asian, non-Hispanic/Latino; 1 Hispanic/Latino; 1 Two or more races, non-Hispanic/Latino), 1 international. Average age 31. 14 applicants, 71% accepted, 6 enrolled. In 2019, 1 master's, 5 doctorates awarded. *Entrance requirements:* For master's, GRE General Test; for doctorate, GRE General Test, master's thesis or research. Additional exam requirements/recommendations for international students: required—TOEFL (minimum score 550 paper-based; 80 iBT), IELTS, PTE. *Application deadline:* For fall admission, 7/1 for domestic students, 4/1 for international students. Application fee: $65. Electronic applications accepted. *Financial support:* In 2019–20, 17 students received support, including 1 fellowship, 14 teaching assistantships; research assistantships, career-related internships or fieldwork, Federal Work-Study, scholarships/grants, and tuition waivers (full and partial) also available. Support available to part-time students. Financial award application deadline: 2/15. *Unit head:* Cesar Rebellon, Chair, 603-862-2500. *Application contact:* Brenda Worden, Administrative Assistant, 603-862-2500, E-mail: sociology.dept@unh.edu.
Website: http://www.cola.unh.edu/sociology

University of New Mexico, Graduate Studies, College of Arts and Sciences, Program in Sociology, Albuquerque, NM 87131-2039. Offers MA, PhD. *Program availability:* Part-time. Terminal master's awarded for partial completion of doctoral program. *Degree requirements:* For master's, thesis; for doctorate, comprehensive exam, thesis/dissertation. *Entrance requirements:* For master's and doctorate, GRE General Test, 2 writing samples, 3 letters of reference, letter of intent. Additional exam requirements/recommendations for international students: required—TOEFL (minimum score 550 paper-based; 79 iBT), IELTS (minimum score 7). Electronic applications accepted. *Expenses:* Tuition, state resident: full-time $7633; part-time $972 per year. Tuition, nonresident: full-time $22,586; part-time $3840 per year. *International tuition:* $23,292 full-time. *Required fees:* $8608. Tuition and fees vary according to course level, course load, degree level, program and student level.

University of New Orleans, Graduate School, College of Liberal Arts, Education and Human Development, Department of Sociology, New Orleans, LA 70148. Offers MA. *Program availability:* Part-time, evening/weekend. *Degree requirements:* For master's, thesis (for some programs). *Entrance requirements:* For master's, GRE General Test. Additional exam requirements/recommendations for international students: required—TOEFL (minimum score 550 paper-based; 79 iBT), IELTS (minimum score 6.5). Electronic applications accepted.

The University of North Carolina at Chapel Hill, Graduate School, College of Arts and Sciences, Department of Sociology, Chapel Hill, NC 27599. Offers MA, PhD. *Degree requirements:* For master's, comprehensive exam, thesis; for doctorate, comprehensive exam, thesis/dissertation. *Entrance requirements:* For master's and doctorate, GRE General Test, minimum GPA of 3.0. Additional exam requirements/recommendations for international students: required—TOEFL (minimum score 550 paper-based). Electronic applications accepted.

The University of North Carolina at Charlotte, College of Liberal Arts and Sciences, Department of Sociology, Charlotte, NC 28223-0001. Offers sociology (MA). *Program availability:* Part-time, evening/weekend. *Faculty:* 19 full-time (13 women), 1 (woman) part-time/adjunct. *Students:* 10 full-time (6 women), 3 part-time (1 woman); includes 3 minority (2 Black or African American, non-Hispanic/Latino; 1 Two or more races, non-Hispanic/Latino). Average age 24. 17 applicants, 71% accepted, 6 enrolled. In 2019, 7 master's awarded. *Degree requirements:* For master's, thesis optional. *Entrance requirements:* For master's, GRE, minimum undergraduate GPA of 3.0; minimum of 18 hours of undergraduate course work in the social sciences, including social theory; demonstrated undergraduate competence in research methods and statistics; acceptable score on GRE exam. Additional exam requirements/recommendations for international students: required—TOEFL (minimum score 557 paper-based; 83 iBT), IELTS (minimum score 6.5), TOEFL (minimum score 557 paper-based, 83 iBT) or IELTS (6.5). *Application deadline:* For fall admission, 5/1 for domestic students. Applications are processed on a rolling basis. Application fee: $75. Electronic applications accepted. *Expenses:* Tuition, state resident: full-time $4337. Tuition, nonresident: full-time $17,771. *Required fees:* $3093. Tuition and fees vary according to course load, degree level and program. *Financial support:* In 2019–20, 21 students received support, including 1 fellowship (averaging $47,476 per year), 13 research assistantships (averaging $11,667 per year), 7 teaching assistantships (averaging $8,929 per year); career-related internships or fieldwork, institutionally sponsored loans, scholarships/grants, and unspecified assistantships also available. Support available to part-time students. Financial award application deadline: 3/1; financial award applicants required to submit FAFSA. *Unit head:* Dr. Scott Fitzgerald, Professor and Department Chair, 704-687-7805, E-mail: sfitzger@uncc.edu. *Application contact:* Kathy B. Giddings, Director of Graduate Admissions, 704-687-5503, Fax: 704-687-1668, E-mail: gradadm@uncc.edu.
Website: http://sociology.uncc.edu/

The University of North Carolina at Greensboro, Graduate School, College of Arts and Sciences, Department of Sociology, Greensboro, NC 27412-5001. Offers criminology (MA); sociology (MA). *Program availability:* Part-time. *Degree requirements:* For master's, comprehensive exam, thesis. *Entrance requirements:* For master's, GRE General Test. Additional exam requirements/recommendations for international students: required—TOEFL. Electronic applications accepted.

The University of North Carolina Wilmington, College of Arts and Sciences, Department of Sociology and Criminology, Wilmington, NC 28403-3297. Offers MA. *Faculty:* 13 full-time (8 women). *Students:* 10 full-time (8 women), 4 part-time (3 women); includes 3 minority (all Black or African American, non-Hispanic/Latino). Average age 24. 20 applicants, 65% accepted, 5 enrolled. In 2019, 8 master's awarded. *Degree requirements:* For master's, thesis or alternative, thesis or internship. *Entrance requirements:* For master's, GRE General Test, 3 letters of recommendation, statement of interest. Additional exam requirements/recommendations for international students: required—TOEFL (minimum score 79 iBT), IELTS (minimum score 6.5). *Application deadline:* For fall admission, 7/1 for domestic students. Applications are processed on a rolling basis. Application fee: $75. Electronic applications accepted. *Expenses: Tuition, area resident:* Full-time $4719; part-time $326 per credit hour. Tuition, state resident: full-time $4719; part-time $326 per credit hour. Tuition, nonresident: full-time $18,548; part-time $1099 per credit hour. *Required fees:* $2738. Tuition and fees vary according to program. *Financial support:* Research assistantships, teaching assistantships, scholarships/grants, and out-of-state tuition awards available. Financial award application deadline: 1/1; financial award applicants required to submit FAFSA. *Unit head:* Dr. Mike Maume, Chair, 910-962-7749, Fax: 910-962-7385, E-mail: maume@uncw.edu. *Application contact:* Dr. Jake Day, Graduate Coordinator, 910-962-7024, Fax: 910-962-7385, E-mail: dayj@uncw.edu.
Website: http://www.uncw.edu/socgrad/index.html

University of North Dakota, Graduate School, College of Arts and Sciences, Department of Sociology, Grand Forks, ND 58202. Offers MA. *Degree requirements:* For master's, thesis, final examination. *Entrance requirements:* For master's, minimum GPA of 3.0. Additional exam requirements/recommendations for international students: required—TOEFL (minimum score 550 paper-based; 79 iBT), IELTS (minimum score 6.5). Electronic applications accepted.

University of Northern Colorado, Graduate School, College of Humanities and Social Sciences, Department of Sociology, Greeley, CO 80639. Offers MA. *Program availability:* Part-time. *Degree requirements:* For master's, comprehensive exam. *Entrance requirements:* For master's, 2 letters of recommendation. Electronic applications accepted.

University of North Texas, Toulouse Graduate School, Denton, TX 76203-5459. Offers accounting (MS); applied anthropology (MA, MS); applied behavior analysis (Certificate); applied geography (MA); applied technology and performance improvement (M Ed, MS); art education (MA); art history (MA); arts leadership (Certificate); audiology (Au D); behavior analysis (MS); behavioral science (PhD); biochemistry and molecular biology (MS); biology (MA, MS); biomedical engineering (MS); business analysis (MS); chemistry (MS); clinical health psychology (PhD); communication studies (MA, MS); computer engineering (MS); computer science (MS); counseling (M Ed, MS), including clinical mental health counseling (MS), college and university counseling, elementary school counseling, secondary school counseling; creative writing (MA); criminal justice (MS); curriculum and instruction (M Ed); decision sciences (MBA); design (MA, MFA), including fashion design (MFA), innovation studies, interior design (MFA); early childhood studies (MS); economics (MS); educational leadership (M Ed, Ed D); educational psychology (MS, PhD), including family studies (MS), gifted and talented (MS), human development (MS), learning and cognition (MS), research, measurement and evaluation (MS); electrical engineering (MS); emergency management (MPA); engineering technology (MS); English (MA); English as a second language (MA); environmental science (MS); finance (MBA, MS); financial management (MPA); French (MA); health services management (MBA); higher education (M Ed, Ed D); history (MA, MS); hospitality management (MS); human resources management (MPA); information science (MS); information systems (PhD); information technologies (MBA); interdisciplinary studies (MA, MS); international studies (MA); international sustainable tourism (MS); jazz studies (MM); journalism (MA, MJ, Graduate Certificate), including interactive and virtual digital communication (Graduate Certificate), narrative journalism (Graduate Certificate); public relations (Graduate Certificate); kinesiology (MS); linguistics (MA); local government management (MPA); logistics (PhD); logistics and supply chain management (MBA); long-term care, senior housing, and aging services (MA); management (PhD); marketing (MBA); mathematics (MA, MS); mechanical and energy engineering (MS, PhD); music (MA), including ethnomusicology, music theory, musicology, performance; music composition (PhD); music education (MM Ed, PhD); nonprofit management (MPA); operations and supply chain management (MBA); performance (MM, DMA); philosophy (MA); political science (MA); professional and technical communication (MA); radio, television and film (MA, MFA); rehabilitation counseling (Certificate); sociology (MA); Spanish (MA); special education (M Ed); speech-language pathology (MA); strategic management (MBA); studio art (MFA); teaching (M Ed); MBA/MS. *Program availability:* Part-time, evening/weekend, online learning. Terminal master's awarded for partial completion of doctoral program. *Degree requirements:* For master's, variable foreign language requirement, comprehensive exam (for some programs), thesis (for some programs); for doctorate, variable foreign language requirement, comprehensive exam (for some programs), thesis/dissertation; for other advanced degree, variable foreign language requirement, comprehensive exam (for some programs). *Entrance requirements:* For master's and doctorate, GRE, GMAT. Additional exam requirements/recommendations for international students: required—TOEFL (minimum score 550 paper-based; 79 iBT). Electronic applications accepted.

University of Notre Dame, The Graduate School, College of Arts and Letters, Division of Social Sciences, Department of Sociology, Notre Dame, IN 46556. Offers PhD. *Degree requirements:* For doctorate, thesis/dissertation, 2 area specialty exams. *Entrance requirements:* For doctorate, GRE General Test, GRE Subject Test (strongly recommended). Additional exam requirements/recommendations for international students: required—TOEFL (minimum score 600 paper-based; 80 iBT). Electronic applications accepted.

University of Oklahoma, College of Arts and Sciences, Department of Sociology, Norman, OK 73019. Offers MA, PhD. *Program availability:* Part-time. Terminal master's awarded for partial completion of doctoral program. *Degree requirements:* For master's, thesis, 3 courses in statistics, 1 course in theory, 1 course in research methods, professionalization seminar; for doctorate, comprehensive exam, thesis/dissertation, 3 semesters of statistics, 2 semesters of theory, 1 semester of research methods, professionalization seminar, teaching seminar. *Entrance requirements:* For master's and doctorate, GRE. Additional exam requirements/recommendations for international students: required—TOEFL (minimum score 79 iBT) or IELTS (minimum score 6.5). Electronic applications accepted. *Expenses:* Tuition, state resident: full-time $6583.20; part-time $274.30 per credit hour. Tuition, nonresident: full-time $21,242; part-time $885.10 per credit hour. *International tuition:* $21,242.40 full-time. *Required fees:* $1994.20; $72.55 per credit hour. $126.50 per semester. Tuition and fees vary according to course load and degree level.

University of Oregon, Graduate School, College of Arts and Sciences, Department of Sociology, Eugene, OR 97403. Offers MA, MS, PhD. *Program availability:* Part-time. Terminal master's awarded for partial completion of doctoral program. *Degree requirements:* For doctorate, thesis/dissertation. *Entrance requirements:* For master's and doctorate, GRE General Test, minimum GPA of 3.0. Additional exam requirements/recommendations for international students: required—TOEFL.

University of Ottawa, Faculty of Graduate and Postdoctoral Studies, Faculty of Social Sciences, Department of Sociology and Anthropology, Ottawa, ON K1N 6N5, Canada. Offers MA. *Degree requirements:* For master's, thesis or alternative. *Entrance requirements:* For master's, honors bachelor's degree or equivalent, minimum B average. Electronic applications accepted.

University of Pennsylvania, School of Arts and Sciences, Graduate Group in Sociology, Philadelphia, PA 19104. Offers AM, PhD. *Faculty:* 35 full-time (17 women), 10 part-time/adjunct (4 women). *Students:* 50 full-time (36 women); includes 20 minority (8 Black or African American, non-Hispanic/Latino; 4 Asian, non-Hispanic/Latino; 7 Hispanic/Latino; 1 Two or more races, non-Hispanic/Latino), 13 international. Average age 29. 230 applicants, 6% accepted, 4 enrolled. In 2019, 4 master's, 6 doctorates awarded. Terminal master's awarded for partial completion of doctoral program. Application fee: $90.
Website: http://sociology.sas.upenn.edu/graduate_resources

University of Pittsburgh, Kenneth P. Dietrich School of Arts and Sciences, Department of Sociology, Pittsburgh, PA 15260. Offers MA, PhD. *Program availability:* Part-time, online learning. *Faculty:* 15 full-time (7 women). *Students:* 31 full-time (21 women); includes 10 minority (5 Black or African American, non-Hispanic/Latino; 1 American Indian or Alaska Native, non-Hispanic/Latino; 1 Asian, non-Hispanic/Latino; 1 Hispanic/Latino; 2 Two or more races, non-Hispanic/Latino), 6 international. Average age 31. 52 applicants, 12% accepted, 4 enrolled. In 2019, 2 master's, 3 doctorates awarded. Terminal master's awarded for partial completion of doctoral program. *Degree requirements:* For master's, thesis; for doctorate, comprehensive exam, Preliminary Exam. *Entrance requirements:* For master's and doctorate, statement of purpose, career statement, writing sample. Additional exam requirements/recommendations for international students: required—TOEFL (minimum score 90 iBT), IELTS (minimum score 7). *Application deadline:* For fall admission, 1/15 priority date for domestic and international students. Application fee: $50. Electronic applications accepted. *Expenses:* Contact institution. *Financial support:* In 2019–20, 20 students received support, including 7 fellowships with full tuition reimbursements available, 2 research assistantships with full tuition reimbursements available, 9 teaching assistantships with full tuition reimbursements available; scholarships/grants, health care benefits, tuition waivers (full and partial), unspecified assistantships, and part-time instructor positions also available. Financial award application deadline: 1/15; financial award applicants required to submit CSS PROFILE or FAFSA. *Unit head:* Dr. Mohammed Bamyeh, Professor of Sociology & Chair, 412-648-7582, Fax: 412-648-2799, E-mail: mab205@pitt.edu. *Application contact:* Meg R. Caruso, Academic Administrator, Graduate & Undergradute, 412-648-7588, Fax: 412-648-2799, E-mail: mlr58@pitt.edu.
Website: http://www.sociology.pitt.edu/graduate/

University of Puerto Rico at Río Piedras, College of Social Sciences, Department of Sociology, San Juan, PR 00931-3300. Offers MA. *Degree requirements:* For master's, comprehensive exam, thesis. *Entrance requirements:* For master's, GRE or PAEG, interview, minimum GPA of 3.0, letter of recommendation.

University of Regina, Faculty of Graduate Studies and Research, Faculty of Arts, Department of Sociology and Social Studies, Regina, SK S4S 0A2, Canada. Offers social studies (MA); sociology (MA). *Program availability:* Part-time. *Faculty:* 8 full-time (4 women), 4 part-time/adjunct (1 woman). *Students:* 4 full-time (3 women), 3 part-time (all women). Average age 30. 26 applicants, 35% accepted. In 2019, 4 master's awarded. *Degree requirements:* For master's, thesis. *Entrance requirements:* For master's, post secondary transcripts and 2 letters of recommendation; BA Honours degree or equivalent in sociology. Additional exam requirements/recommendations for international students: required—TOEFL (minimum score 580 paper-based; 80 iBT), IELTS (minimum score 6.5), PTE (minimum score 59), other options are CAEL, MELAB, Cantest and U of R ESL. *Application deadline:* Applications are processed on a rolling basis. Application fee: $100. Electronic applications accepted. *Expenses: Tuition:* Full-time $6684 Canadian dollars. *Required fees:* $100 Canadian dollars; $3351.45 Canadian dollars per trimester. $1117.15 Canadian dollars per semester. Tuition and fees vary according to course level, course load, degree level and program. *Financial support:* Fellowships, research assistantships, teaching assistantships, career-related internships or fieldwork, Federal Work-Study, scholarships/grants, unspecified assistantships, and travel award and Graduate Scholarship and Base funds available. Support available to part-time students. Financial award application deadline: 9/30. *Unit head:* Dr. Rozzete Jurdi-Hage, Department Head, 306-585-4196, Fax: 306-585-4815, E-mail: Rozzet.Jurdi@uregina.ca. *Application contact:* Dr. JoAnn Jaffe, Graduate Coordinator, 306-585-4198, Fax: 306-585-4815, E-mail: JoAnn.Jaffe@uregina.ca.
Website: http://www.uregina.ca/arts/sociology-social-studies

University of Saskatchewan, College of Graduate and Postdoctoral Studies, College of Arts and Science, Department of Sociology, Saskatoon, SK S7N 5A2, Canada. Offers MA, PhD. *Degree requirements:* For master's, thesis; for doctorate, comprehensive exam (for some programs), thesis/dissertation. *Entrance requirements:* Additional exam requirements/recommendations for international students: required—TOEFL (minimum score 80 iBT); recommended—IELTS (minimum score 6.5). Electronic applications accepted.

University of South Africa, College of Human Sciences, Pretoria, South Africa. Offers adult education (M Ed); African languages (MA, PhD); African politics (MA, PhD); Afrikaans (MA, PhD); ancient history (MA, PhD); ancient Near Eastern studies (MA, PhD); anthropology (MA, PhD); applied linguistics (MA); Arabic (MA, PhD); archaeology (MA); art history (MA); Biblical archaeology (MA); Biblical studies (M Th, D Th, PhD); Christian spirituality (M Th, D Th); church history (M Th, D Th); classical studies (MA, PhD); clinical psychology (MA); communication (MA, PhD); comparative education (M Ed, Ed D); consulting psychology (D Admin, D Com, PhD); curriculum studies (M Ed, Ed D); development studies (M Admin, MA, D Admin, PhD); didactics (M Ed, Ed D); education (M Tech); education management (M Ed, Ed D); educational psychology (M Ed); English (MA); environmental education (M Ed); French (MA, PhD); German (MA, PhD); Greek (MA); guidance and counseling (M Ed); health studies (MA, PhD), including health sciences education (MA), health services management (MA), medical and surgical nursing science (critical care general) (MA), midwifery and neonatal nursing science (MA), trauma and emergency care (MA); history (MA, PhD); history of education (Ed D); inclusive education (M Ed, Ed D); information and communications technology policy and regulation (MA); information science (MA, MIS, PhD); international politics (MA, PhD); Islamic studies (MA, PhD); Italian (MA, PhD); Judaica (MA, PhD); linguistics (MA, PhD); mathematical education (M Ed); mathematics education (MA); missiology (M Th, D Th); modern Hebrew (MA, PhD); musicology (MA, MMus, D Mus, PhD); natural science education (M Ed); New Testament (M Th, D Th); Old Testament (D Th); pastoral therapy (M Th, D Th); philosophy (MA); philosophy of education (M Ed, Ed D); politics (MA, PhD); Portuguese (MA, PhD); practical theology (M Th, D Th); psychology (MA, MS, PhD); psychology of education (M Ed, Ed D); public health (MA); religious studies (MA, D Th, PhD); Romance languages (MA); Russian (MA, PhD); Semitic languages (MA, PhD); social behavior studies in HIV/AIDS (MA); social science (mental health) (MA); social science in development studies (MA); social science in psychology (MA); social science in social work (MA); social science in sociology (MA); social work (MSW, DSW, PhD); socio-education (M Ed, Ed D); sociolinguistics (MA); sociology (MA, PhD); Spanish (MA, PhD); systematic theology (M Th, D Th); TESOL (teaching English to speakers of other languages) (MA); theological ethics (M Th, D Th); theory of literature (MA, PhD); urban ministries (D Th); urban ministry (M Th).

University of South Alabama, College of Arts and Sciences, Department of Sociology, Anthropology and Social Work, Mobile, AL 36688-0002. Offers sociology (MA). *Program availability:* Part-time, evening/weekend. *Faculty:* 3 full-time (1 woman). *Students:* 4 full-time (3 women); includes 1 minority (Black or African American, non-Hispanic/Latino). Average age 32. 1 applicant, 100% accepted, 1 enrolled. In 2019, 4 master's awarded. *Degree requirements:* For master's, comprehensive exam, thesis optional. *Entrance requirements:* For master's, GRE. Additional exam requirements/recommendations for international students: required—TOEFL (minimum score 525 paper-based; 71 iBT), IELTS (minimum score 6). *Application deadline:* For fall admission, 7/15 priority date for domestic students, 6/15 priority date for international students; for spring admission, 12/1 priority date for domestic students, 5/1 priority date for international students; for summer admission, 5/1 for domestic students, 4/1 for international students. Applications are processed on a rolling basis. Application fee: $35. Electronic applications accepted. *Expenses: Tuition, area resident:* Part-time $442 per credit hour. Tuition, state resident: full-time $10,608; part-time $442 per credit hour. Tuition, nonresident: full-time $21,216; part-time $884 per credit hour. *Financial support:* In 2019–20, teaching assistantships with tuition reimbursements (averaging $9,000 per year) were awarded; fellowships, research assistantships, career-related internships or fieldwork, Federal Work-Study, institutionally sponsored loans, scholarships/grants, and unspecified assistantships also available. Support available to part-time students. Financial award application deadline: 3/15; financial award applicants required to submit FAFSA. *Unit head:* Dr. Roma S. Hanks, Chair, 251-460-6347, Fax: 251-460-7925, E-mail: rhanks@southalabama.edu. *Application contact:* Dr. Christopher Freed, Graduate Coordinator, Sociology, 251-460-6348, Fax: 251-460-7925, E-mail: cfreed@southalabama.edu.
Website: http://www.southalabama.edu/colleges/artsandsci/syansw

University of South Carolina, The Graduate School, College of Arts and Sciences, Department of Sociology, Columbia, SC 29208. Offers MA, PhD. *Program availability:* Part-time. Terminal master's awarded for partial completion of doctoral program. *Degree requirements:* For master's, thesis; for doctorate, comprehensive exam, thesis/dissertation. *Entrance requirements:* For master's and doctorate, GRE General Test. Additional exam requirements/recommendations for international students: required—TOEFL (minimum score 570 paper-based; 75 iBT). Electronic applications accepted.

University of Southern California, Graduate School, Dana and David Dornsife College of Letters, Arts and Sciences, Department of Sociology, Los Angeles, CA 90089. Offers PhD. *Degree requirements:* For doctorate, comprehensive exam, thesis/dissertation. *Entrance requirements:* For doctorate, GRE. Additional exam requirements/recommendations for international students: required—TOEFL. Electronic applications accepted.

University of South Florida, College of Arts and Sciences, Department of Sociology, Tampa, FL 33620-9951. Offers MA, PhD. *Program availability:* Part-time. *Faculty:* 11 full-time (7 women). *Students:* 36 full-time (21 women), 2 part-time (1 woman); includes 14 minority (3 Black or African American, non-Hispanic/Latino; 3 Asian, non-Hispanic/Latino; 4 Hispanic/Latino; 4 Two or more races, non-Hispanic/Latino), 6 international. Average age 31. 29 applicants, 62% accepted, 11 enrolled. In 2019, 6 master's, 3 doctorates awarded. *Degree requirements:* For master's, comprehensive exam, thesis; for doctorate, comprehensive exam, thesis/dissertation. *Entrance requirements:* For master's, GRE (preferred scores of 153V - 61st percentile, 144Q - 17th percentile), 3 letters of recommendation, personal statement, writing sample; for doctorate, GRE (preferred scores 160V - 86th percentile, 144Q - 17th percentile), 3 letters of recommendation, personal statement, writing sample. Additional exam requirements/recommendations for international students: required—TOEFL, TOEFL minimum score 550 paper-based; 79 iBT or IELTS minimum score 6.5 (for PhD); TOEFL minimum score 600 paper-based (for MA). *Application deadline:* For fall admission, 1/15 priority date for domestic and international students. Application fee: $30. Electronic applications accepted. *Financial support:* In 2019–20, 13 students received support, including 21 teaching assistantships with tuition reimbursements available (averaging $12,581 per year); unspecified assistantships also available. Financial award application deadline: 3/1. *Unit head:* Dr. James Cavendish, Associate Professor and Chairperson, 813-974-2633, Fax: 813-974-6455, E-mail: jcavendi@usf.edu. *Application contact:* Dr. Sara Crawley, Associate Professor and Graduate Program Director, 813-974-0977, Fax: 813-974-6455, E-mail: scrawley@usf.edu.
Website: http://sociology.usf.edu

The University of Tennessee, Graduate School, College of Arts and Sciences, Department of Sociology, Knoxville, TN 37996. Offers criminology (MA, PhD); energy, environment, and resource policy (MA, PhD); political economy (MA, PhD). *Program availability:* Part-time. *Degree requirements:* For master's, thesis or alternative; for doctorate, thesis/dissertation. *Entrance requirements:* For master's, GRE General Test, minimum GPA of 3.0; for doctorate, GRE General Test, minimum GPA of 3.5. Additional exam requirements/recommendations for international students: required—TOEFL. Electronic applications accepted.

The University of Texas at Arlington, Graduate School, College of Liberal Arts, Department of Sociology and Anthropology, Program in Sociology, Arlington, TX 76019. Offers MA. *Program availability:* Part-time, evening/weekend. *Degree requirements:* For master's, comprehensive exam, thesis or alternative. *Entrance requirements:* For master's, GRE General Test, 12 hours of undergraduate course work in sociology. Additional exam requirements/recommendations for international students: required—TOEFL (minimum score 550 paper-based). Electronic applications accepted.

The University of Texas at Austin, Graduate School, College of Liberal Arts, Department of Sociology, Austin, TX 78712-1111. Offers MA, PhD. *Degree requirements:* For master's, thesis; for doctorate, thesis/dissertation. *Entrance requirements:* For master's and doctorate, GRE General Test. Additional exam requirements/recommendations for international students: required—TOEFL. Electronic applications accepted.

The University of Texas at El Paso, Graduate School, College of Liberal Arts, Department of Sociology and Anthropology, El Paso, TX 79968-0001. Offers applied anthropology (Certificate); applied social sciences (Certificate); sociology (MA). *Program availability:* Part-time, evening/weekend. *Degree requirements:* For master's, thesis. *Entrance requirements:* For master's, GRE General Test, minimum GPA of 3.0. Additional exam requirements/recommendations for international students: required—TOEFL. Electronic applications accepted.

The University of Texas at San Antonio, College of Liberal and Fine Arts, Department of Sociology, San Antonio, TX 78249-0617. Offers MS. *Program availability:* Part-time. *Degree requirements:* For master's, comprehensive exam, internship or thesis. *Entrance requirements:* For master's, GRE (waived if GPA 3.5 or above), BA/BS with 18 credit hours in field of study or other appropriate field of study; official transcripts; statement of purpose; academic writing sample; 3 letters of recommendation; minimum GPA of 3.0. Additional exam requirements/recommendations for international students: required—TOEFL (minimum score 550 paper-based; 79 iBT), IELTS (minimum score 6.5). Electronic applications accepted. *Expenses:* Contact institution.

The University of Texas at Tyler, College of Arts and Sciences, Department of Social Sciences, Tyler, TX 75799-0001. Offers criminal justice (MS); public administration (MPA); sociology (MS). *Program availability:* Part-time, evening/weekend. *Faculty:* 5 full-time (2 women), 5 part-time/adjunct (1 woman). *Students:* 17 full-time (12 women), 36 part-time (25 women); includes 22 minority (7 Black or African American, non-Hispanic/Latino; 1 Asian, non-Hispanic/Latino; 12 Hispanic/Latino; 2 Two or more races, non-Hispanic/Latino), 2 international. Average age 36. 27 applicants, 89% accepted, 16 enrolled. In 2019, 19 master's awarded. *Degree requirements:* For master's, comprehensive exam, thesis optional. *Entrance requirements:* For master's, GRE General Test, minimum GPA of 3.0. Additional exam requirements/recommendations for international students: required—TOEFL. *Application deadline:* For fall admission, 8/17 priority date for domestic students, 7/1 priority date for international students; for spring admission, 12/21 priority date for domestic students, 11/1 priority date for international students. Applications are processed on a rolling basis. Application fee: $25 ($50 for international students). *Financial support:* In 2019–20, 1 fellowship (averaging $1,000 per year) was awarded; research assistantships, teaching assistantships, career-related internships or fieldwork, Federal Work-Study, and scholarships/grants also available. Support available to part-time students. Financial award application deadline: 7/1; financial award applicants required to submit FAFSA. *Unit head:* Dr. Thomas Guderjan, Chair, 903-566-7418, E-mail: tguderjan@uttyler.edu. *Application contact:* Dr. Thomas Guderjan, Chair, 903-566-7418, E-mail: tguderjan@uttyler.edu. Website: https://www.uttyler.edu/socialsciences/

The University of Texas Rio Grande Valley, College of Liberal Arts, Department of Sociology and Anthropology, Edinburg, TX 78539. Offers disaster studies (MA); sociology (MS). *Faculty:* 9 full-time (3 women). *Students:* 28 full-time (16 women), 19 part-time (14 women); includes 40 minority (1 Black or African American, non-Hispanic/Latino; 1 Asian, non-Hispanic/Latino; 38 Hispanic/Latino), 6 international. Average age 32. 21 applicants, 86% accepted, 12 enrolled. In 2019, 12 master's awarded. *Entrance requirements:* Additional exam requirements/recommendations for international students: required—TOEFL or IELTS. *Expenses:* Tuition, area resident: Full-time $5959; part-time $440 per credit hour. Tuition, state resident: full-time $5959. Tuition, nonresident: full-time $5959. *International tuition:* $13,321 full-time. *Required fees:* $1169; $185 per credit hour. Website: utrgv.edu/sociology/index.htm

The University of Toledo, College of Graduate Studies, College of Languages, Literature and Social Sciences, Department of Sociology and Anthropology, Toledo, OH 43606-3390. Offers sociology (MA). *Program availability:* Part-time. *Degree requirements:* For master's, thesis or alternative. *Entrance requirements:* For master's, GRE, minimum cumulative point-hour ratio of 2.7 for all previous academic work, three letters of recommendation, statement of purpose, transcripts from all prior institutions attended. Additional exam requirements/recommendations for international students: required—TOEFL (minimum score 550 paper-based; 80 iBT). Electronic applications accepted.

University of Toronto, School of Graduate Studies, Faculty of Arts and Science, Department of Sociology, Toronto, ON M5S 1A1, Canada. Offers MA, PhD. *Program availability:* Part-time. *Degree requirements:* For doctorate, thesis/dissertation. *Entrance requirements:* For master's, GRE (for applicants from non-Canadian universities, recommended for those from Canadian universities), 5 full-year courses in sociology, basic research and statistical skills; 2 letters of reference; minimum B+ average in each of last two years of post-secondary education; for doctorate, GRE (for applicants from non-Canadian universities; recommended for those from Canadian universities), MA in sociology, minimum A- average, 2 letters of reference, statement of interest. Additional exam requirements/recommendations for international students: required—TOEFL (minimum score 580 paper-based; 93 iBT), TWE (minimum score 5). Electronic applications accepted.

University of Utah, Graduate School, College of Social and Behavioral Science, Department of Sociology, Salt Lake City, UT 84112-1107. Offers M Stat, MA, MS, PhD. *Program availability:* Part-time. *Faculty:* 9 full-time (5 women). *Students:* 24 full-time (17 women), 3 part-time (2 women); includes 5 minority (1 Black or African American, non-Hispanic/Latino; 4 Hispanic/Latino), 5 international. Average age 32. 26 applicants, 35% accepted, 8 enrolled. In 2019, 5 master's, 1 doctorate awarded. Terminal master's awarded for partial completion of doctoral program. *Degree requirements:* For master's, thesis; for doctorate, comprehensive exam, thesis/dissertation, Qualifying Exam. *Entrance requirements:* For master's and doctorate, GRE, minimum undergraduate GPA of 3.0. Additional exam requirements/recommendations for international students: required—TOEFL (minimum score 80 paper-based), IELTS (minimum score 6.5), either TOEFL or IELTS. *Application deadline:* For fall admission, 12/15 for domestic and international students. Application fee: $55 ($65 for international students). Electronic applications accepted. *Expenses:* Tuition, state resident: full-time $7085; part-time $272.51 per credit hour. Tuition, nonresident: full-time $24,937; part-time $959.12 per

credit hour. *Required fees:* $880.52; $880.52 per semester. Tuition and fees vary according to degree level, program and student level. *Financial support:* In 2019–20, 1 fellowship (averaging $31,000 per year), 3 research assistantships (averaging $26,333 per year), 19 teaching assistantships (averaging $14,105 per year) were awarded; scholarships/grants and unspecified assistantships also available. Financial award application deadline: 12/15; financial award applicants required to submit FAFSA. *Unit head:* Dr. Ming Wen, Chair, 801-581-6153, Fax: 801-585-3784, E-mail: ming.wen@soc.utah.edu. *Application contact:* Alana Robinson, Graduate Records Secretary, 801-581-6153, Fax: 801-585-3784, E-mail: alana.robison@soc.utah.edu. Website: http://www.soc.utah.edu/

University of Victoria, Faculty of Graduate Studies, Faculty of Social Sciences, Department of Sociology, Victoria, BC V8W 2Y2, Canada. Offers MA, PhD. *Program availability:* Part-time. *Degree requirements:* For master's, thesis; for doctorate, thesis/dissertation, candidacy exam. *Entrance requirements:* For master's, minimum B+ average. Additional exam requirements/recommendations for international students: required—TOEFL (minimum score 575 paper-based), IELTS (minimum score 7), TWE (minimum score 4).

University of Virginia, College and Graduate School of Arts and Sciences, Department of Sociology, Charlottesville, VA 22903. Offers MA, PhD. *Degree requirements:* For master's, thesis; for doctorate, comprehensive exam, thesis/dissertation. *Entrance requirements:* For master's and doctorate, GRE General Test, GRE Subject Test, 2 letters of recommendation. Additional exam requirements/recommendations for international students: required—TOEFL (minimum score 600 paper-based; 90 iBT), IELTS (minimum score 7). Electronic applications accepted.

University of Washington, Graduate School, College of Arts and Sciences, Department of Sociology, Seattle, WA 98195. Offers MA, PhD. *Degree requirements:* For master's, thesis; for doctorate, thesis/dissertation. *Entrance requirements:* For master's and doctorate, GRE General Test, minimum GPA of 3.0. Additional exam requirements/recommendations for international students: required—TOEFL. Electronic applications accepted.

University of Waterloo, Graduate Studies and Postdoctoral Affairs, Faculty of Arts, Department of Sociology and Legal Studies, Waterloo, ON N2L 3G1, Canada. Offers MA, PhD. *Program availability:* Part-time. *Degree requirements:* For master's, thesis (for some programs); for doctorate, one foreign language, thesis/dissertation. *Entrance requirements:* For master's, honors degree, minimum B+ average, resume, writing sample; for doctorate, master's degree, minimum A- average, resume, writing sample. Additional exam requirements/recommendations for international students: required—TOEFL, IELTS, PTE. Electronic applications accepted.

The University of Western Ontario, School of Graduate and Postdoctoral Studies, Faculty of Social Science, Department of Sociology, London, ON N6A 3K7, Canada. Offers MA, PhD. Terminal master's awarded for partial completion of doctoral program. *Degree requirements:* For master's, thesis (for some programs); for doctorate, one foreign language, comprehensive exam, thesis/dissertation. *Entrance requirements:* For master's, minimum B+ average, honors degree; for doctorate, minimum A- average. Additional exam requirements/recommendations for international students: required—TOEFL. Electronic applications accepted.

University of Windsor, Faculty of Graduate Studies, Faculty of Arts and Social Sciences, Department of Sociology and Anthropology, Windsor, ON N9B 3P4, Canada. Offers criminology (MA); sociology (MA); sociology-social justice (PhD). *Program availability:* Part-time. *Degree requirements:* For master's, thesis; for doctorate, comprehensive exam, thesis/dissertation. *Entrance requirements:* For master's, minimum B+ average; for doctorate, writing sample, minimum B+ average. Additional exam requirements/recommendations for international students: required—TOEFL (minimum score 560 paper-based). Electronic applications accepted.

University of Wisconsin–Madison, Graduate School, College of Letters and Science, Department of Sociology, Madison, WI 53706-1380. Offers rural sociology (MS); sociology (MS, PhD). *Program availability:* Part-time. Terminal master's awarded for partial completion of doctoral program. *Degree requirements:* For master's, thesis, oral exam; for doctorate, thesis/dissertation, preliminary and final oral exams, 4 seminars. *Entrance requirements:* For master's and doctorate, GRE General Test. Additional exam requirements/recommendations for international students: required—TOEFL. Electronic applications accepted.

University of Wisconsin–Milwaukee, Graduate School, College of Letters and Science, Department of Sociology, Milwaukee, WI 53201-0413. Offers MA, PhD. *Program availability:* Part-time. *Entrance requirements:* For master's, GRE. Electronic applications accepted.

University of Wyoming, College of Arts and Sciences, Department of Sociology, Laramie, WY 82071. Offers MA. *Program availability:* Part-time. *Degree requirements:* For master's, thesis. *Entrance requirements:* For master's, GRE General Test, minimum GPA of 3.0. Additional exam requirements/recommendations for international students: required—TOEFL (minimum score 525 paper-based). Electronic applications accepted.

Université Laval, Faculty of Social Sciences, Department of Sociology, Programs in Sociology, Québec, QC G1K 7P4, Canada. Offers MA, PhD. Terminal master's awarded for partial completion of doctoral program. *Degree requirements:* For master's, thesis; for doctorate, comprehensive exam, thesis/dissertation. *Entrance requirements:* For master's, English exam (comprehension of written English), French exam (for some), knowledge of French; for doctorate, English exam (comprehension of written English), French exam may be required, knowledge of French. Electronic applications accepted.

Utah State University, School of Graduate Studies, College of Humanities and Social Sciences, Department of Sociology, Social Work, and Anthropology, Logan, UT 84322. Offers anthropology (MS); social work (MSW); sociology (MS, PhD). *Accreditation:* CSWE. *Degree requirements:* For master's, thesis; for doctorate, comprehensive exam, thesis/dissertation. *Entrance requirements:* For master's, GRE General Test, minimum GPA of 3.0, recommendation letters; for doctorate, GRE General Test, minimum GPA of 3.0, recommendation letters, transcripts, personal statement, MS degree. Additional exam requirements/recommendations for international students: required—TOEFL; recommended—TWE.

Vanderbilt University, Department of Sociology, Nashville, TN 37240-1001. Offers MA, PhD. *Faculty:* 16 full-time (6 women). *Students:* 32 full-time (27 women); includes 11 minority (6 Black or African American, non-Hispanic/Latino; 4 Asian, non-Hispanic/Latino; 1 Hispanic/Latino), 2 international. Average age 28. 95 applicants, 11% accepted, 4 enrolled. In 2019, 6 master's, 2 doctorates awarded. *Degree requirements:* For master's, thesis; for doctorate, comprehensive exam, thesis/dissertation, area, qualifying, and final exams. *Entrance requirements:* For master's and doctorate, GRE General Test. Additional exam requirements/recommendations for international students: required—TOEFL (minimum score 570 paper-based; 88 iBT). *Application deadline:* For fall admission, 1/15 for domestic and international students. Electronic applications accepted. *Expenses:* Tuition: Full-time $51,018; part-time $2087 per hour. *Required fees:* $542. Tuition and fees vary according to program. *Financial support:* Fellowships with full tuition reimbursements, research assistantships, teaching assistantships with full tuition reimbursements, Federal Work-Study, institutionally

sponsored loans, scholarships/grants, and health care benefits available. Financial award application deadline: 1/15; financial award applicants required to submit CSS PROFILE or FAFSA. *Unit head:* Dr. Larry Isaac, Chair, 615-322-7626, Fax: 615-322-7505, E-mail: larry.isaac@vanderbilt.edu. *Application contact:* Lijun Song, Director of Graduate Studies, 615-322-1731, Fax: 615-322-7505, E-mail: lijun.song@vanderbilt.edu.
Website: http://www.vanderbilt.edu/sociology/VDOS_Home.shtml

Virginia Commonwealth University, Graduate School, College of Humanities and Sciences, Department of Sociology, Richmond, VA 23284-9005. Offers digital sociology (MS). *Degree requirements:* For master's, thesis optional. *Entrance requirements:* For master's, GRE General Test. Additional exam requirements/recommendations for international students: required—TOEFL (minimum score 600 paper-based; 100 iBT); recommended—IELTS (minimum score 6.5). Electronic applications accepted.

Washington State University, College of Arts and Sciences, Department of Sociology, Pullman, WA 99164. Offers MA, PhD. *Program availability:* Part-time. Terminal master's awarded for partial completion of doctoral program. *Degree requirements:* For master's, thesis; for doctorate, comprehensive exam, thesis/dissertation. *Entrance requirements:* For master's, bachelor's degree, minimum GPA of 3.0; for doctorate, MA in sociology, minimum GPA of 3.0. Additional exam requirements/recommendations for international students: required—TOEFL (minimum score 550 paper-based). Electronic applications accepted.

Wayne State University, College of Liberal Arts and Sciences, Department of Sociology, Detroit, MI 48202. Offers applied sociological research methodology (MA); medical sociology/health (PhD); race/gender inequality (PhD); sociology (MA); urban/labor studies (PhD). *Faculty:* 13. *Students:* 22 full-time (17 women), 9 part-time (3 women); includes 6 minority (4 Black or African American, non-Hispanic/Latino; 1 Hispanic/Latino; 1 Two or more races, non-Hispanic/Latino), 2 international. Average age 35. 36 applicants, 25% accepted, 2 enrolled. In 2019, 1 master's, 3 doctorates awarded. *Degree requirements:* For master's, thesis (for some programs), oral exam, public defense of thesis/essay; for doctorate, comprehensive exam, thesis/dissertation, oral exam, public defense of the dissertation. *Entrance requirements:* For master's, minimum GPA of 3.3 in upper-division courses; substantial background in sociology, social science research methods, sociological theory, and basic statistics; three letters of reference (at least 2 from college/university faculty); writing sample; statement of interest; for doctorate, minimum GPA of 3.5 in master's work; three letters of reference (at least 2 from college/university faculty); statement of interest; sample of written work. Additional exam requirements/recommendations for international students: required—TOEFL (minimum score 600 paper-based; 100 iBT), TWE, Michigan English Language Assessment Battery (minimum score 85); recommended—IELTS. *Application deadline:* For fall admission, 1/15 for domestic and international students. Application fee: $50. Electronic applications accepted. *Expenses: Tuition:* Full-time $34,567. *Financial support:* In 2019–20, 21 students received support, including 3 fellowships with tuition reimbursements available (averaging $20,000 per year), 8 teaching assistantships with tuition reimbursements available (averaging $19,967 per year); research assistantships with tuition reimbursements available, scholarships/grants, health care benefits, and unspecified assistantships also available. Financial award applicants required to submit FAFSA. *Unit head:* Dr. Jeffrey Kentor, Chair and Professor, 313-577-8131, E-mail: jeffrey.kentor@wayne.edu. *Application contact:* Dr. David Merolla, Director of Graduate Studies, 313-577-2930, E-mail: dmerolla@wayne.edu.
Website: http://clas.wayne.edu/Sociology/

Western Illinois University, School of Graduate Studies, College of Arts and Sciences, Department of Sociology and Anthropology, Macomb, IL 61455-1390. Offers sociology (MA). *Program availability:* Part-time. *Degree requirements:* For master's, thesis or alternative. *Entrance requirements:* Additional exam requirements/recommendations for international students: required—TOEFL (minimum score 550 paper-based; 80 iBT). Electronic applications accepted.

Western Kentucky University, Graduate School, Potter College of Arts and Letters, Department of Sociology, Bowling Green, KY 42101. Offers criminology (MA); sociology (MA). *Program availability:* Online learning. *Degree requirements:* For master's, comprehensive exam, thesis optional, final exam. *Entrance requirements:* For master's, GRE General Test, minimum GPA of 3.0. Additional exam requirements/recommendations for international students: required—TOEFL (minimum score 555 paper-based; 79 iBT).

Western Michigan University, Graduate College, College of Arts and Sciences, Department of Sociology, Kalamazoo, MI 49008. Offers MA, PhD. *Degree requirements:* For master's, thesis; for doctorate, one foreign language, thesis/dissertation.

West Virginia University, Eberly College of Arts and Sciences, Morgantown, WV 26506. Offers biology (MS, PhD); chemistry (MS, PhD); communication studies (MA, PhD); computational statistics (PhD); creative writing (MFA); English (MA, PhD); forensic and investigative science (MS); forensic science (PhD); geography (MA); geology (MA, PhD); history (MA, PhD); legal studies (MLS); mathematics (MS); physics (MS, PhD); political science (MA, PhD); professional writing and editing (MA); psychology (MA); public administration (MPA); social work (MSW); sociology (MA, PhD); statistics (MS). *Program availability:* Part-time, evening/weekend, online learning. Terminal master's awarded for partial completion of doctoral program. *Degree requirements:* For master's, thesis (for some programs); for doctorate, comprehensive exam, thesis/dissertation. *Entrance requirements:* For master's and doctorate, GRE. Additional exam requirements/recommendations for international students: required—TOEFL (minimum score 600 paper-based); recommended—TWE. Electronic applications accepted.

Wichita State University, Graduate School, Fairmount College of Liberal Arts and Sciences, Department of Sociology, Wichita, KS 67260. Offers MA. *Program availability:* Part-time.

Wilfrid Laurier University, Faculty of Graduate and Postdoctoral Studies, Faculty of Arts, Department of Sociology, Waterloo, ON N2L 3C5, Canada. Offers health, family and well-being (MA); internationalization, migration and human rights (MA). *Entrance requirements:* For master's, honours BA with minimum B+ average and major in sociology. Additional exam requirements/recommendations for international students: required—TOEFL (minimum score 89 iBT). Electronic applications accepted.

Yale University, Graduate School of Arts and Sciences, Department of Sociology, New Haven, CT 06520. Offers comparative and historical sociology (PhD); cultural sociology and social theory (PhD); social stratification and the life course (PhD). *Degree requirements:* For doctorate, thesis/dissertation. *Entrance requirements:* For doctorate, GRE General Test.

York University, Faculty of Graduate Studies, Faculty of Liberal Arts and Professional Studies, Program in Sociology, Toronto, ON M3J 1P3, Canada. Offers MA, PhD. *Program availability:* Part-time. *Degree requirements:* For master's, thesis or alternative; for doctorate, one foreign language, comprehensive exam, thesis/dissertation, analytical paper. Electronic applications accepted.

York University, Faculty of Graduate Studies, Program in Social and Political Thought, Toronto, ON M3J 1P3, Canada. Offers MA, PhD. *Program availability:* Part-time. *Degree requirements:* For master's, one foreign language, thesis or alternative, oral exams; for doctorate, one foreign language, comprehensive exam, thesis/dissertation. Electronic applications accepted.

Survey Methodology

University of Maryland, College Park, Academic Affairs, College of Behavioral and Social Sciences, Joint Program in Survey Methodology, College Park, MD 20742. Offers MS, PhD. *Degree requirements:* For master's, thesis (for some programs), scholarly paper; for doctorate, thesis/dissertation. *Entrance requirements:* For master's, GRE General Test (recommended), minimum GPA of 3.0, 3 letters of recommendation; for doctorate, GRE General Test, minimum GPA of 3.0, 3 letters of recommendation. Electronic applications accepted.

University of Michigan, Rackham Graduate School, Program in Survey Methodology, Ann Arbor, MI 48109. Offers data science (MS, PhD); social and psychological (MS, PhD); statistical (MS, PhD); survey methodology (Certificate). *Program availability:* Part-time. Terminal master's awarded for partial completion of doctoral program. *Degree requirements:* For master's, internships; for doctorate, comprehensive exam, thesis/dissertation. *Entrance requirements:* For master's and doctorate, GRE, 3 letters of recommendation, academic statement of purpose, personal statement, resume or curriculum vitae, academic transcripts; for Certificate, 3 letters of recommendation, academic statement of purpose, personal statement, resume or curriculum vitae, academic transcripts. Additional exam requirements/recommendations for international students: required—TOEFL (minimum score 560 paper-based; 84 iBT). Electronic applications accepted. *Expenses:* Contact institution.

University of Nebraska–Lincoln, Graduate College, Interdepartmental Area of Survey Research and Methodology, Lincoln, NE 68588. Offers MS, PhD. *Degree requirements:* For master's, comprehensive exam. *Entrance requirements:* For master's, GRE General Test or GMAT. Additional exam requirements/recommendations for international students: required—TOEFL (minimum score 550 paper-based). Electronic applications accepted.

APPENDIXES

Institutional Changes
Since the 2020 Edition (Graduate)

Following is an alphabetical listing of institutions that have recently closed, merged with other institutions, or changed their names or status. In the case of a name change, the former name appears first, followed by the new name.

Antioch University (Midwest Yellow Springs, OH): *closed.*

Argosy University, Atlanta (Atlanta, GA): *closed.*

Argosy University, Chicago (Chicago, IL): *closed.*

Argosy University, Hawaii (Honolulu, HI): *closed.*

Argosy University, Los Angeles (Los Angeles, CA): *closed.*

Argosy University, Northern Virginia (Arlington, VA): *closed.*

Argosy University, Orange County (Orange, CA): *closed.*

Argosy University, Phoenix (Phoenix, AZ): *closed.*

Argosy University, Seattle (Seattle, WA): *closed.*

Argosy University, Tampa (Tampa, FL): *closed.*

Argosy University, Twin Cities (Eagan, MN): *closed.*

College of Saint Elizabeth (Morristown, NJ): *name changed to Saint Elizabeth University.*

College of St. Joseph (Rutland, VT): *closed.*

Concordia University (Portland, OR): *closed.*

Elmhurst College (Elmhurst, IL): *name changed to Elmhurst University.*

The John Marshall Law School (Chicago, IL): *closed; acquired by University of Illinois at Chicago; name changed to UIC John Marshall Law School.*

Marygrove College (Detroit, MI): *closed.*

Nebraska Christian College of Hope International University (Papillion, NE): *closed.*

Northwest Christian University (Eugene, OR): *name changed to Bushnell University.*

Notre Dame de Namur University (Belmont, CA): *closed.*

Silver Lake College of the Holy Family (Manitowoc, WI): *closed.*

University of South Florida Sarasota-Manatee (Sarasota, FL): *to merge with University of South Florida Main Campus.*

University of South Florida, St. Petersburg (St. Petersburg, FL): *to merge with University of South Florida Main Campus.*

Watkins College of Art, Design, and Film (Nashville, TN): *to merge with Belmont University.*

Abbreviations Used in the Guides

The following list includes abbreviations of degree names used in the profiles in the 2020 edition of the guides. Because some degrees (e.g., Doctor of Education) can be abbreviated in more than one way (e.g., D.Ed. or Ed.D.), and because the abbreviations used in the guides reflect the preferences of the individual colleges and universities, the list may include two or more abbreviations for a single degree.

DEGREES

A Mus D	Doctor of Musical Arts
AC	Advanced Certificate
AD	Artist's Diploma
	Doctor of Arts
ADP	Artist's Diploma
Adv C	Advanced Certificate
AGC	Advanced Graduate Certificate
AGSC	Advanced Graduate Specialist Certificate
ALM	Master of Liberal Arts
AM	Master of Arts
AMBA	Accelerated Master of Business Administration
APC	Advanced Professional Certificate
APMPH	Advanced Professional Master of Public Health
App Sc	Applied Scientist
App Sc D	Doctor of Applied Science
AstE	Astronautical Engineer
ATC	Advanced Training Certificate
Au D	Doctor of Audiology
B Th	Bachelor of Theology
CAES	Certificate of Advanced Educational Specialization
CAGS	Certificate of Advanced Graduate Studies
CAL	Certificate in Applied Linguistics
CAPS	Certificate of Advanced Professional Studies
CAS	Certificate of Advanced Studies
CATS	Certificate of Achievement in Theological Studies
CE	Civil Engineer
CEM	Certificate of Environmental Management
CET	Certificate in Educational Technologies
CGS	Certificate of Graduate Studies
Ch E	Chemical Engineer
Clin Sc D	Doctor of Clinical Science
CM	Certificate in Management
CMH	Certificate in Medical Humanities
CMM	Master of Church Ministries
CMS	Certificate in Ministerial Studies
CNM	Certificate in Nonprofit Management
CPC	Certificate in Publication and Communication
CPH	Certificate in Public Health
CPS	Certificate of Professional Studies
CScD	Doctor of Clinical Science
CSD	Certificate in Spiritual Direction
CSS	Certificate of Special Studies
CTS	Certificate of Theological Studies
D Ac	Doctor of Acupuncture
D Admin	Doctor of Administration
D Arch	Doctor of Architecture
D Be	Doctor in Bioethics
D Com	Doctor of Commerce
D Couns	Doctor of Counseling
D Des	Doctorate of Design
D Div	Doctor of Divinity
D Ed	Doctor of Education
D Ed Min	Doctor of Educational Ministry
D Eng	Doctor of Engineering
D Engr	Doctor of Engineering
D Ent	Doctor of Enterprise

D Env	Doctor of Environment
D Law	Doctor of Law
D Litt	Doctor of Letters
D Med Sc	Doctor of Medical Science
D Mgt	Doctor of Management
D Min	Doctor of Ministry
D Miss	Doctor of Missiology
D Mus	Doctor of Music
D Mus A	Doctor of Musical Arts
D Phil	Doctor of Philosophy
D Prof	Doctor of Professional Studies
D Ps	Doctor of Psychology
D Sc	Doctor of Science
D Sc D	Doctor of Science in Dentistry
D Sc IS	Doctor of Science in Information Systems
D Sc PA	Doctor of Science in Physician Assistant Studies
D Th	Doctor of Theology
D Th P	Doctor of Practical Theology
DA	Doctor of Accounting
	Doctor of Arts
DACM	Doctor of Acupuncture and Chinese Medicine
DAIS	Doctor of Applied Intercultural Studies
DAOM	Doctorate in Acupuncture and Oriental Medicine
DAT	Doctorate of Athletic Training
	Professional Doctor of Art Therapy
DBA	Doctor of Business Administration
DBH	Doctor of Behavioral Health
DBL	Doctor of Business Leadership
DC	Doctor of Chiropractic
DCC	Doctor of Computer Science
DCD	Doctor of Communications Design
DCE	Doctor of Computer Engineering
DCJ	Doctor of Criminal Justice
DCL	Doctor of Civil Law
	Doctor of Comparative Law
DCM	Doctor of Church Music
DCN	Doctor of Clinical Nutrition
DCS	Doctor of Computer Science
DDN	Diplôme du Droit Notarial
DDS	Doctor of Dental Surgery
DE	Doctor of Education
	Doctor of Engineering
DED	Doctor of Economic Development
DEIT	Doctor of Educational Innovation and Technology
DEL	Doctor of Executive Leadership
DEM	Doctor of Educational Ministry
DEPD	Diplôme Études Spécialisées
DES	Doctor of Engineering Science
DESS	Diplôme Études Supérieures Spécialisées
DET	Doctor of Educational Technology
DFA	Doctor of Fine Arts
DGP	Diploma in Graduate and Professional Studies
DGS	Doctor of Global Security
DH Sc	Doctor of Health Sciences
DHA	Doctor of Health Administration
DHCE	Doctor of Health Care Ethics
DHL	Doctor of Hebrew Letters
DHPE	Doctorate of Health Professionals Education
DHS	Doctor of Health Science
DHSc	Doctor of Health Science
DIT	Doctor of Industrial Technology
	Doctor of Information Technology
DJS	Doctor of Jewish Studies
DLS	Doctor of Liberal Studies

DM	Doctor of Management	EMIB	Executive Master of International Business
	Doctor of Music	EMIR	Executive Master in International Relations
DMA	Doctor of Musical Arts	EML	Executive Master of Leadership
DMD	Doctor of Dental Medicine	EMPA	Executive Master of Public Administration
DME	Doctor of Manufacturing Management	EMPL	Executive Master in Policy Leadership
	Doctor of Music Education		Executive Master in Public Leadership
DMFT	Doctor of Marital and Family Therapy	EMS	Executive Master of Science
DMH	Doctor of Medical Humanities	EMTM	Executive Master of Technology Management
DML	Doctor of Modern Languages	Eng	Engineer
DMP	Doctorate in Medical Physics	Eng Sc D	Doctor of Engineering Science
DMPNA	Doctor of Management Practice in Nurse Anesthesia	Engr	Engineer
		Exec MHA	Executive Master of Health Administration
DN Sc	Doctor of Nursing Science	Exec Ed D	Executive Doctor of Education
DNAP	Doctor of Nurse Anesthesia Practice	Exec MBA	Executive Master of Business Administration
DNP	Doctor of Nursing Practice	Exec MPA	Executive Master of Public Administration
DNP-A	Doctor of Nursing Practice - Anesthesia	Exec MPH	Executive Master of Public Health
DNS	Doctor of Nursing Science	Exec MS	Executive Master of Science
DO	Doctor of Osteopathy	Executive MA	Executive Master of Arts
DOL	Doctorate of Organizational Leadership	G Dip	Graduate Diploma
DOM	Doctor of Oriental Medicine	GBC	Graduate Business Certificate
DOT	Doctor of Occupational Therapy	GDM	Graduate Diploma in Management
DPA	Diploma in Public Administration	GDPA	Graduate Diploma in Public Administration
	Doctor of Public Administration	GEMBA	Global Executive Master of Business Administration
DPDS	Doctor of Planning and Development Studies		
DPH	Doctor of Public Health	GM Acc	Graduate Master of Accountancy
DPM	Doctor of Plant Medicine	GMBA	Global Master of Business Administration
	Doctor of Podiatric Medicine	GP LL M	Global Professional Master of Laws
DPPD	Doctor of Policy, Planning, and Development	GPD	Graduate Performance Diploma
DPS	Doctor of Professional Studies	GSS	Graduate Special Certificate for Students in Special Situations
DPT	Doctor of Physical Therapy		
DPTSc	Doctor of Physical Therapy Science	IEMBA	International Executive Master of Business Administration
Dr DES	Doctor of Design		
Dr NP	Doctor of Nursing Practice	IMA	Interdisciplinary Master of Arts
Dr OT	Doctor of Occupational Therapy	IMBA	International Master of Business Administration
Dr PH	Doctor of Public Health	IMES	International Master's in Environmental Studies
Dr Sc PT	Doctor of Science in Physical Therapy	Ingeniero	Engineer
DRSc	Doctor of Regulatory Science	JCD	Doctor of Canon Law
DS	Doctor of Science	JCL	Licentiate in Canon Law
DS Sc	Doctor of Social Science	JD	Juris Doctor
DScPT	Doctor of Science in Physical Therapy	JM	Juris Master
DSI	Doctor of Strategic Intelligence	JSD	Doctor of Juridical Science
DSJS	Doctor of Science in Jewish Studies		Doctor of Jurisprudence
DSL	Doctor of Strategic Leadership		Doctor of the Science of Law
DSNS	Doctorate of Statecraft and National Security	JSM	Master of the Science of Law
DSS	Doctor of Strategic Security	L Th	Licentiate in Theology
DSW	Doctor of Social Work	LL B	Bachelor of Laws
DTL	Doctor of Talmudic Law	LL CM	Master of Comparative Law
	Doctor of Transformational Leadership	LL D	Doctor of Laws
DV Sc	Doctor of Veterinary Science	LL M	Master of Laws
DVM	Doctor of Veterinary Medicine	LL M in Tax	Master of Laws in Taxation
DWS	Doctor of Worship Studies	LL M CL	Master of Laws in Common Law
EAA	Engineer in Aeronautics and Astronautics	M Ac	Master of Accountancy
EASPh D	Engineering and Applied Science Doctor of Philosophy		Master of Accounting
			Master of Acupuncture
ECS	Engineer in Computer Science	M Ac OM	Master of Acupuncture and Oriental Medicine
Ed D	Doctor of Education	M Acc	Master of Accountancy
Ed DCT	Doctor of Education in College Teaching		Master of Accounting
Ed L D	Doctor of Education Leadership	M Acct	Master of Accountancy
Ed M	Master of Education		Master of Accounting
Ed S	Specialist in Education	M Accy	Master of Accountancy
Ed Sp	Specialist in Education	M Actg	Master of Accounting
EDB	Executive Doctorate in Business	M Acy	Master of Accountancy
EDM	Executive Doctorate in Management	M Ad	Master of Administration
EE	Electrical Engineer	M Ad Ed	Master of Adult Education
EJD	Executive Juris Doctor	M Adm	Master of Administration
EMBA	Executive Master of Business Administration	M Adm Mgt	Master of Administrative Management
EMFA	Executive Master of Forensic Accounting	M Admin	Master of Administration
EMHA	Executive Master of Health Administration	M ADU	Master of Architectural Design and Urbanism
EMHCL	Executive Master in Healthcare Leadership	M Adv	Master of Advertising

M Ag	Master of Agriculture
M Ag Ed	Master of Agricultural Education
M Agr	Master of Agriculture
M App Comp Sc	Master of Applied Computer Science
M App St	Master of Applied Statistics
M Appl Stat	Master of Applied Statistics
M Aq	Master of Aquaculture
M Ar	Master of Architecture
M Arch	Master of Architecture
M Arch I	Master of Architecture I
M Arch II	Master of Architecture II
M Arch E	Master of Architectural Engineering
M Arch H	Master of Architectural History
M Bioethics	Master in Bioethics
M Cat	Master of Catechesis
M Ch E	Master of Chemical Engineering
M Cl D	Master of Clinical Dentistry
M Cl Sc	Master of Clinical Science
M Comm	Master of Communication
M Comp	Master of Computing
M Comp Sc	Master of Computer Science
M Coun	Master of Counseling
M Dent	Master of Dentistry
M Dent Sc	Master of Dental Sciences
M Des	Master of Design
M Des S	Master of Design Studies
M Div	Master of Divinity
M E Sci	Master of Earth Science
M Ec	Master of Economics
M Econ	Master of Economics
M Ed	Master of Education
M Ed T	Master of Education in Teaching
M En	Master of Engineering
M En S	Master of Environmental Sciences
M Eng	Master of Engineering
M Eng Mgt	Master of Engineering Management
M Engr	Master of Engineering
M Ent	Master of Enterprise
M Env	Master of Environment
M Env Des	Master of Environmental Design
M Env E	Master of Environmental Engineering
M Env Sc	Master of Environmental Science
M Ext Ed	Master of Extension Education
M Fin	Master of Finance
M Geo E	Master of Geological Engineering
M Geoenv E	Master of Geoenvironmental Engineering
M Geog	Master of Geography
M Hum	Master of Humanities
M IDST	Master's in Interdisciplinary Studies
M Jur	Master of Jurisprudence
M Kin	Master of Kinesiology
M Land Arch	Master of Landscape Architecture
M Litt	Master of Letters
M Mark	Master of Marketing
M Mat SE	Master of Material Science and Engineering
M Math	Master of Mathematics
M Mech E	Master of Mechanical Engineering
M Med Sc	Master of Medical Science
M Mgmt	Master of Management
M Mgt	Master of Management
M Min	Master of Ministries
M Mtl E	Master of Materials Engineering
M Mu	Master of Music
M Mus	Master of Music
M Mus Ed	Master of Music Education
M Music	Master of Music
M Pet E	Master of Petroleum Engineering
M Pharm	Master of Pharmacy
M Phil	Master of Philosophy
M Phil F	Master of Philosophical Foundations
M Pl	Master of Planning
M Plan	Master of Planning
M Pol	Master of Political Science
M Pr Met	Master of Professional Meteorology
M Prob S	Master of Probability and Statistics
M Psych	Master of Psychology
M Pub	Master of Publishing
M Rel	Master of Religion
M Sc	Master of Science
M Sc A	Master of Science (Applied)
M Sc AC	Master of Science in Applied Computing
M Sc AHN	Master of Science in Applied Human Nutrition
M Sc BMC	Master of Science in Biomedical Communications
M Sc CS	Master of Science in Computer Science
M Sc E	Master of Science in Engineering
M Sc Eng	Master of Science in Engineering
M Sc Engr	Master of Science in Engineering
M Sc F	Master of Science in Forestry
M Sc FE	Master of Science in Forest Engineering
M Sc Geogr	Master of Science in Geography
M Sc N	Master of Science in Nursing
M Sc OT	Master of Science in Occupational Therapy
M Sc P	Master of Science in Planning
M Sc Pl	Master of Science in Planning
M Sc PT	Master of Science in Physical Therapy
M Sc T	Master of Science in Teaching
M SEM	Master of Sustainable Environmental Management
M Serv Soc	Master of Social Service
M Soc	Master of Sociology
M Sp Ed	Master of Special Education
M Stat	Master of Statistics
M Sys E	Master of Systems Engineering
M Sys Sc	Master of Systems Science
M Tax	Master of Taxation
M Tech	Master of Technology
M Th	Master of Theology
M Trans E	Master of Transportation Engineering
M U Ed	Master of Urban Education
M Urb	Master of Urban Planning
M Vet Sc	Master of Veterinary Science
MA	Master of Accounting
	Master of Administration
	Master of Arts
MA Comm	Master of Arts in Communication
MA Ed	Master of Arts in Education
MA Ed/HD	Master of Arts in Education and Human Development
MA Islamic	Master of Arts in Islamic Studies
MA Min	Master of Arts in Ministry
MA Miss	Master of Arts in Missiology
MA Past St	Master of Arts in Pastoral Studies
MA Ph	Master of Arts in Philosophy
MA Psych	Master of Arts in Psychology
MA Sc	Master of Applied Science
MA Sp	Master of Arts (Spirituality)
MA Th	Master of Arts in Theology
MA-R	Master of Arts (Research)
MAA	Master of Applied Anthropology
	Master of Applied Arts
	Master of Arts in Administration
MAAA	Master of Arts in Arts Administration
MAAD	Master of Advanced Architectural Design
MAAE	Master of Arts in Art Education
MAAPPS	Master of Arts in Asia Pacific Policy Studies
MAAS	Master of Arts in Aging and Spirituality
MAASJ	Master of Arts in Applied Social Justice

MAAT	Master of Arts in Applied Theology
MAB	Master of Agribusiness
	Master of Applied Bioengineering
	Master of Arts in Business
MABA	Master's in Applied Behavior Analysis
MABC	Master of Arts in Biblical Counseling
MABE	Master of Arts in Bible Exposition
MABL	Master of Arts in Biblical Languages
MABM	Master of Agribusiness Management
MABS	Master of Arts in Biblical Studies
MABT	Master of Arts in Bible Teaching
MAC	Master of Accountancy
	Master of Accounting
	Master of Arts in Communication
	Master of Arts in Counseling
MACC	Master of Arts in Christian Counseling
MACCT	Master of Accounting
MACD	Master of Arts in Christian Doctrine
MACE	Master of Arts in Christian Education
MACH	Master of Arts in Church History
MACI	Master of Arts in Curriculum and Instruction
MACIS	Master of Accounting and Information Systems
MACJ	Master of Arts in Criminal Justice
MACL	Master of Arts in Christian Leadership
	Master of Arts in Community Leadership
MACM	Master of Arts in Christian Ministries
	Master of Arts in Christian Ministry
	Master of Arts in Church Music
	Master of Arts in Counseling Ministries
MACML	Master of Arts in Christian Ministry and Leadership
MACN	Master of Arts in Counseling
MACO	Master of Arts in Counseling
MAcOM	Master of Acupuncture and Oriental Medicine
MACP	Master of Arts in Christian Practice
	Master of Arts in Church Planting
	Master of Arts in Counseling Psychology
MACS	Master of Applied Computer Science
	Master of Arts in Catholic Studies
	Master of Arts in Christian Studies
MACSE	Master of Arts in Christian School Education
MACT	Master of Arts in Communications and Technology
MAD	Master in Educational Institution Administration
	Master of Art and Design
MADR	Master of Arts in Dispute Resolution
MADS	Master of Applied Disability Studies
MAE	Master of Aerospace Engineering
	Master of Agricultural Economics
	Master of Agricultural Education
	Master of Applied Economics
	Master of Architectural Engineering
	Master of Art Education
	Master of Arts in Education
	Master of Arts in English
MAEd	Master of Arts Education
MAEE	Master of Agricultural and Extension Education
MAEL	Master of Arts in Educational Leadership
MAEM	Master of Arts in Educational Ministries
MAEP	Master of Arts in Economic Policy
	Master of Arts in Educational Psychology
MAES	Master of Arts in Environmental Sciences
MAET	Master of Arts in English Teaching
MAF	Master of Arts in Finance
MAFE	Master of Arts in Financial Economics
MAFM	Master of Accounting and Financial Management
MAFS	Master of Arts in Family Studies
MAG	Master of Applied Geography
MAGU	Master of Urban Analysis and Management
MAH	Master of Arts in Humanities
MAHA	Master of Arts in Humanitarian Assistance
MAHCM	Master of Arts in Health Care Mission
MAHG	Master of American History and Government
MAHL	Master of Arts in Hebrew Letters
MAHN	Master of Applied Human Nutrition
MAHR	Master of Applied Historical Research
MAHS	Master of Arts in Human Services
MAHSR	Master in Applied Health Services Research
MAIA	Master of Arts in International Administration
	Master of Arts in International Affairs
MAICS	Master of Arts in Intercultural Studies
MAIDM	Master of Arts in Interior Design and Merchandising
MAIH	Master of Arts in Interdisciplinary Humanities
MAIOP	Master of Applied Industrial/Organizational Psychology
MAIS	Master of Arts in Intercultural Studies
	Master of Arts in Interdisciplinary Studies
	Master of Arts in International Studies
MAIT	Master of Administration in Information Technology
MAJ	Master of Arts in Journalism
MAJCS	Master of Arts in Jewish Communal Service
MAJPS	Master of Arts in Jewish Professional Studies
MAJS	Master of Arts in Jewish Studies
MAL	Master of Athletic Leadership
MALA	Master of Arts in Liberal Arts
MALCM	Master in Arts Leadership and Cultural Management
MALD	Master of Arts in Law and Diplomacy
MALER	Master of Arts in Labor and Employment Relations
MALL	Master of Arts in Language Learning
MALLT	Master of Arts in Language, Literature, and Translation
MALP	Master of Arts in Language Pedagogy
MALS	Master of Arts in Liberal Studies
MAM	Master of Acquisition Management
	Master of Agriculture and Management
	Master of Applied Mathematics
	Master of Arts in Management
	Master of Arts in Ministry
	Master of Arts Management
	Master of Aviation Management
MAMC	Master of Arts in Mass Communication
	Master of Arts in Ministry and Culture
	Master of Arts in Ministry for a Multicultural Church
MAME	Master of Arts in Missions/Evangelism
MAMFC	Master of Arts in Marriage and Family Counseling
MAMFT	Master of Arts in Marriage and Family Therapy
MAMHC	Master of Arts in Mental Health Counseling
MAMS	Master of Applied Mathematical Sciences
	Master of Arts in Ministerial Studies
	Master of Arts in Ministry and Spirituality
MAMT	Master of Arts in Mathematics Teaching
MAN	Master of Applied Nutrition
MANT	Master of Arts in New Testament
MAOL	Master of Arts in Organizational Leadership
MAOM	Master of Acupuncture and Oriental Medicine
	Master of Arts in Organizational Management
MAOT	Master of Arts in Old Testament
MAP	Master of Applied Politics
	Master of Applied Psychology
	Master of Arts in Planning
	Master of Psychology
	Master of Public Administration
MAP Min	Master of Arts in Pastoral Ministry
MAPA	Master of Arts in Public Administration
MAPC	Master of Arts in Pastoral Counseling

MAPE	Master of Arts in Physics Education
MAPM	Master of Arts in Pastoral Ministry
	Master of Arts in Pastoral Music
	Master of Arts in Practical Ministry
MAPP	Master of Arts in Public Policy
MAPS	Master of Applied Psychological Sciences
	Master of Arts in Pastoral Studies
	Master of Arts in Public Service
MAPW	Master of Arts in Professional Writing
MAQRM	Master's of Actuarial and Quantitative Risk Management
MAR	Master of Arts in Reading
	Master of Arts in Religion
Mar Eng	Marine Engineer
MARC	Master of Arts in Rehabilitation Counseling
MARE	Master of Arts in Religious Education
MARL	Master of Arts in Religious Leadership
MARS	Master of Arts in Religious Studies
MAS	Master of Accounting Science
	Master of Actuarial Science
	Master of Administrative Science
	Master of Advanced Study
	Master of American Studies
	Master of Animal Science
	Master of Applied Science
	Master of Applied Statistics
	Master of Archival Studies
MASA	Master of Advanced Studies in Architecture
MASC	Master of Arts in School Counseling
MASD	Master of Arts in Spiritual Direction
MASE	Master of Arts in Special Education
MASF	Master of Arts in Spiritual Formation
MASJ	Master of Arts in Systems of Justice
MASLA	Master of Advanced Studies in Landscape Architecture
MASM	Master of Aging Services Management
	Master of Arts in Specialized Ministries
MASS	Master of Applied Social Science
MASW	Master of Aboriginal Social Work
MAT	Master of Arts in Teaching
	Master of Arts in Theology
	Master of Athletic Training
	Master's in Administration of Telecommunications
Mat E	Materials Engineer
MATCM	Master of Acupuncture and Traditional Chinese Medicine
MATDE	Master of Arts in Theology, Development, and Evangelism
MATDR	Master of Territorial Management and Regional Development
MATE	Master of Arts for the Teaching of English
MATESL	Master of Arts in Teaching English as a Second Language
MATESOL	Master of Arts in Teaching English to Speakers of Other Languages
MATF	Master of Arts in Teaching English as a Foreign Language/Intercultural Studies
MATFL	Master of Arts in Teaching Foreign Language
MATH	Master of Arts in Therapy
MATI	Master of Administration of Information Technology
MATL	Master of Arts in Teaching of Languages
	Master of Arts in Transformational Leadership
MATM	Master of Arts in Teaching of Mathematics
MATRN	Master of Athletic Training
MATS	Master of Arts in Theological Studies
	Master of Arts in Transforming Spirituality
MAUA	Master of Arts in Urban Affairs
MAUD	Master of Arts in Urban Design
MAURP	Master of Arts in Urban and Regional Planning

MAW	Master of Arts in Worship
MAWSHP	Master of Arts in Worship
MAYM	Master of Arts in Youth Ministry
MB	Master of Bioinformatics
MBA	Master of Business Administration
MBA-AM	Master of Business Administration in Aviation Management
MBA-EP	Master of Business Administration–Experienced Professionals
MBAA	Master of Business Administration in Aviation
MBAE	Master of Biological and Agricultural Engineering
	Master of Biosystems and Agricultural Engineering
MBAH	Master of Business Administration in Health
MBAi	Master of Business Administration–International
MBAICT	Master of Business Administration in Information and Communication Technology
MBC	Master of Building Construction
MBE	Master of Bilingual Education
	Master of Bioengineering
	Master of Bioethics
	Master of Biomedical Engineering
	Master of Business Economics
	Master of Business Education
MBEE	Master in Biotechnology Enterprise and Entrepreneurship
MBET	Master of Business, Entrepreneurship and Technology
MBI	Master in Business Informatics
MBIOT	Master of Biotechnology
MBiotech	Master of Biotechnology
MBL	Master of Business Leadership
MBLE	Master in Business Logistics Engineering
MBME	Master's in Biomedical Engineering
MBMSE	Master of Business Management and Software Engineering
MBOE	Master of Business Operational Excellence
MBS	Master of Biblical Studies
	Master of Biological Science
	Master of Biomedical Sciences
	Master of Bioscience
	Master of Building Science
	Master of Business and Science
	Master of Business Statistics
MBST	Master of Biostatistics
MBT	Master of Biomedical Technology
	Master of Biotechnology
	Master of Business Taxation
MBV	Master of Business for Veterans
MC	Master of Classics
	Master of Communication
	Master of Counseling
MC Ed	Master of Continuing Education
MC Sc	Master of Computer Science
MCA	Master of Commercial Aviation
	Master of Communication Arts
	Master of Criminology (Applied)
MCAM	Master of Computational and Applied Mathematics
MCC	Master of Computer Science
MCD	Master of Communications Disorders
	Master of Community Development
MCE	Master in Electronic Commerce
	Master of Chemistry Education
	Master of Christian Education
	Master of Civil Engineering
	Master of Control Engineering
MCEM	Master of Construction Engineering Management
MCEPA	Master of Chinese Economic and Political Affairs
MCHE	Master of Chemical Engineering
MCIS	Master of Communication and Information Studies

	Master of Computer and Information Science	ME Sc	Master of Engineering Science
	Master of Computer Information Systems	ME-PD	Master of Education–Professional Development
MCIT	Master of Computer and Information Technology	MEA	Master of Educational Administration
MCJ	Master of Criminal Justice		Master of Engineering Administration
MCL	Master in Communication Leadership	MEAE	Master of Entertainment Arts and Engineering
	Master of Canon Law	MEAP	Master of Environmental Administration and Planning
	Master of Christian Leadership		
	Master of Comparative Law	MEB	Master of Energy Business
MCM	Master of Christian Ministry	MEBD	Master in Environmental Building Design
	Master of Church Music	MEBT	Master in Electronic Business Technologies
	Master of Communication Management	MEC	Master of Electronic Commerce
	Master of Community Medicine	Mech E	Mechanical Engineer
	Master of Construction Management	MEDS	Master of Environmental Design Studies
	Master of Contract Management	MEE	Master in Education
MCMin	Master of Christian Ministry		Master of Electrical Engineering
MCMM	Master in Communications and Media Management		Master of Energy Engineering
MCMP	Master of City and Metropolitan Planning		Master of Environmental Engineering
MCMS	Master of Clinical Medical Science	MEECON	Master of Energy Economics
MCN	Master of Clinical Nutrition	MEEM	Master of Environmental Engineering and Management
MCOL	Master of Arts in Community and Organizational Leadership		
		MEENE	Master of Engineering in Environmental Engineering
MCP	Master of City Planning		
	Master of Community Planning	MEEP	Master of Environmental and Energy Policy
	Master of Counseling Psychology	MEERM	Master of Earth and Environmental Resource Management
	Master of Cytopathology Practice		
	Master of Science in Quality Systems and Productivity	MEH	Master in Humanistic Studies
			Master of Environmental Health
MCPD	Master of Community Planning and Development		Master of Environmental Horticulture
MCR	Master in Clinical Research	MEHS	Master of Environmental Health and Safety
MCRP	Master of City and Regional Planning	MEIM	Master of Entertainment Industry Management
	Master of Community and Regional Planning		Master of Equine Industry Management
MCRS	Master of City and Regional Studies	MEL	Master of Educational Leadership
MCS	Master of Chemical Sciences		Master of Engineering Leadership
	Master of Christian Studies		Master of English Literature
	Master of Clinical Science	MELP	Master of Environmental Law and Policy
	Master of Combined Sciences	MEM	Master of Engineering Management
	Master of Communication Studies		Master of Environmental Management
	Master of Computer Science		Master of Marketing
	Master of Consumer Science	MEME	Master of Engineering in Manufacturing Engineering
MCSE	Master of Computer Science and Engineering		
MCSL	Master of Catholic School Leadership		Master of Engineering in Mechanical Engineering
MCSM	Master of Construction Science and Management	MENR	Master of Environment and Natural Resources
MCT	Master of Commerce and Technology	MENVEGR	Master of Environmental Engineering
MCTM	Master of Clinical Translation Management	MEP	Master of Engineering Physics
MCTP	Master of Communication Technology and Policy	MEPC	Master of Environmental Pollution Control
MCTS	Master of Clinical and Translational Science	MEPD	Master of Environmental Planning and Design
MCVS	Master of Cardiovascular Science	MER	Master of Employment Relations
MD	Doctor of Medicine	MERE	Master of Entrepreneurial Real Estate
MDA	Master of Dietetic Administration	MERL	Master of Energy Regulation and Law
MDB	Master of Design-Build	MES	Master of Education and Science
MDE	Master in Design Engineering		Master of Engineering Science
	Master of Developmental Economics		Master of Environment and Sustainability
	Master of Distance Education		Master of Environmental Science
	Master of the Education of the Deaf		Master of Environmental Studies
MDH	Master of Dental Hygiene		Master of Environmental Systems
MDI	Master of Disruptive Innovation	MESM	Master of Environmental Science and Management
MDM	Master of Design Methods	MET	Master of Educational Technology
	Master of Digital Media		Master of Engineering Technology
MDP	Master in Sustainable Development Practice		Master of Entertainment Technology
	Master of Development Practice		Master of Environmental Toxicology
MDR	Master of Dispute Resolution	METM	Master of Engineering and Technology Management
MDS	Master in Data Science		
	Master of Dental Surgery	MEVE	Master of Environmental Engineering
	Master of Design Studies	MF	Master of Finance
	Master of Digital Sciences		Master of Forestry
MDSPP	Master in Data Science for Public Policy	MFA	Master of Financial Administration
ME	Master of Education		Master of Fine Arts
	Master of Engineering	MFALP	Master of Food and Agriculture Law and Policy
	Master of Entrepreneurship	MFAS	Master of Fisheries and Aquatic Science

MFC	Master of Forest Conservation
MFCS	Master of Family and Consumer Sciences
MFE	Master of Financial Economics
	Master of Financial Engineering
	Master of Forest Engineering
MFES	Master of Fire and Emergency Services
MFG	Master of Functional Genomics
MFHD	Master of Family and Human Development
MFM	Master of Financial Management
	Master of Financial Mathematics
MFPE	Master of Food Process Engineering
MFR	Master of Forest Resources
MFRC	Master of Forest Resources and Conservation
MFRE	Master of Food and Resource Economics
MFS	Master of Food Science
	Master of Forensic Sciences
	Master of Forest Science
	Master of Forest Studies
	Master of French Studies
MFST	Master of Food Safety and Technology
MFT	Master of Family Therapy
MFWCB	Master of Fish, Wildlife and Conservation Biology
MFYCS	Master of Family, Youth and Community Sciences
MGA	Master of Global Affairs
	Master of Government Administration
	Master of Governmental Administration
MGBA	Master of Global Business Administration
MGC	Master of Genetic Counseling
MGCS	Master of Genetic Counselor Studies
MGD	Master of Graphic Design
MGE	Master of Geotechnical Engineering
MGEM	Master of Geomatics for Environmental Management
	Master of Global Entrepreneurship and Management
MGIS	Master of Geographic Information Science
	Master of Geographic Information Systems
MGM	Master of Global Management
MGMA	Master of Greenhouse Gas Management and Accounting
MGP	Master of Gestion de Projet
MGPS	Master of Global Policy Studies
MGREM	Master of Global Real Estate Management
MGS	Master of Gender Studies
	Master of Gerontological Studies
	Master of Global Studies
MH	Master of Humanities
MH Sc	Master of Health Sciences
MHA	Master of Health Administration
	Master of Healthcare Administration
	Master of Hospital Administration
	Master of Hospitality Administration
MHB	Master of Human Behavior
MHC	Master of Mental Health Counseling
MHCA	Master of Health Care Administration
MHCD	Master of Health Care Design
MHCI	Master of Human-Computer Interaction
MHCL	Master of Health Care Leadership
MHCM	Master of Health Care Management
MHE	Master of Health Education
	Master of Higher Education
	Master of Human Ecology
MHE Ed	Master of Home Economics Education
MHEA	Master of Higher Education Administration
MHHS	Master of Health and Human Services
MHI	Master of Health Informatics
	Master of Healthcare Innovation
MHID	Master of Healthcare Interior Design

MHIHIM	Master of Health Informatics and Health Information Management
MHIIM	Master of Health Informatics and Information Management
MHK	Master of Human Kinetics
MHM	Master of Healthcare Management
MHMS	Master of Health Management Systems
MHP	Master of Health Physics
	Master of Heritage Preservation
	Master of Historic Preservation
MHPA	Master of Heath Policy and Administration
MHPCTL	Master of High Performance Coaching and Technical Leadership
MHPE	Master of Health Professions Education
MHR	Master of Human Resources
MHRD	Master in Human Resource Development
MHRIR	Master of Human Resources and Industrial Relations
MHRLR	Master of Human Resources and Labor Relations
MHRM	Master of Human Resources Management
MHS	Master of Health Science
	Master of Health Sciences
	Master of Health Studies
	Master of Hispanic Studies
	Master of Human Services
	Master of Humanistic Studies
MHSA	Master of Health Services Administration
MHSM	Master of Health Systems Management
MI	Master of Information
	Master of Instruction
MI Arch	Master of Interior Architecture
MIA	Master of Interior Architecture
	Master of International Affairs
MIAA	Master of International Affairs and Administration
MIAM	Master of International Agribusiness Management
MIAPD	Master of Interior Architecture and Product Design
MIB	Master of International Business
MIBS	Master of International Business Studies
MICLJ	Master of International Criminal Law and Justice
MICM	Master of International Construction Management
MID	Master of Industrial Design
	Master of Industrial Distribution
	Master of Innovation Design
	Master of Interior Design
	Master of International Development
MIDA	Master of International Development Administration
MIDP	Master of International Development Policy
MIDS	Master of Information and Data Science
MIE	Master of Industrial Engineering
MIF	Master of International Forestry
MIHTM	Master of International Hospitality and Tourism Management
MIJ	Master of International Journalism
MILR	Master of Industrial and Labor Relations
MIM	Master in Ministry
	Master of Information Management
	Master of International Management
	Master of International Marketing
MIMFA	Master of Investment Management and Financial Analysis
MIMLAE	Master of International Management for Latin American Executives
MIMS	Master of Information Management and Systems
	Master of Integrated Manufacturing Systems
MIP	Master of Infrastructure Planning
	Master of Intellectual Property
	Master of International Policy
MIPA	Master of International Public Affairs
MIPD	Master of Integrated Product Design

MIPER	Master of International Political Economy of Resources
MIPM	Master of International Policy Management
MIPP	Master of International Policy and Practice
	Master of International Public Policy
MIPS	Master of International Planning Studies
MIR	Master of Industrial Relations
	Master of International Relations
MIRD	Master of International Relations and Diplomacy
MIRHR	Master of Industrial Relations and Human Resources
MIS	Master of Imaging Science
	Master of Industrial Statistics
	Master of Information Science
	Master of Information Systems
	Master of Integrated Science
	Master of Interdisciplinary Studies
	Master of International Service
	Master of International Studies
MISE	Master of Industrial and Systems Engineering
MISKM	Master of Information Sciences and Knowledge Management
MISM	Master of Information Systems Management
MISW	Master of Indigenous Social Work
MIT	Master in Teaching
	Master of Industrial Technology
	Master of Information Technology
	Master of Initial Teaching
	Master of International Trade
MITA	Master of Information Technology Administration
MITM	Master of Information Technology and Management
MJ	Master of Journalism
	Master of Jurisprudence
MJ Ed	Master of Jewish Education
MJA	Master of Justice Administration
MJM	Master of Justice Management
MJS	Master of Judaic Studies
	Master of Judicial Studies
	Master of Juridical Studies
MK	Master of Kinesiology
MKM	Master of Knowledge Management
ML	Master of Latin
	Master of Law
ML Arch	Master of Landscape Architecture
MLA	Master of Landscape Architecture
	Master of Liberal Arts
MLAS	Master of Laboratory Animal Science
	Master of Liberal Arts and Sciences
MLAUD	Master of Landscape Architecture in Urban Development
MLD	Master of Leadership Development
	Master of Leadership Studies
MLE	Master of Applied Linguistics and Exegesis
MLER	Master of Labor and Employment Relations
MLI Sc	Master of Library and Information Science
MLIS	Master of Library and Information Science
	Master of Library and Information Studies
MLM	Master of Leadership in Ministry
MLPD	Master of Land and Property Development
MLRHR	Master of Labor Relations and Human Resources
MLS	Master of Leadership Studies
	Master of Legal Studies
	Master of Liberal Studies
	Master of Library Science
	Master of Life Sciences
	Master of Medical Laboratory Sciences
MLSCM	Master of Logistics and Supply Chain Management
MLT	Master of Language Technologies

MLTCA	Master of Long Term Care Administration
MLW	Master of Studies in Law
MLWS	Master of Land and Water Systems
MM	Master of Management
	Master of Mediation
	Master of Ministry
	Master of Music
MM Ed	Master of Music Education
MM Sc	Master of Medical Science
MM St	Master of Museum Studies
MMA	Master of Marine Affairs
	Master of Media Arts
	Master of Musical Arts
MMAL	Master of Maritime Administration and Logistics
MMAS	Master of Military Art and Science
MMB	Master of Microbial Biotechnology
MMC	Master of Manufacturing Competitiveness
	Master of Mass Communications
MMCM	Master of Music in Church Music
MMCSS	Master of Mathematical Computational and Statistical Sciences
MME	Master of Management in Energy
	Master of Manufacturing Engineering
	Master of Mathematics Education
	Master of Mathematics for Educators
	Master of Mechanical Engineering
	Master of Mining Engineering
	Master of Music Education
MMEL	Master's in Medical Education Leadership
MMF	Master of Mathematical Finance
MMFC/T	Master of Marriage and Family Counseling/Therapy
MMFT	Master of Marriage and Family Therapy
MMG	Master of Management
MMH	Master of Management in Hospitality
	Master of Medical Humanities
MMI	Master of Management of Innovation
MMIS	Master of Management Information Systems
MML	Master of Managerial Logistics
MMM	Master of Manufacturing Management
	Master of Marine Management
	Master of Medical Management
MMP	Master of Marine Policy
	Master of Medical Physics
	Master of Music Performance
MMPA	Master of Management and Professional Accounting
MMQM	Master of Manufacturing Quality Management
MMR	Master of Marketing Research
MMRM	Master of Marine Resources Management
MMS	Master in Migration Studies
	Master of Management Science
	Master of Management Studies
	Master of Manufacturing Systems
	Master of Marine Studies
	Master of Materials Science
	Master of Mathematical Sciences
	Master of Medical Science
	Master of Medieval Studies
MMSE	Master of Manufacturing Systems Engineering
MMSM	Master of Music in Sacred Music
MMT	Master in Marketing
	Master of Math for Teaching
	Master of Music Therapy
	Master's in Marketing Technology
MMus	Master of Music
MN	Master of Nursing
	Master of Nutrition
MN NP	Master of Nursing in Nurse Practitioner

MNA	Master of Nonprofit Administration	MPM	Master of Pastoral Ministry
	Master of Nurse Anesthesia		Master of Pest Management
MNAE	Master of Nanoengineering		Master of Policy Management
MNAL	Master of Nonprofit Administration and Leadership		Master of Practical Ministries
MNAS	Master of Natural and Applied Science		Master of Professional Management
MNCL	Master of Nonprofit and Civic Leadership		Master of Project Management
MNCM	Master of Network and Communications Management		Master of Public Management
		MPNA	Master of Public and Nonprofit Administration
MNE	Master of Nuclear Engineering	MPNL	Master of Philanthropy and Nonprofit Leadership
MNL	Master in International Business for Latin America	MPO	Master of Prosthetics and Orthotics
MNM	Master of Nonprofit Management	MPOD	Master of Positive Organizational Development
MNO	Master of Nonprofit Organization	MPP	Master of Public Policy
MNPL	Master of Not-for-Profit Leadership	MPPA	Master of Public Policy Administration
MNpS	Master of Nonprofit Studies		Master of Public Policy and Administration
MNR	Master of Natural Resources	MPPAL	Master of Public Policy, Administration and Law
MNRD	Master of Natural Resources Development	MPPGA	Master of Public Policy and Global Affairs
MNRES	Master of Natural Resources and Environmental Studies	MPPM	Master of Public Policy and Management
		MPR	Master of Public Relations
MNRM	Master of Natural Resource Management	MPRTM	Master of Parks, Recreation, and Tourism Management
MNRMG	Master of Natural Resource Management and Geography	MPS	Master of Pastoral Studies
MNRS	Master of Natural Resource Stewardship		Master of Perfusion Science
MNS	Master of Natural Science		Master of Planning Studies
MNSE	Master of Natural Sciences Education		Master of Political Science
MO	Master of Oceanography		Master of Preservation Studies
MOD	Master of Organizational Development		Master of Prevention Science
MOGS	Master of Oil and Gas Studies		Master of Professional Studies
MOL	Master of Organizational Leadership		Master of Public Service
MOM	Master of Organizational Management	MPSA	Master of Public Service Administration
	Master of Oriental Medicine	MPSG	Master of Population and Social Gerontology
MOR	Master of Operations Research	MPSIA	Master of Political Science and International Affairs
MOT	Master of Occupational Therapy	MPSL	Master of Public Safety Leadership
MP	Master of Physiology	MPT	Master of Pastoral Theology
	Master of Planning		Master of Physical Therapy
MP Ac	Master of Professional Accountancy		Master of Practical Theology
MP Acc	Master of Professional Accountancy	MPVM	Master of Preventive Veterinary Medicine
	Master of Professional Accounting	MPW	Master of Professional Writing
	Master of Public Accounting		Master of Public Works
MP Aff	Master of Public Affairs	MQF	Master of Quantitative Finance
MP Th	Master of Pastoral Theology	MQM	Master of Quality Management
MPA	Master of Performing Arts		Master of Quantitative Management
	Master of Physician Assistant	MQS	Master of Quality Systems
	Master of Professional Accountancy	MR	Master of Recreation
	Master of Professional Accounting		Master of Retailing
	Master of Public Administration	MRA	Master in Research Administration
	Master of Public Affairs		Master of Regulatory Affairs
MPAC	Master of Professional Accounting	MRC	Master of Rehabilitation Counseling
MPAID	Master of Public Administration and International Development	MRCP	Master of Regional and City Planning
			Master of Regional and Community Planning
MPAP	Master of Physician Assistant Practice	MRD	Master of Rural Development
	Master of Public Administration and Policy	MRE	Master of Real Estate
	Master of Public Affairs and Politics		Master of Religious Education
MPAS	Master of Physician Assistant Science	MRED	Master of Real Estate Development
	Master of Physician Assistant Studies	MREM	Master of Resource and Environmental Management
MPC	Master of Professional Communication		
MPD	Master of Product Development	MRLS	Master of Resources Law Studies
	Master of Public Diplomacy	MRM	Master of Resources Management
MPDS	Master of Planning and Development Studies	MRP	Master of Regional Planning
MPE	Master of Physical Education	MRRD	Master in Recreation Resource Development
MPEM	Master of Project Engineering and Management	MRS	Master of Religious Studies
MPFM	Master of Public Financial Management	MRSc	Master of Rehabilitation Science
MPH	Master of Public Health	MRUD	Master of Resilient Design
MPHE	Master of Public Health Education	MS	Master of Science
MPHM	Master in Plant Health Management	MS Cmp E	Master of Science in Computer Engineering
MPHS	Master of Population Health Sciences	MS Kin	Master of Science in Kinesiology
MPHTM	Master of Public Health and Tropical Medicine	MS Acct	Master of Science in Accounting
MPI	Master of Public Informatics	MS Accy	Master of Science in Accountancy
MPIA	Master of Public and International Affairs	MS Aero E	Master of Science in Aerospace Engineering
MPL	Master of Pastoral Leadership	MS Ag	Master of Science in Agriculture

MS Arch	Master of Science in Architecture
MS Arch St	Master of Science in Architectural Studies
MS Bio E	Master of Science in Bioengineering
MS Bm E	Master of Science in Biomedical Engineering
MS Ch E	Master of Science in Chemical Engineering
MS Cp E	Master of Science in Computer Engineering
MS Eco	Master of Science in Economics
MS Econ	Master of Science in Economics
MS Ed	Master of Science in Education
MS Ed Admin	Master of Science in Educational Administration
MS El	Master of Science in Educational Leadership and Administration
MS En E	Master of Science in Environmental Engineering
MS Eng	Master of Science in Engineering
MS Engr	Master of Science in Engineering
MS Env E	Master of Science in Environmental Engineering
MS Exp Surg	Master of Science in Experimental Surgery
MS Mat SE	Master of Science in Material Science and Engineering
MS Met E	Master of Science in Metallurgical Engineering
MS Mgt	Master of Science in Management
MS Min	Master of Science in Mining
MS Min E	Master of Science in Mining Engineering
MS Mt E	Master of Science in Materials Engineering
MS Otol	Master of Science in Otolaryngology
MS Pet E	Master of Science in Petroleum Engineering
MS Sc	Master of Social Science
MS Sp Ed	Master of Science in Special Education
MS Stat	Master of Science in Statistics
MS Surg	Master of Science in Surgery
MS Tax	Master of Science in Taxation
MS Tc E	Master of Science in Telecommunications Engineering
MS-R	Master of Science (Research)
MSA	Master of School Administration
	Master of Science in Accountancy
	Master of Science in Accounting
	Master of Science in Administration
	Master of Science in Aeronautics
	Master of Science in Agriculture
	Master of Science in Analytics
	Master of Science in Anesthesia
	Master of Science in Architecture
	Master of Science in Aviation
	Master of Sports Administration
	Master of Surgical Assisting
MSAA	Master of Science in Astronautics and Aeronautics
MSABE	Master of Science in Agricultural and Biological Engineering
MSAC	Master of Science in Acupuncture
MSACC	Master of Science in Accounting
MSACS	Master of Science in Applied Computer Science
MSAE	Master of Science in Aeronautical Engineering
	Master of Science in Aerospace Engineering
	Master of Science in Applied Economics
	Master of Science in Applied Engineering
	Master of Science in Architectural Engineering
MSAEM	Master of Science in Aerospace Engineering and Mechanics
MSAF	Master of Science in Aviation Finance
MSAG	Master of Science in Applied Geosciences
MSAH	Master of Science in Allied Health
MSAL	Master of Sport Administration and Leadership
MSAM	Master of Science in Applied Mathematics
MSANR	Master of Science in Agriculture and Natural Resources
MSAS	Master of Science in Administrative Studies
	Master of Science in Applied Statistics
	Master of Science in Architectural Studies

MSAT	Master of Science in Accounting and Taxation
	Master of Science in Advanced Technology
	Master of Science in Athletic Training
MSB	Master of Science in Biotechnology
MSBA	Master of Science in Business Administration
	Master of Science in Business Analysis
MSBAE	Master of Science in Biological and Agricultural Engineering
	Master of Science in Biosystems and Agricultural Engineering
MSBCB	Master's in Bioinformatics and Computational Biology
MSBE	Master of Science in Biological Engineering
	Master of Science in Biomedical Engineering
MSBENG	Master of Science in Bioengineering
MSBH	Master of Science in Behavioral Health
MSBM	Master of Sport Business Management
MSBME	Master of Science in Biomedical Engineering
MSBMS	Master of Science in Basic Medical Science
MSBS	Master of Science in Biomedical Sciences
MSBTM	Master of Science in Biotechnology and Management
MSC	Master of Science in Commerce
	Master of Science in Communication
	Master of Science in Counseling
	Master of Science in Criminology
	Master of Strategic Communication
MSCC	Master of Science in Community Counseling
MSCD	Master of Science in Communication Disorders
	Master of Science in Community Development
MSCE	Master of Science in Chemistry Education
	Master of Science in Civil Engineering
	Master of Science in Clinical Epidemiology
	Master of Science in Computer Engineering
	Master of Science in Continuing Education
MSCEE	Master of Science in Civil and Environmental Engineering
MSCF	Master of Science in Computational Finance
MSCH	Master of Science in Chemical Engineering
MSChE	Master of Science in Chemical Engineering
MSCI	Master of Science in Clinical Investigation
MSCID	Master of Science in Community and International Development
MSCIS	Master of Science in Computer and Information Science
	Master of Science in Computer and Information Systems
	Master of Science in Computer Information Science
	Master of Science in Computer Information Systems
MSCIT	Master of Science in Computer Information Technology
MSCJ	Master of Science in Criminal Justice
MSCJA	Master of Science in Criminal Justice Administration
MSCJS	Master of Science in Crime and Justice Studies
MSCLS	Master of Science in Clinical Laboratory Studies
MSCM	Master of Science in Church Management
	Master of Science in Conflict Management
	Master of Science in Construction Management
	Master of Supply Chain Management
MSCMP	Master of Science in Cybersecurity Management and Policy
MSCNU	Master of Science in Clinical Nutrition
MSCP	Master of Science in Clinical Psychology
	Master of Science in Community Psychology
	Master of Science in Computer Engineering
	Master of Science in Counseling Psychology
MSCPE	Master of Science in Computer Engineering
MSCPharm	Master of Science in Pharmacy
MSCR	Master of Science in Clinical Research

MSCRP	Master of Science in City and Regional Planning
	Master of Science in Community and Regional Planning
MSCS	Master of Science in Clinical Science
	Master of Science in Computer Science
	Master of Science in Cyber Security
MSCSD	Master of Science in Communication Sciences and Disorders
MSCSE	Master of Science in Computer Science and Engineering
MSCTE	Master of Science in Career and Technical Education
MSD	Master of Science in Dentistry
	Master of Science in Design
	Master of Science in Dietetics
MSDM	Master of Security and Disaster Management
MSE	Master of Science Education
	Master of Science in Economics
	Master of Science in Education
	Master of Science in Engineering
	Master of Science in Engineering Management
	Master of Software Engineering
	Master of Special Education
	Master of Structural Engineering
MSECE	Master of Science in Electrical and Computer Engineering
MSED	Master of Sustainable Economic Development
MSEE	Master of Science in Electrical Engineering
	Master of Science in Environmental Engineering
MSEH	Master of Science in Environmental Health
MSEL	Master of Science in Educational Leadership
MSEM	Master of Science in Engineering and Management
	Master of Science in Engineering Management
	Master of Science in Engineering Mechanics
	Master of Science in Environmental Management
MSENE	Master of Science in Environmental Engineering
MSEO	Master of Science in Electro-Optics
MSES	Master of Science in Embedded Software Engineering
	Master of Science in Engineering Science
	Master of Science in Environmental Science
	Master of Science in Environmental Studies
	Master of Science in Exercise Science
MSESE	Master of Science in Energy Systems Engineering
MSET	Master of Science in Educational Technology
	Master of Science in Engineering Technology
MSEV	Master of Science in Environmental Engineering
MSF	Master of Science in Finance
	Master of Science in Forestry
MSFA	Master of Science in Financial Analysis
MSFCS	Master of Science in Family and Consumer Science
MSFE	Master of Science in Financial Engineering
MSFM	Master of Sustainable Forest Management
MSFOR	Master of Science in Forestry
MSFP	Master of Science in Financial Planning
MSFS	Master of Science in Financial Sciences
	Master of Science in Forensic Science
MSFSB	Master of Science in Financial Services and Banking
MSFT	Master of Science in Family Therapy
MSGC	Master of Science in Genetic Counseling
MSH	Master of Science in Health
	Master of Science in Hospice
MSHA	Master of Science in Health Administration
MSHCA	Master of Science in Health Care Administration
MSHCPM	Master of Science in Health Care Policy and Management
MSHE	Master of Science in Health Education
MSHES	Master of Science in Human Environmental Sciences

MSHFID	Master of Science in Human Factors in Information Design
MSHFS	Master of Science in Human Factors and Systems
MSHI	Master of Science in Health Informatics
MSHP	Master of Science in Health Professions
MSHR	Master of Science in Human Resources
MSHRL	Master of Science in Human Resource Leadership
MSHRM	Master of Science in Human Resource Management
MSHROD	Master of Science in Human Resources and Organizational Development
MSHS	Master of Science in Health Science
	Master of Science in Health Services
	Master of Science in Homeland Security
MSHSR	Master of Science in Human Security and Resilience
MSI	Master of Science in Information
	Master of Science in Instruction
	Master of System Integration
MSIA	Master of Science in Industrial Administration
	Master of Science in Information Assurance
MSIDM	Master of Science in Interior Design and Merchandising
MSIE	Master of Science in Industrial Engineering
MSIEM	Master of Science in Information Engineering and Management
MSIM	Master of Science in Industrial Management
	Master of Science in Information Management
	Master of Science in International Management
MSIMC	Master of Science in Integrated Marketing Communications
MSIMS	Master of Science in Identity Management and Security
MSIS	Master of Science in Information Science
	Master of Science in Information Studies
	Master of Science in Information Systems
	Master of Science in Interdisciplinary Studies
MSISE	Master of Science in Infrastructure Systems Engineering
MSISM	Master of Science in Information Systems Management
MSISPM	Master of Science in Information Security Policy and Management
MSIST	Master of Science in Information Systems Technology
MSIT	Master of Science in Industrial Technology
	Master of Science in Information Technology
	Master of Science in Instructional Technology
MSITM	Master of Science in Information Technology Management
MSJ	Master of Science in Journalism
	Master of Science in Jurisprudence
MSJC	Master of Social Justice and Criminology
MSJFP	Master of Science in Juvenile Forensic Psychology
MSJJ	Master of Science in Juvenile Justice
MSJPS	Master of Science in Justice and Public Safety
MSK	Master of Science in Kinesiology
MSL	Master in the Study of Law
	Master of School Leadership
	Master of Science in Leadership
	Master of Science in Limnology
	Master of Sports Leadership
	Master of Strategic Leadership
	Master of Studies in Law
MSLA	Master of Science in Legal Administration
MSLB	Master of Sports Law and Business
MSLFS	Master of Science in Life Sciences
MSLP	Master of Speech-Language Pathology
MSLS	Master of Science in Library Science
MSLSCM	Master of Science in Logistics and Supply Chain Management
MSLT	Master of Second Language Teaching

MSM	Master of Sacred Ministry	
	Master of Sacred Music	
	Master of School Mathematics	
	Master of Science in Management	
	Master of Science in Medicine	
	Master of Science in Organization Management	
	Master of Security Management	
	Master of Strategic Ministry	
	Master of Supply Management	
MSMA	Master of Science in Marketing Analysis	
MSMAE	Master of Science in Materials Engineering	
MSMC	Master of Science in Management and Communications	
	Master of Science in Mass Communications	
MSME	Master of Science in Mathematics Education	
	Master of Science in Mechanical Engineering	
	Master of Science in Medical Ethics	
MSMHC	Master of Science in Mental Health Counseling	
MSMIT	Master of Science in Management and Information Technology	
MSMLS	Master of Science in Medical Laboratory Science	
MSMOT	Master of Science in Management of Technology	
MSMP	Master of Science in Medical Physics	
	Master of Science in Molecular Pathology	
MSMS	Master of Science in Management Science	
	Master of Science in Marine Science	
	Master of Science in Medical Sciences	
MSMSE	Master of Science in Manufacturing Systems Engineering	
	Master of Science in Material Science and Engineering	
	Master of Science in Material Science Engineering	
	Master of Science in Mathematics and Science Education	
MSMus	Master of Sacred Music	
MSN	Master of Science in Nursing	
MSNA	Master of Science in Nurse Anesthesia	
MSNE	Master of Science in Nuclear Engineering	
MSNS	Master of Science in Natural Science	
	Master of Science in Nutritional Science	
MSOD	Master of Science in Organization Development	
	Master of Science in Organizational Development	
MSOEE	Master of Science in Outdoor and Environmental Education	
MSOES	Master of Science in Occupational Ergonomics and Safety	
MSOH	Master of Science in Occupational Health	
MSOL	Master of Science in Organizational Leadership	
MSOM	Master of Science in Oriental Medicine	
MSOR	Master of Science in Operations Research	
MSOT	Master of Science in Occupational Technology	
	Master of Science in Occupational Therapy	
MSP	Master of Science in Pharmacy	
	Master of Science in Planning	
	Master of Speech Pathology	
	Master of Sustainable Peacebuilding	
MSPA	Master of Science in Physician Assistant	
MSPAS	Master of Science in Physician Assistant Studies	
MSPC	Master of Science in Professional Communications	
MSPE	Master of Science in Petroleum Engineering	
MSPH	Master of Science in Public Health	
MSPHR	Master of Science in Pharmacy	
MSPM	Master of Science in Professional Management	
	Master of Science in Project Management	
MSPNGE	Master of Science in Petroleum and Natural Gas Engineering	
MSPPM	Master of Science in Public Policy and Management	
MSPS	Master of Science in Pharmaceutical Science	
	Master of Science in Political Science	

	Master of Science in Psychological Services	
MSPT	Master of Science in Physical Therapy	
MSRA	Master of Science in Recreation Administration	
MSRE	Master of Science in Real Estate	
	Master of Science in Religious Education	
MSRED	Master of Science in Real Estate Development	
	Master of Sustainable Real Estate Development	
MSRLS	Master of Science in Recreation and Leisure Studies	
MSRM	Master of Science in Risk Management	
MSRMP	Master of Science in Radiological Medical Physics	
MSRS	Master of Science in Radiological Sciences	
	Master of Science in Rehabilitation Science	
MSS	Master of Security Studies	
	Master of Social Science	
	Master of Social Services	
	Master of Sports Science	
	Master of Strategic Studies	
	Master's in Statistical Science	
MSSA	Master of Science in Social Administration	
MSSCM	Master of Science in Supply Chain Management	
MSSD	Master of Arts in Software Driven Systems Design	
	Master of Science in Sustainable Design	
MSSE	Master of Science in Software Engineering	
	Master of Science in Special Education	
MSSEM	Master of Science in Systems and Engineering Management	
MSSI	Master of Science in Security Informatics	
	Master of Science in Strategic Intelligence	
MSSIS	Master of Science in Security and Intelligence Studies	
MSSL	Master of Science in School Leadership	
MSSLP	Master of Science in Speech-Language Pathology	
MSSM	Master of Science in Sports Medicine	
	Master of Science in Systems Management	
MSSP	Master of Science in Social Policy	
MSSS	Master of Science in Safety Science	
	Master of Science in Systems Science	
MSST	Master of Science in Security Technologies	
MSSW	Master of Science in Social Work	
MSSWE	Master of Science in Software Engineering	
MST	Master of Science and Technology	
	Master of Science in Taxation	
	Master of Science in Teaching	
	Master of Science in Technology	
	Master of Science in Telecommunications	
	Master of Science Teaching	
MSTC	Master of Science in Technical Communication	
	Master of Science in Telecommunications	
MSTCM	Master of Science in Traditional Chinese Medicine	
MSTE	Master of Science in Telecommunications Engineering	
	Master of Science in Transportation Engineering	
MSTL	Master of Science in Teacher Leadership	
MSTM	Master of Science in Technology Management	
	Master of Science in Transfusion Medicine	
MSTOM	Master of Science in Traditional Oriental Medicine	
MSUASE	Master of Science in Unmanned and Autonomous Systems Engineering	
MSUD	Master of Science in Urban Design	
MSUS	Master of Science in Urban Studies	
MSW	Master of Social Work	
MSWE	Master of Software Engineering	
MSWREE	Master of Science in Water Resources and Environmental Engineering	
MT	Master of Taxation	
	Master of Teaching	
	Master of Technology	
	Master of Textiles	
MTA	Master of Tax Accounting	

	Master of Teaching Arts	PC	Performer's Certificate
	Master of Tourism Administration	PD	Professional Diploma
MTC	Master of Technical Communications	PGC	Post-Graduate Certificate
MTCM	Master of Traditional Chinese Medicine	PGD	Postgraduate Diploma
MTD	Master of Training and Development	Ph L	Licentiate of Philosophy
MTE	Master in Educational Technology	Pharm D	Doctor of Pharmacy
	Master of Technological Entrepreneurship	PhD	Doctor of Philosophy
MTESOL	Master in Teaching English to Speakers of Other Languages	PhD Otol	Doctor of Philosophy in Otolaryngology
		PhD Surg	Doctor of Philosophy in Surgery
MTHM	Master of Tourism and Hospitality Management	PhDEE	Doctor of Philosophy in Electrical Engineering
MTI	Master of Information Technology	PMBA	Professional Master of Business Administration
MTID	Master of Tangible Interaction Design	PMC	Post Master Certificate
MTL	Master of Talmudic Law	PMD	Post-Master's Diploma
MTM	Master of Technology Management	PMS	Professional Master of Science
	Master of Telecommunications Management		Professional Master's
	Master of the Teaching of Mathematics	Post-Doctoral MS	Post-Doctoral Master of Science
	Master of Transformative Ministry	Post-MSN Certificate	Post-Master of Science in Nursing Certificate
	Master of Translational Medicine	PPDPT	Postprofessional Doctor of Physical Therapy
MTMH	Master of Tropical Medicine and Hygiene	Pro-MS	Professional Science Master's
MTMS	Master in Teaching Mathematics and Science	Professional MA	Professional Master of Arts
MTOM	Master of Traditional Oriental Medicine	Professional MBA	Professional Master of Business Administration
MTPC	Master of Technical and Professional Communication	Professional MS	Professional Master of Science
MTR	Master of Translational Research	PSM	Professional Master of Science
MTS	Master of Theatre Studies		Professional Science Master's
	Master of Theological Studies	Psy D	Doctor of Psychology
MTW	Master of Teaching Writing	Psy M	Master of Psychology
MTWM	Master of Trust and Wealth Management	Psy S	Specialist in Psychology
MUA	Master of Urban Affairs	Psya D	Doctor of Psychoanalysis
MUAP	Master's of Urban Affairs and Policy	S Psy S	Specialist in Psychological Services
MUCD	Master of Urban and Community Design	Sc D	Doctor of Science
MUD	Master of Urban Design	Sc M	Master of Science
MUDS	Master of Urban Design Studies	SCCT	Specialist in Community College Teaching
MUEP	Master of Urban and Environmental Planning	ScDPT	Doctor of Physical Therapy Science
MUP	Master of Urban Planning	SD	Specialist Degree
MUPD	Master of Urban Planning and Development	SJD	Doctor of Juridical Sciences
MUPP	Master of Urban Planning and Policy	SLPD	Doctor of Speech-Language Pathology
MUPRED	Master of Urban Planning and Real Estate Development	SM	Master of Science
		SM Arch S	Master of Science in Architectural Studies
MURP	Master of Urban and Regional Planning	SMACT	Master of Science in Art, Culture and Technology
	Master of Urban and Rural Planning	SMBT	Master of Science in Building Technology
MURPL	Master of Urban and Regional Planning	SP	Specialist Degree
MUS	Master of Urban Studies	Sp Ed	Specialist in Education
Mus M	Master of Music	Sp LIS	Specialist in Library and Information Science
MUSA	Master of Urban Spatial Analytics	SPA	Specialist in Arts
MVP	Master of Voice Pedagogy	Spec	Specialist's Certificate
MVS	Master of Visual Studies	Spec M	Specialist in Music
MWBS	Master of Won Buddhist Studies	Spt	Specialist Degree
MWC	Master of Wildlife Conservation	SSP	Specialist in School Psychology
MWR	Master of Water Resources	STB	Bachelor of Sacred Theology
MWS	Master of Women's Studies	STD	Doctor of Sacred Theology
	Master of Worship Studies	STL	Licentiate of Sacred Theology
MWSc	Master of Wildlife Science	STM	Master of Sacred Theology
Nav Arch	Naval Architecture	tDACM	Transitional Doctor of Acupuncture and Chinese Medicine
Naval E	Naval Engineer		
ND	Doctor of Naturopathic Medicine	TDPT	Transitional Doctor of Physical Therapy
	Doctor of Nursing	Th D	Doctor of Theology
NE	Nuclear Engineer	Th M	Master of Theology
Nuc E	Nuclear Engineer	TOTD	Transitional Doctor of Occupational Therapy
OD	Doctor of Optometry	VMD	Doctor of Veterinary Medicine
OTD	Doctor of Occupational Therapy	WEMBA	Weekend Executive Master of Business Administration
PBME	Professional Master of Biomedical Engineering	XMA	Executive Master of Arts

INDEXES

Displays and Close-Ups

Directories and Subject Areas

Following is an alphabetical listing of directories and subject areas. Also listed are cross-references for subject area names not used in the directory structure of the guides, for example, "City and Regional Planning (*see* Urban and Regional Planning)"

Graduate Programs in the Humanities, Arts & Social Sciences

Addictions/Substance Abuse Counseling
Administration (*see* Arts Administration; Public Administration)
African-American Studies
African Languages and Literatures (*see* African Studies)
African Studies
Agribusiness (*see* Agricultural Economics and Agribusiness)
Agricultural Economics and Agribusiness
Alcohol Abuse Counseling (*see* Addictions/Substance Abuse Counseling)
American Indian/Native American Studies
American Studies
Anthropology
Applied Arts and Design—General
Applied Behavior Analysis
Applied Economics
Applied History (*see* Public History)
Applied Psychology
Applied Social Research
Arabic (*see* Near and Middle Eastern Languages)
Arab Studies (*see* Near and Middle Eastern Studies)
Archaeology
Architectural History
Architecture
Archives Administration (*see* Public History)
Area and Cultural Studies (*see* African-American Studies; African Studies; American Indian/Native American Studies; American Studies; Asian-American Studies; Asian Studies; Canadian Studies; Cultural Studies; East European and Russian Studies; Ethnic Studies; Folklore; Gender Studies; Hispanic Studies; Holocaust Studies; Jewish Studies; Latin American Studies; Near and Middle Eastern Studies; Northern Studies; Pacific Area/Pacific Rim Studies; Western European Studies; Women's Studies)
Art/Fine Arts
Art History
Arts Administration
Arts Journalism
Art Therapy
Asian-American Studies
Asian Languages
Asian Studies
Behavioral Sciences (*see* Psychology)
Bible Studies (*see* Religion; Theology)
Biological Anthropology
Black Studies (*see* African-American Studies)
Broadcasting (*see* Communication; Film, Television, and Video Production)
Broadcast Journalism
Building Science
Canadian Studies
Celtic Languages
Ceramics (*see* Art/Fine Arts)
Child and Family Studies
Child Development
Chinese
Chinese Studies (*see* Asian Languages; Asian Studies)
Christian Studies (*see* Missions and Missiology; Religion; Theology)
Cinema (*see* Film, Television, and Video Production)
City and Regional Planning (*see* Urban and Regional Planning)
Classical Languages and Literatures (*see* Classics)
Classics
Clinical Psychology

Clothing and Textiles
Cognitive Psychology (*see* Psychology—General; Cognitive Sciences)
Cognitive Sciences
Communication—General
Community Affairs (*see* Urban and Regional Planning; Urban Studies)
Community Planning (*see* Architecture; Environmental Design; Urban and Regional Planning; Urban Design; Urban Studies)
Community Psychology (*see* Social Psychology)
Comparative and Interdisciplinary Arts
Comparative Literature
Composition (*see* Music)
Computer Art and Design
Conflict Resolution and Mediation/Peace Studies
Consumer Economics
Corporate and Organizational Communication
Corrections (*see* Criminal Justice and Criminology)
Counseling (*see* Counseling Psychology; Pastoral Ministry and Counseling)
Counseling Psychology
Crafts (*see* Art/Fine Arts)
Creative Arts Therapies (*see* Art Therapy; Therapies—Dance, Drama, and Music)
Criminal Justice and Criminology
Cultural Anthropology
Cultural Studies
Dance
Decorative Arts
Demography and Population Studies
Design (*see* Applied Arts and Design; Architecture; Art/Fine Arts; Environmental Design; Graphic Design; Industrial Design; Interior Design; Textile Design; Urban Design)
Developmental Psychology
Diplomacy (*see* International Affairs)
Disability Studies
Drama Therapy (*see* Therapies—Dance, Drama, and Music)
Dramatic Arts (*see* Theater)
Drawing (*see* Art/Fine Arts)
Drug Abuse Counseling (*see* Addictions/Substance Abuse Counseling)
Drug and Alcohol Abuse Counseling (*see* Addictions/Substance Abuse Counseling)
East Asian Studies (*see* Asian Studies)
East European and Russian Studies
Economic Development
Economics
Educational Theater (*see* Theater; Therapies—Dance, Drama, and Music)
Emergency Management
English
Environmental Design
Ethics
Ethnic Studies
Ethnomusicology (*see* Music)
Experimental Psychology
Family and Consumer Sciences—General
Family Studies (*see* Child and Family Studies)
Family Therapy (*see* Child and Family Studies; Clinical Psychology; Counseling Psychology; Marriage and Family Therapy)
Filmmaking (*see* Film, Television, and Video Production)
Film Studies (*see* Film, Television, and Video Production)
Film, Television, and Video Production
Film, Television, and Video Theory and Criticism
Fine Arts (*see* Art/Fine Arts)
Folklore
Foreign Languages (*see* specific language)
Foreign Service (*see* International Affairs; International Development)
Forensic Psychology
Forensic Sciences
Forensics (*see* Speech and Interpersonal Communication)
French
Gender Studies

General Studies (*see* Liberal Studies)
Genetic Counseling
Geographic Information Systems
Geography
German
Gerontology
Graphic Design
Greek (*see* Classics)
Health Communication
Health Psychology
Hebrew (*see* Near and Middle Eastern Languages)
Hebrew Studies (*see* Jewish Studies)
Hispanic and Latin American Languages
Hispanic Studies
Historic Preservation
History
History of Art (*see* Art History)
History of Medicine
History of Science and Technology
Holocaust and Genocide Studies
Home Economics (*see* Family and Consumer Sciences—General)
Homeland Security
Household Economics, Sciences, and Management
(*see* Family and Consumer Sciences—General)
Human Development
Humanities
Illustration
Industrial and Labor Relations
Industrial and Organizational Psychology
Industrial Design
Interdisciplinary Studies
Interior Design
International Affairs
International Development
International Economics
International Service (*see* International Affairs; International Development)
International Trade Policy
Internet and Interactive Multimedia
Interpersonal Communication (*see* Speech and Interpersonal Communication)
Interpretation (*see* Translation and Interpretation)
Islamic Studies (*see* Near and Middle Eastern Studies; Religion)
Italian
Japanese
Japanese Studies (*see* Asian Languages; Asian Studies; Japanese)
Jewelry (*see* Art/Fine Arts)
Jewish Studies
Journalism
Judaic Studies (*see* Jewish Studies; Religion)
Labor Relations (*see* Industrial and Labor Relations)
Landscape Architecture
Latin American Studies
Latin (*see* Classics)
Law Enforcement (*see* Criminal Justice and Criminology)
Liberal Studies
Lighting Design
Linguistics
Literature (*see* Classics; Comparative Literature; specific language)
Marriage and Family Therapy
Mass Communication
Media Studies
Medical Illustration
Medieval and Renaissance Studies
Metalsmithing (*see* Art/Fine Arts)
Middle Eastern Studies (*see* Near and Middle Eastern Studies)
Military and Defense Studies
Mineral Economics
Ministry (*see* Pastoral Ministry and Counseling; Theology)
Missions and Missiology
Motion Pictures (*see* Film, Television, and Video Production)
Museum Studies
Music
Musicology (*see* Music)
Music Therapy (*see* Therapies—Dance, Drama, and Music)
National Security

Native American Studies (*see* American Indian/Native American Studies)
Near and Middle Eastern Languages
Near and Middle Eastern Studies
Northern Studies
Organizational Psychology (*see* Industrial and Organizational Psychology)
Oriental Languages (*see* Asian Languages)
Oriental Studies (*see* Asian Studies)
Pacific Area/Pacific Rim Studies
Painting (*see* Art/Fine Arts)
Pastoral Ministry and Counseling
Philanthropic Studies
Philosophy
Photography
Playwriting (*see* Theater; Writing)
Policy Studies (*see* Public Policy)
Political Science
Population Studies (*see* Demography and Population Studies)
Portuguese
Printmaking (*see* Art/Fine Arts)
Product Design (*see* Industrial Design)
Psychoanalysis and Psychotherapy
Psychology—General
Public Administration
Public Affairs
Public History
Public Policy
Public Speaking (*see* Mass Communication; Rhetoric; Speech and Interpersonal Communication)
Publishing
Regional Planning (*see* Architecture; Urban and Regional Planning; Urban Design; Urban Studies)
Rehabilitation Counseling
Religion
Renaissance Studies (*see* Medieval and Renaissance Studies)
Rhetoric
Romance Languages
Romance Literatures (*see* Romance Languages)
Rural Planning and Studies
Rural Sociology
Russian
Scandinavian Languages
School Psychology
Sculpture (*see* Art/Fine Arts)
Security Administration (*see* Criminal Justice and Criminology)
Slavic Languages
Slavic Studies (*see* East European and Russian Studies; Slavic Languages)
Social Psychology
Social Sciences
Sociology
Southeast Asian Studies (*see* Asian Studies)
Soviet Studies (*see* East European and Russian Studies; Russian)
Spanish
Speech and Interpersonal Communication
Sport Psychology
Studio Art (*see* Art/Fine Arts)
Substance Abuse Counseling (*see* Addictions/Substance Abuse Counseling)
Survey Methodology
Sustainable Development
Technical Communication
Technical Writing
Telecommunications (*see* Film, Television, and Video Production)
Television (*see* Film, Television, and Video Production)
Textile Design
Textiles (*see* Clothing and Textiles; Textile Design)
Thanatology
Theater
Theater Arts (*see* Theater)
Theology
Therapies—Dance, Drama, and Music
Translation and Interpretation
Transpersonal and Humanistic Psychology
Urban and Regional Planning

Urban Design

Urban Planning (*see* Architecture; Urban and Regional Planning; Urban Design; Urban Studies)

Urban Studies

Video (*see* Film, Television, and Video Production)

Visual Arts (*see* Applied Arts and Design; Art/Fine Arts; Film, Television, and Video Production; Graphic Design; Illustration; Photography)

Western European Studies

Women's Studies

World Wide Web (*see* Internet and Interactive Multimedia)

Writing

Graduate Programs in the Biological/ Biomedical Sciences & Health-Related Medical Professions

Acupuncture and Oriental Medicine

Acute Care/Critical Care Nursing Administration (*see* Health Services Management and Hospital Administration; Nursing and Healthcare Administration; Pharmaceutical Administration)

Adult Nursing

Advanced Practice Nursing (*see* Family Nurse Practitioner Studies)

Allied Health—General

Allied Health Professions (*see* Clinical Laboratory Sciences/Medical Technology; Clinical Research; Communication Disorders; Dental Hygiene; Emergency Medical Services; Occupational Therapy; Physical Therapy; Physician Assistant Studies; Rehabilitation Sciences)

Allopathic Medicine

Anatomy

Anesthesiologist Assistant Studies

Animal Behavior

Bacteriology

Behavioral Sciences (*see* Biopsychology; Neuroscience; Zoology)

Biochemistry

Bioethics

Biological and Biomedical Sciences—General Biological Chemistry (*see* Biochemistry)

Biological Oceanography (*see* Marine Biology)

Biophysics

Biopsychology

Botany

Breeding (*see* Botany; Plant Biology; Genetics)

Cancer Biology/Oncology

Cardiovascular Sciences

Cell Biology

Cellular Physiology (*see* Cell Biology; Physiology)

Child-Care Nursing (*see* Maternal and Child/Neonatal Nursing)

Chiropractic

Clinical Laboratory Sciences/Medical Technology

Clinical Research

Community Health

Community Health Nursing

Computational Biology

Conservation (*see* Conservation Biology; Environmental Biology)

Conservation Biology

Crop Sciences (*see* Botany; Plant Biology)

Cytology (*see* Cell Biology)

Dental and Oral Surgery (*see* Oral and Dental Sciences)

Dental Assistant Studies (*see* Dental Hygiene)

Dental Hygiene

Dental Services (*see* Dental Hygiene)

Dentistry

Developmental Biology Dietetics (*see* Nutrition)

Ecology

Embryology (*see* Developmental Biology)

Emergency Medical Services

Endocrinology (*see* Physiology)

Entomology

Environmental Biology

Environmental and Occupational Health

Epidemiology

Evolutionary Biology

Family Nurse Practitioner Studies

Foods (*see* Nutrition)

Forensic Nursing

Genetics

Genomic Sciences

Gerontological Nursing

Health Physics/Radiological Health

Health Promotion

Health-Related Professions (*see* individual allied health professions)

Health Services Management and Hospital Administration

Health Services Research

Histology (*see* Anatomy; Cell Biology)

HIV/AIDS Nursing

Hospice Nursing

Hospital Administration (*see* Health Services Management and Hospital Administration)

Human Genetics

Immunology

Industrial Hygiene

Infectious Diseases

International Health

Laboratory Medicine (*see* Clinical Laboratory Sciences/Medical Technology; Immunology; Microbiology; Pathology)

Life Sciences (*see* Biological and Biomedical Sciences)

Marine Biology

Maternal and Child Health

Maternal and Child/Neonatal Nursing

Medical Imaging

Medical Microbiology

Medical Nursing (*see* Medical/Surgical Nursing)

Medical Physics

Medical/Surgical Nursing

Medical Technology (*see* Clinical Laboratory Sciences/Medical Technology)

Medical Sciences (*see* Biological and Biomedical Sciences)

Medical Science Training Programs (*see* Biological and Biomedical Sciences)

Medicinal and Pharmaceutical Chemistry

Medicinal Chemistry (*see* Medicinal and Pharmaceutical Chemistry)

Medicine (*see* Allopathic Medicine; Naturopathic Medicine; Osteopathic Medicine; Podiatric Medicine)

Microbiology

Midwifery (*see* Nurse Midwifery)

Molecular Biology

Molecular Biophysics

Molecular Genetics

Molecular Medicine

Molecular Pathogenesis

Molecular Pathology

Molecular Pharmacology

Molecular Physiology

Molecular Toxicology

Naturopathic Medicine

Neural Sciences (*see* Biopsychology; Neurobiology; Neuroscience)

Neurobiology

Neuroendocrinology (*see* Biopsychology; Neurobiology; Neuroscience; Physiology)

Neuropharmacology (*see* Biopsychology; Neurobiology; Neuroscience; Pharmacology)

Neurophysiology (*see* Biopsychology; Neurobiology; Neuroscience; Physiology)

Neuroscience

Nuclear Medical Technology (*see* Clinical Laboratory Sciences/ Medical Technology)

Nurse Anesthesia

Nurse Midwifery

Nurse Practitioner Studies (*see* Family Nurse Practitioner Studies)

Nursing Administration (*see* Nursing and Healthcare Administration)

Nursing and Healthcare Administration

Nursing Education

Nursing—General

Nursing Informatics

Nutrition
Occupational Health (*see* Environmental and Occupational Health;
    Occupational Health Nursing)
Occupational Health Nursing
Occupational Therapy
Oncology (*see* Cancer Biology/Oncology)
Oncology Nursing
Optometry
Oral and Dental Sciences
Oral Biology (*see* Oral and Dental Sciences)
Oral Pathology (*see* Oral and Dental Sciences)
Organismal Biology (*see* Biological and Biomedical Sciences; Zoology)
Oriental Medicine and Acupuncture (*see* Acupuncture and Oriental
    Medicine)
Orthodontics (*see* Oral and Dental Sciences)
Osteopathic Medicine
Parasitology
Pathobiology
Pathology
Pediatric Nursing
Pedontics (*see* Oral and Dental Sciences)
Perfusion
Pharmaceutical Administration
Pharmaceutical Chemistry (*see* Medicinal and Pharmaceutical
    Chemistry)
Pharmaceutical Sciences
Pharmacology
Pharmacy
Photobiology of Cells and Organelles
    (*see* Botany; Cell Biology; Plant Biology)
Physical Therapy
Physician Assistant Studies
Physiological Optics (*see* Vision Sciences)
Podiatric Medicine
Preventive Medicine (*see* Community Health and Public Health)
Physiological Optics (*see* Physiology)
Physiology
Plant Biology
Plant Molecular Biology
Plant Pathology
Plant Physiology
Pomology (*see* Botany; Plant Biology)
Psychiatric Nursing
Public Health—General
Public Health Nursing (*see* Community Health Nursing)
Psychiatric Nursing
Psychobiology (*see* Biopsychology)
Psychopharmacology (*see* Biopsychology;
    Neuroscience; Pharmacology)
Radiation Biology
Radiological Health (*see* Health Physics/Radiological Health)
Rehabilitation Nursing
Rehabilitation Sciences
Rehabilitation Therapy (*see* Physical Therapy)
Reproductive Biology
School Nursing
Sociobiology (*see* Evolutionary Biology)
Structural Biology
Surgical Nursing (*see* Medical/Surgical Nursing)
Systems Biology
Teratology
Therapeutics
Theoretical Biology (*see* Biological and Biomedical Sciences)
Therapeutics (*see* Pharmaceutical Sciences;
    Pharmacology; Pharmacy)
Toxicology
Transcultural Nursing
Translational Biology
Tropical Medicine (*see* Parasitology)
Veterinary Medicine
Veterinary Sciences
Virology
Vision Sciences
Wildlife Biology (*see* Zoology)
Women's Health Nursing
Zoology

Graduate Programs in the Physical Sciences, Mathematics, Agricultural Sciences, the Environment & Natural Resources

Acoustics
Agricultural Sciences
Agronomy and Soil Sciences
Analytical Chemistry
Animal Sciences
Applied Mathematics
Applied Physics
Applied Statistics
Aquaculture
Astronomy
Astrophysical Sciences (*see* Astrophysics; Atmospheric Sciences;
    Meteorology; Planetary and Space Sciences)
Astrophysics
Atmospheric Sciences
Biological Oceanography (*see* Marine Affairs; Marine Sciences;
    Oceanography)
Biomathematics
Biometry
Biostatistics
Chemical Physics
Chemistry
Computational Sciences
Condensed Matter Physics
Dairy Science (*see* Animal Sciences)
Earth Sciences (*see* Geosciences)
Environmental Management and Policy
Environmental Sciences
Environmental Studies (*see* Environmental Management and Policy)
Experimental Statistics (*see* Statistics)
Fish, Game, and Wildlife Management
Food Science and Technology
Forestry
General Science (*see* specific topics)
Geochemistry
Geodetic Sciences
Geological Engineering (*see* Geology)
Geological Sciences (*see* Geology)
Geology
Geophysical Fluid Dynamics (*see* Geophysics)
Geophysics
Geosciences
Horticulture
Hydrogeology
Hydrology
Inorganic Chemistry
Limnology
Marine Affairs
Marine Geology
Marine Sciences
Marine Studies (*see* Marine Affairs; Marine Geology;
    Marine Sciences; Oceanography)
Mathematical and Computational Finance
Mathematical Physics
Mathematical Statistics (*see* Applied Statistics; Statistics)
Mathematics
Meteorology
Mineralogy
Natural Resource Management (*see* Environmental Management
    and Policy; Natural Resources)
Natural Resources
Nuclear Physics (*see* Physics)
Ocean Engineering (*see* Marine Affairs; Marine Geology;
    Marine Sciences; Oceanography)
Oceanography
Optical Sciences
Optical Technologies (*see* Optical Sciences)
Optics (*see* Applied Physics; Optical Sciences; Physics)
Organic Chemistry

Paleontology
Paper Chemistry (*see* Chemistry)
Photonics
Physical Chemistry
Physics
Planetary and Space Sciences
Plant Sciences
Plasma Physics
Poultry Science (*see* Animal Sciences)
Radiological Physics (*see* Physics)
Range Management (*see* Range Science)
Range Science
Resource Management (*see* Environmental Management and Policy; Natural Resources)
Solid-Earth Sciences (*see* Geosciences)
Space Sciences (*see* Planetary and Space Sciences)
Statistics
Theoretical Chemistry
Theoretical Physics
Viticulture and Enology
Water Resources

Graduate Programs in Engineering & Applied Sciences

Aeronautical Engineering (*see* Aerospace/Aeronautical Engineering)
Aerospace/Aeronautical Engineering
Aerospace Studies (*see* Aerospace/Aeronautical Engineering)
Agricultural Engineering
Applied Mechanics (*see* Mechanics)
Applied Science and Technology
Architectural Engineering
Artificial Intelligence/Robotics
Astronautical Engineering (*see* Aerospace/Aeronautical Engineering)
Automotive Engineering
Aviation
Biochemical Engineering
Bioengineering
Bioinformatics
Biological Engineering (*see* Bioengineering)
Biomedical Engineering
Biosystems Engineering
Biotechnology
Ceramic Engineering (*see* Ceramic Sciences and Engineering)
Ceramic Sciences and Engineering
Ceramics (*see* Ceramic Sciences and Engineering)
Chemical Engineering
Civil Engineering
Computer and Information Systems Security
Computer Engineering
Computer Science
Computing Technology (*see* Computer Science)
Construction Engineering
Construction Management
Database Systems
Electrical Engineering
Electronic Materials
Electronics Engineering (*see* Electrical Engineering)
Energy and Power Engineering
Energy Management and Policy
Engineering and Applied Sciences
Engineering and Public Affairs (*see* Technology and Public Policy)
Engineering and Public Policy (*see* Energy Management and Policy; Technology and Public Policy)
Engineering Design
Engineering Management
Engineering Mechanics (*see* Mechanics)
Engineering Metallurgy (*see* Metallurgical Engineering and Metallurgy)

Engineering Physics
Environmental Design (*see* Environmental Engineering)
Environmental Engineering
Ergonomics and Human Factors
Financial Engineering
Fire Protection Engineering
Food Engineering (*see* Agricultural Engineering)
Game Design and Development
Gas Engineering (*see* Petroleum Engineering)
Geological Engineering
Geophysics Engineering (*see* Geological Engineering)
Geotechnical Engineering
Hazardous Materials Management
Health Informatics
Health Systems (*see* Safety Engineering; Systems Engineering)
Highway Engineering (*see* Transportation and Highway Engineering)
Human-Computer Interaction
Human Factors (*see* Ergonomics and Human Factors)
Hydraulics
Hydrology (*see* Water Resources Engineering)
Industrial Engineering (*see* Industrial/Management Engineering)
Industrial/Management Engineering
Information Science
Internet Engineering
Macromolecular Science (*see* Polymer Science and Engineering)
Management Engineering (*see* Engineering Management; Industrial/Management Engineering)
Management of Technology
Manufacturing Engineering
Marine Engineering (*see* Civil Engineering)
Materials Engineering
Materials Sciences
Mechanical Engineering
Mechanics
Medical Informatics
Metallurgical Engineering and Metallurgy
Metallurgy (*see* Metallurgical Engineering and Metallurgy)
Mineral/Mining Engineering
Modeling and Simulation
Nanotechnology
Nuclear Engineering
Ocean Engineering
Operations Research
Paper and Pulp Engineering
Petroleum Engineering
Pharmaceutical Engineering
Plastics Engineering (*see* Polymer Science and Engineering)
Polymer Science and Engineering
Public Policy (*see* Energy Management and Policy; Technology and Public Policy)
Reliability Engineering
Robotics (*see* Artificial Intelligence/Robotics)
Safety Engineering
Software Engineering
Solid-State Sciences (*see* Materials Sciences)
Structural Engineering
Surveying Science and Engineering
Systems Analysis (*see* Systems Engineering)
Systems Engineering
Systems Science
Technology and Public Policy
Telecommunications
Telecommunications Management
Textile Sciences and Engineering
Textiles (*see* Textile Sciences and Engineering)
Transportation and Highway Engineering
Urban Systems Engineering (*see* Systems Engineering)
Waste Management (*see* Hazardous Materials Management)
Water Resources Engineering

Graduate Programs in Business, Education, Information Studies, Law & Social Work

Accounting
Actuarial Science
Adult Education
Advertising and Public Relations
Agricultural Education
Alcohol Abuse Counseling (*see* Counselor Education)
Archival Management and Studies
Art Education
Athletics Administration (*see* Kinesiology and Movement Studies)
Athletic Training and Sports Medicine
Audiology (*see* Communication Disorders)
Aviation Management
Banking (*see* Finance and Banking)
Business Administration and Management—General
Business Education
Communication Disorders
Community College Education
Computer Education
Continuing Education (*see* Adult Education)
Counseling (*see* Counselor Education)
Counselor Education
Curriculum and Instruction
Developmental Education
Distance Education Development
Drug Abuse Counseling (*see* Counselor Education)
Early Childhood Education
Educational Leadership and Administration
Educational Measurement and Evaluation
Educational Media/Instructional Technology
Educational Policy
Educational Psychology
Education—General
Education of the Blind (*see* Special Education)
Education of the Deaf (*see* Special Education)
Education of the Gifted
Education of the Hearing Impaired (*see* Special Education)
Education of the Learning Disabled (*see* Special Education)
Education of the Mentally Retarded (*see* Special Education)
Education of the Physically Handicapped (*see* Special Education)
Education of Students with Severe/Multiple Disabilities
Education of the Visually Handicapped (*see* Special Education)
Electronic Commerce
Elementary Education
English as a Second Language
English Education
Entertainment Management
Entrepreneurship
Environmental Education
Environmental Law
Exercise and Sports Science
Exercise Physiology (*see* Kinesiology and Movement Studies)
Facilities and Entertainment Management
Finance and Banking
Food Services Management (*see* Hospitality Management)
Foreign Languages Education
Foundations and Philosophy of Education
Guidance and Counseling (*see* Counselor Education)
Health Education
Health Law
Hearing Sciences (*see* Communication Disorders)
Higher Education
Home Economics Education
Hospitality Management
Hotel Management (*see* Travel and Tourism)
Human Resources Development
Human Resources Management
Human Services
Industrial Administration (*see* Industrial and Manufacturing Management)
Industrial and Manufacturing Management

Industrial Education (*see* Vocational and Technical Education)
Information Studies
Instructional Technology (*see* Educational Media/Instructional Technology)
Insurance
Intellectual Property Law
International and Comparative Education
International Business
International Commerce (*see* International Business)
International Economics (*see* International Business)
International Trade (*see* International Business)
Investment and Securities (*see* Business Administration and Management; Finance and Banking; Investment Management)
Investment Management
Junior College Education (*see* Community College Education)
Kinesiology and Movement Studies
Law
Legal and Justice Studies
Leisure Services (*see* Recreation and Park Management)
Leisure Studies
Library Science
Logistics
Management (*see* Business Administration and Management)
Management Information Systems
Management Strategy and Policy
Marketing
Marketing Research
Mathematics Education
Middle School Education
Movement Studies (*see* Kinesiology and Movement Studies)
Multilingual and Multicultural Education
Museum Education
Music Education
Nonprofit Management
Nursery School Education (*see* Early Childhood Education)
Occupational Education (*see* Vocational and Technical Education)
Organizational Behavior
Organizational Management
Parks Administration (*see* Recreation and Park Management)
Personnel (*see* Human Resources Development; Human Resources Management; Organizational Behavior; Organizational Management; Student Affairs)
Philosophy of Education (*see* Foundations and Philosophy of Education)
Physical Education
Project Management
Public Relations (*see* Advertising and Public Relations)
Quality Management
Quantitative Analysis
Reading Education
Real Estate
Recreation and Park Management
Recreation Therapy (*see* Recreation and Park Management)
Religious Education
Remedial Education (*see* Special Education)
Restaurant Administration (*see* Hospitality Management)
Science Education
Secondary Education
Social Sciences Education
Social Studies Education (*see* Social Sciences Education)
Social Work
Special Education
Speech-Language Pathology and Audiology (*see* Communication Disorders)
Sports Management
Sports Medicine (*see* Athletic Training and Sports Medicine)
Sports Psychology and Sociology (*see* Kinesiology and Movement Studies)
Student Affairs
Substance Abuse Counseling (*see* Counselor Education)
Supply Chain Management
Sustainability Management
Systems Management (*see* Management Information Systems)
Taxation
Teacher Education (*see* specific subject areas)

Teaching English as a Second Language (*see* English as a Second Language)
Technical Education (*see* Vocational and Technical Education)
Transportation Management

Travel and Tourism
Urban Education
Vocational and Technical Education
Vocational Counseling (*see* Counselor Education)

Directories and Subject Areas in This Book

NOTES

NOTES

NOTES

NOTES

NOTES

NOTES

NOTES

NOTES

NOTES